State Alpha Code Table

Code	State	Code	State	Code	State
AL	Alabama	LA	Louisiana	OK	Oklahoma
AK	Alaska	ME	Maine	OR	Oregon
AZ	Arizona	MD	Maryland	PA	Pennsylvania
AR	Arkansas	MA	Massachusetts	PR	Puerto Rico
CA	California	MI	Michigan	RI	Rhode Island
CO	Colorado	MN	Minnesota	SC	South Carolina
CT	Connecticut	MS	Mississippi	SD	South Dakota
DE	Delaware	MO	Missouri	TN	Tennessee
DC	District of Columbia	MT	Montana	TX	Texas
FL	Florida	NE	Nebraska	UT	Utah
GA	Georgia	NV	Nevada	VT	Vermont
HI	Hawaii	NH	New Hampshire	VA	Virginia
ID	Idaho	NJ	New Jersey	WA	Washington
IL	Illinois	NM	New Mexico	WV	West Virginia
IN	Indiana	NY	New York	WI	Wisconsin
IA	Iowa	NC	North Carolina	WY	Wyoming
KS	Kansas	ND	North Dakota		
KY	Kentucky	OH	Ohio		

Time Zones and Abbreviations

Abbr.	Name	Standard Meridian	**Hours from Greenwich Mean Time** Standard	Daylight (War)
A	Atlantic	60°	4:00	3:00
E	Eastern	75°	5:00	4:00
C	Central	90°	6:00	5:00
M	Mountain	105°	7:00	6:00
P	Pacific	120°	8:00	7:00
Y	Yukon	135°	9:00	8:00
AH	Alaska-Hawaii	150°	10:00	9:00
H	Hawaiian	157°30′	10:30	9:30
B	Bering	165°	11:00	10:00

Abbr.	Time Type
S	Standard
D	Daylight
W	War

THE AMERICAN ATLAS

REVISED

US Latitudes and Longitudes
Time Changes and Time Zones

Compiled and Programmed by
Thomas G. Shanks

Published by
ACS Publications, Inc.
P.O. Box 16430
San Diego, California 92116-0430

First Edition published 1978. Fourth Edition 1987

International Standard Book Number 0-917086-91-0

Printed in the United States of America

Published by ACS Publications, Inc.
P.O. Box 16430
San Diego, CA 92116-0430

PREFACE

The information contained in this book was originally assembled as an on-line data base for an astrological calculation service, for, as a group, astrologers are most concerned with precision in geographical place coordinates and the history of time changes. As the data accumulated from a variety of sources, the desirability of making the information available to the public in the form of a book became apparent. *The American Atlas*, first printed in 1978, is the result of this effort.

The original place names and geographical coordinates came from four main sources. Although much time was spent in integrating and condensing the information, no individual or computer procedures could edit and resolve all conflicts and redundant information.

The major early sources for time changes were the pioneering works of Doris Chase Doane's *Time Changes in the U.S.A.* and Curran & Taylor's *World Daylight Saving Time*. To this base were added the results of primary research, as well as the contributions of individuals who researched the history of time changes at local libraries using newspaper microfilm collections. The time change information will continue to be refined in future editions.

More than a year has been spent preparing this fourth edition, which contains many significant improvements in the time change tables. New results of primary research and further individual contributions have been integrated into the tables, making them substantially different and more correct than previous editions. In particular a collection of *The Official Guide of the Railways...of the United States...* published by the National Railway Publication Co., dating from 1931 has been obtained, and the wealth of time change information it contains has enriched this edition. Further, a more general effort has been made to show small towns near larger ones as following the time changes of the larger neighbor. Though this will be incorrect in a few cases, the general rule is usually correct.

Critics have raised the issue of early observance of sundial time vs. local mean time and have suggested a more gradual adoption of standard time at the close of the 19th century. These issues have been tabled for attention in a subsequent edition.

Thomas Shanks
October, 1987

ACKNOWLEDGMENTS

Major contributions have been made by the following published materials and journals: Doris Chase Doane, *Time Changes in the U.S.A.*; Curran and Taylor, *World Daylight Saving Time*; documents published by the Interstate Commerce Commission; National Railway Publication Co., *The Official Guide of the Railways ... of the United States...; The Mercury Hour; AFA Bulletin*; and *Astro Psychological Problems*.

Individuals making major contributions include: Mark Pottenger, Mary Brandes, Don Borkowski, Eugene Seger, Wayne Lee Holt, Mary Frances Wood and Arthur Blackwell.

Significant material was also provided by: Dorothy Pierce, John Adkins, Lillian Celic, Edith Custer, Gary Duncan, Lynne Burmyn, Liz Anderson, and Susan Aiu.

Contents

SUBMITTING CORRECTIONS

Additions or corrections to the material presented in the *Atlas* are requested. We ask that copies of printed documentation be submitted supporting the suggested change. Submit such material to:

The American Atlas
ACS Publications, Inc.
P O Box 16430
San Diego, CA 92116-0430

How To Use This Book

Turn to the state desired. For each state there are time tables, a list of counties with each county numbered, and a list of cities and towns. Any comments are noted before a state's time tables. Cities are arranged alphabetically with city name, county number, time table number, latitude, longitude and longitude time equivalent (hours, minutes and seconds from Greenwich), in that order.

LATITUDE AND LONGITUDE
Find the target city. If there is more than one with the same name, check the county. For cities with no county shown, none was given in the sources used in compiling this reference. Once you have found your city, the latitude, longitude and time equivalent of the longitude can be read right from that line.

TIME CHANGE TABLES
The Time Tables have a single entry for each change of time zone or time type. That entry is effective until the next time change, whether the period is one day or thirty-five years.

The first letter gives the time zone (two letters for Alaska-Hawaii); see the Table of Time Zones and Abbreviations. The next letter gives the time type: D for Daylight, S for Standard, W for War (which has the same effect as Daylight). The last letter is T for time. An entry of EST spells out Eastern Standard Time, CDT is Central Daylight Time, MWT is Mountain War Time, and so on. LMT is the abbreviation for Local Mean Time.

The appropriate time table for each location is designated in the column preceding the latitude. Find the time table number for your target city and then locate the time table with that number in the 'Time Tables' section for that state. (If there is only one time table for the whole state, then no time table number is given after the city and county number.) Scan down the column of dates to the date you want. The last date entry before the target date and time gives the time zone and standard/daylight time observance in effect at the target date and time.

The following example shows that clocks in a certain part of Delaware were set ahead to Eastern War Time at 2:00 AM on March 31, 1918, and were set back to Eastern Standard time at 2:00 AM on October 27, 1918. Any birth that took place between those times would have been recorded in EWT.

DE #11

Before 11/18/1883		**LMT**
11/18/1883	**12:00**	**EST**
3/31/1918	**02:00**	**EWT**
10/27/1918	**02:00**	**EST**

Some time tables give a reference to another table in the same state instead of a time change. Refer to the second table for time changes if your date is in the period before the next entry in the first table.

US TABLES
Most time tables end with "US#x". This is a reference to one of the US Time Tables at the front of the book, which give the more common time observance shifts without reference to zone as well as the daylight time shifts to the year 2000, assuming continued use of the Uniform Time Act. The time type from the US table is combined with the last time zone specified in the state table.

If the last entry in a state table is not a reference to a US Table but indicates a regular time shift, then there has been no change since that date; the time zone and observance last listed continue to be in effect. For example, the last Arizona entry is:

10/29/1967 02:00 MST

meaning that Arizona has been on Mountain Standard Time continuously since 2:00 AM October 29, 1967.

Table I

How To Calculate Sidereal Time

	Example 1	Example 2	Example 3
	May 11, 1931 1:30 PM New York City	November 11, 1931 6:15 PM Honolulu, HI	May 11, 1931 12:15 AM San Francisco, CA
1) Convert the time of birth to the 24-hour clock.	13:30	18:15	00:15
2) Find the time zone and daylight/standard time observance from *The American Atlas* and then use the table of **Time Zones and Abbreviations** to convert to Universal Time (UT).	EDT 4:00 17:30	HST 10:00 28:45	PST 8:00 8:15
3) Reduce to less than 24 hours and add 1 day to obtain the Greenwich birth date, if necessary. Greenwich birth date is used to enter the ephemeris to obtain the sidereal time as in step 5 below.	17:30 *May 11, 1931*	−24:00 4:45 *Nov. 12, 1931*	8:15 *May 11, 1931*
4) Use the UT of birth and Table II to determine the solar/sidereal time correction (acceleration).	00:02:52 17:32:52	00:00:47 4:45:47	00:01:21 8:16:21
5) Find the midnight sidereal time for birthdate from *The American Ephemeris* or other reference and add to the birthtime UT.	15:11:16 32:44:08	3:20:39 8:06:26	15:11:16 23:27:37
6) Subtract the longitude time equivalent obtained from *The American Atlas* to get the sidereal time of birth.	−4:55:48 27:48:20	−10:31:28 −2:25:02	−8:09:40 15:17:57
7) Add or subract 24 hours, if necessary, to put sidereal time in the range between 0 to 24 hours.	−24:00:00 3:48:20	+24:00:00 21:34:58	15:17:57

Table II

Solar-Sidereal Time Correction (Acceleration)

	0h		1h		2h		3h		4h		5h		6h		7h		8h		9h		10h		11h	
MIN	m	s	m	s	m	s	m	s	m	s	m	s	m	s	m	s	m	s	m	s	m	s	m	s
0	0	0	0	10	0	20	0	30	0	39	0	49	0	59	1	9	1	19	1	29	1	39	1	48
1	0	0	0	10	0	20	0	30	0	40	0	49	0	59	1	9	1	19	1	29	1	39	1	49
2	0	0	0	10	0	20	0	30	0	40	0	50	0	59	1	9	1	19	1	29	1	39	1	49
3	0	0	0	10	0	20	0	30	0	40	0	50	0	60	1	9	1	19	1	29	1	39	1	49
4	0	1	0	11	0	20	0	30	0	40	0	50	0	60	1	10	1	20	1	29	1	39	1	49
5	0	1	0	11	0	21	0	30	0	40	0	50	0	60	1	10	1	20	1	30	1	39	1	49
6	0	1	0	11	0	21	0	31	0	40	0	50	1	0	1	10	1	20	1	30	1	40	1	49
7	0	1	0	11	0	21	0	31	0	41	0	50	1	0	1	10	1	20	1	30	1	40	1	50
8	0	1	0	11	0	21	0	31	0	41	0	51	1	0	1	10	1	20	1	30	1	40	1	50
9	0	1	0	11	0	21	0	31	0	41	0	51	1	1	1	10	1	20	1	30	1	40	1	50
10	0	2	0	11	0	21	0	31	0	41	0	51	1	1	1	11	1	20	1	30	1	40	1	50
11	0	2	0	12	0	22	0	31	0	41	0	51	1	1	1	11	1	21	1	31	1	40	1	50
12	0	2	0	12	0	22	0	32	0	41	0	51	1	1	1	11	1	21	1	31	1	41	1	50
13	0	2	0	12	0	22	0	32	0	42	0	51	1	1	1	11	1	21	1	31	1	41	1	51
14	0	2	0	12	0	22	0	32	0	42	0	52	1	1	1	11	1	21	1	31	1	41	1	51
15	0	2	0	12	0	22	0	32	0	42	0	52	1	2	1	11	1	21	1	31	1	41	1	51
16	0	3	0	12	0	22	0	32	0	42	0	52	1	2	1	12	1	21	1	31	1	41	1	51
17	0	3	0	13	0	23	0	32	0	42	0	52	1	2	1	12	1	22	1	32	1	41	1	51
18	0	3	0	13	0	23	0	33	0	42	0	52	1	2	1	12	1	22	1	32	1	42	1	51
19	0	3	0	13	0	23	0	33	0	43	0	52	1	2	1	12	1	22	1	32	1	42	1	52
20	0	3	0	13	0	23	0	33	0	43	0	53	1	2	1	12	1	22	1	32	1	42	1	52
21	0	3	0	13	0	23	0	33	0	43	0	53	1	3	1	12	1	22	1	32	1	42	1	52
22	0	4	0	13	0	23	0	33	0	43	0	53	1	3	1	13	1	22	1	32	1	42	1	52
23	0	4	0	14	0	23	0	33	0	43	0	53	1	3	1	13	1	23	1	32	1	42	1	52
24	0	4	0	14	0	24	0	34	0	43	0	53	1	3	1	13	1	23	1	33	1	43	1	52
25	0	4	0	14	0	24	0	34	0	44	0	53	1	3	1	13	1	23	1	33	1	43	1	53
26	0	4	0	14	0	24	0	34	0	44	0	54	1	3	1	13	1	23	1	33	1	43	1	53
27	0	4	0	14	0	24	0	34	0	44	0	54	1	4	1	13	1	23	1	33	1	43	1	53
28	0	5	0	14	0	24	0	34	0	44	0	54	1	4	1	14	1	23	1	33	1	43	1	53
29	0	5	0	15	0	24	0	34	0	44	0	54	1	4	1	14	1	24	1	33	1	43	1	53
30	0	5	0	15	0	25	0	34	0	44	0	54	1	4	1	14	1	24	1	34	1	43	1	53
31	0	5	0	15	0	25	0	35	0	45	0	54	1	4	1	14	1	24	1	34	1	44	1	54
32	0	5	0	15	0	25	0	35	0	45	0	55	1	4	1	14	1	24	1	34	1	44	1	54
33	0	5	0	15	0	25	0	35	0	45	0	55	1	5	1	14	1	24	1	34	1	44	1	54
34	0	6	0	15	0	25	0	35	0	45	0	55	1	5	1	15	1	24	1	34	1	44	1	54
35	0	6	0	16	0	25	0	35	0	45	0	55	1	5	1	15	1	25	1	34	1	44	1	54
36	0	6	0	16	0	26	0	35	0	45	0	55	1	5	1	15	1	25	1	35	1	44	1	54
37	0	6	0	16	0	26	0	36	0	46	0	55	1	5	1	15	1	25	1	35	1	45	1	54
38	0	6	0	16	0	26	0	36	0	46	0	56	1	5	1	15	1	25	1	35	1	45	1	55
39	0	6	0	16	0	26	0	36	0	46	0	56	1	6	1	15	1	25	1	35	1	45	1	55
40	0	7	0	16	0	26	0	36	0	46	0	56	1	6	1	16	1	25	1	35	1	45	1	55
41	0	7	0	17	0	26	0	36	0	46	0	56	1	6	1	16	1	26	1	35	1	45	1	55
42	0	7	0	17	0	27	0	36	0	46	0	56	1	6	1	16	1	26	1	36	1	45	1	55
43	0	7	0	17	0	27	0	37	0	46	0	56	1	6	1	16	1	26	1	36	1	46	1	55
44	0	7	0	17	0	27	0	37	0	47	0	57	1	6	1	16	1	26	1	36	1	46	1	56
45	0	7	0	17	0	27	0	37	0	47	0	57	1	7	1	16	1	26	1	36	1	46	1	56
46	0	8	0	17	0	27	0	37	0	47	0	57	1	7	1	17	1	26	1	36	1	46	1	56
47	0	8	0	18	0	27	0	37	0	47	0	57	1	7	1	17	1	27	1	36	1	46	1	56
48	0	8	0	18	0	28	0	37	0	47	0	57	1	7	1	17	1	27	1	37	1	46	1	56
49	0	8	0	18	0	28	0	38	0	47	0	57	1	7	1	17	1	27	1	37	1	47	1	56
50	0	8	0	18	0	28	0	38	0	48	0	57	1	7	1	17	1	27	1	37	1	47	1	57
51	0	8	0	18	0	28	0	38	0	48	0	58	1	8	1	17	1	27	1	37	1	47	1	57
52	0	9	0	18	0	28	0	38	0	48	0	58	1	8	1	18	1	27	1	37	1	47	1	57
53	0	9	0	19	0	28	0	38	0	48	0	58	1	8	1	18	1	28	1	37	1	47	1	57
54	0	9	0	19	0	29	0	38	0	48	0	58	1	8	1	18	1	28	1	38	1	47	1	57
55	0	9	0	19	0	29	0	39	0	48	0	58	1	8	1	18	1	28	1	38	1	48	1	57
56	0	9	0	19	0	29	0	39	0	49	0	58	1	8	1	18	1	28	1	38	1	48	1	58
57	0	9	0	19	0	29	0	39	0	49	0	59	1	9	1	18	1	28	1	38	1	48	1	58
58	0	10	0	19	0	29	0	39	0	49	0	59	1	9	1	19	1	28	1	38	1	48	1	58
59	0	10	0	20	0	29	0	39	0	49	0	59	1	9	1	19	1	29	1	38	1	48	1	58
60	0	10	0	20	0	30	0	39	0	49	0	59	1	9	1	19	1	29	1	39	1	48	1	58

12h		13h		14h		15h		16h		17h		18h		19h		20h		21h		22h		23h		
m	s	m	s	m	s	m	s	m	s	m	s	m	s	m	s	m	s	m	s	m	s	m	s	MIN
1	58	2	8	2	18	2	28	2	38	2	48	2	57	3	7	3	17	3	27	3	37	3	47	0
1	58	2	8	2	18	2	28	2	38	2	48	2	58	3	7	3	17	3	27	3	37	3	47	1
1	59	2	8	2	18	2	28	2	38	2	48	2	58	3	8	3	17	3	27	3	37	3	47	2
1	59	2	9	2	18	2	28	2	38	2	48	2	58	3	8	3	18	3	27	3	37	3	47	3
1	59	2	9	2	19	2	29	2	38	2	48	2	58	3	8	3	18	3	28	3	37	3	47	4
1	59	2	9	2	19	2	29	2	39	2	48	2	58	3	8	3	18	3	28	3	38	3	48	5
1	59	2	9	2	19	2	29	2	39	2	49	2	58	3	8	3	18	3	28	3	38	3	48	6
1	59	2	9	2	19	2	29	2	39	2	49	2	59	3	8	3	18	3	28	3	38	3	48	7
1	60	2	9	2	19	2	29	2	39	2	49	2	59	3	9	3	18	3	28	3	38	3	48	8
1	60	2	10	2	19	2	29	2	39	2	49	2	59	3	9	3	19	3	28	3	38	3	48	9
1	60	2	10	2	20	2	29	2	39	2	49	2	59	3	9	3	19	3	29	3	38	3	48	10
2	0	2	10	2	20	2	30	2	40	2	49	2	59	3	9	3	19	3	29	3	39	3	49	11
2	0	2	10	2	20	2	30	2	40	2	50	2	59	3	9	3	19	3	29	3	39	3	49	12
2	0	2	10	2	20	2	30	2	40	2	50	2	60	3	9	3	19	3	29	3	39	3	49	13
2	1	2	10	2	20	2	30	2	40	2	50	2	60	3	10	3	19	3	29	3	39	3	49	14
2	1	2	11	2	20	2	30	2	40	2	50	2	60	3	10	3	20	3	29	3	39	3	49	15
2	1	2	11	2	21	2	30	2	40	2	50	3	0	3	10	3	20	3	30	3	39	3	49	16
2	1	2	11	2	21	2	31	2	40	2	50	3	0	3	10	3	20	3	30	3	40	3	49	17
2	1	2	11	2	21	2	31	2	41	2	51	3	0	3	10	3	20	3	30	3	40	3	50	18
2	1	2	11	2	21	2	31	2	41	2	51	3	1	3	10	3	20	3	30	3	40	3	50	19
2	2	2	11	2	21	2	31	2	41	2	51	3	1	3	11	3	20	3	30	3	40	3	50	20
2	2	2	12	2	21	2	31	2	41	2	51	3	1	3	11	3	21	3	30	3	40	3	50	21
2	2	2	12	2	22	2	31	2	41	2	51	3	1	3	11	3	21	3	31	3	40	3	50	22
2	2	2	12	2	22	2	32	2	41	2	51	3	1	3	11	3	21	3	31	3	41	3	50	23
2	2	2	12	2	22	2	32	2	42	2	52	3	1	3	11	3	21	3	31	3	41	3	51	24
2	2	2	12	2	22	2	32	2	42	2	52	3	2	3	11	3	21	3	31	3	41	3	51	25
2	3	2	12	2	22	2	32	2	42	2	52	3	2	3	12	3	21	3	31	3	41	3	51	26
2	3	2	13	2	22	2	32	2	42	2	52	3	2	3	12	3	22	3	31	3	41	3	51	27
2	3	2	13	2	23	2	32	2	42	2	52	3	2	3	12	3	22	3	32	3	41	3	51	28
2	3	2	13	2	23	2	33	2	42	2	52	3	2	3	12	3	22	3	32	3	42	3	51	29
2	3	2	13	2	23	2	33	2	43	2	52	3	2	3	12	3	22	3	32	3	42	3	52	30
2	3	2	13	2	23	2	33	2	43	2	53	3	3	3	12	3	22	3	32	3	42	3	52	31
2	4	2	13	2	23	2	33	2	43	2	53	3	3	3	13	3	22	3	32	3	42	3	52	32
2	4	2	14	2	23	2	33	2	43	2	53	3	3	3	13	3	23	3	32	3	42	3	52	33
2	4	2	14	2	24	2	33	2	43	2	53	3	3	3	13	3	23	3	33	3	42	3	52	34
2	4	2	14	2	24	2	34	2	43	2	53	3	3	3	13	3	23	3	33	3	43	3	52	35
2	4	2	14	2	24	2	34	2	44	2	53	3	3	3	13	3	23	3	33	3	43	3	53	36
2	4	2	14	2	24	2	34	2	44	2	54	3	3	3	13	3	23	3	33	3	43	3	53	37
2	5	2	14	2	24	2	34	2	44	2	54	3	4	3	14	3	23	3	33	3	43	3	53	38
2	5	2	15	2	24	2	34	2	44	2	54	3	4	3	14	3	24	3	33	3	43	3	53	39
2	5	2	15	2	25	2	34	2	44	2	54	3	4	3	14	3	24	3	34	3	43	3	53	40
2	5	2	15	2	25	2	35	2	44	2	54	3	4	3	14	3	24	3	34	3	44	3	53	41
2	5	2	15	2	25	2	35	2	45	2	54	3	4	3	14	3	24	3	34	3	44	3	54	42
2	5	2	15	2	25	2	35	2	45	2	55	3	4	3	14	3	24	3	34	3	44	3	54	43
2	6	2	15	2	25	2	35	2	45	2	55	3	5	3	15	3	24	3	34	3	44	3	54	44
2	6	2	16	2	25	2	35	2	45	2	55	3	5	3	15	3	25	3	34	3	44	3	54	45
2	6	2	16	2	26	2	35	2	45	2	55	3	5	3	15	3	25	3	35	3	44	3	54	46
2	6	2	16	2	26	2	36	2	45	2	55	3	5	3	15	3	25	3	35	3	45	3	54	47
2	6	2	16	2	26	2	36	2	46	2	55	3	5	3	15	3	25	3	35	3	45	3	55	48
2	6	2	16	2	26	2	36	2	46	2	56	3	5	3	15	3	25	3	35	3	45	3	55	49
2	6	2	16	2	26	2	36	2	46	2	56	3	6	3	15	3	25	3	35	3	45	3	55	50
2	7	2	17	2	26	2	36	2	46	2	56	3	6	3	16	3	26	3	35	3	45	3	55	51
2	7	2	17	2	27	2	36	2	46	2	56	3	6	3	16	3	26	3	36	3	45	3	55	52
2	7	2	17	2	27	2	37	2	46	2	56	3	6	3	16	3	26	3	36	3	46	3	55	53
2	7	2	17	2	27	2	37	2	47	2	56	3	6	3	16	3	26	3	36	3	46	3	56	54
2	7	2	17	2	27	2	37	2	47	2	57	3	6	3	16	3	26	3	36	3	46	3	56	55
2	7	2	17	2	27	2	37	2	47	2	57	3	7	3	16	3	26	3	36	3	46	3	56	56
2	8	2	17	2	27	2	37	2	47	2	57	3	7	3	17	3	26	3	36	3	46	3	56	57
2	8	2	18	2	28	2	37	2	47	2	57	3	7	3	17	3	27	3	37	3	46	3	56	58
2	8	2	18	2	28	2	38	2	47	2	57	3	7	3	17	3	27	3	37	3	47	3	56	59
2	8	2	18	2	28	2	38	2	48	2	57	3	7	3	17	3	27	3	37	3	47	3	57	60

ALABAMA

TIME TABLES

AL # 1

Before 11/18/1883		LMT
11/18/1883	12:00	CST
3/31/1918	02:00	CWT
10/27/1918	02:00	CST
3/30/1919	02:00	CWT
10/26/1919	02:00	CST
7/21/1941	00:01	CDT
10/01/1941	00:01	CST
2/09/1942	02:00	CWT
9/30/1945	02:00	CST
4/30/1967	02:00	US#1

AL # 2

Before 11/18/1883		LMT
11/18/1883	12:00	CST
3/31/1918	02:00	CWT
10/27/1918	02:00	CST
3/30/1919	02:00	CWT
10/26/1919	02:00	CST
7/21/1941	00:01	CDT
10/01/1941	00:01	CST
2/09/1942	02:00	CWT
9/30/1945	02:00	CST
4/27/1958	02:00	CDT
10/25/1958	02:00	CST
4/26/1959	02:00	CDT
9/27/1959	02:00	CST
4/24/1960	02:00	CDT
9/25/1960	02:00	CST
4/30/1967	02:00	US#1

AL # 3

Before 11/18/1883		LMT
11/18/1883	12:00	CST
3/31/1918	02:00	CWT
10/27/1918	02:00	CST
3/30/1919	02:00	CWT
10/26/1919	02:00	CST
7/21/1941	00:01	CDT
10/01/1941	00:01	CST
2/09/1942	02:00	CWT
9/30/1945	02:00	CST
4/27/1958	00:01	CDT
10/25/1958	00:01	CST
4/30/1967	02:00	US#1

AL # 4

Before 11/18/1883		LMT
11/18/1883	12:00	CST
3/31/1918	02:00	CWT
10/27/1918	02:00	CST
3/30/1919	02:00	CWT
10/26/1919	02:00	CST
5/18/1935	00:01	CDT
9/02/1935	00:01	CST
4/28/1940	02:00	CDT
9/29/1940	02:00	CST
7/21/1941	00:01	CDT
10/01/1941	00:01	CST
2/09/1942	02:00	CWT
9/30/1945	02:00	CST
4/30/1967	02:00	US#1

AL # 5

Before 11/18/1883		LMT
11/18/1883	12:00	CST
3/31/1918	02:00	CWT
10/27/1918	02:00	CST
3/30/1919	02:00	CWT
10/26/1919	02:00	CST
7/21/1941	00:01	CDT
10/01/1941	00:01	CST
2/09/1942	02:00	CWT
9/30/1945	02:00	CST
4/24/1966	02:00	US#1

AL # 6

Before 11/18/1883		LMT
11/18/1883	12:00	CST
3/31/1918	02:00	CWT
10/27/1918	02:00	CST
3/30/1919	02:00	CWT
10/26/1919	02:00	CST
4/28/1940	02:00	CDT
9/29/1940	02:00	CST
7/21/1941	00:01	CDT
10/01/1941	00:01	CST
2/09/1942	02:00	CWT
9/30/1945	02:00	CST
4/30/1967	02:00	US#1

AL # 7

Before 1/01/1903		LMT
1/01/1903	12:00	CST
3/31/1918	02:00	CWT
10/27/1918	02:00	CST
3/30/1919	02:00	CWT
10/26/1919	02:00	CST
3/23/1941	12:00	EST
2/09/1942	02:00	EWT
2/14/1943	02:00	CWT
9/30/1945	02:00	EST
4/30/1967	02:00	US#1

COUNTIES

1 Autauga
2 Baldwin
3 Barbour
4 Bibb
5 Blount
6 Bullock
7 Butler
8 Calhoun
9 Chambers
10 Cherokee
11 Chilton
12 Choctaw
13 Clarke
14 Clay
15 Cleburne
16 Coffee
17 Colbert
18 Conecuh
19 Coosa
20 Covington
21 Crenshaw
22 Cullman
23 Dale
24 Dallas
25 De Kalb
26 Elmore
27 Escambia
28 Etowah
29 Fayette
30 Franklin
31 Geneva
32 Greene
33 Hale
34 Henry
35 Houston
36 Jackson
37 Jefferson
38 Lamar
39 Lauderdale
40 Lawrence
41 Lee
42 Limestone
43 Lowndes
44 Macon
45 Madison
46 Marengo
47 Marion
48 Marshall
49 Mobile
50 Monroe
51 Montgomery
52 Morgan
53 Perry
54 Pickens
55 Pike
56 Randolph
57 Russell
58 St Clair
59 Shelby
60 Sumter
61 Talladega
62 Tallapoosa
63 Tuscaloosa
64 Walker
65 Washington
66 Wilcox
67 Winston

Place	Table	Lat	Long	Time
Abanda 9	1	33N09	85w22	5:41:28
Abbeville 34	1	31N34	85w15	5:41:00
Abel 15	1	33N26	85w41	5:42:44
Abercrombie 4	1	32N57	87w08	5:48:32
Aberfoil 6	1	32N04	85w41	5:42:44
Abernant 63	1	33N17	87w14	5:48:56
Abernathy 15	1	33N38	85w35	5:42:20
Ackerville 66	1	31N53	87w00	5:48:00
Acmar 58	1	33N37	86w30	5:46:00
Active 4	1	32N45	86w59	5:47:56
Ada 51	1	32N03	86w13	5:44:52
Adamsburg 25	1	34N27	85w43	5:42:52
Adamsville 37	1	33N40	86w59	5:47:56
Addison 67	1	34N12	87w11	5:48:44
Adger 37	1	33N23	87w06	5:48:24
Adler 53	1	32N41	87w13	5:48:52
Ai 15	1	33N38	85w35	5:42:20
Aimwell 46	1	32N06	87w52	5:51:28
Airport Highlands 37	6	33N34	86w44	5:46:56
Akron 33	1	32N53	87w45	5:51:00
Alabama City 28	6	34N01	86w03	5:44:12
Alabama Port 49	1	30N23	88w14	5:52:56
Alabama Shores 17	1	34N45	87w41	5:50:44
Alabaster 59	1	33N15	86w49	5:47:16
Alberta 66	1	32N14	87w25	5:49:40
Alberta City 63	6	33N12	87w32	5:50:08
Alberton 16	1	31N13	86w10	5:44:40
Albertville 48	1	34N16	86w13	5:44:52
Alden 37	1	33N38	86w58	5:47:52
Alder Springs 48	1	34N16	86w12	5:44:48
Aldrich 59	1	33N05	86w51	5:47:24
Aldridge Grove 40	1	34N29	87w17	5:49:08
Aldrige 64	1	33N44	87w17	5:49:08
Alexander City 62	1	32N56	85w58	5:43:52
Alexander Heights 39	1	34N49	87w40	5:50:40
Alexandria 8	1	33N46	85w53	5:43:32
Alexis 10	1	34N09	85w41	5:42:44
Aliceville 54	1	33N08	88w09	5:52:36
Allen 13	1	31N36	87w44	5:50:56
Allens Crossroads 48	1	34N24	86w27	5:45:48
Allenton 66	1	31N53	87w00	5:48:00
Allenville 46	1	32N28	87w36	5:50:24
Allgood 5	1	33N55	86w31	5:46:04
Allsboro 17	1	34N46	87w58	5:51:52
Alma 13	1	31N28	87w45	5:51:00
Almeria 6	1	32N08	85w43	5:42:52
Almond 56	1	33N07	85w34	5:42:16
Alpine 61	1	33N21	86w14	5:44:56
Altadena Valley 37	6	33N28	86w45	5:47:00
Alton 37	1	33N35	86w38	5:46:32
Altoona 28	1	34N02	86w20	5:45:20
America 64	1	33N44	87w17	5:49:08
Andalusia 20	1	31N18	86w29	5:45:56
Anderson 28	6	33N57	86w01	5:44:04
Anderson 39	1	34N55	87w16	5:49:04
Andrews Chapel 52	1	34N25	87w05	5:48:20
Angel 8	1	33N49	85w46	5:43:04
Annemanie 66	1	32N03	87w34	5:50:16
Anniston 8	6	33N39	85w50	5:43:20
Anniston Army Depot 8	6	33N40	85w50	5:43:20
Ansley 55	1	31N53	86w07	5:44:28
Antioch 8	1	33N36	86w01	5:44:04
Antioch 20	1	31N17	86w27	5:45:48
Antioch 55	1	31N48	85w56	5:43:44
Appleton 27	1	31N05	87w04	5:48:16
Aqua Vista 39	1	34N52	87w32	5:50:08
Aquilla 65	1	31N38	88w20	5:53:20
Arab 48	1	34N19	86w30	5:46:00
Ararat 12	1	31N55	88w19	5:53:16
Arbacoochee 15	1	33N38	85w35	5:42:20
Ardell 22	1	34N06	87w04	5:48:16
Ardilla 35	1	31N15	85w26	5:41:44
Ardmore 42	1	34N59	86w51	5:47:24
Ardmore Highway 45	2	34N43	86w38	5:46:32
Argo 37	1	33N41	86w32	5:46:08
Argo Heights 64	1	33N46	87w11	5:48:44
Arguta 23	1	31N24	85w41	5:42:44
Ariton 23	1	31N36	85w43	5:42:52
Arkadelphia 22	1	33N54	86w58	5:47:52
Arkwright 59	1	33N24	86w25	5:45:40
Arley 67	1	34N04	87w13	5:48:52
Arlington 66	1	32N04	87w35	5:50:20
Armstead 5	1	33N55	86w27	5:45:48
Armstrong 44	1	32N14	85w39	5:42:36
Arona 25	1	34N10	86w09	5:44:36
Arrowhead 51	4	32N23	86w15	5:45:00
Arsenal 45	2	34N41	86w39	5:46:36
Asbury 23	1	31N24	85w41	5:42:44
Asbury 48	1	34N16	86w12	5:44:48
Ashbank 64	1	33N59	87w29	5:49:56
Ashby 4	1	33N01	86w55	5:47:40
Ashford 35	1	31N11	85w14	5:40:56
Ashland 14	1	33N16	85w50	5:43:20
Ashridge 67	1	34N14	87w37	5:50:28
Ashville 58	1	33N50	86w15	5:45:00
Aspel 36	1	34N39	86w01	5:44:04
Athens 42	1	34N48	86w58	5:47:52
Atkinson 13	1	31N55	87w45	5:51:00
Atmore 27	1	31N02	87w29	5:49:56
Attalla 28	1	34N01	86w06	5:44:24
Atwood 30	1	34N20	87w56	5:51:44
Auburn 41	5	32N36	85w29	5:41:56
Augustin 53	1	32N23	87w00	5:48:00
Aurora 28	1	34N10	86w09	5:44:36
Aurora Springs 17	1	34N46	87w58	5:51:52
Austinville 52	3	34N33	86w59	5:47:56
Autaugaville 1	1	32N26	86w39	5:46:36
Avalon Park 37	1	33N26	86w57	5:47:48
Avant 7	1	31N38	86w44	5:46:56
Avery 36	1	34N53	85w50	5:43:20
Avoca 40	1	34N30	87w44	5:50:56
Avon 35	1	31N11	85w17	5:41:08
Avondale 37	6	33N32	86w47	5:47:08
Avondale Village 58	1	33N35	86w23	5:45:32
Awin 66	1	31N53	87w00	5:48:00
Axis 49	1	30N56	88w02	5:52:08
Ayres 37	1	33N41	86w41	5:46:44
Babbie 20	1	31N17	86w19	5:45:16
Bacon Level 56	1	33N09	85w22	5:41:28
Bagley 37	1	33N44	87w07	5:48:28
Baileyton 22	1	34N16	86w37	5:46:28
Baker Hill 3	1	31N47	85w18	5:41:12
Bald Hill 31	1	31N06	85w36	5:42:24
Baldwin Farms 44	1	32N17	85w51	5:43:24
Balkum 34	1	31N22	85w20	5:41:20
Ballplay 28	6	33N57	86w01	5:44:04
Bangor 5	1	33N58	86w46	5:47:04
Bankhead 25	1	34N34	85w35	5:42:20
Bankhead 64	1	33N44	87w17	5:49:08
Banks 55	1	31N49	85w51	5:43:24
Bankston 29	1	33N40	87w40	5:50:40
Barachais 51	1	32N17	86w06	5:44:24
Barber 35	1	31N11	85w15	5:41:00
Barfield 14	1	33N18	85w45	5:43:00
Barlow 65	1	31N38	88w20	5:53:20
Barlow Bend 13	1	31N32	87w53	5:51:32
Barnesville 47	1	34N08	87w59	5:51:56
Barnett Chapel 35	1	34N08	87w15	5:49:00
Barnett Crossroads 27	1	31N05	87w04	5:48:16
Barney 64	1	33N46	87w11	5:48:44
Barnwell 2	1	30N31	87w54	5:51:36
Barrytown 12	1	31N53	88w20	5:53:20
Barton 17	1	34N44	87w54	5:51:36
Bartonville 37	6	33N35	86w46	5:47:04
Basham 52	1	34N27	86w57	5:47:48
Bashi 13	1	31N55	87w45	5:51:00
Basin 16	1	31N25	86w04	5:44:16
Bass 36	1	34N53	85w50	5:43:20
Bassetts Creek 65	1	31N27	88w02	5:52:08
Batesville 3	1	32N01	85w19	5:41:16
Battens Crossroads 16	1	31N11	85w52	5:43:28
Battleground 22	1	34N14	86w52	5:47:28
Battles Wharf 2	1	30N31	87w54	5:51:36
Bay Minette 2	1	30N53	87w46	5:51:04
Bayou La Batre 49	1	30N24	88w15	5:53:00
Bay Springs 10	1	34N09	85w41	5:42:44
Bayview 37	1	33N36	86w57	5:47:48
Bazemore 29	1	33N53	87w42	5:50:48
Beamon 23	1	31N24	85w41	5:42:44
Bean Rock 48	1	34N24	86w27	5:45:48
Bear Creek 47	1	34N13	87w43	5:50:52
Beasons Mill 15	1	33N38	85w35	5:42:20
Beatrice 50	1	31N44	87w13	5:48:52
Beaty Crossroads 25	1	34N38	85w45	5:43:00
Beaverton 38	1	33N56	88w01	5:52:04
Beaver Town 54	1	33N08	88w10	5:52:40
Beck 20	1	31N17	86w27	5:45:48
Bel Air 49	1	30N40	88w06	5:52:24
Belforest 2	1	30N36	87w54	5:51:36
Belfountain 2	1	30N37	87w20	5:49:20
Belgreen 30	1	34N30	87w44	5:50:56
Belk 29	1	33N39	87w56	5:51:44
Bellamy 60	1	32N27	88w08	5:52:32
Bellefonte 36	1	34N43	85w58	5:43:52
Bellefountaine 49	1	30N37	88w12	5:52:48
Belle Mina 42	1	34N39	86w53	5:47:32
Belleville 18	1	31N26	86w56	5:47:44
Bellevue 28	6	33N57	86w01	5:44:04
Bell Springs 52	1	34N22	86w54	5:47:36
Bellview 66	1	31N50	87w23	5:49:32
Bellwood 31	1	31N10	85w48	5:43:12
Bellwood 37	1	33N28	86w56	5:47:44
Belmont 60	1	32N32	87w59	5:51:56
Beloit 24	1	32N26	87w14	5:48:56
Belview Heights 17	1	34N44	87w42	5:50:48
Bemiston 61	1	33N26	86w06	5:44:24
Benevola 54	1	33N20	87w54	5:51:36
Benoit 64	1	33N46	87w11	5:48:44
Bentley Hills 37	6	33N29	86w46	5:47:04
Benton 43	1	32N19	86w49	5:47:16
Ben Vines Gap 37	1	33N33	86w59	5:47:56
Berkley 45	2	34N42	86w22	5:45:28
Berlin 22	1	34N11	86w48	5:47:12

ALABAMA

Bermuda 18	1	31N26	86w56	5:47:44
Bermuda 50	1	31N31	87w20	5:49:20
Berry 29	1	33N40	87w36	5:50:24
Bertha 23	1	31N25	85w20	5:41:20
Bessemer 37	1	33N24	86w58	5:47:52
Bessemer Gardens 37	1	33N26	86w57	5:47:48
Bessemer Homestead 37	1	33N26	86w57	5:47:48
Bethany 63	1	33N15	87w41	5:50:44
Bethel 22	1	34N11	86w48	5:47:12
Bethel 42	1	34N56	86w59	5:47:56
Bethel Grove 1	1	32N33	86w50	5:47:20
Bethlehem 51	1	31N58	86w17	5:45:08
Beulah 20	1	31N17	86w15	5:45:00
Beulah 32	1	32N54	87w47	5:51:08
Beulah 41	5	32N47	85w09	5:40:36
Bevelle 62	1	32N59	85w52	5:43:28
Bexar 47	1	34N11	88w09	5:52:36
Bibbville 4	1	33N13	87w09	5:48:36
Biddle Crossroads 25	1	34N38	85w45	5:43:00
Bigbee 65	1	31N37	88w10	5:52:40
Big Creek 35	1	31N15	85w26	5:41:44
Big Springs 4	1	33N13	87w09	5:48:36
Billingsley 1	1	32N37	86w46	5:47:04
Billy Goat Hill 10	1	34N09	85w41	5:42:44
Birdine 32	1	32N39	87w53	5:51:32
Birdsong 22	1	34N11	86w48	5:47:12
Birmingham 37	6	33N31	86w48	5:47:12
Bishop 17	1	34N46	87w58	5:51:52
Biven 37	6	33N34	86w52	5:47:28
Black 31	1	31N01	85w44	5:42:56
Black Diamond 37	1	33N26	86w57	5:47:48
Black Rock 21	1	31N44	86w19	5:45:16
Blacksher 2	1	30N54	87w47	5:51:08
Blackwood 34	1	31N22	85w20	5:41:20
Bladon Springs 12	1	31N44	88w12	5:52:48
Blanche 10	1	34N22	85w37	5:42:28
Blanton 41	5	32N47	85w09	5:40:36
Bleecker 41	7	32N35	85w10	5:40:40
Blossburg 37	1	33N36	86w58	5:47:52
Blount Springs 5	1	33N53	86w45	5:47:00
Blountsville 5	1	34N05	86w35	5:46:20
Blow Gourd 5	1	33N59	86w35	5:46:20
Blue Creek 37	1	33N26	86w57	5:47:48
Blue Creek Junction 37	1	33N26	86w57	5:47:48
Blue Mountain 8	6	33N41	85w50	5:43:20
Blue Pond 10	1	34N13	85w36	5:42:24
Blue Ridge Estates 37	6	33N25	86w48	5:47:12
Blues Old Stand 6	1	31N57	85w42	5:42:48
Blue Spring 45	2	34N46	86w37	5:46:28
Blue Springs 3	1	31N40	85w31	5:42:04
Blue Springs 5	1	34N05	86w35	5:46:20
Blue Springs 20	1	31N17	86w15	5:45:00
Bluff 29	1	33N41	87w50	5:51:20
Bluff Park 37	1	33N25	86w50	5:47:20
Bluff Spring 14	1	33N16	85w50	5:43:20
Bluff Springs 16	1	31N25	86w04	5:44:16
Bluffton 10	1	33N57	85w23	5:41:32
Boar Tush 67	1	34N14	87w37	5:50:28
Boaz 48	1	34N12	86w10	5:44:40
Bobo 29	1	33N55	87w48	5:51:12
Bobo 45	2	34N54	86w44	5:46:56
Boiling Springs 8	1	33N47	86w01	5:44:04
Boldo 64	1	33N50	87w17	5:49:08
Boley Springs 29	1	33N40	87w36	5:50:24
Boligee 32	1	32N45	88w02	5:52:08
Bolinger 12	1	31N47	88w20	5:53:20
Bolivar 36	1	34N59	85w46	5:43:04
Bolling 7	1	31N43	86w42	5:46:48
Bomar 10	1	34N09	85w41	5:42:44
Bon-air 37	1	33N26	86w57	5:47:48
Bon Air 61	1	33N16	86w20	5:45:20
Bon Secour 2	1	30N19	87w44	5:50:56
Booth 1	1	32N30	86w35	5:46:20
Boot Hill 55	1	31N47	85w33	5:42:12
Boozer Heights 8	6	33N40	85w50	5:43:20
Borden Springs 15	1	33N56	85w28	5:41:52
Borden Wheeler Springs 15	1	33N44	85w26	5:41:44
Borom 44	1	32N14	85w25	5:41:40
Boston 47	1	34N01	87w46	5:51:04
Boswell 6	1	31N48	85w56	5:43:44
Bowles 18	1	31N26	86w56	5:47:44
Bowmans Crossroads 25	1	34N36	85w55	5:43:40
Boyd 60	1	32N36	88w12	5:52:48
Boyd Crossing 63	1	33N05	87w14	5:48:56
Boykin 27	1	31N05	87w04	5:48:16
Boykin 66	1	32N05	87w17	5:49:08
Boylston 51	4	32N25	86w17	5:45:08
Boys Ranch 24	1	32N05	87w00	5:48:00
Bradford 19	1	32N59	86w08	5:44:32
Bradley 27	1	31N02	86w43	5:46:52
Bradleyton 21	1	31N57	86w19	5:45:16
Braggs 43	1	32N05	87w00	5:48:00
Branchville 58	1	33N40	86w26	5:45:44
Brandontown 45	2	34N43	86w38	5:46:32
Brannon Springs 28	1	33N47	86w01	5:44:04
Brannon Stand 35	1	31N15	85w26	5:41:44
Brantley 21	1	31N35	86w16	5:45:04
Brantley 24	1	32N23	87w00	5:48:00
Brantleyville 59	1	33N12	86w52	5:47:28
Brassell 51	1	32N17	86w06	5:44:24
Bremen 22	1	33N59	86w58	5:47:52
Brent 4	1	32N56	87w10	5:48:40
Brentwood Hills 37	6	33N25	86w48	5:47:12
Brewersville 60	1	32N29	88w04	5:52:16
Brewton 27	1	31N07	87w04	5:48:16
Briar Hill 55	1	31N43	86w07	5:44:28
Brick 17	1	34N45	87w41	5:50:44
Brickyard 57	7	32N24	85w01	5:40:04
Bridgeport 36	1	34N57	85w43	5:42:52
Bridlewood Forest Estates 37	1	33N37	86w41	5:46:44
Brierfield 4	1	33N02	86w55	5:47:40
Brighton 37	1	33N27	86w56	5:47:44
Brilliant 47	1	34N01	87w46	5:51:04
Brisco Store 36	1	34N53	85w50	5:43:20
Broadmoor 37	1	33N26	86w57	5:47:48
Brompton 58	1	33N33	86w32	5:46:08
Brookland 16	1	31N13	86w10	5:44:40
Brooklyn 16	1	31N17	86w15	5:45:00
Brooklyn 18	1	31N16	86w46	5:47:04
Brooklyn 22	1	34N10	86w37	5:46:28
Brooks 20	1	31N29	86w41	5:46:44
Brookside 37	1	33N38	86w55	5:47:40
Brooksville 5	1	34N10	86w29	5:45:56
Brooksville 52	1	34N28	86w48	5:47:12
Brookwood 63	1	33N17	87w18	5:49:12
Brookwood Forest 42	1	34N48	86w58	5:47:52
Brookwood Village Mall 37	6	33N27	86w49	5:47:16
Broomtown 10	1	34N16	85w34	5:42:16
Broughton 56	1	33N09	85w22	5:41:28
Browns 24	1	32N26	87w23	5:49:32
Brownsboro 45	2	34N45	86w27	5:45:48
Browns Corner 45	2	34N54	86w44	5:46:56
Browns Crossroads 23	1	31N24	85w41	5:42:44
Browntown 36	1	34N38	85w45	5:43:00
Brownville 14	1	33N04	86w03	5:44:12
Brownville 18	1	31N26	86w56	5:47:44
Brownville 37	1	33N27	86w54	5:47:36
Brownville 63	6	33N14	87w36	5:50:24
Bruceville 6	1	32N08	85w43	5:42:52
Brundidge 55	1	31N43	85w49	5:43:16
Brunnet Heights 37	6	33N35	86w46	5:47:04
Bryant 36	1	34N24	85w42	5:42:48
Buchanan Peninsula 17	1	34N46	87w58	5:51:52
Buckhorn 45	2	34N55	86w26	5:45:44
Buckhorn 55	1	31N49	85w51	5:43:24
Bucks 49	1	31N01	88w01	5:52:04
Bucksnort 48	1	34N31	86w15	5:45:00
Buena Vista 50	1	31N48	87w15	5:49:00
Buena Vista Highlands 37	6	33N27	86w49	5:47:16
Buffalo 9	5	32N54	85w24	5:41:36
Buggs Chapel 45	2	34N35	86w28	5:45:52
Buhl 63	1	33N10	87w51	5:51:24
Bullock 21	1	31N35	86w15	5:45:00
Burchfield 63	1	33N19	87w19	5:49:16
Burgreen Corners 42	1	34N41	86w41	5:46:44
Burks Gardens 63	6	33N12	87w32	5:50:08
Burkville 43	1	32N20	86w32	5:46:08
Burl 66	1	31N50	87w06	5:48:24
Burlington 26	1	32N31	85w53	5:43:32
Burns 8	1	33N56	85w37	5:42:28
Burnsville 24	1	32N28	86w53	5:47:32
Burnt Corn 50	1	31N33	87w10	5:48:40
Burntout 30	1	34N22	88w03	5:52:12
Burnwell 64	1	33N42	87w05	5:48:20
Bushy Creek 7	1	31N38	86w44	5:46:56
Bushy Pond 22	1	33N54	86w58	5:47:52
Butler 12	1	32N05	88w13	5:52:52
Butler Springs 7	1	31N52	86w50	5:47:20
Buttston 62	1	32N50	85w45	5:43:00
Buyck 26	1	32N43	86w19	5:45:16
Bynum 8	1	33N37	85w58	5:43:52
Caddo 40	1	34N35	87w06	5:48:24
Caffee Junction 63	1	33N20	87w01	5:48:04
Cahaba 24	1	32N19	87w17	5:49:08
Cahaba Crest 37	1	33N37	86w37	5:46:28
Cahaba Heights 37	6	33N28	86w45	5:47:00
Cahaba Hills 37	1	33N33	86w32	5:46:08
Cahaba Mall 37	6	33N28	86w45	5:47:00
Cahaba River Estates 59	1	33N26	86w57	5:47:48
Calcis 59	1	33N24	86w25	5:45:40
Caldwell 58	1	33N46	86w29	5:45:56
Caledonia 66	1	31N50	87w06	5:48:24
Calera 59	1	33N06	86w45	5:47:00
Calhoun 43	1	32N03	86w33	5:46:12
Calumet 64	1	33N44	87w17	5:49:08
Calvert 65	1	31N09	88w01	5:52:04
Camden 66	1	31N59	87w17	5:49:08
Cameronsville 36	1	34N53	85w50	5:43:20
Campbell 13	1	31N55	87w59	5:51:56
Campbells Crossroads 14	1	33N18	85w45	5:43:00
Campbellville 64	1	33N43	87w00	5:48:00
Camp Hill 62	1	32N48	85w39	5:42:36
Camp Oliver 37	1	33N46	87w20	5:49:20
Canoe 27	1	31N02	87w31	5:50:04
Canton Bend 66	1	32N00	87w18	5:49:12
Capell 66	1	32N00	87w18	5:49:12
Capital Heights 51	4	32N23	86w16	5:45:04
Capps 34	1	31N25	85w20	5:41:20
Capshaw 42	1	34N48	86w51	5:47:24
Carbon Hill 64	1	33N53	87w32	5:50:08
Cardiff 37	1	33N39	86w56	5:47:44
Carlisle 28	1	34N10	86w09	5:44:36
Carlowville 24	1	32N08	87w00	5:48:00
Carlton 13	1	31N21	87w51	5:51:24
Carns 36	1	34N47	85w55	5:43:40
Carolina 20	1	31N14	86w31	5:46:04
Carolyn 51	4	32N21	86w17	5:45:08
Carpenter 2	1	30N54	87w47	5:51:08
Carriger 42	1	34N48	86w58	5:47:52
Carr Mill 14	1	33N16	85w50	5:43:20
Carrollton 54	1	33N16	88w06	5:52:24
Carrville 62	1	32N32	85w52	5:43:28
Carson 65	1	31N30	87w59	5:51:56
Carter Grove 45	2	34N56	86w34	5:46:16
Cartwright 42	1	34N56	86w59	5:47:56
Carver Court 44	1	32N25	85w42	5:42:48
Casemore 33	1	32N30	87w43	5:50:52
Casey 24	1	32N23	87w00	5:48:00
Castleberry 18	1	31N18	87w01	5:48:04
Catalpa 55	1	31N48	85w56	5:43:44
Catherine 66	1	32N11	87w28	5:49:52
Catherwood Park 37	1	33N32	86w57	5:47:48
Catoma 51	4	32N22	86w20	5:45:20
Cave Spring 28	6	34N01	86w04	5:44:16
Cave Spring 45	2	34N35	86w28	5:45:52
Cave Springs 17	1	34N44	87w42	5:50:48
Cecil 51	1	32N18	86w01	5:44:04
Cedar Bluff 10	1	34N13	85w37	5:42:28
Cedar Cove 63	1	33N11	87w27	5:49:48
Cedar Fork 13	1	31N39	87w42	5:50:48
Cedar Grove 20	1	31N17	86w27	5:45:48
Cedar Grove 36	1	34N53	85w50	5:43:20
Cedar Hill 29	1	33N41	87w50	5:51:20
Cedar Hill 42	1	34N59	86w51	5:47:24
Cedar Hill Estates 17	1	34N44	87w42	5:50:48
Cedar Lake 52	3	34N33	86w59	5:47:56
Cedar Plains 52	1	34N22	86w54	5:47:36
Cedar Point 45	2	34N33	86w24	5:45:36
Cedar Springs 8	1	33N49	85w46	5:43:04
Center 67	1	34N14	87w37	5:50:28
Centercrest 37	1	33N37	86w41	5:46:44
Centergrove 52	1	34N28	86w48	5:47:12
Center Hill 22	1	34N04	86w46	5:47:04
Center Hill 39	1	34N58	87w22	5:49:28
Center Hill 42	1	34N54	86w44	5:46:56
Center Point 13	1	31N46	88w05	5:52:20
Center Point 37	1	33N38	86w41	5:46:44
Center Point Gardens 37	1	33N37	86w41	5:46:44
Center Springs 5	1	33N49	86w44	5:46:56
Center Star 39	1	34N52	87w32	5:50:08
Centerville 18	1	31N26	86w56	5:47:44
Centerwood Estates 37	1	33N37	86w41	5:46:44
Central 22	1	34N11	86w48	5:47:12
Central 26	1	32N41	86w06	5:44:24
Central City 16	1	31N19	85w49	5:43:16
Central Crossroads 36	1	34N38	85w45	5:43:00
Central Heights 39	1	34N49	87w40	5:50:40
Central Mills 24	1	32N17	87w22	5:49:28
Centre 10	1	34N09	85w41	5:42:44
Centreville 4	1	32N57	87w08	5:48:32
Ceramic 57	7	32N28	85w01	5:40:04
Chalkville 37	1	33N37	86w41	5:46:44
Chalybeate Springs 40	1	34N38	87w12	5:48:48
Champion 5	1	33N55	86w27	5:45:48
Chance 13	1	31N45	87w32	5:50:08
Chancellor 31	1	31N11	85w53	5:43:32
Chandler Springs 61	1	33N19	86w00	5:44:00
Chapel Hill 9	5	32N54	85w24	5:41:36
Chapel Hill 37	6	33N25	86w48	5:47:12
Chapman 7	1	31N40	86w43	5:46:52
Chase 45	2	34N47	86w33	5:46:12
Chastang 49	1	31N02	88w01	5:52:04
Chatom 65	1	31N28	88w16	5:53:04
Chelsea 59	1	33N20	86w38	5:46:32
Cherokee 17	1	34N45	87w58	5:51:52
Cherokee Bluffs 62	1	32N31	85w53	5:43:32
Cherokee Forest 37	6	33N29	86w46	5:47:04
Cherry Grove 42	1	34N48	86w58	5:47:52
Chesson 44	1	32N13	85w53	5:43:32
Chesterfield 10	1	34N29	85w29	5:41:56
Chestnut 50	1	31N45	87w13	5:48:52
Chestnut Grove 16	1	31N43	85w49	5:43:16
Chickasaw 49	1	30N46	88w05	5:52:20
Chickasaw Terrace 49	1	30N44	88w05	5:52:20
Chigger Hill 25	1	34N21	86w00	5:44:00
Childersburg 61	1	33N16	86w21	5:45:24
Chilton 13	1	31N42	87w46	5:51:04
China 18	1	31N26	86w56	5:47:44
China Grove 55	1	31N48	85w56	5:43:44
Chinneby 61	1	33N32	85w57	5:43:48
Choccolocco 8	1	33N41	85w41	5:42:44
Choctaw Bluff 13	1	31N22	87w46	5:51:04
Choctaw City 12	1	32N05	88w17	5:53:08
Choctow Corner 13	1	31N55	87w45	5:51:00
Chosea Springs 8	6	33N40	85w50	5:43:20
Christiana 56	1	33N26	85w41	5:42:44
Chrysler 50	1	31N18	87w42	5:50:48
Chulafinnee 15	1	33N38	85w35	5:42:20
Chunchula 49	1	30N55	88w12	5:52:48
Church Hill 62	1	32N44	85w37	5:42:28
Circlewood 63	6	33N12	87w32	5:50:08
Citronelle 49	1	31N06	88w14	5:52:56
Claiborne 50	1	31N33	87w31	5:50:04
Clairmont Springs 14	1	33N26	86w06	5:44:24
Clanton 11	1	32N51	86w38	5:46:32
Clarence 5	1	34N05	86w24	5:45:36
Clarksville 13	1	31N46	88w05	5:52:20
Claud 26	1	32N37	86w02	5:44:08
Clay 37	1	33N42	86w36	5:46:24
Clay City 2	1	30N31	87w54	5:51:36
Clayhatchee 23	1	31N19	85w43	5:42:52

Clayhill 46 1 31N55 87w45 5:51:00
Claysville 48 1 34N21 86w19 5:45:16
Clayton 3 1 31N53 85w27 5:41:48
Clear Springs 5 1 33N55 86w27 5:45:48
Clearview 20 1 31N30 86w22 5:45:28
Clearview 21 1 31N57 86w19 5:45:16
Cleveland 5 1 33N59 86w35 5:46:20
Cleveland 29 1 33N40 87w40 5:50:40
Cleveland Crossroads 14 1 33N04 86w03 5:44:12
Cliff Haven 17 1 34N45 87w41 5:50:44
Clinton 32 1 32N55 88w00 5:52:00
Clintonville 16 1 31N23 85w56 5:43:44
Clio 3 1 31N43 85w37 5:42:28
Clopton 23 1 31N37 85w26 5:41:44
Cloverdale 39 1 34N56 87w46 5:51:04
Cloverdale 63 6 33N12 87w32 5:50:08
Cloverdale Heights 39 1 34N49 87w40 5:50:40
Cloverland 51 4 32N20 86w19 5:45:16
Clubview Heights 28 6 33N57 86w01 5:44:04
Cluttsville 45 2 34N51 86w45 5:47:00
Coal Bluff 66 1 31N58 87w38 5:50:32
Coalburg 37 6 33N35 86w52 5:47:28
Coal City 58 1 33N40 86w17 5:45:08
Coal Fire 54 1 33N23 88w01 5:52:04
Coaling 63 1 33N10 87w20 5:49:20
Coalmont 59 1 33N12 86w52 5:47:28
Coal Valley 64 1 33N46 87w23 5:49:32
Coatopa 60 1 32N29 88w04 5:52:16
Cobb City 8 1 33N59 85w55 5:43:40
Cobbs Ford 26 4 32N27 86w19 5:45:16
Cobb Town 8 6 33N40 85w50 5:43:20
Cochrane 54 1 33N04 88w15 5:53:00
Coden 49 1 30N23 88w14 5:52:56
Cody 38 1 33N41 87w50 5:51:20
Coffee Springs 31 1 31N10 85w55 5:43:40
Coffeeville 13 1 31N45 88w05 5:52:20
Cohasset 18 1 31N24 86w37 5:46:28
Coker 63 1 33N15 87w41 5:50:44
Colbert Heights 17 1 34N44 87w42 5:50:48
Cold Springs 22 1 33N54 86w58 5:47:52
Cold Springs 26 1 32N37 86w24 5:45:36
Cold Springs 52 1 34N22 86w54 5:47:36
Coldwater 8 1 33N36 86w01 5:44:04
Coldwater 15 1 33N44 85w26 5:41:44
Collbran 25 1 34N23 85w47 5:43:08
Collins Chapel 11 1 32N51 86w38 5:46:32
Collinsville 25 1 34N16 85w52 5:43:28
Collirene 43 1 32N19 86w49 5:47:16
Coloma 10 1 34N09 85w41 5:42:44
Colonial Heights 17 1 34N44 87w42 5:50:48
Colony 63 6 33N14 87w36 5:50:24
Columbia 35 1 31N18 85w07 5:40:28
Columbiana 59 1 33N11 86w36 5:46:24
Columbus City 48 1 34N21 86w19 5:45:16
Colwell 8 1 33N59 85w55 5:43:40
Comer 3 1 32N02 85w23 5:41:32
Concord 5 1 33N59 86w35 5:46:20
Concord 37 1 33N26 86w57 5:47:48
Congo 10 1 34N13 85w36 5:42:24
Conifer 26 1 32N31 85w53 5:43:32
Consul 46 1 32N13 87w26 5:49:44
Cooks Springs 58 1 33N36 86w23 5:45:32
Cool Springs 58 1 33N43 86w24 5:45:36
Coon Creek 64 1 33N43 87w00 5:48:00
Cooper 11 1 32N47 86w33 5:46:12
Coosa Court 61 1 33N16 86w21 5:45:24
Coosada 26 1 32N30 86w20 5:45:20
Coosa River 26 1 32N37 86w24 5:45:36
Copeland 65 1 31N38 88w20 5:53:20
Copeland Bridge 25 1 34N14 85w51 5:43:24
Copper Springs 58 1 33N40 86w25 5:45:40
Coppinville 16 1 31N19 85w49 5:43:16
Corcoran 55 1 31N48 85w56 5:43:44
Cordova 64 1 33N46 87w11 5:48:44
Corinth 6 1 31N48 85w56 5:43:44
Corinth 22 1 34N14 86w52 5:47:28
Corinth 56 1 33N18 85w29 5:41:56
Corner 37 1 33N15 86w48 5:47:12
Cornhouse 56 1 33N09 85w22 5:41:28
Cornwall Furnace 10 1 34N13 85w36 5:42:24
Corona 64 1 33N40 87w36 5:50:24
Cortelyou 65 1 31N27 88w02 5:52:08
Cotaco 52 1 34N28 86w48 5:47:12
Cottage Grove 19 1 34N18 86w33 5:46:12
Cottage Hill 37 1 33N30 86w58 5:47:52
Cottage Hill 49 1 30N39 88w09 5:52:36
Cottondale 63 1 33N11 87w27 5:49:48
Cottonton 57 7 32N09 85w04 5:40:16
Cottontown 17 1 34N42 87w34 5:50:16
Cotton Valley 44 1 32N26 85w42 5:42:48
Cottonwood 35 1 31N03 85w18 5:41:12
Country Club Acres 42 1 34N48 86w58 5:47:52
Country Club Highlands 37 6 33N25 86w48 5:47:12
County Line 5 1 33N49 86w43 5:46:52
County Line 20 1 31N13 86w10 5:44:40
County Line 55 1 31N40 86w10 5:44:40
Courtland 40 1 34N40 87w19 5:49:16
Covin 29 1 33N41 87w50 5:51:20
Cowarts 35 1 31N12 85w18 5:41:12
Coxey 42 1 34N48 86w58 5:47:52
Coy 66 1 31N54 87w28 5:49:52
Cragford 14 1 33N15 85w40 5:42:40
Craig 24 1 32N22 86w59 5:47:56
Craig Air Force Base 24 1 32N23 87w00 5:48:00
Crane Hill 22 1 34N04 87w03 5:48:12

ALABAMA

Crawford 57 7 32N27 85w11 5:40:44
Creek Stand 44 1 32N08 85w43 5:42:52
Creel Town 64 1 33N43 87w00 5:48:00
Creola 49 1 30N54 88w03 5:52:12
Crescent Heights 37 1 33N26 86w57 5:47:48
Crestline 37 6 33N29 86w46 5:47:04
Crestline Heights 37 6 33N31 86w45 5:47:00
Crestview Gardens 58 1 33N35 86w23 5:45:32
Creswell 59 1 33N21 86w27 5:45:48
Crews 38 1 33N54 88w08 5:52:32
Crichton 49 1 30N42 88w06 5:52:24
Cromwell 12 1 32N14 88w17 5:53:08
Crooked Oak 17 1 34N44 87w42 5:50:48
Cropwell 58 1 33N33 86w16 5:45:04
Crosby 35 1 31N09 85w06 5:40:24
Cross Key 42 1 34N56 86w59 5:47:56
Crossroads 2 1 30N54 87w47 5:51:08
Cross Roads 13 1 31N37 88w01 5:52:04
Crossroads 48 1 34N21 86w19 5:45:16
Crosston 37 1 33N41 86w41 5:46:44
Crossville 38 1 33N45 88w00 5:52:00
Crudup 28 6 34N01 86w04 5:44:16
Crumley Chapel 37 6 33N34 86w52 5:47:28
Cuba 60 1 32N26 88w23 5:53:32
Cullman 22 1 34N11 86w51 5:47:24
Cullomburg 12 1 31N43 88w18 5:53:12
Cunningham 13 1 31N55 87w59 5:51:56
Cunningham 54 1 33N08 88w10 5:52:40
Curry 61 1 33N29 86w01 5:44:04
Curry 64 1 33N50 87w17 5:49:08
Currytown 23 1 31N19 85w29 5:41:56
Curtis 16 1 31N25 86w04 5:44:16
Curtiston 28 6 34N01 86w04 5:44:16
Cusseta 9 5 32N47 85w19 5:41:16
Cypress 33 1 32N57 87w40 5:50:40
Cypress Heights 39 1 34N49 87w40 5:50:40
Cyril 12 1 32N15 88w23 5:53:32
Dadeville 62 1 32N50 85w46 5:43:04
Daleville 23 1 31N19 85w43 5:42:52
Dallas 5 1 33N49 86w44 5:46:56
Damascus 16 1 31N25 86w04 5:44:16
Damascus 27 1 31N05 87w04 5:48:16
Dancy 54 1 33N08 88w10 5:52:40
Danley 16 1 31N25 86w04 5:44:16
Danville 37 6 33N35 86w46 5:47:04
Danville 52 1 34N25 87w03 5:48:12
Danway 9 5 32N38 85w23 5:41:32
Daphne 2 1 30N36 87w54 5:51:36
Dargin 59 1 33N06 86w45 5:47:00
Darlington 66 1 31N59 87w08 5:48:32
Dauphin Island 49 1 30N15 88w07 5:52:28
Daviston 62 1 33N01 85w38 5:42:32
Davisville 44 1 32N26 85w42 5:42:48
Dawes 49 1 30N41 88w06 5:52:24
Dawson 25 1 34N18 85w56 5:43:44
Dayton 46 1 32N21 87w38 5:50:32
De Armanville 8 1 33N38 85w45 5:43:00
Deason Hill 64 1 33N46 87w11 5:48:44
Deatsville 26 1 32N37 86w24 5:45:36
Deavertown 5 1 33N59 86w35 5:46:20
Decatur 52 3 34N36 86w59 5:47:56
Deer Park 65 1 31N13 88w02 5:52:08
Defoor 67 1 34N14 87w37 5:50:28
Delchamps 49 1 30N23 88w14 5:52:56
Delmar 67 1 34N05 87w36 5:50:24
Delta 14 1 33N26 85w42 5:42:48
Demopolis 46 1 32N31 87w50 5:51:20
Dempsey 30 1 34N30 87w44 5:50:56
Deposit 45 2 34N55 86w26 5:45:44
Detroit 38 1 34N02 88w10 5:52:40
Devenport 43 1 32N08 86w29 5:45:56
Dexter 26 1 32N31 86w12 5:44:48
Diamond 48 1 34N21 86w19 5:45:16
Dickert 56 1 33N07 85w34 5:42:16
Dickinson 13 1 31N46 87w43 5:50:52
Dillard 23 1 31N24 85w41 5:42:44
Dilworth 64 1 33N43 87w00 5:48:00
Dime 30 1 31N55 87w59 5:51:56
Dixiana 37 1 33N44 86w42 5:46:48
Dixie 27 1 31N09 86w44 5:46:56
Dixieland 57 7 32N28 85w01 5:40:04
Dixon Corner 49 1 30N31 88w14 5:52:56
Dixons Mills 46 1 32N04 87w47 5:51:08
Dixonville 27 1 31N05 87w04 5:48:16
Docena 37 1 33N34 86w55 5:47:40
Dock 7 1 31N50 86w38 5:46:32
Dog 25 1 34N24 85w41 5:42:44
Dogtown 64 1 33N54 87w31 5:50:04
Dogwood 25 1 34N27 85w43 5:42:52
Dolcito 37 6 33N35 86w46 5:47:04
Doliska 64 1 33N46 87w20 5:49:20
Dolomite 37 1 33N27 86w58 5:47:52
Dolonah 37 1 33N26 86w57 5:47:48
Dora 64 1 33N44 87w05 5:48:20
Doster 3 1 31N36 85w43 5:42:52
Dothan 35 1 31N13 85w24 5:41:36
Double Bridges 34 1 31N33 85w15 5:41:00
Double Bridges 48 1 34N10 86w09 5:44:36
Doublehead 9 5 33N01 85w21 5:41:24
Double Springs 67 1 34N09 87w24 5:49:36
Douglas 25 1 34N27 85w43 5:42:52
Douglas 48 1 34N11 86w21 5:45:24
Downing 51 1 32N10 86w00 5:44:00
Downs 44 1 32N17 85w51 5:43:24
Dozier 21 1 31N30 86w22 5:45:28
Drewry 50 1 31N31 87w20 5:49:20
Drummond 64 1 33N43 87w00 5:48:00
Dry Forks 66 1 32N00 87w18 5:49:12
Dry Valley 61 1 33N37 86w07 5:44:28
Dublin 51 1 32N03 86w13 5:44:52
Ducksprings 28 6 34N01 86w04 5:44:16

Dudley 63 1 33N05 87w14 5:48:56
Dudleyville 62 1 32N48 85w39 5:42:36
Duke 8 1 33N49 85w54 5:43:36
Dulin 47 1 33N55 87w48 5:51:12
Duncan Crossroads 36 1 34N35 85w59 5:43:56
Duncanville 63 1 33N04 87w27 5:49:48
Dundee 31 1 31N06 85w42 5:42:48
Dunn 55 1 31N48 85w56 5:43:44
Dunns 20 1 31N17 86w27 5:45:48
Dupree 35 1 31N11 85w15 5:41:00
Dutton 36 1 34N36 85w55 5:43:40
Duval 20 1 31N17 86w15 5:45:00
Dyas 2 1 30N58 87w41 5:50:44
Dyers Crossroads 22 1 34N11 86w48 5:47:12
Eady City 9 5 32N49 85w10 5:40:40
Earlytown 31 1 31N13 86w10 5:44:40
Eastaboga 8 1 33N36 86w01 5:44:04
East Brewton 27 1 31N06 87w04 5:48:16
Eastbrook 51 4 32N23 86w15 5:45:00
East Brookwood 63 1 33N17 87w17 5:49:08
Eastern Valley 37 1 33N26 86w57 5:47:48
East Escambia 27 1 31N06 86w55 5:47:40
East Florence 39 1 34N49 87w40 5:50:40
East Gadsden 28 1 33N59 85w57 5:43:48
East Hampton 42 1 34N48 86w58 5:47:52
East Haven 37 1 33N37 86w41 5:46:44
East Irondale 37 1 33N32 86w42 5:46:48
East Jasper 64 1 33N50 87w14 5:48:56
East Killen 39 1 34N52 87w32 5:50:08
East Lake 37 6 33N34 86w44 5:46:56
East Point 22 1 34N11 86w48 5:47:12
East Side 63 6 33N12 87w32 5:50:08
East Tallassee 62 1 32N32 85w53 5:43:32
Eastwood 5 1 33N55 86w27 5:45:48
Ebenezer 22 1 34N14 86w52 5:47:28
Echo 23 1 31N29 85w28 5:41:52
Echola 63 1 33N21 87w41 5:50:44
Echols Crossroads 52 1 34N28 86w48 5:47:12
Eclectic 26 1 32N39 86w02 5:44:08
Eddy 48 1 34N19 86w30 5:46:00
Eden 58 1 33N35 86w23 5:45:32
Edgefield 3 1 31N52 85w27 5:41:48
Edgefield 36 1 34N53 85w50 5:43:20
Edgemont 37 6 33N27 86w49 5:47:16
Edgemont Park 37 6 33N27 86w49 5:47:16
Edgemoor Estates 37 6 33N27 86w49 5:47:16
Edgewater 37 1 33N31 86w56 5:47:44
Edgewood 37 6 33N27 86w49 5:47:16
Edna 12 1 32N22 88w17 5:53:08
Edwardsville 15 1 33N43 85w31 5:42:04
Edwin 34 1 31N37 85w26 5:41:44
Egypt 28 1 34N04 86w21 5:45:24
Eight Mile 49 1 30N50 88w13 5:52:52
Elamville 3 1 31N36 85w43 5:42:52
Elba 16 1 31N25 86w04 5:44:16
Elberta 2 1 30N25 87w31 5:50:04
Eldridge 64 1 33N55 87w37 5:50:28
Elgin 39 1 34N50 87w20 5:49:20
Eliska 50 1 31N18 87w30 5:50:00
Elkmont 42 1 34N56 86w58 5:47:52
Elkwood 45 1 34N59 86w51 5:47:24
Ellards 53 1 32N56 87w10 5:48:40
Elliotsville 59 1 33N12 86w47 5:47:08
Ellisville 2 1 30N37 87w45 5:51:00
Ellisville 10 1 34N09 85w41 5:42:44
Elmore 26 1 32N32 86w19 5:45:16
Elrod 63 1 33N15 87w48 5:51:12
Elsanor 2 1 30N33 87w42 5:50:48
Elsmeade 51 4 32N20 86w16 5:45:04
Elting 39 1 34N49 87w40 5:50:40
Emelle 60 1 32N44 88w19 5:53:16
Emerald Shores 39 1 34N49 87w40 5:50:40
Empire 64 1 33N49 87w00 5:48:00
Englewood 63 6 33N09 87w35 5:50:20
English Village 37 6 33N29 86w46 5:47:04
Enon 6 1 32N05 85w31 5:42:04
Enon 22 1 34N14 86w52 5:47:28
Enon 35 1 31N16 85w16 5:41:04
Enon 55 1 31N49 85w51 5:43:24
Ensley 37 6 33N31 86w53 5:47:32
Enterprise 11 1 32N45 86w31 5:46:04
Enterprise 16 1 31N19 85w51 5:43:24
Eoda 20 1 31N17 86w27 5:45:48
Eoline 4 1 33N00 87w14 5:48:56
Epes 60 1 32N42 88w07 5:52:28
Equality 19 1 32N46 86w06 5:44:24
Erin 14 1 33N18 85w45 5:43:00
Escatawpa 65 1 31N16 88w21 5:53:24
Estelle 66 1 32N00 87w18 5:49:12
Estes Crossroads 10 1 33N56 85w37 5:42:28
Estillfork 36 1 34N55 86w10 5:44:40
Ethel 55 1 31N49 85w51 5:43:24
Ethelsville 54 1 33N25 88w13 5:52:52
Euclid Estates 37 6 33N29 86w46 5:47:04
Eufaula 3 1 31N54 85w09 5:40:36
Eulaton 8 1 33N39 85w55 5:43:40
Eunola 31 1 31N02 85w50 5:43:20
Eureka 36 1 34N53 85w50 5:43:20
Eutaw 32 1 32N50 87w53 5:51:32
Eva 52 1 34N20 86w46 5:47:04
Evansboro 12 1 31N56 88w28 5:53:52
Evansville 33 1 32N53 87w44 5:50:56
Evergreen 1 1 32N39 86w43 5:46:52
Evergreen 18 1 31N26 86w57 5:47:48
Ewell 23 1 31N24 85w41 5:42:44
Excel 50 1 31N26 87w21 5:49:24
Exmoor 46 1 32N06 87w52 5:51:28
Fabius 36 1 34N49 85w47 5:43:08
Fackler 36 1 34N47 85w55 5:43:40

ALABAMA

Fadette 31	1	31N06	85w36	5:42:24
Fairdale 4	1	32N57	87w08	5:48:32
Fairfax 9	5	32N48	85w11	5:40:44
Fairfield 20	1	31N17	86w27	5:45:48
Fairfield 37	1	33N29	86w55	5:47:40
Fairfield 40	1	34N29	87w17	5:49:08
Fairfield Highlands 37	1	33N28	86w55	5:47:40
Fairfield Village 37	1	33N28	86w56	5:47:44
Fairford 65	1	31N16	88w02	5:52:08
Fairhope 2	1	30N31	87w54	5:51:36
Fairmont 42	1	34N48	86w58	5:47:52
Fairoaks 60	1	32N57	88w16	5:53:04
Fairview 11	1	32N51	86w38	5:46:32
Fairview 18	1	31N26	86w56	5:47:44
Fairview 22	1	34N11	86w48	5:47:12
Fairview 25	1	34N18	85w56	5:43:44
Fairview 37	6	33N30	86w52	5:47:28
Fairview 42	1	34N48	86w58	5:47:52
Fairview 45	2	34N55	86w26	5:45:44
Fairview 47	1	34N16	87w50	5:51:20
Fairview 52	3	34N33	86w59	5:47:56
Fairview 58	1	33N45	86w09	5:44:36
Fairview 67	1	34N12	87w11	5:48:44
Fairview West 22	1	34N04	86w46	5:47:04
Falco 20	1	31N06	86w36	5:46:24
Falkville 52	1	34N22	86w55	5:47:40
Fannie 27	1	31N00	87w15	5:49:00
Farill 10	1	34N13	85w36	5:42:24
Farley 45	2	34N41	86w34	5:46:16
Farmersville 43	1	32N05	86w54	5:47:36
Farmville 41	5	32N38	85w23	5:41:32
Fatama 66	1	32N00	87w18	5:49:12
Faunsdale 46	1	32N25	87w36	5:50:24
Fayette 29	1	33N41	87w50	5:51:20
Fayetteville 61	1	33N09	86w24	5:45:36
Fergusons Cross Roads 58	1	34N00	86w15	5:45:00
Fernbank 38	1	33N35	88w09	5:52:36
Fernland 49	1	30N29	88w21	5:53:24
Fernwood Estates 37	1	33N37	86w41	5:46:44
Finchburg 50	1	31N43	87w25	5:49:40
Finley Crossing 13	1	31N55	87w45	5:51:00
Fisher Crossroads 25	1	34N27	85w43	5:42:52
Fishhead 14	1	33N26	85w41	5:42:44
Fish Pond 40	1	34N38	87w12	5:48:48
Fisk 45	2	34N56	86w34	5:46:16
Fitzpatrick 6	1	32N09	85w56	5:43:44
Five Points 5	1	33N59	86w35	5:46:20
Five Points 9	5	33N03	85w20	5:41:20
Five Points 15	1	33N38	85w35	5:42:20
Five Points 23	1	31N20	85w36	5:42:24
Five Points 24	1	32N19	87w17	5:49:08
Five Points 26	4	32N27	86w19	5:45:16
Five Points 35	1	31N02	85w24	5:41:36
Five Points 40	1	34N29	87w17	5:49:08
Five Points 45	2	34N54	86w44	5:46:56
Five Points 48	1	34N21	86w19	5:45:16
Five Points 64	1	33N50	87w17	5:49:08
Five Points East 37	1	33N32	86w42	5:46:48
Flat Creek 64	1	33N46	87w20	5:49:20
Flat Rock 14	1	33N18	85w45	5:43:00
Flat Rock 36	1	34N46	85w42	5:42:48
Flatwood 51	4	32N25	86w17	5:45:08
Flatwood 64	1	33N54	87w31	5:50:04
Flatwood 66	1	32N09	87w31	5:50:04
Fleetwood 63	1	33N11	87w27	5:49:48
Fleta 51	1	32N16	86w23	5:45:32
Flint City 52	1	34N31	86w58	5:47:52
Flomaton 27	1	31N00	87w16	5:49:04
Florala 20	1	31N00	86w20	5:45:20
Floral Crest 36	1	34N24	85w42	5:42:48
Florence 39	1	34N48	87w41	5:50:44
Florette 52	1	34N28	86w48	5:47:12
Flower Hill 40	1	34N38	87w12	5:48:48
Floyd 26	1	32N37	86w02	5:44:08
Foley 2	1	30N24	87w41	5:50:44
Folsom 56	1	33N25	85w30	5:42:00
Ford City 17	1	34N45	87w41	5:50:44
Forest 54	1	33N25	88w13	5:52:52
Forest Brook Estates 37	6	33N25	86w48	5:47:12
Forestdale 37	1	33N35	86w55	5:47:40
Forester 1	1	32N28	86w27	5:45:48
Forester Chapel 56	1	33N07	85w34	5:42:16
Forest Hills 8	6	33N40	85w50	5:43:20
Forest Hills 37	1	33N28	86w56	5:47:44
Forest Hills 39	1	34N49	87w40	5:50:40
Forest Hills 61	1	33N16	86w21	5:45:24
Forest Home 7	1	31N52	86w50	5:47:20
Forkland 32	1	32N39	87w53	5:51:32
Forkville 67	1	34N14	87w37	5:50:28
Forney 10	1	34N05	85w28	5:41:52
Fort Benning 57	7	32N26	84w57	5:39:48
Fort Dale 7	1	31N50	86w38	5:46:32
Fort Davis 44	1	32N15	85w43	5:42:52
Fort Deposit 43	1	31N59	86w35	5:46:20
Fort McClellan 8	1	33N43	85w47	5:43:08
Fort Mitchell 57	7	32N20	85w01	5:40:04
Fort Morgan 2	1	30N14	88w01	5:52:04
Fort Payne 25	1	34N26	85w43	5:42:52
Fort Rucker 23	5	31N20	85w43	5:42:52
Fosheeton 62	1	33N46	85w53	5:43:32
Fosters 63	1	33N06	87w41	5:50:44
Fostoria 43	1	32N05	86w54	5:47:36
Fountain 50	1	31N36	87w25	5:49:40
Four Mile 59	1	33N15	86w30	5:46:00
Fowlers Crossroads 29	1	33N40	87w40	5:50:40
Fowl River 49	1	30N37	88w12	5:52:48
Fox 63	6	33N12	87w32	5:50:08
Frances Heights 37	6	33N37	86w48	5:47:12
Francisco 36	1	35N03	86w16	5:45:04
Francis Mill 8	1	33N47	86w01	5:44:04
Frankfort 30	1	34N30	87w44	5:50:56
Franklin 50	1	31N43	87w25	5:49:40
Frankville 65	1	31N39	88w09	5:52:36
Fredonia 9	5	33N01	85w21	5:41:24
Freemanville 27	1	31N01	87w30	5:50:00
Fremont 1	1	32N33	86w50	5:47:20
French Mill 42	1	34N48	86w58	5:47:52
Fresco 16	1	31N43	85w49	5:43:16
Fridays Crossing 5	1	33N55	86w27	5:45:48
Friendship 20	1	31N17	86w15	5:45:00
Friendship 26	1	32N31	85w53	5:43:32
Frisco City 50	1	31N26	87w24	5:49:36
Frost 4	1	32N57	87w08	5:48:32
Fruitdale 65	1	31N21	88w25	5:53:40
Fruithurst 15	1	33N44	85w26	5:41:44
Fullers Crossroads 21	1	31N43	86w16	5:45:04
Fullerton 10	1	34N16	85w34	5:42:16
Fulton 13	1	31N47	87w44	5:50:56
Fulton Bridge 47	1	34N08	87w59	5:51:56
Fultondale 37	6	33N37	86w48	5:47:12
Fulton Road 49	1	30N38	88w05	5:52:20
Fulton Springs 37	6	33N37	86w48	5:47:12
Furman 66	1	31N55	86w58	5:47:52
Fyffe 25	1	34N26	85w58	5:43:52
Gadsden 28	6	34N01	86w01	5:44:04
Gainer 31	1	31N07	86w02	5:44:08
Gainestown 13	1	31N27	87w42	5:50:48
Gainesville 60	1	32N47	88w13	5:52:52
Gallant 28	1	34N00	86w15	5:45:00
Gallion 33	1	32N30	87w43	5:50:52
Gamble 64	1	33N50	87w17	5:49:08
Gandys Cove 52	1	34N22	86w54	5:47:36
Gantt	1	31N25	86w29	5:45:56
Gantts Junction 61	1	33N10	86w19	5:45:16
Gantts Quarry 61	1	33N08	86w18	5:45:12
Garden 54	1	33N08	88w10	5:52:40
Garden City 22	1	34N01	86w45	5:47:00
Gardendale 37	1	33N39	86w49	5:47:16
Garden Highlands 37	6	33N28	86w52	5:47:28
Gardiners Gin 64	1	33N46	87w11	5:48:44
Garland 7	1	31N33	86w50	5:47:20
Garrards Crossroads 35	1	30N58	85w31	5:42:04
Garth 36	1	34N47	86w20	5:45:20
Garywood 37	1	33N26	86w57	5:47:48
Gasque 2	1	30N15	87w49	5:51:16
Gastonburg 66	1	32N11	87w28	5:49:52
Gaylesville 10	1	34N16	85w34	5:42:16
Geiger 60	1	32N52	88w18	5:53:12
Genery 37	1	33N26	86w57	5:47:48
Geneva 31	1	31N02	85w52	5:43:28
Gentilly Forest 37	6	33N27	86w47	5:47:08
Georgetown 49	1	30N55	88w12	5:52:48
Georgia 42	1	34N48	87w07	5:48:28
Georgia 52	1	34N27	86w57	5:47:48
Georgiana 7	1	31N38	86w44	5:46:56
Geraldine 25	1	34N20	86w00	5:44:00
Gibsonville 14	1	33N16	85w50	5:43:20
Gilbert Crossroads 25	1	34N18	85w56	5:43:44
Gilbertown 12	1	31N53	88w19	5:53:16
Gilbertsboro 42	1	34N59	87w09	5:48:36
Giles 4	1	33N13	87w09	5:48:36
Gilliam Springs 48	1	34N19	86w30	5:46:00
Gilmore 37	1	33N26	86w57	5:47:48
Gipsy 42	1	34N56	86w59	5:47:56
Girard 57	7	32N28	85w01	5:40:04
Gladstone 45	2	34N43	86w40	5:46:40
Glass 9	5	32N48	85w11	5:40:44
Gleandean 41	5	32N36	85w27	5:41:48
Glen Allen 29	1	33N52	87w45	5:51:00
Glen City 58	1	33N35	86w23	5:45:32
Glencoe 28	1	33N57	85w56	5:43:44
Glencoe 37	6	33N29	86w46	5:47:04
Glendale 37	6	33N37	86w48	5:47:12
Glen Hills 37	1	33N26	86w57	5:47:48
Glen Oaks 37	1	33N28	86w56	5:47:44
Glenville 57	7	32N08	85w11	5:40:44
Glenwood 21	1	31N40	86w10	5:44:40
Gnatville 10	1	33N56	85w37	5:42:28
Godwin Estates 37	1	33N37	86w41	5:46:44
Goldbranch 19	1	33N01	86w19	5:45:16
Golden Springs 8	6	33N40	85w50	5:43:20
Gold Mine 47	1	34N01	87w46	5:51:04
Gold Ridge 22	1	34N11	86w48	5:47:12
Gold Ridge 41	5	32N44	85w37	5:42:28
Goldville 62	1	33N07	85w34	5:42:16
Gonce 36	1	34N53	85w50	5:43:20
Good Hope 22	1	34N07	86w52	5:47:28
Good Hope 26	1	32N37	86w02	5:44:08
Goodman 16	1	31N15	86w01	5:44:04
Goodson 4	1	32N56	87w10	5:48:40
Good Springs 42	1	34N50	87w16	5:49:04
Goodsprings 64	1	33N40	87w15	5:49:00
Goodwater 19	1	33N04	86w03	5:44:12
Goodway 50	1	31N20	87w25	5:49:40
Goose Pond Crossroads 36	1	34N39	86w01	5:44:04
Gordo 54	1	33N19	87w54	5:51:36
Gordon 35	1	31N05	85w08	5:40:32
Gordon Heights 37	1	33N26	86w57	5:47:48
Gordonsville 43	1	32N19	86w49	5:47:16
Gorgas 64	1	33N39	87w12	5:48:48
Goshen 55	1	31N43	86w07	5:44:28
Gosport 13	1	31N39	87w42	5:50:48
Graball 34	1	31N33	85w15	5:41:00
Grady 51	1	32N00	86w12	5:44:48
Graham 56	1	33N27	85w19	5:41:16
Grand Bay 49	1	30N29	88w21	5:53:24
Grangeburg 35	1	31N09	85w06	5:40:24
Grant 48	1	34N31	86w16	5:45:04
Granttown 61	1	33N32	85w57	5:43:48
Grasselli 37	1	33N26	86w57	5:47:48
Grassy 48	1	34N19	86w30	5:46:00
Gravel Hill 30	1	34N30	87w44	5:50:56
Gravelly Springs 39	1	34N49	87w40	5:50:40
Gravleeton 64	1	33N46	87w03	5:48:12
Grays Chapel 36	1	34N55	86w10	5:44:40
Grayson 67	1	34N17	87w20	5:49:20
Graystone 5	1	33N55	86w31	5:46:04
Graysville 37	1	33N38	86w58	5:47:52
Grayton 8	1	33N47	86w01	5:44:04
Greeley 63	1	33N20	87w01	5:48:04
Greenbrier 39	1	34N49	87w40	5:50:40
Greenbrier 42	1	34N41	86w41	5:46:44
Green Chapel 25	1	34N27	85w54	5:43:36
Green Lantern 51	4	32N20	86w16	5:45:04
Green Pond 4	1	33N13	87w07	5:48:28
Greensboro 33	1	32N42	87w36	5:50:24
Greens Chapel 5	1	33N59	86w35	5:46:20
Greensport 58	1	33N43	86w24	5:45:36
Green Valley 28	6	33N57	86w01	5:44:04
Green Valley 37	6	33N27	86w47	5:47:08
Greenview Estate 37	6	33N25	86w48	5:47:12
Greenville 7	1	31N50	86w38	5:46:32
Greenwood 13	1	31N42	87w46	5:51:04
Greenwood 37	1	33N21	87w54	5:51:36
Greenwood 44	1	32N25	85w42	5:42:48
Grimes 23	1	31N18	85w27	5:41:48
Grove Hill 13	1	31N42	87w47	5:51:08
Groveoak 25	1	34N26	86w04	5:44:16
Grove Park 37	6	33N27	86w49	5:47:16
Grove Park 61	1	33N16	86w21	5:45:24
Guerryton 6	1	32N14	85w25	5:41:40
Guest 25	1	34N27	85w43	5:42:52
Guin 47	1	33N58	87w55	5:51:40
Gulfcrest 49	1	31N01	88w14	5:52:56
Gulf Shores 2	1	30N17	87w41	5:50:44
Gum Pond 52	1	34N20	86w46	5:47:04
Gum Spring 5	1	34N05	86w35	5:46:20
Gum Spring 52	1	34N27	86w57	5:47:48
Gunter Air Force Base 51	4	32N24	86w17	5:45:08
Guntersville 48	1	34N21	86w18	5:45:12
Gurley 45	2	34N39	86w26	5:45:44
Guthery Crossroads 22	1	34N06	87w04	5:48:16
Gu-Win 47	1	33N57	87w52	5:51:28
Hackleburg 47	1	34N17	87w50	5:51:20
Hackneyville 62	1	32N59	85w52	5:43:28
Hacoda 31	1	31N04	86w10	5:44:40
Hagler 63	1	33N04	87w27	5:49:48
Haleburg 34	1	31N24	85w08	5:40:32
Haleys 47	1	34N14	87w37	5:50:28
Haleyville 67	1	34N14	87w37	5:50:28
Half Acre 46	1	32N15	87w57	5:51:48
Halltown 30	1	34N27	88w08	5:52:32
Halsell 12	1	32N05	88w17	5:53:08
Hamburg 53	1	32N33	87w18	5:49:12
Hamilton 47	1	34N09	87w59	5:51:56
Hamilton Crossroads 55	1	31N43	85w49	5:43:16
Hammondville 25	1	34N35	85w38	5:42:32
Hamner 60	1	32N42	88w07	5:52:28
Hampden 46	1	32N04	87w35	5:50:20
Hanceville 22	1	34N04	86w46	5:47:04
Hancock Crossroads 36	1	34N35	85w59	5:43:56
Hannah 42	1	34N48	86w58	5:47:52
Hannon 44	1	32N14	85w25	5:41:40
Hanover 19	1	32N53	86w13	5:44:52
Hardaway 44	1	32N17	85w51	5:43:24
Harkins Crossroads 14	1	33N16	85w50	5:43:20
Harlem Heights 37	1	33N26	86w57	5:47:48
Harmony 20	1	31N17	86w27	5:45:48
Harmony 40	1	34N29	87w17	5:49:08
Harmony 48	1	34N16	86w12	5:44:48
Harpersville 59	1	33N21	86w26	5:45:44
Harrell 24	1	32N26	87w14	5:48:56
Harrisburg 4	1	32N56	87w10	5:48:40
Harrisburg 58	1	33N35	86w23	5:45:32
Harrisville 28	1	34N04	86w21	5:45:24
Hartford 31	1	31N06	85w42	5:42:48
Hartselle 52	1	34N27	86w56	5:47:44
Harvest 45	2	34N51	86w45	5:47:00
Hatchechubbee 57	7	32N16	85w17	5:41:08
Hatton 40	1	34N34	87w25	5:49:40
Havana 33	1	32N48	87w37	5:50:28
Hawk 56	1	33N22	85w24	5:41:36
Hawthorn 65	1	31N27	88w02	5:52:08
Hayden 5	1	33N53	86w49	5:47:16
Haynes 1	1	32N28	86w27	5:45:48
Haynes Crossing 36	1	34N53	85w50	5:43:20
Hayneville 43	1	32N11	86w35	5:46:20
Hays Mill 42	1	34N56	86w59	5:47:56
Haywood 56	1	33N18	85w29	5:41:56
Hazel Green 45	2	34N56	86w34	5:46:16
Hazen 24	1	32N20	87w12	5:48:48
Headland 34	1	31N21	85w21	5:41:24
Healing Springs 65	1	31N38	88w20	5:53:20
Heath 20	1	31N21	86w28	5:45:52
Hebron 48	1	34N31	86w15	5:45:00
Hector 6	1	32N13	85w53	5:43:32

ALABAMA

Heflin 15	1	33N39	85w35	5:42:20
Heiberger 53	1	32N46	87w17	5:49:08
Helena 59	1	33N18	86w51	5:47:24
Helicon 21	1	32N00	86w12	5:44:48
Helicon 67	1	34N05	87w13	5:48:52
Henagar 25	1	34N38	85w46	5:43:04
Henderson 55	1	31N43	86w07	5:44:28
Hendricks 5	1	33N55	86w27	5:45:48
Hendrix 5	1	34N02	86w27	5:45:48
Henryville 48	1	34N21	86w19	5:45:16
Henson Springs 38	1	33N56	88w01	5:52:04
Herbert 18	1	31N26	86w56	5:47:44
Heron Bay 49	1	30N21	88w08	5:52:32
Hester Heights 30	1	34N30	87w44	5:50:56
Hickory Flat 9	1	33N09	85w22	5:41:28
Hickory Hills 39	1	34N49	87w40	5:50:40
Hideaway Hills 39	1	34N52	87w32	5:50:08
Higdon 36	1	34N51	85w37	5:42:28
Highbluff 31	1	31N06	85w42	5:42:48
Highland 14	1	33N18	85w45	5:43:00
Highland Home 21	1	31N57	86w19	5:45:16
Highland Lake 5	1	33N53	86w25	5:45:40
Highmound 5	1	34N12	86w18	5:45:12
High Point 25	1	34N35	85w37	5:42:28
High Point 48	1	34N16	86w12	5:44:48
High Ridge 6	1	32N08	85w43	5:42:52
Hightogy 38	1	33N45	88w07	5:52:28
Hightower 15	1	33N27	85w19	5:41:16
Hillard 64	1	33N50	87w32	5:50:08
Hillman 37	1	33N26	86w57	5:47:48
Hillman Gardens 37	1	33N26	86w57	5:47:48
Hillman Park 37	1	33N26	86w57	5:47:48
Hillsboro 40	1	34N39	87w12	5:48:48
Hillsboro 45	2	34N55	86w26	5:45:44
Hilltop 37	1	33N26	86w57	5:47:48
Hillview 37	6	33N34	86w52	5:47:28
Hirsch 57	7	32N11	85w10	5:40:40
Hissop 19	1	32N54	86w09	5:44:36
Hobbs Island 45	2	34N38	86w34	5:46:16
Hobgood 17	1	34N44	87w42	5:50:48
Hoboken 3	1	31N53	85w09	5:40:36
Hoboken 46	1	32N06	87w52	5:51:28
Hobson City 8	6	33N37	85w51	5:43:24
Hodge 36	1	34N36	85w55	5:43:40
Hodges 30	1	34N20	87w56	5:51:44
Hodges Store 52	1	34N25	87w05	5:48:20
Hodgesville 35	1	31N15	85w26	5:41:44
Hodgewood 12	1	31N55	88w19	5:53:16
Hogglesville 33	1	33N00	87w39	5:50:36
Hogjaw 48	1	34N19	86w30	5:46:00
Hokes Bluff 28	1	34N00	85w52	5:43:28
Holiday Park Estates 37	1	33N37	86w41	5:46:44
Holland Gin 42	1	34N56	86w59	5:47:56
Holley Crossroads 8	1	33N49	85w46	5:43:04
Hollins 14	1	33N07	86w09	5:44:36
Hollis Crossroads 15	1	33N38	85w35	5:42:20
Holly Pond 22	1	34N10	86w37	5:46:28
Holly Springs 5	1	33N46	86w29	5:45:56
Hollytree 36	1	34N48	86w15	5:45:00
Hollywood 36	1	34N44	85w59	5:43:56
Hollywood 37	6	33N27	86w49	5:47:16
Holt 63	6	33N12	87w32	5:50:08
Holtville 26	1	32N37	86w24	5:45:36
Holy Trinity 57	7	32N12	84w59	5:39:56
Homewood 37	6	33N29	86w47	5:47:08
Honoraville 21	1	31N51	86w24	5:45:36
Hoods Crossroads 5	1	33N55	86w27	5:45:48
Hoover 37	6	33N26	86w50	5:47:20
Hope Hull 51	1	32N15	86w20	5:45:20
Hopewell 10	1	34N13	85w36	5:42:24
Hopewell 15	1	33N38	85w35	5:42:20
Hopewell 25	1	34N16	86w12	5:44:48
Hopewell 37	1	33N26	86w57	5:47:48
Horn Hill 20	1	31N17	86w15	5:45:00
Horton 48	1	34N12	86w18	5:45:12
Hortons Mill 5	1	33N55	86w27	5:45:48
Houston 67	1	34N08	87w15	5:49:00
Howard 29	1	33N54	87w31	5:50:04
Howells Cross Roads 10	1	34N09	85w41	5:42:44
Howelton 28	1	34N04	86w21	5:45:24
Howton 63	1	33N11	87w27	5:49:48
Hubbertville 29	1	33N41	87w50	5:51:20
Hudson Gardens 37	1	33N26	86w57	5:47:48
Hueytown 37	1	33N26	86w59	5:47:56
Hueytown Crest 37	1	33N26	86w57	5:47:48
Hugo 46	1	32N16	87w37	5:50:28
Huguley 9	5	32N51	85w12	5:40:48
Hulaco 52	1	34N18	86w33	5:46:12
Hull 64	1	33N43	87w00	5:48:00
Humpton 48	1	34N38	86w16	5:45:04
Hunter 51	4	32N24	86w24	5:45:36
Huntsville 45	2	34N44	86w35	5:46:20
Hurricane 2	1	30N54	87w47	5:51:08
Hurtsboro 57	7	32N15	85w25	5:41:40
Hustlerville 48	1	34N16	86w12	5:44:48
Hustontown 39	1	34N52	87w32	5:50:08
Huxford 27	1	31N13	87w28	5:49:52
Hyatt 48	1	34N12	86w18	5:45:12
Hybart 50	1	31N50	87w23	5:49:32
Hytop 36	1	34N55	86w05	5:44:20
Idaho 14	1	33N16	85w50	5:43:20
Ider 25	1	34N44	85w39	5:42:36
Independence 1	1	32N28	86w27	5:45:48
Indian Creek 6	1	31N57	85w42	5:42:48
Indian Hill 61	1	33N16	86w21	5:45:24
Indian Springs 39	1	34N49	87w40	5:50:40
Industrial City 37	1	33N26	86w57	5:47:48
Industry 7	1	31N38	86w44	5:46:56
Ingram 33	1	33N00	87w39	5:50:36
Inland 5	1	33N55	86w27	5:45:48
Inmanfield 67	1	34N12	87w11	5:48:44
Ino 16	1	31N13	86w10	5:44:40
Institute 66	1	32N00	87w00	5:48:00
Interburan Heights 37	1	33N28	86w56	5:47:44
Inverness 6	1	32N01	85w45	5:43:00
Ireland Hill 47	1	34N14	87w37	5:50:28
Ironaton 61	1	33N26	85w59	5:43:56
Iron City 8	6	33N40	85w50	5:43:20
Irondale 37	1	33N32	86w42	5:46:48
Irvington 49	1	30N31	88w14	5:52:56
Isabella 11	1	32N47	86w52	5:47:28
Isbell 30	1	34N27	87w45	5:51:00
Ishkooda 37	1	33N26	86w53	5:47:32
Isney 12	1	31N46	88w20	5:53:20
Ivalee 28	6	34N01	86w04	5:44:16
Jachin 12	1	32N14	88w10	5:52:40
Jack 16	1	31N33	86w04	5:44:16
Jackson 12	1	31N55	88w19	5:53:16
Jackson 13	1	31N31	87w53	5:51:32
Jackson Oak 2	1	30N36	87w54	5:51:36
Jacksons Gap 62	1	32N53	85w49	5:43:16
Jacksonville 8	1	33N49	85w46	5:43:04
Jack Springs 27	1	31N10	87w32	5:50:08
Jagger 64	1	33N59	87w29	5:49:56
Jamestown 10	1	34N16	85w34	5:42:16
Jamesville 41	5	32N44	85w37	5:42:28
Jarrett 9	5	32N48	85w11	5:40:44
Jasper 64	1	33N50	87w17	5:49:08
Java 16	1	31N43	85w49	5:43:16
Jeddo 50	1	31N18	87w30	5:50:00
Jeff 45	2	34N43	86w40	5:46:40
Jefferson 46	1	32N23	87w54	5:51:36
Jefferson Park 37	1	33N32	86w42	5:46:48
Jemison 11	1	32N58	86w45	5:47:00
Jena 32	1	33N03	87w46	5:51:04
Jenifer 61	1	33N33	85w56	5:43:44
Jericho 53	1	32N38	87w21	5:49:24
Jernigan 57	7	32N09	85w04	5:40:16
Jerusalem Heights 63	6	33N12	87w32	5:50:08
Joe Wheeler Dam 40	1	34N41	87w24	5:49:36
Johnsons Crossing 22	1	34N04	86w46	5:47:04
Johnsonville 18	1	31N26	86w56	5:47:44
Jones 1	1	32N35	86w54	5:47:36
Jonesboro 2	1	30N36	87w54	5:51:36
Jonesboro 30	1	34N30	87w44	5:50:56
Jonesboro 37	1	33N26	86w57	5:47:48
Jones Chapel 22	1	34N13	87w03	5:48:12
Jones Crossroads 42	1	34N48	86w58	5:47:52
Joppa 22	1	34N18	86w33	5:46:12
Joquin 55	1	31N43	86w07	5:44:28
Jordan 26	1	32N31	86w12	5:44:48
Jordan 65	1	31N28	88w16	5:53:04
Jordans Mill 30	1	34N22	88w03	5:52:12
Josephine 2	1	30N25	87w36	5:50:24
Joseph Springs 8	6	33N40	85w50	5:43:20
Josie 55	1	31N49	85w51	5:43:24
Kansas 64	1	33N54	87w33	5:50:12
Kaolin 57	7	32N28	85w01	5:40:04
Kaulton 63	6	33N12	87w32	5:50:08
Keego 27	1	31N05	87w04	5:48:16
Keener 28	6	34N01	86w04	5:44:16
Kellerman 63	1	33N20	87w19	5:49:16
Kelly 23	1	31N19	85w40	5:42:40
Kellyton 19	1	32N59	86w08	5:44:32
Kendale Gardens 39	1	34N49	87w40	5:50:40
Kennedy 38	1	33N35	87w59	5:51:56
Kent 26	1	32N37	85w57	5:43:48
Kent 55	1	31N43	86w07	5:44:28
Kenwood 37	6	33N25	86w48	5:47:12
Ketona 37	6	33N35	86w46	5:47:04
Key 10	1	34N09	85w41	5:42:44
Keys Mill 45	2	34N55	86w26	5:45:44
Keystone 59	1	33N12	86w47	5:47:08
Keyton 16	1	31N19	85w49	5:43:16
Killen 39	1	34N52	87w32	5:50:08
Kilpatrick 25	1	34N16	86w12	5:44:48
Kimberly 37	1	33N46	86w48	5:47:12
Kimbrel 37	1	33N20	87w01	5:48:04
Kimbrough 66	1	32N02	87w34	5:50:16
Kincheon 11	1	32N51	86w38	5:46:32
Kings Landing 24	1	32N17	86w59	5:47:56
Kingtown 39	1	34N50	87w20	5:49:20
Kingville 38	1	33N35	87w59	5:51:56
Kinsey 35	1	31N18	85w21	5:41:24
Kinston 16	1	31N13	86w10	5:44:40
Kinterbish 60	1	32N25	88w24	5:53:36
Kirbytown 48	1	34N32	86w04	5:44:16
Kirk 54	1	33N20	87w54	5:51:36
Kirkland 27	1	31N05	87w04	5:48:16
Kirklands Crossroads 34	1	31N22	85w20	5:41:20
Kirks Grove 10	1	34N07	85w20	5:41:20
Klein 59	1	33N21	86w27	5:45:48
Klondike 64	1	33N44	87w17	5:49:08
Knightens Crossroads 8	1	33N56	85w37	5:42:28
Knoxville 32	1	33N00	87w47	5:51:08
Koenton 65	1	31N38	88w20	5:53:20
Kowaliga Beach 26	1	32N59	85w52	5:43:28
Krafton 49	1	30N44	88w05	5:52:20
Kyles 36	1	34N47	85w55	5:43:40
Kymulga 61	1	33N21	86w14	5:44:56
Laceys Chapel 37	1	33N26	86w57	5:47:48
Laceys Spring 52	1	34N31	86w38	5:46:32
Lacon 52	1	34N22	86w54	5:47:36
Ladiga 8	1	33N56	85w37	5:42:28
Ladonia 57	7	32N24	85w03	5:40:12
Lafayette 9	5	32N54	85w24	5:41:36
Lake Coves 39	1	34N49	87w40	5:50:40
Lake Drive Estates 37	6	33N27	86w49	5:47:16
Lake Forest 2	1	30N36	87w54	5:51:36
Lake Shore Estates 37	6	33N27	86w49	5:47:16
Lakeside Acres 39	1	34N52	87w32	5:50:08
Lakeside Highlands 39	1	34N49	87w40	5:50:40
Lakeview 25	1	34N28	85w52	5:43:28
Lakeview 48	1	34N21	86w19	5:45:16
Lakeview Estates 37	6	33N27	86w49	5:47:16
Lakeview Highlands 17	1	34N45	87w41	5:50:44
Lakeview Park 37	6	33N27	86w49	5:47:16
Lakewood 42	1	34N48	86w58	5:47:52
Lakewood Estates 37	1	33N26	86w57	5:47:48
Lamison 66	1	32N07	87w34	5:50:16
Land 12	1	32N02	88w20	5:53:20
Landersville 40	1	34N29	87w17	5:49:08
Lands Crossroads 25	1	34N29	85w52	5:43:28
Lane Springs 17	1	34N46	87w58	5:51:52
Lanett 9	5	32N52	85w12	5:40:48
Langdale 9	5	32N47	85w12	5:40:48
Langston 36	1	34N32	86w04	5:44:16
Langtown 40	1	34N40	87w19	5:49:16
Laniers 61	1	33N21	86w14	5:44:56
Lapine 21	1	31N57	86w19	5:45:16
Lapine 51	1	31N58	86w17	5:45:08
La Place 44	1	32N24	85w56	5:43:44
Lardent 8	6	33N40	85w50	5:43:20
Larkinsville 36	1	34N39	86w01	5:44:04
Larkwood 37	1	33N37	86w41	5:46:44
Lasca 46	1	31N55	87w45	5:51:00
Latham 2	1	31N00	87w52	5:51:28
Lathamville 25	1	34N17	85w59	5:43:56
Lattiwood 48	1	34N16	86w12	5:44:48
Lauderdale Beach 39	1	34N49	87w40	5:50:40
Laurendine 49	1	30N37	88w12	5:52:48
Lavaca 12	1	32N08	88w05	5:52:20
Lawley 4	1	32N52	86w57	5:47:48
Lawrence 10	1	34N13	85w36	5:42:24
Lawrence Cove 52	1	34N20	86w46	5:47:04
Lawrence Mill 29	1	33N41	87w50	5:51:20
Lawrenceville 34	1	31N33	85w15	5:41:00
Leatherwood 8	6	33N40	85w50	5:43:20
Lebanon 15	1	33N44	85w23	5:41:32
Lebanon 25	1	34N14	85w51	5:43:24
Lecta 15	1	33N38	85w35	5:42:20
Leeds 37	1	33N33	86w33	5:46:12
Leeds Mineral Well 37	1	33N33	86w32	5:46:08
Leesburg 10	1	34N11	85w46	5:43:04
Leesdale 52	1	34N22	86w54	5:47:36
Leggtown 42	1	34N56	86w59	5:47:56
Lehigh	1	33N52	86w41	5:46:44
Leighton 17	1	34N42	87w32	5:50:08
Lenlock 8	6	33N40	85w50	5:43:20
Lenox 18	1	31N20	87w11	5:48:44
Leon 21	1	31N30	86w22	5:45:28
Leroy 65	1	31N30	87w59	5:51:56
Leslie 11	1	32N40	86w55	5:47:40
Lester 42	1	34N59	87w09	5:48:36
Letcher 36	1	34N38	86w16	5:45:04
Letchers 8	6	33N40	85w50	5:43:20
Letohatchee 43	1	32N08	86w29	5:45:56
Level Plains 23	1	31N18	85w46	5:43:04
Levelroad 56	1	33N07	85w34	5:42:16
Levert 53	1	32N41	87w13	5:48:52
Lewis 23	1	31N19	85w29	5:41:56
Lewiston 32	1	32N50	87w53	5:51:32
Lexington 39	1	34N58	87w22	5:49:28
Liberty 5	1	34N05	86w35	5:46:20
Liberty 7	1	32N28	86w27	5:45:48
Liberty 25	1	34N10	86w09	5:44:36
Liberty City 44	1	32N34	85w39	5:42:36
Liberty Highlands 37	1	33N32	86w42	5:46:48
Liberty Hill 30	1	34N21	87w42	5:50:48
Libertyville 20	1	31N15	86w28	5:45:52
Lightwood 26	1	32N37	86w24	5:45:36
Lilita	1	32N27	88w08	5:52:32
Lillian 2	1	30N25	87w26	5:49:44
Lily Flag 45	2	34N41	86w34	5:46:16
Lime 56	1	33N09	85w22	5:41:28
Lime Kiln 17	1	34N46	87w58	5:51:52
Limestone 50	1	31N31	87w20	5:49:20
Lim Rock 36	1	34N40	86w11	5:44:44
Lincoln 61	1	33N37	86w07	5:44:28
Lincoln Park 63	6	33N12	87w32	5:50:08
Lincoya Estates 37	6	33N27	86w47	5:47:08
Lindbergh 37	1	33N36	86w58	5:47:52
Linden 46	1	32N18	87w48	5:51:12
Lineville 14	1	33N19	85w45	5:43:00
Linn Crossing 37	1	33N36	86w58	5:47:52
Linwood 55	1	31N56	85w52	5:43:28
Lipscomb 37	1	33N27	86w54	5:47:36
Lisman 12	1	32N15	88w13	5:52:52
Little Oak 55	1	31N48	85w56	5:43:44
Little River 2	1	31N18	87w44	5:50:56
Little River 10	1	34N13	85w36	5:42:24
Little Rock 27	1	31N01	87w30	5:50:00
Little Shawmut 9	5	32N51	85w13	5:40:52
Little Texas 44	1	32N26	85w42	5:42:48
Littleton 28	6	34N01	86w04	5:44:16
Littleton 37	1	33N36	86w58	5:47:52
Littleville 17	1	34N36	87w41	5:50:44
Littleville 67	1	34N14	87w37	5:50:28
Livingston 60	1	32N35	88w11	5:52:44

ALABAMA

Place		Lat.	Long.	Time
Loachapoka 41	5	32N36	85W36	5:42:24
Loango 20	1	31N24	86W37	5:46:28
Locke Crossroads 42	1	34N56	86W59	5:47:56
Lockhart 20	1	31N01	86W21	5:45:24
Lock Six 39	1	34N52	87W32	5:50:08
Lock Three 39	1	34N50	87W20	5:49:20
Locust Fork 5	1	33N52	86W39	5:46:36
Logan 22	1	34N10	86W58	5:47:52
Logton 55	1	31N48	85W56	5:43:44
Lomax 11	1	32N53	86W40	5:46:40
London 18	1	31N18	87W00	5:48:00
London 51	1	32N17	86W06	5:44:24
London 58	1	33N33	86W16	5:45:04
Long Island 36	1	34N58	85W40	5:42:40
Longview 22	1	34N14	86W52	5:47:28
Longview 59	1	33N12	86W47	5:47:08
Lookout Mountain 28	1	34N07	85W47	5:43:08
Loop 10	1	34N13	85W36	5:42:24
Loop 49	1	30N40	88W06	5:52:24
Loree 18	1	31N26	86W56	5:47:44
Lottie 2	1	31N01	87W30	5:50:00
Louisville 3	1	31N47	85W33	5:42:12
Lovelace Crossroads 39	1	34N49	87W40	5:50:40
Loveless 25	1	34N27	85W43	5:42:52
Loveless Park 37	1	33N26	86W57	5:47:48
Lovick 37	1	33N37	86W37	5:46:28
Lower Peach Tree 66	1	31N50	87W33	5:50:12
Lowery 31	1	31N13	86W10	5:44:40
Low Gap 58	1	33N40	86W25	5:45:40
Lowndesboro 43	1	32N17	86W37	5:46:28
Lowry Mill 16	1	31N32	86W02	5:44:08
Loxley 2	1	30N37	87W45	5:51:00
Lucille 4	1	33N07	87W07	5:48:28
Lugo 3	1	31N53	85W09	5:40:36
Lumbull 47	1	34N17	87W42	5:50:48
Luttrell 25	1	34N27	85W54	5:43:36
Luverne 21	1	31N43	86W16	5:45:04
Lydia 25	1	34N27	85W43	5:42:52
Lyeffion 18	1	31N35	86W59	5:47:56
Lynn 67	1	34N03	87W33	5:50:12
Lynn Crossing 37	1	33N36	86W58	5:47:52
Lynn Haven 63	6	33N12	87W32	5:50:08
Lynns Park 64	1	33N46	87W11	5:48:44
Lytle 31	1	31N07	86W02	5:44:08
Mabson 23	1	31N24	85W41	5:42:44
Macedonia 15	1	33N32	85W21	5:41:24
Macedonia 36	1	34N35	85W59	5:43:56
Macedonia 51	1	32N03	86W13	5:44:52
Macedonia 64	1	33N50	87W17	5:49:08
Macon 8	1	33N47	86W01	5:44:04
Madison 45	2	34N42	86W45	5:47:00
Madison 51	4	32N25	86W17	5:45:08
Madison Crossroads 45	2	34N58	86W43	5:46:52
Madrid 35	1	31N02	85W24	5:41:36
Magazine 49	1	30N41	88W06	5:52:24
Magnolia 46	1	32N08	87W40	5:50:40
Magnolia Beach 2	1	30N31	87W54	5:51:36
Magnolia Springs 2	1	30N24	87W46	5:51:04
Magnolia Terminal 46	1	32N04	87W35	5:50:20
Majestic 37	1	33N45	86W49	5:47:16
Malbis 2	1	30N36	87W54	5:51:36
Malcolm 65	1	31N12	88W01	5:52:04
Malone 56	1	33N12	85W35	5:42:20
Malta 27	1	31N01	87W30	5:50:00
Malvern 31	1	31N08	85W31	5:42:04
Mamie 51	1	32N10	86W00	5:44:00
Manack 43	1	32N20	86W31	5:46:04
Manchester 64	1	33N57	87W19	5:49:16
Manila 13	1	31N32	87W47	5:51:08
Manley Crossroads 45	2	34N41	86W41	5:46:44
Manningham 7	1	31N50	86W38	5:46:32
Mansion View 39	1	34N49	87W40	5:50:40
Mantua 32	1	33N03	87W56	5:51:44
Maple Hill 45	1	34N59	86W51	5:47:24
Maplesville 11	1	32N47	86W52	5:47:28
Maplewood 37	1	33N33	86W32	5:46:08
Marble City Heights 61	1	33N10	86W19	5:45:16
Marble Valley 19	1	33N10	86W19	5:45:16
Marbury 1	1	32N39	86W31	5:46:04
Marcoot 9	5	32N54	85W24	5:41:36
Margaret 58	1	33N41	86W29	5:45:56
Margerum 17	1	34N46	87W58	5:51:52
Marietta 64	1	33N46	87W23	5:49:32
Marion 53	1	32N38	87W19	5:49:16
Marion Junction 24	1	32N26	87W14	5:48:56
Markeeta 58	1	33N33	86W32	5:46:08
Marl 31	1	31N07	86W02	5:44:08
Marley Mill 23	1	31N24	85W41	5:42:44
Marlow 2	1	30N30	87W42	5:50:48
Marshall Space Flight Center 45	2	34N44	86W36	5:46:24
Mars Hill 39	1	34N49	87W40	5:50:40
Martintown 36	1	34N43	85W58	5:43:52
Martinville 27	1	31N01	87W30	5:50:00
Martling 48	1	34N16	86W12	5:44:48
Marvel 4	1	33N09	87W00	5:48:00
Marvyn 41	5	32N38	85W23	5:41:32
Marylee 64	1	33N50	87W17	5:49:08
Maryville 28	6	34N01	86W04	5:44:16
Massey 52	1	34N25	87W05	5:48:20
Masterson Mill 40	1	34N29	87W17	5:49:08
Mathews 51	1	32N10	86W00	5:44:00
Mattawana 5	1	33N55	86W27	5:45:48
Maud 17	1	34N46	87W58	5:51:52
Maxine 37	1	33N46	87W20	5:49:20
Maxwell 63	6	33N12	87W32	5:50:08
Maxwell Air Force Base 51	4	32N22	86W18	5:45:12
Maxwellborn 8	1	33N56	85W37	5:42:28
Mayfair 37	6	33N27	86W49	5:47:16
Maylene 59	1	33N12	86W52	5:47:28
Maynards Cove 36	1	34N39	86W01	5:44:04
Maysville 45	2	34N42	86W22	5:45:28
Maytown 37	1	33N32	87W00	5:48:00
McCalla 37	1	33N20	87W01	5:48:04
McClure Town 55	1	31N48	85W56	5:43:44
McCrory Village 63	6	33N14	87W36	5:50:24
McCulley Hill 4	1	33N07	87W07	5:48:28
McCullough 27	1	31N10	87W32	5:50:08
McCullum 64	1	33N50	87W17	5:49:08
McDonald Chapel 37	1	33N31	86W56	5:47:44
McDowell 60	1	32N29	88W04	5:52:16
McElderry 61	1	33N32	85W57	5:43:48
McFarland 63	6	33N12	87W32	5:50:08
McGhees Bend 10	1	34N09	85W41	5:42:44
McGinty 9	5	32N47	85W09	5:40:36
McIntosh 65	1	31N16	88W02	5:52:08
McKenzie 7	1	31N33	86W43	5:46:52
McKestes 25	1	34N18	85W56	5:43:44
McKinley 46	1	32N13	87W26	5:49:44
McLarty 5	1	34N12	86W18	5:45:12
McLendon 57	7	32N09	85W04	5:40:16
McMullen 54	1	33N08	88W10	5:52:40
McShan 54	1	33N23	88W09	5:52:36
McVay 13	1	31N42	87W46	5:51:04
McVille 48	1	34N16	86W12	5:44:48
McWilliams 66	1	31N50	87W06	5:48:24
Megargel 50	1	31N23	87W26	5:49:44
Mehama 40	1	34N30	87W44	5:50:56
Mellow Valley 14	1	33N15	85W39	5:42:36
Melrose 18	1	31N26	86W56	5:47:44
Melrose 54	1	33N23	88W09	5:52:36
Melton 33	1	32N45	87W44	5:50:56
Meltonsville 48	1	34N32	86W04	5:44:16
Melville 67	1	34N05	87W13	5:48:52
Melvin 12	1	31N56	88W28	5:53:52
Mentone 25	1	34N34	85W35	5:42:20
Mercury 45	2	34N47	86W33	5:46:12
Meridianville 45	2	34N51	86W34	5:46:16
Merry 51	1	32N17	86W06	5:44:24
Mexboro 50	1	31N26	87W24	5:49:36
Mexia 50	1	31N30	87W23	5:49:32
Micaville 15	1	33N38	85W35	5:42:20
Middle Brooks Cross Roads 41	5	32N44	85W37	5:42:28
Middleton 8	1	33N47	86W01	5:44:04
Midfield 37	1	33N27	86W55	5:47:40
Midland City 23	1	31N19	85W29	5:41:56
Midway 6	1	32N05	85W31	5:42:04
Midway 7	1	31N51	86W24	5:45:36
Midway 11	1	32N43	86W29	5:45:56
Midway 14	1	33N04	86W03	5:44:12
Midway 40	1	34N29	87W17	5:49:08
Midway 50	1	31N53	87W00	5:48:00
Midway Plaza 41	5	32N38	85W23	5:41:32
Miflin 2	1	30N25	87W36	5:50:24
Mignon 61	1	33N11	86W18	5:45:12
Miles 37	1	33N28	86W56	5:47:44
Millbrook 26	1	32N29	86W22	5:45:28
Miller 46	1	32N09	87W47	5:51:08
Millers Ferry 66	1	32N06	87W22	5:49:28
Millerville 14	1	33N12	85W56	5:43:44
Millport 38	1	33N34	88W05	5:52:20
Millry 65	1	31N38	88W19	5:53:16
Milltown 9	5	33N01	85W29	5:41:56
Mill Village 48	1	34N21	86W19	5:45:16
Milstead 44	1	32N27	85W54	5:43:36
Milton 1	1	32N33	86W50	5:47:20
Mineral Springs 11	1	32N58	86W37	5:46:28
Minooka 11	1	33N06	86W45	5:47:00
Minor 37	1	33N31	86W56	5:47:44
Minor Terrace 61	1	33N16	86W21	5:45:24
Minter 24	1	32N05	87W00	5:48:00
Minvale 25	1	34N27	85W43	5:42:52
Mitchell 6	1	32N15	85W56	5:43:44
Mitchell Town 39	1	34N52	87W32	5:50:08
Mitylene 51	1	32N23	86W11	5:44:44
Mobile 49	1	30N41	88W03	5:52:12
Moffett 49	1	30N44	88W28	5:53:52
Molder 45	2	34N42	86W22	5:45:28
Mollie 12	1	32N14	88W17	5:53:08
Molloy 38	1	33N54	88W08	5:52:32
Mon Louis 49	1	30N23	88W14	5:52:56
Monroeville 50	1	31N31	87W20	5:49:20
Monrovia 45	2	34N43	86W40	5:46:40
Montague 36	1	34N59	85W46	5:43:04
Monterey 7	1	31N52	86W50	5:47:20
Montevallo 59	1	33N06	86W52	5:47:28
Monte Vista 28	6	33N57	86W01	5:44:04
Montgomery 51	4	32N23	86W19	5:45:16
Monticello 55	1	31N49	85W51	5:43:24
Montrose 2	1	30N34	87W54	5:51:36
Moody 58	1	33N36	86W27	5:45:48
Moorefield 9	5	32N54	85W24	5:41:36
Moores Bridge 63	1	33N27	87W47	5:51:08
Moores Crossroad 25	1	34N27	85W54	5:43:36
Moores Crossroads 56	1	33N09	85W22	5:41:28
Moores Mill 45	2	34N47	86W33	5:46:12
Mooresville 42	1	34N38	86W53	5:47:32
Moreland 67	1	34N08	87W15	5:49:00
Morgan 37	1	33N26	86W57	5:47:48
Morgan City 52	1	34N28	86W34	5:46:16
Moriah 19	1	32N53	86W13	5:44:52
Morningside 37	1	33N37	86W41	5:46:44
Morris 37	1	33N46	86W44	5:46:56
Morris Chapel 40	1	34N32	87W11	5:48:44
Morvin 13	1	31N59	87W59	5:51:56
Moshat 10	1	34N09	85W41	5:42:44
Mossy Grove 55	1	31N48	85W56	5:43:44
Mostellers 59	1	33N07	86W35	5:46:20
Motley 14	1	33N07	85W34	5:42:16
Moulton 40	1	34N29	87W18	5:49:12
Moulton Heights 52	3	34N36	87W01	5:48:04
Moundville 33	1	33N00	87W38	5:50:32
Mountainboro 28	1	34N08	86W05	5:44:20
Mountain Brook 37	6	33N30	86W45	5:47:00
Mountain Brook Village 37	6	33N29	86W46	5:47:04
Mountain Chest 48	1	34N21	86W19	5:45:16
Mountain Creek 11	1	32N43	86W29	5:45:56
Mountain Grove 5	1	34N05	86W35	5:46:20
Mountain Home 40	1	34N40	87W19	5:49:16
Mountain View 48	1	34N21	86W19	5:45:16
Mountain Woods Park 37	6	33N27	86W47	5:47:08
Mount Andrew 3	1	31N58	85W32	5:42:08
Mount Carmel 36	1	34N59	85W46	5:43:04
Mount Carmel 48	1	34N21	86W19	5:45:16
Mount Carmel 51	1	31N58	86W17	5:45:08
Mount Hebron 32	1	32N45	88W01	5:52:04
Mount Hebron 48	1	34N10	86W09	5:44:36
Mount Herman Valley 33	1	32N47	87W31	5:50:04
Mount Hester 17	1	34N46	87W58	5:51:52
Mount Hope 40	1	34N29	87W27	5:49:48
Mount Ida 21	1	31N35	86W15	5:45:00
Mount Jefferson 41	5	32N38	85W23	5:41:32
Mount Meigs 51	1	32N22	86W04	5:44:16
Mount Nebo 24	1	32N19	86W49	5:47:16
Mount Olive 19	1	33N04	86W03	5:44:12
Mount Olive 37	1	33N41	86W52	5:47:28
Mount Pinson 37	1	33N43	86W40	5:46:40
Mount Pleasant 16	1	31N19	85W49	5:43:16
Mount Pleasant 50	1	31N18	87W30	5:50:00
Mount Rozell 42	1	34N59	87W09	5:48:36
Mount Star 30	1	34N30	87W44	5:50:56
Mount Sterling 12	1	32N16	88W13	5:52:52
Mount Union 18	1	31N26	86W56	5:47:44
Mount Vernon 22	1	34N14	86W52	5:47:28
Mount Vernon 25	1	34N27	85W43	5:42:52
Mount Vernon 29	1	33N41	87W50	5:51:20
Mount Vernon 49	1	31N05	88W01	5:52:04
Mount Willing 43	1	31N59	86W35	5:46:20
Mount Zion 51	1	32N03	86W13	5:44:52
Mud Creek 10	1	34N05	85W31	5:42:04
Mud Creek 36	1	34N43	85W58	5:43:52
Mud Creek 37	1	33N23	87W06	5:48:24
Mulga 37	1	33N33	86W59	5:47:56
Mulga Mine 37	1	33N33	86W59	5:47:56
Mullins Flat 45	2	34N39	86W41	5:46:44
Munford 61	1	33N33	85W55	5:43:40
Munk City 40	1	34N29	87W17	5:49:08
Murphy 39	1	34N55	88W04	5:52:16
Murrays Chapel 58	1	33N46	86W29	5:45:56
Muscadine 15	1	33N44	85W23	5:41:32
Muscadine Junction 15	1	33N44	85W23	5:41:32
Muscle Shoals 17	1	34N43	87W37	5:50:28
Muscoda 37	1	33N26	86W57	5:47:48
Mynot 17	1	34N46	87W58	5:51:52
Myrtlewood 46	1	32N16	87W57	5:51:48
Nadawah 50	1	32N00	87W18	5:49:12
Naftel 51	1	31N58	86W17	5:45:08
Nanafalia 46	1	32N07	87W59	5:51:56
Nances Creek 8	1	33N56	85W37	5:42:28
Napier 23	1	31N15	85W26	5:41:44
Napoleon 56	1	33N18	85W29	5:41:56
Nat 36	1	34N38	86W16	5:45:04
Natchez 50	1	31N45	87W13	5:48:52
Nathan 67	1	34N05	87W13	5:48:52
Natural Bridge 67	1	34N06	87W36	5:50:24
Nauvoo 64	1	34N00	87W29	5:49:56
Nectar 5	1	33N59	86W35	5:46:20
Needham 12	1	31N59	88W21	5:53:24
Needmore 48	1	34N10	86W09	5:44:36
Needmore 55	1	31N55	85W57	5:43:48
Needmore 67	1	34N14	87W37	5:50:28
Neel 52	1	34N27	86W57	5:47:48
Neenah 66	1	32N00	87W18	5:49:12
Nellie 66	1	32N00	87W18	5:49:12
Nesmith 22	1	34N11	86W48	5:47:12
Ne Smith 40	1	34N41	87W24	5:49:36
Nettleboro 13	1	31N46	87W43	5:50:52
Newbern 33	1	32N36	87W32	5:50:08
Newberry Crossroads 10	1	34N09	85W41	5:42:44
New Brashier Chapel 48	1	34N16	86W12	5:44:48
New Brockton 16	1	31N23	85W56	5:43:44
Newburg 30	1	34N30	87W44	5:50:56
New Castle 37	1	33N39	86W46	5:47:04
New Center 52	1	34N27	86W57	5:47:48
New Dora 64	1	33N44	87W07	5:48:28
Newell 56	1	33N26	85W26	5:41:44
New Georgia 67	1	34N12	87W11	5:48:44
New Haven 45	2	34N41	86W41	5:46:44
New Hill 37	1	33N26	86W57	5:47:48
New Home 25	1	34N38	85W45	5:43:00
New Hope 16	1	31N43	85W49	5:43:16
New Hope 22	1	34N10	86W37	5:46:28
New Hope 36	1	34N39	86W01	5:44:04
New Hope 45	2	34N32	86W24	5:45:36
New Hope 59	6	33N28	86W45	5:47:00
New Hopewell 15	1	33N38	85W35	5:42:20
New Lexington 63	1	33N40	87W36	5:50:24
New London 58	1	33N33	86W16	5:45:04
New Market 45	2	34N55	86W26	5:45:44
New Moon 10	1	34N16	85W34	5:42:16

ALABAMA

New Prospect 1 1 32N43 86w29 5:45:56
New Prospect 33 1 32N53 87w44 5:50:56
New Sharon 45 2 34N56 86w34 5:46:16
New Site 62 1 33N02 85w47 5:43:08
Newsome 25 1 34N32 85w49 5:43:16
Newton 23 1 31N17 85w43 5:42:52
Newton Springs 35 1 31N15 85w26 5:41:44
Newtonville 29 1 33N33 87w48 5:51:12
Newtown 30 1 34N30 87w44 5:50:56
New Town 36 1 34N53 85w50 5:43:20
Newville 34 1 31N26 85w20 5:41:20
Nichburg 18 1 31N24 87w15 5:49:00
Nicholsville 46 1 31N55 87w45 5:51:00
Nitrate City 17 1 34N45 87w41 5:50:44
Nixburg 19 1 32N50 86w07 5:44:28
Nix Mill 30 1 34N21 87w42 5:50:48
Nixons Chapel 48 1 34N12 86w18 5:45:12
Noah 10 1 34N09 85w41 5:42:44
Nokomis 27 1 31N01 87w30 5:50:00
Nolandale 45 2 34N41 86w41 5:46:44
Normal 45 2 34N47 86w34 5:46:16
North Arab 48 1 34N19 86w30 5:46:00
North Athens 42 1 34N48 86w58 5:47:52
North Birmingham 37
6 33N34 86w49 5:47:16
North Carrollton 37
1 33N24 87w02 5:48:08
North Elmore 26 4 32N27 86w19 5:45:16
North Florence 39 1 34N49 87w40 5:50:40
North Highlands 37
1 33N27 87w03 5:48:12
North Johns 37 1 33N22 87w06 5:48:24
North Mobile 49 1 30N47 88w04 5:52:16
Northport 63 6 33N16 87w34 5:50:16
North River 29 1 33N50 87w42 5:50:48
North Selma 24 1 32N23 87w00 5:48:00
Northside 35 1 31N15 85w26 5:41:44
North Smithfield Estates 37
6 33N34 86w52 5:47:28
North Vinemont 22 1 34N14 86w52 5:47:28
North Walter 22 1 34N11 86w48 5:47:12
Northwood Hills 39
1 34N49 87w40 5:50:40
Norton 45 2 34N41 86w40 5:46:40
Notasulga 44 5 32N34 85w41 5:42:44
Nottingham 61 1 33N21 86w14 5:44:56
Nuckols 57 7 32N20 85w01 5:40:04
Nymph 11 1 31N26 86w56 5:47:44
Oak Bowery 9 5 32N54 85w24 5:41:36
Oak Crossing 37 1 33N33 86w32 5:46:08
Oakdale 42 1 34N48 86w58 5:47:52
Oak Grove 11 1 32N57 86w45 5:47:00
Oak Grove 30 1 34N30 87w44 5:50:56
Oak Grove 37 1 33N23 87w06 5:48:24
Oak Grove 42 1 34N59 86w51 5:47:24
Oak Grove 49 1 30N48 88w07 5:52:28
Oak Grove 61 1 33N11 86w18 5:45:12
Oak Hill 25 1 34N17 85w59 5:43:56
Oakhill 66 1 31N55 87w05 5:48:20
Oakland 39 1 34N50 87w48 5:51:12
Oaklevel 15 1 33N44 85w26 5:41:44
Oakman 64 1 33N43 87w23 5:49:32
Oakmulgee 53 1 32N45 86w59 5:47:56
Oak Park 37 6 33N35 86w46 5:47:04
Oak Ridge 52 1 34N27 86w57 5:47:48
Oak Ridge 58 1 33N35 86w23 5:45:32
Oakville 40 1 34N25 87w05 5:48:20
Oakwood 37 1 33N26 86w57 5:47:48
Oakwood College 45
2 34N43 86w35 5:46:20
Oakworth 52 3 34N33 86w59 5:47:56
Oaky Grove 34 1 31N25 85w20 5:41:20
Oaky Streak 7 1 31N40 86w30 5:46:00
Octagon 46 1 32N18 87w47 5:51:08
Odena 61 1 33N10 86w19 5:45:16
Oden Ridge 52 1 34N20 86w46 5:47:04
Odenville 58 1 33N41 86w24 5:45:36
Odom 7 1 31N32 86w43 5:46:52
Ofelia 56 1 33N18 85w45 5:43:00
Ohatchee 8 1 33N47 86w00 5:44:00
Old Bethel 17 1 34N42 87w34 5:50:16
Old Burleson 30 1 34N22 88w03 5:52:12
Old Davistown 8 6 33N40 85w50 5:43:20
Oldfield 61 1 33N10 86w19 5:45:16
Old Kingston 1 1 32N28 86w27 5:45:48
Old Maylene 59 1 33N12 86w52 5:47:28
Old Monrovia 45 2 34N43 86w40 5:46:40
Old Nauvoo 30 1 34N30 87w44 5:50:56
Old Samuel 12 1 31N53 88w20 5:53:20
Old Spring Hill 46
1 32N30 87w43 5:50:52
Old Texas 50 1 31N53 87w00 5:48:00
Old Town 18 1 31N26 86w56 5:47:44
Old Town 24 1 32N19 86w49 5:47:16
Oleander 48 1 34N24 86w27 5:45:48
Oliver 39 1 34N50 87w20 5:49:20
Olmsted 63 1 33N11 87w27 5:49:48
Olustee 55 1 31N53 86w07 5:44:28
Omaha 56 1 33N21 85w04 5:40:16
Oneal 42 1 34N48 86w58 5:47:52
Oneonta 5 1 33N57 86w28 5:45:52
Onycha 20 1 31N17 86w27 5:45:48
Opelika 41 5 32N39 85w23 5:41:32
Opine 13 1 31N55 87w45 5:51:00
Opine 20 1 31N17 86w15 5:45:00
Opp 20 1 31N17 86w16 5:45:04
Orange Beach 2 1 30N18 87w34 5:50:16
Orion 55 1 31N58 86w00 5:44:00
Orrville 42 1 34N44 86w58 5:47:52
Osanippa 9 5 32N47 85w09 5:40:36
Osborn 53 1 32N41 87w13 5:48:52
Oswichee 57 7 32N20 85w01 5:40:04
Our Town 62 1 32N59 85w52 5:43:28
Overbrook 61 1 33N07 86w12 5:44:48
Overton 37 6 33N28 86w43 5:46:52
Owassa 18 1 31N24 86w56 5:47:44
Owens Cross Roads 45
2 34N35 86w28 5:45:52
Oxanna 8 6 33N40 85w50 5:43:20
Oxford 8 6 33N36 85w51 5:43:24
Oxford Lake 8 6 33N40 85w50 5:43:20
Oxmoor 37 6 33N28 86w52 5:47:28
Ozark 23 1 31N28 85w39 5:42:36
Painter 25 1 34N17 85w59 5:43:56
Paint Rock 36 1 34N40 86w20 5:45:20
Palestine 15 1 33N44 85w26 5:41:44
Palmerdale 37 1 33N44 86w39 5:46:36
Palmers Crossroads 50
1 31N18 87w30 5:50:00
Palmetto 54 1 33N23 88w01 5:52:04
Palmetto Beach 2 1 30N16 87w41 5:50:44
Palos 37 1 33N46 87w20 5:49:20
Panola 21 1 31N58 86w17 5:45:08
Panola 60 1 32N57 88w16 5:53:04
Pansey 35 1 31N09 85w11 5:40:44
Paran 56 1 33N09 85w22 5:41:28
Park City 2 1 30N36 87w54 5:51:36
Parkdale 19 1 33N04 86w03 5:44:12
Park Hill 58 1 33N35 86w23 5:45:32
Parkland 64 1 33N50 87w17 5:49:08
Parkwood 37 1 33N26 86w57 5:47:48
Parrish 64 1 33N44 87w17 5:49:08
Partridge Crossroads 37
1 33N15 86w48 5:47:12
Patsburg 21 1 31N43 86w16 5:45:04
Patton 64 1 33N46 87w23 5:49:32
Patton Chapel 37 6 33N27 86w47 5:47:08
Paul 18 1 31N19 86w44 5:46:56
Pauls Hill 37 1 33N26 86w57 5:47:48
Pawnee 37 6 33N35 86w46 5:47:04
Peachburg 1 32N10 85w38 5:42:32
Peacock 13 1 31N42 87w46 5:51:04
Pea Ridge 27 1 31N05 87w04 5:48:16
Pea Ridge 29 1 33N40 87w36 5:50:24
Pea Ridge 47 1 33N57 87w53 5:51:32
Pea Ridge 59 1 33N09 87w00 5:48:00
Pearson 63 1 33N04 87w27 5:49:48
Peavy 56 1 33N09 85w22 5:41:28
Pebble 67 1 34N14 87w37 5:50:28
Peeks Corner 25 1 34N14 85w51 5:43:24
Peeks Hill 8 1 33N47 86w01 5:44:04
Peets Corner 42 1 34N48 86w58 5:47:52
Pelham 59 1 33N13 86w47 5:47:08
Pelham Heights 8 6 33N40 85w50 5:43:20
Pell City 58 1 33N35 86w17 5:45:08
Penfield Heights 37
6 33N35 86w46 5:47:04
Penn 52 1 34N25 87w05 5:48:20
Pennington 12 1 32N13 88w03 5:52:12
Pennsylvania 49 1 30N54 88w03 5:52:12
Penton 9 5 32N54 85w24 5:41:36
Pepperell 41 5 32N38 85w23 5:41:32
Perdido 2 1 31N00 87w38 5:50:32
Perdido Beach 2 1 30N25 87w36 5:50:24
Perdue Hill 50 1 31N31 87w30 5:50:00
Perote 6 1 31N57 85w42 5:42:48
Perrys Mill 51 1 32N17 86w06 5:44:24
Perry Store 16 1 31N13 86w10 5:44:40
Perryville 53 1 32N23 87w00 5:48:00
Peterman 50 1 31N36 87w16 5:49:04
Peterson 63 1 33N14 87w25 5:49:40
Petersville 39 1 34N51 87w41 5:50:44
Petey 42 1 34N48 86w58 5:47:52
Petrey 21 1 31N51 86w13 5:44:52
Petronia 43 1 32N19 86w49 5:47:16
Pettusville 42 1 34N56 86w59 5:47:56
Peytonia Points 17
1 34N45 87w41 5:50:44
Phalin 63 1 33N04 87w27 5:49:48
Phelan 22 1 34N11 86w48 5:47:12
Phenix City 57 7 32N28 85w00 5:40:00
Phil Campbell 30 1 34N21 87w42 5:50:48
Phillipsville 2 1 30N54 87w47 5:51:08
Pickensville 54 1 33N14 88w16 5:53:04
Pickering 24 1 32N34 86w55 5:47:40
Piedmont 8 1 33N55 85w37 5:42:28
Piedmont Springs 8
1 33N56 85w37 5:42:28
Pierce 49 1 30N44 88w28 5:53:52
Pigeon Creek 7 1 31N50 86w38 5:46:32
Pike Road 51 1 32N17 86w06 5:44:24
Pikeville 36 1 34N39 86w01 5:44:04
Pilgrims Rest 28 6 33N57 86w01 5:44:04
Pinckard 23 1 31N19 85w33 5:42:12
Pinder Hill 36 1 34N53 85w50 5:43:20
Pine Apple 66 1 31N52 86w59 5:47:56
Pine Beach 2 1 30N16 87w41 5:50:44
Pinebelt 24 1 32N19 87w17 5:49:08
Pine Dale 42 1 34N59 86w51 5:47:24
Pinedale 51 4 32N21 86w17 5:45:08
Pinedale Acres 39 1 34N52 87w32 5:50:08
Pinedale Acres 42 1 34N48 86w58 5:47:52
Pinedale Shores 58
1 33N43 86w24 5:45:36
Pine Flat 1 1 32N37 86w24 5:45:36
Pine Grove 6 1 32N05 85w31 5:42:04
Pine Grove 10 1 34N09 85w41 5:42:44
Pine Grove 62 1 32N48 85w39 5:42:36
Pine Hill 56 1 33N27 85w19 5:41:16
Pine Hill 66 1 32N00 87w34 5:50:16
Pine Level 1 1 32N37 86w24 5:45:36
Pine Level 16 1 31N25 86w04 5:44:16
Pine Level 51 1 32N04 86w04 5:44:16
Pine Mountain 5 1 33N49 86w36 5:46:24
Pine Orchard 50 1 31N35 87w16 5:49:04
Pineview 37 1 33N32 86w42 5:46:48
Pinewood Terrace 61
1 33N16 86w21 5:45:24
Piney 10 1 34N09 85w41 5:42:44
Piney Bend 30 1 34N22 88w03 5:52:12
Piney Chapel 42 1 34N48 86w58 5:47:52
Piney Grove 40 1 34N25 87w05 5:48:20
Piney Grove 47 1 34N01 87w46 5:51:04
Piney Woods 15 1 33N44 85w26 5:41:44
Pinkney City 37 6 33N34 86w52 5:47:28
Pinkneyville 14 1 33N04 86w03 5:44:12
Pinnell 62 1 32N48 85w39 5:42:36
Pinson 37 1 33N41 86w41 5:46:44
Pintlala 51 1 32N16 86w23 5:45:32
Pisgah 36 1 34N41 85w47 5:43:08
Pisgah 42 1 34N54 86w44 5:46:56
Pittsview 57 7 32N11 85w10 5:40:40
Plainview 25 1 34N29 85w52 5:43:28
Plain View 37 6 33N35 86w46 5:47:04
Plant City 9 5 32N51 85w12 5:40:48
Plantersville 24 1 32N40 86w56 5:47:44
Plantersville 61 1 33N21 86w14 5:44:56
Plateau 49 1 30N44 88w05 5:52:20
Pleasant Gap 10 1 33N59 85w31 5:42:04
Pleasant Grove 11 1 32N57 86w45 5:47:00
Pleasant Grove 36 1 34N53 85w50 5:43:20
Pleasant Grove 37 1 33N32 87w02 5:48:08
Pleasant Grove Estates 37
1 33N20 87w54 5:51:36
Pleasant Hill 12 1 31N53 88w20 5:53:20
Pleasant Hill 24 1 32N17 86w59 5:47:56
Pleasant Hill 27 1 31N01 87w30 5:50:00
Pleasant Hill 30 1 34N23 87w44 5:50:56
Pleasant Hill 37 1 33N26 86w57 5:47:48
Pleasant Home 20 1 31N17 86w27 5:45:48
Pleasant Ridge 30 1 34N30 87w44 5:50:56
Pleasant Ridge 32 1 32N50 87w53 5:51:32
Pleasant Ridge 55 1 31N40 86w10 5:44:40
Pleasant Site 30 1 34N33 88w04 5:52:16
Pletcher 11 1 32N42 86w47 5:47:08
Plevna 45 2 34N58 86w25 5:45:40
Poarch 27 1 31N01 87w30 5:50:00
Pocahontas 64 1 33N54 87w31 5:50:04
Pogo 30 1 34N31 88w13 5:52:52
Point Clear 2 1 30N28 87w55 5:51:40
Polk 24 1 32N19 86w49 5:47:16
Pollard 27 1 31N02 87w10 5:48:40
Pollards Bend 10 1 34N11 85w46 5:43:04
Ponders 62 1 32N50 85w45 5:43:00
Pondville 4 1 32N56 87w10 5:48:40
Pool 40 1 34N25 87w05 5:48:20
Pooles Crossroads 56
1 33N09 85w22 5:41:28
Pools Crossroads 11
1 32N51 86w38 5:46:32
Pope 46 1 32N04 87w38 5:50:32
Poplarridge 45 2 34N33 86w24 5:45:36
Poplar Springs 48 1 34N16 86w12 5:44:48
Poplar Springs 67 1 33N59 87w29 5:49:56
Port Birmingham 37
1 33N33 86w59 5:47:56
Porter 37 1 33N36 86w57 5:47:48
Porter Square 35 1 31N15 85w26 5:41:44
Portersville 25 1 34N19 85w49 5:43:16
Posey Mill 30 1 34N14 87w37 5:50:28
Poseys Crossroads 1
1 32N28 86w27 5:45:48
Postoak 6 1 32N08 85w43 5:42:52
Potash 56 1 33N09 85w22 5:41:28
Potter 24 1 32N23 87w00 5:48:00
Powderly 37 6 33N28 86w53 5:47:32
Powell's Crossroads 25
1 34N27 85w54 5:43:36
Powers 33 1 33N00 87w39 5:50:36
Powhatan 37 1 33N35 87w06 5:48:24
Powledge 41 7 32N36 85w14 5:40:56
Praco 37 1 33N38 87w07 5:48:28
Prairie 66 1 32N10 87w26 5:49:44
Prairieville 33 1 32N30 87w43 5:50:52
Pratt City 37 6 33N34 86w52 5:47:28
Prattmont 1 1 32N28 86w27 5:45:48
Pratts 3 1 31N52 85w27 5:41:48
Prattville 1 1 32N28 86w29 5:45:56
Prescott 58 1 33N35 86w23 5:45:32
Preston 48 1 34N39 86w01 5:44:04
Prestwick 65 1 31N30 87w59 5:51:56
Priceville 52 3 34N33 86w59 5:47:56
Prichard 49 1 30N44 88w05 5:52:20
Pride 17 1 34N44 87w42 5:50:48
Primitive Ridge 4 1 33N07 87w07 5:48:28
Princeton 36 1 34N50 86w09 5:44:36
Pronto 55 1 31N48 85w56 5:43:44
Prospect 64 1 33N59 87w29 5:49:56
Providence 7 1 31N38 86w44 5:46:56
Providence 22 1 34N14 86w52 5:47:28
Providence 46 1 32N30 87w43 5:50:52
Providence 64 1 33N46 87w23 5:49:32
Prudence 57 7 32N11 85w10 5:40:40
Pruitton 39 1 35N02 87w30 5:50:00
Pulltight 47 1 34N01 87w46 5:51:04
Pumpkin Center 25 1 34N27 85w43 5:42:52
Pumpkin Center 52 1 34N25 87w05 5:48:20
Pumpkin Center 64 1 33N46 87w20 5:49:20
Pushmataha 12 1 32N15 88w23 5:53:32
Putnam 46 1 32N01 88w02 5:52:08
Pyriton 14 1 33N22 85w50 5:43:20
Queenstown 37 1 33N37 86w37 5:46:28
Quintard Mall 8 6 33N40 85w50 5:43:20
Quinton 64 1 33N46 87w20 5:49:20
Rabb 18 1 31N26 86w56 5:47:44
Rabbittown 8 1 33N56 85w37 5:42:28
Rabbit Town 48 1 34N16 86w12 5:44:48
Rabbittown 67 1 34N14 87w37 5:50:28
Rabun 2 1 30N54 87w47 5:51:08
Ragland 58 1 33N45 86w09 5:44:36
Rahatchie 61 1 33N16 86w21 5:45:24
Raimund 37 1 33N26 86w57 5:47:48
Rainbow City 28 6 33N57 86w01 5:44:04
Rainsville 25 1 34N30 85w51 5:43:24
Raleigh 54 1 33N12 87w58 5:51:52

Ralph 63 1 33N03 87w46 5:51:04
Ramer 51 1 32N03 86w13 5:44:52
Ranburne 15 1 33N35 85w24 5:41:36
Randolph 4 1 32N54 86w55 5:47:40
Range 18 1 31N19 87w14 5:48:56
Rash 36 1 34N53 85w50 5:43:20
Rayburn 48 1 34N21 86w19 5:45:16
Reads Mill 8 1 33N49 85w54 5:43:36
Red Bank 40 1 34N41 87w24 5:49:36
Red Bay 30 1 34N28 88w04 5:52:16
Reddock Springs 7 1 31N50 86w38 5:46:32
Red Gap Junction 37 1 33N32 86w42 5:46:48
Red Hill 5 1 33N43 87w00 5:48:00
Red Hill 26 1 32N41 85w57 5:43:48
Red Hill 48 1 34N21 86w19 5:45:16
Redland Heights 9 5 32N49 85w10 5:40:40
Red Level 20 1 31N24 86w36 5:46:24
Redmont Park 37 6 33N29 86w46 5:47:04
Red Ore 37 1 33N26 86w57 5:47:48
Red Rock 17 1 34N44 87w42 5:50:48
Red Rock Junction 17 1 34N46 87w58 5:51:52
Redstone Arsenal 45 2 34N44 86w36 5:46:24
Red Wine 37 1 33N36 86w58 5:47:52
Reece City 28 6 34N04 86w02 5:44:08
Reedtown 30 1 34N30 87w44 5:50:56
Reform 54 1 33N23 88w01 5:52:04
Regent Forest 37 6 33N25 86w48 5:47:12
Rehobeth 35 1 31N15 85w26 5:41:44
Rehoboth 66 1 32N14 87w25 5:49:40
Reid 42 1 34N48 86w58 5:47:52
Remlap 5 1 33N49 86w36 5:46:24
Renfroe 61 1 33N26 86w06 5:44:24
Reno 63 1 33N20 87w01 5:48:04
Repton 18 1 31N25 87w14 5:48:56
Republic 37 6 33N34 86w52 5:47:28
Rhoades 16 1 31N13 86w10 5:44:40
Rhodesville 39 1 34N49 87w40 5:50:40
Richmond 24 1 32N05 87w00 5:48:00
Riderwood 12 1 32N16 88w13 5:52:52
Ridgeville 7 1 31N52 86w50 5:47:20
Ridgeville 28 6 34N01 86w04 5:44:16
Ringgold 10 1 34N16 85w34 5:42:16
Ripley 42 1 34N48 86w58 5:47:52
Riverbend 4 1 33N07 87w07 5:48:28
River Bend 33 1 32N39 87w39 5:50:36
Riverdale 25 1 34N34 85w35 5:42:20
River Falls 20 1 31N21 86w34 5:46:16
Rivermont 17 1 34N45 87w41 5:50:44
Rivermont 39 1 34N49 87w40 5:50:40
River Park 2 1 30N31 87w54 5:51:36
River Park 25 1 34N34 85w35 5:42:20
Riverside 5 1 34N05 86w35 5:46:20
Riverside 58 1 33N37 86w12 5:44:48
Riverton 17 1 34N46 87w58 5:51:52
River View 9 5 32N47 85w09 5:40:36
Riverview 27 1 31N05 87w04 5:48:16
Roanoke 56 1 33N09 85w22 5:41:28
Roanoke Junction 41 5 32N38 85w23 5:41:32
Roba 44 1 32N15 85w36 5:42:24
Robbins Crossroads 37 1 33N43 86w58 5:47:52
Roberts 27 1 31N17 86w27 5:45:48
Robertsdale 2 1 30N33 87w43 5:50:52
Robertsville 64 1 34N52 85w23 5:41:32
Robinsons 43 1 32N20 86w32 5:46:08
Robinson Springs 26 4 32N27 86w19 5:45:16
Robinsonville 27 1 31N01 87w30 5:50:00
Robinwood 37 6 33N35 86w46 5:47:04
Rock City 36 1 34N35 85w59 5:43:56
Rock City 47 1 33N55 87w48 5:51:12
Rockdale 37 1 33N26 86w57 5:47:48
Rocket 45 2 34N41 86w40 5:46:40
Rockford 19 1 32N53 86w13 5:44:52
Rock Hill 27 1 31N05 87w04 5:48:16
Rock House 36 1 34N35 85w59 5:43:56
Rockledge 28 1 34N05 86w07 5:44:28
Rock Mills 56 1 33N09 85w22 5:41:28
Rock Run 10 1 33N56 85w37 5:42:28
Rock Spring 28 1 33N59 85w55 5:43:40
Rock Springs 5 1 34N05 86w35 5:46:20
Rock Springs 12 1 32N16 88w13 5:52:52
Rock Stand 56 1 33N09 85w22 5:41:28
Rockwest 66 1 32N00 87w18 5:49:12
Rockwood 30 1 34N30 87w44 5:50:56
Rocky Head 23 1 31N36 85w43 5:42:52
Rocky Hill 40 1 34N41 87w24 5:49:36
Rocky Hollow 64 1 33N50 87w17 5:49:08
Rocky Ridge 37 6 33N28 86w45 5:47:00
Rodentown 25 1 34N10 86w09 5:44:36
Roebuck Plaza 37 1 33N36 86w40 5:46:40
Roeton 16 1 31N43 85w49 5:43:16
Rogersville 39 1 34N50 87w18 5:49:12
Romar Beach 2 1 30N18 87w34 5:50:16
Rome 20 1 31N17 86w27 5:45:48
Romulus 63 1 33N10 87w51 5:51:24
Roosevelt 37 1 33N27 86w56 5:47:44
Roper 37 1 33N37 86w37 5:46:28
Rosa 5 1 33N55 86w27 5:45:48
Rosalie 36 1 34N42 85w46 5:43:04
Roseboro 45 2 35N01 86w21 5:45:24
Rosebud 66 1 31N55 87w05 5:48:20
Rosedale 37 6 33N27 86w49 5:47:16
Rosedale 63 6 33N12 87w32 5:50:08
Rose Hill 20 1 31N30 86w22 5:45:28
Rose Hill 37 1 33N32 86w42 5:46:48
Rose Park 39 1 34N49 87w40 5:50:40
Rosinton 2 1 30N33 87w42 5:50:48
Rossland City 29 1 33N41 87w50 5:51:20
Round Hill 13 1 31N55 87w45 5:51:00
Round Mountain 10 1 32N44 85w37 5:42:28
Rowells Crossroad 41 5 32N44 85w37 5:42:28
Roxana 41 5 32N44 85w37 5:42:28
Royal 5 1 34N05 86w35 5:46:20
Ruffner 37 1 33N32 86w42 5:46:48
Russell 29 1 33N50 87w50 5:51:20
Russell 49 1 31N07 88w14 5:52:56
Russell Heights 37 1 33N33 86w32 5:46:08
Russell Mill 62 1 32N59 85w52 5:43:28
Russellville 30 1 34N30 87w44 5:50:56
Rutan 65 1 31N28 88w16 5:53:04
Ruth 48 1 34N19 86w30 5:46:00
Rutherford 57 7 32N14 85w25 5:41:40
Rutledge 21 1 31N46 86w25 5:45:40
Rutledge 37 1 33N28 86w55 5:47:40
Ryan 59 1 33N05 86w51 5:47:24
Ryan Crossroads 52 1 34N18 86w33 5:46:12
Ryland 45 2 34N46 86w29 5:45:56
Saco 55 1 31N48 85w56 5:43:44
Safford 24 1 32N17 87w22 5:49:28
Saginaw 59 1 33N12 86w47 5:47:08
Sahama Village 63 6 33N12 87w32 5:50:08
Saint Bernard 22 1 34N10 86w49 5:47:16
Saint Clair 43 1 32N19 86w37 5:46:28
Saint Clair Springs 58 1 33N46 86w29 5:45:56
Saint Elmo 49 1 30N30 88w15 5:53:00
Saint Florian 39 1 34N53 87w39 5:50:36
Saints Crossroads 30 1 34N30 87w44 5:50:56
Saint Stephens 65 1 31N32 88w03 5:52:12
Saks 8 6 33N40 85w50 5:43:20
Salem 24 1 32N19 87w17 5:49:08
Salem 41 7 32N36 85w14 5:40:56
Salem 42 1 34N56 86w59 5:47:56
Salitpa 13 1 31N37 88w01 5:52:04
Samantha 63 1 33N25 87w36 5:50:24
Samford University 37 6 33N27 86w49 5:47:16
Samson 31 1 31N07 86w03 5:44:12
Samuels Chapel 28 1 34N04 86w21 5:45:24
Sandfield 55 1 31N48 85w56 5:43:44
Sandfort 57 7 32N18 85w10 5:40:40
Sand Rock 10 1 34N14 85w51 5:43:24
Sand Springs 42 1 34N55 86w51 5:47:24
Sandusky 37 6 33N34 86w52 5:47:28
Sandy Creek 9 5 32N48 85w39 5:42:36
Sandy Ridge 43 1 32N08 86w29 5:45:56
Sanford 20 1 31N18 86w24 5:45:36
Sanie 58 1 33N40 86w25 5:45:40
San Souci Beach 49 1 30N25 88w17 5:53:08
Santuck 26 1 32N31 86w12 5:44:48
Sapps 54 1 33N16 88w06 5:52:24
Saragossa 64 1 33N59 87w29 5:49:56
Saraland 49 1 30N50 88w04 5:52:16
Saratoga 48 1 34N16 86w12 5:44:48
Sardine 27 1 31N00 87w15 5:49:00
Sardis 6 1 32N59 86w08 5:44:32
Sardis 24 1 32N17 86w59 5:47:56
Sardis City 28 1 34N10 86w09 5:44:36
Sardis Springs 42 1 34N48 86w58 5:47:52
Satsuma 49 1 30N51 88w04 5:52:16
Saucer 7 1 31N52 86w50 5:47:20
Saville 21 1 31N57 86w19 5:45:16
Sawyerville 33 1 32N45 87w44 5:50:56
Sayre 37 1 33N43 86w58 5:47:52
Sayreton 37 6 33N34 86w49 5:47:16
Scant City 48 1 34N19 86w30 5:46:00
Scarce Grease 42 1 34N59 87w09 5:48:36
Scenic Heights 28 6 33N57 86w01 5:44:04
Schenks 8 1 33N49 85w54 5:43:36
Schmits Mill 61 1 33N37 86w07 5:44:28
Scotland 50 1 31N35 87w16 5:49:04
Scott City 37 1 33N33 86w32 5:46:08
Scottsboro 36 1 34N40 86w02 5:44:08
Scrange 2 1 31N10 87w32 5:50:08
Scyrene 13 1 31N46 87w43 5:50:52
Seaboard 65 1 31N20 88w12 5:52:48
Seacliff 2 1 30N31 87w54 5:51:36
Seale 57 7 32N18 85w10 5:40:40
Sealy Springs 35 1 31N03 85w18 5:41:12
Searight 21 1 31N30 86w22 5:45:28
Searles 63 1 33N20 87w19 5:49:16
Section 36 1 34N35 85w59 5:43:56
Segco 64 1 33N44 87w17 5:49:08
Selfville 5 1 33N49 86w44 5:46:56
Sellers 51 1 31N58 86w17 5:45:08
Sellersville 31 1 31N10 85w55 5:43:40
Selma 24 1 32N25 87w01 5:48:04
Selma Mall 24 1 32N23 87w00 5:48:00
Selmont 24 1 32N23 87w00 5:48:00
Seman 26 1 32N41 86w06 5:44:24
Seminole 2 1 30N31 87w28 5:49:52
Semmes 49 1 30N47 88w16 5:53:04
Service 12 1 31N44 88w12 5:52:48
Seven Hills 49 1 30N41 88w06 5:52:24
Shacklesville 7 1 31N38 86w44 5:46:56
Shades Creek 37 6 33N27 86w49 5:47:16
Shades Crest Estates 37 6 33N25 86w48 5:47:12
Shady Brook 37 1 33N26 86w57 5:47:48
Shady Grove 14 1 33N04 86w03 5:44:12
Shady Grove 16 1 31N25 86w04 5:44:16
Shady Grove 30 1 34N21 87w42 5:50:48
Shady Grove 55 1 31N55 86w10 5:44:40
Shannon 37 1 33N24 86w52 5:47:28
Shawmut 9 5 32N50 85w10 5:40:40
Shawnee 66 1 32N00 87w18 5:49:12
Sheffield 17 1 34N45 87w44 5:50:56
Shelby 59 1 33N07 86w35 5:46:20
Shellhorn 55 1 31N53 86w07 5:44:28
Sherman Heights 8 6 33N40 85w50 5:43:20

ALABAMA

Sherwood Forest 39 1 34N49 87w40 5:50:40
Shiloh 25 1 34N27 85w43 5:42:52
Shiloh 46 1 32N08 87w40 5:50:40
Shiloh 55 1 31N49 85w51 5:43:24
Shinebone 14 1 33N18 85w45 5:43:00
Shingle 30 1 34N21 87w42 5:50:48
Shoals Acres 39 1 34N52 87w32 5:50:08
Shopton 6 1 32N07 85w57 5:43:48
Short Creek 37 1 33N33 87w06 5:48:24
Shorter 44 1 32N24 85w57 5:43:48
Shorterville 34 1 31N37 85w09 5:40:36
Shortleaf 46 1 32N31 87w51 5:51:24
Shottsville 47 1 34N08 87w59 5:51:56
Shreve 18 1 31N26 86w41 5:46:44
Sico 61 1 33N10 86w19 5:45:16
Siddonsville 46 1 32N28 87w36 5:50:24
Sidney 49 1 31N07 88w14 5:52:56
Sigma 35 1 31N15 85w26 5:41:44
Sikesville 14 1 33N07 85w34 5:42:16
Silas 12 1 31N46 88w20 5:53:20
Siloam 60 1 32N25 88w24 5:53:36
Siluria 59 1 33N11 86w46 5:47:04
Silver Cross 65 1 31N39 88w09 5:52:36
Silverhill 2 1 30N33 87w45 5:51:00
Silver Run 61 1 33N32 85w57 5:43:48
Simcoe 22 1 34N15 86w44 5:46:56
Simmsville 59 1 33N20 86w38 5:46:32
Simsville 6 1 32N08 85w43 5:42:52
Sipsey 64 1 33N55 87w10 5:48:40
Six Mile 4 1 33N02 86w55 5:47:40
Skaggs Corner 25 1 34N38 85w45 5:43:00
Skegg Crossroads 14 1 33N04 86w03 5:44:12
Skinem 45 2 34N56 86w34 5:46:16
Skinnerton 18 1 31N26 86w56 5:47:44
Skipperville 23 1 31N33 85w33 5:42:12
Skirum 25 1 34N18 85w56 5:43:44
Skyline 36 1 34N39 86w01 5:44:04
Skyline Estates 37 6 33N25 86w48 5:47:12
Sky Ranch 37 6 33N25 86w48 5:47:12
Skyview 37 1 33N26 86w57 5:47:48
Slackland 10 6 33N57 86w01 5:44:04
Slocomb 31 1 31N07 85w36 5:42:24
Smith Hill 4 1 33N07 87w07 5:48:28
Smith Institute 28 1 34N10 86w09 5:44:36
Smiths 41 7 32N32 85w06 5:40:24
Smithson 37 1 33N26 86w57 5:47:48
Smithsonia 39 1 34N49 87w40 5:50:40
Smut Eye 6 1 31N57 85w42 5:42:48
Smyer 13 1 31N55 87w59 5:51:56
Smyrna 35 1 31N15 85w26 5:41:44
Snead 5 1 34N07 86w24 5:45:36
Snoddy 32 1 32N50 87w53 5:51:32
Snowdoun 51 1 32N15 86w18 5:45:12
Snow Hill 66 1 32N00 87w00 5:48:00
Snowtown 37 1 33N44 87w07 5:48:28
Socapatoy 19 1 32N59 86w08 5:44:32
Society Hill 44 1 32N26 85w27 5:41:48
Soleo 19 1 33N04 86w03 5:44:12
Somerville 52 1 34N28 86w48 5:47:12
South 20 1 31N24 86w37 5:46:28
South Calera 59 1 33N06 86w45 5:47:00
South Gate Mall 17 1 34N45 87w41 5:50:44
South Guntersville 48 1 34N21 86w19 5:45:16
South Haleyville 67 1 34N14 87w37 5:50:28
South Highlands 37 6 33N30 86w48 5:47:12
South Holt 63 6 33N12 87w32 5:50:08
South Lowell 64 1 33N50 87w17 5:49:08
South Sheffield 17 1 34N44 87w42 5:50:48
Southside 28 1 33N55 86w01 5:44:04
Southtown 48 1 34N21 86w19 5:45:16
Southwood 37 6 33N27 86w49 5:47:16
Souwilpa 12 1 31N46 88w20 5:53:20
Spanish Fort 2 1 30N40 87w54 5:51:36
Speake 40 1 34N25 87w05 5:48:20
Speed 19 1 32N46 86w06 5:44:24
Speeds Water Mill 54 1 33N20 87w54 5:51:36
Speigner 26 1 32N35 86w21 5:45:24
Sprague 51 1 32N08 86w17 5:45:08
Springbrook 63 6 33N12 87w32 5:50:08
Springdale 37 6 33N35 86w46 5:47:04
Springfield 13 1 31N55 87w45 5:51:00
Springfield 39 1 34N50 87w20 5:49:20
Springfield 56 1 33N09 85w22 5:41:28
Spring Garden 10 1 33N58 85w33 5:42:12
Spring Hill 3 1 32N02 85w23 5:41:32
Spring Hill 49 1 30N42 88w10 5:52:40
Spring Hill 55 1 31N42 85w58 5:43:52
Spring Hill 64 1 33N54 87w31 5:50:04
Spring Valley 17 1 34N44 87w42 5:50:48
Springville 58 1 33N46 86w29 5:45:56
Springville Lake Estates 58 1 33N46 86w29 5:45:56
Sprott 53 1 32N41 87w13 5:48:52
Spruce Pine 30 1 34N23 87w44 5:50:56
Standard 64 1 33N44 87w17 5:49:08
Standing Rock 9 5 33N05 85w15 5:41:00
Stanley 20 1 31N17 86w27 5:45:48
Stansel 54 1 33N23 88w01 5:52:04
Stanton 11 1 32N44 86w54 5:47:36
Stapleton 2 1 30N44 87w48 5:51:12
State Line 35 1 30N57 85w24 5:41:36
Statesville 1 1 32N23 87w00 5:48:00
Steele 58 1 33N56 86w12 5:44:48
Steelwood 2 1 30N37 87w45 5:51:00

ALABAMA

Place		Lat	Long	Time
Steenson Hollow 17	1	34N45	87w41	5:50:44
Steppville 22	1	34N04	86w46	5:47:04
Sterrett 59	1	33N27	86w29	5:45:56
Stevenson 36	1	34N52	85w50	5:43:20
Stewart 33	1	32N55	87w42	5:50:48
Stewartville	1	33N05	86w15	5:45:00
Stills Cross Road 6	1	31N48	85w56	5:43:44
Stockdale 61	1	33N32	85w57	5:43:48
Stockton 2	1	31N00	87w52	5:51:28
Stokeley 20	1	31N17	86w27	5:45:48
Stokes 63	1	33N04	87w27	5:49:48
Stoney Point 1	1	32N37	86w24	5:45:36
Stotesville 4	1	33N07	87w07	5:48:28
Stough 29	1	33N41	87w50	5:51:20
Straight Mountain 5	1	33N55	86w27	5:45:48
Strawberry 5	1	34N19	86w30	5:46:00
Stroud 9	5	33N03	85w20	5:41:20
Stroups Crossroads 52	1	34N25	87w05	5:48:20
Studdards Crossroads 29	1	33N54	87w31	5:50:04
Sturkie 9	5	32N54	85w24	5:41:36
Suggsville 13	1	31N39	87w42	5:50:48
Sulligent 38	1	33N54	88w08	5:52:32
Sulphur Springs 5	1	33N53	86w45	5:47:00
Sulphur Springs 25	1	34N46	85w32	5:42:08
Sulphur Springs 45	2	34N55	86w26	5:45:44
Sumiton 64	1	33N46	87w03	5:48:12
Summerdale 2	1	30N29	87w42	5:50:48
Summerfield 24	1	32N23	87w00	5:48:00
Summit 5	1	34N12	86w30	5:46:00
Sumterville 60	1	32N42	88w07	5:52:28
Sunflower 65	1	31N23	88w02	5:52:08
Sunny South 66	1	31N58	87w38	5:50:32
Sunset Mill Village 24	1	32N23	87w00	5:48:00
Sun Valley 37	1	33N37	86w41	5:46:44
Surginer 46	1	32N08	87w40	5:50:40
Suttle 53	1	32N32	87w11	5:48:44
Swaim 36	1	34N47	86w20	5:45:20
Swancott 42	1	34N41	86w41	5:46:44
Swearengin 48	1	34N39	86w01	5:44:04
Sweet Water 46	1	32N04	87w57	5:51:48
Sycamore 61	1	33N15	86w12	5:44:48
Sylacauga 61	1	33N10	86w15	5:45:00
Sylvania 25	1	34N34	85w49	5:43:16
Sylvan Springs 37	1	33N31	87w01	5:48:04
Tabernacle 16	1	31N23	85w56	5:43:44
Tabernacle 35	1	31N15	85w26	5:41:44
Tabor 28	6	33N57	86w01	5:44:04
Taff 10	1	34N16	85w34	5:42:16
Taits Gap 5	1	33N55	86w27	5:45:48
Talladega 61	1	33N26	86w06	5:44:24
Talladega Springs 61	1	33N07	86w26	5:45:44
Tallahatta Springs 13	1	31N55	87w45	5:51:00
Tallapoosa City 62	1	32N32	85w53	5:43:32
Tallassee 26	1	32N32	85w54	5:43:36
Tallaweka 26	1	32N31	85w53	5:43:32
Talucah 52	1	34N30	86w41	5:46:44
Tanner 42	1	34N44	86w58	5:47:52
Tanner Crossroads 42	1	34N44	86w58	5:47:52
Tanner Heights 52	1	34N27	86w57	5:47:48
Tanner Williams 49	1	30N41	88w14	5:52:56
Tanyard 6	1	31N57	85w42	5:42:48
Tanyard 58	1	33N40	86w17	5:45:08
Tarentum 55	1	31N43	85w49	5:43:16
Tarpley 37	6	33N28	86w52	5:47:28
Tarrant 37	6	33N35	86w46	5:47:04
Tarrant Heights 37	6	33N35	86w46	5:47:04
Tasso 24	1	32N19	87w17	5:49:08
Tattlersville 13	1	31N46	88w05	5:52:20
Taylor 35	1	31N10	85w28	5:41:52
Taylors Crossroads 56	1	33N09	85w22	5:41:28
Taylorville 63	6	33N12	87w32	5:50:08
Teals Crossroads 3	1	31N36	85w43	5:42:52
Teasleys Mill 51	1	32N10	86w00	5:44:00
Tecumseh 10	1	33N57	85w23	5:41:32
Teddy 27	1	31N05	87w04	5:48:16
Tenant 56	1	33N16	85w27	5:41:48
Ten Broeck 25	1	34N27	85w54	5:43:36
Tennala 10	1	34N09	85w41	5:42:44
Tennille 55	1	31N43	85w49	5:43:16
Tensaw 2	1	31N09	87w48	5:51:12
Terese 3	1	31N53	85w09	5:40:36
Texasville 3	1	31N43	85w26	5:41:44
Thach 42	1	34N56	86w59	5:47:56
Thack 64	1	34N55	86w54	5:47:36
Thaddeus 62	1	32N34	85w39	5:42:36
Tharptown 30	1	34N30	87w44	5:50:56
The Cedars 39	1	34N49	87w40	5:50:40
The Highlands 28	6	33N57	86w01	5:44:04
Theodore 49	1	30N33	88w10	5:52:40
The Ridge 50	1	31N31	87w20	5:49:20
Thomas Acres 37	1	33N26	86w57	5:47:48
Thomas Hill 61	1	33N10	86w19	5:45:16
Thomaston 46	1	32N16	87w38	5:50:32
Thomasville 13	1	31N55	87w44	5:50:56
Thompson 6	1	32N08	85w43	5:42:52
Thorn Hill 47	1	34N14	87w37	5:50:28
Thornton 62	1	32N50	85w45	5:43:00
Thorntontown 39	1	34N50	87w20	5:49:20
Thorsby 11	1	32N55	86w43	5:46:52
Three Notch 6	1	32N05	85w31	5:42:04
Three Notches 49	1	30N36	88w10	5:52:40
Threet 39	1	34N56	87w46	5:51:04
Thurston 31	1	31N02	85w51	5:43:24
Tibbie 65	1	31N22	88w15	5:53:00
Tilden 24	1	32N05	87w00	5:48:00
Till 7	1	31N38	86w44	5:46:56
Tiller Crossroads 9	5	32N48	85w39	5:42:36
Tillery Crossroads 41	5	32N47	85w09	5:40:36
Tillmans Corner 49	1	30N36	88w10	5:52:40
Tinela 50	1	31N50	87w23	5:49:32
Titus 26	1	32N41	86w15	5:45:00
Toadvine 37	1	33N26	86w57	5:47:48
Toddtown 13	1	31N42	87w46	5:51:04
Tompkinsville 12	1	32N13	88w10	5:52:40
Toney 45	2	34N54	86w44	5:46:56
Toonersville 39	1	34N50	87w20	5:49:20
Town Creek 40	1	34N41	87w24	5:49:36
Townley 64	1	33N52	87w26	5:49:44
Toxey 12	1	31N55	88w19	5:53:16
Trade 22	1	34N06	87w04	5:48:16
Trafford 37	1	33N49	86w45	5:47:00
Travis Bridge 18	1	31N26	86w56	5:47:44
Tredegar 8	1	33N49	85w46	5:43:04
Trenton 36	1	34N45	86w15	5:45:00
Triana 45	2	34N35	86w44	5:46:56
Trimble 22	1	34N11	86w48	5:47:12
Trinity 52	1	34N35	87w06	5:48:24
Troy 55	1	31N48	85w58	5:43:52
Trussville 37	1	33N37	86w36	5:46:24
Tuckabatchie 26	1	32N31	85w53	5:43:32
Tucker Crossroads 10	1	34N13	85w36	5:42:24
Tumbleton 34	1	31N22	85w20	5:41:20
Tunnel Springs 50	1	31N38	87w14	5:48:56
Tupelo 36	1	34N39	86w01	5:44:04
Turkestan 50	1	31N50	87w06	5:48:24
Turkey Branch 2	1	30N24	87w46	5:51:04
Turkeytown 28	1	34N04	85w53	5:43:32
Turner Crossroads 16	1	31N23	85w56	5:43:44
Tuscaloosa 63	6	33N12	87w34	5:50:16
Tuscumbia 17	1	34N44	87w42	5:50:48
Tuskegee 44	1	32N25	85w42	5:42:48
Tuskegee Institute 44	1	32N25	85w42	5:42:48
Twin 47	1	33N57	87w53	5:51:32
Twinsprings 3	1	31N53	85w09	5:40:36
Tyler 24	1	32N21	86w53	5:47:32
Tyler Crossroads 3	1	31N47	85w33	5:42:12
Tyson 43	1	32N16	86w23	5:45:32
Tysonville 44	1	32N24	85w56	5:43:44
Uchee 57	7	32N16	85w17	5:41:08
Underwood 39	1	34N49	87w40	5:50:40
Underwood 59	1	33N05	86w51	5:47:24
Underwood Crossroads 17	1	34N42	87w34	5:50:16
Union 28	1	34N10	86w09	5:44:36
Union 32	1	32N50	87w53	5:51:32
Union 34	1	31N33	85w15	5:41:00
Union 52	1	34N28	86w48	5:47:12
Union 62	1	32N50	85w45	5:43:00
Union Academy 16	1	31N19	85w49	5:43:16
Union Grove 11	1	32N57	86w45	5:47:00
Union Grove 22	1	34N10	86w37	5:46:28
Union Grove 48	1	34N25	86w27	5:45:48
Union Hill 15	1	33N38	85w35	5:42:20
Union Hill 42	1	34N50	87w16	5:49:04
Union Hill 52	1	34N22	86w54	5:47:36
Union Springs 6	1	32N09	85w43	5:42:52
Uniontown 53	1	32N27	87w31	5:50:04
Unity 19	1	33N01	86w19	5:45:16
Unity 63	6	33N12	87w32	5:50:08
Universal Heights 63	6	33N12	87w32	5:50:08
University 63	6	33N13	87w33	5:50:12
University Of South Alabama 49	1	30N42	88w10	5:52:40
Upper Coalburg 37	6	33N37	86w48	5:47:12
Upshaw 67	1	34N12	87w11	5:48:44
Uptown 37	1	33N26	86w57	5:47:48
Uriah 50	1	31N19	87w36	5:50:24
Valdosta 17	1	34N44	87w42	5:50:48
Valhermoso Springs 52	1	34N30	86w41	5:46:44
Vallegrande 24	1	32N23	87w00	5:48:00
Valley Creek 37	1	33N23	87w04	5:48:16
Valley Head 25	1	34N34	85w37	5:42:28
Vance 63	1	33N11	87w14	5:48:56
Vandiver 59	1	33N28	86w31	5:46:04
Vangale 46	1	32N06	87w52	5:51:28
Vaughn 2	1	31N00	87w52	5:51:28
Verbena 11	1	32N45	86w31	5:46:04
Vernledge 21	1	31N43	86w16	5:45:04
Vernon 38	1	33N45	88w07	5:52:28
Vernontown 4	1	33N07	87w07	5:48:28
Vestavia Hills 37	1	33N25	86w47	5:47:08
Vesthaven 37	6	33N27	86w47	5:47:08
Veterans Hospital 63	6	33N12	87w32	5:50:08
Veto 42	1	34N56	86w59	5:47:56
Victoria 16	1	31N33	85w53	5:43:32
Vida 1	1	32N28	86w27	5:45:48
Vidette 21	1	31N43	86w16	5:45:04
Viewpoint 25	1	34N18	85w56	5:43:44
Vigo 8	1	33N56	85w37	5:42:28
Village Springs 5	1	33N46	86w38	5:46:32
Villula 57	7	32N11	85w10	5:40:40
Vina 30	1	34N23	88w04	5:52:16
Vincent 59	1	33N23	86w25	5:45:40
Vinegar Bend 65	1	31N16	88w21	5:53:24
Vine Hill 1	1	32N34	86w55	5:47:40
Vineland 46	1	31N55	87w45	5:51:00
Vineland Park 37	1	33N26	86w57	5:47:48
Vinemont 22	1	34N15	86w52	5:47:28
Virginia 37	1	33N26	86w57	5:47:48
Virginia Shores 17	1	34N45	87w41	5:50:44
Vocation 50	1	31N01	87w30	5:50:00
Volanta 2	1	30N31	87w54	5:51:36
Vredenburgh 50	1	31N53	87w19	5:49:16
Waco 30	1	34N30	87w44	5:50:56
Wadley 56	1	33N07	85w34	5:42:16
Wadsworth 1	1	32N41	86w27	5:45:48
Wagar 65	1	31N27	88w02	5:52:08
Wagarville 65	1	31N27	88w02	5:52:08
Walco 61	1	33N10	86w19	5:45:16
Waldo 61	1	33N26	86w06	5:44:24
Walker Chapel 37	6	33N37	86w48	5:47:12
Walkers Corner 22	1	34N11	86w48	5:47:12
Walker Springs 13	1	31N32	87w47	5:51:08
Walkerton 58	1	33N35	86w23	5:45:32
Wallace 27	1	31N05	87w04	5:48:16
Walley 65	1	31N16	88w21	5:53:24
Wallsboro 26	1	32N31	86w12	5:44:48
Wallsburg 26	1	32N37	86w14	5:44:56
Wall Street 42	1	34N41	86w41	5:46:44
Walnut Grove 28	1	34N04	86w18	5:45:12
Walnut Grove 37	1	33N28	86w55	5:47:40
Walnut Hill 62	1	32N50	85w45	5:43:00
Walter 22	1	34N04	86w46	5:47:04
Wannville 36	1	34N43	85w58	5:43:52
Ward 60	1	32N22	88w17	5:53:08
Ware 26	1	32N31	85w53	5:43:32
Warrenton 48	1	34N21	86w19	5:45:16
Warrior 37	1	33N49	86w49	5:47:16
Warriorstand 44	1	32N15	85w36	5:42:24
Warsaw 60	1	32N57	88w16	5:53:04
Waterford 23	1	31N20	85w36	5:42:24
Waterloo 39	1	34N55	88w04	5:52:16
Water Valley 12	1	31N53	88w20	5:53:20
Watson 10	1	34N16	85w34	5:42:16
Watson 37	1	33N38	86w53	5:47:32
Watsonville 66	1	31N50	87w06	5:48:24
Watts Mill 14	1	33N18	85w45	5:43:00
Wattsville 58	1	33N40	86w17	5:45:08
Waugh 51	4	32N23	86w15	5:45:00
Waverly 41	5	32N44	85w35	5:42:20
Wawbeek 27	1	31N01	87w30	5:50:00
Wayne 46	1	32N06	87w52	5:51:28
Weaver 8	1	33N45	85w49	5:43:16
Webb 35	1	31N17	85w16	5:41:04
Webb Addition 36	1	34N39	86w01	5:44:04
Webster Chapel 8	6	33N57	86w01	5:44:04
Wedgworth 33	1	32N45	87w44	5:50:56
Wedowee 56	1	33N19	85w29	5:41:56
Weed Crossroad 21	1	31N35	86w15	5:45:00
Weeden Heights 39	1	34N49	87w40	5:50:40
Weeks 31	1	31N13	86w10	5:44:40
Wegra 64	1	33N38	87w07	5:48:28
Wehadkee 56	1	33N09	85w22	5:41:28
Wellington 8	1	33N49	85w54	5:43:36
Welti 22	1	34N08	86w44	5:46:56
Wende 57	7	32N14	85w25	5:41:40
Wenonah 37	6	33N28	86w52	5:47:28
Weogufka 19	1	33N01	86w19	5:45:16
Weoka 26	1	32N31	86w12	5:44:48
Wessington 11	1	33N06	86w45	5:47:00
West 45	2	34N44	86w36	5:46:24
West Alexandria 8	1	33N46	85w53	5:43:32
West Anniston 8	6	33N40	85w50	5:43:20
West Bend 13	1	31N46	88w05	5:52:20
West Blocton 4	1	33N07	87w07	5:48:28
West Decatur 52	3	34N33	86w59	5:47:56
West End 8	1	33N40	85w55	5:43:40
West End 37	6	33N28	86w52	5:47:28
West End Anniston 8	6	33N40	85w50	5:43:20
West Ensley 37	1	33N31	86w56	5:47:44
Western Hills 49	1	30N42	88w10	5:52:40
Western Hills Mall 37	1	33N28	86w55	5:47:40
West Fairfield 37	1	33N28	86w55	5:47:40
West Greene 32	1	32N56	88w05	5:52:20
West Highlands 37	1	33N26	86w57	5:47:48
West Jasper 64	1	33N48	87w20	5:49:20
West Jefferson 37	1	33N39	87w03	5:48:12
West Lake Highlands 37	1	33N26	86w57	5:47:48
West Monroeville 50	1	31N31	87w20	5:49:20
Weston 47	1	34N09	88w02	5:52:08
Westover 59	1	33N21	86w32	5:46:08
West Point 22	1	34N14	86w52	5:47:28
West Pratt 64	1	33N44	87w07	5:48:28
West Sayre 37	1	33N44	87w07	5:48:28
West Selmont 24	1	32N23	87w00	5:48:00
West Side 37	1	33N26	86w57	5:47:48
West Side 51	4	32N22	86w20	5:45:20
West Wellington 8	1	33N49	85w54	5:43:36
Westwood 37	6	33N34	86w52	5:47:28
Wetumpka 26	1	32N32	86w13	5:44:52
Whatley 13	1	31N39	87w42	5:50:48
Wheat 22	1	34N06	87w04	5:48:16
Wheeler 40	1	34N40	87w19	5:49:16
White City 1	1	32N43	86w29	5:45:56
White City 22	1	34N04	86w46	5:47:04
White Hall 43	1	32N20	86w43	5:46:52
Whitehead 39	1	34N50	87w20	5:49:20
Whitehouse 47	1	34N14	87w37	5:50:28
Whitehouse Forks 2	1	30N54	87w47	5:51:08
Whiteoak 17	1	34N42	87w34	5:50:16
White Oak 34	1	31N33	85w15	5:41:00
Whiteoak 48	1	34N16	86w12	5:44:48
White Plains 8	6	33N40	85w50	5:43:20

ALABAMA

Place		Lat.	Long.	Time
White Plains 9	5	32N54	85w24	5:41:36
Whites Bluff 24	1	32N19	87w17	5:49:08
Whitesboro 28	1	34N10	86w09	5:44:36
Whites Chapel 58	1	33N36	86w32	5:46:08
Whites Gap 8	1	33N49	85w46	5:43:04
Whiteside	3	34N38	86w57	5:47:48
White Signboard Crossroads 56	1	33N09	85w22	5:41:28
Whitesville 48	1	34N10	86w09	5:44:36
Whitfield 60	1	32N29	88w19	5:53:16
Whitney 58	1	33N50	86w15	5:45:00
Whiton 25	1	34N17	85w59	5:43:56
Whitson 63	6	33N12	87w32	5:50:08
Whorton 10	1	34N09	85w41	5:42:44
Wicksburg 35	1	31N14	85w32	5:42:08
Wiggins 20	1	31N17	86w27	5:45:48
Wigginsville 42	1	34N48	86w58	5:47:52
Wiginton 47	1	34N16	87w50	5:51:20
Wilburn 22	1	33N54	86w58	5:47:52
Wilkes 37	1	33N28	86w55	5:47:40
Wilkinstown 16	1	31N48	85w56	5:43:44
Willow Springs 26	1	32N31	86w12	5:44:48
Wills Crossroads 34	1	31N33	85w15	5:41:00
Wills Valley 28	1	34N08	86w01	5:44:04
Wilmer 49	1	30N44	88w28	5:53:52
Wilsonia	1	34N06	85w54	5:43:36
Wilson Lake Shores 17	1	34N45	87w41	5:50:44
Wilsonville 59	1	33N15	86w32	5:46:08
Wilton 59	1	33N03	86w52	5:47:28
Wimberly 12	1	31N55	88w19	5:53:16
Windham Springs 63	1	33N24	87w30	5:50:00
Windsor Highlands 37	6	33N27	86w49	5:47:16
Winfield 47	1	33N56	87w49	5:51:16
Wing 20	1	31N02	86w37	5:46:28
Wingaro 55	1	31N53	86w07	5:44:28
Winn 13	1	31N32	87w53	5:51:32
Winninger 36	1	34N38	86w16	5:45:04
Winslow 1	1	32N26	86w39	5:46:36
Winterboro 61	1	33N19	86w12	5:44:48
Winton 52	1	34N28	86w48	5:47:12
Wolf Creek 58	1	33N35	86w23	5:45:32
Wolf Springs 40	1	34N41	87w24	5:49:36
Womack Hill 12	1	31N53	88w20	5:53:20
Woodaire Estates 37	1	33N37	86w41	5:46:44
Woodbluff 13	1	31N55	87w59	5:51:56
Woodford 60	1	32N29	88w04	5:52:16
Woodland 44	1	32N34	85w39	5:42:36
Woodland 56	1	33N22	85w20	5:41:20
Woodlawn 37	6	33N33	86w45	5:47:00
Woodlawn Heights 30	1	34N30	87w44	5:50:56
Woodmeadow 37	6	33N25	86w48	5:47:12
Woodmont 37	1	33N26	86w57	5:47:48
Woodstock 4	1	33N13	87w09	5:48:36
Woodville 36	1	34N38	86w17	5:45:08
Woodward 37	1	33N26	86w57	5:47:48
Woolfolk 61	1	33N32	85w57	5:43:48
Wren 40	1	34N26	87w18	5:49:12
Wright 39	1	34N55	88w04	5:52:16
Wyatt 64	1	33N46	87w20	5:49:20
Wylam 37	1	33N31	86w56	5:47:44
Wynnville 5	1	34N04	86w21	5:45:24
Yantley 12	1	32N15	88w23	5:53:32
Yarbo 65	1	31N32	88w17	5:53:08
Yelling Settlement 2	1	30N36	87w54	5:51:36
Yellow Bluff 66	1	31N58	87w32	5:50:08
Yellow Creek Falls 10	1	34N13	85w36	5:42:24
Yellowleaf 59	1	33N15	86w30	5:46:00
Yellow Pine 65	1	31N24	88w26	5:53:44
York 60	1	32N29	88w18	5:53:12
Youngblood 55	1	31N48	85w56	5:43:44
Youngs Chapel 28	6	33N57	86w01	5:44:04
Yupon 2	1	30N24	87w46	5:51:04
Zimco 13	1	31N42	87w46	5:51:04
Zion 54	1	33N20	87w54	5:51:36
Zip City 39	1	34N49	87w40	5:50:40
Zoar 16	1	31N25	86w04	5:44:16

TIME TABLES

On October 30, 1983, the entire state of Alaska went on Yukon time (9 hours west), replacing four time zones with one. Islands west of 169w30 longitude observe AHST standard time (10 hours west).

AK # 1

Date	Time	Zone
Before 8/20/1900		LMT
8/20/1900	12:00	YST
2/09/1942	02:00	YWT
9/30/1945	02:00	YST
4/27/1969	02:00	YDT
10/26/1969	02:00	YST
4/26/1970	02:00	YDT
10/25/1970	02:00	YST
4/25/1971	02:00	YDT
10/31/1971	02:00	YST
4/30/1972	02:00	YDT
10/29/1972	02:00	YST
4/29/1973	02:00	YDT
10/28/1973	02:00	YST
1/06/1974	02:00	YDT
10/27/1974	02:00	YST
2/23/1975	02:00	YDT
10/26/1975	02:00	YST
4/25/1976	02:00	YDT
10/31/1976	02:00	YST
4/24/1977	02:00	YDT
10/30/1977	02:00	YST
4/30/1978	02:00	YDT
10/29/1978	02:00	YST
4/29/1979	02:00	YDT
10/28/1979	02:00	YST
4/27/1980	02:00	YDT
10/26/1980	02:00	YST
4/26/1981	02:00	YDT
10/25/1981	02:00	YST
4/25/1982	02:00	YDT
10/31/1982	02:00	YST
4/24/1983	02:00	YDT
10/30/1983	02:00	YST
4/29/1984	02:00	US#1

AK # 2

Date	Time	Zone
Before 8/20/1900		LMT
8/20/1900	12:00	BST
2/09/1942	02:00	BWT
9/30/1945	02:00	BST
9/22/1968	02:00	AHST
4/27/1969	02:00	AHDT
10/26/1969	02:00	AHST
4/26/1970	02:00	AHDT
10/25/1970	02:00	AHST
4/25/1971	02:00	AHDT
10/31/1971	02:00	AHST
4/30/1972	02:00	AHDT
10/29/1972	02:00	AHST
4/29/1973	02:00	AHDT
10/28/1973	02:00	AHST
1/06/1974	02:00	AHDT
10/27/1974	02:00	AHST
2/23/1975	02:00	AHDT
10/26/1975	02:00	AHST
4/25/1976	02:00	AHDT
10/31/1976	02:00	AHST
4/24/1977	02:00	AHDT
10/30/1977	02:00	AHST
4/30/1978	02:00	AHDT
10/29/1978	02:00	AHST
4/29/1979	02:00	AHDT
10/28/1979	02:00	AHST
4/27/1980	02:00	AHDT
10/26/1980	02:00	AHST
4/26/1981	02:00	AHDT
10/25/1981	02:00	AHST
4/25/1982	02:00	AHDT
10/31/1982	02:00	AHST
4/24/1983	02:00	AHDT
10/30/1983	02:00	YST
4/29/1984	02:00	US#1

AK # 3

Date	Time	Zone
Before 8/20/1900		LMT
8/20/1900	12:00	BST
2/09/1942	02:00	BWT
9/30/1945	02:00	BST
10/27/1968	02:00	AHST
4/27/1969	02:00	AHDT
10/26/1969	02:00	AHST
4/26/1970	02:00	AHDT
10/25/1970	02:00	AHST
4/25/1971	02:00	AHDT
10/31/1971	02:00	AHST
4/30/1972	02:00	AHDT
10/29/1972	02:00	AHST
4/29/1973	02:00	AHDT
10/28/1973	02:00	AHST
1/06/1974	02:00	AHDT
10/27/1974	02:00	AHST
2/23/1975	02:00	AHDT
10/26/1975	02:00	AHST
4/25/1976	02:00	AHDT
10/31/1976	02:00	AHST
4/24/1977	02:00	AHDT
10/30/1977	02:00	AHST
4/30/1978	02:00	AHDT
10/29/1978	02:00	AHST
4/29/1979	02:00	AHDT
10/28/1979	02:00	AHST
4/27/1980	02:00	AHDT
10/26/1980	02:00	AHST
4/26/1981	02:00	AHDT
10/25/1981	02:00	AHST
4/25/1982	02:00	AHDT
10/31/1982	02:00	AHST
4/24/1983	02:00	AHDT
10/30/1983	02:00	YST
4/29/1984	02:00	US#1

AK # 4

Date	Time	Zone
Before 8/20/1900		LMT
8/20/1900	12:00	PST
2/09/1942	02:00	PWT
9/30/1945	02:00	PST
4/27/1969	02:00	PDT
10/26/1969	02:00	PST
4/26/1970	02:00	PDT
10/25/1970	02:00	PST
4/25/1971	02:00	PDT
10/31/1971	02:00	PST
4/30/1972	02:00	PDT
10/29/1972	02:00	PST
4/29/1973	02:00	PDT
10/28/1973	02:00	PST
1/06/1974	02:00	PDT
10/27/1974	02:00	PST
2/23/1975	02:00	PDT
10/26/1975	02:00	PST
4/25/1976	02:00	PDT
10/31/1976	02:00	PST
4/24/1977	02:00	PDT
10/30/1977	02:00	PST
4/30/1978	02:00	PDT
10/29/1978	02:00	PST
4/29/1979	02:00	PDT
10/28/1979	02:00	PST
4/27/1980	02:00	PDT
10/26/1980	02:00	PST
4/26/1981	02:00	PDT
10/25/1981	02:00	PST
4/25/1982	02:00	PDT
10/31/1982	02:00	PST
4/24/1983	02:00	PDT
10/30/1983	02:00	YST
4/29/1984	02:00	US#1

AK # 5

Date	Time	Zone
Before 8/20/1900		LMT
8/20/1900	12:00	AHST
2/09/1942	02:00	AHWT
9/30/1945	02:00	AHST
4/27/1969	02:00	AHDT
10/26/1969	02:00	AHST
4/26/1970	02:00	AHDT
10/25/1970	02:00	AHST
4/25/1971	02:00	AHDT
10/31/1971	02:00	AHST
4/30/1972	02:00	AHDT
10/29/1972	02:00	AHST
4/29/1973	02:00	AHDT
10/28/1973	02:00	AHST
1/06/1974	02:00	AHDT
10/27/1974	02:00	AHST
2/23/1975	02:00	AHDT
10/26/1975	02:00	AHST
4/25/1976	02:00	AHDT
10/31/1976	02:00	AHST
4/24/1977	02:00	AHDT
10/30/1977	02:00	AHST
4/30/1978	02:00	AHDT
10/29/1978	02:00	AHST
4/29/1979	02:00	AHDT
10/28/1979	02:00	AHST
4/27/1980	02:00	AHDT
10/26/1980	02:00	AHST
4/26/1981	02:00	AHDT
10/25/1981	02:00	AHST
4/25/1982	02:00	AHDT
10/31/1982	02:00	AHST
4/24/1983	02:00	AHDT
10/30/1983	02:00	YST
4/29/1984	02:00	US#1

AK # 6

Date	Time	Zone
Before 8/20/1900		LMT
8/20/1900	12:00	BST
2/09/1942	02:00	BWT
9/30/1945	02:00	BST
4/27/1969	02:00	BDT
10/26/1969	02:00	BST
4/26/1970	02:00	BDT
10/25/1970	02:00	BST
4/25/1971	02:00	BDT
10/31/1971	02:00	BST
4/30/1972	02:00	BDT
10/29/1972	02:00	BST
4/29/1973	02:00	BDT
10/28/1973	02:00	BST
1/06/1974	02:00	BDT
10/27/1974	02:00	BST
2/23/1975	02:00	BDT
10/26/1975	02:00	BST
4/25/1976	02:00	BDT
10/31/1976	02:00	BST
4/24/1977	02:00	BDT
10/30/1977	02:00	BST
4/30/1978	02:00	BDT
10/29/1978	02:00	BST
4/29/1979	02:00	BDT
10/28/1979	02:00	BST
4/27/1980	02:00	BDT
10/26/1980	02:00	BST
4/26/1981	02:00	BDT
10/25/1981	02:00	BST
4/25/1982	02:00	BDT
10/31/1982	02:00	BST
4/24/1983	02:00	BDT
10/30/1983	02:00	YST
4/29/1984	02:00	US#1

AK # 7

Date	Time	Zone
Before 8/20/1900		LMT
8/20/1900	12:00	BST
2/09/1942	02:00	BWT
9/30/1945	02:00	BST
4/27/1969	02:00	BDT
10/26/1969	02:00	BST
4/26/1970	02:00	BDT
10/25/1970	02:00	BST
4/25/1971	02:00	BDT
10/31/1971	02:00	BST
4/30/1972	02:00	BDT
10/29/1972	02:00	BST
4/29/1973	02:00	BDT
10/28/1973	02:00	BST
1/06/1974	02:00	BDT
10/27/1974	02:00	BST
2/23/1975	02:00	BDT
10/26/1975	02:00	BST
4/25/1976	02:00	BDT
10/31/1976	02:00	BST
4/24/1977	02:00	BDT
10/30/1977	02:00	BST
4/30/1978	02:00	BDT
10/29/1978	02:00	BST
4/29/1979	02:00	BDT
10/28/1979	02:00	BST
4/27/1980	02:00	BDT
10/26/1980	02:00	BST
4/26/1981	02:00	BDT
10/25/1981	02:00	BST
4/25/1982	02:00	BDT
10/31/1982	02:00	BST
4/24/1983	02:00	BDT
10/30/1983	02:00	AHST
4/29/1984	02:00	US#1

COUNTIES

1 Aleutian Islands
2 Anchorage
3 Angoon
4 Barrow-North Slope
5 Bethel
6 Bristol Bay Borough
7 Bristol Bay
8 Cordova-McCarthy
9 Fairbanks
10 Haines
11 Juneau
12 Kenai-Cook Inlet
13 Ketchikan
14 Kobuk
15 Kodiak
16 Kuskokwim
17 Matanuska-Susitna
18 Nome
19 Outer Ketchikan
20 Prince of Wales
21 Seward
22 Sitka
23 Skagway-Yakutat
24 Southeast Fairbanks
25 Upper Yukon
26 Valdez-Chitina-Whittier
27 Wade Hampton
28 Wrangell-Petersburg
29 Yukon-Koykuk

Place		Lat	Long	Time
Ac	2	61N00	159w57	10:39:48
Adak	7	51N52	176w39	11:46:36
Adak Naval Station 1	7	51N52	176w39	11:46:36
Akhiok 15	5	56N57	154w10	10:16:40
Akiachak 5	3	60N55	161w26	10:45:44
Akiak 5	3	60N55	161w13	10:44:52
Akolmiut 5	6	60N54	162w30	10:50:00
Akutan 1	6	54N08	165w46	11:03:04
Alakanuk 27	6	62N41	164w37	10:58:28
Alatna 29	5	66N34	152w39	10:10:36
Aleknagik 7	2	59N17	158w36	10:34:24
Aleknagik Mission 7	2	59N17	158w36	10:34:24
Aleutian Islands 1	7	52N07	176w36	11:46:24
Alexander	5	61N25	150w36	10:02:24
Alexander 17	2	58N03	158w49	10:35:16
Alitak 15	5	57N21	153w10	10:12:40
Allakaket 29	5	66N34	152w39	10:10:36
Ambler 14	2	67N05	157w52	10:31:28
Anaktuvuk Pass 4	5	68N08	151w45	10:07:00
Anchorage 2	5	61N13	149w54	9:59:36
Anchor Point 12	5	59N47	151w50	10:07:20
Anderson 29	5	64N25	149w15	9:57:00
Andreafsky	6	62N03	163w10	10:52:40
Angoon 3	4	57N30	134w35	8:58:20
Aniak 16	2	61N35	159w32	10:38:08
Annette 19	4	55N04	131w33	8:46:12
Anvik 16	2	62N39	160w13	10:40:52
Arctic Village 25	5	68N08	145w32	9:42:08
Atka 1	7	52N12	174w12	11:36:48
Atmautluak 5	6	60N49	162w43	10:50:52
Auke Bay 11	4	58N23	134w40	8:58:40
Aurora 9	5	64N51	147w47	9:51:08
Aurora Lodge 9	5	64N29	146w59	9:47:56
Baranof 22	4	57N05	134w50	8:59:20
Barrow 4	5	71N18	156w47	10:27:08
Bartlett Cove 23	4	58N25	135w44	9:02:56
Basher	5	61N10	149w41	9:58:44
Beaver 25	5	66N22	147w24	9:49:36
Belkofski 1	6	55N05	162w02	10:48:08
Bell Island Hot Springs 19	4	55N24	132w08	8:48:32
Bethel 5	3	60N48	161w45	10:47:00
Bettles 29	5	66N55	151w42	10:06:48
Big Delta 24	5	64N10	145w51	9:43:24
Big Lake 17	5	67N30	149w27	9:57:48
Big Mountain Radio Relay 6	2	58N03	158w49	10:35:16
Bill Moores	6	62N57	163w46	10:55:04
Biorka	6	53N50	166w13	11:04:52
Birch Creek 25	5	69N00	147w22	9:49:28
Birch Estates 9	5	64N51	147w47	9:51:08
Birch Lake 24	5	64N51	147w47	9:51:08
Birchwood 2	5	61N24	149w29	9:57:56
Bjerremark 9	5	64N51	147w47	9:51:08
Border 24	5	63N07	143w22	9:33:28
Boswell Bay 8	5	60N33	145w45	9:43:00
Boundary	5	64N04	141w06	9:24:24
Boundary 25	5	64N51	147w47	9:51:08
Boyd 9	5	64N51	147w47	9:51:08
Brevig Mission 18	6	65N20	166w29	11:05:56
Bristol Bay	2	59N19	157w44	10:30:56
Broadmoor Acres 9	5	64N51	147w47	9:51:08
Broad Pass	5	63N14	149w16	9:57:04
Browerville 4	5	71N18	156w47	10:27:08
Buckland 14	3	65N59	161w08	10:44:32
Butte 17	5	61N33	149w03	9:56:12
Campbell 2	5	61N12	149w53	9:59:32
Campbell 20	4	55N22	132w43	8:50:52
Candle 14	3	65N55	161w56	10:47:44
Cantwell 29	5	63N24	148w57	9:55:48
Cape Fanshaw	4	57N13	133w30	8:54:00
Cape Lisburne 4	6	68N52	166w05	11:04:20
Cape Newenham Air Force Sta 5	3	59N01	161w49	10:47:16
Cape Pole 20	4	55N58	133w48	8:55:12
Cape Romanzof 27	6	60N49	162w43	10:50:52
Cape Sarichef Radio Relay 1	6	53N53	166w32	11:06:08
Cape Yakataga 8	5	60N04	142w26	9:29:44
Carlanna 13	4	55N24	132w08	8:48:32
Central 25	5	65N35	144w48	9:39:12
Chalkyitsik 25	5	66N39	143w43	9:34:52
Chandalar	5	67N30	148w30	9:54:00
Chaniliut	6	63N02	163w25	10:53:40
Charcoal Point 13	4	55N24	132w08	8:48:32
Chase 17	5	62N28	150w07	10:00:28
Chatanika 9	5	65N07	147w28	9:49:52
Chatham	4	57N31	134w56	8:59:44
Chefornak 5	6	60N13	164w12	10:56:48
Chena Hot Springs 9	5	64N51	147w47	9:51:08
Chernofski 1	6	53N25	167w33	11:10:12
Chevak 27	6	61N32	165w35	11:02:20
Chickaloon	5	61N48	148w28	9:53:52
Chickaloon 17	5	59N47	154w07	10:16:28
Chicken 25	5	64N05	141w56	9:27:44
Chignik 1	2	56N18	158w24	10:33:36
Chignik Lagoon	2	56N20	158w29	10:33:56
Chignik Lake 1	2	56N14	158w47	10:35:08
Chisana 24	5	62N04	142w03	9:28:12
Chistochina 26	5	62N34	144w40	9:38:40
Chitina 26	5	61N31	144w26	9:37:44
Chuathbaluk 16	2	61N34	159w16	10:37:04
Chugiak 2	5	61N24	149w29	9:57:56

ALASKA

Circle 25 5 65N50 144w04 9:36:16
Circle Hot Springs 25 5 65N29 144w38 9:38:32
Clam Gulch 12 5 60N15 151w23 10:05:32
Clarks Point 6 2 58N51 158w33 10:34:12
Clear 29 5 64N25 149w15 9:57:00
Clearwater Ranch 24 5 63N47 145w14 9:40:56
Clover Pass 13 4 55N25 131w48 8:47:12
Coal Creek 25 5 64N51 147w47 9:51:08
Cohoe 12 5 60N22 151w18 10:05:12
Cold Bay 1 6 55N12 162w42 10:50:48
College 9 5 64N52 147w49 9:51:16
Colorado 5 63N10 149w26 9:57:44
Colorado 17 2 58N03 158w49 10:35:16
Colville River 4 5 71N18 156w47 10:27:08
Cooper Landing 21 5 60N29 149w50 9:59:20
Copper Center 26 5 61N58 145w18 9:41:12
Cordova 8 5 60N33 145w45 9:43:00
Cottonwood 17 5 61N34 149w43 9:58:52
Craig 20 4 55N29 133w09 8:52:36
Crooked Creek 16 5 64N56 141w40 9:26:40
Curry 17 5 62N37 150w01 10:00:04
Curry's Corner 9 5 64N51 147w47 9:51:08
Deadhorse 25 5 70N11 148w29 9:53:56
Deering 14 6 66N04 162w42 10:50:48
Delta Junction 24 5 64N02 145w44 9:42:56
Denali 5 63N11 147w28 9:49:52
Derby Tract 9 5 64N51 147w47 9:51:08
Dillingham 6 2 59N03 158w28 10:33:52
Diomede 18 6 65N47 169w00 11:16:00
Donnelly 24 5 63N41 145w53 9:43:32
Dot Lake 24 5 63N40 144w04 9:36:16
Douglas 11 4 58N17 134w24 8:57:36
Duncan Canal 28 4 56N48 132w58 8:51:52
Dutch Harbor 1 6 53N53 166w32 11:06:08
Eagle 25 5 64N47 141w12 9:24:48
Eagle River 2 5 61N19 149w34 9:58:16
Eagle Village 25 5 64N47 141w07 9:24:28
Eastchester 2 2 58N03 158w49 10:35:16
Edelta Junction 5 64N02 145w44 9:42:56
Edna Bay 4 55N57 133w40 8:54:40
Eek 5 6 60N14 162w02 10:48:08
Egegik 6 5 58N13 157w22 10:29:28
Eielson 5 5 64N38 147w06 9:48:24
Eielson Air Force Base 9 5 64N38 147w06 9:48:24
Eklutna 2 5 61N28 149w22 9:57:28
Eklutna Housing Project 2 5 61N36 149w20 9:57:20
Ekuk 6 2 58N49 158w34 10:34:16
Ekwok 6 5 59N22 157w30 10:30:00
Elfin Cove 23 4 58N12 136w22 9:05:28
Elim 18 6 64N37 162w15 10:49:00
Ellamar 5 60N54 146w43 9:46:52
Elmendorf 5 61N15 149w49 9:59:16
Elmendorf Air Force Base 2 5 61N15 149w49 9:59:16
Elmendorf Reservation 1 5 61N17 149w49 9:59:16
Emanguk 14 6 62N45 164w30 10:58:00
Emmonak 27 6 62N45 164w30 10:58:00
English Bay 12 5 59N22 151w55 10:07:40
Entrance Island 4 57N25 133w27 8:53:48
Eska 17 5 61N44 148w54 9:55:36
Ester 9 5 64N51 148w01 9:52:04
Eureka 17 5 61N36 149w20 9:57:20
Eureka 29 5 65N00 150w38 10:02:32
Eureka Roadhouse 5 61N56 147w10 9:48:40
Evansville 15 5 66N56 151w30 10:06:00
Excursion Inlet 23 4 58N25 135w27 9:01:48
Eyak 5 60N32 145w36 9:42:24
Eyak River Cabins 8 5 60N33 145w45 9:43:00
Fairbanks 9 5 64N51 147w43 9:50:52
Fairbanks North Star 5 5 64N48 148w21 9:53:24
False Pass 1 6 54N51 163w25 10:53:40
Farewell 16 5 63N06 154w44 10:18:56
Farewell Lake Lodge 5 62N31 153w54 10:15:36
Federal 2 2 58N03 158w49 10:35:16
Federal 9 5 64N51 147w47 9:51:08
Fire Lake 2 5 61N21 149w32 9:58:08
Flat 16 2 62N28 158w01 10:32:04
Fort Greely 24 5 64N00 145w44 9:42:56
Fort Richardson 2 5 61N16 149w41 9:58:44
Fortuna Ledge 27 6 61N53 162w05 10:48:20
Fort Wainwright 9 5 64N50 147w38 9:50:32
Fortymile Roadhouse 24 5 63N47 145w14 9:40:56
Fort Yukon 25 5 66N34 145w16 9:41:04
Fox 9 5 64N58 147w38 9:50:32
Fritz Cove 11 4 58N22 134w39 8:58:36
Fritz Creek 12 5 59N42 151w21 10:05:24
Funter 4 58N15 134w51 8:59:24
Funter Bay 3 4 58N21 134w33 8:58:12
Gakona 26 5 62N18 145w18 9:41:12
Galena 29 5 64N44 156w56 10:27:44
Gambell 18 7 63N47 171w45 11:27:00
Ganes Creek 16 5 62N56 156w04 10:24:16
Garner 5 63N50 148w59 9:55:56
Geist 9 5 64N51 147w47 9:51:08
Girdwood 2 5 60N57 149w10 9:56:40
Glen Alps 2 5 61N06 149w42 9:58:48
Glennallen 26 5 62N07 145w33 9:42:12
Goat Creek 17 5 61N25 149w26 9:57:44
Gold Creek 17 5 62N46 149w41 9:58:44
Golovin 18 6 64N33 163w02 10:52:08
Goodnews 3 59N07 161w35 10:46:20
Goodnews Bay 5 3 59N07 161w35 10:46:20
Goodnews Mining Camp 5 3 59N01 161w49 10:47:16
Gost Creek 2 62N13 159w47 10:39:08
Graehl 9 5 64N51 147w44 9:50:56
Granite Mountain 14 6 64N57 165w49 11:03:16
Grayling 16 2 62N57 160w03 10:40:12
Gulkana 26 5 62N16 145w23 9:41:32
Gulkana Airport 26 5 62N12 145w28 9:41:52
Gustavus 23 4 58N25 135w44 9:02:56
Haines 10 4 59N14 135w26 9:01:44
Halibut Cove 12 5 59N35 151w14 10:04:56
Hamilton 27 6 62N54 163w53 10:55:32
Hamilton Acres 9 5 64N51 147w47 9:51:08
Happy Valley 12 5 59N47 151w50 10:07:20
Harding Lake 9 5 64N51 147w47 9:51:08
Hawk Inlet 3 4 58N21 134w33 8:58:12
Healy 29 5 63N52 148w58 9:55:52
Herendeen Bay 2 55N50 160w50 10:43:20
Herring Cove 13 4 55N20 131w31 8:46:04
Hogatza 29 5 66N13 155w41 10:22:44
Hollis 20 4 55N24 132w08 8:48:32
Holy Cross 16 2 62N12 159w46 10:39:04
Homer 12 5 59N39 151w33 10:06:12
Hoonah 23 4 58N07 135w27 9:01:48
Hooper Bay 27 6 61N32 166w06 11:04:24
Hope 21 5 60N55 149w39 9:58:36
Houston 17 5 61N38 149w51 9:59:24
Hughes 29 5 66N03 154w15 10:17:00
Huslia 29 5 65N41 156w24 10:25:36
Hydaburg 20 4 55N12 132w50 8:51:20
Hyder 19 4 55N55 130w02 8:40:08
Iguigig 6 5 59N16 155w53 10:23:32
Ikatan 1 6 54N45 163w19 10:53:16
Iliamna 6 5 59N45 154w55 10:19:40
Indian River 29 5 66N34 152w39 10:10:36
Island Homes 9 5 64N51 147w47 9:51:08
Ivanof Bay 1 2 55N54 159w29 10:37:56
Jennie M. Fairbanks 9 5 64N51 147w47 9:51:08
Joe Ward Camp 5 66N52 143w42 9:34:48
Johnston 9 5 64N51 147w47 9:51:08
Juneau 11 4 58N18 134w25 8:57:40
Kachemak 12 5 59N40 151w26 10:05:44
Kaguyak 8 5 56N52 153w46 10:15:04
Kake 28 4 56N59 133w57 8:55:48
Kakhonak 4 5 59N26 154w51 10:19:24
Kaktovik 4 5 70N08 143w38 9:34:32
Kalakaket Creek Radio Relay 29 5 64N44 156w56 10:27:44
Kalskag 16 2 61N32 160w18 10:41:12
Kaltag 29 2 64N20 158w43 10:34:52
Karluk 15 5 57N34 154w28 10:17:52
Kasaan 20 4 55N32 132w24 8:49:36
Kashega 6 53N28 167w10 11:08:40
Kashegelok 16 5 61N42 157w10 10:28:40
Kasigluk 5 6 60N54 162w30 10:50:00
Kasilof 12 5 60N23 151w18 10:05:12
Katalla 5 60N12 144w31 9:38:04
Kenai 12 5 60N33 151w16 10:05:04
Kenai Lake 21 5 60N29 149w50 9:59:20
Kenai Packers Cannery 12 5 60N33 151w16 10:05:04
Kennicott 8 5 61N31 144w26 9:37:44
Ketchikan 13 4 55N21 131w39 8:46:36
Ketchikan Gateway 7 4 55N33 131w28 8:45:52
Kiana 14 2 66N58 160w26 10:41:44
King Cove 1 6 55N03 162w19 10:49:16
King Salmon 6 5 58N42 156w40 10:26:40
Kipnuk 5 6 59N56 164w03 10:56:12
Kivalina 14 6 67N44 164w33 10:58:12
Kiwalik 3 66N02 161w50 10:47:20
Klatt Road 2 2 58N03 158w49 10:35:16
Klawock 20 4 55N33 133w06 8:52:24
Klukwan 10 4 59N24 135w54 9:03:36
Knik 17 5 61N28 149w43 9:58:52
Knudson Cove 13 4 55N24 132w08 8:48:32
Kobuk 14 5 66N55 156w52 10:27:28
Kodiak 15 5 57N48 152w24 10:09:36
Kodiak Island 5 57N54 153w03 10:12:12
Kodiak Naval Station 15 5 57N45 152w29 10:09:56
Kokhanok 6 5 59N38 154w53 10:19:32
Kokiak 5 57N47 152w24 10:09:36
Kokrines 29 5 64N56 154w42 10:18:48
Koliganek 6 5 59N48 157w25 10:29:40
Kongiganak 5 6 59N52 163w02 10:52:08
Kotlik 27 6 63N02 163w33 10:54:12
Kotzebue 14 6 66N54 162w35 10:50:20
Koyuk 18 3 64N56 161w09 10:44:36
Koyukuk 29 2 64N53 157w42 10:30:48
Kupreanof 28 4 56N48 132w58 8:51:52
Kuskokwim 5 62N12 156w49 10:27:16
Kustatan 12 5 61N04 151w08 10:04:32
Kwethluk 5 3 60N49 161w26 10:45:44
Kwigillingok 5 6 59N51 163w08 10:52:32
Kwiguk 6 62N46 164w30 10:58:00
Kwinhagak 3 3 59N45 161w54 10:47:36
Lake Minchumina 29 5 63N53 152w19 10:09:16
Larsen Bay 15 5 57N32 153w59 10:15:56
Lawing 21 5 60N07 149w26 9:57:44
Lemeta 9 5 64N52 147w44 9:50:56
Lemon Creek 11 4 58N21 134w29 8:57:56
Lena Cove 11 4 58N24 134w46 8:59:04
Levelock 6 5 59N07 156w51 10:27:24
Lignite 5 63N55 149w01 9:56:04
Lime Village 16 5 61N21 155w28 10:21:52
Livengood 29 5 65N32 148w33 9:54:12
Long 29 5 64N45 155w30 10:22:00
Long Island 17 5 61N33 149w52 9:59:28
Loring 4 55N36 131w38 8:46:32
Lost River 23 1 59N33 139w44 9:18:56
Lower Kalskag 16 2 61N31 160w21 10:41:24
Lower Mendenhall Valley 11 4 58N22 134w35 8:58:20
Lower Tonsina 26 5 61N57 145w36 9:42:24
Mack 9 5 64N51 147w47 9:51:08
Manley Hot Springs 29 5 65N00 150w38 10:02:32
Manokotak 6 2 58N59 159w03 10:36:12
Marshall 14 6 61N53 162w05 10:48:20
Marvel Creek 5 2 61N34 159w24 10:37:36
Marys Igloo 18 6 65N09 165w04 11:00:16
Matanuska 17 5 61N33 149w14 9:56:56
May Creek 8 5 61N21 142w42 9:30:48
McCarthy 5 61N26 142w56 9:31:44
McCord 5 57N09 153w12 10:12:48
McGrath 16 5 62N58 155w36 10:22:24
McKinley Acres 9 5 64N51 147w47 9:51:08
McKinley Park 29 5 63N44 148w55 9:55:40
Meakerville 8 5 60N33 145w44 9:42:56
Medfra 16 5 63N06 154w44 10:18:56
Mekoryuk 5 6 60N23 166w11 11:04:44
Mellicks Trading Post 16 5 61N42 157w10 10:28:40
Mendeltna Lodge 17 5 61N36 149w20 9:57:20
Mendenhall Flats 11 4 58N22 134w38 8:58:32
Mentasta Lake 26 5 62N55 143w45 9:35:00
Metlakatla 19 4 55N08 131w35 8:46:20
Meyers Chuck 19 4 55N45 132w15 8:49:00
Miller House 5 65N32 145w13 9:40:52
Minto 29 5 64N53 149w11 9:56:44
Montana 17 5 62N05 150w04 10:00:16
Moose Creek 5 61N41 149w02 9:56:08
Moose Pass 21 5 60N29 149w22 9:57:28
Morzhovoi 1 6 54N55 163w18 10:53:12
Moses Point 18 6 64N42 162w02 10:48:08
Mountain Point 13 4 55N18 131w32 8:46:08
Mountain View 2 5 61N13 149w52 9:59:28
Mountain Village 27 6 62N05 163w43 10:54:52
Mount Edgecumbe 22 4 57N03 135w21 9:01:24
Mud Bay 13 4 55N25 131w46 8:47:04
Mumtrak 3 3 59N07 161w35 10:46:20
Myers Chuck 10 4 55N45 132w15 8:49:00
Nabesna 5 62N22 143w00 9:32:00
Naknek 6 5 58N44 157w01 10:28:04
Nancy 17 5 61N45 150w03 10:00:12
Napaimiut 2 61N33 158w42 10:34:48
Napaiskak 3 3 60N43 161w55 10:47:40
Napakiak 5 3 60N42 161w57 10:47:48
Nelson Lagoon 1 2 55N55 161w00 10:44:00
Nenana 29 5 64N34 149w05 9:56:20
Newhalen 6 5 59N43 154w54 10:19:36
New Stuyahok 6 5 59N29 157w20 10:29:20
Newtok 5 6 60N56 164w38 10:58:32
Nightmute 5 6 60N29 164w44 10:58:56
Nikishka 12 5 60N33 151w16 10:05:04
Nikolai 16 5 62N58 154w10 10:16:40
Nikolski 1 6 52N56 168w52 11:15:28
Nilak 27 6 62N32 164w52 10:59:28
Ninilchik 12 5 60N03 151w40 10:06:40
Noatak 14 6 67N34 162w58 10:51:52
Nolan 5 67N29 150w14 10:00:56
Nome 18 6 64N30 165w25 11:01:40
Nondalton 6 5 59N58 154w51 10:19:24
Noorvik 14 3 66N50 161w03 10:44:12
North Douglas 11 4 58N19 134w28 8:57:52
North Kenai 12 5 60N33 151w16 10:05:04
North Pole 9 5 64N45 147w21 9:49:24
Northway 24 5 62N58 141w56 9:27:44
Nulato 29 2 64N43 158w06 10:32:24
Nunaka Valley 2 5 61N12 149w46 9:59:04
Nunapitchuk 5 6 60N54 162w30 10:50:00
Nushagak 2 58N57 158w23 10:33:32
Odiak Slough 8 5 60N33 145w45 9:43:00
Old Andreafski 27 6 62N03 163w14 10:52:56
Old Harbor 15 5 57N12 153w18 10:13:12
Old Ninilchik 12 5 60N03 151w40 10:06:40
Old Tyonek 12 5 61N04 151w08 10:04:32
Olnes 9 5 65N05 147w40 9:50:40
Ophir 5 63N10 156w31 10:26:04
Orca 8 5 60N40 145w43 9:42:52
Oscarville 5 3 60N44 161w46 10:47:04
Otter 2 62N28 158w13 10:32:52
Outer Ketchikan 4 55N05 131w32 8:46:08
Ouzinki 15 5 57N56 152w30 10:10:00
Palmer 17 5 61N36 149w07 9:56:28
Paradise 2 62N25 160w03 10:40:12
Paradise Hill 16 2 62N12 159w46 10:39:04
Pauloff Harbor 1 6 54N28 162w42 10:50:48
Paxson 26 5 63N02 145w30 9:42:00
Pederson Point 7 5 58N44 157w01 10:28:04
Pedro Bay 7 5 59N47 154w07 10:16:28
Pelican 23 4 57N58 136w14 9:04:56
Peninsula Point 13 4 55N23 131w44 8:46:56
Pennock Island 13 4 55N20 131w38 8:46:32
Perryville 1 2 55N55 159w09 10:36:36
Petersburg 28 4 56N48 132w58 8:51:52
Peters Creek 2 5 61N25 149w26 9:57:44
Pile Bay Village 5 59N47 153w53 10:15:32
Pilot Point 6 2 57N34 157w35 10:30:20
Pilot Station 27 6 61N56 162w53 10:51:32
Pitkas Point 27 6 62N02 163w17 10:53:08
Platinum 5 3 59N01 161w49 10:47:16
Point Baker 26 4 56N21 133w37 8:54:28
Point Barrow Dew Station 4 5 71N18 156w47 10:27:08
Point Hope 4 6 68N21 166w47 11:07:08

ALASKA

Place		Lat	Long	Time
Point Lay	6	69N46	163w03	10:52:12
Point Retreat 3	4	58N21	134w33	8:58:12
Point Whiteshed 8	5	60N33	145w45	9:43:00
Portage	5	60N50	148w59	9:55:56
Portage Creek 7	2	59N24	158w38	10:34:32
Port Alexander 22	4	56N15	134w39	8:58:36
Port Alsworth 6	5	60N12	154w19	10:17:16
Port Ashton	5	60N04	148w03	9:52:12
Port Chilkoot	4	59N14	135w26	9:01:44
Port Clarence 18	6	64N57	165w49	11:03:16
Port Graham 12	5	59N21	151w50	10:07:20
Port Heiden 6	2	56N55	158w41	10:34:44
Port Higgins 13	4	55N27	131w49	8:47:16
Port Lions 15	5	57N52	152w53	10:11:32
Port Moller	2	56N00	160w35	10:42:20
Port Nellie Juan	5	60N33	148w10	9:52:40
Port Wakefield	5	58N03	153w03	10:12:12
Pounrevik 27	6	62N32	164w52	10:59:28
Prince Of Wales 10	4	55N44	133w15	8:53:00
Prudhoe Bay 4	5	70N15	148w22	9:53:28
Quartz Creek 12	5	60N29	149w50	9:59:20
Quinhagak 5	3	59N45	161w54	10:47:36
Rainbow	5	61N00	149w39	9:58:36
Rampart 29	5	65N30	150w10	10:00:40
Red Devil 16	5	61N46	157w19	10:29:16
Red Salmon 7	5	58N44	157w01	10:28:04
Rego 9	5	64N51	147w47	9:51:08
Rodman 22	4	57N03	135w20	9:01:20
Ruby 29	5	64N45	155w30	10:22:00
Russian Mission 27	3	61N47	161w19	10:45:16
Saint George 1	7	56N36	169w33	11:18:12
Saint Marys 27	6	62N03	163w10	10:52:40
Saint Michael 18	6	63N29	162w02	10:48:08
Saint Paul 1	7	57N07	170w17	11:21:08
Salmon Creek 11	4	58N20	134w28	8:57:52
Salt Chuck	4	55N38	132w33	8:50:12
Sanak	6	54N30	162w49	10:51:16
Sand Lake	5	61N09	149w57	9:59:48
Sand Point 1	2	55N20	160w30	10:42:00
San Juan Cannery	5	60N03	148w04	9:52:16
Savoonga 18	7	63N42	170w29	11:21:56
Saxman 13	4	55N19	131w36	8:46:24
Scammon Bay 27	6	61N51	165w35	11:02:20
Scow Bay 28	4	56N46	132w58	8:51:52
Seatons Stop 24	5	62N58	141w56	9:27:44
Selawik 14	2	66N36	160w00	10:40:00
Seldovia 12	5	59N26	151w43	10:06:52
Seward 21	5	60N07	149w27	9:57:48
Shageluk 16	2	62N41	159w34	10:38:16
Shaktoolik 18	3	64N20	161w09	10:44:36
Shanly 9	5	64N51	147w47	9:51:08
Sheldon Point 27	6	62N32	164w52	10:59:28
Shemya Station 1	2	58N03	158w49	10:35:16
Shishmaref 18	6	66N15	166w04	11:04:16
Shoreline Drive 13	4	55N24	132w08	8:48:32
Shuman House	5	66N54	143w46	9:35:04
Shungnak 14	5	66N52	157w09	10:28:36
Shungnak Village	5	66N55	156w52	10:27:28
Silvertip	5	60N45	149w22	9:57:28
Sitka 22	4	57N03	135w20	9:01:20
Skagway 23	4	59N28	135w19	9:01:16
Skagway Portion	4	59N29	135w18	9:01:12
Skwentna 17	5	61N58	151w11	10:04:44
Sleetmute 16	5	61N42	157w10	10:28:40
Snowball 9	5	64N51	147w47	9:51:08
Snug Harbor 21	5	60N29	149w50	9:59:20
Soldotna 12	5	60N29	151w03	10:04:12
Sourdough 26	5	62N26	144w59	9:39:56
South Bjerremark 9	5	64N50	147w53	9:51:32
South Fairbanks 9	5	64N51	147w47	9:51:08
South Naknek 6	5	58N41	157w00	10:28:00
Spenard 2	5	61N11	149w55	9:59:40
Sprucewood 9	5	64N51	147w47	9:51:08
Squaw Harbor 1	2	55N15	160w33	10:42:12
Standard	5	64N47	148w32	9:54:08
Stebbins 18	6	63N31	162w17	10:49:08
Sterling 12	5	60N32	150w46	10:03:04
Stevens Village 25	5	66N01	149w06	9:56:24
Stony River 16	5	61N47	156w35	10:26:20
Summit 17	5	63N20	149w07	9:56:28
Summit Lodge 26	5	62N26	144w59	9:39:56
Sunnyside 23	4	57N59	136w15	9:05:00
Sunshine	5	62N10	150w04	10:00:16
Sunshine 17	2	58N03	158w49	10:35:16
Suntrana 29	5	63N52	148w51	9:55:24
Susitna	5	61N33	150w31	10:02:04
Sutton 17	5	61N43	148w54	9:55:36
Takotna 16	5	62N59	156w04	10:24:16
Taku Lodge 11	4	58N21	134w33	8:58:12
Talkeetna 17	5	62N20	150w06	10:00:24
Tanacross 24	5	63N23	143w21	9:33:24
Tanana 29	5	65N10	152w04	10:08:16
Tanunak 3	6	60N37	165w15	11:01:00
Taslina 26	5	62N12	145w28	9:41:52
Tatitlek 26	5	60N53	146w41	9:46:44
Tazlina	5	62N04	146w27	9:45:48
Tee Harbor 11	4	58N25	134w46	8:59:04
Telida 16	5	63N23	153w16	10:13:04
Teller 18	6	65N16	166w22	11:05:28
Teller Mission	6	65N20	166w29	11:05:56
Tenakee Springs 3	4	57N47	135w13	9:00:52
Terminal Reservation	4	59N30	135w26	9:01:44
Tetlin 24	5	63N08	142w31	9:30:04
Thane 11	4	58N16	134w20	8:57:20
Thorne Bay 20	4	55N41	132w27	8:49:48
Tin City	6	65N33	167w51	11:11:24
Todd	4	57N28	135w03	9:00:12
Togiak 6	2	59N04	160w24	10:41:36
Tok 24	5	63N20	142w59	9:31:56
Tokeen 20	4	55N56	133w20	8:53:20
Toksook Bay 5	6	60N32	165w00	11:00:00
Tonsina 26	5	61N57	145w36	9:42:24
Totem Bight 13	4	55N24	132w08	8:48:32
Totem Park 9	5	64N51	147w47	9:51:08
Tuluksak 5	2	61N06	160w58	10:43:52
Tuntutuliak 5	6	60N22	162w38	10:50:32
Tununak 5	6	60N37	165w15	11:01:00
Turnagain Heights 2	5	61N12	149w53	9:59:32
Twin Hills 7	2	59N21	160w00	10:40:00
Tyonek 12	5	61N04	151w08	10:04:32
Ugashik 6	5	57N31	157w24	10:29:36
Umiat	5	69N22	152w08	10:08:32
Umkumute 5	6	60N32	165w06	11:00:24
Unalakleet 18	2	63N52	160w47	10:43:08
Unalaska 1	6	53N53	166w32	11:06:08
Unga	2	55N11	160w30	10:42:00
Ungalik 18	2	63N52	160w47	10:43:08
University Park 9	5	64N51	147w47	9:51:08
Upper Kalskag 16	2	61N32	160w18	10:41:12
Upper Mendenhall Valley 11	4	58N24	134w34	8:58:16
Upper Nickeyville 13	4	55N24	132w08	8:48:32
Upper Yukon	5	66N27	144w19	9:37:16
Usibelli 29	5	63N51	148w47	9:55:08
Usibelli Mine 29	5	63N52	148w43	9:54:52
Uyak	5	57N38	154w00	10:16:00
Valdez 26	5	61N07	146w16	9:45:04
Vank Island 28	4	56N28	132w23	8:49:32
Venetie 25	5	67N01	146w25	9:45:40
Wacker 13	4	55N25	131w44	8:46:56
Wade Hampton	6	62N18	164w41	10:58:44
Wainwright 4	2	70N38	160w02	10:40:08
Wales 18	6	65N37	168w05	11:12:20
Ward Cove 13	4	55N25	131w44	8:46:56
Wasilla 17	5	61N35	149w26	9:57:44
Waterfall 20	4	55N24	132w08	8:48:32
West Fairwest 9	5	64N51	147w47	9:51:08
Westgate 9	5	64N51	147w47	9:51:08
West Juneau 11	4	58N21	134w33	8:58:12
West Petersburg	4	56N49	132w58	8:51:52
Westwood 9	5	64N51	147w47	9:51:08
White Mountain 18	6	64N41	163w24	10:53:36
Whitney 2	5	61N15	149w49	9:59:16
Whitshed	5	60N28	145w57	9:43:48
Whittier 26	5	60N47	148w41	9:54:44
Wilburs Place	6	62N05	163w28	10:53:52
Wilcox 9	5	64N51	147w47	9:51:08
Wilcox Estates 9	5	64N51	147w47	9:51:08
Wild Lake 29	5	66N56	151w30	10:06:00
Wildwood Station	5	60N35	151w18	10:05:12
Willow 17	5	61N45	150w03	10:00:12
Wiseman 29	5	67N25	150w06	10:00:24
Woodchopper 25	5	64N51	147w47	9:51:08
Woodland Park 2	5	61N12	149w53	9:59:32
Wood River 6	2	59N04	158w26	10:33:44
Woody Island 15	5	57N47	152w21	10:09:24
Wrangell 28	4	56N28	132w23	8:49:32
Yakutat 23	1	59N33	139w44	9:18:56
Yakutat Portion 12	1	59N27	138w06	9:12:24
Yankee Creek 16	5	62N56	156w04	10:24:16

TIME TABLES

Arizona has declined to observe daylight time, except as noted in the time tables. During World War II wartime ended early in the MST portions of Arizona. The shift to MST for Yuma County (Table #3) has been estimated from incomplete information. Some publications circa 1900 show southern Arizona as far north as Phoenix on Pacific time.

AZ # 1

Before 11/18/1883		LMT
11/18/1883	12:00	MST
3/31/1918	02:00	MWT
10/27/1918	02:00	MST
3/30/1919	02:00	MWT
10/26/1919	02:00	MST
2/09/1942	02:00	MWT
1/01/1944	00:01	MST
3/17/1944	00:01	MWT
10/01/1944	00:01	MST
4/30/1967	02:00	MDT
10/29/1967	02:00	MST

....

AZ # 2

Before 11/18/1883		LMT
11/18/1883	12:00	PST
3/31/1918	02:00	PWT
10/27/1918	02:00	PST
3/30/1919	02:00	PWT
10/26/1919	02:00	PST
2/09/1942	02:00	PWT
3/07/1945	00:01	MST
4/30/1967	02:00	MDT
10/29/1967	02:00	MST

....

AZ # 3

Before 11/18/1883		LMT
11/18/1883	12:00	PST
3/31/1918	02:00	PWT
10/27/1918	02:00	PST
3/30/1919	02:00	PWT
10/26/1919	02:00	PST
3/06/1921	02:00	PDT
10/30/1921	02:00	PST
1/01/1929	00:00	MST
2/09/1942	02:00	MWT
1/01/1944	00:01	MST
3/17/1944	00:01	MWT
10/01/1944	00:01	MST
4/30/1967	02:00	MDT
10/29/1967	02:00	MST

COUNTIES

1 Apache
2 Cochise
3 Coconino
4 Gila
5 Graham
6 Greenlee
7 Maricopa
8 Mohave
9 Navajo
10 Pima
11 Pinal
12 Santa Cruz
13 Yavapai
14 Yuma

Place	Table	Lat.	Long.	LMT
Adamsville 11	1	33N02	111w23	7:25:32
Agua Caliente 7	1	32N48	113w33	7:34:12
Agua Fria 7	1	33N37	112w19	7:29:16
Agua Fria 13	1	34N32	112w28	7:29:52
Agua Linda 12	1	31N42	111w04	7:24:16
Aguila 7	1	33N56	113w11	7:32:44
Ajo 10	1	32N22	112w52	7:31:28
Ak	1	31N55	112w02	7:28:08
Akchin 10	1	31N55	111w53	7:27:32
Akchin 11	1	33N04	112w03	7:28:12
Alamo Crossing 14	3	33N49	113w32	7:34:08
Alchesay Flat 9	1	33N50	109w58	7:19:52
Allentown 1	1	35N17	109w12	7:16:48
Allenville 7	1	33N22	112w35	7:30:20
Alpine 1	1	33N51	109w09	7:16:36
Amado 12	1	31N43	111w04	7:24:16
Anegam 10	1	32N22	112w02	7:28:08
Apache 2	1	31N50	109w02	7:16:08
Apache 9	1	33N57	110w05	7:20:20
Apache Flats 2	1	31N33	110w21	7:21:24
Apache Ho 11	1	33N25	111w34	7:26:16
Apache Junction 11	1	33N25	111w33	7:26:12
Apache Wells 7	1	33N26	111w44	7:26:56
Arcadia 7	1	33N30	112w00	7:28:00
Arivaca 10	1	31N35	111w20	7:25:20
Arizola 11	1	32N53	111w44	7:26:56
Arizona City 11	1	32N53	111w44	7:26:56
Arizona Shores 14	3	34N09	114w17	7:37:08
Arizona State Teachers Coll. 3	1	35N12	111w37	7:26:28
Arizona Sunsites 2	1	31N54	109w49	7:19:16
Arlington 7	1	33N20	112w46	7:31:04
Arrowhead Mall 7	1	33N33	112w13	7:28:52
Artesa 10	1	31N55	111w53	7:27:32
Artesia 5	1	32N49	109w43	7:18:52
Asher 14	3	32N40	114w08	7:36:32
Ash Fork 13	1	35N13	112w29	7:29:56
Avondale 7	1	33N26	112w21	7:29:24
Aztec 14	3	32N49	113w27	7:33:48
Baby Rock 9	1	36N44	110w15	7:21:00
Bacobi 9	1	35N56	110w41	7:22:44
Bagdad 13	1	34N34	113w11	7:32:44
Bakerville 2	1	31N25	109w54	7:19:36
Bapchule 11	1	33N12	111w50	7:27:20
Bayless Shopping Center 11	1	33N25	111w34	7:26:16
Beardsley 7	1	33N33	112w13	7:28:52
Beaver Dam 8	2	36N53	113w56	7:35:44
Bella Vista Estates 2	1	31N33	110w17	7:21:08
Bellemont 3	1	35N14	111w50	7:27:20
Benson 2	1	31N58	110w18	7:21:12
Benson Highway 10	1	32N03	110w51	7:23:24
Big Springs 3	1	36N57	112w31	7:30:04
Bisbee 2	1	31N27	109w55	7:19:40
Bitahochee 9	1	35N24	110w05	7:20:20
Bitter Springs 3	1	36N49	111w38	7:26:32
Black Canyon City 13	1	34N58	112w09	7:28:36
Blackwater 11	1	32N59	111w31	7:26:04
Blue 6	1	33N37	109w06	7:16:24
Bonita 5	1	32N15	109w50	7:19:20
Borrees Corner 11	1	32N59	111w31	7:26:04
Bouse 14	3	33N56	114w00	7:36:00
Bowie 2	1	32N19	109w29	7:17:56
Boys Ranch 7	1	33N18	111w46	7:27:04
Brenda 14	3	33N47	113w37	7:34:28
Bridge Canyon Country Estate 13	1	35N20	112w53	7:31:32
Bridgeport 13	1	34N44	112w01	7:28:04
Briggs Townsite 2	1	31N25	109w54	7:19:36
Buckeye 7	1	33N22	112w35	7:30:20
Buckhorn 7	1	33N26	111w44	7:26:56
Buena Vista 5	1	32N49	109w43	7:18:52
Bullhead City 8	2	35N09	114w34	7:38:16
Bumble Bee 13	1	34N12	112w09	7:28:36
Burnt Water 1	1	35N13	109w20	7:17:20
Bushman Acres 9	1	35N02	110w42	7:22:48
Bylas 5	1	33N08	110w07	7:20:28
Cactus Flat 5	1	32N49	109w43	7:18:52
Cactus Forest 11	1	33N02	111w23	7:25:32
Calva 5	1	33N07	110w07	7:20:28
Camel View Plaza 7	1	33N29	111w56	7:27:44
Cameron 3	1	35N53	111w25	7:25:40
Camp Creek 7	1	33N50	111w57	7:27:48
Camp Verde 13	1	34N34	111w51	7:27:24
Camp Verde Indian Res 13	1	34N34	111w51	7:27:24
Cane Beds 8	1	36N57	112w31	7:30:04
Canelo 12	1	31N40	110w32	7:22:08
Canyon Day 4	1	33N47	109w59	7:19:56
Capitol 7	1	33N30	112w05	7:28:20
Carefree 7	1	33N50	111w57	7:27:48
Carmen 12	1	31N42	111w04	7:24:16
Carrizo 4	1	34N15	110w02	7:20:08
Casa Blanca 11	1	33N12	111w50	7:27:20
Casa Grande 11	1	32N53	111w45	7:27:00
Casas Adobes 10	1	32N19	110w57	7:23:48
Casas Grande Mall 11	1	32N53	111w44	7:26:56
Cashion 7	1	33N26	112w18	7:29:12
Castle Hot Springs 13	1	33N51	112w37	7:30:28
Castle Rock Shores 14	3	34N09	114w17	7:37:08
Catalina 10	1	32N20	110w58	7:23:52
Catalina Foothills 10	1	32N18	110w56	7:23:44
Cave Creek 7	1	33N50	111w57	7:27:48
Cedar Creek 4	1	33N47	109w59	7:19:56
Cedar Ridge 3	1	35N53	111w25	7:25:40
Centerville 13	1	34N46	112w04	7:28:16
Central 5	1	32N52	109w48	7:19:12
Central Heights 4	1	33N25	110w49	7:23:16
Chambers 1	1	35N11	109w26	7:17:44
Chandler 7	1	33N18	111w50	7:27:20
Chandler Heights 7	1	33N13	111w41	7:26:44
Cherry 13	1	34N32	112w15	7:29:00
Chevelon 3	1	35N12	111w37	7:26:28
Chiawuli Tak 10	1	31N56	111w47	7:27:08
Chilchinbito 9	1	36N31	110w05	7:20:20
Childs 10	1	32N22	112w51	7:31:24
Chinle 1	1	36N09	109w33	7:18:12
Chino Valley 13	1	34N45	112w27	7:29:48
Chloride 8	2	35N25	114w12	7:36:48
Choulic 10	1	31N55	111w53	7:27:32
Christmas 4	1	33N04	110w44	7:22:56
Chuichu 11	1	32N45	111w47	7:27:08
Cibecue 9	1	34N15	110w02	7:20:08
Cibola 14	3	33N37	114w35	7:38:20
Cienega Springs 14	3	34N09	114w17	7:37:08
Circle City 7	1	33N51	112w37	7:30:28
Citrus Gardens 7	1	33N26	111w50	7:27:20
Citrus Park 7	1	33N30	112w21	7:29:24
Clarkdale 13	1	34N46	112w03	7:28:12
Claypool 4	1	33N25	110w51	7:23:24
Clay Springs 9	1	34N22	110w18	7:21:12
Clearwater Hills 7	1	33N29	111w56	7:27:44
Cleator 13	1	34N24	112w14	7:28:56
Clemenceau 13	1	34N44	112w01	7:28:04
Clifton 6	1	33N03	109w18	7:17:12
Coal Mine Mesa 3	1	36N08	111w14	7:24:56
Cochise 2	1	32N07	109w55	7:19:40
Coconino 3	1	35N12	111w37	7:26:28
Cocopah Indian Reservation 14	3	34N34	111w51	7:27:24
Colorado City 8	1	37N01	112w58	7:31:52
Colorado River Indian Res 14	3	34N09	114w17	7:37:08
Commerce 7	1	33N27	112w04	7:28:16
Comobabi 10	1	32N03	111w48	7:27:12
Concho 1	1	34N28	109w36	7:18:24
Congress 13	1	34N09	112w51	7:31:24
Continental 10	1	31N51	110w59	7:23:56
Coolidge 11	1	32N59	111w31	7:26:04
Co-op Village 7	1	33N22	112w10	7:28:40
Copper Mines 3	1	35N53	111w25	7:25:40
Copper Queen 2	1	31N25	109w54	7:19:36
Cork 5	1	33N02	109w58	7:19:52
Cornfields 1	1	35N43	109w33	7:18:12
Cornville 13	1	34N43	111w55	7:27:40
Coronada Foothills Estates 10	1	32N18	110w56	7:23:44
Coronado 10	1	32N13	110w53	7:23:32
Cortaro 10	1	32N22	111w05	7:24:20
Cottonwood 13	1	34N45	112w01	7:28:04
Cottonwood Station 1	1	36N09	109w33	7:18:12
Country Life 7	1	33N26	111w50	7:27:20
Cove 1	1	36N47	108w41	7:14:44
Covered Wells 10	1	31N55	111w53	7:27:32
Cowlic 10	1	31N48	111w59	7:27:56
Cow Springs 3	1	36N19	110w56	7:23:44
Crestview 2	1	31N25	109w54	7:19:36
Cross Canyon 1	1	35N39	109w06	7:16:24
Crown King 13	1	34N24	112w14	7:28:56
Cuckelbur 11	1	32N53	111w44	7:26:56
Cutter 4	1	33N24	110w48	7:23:12
Dam View 14	3	34N09	114w17	7:37:08
Date 13	1	34N09	112w51	7:31:24
Dateland 14	3	32N48	113w33	7:34:12
Davis Dam 8	2	35N09	114w34	7:38:16
Davis-Monthan Air For 10	1	32N11	110w53	7:23:32
Deer Valley 7	1	33N45	112w03	7:28:12
Del Rio 13	1	34N45	112w27	7:29:48
Dennehotso 1	1	36N44	110w15	7:21:00
Desert Carmel 11	1	32N53	111w44	7:26:56
Desert Sands 7	1	33N26	111w50	7:27:20
Desert View 3	1	36N03	112w08	7:28:32
Dewey 13	1	34N32	112w15	7:29:00
Diamond Valley 13	1	34N32	112w28	7:29:52
Dilkon 9	1	35N02	110w42	7:22:48
Dinnehotso	1	36N51	109w51	7:19:24
Dolan Springs 8	2	34N52	114w09	7:36:36
Dome 14	3	32N44	114w35	7:38:20
Don Luis 2	1	31N25	109w54	7:19:36
Dos Cabezas 2	1	32N10	109w37	7:18:28
Double Adobe 2	1	31N36	109w40	7:18:40
Douglas 2	1	31N21	109w33	7:18:12
Dragoon 2	1	32N02	110w02	7:20:08
Drake 13	1	34N59	112w23	7:29:32
Dreamland Villa 7	1	33N26	111w44	7:26:56
Drexel Heights 10	1	32N08	110w56	7:23:44
Dudleyville 11	1	32N59	110w46	7:23:04
Duncan 6	1	32N43	109w06	7:16:24
Dysart 7	1	33N33	112w13	7:28:52
Eagar 1	1	34N06	109w17	7:17:08
Eagle Creek 6	1	33N03	109w18	7:17:12
East Flagstaff 3	1	35N12	111w37	7:26:28
East Fork 9	1	33N50	109w58	7:19:52
East Plantsite 6	1	33N04	109w21	7:17:24
Eden 5	1	32N58	109w54	7:19:36
Ehrenberg 14	3	33N36	114w31	7:38:04

Eleven Mile Corner 11
1 32N53 111w44 7:26:56
Elfrida 2 1 31N41 109w41 7:18:44
Elgin 12 1 31N40 110w32 7:22:08
Elik 1 32N31 111w57 7:27:48
El Mirage 7 1 33N36 112w19 7:29:16
Eloy 11 1 32N45 111w33 7:26:12
El Pueblecito 14 3 32N44 114w35 7:38:20
Emery Park 10 1 32N08 110w56 7:23:44
Empire Landing 14
3 34N09 114w17 7:37:08
Fairbank 2 1 31N43 110w11 7:20:44
Falcon Estates 7 1 33N26 111w50 7:27:20
Fiesta Park 7 1 33N26 111w50 7:27:20
Fishers Landing 14
3 32N44 114w35 7:38:20
Flagstaff 3 1 35N12 111w39 7:26:36
Flecha Caida Estates 10
1 32N18 110w56 7:23:44
Florence 11 1 33N02 111w23 7:25:32
Florence Junction 11
1 33N16 111w20 7:25:20
Forbing Park 13 1 34N32 112w28 7:29:52
Fort Apache 9 1 33N47 109w59 7:19:56
Fort Apache Indian Res 1
1 33N50 109w58 7:19:52
Fort Apache Junction 4
1 33N50 109w58 7:19:52
Fort Defiance 1 1 35N45 109w05 7:16:20
Fort Huachuca 2 1 31N33 110w21 7:21:24
Fort McDowell 7 1 33N28 111w55 7:27:40
Fort Mcdowell Indian Res 7
1 33N05 111w44 7:26:56
Fort Thomas 5 1 33N02 109w58 7:19:52
Fountain East 7 1 33N26 111w50 7:27:20
Fountain of the Sun 7
1 33N26 111w50 7:27:20
Franklin 6 1 32N41 109w05 7:16:20
Fredonia 3 1 36N57 112w32 7:30:08
Fresnal Canyon 10
1 31N55 111w53 7:27:32
Friendly Corners 11
1 32N45 111w33 7:26:12
Fry 2 1 31N33 110w17 7:21:08
Gadsden 14 3 32N33 114w47 7:39:08
Galena 2 1 31N25 109w54 7:19:36
Ganado 1 1 35N43 109w33 7:18:12
Geronimo 5 1 33N02 109w58 7:19:52
Gibson 10 1 32N22 112w51 7:31:24
Gila Bend 7 1 32N57 112w43 7:30:52
Gila Bend Indian Reservation 7
1 31N55 111w53 7:27:32
Gila Crossing 7 1 33N22 112w10 7:28:40
Gila River Indian Res 7
1 33N05 111w44 7:26:56
Gilbert 7 1 33N21 111w47 7:27:08
Gisela 4 1 34N14 111w20 7:25:20
Gladden 7 1 33N56 113w11 7:32:44
Gleeson 2 1 31N41 109w41 7:18:44
Glendale 7 1 33N32 112w11 7:28:44
Glen Ilah 13 1 34N13 112w45 7:31:00
Globe 4 1 33N24 110w47 7:23:08
Golden Hills 7 1 33N26 111w50 7:27:20
Goldfield 11 1 33N25 111w34 7:26:16
Goodyear 7 1 33N27 112w21 7:29:24
Goodyear Farms 7 1 34N30 112w41 7:30:44
Graham 5 1 32N50 109w45 7:19:00
Grand Canyon 3 1 36N03 112w09 7:28:36
Grand Canyon Caverns 3
2 35N32 113w25 7:33:40
Grand Canyon Estates 3
1 36N03 112w08 7:28:32
Grand View 13 1 34N32 112w28 7:29:52
Grasshopper Junction 8
2 35N12 114w02 7:36:08
Gray Mountain 3 1 35N45 111w28 7:25:52
Greasewood 9 1 35N43 109w33 7:18:12
Greasewood Springs 1
1 36N35 109w05 7:16:20
Greaterville 10 1 31N40 110w39 7:22:36
Greenlaw Village 3
1 35N12 111w37 7:26:28
Green Valley 10 1 31N50 111w00 7:24:00
Greenway Center 7
1 33N35 112w23 7:29:32
Greer 1 1 34N01 109w27 7:17:48
Groom Creek 13 1 34N32 112w28 7:29:52
Gu Achi 10 1 31N55 111w53 7:27:32
Gu Komelik 11 1 31N55 111w53 7:27:32
Gunsight 10 1 32N22 112w51 7:31:24
Gu Oidak 10 1 31N55 111w53 7:27:32
Guthrie 6 1 33N03 109w18 7:17:12
Gu Vo 10 1 31N55 111w53 7:27:32
Hacienda De Valencia 7
1 33N26 111w50 7:27:20
Hackberry 8 2 35N22 113w44 7:34:56
Hamilton Corner 7
1 33N18 111w46 7:27:04
Hano 9 1 35N50 110w23 7:21:32
Happy Jack 3 1 34N45 111w24 7:25:36
Harcuvar 14 3 33N47 113w37 7:34:28
Harshaw 12 1 31N33 110w45 7:23:00
Hassayampa 7 1 33N21 112w41 7:30:44
Havana Nakya 10 1 31N55 111w53 7:27:32
Havasupai Indian Reservation 3
1 34N09 114w17 7:37:08
Hawkins 13 1 34N09 112w51 7:31:24
Hawley Lake 1 1 34N04 109w51 7:19:24
Hayden 4 1 33N00 110w47 7:23:08
Heber 9 1 34N26 110w36 7:22:24
Hereford 2 1 31N26 110w06 7:20:24
Hickiwan 10 1 31N55 111w53 7:27:32
Hidden Springs 3 1 35N53 111w25 7:25:40
Hightown 7 1 33N18 111w46 7:27:04
Higley 7 1 33N18 111w43 7:26:52
Hillside 13 1 34N25 112w55 7:31:40

Hilltop 2 1 32N16 109w14 7:16:56
Ho-Kay-Gan 13 1 34N32 112w28 7:29:52
Holbrook 9 1 34N54 110w10 7:20:40
Holiday 14 3 34N09 114w17 7:37:08
Hollywood 5 1 32N49 109w43 7:18:52
Hopi 9 1 35N56 110w22 7:21:28
Hopi Indian Reservation 3
1 35N49 110w12 7:20:48
Horn 14 3 32N57 113w30 7:34:00
Horse Mesa 7 1 33N32 111w23 7:25:32
Horse Thief 13 1 34N24 112w14 7:28:56
Hotevilla 9 1 35N56 110w41 7:22:44
Houck 1 1 35N17 109w12 7:16:48
House Rock 3 1 36N57 112w31 7:30:04
Huachuca 2 1 31N37 110w19 7:21:16
Huachuca Terrace 2
1 36N09 109w33 7:18:12
Hualapai 8 2 35N12 114w02 7:36:08
Hualapai Indian Reservation 3
1 34N34 111w51 7:27:24
Hubbell 1 1 35N43 109w33 7:18:12
Humboldt 13 1 34N30 112w14 7:28:56
Hunt 1 1 34N28 109w36 7:18:24
Hunters Point 1 1 35N39 109w06 7:16:24
Hyder 14 3 32N48 113w33 7:34:12
Immanuel Mission 1
1 36N58 109w02 7:16:08
Indian Gardens 3 1 34N52 111w47 7:27:08
Indian Ridge Estates 10
1 32N14 110w49 7:23:16
Indian School 7 1 33N30 112w05 7:28:20
Indian Wells 9 1 35N22 110w09 7:20:36
Inscription House 3
1 36N19 110w56 7:23:44
Inspiration 4 1 33N25 110w53 7:23:32
Iron Springs 13 1 34N35 112w34 7:30:16
Jackrabbit 11 1 32N53 111w44 7:26:56
Jackson Acres 13 1 34N32 112w28 7:29:52
Jacob Lake 3 1 36N43 112w13 7:28:52
Jakes Corner 4 1 34N14 111w20 7:25:20
Jeddito 9 1 35N49 110w12 7:20:48
Jerome 13 1 34N45 112w07 7:28:28
Johnson 2 1 32N02 110w02 7:20:08
Joseph City 9 1 34N57 110w20 7:21:20
Kaibab 8 1 36N54 112w44 7:30:56
Kaibab Indian Reservation 8
1 35N49 110w12 7:20:48
Kaibito 3 1 36N19 110w56 7:23:44
Kaihon Kug 10 1 31N55 111w53 7:27:32
Kaka 7 1 31N55 111w53 7:27:32
Kansas Settlement 2
1 32N15 109w50 7:19:20
Katherine 8 2 35N09 114w34 7:38:16
Kayenta 9 1 36N44 110w15 7:21:00
Keams Canyon 9 1 35N49 110w12 7:20:48
Kearny 11 1 33N03 110w54 7:23:36
Kelvin 11 1 33N03 110w54 7:23:36
Kerwo 10 1 31N55 111w53 7:27:32
Kingman 8 2 35N12 114w04 7:36:16
Kin-li-chee 1 1 35N43 109w33 7:18:12
Kino 10 1 32N15 110w59 7:23:56
Kinsley Ranch 10 1 31N42 111w04 7:24:16
Kirkland 13 1 34N25 112w43 7:30:52
Kirkland Junction 13
1 34N22 112w40 7:30:40
Klagetoh 1 1 35N43 109w33 7:18:12
Klondyke 5 1 32N15 109w50 7:19:20
Kofa 14 3 32N44 114w35 7:38:20
Kohatk 11 1 31N55 111w53 7:27:32
Komatke 7 1 33N22 112w10 7:28:40
Komelik 10 1 31N55 111w53 7:27:32
Ko Vaya 10 1 31N55 111w53 7:27:32
Laguna 14 3 32N44 114w35 7:38:20
Lake Havasu City 8
2 34N30 114w20 7:37:20
Lake Mary 3 1 35N12 111w37 7:26:28
Lake Mead Rancheros 8
2 35N12 114w02 7:36:08
Lake Mohave 8 2 35N09 114w34 7:38:16
Lake Montezuma 13
1 34N30 112w41 7:30:44
Lakeside 9 1 34N09 109w58 7:19:52
Lakeside 14 3 34N09 114w17 7:37:08
Lakeview 3 1 34N55 111w28 7:25:52
La Palma 11 1 32N53 111w31 7:26:04
La Ronde Shopping Center 7
1 33N35 112w23 7:29:32
Laveen 7 1 33N22 112w10 7:28:40
Leisure World 7 1 33N26 111w50 7:27:20
Leupp 3 1 35N17 110w58 7:23:52
Leupp Corner 3 1 35N05 110w52 7:23:28
Liberty 7 1 33N22 112w35 7:30:20
Ligurta 14 3 32N40 114w08 7:36:32
Lincon 10 1 31N55 111w53 7:27:32
Litchfield 7 1 33N31 112w24 7:29:36
Litchfield Park 7
1 33N30 112w21 7:29:24
Little Acres 4 1 33N24 110w48 7:23:12
Little Colorado 9
1 34N56 110w29 7:21:56
Littlefield 8 2 36N53 113w56 7:35:44
Little Tucson 10 1 31N55 111w53 7:27:32
Lizard Acres 7 1 33N33 112w13 7:28:52
Lochiel 12 1 31N20 110w38 7:22:32
Lone Star 5 1 32N49 109w43 7:18:52
Long Valley 3 1 35N12 111w37 7:26:28
Los Gatos 7 1 33N29 111w56 7:27:44
Lowell 2 1 31N25 109w54 7:19:36
Lower Miami 4 1 33N24 110w52 7:23:28
Low Mountain 9 1 36N09 109w33 7:18:12
Lukachukai 1 1 36N25 109w15 7:17:00
Luke 7 1 33N33 112w21 7:29:24
Luke Air Force Base 7
1 33N33 112w11 7:28:44
Lukeville 10 1 31N53 112w49 7:31:16
Lupton 1 1 35N21 109w04 7:16:16

ARIZONA

Lynx Estates 13 1 34N32 112w28 7:29:52
Madera Canyon 12 1 32N08 110w56 7:23:44
Mammoth 11 1 32N43 110w39 7:22:36
Manila 1 34N58 110w25 7:21:40
Marana 10 1 32N27 111w13 7:24:52
Marble Canyon 3 1 36N49 111w38 7:26:32
Maricopa 11 1 33N04 112w03 7:28:12
Maricopa Indian Reservation 11
1 33N05 111w44 7:26:56
Maricopa Village 7
1 33N22 112w10 7:28:40
Marine Corps Air Station 14
3 32N44 114w35 7:38:20
Marinette 1 33N36 112w17 7:29:08
Martinez Lake 14 3 32N44 114w35 7:38:20
Maryvale 7 1 33N30 112w10 7:28:40
Maverick 1 1 34N15 110w02 7:20:08
Mayer 13 1 34N24 112w14 7:28:56
McDowell 7 1 33N28 112w00 7:28:00
McGuireville 13 1 34N39 111w44 7:26:56
McNary 1 1 34N04 109w51 7:19:24
McNeal 2 1 31N36 109w40 7:18:40
Meadow Brook 14 3 32N44 114w35 7:38:20
Mennonite Mission 1
1 35N43 109w33 7:18:12
Mesa 7 1 33N25 111w50 7:27:20
Mexican Town 10 1 32N22 112w51 7:31:24
Mexican Water 1 1 36N58 109w02 7:16:08
Miami 4 1 33N24 110w52 7:23:28
Miami Gardens 4 1 33N24 110w52 7:23:28
Middle Verde 13 1 34N34 111w51 7:27:24
Midland City 4 1 33N24 110w52 7:23:28
Miller Valley 13 1 34N32 112w28 7:29:52
Mineral Creek 11 1 33N03 110w54 7:23:36
Mingus Mountain 13
1 34N41 112w07 7:28:28
Miracle Valley 2 1 31N26 110w06 7:20:24
Miramonte Acres 2
1 31N25 109w54 7:19:36
Mishongnovi 9 1 35N50 110w33 7:22:12
Mobile 7 1 33N03 112w16 7:29:04
Moccasin 8 1 36N55 112w46 7:31:04
Moenave 3 1 36N08 111w14 7:24:56
Moenkopi 3 1 36N07 111w13 7:24:52
Mohave Valley 8 2 34N52 114w09 7:36:36
Mohawk 14 3 32N44 113w45 7:35:00
Morenci 6 1 33N05 109w22 7:17:28
Mormon Lake 3 1 34N55 111w28 7:25:52
Morristown 7 1 33N51 112w37 7:30:28
Mountainaire 3 1 35N12 111w37 7:26:28
Mountain View 2 1 31N25 109w54 7:19:36
Mount Elden 3 1 35N12 111w37 7:26:28
Mount Lemmon 10 1 32N27 110w45 7:23:00
Munds Park 3 1 35N12 111w37 7:26:28
Na-Ab-Tee Canyon 9
1 35N24 110w05 7:20:20
Naco 2 1 31N20 109w57 7:19:48
N.A.J. 3 1 35N12 111w37 7:26:28
Navajo 1 1 35N07 109w32 7:18:08
Navajo Indian Reservation 1
1 35N41 109w03 7:16:12
Navajo Monument 9
1 36N41 110w21 7:21:24
Navajo Mountain Trading Post 3
1 36N19 110w56 7:23:44
Navajo Station 1 1 35N43 109w33 7:18:12
Nazlini 1 1 35N43 109w33 7:18:12
Ndavis Dam 2 35N11 114w34 7:38:16
Nelson 13 2 35N31 113w19 7:33:16
New Hope 7 1 33N26 111w50 7:27:20
New Oraibi 9 1 35N53 110w37 7:22:28
New River 7 1 33N30 112w05 7:28:20
New Tucson 10 1 32N08 110w57 7:23:48
Nicksville 2 1 31N26 110w06 7:20:24
Nogales 12 1 31N20 110w56 7:23:44
Nolia 10 1 31N55 111w53 7:27:32
Northeast 7 1 33N31 112w02 7:28:08
Northern Hills 10
1 32N19 110w57 7:23:48
North Rim 3 1 36N57 112w31 7:30:04
Northwest 7 1 33N30 112w08 7:28:32
Nutrioso 1 1 33N57 109w13 7:16:52
Oak Springs 1 1 35N17 109w12 7:16:48
Oasis Park 7 1 33N25 111w34 7:26:16
Oatman 8 2 35N02 114w23 7:37:32
Ocotillo 7 1 33N18 111w46 7:27:04
Octave 13 1 34N09 112w51 7:31:24
Olberg 11 1 33N06 111w41 7:26:44
Old Columbine 5 1 32N49 109w43 7:18:52
Old Oraibi 9 1 35N53 110w37 7:22:28
Oracle 11 1 32N37 110w46 7:23:04
Oracle Foot Hill Estates 10
1 32N19 110w57 7:23:48
Oraibi 9 1 35N53 110w37 7:22:28
Orange Grove Estates 10
1 32N19 110w57 7:23:48
Oro Valley 10 1 32N19 110w57 7:23:48
Page 3 1 36N57 111w27 7:25:48
Page Springs 13 1 34N43 111w55 7:27:40
Palamino Acres 7 1 33N21 111w47 7:27:08
Palm Springs 11 1 33N25 111w34 7:26:16
Palominas 2 1 31N26 110w06 7:20:24
Palo Verde 7 1 33N21 112w41 7:30:44
Papago 7 1 33N28 111w55 7:27:40
Papago 10 1 31N59 112w00 7:28:00
Papago Indian Reservation 7
1 31N55 111w53 7:27:32
Paradise 2 1 32N16 109w14 7:16:56
Paradise Valley 7
1 33N32 111w57 7:27:48
Park 1 35N16 111w57 7:27:48
Parker 14 3 34N09 114w17 7:37:08
Parker Creek 4 1 33N24 110w48 7:23:12
Parks 3 1 35N12 111w37 7:26:28
Patagonia 12 1 31N33 110w45 7:23:00
Paulden 13 1 34N53 112w28 7:29:52

Paul Spur 2 1 31N22 109w44 7:18:56
Payson 4 1 34N14 111w20 7:25:20
Peach Springs 8 2 35N32 113w25 7:33:40
Pearce 2 1 31N54 109w49 7:19:16
Peeples Valley 13
1 34N25 112w43 7:30:52
Penzance 1 34N54 110w15 7:21:00
Peoria 7 1 33N35 112w14 7:28:56
Peralta Estates 11
1 33N25 111w34 7:26:16
Peridot 4 1 33N18 110w28 7:21:52
Perkinsville 13 1 34N45 112w27 7:29:48
Perryville 7 1 33N22 112w35 7:30:20
Petrified Forest National Pa 9
1 34N55 110w09 7:20:36
Phoenix 7 1 33N27 112w04 7:28:16
Pia Oik 10 1 31N55 111w53 7:27:32
Picacho 11 1 32N43 111w30 7:26:00
Pima 5 1 32N54 109w50 7:19:20
Pine 4 1 34N23 111w27 7:25:48
Pinecrest 5 1 32N49 109w43 7:18:52
Pinedale 9 1 34N18 110w15 7:21:00
Pineon 1 36N06 110w14 7:20:56
Pine Springs 1 1 35N17 109w12 7:16:48
Pinetop 9 1 34N08 109w56 7:19:44
Pinnacle Peak Village 7
1 33N36 111w55 7:27:40
Pinon 9 1 36N06 110w14 7:20:56
Pirtleville 2 1 31N22 109w34 7:18:16
Pisinemo 10 1 31N55 111w53 7:27:32
Pisinimo 1 32N02 112w19 7:29:16
Plantsite 6 1 33N03 109w20 7:17:20
Plaza 3 1 35N12 111w37 7:26:28
Polacca 9 1 35N50 110w23 7:21:32
Poland Junction 13
1 34N24 112w14 7:28:56
Pomerene 2 1 32N00 110w17 7:21:08
Portal 2 1 31N55 109w09 7:16:36
Poston 14 3 34N09 114w17 7:37:08
Prescott 13 1 34N33 112w28 7:29:52
Presidential Estates 2
1 31N37 110w19 7:21:16
Prinston Park 7 1 33N21 111w47 7:27:08
Pueblo Alto 7 1 33N18 111w46 7:27:04
Pumpkin Center 4 1 33N52 111w19 7:25:16
Quartzsite 14 3 33N40 114w13 7:36:52
Queen Creek 7 1 33N15 111w33 7:26:12
Queen Valley 11 1 33N25 111w34 7:26:16
Querino 1 1 35N17 109w12 7:16:48
Quijotoa 1 32N10 112w07 7:28:28
Rainbow Valley 7 1 33N22 112w35 7:30:20
Ranch del Sol 7 1 33N21 111w47 7:27:08
Rancho del Rio 14
3 34N09 114w17 7:37:08
Randolph 11 1 32N55 111w31 7:26:04
Rare Metals 3 1 36N08 111w14 7:24:56
Ray 1 33N11 111w00 7:24:00
Redington 10 1 31N57 110w18 7:21:12
Red Lake 3 1 35N15 112w11 7:28:44
Red Mesa 1 1 36N58 109w02 7:16:08
Red Rock 1 1 36N36 109w04 7:16:16
Red Rock 11 1 32N35 111w20 7:25:20
Richville 1 1 34N31 109w22 7:17:28
Rillito 10 1 32N25 111w09 7:24:36
Rimmy Jims 3 1 35N02 110w42 7:22:48
Rimrock 13 1 34N39 111w44 7:26:56
Rincon 10 1 32N13 110w49 7:23:16
Rio Rico 12 1 31N21 110w56 7:23:44
Rio Verde 7 1 33N36 111w55 7:27:40
Riverside Stage Stop 11
1 33N03 110w54 7:23:36
Riverside Terrace 10
1 32N19 110w57 7:23:48
Riviera 8 2 34N52 114w09 7:36:36
Rock Point 1 1 36N09 109w33 7:18:12
Rock Springs 13 1 33N30 112w05 7:28:20
Roll 14 3 32N45 113w59 7:35:56
Roosevelt 4 1 33N41 111w09 7:24:36
Rough Rock 1 1 36N09 109w33 7:18:12
Round Rock 1 1 36N31 109w28 7:17:52
Rye 4 1 34N14 111w20 7:25:20
Sacate 11 1 33N12 111w50 7:27:20
Sacaton 11 1 33N06 111w47 7:27:08
Sacaton Flats 11 1 33N05 111w44 7:26:56
Sacred Mountain 3
1 35N12 111w37 7:26:28
Safford 5 1 32N50 109w43 7:18:52
Saginaw 2 1 31N25 109w54 7:19:36
Sahuarita 10 1 31N57 110w58 7:23:52
Saint David 2 1 31N54 110w13 7:20:52
Saint Johns 1 1 34N30 109w22 7:17:28
Saint Michaels 1 1 35N39 109w06 7:16:24
Salado 1 1 34N31 109w22 7:17:28
Salina 1 1 36N01 109w52 7:19:28
Salome 14 3 33N47 113w37 7:34:28
Salt River 7 1 33N32 111w45 7:27:00
Salt River Indian Res 7
1 33N05 111w44 7:26:56
Salt River Powder District C 4
1 33N40 111w09 7:24:36
San Carlos 4 1 33N21 110w27 7:21:48
San Carlos Indian Res 4
1 33N20 110w27 7:21:48
Sanders 1 1 35N13 109w20 7:17:20
Sand Springs 3 1 35N53 110w37 7:22:28
San Jose 2 1 31N25 109w54 7:19:36
San Jose 5 1 32N49 109w43 7:18:52
San Lucy Village 7
1 32N57 112w43 7:30:52
San Luis 10 1 31N55 111w53 7:27:32
San Luis 14 3 32N29 114w47 7:39:08
San Manuel 11 1 32N36 110w38 7:22:32
San Miguel 10 1 31N37 111w47 7:27:08
San Rafael Terrace 2
1 31N25 109w54 7:19:36
San Simon 2 1 32N16 109w14 7:16:56
Santa Cruz 11 1 33N22 112w10 7:28:40
Santa Maria 7 1 33N27 112w08 7:28:32
Santan 11 1 33N05 111w44 7:26:56
Santa Rita 12 1 31N42 111w04 7:24:16
San Xavier 10 1 32N08 110w56 7:23:44
San Xavier Indian Reservatio 10
1 31N55 111w53 7:27:32
Sasabe 10 1 31N29 111w33 7:26:12
Sawmill 1 1 35N45 109w05 7:16:20
Schuchk 10 1 32N07 111w41 7:26:44
Schuchuli 10 1 31N55 111w53 7:27:32
Scottsdale 7 1 33N29 111w56 7:27:44
Second Mesa 9 1 35N50 110w33 7:22:12
Sedona 3 1 34N52 111w46 7:27:04
Seligman 13 1 35N20 112w53 7:31:32
Sells 10 1 31N55 111w53 7:27:32
Sentinel 7 1 32N52 113w13 7:32:52
Sherwood 7 1 33N26 111w50 7:27:20
Shipolovi 9 1 35N50 110w33 7:22:12
Shongopovi 9 1 35N48 110w32 7:22:08
Shonto 9 1 36N19 110w56 7:23:44
Shopishk 11 1 31N55 111w53 7:27:32
Short Creek 1 36N59 112w59 7:31:56
Show Low 9 1 34N15 110w02 7:20:08
Shumway 9 1 34N15 110w02 7:20:08
Sichomovi 9 1 35N50 110w23 7:21:32
Sierra Bonita 5 1 32N15 109w50 7:19:20
Sierra Vista 2 1 31N33 110w18 7:21:12
Sil Murk 7 1 32N57 112w43 7:30:52
Sil Nakya 10 1 32N13 111w49 7:27:16
Silver Bell 10 1 32N23 111w30 7:26:00
Site Six 8 2 34N30 114w20 7:37:20
Skull Valley 13 1 34N30 112w41 7:30:44
Skyline Bel Aire Estates 10
1 32N18 110w56 7:23:44
Skyway Village 7 1 33N26 111w50 7:27:20
Smelter City 13 1 34N44 112w01 7:28:04
Smoke Signal 9 1 36N09 109w33 7:18:12
Snowflake 9 1 34N30 110w05 7:20:20
Soap Creek 3 1 36N49 111w38 7:26:32
Solomon 5 1 32N49 109w38 7:18:32
Somerton 14 3 32N34 114w45 7:39:00
Sonoita 12 1 31N40 110w39 7:22:36
Sonora Town 7 1 33N18 111w46 7:27:04
South Bisbee 2 1 31N25 109w54 7:19:36
South Central 7 1 33N24 112w03 7:28:12
Southgate Mall 14
3 32N44 114w35 7:38:20
South Tucson 10 1 32N12 110w58 7:23:52
Speedway 10 1 32N15 110w55 7:23:40
Springerville 1 1 34N08 109w17 7:17:08
Spring Valley 13 1 34N24 112w14 7:28:56
Stanfield 11 1 32N53 111w58 7:27:52
Stanton 13 1 34N09 112w51 7:31:24
Stargo 6 1 33N04 109w22 7:17:28
Star Valley 4 1 34N14 111w20 7:25:20
Steamboat 1 1 35N45 109w51 7:19:24
Stoneman Lake 3 1 34N45 111w11 7:24:44
Strawberry 4 1 34N23 111w27 7:25:48
Student Union 10 1 32N14 110w57 7:23:48
Summerhaven 1 32N26 110w46 7:23:04
Sun City 7 1 33N35 112w23 7:29:32
Sunflower 7 1 33N52 111w28 7:25:52
Sunizona 2 1 31N54 109w49 7:19:16
Sun Lakes 7 1 33N18 111w46 7:27:04
Sunnyslope 7 1 33N34 112w03 7:28:12
Sunrise 3 1 35N02 110w42 7:22:48
Sunrise Springs 1
1 35N43 109w33 7:18:12
Sunset 5 1 32N15 109w50 7:19:20
Sunset Acres 2 1 31N25 109w54 7:19:36
Sun Terra Acres 7
1 33N21 111w47 7:27:08
Sun Valley 9 1 34N55 110w09 7:20:36
Supai 3 1 35N14 112w14 7:28:56
Superior 11 1 33N18 111w06 7:24:24
Superstition Estates 11
1 33N25 111w34 7:26:16
Supi Oidak 10 1 31N55 111w53 7:27:32
Surprise 7 1 33N38 112w20 7:29:20
Swift Trail Junction 5
1 32N49 109w43 7:18:52
Tacna 14 3 32N41 114w01 7:36:04
Tahchee 1 1 36N09 109w33 7:18:12
Tanque Verde 10 1 32N15 110w45 7:23:00
Tapco 13 1 34N46 112w04 7:28:16
Tat Momoli 11 1 31N55 111w53 7:27:32
Tatria Toak 10 1 31N55 111w53 7:27:32
Taylor 9 1 34N28 110w05 7:20:20
Teec Nos Pas 1 1 36N55 109w06 7:16:24
Tees To 9 1 35N02 110w42 7:22:48
Tempe 7 1 33N25 111w56 7:27:44
Temple Bar Marina 8
2 34N52 114w09 7:36:36
Tes Nez Iah 1 1 36N44 110w15 7:21:00
Thatcher 5 1 32N51 109w46 7:19:04
Theba 7 1 32N55 112w53 7:31:32
The Gap 3 1 35N53 111w25 7:25:40
Three Points 10 1 32N08 110w57 7:23:48
Tierra Madre 7 1 33N21 111w47 7:27:08
Tintown 2 1 31N25 109w54 7:19:36
Tolacon 1 1 36N58 109w02 7:16:08
Tolani 3 1 35N02 110w42 7:22:48
Tolleson 7 1 33N27 112w16 7:29:04
Toltec 11 1 32N47 111w37 7:26:28
Tombstone 2 1 31N43 110w04 7:20:16
Tonalea 3 1 36N19 110w56 7:23:44
Tonopah 7 1 33N30 112w56 7:31:44
Tonto Basin 4 1 33N52 111w19 7:25:16
Topawa 10 1 31N48 111w51 7:27:24
Topock 8 2 34N43 114w29 7:37:56
Toreva 9 1 35N50 110w33 7:22:12

ARIZONA

Tortilla Flat 7 1 33N32 111w23 7:25:32
Totopitk 7 1 31N55 111w53 7:27:32
Toyei 1 1 35N43 109w33 7:18:12
Tremaine 7 1 33N13 111w41 7:26:44
Truxton 8 2 35N29 113w34 7:34:16
Tsail 1 1 36N09 109w33 7:18:12
Tse Bonita 1 1 35N41 109w03 7:16:12
Tsegi 9 1 36N19 110w56 7:23:44
Tubac 12 1 31N42 111w04 7:24:16
Tuba City 3 1 36N08 111w14 7:24:56
Tucson 10 1 32N13 110w58 7:23:52
Tucson Country Club Estates 10
1 32N14 110w49 7:23:16
Tucson National Estates 10
1 32N19 110w57 7:23:48
Tumacacori 12 1 31N42 111w04 7:24:16
Turkey Flat 5 1 32N49 109w43 7:18:52
Tusayan 3 1 36N03 112w08 7:28:32
Tusconita 10 1 32N08 110w56 7:23:44
Twin Arrows 3 1 35N12 111w37 7:26:28
Twin Buttes 10 1 32N08 110w56 7:23:44
Twin Knolls 7 1 33N25 111w50 7:27:20
Two Guns 1 35N07 111w06 7:24:24
Two Story 1 1 35N39 109w06 7:16:24
University 10 1 32N13 110w55 7:23:40
Upper Greasewood Trading Pos 1
1 36N35 109w05 7:16:20
Upper Wheatfields 1
1 36N35 109w05 7:16:20
Utting 14 3 33N47 113w37 7:34:28
Vahki 11 1 33N12 111w50 7:27:20
Vail 10 1 32N03 110w43 7:22:52
Vaiva Vo 11 1 31N55 111w53 7:27:32
Valencia 7 1 33N22 112w35 7:30:20
Valentine 8 2 35N23 113w40 7:34:40
Valley Farms 11 1 32N59 111w27 7:25:48
Vamori 10 1 31N55 111w53 7:27:32
Vandenberg Village 10
1 32N11 110w53 7:23:32
Vaya Chin 10 1 31N55 111w53 7:27:32
Velda Rose Estates 7
1 33N26 111w50 7:27:20
Velda Rose Gardens 7
1 33N26 111w50 7:27:20
Ventana 10 1 31N55 111w53 7:27:32
Venture Out 7 1 33N26 111w50 7:27:20
Verde 13 1 34N38 111w47 7:27:08
Vernon 1 1 34N15 109w41 7:18:44
Vicksburg 14 3 33N47 113w37 7:34:28
Village Meadows 2
1 31N33 110w17 7:21:08
Waddell 7 1 33N37 112w26 7:29:44
Wagoner 13 1 34N13 112w32 7:30:08
Wahak Hotrontk 10
1 31N55 111w53 7:27:32
Wahweap 3 1 36N53 111w36 7:26:24
Walker 13 1 34N32 112w28 7:29:52
Walnut Grove 13 1 34N25 112w43 7:30:52
Walpi 9 1 35N50 110w23 7:21:32
Warren 2 1 31N25 109w54 7:19:36
Washington Camp 12
1 31N33 110w45 7:23:00
Weedville 7 1 33N33 112w11 7:28:44
Wellton 14 3 32N40 114w08 7:36:32
Wenden 14 3 33N49 113w33 7:34:12
West Chandler 7 1 33N18 111w46 7:27:04
West Sedona 13 1 34N30 112w41 7:30:44
Westward Quest 7 1 33N26 111w50 7:27:20
West Yuma 14 3 32N43 114w40 7:38:40
Whipple 13 1 34N32 112w28 7:29:52
Whispering Hills 2
1 31N33 110w17 7:21:08
White Clay 1 1 35N45 109w05 7:16:20
White Cone 9 1 35N24 110w05 7:20:20
White Mountain Lake 9
1 34N15 110w02 7:20:08
Whiteriver 9 1 33N50 109w58 7:19:52
White Tanks 7 1 33N22 112w35 7:30:20
Why 10 1 32N22 112w51 7:31:24
Wickenburg 7 1 33N58 112w44 7:30:56
Wide Ruins 1 1 35N20 109w20 7:17:20
Wikieup 8 2 34N42 113w37 7:34:28
Wilhoit 13 1 34N25 112w43 7:30:52
Willcox 2 1 32N15 109w50 7:19:20
Williams 3 1 35N15 112w11 7:28:44
Williams Air Force Base 7
1 33N21 111w50 7:27:20
Willow Beach 8 2 35N58 114w50 7:39:20
Willow Valley Estates 8
2 34N52 114w09 7:36:36
Window Rock 1 1 35N41 109w03 7:16:12
Winkelman 4 1 32N59 110w46 7:23:04
Winona 3 1 35N12 111w37 7:26:28
Winslow 9 1 35N02 110w42 7:22:48
Wintersburg 7 1 33N19 112w46 7:31:04
Winwood 2 1 31N25 109w54 7:19:36
Wittmann 7 1 33N47 112w32 7:30:08
Woodruff 9 1 34N47 110w03 7:20:12
Woodsprings 1 1 35N43 109w33 7:18:12
Yaqui Indian Settlement 7
1 33N25 112w00 7:28:00
Yarnell 13 1 34N13 112w45 7:31:00
Yava 13 1 34N32 112w28 7:29:52
Yavapai Indian Reservation 13
1 34N32 112w28 7:29:52
York 6 1 32N42 109w03 7:16:12
Young 4 1 34N06 110w57 7:23:48
Youngtown 7 1 33N36 112w18 7:29:12
Yucca 8 2 34N52 114w09 7:36:36
Yuma 14 3 32N43 114w37 7:38:28
Yuma Proving Ground 14
3 32N52 114w26 7:37:44
Yuma Station 14 3 32N39 114w35 7:38:20

ARKANSAS

TIME TABLES

Before 11/18/1883 LMT
11/18/1883 12:00 CST
3/31/1918 02:00 CWT
10/27/1918 02:00 CST
3/30/1919 02:00 CWT
10/26/1919 02:00 CST
2/09/1942 02:00 CWT
9/30/1945 02:00 CST
4/30/1967 02:00 US#1

COUNTIES

1 Arkansas
2 Ashley
3 Baxter
4 Benton
5 Boone
6 Bradley
7 Calhoun
8 Carroll
9 Chicot
10 Clark
11 Clay
12 Cleburne
13 Cleveland
14 Columbia
15 Conway
16 Craighead
17 Crawford
18 Crittenden
19 Cross
20 Dallas
21 Desha
22 Drew
23 Faulkner
24 Franklin
25 Fulton
26 Garland
27 Grant
28 Greene
29 Hempstead
30 Hot Spring
31 Howard
32 Independence
33 Izard
34 Jackson
35 Jefferson
36 Johnson
37 Lafayette
38 Lawrence
39 Lee
40 Lincoln
41 Little River
42 Logan
43 Lonoke
44 Madison
45 Marion
46 Miller
47 Mississippi
48 Monroe
49 Montgomery
50 Nevada
51 Newton
52 Ouachita
53 Perry
54 Phillips
55 Pike
56 Poinsett
57 Polk
58 Pope
59 Prairie
60 Pulaski
61 Randolph
62 St Francis
63 Saline
64 Scott
65 Searcy
66 Sebastian
67 Sevier
68 Sharp
69 Stone
70 Union
71 Van Buren
72 Washington
73 White
74 Woodruff
75 Yell

Abbott 64 35N05 94w12 6:16:48
Aberdeen 48 34N38 91w23 6:05:32
Acorn 57 34N37 94w12 6:16:48
Ada 15 35N02 92w54 6:11:36
Adona 53 35N02 92w54 6:11:36
Afton 25 36N23 91w31 6:06:04
Agnos 25 36N17 91w41 6:06:44
Air Base 60 34N55 92w07 6:08:28
Alabam 44 36N09 93w41 6:14:44
Alabama 50 33N29 93w24 6:13:36
Albany 50 33N40 93w22 6:13:28
Albert Pike 26 34N30 93w03 6:12:12
Albion 73 35N21 91w47 6:07:08
Alco 69 35N53 92w22 6:09:28
Alexander 28 36N04 90w32 6:02:08
Alexander 60 34N38 92w27 6:09:48
Alfrey 48 34N48 91w09 6:04:36
Algoa 34 35N37 91w16 6:05:04
Alicia 38 35N54 91w05 6:04:20
Alix 24 35N25 93w44 6:14:56
Allbrook 31 33N53 93w55 6:15:40
Alleene 41 33N46 94w16 6:17:04
Allen 58 35N36 93w08 6:12:32
Allfriend 51 36N11 93w24 6:13:36
Allison 69 35N56 92w07 6:08:28
Allport 43 34N32 91w47 6:07:08
Alma 17 35N29 94w13 6:16:52
Almond 12 35N42 91w48 6:07:12
Almyra 1 34N24 91w25 6:05:40
Alpena 5 36N18 93w18 6:13:12
Alpine 10 34N14 93w23 6:13:32
Alread 71 35N35 92w28 6:09:52
Altheimer 35 34N19 91w51 6:07:24
Alto 56 35N37 90w20 6:01:20
Altus 24 35N27 93w46 6:15:04
Aly 75 34N59 93w18 6:13:12
Amagon 34 35N34 91w06 6:04:24
Amanca 18 35N06 90w22 6:01:28
Amity 10 34N16 93w28 6:13:52
Amy 52 33N44 92w49 6:11:16
Anderson 4 36N18 94w17 6:17:08
Annieville 38 36N09 91w14 6:04:56
Anthony 29 33N42 93w35 6:14:20
Antioch 53 35N02 92w42 6:10:48
Antioch 73 35N04 91w53 6:07:32
Antoine 55 34N02 93w25 6:13:40
Apex 66 35N01 94w23 6:17:32
Aplin 53 34N58 92w59 6:11:56
Apple Glenn 4 36N27 94w32 6:18:08
Appleton 58 35N25 92w53 6:11:32
Arbaugh 51 35N41 93w35 6:14:20
Arbor Grove 38 36N03 90w59 6:03:56
Arcadia 29 33N48 93w23 6:13:32
Archey Valley 71 35N42 92w44 6:10:56
Ard 75 35N14 93w10 6:12:40
Arden 41 33N41 94w17 6:17:08
Arkadelphia 10 34N07 93w04 6:12:16
Arkana 36N14 92w18 6:09:12
Arkana 37 33N06 93w39 6:14:36
Arkansas 1 34N04 91w22 6:05:28
Arkansas City 21 33N37 91w12 6:04:48
Arkansas Fuel Oil Company Vi 14
33N16 93w14 6:12:56
Arkansas Post 34N01 91w21 6:05:24
Arkinda 41 33N47 94w28 6:17:52
Arkoal 66 35N06 94w21 6:17:24
Armorel 47 35N55 89w48 5:59:12
Armstrong 68 36N15 91w22 6:05:28
Arthur 15 35N15 92w41 6:10:44
Ashdown 41 33N40 94w08 6:16:32
Asher 44 36N00 94w01 6:16:04
Asher 60 34N44 92w20 6:09:20
Ash Flat 68 36N13 91w37 6:06:28
Ashland 38 35N58 91w01 6:04:04
Ashley 32 35N51 91w37 6:06:28
Ashton 9 33N20 91w17 6:05:08
Athelstan 47 35N42 89w58 5:59:52
Athens 31 34N17 94w03 6:16:12
Atkins 58 35N14 92w56 6:11:44
Atlanta 14 33N07 93w06 6:12:24
Attica 61 36N16 90w58 6:03:52
Aubrey 39 34N43 90w54 6:03:36
Auburn 40 34N02 91w31 6:06:04
Augusta 74 35N17 91w22 6:05:28
Aurelle 70 33N06 92w22 6:09:28
Aurora 44 36N05 93w44 6:14:56
Austin 15 35N22 92w34 6:10:16
Austin 43 35N00 91w59 6:07:56
Auvergne 34 35N31 91w14 6:04:56
Avery 40 33N54 91w30 6:06:00
Avilla 63 34N38 92w27 6:09:48
Avoca 4 36N24 94w04 6:16:16
Avon 67 34N02 94w21 6:17:24
Azor 50 33N44 93w28 6:13:52
Back Gate 21 33N54 91w30 6:06:00
Bain 26 34N32 93w09 6:12:36
Baker 65 35N55 92w38 6:10:32
Baker 68 36N15 91w22 6:05:28
Balch 34 35N32 91w04 6:04:16
Bald Knob 73 35N19 91w34 6:06:16
Baldwin 72 36N04 94w09 6:16:36
Ball 4 36N07 94w28 6:17:52
Ballard 68 36N13 91w36 6:06:24
Band Mill 33 36N09 91w55 6:07:40
Banks 6 33N35 92w16 6:09:04
Banner 12 35N39 91w50 6:07:20
Barber 42 35N07 94w05 6:16:20
Bard 28 36N04 90w32 6:02:08
Bardstown 47 35N30 90w09 6:00:36
Barfield 47 35N57 89w57 5:59:48
Barham 24 35N26 93w57 6:15:48
Barling 66 35N20 94w18 6:17:12
Barnes 24 35N29 93w50 6:15:20
Barnes 74 35N19 91w11 6:04:44
Barnett 71 35N23 92w25 6:09:40
Barney 23 35N12 92w12 6:08:48
Barraque 35 34N27 92w10 6:08:40
Barren Fork 33 35N58 91w44 6:06:56
Barrentine Corner 73
35N04 91w53 6:07:32
Barringer 10 33N55 93w09 6:12:36
Barton 54 34N33 90w46 6:03:04
Bass 51 35N54 93w00 6:12:00
Bassett 47 35N32 90w08 6:00:32
Bass Little 66 35N12 94w19 6:17:16
Batavia 5 36N17 93w14 6:12:56
Bateman 34 35N36 91w20 6:05:20
Bates 64 34N55 94w23 6:17:32
Batesville 32 35N46 91w39 6:06:36
Batson 36 35N37 93w39 6:14:36
Baucum 60 34N47 92w12 6:08:48
Bauxite 63 34N33 92w30 6:10:00
Baxter 22 33N32 91w26 6:05:44
Baxter 26 34N42 93w18 6:13:12
Bay 16 35N45 90w34 6:02:16
Bayliss 58 35N24 93w14 6:12:56
Bayou Meto 1 34N13 91w31 6:06:04
Bayou Metro 43 34N47 91w54 6:07:36
Bay Village 19 35N24 90w45 6:03:00
Bear 26 34N31 93w14 6:12:56
Bear Creek 65 35N55 92w38 6:10:32
Bear Creek Springs 5
36N14 93w04 6:12:16
Bearden 52 33N43 92w37 6:10:28
Bear Hollow Village 66
35N22 94w23 6:17:32
Bear Wallow 42 35N12 93w32 6:14:08
Beatie 4 36N25 94w35 6:18:20
Beaudry 26 34N42 93w04 6:12:16
Beaver 8 36N28 93w46 6:15:04
Beck 18 34N57 90w28 6:01:52
Bedford 19 35N13 90w52 6:03:28
Beebe 73 35N04 91w53 6:07:32
Bee Branch 71 35N27 92w24 6:09:36
Beech 46 33N14 93w52 6:15:28
Beech Creek 2 33N08 91w38 6:06:32
Beech Grove 28 36N10 90w37 6:02:28
Beedeville 34 35N26 91w06 6:04:24
Behestian 52 33N44 92w57 6:11:48
Beirne 10 33N53 93w12 6:12:48
Belcher 59 34N34 91w36 6:06:24
Belfast 34N25 92w28 6:09:52
Bellaire 9 33N32 91w26 6:05:44
Bella Vista 4 36N22 94w13 6:16:52
Bell City 11 36N16 90w18 6:01:12
Bellefonte 5 36N12 93w03 6:12:12
Belle Meade 62 34N57 90w28 6:01:52
Belleville 75 35N06 93w27 6:13:48
Bellmore 69 35N44 91w52 6:07:28
Bells Chapel 58 35N14 92w55 6:11:40
Bellville 67 33N53 94w05 6:16:20
Belton 29 33N57 93w51 6:15:24
Ben 69 35N38 91w57 6:07:48
Benedict 23 35N00 92w32 6:10:08
Bengall 34 35N37 91w16 6:05:04
Ben Gay 68 36N05 91w29 6:05:56
Ben Hur 51 35N44 92w58 6:11:52
Ben Lomond 67 33N50 94w07 6:16:28
Bennett 11 36N28 90w24 6:01:36
Bennett Bayou 25 36N26 92w04 6:08:16
Bentley 15 35N06 92w46 6:11:04
Benton 63 34N34 92w35 6:10:20
Bentonville 4 36N22 94w13 6:16:52
Berea 2 33N14 91w48 6:07:12
Bergman 5 36N19 93w01 6:12:04
Berlin 2 33N14 91w48 6:07:12
Bernice 58 35N17 93w09 6:12:36
Berryville 8 36N22 93w34 6:14:16
Beryl 23 35N05 92w27 6:09:48
Bethany 31 34N07 94w01 6:16:04
Bethel 28 36N04 90w32 6:02:08
Bethel Grove 72 36N02 94w15 6:17:00
Bethel Heights 4 36N13 94w07 6:16:28
Bethesda 32 35N48 91w47 6:07:08
Beulah 59 34N49 91w24 6:05:36
Beverage Town 71 35N25 92w43 6:10:52
Beverly 66 35N21 94w07 6:16:28
Bexar 25 36N17 92w00 6:08:00
Bidville 17 35N48 94w08 6:16:32
Big Bottom 32 35N41 91w27 6:05:48
Bigelow 53 35N00 92w38 6:10:32
Bigflat 3 36N01 92w24 6:09:36
Big Fork 34N29 93w58 6:15:52
Biggers 61 36N20 90w49 6:03:16
Big Lake 47 35N51 90w12 6:00:48
Big Rock 60 34N41 92w20 6:09:20
Big Springs 45 36N11 92w45 6:11:00
Big Springs 69 35N52 92w07 6:08:28
Billingsleys Corner 41
33N50 94w21 6:17:24
Billstown 55 34N04 93w42 6:14:48
Bingen 29 33N57 93w51 6:15:24
Birdeye 19 35N23 90w41 6:02:44
Birdsong 47 35N29 90w21 6:01:24
Bird Town 15 35N16 92w34 6:10:16
Birta 75 35N01 93w08 6:12:32
Biscoe 59 34N49 91w25 6:05:40
Bismarck 30 34N19 93w10 6:12:40
Blackburn 72 35N48 94w08 6:16:32
Blackfish 62 34N57 90w33 6:02:12
Black Fork 64 34N46 94w25 6:17:40
Blackland 31 33N49 93w53 6:15:32
Blackland 41 33N43 94w24 6:17:36
Black Oak 16 35N50 90w22 6:01:28
Black Oak 56 35N29 90w21 6:01:24
Black Oak 72 36N04 94w09 6:16:36
Black Rock 38 36N07 91w06 6:04:24
Black Springs 49 34N28 93w43 6:14:52
Blackton 48 34N40 91w06 6:04:24
Blackville 34 35N37 91w16 6:05:04
Blackwell 15 35N13 92w50 6:11:20

ARKANSAS

Place	Lat.	Long.	Time
Blakely 26	34n42	93w04	6:12:16
Blakemore 43	34n33	91w53	6:07:32
Blanchard Springs 70	33n01	92w43	6:10:52
Blansett 64	34n46	94w14	6:16:56
Blanville 68	36n04	91w37	6:06:28
Blevins 29	33n52	93w35	6:14:20
Bloomer 66	35n18	94w07	6:16:28
Blossom 62	34n55	91w07	6:04:28
Blue Ball	34n58	93w43	6:14:52
Blue Bayou 31	33n53	94w00	6:16:00
Blue Cane 11	36n14	90w13	6:00:52
Blue Eye 8	36n30	93w24	6:13:36
Blue Mountain 42	35n08	93w43	6:14:52
Blue Ridge 31	34n11	94w02	6:16:08
Blue Springs 26	34n30	93w03	6:12:12
Bluff City 50	33n43	93w08	6:12:32
Bluffton 75	34n54	93w36	6:14:24
Blytheville 47	35n56	89w55	5:59:40
Blytheville Air Force Base 47	35n57	89w57	5:59:48
Blytheville Junction 47	35n57	89w57	5:59:48
Board Camp 57	34n32	94w06	6:16:24
Boas 38	36n02	90w57	6:03:48
Bob Ward 18	35n05	90w20	6:01:20
Bodcaw 50	33n33	93w25	6:13:40
Bogy 35	34n13	91w45	6:07:00
Bohannon 44	36n05	93w50	6:15:20
Bois D Arc 29	33n38	93w48	6:15:12
Bolding 70	33n02	92w11	6:08:44
Boles 64	34n47	94w03	6:16:12
Bonanza 66	35n14	94w26	6:17:44
Bondsville 47	35n37	90w20	6:01:20
Bonnerdale 30	34n23	93w23	6:13:32
Bono 16	35n55	90w48	6:03:12
Bono 23	35n14	92w23	6:09:32
Booker 60	34n47	92w12	6:08:48
Booneville 42	35n08	93w55	6:15:40
Booster 65	35n50	92w33	6:10:12
Boothe 64	35n08	94w03	6:16:12
Boston 44	35n49	93w39	6:14:36
Boswell 33	36n02	92w04	6:08:16
Botkinburg 71	35n35	92w28	6:09:52
Boueff 9	33n07	91w16	6:05:04
Boughton 50	33n52	93w21	6:13:24
Bovine 2	33n14	91w48	6:07:12
Bowen 55	34n02	93w30	6:14:00
Bowman 13	34n01	92w07	6:08:28
Bowman 16	35n49	90w26	6:01:44
Boxelder 47	35n56	90w15	6:01:00
Boxley 51	36n03	93w31	6:14:04
Boyd 37	33n22	93w35	6:14:20
Boyd 46	33n16	93w53	6:15:32
Boydell 2	33n22	91w29	6:05:56
Boydsville 11	36n20	90w23	6:01:32
Boynton 47	35n56	90w15	6:01:00
Bradford 73	35n25	91w27	6:05:48
Bradley 37	33n06	93w39	6:14:36
Bradley Quarters 6	33n37	92w04	6:08:16
Bradshaw 11	36n24	90w21	6:01:24
Brady 60	34n45	92w22	6:09:28
Bragg 52	33n36	92w58	6:11:52
Branch 24	35n18	93w57	6:15:48
Brasfield 59	34n49	91w24	6:05:36
Brashears 44	35n50	93w50	6:15:20
Brawley 64	34n51	94w19	6:17:16
Bredlow Corner 60	34n33	91w53	6:07:32
Brentwood 72	35n51	94w06	6:16:24
Brewer 12	35n36	92w11	6:08:44
Brickeys 39	34n52	90w36	6:02:24
Bridge Creek 52	33n25	92w52	6:11:28
Briggsville 75	34n56	93w30	6:14:00
Brighton 28	36n04	90w21	6:01:24
Bright Star 31	33n53	93w55	6:15:40
Brightstar 46	33n08	94w03	6:16:12
Brightwater 4	36n25	94w04	6:16:16
Brinkley 48	34n53	91w12	6:04:48
Brister 14	33n06	93w12	6:12:48
Bristol 23	35n09	92w08	6:08:32
Bristow 61	36n11	90w59	6:03:56
Brockett 61	36n16	90w58	6:03:52
Brockwell 33	36n09	91w55	6:07:40
Brookings 11	36n17	90w40	6:02:40
Brookland 16	35n54	90w35	6:02:20
Brown 47	35n53	90w10	6:00:40
Brown Springs 30	34n10	92w55	6:11:40
Brownstown 67	33n53	94w05	6:16:20
Bruins 18	34n57	90w28	6:01:52
Bruins Landing 18	34n57	90w28	6:01:52
Brumley 23	35n05	92w27	6:09:48
Brummitt 43	34n29	91w33	6:06:12
Bruno 45	36n09	92w47	6:11:08
Brush Creek 27	34n10	92w36	6:10:24
Brush Creek 72	36n11	93w58	6:15:52
Brushy 64	34n51	93w52	6:15:28
Brushy Lake 19	35n19	90w57	6:03:48
Brutonville 34	35n37	90w54	6:03:36
Bryant 63	34n36	92w29	6:09:56
Brymar 47	35n42	89w58	5:59:52
Buckeye 47	35n56	90w15	6:01:00
Buckner 37	33n22	93w26	6:13:44
Buck Range 31	33n52	93w52	6:15:28
Buckville 26	34n39	93w20	6:13:20
Buena Vista 52	33n29	92w58	6:11:52
Buffalo City 3	36n18	92w20	6:09:20
Buford 3	36n14	92w25	6:09:40
Buie 27	34n19	92w33	6:10:12
Bullard 59	35n00	91w39	6:06:36
Bullfrog Valley 58	35n24	93w07	6:12:28
Bull Shoals 45	36n23	92w35	6:10:20
Bunn 20	34n00	92w30	6:10:00
Bunney 16	35n50	90w22	6:01:28
Burdette 47	35n49	89w56	5:59:44
Burg 31	34n14	94w04	6:16:16
Burke 41	33n46	94w16	6:17:04
Burlington 5	36n14	93w04	6:12:16
Burma 66	35n05	94w16	6:17:04
Burnett 58	35n19	92w52	6:11:28
Burnville 66	35n13	94w15	6:17:00
Burton Mill 37	33n22	93w42	6:14:48
Busch 8	36n28	93w50	6:15:20
Bussey 14	33n22	93w30	6:14:00
Butler 47	35n42	89w58	5:59:52
Butlerville 43	34n59	91w50	6:07:20
Butterfield 30	34n26	92w49	6:11:16
Byron 25	36n19	91w58	6:07:52
Cabanal 8	36n17	93w32	6:14:08
Cabot 43	34n59	92w01	6:08:04
Caddo Gap 49	34n24	93w37	6:14:28
Caddo Valley 10	34n05	93w02	6:12:08
Cain 17	35n38	94w10	6:16:40
Calamine 68	36n01	91w24	6:05:36
Caldwell 62	35n05	90w49	6:03:16
Cale 50	33n38	93w14	6:12:56
Caledonia 70	33n01	92w43	6:10:52
Calf Creek 65	35n55	92w49	6:11:16
Calhoun 14	33n16	93w14	6:12:56
Calhoun 59	35n00	91w26	6:05:44
Calico Rock 33	36n07	92w09	6:08:36
Calion 70	33n20	92w32	6:10:08
Calmer 13	33n58	92w11	6:08:44
Calumet 47	35n57	89w57	5:59:48
Calvert 27	34n13	92w25	6:09:40
Calvin 38	35n54	91w05	6:04:20
Camden 52	33n35	92w50	6:11:20
Cammack Village 60	34n47	92w21	6:09:24
Camp 25	36n25	91w44	6:06:56
Campbell 65	35n55	92w38	6:10:32
Campbell Station 34	35n40	91w15	6:05:00
Camp Joseph T. Robinson 23	34n45	92w22	6:09:28
Canaan 65	35n55	92w38	6:10:32
Canadian 47	35n54	89w47	5:59:08
Canale 37	33n06	93w39	6:14:36
Cane 73	35n10	91w51	6:07:24
Cane Creek 27	34n19	92w24	6:09:36
Canehill 72	35n55	94w23	6:17:32
Caney 23	35n05	92w27	6:09:48
Caney 30	34n19	93w10	6:12:40
Caney 45	36n14	92w41	6:10:44
Caney 50	33n34	93w24	6:13:36
Caney Fork 55	34n13	93w31	6:14:04
Caney Valley 55	34n16	93w28	6:13:52
Canfield 37	33n11	93w38	6:14:32
Capps 5	36n14	93w04	6:12:16
Capps City 46	33n08	94w03	6:16:12
Caraway 16	35n46	90w19	6:01:16
Carbon City 42	35n18	93w43	6:14:52
Carden Bottoms 75	35n14	93w10	6:12:40
Cargile 71	35n23	92w18	6:09:12
Carlisle 43	34n47	91w45	6:07:00
Carlton 9	33n19	91w19	6:05:16
Carmel 6	33n37	92w04	6:08:16
Carmi 47	35n56	90w15	6:01:00
Carolan 42	35n08	93w55	6:15:40
Caroline 43	34n59	91w58	6:07:52
Carpenter 11	36n28	90w44	6:02:56
Carroll 52	33n44	92w50	6:11:20
Carroll's Corner 47	35n53	90w10	6:00:40
Carrollton 8	36n17	93w16	6:13:04
Carryville 11	36n23	90w12	6:00:48
Carson 47	35n42	89w58	5:59:52
Carson Lake 47	35n38	90w03	6:00:12
Carter 2	33n14	91w47	6:07:08
Carter Cove Use Area 75	34n59	93w18	6:13:12
Carthage 20	34n04	92w33	6:10:12
Carver 51	36n01	93w03	6:12:12
Casa 53	35n02	93w03	6:12:12
Cash 16	35n48	90w56	6:03:44
Cass 24	35n29	93w50	6:15:20
Casscoe 1	34n32	91w20	6:05:20
Caswell 7	33n45	92w32	6:10:08
Catalpa 36	35n38	93w27	6:13:48
Catcher 17	35n29	94w20	6:17:20
Catholic Point 15	35n21	92w32	6:10:08
Cato 23	34n56	92w16	6:09:04
Catron 54	34n13	90w57	6:03:48
Caulksville 42	35n18	93w52	6:15:28
Cauthron 64	34n55	94w18	6:17:12
Cavanaugh 66	35n22	94w23	6:17:32
Cave City 68	35n57	91w33	6:06:12
Cavecreek 51	35n55	93w03	6:12:12
Cave Springs 4	36n16	94w14	6:16:56
Cecil 24	35n26	93w57	6:15:48
Cedar Creek 64	34n47	93w51	6:15:24
Cedar Falls 15	35n08	92w55	6:11:40
Cedar Grove 32	35n35	91w45	6:07:00
Cedar Grove 61	36n16	90w58	6:03:52
Cedarville 17	35n35	94w22	6:17:28
Center 68	36n09	91w31	6:06:04
Center Grove 27	34n19	92w24	6:09:36
Center Hill 28	35n16	91w53	6:07:32
Center Point 10	33n55	93w09	6:12:36
Center Point 31	34n01	93w59	6:15:56
Center Point 59	34n47	91w34	6:06:16
Center Post 12	35n29	92w12	6:08:48
Center Ridge 10	34n16	93w28	6:13:52
Center Ridge 15	35n22	92w34	6:10:16
Centerton 4	36n22	94w17	6:17:08
Center Valley 58	35n17	93w09	6:12:36
Centerville 23	35n14	92w23	6:09:32
Centerville 29	33n44	93w28	6:13:52
Centerville 75	35n07	93w10	6:12:40
Central 10	34n05	93w02	6:12:08
Central 30	34n23	92w49	6:11:16
Central 67	33n57	94w21	6:17:24
Central Baptist College 23	35n05	92w27	6:09:48
Central City 26	34n30	93w03	6:12:12
Central City 66	35n20	94w11	6:16:44
Cerrogordo 41	33n50	94w21	6:17:24
Chalk Bluff 11	36n27	90w12	6:00:48
Chalybeate Springs 69	35n46	92w00	6:08:00
Chalybeate Springs 75	35n03	93w23	6:13:32
Champagnolle 7	33n28	92w34	6:10:16
Chanticleer 9	33n20	91w17	6:05:08
Chapel Hill 67	34n02	94w21	6:17:24
Charleston 24	35n18	94w05	6:16:20
Charlotte 32	35n49	91w26	6:05:44
Chatfield 18	35n00	90w24	6:01:36
Chelford 47	35n29	90w21	6:01:24
Cherokee 4	36n18	94w34	6:18:16
Cherokee City 4	36n16	94w25	6:17:40
Cherry Hill 53	34n59	92w53	6:11:32
Cherry Valley 19	35n24	90w45	6:03:00
Chester 17	35n41	94w11	6:16:44
Chickalah 75	35n10	93w17	6:13:08
Chickasawba 47	35n56	89w51	5:59:24
Chicot 9	33n12	91w17	6:05:08
Chicot Terrace 60	34n41	92w21	6:09:24
Chidester 52	33n42	93w01	6:12:04
Childress 16	35n54	90w21	6:01:24
Childress 59	34n58	91w30	6:06:00
Chilson 16	35n48	90w56	6:03:44
Chimes 71	35n50	92w33	6:10:12
Chismville 42	35n13	93w56	6:15:44
Choctaw 71	35n33	92w24	6:09:36
Chrisp 73	35n07	91w53	6:07:32
Christian 32	35n36	91w29	6:05:56
Cincinnati 72	35n59	94w29	6:17:56
Claiborne 33	36n06	92w05	6:08:20
Clarendon 48	34n42	91w19	6:05:16
Clarkedale 18	35n19	90w14	6:00:56
Clarkridge 3	36n29	92w21	6:09:24
Clarks Corner 62	35n01	90w41	6:02:44
Clarksville 36	35n28	93w28	6:13:52
Clay 73	35n15	91w43	6:06:52
Clear Lake 47	35n52	89w51	5:59:24
Cleveland 15	35n25	92w43	6:10:52
Clifton 23	35n12	92w28	6:09:52
Clifty 44	36n14	93w48	6:15:12
Clinton 71	35n36	92w28	6:09:52
Cloar 18	35n16	90w28	6:01:52
Clover Bend 38	36n03	90w59	6:03:56
Clow 29	33n53	93w46	6:15:04
Clyde 72	35n55	94w24	6:17:36
Coal 64	34n55	94w23	6:17:32
Coaldale 64	34n53	94w36	6:18:24
Coal Hill 36	35n26	93w40	6:14:40
Cobbs 43	34n33	91w53	6:07:32
Cody 39	34n46	90w46	6:03:04
Coffeeville 34	35n25	91w27	6:05:48
Coffey 73	35n12	91w58	6:07:52
Coffman 28	36n04	90w32	6:02:08
Coffman 38	36n03	90w59	6:03:56
Coin 8	36n20	93w20	6:13:20
Coldwater 19	35n24	90w37	6:02:28
Coldwell 73	35n23	91w37	6:06:28
Cole 66	35n12	94w24	6:17:36
Coleman 22	33n33	91w47	6:07:08
Cole Spur 40	33n59	91w34	6:06:16
Colfax 3	36n18	92w20	6:09:20
College City 38	36n08	90w56	6:03:44
College Heights	33n53	91w48	6:07:12
Collegehill 14	33n21	93w12	6:12:48
Collegeville 63	34n38	92w27	6:09:48
Collier 28	36n01	90w29	6:01:56
Collins 22	33n32	91w34	6:06:16
Colt 62	35n08	90w49	6:03:16
Columbia 61	36n22	90w56	6:03:44
Columbus 29	33n46	93w49	6:15:16
Colville 4	36n15	94w12	6:16:48
Combs 44	35n50	93w50	6:15:20
Cominto 22	33n34	91w39	6:06:36
Compton 51	36n06	93w18	6:13:12
Concord 12	35n40	91w51	6:07:24
Congo 63	34n30	92w35	6:10:20
Connor 8	36n16	93w28	6:13:52
Convenience 58	35n20	92w57	6:11:48
Conway 23	35n05	92w26	6:09:44
Cord 32	35n49	91w21	6:05:24
Corinth 75	35n06	93w27	6:13:48
Corley 42	35n18	93w43	6:14:52
Cornerstone 35	34n14	91w45	6:07:00
Cornerville 40	33n51	91w56	6:07:44
Cornhill 67	33n53	94w05	6:16:20
Cornie 70	33n06	92w51	6:11:24
Corning 11	36n25	90w35	6:02:20
Cotter 3	36n16	92w32	6:10:08
Cotton Belt Junction 48	34n48	91w09	6:04:36
Cotton Plant 74	35n00	91w15	6:05:00
Cotton Town 75	35n14	93w10	6:12:40
Cottonwood Corner 16	35n54	90w21	6:01:24
Cottonwood Corner 47	35n42	89w58	5:59:52
Council 39	34n52	90w30	6:02:00
County Line 31	33n57	93w56	6:15:44
Cove 57	34n26	94w25	6:17:40
Cove City 17	35n41	94w21	6:17:24
Cove Creek 72	35n50	94w18	6:17:12
Cowell 51	35n50	93w12	6:12:48
Cow Lake 34	35n25	91w05	6:04:20
Cowlingsville 67	33n53	94w05	6:16:20
Coy 43	34n32	91w53	6:07:32
Cozahome 65	36n03	92w31	6:10:04
Crabtree 71	35n35	92w28	6:09:52
Craig 71	35n32	92w36	6:10:24
Cravens 24	35n33	93w54	6:15:36
Crawfordsville 18	35n14	90w20	6:01:20

ARKANSAS

Place	Latitude	Longitude	Time
Creigh 48	34N33	90w55	6:03:40
Crigler 40	33N56	91w50	6:07:20
Critten Ridge 41	33N43	94w24	6:17:36
Crockett 11	36N23	90w12	6:00:48
Crocketts Bluff 1	34N27	91w13	6:04:52
Crook 22	33N28	91w57	6:07:48
Crosby 73	35N17	91w50	6:07:20
Cross 8	36N29	93w38	6:14:32
Crosses 44	36N04	94w09	6:16:36
Crossett 2	33N08	91w58	6:07:52
Crossroads 12	35N23	92w13	6:08:52
Crossroads 27	34N19	92w24	6:09:36
Cross Roads 29	33N46	93w41	6:14:44
Cross Roads 30	34N23	93w23	6:13:32
Cross Roads 33	36N09	92w07	6:08:28
Cross Roads 41	33N50	94w21	6:17:24
Cross Roads 42	35N22	93w32	6:14:08
Cross Roads 44	36N09	93w52	6:15:28
Cross Roads 48	34N36	91w12	6:04:48
Cross Roads 52	33N23	92w47	6:11:08
Crossroads 59	34N58	91w30	6:06:00
Crow Creek 62	35N01	90w47	6:03:08
Crowley 28	36N12	90w37	6:02:28
Crumrod 54	34N09	90w59	6:03:56
Crystal Springs 26	34N31	93w20	6:13:20
Crystal Springs Landing 26	34N31	93w20	6:13:20
Cullendale 52	33N35	92w47	6:11:08
Culp 3	36N07	92w08	6:08:32
Culpepper 71	35N30	92w32	6:10:08
Cumi 3	36N22	92w14	6:08:56
Current River 61	36N19	90w49	6:03:16
Curtis 10	34N00	93w06	6:12:24
Cushman 32	35N53	91w45	6:07:00
Cut Off 46	33N14	93w45	6:15:00
Cypert 54	34N29	90w57	6:03:48
Cypress Corner 39	34N36	90w45	6:03:00
Cypress Ridge 48	34N45	91w09	6:04:36
Cypress Valley 15	35N15	92w41	6:10:44
Dabney 71	35N08	92w45	6:11:00
Dacus 18	35N08	90w11	6:00:44
Daisy 55	34N14	93w45	6:15:00
Dalark 20	34N02	92w53	6:11:32
Dallas 7	33N35	92w24	6:09:36
Dalton 61	36N25	91w08	6:04:32
Damascus 23	35N22	92w25	6:09:40
Danley 23	34N58	92w24	6:09:36
Danville 75	35N03	93w24	6:13:36
Darcy 12	35N32	92w06	6:08:24
Dardanelle 75	35N13	93w09	6:12:36
Darysaw 27	34N13	92w18	6:09:12
Datto 11	36N24	90w44	6:02:56
Davenport 73	35N26	91w50	6:07:20
Day 33	36N13	91w36	6:06:24
Days Creek 46	33N19	94w00	6:16:00
Dayton 66	35N07	94w12	6:16:48
Deaneyville 29	33N48	93w23	6:13:32
De Ann 29	33N47	93w34	6:14:16
Deans Market 17	35N29	94w14	6:16:56
Dean Spring 17	35N29	94w14	6:16:56
De Bastrop 2	33N07	91w31	6:06:04
Deberrie 53	35N00	92w48	6:11:12
Decatur 4	36N20	94w28	6:17:52
Deckerville 56	35N27	90w18	6:01:12
Deep Elm 9	33N20	91w17	6:05:08
Deep Elm 48	34N36	91w12	6:04:48
Deer 51	35N50	93w13	6:12:52
Deerfield 21	34N04	91w01	6:04:04
Degray 10	34N05	93w02	6:12:08
Dekalb 27	34N24	92w31	6:10:04
Delaney 44	36N00	94w01	6:16:04
Delaplaine 28	36N14	90w44	6:02:56
Delaware 42	35N17	93w19	6:13:16
Delfore 16	35N56	90w15	6:01:00
Delight 55	34N02	93w31	6:14:04
Dell 47	35N51	90w02	6:00:08
Delmar 8	36N10	93w20	6:13:20
De Luce 1	34N17	91w20	6:05:20
Demun 61	36N17	90w58	6:03:52
Denmark 34	35N29	91w37	6:06:28
Dennard 71	35N46	92w31	6:10:04
Denning 24	35N25	93w45	6:15:00
Denton 64	34N53	94w11	6:16:44
Denver 8	36N23	93w19	6:13:16
Denwood 47	35N29	90w21	6:01:24
Departee 32	35N34	91w25	6:05:40
De Queen 67	34N02	94w21	6:17:24
Dermott 9	33N32	91w26	6:05:44
De Roane 29	33N39	93w34	6:14:16
De Roche 30	34N19	93w05	6:12:20
Des Arc 59	34N58	91w30	6:06:00
Desha 32	35N44	91w41	6:06:44
De Soto 45	36N05	92w36	6:10:24
Detonti 63	34N30	92w31	6:10:04
De Valls Bluff 59	34N47	91w28	6:05:52
De View 74	35N13	91w11	6:04:44
Dewey 73	35N26	91w50	6:07:20
De Witt 1	34N18	91w20	6:05:20
Dialion 13	33N58	92w11	6:08:44
Diamond 66	35N05	94w17	6:17:08
Diamond City 5	36N27	92w55	6:11:40
Diamondhead 26	34N30	93w03	6:12:12
Dian 50	33N48	93w23	6:13:32
Diaz 34	35N38	91w16	6:05:04
Dickerson 36	35N41	93w39	6:14:36
Dickson 4	36N26	94w20	6:17:20
Dierks 31	34N07	94w01	6:16:04
Dill 12	35N34	91w56	6:07:44
Dillard 31	33N54	93w56	6:15:44
Dillen 36	35N44	93w24	6:13:36
Divide 15	35N02	93w03	6:12:12
Dixie 16	35N49	90w26	6:01:44
Dixie 74	35N05	91w22	6:05:28
Dixon 48	34N52	91w08	6:04:32
Dobson 56	35N41	91w00	6:04:00
Dodd City 45	36N19	92w47	6:11:08
Doddridge 46	33N06	93w55	6:15:40
Dodson 14	33N16	93w14	6:12:56
Dodsons Corner 62	35N01	90w47	6:03:08
Dogpatch 51	36N06	93w08	6:12:32
Dogwood 47	35N57	89w57	5:59:48
Dogwood 73	35N06	91w36	6:06:24
Dollarway 35	34N13	92w02	6:08:08
Dolph 33	36N15	92w06	6:08:24
Donald 24	35N19	93w56	6:15:44
Donaldson 30	34N14	92w55	6:11:40
Dongola 65	35N55	92w38	6:10:32
Doniphan 73	35N15	91w43	6:06:52
Dora 17	35N28	94w26	6:17:44
Dortch 43	34N43	92w03	6:08:12
Dota 32	35N50	91w24	6:05:36
Dover 58	35N24	93w07	6:12:28
Dowdy 32	35N49	91w21	6:05:24
Dowell 38	35N56	90w57	6:03:48
Drakes Creek 44	36N05	93w44	6:14:56
Drasco 12	35N38	91w57	6:07:48
Driggs 42	35N14	93w46	6:15:04
Driver 47	35N37	90w01	6:00:04
Dryden 16	35N50	90w54	6:03:36
Dryfork 8	36N09	93w29	6:13:56
Dry Run 20	33N49	92w22	6:09:28
Drytown 33	35N58	91w48	6:07:12
Dublin 42	35N22	93w32	6:14:08
Duckett 31	34N17	94w13	6:16:52
Dudley Lake 35	34N27	91w52	6:07:28
Duff 65	36N02	92w48	6:11:12
Dumas 21	33N53	91w30	6:06:00
Duncan 48	34N36	91w13	6:04:52
Dunnington 32	35N38	91w28	6:05:52
Dunnington 35	34N22	91w47	6:07:08
Durham 72	35N57	93w59	6:15:56
Durian 30	34N23	92w49	6:11:16
Dutch Creek 75	35N00	93w39	6:14:36
Dutch Mills 72	35N53	94w29	6:17:56
Dutton 44	35N49	93w42	6:14:48
Duty 38	36N04	91w04	6:04:16
Dyer 17	35N30	94w08	6:16:32
Dyess 47	35N36	90w13	6:00:52
Eagle Mills 52	33N41	92w43	6:10:52
Eagleton 57	34N46	94w25	6:17:40
Earle 18	35N16	90w28	6:01:52
East Black Oak 18	35N29	90w21	6:01:24
East Camden 52	33N36	92w44	6:10:56
East End 63	34N30	92w12	6:08:48
East Fork 23	35N11	92w23	6:09:32
East Pocahontas 61	36N16	90w58	6:03:52
East Richwoods 69	35N52	92w07	6:08:28
East Sullivan 68	35N59	91w36	6:06:24
East Wilson 47	35N36	90w03	6:00:12
Eaton 38	36N03	91w13	6:04:52
Ebenezer 14	33N25	93w04	6:12:16
Ebony 18	35N13	90w12	6:00:48
Echo 42	35N08	94w03	6:16:12
Economy 58	35N14	92w55	6:11:40
Ecore Fabre 52	33N34	92w53	6:11:32
Eden Isle 12	35N32	92w06	6:08:24
Edgemont 12	35N36	92w11	6:08:44
Edmondson 18	35N06	90w19	6:01:16
Efay 72	36N04	94w09	6:16:36
Eglantine 71	35N39	92w19	6:09:16
Egypt 16	35N52	90w57	6:03:48
Elaine 54	34N19	90w51	6:03:24
Elberta 65	35N50	92w33	6:10:12
El Dorado 70	33N12	92w40	6:10:40
Eleven Points 61	36N22	91w04	6:04:16
Elixir 5	36N20	93w01	6:12:04
Elizabeth 25	36N20	92w06	6:08:24
Elkins 72	36N00	94w01	6:16:04
Elk Ranch 8	36N24	93w44	6:14:56
Elliott	33N27	92w50	6:11:20
Ellis 3	36N18	92w20	6:09:20
Ellis 19	35N13	90w56	6:03:44
Ellison 35	34N23	91w57	6:07:48
Ellsworth 42	35N17	93w33	6:14:12
Elm 10	34N16	93w28	6:13:52
Elm Grove 16	35N49	90w26	6:01:44
Elm Park 64	35N08	94w03	6:16:12
Elm Springs 72	36N12	94w16	6:17:04
Elm Store 61	36N28	91w12	6:04:48
Elmwood 5	36N09	93w06	6:12:24
Elnora 61	36N16	90w58	6:03:52
Elon 2	33N03	91w54	6:07:36
El Paso 73	35N08	92w06	6:08:24
Emanuel 1	34N24	91w25	6:05:40
Emerson 14	33N06	93w11	6:12:44
Emmet 50	33N44	93w28	6:13:52
Empire 9	33N07	91w33	6:06:12
Enders 23	35N23	92w13	6:08:52
Engelberg 61	36N16	90w58	6:03:52
England 43	34N33	91w58	6:07:52
England Junction 35	34N45	92w21	6:09:24
English 35	34N45	92w21	6:09:24
Enola 23	35N12	92w12	6:08:48
Enright 73	35N15	91w43	6:06:52
Enterprise 66	35N22	94w23	6:17:32
Erbie 51	36N06	93w08	6:12:32
Eros 45	36N09	92w55	6:11:40
Erwin 34	35N37	91w16	6:05:04
Erwin 59	34N58	91w30	6:06:00
Esculapia 4	36N21	94w06	6:16:24
Estes 60	34N33	91w53	6:07:32
Ethel 1	34N17	91w10	6:04:40
Etna 24	35N29	93w50	6:15:20
Etowah 47	35N44	90w14	6:00:56
Euclid Heights 26	34N30	93w03	6:12:12
Eudora 9	33N07	91w16	6:05:04
Eula 65	35N55	92w49	6:11:16
Eureka Springs 8	36N24	93w44	6:14:56
Evansville 72	35N48	94w30	6:18:00
Evelyn Hills 72	36N04	94w09	6:16:36
Evening Shade 68	36N04	91w37	6:06:28
Evening Star 28	36N14	90w43	6:02:52
Everton 5	36N09	92w54	6:11:36
Ewing 5	36N09	93w03	6:12:12
Excelsior 66	35N13	94w15	6:17:00
Extra 2	33N06	91w45	6:07:00
Fairbanks 71	35N23	92w13	6:08:52
Fairfield 60	34N41	92w21	6:09:24
Fairfield Bay 71	35N39	92w19	6:09:16
Fairindale 20	34N04	92w33	6:10:12
Fair Oaks 19	35N15	91w02	6:04:08
Fairplay 63	34N30	92w42	6:10:48
Fairview 9	33N20	91w17	6:05:08
Fairview 20	33N58	92w53	6:11:32
Fairview 43	34N47	91w54	6:07:36
Fairview 45	36N17	92w36	6:10:24
Fairview 52	33N35	92w47	6:11:08
Fairview 65	35N56	92w26	6:09:44
Fairview 67	34N10	94w19	6:17:16
Faith	34N06	92w06	6:08:24
Falcon 50	33N28	93w25	6:13:40
Falls Chapel 67	33N53	94w05	6:16:20
Fallsville 51	35N44	93w24	6:13:36
Fancy Hill 49	34N24	93w37	6:14:28
Farelly Lake 35	34N29	91w33	6:06:12
Fargo 48	34N57	91w11	6:04:44
Farmington 72	36N03	94w15	6:17:00
Farmville 6	33N37	92w04	6:08:16
Farris 69	35N57	92w22	6:09:28
Faulknerville 28	36N10	90w37	6:02:28
Fayette 7	33N21	92w27	6:09:48
Fayetteville 72	36N04	94w10	6:16:40
Felker 4	36N14	94w28	6:17:52
Felsenthal 70	33N03	92w09	6:08:36
Felton 39	34N48	90w48	6:03:12
Fender 61	36N06	90w57	6:03:48
Fendley 10	34N16	93w28	6:13:52
Fenter 27	34N27	92w39	6:10:36
Ferda 35	34N33	91w53	6:07:32
Ferguson 54	34N09	90w59	6:03:56
Ferguson 75	35N07	93w26	6:13:44
Ferguson Crossroads 46	33N16	93w53	6:15:32
Fern 24	35N38	94w10	6:16:40
Ferndale	34N47	92w34	6:10:16
Fiftysix 69	35N57	92w13	6:08:52
Figure Five 17	35N29	94w20	6:17:20
Finch 28	36N04	90w32	6:02:08
Fir 49	34N37	93w28	6:13:52
Fisher 16	35N48	90w56	6:03:44
Fisher 56	35N30	90w58	6:03:52
Fitzgerald 34	35N37	91w16	6:05:04
Fitzhugh 74	35N22	91w19	6:05:16
Fivemile 12	35N38	91w57	6:07:48
Flag 69	35N49	92w24	6:09:36
Flat Creek 38	36N06	91w13	6:04:52
Flat Rock 36	35N20	93w15	6:13:00
Fleener 39	34N52	91w01	6:04:04
Flint 4	36N16	94w25	6:17:40
Flippin 45	36N17	92w36	6:10:24
Floodway 47	35N53	90w10	6:00:40
Floral 32	35N36	91w45	6:07:00
Florence 22	33N46	91w39	6:06:36
Floyd 73	35N12	91w58	6:07:52
Fogleman 18	35N24	90w15	6:01:00
Fomby 41	33N41	94w08	6:16:32
Fontaine 28	36N04	90w32	6:02:08
Fordyce 20	33N49	92w25	6:09:40
Foreman 41	33N43	94w24	6:17:36
Forest Grove 14	36N05	93w44	6:14:56
Forest Grove 37	33N06	93w28	6:13:52
Forest Park 60	34N46	92w23	6:09:32
Formosa 71	35N28	92w31	6:10:04
Forrest City 62	35N01	90w47	6:03:08
Fort Chaffee 66	35N22	94w23	6:17:32
Fort Douglas 36	35N41	93w15	6:13:00
Fort Lynn 46	33N16	93w53	6:15:32
Fort Smith 66	35N23	94w25	6:17:40
Forty Four 33	36N09	92w05	6:08:20
Forum 44	36N05	93w44	6:14:56
Foster 61	36N21	90w59	6:03:56
Fouke 46	33N16	93w53	6:15:32
Fountain Hill 2	33N21	91w51	6:07:24
Fountain Lake 26	34N30	93w03	6:12:12
Fountain Prairie 2	33N14	91w48	6:07:12
Fourche 53	35N00	92w37	6:10:28
Fourche Lafave 53	35N00	92w49	6:11:16
Four Forks 39	34N46	90w46	6:03:04
Four Mile Corner 59	34N58	91w30	6:06:00
Fourmile Hill 73	35N15	91w43	6:06:52
Fowler 75	35N14	93w10	6:12:40
Fox 69	35N47	92w18	6:09:12
Fox Hill 66	35N05	94w16	6:17:04
Francis 5	36N14	93w04	6:12:16
Francis 12	35N35	92w04	6:08:16
Francure 73	35N09	91w29	6:05:56
Franklin 33	36N11	91w45	6:07:00
Fredonia 59	34N49	91w24	6:05:36
Freedom 57	34N38	94w23	6:17:32
Free Hope 14	33N16	93w14	6:12:56
Freeo 52	33N46	92w41	6:10:44
French 37	33N04	93w33	6:14:12
Frenchmans Bayou 47	35N28	90w11	6:00:44
Friendship 14	33N22	93w30	6:14:00
Friendship 30	34N13	93w00	6:12:00
Friley 36	35N49	93w39	6:14:36
Frisco Junction 47	35N56	90w15	6:01:00
Frog Town 66	35N01	94w23	6:17:32
Frys Mill 56	35N32	90w25	6:01:40
Fulton 29	33N37	93w49	6:15:16
Furlow 43	34N50	91w59	6:07:56
Gainesboro 32	35N46	91w37	6:06:28
Gaines Landing 9	33N20	91w17	6:05:08
Gainesville 28	36N10	90w31	6:02:04
Gainsboro 32	35N50	91w30	6:06:00

ARKANSAS

Gaither 5	36N09	93w10	6:12:40
Galla Creek 58	35N14	93w03	6:12:12
Galla Rock 58	35N08	93w06	6:12:24
Gallitin 4	36N11	94w34	6:18:16
Galloway 60	34N47	92w12	6:08:48
Gamaliel 3	36N27	92w14	6:08:56
Gammon 18	35N13	90w12	6:00:48
Gap 49	34N25	93w37	6:14:28
Gap Springs 57	34N27	94w07	6:16:28
Garden 74	35N05	91w23	6:05:32
Gardner 70	33N06	92w22	6:09:28
Garfield 4	36N27	93w58	6:15:52
Garland 46	33N22	93w43	6:14:52
Garland Springs 23	35N14	92w07	6:08:28
Garlandville 29	33N48	93w23	6:13:32
Garner 73	35N09	91w47	6:07:08
Garret Grove 39	34N48	91w00	6:04:00
Garrett 36	35N26	93w23	6:13:32
Garrett Bridge 40	33N54	91w30	6:06:00
Gassett 39	34N52	90w35	6:02:20
Gassville 3	36N17	92w30	6:10:00
Gaston 49	34N33	93w46	6:15:04
Gateway 4	36N29	93w56	6:15:44
Gaylor 69	35N52	92w07	6:08:28
Geneva 67	34N02	94w21	6:17:24
Genevia 60	33N35	91w48	6:07:12
Genoa 46	33N23	93w54	6:15:36
Gentry 4	36N16	94w29	6:17:56
George 51	36N11	93w24	6:13:36
Georgetown 44	36N02	93w55	6:15:40
Georgetown 58	35N20	93w15	6:13:00
Georgetown 73	35N08	91w27	6:05:48
Georgia 50	33N41	93w16	6:13:04
Gepp 25	36N23	92w07	6:08:28
Geridge 43	34N33	91w53	6:07:32
Gernada Chapel 24	35N29	93w50	6:15:20
Gethsemane 35	34N45	92w21	6:09:24
Gibbs 49	34N40	93w41	6:14:44
Gibson 16	35N50	90w48	6:03:12
Gibson 60	34N48	92w14	6:08:56
Gid 33	35N58	91w51	6:07:24
Gieseck 19	35N16	90w28	6:01:52
Gifford 30	34N23	92w45	6:11:00
Gilbert 65	35N59	92w43	6:10:52
Gilchrist 47	35N45	89w56	5:59:44
Giles 12	35N35	92w08	6:08:32
Giles Spur 38	36N06	90w57	6:03:48
Gilkerson 16	35N47	90w47	6:03:08
Gilkey 75	34N59	93w21	6:13:24
Gill 39	34N58	90w54	6:03:36
Gillett 1	34N07	91w23	6:05:32
Gillham 67	34N10	94w19	6:17:16
Gilmore 18	35N25	90w17	6:01:08
Gin City 37	33N06	93w39	6:14:36
Gladden 19	35N16	90w28	6:01:52
Glaize 34	35N29	91w25	6:05:40
Glass 34	35N51	91w07	6:04:28
Gleason 23	35N05	92w27	6:09:48
Gleghorn 11	36N23	90w31	6:02:04
Glencoe 25	36N18	91w45	6:07:00
Glendale 40	33N58	91w58	6:07:52
Glen Rose 30	34N23	92w49	6:11:16
Glenwood 55	34N20	93w33	6:14:12
Gobbler 8	36N22	93w34	6:14:16
Gobblers Point 15	35N24	92w49	6:11:16
Gold Creek 23	35N05	92w27	6:09:48
Golden City 42	35N08	93w55	6:15:40
Golden Lake 47	35N34	90w04	6:00:16
Gold Lake Estates 23	35N05	92w27	6:09:48
Goobertown 16	35N54	90w35	6:02:20
Goodhope 52	33N44	93w04	6:12:16
Goodrum 43	34N53	92w00	6:08:00
Goodwin 62	34N56	91w01	6:04:04
Goose Camp 36	35N26	93w37	6:14:28
Goshen 72	36N06	93w59	6:15:56
Gosnell 47	35N58	89w58	5:59:52
Gould 40	33N59	91w34	6:06:16
Gourd 40	33N38	91w24	6:05:36
Grady 40	34N05	91w42	6:06:48
Grand Glaise 34	35N29	91w25	6:05:40
Grand Lake 9	33N07	91w16	6:05:04
Grandview 8	36N26	93w37	6:14:28
Grange 68	35N56	91w33	6:06:12
Grannis 57	34N14	94w20	6:17:20
Grapevine 27	34N09	92w19	6:09:16
Graphic 17	35N29	94w14	6:16:56
Grassy 12	35N39	91w50	6:07:20
Grassy Lake 18	35N16	90w28	6:01:52
Gravel Hill 58	35N24	93w07	6:12:28
Gravel Hill 71	35N25	92w43	6:10:52
Gravel Hill 73	35N15	91w59	6:07:56
Gravelly 75	34N53	93w41	6:14:44
Gravelly Hill 75	34N53	93w41	6:14:44
Gravelridge 6	33N35	92w16	6:09:04
Gravel Ridge 60	34N55	92w07	6:08:28
Graves Chapel 67	33N53	94w05	6:16:20
Gravesville 71	35N22	92w24	6:09:36
Gravette 4	36N25	94w27	6:17:48
Gray Rock 42	35N18	93w43	6:14:52
Grays 74	35N14	91w14	6:04:56
Greasy Corner 62	35N04	90w30	6:02:00
Greenbrier 23	35N14	92w23	6:09:32
Greene High 28	36N04	90w32	6:02:08
Greenfield 56	35N38	90w43	6:02:52
Green Forest 8	36N20	93w26	6:13:44
Green Hill 22	33N37	91w56	6:07:44
Greenland 72	36N00	94w10	6:16:40
Greenway 11	36N21	90w13	6:00:52
Greenwood 24	35N29	93w50	6:15:20
Greenwood 66	35N13	94w16	6:17:04
Greers Ferry 12	35N34	92w11	6:08:44
Gregory 74	35N09	91w21	6:05:24
Grider 47	35N38	89w59	5:59:56
Griffin 15	35N24	92w49	6:11:16
Griffith Spring 40	33N56	91w50	6:07:20
Griffithtown 10	34N05	93w02	6:12:08
Griffithville 73	35N08	91w39	6:06:36
Grove 51	36N05	92w58	6:11:52
Grubbs 34	35N39	91w04	6:04:16
Guernsey 29	33N42	93w35	6:14:20
Guion 33	35N56	91w57	6:07:48
Gulledge 2	33N14	91w48	6:07:12
Gum Log 58	35N17	92w59	6:11:56
Gum Pond 1	34N32	91w32	6:06:08
Gum Springs 10	34N05	93w02	6:12:08
Gum Woods 43	34N32	91w58	6:07:52
Gurdon 10	33N55	93w09	6:12:36
Guy 23	35N20	92w20	6:09:20
Habberton 72	36N04	94w09	6:16:36
Hackett 66	35N11	94w25	6:17:40
Hadley 37	33N22	93w26	6:13:44
Hagarville 36	35N31	93w19	6:13:16
Hale 26	34N35	93w10	6:12:40
Half Moon 47	35N57	89w57	5:59:48
Half Moon Lake 47	35N55	90w01	6:00:04
Halley 21	33N32	91w20	6:05:20
Halley Junction 9	33N32	91w26	6:05:44
Halliday 28	36N08	90w26	6:01:44
Halstead 60	34N45	92w22	6:09:28
Hamburg 2	33N14	91w48	6:07:12
Hamilton 43	34N39	91w44	6:06:56
Hamiter 43	34N42	92w06	6:08:24
Hammonsville 73	35N14	92w07	6:08:28
Hampton 7	33N32	92w28	6:09:52
Hancock 16	35N54	90w21	6:01:24
Hand 3	36N20	92w06	6:08:24
Hand Valley 45	36N17	92w36	6:10:24
Hanover 69	35N48	92w07	6:08:28
Happy 73	35N15	91w43	6:06:52
Happy Bend 58	35N14	92w55	6:11:40
Happy Corners 47	35N56	90w15	6:01:00
Hardin 23	35N14	92w21	6:09:24
Hardin 35	34N13	92w02	6:08:08
Hardy 68	36N19	91w29	6:05:56
Hargraves Junction 11	36N16	90w18	6:01:12
Harmon 72	36N09	94w16	6:17:04
Harmontown 32	35N46	91w37	6:06:28
Harmony 5	36N14	93w04	6:12:16
Harmony 6	33N37	92w04	6:08:16
Harmony 14	33N16	93w14	6:12:56
Harmony 36	35N33	93w33	6:14:12
Harmony 44	36N05	93w44	6:14:56
Harmony 73	35N15	91w43	6:06:52
Harmony Grove 52	33N35	92w47	6:11:08
Harper 13	33N49	92w02	6:08:08
Harrell 7	33N31	92w24	6:09:36
Harriet 65	36N00	92w31	6:10:04
Harris 69	35N57	92w09	6:08:36
Harris 72	36N04	94w09	6:16:36
Harrisburg 56	35N34	90w43	6:02:52
Harrison 5	36N14	93w07	6:12:28
Hartford 66	35N01	94w23	6:17:32
Hartman 36	35N26	93w37	6:14:28
Hartsell 73	35N28	91w41	6:06:44
Hartsugg 71	35N41	92w37	6:10:28
Hartwell 44	36N05	93w44	6:14:56
Harve 23	35N10	92w16	6:09:04
Harvey 64	34N51	93w47	6:15:08
Haskell 63	34N30	92w38	6:10:32
Hasty 51	36N01	93w03	6:12:12
Hatfield 57	34N29	94w23	6:17:32
Hattieville 15	35N17	92w47	6:11:08
Hatton 57	34N21	94w22	6:17:28
Havana 75	35N07	93w32	6:14:08
Hayley 59	34N58	91w30	6:06:00
Haynes 39	34N53	90w47	6:03:08
Hays 28	36N03	90w23	6:01:32
Haywood 11	36N20	90w13	6:00:52
Haywood 35	34N23	91w57	6:07:48
Hazel 49	34N31	93w40	6:14:40
Hazen 59	34N47	91w35	6:06:20
Heafer 18	35N16	90w28	6:01:52
Healing Springs 4	36N22	94w13	6:16:52
Healing Springs 12	35N40	91w56	6:07:44
Hearn 10	34N05	93w02	6:12:08
Heart 25	36N18	91w45	6:07:00
Heber 12	35N30	92w00	6:08:00
Heber Springs 12	35N30	92w02	6:08:08
Hebron 13	33N46	92w14	6:08:56
Hector 58	35N28	92w59	6:11:56
Helena 54	34N32	90w36	6:02:24
Helena Crossing 54	34N32	90w37	6:02:28
Henderson 3	36N23	92w14	6:08:56
Henderson College 10	34N05	93w02	6:12:08
Hendrix College 23	35N05	92w27	6:09:48
Hensley 60	34N30	92w12	6:08:48
Henton 1	34N25	91w40	6:06:40
Herbert 52	33N35	92w47	6:11:08
Herbine 13	33N58	92w11	6:08:44
Herd 69	36N04	92w11	6:08:44
Hermitage 6	33N27	92w10	6:08:40
Hermitage 60	34N43	92w16	6:09:04
Herndon 16	35N56	90w43	6:02:52
Herpel 69	35N52	92w07	6:08:28
Herring 75	35N00	93w31	6:14:04
Hervey 46	33N26	94w04	6:16:16
Heth 62	35N05	90w28	6:01:52
Hickey 36	35N30	93w15	6:13:00
Hickeytown 36	35N20	93w15	6:13:00
Hickman 47	35N57	89w57	5:59:48
Hickoria 11	36N25	90w35	6:02:20
Hickory 8	36N21	93w26	6:13:44
Hickory Flat 73	35N26	91w50	6:07:20
Hickory Grove 51	35N50	93w17	6:13:08
Hickory Hill 15	35N08	92w45	6:11:00
Hickory Plains 59	34N59	91w44	6:06:56
Hickory Ridge 19	35N24	91w00	6:04:00
Hickory Valley 32	35N56	91w33	6:06:12
Hicks 54	34N33	90w55	6:03:40
Hicks 72	36N04	94w09	6:16:36
Hicks Station 62	35N01	90w41	6:02:44
Hicksville 54	34N35	91w01	6:04:04
Hico 4	36N11	94w31	6:18:04
Hidden Valley 68	36N18	91w31	6:06:04
Higden 12	35N35	92w12	6:08:48
Higgins 15	35N06	92w52	6:11:28
Higgins 60	34N43	92w16	6:09:04
Higginson 73	35N12	91w43	6:06:52
Highfill 4	36N16	94w21	6:17:24
Highland 68	36N16	91w30	6:06:00
Hightower 47	35N45	89w56	5:59:44
Hilburn 44	35N48	93w47	6:15:08
Hill Creek 15	35N10	92w38	6:10:32
Hillcrest 36	35N28	93w30	6:14:00
Hillcrest 60	34N45	92w22	6:09:28
Hillemann 74	35N08	91w05	6:04:20
Hindman 48	34N40	91w05	6:04:20
Hindsville 44	36N09	93w52	6:15:28
Hiram 12	35N28	91w52	6:07:28
Hiwasse 4	36N26	94w20	6:17:20
Hixson 69	36N02	92w08	6:08:32
Hobbs 17	35N32	94w16	6:17:04
Hogeye 72	35N55	94w11	6:16:44
Holiday Island 8	36N24	93w44	6:14:56
Holland 23	35N10	92w16	6:09:04
Hollis 53	34N52	93w07	6:12:28
Holly 71	35N40	92w24	6:09:36
Holly Corner 11	36N16	90w18	6:01:12
Holly Creek 31	34N08	93w57	6:15:48
Holly Grove 48	34N36	91w12	6:04:48
Holly Island 11	36N16	90w18	6:01:12
Holly Springs 20	33N49	92w43	6:10:52
Holly Springs 73	35N15	91w43	6:06:52
Hollywood 10	34N05	93w02	6:12:08
Holman 36	35N26	93w23	6:13:32
Holmes 61	36N16	90w58	6:03:52
Holub 39	34N46	90w46	6:03:04
Homan 46	33N33	93w53	6:15:32
Homewood 53	35N02	93w03	6:12:12
Hon 64	34N56	94w11	6:16:44
Hooker 28	36N04	90w32	6:02:08
Hooker 35	34N13	92w02	6:08:08
Hoover 4	36N15	94w20	6:17:20
Hope 29	33N40	93w36	6:14:24
Hopewell 28	36N14	90w22	6:01:28
Hopewell 38	36N03	90w59	6:03:56
Hopper 49	34N22	93w41	6:14:44
Horatio 67	33N56	94w21	6:17:24
Hornor 54	34N33	90w41	6:02:44
Horsehead 36	35N33	93w34	6:14:16
Horseshoe 34	35N37	91w16	6:05:04
Horseshoe Bend 33	36N12	91w43	6:06:52
Hot Springs 26	34N31	93w03	6:12:12
Hot Springs National Park 26	34N30	93w03	6:12:12
Houston 53	35N02	92w42	6:10:48
Howard 15	35N09	92w37	6:10:28
Howell 74	35N07	91w15	6:05:00
Hoxie 38	36N03	90w59	6:03:56
Hubbard 72	35N59	94w19	6:17:16
Huddleston 49	34N37	93w47	6:15:08
Hudgin 13	33N59	91w59	6:07:56
Hudson 51	35N56	93w14	6:12:56
Huey 7	33N39	92w28	6:09:52
Huff 32	35N39	91w37	6:06:28
Huffman 47	35N57	89w57	5:59:48
Hughes 62	34N57	90w28	6:01:52
Hulbert 18	35N08	90w11	6:00:44
Humnoke 43	34N33	91w45	6:07:00
Humphrey 1	34N25	91w43	6:06:52
Hunt 36	35N32	93w39	6:14:36
Hunt 64	34N57	93w45	6:15:00
Hunter 74	35N03	91w08	6:04:32
Huntington 66	35N05	94w16	6:17:04
Huntsville 44	36N05	93w44	6:14:56
Hurricane Grove 49	34N33	93w38	6:14:32
Hutchinson 32	35N35	91w45	6:07:00
Hutson 32	35N38	91w28	6:05:52
Huttig 70	33N02	92w11	6:08:44
Ida 12	35N35	91w56	6:07:44
Imboden 38	36N12	91w11	6:04:44
Indian 9	33N07	91w16	6:05:04
Indian Bayou 43	34N32	91w52	6:07:28
Indianhead Lake Estates 60	34N48	92w14	6:08:56
Industrial 60	34N41	92w21	6:09:24
Ingalls 6	33N23	92w09	6:08:36
Ingleside 34	35N37	91w16	6:05:04
Ingram 61	36N24	91w00	6:04:00
Ione 42	35N08	93w55	6:15:40
Ions Creek 75	34N48	93w36	6:14:24
Ironton 60	34N44	92w20	6:09:20
Isbell 43	34N34	91w42	6:06:48
Island 66	35N24	94w07	6:16:28
Iuka 33	36N14	92w11	6:08:44
Ivan 20	33N55	92w26	6:09:44
Ivesville 60	34N46	92w23	6:09:32
Ivy 20	34N04	92w33	6:10:12
Ivy 24	35N30	94w00	6:16:00
Jackson Heights 60	34N55	92w07	6:08:28
Jacksonport 34	35N39	91w19	6:05:16
Jacksonville 60	34N52	92w07	6:08:28
James 64	34N55	93w51	6:15:24
James Creek 45	36N20	92w36	6:10:24
James R Bush 54	34N27	90w44	6:02:56
Jamestown 32	35N42	91w42	6:06:48
Jamestown 36	35N28	93w30	6:14:00
Janes Creek 61	36N19	91w13	6:04:52
Japton 44	35N58	93w48	6:15:12
Jasper 51	36N01	93w11	6:12:44
Jeannette 18	35N04	90w30	6:02:00
Jeff Davis 41	33N48	94w23	6:17:32

ARKANSAS

Place	Lat.	Long.	Time
Jefferson 35	34N23	92w10	6:08:40
Jefferson Square 35	34N13	92w02	6:08:08
Jennie 9	33N15	91w17	6:05:08
Jenny Lind	35N15	94w19	6:17:16
Jenson 66	35N11	94w25	6:17:40
Jericho 18	35N17	90w14	6:00:56
Jerome 22	33N24	91w28	6:05:52
Jerrett 61	36N25	90w54	6:03:36
Jersey 6	33N26	92w19	6:09:16
Jerusalem 15	35N24	92w49	6:11:16
Jessieville 26	34N42	93w04	6:12:16
Jesup 38	36N02	91w20	6:05:20
Jethro 24	35N29	93w50	6:15:20
Jewell 41	33N51	94w25	6:17:40
Jim Fork 66	35N07	94w21	6:17:24
Joan 10	34N05	93w02	6:12:08
Joe Burleson 45	36N15	92w45	6:11:00
Johnson 72	36N10	94w08	6:16:32
Johnstown 34	35N37	91w16	6:05:04
Johnsville 6	33N23	92w09	6:08:36
Joiner 47	35N31	90w09	6:00:36
Jolliff Store 47	35N56	90w15	6:01:00
Jonesboro 16	35N50	90w42	6:02:48
Jones Mill 30	34N23	92w49	6:11:16
Jonesville 46	33N16	93w53	6:15:32
Joplin 49	34N33	93w38	6:14:32
Jordan 3	36N14	92w11	6:08:44
Joy 73	35N18	91w58	6:07:52
Joyce City 52	33N23	92w47	6:11:08
Joyland 56	35N32	90w25	6:01:40
Joyland Park 42	35N08	93w55	6:15:40
Judd Hill 56	35N41	90w31	6:02:04
Judsonia 73	35N16	91w38	6:06:32
Julius 18	35N14	90w19	6:01:16
Jumbo 33	36N04	91w54	6:07:36
Junction City 70	33N01	92w43	6:10:52
Jurden 62	34N57	90w28	6:01:52
Kahoka 69	35N52	92w07	6:08:28
Kearney 35	34N27	92w11	6:08:44
Keaton 1	34N27	91w20	6:05:20
Kedron 13	34N03	92w08	6:08:32
Keesee 45	36N29	92w50	6:11:20
Keeter 45	36N24	92w43	6:10:52
Keevil 48	34N48	91w14	6:04:56
Keiser 47	35N40	90w06	6:00:24
Kellum 67	34N02	94w21	6:17:24
Kelso 21	33N48	91w16	6:05:04
Kenney 53	34N58	92w39	6:10:36
Kenova 70	33N22	92w44	6:10:56
Kensett 73	35N14	91w40	6:06:40
Kent 52	33N38	92w49	6:11:16
Kentucky 63	34N30	92w35	6:10:20
Kenwood 15	35N14	92w55	6:11:40
Keo 43	34N36	92w01	6:08:04
Kerlin 14	33N16	93w14	6:12:56
Kerr 43	34N42	92w06	6:08:24
Kiblah 46	33N03	93w54	6:15:36
Kibler 17	35N26	94w14	6:16:56
Kilgore 11	36N24	90w39	6:02:36
Kimberley 55	34N04	93w42	6:14:48
Kimbrough 40	34N08	91w41	6:06:44
Kindall 54	34N33	90w51	6:03:24
King 36	35N32	93w29	6:13:56
King Mills 68	36N18	91w31	6:06:04
Kings 67	34N10	94w19	6:17:16
Kingsland 13	33N52	92w18	6:09:12
Kingston 44	36N03	93w31	6:14:04
Kingston 75	35N01	93w11	6:12:44
Kingtown 54	34N33	90w55	6:03:40
Kinton 62	35N01	90w41	6:02:44
Kirby 55	34N15	93w39	6:14:36
Kirkland 52	33N23	92w47	6:11:08
Kittle 25	36N30	91w33	6:06:12
Kizer 37	36N06	93w39	6:14:36
Knob 11	36N17	90w27	6:01:48
Knob Creek 33	36N04	91w54	6:07:36
Knobel 11	36N19	90w36	6:02:24
Knowlton 21	34N09	90w59	6:03:56
Knoxville 36	35N23	93w22	6:13:28
Koch Ridge 71	35N35	92w28	6:09:52
Kokomo 39	34N52	90w35	6:02:20
Kramer 74	35N17	91w22	6:05:28
Kurdo 21	33N50	91w16	6:05:04
Lacey 22	33N33	91w47	6:07:08
Laconia 21	34N04	91w01	6:04:04
LaCrosse 33	36N06	91w50	6:07:20
Ladd 35	34N13	92w02	6:08:08
Ladelle 22	33N28	91w48	6:07:12
La Fave 64	34N51	93w47	6:15:08
Lafe 28	36N12	90w31	6:02:04
Lafferty 33	35N55	91w51	6:07:24
La Grange 39	34N39	90w44	6:02:56
La Grue 1	34N17	91w20	6:05:20
Lake Catherine 26	34N30	93w03	6:12:12
Lake City 16	35N49	90w26	6:01:44
Lake Dick 35	34N45	92w21	6:09:24
Lake Elmdale 72	36N11	94w09	6:16:36
Lake Frances 4	36N08	94w33	6:18:12
Lake Hamilton 26	34N27	93w08	6:12:32
Lakeside 26	34N30	93w03	6:12:12
Lakeside 52	33N35	92w47	6:11:08
Lakeview 3	36N21	92w29	6:09:56
Lake View 16	35N49	90w26	6:01:44
Lake View 54	34N32	90w37	6:02:28
Lakeview 75	35N14	93w10	6:12:40
Lake Village 9	33N20	91w17	6:05:08
Lakeway 45	36N14	92w41	6:10:44
Lakewood 35	34N45	92w21	6:09:24
Lamar 36	35N27	93w23	6:13:32
Lamartine 14	33N21	93w18	6:13:12
Lamb 64	34N52	94w00	6:16:00
Lambert 30	34N19	93w10	6:12:40
Lambrook 54	34N20	90w58	6:03:52
Lamont	34N06	92w17	6:09:08
Lanark 6	33N35	92w16	6:09:04
Lancaster 17	35N34	94w14	6:16:56
Landers 56	35N41	90w31	6:02:04
Landis 65	35N56	92w26	6:09:44
Laneburg 50	33N41	93w21	6:13:24
Lanesport 41	33N43	94w24	6:17:36
Langley 55	34N19	93w51	6:15:24
Lansing 18	35N14	90w19	6:01:16
Lanty 15	35N08	92w45	6:11:00
Lapile 70	33N04	92w16	6:09:04
Larkin 33	36N09	91w51	6:07:24
Larue 4	36N21	93w57	6:15:48
Latour 54	34N36	90w45	6:03:00
Lavaca 66	35N20	94w10	6:16:40
Lave Creek 68	36N08	91w37	6:06:28
Lawrenceville 48	34N36	91w12	6:04:48
Lawson 70	33N12	92w29	6:09:56
Layne 68	36N04	91w37	6:06:28
Leachville 47	35N56	90w16	6:01:04
Lead Hill 5	36N25	92w55	6:11:40
Leake 50	33N30	93w10	6:12:40
Lebanon 65	35N55	92w38	6:10:32
Lebanon 67	33N53	94w05	6:16:20
Leecreek 17	35N41	94w21	6:17:24
Lehi 18	35N13	90w12	6:00:48
Leitner 35	34N13	92w02	6:08:08
Lemmons 11	36N24	90w26	6:01:44
Lennie 47	35N53	90w10	6:00:40
Leola 27	34N10	92w35	6:10:20
Leonard 11	36N16	90w18	6:01:12
Lepanto 56	35N37	90w20	6:01:20
Leslie 65	35N50	92w34	6:10:16
Lester 16	35N54	90w27	6:01:48
Lester 52	33N44	93w04	6:12:16
Letona 73	35N22	91w50	6:07:20
Leverney 49	34N42	93w27	6:13:48
Lewis 64	35N03	94w11	6:16:44
Lewisburg 15	35N08	92w45	6:11:00
Lewisville 37	33N22	93w35	6:14:20
Lexa 54	34N36	90w45	6:03:00
Lexington 69	35N43	92w25	6:09:40
Liberty 52	33N23	92w47	6:11:08
Liberty Hall 75	35N14	93w10	6:12:40
Liberty Valley 73	35N18	91w34	6:06:16
Lick Creek 41	33N44	94w12	6:16:48
Lick Mountain 15	35N23	92w35	6:10:20
Liddell 11	36N27	90w09	6:00:36
Light 28	36N04	90w45	6:03:00
Limedale 32	35N46	91w37	6:06:28
Limestone 51	35N47	93w17	6:13:08
Lincoln 72	35N57	94w25	6:17:40
Linder 23	35N14	92w23	6:09:32
Linn Creek 71	35N45	92w27	6:09:48
Linwood 35	34N09	91w48	6:07:12
Lisbon 70	33N13	92w40	6:10:40
Litteral 72	36N06	94w16	6:17:04
Little Black 61	36N27	90w51	6:03:24
Little Dixie 59	34N58	91w30	6:06:00
Little Flock 4	36N19	94w08	6:16:32
Little Italy 53	35N00	92w37	6:10:28
Little Red 73	35N26	91w50	6:07:20
Little River Country Club 41	33N50	94w21	6:17:24
Little Rock 60	34N45	92w17	6:09:08
Live Oak 22	33N45	91w34	6:06:16
Locke 17	35N38	94w10	6:16:40
Lockesburg 67	33N58	94w10	6:16:40
Locust Bayou 7	33N35	92w47	6:11:08
Locust Grove 32	35N43	91w44	6:06:56
Locust Grove 69	35N54	92w23	6:09:32
Lodge Corner 1	34N29	91w33	6:06:12
Lodi 55	34N20	93w33	6:14:12
Lollie 23	34N57	92w25	6:09:40
London 58	35N20	93w15	6:13:00
Lone Hill 30	34N21	92w55	6:11:40
Lonelm 24	35N31	94w05	6:16:20
Lone Pine 40	33N51	91w49	6:07:16
Lone Pine 65	35N55	92w38	6:10:32
Lone Rock 3	36N10	92w20	6:09:20
Longview 2	33N19	91w54	6:07:36
Lon Norris 66	35N18	94w25	6:17:40
Lono 30	34N12	92w43	6:10:52
Lonoke 43	34N47	91w54	6:07:36
Lonsdale 26	34N33	92w49	6:11:16
Lookout Store 48	34N38	91w23	6:05:32
Lorine 61	36N16	90w58	6:03:52
Lost Corner 58	35N24	92w49	6:11:16
Louann 52	33N23	92w48	6:11:12
Love 33	36N04	91w37	6:06:28
Lowden 47	35N57	89w57	5:59:48
Lowell 4	36N15	94w08	6:16:32
Lower Poplar Ridge 16	35N50	90w22	6:01:28
Lower Surrounded Hill 59	34N50	91w24	6:05:36
Lowes Boydsville 11	36N16	90w18	6:01:12
Low Gap 51	36N00	93w11	6:12:44
Lowry	36N29	93w03	6:12:12
Luber 69	35N45	92w04	6:08:16
Lucas 18	34N56	90w20	6:01:20
Lucas 42	35N08	94w03	6:16:12
Ludwig 36	35N28	93w30	6:14:00
Lumber 14	33N21	93w18	6:13:12
Luna 9	33N20	91w17	6:05:08
Lundell 54	34N11	90w58	6:03:52
Lunenburg 33	36N00	91w56	6:07:44
Lunsford 16	35N33	90w33	6:02:12
Lurton 51	35N46	93w05	6:12:20
Lutherville 36	35N26	93w23	6:13:32
Luxora 47	35N45	89w56	5:59:44
Lydesdale 14	33N16	93w14	6:12:56
Lynn 38	36N00	91w15	6:05:00
Mabelvale 60	34N39	92w23	6:09:32
Maberry 74	35N00	91w15	6:05:00
Macedonia 14	33N16	93w14	6:12:56
Macedonia 15	35N17	92w47	6:11:08
Macedonia 75	35N03	93w23	6:13:32
Macey 16	35N54	90w21	6:01:24
Macks 34	35N37	91w16	6:05:04
Macon 60	34N55	92w07	6:08:28
Macon Lake 9	33N20	91w17	6:05:08
Madding 35	34N45	92w21	6:09:24
Madison 62	35N01	90w43	6:02:52
Magazine 42	35N09	93w48	6:15:12
Magic Springs 65	35N55	92w49	6:11:16
Magness 32	35N42	91w29	6:05:56
Magnet 30	34N27	92w53	6:11:32
Magnet Cove 30	34N23	92w49	6:11:16
Magnolia 14	33N16	93w14	6:12:56
Main Shore 28	36N00	90w25	6:01:40
Main Street 60	34N47	92w15	6:09:00
Mallet Town 15	35N16	92w34	6:10:16
Malvern 30	34N22	92w49	6:11:16
Mammoth Spring 25	36N30	91w33	6:06:12
Manchester 20	34N00	92w52	6:11:28
Mandalay 47	35N53	90w10	6:00:40
Mandeville 46	33N29	93w58	6:15:52
Manfred 49	34N24	93w37	6:14:28
Mangrum 16	35N50	90w22	6:01:28
Manila 47	35N53	90w10	6:00:40
Manning 20	34N01	92w48	6:11:12
Mansfield 64	35N04	94w15	6:17:00
Manson 61	36N16	90w58	6:03:52
Maple Grove 56	35N41	90w31	6:02:04
Marble 44	36N08	93w35	6:14:20
Marble City 51	36N05	93w10	6:12:40
Marcella 69	35N47	91w53	6:07:32
Marche 60	34N52	92w22	6:09:28
Marianna 39	34N46	90w46	6:03:04
Marie 47	35N38	90w03	6:00:12
Marie Saline 2	33N02	92w00	6:08:00
Marion 18	35N13	90w12	6:00:48
Marked Tree 56	35N32	90w25	6:01:40
Marmaduke 28	36N11	90w23	6:01:32
Marrs Hill 72	36N02	94w20	6:17:20
Marshall 65	35N55	92w38	6:10:32
Marshell 32	35N52	91w17	6:05:08
Mars Hill 37	33N16	93w33	6:14:12
Martindale 60	34N45	92w22	6:09:28
Martinville 23	35N20	92w29	6:09:56
Marvell 54	34N33	90w55	6:03:40
Marvinville 75	35N07	93w32	6:14:08
Marysville 70	33N16	93w14	6:12:56
Mason 75	35N02	93w07	6:12:28
Mason Valley 4	36N18	94w21	6:17:24
Masonville 21	33N38	91w24	6:05:36
Massard 66	35N22	94w23	6:17:32
Matney 3	36N08	92w23	6:09:32
Matthews 23	35N15	92w16	6:09:04
Maumee 65	36N03	92w37	6:10:28
Maxey 17	35N33	94w03	6:16:12
Maxville 68	35N56	91w33	6:06:12
Mayfield 72	36N04	94w09	6:16:36
Mayflower 23	34N57	92w26	6:09:44
Maynard 61	36N25	90w54	6:03:36
Maysville 4	36N24	94w36	6:18:24
Mazarn 49	34N23	93w23	6:13:32
McAlmont 60	34N49	92w11	6:08:44
McArthur 21	33N38	91w24	6:05:36
McCaskill 29	33N55	93w39	6:14:36
McClelland 74	35N17	91w22	6:05:28
McCormick 56	35N41	90w31	6:02:04
McCrory 74	35N16	91w12	6:04:48
McDonald 19	35N16	90w33	6:02:12
McDougal 11	36N26	90w23	6:01:32
McFadden 34	35N24	91w00	6:04:00
McFall 1	34N31	91w26	6:05:44
McFerrin 47	35N42	89w58	5:59:52
McGavock 47	35N30	90w08	6:00:32
McGehee 21	33N38	91w24	6:05:36
McGintytown 23	35N14	92w23	6:09:32
McHue 32	35N44	91w38	6:06:32
McIlroy 24	35N41	93w46	6:15:04
McJester 12	35N28	91w49	6:07:16
McKamie 37	33N16	93w30	6:14:00
McKennon 36	35N22	93w19	6:13:16
McKinney 6	33N37	92w04	6:08:16
McLaren 15	35N20	92w40	6:10:40
McMilan Corner 9	33N20	91w17	6:05:08
McNab 29	33N40	93w50	6:15:20
McNeil 14	33N21	93w13	6:12:52
McPhearson 3	36N07	92w08	6:08:32
McRae 73	35N07	91w49	6:07:16
Meadow Cliff 62	35N01	90w47	6:03:08
Meg 24	35N29	93w50	6:15:20
Melbourne 33	36N04	91w54	6:07:36
Mellwood 54	34N13	90w57	6:03:48
Melrose 69	35N43	91w44	6:06:56
Melton 35	34N08	91w53	6:07:32
Mena 57	34N35	94w15	6:17:00
Menifee 15	35N09	92w33	6:10:12
Meridian 2	33N09	91w57	6:07:48
Meroney 40	33N59	91w34	6:06:16
Merrivale 60	34N44	92w20	6:09:20
Merry Green 27	34N19	92w23	6:09:32
Mesa 59	34N47	91w27	6:05:48
Metalton 8	36N22	93w34	6:14:16
Middle 24	35N27	93w50	6:15:20
Middlebrook 61	36N25	90w54	6:03:36
Middleton 15	35N22	92w34	6:10:16
Midland 66	35N06	94w21	6:17:24
Midway 3	36N18	92w25	6:09:40
Midway 30	34N18	92w52	6:11:28
Midway 31	33N57	93w51	6:15:24
Midway 37	33N22	93w35	6:14:20
Midway 42	35N18	93w38	6:14:32
Midway 50	33N48	93w23	6:13:32
Midway Corner 18	35N06	90w22	6:01:28
Milford 67	33N53	94w05	6:16:20
Mill Bayou 1	34N25	91w27	6:05:48
Mill Creek 58	35N17	93w09	6:12:36

 ARKANSAS

Place	Lat	Long	Time
Mill Creek 66	35N22	94w23	6:17:32
Miller 41	33N47	94w28	6:17:52
Millers Bluff 52	33N23	92w47	6:11:08
Milligan Ridge 47	35N53	90w10	6:00:40
Milltown 66	35N13	94w15	6:17:00
Milo 2	33N14	91w48	6:07:12
Mine Creek 29	33N55	93w47	6:15:08
Mineral 67	34N09	94w19	6:17:16
Mineral Springs 31	33N53	93w55	6:15:40
Minorca 61	36N25	90w54	6:03:36
Minturn 38	35N59	91w02	6:04:08
Mist 2	33N17	91w42	6:06:48
Mitchell 19	35N24	90w45	6:03:00
Mitchell 25	36N24	92w00	6:08:00
Mitchellville 21	33N54	91w30	6:06:00
Mixon 42	35N08	93w55	6:15:40
Moark 11	36N29	90w31	6:02:04
Modoc 54	34N19	90w51	6:03:24
Moffit 72	35N59	94w19	6:17:16
Moko 25	36N28	91w50	6:07:20
Monarch 45	36N14	92w41	6:10:44
Monette 16	35N53	90w21	6:01:24
Monkey Run 3	36N17	92w30	6:10:00
Monroe 48	34N44	91w06	6:04:24
Montana 36	35N26	93w37	6:14:28
Monte Ne 4	36N19	94w08	6:16:32
Monterey 19	35N16	90w33	6:02:12
Monticello 22	33N38	91w47	6:07:08
Montongo 22	33N33	91w47	6:07:08
Montreal 66	35N06	94w21	6:17:24
Montrose 2	33N18	91w30	6:06:00
Mont Sandals 66	35N19	94w14	6:16:56
Mooney 54	34N12	91w00	6:04:00
Moore 51	35N43	93w04	6:12:16
Moorefield 32	35N47	91w34	6:06:16
Moreland 58	35N22	93w00	6:12:00
Morganton 71	35N28	92w21	6:09:24
Morning Star 26	34N30	93w03	6:12:12
Morning Star 65	35N55	92w38	6:10:32
Morning Sun 73	35N15	91w43	6:06:52
Moro 39	34N48	90w59	6:03:56
Moro Bay 6	33N19	92w21	6:09:24
Morrilton 15	35N09	92w44	6:10:56
Morris 1	34N26	91w34	6:06:16
Morrison Bluff 42	35N22	93w32	6:14:08
Morriston 25	36N16	91w47	6:07:08
Morrow 72	35N52	94w26	6:17:44
Morton 74	35N16	91w12	6:04:48
Mosby 54	34N13	90w57	6:03:48
Moscow 35	34N09	91w48	6:07:12
Mosley 75	35N14	93w10	6:12:40
Mossville 51	35N54	93w23	6:13:32
Mound City 18	35N14	90w08	6:00:32
Mounds 28	36N04	90w32	6:02:08
Mountainburg 17	35N38	94w10	6:16:40
Mountain Crest 24	36N00	94w01	6:16:04
Mountain Home 3	36N20	92w23	6:09:32
Mountain Home 73	35N26	91w50	6:07:20
Mountain Pine 26	34N34	93w10	6:12:40
Mountain Top 24	35N29	93w50	6:15:20
Mountain Valley 26	34N38	93w04	6:12:16
Mountain View 69	35N52	92w07	6:08:28
Mount Calm 25	36N28	91w59	6:07:56
Mount Gayler 17	35N48	94w08	6:16:32
Mount George 75	35N03	93w23	6:13:32
Mount Hersey 51	36N09	92w55	6:11:40
Mount Holly 70	33N18	92w58	6:11:52
Mount Ida 49	34N34	93w38	6:14:32
Mount Judea 51	35N55	93w04	6:12:16
Mount Moriah 55	34N04	93w42	6:14:48
Mount Olive 6	33N23	92w09	6:08:36
Mount Olive 33	36N00	92w06	6:08:24
Mount Olive 72	36N00	94w01	6:16:04
Mount Pisgah 73	35N19	91w50	6:07:20
Mount Pleasant 33	35N58	91w45	6:07:00
Mount Sherman 51	36N00	93w11	6:12:44
Mount Tabor 22	33N33	91w47	6:07:08
Mount Tabor 26	34N39	93w20	6:13:20
Mount Vernon 23	35N14	92w08	6:08:32
Mount Vernon 36	35N26	93w37	6:14:28
Mozart 69	35N47	92w18	6:09:12
Muddyfork 31	33N57	93w51	6:15:24
Mulberry 17	35N30	94w03	6:16:12
Murfreesboro 55	34N04	93w41	6:14:44
Murphys Corner 34	35N37	91w16	6:05:04
Murray 51	35N56	93w18	6:13:12
Mustin Lake 52	33N35	92w47	6:11:08
Myatt 25	36N23	91w39	6:06:36
Myron 33	36N11	91w42	6:06:48
Nady 1	34N08	91w16	6:05:04
Nail 51	35N49	93w18	6:13:12
Nashville 31	33N57	93w51	6:15:24
Nathan 55	34N06	93w49	6:15:16
Natural Dam 17	35N38	94w23	6:17:32
Natural Steps 60	34N54	92w30	6:10:00
Naylor 23	35N05	92w13	6:08:52
Neal 47	35N58	90w12	6:00:48
Neal Springs 67	33N57	94w21	6:17:24
Nebo 40	33N56	91w50	6:07:20
Needham 16	35N49	90w26	6:01:44
Needmore 64	34N54	94w05	6:16:20
Neely 75	35N14	93w10	6:12:40
Nella 64	34N46	94w25	6:17:40
Nelson 11	36N22	90w44	6:02:56
Nelsonville 68	36N05	91w29	6:05:56
Nettleton 16	35N49	90w35	6:02:20
Newark 32	35N42	91w27	6:05:48
New Augusta 74	35N17	91w22	6:05:28
New Blaine 42	35N17	93w25	6:13:40
Newburg 33	36N08	91w57	6:07:48
New Caledonia 70	33N01	92w43	6:10:52
Newcastle 62	35N01	90w47	6:03:08
Newcomb 63	34N34	92w39	6:10:36
New Dixie 53	35N00	92w37	6:10:28
New Edinburg 13	33N46	92w14	6:08:56
Newell 70	33N13	92w40	6:10:40
New Gascony 35	34N45	92w21	6:09:24
New Hope 22	33N33	91w47	6:07:08
New Hope 32	35N46	91w37	6:06:28
Newhope 55	34N14	93w53	6:15:32
New Hope 58	35N17	93w09	6:12:36
New Hope 62	34N57	90w28	6:01:52
New London 70	33N11	92w20	6:09:20
Newnata 69	35N49	93w18	6:13:12
Newport 34	35N37	91w16	6:05:04
New Salme 74	35N17	91w22	6:05:28
New Spadra 36	35N28	93w30	6:14:00
New Summit 63	34N33	92w30	6:10:00
New Tennessee 53	34N58	93w06	6:12:24
Newton 23	35N09	92w12	6:08:48
New Town 17	35N29	94w14	6:16:56
Newtown 35	34N45	92w21	6:09:24
Nichols 15	35N24	92w42	6:10:48
Nimmons 11	36N18	90w06	6:00:24
Nimrod 53	35N00	92w48	6:11:12
Nix 20	34N00	92w47	6:11:08
Noble Lake 35	34N13	92w02	6:08:08
Nodena 47	35N36	90w03	6:00:12
Nola 64	34N53	93w41	6:14:44
Noland 61	36N16	90w58	6:03:52
Norfork 3	36N13	92w17	6:09:08
Norman 49	34N27	93w41	6:14:44
Norphlet 70	33N19	92w40	6:10:40
Norristown 58	35N16	93w10	6:12:40
North Big Rock 68	36N05	91w29	6:05:56
North Bingen 29	33N57	93w51	6:15:24
North Boothe 64	35N08	94w03	6:16:12
North Brinkley 48	34N48	91w09	6:04:36
North Cedar 35	34N13	92w02	6:08:08
North Crossett 2	33N09	91w56	6:07:44
North Dardanelle 58	35N14	93w10	6:12:40
Northern Ohio 56	35N32	90w25	6:01:40
North Fordyce	33N50	92w25	6:09:40
North Harrison 5	36N15	93w06	6:12:24
North Heights 46	33N26	94w04	6:16:16
North Hughes 62	34N57	90w28	6:01:52
North Lebanon 68	36N11	91w25	6:05:40
North Lewisville 37	33N22	93w35	6:14:20
North Little Rock 60	34N45	92w16	6:09:04
North Pitts 56	35N48	90w56	6:03:44
Northpoint 60	34N54	92w30	6:10:00
North Union 68	36N22	91w19	6:05:16
Northwest 69	36N00	92w15	6:09:00
Norvell 18	35N17	90w28	6:01:52
Nowland 29	33N46	93w30	6:14:00
Number Nine 47	35N57	89w57	5:59:48
Oak Bluff 11	36N17	90w17	6:01:08
Oak Forest 39	34N47	90w54	6:03:36
Oakgrove 8	36N27	93w26	6:13:44
Oak Grove 13	33N58	92w11	6:08:44
Oak Grove 30	34N23	92w49	6:11:16
Oak Grove 43	35N00	91w59	6:07:56
Oak Grove 50	33N34	93w24	6:13:36
Oakgrove 53	35N02	92w42	6:10:48
Oak Grove 58	35N17	93w09	6:12:36
Oak Grove 67	33N53	94w05	6:16:20
Oakhaven 29	33N44	93w37	6:14:28
Oakland 45	36N28	92w35	6:10:20
Oakland Heights 58	35N17	93w09	6:12:36
Oaklawn 26	34N30	93w03	6:12:12
Oak Park 35	34N13	92w02	6:08:08
Oark 36	35N41	93w35	6:14:20
Oconee 61	36N25	91w08	6:04:32
Oden 49	34N37	93w47	6:15:08
O'Donnell Bend 47	35N45	89w56	5:59:44
Ogden 41	33N35	94w03	6:16:12
Ogemaw 52	33N28	93w02	6:12:08
Oil Trough 32	35N38	91w28	6:05:52
O'Kean 61	36N12	90w51	6:03:24
Okolona 10	34N00	93w20	6:13:20
Ola 75	35N02	93w13	6:12:52
Old Alabam 44	36N05	93w44	6:14:56
Old Austin 43	35N00	91w59	6:07:56
Old Grand Glaise 34	35N25	91w27	6:05:48
Old Hickory 15	35N20	92w50	6:11:20
Old Jenny Lind 66	35N22	94w23	6:17:32
Old Joe 3	36N12	92w17	6:09:08
Old Lexington	35N43	92w25	6:09:40
Old Milo 2	33N14	91w48	6:07:12
Old Neeley 75	35N14	93w10	6:12:40
Old River 35	34N11	91w40	6:06:40
Old Union 70	33N13	92w40	6:10:40
Old Weona 56	35N41	90w31	6:02:04
Oliver 64	34N54	94w15	6:17:00
Oliver Springs 17	35N31	94w18	6:17:12
Olmstead 60	34N48	92w14	6:08:56
Olvey 5	36N11	92w58	6:11:52
Olyphant 34	35N32	91w23	6:05:32
Oma 30	34N26	93w18	6:13:12
Omaha 5	36N27	93w11	6:12:44
Omega 8	36N13	93w32	6:14:08
Omega 75	35N14	93w10	6:12:40
Onda 72	35N55	94w11	6:16:44
One Horse Store 1	34N29	91w33	6:06:12
Oneida 54	34N28	90w47	6:03:08
Onia 69	35N55	92w19	6:09:16
Onyx 75	34N51	93w25	6:13:40
Opal 57	34N32	94w06	6:16:24
Opal 73	35N04	91w53	6:07:32
Oppelo 15	35N06	92w46	6:11:04
Optimus 69	36N07	92w08	6:08:32
Orion 27	34N27	92w11	6:08:44
Orlando 13	33N46	92w14	6:08:56
Osage 8	36N11	93w24	6:13:36
Osceola 47	35N42	89w58	5:59:52
Otter 63	34N36	92w24	6:09:36
Otto 23	35N05	92w13	6:08:52
Otwell 16	35N44	90w50	6:03:20
Ouachita 20	33N55	92w51	6:11:24
Ouachita College 10	34N05	93w02	6:12:08
Ouita 58	35N17	93w09	6:12:36
Overcup 15	35N08	92w45	6:11:00
Overcup 74	35N16	91w12	6:04:48
Owensville 63	34N37	92w49	6:11:16
Oxford 33	36N13	91w56	6:07:44
Oxley 65	35N50	92w33	6:10:12
Ozan 29	33N51	93w43	6:14:52
Ozark 24	35N29	93w50	6:15:20
Ozark Acres 68	36N15	91w22	6:05:28
Ozark Lithia 26	34N30	93w03	6:12:12
Ozone 36	35N39	93w27	6:13:48
Pace City 52	33N23	92w47	6:11:08
Packard Springs 8	36N20	93w45	6:15:00
Palarm 23	35N03	92w16	6:09:04
Palatka 11	36N25	90w35	6:02:20
Palestine 62	34N58	90w54	6:03:36
Palmer 48	34N36	91w12	6:04:48
Palmyra 40	33N55	91w56	6:07:44
Pangburn 73	35N26	91w50	6:07:20
Pankey 60	34N46	92w23	6:09:32
Pansy 13	33N58	92w11	6:08:44
Panther Forest 9	33N20	91w17	6:05:08
Paraclifta 67	33N53	94w11	6:16:44
Paradise	33N32	91w48	6:07:12
Paragould 28	36N03	90w29	6:01:56
Paragould Junction 28	36N04	90w32	6:02:08
Paraloma 67	33N48	94w01	6:16:04
Paris 42	35N18	93w44	6:14:56
Park 64	34N48	93w58	6:15:52
Parkdale 2	33N07	91w33	6:06:12
Parker 50	33N34	93w23	6:13:32
Parkers Chapel 70	33N13	92w40	6:10:40
Park Hill 60	34N48	92w14	6:08:56
Parkin 19	35N16	90w34	6:02:16
Park Place 39	34N52	90w35	6:02:20
Parks 64	34N48	93w58	6:15:52
Parma 69	35N36	92w11	6:08:44
Parnell 43	34N59	92w01	6:08:04
Paron 63	34N46	92w46	6:11:04
Partee 14	33N16	93w14	6:12:56
Parthenon 51	35N57	93w14	6:12:56
Pastoria 35	34N22	92w01	6:08:04
Patmos 29	33N31	93w34	6:14:16
Patrick 44	36N00	94w01	6:16:04
Patsville 6	33N27	92w10	6:08:40
Patterson 74	35N16	91w14	6:04:56
Pauls 16	35N55	90w48	6:03:12
Pawheen 47	35N56	90w15	6:01:00
Payne 11	36N17	90w07	6:00:28
Payne 70	33N06	92w22	6:09:28
Payneway 56	35N41	90w31	6:02:04
Peach Orchard 11	36N17	90w40	6:02:40
Pearcy 26	34N26	93w18	6:13:12
Pea Ridge 4	36N27	94w07	6:16:28
Pearson 12	35N27	92w08	6:08:32
Pecan 47	35N29	90w03	6:00:12
Peel 45	36N26	92w46	6:11:04
Pelsor 58	35N43	93w04	6:12:16
Pencil Bluff 49	34N39	93w44	6:14:56
Pendleton 21	33N54	91w30	6:06:00
Pennington 6	33N37	92w06	6:08:24
Pennington 34	35N34	91w06	6:04:24
Pennys 67	33N53	94w05	6:16:20
Penrose 74	35N12	91w03	6:04:12
Perla 30	34N22	92w47	6:11:08
Perry 53	35N03	92w48	6:11:12
Perrytown 29	33N42	93w32	6:14:08
Perryville 53	35N00	92w48	6:11:12
Peter Creek 12	35N35	91w57	6:07:48
Peterpender 24	35N18	94w02	6:16:08
Pettigrew 44	35N49	93w39	6:14:36
Pettus 43	34N37	91w54	6:07:36
Pettyville 47	35N51	90w06	6:00:24
Philadelphia 14	33N16	93w14	6:12:56
Philadelphia 16	35N50	90w48	6:03:12
Philander Smith College 60	34N44	92w19	6:09:16
Phillips 26	34N33	92w50	6:11:20
Phillips Bayou 39	34N46	90w46	6:03:04
Phoenix 58	35N24	93w01	6:12:04
Pickens 21	33N51	91w29	6:05:56
Pickens 73	35N15	91w43	6:06:52
Piercetown 51	36N00	93w11	6:12:44
Pigeon 3	36N27	92w21	6:09:24
Piggott 11	36N23	90w11	6:00:44
Pike 55	34N07	93w35	6:14:20
Pilgrims Rest 72	36N11	94w09	6:16:36
Pilot Rock 36	35N40	93w13	6:12:52
Pinckney 18	34N57	90w28	6:01:52
Pindall 65	36N04	92w53	6:11:32
Pine 12	35N29	91w52	6:07:28
Pine Bluff 35	34N13	92w01	6:08:04
Pine Bluff Arsenal 35	34N13	92w02	6:08:08
Pine City 48	34N36	91w12	6:04:48
Pinecrest 35	34N13	92w02	6:08:08
Pine Grove 20	33N55	92w51	6:11:24
Pine Grove Valley 64	35N04	94w15	6:17:00
Pine Log 4	36N24	93w54	6:15:36
Pine Mountain 23	35N01	92w27	6:09:48
Pine Ridge 48	34N41	91w11	6:04:44
Pine Ridge 49	34N35	93w54	6:15:36
Pine Valley 32	35N56	91w33	6:06:12
Pineville 33	36N09	92w07	6:08:28
Piney 26	34N30	93w03	6:12:12
Piney 36	35N21	93w20	6:13:20
Piney Fork 68	36N04	91w38	6:06:32
Piney Grove 37	33N22	93w35	6:14:20
Piney Grove 55	34N02	93w30	6:14:00
Pinnacle 60	34N50	92w29	6:09:56
Pisgah 55	34N02	93w30	6:14:00
Pisgah 75	35N14	93w10	6:12:40

ARKANSAS

Place	Latitude	Longitude	Time
Pitman 61	36N25	90w54	6:03:36
Pitts 56	35N48	90w56	6:03:44
Pittsburg 36	35N26	93w22	6:13:28
Plainfield 14	33N06	93w12	6:12:48
Plainview 73	35N16	91w38	6:06:32
Plainview 75	34N59	93w18	6:13:12
Plant 71	35N35	92w28	6:09:52
Planters 9	33N08	91w18	6:05:12
Pleasant Grove 16	35N50	90w48	6:03:12
Pleasant Grove 69	35N49	91w54	6:07:36
Pleasant Grove 71	35N25	92w43	6:10:52
Pleasant Hill 17	35N31	94w05	6:16:20
Pleasant Hill 19	35N13	90w47	6:03:08
Pleasant Hill 26	34N30	93w03	6:12:12
Pleasant Hill 50	33N48	93w23	6:13:32
Pleasant Hills 69	35N55	92w19	6:09:16
Pleasant Plains 32	35N33	91w38	6:06:32
Pleasant Ridge 25	36N18	91w39	6:06:36
Pleasant Valley 23	35N14	92w23	6:09:32
Pleasant Valley 37	33N06	93w39	6:14:36
Pleasant Valley 53	35N00	92w37	6:10:28
Pleasant View 24	35N29	93w50	6:15:20
Plum Bayou 35	34N20	91w54	6:07:36
Plumerville 15	35N10	92w38	6:10:32
Plumlee 51	36N05	93w18	6:13:12
Plunketts 59	34N49	91w24	6:05:36
Pocahontas 61	36N16	90w58	6:03:52
Poff 12	35N40	92w11	6:08:44
Point 74	35N09	91w21	6:05:24
Point Cedar 30	34N20	93w19	6:13:16
Point De Luce 1	34N12	91w17	6:05:08
Poland 28	36N00	90w37	6:02:28
Pollard 11	36N27	90w16	6:01:04
Polo 8	36N26	93w33	6:14:12
Ponca 51	36N02	93w22	6:13:28
Pontoon 15	35N02	93w03	6:12:12
Poplar Grove 54	34N33	90w51	6:03:24
Porter 17	35N44	94w08	6:16:32
Portia 38	36N05	91w04	6:04:16
Portland 2	33N14	91w31	6:06:04
Posey 62	34N55	91w07	6:04:28
Possum Fork 21	33N46	91w16	6:05:04
Possum Grape 34	35N25	91w27	6:05:48
Postelle 54	34N34	91w01	6:04:04
Potter 57	34N33	94w20	6:17:20
Pottsville 58	35N15	93w03	6:12:12
Poughkeepsie 68	36N05	91w29	6:05:56
Powell 16	35N56	90w38	6:02:32
Powhatan 38	36N05	91w07	6:04:28
Poyen 27	34N20	92w38	6:10:32
Prague 27	34N19	92w24	6:09:36
Prairie Creek 66	35N01	94w23	6:17:32
Prairie Grove 72	35N58	94w19	6:17:16
Prairie View 42	35N20	93w32	6:14:08
Prattsville 27	34N19	92w33	6:10:12
Prescott 50	33N48	93w23	6:13:32
Preston 23	35N05	92w27	6:09:48
Preston Ferry 1	34N38	91w23	6:05:32
Price 26	34N30	93w03	6:12:12
Price 45	36N27	92w38	6:10:32
Price 72	35N58	94w29	6:17:56
Prim 12	35N42	92w07	6:08:28
Princeton 20	33N59	92w38	6:10:32
Process City 67	34N02	94w21	6:17:24
Proctor 18	35N05	90w14	6:00:56
Promised Land 56	35N41	90w31	6:02:04
Providence 73	35N16	91w38	6:06:32
Provo 67	34N02	94w06	6:16:24
Pruitt 51	36N03	93w08	6:12:32
Pulaski 43	34N47	92w03	6:08:12
Pullman 67	34N02	94w21	6:17:24
Pumpkin Bend 74	35N18	91w06	6:04:24
Purdy 44	36N05	93w34	6:14:16
Pyatt 45	36N15	92w51	6:11:24
Quinn 70	33N13	92w40	6:10:40
Quitman 12	35N23	92w13	6:08:52
Ralph 45	36N14	92w41	6:10:44
Ramsey 20	33N53	92w33	6:10:12
Ramsey Hill 32	35N46	91w37	6:06:28
Randall 13	33N58	92w11	6:08:44
Randolph 21	33N55	91w31	6:06:04
Ranger 75	35N03	93w23	6:13:32
Rankin 53	34N58	92w44	6:10:56
Ratcliff 42	35N18	93w53	6:15:32
Ratio 54	34N16	90w56	6:03:44
Ravanna 46	33N08	94w03	6:16:12
Ravenden 38	36N14	91w15	6:05:00
Ravenden Springs 61	36N19	91w13	6:04:52
Rawlison 62	34N57	90w28	6:01:52
Raymond 48	34N37	91w07	6:04:28
Reader 52	33N46	93w06	6:12:24
Readland 9	33N04	91w13	6:04:52
Rea Valley 45	36N17	92w36	6:10:24
Rector 11	36N16	90w17	6:01:08
Red Colony 67	33N58	94w09	6:16:36
Redemption 53	35N00	92w37	6:10:28
Redfield 35	34N27	92w11	6:08:44
Red Fork 21	33N53	91w18	6:05:12
Red Hill 52	33N42	93w03	6:12:12
Redland 50	33N48	93w23	6:13:32
Red Leaf 9	33N20	91w17	6:05:08
Red Lick 36	35N33	93w25	6:13:40
Red Oak 26	34N30	93w03	6:12:12
Red Springs 10	33N55	93w09	6:12:36
Redstar 44	35N52	93w32	6:14:08
Redstripe 69	35N49	91w55	6:07:40
Red Wing 67	34N02	94w21	6:17:24
Reed 21	33N42	91w27	6:05:48
Reed Keathly 75	35N03	93w29	6:13:56
Reeds Creek 38	35N56	91w18	6:05:12
Reedville 21	33N54	91w30	6:06:00
Relfs Bluff 40	33N56	91w50	6:07:20
Relief 32	35N39	91w42	6:06:48
Remmel 34	35N37	91w16	6:05:04
Rena 17	35N29	94w21	6:17:24
Republican 23	35N14	92w23	6:09:32
Revel 74	35N17	91w22	6:05:28
Revilee 42	35N11	93w47	6:15:08
Rex 71	35N35	92w28	6:09:52
Reydell 35	34N09	91w34	6:06:16
Reyno 61	36N22	90w45	6:03:00
Reynolds 28	36N11	90w20	6:01:20
Rhea 72	36N01	94w24	6:17:36
Rheas Mill 72	36N01	94w24	6:17:36
Rich 48	34N48	91w09	6:04:36
Richardson 61	36N24	90w52	6:03:28
Richland 60	34N43	92w16	6:09:04
Richland View 72	36N00	94w01	6:16:04
Richmond 41	33N38	94w13	6:16:52
Rich Mountain 57	34N42	94w21	6:17:24
Richwood 10	34N05	93w02	6:12:08
Riley 75	35N07	93w32	6:14:08
Rio Vista 73	35N18	91w34	6:06:16
Risher 16	35N48	90w56	6:03:44
Rison 13	33N58	92w11	6:08:44
Ritchie 70	33N13	92w40	6:10:40
Riverdale 66	35N20	94w11	6:16:44
River Mountain 42	35N17	93w19	6:13:16
Riverside 74	35N18	91w14	6:04:56
Rivervale 56	35N41	90w21	6:01:24
Riverview 15	35N08	92w45	6:11:00
Rixey 60	34N47	92w12	6:08:48
Roane 37	33N07	93w41	6:14:44
Roanoke 61	36N13	91w04	6:04:16
Roasting Ear 69	35N56	92w18	6:09:12
Roberts 35	34N27	91w43	6:06:52
Robertsville 15	35N17	92w47	6:11:08
Robinson 4	36N11	94w34	6:18:16
Rob Roy 35	34N45	92w21	6:09:24
Rock Creek 65	36N02	92w31	6:10:04
Rock Hill 28	36N04	90w32	6:02:08
Rock Hill 67	33N53	94w05	6:16:20
Rockhouse 44	36N24	93w44	6:14:56
Rock Island Junction 6	33N27	92w10	6:08:40
Rock Island Quarters 70	33N13	92w40	6:10:40
Rockport 30	34N23	92w49	6:11:16
Rock Spring 65	35N57	92w32	6:10:08
Rock Springs 22	33N37	91w56	6:07:44
Rockwell 26	34N30	93w03	6:12:12
Rocky 47	35N56	90w15	6:01:00
Rocky Hill 71	35N45	92w31	6:10:04
Rocky Mound 14	33N16	93w14	6:12:56
Rocky Mound 29	33N42	93w35	6:14:20
Rocky Mound 46	33N16	93w53	6:15:32
Rodney 3	36N14	92w10	6:08:40
Roe 48	34N38	91w23	6:05:32
Rogers 4	36N20	94w07	6:16:28
Rohwer 21	33N46	91w17	6:05:08
Roland 60	34N54	92w30	6:10:00
Rolla 30	34N23	92w49	6:11:16
Roller Ridge 4	36N29	93w55	6:15:40
Romance 73	35N14	92w03	6:08:12
Rondo 39	34N40	90w49	6:03:16
Rondo 46	33N26	94w04	6:16:16
Rosa 47	35N45	89w56	5:59:44
Rosboro 55	34N18	93w31	6:14:04
Rose Bud 73	35N20	92w05	6:08:20
Rose City 60	34N47	92w12	6:08:48
Rose Creek 53	35N04	93w00	6:12:00
Roseland 47	35N51	90w06	6:00:24
Rose Meadow 60	34N43	92w16	6:09:04
Roseville 42	35N21	93w46	6:15:04
Rosie 32	35N40	91w32	6:06:08
Ross 58	35N26	93w23	6:13:32
Rosston 50	33N34	93w24	6:13:36
Rotan 47	35N42	89w58	5:59:52
Round Mountain 15	35N02	93w03	6:12:12
Round Pond 62	35N04	90w37	6:02:28
Round Prairie 4	36N16	94w33	6:18:12
Rover 75	34N57	93w24	6:13:36
Rowell 13	33N53	92w01	6:08:04
Roxton 44	36N02	93w55	6:15:40
Roy 55	33N57	93w51	6:15:24
Royal 26	34N31	93w14	6:12:56
Royal 73	35N06	92w01	6:08:04
Royal Oak 63	34N40	92w22	6:09:28
Rudd 8	36N22	93w34	6:14:16
Ruddell 32	35N47	91w41	6:06:44
Ruddle Mill 32	35N46	91w37	6:06:28
Rudy 17	35N31	94w16	6:17:04
Rule 8	36N17	93w28	6:13:52
Rumley 65	35N50	92w33	6:10:12
Running Lake 61	36N19	90w53	6:03:32
Rupert 71	35N35	92w28	6:09:52
Rushing 69	35N39	92w19	6:09:16
Russell 73	35N22	91w31	6:06:04
Russellville 58	35N17	93w08	6:12:32
Ryan 43	34N33	91w53	6:07:32
Rye 13	33N45	91w59	6:07:56
Rye Hill 66	35N22	94w23	6:17:32
Sacred Heart 36	35N26	93w37	6:14:28
Saddle 25	36N30	91w33	6:06:12
Saffell 38	35N55	91w18	6:05:12
Sage 33	36N03	91w49	6:07:16
Saginaw 30	34N14	92w55	6:11:40
Saint Charles 1	34N23	91w08	6:04:32
Saint Francis 11	36N27	90w09	6:00:36
Saint James 69	35N50	91w55	6:07:40
Saint Joe 65	36N02	92w48	6:11:12
Saint Paul 44	35N50	93w46	6:15:04
Saint Vincent 15	35N19	92w44	6:10:56
Salado 32	35N42	91w36	6:06:24
Salem 25	36N22	91w50	6:07:20
Salem 55	34N20	93w33	6:14:12
Salesville 3	36N15	92w16	6:09:04
Saline 13	33N52	92w18	6:09:12
Saltillo 23	35N05	92w27	6:09:48
Salus 36	35N44	93w24	6:13:36
Sand Hill 59	34N58	91w30	6:06:00
Sand Point 17	35N39	94w05	6:16:20
Sand Spring 58	35N27	93w16	6:13:04
Sandtown 15	35N08	92w45	6:11:00
Sandtown 32	35N46	91w37	6:06:28
Sandy Bend 70	33N06	92w22	6:09:28
Sandyland 70	33N13	92w40	6:10:40
Sandy Ridge 47	35N57	89w57	5:59:48
Saratoga 31	33N46	93w53	6:15:32
Sardis 63	34N33	92w30	6:10:00
Savoy 72	36N04	94w09	6:16:36
Sayre 52	33N44	93w04	6:12:16
Schaal 31	33N53	93w55	6:15:40
Schaberg 17	35N38	94w10	6:16:40
Schug 16	36N04	90w32	6:02:08
Scotland 71	35N32	92w37	6:10:28
Scott 60	34N42	92w06	6:08:24
Scottsville 58	35N27	93w03	6:12:12
Scranton 42	35N22	93w32	6:14:08
Screeton 59	34N47	91w34	6:06:16
Searcy 73	35N15	91w44	6:06:56
Seaton 43	34N33	91w53	6:07:32
Seaton Dump 43	34N33	91w53	6:07:32
Sedgwick 38	35N59	90w52	6:03:28
Self Creek 55	34N15	93w42	6:14:48
Selma 22	33N42	91w34	6:06:16
Seyppel 18	34N57	90w28	6:01:52
Shady Grove 25	36N24	92w00	6:08:00
Shady Grove 36	35N28	93w30	6:14:00
Shady Grove 47	35N53	90w10	6:00:40
Shady Grove 50	33N48	93w23	6:13:32
Shady Grove 56	35N41	90w31	6:02:04
Shady Grove 60	34N45	92w22	6:09:28
Shannon 40	34N05	91w42	6:06:48
Shannon 61	36N16	90w58	6:03:52
Shannondale 62	34N57	90w28	6:01:52
Shannon Hills 63	34N40	92w22	6:09:28
Sharman 14	33N22	93w30	6:14:00
Sharum 61	36N14	90w43	6:02:52
Shaw 63	34N30	92w32	6:10:08
Shelbyville 68	35N56	91w33	6:06:12
Shell Lake 62	35N04	90w30	6:02:00
Shepherd 17	35N44	93w59	6:15:56
Sheppard 29	33N38	93w44	6:14:56
Sheridan 27	34N19	92w24	6:09:36
Sherman 36	35N40	93w26	6:13:44
Sherrill 35	34N23	91w57	6:07:48
Sherwood 60	34N49	92w13	6:08:52
Sherwood Hills 30	34N23	92w49	6:11:16
Shiloh 31	33N53	93w55	6:15:40
Shiloh 37	33N22	93w26	6:13:44
Shiloh 58	35N17	93w09	6:12:36
Shiloh 61	36N18	91w02	6:04:08
Shirley 71	35N39	92w19	6:09:16
Shives 9	33N20	91w17	6:05:08
Shoal Creek 42	35N17	93w26	6:13:44
Shoffner 34	35N39	92w19	6:09:16
Short Mountain 42	35N18	93w45	6:15:00
Shover Springs 29	33N42	93w35	6:14:20
Shuler 70	33N13	92w40	6:10:40
Sidney 68	36N00	91w40	6:06:40
Sidon 73	35N21	91w56	6:07:44
Signal Hill 69	35N45	92w04	6:08:16
Siloam 61	36N27	90w56	6:03:44
Siloam Springs 4	36N11	94w32	6:18:08
Silver 49	34N33	93w38	6:14:32
Silver Lake 21	33N56	91w26	6:05:44
Silver Ridge 67	33N53	94w05	6:16:20
Simpson 27	34N25	92w18	6:09:12
Sims 49	34N40	93w41	6:14:44
Sitka 68	36N15	91w22	6:05:28
Skunkhollow 23	35N05	92w27	6:09:48
Slaytonville 66	35N11	94w25	6:17:40
Slonikers Mill 62	34N58	90w54	6:03:36
Slovac 59	34N29	91w33	6:06:12
Smackover 70	33N22	92w44	6:10:56
Smale 48	34N43	91w06	6:04:24
Smalley 48	34N25	91w01	6:04:04
Smart 69	35N44	92w09	6:08:36
Smearney 6	33N23	92w09	6:08:36
Smiths Corner 39	34N48	91w00	6:04:00
Smithton 10	33N57	93w08	6:12:32
Smithville 38	36N05	91w18	6:05:12
Smyrna 58	35N39	92w55	6:11:40
Snow 45	36N14	92w41	6:10:44
Snowball 65	35N55	92w49	6:11:16
Snow Hill 52	33N23	92w47	6:11:08
Snow Lake 21	34N04	91w01	6:04:04
Snyder 2	33N18	91w30	6:06:00
Social Hill 30	34N20	92w55	6:11:40
Solgohachia 15	35N15	92w41	6:10:44
Sonora 72	36N11	94w09	6:16:36
Soudan 39	34N46	90w46	6:03:04
Southall 20	33N55	92w26	6:09:44
South Big Rock 68	36N00	91w29	6:05:56
South Crossett 2	33N09	91w57	6:07:48
Southerlands Crossroads 24	35N29	93w50	6:15:20
Southern State College 14	33N16	93w14	6:12:56
South Fort Smith 66	35N22	94w23	6:17:32
South Harrison 5	36N12	93w07	6:12:28
South Hot Springs 26	34N30	93w03	6:12:12
South Jacksonville 60	34N47	92w12	6:08:48
Southland 54	34N36	90w45	6:03:00
South Lead Hill 5	36N14	93w04	6:12:16
South Lebanon 68	36N08	91w25	6:05:40
South Ozark 24	35N29	93w50	6:15:20
South Pine Bluff 35	34N13	92w02	6:08:08
South Sheridan 27	34N19	92w24	6:09:36
South Side 32	35N42	91w36	6:06:24
South Side 60	34N43	92w16	6:09:04
Southside 71	35N27	92w24	6:09:36

South Union 68	36N17	91w18	6:05:12
Southwest Little Rock 60	34N44	92w20	6:09:20
Spadra 36	35N29	93w29	6:13:56
Sparkman 20	33N55	92w51	6:11:24
Spear Lake 56	35N32	90w25	6:01:40
Spirit Lake 37	33N22	93w35	6:14:20
Spotville 14	33N16	93w14	6:12:56
Spring Creek 39	34N46	90w46	6:03:04
Springdale 72	36N11	94w08	6:16:32
Springfield 15	35N16	92w34	6:10:16
Spring Grove 28	36N03	90w34	6:02:16
Springhill 23	35N14	92w23	6:09:32
Spring Hill 29	33N35	93w39	6:14:36
Springtown 4	36N16	94w25	6:17:40
Spring Valley 72	36N11	93w56	6:15:44
Stacy 18	35N23	90w15	6:01:00
Stacy 56	35N41	90w31	6:02:04
Stamps 37	33N22	93w30	6:14:00
Standard-Umsted 52	33N22	92w44	6:10:56
Stanford 28	36N04	90w32	6:02:08
Stanley 1	34N10	91w23	6:05:32
Star City 40	33N56	91w51	6:07:24
Stark 12	35N32	92w06	6:08:24
Starr Hill 72	35N57	94w25	6:17:40
State Capital 60	34N44	92w16	6:09:04
State College Of Arkansas 23	35N05	92w27	6:09:48
State Line 14	33N06	93w12	6:12:48
State Line 37	33N06	93w28	6:13:52
State Services 63	34N45	92w43	6:10:52
State University 16	35N50	90w43	6:02:52
Staves 13	33N58	92w11	6:08:44
Steel 37	33N20	93w38	6:14:32
Steele 15	35N13	92w37	6:10:28
Stephens 52	33N25	93w04	6:12:16
Steprock 73	35N26	91w41	6:06:44
Sterling Spring 16	35N50	90w48	6:03:12
Steve 75	34N59	93w18	6:13:12
Stevens Creek 73	35N18	91w34	6:06:16
Stokes 61	36N16	90w58	6:03:52
Stonewall 28	36N14	90w32	6:02:08
Stony Point 53	35N02	92w42	6:10:48
Stony Point 73	35N04	91w53	6:07:32
Story 49	34N42	93w31	6:14:04
Stoverville 51	36N06	93w18	6:13:12
Strangers Home 38	35N54	91w05	6:04:20
Strawberry 38	35N58	91w19	6:05:16
Strickler 72	35N55	94w11	6:16:44
Stringtown 67	33N57	94w21	6:17:24
Strong 70	33N07	92w21	6:09:24
Stuart 68	36N18	91w31	6:06:04
Sturkie 25	36N27	91w53	6:07:32
Stuttgart 1	34N30	91w33	6:06:12
Subiaco 42	35N18	93w38	6:14:32
Success 11	36N27	90w43	6:02:52
Sugar Camp 12	35N40	92w07	6:08:28
Sugar Grove 42	35N08	93w55	6:15:40
Sugar Hill 72	35N57	94w25	6:17:40
Sugar Loaf 5	36N26	92w55	6:11:40
Sugarloaf Lake 66	35N11	94w25	6:17:40
Sulphur City 72	36N04	94w09	6:16:36
Sulphur Rock 32	35N45	91w30	6:06:00
Sulphur Springs 4	36N29	94w28	6:17:52
Sulphur Springs 35	34N13	92w02	6:08:08
Sulphur Springs 36	35N28	93w30	6:14:00
Sulphur Springs 75	35N14	93w10	6:12:40
Summers 72	35N59	94w29	6:17:56
Summit 45	36N15	92w41	6:10:44
Sumpter 6	33N25	92w18	6:09:12
Sunnydale 73	35N26	91w41	6:06:44
Sunny Hill 73	35N15	91w43	6:06:52
Sunset 18	35N13	90w12	6:00:48
Sunset 72	35N48	94w08	6:16:32
Sunshine 2	33N07	91w33	6:06:12
Sunshine 26	34N31	93w14	6:12:56
Supply 61	36N25	90w54	6:03:36
Sutton 50	33N44	93w28	6:13:52
Swain 51	35N51	93w20	6:13:20
Swan Lake 35	34N45	92w21	6:09:24
Swayne 47	35N48	89w51	5:59:24
Sweden 35	34N45	92w21	6:09:24
Sweet Home 60	34N41	92w15	6:09:00
Swifton 34	35N49	91w08	6:04:32
Sycamore 10	33N55	93w09	6:12:36
Sycamore Bend 62	34N57	90w28	6:01:52
Sylamore 33	36N04	91w54	6:07:36
Sylamore 69	35N54	92w15	6:09:00
Sylvan Hills 60	34N48	92w14	6:08:56
Sylvania 43	35N02	91w57	6:07:48
Tafton 60	34N36	92w13	6:08:52
Talladega 35	34N07	92w07	6:08:28
Tamo 35	34N07	91w46	6:07:04
Tappan 54	34N19	90w55	6:03:40
Tarry 40	34N05	91w50	6:07:20
Tate 42	35N00	93w56	6:15:44
Taylor 14	33N06	93w28	6:13:52
Tech 58	35N17	93w09	6:12:36
Telico 62	35N07	90w48	6:03:12
Tennessee 22	33N33	91w47	6:07:08
Tennessee 27	34N12	92w37	6:10:28
Terre Noire 10	34N04	93w17	6:13:08
Terrytown 60	34N43	92w16	6:09:04
Texarkana 46	33N26	94w03	6:16:12
Thacker 38	36N14	91w16	6:05:04
Thebes 2	33N18	91w30	6:06:00
Thida 32	35N34	91w29	6:05:56
Thompson 55	34N05	93w41	6:14:44
Thornburg 53	35N00	92w48	6:11:12
Thorney 44	36N00	94w01	6:16:04
Thornton 7	33N47	92w29	6:09:56
Three Brothers 3	36N18	92w20	6:09:20
Three Creeks 70	33N01	92w43	6:10:52
Three Forks 18	35N16	90w28	6:01:52
Tichnor 1	34N08	91w16	6:05:04
Tillar 22	33N43	91w27	6:05:48
Tilly 58	35N43	92w50	6:11:20
Tilton 19	35N19	91w01	6:04:04
Timbo 69	35N52	92w19	6:09:16
Tinsman 7	33N38	92w21	6:09:24
Titsworth 42	35N21	93w41	6:14:44
Tobin 55	34N02	93w30	6:14:00
Togo 19	35N16	90w33	6:02:12
Tokio 29	34N00	93w45	6:15:00
Toledo 13	33N58	92w11	6:08:44
Tollette 31	33N53	93w55	6:15:40
Tollville 59	34N47	91w27	6:05:48
Toltec 43	34N42	92w06	6:08:24
Tomahawk 65	36N02	92w43	6:10:52
Tomato 47	35N51	89w44	5:58:56
Tomberlin 43	34N33	91w53	6:07:32
Tomlinson 42	35N05	94w05	6:16:20
Toneyville 60	34N55	92w07	6:08:28
Tongin 39	34N52	90w35	6:02:20
Tontitown 72	36N11	94w14	6:16:56
Topaz 62	35N04	90w30	6:02:00
Totten 43	34N53	91w46	6:07:04
Trammellville 11	36N16	90w18	6:01:12
Traskwood 63	34N27	92w39	6:10:36
Treat 58	35N44	93w24	6:13:36
Trenton 54	34N33	90w51	6:03:24
Trippe 21	33N38	91w24	6:05:36
Troy 47	35N36	89w58	5:59:52
Troy 52	33N25	93w04	6:12:16
Trumann 56	35N41	90w31	6:02:04
Tubal 70	33N04	92w56	6:11:44
Tuck 16	35N50	90w48	6:03:12
Tucker 35	34N26	91w57	6:07:48
Tuckerman 34	35N44	91w12	6:04:48
Tukertown 47	35N49	89w56	5:59:44
Tulip 20	34N04	92w33	6:10:12
Tull 27	34N27	92w35	6:10:20
Tully 56	35N41	90w31	6:02:04
Tulot 56	35N41	90w31	6:02:04
Tumbling Shoals 12	35N32	92w01	6:08:04
Tupelo 34	35N23	91w14	6:04:56
Turkey Creek 69	35N45	92w14	6:08:56
Turner 54	34N29	91w01	6:04:04
Turrell 18	35N23	90w15	6:01:00
Tuttle 72	36N00	94w01	6:16:04
Twentythree 73	35N18	91w34	6:06:16
Twin Creek 33	36N04	91w54	6:07:36
Twin Springs 60	34N45	92w22	6:09:28
Twist 19	35N23	90w31	6:02:04
Tyro 40	33N50	91w43	6:06:52
Tyronza 56	35N30	90w22	6:01:28
Tyronza Junction 56	35N32	90w25	6:01:40
Ulm 59	34N35	91w28	6:05:52
Umpire 31	34N17	94w03	6:16:12
Union 25	36N22	91w50	6:07:20
Union 67	34N02	94w21	6:17:24
Union 70	33N06	92w22	6:09:28
Unionhill 32	35N25	91w27	6:05:48
Union Ridge 66	35N08	94w03	6:16:12
Uniontown 17	35N35	94w27	6:17:48
Union Valley 53	34N58	92w49	6:11:16
University 72	36N04	94w09	6:16:36
University of Arkansas at Mo 22	33N33	91w47	6:07:08
Uno 56	35N37	90w54	6:03:36
Upper Surrounded Hill 59	34N53	91w25	6:05:40
Urbana 70	33N10	92w27	6:09:48
Urbanette 8	36N25	93w32	6:14:08
Ursula 66	35N18	94w02	6:16:08
Vail 16	35N56	90w15	6:01:00
Valley Hill 12	35N32	92w06	6:08:24
Valley Springs 5	36N09	92w59	6:11:56
Valley View 16	35N50	90w48	6:03:12
Van 1	34N20	91w14	6:04:56
Van Buren 17	35N26	94w21	6:17:24
Vandervoort 57	34N23	94w22	6:17:28
Vanity Corner 73	35N15	91w43	6:06:52
Vanndale 19	35N19	90w46	6:03:04
Vaughan 32	35N41	91w23	6:05:32
Vaughn 4	36N22	94w13	6:16:52
Vaugine 35	34N13	92w00	6:08:00
Veasey 22	33N29	91w49	6:07:16
Velie 52	33N35	92w47	6:11:08
Velvet Ridge 73	35N25	91w34	6:06:16
Vendor 51	35N57	93w05	6:12:20
Venus 44	35N54	93w35	6:14:20
Verona 45	36N09	92w47	6:11:08
Vesta 24	35N18	94w02	6:16:08
Vick 6	33N20	92w06	6:08:24
Victoria 47	35N42	89w58	5:59:52
Vidette 25	36N26	92w07	6:08:28
Village 14	33N16	93w03	6:12:12
Villemont 35	34N10	91w34	6:06:16
Vilonia 23	35N05	92w13	6:08:52
Vimy Ridge 63	34N36	92w25	6:09:40
Vincent 18	35N14	90w19	6:01:16
Vine Prairie 17	35N31	94w05	6:16:20
Vineyard 39	34N46	90w46	6:03:04
Vineyard 72	35N48	94w29	6:17:56
Vineygrove 72	35N59	94w19	6:17:16
Viola 25	36N24	91w59	6:07:56
Violet Hill 33	36N09	91w50	6:07:20
Wabash 54	34N23	90w50	6:03:20
Wabbaseka 35	34N22	91w48	6:07:12
Wager 4	36N15	94w17	6:17:08
Walcott 28	36N03	90w40	6:02:40
Waldenburg 56	35N34	90w56	6:03:44
Waldo 14	33N22	93w17	6:13:08
Waldron 64	34N54	94w05	6:16:20
Walker 14	33N16	93w14	6:12:56
Walker 73	35N15	91w43	6:06:52
Walker Creek 37	33N07	93w31	6:14:04
Walkerville 14	33N06	93w12	6:12:48
Wallace 41	33N43	94w24	6:17:36
Wallaceburg 29	33N52	93w30	6:14:00
Walls 43	34N40	91w59	6:07:56
Walnut 51	35N44	93w24	6:13:36
Walnut Corner 28	36N02	90w47	6:03:08
Walnut Corner 54	34N33	90w46	6:03:04
Walnut Grove 11	36N25	90w35	6:02:20
Walnut Grove 32	35N49	91w21	6:05:24
Walnut Grove 41	33N41	94w08	6:16:32
Walnut Grove 56	35N41	90w31	6:02:04
Walnut Grove 71	35N35	92w28	6:09:52
Walnut Grove 72	36N02	94w15	6:17:00
Walnut Grove 75	35N07	93w32	6:14:08
Walnut Hill 37	33N06	93w39	6:14:36
Walnut Lake 21	33N50	91w30	6:06:00
Walnut Ridge 38	36N04	90w57	6:03:48
Walnut Springs 67	33N57	94w21	6:17:24
Walters 47	35N56	90w15	6:01:00
Waltreak 75	34N59	93w37	6:14:28
Wampler 35	34N13	92w02	6:08:08
Wampoo 60	34N33	91w53	6:07:32
Wappanocca 18	35N18	90w16	6:01:04
Ward 43	35N02	91w57	6:07:48
Wardell 47	35N30	90w09	6:00:36
War Eagle	36N16	93w56	6:15:44
Warm Springs 61	36N28	91w02	6:04:08
Warner 52	33N35	92w47	6:11:08
Warren 6	33N37	92w04	6:08:16
Washburn 66	35N10	94w06	6:16:24
Washington 29	33N47	93w41	6:14:44
Washington Square 62	35N01	90w47	6:03:08
Watalula 24	35N32	93w45	6:15:00
Watensaw 59	34N45	91w28	6:05:52
Waterloo 50	33N33	93w15	6:13:00
Water Valley 61	36N20	91w08	6:04:32
Watkins 73	35N15	91w43	6:06:52
Watkins Corner 54	34N33	90w55	6:03:40
Watson 21	33N54	91w15	6:05:00
Watson Chapel 35	34N13	92w02	6:08:08
Wattensaw 43	34N47	91w54	6:07:36
Waveland 75	35N08	93w38	6:14:32
Wayton 51	35N55	93w15	6:13:00
Weathers 44	35N58	93w31	6:14:04
Weaver 24	35N22	94w02	6:16:08
Webb City 24	35N29	93w50	6:15:20
Wedington 72	36N04	94w25	6:17:40
Weeks 64	34N53	94w36	6:18:24
Weiner 56	35N37	90w54	6:03:36
Welborn 15	35N10	92w45	6:11:00
Welcome 14	33N06	93w28	6:13:52
Weldon 34	35N27	91w14	6:04:56
Wells Bayou 40	33N55	91w37	6:06:28
Weona 56	35N33	90w36	6:02:24
Weona Junction 56	35N41	90w31	6:02:04
Wesley 44	36N02	93w55	6:15:40
Wesley Chapel 15	35N08	92w45	6:11:00
Wesson 70	33N07	92w46	6:11:04
West Bauxite 63	34N33	92w30	6:10:00
West Camden Heights 52	33N35	92w47	6:11:08
West Crossett 2	33N09	91w57	6:07:48
West End 35	34N13	92w02	6:08:08
Western Grove 51	36N06	92w57	6:11:48
West Fork 72	35N55	94w11	6:16:44
West Gum Springs 10	34N05	93w02	6:12:08
West Hartford 66	35N01	94w23	6:17:32
West Helena 54	34N33	90w38	6:02:32
West Line 67	34N02	94w34	6:18:16
West Memphis 18	35N09	90w11	6:00:44
Westor 39	34N46	90w46	6:03:04
West Otis 67	34N02	94w21	6:17:24
West Pangburn 12	35N32	92w06	6:08:24
West Point 73	35N12	91w37	6:06:28
West Prairie 56	35N37	90w52	6:03:28
West Richwoods 69	35N52	92w07	6:08:28
West Ridge 47	35N41	90w16	6:01:04
West Sullivan 68	35N59	91w39	6:06:36
Westville 17	35N29	94w20	6:17:20
Wharton 44	36N05	93w44	6:14:56
Wharton Creek 44	36N02	93w37	6:14:28
Wheatley 62	34N55	91w07	6:04:28
Wheeler 71	35N37	92w43	6:10:52
Wheeler 72	36N07	94w16	6:17:04
Wheeling 25	36N22	91w50	6:07:20
Whelen Springs 10	33N50	93w07	6:12:28
Whipple 71	35N27	92w24	6:09:36
Whistleville 47	35N53	90w10	6:00:40
Whitaker 56	35N34	90w43	6:02:52
White 2	33N01	92w00	6:08:00
Whitecliffs 41	33N53	94w05	6:16:20
White Eagle 15	35N06	92w57	6:11:48
Whitehall 39	34N52	90w35	6:02:20
Whitehall 56	35N29	90w44	6:02:56
Whiteoak 24	35N29	93w50	6:15:20
Whiterock 24	35N35	93w58	6:15:52
Whitetown 49	34N37	93w47	6:15:08
Whiteville 3	36N17	92w30	6:10:00
Whitley 17	35N35	94w07	6:16:28
Whitmore 62	35N01	90w41	6:02:44
Whittington 26	34N31	92w56	6:11:44
Whitton 47	35N30	90w15	6:01:00
Wickes 57	34N18	94w20	6:17:20
Wideman 33	36N11	92w01	6:08:04
Widener 62	35N01	90w41	6:02:44
Wilburn 12	35N31	91w52	6:07:28
Wild Cherry 25	36N16	92w04	6:08:16
Wiley 61	36N11	90w55	6:03:40
Wileys Cove 65	35N50	92w34	6:10:16
Williams 43	34N40	92w04	6:08:16
Williams Junction 53	35N00	92w48	6:11:12
Williamson 67	33N57	94w21	6:17:24
Williford 68	36N15	91w21	6:05:24
Willis 56	35N39	90w31	6:02:04
Willisville 50	33N31	93w18	6:13:12

Place	Latitude	Longitude	Time
Willow 20	34N08	92w45	6:11:00
Willow Creek 71	35N27	92w24	6:09:36
Wilmar 22	33N37	91w56	6:07:44
Wilmington 70	33N13	92w26	6:09:44
Wilmot 2	33N04	91w34	6:06:16
Wilson 47	35N34	90w03	6:00:12
Wilson 58	35N14	92w55	6:11:40
Wilton 41	33N45	94w09	6:16:36
Winchester 22	33N47	91w29	6:05:56
Winesburg 16	35N50	90w48	6:03:12
Winfield 64	34N54	94w05	6:16:20
Winfrey 17	35N44	94w06	6:16:24
Wing 75	34N59	93w18	6:13:12
Winona 8	36N22	93w41	6:14:44
Winslow 72	35N48	94w08	6:16:32
Winston Terrace 60	34N44	92w20	6:09:20
Winthrop 41	33N50	94w21	6:17:24
Wirth 68	36N30	91w33	6:06:12
Wiseman 33	36N14	91w49	6:07:16
Witcherville 66	35N05	94w16	6:17:04
Witherspoon 30	34N05	93w02	6:12:08
Witter 44	35N56	93w41	6:14:44
Wittich 24	35N22	93w52	6:15:28
Wittsburg 19	35N13	90w47	6:03:08
Witts Springs 65	35N46	92w52	6:11:28
Wiville 74	35N16	91w12	6:04:48
Wolf Bayou 12	35N39	91w54	6:07:36
Wolf Creek 55	34N02	93w28	6:13:52
Womble 49	34N28	93w40	6:14:40
Woodberry 7	33N35	92w31	6:10:04
Woodland 36	35N28	93w30	6:14:00
Woodland Corner 47	35N57	89w57	5:59:48
Woodland Heights 60	34N46	92w23	6:09:32
Woodland Hills 25	36N18	91w31	6:06:04
Woodrow 12	35N42	92w06	6:08:24
Woodson 60	34N32	92w13	6:08:52
Woolsey 72	35N55	94w11	6:16:44
Woolum 71	35N50	92w33	6:10:12
Wooster 23	35N12	92w27	6:09:48
Worden 73	35N18	91w34	6:06:16
Worthen 58	35N15	93w03	6:12:12
Wright 35	34N26	92w04	6:08:16
Wrightsville 60	34N36	92w13	6:08:52
Wycamp 54	34N33	90w38	6:02:32
Wycough 32	35N45	91w26	6:05:44
Wye 53	34N57	92w38	6:10:32
Wyman 72	36N09	94w07	6:16:28
Wynne 19	35N14	90w47	6:03:08
Wyola 72	35N48	94w08	6:16:32
Yale 36	35N40	93w39	6:14:36
Yancopin 21	33N56	91w13	6:04:52
Yarbro 47	35N57	89w57	5:59:48
Yardelle 51	36N06	92w57	6:11:48
Y City 64	34N38	93w44	6:14:56
Yell 4	36N11	94w23	6:17:32
Yellville 45	36N14	92w41	6:10:44
Yocum 8	36N28	93w27	6:13:48
Yoestown 17	35N29	94w14	6:16:56
York 43	34N57	92w03	6:08:12
Yorktown 40	34N01	91w49	6:07:16
Yukon 21	33N46	91w29	6:05:56
Zack 65	35N55	92w38	6:10:32
Zent 48	34N48	91w09	6:04:36
Zinc 5	36N17	92w55	6:11:40
Zion 33	36N05	91w46	6:07:04

ARKANSAS

TIME TABLES

Before 11/18/1883		LMT
11/18/1883	12:00	PST
3/31/1918	02:00	PWT
10/27/1918	02:00	PST
3/30/1919	02:00	PWT
10/26/1919	02:00	PST
2/09/1942	02:00	PWT
9/30/1945	02:00	PST
3/14/1948	02:00	PDT
1/01/1949	02:00	PST
4/30/1950	02:00	PDT
9/24/1950	02:00	PST
4/29/1951	02:00	PDT
9/30/1951	02:00	PST
4/27/1952	02:00	PDT
9/28/1952	02:00	PST
4/26/1953	02:00	PDT
9/27/1953	02:00	PST
4/25/1954	02:00	PDT
9/26/1954	02:00	PST
4/24/1955	02:00	PDT
9/25/1955	02:00	PST
4/29/1956	02:00	PDT
9/30/1956	02:00	PST
4/28/1957	02:00	PDT
9/29/1957	02:00	PST
4/27/1958	02:00	PDT
9/28/1958	02:00	PST
4/26/1959	02:00	PDT
9/27/1959	02:00	PST
4/24/1960	02:00	PDT
9/25/1960	02:00	PST
4/30/1961	02:00	PDT
9/24/1961	02:00	PST
4/29/1962	02:00	PDT
10/28/1962	02:00	PST
4/28/1963	02:00	PDT
10/27/1963	02:00	PST
4/26/1964	02:00	PDT
10/25/1964	02:00	PST
4/25/1965	02:00	PDT
10/31/1965	02:00	PST
4/24/1966	02:00	PDT
10/30/1966	02:00	PST
4/30/1967	02:00	US#1

COUNTIES

1 Alameda
2 Alpine
3 Amador
4 Butte
5 Calaveras
6 Colusa
7 Contra Costa
8 Del Norte
9 El Dorado
10 Fresno
11 Glenn
12 Humboldt
13 Imperial
14 Inyo
15 Kern
16 Kings
17 Lake
18 Lassen
19 Los Angeles
20 Madera
21 Marin
22 Mariposa
23 Mendocino
24 Merced
25 Modoc
26 Mono
27 Monterey
28 Napa
29 Nevada
30 Orange
31 Placer
32 Plumas
33 Riverside
34 Sacramento
35 San Benito
36 San Bernardino
37 San Diego
38 San Francisco
39 San Joaquin
40 San Luis Obispo
41 San Mateo
42 Santa Barbara
43 Santa Clara
44 Santa Cruz
45 Shasta
46 Sierra
47 Siskiyou
48 Solano
49 Sonoma
50 Stanislaus
51 Sutter
52 Tehama
53 Trinity
54 Tulare
55 Tuolumne
56 Ventura
57 Yolo
58 Yuba

Place	Lat	Long	Time
Abalone Cove 19	33N46	118W21	7:53:24
Aberdeen 14	37N10	118W17	7:53:08
Academy 10	36N49	119W43	7:58:52
Acampo 39	38N10	121W13	8:04:52
Actis Gardens 15	35N08	117W59	7:51:56
Acton 19	34N28	118W12	7:52:48
Adelaida 40	35N38	120W41	8:02:44
Adelanto 36	34N35	117W22	7:49:28
Adin 25	41N12	120W57	8:03:48
Aerial Acres 15	34N56	117W57	7:51:48
Aetna Springs 28	38N37	122W26	8:09:44
Afton 11	39N28	121W59	8:07:56
Agnew 43	37N25	121W57	8:07:48
Agoura 19	34N09	118W45	7:55:00
Agua Caliente 49	38N17	122W28	8:09:52
Agua Caliente Indian Res 33	33N49	116W32	7:46:08
Agua Caliente Springs 37	33N05	116W36	7:46:24
Agua Dulce 19	34N25	118W32	7:54:08
Aguanga 33	33N27	116W51	7:47:24
Ahwahnee 20	37N23	119W44	7:58:56
Airbase 42	34N54	120W26	8:01:44
Airport 1	37N43	122W11	8:08:44
Airport 36	34N04	117W35	7:50:20
Alameda 1	37N46	122W15	8:09:00
Alamo 7	37N51	122W02	8:08:08
Alamo Oaks 7	37N50	121W59	8:07:56
Alamorio 13	32N59	115W32	7:42:08
Albany 1	37N53	122W18	8:09:12
Alberhill 33	33N44	117W24	7:49:36
Albion 23	39N14	123W46	8:15:04
Alderbrook Tract 43	37N19	122W02	8:08:08
Aldercroft Heights 43	37N15	121W58	8:07:52
Alderpoint 12	40N11	123W37	8:14:28
Alder Springs 10	37N05	119W29	7:57:56
Alessandro 33	33N56	117W18	7:49:12
Alexander Valley 49	38N42	122W54	8:11:36
Algerine 55	37N59	120W23	8:01:32
Alhambra 19	34N08	118W06	7:52:24
Alhambra Valley 7	37N59	122W07	8:08:28
Alisal 27	36N41	121W39	8:06:36
All American 43	37N19	122W02	8:08:08
Alleghany 46	39N28	120W51	8:03:24
Allendale 48	38N21	121W59	8:07:56
Allensworth 54	35N52	119W23	7:57:32
Alliance 12	40N52	124W05	8:16:20
Almanor 32	40N07	120W54	8:03:36
Almondale 19	34N30	117W55	7:51:40
Almonte 21	37N53	122W32	8:10:08
Alondra 19	33N54	118W19	7:53:16
Alondra Park 19	33N54	118W20	7:53:20
Alpaugh 54	35N53	119W29	7:57:56
Alpine 37	32N50	116W46	7:47:04
Alpine Heights 37	32N50	116W46	7:47:04
Alpine Hills 41	37N27	122W11	8:08:44
Alpine Village 54	36N08	118W49	7:55:16
Alta 31	39N12	120W49	8:03:16
Altadena 19	34N11	118W08	7:52:32
Alta Hill 29	39N14	121W04	8:04:16
Al Tahoe 9	38N57	119W59	7:59:56
Alta Loma 36	34N08	117W36	7:50:24
Alta Sierra 15	35N42	118W27	7:53:48
Alta Sierra Estates 29	39N13	121W04	8:04:16
Altaville 5	38N05	120W33	8:02:12
Alto 21	37N54	122W32	8:10:08
Alton 12	40N35	124W08	8:16:32
Alturas 25	41N29	120W32	8:02:08
Alum Rock 43	37N23	121W49	8:07:16
Alvarado 1	37N36	122W01	8:08:04
Alviso 43	37N26	121W59	8:07:56
Amador 3	38N25	120W49	8:03:16
Ambassador 19	34N04	118W18	7:53:12
Ambler 54	36N20	119W18	7:57:12
Ambler Park 27	36N41	121W39	8:06:36
Amboy 36	34N33	115W45	7:43:00
Ambrose 7	38N02	121W58	8:07:52
American Canyon 28	38N07	122W14	8:08:56
Amphibious Base 37	32N40	117W10	7:48:40
Anaheim 30	33N50	117W55	7:51:40
Anchor Bay 23	38N46	123W32	8:14:08
Anderson 45	40N27	122W18	8:09:12
Anderson Springs 17	38N45	122W37	8:10:28
Andrade 13	32N43	114W43	7:38:52
Andrew Jackson 37	32N45	117W04	7:48:16
Angels 5	38N05	120W30	8:02:00
Angels Camp 5	38N04	120W32	8:02:08
Angelus Oaks 36	34N09	116W59	7:47:56
Angiola 54	35N59	119W28	7:57:52
Angwin 28	38N34	122W26	8:09:44
Annapolis 49	38N43	123W22	8:13:28
Antelope 34	38N45	121W17	8:05:08
Antelope Acres 19	34N40	118W11	7:52:44
Antelope Center 19	34N35	118W06	7:52:24
Antioch 7	38N01	121W48	8:07:12
Antonio 42	34N41	120W29	8:01:56
Anza 33	33N33	116W43	7:46:52
Anza 37	33N12	116W19	7:45:16
Applegate 31	39N00	120W59	8:03:56
Apple Valley 36	34N31	117W13	7:48:52
Aptos 44	36N59	121W54	8:07:36
Arbolade 56	34N27	119W16	7:57:04
Arbuckle 6	39N01	122W03	8:08:12
Arcade 19	34N05	118W22	7:53:28
Arcade 34	38N37	121W26	8:05:44
Arcadia 19	34N08	118W02	7:52:08
Arcata 12	40N52	124W05	8:16:20
Arch Beach Heights 30	33N32	117W47	7:51:08
Arden 34	38N36	121W23	8:05:32
Ardmore 19	33N56	118W11	7:52:44
Arena 24	37N21	120W36	8:02:24
Argus 36	35N46	117W23	7:49:32
Arlanza Village 33	33N56	117W29	7:49:56
Arleta 19	34N15	118W25	7:53:40
Arlington 33	33N55	117W27	7:49:48
Arlynda Corners 12	40N35	124W16	8:17:04
Armistead 15	35N39	117W49	7:51:16
Armona 16	36N19	119W42	7:58:48
Army Point 48	38N03	122W09	8:08:36
Army Terminal 1	37N48	122W13	8:08:52
Arnold 5	38N15	120W21	8:01:24
Arnold Heights 33	33N56	117W18	7:49:12
Aromas 27	36N54	121W39	8:06:36
Arrowbear Lake	34N13	117W05	7:48:20
Arrowhead 36	34N17	117W14	7:48:56
Arrowhead Highlands 36	34N14	117W17	7:49:08
Arrow Mall 19	34N06	117W53	7:51:32
Arroyo Grande 40	35N07	120W35	8:02:20
Artesia 19	33N52	118W05	7:52:20
Artois 11	39N37	122W12	8:08:48
Arvin 15	35N12	118W50	7:55:20
Arvin Farm Labor Center 15	35N24	119W02	7:56:08
Ashland 1	37N41	122W07	8:08:28
Ashlan Park 10	36N48	119W46	7:59:04
Asilomar 27	36N37	121W56	8:07:44
Aspendell 14	37N22	118W24	7:53:36
Asti 49	38N46	122W58	8:11:52
Atascadero 40	35N29	120W40	8:02:40
Athens 19	33N57	118W18	7:53:12
Atherton 41	37N28	122W12	8:08:48
Athlone 24	37N14	120W15	8:01:00
Atlanta 39	37N44	121W07	8:04:28
Atolia 36	35N19	117W37	7:50:28
Atwater 24	37N21	120W37	8:02:28
Atwood 30	33N52	117W50	7:51:20
Auberry 10	37N05	119W29	7:57:56
Auburn 31	38N54	121W04	8:04:16
August School Area 39	37N59	121W16	8:05:04
Avalon 19	33N21	118W20	7:53:20
Avalon Village 19	33N48	118W16	7:53:04
Avenal 16	36N00	120W08	8:00:32
Avery 5	38N13	120W22	8:01:28
Avila Beach 40	35N11	120W44	8:02:56
Avocado Heights 19	34N02	118W00	7:52:00
Azusa 19	34N08	117W52	7:51:28
Baden 41	37N39	122W26	8:09:44
Badger 54	36N38	119W01	7:56:04
Bagby 22	37N43	120W12	8:00:48
Bagdad 36	34N35	115W53	7:43:32
Bailey 19	33N58	118W01	7:52:04
Baker 36	35N16	116W04	7:44:16
Bakersfield 15	35N23	119W01	7:56:04
Balance Rock 54	35N48	118W39	7:54:36
Balboa 30	33N36	117W54	7:51:36
Balboa Island 30	33N37	117W53	7:51:32
Balch Camp 10	36N47	119W25	7:57:40
Baldwin Lake 36	34N16	116W51	7:47:24
Baldwin Park 19	34N04	117W58	7:51:52
Ballarat 14	35N46	117W23	7:49:32
Ballard 42	34N36	120W10	8:00:40
Ballico 24	37N27	120W42	8:02:48
Ballroad 30	33N49	118W02	7:52:08
Balls Ferry 45	40N27	122W18	8:09:12
Baltimore Park 21	37N56	122W32	8:10:08
Bandini 19	34N01	118W09	7:52:36
Bangor 4	39N23	121W24	8:05:36
Bankhead Springs 37	32N37	116W11	7:44:44
Banning 33	33N56	116W53	7:47:32
Banta 39	37N45	121W22	8:05:28
Barber City 30	33N45	117W59	7:51:56
Bard 13	32N47	114W33	7:38:12
Bardsdale 56	34N24	118W55	7:55:40
Barona Ranch Indian Res 37	33N49	116W32	7:46:08
Barrett 37	32N39	116W47	7:47:08
Barrington 19	34N04	118W29	7:53:56
Barron Park 43	37N25	122W08	8:08:32
Barstow 36	34N54	117W01	7:48:04
Barstow Colony 10	36N48	119W50	7:59:20
Barton 10	36N44	119W45	7:59:00
Base Line 36	34N07	117W18	7:49:12
Bassett 19	34N03	118W00	7:52:00
Bassetts 46	39N34	120W38	8:02:32
Bass Lake 20	37N19	119W33	7:58:12
Batavia 48	38N27	121W50	8:07:20
Baxter 31	39N13	120W47	8:03:08
Bay 36	34N15	116W53	7:47:32
Bayliss 11	39N31	122W01	8:08:04
Bay Meadows Race Track 41	37N33	122W18	8:09:12
Bayo Vista 7	38N01	122W17	8:09:08
Bayshore 41	37N41	122W24	8:09:36
Bayside 12	40N51	124W04	8:16:16
Bayview 12	40N47	124W10	8:16:40
Bay View 38	37N44	122W24	8:09:36
Bayview Park 7	37N58	122W20	8:09:20
Bay View Park 27	36N37	121W50	8:07:20
Beach Center 30	33N41	118W00	7:52:00
Beale Air Force Base 58	39N07	121W22	8:05:28
Beale East 58	39N07	121W22	8:05:28
Beale West 58	39N07	121W25	8:05:40
Bear Creek 24	37N18	120W29	8:01:56
Bear River 29	38N54	121W04	8:04:16
Bear River Lake 3	38N25	120W33	8:02:12
Bear River Pines 29	39N13	121W04	8:04:16
Bear Valley 2	38N15	120W21	8:01:24
Bear Valley 22	37N29	119W58	7:59:52
Beaumont 33	33N56	116W58	7:47:52
Beckwith	39N50	120W22	8:01:28
Beckwourth 32	40N22	120W25	8:01:40
Bee Rock 40	35N52	120W48	8:03:12
Bel Aire Estates 21	37N53	122W29	8:09:56
Belden 32	40N00	121W15	8:05:00
Bell 19	33N59	118W11	7:52:44
Bellaire 7	38N00	121W51	8:07:24
Bella Vista 7	38N00	121W51	8:07:24
Bella Vista 19	34N01	118W09	7:52:36

CALIFORNIA

Bella Vista 45 40N38 122w14 8:08:56
Belle Haven 41 37N27 122w11 8:08:44
Belleview 55 37N59 120w23 8:01:32
Bellevue 49 38N26 122w43 8:10:52
Bellflower 19 33N53 118w09 7:52:36
Bell Gardens 19 33N58 118w10 7:52:40
Bell Mountain 36 34N33 117w21 7:49:24
Bellota 39 38N01 121w05 8:04:20
Bells Station 43 36N51 121w24 8:05:36
Belltown 33 34N01 117w23 7:49:32
Bellview 12 40N30 124w06 8:16:24
Bel Marin Keys 21 38N06 122w34 8:10:16
Belmont 41 37N31 122w17 8:09:08
Belvedere 19 34N01 118w09 7:52:36
Belvedere 21 37N52 122w28 8:09:52
Belvedere Gardens 19 34N01 118w09 7:52:36
Belvernon Gardens 21 37N53 122w29 8:09:56
Benbow 12 40N06 123w48 8:15:12
Bend 52 40N11 122w16 8:09:04
Benicia 48 38N03 122w09 8:08:36
Ben Lomond 44 37N05 122w05 8:08:20
Benton 26 37N48 118w32 7:54:08
Berenda 20 37N02 120w09 8:00:36
Berkeley 1 37N52 122w16 8:09:04
Berkeley Highlands 7 37N54 122w17 8:09:08
Bernal 38 37N45 122w26 8:09:44
Berry Creek 4 39N39 121w24 8:05:36
Berryessa 28 38N40 122w19 8:09:16
Berryessa Park 28 38N18 122w18 8:09:12
Berry Hill Estates 19 33N46 118w21 7:53:24
Berteleda 8 41N46 124w12 8:16:48
Bertsch Terrace 8 41N46 124w12 8:16:48
Bethany 39 37N43 121w26 8:05:44
Bethel Island 7 38N01 121w38 8:06:32
Bethel Tract 10 36N37 119w31 7:58:04
Betteravia 42 34N55 120w31 8:02:04
Beverly Hills 19 34N04 118w25 7:53:40
Bieber 18 41N07 121w08 8:04:32
Big Bar 53 40N45 123w15 8:13:00
Big Basin 44 37N07 122w07 8:08:28
Big Bear 36 34N12 116w58 7:47:52
Big Bear City 36 34N16 116w51 7:47:24
Big Bear Highlands 36 34N15 116w53 7:47:32
Big Bear Lake 36 34N15 116w53 7:47:32
Big Bear Pines 36 34N15 116w53 7:47:32
Big Bear Pinewoods 36 34N15 116w53 7:47:32
Big Bend 45 41N01 121w55 8:07:40
Big Chief 31 39N20 120w12 8:00:48
Big Creek 10 37N12 119w09 7:56:36
Big Flat 47 41N00 122w41 8:10:44
Biggs 4 39N25 121w43 8:06:52
Big Lagoon Park 12 41N04 124w08 8:16:32
Big Meadows 5 38N15 120w21 8:01:24
Big Oak Flat 55 37N49 120w16 8:01:04
Big Pine 14 37N10 118w17 7:53:08
Big Pine Indian Reservation 14 38N33 121w28 8:05:52
Big Springs 47 41N44 122w31 8:10:04
Big Sur 27 36N15 121w48 8:07:12
Big Trees 44 37N03 122w04 8:08:16
Big Valley 18 41N04 121w07 8:04:28
Bijou 9 38N56 119w59 7:59:56
Binghamton 48 38N27 121w50 8:07:20
Biola 10 36N48 120w01 8:00:04
Birch Hill 37 33N20 116w55 7:47:40
Birds Landing 48 38N08 121w52 8:07:28
Bishop 14 37N22 118w24 7:53:36
Bishop Acres 15 35N30 119w16 7:57:04
Bishop Creek 14 37N22 118w24 7:53:36
Bishop Indian Reservation 14 38N36 121w23 8:05:32
Bitterwater 35 36N13 121w07 8:04:28
Bixby 19 33N50 118w11 7:52:44
Black Meadow Landing 36 34N17 114w09 7:36:36
Black Point 21 38N07 122w30 8:10:00
Blairsden 32 39N47 120w37 8:02:28
Blocksburg 12 40N17 123w38 8:14:32
Bloomfield 49 38N13 122w38 8:10:32
Bloomfield Acres 12 40N52 124w05 8:16:20
Bloomington 36 34N04 117w24 7:49:36
Blossom Hill 43 37N15 121w51 8:07:24
Blossom Valley 43 37N23 122w05 8:08:20
Blue Canyon 31 39N16 120w43 8:02:52
Blue Hills 43 37N17 122w01 8:08:04
Blue Jay 36 34N15 117w13 7:48:52
Blue Lake 12 40N53 123w59 8:15:56
Bluff Creek 12 41N03 123w40 8:14:40
Bly 33 34N00 117w26 7:49:44
Blythe 33 33N37 114w36 7:38:24
Bodega 49 38N21 122w58 8:11:52
Bodega Bay 49 38N20 123w03 8:12:12
Bodfish 15 35N36 118w30 7:54:00
Bolinas 21 37N54 122w42 8:10:48
Bolsa 30 33N45 117w59 7:51:56
Bolsa Knolls 27 36N41 121w39 8:06:36
Bombay Beach 13 33N14 115w31 7:42:04
Bonds Corner 13 32N49 115w23 7:41:32
Bonita 37 32N40 117w02 7:48:08
Bonnie Bell 33 33N56 116w38 7:46:32
Bonny Doon 44 36N59 122w00 8:08:00
Bonnyview 45 40N32 122w23 8:09:32
Bonsall 37 33N16 117w14 7:48:56
Boonville 23 39N01 123w22 8:13:28
Border City 19 34N30 117w50 7:51:20
Boron 15 35N00 117w39 7:50:36
Borosolvay 36 35N46 117w23 7:49:32
Borrego 37 33N15 116w23 7:45:32
Bostonia 37 32N48 116w57 7:47:48
Boston Ravine 29 39N13 121w04 8:04:16
Boulder Creek 44 37N07 122w07 8:08:28
Boulder Oaks 37 32N49 116w32 7:46:08
Boulder Park 13 32N37 116w11 7:44:44
Boulevard 37 32N40 116w16 7:45:04
Bowling Green 34 38N36 121w26 8:05:44
Bowman 31 38N54 121w04 8:04:16
Box Springs 33 33N59 117w21 7:49:24
Boyes Hot Springs 49 38N19 122w29 8:09:56
Boyle 19 34N04 118w13 7:52:52
Boys Republic 36 34N01 117w41 7:50:44
Brackney 44 37N05 122w05 8:08:20
Bradbury 19 34N09 117w58 7:51:52
Bradford 1 37N40 122w05 8:08:20
Bradley 27 35N52 120w48 8:03:12
Brandeis 56 34N21 119w04 7:56:16
Branscomb 23 39N39 123w37 8:14:28
Brawley 13 32N59 115w31 7:42:04
Bray 47 41N39 121w58 8:07:52
Brea 30 33N55 117w54 7:51:36
Brentwood 7 37N56 121w42 8:06:48
Briceland 12 40N07 123w54 8:15:36
Bridgehead 7 38N01 121w50 8:07:20
Bridge House 34 38N30 121w12 8:04:48
Bridgeport 22 37N29 119w58 7:59:52
Bridgeport 26 38N15 119w14 7:56:56
Bridgeville 12 40N28 123w48 8:15:12
Briggs 19 34N04 118w22 7:53:28
Briones 7 37N59 122w12 8:08:48
Brisbane 41 37N41 122w24 8:09:36
Bristol 30 33N45 117w55 7:51:40
Broadmoor 41 37N41 122w29 8:09:56
Broadway 34 38N33 121w29 8:05:56
Broadway 41 37N35 122w22 8:09:28
Brockway 31 39N14 120w01 8:00:04
Broderick 57 38N36 121w32 8:06:08
Brookdale 44 37N06 122w06 8:08:24
Brookhurst Center 30 33N49 117w59 7:51:56
Brooks 57 38N45 122w09 8:08:36
Brookside Park 41 37N27 122w11 8:08:44
Browns Flat 55 37N59 120w23 8:01:32
Browns Valley 58 39N15 121w25 8:05:40
Brownsville 58 39N28 121w16 8:05:04
Bryant 19 33N52 118w10 7:52:40
Bryn Mawr 36 34N03 117w14 7:48:56
Bryson 27 35N52 120w48 8:03:12
Bryte 57 38N36 121w32 8:06:08
Buckeye 45 40N33 122w22 8:09:28
Buckhorn 56 34N24 118w55 7:55:40
Buckingham Park 17 38N59 122w50 8:11:20
Buck Meadows 22 37N50 120w14 8:00:56
Bucks Bar 9 38N44 120w48 8:03:12
Bucks Lake 32 39N56 120w55 8:03:40
Buellton 42 34N37 120w12 8:00:48
Buena 37 33N11 117w15 7:49:00
Buena Park 30 33N52 118w00 7:52:00
Buena Vista 3 38N22 120w56 8:03:44
Buena Vista 49 38N17 122w28 8:09:52
Buhach 24 37N18 120w29 8:01:56
Bullard 10 36N49 119w49 7:59:16
Bullock's Fashion Square 19 34N09 118w26 7:53:44
Bummerville 5 38N24 120w32 8:02:08
Burbank 19 34N11 118w19 7:53:16
Burbank 43 37N19 121w56 8:07:44
Burke 19 33N59 118w05 7:52:20
Burkett Acres 39 37N58 121w15 8:05:00
Burkett Gardens 39 37N58 121w15 8:05:00
Burlingame 41 37N35 122w21 8:09:24
Burlingame Hills 41 37N35 122w22 8:09:28
Burney 45 40N53 121w40 8:06:40
Burnt Ranch 53 40N49 123w29 8:13:56
Burrel 10 36N29 119w59 7:59:56
Burrough 10 37N01 119w24 7:57:36
Burson 5 38N11 120w54 8:03:36
Butte City 11 39N28 121w59 8:07:56
Butte Creek 4 39N44 121w50 8:07:20
Butte Meadows 4 39N53 121w40 8:06:40
Butte Valley 47 41N50 121w58 8:07:52
Buttonwillow 15 35N24 119w28 7:57:52
Byron 7 37N52 121w38 8:06:32
Cabazon 33 33N55 116w47 7:47:08
Cabrillo 19 33N50 118w14 7:52:56
Cabrillo Estates 40 35N18 120w45 8:03:00
Cache Creek 15 35N08 117w59 7:51:56
Cachuma Village 42 34N25 119w42 7:58:48
Cadiz 36 34N31 115w31 7:42:04
Cahuilla 33 33N33 116w43 7:46:52
Cahuilla Estates 33 33N33 116w43 7:46:52
Cahuilla Hills 33 33N43 116w19 7:45:16
Cahuilla Indian Reservation 33 33N49 116w32 7:46:08
Cairns Corner 54 36N12 119w05 7:56:20
Cajon Junction 36 34N19 117w28 7:49:52
Calabasas 19 34N06 118w42 7:54:48
Calabasas Highlands 19 34N08 118w39 7:54:36
Calabasas Park 19 34N08 118w39 7:54:36
Calaveras 39 38N00 121w20 8:05:20
Calaveras Yacht and Country 39 37N58 121w19 8:05:16
Calaveritas 5 38N12 120w41 8:02:44
Calavo Gardens 37 32N46 116w58 7:47:52
Caldors Corner 15 35N21 118w59 7:55:56
Calexico 13 32N40 115w30 7:42:00
Calico 36 34N54 116w50 7:47:20
Caliente 15 35N17 118w38 7:54:32
California City 15 35N12 117w47 7:51:08
California Hot Springs 54 35N53 118w41 7:54:44
California Rehabilitation Ce 33 33N53 117w33 7:50:12
California Valley 40 35N23 120w37 8:02:28
Calimesa 33 34N00 117w04 7:48:16
Calipatria 13 33N08 115w31 7:42:04
Calistoga 28 38N35 122w35 8:10:20
Calla 39 37N48 121w11 8:04:44
Callahan 47 41N18 122w48 8:11:12
Calpack 24 37N18 120w29 8:01:56
Calpella 23 39N14 123w12 8:12:48
Calpine 46 39N40 120w27 8:01:48
Calville 12 40N52 124w05 8:16:20
Calwa 10 36N42 119w46 7:59:04
Camarillo 56 34N13 119w02 7:56:08
Camarillo Heights 56 34N15 119w03 7:56:12
Cambria 40 35N34 121w05 8:04:20
Cambrian Park 43 37N15 121w56 8:07:44
Cambrian Park Plaza 43 37N15 121w56 8:07:44
Cambria Pines 40 35N33 121w05 8:04:20
Cambria Pines Manor 40 35N33 121w05 8:04:20
Camden 10 36N26 119w48 7:59:12
Camellia Station 34 38N34 121w26 8:05:44
Cameo Acres 7 37N50 122w00 8:08:00
Cameron Corners 37 32N37 116w28 7:45:52
Cameron Creek Colony 54 36N20 119w18 7:57:12
Cameron Park 9 38N40 120w56 8:03:44
Camino 9 38N44 120w41 8:02:44
Camino Heights 9 38N44 120w41 8:02:44
Campbell 43 37N17 121w57 8:07:48
Camp Connell 5 38N15 120w21 8:01:24
Camp Kaweah 54 36N34 118w46 7:55:04
Camp Meeker 49 38N26 122w57 8:11:48
Camp Nelson 54 36N08 118w37 7:54:28
Campo 37 32N37 116w28 7:45:52
Campo Indian Reservation 37 33N49 116w32 7:46:08
Campo Seco 5 38N14 120w51 8:03:24
Camp Pendleton 37 33N19 117w18 7:49:12
Camp Richardson 9 38N56 119w59 7:59:56
Camp Sabrina 14 37N22 118w24 7:53:36
Camp Sierra 10 37N09 119w18 7:57:12
Campton Heights 12 40N35 124w08 8:16:32
Camptonville 58 39N27 121w03 8:04:12
Camp Wishon 54 36N08 118w49 7:55:16
Camulos 56 34N25 118w48 7:55:12
Canby 25 41N27 120w52 8:03:28
Canoga Annex 19 34N12 118w37 7:54:28
Canoga Park 19 34N12 118w35 7:54:20
Cantil 15 35N18 117w58 7:51:52
Cantua Creek 10 36N30 120w19 8:01:16
Canyon 7 37N50 122w11 8:08:44
Canyon City 37 32N37 116w28 7:45:52
Canyon Country 19 34N25 118w32 7:54:08
Canyon Crest 33 33N59 117w21 7:49:24
Canyondam 32 40N10 121w04 8:04:16
Canyon Lake 33 33N45 117w10 7:48:40
Capay 57 38N32 122w03 8:08:12
Capetown 12 40N35 124w16 8:17:04
Capistrano Beach 30 33N28 117w40 7:50:40
Capistrano Highlands 30 33N34 117w45 7:51:00
Capital Hill 40 35N38 120w41 8:02:44
Capitola 44 36N58 121w58 8:07:52
Carbona 39 37N43 121w26 8:05:44
Carbon Canyon 36 34N01 117w41 7:50:44
Cardiff 37 33N02 117w16 7:49:04
Cardiff By The Sea 37 33N02 117w16 7:49:04
Cardwell 10 36N46 119w47 7:59:08
Caribou 32 39N30 121w33 8:06:12
Carlotta 12 40N32 124w03 8:16:12
Carlsbad 37 33N10 117w21 7:49:24
Carmel 27 36N32 121w53 8:07:32
Carmel By The Sea 27 36N33 121w55 8:07:40
Carmel Highlands 27 36N33 121w53 8:07:32
Carmel Hills 27 36N33 121w53 8:07:32
Carmel Point 27 36N33 121w53 8:07:32
Carmel Valley 27 36N29 121w43 8:06:52
Carmel Valley Village 27 36N29 121w44 8:06:56
Carmel Woods 27 36N33 121w53 8:07:32
Carmenita 19 33N56 118w04 7:52:16
Carmet 49 38N20 123w03 8:12:12
Carmichael 34 38N38 121w19 8:05:16
Carnelian Bay 31 39N14 120w05 8:00:20
Carpinteria 42 34N24 119w31 7:58:04
Carpinteria Valley 42 34N25 119w33 7:58:12
Carquinez Heights 48 38N07 122w14 8:08:56
Carrick Addition 47 41N26 122w23 8:09:32
Carson 19 33N48 118w17 7:53:08
Carson Hill 5 38N04 120w33 8:02:12
Cartago 14 36N19 118w02 7:52:08
Caruthers 10 36N32 119w50 7:59:20
Carwood 19 33N51 118w09 7:52:36
Casa Conejo 56 34N11 118w55 7:55:40
Casa Correo 7 37N58 121w59 8:07:56
Casa de Oro 37 32N45 116w58 7:47:52
Casa Loma 31 39N13 120w47 8:03:08
Casitas Springs 56 34N22 119w19 7:57:16
Casmalia 42 34N50 120w32 8:02:08
Caspar 23 39N22 123w49 8:15:16
Cassel 45 40N55 121w33 8:06:12
Castaic 19 34N30 118w37 7:54:28
Castella 45 41N09 122w19 8:09:16

Place	Lat.	Long.	Time
Castellammare 19	34N05	118w30	7:54:00
Castle 24	37N23	120w34	8:02:16
Castle Air Force Base 24	37N23	120w34	8:02:16
Castle Garden 24	37N23	120w34	8:02:16
Castle Park 37	32N37	117w04	7:48:16
Castlewood 1	37N42	121w54	8:07:36
Castro Valley 1	37N42	122w04	8:08:16
Castroville 27	36N46	121w45	8:07:00
Catalina 19	34N09	118w07	7:52:28
Cathedral City 33	33N47	116w28	7:45:52
Catheys Valley 22	37N26	120w06	8:00:24
Cawelo 15	35N24	119w02	7:56:08
Cayton 45	40N53	121w40	8:06:40
Cayucos 40	35N27	120w54	8:03:36
Cazadero 49	38N32	123w05	8:12:20
Cecilville 47	41N09	123w08	8:12:32
Cedar 19	37N12	119w09	7:56:36
Cedarbrook 10	36N42	119w03	7:56:12
Cedar Crest 10	37N12	119w09	7:56:36
Cedar Flat 31	39N14	120w05	8:00:20
Cedar Glen 36	34N15	117w10	7:48:40
Cedar Grove 9	38N44	120w41	8:02:44
Cedar Grove 10	36N44	118w58	7:55:52
Cedarpines Park 36	34N15	117w20	7:49:20
Cedar Ridge 29	39N12	121w01	8:04:04
Cedar Ridge 55	37N59	120w23	8:01:32
Cedar Slope 54	36N08	118w49	7:55:16
Cedarville 25	41N32	120w10	8:00:40
Cedarville Indian Res 25	38N36	121w23	8:05:32
Centerville 10	36N44	119w30	7:58:00
Central Coast 30	33N39	117w51	7:51:24
Central Colusa 6	39N08	122w06	8:08:24
Central District 19	34N03	117w47	7:51:08
Central Shasta 45	40N37	122w00	8:08:00
Central Valley 45	40N41	122w22	8:09:28
Centre 34	38N35	121w25	8:05:40
Century City 19	34N03	118w25	7:53:40
Ceres 50	37N35	120w57	8:03:48
Cerritos 19	33N52	118w05	7:52:20
Chalfant 26	37N22	118w24	7:53:36
Challenge 58	39N29	121w13	8:04:52
Chambers Lodge 31	39N05	120w10	8:00:40
Chambless 36	34N33	115w32	7:42:08
Champagne Fountain 43	37N17	122w01	8:08:04
Chapmantown 4	39N44	121w50	8:07:20
Chapman Woods 19	34N09	118w05	7:52:20
Chappo 37	33N15	117w18	7:49:12
Charter Oak 19	34N06	117w53	7:51:32
Chatsworth 19	34N15	118w36	7:54:24
Chatsworth Lake Manor 19	34N15	118w35	7:54:20
Chawanakee 10	37N05	119w29	7:57:56
Chemeketa Park 43	37N15	121w58	8:07:52
Cherokee 4	39N30	121w33	8:06:12
Cherokee 29	39N16	121w01	8:04:04
Cherokee Strip 15	35N30	119w16	7:57:04
Cherry Creek Acres 29	38N54	121w04	8:04:16
Cherryland 1	37N42	122w06	8:08:24
Cherry Valley 33	33N58	116w58	7:47:52
Chester 32	40N19	121w14	8:04:56
Chestnut 41	37N39	122w26	8:09:44
Chicago Park 29	39N09	120w58	8:03:52
Chico 4	39N44	121w50	8:07:20
Chico Vecino 4	39N44	121w50	8:07:20
Chilcoot 32	39N48	120w08	8:00:32
Childrens Fairyland 1	37N49	122w14	8:08:56
Childs Meadows 52	40N19	121w32	8:06:08
China 38	37N47	122w26	8:09:44
China Lake 15	35N39	117w39	7:50:36
Chinese Camp 55	37N52	120w26	8:01:44
Chino 36	34N01	117w41	7:50:44
Chinowths Corner 54	36N20	119w18	7:57:12
Chiriaco Summit 33	33N44	116w21	7:45:24
Chittenden 44	36N51	121w32	8:06:08
Cholame 40	35N44	120w18	8:01:12
Chowchilla 20	37N07	120w16	8:01:04
Chrome 11	39N45	122w11	8:08:44
Chualar 27	36N34	121w31	8:06:04
Chuckwalla 33	33N42	115w11	7:40:44
Chula Vista 37	32N38	117w05	7:48:20
Church of God Colony 10	36N37	119w31	7:58:04
Cima 36	35N14	115w30	7:42:00
Cisco 31	39N19	120w16	8:01:04
Citrus Heights 34	38N42	121w17	8:05:08
City Hall 38	37N47	122w26	8:09:44
City of Commerce 19	34N01	118w09	7:52:36
City of Industry 19	34N02	117w56	7:51:44
City Terrace 19	34N03	118w11	7:52:44
Civic Center 19	34N11	118w27	7:53:48
Civic Center 21	38N01	122w33	8:10:12
Civic Center 30	33N45	117w51	7:51:24
Civic Center Annex 1	37N48	122w13	8:08:52
Clairemont 37	32N50	117w11	7:48:44
Clam Beach 12	40N52	124w05	8:16:20
Claremont 19	34N06	117w43	7:50:52
Clarksburg 57	38N25	121w32	8:06:08
Clarksville 9	38N40	120w56	8:03:44
Clay 34	38N18	121w14	8:04:56
Clayton 7	37N56	121w56	8:07:44
Clear Creek 18	40N18	121w01	8:04:04
Clear Creek 47	41N43	123w27	8:13:48
Clearlake Highlands 17	38N57	122w38	8:10:32
Clearlake Oaks 17	39N01	122w41	8:10:44
Clearlake Park 17	38N58	122w39	8:10:36
Clements 39	38N11	121w05	8:04:20
Cleone 23	39N27	123w48	8:15:12
Clifton 19	33N49	118w23	7:53:32
Clinter 10	36N46	119w45	7:59:00
Clinton 3	38N21	120w46	8:03:04
Clio 32	39N50	120w35	8:02:20
Clippergap 31	38N54	121w04	8:04:16
Clipper Mills 4	39N32	121w09	8:04:36
Cloverdale 45	40N27	122w18	8:09:12
Cloverdale 49	38N48	123w01	8:12:04
Clovis 10	36N49	119w42	7:58:48
Clyde 7	38N02	122w02	8:08:08
Coachella 33	33N41	116w10	7:44:40
Coachella Valley 33	33N39	116w11	7:44:44
Coalinga 10	36N09	120w21	8:01:24
Coarsegold 20	37N16	119w42	7:58:48
Coastal 27	36N15	121w44	8:06:56
Cobb 17	38N49	122w43	8:10:52
Coddingtown 49	38N27	122w42	8:10:48
Codora 11	39N24	122w01	8:08:04
Coffee 53	41N00	122w41	8:10:44
Cohasset 4	39N44	121w50	8:07:20
Cole 19	34N06	118w22	7:53:28
Coleville 26	38N34	119w30	7:58:00
Colfax 31	39N06	120w57	8:03:48
College Center 15	35N23	118w59	7:55:56
College City 6	39N00	122w00	8:08:00
College Grove Center 37	32N45	117w04	7:48:16
College Heights 36	34N06	117w41	7:50:44
College Heights 44	36N59	121w54	8:07:36
College Park 56	34N12	118w53	7:55:32
Collegeville 39	37N56	121w16	8:05:04
Collier 19	34N12	118w37	7:54:28
Collierville 39	38N10	121w13	8:04:52
Collinsville 48	38N14	122w02	8:08:08
Colma 41	37N41	122w28	8:09:52
Coloma 9	38N48	120w53	8:03:32
Colonial 34	38N32	121w27	8:05:48
Colonial Juarez 30	33N44	117w57	7:51:48
Colton 36	34N04	117w20	7:49:20
Columbia 55	38N02	120w24	8:01:36
Colusa 6	39N13	122w01	8:08:04
Commerce 19	34N00	118w09	7:52:36
Commonwealth 30	33N53	117w56	7:51:44
Community Center 56	34N17	118w45	7:55:00
Comptche 23	39N16	123w35	8:14:20
Compton 19	33N54	118w13	7:52:52
Concepcion 42	34N42	120w29	8:01:56
Concord 7	37N59	122w02	8:08:08
Concord Naval Weapons Statio 7	37N58	122w01	8:08:04
Conejo 10	36N31	119w43	7:58:52
Conejo Village 56	34N12	118w53	7:55:32
Confidence 55	37N59	120w23	8:01:32
Convict Lake 26	37N22	118w24	7:53:36
Cool 9	38N53	121w01	8:04:04
Coopers Corner 39	38N10	121w13	8:04:52
Copco 47	41N55	122w33	8:10:12
Copperopolis 5	37N59	120w38	8:02:32
Corcoran 16	36N06	119w33	7:58:12
Cordelia 48	38N14	122w02	8:08:08
Cordova Town West 34	38N35	121w20	8:05:20
Cornell 19	34N07	118w47	7:55:08
Corning 52	39N54	122w10	8:08:40
Corona 33	33N53	117w34	7:50:16
Corona del Mar 30	33N36	117w52	7:51:28
Coronado 37	32N41	117w11	7:48:44
Coronita 33	33N53	117w33	7:50:12
Corralitos 44	36N59	121w48	8:07:12
Corte Madera 21	37N55	122w32	8:10:08
Coso Junction 14	35N56	117w54	7:51:36
Costa Mesa 30	33N38	117w55	7:51:40
Cotati 49	38N20	122w42	8:10:48
Cotners Corners 36	34N31	117w12	7:48:48
Cottage Corners 35	36N51	121w24	8:05:36
Cotton Center 54	36N04	119w04	7:56:16
Cottonwood 45	40N23	122w17	8:09:08
Coulterville 22	37N43	120w12	8:00:48
Country Club Estates 40	35N18	120w45	8:03:00
Country Modern 15	35N08	117w59	7:51:56
County Strip 19	34N06	118w23	7:53:32
Court 7	37N59	122w07	8:08:28
Courtland 34	38N20	121w34	8:06:16
Covelo 23	39N48	123w15	8:13:00
Covina 19	34N05	117w52	7:51:28
Covington Mill 53	40N43	122w48	8:11:12
Cowan Heights 30	33N47	117w46	7:51:04
Cowell 7	37N57	122w00	8:08:00
Coyote 43	37N13	121w44	8:06:56
Craf 36	34N05	117w08	7:48:32
Crafton 36	34N05	117w08	7:48:32
Crannell	41N01	124w05	8:16:20
Crenshaw 19	33N59	118w22	7:53:28
Crescent 19	34N06	118w23	7:53:32
Crescent City 8	41N45	124w12	8:16:48
Crescent Mills 32	40N06	120w55	8:03:40
Cressey 24	37N25	120w40	8:02:40
Crest 37	32N48	116w57	7:47:48
Crest Forest 36	34N14	117w17	7:49:08
Crestline 36	34N14	117w18	7:49:12
Crestmore 36	34N05	117w25	7:49:40
Crestmore Heights 33	34N00	117w26	7:49:44
Creston 40	35N31	120w31	8:02:04
Crest Park 36	34N15	117w10	7:48:40
Crestview 26	37N22	118w24	7:53:36
Crockett 7	38N03	122w13	8:08:52
Cromberg 32	39N47	120w37	8:02:28
Cross Roads 36	34N10	114w18	7:37:12
Crowley 54	36N20	119w18	7:57:12
Crowley Lake 26	37N22	118w24	7:53:36
Crows Landing 50	37N24	121w04	8:04:16
Crutcher 19	33N54	118w10	7:52:40
Crystal Cove 30	33N32	117w47	7:51:08
Cucamonga 36	34N06	117w36	7:50:24
Cudahy 19	33N58	118w11	7:52:44
Cuesta-by-the-Sea 40	35N18	120w45	8:03:00
Culver City 19	34N01	118w25	7:53:40
Cummings 23	38N17	122w28	8:09:52
Cunningham 49	38N24	122w50	8:11:20
Cupertino 43	37N19	122w02	8:08:08
Curry Village 22	37N45	119w35	7:58:20
Curtiss Heights 12	40N52	124w05	8:16:20
Cutler 54	36N31	119w17	7:57:08
Cutten 12	40N46	124w09	8:16:36
Cuyama 42	34N54	119w41	7:58:44
Cypress 30	33N50	118w02	7:52:08
Cypress Grove 21	38N10	122w53	8:11:32
Daggett 36	34N52	116w53	7:47:32
Dairyville 52	40N11	122w16	8:09:04
Dales 52	40N11	122w16	8:09:04
Dalewood	33N47	117w59	7:51:56
Daly City 41	37N42	122w28	8:09:52
Dana 45	41N04	121w29	8:05:56
Dana Point 30	33N28	117w42	7:50:48
Danby 36	34N44	115w15	7:41:00
Danville 7	37N49	122w00	8:08:00
Dardanelle 55	38N20	119w50	7:59:20
Darrah 22	37N29	119w58	7:59:52
Darwin 14	36N16	117w36	7:50:24
Date City 13	32N49	115w23	7:41:32
Daulton 20	36N58	120w04	8:00:16
Davenport 44	37N01	122w12	8:08:48
Davis 57	38N33	121w44	8:06:56
Davis Creek 25	41N44	120w22	8:01:28
Day 25	41N03	121w24	8:05:36
Dayton 4	39N44	121w50	8:07:20
Daywalt 49	38N24	122w50	8:11:20
Deane Brothers Subdivision 19	34N25	118w32	7:54:08
Dearborn Park 41	37N15	122w23	8:09:32
Death Valley 14	36N27	116w52	7:47:28
Debon 47	41N26	122w23	8:09:32
Decoto 1	37N36	122w01	8:08:04
Deep Springs 14	37N22	117w59	7:51:56
Deer Creek 52	40N19	121w32	8:06:08
Deer Lick Springs 53	40N22	122w53	8:11:32
Deer Park 28	38N32	122w28	8:09:52
Del Aire 19	33N55	118w22	7:53:28
Delano 15	35N46	119w15	7:57:00
Del Cerro 37	32N47	117w04	7:48:16
Del Dios 37	33N04	117w07	7:48:28
Delevan 6	39N22	122w11	8:08:44
Delft Colony 54	36N32	119w23	7:57:32
Delhi 24	37N26	120w46	8:03:04
Delkern 15	35N21	119w03	7:56:12
Del Loma 53	40N45	123w15	8:13:00
Del Mar 37	32N58	117w16	7:49:04
Del Mar 44	36N59	122w00	8:08:00
Del Mar Heights 40	35N22	120w51	8:03:24
Del Mar Race Track 37	32N59	117w16	7:49:04
Del Mesa 21	37N58	122w31	8:10:04
Del Monte Center 27	36N36	121w53	8:07:32
Del Monte Forest 27	36N35	121w56	8:07:44
Del Monte Heights 27	36N37	121w50	8:07:20
Del Monte Park 27	36N37	121w56	8:07:44
Del Paso Heights 34	38N38	121w26	8:05:44
Del Rey 10	36N40	119w36	7:58:24
Del Rey Oaks 27	36N36	121w50	8:07:20
Del Rio Woods 49	38N37	122w52	8:11:28
Del Rosa 36	34N09	117w15	7:49:00
Del Sur 19	34N40	118w11	7:52:44
Delta 39	38N13	121w33	8:06:12
De Luz 37	33N15	117w18	7:49:12
Del Valle 19	34N02	118w18	7:53:12
Democrat Hot Springs 15	35N23	119w01	7:56:04
Denair 50	37N32	120w48	8:03:12
Denny 53	41N05	123w16	8:13:04
Denverton 48	38N14	122w02	8:08:08
Derby Acres 15	35N11	119w32	7:58:08
Descanso 37	32N51	116w37	7:46:28
Desert 36	35N28	115w16	7:41:04
Desert Beach 33	33N34	116w05	7:44:20
Desert Center 33	33N43	115w24	7:41:36
Desert Hot Springs 33	33N58	116w30	7:46:00
Desert Lake 15	35N00	117w39	7:50:36
Desert Shores 13	33N39	116w09	7:44:36
Desert View Highlands 19	34N36	118w09	7:52:36
Des Moines 30	33N56	117w56	7:51:44
Devils Den 15	35N46	119w58	7:59:52
Devore 36	34N13	117w24	7:49:36
Devore Heights 36	34N10	117w17	7:49:08
Diablo 7	37N50	121w59	8:07:56
Diablo Range 43	37N05	121w25	8:05:40
Diamond 30	33N44	117w54	7:51:36
Diamond Bar 19	33N59	117w50	7:51:20
Diamond Heights 38	37N45	122w26	8:09:44
Diamond Springs 9	38N42	120w49	8:03:16
Diamond Springs Heights 9	38N42	120w49	8:03:16
Di Giorgio 15	35N15	118w51	7:55:24
Dillon Beach 21	38N15	122w58	8:11:52
Dimond 1	37N48	122w13	8:08:52
Dinkey Creek 10	37N09	119w18	7:57:12
Dinsmore 12	40N28	123w48	8:15:12
Dinuba 54	36N32	119w23	7:57:32
Dixon 48	38N27	121w49	8:07:16

CALIFORNIA

Dobbins 58	39N22	121w12	8:04:48
Dockweiler 19	34N02	118w19	7:53:16
Doheny Park 30	33N28	117w40	7:50:40
Dollar Ranch 7	37N53	122w03	8:08:12
Dominguez 19	33N50	118w13	7:52:52
Donlon 56	34N12	119w10	7:56:40
Donner 29	39N22	120w18	8:01:12
Donner Lake 29	39N20	120w12	8:00:48
Don Pedro Camp 55	37N40	120w28	8:01:52
Dorrington 5	38N15	120w21	8:01:24
Dorris 47	41N58	121w55	8:07:40
Dos Palos 24	36N59	120w37	8:02:28
Dos Rios 23	39N43	123w21	8:13:24
Douglas 19	34N01	118w28	7:53:52
Douglas City 53	40N39	122w57	8:11:48
Douglasflat 5	38N07	120w27	8:01:48
Downey 19	33N56	118w08	7:52:32
Downieville 46	39N34	120w50	8:03:20
Doyle 18	40N02	120w06	8:00:24
Drakesbad 32	40N18	121w14	8:04:56
Drytown 3	38N48	121w53	8:07:32
Duarte 19	34N08	117w58	7:51:52
Dublin 1	37N42	121w56	8:07:44
Ducor 54	35N54	119w03	7:56:12
Dulzura 37	32N39	116w47	7:47:08
Duncans Mills 49	38N27	123w03	8:12:12
Dunlap 10	36N44	119w07	7:56:28
Dunlap Acres 36	34N02	117w07	7:48:28
Dunmovin 14	35N56	117w54	7:51:36
Dunneville Corners 35	36N51	121w24	8:05:36
Dunnigan 57	38N53	121w58	8:07:52
Dunsmuir 47	41N13	122w16	8:09:04
Durham 4	39N39	121w48	8:07:12
Dustin Acres 15	35N09	119w28	7:57:52
Dutch Flat 31	39N12	120w51	8:03:24
Dutch Village 19	33N51	118w09	7:52:36
Eagle Lake Resort 18	40N25	120w39	8:02:36
Eagle Mountain 33	33N51	115w29	7:41:56
Eagle Rock 19	34N08	118w12	7:52:48
Eagle Tree 39	38N15	121w31	8:06:04
Eagleville 25	41N19	120w07	8:00:28
Earlimart 54	35N53	119w16	7:57:04
Earp 36	34N10	114w18	7:37:12
East Acres 20	36N51	120w27	8:01:48
East Applegate 31	39N06	120w59	8:03:56
East Blythe 33	33N37	114w34	7:38:16
East Colusa 6	39N14	121w59	8:07:56
East Compton 19	33N54	118w12	7:52:48
East Farmersville 54	36N18	119w12	7:56:48
East Firebaugh 20	36N58	120w04	8:00:16
East Fresno 10	36N46	119w43	7:58:52
East Garrison 27	36N37	121w50	8:07:20
Eastgate 19	34N04	118w23	7:53:32
East Gate 33	33N56	117w14	7:48:56
East Gridley 4	39N22	121w42	8:06:48
East Guernewood 49	38N30	123w00	8:12:00
East Highlands 36	34N07	117w10	7:48:40
East Hopland 23	38N58	123w07	8:12:28
East Imperial 13	32N55	114w49	7:39:16
East Irvine 30	33N41	117w46	7:51:04
East Kern 15	35N13	117w56	7:51:44
East La Mirada 19	33N55	117w59	7:51:56
Eastland 19	34N04	117w56	7:51:44
East Long Beach 19	33N47	118w09	7:52:36
East Los Angeles 19	34N01	118w09	7:52:36
East Lynwood 19	33N55	118w12	7:52:48
East Modesto 50	37N38	120w59	8:03:56
Eastmont 1	37N46	122w11	8:08:44
East Nicolaus 51	38N55	121w33	8:06:12
Easton 10	36N39	119w47	7:59:08
East Orosi 54	36N32	119w17	7:57:08
East Palo Alto 43	37N28	122w08	8:08:32
East Pasadena 19	34N09	118w05	7:52:20
East Porterville 54	36N03	118w59	7:55:56
East Quincy 32	39N56	120w55	8:03:40
East Richmond 7	37N57	122w19	8:09:16
East San Diego 37	32N44	117w05	7:48:20
East San Gabriel Valley 19	34N06	117w53	7:51:32
East Santa Cruz 44	36N59	122w00	8:08:00
East Shasta 45	41N00	121w30	8:06:00
Eastside Acres 20	36N51	120w27	8:01:48
Eastside Ranch 20	36N51	120w27	8:01:48
East Sierra 46	39N36	120w12	8:00:48
East Stockton 39	37N58	121w15	8:05:00
East Tehama 52	40N21	121w49	8:07:16
East Tulare 54	36N13	119w20	7:57:20
East Tustin 30	33N45	117w49	7:51:16
East Vallejo 48	38N07	122w14	8:08:56
East Ventura 56	34N16	119w13	7:56:52
East View 19	33N45	118w19	7:53:16
Eastwood Village 19	34N02	117w56	7:51:44
East Yolo 57	38N33	121w33	8:06:12
Echo Lake 9	38N49	120w03	8:00:12
Echo Park 19	34N05	118w16	7:53:04
Edendale 19	34N05	118w16	7:53:04
Eden Gardens 37	32N59	117w16	7:49:04
Edgemar 41	37N38	122w29	8:09:56
Edgemont 18	40N18	120w32	8:02:08
Edgemont 33	33N56	117w17	7:49:08
Edgemont Acres 15	34N56	117w57	7:51:48
Edgewood 47	41N26	122w23	8:09:32
Edison 15	35N21	118w52	7:55:28
Edmundson Acres 15	35N12	118w50	7:55:20
Edwards 15	34N56	117w57	7:51:48
Edwards Air Force Base 15	34N54	117w52	7:51:28
Edwards Estates 15	34N56	117w57	7:51:48
Edwards Palisades 15	34N56	117w57	7:51:48
Eel Rock 12	40N16	123w53	8:15:32
Eight Mile House 9	38N44	120w41	8:02:44
El Bonita 49	38N30	123w00	8:12:00
El Cajon 37	32N48	116w57	7:47:48
El Camino 52	40N03	122w09	8:08:36
El Centro 13	32N48	115w34	7:42:16
El Cerrito 7	37N55	122w19	8:09:16
El Cerrito 33	33N53	117w33	7:50:12
Elders Corner 31	38N54	121w04	8:04:16
Elderwood 54	36N28	119w08	7:56:32
El Dorado 9	38N41	120w51	8:03:24
El Dorado Hills 9	38N41	121w11	8:04:44
Eldridge 49	38N21	122w31	8:10:04
El Encanto Heights 42	34N26	119w53	7:59:32
El Granada 41	37N30	122w28	8:09:52
Elizabeth Lake 19	34N40	118w21	7:53:24
Elk 23	39N08	123w43	8:14:52
Elk Creek 11	39N36	122w32	8:10:08
Elk Grove 34	38N25	121w22	8:05:28
Elkhorn Village 57	38N36	121w32	8:06:08
Elk River 12	40N47	124w10	8:16:40
El Macero 57	38N37	121w43	8:06:52
Elmhurst 1	37N44	122w10	8:08:40
Elmira 48	38N21	121w55	8:07:40
El Mirage 36	34N35	117w25	7:49:40
El Modena 30	33N49	117w50	7:51:20
El Monte 7	37N58	121w59	8:07:56
El Monte 19	34N04	118w02	7:52:08
Elm View 10	36N32	119w50	7:59:20
Elmwood 1	37N52	122w15	8:09:00
El Nido 24	37N08	120w29	8:01:56
El Paso De Robles 40	35N38	120w41	8:02:44
El Portal 22	37N41	119w47	7:59:08
El Porto Beach 19	33N53	118w24	7:53:36
El Pueblo 7	38N00	121w51	8:07:24
El Rio 56	34N14	119w10	7:56:40
El Rio Villa 57	38N32	121w58	8:07:52
El Segundo 19	33N55	118w25	7:53:40
El Sereno 19	34N05	118w16	7:53:04
Elsinore 33	33N40	117w20	7:49:20
Elsinore Valley 33	33N44	117w26	7:49:44
El Sobrante 7	37N59	122w18	8:09:12
El Toro 30	33N38	117w42	7:50:48
El Toro Marine Corps Air Sta 30	33N41	117w42	7:50:48
El Toro Station 30	33N41	117w42	7:50:48
El Verano 49	38N18	122w29	8:09:56
Elverta 34	38N43	121w27	8:05:48
El Viejo 50	37N40	121w00	8:04:00
Emandal 23	39N25	123w21	8:13:24
Emerald Bay 30	33N33	117w48	7:51:12
Emerald Lake 41	37N28	122w14	8:08:56
Emeryville 1	37N50	122w18	8:09:12
Emigrant Gap 31	39N19	120w38	8:02:32
Empire 50	37N38	120w54	8:03:36
Encanto 37	32N42	117w04	7:48:16
Encinal 43	37N21	122w02	8:08:08
Encinitas 37	33N03	117w17	7:49:08
Encino 19	34N09	118w30	7:54:00
Enterprise 45	40N35	122w20	8:09:20
Escalon 39	37N48	121w00	8:04:00
Escondido 37	33N07	117w05	7:48:20
Escondido Junction 37	33N12	117w20	7:49:20
Escondido Village Mall 37	33N04	117w03	7:48:12
Esparto 57	38N42	122w01	8:08:04
Essex 36	34N44	115w15	7:41:00
Estrella 40	35N45	120w42	8:02:48
Estudillo 1	37N43	122w09	8:08:36
Etiwanda 36	34N08	117w31	7:50:04
Etna 47	41N27	122w54	8:11:36
Ettersburg 12	40N06	123w48	8:15:12
Eucalyptus Hills 37	32N53	116w57	7:47:48
Eugene 50	37N56	121w00	8:04:00
Eureka 12	40N47	124w09	8:16:36
Evergreen Acres 42	34N54	120w26	8:01:44
Exeter 54	36N18	119w09	7:56:36
Fairfax 21	37N59	122w35	8:10:20
Fairfield 48	38N15	122w03	8:08:12
Fairhaven 12	40N49	124w11	8:16:44
Fairmead 20	37N07	120w16	8:01:04
Fairmont 19	34N40	118w11	7:52:44
Fairmont Terrace 1	37N43	122w09	8:08:36
Fairmount 7	37N55	122w18	8:09:12
Fair Oaks 34	38N39	121w16	8:05:04
Fair Oaks 40	35N07	120w35	8:02:20
Fairview 1	37N40	122w03	8:08:12
Fairview 10	36N42	119w33	7:58:12
Fairview 30	33N41	117w54	7:51:36
Fairview 50	37N38	120w59	8:03:56
Fairview 54	35N43	118w26	7:53:44
Falk 12	40N47	124w10	8:16:40
Fallbrook 37	33N23	117w15	7:49:00
Fallbrook Junction 37	33N15	117w18	7:49:12
Fallen Leaf 9	38N53	120w04	8:00:16
Fallon 21	38N15	122w54	8:11:36
Fall River Mills 45	41N00	121w26	8:05:44
Fallsvale 36	34N06	116w57	7:47:48
Fancher 10	36N44	119w45	7:59:00
Farmers Market 19	34N04	118w21	7:53:24
Farmersville 54	36N18	119w12	7:56:48
Farmington 39	37N56	121w00	8:04:00
Fashion Square La Habra 30	33N56	117w56	7:51:44
Fawnskin 36	34N16	116w57	7:47:48
Feather Falls 4	39N36	121w16	8:05:04
Feather River Inn 32	39N47	120w37	8:02:28
Federal 19	34N06	117w53	7:51:32
Federal 30	33N50	117w55	7:51:40
Federal Building 38	37N47	122w26	8:09:44
Federal Building 56	34N12	119w10	7:56:40
Federal Terrace 48	38N07	122w14	8:08:56
Fellows 15	35N11	119w32	7:58:08
Felton 44	37N03	122w04	8:08:16
Felton Grove 44	37N03	122w04	8:08:16
Fenner	34N49	115w11	7:40:44
Fernbridge 12	40N35	124w08	8:16:32
Fernbrook 37	32N58	116w55	7:47:40
Ferndale 12	40N35	124w16	8:17:04
Fern Valley 33	33N45	116w43	7:46:52
Fernwood 19	34N05	118w37	7:54:28
Fetters Hot Springs 49	38N19	122w29	8:09:56
Fiddletown 3	38N30	120w46	8:03:04
Fieldbrook 12	40N52	124w05	8:16:20
Fields Landing 12	40N44	124w13	8:16:52
Fig Garden 10	36N48	119w48	7:59:12
Figueroa 19	34N11	118w08	7:52:32
Fillmore 56	34N24	118w55	7:55:40
Finley 17	39N00	122w52	8:11:28
Firebaugh 10	36N52	120w27	8:01:48
Fire Mountain 52	40N19	121w32	8:06:08
Firestone 19	33N56	118w11	7:52:44
Firestone Park 19	33N59	118w15	7:53:00
First Street 37	33N12	117w20	7:49:20
Fish Camp 22	37N29	119w38	7:58:32
Fisk 38	37N46	122w28	8:09:52
Fitchburg 1	37N46	122w11	8:08:44
Five Brooks 21	38N02	122w47	8:11:08
Five Corners 39	37N48	121w11	8:04:44
Five Mile Terrace 9	38N44	120w48	8:03:12
Five Points 10	36N26	120w06	8:00:24
Fleet 37	32N45	117w09	7:48:36
Flinn Springs 37	32N48	116w57	7:47:48
Flintridge 19	34N11	118w12	7:52:48
Florence 19	33N58	118w15	7:53:00
Florin 34	38N30	121w24	8:05:36
Floriston 29	39N24	120w01	8:00:04
Flosden Acres 48	38N07	122w14	8:08:56
Flournoy 52	39N55	122w26	8:09:44
Flower Village 15	35N23	118w59	7:55:56
Fly In Acres 5	38N15	120w21	8:01:24
Folsom 34	38N42	121w09	8:04:36
Folsom Junction 34	38N41	121w11	8:04:44
Fontana 36	34N06	117w26	7:49:44
Foothill Center 19	34N07	117w54	7:51:36
Foothill Farms 34	38N40	121w20	8:05:20
Forbestown 4	39N31	121w16	8:05:04
Ford City 15	35N09	119w27	7:57:48
Forest 46	39N28	120w51	8:03:24
Foresta 22	37N45	119w35	7:58:20
Forest Falls 36	34N06	116w57	7:47:48
Forest Glen 53	40N23	123w20	8:13:20
Foresthill 31	39N01	120w49	8:03:16
Forest Home 3	38N29	120w51	8:03:24
Forest Home 36	34N06	116w57	7:47:48
Forest Knolls 21	38N01	122w40	8:10:40
Forest Lake 39	38N10	121w13	8:04:52
Forest Park 44	37N07	122w07	8:08:28
Forest Ranch 4	39N53	121w40	8:06:40
Forest Springs 29	39N13	121w04	8:04:16
Forest Springs 44	37N07	122w07	8:08:28
Forestville 49	38N28	122w54	8:11:36
Forks Of Salmon 47	41N16	123w19	8:13:16
Forrest Park 19	34N25	118w32	7:54:08
Fort Baker 21	37N52	122w30	8:10:00
Fort Barry 21	37N52	122w30	8:10:00
Fort Bidwell 25	41N52	120w09	8:00:36
Fort Bidwell Indian Res 25	38N33	121w28	8:05:52
Fort Bragg 23	39N26	123w48	8:15:12
Fort Cronkhite 21	37N52	122w30	8:10:00
Fort Dick	41N52	124w09	8:16:36
Fort Independence Indian Res 14	38N36	121w23	8:05:32
Fort Irwin 36	35N15	116w42	7:46:48
Fort Jones 47	41N36	122w51	8:11:24
Fort Macarthur 19	33N44	118w18	7:53:12
Fort Mohave Indian Res 36	34N09	114w17	7:37:08
Fort Ord 27	36N38	121w46	8:07:04
Fort Ord Village 27	36N37	121w50	8:07:20
Fort Romie 27	36N25	121w19	8:05:16
Fort Rosecrans 37	32N44	117w14	7:48:56
Fort Seward 12	40N06	123w48	8:15:12
Fort Sutter 34	38N34	121w28	8:05:52
Fortuna 12	40N36	124w09	8:16:36
Fort Yuma 13	32N44	114w38	7:38:32
Fort Yuma Indian Reservation 13	34N09	114w17	7:37:08
Foster City 41	37N34	122w15	8:09:00
Fountain Valley 30	33N42	117w58	7:51:52
Four Corners 36	34N11	116w04	7:44:16
Four Corners 36	35N00	117w39	7:50:36
Fouts Springs 6	39N23	122w33	8:10:12
Fowler 10	36N38	119w41	7:58:44
Foy 19	34N00	118w16	7:53:04
Franciscan Park 41	37N42	122w28	8:09:52
Franklin 28	38N18	122w18	8:09:12
Franklin 34	38N22	121w26	8:05:44
Frazier Park 15	34N49	118w56	7:55:44
Fredericksburg 2	38N49	119w41	7:58:44
Freedom 44	36N56	121w46	8:07:04
Freestone 49	38N24	122w50	8:11:20
Fremont 1	37N32	121w57	8:07:48
French Camp 39	37N53	121w16	8:05:04
French Corral 29	39N12	121w18	8:05:12
French Gulch 45	40N42	122w38	8:10:32
Fresh Pond 9	38N46	120w34	8:02:16
Freshwater 12	40N47	124w10	8:16:40
Fresno 10	36N44	119w47	7:59:08

CALIFORNIA

Friant 10 36N59 119w43 7:58:52
Friendly Hills 36 34N08 116w19 7:45:16
Fruitland 12 40N16 123w53 8:15:32
Fruitridge 34 38N32 121w27 8:05:48
Fruitvale 1 37N47 122w13 8:08:52
Fruitvale 15 35N24 119w02 7:56:08
Fruto 11 39N31 122w12 8:08:48
Fullerton 30 33N53 117w56 7:51:44
Fulton 49 38N30 122w46 8:11:04
Gabilan 27 36N42 121w32 8:06:08
Gabilan Acres 27 36N41 121w39 8:06:36
Gallinas 21 38N01 122w33 8:10:12
Galt 34 38N15 121w18 8:05:12
Ganser Bar 32 40N00 121w15 8:05:00
Garberville 12 40N06 123w48 8:15:12
Gardena 19 33N53 118w18 7:53:12
Garden Acres 39 37N58 121w14 8:04:56
Gardena Village 41 37N41 122w29 8:09:56
Garden Farms 40 35N29 120w40 8:02:40
Garden Gate Village 43 37N19 122w02 8:08:08
Garden Grove 30 33N47 117w55 7:51:40
Garden Valley 9 38N51 120w51 8:03:24
Garden Village 41 37N41 122w29 8:09:56
Garey 42 34N53 120w19 8:01:16
Garfield 15 35N36 118w30 7:54:00
Garlock 15 35N24 117w47 7:51:08
Gasoline Alley 31 38N54 121w04 8:04:16
Gas Point 45 32N48 116w57 7:47:48
Gasquet 8 41N51 123w58 8:15:52
Gates 48 38N21 121w59 8:07:56
Gateway 19 34N00 118w24 7:53:36
Gateway 29 39N20 120w12 8:00:48
Gaviota 42 34N29 120w13 8:00:52
Gazelle 47 41N31 122w31 8:10:04
Geary 38 37N47 122w26 8:09:44
Gene 36 34N10 114w18 7:37:12
Genesee 32 40N04 120w50 8:03:20
George 36 34N35 117w23 7:49:32
George Air Force Base 36 34N35 117w22 7:49:28
Georgetown 9 38N54 120w50 8:03:20
George Washington 37 32N45 117w09 7:48:36
Gerber 52 40N04 122w09 8:08:36
Geyser Resort 49 38N48 123w01 8:12:04
Geyserville 49 38N42 122w54 8:11:36
Gilman Hot Springs 33 33N50 116w59 7:47:56
Gilroy 43 37N01 121w34 8:06:16
Gilroy Hot Springs 43 37N01 121w35 8:06:20
Glacier Lodge 14 37N10 118w17 7:53:08
Glamis 13 33N00 115w04 7:40:16
Glassell 19 34N07 118w14 7:52:56
Glen Arbor 44 37N05 122w05 8:08:20
Glen Avon 33 34N01 117w29 7:49:56
Glen Avon Heights 33 34N01 117w29 7:49:56
Glenbrook Heights 29 39N13 121w04 8:04:16
Glenburn 45 41N04 121w29 8:05:56
Glencoe 5 38N21 120w35 8:02:20
Glendale 12 40N52 124w05 8:16:20
Glendale 19 34N09 118w15 7:53:00
Glendora 19 34N08 117w52 7:51:28
Glen Ellen 49 38N22 122w31 8:10:04
Glenhaven 17 39N02 122w44 8:10:56
Glen Martin 36 34N09 116w59 7:47:56
Glenn 11 39N31 122w01 8:08:04
Glennville 15 35N44 118w42 7:54:48
Glenoaks 19 34N11 118w20 7:53:20
Glenshire 29 39N20 120w12 8:00:48
Glenview 19 34N05 118w37 7:54:28
Glenview 37 32N50 116w54 7:47:36
Glorietta 7 37N52 122w08 8:08:32
Goffs 36 34N55 115w04 7:40:16
Golden Gate Race Track 1 37N53 122w19 8:09:16
Golden Hills 37 32N44 117w07 7:48:28
Gold Flat 29 39N16 121w01 8:04:04
Gold Gulch 44 37N03 122w04 8:08:16
Gold Hill 9 38N44 120w48 8:03:12
Gold Run 31 39N10 120w52 8:03:28
Goleta 42 34N27 119w50 7:59:20
Goleta Valley 42 34N27 119w50 7:59:20
Gonzales 27 36N30 121w26 8:05:44
Goodyears Bar 46 39N32 120w53 8:03:32
Gorman 19 34N47 118w51 7:55:24
Goshen 54 36N21 119w25 7:57:40
Government Island 1 37N47 122w16 8:09:04
Graeagle 32 39N47 120w37 8:02:28
Graham 19 33N57 118w14 7:52:56
Granada Hills 19 34N16 118w30 7:54:00
Grand Avenue 33 33N55 117w44 7:50:56
Grand Central 19 34N10 118w16 7:53:04
Grand Lake 1 37N49 122w14 8:08:56
Grand Terrace 36 34N02 117w19 7:49:16
Grandview-Palos Verdes 19 33N46 118w21 7:53:24
Grangeville 16 36N20 119w39 7:58:36
Granite Bay Vista 31 38N45 121w17 8:05:08
Graniteville 29 39N16 121w01 8:04:04
Grantville 37 32N46 117w06 7:48:24
Grass Valley 29 39N13 121w04 8:04:16
Graton 49 38N26 122w52 8:11:28
Grayson 50 37N28 121w08 8:04:32
Greeley 15 35N21 118w59 7:55:56
Green 19 34N00 118w17 7:53:08
Greenacres 15 35N23 119w07 7:56:28
Greenbrae 21 37N57 122w30 8:10:00
Greenbrook 7 37N50 122w00 8:08:00
Greenfield 27 36N19 121w15 8:05:00
Greenmead 19 33N56 118w15 7:53:00
Greenspot 36 34N05 117w08 7:48:32
Green Valley 19 34N25 118w32 7:54:08
Green Valley Estates 48 38N14 122w02 8:08:08
Green Valley Lake 36 34N14 117w04 7:48:16
Greenview 47 41N33 122w54 8:11:36
Greenview Acres 12 40N52 124w05 8:16:20
Greenville 32 40N08 120w57 8:03:48
Greenwich Village 56 34N12 118w53 7:55:32
Greenwood 9 38N54 120w55 8:03:40
Grenada 47 41N39 122w31 8:10:04
Gridley 4 39N22 121w42 8:06:48
Griffith 19 34N06 118w16 7:53:04
Grimes 6 39N04 121w54 8:07:36
Grizzly Flats 9 38N38 120w31 8:02:04
Grossmont 37 32N47 116w59 7:47:56
Grove Highlands 27 36N37 121w56 8:07:44
Groveland 55 37N50 120w14 8:00:56
Grover City 40 35N07 120w37 8:02:28
Guadalupe 42 34N58 120w34 8:02:16
Gualala 23 38N46 123w32 8:14:08
Guasti 36 34N05 117w31 7:50:04
Guatay 37 32N51 116w34 7:46:16
Guerneville 49 38N30 123w00 8:12:00
Guernewood Park 49 38N30 123w00 8:12:00
Guernsey 16 36N20 119w39 7:58:36
Guernsey Mill 54 35N48 118w43 7:54:52
Guinda 57 38N50 122w12 8:08:48
Gustine 24 37N16 121w00 8:04:00
Hacienda 49 38N28 122w53 8:11:32
Hacienda Heights 19 34N00 117w58 7:51:52
Haiwee 14 36N09 117w59 7:51:56
Halcyon 40 35N07 120w35 8:02:20
Half Moon Bay 41 37N28 122w26 8:09:44
Hall 1 37N36 122w01 8:08:04
Halloran Springs 36 35N16 116w04 7:44:16
Halls Corner 16 36N17 119w51 7:59:24
Hallwood 58 39N09 121w32 8:06:08
Hamburg 47 41N49 123w00 8:12:00
Hamilton Air Force Base 21 38N03 122w31 8:10:04
Hamilton City 11 39N45 122w01 8:08:04
Hancock 19 33N57 118w17 7:53:08
Hanford 16 36N20 119w39 7:58:36
Happy Camp 47 41N48 123w23 8:13:32
Harbison Canyon 37 32N49 116w50 7:47:20
Harbor 56 34N12 119w10 7:56:40
Harbor City 19 33N48 118w17 7:53:08
Harbor Side 37 32N37 117w04 7:48:16
Hardman Center 33 33N57 117w24 7:49:36
Hardwick 16 36N20 119w39 7:58:36
Harlem Springs 36 34N08 117w13 7:48:52
Harmony 40 35N31 121w01 8:04:04
Harmony Grove 37 33N04 117w03 7:48:12
Harris 12 40N06 123w48 8:15:12
Hartland 54 36N38 119w01 7:56:04
Harvard 36 34N54 116w50 7:47:20
Haskell Creek Homesites 46 39N34 120w38 8:02:32
Hat Creek 45 40N47 121w30 8:06:00
Hathaway Pines 5 38N07 120w28 8:01:52
Hatton Fields 27 36N33 121w53 8:07:32
Havasu Lake 36 34N50 114w36 7:38:24
Havilah 15 35N17 118w38 7:54:32
Hawaiian Gardens 19 33N50 118w04 7:52:16
Hawkinsville 47 41N44 122w38 8:10:32
Hawthorne 19 33N55 118w21 7:53:24
Hayfork 53 40N33 123w11 8:12:44
Hayward 1 37N40 122w05 8:08:20
Hayward Highlands 1 37N40 122w03 8:08:12
Hazard 19 34N03 118w11 7:52:44
Healdsburg 49 38N37 122w52 8:11:28
Heber 13 32N44 115w32 7:42:08
Helena 53 40N47 123w08 8:12:32
Helendale 36 34N45 117w19 7:49:16
Helm 36N32 120w06 8:00:24
Hemet 33 33N45 116w58 7:47:52
Henderson Center 12 40N47 124w10 8:16:40
Henderson Village 39 38N08 121w17 8:05:08
Henley 47 41N55 122w33 8:10:12
Herald 34 38N18 121w14 8:04:56
Hercules 7 38N01 122w17 8:09:08
Herlong 18 40N09 120w08 8:00:32
Hermosa Beach 19 33N52 118w24 7:53:36
Hernandez 35 36N51 121w24 8:05:36
Herndon 10 36N50 119w55 7:59:40
Hesperia 36 34N25 117w18 7:49:12
Heyer 1 37N39 122w04 8:08:16
Hickman 50 37N37 120w45 8:03:00
Hidden Hills 19 34N10 118w40 7:54:40
Hidden Meadows 37 33N04 117w03 7:48:12
Hidden Valley 31 38N49 121w12 8:04:48
Highgrove 33 34N01 117w20 7:49:20
Highland 36 34N08 117w13 7:48:52
Highland Manor 15 35N24 119w02 7:56:08
Highland Park 15 35N24 119w02 7:56:08
Highland Park 19 34N07 118w12 7:52:48
Highway City 10 36N48 119w50 7:59:20
Hilarita 21 37N53 122w29 8:09:56
Hillcrest 15 35N23 118w57 7:55:48
Hillcrest 37 32N45 117w09 7:48:36
Hillcrest Center 15 35N23 118w57 7:55:48
Hillcrest Park 48 38N07 122w14 8:08:56
Hillgrove 19 34N00 117w57 7:51:48
Hillsborough 41 37N35 122w21 8:09:24
Hillsdale 41 37N32 122w18 8:09:12
Hills Flat 29 39N13 121w04 8:04:16
Hilltop 15 35N23 119w01 7:56:04
Hilmar 24 37N25 120w51 8:03:24
Hilt 47 41N50 122w37 8:10:28
Hilton 49 38N28 122w53 8:11:32
Hinkley 36 34N56 117w12 7:48:48
Hiouchi Valley 8 41N46 124w12 8:16:48
Hi Vista 19 34N40 118w11 7:52:44
Hoaglin 53 40N12 123w30 8:14:00
Hobart 19 34N00 118w14 7:52:56
Hobart Mills 29 39N20 120w12 8:00:48
Hobergs 38N50 122w43 8:10:52
Hodge 36 34N49 117w11 7:48:44
Holcomb Village 37 33N27 116w51 7:47:24
Holiday Forest 36 34N15 116w53 7:47:32
Hollister 35 36N51 121w24 8:05:36
Hollydale 19 33N56 118w11 7:52:44
Hollydale 49 38N28 122w53 8:11:32
Hollywood 19 34N06 118w21 7:53:24
Hollywood Beach 56 34N12 119w10 7:56:40
Hollywood-by-the-Sea 56 34N12 119w10 7:56:40
Hollywood Park Race Track 19 33N57 118w20 7:53:20
Holmes 12 40N21 123w55 8:15:40
Holt 39 37N56 121w26 8:05:44
Holtville 13 32N49 115w23 7:41:32
Holy City 43 37N10 121w59 8:07:56
Home Acres 7 38N00 121w51 8:07:24
Home Gardens 19 33N56 118w11 7:52:44
Home Gardens 33 33N53 117w32 7:50:08
Homeland 33 33N45 117w07 7:48:28
Homestead 33 33N33 116w43 7:46:52
Homestead 39 37N56 121w16 8:05:04
Homestead Valley 21 37N54 122w32 8:10:08
Homewood 31 39N05 120w10 8:00:40
Honby 19 34N25 118w32 7:54:08
Honcut 4 39N20 121w32 8:06:08
Honeydew 12 40N14 124w07 8:16:28
Honey Lake 18 40N05 120w06 8:00:24
Hood 34 38N22 121w31 8:06:04
Hooker 52 40N23 122w17 8:09:08
Hookston 7 37N58 122w05 8:08:20
Hoopa 12 41N03 123w41 8:14:44
Hoopa Valley Indian Res 12 41N03 123w40 8:14:40
Hope Ranch 42 34N26 119w44 7:58:56
Hopeton 24 37N31 120w26 8:01:44
Hope Valley 2 41N54 120w21 8:01:24
Hopland 23 38N58 123w07 8:12:28
Horizon Hills 56 34N12 118w53 7:55:32
Hornbrook 47 41N55 122w33 8:10:12
Hornitos 22 37N30 120w14 8:00:56
Horse Creek 47 41N49 123w00 8:12:00
Howard Landing 34 38N15 121w31 8:06:04
Howest 41 37N35 122w22 8:09:28
Huasna 40 35N07 120w35 8:02:20
Hub City 19 33N53 118w15 7:53:00
Hudson 50 37N38 120w59 8:03:56
Hughson 50 37N36 120w52 8:03:28
Hume 10 36N47 118w55 7:55:40
Humphreys Station 10 36N49 119w43 7:58:52
Hunters Valley 22 37N30 120w14 8:00:56
Huntington Beach 30 33N40 118w05 7:52:20
Huntington Lake 10 37N15 119w14 7:56:56
Huntington Park 19 33N58 118w14 7:52:56
Huron 10 36N12 120w06 8:00:24
Hyampom 53 40N37 123w27 8:13:48
Hydesville 12 40N33 124w06 8:16:24
Idlewild 54 35N48 118w43 7:54:52
Idria 35 36N25 120w41 8:02:44
Idyllwild 33 33N42 116w42 7:46:48
Idylwood Acres 7 37N55 122w03 8:08:12
Ignacio 21 38N04 122w32 8:10:08
Igo 45 40N30 122w32 8:10:08
Imperial 13 32N51 115w34 7:42:16
Imperial Beach 37 32N35 117w07 7:48:28
Imperial Crest 19 33N54 118w05 7:52:20
Incline 22 37N41 119w47 7:59:08
Independence 14 36N48 118w12 7:52:48
Indian Falls 32 40N01 120w58 8:03:52
Indian Mission 10 37N05 119w29 7:57:56
Indianola 12 40N51 124w04 8:16:16
Indian Wells 33 33N43 116w20 7:45:20
Indio 33 33N43 116w13 7:44:52
Industrial 30 33N45 117w49 7:51:16
Industry 19 34N01 117w58 7:51:52
Inglenook 23 39N27 123w48 8:15:12
Inglewood 19 33N58 118w21 7:53:24
Ingot 45 40N44 122w05 8:08:20
Inverness 21 38N06 122w51 8:11:24
Inverness Park 21 38N04 122w48 8:11:12
Inwood 45 40N30 121w53 8:07:32
Inyokern 15 35N39 117w49 7:51:16
Ione 3 38N21 120w56 8:03:44
Iowa Hill 31 39N06 120w57 8:03:48
Iron Mountain 36 34N07 114w31 7:38:04
Irvine 33N41 117w46 7:51:04
Irvington 1 37N32 121w58 8:07:52
Irwin 24 37N25 120w51 8:03:24
Irwindale 19 34N07 117w56 7:51:44
Island Mountain 53 40N02 123w30 8:14:00
Isla Vista 42 34N25 119w51 7:59:24
Isleton 34 38N10 121w37 8:06:28
Italian Swiss Colony 20 36N58 120w04 8:00:16
Ivanhoe 54 36N23 119w13 7:56:52
Ivanpah 36 35N21 115w18 7:41:12
Jacinto Grange 11 39N31 122w01 8:08:04
Jackson 3 38N21 120w46 8:03:04
Jackson Gate 3 38N21 120w46 8:03:04
Jacksonville 55 37N52 120w26 8:01:44
Jacumba 37 32N37 116w11 7:44:44
Jalama 42 34N42 120w29 8:01:56

Place	Latitude	Longitude	Time
Jamacha Junction 37	32N44	117w00	7:48:00
Jamesburg 27	36N29	121w44	8:06:56
Jameson Beach 9	38N55	120w00	8:00:00
Jamestown 55	37N57	120w25	8:01:40
Jamul 37	32N43	116w52	7:47:28
Janesville 18	40N18	120w32	8:02:08
Jarbo 4	39N30	121w33	8:06:12
Jarvis Landing 1	37N32	122w02	8:08:08
Jelly 52	40N11	122w16	8:09:04
Jenner 49	38N27	123w07	8:12:28
Jenny Lind 5	38N12	120w50	8:03:20
Jesmond Dene 37	33N11	117w07	7:48:28
Jimtown 49	38N37	122w52	8:11:28
Johannesburg 15	35N22	117w38	7:50:32
John Adams 37	32N46	117w07	7:48:28
Johnsondale 54	35N58	118w32	7:54:08
Johnson Park 45	40N53	121w40	8:06:40
Johnson Tract 54	36N20	119w18	7:57:12
Johnstonville 18	40N25	120w39	8:02:36
Johnstown 37	32N50	116w54	7:47:36
Johnsville 32	39N47	120w37	8:02:28
Jolon 27	35N58	121w11	8:04:44
Jonesville 4	40N05	121w33	8:06:12
Joshua Tree 36	34N08	116w19	7:45:16
Julian 37	33N05	116w36	7:46:24
Junction City 53	40N44	123w04	8:12:16
June Lake 26	37N47	119w04	7:56:16
June Lake Junction 26	37N47	119w04	7:56:16
Juniper Hills 19	34N31	117w59	7:51:56
Juniper Lake Resort 18	40N18	121w14	8:04:56
Juniper Springs 33	33N45	117w10	7:48:40
Jurupa 33	33N59	117w29	7:49:56
Kaiser Center 1	37N48	122w16	8:09:04
Kaiser's Eagle Mountain 33	33N51	115w29	7:41:56
Kamp Klamath 8	41N32	124w02	8:16:08
Karnak 51	38N48	121w43	8:06:52
Kaweah 54	36N28	118w52	7:55:28
Kearny Mesa 37	32N49	117w09	7:48:36
Keddie 32	40N01	120w58	8:03:52
Keeler 14	36N29	117w52	7:51:28
Keene 15	35N13	118w33	7:54:12
Keene Summit 23	39N16	123w35	8:14:20
Kellog 49	38N35	122w35	8:10:20
Kelsey 9	38N48	120w49	8:03:16
Kelseyville 17	38N59	122w50	8:11:20
Kelso 36	35N01	115w39	7:42:36
Kennedy Meadow 55	37N59	120w23	8:01:32
Kensington 7	37N55	122w17	8:09:08
Kensington 37	32N46	117w06	7:48:24
Kentfield 21	37N58	122w33	8:10:12
Kent Woodlands 21	37N58	122w31	8:10:04
Kenwood 49	38N25	122w33	8:10:12
Keough Hot Springs 14	37N22	118w24	7:53:36
Kerman 10	36N43	120w04	8:00:16
Kern Homes 15	35N24	119w02	7:56:08
Kernvale 15	35N39	118w28	7:53:52
Kernville 15	35N45	118w26	7:53:44
Kester 19	34N12	118w27	7:53:48
Keswick 45	40N33	122w22	8:09:28
Kettleman City 16	36N01	119w58	7:59:52
Keyes 50	37N34	120w55	8:03:40
Keystone 55	37N57	120w25	8:01:40
Kilkare Woods 1	37N38	121w55	8:07:40
King 30	33N46	117w53	7:51:32
King City 27	36N13	121w08	8:04:32
Kings Beach 31	39N14	120w01	8:00:04
Kingsburg 10	36N31	119w33	7:58:12
Kings Canyon National Park 54	36N44	118w58	7:55:52
Kingvale 29	39N19	120w16	8:01:04
Kirkville 51	38N48	121w43	8:06:52
Kirkwood 2	38N42	120w04	8:00:16
Kirkwood 52	39N56	122w11	8:08:44
Kit Carson 3	38N41	120w07	8:00:28
Klamath 8	41N32	124w02	8:16:08
Klamath Glen 8	41N32	124w02	8:16:08
Klamath River 47	41N52	122w50	8:11:20
Kneeland 12	40N45	123w59	8:15:56
Knightsen 7	37N58	121w40	8:06:40
Knights Ferry 50	37N46	120w51	8:03:24
Knights Landing 57	38N48	121w43	8:06:52
Knob 45	40N22	122w53	8:11:32
Knowles 20	37N13	119w54	7:59:36
Komandorski Village 1	37N43	121w55	8:07:40
Korbel 12	40N52	123w58	8:15:52
Kramer Junction 36	35N00	117w35	7:50:20
Krug 28	38N31	122w29	8:09:56
Kyburz 9	38N47	120w18	8:01:12
La Ballona 19	34N00	118w24	7:53:36
La Barr Meadows 29	39N13	121w04	8:04:16
La Canada 19	34N13	118w12	7:52:48
La Costa 19	34N06	118w44	7:54:56
La Crescenta 19	34N13	118w15	7:53:00
La Cresta 15	35N23	118w59	7:55:56
La Cresta 37	32N47	116w58	7:47:52
Ladera 41	37N24	122w12	8:08:48
Ladera Heights 19	33N59	118w22	7:53:28
Lafayette 7	37N53	122w07	8:08:28
La Fetra 19	34N08	117w51	7:51:24
La Grange 50	37N40	120w28	8:01:52
Laguna Beach 30	33N33	117w47	7:51:08
Laguna Dam 13	32N44	114w35	7:38:20
Laguna Hills 30	33N37	117w43	7:50:52
Laguna Lake 40	35N18	120w45	8:03:00
Laguna Niguel 30	33N32	117w42	7:50:48
Lagunitas 21	38N01	122w42	8:10:48
La Habra 30	33N56	117w57	7:51:48
La Habra Heights 19	33N57	117w58	7:51:52
La Honda 41	37N19	122w16	8:09:04
Lairport 19	33N55	118w25	7:53:40
La Jolla 30	33N53	117w51	7:51:24
La Jolla 37	32N51	117w16	7:49:04
La Jolla Indian Reservation 37	33N49	116w32	7:46:08
Lake Alpine 2	38N15	120w21	8:01:24
Lake Arrowhead 36	34N15	117w11	7:48:44
Lake City 25	41N39	120w13	8:00:52
Lake Elsinore 33	33N55	117w44	7:50:56
Lake Forest 31	39N09	120w09	8:00:36
Lakehead 45	40N54	122w23	8:09:32
Lake Henshaw 37	33N07	116w40	7:46:40
Lake Hills Estates 9	38N41	121w11	8:04:44
Lake Hughes 19	34N41	118w26	7:53:44
Lake Isabella 15	35N35	118w31	7:54:04
Lake Kirkwood 9	38N42	120w04	8:00:16
Lakeland Village 33	33N38	117w21	7:49:24
Lake Los Angeles 19	34N35	118w06	7:52:24
Lake Mary 26	37N38	118w58	7:55:52
Lake Mathews 33	33N52	117w19	7:49:16
Lake Morena Village 37	32N37	116w28	7:45:52
Lake Nokopen 18	40N18	121w01	8:04:04
Lake Of The Woods 15	34N49	118w57	7:55:48
Lakeport 17	39N03	122w55	8:11:40
Lake San Marcos 37	33N11	117w13	7:48:52
Lakeshore 10	37N15	119w12	7:56:48
Lakeside 37	32N52	116w55	7:47:40
Lakeside Farms 37	32N50	116w56	7:47:44
Lake Tahoe 31	39N14	120w07	8:00:28
Lake Tamarisk 33	33N43	115w24	7:41:36
Lakeview 15	35N21	118w59	7:55:56
Lakeview 33	33N50	117w07	7:48:28
Lakeview 37	32N50	116w54	7:47:36
Lake View Terrace 19	34N17	118w27	7:53:48
Lakeville 49	38N13	122w38	8:10:32
Lakewood 19	33N51	118w08	7:52:32
La Loma 50	37N38	120w59	8:03:56
Lambert 49	38N37	122w52	8:11:28
La Mesa 37	32N45	117w02	7:48:08
La Mirada 19	33N51	118w02	7:52:08
La Moine	40N59	122w26	8:09:44
Lamont 15	35N15	118w55	7:55:40
Lanare 10	36N26	119w56	7:59:44
Lancaster 19	34N42	118w08	7:52:32
Landers 36	34N07	116w26	7:45:44
Land Park 34	38N32	121w28	8:05:52
Landscape 1	37N54	122w17	8:09:08
Lansdale 21	37N59	122w35	8:10:20
La Palma 30	33N51	118w03	7:52:12
La Panza 40	35N23	120w37	8:02:28
La Patera 42	34N26	119w51	7:59:24
La Porte 32	39N41	120w59	8:03:56
La Presa 37	32N42	117w00	7:48:00
La Puente 19	34N02	117w57	7:51:48
La Quinta 33	33N40	116w19	7:45:16
Larabee Ranch 12	40N21	123w55	8:15:40
Larchmont Riviera 34	38N33	121w22	8:05:28
Larkfield 49	38N26	122w43	8:10:52
Larkspur 21	37N56	122w32	8:10:08
Larwin Plaza-Vallejo 48	38N07	122w14	8:08:56
Larwin Square-Tustin 30	33N45	117w49	7:51:16
Las Cruces 42	34N31	120w14	8:00:56
La Selva Beach 44	36N56	121w50	8:07:20
Las Flores 19	34N06	118w44	7:54:56
Las Flores 52	40N03	122w09	8:08:36
La Sierra 33	33N56	117w29	7:49:56
Las Lomas 27	36N55	121w47	8:07:08
Las Lomas 49	38N42	122w54	8:11:36
Las Posas 56	34N17	119w02	7:56:08
Las Posas Estates 56	34N14	119w02	7:56:08
Lathrop 39	37N49	121w16	8:05:04
La Tijera 19	33N59	118w20	7:53:20
Laton 10	36N26	119w41	7:58:44
Latrobe 9	38N40	120w56	8:03:44
Laurel 1	37N48	122w12	8:08:48
Laurel 44	37N15	121w58	8:07:52
Laurel Canyon 19	34N12	118w24	7:53:36
La Verne 19	34N06	117w46	7:51:04
La Vina 20	36N58	120w04	8:00:16
Lawndale 19	33N54	118w21	7:53:24
Lawndale 49	38N25	122w33	8:10:12
Laws 14	37N24	118w21	7:53:24
Laytonville 23	39N41	123w29	8:13:56
Lebec 15	34N50	118w52	7:55:28
Leesville 6	39N09	122w09	8:08:36
Lee Vining 26	37N58	119w07	7:56:28
Leggett 23	39N52	123w43	8:14:52
Le Grand 24	37N14	120w15	8:01:00
Leisure World 30	33N46	118w05	7:52:20
Lemoncove 54	36N23	119w01	7:56:04
Lemon Grove 37	32N44	117w01	7:48:04
Lemon Heights 30	33N46	117w47	7:51:08
Lemoore 16	36N18	119w46	7:59:04
Lemoore Station 16	36N16	119w54	7:59:36
Lennox 19	33N56	118w21	7:53:24
Lenwood 36	34N53	117w07	7:48:28
Leona Valley 19	34N35	118w06	7:52:24
Letterman 38	37N47	122w27	8:09:48
Leucadia 37	33N05	117w18	7:49:12
Lewiston 53	40N43	122w48	8:11:12
Lexington 43	37N10	121w58	8:07:52
Liberty Acres 19	33N55	118w21	7:53:24
Liberty Farms 48	38N19	121w42	8:06:48
Libfarm 48	38N19	121w42	8:06:48
Likely 25	41N14	120w30	8:02:00
Limco 56	34N21	119w04	7:56:16
Lincoln 31	38N54	121w17	8:05:08
Lincoln Acres 37	32N40	117w04	7:48:16
Lincoln Heights 19	34N05	118w13	7:52:52
Lincoln Village 19	33N50	118w14	7:52:56
Lincoln Village 34	38N35	121w20	8:05:20
Lincoln Village 39	38N00	121w20	8:05:20
Linda 58	39N09	121w27	8:05:48
Linda Mar 41	37N38	122w29	8:09:56
Linda Mar Gardens 37	32N59	117w16	7:49:04
Linda Vista 37	32N45	117w10	7:48:40
Linda Vista 43	37N22	121w49	8:07:16
Lindbergh Field 37	32N44	117w11	7:48:44
Lind Cove 54	36N22	119w04	7:56:16
Linden 39	38N01	121w05	8:04:20
Linden Avenue 41	37N39	122w26	8:09:44
Lindenwood 41	37N27	122w11	8:08:44
Lindsay 54	36N12	119w05	7:56:20
Lingard 24	37N18	120w29	8:01:56
Linnell 54	36N20	119w18	7:57:12
Litchfield 18	40N23	120w23	8:01:32
Little Lake 14	35N56	117w55	7:51:40
Little Lake 33	33N45	116w56	7:47:44
Little Morongo Heights 36	34N03	116w35	7:46:20
Little Norway 9	38N49	120w03	8:00:12
Little Reed Heights 21	37N53	122w29	8:09:56
Littleriver 23	39N17	123w47	8:15:08
Littlerock 19	34N31	117w59	7:51:56
Little Shasta 47	41N44	122w31	8:10:04
Little Valley 18	40N54	121w11	8:04:44
Live Oak 51	39N17	121w40	8:06:40
Live Oak Acres 56	34N24	119w18	7:57:12
Live Oak Canyon 19	34N07	117w46	7:51:04
Live Oak Springs 37	32N41	116w20	7:45:20
Livermore 1	37N41	121w47	8:07:08
Livingston 24	37N23	120w43	8:02:52
Llano 19	34N30	117w50	7:51:20
Lobitos 41	37N30	122w28	8:09:52
Lobo 30	33N48	117w59	7:51:56
Loch Lomond 17	38N49	122w43	8:10:52
Locke 34	38N15	121w31	8:06:04
Lockeford 39	38N10	121w09	8:04:36
Lockhart 36	34N56	117w12	7:48:48
Lockwood 27	35N56	121w05	8:04:20
Locust 21	37N54	122w32	8:10:08
Lodge Pole 54	36N34	118w46	7:55:04
Lodi 39	38N08	121w16	8:05:04
Lodi Rural 39	38N09	121w18	8:05:12
Lodoga 6	39N18	122w29	8:09:56
Loftus 45	40N54	122w23	8:09:32
Loleta 12	40N38	124w13	8:16:52
Loma 19	33N46	118w08	7:52:32
Loma Linda 36	34N03	117w16	7:49:04
Loma Mar 41	37N16	122w18	8:09:12
Loma Rica 58	39N09	121w32	8:06:08
Lomas Santa Fe 37	32N59	117w16	7:49:04
Loma Verde 21	38N06	122w34	8:10:16
Lomita 19	33N47	118w19	7:53:16
Lomita Park 41	37N37	122w26	8:09:44
Lomo 51	39N17	121w40	8:06:40
Lompico 44	37N03	122w04	8:08:16
Lompoc 42	34N38	120w28	8:01:52
Lompoc Valley 42	34N40	120w24	8:01:36
London 54	36N32	119w23	7:57:32
Lone Pine 14	36N36	118w04	7:52:16
Lone Pine Indian Reservation 14	38N33	121w28	8:05:52
Long Barn 55	38N05	120w08	8:00:32
Long Beach 19	33N47	118w11	7:52:44
Long Beach Naval Shipyard 19	33N49	118w10	7:52:40
Longvale 23	39N25	123w21	8:13:24
Longview 19	34N30	117w55	7:51:40
Lonoak 35	36N13	121w07	8:04:28
Lonoke 43	37N01	121w35	8:06:20
Lookout 25	41N13	121w09	8:04:36
Loomis 31	38N49	121w12	8:04:48
Loomis Corners 45	40N33	122w22	8:09:28
Loop 19	33N56	118w11	7:52:44
Loraine 15	35N17	118w38	7:54:32
Loree Estates 43	37N19	122w02	8:08:08
Los Alamitos 30	33N48	118w04	7:52:16
Los Alamos 42	34N44	120w17	8:01:08
Los Altos 43	37N23	122w07	8:08:28
Los Altos Hills 43	37N22	122w08	8:08:32
Los Angeles 19	34N04	118w15	7:53:00
Los Banos 24	37N04	120w51	8:03:24
Los Berros 40	35N07	120w35	8:02:20
Los Coyotes Indian Res 37	33N49	116w32	7:46:08
Los Deltos 10	36N51	120w27	8:01:48
Los Feliz 19	34N06	118w18	7:53:12
Los Gatos 43	37N14	121w59	8:07:56
Los Medanos	38N01	121w51	8:07:24
Los Molinos 52	40N03	122w06	8:08:24
Los Nietos 19	33N59	118w04	7:52:16
Los Olivos 42	34N40	120w07	8:00:28
Los Osos 40	35N19	120w50	8:03:20
Los Padres 56	34N41	119w14	7:56:56
Los Posas Park 56	34N14	119w02	7:56:08
Los Ranchitos 21	38N01	122w33	8:10:12
Los Serranos 36	33N58	117w43	7:50:52
Lost Hills 15	35N37	119w41	7:58:44
Lost Lake 33	33N37	114w35	7:38:20
Lotus 9	38N48	120w55	8:03:40
Lower Lake 17	38N55	122w37	8:10:28
Lower Trinity 53	40N49	123w26	8:13:44
Loyalton 46	39N41	120w14	8:00:56
Loyola 43	37N22	122w06	8:08:24
Lucas Valley 21	38N01	122w33	8:10:12
Lucerne 17	39N06	122w48	8:11:12
Lucerne Valley 36	34N27	116w57	7:47:48
Ludlow	34N43	116w10	7:44:40

Lugo 19 34N01 118W12 7:52:48
Lundy 26 37N58 119W07 7:56:28
Lushmeadows Mountain Estates 22 37N29 119W58 7:59:52
Luther Burbank 49 38N27 122W42 8:10:48
Lynwood 19 33N56 118W13 7:52:52
Lynwood Gardens 19 33N55 118W12 7:52:48
Lynwood Hills 37 32N39 117W03 7:48:12
Lyoth 39 37N49 121W17 8:05:08
Lytle Creek 36 34N15 117W30 7:50:00
Lytton 38N40 122W52 8:11:28
Macdoel 47 41N50 122W00 8:08:00
Maclay 19 34N17 118W27 7:53:48
Madeline 18 41N03 120W28 8:01:52
Madeline Plains 18 40N52 120W22 8:01:28
Madera 20 36N57 120W03 8:00:12
Madera Acres 20 36N58 120W04 8:00:16
Madera Rural 20 36N59 120W05 8:00:20
Madera West 20 36N54 120W21 8:01:24
Madison 57 38N41 121W58 8:07:52
Madonna Road Plaza 40 35N18 120W45 8:03:00
Mad River 53 40N18 123W26 8:13:44
Madrone 43 37N08 121W39 8:06:36
Magalia 4 39N49 121W35 8:06:20
Magnolia 13 32N59 115W32 7:42:08
Magnolia Center 33 33N57 117W23 7:49:32
Magnolia Park 19 34N10 118W20 7:53:20
Malaga 10 36N41 119W44 7:58:56
Malibu 19 34N02 118W41 7:54:44
Malibu Beach 19 34N02 118W41 7:54:44
Malibu Canyon Homes 19 34N08 118W39 7:54:36
Malott 7 37N55 122W18 8:09:12
Maltby 38N01 122W04 8:08:16
Mammoth Lakes 26 37N39 118W59 7:55:56
Manchester 23 38N58 123W41 8:14:44
Manhattan Beach 19 33N54 118W25 7:53:40
Manila 12 40N52 124W05 8:16:20
Mankas Corners 48 38N14 122W02 8:08:08
Manor 21 37N59 122W35 8:10:20
Manteca 39 37N48 121W13 8:04:52
Manton 52 40N26 121W52 8:07:28
Manzanita 4 39N22 121W42 8:06:48
Manzanita Indian Reservation 37 33N49 116W32 7:46:08
Maple Creek 12 40N52 123W58 8:15:52
Maravilla Park 19 34N01 118W09 7:52:36
Marcelina 19 33N50 118W19 7:53:16
March 33 33N54 117W16 7:49:04
March Air Force Base 33 33N54 117W15 7:49:00
Mare Island 48 38N06 122W16 8:09:04
Mariani Mall 43 37N19 122W02 8:08:08
Maricopa 15 35N04 119W24 7:57:36
Marigold 36 34N04 117W12 7:48:48
Marina 27 36N41 121W48 8:07:12
Marina 38 37N48 122W26 8:09:44
Marina Del Rey 19 33N58 118W27 7:53:48
Marin City 21 37N52 122W30 8:10:00
Marin Country Club Estates 21 38N06 122W34 8:10:16
Marine Corps Base 36 34N08 116W04 7:44:16
Marine Corps Recruit Depot 37 32N45 117W09 7:48:36
Marine Corps Supply Center 36 34N58 116W55 7:47:40
Mariner 30 33N46 118W05 7:52:20
Marinwood 21 38N02 122W32 8:10:08
Mariposa 22 37N29 119W58 7:59:52
Market 19 34N02 118W15 7:53:00
Markleeville 2 38N42 119W47 7:59:08
Mark West 49 38N27 122W42 8:10:48
Marloma 19 33N46 118W21 7:53:24
Marne 19 34N05 117W31 7:50:04
Marshall 21 38N10 122W53 8:11:32
Marshall Station 10 36N49 119W43 7:58:52
Martell 3 38N22 120W48 8:03:12
Martinez 7 38N01 122W08 8:08:32
Martins Beach 41 37N30 122W28 8:09:52
Mart Of Montebello 19 34N01 118W07 7:52:28
Mar Vista 19 34N00 118W26 7:53:44
Marysville 58 39N16 121W28 8:05:52
Massack 32 39N56 120W55 8:03:40
Mather 34 38N34 121W21 8:05:24
Mather Air Force Base 34 38N33 121W17 8:05:08
Mather Heights 34 38N33 121W17 8:05:08
Maxwell 6 39N17 122W11 8:08:44
Mayflower Village 19 34N08 118W00 7:52:00
Maywood 19 33N59 118W11 7:52:44
McArthur 45 41N03 121W24 8:05:36
McCann 12 40N21 123W55 8:15:40
McClellan Air Force Base 34 38N40 121W23 8:05:32
McCloud 47 41N15 122W08 8:08:32
McFarland 15 35N41 119W14 7:56:56
McKeon 31 38N54 121W04 8:04:16
McKinleyville 12 40N57 124W06 8:16:24
McKittrick 15 35N18 119W37 7:58:28
McKnight Acres 28 38N07 122W14 8:08:56
McLane 10 36N46 119W45 7:59:00
McLaren 38 37N43 122W25 8:09:40
McMillan Manor 56 34N12 119W10 7:56:40
Meadowbrook 33 33N47 117W14 7:48:56
Meadow Lake Park 29 39N20 120W12 8:00:48
Meadow Lakes 10 37N05 119W29 7:57:56
Meadowsweet 21 37N56 122W31 8:10:04
Meadow Valley 32 39N56 121W05 8:04:20
Meadow Vista 31 39N06 121W01 8:04:04
Mead Valley 33 33N47 117W14 7:48:56

Mecca 33 33N34 116W05 7:44:20
Medicine Lake Lodge 47 41N57 121W28 8:05:52
Meeks Bay 9 39N09 120W09 8:00:36
Melody Oaks Trailer Park 3 38N21 120W46 8:03:04
Meloland 13 32N48 115W34 7:42:16
Melones 5 38N04 120W33 8:02:12
Melsons Corner 9 38N40 120W40 8:02:40
Melvin 10 36N49 119W43 7:58:52
Mendocino 23 39N19 123W48 8:15:12
Mendota 10 36N45 120W23 8:01:32
Menifee 33 33N45 117W10 7:48:40
Menlo Park 41 37N27 122W12 8:08:48
Mentone 36 34N04 117W08 7:48:32
Merced 24 37N18 120W29 8:01:56
Merced Falls 24 37N31 120W26 8:01:44
Meridian 51 39N09 121W55 8:07:40
Merrill 36 34N06 117W28 7:49:52
Merritt-Peck Colonies 10 36N36 119W27 7:57:48
Mesa Center 30 33N39 117W55 7:51:40
Mesa Grande 37 33N07 116W40 7:46:40
Mesa Verde 33 33N37 114W35 7:38:20
Metro Main 34 38N33 121W28 8:05:52
Metropolitan 12 40N35 124W08 8:16:32
Metropolitan 19 34N05 118W22 7:53:28
Mettler 15 35N23 119W01 7:56:04
Metz 27 36N25 121W19 8:05:16
Mexican Colony 15 35N30 119W16 7:57:04
Michigan Bluff 31 39N01 120W49 8:03:16
Michillinda 19 34N09 118W05 7:52:20
Mid City 39 37N57 121W17 8:05:08
Midco 42 34N54 120W26 8:01:44
Middlefield Road 41 37N28 122W14 8:08:56
Middle River 39 37N56 121W26 8:05:44
Middletown 17 38N45 122W37 8:10:28
Midlake 17 39N09 123W12 8:12:48
Midland 33N52 114W48 7:39:12
Midpines 22 37N33 119W56 7:59:44
Midtown 4 39N44 121W50 8:07:20
Midtown Center 19 34N03 118W20 7:53:20
Midway City 30 33N45 117W59 7:51:56
Midway Wells 13 33N00 115W04 7:40:16
Mikon 57 38N36 121W32 8:06:08
Milford 18 40N10 120W22 8:01:28
Millbrae 41 37N36 122W24 8:09:36
Millbrae Meadows 41 37N36 122W24 8:09:36
Mill Creek 52 40N19 121W32 8:06:08
Mill Creek Park 36 34N05 117W08 7:48:32
Millers Corners 20 36N58 120W04 8:00:16
Mills 38 37N47 122W25 8:09:40
Mills College 1 37N47 122W11 8:08:44
Millsdale 41 37N35 122W22 8:09:28
Mills Orchard 11 39N45 122W01 8:08:04
Mill Valley 21 37N54 122W32 8:10:08
Millville 45 40N33 122W11 8:08:44
Milo 54 36N08 118W49 7:55:16
Milpas 42 34N26 119W41 7:58:44
Milpitas 43 37N26 121W55 8:07:40
Milton 5 37N56 121W00 8:04:00
Mineral 52 40N21 121W36 8:06:24
Mineralking 54 36N26 118W54 7:55:36
Minkler 10 36N42 119W33 7:58:12
Mint Canyon 19 34N25 118W32 7:54:08
Mirabel Heights 49 38N28 122W53 8:11:32
Mirabel Park 49 38N28 122W53 8:11:32
Miracle Hot Springs 15 35N35 118W32 7:54:08
Miracle Manor 15 35N08 117W59 7:51:56
Miraleste 19 33N46 118W21 7:53:24
Mira Loma 33 34N00 117W31 7:50:04
Miramar 37 32N52 117W08 7:48:32
Miramar 41 37N30 122W28 8:09:52
Mira Mesa 37 32N55 117W08 7:48:32
Miramonte 10 36N42 119W03 7:56:12
Mira Monte 56 34N27 119W16 7:57:04
Miranda 12 40N14 123W49 8:15:16
Mira Vista 7 37N57 122W19 8:09:16
Missile View 42 34N54 120W26 8:01:44
Mission 43 37N21 121W59 8:07:56
Mission Annex 38 37N46 122W26 8:09:44
Mission Bay 37 32N47 117W14 7:48:56
Mission Beach 37 32N47 117W15 7:49:00
Mission Canyon 42 34N27 119W43 7:58:52
Mission Hills 37 32N45 117W10 7:48:40
Mission Hills 42 34N42 120W29 8:01:56
Mission Rafael 21 37N59 122W32 8:10:08
Mission San Jose 1 37N32 121W58 8:07:52
Mission Valley 37 32N46 117W09 7:48:36
Mission Viejo 30 33N36 117W40 7:50:40
Mission Village 37 32N48 117W08 7:48:32
Mitchell Corner 54 36N20 119W18 7:57:12
Mitchell Mill 5 38N23 120W31 8:02:04
Mi-Wuk Village 55 38N05 120W13 8:00:52
Moccasin 55 37N49 120W18 8:01:12
Mococo 7 37N59 122W07 8:08:28
Modesto 50 37N39 121W00 8:04:00
Modjeska 30 33N49 117W50 7:51:20
Moffett Field 43 37N25 122W03 8:08:12
Mojave 15 35N03 118W10 7:52:40
Mojave Heights 36 34N33 117W21 7:49:24
Mojave Valley 36 34N53 117W07 7:48:28
Mokelumne Hill 5 38N18 120W43 8:02:52
Monarch Bay 30 33N31 117W43 7:50:52
Mona Vista 55 37N59 120W23 8:01:32
Monmouth 10 36N34 119W44 7:58:56
Mono Hot Springs 10 37N21 119W01 7:56:04
Mono Lake 38N01 119W09 7:56:36
Monolith 35N07 118W22 7:53:28
Monrovia 19 34N09 118W00 7:52:00
Monson 54 36N32 119W23 7:57:32
Montague 47 41N44 122W32 8:10:08

CALIFORNIA

Montair 7 37N50 122W00 8:08:00
Montalvin Manor 7 37N58 122W20 8:09:20
Montalvo 56 34N15 119W12 7:56:48
Montana 19 34N02 118W30 7:54:00
Montara 41 37N33 122W31 8:10:04
Monta Vista 43 37N19 122W03 8:08:12
Montclair 36 34N03 117W42 7:50:48
Montclair Plaza 36 34N05 117W41 7:50:44
Montebello 19 34N00 118W07 7:52:28
Montebello Gardens 19 33N59 118W05 7:52:20
Montecito 42 34N26 119W40 7:58:40
Monte Nido 19 34N08 118W39 7:54:36
Monterey 27 36N37 121W55 8:07:40
Monterey Park 19 34N04 118W08 7:52:32
Monterey Peninsula 27 36N36 121W56 8:07:44
Monte Rio 49 38N28 123W00 8:12:00
Montesano 49 38N30 123W00 8:12:00
Monte Sereno 43 37N15 121W59 8:07:56
Monte Toyon 44 36N59 121W54 8:07:36
Montgomery Creek 45 40N51 121W55 8:07:40
Montgomery Field 37 32N49 117W08 7:48:32
Montgomery Village 49 38N27 122W42 8:10:48
Montrose 19 34N12 118W14 7:52:56
Moody 30 33N49 118W02 7:52:08
Moonridge 36 34N15 116W53 7:47:32
Moonstone 12 41N04 124W08 8:16:32
Moorpark 56 34N17 118W53 7:55:32
Moorpark Home Acres 56 34N17 118W53 7:55:32
Morada 39 38N02 121W15 8:05:00
Moraga 7 37N50 122W08 8:08:32
Mora Villa 42 34N26 119W42 7:58:48
Morena 37 32N50 116W56 7:47:44
Moreno 33 33N55 117W09 7:48:36
Moreno Valley 33 33N56 117W15 7:49:00
Morgan Hill 43 37N08 121W39 8:06:36
Mormon Bar 22 37N29 119W58 7:59:52
Morningside Park 19 33N58 118W19 7:53:16
Morongo Indian Reservation 33 33N49 116W32 7:46:08
Morongo Valley 36 34N03 116W35 7:46:20
Morro Bay 40 35N22 120W51 8:03:24
Morro Palisades 40 35N18 120W45 8:03:00
Morse 35 36N51 121W32 8:06:08
Moss Beach 41 37N32 122W31 8:10:04
Mossdale 39 37N49 121W17 8:05:08
Moss Landing 27 36N48 121W47 8:07:08
Mountain Center 33 33N42 116W44 7:46:56
Mountain Empire 37 32N42 116W28 7:45:52
Mountain Gate 45 40N33 122W22 8:09:28
Mountain House 1 37N43 121W26 8:05:44
Mountain Mesa 15 35N39 118W28 7:53:52
Mountain Pass 36 35N28 115W16 7:41:04
Mountain Ranch 5 38N14 120W33 8:02:12
Mountain Spring 37 32N37 116W11 7:44:44
Mountain View 15 35N21 118W59 7:55:56
Mountain View 43 37N23 122W05 8:08:20
Mountain View Acres 36 34N33 117W21 7:49:24
Mount Aukum 9 38N33 120W44 8:02:56
Mount Baldy 36 34N14 117W40 7:50:40
Mount Bullion 22 37N29 119W58 7:59:52
Mount Eden 1 37N37 122W06 8:08:24
Mount Hamilton 43 37N21 121W50 8:07:20
Mount Hebron 47 41N47 122W00 8:08:00
Mount Helix 37 32N46 116W59 7:47:56
Mount Hermon 44 37N03 122W04 8:08:16
Mount Laguna 37 32N52 116W25 7:45:40
Mount San Antonio 19 34N00 117W51 7:51:24
Mount Shasta 47 41N19 122W19 8:09:16
Mount Signal 13 32N41 115W29 7:41:56
Mount View 7 37N59 122W07 8:08:28
Mount Wilson 19 34N14 118W04 7:52:16
Mugginsville 47 41N37 122W51 8:11:24
Muir 23 39N25 123W21 8:13:24
Muir Beach 21 38N04 122W48 8:11:12
Muir Woods 21 37N54 122W32 8:10:08
Mulberry 4 39N44 121W49 8:07:16
Murphys 5 38N08 120W28 8:01:52
Murray Park 21 37N56 122W32 8:10:08
Murrieta 33 33N33 117W13 7:48:52
Murrieta Hot Springs 33 33N33 117W13 7:48:52
Muscoy 36 34N10 117W20 7:49:20
Myers Flat 12 40N16 123W53 8:15:32
Myrtletowne 12 40N47 124W10 8:16:40
Nadeau 19 33N59 118W15 7:53:00
Nanceville 54 36N04 119W04 7:56:16
Napa 28 38N18 122W17 8:09:08
Narod 34N04 117W41 7:50:44
Nashville 9 38N41 120W51 8:03:24
National City 37 32N41 117W05 7:48:20
Natomas 34 38N40 121W33 8:06:12
Navajo 37 32N47 117W02 7:48:08
Naval 37 32N45 117W09 7:48:36
Naval 56 34N10 119W12 7:56:48
Naval Air Station 1 37N47 122W16 8:09:04
Naval Air Station 16 36N17 119W51 7:59:24
Naval Hospital 1 37N48 122W13 8:08:52
Naval Hospital 37 32N45 117W09 7:48:36
Naval Supply Center 1 37N48 122W13 8:08:52
Naval Training Center 37 32N45 117W09 7:48:36
Navarro 23 39N09 123W33 8:14:12
Navelencia 10 36N36 119W27 7:57:48
Nebo Center 36 34N52 116W57 7:47:48

CALIFORNIA

Place	Lat	Long	Time
Needles 36	34N51	114w37	7:38:28
Neenach 19	34N40	118w11	7:52:44
Nelson 4	39N33	121w46	8:07:04
Nestor 37	32N45	117w09	7:48:36
Nevada 29	39N19	120w59	8:03:56
Nevada City 29	39N16	121w01	8:04:04
New Almaden 43	37N11	121w49	8:07:16
Newark 1	37N32	122w02	8:08:08
New Auberry 10	37N05	119w29	7:57:56
Newberry Springs 36	34N50	116w41	7:46:44
Newburg 12	40N35	124w08	8:16:32
Newbury Park 56	34N11	118w53	7:55:32
Newcastle 31	38N53	121w08	8:04:32
New Chicago 3	38N25	120w49	8:03:16
New Cuyama 42	34N56	119w39	7:58:36
Newell 25	41N57	121w28	8:05:52
Newhall 19	34N23	118w32	7:54:08
Newhall Ranch 19	34N25	118w32	7:54:08
Newman 50	37N19	121w01	8:04:04
New Monterey 27	36N36	121w53	8:07:32
New Pine Creek 25	42N00	120w18	8:01:12
Newport Beach 30	33N37	117w56	7:51:44
Newtown 9	38N44	120w48	8:03:12
Newtown 29	39N16	121w01	8:04:04
Newville 11	39N45	122w11	8:08:44
Nicasio 21	38N04	122w42	8:10:48
Nice 17	39N07	122w51	8:11:24
Nicolaus 51	38N55	121w35	8:06:20
Nigger Hill 9	38N44	120w48	8:03:12
Nightingale 33	33N48	116w44	7:46:56
Niguel Terrace 30	33N31	117w43	7:50:52
Niland 13	33N14	115w31	7:42:04
Niles 1	37N35	121w58	8:07:52
Nimshew 4	39N49	121w35	8:06:20
Nipomo 40	35N03	120w29	8:01:56
Nipton 36	35N28	115w16	7:41:04
Noe Valley 38	37N45	122w26	8:09:44
Norco 33	33N56	117w33	7:50:12
Nord 4	39N47	121w57	8:07:48
Norden 29	39N20	120w22	8:01:28
Normal Heights 37	32N46	117w07	7:48:28
North Annex 19	34N18	118w26	7:53:44
North Antelope Valley 19	34N42	118w12	7:52:48
North Bay View Park 27	36N37	121w50	8:07:20
North Beach 38	37N48	122w26	8:09:44
North Belridge 15	34N50	120w32	8:02:08
North Berkeley 1	37N53	122w16	8:09:04
North Bloomfield 29	39N16	121w01	8:04:04
North Carlsbad 37	33N12	117w20	7:49:20
North City 37	33N03	117w04	7:48:16
North Coastal 12	41N00	124w04	8:16:16
North Columbia 29	39N16	121w01	8:04:04
Northcrest 8	41N46	124w12	8:16:48
North Cucamonga 36	34N06	117w35	7:50:20
North Downey 19	33N57	118w08	7:52:32
Northeast Modesto 50	37N38	120w59	8:03:56
North Edwards 15	34N56	117w57	7:51:48
North El Dorado 9	38N48	120w44	8:02:56
North Elsinore 33	33N55	117w44	7:50:56
North Fair Oaks 41	37N29	122w12	8:08:48
North Fillmore 56	34N24	118w55	7:55:40
North Fork 20	37N14	119w31	7:58:04
North Gardena 19	33N53	118w17	7:53:08
North Glendale 19	34N10	118w14	7:52:56
North Highlands 34	38N42	121w22	8:05:28
North Hills 19	34N16	118w30	7:54:00
North Hollywood 19	34N10	118w23	7:53:32
North Inglewood 19	33N58	118w21	7:53:24
North Island 37	32N42	117w14	7:48:56
North Loma Linda 36	34N04	117w16	7:49:04
North Long Beach 19	33N52	118w10	7:52:40
North Oaks 19	34N25	118w32	7:54:08
North Palm Springs 33	33N56	116w32	7:46:08
North Park 37	32N45	117w07	7:48:28
North Redondo Beach 19	33N52	118w22	7:53:28
North Richmond 7	37N57	122w22	8:09:28
Northridge 19	34N14	118w33	7:54:12
North Sacramento 34	38N36	121w26	8:05:44
North San Juan 29	39N22	121w06	8:04:24
North Seal Beach 30	33N46	118w05	7:52:20
North Shafter 15	35N30	119w16	7:57:04
North Shore 33	33N34	116w05	7:44:20
North Torrance 19	33N52	118w20	7:53:20
North Turlock 50	37N29	120w50	8:03:20
North Valley Plaza 4	39N44	121w50	8:07:20
Northwest 21	38N13	122w50	8:11:20
North Whittier 19	34N03	117w59	7:51:56
North Whittier Heights 19	34N00	117w57	7:51:48
Norton Air Force Base 36	34N06	117w15	7:49:00
Norwalk 19	33N54	118w05	7:52:20
Norwalk Manor 19	33N54	118w05	7:52:20
Norwood Center 19	34N17	118w27	7:53:48
Novato 21	38N06	122w35	8:10:20
Noyo 23	39N27	123w48	8:15:12
Nubieber 18	41N06	121w11	8:04:44
Nuevo 33	33N48	117w09	7:48:36
Nut Tree 48	38N21	121w59	8:07:56
Nyland Acres 56	34N12	119w10	7:56:40
Oak Bottom 45	40N38	122w33	8:10:12
Oakdale 50	37N46	120w51	8:03:24
Oak Glen 36	34N02	117w05	7:48:20
Oak Grove 4	39N30	121w33	8:06:12
Oak Grove 37	33N27	116w51	7:47:24
Oakhurst 20	37N19	119w40	7:58:40
Oak Knoll Hills 43	37N19	122w02	8:08:08
Oak Knolls 42	34N54	120w26	8:01:44
Oakland 1	37N49	122w16	8:09:04
Oakland Recreational Camp 55	37N50	120w14	8:00:56
Oakley 7	38N00	121w44	8:06:56
Oak Park 34	38N33	121w28	8:05:52
Oak Park 40	35N38	120w41	8:02:44
Oak Run 45	40N41	122w02	8:08:08
Oaks 40	35N07	120w35	8:02:20
Oak Valley 56	34N09	118w48	7:55:12
Oak View 56	34N24	119w18	7:57:12
Oakville 28	38N26	122w24	8:09:36
Oakwood 19	34N05	118w18	7:53:12
Oasis 33	33N39	116w09	7:44:36
O'Brien 45	40N49	122w20	8:09:20
Occidental 49	38N24	122w57	8:11:48
Ocean Beach 37	32N44	117w14	7:48:56
Oceano 40	35N06	120w37	8:02:28
Ocean Park 19	34N01	118w28	7:53:52
Oceanside 37	33N12	117w23	7:49:32
Ocean View 49	38N20	123w03	8:12:12
Ocotillo Wells 37	33N13	116w20	7:45:20
Oildale 15	35N25	119w01	7:56:04
Ojai 56	34N27	119w15	7:57:00
Olancha 14	36N17	118w01	7:52:04
Old Fellows Park 49	38N30	123w00	8:12:00
Old Fort Jim 9	38N44	120w48	8:03:12
Old Gilroy 43	37N01	121w35	8:06:20
Old Mammoth 26	37N38	118w58	7:55:52
Old River 15	35N21	119w03	7:56:12
Old San Diego 37	32N46	117w11	7:48:44
Old Station 45	40N41	121w26	8:05:44
Oleander 10	36N43	119w48	7:59:12
Olema 21	38N02	122w47	8:11:08
Olinda 30	33N55	117w53	7:51:32
Olinda 45	40N27	122w18	8:09:12
Olive 30	33N50	117w50	7:51:20
Olivehurst 58	39N06	121w34	8:06:16
Olivenhain 37	33N03	117w17	7:49:08
Olympia 44	37N03	122w04	8:08:16
Olympic 19	34N04	118w24	7:53:36
Olympic Valley 31	39N09	120w09	8:00:36
Omo Ranch 9	38N35	120w35	8:02:20
O'Neals 20	37N08	119w42	7:58:48
One Hundred Palms 33	33N39	116w09	7:44:36
Ono 45	40N29	122w37	8:10:28
Ontario 36	34N04	117w39	7:50:36
Onyx 15	35N41	118w14	7:52:56
Opal Cliffs 44	36N58	121w58	8:07:52
Ophir 31	38N54	121w04	8:04:16
Orange 30	33N47	117w51	7:51:24
Orange Cove 10	36N38	119w19	7:57:16
Orange Heights 36	34N06	117w38	7:50:32
Orangehurst 30	33N52	117w58	7:51:52
Orange Park Acres 30	33N48	117w47	7:51:08
Orangevale 34	38N41	121w13	8:04:52
Orcutt 42	34N52	120w27	8:01:48
Ordbend 11	39N31	122w01	8:08:04
Oregon City 4	39N30	121w33	8:06:12
Oregon House 58	39N21	121w17	8:05:08
Orick 12	41N17	124w04	8:16:16
Orinda 7	37N53	122w11	8:08:44
Orland 11	39N45	122w12	8:08:48
Orleans 12	41N18	123w32	8:14:08
Ormand 33	34N00	117w26	7:49:44
Oro Fino 47	41N37	122w51	8:11:24
Oro Grande 36	34N36	117w21	7:49:24
Oro Loma 10	36N51	120w27	8:01:48
Orosi 54	36N33	119w17	7:57:08
Oroville 4	39N31	121w33	8:06:12
Osbourne 19	34N06	118w20	7:53:20
Otay 37	32N36	117w04	7:48:16
Otterbein 19	34N00	117w53	7:51:32
Outingdale 9	38N40	120w40	8:02:40
Oval 54	36N20	119w18	7:57:12
Owenyo	36N38	118w04	7:52:16
Oxnard 56	34N12	119w10	7:56:40
Oxnard Beach 56	34N12	119w10	7:56:40
Pabrico 1	38N16	122w26	8:09:44
Pacheco 7	37N59	122w04	8:08:16
Pacific 19	33N48	118w11	7:52:44
Pacifica 41	37N36	122w30	8:10:00
Pacific Beach 37	32N48	117w14	7:48:56
Pacific Gardens 39	37N58	121w19	8:05:16
Pacific Grove 27	36N37	121w55	8:07:40
Pacific House 9	38N46	120w30	8:02:00
Pacific Manor 12	40N52	124w05	8:16:20
Pacific Manor 41	37N38	122w29	8:09:56
Pacific Palisades 19	34N05	118w30	7:54:00
Pacific Villas 39	37N58	121w19	8:05:16
Pacoima 19	34N16	118w26	7:53:44
Paddison Square 19	33N54	118w05	7:52:20
Paddon 48	38N21	121w59	8:07:56
Paicines 35	36N44	121w17	8:05:08
Paintersville 34	38N20	121w34	8:06:16
Pajaro 27	36N55	121w47	8:07:08
Pala 37	33N22	117w05	7:48:20
Pala Mesa Village 37	33N23	117w21	7:49:24
Palermo 4	39N26	121w33	8:06:12
Pallett 19	34N26	117w50	7:51:20
Palm City 33	33N43	116w19	7:45:16
Palmdale 19	34N35	118w07	7:52:28
Palm Desert 33	33N43	116w22	7:45:28
Palmer Creek 12	40N35	124w08	8:16:32
Palms 19	34N02	118w24	7:53:36
Palm Springs 33	33N49	116w32	7:46:08
Palm Wells 36	34N03	116w35	7:46:20
Palo Alto 43	37N27	122w10	8:08:40
Palo Cedro 45	40N34	122w14	8:08:56
Paloma 5	38N12	120w50	8:03:20
Palomares 1	37N42	122w05	8:08:20
Palomar Mountain 37	33N20	116w55	7:47:40
Palomar Park 41	37N28	122w15	8:09:00
Palos Verdes 19	33N43	118w21	7:53:24
Palos Verdes Estates 19	33N48	118w23	7:53:32
Palos Verdes Peninsula 19	33N46	118w22	7:53:28
Palo Verde 13	33N26	114w44	7:38:56
Panama 15	35N21	119w03	7:56:12
Panamint Springs 14	36N36	118w04	7:52:16
Panoche 35	36N44	121w17	8:05:08
Panorama City 19	34N11	118w26	7:53:44
Panorama Heights 30	33N47	117w48	7:51:12
Panorama Heights 54	35N48	118w43	7:54:52
Paradise 4	39N46	121w37	8:06:28
Paradise 50	37N38	121w01	8:04:04
Paradise Camp 26	37N22	118w24	7:53:36
Paradise Cay 21	37N53	122w29	8:09:56
Paradise Park 44	36N59	122w00	8:08:00
Paramount 19	33N53	118w10	7:52:40
Parchers Camp 14	37N22	118w24	7:53:36
Park 1	37N52	122w17	8:09:08
Park Central 1	37N47	122w16	8:09:04
Parker Dam 36	34N17	114w09	7:36:36
Parkfield 27	35N54	120w26	8:01:44
Parkmoor 43	37N19	121w55	8:07:40
Parkside 38	37N45	122w29	8:09:56
Park Siding 49	38N13	122w38	8:10:32
Park Village 14	36N18	116w45	7:47:00
Parkway 34	38N29	121w27	8:05:48
Parkway Estates 34	38N29	121w27	8:05:48
Parkwood 20	36N58	120w04	8:00:16
Parlier 10	36N37	119w32	7:58:08
Pasadena 19	34N09	118w09	7:52:36
Pasatiempo 44	37N00	122w01	8:08:04
Paskenta 52	39N53	122w33	8:10:12
Paso Robles 40	35N42	120w36	8:02:24
Patata 19	33N56	118w11	7:52:44
Patterson 50	37N28	121w08	8:04:32
Patton Village 18	40N09	120w08	8:00:32
Pauma Valley 37	33N19	117w00	7:48:00
Paxton 32	40N01	120w58	8:03:52
Paynes Creek 52	40N20	121w55	8:07:40
Paynesville 2	38N49	119w41	7:58:44
Peanut 53	40N33	123w11	8:12:44
Pearblossom 19	34N30	117w55	7:51:40
Peardale 29	39N13	121w04	8:04:16
Pearland 19	34N35	118w06	7:52:24
Pearsonville 14	35N39	117w49	7:51:16
Pebble Beach 27	36N34	121w57	8:07:48
Pecwan 12	41N03	123w40	8:14:40
Pedley 33	33N58	117w29	7:49:56
Pedro Valley 41	37N38	122w29	8:09:56
Penasquitos 37	32N59	117w07	7:48:28
Pendleton 37	33N22	117w25	7:49:40
Peninsula Center 19	33N46	118w21	7:53:24
Peninsula Village 32	40N18	121w01	8:04:04
Penngrove 49	38N18	122w40	8:10:40
Pennington 51	39N17	121w40	8:06:40
Penn Valley 29	39N13	121w04	8:04:16
Penryn 31	38N51	121w10	8:04:40
Pentz 4	39N30	121w33	8:06:12
Pepperwood 12	40N21	123w55	8:15:40
Perkins 34	38N33	121w22	8:05:28
Perris 33	33N47	117w14	7:48:56
Perris Valley 33	33N48	117w12	7:48:48
Perry 19	33N57	118w00	7:52:00
Perry 43	37N08	121w39	8:06:36
Pescadero 41	37N15	122w23	8:09:32
Petaluma 49	38N14	122w39	8:10:36
Petaluma Rural 49	38N16	122w41	8:10:44
Peters 39	38N01	121w05	8:04:20
Petrolia 12	40N19	124w17	8:17:08
Phelan 36	34N25	117w34	7:50:16
Phillipsville 12	40N13	123w47	8:15:08
Philo 23	39N04	123w26	8:13:44
Pico 19	33N59	118w05	7:52:20
Pico Heights 19	34N03	118w18	7:53:12
Pico Rivera 19	33N59	118w05	7:52:20
Piedmont 1	37N50	122w14	8:08:56
Piedra 10	36N47	119w25	7:57:40
Piercy 23	39N59	123w48	8:15:12
Pike 46	39N22	121w06	8:04:24
Pilot Hill 9	38N50	121w01	8:04:04
Pine Bluff 34	38N41	121w11	8:04:44
Pine Cove 33	33N45	116w43	7:46:52
Pinecrest 55	38N11	120w00	8:00:00
Pinedale 10	36N50	119w48	7:59:12
Pine Flat 54	35N53	118w41	7:54:44
Pine Grove 3	38N25	120w40	8:02:40
Pine Grove 17	38N49	122w43	8:10:52
Pine Grove 23	39N27	123w48	8:15:12
Pine Grove 45	40N41	122w21	8:09:24
Pine Hills 12	40N47	124w10	8:16:40
Pine Hills 37	33N05	116w36	7:46:24
Pinehurst 10	36N42	119w00	7:56:00
Pineridge 10	37N04	119w22	7:57:28
Pine Valley 37	32N49	116w32	7:46:08
Pinole 7	38N00	122w17	8:09:08
Pinon Hills 36	34N08	117w18	7:49:12
Pinyon Pines 33	33N48	116w44	7:46:56
Pioneer 3	38N25	120w33	8:02:12
Pioneer Point 36	35N46	117w23	7:49:32
Pioneertown 36	34N10	116w30	7:46:00
Piru 56	34N25	118w48	7:55:12
Pismo Beach 40	35N09	120w38	8:02:32
Pittsburg 7	38N02	121w53	8:07:32

Pittville 18 41N03 121w24 8:05:36
Pixley 54 35N58 119w18 7:57:12
Placentia 30 33N53 117w52 7:51:28
Placerville 9 38N44 120w48 8:03:12
Plainsburg 24 37N18 120w29 8:01:56
Plainview 54 36N09 119w03 7:56:12
Planada 24 37N18 120w19 8:01:16
Planehaven 34 38N40 121w23 8:05:32
Plano 54 36N04 119w04 7:56:16
Plantation 49 38N32 123w05 8:12:20
Plaster City 13 32N47 115w51 7:43:24
Platina 45 40N22 122w53 8:11:32
Playa Del Rey 19 33N59 118w27 7:53:48
Playmor 37 32N37 117w04 7:48:16
Plaza 30 33N47 117w50 7:51:20
Plaza Camino Real 37 33N01 117w17 7:49:08
Plaza Center 36 34N03 117w39 7:50:36
Pleasant Grove 51 38N49 121w29 8:05:56
Pleasant Hill 7 37N57 122w04 8:08:16
Pleasant Hill 12 40N52 124w05 8:16:20
Pleasanton 1 37N40 121w52 8:07:28
Pleasant Valley 9 38N44 120w48 8:03:12
Plymouth 3 38N29 120w51 8:03:24
Poinsettia Tract 7 38N00 121w51 8:07:24
Point Arena 23 38N55 123w41 8:14:44
Point Firmin 19 33N44 118w18 7:53:12
Point Loma 37 32N44 117w14 7:48:56
Point Mugu 56 34N07 119w06 7:56:24
Point Pleasant 34 38N25 121w22 8:05:28
Point Reyes Station 21 38N04 122w48 8:11:12
Point Richmond 7 37N56 122w20 8:09:20
Pollock Pines 9 38N46 120w34 8:02:16
Pomona 19 34N04 117w45 7:51:00
Pond 15 35N43 119w20 7:57:20
Pondosa 47 41N12 121w41 8:06:44
Pope Valley 28 38N37 122w26 8:09:44
Poplar 54 36N03 119w09 7:56:36
Port Chicago 7 38N03 122w01 8:08:04
Port Costa 7 38N03 122w11 8:08:44
Porterville 54 36N04 119w01 7:56:04
Port Hueneme 56 34N07 119w12 7:56:48
Port Kenyon 12 40N35 124w16 8:17:04
Portola 32 39N49 120w28 8:01:52
Portola Terrace 41 37N27 122w11 8:08:44
Portola Valley 41 37N23 122w13 8:08:52
Port San Luis 40 35N11 120w44 8:02:56
Portuguese Bend 19 33N46 118w21 7:53:24
Posey 54 35N48 118w43 7:54:52
Poso Park 54 35N48 118w43 7:54:52
Posts 27 36N15 121w48 8:07:12
Potrero 37 32N36 116w37 7:46:28
Potter Valley 23 39N19 123w07 8:12:28
Poway 37 32N58 117w02 7:48:08
Pozo 40 35N23 120w37 8:02:28
Prather 10 37N02 119w31 7:58:04
Prattco 27 36N37 121w50 8:07:20
Prattville 32 40N10 121w04 8:04:16
Presidio 38 37N47 122w27 8:09:48
Presidio Of Monterey 27 36N36 121w53 8:07:32
Preston Heights 12 40N52 124w05 8:16:20
Preuss 19 34N03 118w23 7:53:32
Priest Valley 27 36N08 120w22 8:01:28
Princeton 6 39N24 122w01 8:08:04
Princeton 41 37N30 122w28 8:09:52
Princeton-by-the-Sea 41 37N30 122w28 8:09:52
Proberta 52 40N05 122w10 8:08:40
Project City 45 40N41 122w21 8:09:24
Prosser Lakeview Estates 29 39N20 120w12 8:00:48
Prunedale 27 36N41 121w39 8:06:36
Pudding Creek 23 39N27 123w48 8:15:12
Puente Junction 19 34N02 117w56 7:51:44
Pulga 4 39N30 121w33 8:06:12
Pumpkin Center 15 35N21 119w03 7:56:12
Quail Valley 33 33N42 117w14 7:48:56
Quaking Aspen 54 36N08 118w49 7:55:16
Quartz 55 37N57 120w25 8:01:40
Quartz Hill 19 34N40 118w13 7:52:52
Quincy 32 39N56 120w57 8:03:48
Quito 43 37N17 122w01 8:08:04
Rackerby 58 39N26 121w20 8:05:20
Radec 33 33N45 116w56 7:47:44
Rafael Village 21 38N06 122w34 8:10:16
Rail Road Flat 5 38N20 120w30 8:02:00
Rainbow 37 33N23 117w21 7:49:24
Raisin 10 36N36 119w54 7:59:36
Ralph 55 37N59 120w23 8:01:32
Ramirez 19 34N00 118w17 7:53:08
Ramona 37 33N02 116w52 7:47:28
Ranch Club Estates 33 33N49 116w32 7:46:08
Ranch House 37 33N15 117w18 7:49:12
Ranchita 37 33N13 116w36 7:46:24
Rancho Bernardo 37 33N03 117w03 7:48:12
Rancho California 33 33N46 117w29 7:49:56
Rancho Cordova 34 38N36 121w18 8:05:12
Rancho Cucamonga 36 34N06 117w36 7:50:24
Rancho Del Mar 28 38N07 122w14 8:08:56
Rancho Del Rey 37 32N37 117w04 7:48:16
Rancho La Costa 37 33N05 117w17 7:49:08
Rancho Mirage 33 33N45 116w24 7:45:36
Rancho Palos Verdes 19 33N46 118w21 7:53:24
Rancho Park 19 34N02 118w26 7:53:44
Rancho Penasquitos 37 32N59 117w07 7:48:28
Rancho Rinconado 43 37N19 122w02 8:08:08
Rancho San Fernando Rey 42 34N25 119w42 7:58:48

Rancho Santa Clarita 19 34N26 118w32 7:54:08
Rancho Santa Fe 37 33N01 117w10 7:48:40
Randall 9 38N46 120w30 8:02:00
Randall Island 34 38N20 121w34 8:06:16
Randolph 46 39N36 120w22 8:01:28
Randsburg 15 35N22 117w39 7:50:36
Ravendale 18 40N48 120w22 8:01:28
Ravenswood 41 37N28 122w09 8:08:36
Rawhide 55 37N59 120w23 8:01:32
Rawson 52 40N11 122w16 8:09:04
Raymond 20 37N13 119w54 7:59:36
Rector 54 36N20 119w18 7:57:12
Red Bank 52 40N11 122w16 8:09:04
Red Bluff 52 40N11 122w15 8:09:00
Redcrest 12 40N21 123w55 8:15:40
Redding 45 40N35 122w23 8:09:32
Red Hill 30 33N45 117w49 7:51:16
Redlands 36 34N04 117w11 7:48:44
Redlands Heights 36 34N04 117w12 7:48:48
Red Mountain 36 35N37 117w38 7:50:32
Redondo Beach 19 33N50 118w23 7:53:32
Reds Meadow 26 37N38 118w58 7:55:52
Red Top 20 37N18 120w29 8:01:56
Redway 12 40N07 123w50 8:15:20
Redwood City 41 37N30 122w15 8:09:00
Redwood Estates 43 37N10 121w59 8:07:56
Redwood Grove 44 37N07 122w07 8:08:28
Redwood Lodge 23 39N27 123w48 8:15:12
Redwood Terrace 41 37N19 122w18 8:09:12
Redwood Valley 23 39N16 123w12 8:12:48
Reedley 10 36N36 119w27 7:57:48
Requa 8 41N33 124w04 8:16:16
Rescue 9 38N43 120w57 8:03:48
Reseda 19 34N12 118w32 7:54:08
Reynolds 23 39N59 123w48 8:15:12
Rheem 7 37N58 122w20 8:09:20
Rheem Valley 7 37N52 122w07 8:08:28
Rhodes 39 37N43 121w26 8:05:44
Rialto 36 34N06 117w22 7:49:28
Riccas Corner 49 38N26 122w43 8:10:52
Rice 36 34N07 114w31 7:38:04
Richardson Grove 12 40N06 123w48 8:15:12
Richardson Springs 4 39N50 121w47 8:07:08
Rich Bar 40N01 121w10 8:04:40
Richfield 52 39N56 122w11 8:08:44
Richgrove 54 35N48 119w07 7:56:28
Richmond 7 37N56 122w21 8:09:24
Richmond Square 41 37N36 122w24 8:09:36
Richvale 4 39N30 121w45 8:07:00
Ridgecrest 15 35N38 117w40 7:50:40
Riego 51 38N43 121w27 8:05:48
Rimcrest 33 33N49 116w32 7:46:08
Rimforest 36 34N15 117w14 7:48:56
Rimpau 19 34N03 118w20 7:53:20
Rimrock 36 34N10 116w30 7:46:00
Rincon Annex 38 37N46 122w27 8:09:48
Rio Bonito 4 34N04 118w22 7:53:28
Rio Bravo 15 35N24 119w02 7:56:08
Rio Campo 49 38N28 123w00 8:12:00
Rio Dell 12 40N30 124w06 8:16:24
Rio Dell 49 38N28 122w53 8:11:32
Rio Del Mar 44 36N59 121w54 8:07:36
Rio Linda 34 38N41 121w27 8:05:48
Rio Nido 49 38N31 122w59 8:11:56
Rio Oso 51 38N58 121w33 8:06:12
Rio Vista 48 38N10 121w42 8:06:48
Ripley 33 33N32 114w39 7:38:36
Ripon 39 37N44 121w07 8:04:28
Ripperdan 20 36N58 120w04 8:00:16
Rivera 19 33N59 118w05 7:52:20
Riverbank 50 37N44 120w56 8:03:44
Riverdale 10 36N26 119w52 7:59:28
River Kern 15 35N43 118w26 7:53:44
River Pines 3 38N33 120w45 8:03:00
River Road 50 37N38 120w59 8:03:56
Riverside 33 33N59 117w22 7:49:28
Riverside Grove 44 37N07 122w07 8:08:28
Riverview 15 35N24 119w02 7:56:08
Riverview 37 32N50 116w56 7:47:44
Riverview Farms 37 32N51 116w56 7:47:44
Riviera Cliff 39 37N58 121w19 8:05:16
Roads End 54 35N56 118w30 7:54:00
Robbins 51 38N53 121w43 8:06:52
Robinsons Corner 4 39N30 121w33 8:06:12
Robles Del Rio 27 36N29 121w44 8:06:56
Rockaway Beach 41 37N38 122w29 8:09:56
Rock Creek 32 39N30 121w33 8:06:12
Rock Crest 32 39N55 121w20 8:05:20
Rockhaven 10 37N09 119w18 7:57:12
Rocking Horse Ranchos 19 33N44 118w18 7:53:12
Rocklin 31 38N48 121w14 8:04:56
Rockport 23 39N45 123w49 8:15:16
Rockridge 1 37N50 122w14 8:08:56
Rockville 48 38N14 122w02 8:08:08
Rodeo 7 38N02 122w16 8:09:04
Rogers Flat 32 39N55 121w20 8:05:20
Rogina Heights 23 39N09 123w12 8:12:48
Rohnert Park 49 38N20 122w42 8:10:48
Rohnerville 12 40N34 124w08 8:16:32
Rolinda 10 36N44 119w58 7:59:52
Rolling Hills 19 33N46 118w20 7:53:20
Rolling Hills 33 33N33 116w43 7:46:52
Rolling Hills Estates 19 33N47 118w21 7:53:24
Rolling Hills Estates 40 35N18 120w45 8:03:00
Rolling Hills Riviera 19 33N44 118w18 7:53:12
Rollingwood 7 37N58 122w20 8:09:20
Romie Lane 27 36N41 121w39 8:06:36
Romoland 33 33N45 117w11 7:48:44

Roosevelt Corner 19 34N40 118w11 7:52:44
Roosevelt Terrace 48 38N07 122w14 8:08:56
Rosamond 15 34N52 118w10 7:52:40
Rose Bowl 19 34N10 118w10 7:52:40
Rosedale 15 35N24 119w09 7:56:36
Roseland 49 38N25 122w44 8:10:56
Rosemead 19 34N05 118w04 7:52:16
Rosemont 34 38N33 121w22 8:05:28
Roseville 31 38N45 121w17 8:05:08
Roseville Square 31 38N45 121w17 8:05:08
Rosewood 12 40N47 124w10 8:16:40
Ross 21 37N58 122w33 8:10:12
Ross Corner 13 32N47 114w33 7:38:12
Rossmoor 30 33N48 118w05 7:52:20
Rossmoor Highlands 30 33N48 118w04 7:52:16
Ross Valley 21 37N58 122w32 8:10:08
Rotavele 11 39N45 122w01 8:08:04
Rough And Ready 29 39N14 121w08 8:04:32
Round Hill Country Club 7 37N51 122w01 8:08:04
Round Mountain 45 40N48 121w56 8:07:44
Round Valley 14 37N22 118w24 7:53:36
Round Valley Indian Res 23 38N33 121w28 8:05:52
Rovana 14 37N22 118w24 7:53:36
Rowland 19 34N05 117w31 7:50:04
Rowland Heights 19 33N59 117w53 7:51:32
Rubidoux 33 34N00 117w24 7:49:36
Rucker 43 37N01 121w35 8:06:20
Rumsey 57 38N53 122w14 8:08:56
Running Springs 36 34N12 117w06 7:48:24
Rupert 58 39N09 121w32 8:06:08
Russell City 37N39 122w08 8:08:32
Russian River Terrace 49 38N28 122w53 8:11:32
Ruth 53 40N28 123w48 8:15:12
Rutherford 28 38N28 122w25 8:09:40
Ryans Slough 12 40N47 124w09 8:16:36
Ryde 34 38N14 121w34 8:06:16
Sabre City 31 38N45 121w17 8:05:08
Sacramento 34 38N35 121w29 8:05:56
Sacramento Army Depot 34 38N33 121w28 8:05:52
Sacramento Canyon 45 40N58 122w21 8:09:24
Sacramento South 34 38N32 121w27 8:05:48
Sage 33 33N45 116w56 7:47:44
Saint Francis Heights 41 37N41 122w29 8:09:56
Saint Helena 28 38N30 122w28 8:09:52
Saint James Park 43 37N20 121w53 8:07:32
Saint Lawrence Terrace 40 35N45 120w42 8:02:48
Saint Marys College 7 37N51 122w06 8:08:24
Saint Matthew 41 37N34 122w19 8:09:16
Salida 50 37N42 121w05 8:04:20
Salinas 27 36N40 121w39 8:06:36
Salmon Creek 49 38N20 123w03 8:12:12
Salt Creek 45 40N54 122w23 8:09:32
Saltdale 15 35N22 117w54 7:51:36
Salton City 13 33N39 116w09 7:44:36
Salton Sea Beach 13 33N39 116w09 7:44:36
Saltus 36 34N33 115w45 7:43:00
Salvador 28 38N18 122w18 8:09:12
Salyer 53 40N54 123w35 8:14:20
Samoa 12 40N49 124w11 8:16:44
San Andreas 5 38N12 120w41 8:02:44
San Anselmo 21 37N59 122w34 8:10:16
San Antonio 43 37N23 122w05 8:08:20
San Antonio Heights 36 34N09 117w40 7:50:40
San Ardo 27 35N58 120w59 8:03:56
San Benito 36N30 121w05 8:04:20
San Bernardino 36 34N07 117w19 7:49:16
San Bruno 41 37N38 122w25 8:09:40
San Carlos 37 32N47 117w02 7:48:08
San Carlos 41 37N31 122w16 8:09:04
San Clemente 30 33N26 117w37 7:50:28
Sandberg 19 34N40 118w26 7:53:44
Sand City 27 36N37 121w51 8:07:24
San Diego 37 32N43 117w09 7:48:36
San Dieguito 37 33N03 117w16 7:49:04
San Dimas 19 34N06 117w48 7:51:12
Sandy Korner 33 33N39 116w09 7:44:36
Sandyland 42 34N25 119w33 7:58:12
San Felipe 43 36N51 121w24 8:05:36
San Fernando 19 34N17 118w26 7:53:44
Sanford 19 34N04 118w18 7:53:12
San Francisco 38 37N47 122w25 8:09:40
San Francisco Intl Airport 41 37N37 122w23 8:09:32
San Francisco Recreation Cam 55 38N33 121w17 8:05:08
San Gabriel 19 34N06 118w06 7:52:24
Sanger 10 36N42 119w33 7:58:12
San Geronimo 21 38N01 122w39 8:10:36
San Geronimo Valley 21 38N00 122w39 8:10:36
San Gorgonio Pass 33 33N59 117w02 7:48:08
San Gregorio 41 37N20 122w23 8:09:32
San Jacinto 33 33N47 116w57 7:47:48
San Joaquin 10 36N36 120w11 8:00:44
San Joaquin Bridge 39 37N49 121w17 8:05:08
San Jose 43 37N20 121w53 8:07:32
San Juan Bautista 35 36N51 121w32 8:06:08

San Juan Capistrano 30 33N30 117w40 7:50:40
San Lawrence Terrace 40 35N45 120w42 8:02:48
San Leandro 1 37N44 122w09 8:08:36
San Lorenzo 1 37N41 122w08 8:08:32
San Lorenzo Park 44 37N07 122w07 8:08:28
San Lorenzo Valley 44 37N07 122w06 8:08:24
San Lucas 27 36N08 121w01 8:04:04
San Luis Obispo 40 35N17 120w40 8:02:40
San Luis Obispo Bay 40 35N12 120w41 8:02:44
San Luis Obispo Rural 40 35N17 120w37 8:02:28
San Luis Rey 37 33N14 117w19 7:49:16
San Luis Rey Downs 37 33N14 117w20 7:49:20
San Marcos 37 33N09 117w10 7:48:40
San Marin 21 38N06 122w34 8:10:16
San Marino 19 34N07 118w06 7:52:24
San Martin 43 37N05 121w37 8:06:28
San Mateo 41 37N34 122w19 8:09:16
San Miguel 40 35N45 120w42 8:02:48
San Onofre 37 33N26 117w38 7:50:32
San Pablo 7 37N58 122w21 8:09:24
San Pasqual 37 33N04 117w03 7:48:12
San Pedro 19 33N45 118w19 7:53:16
San Quentin 21 37N56 122w29 8:09:56
San Rafael 21 37N58 122w32 8:10:08
San Ramon 7 37N47 121w59 8:07:56
San Ramon Village 7 37N44 121w57 8:07:48
San Roque 42 34N26 119w44 7:58:56
Sans Crainte 7 37N55 122w03 8:08:12
San Simeon 40 35N39 121w11 8:04:44
Santa Ana 30 33N46 117w52 7:51:28
Santa Ana Air Facility 30 33N42 117w49 7:51:16
Santa Ana Canyon 30 33N53 117w44 7:50:56
Santa Ana Heights 30 33N40 117w52 7:51:28
Santa Anita 19 34N08 118w02 7:52:08
Santa Anita Race Track 19 34N08 118w03 7:52:12
Santa Barbara 42 34N25 119w42 7:58:48
Santa Clara 43 37N21 121w57 8:07:48
Santa Cruz 44 36N58 122w01 8:08:04
Santa Cruz Gardens 44 36N59 122w00 8:08:00
Santa Fe Springs 19 33N57 118w04 7:52:16
Santa Margarita 40 35N23 120w37 8:02:28
Santa Maria 42 34N57 120w26 8:01:44
Santa Maria Valley 42 34N54 120w24 8:01:36
Santa Monica 19 34N01 118w29 7:53:56
Santa Nella 24 37N15 121w00 8:04:00
Santa Paula 56 34N21 119w04 7:56:16
Santa Rita 27 36N44 121w39 8:06:36
Santa Rita 42 34N42 120w29 8:01:56
Santa Rita Park 24 37N03 120w36 8:02:24
Santa Rosa 49 38N26 122w43 8:10:52
Santa Rosa Indian Res 33 33N49 116w32 7:46:08
Santa Rosa Race Track 49 38N26 122w42 8:10:48
Santa Susana 56 34N17 118w43 7:54:52
Santa Venetia 21 38N00 122w31 8:10:04
Santa Western 19 34N05 118w22 7:53:28
Santa Ynez 42 34N37 120w05 8:00:20
Santa Ynez Valley 42 34N37 120w07 8:00:28
Santa Ysabel 37 33N07 116w40 7:46:40
Santa Ysabel Indian Res 37 33N49 116w32 7:46:08
Santee 37 32N50 116w58 7:47:52
San Ysidro 37 32N33 117w02 7:48:08
Saranap 7 37N53 122w05 8:08:20
Saratoga 43 37N16 122w02 8:08:08
Sather Gate 1 37N52 122w16 8:09:04
Saticoy 56 34N17 119w09 7:56:36
Sattley 46 39N37 120w25 8:01:40
Saugus 19 34N25 118w32 7:54:08
Sausalito 21 37N51 122w29 8:09:56
Saviers 56 34N12 119w10 7:56:40
Savoy 19 34N06 117w53 7:51:32
Sawyers Bar 47 41N18 123w07 8:12:28
Scenic Brook Estates 55 37N59 120w23 8:01:32
Scenic Center 50 37N38 120w59 8:03:56
Scheelite 14 37N22 118w24 7:53:36
Scheideck 56 35N04 119w24 7:57:36
Schellville 49 38N17 122w28 8:09:52
Scotia 12 40N29 124w06 8:16:24
Scotland 36 34N15 117w30 7:50:00
Scott Bar 47 41N45 123w00 8:12:00
Scotts Valley 44 37N03 122w00 8:08:00
Scotts Valley Center 44 36N59 122w00 8:08:00
Scripps Ranch 37 32N55 117w06 7:48:24
Seacliff 44 36N59 121w54 8:07:36
Seahaven 21 38N06 122w51 8:11:24
Seal Beach 30 33N44 118w06 7:52:24
Seal Beach Naval Weapons Sta 30 33N46 118w05 7:52:20
Searles Valley 36 35N46 117w23 7:49:32
Seaside 27 36N37 121w50 8:07:20
Sebastiani 49 38N17 122w28 8:09:52
Sebastopol 49 38N24 122w49 8:11:16
Sedco Hills 33 33N39 117w17 7:49:08
Seeley 13 32N48 115w41 7:42:44
Seiad Valley 47 41N51 123w11 8:12:44
Seigler Springs 17 38N45 122w37 8:10:28

Selby 38N03 122w15 8:09:00
Selma 10 36N34 119w37 7:58:28
Seneca 32 40N10 121w04 8:04:16
Sepulveda 19 34N14 118w28 7:53:52
Sequoia Crest 54 36N08 118w49 7:55:16
Sequoia National Park 54 36N30 118w30 7:54:00
Serena Park 42 34N25 119w33 7:58:12
Serra Mesa 37 32N46 117w08 7:48:32
Serramonte 41 37N41 122w29 8:09:56
Sespe 56 34N24 118w57 7:55:48
Seven Oaks 36 34N09 116w59 7:47:56
Seville 54 36N20 119w18 7:57:12
Shady Dell 32N59 116w55 7:47:40
Shafter 15 35N30 119w16 7:57:04
Shandon 40 35N39 120w23 8:01:32
Sharpe Army Depot 39 37N49 121w17 8:05:08
Sharp Park 41 37N38 122w29 8:09:56
Shasta 45 40N36 122w29 8:09:56
Shasta Dam 45 40N40 122w23 8:09:32
Shasta Retreat 47 41N13 122w16 8:09:04
Shaver Lake 10 37N09 119w18 7:57:12
Shaver Lake Heights 10 37N09 119w18 7:57:12
Shaver Lake Point 10 37N09 119w18 7:57:12
Shaws Flat 55 37N59 120w23 8:01:32
Sheepranch 5 38N13 120w28 8:01:52
Sheldon 34 38N25 121w22 8:05:28
Shell Beach 40 35N09 120w40 8:02:40
Shelter Cove 41 37N38 122w29 8:09:56
Sheridan 31 38N59 121w22 8:05:28
Sheridan 49 38N29 123w01 8:12:04
Sherman Island 34 38N10 121w42 8:06:48
Sherman Oaks 19 34N09 118w26 7:53:44
Sherwin Plaza 26 37N38 118w58 7:55:52
Sherwood Forest 7 37N58 122w18 8:09:12
Shingle Springs 9 38N40 120w56 8:03:44
Shingletown 45 40N30 121w53 8:07:32
Shirley 30 33N49 118w02 7:52:08
Shively 12 40N29 124w06 8:16:24
Shore Acres 7 38N02 121w58 8:07:52
Short Acres 16 36N20 119w39 7:58:36
Shoshone 14 35N58 116w16 7:45:04
Sierra 10 36N59 119w20 7:57:20
Sierra City 46 39N34 120w38 8:02:32
Sierra Madre 19 34N10 118w02 7:52:08
Sierra Village No.1 55 38N05 120w13 8:00:52
Sierraville 46 39N36 120w22 8:01:28
Signal Hill 19 33N48 118w10 7:52:40
Silverado 30 33N45 117w38 7:50:32
Silver City 54 36N26 118w54 7:55:36
Silver Fork 9 38N47 120w18 8:01:12
Silver Lake 3 38N21 120w46 8:03:04
Silver Strand 56 34N12 119w10 7:56:40
Simi 34N16 118w47 7:55:08
Simi Valley 56 34N16 118w45 7:55:00
Simmler 40 35N23 120w37 8:02:28
Simms 39 37N44 121w07 8:04:28
Singing Springs 19 34N35 118w06 7:52:24
Sisquoc 42 34N54 120w26 8:01:44
Sites 6 39N23 122w33 8:10:12
Skyforest 36 34N15 117w10 7:48:40
Sky Londa 41 37N23 122w16 8:09:04
Sky Valley 33 33N58 116w30 7:46:00
Sleepy Hollow 21 37N59 122w35 8:10:20
Sleepy Hollow 36 33N57 117w47 7:51:08
Sleepy Valley 19 34N25 118w32 7:54:08
Sloat 32 39N52 120w44 8:02:56
Sloughhouse 34 38N31 121w06 8:04:24
Smartville 58 39N13 121w18 8:05:12
Smiley Heights 36 34N04 117w12 7:48:48
Smiley Park 36 34N12 117w07 7:48:28
Smithflat 9 38N44 120w45 8:03:00
Smith River 8 41N56 124w09 8:16:36
Smoke Tree 33 33N49 116w32 7:46:08
Snelling 24 37N31 120w26 8:01:44
Snow Creek 33 33N56 116w38 7:46:32
Snowline Camp 9 38N44 120w41 8:02:44
Soboba Hot Springs 33 33N47 116w58 7:47:52
Soda Bay 17 38N59 122w50 8:11:20
Soda Springs 29 39N20 120w23 8:01:32
Solana Beach 37 33N00 117w16 7:49:04
Solano Race Track 48 38N08 122w14 8:08:56
Soledad 27 36N26 121w20 8:05:20
Solemint 19 34N25 118w32 7:54:08
Solromar 56 34N03 118w57 7:55:48
Solvang 42 34N36 120w10 8:00:40
Somerset 9 38N40 120w40 8:02:40
Somes Bar 47 41N23 123w29 8:13:56
Somis 56 34N16 119w00 7:56:00
Sonoma 49 38N18 122w28 8:09:52
Sonoma Vista 49 38N17 122w28 8:09:52
Sonora 55 37N59 120w23 8:01:32
Soquel 44 36N59 121w57 8:07:48
Sorensens 2 38N49 119w41 7:58:44
Soto 19 33N58 118w13 7:52:52
Soulsbyville 55 37N59 120w16 8:01:04
South Alhambra 19 34N04 118w08 7:52:32
South Antelope Valley 19 34N31 118w07 7:52:28
South Bay Cities 19 33N51 118w23 7:53:32
South Belridge 15 35N18 119w37 7:58:28
South Berkeley 1 37N52 122w16 8:09:04
South Coast 30 33N34 117w44 7:50:56
South Coastside 41 37N25 122w22 8:09:28
South Corona 33 33N53 117w33 7:50:12
South Coyote 43 37N13 121w44 8:06:56
South Dos Palos 24 36N58 120w39 8:02:36
South Downey 19 33N55 118w09 7:52:36
Southeast 19 34N00 118w14 7:52:56

CALIFORNIA

Southeastern 37 32N42 117w07 7:48:28
South El Dorado 9 38N39 120w51 8:03:24
South El Monte 19 34N03 118w03 7:52:12
South Fontana 36 34N04 117w29 7:49:56
South Fork 12 40N21 123w55 8:15:40
South Fork 20 37N14 119w31 7:58:04
South Fresno 10 36N41 119w48 7:59:12
South Gardena 19 33N53 118w17 7:53:08
South Gate 19 33N57 118w12 7:52:48
South Laguna 30 33N30 117w45 7:51:00
South Lake Tahoe 9 38N57 119w59 7:59:56
Southland 1 37N38 122w07 8:08:28
South Main 30 33N43 117w52 7:51:28
South Modesto 50 37N36 120w59 8:03:56
South Oroville 4 39N29 121w32 8:06:08
South Park 49 38N26 122w43 8:10:52
South Pasadena 19 34N07 118w09 7:52:36
Southport 57 38N34 121w32 8:06:08
South San Francisco 41 37N39 122w24 8:09:36
South San Gabriel 19 34N03 118w06 7:52:24
South San Jose Hills 19 34N01 117w54 7:51:36
South San Leandro 1 37N42 122w08 8:08:32
South Shafter 15 35N30 119w16 7:57:04
South Shores Shopping Center 1 37N47 122w16 8:09:04
South Sutter 51 38N52 121w32 8:06:08
South Taft 15 35N08 119w27 7:57:48
South Turlock 50 37N29 120w50 8:03:20
South Vista 37 33N11 117w15 7:49:00
South Whittier 19 33N56 118w02 7:52:08
South Whittier Heights 19 33N56 118w02 7:52:08
South Yuba City 51 39N07 121w38 8:06:32
Spanish Creek 32 39N56 120w55 8:03:40
Spanish Flat 28 38N18 122w18 8:09:12
Spanish Ranch 32 39N56 121w05 8:04:20
Spaulding 18 40N25 120w39 8:02:36
Spicer City 15 35N24 119w28 7:57:52
Spreckels 27 36N39 121w38 8:06:32
Spreckels Junction 27 36N41 121w39 8:06:36
Spring Garden 32 39N56 120w55 8:03:40
Spring Hill 29 39N13 121w04 8:04:16
Springtowne 48 38N07 122w14 8:08:56
Spring Valley 37 32N45 116w58 7:47:52
Springville 54 36N08 118w49 7:55:16
Springville 56 34N14 119w02 7:56:08
Spruce Point 12 40N47 124w10 8:16:40
Spurgeon 43 33N45 117w53 7:51:32
Squaw Valley 10 36N44 119w15 7:57:00
Squirrel Valley 15 35N39 118w28 7:53:52
Stafford 12 40N29 124w06 8:16:24
Standard 55 37N59 120w20 8:01:20
Standish 18 40N22 120w25 8:01:40
Stanford 43 37N25 122w10 8:08:40
Stanton 30 33N48 118w00 7:52:00
State Capitol 34 38N34 121w29 8:05:56
Stateline 9 38N57 119w57 7:59:48
Steele Park 28 38N18 122w18 8:09:12
Stephens 19 33N56 118w04 7:52:16
Sterling Park 41 37N42 122w28 8:09:52
Stevinson 24 37N20 120w51 8:03:24
Stewarts Point 49 38N39 123w24 8:13:36
Stinson Beach 21 37N54 122w38 8:10:32
Stirling City 4 39N54 121w32 8:06:08
Stockton 39 37N58 121w17 8:05:08
Stokdale 15 35N21 119w03 7:56:12
Stonegate 41 37N27 122w11 8:08:44
Stone Lagoon 12 41N04 124w08 8:16:32
Stonestown 38 37N44 122w28 8:09:52
Stonyford 6 39N23 122w33 8:10:12
Storrie 32 39N55 121w20 8:05:20
Stove Pipe Wells 14 36N18 116w45 7:47:00
Stratford 16 36N11 119w49 7:59:16
Strathmore 54 36N09 119w04 7:56:16
Strawberry 9 38N47 120w18 8:01:12
Strawberry 55 38N13 120w01 8:00:04
Strawberry Manor 21 37N54 122w32 8:10:08
Strawberry Point 21 37N54 122w31 8:10:04
Strawberry Valley 58 39N34 121w06 8:04:24
Stuart 37 33N15 117w18 7:49:12
Studebaker 19 33N54 118w05 7:52:20
Studio City 19 34N09 118w24 7:53:36
Studio Village 19 34N00 118w24 7:53:36
Success 54 36N04 119w04 7:56:16
Sugarloaf 36 34N15 116w53 7:47:32
Sugarloaf 45 40N54 122w23 8:09:32
Sugarloaf Mountain Park 54 35N48 118w43 7:54:52
Sugar Pine 20 37N19 119w40 7:58:40
Sugar Pine 55 38N05 120w13 8:00:52
Suisun 48 38N14 122w02 8:08:08
Suisun City 48 38N14 122w02 8:08:08
Sulphur Springs 56 33N45 117w51 7:51:24
Sultana 54 36N33 119w20 7:57:20
Summer Home 39 37N48 121w11 8:04:44
Summerhome Park 49 38N28 122w53 8:11:32
Summerland 42 34N25 119w36 7:58:24
Summit 36 34N20 117w25 7:49:40
Summit City 45 40N42 122w24 8:09:36
Summit Inn 22 37N29 119w58 7:59:52
Sun City 33 33N42 117w12 7:48:48
Suncrest 32N48 116w52 7:47:28
Sunfair 36 34N08 116w19 7:45:16
Sunkist 30 33N50 117w52 7:51:28
Sunland 19 34N15 118w20 7:53:20
Sunland 54 36N04 119w04 7:56:16
Sunny Brae 12 40N52 124w05 8:16:20

CALIFORNIA

Place	Lat	Long	Time
Sunnybrook 3	38N22	120w56	8:03:44
Sunny Hills 30	33N53	117w56	7:51:44
Sunnymead 33	33N56	117w15	7:49:00
Sunnyside 10	36N44	119w45	7:59:00
Sunnyside 37	32N40	117w01	7:48:04
Sunnyslope 33	34N00	117w26	7:49:44
Sunnyvale 43	37N23	122w02	8:08:08
Sunnyvale Plaza 43	37N23	122w01	8:08:04
Sunny Vista 37	32N38	117w04	7:48:16
Sunol 1	37N36	121w53	8:07:32
Sunrise Oasis 33	33N49	116w32	7:46:08
Sunset 12	40N52	124w05	8:16:20
Sunset 38	37N46	122w28	8:09:52
Sunset Beach 30	33N43	118w04	7:52:16
Sunset Beach 44	36N55	121w47	8:07:08
Sunset Hills 19	34N00	117w57	7:51:48
Sunset Terrace 40	35N18	120w45	8:03:00
Sunset Tract 56	34N24	119w18	7:57:12
Sunset View 29	39N13	121w04	8:04:16
Sunset-Whitney Ranch 31	38N48	121w14	8:04:56
Sunshine Homes 19	34N25	118w32	7:54:08
Sun Valley 19	34N14	118w23	7:53:32
Sun Village 19	34N35	118w06	7:52:24
Surf 42	34N42	120w29	8:01:56
Surfside 30	33N44	118w05	7:52:20
Surprise Valley 25	41N33	120w09	8:00:36
Susana Knolls 56	34N16	118w45	7:55:00
Susanville 18	40N25	120w39	8:02:36
Sutter 51	39N10	121w45	8:07:00
Sutter Creek 3	38N24	120w48	8:03:12
Sutter Hill 3	38N24	120w48	8:03:12
Sutter Island 34	38N20	121w34	8:06:16
Swanton 44	37N01	122w12	8:08:48
Sweet Brier 45	41N09	122w19	8:09:16
Sweetland 29	39N22	121w06	8:04:24
Sycamore 6	39N09	121w55	8:07:40
Sycamore 7	37N50	122w00	8:08:00
Sylmar 19	34N19	118w26	7:53:44
Sylvia Park 19	34N05	118w37	7:54:28
Taft 15	35N08	119w28	7:57:52
Taft Heights 15	35N08	119w28	7:57:52
Tagus 54	36N13	119w20	7:57:20
Tahoe City 31	39N10	120w09	8:00:36
Tahoe Keys 9	38N56	119w59	7:59:56
Tahoe Paradise 9	38N56	119w59	7:59:56
Tahoe Pines 31	39N05	120w10	8:00:40
Tahoe Valley 9	38N55	120w00	8:00:00
Tahoe Vista 31	39N14	120w03	8:00:12
Tahoma 31	39N04	120w08	8:00:32
Talica 37	33N12	117w20	7:49:20
Talmage 23	39N08	123w10	8:12:40
Tamalpais Valley 21	37N53	122w32	8:10:08
Tamarack 5	38N15	120w21	8:01:24
Tambs Station 55	37N59	120w23	8:01:32
Tanforan 41	37N39	122w26	8:09:44
Tangair 42	34N41	120w29	8:01:56
Tanglewood 44	37N03	122w04	8:08:16
Tara Hills 7	37N58	122w20	8:09:20
Tarpey 10	36N46	119w43	7:58:52
Tarzana 19	34N10	118w32	7:54:08
Tassajara Hot Springs 27	36N29	121w44	8:06:56
Taurusa 54	36N20	119w18	7:57:12
Taylorsville 32	40N04	120w50	8:03:20
Tecate 37	32N35	116w37	7:46:28
Tecnor 47	41N47	122w00	8:08:00
Tecopa 14	35N51	116w13	7:44:52
Tecopa Hot Springs 14	35N51	116w13	7:44:52
Tehachapi 15	35N08	118w27	7:53:48
Tehama 52	40N02	122w07	8:08:28
Temecula 33	33N30	117w09	7:48:36
Temescal 1	37N50	122w16	8:09:04
Temple City 19	34N07	118w01	7:52:04
Templeton 40	35N33	120w42	8:02:48
Tennant 47	41N47	122w00	8:08:00
Tent City 37	32N41	117w11	7:48:44
Terminal Island 19	33N44	118w18	7:53:12
Terminous 39	38N08	121w17	8:05:08
Termo 18	40N52	120w27	8:01:48
Terra Bella 54	35N58	119w03	7:56:12
Terra Linda 21	38N01	122w33	8:10:12
Terra Loma 41	37N41	122w29	8:09:56
Tewksbury Heights 7	37N57	122w19	8:09:16
Textile 19	34N02	118w18	7:53:12
The Cedars 31	39N19	120w16	8:01:04
The Forks 23	39N09	123w12	8:12:48
The Geysers 49	38N48	123w01	8:12:04
The Oaks 29	39N13	121w04	8:04:16
Thermal 33	33N39	116w09	7:44:36
Thermalito 4	39N31	121w35	8:06:20
The Sea Ranch 49	40N12	123w30	8:14:00
Thomas Mountain 33	33N48	116w44	7:46:56
Thornton 39	38N14	121w25	8:05:40
Thousand Oaks 56	34N10	118w50	7:55:20
Thousand Palms 33	33N49	116w24	7:45:36
Three Arch Bay 30	33N31	117w43	7:50:52
Three Point 19	34N40	118w26	7:53:44
Three Rivers 54	36N26	118w54	7:55:36
Three Rocks 10	36N30	120w19	8:01:16
Tiburon 21	37N53	122w27	8:09:48
Tierra Buena 51	39N08	121w36	8:06:24
Tierra del Sol 37	32N40	116w16	7:45:04
Tierra Santa 37	32N47	117w06	7:48:24
Timber Lodge 22	37N33	119w56	7:59:44
Tionesta 25	41N39	121w20	8:05:20
Tipton 54	36N04	119w19	7:57:16
Tivy Valley 10	36N42	119w33	7:58:12
Tobin 32	39N30	121w33	8:06:12
Tocaloma 21	38N02	122w47	8:11:08
Todos Santos 7	37N58	122w01	8:08:04
Tolenas 48	38N16	122w01	8:08:04
Tollhouse 10	37N01	119w24	7:57:36
Toluca Lake 19	34N09	118w22	7:53:28
Tomales 21	38N15	122w54	8:11:36
Toms Place 26	37N34	118w41	7:54:44
Tonyville 54	36N12	119w05	7:56:20
Toolville 54	36N17	119w09	7:56:36
Topanga 19	34N05	118w37	7:54:28
Topanga Beach 19	34N06	118w44	7:54:56
Topanga Oaks 19	34N05	118w37	7:54:28
Topanga Park 19	34N05	118w37	7:54:28
Topa Topa 56	34N21	119w04	7:56:16
Topaz 26	38N36	119w30	7:58:00
Top of the World 30	33N33	117w45	7:51:00
Tormey 7	38N03	122w14	8:08:56
Toro 27	36N34	121w40	8:06:40
Torrance 19	33N50	118w19	7:53:16
Torres Martinex Indian Res 33	33N49	116w32	7:46:08
Torrey Pines Homes 37	32N50	117w14	7:48:56
Tower 10	36N46	119w47	7:59:08
Town and Country 7	37N50	122w00	8:08:00
Town and Country Trailer Par 33	33N56	117w14	7:48:56
Town and Country Village 34	38N37	121w23	8:05:32
Town Center 54	36N20	119w18	7:57:12
Town Talk 29	39N16	121w01	8:04:04
Toyon 45	40N33	122w22	8:09:28
Trabuco 30	33N41	117w36	7:50:24
Trabuco Canyon 30	33N40	117w35	7:50:20
Tracy 39	37N44	121w26	8:05:44
Tracy Rural 39	37N44	121w24	8:05:36
Tranquillity 10	36N39	120w15	8:01:00
Traver	36N27	119w29	7:57:56
Travis Air Force Base 48	38N16	121w55	8:07:40
Treasure Island 38	37N46	122w27	8:09:48
Trenton 49	38N26	122w43	8:10:52
Tres Pinos 35	36N48	121w19	8:05:16
Trevarno 1	37N41	121w46	8:07:04
Trigo 20	36N58	120w04	8:00:16
Trimmer 10	36N55	119w18	7:57:12
Trinidad 12	41N04	124w09	8:16:36
Trinity Alps 53	40N43	122w48	8:11:12
Trinity Center 53	41N00	122w41	8:10:44
Triple R Estates 54	36N04	119w04	7:56:16
Trona 36	35N46	117w23	7:49:32
Tropico 19	34N08	118w16	7:53:04
Tropico Village 15	34N52	118w10	7:52:40
Trowbridge 51	38N55	121w31	8:06:04
Truckee 29	39N20	120w11	8:00:44
Tujunga 19	34N15	118w18	7:53:12
Tulare 54	36N13	119w21	7:57:24
Tulelake 47	41N57	121w29	8:05:56
Tule River Indian Res 54	38N33	121w28	8:05:52
Tunitas 41	37N23	122w23	8:09:32
Tuolumne 55	37N58	120w15	8:01:00
Tuolumne Meadows 55	37N45	119w35	7:58:20
Tupman 15	35N18	119w21	7:57:24
Turk 10	36N08	120w22	8:01:28
Turlock 50	37N30	120w51	8:03:24
Turner Station 39	37N48	121w11	8:04:44
Tustin 30	33N44	117w49	7:51:16
Tustin-Foothills 30	33N46	117w48	7:51:12
Tuttle 24	37N18	120w29	8:01:56
Tuttletown 55	37N59	120w23	8:01:32
Tuxedo Country Club Estates 39	37N58	121w19	8:05:16
Tuxedo Park 39	37N58	121w19	8:05:16
T.V. Bell 24	37N18	120w29	8:01:56
Twain 32	40N01	121w03	8:04:12
Twain Harte 55	38N02	120w14	8:00:56
Tweedy 19	33N56	118w11	7:52:44
Twentynine Palms 36	34N08	116w03	7:44:12
Twentynine Palms Base 36	34N14	116w04	7:44:16
Twin Bridges 9	38N49	120w07	8:00:28
Twin Cities 34	38N15	121w18	8:05:12
Twin Lakes 44	36N58	121w58	8:07:52
Twin Oaks 37	33N11	117w13	7:48:52
Twin Peaks 36	34N14	117w14	7:48:56
Ukiah 23	39N09	123w13	8:12:52
Ulmar 1	37N41	121w46	8:07:04
Union City 1	37N36	122w01	8:08:04
Union Hill 29	39N13	121w04	8:04:16
Universal City 19	34N08	118w21	7:53:24
University 42	34N26	119w50	7:59:20
University City 37	32N52	117w12	7:48:48
University Heights 41	37N27	122w11	8:08:44
University of California-Dav 57	38N37	121w43	8:06:52
University Of Santa Clara 43	37N21	121w58	8:07:52
University Park 30	33N37	117w54	7:51:36
Upland 36	34N06	117w39	7:50:36
Upper Lake 17	39N10	122w54	8:11:36
Upper San Gabriel Valley 19	34N06	118w01	7:52:04
Upper Scheelite 14	37N22	118w24	7:53:36
Upper Soda Springs 47	41N13	122w16	8:09:04
Uptown 36	34N08	117w18	7:49:12
U S Naval Hospital 19	33N49	118w10	7:52:40
U S Naval Postgrad School 27	36N36	121w53	8:07:32
Vacation 49	38N30	123w00	8:12:00
Vacaville 48	38N21	121w59	8:07:56
Vade 9	38N49	120w03	8:00:12
Valencia 19	34N23	118w33	7:54:12
Valerie 33	33N39	116w09	7:44:36
Valinda 19	34N02	117w56	7:51:44
Vallecito 5	38N05	120w28	8:01:52
Vallejo 48	38N07	122w15	8:09:00
Vallemar 41	37N38	122w29	8:09:56
Valle Vista 1	37N40	122w05	8:08:20
Valle Vista 33	33N45	116w56	7:47:44
Valley Acres 15	35N09	119w28	7:57:52
Valley Center 37	33N13	117w02	7:48:08
Valleydale 19	34N07	117w54	7:51:36
Valley Fair 43	37N19	121w56	8:07:44
Valley Ford 49	38N19	122w55	8:11:40
Valley Home 50	37N50	120w55	8:03:40
Valley of Enchantment 36	34N14	117w17	7:49:08
Valley of the Moon 36	34N14	117w17	7:49:08
Valley Plaza 19	34N05	118w22	7:53:28
Valley Springs 5	38N12	120w50	8:03:20
Valley View Park 36	34N14	117w19	7:49:16
Valley Village 19	34N10	118w24	7:53:36
Valley Wells 36	35N28	115w16	7:41:04
Valona 7	38N03	122w14	8:08:56
Val Verde Park 19	34N25	118w32	7:54:08
Valyermo 19	34N26	117w50	7:51:20
Van Allen 39	37N48	120w59	8:03:56
Vanden 48	38N21	121w59	8:07:56
Vandenberg Air Force Base 42	34N41	120w29	8:01:56
Vandenberg Village 42	34N42	120w29	8:01:56
Vandenburg 42	34N41	120w29	8:01:56
Van Duzen 12	40N28	123w48	8:15:12
Van Nuys 19	34N11	118w26	7:53:44
Vanowen 19	34N05	118w22	7:53:28
Venice 19	34N00	118w29	7:53:56
Ventucopa 42	35N04	119w24	7:57:36
Ven-tu Park 56	34N11	118w55	7:55:40
Ventura 56	34N17	119w18	7:57:12
Verdemont 36	34N12	117w22	7:49:28
Verdi Sierra Pines 46	39N31	119w59	7:59:56
Verdugo City 19	34N10	118w15	7:53:00
Verdugo Viejo 19	34N10	118w15	7:53:00
Vermont Avenue 19	34N05	118w18	7:53:12
Vernalis 39	37N38	121w17	8:05:08
Vernon 19	34N00	118w14	7:52:56
Verona 51	38N54	121w35	8:06:20
Verona Landing 51	38N54	121w35	8:06:20
Veterans Administration Hosp 19	33N49	118w10	7:52:40
Veterans Bureau Hospital 43	37N24	122w09	8:08:36
Veterans Home 28	38N24	122w22	8:09:28
Vichy Springs 23	39N09	123w12	8:12:48
Victor 39	38N08	121w12	8:04:48
Victoria Park 19	33N53	118w17	7:53:08
Victorville 36	34N32	117w18	7:49:12
Victory Center Annex 19	34N05	118w22	7:53:28
Vidal 36	34N11	114w34	7:38:16
View Park 19	33N59	118w20	7:53:20
Viking 19	33N49	118w07	7:52:28
Village 19	34N04	118w26	7:53:44
Villa Grande 49	38N29	123w01	8:12:04
Villa Park 30	33N49	117w49	7:51:16
Villa Verona 4	39N30	121w33	8:06:12
Vina 52	39N56	122w03	8:08:12
Vincent 19	34N35	118w06	7:52:24
Vineburg 49	38N16	122w26	8:09:44
Vine Hill 7	38N01	122w06	8:08:24
Vineyard 36	34N05	117w31	7:50:04
Vinton 32	39N48	120w10	8:00:40
Vinvale 19	33N56	118w11	7:52:44
Viola 45	40N31	121w41	8:06:44
Virginia Colony 56	34N17	118w53	7:55:32
Virner 9	38N54	120w50	8:03:20
Visalia 54	36N20	119w18	7:57:12
Visitacion 38	37N43	122w25	8:09:40
Vista 37	33N12	117w14	7:48:56
VistaDel Morro 40	35N18	120w45	8:03:00
Vista Grande 41	37N41	122w27	8:09:48
Vista La Mesa 37	32N46	117w00	7:48:00
Vista Park 15	35N21	118w59	7:55:56
Volcano 3	38N26	120w37	8:02:28
Volta 24	37N06	120w56	8:03:44
Vorden 34	38N15	121w31	8:06:04
Waddington 12	40N35	124w16	8:17:04
Wagner 19	33N57	118w18	7:53:12
Wagy Flats 15	35N39	118w28	7:53:52
Wahtoke 10	36N36	119w27	7:57:48
Walerga 34	38N41	121w23	8:05:32
Walker 19	33N58	118w10	7:52:40
Walker 26	38N33	119w30	7:58:00
Walker 47	41N52	122w44	8:10:56
Walker Landing 34	38N15	121w31	8:06:04
Wallace 5	38N12	120w59	8:03:56
Walnut 19	34N01	117w52	7:51:28
Walnut Creek 7	37N54	122w04	8:08:16
Walnut Grove 34	38N15	121w31	8:06:04
Walnut Heights 7	37N53	122w03	8:08:12
Walnut Park 19	33N58	118w13	7:52:52
Walsh Station 34	38N33	121w22	8:05:28
Walteria 19	33N49	118w21	7:53:24
Warm Springs 1	37N34	121w59	8:07:56
Warner Ranch 33	33N56	117w14	7:48:56
Warner Springs 37	33N17	116w38	7:46:32
Wasco 15	35N36	119w20	7:57:20
Washington 19	34N01	118w16	7:53:04
Washington 29	39N22	120w48	8:03:12
Washington Manor 1	37N42	122w08	8:08:32
Waterford 50	37N38	120w46	8:03:04
Waterloo 39	37N58	121w18	8:05:12
Watson 19	33N48	118w16	7:53:04

CALIFORNIA

Place	Lat.	Long.	Time
Watsonville 44	36N55	121w45	8:07:00
Watts 19	33N57	118w14	7:52:56
Watts Valley 10	37N01	119w24	7:57:36
Waukena 54	36N08	119w30	7:58:00
Waverly Park 56	34N12	118w53	7:55:32
Wawona 22	37N32	119w39	7:58:36
Weaverville 53	40N44	122w56	8:11:44
Webster Street 1	37N47	122w16	8:09:04
Weed 47	41N25	122w23	8:09:32
Weed Patch 15	35N16	118w55	7:55:40
Weimar 31	39N02	120w58	8:03:52
Weitchpec 12	41N03	123w40	8:14:40
Weldon 15	35N40	118w18	7:53:12
Wendel 18	40N21	120w14	8:00:56
Weott 12	40N20	123w55	8:15:40
West 21	37N59	122w45	8:11:00
West Adams 19	34N02	118w19	7:53:16
West Arcadia 19	34N08	118w02	7:52:08
West Athens 19	33N55	118w18	7:53:12
West Butte 51	39N17	121w40	8:06:40
West Carson 19	33N50	118w18	7:53:12
Westchester 19	33N55	118w25	7:53:40
West Colusa 6	39N12	122w25	8:09:40
West Compton 19	33N54	118w16	7:53:04
West Covina 19	34N04	117w54	7:51:36
Westend 36	35N42	117w24	7:49:36
Western Avenue 19	33N45	118w19	7:53:16
Western Village 15	35N08	117w59	7:51:56
Westfield 19	33N46	118w21	7:53:24
West Fresno 10	36N45	119w50	7:59:20
West Garden Grove 30	33N47	117w59	7:51:56
Westgate 43	37N19	121w58	8:07:52
Westgate 56	34N12	118w53	7:55:32
West Guernewood 49	38N30	123w00	8:12:00
Westhaven 10	36N17	119w51	7:59:24
Westhaven 12	41N04	124w08	8:16:32
West Hills 56	34N27	119w16	7:57:04
West Hollywood 19	34N05	118w22	7:53:28
West Imperial 13	32N50	115w45	7:43:00
Westlake 41	37N42	122w28	8:09:52
Westlake Village 56	34N12	118w53	7:55:32
Westley 50	37N33	121w12	8:04:48
West Los Angeles 19	34N03	118w28	7:53:52
West Manteca 39	37N48	121w11	8:04:44
West Menlo Park 41	37N27	122w11	8:08:44
Westminster 30	33N47	118w00	7:52:00
West Modesto 50	37N37	121w01	8:04:04
Westmont 19	33N57	118w18	7:53:12
Westmorland 13	33N02	115w37	7:42:28
West Napa 28	38N18	122w18	8:09:12
West Orange 30	33N47	117w53	7:51:32
West Palm Springs 33	33N56	116w38	7:46:32
West Pittsburg 7	38N02	121w55	8:07:40
West Point 5	38N24	120w32	8:02:08
Westport 23	39N38	123w47	8:15:08
West Portal 38	37N44	122w27	8:09:48
West Puente Valley 19	34N03	117w58	7:51:52
Westridge 41	37N41	122w29	8:09:56
West Sacramento 57	38N35	121w32	8:06:08
Westside 15	35N09	119w23	7:57:32
Westside 50	37N38	120w59	8:03:56
West Sierra 46	39N35	120w45	8:03:00
West Tehama 52	40N03	122w30	8:10:00
West Valley 31	38N55	121w19	8:05:16
Westvern 19	34N00	118w19	7:53:16
West Whittier 19	33N59	118w04	7:52:16
Westwood 18	40N18	121w00	8:04:00
Westwood 19	34N04	118w27	7:53:48
Westwood Acres 43	37N01	121w35	8:06:20
Westwood Village 12	40N52	124w05	8:16:20
Wheatland 58	39N01	121w25	8:05:40
Wheeler Ridge 15	35N00	118w57	7:55:48
Wheeler Springs 56	34N27	119w16	7:57:04
Whiskeytown 45	40N38	122w33	8:10:12
Whispering Pines 17	38N45	122w37	8:10:28
White Hall 9	38N46	120w30	8:02:00
White Pines 5	38N16	120w21	8:01:24
White River 54	36N04	119w04	7:56:16
White Rock 34	38N41	121w11	8:04:44
Whitethorn	40N01	123w57	8:15:48
White Water 33	33N56	116w38	7:46:32
Whitley Gardens 40	35N38	120w41	8:02:44
Whitlow 12	40N16	123w53	8:15:32
Whitmore 45	40N38	121w55	8:07:40
Whitner Heights 10	36N37	119w31	7:58:04
Whittier 19	33N58	118w03	7:52:12
Whittier Downs 19	33N59	118w04	7:52:16
Wiest 13	32N59	115w32	7:42:08
Wilbur Springs 6	39N09	122w09	8:08:36
Wilcox 19	34N05	118w20	7:53:20
Wildflower 10	36N34	119w37	7:58:28
Wildomar 33	33N36	117w17	7:49:08
Wildrose 14	35N46	117w23	7:49:32
Wildwood 12	40N30	124w06	8:16:24
Wildwood 44	37N07	122w07	8:08:28
Wildwood 53	40N22	122w53	8:11:32
Wilfred 49	38N26	122w43	8:10:52
Willaura Estates 29	39N13	121w04	8:04:16
William H. Taft 37	32N48	117w11	7:48:44
Williams 6	39N09	122w09	8:08:36
Willits 23	39N25	123w21	8:13:24
Willow Brook 19	33N56	118w15	7:53:00
Willow Creek 12	40N56	123w38	8:14:32
Willow Ranch 25	41N54	120w21	8:01:24
Willows 11	39N31	122w12	8:08:48
Willow Springs 15	34N52	118w10	7:52:40
Willow Springs 55	37N59	120w16	8:01:04
Willow Valley 29	39N16	121w01	8:04:04
Will Rogers 19	34N01	118w29	7:53:56
Wilmar 19	34N04	118w05	7:52:20
Wilmington 19	33N48	118w16	7:53:04
Wilseyville 5	38N23	120w31	8:02:04
Wilshire-La Brea 19	34N04	118w21	7:53:24
Wilsona 19	34N40	118w11	7:52:44
Wilsona Gardens 19	34N40	118w11	7:52:44
Wilsonia 54	36N44	118w57	7:55:48
Wilton 34	38N25	121w17	8:05:08
Winchester 33	33N43	117w05	7:48:20
Windsor 49	38N33	122w49	8:11:16
Windsor Hills 19	33N59	118w22	7:53:28
Winnetka 19	34N12	118w34	7:54:16
Winter Gardens 37	32N50	116w56	7:47:44
Winterhaven 13	32N44	114w38	7:38:32
Winters 57	38N32	121w58	8:07:52
Winterwarm 37	33N23	117w21	7:49:24
Winton 24	37N23	120w37	8:02:28
Wise 19	33N55	118w25	7:53:40
Wiseburn 19	33N55	118w21	7:53:24
Wishon 20	37N18	119w32	7:58:08
Witch Creek 37	33N03	116w54	7:47:36
Witter Springs 17	39N11	122w58	8:11:52
Wofford Heights 15	35N42	118w27	7:53:48
Wonderland 32	40N33	122w22	8:09:28
Woodacre 21	38N05	122w36	8:10:24
Woodbridge 39	38N09	121w18	8:05:12
Woodcrest 33	33N53	117w22	7:49:28
Woodfords 2	38N47	119w50	7:59:20
Woodlake 54	36N25	119w06	7:56:24
Woodland 57	38N41	121w46	8:07:04
Woodland Acres 56	34N27	119w16	7:57:04
Woodland Hills 19	34N11	118w35	7:54:20
Woodleaf 58	39N29	121w13	8:04:52
Woodruff Avenue 19	33N53	118w08	7:52:32
Woodside 41	37N26	122w16	8:09:04
Woodside Highlands 41	37N28	122w15	8:09:00
Woodville 54	36N06	119w12	7:56:48
Woody 15	35N42	118w50	7:55:20
Workfield 27	36N37	121w50	8:07:20
Workman 19	33N56	118w11	7:52:44
Worldway Postal Center 19	34N05	118w19	7:53:16
Worth	36N03	118w55	7:55:40
Wrightwood 36	34N21	117w38	7:50:32
Wyandotte 4	39N30	121w33	8:06:12
Wynola 37	33N07	116w40	7:46:40
Yale 33	33N45	116w56	7:47:44
Yankee Hill 4	39N30	121w33	8:06:12
Yermo 36	34N54	116w50	7:47:20
Yettem 54	36N29	119w16	7:57:04
Ygnacio Valley 7	37N56	122w02	8:08:08
Yolanda 21	37N59	122w35	8:10:20
Yolano 48	38N27	121w50	8:07:20
Yolo 57	38N44	121w48	8:07:12
Yorba 19	34N05	117w45	7:51:00
Yorba Linda 30	33N53	117w49	7:51:16
York 19	34N05	118w22	7:53:28
Yorkville 23	38N55	123w16	8:13:04
Yosemite 22	37N45	119w35	7:58:20
Yosemite Lodge 22	37N45	119w35	7:58:20
Yosemite National Park 22	37N45	119w35	7:58:20
Yountville 28	38N24	122w22	8:09:28
Yreka 47	41N44	122w38	8:10:32
Yreka City 47	41N40	122w36	8:10:24
Yuba City 51	39N08	121w37	8:06:28
Yuba Foothills 58	39N25	121w13	8:04:52
Yucaipa 36	34N02	117w02	7:48:08
Yucca Valley 36	34N08	116w27	7:45:48
Zamora 57	38N48	121w53	8:07:32
Zante 54	36N04	119w04	7:56:16
Zenia 53	40N12	123w30	8:14:00
Zzyzx 36	35N16	116w04	7:44:16

TIME TABLES

CO # 1
Before 11/18/1883 LMT
11/18/1883 12:00 MST
3/31/1918 02:00 MWT
10/27/1918 02:00 MST
3/30/1919 02:00 MWT
10/26/1919 02:00 MST
2/09/1942 02:00 MWT
9/30/1945 02:00 MST
4/25/1965 02:00 MDT
10/31/1965 02:00 MST
4/24/1966 02:00 MDT
10/30/1966 02:00 MST
4/30/1967 02:00 US#1
....

CO # 2
Before 11/18/1883 LMT
11/18/1883 12:00 MST
3/31/1918 02:00 MWT
10/27/1918 02:00 MST
3/30/1919 02:00 MWT
10/26/1919 02:00 MST
3/28/1920 02:00 MDT
10/31/1920 02:00 MST
3/27/1921 02:00 MDT
5/22/1921 02:00 MST
2/09/1942 02:00 MWT
9/30/1945 02:00 MST
4/25/1965 02:00 MDT
10/31/1965 02:00 MST
4/24/1966 02:00 MDT
10/30/1966 02:00 MST
4/30/1967 02:00 US#1
....

CO # 3
Before 11/18/1883 LMT
11/18/1883 12:00 MST
3/31/1918 02:00 MWT
10/27/1918 02:00 MST
3/30/1919 02:00 MWT
10/26/1919 02:00 MST
2/09/1942 02:00 MWT
9/30/1945 02:00 MST
5/02/1964 02:00 MDT
9/27/1964 02:00 MST
4/25/1965 02:00 MDT
10/31/1965 02:00 MST
4/24/1966 02:00 MDT
10/30/1966 02:00 MST
4/30/1967 02:00 US#1

COUNTIES

1 Adams
2 Alamosa
3 Arapahoe
4 Archuleta
5 Baca
6 Bent
7 Boulder
8 Chaffee
9 Cheyenne
10 Clear Creek
11 Conejos
12 Costilla
13 Crowley
14 Custer
15 Delta
16 Denver
17 Dolores
18 Douglas
19 Eagle
20 Elbert
21 El Paso
22 Fremont
23 Garfield
24 Gilpin
25 Grand
26 Gunnison
27 Hinsdale
28 Huerfano
29 Jackson
30 Jefferson
31 Kiowa
32 Kit Carson
33 Lake
34 La Plata
35 Larimer
36 Las Animas
37 Lincoln
38 Logan
39 Mesa
40 Mineral
41 Moffat
42 Montezuma
43 Montrose
44 Morgan
45 Otero
46 Ouray
47 Park
48 Phillips
49 Pitkin
50 Prowers
51 Pueblo
52 Rio Blanco
53 Rio Grande
54 Routt
55 Saguache
56 San Juan
57 San Miguel
58 Sedgwick
59 Summit
60 Teller
61 Washington
62 Weld
63 Yuma

Acres Green Homes 18 2 39N37 105w00 7:00:00
Adams City 1 2 39N50 104w56 6:59:44
Adobe Park 8 1 38N32 106w00 7:04:00
Agate 20 1 39N28 103w57 6:55:48
Aguilar 36 1 37N24 104w39 6:58:36
Akron 61 1 40N10 103w13 6:52:52
Alamosa 2 1 37N28 105w52 7:03:28
Alcott 16 2 39N47 105w03 7:00:12
Allenspark 7 1 40N12 105w32 7:02:08
Allison 34 1 37N02 107w29 7:09:56
Alma 47 1 39N17 106w04 7:04:16
Almont 26 1 38N40 106w51 7:07:24
Alpine 53 1 37N40 106w37 7:06:28
Altura 1 2 39N43 104w51 6:59:24
Alvin 63 1 40N04 102w13 6:48:52
American City 24 1 39N49 105w31 7:02:04
Amherst 48 1 40N41 102w10 6:48:40
Andersonville 35 1 40N35 105w06 7:00:24
Angel Acres 30 1 39N30 105w20 7:01:20
Animas City 34 1 37N17 107w52 7:11:28
Antlers 23 1 39N32 107w47 7:11:08
Anton 61 1 39N45 103w13 6:52:52
Antonito 11 1 37N05 105w54 7:03:36
Apache City 28 1 37N37 104w47 6:59:08
Apex 24 1 39N49 105w31 7:02:04
Appleton 39 1 39N03 108w33 7:14:12
Applewood 30 2 39N45 105w10 7:00:40
Aqua Ramon 53 1 37N32 106w21 7:05:24
Arabian Acres 60 1 38N57 105w17 7:01:08
Arapahoe 9 1 38N51 102w11 6:48:44
Arboles 4 1 37N07 107w22 7:09:28
Aristocrat Ranchettes 62 1 40N05 104w49 6:59:16
Arlington 31 1 38N20 103w21 6:53:24
Arlington Park 62 1 40N24 104w42 6:58:48
Aroya 9 1 38N49 103w00 6:52:00
Arriba 37 1 39N17 103w17 6:53:08
Arriola 42 1 37N21 108w34 7:14:16
Artesia 40 1 40N20 108w34 7:14:16
Arvada 1 2 39N50 105w05 7:00:20
Arvada Heights 30 2 39N48 105w06 7:00:24
Aspen 49 3 39N11 106w49 7:07:16
Aspen Park 30 1 39N30 105w20 7:01:20
Association Camp 35 1 40N20 105w34 7:02:16
Atwood 38 1 40N33 103w16 6:53:04
Ault 62 1 40N35 104w44 6:58:56
Aurora 1 2 39N44 104w51 6:59:24
Austin 15 1 38N48 107w58 7:11:52
Avon 19 1 39N38 106w31 7:06:04
Avondale 51 1 38N14 104w21 6:57:24
Axial 1 40N17 107w47 7:11:08
Bailey 47 1 39N25 105w29 7:01:56
Bald Mountain 7 1 40N02 105w25 7:01:40
Balltown 33 1 39N03 106w16 7:05:04
Barnesville 62 1 40N27 104w33 6:58:12
Barr 1 2 39N57 104w58 6:59:52
Bartlett 5 1 37N23 102w16 6:49:04
Barton 50 1 38N04 102w18 6:49:12
Basalt 19 1 39N22 107w02 7:08:08
Baxterville 53 1 37N32 106w21 7:05:24
Bayfield 34 1 37N14 107w36 7:10:24
Bear Mine 26 1 38N56 107w16 7:09:04
Beaver Point 35 1 40N22 105w31 7:02:04
Beaver Ridge 47 1 39N14 106w00 7:04:00
Bedrock 43 1 38N19 108w54 7:15:36
Beecher Island 63 1 40N04 102w13 6:48:52
Belle Plain 51 1 38N17 104w35 6:58:20
Bellvue 35 1 40N38 105w10 7:00:40
Belmar 30 2 39N42 105w05 7:00:20
Belmont 51 1 38N17 104w35 6:58:20
Bendemeer Valley 10 1 39N38 105w20 7:01:20
Bennett 1 1 39N46 104w26 6:57:44
Bergen Park 30 1 39N41 105w22 7:01:28
Berthoud 35 1 40N19 105w05 7:00:20
Berthoud Falls 10 1 39N46 105w42 7:02:48
Berthoud Pass 10 1 39N45 105w32 7:02:08
Bethune 32 1 39N18 102w26 6:49:44
Beulah 51 1 38N05 104w59 6:59:56
Beverly Hills 18 1 39N22 104w52 6:59:28
Big Bend 6 1 38N09 102w43 6:50:52
Big Elk Meadows 35 1 40N14 105w17 7:01:08
Black Forest 21 1 38N51 104w48 6:59:12
Black Hawk 24 1 39N49 105w30 7:02:00
Blanca 12 1 37N27 105w31 7:02:04
Blende 51 1 38N15 104w36 6:58:24
Blue Mountain 41 1 40N15 108w52 7:15:28
Blue Mountain Estates 30 2 39N45 105w11 7:00:44
Blue River 59 1 39N26 106w03 7:04:12
Blue Valley Acres 10 1 39N45 105w32 7:02:08
Bonanza 55 1 38N18 106w08 7:04:32
Boncarbo 36 1 37N13 104w41 6:58:44
Bond 19 1 39N52 106w42 7:06:48
Bondad 34 1 37N17 107w52 7:11:28
Boone 51 1 38N15 104w15 6:57:00
Boulder 7 1 40N01 105w17 7:01:08
Bountiful 11 1 37N16 105w58 7:03:52
Bovina 37 1 39N17 103w30 6:54:00
Bowie 15 1 38N55 107w33 7:10:12
Bow Mar 3 2 39N38 105w03 7:00:12
Boxelder Estates 35 1 40N35 105w06 7:00:24
Boyero 37 1 38N57 103w16 6:53:04
Brandon 9 1 38N27 102w26 6:49:44
Brandon 31 1 38N15 104w16 6:57:04
Branson 36 1 37N01 103w53 6:55:32
Breckenridge 59 1 39N29 106w03 7:04:12
Breen 34 1 37N17 108w02 7:12:08
Brewster 22 1 38N23 105w08 7:00:32
Briggsdale 62 1 40N38 104w20 6:57:20
Brighton 1 2 39N59 104w49 6:59:16
Bristol 50 1 38N07 102w19 6:49:16
Broadmoor 21 1 38N50 104w50 6:59:20
Broadway Estates 3 2 39N37 105w00 7:00:00
Broken Arrow Acres 30 1 39N30 105w20 7:01:20
Brook Forest 30 1 39N38 105w20 7:01:20
Brook Forest Estates 10 1 39N38 105w20 7:01:20
Brookridge 3 2 39N37 105w00 7:00:00
Brookside 22 1 38N25 105w11 7:00:44
Brookvale 10 1 39N38 105w26 7:01:44
Brookwood 21 1 38N53 104w48 6:59:12
Broomfield 7 2 39N55 105w05 7:00:20
Brownlee 29 1 40N44 106w17 7:05:08
Brush 44 1 40N15 103w37 6:54:28
Buckeye 35 1 40N42 105w01 7:00:04
Buckingham 35 1 40N35 105w06 7:00:24
Buckingham 44 1 40N37 103w58 6:55:52
Buckingham Square 3 2 39N43 104w51 6:59:24
Buda 62 1 40N19 105w05 7:00:20
Buena Vista 8 1 38N51 106w08 7:04:32
Buffalo Creek 30 1 39N23 105w17 7:01:08
Buford 52 1 40N02 107w55 7:11:40
Burland Ranchettes 47 1 39N25 105w20 7:01:20
Burlington 32 1 39N18 102w16 6:49:04
Burlington Square 7 1 40N11 105w07 7:00:28
Burns 19 1 39N52 106w53 7:07:32
Byers 3 1 39N43 104w14 6:56:56
Caddoa 6 1 38N04 102w56 6:51:44
Cahone 17 1 37N39 108w49 7:15:16
Calhan 21 1 39N02 104w18 6:57:12
California Oil Camp 52 1 40N05 108w47 7:15:08
Cameo 1 39N09 108w19 7:13:16
Camp Bird 46 1 37N58 107w44 7:10:56
Camp George West 30 2 39N45 105w11 7:00:44
Campion 35 1 40N21 105w05 7:00:20
Campo 5 1 37N06 102w35 6:50:20
Canfield 7 2 40N00 105w07 7:00:28
Canon 11 1 37N05 106w01 7:04:04
Canon City 22 1 38N27 105w14 7:00:56
Capitol Hill 16 2 39N44 104w58 6:59:52
Carbondale 23 1 39N24 107w13 7:08:52
Cardiff 23 1 39N31 107w19 7:09:16
Carr 62 1 40N54 104w53 6:59:32
Cascade 21 1 38N54 104w58 6:59:52
Castle Oaks 18 1 39N22 104w52 6:59:28
Castle Rock 18 1 39N22 104w51 6:59:24
Cattle Creek 23 1 39N24 107w13 7:08:52
Cedar 57 1 38N10 108w25 7:13:40
Cedar Cove 35 1 40N24 105w05 7:00:20
Cedaredge 15 1 38N54 107w56 7:11:44
Cedarwood 51 1 37N57 104w37 6:58:28
Centennial 3 2 39N38 104w59 6:59:56
Center 55 1 37N45 106w06 7:04:24
Central City 24 1 39N48 105w31 7:02:04
Chaddsford 3 2 39N43 104w51 6:59:24
Chama 12 1 37N10 105w23 7:01:32
Chapel Hills 21 1 38N53 104w48 6:59:12
Chautauqua 7 1 40N00 105w16 7:01:04
Cheraw 45 1 38N06 103w31 6:54:04
Cherrelyn 3 2 39N38 104w59 6:59:56
Cherry 18 1 39N22 104w52 6:59:28
Cherry Creek 16 2 39N36 104w53 6:59:32
Cherry Hills Crest 3 2 39N37 105w00 7:00:00
Cherry Hills Manor 3 2 39N37 105w00 7:00:00
Cherry Hills Village 3 2 39N38 104w56 6:59:44
Cherry Knolls 3 2 39N37 105w00 7:00:00
Cherry Ridge 3 2 39N38 104w59 6:59:56
Cherry Valley 18 1 39N23 104w45 6:59:00
Cherrywood Village 3 2 39N37 105w00 7:00:00
Cheyenne Canon 21 1 38N53 104w48 6:59:12
Cheyenne Wells 9 1 38N49 102w21 6:49:24
Chimney Rock 4 1 37N13 107w18 7:09:12
Chipita Park 21 1 38N54 104w58 6:59:52
Chivington 31 1 38N26 102w32 6:50:08
Chromo 4 1 37N02 106w50 7:07:20
Chula Vista 24 2 39N45 105w11 7:00:44
Cimarron 43 1 38N27 107w34 7:10:16
Cinderella City 3 2 39N38 104w59 6:59:56
Circle East Mall 21 1 38N51 104w47 6:59:08
Citadel 21 1 38N51 104w47 6:59:08
Clark 54 1 40N43 106w55 7:07:40
Clifton 39 1 39N06 108w26 7:13:44
Climax 33 1 39N22 106w11 7:04:44
Coal Creek 22 1 38N22 105w09 7:00:36
Coaldale 22 1 38N22 105w45 7:03:00
Coalmont 29 1 40N34 106w27 7:05:48
Cochetopa 55 1 38N13 106w45 7:07:00
Cokedale 36 1 37N08 104w37 6:58:28
Collbran 39 1 39N14 107w58 7:11:52
College 62 1 40N24 104w42 6:58:48
College Heights 34 1 37N17 107w52 7:11:28
Colona 46 1 38N20 107w47 7:11:08
Colorado Mountain Estates 60 1 38N57 105w17 7:01:08
Colorado Springs 21 1 38N50 104w49 6:59:16
Columbine 3 2 39N37 105w00 7:00:00
Columbine 54 1 40N43 106w55 7:07:40
Columbine Hills 30 2 39N37 105w00 7:00:00
Columbine Knolls 3 2 39N37 105w00 7:00:00

Columbine Manor 3 2 39N37 105w00 7:00:00
Columbine Valley 3 2 39N36 105w02 7:00:08
Commerce City 1 2 39N49 104w56 6:59:44
Como 47 1 39N19 105w54 7:03:36
Conejos 11 1 37N05 106w01 7:04:04
Conifer 30 1 39N31 105w18 7:01:12
Conifer Mountain 30 1 39N30 105w20 7:01:20
Conifer Park 30 1 39N30 105w20 7:01:20
Cope 61 1 39N40 102w51 6:51:24
Cornish 62 1 40N31 104w25 6:57:40
Coronado 1 2 39N50 104w57 6:59:48
Cortez 42 1 37N21 108w35 7:14:20
Cory 15 1 38N47 107w59 7:11:56
Cotopaxi 22 1 38N22 105w41 7:02:44
Country Club Estates 35 1 40N35 105w06 7:00:24
Country Club Park 7 1 40N00 105w16 7:01:04
Cowdrey 29 1 40N52 106w19 7:05:16
Cragmor 21 1 38N53 104w48 6:59:12
Craig 41 1 40N31 107w33 7:10:12
Craig South Highlands 41 1 40N31 107w33 7:10:12
Crawford 15 1 38N42 107w37 7:10:28
Creede 40 1 37N51 106w56 7:07:44
Crescent 7 1 39N56 105w21 7:01:24
Cresta Vista 21 1 38N48 104w49 6:59:16
Crested Butte 26 1 38N52 106w59 7:07:56
Crestmoor 3 2 39N41 104w56 6:59:44
Crestone 55 1 38N00 105w42 7:02:48
Cripple Creek 60 1 38N45 105w11 7:00:44
Crisman 7 1 40N00 105w16 7:01:04
Crook 38 1 40N52 102w48 6:51:12
Crowley 13 1 38N12 103w51 6:55:24
Crystola 60 1 38N57 105w02 7:00:08
Cuchara 28 1 37N23 105w06 7:00:24
Dacono 62 1 40N05 104w57 6:59:48
Dailey 38 1 40N39 102w43 6:50:52
Dalerose 36 1 37N15 103w21 6:53:24
De Beque 39 1 39N20 108w13 7:12:52
Deckers 18 2 39N26 104w58 6:59:52
Deepcreek 54 1 40N43 106w55 7:07:40
Deer Creek Valley Ranchos 47 1 39N25 105w20 7:01:20
Deer Park 54 1 40N16 106w57 7:07:48
Deer Trail 3 1 39N37 104w02 6:56:08
Delhi 36 1 37N39 104w01 6:56:04
Del Norte 53 1 37N41 106w21 7:05:24
Delta 15 1 38N44 108w04 7:12:16
Denver 16 2 39N44 104w59 6:59:56
Denver Merchandise Mart 1 2 39N48 104w57 6:59:48
Deora 5 1 37N38 102w56 6:51:44
Derby 1 2 39N50 104w55 6:59:40
Devine 51 1 38N17 104w35 6:58:20
Dillon 59 1 39N37 106w04 7:04:16
Dinosaur 41 1 40N15 109w01 7:16:04
Divide 60 1 38N57 105w10 7:00:40
Dolores 42 1 37N28 108w30 7:14:00
Dome Rock 30 1 39N25 105w14 7:00:56
Dorey Lakes 24 2 39N45 105w11 7:00:44
Dory Hill 24 2 39N45 105w11 7:00:44
Dotsero 19 1 39N39 106w57 7:07:48
Dove Creek 17 1 37N46 108w54 7:15:36
Downieville 10 1 39N46 105w36 7:02:24
Downtown 3 2 39N38 104w59 6:59:56
Doyleville 1 38N27 106w37 7:06:28
Drake 35 1 40N26 105w21 7:01:24
Dream House Acres 3 2 39N37 105w00 7:00:00
Dry Creek Basin 57 1 38N10 108w25 7:13:40
Dumont 10 1 39N46 105w36 7:02:24
Dunton 1 37N46 108w05 7:12:20
Dupont 1 2 39N51 104w55 6:59:40
Durango 34 1 37N17 107w53 7:11:32
Eads 31 1 38N29 102w47 6:51:08
Eagle 19 1 39N39 106w50 7:07:20
East Adams 1 1 39N53 104w11 6:56:44
East Alamosa 2 1 37N28 105w51 7:03:24
East Arapahoe 3 1 39N41 104w17 6:57:08
East Canon 22 1 38N29 105w14 7:00:56
Eastlake 1 2 39N55 104w58 6:59:52
Eastlake 51 1 38N14 104w38 6:58:32
East Portal 24 1 39N54 105w39 7:02:36
Eastridge 3 2 39N39 104w51 6:59:24
Eastridge South 3 2 39N39 104w51 6:59:24
East Weston 36 1 37N08 104w48 6:59:12
Eaton 62 1 40N32 104w42 6:58:48
Echo Lake 10 1 39N45 105w32 7:02:08
Eckert 15 1 38N51 107w58 7:11:52
Eckley 63 1 40N07 102w29 6:49:56
Eden 51 1 38N16 104w33 6:58:12
Edgemont 30 2 39N44 105w08 7:00:32
Edgewater 30 2 39N46 105w04 7:00:16
Edison 21 1 38N50 104w13 6:56:52
Edler 5 1 37N11 102w47 6:51:08
Edwards 19 1 39N39 106w36 7:06:24
Egnar 57 1 37N55 108w56 7:15:44
Elbert 20 1 39N13 104w32 6:58:08
Eldora 7 1 39N57 105w34 7:02:16
Eldorado Springs 7 1 39N56 105w17 7:01:08
Eleven Mile Village 47 1 38N59 105w22 7:01:28
Elizabeth 20 1 39N22 104w36 6:58:24
El Jebel 19 1 40N31 107w33 7:10:12
Elk Creek Acres 30 1 39N25 105w20 7:01:20
Elk Creek Highlands 47 1 39N25 105w20 7:01:20

Elkhorn Acres 47 1 39N25 105w20 7:01:20
Elk River 54 1 40N30 106w50 7:07:20
Elk Springs 41 1 40N21 108w27 7:13:48
Elkton 60 1 38N42 105w08 7:00:32
Ellicott 21 1 38N50 104w23 6:57:32
El Moro 36 1 37N10 104w30 6:58:00
El Rancho 30 2 39N45 105w11 7:00:44
Elsmere 21 1 38N53 104w42 6:58:48
El Vado 7 1 40N00 105w16 7:01:04
Elwell 62 1 40N20 104w55 6:59:40
Emma 19 1 39N24 107w13 7:08:52
Empire 10 1 39N46 105w41 7:02:44
Englewood 3 2 39N39 104w59 6:59:56
Erie 62 2 40N03 105w03 7:00:12
Escalante Forks 39 1 38N44 108w04 7:12:16
Estabrook 47 1 39N25 105w29 7:01:56
Estes Park 35 1 40N23 105w31 7:02:04
Estrella 2 1 37N28 105w51 7:03:24
Evans 62 1 40N23 104w41 6:58:44
Evanston 62 1 40N06 104w57 6:59:48
Evergreen 30 1 39N38 105w19 7:01:16
Ever Green Hills 30 1 39N38 105w20 7:01:20
Evergreen West 10 1 39N38 105w20 7:01:20
Fairplay 47 1 39N14 106w00 7:04:00
Fairview 14 1 37N55 104w56 6:59:44
Fairview 23 1 39N33 107w39 7:10:36
Fairway Estates 35 1 40N35 105w06 7:00:24
Falcon 21 1 38N56 104w37 6:58:28
Falcon Estates 21 1 38N51 104w48 6:59:12
Falfa 34 1 37N17 107w52 7:11:28
Fall Creek 57 1 38N00 108w00 7:12:00
Farisita 28 1 37N45 105w04 7:00:16
Farmers 62 1 40N24 104w42 6:58:48
Federal Heights 1 2 39N52 105w02 7:00:08
Fenders 2 39N34 105w13 7:00:52
Ferncliffe 7 1 40N12 105w32 7:02:08
Ferndale 30 1 39N23 105w17 7:01:08
Firestone 62 1 40N07 104w57 6:59:48
First View 9 1 38N49 102w21 6:49:24
Fitzsimons 1 2 39N45 104w48 6:59:12
Flagler 32 1 39N18 103w04 6:52:16
Fleming 38 1 40N35 102w53 6:51:32
Flintwood Hills 18 1 39N23 104w45 6:59:00
Florence 22 1 38N23 105w08 7:00:32
Florissant 60 1 38N57 105w17 7:01:08
Florissant Heights 60 1 38N57 105w17 7:01:08
Fondis 20 1 39N13 104w21 6:57:24
Forest Hills 24 2 39N45 105w11 7:00:44
Fort Carson 21 1 38N45 104w47 6:59:08
Fort Collins 35 1 40N35 105w05 7:00:20
Fort Garland 12 1 37N26 105w26 7:01:44
Fort Logan 3 2 39N39 105w02 7:00:08
Fort Lupton 62 1 40N05 104w49 6:59:16
Fort Morgan 44 1 40N15 103w48 6:55:12
Fountain 21 1 38N41 104w42 6:58:48
Fowler 45 1 38N08 104w02 6:56:08
Foxborough 7 2 39N55 105w06 7:00:24
Fox Creek 11 1 37N05 106w01 7:04:04
Foxton 30 1 39N25 105w14 7:00:56
Franktown 18 1 39N24 104w45 6:59:00
Fraser 25 1 39N57 105w49 7:03:16
Frederick 62 1 40N06 104w56 6:59:44
Freeman 53 1 37N32 106w21 7:05:24
Freshwater 47 1 38N46 105w32 7:02:08
Friendship Ranch 47 1 39N25 105w20 7:01:20
Frisco 59 1 39N35 106w06 7:04:24
Fruita 39 1 39N09 108w44 7:14:56
Fruitvale 39 1 39N05 108w30 7:14:00
Galeton 62 1 40N31 104w35 6:58:20
Garcia 12 1 37N00 105w32 7:02:08
Garden City 62 1 40N24 104w42 6:58:48
Gardner 28 1 37N47 105w10 7:00:40
Garfield 8 1 38N33 106w18 7:05:12
Gateway 39 1 38N41 108w59 7:15:56
Gato 4 1 37N03 107w12 7:08:48
Gem Village 34 1 37N13 107w38 7:10:32
Genesee 30 2 39N45 105w11 7:00:44
Genoa 37 1 39N17 103w30 6:54:00
Georgetown 10 1 39N42 105w42 7:02:48
Gilcrest 62 1 40N17 104w47 6:59:08
Gill 62 1 40N27 104w33 6:58:12
Gilman 19 1 39N32 106w24 7:05:36
Gilsonite 39 1 39N09 108w44 7:14:56
Gladel 56 1 38N01 108w47 7:15:08
Glade Park 39 1 39N00 108w44 7:14:56
Glendale 3 2 39N43 104w56 6:59:44
Glendevey 35 1 40N48 105w56 7:03:44
Glen Echo 35 1 40N38 105w10 7:00:40
Glenelk 30 1 39N25 105w20 7:01:20
Glen Haven 35 1 40N27 105w27 7:01:48
Glenisle 47 1 39N25 105w29 7:01:56
Glen Park 21 1 39N07 104w55 6:59:40
Glentivar 47 1 39N14 106w00 7:04:00
Glenwood Springs 23 1 39N33 107w19 7:09:16
Golden 30 2 39N46 105w13 7:00:52
Goldfield 60 1 38N42 105w08 7:00:32
Gold Hill 7 1 40N04 105w25 7:01:40
Goodale 50 1 38N07 102w19 6:49:16
Goodnight 51 1 38N15 104w39 6:58:36
Goodrich 44 1 40N21 104w04 6:56:16
Gould 29 1 40N44 106w17 7:05:08
Granada 50 1 38N04 102w19 6:49:16
Granby 25 1 40N05 105w56 7:03:44
Grand Junction 39 1 39N04 108w33 7:14:12

COLORADO

Grand Lake 25 1 40N15 105w49 7:03:16
Grand Mesa 15 1 38N54 107w55 7:11:40
Grand Valley 23 1 39N27 108w03 7:12:12
Grandview 34 1 37N17 107w52 7:11:28
Grandview Estates 18 2 39N31 104w46 6:59:04
Granite 8 1 39N03 106w16 7:05:04
Grant 47 1 39N28 105w40 7:02:40
Greeley 62 1 40N25 104w42 6:58:48
Greeley Mall 62 1 40N24 104w42 6:58:48
Greenland 18 1 39N14 104w53 6:59:32
Green Mountain 30 2 39N41 105w08 7:00:32
Green Mountain Camp 59 1 40N04 106w24 7:05:36
Green Mountain Estates 30 2 39N41 105w08 7:00:32
Green Mountain Falls 21 1 38N56 105w02 7:00:08
Green Mountain Village 30 2 39N41 105w08 7:00:32
Green Towers 51 1 37N55 104w56 6:59:44
Green Valley Acres 30 1 39N30 105w20 7:01:20
Greenway Park 30 2 39N55 105w06 7:00:24
Greenwood 14 1 38N12 105w06 7:00:24
Greenwood 51 1 37N55 104w56 6:59:44
Greenwood Village 3 2 39N37 104w56 6:59:44
Greystone 41 1 40N37 108w41 7:14:44
Grover 62 1 40N52 104w14 6:56:56
Guadalupe 11 1 37N05 106w01 7:04:04
Guffey 47 1 38N45 105w31 7:02:04
Gulnare 36 1 37N19 104w45 6:59:00
Gunbarrel Estates 7 1 40N11 105w07 7:00:28
Gunbarrel Meadows 7 1 40N00 105w16 7:01:04
Gunnison 26 1 38N33 106w56 7:07:44
Gypsum 19 1 39N39 106w57 7:07:48
Hahns Peak 54 1 40N43 106w55 7:07:40
Hale 63 1 39N38 102w09 6:48:36
Hallcraft Town Houses 30 2 39N41 105w08 7:00:32
Hamilton 41 1 40N22 107w37 7:10:28
Hanover 21 1 38N51 104w47 6:59:08
Hardin 62 1 40N24 104w34 6:58:16
Harmony 35 1 40N35 105w06 7:00:24
Harris Park 47 1 39N25 105w20 7:01:20
Hartman 50 1 38N07 102w13 6:48:52
Hartsel 47 1 39N01 105w48 7:03:12
Hasty 6 1 38N07 102w58 6:51:52
Haswell 31 1 38N27 103w10 6:52:40
Hawley 45 1 38N03 103w43 6:54:52
Haxtun 48 1 40N39 102w38 6:50:32
Hayden 54 1 40N30 107w16 7:09:04
Hazeltine Heights 1 2 39N55 104w51 6:59:24
Heatherwood 7 1 40N00 105w16 7:01:04
Heeney 59 1 40N04 106w24 7:05:36
Henderson 1 2 39N55 104w51 6:59:24
Hereford 62 1 40N57 104w18 6:57:12
Hermosa 34 1 37N17 107w52 7:11:28
Herzman Mesa 30 1 39N37 105w19 7:01:16
Hesperus 34 1 37N17 108w02 7:12:08
Hiawatha 41 1 40N59 108w37 7:14:28
Hidden Valley 30 1 39N41 105w20 7:01:20
Hideaway Park 25 1 39N53 105w46 7:03:04
High Chateau Ranches 60 1 38N57 105w17 7:01:08
Highland Acres 62 1 40N24 104w42 6:58:48
Highland Lake 62 1 40N13 104w50 6:59:20
Highland Lakes 60 1 38N56 105w09 7:00:36
Highland Park 39 1 39N03 108w33 7:14:12
Highland Park 47 1 39N25 105w20 7:01:20
Highlands 16 2 39N46 105w01 7:00:04
High-mar 7 1 40N00 105w16 7:01:04
Hi-Land Acres 1 2 39N57 104w58 6:59:52
Hill and Park 62 1 40N24 104w42 6:58:48
Hillrose 44 1 40N20 103w31 6:54:04
Hillside 22 1 38N16 105w37 7:02:28
Hilltop 18 2 39N31 104w46 6:59:04
Hitchens 54 1 40N30 106w50 7:07:20
Hoehne 36 1 37N17 104w23 6:57:32
Hoffman Heights 3 2 39N43 104w51 6:59:24
Holiday Hills 60 1 39N00 105w04 7:00:16
Holly 50 1 38N03 102w07 6:48:28
Holyoke 48 1 40N35 102w18 6:49:12
Homelake 53 1 37N35 106w07 7:04:28
Hooper 2 1 37N45 105w53 7:03:32
Hoopup 36 1 37N15 103w21 6:53:24
Horsetooth Heights 35 1 40N35 105w06 7:00:24
Hotchkiss 15 1 38N48 107w43 7:10:52
Hot Creek 11 1 37N16 106w15 7:05:00
Hot Sulphur"springs 1 40N04 106w06 7:04:24
Hot Sulphur Springs 25 1 40N04 106w06 7:04:24
Howard 22 1 38N27 105w50 7:03:20
Hoyt 44 1 40N01 104w05 6:56:20
Hudson 62 1 40N04 104w39 6:58:36
Huerfano Valley 51 1 38N02 104w17 6:57:08
Hugo 37 1 39N08 103w28 6:53:52
Husted 21 1 38N59 104w52 6:59:28
Hyde 61 1 40N09 102w58 6:51:52
Hygiene 7 1 40N11 105w11 7:00:44
Hyland Hills 10 1 39N38 105w20 7:01:20
Idaho Springs 10 1 39N45 105w31 7:02:04
Idalia 63 1 39N42 102w18 6:49:12
Idledale 30 2 39N40 105w15 7:01:00

COLORADO

Ignacio 34	1	37N07	107w38	7:10:32
Iliff 38	1	40N45	103w04	6:52:16
Ilse 14	1	38N26	105w13	7:00:52
Indian Agency 34	1	37N07	107w38	7:10:32
Indian Creek 60	1	38N57	105w17	7:01:08
Indian Hills 30	2	39N37	105w14	7:00:56
Iola	1	38N29	107w06	7:08:24
Ione 62	1	40N09	104w49	6:59:16
Irondale 1	2	39N51	104w53	6:59:32
Ironton 46	1	38N01	107w41	7:10:44
Ivywild 21	1	38N48	104w49	6:59:16
Jamestown 7	1	40N07	105w23	7:01:32
Jansen 36	1	37N09	104w32	6:58:08
Jaroso 12	1	37N00	105w38	7:02:32
Jefferson 47	1	39N23	105w48	7:03:12
Jefferson Heights 47	1	39N23	105w48	7:03:12
Joes 63	1	39N39	102w41	6:50:44
Johnson Village 8	1	38N50	106w08	7:04:32
Johnstown 62	1	40N20	104w54	6:59:36
Juanita 4	1	37N16	107w00	7:08:00
Julesburg 58	1	40N59	102w16	6:49:04
Kahler 62	1	40N19	105w05	7:00:20
Kaibab 19	1	39N39	106w50	7:07:20
Karval 37	1	38N44	103w32	6:54:08
Keenesburg 62	1	40N07	104w31	6:58:04
Kelim 35	1	40N24	105w05	7:00:20
Keota 62	1	40N42	104w05	6:56:20
Kersey 62	1	40N23	104w34	6:58:16
Kim 36	1	37N15	103w21	6:53:24
Kings Canyon	1	40N56	106w14	7:04:56
Kiowa 20	1	39N21	104w28	6:57:52
Kirk 63	1	39N37	102w36	6:50:24
Kit Carson 9	1	38N46	102w48	6:51:12
Kittredge 30	2	39N39	105w18	7:01:12
Kline 34	1	37N09	108w08	7:12:32
Knob Hill 21	1	38N51	104w47	6:59:08
Koen 50	1	38N04	102w18	6:49:12
Kokomo	1	39N26	106w11	7:04:44
Kremmling 25	1	40N04	106w24	7:05:36
Kuhlmann Heights 7	2	39N45	105w11	7:00:44
Kutch 20	1	39N07	104w11	6:56:44
K-z Ranchettes 47	1	39N25	105w20	7:01:20
Lafayette 7	2	40N00	105w05	7:00:20
La Garita 55	1	37N50	106w15	7:05:00
Laird 63	1	40N05	102w06	6:48:24
La Jara 11	1	37N16	105w58	7:03:52
La Junta 45	1	37N59	103w33	6:54:12
La Junta Gardens 45	1	37N59	103w31	6:54:04
Lakeborough 30	2	39N38	105w04	7:00:16
Lake City 27	1	38N02	107w19	7:09:16
Lake George 47	1	38N59	105w22	7:01:28
Lakeside 30	2	39N47	105w03	7:00:12
Lake View 24	2	39N45	105w11	7:00:44
Lakewood 30	2	39N44	105w05	7:00:20
Lamar 50	1	38N05	102w37	6:50:28
La Montana Mesa 60	1	38N57	105w17	7:01:08
Laporte 35	1	40N38	105w08	7:00:32
La Posta 34	1	37N17	107w52	7:11:28
Lariat 53	1	37N34	106w09	7:04:36
Larkspur 18	1	39N14	104w53	6:59:32
La Salle 62	1	40N21	104w42	6:58:48
Las Animas 6	1	38N04	103w13	6:52:52
Lasauses 11	1	37N15	105w54	7:03:36
Las Mesitas 11	1	37N05	106w01	7:04:04
Last Chance 61	1	39N59	103w36	6:54:24
La Valley 12	1	37N09	105w24	7:01:36
La Veta 28	1	37N31	105w00	7:00:00
Lawson 10	1	39N45	105w32	7:02:08
Lay 41	1	40N32	107w53	7:11:32
Lazear 15	1	38N47	107w47	7:11:08
Leadville 33	1	39N15	106w18	7:05:12
Lebanon 42	1	37N29	108w30	7:14:00
Leisure Living 62	2	40N03	105w04	7:00:16
Lewis 42	1	37N30	108w40	7:14:40
Leyden 30	2	39N51	105w11	7:00:44
Liberty Bell Village 57	1	37N56	107w48	7:11:12
Limon 37	1	39N16	103w41	6:54:44
Lincoln Park 22	1	38N25	105w12	7:00:48
Lindon 61	1	39N44	103w24	6:53:36
Littleton 3	2	39N37	105w01	7:00:04
Livengood Hills 18	2	39N31	104w46	6:59:04
Livermore 35	1	40N47	105w16	7:01:04
Lobatos 11	1	37N05	106w01	7:04:04
Lochbuie 62	2	39N57	104w58	6:59:52
Lochwood 30	2	39N41	105w00	7:00:00
Log Lane Village 44	1	40N16	103w50	6:55:20
Loma 39	1	39N12	108w49	7:15:16
Loma Linda 34	1	37N17	107w52	7:11:28
Lombard Village 51	1	38N15	104w36	6:58:24
Lone Pine Estates 30	2	39N40	105w07	7:00:28
Longmont 7	1	40N10	105w06	7:00:24
Longview 30	1	39N25	105w14	7:00:56
Lookout Mountain 30	2	39N45	105w11	7:00:44
Loretto Heights 16	2	39N39	105w02	7:00:08
Los Fuertes 12	1	37N09	105w24	7:01:36
Louisville 7	2	39N59	105w08	7:00:32
Louviers 18	2	39N28	105w01	7:00:04
Loveland 35	1	40N24	105w05	7:00:20
Loveland Heights 35	1	40N26	105w21	7:01:24
Lowery Air Force Base 16	2	39N43	104w53	6:59:32
Lubers 6	1	38N08	102w51	6:51:24
Lucerne 62	1	40N29	104w42	6:58:48
Ludlow 36	1	37N20	104w35	6:58:20
Lycan	1	37N37	102w12	6:48:48
Lyons 7	1	40N14	105w16	7:01:04
Lyons Park Estates 7	1	40N14	105w17	7:01:08
Mack 39	1	39N13	108w52	7:15:28
Madison Hill 30	2	39N50	105w01	7:00:04
Madrid 36	1	37N10	104w30	6:58:00
Magnolia 7	1	39N58	105w31	7:02:04
Maher 43	1	38N39	107w35	7:10:20
Manassa 11	1	37N11	105w56	7:03:44
Mancos 42	1	37N21	108w18	7:13:12
Mancos Creek 42	1	37N21	108w34	7:14:16
Mandalay Gardens 30	2	39N55	105w06	7:00:24
Manitou Springs 21	1	38N52	104w55	6:59:40
Manzanola 45	1	38N06	103w52	6:55:28
Marble 26	1	39N04	107w12	7:08:48
Marshall 7	2	39N57	105w14	7:00:56
Marshdale	1	39N36	105w19	7:01:16
Marshdale Park 30	1	39N38	105w20	7:01:20
Marvel 34	1	37N07	108w08	7:12:32
Masonic Park 53	1	37N40	106w37	7:06:28
Masonville 35	1	40N29	105w13	7:00:52
Massadona 41	1	40N15	108w38	7:14:32
Masters 62	1	40N18	104w15	6:57:00
Matheson 20	1	39N10	103w59	6:55:56
Maxeyville 53	1	37N34	106w09	7:04:36
Maybell 41	1	40N31	108w05	7:12:20
Mayday	1	37N21	108w05	7:12:20
Maysville 8	1	38N32	106w11	7:04:44
McClave 6	1	38N08	102w51	6:51:24
McCoy 19	1	39N55	106w44	7:06:56
McCoy Hills 1	2	39N50	104w57	6:59:48
McCoy Subdivision 8	1	38N32	106w00	7:04:00
McElmo 42	1	37N21	108w34	7:14:16
Mead 62	1	40N14	105w00	7:00:00
Meadow Brook Heights 30	2	39N37	105w00	7:00:00
Meeker 52	1	40N02	107w55	7:11:40
Meeker Park 7	1	40N12	105w32	7:02:08
Meredith 49	1	39N22	106w44	7:06:56
Merino 38	1	40N32	103w23	6:53:32
Mesa 39	1	39N10	108w08	7:12:32
Mesa 51	1	38N15	104w39	6:58:36
Mesa Verde National Park 42	1	37N11	108w29	7:13:56
Mesita 12	1	37N06	105w36	7:02:24
Messex 61	1	40N29	103w21	6:53:24
Milliken 62	1	40N20	104w51	6:59:24
Milner 54	1	40N29	107w01	7:08:04
Minturn 19	1	39N35	106w26	7:05:44
Mirage 55	1	38N00	105w54	7:03:36
Missouri Park 8	1	38N32	106w00	7:04:00
Model 36	1	37N22	104w15	6:57:00
Moffat 41	1	40N20	107w36	7:10:24
Moffat 55	1	38N00	105w54	7:03:36
Mogote 11	1	37N04	106w06	7:04:24
Molina 39	1	39N11	108w04	7:12:16
Montclair 16	2	39N44	104w54	6:59:36
Monte Vista 53	1	37N35	106w09	7:04:36
Montezuma 59	1	39N35	105w52	7:03:28
Montrose 43	1	38N29	107w53	7:11:32
Monument 21	1	39N06	104w52	6:59:28
Monument Lake Park 36	1	37N08	104w48	6:59:12
Moore Dale 47	1	39N25	105w29	7:01:56
Morgan 11	1	37N16	105w58	7:03:52
Morrison 30	2	39N39	105w12	7:00:48
Mosca 2	1	37N39	105w52	7:03:28
Mountain Park 30	2	39N45	105w11	7:00:44
Mountain View 30	2	39N46	105w03	7:00:12
Mountain View 35	1	40N35	105w06	7:00:24
Mountain View Acres 2	1	37N28	105w51	7:03:24
Mountain View Lakes 30	1	39N25	105w20	7:01:20
Mount Crested Butte 26	1	38N52	106w59	7:07:56
Mount Massive Lakes 33	1	39N15	106w18	7:05:12
Mount Princeton 8	1	38N45	106w05	7:04:20
Mount Vernon Club Place 30	2	39N45	105w11	7:00:44
Mutual 28	1	37N37	104w47	6:59:08
Nast 49	1	39N22	106w44	7:06:56
Nathrop 8	1	38N45	106w05	7:04:20
Naturita 43	1	38N14	108w34	7:14:16
Nederland 7	1	39N58	105w31	7:02:04
Nevadaville 24	1	39N49	105w31	7:02:04
New Castle 23	1	39N34	107w32	7:10:08
New Raymer 62	1	40N36	103w51	6:55:24
Nighthawk 18	2	39N26	104w58	6:59:52
Ninaview 6	1	38N04	103w13	6:52:52
Ninemile Corner 44	1	40N15	103w38	6:54:32
Niwot 7	1	40N06	105w10	7:00:40
Norfolk 35	1	40N55	104w58	6:59:52
Norrie 49	1	39N22	106w44	7:06:56
North Aurora 1	2	39N45	104w47	6:59:08
North Avondale 51	1	38N16	104w21	6:57:24
North Boulder 7	1	40N00	105w16	7:01:04
North Cherry Creek Valley 3	2	39N42	104w53	6:59:32
North Delta 15	1	38N44	108w04	7:12:16
North End 21	1	38N53	104w48	6:59:12
Northglenn 1	2	39N53	104w58	6:59:52
North La Junta 45	1	37N59	103w31	6:54:04
North Pecos 1	2	39N50	105w01	7:00:04
North Pole 21	1	38N54	104w58	6:59:52
North Valley 1	2	39N50	104w57	6:59:48
North Washington Heights 1	2	39N50	104w57	6:59:48
Norwood 57	1	38N08	108w20	7:13:20
Nucla 43	1	38N16	108w33	7:14:12
Numa 13	1	38N13	103w45	6:55:00
Nunn 62	1	40N42	104w47	6:59:08
Nutria 4	1	37N16	107w00	7:08:00
Oak Creek 54	1	40N16	106w57	7:07:48
Oak Grove 43	1	38N29	107w52	7:11:28
Oehlmann Park 30	1	39N30	105w20	7:01:20
Ohio 26	1	38N34	106w37	7:06:28
Olathe 43	1	38N36	107w59	7:11:56
Olinger Gardens 30	2	39N45	105w03	7:00:12
Oliver 26	1	38N56	107w16	7:09:04
Olney Springs 13	1	38N10	103w57	6:55:48
Olympus Heights 35	1	40N26	105w21	7:01:24
Ophir 57	1	37N52	107w52	7:11:28
Orchard 44	1	40N20	104w07	6:56:28
Orchard City 15	1	38N50	107w58	7:11:52
Orchard Mesa 39	1	39N03	108w26	7:13:44
Ordway 13	1	38N13	103w45	6:55:00
Ormandale 51	1	38N15	104w39	6:58:36
Ortiz 11	1	37N05	106w01	7:04:04
Otis 61	1	40N09	102w58	6:51:52
Ouray 46	1	38N01	107w40	7:10:40
Ovid 58	1	40N58	102w23	6:49:32
Oxford 34	1	37N07	107w38	7:10:32
Pactolus 24	2	39N45	105w11	7:00:44
Padroni 38	1	40N47	103w10	6:52:40
Pagosa 4	1	37N16	107w00	7:08:00
Pagosa Springs 4	1	37N16	107w01	7:08:04
Paisaje 11	1	37N05	106w01	7:04:04
Palisade 39	1	39N07	108w21	7:13:24
Palmer Lake 21	1	39N07	104w55	6:59:40
Pandora 57	1	37N56	107w48	7:11:12
Paoli 48	1	40N37	102w28	6:49:52
Paonia 15	1	38N52	107w36	7:10:24
Papeton	1	38N54	104w49	6:59:16
Paradox 43	1	38N22	108w58	7:15:52
Park Center 22	1	38N26	105w13	7:00:52
Parkdale 22	1	38N29	105w23	7:01:32
Parker 18	2	39N31	104w46	6:59:04
Park Hill 16	2	39N45	104w55	6:59:40
Parlin 26	1	38N31	106w43	7:06:52
Parshall 25	1	40N03	106w11	7:04:44
Patt 36	1	37N15	103w21	6:53:24
Peaceful Valley 7	1	40N14	105w17	7:01:08
Peagreen 43	1	38N44	108w04	7:12:16
Pear Park 39	1	39N03	108w33	7:14:12
Peckham 62	1	40N21	104w42	6:58:48
Peetz 38	1	40N58	103w07	6:52:28
Penitentiary 22	1	38N26	105w13	7:00:52
Penrose 22	1	38N26	105w01	7:00:04
Peoples 1	2	39N43	104w51	6:59:24
Perl-Mack 1	2	39N50	105w01	7:00:04
Peterson Field 21	1	38N49	104w43	6:58:52
Peyton 21	1	39N02	104w29	6:57:56
Pheasant Run 3	2	39N43	104w51	6:59:24
Phippsburg 54	1	40N14	106w57	7:07:48
Piedmont 46	1	38N09	107w45	7:11:00
Piedra 4	1	37N12	107w18	7:09:12
Pierce 62	1	40N38	104w45	6:59:00
Pikes Peak 21	1	38N54	104w58	6:59:52
Pikeview	1	38N55	104w49	6:59:16
Pine 30	1	39N25	105w20	7:01:20
Pinecliff 7	1	39N56	105w26	7:01:44
Pine Crest 21	1	39N07	104w55	6:59:40
Pine Park Estates 30	2	39N40	105w07	7:00:28
Pinewood Springs 35	1	40N14	105w17	7:01:08
Pinnacle Park 62	1	40N24	104w42	6:58:48
Pinon 51	1	38N38	104w40	6:58:40
Pinon Canyon 36	1	37N10	104w30	6:58:00
Pitkin 26	1	38N37	106w31	7:06:04
Placerville 57	1	38N01	108w03	7:12:12
Plateau City 39	1	39N14	107w58	7:11:52
Platner 61	1	40N09	103w04	6:52:16
Platoro 11	1	37N34	106w09	7:04:36
Platteville 62	1	40N13	104w49	6:59:16
Plaza 53	1	37N32	106w21	7:05:24
Pleasant View 30	2	39N45	105w11	7:00:44
Pleasant View 42	1	37N35	108w46	7:15:04
Poncha Springs 8	1	38N31	106w05	7:04:20
Ponderosa Park 20	1	39N22	104w36	6:58:24
Portland 22	1	38N23	105w01	7:00:04
Poudre Park 35	1	40N41	105w18	7:01:12
Powderhorn 26	1	38N17	107w07	7:08:28
Powder Wash	1	40N57	108w19	7:13:16
Powder Wash 41	1	38N51	104w48	6:59:12
Pritchett 5	1	37N22	102w52	6:51:28
Proctor 38	1	40N48	102w57	6:51:48
Prospect 62	1	40N07	104w31	6:58:04
Prospect Heights 22	1	38N26	105w14	7:00:56
Prospect Valley 30	1	40N05	104w25	6:57:40
Prowers 6	1	38N05	102w37	6:50:28
Pryor 28	1	37N31	104w43	6:58:52
Pueblo 51	1	38N14	104w36	6:58:24
Pueblo Army Depot 51	1	38N17	104w35	6:58:20
Purcell 62	1	40N35	104w44	6:58:56

Place		Lat	Long	Time
Purgatoire Valley 6	1	37N52	103w06	6:52:24
Quimby 1	2	39N50	104w57	6:59:48
Radium 25	1	39N57	106w34	7:06:16
Ragged Mountain 26	1	38N56	107w16	7:09:04
Rainbow Valley 60	1	38N56	105w09	7:00:36
Ramah 21	1	39N07	104w10	6:56:40
Rand 29	1	40N27	106w11	7:04:44
Rangely 52	1	40N05	108w48	7:15:12
Range View Estates 62	1	40N24	104w42	6:58:48
Rattlesnake Buttes 28	1	37N37	104w47	6:59:08
Raymer 62	1	40N41	103w56	6:55:44
Raymond 7	1	40N14	105w17	7:01:08
Redcliff 19	1	39N31	106w22	7:05:28
Red Feather Lakes 35	1	40N48	105w35	7:02:20
Redlands 39	1	39N04	108w37	7:14:28
Redmesa 34	1	37N06	108w11	7:12:44
Red Mountain 46	1	38N01	107w41	7:10:44
Redstone 49	1	39N11	107w14	7:08:56
Redvale 43	1	38N10	108w25	7:13:40
Red Wing 28	1	37N44	105w17	7:01:08
Rembrandt Place 3	2	39N35	104w56	6:59:44
Rezago 36	1	37N10	104w30	6:58:00
Richfield 11	1	37N16	105w58	7:03:52
Rico 17	1	37N42	108w02	7:12:08
Ridgway 46	1	38N09	107w46	7:11:04
Rifle 23	1	39N32	107w47	7:11:08
Rinn 62	1	40N11	105w07	7:00:28
Rio Blanco 52	1	39N44	107w57	7:11:48
Riverside 7	1	40N14	105w17	7:01:08
Riverview 30	1	39N23	105w17	7:01:08
Roberta 45	1	37N59	103w31	6:54:04
Rockvale 22	1	38N22	105w10	7:00:40
Rocky Ford 45	1	38N03	103w43	6:54:52
Rocky Mountain Arsenal 1	2	39N45	104w48	6:59:12
Rogers Mesa 15	1	38N48	107w43	7:10:52
Roggen 62	1	40N10	104w22	6:57:28
Roland Valley 47	1	39N25	105w20	7:01:20
Rolling Hills 7	1	40N00	105w16	7:01:04
Rollinsville 24	1	39N55	105w30	7:02:00
Romeo 11	1	37N10	105w59	7:03:56
Rosedale 62	1	40N24	104w42	6:58:48
Rosita	1	38N06	105w20	7:01:20
Roswell 21	1	38N53	104w48	6:59:12
Rowena 7	1	40N07	105w24	7:01:36
Royal Gorge 22	1	38N28	105w19	7:01:16
Royal Ranch 47	1	39N25	105w20	7:01:20
Ruedi 19	1	39N22	107w02	7:08:08
Rulison 23	1	39N27	108w03	7:12:12
Rush 21	1	38N50	104w05	6:56:20
Russell Gulch 24	1	39N49	105w31	7:02:04
Rustic 35	1	40N38	105w10	7:00:40
Rye 51	1	37N55	104w56	6:59:44
Saguache 55	1	38N05	106w08	7:04:32
Saint Charles Mesa 51	1	38N14	104w33	6:58:12
Saint Peters 38	1	40N41	102w50	6:51:20
Salida 8	1	38N32	106w00	7:04:00
Salina 7	1	40N00	105w16	7:01:04
Salt Creek 51	1	38N15	104w36	6:58:24
San Acacio 12	1	37N13	105w34	7:02:16
San Antonio 11	1	37N01	106w01	7:04:04
Sand Park 8	1	38N32	106w00	7:04:00
Sanford 11	1	37N16	105w54	7:03:36
San Francisco 12	1	37N09	105w24	7:01:36
Sangre De Cristo Ranches 12	1	37N26	105w26	7:01:44
San Isabel 14	1	37N55	104w56	6:59:44
San Juan 36	1	37N07	104w45	6:59:00
San Luis 12	1	37N12	105w25	7:01:40
San Pablo 12	1	37N09	105w24	7:01:36
San Pedro 12	1	37N09	105w24	7:01:36
Santa Fe Drive 16	2	39N44	105w01	7:00:04
Sapinero 26	1	38N27	107w17	7:09:08
Sarcillo 36	1	37N10	104w30	6:58:00
Sarcillo Canon 36	1	37N08	104w48	6:59:12
Sargent 53	1	37N41	106w08	7:04:32
Sargents 55	1	38N25	106w24	7:05:36
Sargents School 53	1	37N34	106w09	7:04:36
Sawpit 57	1	38N00	108w00	7:12:00
Security 21	1	38N45	104w45	6:59:00
Sedalia 18	2	39N27	105w01	7:00:04
Sedgwick 58	1	40N56	102w32	6:50:08
Segundo 36	1	37N08	104w45	6:59:00
Seibert 32	1	39N18	102w53	6:51:32
Semper 30	2	39N55	105w06	7:00:24
Severance 62	1	40N31	104w51	6:59:24
Shadow Mountain 25	1	40N15	105w50	7:03:20
Shamballa Ashrama 18	2	39N26	104w58	6:59:52
Shauano Vista 8	1	38N32	106w00	7:04:00
Shaw 37	1	39N17	103w30	6:54:00
Shaw Heights 1	2	39N50	105w01	7:00:04
Shaw Heights Mesa 1	2	39N50	105w01	7:00:04
Shawnee 47	1	39N25	105w33	7:02:12
Sheridan 3	2	39N38	105w02	7:00:08
Sheridan Lake 31	1	38N28	102w18	6:49:12
Sherrelwood 1	2	39N50	105w00	7:00:00
Sherrelwood Estates 1	2	39N50	105w01	7:00:04
Sierra Vista 51	1	37N55	104w56	6:59:44
Silt 23	1	39N33	107w40	7:10:40
Silver Cliff 14	1	38N08	105w27	7:01:48
Silver Heights 18	1	39N22	104w52	6:59:28
Silver Plume 10	1	39N42	105w44	7:02:56
Silver Springs 30	1	39N25	105w20	7:01:20
Silverthorne 59	1	39N38	106w04	7:04:16
Silverton 56	1	37N49	107w40	7:10:40
Simla 20	1	39N09	104w05	6:56:20
Simpson 1	1	39N35	104w03	6:56:12
Singleton 47	1	39N26	105w37	7:02:28
Skyland Village 1	2	39N50	105w01	7:00:04
Skyline 3	2	39N41	104w56	6:59:44
Sky Village 30	2	39N40	105w07	7:00:28
Skyway 21	1	38N48	104w49	6:59:16
Skyway 39	1	39N10	108w08	7:12:32
Skyway Estates 21	1	38N48	104w49	6:59:16
Skyway Park 21	1	38N48	104w49	6:59:16
Slater 41	1	41N00	107w23	7:09:32
Slick Rock 57	1	38N03	108w54	7:15:36
Smeltertown 8	1	38N32	106w00	7:04:00
Snowmass 49	1	39N20	106w59	7:07:56
Snyder 44	1	40N20	103w36	6:54:24
Somerset 26	1	38N56	107w28	7:09:52
Sopris	1	37N08	104w34	6:58:16
South 63	1	39N40	102w25	6:49:40
South Aurora 3	2	39N40	104w53	6:59:32
South Boulder 7	1	40N00	105w16	7:01:04
South Canon 22	1	38N22	105w17	7:01:08
South Denver 16	2	39N43	104w58	6:59:52
Southern Ute Indian Res 34	1	37N07	107w38	7:10:32
South Fork 53	1	37N40	106w37	7:06:28
South Forty 59	1	39N38	106w04	7:04:16
Southglenn 3	2	39N37	105w00	7:00:00
South Jefferson 30	2	39N35	105w12	7:00:48
South Park City 47	1	39N14	106w00	7:04:00
South Platte 30	1	39N25	105w10	7:00:40
Southwind 3	2	39N37	105w00	7:00:00
Southwood 3	2	39N37	105w00	7:00:00
Spanish Colony 62	1	40N24	104w42	6:58:48
Spanish Village 62	1	40N24	104w34	6:58:16
Spar City 40	1	37N51	106w56	7:07:44
Sphinx Park 30	1	39N25	105w20	7:01:20
Spivak 30	2	39N45	105w03	7:00:12
Springfield 5	1	37N24	102w37	6:50:28
Spring Valley 60	1	38N56	105w09	7:00:36
Sprucedale 30	1	39N38	105w20	7:01:20
Squaw Point 17	1	37N46	108w54	7:15:36
Stanley Park 30	2	39N37	105w17	7:01:08
Starkville 36	1	37N07	104w31	6:58:04
State Bridge	1	39N51	106w39	7:06:36
Steamboat Springs 54	1	40N29	106w50	7:07:20
Steamboat Village 54	1	40N09	106w54	7:07:36
Sterling 38	1	40N37	103w13	6:52:52
Stockyards 16	2	39N48	104w57	6:59:48
Stone City	1	38N12	104w51	6:59:24
Stoneham 62	1	40N36	103w40	6:54:40
Stoner 42	1	37N35	108w19	7:13:16
Stonewall 36	1	37N09	105w01	7:00:04
Stonington 5	1	37N18	102w11	6:48:44
Strasburg 1	1	39N44	104w20	6:57:20
Stratmoor Hills 21	1	38N48	104w49	6:59:16
Stratton 32	1	39N19	102w36	6:50:24
Stratton Meadows 21	1	38N48	104w49	6:59:16
Stratton Park 21	1	38N53	104w48	6:59:12
Stringtown 33	1	39N15	106w18	7:05:12
Sugar City 13	1	38N14	103w40	6:54:40
Sugarloaf 7	1	40N01	105w25	7:01:40
Sullivan	2	39N40	104w54	6:59:36
Summit Cove 59	1	39N38	106w04	7:04:16
Summitville 53	1	37N32	106w21	7:05:24
Sunbeam 41	1	40N31	108w05	7:12:20
Sunnyside 34	1	37N17	107w52	7:11:28
Sunnyslopes 1	2	39N55	105w06	7:00:24
Sunshine 7	1	40N00	105w16	7:01:04
Superior 7	2	39N57	105w10	7:00:40
Surrey Ridge 18	1	39N22	104w52	6:59:28
Sutank 23	1	39N24	107w13	7:08:52
Swallows 51	1	38N57	104w42	6:58:48
Swede Corners 55	1	38N05	106w09	7:04:36
Sweetwater 19	1	39N39	106w57	7:07:48
Swink 45	1	38N01	103w38	6:54:32
Switzerland Village 30	1	39N25	105w20	7:01:20
Sylvan 42	1	37N35	108w46	7:15:04
Tabernash 25	1	40N00	105w51	7:03:24
Table Land 58	1	40N50	102w17	6:49:08
Tacoma 34	1	37N31	107w47	7:11:08
Tamarron 34	1	37N17	107w52	7:11:28
Tanglewood Acres 14	1	38N08	105w28	7:01:52
Tarryall 47	1	39N07	105w29	7:01:56
Taylor Park 26	1	38N40	106w51	7:07:24
Telluride 57	1	37N56	107w49	7:11:16
Tennyson Heights 35	1	40N35	105w06	7:00:24
Terminal Annex 16	2	39N43	104w59	6:59:56
Texas Creek 22	1	38N25	105w35	7:02:20
Texas Oil Camp 52	1	40N05	108w47	7:15:08
Thatcher 36	1	37N33	104w07	6:56:28
The Mesa 21	1	38N51	104w52	6:59:28
The Pinery 18	2	39N31	104w46	6:59:04
Thornton 1	2	39N51	104w58	6:59:52
Thurman 61	1	39N18	103w04	6:52:16
Tiffany 34	1	37N02	107w32	7:10:08
Timbers 3	2	39N39	104w51	6:59:24
Timnath 35	1	40N32	104w59	6:59:56
Timpas 45	1	37N49	103w46	6:55:04
Tincup 26	1	38N40	106w51	7:07:24
Tiny Town	2	39N36	105w14	7:00:56
Tolland 24	1	39N55	105w30	7:02:00
Toltec 28	1	37N37	104w47	6:59:08
Tonnerville 6	1	38N04	103w13	6:52:52
Toponas 54	1	40N04	106w48	7:07:12
Torres 36	1	37N08	104w48	6:59:12
Torres 53	1	37N34	106w09	7:04:36
Towaoc 42	1	37N12	108w44	7:14:56
Towner 31	1	38N28	102w05	6:48:20
Tranquil Acres 60	1	39N00	105w04	7:00:16
Trimble 34	1	37N23	107w51	7:11:24
Trinchera 36	1	37N02	104w03	6:56:12
Trinidad 36	1	37N10	104w31	6:58:04
Troutdale 30	1	39N38	105w20	7:01:20
Trout Haven 60	1	38N56	105w09	7:00:36
Trout Lake 57	1	37N52	107w52	7:11:28
Troy 36	1	37N15	103w21	6:53:24
Truckton 21	1	38N50	104w13	6:56:52
Trujillo 4	1	37N16	107w00	7:08:00
Trumbull 30	2	39N26	104w58	6:59:52
Turkey Creek 51	1	38N23	104w46	6:59:04
Twin Lakes	1	39N05	106w23	7:05:32
Twin Rock 60	1	38N57	105w17	7:01:08
Twin Spruce 30	2	39N45	105w11	7:00:44
Two Butte Creek 50	1	37N52	102w19	6:49:16
Two Buttes 5	1	37N34	102w24	6:49:36
Tyrone 36	1	37N27	104w13	6:56:52
Unaweep 39	1	38N59	108w27	7:13:48
Uncompahgre 43	1	38N29	107w52	7:11:28
Union 44	1	40N20	103w36	6:54:24
University Park 16	2	39N41	104w58	6:59:52
Upper St Vrain 7	1	40N12	105w30	7:02:00
Uravan 43	1	38N22	108w44	7:14:56
U S Air Force Academy 21	1	38N59	104w52	6:59:28
Ute Heights 8	1	38N32	106w00	7:04:00
Ute Mountain 42	1	37N10	108w40	7:14:40
Ute Mountain Indian Res 42	1	37N12	108w44	7:14:56
Utleyville	1	37N17	103w04	6:52:16
Vail 19	1	39N39	106w23	7:05:32
Vallecito 34	1	37N23	107w35	7:10:20
Valley Hi Mountain Estates 60	1	38N57	105w17	7:01:08
Vancorum 43	1	38N14	108w36	7:14:24
Venetian Village 21	1	38N53	104w48	6:59:12
Vernon 63	1	39N57	102w19	6:49:16
Victor 60	1	38N43	105w09	7:00:36
Viejo San Acacio 12	1	37N13	105w34	7:02:16
Vigil 36	1	37N10	104w57	6:59:48
Vilas 5	1	37N22	102w27	6:49:48
Village East 3	2	39N43	104w51	6:59:24
Villa Grove 55	1	38N15	105w59	7:03:56
Villa Italia 30	2	39N42	105w05	7:00:20
Villegreen 36	1	37N18	103w31	6:54:04
Vineland 51	1	38N17	104w35	6:58:20
Virginia Dale 35	1	40N57	105w21	7:01:24
Vista Verde 3	2	39N37	105w00	7:00:00
Vollmar 62	1	40N07	104w51	6:59:24
Vona 32	1	39N18	102w45	6:51:00
Vroman 45	1	38N03	103w43	6:54:52
Wagner Manor 7	1	40N00	105w16	7:01:04
Wagon Wheel Gap 40	1	37N46	106w49	7:07:16
Wahatoya 28	1	37N30	105w00	7:00:00
Wah Keeney Park 30	1	39N40	105w21	7:01:24
Wahketa Village 44	1	40N16	103w49	6:55:16
Walden 29	1	40N44	106w17	7:05:08
Wallstreet 7	1	40N00	105w16	7:01:04
Walnut Hills 3	2	39N38	104w59	6:59:56
Walsenburg 28	1	37N38	104w47	6:59:08
Walsh 5	1	37N23	102w17	6:49:08
Waltonia 35	1	40N26	105w21	7:01:24
Wamblee Park 30	1	39N30	105w20	7:01:20
Wamblee Valley 30	1	39N30	105w20	7:01:20
Wandcrest Park 30	1	39N25	105w20	7:01:20
Ward 7	1	40N04	105w31	7:02:04
Watkins 1	1	39N45	104w36	6:58:24
Wattenberg 62	1	40N02	104w50	6:59:20
Waverly 2	1	37N28	105w51	7:03:24
Welby 1	2	39N51	104w58	6:59:52
Weldona 44	1	40N21	103w58	6:55:52
Wellington 35	1	40N46	105w05	7:00:20
Wellshire 16	2	39N41	104w56	6:59:44
Wellsville 22	2	39N26	104w58	6:59:52
Welty 62	1	40N19	105w05	7:00:20
Westcliffe 14	1	38N09	105w28	7:01:52
Westcreek	1	39N09	105w10	7:00:40
West End 21	1	38N51	104w52	6:59:28
Western Hills 1	2	39N50	104w59	6:59:56
West Farm 50	1	38N05	102w37	6:50:28
Westland 30	2	39N45	105w06	7:00:24
Westminster 1	2	39N50	105w02	7:00:08
Westminster Plaza 1	2	39N50	105w01	7:00:04
Weston 36	1	37N08	104w48	6:59:12
West Village 49	1	39N12	106w50	7:07:20
Westwood 16	2	39N42	105w02	7:00:08
Westwood Lake 60	1	39N00	105w04	7:00:16
Wetmore 14	1	38N14	105w05	7:00:20

COLORADO

Place	Zone	Lat.	Long.	Time
Wheat Ridge 30	2	39N46	105W07	7:00:28
Wheeler 24	2	39N45	105W11	7:00:44
White Pine 26	1	38N25	106W24	7:05:36
Whitewater 39	1	38N59	108W27	7:13:48
Widefield 21	1	38N45	104W44	6:58:56
Wiggins 44	1	40N14	104W04	6:56:16
Wild Horse 9	1	38N50	103W00	6:52:00
Wiley 50	1	38N09	102W43	6:50:52
Willard 38	1	40N33	103W29	6:53:56
Williamsburg 22	1	38N23	105W09	7:00:36
Willowbrook 30	2	39N40	105W07	7:00:28
Willow Creek 3	2	39N38	104W59	6:59:56
Willow Gulch 17	1	38N08	108W17	7:13:08
Wilson Lake Estates 60	1	38N57	105W17	7:01:08
Windsor 62	1	40N29	104W54	6:59:36
Winter Park 25	1	39N53	105W46	7:03:04
Wolcott 19	1	39N42	106W40	7:06:40
Wondervu 7	1	39N56	105W24	7:01:36
Woodglen 1	2	39N53	104W58	6:59:52
Woodland Acres 51	1	37N55	104W56	6:59:44
Woodland Park 60	1	39N00	105W03	7:00:12
Woodrow 61	1	39N59	103W36	6:54:24
Woody Creek 49	1	39N17	106W54	7:07:36
Wray 63	1	40N05	102W13	6:48:52
Yampa 54	1	40N09	106W55	7:07:40
Yellow Jacket 42	1	37N32	108W43	7:14:52
Yoder 21	1	38N50	104W13	6:56:52
Yorkborough 1	2	39N50	104W57	6:59:48
Yuma 63	1	40N08	102W43	6:50:52

TIME TABLES

Standard time was 'obligatory' in Connecticut until 1938. Nevertheless, daylight time was generally observed, beginning in 1920 in the larger cities, and generally after 1926. Caution is advised from 1920 to 1930.

CT # 1

Before 11/18/1883		LMT
11/18/1883	12:00	EST
3/31/1918	02:00	EWT
10/27/1918	02:00	EST
3/30/1919	02:00	EWT
10/26/1919	02:00	EST
4/25/1926	02:00	EDT
9/26/1926	02:00	EST
4/24/1927	02:00	EDT
9/25/1927	02:00	EST
4/29/1928	02:00	EDT
9/30/1928	02:00	EST
4/28/1929	02:00	EDT
9/29/1929	02:00	EST
4/27/1930	02:00	EDT
9/28/1930	02:00	EST
4/26/1931	02:00	EDT
9/27/1931	02:00	EST
4/24/1932	02:00	EDT
9/25/1932	02:00	EST
4/30/1933	02:00	EDT
9/24/1933	02:00	EST
4/29/1934	02:00	EDT
9/30/1934	02:00	EST
4/28/1935	02:00	EDT
9/29/1935	02:00	EST
4/26/1936	02:00	EDT
9/27/1936	02:00	EST
4/25/1937	02:00	EDT
9/26/1937	02:00	EST
4/24/1938	02:00	EDT
10/02/1938	02:00	EST
4/30/1939	02:00	EDT
9/24/1939	02:00	EST
4/28/1940	02:00	EDT
9/29/1940	02:00	EST
4/27/1941	02:00	EDT
9/28/1941	02:00	EST
2/09/1942	02:00	EWT
12/31/1945	24:00	EST
4/28/1946	02:00	US#2

CT # 2

Before 11/18/1883		LMT
11/18/1883	12:00	EST
3/31/1918	02:00	EWT
10/27/1918	02:00	EST
3/30/1919	02:00	EWT
10/26/1919	02:00	EST
4/25/1920	02:00	EDT
10/31/1920	02:00	EST
4/24/1921	02:00	EDT
9/25/1921	02:00	EST
4/30/1922	02:00	EDT
9/24/1922	02:00	EST
4/29/1923	02:00	EDT
9/30/1923	02:00	EST
4/27/1924	02:00	EDT
9/28/1924	02:00	EST
4/26/1925	02:00	EDT
9/27/1925	02:00	EST
4/25/1926	02:00	EDT
9/26/1926	02:00	EST
4/24/1927	02:00	EDT
9/25/1927	02:00	EST
4/29/1928	02:00	EDT
9/30/1928	02:00	EST
4/28/1929	02:00	EDT
9/29/1929	02:00	EST
4/27/1930	02:00	EDT
9/28/1930	02:00	EST
4/26/1931	02:00	EDT
9/27/1931	02:00	EST
4/24/1932	02:00	EDT
9/25/1932	02:00	EST
4/30/1933	02:00	EDT
9/24/1933	02:00	EST
4/29/1934	02:00	EDT
9/30/1934	02:00	EST
4/28/1935	02:00	EDT
9/29/1935	02:00	EST
4/26/1936	02:00	EDT
9/27/1936	02:00	EST
4/25/1937	02:00	EDT
9/26/1937	02:00	EST
4/24/1938	02:00	EDT
10/02/1938	02:00	EST
4/30/1939	02:00	EDT
9/24/1939	02:00	EST
4/28/1940	02:00	EDT
9/29/1940	02:00	EST
4/27/1941	02:00	EDT
9/28/1941	02:00	EST
2/09/1942	02:00	EWT
12/31/1945	24:00	EST
4/28/1946	02:00	US#2

CT # 3

Before 11/18/1883		LMT
11/18/1883	12:00	EST
3/31/1918	02:00	EWT
10/27/1918	02:00	EST
3/30/1919	02:00	EWT
10/26/1919	02:00	EST
4/25/1920	02:00	EDT
10/31/1920	02:00	EST
4/25/1926	02:00	EDT
9/26/1926	02:00	EST
4/24/1927	02:00	EDT
9/25/1927	02:00	EST
4/29/1928	02:00	EDT
9/30/1928	02:00	EST
4/28/1929	02:00	EDT
9/29/1929	02:00	EST
4/27/1930	02:00	EDT
9/28/1930	02:00	EST
4/26/1931	02:00	EDT
9/27/1931	02:00	EST
4/24/1932	02:00	EDT
9/25/1932	02:00	EST
4/30/1933	02:00	EDT
9/24/1933	02:00	EST
4/29/1934	02:00	EDT
9/30/1934	02:00	EST
4/28/1935	02:00	EDT
9/29/1935	02:00	EST
4/26/1936	02:00	EDT
9/27/1936	02:00	EST
4/25/1937	02:00	EDT
9/26/1937	02:00	EST
4/24/1938	02:00	EDT
10/02/1938	02:00	EST
4/30/1939	02:00	EDT
9/24/1939	02:00	EST
4/28/1940	02:00	EDT
9/29/1940	02:00	EST
4/27/1941	02:00	EDT
9/28/1941	02:00	EST
2/09/1942	02:00	EWT
12/31/1945	24:00	EST
4/28/1946	02:00	US#2

CT # 4

Before 11/18/1883		LMT
11/18/1883	12:00	EST
3/31/1918	02:00	EWT
10/27/1918	02:00	EST
3/30/1919	02:00	EWT
10/26/1919	02:00	EST
4/24/1921	02:00	EDT
9/25/1921	02:00	EST
4/25/1926	02:00	EDT
9/26/1926	02:00	EST
4/24/1927	02:00	EDT
9/25/1927	02:00	EST
4/29/1928	02:00	EDT
9/30/1928	02:00	EST
4/28/1929	02:00	EDT
9/29/1929	02:00	EST
4/27/1930	02:00	EDT
9/28/1930	02:00	EST
4/26/1931	02:00	EDT
9/27/1931	02:00	EST
4/24/1932	02:00	EDT
9/25/1932	02:00	EST
4/30/1933	02:00	EDT
9/24/1933	02:00	EST
4/29/1934	02:00	EDT
9/30/1934	02:00	EST
4/28/1935	02:00	EDT
9/29/1935	02:00	EST
4/26/1936	02:00	EDT
9/27/1936	02:00	EST
4/25/1937	02:00	EDT
9/26/1937	02:00	EST
4/24/1938	02:00	EDT
10/02/1938	02:00	EST
4/30/1939	02:00	EDT
9/24/1939	02:00	EST
4/28/1940	02:00	EDT
9/29/1940	02:00	EST
4/27/1941	02:00	EDT
9/28/1941	02:00	EST
2/09/1942	02:00	EWT
12/31/1945	24:00	EST
4/28/1946	02:00	US#2

CT # 5

Before 11/18/1883		LMT
11/18/1883	12:00	EST
3/31/1918	02:00	EWT
10/27/1918	02:00	EST
3/30/1919	02:00	EWT
10/26/1919	02:00	EST
4/24/1921	02:00	EDT
9/25/1921	02:00	EST
4/30/1922	02:00	EDT
9/24/1922	02:00	EST
4/29/1923	02:00	EDT
9/30/1923	02:00	EST
4/27/1924	02:00	EDT
9/28/1924	02:00	EST
4/26/1925	02:00	EDT
9/27/1925	02:00	EST
4/25/1926	02:00	EDT
9/26/1926	02:00	EST
4/24/1927	02:00	EDT
9/25/1927	02:00	EST
4/29/1928	02:00	EDT
9/30/1928	02:00	EST
4/28/1929	02:00	EDT
9/29/1929	02:00	EST
4/27/1930	02:00	EDT
9/28/1930	02:00	EST
4/26/1931	02:00	EDT
9/27/1931	02:00	EST
4/24/1932	02:00	EDT
9/25/1932	02:00	EST
4/30/1933	02:00	EDT
9/24/1933	02:00	EST
4/29/1934	02:00	EDT
9/30/1934	02:00	EST
4/28/1935	02:00	EDT
9/29/1935	02:00	EST
4/26/1936	02:00	EDT
9/27/1936	02:00	EST
4/25/1937	02:00	EDT
9/26/1937	02:00	EST
4/24/1938	02:00	EDT
10/02/1938	02:00	EST
4/30/1939	02:00	EDT
9/24/1939	02:00	EST
4/28/1940	02:00	EDT
9/29/1940	02:00	EST
4/27/1941	02:00	EDT
9/28/1941	02:00	EST
2/09/1942	02:00	EWT
12/31/1945	24:00	EST
4/28/1946	02:00	US#2

COUNTIES

1 Fairfield
2 Hartford
3 Litchfield
4 Middlesex
5 New Haven
6 New London
7 Tolland
8 Windham

Abington 8	1	41n52	72w01	4:48:04
Addison 2	2	41n41	72w35	4:50:20
Agua Vista 1	4	41n24	73w27	4:53:48
Aljen Heights 6	1	41n34	71w53	4:47:32
Allerton Farms 5	1	41n30	73w03	4:52:12
Allington 5	2	41n16	72w58	4:51:52
Almyville 8	1	41n43	71w53	4:47:32
Amenia Union 3	1	41n53	73w29	4:53:56
Amesville 3	1	42n02	73w20	4:53:20
Amity 5	2	41n23	73w00	4:52:00
Amston 7	1	41n38	72w21	4:49:24
Andover 7	1	41n44	72w22	4:49:28
Ansonia 5	1	41n21	73w05	4:52:20
Ansonia Mall 5	1	41n21	73w04	4:52:16
Ashford 8	1	41n53	72w11	4:48:44
Ashford Lake 8	1	41n50	72w16	4:49:04
Aspetuck 1	3	41n08	73w21	4:53:24
Attawan Beach 6	1	41n19	72w12	4:48:48
Attawaugan 8	1	41n51	71w53	4:47:32
Atwoodville 7	1	41n50	72w16	4:49:04
Avery Heights 3	1	41n35	73w25	4:53:40
Avery Hill 6	1	41n34	71w53	4:47:32
Avon 2	1	41n48	72w52	4:51:28
Baccus Corner 6	1	41n32	72w05	4:48:20
Baileyville 4	1	41n31	72w43	4:50:52
Bakersville 3	1	41n53	72w59	4:51:56
Ballouville 8	1	41n52	71w52	4:47:28
Ball Pond 1	4	41n24	73w27	4:53:48
Baltic 6	1	41n37	72w05	4:48:20
Banksville 1	1	41n02	73w37	4:54:28
Bantam 3	1	41n44	73w14	4:52:56
Barkhamsted 3	1	41n56	72w59	4:51:56
Barnum 1	2	41n10	73w13	4:52:52
Barry Square 2	2	41n45	72w41	4:50:44
Bashan 4	1	41n27	72w28	4:49:52
Bayview 5	2	41n13	73w03	4:52:12
Beacon Falls 5	1	41n26	73w03	4:52:12
Beardsley 1	2	41n12	73w12	4:52:48
Beaverbrook 1	4	41n24	73w27	4:53:48
Beckettville 1	4	41n24	73w27	4:53:48
Bel Aire Estates 6	1	41n21	71w59	4:47:56
Belden 1	1	41n07	73w26	4:53:44
Belle Haven 1	1	41n02	73w37	4:54:28
Berkshire 1	1	41n25	73w17	4:53:08
Berkshire Estates 5	1	41n29	73w13	4:52:52
Berkshire Shopping Center 1	4	41n24	73w27	4:53:48
Berlin 2	1	41n37	72w46	4:51:04
Best View 6	2	41n24	72w07	4:48:28
Bethany 5	1	41n25	73w00	4:52:00
Bethel 1	1	41n23	73w24	4:53:36
Bethlehem 3	1	41n39	73w16	4:53:04
Birch Groves 3	1	41n35	73w25	4:53:40
Birch Hill 3	1	41n43	73w29	4:53:56
Birch Mountain 7	1	41n47	72w31	4:50:04
Birchwood 2	2	41n51	72w39	4:50:36
Birdland 2	1	41n59	72w34	4:50:16
Bishops Corner 2	2	41n47	72w45	4:51:00
Bissell 2	2	41n49	72w37	4:50:28
Black Point 6	1	41n19	72w12	4:48:48
Blackstone Acres 5	2	41n17	72w48	4:51:12
Bloomfield 2	2	41n50	72w43	4:50:52
Blue Hills 2	2	41n47	72w41	4:50:44
Boardmans Bridge 3	1	41n35	73w25	4:53:40
Bolton 7	1	41n46	72w26	4:49:44
Bolton Center 7	1	41n47	72w31	4:50:04
Bonny Brook 3	1	41n35	73w25	4:53:40
Borough 6	2	41n21	72w03	4:48:12
Botsford 1	1	41n22	73w15	4:53:00
Boulder Lake 4	1	41n17	72w32	4:50:08
Bozrah 6	1	41n33	72w10	4:48:40
Bradford Hill 8	1	41n41	71w55	4:47:40
Branchville 1	1	41n16	73w26	4:53:44
Brandy Hill 8	1	41n40	73w21	4:53:24
Branford 5	2	41n17	72w48	4:51:12
Branford Hills 5	2	41n17	72w48	4:51:12
Branford Point 5	2	41n17	72w48	4:51:12
Branhaven Shopping Center 5	2	41n17	72w48	4:51:12
Brendan Heights 7	1	41n59	72w39	4:50:36
Bretton Heights 4	3	41n33	72w39	4:50:36
Bridgeport 1	2	41n11	73w12	4:52:48
Bridgewater 3	1	41n32	73w22	4:53:28
Brighton Beach 6	1	41n19	72w20	4:49:20
Bristol 2	3	41n40	72w57	4:51:48
Bristol Terrace 5	1	41n30	73w03	4:52:12
Broad Brook 2	1	41n55	72w33	4:50:12
Bromica 3	1	41n43	73w29	4:53:56
Brookfield 1	1	41n28	73w24	4:53:36
Brooklyn 8	1	41n47	71w57	4:47:48
Bruce Park 1	1	41n02	73w37	4:54:28
Brush Island 1	1	41n05	73w29	4:53:56
Buckingham 2	2	41n41	72w35	4:50:20
Buckland 2	1	41n47	72w31	4:50:04
Bucks Corners 2	2	41n41	72w35	4:50:20
Bulls Bridge 3	1	41n41	73w28	4:53:52
Bundy Hill 6	1	41n37	71w59	4:47:56
Bungay 5	1	41n24	73w04	4:52:16
Burlington 2	1	41n45	72w56	4:51:44
Burnside 2	2	41n47	72w37	4:50:28
Burr Hill 4	1	41n23	72w26	4:49:44
Burrville 3	1	41n49	73w07	4:52:28
Burwells Beach 5	2	41n13	73w03	4:52:12
Byram 1	1	41n00	73w40	4:54:40
Camp Bethel 4	1	41n29	72w31	4:50:04
Camptown 5	1	41n19	73w04	4:52:16
Canaan 3	1	42n02	73w20	4:53:20
Candleset Cove 3	1	41n35	73w25	4:53:40
Candlewood Hill 1	4	41n24	73w27	4:53:48
Candlewood Hill 4	1	41n30	72w34	4:50:16
Candlewood Isle 1	4	41n24	73w27	4:53:48
Candlewood Knolls 1	4	41n24	73w27	4:53:48
Candlewood Lake Club 1	1	41n29	73w25	4:53:40
Candlewood Lake Estates 1	1	41n35	73w30	4:54:00
Candlewood Orchards 1	1	41n29	73w25	4:53:40
Candlewood Point 3	1	41n35	73w25	4:53:40
Candlewood Shores 1	1	41n29	73w25	4:53:40
Candlewood Springs 3	1	41n35	73w25	4:53:40
Candlewood Trails 3	1	41n35	73w25	4:53:40
Cannondale 1	1	41n13	73w26	4:53:44
Canterbury 8	1	41n43	72w00	4:48:00
Canton 2	1	41n51	72w54	4:51:36
Cedar Beach 5	2	41n13	73w03	4:52:12
Cedar Heights 1	4	41n24	73w27	4:53:48
Cedarhurst 1	1	41n25	73w17	4:53:08
Cedar Knolls 3	1	41n35	73w25	4:53:40
Cedar Lake 2	3	41n41	72w56	4:51:44
Cedar Land 5	1	41n29	73w13	4:52:52
Cedar Springs 2	1	41n36	72w53	4:51:32

CONNECTICUT

Center 1 2 41N15 73w13 4:52:52
Centerbrook 4 1 41N21 72w25 4:49:40
Center Groton 6 2 41N21 72w03 4:48:12
Center Hill 2 1 41N53 72w59 4:51:56
Centerville 5 2 41N24 72w54 4:51:36
Central 2 2 41N46 72w41 4:50:44
Central Village 8 1 41N43 71w54 4:47:36
Chaffeeville 7 1 41N48 72w15 4:49:00
Chalkers Beach 4 1 41N17 72w22 4:49:28
Chaplin 8 1 41N47 72w08 4:48:32
Chapman Beach 4 1 41N17 72w26 4:49:44
Cherry Brook 2 1 41N51 72w55 4:51:40
Cherry Hill 3 1 41N52 73w22 4:53:28
Cheshire 5 1 41N30 72w54 4:51:36
Chester 4 1 41N24 72w30 4:50:00
Chesterfield 6 1 41N28 72w10 4:48:40
Chickahominy 1 1 41N02 73w37 4:54:28
Chippens Hill 2 3 41N41 72w56 4:51:44
Christy Hill Estates 6
2 41N26 72w05 4:48:20
Churchwood 6 1 41N19 72w12 4:48:48
Circle Beach 5 1 41N17 72w36 4:50:24
Clarks Corner 8 1 41N45 72w09 4:48:36
Clarks Falls 6 1 41N21 71w58 4:47:52
Clarks Village 6 1 41N22 71w50 4:47:20
Clearview Heights 7
1 41N57 72w18 4:49:12
Clifton 5 1 41N24 73w04 4:52:16
Clinton 4 1 41N17 72w32 4:50:08
Clinton Beach 4 1 41N17 72w32 4:50:08
Clintonville 5 2 41N23 72w52 4:51:28
Cobalt 4 1 41N34 72w34 4:50:16
Colburn Hill 7 1 41N57 72w18 4:49:12
Colchester 6 1 41N35 72w20 4:49:20
Colebrook 3 1 42N00 73w05 4:52:20
Collinsville 2 1 41N49 72w55 4:51:40
Colonial Manor 6 1 41N32 72w05 4:48:20
Colonial Plaza 5 1 41N34 73w04 4:52:16
Columbia 7 1 41N42 72w18 4:49:12
Compo Beach 1 3 41N08 73w21 4:53:24
Compo Hill 1 3 41N08 73w21 4:53:24
Conantville 7 1 41N43 72w13 4:48:52
Congamond Lakes 2 1 42N00 72w42 4:50:48
Connecticut Post Shopping Ce 5
2 41N13 73w03 4:52:12
Connings Park 6 2 41N23 72w04 4:48:16
Conning Towers 6 2 41N21 72w03 4:48:12
Copaco Shopping Center 2
2 41N49 72w42 4:50:48
Corbin's Corner Shopping Par 2
2 41N44 72w44 4:50:56
Cornwall 3 1 41N51 73w19 4:53:16
Cornwall Bridge 3 1 41N49 73w22 4:53:28
Cornwall Center 3 1 41N52 73w22 4:53:28
Cornwall Hollow 3 1 42N02 73w20 4:53:20
Cos Cob 1 1 41N02 73w36 4:54:24
Cottage Grove 2 2 41N49 72w42 4:50:48
Country Club Heights 2
1 41N35 72w53 4:51:32
Coventry 7 1 41N47 72w21 4:49:24
Cranska Village 8 1 41N43 71w53 4:47:32
Crescent Beach 6 1 41N19 72w12 4:48:48
Cromwell 4 3 41N37 72w40 4:50:40
Crystal Lake 7 1 41N51 72w28 4:49:52
Daleville 7 1 41N53 72w18 4:49:12
Damascus 5 2 41N17 72w48 4:51:12
Danbury 1 4 41N24 73w28 4:53:52
Danbury Quarter 3 1 41N55 73w04 4:52:16
Danielson 8 1 41N48 71w53 4:47:32
Darien 1 1 41N05 73w28 4:53:52
Dayville 8 1 41N51 71w53 4:47:32
Deep River 4 1 41N23 72w26 4:49:44
Deerfield 2 2 41N51 72w39 4:50:36
Deer Island 3 1 41N41 73w15 4:53:00
Deer Run Shores 1 1 41N35 73w30 4:54:00
Derby 5 1 41N19 73w05 4:52:20
Derby Neck 5 1 41N19 73w04 4:52:16
Devil's Backbone 3
1 41N38 73w13 4:52:52
Devon 5 2 41N13 73w03 4:52:12
Diamond Lake 2 2 41N41 72w35 4:50:20
Dibble Hill 3 1 41N52 73w22 4:53:28
Dickerman's Corner 2
1 41N35 72w53 4:51:32
Doanville 6 1 41N34 71w52 4:47:28
Dodgingtown 1 1 41N25 73w19 4:53:16
Dolphin Gardens 6 2 41N21 72w03 4:48:12
Double Beach 5 2 41N17 72w48 4:51:12
Dowd's Corner 2 1 41N49 72w54 4:51:36
Drakeville 3 1 41N49 73w07 4:52:28
Durham 4 1 41N27 72w41 4:50:44
Eagleville 7 1 41N48 72w15 4:49:00
East Berlin 2 1 41N37 72w43 4:50:52
East Brooklyn 8 1 41N48 71w54 4:47:36
East Canaan 3 1 42N01 73w17 4:53:08
East Cornwall 3 1 41N45 73w11 4:52:44
East Derby 5 1 41N19 73w04 4:52:16
East End 5 1 41N33 73w01 4:52:04
Eastern Point 6 2 41N21 72w03 4:48:12
East Farmington Heights 2
1 41N43 72w50 4:51:20
Eastford 8 1 41N53 72w05 4:48:20
East Glastonbury 2
2 41N41 72w35 4:50:20
East Granby 2 1 41N55 72w45 4:51:00
East Great Plain 6
1 41N32 72w05 4:48:20
East Haddam 4 1 41N29 72w24 4:49:36
East Haddam Landing 4
1 41N27 72w28 4:49:52
East Hampton 4 1 41N33 72w32 4:50:08
East Hartford 2 2 41N46 72w37 4:50:28
East Hartland 2 1 42N00 72w58 4:51:52
East Haven 5 2 41N17 72w52 4:51:28
East Hill 2 1 41N49 72w54 4:51:36
East Killingly 8 1 41N49 71w52 4:47:28
East Litchfield 3 1 41N45 73w11 4:52:44
East Lyme 6 1 41N21 72w14 4:48:56
East Morris 3 1 41N43 73w15 4:53:00
East New London 6 2 41N21 72w06 4:48:24
Easton 1 2 41N15 73w18 4:53:12
East Plymouth 3 3 41N40 73w01 4:52:04
East Port Chester 1
1 41N02 73w37 4:54:28
East Putnam 8 1 41N55 71w55 4:47:40
East River 5 1 41N17 72w36 4:50:24
East River Beach 5
1 41N17 72w36 4:50:24
East Thompson 8 1 41N57 71w52 4:47:28
Eastview Acres 5 1 41N24 73w04 4:52:16
East Village 1 1 41N19 73w15 4:53:00
East Wallingford 5
1 41N28 72w49 4:51:16
East Willington 7 1 41N53 72w18 4:49:12
East Windsor 2 1 41N55 72w35 4:50:20
East Windsor Hill 2
2 41N51 72w39 4:50:36
East Woodstock 8 1 41N57 71w59 4:47:56
Ebbs Corner 2 1 42N00 72w42 4:50:48
Edgewood 7 1 41N57 72w18 4:49:12
Ekonk 8 1 41N43 71w53 4:47:32
Ekonk Hill 6 1 41N34 71w52 4:47:28
Ellington 7 1 41N54 72w27 4:49:48
Elliot 8 1 41N52 71w58 4:47:52
Ellsworth 3 1 41N53 73w29 4:53:56
Elm Hill 2 2 41N41 72w44 4:50:56
Elmville 8 1 41N51 71w53 4:47:32
Elmwood 1 4 41N22 73w25 4:53:40
Elmwood 2 2 41N44 72w44 4:50:56
Enders Island 6 1 41N21 71w58 4:47:52
Enfield 2 1 41N59 72w34 4:50:16
Essex 4 1 41N21 72w26 4:49:44
Ethel Acres 6 1 41N37 71w59 4:47:56
Ettadore Park 5 2 41N13 73w03 4:52:12
Fabyan 8 1 42N01 71w56 4:47:44
Fairfield 1 2 41N09 73w16 4:53:04
Fairground 6 1 41N32 72w05 4:48:20
Fair Haven 5 2 41N19 72w53 4:51:32
Fairy Lake 6 1 41N28 72w10 4:48:40
Fall Mountain 2 3 41N41 72w56 4:51:44
Fall Mountain Lake 3
3 41N40 73w01 4:52:04
Falls Switch 6 1 41N32 72w05 4:48:20
Falls Village 3 1 42N02 73w20 4:53:20
Farmington 2 1 41N44 72w51 4:51:24
Far View Beach 5 2 41N13 73w03 4:52:12
Fenwick 4 1 41N16 72w21 4:49:24
Fenwood 4 1 41N17 72w22 4:49:28
Ferris Estates 3 1 41N35 73w25 4:53:40
Ferry Point 4 1 41N17 72w22 4:49:28
Ferry View Heights 6
2 41N26 72w05 4:48:20
Field Crest Estates 6
1 41N21 71w59 4:47:56
Firetown 2 1 41N52 72w48 4:51:12
Fitchville 6 1 41N34 72w09 4:48:36
Five City Plaza Shopping Cen 2
2 41N46 72w45 4:51:00
Five Points 2 1 41N57 72w47 4:51:08
Flanders 3 1 41N43 73w29 4:53:56
Flat Rock 8 1 41N41 71w55 4:47:40
Flax Hill 1 1 41N07 73w26 4:53:44
Floral Park 4 1 41N17 72w22 4:49:28
Floydville 2 1 41N57 72w47 4:51:08
Forbes Village 2 2 41N47 72w37 4:50:28
Forest Glen 4 1 41N17 72w22 4:49:28
Forest Heights 5 2 41N13 73w03 4:52:12
Forest Hills 2 1 41N36 72w53 4:51:32
Forest Park 7 1 41N39 72w22 4:49:28
Forestville 2 3 41N41 72w56 4:51:44
Forestville 7 1 41N57 72w18 4:49:12
Fort Hill 3 1 41N35 73w25 4:53:40
Fort Trumbull Beach 5
2 41N13 73w03 4:52:12
Fox Den 2 1 41N49 72w50 4:51:20
Foxon 5 2 41N17 72w53 4:51:32
Foxtown 4 1 41N34 72w20 4:49:20
Fox Village 7 1 41N57 72w18 4:49:12
Franklin 6 1 41N37 72w08 4:48:32
Franklin Square 6 1 41N32 72w05 4:48:20
Frog Hollow 7 1 41N54 72w28 4:49:52
Furnace Hollow 7 1 41N57 72w18 4:49:12
Gales Ferry 6 2 41N26 72w05 4:48:20
Gallows Hill 1 1 41N20 73w26 4:53:44
Garden City 5 1 41N24 73w04 4:52:16
Gaylordsville 3 1 41N39 73w29 4:53:56
Georgetown 1 1 41N16 73w26 4:53:44
Germantown 1 4 41N24 73w27 4:53:48
Giants Neck 6 1 41N19 72w12 4:48:48
Gildersleeve 4 3 41N34 72w38 4:50:32
Gilead 7 1 41N39 72w22 4:49:28
Gilman 6 1 41N34 72w16 4:49:04
Glasgo 6 1 41N34 71w53 4:47:32
Glastonbury 2 2 41N42 72w35 4:50:20
Glen 1 1 41N20 73w26 4:53:44
Glenbrook 1 1 41N04 73w31 4:54:04
Glen Ridge 5 1 41N30 73w03 4:52:12
Glenville 1 1 41N02 73w37 4:54:28
Glynville 7 1 41N57 72w18 4:49:12
Golden Spur 6 2 41N20 72w09 4:48:36
Good Hill 3 1 41N33 73w12 4:52:48
Good Hill 5 1 41N24 73w04 4:52:16
Goodsell Point 5 2 41N17 72w48 4:51:12
Goodwives Shopping Plaza 1
1 41N05 73w29 4:53:56
Goshen 3 1 41N51 73w14 4:52:56
Goshen Hills 6 1 41N38 72w13 4:48:52
Governor's Hill 5 1 41N24 73w04 4:52:16
Granby 2 1 41N58 72w49 4:51:16
Granite Bay 5 2 41N17 72w48 4:51:12
Grappaville 3 1 41N44 73w14 4:52:56
Grasmere 1 2 41N10 73w15 4:53:00
Grassy Hill 3 1 41N33 73w12 4:52:48
Grassy Plain 1 4 41N22 73w25 4:53:40
Great Hammock 4 1 41N17 72w22 4:49:28
Great Harbor 5 2 41N23 72w51 4:51:24
Great Meadows 1 4 41N24 73w27 4:53:48
Greenfield Hill 1 2 41N10 73w15 4:53:00
Green Manorville 2
1 41N59 72w34 4:50:16
Greens Farms 1 2 41N07 73w19 4:53:16
Greenville 6 1 41N32 72w05 4:48:20
Greenwich 1 1 41N02 73w38 4:54:32
Greystone 3 3 41N40 73w01 4:52:04
Griswold 6 1 41N35 71w56 4:47:44
Griswoldville 2 2 41N43 72w41 4:50:44
Grosvenor Dale 8 1 41N58 71w54 4:47:36
Groton 6 2 41N21 72w05 4:48:20
Groton Heights 6 2 41N21 72w03 4:48:12
Groton Lake Shores 6
1 41N19 72w12 4:48:48
Groton Long Point 6
2 41N21 72w03 4:48:12
Groton Shopping Mall 6
2 41N21 72w03 4:48:12
Grove Beach 4 1 41N17 72w32 4:50:08
Grove Beach Point 4
1 41N17 72w26 4:49:44
Grove Beach Terrace 4
1 41N17 72w26 4:49:44
Guilford 5 1 41N19 72w42 4:50:48
Gurleyville 7 1 41N48 72w15 4:49:00
Haddam 4 1 41N28 72w33 4:50:12
Haddam Neck 4 1 41N35 72w30 4:50:00
Hadlyme 6 1 41N25 72w25 4:49:40
Hale Court 1 3 41N08 73w21 4:53:24
Hallville 6 1 41N32 72w05 4:48:20
Hamburg 6 1 41N19 72w20 4:49:20
Hamden 5 2 41N23 72w54 4:51:36
Hampton 8 1 41N47 72w03 4:48:12
Hank Hill 7 1 41N48 72w15 4:49:00
Hanover 6 1 41N38 72w04 4:48:16
Happyland 6 1 41N32 72w05 4:48:20
Harbor View 4 1 41N17 72w32 4:50:08
Harrisville 8 1 41N57 71w59 4:47:56
Hartford 2 2 41N46 72w41 4:50:44
Hartland 2 1 42N00 72w57 4:51:48
Harwinton 3 1 41N46 73w04 4:52:16
Hattertown 1 1 41N25 73w19 4:53:16
Hawks Nest Beach 6
1 41N19 72w20 4:49:20
Hawleyville 1 1 41N26 73w21 4:53:24
Hawthorne Terrace 1
4 41N24 73w27 4:53:48
Hayden 2 2 41N51 72w39 4:50:36
Hayestown 1 4 41N24 73w27 4:53:48
Hazardville 2 1 41N59 72w34 4:50:16
Hebron 7 1 41N39 72w23 4:49:32
Hidden Lake 4 1 41N30 72w34 4:50:16
Higganum 4 1 41N30 72w33 4:50:12
Highland Park 2 1 41N47 72w31 4:50:04
Highwood 5 2 41N22 72w55 4:51:40
Hillcrest 5 1 41N32 73w07 4:52:28
Hillside 1 2 41N12 73w10 4:52:40
Hitchcock Lake 5 1 41N36 72w59 4:51:56
Hockanum 2 2 41N45 72w37 4:50:28
Holiday Homes 6 1 41N34 72w20 4:49:20
Hollywyle Park 1 4 41N24 73w27 4:53:48
Honeypot Glen 5 1 41N30 72w54 4:51:36
Hopeville 6 1 41N37 71w59 4:47:56
Hotchkissville 3 1 41N33 73w12 4:52:48
Huckleberry Hill 2
1 41N49 72w50 4:51:20
Hungary Hill 8 1 41N42 71w50 4:47:20
Huntington 1 1 41N19 73w08 4:52:32
Huntingtown 1 1 41N25 73w19 4:53:16
Hydeville 7 1 41N59 72w17 4:49:08
Indian Cove 5 2 41N23 72w51 4:51:24
Indian Neck 5 2 41N17 72w48 4:51:12
Ivoryton 4 1 41N21 72w27 4:49:48
Jericho Hill 6 1 41N19 72w20 4:49:20
Jewett City 6 1 41N36 71w59 4:47:56
Jordan Village 6 2 41N20 72w09 4:48:36
Kensington 2 3 41N38 72w46 4:51:04
Kent 3 1 41N44 73w29 4:53:56
Kent Furnace 3 1 41N43 73w29 4:53:56
Kilby 5 2 41N18 72w56 4:51:44
Killingly 8 1 41N50 71w52 4:47:28
Killingworth 4 1 41N23 72w34 4:50:16
Kings Corner 2 1 41N56 72w37 4:50:28
Knollcrest 1 4 41N24 73w27 4:53:48
Knollwood 4 1 41N17 72w22 4:49:28
Lake Bashan 4 1 41N27 72w28 4:49:52
Lake Beseck 4 1 41N31 72w43 4:50:52
Lake Garda 2 1 41N45 72w53 4:51:32
Lake Hayward 4 1 41N34 72w20 4:49:20
Lake Pocotopaug 4 1 41N36 72w31 4:50:04
Lakeridge Heights 4
3 41N33 72w39 4:50:36
Lakeside 3 1 41N41 73w15 4:53:00
Lakeside 5 1 41N29 73w13 4:52:52
Lakeview Terrace 7
1 41N57 72w18 4:49:12
Lakeville 3 1 41N58 73w26 4:53:44
Lattins Landing 1 4 41N24 73w27 4:53:48
Laurel Beach 5 2 41N13 73w03 4:52:12
Laurel Hill 6 1 41N55 71w55 4:47:40
Laysville 6 1 41N19 72w20 4:49:20
Lebanon 6 1 41N37 72w14 4:48:56
Ledyard 6 2 41N26 72w03 4:48:12
Leesville 4 1 41N30 72w27 4:49:48
Leetes Island 5 2 41N23 72w51 4:51:24
Leffingwell 6 1 41N32 72w05 4:48:20
Liberty Hill 6 1 41N38 72w13 4:48:52
Lime Rock 3 1 41N58 73w27 4:53:48

CONNECTICUT

Lisbon 6	1	41N35	72W01	4:48:04
Litchfield 3	1	41N45	73W11	4:52:44
Little Boston 1	1	41N18	73W23	4:53:32
Little City 4	1	41N30	72W34	4:50:16
Long Hill 1	2	41N15	73W13	4:52:52
Long Hill 4	3	41N33	72W39	4:50:36
Long Hill 6	2	41N21	72W03	4:48:12
Long Society 6	1	41N32	72W05	4:48:20
Lordship 1	2	41N12	73W08	4:52:32
Lords Point 6	1	41N21	71W58	4:47:52
Lyme 6	1	41N24	72W21	4:49:24
Lyons Plain	1	41N13	73W21	4:53:24
Macedonia 3	1	41N43	73W29	4:53:56
Madison 5	1	41N19	72W38	4:50:32
Manchester 2	1	41N47	72W31	4:50:04
Manchester Green 2	1	41N47	72W31	4:50:04
Mansfield 7	1	41N47	72W15	4:49:00
Mansfield Hollow 7	1	41N50	72W16	4:49:04
Maple Hill 2	2	41N41	72W44	4:50:56
Marble Dale 3	1	41N40	73W21	4:53:24
Margerie Manor 1	4	41N24	73W27	4:53:48
Marion 2	1	41N34	72W56	4:51:44
Marlborough 2	1	41N38	72W27	4:49:48
Maromas 4	3	41N33	72W39	4:50:36
Mashapaug 7	1	41N57	72W18	4:49:12
Massapeag 6	2	41N26	72W07	4:48:28
Mayberry Village 2	2	41N47	72W37	4:50:28
Mechanicsville 8	1	41N56	71W54	4:47:36
Melrose 2	1	41N56	72W32	4:50:08
Melville Village 1	2	41N10	73W15	4:53:00
Meriden 5	3	41N32	72W48	4:51:12
Merrow 7	1	41N49	72W19	4:49:16
Mianus 1	1	41N02	73W36	4:54:24
Middle Beach 5	1	41N17	72W36	4:50:24
Middlebury 5	1	41N32	73W07	4:52:28
Middlefield 4	1	41N31	72W43	4:50:52
Middle Haddam 4	1	41N33	72W33	4:50:12
Middletown 4	3	41N34	72W39	4:50:36
Milbrook 1	1	41N02	73W37	4:54:28
Milford 5	2	41N14	73W04	4:52:16
Milford Lawns 5	2	41N13	73W03	4:52:12
Millbrook 5	2	41N24	72W54	4:51:36
Milldale 2	1	41N34	72W53	4:51:32
Millington 4	1	41N27	72W28	4:49:52
Mill Plain 1	4	41N24	73W27	4:53:48
Millville 5	1	41N30	73W03	4:52:12
Milton 3	1	41N45	73W11	4:52:44
Minortown 3	1	41N33	73W12	4:52:48
Mixville 5	1	41N30	72W54	4:51:36
Mohegan 6	2	41N26	72W07	4:48:28
Momauguin 5	2	41N17	72W53	4:51:32
Monroe 1	1	41N20	73W14	4:52:56
Montowese 5	2	41N23	72W52	4:51:28
Montville 6	1	41N28	72W09	4:48:36
Moodus 4	1	41N30	72W27	4:49:48
Moosup 8	1	41N43	71W53	4:47:32
Morningside 5	2	41N13	73W03	4:52:12
Morningside Park 6	2	41N21	72W08	4:48:32
Morris 3	1	41N41	73W12	4:52:48
Morris Cove 5	2	41N17	72W53	4:51:32
Mount Carmel 5	2	41N24	72W54	4:51:36
Mount Hope 7	1	41N50	72W16	4:49:04
Myrtle Beach 5	2	41N13	73W03	4:52:12
Mystic 6	1	41N21	71W58	4:47:52
Naugatuck 5	1	41N30	73W03	4:52:12
Naugatuck Gardens 5	2	41N13	73W03	4:52:12
Naugatuck Valley Mall 5	1	41N33	73W01	4:52:04
Nautilus Park 6	2	41N21	72W03	4:48:12
Nepaug 3	1	41N53	72W59	4:51:56
Newberry Corner 3	1	41N49	73W07	4:52:28
New Britain 2	3	41N40	72W47	4:51:08
New Canaan 1	1	41N09	73W30	4:54:00
Newent 6	1	41N37	71W59	4:47:56
New Fairfield 1	1	41N28	73W30	4:54:00
Newfield 1	2	41N11	73W10	4:52:40
Newfield 3	1	41N49	73W07	4:52:28
Newfield Heights 4	3	41N33	72W39	4:50:36
New Hartford 3	1	41N51	73W01	4:52:04
New Haven 5	2	41N18	72W55	4:51:40
Newington 2	2	41N41	72W44	4:50:56
New London 6	2	41N22	72W06	4:48:24
New Milford 3	1	41N35	73W25	4:53:40
New Preston 3	1	41N40	73W21	4:53:24
Newtown 1	1	41N24	73W17	4:53:08
New Village 8	1	41N41	71W55	4:47:40
Niantic 6	2	41N20	72W11	4:48:44
Nichols 1	2	41N15	73W13	4:52:52
Noank 6	2	41N21	72W03	4:48:12
Noble 1	2	41N11	73W11	4:52:44
Norfolk 3	1	41N59	73W12	4:52:48
Noroton 1	1	41N05	73W29	4:53:56
Noroton Heights 1	1	41N05	73W29	4:53:56
North Ashford 8	1	41N56	72W04	4:48:16
North Bloomfield 2	2	41N49	72W42	4:50:48
North Branford 5	1	41N21	72W47	4:51:08
North Canaan 3	1	42N01	73W18	4:53:12
North Canton 2	1	41N49	72W54	4:51:36
North Cornwall 3	1	41N52	73W22	4:53:28
Northfield 3	1	41N42	73W07	4:52:28
Northford 5	1	41N24	72W48	4:51:12
North Franklin 6	1	41N37	72W08	4:48:32
North Glenwood 6	2	41N26	72W05	4:48:20
North Granby 2	1	42N00	72W50	4:51:20
North Grosvenordale 8	1	41N59	71W54	4:47:36
North Guilford 5	2	41N23	72W51	4:51:24
North Haven 5	2	41N23	72W52	4:51:28
North Kent 3	1	41N43	73W29	4:53:56
North Mianus 1	1	41N02	73W36	4:54:24
North Sterling 8	1	41N42	71W50	4:47:20
North Stonington 6	1	41N27	71W52	4:47:28
North Thompsonville 2	1	41N59	72W34	4:50:16
Northville 3	1	41N35	73W25	4:53:40
North Westchester 6	1	41N34	72W20	4:49:20
North Windham 8	1	41N45	72W09	4:48:36
North Woodbury 3	1	41N33	73W12	4:52:48
North Woodstock 8	1	42N00	72W00	4:48:00
Norwalk 1	3	41N07	73W22	4:53:28
Norwalk Mall 1	3	41N08	73W24	4:53:36
Norwich 6	1	41N31	72W05	4:48:20
Norwichtown 6	1	41N32	72W05	4:48:20
Nut Plains 5	2	41N23	72W51	4:51:24
Oakdale 6	1	41N28	72W10	4:48:40
Oakdale Manor 5	1	41N29	73W13	4:52:52
Oakland Gardens 2	1	41N43	72W50	4:51:20
Oakville 3	1	41N35	73W06	4:52:24
Occum 6	1	41N32	72W05	4:48:20
Olde Mistick Village 6	1	41N21	71W59	4:47:56
Old Greenwich 1	1	41N03	73W35	4:54:20
Old Lyme 6	1	41N20	72W18	4:49:12
Old Lyme Shores 6	1	41N19	72W20	4:49:20
Old Mystic 6	1	41N23	71W58	4:47:52
Old Saybrook 4	1	41N18	72W23	4:49:32
Oneco 8	1	41N42	71W48	4:47:12
Orange 5	2	41N17	73W02	4:52:08
Orcutts 7	1	41N57	72W18	4:49:12
Oronoque 1	2	41N12	73W08	4:52:32
Oswegatchie 6	2	41N20	72W09	4:48:36
Oswegatchie Hills 6	1	41N19	72W12	4:48:48
Owenoke 1	3	41N08	73W21	4:53:24
Oxford 5	1	41N25	73W08	4:52:32
Ox Hill 6	1	41N32	72W05	4:48:20
Oxoboxo Lake 6	1	41N28	72W10	4:48:40
Pachaug 6	1	41N37	71W59	4:47:56
Packerville 8	1	41N42	71W58	4:47:52
Palestine 1	1	41N25	73W19	4:53:16
Palmertown 6	2	41N27	72W08	4:48:32
Paradise Green 1	2	41N12	73W08	4:52:32
Pawcatuck 6	1	41N23	71W50	4:47:20
Pemberwick 1	1	41N00	73W40	4:54:40
Pequabuck 3	3	41N40	72W59	4:51:56
Perkins Corner 7	1	41N43	72W13	4:48:52
Phoenixville 8	1	41N48	72W08	4:48:32
Pine Bridge 5	1	41N26	73W03	4:52:12
Pine Grove 3	1	42N02	73W20	4:53:20
Pine Grove 6	1	41N19	72W12	4:48:48
Pine Meadow 3	1	41N52	72W58	4:51:52
Pine Orchard 5	2	41N17	72W48	4:51:12
Pine Rock Park 1	1	41N19	73W08	4:52:32
Plainfield 8	1	41N41	71W56	4:47:44
Plainville 2	1	41N40	72W52	4:51:28
Plantsville 2	1	41N35	72W53	4:51:32
Plaza 5	1	41N34	73W02	4:52:08
Pleasant Acres 1	4	41N24	73W27	4:53:48
Pleasant Valley 3	1	41N55	72W59	4:51:56
Pleasure Beach 6	2	41N19	72W09	4:48:36
Plymouth 3	3	41N40	73W01	4:52:04
Point Beach 5	2	41N13	73W03	4:52:12
Point O'Woods 6	1	41N19	72W15	4:49:00
Pomfret 8	1	41N52	71W59	4:47:56
Pomperaug 3	1	41N33	73W12	4:52:48
Pond Point 5	2	41N13	73W03	4:52:12
Ponset 4	1	41N30	72W34	4:50:16
Pootatuck Park 1	1	41N25	73W17	4:53:08
Poquetanuck 6	1	41N32	72W05	4:48:20
Poquonock 2	2	41N54	72W41	4:50:44
Poquonock Bridge 6	2	41N21	72W02	4:48:08
Portland 4	3	41N35	72W37	4:50:28
Pratts Corner 2	1	41N36	72W53	4:51:32
Presidential 2	1	41N59	72W34	4:50:16
Preston 6	1	41N31	72W01	4:48:04
Prospect 5	1	41N30	72W59	4:51:56
Prospect Beach 5	2	41N16	72W58	4:51:52
Prospect Hill 2	1	41N56	72W37	4:50:28
Puddle Town 3	1	41N49	72W55	4:51:40
Putnam 8	2	41N55	71W55	4:47:40
Putnam Heights 8	1	41N55	71W55	4:47:40
Putney 1	2	41N12	73W08	4:52:32
Quaddick 8	1	41N57	71W52	4:47:28
Quaker Farms 5	1	41N24	73W04	4:52:16
Quaker Hill 6	2	41N24	72W07	4:48:28
Quarryville 7	1	41N47	72W31	4:50:04
Quebec 8	1	41N48	71W54	4:47:36
Quinebaug 8	1	42N01	71W57	4:47:48
Rainbow 2	2	41N51	72W39	4:50:36
Redding 1	1	41N18	73W24	4:53:36
Redding Ridge 1	1	41N19	73W21	4:53:24
Reynolds Bridge 3	1	41N41	73W04	4:52:16
Ridgebury 1	1	41N17	73W30	4:54:00
Ridgefield 1	1	41N17	73W30	4:54:00
Ridgeway 1	1	41N05	73W33	4:54:12
Ridgewood 4	1	41N17	72W32	4:50:08
Ridgewood Park 6	2	41N20	72W09	4:48:36
Rising Corner 2	1	42N00	72W42	4:50:48
Rivercliff 5	2	41N13	73W03	4:52:12
River Glen 2	1	41N43	72W50	4:51:20
Riverside 1	1	41N03	73W36	4:54:24
Riverside 2	1	41N49	72W55	4:51:40
Riverside 5	1	41N24	73W04	4:52:16
Riversville 1	1	41N02	73W37	4:54:28
Riverton 3	1	41N58	73W01	4:52:04
Robertsville 3	1	41N58	73W01	4:52:04
Rockfall 4	3	41N32	72W42	4:50:48
Rock Ridge 1	1	41N02	73W37	4:54:28
Rockville 7	3	41N52	72W28	4:49:52
Rocky Glen 1	1	41N25	73W17	4:53:08
Rocky Hill 2	2	41N40	72W39	4:50:36
Rogers 8	1	41N50	71W54	4:47:36
Round Hill 1	1	41N02	73W37	4:54:28
Rowayton 1	1	41N05	73W26	4:53:44
Roxbury 3	1	41N34	73W18	4:53:12
Roxbury Falls 3	1	41N45	73W11	4:52:44
Sachem Head 5	2	41N23	72W51	4:51:24
Salem 6	1	41N29	72W15	4:49:00
Salem Four Corners 6	1	41N34	72W20	4:49:20
Salisbury 3	1	41N58	73W26	4:53:44
Sandy Beach 3	1	41N41	73W15	4:53:00
Sandy Hook 1	1	41N25	73W17	4:53:08
Saugatuck 1	3	41N08	73W21	4:53:24
Saugatuck Shores 1	3	41N08	73W21	4:53:24
Saunders Point 6	1	41N19	72W12	4:48:48
Savin Rock 5	2	41N16	72W58	4:51:52
Saybrook Manor 4	1	41N17	72W22	4:49:28
Saybrook Point 4	1	41N17	72W22	4:49:28
Scantic 2	1	41N56	72W37	4:50:28
Scitico 2	1	41N59	72W34	4:50:16
Scotland 8	1	41N42	72W05	4:48:20
Seaview Beach 5	1	41N17	72W36	4:50:24
Secret Lake 2	1	41N49	72W50	4:51:20
Seymour 5	1	41N24	73W04	4:52:16
Shady Rest 1	1	41N25	73W17	4:53:08
Shailerville 4	1	41N29	72W31	4:50:04
Sharon 3	1	41N52	73W27	4:53:48
Sharon Valley 3	1	41N53	73W29	4:53:56
Shelton 1	1	41N19	73W05	4:52:20
Sherman 1	1	41N34	73W30	4:54:00
Sherman Corner 8	1	41N45	72W09	4:48:36
Sherwood Manor 2	1	41N59	72W34	4:50:16
Short Beach 5	2	41N17	72W48	4:51:12
Silver Beach 5	2	41N13	73W03	4:52:12
Simsbury 2	1	41N53	72W48	4:51:12
Skiff Mountain 3	1	41N43	73W29	4:53:56
Somers 7	1	42N00	72W28	4:49:52
Somersville 7	1	41N59	72W29	4:49:56
Sound View 6	1	41N19	72W20	4:49:20
South Britain 5	1	41N28	73W15	4:53:00
Southbury 5	1	41N29	73W14	4:52:56
South Canaan 3	1	42N02	73W20	4:53:20
South Canterbury 8	1	41N42	71W58	4:47:52
South Chaplin 8	1	41N45	72W09	4:48:36
South Coventry 7	1	41N46	72W19	4:49:16
South Ellsworth 3	1	41N53	73W29	4:53:56
South End 5	2	41N17	72W53	4:51:32
South Farms 4	3	41N33	72W39	4:50:36
South Glastonbury 2	2	41N41	72W35	4:50:20
South Glenwoods 6	2	41N26	72W05	4:48:20
Southington 2	1	41N36	72W53	4:51:32
South Kent 3	1	41N41	73W28	4:53:52
South Killingly 8	1	41N48	71W54	4:47:36
South Lyme 6	1	41N19	72W15	4:49:00
South Manchester 2	1	41N47	72W31	4:50:04
South Meriden 5	3	41N32	72W48	4:51:12
Southport 1	2	41N08	73W17	4:53:08
South Wethersfield 2	2	41N43	72W41	4:50:44
South Willington 7	1	41N53	72W18	4:49:12
South Windham 8	1	41N41	72W10	4:48:40
South Windsor 2	1	41N50	72W33	4:50:12
Southwood Acres 2	1	41N59	72W34	4:50:16
South Woodstock 8	1	41N56	71W58	4:47:52
Sport Hill 1	2	41N14	73W16	4:53:04
Sprague 6	1	41N37	72W05	4:48:20
Springdale 1	1	41N05	73W32	4:54:08
Spring Glen 5	2	41N22	72W55	4:51:40
Spring Hill 7	1	41N48	72W15	4:49:00
Stafford 7	1	41N59	72W19	4:49:16
Stafford Springs 7	1	41N57	72W18	4:49:12
Staffordville 7	1	42N00	72W16	4:49:04
Stamford 1	1	41N03	73W32	4:54:08
Stanwich 1	1	41N02	73W37	4:54:28
State Line 7	1	41N57	72W18	4:49:12
Sterling 8	1	41N43	71W50	4:47:20
Sterling Hill 8	1	41N43	71W53	4:47:32
Stevenson 1	1	41N23	73W11	4:52:44
Stillmans Corner 2	1	41N36	72W53	4:51:32
Stonington 6	1	41N22	71W54	4:47:36
Stony Corners 2	1	41N49	72W50	4:51:20
Stony Creek 5	2	41N17	72W48	4:51:12
Storrs 7	1	41N49	72W15	4:49:00
Straitsville 5	1	41N30	73W03	4:52:12
Stratfield 1	2	41N10	73W15	4:53:00
Stratford 1	2	41N12	73W08	4:52:32
Submarine Base 6	2	41N21	72W03	4:48:12
Suffield 2	1	42N00	72W40	4:50:40
Sunrise Hill 5	2	41N23	73W00	4:52:00
Taconic 3	1	42N02	73W25	4:53:40
Taftville 6	1	41N33	72W03	4:48:12
Talcott Village 2	1	41N43	72W50	4:51:20
Talcottville 7	1	41N51	72W28	4:49:52
Talmadge Hill 1	1	41N09	73W30	4:54:00
Tariffville 2	1	41N54	72W46	4:51:04
Terminal 5	2	41N19	72W55	4:51:40
Terryville 3	3	41N40	73W01	4:52:04
Thames View 6	2	41N24	72W07	4:48:28
Thamesville 6	1	41N32	72W05	4:48:20
The Dock 1	2	41N12	73W08	4:52:32
Thomaston 3	1	41N41	73W04	4:52:16
Thompson 8	1	41N59	71W53	4:47:32
Thompsonville	1	42N00	72W36	4:50:24
Titicus 1	1	41N17	73W30	4:54:00
Toilsome Hill 1	2	41N10	73W15	4:53:00
Tokeneke 1	1	41N05	73W29	4:53:56

CONNECTICUT

Tolland 7 1 41N52 72w22 4:49:28
Torringford 3 1 41N49 73w07 4:52:28
Torrington 3 1 41N48 73w07 4:52:28
Town Hill 3 1 41N53 72w59 4:51:56
Town Line Plaza 2 2 41N40 72w39 4:50:36
Tracy 5 1 41N28 72w49 4:51:16
Trails Corner 6 2 41N21 72w03 4:48:12
Tri-City Shopping Plaza 7 1 41N51 72w28 4:49:52
Trumbull 1 2 41N15 73w12 4:52:48
Tunxis Hill 1 2 41N10 73w15 4:53:00
Twin Lakes 3 1 42N02 73w25 4:53:40
Tyler Lake Heights 3 1 41N50 73w14 4:52:56
Uncasville 6 2 41N26 72w06 4:48:24
Union 7 1 42N00 72w10 4:48:40
Union City 5 1 41N30 73w03 4:52:12
Unionville 2 1 41N45 72w53 4:51:32
Upper Stepney 1 1 41N19 73w15 4:53:00
U S Coast Guard Academy 6 2 41N21 72w06 4:48:24
Vernon 7 1 41N51 72w28 4:49:52
Versailles 6 1 41N34 72w03 4:48:12
Voluntown 6 1 41N34 71w50 4:47:20
Wallingford 5 1 41N27 72w50 4:51:20
Wallingford Plaza 5 1 41N28 72w49 4:51:16
Walnut Beach 5 2 41N13 73w03 4:52:12
Walnut Hill 6 1 41N22 72w13 4:48:52
Walnut Tree Hill 1 1 41N25 73w17 4:53:08
Wamphassuc Point 6 1 41N21 71w58 4:47:52
Wapping 2 2 41N49 72w37 4:50:28
Warehouse Point 2 1 41N56 72w37 4:50:28
Warren 3 1 41N44 73w21 4:53:24
Warrenville 8 1 41N52 72w10 4:48:40
Washington 3 1 41N39 73w19 4:53:16
Washington Hill 3 1 41N49 72w54 4:51:36
Washington Square 6 1 41N32 72w05 4:48:20
Waterbury 5 1 41N33 73w03 4:52:12
Waterford 6 2 41N21 72w09 4:48:36
Watertown 3 1 41N36 73w06 4:52:24
Wauregan 8 1 41N45 71w55 4:47:40
Wauwecus Hill 6 1 41N32 72w05 4:48:20
Weatogue 2 1 41N51 72w50 4:51:20
Webster Square Shopping Cent 2 3 41N38 72w46 4:51:04
Weekeempee 3 1 41N33 73w12 4:52:48
Welles Village 2 2 41N41 72w35 4:50:20
Wells Quarter Village 2 2 41N43 72w41 4:50:44
Wequetequock 6 1 41N22 71w50 4:47:20
Wesleyan 4 3 41N33 72w39 4:50:36
West Ashford 8 1 41N50 72w16 4:49:04
West Avon 2 1 41N49 72w50 4:51:20
West Bantam 3 1 41N44 73w14 4:52:56
Westbrook 4 1 41N18 72w28 4:49:52
West Cheshire 5 1 41N30 72w54 4:51:36
Westchester 6 1 41N34 72w20 4:49:20
West Cornwall 3 1 41N52 73w22 4:53:28
West End 2 3 41N41 72w56 4:51:44
West Farms Mall 2 1 41N43 72w50 4:51:20
Westfield 4 3 41N33 72w39 4:50:36
Westford 8 1 41N57 72w18 4:49:12
West Goshen 3 1 41N50 73w14 4:52:56
West Granby 2 1 41N57 72w50 4:51:20
West Hartford 2 2 41N45 72w44 4:50:56
West Hartland 2 1 42N00 72w58 4:51:52
West Haven 5 2 41N17 72w57 4:51:48
West Lakes 5 2 41N23 72w51 4:51:24
Westminster 8 1 41N42 71w58 4:47:52
West Mystic 6 1 41N21 71w59 4:47:56
Weston 1 1 41N12 73w23 4:53:32
Westport 1 5 41N09 73w22 4:53:28
West Putnam Avenue 1 1 41N02 73w37 4:54:28
West Redding 1 1 41N20 73w26 4:53:44
West Shore 5 2 41N16 72w58 4:51:52
West Side 6 1 41N32 72w05 4:48:20
West Simsbury 2 1 41N52 72w50 4:51:20
West Stafford 7 1 41N57 72w18 4:49:12
West Suffield 2 1 42N00 72w42 4:50:48
West Thompson 8 1 41N59 71w54 4:47:36
West Torrington 3 1 41N49 73w07 4:52:28
Westview Acres 5 1 41N24 73w04 4:52:16
Westview Heights 5 1 41N32 73w07 4:52:28
Westville 5 2 41N19 72w58 4:51:52
West Wauregan 8 1 41N45 71w55 4:47:40
West Willington 7 1 41N53 72w18 4:49:12
Westwood Park 6 1 41N32 72w05 4:48:20
West Woods 3 1 41N53 73w29 4:53:56
West Woodstock 8 1 41N57 71w59 4:47:56
Wethersfield 2 2 41N42 72w40 4:50:40
Wheeler Farms 5 2 41N13 73w03 4:52:12
Whigville 2 3 41N41 72w56 4:51:44
Whipstick 1 1 41N17 73w30 4:54:00
Whisconier 1 1 41N28 73w23 4:53:32
Whitacres 2 1 41N59 72w34 4:50:16
Whitcomb Hill 3 1 41N49 73w22 4:53:28
White Sands Beach 6 1 41N19 72w20 4:49:20
Whitneyville 5 2 41N22 72w54 4:51:36
Wildermere Beach 5 2 41N13 73w03 4:52:12
Willimantic 8 1 41N43 72w13 4:48:52
Willington 7 1 41N52 72w16 4:49:04
Willington Hill 7 1 41N53 72w18 4:49:12
Willow Point 6 1 41N21 71w58 4:47:52
Wilson 2 2 41N51 72w39 4:50:36
Wilsonville 8 1 41N59 71w54 4:47:36
Wilton 1 1 41N12 73w26 4:53:44
Winchester 3 1 41N55 73w06 4:52:24
Windham 8 1 41N42 72w10 4:48:40
Winding Lanes 2 1 41N49 72w50 4:51:20
Windsor 2 2 41N50 72w39 4:50:36
Windsor Locks 2 1 41N56 72w38 4:50:32
Windsorville 2 1 41N53 72w32 4:50:08
Winsted 3 1 41N55 73w04 4:52:16
Winthrop 4 1 41N23 72w26 4:49:44
Wolcott 5 1 41N36 72w59 4:51:56
Woodbridge 5 2 41N21 73w01 4:52:04
Woodbury 3 1 41N33 73w13 4:52:52
Woodmont 5 2 41N13 73w03 4:52:12
Woodstock 8 1 41N57 72w00 4:48:00
Woodstock Valley 8 1 41N56 72w04 4:48:16
Woodtick 5 1 41N36 72w59 4:51:56
Woodville 3 1 41N40 73w21 4:53:24
Yale 5 2 41N19 72w56 4:51:44
Yale University 5 2 41N19 72w56 4:51:44
Yalesville 5 1 41N28 72w49 4:51:16
Yantic 6 1 41N33 72w07 4:48:28
Zoar 1 1 41N25 73w17 4:53:08

DELAWARE

TIME TABLES

DE # 1

Before 11/18/1883 LMT
11/18/1883 12:00 EST
3/31/1918 02:00 EWT
10/27/1918 02:00 EST
3/30/1919 02:00 EWT
10/26/1919 02:00 EST
3/28/1920 02:00 EDT
10/31/1920 02:00 EST
4/24/1921 02:00 EDT
9/25/1921 02:00 EST
4/30/1922 02:00 EDT
9/24/1922 02:00 EST
4/29/1923 02:00 EDT
9/30/1923 02:00 EST
4/27/1924 02:00 EDT
9/28/1924 02:00 EST
4/26/1925 02:00 EDT
9/27/1925 02:00 EST
4/25/1926 02:00 EDT
9/26/1926 02:00 EST
4/24/1927 02:00 EDT
9/25/1927 02:00 EST
4/29/1928 02:00 EDT
9/30/1928 02:00 EST
4/28/1929 02:00 EDT
9/29/1929 02:00 EST
4/27/1930 02:00 EDT
9/28/1930 02:00 EST
4/26/1931 02:00 EDT
9/27/1931 02:00 EST
4/24/1932 02:00 EDT
9/25/1932 02:00 EST
4/30/1933 02:00 EDT
9/24/1933 02:00 EST
4/29/1934 02:00 EDT
9/30/1934 02:00 EST
4/28/1935 02:00 EDT
9/29/1935 02:00 EST
4/26/1936 02:00 EDT
9/27/1936 02:00 EST
4/25/1937 02:00 EDT
9/26/1937 02:00 EST
4/24/1938 02:00 EDT
9/25/1938 02:00 EST
4/30/1939 02:00 EDT
9/24/1939 02:00 EST
4/28/1940 02:00 EDT
9/29/1940 02:00 EST
4/27/1941 02:00 EDT
9/28/1941 02:00 EST
2/09/1942 02:00 EWT
9/30/1945 02:00 EST
4/28/1946 02:00 EDT
9/29/1946 02:00 EST
4/27/1947 02:00 EDT
9/28/1947 02:00 EST
4/25/1948 02:00 EDT
9/26/1948 02:00 EST
4/24/1949 02:00 EDT
9/25/1949 02:00 EST
4/30/1950 02:00 EDT
9/24/1950 02:00 EST
4/29/1951 02:00 EDT
9/30/1951 02:00 EST
4/27/1952 02:00 EDT
9/28/1952 02:00 EST
4/26/1953 02:00 EDT
9/27/1953 02:00 EST
4/25/1954 02:00 EDT
9/26/1954 02:00 EST
4/24/1955 02:00 EDT
9/25/1955 02:00 EST
4/29/1956 02:00 US#2

DE # 2

Before 11/18/1883 LMT
11/18/1883 12:00 EST
3/31/1918 02:00 EWT
10/27/1918 02:00 EST
3/30/1919 02:00 EWT
10/26/1919 02:00 EST
2/09/1942 02:00 EWT
9/30/1945 02:00 EST
4/28/1946 02:00 DE#1
4/29/1956 02:00 US#2

DE # 3

Before 11/18/1883 LMT
11/18/1883 12:00 EST
3/31/1918 02:00 EWT
10/27/1918 02:00 EST
3/30/1919 02:00 EWT
10/26/1919 02:00 EST
2/09/1942 02:00 EWT
9/30/1945 02:00 EST
4/27/1947 02:00 US#3

DE # 4

Before 11/18/1883 LMT
11/18/1883 12:00 EST
3/31/1918 02:00 EWT
10/27/1918 02:00 EST
3/30/1919 02:00 EWT
10/26/1919 02:00 EST
2/09/1942 02:00 EWT
9/30/1945 02:00 EST
4/25/1948 02:00 US#3

DE # 5

Before 11/18/1883 LMT
11/18/1883 12:00 EST
3/31/1918 02:00 EWT
10/27/1918 02:00 EST
3/30/1919 02:00 EWT
10/26/1919 02:00 EST
2/09/1942 02:00 EWT
9/30/1945 02:00 EST
4/29/1951 02:00 DE#1
4/29/1956 02:00 US#2

DE # 6

Before 11/18/1883 LMT
11/18/1883 12:00 EST
3/31/1918 02:00 EWT
10/27/1918 02:00 EST
3/30/1919 02:00 EWT
10/26/1919 02:00 EST
2/09/1942 02:00 EWT
9/30/1945 02:00 EST
4/26/1953 02:00 US#3

DE # 7

Before 11/18/1883 LMT
11/18/1883 12:00 EST
3/31/1918 02:00 EWT
10/27/1918 02:00 EST
3/30/1919 02:00 EWT
10/26/1919 02:00 EST
2/09/1942 02:00 EWT
9/30/1945 02:00 EST
4/28/1946 02:00 EDT
9/29/1946 02:00 EST
4/27/1947 02:00 EDT
9/28/1947 02:00 EST
4/25/1948 02:00 EDT
9/26/1948 02:00 EST
4/24/1949 02:00 EDT
9/25/1949 02:00 EST
4/30/1950 02:00 EDT
9/24/1950 02:00 EST
4/29/1951 02:00 EDT
9/30/1951 02:00 EST
4/27/1952 02:00 EDT
9/28/1952 02:00 EST
4/24/1955 02:00 EDT
9/25/1955 02:00 EST
4/29/1956 02:00 US#2

DE # 8

Before 11/18/1883 LMT
11/18/1883 12:00 EST
3/31/1918 02:00 EWT
10/27/1918 02:00 EST
3/30/1919 02:00 EWT
10/26/1919 02:00 EST
2/09/1942 02:00 EWT
9/30/1945 02:00 EST
4/27/1947 02:00 EDT
9/28/1947 02:00 EST
4/25/1948 02:00 EDT
9/26/1948 02:00 EST
4/24/1949 02:00 EDT
9/25/1949 02:00 EST
4/30/1950 02:00 EDT
9/24/1950 02:00 EST
4/29/1951 02:00 EDT
9/30/1951 02:00 EST
4/27/1952 02:00 EDT
9/28/1952 02:00 EST
4/24/1955 02:00 EDT
9/25/1955 02:00 EST
4/29/1956 02:00 US#2

DE # 9

Before 11/18/1883 LMT
11/18/1883 12:00 EST
3/31/1918 02:00 EWT
10/27/1918 02:00 EST
3/30/1919 02:00 EWT
10/26/1919 02:00 EST
2/09/1942 02:00 EWT
9/30/1945 02:00 EST
4/28/1946 02:00 EDT
9/29/1946 02:00 EST
4/25/1948 02:00 DE#1
4/29/1956 02:00 US#2

DE # 10

Before 11/18/1883 LMT
11/18/1883 12:00 EST
3/31/1918 02:00 EWT
10/27/1918 02:00 EST
3/30/1919 02:00 EWT
10/26/1919 02:00 EST
4/26/1931 02:00 DE#1
4/29/1956 02:00 US#2

DE # 11

Before 11/18/1883 LMT
11/18/1883 12:00 EST
3/31/1918 02:00 EWT
10/27/1918 02:00 EST
3/30/1919 02:00 EWT
10/26/1919 02:00 EST
2/09/1942 02:00 EWT
9/30/1945 02:00 EST
4/28/1946 02:00 EDT
9/29/1946 02:00 EST
4/26/1953 02:00 DE#1
4/29/1956 02:00 US#2

DE # 12

Before 11/18/1883 LMT
11/18/1883 12:00 EST
3/31/1918 02:00 EWT
10/27/1918 02:00 EST
3/30/1919 02:00 EWT
10/26/1919 02:00 EST
4/24/1938 02:00 DE#1
4/29/1956 02:00 US#2

DE # 13

Before 11/18/1883 LMT
11/18/1883 12:00 DE#2
4/27/1947 02:00 DE#1
4/29/1956 02:00 US#2

DE # 14

Before 11/18/1883 LMT
11/18/1883 12:00 DE#2
4/25/1948 02:00 DE#1
4/29/1956 02:00 US#2

DE # 15

Before 11/18/1883 LMT
11/18/1883 12:00 DE#2
4/26/1953 02:00 DE#1
4/29/1956 02:00 US#2

DE # 16

Before 11/18/1883 LMT
11/18/1883 12:00 EST
3/31/1918 02:00 EWT
10/27/1918 02:00 EST
3/30/1919 02:00 EWT
10/26/1919 02:00 EST
2/09/1942 02:00 EWT
9/30/1945 02:00 EST
4/24/1955 02:00 EDT
9/25/1955 02:00 EST
4/29/1956 02:00 US#2

COUNTIES

1 Kent   2 New Castle   3 Sussex

Place	Table	Lat	Long	Time
Adamsville 1	7	38N48	75W36	5:02:24
Afton 2	1	39N45	75W33	5:02:12
Airport Villa 2	1	39N41	75W34	5:02:16
Alapocas 2	1	39N48	75W31	5:02:04
Albertson Park 2	1	39N44	75W39	5:02:36
Analine Village 2	1	39N48	75W28	5:01:52
Andrewsville 1	7	38N48	75W36	5:02:24
Anglesey 2	1	39N46	75W35	5:02:20
Angola Beach 3	16	38N43	75W17	5:01:08
Anna Acres 3	16	38N43	75W05	5:00:20
Arden 2	1	39N49	75W29	5:01:56
Arden Croft 2	1	39N45	75W33	5:02:12
Argo Corner 3	9	38N55	75W22	5:01:28
Arundel 2	1	39N44	75W39	5:02:36
Ashbourne Hills 2	1	39N48	75W28	5:01:52
Ashland 2	1	39N46	75W35	5:02:20
Ashley 2	1	39N43	75W37	5:02:28
Atlanta 3	16	38N44	75W36	5:02:24
Atlanta Estates 3	16	38N37	75W39	5:02:36
Augustine Beach 2	12	39N31	75W35	5:02:20
Avalon 2	1	39N44	75W39	5:02:36
Bacon 3	4	38N27	75W35	5:02:20
Baldton 2	1	39N41	75W34	5:02:16
Barkers Landing 1	6	39N04	75W28	5:01:52
Bayard 3	4	38N31	75W14	5:00:56
Bay View Park 3	16	38N32	75W04	5:00:16
Bayville 3	3	38N28	75W13	5:00:52
Bear 2	12	39N38	75W40	5:02:40
Beaver Brook 2	1	39N41	75W34	5:02:16
Beaverdam Heights 3	16	38N37	75W39	5:02:36
Bellefonte 2	1	39N47	75W30	5:02:00
Bellemoor 2	1	39N45	75W32	5:02:08
Bellevue Manor 2	1	39N46	75W30	5:02:00
Belltown 3	16	38N47	75W09	5:00:36
Belvidere 2	1	39N43	75W37	5:02:28
Bestfield 2	1	39N43	75W37	5:02:28
Bethany Beach 3	16	38N32	75W04	5:00:16
Bethel 3	16	38N34	75W37	5:02:28
Big Stone Beach 1	9	38N55	75W22	5:01:28
Binns Village 2	10	39N41	75W43	5:02:52
Birchwood Park 2	10	39N41	75W43	5:02:52
Blackbird 2	14	39N24	75W41	5:02:44
Blackiston 1	2	39N17	75W38	5:02:32
Blades 3	16	38N38	75W37	5:02:28
Blue Hen Mall 1	1	39N09	75W31	5:02:04
Blue Rock Manor 2	1	39N48	75W31	5:02:04
Bowers 1	6	39N04	75W24	5:01:36
Boxwood 2	1	39N43	75W37	5:02:28
Brack-Ex 2	1	39N45	75W35	5:02:20
Brandywine 2	1	39N48	75W30	5:02:00
Brandywine Estates 2	1	39N48	75W28	5:01:52
Brandywine Springs Manor 2	1	39N44	75W39	5:02:36
Brandywood 2	1	39N45	75W33	5:02:12
Breezewood 2	10	39N41	75W43	5:02:52
Brenford 1	11	39N18	75W36	5:02:24
Briar Park 1	1	39N09	75W31	5:02:04
Bridgeville 3	3	38N45	75W36	5:02:24
Broadacres 3	16	38N37	75W39	5:02:36
Broad Creek 3	6	38N33	75W34	5:02:16
Broadkill Beach 3	16	38N47	75W19	5:01:16
Brookbend 2	10	39N41	75W43	5:02:52
Brookdale Heights 1	1	39N07	75W33	5:02:12
Brookhaven 2	10	39N41	75W43	5:02:52
Brookland Terrace 2	1	39N44	75W38	5:02:32
Brookside 2	10	39N40	75W43	5:02:52
Brookside Park 2	10	39N40	75W43	5:02:52
Brookview Apartments 2	1	39N48	75W28	5:01:52
Brownsville 1	16	38N55	75W35	5:02:20
Bunting 3	3	38N28	75W13	5:00:52
Bush Manor 1	1	39N09	75W31	5:02:04
Buttonwood 2	1	39N41	75W34	5:02:16
Camden 1	1	39N07	75W33	5:02:12
Cannon 3	6	38N44	75W36	5:02:24
Canterbury 1	3	39N00	75W35	5:02:20
Capitol Green 1	1	39N09	75W31	5:02:04
Capitol Park 1	1	39N09	75W31	5:02:04
Cardiff 2	1	39N45	75W33	5:02:12
Carlisle Village 1	1	39N09	75W31	5:02:04
Carpenter 2	1	39N48	75W31	5:02:04
Carrcroft 2	1	39N48	75W31	5:02:04
Carrcroft Crest 2	1	39N48	75W31	5:02:04
Carter 1	1	39N09	75W31	5:02:04
Castle Hills 2	1	39N41	75W34	5:02:16
Catalina Gardens 2	10	39N41	75W43	5:02:52
Cedar Heights 2	1	39N43	75W37	5:02:28
Center Green 2	1	39N48	75W28	5:01:52
Centerville 2	12	39N49	75W37	5:02:28
Central Kent 1	6	39N04	75W33	5:02:12
Central Pencader 2	15	39N35	75W44	5:02:56
Centreville 2	1	39N46	75W35	5:02:20
Chalfonte 2	1	39N45	75W33	5:02:12
Channin 2	1	39N48	75W31	5:02:04
Chapel Hill 2	10	39N41	75W43	5:02:52
Chatham 2	1	39N45	75W33	5:02:12
Chelsea Estates 2	1	39N41	75W34	5:02:16
Cherokee Woods 2	10	39N41	75W43	5:02:52
Chestnut Hill Estates 2	10	39N41	75W43	5:02:52
Chestnut Knoll 3	9	38N55	75W22	5:01:28
Cheswold 1	6	39N13	75W35	5:02:20
Christiana 2	10	39N40	75W40	5:02:40
Christiana Acres 2	1	39N41	75W34	5:02:16
Christine Manor 2	10	39N41	75W43	5:02:52
Clarksville 3	16	38N33	75W09	5:00:36
Claymont 2	1	39N48	75W27	5:01:48
Clayton 1	2	39N17	75W38	5:02:32
Clearfield 2	1	39N48	75W28	5:01:52
Clearview Manor 2	1	39N41	75W34	5:02:16
Cleland Heights 2	1	39N45	75W35	5:02:20
Clifton Park Manor 2	1	39N45	75W32	5:02:08
Cocked Hat 3	16	38N44	75W36	5:02:24
College Park 2	10	39N41	75W43	5:02:52
Collins Park 2	1	39N41	75W33	5:02:12
Colonial Heights 2	1	39N45	75W35	5:02:20
Colonial Park 2	1	39N45	75W35	5:02:20
Columbia 3	4	38N27	75W35	5:02:20
Concord 3	16	38N37	75W39	5:02:36
Concord Manor 2	1	39N48	75W31	5:02:04
Cool Spring 3	6	38N47	75W19	5:01:16
Cooper Farm 2	1	39N44	75W39	5:02:36
Cottonpatch Hill 3	16	38N32	75W04	5:00:16
Coventry 2	1	39N41	75W34	5:02:16
Coverdales Crossroads 3	16	38N44	75W36	5:02:24
Covered Bridge Farms 2	10	39N41	75W43	5:02:52
Cragmere 2	1	39N46	75W30	5:02:00
Cragmere Woods 2	1	39N46	75W30	5:02:00
Craigs Mill 3	16	38N37	75W39	5:02:36
Cranston Heights 2	1	39N44	75W39	5:02:36
Crossgates 1	1	39N09	75W31	5:02:04
Dagsboro 3	4	38N33	75W15	5:01:00
Darley Woods 2	1	39N45	75W33	5:02:12
Dartmouth Woods 2	1	39N45	75W33	5:02:12
Deerhurst 2	1	39N48	75W31	5:02:04
Delaplane Manor 2	10	39N41	75W43	5:02:52
Delaware City 2	15	39N35	75W36	5:02:24

DELAWARE

Delaware Heights 2 1 39N46 75w35 5:02:20
Del Haven Estates 1 6 39N04 75w28 5:01:52
Delmar 3 4 38N27 75w35 5:02:20
Del Park Manor 2 1 39N44 75w39 5:02:36
Devon 2 1 39N45 75w33 5:02:12
Devonshire 2 1 39N45 75w33 5:02:12
Dewey Beach 3 3 38N43 75w05 5:00:20
Dobbinsville 2 1 39N41 75w34 5:02:16
Dover 1 1 39N10 75w32 5:02:08
Dover Air Force Base 1 1 39N07 75w29 5:01:56
Doverbrook Gardens 1 1 39N09 75w31 5:02:04
Downs Chapel 1 2 39N17 75w38 5:02:32
Drummond North 2 10 39N41 75w43 5:02:52
Dunleith 2 1 39N45 75w33 5:02:12
Dunlinden Acres 2 1 39N45 75w35 5:02:20
Dupont Manor 1 1 39N12 75w33 5:02:12
Du Ross Heights 2 1 39N41 75w37 5:02:28
Eastover Hills 1 1 39N09 75w31 5:02:04
Eberton 1 1 39N09 75w31 5:02:04
Eden Park 2 1 39N41 75w34 5:02:16
Edge Hill 1 1 39N09 75w31 5:02:04
Edgehill Acres 1 1 39N09 75w31 5:02:04
Edgemoor 2 1 39N45 75w32 5:02:08
Edgemoor Gardens 2 1 39N45 75w32 5:02:08
Edgemoor Terrace 2 1 39N45 75w32 5:02:08
Edgewater Acres 3 3 38N28 75w13 5:00:52
Edgewood Hills 2 1 39N45 75w32 5:02:08
Edwardsville 1 3 39N00 75w35 5:02:20
Ellendale 3 4 38N48 75w26 5:01:44
Elliott Heights 2 10 39N41 75w43 5:02:52
Elmhurst 2 1 39N43 75w37 5:02:28
Elsmere 2 1 39N44 75w35 5:02:20
Elsmere Junction 2 1 39N45 75w35 5:02:20
English Village 2 10 39N41 75w43 5:02:52
Evergreen Acres 3 9 38N55 75w22 5:01:28
Fairfax 2 1 39N47 75w33 5:02:12
Fairfield 2 10 39N41 75w43 5:02:52
Fairfield Crest 2 10 39N41 75w43 5:02:52
Fairfield Farms 1 1 39N09 75w31 5:02:04
Fairmount 3 16 38N43 75w17 5:01:08
Fairwinds 2 12 39N38 75w40 5:02:40
Farmington 1 6 38N52 75w35 5:02:20
Faulkland 2 1 39N44 75w39 5:02:36
Faulkland Heights 2 1 39N44 75w39 5:02:36
Faulkwoods 2 1 39N45 75w33 5:02:12
Federal 2 10 39N41 75w43 5:02:52
Felton 3 3 39N01 75w35 5:02:20
Felton Manor 1 3 39N00 75w35 5:02:20
Fenwick Island 3 16 38N27 75w03 5:00:12
Fieldsboro 2 14 39N24 75w41 5:02:44
Fireside Park 2 10 39N41 75w43 5:02:52
Flemings Corner 1 16 38N55 75w35 5:02:20
Flemings Landings 2 14 39N24 75w41 5:02:44
Forest Brook Glen 2 1 39N43 75w37 5:02:28
Forest Hills Park 2 1 39N48 75w31 5:02:04
Forest Park 2 1 39N45 75w35 5:02:20
Four Seasons 2 10 39N41 75w43 5:02:52
Frankford 3 4 38N31 75w14 5:00:56
Frederica 1 16 39N01 75w28 5:01:52
Galewood 2 1 39N48 75w31 5:02:04
Garfield Park 2 1 39N41 75w34 5:02:16
Gateway Farms 2 12 39N47 75w42 5:02:48
George Read Village 2 10 39N41 75w43 5:02:52
Georgetown 3 4 38N41 75w23 5:01:32
Ginns Corner 2 14 39N24 75w41 5:02:44
Glasgow 2 10 39N41 75w43 5:02:52
Glen Burne Estates 2 1 39N43 75w37 5:02:28
Glendale 2 10 39N41 75w43 5:02:52
Glenville 2 1 39N43 75w37 5:02:28
Gordon Heights 2 1 39N45 75w32 5:02:08
Gordy Estates 2 1 39N43 75w37 5:02:28
Granogue 2 1 39N46 75w35 5:02:20
Gravel Hill 3 4 38N41 75w23 5:01:32
Graylyn Crest 2 1 39N45 75w33 5:02:12
Greater Newark 2 10 39N41 75w44 5:02:56
Green Acres 2 1 39N48 75w31 5:02:04
Green Bank 2 1 39N44 75w39 5:02:36
Greenbriar 2 1 39N41 75w34 5:02:16
Greentop 3 16 38N52 75w25 5:01:40
Greentree 2 1 39N48 75w28 5:01:52
Greenview 1 1 39N09 75w31 5:02:04
Greenville 2 1 39N46 75w35 5:02:20
Greenwood 3 7 38N48 75w36 5:02:24
Gumboro 3 4 38N31 75w14 5:00:56
Gumwood 2 1 39N48 75w31 5:02:04
Guyencourt 2 1 39N46 75w35 5:02:20
Gwinhurst 2 1 39N46 75w30 5:02:00
Hall Estates 1 9 38N55 75w22 5:01:28
Hamby's Corner 2 1 39N45 75w33 5:02:12
Hamilton Park 2 1 39N41 75w34 5:02:16
Harbeson 3 16 38N43 75w17 5:01:08
Hardscrabble 3 16 38N37 75w39 5:02:36
Harmony Hills 2 10 39N41 75w43 5:02:52
Harrington 1 4 38N56 75w35 5:02:20
Hartly 1 6 39N10 75w43 5:02:52
Hayden Park 2 1 39N43 75w37 5:02:28
Hazlettville 1 6 39N10 75w43 5:02:52
Hearns Mill 3 16 38N37 75w39 5:02:36
Henlopen Acres 3 16 38N43 75w05 5:00:20
Henry Clay 2 1 39N46 75w35 5:02:20
Hickman 1 16 38N53 75w50 5:03:20
Hickory Hill 3 16 38N35 75w17 5:01:08
Hickory Ridge 1 11 39N18 75w36 5:02:24
Highland Acres 1 1 39N07 75w32 5:02:08
Highland Acres 3 16 38N47 75w09 5:00:36
Highland West 2 1 39N44 75w39 5:02:36
Hillcrest 2 1 39N45 75w32 5:02:08
Hilldale 1 1 39N09 75w31 5:02:04
Hillside Heights 2 10 39N41 75w43 5:02:52
Hilltop Manor 2 1 39N46 75w30 5:02:00
Hockessin 2 12 39N47 75w42 5:02:48
Hollandsville 1 3 39N00 75w35 5:02:20
Holloway Terrace 2 1 39N42 75w33 5:02:12
Holly Oak 2 1 39N47 75w29 5:01:56
Holly Oak 3 16 38N37 75w39 5:02:36
Holly Oak Terrace 2 1 39N46 75w30 5:02:00
Hollyville 3 16 38N43 75w17 5:01:08
Houston 1 4 38N55 75w30 5:02:00
Huntley 1 1 39N09 75w31 5:02:04
Hyde Park 2 1 39N44 75w39 5:02:36
Idela 2 1 39N43 75w37 5:02:28
Indian Beach 3 16 38N43 75w05 5:00:20
Indian Field 2 1 39N45 75w33 5:02:12
Indian River Acres 3 4 38N33 75w15 5:01:00
Ivy Ridge 2 1 39N41 75w34 5:02:16
Jefferson Farms 2 1 39N41 75w34 5:02:16
Jimtown 3 16 38N47 75w09 5:00:36
Johnson Corner 3 3 38N28 75w13 5:00:52
Keen-Wik 3 3 38N28 75w13 5:00:52
Kenilworth 2 1 39N48 75w28 5:01:52
Kenmore Park 3 16 38N37 75w39 5:02:36
Kent Acres 1 1 39N09 75w31 5:02:04
Kenton 1 6 39N13 75w40 5:02:40
Kiamensi 2 1 39N43 75w37 5:02:28
Killens Addition 3 16 38N43 75w05 5:00:20
Kirkwood 2 13 39N34 75w42 5:02:48
Kitts Hummock 1 1 39N09 75w31 5:02:04
Klair Estates 2 1 39N44 75w39 5:02:36
Kynlyn Apartments 2 1 39N46 75w30 5:02:00
Lake Pines 3 2 38N33 75w34 5:02:16
Lamatan 2 10 39N41 75w43 5:02:52
Lancashire 2 1 39N45 75w33 5:02:12
Lancaster Court 2 1 39N45 75w35 5:02:20
Lancaster Village 2 1 39N45 75w35 5:02:20
Laurel 3 2 38N33 75w34 5:02:16
Lebanon 1 1 39N09 75w31 5:02:04
Leedom Estates 2 1 39N41 75w34 5:02:16
Leipsic 1 1 39N14 75w31 5:02:04
Lewes 3 5 38N46 75w09 5:00:36
Lewes Beach 3 5 38N47 75w09 5:00:36
Liftwood 2 1 39N48 75w31 5:02:04
Limestone Acres 2 1 39N44 75w39 5:02:36
Limestone Gardens 2 1 39N44 75w39 5:02:36
Lincoln 3 6 38N52 75w25 5:01:40
Lindenmere 2 1 39N46 75w30 5:02:00
Little Creek 1 1 39N10 75w27 5:01:48
Llangollen Estates 2 1 39N41 75w34 5:02:16
Longview Farms 2 1 39N45 75w33 5:02:12
Lower Christiana 2 1 39N44 75w36 5:02:24
Lowes Crossroads 3 16 38N35 75w17 5:01:08
Lumbrook 2 10 39N41 75w43 5:02:52
Lynch Heights 1 9 38N55 75w22 5:01:28
Lyndalia 2 1 39N43 75w37 5:02:28
Lynnfield 2 1 39N48 75w31 5:02:04
Magnolia 1 6 39N04 75w28 5:01:52
Manor 2 1 39N41 75w34 5:02:16
Manor Park 2 1 39N41 75w34 5:02:16
Maplecrest 2 1 39N44 75w39 5:02:36
Maplewood 2 10 39N41 75w43 5:02:52
Marshallton 2 1 39N44 75w39 5:02:36
Marvels Crossroad 1 16 38N55 75w35 5:02:20
Marydel 1 8 39N07 75w45 5:03:00
Masten's Corner 1 3 39N00 75w35 5:02:20
Mayfair 1 1 39N09 75w31 5:02:04
Mayfield 2 1 39N48 75w31 5:02:04
Mayview Manor 2 1 39N41 75w34 5:02:16
McClellandville 2 10 39N41 75w43 5:02:52
McDaniel Heights 2 1 39N48 75w31 5:02:04
Meadowbrook 2 1 39N43 75w37 5:02:28
Meadowood 2 10 39N41 75w43 5:02:52
Mechanicsville 2 10 39N41 75w43 5:02:52
Meeting House Hill 2 10 39N41 75w43 5:02:52
Middleford 3 16 38N37 75w39 5:02:36
Middlesex Beach 3 16 38N32 75w04 5:00:16
Middletown 2 12 39N27 75w43 5:02:52
Midvale 2 1 39N41 75w34 5:02:16
Midway 3 16 38N43 75w05 5:00:20
Milford 3 9 38N55 75w26 5:01:44
Milford Cross Roads 2 10 39N41 75w43 5:02:52
Milford Plaza 3 9 38N55 75w22 5:01:28
Millpond Acres 3 16 38N47 75w09 5:00:36
Millsboro 3 3 38N36 75w18 5:01:12
Millville 3 16 38N33 75w07 5:00:28
Milton 3 16 38N47 75w19 5:01:16
Minquadale 2 1 39N43 75w34 5:02:16
Mispillion Light 3 9 38N55 75w22 5:01:28
Mission 3 16 38N35 75w17 5:01:08
Monroe Park 2 1 39N46 75w35 5:02:20
Montchanin 2 1 39N47 75w35 5:02:20
Monterey Farms 2 1 39N41 75w34 5:02:16
Morris Estates 1 1 39N09 75w31 5:02:04
Mount Cuba 2 1 39N46 75w35 5:02:20
Naamans Gardens 2 1 39N45 75w33 5:02:12
Naamans Manor 2 1 39N45 75w33 5:02:12
Nanticoke Acres 3 16 38N37 75w39 5:02:36
Nassau 3 6 38N45 75w11 5:00:44
Newark 2 10 39N41 75w46 5:03:04
New Castle 2 1 39N40 75w34 5:02:16
New Castle Manor 2 1 39N41 75w34 5:02:16
Newkirk Estates 2 10 39N41 75w43 5:02:52
Newport 2 1 39N43 75w37 5:02:28
Northcrest 2 1 39N45 75w33 5:02:12
North Hills 2 1 39N46 75w30 5:02:00
North Ridge 2 1 39N48 75w28 5:01:52
North Seaford Heights 3 2 38N37 75w39 5:02:36
Northshire 2 1 39N45 75w33 5:02:12
North Shores 3 16 38N47 75w19 5:01:16
North Shores 3 16 38N43 75w05 5:00:20
North Shores 3 16 38N37 75w39 5:02:36
North Star 2 10 39N41 75w43 5:02:52
Northwest Dover Heights 1 1 39N09 75w31 5:02:04
Northwood 2 1 39N48 75w31 5:02:04
Nottingham Green 2 10 39N41 75w43 5:02:52
Oak Grove 1 1 39N09 75w31 5:02:04
Oak Grove 2 1 39N45 75w35 5:02:20
Oak Grove 3 16 38N37 75w39 5:02:36
Oak Hill 2 1 39N45 75w35 5:02:20
Oak Lane Manor 2 1 39N48 75w31 5:02:04
Oakmont 2 1 39N41 75w34 5:02:16
Oak Orchard 3 16 38N35 75w17 5:01:08
Ocean View 3 16 38N33 75w05 5:00:20
Odessa 2 12 39N27 75w39 5:02:36
Ogletown 2 10 39N41 75w43 5:02:52
Omar 3 4 38N31 75w14 5:00:56
Overlook 2 1 39N48 75w28 5:01:52
Overview Gardens 2 1 39N41 75w34 5:02:16
Owls Nest Estates 2 1 39N46 75w35 5:02:20
Palm Spring Manor 2 10 39N41 75w43 5:02:52
Paris Villa 1 6 39N04 75w28 5:01:52
Pembrey 2 1 39N48 75w31 5:02:04
Penarth 2 1 39N48 75w31 5:02:04
Penn Acres 2 1 39N41 75w34 5:02:16
Pennrock 2 1 39N46 75w30 5:02:00
Penny Hill 2 1 39N47 75w30 5:02:00
Perry Park 2 1 39N45 75w33 5:02:12
Perth 2 1 39N48 75w31 5:02:04
Petersburg 1 3 39N02 75w34 5:02:16
Phillips Hill 3 16 38N35 75w17 5:01:08
Pickering Beach 1 1 39N09 75w31 5:02:04
Piedmont 2 12 39N47 75w39 5:02:36
Pilottown 3 16 38N47 75w09 5:00:36
Pinetown 3 16 38N47 75w09 5:00:36
Pine Tree Corners 2 14 39N24 75w41 5:02:44
Piney Grove 3 4 38N41 75w23 5:01:32
Pleasant Hill 2 1 39N43 75w37 5:02:28
Pleasanton Acres 1 1 39N09 75w31 5:02:04
Pleasantville 2 10 39N40 75w38 5:02:32
Plymouth 1 3 39N00 75w35 5:02:20
Point Breeze 2 14 39N24 75w41 5:02:44
Polly Drummond 2 10 39N41 75w43 5:02:52
Porter 2 12 39N38 75w40 5:02:40
Port Mahon 1 1 39N09 75w31 5:02:04
Port Penn 2 12 39N31 75w35 5:02:20
Portsville 3 2 38N33 75w34 5:02:16
Prime Hook Beach 1 9 38N55 75w22 5:01:28
Quakertown 3 16 38N47 75w09 5:00:36
Radnor Green 2 1 39N48 75w28 5:01:52
Radnor Woods 2 1 39N48 75w28 5:01:52
Rambleton Acres 2 1 39N41 75w34 5:02:16
Ramblewood 2 1 39N45 75w33 5:02:12
Redden 3 4 38N41 75w23 5:01:32
Red Lion 2 15 39N35 75w38 5:02:32
Reeves Crossing 1 3 39N00 75w35 5:02:20
Rehoboth Beach 3 3 38N43 75w05 5:00:20
Rehoboth Manor 3 3 38N43 75w05 5:00:20
Reliance 3 16 38N37 75w39 5:02:36
Richardson Park 2 1 39N43 75w37 5:02:28
Rising Sun 1 1 39N07 75w33 5:02:12
Riverdale 3 16 38N35 75w17 5:01:08
Riverside Gardens 2 1 39N48 75w28 5:01:52
Rockland 2 1 39N48 75w34 5:02:16
Rodney Village 1 1 39N07 75w32 5:02:08
Rodric Village 1 1 39N09 75w31 5:02:04
Rogers Haven 3 16 38N33 75w07 5:00:28
Rogers Manor 2 1 39N41 75w34 5:02:16
Rolling Hills 2 1 39N43 75w37 5:02:28
Rolling Park 2 1 39N48 75w28 5:01:52
Rosedale Beach 3 16 38N35 75w17 5:01:08
Rose Gate 2 1 39N41 75w34 5:02:16
Rose Hill 2 1 39N41 75w34 5:02:16
Rose Hill Gardens 2 1 39N41 75w34 5:02:16
Roselle 2 1 39N45 75w35 5:02:20
Roseville Park 2 10 39N42 75w43 5:02:52
Roxana 3 4 38N31 75w14 5:00:56
Rutherford 2 10 39N41 75w43 5:02:52

DELAWARE

Saint Georges 2 12 39N33 75w39 5:02:36
Sandtown 1 3 39N00 75w35 5:02:20
Scottfield 2 10 39N41 75w43 5:02:52
Seabreeze 3 16 38N43 75w05 5:00:20
Seaford 3 2 38N39 75w37 5:02:28
Seaford Heights 3 2 38N37 75w39 5:02:36
Sedgley Farms 2 1 39N46 75w35 5:02:20
Seeneytown 1 2 39N17 75w38 5:02:32
Selbyville 3 3 38N28 75w14 5:00:56
Shady Lane 1 1 39N09 75w31 5:02:04
Sharpley 2 1 39N48 75w31 5:02:04
Shawtown 2 1 39N41 75w34 5:02:16
Shellburne 2 1 39N48 75w31 5:02:04
Sherwood 1 1 39N09 75w31 5:02:04
Sherwood Park 2 1 39N44 75w39 5:02:36
Shortly 3 4 38N41 75w23 5:01:32
Silverbrook 2 1 39N45 75w35 5:02:20
Silver Lake Shores 3 16 38N43 75w05 5:00:20
Silverside Heights 2 1 39N46 75w30 5:02:00
Silview 2 1 39N43 75w37 5:02:28
Simonds Gardens 2 1 39N41 75w34 5:02:16
Slaughter Beach 3 6 38N54 75w18 5:01:12
Slaytonville 3 16 38N55 75w35 5:02:20
Smyrna 1 11 39N18 75w36 5:02:24
Snug Harbor 3 16 38N37 75w39 5:02:36
South Bethany 3 16 38N32 75w04 5:00:16
South Bowers 1 9 38N55 75w22 5:01:28
South Dover Acres 1 1 39N09 75w31 5:02:04
Stanton 2 1 39N43 75w39 5:02:36
Star Hill 1 1 39N09 75w31 5:02:04
Staytonville 3 16 38N55 75w35 5:02:20
Stockdale 2 1 39N48 75w28 5:01:52
Stockly 3 4 38N41 75w23 5:01:32
Stockton 2 1 39N41 75w34 5:02:16
Stratford 2 1 39N41 75w34 5:02:16
Surrey Park 2 1 39N48 75w31 5:02:04
Sussex Shores 3 16 38N32 75w04 5:00:16
Swann Keys 3 3 38N28 75w13 5:00:52
Swanwyck 2 1 39N41 75w34 5:02:16
Swanwyck Estates 2 1 39N41 75w34 5:02:16
Swanwyck Gardens 2 1 39N41 75w34 5:02:16
Sycamore 3 2 38N33 75w34 5:02:16
Sycamore Gardens 2 10 39N41 75w43 5:02:52
Talleyville 2 1 39N48 75w33 5:02:12
Tanglewood 2 10 39N41 75w43 5:02:52
Tarleton 2 1 39N48 75w31 5:02:04
Taylor Estates 1 1 39N09 75w31 5:02:04
Taylors Bridge 2 14 39N24 75w41 5:02:44
The Beeches 1 1 39N09 75w31 5:02:04
The Cedars 2 1 39N44 75w39 5:02:36
The Island 3 16 38N37 75w39 5:02:36
The Timbers 2 1 39N48 75w31 5:02:04
Thompsonville 1 9 38N55 75w22 5:01:28
Tidbury Manor 1 1 39N09 75w31 5:02:04
Todd Estates 2 10 39N41 75w43 5:02:52
Tower Trailer Park 2 1 39N48 75w28 5:01:52
Towne Point 1 1 39N09 75w31 5:02:04
Townsend 2 14 39N24 75w41 5:02:44
Tuxedo Park 2 1 39N43 75w37 5:02:28
Tybrook 2 1 39N44 75w39 5:02:36
Union Street 2 1 39N45 75w35 5:02:20
Upper Christiana 2 10 39N41 75w41 5:02:44
Vagabond Trailer Park 2 1 39N48 75w28 5:01:52
Valley Run 2 1 39N45 75w33 5:02:12
Van Dyke Village 2 1 39N41 75w34 5:02:16
Vernon 1 16 38N55 75w35 5:02:20
Village of Drummond Hill 2 10 39N41 75w43 5:02:52
Villa Monterey 2 1 39N46 75w30 5:02:00
Viola 1 3 39N02 75w34 5:02:16
Voshels Cove 1 1 39N09 75w31 5:02:04
Washington Heights 3 16 38N43 75w05 5:00:20
Washington Park 2 1 39N41 75w34 5:02:16
Webb Manor 3 9 38N55 75w22 5:01:28
Webster Farms 2 1 39N48 75w31 5:02:04
Wedgewood Acres 2 1 39N41 75w34 5:02:16
Weisman Acres 3 9 38N55 75w22 5:01:28
Welshire 2 1 39N48 75w31 5:02:04
West Beach 3 4 38N33 75w15 5:01:00
Westfield 2 1 39N43 75w37 5:02:28
West Haven 2 1 39N46 75w35 5:02:20
West Meadow 2 10 39N41 75w43 5:02:52
Westover Hills 2 1 39N46 75w35 5:02:20
West Park 2 1 39N46 75w35 5:02:20
Westview 2 1 39N43 75w37 5:02:28
Westwood Manor 2 1 39N45 75w33 5:02:12
Whiteleysburg 1 3 39N00 75w35 5:02:20
White Oak Farms 1 1 39N09 75w31 5:02:04
Whitesville 3 4 38N27 75w35 5:02:20
Williamsville 1 4 38N55 75w30 5:02:00
Williamsville 3 3 38N28 75w13 5:00:52
Willow Grove 1 1 39N07 75w33 5:02:12
Willow Run 2 1 39N45 75w35 5:02:20
Wilmington 2 1 39N45 75w33 5:02:12
Wilmington Manor Gardens 2 1 39N41 75w34 5:02:16
Wilmont 2 1 39N45 75w33 5:02:12
Windermer 2 1 39N43 75w37 5:02:28
Windy Bush 2 1 39N45 75w33 5:02:12
Windy Hills 2 10 39N41 75w43 5:02:52
Winterthur 2 1 39N48 75w36 5:02:24
Woodbine 2 1 39N48 75w31 5:02:04
Woodbrook 1 1 39N09 75w31 5:02:04
Woodbrook 2 1 39N48 75w31 5:02:04
Woodcrest 1 1 39N09 75w31 5:02:04
Woodcrest 2 1 39N43 75w37 5:02:28
Wooddale 2 1 39N46 75w35 5:02:20
Woodenhawk 3 7 38N48 75w36 5:02:24
Woodland 3 16 38N37 75w39 5:02:36
Woodland Beach 1 11 39N18 75w36 5:02:24
Woodland Homes 2 1 39N43 75w37 5:02:28
Woods Haven 1 9 38N55 75w22 5:01:28
Woodside 1 3 39N04 75w34 5:02:16
Woodside Hills 2 1 39N46 75w30 5:02:00
Woods Manor 1 1 39N09 75w31 5:02:04
Worthland 2 1 39N48 75w28 5:01:52
Wyoming 1 1 39N07 75w33 5:02:12
York Beach 3 16 38N32 75w04 5:00:16
Yorklyn 2 12 39N49 75w41 5:02:44

DISTRICT OF COLUMBIA

TIME TABLES

Before 3/13/1884		LMT	9/28/1947	02:00	EST	4/30/1953	02:00	EDT	10/26/1958	02:00	EST	4/26/1964	02:00	EDT
3/13/1884	12:00	EST	5/02/1948	02:00	EDT	9/27/1953	02:00	EST	4/26/1959	02:00	EDT	10/25/1964	02:00	EST
3/31/1918	02:00	EWT	9/26/1948	02:00	EST	4/25/1954	02:00	EDT	10/25/1959	02:00	EST	4/25/1965	02:00	EDT
10/27/1918	02:00	EST	4/24/1949	02:00	EDT	9/26/1954	02:00	EST	4/24/1960	02:00	EDT	10/31/1965	02:00	EST
3/30/1919	02:00	EWT	9/25/1949	02:00	EST	4/24/1955	02:00	EDT	10/30/1960	02:00	EST	4/24/1966	02:00	EDT
10/26/1919	02:00	EST	5/04/1950	02:00	EDT	9/25/1955	02:00	EST	4/30/1961	02:00	EDT	10/30/1966	02:00	EST
5/02/1922	02:00	EDT	9/24/1950	02:00	EST	4/29/1956	02:00	EDT	10/29/1961	02:00	EST	4/30/1967	02:00	US#1
9/04/1922	02:00	EST	4/29/1951	02:00	EDT	10/28/1956	02:00	EST	4/29/1962	02:00	EDT			
2/09/1942	02:00	EWT	9/30/1951	02:00	EST	4/28/1957	02:00	EDT	10/28/1962	02:00	EST			
9/30/1945	02:00	EST	4/27/1952	02:00	EDT	10/27/1957	02:00	EST	4/28/1963	02:00	EDT			
5/11/1947	02:00	EDT	9/28/1952	02:00	EST	4/27/1958	02:00	EDT	10/27/1963	02:00	EST			

COUNTIES

1 Washington

Anacostia 1	38N52	76W59	5:07:56
Benjamin Franklin 1	38N53	77W00	5:08:00
Benning 1	38N53	76W56	5:07:44
Bolling Air Force Base 1	38N51	77W01	5:08:04
Brightwood 1	38N57	77W01	5:08:04
Brookland 1	38N56	77W00	5:08:00
Calvert 1	38N55	77W04	5:08:16
Capitol Building 1	38N53	77W01	5:08:04
Cardinal 1	38N56	77W00	5:08:00
Cleveland Park 1	38N56	77W03	5:08:12
Columbia Heights 1	38N55	77W02	5:08:08
Congress Heights 1	38N50	77W00	5:08:00
Customs House 1	38N56	76W59	5:07:56
Eagle 1	38N57	77W06	5:08:24
Fort Davis 1	38N52	76W59	5:07:56
Friendship 1	38N57	77W06	5:08:24
Georgetown 1	38N55	77W04	5:08:16
Hoya 1	38N55	77W04	5:08:16
Kendall Green 1	38N54	77W00	5:08:00
L'Enfant Plaza 1	38N53	77W01	5:08:04
Naval Research Laboratory 1	38N52	77W00	5:08:00
Naval Station 1	38N52	77W00	5:08:00
Palisades 1	38N57	77W06	5:08:24
Petworth 1	38N57	77W01	5:08:04
Randle 1	38N52	76W59	5:07:56
State Department 1	38N53	77W00	5:08:00
Temple Heights 1	38N55	77W02	5:08:08
Treasury 1	38N53	77W00	5:08:00
Truxton Circle 1	38N54	77W00	5:08:00
Walter Reed 1	38N59	77W01	5:08:04
Washington 1	38N54	77W02	5:08:08
Watergate 1	38N54	77W03	5:08:12
West End 1	38N54	77W03	5:08:12
White House 1	38N54	77W02	5:08:08
Woodley Road 1	38N56	77W03	5:08:12
Woodridge 1	38N56	76W59	5:07:56

FLORIDA

TIME TABLES

FL # 1

Before 5/30/1889		LMT
5/30/1889	12:00	CST
3/31/1918	02:00	CWT
10/27/1918	02:00	CST
3/30/1919	02:00	CWT
10/26/1919	02:00	CST
2/09/1942	02:00	CWT
9/30/1945	02:00	CST
4/30/1967	02:00	US#1

FL # 2

Before 5/30/1889		LMT
5/30/1889	12:00	CST
3/31/1918	02:00	CWT
10/27/1918	02:00	CST
3/30/1919	02:00	CWT
10/26/1919	02:00	CST
2/09/1942	02:00	CWT
9/30/1945	02:00	CST
4/28/1946	02:00	CDT
9/29/1946	02:00	CST
4/27/1947	02:00	CDT
9/28/1947	02:00	CST
4/25/1948	02:00	CDT
9/26/1948	02:00	CST
4/24/1949	02:00	CDT
9/25/1949	02:00	CST
4/30/1950	02:00	CDT
9/24/1950	02:00	CST
4/29/1951	02:00	CDT
9/30/1951	02:00	CST
4/27/1952	02:00	CDT
9/28/1952	02:00	CST
4/26/1953	02:00	CDT
9/27/1953	02:00	CST
4/25/1954	02:00	CDT
9/26/1954	02:00	CST
4/24/1955	02:00	CDT
9/25/1955	02:00	CST
4/29/1956	02:00	CDT
10/28/1956	02:00	CST
4/28/1957	02:00	CDT
10/27/1957	02:00	CST
4/27/1958	02:00	CDT
10/26/1958	02:00	CST
4/26/1959	02:00	CDT
10/25/1959	02:00	CST
4/24/1960	02:00	CDT
10/30/1960	02:00	CST
4/30/1961	02:00	CDT
10/29/1961	02:00	CST
4/29/1962	02:00	CDT
10/28/1962	02:00	CST
4/28/1963	02:00	CDT
10/27/1963	02:00	CST
4/26/1964	02:00	CDT
10/25/1964	02:00	CST
4/25/1965	02:00	CDT
10/31/1965	02:00	CST
4/30/1967	02:00	US#1

FL # 3

Before 5/30/1889		LMT
5/30/1889	12:00	CST
3/31/1918	02:00	CWT
10/27/1918	02:00	CST
3/30/1919	02:00	CWT
10/26/1919	02:00	CST
4/27/1941	02:00	CDT
9/28/1941	02:00	CST
2/09/1942	02:00	CWT
9/30/1945	02:00	CST
4/28/1946	02:00	CDT
9/29/1946	02:00	CST
5/04/1947	02:00	CDT
9/28/1947	02:00	CST
4/25/1948	02:00	CDT
9/26/1948	02:00	CST
4/24/1949	02:00	CDT
9/25/1949	02:00	CST
4/30/1950	02:00	CDT
9/24/1950	02:00	CST
4/29/1951	02:00	CDT
9/30/1951	02:00	CST
4/27/1952	02:00	CDT
9/28/1952	02:00	CST
4/26/1953	02:00	CDT
9/27/1953	02:00	CST
4/25/1954	02:00	CDT
9/26/1954	02:00	CST
4/24/1955	02:00	CDT
10/30/1955	02:00	CST
4/29/1956	02:00	CDT
10/28/1956	02:00	CST
4/28/1957	02:00	CDT
10/27/1957	02:00	CST
4/27/1958	02:00	CDT
9/01/1958	02:00	CST
4/26/1959	02:00	CDT
10/25/1959	02:00	CST
4/24/1960	02:00	CDT
10/30/1960	02:00	CST
4/30/1961	02:00	CDT
10/29/1961	02:00	CST
4/29/1962	02:00	CDT
10/28/1962	02:00	CST
4/28/1963	02:00	CDT
10/27/1963	02:00	CST
4/26/1964	02:00	CDT
10/25/1964	02:00	CST
4/25/1965	02:00	CDT
10/31/1965	02:00	CST
4/30/1967	02:00	US#1

FL # 4

Before 5/30/1889		LMT
5/30/1889	12:00	CST
3/31/1918	02:00	CWT
10/27/1918	02:00	CST
3/30/1919	02:00	CWT
10/26/1919	02:00	CST
4/26/1931	02:00	CDT
9/27/1931	02:00	CST
4/27/1941	02:00	CDT
9/28/1941	02:00	CST
2/09/1942	02:00	CWT
9/30/1945	02:00	CST
4/28/1946	02:00	CDT
9/29/1946	02:00	CST
5/04/1947	02:00	CDT
9/28/1947	02:00	CST
4/25/1948	02:00	CDT
9/26/1948	02:00	CST
4/24/1949	02:00	CDT
9/25/1949	02:00	CST
4/30/1950	02:00	CDT
9/24/1950	02:00	CST
4/29/1951	02:00	CDT
9/30/1951	02:00	CST
4/27/1952	02:00	CDT
9/28/1952	02:00	CST
4/26/1953	02:00	CDT
9/27/1953	02:00	CST
4/25/1954	02:00	CDT
9/26/1954	02:00	CST
4/24/1955	02:00	CDT
10/30/1955	02:00	CST
4/29/1956	02:00	CDT
10/28/1956	02:00	CST
4/28/1957	02:00	CDT
10/27/1957	02:00	CST
4/27/1958	02:00	CDT
9/01/1958	02:00	CST
4/26/1959	02:00	CDT
10/25/1959	02:00	CST
4/24/1960	02:00	CDT
10/30/1960	02:00	CST
4/30/1961	02:00	CDT
10/29/1961	02:00	CST
4/29/1962	02:00	CDT
10/28/1962	02:00	CST
4/28/1963	02:00	CDT
10/27/1963	02:00	CST
4/26/1964	02:00	CDT
10/25/1964	02:00	CST
4/25/1965	02:00	CDT
10/31/1965	02:00	CST
4/30/1967	02:00	US#1

FL # 5

Before 5/30/1889		LMT
5/30/1889	12:00	CST
3/31/1918	02:00	CWT
10/27/1918	02:00	CST
1/01/1919	02:00	EST
3/30/1919	02:00	EWT
10/26/1919	02:00	EST
2/09/1942	02:00	EWT
9/30/1945	02:00	EST
4/30/1967	02:00	US#1

FL # 6

Before 5/30/1889		LMT
5/30/1889	12:00	CST
3/31/1918	02:00	CWT
10/27/1918	02:00	CST
1/01/1919	02:00	EST
3/30/1919	02:00	EWT
10/26/1919	02:00	EST
2/09/1942	02:00	EWT
9/30/1945	02:00	EST
4/28/1946	02:00	EDT
9/29/1946	02:00	EST
4/30/1967	02:00	US#1

COUNTIES

1 Alachua
2 Baker
3 Bay
4 Bradford
5 Brevard
6 Broward
7 Calhoun
8 Charlotte
9 Citrus
10 Clay
11 Collier
12 Columbia
13 Dade
14 De Soto
15 Dixie
16 Duval
17 Escambia
18 Flagler
19 Franklin
20 Gadsden
21 Gilchrist
22 Glades
23 Gulf
24 Hamilton
25 Hardee
26 Hendry
27 Hernando
28 Highlands
29 Hillsborough
30 Holmes
31 Indian River
32 Jackson
33 Jefferson
34 Lafayette
35 Lake
36 Lee
37 Leon
38 Levy
39 Liberty
40 Madison
41 Manatee
42 Marion
43 Martin
44 Monroe
45 Nassau
46 Okaloosa
47 Okeechobee
48 Orange
49 Osceola
50 Palm Beach
51 Pasco
52 Pinellas
53 Polk
54 Putnam
55 St Johns
56 St Lucie
57 Santa Rosa
58 Sarasota
59 Seminole
60 Sumter
61 Suwannee
62 Taylor
63 Union
64 Volusia
65 Wakulla
66 Walton
67 Washington

Acline 8	5	26N57	82w00	5:28:00
Acres of Diamond 5	5	28N05	80w38	5:22:32
Adamsville 29	5	27N51	82w23	5:29:32
Airport 13	6	25N48	80w15	5:21:00
Airport Siding 16	5	30N27	81w34	5:26:16
Alachua 1	5	29N47	82w30	5:30:00
Aladdin City 13	5	25N29	80w30	5:22:00
Alafia 29	5	28N01	82w08	5:28:32
Alameda 13	6	25N46	80w19	5:21:16
Alaqua 66	1	30N43	86w07	5:44:28
Alderman Park 16	5	30N20	81w35	5:26:20
Alford 32	1	30N42	85w24	5:41:36
Allandale 64	5	29N13	81w02	5:24:08
Allanton 3	1	30N09	85w39	5:42:36
Allapattah 13	6	25N50	80w14	5:20:56
Allentown 57	1	30N39	87w05	5:48:20
Alliance 32	1	30N37	85w07	5:40:28
Alligator Lake 49	5	28N15	81w17	5:25:08
Alligator Point Marina 19	5	30N11	84w23	5:37:32
Altamonte Springs 59	5	28N40	81w24	5:25:36
Alta Vista 8	5	26N57	82w00	5:28:00
Altha 7	1	30N34	85w08	5:40:32
Alton 34	5	30N03	83w08	5:32:32
Altoona 35	5	28N58	81w39	5:26:36
Altschul 20	5	30N37	84w25	5:37:40
Alturas 53	5	27N52	81w43	5:26:52
Alva 36	5	26N43	81w37	5:26:28
Amelia City 45	5	30N35	81w28	5:25:52
American Beach 45	5	30N34	81w27	5:25:48
Anastasia 55	5	29N48	81w16	5:25:04
Anclote 51	5	28N15	82w45	5:31:00
Anclote Acres 51	5	28N13	82w43	5:30:52
Andalusia 18	5	29N28	81w15	5:25:00
Andover Golf Estates 13	6	25N56	80w13	5:20:52
Andover Lake Estates 13	6	25N56	80w13	5:20:52
Angel City 5	5	28N20	80w40	5:22:40
Angler Park 44	5	25N08	80w25	5:21:40
Ankona	5	27N21	80w17	5:21:08
Anna Maria 41	5	27N32	82w44	5:30:56
Anona 52	5	27N53	82w46	5:31:04
Anthony 42	5	29N18	82w07	5:28:28
Antioch 29	5	28N01	82w08	5:28:32
Apalachicola 19	5	29N43	84w59	5:39:56
Apollo Beach 29	5	27N46	82w24	5:29:36
Apopka 48	5	28N40	81w31	5:26:04
Araguey Park 55	5	29N48	81w16	5:25:04
Arcadia 14	5	27N13	81w52	5:27:28
Arcadia West 14	5	27N38	82w08	5:28:32
Archer 1	5	29N32	82w32	5:30:08
Argyle 66	1	30N43	86w02	5:44:08
Ariel	5	28N54	80w52	5:23:28
Aripeka 51	5	28N26	82w40	5:30:40
Arlington 16	5	30N20	81w36	5:26:24
Arlington Green 16	5	30N20	81w35	5:26:20
Arlington Heights 16	5	30N20	81w35	5:26:20
Arlington Park 6	6	26N18	80w10	5:20:40
Arlingwood 16	5	30N20	81w35	5:26:20
Armstrong 55	5	29N46	81w27	5:25:48
Arran 65	5	30N11	84w23	5:37:32
Arredondo	5	29N36	82w25	5:29:40
Ashton 49	5	28N15	81w17	5:25:08
Ashville 33	5	30N28	83w38	5:34:32
Astatula 35	5	28N43	81w44	5:26:56
Astor 35	5	29N10	81w32	5:26:08
Astor Park 35	5	29N09	81w34	5:26:16
Astronaut Trail 5	5	28N36	80w49	5:23:16
Athena 62	5	29N59	83w30	5:34:00
Atlantic Beach 16	5	30N20	81w24	5:25:36
Atlantic Boulevard Estates 16	5	30N20	81w35	5:26:20
Atlantic Heights 13	6	25N48	80w09	5:20:36
Atlantis 50	6	26N37	80w06	5:20:24
Auburn 46	1	30N49	86w32	5:46:08
Auburndale 53	5	28N04	81w48	5:27:12
Aucilla 33	5	30N33	83w52	5:35:28
Audubon 5	5	28N14	80w40	5:22:40
Aurantia 5	5	28N36	80w49	5:23:16
Auxiliary Field No. 9 46	1	30N26	86w37	5:46:28
Avalon Beach 57	1	30N39	87w05	5:48:20
Avondale 16	5	30N20	81w41	5:26:44
Avon Park 28	5	27N36	81w31	5:26:04
Avon Park Lakes 28	5	27N36	81w30	5:26:00
Azalea Park 48	5	28N35	81w18	5:25:12
Azalea Terrace 16	5	30N17	81w35	5:26:20
Babson Park 53	5	27N49	81w32	5:26:08
Bagdad 57	3	30N36	87w02	5:48:08
Bahama Beach 3	1	30N09	85w39	5:42:36
Bahia Beach 29	5	27N44	82w24	5:29:36
Bahia-mar 6	6	26N05	80w09	5:20:36
Bahoma 67	1	30N47	85w32	5:42:08
Baker 3	1	30N09	85w39	5:42:36
Baker 46	1	30N48	86w41	5:46:44
Baker Settlement 30	1	30N46	85w51	5:43:24
Bakers Mill 24	5	30N35	82w56	5:31:44
Bakersville 55	5	29N48	81w16	5:25:04
Baldwin 16	5	30N18	81w59	5:27:56
Bal Harbour 13	6	25N54	80w08	5:20:32
Ballantine Manor 41	5	27N20	82w32	5:30:08
Balm 29	5	27N46	82w16	5:29:04
Bamboo 60	5	28N49	81w53	5:27:32
Barberville 64	5	29N11	81w26	5:25:44
Bar Dee Homes 52	5	27N53	82w46	5:31:04
Bardin 54	5	29N39	81w39	5:26:36
Bare Beach 50	5	26N45	80w58	5:23:52
Barefoot Bay 5	5	27N47	80w29	5:21:56
Barrineau Park 17	1	30N42	87w26	5:49:44
Barry College 13	6	25N53	80w11	5:20:44
Barth 17	1	30N37	87w20	5:49:20
Bartow 53	5	27N54	81w50	5:27:20
Barwal 6	6	26N18	80w10	5:20:40
Bascom 32	1	30N56	85w07	5:40:28
Basinger 47	5	27N23	81w02	5:24:08
Baskins 52	5	27N53	82w46	5:31:04
Bassville Park 35	5	28N49	81w53	5:27:32
Bay Acres 58	5	27N12	82w30	5:30:00
Bayard 16	5	30N09	81w31	5:26:04
Bay City 19	1	29N44	85w00	5:40:00
Bay Harbor 3	1	30N09	85w39	5:42:36
Bay Harbor Islands 13	6	25N53	80w08	5:20:32
Bayhead 3	1	30N22	85w27	5:41:48
Bayhill 60	5	28N40	82w07	5:28:28
Bay Lake 35	5	28N34	81w52	5:27:28
Bay Lake 42	5	29N25	82w06	5:28:24
Bay Lake 48	5	28N33	81w23	5:25:32
Bayou George 3	1	30N16	85w33	5:42:12
Bay Pines 52	5	27N49	82w47	5:31:08
Bayport 27	5	28N32	82w39	5:30:36
Bayridge 48	5	28N41	81w28	5:25:52
Bayshore 36	5	26N43	81w50	5:27:20
Bay Shore Estates 58	5	27N04	82w20	5:29:20

 FLORIDA

Bayshore Gardens 41
5 27N26 82w35 5:30:20
Bayshore Manor 36 5 26N39 81w53 5:27:32
Bayshore Park 8 5 26N57 82w00 5:28:00
Bay Springs 17 1 31N01 87w30 5:50:00
Bayview 3 1 30N12 85w43 5:42:52
Bay Vista 52 5 27N45 82w39 5:30:36
Baywood 54 5 29N44 81w53 5:27:32
Beach 31 5 27N40 80w24 5:21:36
Beachwood 16 5 30N20 81w29 5:25:56
Beacon Hill 23 1 29N55 85w23 5:41:32
Beacon Light 6 6 26N17 80w09 5:20:36
Beacon Squier 51 5 28N13 82w45 5:31:00
Bealsville 29 5 28N01 82w08 5:28:32
Bean City 50 5 26N42 80w48 5:23:12
Bear Creek 3 1 30N09 85w39 5:42:36
Bear Head 66 1 30N43 86w07 5:44:28
Bear Lake 59 5 28N41 81w28 5:25:52
Beauclere Manor 16
5 30N14 81w38 5:26:32
Beaver Creek 46 1 30N48 86w40 5:46:40
Becker 45 5 30N40 81w38 5:26:32
Beeghly Heights 16
5 30N26 81w39 5:26:36
Bee Ridge 58 5 27N19 82w31 5:30:04
Bel Air 59 5 28N48 81w15 5:25:00
Bell 21 5 29N45 82w52 5:31:28
Bellair 10 5 30N08 81w42 5:26:48
Belleair 52 5 27N56 82w49 5:31:16
Belleair Beach 52 5 26N55 82w51 5:31:24
Belleair Bluffs 52
5 27N55 82w49 5:31:16
Belleair Shores 52
5 27N55 82w51 5:31:24
Belle Ayre Estates 35
5 28N48 81w39 5:26:36
Belle Glade 50 5 26N41 80w40 5:22:40
Belle Glade Camp 50
5 26N39 80w41 5:22:44
Belle Haven 52 5 28N00 82w46 5:31:04
Belle Isle 48 5 28N28 81w22 5:25:28
Belleview 17 4 30N26 87w17 5:49:08
Belleview 42 5 29N04 82w03 5:28:12
Belleview Heights 42
5 29N04 82w03 5:28:12
Bellwood 5 5 28N30 80w47 5:23:08
Belmont 52 5 27N56 82w46 5:31:04
Belvedere Homes 50
6 26N42 80w05 5:20:20
Benbow 22 5 26N45 80w58 5:23:52
Bennett 3 1 30N22 85w27 5:41:48
Ben's Lake 46 1 30N28 86w32 5:46:08
Benson Junction 64
5 28N53 81w18 5:25:12
Bereah 53 5 27N45 81w48 5:27:12
Beresford 64 5 29N02 81w18 5:25:12
Beresford Manor 64
5 29N02 81w18 5:25:12
Berkeley 27 5 28N30 82w36 5:30:24
Berrydale 57 1 30N53 87w03 5:48:12
Bethany 41 5 27N21 82w10 5:28:40
Bethel 65 5 30N26 84w17 5:37:08
Bethlehem 30 1 30N53 85w40 5:42:40
Bethune Beach 64 5 29N02 80w55 5:23:40
Betty Lou Beach 3 1 30N09 85w39 5:42:36
Beulah 48 5 28N34 81w35 5:26:20
Beverly Beach 18 5 29N31 81w09 5:24:36
Beverly Hills 9 5 28N51 82w29 5:29:56
Beverly Hills 16 5 30N23 81w41 5:26:44
Beverly Terrace 58
5 27N21 82w31 5:30:04
Bevilles Corner 60
5 28N40 82w07 5:28:28
Bid-a-wee 3 1 30N09 85w39 5:42:36
Big Bayou 52 5 27N47 82w40 5:30:40
Big Bend Farm 37 5 30N25 84w20 5:37:20
Big Coppitt Key 44
5 24N34 81w44 5:26:56
Big Cypress 26 5 26N45 80w58 5:23:52
Big Cypress Seminole Indian 6
6 26N01 80w13 5:20:52
Big Pine Key 44 5 24N40 81w21 5:25:24
Biltmore 16 5 30N19 81w43 5:26:52
Biltmore Beach 3 1 30N09 85w39 5:42:36
Biscayne Facility 13
6 25N47 80w13 5:20:52
Biscayne Gardens 13
6 25N54 80w13 5:20:52
Biscayne Park 13 6 25N53 80w11 5:20:44
Bithlo 48 5 28N33 81w06 5:24:24
Black Acres 1 5 29N40 82w20 5:29:20
Blackman 46 1 30N56 86w38 5:46:32
Bland 1 5 29N47 82w30 5:30:00
Blanton 51 5 28N25 82w15 5:29:00
Blichton 42 5 29N11 82w09 5:28:36
Bloody Bluff 19 5 30N23 84w48 5:39:12
Bloomingdale 29 5 27N54 82w16 5:29:04
Blountstown 7 1 30N27 85w03 5:40:12
Bloxham 37 5 30N26 84w18 5:37:12
Blue Inlet 50 6 26N23 80w05 5:20:20
Blue Lake 64 5 29N02 81w18 5:25:12
Blue Lakes Ridge 35
5 29N00 81w32 5:26:08
Blue Mountain 66 1 30N20 86w12 5:44:48
Blue Mountain Beach 66
1 30N22 86w07 5:44:28
Blue Springs 35 5 28N44 81w49 5:27:16
Blue Springs 64 5 28N55 81w17 5:25:08
Bluff Springs 17 1 30N56 87w17 5:49:08
Boardman 42 5 29N30 82w14 5:28:56
Boca Chica 44 5 24N34 81w42 5:26:48
Boca Ciega 52 5 27N51 82w48 5:31:12
Boca Grande 36 5 26N45 82w16 5:29:04
Boca Harbour 50 6 26N23 80w05 5:20:20
Boca Raton 50 6 26N21 80w05 5:20:20
Bogia 17 1 30N51 87w19 5:49:16
Bokeelia 36 5 26N42 82w10 5:28:40
Bonifay 30 1 30N47 85w41 5:42:44
Bonita Beach 36 5 26N20 81w47 5:27:08
Bonita Shores 11 5 26N20 81w47 5:27:08
Bonita Springs 36 5 26N21 81w47 5:27:08
Bookertown 59 5 28N48 81w15 5:25:00
Bostwick 54 5 29N46 81w38 5:26:32
Botts 57 1 30N39 87w05 5:48:20
Boulevard 52 5 28N00 82w46 5:31:04
Boulogne 45 5 30N47 81w59 5:27:56
Bowden 16 5 30N17 81w35 5:26:20
Bowling Green 25 5 27N38 81w50 5:27:20
Boyd 5 30N11 83w37 5:34:28
Boynton Beach 50 6 26N32 80w04 5:20:16
Boys Ranch 61 5 30N18 82w59 5:31:56
Braden Castle 41 5 27N28 82w35 5:30:20
Bradenton 41 5 27N30 82w34 5:30:16
Bradenton Beach 41
5 27N29 82w42 5:30:48
Bradford 67 1 30N47 85w32 5:42:08
Bradfordville 37 5 30N34 84w13 5:36:52
Bradley 53 5 27N48 81w59 5:27:56
Brandon 29 5 27N55 82w17 5:29:08
Branford 61 5 29N58 82w56 5:31:44
Brannonville 3 1 30N09 85w39 5:42:36
Braswells 33 5 30N33 83w52 5:35:28
Bratt 17 1 30N58 87w26 5:49:44
Breezeswept Park Estates 6
6 26N07 80w13 5:20:52
Brent 17 4 30N26 87w15 5:49:00
Brentwood 16 5 30N23 81w41 5:26:44
Brentwood Estates 6
6 26N09 80w12 5:20:48
Bright 13 6 25N50 80w17 5:21:08
Brighton 28 5 27N14 81w06 5:24:24
Brighton Indian Reservation 22
6 26N01 80w13 5:20:52
Briney Breezes 6 26N31 80w03 5:20:12
Bristol 39 5 30N26 84w59 5:39:56
Broadview Country Club Estat 6
6 26N09 80w13 5:20:52
Broadview Park 6 6 26N07 80w13 5:20:52
Bronson 38 5 29N27 82w39 5:30:36
Brooker 4 5 29N54 82w18 5:29:12
Brooklyn 16 5 30N20 81w41 5:26:44
Brooksville 27 5 28N33 82w23 5:29:32
Brooksville West 27
5 28N31 82w29 5:29:56
Browardale 6 6 26N08 80w14 5:20:56
Broward Highlands 6
6 26N18 80w10 5:20:40
Brownsdale 57 1 30N57 87w09 5:48:36
Browns Still 63 5 30N01 82w20 5:29:20
Browns Village 13 6 25N49 80w14 5:20:56
Brownsville 13 6 25N49 80w14 5:20:56
Brownsville 17 4 30N26 87w15 5:49:00
Browntown 32 1 30N58 85w31 5:42:04
Brownville 14 5 27N13 81w52 5:27:28
Bruce 66 1 30N28 85w58 5:43:52
Bryant 50 5 26N49 80w40 5:22:40
Bryceville 45 5 30N23 81w56 5:27:44
Brynwood 36 5 26N36 81w52 5:27:28
Buccaneer Estates 13
6 25N55 80w15 5:21:00
Buchanan 25 5 27N29 81w48 5:27:12
Buckhorn 65 5 30N04 84w30 5:38:00
Buckingham 36 5 26N39 81w50 5:27:20
Buena Vista 13 6 25N49 80w12 5:20:48
Buena Vista 51 5 28N11 82w45 5:31:00
Bunche Park 13 6 25N55 80w15 5:21:00
Bunker 14 5 27N13 81w52 5:27:28
Bunnell 18 5 29N28 81w16 5:25:04
Burbank 42 5 29N22 81w58 5:27:52
Bushnell 60 5 28N40 82w07 5:28:28
Byrnville 17 1 30N58 87w16 5:49:04
Calhoun West 7 1 30N26 85w16 5:41:04
Callahan 45 5 30N34 81w50 5:27:20
Callaway 3 1 30N08 85w35 5:42:20
Camellia Gardens 48
5 28N29 81w22 5:25:28
Cameron City 59 5 28N48 81w15 5:25:00
Campbell 49 5 28N18 81w25 5:25:40
Campbellton 32 1 30N57 85w24 5:41:36
Camp Blanding 10 5 29N57 82w06 5:28:24
Camp Roosevelt 42 5 29N11 82w09 5:28:36
Camps Mine 27 5 28N32 82w29 5:29:56
Campton 46 1 30N53 86w31 5:46:04
Campville 1 5 29N40 82w07 5:28:28
Canaan 59 5 28N48 81w15 5:25:00
Canal Point 50 5 26N52 80w38 5:22:32
Candler 42 5 29N04 81w58 5:27:52
Cannon Town 46 1 30N51 86w41 5:46:44
Canova Beach 5 5 28N08 80w35 5:22:20
Cantonment 17 1 30N37 87w20 5:49:20
Cape Canaveral 5 5 28N24 80w36 5:22:24
Cape Coral 36 5 26N34 81w57 5:27:48
Cape Haze 8 5 26N50 82w16 5:29:04
Cape Sable 44 5 25N33 81w01 5:24:04
Cape Vista 41 5 27N28 82w35 5:30:20
Capitola 37 5 30N27 84w05 5:36:20
Capps 33 5 30N25 83w55 5:35:40
Captiva 36 5 26N31 82w11 5:28:44
Caribbean Key 50 6 26N23 80w05 5:20:20
Carleton 54 5 29N36 82w05 5:28:20
Carl Fisher 13 6 25N48 80w09 5:20:36
Carlton 52 5 28N00 82w46 5:31:04
Carlton Village 35
5 28N49 81w53 5:27:32
Carol City 13 6 25N56 80w16 5:21:04
Carr 7 1 30N34 85w08 5:40:32
Carrabelle 19 5 29N51 84w40 5:38:40
Carrabelle Beach 19
5 29N51 84w40 5:38:40
Carraway 54 5 29N39 81w39 5:26:36
Carrollwood 29 5 28N04 82w29 5:29:56
Carters 53 5 28N03 81w56 5:27:44
Carver 16 5 30N22 81w41 5:26:44
Carver Heights 6 6 26N18 80w10 5:20:40
Carver Ranch Estates 6
6 25N59 80w12 5:20:48
Carver Village 6 6 26N15 80w09 5:20:36
Caryville 67 1 30N41 85w47 5:43:08
Casa Blanco 33 5 30N33 83w52 5:35:28
Cassadaga 64 5 28N58 81w14 5:24:56
Casselberry 59 5 28N40 81w20 5:25:20
Cassia 35 5 28N51 81w41 5:26:44
Cassia Station 35 5 28N49 81w34 5:26:16
Cecil Field Naval Air Statio 16
5 30N19 81w39 5:26:36
Cedar Grove 3 1 30N10 85w37 5:42:28
Cedar Hammock 41 5 27N28 82w35 5:30:20
Cedar Hills 16 5 30N16 81w43 5:26:52
Cedar Key 38 5 29N08 83w02 5:32:08
Cedar Point 16 5 30N26 81w39 5:26:36
Center City 52 5 27N53 82w46 5:31:04
Center Hill 60 5 28N39 82w00 5:28:00
Central Pasco 51 5 28N18 82w24 5:29:36
Central Volusia 64
5 29N06 81w06 5:24:24
Century 17 1 30N58 87w16 5:49:04
Century 21 36 5 26N36 81w52 5:27:28
Century Corners 50
6 26N42 80w05 5:20:20
Cerrogordo 30 1 30N46 85w51 5:43:24
Chain o'Lakes 35 5 29N00 81w32 5:26:08
Chaires 37 5 30N26 84w07 5:36:28
Chaires Cross Roads 37
5 30N26 84w17 5:37:08
Channell 35 5 28N48 81w39 5:26:36
Charlotte Beach 5 26N56 82w14 5:28:56
Charlotte Harbor 8
5 26N57 82w00 5:28:00
Charlotte Park 8 5 26N57 82w00 5:28:00
Chaseville 16 5 30N20 81w35 5:26:20
Chassahowitzka 9 5 28N43 82w34 5:30:16
Chatmar 42 5 29N03 82w27 5:29:48
Chattahoochee 20 5 30N42 84w51 5:39:24
Cherry Lake 40 5 30N28 83w25 5:33:40
Chester 45 5 30N38 81w36 5:26:24
Chiefland 38 5 29N29 82w52 5:31:28
Chipley 67 1 30N47 85w32 5:42:08
Chipola 7 1 30N34 85w08 5:40:32
Chipola 32 1 30N47 85w14 5:40:56
Chipola Park 7 1 30N47 85w14 5:40:56
Choctaw 66 1 30N22 86w07 5:44:28
Choctaw Beach 46 1 30N30 86w08 5:44:32
Chokoloskee 11 5 25N49 81w22 5:25:28
Chosen 50 5 26N40 80w41 5:22:44
Chosen Labor Camp 50
5 26N40 80w41 5:22:44
Christina 53 5 28N03 81w56 5:27:44
Christmas 48 5 28N32 81w01 5:24:04
Chuluota 59 5 28N39 81w08 5:24:32
Chumuckla 57 1 30N39 87w05 5:48:20
Cinco Bayou 46 1 30N25 86w36 5:46:24
Citra 42 5 29N25 82w07 5:28:28
Citronelle 9 5 28N54 82w35 5:30:20
Citrus Center 22 5 26N50 81w06 5:24:24
Citrus Park 29 5 27N58 82w47 5:31:08
Citrus Springs 9 5 29N03 82w27 5:29:48
Citrus Tower 35 5 28N33 81w45 5:27:00
City Point 5 5 28N24 80w45 5:23:00
City View 36 5 26N36 81w52 5:27:28
Clair-Mel City 29 5 27N57 82w24 5:29:36
Clarcona 48 5 28N37 81w30 5:26:00
Clark 1 5 29N50 82w36 5:30:24
Clarksville 7 1 30N26 85w11 5:40:44
Clear Lake 1 5 29N40 82w20 5:29:20
Clear Springs 66 1 31N00 86w19 5:45:16
Clearview 52 5 27N49 82w41 5:30:44
Clearwater 52 5 27N58 82w48 5:31:12
Clearwater Beach 52
5 28N00 82w46 5:31:04
Clermont 35 5 28N32 81w45 5:27:00
Cleveland 8 5 26N58 82w00 5:28:00
Cleveland Street 52
5 27N58 82w47 5:31:08
Clewiston 26 5 26N45 80w56 5:23:44
Clifton 16 5 30N20 81w35 5:26:20
Cloud Lake 50 6 26N41 80w05 5:20:20
Coach Light Manor 36
5 26N36 81w52 5:27:28
Cobbtown 57 1 30N57 87w09 5:48:36
Cocoa 5 5 28N21 80w44 5:22:56
Cocoa Beach 5 5 28N20 80w37 5:22:28
Coconut 36 5 26N24 81w51 5:27:24
Coconut Creek 6 6 26N15 80w11 5:20:44
Coconut Grove 13 6 25N44 80w15 5:21:00
Codys Corner 18 5 29N28 81w15 5:25:00
Coldwater 57 1 30N39 87w05 5:48:20
Colee 6 6 26N08 80w11 5:20:44
Coleman 60 5 28N48 82w04 5:28:16
College Park 5 29N53 81w21 5:25:24
College Park 6 6 26N18 80w10 5:20:40
College Park 48 5 28N35 81w24 5:25:36
College Point 3 1 30N09 85w39 5:42:36
Collier City 6 6 26N15 80w09 5:20:36
Collier Manor 6 6 26N17 80w09 5:20:36
Colonial Hills 51 5 28N13 82w44 5:30:56
Colonial Manor 16 5 30N19 81w43 5:26:52
Colonialtown 48 5 28N33 81w21 5:25:24
Columbia 12 5 30N17 81w24 5:25:36
Combee Settlement 53
5 28N04 81w54 5:27:36
Compass Lake 32 1 30N36 85w24 5:41:36
Conch Key 44 5 24N49 80w49 5:23:16
Concord 20 5 30N37 84w25 5:37:40
Connersville 53 5 27N54 81w50 5:27:20
Conway 48 5 28N31 81w21 5:25:24
Cooks Hammock 34 5 29N56 83w17 5:33:08
Cooper City 6 6 26N34 80w16 5:21:04
Copeland 11 5 25N57 81w22 5:25:28

Cora 57 1 30N57 87w09 5:48:36
Coral Cove 58 5 27N15 82w31 5:30:04
Coral Estates 6 6 26N09 80w11 5:20:44
Coral Gables 13 6 25N45 80w16 5:21:04
Coral Gardens 43 5 27N12 80w15 5:21:00
Coral Heights 6 6 26N09 80w12 5:20:48
Coral Point 6 6 26N09 80w11 5:20:44
Coral Ridge 6 6 26N10 80w10 5:20:40
Coral Springs 6 6 26N16 80w15 5:21:00
Coral Way Village 13 6 25N44 80w18 5:21:12
Coral Woods 6 6 26N09 80w12 5:20:48
Corkscrew 11 5 26N25 81w25 5:25:40
Cornwell 28 5 27N23 81w06 5:24:24
Coronado 64 5 29N02 80w55 5:23:40
Coronet 29 5 27N58 82w08 5:28:32
Corry Field 17 1 30N04 87w12 5:48:48
Cortez 41 5 27N28 82w41 5:30:44
Cottage Hill 17 1 30N38 87w19 5:49:16
Cottage Point 36 5 26N36 81w52 5:27:28
Cottondale 32 1 30N48 85w23 5:41:32
Cottonplant 42 5 29N11 82w09 5:28:36
Country Club Acres 50 6 26N27 80w05 5:20:20
Country Club Estates 12 5 30N17 81w24 5:25:36
Country Club Estates 53 5 28N32 81w22 5:25:28
Country Estates 51 5 28N11 82w44 5:30:56
Courtenay 5 5 28N14 80w40 5:22:40
Cove 3 1 30N09 85w39 5:42:36
Cox 7 1 30N27 85w03 5:40:12
Coytown 48 5 28N33 81w21 5:25:24
Crackertown 38 5 29N02 82w40 5:30:40
Crawfordville 65 5 30N11 84w23 5:37:32
Crescent Beach 55 5 29N46 81w15 5:25:00
Crescent Beach 58 5 27N19 82w31 5:30:04
Crescent City 54 5 29N26 81w31 5:26:04
Cresthaven 6 6 26N17 80w09 5:20:36
Cresthaven Villas 50 6 26N40 80w06 5:20:24
Crestview 13 6 25N55 80w15 5:21:00
Crestview 46 1 30N46 86w34 5:46:16
Crewsville 25 5 27N29 81w48 5:27:12
Cross City 15 5 29N38 83w07 5:32:28
Cross Creek 1 5 29N36 82w05 5:28:20
Crown Point 48 5 28N34 81w35 5:26:20
Crows Bluff 35 5 29N00 81w23 5:25:32
Crystal Beach 5 28N05 82w47 5:31:08
Crystal Lake 53 5 28N02 81w57 5:27:48
Crystal Lake 67 1 30N38 85w35 5:42:20
Crystal River 9 5 28N54 82w35 5:30:20
Crystal Springs 51 5 28N11 82w10 5:28:40
Cubitis 14 5 27N13 81w52 5:27:28
Cudjoe 44 5 24N45 81w20 5:25:20
Cumbee 53 5 28N03 81w56 5:27:44
Curlew 52 5 28N04 82w44 5:30:56
Curtis 21 5 29N45 82w52 5:31:28
Curtis Mill 65 5 30N04 84w30 5:38:00
Cutler Ridge 13 5 25N35 80w20 5:21:20
Cypress 32 1 30N42 85w05 5:40:20
Cypress Gardens 53 5 28N01 81w42 5:26:48
Cypress Lake Estates 64 5 29N02 81w18 5:25:12
Cypress Quarters 47 5 27N15 80w49 5:23:16
Dade City 51 5 28N22 82w11 5:28:44
Dalkeith 23 1 30N00 85w09 5:40:36
Dallas 5 28N58 82w03 5:28:12
Dames Point 16 5 30N27 81w34 5:26:16
Dania 6 6 26N03 80w09 5:20:36
Dania Indian Reservation 6 6 26N01 80w13 5:20:52
Danks Corner 42 5 29N00 82w02 5:28:08
Darby 51 5 28N22 82w11 5:28:44
Darlington 66 1 30N57 86w03 5:44:12
Davenport 53 5 28N10 81w36 5:26:24
Davie 6 6 26N04 80w14 5:20:56
Day 34 5 30N12 83w17 5:33:08
Daytona Beach 64 5 29N13 81w01 5:24:04
Daytona Beach Shores 64 5 29N10 80w58 5:23:52
Daytona Highbridge Estates 64 5 29N13 81w02 5:24:08
Daytona Park Estates 64 5 29N02 81w18 5:25:12
De Bary 64 5 28N54 81w18 5:25:12
Deerfield Beach 6 6 26N19 80w06 5:20:24
Deerland 46 1 30N46 86w34 5:46:16
Deer Park 49 5 28N06 80w54 5:23:36
De Funiak Springs 66 1 30N43 86w07 5:44:28
Dekle Beach 62 5 30N07 83w35 5:34:20
Delaco 46 1 30N46 86w34 5:46:16
De Land 64 5 29N02 81w18 5:25:12
De Land Highlands 64 5 29N02 81w18 5:25:12
De Land Rural 64 5 29N02 81w19 5:25:16
De Leon Springs 64 5 29N07 81w21 5:25:24
Delespine 5 5 28N36 80w49 5:23:16
Dellwood 32 1 30N49 85w03 5:40:12
Delray Beach 50 6 26N28 80w04 5:20:16
Delray Gardens 50 6 26N27 80w05 5:20:20
Delray Shores 50 6 26N27 80w05 5:20:20
Deltona 64 5 28N53 81w16 5:25:04
Denaud 26 5 26N45 81w31 5:26:04
De Soto City 28 5 27N27 81w24 5:25:36
Desoto Lakes 58 5 27N20 82w32 5:30:08
Destin 46 1 30N24 86w30 5:46:00
Devils Garden 26 5 26N45 80w58 5:23:52
Dewey Park 16 5 30N19 81w39 5:26:36
Dickerson City 57 1 30N39 87w05 5:48:20
Dills 33 5 30N33 83w52 5:35:28
Dinsmore 16 5 30N26 81w46 5:27:04
Dirego Park 3 1 30N09 85w39 5:42:36
Disston Plaza 52 5 27N47 82w43 5:30:52
Dixie Grove 51 5 28N15 82w45 5:31:00
Dixieland 53 5 28N02 81w57 5:27:48
Dixie Ranch Acres 47 5 27N14 80w49 5:23:16
Dixie Village 48 5 28N31 81w21 5:25:24
Doctors Inlet 10 5 30N06 81w47 5:27:08
Doctor's Lake Estates 10 5 30N08 81w42 5:26:48
Dogtown 20 5 30N35 84w35 5:38:20
Dogwood Lake Estates 30 1 30N53 85w40 5:42:40
Dona Vista 35 5 28N56 81w40 5:26:40
Dorcas 46 1 30N46 86w34 5:46:16
Dorset 50 5 26N49 80w40 5:22:40
Douglas City 20 5 30N35 84w35 5:38:20
Douglas Crossroads 66 1 30N43 85w57 5:43:48
Dover 29 5 28N00 82w13 5:28:52
Dover Shores 48 5 28N31 81w21 5:25:24
Dowling Park 61 5 30N15 83w14 5:32:56
Drayton Island 54 5 29N23 81w38 5:26:32
Drexel 51 5 28N15 82w28 5:29:52
Drifton 33 5 30N30 83w53 5:35:32
Druid Hills 59 5 28N38 81w22 5:25:28
Duck Key 44 5 24N42 81w05 5:24:20
Duette 41 5 27N38 81w50 5:27:20
Dukes 63 5 30N01 82w20 5:29:20
Dundee 53 5 28N02 81w37 5:26:28
Dunedin 52 5 28N01 82w47 5:31:08
Dunedin Isles 52 5 28N14 82w47 5:31:08
Dunlawton 64 5 29N09 80w59 5:23:56
Dunnellon 42 5 29N03 82w28 5:29:52
Dupont 18 5 29N26 81w13 5:24:52
Durant 29 5 27N54 82w11 5:28:44
Durbin 5 30N05 81w28 5:25:52
Durham 7 1 30N27 85w03 5:40:12
Duval 16 5 30N26 81w39 5:26:36
Eagle Lake 53 5 27N59 81w45 5:27:00
Earleton 1 5 29N45 82w06 5:28:24
East Alachua 1 5 29N47 82w30 5:30:00
East Auburndale 53 5 28N04 81w46 5:27:04
East Avenue 58 5 27N19 82w31 5:30:04
Eastbrook 48 5 28N34 81w35 5:26:20
Eastern Shores 13 6 25N56 80w11 5:20:44
East Flagler 18 5 29N32 81w14 5:24:56
Eastgate 48 5 28N36 81w21 5:25:24
East Hill 17 4 30N26 87w15 5:49:00
East Lake Park 29 5 28N00 82w25 5:29:40
Eastlake Weir 42 5 29N01 81w55 5:27:40
East Liberty 39 5 30N21 84w48 5:39:12
East Marion 42 5 29N12 81w50 5:27:20
East Mulberry 53 5 27N54 81w58 5:27:52
East Naples 11 5 26N08 81w46 5:27:04
East Okeechobee 47 5 27N18 80w45 5:23:00
East Orange 48 5 28N33 81w11 5:24:44
East Palatka 54 5 29N39 81w36 5:26:24
Eastpoint 19 5 29N44 84w53 5:39:32
East Rockland Key 44 5 24N34 81w44 5:26:56
East Venice 58 5 27N04 82w20 5:29:20
Eastway Park 6 6 26N18 80w10 5:20:40
East Williston 38 5 29N23 82w27 5:29:48
East Winter Haven 53 5 28N02 81w42 5:26:48
Eaton Park 53 5 28N00 81w55 5:27:40
Eatonville 48 5 28N37 81w23 5:25:32
Eau Gallie 5 5 28N08 80w38 5:22:32
Ebro 67 1 30N27 85w53 5:43:32
Econfina 1 30N25 85w32 5:42:08
Edgar 54 5 29N38 81w54 5:27:36
Edgewater 64 5 28N59 80w54 5:23:36
Edgewater Gulf Beach 3 1 30N11 85w49 5:43:16
Edgewood 16 5 30N18 81w38 5:26:32
Edgewood 48 5 28N29 81w22 5:25:28
Edison 29 5 28N00 82w31 5:30:04
Edison Center 13 6 25N47 80w13 5:20:52
Eglin 46 2 30N32 86w36 5:46:24
Eglin Air Force Base 46 2 30N29 86w30 5:46:00
Eglin Village 46 2 30N26 86w37 5:46:28
Egypt Lake 29 5 28N00 82w30 5:30:00
Elder Springs 59 5 28N48 81w15 5:25:00
El Dorado Acres 36 5 26N20 81w47 5:27:08
Eldridge 5 29N12 81w27 5:25:48
Eleven Mile 19 5 29N48 85w18 5:41:12
Elfers 51 5 28N13 82w43 5:30:52
El Jobean 8 5 26N58 82w13 5:28:52
Elkton 55 5 29N47 81w26 5:25:44
Ellaville 40 5 30N23 83w11 5:32:44
Ellenton 41 5 27N31 82w32 5:30:08
Ellinor Village 64 5 29N18 81w03 5:24:12
Ellison Acres 64 5 29N02 80w55 5:23:40
Ellisville 12 5 30N17 81w24 5:25:36
Ellyson Field 17 3 30N31 87w12 5:48:48
Ellzey 38 5 29N19 82w48 5:31:12
Eloise 53 5 27N59 81w44 5:26:56
Eloise Woods 53 5 28N01 81w44 5:26:56
El Portal 13 6 25N51 80w12 5:20:48
El Rancho Village 41 5 27N28 82w35 5:30:20
Elwood Park 41 5 27N28 82w35 5:30:20
Empire Point 16 5 30N19 81w39 5:26:36
Emporia 64 5 29N14 81w28 5:25:52
Enchanted Park 16 5 30N16 81w43 5:26:52
Englewood 58 5 26N58 82w21 5:29:24
Englewood Beach 58 5 26N56 82w16 5:29:04

FLORIDA

Englewood Manor 50 6 26N36 80w05 5:20:20
Enon 17 1 31N01 87w30 5:50:00
Ensley 17 3 30N31 87w16 5:49:04
Enterprise 64 5 28N52 81w16 5:25:04
Eridu 62 5 30N18 83w45 5:35:00
Errol Estates 48 5 28N58 81w39 5:26:36
Escambia Farms 46 1 30N48 86w40 5:46:40
Espanola 18 5 29N31 81w19 5:25:16
Estero 36 5 26N26 81w49 5:27:16
Estero River Heights 36 5 26N26 81w49 5:27:16
Estiffanulga 39 5 30N26 84w59 5:39:56
Esto 30 1 30N59 85w39 5:42:36
Eucheeanna 66 1 30N43 86w07 5:44:28
Euclid 52 5 27N47 82w40 5:30:40
Eureka 42 5 29N22 81w55 5:27:40
Eustis 35 5 28N51 81w41 5:26:44
Eva 53 5 28N11 81w50 5:27:20
Everglades 11 5 25N52 81w23 5:25:32
Evergreen 45 5 30N38 81w36 5:26:24
Evinston 1 5 29N30 82w14 5:28:56
Facil 24 5 30N20 82w44 5:30:56
Fairbanks 1 5 29N44 82w16 5:29:04
Fairfield 16 5 30N21 81w39 5:26:36
Fairfield 42 5 29N22 82w15 5:29:00
Fair Gate 6 6 26N14 80w12 5:20:48
Fairmont 16 5 30N17 81w35 5:26:20
Fairview Shores 48 5 28N35 81w24 5:25:36
Fairvilla 48 5 28N35 81w24 5:25:36
Fairyland 5 5 28N14 80w40 5:22:40
Falmouth 61 5 30N21 83w08 5:32:32
Fannin 38 5 29N36 82w55 5:31:40
Farmton 64 5 28N51 81w10 5:24:40
Fatio 64 5 29N02 81w18 5:25:12
Favorita 18 5 29N22 81w11 5:24:44
Federal Point 54 5 29N39 81w36 5:26:24
Fedhaven 53 5 27N53 81w34 5:26:16
Felda 26 5 26N34 81w26 5:25:44
Felica 9 5 28N54 82w22 5:29:28
Fellowship 42 5 29N11 82w09 5:28:36
Fellsmere 31 5 27N46 80w36 5:22:24
Fenholloway 62 5 30N07 83w35 5:34:20
Fernandina 5 30N40 81w27 5:25:48
Fernandina Beach 45 5 30N40 81w27 5:25:48
Fern Crest Village 6 6 26N05 80w13 5:20:52
Ferndale 35 5 28N37 81w42 5:26:48
Fern Park 59 5 28N39 81w21 5:25:24
Ferry Pass 17 4 30N29 87w12 5:48:48
Festus 33 5 30N33 83w52 5:35:28
Fidelis 57 1 30N57 87w09 5:48:36
Fisher Island 13 6 25N48 80w09 5:20:36
Fish Lake 49 5 28N18 81w25 5:25:40
Five Points 5 5 28N22 80w45 5:23:00
Five Points 12 5 30N13 82w38 5:30:32
Flagler 13 5 25N36 80w13 5:20:52
Flagler 44 5 24N34 81w44 5:26:56
Flagler Beach 18 5 29N29 81w08 5:24:32
Flamingo 44 5 25N08 80w57 5:23:48
Flamingo Bay 36 5 26N30 82w04 5:28:16
Fleming Heights 48 5 28N34 81w27 5:25:48
Flemington 42 5 29N22 82w12 5:28:48
Florahome 54 5 29N44 81w54 5:27:36
Floral Bluff 16 5 30N20 81w35 5:26:20
Floral City 9 5 28N45 82w17 5:29:08
Floral Park 50 6 26N36 80w05 5:20:20
Flordale 16 5 30N22 81w41 5:26:44
Florence Villa 53 5 28N01 81w44 5:26:56
Floresta 50 6 26N23 80w05 5:20:20
Floresta Estates 6 6 26N18 80w10 5:20:40
Florida Beach 3 1 30N09 85w39 5:42:36
Florida City 13 5 25N27 80w29 5:21:56
Florida Gardens 50 6 26N36 80w05 5:20:20
Floridana Beach 5 5 28N05 80w36 5:22:24
Florida Ridge 31 5 27N35 80w25 5:21:40
Florida Southern College 53 5 28N33 81w23 5:25:32
Florosa 46 1 30N25 86w39 5:46:36
Flower Bluff 38 5 29N29 82w52 5:31:28
Flowersville 66 1 30N57 86w20 5:45:20
Footman 5 5 28N14 80w40 5:22:40
Forest City 59 5 28N38 81w22 5:25:28
Forest Grove 1 5 29N47 82w30 5:30:00
Forest Hills 29 5 28N03 82w27 5:29:48
Forest Hills 51 5 28N11 82w44 5:30:56
Forest Ridge 1 5 29N40 82w20 5:29:20
Forrest Hills 64 5 29N18 81w03 5:24:12
Fort Barrancas 17 4 30N21 87w16 5:49:04
Fort Basinger 28 5 27N22 81w03 5:24:12
Fort Caroline Club Estates 16 5 30N20 81w35 5:26:20
Fort Drum 47 5 27N14 80w49 5:23:16
Fort George Island 16 5 30N27 81w34 5:26:16
Fort Green 25 5 27N37 81w57 5:27:48
Fort Green Springs 25 5 27N38 81w50 5:27:20
Fort Lauderdale 6 6 26N07 80w08 5:20:32
Fort Lonesome 29. 5 28N00 82w31 5:30:04
Fort McCoy 42 5 29N22 81w58 5:27:52
Fort Meade 53 5 27N45 81w48 5:27:12
Fort Myers 36 5 26N39 81w52 5:27:28
Fort Myers Beach 36 5 26N27 81w56 5:27:44
Fort Myers Shores 36 5 26N42 81w45 5:27:00
Fort Myers Villas 36 5 26N36 81w52 5:27:28
Fort Ogden 14 5 27N05 81w57 5:27:48
Fort Pierce 56 5 27N27 80w20 5:21:20

Place	Zone	Latitude	Longitude	Time
Fort Pierce Beach 56	5	27N21	80w19	5:21:16
Fort Pierce Shores 56	5	27N21	80w19	5:21:16
Fort Taylor 44	5	24N34	81w44	5:26:56
Fort Union 61	5	30N18	82w59	5:31:56
Fort Walton Beach 46	1	30N25	86w36	5:46:24
Fort White 12	5	29N55	82w43	5:30:52
Forty Ninth Street 52	5	27N45	82w42	5:30:48
Fountain 3	1	30N29	85w25	5:41:40
Fountain Heights 53	5	28N02	81w57	5:27:48
Four Mile Village 66	1	30N23	86w14	5:44:56
Four Points 50	6	26N40	80w06	5:20:24
Francis 54	5	29N39	81w39	5:26:36
Franklinton 45	5	30N40	81w27	5:25:48
Franwood Pines 50	6	26N27	80w05	5:20:20
Freeport 66	1	30N30	86w08	5:44:32
Frink 7	1	30N26	85w11	5:40:44
Frontenac 5	5	28N28	80w46	5:23:04
Frostproof 53	5	27N45	81w32	5:26:08
Fruit Cove 55	5	30N12	81w35	5:26:20
Fruitland 54	5	29N26	81w31	5:26:04
Fruitland Park 35	5	28N51	81w54	5:27:36
Fruitville 58	5	27N20	82w29	5:29:56
Fuller Heights 53	5	27N54	81w58	5:27:52
Fullerton 64	5	28N52	80w51	5:23:24
Fullerville 35	5	29N02	81w18	5:25:12
Fulton 16	5	30N18	81w38	5:26:32
Fussels Corner 53	5	28N04	81w48	5:27:12
Gainesville 1	5	29N40	82w20	5:29:20
Galliver 46	1	30N43	86w45	5:47:00
Galloway 53	5	28N03	81w56	5:27:44
Galt City 57	1	30N36	87w02	5:48:08
Gardena 59	5	28N40	81w12	5:24:48
Garden City 16	5	30N26	81w39	5:26:36
Garden City 46	1	30N46	86w34	5:46:16
Garden Grove 27	5	28N32	82w29	5:29:56
Gardenville 29	5	27N51	82w23	5:29:32
Gardner 25	5	27N21	81w48	5:27:12
Garnier 46	1	30N36	86w36	5:46:24
Gaskin 66	1	30N58	86w08	5:44:32
Gateway Mall 52	5	27N51	82w40	5:30:40
General Mail Center 16	5	30N19	81w39	5:26:36
Geneva 59	5	28N44	81w07	5:24:28
Genoa	5	30N24	82w50	5:31:20
Georgetown 54	5	29N23	81w38	5:26:32
Georgiana 5	5	28N14	80w40	5:22:40
Gibson 20	5	30N37	84w25	5:37:40
Gibsonia 53	5	28N03	81w56	5:27:44
Gibsonton 29	5	27N51	82w23	5:29:32
Gifford 31	5	27N40	80w25	5:21:40
Gillett 41	5	27N32	82w34	5:30:16
Gilmore 16	5	30N20	81w35	5:26:20
Glades 50	5	26N41	80w32	5:22:08
Glencoe 64	5	29N02	80w55	5:23:40
Glendale 66	1	30N52	86w07	5:44:28
Glen Ridge 50	6	26N41	80w05	5:20:20
Glen Saint Mary 2	5	30N16	82w10	5:28:40
Glen St Mary 2	5	30N16	82w10	5:28:40
Glenvar Heights 13	6	25N42	80w19	5:21:16
Glenwood 3	1	30N09	85w39	5:42:36
Glenwood 64	5	29N02	81w18	5:25:12
Glory 20	5	30N35	84w35	5:38:20
Glynlea 16	5	30N17	81w35	5:26:20
Golden Beach 13	6	25N58	80w07	5:20:28
Golden Beach 58	5	27N04	82w20	5:29:20
Golden Gate 11	5	26N11	81w48	5:27:12
Golden Gate 43	5	27N12	80w15	5:21:00
Golden Heights 35	5	28N48	81w39	5:26:36
Golden Isles 6	6	25N59	80w09	5:20:36
Goldenrod 48	5	28N37	81w19	5:25:16
Golden Shores 13	6	25N56	80w09	5:20:36
Golf 50	6	26N30	80w06	5:20:24
Golfair Manor 16	5	30N26	81w39	5:26:36
Golf Lake Estates 41	5	27N28	82w35	5:30:20
Golfview 50	6	26N41	80w07	5:20:28
Golfview Heights 50	6	26N40	80w06	5:20:24
Gomez 43	5	27N05	80w09	5:20:36
Gonzalez 17	3	30N35	87w18	5:49:12
Goodbys 16	5	30N14	81w38	5:26:32
Good Hope 46	1	30N48	86w40	5:46:40
Goodland 11	5	25N55	81w39	5:26:36
Goodno 22	5	26N50	81w06	5:24:24
Gordon 66	1	31N00	86w19	5:45:16
Gordon Chapel 54	5	29N36	82w05	5:28:20
Gordonville 53	5	27N54	81w50	5:27:20
Gotha 48	5	28N32	81w31	5:26:04
Goulding 17	4	30N27	87w14	5:48:56
Goulds 13	5	25N33	80w23	5:21:32
Graceville 32	1	30N58	85w31	5:42:04
Graham 4	5	29N52	82w13	5:28:52
Grandin 54	5	29N44	81w55	5:27:40
Grand Island 35	5	28N53	81w44	5:26:56
Grand Park 16	5	30N24	81w45	5:27:00
Grand Ridge 32	1	30N43	85w01	5:40:04
Grangers Mill 12	5	30N17	81w24	5:25:36
Grant 5	5	27N56	80w32	5:22:08
Gratigny 13	6	25N54	80w13	5:20:52
Grayton Beach 66	1	30N22	86w07	5:44:28
Greenacres City 50	6	26N38	80w07	5:20:28
Greenbriar 59	5	28N48	81w15	5:25:00
Green Cove Springs 10	5	29N59	81w42	5:26:48
Greenfield Manor 16	5	30N17	81w35	5:26:20
Green Hills 3	1	30N29	85w35	5:41:40
Green Hills 13	5	25N36	80w22	5:21:28
Greenland 16	5	30N10	81w33	5:26:12
Greensboro 20	5	30N34	84w45	5:39:00
Greenville 40	5	30N28	83w38	5:34:32
Greenwood 32	1	30N52	85w10	5:40:40
Greenwood 57	1	30N57	87w09	5:48:36
Gretna 20	5	30N37	84w40	5:38:40
Greyhound Key	5	24N51	80w47	5:23:08
Griffin 53	5	28N03	81w56	5:27:44
Griffins Corner 25	5	27N33	81w49	5:27:16
Gross 45	5	30N38	81w36	5:26:24
Grove City 8	5	26N54	82w14	5:28:56
Groveland 35	5	28N34	81w51	5:27:24
Grove Park 1	5	29N36	82w05	5:28:20
Grove Park 16	5	30N17	81w35	5:26:20
Grove Park 29	5	28N00	82w30	5:30:00
Grove Park 53	5	28N02	81w57	5:27:48
Grove Park Estates 29	5	28N00	82w30	5:30:00
Gulf Beach 17	4	30N25	87w17	5:49:08
Gulf Breeze 57	4	30N22	87w09	5:48:36
Gulf City 29	5	27N44	82w24	5:29:36
Gulf Gate Estates 58	5	27N16	82w31	5:30:04
Gulf Hammock 38	5	29N15	82w44	5:30:56
Gulf Harbors 51	5	28N14	82w45	5:31:00
Gulf Lagoon Beach 3	1	30N09	85w39	5:42:36
Gulfport 52	5	27N45	82w43	5:30:52
Gulf Resort Beach 3	1	30N09	85w39	5:42:36
Gulf Shores 58	5	27N04	82w20	5:29:20
Gulf Stream 50	6	26N29	80w03	5:20:12
Hacienda 6	6	26N05	80w12	5:20:48
Hague 1	5	29N40	82w20	5:29:20
Haile 1	5	29N39	82w36	5:30:24
Haines City 53	5	28N07	81w38	5:26:32
Half Moon 1	5	29N39	82w36	5:30:24
Hallandale 6	6	25N59	80w08	5:20:32
Hamilton 6	6	26N15	80w09	5:20:36
Hammond 54	5	29N26	81w31	5:26:04
Hampton 4	5	29N52	82w08	5:28:32
Hampton Springs 62	5	30N05	83w40	5:34:40
Hanson 40	5	30N34	83w21	5:33:24
Harbor Bluffs 52	5	27N53	82w46	5:31:04
Harbor East 50	6	26N23	80w05	5:20:20
Harbor Oaks 64	5	29N09	80w59	5:23:56
Harbor Point 64	5	29N13	81w02	5:24:08
Harbor View 8	5	26N57	82w00	5:28:00
Harborview 16	5	30N23	81w41	5:26:44
Harbour Heights 8	5	26N57	82w00	5:28:00
Hardaway 20	5	30N38	84w44	5:38:56
Hardeetown 38	5	29N29	82w52	5:31:28
Hardin Heights 20	5	30N42	84w51	5:39:24
Harlem 26	5	26N44	80w57	5:23:48
Harlem Heights 48	5	28N34	81w35	5:26:20
Harold 57	1	30N40	86w53	5:47:32
Harrisburg 22	5	26N57	81w19	5:25:16
Hart Haven 16	5	30N19	81w43	5:26:52
Harvey Heights 36	5	26N36	81w52	5:27:28
Hastings 55	5	29N43	81w31	5:26:04
Hatchbend 34	5	29N58	82w55	5:31:40
Havana 20	5	30N37	84w25	5:37:40
Haven Beach 52	5	27N54	82w51	5:31:24
Haverhill 50	6	26N42	80w07	5:20:28
Hawthorne 1	5	29N36	82w05	5:28:20
Hedges 45	5	30N38	81w36	5:26:24
Heilbron Springs 4	5	29N57	82w06	5:28:24
Hercules 16	5	30N14	81w57	5:27:48
Hermitage 20	5	28N14	80w36	5:22:24
Hernando 9	5	28N54	82w23	5:29:32
Herndon 48	5	28N33	81w23	5:25:32
Hero 45	5	30N38	81w36	5:26:24
Hesperides 53	5	27N53	81w34	5:26:16
Hialeah 13	6	25N50	80w17	5:21:08
Hialeah Gardens 13	6	25N52	80w21	5:21:24
Hialeah Lakes 13	6	25N54	80w18	5:21:12
Hibernia 10	5	29N59	81w41	5:26:44
Hibiscus Mobile Park 35	5	28N48	81w39	5:26:36
Hickory Hill 30	1	30N46	85w51	5:43:24
Highland 10	5	30N07	82w03	5:28:12
Highland Beach 50	6	26N25	80w04	5:20:16
Highland City 53	5	27N58	81w53	5:27:32
Highland Court Manor 1	5	29N40	82w20	5:29:20
Highland Lakes 28	5	27N36	81w30	5:26:00
Highland Park 52	5	27N53	82w46	5:31:04
Highland Park 53	5	27N52	81w34	5:26:16
Highland Park 59	5	28N48	81w15	5:25:00
Highlands 6	6	26N17	80w09	5:20:36
Highlands 16	5	30N26	81w39	5:26:36
Highland View 23	5	29N50	85w19	5:41:16
High Point 52	5	27N56	82w46	5:31:04
High Springs 1	5	29N50	82w36	5:30:24
Hiland Park 3	1	30N12	85w38	5:42:32
Hilden	5	30N04	81w26	5:25:44
Hildreth 61	5	29N58	82w55	5:31:40
Hillcrest Heights 53	5	27N50	81w32	5:26:08
Hilldale 29	5	28N00	82w30	5:30:00
Hilliard 45	5	30N41	81w55	5:27:40
Hilliardville 65	5	30N26	84w17	5:37:08
Hill N Dale 27	5	28N32	82w29	5:29:56
Hillsboro Beach 6	6	26N18	80w05	5:20:20
Hines	5	29N45	83w14	5:32:56
Hinson 20	5	30N39	84w25	5:37:40
Hinson Cross Roads 67	1	30N47	85w49	5:43:16
Hobe Sound 43	5	27N04	80w08	5:20:32
Hogan 16	5	30N17	81w35	5:26:20
Holden Heights 48	5	28N31	81w24	5:25:36
Holder 9	5	28N58	82w25	5:29:40
Holiday 51	5	28N15	82w45	5:31:00
Holiday Gardens 51	5	28N12	82w44	5:30:56
Holiday Harbor 16	5	30N17	81w35	5:26:20
Holiday Heights 44	5	25N08	80w25	5:21:40
Holiday Hills 51	5	28N14	82w45	5:31:00
Holiday Manor 53	5	28N07	81w37	5:26:28
Holiday Plaza 3	1	30N09	85w39	5:42:36
Holland Crossroads 30	1	30N53	85w40	5:42:40
Holley 57	1	30N27	86w54	5:47:36
Hollister 54	5	29N37	81w49	5:27:16
Holly Ford 16	5	30N26	81w39	5:26:36
Holly Hill 64	5	29N16	81w03	5:24:12
Holly Point 10	5	30N08	81w42	5:26:48
Hollywood 6	6	26N01	80w09	5:20:36
Hollywood Beach 3	1	30N15	85w57	5:43:48
Hollywood Hills 6	6	26N01	80w11	5:20:44
Hollywood Ridge Farms 6	6	25N59	80w12	5:20:48
Hollywood Seminole Indian Re 6	6	26N01	80w13	5:20:52
Holmes Beach 41	5	27N31	82w43	5:30:52
Holmes West 30	1	30N52	85w56	5:43:44
Holopaw 49	5	28N08	81w05	5:24:20
Holt 46	1	30N43	86w45	5:47:00
Homeland 53	5	27N49	81w50	5:27:20
Homestead 13	5	25N28	80w29	5:21:56
Homestead Air Force Base 13	5	25N30	80w24	5:21:36
Homosassa Springs 9	5	28N48	82w35	5:30:20
Honeyville 23	1	30N03	85w11	5:40:44
Hopewell 29	5	28N01	82w08	5:28:32
Hopewell 40	5	30N28	83w25	5:33:40
Hopkins 5	5	28N05	80w38	5:22:32
Hornsville 32	1	30N42	84w56	5:39:44
Horseshoe Beach 15	5	29N26	83w17	5:33:08
Hosford 39	5	30N23	84w48	5:39:12
Houston 61	5	30N15	82w54	5:31:36
Howey In The Hills 35	5	28N43	81w46	5:27:04
Hudson 51	5	28N22	82w42	5:30:48
Hugh 10	5	30N10	82w02	5:28:08
Hull 14	5	27N13	81w52	5:27:28
Hurlburt 46	1	30N25	86w41	5:46:44
Hyde Grove 16	5	30N14	81w57	5:27:48
Hyde Park 16	5	30N14	81w57	5:27:48
Hyde Park 65	5	30N26	84w17	5:37:08
Hypoluxo 50	6	26N34	80w03	5:20:12
Iddo 62	5	30N28	83w38	5:34:32
Idylwild 1	5	29N40	82w20	5:29:20
Ilexhurst 41	5	27N29	82w42	5:30:48
Immokalee 11	5	26N25	81w25	5:25:40
Imperial Estates 48	5	28N29	81w22	5:25:28
Indialantic 5	5	28N06	80w34	5:22:16
Indian Creek 13	6	25N52	80w08	5:20:32
Indian Harbour Beach 5	5	28N09	80w36	5:22:24
Indian Lake Estates 53	5	27N53	81w34	5:26:16
Indianola 5	5	28N14	80w40	5:22:40
Indian Pass 23	5	29N41	85w16	5:41:04
Indian River City 5	5	28N36	80w49	5:23:16
Indian River Shores 31	5	27N42	80w23	5:21:32
Indian Rocks Beach 52	5	27N53	82w51	5:31:24
Indian Shores 52	5	27N54	82w51	5:31:24
Indiantown 43	5	27N01	80w28	5:21:52
Indrio 56	5	27N31	80w21	5:21:24
Inglis 38	5	29N02	82w40	5:30:40
Inlet Beach 3	1	30N15	85w57	5:43:48
Interbay 29	5	27N53	82w31	5:30:04
Intercession City 49	5	28N16	81w31	5:26:04
Interior County 58	5	27N10	82w21	5:29:24
Interlachen 54	5	29N37	81w53	5:27:32
Inverness 9	5	28N50	82w20	5:29:20
Inverrary 6	6	26N09	80w13	5:20:52
Inwood 53	5	28N01	81w44	5:26:56
Iona Gardens 36	5	26N36	81w52	5:27:28
Irvine 42	5	29N22	82w12	5:28:48
Islamorada 44	5	24N56	80w37	5:22:28
Island Grove 1	5	29N27	82w07	5:28:28
Islandia 13	5	25N25	80w13	5:20:52
Isleboro 64	5	29N02	80w55	5:23:40
Isle Of Palms 16	5	30N17	81w35	5:26:20
Isleworth 48	5	28N30	81w32	5:26:08
Istachatta 27	5	28N39	82w02	5:28:08
Istokpoga Shores 28	5	27N27	81w15	5:25:00
Ivan 65	5	30N26	84w17	5:37:08
Ives Estates 13	6	25N56	80w11	5:20:44
Izagora 30	1	30N47	85w49	5:43:16
Jackson Still 66	1	30N43	86w07	5:44:28
Jacksonville 16	5	30N20	81w39	5:26:36
Jacksonville Beach 16	5	30N17	81w24	5:25:36
Jacksonville Heights 16	5	30N16	81w43	5:26:52
Jacksonville Naval Air Stati 16	5	30N19	81w39	5:26:36
Jacksonville Navy Fuel Depot 16	5	30N23	81w41	5:26:44
Jacksonville University 16	5	30N20	81w35	5:26:20
Jacob 32	1	30N54	85w24	5:41:36
Jamestown 59	5	28N40	81w12	5:24:48
Jamieson	5	30N40	84w27	5:37:48

Jan-phyl Village 53	5	28N01	81w46	5:27:04
Jarrott 33	5	30N33	83w52	5:35:28
Jasmine Estates 51	5	28N19	82w42	5:30:48
Jasper 24	5	30N31	82w57	5:31:48
Jassamine 51	5	28N22	82w11	5:28:44
Jay 57	1	30N57	87w09	5:48:36
Jena 15	5	29N40	83w22	5:33:28
Jenada Isles 6	6	26N09	80w11	5:20:44
Jennings 24	5	30N36	83w06	5:32:24
Jensen Beach 43	5	27N15	80w14	5:20:56
Jerome 11	5	26N00	81w21	5:25:24
Johnson 54	5	29N36	82w05	5:28:20
Johns Pass 52	5	27N50	82w48	5:31:12
Jonesville 1	5	29N40	82w20	5:29:20
Joshua 14	5	27N13	81w52	5:27:28
Judson 38	5	29N37	82w49	5:31:16
June Park 5	5	28N04	80w41	5:22:44
Juno Beach 50	6	26N52	80w03	5:20:12
Jupiter 50	6	26N57	80w06	5:20:24
Jupiter Island 43	5	27N05	80w07	5:20:28
Kathleen 53	5	28N07	82w02	5:28:08
Keaton Beach 62	5	30N07	83w35	5:34:20
Kelly Park	5	28N46	81w30	5:26:00
Kenansville 49	5	27N53	80w59	5:23:56
Kendall 13	6	25N41	80w19	5:21:16
Kendrick 42	5	29N15	82w10	5:28:40
Kenneth City 52	5	27N49	82w43	5:30:52
Kensington Park 58	5	27N22	82w30	5:30:00
Kerr City 42	5	29N25	82w06	5:28:24
Keuka 54	5	29N36	82w05	5:28:20
Key Biscayne 13	6	25N42	80w10	5:20:40
Key Colony Beach 44	5	24N45	80w57	5:23:48
Key Largo 44	5	25N08	80w25	5:21:40
Key Largo Park 44	5	25N08	80w25	5:21:40
Key Largo Village 44	5	25N08	80w25	5:21:40
Keystone Heights 10	5	29N47	82w02	5:28:08
Keystone Islands 13	6	25N53	80w11	5:20:44
Keysville 29	5	27N52	82w06	5:28:24
Key West 44	5	24N33	81w47	5:27:08
Kilarney Shores 16	5	30N17	81w35	5:26:20
Killarney 48	5	28N33	81w39	5:26:36
Killearn Estates 37	5	30N28	84w18	5:37:12
Kinard 7	1	30N16	85w15	5:41:00
Kings Bay 13	5	25N38	80w21	5:21:24
Kings Ferry 45	5	30N41	81w56	5:27:44
Kingsley Lake 10	5	29N57	82w06	5:28:24
Kingsley Village 10	5	29N57	82w06	5:28:24
Kings Road 16	5	30N19	81w43	5:26:52
Kingswood Manor 48	5	28N35	81w24	5:25:36
Kirby Loop 56	5	27N21	80w19	5:21:16
Kirkwood 1	5	29N30	82w17	5:29:08
Kissimmee 49	5	28N18	81w24	5:25:36
Kissimmee Park 49	5	28N15	81w17	5:25:08
Knights 29	5	28N05	82w08	5:28:32
Knoxhill 66	1	30N43	85w57	5:43:48
Korona 18	5	29N25	81w12	5:24:48
Kossuthville 53	5	28N04	81w48	5:27:12
Kynesville 32	1	30N48	85w22	5:41:28
La Belle 26	5	26N46	81w26	5:25:44
Lackawanna 16	5	30N16	81w43	5:26:52
Lacoochee 51	5	28N28	82w11	5:28:44
La Crosse 1	5	29N51	82w24	5:29:36
Lady Lake 35	5	28N55	81w55	5:27:40
Lafayette 37	5	30N26	84w16	5:37:04
La Gorce Island 13	6	25N48	80w09	5:20:36
La Grange 5	5	28N36	80w49	5:23:16
Laguna Beach 3	1	30N14	85w56	5:43:44
Lake Alfred 53	5	28N06	81w44	5:26:56
Lake Bird 62	5	30N14	83w37	5:34:28
Lake Bradford 37	5	30N26	84w17	5:37:08
Lake Brantley 59	5	28N42	81w20	5:25:20
Lake Buena Vista 48	5	28N33	81w23	5:25:32
Lake Butler 63	5	30N01	82w21	5:29:24
Lake Cain Hills 48	5	28N31	81w24	5:25:36
Lake Carroll 29	5	28N03	82w30	5:30:00
Lake Charm 59	5	28N40	81w12	5:24:48
Lake City 12	5	30N11	82w38	5:30:32
Lake Clarke Shores 50	6	26N39	80w05	5:20:20
Lake Como 54	5	29N29	81w34	5:26:16
Lake Forest 16	5	30N23	81w41	5:26:44
Lake Frances 35	5	28N48	81w44	5:26:56
Lake Garfield 53	5	27N54	81w50	5:27:20
Lake Geneva 10	5	29N46	82w01	5:28:04
Lake Hamilton 53	5	28N03	81w37	5:26:28
Lake Harbor 50	5	26N42	80w48	5:23:12
Lake Helen 64	5	28N59	81w14	5:24:56
Lake Holloway 53	5	28N02	81w55	5:27:40
Lake Jem 35	5	28N45	81w40	5:26:40
Lake Joanna 35	5	28N51	81w41	5:26:44
Lake Juniata 35	5	28N48	81w44	5:26:56
Lake Kathryn Estates 59	5	28N40	81w20	5:25:20
Lake Kathryn Heights 35	5	29N02	81w18	5:25:12
Lake Kathryn Village 59	5	28N40	81w20	5:25:20
Lakeland 53	5	28N03	81w57	5:27:48
Lake Lindsey 27	5	28N32	82w29	5:29:56
Lake Lucerne 13	6	25N55	80w15	5:21:00
Lake Lucina 16	5	30N20	81w35	5:26:20
Lake Magdalene 29	5	28N04	82w28	5:29:52
Lake Maitland 48	5	28N37	81w23	5:25:32
Lake Marian Highlands 49'	5	27N53	80w59	5:23:56
Lake Mary 59	5	28N46	81w19	5:25:16
Lake Maude 53	5	28N01	81w44	5:26:56
Lake Mendelin Estates 48	5	28N41	81w28	5:25:52
Lake Monroe 59	5	28N50	81w19	5:25:16
Lake of the Hills 53	5	27N57	81w36	5:26:24
Lake Ola 35	5	28N48	81w39	5:26:36
Lake Panasoffkee 60	5	28N45	82w06	5:28:24
Lake Park 50	6	26N48	80w03	5:20:12
Lake Placid 28	5	27N18	81w22	5:25:28
Lakeport 22	5	26N50	81w06	5:24:24
Lake Rogers Isle 50	6	26N23	80w05	5:20:20
Lake Saunders Trailer Park 35	5	28N48	81w39	5:26:36
Lake Ship Heights 53	5	28N00	81w44	5:26:56
Lake Shore 16	5	30N17	81w44	5:26:56
Lake Shore Estates 52	5	27N57	82w45	5:31:00
Lake Tarpon 52	5	27N57	82w45	5:31:00
Lake Tarpon Mobile Homes 52	5	27N57	82w45	5:31:00
Lake View 6	6	26N19	80w09	5:20:36
Lake Wales 53	5	27N54	81w35	5:26:20
Lake Weir 42	5	29N03	81w56	5:27:44
Lakewood 16	5	30N14	81w38	5:26:32
Lakewood 37	5	30N26	84w17	5:37:08
Lakewood 66	1	30N59	86w17	5:45:08
Lake Worth 50	6	26N37	80w03	5:20:12
Lamont 33	5	30N23	83w49	5:35:16
Lanair Park 50	6	26N36	80w05	5:20:20
Lanark 19	5	29N53	84w36	5:38:24
Lancaster 61	5	30N18	82w59	5:31:56
Land o'Lakes 51	5	28N11	82w34	5:30:16
Lane Park 35	5	28N48	81w44	5:26:56
Lantana 50	6	26N35	80w03	5:20:12
Largo 52	5	27N55	82w47	5:31:08
Larsen 16	5	30N17	81w35	5:26:20
Lauderdale-by-the-Sea 6	6	26N11	80w06	5:20:24
Lauderdale Isles 6	6	26N06	80w12	5:20:48
Lauderdale Lakes 6	6	26N10	80w13	5:20:52
Lauderhill 6	6	26N08	80w13	5:20:52
Laurel 58	5	27N08	82w27	5:29:48
Laurel Grove 10	5	30N08	81w42	5:26:48
Laurel Hill 46	1	30N56	86w28	5:45:52
Laurel Park 17	4	30N26	87w15	5:49:00
Lawtey 4	5	30N03	82w05	5:28:20
Layton 44	5	24N49	80w49	5:23:16
Lazy Lake 6	6	26N09	80w13	5:20:52
Lealman 52	5	27N49	82w41	5:30:44
Lebanon 38	5	29N06	82w38	5:30:32
Lecanto 9	5	28N51	82w29	5:29:56
Lee 40	5	30N25	83w18	5:33:12
Leesburg 35	5	28N49	81w53	5:27:32
Lehigh Acres 36	5	26N36	81w38	5:26:32
Leisure City 13	5	25N29	80w30	5:22:00
Lely Golf Estates 11	5	26N11	81w48	5:27:12
Lelyland 11	5	26N11	81w48	5:27:12
Lely Tropical Estates 11	5	26N11	81w48	5:27:12
Lemon Grove 25	5	27N33	81w49	5:27:16
Leon 37	5	30N28	84w18	5:37:12
Leonards 7	1	30N27	85w03	5:40:12
Leonia 30	1	30N55	86w01	5:44:04
Leonton 33	5	30N33	83w52	5:35:28
Lessie 45	5	30N41	81w56	5:27:44
Leto 29	5	28N00	82w31	5:30:04
Libby Heights 1	5	29N40	82w20	5:29:20
Liberty 66	1	30N43	86w07	5:44:28
Lido Beach 52	5	27N45	82w42	5:30:48
Lighthouse Point 6	6	26N16	80w10	5:20:40
Lighthouse Point 43	5	27N12	80w15	5:21:00
Lily 25	5	27N29	81w55	5:27:40
Limestone 25	5	27N22	81w54	5:27:36
Limestone 33	5	30N33	83w52	5:35:28
Limona 29	5	27N56	82w17	5:29:08
Lincoln 13	6	25N48	80w09	5:20:36
Lincoln City 4	5	29N57	82w06	5:28:24
Lincoln Estates 1	5	29N40	82w20	5:29:20
Linda Loma 36	5	26N36	81w52	5:27:28
Linden 60	5	28N37	82w03	5:28:12
Lisbon 35	5	28N49	81w53	5:27:32
Lithia 29	5	28N00	82w31	5:30:04
Little River 13	6	25N52	80w13	5:20:52
Little Torch Key 44	5	24N45	81w20	5:25:20
Live Oak 61	5	30N18	82w59	5:31:56
Live Oak 67	1	30N38	85w43	5:42:52
Live Oak Point 65	5	30N11	84w23	5:37:32
Lloyd 33	5	30N28	84w01	5:36:04
Lochloosa 1	5	29N30	82w06	5:28:24
Lock Arbor 59	5	28N48	81w15	5:25:00
Lockhart 48	5	28N37	81w28	5:25:52
Lockwood Ridge 58	5	27N19	82w31	5:30:04
Lona 12	5	30N12	82w44	5:30:56
Londonderry 48	5	28N34	81w27	5:25:48
Long Beach Resort 3	1	30N11	85w49	5:43:16
Longboat Key 41	5	27N26	82w40	5:30:40
Longdale 59	5	28N42	81w20	5:25:20
Long Key 44	5	24N49	80w49	5:23:16
Longwood 46	1	30N36	86w35	5:46:20
Longwood 59	5	28N42	81w21	5:25:24
Loretto 16	5	30N12	81w35	5:26:20
Lorida 28	5	27N27	81w15	5:25:00
Lottieville 21	5	29N37	82w49	5:31:16
Lotus 5	5	28N14	80w40	5:22:40
Loughman 53	5	28N14	81w34	5:26:16
Louise 1	5	29N47	82w10	5:28:40
Lovedale 32	1	30N56	85w07	5:40:28
Loveridge Heights 5	5	28N10	80w38	5:22:32
Lovett 40	5	30N28	83w38	5:34:32
Lovewood 32	1	30N48	85w22	5:41:28
Lowell 42	5	29N20	82w12	5:28:48
Lower Boca Ciega 52	5	27N45	82w44	5:30:56
Lower Keys 44	5	24N37	81w39	5:26:36
Loxahatchee 50	6	26N41	80w18	5:21:12
Lucerne Park 53	5	28N01	81w44	5:26:56
Ludlam 13	6	25N44	80w18	5:21:12
Lullwater Beach 3	1	30N09	85w39	5:42:36
Lulu 12	5	30N07	82w29	5:29:56
Lumberton 51	5	28N16	82w08	5:28:32
Lundy 54	5	29N38	81w38	5:26:32
Luraville 61	5	30N07	83w10	5:32:40
Lutz 29	5	28N09	82w28	5:29:52
Lynne 42	5	29N12	81w55	5:27:40
Lynn Haven 3	1	30N15	85w39	5:42:36
Mabel 60	5	28N39	82w00	5:28:00
MacClenny 2	5	30N17	82w07	5:28:28
MacDill Air Force Base 29	5	27N51	82w30	5:30:00
Mack Bayou 66	1	30N23	86w14	5:44:56
Madeira Beach 52	5	27N48	82w48	5:31:12
Madison 40	5	30N28	83w25	5:33:40
Magnet Cove 20	5	30N37	84w25	5:37:40
Magnolia Beach 3	1	30N09	85w39	5:42:36
Magnolia Gardens 16	5	30N22	81w41	5:26:44
Magnolia Springs 10	5	29N59	81w41	5:26:44
Mainland 64	5	29N18	81w03	5:24:12
Maitland 48	5	28N38	81w22	5:25:28
Malabar 5	5	28N00	80w34	5:22:16
Malone 32	1	30N57	85w10	5:40:40
Manalapan 50	6	26N34	80w02	5:20:08
Manasota Key 58	5	26N56	82w16	5:29:04
Manatee 41	5	27N28	82w35	5:30:20
Mandarin 16	5	30N14	81w38	5:26:32
Mango 29	5	27N59	82w19	5:29:16
Mango Hills 29	5	27N59	82w17	5:29:08
Mangonia Park 50	6	26N45	80w04	5:20:16
Mannville 54	5	29N38	81w54	5:27:36
Marathon 44	5	24N43	81w05	5:24:20
Marathon Shores 44	5	24N42	81w05	5:24:20
Maravilla 56	5	27N21	80w19	5:21:16
Marco 11	5	25N58	81w44	5:26:56
Margate 6	6	26N15	80w12	5:20:48
Margate Estates 6	6	26N14	80w12	5:20:48
Marianna 32	1	30N46	85w14	5:40:56
Marietta 16	5	30N19	81w43	5:26:52
Marineland 18	5	29N40	81w13	5:24:52
Marion Oaks 42	5	29N11	82w09	5:28:36
Martel 42	5	29N11	82w16	5:29:04
Martin 42	5	29N11	82w09	5:28:36
Mary Esther 46	1	30N25	86w39	5:46:36
Masaryktown 27	5	28N27	82w27	5:29:48
Mascotte 35	5	28N35	81w54	5:27:36
Mason 12	5	30N17	81w24	5:25:36
Matanzas 55	5	29N49	81w18	5:25:12
Matlacha 36	5	26N38	82w04	5:28:16
Matoaka 41	5	27N24	82w32	5:30:08
Maxcy Quarters 53	5	27N45	81w32	5:26:08
Maxville 16	5	30N12	82w01	5:28:04
Mayo 34	5	30N03	83w10	5:32:40
Mayo Junction 34	5	30N03	83w11	5:32:44
Mayo West 34	5	30N08	83w16	5:33:04
Mayport 16	5	30N24	81w26	5:25:44
Mayport Naval Housing 16	5	30N23	81w25	5:25:40
Mayport Naval Station 16	5	30N19	81w39	5:26:36
McAllister 42	5	29N20	82w12	5:28:48
McAlpin 61	5	30N08	82w57	5:31:48
McCoy Air Force Base 48	5	28N26	81w21	5:25:24
McDavid 17	1	30N52	87w19	5:49:16
McGregor Gardens 36	5	26N36	81w52	5:27:28
McGregor Groves 36	5	26N36	81w52	5:27:28
McIntosh 42	5	29N27	82w13	5:28:52
McKinnon 17	1	30N47	87w28	5:49:52
McLellen 57	1	30N39	87w05	5:48:20
McMeekin 54	5	29N36	82w05	5:28:20
McRae 10	5	29N47	82w02	5:28:08
Meadowbrook 10	5	30N08	81w42	5:26:48
Meadowbrook 48	5	28N34	81w27	5:25:48
Meadowbrook Terrace 10	5	30N08	81w42	5:26:48
Mecca 59	5	28N48	81w15	5:25:00
Medart 65	5	30N05	84w23	5:37:32
Medley 13	6	25N50	80w19	5:21:16
Medulla 53	5	27N58	81w59	5:27:56
Melaleuca Isle 6	6	26N07	80w13	5:20:52
Melbourne 5	5	28N05	80w37	5:22:28
Melbourne Beach 5	5	28N04	80w34	5:22:16
Melbourne Gardens 5	5	28N05	80w38	5:22:32
Melbourne Shores 5	5	28N05	80w36	5:22:24
Melbourne Village 5	5	28N05	80w40	5:22:40
Melrose 1	5	29N43	82w03	5:28:12
Melrose Park 6	6	26N08	80w12	5:20:48
Melrose Park 12	5	30N17	81w24	5:25:36
Memphis 41	5	27N32	82w33	5:30:12
Meredith Manor 59	5	28N42	81w20	5:25:20

Meridan 37 5 30N26 84w17 5:37:08
Merritt Island 5 5 28N21 80w42 5:22:48
Mexico Beach 3 1 29N57 85w25 5:41:40
Miami 13 6 25N47 80w11 5:20:44
Miami Beach 13 6 25N47 80w08 5:20:32
Miami Gardens 6 6 25N59 80w12 5:20:48
Miami Gardens 13 6 25N52 80w06 5:20:24
Miami Lakes 13 6 25N54 80w18 5:21:12
Miami Shores 13 6 25N52 80w11 5:20:44
Miami Springs 13 6 25N49 80w18 5:21:12
Micanopy 1 5 29N30 82w17 5:29:08
Micco 5 5 27N53 80w30 5:22:00
Miccosukee 37 5 30N36 84w03 5:36:12
Middleburg 10 5 30N04 81w52 5:27:28
Middle Keys 44 5 24N46 80w57 5:23:48
Midway 20 5 30N30 84w27 5:37:48
Midway 29 5 28N01 82w08 5:28:32
Midway 59 5 28N48 81w15 5:25:00
Midway West 13 6 25N51 80w15 5:21:00
Mikesville 12 5 30N17 81w24 5:25:36
Millcreek 55 5 29N48 81w16 5:25:04
Milligan 46 1 30N45 86w38 5:46:32
Millspring 32 1 30N43 85w01 5:40:04
Milltown 23 1 29N48 85w18 5:41:12
Millview 17 4 30N26 87w17 5:49:08
Millville 3 1 30N09 85w39 5:42:36
Milton 57 3 30N38 87w03 5:48:12
Mims 5 5 28N40 80w51 5:23:24
Mineral Springs 57
1 30N57 87w09 5:48:36
Minneola 35 5 28N35 81w45 5:27:00
Mintons Corner 5 5 28N05 80w38 5:22:32
Miracle Mile 36 5 26N36 81w52 5:27:28
Miramar 6 6 25N59 80w15 5:21:00
Miramar Beach 66 1 30N25 86w33 5:46:12
Miramar Terrace 16
5 30N27 81w34 5:26:16
Mission City 64 5 29N02 80w55 5:23:40
Mobile Haven Estates 36
5 26N36 81w52 5:27:28
Mobile Home Park 58
5 27N19 82w31 5:30:04
Mobile Manor 59 5 28N42 81w20 5:25:20
Modello 13 5 25N29 80w30 5:22:00
Moffitt 25 5 27N29 81w48 5:27:12
Molino 17 1 30N43 87w20 5:49:20
Molino Crossroads 17
1 30N37 87w20 5:49:20
Money Bayou 23 1 29N48 85w18 5:41:12
Monroe 11 5 25N54 81w17 5:25:08
Monroes Corner 42 5 29N00 82w02 5:28:08
Montbrook 38 5 29N20 82w27 5:29:48
Montclair 35 5 28N49 81w53 5:27:32
Monteocha 1 5 29N40 82w20 5:29:20
Monterey 16 5 30N20 81w35 5:26:20
Monticello 33 5 30N33 83w52 5:35:28
Montverde 35 5 28N36 81w41 5:26:44
Moore Haven 22 5 26N50 81w06 5:24:24
Moreland Park 60 5 28N53 82w02 5:28:08
Morningside Park 48
5 28N29 81w22 5:25:28
Morrison Home 50 6 26N40 80w06 5:20:24
Morriston 38 5 29N17 82w27 5:29:48
Morse Shores 36 5 26N39 81w50 5:27:20
Mosley Hall 40 5 30N28 83w38 5:34:32
Moss Bluff 42 5 29N03 81w56 5:27:44
Mossy Head 66 1 30N45 86w19 5:45:16
Moultrie 55 5 29N48 81w16 5:25:04
Moultrie Junction 55
5 29N48 81w16 5:25:04
Mountain Lake 53 5 27N53 81w34 5:26:16
Mount Carmel 57 1 30N59 87w07 5:48:28
Mount Dora 35 5 28N49 81w38 5:26:32
Mount Pleasant 20 5 30N35 84w35 5:38:20
Mount Plymouth 35 5 28N49 81w34 5:26:16
Mount Royal 54 5 29N29 81w41 5:26:44
Mulat 57 1 30N39 87w05 5:48:20
Mulberry 53 5 27N54 81w59 5:27:56
Mullinsville 53 5 27N45 81w32 5:26:08
Mullis City 29 5 28N04 82w29 5:29:56
Munson 57 1 30N52 86w52 5:47:28
Munson Island 44 5 24N34 81w44 5:26:56
Murdock 8 5 27N01 82w09 5:28:36
Murray Hill 16 5 30N19 81w43 5:26:52
Myakka 41 5 27N26 82w21 5:29:24
Myakka City 41 5 27N21 82w10 5:28:40
Myakka Head 41 5 27N29 81w55 5:27:40
Myakka River Manor 58
5 27N04 82w20 5:29:20
Myerlee 36 5 26N36 81w52 5:27:28
Myrtis 12 5 30N17 81w24 5:25:36
Myrtle Grove 17 4 30N26 87w17 5:49:08
Nalcrest 53 5 27N53 81w34 5:26:16
Naples 11 5 26N08 81w48 5:27:12
Naples Manor 11 5 26N11 81w48 5:27:12
Naples Park 11 5 26N16 81w48 5:27:12
Naranja 13 5 25N31 80w26 5:21:44
Narcoossee 49 5 28N18 81w14 5:24:56
Nash 33 5 30N23 83w49 5:35:16
Nassauville 45 5 30N40 81w27 5:25:48
National Gardens 64
5 29N18 81w03 5:24:12
Naval Air Medical Center 17
4 30N30 87w15 5:49:00
Naval Air Station 17
4 30N21 87w16 5:49:04
Naval Hospital 16 5 30N19 81w39 5:26:36
Naval Technical Training Cen 17
1 30N04 87w12 5:48:48
Naval Training Center 48
5 28N34 81w19 5:25:16
Navarre 57 1 30N24 86w52 5:47:28
Neptune Beach 16 5 30N21 81w25 5:25:40
New Berlin 16 5 30N27 81w34 5:26:16
Newbern 29 5 28N09 82w28 5:29:52
Newberry 1 5 29N39 82w37 5:30:28
Newburn 61 5 30N16 83w09 5:32:36
New Harmony 66 1 31N00 86w19 5:45:16
New Hope 30 1 30N46 85w51 5:43:24
New Hope 67 1 30N38 85w43 5:42:52
New Liberty City 13
6 25N55 80w15 5:21:00
New Pierce 41 5 27N24 82w32 5:30:08
New Point Comfort 8
5 26N56 82w16 5:29:04
Newport 44 5 25N08 80w25 5:21:40
Newport 65 5 30N12 84w11 5:36:44
New Port Richey 51
5 28N16 82w43 5:30:52
New River 4 5 29N58 82w16 5:29:04
New River 6 6 26N08 80w11 5:20:44
New Smyrna 64 5 28N59 80w56 5:23:44
New Smyrna Beach 64
5 29N01 80w56 5:23:44
Newtown Heights 58
5 27N19 82w31 5:30:04
New Upsala 59 5 28N48 81w15 5:25:00
New York 57 1 30N50 87w12 5:48:48
Niceville 46 1 30N31 86w30 5:46:00
Nichols 53 5 27N54 82w02 5:28:08
Nobles 17 4 30N29 87w12 5:48:48
Nobleton 27 5 28N39 82w16 5:29:04
Nocatee 14 5 27N10 81w53 5:27:32
Nokomis 58 5 27N08 82w27 5:29:48
Noma 30 1 30N59 85w37 5:42:28
Norfleet 37 5 30N26 84w18 5:37:12
Norin Plaza 13 6 25N53 80w11 5:20:44
Norland 13 6 25N56 80w13 5:20:52
Normandy 13 6 25N51 80w08 5:20:32
Normandy 16 5 30N19 81w43 5:26:52
Normandy Isle 13 6 25N48 80w09 5:20:36
Normandy Manor 16 5 30N19 81w43 5:26:52
Normandy Village 16
5 30N14 81w57 5:27:48
North Andrews Gardens 6
6 26N11 80w09 5:20:36
North Andrews Terrace 6
6 26N12 80w09 5:20:36
North Babcock 5 5 28N05 80w38 5:22:32
North Bay Village 13
6 25N51 80w10 5:20:40
North Columbia 12 5 30N23 82w35 5:30:20
North Crest 48 5 28N41 81w28 5:25:52
Northeast Park 52 5 27N48 82w39 5:30:36
North Fort Myers 36
5 26N40 81w54 5:27:36
North Lauderdale 6
6 26N13 80w13 5:20:52
North Miami 13 6 25N54 80w11 5:20:44
North Miami Beach 13
6 25N56 80w10 5:20:40
North Naples 11 5 26N12 81w48 5:27:12
North Oak Hill 16 5 30N16 81w43 5:26:52
North Orlando 59 5 28N41 81w17 5:25:08
North Palm Beach 50
6 26N49 80w04 5:20:16
North Peninsula 64
5 29N23 81w05 5:24:20
North Port 58 5 27N04 82w20 5:29:20
North Port Charlotte 58
5 27N03 82w14 5:28:56
North Redington Beach 52
5 27N49 82w49 5:31:16
North River Shores 43
5 27N12 80w15 5:21:00
North Saint Johns 55
5 30N08 81w29 5:25:56
North Shore 16 5 30N23 81w41 5:26:44
Northside 58 5 27N19 82w31 5:30:04
Northwest 13 6 25N51 80w14 5:20:56
North Westside 13 6 25N48 80w19 5:21:16
North Winter Haven 53
5 28N03 81w44 5:26:56
Northwood 1 5 29N40 82w20 5:29:20
Northwood 50 6 26N45 80w05 5:20:20
Norwood 13 6 25N57 80w13 5:20:52
Nova Road 64 5 29N18 81w03 5:24:12
NTC Annex 48 5 28N26 81w21 5:25:24
Nutall Rise 62 5 30N07 83w35 5:34:20
Oak 42 5 29N11 82w09 5:28:36
Oak Crest 1 5 29N36 82w05 5:28:20
Oakdale 32 1 30N47 85w14 5:40:56
Oak Grove 17 1 30N55 87w27 5:49:48
Oak Grove 20 5 30N42 84w51 5:39:24
Oak Grove 23 1 29N48 85w18 5:41:12
Oak Grove 25 5 27N33 81w49 5:27:16
Oak Grove 46 1 30N48 86w40 5:46:40
Oak Habor 16 5 30N21 81w25 5:25:40
Oak Haven 16 5 30N17 81w35 5:26:20
Oak Hill 64 5 28N52 80w51 5:23:24
Oak Hill Park 16 5 30N16 81w43 5:26:52
Oakhurst 52 5 27N53 82w46 5:31:04
Oakland 48 5 28N33 81w38 5:26:32
Oakland Hills 59 5 28N37 81w25 5:25:40
Oakland Park 6 6 26N10 80w08 5:20:32
Oakland Park 35 5 28N48 81w39 5:26:36
Oakland Shores 48 5 28N38 81w22 5:25:28
Oak Terrace 53 5 27N54 81w58 5:27:52
Oakwood Villa 16 5 30N20 81w35 5:26:20
O'Brien 61 5 30N02 82w57 5:31:48
Ocala 42 5 29N11 82w08 5:28:32
Ocala Ridge 42 5 29N11 82w09 5:28:36
Ocean Beach 5 5 28N20 80w37 5:22:28
Ocean Breeze 43 5 27N15 80w13 5:20:52
Ocean Breeze Park 43
5 27N13 80w12 5:20:48
Ocean City 46 1 30N26 86w36 5:46:24
Ocean Ridge 50 6 26N32 80w03 5:20:12
Ocean View 13 6 25N50 80w08 5:20:32
Oceanway 16 5 30N28 81w38 5:26:32
Ochopee 11 5 25N54 81w18 5:25:12
Ocoee 48 5 28N34 81w33 5:26:12
Odessa 51 5 28N11 82w36 5:30:24
Ojus 13 6 25N57 80w09 5:20:36
Okahumpka 35 5 28N45 81w54 5:27:36
Okeechobee 47 5 27N15 80w50 5:23:20
Okeelanta 50 5 26N37 80w43 5:22:52
Oklawaha 42 5 29N03 81w56 5:27:44
Old Calloway 3 1 30N09 85w39 5:42:36
Oldsmar 52 5 28N02 82w40 5:30:40
Old Town 15 5 29N36 82w59 5:31:56
Olustee 2 5 30N12 82w26 5:29:44
Olympia Heights 13
6 25N43 80w21 5:21:24
Ona 25 5 27N29 81w55 5:27:40
Oneco 41 5 27N27 82w33 5:30:12
O'Neil 45 5 30N40 81w27 5:25:48
Opa Locka 13 6 25N55 80w14 5:20:56
Open Air 52 5 27N47 82w40 5:30:40
Orange 39 5 30N26 84w59 5:39:56
Orange Bend 35 5 28N49 81w53 5:27:32
Orange Blossom 35 5 28N43 81w46 5:27:04
Orange Blossom 48 5 28N31 81w24 5:25:36
Orange Blossom Hills 42
5 29N00 82w02 5:28:08
Orange City 64 5 28N57 81w18 5:25:12
Orange City Hills 64
5 28N55 81w17 5:25:08
Orangedale 53 5 28N03 81w56 5:27:44
Orangedale 55 5 29N59 81w41 5:26:44
Orange Hammock 18 5 29N28 81w15 5:25:00
Orange Heights 1 5 29N43 82w08 5:28:32
Orange Hill 67 1 30N47 85w32 5:42:08
Orange Home 60 5 28N30 81w32 5:26:08
Orange Lake 42 5 29N25 82w13 5:28:52
Orange Mills 54 5 29N39 81w36 5:26:24
Orange Park 10 5 30N10 81w42 5:26:48
Orange Springs 42 5 29N30 81w57 5:27:48
Orchid 31 5 27N46 80w25 5:21:40
Orienta Gardens 59
5 28N40 81w22 5:25:28
Orient Park 29 5 28N00 82w30 5:30:00
Oriole Beach 57 4 30N22 87w11 5:48:44
Orlando 48 5 28N33 81w23 5:25:32
Orlando Naval Hospital 48
5 28N34 81w19 5:25:16
Orlovista 48 5 28N32 81w26 5:25:44
Ormond Beach 64 5 29N17 81w03 5:24:12
Ormond By The Sea 64
5 29N20 81w04 5:24:16
Ortega 16 5 30N16 81w43 5:26:52
Ortega Forest 16 5 30N19 81w39 5:26:36
Ortega Hills 16 5 30N19 81w39 5:26:36
Osceola Forest 16 5 30N23 81w41 5:26:44
Oslo 5 27N35 80w23 5:21:32
Osprey 58 5 27N12 82w29 5:29:56
Osteen 64 5 28N51 81w10 5:24:40
Otis 16 5 30N19 81w50 5:27:20
Otter Creek 38 5 29N19 82w46 5:31:04
Outer West 13 6 25N47 80w24 5:21:36
Overbrook Gardens 58
5 26N56 82w16 5:29:04
Overstreet 23 1 30N00 85w22 5:41:28
Oviedo 59 5 28N40 81w13 5:24:52
Oxford 60 5 28N56 82w02 5:28:08
Oyster Bayou 51 5 28N14 82w44 5:30:56
Ozello 9 5 28N54 82w35 5:30:20
Ozona 52 5 28N04 82w47 5:31:08
Pace 57 3 30N36 87w10 5:48:40
Page Park 36 5 26N35 81w52 5:27:28
Pahokee 50 5 26N50 80w40 5:22:40
Painters Hill 18 5 29N32 81w09 5:24:36
Paisley 35 5 29N00 81w32 5:26:08
Palatka 54 5 29N39 81w38 5:26:32
Palma Ceia 29 5 27N56 82w30 5:30:00
Palm Acres 36 5 26N36 81w52 5:27:28
Palma Sola 41 5 27N30 82w38 5:30:32
Palma Sola Park 41
5 27N28 82w35 5:30:20
Palm Bay 5 5 28N02 80w35 5:22:20
Palm Beach 50 6 26N43 80w02 5:20:08
Palm Beach Air Force Base 50
6 26N40 80w06 5:20:24
Palm Beach Gardens 50
6 26N50 80w06 5:20:24
Palm Beach Shores 50
6 26N47 80w02 5:20:08
Palm City 43 5 27N09 80w16 5:21:04
Palmdale 22 5 26N57 81w19 5:25:16
Palmetto 41 5 27N31 82w34 5:30:16
Palmetto Estates 13
5 25N36 80w22 5:21:28
Palm Harbor 52 5 27N57 82w45 5:31:00
Palm River 29 5 27N57 82w24 5:29:36
Palm River Estates 11
5 26N11 81w48 5:27:12
Palm Shores 5 5 28N12 80w41 5:22:44
Palm Springs 50 6 26N37 80w06 5:20:24
Palm Springs North 13
6 25N53 80w17 5:21:08
Palm Valley 55 5 30N15 81w23 5:25:32
Palm View 41 5 27N32 82w34 5:30:16
Palm Village 13 6 25N53 80w17 5:21:08
Paloma Park 36 5 26N39 81w53 5:27:32
Panacea 65 5 30N02 84w23 5:37:32
Panacea Park 65 5 30N02 84w23 5:37:32
Panacoochee Retreats 60
5 28N45 82w05 5:28:20
Panama City 3 1 30N10 85w40 5:42:40
Panama City Beach 3
1 30N10 85w48 5:43:12
Panama Park 16 5 30N12 81w35 5:26:20
Paola 59 5 28N48 81w15 5:25:00
Paolita Station 11
5 25N52 81w23 5:25:32
Paradise 5 29N42 82w21 5:29:24
Paradise Bay 41 5 27N28 82w35 5:30:20
Paradise Beach 17 1 30N24 87w25 5:49:40

Paradise Palms 50 6 26N23 80W05 5:20:20
Paradise Park 56 5 27N21 80W19 5:21:16
Paradise Point 9 5 28N54 82W35 5:30:20
Paradise Shores 36
5 26N39 81W50 5:27:20
Park City 6 6 26N07 80W13 5:20:52
Parker 3 1 30N08 85W36 5:42:24
Parkland 6 6 26N19 80W15 5:21:00
Parmalee 41 5 27N21 82W10 5:28:40
Paront 32 1 30N43 85W01 5:40:04
Parrish 41 5 27N35 82W26 5:29:44
Pasco 51 5 28N19 82W20 5:29:20
Pass-a-Grille Beach 52
5 27N44 82W45 5:31:00
Patrick Air Force Base 5
5 28N14 80W36 5:22:24
Paxon 16 5 30N19 81W43 5:26:52
Paxton 66 1 30N59 86W18 5:45:12
Peace River Shores 8
5 26N57 82W00 5:28:00
Peach Orchard 1 5 29N32 82W31 5:30:04
Pecan Park 16 5 30N26 81W39 5:26:36
Peddys Mill 53 5 27N54 81W58 5:27:52
Pedro 42 5 29N00 82W02 5:28:08
Pelican Lake 50 5 26N45 80W41 5:22:44
Pembroke 53 5 27N47 81W48 5:27:12
Pembroke Park 6 6 25N59 80W10 5:20:40
Pembroke Pines 6 6 26N00 80W14 5:20:56
Peniel 54 5 29N39 81W39 5:26:36
Peninsula 29 5 27N56 82W30 5:30:00
Peninsula 64 5 29N11 81W00 5:24:00
Penney Farms 10 5 30N01 81W48 5:27:12
Pennsuco 13 6 25N54 80W23 5:21:32
Pensacola 17 4 30N25 87W13 5:48:52
Pensacola Beach 17
4 30N22 87W11 5:48:44
Pensacola Shores 57
4 30N22 87W11 5:48:44
Peoples City 42 5 29N25 82W13 5:28:52
Peppertree Bay 58 5 27N20 82W32 5:30:08
Perrine 13 5 25N36 80W21 5:21:24
Perry 62 5 30N07 83W35 5:34:20
Peters 13 5 25N36 80W22 5:21:28
Philips Plaza 16 5 30N18 81W38 5:26:32
Phillipi Gardens 58
5 27N17 82W31 5:30:04
Picketville 16 5 30N19 81W43 5:26:52
Picnic 29 5 28N00 82W31 5:30:04
Picolata 55 5 29N48 81W16 5:25:04
Pierce 53 5 27N54 81W58 5:27:52
Pierson 64 5 29N14 81W28 5:25:52
Pine Air 50 6 26N40 80W06 5:20:24
Pine Castle 48 5 28N28 81W22 5:25:28
Pine Crest 29 5 28N00 82W30 5:30:00
Pineda 5 5 28N14 80W40 5:22:40
Pine Dale 53 5 27N50 81W58 5:27:52
Pine Forest 17 4 30N29 87W12 5:48:48
Pine Grove 5 5 28N05 80W38 5:22:32
Pine Grove 49 5 28N15 81W17 5:25:08
Pine Grove 61 5 30N18 82W59 5:31:56
Pine Hill Estates 1
5 29N40 82W20 5:29:20
Pine Hills 48 5 28N35 81W27 5:25:48
Pine Island Center 36
5 26N36 81W52 5:27:28
Pineland 36 5 26N39 82W09 5:28:36
Pineland 62 5 30N07 83W35 5:34:20
Pineland Gardens 16
5 30N17 81W35 5:26:20
Pine Level 14 5 27N13 81W52 5:27:28
Pinellas Park 52 5 27N50 82W43 5:30:52
Pine Log 3 1 30N24 85W55 5:43:40
Pine Manor 36 5 26N36 81W52 5:27:28
Pineola 9 5 28N41 82W17 5:29:08
Pine Ridge Country Estates 9
5 28N51 82W29 5:29:56
Pine Shores 58 5 27N16 82W32 5:30:08
Pinesville 1 5 29N32 82W31 5:30:04
Pinetta 40 5 30N36 83W21 5:33:24
Pineville 17 1 31N01 87W30 5:50:00
Pinewood 13 6 25N54 80W13 5:20:52
Piney Point 41 5 27N38 82W32 5:30:08
Pioneer Village 36
5 26N39 81W53 5:27:32
Pirate Harbor 8 5 26N57 82W00 5:28:00
Pittman 30 1 30N47 85W49 5:43:16
Placida 8 5 26N50 82W16 5:29:04
Plantation 6 6 26N08 80W15 5:21:00
Plantation 44 5 25N01 80W31 5:22:04
Plantation Acres 6
6 26N07 80W13 5:20:52
Plantation Isles 6
6 26N07 80W13 5:20:52
Plantation Park 6 6 26N07 80W13 5:20:52
Plant City 29 5 28N01 82W07 5:28:28
Platt 14 5 27N13 81W52 5:27:28
Playland Isles 6 6 26N07 80W13 5:20:52
Playland Village 6
6 26N07 80W13 5:20:52
Plaza 42 5 29N11 82W09 5:28:36
Pleasant Grove 17 4 30N25 87W17 5:49:08
Pleasant Grove 29 5 27N54 82W11 5:28:44
Pleasant Grove 66 1 30N43 86W07 5:44:28
Pleasant Ridge 66 1 30N43 86W07 5:44:28
Plummer 16 5 30N24 81W45 5:27:00
Plymouth 48 5 28N42 81W33 5:26:12
Poinciana 49 5 28N18 81W25 5:25:40
Point Washington 66
1 30N22 86W07 5:44:28
Polk City 53 5 28N11 81W50 5:27:20
Polly Town 16 5 30N26 81W39 5:26:36
Polo Club Estates 50
6 26N40 80W06 5:20:24
Pomona Park 54 5 29N30 81W36 5:26:24
Pompano Beach 6 6 26N14 80W08 5:20:32

Pompano Beach Highlands 6
6 26N17 80W10 5:20:40
Ponce 13 6 25N45 80W16 5:21:04
Ponce de Leon 30 1 30N44 85W56 5:43:44
Ponce Inlet 64 5 29N05 80W56 5:23:44
Ponce Park 5 29N05 80W55 5:23:40
Ponte Vedra 55 5 30N15 81W23 5:25:32
Ponte Vedra Beach 55
5 30N15 81W23 5:25:32
Port Charlotte 8 5 26N59 82W06 5:28:24
Port Everglades 6 6 26N05 80W09 5:20:36
Portland 66 1 30N31 86W12 5:44:48
Port Malabar 5 5 28N04 80W37 5:22:28
Port Mayaca 5 26N59 80W36 5:22:24
Port of Palm Beach Junction 50
6 26N47 80W04 5:20:16
Port Orange 64 5 29N09 80W59 5:23:56
Port Richey 51 5 28N24 82W35 5:30:20
Port Saint Joe 23 5 29N49 85W18 5:41:12
Port Saint John 5 5 28N22 80W45 5:23:00
Port Saint Lucie 56
5 27N21 80W19 5:21:16
Port Salerno 43 5 27N09 80W12 5:20:48
Port Sewall 43 5 27N11 80W12 5:20:48
Port Tampa City 29
5 27N52 82W31 5:30:04
Pottsburg 16 5 30N17 81W35 5:26:20
Powell 27 5 28N32 82W29 5:29:56
Princeton 5 25N32 80W25 5:21:40
Prine 53 5 28N07 81W37 5:26:28
Produce 29 5 28N00 82W25 5:29:40
Progress Village 29
5 27N54 82W22 5:29:28
Prospect Road 6 6 26N09 80W12 5:20:48
Prosperity 30 1 30N51 85W57 5:43:48
Providence 53 5 28N09 81W58 5:27:52
Providence 63 5 30N07 82W29 5:29:56
Pumpkin Center 35 5 28N44 81W49 5:27:16
Punta Gorda 8 5 26N56 82W03 5:28:12
Punta Gorda Isles 8
5 26N57 82W00 5:28:00
Punta Rassa 36 5 26N29 82W01 5:28:04
Purvis Still 24 5 30N31 82W56 5:31:44
Putnam Hall 54 5 29N44 81W58 5:27:52
Quincy 20 5 30N35 84W34 5:38:16
Quinlan 16 5 30N26 81W39 5:26:36
Raccoon Key 44 5 24N34 81W44 5:26:56
Raiford 63 5 30N04 82W14 5:28:56
Rainbow Homes 50 6 26N27 80W05 5:20:20
Rainbow Lakes 42 5 29N03 82W27 5:29:48
Raleigh 38 5 29N27 82W28 5:29:52
Ralston Beach 29 5 28N00 82W30 5:30:00
Ramrod Key 44 5 24N45 81W20 5:25:20
Ravenna Park 59 5 28N48 81W15 5:25:00
Rawls Park 53 5 28N03 81W56 5:27:44
Redbay 66 1 30N39 85W59 5:43:56
Reddick 42 5 29N22 82W12 5:28:48
Red Head 67 1 30N29 85W51 5:43:24
Redington Beach 52
5 27N49 82W49 5:31:16
Redington Shores 52
5 27N50 82W50 5:31:20
Redland 13 5 25N29 80W30 5:22:00
Red Level 9 5 28N54 82W35 5:30:20
Remley Heights 35 5 28N48 81W39 5:26:36
Remuda Ranch Grants 11
5 25N55 81W39 5:26:36
Rerdell 27 5 28N34 82W09 5:28:36
Resota Beach 3 1 30N18 85W36 5:42:24
Rex 1 5 29N36 82W05 5:28:20
Ribault Manor 16 5 30N23 81W41 5:26:44
Richey Lakes 51 5 28N14 82W44 5:30:56
Richloam 27 5 28N37 82W03 5:28:12
Richmond Heights 13
5 25N38 80W23 5:21:32
Rideout 10 5 30N06 81W47 5:27:08
Ridge Harbor 8 5 26N57 82W00 5:28:00
Ridge Manor 27 5 28N31 82W10 5:28:40
Ridgewood 1 5 29N40 82W20 5:29:20
Ridgewood 10 5 30N08 81W42 5:26:48
Ridge Wood Heights 58
5 27N17 82W31 5:30:04
Rileys Park 35 5 28N48 81W39 5:26:36
Rio 43 5 27N13 80W12 5:20:48
Rital 27 5 28N28 82W12 5:28:48
Ritta 50 5 26N45 80W58 5:23:52
Riverdale 27 5 28N22 82W11 5:28:44
River Junction 20 5 30N42 84W51 5:39:24
Riverland Village 6
6 26N06 80W12 5:20:48
River Lawn 36 5 26N39 81W50 5:27:20
River Ranch 53 5 27N53 81W34 5:26:16
River Ranch Shores 53
5 27N53 81W34 5:26:16
Riverside 13 6 25N46 80W14 5:20:56
Riverside 16 5 30N20 81W41 5:26:44
Riverview 16 5 30N23 81W41 5:26:44
Riverview 17 4 30N26 87W13 5:48:52
Riverview 29 3 30N32 87W12 5:48:48
Riviera Beach 50 6 26N47 80W03 5:20:12
Riviera Colony 11 5 26N11 81W48 5:27:12
Rixsford 61 5 30N18 82W59 5:31:56
Robin Hill 59 5 28N40 81W22 5:25:28
Robinson Point 57 1 30N39 87W05 5:48:20
Rochelle 1 5 29N36 82W14 5:28:56
Rock Bluff 39 5 30N26 84W59 5:39:56
Rockdale Keys 13 5 25N36 80W22 5:21:28
Rock Harbor 44 5 24N45 81W20 5:25:20
Rock Hill 6 6 26N07 80W13 5:20:52
Rock Hill 66 1 30N43 86W07 5:44:28
Rock Island Village 6
6 26N07 80W13 5:20:52
Rockledge 5 5 28N20 80W44 5:22:56
Rock Springs 48 5 28N41 81W28 5:25:52
Rocky Creek 29 5 28N00 82W34 5:30:16

Ro-len Lake Gardens 6
6 25N59 80W09 5:20:36
Rolling Acres 27 5 28N32 82W29 5:29:56
Rolling Hills 16 5 30N19 81W43 5:26:52
Rolling Hills 53 5 27N50 81W58 5:27:52
Rolling Oak Acres 6
6 26N07 80W13 5:20:52
Romeo 42 5 29N03 82W27 5:29:48
Roosevelt Estates 50
6 26N40 80W06 5:20:24
Rosedale 20 5 30N42 84W51 5:39:24
Roseland 31 5 27N50 80W30 5:22:00
Rosemont Hills 48 5 28N35 81W24 5:25:36
Rotonda West 8 5 26N50 82W16 5:29:04
Round Lake 32 1 30N39 85W24 5:41:36
Roy 5 29N37 81W29 5:25:56
Royal 60 5 28N53 82W02 5:28:08
Royal Gardens Estates 41
5 27N28 82W35 5:30:20
Royal Oak Hills 50
6 26N23 80W05 5:20:20
Royal Palm Beach 50
6 26N41 80W15 5:21:00
Royal Palm Beach Plaza 50
6 26N40 80W06 5:20:24
Royal Pal Village 36
5 26N36 81W52 5:27:28
Royals Cross Roads 30
1 30N46 85W51 5:43:24
Rubonia 41 5 27N35 82W33 5:30:12
Ruskin 29 5 27N43 82W26 5:29:44
Russell 10 5 30N03 81W45 5:27:00
Rutland 60 5 28N45 82W05 5:28:20
Rutledge 1 5 29N40 82W20 5:29:20
Safety Harbor 52 5 28N00 82W43 5:30:52
Saint Andrews 3 1 30N09 85W39 5:42:36
Saint Armand's 58 5 27N19 82W31 5:30:04
Saint Augustine 55
5 29N54 81W19 5:25:16
Saint Augustine Beach 55
5 29N51 81W16 5:25:04
Saint Augustine Shores 55
5 29N48 81W16 5:25:04
Saint Catherine 60
5 28N37 82W08 5:28:32
Saint Cloud 49 5 28N15 81W17 5:25:08
Saint Georges Island 19
5 29N45 84W53 5:39:32
Saint James City 36
5 26N29 82W05 5:28:20
Saint Johns Park 16
5 30N16 81W43 5:26:52
Saint Johns Park 18
5 29N28 81W15 5:25:00
Saint Joseph 51 5 28N22 82W11 5:28:44
Saint Leo 51 5 28N20 82W15 5:29:00
Saint Lucie 56 5 27N29 80W20 5:21:20
Saint Marks 65 5 30N09 84W12 5:36:48
Saint Nicholas 16 5 30N21 81W31 5:26:04
Saint Petersburg 52
5 27N46 82W39 5:30:36
Saint Petersburg Beach 19
5 27N45 82W45 5:31:00
Salem 62 5 29N53 83W25 5:33:40
Salerno 43 5 27N09 80W12 5:20:48
Salt Springs 42 5 29N21 81W44 5:26:56
Salvista 36 5 26N39 81W53 5:27:32
Samoset 41 5 27N28 82W33 5:30:12
Sampson 4 5 29N55 82W13 5:28:52
Samsula 64 5 29N02 80W55 5:23:40
San Antonio 51 5 28N21 82W17 5:29:08
Sanborn 65 5 30N05 84W36 5:38:24
San Carlos Park 36
5 26N36 81W52 5:27:28
Sandalfoot Cove 50
6 26N23 80W05 5:20:20
Sandalwood 16 5 30N17 81W35 5:26:20
Sand Cut 50 5 26N49 80W40 5:22:40
Sanderson 2 5 30N15 82W16 5:29:04
Sandestin 66 1 30N25 86W33 5:46:12
Sandpiper Cove 46 1 30N25 86W33 5:46:12
Sandy 41 5 27N21 82W10 5:28:40
Sanford 59 5 28N48 81W16 5:25:04
Sangully 53 5 28N03 81W56 5:27:44
Sanibel 36 5 26N27 82W01 5:28:04
San Jose 16 5 30N15 81W38 5:26:32
San Jose Estates 16
5 30N14 81W38 5:26:32
San Marco 16 5 30N20 81W35 5:26:20
San Mateo 16 5 30N26 81W39 5:26:36
San Mateo 54 5 29N36 81W35 5:26:20
San Pablo 16 5 30N20 81W29 5:25:56
San Souci 16 5 30N17 81W35 5:26:20
San Souci Estates 13
6 25N53 80W11 5:20:44
Santa Fe 1 5 29N53 82W26 5:29:44
Santa Fe Lake 1 5 29N45 82W06 5:28:24
Santa Monica 3 1 30N15 85W57 5:43:48
Santa Monica 16 5 30N17 81W35 5:26:20
Santa Rosa Beach 66
1 30N22 86W14 5:44:56
Santos 42 5 29N06 82W06 5:28:24
Sarabay Acres 58 5 27N12 82W30 5:30:00
Sarasota 58 5 27N20 82W32 5:30:08
Sarasota Beach 58 5 27N16 82W33 5:30:12
Sarasota Springs 58
5 27N18 82W28 5:29:52
Saratoga 54 5 29N33 81W39 5:26:36
Sarno Plaza 5 5 28N10 80W38 5:22:32
Satellite Beach 5 5 28N10 80W36 5:22:24
Satsuma 5 29N33 81W39 5:26:36
Saufley Field 17 3 30N28 87W21 5:49:24
Sawdust 20 5 30N35 84W35 5:38:20
Sawgrass 55 5 30N15 81W23 5:25:32
Scotland 20 5 30N37 84W25 5:37:40
Scotts Ferry 7 1 30N27 85W03 5:40:12

FLORIDA

Scottsmoor 5	5	28N46	80w53	5:23:32
Seaglades 17	4	30N25	87w17	5:49:08
Seagrove Beach 66	1	30N19	86w08	5:44:32
Sea Ranch Lakes 6	6	26N12	80w06	5:20:24
Searstown 53	5	28N03	81w56	5:27:44
Seaside 44	5	25N08	80w25	5:21:40
Sebastian 31	5	27N49	80w28	5:21:52
Sebastian Highlands 31	5	27N47	80w29	5:21:56
Sebring 28	5	27N27	81w24	5:25:36
Sebring Southgate 28	5	27N30	81w27	5:25:48
Seffner 29	5	27N59	82w17	5:29:08
Seminole	5	27N50	82w47	5:31:08
Seminole 46	1	30N31	86w29	5:45:56
Seminole Heights 29	5	27N59	82w28	5:29:52
Seminole Lake Country Club 52	5	27N53	82w46	5:31:04
Seminole Manor 50	6	26N36	80w05	5:20:20
Seminole Park 52	5	27N53	82w46	5:31:04
Seville 64	5	29N19	81w30	5:26:00
Sewall's Point 43	5	27N11	80w10	5:20:40
Shackleford 17	4	30N27	87w13	5:48:52
Shadeville 65	5	30N11	84w23	5:37:32
Shady 42	5	29N11	82w09	5:28:36
Shady Grove 32	1	30N43	85w01	5:40:04
Shady Grove 62	5	30N17	83w38	5:34:32
Shady Rest 20	5	30N37	84w25	5:37:40
Shalimar 46	1	30N27	86w36	5:46:24
Shamrock 15	5	29N39	83w09	5:32:36
Shangri-la 52	5	27N53	82w46	5:31:04
Sharpes 5	5	28N26	80w46	5:23:04
Shawnee 22	5	26N45	80w58	5:23:52
Shell Bluff 18	5	29N28	81w15	5:25:00
Shell Land 52	5	27N56	82w46	5:31:04
Shell Point Village 36	5	26N36	81w52	5:27:28
Sheltering Pines 36	5	26N36	81w52	5:27:28
Shenandoah 13	6	25N45	80w14	5:20:56
Sherman 47	5	27N14	80w49	5:23:16
Sherwood Park 50	6	26N27	80w05	5:20:20
Shiloh 1	5	29N47	82w30	5:30:00
Shiloh 5	5	28N36	80w49	5:23:16
Shilow 29	5	28N01	82w08	5:28:32
Shingle Creek 49	5	28N18	81w25	5:25:40
Shorewood 6	6	26N18	80w10	5:20:40
Siesta 58	5	27N18	82w33	5:30:12
Siesta Key 58	5	27N17	82w33	5:30:12
Sills 32	1	30N47	85w14	5:40:56
Silver Beach Heights 35	5	28N56	81w40	5:26:40
Silver Sands 3	1	30N09	85w39	5:42:36
Silver Shores 6	6	26N11	80w09	5:20:36
Silver Springs 42	5	29N13	82w03	5:28:12
Silver Springs 46	1	30N46	86w34	5:46:16
Silver Springs Shores 42	5	29N11	82w09	5:28:36
Simpson Yard 16	5	30N21	81w39	5:26:36
Simsville 32	1	30N47	85w14	5:40:56
Singer Island 50	6	26N47	80w04	5:20:16
Sink Creek 32	1	30N37	85w09	5:40:36
Sipes 59	5	28N48	81w15	5:25:00
Sirmans 40	5	30N21	83w39	5:34:36
Sisco 54	5	29N30	81w36	5:26:24
Skycrest 52	5	28N00	82w46	5:31:04
Sky Lake 48	5	28N29	81w22	5:25:28
Skyland Heights 1	5	29N40	82w20	5:29:20
Slaughter 51	5	28N37	82w03	5:28:12
Slavia 59	5	28N40	81w12	5:24:48
Slones Ridge 35	5	28N34	81w52	5:27:28
Smith Creek 65	5	30N11	84w39	5:38:36
Smiths Corner 30	1	30N53	85w40	5:42:40
Smiths Crossroads 30	1	31N01	85w44	5:42:56
Snake Creek 6	6	25N59	80w12	5:20:48
Snapper Creek Park 13	6	25N42	80w19	5:21:16
Sneads 32	1	30N43	84w56	5:39:44
Snow Hill 59	5	28N40	81w12	5:24:48
Snug Harbor 43	5	27N12	80w15	5:21:00
Socrum 53	5	28N03	81w56	5:27:44
Solana 8	5	26N56	81w58	5:27:52
Sopchoppy 65	5	30N04	84w30	5:38:00
Sorrento 35	5	28N49	81w34	5:26:16
Sorrento Shores 58	5	27N12	82w30	5:30:00
South And East Junction 59	5	28N48	81w15	5:25:00
South And East Osceola 49	5	28N06	81w04	5:24:16
South Apopka 48	5	28N39	81w31	5:26:04
South Bay 50	5	26N40	80w43	5:22:52
Southboro 50	6	26N41	80w04	5:20:16
South Boyette 29	5	28N00	82w31	5:30:04
South Clewiston 26	5	26N45	80w58	5:23:52
South Daytona 64	5	29N10	81w00	5:24:00
Southeast 53	5	28N01	81w44	5:26:56
South Flomaton 17	1	30N53	87w22	5:49:28
South Fort Myers 36	5	26N36	81w52	5:27:28
Southgate 58	5	27N19	82w32	5:30:08
South Gate Ridge 58	5	27N17	82w30	5:30:00
South Jacksonville 16	5	30N18	81w38	5:26:32
South Miami 13	6	25N42	80w18	5:21:12
South Miami Heights 13	5	25N36	80w23	5:21:32
South Mulberry 53	5	27N54	81w58	5:27:52
South Ocala 42	5	29N11	82w09	5:28:36
South Palm Beach 50	6	26N35	80w02	5:20:08
South Pasadena 52	5	27N46	82w44	5:30:56
South Patrick 5	5	28N10	80w36	5:22:24
South Patrick Shores 5	5	28N12	80w36	5:22:24
South Peninsula 64	5	29N08	80w57	5:23:48
South Ponte Vedra Beach 55	5	30N03	81w20	5:25:20
Southport 3	1	30N17	85w39	5:42:36
South Punta Gorda Heights 8	5	26N52	82w00	5:28:00
Southridge 16	5	30N17	81w35	5:26:20
South Shore 50	5	26N45	80w58	5:23:52
Southside 6	6	26N05	80w09	5:20:36
Southside 35	5	28N56	81w40	5:26:40
Southside 53	5	28N02	81w57	5:27:48
Southside 58	5	27N19	82w31	5:30:04
Southside Estates 16	5	30N17	81w35	5:26:20
South Trail 58	5	27N19	82w31	5:30:04
South Venice 58	5	27N03	82w25	5:29:40
Southwest 50	6	26N40	80w06	5:20:24
South Westside 13	6	25N44	80w21	5:21:24
Southwood 48	5	28N29	81w22	5:25:28
Sparr 42	5	29N20	82w07	5:28:28
Spaulding 16	5	30N26	81w39	5:26:36
Spring Creek 65	5	30N26	84w17	5:37:08
Springfield 3	1	30N10	85w37	5:42:28
Spring Glen 16	5	30N18	81w38	5:26:32
Springhead 29	5	28N01	82w08	5:28:32
Spring Hill 27	5	28N32	82w29	5:29:56
Spring Lake 27	5	28N32	82w29	5:29:56
Spring Lake 28	5	27N30	81w27	5:25:48
Spring Park 16	5	30N18	81w38	5:26:32
Springside 54	5	29N39	81w39	5:26:36
Spuds 55	5	29N47	81w26	5:25:44
Stanton 42	5	28N59	81w55	5:27:40
Starke 4	5	29N57	82w07	5:28:28
State Highway 59	5	28N37	81w19	5:25:16
Steele Church 66	1	30N43	86w07	5:44:28
Steinhatchee 62	5	29N40	83w23	5:33:32
Stemper 29	5	28N09	82w28	5:29:52
Stephensville 62	5	29N41	83w23	5:33:32
Stetson 64	5	29N02	81w18	5:25:12
Stock Island 44	5	24N34	81w44	5:26:56
Streamline 50	5	26N49	80w40	5:22:40
Stuart 43	5	27N12	80w15	5:21:00
Suburban Heights 1	5	29N40	82w20	5:29:20
Sugar Loaf Shores 44	5	24N45	81w20	5:25:20
Sugarmill Woods 9	5	28N47	82w37	5:30:28
Sulphur Springs 29	5	28N01	82w27	5:29:48
Sumatra 39	5	30N01	84w59	5:39:56
Summerfield 42	5	29N01	82w02	5:28:08
Summer Haven 55	5	29N42	81w13	5:24:52
Summerland Key 44	5	24N40	81w27	5:25:48
Summerport Beach 48	5	28N34	81w35	5:26:20
Sumterville 60	5	28N45	82w04	5:28:16
Sunbeam 16	5	30N12	81w35	5:26:20
Sun City 29	5	27N41	82w28	5:29:52
Sun City Center 29	5	27N43	82w21	5:29:24
Suncoast Estates 36	5	26N39	81w53	5:27:32
Sun Garden 10	5	29N59	81w41	5:26:44
Sun Haven 58	5	27N21	82w31	5:30:04
Suniland 13	6	25N40	80w20	5:21:20
Sunland 59	5	28N48	81w15	5:25:00
Sunland Gardens 56	5	27N21	80w19	5:21:16
Sunniland 11	5	26N25	81w25	5:25:40
Sun 'n Lakes Estates 28	5	27N18	81w22	5:25:28
Sunny Hills 67	1	30N47	85w32	5:42:08
Sunny Isles 13	6	25N56	80w07	5:20:28
Sunnyland 58	6	26N34	80w03	5:20:12
Sunnyside 3	1	30N15	85w57	5:43:48
Sunnyside 35	5	28N49	81w53	5:27:32
Sun Ray Homes 53	5	27N45	81w32	5:26:08
Sunrise 6	6	26N09	80w13	5:20:52
Sunrise Golf Village 6	6	26N08	80w14	5:20:56
Sunrise Heights 6	6	26N07	80w13	5:20:52
Sunset Beach 52	5	27N47	82w46	5:31:04
Sunset Gardens 5	5	28N05	80w38	5:22:32
Sunset Harbor 42	5	29N00	82w02	5:28:08
Sunset Island 13	6	25N48	80w09	5:20:36
Sunset Point 44	5	25N01	80w31	5:22:04
Sunshine 29	5	28N00	82w34	5:30:16
Sunshine Beach 52	5	27N50	82w48	5:31:12
Sunshine Parkway 50	6	26N36	80w13	5:20:52
Sunshine Ranches 6	6	26N07	80w13	5:20:52
Suntree 5	5	28N05	80w38	5:22:32
Surfside 13	6	25N53	80w08	5:20:32
Suwanee Valley 12	5	30N17	81w24	5:25:36
Suwannee 15	5	29N20	83w09	5:32:36
Suwannee River 21	5	29N36	82w56	5:31:44
Suwannee Springs 61	5	30N18	82w59	5:31:56
Svea 46	1	30N58	86w27	5:45:48
Sweet Gum Head 30	1	30N46	85w51	5:43:24
Sweetwater 13	6	25N46	80w22	5:21:28
Sweetwater 16	5	30N14	81w57	5:27:48
Sweetwater 39	5	30N26	84w59	5:39:56
Sweetwater Creek 29	5	28N00	82w34	5:30:16
Sweetwater Oaks 59	5	28N42	81w20	5:25:20
Switzerland 55	5	29N59	81w41	5:26:44
Sycamore 20	5	30N35	84w35	5:38:20
Sydney 29	5	27N58	82w12	5:28:48
Sylvan Shores 35	5	28N48	81w39	5:26:36
Tacoma 1	5	29N30	82w17	5:29:08
Taft 48	5	28N26	81w22	5:25:28
Tahitian Gardens 51	5	28N12	82w45	5:31:00
Tallahassee 37	5	30N27	84w17	5:37:08
Tallevast 41	5	27N24	82w33	5:30:12
Talleyrand 16	5	30N27	81w34	5:26:16
Tamarac 6	6	26N11	80w13	5:20:52
Tamiami 13	6	25N46	80w19	5:21:16
Tampa 29	5	27N57	82w27	5:29:48
Tangelo Park 48	5	28N29	81w22	5:25:28
Tangerine 48	5	28N47	81w38	5:26:32
Tang-O-Mar Beach 66	1	30N25	86w33	5:46:12
Tarpon Springs 52	5	28N09	82w45	5:31:00
Tarrytown 60	5	28N37	82w03	5:28:12
Tavares 35	5	28N48	81w44	5:26:56
Tavernier 44	5	25N01	80w31	5:22:04
Taylor 2	5	30N15	82w16	5:29:04
Tee and Green Estates 8	5	26N57	82w00	5:28:00
Telogia 39	5	30N21	84w49	5:39:16
Temple Terrace 29	5	28N02	82w23	5:29:32
Tenille 62	5	29N47	83w20	5:33:20
Tensulate 16	5	30N14	81w57	5:27:48
Tequesta 50	6	26N58	80w06	5:20:24
Terra Ceia 41	5	27N35	82w35	5:30:20
Theressa 4	5	29N50	82w04	5:28:16
Thomas City 33	5	30N33	83w52	5:35:28
Thompson 44	5	25N01	80w31	5:22:04
Thonotosassa 29	5	28N04	82w18	5:29:12
Thunderbird 36	5	26N36	81w52	5:27:28
Tice 36	5	26N40	81w49	5:27:16
Tierra Verda 52	5	27N43	82w42	5:30:48
Tildenville 48	5	28N34	81w35	5:26:20
Tisonia 16	5	30N26	81w39	5:26:36
Titusville 5	5	28N37	80w49	5:23:16
Tocoi Junction 55	5	29N47	81w26	5:25:44
Tomoka Estates 64	5	29N18	81w03	5:24:12
Torrey 25	5	27N38	81w50	5:27:20
Towers 48	5	28N36	81w21	5:25:24
Town and Country Plaza 17	4	30N26	87w15	5:49:00
Townsend 34	5	30N12	83w17	5:33:08
Trailer City 37	5	30N26	84w17	5:37:08
Trailer Estates 41	5	27N25	82w35	5:30:20
Trailer Haven 5	5	28N05	80w38	5:22:32
Tranquility Park 53	5	28N01	81w44	5:26:56
Trapnell 29	5	28N01	82w08	5:28:32
Treasure Island 13	6	25N51	80w08	5:20:32
Treasure Island 52	5	27N46	82w46	5:31:04
Trenton 21	5	29N37	82w49	5:31:16
Triangle 35	5	28N48	81w39	5:26:36
Triangle Acres 35	5	28N48	81w39	5:26:36
Trilby 51	5	28N28	82w12	5:28:48
Tri Par Estates 58	5	27N23	82w32	5:30:08
Tropic 5	5	28N14	80w40	5:22:40
Tropical Gulf Acres 8	5	26N57	82w00	5:28:00
Tropical Shores Manor 35	5	28N48	81w44	5:26:56
Tropicanna Mobile Manor 36	5	26N36	81w52	5:27:28
Tropic Heights 8	5	26N57	82w00	5:28:00
Tropic Isle 50	6	26N27	80w05	5:20:20
Turkey Creek 29	5	28N01	82w08	5:28:32
Turner River 11	5	25N54	81w17	5:25:08
Tuscanooga 35	5	28N34	81w52	5:27:28
Twin Lake 29	5	28N01	82w27	5:29:48
Twin Palms 36	5	26N36	81w52	5:27:28
Two Egg 32	1	30N56	85w07	5:40:28
Tyndall 3	1	30N05	85w37	5:42:28
Tyndall Air Force Base 3	1	30N09	85w39	5:42:36
Uleta 13	6	25N47	80w13	5:20:52
Umatilla 35	5	28N59	81w35	5:26:20
Union Park 48	5	28N34	81w17	5:25:08
University 1	5	29N40	82w20	5:29:20
University 29	5	28N04	82w25	5:29:40
University of Miami 13	6	25N44	80w16	5:21:04
University of South Florida 29	5	28N04	82w25	5:29:40
University Of Tampa 29	5	27N56	82w29	5:29:56
University of West Florida 17	4	30N29	87w12	5:48:48
University Park 16	5	30N20	81w35	5:26:20
University Park 50	6	26N23	80w08	5:20:32
Upper Key Largo 44	5	25N08	80w25	5:21:40
Upper Keys 44	5	25N01	80w32	5:22:08
U.S.A.F. Hospital 46	1	30N28	86w32	5:46:08
Useppa Island 36	5	26N45	82w16	5:29:04
U.S. Navy Mine Defense Labor 3	1	30N09	85w39	5:42:36
Valkaria 5	5	27N58	80w33	5:22:12
Valley Church 66	1	30N43	86w07	5:44:28
Valparaiso 46	2	30N29	86w30	5:46:00
Valrico 29	5	27N56	82w17	5:29:08
Vamo 58	5	27N14	82w29	5:29:56
Venetia 16	5	30N19	81w39	5:26:36
Venetian Gardens 58	5	27N08	82w27	5:29:48
Venetian Islands 13	6	25N48	80w09	5:20:36
Venice 58	5	27N06	82w27	5:29:48

FLORIDA

Venice Beach Park 58 5 27N04 82w20 5:29:20
Venice Gardens 58 5 27N04 82w20 5:29:20
Venus 28 5 27N04 81w22 5:25:28
Verdie 45 5 30N14 81w57 5:27:48
Vermont Heights 55 5 29N49 81w24 5:25:36
Verna 41 5 27N21 82w10 5:28:40
Vernon 67 1 30N37 85w43 5:42:52
Vero Beach 31 5 27N38 80w24 5:21:36
Vero Beach Highlands 31 5 27N40 80w24 5:21:36
Vero Beach South 31 5 27N40 80w24 5:21:36
Vero Lake Estates 31 5 27N40 80w24 5:21:36
Vero Shores 31 5 27N40 80w24 5:21:36
Vicksburg 3 1 30N19 85w40 5:42:40
Victory Gardens 13 5 25N34 80w22 5:21:28
Vilano Beach 55 5 29N55 81w18 5:25:12
Vilas 39 5 30N13 84w53 5:39:32
Village Green 1 5 29N40 82w20 5:29:20
Village Green 5 5 28N20 80w44 5:22:56
Villa Rica 50 6 26N23 80w05 5:20:20
Villa Sabine 17 4 30N22 87w11 5:48:44
Vineland 48 5 28N34 81w35 5:26:20
Virginia Gardens 13 6 25N49 80w18 5:21:12
Vitis 51 5 28N14 82w11 5:28:44
Wabasso 31 5 27N45 80w26 5:21:44
Wacahotta 1 5 29N30 82w17 5:29:08
Wacissa 33 5 30N22 83w59 5:35:56
Wadesboro 37 5 30N26 84w17 5:37:08
Wahneta 53 5 27N57 81w44 5:26:56
Wahoo 60 5 29N28 81w15 5:25:00
Wakulla 65 5 30N14 84w14 5:36:56
Wakulla Beach 65 5 30N11 84w23 5:37:32
Wakulla Springs 65 5 30N26 84w17 5:37:08
Walden Lake 29 5 28N01 82w08 5:28:32
Waldo 1 5 29N48 82w10 5:28:40
Walkill 10 5 29N59 81w41 5:26:44
Wallace 57 1 30N39 87w05 5:48:20
Wall Springs 52 5 27N57 82w45 5:31:00
Walnut Hill 17 1 30N53 87w30 5:50:00
Walton 56 5 27N18 80w16 5:21:04
Wannee 21 5 29N43 82w56 5:31:44
Ward Ridge 23 5 29N47 85w17 5:41:08
Warm Mineral Springs 58 5 27N04 82w20 5:29:20
Warrington 17 4 30N23 87w17 5:49:08
Washington Park 6 6 26N07 80w13 5:20:52
Watertown 12 5 30N11 82w36 5:30:24
Wauchula 25 5 27N33 81w49 5:27:16
Wauchula Hills 25 5 27N33 81w49 5:27:16
Waukeenah 33 5 30N25 83w57 5:35:48
Wausau 67 1 30N38 85w35 5:42:20
Waverly 53 5 27N59 81w37 5:26:28
Weathersfield 59 5 28N40 81w22 5:25:28
Webb's City 52 5 27N46 82w38 5:30:32
Webster 60 5 28N37 82w03 5:28:12
Weeki Wachee 27 5 28N31 82w34 5:30:16
Weirsdale 42 5 28N59 81w55 5:27:40
Wekiwa Manor 48 5 28N41 81w28 5:25:52
Wekiwa Springs 48 5 28N41 81w28 5:25:52
Welaka 54 5 29N29 81w41 5:26:44
Welcome 29 5 28N00 82w31 5:30:04
Wellborn 61 5 30N14 82w49 5:31:16
Wesley Chapel 51 5 28N14 82w11 5:28:44
Wesley Manor 55 5 30N12 81w35 5:26:20
West Auburndale 53 5 28N04 81w49 5:27:16
West Augustine 55 5 29N48 81w16 5:25:04
Westbay 3 1 30N18 85w52 5:43:28
West Bay 16 5 30N24 81w45 5:27:00
West Bradenton 41 5 27N29 82w37 5:30:28
Westchester 13 6 25N44 80w18 5:21:12
West Eau Gallie 5 5 28N08 80w39 5:22:36
West End 32 1 30N47 85w14 5:40:56
West End 42 5 29N11 82w10 5:28:40
Western Acres 36 5 26N39 81w53 5:27:32
West Farm 40 5 30N28 83w25 5:33:40
West Flagler 18 5 29N26 81w20 5:25:20
West Frost Proof 53 5 27N44 81w35 5:26:20
Westgate 6 26N43 80w06 5:20:24
Westgate 50 1 30N09 85w39 5:42:36
West Hills 1 5 29N40 82w20 5:29:20
West Holly Hill 64 5 29N14 81w02 5:24:08
West Hollywood 6 6 26N01 80w12 5:20:48
West Jacksonville 16 5 30N19 81w50 5:27:20
West Lake Wales 53 5 27N54 81w39 5:26:36
West Lantana 50 6 26N35 80w04 5:20:16
West Liberty 39 5 30N25 84w59 5:39:56
West Melbourne 5 5 28N04 80w39 5:22:36
West Miami 13 6 25N46 80w17 5:21:08
Westmoreland Estates 1 5 29N40 82w20 5:29:20
West Okeechobee 47 5 27N19 80w54 5:23:36
West Palm Beach 50 6 26N43 80w03 5:20:12
West Palmetto Park 50 6 26N23 80w05 5:20:20
West Panama City Beach 3 1 30N13 85w53 5:43:32
West Pensacola 17 4 30N25 87w16 5:49:04
West Scenic Park 53 5 27N53 81w34 5:26:16
Westside 64 5 29N13 81w02 5:24:08
West St Lucie 56 5 27N28 80w27 5:21:48
West Tampa 29 5 27N58 82w29 5:29:56
West Tocoi 10 5 29N59 81w41 5:26:44
West Vero Beach 31 5 27N40 80w24 5:21:36
Westview 13 6 25N54 80w13 5:20:52
Westville 30 1 30N46 85w51 5:43:24
West Wakulla County 65 5 30N05 84w26 5:37:44
West Winter Haven 53 5 28N03 81w47 5:27:08
Westwood 16 5 30N27 81w34 5:26:16
Westwood 48 5 28N34 81w27 5:25:48
Westwood Lakes 13 6 25N44 80w23 5:21:32
Wewahitchka 23 1 30N07 85w12 5:40:48
Whispering Palms 50 6 26N36 80w05 5:20:20
White City 23 5 29N53 85w13 5:40:52
Whitehead Cross Roads 67 1 30N47 85w49 5:43:16
Whitehouse 16 5 30N19 81w50 5:27:20
Whites Landing 59 5 28N40 81w12 5:24:48
White Springs 24 5 30N20 82w45 5:31:00
White Springs 39 5 30N26 84w59 5:39:56
Whitfield Estates 41 5 27N25 82w34 5:30:16
Whiting Field 57 3 30N43 87w01 5:48:04
Whitney 35 5 28N49 81w53 5:27:32
Whitney Beach 41 5 27N24 82w39 5:30:36
Wilbur-By-The-Sea 64 5 29N11 81w00 5:24:00
Wildwood 60 5 28N52 82w02 5:28:08
Williams Point 5 5 28N22 80w45 5:23:00
Willis Landing 23 1 30N07 85w12 5:40:48
Williston 38 5 29N23 82w27 5:29:48
Willow 41 5 27N35 82w25 5:29:40
Wilma 5 30N09 84w58 5:39:52
Wilson 5 28N39 80w42 5:22:48
Wilson Haven 51 5 28N32 82w29 5:29:56
Wilton Manors 6 6 26N10 80w08 5:20:32
Wimauma 29 5 27N43 82w18 5:29:12
Windermere 48 5 28N30 81w32 5:26:08
Windmill Village Trailer Par 11 5 26N11 81w48 5:27:12
Windsor 1 5 29N40 82w20 5:29:20
Windy Hill 16 5 30N17 81w35 5:26:20
Winfield 12 5 30N17 81w24 5:25:36
Winslow Beach 5 5 28N20 80w37 5:22:28
Winston 53 5 28N02 81w59 5:27:56
Winter Beach 31 5 27N43 80w25 5:21:40
Winter Garden 48 5 28N34 81w35 5:26:20
Winter Haven 53 5 28N01 81w44 5:26:56
Winter Park 48 5 28N36 81w20 5:25:20
Winter Springs 59 5 28N40 81w20 5:25:20
Wonderwood 16 5 30N21 81w25 5:25:40
Woodland Acres 16 5 30N20 81w35 5:26:20
Woodland Park 36 5 26N38 81w52 5:27:28
Woodlawn 3 1 30N09 85w39 5:42:36
Woodlawn Beach 57 4 30N22 87w11 5:48:44
Woodruff Springs 59 5 28N48 81w15 5:25:00
Woods 39 5 30N26 84w59 5:39:56
Woodside Heights 37 5 30N26 84w17 5:37:08
Woodville 3 1 30N09 85w39 5:42:36
Woodville 37 5 30N19 84w15 5:37:00
Worthington 63 5 29N58 82w29 5:29:56
Worthington Springs 63 5 29N56 82w25 5:29:40
Wright 46 1 30N36 86w36 5:46:24
Wynnehaven Beach 46 1 30N25 86w39 5:46:36
Wynwood 59 5 28N48 81w15 5:25:00
Yacht Harbor 50 6 26N47 80w04 5:20:16
Yalaha 35 5 28N44 81w49 5:27:16
Yankeetown 38 5 29N02 82w43 5:30:52
Ybor City 29 5 27N58 82w26 5:29:44
Yeehaw Junction 49 5 27N14 80w49 5:23:16
Yelvington 55 5 29N38 81w31 5:26:04
Yon's Lakeside Estates 37 5 30N26 84w17 5:37:08
Yon's Subdivision 23 1 29N48 85w18 5:41:12
York 42 5 29N11 82w09 5:28:36
Youmans 29 5 28N01 82w08 5:28:32
Youngstown 3 1 30N22 85w26 5:41:44
Yukon 16 5 30N14 81w42 5:26:48
Yulee 45 5 30N38 81w36 5:26:24
Zellwood 48 5 28N44 81w36 5:26:24
Zephyrhills 51 5 28N14 82w11 5:28:44
Zolfo Springs 25 5 27N30 81w48 5:27:12
Zuber 42 5 29N11 82w09 5:28:36

TIME TABLES

There is considerable confusion about shifts from Central to Eastern time, and the reverse. These shifts for rural areas have not been documented and may not always be correct, particularly at the boundaries between Eastern and Central time zone areas.

GA # 1		
Before	1/01/1903	LMT
1/01/1903	12:00	EST
3/31/1918	02:00	EWT
10/27/1918	02:00	EST
3/30/1919	02:00	EWT
10/26/1919	02:00	EST
2/09/1942	02:00	EWT
9/30/1945	02:00	EST
4/30/1967	02:00	US#1

GA # 2		
Before	1/01/1903	LMT
1/01/1903	12:00	EST
3/31/1918	02:00	EWT
10/27/1918	02:00	EST
3/30/1919	02:00	EWT
10/26/1919	02:00	EST
8/04/1941	02:00	EDT
2/09/1942	02:00	EWT
9/30/1945	02:00	EST
4/30/1967	02:00	US#1

GA # 3		
Before	1/01/1888	LMT
1/01/1888	12:00	EST
3/31/1918	02:00	EWT
10/27/1918	02:00	EST
3/30/1919	02:00	EWT
10/26/1919	02:00	EST
2/09/1942	02:00	EWT
9/30/1945	02:00	EST
4/30/1967	02:00	US#1

GA # 4		
Before	3/25/1888	LMT
3/25/1888	12:00	EST
3/31/1918	02:00	EWT
10/27/1918	02:00	EST
3/30/1919	02:00	EWT
10/26/1919	02:00	EST
2/09/1942	02:00	EWT
9/30/1945	02:00	EST
4/30/1967	02:00	US#1

GA # 5		
Before	1/01/1903	LMT
1/01/1903	12:00	CST
3/31/1918	02:00	CWT
10/27/1918	02:00	CST
3/30/1919	02:00	CWT
10/26/1919	02:00	CST
3/22/1941	00:00	EST
2/09/1942	02:00	EWT
1/29/1943	00:01	CWT
9/30/1945	02:00	EST
4/30/1967	02:00	US#1

GA # 6		
Before	1/01/1903	LMT
1/01/1903	12:00	EST
1/01/1918	12:00	CST
3/31/1918	02:00	CWT
10/27/1918	02:00	CST
3/30/1919	02:00	CWT
10/26/1919	02:00	CST
3/22/1941	00:00	EST
2/09/1942	02:00	EWT
1/29/1943	00:01	CWT
9/30/1945	02:00	EST
4/30/1967	02:00	US#1

GA # 7		
Before	1/01/1903	LMT
1/01/1903	12:00	EST
1/01/1918	12:00	CST
3/31/1918	02:00	CWT
10/27/1918	02:00	CST
3/30/1919	02:00	CWT
10/26/1919	02:00	CST
4/28/1935	01:00	CDT
9/29/1935	02:00	CST
4/26/1936	00:00	CDT
9/27/1936	02:00	CST
4/25/1937	00:00	CDT
9/26/1937	00:00	CST
4/24/1938	00:00	CDT
9/25/1938	00:00	CST
4/30/1939	00:00	CDT
9/24/1939	00:00	CST
4/28/1940	00:00	CDT
9/29/1940	00:00	CST
3/22/1941	00:00	EST
2/09/1942	02:00	EWT
1/29/1943	00:01	CWT
9/30/1945	02:00	EST
4/30/1967	02:00	US#1

GA # 8		
Before	1/01/1903	LMT
1/01/1903	12:00	CST
3/31/1918	02:00	CWT
10/27/1918	02:00	CST
3/30/1919	02:00	CWT
10/26/1919	02:00	CST
3/21/1941	11:35	EST
2/09/1942	02:00	EWT
1/28/1943	12:30	CWT
9/30/1945	02:00	EST
4/30/1967	02:00	US#1

GA # 9		
Before	1/01/1903	LMT
1/01/1903	12:00	CST
3/31/1918	02:00	CWT
10/27/1918	02:00	CST
3/30/1919	02:00	CWT
10/26/1919	02:00	CST
4/25/1937	00:00	CDT
9/26/1937	00:00	CST
4/24/1938	00:00	CDT
9/25/1938	00:00	CST
4/30/1939	00:00	CDT
9/24/1939	00:00	CST
4/28/1940	00:00	CDT
9/29/1940	00:00	CST
3/21/1941	11:35	EST
2/09/1942	02:00	EWT
1/28/1943	12:30	CWT
9/30/1945	02:00	EST
4/30/1967	02:00	US#1

GA # 10		
Before	1/01/1903	LMT
1/01/1903	12:00	CST
3/31/1918	02:00	CWT
10/27/1918	02:00	CST
3/30/1919	02:00	CWT
10/26/1919	02:00	CST
4/28/1935	01:00	CDT
9/29/1935	02:00	CST
4/26/1936	00:00	CDT
9/27/1936	02:00	CST
4/25/1937	00:00	CDT
9/26/1937	00:00	CST
4/24/1938	00:00	CDT
9/25/1938	00:00	CST
4/30/1939	00:00	CDT
9/24/1939	00:00	CST
4/28/1940	00:00	CDT
9/29/1940	00:00	CST
3/21/1941	11:35	EST
2/09/1942	02:00	EWT
1/28/1943	12:30	CWT
9/30/1945	02:00	EST
4/30/1967	02:00	US#1

GA # 11		
Before	1/01/1903	LMT
1/01/1903	12:00	CST
3/31/1918	02:00	CWT
10/27/1918	02:00	CST
3/30/1919	02:00	CWT
10/26/1919	02:00	CST
4/19/1936	00:00	CDT
9/12/1936	00:00	CST
4/25/1937	00:00	CDT
8/29/1937	00:00	CST
5/29/1938	00:00	CDT
9/10/1938	00:00	CST
5/27/1939	00:00	CDT
9/09/1939	00:00	CST
5/27/1940	00:00	CDT
9/08/1940	00:00	CST
3/21/1941	11:35	EST
2/09/1942	02:00	EWT
1/28/1943	12:30	CWT
9/30/1945	02:00	EST
4/30/1967	02:00	US#1

GA # 12		
Before	1/01/1903	LMT
1/01/1903	12:00	CST
3/31/1918	02:00	CWT
10/27/1918	02:00	CST
3/30/1919	02:00	CWT
10/26/1919	02:00	CST
2/09/1942	02:00	CWT
9/30/1945	02:00	EST
4/30/1967	02:00	US#1

GA # 13		
Before	1/01/1903	LMT
1/01/1903	12:00	CST
3/31/1918	02:00	CWT
10/27/1918	02:00	CST
3/30/1919	02:00	CWT
10/26/1919	02:00	CST
7/20/1941	02:00	CDT
2/09/1942	02:00	CWT
9/30/1945	02:00	EST
4/30/1967	02:00	US#1

GA # 14		
Before	1/01/1903	LMT
1/01/1903	12:00	CST
3/31/1918	02:00	CWT
10/27/1918	02:00	CST
3/30/1919	02:00	CWT
10/26/1919	02:00	CST
3/22/1941	00:00	EST
2/09/1942	02:00	EWT
1/28/1943	12:30	CWT
9/30/1945	02:00	EST
4/30/1967	02:00	US#1

GA # 15		
Before	1/01/1903	LMT
1/01/1903	12:00	CST
3/31/1918	02:00	CWT
10/27/1918	02:00	CST
3/30/1919	02:00	CWT
10/26/1919	02:00	CST
4/25/1937	00:00	CDT
9/26/1937	00:00	CST
4/24/1938	00:00	CDT
9/25/1938	00:00	CST
6/01/1939	00:00	CDT
9/01/1939	00:00	CST
4/28/1940	00:00	CDT
9/29/1940	00:00	CST
3/22/1941	00:00	EST
2/09/1942	02:00	EWT
1/28/1943	12:30	CWT
9/30/1945	02:00	EST
4/30/1967	02:00	US#1

GA # 16		
Before	1/01/1903	LMT
1/01/1903	12:00	CST
3/31/1918	02:00	CWT
10/27/1918	02:00	CST
3/30/1919	02:00	CWT
10/26/1919	02:00	CST
3/23/1941	12:00	EST
2/09/1942	02:00	EWT
2/14/1943	02:00	CWT
9/30/1945	02:00	EST
4/30/1967	02:00	US#1

GA # 17		
Before	1/01/1903	LMT
1/01/1903	12:00	CST
3/31/1918	02:00	CWT
10/27/1918	02:00	CST
3/30/1919	02:00	CWT
10/26/1919	02:00	CST
4/30/1939	00:00	CDT
9/24/1939	00:00	CST
3/23/1941	12:00	EST
2/09/1942	02:00	EWT
2/14/1943	02:00	CWT
9/30/1945	02:00	EST
4/30/1967	02:00	US#1

GA # 18		
Before	1/01/1903	LMT
1/01/1903	12:00	CST
3/31/1918	02:00	CWT
10/27/1918	02:00	CST
3/30/1919	02:00	CWT
10/26/1919	02:00	CST
4/26/1936	00:00	CDT
9/27/1936	02:00	CST
4/25/1937	00:00	CDT
9/26/1937	00:00	CST
3/24/1941	02:00	EST
2/09/1942	02:00	EWT
1/28/1943	12:30	CWT
9/30/1945	02:00	EST
4/30/1967	02:00	US#1

GA # 19		
Before	1/01/1903	LMT
1/01/1903	12:00	CST
3/31/1918	02:00	CWT
10/27/1918	02:00	CST
3/30/1919	02:00	CWT
10/26/1919	02:00	CST
3/21/1941	11:35	EST
2/09/1942	02:00	EWT
9/27/1942	02:00	CWT
9/30/1945	02:00	EST
4/30/1967	02:00	US#1

GA # 20		
Before	1/01/1903	LMT
1/01/1903	12:00	EST
3/31/1918	02:00	EWT
10/27/1918	02:00	EST
3/30/1919	02:00	EWT
10/26/1919	02:00	EST
2/09/1942	02:00	EWT
1/28/1943	12:30	CWT
9/30/1945	02:00	EST
4/30/1967	02:00	US#1

GA # 21		
Before	1/01/1903	LMT
1/01/1903	12:00	EST
3/31/1918	02:00	EWT
10/27/1918	02:00	EST
3/30/1919	02:00	EWT
10/26/1919	02:00	EST
4/25/1937	00:00	EDT
9/26/1937	00:00	EST
4/24/1938	00:00	EDT
9/25/1938	00:00	EST
4/30/1939	00:00	EDT
9/24/1939	00:00	EST
4/28/1940	00:00	EDT
9/29/1940	00:00	EST
2/09/1942	02:00	EWT
1/28/1943	12:30	CWT
9/30/1945	02:00	EST
4/30/1967	02:00	US#1

GA # 22		
Before	1/01/1903	LMT
1/01/1903	12:00	EST
3/31/1918	02:00	EWT
10/27/1918	02:00	EST
3/30/1919	02:00	EWT
10/26/1919	02:00	EST
8/04/1941	02:00	EDT
2/09/1942	02:00	EWT
1/28/1943	12:30	CWT
9/30/1945	02:00	EST
4/30/1967	02:00	US#1

GA # 23		
Before	5/01/1888	LMT
5/01/1888	12:00	EST
3/31/1918	02:00	EWT
10/27/1918	02:00	EST
3/30/1919	02:00	EWT
10/26/1919	02:00	EST
2/09/1942	02:00	EWT
1/28/1943	12:30	CWT
9/30/1945	02:00	EST
4/30/1967	02:00	US#1

GA # 24		
Before	1/01/1903	LMT
1/01/1903	12:00	EST
3/31/1918	02:00	EWT
10/27/1918	02:00	EST
3/30/1919	02:00	EWT
10/26/1919	02:00	EST
2/09/1942	02:00	EWT
1/28/1943	12:00	CWT
2/04/1943	12:00	EWT
9/30/1945	02:00	EST
4/30/1967	02:00	US#1

GA # 25		
Before	1/01/1903	LMT
1/01/1903	12:00	EST
3/31/1918	02:00	EWT
10/27/1918	02:00	EST
3/30/1919	02:00	EWT
10/26/1919	02:00	EST
2/09/1942	02:00	EWT
2/05/1943	02:00	CWT
9/30/1945	02:00	EST
4/30/1967	02:00	US#1

COUNTIES

1 Appling
2 Atkinson
3 Bacon
4 Baker
5 Baldwin
6 Banks
7 Barrow
8 Bartow
9 Ben Hill
10 Berrien
11 Bibb
12 Bleckley
13 Brantley
14 Brooks
15 Bryan
16 Bulloch
17 Burke
18 Butts
19 Calhoun
20 Camden
21 Candler
22 Carroll
23 Catoosa
24 Charlton
25 Chatham
26 Chattahoochee
27 Chattooga
28 Cherokee
29 Clarke
30 Clay
31 Clayton
32 Clinch
33 Cobb
34 Coffee
35 Colquitt
36 Columbia
37 Cook
38 Coweta
39 Crawford
40 Crisp
41 Dade
42 Dawson
43 Decatur
44 De Kalb
45 Dodge
46 Dooly
47 Dougherty
48 Douglas
49 Early
50 Echols
51 Effingham
52 Elbert
53 Emanuel
54 Evans
55 Fannin
56 Fayette
57 Floyd
58 Forsyth
59 Franklin
60 Fulton
61 Gilmer
62 Glascock
63 Glynn
64 Gordon
65 Grady
66 Greene
67 Gwinnett
68 Habersham
69 Hall
70 Hancock
71 Haralson
72 Harris
73 Hart
74 Heard
75 Henry
76 Houston
77 Irwin
78 Jackson
79 Jasper
80 Jeff Davis
81 Jefferson
82 Jenkins
83 Johnson
84 Jones
85 Lamar
86 Lanier
87 Laurens
88 Lee
89 Liberty
90 Lincoln
91 Long
92 Lowndes
93 Lumpkin
94 McDuffie
95 McIntosh
96 Macon
97 Madison
98 Marion
99 Meriwether
100 Miller
101 Mitchell
102 Monroe
103 Montgomery
104 Morgan
105 Murray
106 Newton
107 Oconee
108 Oglethorpe
109 Paulding
110 Peach
111 Pickens
112 Pierce
113 Pike
114 Polk
115 Pulaski
116 Putnam
117 Quitman
118 Rabun
119 Randolph
120 Richmond
121 Rockdale
122 Schley
123 Screven
124 Seminole
125 Spalding
126 Stephens
127 Stewart
128 Sumter
129 Talbot
130 Taliaferro
131 Tattnall
132 Taylor
133 Telfair
134 Terrell
135 Thomas
136 Tift
137 Toombs
138 Towns
139 Treutlen
140 Troup
141 Turner
142 Twiggs
143 Union
144 Upson
145 Walker
146 Walton
147 Ware
148 Warren
149 Washington
150 Wayne
151 Webster
152 Wheeler
153 White
154 Whitfield
155 Wilcox
156 Wilkes
157 Wilkinson
158 Worth
159 Columbus

Aaron 16 20 32N32 81w56 5:27:44
Abac 136 20 31N27 83w31 5:34:04
Abba 77 20 31N43 83w15 5:33:00
Abbeville 155 20 31N59 83w18 5:33:12
Abbottsford 140 8 33N03 85w11 5:40:44
Aberdeen 56 8 33N19 84w17 5:37:08
Acree 47 20 31N33 84w00 5:36:00
Acworth 33 8 34N04 84w41 5:38:44
Adairsville 8 8 34N22 84w56 5:39:44
Adams Park 142 20 32N48 83w30 5:34:00
Adasburg 156 20 33N44 82w45 5:31:00
Adel 37 20 31N08 83w25 5:33:40
Adgateville 79 20 33N11 83w38 5:34:32
Adrian 53 20 32N33 82w35 5:30:20
Agnes 90 20 33N48 82w29 5:29:56
Agnes Scott College 44 20 33N47 84w17 5:37:08
Aid 59 20 34N22 83w14 5:32:56
Ailey 103 20 32N11 82w34 5:30:16
Airline 73 20 34N22 83w05 5:32:20
Akin 16 20 32N23 81w40 5:26:40
Alamo 152 20 32N09 82w47 5:31:08
Alapaha 10 20 31N23 83w13 5:32:52
Albany 47 11 31N35 84w10 5:36:40
Albion Acres 120 20 33N26 82w01 5:28:04
Alcovy 106 20 33N40 83w52 5:35:28
Alcovy Shores 79 20 33N18 83w41 5:34:44
Aldora 85 15 33N03 84w11 5:36:44
Alexander 17 20 33N01 81w53 5:27:32
Alford 73 20 34N21 82w56 5:31:44
Alfords 158 20 31N32 83w50 5:35:20
Aline 21 20 32N21 82w09 5:28:36
Allen City 67 20 34N00 84w10 5:36:40
Allendale 67 20 33N57 83w59 5:35:56
Allenhurst 89 20 31N47 81w37 5:26:28
Allentown 157 20 32N41 83w20 5:33:20
Allenville 10 20 31N12 83w15 5:33:00
Allenwood 5 20 33N05 83w14 5:32:56
Allie 99 8 33N04 84w45 5:39:00
Alma 3 20 31N33 82w28 5:29:52
Almon 106 20 33N37 83w56 5:35:44
Alpharetta 60 7 34N04 84w18 5:37:12
Alpine 27 8 34N29 85w29 5:41:56
Alps 99 8 33N10 84w35 5:38:20
Alps Road 29 20 33N55 83w20 5:33:20
Alston 103 20 32N05 82w29 5:29:56
Altamaha 131 20 32N05 82w07 5:28:28
Altamaha River 1 20 31N53 82w18 5:29:12
Altman 123 20 32N49 81w39 5:26:36
Alto 68 20 34N28 83w35 5:34:20
Alto Park 57 8 34N17 85w12 5:40:48
Alvaton 99 8 33N10 84w35 5:38:20
Amboy 141 20 31N43 83w39 5:34:36
Ambrose 34 20 31N36 83w01 5:32:04
Americus 128 18 32N03 84w13 5:36:52
Amity 90 20 33N48 82w29 5:29:56
Amsterdam 43 8 30N53 84w26 5:37:44
Amzi 105 8 34N46 84w48 5:39:12
Anderson City 158 20 31N19 83w55 5:35:40
Andersonville 128 8 32N12 84w09 5:36:36
Anguilla 63 20 31N12 81w29 5:25:56
Antioch 114 8 34N01 85w15 5:41:00
Antioch 140 8 33N02 85w02 5:40:08
Aonia 156 20 33N44 82w45 5:31:00
Apalachee 104 20 33N41 83w26 5:33:44
Apple Valley 78 20 34N12 83w27 5:33:48
Appling 36 20 33N35 82w18 5:29:12
Arabi 40 20 31N50 83w44 5:34:56
Aragon 114 8 34N02 85w03 5:40:12
Aragon Park 120 20 33N28 81w59 5:27:56
Arcade 78 20 34N05 83w34 5:34:16
Arch City 64 8 34N30 84w57 5:39:48
Archery 151 8 32N02 84w24 5:37:36
Arco 63 20 31N12 81w29 5:25:56
Arcola 16 20 32N20 81w36 5:26:24
Ardmore 51 20 32N22 81w18 5:25:12
Argyle 32 20 31N05 82w39 5:30:36
Arkwright 11 25 32N51 83w41 5:34:44
Arlington 19 8 31N26 84w44 5:38:56
Armuchee 57 8 34N23 85w10 5:40:40
Arnco Mills 38 8 33N22 84w47 5:39:08
Arnoldsville 108 20 33N54 83w13 5:32:52
Arp 77 20 31N48 83w29 5:33:56
Arrowhead Village 31 8 33N31 84w21 5:37:24
Ashburn 141 20 31N43 83w39 5:34:36
Ashford Park 44 20 33N52 84w20 5:37:20
Ashintilly 95 20 31N32 81w31 5:26:04
Ashland 59 20 34N22 83w14 5:32:56
Atco 8 8 34N10 84w48 5:39:12
Athens 29 3 33N57 83w23 5:33:32
Atkinson 13 20 31N13 81w47 5:27:08
Atlanta 60 7 33N45 84w23 5:37:32
Attapulgus 43 8 30N45 84w29 5:37:56
Attica 78 3 33N59 83w23 5:33:32
Atwater 144 8 32N57 84w21 5:37:24
Auburn 7 20 34N01 83w50 5:35:20
Audubon 64 8 34N35 84w56 5:39:44
Augusta 120 2 33N28 81w58 5:27:52
Auraria 93 8 34N25 84w07 5:36:28
Austell 33 8 33N49 84w38 5:38:32
Austin 104 20 33N38 83w37 5:34:28
Autreyville 35 20 31N11 83w48 5:35:12
Autry 69 1 34N18 83w49 5:35:16
Avalon 25 20 32N00 81w05 5:24:20
Avalon 126 20 34N30 83w12 5:32:48
Avans 41 8 34N52 85w31 5:42:04
Avera 81 20 33N12 82w32 5:30:08
Avert Acres 47 11 31N34 84w11 5:36:44
Avery 28 8 34N14 84w29 5:37:56
Avondale 11 25 32N49 83w41 5:34:44
Avondale 94 20 33N25 82w19 5:29:16
Avondale Estates 44 20 33N47 84w16 5:37:04
Axson 2 20 31N17 82w44 5:30:56
Ayersville 126 20 34N35 83w20 5:33:20
Bacon Park 25 20 32N00 81w05 5:24:20
Baconton 101 20 31N23 84w10 5:36:40
Bainbridge 43 8 30N55 84w35 5:38:20
Bairdstown 108 20 33N37 83w04 5:32:16
Baker Village 159 17 32N29 84w57 5:39:48
Baldwin 6 20 34N30 83w32 5:34:08
Baldwinville 129 8 32N36 84w28 5:37:52
Ball Ground 28 8 34N20 84w23 5:37:32
Ball Ground 105 8 34N46 84w48 5:39:12
Balls Ferry 83 20 32N43 82w47 5:31:08
Baltimore 156 20 33N44 82w45 5:31:00
Banning 22 8 33N29 84w55 5:39:40
Bannockburn 10 20 31N12 83w15 5:33:00
Barkers Crossroads 74 8 33N21 85w04 5:40:16
Barker Spring 144 8 32N53 84w20 5:37:20
Barksdale 149 20 33N00 82w53 5:31:32
Barnesville 85 8 33N03 84w09 5:36:36
Barnett 148 20 33N28 82w42 5:30:48
Barnett Shoals 107 3 33N59 83w23 5:33:32
Barney 14 20 31N01 83w31 5:34:04
Barnsley 8 8 34N14 84w57 5:39:48
Barretts 92 20 31N00 83w12 5:32:48
Barrettsville 42 8 34N25 84w07 5:36:28
Barrow Heights 7 20 33N59 83w43 5:34:52
Bartletts Ferry 72 17 32N29 84w57 5:39:48
Bartonwoods 44 7 33N46 84w21 5:37:24
Bartow 81 20 32N53 82w29 5:29:56
Barwick 14 20 30N54 83w44 5:34:56
Bascom 123 20 32N49 81w39 5:26:36
Bass Crossroads 140 8 33N11 84w52 5:39:28
Batesville 68 20 34N40 83w27 5:33:48
Bath 120 20 33N17 82w12 5:28:48
Battery Point 25 20 32N03 81w04 5:24:16
Battle Park 159 17 32N26 84w57 5:39:48
Baughs Crossroads 140 8 32N52 85w11 5:40:44
Baxley 1 20 31N47 82w21 5:29:24
Baxter 143 8 34N41 84w01 5:36:04
Bay 35 20 31N13 83w59 5:35:56
Bayview 91 20 31N43 81w45 5:27:00
Beach 147 20 31N26 82w30 5:30:00
Beachton 65 8 30N50 83w59 5:35:56
Beacon Heights 104 20 33N36 83w28 5:33:52
Beallwood 159 17 32N29 84w57 5:39:48
Beatrice 127 8 32N03 84w48 5:39:12
Beaulieu 25 20 32N00 81w05 5:24:20
Beaverdale 154 8 34N46 84w58 5:39:52
Beechwood Hills 29 3 33N59 83w23 5:33:32
Belair 120 20 33N29 82w02 5:28:08
Belfast 15 20 31N57 81w19 5:25:16
Bellton 69 1 34N23 83w40 5:34:40
Bellview 100 8 31N10 84w36 5:38:24
Bellville 54 20 32N09 81w59 5:27:56
Bellville Bluff 95 20 31N32 81w31 5:26:04
Belmont 44 20 33N44 84w11 5:36:44
Belmont 69 1 34N18 83w49 5:35:16
Belmont Hills 33 8 33N53 84w32 5:38:08
Belvedere Park 44 20 33N44 84w16 5:37:04
Belvedere Plaza 44 20 33N44 84w16 5:37:04
Belvins Acres 23 8 35N01 85w11 5:40:44
Bemiss 92 20 30N56 83w15 5:33:00
Bender 87 20 32N33 83w04 5:32:16
Benedict 114 8 34N01 85w15 5:41:00
Benevolence 119 8 31N53 84w44 5:38:56
Ben Hill 60 10 33N43 84w31 5:38:04
Bentley Place 145 8 34N57 85w18 5:41:12
Benton 57 8 34N17 85w12 5:40:48
Berkeley Lake 67 20 33N59 84w11 5:36:44
Berkshire Woods 25 20 32N00 81w05 5:24:20
Berlin 35 20 31N04 83w37 5:34:28
Berry Hill 57 8 34N19 85w14 5:40:56
Berryton 27 8 34N29 85w21 5:41:24
Berzelia 36 20 33N25 82w19 5:29:16
Bethany 4 8 31N29 84w31 5:38:04
Bethel 79 20 33N18 83w41 5:34:44
Bethel 119 8 31N46 84w48 5:39:12
Bethesda 25 20 32N00 81w05 5:24:20
Bethesda 67 20 33N57 83w59 5:35:56

GEORGIA

Bethlehem 7 20 33N56 83W44 5:34:56
Between 146 20 33N49 83W48 5:35:12
Beulah 90 20 33N52 82W39 5:30:36
Beulah 109 8 34N00 85W00 5:40:00
Beverly Heights 159 17 32N29 84W57 5:39:48
Beverly Hills 145 8 34N56 85W17 5:41:08
Bexton 38 8 33N17 84W46 5:39:04
Bibb City 159 17 32N30 85W00 5:40:00
Bibb Mills 102 8 33N02 83W56 5:35:44
Bickley 147 20 31N31 82W38 5:30:32
Big Canoe 111 8 34N28 84W26 5:37:44
Big Creek 58 8 34N07 84W11 5:36:44
Big Springs 140 8 33N02 85W02 5:40:08
Billarp 48 8 33N41 84W46 5:39:04
Bill Davis 17 20 32N58 81W45 5:27:00
Birdie 125 8 33N15 84W15 5:37:00
Birmingham 60 7 34N04 84W18 5:37:12
Bishop 107 20 33N49 83W26 5:33:44
Blackjack 38 8 33N18 84W33 5:38:12
Blackshear 112 20 31N18 82W14 5:28:56
Blackshear Place 69 1 34N18 83W49 5:35:16
Blacksville 75 20 33N27 84W09 5:36:36
Blackwells 33 8 34N02 84W32 5:38:08
Blackwood 64 8 34N30 84W57 5:39:48
Blaine 111 8 34N31 84W30 5:38:00
Blairsville 143 8 34N53 83W58 5:35:52
Blair Village 60 7 33N40 84W23 5:37:32
Blakely 49 8 31N23 84W56 5:39:44
Blandford 51 20 32N18 81W14 5:24:56
Bland Villa 40 20 31N58 83W47 5:35:08
Blitch 16 20 32N26 81W47 5:27:08
Blitchton 15 20 32N12 81W26 5:25:44
Bloomingdale 25 20 32N08 81W18 5:25:12
Blowing Springs 145 8 35N00 85W20 5:41:20
Blue Ridge 55 8 34N52 84W20 5:37:20
Bluffton 30 8 31N31 84W52 5:39:28
Blun 53 20 32N31 82W19 5:29:16
Blundale 53 20 32N31 82W19 5:29:16
Blythe 120 20 33N17 82W12 5:28:48
Bogart 107 20 33N57 83W31 5:34:04
Bold Spring 146 20 33N48 83W46 5:35:04
Bolingbroke 102 8 32N57 83W48 5:35:12
Bolton 60 7 33N47 84W26 5:37:44
Bona Bella 25 20 32N00 81W05 5:24:20
Bonaire 76 20 32N33 83W36 5:34:24
Bonds 142 20 32N48 83W30 5:34:00
Boneville 94 20 33N26 82W27 5:29:48
Boozeville 57 8 34N11 85W11 5:40:44
Boston 135 20 30N47 83W47 5:35:08
Bostwick 104 20 33N44 83W31 5:34:04
Bowdon 22 8 33N32 85W15 5:41:00
Bowdon Junction 22 8 33N40 85W09 5:40:36
Bowersville 73 20 34N22 83W05 5:32:20
Bowman 52 20 34N12 83W02 5:32:08
Box Springs 129 8 32N32 84W40 5:38:40
Boyd Highlands 23 8 35N01 85W11 5:40:44
Boydville 126 20 34N35 83W20 5:33:20
Boykin 100 8 31N06 84W41 5:38:44
Boynton 23 8 35N01 85W11 5:40:44
Boynton Ridge 23 8 34N55 85W12 5:40:48
Boys Estate 63 20 31N12 81W29 5:25:56
Bradley 84 20 33N01 83W32 5:34:08
Branchville 101 8 31N09 84W23 5:37:32
Brantley 98 8 32N22 84W28 5:37:52
Braselton 78 20 34N07 83W46 5:35:04
Braswell 109 8 33N59 84W58 5:39:52
Bremen 71 8 33N43 85W09 5:40:36
Brentwood 47 11 31N34 84W11 5:36:44
Brest 101 20 31N23 84W10 5:36:40
Brewton 87 20 32N36 82W48 5:31:12
Briarcliff 44 20 33N50 84W19 5:37:16
Briarwood 60 7 33N41 84W27 5:37:48
Briar Wood Estates 33 8 33N56 84W32 5:38:08
Brick Store 106 20 33N39 83W43 5:34:52
Bridgeboro 158 20 31N24 83W59 5:35:56
Bridgeman Heights 11 25 32N50 83W37 5:34:28
Brighton 136 20 31N27 83W31 5:34:04
Brinson 43 8 30N59 84W44 5:38:56
Brisbon 15 20 31N57 81W19 5:25:16
Bristol 112 20 31N26 82W15 5:29:00
Broad 156 20 33N52 82W44 5:30:56
Broadhurst 150 20 31N28 81W55 5:27:40
Brockton 78 20 34N06 83W34 5:34:16
Bronco 145 8 34N42 85W22 5:41:28
Bronwood 134 8 31N50 84W22 5:37:28
Brookfield 136 20 31N25 83W23 5:33:32
Brookhaven 11 25 32N49 83W41 5:34:44
Brooklet 16 20 32N23 81W40 5:26:40
Brooklyn 127 8 32N10 84W43 5:38:52
Brooks 56 8 33N20 84W27 5:37:48
Brooks Crossing 29 3 33N59 83W23 5:33:32
Brooksville 119 8 31N53 84W44 5:38:56
Brookton 69 1 34N18 83W49 5:35:16
Brookvale Estates 23 8 35N01 85W11 5:40:44
Brookwood 58 8 34N04 84W18 5:37:12
Brookwood 87 20 32N33 82W54 5:31:36
Browndale 115 20 32N17 83W28 5:33:52
Browns 5 20 33N05 83W14 5:32:56
Brownwood 104 20 33N36 83W28 5:33:52
Broxton 34 20 31N38 82W53 5:31:32
Brunswick 63 23 31N10 81W30 5:26:00
Buchanan 71 8 33N48 85W11 5:40:44
Buckhead 104 20 33N32 83W21 5:33:24
Budapest 71 8 33N45 85W17 5:41:08
Buena Vista 98 8 32N19 84W31 5:38:04
Buffington 28 8 34N14 84W29 5:37:56
Buford 67 20 34N06 84W02 5:36:08
Bullard 142 20 32N48 83W30 5:34:00
Bulloch Crossroads 99 8 32N51 84W36 5:38:24
Bunker Hill 143 8 34N53 83W58 5:35:52
Burning Bush 23 8 35N01 85W11 5:40:44
Burnside 25 20 32N00 81W05 5:24:20
Burroughs 25 20 31N59 81W15 5:25:00
Burwell 22 8 33N35 85W05 5:40:20
Bushnell 34 20 31N34 82W58 5:31:52
Bussey Crossroads 99 8 32N54 84W44 5:38:56
Butler 132 8 32N33 84W14 5:36:56
Butler Subdivision 47 11 31N34 84W11 5:36:44
Butts 82 20 32N48 81W57 5:27:48
Byers Crossroads 22 8 33N29 84W55 5:39:40
Byromville 46 20 32N11 83W54 5:35:36
Byron 110 8 32N39 83W46 5:35:04
Cabaniss 102 8 33N02 83W56 5:35:44
Cadley 148 20 33N32 82W40 5:30:40
Cadwell 87 20 32N20 83W03 5:32:12
Cagle 111 8 34N28 84W26 5:37:44
Cairo 65 8 30N52 84W13 5:36:52
Caleb 67 20 33N43 84W06 5:36:24
Calhoun 64 8 34N30 84W57 5:39:48
Calvary 65 8 30N44 84W21 5:37:24
Camak 148 20 33N27 82W39 5:30:36
Camelot 29 3 33N59 83W23 5:33:32
Camelot 31 8 33N31 84W21 5:37:24
Camilla 101 20 31N14 84W12 5:36:48
Campania 36 20 33N25 82W19 5:29:16
Campton 146 20 33N52 83W43 5:34:52
Canal Lake 143 8 34N53 83W58 5:35:52
Candler 69 1 34N18 83W49 5:35:16
Cannon Gate 36 20 33N29 82W02 5:28:08
Cannonville 140 8 33N02 85W02 5:40:08
Canon 59 20 34N21 83W07 5:32:28
Canoochee 53 20 32N40 82W11 5:28:44
Canoochee 54 20 32N13 81W55 5:27:40
Canton 28 8 34N14 84W29 5:37:56
Capel 65 8 30N50 84W12 5:36:48
Capitol Hill 60 7 33N45 84W23 5:37:32
Captolo 123 20 32N49 81W39 5:26:36
Carbondale 154 8 34N46 84W58 5:39:52
Carl 7 20 34N00 83W49 5:35:16
Carlton 97 20 34N03 83W02 5:32:08
Carmel 99 8 33N06 84W35 5:38:20
Carmichael Crossroads 28 8 34N14 84W29 5:37:56
Carnegie 119 8 31N39 84W47 5:39:08
Carnes Creek 126 20 34N35 83W20 5:33:20
Carnesville 59 20 34N22 83W14 5:32:56
Carnigan 95 20 31N27 81W23 5:25:32
Carns Mill 111 8 34N31 84W30 5:38:00
Carrollton 22 8 33N35 85W05 5:40:20
Carrs 70 20 33N17 82W58 5:31:52
Carsonville 132 8 32N43 84W18 5:37:12
Cartecay 61 8 34N39 84W22 5:37:28
Carters 105 8 34N37 84W42 5:38:48
Carters Grove 130 20 33N48 82W54 5:31:36
Cartersville 8 8 34N10 84W48 5:39:12
Cary 12 20 32N23 83W21 5:33:24
Cascade Heights 60 10 33N43 84W29 5:37:56
Casey Springs 105 8 34N40 84W51 5:39:24
Cash 64 8 34N30 84W57 5:39:48
Cass 8 8 34N13 84W51 5:39:24
Cassandra 145 8 34N52 85W23 5:41:32
Cassville 8 8 34N15 84W51 5:39:24
Cataula 72 8 32N39 84W52 5:39:28
Catlett 145 8 34N42 85W22 5:41:28
Catoosa Springs 23 8 34N55 85W03 5:40:12
Cave Spring 57 8 34N06 85W20 5:41:20
Cecil 37 20 31N03 83W24 5:33:36
Cedar Creek Park 29 3 33N59 83W23 5:33:32
Cedar Crossing 137 20 32N11 82W17 5:29:08
Cedar Grove 25 20 32N00 81W05 5:24:20
Cedar Grove 44 20 33N37 84W17 5:37:08
Cedar Grove 60 10 33N35 84W34 5:38:16
Cedar Grove 87 20 32N17 82W50 5:31:20
Cedar Grove 145 8 34N52 85W23 5:41:32
Cedar Hammock 25 20 32N00 81W05 5:24:20
Cedar Point 95 20 31N29 81W21 5:25:24
Cedar Springs 49 8 31N11 85W02 5:40:08
Cedartown 114 8 34N01 85W15 5:41:00
Celeste 156 20 33N44 82W45 5:31:00
Centennial 104 20 33N38 83W37 5:34:28
Center 8 8 34N10 84W48 5:39:12
Center 78 20 34N03 83W25 5:33:40
Center 137 20 32N15 82W24 5:29:36
Center Point 22 8 33N44 85W02 5:40:08
Center Post 145 8 34N36 85W21 5:41:24
Centerville 44 20 33N43 84W06 5:36:24
Centerville 52 20 34N08 82W50 5:31:20
Centerville 76 8 32N38 83W41 5:34:44
Centerville 129 8 32N36 84W28 5:37:52
Centralhatchee 74 8 33N22 85W06 5:40:24
Central Junction 25 20 32N04 81W07 5:24:28
Central Toombs 137 20 32N01 82W21 5:29:24
Century 88 20 31N44 84W10 5:36:40
Chalybeate Springs 99 8 32N51 84W35 5:38:20
Chamberlain 145 8 34N42 85W22 5:41:28
Chamblee 44 20 33N53 84W18 5:37:12
Chambliss 128 18 32N04 84W14 5:36:56
Chapel Hill 48 8 33N45 84W45 5:39:00
Chappel 85 8 33N07 84W12 5:36:48
Charing 132 8 32N30 84W25 5:37:40
Charles 127 8 32N08 84W50 5:39:20
Charles 137 20 32N15 82W24 5:29:36
Charlotteville 103 20 32N02 82W31 5:30:04
Chastain 135 20 31N01 83W52 5:35:28
Chatham City 25 20 32N06 81W09 5:24:36
Chatham Villas 25 20 32N06 81W09 5:24:36
Chatsworth 105 8 34N46 84W46 5:39:04
Chattahoochee 44 8 33N57 84W25 5:37:40
Chattahoochee Plantation 33 8 33N56 84W32 5:38:08
Chattanooga Valley 145 8 34N57 85W19 5:41:16
Chatterton 34 20 31N31 82W38 5:30:32
Chattoogaville 27 8 34N24 85W24 5:41:36
Chauncey 45 20 32N06 83W04 5:32:16
Checkero 118 20 34N53 83W24 5:33:36
Chelsea 27 8 34N29 85W29 5:41:56
Chennault 90 20 33N52 82W39 5:30:36
Cherrylog 61 8 34N47 84W24 5:37:36
Chestatee 58 8 34N17 84W00 5:36:00
Chester 45 20 32N24 83W09 5:32:36
Chestnutflat 145 8 34N42 85W22 5:41:28
Chestnut Mountain 69 1 34N10 83W50 5:35:20
Chickamauga 145 8 34N52 85W18 5:41:12
Chickasawhatchee 134 8 31N46 84W26 5:37:44
Chicopee 69 1 34N15 83W51 5:35:24
China Hill 133 20 31N59 83W12 5:32:48
Chipley 72 8 32N50 85W00 5:40:00
Chippewa Terrace 25 20 32N00 81W05 5:24:20
Choestoe 143 8 34N53 83W58 5:35:52
Chubtown 57 8 34N07 85W20 5:41:20
Chula 136 20 31N33 83W32 5:34:08
Cinderella Hills 23 8 35N01 85W11 5:40:44
Cisco 105 8 34N57 84W44 5:38:56
Civic Center 60 7 33N47 84W23 5:37:32
Clarkdale 33 8 33N50 84W39 5:38:36
Clarke Dale 29 3 33N59 83W23 5:33:32
Clarkesville 68 20 34N37 83W31 5:34:04
Clarksboro 78 3 33N59 83W23 5:33:32
Clarkston 44 20 33N49 84W14 5:36:56
Claxton 54 20 32N10 81W55 5:27:40
Clayfields 157 20 32N51 83W12 5:32:48
Clayton 118 20 34N53 83W23 5:33:32
Clem 22 8 33N32 85W01 5:40:04
Clermont 69 1 34N29 83W47 5:35:08
Cleveland 153 20 34N36 83W46 5:35:04
Cliftondale 60 10 33N38 84W26 5:37:44
Climax 43 8 30N53 84W26 5:37:44
Clinchfield 76 20 32N25 83W38 5:34:32
Clinton 84 20 33N01 83W32 5:34:08
Cloudland 27 8 34N31 85W30 5:42:00
Cloverdale 41 8 34N46 85W32 5:42:08
Clyattville 92 20 30N42 83W19 5:33:16
Clyo 51 20 32N29 81W16 5:25:04
Coal Mountain 58 8 34N16 84W06 5:36:24
Cobb 128 20 31N57 83W59 5:35:56
Cobbtown 131 20 32N17 82W08 5:28:32
Cobbville 133 20 32N02 82W50 5:31:20
Cochran 12 20 32N23 83W21 5:33:24
Coffee 3 20 31N28 82W15 5:29:00
Coffee Bluff 25 20 32N00 81W05 5:24:20
Cogdell 32 20 31N10 82W43 5:30:52
Cohutta 154 8 34N58 84W57 5:39:48
Cohutta Springs 105 8 34N53 84W45 5:39:00
Colbert 97 20 34N02 83W13 5:32:52
Coldwater Creek 52 20 34N12 82W50 5:31:20
Coleman 119 8 31N40 84W54 5:39:36
Colemans Lake 53 20 32N19 82W17 5:29:08
Colesburg 20 20 30N58 81W43 5:26:52
Colfax 16 20 32N26 81W47 5:27:08
College 110 8 32N33 83W53 5:35:32
Collegeboro 16 20 32N25 81W47 5:27:08
College Heights 47 11 31N34 84W11 5:36:44
College Park 60 7 33N40 84W27 5:37:48
Collins 131 20 32N11 82W07 5:28:28
Colomokee 49 8 31N25 84W58 5:39:52
Colonial Oaks 25 20 32N00 81W05 5:24:20
Colonial Place 47 11 31N34 84W10 5:36:40
Colquitt 100 8 31N10 84W44 5:38:56
Colson Store 68 20 34N34 83W33 5:34:12
Columbia Heights 36 20 33N29 82W02 5:28:08
Columbus 159 17 32N28 84W59 5:39:56
Colwell 55 8 34N58 84W23 5:37:32
Comer 97 20 34N04 83W08 5:32:32
Commerce 78 20 34N12 83W28 5:33:52
Comolli 52 20 34N08 82W50 5:31:20
Concord 113 8 33N05 84W27 5:37:48
Concord 122 8 32N14 84W18 5:37:12
Coney 40 20 31N58 83W47 5:35:08
Conley 31 20 33N39 84W20 5:37:20
Constitution 44 7 33N42 84W21 5:37:24
Conyers 121 20 33N40 84W01 5:36:04
Cooksville 74 8 33N11 84W52 5:39:28
Coolidge 135 20 31N01 83W52 5:35:28
Cool Spring 35 20 31N17 83W40 5:34:40
Cooper Heights 145 8 34N48 85W23 5:41:32
Coopers 5 20 33N01 83W18 5:33:12
Coosa 57 8 34N15 85W21 5:41:24
Copeland 45 20 31N59 83W12 5:32:48
Cordele 40 20 31N58 83W47 5:35:08
Corinth 38 8 33N14 84W57 5:39:48
Cornelia 68 20 34N31 83W32 5:34:08
Cotton 101 20 31N10 84W04 5:36:16
Cotton Hill 30 8 31N48 84W57 5:39:48
Council 32 20 30N37 82W31 5:30:04
County Line 7 20 33N59 83W43 5:34:52

GEORGIA

Place	Zone	Lat.	Long.	Time
County Line 127	8	32N03	84w48	5:39:12
Court Square 87	20	32N33	82w54	5:31:36
Covena 53	20	32N30	82w27	5:29:48
Coverdale 141	20	31N38	83w58	5:35:52
Covington 106	20	33N36	83w51	5:35:24
Covington Mills 106	20	33N40	83w52	5:35:28
Cox 95	20	31N27	81w34	5:26:16
Coxs Crossing 31	8	33N38	84w22	5:37:28
Crabapple 60	8	34N05	84w20	5:37:20
Crandall 105	8	34N53	84w45	5:39:00
Craneeater 64	8	34N30	84w57	5:39:48
Cravey 133	20	32N01	83w04	5:32:16
Crawford 108	20	33N53	83w09	5:32:36
Crawfordville 130	20	33N33	82w54	5:31:36
Crescent 95	20	31N31	81w22	5:25:28
Crest 144	8	32N53	84w20	5:37:20
Crest Hill Gardens 25	20	32N00	81w05	5:24:20
Crestview 4	8	31N26	84w44	5:38:56
Crestwell Heights 11	25	32N51	83w41	5:34:44
Cromers 59	20	34N17	83w07	5:32:28
Crosland 35	20	31N18	83w38	5:34:32
Cross Keys 11	25	32N50	83w37	5:34:28
Crossroads 73	20	34N22	83w05	5:32:20
Crossroads 89	20	31N44	81w26	5:25:44
Crowders Crossing 99	8	32N54	84w44	5:38:56
Cruse 67	20	34N00	84w10	5:36:40
Crystal Springs 11	25	32N50	83w37	5:34:28
Crystal Springs 57	8	34N22	85w11	5:40:44
Crystal Valley 159	16	32N31	84w52	5:39:28
Cuba 49	8	31N19	84w55	5:39:40
Culloden 102	8	32N52	84w06	5:36:24
Culverton 70	20	33N19	82w54	5:31:36
Cumming 58	8	34N12	84w10	5:36:40
Curryville 64	8	34N30	84w57	5:39:48
Curtis 55	8	34N52	84w19	5:37:16
Cusseta 26	8	32N18	84w47	5:39:08
Custer Terrace 159	17	32N26	84w57	5:39:48
Cuthbert 119	8	31N46	84w48	5:39:12
Cypress Mills 63	20	31N12	81w29	5:25:56
Dacula 67	20	33N59	83w54	5:35:36
Dahlonega 93	8	34N32	83w59	5:35:56
Daisy 54	20	32N09	81w50	5:27:20
Dakota 141	20	31N47	83w57	5:35:48
Dallas 109	8	33N55	84w51	5:39:24
Dallondale 23	8	34N57	85w18	5:41:12
Dalton 154	19	34N46	84w58	5:39:52
Damascus 49	8	31N18	84w43	5:38:52
Damascus 64	8	34N30	84w57	5:39:48
Dames Ferry 102	20	33N01	83w44	5:34:56
Danburg 156	20	33N52	82w39	5:30:36
Daniel 15	20	31N57	81w19	5:25:16
Daniel Springs 66	20	33N37	83w04	5:32:16
Danielsville 97	20	34N08	83w13	5:32:52
Danville 142	20	32N37	83w15	5:33:00
Darien 95	20	31N23	81w26	5:25:44
Dasher 92	20	30N45	83w13	5:32:52
David 62	20	33N13	82w28	5:29:52
Davis Academy 6	20	34N16	83w25	5:33:40
Davisboro 149	20	32N59	82w36	5:30:24
Davis Crossroads 145	8	34N52	85w23	5:41:32
Dawesville 135	20	30N55	84w01	5:36:04
Dawnville 154	8	34N46	84w58	5:39:52
Dawson 134	8	31N46	84w27	5:37:48
Dawsonville 42	8	34N25	84w07	5:36:28
Days Crossroads 30	8	31N37	85w03	5:40:12
Dearing 94	20	33N23	82w24	5:29:36
Decatur 44	7	33N47	84w18	5:37:12
Deenwood 147	20	31N14	82w23	5:29:32
Deepstep 149	20	33N01	82w58	5:31:52
Deerwood Park 44	20	33N44	84w16	5:37:04
Delhi 156	20	33N52	82w44	5:30:56
Dellwood 53	20	32N31	82w19	5:29:16
Delowe 60	7	33N41	84w27	5:37:48
Demorest 68	20	34N34	83w33	5:34:12
Denmark 16	20	32N23	81w40	5:26:40
Dennis 116	20	33N19	83w23	5:33:32
Denton 80	20	31N44	82w42	5:30:48
Denver 74	8	33N21	85w04	5:40:16
De Soto 128	20	31N57	84w04	5:36:16
De Soto Park 57	8	34N12	85w13	5:40:52
Desser 124	8	31N03	84w53	5:39:32
Devereux 70	20	33N13	83w05	5:32:20
Dewberry 69	1	34N18	83w49	5:35:16
Dewberry 145	8	34N57	85w18	5:41:12
Dewey Crossroads 8	8	34N17	84w45	5:39:00
Dewitt 47	20	31N25	84w09	5:36:36
Dewy Rose 52	20	34N10	82w57	5:31:48
Dexter 87	20	32N27	83w04	5:32:16
Dial 55	8	34N52	84w19	5:37:16
Dialtown 106	20	33N38	83w52	5:35:28
Diamond Hill 97	20	34N01	83w12	5:32:48
Dickey 19	8	31N33	84w40	5:38:40
Dicks Hill 68	20	34N31	83w30	5:34:00
Digbey 125	8	33N17	84w28	5:37:52
Dillard 118	20	34N58	83w23	5:33:32
Dillon 135	20	30N50	83w59	5:35:56
Dixie 14	20	30N46	83w41	5:34:44
Dixie 106	20	33N40	83w52	5:35:28
Dixie Union 147	20	31N20	82w28	5:29:52
Dobbins Air Force Base 33	8	33N56	84w32	5:38:08
Dock Junction 63	20	31N12	81w30	5:26:00
Doctortown 150	20	31N39	81w50	5:27:20
Doerun 35	20	31N19	83w55	5:35:40
Doles 158	20	31N42	83w53	5:35:32
Donald 91	20	31N43	81w45	5:27:00
Donalsonville 124	8	31N03	84w53	5:39:32
Donegal 16	20	32N26	81w47	5:27:08
Donovan 83	20	32N46	82w44	5:30:56
Doogan 105	8	34N57	84w44	5:38:56
Dooling 46	20	32N18	84w01	5:36:04
Doraville 44	20	33N54	84w17	5:37:08
Dorchester 89	20	31N50	81w31	5:26:04
Dorsey 104	20	33N36	83w28	5:33:52
Dosia 136	20	31N27	83w31	5:34:04
Dot 22	8	33N32	85w15	5:41:00
Double Branches 90	20	33N48	82w29	5:29:56
Doublegate 47	11	31N34	84w11	5:36:44
Double Run 155	20	31N57	83w33	5:34:12
Dougherty 42	8	34N25	84w07	5:36:28
Douglas 34	20	31N31	82w51	5:31:24
Douglasville 48	8	33N45	84w45	5:39:00
Dove Creek 52	20	34N07	82w55	5:31:40
Dover 123	20	32N35	81w43	5:26:52
Doverel 134	8	31N46	84w26	5:37:44
Downtown 60	7	33N45	84w20	5:37:20
Doyle 98	8	32N17	84w27	5:37:48
Draketown 71	8	33N50	85w03	5:40:12
Dranesville 98	8	32N22	84w28	5:37:52
Drayton 46	20	32N06	83w48	5:35:12
Dresden 38	8	33N22	84w47	5:39:08
Drew 58	8	34N14	84w12	5:36:48
Drexel 104	20	33N38	83w37	5:34:28
Druid Hills 44	7	33N47	84w20	5:37:20
Dry Branch 82	20	32N55	81w57	5:27:48
Dry Branch 142	20	32N48	83w30	5:34:00
Drypond 78	20	34N12	83w27	5:33:48
Dublin 87	20	32N32	82w54	5:31:36
Dubois 45	20	32N21	83w18	5:33:12
Ducktown 58	8	34N15	84w15	5:37:00
Dudley 87	20	32N33	83w04	5:32:16
Due West 33	8	33N56	84w32	5:38:08
Duffee 101	20	31N14	84w13	5:36:52
Dugdown 71	8	33N53	85w13	5:40:52
Duluth 67	20	34N00	84w09	5:36:36
Dumas 151	8	32N04	84w32	5:38:08
Dunaire 44	20	33N44	84w16	5:37:04
Duncan Park 23	8	35N01	85w14	5:40:56
Duncanville 65	8	30N44	84w08	5:36:32
Dunn Store 105	8	34N53	84w45	5:39:00
Dunwoody 44	20	33N57	84w20	5:37:20
Du Pont 32	20	31N00	82w52	5:31:28
Durand 99	8	32N55	84w46	5:39:04
Dye 52	20	34N12	83w02	5:32:08
Dyke 61	8	34N42	84w29	5:37:56
Eagle Cliff 145	8	35N00	85w20	5:41:20
Eagle Grove 73	20	34N21	83w06	5:32:24
Eagle Pond 88	20	31N55	84w15	5:37:00
Eastanollee 126	20	34N31	83w15	5:33:00
East Armuchee 145	8	34N42	85w22	5:41:28
East Atlanta 44	7	33N44	84w20	5:37:20
East Boynton 23	8	35N01	85w11	5:40:44
East Crisp 40	20	31N58	83w42	5:34:48
East Dougherty 47	20	31N33	84w04	5:36:16
East Dublin 87	20	32N33	82w52	5:31:28
East Ellijay 61	8	34N37	84w30	5:38:00
East Griffin 125	8	33N14	84w14	5:36:56
East Juliette 84	20	33N06	83w48	5:35:12
Eastland Heights 44	7	33N43	84w20	5:37:20
Eastman 45	20	32N12	83w11	5:32:44
Eastman Mills 45	20	32N12	83w11	5:32:44
East Marietta 33	8	33N56	84w32	5:38:08
East Meadow 29	3	33N59	83w23	5:33:32
East Moultrie 35	20	31N11	83w48	5:35:12
East Newnan 38	8	33N21	84w46	5:39:04
East Point 60	7	33N41	84w27	5:37:48
East River 86	20	31N01	83w00	5:32:00
East Thomaston 144	8	32N53	84w20	5:37:20
East Trion 27	8	34N33	85w18	5:41:12
Eastville 107	20	33N53	83w30	5:34:00
Eastwood 44	7	33N44	84w20	5:37:20
Eastwood 44	7	33N45	84w19	5:37:16
Eastwood Apartments 11	25	32N49	83w41	5:34:44
Eatonton 116	20	33N20	83w23	5:33:32
Ebernezer 146	20	33N39	83w43	5:34:52
Echeconnee 110	8	32N39	83w45	5:35:00
Echota 64	8	34N31	84w55	5:39:40
Eden 51	20	32N11	81w24	5:25:36
Edge Hill 62	20	33N04	82w37	5:30:28
Edgewater Park 25	20	32N00	81w05	5:24:20
Edgewood 36	20	33N29	82w02	5:28:08
Edison 19	8	31N34	84w44	5:38:56
Edith 32	20	30N41	82w33	5:30:12
Egypt 51	20	32N22	81w18	5:25:12
Elberta 76	20	32N37	83w39	5:34:36
Elberton 52	20	34N07	82w52	5:31:28
Elder 107	20	33N46	83w20	5:33:20
Eldora 15	20	32N07	81w29	5:25:56
Eldorendo 43	8	31N03	84w39	5:38:36
Eleanor Village 47	11	31N34	84w11	5:36:44
Elery 74	8	33N21	85w04	5:40:16
Elim 91	20	31N43	81w45	5:27:00
Elizabeth 33	8	33N59	84w34	5:38:16
Elko 76	20	32N20	83w42	5:34:48
Ellabell 15	20	32N07	81w29	5:25:56
Ellaville 122	8	32N14	84w19	5:37:16
Ellenton 35	20	31N11	83w35	5:34:20
Ellenwood 31	20	33N37	84w17	5:37:08
Ellerslie 72	8	32N38	84w48	5:39:12
Ellijay 61	8	34N42	84w29	5:37:56
Ellwood 120	20	33N17	82w12	5:28:48
Elmodel 4	8	31N21	84w29	5:37:56
Elmwood 87	20	32N33	82w54	5:31:36
Elza 131	20	32N05	82w07	5:28:28
Ematia Island 79	20	33N13	83w40	5:34:40
Embry 109	8	33N55	84w50	5:39:20
Embry Hills 44	20	33N53	84w18	5:37:12
Emerson 8	8	34N08	84w45	5:39:00
Emerson Park 147	20	31N14	82w22	5:29:28
Emit 16	20	32N26	81w47	5:27:08
Emma 42	8	34N29	84w12	5:36:48
Emmalane 82	20	32N46	82w00	5:28:00
Emory University 44	7	33N47	84w21	5:37:24
Empire 45	20	32N21	83w18	5:33:12
Empress 14	20	30N41	83w31	5:34:04
Enigma 10	20	31N21	83w21	5:33:24
Enongrove 74	8	33N21	85w04	5:40:16
Enterprise 108	20	34N03	83w02	5:32:08
Ephesus 74	8	33N25	85w00	5:40:00
Epworth 55	8	34N58	84w23	5:37:32
Esom Hill 114	8	33N57	85w23	5:41:32
Etna 114	8	33N57	85w23	5:41:32
Eton 105	8	34N50	84w46	5:39:04
Eudora 79	20	33N25	83w43	5:34:52
Euharlee 8	8	34N10	84w48	5:39:12
Eulonia 95	20	31N32	81w26	5:25:44
Evans 36	20	33N32	82w08	5:28:32
Evansville 140	8	33N04	85w14	5:40:56
Everett 63	20	31N17	81w31	5:26:04
Everett City 63	20	31N24	81w38	5:26:32
Everett Springs 57	8	34N22	85w11	5:40:44
Evermay 99	8	33N06	84w35	5:38:20
Excelsior 21	20	32N19	81w58	5:27:52
Experiment 125	8	33N17	84w17	5:37:08
Faceville 43	8	30N45	84w38	5:38:32
Fairburn 60	10	33N34	84w35	5:38:20
Fairfax 147	20	31N16	82w40	5:30:40
Fairlawn Acres 23	8	34N57	85w18	5:41:12
Fairmount 64	8	34N26	84w42	5:38:48
Fair Oaks 33	8	33N55	84w33	5:38:12
Fairplay 48	8	33N38	84w51	5:39:24
Fairplay 104	20	33N38	83w37	5:34:28
Fairview 68	20	34N34	83w33	5:34:12
Fairview 145	8	34N57	85w18	5:41:12
Fairyland 145	8	34N53	85w24	5:41:36
Fargo 32	20	30N41	82w34	5:30:16
Farmdale 123	20	32N49	81w39	5:26:36
Farmers High 22	8	33N35	85w05	5:40:20
Farmington 107	20	33N47	83w26	5:33:44
Farmville 64	8	34N30	84w57	5:39:48
Farrar 79	20	33N28	83w38	5:34:32
Fashion 105	8	34N46	84w48	5:39:12
Faulkner 111	8	34N20	84w23	5:37:32
Fayetteville 56	8	33N27	84w27	5:37:48
Federal 47	11	31N35	84w10	5:36:40
Federal Annex 60	7	33N45	84w20	5:37:20
Federal Reserve 60	7	33N45	84w23	5:37:32
Felton 71	8	33N53	85w13	5:40:52
Fence 67	20	34N01	83w49	5:35:16
Fender 136	20	31N22	83w29	5:33:56
Ficklin 156	20	33N44	82w45	5:31:00
Ficklings Mill 132	8	32N33	84w14	5:36:56
Fidele 64	8	34N35	84w56	5:39:44
Fife 60	10	33N35	84w34	5:38:16
Fincherville 18	20	33N18	83w58	5:35:52
Findlay 46	20	32N12	83w46	5:35:04
Finleyson 115	20	32N11	83w31	5:34:04
Fish Creek 114	8	34N01	85w15	5:41:00
Fitzgerald 9	20	31N43	83w15	5:33:00
Fitzgerald Cotton Mill 9	20	31N43	83w15	5:33:00
Fitzpatrick 142	20	32N41	83w20	5:33:20
Five Forks 67	20	33N57	83w59	5:35:56
Five Forks 135	20	30N48	83w48	5:35:12
Five Points 96	8	32N18	84w01	5:36:04
Five Points 119	8	31N45	84w37	5:38:28
Five Points 132	8	32N33	84w14	5:36:56
Five Points 139	20	32N23	82w36	5:30:24
Five Springs 154	8	34N46	84w58	5:39:52
Flat Rock 116	20	33N19	83w23	5:33:32
Flat Rock 159	17	32N29	84w57	5:39:48
Flat Shoals 73	20	34N22	83w05	5:32:20
Fleming 89	20	31N52	81w34	5:26:16
Flemington 89	20	31N52	81w34	5:26:16
Flint 101	20	31N23	84w10	5:36:40
Flint Hill 129	8	32N48	84w42	5:38:48
Flintside 128	20	31N57	84w01	5:36:04
Flintstone 145	8	34N53	85w18	5:41:12
Flippen 75	20	33N29	84w11	5:36:44
Floralhill 156	20	33N52	82w39	5:30:36
Flovilla 18	20	33N15	83w53	5:35:32
Flowery Branch 69	1	34N10	83w56	5:35:44
Floyd 33	8	33N51	84w35	5:38:20
Floyd Springs 57	8	34N22	85w11	5:40:44
Folkston 24	20	30N50	82w00	5:28:00
Folsom 8	8	34N22	84w56	5:39:44
Forest Lake 11	25	32N51	83w41	5:34:44
Forest Park 31	20	33N37	84w22	5:37:28
Forest Park 47	11	31N34	84w11	5:36:44
Forest River Farms 25	20	32N00	81w05	5:24:20
Forsyth 102	8	33N02	83w56	5:35:44
Fort Benning 26	16	32N22	84w50	5:39:20
Fort Gaines 30	8	31N36	85w03	5:40:12
Fort Gordon 120	20	33N25	82w09	5:28:36
Fort Lamar 97	20	34N10	83w15	5:33:00
Fort McAllister 15	20	31N57	81w19	5:25:16
Fort McPherson 60	7	33N42	84w27	5:37:48
Fort Oglethorpe 23	8	34N57	85w16	5:41:04
Fort Screven 25	20	32N00	80w51	5:23:24
Fortson 159	8	32N37	84w58	5:39:44
Fortsonia 52	20	34N08	82w50	5:31:20

GEORGIA

Fort Stewart 89 20 31N52 81w35 5:26:20
Fort Valley 110 8 32N33 83w53 5:35:32
Foster Hills 23 8 35N01 85w11 5:40:44
Fosters Mills 57 8 34N17 85w12 5:40:48
Four Points 47 11 31N34 84w10 5:36:40
Fowlstown 43 8 30N48 84w33 5:38:12
Franklin 74 8 33N17 85w06 5:40:24
Franklin Springs 59 20 34N17 83w09 5:32:36
Franklinton 11 20 32N48 83w30 5:34:00
Frazier 12 20 32N23 83w21 5:33:24
Free Home 28 8 34N14 84w16 5:37:04
Friendship 114 8 34N01 85w15 5:41:00
Friendship 128 8 32N09 84w25 5:37:40
Frolona 74 8 33N21 85w04 5:40:16
Fruitland 50 20 30N59 82w52 5:31:28
Fry 55 8 34N59 84w22 5:37:28
Fullerville 22 8 33N44 84w55 5:39:40
Funkhouser 8 8 34N26 84w42 5:38:48
Funston 35 20 31N12 83w52 5:35:28
Furniture City 33 8 33N48 84w37 5:38:28
Gabbettville 140 8 32N57 85w08 5:40:32
Gaddistown 143 8 34N41 84w01 5:36:04
Gaillard 39 8 32N43 84w01 5:36:04
Gaines Community 29 3 33N59 83w23 5:33:32
Gainesville 69 1 34N18 83w50 5:35:20
Galloway 55 8 34N52 84w19 5:37:16
Garden City 25 20 32N06 81w09 5:24:36
Garden Lakes 57 8 34N17 85w12 5:40:48
Garden Valley 96 8 32N22 84w11 5:36:44
Gardi 150 20 31N32 81w48 5:27:12
Garfield 53 20 32N39 82w05 5:28:20
Garnersville 30 8 31N48 84w57 5:39:48
Garretta 87 20 32N33 82w54 5:31:36
Gary 53 20 32N31 82w19 5:29:16
Gates City 60 7 33N45 84w23 5:37:32
Gay 99 8 33N06 84w35 5:38:20
Geneva 129 8 32N35 84w33 5:38:12
Georgetown 106 20 33N38 83w52 5:35:28
Georgetown 117 8 31N53 85w06 5:40:24
Georgia Southern 16 20 32N26 81w47 5:27:08
Georgia Southwestern College 128 18 32N04 84w14 5:36:56
Germany 118 20 34N53 83w24 5:33:36
Gibson 62 20 33N14 82w36 5:30:24
Gill 90 20 33N52 82w39 5:30:36
Gillis Springs 139 20 32N28 82w30 5:30:00
Gillsville 69 20 34N18 83w38 5:34:32
Gilmore 33 8 33N53 84w32 5:38:08
Girard 17 20 33N03 81w43 5:26:52
Glades 116 20 33N23 83w26 5:33:44
Gladesville 79 20 33N18 83w41 5:34:44
Gladys 10 20 31N23 83w13 5:32:52
Glasgow 135 20 30N48 83w48 5:35:12
Glencliff 144 8 32N53 84w20 5:37:20
Glendale 120 20 33N28 81w59 5:27:56
Glen Haven 44 20 33N45 84w13 5:36:52
Glenloch 74 8 33N21 85w04 5:40:16
Glenloch Village 56 8 33N19 84w17 5:37:08
Glenmore 147 20 31N14 82w22 5:29:28
Glenn 74 8 33N09 85w12 5:40:48
Glennville 131 20 31N56 81w56 5:27:44
Glenwood 57 8 34N17 85w12 5:40:48
Glenwood 152 20 32N11 82w40 5:30:40
Glenwood Hills 44 20 33N44 84w16 5:37:04
Gloster 67 20 33N55 84w04 5:36:16
Glynco 63 20 31N15 81w28 5:25:52
Glynn Haven 63 20 31N09 81w23 5:25:32
Goat Town 149 20 33N00 82w53 5:31:32
Gobblers Hill 26 8 32N18 84w47 5:39:08
Gober 28 8 34N20 84w23 5:37:32
Godfrey 104 20 33N27 83w30 5:34:00
Godwinsville 45 20 32N08 83w08 5:32:32
Goggins 85 8 33N03 84w10 5:36:40
Goldmine 73 20 34N21 83w06 5:32:24
Goldsboro 12 20 32N23 83w21 5:33:24
Goldson 132 8 32N33 84w14 5:36:56
Goodes 60 10 33N31 84w40 5:38:40
Good Hope 146 20 33N48 83w37 5:34:28
Goose Island 61 8 34N47 84w23 5:37:32
Gorday 158 20 31N29 83w53 5:35:32
Gordon 157 20 32N54 83w20 5:33:20
Gordon Road 60 7 33N44 84w25 5:37:40
Gordon Springs 154 8 34N48 85w01 5:40:04
Gordy 158 20 31N29 83w53 5:35:32
Gore 27 8 34N29 85w21 5:41:24
Goss 52 20 34N08 82w50 5:31:20
Gough 17 20 33N06 82w14 5:28:56
Gracewood 120 20 33N22 82w02 5:28:08
Grady 114 8 34N01 85w15 5:41:00
Graham 1 20 31N50 82w30 5:30:00
Grange 81 20 33N00 82w24 5:29:36
Grangerville 158 20 31N29 81w44 5:26:56
Granite Hill 70 20 33N17 82w58 5:31:52
Grantville 38 8 33N14 84w50 5:39:20
Gratis 146 20 33N53 83w40 5:34:40
Graves 134 8 31N46 84w31 5:38:04
Gray 84 20 33N01 83w32 5:34:08
Gray Hill 140 8 32N52 85w11 5:40:44
Graymont 53 20 32N35 82w09 5:28:36
Grayson 67 20 33N54 83w57 5:35:48
Graysville 23 8 34N59 85w08 5:40:32
Greeley 28 8 34N19 84w33 5:38:12
Green Acres 23 8 34N57 85w18 5:41:12
Green Acres 29 3 33N59 83w23 5:33:32
Green Acres Estate 87 20 32N33 82w54 5:31:36
Greenough 101 20 31N23 84w10 5:36:40
Greensboro 66 20 33N35 83w11 5:32:44
Greens Crossing 92 20 30N54 83w05 5:32:20
Greens Cut 17 20 33N10 81w59 5:27:56
Greens Mill 55 8 34N52 84w19 5:37:16
Greenville 20 20 30N48 81w41 5:26:44
Greenville 99 8 33N02 84w43 5:38:52
Greenway 53 20 32N34 82w15 5:29:00
Greenway 60 7 34N01 84w21 5:37:24
Greenwood 75 20 33N27 84w09 5:36:36
Greenwood 101 20 31N14 84w13 5:36:52
Greenwood Forest 32 20 30N56 83w00 5:32:00
Gresham Park 44 7 33N44 84w20 5:37:20
Greshamville 66 20 33N37 83w19 5:33:16
Gresston 45 20 32N17 83w15 5:33:00
Griffin 125 15 33N01 84w16 5:37:04
Grimball Park 25 20 32N00 81w05 5:24:20
Griswold 84 25 32N50 83w37 5:34:28
Grizzletown 8 8 34N04 84w40 5:38:40
Grooverville 14 20 30N48 83w48 5:35:12
Grovania 76 20 32N22 83w40 5:34:40
Groveland 15 20 32N08 81w45 5:27:00
Grove Park 25 20 32N00 81w05 5:24:20
Grove Point 25 20 32N03 81w07 5:24:28
Grovetown 36 20 33N27 82w12 5:28:48
Guild 145 8 34N42 85w22 5:41:28
Gum Branch 89 20 31N52 81w35 5:26:20
Gum Log 143 8 34N53 83w58 5:35:52
Guysie 3 20 31N32 82w28 5:29:52
Guyton 51 20 32N20 81w24 5:25:36
Habersham 68 20 34N36 83w34 5:34:16
Haddock 84 20 33N02 83w26 5:33:44
Hagan 54 20 32N09 81w56 5:27:44
Hahira 92 20 30N59 83w22 5:33:28
Halcyondale 123 20 32N49 81w39 5:26:36
Halfmoon Landing 89 20 31N42 81w16 5:25:04
Halls 8 8 34N18 84w56 5:39:44
Hallwood 116 20 33N19 83w23 5:33:32
Halycon Bluff 25 20 32N04 81w07 5:24:28
Hamilton 72 8 32N45 84w53 5:39:32
Hammett 39 8 32N43 84w01 5:36:04
Hampton 75 8 33N23 84w17 5:37:08
Handy 38 8 33N22 84w47 5:39:08
Haney 57 8 34N07 85w20 5:41:20
Hannah 48 8 33N44 84w49 5:39:16
Hannah Mill 144 8 32N53 84w20 5:37:20
Hannatown 43 8 30N54 84w34 5:38:16
Hapeville 60 7 33N40 84w25 5:37:40
Happy Hollow 155 20 31N58 83w36 5:34:24
Haralson 38 8 33N14 84w34 5:38:16
Harbins 67 20 33N56 83w43 5:34:52
Harding 136 20 31N27 83w31 5:34:04
Hardwick 5 20 33N04 83w14 5:32:56
Harlem 36 22 33N25 82w19 5:29:16
Harllee 116 20 33N05 83w14 5:32:56
Harmony 116 20 33N19 83w23 5:33:32
Harmony Church 159 17 32N26 84w57 5:39:48
Harrietts Bluff 20 20 30N58 81w43 5:26:52
Harrington 63 20 31N09 81w23 5:25:32
Harris 99 8 33N04 84w45 5:39:00
Harrisburg 145 8 34N29 85w21 5:41:24
Harrison 149 20 32N50 82w43 5:30:52
Harrisonville 140 8 33N11 84w52 5:39:28
Harrock Hall 25 20 32N00 81w05 5:24:20
Hartford 115 20 32N17 83w28 5:33:52
Hartsfield 35 20 31N13 83w59 5:35:56
Hartwell 73 20 34N21 82w56 5:31:44
Harvest 68 20 34N40 83w27 5:33:48
Haskins 87 20 32N33 83w04 5:32:16
Hassler Mill 154 8 34N48 85w01 5:40:04
Hatcher 117 8 31N53 85w07 5:40:28
Hatley 40 20 31N54 83w37 5:34:28
Hawkinsville 115 20 32N17 83w28 5:33:52
Haylow 50 20 30N50 82w54 5:31:36
Hayneville 76 20 32N23 83w37 5:34:28
Hayston 106 20 33N31 83w44 5:34:56
Hazlehurst 80 20 31N52 82w36 5:30:24
Head River 41 8 34N31 85w30 5:42:00
Heardville 58 8 34N14 84w12 5:36:48
Hebardville 147 20 31N14 82w22 5:29:28
Helen 153 20 34N42 83w42 5:34:48
Helena 133 20 32N04 82w55 5:31:40
Hemp 55 8 34N52 84w15 5:37:00
Henderson 76 20 32N21 83w47 5:35:08
Hendrick 144 8 32N53 84w20 5:37:20
Hentown 49 8 31N23 84w57 5:39:48
Hephzibah 120 20 33N19 82w06 5:28:24
Herndon 82 20 32N34 82w15 5:29:00
Herod 134 8 31N42 84w26 5:37:44
Hiawassee 138 20 34N58 83w46 5:35:04
Hickory Bluff 20 20 31N06 81w43 5:26:52
Hickory Flat 6 20 34N23 83w40 5:34:40
Hickory Flat 28 8 34N14 84w29 5:37:56
Hickory Level 22 8 33N35 85w05 5:40:20
Hickox 13 20 31N09 82w00 5:28:00
Higdon 55 8 34N58 84w23 5:37:32
Higgston 103 20 32N13 82w28 5:29:52
Highfalls 102 8 33N18 83w58 5:35:52
Highland Heights 92 20 30N51 83w15 5:33:00
Highland Mills 125 8 33N17 84w17 5:37:08
Highland Park 25 20 32N00 81w05 5:24:20
Highland Pines 159 17 32N29 84w57 5:39:48
High Point 106 20 33N40 83w52 5:35:28
High Point 145 8 34N52 85w23 5:41:32
High Shoals 104 20 33N49 83w30 5:34:00
Hightower 58 8 34N14 84w12 5:36:48
Hill City 64 8 34N35 84w56 5:39:44
Hillcrest 140 8 33N06 85w01 5:40:04
Hillman 130 20 33N33 82w54 5:31:36
Hills 68 20 34N40 83w27 5:33:48
Hillsboro 79 20 33N11 83w38 5:34:32
Hilltonia 123 20 32N53 81w40 5:26:40
Hilton 49 8 31N23 84w57 5:39:48
Hilyer 140 8 33N02 85w02 5:40:08
Hinesville 89 20 31N51 81w36 5:26:24
Hinkles 145 8 34N46 85w32 5:42:08
Hinsonton 101 20 31N05 84w05 5:36:20
Hinton 111 8 34N28 84w26 5:37:44
Hiram 109 8 33N50 84w48 5:39:12
Hi Roc Shores 121 20 33N41 84w00 5:36:00
Hobby 141 20 31N43 83w39 5:34:36
Hoboken 13 20 31N11 82w08 5:28:32
Hogansville 140 8 33N10 84w55 5:39:40
Hog Mountain 67 20 34N07 84w00 5:36:00
Holbrook 28 8 34N14 84w12 5:36:48
Holland 27 8 34N21 85w22 5:41:28
Hollingsworth 6 20 34N28 83w34 5:34:16
Hollis 135 20 30N58 83w44 5:34:56
Hollonville 113 8 33N11 84w21 5:37:24
Holly Springs 28 8 34N10 84w30 5:38:00
Holly Springs 78 20 34N15 83w34 5:34:16
Hollywood 68 20 34N39 83w27 5:33:48
Holt 77 20 31N36 83w07 5:32:28
Homeland 24 20 30N51 82w01 5:28:04
Homer 6 20 34N20 83w30 5:34:00
Homerville 32 20 31N02 82w45 5:31:00
Honora 90 20 33N48 82w29 5:29:56
Hooker 41 8 34N52 85w31 5:42:04
Hopeful 101 20 31N14 84w13 5:36:52
Hopewell 28 8 34N14 84w29 5:37:56
Hopewell 72 8 32N53 84w50 5:39:20
Horns 39 8 32N41 84w00 5:36:00
Horseleg Estates 57 8 34N17 85w12 5:40:48
Hortense 13 20 31N20 81w57 5:27:48
Hoschton 78 20 34N06 83w46 5:35:04
Houston Lake 76 20 32N30 83w36 5:34:24
Howard 132 8 32N36 84w23 5:37:32
Howell 50 20 30N50 83w03 5:32:12
Huber 142 20 32N42 83w33 5:34:12
Hubert 16 20 32N23 81w40 5:26:40
Hudson Mill 72 8 32N39 84w51 5:39:24
Huffaker 57 8 34N17 85w12 5:40:48
Huffer 34 20 31N30 82w51 5:31:24
Hughland 131 20 32N10 82w01 5:28:04
Hulett 22 8 33N35 85w05 5:40:20
Hull 97 20 34N01 83w18 5:33:12
Hulmeville 52 20 34N08 82w50 5:31:20
Hunter 123 20 32N39 81w33 5:26:12
Hunter Army Airfield 25 20 32N01 81w06 5:24:24
Huntington 128 18 32N04 84w14 5:36:56
Huntsville 109 8 34N00 84w49 5:39:16
Hurst 55 8 34N52 84w15 5:37:00
Hutchings 108 20 33N51 83w10 5:32:40
Ideal 96 8 32N22 84w11 5:36:44
Ila 97 20 34N10 83w19 5:33:16
Imlac 99 8 32N58 84w37 5:38:28
Imperial 116 20 33N19 83w23 5:33:32
Indianola 92 20 30N51 83w15 5:33:00
Indian Springs 18 8 33N15 83w55 5:35:40
Indian Springs 23 8 35N01 85w11 5:40:44
Industrial 60 10 33N44 84w32 5:38:08
Inman 56 8 33N23 84w25 5:37:40
International 68 20 34N31 83w32 5:34:08
International Office Park 60 7 33N40 84w23 5:37:32
Ione 14 20 30N58 83w44 5:34:56
Iron City 124 8 31N01 84w49 5:39:16
Irwins 149 20 32N56 82w49 5:31:16
Irwinton 157 20 32N49 83w10 5:32:40
Irwinville 77 20 31N39 83w23 5:33:32
Isabella 158 20 31N32 83w50 5:35:20
Isle of Hope 25 20 32N00 81w05 5:24:20
Ivanhoe 18 20 32N23 81w40 5:26:40
Ivey 157 20 32N55 83w18 5:33:12
Ivy Log 143 8 34N53 83w58 5:35:52
Jackson 18 20 33N18 83w58 5:35:52
Jacksons Crossroads 156 20 33N52 82w44 5:30:56
Jacksonville 133 20 31N49 82w59 5:31:56
Jacksonville 138 20 34N56 83w51 5:35:24
Jake 22 8 33N42 85w11 5:40:44
Jakin 49 8 31N06 84w59 5:39:56
James 84 20 32N58 83w29 5:33:56
Jamestown 147 20 31N14 82w22 5:29:28
Jarrell 132 8 32N33 84w14 5:36:56
Jasper 111 8 34N28 84w26 5:37:44
Jay Bird Springs 45 20 32N06 83w04 5:32:16
Jefferson 78 20 34N07 83w35 5:34:20
Jefferson 116 20 33N19 83w23 5:33:32
Jefferson Mill 108 20 33N53 83w09 5:32:36
Jeffersonville 142 20 32N41 83w20 5:33:20
Jekyll Island 63 20 31N12 81w29 5:25:56
Jenkinsburg 18 20 33N20 84w02 5:36:08
Jersey 146 20 33N43 83w47 5:35:08
Jerusalem 20 20 30N58 81w50 5:27:20
Jerusalem 111 8 34N28 84w26 5:37:44
Jesup 150 20 31N36 81w53 5:27:32
Jewell 148 20 33N18 82w47 5:31:08
Jewtown 63 20 31N09 81w23 5:25:32
Jimps 16 20 32N26 81w47 5:27:08
Johnson Corner 137 20 32N04 82w18 5:29:12
Johnstonville 85 8 33N03 84w10 5:36:40
Jolly 113 8 33N11 84w21 5:37:24
Jones 95 20 31N44 81w26 5:25:44
Jones Acres 84 25 32N50 83w37 5:34:28
Jonesboro 31 9 33N31 84w22 5:37:28
Jones Crossroads 72 8 32N53 84w50 5:39:20
Jonesville 22 8 33N32 85w15 5:41:00

Jot Em Down Store 112 20 31N18 82W15 5:29:00
Juliette 102 20 33N06 83W48 5:35:12
Junction City 129 8 32N36 84W28 5:37:52
Juniper 98 8 32N32 84W36 5:38:24
Juno 42 8 34N29 84W12 5:36:48
Kansas 22 8 33N42 85W11 5:40:44
Kathleen 76 20 32N30 83W36 5:34:24
Keith 23 8 34N50 85W03 5:40:12
Keithsburg 28 8 34N16 84W27 5:37:48
Keller 15 20 31N50 81W15 5:25:00
Kelley Hill 159 17 32N26 84W57 5:39:48
Kelly 79 20 33N24 83W35 5:34:20
Kellytown 75 20 33N27 84W09 5:36:36
Kemp 53 20 32N31 82W19 5:29:16
Kennesaw 33 8 34N01 84W37 5:38:28
Kensington 145 8 34N45 85W28 5:41:52
Kenwood 56 8 33N25 84W31 5:38:04
Kenzie 144 8 32N53 84W20 5:37:20
Keysville 17 20 33N14 82W14 5:28:56
Kibbee 103 20 32N17 82W31 5:30:04
Kiker 61 8 34N42 84W29 5:37:56
Kildare 51 20 32N32 81W27 5:25:48
Killarney 49 8 31N05 84W59 5:39:56
Kimbrough 151 8 32N05 84W40 5:38:40
Kinderlou 92 20 30N48 83W22 5:33:28
Kings 106 20 33N40 83W52 5:35:28
Kingsboro 72 8 32N45 84W52 5:39:28
Kingsland 20 20 30N48 81W41 5:26:44
Kingston 8 8 34N14 84W57 5:39:48
King's Wood 25 20 32N04 81W07 5:24:28
Kingwood 35 20 31N11 83W48 5:35:12
Kinseytown 153 20 34N36 83W46 5:35:04
Kirkland 2 20 31N19 82W35 5:30:20
Kirkland 80 20 31N52 82W36 5:30:24
Kite 83 20 32N44 82W32 5:30:08
Klondike 44 20 33N43 84W06 5:36:24
Klondike 69 1 34N18 83W49 5:35:16
Klondike 76 20 32N17 83W28 5:33:52
Knott 140 8 33N02 85W02 5:40:08
Knoxville 39 8 32N44 84W00 5:36:00
Kramer 155 20 31N59 83W19 5:33:16
Laboon 146 20 33N47 83W37 5:34:28
La Crosse 122 8 32N14 84W18 5:37:12
Ladds 8 8 34N12 84W51 5:39:24
Lafayette 145 8 34N42 85W17 5:41:08
La Grange 140 8 33N02 85W02 5:40:08
Lake 114 8 34N01 85W15 5:41:00
Lake Arrowhead 28 8 34N19 84W33 5:38:12
Lake Capri Estates 121 20 33N43 84W06 5:36:24
Lake Cindy 75 8 33N23 84W17 5:37:08
Lake City 31 8 33N37 84W21 5:37:24
Lake Creek 114 8 34N01 85W15 5:41:00
Lake Howard 145 8 34N42 85W22 5:41:28
Lakeland 86 20 31N02 83W04 5:32:16
Lake Lucerne 67 20 33N53 84W08 5:36:32
Lakemont 118 20 34N47 83W25 5:33:40
Lakemount 118 20 34N47 83W25 5:33:40
Lake Park 92 20 30N41 83W11 5:32:44
Lakeshore Estates 69 1 34N18 83W49 5:35:16
Lakeside Park 25 20 32N00 81W05 5:24:20
Lake Talmadge 75 8 33N23 84W17 5:37:08
Lake Tara 31 8 33N31 84W21 5:37:24
Lakeview 12 20 32N23 83W21 5:33:24
Lakeview 23 8 34N58 85W15 5:41:00
Lakeview 110 8 32N33 83W53 5:35:32
Lakeview Estates 121 20 33N41 84W00 5:36:00
Lakewood 60 7 33N43 84W23 5:37:32
Lamarville 25 20 32N03 81W07 5:24:28
Landrum 42 8 34N25 84W07 5:36:28
Laney 101 20 31N13 84W02 5:36:08
Lanier 15 20 32N08 81W37 5:26:28
Lashley 76 20 32N33 83W36 5:34:24
Lathemtown 28 8 34N15 84W19 5:37:16
Laurens Hill 87 20 32N34 83W09 5:32:36
Lavender 57 8 34N17 85W12 5:40:48
La Vista 44 7 33N49 84W20 5:37:20
Lavonia 59 20 34N26 83W06 5:32:24
Lawrenceville 67 20 33N57 83W59 5:35:56
Lax 34 20 31N36 83W15 5:33:00
Leaf 153 20 34N36 83W46 5:35:04
Leah 36 20 33N33 82W19 5:29:16
Leary 19 8 31N29 84W31 5:38:04
Leathersville 90 20 33N42 82W27. 5:29:48
Lebanon 28 8 34N09 84W31 5:38:04
Leefield 16 20 32N26 81W47 5:27:08
Lee Pope 39 8 32N37 83W58 5:35:52
Leesburg 88 20 31N44 84W10 5:36:40
Lees Crossing 140 8 33N02 85W02 5:40:08
Lees Mill 56 8 33N25 84W31 5:38:04
Leland 33 8 33N49 84W34 5:38:16
Leliaton 2 20 31N20 83W03 5:32:12
Lena 33 8 34N04 84W40 5:38:40
Lenox 37 20 31N16 83W28 5:33:52
Lenox Square 60 7 33N51 84W22 5:37:28
Leslie 128 20 31N57 84W05 5:36:20
Lewis 123 20 32N49 81W39 5:26:36
Lewistown 36 20 33N32 82W08 5:28:32
Lexington 108 20 33N52 83W07 5:32:28
Lexsy 53 20 32N31 82W19 5:29:16
Liberty City 25 20 32N03 81W07 5:24:28
Libertyhill 85 8 33N07 84W12 5:36:48
Lifsey 113 8 33N06 84W20 5:37:20
Lightfoot 157 20 32N49 83W05 5:32:20
Lilburn 67 20 33N53 84W08 5:36:32
Lilly 46 20 32N09 83W53 5:35:32
Lillypond 64 8 34N26 84W57 5:39:48
Lime Sink 65 8 31N02 84W19 5:37:16
Limestone 12 20 32N23 83W21 5:33:24
Lincoln Park 144 8 32N52 84W20 5:37:20
Lincolnton 90 20 33N48 82W29 5:29:56
Lindale 57 8 34N11 85W11 5:40:44
Lindsey Creek 159 17 32N29 84W57 5:39:48
Linesville 156 20 33N33 82W54 5:31:36
Linton 70 20 33N07 83W00 5:32:00
Linwood 145 8 34N43 85W22 5:41:28
Listonia 40 20 31N58 83W47 5:35:08
Lithia Springs 48 8 33N47 84W40 5:38:40
Little House Creek 9 20 31N45 83W18 5:33:12
Little Miami 92 20 30N51 83W15 5:33:00
Little River 116 20 33N16 83W25 5:33:40
Little Sand Mountain 27 8 34N29 85W14 5:40:56
Livingston 57 8 34N17 85W12 5:40:48
Lizella 11 8 32N48 83W49 5:35:16
Loco 90 20 33N48 82W29 5:29:56
Locust Grove 75 20 33N21 84W07 5:36:28
Loganville 146 20 33N50 83W54 5:35:36
Lollie 87 20 32N29 82W46 5:31:04
Lone Oak 99 8 33N10 84W49 5:39:16
Long Cane 140 8 32N57 85W08 5:40:32
Longstreet Bleckley 12 20 32N23 83W21 5:33:24
Lookout Mountain 145 8 34N58 85W21 5:41:24
Lorane 11 25 32N50 83W37 5:34:28
Lorenzo 51 20 32N22 81W18 5:25:12
Lorwood 25 20 32N00 81W05 5:24:20
Lost Mountain 33 8 33N52 84W41 5:38:44
Lothair 139 20 32N23 82W36 5:30:24
Lotts 34 20 31N38 82W53 5:31:32
Louise 140 8 33N05 84W56 5:39:44
Louisville 81 20 33N00 82W25 5:29:40
Louvale 127 8 32N10 84W50 5:39:20
Lovejoy 31 8 33N26 84W19 5:37:16
Lovett 87 20 32N38 82W46 5:31:04
Lowell 22 8 33N35 85W05 5:40:20
Lowry 56 8 33N25 84W31 5:38:04
Lucile 49 8 31N23 84W57 5:39:48
Lucius 61 8 34N47 84W23 5:37:32
Ludowici 91 20 31N43 81W45 5:27:00
Ludville 111 8 34N28 84W36 5:38:24
Luella 75 8 33N21 84W11 5:36:44
Lula 69 20 34N23 83W40 5:34:40
Lulaton 13 20 31N12 81W59 5:27:56
Lumber City 133 20 31N56 82W41 5:30:44
Lumpkin 127 8 32N03 84W48 5:39:12
Luthersville 99 8 33N13 84W45 5:39:00
Luvdale 47 11 31N34 84W11 5:36:44
Luxomni 67 20 33N53 84W08 5:36:32
Lyerly 27 8 34N24 85W24 5:41:36
Lynn 43 8 30N54 84W34 5:38:16
Lynnwood 23 8 34N57 85W18 5:41:12
Lyons 137 20 32N12 82W19 5:29:16
Lytle 145 8 34N52 85W23 5:41:32
Mableton 33 8 33N49 84W35 5:38:20
Macedonia 28 8 34N14 84W29 5:37:56
Machen 79 20 33N18 83W41 5:34:44
MacLand 33 8 33N54 84W40 5:38:40
Macon 11 25 32N51 83W38 5:34:32
Madison 104 20 33N36 83W28 5:33:52
Madola 55 8 34N58 84W23 5:37:32
Madras 38 8 33N27 84W44 5:38:56
Madray Springs 150 20 31N36 81W53 5:27:32
Magby Gap 41 8 34N52 85W31 5:42:04
Magnet 121 20 33N41 84W00 5:36:00
Mallorysville 156 20 33N52 82W44 5:30:56
Malvern 53 20 32N48 81W57 5:27:48
Manassas 131 20 32N10 82W01 5:28:04
Manchester 99 8 32N51 84W37 5:38:28
Manor 147 20 31N06 82W34 5:30:16
Mansfield 106 20 33N31 83W44 5:34:56
Manta 26 8 32N18 84W47 5:39:08
Marblehill 111 8 34N26 84W20 5:37:20
Maretts 73 20 34N26 83W06 5:32:24
Marietta 33 10 33N57 84W33 5:38:12
Marine Corps Center 47 20 31N33 84W03 5:36:12
Marion 142 20 32N48 83W30 5:34:00
Marlow 51 20 32N16 81W23 5:25:32
Marshallville 96 8 32N26 83W56 5:35:44
Mars Hill 33 8 34N04 84W40 5:38:40
Martech 60 7 33N47 84W26 5:37:44
Martin 126 20 34N29 83W11 5:32:44
Martinez 36 20 33N31 82W05 5:28:20
Massee 37 20 31N08 83W26 5:33:44
Match 52 20 34N12 83W02 5:32:08
Matt 58 8 34N14 84W12 5:36:48
Matthews 81 20 33N13 82W18 5:29:12
Mattox 24 20 31N52 82W36 5:30:24
Mauk 132 8 32N30 84W25 5:37:40
Maxeys 108 20 33N45 83W11 5:32:44
Maxim 90 20 33N48 82W29 5:29:56
Maxwell 79 20 33N24 83W35 5:34:20
Mayday 50 8 33N35 84W21 5:37:24
Mayfair 25 20 32N04 81W07 5:24:28
Mayfield 70 20 33N21 82W48 5:31:12
Mayhaw 100 8 31N09 84W51 5:39:24
Maysville 6 20 34N15 83W34 5:34:16
McAfee 44 20 33N44 84W16 5:37:04
McBean 120 20 33N15 81W57 5:27:48
McBride 38 8 33N22 84W47 5:39:08
McCaysville 55 8 34N57 84W22 5:37:28
McCollum 38 8 33N26 84W42 5:38:48
McCrary Settlement 144 8 33N01 84W30 5:38:00
McCutchen 154 8 34N48 85W01 5:40:04
McDaniels 64 8 34N27 84W58 5:39:52
McDonald Acres 23 8 34N57 85W18 5:41:12
McDonough 75 21 33N27 84W09 5:36:36
McElroys Mill 121 20 33N51 83W54 5:35:36
McGregor 103 20 32N12 82W31 5:30:04
McIntosh 89 20 31N48 81W26 5:25:44
McIntosh Mill Village 38 8 33N22 84W47 5:39:08
McIntyre 157 20 32N51 83W12 5:32:48
McKinney 144 15 32N56 84W17 5:37:08
McKinnon 150 20 31N25 81W56 5:27:44
McPherson 109 8 33N55 84W50 5:39:20
McRae 133 20 32N04 82W54 5:31:36
McWhorter 48 8 33N45 84W45 5:39:00
Meansville 113 15 33N03 84W18 5:37:12
Mechanicsville 67 20 33N55 84W15 5:37:00
Meeks 83 20 32N42 82W31 5:30:04
Meigs 135 20 31N04 84W06 5:36:24
Meinhard 25 20 32N12 81W13 5:24:52
Meldrim 51 20 32N09 81W23 5:25:32
Melrose 92 8 33N35 84W21 5:37:24
Melson 57 8 34N07 85W20 5:41:20
Mendes 131 20 31N56 81W56 5:27:44
Menlo 27 8 34N29 85W29 5:41:56
Meridian 95 20 31N27 81W23 5:25:32
Meriwether 5 20 33N07 83W17 5:33:08
Meriwether White Sulphur Spr 99 8 32N53 84W50 5:39:20
Merrillville 135 20 30N57 83W53 5:35:32
Mershon 112 20 31N28 82W15 5:29:00
Mesena 148 20 33N28 82W36 5:30:24
Metasville 156 20 33N44 82W45 5:31:00
Metcalf 135 20 30N42 84W00 5:36:00
Metter 21 20 32N24 82W03 5:28:12
Mica 28 8 34N20 84W23 5:37:32
Middle Oconee 29 20 33N57 83W27 5:33:48
Middle Rockdale 121 20 33N40 84W02 5:36:08
Middleton 52 20 34N04 82W47 5:31:08
Midland 159 8 32N34 84W48 5:39:12
Midville 17 20 32N49 82W14 5:28:56
Midway 23 8 34N57 85W18 5:41:12
Midway 68 20 34N31 83W32 5:34:08
Midway 89 20 31N48 81W26 5:25:44
Midway 131 20 34N53 83W24 5:33:36
Milan 133 20 32N01 83W04 5:32:16
Milford 4 8 31N23 84W33 5:38:12
Mill Creek 154 8 34N48 85W01 5:40:04
Milledgeville 5 20 33N05 83W14 5:32:56
Millen 82 20 32N48 81W57 5:27:48
Millhaven 123 20 32N56 81W39 5:26:36
Millwood 147 20 31N16 82W40 5:30:40
Milner 85 8 33N07 84W12 5:36:48
Milner Cross Roads 85 8 33N03 84W10 5:36:40
Milstead 121 20 33N41 83W59 5:35:56
Mineola 92 20 30N51 83W15 5:33:00
Mineral Bluff 55 8 34N55 84W17 5:37:08
Minnesota 35 20 31N19 83W55 5:35:40
Minter 87 20 32N29 82W46 5:31:04
Mission Ridge 145 8 34N57 85W18 5:41:12
Mitchell 62 20 33N13 82W42 5:30:48
Mize 126 20 34N35 83W20 5:33:20
Mizell 132 8 32N33 84W14 5:36:56
Modoc 53 20 32N37 82W19 5:29:16
Molena 113 8 33N01 84W30 5:38:00
Moncrief 65 8 30N26 84W17 5:37:08
Moniac 24 20 30N31 82W14 5:28:56
Monroe 146 20 33N47 83W43 5:34:52
Montclair 120 20 33N29 82W02 5:28:08
Monteith 25 20 32N04 81W07 5:24:28
Montevideo 52 20 34N08 82W50 5:31:20
Montezuma 96 8 32N18 84W02 5:36:08
Montgomery 25 20 31N57 81W07 5:24:28
Monticello 79 20 33N18 83W40 5:34:40
Montreal 44 20 33N49 84W17 5:37:08
Montrose 87 20 32N34 83W09 5:32:36
Moody 92 20 30N59 83W12 5:32:48
Moody Field 86 20 30N51 83W15 5:33:00
Moons 145 8 34N53 85W18 5:41:12
Moores 87 20 32N33 82W54 5:31:36
Mora 2 20 31N25 82W57 5:31:48
Moreland 38 8 33N17 84W46 5:39:04
Morgan 19 8 31N32 84W36 5:38:24
Morganton 55 8 34N53 84W15 5:37:00
Morganville 41 8 34N56 85W27 5:41:48
Morningside Heights 69 1 34N18 83W49 5:35:16
Morris 117 8 31N48 84W57 5:39:48
Morris Brown 60 7 33N45 84W25 5:37:40
Morris Estates 23 8 35N01 85W11 5:40:44
Morrow 31 8 33N35 84W20 5:37:20
Morven 14 20 30N57 83W30 5:34:00
Mossy Creek 153 20 34N33 83W41 5:34:44
Moultrie 35 20 31N11 83W47 5:35:08
Mountainbrook 72 8 32N53 84W50 5:39:20
Mountain City 118 20 34N55 83W23 5:33:32
Mountain Hill 72 8 32N45 84W52 5:39:28
Mountain Park 28 8 34N05 84W25 5:37:40
Mountain Scene 138 20 34N57 83W45 5:35:00
Mountain View 31 8 33N38 84W23 5:37:32
Mountain View 145 8 34N57 85W18 5:41:12
Mount Airy 68 20 34N31 83W30 5:34:00
Mount Berry 57 8 34N17 85W11 5:40:44
Mount Bethel 33 8 33N56 84W32 5:38:08
Mount Carmel 145 8 34N40 85W19 5:41:16
Mount Olivet 73 20 34N21 82W56 5:31:44
Mount Park 67 20 33N53 84W08 5:36:32
Mount Pleasant 6 20 34N20 83W34 5:34:00
Mount Pleasant 150 20 31N20 81W57 5:27:48
Mount Vernon 103 20 32N11 82W36 5:30:24
Mount Vernon 146 20 33N48 83W46 5:35:04
Mount Vernon 154 8 34N48 85W01 5:40:04
Mountville 140 8 33N02 84W55 5:39:40
Mount Zion 22 8 33N38 85W11 5:40:44
Moxley 81 20 32N55 82W24 5:29:36
Moye 19 8 31N33 84W42 5:38:48
Mud Creek 68 20 34N30 83W36 5:34:24

GEORGIA

Mulberry 7 20 33N59 83W43 5:34:52
Mulberry Grove 72 8 32N39 84W51 5:39:24
Munnerlyn 17 20 32N57 81W57 5:27:48
Murphy 35 20 31N01 83W52 5:35:28
Murrays Crossroads 122 8 32N14 84W18 5:37:12
Murray's Lake 31 8 33N37 84W22 5:37:28
Murrayville 69 1 34N23 83W55 5:35:40
Musella 39 8 32N48 84W02 5:36:08
Myrtle Grove 15 20 31N57 81W19 5:25:16
Mystic 77 20 31N38 83W20 5:33:20
Nahunta 13 20 31N12 81W59 5:27:56
Nails Creek 6 20 34N22 83W14 5:32:56
Nankipooh 159 17 32N29 84W57 5:39:48
Naomi 145 8 34N42 85W22 5:41:28
Nashville 10 20 31N12 83W15 5:33:00
National Colony Apartments 31 8 33N31 84W21 5:37:24
National Hills 120 20 33N28 82W01 5:28:04
Naylor 92 20 30N52 83W10 5:32:40
Neal 113 8 33N06 84W26 5:37:44
Nebo 109 8 33N55 84W50 5:39:20
Neco 120 20 33N25 82W02 5:28:08
Needmore 50 20 30N41 82W43 5:30:52
Neese 97 20 34N01 83W18 5:33:12
Nelson 28 8 34N23 84W22 5:37:28
Nevils 16 20 32N08 81W37 5:26:28
Newark 135 20 30N50 83W59 5:35:56
Newborn 106 20 33N31 83W41 5:34:44
New Branch 137 20 32N11 82W17 5:29:08
New Cotton Mill 28 8 34N14 84W29 5:37:56
New Elm 35 20 31N11 83W48 5:35:12
New England 41 8 34N52 85W31 5:42:04
New Era 128 18 32N04 84W14 5:36:56
New Georgia 109 8 33N55 84W50 5:39:20
New Holland 69 1 34N18 83W49 5:35:16
New Home 41 8 34N52 85W31 5:42:04
New Hope 67 20 33N57 83W59 5:35:56
New Hope 90 20 33N48 82W29 5:29:56
New Hope 109 8 33N52 84W48 5:39:12
Newington 123 20 32N35 81W30 5:26:00
Newnan 38 14 33N23 84W48 5:39:12
New Point 128 8 32N02 84W24 5:37:36
New Salem 6 20 34N20 83W30 5:34:00
New Sirmans 32 20 31N02 83W04 5:32:16
Newton 4 8 31N19 84W20 5:37:20
Newton Factory 106 20 33N40 83W52 5:35:28
Newtown 60 7 34N04 84W18 5:37:12
Newtown 156 20 33N44 82W45 5:31:00
New York 114 8 34N03 85W03 5:40:12
Neyami 88 20 31N44 84W10 5:36:40
Nicholasville 49 8 31N26 84W44 5:38:56
Nicholls 34 20 31N31 82W38 5:30:32
Nicholson 78 20 34N07 83W26 5:33:44
Nickelsville 64 8 34N35 84W56 5:39:44
Nickelsville 157 20 32N49 83W10 5:32:40
Nickleville 65 8 30N53 84W19 5:37:16
Nickville 52 20 34N10 82W57 5:31:48
Noah 81 20 33N13 82W19 5:29:16
Noble 145 8 34N42 85W22 5:41:28
Noonday 33 8 33N56 84W32 5:38:08
Norcross 67 20 33N56 84W13 5:36:52
Norman 156 20 33N52 82W44 5:30:56
Norman Park 35 20 31N16 83W41 5:34:44
Normantown 137 20 32N18 82W22 5:29:28
Norris 148 20 33N21 82W44 5:30:56
Norristown 53 20 32N30 82W30 5:30:00
North Atlanta 44 6 33N52 84W21 5:37:24
North Buena Vista 98 8 32N26 84W31 5:38:04
North Canton 28 8 34N14 84W29 5:37:56
North Central 154 8 34N49 84W55 5:39:40
North Dade 41 8 34N55 85W27 5:41:48
North Decatur 44 7 33N47 84W19 5:37:16
North Druid Hills 44 20 33N50 84W19 5:37:16
North Dublin 87 20 32N33 82W54 5:31:36
North Echols 50 20 30N46 82W57 5:31:48
North Elberton 52 20 34N08 82W50 5:31:20
North High Shoals 107 20 33N49 83W30 5:34:00
North Ogeechee 82 20 32N51 81W55 5:27:40
North Rockdale 121 20 33N44 83W59 5:35:56
North Roswell 60 7 34N01 84W21 5:37:24
North Side 60 7 33N50 84W23 5:37:32
North West Point 140 8 32N52 85W11 5:40:44
North Whitfield 154 8 34N55 84W56 5:39:44
Northwoods 44 20 33N54 84W16 5:37:04
Norwood 148 20 33N28 82W45 5:31:00
Note 116 20 33N19 83W23 5:33:32
Nuberg 73 20 34N10 82W57 5:31:48
Nunez 53 20 32N30 82W21 5:29:24
Oakdale 33 8 33N49 84W30 5:38:00
Oakfield 158 20 31N47 83W58 5:35:52
Oak Grove 28 8 34N06 84W31 5:38:04
Oak Grove 44 20 33N50 84W18 5:37:12
Oak Grove 140 8 32N53 84W50 5:39:20
Oak Hill 61 8 34N42 84W29 5:37:56
Oak Hill 106 20 33N40 83W52 5:35:28
Oakhurst 25 20 32N00 81W05 5:24:20
Oakland 88 20 31N44 84W10 5:36:40
Oakland 99 8 33N06 84W35 5:38:20
Oakland Heights 8 8 34N13 84W48 5:39:12
Oakland Park 159 17 32N29 84W57 5:39:48
Oaklawn 14 20 30N48 83W48 5:35:12
Oakman 64 8 34N34 84W43 5:38:52
Oak Mountain 72 8 32N48 84W42 5:38:48
Oak Park 53 20 32N22 82W19 5:29:16
Oak Ridge 136 20 31N24 83W30 5:34:00
Oakwood 69 1 34N15 83W54 5:35:36
Oasis 55 8 34N52 84W19 5:37:16
Ocee 60 8 34N04 84W13 5:36:52
Ochillee 26 17 32N26 84W57 5:39:48
Ochlocknee 135 20 30N58 84W01 5:36:04
Ochwalkee 152 20 32N11 82W40 5:30:40
Ocilla 77 20 31N36 83W15 5:33:00
Oconee 149 20 32N51 82W58 5:31:52
Oconee Heights 29 3 33N59 83W23 5:33:32
Odessadale 99 8 33N01 84W49 5:39:16
Odum 150 20 31N40 82W02 5:28:08
Offerman 112 20 31N25 82W07 5:28:28
Ogeechee 123 20 32N49 81W39 5:26:36
Ogeecheeton 25 20 32N04 81W07 5:24:28
Oglesby 149 20 33N05 82W58 5:31:52
Oglethorpe 25 20 32N00 81W05 5:24:20
Oglethorpe 96 8 32N18 84W04 5:36:16
Oglethorpe Park 25 20 32N03 81W07 5:24:28
Oglethorpe University 44 20 33N52 84W20 5:37:20
Ohoopee 137 20 32N11 82W13 5:28:52
Okefenokee 147 20 31N14 82W22 5:29:28
Ola 75 20 33N27 84W09 5:36:36
Old Airport Community 57 8 34N17 85W12 5:40:48
Old Damascus 49 8 31N18 84W43 5:38:52
Olive Branch 129 8 32N41 84W32 5:38:08
Oliver 123 20 32N31 81W32 5:26:08
Olney 16 20 32N07 81W29 5:25:56
Omaha 127 8 32N09 84W54 5:39:36
Omega 136 20 31N21 83W36 5:34:24
Oostanaula 64 8 34N30 84W57 5:39:48
Ophir 28 8 34N20 84W23 5:37:32
Orange 28 8 34N14 84W29 5:37:56
Orchard Hill 125 8 33N11 84W13 5:36:52
Orchard Hills 145 8 34N57 85W18 5:41:12
Ordway 159 17 32N29 84W57 5:39:48
Orianna 87 20 32N32 82W35 5:30:20
Orland 139 20 32N23 82W36 5:30:24
Oscarville 58 8 34N18 83W49 5:35:16
Osierfield 77 20 31N40 83W07 5:32:28
Ousley 92 20 30N51 83W15 5:33:00
Owensboro 155 20 31N57 83W27 5:33:48
Owltown 143 8 34N53 83W58 5:35:52
Oxford 106 20 33N37 83W52 5:35:28
Pace 106 20 33N40 83W52 5:35:28
Pachitta 119 8 31N46 84W48 5:39:12
Palmetto 60 10 33N31 84W40 5:38:40
Palmetto 108 20 33N55 82W55 5:31:40
Palmyra 88 20 31N44 84W10 5:36:40
Paneras 5 20 33N05 83W14 5:32:56
Panhandle 132 8 32N34 84W06 5:36:24
Panhandle 148 20 33N19 82W29 5:29:56
Pannell 146 20 33N48 83W46 5:35:04
Pantertown 55 8 34N55 84W17 5:37:08
Panthersville 44 6 33N43 84W16 5:37:04
Paoli 97 20 34N04 83W08 5:32:32
Paradise Park 25 20 32N00 81W05 5:24:20
Parhams 59 20 34N22 83W14 5:32:56
Park City 145 8 34N57 85W18 5:41:12
Parkers 43 8 31N01 84W28 5:37:52
Parkersburg 25 20 32N00 81W05 5:24:20
Parkerville 158 20 31N19 83W55 5:35:40
Park Hill 69 1 34N18 83W49 5:35:16
Parrott 134 8 31N54 84W31 5:38:04
Patillo 85 8 33N18 83W58 5:35:52
Patten 135 20 30N48 83W48 5:35:12
Patterson 112 20 31N23 82W08 5:28:32
Pavo 135 20 30N58 83W45 5:35:00
Payne 11 25 32N51 83W41 5:34:44
Payne 28 8 34N04 84W40 5:38:40
Paynes Mill 144 8 32N53 84W20 5:37:20
Peach Orchard 120 20 33N26 82W01 5:28:04
Peachtree Center 60 7 33N45 84W20 5:37:20
Peachtree City 56 8 33N24 84W35 5:38:20
Pearly 87 20 32N33 82W54 5:31:36
Pearson 2 20 31N18 82W51 5:31:24
Pebblebrook Estates 33 8 33N49 84W35 5:38:20
Pebble City 101 20 31N16 84W01 5:36:04
Pedenville 113 8 33N06 84W26 5:37:44
Pelham 101 20 31N08 84W09 5:36:36
Pembroke 15 20 32N08 81W37 5:26:28
Pendergrass 78 20 34N10 83W41 5:34:44
Pendley Hills 44 20 33N44 84W16 5:37:04
Penfield 66 20 33N40 83W11 5:32:44
Penia 40 20 31N58 83W47 5:35:08
Pennick 63 20 31N12 81W29 5:25:56
Pennington 104 20 33N36 83W28 5:33:52
Pennville 27 8 34N29 85W21 5:41:24
Peoples Still 65 8 30N53 84W19 5:37:16
Pepperton 18 8 33N18 83W58 5:35:52
Perkins 82 20 32N55 81W57 5:27:48
Perry 76 20 32N28 83W44 5:34:56
Perry Homes 60 7 33N47 84W26 5:37:44
Persimmon 118 20 34N53 83W24 5:33:36
Petross 103 20 32N15 82W24 5:29:36
Phelps 154 8 34N42 84W59 5:39:56
Philema 88 20 31N44 84W03 5:36:12
Phillipsburg 136 20 31N26 83W31 5:34:04
Phillips Subdivision 120 20 33N29 82W02 5:28:08
Philomath 108 20 33N44 82W59 5:31:56
Phinizy 36 20 33N33 82W19 5:29:16
Phoenix 116 20 33N21 83W17 5:33:08
Pickard 144 8 32N53 84W20 5:37:20
Piedmont 85 15 33N01 84W15 5:37:00
Pierceville 55 8 34N59 84W22 5:37:28
Pineboro 35 20 31N11 83W48 5:35:12
Pine Chapel 64 8 34N30 84W57 5:39:48
Pine Grove 1 20 31N47 82W21 5:29:24
Pine Grove 92 20 30N56 83W15 5:33:00
Pine Harbor 95 20 31N32 81W31 5:26:04
Pinehurst 46 20 32N12 83W46 5:35:04
Pinehurst 75 20 33N33 84W14 5:36:56
Pine Lake 44 20 33N47 84W12 5:36:48
Pineland 50 20 30N59 82W52 5:31:28
Pine Log 8 8 34N21 84W44 5:38:56
Pine Mountain 72 8 32N52 84W51 5:39:24
Pine Mountain 118 20 34N54 83W09 5:32:36
Pine Mountain Valley 72 8 32N48 84W50 5:39:20
Pineora 51 20 32N17 81W24 5:25:36
Pine Park 65 8 30N51 84W06 5:36:24
Pinetree Plaza 44 20 33N54 84W16 5:37:04
Pine Valley 120 20 33N28 81W59 5:27:56
Pineview 155 20 32N07 83W30 5:34:00
Piney Bluff 20 20 31N06 81W43 5:26:52
Piney Grove 72 17 32N29 84W57 5:39:48
Pin Point 25 20 32N00 81W05 5:24:20
Pinson 57 8 34N17 85W12 5:40:48
Pio Nono 11 25 32N51 83W36 5:34:24
Pirkle Woods 58 8 34N14 84W12 5:36:48
Pittman 67 20 33N58 84W10 5:36:40
Pitts 155 20 31N57 83W34 5:34:16
Pittsburg 44 20 33N52 84W16 5:37:04
Plainfield 45 20 32N17 83W07 5:32:28
Plains 128 8 32N02 84W24 5:37:36
Plainview 59 20 34N22 83W14 5:32:56
Plainville 64 8 34N24 85W02 5:40:08
Plaza 31 8 33N37 84W22 5:37:28
Pleasant Grove 140 8 32N58 85W00 5:40:00
Pleasant Hill 60 10 33N38 84W26 5:37:44
Pleasant Hill 67 20 34N00 84W10 5:36:40
Pleasant Hill 129 8 32N47 84W34 5:38:16
Pleasant Hill 134 8 31N46 84W26 5:37:44
Pleasant Valley 8 8 34N22 84W56 5:39:44
Pleasant Valley 46 20 32N06 83W48 5:35:12
Pocotalago 97 20 34N12 83W17 5:33:08
Point Peter 108 20 34N03 83W02 5:32:08
Pollards Corner 36 20 33N33 82W19 5:29:16
Pomona 125 8 33N15 84W15 5:37:00
Pond Spring 145 8 34N52 85W23 5:41:32
Pooler 25 20 32N07 81W15 5:25:00
Pope City 155 20 31N57 83W27 5:33:48
Popes Ferry 102 8 33N07 83W48 5:35:12
Poplar Springs 71 8 33N48 85W11 5:40:44
Portal 16 20 32N33 81W56 5:27:44
Porterdale 106 20 33N33 83W57 5:35:48
Porter Springs 93 8 34N32 83W59 5:35:56
Portland 114 8 34N03 85W03 5:40:12
Port Wentworth 25 20 32N09 81W10 5:24:40
Postell 84 25 32N50 83W37 5:34:28
Potterville 132 8 32N31 84W07 5:36:28
Poulan 158 20 31N31 83W47 5:35:08
Powder Springs 33 8 33N52 84W41 5:38:44
Powell Place 47 11 31N34 84W11 5:36:44
Powelton 70 20 33N26 82W52 5:31:28
Powersville 110 8 32N37 83W48 5:35:12
Prather 156 20 33N44 82W45 5:31:00
Prattsburg 129 8 32N36 84W23 5:37:32
Presley 138 20 34N57 83W45 5:35:00
Preston 151 8 32N04 84W32 5:38:08
Pretoria 47 11 31N34 84W11 5:36:44
Price 69 1 34N18 83W49 5:35:16
Pridgen 34 20 31N42 82W56 5:31:44
Primrose 99 8 33N09 84W44 5:38:56
Princeton 29 3 33N59 83W23 5:33:32
Pringle 149 20 32N50 82W43 5:30:52
Prior 114 8 33N57 85W23 5:41:32
Pritchetts 158 20 31N19 83W55 5:35:40
Privette Heights 33 8 33N56 84W32 5:38:08
Pulaski 21 20 32N23 81W59 5:27:56
Pumpkin Center 36 20 33N25 82W19 5:29:16
Putnam 98 8 32N22 84W28 5:37:52
Putney 47 20 31N29 84W08 5:36:32
Pyles Marsh 63 20 31N12 81W29 5:25:56
Pyne 140 8 33N02 85W02 5:40:08
Queensland 9 20 31N48 83W15 5:33:00
Quitman 14 20 30N47 83W34 5:34:16
Rabbit Hill 15 20 31N57 81W19 5:25:16
Rabun Gap 118 20 34N58 83W23 5:33:32
Racepond 24 20 31N00 82W08 5:28:32
Radium Springs 47 11 31N35 84W10 5:36:40
Raines 40 20 31N53 83W52 5:35:28
Raleigh 99 8 32N56 84W38 5:38:32
Ramhurst 105 8 34N42 84W44 5:38:56
Randall 127 8 32N03 84W48 5:39:12
Ranger 64 8 34N30 84W43 5:38:52
Raoul 68 20 34N28 83W34 5:34:16
Raulerson 13 20 31N23 82W08 5:28:32
Ravenwood 120 20 33N29 82W02 5:28:08
Raybon 13 20 31N12 81W59 5:27:56
Ray City 10 20 31N05 83W11 5:32:44
Rayle 156 20 33N48 82W54 5:31:36
Raymond 38 8 33N20 84W43 5:38:52
Raytown 130 20 33N33 82W54 5:31:36
Rebecca 141 20 31N48 83W29 5:33:56
Rebie 12 20 32N24 83W09 5:32:36
Recovery 43 8 30N42 84W51 5:39:24
Redan 44 20 33N45 84W09 5:36:36
Red Bluff 20 20 31N02 81W43 5:26:52
Redbud 64 8 34N32 84W46 5:39:04
Redclay 154 8 34N57 84W57 5:39:48
Red Hill 59 20 34N30 83W11 5:32:44
Red Hill 127 8 32N05 84W40 5:38:40
Redland 150 20 31N36 81W53 5:27:32
Red Lane 69 1 34N18 83W49 5:35:16
Red Oak 60 8 33N38 84W30 5:38:00

Red Rock 109 8 34N04 84W40 5:38:40
Red Rock 158 20 31N32 83W50 5:35:20
Red Stone 78 20 34N06 83W34 5:34:16
Reed Creek 73 20 34N21 82W56 5:31:44
Reese 148 20 33N25 82W40 5:30:40
Reeves 64 8 34N28 85W01 5:40:04
Register 16 20 32N22 81W53 5:27:32
Rehobeth 72 8 32N39 84W51 5:39:24
Rehoboth 44 20 33N49 84W17 5:37:08
Reidsboro 113 8 33N11 84W21 5:37:24
Reidsville 131 20 32N06 82W07 5:28:28
Reka 15 20 32N08 81W37 5:26:28
Relay 57 8 34N01 85W15 5:41:00
Remerton 92 20 30N50 83W18 5:33:12
Renfroe 26 8 32N14 84W43 5:38:52
Reno 65 8 30N46 84W18 5:37:12
Rentz 87 20 32N23 83W00 5:32:00
Reo 145 8 34N48 85W01 5:40:04
Resaca 64 8 34N35 84W56 5:39:44
Resseaus Crossroads 116 20 33N19 83W23 5:33:32
Rest Haven 67 20 34N08 83W59 5:35:56
Retreat 89 20 31N44 81W26 5:25:44
Rex 31 20 33N36 84W16 5:37:04
Reynolds 132 8 32N33 84W06 5:36:24
Reynoldsville 124 8 31N03 84W53 5:39:32
Rhine 45 20 31N59 83W12 5:32:48
Riceboro 89 20 31N44 81W26 5:25:44
Richfield 25 20 32N03 81W07 5:24:28
Richland 127 8 32N05 84W40 5:38:40
Richmond Hill 15 20 31N56 81W18 5:25:12
Richwood 46 20 32N03 83W48 5:35:12
Ricks Place 30 8 31N37 85W03 5:40:12
Rico 60 10 33N31 84W40 5:38:40
Riddleville 149 20 32N54 82W40 5:30:40
Ridgeville 95 20 31N32 81W31 5:26:04
Ridley 74 8 33N21 85W04 5:40:16
Rincon 51 20 32N18 81W14 5:24:56
Ringgold 23 8 34N55 85W07 5:40:28
Rio 125 8 33N15 84W15 5:37:00
Rio Vista 25 20 32N03 81W04 5:24:16
Rising Fawn 41 8 34N46 85W32 5:42:08
Riverdale 31 8 33N34 84W25 5:37:40
Rivers End 25 20 32N00 81W05 5:24:20
Riverside 11 25 32N51 83W41 5:34:44
Riverside 25 20 32N03 81W04 5:24:16
Riverside 35 20 31N11 83W48 5:35:12
Riverside 57 8 34N17 85W12 5:40:48
Rivertown 60 10 33N35 84W34 5:38:16
Riverturn 124 8 31N03 84W53 5:39:32
Roanoke 9 20 31N43 83W15 5:33:00
Roberta 39 8 32N43 84W01 5:36:04
Roberts Cross Road 69 1 34N07 84W00 5:36:00
Robertstown 153 20 34N42 83W44 5:34:56
Robinson 130 20 33N37 83W04 5:32:16
Rochelle 155 20 31N57 83W27 5:33:48
Rockalo 74 8 33N21 85W04 5:40:16
Rock Branch 52 20 34N08 82W50 5:31:20
Rock Creek 126 20 34N34 83W16 5:33:04
Rock Cut 31 8 33N36 84W20 5:37:20
Rock Hill 49 8 31N23 84W57 5:39:48
Rockingham 3 20 31N34 82W24 5:29:36
Rockledge 87 20 32N27 82W41 5:30:44
Rockmart 114 8 34N00 85W03 5:40:12
Rock Spring 145 8 34N50 85W14 5:40:56
Rockville 116 20 33N19 83W23 5:33:32
Rocky Creek 64 8 34N30 84W57 5:39:48
Rocky Face 154 8 34N48 85W01 5:40:04
Rocky Ford 123 20 32N40 81W50 5:27:20
Rocky Mount 99 8 33N10 84W40 5:38:40
Rocky Plains 106 20 33N40 83W52 5:35:28
Roddy 45 20 32N23 83W21 5:33:24
Rogers 97 20 34N12 83W27 5:33:48
Rome 57 5 34N15 85W10 5:40:40
Roopville 22 8 33N27 85W08 5:40:32
Roosterville 74 8 33N27 85W08 5:40:32
Roper 32 20 30N49 82W39 5:30:36
Roscoe 38 8 33N22 84W47 5:39:08
Rosebud 67 20 33N51 83W54 5:35:36
Rosedale 57 8 34N30 84W57 5:39:48
Rose Dhu 25 20 32N00 81W05 5:24:20
Rose Hill 25 20 32N00 81W05 5:24:20
Rose Hill 113 15 33N03 84W18 5:37:12
Rose Hill 159 17 32N29 84W57 5:39:48
Rosemont 36 20 33N33 82W19 5:29:16
Rosemont Park 57 8 34N17 85W12 5:40:48
Rosier 17 20 32N59 82W15 5:29:00
Rossignol Hill 25 20 32N06 81W09 5:24:36
Rossville 145 12 34N58 85W18 5:41:12
Roswell 60 7 34N02 84W22 5:37:28
Round Oak 84 20 33N07 83W37 5:34:28
Rover 125 8 33N11 84W21 5:37:24
Rowena 49 8 31N26 84W44 5:38:56
Roxanna 109 8 33N55 84W50 5:39:20
Royston 59 20 34N17 83W07 5:32:28
Ruckersville 52 20 34N10 82W47 5:31:08
Rudden 116 20 33N19 83W23 5:33:32
Rupert 132 8 32N27 84W17 5:37:08
Russell 7 20 33N59 83W42 5:34:48
Russellville 102 8 32N52 84W06 5:36:24
Rutland 11 8 32N44 83W40 5:34:40
Rutledge 104 20 33N38 83W37 5:34:28
Rydal 8 8 34N20 84W43 5:38:52
Ryo 64 8 34N26 84W42 5:38:48
Saint Charles 38 8 33N17 84W46 5:39:04
Saint Clair 17 20 33N09 82W13 5:28:52
Saint George 24 20 30N31 82W02 5:28:08
Saint Marks 99 8 33N07 84W49 5:39:16
Saint Marys 20 20 30N44 81W33 5:26:12
Saint Simons Island 63 20 31N08 81W24 5:25:36
Sale City 101 20 31N16 84W01 5:36:04
Salem 12 20 32N29 83W15 5:33:00
Salem 107 20 33N47 83W25 5:33:40

Sanborn 47 11 31N34 84W11 5:36:44
Sandalwood 47 11 31N34 84W11 5:36:44
Sandersville 149 20 32N59 82W48 5:31:12
Sandersville Rural 149 20 33N01 82W47 5:31:08
Sandfly 25 20 32N00 81W05 5:24:20
Sand Hill 22 8 33N44 84W55 5:39:40
Sand Hill 147 20 31N06 82W34 5:30:16
Sand Mountain 41 8 34N55 85W33 5:42:12
Sand Town 33 8 33N56 84W32 5:38:08
Sandtown 156 20 33N44 82W45 5:31:00
Sandy Cross 59 20 34N18 83W16 5:33:04
Sandy Cross 108 20 34N03 83W02 5:32:08
Sandy Plains 33 8 34N01 84W30 5:38:00
Sandy Springs 60 20 33N56 84W23 5:37:32
Sanford 97 20 34N01 83W18 5:33:12
Sanford 127 8 32N03 84W48 5:39:12
Santa Claus 137 20 32N10 82W20 5:29:20
Sapelo 95 20 31N23 81W17 5:25:08
Sapp 12 20 32N23 83W21 5:33:24
Sardis 17 20 32N58 81W46 5:27:04
Sargent 38 8 33N26 84W52 5:39:28
Sasser 134 8 31N43 84W21 5:37:24
Satilla Creek 1 20 31N42 82W23 5:29:32
Satolah 118 20 34N59 83W11 5:32:44
Sautee-Nacoochee 153 20 34N41 83W40 5:34:40
Savannah 25 4 32N05 81W06 5:24:24
Savannah Beach 25 20 32N01 80W51 5:23:24
Scarboro 82 20 32N48 81W57 5:27:48
Scarbrough Cross Roads 75 20 33N37 84W17 5:37:08
Schatulga 159 17 32N29 84W57 5:39:48
Schlatterville 13 20 31N11 82W08 5:28:32
Schley 35 20 31N11 83W48 5:35:12
Scotland 133 20 32N03 82W49 5:31:16
Scott 83 20 32N33 82W40 5:30:40
Scottdale 44 20 33N47 84W16 5:37:04
Scottsboro 5 20 33N05 83W14 5:32:56
Screven 150 20 31N29 82W01 5:28:04
Sea Island 63 20 31N12 81W21 5:25:24
Sells 78 20 34N06 83W46 5:35:04
Seney 114 8 34N03 85W03 5:40:12
Senoia 38 8 33N18 84W33 5:38:12
Sessoms 3 20 31N31 82W38 5:30:32
Seville 155 20 31N58 83W36 5:34:24
Seymour 116 20 33N19 83W23 5:33:32
Shady Dale 79 20 33N24 83W36 5:34:24
Shake Rag 56 8 33N19 84W17 5:37:08
Shake Rag 60 7 34N03 84W04 5:36:16
Shannon 57 8 34N20 85W04 5:40:16
Sharon 130 20 33N34 82W48 5:31:12
Sharon Park 25 20 32N04 81W07 5:24:28
Sharpsburg 38 8 33N20 84W39 5:38:36
Sharps Spur 103 20 32N12 82W31 5:30:04
Sharp Top 28 8 34N14 84W29 5:37:56
Shawnee 51 20 32N29 81W25 5:25:40
Shell Bluff 17 20 33N06 82W01 5:28:04
Shellman 119 8 31N46 84W37 5:38:28
Shellman Bluff 95 20 31N35 81W19 5:25:16
Shelly 135 20 30N58 83W44 5:34:56
Sheppards 123 20 32N49 81W39 5:26:36
Sherwood 31 8 33N31 84W21 5:37:24
Sherwood Forest 38 8 33N22 84W47 5:39:08
Sherwood Forest 57 8 34N17 85W12 5:40:48
Shields Crossroads 145 8 34N52 85W23 5:41:32
Shiloh 72 8 32N49 84W42 5:38:48
Shiloh 92 20 31N04 82W39 5:30:36
Shingler 158 20 31N35 83W47 5:35:08
Shoal Creek 73 20 34N26 83W06 5:32:24
Shoals 148 20 33N08 82W42 5:30:48
Shurlington 11 25 32N50 83W37 5:34:28
Sigsbee 35 20 31N16 83W52 5:35:28
Silco 20 20 30N52 81W50 5:27:20
Silica Hills 47 11 31N34 84W10 5:36:40
Silk Hope 25 20 32N03 81W11 5:24:44
Silk Mills 52 20 34N08 82W50 5:31:20
Siloam 66 20 33N32 83W05 5:32:20
Silver City 58 8 34N20 84W07 5:36:28
Silver Creek 57 8 34N11 85W10 5:40:40
Silver Pines 11 25 32N49 83W41 5:34:44
Silvertown 144 8 32N53 84W20 5:37:20
Simpson 74 8 33N21 85W04 5:40:16
Sirmans 32 20 31N05 82W58 5:31:52
Six Mile 57 8 34N10 85W13 5:40:52
Skipperton 11 8 32N45 83W42 5:34:48
Skyland 44 20 33N52 84W20 5:37:20
Skyland Terrace 25 20 32N04 81W07 5:24:28
Smarr 102 8 32N59 83W53 5:35:32
Smithonia 108 20 34N00 83W11 5:32:44
Smiths Crossroads 72 8 32N48 84W49 5:39:16
Smithsonia 108 20 34N01 83W12 5:32:48
Smithville 88 20 31N54 84W15 5:37:00
Smyrna 33 8 33N53 84W31 5:38:04
Snake Nation 55 8 34N52 84W19 5:37:16
Snapping Shoals 106 20 33N40 83W52 5:35:28
Snead 36 20 33N32 82W08 5:28:32
Snellville 67 20 33N51 84W01 5:36:04
Snipesville 80 20 31N43 82W42 5:30:48
Social Circle 146 20 33N39 83W43 5:34:52
Sofkee 11 25 32N49 83W41 5:34:44
Somerset Park 25 20 32N00 81W05 5:24:20
Sonoraville 64 8 34N30 84W57 5:39:48
Soperton 139 20 32N23 82W35 5:30:20
South Base 76 20 32N37 83W39 5:34:36
South Cobb 33 8 33N48 84W38 5:38:32

GEORGIA

South Decatur 44 20 33N44 84W16 5:37:04
South De Kalb 44 20 33N43 84W17 5:37:08
South Echols 50 20 30N39 82W56 5:31:44
Southern Tech 33 8 33N56 84W32 5:38:08
South Jackson 78 20 34N03 83W30 5:34:00
Southland 120 20 33N26 82W01 5:28:04
South Lincolnton 90 20 33N45 82W25 5:29:40
South Macon 11 25 32N47 83W41 5:34:44
South Moultrie 35 20 31N11 83W48 5:35:12
South Nellsville 120 20 33N27 81W57 5:27:48
South Newport 95 20 31N38 81W24 5:25:36
South Ogeechee 82 20 32N43 82W00 5:28:00
Southover 25 20 32N03 81W07 5:24:28
South Rockdale 121 20 33N35 84W04 5:36:16
South Rossville 145 8 34N57 85W18 5:41:12
Spann 83 20 32N44 82W43 5:30:52
Sparks 37 20 31N12 83W26 5:33:44
Sparta 70 20 33N17 82W58 5:31:52
Spence 65 8 31N02 84W12 5:36:48
Spencer Hills 145 8 34N57 85W18 5:41:12
Spilo 143 8 34N53 83W58 5:35:52
Split Silk 146 20 33N51 83W54 5:35:36
Spout Spring Crossroads 69 1 34N11 83W56 5:35:44
Spring Bluff 20 20 31N06 81W43 5:26:52
Spring Creek 57 8 34N10 85W08 5:40:32
Springfield 51 20 32N22 81W18 5:25:12
Spring Place 105 8 34N46 84W49 5:39:16
Springvale 119 8 31N50 84W53 5:39:32
Springvale, 119 8 31N50 84W52 5:39:28
Standleys Store 30 8 31N37 85W03 5:40:12
Stanleys Store 137 20 32N11 82W17 5:29:08
Stapleton 81 20 33N13 82W28 5:29:52
Stark 18 8 33N18 83W58 5:35:52
Starrs Mill 56 8 33N19 84W31 5:38:04
Starrsville 106 20 33N32 83W49 5:35:16
State College 25 20 32N03 81W04 5:24:16
Statenville 50 20 30N42 83W02 5:32:08
Statesboro 16 20 32N27 81W47 5:27:08
Statham 7 20 33N58 83W35 5:34:20
Steadman 71 8 33N45 85W17 5:41:08
Steam Mill 124 8 30N58 84W55 5:39:40
Stellaville 81 20 33N12 82W23 5:29:32
Stephens 108 20 33N48 83W09 5:32:36
Stephensville 41 8 34N52 85W31 5:42:04
Stergeon Creek 9 20 31N44 83W11 5:32:44
Sterling 63 20 31N16 81W34 5:26:16
Stevens Pottery 5 20 32N57 83W17 5:33:08
Stewart 106 20 33N25 83W52 5:35:28
Stewartville 85 8 33N06 84W20 5:37:20
Stilesboro 8 8 34N10 84W48 5:39:12
Stillmore 53 20 32N27 82W13 5:28:52
Stillwell 51 20 32N23 81W15 5:25:00
Stilson 16 20 32N23 81W40 5:26:40
Stockbridge 75 20 33N33 84W14 5:36:56
Stocks 88 20 31N44 84W10 5:36:40
Stockton 86 20 30N57 83W00 5:32:00
Stone Mountain 44 20 33N49 84W10 5:36:40
Stonewall 60 8 33N36 84W33 5:38:12
Stoney Point 22 8 33N27 85W08 5:40:32
Stovall 68 20 34N31 83W32 5:34:08
Stovall 99 8 32N58 84W51 5:39:24
Stuckey 152 20 32N11 82W40 5:30:40
Subligna 27 8 34N29 85W21 5:41:24
Suches 143 8 34N42 84W01 5:36:04
Sudie 109 8 33N55 84W50 5:39:20
Sugar Hill 67 20 34N06 84W02 5:36:08
Sugar Hill 69 1 34N18 83W49 5:35:16
Sugartown 23 8 34N50 85W03 5:40:12
Sugar Valley 64 8 34N33 85W01 5:40:04
Sulphur Springs 41 8 34N46 85W32 5:42:08
Sumac 105 8 34N53 84W48 5:39:12
Summertown 53 20 32N45 82W16 5:29:04
Summerville 27 8 34N29 85W21 5:41:24
Summit 53 20 32N35 82W09 5:28:36
Sumner 158 20 31N33 83W44 5:34:56
Sumter 128 20 31N57 84W15 5:37:00
Sunbury 89 20 31N48 81W26 5:25:44
Sunlight Park 120 20 33N28 81W59 5:27:56
Sunny Side 125 8 33N21 84W18 5:37:12
Sunnyside 147 20 31N14 82W22 5:29:28
Sunset 35 20 31N11 83W48 5:35:12
Sunset Heights 69 1 34N18 83W49 5:35:16
Sunset Village 144 8 32N53 84W20 5:37:20
Sunsweet 136 20 31N27 83W31 5:34:04
Suomi 45 20 32N06 83W04 5:32:16
Surrency 1 20 31N44 82W12 5:28:48
Sutalee 28 8 34N17 84W45 5:39:00
Suttons Corner 30 8 31N33 84W42 5:38:48
Suwanee 67 20 34N03 84W04 5:36:16
Swainsboro 53 20 32N36 82W20 5:29:20
Swan Lake 75 20 33N33 84W14 5:36:56
Swift Creek 11 25 32N49 83W33 5:34:12
Swords 104 20 33N33 83W18 5:33:12
Sybert 90 20 33N48 82W29 5:29:56
Sycamore 141 20 31N40 83W38 5:34:32
Sylvania 123 20 32N45 81W38 5:26:32
Sylvester 158 20 31N32 83W49 5:35:16
Sylvester Drive 35 20 31N11 83W48 5:35:12
Tadmore 69 1 34N14 83W46 5:35:04
Talbotton 129 8 32N41 84W32 5:38:08
Talking Rock 111 8 34N31 84W30 5:38:00

GEORGIA

Tallapoosa 71 8 33N45 85w17 5:41:08
Tallulah Falls 118 20 34N44 83w24 5:33:36
Talmo 78 20 34N11 83w43 5:34:52
Talona 61 8 34N34 84w31 5:38:04
Tarboro 20 20 31N01 81w48 5:27:12
Tarrytown 103 20 32N19 82w34 5:30:16
Tarver 50 20 30N42 82w56 5:31:44
Tate 111 8 34N25 84w23 5:37:32
Tate City 138 20 34N53 83w24 5:33:36
Tatum 140 8 33N01 85w06 5:40:24
Tax 129 8 32N48 84w42 5:38:48
Taylorsville 8 8 34N05 84w59 5:39:56
Tazewell 98 8 32N23 84w26 5:37:44
Tell 60 8 33N39 84w36 5:38:24
Teloga 27 8 34N29 85w21 5:41:24
Temperance 133 20 31N59 83w12 5:32:48
Temple 22 8 33N44 85w02 5:40:08
Tennga 105 8 34N59 84w44 5:38:56
Tennille 149 20 32N56 82w48 5:31:12
Terrell 158 20 31N31 83w44 5:34:56
Texas 74 8 33N14 85w11 5:40:44
Thalmann 63 20 31N18 81w41 5:26:44
The Hill 120 20 33N28 82w01 5:28:04
The Rock 144 15 32N58 84w15 5:37:00
Thomasboro 123 20 32N40 81w50 5:27:20
Thomaston 144 14 32N53 84w20 5:37:20
Thomasville 135 20 30N50 83w59 5:35:56
Thompsons Mills 78 20 34N06 83w46 5:35:04
Thomson 94 20 33N28 82w30 5:30:00
Three Sisters Mountain 93 8 34N33 83w56 5:35:44
Thrift 82 20 32N48 81w57 5:27:48
Thunder 144 8 33N01 84w30 5:38:00
Thunderbolt 25 20 32N03 81w04 5:24:16
Thurston 66 20 33N35 83w11 5:32:44
Thurston 144 8 32N55 84w26 5:37:44
Thyatira 78 20 34N06 83w34 5:34:16
Ticknor 35 20 31N19 83w55 5:35:40
Tifton 136 20 31N27 83w31 5:34:04
Tiger 118 20 34N51 83w26 5:33:44
Tignall 156 20 33N52 82w44 5:30:56
Tilton 154 8 34N40 84w56 5:39:44
Timothy 29 3 33N59 83w23 5:33:32
Tippettville 46 20 32N06 83w48 5:35:12
Tison 131 20 31N56 81w56 5:27:44
Titus 138 20 34N57 83w45 5:35:00
Toccoa 126 20 34N35 83w19 5:33:16
Toccoa Creek 126 20 34N36 83w20 5:33:20
Toccoa Falls 126 20 34N35 83w20 5:33:20
Toco Hills 44 20 33N50 84w19 5:37:16
Toledo 24 20 30N31 82w02 5:28:08
Tom 83 20 32N42 82w31 5:30:04
Toms Creek 126 20 34N30 83w11 5:32:44
Toomsboro 157 20 32N50 83w05 5:32:20
Topeka Junction 144 15 32N59 84w13 5:36:52
Towaliga 18 8 33N14 84w03 5:36:12
Town and Country 33 8 33N56 84w32 5:38:08
Towns 133 20 32N00 82w45 5:31:00
Townsend 95 20 31N33 81w31 5:26:04
Traders Hill 24 20 31N52 82w36 5:30:24
Trans 145 8 34N42 85w22 5:41:28
Tremont 120 20 33N29 82w02 5:28:08
Tremont Park 25 20 32N04 81w07 5:24:28
Trenton 41 8 34N52 85w31 5:42:04
Trice 144 8 32N53 84w20 5:37:20
Trickum 154 8 34N50 85w03 5:40:12
Trimble 140 8 33N11 84w52 5:39:28
Trion 27 8 34N33 85w19 5:41:16
Troupville 92 20 30N51 83w15 5:33:00
Troutman 127 8 31N53 84w44 5:38:56
Trudie 13 20 31N23 82w08 5:28:32
Tucker 44 20 33N51 84w13 5:36:52
Tugalo 126 20 34N35 83w20 5:33:20
Tugaloo 68 20 34N44 83w23 5:33:32
Tunnel Hill 154 8 34N50 85w03 5:40:12
Turin 38 8 33N20 84w38 5:38:32
Turners Rock 25 20 32N03 81w04 5:24:16
Turnerville 68 20 34N42 83w26 5:33:44
Turpin Place 120 20 33N27 82w00 5:28:00
Tusculum 51 20 32N22 81w18 5:25:12
Tuxedo Park 120 20 33N27 82w01 5:28:04
Twin City 53 20 32N35 82w10 5:28:40
Twin Lakes 92 20 30N43 83w13 5:32:52
Tyrone 56 8 33N28 84w36 5:38:24
Tyrone 156 20 33N44 82w45 5:31:00
Ty Ty 136 20 31N28 83w39 5:34:36
Tyus 22 8 33N32 85w15 5:41:00
Unadilla 46 20 32N16 83w44 5:34:56
Union 98 8 32N22 84w28 5:37:52
Union 109 8 33N44 85w02 5:40:08
Union 117 8 31N53 85w07 5:40:28
Union 127 8 32N09 85w01 5:40:04
Unionburg 136 20 31N27 83w31 5:34:04
Union City 60 10 33N35 84w33 5:38:12
Union Hill 28 8 34N04 84w18 5:37:12
Union Point 66 20 33N37 83w04 5:32:16
Unionville 85 8 33N03 84w10 5:36:40
Unionville 136 20 31N26 83w30 5:34:00
Unity 59 20 34N22 83w14 5:32:56
University 11 25 32N51 83w36 5:34:24
Upatoi 159 8 32N33 84w44 5:38:56
Upper Lookout Creek 41 8 34N46 85w30 5:42:00
Upton 34 20 31N30 82w51 5:31:24
Upton Mill 132 8 32N33 84w14 5:36:56
Uptonville 24 20 31N52 82w36 5:30:24
Uvalda 103 20 32N02 82w31 5:30:04
Vada 19 8 30N53 84w26 5:37:44
Valdosta 92 24 30N50 83w17 5:33:08
Valley 118 20 34N57 83w23 5:33:32
Valley Point 154 8 34N43 84w58 5:39:52
Valley View 145 8 35N00 85w20 5:41:20
Valona 95 20 31N29 81w21 5:25:24
Vandiver Heights 33 8 33N56 84w32 5:38:08
Vanna 73 20 34N14 83w04 5:32:16
Vans Valley 57 8 34N17 85w12 5:40:48
Van Wert 114 8 34N00 85w00 5:40:00
Varnell 154 8 34N54 84w59 5:39:56
Vaughn 125 8 33N15 84w15 5:37:00
Veal 22 8 33N26 85w14 5:40:56
Veazey 66 20 33N35 83w11 5:32:44
Vega 113 15 33N03 84w18 5:37:12
Veribest 108 20 34N03 83w02 5:32:08
Vernonburg 25 20 31N58 81w07 5:24:28
Vernon View 25 20 32N00 81w05 5:24:20
Vesta 108 20 33N58 82w56 5:31:44
Veterans Hospital 120 20 33N28 82w01 5:28:04
Victoria 28 8 34N06 84w31 5:38:04
Victory 22 8 33N32 85w15 5:41:00
Vidalia 137 20 32N13 82w25 5:29:40
Vidette 17 20 33N02 82w15 5:29:00
Vienna 46 20 32N06 83w47 5:35:08
View 68 20 34N31 83w32 5:34:08
Villanow 145 8 34N40 85w05 5:40:20
Villa Rica 22 8 33N44 84w55 5:39:40
Vinings 33 8 33N52 84w28 5:37:52
Vista-Grove 44 20 33N47 84w17 5:37:08
Vulcan 145 8 34N46 85w32 5:42:08
Waco 71 8 33N42 85w11 5:40:44
Wadley 81 20 32N52 82w24 5:29:36
Wahoo 93 8 34N32 83w59 5:35:56
Walden 11 25 32N49 83w41 5:34:44
Waleska 28 8 34N19 84w32 5:38:08
Walker Park 146 20 33N48 83w46 5:35:04
Wallace 115 20 32N17 83w28 5:33:52
Wallaceville 145 8 34N57 85w18 5:41:12
Walls Crossing 122 8 32N14 84w18 5:37:12
Walnut Grove 145 8 34N42 85w22 5:41:28
Walnutgrove 146 20 33N45 83w51 5:35:24
Walthourville 89 20 31N47 81w36 5:26:24
Waresboro 147 20 31N15 82w29 5:29:56
Wares Crossroads 140 8 33N02 85w02 5:40:08
Waresville 74 8 33N21 85w04 5:40:16
Waring 154 8 34N46 84w58 5:39:52
Warm Springs 99 8 32N53 84w41 5:38:44
Warner Robins 76 20 32N37 83w36 5:34:24
Warren Terrace 145 8 34N57 85w18 5:41:12
Warrenton 148 20 33N24 82w40 5:30:40
Warsaw 60 20 34N01 84w12 5:36:48
Warthen 149 20 33N06 82w48 5:31:12
Warwick 158 20 31N50 83w57 5:35:48
Washington 156 20 33N44 82w44 5:30:56
Waterloo 77 20 31N33 83w32 5:34:08
Waterport 146 20 33N51 83w54 5:35:36
Watkinsville 107 20 33N52 83w25 5:33:40
Waverly 20 20 31N06 81w43 5:26:52
Waverly Hall 72 8 32N39 84w49 5:39:16
Waverly Park 23 8 34N57 85w18 5:41:12
Wax 57 8 34N03 85w03 5:40:12
Wayback 19 8 31N33 84w42 5:38:48
Waycross 147 1 31N13 82w21 5:29:24
Waynesboro 17 20 33N06 82w01 5:28:04
Waynesville 13 20 31N14 81w49 5:27:16
Wayside 84 20 33N04 83w37 5:34:28
Weaver 113 8 33N06 84w20 5:37:20
Webb 60 7 34N04 84w18 5:37:12
Weber 10 20 31N15 83w09 5:32:36
Welcome 38 8 33N22 84w47 5:39:08
Welcome Hill 27 8 34N33 85w18 5:41:12
Wenona 40 20 31N54 83w46 5:35:04
Wesley 53 20 32N29 82w20 5:29:20
Wesley 132 8 32N36 84w28 5:37:52
Wesleyan 11 25 32N50 83w37 5:34:28
Wesleyan Estates 11 25 32N51 83w41 5:34:44
West Bainbridge 43 8 30N54 84w34 5:38:16
West Brow 41 8 34N46 85w32 5:42:08
West Cordele 40 20 31N58 83w47 5:35:08
West Crisp 40 20 31N56 83w50 5:35:20
West Crossing 71 8 33N45 85w17 5:41:08
West Dougherty 47 11 31N32 84w14 5:36:56
West Dublin 87 20 32N33 82w54 5:31:36
West End 57 8 34N17 85w12 5:40:48
Wester 52 20 34N08 82w50 5:31:20
Westgate Park 29 3 33N59 83w23 5:33:32
West Georgia College 22 8 33N35 85w05 5:40:20
West Green 34 20 31N37 82w44 5:30:56
West Jackson 78 20 34N09 83w43 5:34:52
Westoak 33 8 33N59 84w32 5:38:08
Weston 151 8 31N59 84w37 5:38:28
West Point 140 13 32N53 85w11 5:40:44
West Savannah 25 20 32N03 81w09 5:24:36
Westside 23 8 34N48 85w03 5:40:12
Westside 69 1 34N18 83w49 5:35:16
West Vidalia 137 20 32N15 82w24 5:29:36
Westwood 9 20 31N43 83w15 5:33:00
Wheat Hill 25 20 32N06 81w09 5:24:36
Wheeler Heights 11 25 32N50 83w37 5:34:28
Whigham 65 8 30N53 84w19 5:37:16
Whistleville 7 20 33N59 83w43 5:34:52
White 8 8 34N17 84w45 5:39:00
White Bluff 25 20 32N00 81w05 5:24:20
White Hall 29 20 33N54 83w22 5:33:28
Whitehouse 75 20 33N27 84w09 5:36:36
Whitemarsh Island 25 20 32N03 81w04 5:24:16
White Oak 20 20 31N02 81w43 5:26:52
White Plains 66 20 33N28 83w01 5:32:04
Whitesburg 22 8 33N30 84w55 5:39:40
Whitestone 61 8 34N34 84w31 5:38:04
White Sulphur 69 1 34N18 83w49 5:35:16
White Sulphur Springs 99 8 32N54 84w48 5:39:12
Whitesville 72 8 32N49 85w02 5:40:08
Whitworth 59 20 34N26 83w06 5:32:24
Wildwood 41 8 34N58 85w25 5:41:40
Wiley 118 20 34N48 83w25 5:33:40
Willacoochee 2 20 31N20 83w03 5:32:12
Willard 116 20 33N19 83w23 5:33:32
Williamson 113 8 33N11 84w22 5:37:28
Wilmington Island 25 20 32N00 80w59 5:23:56
Wilshire 25 20 32N00 81w05 5:24:20
Wilshire Estates 25 20 32N00 81w05 5:24:20
Wilsons Church 78 20 34N12 83w27 5:33:48
Wilsonville 34 20 31N31 82w38 5:30:32
Winchester 96 8 32N27 83w57 5:35:48
Winder 7 20 34N00 83w43 5:34:52
Windsor 146 20 33N51 83w54 5:35:36
Windsor Estates 38 8 33N22 84w47 5:39:08
Windsor Forest 25 20 31N58 81w09 5:24:36
Windsor Park 159 17 32N29 84w57 5:39:48
Windward 25 20 32N03 81w07 5:24:28
Windy Ridge 55 8 34N55 84w17 5:37:08
Winfield 36 20 33N28 82w30 5:30:00
Winokur 24 20 31N02 82w01 5:28:04
Winona Park 147 20 31N14 82w22 5:29:28
Winston 48 8 33N44 84w50 5:39:20
Winterville 29 20 33N59 83w19 5:33:16
Withers 32 20 30N51 82w54 5:31:36
Wofford Crossroads 8 8 34N17 84w45 5:39:00
Woodbine 20 20 30N58 81w44 5:26:56
Woodbury 99 8 32N59 84w35 5:38:20
Woodcliff 123 20 32N49 81w39 5:26:36
Woodland 129 8 32N47 84w34 5:38:16
Woodland Hills 87 20 32N33 82w54 5:31:36
Woodland Hills 145 8 34N57 85w18 5:41:12
Woodlawn Terrace 25 20 32N04 81w07 5:24:28
Woods Grove 138 20 34N56 83w51 5:35:24
Woods Station 23 8 35N01 85w11 5:40:44
Woodstock 28 8 34N06 84w31 5:38:04
Woodville 25 20 32N04 81w07 5:24:28
Woodville 66 20 33N40 83w07 5:32:28
Woolsey 56 8 33N22 84w25 5:37:40
Wooster 99 8 33N06 84w35 5:38:20
Wormsloe 25 20 32N00 81w05 5:24:20
Worth 141 20 32N25 83w30 5:34:00
Worthville 18 20 33N22 83w55 5:35:40
Wray 77 20 31N38 83w03 5:32:12
Wrens 81 20 33N11 82w23 5:29:32
Wright Square 25 20 32N03 81w06 5:24:24
Wrightsville 83 20 32N44 82w43 5:30:52
Wymberley 25 20 32N00 81w05 5:24:20
Wynnton 159 17 32N29 84w57 5:39:48
Yahoola 93 8 34N32 83w59 5:35:56
Yates 38 8 33N22 84w47 5:39:08
Yates Crossroads 74 8 33N21 85w04 5:40:16
Yatesville 144 8 32N55 84w09 5:36:36
Yellow Bluff Fishing Village 89 20 31N48 81w26 5:25:44
Yellow Dirt 74 8 33N21 85w04 5:40:16
Yellow River 106 20 33N28 83w52 5:35:28
Yeomans 134 8 31N46 84w26 5:37:44
Yonah 69 1 34N28 83w34 5:34:16
Yonkers 45 20 32N23 83w21 5:33:24
Yorkville 109 8 33N56 85w00 5:40:00
Youngcane 143 8 34N53 83w58 5:35:52
Young Harris 138 20 34N56 83w51 5:35:24
Youngs 114 8 34N01 85w15 5:41:00
Youngstown 143 8 34N53 83w58 5:35:52
Youth 146 20 33N51 83w54 5:35:36
Zaidee 139 20 32N23 82w36 5:30:24
Zebina 81 20 33N10 82w21 5:29:24
Zebulon 113 8 33N06 84w21 5:37:24
Zenith 39 8 32N41 83w57 5:35:48
Zetella 125 8 33N15 84w15 5:37:00
Zetto 30 8 31N31 84w53 5:39:32
Zingara 121 20 33N41 84w00 5:36:00

HAWAII

TIME TABLES

Hawaii has not observed daylight time, except for the period shown in 1933 and during World War II.

Before 1/01/1900		LMT
1/01/1900	12:00	HST
4/30/1933	02:00	HDT
5/21/1933	02:00	HST
2/09/1942	02:00	HWT
9/30/1945	02:00	HST
6/08/1947	02:00	AHST

COUNTIES

1 Hawaii　2 Honolulu (Oahu)　3 Kauai　4 Maui (incl. Molokai)

Place	Latitude	Longitude	Time
Ahualoa 1	20N05	155w28	10:21:52
Aiea 2	21N23	157w56	10:31:44
Alabama Village 4	20N52	156w27	10:25:48
Alasaki Camp 1	20N01	155w17	10:21:08
Amauulu Camps 1	19N42	155w05	10:20:20
Anahola 3	22N09	159w19	10:37:16
Andrade 1	19N51	155w06	10:20:24
Barbers Point Housing 2	21N20	158w05	10:32:20
Camp H.M. Smith 2	21N23	157w56	10:31:44
Captain Cook 1	19N30	155w55	10:23:40
Cch 2	21N39	157w56	10:31:44
Central Power Plant Village 4	20N57	156w40	10:26:40
Chinatown 2	21N20	157w52	10:31:28
Chin Chuck 1	19N54	155w08	10:20:32
City of Refuge 1	19N26	155w55	10:23:40
Coconut Grove 2	21N24	157w47	10:31:08
Cod Fish Village 4	20N55	156w21	10:25:24
Coral Gardens 2	21N25	157w48	10:31:12
Crater Maui 4	20N57	156w40	10:26:40
Crestview 2	21N24	158w01	10:32:04
Dillingham Ranch	21N34	158w10	10:32:40
East Molokai 4	21N05	156w57	10:27:48
Eleele 3	21N54	159w35	10:38:20
Elevenmile Homestead 1	19N36	155w04	10:20:16
Ewa 2	21N20	158w03	10:32:12
Ewa Beach 2	21N19	158w01	10:32:04
Fernandez Village 2	21N21	158w02	10:32:08
Ford Island 2	21N21	157w56	10:31:44
Fort Shafter 2	21N19	157w50	10:31:20
Foster Village 2	21N22	157w56	10:31:44
Glenwood 1	19N29	155w09	10:20:36
Haaheo 1	19N42	155w05	10:20:20
Haena 3	22N14	159w34	10:38:16
Haiku 4	20N55	156w19	10:25:16
Haina 1	20N05	155w28	10:21:52
Hakalau 1	19N54	155w08	10:20:32
Halaula 1	20N14	155w47	10:23:08
Halawa 1	20N14	155w45	10:23:00
Halawa 2	21N23	157w56	10:31:44
Halawa Heights 2	21N23	157w55	10:31:40
Halawa Hills 2	21N23	157w56	10:31:44
Haleaha 2	21N37	157w55	10:31:40
Haleiwa 2	21N36	158w06	10:32:24
Haliimaile 4	20N52	156w20	10:25:20
Hamoa 4	20N46	156w00	10:24:00
Hana 4	20N45	155w59	10:23:56
Hanalei 3	22N12	159w30	10:38:00
Hanamaulu 3	22N00	159w21	10:37:24
Hanapepe 3	21N55	159w35	10:38:20
Hanapepe Heights 3	21N55	159w35	10:38:20
Haou 4	20N46	156w00	10:24:00
Happy Valley 4	20N54	156w30	10:26:00
Hauula 2	21N37	157w55	10:31:40
Hawaiian Ocean View Estates 1	19N30	155w55	10:23:40
Hawaiian-spanish Village 4	20N55	156w21	10:25:24
Hawaiian Village 2	21N19	157w51	10:31:24
Hawaiian Village 4	20N55	156w21	10:25:24
Hawaii Kai 2	21N17	157w45	10:31:00
Hawaii National Park 1	19N26	155w15	10:21:00
Hawi 1	20N14	155w50	10:23:20
Heeia 2	21N25	157w48	10:31:12
Hickam Air Force Base 2	21N20	157w54	10:31:36
Hickam Housing 2	21N21	157w58	10:31:52
Highway Village 1	19N52	155w07	10:20:28
Hilo 1	19N44	155w05	10:20:20
Hoaeae 2	21N24	158w01	10:32:04
Hoea 1	20N14	155w50	10:23:20
Hokamahoe House Lot 1	19N59	155w14	10:20:56
Holualoa 1	19N37	155w57	10:23:48
Honaunau 1	19N26	155w55	10:23:40
Honohina 1	19N54	155w08	10:20:32
Honokaa 1	20N05	155w28	10:21:52
Honokahua 4	21N00	156w40	10:26:40
Honokohau 1	19N37	155w57	10:23:48
Honokowai 4	20N57	156w40	10:26:40
Honolulu 2	21N19	157w52	10:31:28
Honolulu Intl Airport 2	21N24	157w54	10:31:36
Honomakau 1	20N14	155w47	10:23:08
Honomalino 1	19N30	155w55	10:23:40
Honomu 1	19N52	155w07	10:20:28
Honouliuli 2	21N22	158w02	10:32:08
Honuapo 1	19N04	155w35	10:22:20
Hookena 1	19N30	155w55	10:23:40
Hoolehua 4	21N10	157w05	10:28:20
Hopoi 4	20N54	156w30	10:26:00
Hospital Village 4	20N52	156w27	10:25:48
Huehue 1	19N37	155w57	10:23:48
Huelo 4	20N55	156w19	10:25:16
Iroquis Point 2	21N21	158w02	10:32:08
Iroquois Point 2	21N20	157w59	10:31:56
Iwasaki Camp 1	19N36	155w04	10:20:16
Kaaawa 2	21N33	157w51	10:31:24
Kaalaea 2	21N29	157w51	10:31:24
Kaanapali 4	20N57	156w40	10:26:40
Kaapahu 1	20N03	155w22	10:21:28
Kaauhuhu Homesteads 1	20N14	155w50	10:23:20
Kaawanui 3	21N55	159w38	10:38:32
Kahakuloa 4	21N00	156w33	10:26:12
Kahaluu 1	19N37	155w57	10:23:48
Kahaluu 2	21N28	157w50	10:31:20
Kahana 2	21N34	157w53	10:31:32
Kahana 4	20N57	156w40	10:26:40
Kahei Homesteads 1	20N14	155w50	10:23:20
Kaheka Village 4	20N55	156w21	10:25:24
Kahua 1	20N08	155w48	10:23:12
Kahuku 2	21N41	157w57	10:31:48
Kahului 4	20N53	156w30	10:26:00
Kaiaakea 1	19N56	155w11	10:20:44
Kailua 1	19N39	155w59	10:23:56
Kailua 2	21N24	157w47	10:31:08
Kailua 4	20N55	156w19	10:25:16
Kailua Kona 1	19N39	155w59	10:23:56
Kai Malino 1	19N30	155w55	10:23:40
Kaimu 1	19N30	154w57	10:19:48
Kaimuki 2	21N17	157w48	10:31:12
Kainaliu 1	19N31	155w55	10:23:40
Kainalu 4	21N06	157w01	10:28:04
Kaiwiki 1	19N42	155w05	10:20:20
Kalae 4	21N10	157w06	10:28:24
Kalaheo 3	21N56	159w32	10:38:08
Kalamaula 4	21N06	157w01	10:28:04
Kalaoa 1	19N48	155w06	10:20:24
Kalaoa Homesteads 1	19N37	155w57	10:23:48
Kalapana 1	19N21	154w59	10:19:56
Kalauao 2	21N23	157w56	10:31:44
Kalaupapa 4	21N11	156w59	10:27:56
Kalawao 4	21N12	156w59	10:27:56
Kalepoleopo 4	20N47	156w28	10:25:52
Kalihiwai 3	22N13	159w25	10:37:40
Kalopa Mauka 1	20N05	155w28	10:21:52
Kaluaaha 4	21N04	156w49	10:27:16
Kamaili 1	19N30	154w57	10:19:48
Kamalo 4	21N06	157w01	10:28:04
Kamiloloa 4	21N06	157w01	10:28:04
Kamooloa 2	21N34	158w07	10:32:28
Kamuela 1	20N02	155w40	10:22:40
Kaneohe 2	21N25	157w48	10:31:12
Kaneohe Marine Corps Air Sta 2	21N24	157w47	10:31:08
Kapaa 3	22N05	159w19	10:37:16
Kapaau 1	20N14	155w48	10:23:12
Kapaia 3	22N00	159w21	10:37:24
Kapaka 3	21N55	159w38	10:38:32
Kapalama 2	21N20	157w52	10:31:28
Kapapala 1	19N12	155w29	10:21:56
Kapehu 1	19N59	155w14	10:20:56
Kapunakea 4	20N57	156w40	10:26:40
Kau 1	19N19	155w25	10:21:40
Kaumakani 3	21N55	159w38	10:38:32
Kaumalapau 4	20N47	156w59	10:27:56
Kaumana 1	19N42	155w05	10:20:20
Kaunakakai 4	21N06	157w01	10:28:04
Kaupakulua 4	20N55	156w19	10:25:16
Kaupo 4	20N46	156w00	10:24:00
Kawaihae 1	20N03	155w50	10:23:20
Kawaihua 3	22N04	159w20	10:37:20
Kawailoa 2	21N36	158w05	10:32:20
Kawainui 1	19N51	155w06	10:20:24
Kawanui 1	19N31	155w55	10:23:40
Kawela 2	21N40	157w59	10:31:56
Keaau 1	19N39	154w59	10:19:56
Keaau Camp 1	19N38	155w02	10:20:08
Keaau Ranch 1	19N38	155w02	10:20:08
Kealahou 4	20N46	156w20	10:25:20
Kealakehe Homesteads 1	20N31	156w52	10:27:28
Kealakekua 1	19N31	155w55	10:23:40
Kealia 1	19N24	155w53	10:23:32
Kealia 3	22N06	159w19	10:37:16
Keanae 4	20N55	156w19	10:25:16
Keauhou 1	19N34	155w58	10:23:52
Keaukaha 1	19N42	155w05	10:20:20
Keawakapu 4	20N43	156w27	10:25:48
Keehia 1	20N01	155w17	10:21:08
Keei 1	19N26	155w55	10:23:40
Kehena 1	19N30	154w57	10:19:48
Kekaha 3	21N58	159w43	10:38:52
Kelawea 4	20N57	156w40	10:26:40
Keokea 1	19N30	155w55	10:23:40
Keokea 4	20N43	156w22	10:25:28
Keolu Hills 2	21N24	157w47	10:31:08
Kihalani Homestead 1	19N59	155w14	10:20:56
Kihei 4	20N47	156w28	10:25:52
Kilauea 3	22N13	159w25	10:37:40
Kilauea Military Camp 1	19N26	155w15	10:21:00
Kilauea Settlement 1	19N26	155w16	10:21:04
Kiolakaa Keaa Homesteads 1	19N04	155w35	10:22:20
Kipahulu 4	20N46	156w00	10:24:00
Kipu 3	21N58	159w23	10:37:32
Kipu 4	21N10	157w02	10:28:08
Koali 4	20N46	156w00	10:24:00
Koele 4	20N50	156w55	10:27:40
Kohala 1	20N14	155w48	10:23:12
Kokee 3	21N58	159w43	10:38:52
Kokohahi 2	21N25	157w48	10:31:12
Kokomo 4	20N55	156w19	10:25:16
Kolo 1	19N30	155w55	10:23:40
Koloa 3	21N55	159w28	10:37:52
Kona 1	19N25	155w55	10:23:40
Kona Coast 1	19N25	155w55	10:23:40
Koolauloa 2	21N38	158w00	10:32:00
Koolaupoko 2	21N24	157w49	10:31:16
Kualapuu 4	21N10	157w02	10:28:08
Kualoa 2	21N32	157w53	10:31:32
Kuau 4	20N55	156w21	10:25:24
Kuhio Village 1	20N02	155w40	10:22:40
Kuhua 4	20N57	156w40	10:26:40
Kukaiau 1	20N03	155w22	10:21:28
Kukanono 2	21N24	157w47	10:31:08
Kukui 1	19N33	155w06	10:20:24
Kukuihaele 1	20N07	155w35	10:22:20
Kukuiula 3	21N54	159w28	10:37:52
Kukui Village 1	20N01	155w17	10:21:08
Kula 4	20N45	156w20	10:25:20
Kumukumu 3	22N06	159w19	10:37:16
Kunia 2	21N29	158w07	10:32:28
Kunia Camp 2	21N29	158w07	10:32:28
Kupolo 3	21N58	159w23	10:37:32
Kurtistown 1	19N36	155w04	10:20:16
Lahaina 4	20N53	156w41	10:26:44
Laie 2	21N39	157w56	10:31:44
Lanai City 4	20N50	156w55	10:27:40
Lanikai 2	21N24	157w47	10:31:08
Lanikai Heights 2	21N24	157w47	10:31:08
Laupahoehoe 1	19N59	155w14	10:20:56
Laupahoehoe Point 1	19N59	155w14	10:20:56
Lawai 3	21N55	159w31	10:38:04
Lihue 3	21N59	159w23	10:37:32
Lower Paia 4	20N55	156w23	10:25:32
Lower Village 2	21N21	158w02	10:32:08
Lualualei 2	21N24	158w10	10:32:40
Lualualei Homesteads 2	21N26	158w11	10:32:44
Lunaville 4	20N57	156w40	10:26:40
Maalaea 4	20N48	156w31	10:26:04
Mahukona 1	20N11	155w54	10:23:36
Maili 2	21N25	158w11	10:32:44
Makaha 2	21N29	158w13	10:32:52
Makakilo 2	21N21	158w02	10:32:08
Makakilo City 2	21N21	158w05	10:32:20
Makapala 1	20N14	155w45	10:23:00
Makawao 4	20N51	156w19	10:25:16
Makaweli 3	21N55	159w38	10:38:32
Makena 4	20N47	156w28	10:25:52
Mala 4	20N57	156w40	10:26:40
Mana 3	22N02	159w47	10:39:08
Marconi Area 2	21N40	157w59	10:31:56
Mauka Loa 1	19N51	155w06	10:20:24
Maulua 1	19N59	155w14	10:20:56
Maunaloa 4	21N08	157w13	10:28:52
Maunawili 2	21N22	157w46	10:31:04
McGerrow Village 4	20N52	156w27	10:25:48
McGrew Point 2	21N23	157w56	10:31:44
Mikilua 2	21N26	158w11	10:32:44
Mililani Town 2	21N27	158w01	10:32:04
Mill Camps 2	21N35	158w06	10:32:24

Milolii 1 19N11 155w55 10:23:40
Milo Village 1 20N01 155w17 10:21:08
Moiliili 2 21N18 157w50 10:31:20
Mokaoku 1 19N42 155w05 10:20:20
Mokapu 2 21N27 157w45 10:31:00
Mokuleia 2 21N35 158w10 10:32:40
Moloaa 3 22N11 159w21 10:37:24
Mountainview 1 19N33 155w07 10:20:28
Muolea 4 20N46 156w00 10:24:00
Naalehu 1 19N04 155w35 10:22:20
Nanakuli 2 21N24 158w09 10:32:36
Napili 4 20N57 156w40 10:26:40
Napoopoo 1 19N30 155w55 10:23:40
Nashiwa Village 4 20N55 156w21 10:25:24
Nawiliwili 3 21N58 159w23 10:37:32
Niihau 3 21N54 160w08 10:40:32
Nine Miles 1 19N38 155w02 10:20:08
Ninole 1 19N56 155w11 10:20:44
Niulii 1 20N14 155w45 10:23:00
Niumalu 3 21N58 159w23 10:37:32
Niu Village 1 21N25 157w48 10:31:12
Nonopahu 3 21N55 159w38 10:38:32
North Hilo 1 19N42 155w18 10:21:12
North Kohala 1 20N11 155w49 10:23:16
North Kona 1 19N38 155w53 10:23:32
Numila 3 21N54 159w35 10:38:20
Okoe 1 19N30 155w55 10:23:40
Olaa 1 19N38 155w02 10:20:08
Olaa Summer Lots 1 19N26 155w16 10:21:04
Olinda 4 20N51 156w19 10:25:16
Olomana 2 21N24 157w47 10:31:08
Olowalu 4 20N49 156w38 10:26:32
Omao 3 21N54 159w28 10:37:52
Omapio 4 20N46 156w20 10:25:20
Onomea 1 19N48 155w06 10:20:24
Ookala 1 20N01 155w17 10:21:08
Opaeula Camp 2 21N35 158w06 10:32:24
Opihikao 1 19N26 154w53 10:19:32
Orpheum Village 4 20N55 156w21 10:25:24
Paauhau 1 20N05 155w26 10:21:44
Paauhau Mauka 1 20N05 155w28 10:21:52
Paauilo 1 20N02 155w22 10:21:28
Pacific Palisades 2 21N26 157w57 10:31:48
Pahala 1 19N12 155w29 10:21:56
Pahoa 1 19N30 154w57 10:19:48
Pahoehoe 1 19N30 155w55 10:23:40
Paia 4 20N54 156w22 10:25:28
Palani Junction 1 19N37 155w57 10:23:48
Panaewa 1 19N42 155w05 10:20:20
Papa 1 19N13 155w52 10:23:28
Papaaloa 1 19N59 155w13 10:20:52
Papaikou 1 19N48 155w06 10:20:24
Paukaa 1 19N42 155w05 10:20:20
Paukukalo 4 20N54 156w30 10:26:00
Paumalu 2 21N36 158w05 10:32:20
Pauwela 4 20N56 156w19 10:25:16
Pawaa 2 21N18 157w50 10:31:20
Peahi 4 20N55 156w19 10:25:16
Pearl City 2 21N24 157w59 10:31:56
Pearl City Heights 2 21N24 157w58 10:31:52
Pearl Harbor Naval Sta 2 21N21 157w56 10:31:44
Pepeekeo 1 19N51 155w06 10:20:24
Pepeekeo Mill Camp 1 19N51 155w06 10:20:24
Pihana 4 20N54 156w30 10:26:00
Piihonua 1 19N42 155w05 10:20:20
Poamoho Camp 2 21N31 158w02 10:32:08
Pohakea Homesteads 1 20N03 155w22 10:21:28
Pohakupu 2 21N24 157w47 10:31:08
Poipu 3 21N53 159w27 10:37:48
Pomoho 2 21N30 158w03 10:32:12
Port Allen 3 21N54 159w35 10:38:20
Puako 1 19N59 155w50 10:23:20
Pualaea Homestead 1 19N59 155w14 10:20:56
Pualoke 3 21N58 159w23 10:37:32
Puhi 3 21N58 159w24 10:37:36
Pukalani 4 20N50 156w20 10:25:20
Pukoo 4 21N06 157w01 10:28:04
Pulehu 4 20N46 156w20 10:25:20
Punaluu 1 19N08 155w31 10:22:04
Punaluu 2 21N37 157w55 10:31:40
Puohala 2 21N25 157w48 10:31:12
Pupukea 2 21N45 157w57 10:31:48
Puuanahulu 1 19N49 155w51 10:23:24
Puueo 1 19N42 155w05 10:20:20
Puu Hue 1 20N14 155w50 10:23:20
Puuiki 4 20N46 156w00 10:24:00
Puukolii 4 20N57 156w40 10:26:40
Puunene 4 20N52 156w28 10:25:52
Puunoa 4 20N57 156w40 10:26:40
Puuohala 4 20N54 156w30 10:26:00
Puu Waawaa Ranch 1 20N31 156w52 10:27:28
Puuwai 3 21N55 159w38 10:38:32
Renton 2 21N21 158w02 10:32:08
Schofield Barracks 2 21N30 158w04 10:32:16
School Village 4 20N55 156w21 10:25:24
South Kohala 1 20N04 155w43 10:22:52
South Kona 1 19N21 155w49 10:23:16
Spanish Village B 4 20N52 156w27 10:25:48
Spreckleaville 4 20N54 156w26 10:25:44
Store Village 4 20N55 156w21 10:25:24
Submarine Base 2 21N21 157w56 10:31:44
Sunset Beach 2 21N40 158w03 10:32:12
Tenney 2 21N21 158w02 10:32:08
Tripler Army Hospital 2 21N21 157w53 10:31:32
Ualapue 4 21N06 157w01 10:28:04
Ulumalu 4 20N55 156w19 10:25:16
Ulupalakua 4 20N39 156w24 10:25:36

HAWAII

Umikoa 1 19N59 155w23 10:21:32
Union Mill 1 20N14 155w47 10:23:08
University 2 21N19 157w50 10:31:20
Varona Village 2 21N21 158w02 10:32:08
Volcano 1 19N26 155w16 10:21:04
Wahiawa 2 21N30 158w02 10:32:08
Wahiawa 3 21N54 159w35 10:38:20
Waiahole 2 21N25 157w48 10:31:12
Waiakea 1 19N42 155w05 10:20:20
Waiakoa 4 20N46 156w20 10:25:20
Waialae-kahala 2 21N17 157w48 10:31:12
Waialee 2 21N36 158w05 10:32:20
Waialua 2 21N34 158w07 10:32:28
Waialua 4 21N06 157w01 10:28:04
Waialua Mill 2 21N35 158w06 10:32:24
Waianae 2 21N26 158w09 10:32:36
Waianae Homesteads 2 21N26 158w11 10:32:44
Waianae Uka 2 21N26 158w11 10:32:44
Waiau 2 21N24 157w58 10:31:52
Waiehu 4 20N54 156w30 10:26:00
Waiehu Village 4 20N54 156w30 10:26:00
Waihee 4 20N56 156w31 10:26:04
Waikane 2 21N30 157w51 10:31:24
Waikapu 4 20N52 156w31 10:26:04
Waikapu Reservoir Village 4 20N54 156w30 10:26:00
Waikele 2 21N24 158w01 10:32:04
Waikii 1 19N52 155w39 10:22:36
Waikiki 2 21N17 157w49 10:31:16
Wailea 1 19N54 155w08 10:20:32
Wailua 3 20N51 156w08 10:24:32
Wailua 4 20N55 156w19 10:25:16
Wailuku 4 20N53 156w30 10:26:00
Waimalu 2 21N24 157w57 10:31:48
Waimanalo 2 21N21 157w43 10:30:52
Waimanalo Beach 2 21N20 157w42 10:30:48
Waimea 1 20N01 155w40 10:22:40
Waimea 2 21N36 158w05 10:32:20
Waimea 3 21N58 159w40 10:38:40
Wainaku 1 19N42 155w05 10:20:20
Wainee 4 20N57 156w40 10:26:40
Wainiha 3 22N12 159w30 10:38:00
Waiohinu 1 19N04 155w35 10:22:20
Waipahu 2 21N23 158w01 10:32:04
Waipio Acres 2 21N28 158w01 10:32:04
Waipouli 3 22N04 159w20 10:37:20
Waipunalei Homesteads 1 22N04 159w20 10:37:20
Weloka 1 19N58 155w12 10:20:48
West Molokai 4 21N11 157w06 10:28:24
Wheeler Air Force Base 2 21N30 158w03 10:32:12
Whitmore Village 2 21N31 158w01 10:32:04
Wood Valley Homesteads 1 19N12 155w29 10:21:56

TIME TABLES

Some informal reports show Pacific time observed in southern Idaho later than most sources indicate, but this has not been documented. Southern Idaho changed to daylight time on February 3, 1974, rather than January 6, 1974 with the rest of the country.

ID # 1		
Before 11/18/1883		LMT
11/18/1883	12:00	PST
3/31/1918	02:00	PWT
10/27/1918	02:00	PST
3/30/1919	02:00	PWT
10/26/1919	02:00	PST
2/09/1942	02:00	PWT
9/30/1945	02:00	PST
4/30/1961	02:00	PDT
10/29/1961	02:00	PST
4/29/1962	02:00	PDT
10/28/1962	02:00	PST
4/28/1963	02:00	PDT
10/27/1963	02:00	PST
4/26/1964	02:00	PDT
10/25/1964	02:00	PST
4/25/1965	02:00	PDT
10/31/1965	02:00	PST
4/24/1966	02:00	PDT
10/30/1966	02:00	PST
4/30/1967	02:00	US#1

ID # 2		
Before 11/18/1883		LMT
11/18/1883	12:00	PST
3/31/1918	02:00	PWT
10/27/1918	02:00	PST
3/30/1919	02:00	PWT
10/26/1919	02:00	PST
2/09/1942	02:00	PWT
9/30/1945	02:00	PST
4/26/1964	02:00	PDT
10/25/1964	02:00	PST
4/24/1966	02:00	US#1

ID # 3		
Before 11/18/1883		LMT
11/18/1883	12:00	PST
3/31/1918	02:00	PWT
10/27/1918	02:00	PST
3/30/1919	02:00	PWT
10/26/1919	02:00	PST
5/01/1938	02:00	PDT
10/01/1938	02:00	PST
5/07/1939	02:00	PDT
10/01/1939	02:00	PST
5/05/1940	02:00	PDT
9/29/1940	02:00	PST
5/04/1941	02:00	PDT
9/28/1941	02:00	PST
2/09/1942	02:00	PWT
9/30/1945	02:00	PST
4/26/1964	02:00	PDT
10/25/1964	02:00	PST
4/24/1966	02:00	US#1

ID # 4		
Before 11/18/1883		LMT
11/18/1883	12:00	PST
3/31/1918	02:00	PWT
10/27/1918	02:00	PST
3/30/1919	02:00	PWT
10/26/1919	02:00	PST
2/09/1942	02:00	PWT
9/30/1945	02:00	PST
4/30/1961	02:00	PDT
10/29/1961	02:00	PST
4/29/1962	02:00	PDT
10/28/1962	02:00	PST
4/28/1963	02:00	PDT
10/27/1963	02:00	PST
4/26/1964	02:00	PDT
10/25/1964	02:00	PST
4/24/1966	02:00	US#1

ID # 5		
Before 11/18/1883		LMT
11/18/1883	12:00	PST
3/31/1918	02:00	PWT
10/27/1918	02:00	PST
3/30/1919	02:00	PWT
10/26/1919	02:00	PST
2/09/1942	02:00	PWT
9/30/1945	02:00	PST
4/26/1964	02:00	PDT
10/25/1964	02:00	PST
4/25/1965	02:00	PDT
10/31/1965	02:00	PST
4/24/1966	02:00	PDT
10/30/1966	02:00	PST
4/30/1967	02:00	US#1

ID # 6		
Before 11/18/1883		LMT
11/18/1883	12:00	PST
3/31/1918	02:00	PWT
10/27/1918	02:00	PST
3/30/1919	02:00	PWT
10/26/1919	02:00	PST
5/01/1938	02:00	PDT
10/01/1938	02:00	PST
5/07/1939	02:00	PDT
10/01/1939	02:00	PST
5/05/1940	02:00	PDT
9/29/1940	02:00	PST
5/04/1941	02:00	PDT
9/28/1941	02:00	PST
2/09/1942	02:00	PWT
9/30/1945	02:00	PST
4/30/1961	02:00	PDT
10/29/1961	02:00	PST
4/29/1962	02:00	PDT
10/28/1962	02:00	PST
4/28/1963	02:00	PDT
10/27/1963	02:00	PST
4/26/1964	02:00	PDT
10/25/1964	02:00	PST
4/24/1966	02:00	US#1

ID # 7		
Before 11/18/1883		LMT
11/18/1883	12:00	PST
3/31/1918	02:00	PWT
10/27/1918	02:00	PST
3/30/1919	02:00	PWT
10/26/1919	02:00	PST
2/09/1942	02:00	PWT
9/30/1945	02:00	PST
4/27/1952	02:00	PDT
9/01/1952	02:00	PST
4/30/1961	02:00	PDT
10/29/1961	02:00	PST
4/29/1962	02:00	PDT
10/28/1962	02:00	PST
4/28/1963	02:00	PDT
10/27/1963	02:00	PST
4/26/1964	02:00	PDT
10/25/1964	02:00	PST
4/25/1965	02:00	PDT
10/31/1965	02:00	PST
4/24/1966	02:00	PDT
10/30/1966	02:00	PST
4/30/1967	02:00	US#1

ID # 8		
Before 4/01/1893		LMT
4/01/1893	12:00	PST
3/31/1918	02:00	PWT
10/27/1918	02:00	PST
3/30/1919	02:00	PWT
10/26/1919	02:00	PST
5/15/1931	02:00	PDT
10/15/1931	02:00	PST
4/30/1933	02:00	PDT
9/24/1933	02:00	PST
4/29/1934	02:00	PDT
9/30/1934	02:00	PST
4/28/1935	02:00	PDT
9/29/1935	02:00	PST
4/26/1936	02:00	PDT
9/27/1936	02:00	PST
4/25/1937	02:00	PDT
9/26/1937	02:00	PST
5/01/1938	02:00	PDT
10/01/1938	02:00	PST
5/07/1939	02:00	PDT
10/01/1939	02:00	PST
5/05/1940	02:00	PDT
9/29/1940	02:00	PST
5/04/1941	02:00	PDT
9/28/1941	02:00	PST
2/09/1942	02:00	PWT
9/30/1945	02:00	PST
4/30/1961	02:00	PDT
10/29/1961	02:00	PST
4/29/1962	02:00	PDT
10/28/1962	02:00	PST
4/28/1963	02:00	PDT
10/27/1963	02:00	PST
4/26/1964	02:00	PDT
10/25/1964	02:00	PST
4/24/1966	02:00	US#1

ID # 9		
Before 4/01/1893		LMT
4/01/1893	12:00	PST
3/31/1918	02:00	PWT
10/27/1918	02:00	PST
3/30/1919	02:00	PWT
10/26/1919	02:00	PST
4/30/1933	02:00	PDT
9/24/1933	02:00	PST
4/29/1934	02:00	PDT
9/30/1934	02:00	PST
4/28/1935	02:00	PDT
9/29/1935	02:00	PST
4/26/1936	02:00	PDT
9/27/1936	02:00	PST
4/25/1937	02:00	PDT
9/26/1937	02:00	PST
4/24/1938	02:00	PDT
9/24/1938	02:00	PST
5/07/1939	02:00	PDT
10/01/1939	02:00	PST
5/05/1940	02:00	PDT
9/29/1940	02:00	PST
5/04/1941	02:00	PDT
9/28/1941	02:00	PST
2/09/1942	02:00	PWT
9/30/1945	02:00	PST
4/26/1964	02:00	PDT
10/25/1964	02:00	PST
4/24/1966	02:00	US#1

ID # 10		
Before 4/01/1893		LMT
4/01/1893	12:00	PST
3/31/1918	02:00	PWT
10/27/1918	02:00	PST
3/30/1919	02:00	PWT
10/26/1919	02:00	PST
4/26/1936	02:00	PDT
9/27/1936	02:00	PST
4/25/1937	02:00	PDT
9/26/1937	02:00	PST
4/24/1938	02:00	PDT
9/24/1938	02:00	PST
5/07/1939	02:00	PDT
10/01/1939	02:00	PST
5/05/1940	02:00	PDT
9/29/1940	02:00	PST
5/04/1941	02:00	PDT
9/28/1941	02:00	PST
2/09/1942	02:00	PWT
9/30/1945	02:00	PST
4/30/1961	02:00	PDT
10/29/1961	02:00	PST
4/29/1962	02:00	PDT
10/28/1962	02:00	PST
4/28/1963	02:00	PDT
10/27/1963	02:00	PST
4/26/1964	02:00	PDT
10/25/1964	02:00	PST
4/24/1966	02:00	US#1

ID # 11		
Before 4/01/1893		LMT
4/01/1893	12:00	PST
3/31/1918	02:00	PWT
10/27/1918	02:00	PST
3/30/1919	02:00	PWT
10/26/1919	02:00	PST
5/10/1931	02:00	PDT
10/04/1931	02:00	PST
4/29/1934	02:00	PDT
9/30/1934	02:00	PST
4/28/1935	02:00	PDT
9/29/1935	02:00	PST
4/26/1936	02:00	PDT
9/27/1936	02:00	PST
4/25/1937	02:00	PDT
10/02/1937	02:00	PST
5/01/1938	02:00	PDT
10/01/1938	02:00	PST
5/07/1939	02:00	PDT
10/01/1939	02:00	PST
5/05/1940	02:00	PDT
9/29/1940	02:00	PST
5/04/1941	02:00	PDT
9/28/1941	02:00	PST
2/09/1942	02:00	PWT
9/30/1945	02:00	PST
4/26/1964	02:00	PDT
10/25/1964	02:00	PST
4/24/1966	02:00	US#1

ID # 12		
Before 11/18/1883		LMT
11/18/1883	12:00	PST
3/31/1918	02:00	PWT
10/27/1918	02:00	PST
3/30/1919	02:00	PWT
10/26/1919	02:00	PST
2/09/1942	02:00	PWT
9/30/1945	02:00	PST
4/30/1950	02:00	PDT
9/24/1950	02:00	PST
4/30/1961	02:00	PDT
10/29/1961	02:00	PST
4/29/1962	02:00	PDT
10/28/1962	02:00	PST
4/28/1963	02:00	PDT
10/27/1963	02:00	PST
4/26/1964	02:00	PDT
10/25/1964	02:00	PST
4/24/1966	02:00	US#1

ID # 13		
Before 11/18/1883		LMT
11/18/1883	12:00	PST
3/31/1918	02:00	PWT
10/27/1918	02:00	PST
1/01/1919	02:00	MST
3/30/1919	02:00	MWT
10/26/1919	02:00	MST
2/09/1942	02:00	MWT
9/30/1945	02:00	MST
4/30/1961	02:00	MDT
10/29/1961	02:00	MST
4/29/1962	02:00	MDT
10/28/1962	02:00	MST
4/28/1963	02:00	MDT
10/27/1963	02:00	MST
4/30/1967	02:00	MDT
10/29/1967	02:00	MST
4/28/1968	02:00	MDT
10/27/1968	02:00	MST
4/27/1969	02:00	MDT
10/26/1969	02:00	MST
4/26/1970	02:00	MDT
10/25/1970	02:00	MST
4/25/1971	02:00	MDT
10/31/1971	02:00	MST
4/30/1972	02:00	MDT
10/29/1972	02:00	MST
4/29/1973	02:00	MDT
10/28/1973	02:00	MST
2/03/1974	02:00	MDT
10/27/1974	02:00	US#1

ID # 14		
Before 11/18/1883		LMT
11/18/1883	12:00	PST
3/31/1918	02:00	PWT
10/27/1918	02:00	PST
1/01/1919	02:00	MST
3/30/1919	02:00	MWT
10/26/1919	02:00	MST
2/09/1942	02:00	MWT
9/30/1945	02:00	MST
4/30/1967	02:00	MDT
10/29/1967	02:00	MST
4/28/1968	02:00	MDT
10/27/1968	02:00	MST
4/27/1969	02:00	MDT
10/26/1969	02:00	MST
4/26/1970	02:00	MDT
10/25/1970	02:00	MST
4/25/1971	02:00	MDT
10/31/1971	02:00	MST
4/30/1972	02:00	MDT
10/29/1972	02:00	MST
4/29/1973	02:00	MDT
10/28/1973	02:00	MST
2/03/1974	02:00	MDT
10/27/1974	02:00	US#1

ID # 15		
Before 11/18/1883		LMT
11/18/1883	12:00	PST
3/31/1918	02:00	PWT
10/27/1918	02:00	PST
3/30/1919	02:00	PWT
6/01/1919	02:00	MWT
10/26/1919	02:00	MST
2/09/1942	02:00	MWT
9/30/1945	02:00	MST
4/26/1964	02:00	MDT
10/25/1964	02:00	MST
4/25/1965	02:00	MDT
10/31/1965	02:00	MST
4/30/1967	02:00	MDT
10/29/1967	02:00	MST
4/28/1968	02:00	MDT
10/27/1968	02:00	MST
4/27/1969	02:00	MDT
10/26/1969	02:00	MST
4/26/1970	02:00	MDT
10/25/1970	02:00	MST
4/25/1971	02:00	MDT
10/31/1971	02:00	MST
4/30/1972	02:00	MDT
10/29/1972	02:00	MST
4/29/1973	02:00	MDT
10/28/1973	02:00	MST
2/03/1974	02:00	MDT
10/27/1974	02:00	US#1

ID # 16		
Before 11/18/1883		LMT
11/18/1883	12:00	PST
3/31/1918	02:00	PWT
10/27/1918	02:00	PST
3/30/1919	02:00	PWT
6/01/1919	02:00	MWT
10/26/1919	02:00	MST
2/09/1942	02:00	MWT
9/30/1945	02:00	MST
4/30/1967	02:00	MDT
10/29/1967	02:00	MST
4/28/1968	02:00	MDT
10/27/1968	02:00	MST
4/27/1969	02:00	MDT
10/26/1969	02:00	MST
4/26/1970	02:00	MDT
10/25/1970	02:00	MST
4/25/1971	02:00	MDT
10/31/1971	02:00	MST
4/30/1972	02:00	MDT
10/29/1972	02:00	MST
4/29/1973	02:00	MDT
10/28/1973	02:00	MST
2/03/1974	02:00	MDT
10/27/1974	02:00	US#1

ID # 17		
Before 11/18/1883		LMT
11/18/1883	12:00	PST
3/31/1918	02:00	PWT
10/27/1918	02:00	PST
3/30/1919	02:00	PWT
10/26/1919	02:00	PST
5/13/1923	02:00	MST
2/09/1942	02:00	MWT
9/30/1945	02:00	MST
4/30/1961	02:00	MDT
10/29/1961	02:00	MST
4/29/1962	02:00	MDT
10/28/1962	02:00	MST
4/28/1963	02:00	MDT
10/27/1963	02:00	MST
4/30/1967	02:00	MDT
10/29/1967	02:00	MST
4/28/1968	02:00	MDT
10/27/1968	02:00	MST
4/27/1969	02:00	MDT
10/26/1969	02:00	MST
4/26/1970	02:00	MDT
10/25/1970	02:00	MST
4/25/1971	02:00	MDT
10/31/1971	02:00	MST
4/30/1972	02:00	MDT
10/29/1972	02:00	MST
4/29/1973	02:00	MDT
10/28/1973	02:00	MST
2/03/1974	02:00	MDT
10/27/1974	02:00	US#1

ID # 18		
Before 11/18/1883		LMT
11/18/1883	12:00	PST
3/31/1918	02:00	PWT
10/27/1918	02:00	PST
3/30/1919	02:00	PWT
10/26/1919	02:00	PST
5/13/1923	02:00	MST
2/09/1942	02:00	MWT
9/30/1945	02:00	MST
4/30/1967	02:00	MDT
10/29/1967	02:00	MST
4/28/1968	02:00	MDT
10/27/1968	02:00	MST
4/27/1969	02:00	MDT
10/26/1969	02:00	MST
4/26/1970	02:00	MDT
10/25/1970	02:00	MST
4/25/1971	02:00	MDT
10/31/1971	02:00	MST
4/30/1972	02:00	MDT
10/29/1972	02:00	MST
4/29/1973	02:00	MDT
10/28/1973	02:00	MST
2/03/1974	02:00	MDT
10/27/1974	02:00	US#1

COUNTIES

1 Ada
2 Adams
3 Bannock
4 Bear Lake
5 Benewah
6 Bingham
7 Blaine
8 Boise
9 Bonner
10 Bonneville
11 Boundary
12 Butte
13 Camas
14 Canyon
15 Caribou
16 Cassia
17 Clark
18 Clearwater
19 Custer
20 Elmore
21 Franklin
22 Fremont
23 Gem
24 Gooding
25 Idaho
26 Jefferson
27 Jerome
28 Kootenai
29 Latah
30 Lemhi
31 Lewis
32 Lincoln
33 Madison
34 Minidoka
35 Nez Perce
36 Oneida
37 Owyhee
38 Payette
39 Power
40 Shoshone
41 Teton
42 Twin Falls
43 Valley
44 Washington

Aberdeen 6	16	42N57	112w50	7:31:20
Acequia 34	18	42N10	113w36	7:34:24
Ahsahka 18	2	46N30	116w20	7:45:20
Alameda 3	16	42N57	112w28	7:29:52
Albion 16	18	42N25	113w35	7:34:20
Algoma 9	2	48N12	116w33	7:46:12
Almo 16	18	42N06	113w38	7:34:32
Alpha 43	18	44N31	116w03	7:44:12
Alpine 2	18	44N34	116w40	7:46:40
Alridge 6	14	43N11	111w47	7:27:08
American Falls 39	18	42N47	112w51	7:31:24
Ammon 10	14	43N28	111w58	7:27:52
Anderson Dam 20	18	43N08	115w42	7:42:48
Annis 26	14	43N40	111w55	7:27:40
Antelope 10	14	43N38	111w45	7:27:00
Appleton 24	18	42N43	114w31	7:38:04
Apple Valley 14	18	43N47	116w57	7:47:48
Arbon 39	18	42N27	112w34	7:30:16
Archer 33	14	43N49	111w47	7:27:08
Arco 12	16	43N38	113w18	7:33:12
Argora 17	14	44N10	112w14	7:28:56
Arimo 3	14	42N34	112w10	7:28:40
Ashton 22	13	44N04	111w27	7:25:48
Athol 28	4	47N57	116w42	7:46:48
Atlanta 20	18	43N48	115w08	7:40:32
Atomic City 6	16	43N27	112w49	7:31:16
Avery 40	2	47N15	115w49	7:43:16
Avon 29	2	46N48	116w33	7:46:12
Baker 30	16	45N06	113w44	7:34:56
Bancroft 15	14	42N43	111w53	7:27:32
Banida 21	14	42N14	111w57	7:27:48
Banks 8	18	44N05	116w08	7:44:32
Bannock 3	14	42N54	112w27	7:29:48
Barber 1	18	43N34	116w07	7:44:28
Basalt 6	14	43N19	112w10	7:28:40
Basin 16	18	42N15	113w53	7:35:32
Bates 41	14	43N43	111w06	7:24:24
Bayview 28	2	47N59	116w34	7:46:16
Beachs Corner 10	14	43N29	112w00	7:28:00
Bear 2	18	44N44	116w26	7:45:44
Bellevue 7	18	43N28	114w16	7:37:04
Belmont 28	2	47N57	116w42	7:46:48
Bench 15	14	42N35	111w44	7:26:56
Benewah 5	2	47N19	116w34	7:46:16
Bennington 4	14	42N24	111w19	7:25:16
Bern 4	14	42N20	111w23	7:25:32
Big Creek 43	18	45N08	115w20	7:41:20
Big Springs 22	14	44N31	111w20	7:25:20
Black Cloud 40	2	47N28	115w55	7:43:40
Blackfoot 6	13	43N11	112w21	7:29:24
Black Lake 28	2	47N19	116w34	7:46:16
Blaine 29	2	46N44	117w00	7:48:00
Blanchard 9	2	48N01	116w59	7:47:56
Bliss 24	18	42N56	114w57	7:39:48
Bloomington 4	14	42N11	111w24	7:25:36
Blue Dome 17	16	44N41	113w21	7:33:24
Boise 1	18	43N37	116w13	7:44:52
Boise City 1	18	43N37	116w16	7:45:04
Boise Hills 1	14	43N12	111w46	7:27:04
Bonanza 19	18	44N13	114w56	7:39:44
Bone 10	14	43N29	112w00	7:28:00
Bonners Ferry 11	1	48N42	116w19	7:45:16
Borah 1	18	43N38	116w13	7:44:52
Bovill 29	2	46N51	116w24	7:45:36
Bowmont 14	18	43N27	116w32	7:46:08
Box Canyon 22	14	44N31	111w20	7:25:20
Bradley 40	6	47N32	116w08	7:44:32
Bridge 16	18	42N08	113w20	7:33:20
Broadford 7	18	43N28	114w15	7:37:00
Broten 9	2	48N16	116w33	7:46:12
Bruneau 37	18	42N53	115w48	7:43:12
Bruneau Valley 37	18	42N53	115w48	7:43:12
Buhl 42	18	42N36	114w46	7:39:04
Buist 36	18	42N10	112w39	7:30:36
Burgdorf 25	18	44N55	116w06	7:44:24
Burke 40	8	47N31	115w49	7:43:16
Burley 16	18	42N32	113w48	7:35:12
Burmah 32	18	43N03	114w09	7:36:36
Burton 33	14	43N49	111w47	7:27:08
Butler Bay 5	2	47N19	116w34	7:46:16
Butte City 12	16	43N37	113w14	7:32:56
Cabinet 9	2	48N09	116w10	7:44:40
Caldwell 14	18	43N40	116w41	7:46:44
Caldwell Labor Camp 14	18	43N40	116w41	7:46:44
Camas 26	13	44N00	112w13	7:28:52
Cambridge 44	18	44N34	116w41	7:46:44
Cameron 35	2	46N37	116w39	7:46:36
Canyon Creek 33	14	43N53	111w36	7:26:24
Carey 7	18	43N19	113w57	7:35:48
Careywood 9	2	48N02	116w38	7:46:32
Carlin Bay 28	2	47N27	116w47	7:47:08
Carmen 30	16	45N15	113w54	7:35:36
Cascade 43	18	44N31	116w02	7:44:08
Castleford 42	18	42N31	114w52	7:39:28
Cataldo 28	2	47N33	116w20	7:45:20
Challis 19	18	44N30	114w14	7:36:56
Chatcolet 5	2	47N22	116w47	7:47:08
Cherry Creek 36	18	42N11	112w14	7:28:56
Chester 22	14	44N00	111w35	7:26:20
Chesterfield 15	14	42N52	111w54	7:27:36
Chilco 28	2	47N57	116w42	7:46:48
Chilly 19	16	43N55	113w37	7:34:28
Chubbuck 3	14	42N55	112w28	7:29:52
Churchill 16	18	42N15	113w53	7:35:32
Clagstone 9	2	48N15	116w54	7:47:36
Clark Fork 9	2	48N09	116w11	7:44:44
Clarkia 40	2	47N01	116w15	7:45:00
Clarks Fork 9	2	48N11	116w10	7:44:40
Clarkville 28	1	47N46	116w46	7:47:04
Clawson 41	14	43N49	111w10	7:24:40
Clayton 19	18	44N16	114w24	7:37:36
Clearwater 25	2	46N01	115w53	7:43:32
Clementsville 41	14	43N53	111w36	7:26:24
Cleveland 21	14	42N25	111w44	7:26:56
Cliffs 37	18	42N59	117w03	7:48:12
Clifton 21	14	42N11	112w00	7:28:00
Clover 42	18	42N36	114w46	7:39:04
Clyde 12	15	43N47	113w00	7:32:00
Cobalt 30	18	45N06	114w14	7:36:56
Cocolalla 9	2	48N06	116w37	7:46:28
Coeur d'Alene 28	1	47N41	116w46	7:47:04
Coeur d'Alene Indian Reserva 5	2	46N24	116w48	7:47:12
Colburn 9	2	48N24	116w32	7:46:08
Collister 1	18	43N36	115w39	7:42:36
Coltman 10	14	43N29	112w00	7:28:00
Conda 15	14	42N44	111w32	7:26:08
Conkling Park 28	2	47N24	116w55	7:47:40
Conner 16	18	42N19	113w22	7:33:28
Coolin 9	2	48N29	116w51	7:47:24
Cooperville 25	2	45N46	116w18	7:45:12
Copeland 11	2	48N54	116w23	7:45:32
Corral 13	18	43N21	114w57	7:39:48
Cotterel 16	18	42N31	113w38	7:34:32
Cottonwood 25	4	46N03	116w21	7:45:24
Council 2	18	44N44	116w26	7:45:44
Craigmont 31	2	46N15	116w29	7:45:56
Crouch 8	18	44N07	115w58	7:43:52
Crystal 44	18	44N15	116w58	7:47:52
Culdesac 35	2	46N23	116w40	7:46:40
Culver 9	2	48N16	116w33	7:46:12
Cuprum 2	18	44N44	116w26	7:45:44
Curry 42	18	42N34	114w36	7:38:24
Dalton Gardens 28	1	47N44	116w46	7:47:04
Daniels 36	18	42N11	112w14	7:28:56
Darlington 12	16	43N49	113w25	7:33:40
Dayton 21	14	42N07	112w00	7:28:00
Deary 29	2	46N48	116w33	7:46:12
Declo 16	17	42N31	113w39	7:34:36
Deep Creek 42	18	42N36	114w46	7:39:04
Delta 40	3	47N28	115w55	7:43:40
Desmet 5	2	47N09	116w55	7:47:40
Dietrich 32	18	42N55	114w16	7:37:04
Dingle 4	14	42N13	111w16	7:25:04
Dixie 25	2	45N50	115w26	7:41:44
Doles 14	18	43N40	116w41	7:46:44
Donnelly 43	18	44N44	116w05	7:44:20
Dover 9	2	48N15	116w36	7:46:24
Downey 3	14	42N26	112w07	7:28:28
Driggs 41	14	43N44	111w06	7:24:24
Drummond 22	14	44N00	111w20	7:25:20
Dubois 17	14	44N10	112w14	7:28:56
Dwight 41	14	43N49	111w10	7:24:40
Eagle 1	18	43N42	116w21	7:45:24
Eagle 40	2	47N28	115w55	7:43:40
Eagle Rock 10	14	43N29	112w00	7:28:00
East Camas 13	18	43N20	114w42	7:38:48
East Clark 17	14	44N23	111w55	7:27:40
East Hope 9	2	48N14	116w17	7:45:08
East Lewiston 35	12	46N24	116w59	7:47:56
Eastport 11	4	49N00	116w11	7:44:44
Eaton 44	18	44N15	116w58	7:47:52
Echo Beach 28	2	47N49	116w54	7:47:36
Eddiville 28	1	47N42	116w47	7:47:08
Eden 27	18	42N36	114w13	7:36:52
Edmonds 33	14	43N49	111w47	7:27:08
Egin 22	14	43N58	111w41	7:26:44
Elba 16	18	42N15	113w34	7:34:16
Elk City 25	2	45N50	115w26	7:41:44
Elk River 18	2	46N47	116w11	7:44:44
Ellis 19	18	44N42	114w03	7:36:12
Elmira 9	2	48N29	116w27	7:45:48
Emida 5	2	47N07	116w36	7:46:24
Emmett 23	17	43N52	116w30	7:46:00
Enaville 40	3	47N34	116w15	7:45:00
Enrose 14	18	43N40	116w41	7:46:44
Excelsior Beach 28	2	47N49	116w54	7:47:36
Fairfield 13	18	43N21	114w44	7:38:56
Fairview 21	14	42N01	111w53	7:27:32
Fairview 42	18	42N36	114w46	7:39:04
Fall Creek 25	2	45N55	116w07	7:44:28
Falls City 27	18	42N43	114w31	7:38:04
Featherville 20	18	43N08	115w42	7:42:48
Felt 41	14	43N52	111w11	7:24:44
Fenn 25	2	45N58	116w16	7:45:04
Ferdinand 25	2	46N09	116w24	7:45:36
Fernan Lake 28	1	47N41	116w45	7:47:00
Fernwood 5	2	47N07	116w24	7:45:36
Filer 42	18	42N34	114w37	7:38:28
Firth 6	14	43N18	112w11	7:28:44
Fish Haven 4	14	42N02	111w24	7:25:36
Forney 30	18	45N13	114w16	7:37:04
Fort Hall 6	14	43N02	112w26	7:29:44
Fort Hall Indian Reservation 3	14	42N52	112w27	7:29:48
Fox Creek 41	14	43N36	111w07	7:24:28
Franklin 21	14	42N01	111w48	7:27:12
Fruitland 38	18	44N00	116w55	7:47:40
Fruitvale 2	18	44N49	116w26	7:45:44
Gannett 7	18	43N22	114w11	7:36:44
Gardena 8	18	43N58	116w12	7:44:48
Garden City 1	18	43N38	116w16	7:45:04
Garden Valley 8	18	44N06	115w57	7:43:48
Garfield 26	14	43N29	112w00	7:28:00
Garwood 28	1	47N46	116w46	7:47:04
Gem 40	3	47N31	115w52	7:43:28
Genesee 29	2	46N33	116w56	7:47:44
Geneva 4	14	42N22	111w04	7:24:16
Georgetown 4	14	42N29	111w22	7:25:28
Gibbonsville 30	16	45N33	113w56	7:35:44
Gibson 6	14	43N11	112w21	7:29:24
Gibson City 40	2	47N32	116w14	7:44:56
Gifford 35	2	46N27	116w33	7:46:12
Gilmore 30	16	44N28	113w16	7:33:04
Glencoe 4	14	42N14	111w24	7:25:36
Glendale 21	14	42N11	111w57	7:27:48
Glengary 9	2	48N16	116w33	7:46:12
Glenns Ferry 20	18	42N57	115w18	7:41:12
Glenwood 18	2	46N29	116w15	7:45:00
Glenwood 25	2	46N13	116w02	7:44:08
Golden 25	2	45N55	116w07	7:44:28
Gooding 24	18	42N57	114w42	7:38:48
Goodrich 2	18	44N44	116w26	7:45:44
Goshen 6	14	43N23	112w08	7:28:32
Grace 15	14	42N35	111w44	7:26:56
Grand View 37	18	42N59	116w06	7:44:24
Grangemont 18	2	46N29	116w15	7:45:00
Grangeville 25	4	45N56	116w07	7:44:28
Granite 9	2	47N57	116w42	7:46:48
Grant 26	14	43N29	112w00	7:28:00
Grasmere 37	18	42N23	115w53	7:43:32
Gray 10	14	42N58	111w23	7:25:32
Greencreek 25	2	46N06	116w16	7:45:04
Greenleaf 14	18	43N40	116w49	7:47:16
Greenwood 27	18	42N36	114w08	7:36:32
Greer 18	2	46N24	116w11	7:44:44
Gross 23	18	44N11	116w18	7:45:12
Grouse 19	16	43N41	113w37	7:34:28
Groveland 6	14	43N11	112w21	7:29:24
Gwenford 36	18	42N11	112w14	7:28:56
Hagerman 24	18	42N49	114w54	7:39:36
Hailey 7	18	43N31	114w19	7:37:16
Hamer 26	14	43N56	112w12	7:28:48
Hamilton Corner 38	18	43N58	116w49	7:47:16
Hammett 20	18	42N57	115w28	7:41:52
Hampton 29	2	46N55	116w50	7:47:20
Hansen 42	18	42N32	114w18	7:37:12
Harpster 25	2	46N01	115w53	7:43:32
Harrison 28	2	47N27	116w47	7:47:08
Harvard 29	2	46N55	116w44	7:46:56
Hatwai 35	12	46N24	116w59	7:47:56
Hauser 28	2	47N46	117w01	7:48:04
Hauser Lake 28	2	47N44	117w00	7:48:00
Hawkins 3	14	42N34	112w10	7:28:40
Hayden 28	5	47N46	116w47	7:47:08
Hazelton 27	18	42N36	114w08	7:36:32
Headquarters 18	4	46N38	115w48	7:43:12
Heglar 16	18	42N47	112w51	7:31:24
Heise 26	14	43N39	111w43	7:26:52
Helmer 29	2	46N48	116w28	7:45:52
Heman 22	14	43N58	111w41	7:26:44
Henry 15	14	42N44	111w32	7:26:08
Heyburn 34	18	42N34	113w47	7:35:08
Hibbard 33	14	43N49	111w47	7:27:08
Hill City 13	18	43N18	115w03	7:40:12
Hillview 10	14	43N29	112w00	7:28:00
Holbrook 36	18	42N10	112w39	7:30:36
Hollister 42	18	42N21	114w35	7:38:20
Homedale 37	18	43N37	116w56	7:47:44
Honeysuckle Hills 28	1	47N46	116w46	7:47:04
Hope 9	2	48N15	116w18	7:45:12
Hornet 2	18	44N44	116w26	7:45:44
Horseshoe Bend 8	18	43N55	116w12	7:44:48

Hot Spring Landing 7
18 43N31 114w19 7:37:16
Howe 12 16 43N54 113w06 7:32:24
Huetter 28 2 47N42 116w51 7:47:24
Humphrey 17 14 44N29 112w14 7:28:56
Hunt 27 18 42N40 114w06 7:36:24
Huston 14 18 43N37 116w47 7:47:08
Idaho City 8 18 43N50 115w50 7:43:20
Idaho Falls 10 13 43N30 112w02 7:28:08
Idahome 16 18 42N31 113w38 7:34:32
Idman 17 14 44N10 112w14 7:28:56
Indian Cove 37 18 42N57 115w28 7:41:52
Indian Valley 2 18 44N34 116w26 7:45:44
Inkom 3 14 42N48 112w15 7:29:00
Iona 10 14 43N32 111w56 7:27:44
Irwin 10 14 43N24 111w18 7:25:12
Island Park 22 14 44N24 111w19 7:25:16
Jackson 16 18 42N37 113w40 7:34:40
Jacques 35 2 46N22 116w40 7:46:40
Jamestown 6 14 43N23 112w08 7:28:32
Jerome 27 18 42N44 114w31 7:38:04
Joel 29 5 46N44 117w00 7:48:00
Jonathan 44 18 44N15 116w58 7:47:52
Judge Town 18 2 46N30 115w48 7:43:12
Juliaetta 29 2 46N35 116w42 7:46:48
Juniper 36 18 41N58 112w43 7:30:52
Kamiah 31 2 46N14 116w02 7:44:08
Kellogg 40 9 47N31 116w12 7:44:48
Kendrick 29 2 46N37 116w39 7:46:36
Ketchum 7 18 43N41 114w22 7:37:28
Keuterville 25 2 46N02 116w26 7:45:44
Kidder 25 2 46N09 115w59 7:43:56
Kilgore 17 14 44N24 111w54 7:27:36
Kimball 6 14 43N18 112w12 7:28:48
Kimberly 42 18 42N32 114w22 7:37:28
King Hill 20 18 43N00 115w12 7:40:48
Kingston 40 3 47N33 116w16 7:45:04
Knowlton Heights 14
18 43N40 116w41 7:46:44
Kooskia 25 2 46N09 115w59 7:43:56
Kootenai 9 2 48N19 116w31 7:46:04
Kuna 1 18 43N30 116w25 7:45:40
Labelle 26 14 43N40 111w55 7:27:40
Laclede 9 2 48N12 116w45 7:47:00
Lake Creek 28 2 47N27 117w08 7:48:32
Lake Fork 43 18 44N50 116w05 7:44:20
Lakeview 9 2 47N58 116w27 7:45:48
Lamont 22 14 43N58 111w13 7:24:52
Lanark 4 14 42N17 111w24 7:25:36
Lane 28 2 47N33 116w20 7:45:20
Lapwai 35 2 46N24 116w48 7:47:12
Lardo 43 18 44N55 116w08 7:44:32
Last Chance Resort 22
14 44N31 111w20 7:25:20
Lava Hot Springs 3
13 42N37 112w01 7:28:04
Leadore 30 16 44N41 113w21 7:33:24
Leland 35 2 46N37 116w39 7:46:36
Lemhi 30 16 44N52 113w38 7:34:32
Lenore 35 2 46N31 116w33 7:46:12
Leslie 19 16 43N52 113w28 7:33:52
Letha 23 18 43N54 116w39 7:46:36
Lewiston 35 12 46N25 117w01 7:48:04
Lewiston Orchards 35
12 46N23 116w58 7:47:52
Lewisville 26 14 43N42 112w01 7:28:04
Liberty 4 14 42N17 111w24 7:25:36
Lidy Hot Springs 17
14 44N10 112w14 7:28:56
Lincoln 10 14 43N31 111w58 7:27:52
Linrose 21 14 42N02 111w59 7:27:56
Lone Pine 17 16 44N41 113w21 7:33:24
Lone Star 32 18 42N56 114w24 7:37:36
Lookout 35 2 46N31 116w33 7:46:12
Lorenzo 26 14 43N44 111w52 7:27:28
Lowell 25 2 46N09 115w59 7:43:56
Lower Stanley 19
18 44N13 114w56 7:39:44
Lowman 8 18 44N05 115w37 7:42:28
Lucile 25 2 45N32 116w18 7:45:12
Lund 15 14 42N39 111w53 7:27:32
Lyman 33 14 43N49 111w47 7:27:08
Mackay 19 16 43N55 113w37 7:34:28
Mackey Bar 25 18 44N55 116w06 7:44:24
Macks Inn 22 14 44N31 111w20 7:25:20
Magic City 7 18 43N31 114w19 7:37:16
Magic Resort 7 18 42N56 114w24 7:37:36
Malad 36 17 42N12 112w19 7:29:16
Malad City 36 18 42N12 112w15 7:29:00
Malta 16 18 42N18 113w22 7:33:28
Mapleton 21 14 42N11 111w57 7:27:48
Marion 16 18 42N15 113w53 7:35:32
Marsing 37 18 43N32 116w51 7:47:24
Marysville 22 14 44N04 111w22 7:25:28
May 30 16 44N36 113w55 7:35:40
Mayfield 20 18 43N08 115w42 7:42:48
McArthur 11 2 48N34 116w24 7:45:36
McCall 43 17 44N55 116w06 7:44:24
McCammon 3 13 42N39 112w12 7:28:48
McGuires 28 2 47N44 117w00 7:48:00
Meadow Creek 11 2 48N41 116w19 7:45:16
Meadows 2 18 44N58 116w15 7:45:00
Medimont 28 2 47N29 116w36 7:46:24
Melba 14 18 43N23 116w32 7:46:08
Menan 26 14 43N43 111w59 7:27:56
Meridian 1 18 43N37 116w24 7:45:36
Mesa 2 18 44N38 116w27 7:45:48
Midas 9 2 48N16 116w33 7:46:12
Middleton 14 18 43N42 116w37 7:46:28
Midvale 44 18 44N28 116w44 7:46:56
Minidoka 34 17 42N45 113w29 7:33:56
Mink Creek 21 14 42N14 111w43 7:26:52
Mohler 31 2 46N14 116w28 7:45:52
Montana Junction 3
14 42N54 112w27 7:29:48
Monteview 26 16 43N56 112w32 7:30:08

Montour 23 18 43N55 116w20 7:45:20
Montpelier 4 13 42N19 111w18 7:25:12
Moody Creek 33 14 43N47 111w28 7:25:52
Moore 12 16 43N44 113w22 7:33:28
Mora 1 18 43N29 116w25 7:45:40
Moravia 11 2 48N34 116w24 7:45:36
Moreland 6 16 43N12 112w27 7:29:48
Moscow 29 1 46N44 117w00 7:48:00
Mountain Home 20
18 43N08 115w41 7:42:44
Mountain Home Air Force Base 20
18 43N03 115w52 7:43:28
Mountain View 1 18 43N37 116w15 7:45:00
Mount Idaho 25 2 45N55 116w07 7:44:28
Moyie Springs 11 2 48N44 116w11 7:44:44
Mud Lake 26 16 43N51 112w29 7:29:56
Muldoon 7 18 43N18 113w57 7:35:48
Mullan 40 10 47N28 115w48 7:43:12
Murphy 37 18 43N13 116w33 7:46:12
Murray 40 3 47N38 115w36 7:42:24
Murtaugh 42 18 42N30 114w10 7:36:40
Myrtle 35 2 46N35 116w42 7:46:48
Naf 16 18 42N01 113w17 7:33:08
Nampa 14 18 43N34 116w34 7:46:16
Naples 11 2 48N34 116w24 7:45:36
Neeley 39 18 42N47 112w51 7:31:24
New Centerville 8
18 43N50 115w50 7:43:20
Newdale 22 14 43N53 111w36 7:26:24
New Meadows 2 17 44N58 116w18 7:45:12
New Plymouth 38 18 43N58 116w49 7:47:16
New Sweden 10 14 43N29 112w00 7:28:00
Nezperce 31 4 46N14 116w14 7:44:56
Nez Perce Indian Reservation 18
2 46N24 116w48 7:47:12
Niter 3 14 42N35 111w44 7:26:56
Nordman 9 2 48N38 116w57 7:47:48
North Fork 30 16 45N24 114w00 7:36:00
North Lewiston 35
12 46N24 116w59 7:47:56
Notus 14 18 43N43 116w48 7:47:12
Nounan 4 14 42N19 111w18 7:25:12
Oakley 16 17 42N15 113w53 7:35:32
Ola 23 18 44N11 116w18 7:45:12
Oldtown 9 2 48N11 117w02 7:48:08
Onaway 29 2 46N56 116w53 7:47:32
Orchard 1 17 43N19 116w02 7:44:08
Oreana 37 18 43N03 116w24 7:45:36
Orofino 18 4 46N29 116w15 7:45:00
Orogrande 25 2 45N50 115w26 7:41:44
Osburn 40 4 47N30 116w00 7:44:00
Osgood 10 14 43N29 112w00 7:28:00
Ovid 4 14 42N18 111w24 7:25:36
Oxford 21 14 42N16 112w01 7:28:04
Page 40 3 47N33 116w10 7:44:40
Palisades 10 14 43N21 111w13 7:24:52
Paradise Hot Springs 20
18 43N08 115w42 7:42:48
Paris 4 14 42N14 111w24 7:25:36
Park 29 2 46N48 116w33 7:46:12
Parker 22 14 43N58 111w46 7:27:04
Parma 14 18 43N47 116w57 7:47:48
Patterson 30 16 44N32 113w43 7:34:52
Paul 34 18 42N36 113w47 7:35:08
Payette 38 17 44N05 116w56 7:47:44
Pearl 23 18 43N51 116w19 7:45:16
Peck 35 2 46N26 116w32 7:46:08
Pedee 5 2 47N21 116w50 7:47:20
Pegram 4 14 42N19 111w18 7:25:12
Pella 16 18 42N33 113w48 7:35:12
Peterson 18 16 43N14 112w23 7:29:32
Picabo 7 18 43N18 114w04 7:36:16
Pierce 18 2 46N30 115w48 7:43:12
Pine 20 18 43N08 115w42 7:42:48
Pinehurst 2 18 44N58 116w17 7:45:08
Pinehurst 40 2 47N32 116w14 7:44:56
Pine Ridge 2 18 44N44 116w26 7:45:44
Pingree 6 16 43N07 112w36 7:30:24
Pioneerville 8 18 43N50 115w50 7:43:20
Placerville 8 18 43N57 115w57 7:43:48
Plano 33 14 43N49 111w47 7:27:08
Pleasantview 36 18 42N11 112w14 7:28:56
Plummer 5 4 47N20 116w53 7:47:32
Pocatello 3 13 42N52 112w27 7:29:48
Polaris 40 2 47N30 116w00 7:44:00
Pollock 25 18 45N19 116w21 7:45:24
Ponderay 9 2 48N18 116w31 7:46:04
Ponds Resort 22 14 44N31 111w20 7:25:20
Porthill 11 2 49N00 116w30 7:46:00
Post Falls 28 5 47N43 116w57 7:47:48
Potlatch 29 2 46N55 116w54 7:47:36
Potlatch Junction 29
2 46N56 116w54 7:47:36
Prairie 20 18 43N08 115w42 7:42:48
Preston 21 13 42N06 111w53 7:27:32
Prichard 40 3 47N28 115w55 7:43:40
Priest River 9 2 48N26 116w54 7:47:36
Princeton 29 2 46N55 116w50 7:47:20
Raft River 16 18 42N47 112w51 7:31:24
Ramsdell 5 2 47N21 116w50 7:47:20
Rathdrum 28 2 47N49 116w54 7:47:36
Redfish Lake 19 18 44N13 114w56 7:39:44
Red River Hot Springs 25
2 45N50 115w26 7:41:44
Reno 17 14 44N10 112w14 7:28:56
Reubens 31 2 46N20 116w33 7:46:12
Rexburg 33 14 43N49 111w47 7:27:08
Reynolds 37 18 43N13 116w33 7:46:12
Richfield 32 18 43N03 114w09 7:36:36
Riddle 37 18 42N11 116w07 7:44:28
Rigby 26 14 43N40 111w55 7:27:40
Riggins 25 18 45N25 116w19 7:45:16
Ririe 26 14 43N38 111w47 7:27:08
Riverdale 5 2 47N19 116w34 7:46:16
Riverdale 21 14 42N11 111w57 7:27:48
Riverside 6 14 43N11 112w21 7:29:24

IDAHO

Riverside 14 18 43N40 116w41 7:46:44
Riverside 18 2 46N29 116w15 7:45:00
Roberts 26 14 43N43 112w08 7:28:32
Robin 3 14 42N34 112w10 7:28:40
Rockaway Beach 28
1 47N46 116w46 7:47:04
Rock Creek 42 18 42N32 114w18 7:37:12
Rockford 6 14 43N11 112w21 7:29:24
Rockford Bay 28 1 47N42 116w47 7:47:08
Rockland 39 18 42N34 112w53 7:31:32
Rocky Bar 20 18 43N08 115w42 7:42:48
Rocky Point 5 2 47N21 116w50 7:47:20
Rogerson 42 18 42N13 114w36 7:38:24
Rose 6 14 43N11 112w21 7:29:24
Roseberry 43 18 44N44 116w05 7:44:20
Rose Lake 28 2 47N33 116w20 7:45:20
Roseworth 42 18 42N31 114w52 7:39:28
Roswell 14 18 43N47 116w57 7:47:48
Roy 39 18 42N34 112w52 7:31:28
Rupert 34 18 42N37 113w41 7:34:44
Sagle 9 2 48N12 116w33 7:46:12
Saint Anthony 22
13 43N58 111w41 7:26:44
Saint Charles 4 14 42N07 111w23 7:25:32
Saint Joe 5 2 47N19 116w21 7:45:24
Saint John 36 18 42N11 112w14 7:28:56
Saint Leon 10 14 43N29 112w00 7:28:00
Saint Maries 5 2 47N19 116w35 7:46:20
Salem 33 14 43N49 111w47 7:27:08
Salmon 30 16 45N11 113w54 7:35:36
Samaria 36 18 42N07 112w20 7:29:20
Samuels 9 2 48N25 116w29 7:45:56
Sanders 5 2 47N10 116w55 7:47:40
Sandpoint 9 7 48N17 116w33 7:46:12
Santa 5 2 47N09 116w27 7:45:48
Selle 9 2 48N16 116w33 7:46:12
Sharon 4 14 42N21 111w29 7:25:56
Shelley 6 14 43N23 112w07 7:28:28
Shelton 26 14 43N29 112w00 7:28:00
Shoshone 32 18 42N56 114w25 7:37:40
Shoup 30 18 45N23 114w17 7:37:08
Silver City 37 18 43N13 116w33 7:46:12
Silver Creek Plunge 43
18 44N07 115w58 7:43:52
Silver Sands Beach 28
2 47N49 116w54 7:47:36
Silverton 40 2 47N30 115w57 7:43:48
Skyline 10 14 43N29 112w00 7:28:00
Slate Creek 25 2 45N46 116w18 7:45:12
Small 17 14 44N10 112w14 7:28:56
Smelter Heights 40
2 47N32 116w08 7:44:32
Smelterville 40 2 47N33 116w10 7:44:40
Smiths Ferry 43 18 44N18 116w05 7:44:20
South Gate Plaza 35
12 46N24 116w59 7:47:56
Southside 1 18 43N36 116w12 7:44:48
Southwick 35 2 46N36 116w28 7:45:52
Spalding 35 2 46N27 116w49 7:47:16
Spencer 17 14 44N22 112w11 7:28:44
Spirit Lake 28 2 47N58 116w52 7:47:28
Springdale 16 18 42N33 113w48 7:35:12
Springfield 6 16 43N05 112w41 7:30:44
Squaw Bay 28 2 47N27 116w47 7:47:08
Squirrel 22 14 44N02 111w18 7:25:12
Standrod 16 18 42N01 113w17 7:33:08
Stanley 19 18 44N13 114w56 7:39:44
Star 1 18 43N42 116w30 7:46:00
Starrhs Ferry 16
18 42N33 113w48 7:35:12
State Line 28 2 47N42 117w02 7:48:08
Steirman 8 18 43N50 115w50 7:43:20
Sterling 6 16 43N02 112w44 7:30:56
Stibnite 43 18 44N50 115w07 7:40:28
Stites 25 4 46N06 115w59 7:43:56
Stoddard 14 17 43N23 116w32 7:46:08
Stone 36 18 42N01 112w42 7:30:48
Strevell 16 18 42N01 113w17 7:33:08
Sublett 16 18 42N19 113w22 7:33:28
Suckpoo 31 2 46N22 116w40 7:46:40
Sugar City 33 14 43N52 111w45 7:27:00
Sunbeam 19 18 44N13 114w56 7:39:44
Sunnydell 33 14 43N49 111w47 7:27:08
Sunnyside 9 2 48N16 116w33 7:46:12
Sunnyside 40 2 47N32 116w08 7:44:32
Sunnyslope 14 18 43N40 116w41 7:46:44
Sun Valley 7 18 43N42 114w21 7:37:24
Swanlake 3 14 42N19 112w00 7:28:00
Swan Valley 10 14 43N27 111w20 7:25:20
Sweet 23 18 43N58 116w20 7:45:20
Sweetwater 35 2 46N24 116w48 7:47:12
Syringa 25 2 46N09 115w59 7:43:56
Taber 6 14 43N11 112w21 7:29:24
Talache 9 2 48N12 116w33 7:46:12
Tamarack 2 18 44N44 116w26 7:45:44
Taylor 10 14 43N29 112w00 7:28:00
Teakean 18 2 46N30 116w20 7:45:20
Tendoy 30 16 44N57 113w38 7:34:32
Ten Mile 1 14 43N18 112w09 7:28:36
Tensed 5 2 47N10 116w55 7:47:40
Terreton 26 16 43N51 112w26 7:29:44
Teton 22 14 43N53 111w40 7:26:40
Tetonia 41 14 43N49 111w10 7:24:40
Thain Road 35 12 46N24 116w59 7:47:56
Thatcher 21 14 42N25 111w44 7:26:56
Thomas 6 14 43N11 112w21 7:29:24
Thomas Junction 6
14 43N11 112w21 7:29:24
Thornton 33 14 43N45 111w51 7:27:24
Three Creek 37 18 42N28 114w31 7:38:04
Threemile Corner 11
2 48N41 116w19 7:45:16
Topaz 3 14 42N37 112w01 7:28:04
Torrey 19 18 44N16 114w24 7:37:36
Transfer 35 12 46N24 116w59 7:47:56
Treasureton 21 14 42N11 111w57 7:27:48

IDAHO

Place		Lat	Long	Time
Trestle Creek 9	2	48N15	116w18	7:45:12
Triumph 7	18	43N31	114w19	7:37:16
Troy 29	5	46N44	116w46	7:47:04
Turner 15	14	42N35	111w49	7:27:16
Turner Bay 28	2	47N27	116w47	7:47:08
Tuttle 24	18	42N52	114w51	7:39:24
Twin Falls 42	18	42N34	114w28	7:37:52
Twin Groves 22	14	43N58	111w41	7:26:44
Twin Lakes 28	2	47N49	116w54	7:47:36
Twinlow 28	2	47N49	116w54	7:47:36
Tyhee 3	14	42N57	112w28	7:29:52
Ucon 10	14	43N36	111w58	7:27:52
Unity 16	18	42N33	113w48	7:35:12
University 29	5	46N44	117w00	7:48:00
Ustick 1	18	43N38	116w13	7:44:52
Valley View Heights 35	12	46N24	116w59	7:47:56
Victor 41	13	43N36	111w07	7:24:28
View 16	18	42N33	113w48	7:35:12
Viola 29	5	46N50	117w01	7:48:04
Virginia 3	14	42N30	112w10	7:28:40
Waha 35	12	46N24	116w59	7:47:56
Wallace 40	11	47N28	115w56	7:43:44
Wapello 6	14	43N11	112w21	7:29:24
Wardboro 4	14	42N19	111w18	7:25:12
Wardner 40	3	47N31	116w08	7:44:32
Warm Lake 43	18	44N31	116w03	7:44:12
Warm River 22	14	44N07	111w19	7:25:16
Warren 25	18	45N16	115w41	7:42:44
Wayan 15	14	42N58	111w23	7:25:32
Webb 35	2	46N24	116w48	7:47:12
Weippe 18	2	46N23	115w56	7:43:44
Weiser 44	17	44N45	116w58	7:47:52
Weitz 14	18	43N40	116w41	7:46:44
Wendell 24	18	42N47	114w42	7:38:48
West Camas 13	18	43N19	115w01	7:40:04
West Clark 17	16	44N17	112w34	7:30:16
Western Shoshone 37	18	42N05	116w11	7:44:44
Westlake 25	2	46N09	116w24	7:45:36
Westmond 9	2	48N12	116w33	7:46:12
West Mountain 43	18	44N31	116w03	7:44:12
Weston 21	14	42N02	111w59	7:27:56
West Salmon Falls 42	18	42N33	114w57	7:39:48
White Bird 25	2	45N46	116w18	7:45:12
Whitney 1	18	43N35	116w15	7:45:00
Whitney 21	14	42N04	111w50	7:27:20
Wilder 14	17	43N41	116w55	7:47:40
Wilford 22	14	43N58	111w41	7:26:44
Willow 38	18	44N06	116w44	7:46:56
Winchester 31	4	46N14	116w38	7:46:32
Woodland 25	2	46N13	116w02	7:44:08
Woodland Park 40	2	47N28	115w55	7:43:40
Woodruff 36	18	42N11	112w14	7:28:56
Woodville 6	14	43N23	112w08	7:28:32
Worley 28	2	47N24	116w55	7:47:40
Yellow Pine 43	18	44N58	115w30	7:42:00

ILLINOIS

TIME TABLES

State law required all birth times to be recorded in CST until July 1, 1959, except during World War II when CWT was recorded officially. But this law was not always observed, leading to considerable confusion about actual time of birth for summer births. In 1936 the greater Chicago area is shown as CDT instead of the official EST. However, these are equivalent in their effect. Small towns are assumed to follow nearby larger towns, which may not always be correct.

IL # 1

Before 11/18/1883 LMT
11/18/1883 12:00 CST
3/31/1918 02:00 CWT
10/27/1918 02:00 CST
3/30/1919 02:00 CWT
10/26/1919 02:00 CST
6/13/1920 02:00 CDT
10/31/1920 02:00 CST
3/27/1921 02:00 CDT
10/30/1921 02:00 CST
4/30/1922 02:00 CDT
9/24/1922 02:00 CST
4/29/1923 02:00 CDT
9/30/1923 02:00 CST
4/27/1924 02:00 CDT
9/28/1924 02:00 CST
4/26/1925 02:00 CDT
9/27/1925 02:00 CST
4/25/1926 02:00 CDT
9/26/1926 02:00 CST
4/24/1927 02:00 CDT
9/25/1927 02:00 CST
4/29/1928 02:00 CDT
9/30/1928 02:00 CST
4/28/1929 02:00 CDT
9/29/1929 02:00 CST
4/27/1930 02:00 CDT
9/28/1930 02:00 CST
4/26/1931 02:00 CDT
9/27/1931 02:00 CST
4/24/1932 02:00 CDT
9/25/1932 02:00 CST
4/30/1933 02:00 CDT
9/24/1933 02:00 CST
4/29/1934 02:00 CDT
9/30/1934 02:00 CST
4/28/1935 02:00 CDT
9/29/1935 02:00 CST
3/01/1936 02:00 CDT
11/15/1936 02:00 CST
4/25/1937 02:00 US#2

IL # 2

Before 11/18/1883 LMT
11/18/1883 12:00 CST
3/31/1918 02:00 CWT
10/27/1918 02:00 CST
3/30/1919 02:00 CWT
10/26/1919 02:00 CST
6/13/1920 02:00 CDT
10/31/1920 02:00 CST
3/27/1921 02:00 CDT
10/30/1921 02:00 CST
4/30/1922 02:00 CDT
9/24/1922 02:00 CST
4/29/1923 02:00 CDT
9/30/1923 02:00 CST
4/27/1924 02:00 CDT
9/28/1924 02:00 CST
4/26/1925 02:00 CDT
9/27/1925 02:00 CST
4/25/1926 02:00 CDT
9/26/1926 02:00 CST
4/24/1927 02:00 CDT
9/25/1927 02:00 CST
4/29/1928 02:00 CDT
9/30/1928 02:00 CST
4/28/1929 02:00 CDT
9/29/1929 02:00 CST
4/27/1930 02:00 CDT
9/28/1930 02:00 CST
4/26/1931 02:00 CDT
9/27/1931 02:00 CST
4/24/1932 02:00 CDT
9/25/1932 02:00 CST
4/30/1933 02:00 CDT
9/24/1933 02:00 CST
4/29/1934 02:00 CDT
9/30/1934 02:00 CST
4/28/1935 02:00 CDT
9/29/1935 02:00 CST
3/01/1936 02:00 CDT
11/15/1936 02:00 CST
4/25/1937 02:00 CDT
9/26/1937 02:00 CST
4/24/1938 02:00 CDT
9/25/1938 02:00 CST
4/30/1939 02:00 CDT
9/24/1939 02:00 CST
4/28/1940 02:00 CDT
9/29/1940 02:00 CST
4/27/1941 02:00 CDT
9/28/1941 02:00 CST
2/09/1942 02:00 CWT
9/30/1945 02:00 CST
4/28/1946 02:00 CDT
9/29/1946 02:00 CST
4/27/1947 02:00 CDT
9/28/1947 02:00 CST
4/25/1948 02:00 CDT
9/26/1948 02:00 CST
4/24/1949 02:00 CDT
9/25/1949 02:00 CST
4/30/1950 02:00 CDT
9/24/1950 02:00 CST
4/29/1951 02:00 CDT
9/30/1951 02:00 CST
4/27/1952 02:00 CDT
9/28/1952 02:00 CST
4/26/1953 02:00 CDT
9/27/1953 02:00 CST
4/25/1954 02:00 CDT
9/26/1954 02:00 CST
4/24/1955 02:00 CDT
9/25/1955 02:00 CST
4/29/1956 02:00 US#2

IL # 3

Before 11/18/1883 LMT
11/18/1883 12:00 CST
3/31/1918 02:00 CWT
10/27/1918 02:00 CST
3/30/1919 02:00 CWT
10/26/1919 02:00 CST
6/13/1920 02:00 CDT
10/31/1920 02:00 CST
3/27/1921 02:00 CDT
10/30/1921 02:00 CST
4/30/1922 02:00 CDT
9/24/1922 02:00 CST
4/29/1923 02:00 CDT
9/30/1923 02:00 CST
4/27/1924 02:00 CDT
9/28/1924 02:00 CST
4/26/1925 02:00 CDT
9/27/1925 02:00 CST
4/25/1926 02:00 CDT
9/26/1926 02:00 CST
4/24/1927 02:00 CDT
9/25/1927 02:00 CST
4/29/1928 02:00 CDT
9/30/1928 02:00 CST
4/28/1929 02:00 CDT
9/29/1929 02:00 CST
4/27/1930 02:00 CDT
9/28/1930 02:00 CST
4/26/1931 02:00 CDT
9/27/1931 02:00 CST
4/24/1932 02:00 CDT
9/25/1932 02:00 CST
4/30/1933 02:00 CDT
9/24/1933 02:00 CST
4/29/1934 02:00 CDT
9/30/1934 02:00 CST
4/28/1935 02:00 CDT
9/29/1935 02:00 CST
3/01/1936 02:00 CDT
11/15/1936 02:00 CST
4/25/1937 02:00 CDT
9/26/1937 02:00 CST
4/24/1938 02:00 CDT
9/25/1938 02:00 CST
4/30/1939 02:00 CDT
9/24/1939 02:00 CST
4/28/1940 02:00 CDT
9/29/1940 02:00 CST
4/27/1941 02:00 CDT
9/28/1941 02:00 CST
2/09/1942 02:00 CWT
9/30/1945 02:00 CST
4/28/1946 02:00 CDT
9/29/1946 02:00 CST
4/27/1947 02:00 CDT
9/28/1947 02:00 CST
4/25/1948 02:00 CDT
9/26/1948 02:00 CST
4/24/1949 02:00 CDT
9/25/1949 02:00 CST
4/30/1950 02:00 CDT
9/24/1950 02:00 CST
4/29/1951 02:00 CDT
9/30/1951 02:00 CST
4/27/1952 02:00 CDT
9/28/1952 02:00 CST
4/26/1953 02:00 CDT
9/27/1953 02:00 CST
4/25/1954 02:00 CDT
9/26/1954 02:00 CST
4/24/1955 02:00 CDT
9/25/1955 02:00 CST
4/29/1956 02:00 CDT
9/30/1956 02:00 CST
4/28/1957 02:00 CDT
9/29/1957 02:00 CST
4/27/1958 02:00 CDT
9/28/1958 02:00 CST
4/26/1959 02:00 US#2

IL # 4

Before 11/18/1883 LMT
11/18/1883 12:00 CST
3/31/1918 02:00 CWT
10/27/1918 02:00 CST
3/30/1919 02:00 CWT
10/26/1919 02:00 CST
2/09/1942 02:00 CWT
9/30/1945 02:00 CST
7/01/1959 02:00 US#2

IL # 5

Before 11/18/1883 LMT
11/18/1883 12:00 CST
3/31/1918 02:00 CWT
10/27/1918 02:00 CST
3/30/1919 02:00 CWT
10/26/1919 02:00 CST
2/09/1942 02:00 CWT
9/30/1945 02:00 CST
4/27/1947 02:00 US#2

IL # 6

Before 11/18/1883 LMT
11/18/1883 12:00 CST
3/31/1918 02:00 CWT
10/27/1918 02:00 CST
3/30/1919 02:00 CWT
10/26/1919 02:00 CST
2/09/1942 02:00 CWT
9/30/1945 02:00 CST
4/28/1946 02:00 US#2

IL # 7

Before 11/18/1883 LMT
11/18/1883 12:00 CST
3/31/1918 02:00 CWT
10/27/1918 02:00 CST
3/30/1919 02:00 CWT
10/26/1919 02:00 CST
2/09/1942 02:00 CWT
9/30/1945 02:00 CST
4/28/1946 02:00 CDT
9/29/1946 02:00 CST
4/27/1947 02:00 CDT
9/28/1947 02:00 CST
4/25/1948 02:00 CDT
9/26/1948 02:00 CST
4/24/1949 02:00 CDT
9/25/1949 02:00 CST
4/30/1950 02:00 CDT
9/24/1950 02:00 CST
4/29/1951 02:00 CDT
9/30/1951 02:00 CST
4/27/1952 02:00 CDT
9/28/1952 02:00 CST
4/26/1953 02:00 CDT
9/27/1953 02:00 CST
4/25/1954 02:00 CDT
9/26/1954 02:00 CST
4/24/1955 02:00 CDT
9/25/1955 02:00 CST
4/29/1956 02:00 CDT
9/30/1956 02:00 CST
4/28/1957 02:00 CDT
9/29/1957 02:00 CST
4/27/1958 02:00 CDT
9/28/1958 02:00 CST
4/26/1959 02:00 US#2

IL # 8

Before 11/18/1883 LMT
11/18/1883 12:00 CST
3/31/1918 02:00 CWT
10/27/1918 02:00 CST
3/30/1919 02:00 CWT
10/26/1919 02:00 CST
2/09/1942 02:00 CWT
9/30/1945 02:00 CST
4/27/1952 02:00 CDT
9/28/1952 02:00 CST
4/26/1953 02:00 CDT
9/27/1953 02:00 CST
4/25/1954 02:00 CDT
9/26/1954 02:00 CST
4/24/1955 02:00 CDT
9/25/1955 02:00 CST
4/29/1956 02:00 CDT
9/30/1956 02:00 CST
4/28/1957 02:00 CDT
9/29/1957 02:00 CST
4/27/1958 02:00 CDT
9/28/1958 02:00 CST
4/26/1959 02:00 US#2

IL # 9

Before 11/18/1883 LMT
11/18/1883 12:00 IL#1
9/29/1935 02:00 CST
4/26/1936 02:00 CDT
9/27/1936 02:00 CST
4/25/1937 02:00 IL#2
4/29/1956 02:00 US#2

IL # 10

Before 11/18/1883 LMT
11/18/1883 12:00 IL#1
10/31/1920 02:00 CST
4/30/1933 02:00 IL#2
4/29/1956 02:00 US#2

IL # 11

Before 11/18/1883 LMT
11/18/1883 12:00 IL#1
9/27/1931 02:00 CST
4/24/1938 02:00 CDT
9/25/1938 02:00 CST
4/30/1939 02:00 CDT
9/24/1939 02:00 CST
4/28/1940 02:00 CDT
9/29/1940 02:00 CST
4/27/1941 02:00 CDT
9/28/1941 02:00 IL#2
4/29/1956 02:00 US#2

IL # 12

Before 11/18/1883 LMT
11/18/1883 12:00 CST
3/31/1918 02:00 CWT
10/27/1918 02:00 CST
3/30/1919 02:00 CWT
10/26/1919 02:00 CST
4/26/1931 02:00 IL#1
9/28/1941 02:00 US#2

IL # 13

Before 11/18/1883 LMT
11/18/1883 12:00 CST
3/31/1918 02:00 CWT
10/27/1918 02:00 CST
3/30/1919 02:00 CWT
10/26/1919 02:00 CST
4/24/1938 02:00 CDT
9/25/1938 02:00 IL#4
7/01/1959 02:00 US#2

IL # 14

Before 11/18/1883 LMT
11/18/1883 12:00 CST
3/31/1918 02:00 CWT
10/27/1918 02:00 CST
3/30/1919 02:00 CWT
10/26/1919 02:00 CST
4/26/1931 02:00 CDT
9/27/1931 02:00 CST
4/24/1932 02:00 CDT
9/25/1932 02:00 CST
4/30/1933 02:00 CDT
9/24/1933 02:00 CST
4/29/1934 02:00 CDT
9/30/1934 02:00 CST
4/28/1935 02:00 CDT
9/29/1935 02:00 CST
3/01/1936 02:00 CDT
11/15/1936 02:00 CST
4/25/1937 02:00 CDT
9/26/1937 02:00 CST
4/24/1938 02:00 CDT
9/25/1938 02:00 IL#3
4/26/1959 02:00 US#2

IL # 15

Before 11/18/1883 LMT
11/18/1883 12:00 CST
3/31/1918 02:00 CWT
10/27/1918 02:00 CST
3/30/1919 02:00 CWT
10/26/1919 02:00 CST
4/24/1938 02:00 CDT
9/25/1938 02:00 CST
4/30/1939 02:00 CDT
9/24/1939 02:00 CST
4/28/1940 02:00 CDT
9/29/1940 02:00 CST
4/27/1941 02:00 CDT
9/28/1941 02:00 IL#2
4/29/1956 02:00 US#2

IL # 16

Before 11/18/1883 LMT
11/18/1883 12:00 CST
3/31/1918 02:00 CWT
10/27/1918 02:00 CST
3/30/1919 02:00 CWT
10/26/1919 02:00 CST
4/26/1931 02:00 IL#3
4/26/1959 02:00 US#2

IL # 17

Before 11/18/1883 LMT
11/18/1883 12:00 IL#4
4/24/1932 02:00 CDT
9/25/1932 02:00 CST
4/30/1933 02:00 CDT
9/24/1933 02:00 CST
4/29/1934 02:00 CDT
9/30/1934 02:00 CST
4/28/1935 02:00 CDT
9/29/1935 02:00 CST
3/01/1936 02:00 CDT
11/15/1936 02:00 CST
4/25/1937 02:00 CDT
9/26/1937 02:00 CST
4/24/1938 02:00 CDT
9/25/1938 02:00 CST
4/30/1939 02:00 CDT
9/24/1939 02:00 CST
4/28/1940 02:00 CDT
9/29/1940 02:00 CST
4/27/1941 02:00 CDT
9/28/1941 02:00 IL#2
4/29/1956 02:00 US#2

IL # 18

Before 11/18/1883 LMT
11/18/1883 12:00 CST
3/31/1918 02:00 CWT
10/27/1918 02:00 CST
3/30/1919 02:00 CWT
10/26/1919 02:00 CST
4/24/1938 02:00 CDT
9/25/1938 02:00 CST
4/30/1939 02:00 CDT
9/24/1939 02:00 CST
4/28/1940 02:00 CDT
9/29/1940 02:00 CST
4/27/1941 02:00 CDT
9/28/1941 02:00 CST
2/09/1942 02:00 CWT
9/30/1945 02:00 CST
4/28/1946 02:00 IL#2
4/29/1956 02:00 US#2

IL # 19

Before 11/18/1883 LMT
11/18/1883 12:00 IL#4
4/26/1931 02:00 CDT
9/27/1931 02:00 CST
4/24/1932 02:00 CDT
9/25/1932 02:00 CST
4/30/1933 02:00 CDT
9/24/1933 02:00 CST
4/29/1934 02:00 CDT
9/30/1934 02:00 CST
4/28/1935 02:00 CDT
9/29/1935 02:00 CST
3/01/1936 02:00 CDT
11/15/1936 02:00 CST
4/25/1937 02:00 CDT
9/26/1937 02:00 CST
4/24/1938 02:00 CDT
9/25/1938 02:00 CST
4/30/1939 02:00 CDT
9/24/1939 02:00 CST
4/28/1940 02:00 CDT
9/29/1940 02:00 CST
4/27/1941 02:00 CDT
9/28/1941 02:00 IL#2
4/29/1956 02:00 US#2

IL # 20

Before 11/18/1883 LMT
11/18/1883 12:00 CST
3/31/1918 02:00 CWT
10/27/1918 02:00 CST
3/30/1919 02:00 CWT
10/26/1919 02:00 CST
5/05/1940 02:00 CDT
9/29/1940 02:00 CST
2/09/1942 02:00 CWT
9/30/1945 02:00 CST
4/28/1946 02:00 US#2

IL # 21

Before 11/18/1883 LMT
11/18/1883 12:00 CST
3/31/1918 02:00 CWT
10/27/1918 02:00 CST
3/30/1919 02:00 CWT
10/26/1919 02:00 CST
4/27/1941 02:00 CDT
9/28/1941 02:00 IL#2
4/29/1956 02:00 US#2

IL # 22

Before 11/18/1883 LMT
11/18/1883 12:00 CST
3/31/1918 02:00 CWT
10/27/1918 02:00 CST
3/30/1919 02:00 CWT
10/26/1919 02:00 CST
4/27/1941 02:00 US#2

IL # 23

Before 11/18/1883 LMT
11/18/1883 12:00 IL#6
9/29/1946 02:00 CST
7/01/1959 02:00 US#2

IL # 24

Before 11/18/1883 LMT

TIME TABLES

11/18/1883 12:00 IL#6
10/27/1957 02:00 CST
7/01/1959 02:00 US#2

IL # 25
Before 11/18/1883 LMT
11/18/1883 12:00 CST
3/31/1918 02:00 CWT
10/27/1918 02:00 CST
3/30/1919 02:00 CWT
10/26/1919 02:00 CST
2/09/1942 02:00 CWT
9/30/1945 02:00 CST
4/29/1946 02:00 US#4

IL # 26
Before 11/18/1883 LMT
11/18/1883 12:00 IL#6
4/28/1946 02:00 IL#2
4/29/1956 02:00 US#2

IL # 27
Before 11/18/1883 LMT
11/18/1883 12:00 IL#4
4/29/1934 02:00 IL#2
4/29/1956 02:00 US#2

IL # 28
Before 11/18/1883 LMT
11/18/1883 12:00 CST
3/31/1918 02:00 CWT
10/27/1918 02:00 CST
3/30/1919 02:00 CWT
10/26/1919 02:00 CST
2/09/1942 02:00 CWT
9/30/1945 02:00 CST
4/28/1946 02:00 CDT
9/29/1946 02:00 CST
4/27/1947 02:00 CDT
9/28/1947 02:00 CST
4/25/1948 02:00 CDT
9/26/1948 02:00 CST
4/24/1949 02:00 CDT
9/25/1949 02:00 CST
4/30/1950 02:00 CDT
9/24/1950 02:00 CST
4/29/1951 02:00 CDT
9/30/1951 02:00 CST
4/27/1952 02:00 CDT
9/28/1952 02:00 CST
4/26/1953 02:00 CDT
9/27/1953 02:00 CST
4/25/1954 02:00 CDT
9/26/1954 02:00 CST
4/24/1955 02:00 CDT
9/25/1955 02:00 CST
4/29/1956 02:00 CDT
10/28/1956 02:00 CST
4/28/1957 02:00 CDT
10/27/1957 02:00 CST
4/27/1958 02:00 CDT
9/28/1958 02:00 CST
4/26/1959 02:00 US#2

IL # 29
Before 11/18/1883 LMT
11/18/1883 12:00 IL#5
4/27/1947 02:00 IL#3
4/26/1959 02:00 US#2

IL # 30
Before 11/18/1883 LMT
11/18/1883 12:00 CST
3/31/1918 02:00 CWT
10/27/1918 02:00 CST
3/30/1919 02:00 CWT
10/26/1919 02:00 CST
2/09/1942 02:00 CWT
9/30/1945 02:00 CST
4/27/1947 02:00 IL#2
4/29/1956 02:00 US#2

IL # 31
Before 11/18/1883 LMT
11/18/1883 12:00 IL#5
4/24/1955 02:00 CDT
9/25/1955 02:00 CST
4/29/1956 02:00 CDT
10/28/1956 02:00 CST
4/28/1957 02:00 CDT
10/27/1957 02:00 CST
4/27/1958 02:00 CDT
9/28/1958 02:00 CST
4/26/1959 02:00 US#2

IL # 32
Before 11/18/1883 LMT
11/18/1883 12:00 IL#5
9/28/1947 02:00 CST
7/01/1959 02:00 US#2

IL # 33
Before 11/18/1883 LMT
11/18/1883 12:00 IL#5
9/26/1948 02:00 CST
7/01/1959 02:00 US#2

IL # 34
Before 11/18/1883 LMT
11/18/1883 12:00 IL#4
4/24/1932 02:00 IL#1
9/28/1941 02:00 US#2

IL # 35
Before 11/18/1883 LMT
11/18/1883 12:00 IL#5
4/24/1955 02:00 US#4

IL # 36
Before 11/18/1883 LMT
11/18/1883 12:00 CST
3/31/1918 02:00 CWT
10/27/1918 02:00 CST
3/30/1919 02:00 CWT
10/26/1919 02:00 CST
2/09/1942 02:00 CWT
9/30/1945 02:00 CST
4/25/1948 02:00 IL#2
4/29/1956 02:00 US#2

IL # 37
Before 11/18/1883 LMT
11/18/1883 12:00 CST
3/31/1918 02:00 CWT
10/27/1918 02:00 CST
3/30/1919 02:00 CWT
10/26/1919 02:00 CST
2/09/1942 02:00 CWT
9/30/1945 02:00 CST
4/25/1948 02:00 IL#3
4/26/1959 02:00 US#2

IL # 38
Before 11/18/1883 LMT
11/18/1883 12:00 CST
3/31/1918 02:00 CWT
10/27/1918 02:00 CST
3/30/1919 02:00 CWT
10/26/1919 02:00 CST
2/09/1942 02:00 CWT
9/30/1945 02:00 CST
4/30/1950 02:00 US#4

IL # 39
Before 11/18/1883 LMT
11/18/1883 12:00 CST
3/31/1918 02:00 CWT
10/27/1918 02:00 CST
3/30/1919 02:00 CWT
10/26/1919 02:00 CST
2/09/1942 02:00 CWT
9/30/1945 02:00 CST
4/30/1950 02:00 IL#3
4/26/1959 02:00 US#2

IL # 40
Before 11/18/1883 LMT
11/18/1883 12:00 CST
3/31/1918 02:00 CWT
10/27/1918 02:00 CST
3/30/1919 02:00 CWT
10/26/1919 02:00 CST
2/09/1942 02:00 CWT
9/30/1945 02:00 CST
4/30/1950 02:00 CDT
9/24/1950 02:00 CST
4/29/1951 02:00 CDT
9/30/1951 02:00 CST
4/27/1952 02:00 CDT
9/28/1952 02:00 CST
4/26/1953 02:00 CDT
9/27/1953 02:00 CST
4/25/1954 02:00 CDT
9/26/1954 02:00 CST
4/24/1955 02:00 CDT
9/25/1955 02:00 CST
4/29/1956 02:00 CDT
10/28/1956 02:00 CST
4/28/1957 02:00 CDT
4/29/1957 02:00 IL#3
4/26/1959 02:00 US#2

IL # 41
Before 11/18/1883 LMT
11/18/1883 12:00 CST
3/31/1918 02:00 CWT
10/27/1918 02:00 CST
3/30/1919 02:00 CWT
10/26/1919 02:00 CST
2/09/1942 02:00 CWT
9/30/1945 02:00 CST
4/29/1951 02:00 IL#3
4/26/1959 02:00 US#2

IL # 42
Before 11/18/1883 LMT
11/18/1883 12:00 IL#4
4/29/1934 02:00 IL#1
9/28/1941 02:00 US#2

IL # 43
Before 11/18/1883 LMT
11/18/1883 12:00 CST
3/31/1918 02:00 CWT
10/27/1918 02:00 CST
3/30/1919 02:00 CWT
10/26/1919 02:00 CST
2/09/1942 02:00 CWT
9/30/1945 02:00 CST
4/29/1951 02:00 IL#2
4/29/1956 02:00 US#2

IL # 44
Before 11/18/1883 LMT
11/18/1883 12:00 CST
3/31/1918 02:00 CWT
10/27/1918 02:00 CST
3/30/1919 02:00 CWT
10/26/1919 02:00 CST
2/09/1942 02:00 CWT
9/30/1945 02:00 CST
4/29/1951 02:00 US#4

IL # 45
Before 11/18/1883 LMT
11/18/1883 12:00 IL#8
9/26/1954 02:00 CST
7/01/1959 02:00 US#2

IL # 46
Before 11/18/1883 LMT
11/18/1883 12:00 CST
3/31/1918 02:00 CWT
10/27/1918 02:00 CST
3/30/1919 02:00 CWT
10/26/1919 02:00 CST
2/09/1942 02:00 CWT
9/30/1945 02:00 CST
4/27/1952 02:00 US#4

IL # 47
Before 11/18/1883 LMT
11/18/1883 12:00 IL#8
8/28/1955 02:00 CST
4/29/1956 02:00 IL#3
4/26/1959 02:00 US#2

IL # 48
Before 11/18/1883 LMT
11/18/1883 12:00 CST
3/31/1918 02:00 CWT
10/27/1918 02:00 CST
3/30/1919 02:00 CWT
10/26/1919 02:00 CST
2/09/1942 02:00 CWT
9/30/1945 02:00 CST
4/27/1952 02:00 US#3

IL # 49
Before 11/18/1883 LMT
11/18/1883 12:00 CST
3/31/1918 02:00 CWT
10/27/1918 02:00 CST
3/30/1919 02:00 CWT
10/26/1919 02:00 CST
2/09/1942 02:00 CWT
9/30/1945 02:00 CST
4/26/1953 02:00 CDT
9/27/1953 02:00 CST
4/25/1954 02:00 CDT
9/26/1954 02:00 CST
4/24/1955 02:00 CDT
9/25/1955 02:00 CST
4/29/1956 02:00 CDT
9/30/1956 02:00 CST
4/28/1957 02:00 CDT
9/29/1957 02:00 CST
7/01/1959 02:00 US#2

IL # 50
Before 11/18/1883 LMT
11/18/1883 12:00 CST
3/31/1918 02:00 CWT
10/27/1918 02:00 CST
3/30/1919 02:00 CWT
10/26/1919 02:00 CST
2/09/1942 02:00 CWT
9/30/1945 02:00 CST
4/26/1953 02:00 IL#3
4/26/1959 02:00 US#2

IL # 51
Before 11/18/1883 LMT
11/18/1883 12:00 CST
3/31/1918 02:00 CWT
10/27/1918 02:00 CST
3/30/1919 02:00 CWT
10/26/1919 02:00 CST
2/09/1942 02:00 CWT
9/30/1945 02:00 CST
4/25/1954 02:00 US#2

IL # 52
Before 11/18/1883 LMT
11/18/1883 12:00 CST
3/31/1918 02:00 CWT
10/27/1918 02:00 CST
3/30/1919 02:00 CWT
10/26/1919 02:00 CST
2/09/1942 02:00 CWT
9/30/1945 02:00 CST
4/25/1954 02:00 CDT
9/26/1954 02:00 CST
7/01/1959 02:00 US#2

IL # 53
Before 11/18/1883 LMT
11/18/1883 12:00 CST
3/31/1918 02:00 CWT
10/27/1918 02:00 CST
3/30/1919 02:00 CWT
10/26/1919 02:00 CST
2/09/1942 02:00 CWT
9/30/1945 02:00 CST
4/25/1954 02:00 IL#3
4/26/1959 02:00 US#2

IL # 54
Before 11/18/1883 LMT
11/18/1883 12:00 CST
3/31/1918 02:00 CWT
10/27/1918 02:00 CST
3/30/1919 02:00 CWT
10/26/1919 02:00 CST
2/09/1942 02:00 CWT
9/30/1945 02:00 CST
4/24/1955 02:00 US#2

IL # 55
Before 11/18/1883 LMT
11/18/1883 12:00 CST
3/31/1918 02:00 CWT
10/27/1918 02:00 CST
3/30/1919 02:00 CWT
10/26/1919 02:00 CST
2/09/1942 02:00 CWT
9/30/1945 02:00 CST
4/24/1955 02:00 IL#3
4/26/1959 02:00 US#2

IL # 56
Before 11/18/1883 LMT
11/18/1883 12:00 CST
3/31/1918 02:00 CWT
10/27/1918 02:00 CST
3/30/1919 02:00 CWT
10/26/1919 02:00 CST
2/09/1942 02:00 CWT
9/30/1945 02:00 CST
4/24/1955 02:00 US#4

IL # 57
Before 11/18/1883 LMT
11/18/1883 12:00 CST
3/31/1918 02:00 CWT
10/27/1918 02:00 CST
3/30/1919 02:00 CWT
10/26/1919 02:00 CST
2/09/1942 02:00 CWT
9/30/1945 02:00 CST
4/24/1955 02:00 IL#2
4/29/1956 02:00 US#2

IL # 58
Before 11/18/1883 LMT
11/18/1883 12:00 CST
3/31/1918 02:00 CWT
10/27/1918 02:00 CST
3/30/1919 02:00 CWT
10/26/1919 02:00 CST
2/09/1942 02:00 CWT
9/30/1945 02:00 CST
4/24/1955 02:00 CDT
9/25/1955 02:00 CST
4/29/1956 02:00 CDT
10/28/1956 02:00 CST
4/28/1957 02:00 CDT
10/27/1957 02:00 CST
4/27/1958 02:00 CDT
9/28/1958 02:00 CST
4/26/1959 02:00 US#2

IL # 59
Before 11/18/1883 LMT
11/18/1883 12:00 CST
3/31/1918 02:00 CWT
10/27/1918 02:00 CST
3/30/1919 02:00 CWT
10/26/1919 02:00 CST
2/09/1942 02:00 CWT
9/30/1945 02:00 CST
4/24/1955 02:00 CDT
9/25/1955 02:00 CST
7/01/1959 02:00 US#2

IL # 60
Before 11/18/1883 LMT
11/18/1883 12:00 CST
3/31/1918 02:00 CWT
10/27/1918 02:00 CST
3/30/1919 02:00 CWT
10/26/1919 02:00 CST
2/09/1942 02:00 CWT
9/30/1945 02:00 CST
4/30/1950 02:00 US#3

IL # 61
Before 11/18/1883 LMT
11/18/1883 12:00 CST
3/31/1918 02:00 CWT
10/27/1918 02:00 CST
3/30/1919 02:00 CWT
10/26/1919 02:00 CST
2/09/1942 02:00 CWT
9/30/1945 02:00 CST
4/24/1955 02:00 CDT
9/25/1955 02:00 CST
4/29/1956 02:00 CDT
10/28/1956 02:00 CST
4/28/1957 02:00 CDT
9/29/1957 02:00 IL#3
4/26/1959 02:00 US#2

IL # 62
Before 11/18/1883 LMT
11/18/1883 12:00 CST
3/31/1918 02:00 CWT
10/27/1918 02:00 CST
3/30/1919 02:00 CWT
10/26/1919 02:00 CST
2/09/1942 02:00 CWT
9/30/1945 02:00 CST
4/29/1956 02:00 US#2

IL # 63
Before 11/18/1883 LMT
11/18/1883 12:00 CST
3/31/1918 02:00 CWT
10/27/1918 02:00 CST
3/30/1919 02:00 CWT
10/26/1919 02:00 CST
2/09/1942 02:00 CWT
9/30/1945 02:00 CST
4/29/1956 02:00 IL#3
4/26/1959 02:00 US#2

IL # 64
Before 11/18/1883 LMT
11/18/1883 12:00 CST
3/31/1918 02:00 CWT
10/27/1918 02:00 CST
3/30/1919 02:00 CWT
10/26/1919 02:00 CST
2/09/1942 02:00 CWT
9/30/1945 02:00 CST
4/28/1957 02:00 US#2

IL # 65
Before 11/18/1883 LMT
11/18/1883 12:00 CST
3/31/1918 02:00 CWT
10/27/1918 02:00 CST
3/30/1919 02:00 CWT
10/26/1919 02:00 CST
2/09/1942 02:00 CWT
9/30/1945 02:00 CST
4/28/1957 02:00 IL#3
4/26/1959 02:00 US#2

IL # 66
Before 11/18/1883 LMT
11/18/1883 12:00 CST
3/31/1918 02:00 CWT
10/27/1918 02:00 CST
3/30/1919 02:00 CWT
10/26/1919 02:00 CST
2/09/1942 02:00 CWT
9/30/1945 02:00 CST
4/27/1958 02:00 CDT
9/28/1958 02:00 CST
4/26/1959 02:00 US#2

IL # 67
Before 11/18/1883 LMT
11/18/1883 12:00 CST
3/31/1918 02:00 CWT
10/27/1918 02:00 CST
3/30/1919 02:00 CWT
10/26/1919 02:00 CST
2/09/1942 02:00 CWT
9/30/1945 02:00 CST
4/27/1958 02:00 US#2

IL # 68
Before 11/18/1883 LMT
11/18/1883 12:00 CST
3/31/1918 02:00 CWT
10/27/1918 02:00 CST
3/30/1919 02:00 CWT
10/26/1919 02:00 CST
2/09/1942 02:00 CWT
9/30/1945 02:00 CST
4/25/1948 02:00 CDT
9/26/1948 02:00 CST
4/24/1949 02:00 CDT
9/25/1949 02:00 CST
4/30/1950 02:00 CDT
9/24/1950 02:00 CST
4/29/1951 02:00 CDT
9/30/1951 02:00 CST
4/27/1952 02:00 CDT
9/28/1952 02:00 CST
4/26/1953 02:00 CDT
9/27/1953 02:00 CST
4/25/1954 02:00 CDT
9/26/1954 02:00 CST
4/24/1955 02:00 CDT
9/25/1955 02:00 CST
4/29/1956 02:00 CDT
9/30/1956 02:00 CST
4/28/1957 02:00 US#2

IL # 69
Before 11/18/1883 LMT
11/18/1883 12:00 CST
3/31/1918 02:00 CWT
10/27/1918 02:00 CST
3/30/1919 02:00 CWT
10/26/1919 02:00 CST
5/04/1941 02:00 CDT
9/28/1941 02:00 CST
2/09/1942 02:00 CWT
9/30/1945 02:00 CST
4/24/1955 02:00 IL#2
4/29/1956 02:00 US#2

IL # 70
Before 11/18/1883 LMT
11/18/1883 12:00 CST
3/31/1918 02:00 CWT
10/27/1918 02:00 CST
3/30/1919 02:00 CWT
10/26/1919 02:00 CST
5/04/1941 02:00 CDT
9/28/1941 02:00 CST

TIME TABLES

2/09/1942 02:00 CWT
9/30/1945 02:00 CST
4/25/1948 02:00 IL#2
4/29/1956 02:00 US#2

IL # 71
Before 11/18/1883 LMT
11/18/1883 12:00 CST
3/31/1918 02:00 CWT
10/27/1918 02:00 CST
3/30/1919 02:00 CWT
10/26/1919 02:00 CST
4/27/1941 02:00 CDT
9/28/1941 02:00 CST
2/09/1942 02:00 CWT
9/30/1945 02:00 CST
4/24/1955 02:00 US#2

IL # 72
Before 11/18/1883 LMT
11/18/1883 12:00 CST
3/31/1918 02:00 CWT
10/27/1918 02:00 CST
3/30/1919 02:00 CWT
10/26/1919 02:00 CST
4/24/1929 02:00 US#3

IL # 73
Before 11/18/1883 LMT
11/18/1883 12:00 CST
3/31/1918 02:00 CWT
10/27/1918 02:00 CST
3/30/1919 02:00 CWT
10/26/1919 02:00 CST
2/09/1942 02:00 CWT
9/30/1945 02:00 CST
4/25/1954 02:00 CDT
9/26/1954 02:00 CST
4/24/1955 02:00 CDT
9/25/1955 02:00 CST
7/01/1959 02:00 US#2

IL # 74
Before 11/18/1883 LMT
11/18/1883 12:00 IL#6
9/25/1949 02:00 CST
7/01/1959 02:00 US#2

IL # 75
Before 11/18/1883 LMT
11/18/1883 12:00 CST
3/31/1918 02:00 CWT
10/27/1918 02:00 CST
3/30/1919 02:00 CWT
10/26/1919 02:00 CST
2/09/1942 02:00 CWT
9/30/1945 02:00 CST
4/28/1946 02:00 CDT
9/29/1946 02:00 CST
4/24/1955 02:00 IL#3
4/26/1959 02:00 US#2

IL # 76
Before 11/18/1883 LMT
11/18/1883 12:00 CST
3/31/1918 02:00 CWT
10/27/1918 02:00 CST
3/30/1919 02:00 CWT
10/26/1919 02:00 CST
2/09/1942 02:00 CWT
9/30/1945 02:00 CST
4/28/1957 02:00 CDT
9/29/1957 02:00 CST
5/25/1958 02:00 CDT
9/28/1958 02:00 CST
4/26/1959 02:00 US#2

IL # 77
Before 11/18/1883 LMT
11/18/1883 12:00 CST
3/31/1918 02:00 CWT
10/27/1918 02:00 CST
3/30/1919 02:00 CWT
10/26/1919 02:00 CST
5/01/1938 02:00 IL#3
4/26/1959 02:00 US#2

IL # 78
Before 11/18/1883 LMT
11/18/1883 12:00 CST
3/31/1918 02:00 CWT
10/27/1918 02:00 CST
3/30/1919 02:00 CWT
10/26/1919 02:00 CST
2/09/1942 02:00 CWT
9/30/1945 02:00 CST
4/25/1954 02:00 CDT
9/26/1954 02:00 CST
4/24/1955 02:00 CDT
9/25/1955 02:00 CST
4/29/1956 02:00 US#2

IL # 79
Before 11/18/1883 LMT
11/18/1883 12:00 CST
3/31/1918 02:00 CWT
10/27/1918 02:00 CST
3/30/1919 02:00 CWT
10/26/1919 02:00 CST
2/09/1942 02:00 CWT
9/30/1945 02:00 CST
4/24/1949 02:00 CDT
9/25/1949 02:00 CST
4/30/1950 02:00 CDT
9/24/1950 02:00 CST
4/29/1951 02:00 CDT
9/30/1951 02:00 CST
4/27/1952 02:00 CDT
9/28/1952 02:00 CST
4/26/1953 02:00 CDT
9/27/1953 02:00 CST
4/25/1954 02:00 CDT
9/26/1954 02:00 CST
4/24/1955 02:00 CDT
9/25/1955 02:00 CST
4/29/1956 02:00 CDT
10/28/1956 02:00 CST
4/28/1957 02:00 CDT
9/29/1957 02:00 IL#3
4/26/1959 02:00 US#2

IL # 80
Before 11/18/1883 LMT
11/18/1883 12:00 CST
3/31/1918 02:00 CWT
10/27/1918 02:00 CST
3/30/1919 02:00 CWT
10/26/1919 02:00 CST
2/09/1942 02:00 CWT
9/30/1945 02:00 CST
4/28/1946 02:00 CDT
9/29/1946 02:00 CST
4/27/1947 02:00 CDT
9/28/1947 02:00 CST
4/25/1948 02:00 CDT
9/26/1948 02:00 CST
4/24/1949 02:00 CDT
9/25/1949 02:00 CST
4/30/1950 02:00 CDT
9/24/1950 02:00 CST
4/29/1951 02:00 CDT
9/30/1951 02:00 CST
4/27/1952 02:00 CDT
9/28/1952 02:00 CST
4/26/1953 02:00 CDT
9/27/1953 02:00 CST
4/25/1954 02:00 CDT
9/26/1954 02:00 CST
4/24/1955 02:00 CDT
9/25/1955 02:00 CST
4/29/1956 02:00 CDT
10/28/1956 02:00 CST
4/28/1957 02:00 IL#3
4/26/1959 02:00 US#2

IL # 81
Before 11/18/1883 LMT
11/18/1883 12:00 CST
3/31/1918 02:00 CWT
10/27/1918 02:00 CST
3/30/1919 02:00 CWT
10/26/1919 02:00 CST
2/09/1942 02:00 CWT
9/30/1945 02:00 CST
4/29/1951 02:00 CDT
9/30/1951 02:00 CST
4/27/1952 02:00 CDT
9/28/1952 02:00 CST
4/26/1953 02:00 CDT
9/27/1953 02:00 CST
4/25/1954 02:00 CDT
9/26/1954 02:00 CST
4/24/1955 02:00 CDT
9/25/1955 02:00 CST
4/29/1956 02:00 CDT
10/28/1956 02:00 CST
4/28/1957 02:00 IL#3
4/26/1959 02:00 US#2

IL # 82
Before 11/18/1883 LMT
11/18/1883 12:00 CST
3/31/1918 02:00 CWT
10/27/1918 02:00 CST
3/30/1919 02:00 CWT
10/26/1919 02:00 CST
4/27/1941 02:00 CDT
9/28/1941 02:00 CST
2/09/1942 02:00 IL#3
4/26/1959 02:00 US#2

IL # 83
Before 11/18/1883 LMT
11/18/1883 12:00 CST
3/31/1918 02:00 CWT
10/27/1918 02:00 CST
3/30/1919 02:00 CWT
10/26/1919 02:00 CST
4/27/1941 02:00 CDT
9/28/1941 02:00 CST
2/09/1942 02:00 CWT
9/30/1945 02:00 CST
4/28/1946 02:00 CDT
9/29/1946 02:00 CST
4/27/1947 02:00 CDT
9/28/1947 02:00 CST
4/25/1948 02:00 CDT
9/26/1948 02:00 CST
4/24/1949 02:00 CDT
9/25/1949 02:00 CST
4/30/1950 02:00 CDT
9/24/1950 02:00 CST
4/29/1951 02:00 CDT
9/30/1951 02:00 CST
4/27/1952 02:00 CDT
9/28/1952 02:00 CST
4/26/1953 02:00 CDT
9/27/1953 02:00 CST
4/25/1954 02:00 CDT
9/26/1954 02:00 CST
4/24/1955 02:00 CDT
9/25/1955 02:00 CST
4/29/1956 02:00 CDT
10/28/1956 02:00 CST
4/28/1957 02:00 IL#3
4/26/1959 02:00 US#2

IL # 84
Before 11/18/1883 LMT
11/18/1883 12:00 CST
3/31/1918 02:00 CWT
10/27/1918 02:00 CST
3/30/1919 02:00 CWT
10/26/1919 02:00 CST
2/09/1942 02:00 CWT
9/30/1945 02:00 CST
4/27/1947 02:00 US#5

IL # 85
Before 11/18/1883 LMT
11/18/1883 12:00 CST
3/31/1918 02:00 CWT
10/27/1918 02:00 CST
3/30/1919 02:00 CWT
10/26/1919 02:00 CST
2/09/1942 02:00 CWT
9/30/1945 02:00 CST
4/29/1956 02:00 CDT
9/30/1956 02:00 CST
4/27/1958 02:00 CDT
9/28/1958 02:00 CST
4/26/1959 02:00 US#2

IL # 86
Before 11/18/1883 LMT
11/18/1883 12:00 CST
3/31/1918 02:00 CWT
10/27/1918 02:00 CST
3/30/1919 02:00 CWT
10/26/1919 02:00 CST
2/09/1942 02:00 CWT
9/30/1945 02:00 CST
4/27/1947 02:00 CDT
9/28/1947 02:00 CST
4/25/1948 02:00 CDT
9/26/1948 02:00 CST
4/24/1949 02:00 CDT
9/25/1949 02:00 CST
4/30/1950 02:00 CDT
9/24/1950 02:00 CST
4/29/1951 02:00 CDT
9/30/1951 02:00 CST
4/27/1952 02:00 CDT
9/28/1952 02:00 CST
4/26/1953 02:00 CDT
9/27/1953 02:00 CST
4/25/1954 02:00 CDT
9/26/1954 02:00 CST
4/24/1955 02:00 CDT
9/25/1955 02:00 CST
4/29/1956 02:00 CDT
10/28/1956 02:00 CST
4/28/1957 02:00 IL#3
4/26/1959 02:00 US#2

IL # 87
Before 11/18/1883 LMT
11/18/1883 12:00 CST
3/31/1918 02:00 CWT
10/27/1918 02:00 CST
3/30/1919 02:00 CWT
10/26/1919 02:00 CST
4/27/1941 02:00 CDT
9/28/1941 02:00 IL#4
7/01/1959 02:00 US#2

IL # 88
Before 11/18/1883 LMT
11/18/1883 12:00 CST
3/31/1918 02:00 CWT
10/27/1918 02:00 CST
3/30/1919 02:00 CWT
10/26/1919 02:00 CST
2/09/1942 02:00 CWT
9/30/1945 02:00 CST
4/29/1956 02:00 CDT
9/30/1956 02:00 CST
7/01/1959 02:00 US#2

IL # 89
Before 11/18/1883 LMT
11/18/1883 12:00 CST
3/31/1918 02:00 CWT
10/27/1918 02:00 CST
3/30/1919 02:00 CWT
10/26/1919 02:00 CST
2/09/1942 02:00 CWT
9/30/1945 02:00 CST
4/24/1955 02:00 CDT
10/30/1955 02:00 CST
4/29/1956 02:00 CDT
10/28/1956 02:00 CST
4/28/1957 02:00 CDT
10/27/1957 02:00 CST
4/27/1958 02:00 CDT
9/28/1958 02:00 CST
4/26/1959 02:00 US#2

IL # 90
Before 11/18/1883 LMT
11/18/1883 12:00 CST
3/31/1918 02:00 CWT
10/27/1918 02:00 CST
3/30/1919 02:00 CWT
10/26/1919 02:00 CST
2/09/1942 02:00 CWT
9/30/1945 02:00 CST
4/24/1955 02:00 CDT
9/25/1955 02:00 CST
4/29/1956 02:00 CDT
9/30/1956 02:00 CST
4/28/1957 02:00 CDT
9/29/1957 02:00 CST
4/27/1958 02:00 US#2

IL # 91
Before 11/18/1883 LMT
11/18/1883 12:00 CST
3/31/1918 02:00 CWT
10/27/1918 02:00 CST
3/30/1919 02:00 CWT
10/26/1919 02:00 CST
2/09/1942 02:00 CWT
9/30/1945 02:00 CST
4/27/1952 02:00 CDT
9/28/1952 02:00 CST
4/26/1953 02:00 CDT
9/27/1953 02:00 CST
4/25/1954 02:00 CDT
9/26/1954 02:00 CST
4/24/1955 02:00 CDT
9/25/1955 02:00 CST
4/29/1956 02:00 CDT
10/28/1956 02:00 CST
4/28/1957 02:00 CDT
10/27/1957 02:00 CST
4/27/1958 02:00 CDT
9/28/1958 02:00 CST
4/26/1959 02:00 US#2

IL # 92
Before 11/18/1883 LMT
11/18/1883 12:00 CST
3/31/1918 02:00 CWT
10/27/1918 02:00 CST
3/30/1919 02:00 CWT
10/26/1919 02:00 CST
4/27/1941 02:00 CDT
9/28/1941 02:00 CST
2/09/1942 02:00 CWT
9/30/1945 02:00 CST
4/28/1946 02:00 CDT
9/29/1946 02:00 CST
4/27/1947 02:00 CDT
9/28/1947 02:00 CST
4/25/1948 02:00 CDT
9/26/1948 02:00 CST
4/24/1949 02:00 CDT
9/25/1949 02:00 CST
4/30/1950 02:00 CDT
9/24/1950 02:00 CST
4/29/1951 02:00 CDT
9/30/1951 02:00 CST
4/27/1952 02:00 CDT
9/28/1952 02:00 CST
4/26/1953 02:00 CDT
9/27/1953 02:00 CST
4/25/1954 02:00 CDT
9/26/1954 02:00 CST
4/24/1955 02:00 US#4

IL # 93
Before 11/18/1883 LMT
11/18/1883 12:00 CST
3/31/1918 02:00 CWT
10/27/1918 02:00 CST
3/30/1919 02:00 CWT
10/26/1919 02:00 CST
2/09/1942 02:00 CWT
9/30/1945 02:00 CST
4/26/1953 02:00 CDT
9/27/1953 02:00 CST
4/25/1954 02:00 CDT
9/26/1954 02:00 CST
4/24/1955 02:00 CDT
9/25/1955 02:00 CST
4/29/1956 02:00 US#2

IL # 94
Before 11/18/1883 LMT
11/18/1883 12:00 CST
3/31/1918 02:00 CWT
10/27/1918 02:00 CST
3/30/1919 02:00 CWT
10/26/1919 02:00 CST
2/09/1942 02:00 CWT
9/30/1945 02:00 CST
4/24/1955 02:00 CDT
9/25/1955 02:00 CST
4/29/1956 02:00 CDT
9/30/1956 02:00 CST
7/01/1959 02:00 US#2

IL # 95
Before 11/18/1883 LMT
11/18/1883 12:00 CST
3/31/1918 02:00 CWT
10/27/1918 02:00 CST
3/30/1919 02:00 CWT
10/26/1919 02:00 CST
6/13/1920 02:00 CDT
10/31/1920 02:00 CST
3/27/1921 02:00 CDT
10/30/1921 02:00 CST
4/30/1922 02:00 CDT
9/24/1922 02:00 CST
4/29/1923 02:00 CDT
9/30/1923 02:00 CST
4/27/1924 02:00 CDT
9/28/1924 02:00 CST
4/26/1925 02:00 CDT
9/27/1925 02:00 CST
4/25/1926 02:00 CDT
9/26/1926 02:00 CST
4/24/1927 02:00 CDT
9/25/1927 02:00 CST
4/29/1928 02:00 CDT
9/30/1928 02:00 CST
4/28/1929 02:00 CDT
9/29/1929 02:00 CST
4/27/1930 02:00 CDT
9/28/1930 02:00 CST
4/26/1931 02:00 CDT
9/27/1931 02:00 CST
4/24/1932 02:00 CDT
9/25/1932 02:00 CST
4/30/1933 02:00 CDT
9/24/1933 02:00 CST
4/29/1934 02:00 CDT
9/30/1934 02:00 CST
4/28/1935 02:00 CDT
9/29/1935 02:00 CST
4/26/1936 02:00 CDT
9/27/1936 02:00 CST
4/25/1937 02:00 CDT
9/26/1937 02:00 CST
4/24/1938 02:00 CDT
9/25/1938 02:00 CST
4/30/1939 02:00 CDT
9/24/1939 02:00 CST
4/28/1940 02:00 CDT
9/29/1940 02:00 CST
4/27/1941 02:00 CDT
9/28/1941 02:00 IL#3
4/26/1959 02:00 US#2

IL # 96
Before 11/18/1883 LMT
11/18/1883 12:00 CST
3/31/1918 02:00 CWT
10/27/1918 02:00 CST
3/30/1919 02:00 CWT
10/26/1919 02:00 CST
2/09/1942 02:00 CWT
9/30/1945 02:00 CST
4/24/1949 02:00 CDT
9/25/1949 02:00 CST
4/30/1950 02:00 CDT
9/24/1950 02:00 CST
4/29/1951 02:00 CDT
9/30/1951 02:00 CST
4/27/1952 02:00 CDT
9/28/1952 02:00 CST
4/26/1953 02:00 CDT
9/27/1953 02:00 CST
4/25/1954 02:00 CDT
9/26/1954 02:00 CST
4/24/1955 02:00 IL#3
4/26/1959 02:00 US#2

IL # 97
Before 11/18/1883 LMT
11/18/1883 12:00 CST
3/31/1918 02:00 CWT
10/27/1918 02:00 CST
3/30/1919 02:00 CWT
10/26/1919 02:00 CST
2/09/1942 02:00 CWT
9/30/1945 02:00 CST
4/27/1947 02:00 CDT
9/28/1947 02:00 CST
4/25/1948 02:00 CDT
9/26/1948 02:00 CST
4/24/1949 02:00 CDT
9/25/1949 02:00 CST
4/30/1950 02:00 CDT
9/30/1950 02:00 IL#2
4/29/1956 02:00 US#2

IL # 98
Before 11/18/1883 LMT
11/18/1883 12:00 CST
3/31/1918 02:00 CWT
10/27/1918 02:00 CST
3/30/1919 02:00 CWT
10/26/1919 02:00 CST
5/05/1940 02:00 CDT
9/29/1940 02:00 CST
4/27/1941 02:00 CDT
9/28/1941 02:00 IL#2
4/29/1956 02:00 US#2

IL # 99
Before 11/18/1883 LMT
11/18/1883 12:00 CST
3/31/1918 02:00 CWT
10/27/1918 02:00 CST
3/30/1919 02:00 CWT
10/26/1919 02:00 CST
5/05/1940 02:00 CDT
9/29/1940 02:00 CST
4/27/1941 02:00 CDT
9/28/1941 02:00 CST
2/09/1942 02:00 US#4

TIME TABLES

IL # 100
Before 11/18/1883 LMT
11/18/1883 12:00 IL#1
4/26/1931 02:00 CDT
10/25/1931 02:00 IL#1
9/28/1941 02:00 US#2
....
IL # 101
Before 11/18/1883 LMT
11/18/1883 12:00 CST
3/31/1918 02:00 CWT
10/27/1918 02:00 CST
3/30/1919 02:00 CWT
10/26/1919 02:00 CST
6/13/1920 00:01 CDT
10/31/1920 00:01 CST
3/27/1921 00:01 CDT
10/30/1921 00:01 CST
4/30/1922 00:01 CDT
9/24/1922 00:01 CST
4/29/1923 00:01 CDT
9/30/1923 00:01 CST
4/27/1924 00:01 CDT
9/28/1924 00:01 CST
4/26/1925 00:01 CDT
9/27/1925 00:01 CST
4/25/1926 00:01 CDT
9/26/1926 00:01 CST
4/24/1927 00:01 CDT
9/25/1927 00:01 CST
4/29/1928 00:01 CDT
9/30/1928 00:01 CST
4/28/1929 00:01 CDT
9/29/1929 00:01 CST
4/27/1930 00:01 CDT
9/28/1930 00:01 CST
4/26/1931 00:01 CDT
9/27/1931 00:01 CST
4/24/1932 00:01 CDT
9/25/1932 00:01 CST
4/30/1933 00:01 CDT
9/24/1933 00:01 CST
4/29/1934 00:01 CDT
9/30/1934 00:01 CST
4/28/1935 00:01 CDT
9/29/1935 00:01 CST
3/01/1936 00:01 CDT
11/01/1936 00:01 CST
5/08/1937 00:01 CDT
9/26/1937 00:01 CST
5/01/1938 00:01 CDT
9/25/1938 00:01 CST
5/07/1939 00:01 CDT
9/24/1939 00:01 CST
5/05/1940 00:01 CDT
9/29/1940 00:01 CST
5/04/1941 00:01 CDT
9/28/1941 00:01 CST
9/28/1941 02:00 IL#3
4/26/1959 02:00 US#2
....
IL # 102
Before 11/18/1883 LMT
11/18/1883 12:00 CST
3/31/1918 02:00 CWT
10/27/1918 02:00 CST
3/30/1919 02:00 CWT
10/26/1919 02:00 CST
4/30/1933 00:01 CDT
9/24/1933 00:01 CST
4/29/1934 00:01 CDT
9/30/1934 00:01 CST
4/28/1935 00:01 CDT
9/29/1935 00:01 CST
4/26/1936 00:01 CDT
9/27/1936 00:01 CST
5/08/1937 00:01 CDT
9/26/1937 00:01 CST
5/01/1938 00:01 CDT
9/25/1938 00:01 CST
5/07/1939 00:01 CDT
9/24/1939 00:01 CST
5/05/1940 00:01 CDT
9/29/1940 00:01 CST
5/04/1941 00:01 CDT
9/28/1941 00:01 CST
9/28/1941 02:00 US#3
....
IL # 103
Before 11/18/1883 LMT
11/18/1883 12:00 CST
3/31/1918 02:00 CWT
10/27/1918 02:00 CST
3/30/1919 02:00 CWT
10/26/1919 02:00 CST
4/29/1928 02:00 CDT
9/30/1928 02:00 CST
4/24/1932 02:00 CDT
9/25/1932 02:00 CST
4/30/1933 02:00 CDT
9/24/1933 02:00 CST
4/29/1934 02:00 CDT
9/30/1934 02:00 CST
4/28/1935 02:00 CDT
9/29/1935 02:00 CST
4/26/1936 02:00 CDT
9/27/1936 02:00 CST
4/25/1937 02:00 CDT
9/26/1937 02:00 CST
4/24/1938 02:00 CDT
9/25/1938 02:00 CST
4/30/1939 02:00 CDT
9/24/1939 02:00 CST
4/28/1940 02:00 CDT
9/29/1940 02:00 CST
4/27/1941 02:00 CDT
9/28/1941 02:00 CST
2/09/1942 02:00 CWT
9/30/1945 02:00 CST
4/28/1946 02:00 CDT
9/29/1946 02:00 CST
4/27/1947 02:00 CDT
9/28/1947 02:00 CST
4/25/1948 02:00 CDT
9/26/1948 02:00 CST
4/24/1949 02:00 CDT
9/25/1949 02:00 CST
4/30/1950 02:00 CDT
9/24/1950 02:00 CST
4/29/1951 02:00 CDT
9/30/1951 02:00 CST
4/27/1952 02:00 CDT
9/28/1952 02:00 CST
4/26/1953 02:00 CDT
9/27/1953 02:00 CST
4/25/1954 02:00 CDT
9/26/1954 02:00 CST
4/24/1955 02:00 CDT
9/25/1955 02:00 CST
4/29/1956 02:00 US#2
....
IL # 104
Before 11/18/1883 LMT
11/18/1883 12:00 CST
3/31/1918 02:00 CWT
10/27/1918 02:00 CST
3/30/1919 02:00 CWT
10/26/1919 02:00 CST
5/17/1940 02:00 CDT
9/29/1940 02:00 CST
4/27/1941 02:00 CDT
9/28/1941 02:00 IL#2
4/29/1956 02:00 US#2
....
IL # 105
Before 11/18/1883 LMT
11/18/1883 12:00 CST
3/31/1918 02:00 CWT
10/27/1918 02:00 CST
3/30/1919 02:00 CWT
10/26/1919 02:00 CST
6/13/1920 02:00 CDT
10/31/1920 02:00 CST
4/30/1933 00:01 CDT
9/24/1933 00:01 CST
4/29/1934 00:01 CDT
9/30/1934 00:01 CST
4/28/1935 00:01 CDT
9/29/1935 00:01 CST
4/26/1936 00:01 CDT
9/27/1936 00:01 CST
5/08/1937 00:01 CDT
9/26/1937 00:01 CST
5/01/1938 00:01 CDT
9/25/1938 00:01 CST
5/07/1939 00:01 CDT
9/24/1939 00:01 CST
5/05/1940 00:01 CDT
9/29/1940 00:01 CST
4/27/1941 00:01 CDT
9/28/1941 00:01 IL#7
4/26/1959 02:00 US#2
....
IL # 106
Before 11/18/1883 LMT
11/18/1883 12:00 CST
3/31/1918 02:00 CWT
10/27/1918 02:00 CST
3/30/1919 02:00 CWT
10/26/1919 02:00 CST
2/09/1942 02:00 CWT
9/30/1945 02:00 CST
5/05/1946 02:00 CDT
9/29/1946 02:00 CST
4/27/1947 02:00 IL#3
4/26/1959 02:00 US#2
....
IL # 107
Before 11/18/1883 LMT
11/18/1883 12:00 IL#1
10/31/1920 02:00 CST
4/30/1933 00:01 CDT
9/24/1933 00:01 CST
4/29/1934 00:01 CDT
9/30/1934 00:01 CST
4/28/1935 00:01 CDT
9/29/1935 00:01 CST
4/26/1936 00:01 CDT
9/27/1936 00:01 CST
4/25/1937 00:01 CDT
9/26/1937 00:01 CST
4/24/1938 00:01 CDT
9/25/1938 00:01 CST
4/30/1939 00:01 CDT
9/24/1939 00:01 CST
4/28/1940 00:01 CDT
9/29/1940 00:01 CST
4/27/1941 00:01 CDT
9/28/1941 00:01 CST
2/09/1942 02:00 CWT
9/30/1945 02:00 CST
4/28/1946 02:00 IL#2
4/29/1956 02:00 US#2
....
IL # 108
Before 11/18/1883 LMT
11/18/1883 12:00 CST
3/31/1918 02:00 CWT
10/27/1918 02:00 CST
3/30/1919 02:00 CWT
10/26/1919 02:00 CST
2/09/1942 02:00 CWT
9/30/1945 02:00 CST
4/28/1946 02:00 CDT
9/29/1946 02:00 CST
4/27/1947 02:00 CDT
10/25/1947 02:00 CST
4/25/1948 02:00 IL#2
4/29/1956 02:00 US#2
....
IL # 109
Before 11/18/1883 LMT
11/18/1883 12:00 IL#1
4/27/1941 02:00 CDT
9/28/1941 02:00 CST
2/09/1942 02:00 CWT
9/30/1945 02:00 CST
4/28/1946 02:00 CDT
9/29/1946 02:00 CST
4/27/1947 02:00 CDT
10/29/1947 02:00 IL#2
4/29/1956 02:00 US#2
....
IL # 110
Before 11/18/1883 LMT
11/18/1883 12:00 CST
3/31/1918 02:00 CWT
10/27/1918 02:00 CST
3/30/1919 02:00 CWT
10/26/1919 02:00 CST
2/09/1942 02:00 CWT
9/30/1945 02:00 CST
4/27/1947 02:00 CDT
10/29/1947 02:00 CST
4/25/1948 02:00 CDT
9/26/1948 02:00 CST
4/24/1949 02:00 CDT
9/25/1949 02:00 CST
4/30/1950 02:00 CDT
9/24/1950 02:00 CST
4/29/1951 02:00 CDT
9/30/1951 02:00 CST
4/27/1952 02:00 CDT
9/28/1952 02:00 CST
4/26/1953 02:00 CDT
9/27/1953 02:00 CST
4/25/1954 02:00 CDT
9/26/1954 02:00 CST
4/24/1955 02:00 CDT
9/25/1955 02:00 CST
4/29/1956 02:00 IL#3
4/26/1959 02:00 US#2
....
IL # 111
Before 11/18/1883 LMT
11/18/1883 12:00 IL#7
9/26/1948 02:00 CST
5/29/1949 02:00 CDT
9/03/1949 02:00 CST
4/30/1950 02:00 IL#7
4/26/1959 02:00 US#2
....
IL # 112
Before 11/18/1883 LMT
11/18/1883 12:00 CST
3/31/1918 02:00 CWT
10/27/1918 02:00 CST
3/30/1919 02:00 CWT
10/26/1919 02:00 CST
2/09/1942 02:00 CWT
9/30/1945 02:00 CST
4/27/1947 02:00 CDT
9/28/1947 02:00 CST
4/25/1948 02:00 CDT
10/30/1948 02:00 IL#3
4/26/1959 02:00 US#2
....
IL # 113
Before 11/18/1883 LMT
11/18/1883 12:00 CST
3/31/1918 02:00 CWT
10/27/1918 02:00 CST
3/30/1919 02:00 CWT
10/26/1919 02:00 CST
5/05/1940 02:00 CDT
9/29/1940 02:00 CST
2/09/1942 02:00 CWT
9/30/1945 02:00 CST
4/28/1946 02:00 CDT
9/29/1946 02:00 CST
4/27/1947 02:00 CDT
9/28/1947 02:00 CST
4/25/1948 02:00 CDT
9/26/1948 02:00 CST
4/24/1949 02:00 CDT
9/26/1949 02:00 US#4
....
IL # 114
Before 11/18/1883 LMT
11/18/1883 12:00 CST
3/31/1918 02:00 CWT
10/27/1918 02:00 CST
3/30/1919 02:00 CWT
10/26/1919 02:00 CST
4/28/1935 02:00 CDT
9/29/1935 02:00 CST
4/26/1936 02:00 CDT
9/27/1936 02:00 CST
4/25/1937 02:00 CDT
9/26/1937 02:00 CST
4/24/1938 02:00 CDT
9/25/1938 02:00 CST
4/30/1939 02:00 CDT
9/24/1939 02:00 CST
4/28/1940 02:00 CDT
9/29/1940 02:00 CST
4/27/1941 02:00 CDT
10/26/1941 02:00 CST
2/09/1942 02:00 CWT
9/30/1945 02:00 CST
4/28/1946 02:00 IL#2
4/29/1956 02:00 US#2
....
IL # 115
Before 11/18/1883 LMT
11/18/1883 12:00 CST
3/31/1918 02:00 CWT
10/27/1918 02:00 CST
3/30/1919 02:00 CWT
10/26/1919 02:00 CST
4/27/1941 02:00 CDT
10/26/1941 02:00 CST
2/09/1942 02:00 CWT
9/30/1945 02:00 CST
4/28/1946 02:00 IL#2
4/29/1956 02:00 US#2
....
IL # 116
Before 11/18/1883 LMT
11/18/1883 12:00 IL#1
10/04/1936 02:00 CST
4/25/1937 02:00 CDT
9/26/1937 02:00 CST
4/24/1938 02:00 CDT
9/25/1938 02:00 CST
4/30/1939 02:00 CDT
9/24/1939 02:00 CST
4/28/1940 02:00 CDT
9/29/1940 02:00 CST
4/27/1941 02:00 CDT
9/28/1941 02:00 CST
2/09/1942 02:00 CWT
9/30/1945 02:00 CST
4/28/1946 02:00 CDT
9/29/1946 02:00 CST
4/27/1947 02:00 CDT
9/28/1947 02:00 CST
4/25/1948 02:00 CDT
9/26/1948 02:00 CST
4/24/1949 02:00 CDT
9/25/1949 02:00 CST
4/30/1950 02:00 CDT
9/24/1950 02:00 CST
4/29/1951 02:00 CDT
9/30/1951 02:00 CST
4/27/1952 02:00 CDT
9/28/1952 02:00 CST
4/26/1953 02:00 CDT
9/27/1953 02:00 CST
4/25/1954 02:00 CDT
9/26/1954 02:00 CST
4/24/1955 02:00 CDT
9/25/1955 02:00 CST
4/29/1956 02:00 US#2
....
IL # 117
Before 11/18/1883 LMT
11/18/1883 12:00 CST
3/31/1918 02:00 CWT
10/27/1918 02:00 CST
3/30/1919 02:00 CWT
10/26/1919 02:00 CST
5/25/1941 02:00 CDT
9/28/1941 02:00 IL#6
4/28/1946 02:00 US#2
....
IL # 118
Before 11/18/1883 LMT
11/18/1883 12:00 CST
3/31/1918 02:00 CWT
10/27/1918 02:00 CST
3/30/1919 02:00 CWT
10/26/1919 02:00 CST
5/13/1940 02:00 CDT
9/29/1940 02:00 CST
4/27/1941 02:00 CDT
9/28/1941 02:00 IL#2
4/29/1956 02:00 US#2
....
IL # 119
Before 11/18/1883 LMT
11/18/1883 12:00 CST
3/31/1918 02:00 CWT
10/27/1918 02:00 CST
3/30/1919 02:00 CWT
10/26/1919 02:00 CST
5/12/1941 02:00 CDT
10/26/1941 02:00 CST
2/09/1942 02:00 CWT
9/30/1945 02:00 CST
4/28/1946 02:00 IL#2
4/29/1956 02:00 US#2
....
IL # 120
Before 11/18/1883 LMT
11/18/1883 12:00 CST
3/31/1918 02:00 CWT
10/27/1918 02:00 CST
3/30/1919 02:00 CWT
10/26/1919 02:00 CST
5/25/1941 02:00 CDT
9/25/1941 02:00 IL#7
4/26/1959 02:00 US#2
....
IL # 121
Before 11/18/1883 LMT
11/18/1883 12:00 CST
3/31/1918 02:00 CWT
10/27/1918 02:00 CST
3/30/1919 02:00 CWT
10/26/1919 02:00 CST
2/09/1942 02:00 CWT
9/30/1945 02:00 CST
4/27/1947 02:00 CDT
9/28/1947 02:00 CST
4/25/1948 02:00 CDT
9/26/1948 02:00 CST
4/24/1949 02:00 CDT
9/25/1949 02:00 CST
4/30/1950 02:00 CDT
9/24/1950 02:00 CST
4/29/1951 02:00 CDT
9/30/1951 02:00 CST
4/27/1952 02:00 CDT
9/28/1952 02:00 CST
4/26/1953 02:00 CDT
9/27/1953 02:00 CST
4/25/1954 02:00 CDT
9/26/1954 02:00 CST
4/24/1955 02:00 CDT
9/25/1955 02:00 CST
6/01/1956 02:00 CDT
9/01/1956 02:00 CST
4/28/1957 02:00 IL#3
4/26/1959 02:00 US#2
....
IL # 122
Before 11/18/1883 LMT
11/18/1883 12:00 CST
3/31/1918 02:00 CWT
10/27/1918 02:00 CST
3/30/1919 02:00 CWT
10/26/1919 02:00 CST
2/09/1942 02:00 CWT
9/30/1945 02:00 CST
4/25/1954 02:00 CDT
9/26/1954 02:00 CST
4/24/1955 02:00 CDT
9/25/1955 02:00 CST
4/29/1956 02:00 CDT
9/30/1956 02:00 CST
4/28/1957 02:00 CDT
9/29/1957 02:00 CST
5/01/1958 02:00 CDT
10/01/1958 02:00 CST
4/26/1959 02:00 US#2
....
IL # 123
Before 11/18/1883 LMT
11/18/1883 12:00 CST
3/31/1918 02:00 CWT
10/27/1918 02:00 CST
3/30/1919 02:00 CWT
10/26/1919 02:00 CST
6/04/1941 02:00 CDT
9/28/1941 02:00 CST
2/09/1942 02:00 CWT
9/30/1945 02:00 CST
4/28/1946 02:00 IL#2
4/29/1956 02:00 US#2
....
IL # 124
Before 11/18/1883 LMT
11/18/1883 12:00 CST
3/31/1918 02:00 CWT
10/27/1918 02:00 CST
3/30/1919 02:00 CWT
10/26/1919 02:00 CST
6/01/1941 02:00 CDT
9/18/1941 02:00 IL#7
4/26/1959 02:00 US#2
....
IL # 125
Before 11/18/1883 LMT
11/18/1883 12:00 CST
3/31/1918 02:00 CWT
10/27/1918 02:00 CST
3/30/1919 02:00 CWT
10/26/1919 02:00 CST
5/11/1941 02:00 CDT
10/26/1941 02:00 CST
2/09/1942 02:00 CWT
9/30/1945 02:00 CST
4/28/1946 02:00 IL#2
4/29/1956 02:00 US#2
....
IL # 126
Before 11/18/1883 LMT
11/18/1883 12:00 CST
3/31/1918 02:00 CWT
10/27/1918 02:00 CST
3/30/1919 02:00 CWT
10/26/1919 02:00 CST
4/24/1938 02:00 CDT
9/25/1938 02:00 CST
4/30/1939 02:00 CDT
9/24/1939 02:00 CST
4/28/1940 02:00 CDT
9/29/1940 02:00 CST
4/27/1941 02:00 CDT
10/26/1941 02:00 CST
2/09/1942 02:00 CWT
9/30/1945 02:00 CST
4/28/1946 02:00 US#2
....

TIME TABLES

IL # 127
Before 11/18/1883 LMT
11/18/1883 12:00 CST
3/31/1918 02:00 CWT
10/27/1918 02:00 CST
3/30/1919 02:00 CWT
10/26/1919 02:00 CST
6/08/1941 02:00 CDT
9/28/1941 02:00 IL#7
4/26/1959 02:00 US#2

IL # 128
Before 11/18/1883 LMT
11/18/1883 12:00 IL#6
9/27/1953 02:00 CST
5/01/1954 02:00 CDT
10/02/1954 02:00 CST
4/24/1955 02:00 IL#3
4/26/1959 02:00 US#2

IL # 129
Before 11/18/1883 LMT
11/18/1883 12:00 IL#6
9/26/1948 02:00 CST
5/29/1949 02:00 CDT
9/03/1949 02:00 CST
4/30/1950 02:00 CDT
9/01/1950 02:00 CST
4/29/1951 02:00 IL#2
4/29/1956 02:00 US#2

IL # 130
Before 11/18/1883 LMT
11/18/1883 12:00 CST
3/31/1918 02:00 CWT
10/27/1918 02:00 CST
3/30/1919 02:00 CWT
10/26/1919 02:00 CST
6/01/1941 00:01 CDT
9/28/1941 00:01 IL#6
4/28/1946 02:00 US#2

IL # 131
Before 11/18/1883 LMT
11/18/1883 12:00 IL#7
9/07/1958 02:00 CST
1/01/1959 02:00 US#2

IL # 132
Before 11/18/1883 LMT
11/18/1883 12:00 CST
3/31/1918 02:00 CWT
10/27/1918 02:00 CST
3/30/1919 02:00 CWT
10/26/1919 02:00 CST
2/09/1942 02:00 CWT
9/30/1945 02:00 CST
4/27/1947 02:00 CDT
9/28/1947 02:00 CST
4/25/1948 02:00 CDT
9/26/1948 02:00 CST
4/24/1949 02:00 CDT
9/03/1949 02:00 CST
4/30/1950 02:00 CDT
9/03/1950 02:00 CST
4/29/1951 02:00 IL#2
4/29/1956 02:00 US#2

IL # 133
Before 11/18/1883 LMT
11/18/1883 12:00 CST
3/31/1918 02:00 CWT
10/27/1918 02:00 CST
3/30/1919 02:00 CWT
10/26/1919 02:00 CST
5/24/1940 02:00 CDT
9/29/1940 02:00 CST
2/09/1942 02:00 CWT
9/30/1945 02:00 CST
4/28/1946 02:00 CDT
9/29/1946 02:00 CST
4/27/1947 02:00 CDT
9/28/1947 02:00 CST
4/25/1948 02:00 CDT
9/26/1948 02:00 CST
4/24/1949 02:00 CDT
10/02/1949 02:00 CST
4/30/1950 02:00 CDT
9/24/1950 02:00 CST
4/29/1951 02:00 CDT
9/30/1951 02:00 CST
4/27/1952 02:00 CDT
9/28/1952 02:00 CST
4/26/1953 02:00 CDT
9/27/1953 02:00 CST
4/25/1954 02:00 CDT
9/26/1954 02:00 CST
4/24/1955 02:00 CDT
10/30/1955 02:00 CST
4/29/1956 02:00 IL#3
4/26/1959 02:00 US#2

IL # 134
Before 11/18/1883 LMT
11/18/1883 12:00 CST
3/31/1918 02:00 CWT
10/27/1918 02:00 CST
3/30/1919 02:00 CWT
10/26/1919 02:00 CST
6/01/1941 02:00 CDT
9/28/1941 02:00 CST
2/09/1942 02:00 CWT
9/30/1945 02:00 CST
4/28/1946 02:00 IL#2
4/29/1956 02:00 US#2

IL # 135
Before 11/18/1883 LMT
11/18/1883 12:00 CST
3/31/1918 02:00 CWT
10/27/1918 02:00 CST
3/30/1919 02:00 CWT
10/26/1919 02:00 CST
5/25/1941 02:00 CDT
9/28/1941 02:00 CST
2/09/1942 02:00 CWT
9/30/1945 02:00 CST
4/28/1946 02:00 CDT
9/29/1946 02:00 CST
4/27/1947 02:00 CDT
9/28/1947 02:00 CST
4/25/1948 02:00 CDT
9/26/1948 02:00 CST
4/24/1949 02:00 CDT
9/25/1949 02:00 CST
4/30/1950 02:00 CDT
9/24/1950 02:00 CST
4/29/1951 02:00 CDT
9/30/1951 02:00 CST
4/27/1952 02:00 CDT
9/28/1952 02:00 CST
4/26/1953 02:00 CDT
9/27/1953 02:00 CST
4/25/1954 02:00 CDT
9/26/1954 02:00 CST
4/24/1955 02:00 US#4

IL # 136
Before 11/18/1883 LMT
11/18/1883 12:00 CST
3/31/1918 02:00 CWT
10/27/1918 02:00 CST
3/30/1919 02:00 CWT
10/26/1919 02:00 CST
6/08/1941 02:00 CDT
9/28/1941 02:00 CST
2/09/1942 02:00 CWT
9/30/1945 02:00 CST
4/28/1946 02:00 CDT
9/29/1946 02:00 CST
4/27/1947 02:00 CDT
9/28/1947 02:00 CST
4/25/1948 02:00 CDT
9/26/1948 02:00 CST
4/24/1949 02:00 CDT
9/25/1949 02:00 CST
4/30/1950 02:00 CDT
9/24/1950 02:00 CST
4/29/1951 02:00 CDT
9/30/1951 02:00 CST
4/27/1952 02:00 CDT
9/28/1952 02:00 CST
4/26/1953 02:00 CDT
9/27/1953 02:00 CST
4/25/1954 02:00 CDT
9/26/1954 02:00 CST
4/24/1955 02:00 IL#2
4/29/1956 02:00 US#2

IL # 137
Before 11/18/1883 LMT
11/18/1883 12:00 CST
3/31/1918 02:00 CWT
10/27/1918 02:00 CST
3/30/1919 02:00 CWT
10/26/1919 02:00 CST
2/09/1942 02:00 CWT
9/30/1945 02:00 CST
4/29/1956 02:00 CDT
9/30/1956 02:00 CST
4/28/1957 02:00 CDT
9/29/1957 02:00 CST
5/01/1958 02:00 CDT
8/31/1958 02:00 CST
1/01/1959 02:00 US#2

IL # 138
Before 11/18/1883 LMT
11/18/1883 12:00 CST
3/31/1918 02:00 CWT
10/27/1918 02:00 CST
3/30/1919 02:00 CWT
10/26/1919 02:00 CST
5/26/1940 02:00 CDT
9/29/1940 02:00 IL#6
4/28/1946 02:00 US#2

IL # 139
Before 11/18/1883 LMT
11/18/1883 12:00 CST
3/31/1918 02:00 CWT
10/27/1918 02:00 CST
3/30/1919 02:00 CWT
10/26/1919 02:00 CST
2/09/1942 02:00 CWT
9/30/1945 02:00 CST
4/28/1946 02:00 CDT
9/29/1946 02:00 CST
5/01/1947 02:00 CDT
9/01/1947 02:00 CST
4/24/1955 02:00 CDT
10/30/1955 02:00 CST
4/29/1956 02:00 CDT
10/28/1956 02:00 CST
4/25/1957 02:00 IL#3
4/26/1959 02:00 US#2

IL # 140
Before 11/18/1883 LMT
11/18/1883 12:00 IL#1
10/26/1919 02:00 CST
4/27/1921 02:00 CDT
10/03/1921 02:00 CST
4/30/1922 02:00 IL#2
4/29/1956 02:00 US#2

IL # 141
Before 11/18/1883 LMT
11/18/1883 12:00 CST
3/31/1918 02:00 CWT
10/27/1918 02:00 CST
3/30/1919 02:00 CWT
10/26/1919 02:00 CST
2/09/1942 02:00 CWT
9/30/1945 02:00 CST
4/27/1952 02:00 CDT
9/28/1952 02:00 CST
5/01/1955 02:00 CDT
9/25/1955 02:00 CST
4/29/1956 02:00 IL#3
4/26/1959 02:00 US#2

IL # 142
Before 11/18/1883 LMT
11/18/1883 12:00 CST
3/31/1918 02:00 CWT
10/27/1918 02:00 CST
3/30/1919 02:00 CWT
10/26/1919 02:00 CST
6/21/1920 00:01 CDT
10/04/1920 00:01 CST
3/27/1921 02:00 IL#2
4/29/1956 02:00 US#2

COUNTIES

1 Adams
2 Alexander
3 Bond
4 Boone
5 Brown
6 Bureau
7 Calhoun
8 Carroll
9 Cass
10 Champaign
11 Christian
12 Clark
13 Clay
14 Clinton
15 Coles
16 Cook
17 Crawford
18 Cumberland
19 De Kalb
20 De Witt
21 Douglas
22 Du Page
23 Edgar
24 Edwards
25 Effingham
26 Fayette
27 Ford
28 Franklin
29 Fulton
30 Gallatin
31 Greene
32 Grundy
33 Hamilton
34 Hancock
35 Hardin
36 Henderson
37 Henry
38 Iroquois
39 Jackson
40 Jasper
41 Jefferson
42 Jersey
43 Jo Daviess
44 Johnson
45 Kane
46 Kankakee
47 Kendall
48 Knox
49 Lake
50 La Salle
51 Lawrence
52 Lee
53 Livingston
54 Logan
55 McDonough
56 McHenry
57 McLean
58 Macon
59 Macoupin
60 Madison
61 Marion
62 Marshall
63 Mason
64 Massac
65 Menard
66 Mercer
67 Monroe
68 Montgomery
69 Morgan
70 Moultrie
71 Ogle
72 Peoria
73 Perry
74 Piatt
75 Pike
76 Pope
77 Pulaski
78 Putnam
79 Randolph
80 Richland
81 Rock Island
82 St Clair
83 Saline
84 Sangamon
85 Schuyler
86 Scott
87 Shelby
88 Stark
89 Stephenson
90 Tazewell
91 Union
92 Vermilion
93 Wabash
94 Warren
95 Washington
96 Wayne
97 White
98 Whiteside
99 Will
100 Williamson
101 Winnebago
102 Woodford

Place		Lat	Long	
Abingdon 48	24	40N48	90w24	6:01:36
Abington 66	4	41N07	90w50	6:03:20
Acacia Acres 16	1	41N48	87w52	5:51:28
Acme Station 72	98	40N40	89w40	5:58:40
Adair 55	4	40N25	90w30	6:02:00
Adams 1	66	39N53	91w06	6:04:24
Adams 50	26	41N35	88w45	5:55:00
Adams Corner 93	4	38N32	87w43	5:50:52
Addieville 95	4	38N23	89w29	5:57:56
Addison 22	17	41N56	87w59	5:51:56
Addison Lake Manor 22	17	41N56	88w00	5:52:00
Adeline 71	63	42N08	89w30	5:58:00
Aden 33	4	38N21	88w35	5:54:20
Adrian 34	4	40N31	91w10	6:04:40
Aero Estates 22	12	41N47	88w09	5:52:36
Aetna 15	63	39N24	88w19	5:53:16
Aetna 54	55	40N05	89w12	5:56:48
Afolkey 89	4	42N23	89w32	5:58:08
Afton 19	60	41N51	88w46	5:55:04
Agnew 98	26	41N48	89w43	5:58:52
Akin 28	4	37N59	88w45	5:55:00
Akron 72	57	40N56	89w42	5:58:48
Alan Dale 60	7	38N57	90w11	6:00:44
Alba 37	4	41N26	89w55	5:59:40
Albany 98	4	41N44	90w13	6:00:52
Albers 14	49	38N33	89w37	5:58:28
Albion 24	4	38N23	88w04	5:52:16
Albright 12	55	39N23	87w42	5:50:48
Alden 56	7	42N27	88w32	5:54:08
Aldridge 91	4	37N30	89w26	5:57:44
Aledo 66	4	41N12	90w45	6:03:00
Alexander 69	4	39N43	90w02	6:00:08
Alexis 94	4	41N04	90w33	6:02:12
Algonquin 56	1	42N12	88w16	5:53:04
Algonquin Trails 16	6	42N04	87w57	5:51:48
Alhambra 60	37	38N52	89w46	5:59:04
Allen 50	56	41N09	88w38	5:54:32
Allen 63	29	40N18	89w36	5:58:24
Allendale 60	7	38N57	90w11	6:00:44
Allendale 93	4	38N32	87w43	5:50:52
Allen Grove 63	29	40N16	89w40	5:58:40
Allens Corners 45	29	42N05	88w28	5:53:52
Allentown 90	98	40N32	89w30	5:58:00
Allenville 70	7	39N33	88w32	5:54:08
Allerton 92	55	39N55	87w56	5:51:44
Allin 57	4	40N27	89w12	5:56:48
Allison 51	4	38N44	87w34	5:50:16
Alma 61	4	38N38	88w51	5:55:24
Alorton 82	25	38N35	90w07	6:00:28
Alpha 37	4	41N12	90w23	6:01:32
Alsey 86	63	39N34	90w26	6:01:44
Alsip 16	1	41N40	87w44	5:50:56
Alsip Woods 16	1	41N40	87w43	5:50:52
Alta 72	98	40N45	89w37	5:58:28
Altamont 25	56	39N04	88w45	5:55:00
Altamont 60	7	38N57	90w11	6:00:44
Alto 52	56	41N51	89w00	5:56:00
Alton 60	7	38N53	90w10	6:00:40
Altona 48	4	41N07	90w10	6:00:40
Alton Siding 59	47	39N18	89w52	5:59:28
Alto Pass 91	4	37N34	89w19	5:57:16
Altorf 46	115	41N10	87w53	5:51:32
Alvan 92	26	40N18	87w36	5:50:24
Amboy 52	29	41N44	89w20	5:57:20
America 77	4	37N09	89w08	5:56:32
Americana Village 22	2	41N53	88w04	5:52:16
Ames 67	55	38N05	90w06	6:00:24
Amity 53	55	40N58	88w45	5:55:00
Anchor 57	55	40N34	88w32	5:54:08
Anchorage 16	1	42N06	87w50	5:51:20
Ancient Tree 16	2	42N07	87w49	5:51:16
Ancona 53	55	41N02	88w52	5:55:28
Andalusia 81	4	41N26	90w43	6:02:52

ILLINOIS

Anderman Acres 99 82 41N35 88w11 5:52:44
Anderson 12 55 39N19 87w44 5:50:56
Andover 37 4 41N17 90w16 6:01:04
Andres 99 30 41N20 87w47 5:51:08
Andrew 84 133 39N48 89w38 5:58:32
Anna 91 4 37N28 89w15 5:57:00
Annapolis 17 4 39N09 87w49 5:51:16
Annawan 37 4 41N24 89w55 5:59:40
Antioch 49 22 42N29 88w06 5:52:24
Appanoose 34 4 40N35 91w18 6:05:12
Apple Canyon Lake 43 4 42N30 90w06 6:00:24
Apple River 43 66 42N29 90w09 6:00:36
Appleton 48 4 40N55 90w07 6:00:28
Appletree 16 6 41N35 87w46 5:51:04
Apple Valley 16 1 42N04 87w48 5:51:12
Aptakisic 49 26 42N11 87w57 5:51:48
Arboretum Villages 22 12 41N47 88w05 5:52:20
Arbor Trails 99 1 41N30 87w41 5:50:44
Arbury Hills 99 4 41N32 87w51 5:51:24
Arcadia 16 1 41N31 87w42 5:50:48
Arcadia 69 63 39N50 90w16 6:01:04
Archer 84 133 39N48 89w38 5:58:32
Archie 92 96 39N55 87w50 5:51:20
Arcola 21 63 39N41 88w19 5:53:16
Arden Shores 49 116 42N17 87w51 5:51:24
Arenzville 9 66 39N53 90w22 6:01:28
Argenta 58 57 39N59 88w49 5:55:16
Argo 8 4 42N06 89w58 5:59:52
Argo 16 1 41N47 87w50 5:51:20
Argyle 4 28 42N19 89w01 5:56:04
Arispie 6 4 41N16 89w27 5:57:48
Arlington 6 54 41N29 89w15 5:57:00
Arlington Heights 16 100 42N05 87w59 5:51:56
Arlington Ridge 16 6 42N06 87w58 5:51:52
Armington 90 55 40N20 89w19 5:57:16
Armstrong 92 54 40N18 87w53 5:51:32
Aroma 46 5 41N05 87w47 5:51:08
Aroma Park 46 5 41N05 87w48 5:51:12
Arrington 96 4 38N22 88w31 5:54:04
Arrowhead 22 2 41N53 88w05 5:52:20
Arrowhead 55 4 40N28 90w41 6:02:44
Arrowsmith 57 97 40N27 88w38 5:54:32
Arrow Wood 60 7 38N57 90w11 6:00:44
Arsenal 99 114 41N31 88w07 5:52:28
Artesia 38 4 40N37 88w03 5:52:12
Arthur 70 50 39N43 88w28 5:53:52
Asbury 30 4 37N53 88w12 5:52:48
Ashburn 16 14 41N45 87w44 5:50:56
Ashkum 38 31 40N53 87w57 5:51:48
Ashland 9 65 39N53 90w01 6:00:04
Ashley 95 4 38N20 89w11 5:56:44
Ashmore 15 63 39N32 88w01 5:52:04
Ashton 52 31 41N52 89w13 5:56:52
Assumption 11 61 39N31 89w03 5:56:12
Astoria 29 66 40N14 90w21 6:01:24
Athenia 16 1 41N31 87w42 5:50:48
Athens 65 55 39N58 89w44 5:58:56
Athensville 31 63 39N29 90w13 6:00:52
Atkinson 37 4 41N25 90w01 6:00:04
Atlanta 54 37 40N16 89w14 5:56:56
Atlas 75 4 39N32 90w59 6:03:56
Atlee Ogles 82 25 38N31 89w59 5:59:56
Atrium 22 27 41N54 87w57 5:51:48
Atterberry 65 4 40N03 89w57 5:59:48
Attila 100 4 37N47 88w51 5:55:24
Atwater 59 4 39N20 89w44 5:58:56
Atwood 74 55 39N48 88w28 5:53:52
Atwood Heights 16 1 41N40 87w43 5:50:52
Auburn 84 101 39N36 89w45 5:59:00
Auburn Park 16 1 41N44 87w39 5:50:36
Audubon 68 7 39N17 89w12 5:56:48
Augsburg 26 4 38N52 89w05 5:56:20
Augusta 34 4 40N14 90w57 6:03:48
Aurora 45 102 41N45 88w19 5:53:16
Austin 16 1 41N58 87w40 5:50:40
Austin 58 55 40N00 89w05 5:56:20
Austin View 16 12 41N40 87w47 5:51:08
Aux Sable 32 48 41N25 88w18 5:53:12
Ava 39 4 37N53 89w30 5:58:00
Avena 26 56 39N03 88w51 5:55:24
Avery Hill 82 25 38N32 90w00 6:00:00
Aviston 14 55 38N36 89w36 5:58:24
Avoca 53 72 40N48 88w31 5:54:04
Avon 29 4 40N40 90w26 6:01:44
Ayers 10 54 39N55 87w58 5:51:52
Babcock 81 87 41N30 90w26 6:01:44
Babson 45 95 41N54 88w19 5:53:16
Baden Baden 3 63 38N52 89w33 5:58:12
Bader 85 66 40N08 90w22 6:01:28
Baileyville 71 63 42N12 89w36 5:58:24
Bainbridge 85 7 40N03 90w30 6:02:00
Baker 50 26 41N34 88w49 5:55:16
Bakerville 41 4 38N18 88w55 5:55:40
Balcom 91 4 37N28 89w15 5:57:00
Bald Bluff 36 4 41N02 90w50 6:03:20
Bald Hill 41 4 38N10 89w06 5:56:24
Baldwin 79 55 38N11 89w51 5:59:24
Baldwin Beach 63 55 40N18 90w04 6:00:16
Bales Lake 38 43 40N31 88w05 5:52:20
Ball 84 30 39N40 89w39 5:58:36
Ballou 99 7 41N19 88w06 5:52:24
Banner 29 4 40N32 89w58 5:59:52
Bannister 61 4 38N36 88w57 5:55:48
Bannockburn 49 2 42N11 87w52 5:51:28
Barclay 84 29 39N51 89w32 5:58:08
Bardolph 55 4 40N30 90w34 6:02:16
Bargerville 64 4 37N09 88w44 5:54:56
Barnett 20 55 40N11 89w05 5:56:20
Barnett 68 37 39N11 89w39 5:58:36
Barnhill 96 4 38N17 88w22 5:53:28
Barr 59 63 39N23 90w05 6:00:20
Barren 28 4 38N05 88w59 5:55:56
Barrington 49 1 42N09 88w08 5:52:32
Barrington Highlands 49 1 42N09 88w06 5:52:24
Barrington Hills 16 1 42N08 88w13 5:52:52
Barrington Woods 16 1 42N09 88w04 5:52:16
Barrow 31 4 39N29 90w22 6:01:28
Barry 75 4 39N42 91w02 6:04:08
Barstow 81 63 41N31 90w21 6:01:24
Bartelso 14 55 38N32 89w28 5:57:52
Bartlett 16 27 42N00 88w11 5:52:44
Bartonville 72 98 40N39 89w39 5:58:36
Basco 34 4 40N20 91w12 6:04:48
Base 10 29 40N19 88w08 5:52:32
Batavia 45 103 41N50 88w19 5:53:16
Batavia Highlands 45 103 41N52 88w19 5:53:16
Batchtown 7 65 39N02 90w39 6:02:36
Bates 84 55 39N45 89w54 5:59:36
Batestown 92 54 40N17 87w41 5:50:44
Bath 63 63 40N11 90w08 6:00:32
Battery Rock 35 4 37N32 88w07 5:52:28
Bay City 76 4 37N22 88w29 5:53:56
Bay Colony 16 6 42N03 87w55 5:51:40
Bayle 26 4 39N09 89w06 5:56:24
Baylestown 59 55 39N08 89w49 5:59:16
Baylis 75 4 39N44 90w55 6:03:40
Bayview Gardens 102 4 40N49 89w31 5:58:04
Beach 49 140 42N25 87w49 5:51:16
Beacon Hill 16 1 41N31 87w38 5:50:32
Beardstown 9 7 40N01 90w26 6:01:44
Bear Grove 26 139 38N58 89w11 5:56:44
Bearsdale 58 26 39N52 88w57 5:55:48
Beason 54 55 40N09 89w12 5:56:48
Beau Bien 22 12 41N47 88w05 5:52:20
Beaucoup 95 4 38N21 89w23 5:57:32
Beaver 38 57 40N54 87w36 5:50:24
Beaver Creek 3 55 38N54 89w24 5:57:36
Beaver Creek 33 4 38N10 88w26 5:53:44
Beaver Valley 16 12 41N38 87w51 5:51:24
Beaverville 38 55 40N58 87w37 5:50:28
Beckemeyer 14 55 38N36 89w26 5:57:44
Bedford 75 63 39N28 90w37 6:02:28
Bedford 96 4 38N31 88w25 5:53:40
Bedford Park 16 1 41N46 87w47 5:51:08
Beecher 99 22 41N21 87w38 5:50:32
Beecher City 25 4 39N11 88w47 5:55:08
Beechville 7 65 39N02 90w39 6:02:36
Beecreek 75 63 39N28 90w37 6:02:28
Bel Air Gardens 16 1 42N04 87w48 5:51:12
Belgium 92 26 40N04 87w38 5:50:32
Belgium Row 92 54 40N07 87w47 5:51:08
Belknap 44 4 37N19 88w56 5:55:44
Bellair 17 4 39N00 87w54 5:51:36
Belle Prairie 53 55 40N39 88w31 5:54:04
Belle Prairie City 33 4 38N13 88w33 5:54:12
Belle Rive 41 4 38N14 88w45 5:55:00
Belleview 7 4 39N14 90w43 6:02:52
Belleville 82 25 38N31 89w59 5:59:56
Bellevue 72 98 40N41 89w40 5:58:40
Bellflower 57 56 40N20 88w32 5:54:08
Bellmont 93 13 38N24 87w54 5:51:36
Bell Plain 62 56 41N02 89w13 5:56:52
Belltown 31 4 39N26 90w24 6:01:36
Bellwood 16 2 41N53 87w53 5:51:32
Belmont 38 16 40N44 87w43 5:50:52
Belmont Village 60 7 38N57 90w11 6:00:44
Beltrees 42 4 38N56 90w21 6:01:24
Belvidere 4 26 42N15 88w50 5:55:20
Bement 74 30 39N55 88w34 5:54:16
Benedale Green 22 12 41N47 88w05 5:52:20
Benevolent Heights 82 25 38N31 89w59 5:59:56
Benld 59 55 39N06 89w48 5:59:12
Bennington 24 4 38N31 88w00 5:52:00
Bennington 62 54 41N02 89w06 5:56:24
Bensenville 22 17 41N58 87w58 5:51:52
Benson 102 21 40N51 89w07 5:56:28
Bently 34 4 40N20 91w06 6:04:24
Benton 28 4 38N00 88w55 5:55:40
Benton City Park 28 4 38N00 88w56 5:55:44
Ben Town 57 104 40N29 88w59 5:55:56
Berdan 31 55 39N18 90w24 6:01:36
Berger 16 1 41N37 87w40 5:50:40
Berkeley 16 2 41N53 87w54 5:51:36
Berlin 84 55 39N45 89w54 5:59:36
Bernadotte 29 63 40N25 90w16 6:01:04
Bernice 16 19 41N34 87w34 5:50:16
Berreman 43 4 42N14 89w57 5:59:48
Berry 84 55 39N45 89w32 5:58:08
Berry 96 4 38N26 88w32 5:54:08
Berryville 80 4 38N39 88w03 5:52:12
Berwick 94 4 40N45 90w30 6:02:00
Berwyn 16 1 41N51 87w47 5:51:08
Bethalto 60 55 38N55 90w02 6:00:08
Bethany 70 56 39N39 88w45 5:55:00
Bethel 13 4 39N38 88w38 5:54:32
Bethel 55 4 40N20 90w44 6:02:56
Bethel 69 4 39N46 90w24 6:01:36
Bethel 92 54 39N54 87w39 5:50:36
Bethlehem 25 4 39N04 88w45 5:55:00
Beulah Heights 83 4 37N49 88w27 5:53:48
Beverly 1 66 39N48 91w00 6:04:00
Beverly Manor 90 98 40N42 89w25 5:57:40
Bible Grove 13 4 38N52 88w25 5:53:40
Biddleborn 95 55 38N15 89w45 5:59:00
Big Bay 64 4 37N09 88w44 5:54:56
Big Foot 56 7 42N25 88w37 5:54:28
Big Grove 47 55 41N30 88w32 5:54:08
Biggs 63 63 40N14 89w51 5:59:24
Biggsville 36 4 40N51 90w52 6:03:28
Big Hollow 49 27 42N23 88w09 5:52:36
Big Mound 96 4 38N20 88w25 5:53:40
Bigneck 1 53 40N09 91w13 6:04:52
Big Rock 45 25 41N45 88w33 5:54:12
Big Spring 87 1 39N19 88w32 5:54:08
Billett 51 4 38N40 87w39 5:50:36
Bingham 26 4 39N07 89w13 5:56:52
Binghampton 52 29 41N43 89w20 5:57:20
Binney 60 7 38N58 89w40 5:58:40
Bird 59 63 39N19 89w59 5:59:56
Birds 51 4 38N50 87w40 5:50:40
Birkbeck 20 8 40N09 88w57 5:55:48
Birmingham 85 4 40N14 90w51 6:03:24
Bishop 25 4 39N03 88w25 5:53:40
Bishop 63 7 40N22 89w50 5:59:20
Bishop Hill 37 4 41N12 90w07 6:00:28
Bismarck 92 26 40N16 87w37 5:50:28
Bissell 84 133 39N48 89w38 5:58:32
Black 24 4 38N23 88w03 5:52:12
Blackberry 45 55 41N49 88w27 5:53:48
Blackberry Heights 45 102 41N46 88w20 5:53:20
Blackberry Woods 45 41 41N45 88w27 5:53:48
Black Hawk 81 87 41N27 90w34 6:02:16
Blackhawk Heights 22 2 41N47 87w57 5:51:48
Blackstone 53 55 41N05 88w42 5:54:48
Blaine 4 91 42N22 88w49 5:55:16
Blair 53 36 41N06 88w15 5:53:00
Blair 79 63 38N07 89w42 5:58:48
Blairsville 33 4 38N06 88w32 5:54:08
Blairsville 100 4 37N48 89w05 5:56:20
Blandinsville 55 4 40N33 90w52 6:03:28
Blissville 41 4 38N15 89w06 5:56:24
Blodgett 49 1 42N11 87w49 5:51:16
Bloom 16 1 41N31 87w35 5:50:20
Bloomfield 44 4 37N25 88w54 5:55:36
Bloomingdale 22 27 41N58 88w05 5:52:20
Bloomington 57 104 40N29 89w00 5:56:00
Bloomington Heights 57 104 40N29 88w59 5:55:56
Blossom Hill 56 1 42N14 88w15 5:53:00
Blount 92 26 40N12 87w41 5:50:44
Blue Fountain 60 7 38N57 90w11 6:00:44
Blue Island 16 2 41N40 87w41 5:50:44
Blue Island Junction 16 1 41N39 87w42 5:50:48
Blue Mound 58 58 39N42 89w07 5:56:28
Blue Point 25 4 39N07 88w33 5:54:12
Blue Ridge 74 55 40N14 88w32 5:54:08
Bluff 67 55 38N17 90w15 6:01:00
Bluff City 26 139 38N58 89w03 5:56:12
Bluff City 85 66 40N08 90w22 6:01:28
Bluffdale 31 63 39N19 90w33 6:02:12
Bluff Hall 1 85 39N49 91w15 6:05:00
Bluffs 86 65 39N45 90w32 6:02:08
Bluffside 82 46 38N27 90w12 6:00:48
Bluff Springs 9 7 40N01 90w20 6:01:20
Bluff View Park 82 25 38N37 90w01 6:00:04
Bluford 41 4 38N20 88w45 5:55:00
Blyton 29 63 40N28 90w18 6:01:12
Boaz 64 4 37N18 88w59 5:55:56
Boden 66 4 41N20 90w30 6:02:00
Bogan's 25 4 39N07 88w33 5:54:12
Bogota 40 4 38N55 88w15 5:53:00
Bohleysville 82 55 38N28 90w06 6:00:24
Bois d'Arc 68 63 39N29 89w37 5:58:28
Boles 44 4 37N26 88w58 5:55:52
Bolingbrook 99 4 41N42 88w03 5:52:12
Boling Green 99 1 41N40 88w00 5:52:00
Bolivia 11 8 39N48 89w24 5:57:36
Bolo 95 4 38N15 89w19 5:57:16
Bolton 89 4 42N18 89w38 5:58:32
Bond 51 4 38N49 87w42 5:50:48
Bondville 10 23 40N07 88w22 5:53:28
Bone Gap 24 4 38N27 88w00 5:52:00
Bonfield 46 55 41N09 88w03 5:52:12
Bongard 10 54 40N00 88w09 5:52:36
Bonnie 41 4 38N12 88w54 5:55:36
Bonnie Brea 99 114 41N35 88w03 5:52:12
Bonpas 80 4 38N37 87w58 5:51:52
Bonus 4 26 42N16 88w46 5:55:04
Boody 58 57 39N46 89w03 5:56:12
Boone 4 8 42N22 88w45 5:55:00
Boos 40 4 38N59 88w10 5:52:40
Booster Station 82 25 38N36 89w58 5:59:52
Borton 23 65 39N39 87w56 5:51:44
Boskydell 39 4 37N43 89w14 5:56:56
Boulder 14 4 38N42 89w13 5:56:52
Boulder Hill 47 102 41N44 88w19 5:53:16
Boulevard Manor 16 1 41N51 87w46 5:51:04
Bourbon 21 55 39N45 88w23 5:53:32
Bourbonnais 46 115 41N11 87w52 5:51:28
Bowdre 21 65 39N44 88w09 5:52:36
Bowen 34 4 40N14 91w04 6:04:16
Bowlesville 30 4 37N39 88w12 5:52:48
Bowling 81 4 41N23 90w37 6:02:28
Bowling Green 26 63 39N11 88w57 5:55:48
Boyd 41 4 38N26 88w56 5:55:44
Boyleston 96 4 38N23 88w22 5:53:28
Boynton 90 72 40N22 89w26 5:57:44
Braceville 32 37 41N14 88w16 5:53:04
Bradbury 18 4 39N17 88w15 5:53:00
Bradford 88 4 41N11 89w39 5:58:36
Bradfordton 84 133 39N48 89w38 5:58:32
Bradley 32 125 41N22 88w25 5:53:40
Bradley 46 7 41N09 87w52 5:51:28
Braeside 49 3 42N11 87w49 5:51:16
Braidwood 99 36 41N16 88w13 5:52:52

ILLINOIS

Branding 7	65	38N57	90w36	6:02:24
Brandywine 22	21	41N53	87w58	5:51:52
Branigar Estates 16	27	42N01	88w00	5:52:00
Breckenridge 84	55	39N45	89w32	5:58:08
Breeds 29	4	40N32	89w58	5:59:52
Breese 14	55	38N37	89w32	5:58:08
Bremen 79	66	37N55	89w49	5:59:16
Brenton 27	30	40N43	88w11	5:52:44
Brentwood Estates 16	6	42N06	88w02	5:52:08
Brereton 29	4	40N32	89w58	5:59:52
Brettwood 58	26	39N52	88w57	5:55:48
Brewerville 79	63	38N02	90w00	6:00:00
Briar Bluff 37	87	41N28	90w28	6:01:52
Briarbrook Village 22	2	41N53	88w05	5:52:20
Briarcliffe 22	2	41N53	88w05	5:52:20
Briarwoods Estates 49	6	42N10	87w53	5:51:32
Briarwood Trace 100	4	37N43	89w14	5:56:56
Brickman Manor 16	6	42N04	87w57	5:51:48
Bridgelane 81	87	41N30	90w30	6:02:00
Bridgeport 51	4	38N43	87w46	5:51:04
Bridgeview 16	1	41N45	87w48	5:51:12
Bridgeway Addition 81	87	41N30	90w30	6:02:00
Bright Oaks 56	1	42N14	88w15	5:53:00
Brighton 59	37	39N02	90w08	6:00:32
Brimfield 72	58	40N50	89w53	5:59:32
Brisbane 99	1	41N31	87w58	5:51:52
Bristol 47	7	41N42	88w25	5:53:40
Bristol Lake 47	25	41N39	88w27	5:53:48
Bristol Ridge 47	25	41N39	88w27	5:53:48
Broadlands 10	54	39N54	88w00	5:52:00
Broadmoor 62	4	41N11	89w39	5:58:36
Broadview 16	2	41N52	87w50	5:51:20
Broadway 101	28	42N17	89w04	5:56:16
Broadwell 54	29	40N04	89w27	5:57:48
Brocton 23	55	39N43	87w56	5:51:44
Brooke Estates 49	1	42N11	87w49	5:51:16
Brookeridge 22	12	41N48	88w01	5:52:04
Brookfield 16	1	41N50	87w51	5:51:24
Brook Forest 22	2	41N48	87w56	5:51:44
Brookforest North 99	114	41N33	88w07	5:52:28
Brookhaven 98	4	41N40	89w56	5:59:44
Brookhaven Manor 22	19	41N47	87w59	5:51:56
Brookhill 49	42	42N16	87w56	5:51:44
Brooklyn 82	25	38N39	90w10	6:00:40
Brooklyn 85	4	40N17	90w56	6:03:44
Brookport 64	62	37N08	88w38	5:54:32
Brooks 60	4	38N43	90w07	6:00:28
Brookside 14	4	38N32	89w12	5:56:48
Brooks Isle 71	28	42N01	89w20	5:57:20
Brookview 72	98	40N45	89w37	5:58:28
Brookville 71	63	42N04	89w39	5:58:36
Brookwood 16	1	42N07	87w56	5:51:44
Brookwood Estates 22	17	41N57	87w59	5:51:56
Brothers 92	54	40N07	87w47	5:51:08
Broughton 33	4	37N56	88w27	5:53:48
Brouilletts Creek 23	4	39N45	87w35	5:50:20
Brown 10	54	40N21	88w24	5:53:36
Brownfield 76	4	37N21	88w36	5:54:24
Browning 85	66	40N08	90w22	6:01:28
Browns 24	4	38N23	87w59	5:51:56
Brownstown 26	56	39N00	88w57	5:55:48
Brownsville 97	4	38N06	88w09	5:52:36
Brownwood 90	72	40N25	89w25	5:57:40
Brubaker 61	4	38N40	88w55	5:55:40
Bruce 50	135	41N10	88w50	5:55:20
Bruce 70	7	39N36	88w36	5:54:24
Brunning 99	114	41N35	88w03	5:52:12
Brunswick 87	63	39N31	88w45	5:55:00
Brushy 83	4	37N47	88w39	5:54:36
Brushy Mound 59	47	39N13	89w53	5:59:32
Brussels 7	65	38N57	90w36	6:02:24
Bryant 29	7	40N28	90w06	6:00:24
Bryce 38	7	40N38	87w42	5:50:48
Buck 23	67	39N39	87w50	5:51:20
Buckeye 89	61	42N25	89w39	5:58:36
Buckhart 84	55	39N39	89w21	5:57:24
Buckheart 29	7	40N30	90w03	6:00:12
Buckhorn 5	66	39N53	90w51	6:03:24
Buckingham 46	36	41N03	88w10	5:52:40
Buckley 38	43	40N36	88w02	5:52:08
Buckner 28	4	37N59	89w01	5:56:04
Bucks 20	35	40N19	88w58	5:55:52
Buda 6	63	41N20	89w41	5:58:44
Buena Vista 83	4	37N44	88w33	5:54:12
Buena Vista 85	65	40N09	90w37	6:02:28
Buena Vista 89	4	42N18	89w38	5:58:32
Buffalo 84	8	39N51	89w25	5:57:40
Buffalo Grove 16	6	42N09	87w58	5:51:52
Buffalo Grove 71	4	41N59	89w35	5:58:20
Buffalo Hart 84	8	39N54	89w26	5:57:44
Buffalo Prairie 81	4	41N20	90w51	6:03:24
Bull Creek 49	42	42N16	87w56	5:51:44
Bulpitt 11	26	39N35	89w25	5:57:40
Buncombe 44	4	37N28	88w58	5:55:52
Bungay 33	4	38N11	88w21	5:53:24
Bunker Hill 59	55	39N03	89w57	5:59:48
Bunker Hill Estates 16	1	42N02	87w49	5:51:16
Bunkum 82	4	39N21	90w47	6:03:08
Bunsenville 92	54	39N58	87w38	5:50:32
Burbank 16	1	41N44	87w45	5:51:00
Bureau 6	55	41N27	89w34	5:58:16
Burgess 66	4	41N08	90w38	6:02:32
Burksville 67	8	38N20	90w09	6:00:36
Burlington 45	41	42N03	88w33	5:54:12
Burnham 16	6	41N38	87w34	5:50:16
Burnham Mill 45	107	42N02	88w17	5:53:08
Burns 37	4	41N16	90w02	6:00:08
Burnside 34	4	40N30	91w06	6:04:24
Burnside 44	4	37N33	88w46	5:55:04
Burnside's Lakewood 16	29	41N29	87w43	5:50:52
Burnt Prairie 97	4	38N12	88w12	5:52:48
Burritt 101	4	42N20	89w13	5:56:52
Burr Oak 16	1	41N39	87w42	5:50:48
Burr Oaks 99	114	41N33	88w07	5:52:28
Burr Ridge 16	2	41N47	87w55	5:51:40
Burt 90	86	40N20	89w19	5:57:16
Burton 1	92	39N55	91w23	6:05:32
Burtons Bridge 56	1	42N17	88w14	5:52:56
Burtonview 54	29	40N09	89w22	5:57:28
Bush 100	4	37N51	89w08	5:56:32
Bushnell 55	4	40N33	90w31	6:02:04
Bushton 15	106	39N29	88w13	5:52:52
Butler 68	7	39N12	89w32	5:58:08
Butler Grove 68	7	39N13	89w32	5:58:08
Butterfield 22	83	41N53	88w01	5:52:04
Butterfield West 22	2	41N53	88w04	5:52:16
Button 27	43	40N27	88w00	5:52:00
Buzzville 63	55	40N18	90w04	6:00:16
Byron 71	57	42N08	89w15	5:57:00
Byron Hills 81	4	41N37	90w20	6:01:20
Cabery 46	38	41N00	88w12	5:52:48
Cable 66	4	41N20	90w30	6:02:00
Cache 2	4	37N22	88w59	5:55:56
Cadwell 70	50	39N43	88w28	5:53:52
Cahokia 82	25	38N34	90w11	6:00:44
Cairo 2	4	37N00	89w11	5:56:44
Caledonia 4	45	42N22	88w54	5:55:36
Calhoun 80	4	38N39	88w03	5:52:12
Calumet 16	1	41N40	87w39	5:50:36
Calumet City 16	21	41N37	87w32	5:50:08
Calumet Park 16	1	41N42	87w40	5:50:40
Calvin 97	4	38N13	88w01	5:52:04
Camargo 21	65	39N49	88w10	5:52:40
Cambria 100	4	37N47	89w07	5:56:28
Cambridge 37	4	41N18	90w12	6:00:48
Cambridge 49	42	42N16	87w56	5:51:44
Cambridge-on-the-Lake 16	6	42N09	87w57	5:51:48
Camden 85	4	40N09	90w46	6:03:04
Cameo Terrace 16	6	42N09	87w57	5:51:48
Cameron 94	4	40N53	90w31	6:02:04
Campbell 15	63	39N25	88w18	5:53:12
Campbell Hill 39	63	37N56	89w33	5:58:12
Campbells Island 81	87	41N30	90w26	6:01:44
Camp Epworth 4	26	42N15	88w44	5:54:56
Camp Ground 41	4	38N18	88w55	5:55:40
Camp Grove 62	4	41N05	89w38	5:58:32
Camp Point 1	66	40N03	91w04	6:04:16
Campton 45	60	41N54	88w26	5:53:44
Campus 53	36	41N01	88w18	5:53:12
Campus Walk 45	107	42N02	88w17	5:53:08
Candlewood Estates 10	54	40N12	88w24	5:53:36
Canoe Creek 81	4	41N37	90w12	6:00:48
Canteen 82	25	38N38	90w04	6:00:16
Canterbury Lane 16	1	42N04	87w48	5:51:12
Canton 29	7	40N33	90w02	6:00:08
Cantrall 84	55	39N56	89w41	5:58:44
Capitol 84	133	39N48	89w39	5:58:36
Capitol Oaks 82	25	38N35	89w58	5:59:52
Capri Gardens 16	6	42N06	88w02	5:52:08
Capri Village 16	6	42N06	88w02	5:52:08
Capron 4	8	42N24	88w44	5:54:56
Carbon 82	25	38N36	89w58	5:59:52
Carbon Cliff 81	87	41N30	90w23	6:01:32
Carbondale 39	4	37N44	89w13	5:56:52
Carbon Hill 32	30	41N18	88w18	5:53:12
Cardiff 53	26	41N06	88w26	5:53:44
Carlin Prec 7	4	39N21	90w39	6:02:36
Carlinville 59	47	39N17	89w53	5:59:32
Carlock 57	32	40N35	89w08	5:56:32
Carlyle 14	55	38N37	89w22	5:57:28
Carman 36	4	40N46	91w03	6:04:12
Carmi 97	4	38N05	88w10	5:52:40
Carol Stream 22	2	41N55	88w07	5:52:28
Carpenter 60	25	38N48	89w57	5:59:48
Carpentersville 45	105	42N07	88w17	5:53:08
Carriage Creek 16	29	41N29	87w43	5:50:52
Carrier Mills 83	4	37N41	88w38	5:54:32
Carrigan 61	4	38N38	89w05	5:56:20
Carroll 92	72	39N55	87w45	5:51:00
Carrollton 31	55	39N18	90w24	6:01:36
Carrollwood 60	29	38N52	90w05	6:00:20
Carson 26	63	39N09	89w00	5:56:00
Carterville 100	4	37N44	89w06	5:56:24
Carthage 34	23	40N25	91w08	6:04:32
Carthage Lake 36	4	40N44	91w04	6:04:16
Cartter 61	4	38N30	88w54	5:55:36
Cartwright 84	29	39N51	89w54	5:59:36
Cary 56	1	42N13	88w14	5:52:56
Casey 12	56	39N18	88w00	5:52:00
Caseyville 82	25	38N38	90w02	6:00:08
Casner 41	4	38N21	89w05	5:56:20
Casner 58	54	39N53	88w48	5:55:12
Cass 29	63	40N30	90w16	6:01:04
Castleton 88	4	41N07	89w42	5:58:48
Catlin 92	54	40N04	87w42	5:50:48
Cave 28	4	37N54	88w46	5:55:04
Cave In Rock 35	4	37N28	88w10	5:52:40
Cayuga 53	127	40N53	88w38	5:54:32
Cazenovia 102	4	40N53	89w19	5:57:16
Cedar 48	4	40N51	90w23	6:01:32
Cedar Glen 47	4	41N41	88w21	5:53:24
Cedar Grove 100	4	37N46	88w56	5:55:44
Cedar Island 49	6	42N24	88w11	5:52:44
Cedar Point 50	57	41N16	89w07	5:56:28
Cedar Run 16	6	42N09	87w57	5:51:48
Cedarville 89	61	42N23	89w38	5:58:32
Center Hill 8	4	42N06	89w58	5:59:52
Centerville 7	65	38N57	90w36	6:02:24
Centerville 59	4	39N07	90w03	6:00:12
Centerville 69	63	39N33	90w01	6:00:04
Centerville 74	55	40N13	88w31	5:54:04
Centerville 97	4	38N06	88w09	5:52:36
Central City 61	55	38N33	89w08	5:56:32
Centralia 61	4	38N32	89w08	5:56:32
Central Park 92	54	40N17	87w41	5:50:44
Centreville 82	25	38N33	90w07	6:00:28
Century Oaks West 45	107	42N02	88w17	5:53:08
Cermak Plaza 16	1	41N51	87w48	5:51:12
Cerro Gordo 74	54	39N53	88w44	5:54:56
Chadwick 8	4	42N01	89w53	5:59:32
Chalfin Bridge 67	63	38N10	90w13	6:00:52
Chalmers 55	4	40N25	90w43	6:02:52
Chambersburg 75	65	39N48	90w38	6:02:32
Chambord 22	2	41N48	87w56	5:51:44
Champaign 10	21	40N07	88w15	5:53:00
Chana 71	4	41N59	89w13	5:56:52
Chandlerville 9	29	40N03	90w09	6:00:36
Channahon 99	48	41N26	88w14	5:52:56
Channel Lake 49	6	42N29	88w09	5:52:36
Chantilly 49	1	42N11	87w49	5:51:16
Chanute Air Force Base 10	29	40N18	88w09	5:52:36
Chapin 69	65	39N46	90w24	6:01:36
Chapman 68	4	39N07	89w16	5:57:04
Charleston 15	106	39N30	88w10	5:52:40
Charlotte 53	44	40N48	88w18	5:53:12
Charter Grove 19	6	41N59	88w42	5:54:48
Chasco 44	4	37N22	89w01	5:56:04
Chateau Terrace 82	25	38N32	90w00	6:00:00
Chatham 84	30	39N40	89w42	5:58:48
Chatsworth 53	58	40N45	88w18	5:53:12
Chauncey 51	4	38N50	87w52	5:51:28
Chautauqua 42	4	38N57	90w21	6:01:24
Chautauqua Park 63	55	40N18	90w04	6:00:16
Chautauqua Park 65	29	40N01	89w51	5:59:24
Chebanse 38	57	41N00	87w54	5:51:36
Check Row 29	4	40N40	90w26	6:01:44
Chelsea Cove 16	6	42N09	87w57	5:51:48
Chemung 56	7	42N27	88w39	5:54:36
Cheney Grove 57	36	40N26	88w31	5:54:04
Cheneyville 92	80	40N28	87w35	5:50:20
Chenoa 57	35	40N45	88w43	5:54:52
Chenot Place 82	25	38N31	89w59	5:59:56
Cherry 6	58	41N26	89w13	5:56:52
Cherry Grove 8	4	42N09	89w48	5:59:12
Cherry Hill 99	114	41N31	88w00	5:52:00
Cherry Point 23	7	39N48	87w41	5:50:44
Cherry Valley 101	28	42N13	89w01	5:56:04
Cherrywood 11	7	39N34	89w21	5:57:24
Cherrywood 99	1	41N40	88w00	5:52:00
Chester 79	66	37N55	89w49	5:59:16
Chesterfield 59	63	39N15	90w04	6:00:16
Chesterville 21	50	39N42	88w24	5:53:36
Chestnut 48	33	40N46	90w17	6:01:08
Chestnut 54	55	40N03	89w11	5:56:44
Chicago 16	1	41N52	87w39	5:50:36
Chicago Heights 16	1	41N31	87w38	5:50:32
Chicago Lawn 16	1	41N47	87w43	5:50:52
Chicago Ridge 16	1	41N42	87w47	5:51:08
Chili 34	4	40N14	91w06	6:04:24
Chillicothe 72	51	40N55	89w29	5:57:56
Chilon Chalet 16	1	41N31	87w38	5:50:32
China 52	37	41N49	89w19	5:57:16
Chinatown 60	7	38N43	89w57	5:59:48
Chippendale 49	6	42N09	88w06	5:52:24
Chippewa 16	1	41N40	87w43	5:50:52
Chittenden 49	140	42N22	87w53	5:51:32
Chittyville 100	4	37N48	89w02	5:56:08
Chouteau 60	4	38N47	90w05	6:00:20
Chrisman 23	7	39N48	87w41	5:50:44
Christopher 28	4	37N59	89w03	5:56:12
Christy 51	4	38N42	87w51	5:51:24
Churchville 22	27	41N54	87w57	5:51:48
Cicero 16	1	41N51	87w45	5:51:00
Cimic 84	37	39N34	89w39	5:58:36
Cinnamon Creek 99	1	41N40	88w00	5:52:00
Cisco 74	57	40N01	88w44	5:54:56
Cisne 96	4	38N31	88w26	5:53:44
Cissna Park 38	132	40N34	87w54	5:51:36
Citation Lake Estates 16	2	42N07	87w49	5:51:16
City Park 11	7	39N34	89w21	5:57:24
Clare 19	40	42N01	88w50	5:55:20
Claremont 80	4	38N43	87w58	5:51:52
Clarence 27	132	40N28	87w58	5:51:52
Clarendon Hills 22	2	41N48	87w57	5:51:48
Clarion 6	54	41N32	89w13	5:56:52
Clark Center 12	55	39N22	87w47	5:51:08
Clarksburg 87	7	39N19	88w45	5:55:00
Clarksdale 11	63	39N27	89w24	5:57:36
Clarksville 12	55	39N23	87w42	5:50:48
Clarksville 57	7	40N39	88w47	5:55:08
Clarmin 95	55	38N15	89w45	5:59:00
Clay City 13	4	38N41	88w21	5:53:24
Claypool 32	125	41N22	88w25	5:53:40
Clays Prairie 23	128	39N37	87w42	5:50:48
Clayton 1	63	40N02	90w57	6:03:48
Claytonville 38	7	40N34	87w49	5:51:16
Clearing 16	1	41N47	87w46	5:51:04

Clear Lake 84	29	39N50	89w33	5:58:12
Cleburne 28	4	37N58	89w07	5:56:28
Clement 14	55	38N36	89w18	5:57:12
Cleone 12	4	39N20	87w53	5:51:32
Cleveland 37	63	41N30	90w19	6:01:16
Clifton 38	35	40N56	87w56	5:51:44
Clifton Terrace 60	7	38N57	90w11	6:00:44
Clifty Heights 100	4	37N46	88w56	5:55:44
Clinch 73	4	38N01	89w14	5:56:56
Clinton 20	8	40N09	88w57	5:55:48
Clintonia 20	8	40N10	88w59	5:55:56
Clover 37	4	41N12	90w16	6:01:04
Cloverdale 22	1	41N56	88w07	5:52:28
Cloverdale 90	98	40N39	89w34	5:58:16
Cloverleaf 60	25	38N41	90w07	6:00:28
Cloverleaf 81	87	41N30	90w30	6:02:00
Clyde 16	1	41N51	87w46	5:51:04
Clyde 98	55	41N53	89w55	5:59:40
Coach Light Manor 16	6	42N04	87w57	5:51:48
Coal City 32	30	41N17	88w17	5:53:08
Coal Hollow 6	41	41N22	89w23	5:57:32
Coalton 68	7	39N17	89w18	5:57:12
Coal Valley 81	87	41N27	90w28	6:01:52
Coatsburg 1	63	40N02	91w10	6:04:40
Cobblestone 16	1	42N04	87w48	5:51:12
Cobblewood 16	2	42N07	87w49	5:51:16
Cobden 91	4	37N32	89w15	5:57:00
Coe 81	4	41N37	90w16	6:01:04
Coello 28	4	38N00	89w04	5:56:16
Coffee 93	4	38N20	87w52	5:51:28
Coffeen 68	63	39N05	89w24	5:57:36
Colby Point 56	27	42N21	88w14	5:52:56
Colchester 55	4	40N25	90w48	6:03:12
Coldbrook 94	4	40N56	90w29	6:01:56
Cold Spring 87	63	39N18	88w58	5:55:52
Coleta 98	4	41N39	89w55	5:59:40
Colfax 57	55	40N34	88w37	5:54:28
College Heights 83	4	37N49	88w27	5:53:48
College Park 45	107	42N02	88w17	5:53:08
College View 99	114	41N35	88w03	5:52:12
Collins 99	82	41N35	88w11	5:52:44
Collins 101	4	42N29	89w02	5:56:08
Collinsville 60	7	38N40	89w59	5:59:56
Collison 92	38	40N14	87w48	5:51:12
Colmar 55	4	40N21	90w53	6:03:32
Coloma 98	26	41N47	89w41	5:58:44
Colona 37	63	41N28	90w21	6:01:24
Colonial Gardens 101	55	42N19	89w02	5:56:08
Colonial Heights 16	6	42N04	87w57	5:51:48
Colonial Ridge 16	6	42N03	87w53	5:51:32
Colonial Village 60	7	38N57	90w11	6:00:44
Colonial Village 99	1	41N40	88w00	5:52:00
Colony Park 22	2	41N53	88w05	5:52:20
Colony Point 49	6	42N10	87w53	5:51:32
Colp 100	4	37N48	89w05	5:56:20
Columbia 67	46	38N27	90w12	6:00:48
Columbus 1	63	39N59	91w09	6:04:36
Colusa 34	4	40N34	91w10	6:04:40
Como 98	26	41N48	89w43	5:58:52
Compromise 10	54	40N16	88w00	5:52:00
Compton 52	57	41N42	89w05	5:56:20
Conant 73	4	38N05	89w23	5:57:32
Concord 69	66	39N49	90w22	6:01:28
Concord Green 49	42	42N16	87w56	5:51:44
Condit 10	54	40N16	88w17	5:53:08
Confidence 26	4	39N00	88w57	5:55:48
Congerville 102	5	40N37	89w13	5:56:52
Congress Park 16	1	41N50	87w51	5:51:24
Conlogue 23	128	39N37	87w42	5:50:48
Conover 47	25	41N39	88w27	5:53:48
Continental Village 49	140	42N23	87w52	5:51:28
Cooks Mills 15	65	39N36	88w19	5:53:16
Cooksville 57	57	40N33	88w43	5:54:52
Cooper 84	8	39N45	89w26	5:57:44
Cooperstown 5	65	39N58	90w37	6:02:28
Copley 48	4	41N01	90w09	6:00:36
Cora 39	50	37N50	89w41	5:58:44
Coral 56	29	42N12	88w32	5:54:08
Coral Gable 82	25	38N36	89w58	5:59:52
Cordova 81	4	41N41	90w19	6:01:16
Corinth 100	4	37N49	88w46	5:55:04
Cornell 53	55	41N00	88w44	5:54:56
Cornerville 83	4	37N50	88w37	5:54:28
Cornland 54	4	39N56	89w24	5:57:36
Cornwall 37	4	41N22	90w02	6:00:08
Cortese 46	115	41N05	87w53	5:51:32
Cortland 19	6	41N56	88w39	5:54:36
Corwin 54	63	40N06	89w32	5:58:08
Costin 57	104	40N29	88w59	5:55:56
Cottage 83	4	37N44	88w25	5:53:40
Cottagegrove 83	4	37N49	88w27	5:53:48
Cottage Hills 60	29	38N54	90w04	6:00:16
Cotton Hill 84	55	39N40	89w33	5:58:12
Cottonwood 30	4	37N53	88w13	5:52:52
Coulterville 79	55	38N11	89w36	5:58:24
Council Hill 43	4	42N29	90w21	6:01:24
Country Acres 82	25	38N31	89w59	5:59:56
Country Aire 45	107	42N02	88w17	5:53:08
Country Club Hills 16	6	41N34	87w44	5:50:56
Country Club Manor 16	6	41N35	87w46	5:51:04
Country Club Place 82	25	38N31	89w59	5:59:56
Country Club Terrace 82	25	38N31	89w59	5:59:56
Country Courts 81	87	41N30	90w30	6:02:00
Country Esquire 10	138	40N06	88w12	5:52:48
Country Fair 10	21	40N07	88w15	5:53:00
Country Gardens 16	1	42N07	87w56	5:51:44
Country Heights 41	4	38N18	88w55	5:55:40
Country Knolls 45	107	42N02	88w17	5:53:08
Country Lake 22	12	41N47	88w09	5:52:36
Country Manor 25	4	39N07	88w33	5:54:12
Countryside 16	1	41N47	87w52	5:51:28
Countryside 45	25	41N39	88w27	5:53:48
Countryside 47	25	41N39	88w27	5:53:48
Countryside 49	6	42N12	88w03	5:52:12
Countryside Lake 49	126	42N14	87w59	5:51:56
Countryside Manor 49	42	42N16	87w56	5:51:44
Country View Estates 99	12	41N47	88w09	5:52:36
Covel 57	104	40N29	88w59	5:55:56
Coventry 56	9	42N14	88w21	5:53:24
Covington 95	4	38N27	89w26	5:57:44
Cowden 87	63	39N15	88w52	5:55:28
Cowling 93	4	38N25	87w46	5:51:04
Crab Orchard 100	4	37N44	88w46	5:55:04
Crab Orchard Estates 100	4	37N43	89w14	5:56:56
Cragin 16	2	41N55	87w45	5:51:00
Craig Place 22	83	41N53	88w01	5:52:04
Crainville 100	4	37N45	89w04	5:56:16
Cramers 72	60	40N47	89w58	5:59:52
Crane Creek 63	63	40N10	89w53	5:59:32
Crater Prec 7	63	39N16	90w38	6:02:32
Cravat 41	4	38N31	89w08	5:56:32
Crawford Countryside 16	29	41N30	87w42	5:50:48
Creal Springs 100	4	37N37	88w50	5:55:20
Creek 20	4	40N06	88w51	5:55:24
Creekside 16	29	41N30	87w42	5:50:48
Creekwood 16	1	41N40	88w00	5:52:00
Crenshaw 100	4	37N46	88w56	5:55:44
Crescent 38	7	40N44	87w50	5:51:20
Crescent City 38	55	40N46	87w52	5:51:28
Cress Creek 22	12	41N47	88w09	5:52:36
Crest Haven 82	25	38N31	89w59	5:59:56
Crest Hill 99	114	41N33	88w06	5:52:24
Creston 71	6	41N56	88w58	5:55:52
Crestview Terrace 96	4	38N23	88w22	5:53:28
Crestwood 16	26	41N38	87w44	5:50:56
Crestwood Estates 100	4	37N46	88w56	5:55:44
Crete 99	1	41N27	87w38	5:50:32
Creve Coeur 90	98	40N39	89w35	5:58:20
Cricket Hill 16	29	41N30	87w42	5:50:48
Crisp 96	4	38N21	88w35	5:54:20
Crittenden 10	54	39N55	88w11	5:52:44
Crocketts Estates 49	27	42N23	88w09	5:52:36
Crook 33	4	38N05	88w26	5:53:44
Crooked Lake 49	6	42N25	88w04	5:52:16
Crooked Lake Oaks 49	6	42N25	88w04	5:52:16
Cropsey 57	55	40N37	88w29	5:53:56
Crossroads 44	4	37N25	88w54	5:55:36
Crossroads 82	25	38N37	90w01	6:00:04
Crossroad Terrace 82	25	38N37	90w01	6:00:04
Crossville 97	4	38N10	88w04	5:52:16
Crouch 33	4	38N13	88w31	5:54:04
Crown Estates 22	27	41N54	87w57	5:51:48
Cruger 102	71	40N42	89w18	5:57:12
Crystal Gardens 56	9	42N14	88w21	5:53:24
Crystal Lake 56	9	42N14	88w19	5:53:16
Crystal Lake 60	7	38N57	90w11	6:00:44
Crystal Lake Estates 56	9	42N14	88w21	5:53:24
Crystal Lawns 99	114	41N32	88w05	5:52:20
Crystal Manor 56	9	42N14	88w21	5:53:24
Crystal Vista 56	9	42N14	88w21	5:53:24
Cuba 29	62	40N30	90w12	6:00:48
Cufty Heights 100	4	37N46	88w56	5:55:44
Cullom 53	44	40N53	88w16	5:53:04
Cumberland Green 45	95	41N54	88w19	5:53:16
Cumberland Heights 96	4	38N23	88w22	5:53:28
Cunningham Courts 16	6	42N06	88w02	5:52:08
Curran 84	55	39N45	89w45	5:59:00
Custer 99	37	41N14	88w09	5:52:36
Custer Park 99	37	41N15	88w08	5:52:32
Cutler 73	63	38N02	89w34	5:58:16
Cypress 44	4	37N22	89w01	5:56:04
d'Adrian Gardens 60	7	38N57	90w11	6:00:44
Daggetts 8	4	42N06	89w58	5:59:52
Dahinda 48	4	40N55	90w07	6:00:28
Dahlgren 33	4	38N12	88w41	5:54:44
Dakota 89	67	42N23	89w32	5:58:08
Dale 33	4	38N00	88w29	5:53:56
Dale 57	4	40N26	89w05	5:56:20
Dallasania 83	4	37N41	88w38	5:54:32
Dallas City 34	4	40N38	91w10	6:04:40
Dalton City 70	55	39N43	88w48	5:55:12
Dalzell 6	134	41N22	89w11	5:56:44
Damiansville 14	49	38N33	89w37	5:58:28
Dana 50	55	40N57	88w57	5:55:48
Danforth 38	29	40N49	87w59	5:51:56
Danvers 57	20	40N32	89w11	5:56:44
Danville 92	26	40N08	87w37	5:50:28
Danville Junction 92	54	40N17	87w41	5:50:44
Danway 50	120	41N21	88w42	5:54:48
Dareville 41	4	38N12	88w54	5:55:36
Darien 22	54	41N45	87w58	5:51:52
Darmstadt 82	39	38N17	89w49	5:59:16
Darrow 38	56	40N46	87w34	5:50:16
Darwin 12	4	39N17	87w37	5:50:28
Davis 89	65	42N25	89w25	5:57:40
Davis Junction 71	57	42N06	89w06	5:56:24
Dawson 84	29	39N51	89w28	5:57:52
Daysville 71	28	42N01	89w20	5:57:20
Dayton 50	6	41N25	88w49	5:55:16
Dearborn Heights 16	1	41N43	87w45	5:51:00
Decatur 58	26	39N51	88w57	5:55:48
Decker 80	4	38N38	88w13	5:52:52
Decorra 36	4	40N45	90w54	6:03:36
Deep Lake 49	6	42N25	88w04	5:52:16
Deep Spring Woods 56	15	42N23	88w26	5:53:44
Deep Woods 49	126	42N14	87w59	5:51:56
Deer Creek 90	112	40N38	89w20	5:57:20
Deerfield 49	2	42N10	87w51	5:51:24
Deer Grove 98	29	41N37	89w42	5:58:48
Deering City 28	59	37N54	88w55	5:55:40
Dee Road 16	1	42N02	87w51	5:51:24
Deer Park 49	6	42N10	88w05	5:52:20
Deer Plain 7	65	38N57	90w36	6:02:24
Degognia 39	50	37N49	89w38	5:58:32
De Kalb 19	36	41N56	88w46	5:55:04
Delafield 33	4	38N09	88w37	5:54:28
De Land 74	55	40N07	88w39	5:54:36
Delavan 90	35	40N22	89w33	5:58:12
Delhi 42	25	39N05	90w22	6:01:28
Dellwood Highlands 99	114	41N35	88w03	5:52:12
Del Mar Woods 49	2	42N12	87w51	5:51:24
Delong 48	4	40N52	90w12	6:00:48
Delrey 38	29	40N41	88w01	5:52:04
Del Rey 38	30	40N41	88w07	5:52:28
Delwood 76	4	37N44	88w33	5:54:12
Dement 71	6	41N56	89w00	5:56:00
Denison 51	4	38N38	87w42	5:50:48
Denmark 73	63	38N02	89w34	5:58:16
Denning 28	4	37N54	88w58	5:55:52
Dennison 12	56	39N28	87w36	5:50:24
Denny 73	4	38N01	89w14	5:56:56
Denver 34	4	40N25	91w09	6:04:36
Denver 80	4	38N48	88w12	5:52:48
Depue 6	48	41N19	89w19	5:57:16
Derby 27	111	40N28	88w23	5:53:32
Derby 83	4	37N44	88w21	5:53:24
Derinda 43	4	42N14	90w09	6:00:36
Derinda Center 43	4	42N19	90w13	6:00:52
Derry 75	4	39N37	90w58	6:03:52
Deselm 46	26	41N15	87w51	5:51:24
De Soto 39	4	37N49	89w14	5:56:56
Des Plaines 16	1	42N03	87w52	5:51:28
Detroit 75	4	39N37	90w39	6:02:36
Devereux Heights 84	133	39N48	89w38	5:58:32
Dewey 10	54	40N19	88w17	5:53:08
Dewey Park 60	25	38N48	89w57	5:59:48
Dewitt 20	63	40N11	88w47	5:55:08
Dewmaine 100	4	37N46	89w04	5:56:16
Dexter 25	56	39N04	88w45	5:55:00
Diamond 32	37	41N17	88w15	5:53:00
Diamond City 33	4	38N06	88w32	5:54:08
Diamond Lake 49	6	42N15	88w00	5:52:00
Dieterich 25	4	39N04	88w23	5:53:32
Dillon 90	35	40N26	89w33	5:58:12
Dillsburg 10	29	40N19	88w08	5:52:32
Dimmick 50	55	41N25	89w06	5:56:24
Diona 15	4	39N15	88w10	5:52:40
Disco 34	4	40N38	91w07	6:04:28
Divernon 84	37	39N34	89w39	5:58:36
Divide 41	4	38N26	88w54	5:55:36
Dix 41	4	38N27	88w56	5:55:44
Dixmoor 16	2	41N38	87w41	5:50:44
Dixon 52	25	41N50	89w29	5:57:56
Dixon Springs 76	4	37N24	88w45	5:55:00
Dobbins Downs 10	138	40N06	88w12	5:52:48
Dodds 41	4	38N15	88w53	5:55:32
Doddsville 55	4	40N14	90w37	6:02:28
Dollville 87	63	39N23	88w57	5:55:48
Dolson 12	4	39N26	87w51	5:51:24
Dolton 16	1	41N38	87w36	5:50:24
Dongola 91	23	37N22	89w09	5:56:36
Donnellson 68	63	39N02	89w28	5:57:52
Donovan 38	57	40N53	87w37	5:50:28
Dora 70	55	39N43	88w44	5:54:56
Dorans 15	63	39N24	88w19	5:53:16
Dorchester 59	55	39N03	89w53	5:59:32
Dorr 56	15	42N17	88w24	5:53:36
Dorris Heights 83	4	37N44	88w33	5:54:12
Dorrisville 83	4	37N44	88w33	5:54:12
Dorsey 60	4	38N59	90w00	6:00:00
Douglas 48	60	40N47	90w01	6:00:04
Douglas 82	29	38N26	89w54	5:59:36
Dover 6	55	41N26	89w23	5:57:32
Dow 42	37	39N01	90w21	6:01:24
Dowell 39	4	37N57	89w15	5:57:00
Downers Fairview 22	12	41N48	88w01	5:52:04
Downers Grove 22	12	41N49	88w01	5:52:04
Downers Grove Estates 22	12	41N48	88w01	5:52:04
Downey 49	140	42N19	87w51	5:51:24
Downs 57	79	40N24	88w52	5:55:28
Downtown 84	133	39N48	89w39	5:58:36
Drake 31	4	39N26	90w24	6:01:36

Dresden Acres 32	125	41N22	88w25	5:53:40
Drew Dell Acres 60	7	38N57	90w11	6:00:44
Drexel 16	1	41N51	87w46	5:51:04
Drivers 41	4	38N20	89w02	5:56:08
Druce Lake 49	6	42N22	88w00	5:52:00
Drummer 27	111	40N28	88w24	5:53:36
Drury 81	4	41N23	90w58	6:03:52
Dry Grove 57	4	40N32	89w06	5:56:24
Dry Point 87	63	39N14	88w52	5:55:28
Dubois 95	4	38N13	89w13	5:56:52
Duck Lake Woods 49	27	42N23	88w09	5:52:36
Dudley 23	128	39N37	87w42	5:50:48
Dudleyville 3	55	38N54	89w24	5:57:36
Duncan 66	4	41N17	90w51	6:03:24
Duncan 88	55	40N56	89w45	5:59:00
Duncans Mills 29	7	40N24	90w09	6:00:36
Duncanville 17	4	38N57	87w42	5:50:48
Dundas 80	4	38N50	88w05	5:52:20
Dunfermline 29	7	40N29	90w02	6:00:08
Dunham 56	7	42N23	88w38	5:54:32
Dunham Woods 45	2	41N57	88w16	5:53:04
Dunhurst 16	6	42N09	87w57	5:51:48
Dunlap 72	57	40N52	89w40	5:58:40
Dunlap Lake 60	25	38N48	89w57	5:59:48
Dunleith 43	4	42N29	90w37	6:02:28
Dunning 16	1	41N57	87w47	5:51:08
Du Page 99	4	41N41	88w04	5:52:16
Dupo 82	46	38N31	90w13	6:00:52
Du Quoin 73	4	38N01	89w14	5:56:56
Durand 101	55	42N26	89w20	5:57:20
Durham 34	4	40N35	91w10	6:04:40
Dutch Creek Woodlands 56	27	42N21	88w14	5:52:56
Dutch Hollow 82	25	38N34	90w02	6:00:08
Duvall 87	7	39N24	88w48	5:55:12
Dwight 53	26	41N05	88w26	5:53:44
Dykersburg 100	4	37N37	88w42	5:54:48
Eagarville 59	55	39N07	89w48	5:59:12
Eagle 50	4	41N09	88w54	5:55:36
Eagle Creek 30	4	37N39	88w19	5:53:16
Eagle Heights 45	107	42N02	88w17	5:53:08
Eagle Lake 99	22	41N21	87w37	5:50:28
Eagle Park 60	25	38N41	90w07	6:00:28
Eagle Point 71	4	41N59	89w39	5:58:36
Eagle Point Bay 44	4	37N33	88w58	5:55:52
Earl 50	28	41N35	88w52	5:55:28
Earlville 50	28	41N35	88w55	5:55:40
East Alton 60	29	38N53	90w07	6:00:28
East Bend 10	54	40N21	88w17	5:53:08
East Brooklyn 32	36	41N10	88w16	5:53:04
East Cape Girardeau 2	4	37N19	89w26	5:57:44
East Carondelet 82	46	38N32	90w14	6:00:56
East Chicago Heights 16	1	41N30	87w35	5:50:20
East Clinton 98	4	41N52	90w09	6:00:36
East Dubuque 43	4	42N30	90w39	6:02:36
East Dundee 45	10	42N06	88w16	5:53:04
East Eldorado 83	4	37N49	88w26	5:53:44
Eastern 28	4	37N59	88w46	5:55:04
East Fulton 98	4	41N52	90w09	6:00:36
East Galena 43	4	42N25	90w23	6:01:32
East Galesburg 48	74	40N57	90w19	6:01:16
East Gillespie 59	55	39N08	89w49	5:59:16
East Grove 52	55	41N38	89w27	5:57:48
East Hannibal 75	4	39N43	91w12	6:04:48
East Hardin 31	55	39N06	90w30	6:02:00
East Hazelcrest 16	2	41N35	87w39	5:50:36
East Keokuk 34	4	40N24	91w24	6:05:36
East Lincoln 54	4	40N11	89w18	5:57:12
East Loon Lake 49	6	42N28	88w07	5:52:28
East Lynn 92	132	40N28	87w48	5:51:12
East Marion 100	4	37N44	88w52	5:55:28
East Meadowbrook 60	25	38N54	90w01	6:00:04
East Meadowview 46	115	41N09	87w52	5:51:28
East Moline 81	87	41N32	90w26	6:01:44
East Monroe 35	4	37N34	88w18	5:53:12
East Nelson 70	7	39N34	88w32	5:54:08
East Newbern 42	4	38N56	90w21	6:01:24
East Oakland 15	65	39N38	88w01	5:52:04
Easton 63	63	40N14	89w50	5:59:20
East Peoria 90	98	40N40	89w34	5:58:16
East River 46	26	41N01	87w43	5:50:52
East Rockford 101	28	42N17	89w04	5:56:16
East Saint Louis 82	25	38N37	90w09	6:00:36
East Wenona 50	29	41N04	89w03	5:56:12
East Winchester 86	63	39N37	90w25	6:01:40
Eastwood Manor 56	27	42N21	88w14	5:52:56
Eaton 17	4	39N00	87w44	5:50:56
Eberle 25	4	39N04	88w23	5:53:32
Echo Lake 49	6	42N12	88w03	5:52:12
Eckard 63	55	40N18	90w04	6:00:16
Eddyville 76	4	37N30	88w35	5:54:20
Edelstein 72	57	40N56	89w38	5:58:32
Eden 50	136	41N14	89w06	5:56:24
Eden 72	57	40N42	89w48	5:59:12
Eden 79	63	38N07	89w42	5:58:48
Eden Park 100	4	37N47	89w01	5:56:04
Edford 37	4	41N27	90w15	6:01:00
Edgar 23	7	39N45	87w42	5:50:48
Edgebrook 16	2	42N00	87w46	5:51:04
Edgemont 82	25	38N35	90w04	6:00:16
Edgewood 10	138	40N06	88w12	5:52:48
Edgewood 25	4	38N55	88w40	5:54:40
Edgewood 60	7	38N57	90w11	6:00:44
Edgewood 102	71	40N43	89w17	5:57:08
Edgewood Heights 4	28	42N16	89w00	5:56:00
Edgington 81	4	41N23	90w44	6:02:56
Edinburg 11	55	39N39	89w23	5:57:32
Edison Square 49	140	42N23	87w52	5:51:28
Edwards 72	4	40N45	89w45	5:59:00
Edwardsville 60	25	38N49	89w58	5:59:52
Effingham 25	59	39N07	88w33	5:54:12
Effner 38	56	40N46	87w34	5:50:16
Egan 71	4	42N11	89w24	5:57:36
Egyptian Hills 100	4	37N37	88w50	5:55:20
Egyptian Shores 100	4	37N37	88w50	5:55:20
Eileen 32	36	41N18	88w16	5:53:04
Ela 49	6	42N12	88w04	5:52:16
Elba 30	4	37N53	88w18	5:53:12
Elba 48	4	40N51	90w03	6:00:12
Elba Center 48	60	40N47	90w01	6:00:04
Elbridge 23	56	39N32	87w35	5:50:20
Elburn 45	84	41N54	88w28	5:53:52
Elco 2	4	37N18	89w16	5:57:04
El Dara 75	4	39N37	91w00	6:04:00
Eldena 52	29	41N46	89w25	5:57:40
Elderville 34	4	40N20	91w12	6:04:48
Eldorado 83	4	37N49	88w26	5:53:44
Eldred 31	63	39N17	90w33	6:02:12
Eleanor 94	4	41N01	90w45	6:03:00
Eleroy 89	4	42N20	89w46	5:59:04
Elgin 45	107	42N02	88w17	5:53:08
Eliza 66	4	41N17	90w59	6:03:56
Elizabeth 43	4	42N19	90w13	6:00:52
Elizabethtown 35	4	37N27	88w18	5:53:12
Elk 39	4	37N54	89w14	5:56:56
Elk Grove 16	27	42N02	87w58	5:51:52
Elk Grove Village 16	27	42N01	87w59	5:51:56
Elkhart 54	29	40N01	89w29	5:57:56
Elk Hart City 54	29	40N01	89w29	5:57:56
Elkhorn 5	65	39N53	90w44	6:02:56
Elkhorn Grove 8	4	41N59	89w43	5:58:52
Elk Prairie 41	4	38N10	88w59	5:55:56
Elk Ridge Villa 16	6	42N04	87w57	5:51:48
Elkton 95	4	38N16	89w30	5:58:00
Elkville 39	4	37N55	89w14	5:56:56
Ellery 24	4	38N22	88w08	5:52:32
Ellington 1	92	39N58	91w20	6:05:20
Elliott 27	39	40N28	88w16	5:53:04
Elliottstown 25	4	39N04	88w23	5:53:32
Ellis 92	38	40N18	87w48	5:51:12
Ellisgrove 79	63	38N01	89w55	5:59:40
Ellison 94	4	40N46	90w43	6:02:52
Ellisville 29	4	40N40	90w18	6:01:12
Ellsworth 57	29	40N27	88w43	5:54:52
Ellwood 19	110	42N06	88w42	5:54:48
Elm Estates 22	27	41N54	87w57	5:51:48
Elm Grove 90	21	40N32	89w34	5:58:16
Elmhurst 22	2	41N53	87w56	5:51:44
Elmira 88	4	41N11	89w49	5:59:16
Elmore 72	58	40N55	89w55	5:59:40
El Morro 16	6	41N36	87w45	5:51:00
Elm River 96	4	38N31	88w19	5:53:16
Elmwood 72	60	40N47	89w58	5:59:52
Elmwood Park 16	2	41N56	87w49	5:51:16
El Paso 102	69	40N44	89w01	5:56:04
El-Rancho 46	115	41N05	87w53	5:51:32
Elsah 42	55	38N57	90w22	6:01:28
Elsdon 16	1	41N48	87w43	5:50:52
El Sierra 22	12	41N48	88w01	5:52:04
Elva 19	36	41N56	88w44	5:54:56
Elvaston 34	4	40N24	91w15	6:05:00
Elvira 44	4	37N28	88w59	5:55:56
El Vista 16	6	41N36	87w45	5:51:00
El Vista 72	98	40N42	89w38	5:58:32
Elwin 58	26	39N47	88w59	5:55:56
Elwood 99	70	41N24	88w07	5:52:28
Embarrass 23	67	39N40	87w55	5:51:40
Emden 54	29	40N18	89w29	5:57:56
Emerald Green 22	26	41N49	88w11	5:52:44
Emerald Park 56	27	42N21	88w14	5:52:56
Emerald Terrace 82	25	38N31	89w59	5:59:56
Emerson 98	26	41N48	89w43	5:58:52
Eminence 54	4	40N17	89w19	5:57:16
Emington 53	36	40N58	88w21	5:53:24
Emma 97	4	37N59	88w05	5:52:20
Emmet 55	4	40N30	90w44	6:02:56
Empire 57	4	40N20	88w45	5:55:00
Enchanted Forest 72	98	40N42	89w38	5:58:32
Energy 100	63	37N47	89w02	5:56:08
Enfield 97	4	38N06	88w20	5:53:20
Englemann 82	55	38N26	89w46	5:59:04
Englewood 16	1	41N47	87w38	5:50:32
English 42	55	39N08	90w26	6:01:44
Enion 29	55	40N18	90w04	6:00:16
Enos 59	47	39N18	89w52	5:59:28
Enright 57	4	40N44	89w01	5:56:04
Enterprise 96	4	38N31	88w26	5:53:44
Eola 22	19	41N47	88w15	5:53:00
Eppards Point 53	127	40N48	88w38	5:54:32
Epworth 97	4	38N06	88w09	5:52:36
Equality 30	4	37N44	88w20	5:53:20
Erie 98	88	41N39	90w05	6:00:20
Erienna 32	46	41N21	88w32	5:54:08
Erin 89	4	42N20	89w46	5:59:04
Esmen 53	55	40N59	88w39	5:54:36
Esmond 19	40	42N02	88w56	5:55:44
Essex 46	29	41N11	88w11	5:52:44
Estate Lane 16	1	42N04	87w48	5:51:12
Etherton 39	4	37N46	89w21	5:57:24
Euclid Lake 16	6	42N04	87w57	5:51:48
Eureka 102	71	40N43	89w16	5:57:04
Evans 62	54	41N04	89w06	5:56:24
Evanston 16	1	42N03	87w41	5:50:44
Evansville 79	63	38N05	89w56	5:59:44
Evarts 89	4	42N18	89w29	5:57:56
Evergreen Park 16	1	41N43	87w41	5:50:44
Ewing 28	4	38N05	88w53	5:55:32
Exeter 86	63	39N43	90w30	6:02:00
Exline 46	115	41N05	87w53	5:51:32
Eylar 53	36	40N54	88w24	5:53:36
Ezra 28	4	37N54	88w55	5:55:40
Fairbanks 70	55	39N43	88w38	5:54:32
Fairbury 53	72	40N45	88w31	5:54:04
Fairdale 19	56	42N05	88w51	5:55:24
Fairfield 96	4	38N23	88w22	5:53:28
Fairgrange 15	106	39N35	88w10	5:52:40
Fair Haven 8	4	41N59	89w55	5:59:40
Fairland 21	65	39N52	88w10	5:52:40
Fairman 61	4	38N34	89w07	5:56:28
Fairmont 99	114	41N34	88w04	5:52:16
Fairmont City 82	25	38N39	90w06	6:00:24
Fairmount 64	4	37N09	88w44	5:54:56
Fairmount 92	54	40N03	87w56	5:51:44
Fair Oaks 16	27	41N58	88w06	5:52:24
Fair Oaks 22	54	41N42	88w11	5:52:44
Fairview 11	7	39N34	89w21	5:57:24
Fairview 16	1	41N59	87w52	5:51:28
Fairview 29	65	40N38	90w10	6:00:40
Fairview 82	25	38N37	90w01	6:00:04
Fairview Addition 83	4	37N49	88w27	5:53:48
Fairview Gardens 16	6	42N04	87w57	5:51:48
Fairview Heights 82	25	38N36	90w00	6:00:00
Fairview Park Plaza 14	4	38N31	89w08	5:56:32
Fairway Estates 22	2	41N53	88w05	5:52:20
Fairway Trace 16	6	42N03	87w53	5:51:32
Fall Creek 1	66	39N47	91w18	6:05:12
Fall River 50	6	41N18	88w46	5:55:04
Falmouth 40	4	38N59	88w10	5:52:40
Fancher 87	63	39N16	88w44	5:54:56
Fancy Creek 84	133	39N54	89w39	5:58:36
Fancy Prairie 65	29	40N00	89w37	5:58:28
Fandon 55	4	40N22	90w46	6:03:04
Fargo 5	66	40N00	90w52	6:03:28
Farina 26	4	38N50	88w46	5:55:04
Farmer City 20	57	40N15	88w39	5:54:36
Farmers 29	63	40N25	90w24	6:01:36
Farmersville 68	63	39N27	89w39	5:58:36
Farmingdale 22	19	41N47	87w59	5:51:56
Farmingdale 84	29	39N52	89w55	5:59:40
Farmingdale South 22	19	41N47	87w59	5:51:56
Farmingdale Terrace 22	19	41N47	87w59	5:51:56
Farmingdale Village 22	19	41N47	87w59	5:51:56
Farmington 29	61	40N42	90w00	6:00:00
Farmington 45	95	41N54	88w19	5:53:16
Farmington 49	6	42N12	88w03	5:52:12
Farm Ridge 50	41	41N15	88w52	5:55:28
Farmsted 22	12	41N47	88w09	5:52:36
Farnsworth 49	140	42N19	87w50	5:51:20
Farrington 41	4	38N26	88w45	5:55:00
Farrow 72	98	40N41	89w37	5:58:28
Fayette 31	55	39N21	90w13	6:00:52
Fayette 53	72	40N42	88w24	5:53:36
Fayetteville 82	55	38N21	89w45	5:59:00
Fayville 2	4	37N13	89w27	5:57:48
Feehanville 16	6	42N04	87w57	5:51:48
Felix 32	30	41N19	88w17	5:53:08
Felker 90	98	40N42	89w25	5:57:40
Fenton 98	8	41N44	90w02	6:00:08
Fergestown 100	4	37N46	88w56	5:55:44
Fernway 16	6	41N34	87w49	5:51:16
Ferrin 14	55	38N37	89w22	5:57:28
Ferris 34	4	40N28	91w10	6:04:40
Fiatt 29	4	40N34	90w11	6:00:44
Ficklin 21	7	39N48	88w17	5:53:08
Fiday View 99	114	41N33	88w07	5:52:28
Fidelity 42	4	39N08	90w12	6:00:48
Field 41	4	38N26	88w52	5:55:28
Fieldcrest 16	6	41N36	87w45	5:51:00
Fieldon 42	55	39N07	90w30	6:02:00
Fillmore 68	66	39N07	89w17	5:57:08
Filson 21	63	39N41	88w18	5:53:12
Findlay 87	63	39N31	88w45	5:55:00
Finney Heights 14	4	38N31	89w08	5:56:32
First Pommier 46	26	41N01	87w43	5:50:52
Fisher 10	57	40N19	88w21	5:53:24
Fishhook 75	4	39N44	90w55	6:03:40
Fithian 92	43	40N07	87w53	5:51:32
Five Islands Park 45	55	42N00	88w18	5:53:12
Flag Center 71	6	41N56	89w04	5:56:16
Flagg 71	6	41N56	89w06	5:56:24
Flanagan 53	55	40N53	88w52	5:55:28
Flannigan 33	4	38N00	88w39	5:54:36
Flat Branch 87	57	39N34	88w58	5:55:52
Flat Rock 17	4	38N54	87w40	5:50:40
Flatville 10	30	40N15	88w11	5:52:44
Flat Woods 44	4	37N28	88w45	5:55:00
Fletcher 57	57	40N33	88w43	5:54:52
Flickerville 46	115	41N10	87w53	5:51:32
Flint 75	4	39N42	90w40	6:02:40
Flora 13	4	38N40	88w29	5:53:56
Floraville 82	55	38N23	90w03	6:00:12
Florence 89	4	42N13	89w40	5:58:40
Florid 78	41	41N15	89w20	5:57:20

Flossmoor 16	1	41N32	87W41	5:50:44
Flossmoor Highlands 16	1	41N32	87W41	5:50:44
Flowerfield Acres 22	83	41N53	88W01	5:52:04
Floyd 94	4	40N51	90W30	6:02:00
Fondulac 90	98	40N42	89W31	5:58:04
Fon-Du-Lac 99	82	41N35	88W11	5:52:44
Foosland 10	54	40N22	88W26	5:53:44
Forest Acres 82	25	38N38	90W08	6:00:32
Forest City 63	7	40N21	89W49	5:59:16
Forest Estates 16	6	42N06	88W02	5:52:08
Forest Gardens 49	6	42N16	88W08	5:52:32
Foresthaven 49	2	42N14	87W53	5:51:32
Forest Heights 16	1	41N31	87W38	5:50:32
Forest Hills 16	1	41N44	87W50	5:51:20
Forest Homes 60	29	38N55	90W05	6:00:20
Forest Lake 49	6	42N13	88W03	5:52:12
Forest Manor 99	114	41N35	88W03	5:52:12
Forest Park 16	1	41N52	87W49	5:51:16
Forest River 16	1	42N05	87W54	5:51:36
Forest View 16	1	41N49	87W48	5:51:12
Forest View Hills 16	6	41N36	87W45	5:51:00
Forrest 53	72	40N45	88W25	5:53:40
Forrestal Village 49	140	42N19	87W50	5:51:20
Forreston 71	58	42N08	89W35	5:58:20
Forsyth 58	26	39N56	88W57	5:55:48
Fort Dearborn 16	1	41N54	87W37	5:50:28
Fort Russell 60	25	38N53	89W59	5:59:56
Fort Sheridan 49	26	42N09	87W58	5:51:52
Foss Acres 49	140	42N19	87W50	5:51:20
Foster Pond 67	8	38N20	90W09	6:00:36
Fountain 67	55	38N18	90W19	6:01:16
Fountain Bluff 39	4	37N44	89W33	5:58:12
Fountain Creek 38	7	40N32	87W48	5:51:12
Fountain Gap 67	46	38N27	90W12	6:00:48
Fountain Green 34	4	40N29	90W59	6:03:56
Four Lakes 22	12	41N47	88W05	5:52:20
Four Mile 96	4	38N19	88W39	5:54:36
Fowler 1	66	40N00	91W15	6:05:00
Fox 47	25	41N39	88W27	5:53:48
Foxcroft 22	2	41N53	88W04	5:52:16
Fox Lake 49	1	42N24	88W11	5:52:44
Fox Lake Hills 49	1	42N24	88W08	5:52:32
Fox Lake Vista 49	1	42N26	88W14	5:52:56
Fox Lawn 47	25	41N39	88W27	5:53:48
Fox Point 16	6	42N09	88W06	5:52:24
Fox River 49	1	42N13	88W12	5:52:48
Fox River Estates 45	95	41N54	88W19	5:53:16
Fox River Grove 56	1	42N12	88W13	5:52:52
Fox River Heights 45	95	41N54	88W19	5:53:16
Fox River Valley Gardens 49	1	42N09	88W06	5:52:24
Frankfort 99	55	41N30	87W51	5:51:24
Frankfort Heights 28	4	37N54	88W55	5:55:40
Franklin 69	63	39N37	90W03	6:00:12
Franklin Grove 52	40	41N51	89W18	5:57:12
Franklin Park 16	1	41N56	87W51	5:51:24
Franklin Square 99	55	41N30	87W51	5:51:24
Franklinville 56	11	42N19	88W27	5:53:48
Franks 19	7	41N38	88W41	5:54:44
Frederick 85	7	40N05	90W25	6:01:40
Freeburg 82	29	38N26	89W55	5:59:40
Freeman Spur 100	4	37N52	89W00	5:56:00
Freeport 89	108	42N17	89W36	5:58:24
Fremont 49	6	42N16	88W03	5:52:12
Fremont Junction 16	27	41N58	88W06	5:52:24
French Creek 24	4	38N18	88W01	5:52:04
Frenchman's Cove 16	6	42N06	87W58	5:51:52
French Village 82	7	38N36	90W03	6:00:12
Friends Creek 58	57	40N00	88W49	5:55:16
Friendsville 93	4	38N31	87W48	5:51:12
Frisco 28	4	38N05	88W51	5:55:24
Frog City 2	4	37N06	89W16	5:57:04
Frogtown 95	4	38N26	89W33	5:58:12
Frontenac 22	12	41N47	88W09	5:52:36
Frontenac Place 60	7	38N57	90W11	6:00:44
Fruit 60	25	38N48	89W57	5:59:48
Fruitland 81	87	41N30	90W30	6:02:00
Fry's Wheatland View 99	12	41N47	88W09	5:52:36
Fulton 98	4	41N52	90W11	6:00:44
Fults 67	63	38N10	90W13	6:00:52
Funkhouser 25	56	39N07	88W33	5:54:12
Funks Grove 57	73	40N20	89W06	5:56:24
Future City 2	4	37N00	89W11	5:56:44
Gages Lake 49	27	42N21	88W01	5:52:04
Galatia 83	4	37N51	88W37	5:54:28
Gale 2	4	37N15	89W27	5:57:48
Galena 43	4	42N25	90W26	6:01:44
Galesburg 48	74	40N57	90W22	6:01:28
Galesville 74	55	40N13	88W31	5:54:04
Gallagher 80	4	38N44	88W05	5:52:20
Galt 98	26	41N47	89W46	5:59:04
Galton 21	63	39N41	88W18	5:53:12
Galva 37	4	41N10	90W03	6:00:12
Ganeer 46	82	41N09	87W41	5:50:44
Ganntown 44	4	37N24	88W45	5:55:00
Garber 27	111	40N28	88W23	5:53:32
Gardena 90	98	40N39	89W34	5:58:16
Garden Heights 83	4	37N44	88W33	5:54:12
Garden Hill 96	4	38N35	88W38	5:54:32
Garden Homes 16	1	41N42	87W42	5:50:48
Garden of Eden 46	82	41N10	87W40	5:50:40
Garden Plain 98	4	41N48	90W08	6:00:32
Garden Prairie 4	30	42N15	88W44	5:54:56
Garden Quarter 45	107	42N02	88W17	5:53:08
Gardner 32	72	41N11	88W19	5:53:16
Gardspoint 93	4	38N25	87W46	5:51:04
Garfield 32	36	41N09	88W19	5:53:16
Garfield 50	29	41N04	89W03	5:56:12
Garfield Park 16	1	41N52	87W43	5:50:52
Garland 23	55	39N43	87W56	5:51:44
Garrett 21	55	39N49	88W24	5:53:36
Gary Gardens 22	2	41N53	88W05	5:52:20
Gas Light Village 32	125	41N22	88W25	5:53:40
Gays 70	63	39N28	88W30	5:54:00
Geff 96	4	38N27	88W24	5:53:36
Genesee 98	4	41N53	89W48	5:59:12
Geneseo 37	4	41N27	90W09	6:00:36
Geneva 45	109	41N53	88W18	5:53:12
Genoa 19	110	42N06	88W42	5:54:48
Gent City 100	4	37N46	88W56	5:55:44
Georges Creek 64	4	37N19	88W47	5:55:08
Georgetown 8	4	42N06	89W50	5:59:20
Georgetown 55	4	40N28	90W41	6:02:44
Georgetown 92	57	39N59	87W38	5:50:32
Gerald 92	54	40N18	87W53	5:51:32
Gerlaw 94	4	40N59	90W36	6:02:24
German 80	4	38N48	87W58	5:51:52
Germantown 14	50	38N33	89W32	5:58:08
Germantown 102	57	40N47	89W25	5:57:40
Germantown Hills 102	4	40N46	89W28	5:57:52
German Valley 89	66	42N13	89W29	5:57:56
Germanville 53	4	40N42	88W17	5:53:08
Gibson City 27	111	40N28	88W22	5:53:28
Gibsonia 30	4	37N43	88W14	5:52:56
Gifford 10	54	40N18	88W01	5:52:04
Gilberts 45	8	42N06	88W22	5:53:28
Gilchrist 66	4	41N13	90W35	6:02:20
Gilead 7	65	39N02	90W39	6:02:36
Gillespie 59	55	39N08	89W49	5:59:16
Gillum 57	104	40N29	88W59	5:55:56
Gilman 38	29	40N46	88W00	5:52:00
Gilmer 1	63	39N59	91W12	6:04:48
Gilmore 25	4	38N57	88W38	5:54:32
Gilmore Lake 67	46	38N27	90W12	6:00:48
Gilson 48	4	40N52	90W12	6:00:48
Ginger Creek 22	2	41N48	87W56	5:51:44
Ginger Hill 81	87	41N27	90W35	6:02:20
Girard 59	29	39N27	89W47	5:59:08
Gladstone 36	4	40N51	90W59	6:03:56
Gladstone Commons 16	6	42N04	87W57	5:51:48
Glasford 72	55	40N34	89W49	5:59:16
Glasgow 86	4	39N33	90W31	6:02:04
Glass Works 60	7	38N54	90W10	6:00:40
Glen 60	7	38N45	89W59	5:59:56
Glen Acres 16	1	42N01	87W54	5:51:36
Glenarm 84	30	39N37	89W39	5:58:36
Glen Arms 49	27	42N23	88W09	5:52:36
Glenavon 57	56	40N20	88W31	5:54:04
Glenayre 16	2	42N04	87W48	5:51:12
Glenayre Gardens 16	2	42N04	87W48	5:51:12
Glenbrook Countryside 16	2	42N07	87W49	5:51:16
Glenburn 92	54	40N07	87W47	5:51:08
Glen Carbon 60	7	38N45	90W00	6:00:00
Glencoe 16	1	42N08	87W45	5:51:00
Glendale 76	4	37N27	88W40	5:54:40
Glendale 81	87	41N30	90W24	6:01:36
Glendale Gardens 60	29	38N53	90W05	6:00:20
Glendale Heights 22	2	41N55	88W04	5:52:16
Glen Ellyn 22	26	41N53	88W04	5:52:16
Glen Ellyn Countryside 22	26	41N53	88W04	5:52:16
Glen Ellyn Woods 22	26	41N53	88W04	5:52:16
Glengarry 45	1	41N56	87W53	5:51:32
Glen Hill 22	2	41N53	88W04	5:52:16
Glenn 39	50	37N50	89W41	5:58:44
Glennshire 49	6	42N12	88W03	5:52:12
Glen Oak 22	2	41N53	88W04	5:52:16
Glen Park 50	4	41N31	88W41	5:54:44
Glen Ridge 16	29	41N30	87W42	5:50:48
Glenshire 16	1	42N04	87W48	5:51:12
Glenview 16	1	42N04	87W48	5:51:12
Glen View 82	25	38N36	89W58	5:59:52
Glenview Countryside 16	1	42N04	87W48	5:51:12
Glenview Estates 16	1	42N04	87W48	5:51:12
Glenview Terrace 16	1	42N04	87W48	5:51:12
Glenview Woodlands 16	1	42N04	87W48	5:51:12
Glenwood 16	1	41N33	87W37	5:50:28
Glenwood Estates 16	1	41N33	87W37	5:50:28
Godfrey 60	7	38N58	90W11	6:00:44
Godley 99	37	41N14	88W15	5:53:00
Golconda 76	4	37N22	88W29	5:53:56
Gold 6	63	41N27	89W48	5:59:12
Golden 1	66	40N07	91W01	6:04:04
Golden Acres 16	1	42N04	87W48	5:51:12
Golden Eagle 7	4	38N54	90W34	6:02:16
Golden Gardens 82	25	38N34	90W08	6:00:32
Goldengate 96	4	38N22	88W12	5:52:48
Golden Lilly 2	4	37N00	89W11	5:56:44
Gold Hill 30	4	37N44	88W13	5:52:52
Golena Knolls 72	51	40N55	89W30	5:58:00
Golf 16	1	42N03	87W47	5:51:08
Golf Park Terrace 16	6	42N03	87W55	5:51:40
Golfview Hills 22	2	41N48	87W56	5:51:44
Goode 28	4	38N05	89W04	5:56:16
Goodenow 99	22	41N23	87W38	5:50:32
Goodfarm 32	26	41N09	88W25	5:53:40
Goodfield 102	112	40N38	89W17	5:57:08
Good Hope 55	4	40N33	90W41	6:02:44
Goodrich 46	4	41N09	88W03	5:52:12
Goodwine 38	7	40N34	87W47	5:51:08
Goofy Ridge 63	137	40N20	89W56	5:59:44
Goose Creek 74	4	40N06	88W38	5:54:32
Goose Lake 32	48	41N22	88W18	5:53:12
Gordons 17	4	39N00	87W44	5:50:56
Goreville 44	4	37N33	88W58	5:55:52
Gorham 39	4	37N43	89W29	5:57:56
Goshen 88	4	41N07	89W56	5:59:44
Gossett 97	4	37N59	88W20	5:53:20
Grafton 42	77	38N58	90W26	6:01:44
Grand 39	4	37N39	89W28	5:57:52
Grand Chain 77	4	37N15	89W01	5:56:04
Grand Crossing 16	1	41N45	87W36	5:50:24
Grand Detour 71	25	41N54	89W25	5:57:40
Grand Pier 76	4	37N34	88W27	5:53:48
Grand Prairie 41	4	38N25	89W05	5:56:20
Grand Rapids 50	41	41N14	88W45	5:55:00
Grand Ridge 50	41	41N14	88W50	5:55:20
Grand Tower 39	4	37N38	89W30	5:58:00
Grandview 8	4	41N31	89W55	5:59:40
Grandview 84	55	39N33	87W51	5:51:24
Grandville 40	4	39N08	88W00	5:52:00
Grandwood Park 49	140	42N22	87W53	5:51:32
Grange 10	36	39N58	88W21	5:53:24
Granite City 60	7	38N42	90W09	6:00:36
Grantfork 60	63	38N50	89W40	5:58:40
Grant Park 46	21	41N14	87W39	5:50:36
Grantsburg 44	4	37N22	88W46	5:55:04
Granville 78	41	41N16	89W14	5:56:56
Grape Creek 92	54	40N17	87W41	5:50:44
Grass Lake 49	6	42N26	88W09	5:52:36
Grassy 100	4	37N38	89W06	5:56:24
Gray 97	4	38N14	88W03	5:52:12
Graymont 53	55	40N53	88W47	5:55:08
Graymoor 16	1	41N31	87W42	5:50:48
Grayslake 49	27	42N21	88W02	5:52:08
Grays Siding 92	54	40N07	87W47	5:51:08
Grayville 97	4	38N16	88W00	5:52:00
Great Lakes 49	116	42N18	87W50	5:51:20
Green Acres 55	4	40N28	90W41	6:02:44
Green Acres 84	133	39N48	89W38	5:58:32
Greenbriar 99	1	41N31	87W58	5:51:52
Greenbrook Country 16	27	41N58	88W06	5:52:24
Greenbush 94	4	40N40	90W30	6:02:00
Green Creek 25	4	39N07	88W33	5:54:12
Greenfield 31	55	39N21	90W12	6:00:48
Green Garden 99	30	41N25	87W51	5:51:24
Green Meadows 16	27	41N58	88W06	5:52:24
Green Meadows 45	2	41N52	88W19	5:53:16
Green Oaks 49	27	42N17	87W54	5:51:36
Green River 37	63	41N29	90W20	6:01:20
Green Rock 37	63	41N29	90W22	6:01:28
Greentree 49	42	42N16	87W56	5:51:44
Greenup 18	55	39N15	88W10	5:52:40
Green Valley 22	83	41N53	88W01	5:52:04
Green Valley 90	21	40N24	89W39	5:58:36
Greenview 65	29	40N05	89W44	5:58:56
Greenville 3	55	38N53	89W25	5:57:40
Greenwich 46	115	41N05	87W53	5:51:32
Greenwood 56	11	42N19	88W27	5:53:48
Greenwood Meadows 60	7	38N57	90W11	6:00:44
Greer 38	80	40N32	87W41	5:50:44
Gridley 57	57	40N45	88W53	5:55:32
Grigg 79	93	38N10	90W00	6:00:00
Griggsville 75	53	39N43	90W43	6:02:52
Grimes Addition 98	26	41N48	89W43	5:58:52
Grimsby 39	4	37N43	89W29	5:57:56
Grinnell 64	4	37N19	88W56	5:55:44
Grisham 68	63	39N03	89W32	5:58:08
Griswold 53	44	40N53	88W16	5:53:04
Gross 35	4	37N27	88W18	5:53:12
Grove 40	4	39N07	88W17	5:53:08
Grove City 11	55	39N39	89W23	5:57:32
Groveland 90	98	40N35	89W32	5:58:08
Grover 96	4	38N22	88W19	5:53:16
Guilford 43	4	42N25	90W17	6:01:08
Gulf Port 36	4	40N48	91W05	6:04:20
Gurnee 49	34	42N22	87W55	5:51:40
Guthrie 27	111	40N28	88W23	5:53:32
Hadley 75	4	39N43	90W58	6:03:52
Hafer 100	4	37N46	89W04	5:56:16
Hagaman 59	63	39N15	90W04	6:00:16
Hagarstown 26	139	38N57	89W10	5:56:40
Hagener 9	66	39N55	90W28	6:01:52
Hahnaman 98	29	41N38	89W41	5:58:44
Haines 61	4	38N31	88W52	5:55:28
Hainesville 49	27	42N21	88W04	5:52:16
Haldane 71	63	42N04	89W34	5:58:16
Hale 94	4	40N56	90W43	6:02:52
Half Day 49	2	42N12	87W56	5:51:44
Hall 6	134	41N22	89W13	5:56:52
Hallidayboro 39	4	37N55	89W15	5:57:00
Hallock 38	80	40N32	87W41	5:50:44
Hallock 72	51	40N55	89W34	5:58:16
Hallville 20	8	40N09	88W57	5:55:48
Halsey Village 49	140	42N19	87W50	5:51:20
Hamburg 7	65	39N14	90W43	6:02:52
Hamel 60	29	38N53	89W53	5:59:32
Hamilton 34	4	40N24	91W21	6:05:24
Hamlet 66	4	41N12	90W45	6:03:00
Hamletsburg 76	4	37N08	88W26	5:53:44
Hammond 74	55	39N48	88W36	5:54:24

Place		Lat.	Long.	Time
Hampshire 45	55	42N06	88w32	5:54:08
Hampshire Manor 45	29	42N05	88w28	5:53:52
Hampton 81	4	41N31	90w24	6:01:36
Hampton Court 16	6	41N35	87w46	5:51:04
Hampton Park 99	114	41N35	88w03	5:52:12
Hanaford 28	4	37N57	88w50	5:55:20
Hanna 37	4	41N30	90w16	6:01:04
Hanna City 72	57	40N42	89w48	5:59:12
Hannon 11	7	39N34	89w21	5:57:24
Hanover 43	4	42N15	90w17	6:01:08
Hanover Highlands 16	27	41N58	88w06	5:52:24
Hanover Park 16	27	41N59	88w09	5:52:36
Hanover Park-Ontarioville 16	27	41N58	88w06	5:52:24
Hanover Square 16	27	41N58	88w06	5:52:24
Hanson 87	63	39N09	89w06	5:56:24
Harbor Dell 60	7	38N57	90w11	6:00:44
Harbor Estates 49	6	42N09	88w06	5:52:24
Hardin 7	55	39N10	90w37	6:02:28
Harding 50	28	41N35	88w56	5:55:44
Hardinville 17	4	39N00	87w54	5:51:36
Harlem 101	4	42N20	89w01	5:56:04
Harlem-Irving Plaza 16	1	41N57	87w47	5:51:08
Harmon 52	55	41N43	89w33	5:58:12
Harmony 34	4	40N19	91w07	6:04:28
Harmony 56	29	42N05	88w28	5:53:52
Harmony Village 16	6	42N09	87w57	5:51:48
Harp 20	63	40N11	88w51	5:55:24
Harper 71	63	42N08	89w35	5:58:20
Harpster 27	54	40N22	88w26	5:53:44
Harris 29	63	40N30	90w23	6:01:32
Harris 74	57	40N15	88w38	5:54:32
Harrisburg 83	4	37N44	88w32	5:54:08
Harrison 39	4	37N46	89w21	5:57:24
Harrison 101	4	42N25	89w13	5:56:52
Harrisonville 32	30	41N17	88w17	5:53:08
Harrisonville 67	55	38N17	90w20	6:01:20
Harter 13	4	38N41	88w32	5:54:08
Hartford 60	29	38N50	90w06	6:00:24
Hartland 56	15	42N22	88w31	5:54:04
Hartsburg 54	29	40N15	89w27	5:57:48
Harvard 56	7	42N25	88w37	5:54:28
Harvard Hills 90	98	40N42	89w25	5:57:40
Harvel 68	63	39N22	89w32	5:58:08
Harvey 16	2	41N36	87w50	5:51:20
Harwood 10	30	40N22	88w03	5:52:12
Harwood Heights 16	2	41N58	87w48	5:51:12
Hastings	1	41N41	87w58	5:51:52
Hatcher Woods 32	125	41N22	88w25	5:53:40
Havana 63	55	40N18	90w04	6:00:16
Haw Creek 48	4	40N51	90w10	6:00:40
Hawthorne 16	1	41N51	87w43	5:50:52
Hawthorn Woods 49	6	42N13	88w03	5:52:12
Hayes 21	7	39N48	88w17	5:53:08
Haymarket 16	1	41N53	87w38	5:50:32
Haypress 31	63	39N27	90w32	6:02:08
Hazel Crest 16	2	41N35	87w40	5:50:40
Hazelcrest Highlands 16	2	41N35	87w40	5:50:40
Hazel Dell 18	4	39N12	88w03	5:52:12
Hazel Green 16	1	41N41	87w45	5:51:00
Hazelhurst 71	4	41N59	89w35	5:58:20
Headyville 25	4	39N04	88w23	5:53:32
Heathercrest 16	2	42N07	87w49	5:51:16
Heatherlea 16	6	42N06	88w02	5:52:08
Heatherridge 49	140	42N22	87w53	5:51:32
Heathsville 17	4	38N54	87w40	5:50:40
Hebron 56	48	42N28	88w26	5:53:44
Hecker 67	55	38N18	90w00	6:00:00
Hegeler 92	54	40N17	87w41	5:50:44
Hegewisch 16	26	41N39	87w34	5:50:16
Helena 51	4	38N43	87w52	5:51:28
Helmar 47	55	41N30	88w32	5:54:08
Helvetia 60	56	38N42	89w39	5:58:36
Heman 58	57	39N56	89w04	5:56:16
Henderson 48	74	41N01	90w23	6:01:32
Henderson Grove 48	74	40N57	90w22	6:01:28
Hendryx Manor 72	98	40N45	89w37	5:58:28
Hennepin 78	41	41N15	89w21	5:57:24
Henning 92	26	40N18	87w42	5:50:48
Henry 62	30	41N07	89w22	5:57:28
Hensley 10	54	40N11	88w17	5:53:08
Henton 87	7	39N24	88w48	5:55:12
Herald 97	4	37N58	88w11	5:52:44
Heralds Prairie 97	4	37N58	88w12	5:52:48
Herbert 4	110	42N06	88w45	5:55:00
Herborn 87	63	39N21	88w37	5:54:28
Heritage 81	87	41N30	90w30	6:02:00
Hermon 48	4	40N48	90w10	6:00:40
Herod 76	4	37N35	88w26	5:53:44
Herrick 87	63	39N14	88w58	5:55:52
Herrin 100	4	37N48	89w02	5:56:08
Herscher 46	39	41N03	88w06	5:52:24
Hersman 5	76	39N59	90w46	6:03:04
Hervey City 58	55	39N47	88w52	5:55:28
Hettick 59	63	39N21	90w03	6:00:12
Hewittsville 11	7	39N34	89w21	5:57:24
Heyworth 57	35	40N19	88w59	5:55:56
Hickory 85	66	40N10	90w17	6:01:08
Hickory Falls 56	15	42N23	88w26	5:53:44
Hickory Grove 1	92	39N55	91w23	6:05:32
Hickory Hill 96	4	38N25	88w39	5:54:36
Hickory Hills 16	12	41N43	87w50	5:51:20
Hickory Point 58	26	39N54	88w58	5:55:52
Hicks 35	4	37N35	88w26	5:53:44
Hidalgo 40	4	39N09	88w09	5:52:36
Hidden Cove 16	1	41N45	87w50	5:51:20
Hidden Creek 16	6	42N06	88w02	5:52:08
Hidden Hills 55	4	40N28	90w41	6:02:44
Higginsville 92	38	40N18	87w48	5:51:12
High Lake 22	1	41N53	88w12	5:52:48
Highland 60	56	38N44	89w41	5:58:44
Highland Hills 22	83	41N51	88w01	5:52:04
Highland Lake 49	27	42N21	88w01	5:52:04
Highland Park 49	1	42N11	87w48	5:51:12
Highland Park 83	4	37N49	88w27	5:53:48
Highlands 22	2	41N48	87w56	5:51:44
Highland Shores 56	15	42N23	88w26	5:53:44
Highlawn 16	1	41N38	87w38	5:50:32
High Meadows 72	98	40N40	89w40	5:58:40
Highview Estates 22	2	41N47	87w57	5:51:48
Highway Village 90	98	40N39	89w34	5:58:16
Highwood 49	6	42N12	87w48	5:51:12
Highwood 82	25	38N32	90w00	6:00:00
Highwood Terrace 82	25	38N32	90w00	6:00:00
Hilcrest 68	7	39N08	89w30	5:58:00
Hildreth 23	96	39N55	87w50	5:51:20
Hillcrest 7	4	39N14	90w43	6:02:52
Hillcrest 16	1	41N40	88w00	5:52:00
Hillcrest 71	6	41N57	89w04	5:56:16
Hillerman 64	4	37N14	88w52	5:55:28
Hillery 92	54	40N17	87w41	5:50:44
Hillsboro 68	7	39N09	89w29	5:57:56
Hillsdale 81	4	41N37	90w10	6:00:40
Hillside 16	2	41N53	87w54	5:51:36
Hillside 46	115	41N05	87w53	5:51:32
Hillside-Berkeley 16	2	41N52	87w54	5:51:36
Hillside Manor 46	115	41N05	87w53	5:51:32
Hillview 31	63	39N27	90w32	6:02:08
Hillwood Estates 49	27	42N22	88w06	5:52:24
Hillyard 59	4	39N08	89w59	5:59:56
Himrod 92	26	40N03	87w38	5:50:32
Hinckley 19	43	41N46	88w38	5:54:32
Hindsboro 21	65	39N41	88w08	5:52:32
Hinsdale 22	2	41N48	87w56	5:51:44
Hinswood 22	19	41N47	87w59	5:51:56
Hire 55	4	40N30	90w51	6:03:24
Hittle 90	72	40N22	89w20	5:57:20
Hodgkins 16	1	41N46	87w52	5:51:28
Hoffman 14	4	38N32	89w16	5:57:04
Hoffman Estates 16	6	42N04	88w08	5:52:32
Holbrook 16	1	41N32	87w38	5:50:32
Holcomb 71	57	42N04	89w06	5:56:24
Holden 73	4	38N01	89w14	5:56:56
Holder 57	79	40N27	88w49	5:55:16
Holiday Hills 56	6	42N18	88w13	5:52:52
Holiday Shores 60	25	38N48	89w57	5:59:48
Holland 87	63	39N15	88w45	5:55:00
Hollandia 82	25	38N32	90w00	6:00:00
Hollenback 32	125	41N22	88w25	5:53:40
Hollendale 16	1	41N36	87w38	5:50:32
Holliday 26	4	39N11	88w47	5:55:08
Hollis 72	98	40N36	89w42	5:58:48
Hollowayville 6	134	41N22	89w18	5:57:12
Hollydale 16	2	41N34	87w40	5:50:40
Hollywood 16	1	41N50	87w51	5:51:24
Hollywood Heights 82	25	38N38	90w00	6:00:00
Hollywood Ridge 16	6	42N09	87w57	5:51:48
Holmes Center 72	51	40N55	89w30	5:58:00
Homberg 76	4	37N22	88w29	5:53:56
Home Gardens 92	54	40N17	87w41	5:50:44
Homer 10	57	40N02	87w57	5:51:48
Homestead 82	25	38N36	89w58	5:59:52
Hometown 16	2	41N44	87w43	5:50:52
Homewood 16	2	41N34	87w40	5:50:40
Homewood Acres 16	2	41N34	87w40	5:50:40
Homewood Shores 16	2	41N34	87w40	5:50:40
Homewood Terrace 16	2	41N34	87w40	5:50:40
Honey Bend 68	37	39N11	89w39	5:58:36
Honey Creek 71	4	41N59	89w13	5:56:52
Honey Point 59	4	39N13	89w47	5:59:08
Hononegah Heights 101	4	42N25	89w01	5:56:04
Hookdale 3	4	38N50	89w19	5:57:16
Hoopeston 92	80	40N28	87w40	5:50:40
Hooppole 37	4	41N31	89w55	5:59:40
Hoosier 13	4	38N47	88w25	5:53:40
Hope 50	43	41N09	89w06	5:56:24
Hope 92	54	40N18	87w53	5:51:32
Hopedale 90	72	40N25	89w25	5:57:40
Hopewell 62	30	41N04	89w20	5:57:20
Hop Hollow 60	7	38N57	90w11	6:00:44
Hopkins 98	4	41N48	89w48	5:59:12
Hopkins Park 46	82	41N04	87w33	5:50:12
Hopper 36	4	40N45	90w54	6:03:36
Horace 23	7	39N48	87w41	5:50:44
Horatio Gardens 49	6	42N10	87w57	5:51:48
Hord 13	4	38N46	88w30	5:54:00
Hornsby 59	37	39N11	89w39	5:58:36
Horseshoe 83	4	37N44	88w21	5:53:24
Hospital 46	115	41N05	87w53	5:51:32
Houston 1	66	40N09	91w05	6:04:20
Houston 79	63	38N07	89w42	5:58:48
Howardton 39	4	37N38	89w30	5:58:00
Howe 6	134	41N20	89w18	5:57:12
Hoyleton 95	4	38N27	89w16	5:57:04
Hubbard Woods 16	1	42N06	87w46	5:51:04
Hubbard Woods 61	4	38N31	89w08	5:56:32

Place		Lat.	Long.	Time
Hudgens 100	4	37N46	88w56	5:55:44
Hudson 57	41	40N38	88w59	5:55:56
Huegely 95	4	38N27	89w16	5:57:04
Huey 14	55	38N36	89w18	5:57:12
Hugh's Addition 84	133	39N49	89w37	5:58:28
Hugo 21	7	39N48	88w17	5:53:08
Hull 75	4	39N43	91w13	6:04:52
Humboldt 15	65	39N36	88w19	5:53:16
Hume 23	55	39N48	87w52	5:51:28
Humm Wye 35	4	37N22	88w29	5:53:56
Humrick 92	54	39N54	87w39	5:50:36
Hunt 40	4	39N00	88w01	5:52:04
Hunt City 40	4	39N03	88w01	5:52:04
Hunter 4	28	42N19	89w01	5:56:04
Hunter 23	56	39N40	87w35	5:50:20
Huntington 22	12	41N47	88w09	5:52:36
Huntington Commons 16	6	42N04	87w57	5:51:48
Huntinton Park 60	7	38N57	90w11	6:00:44
Huntley 56	21	42N10	88w26	5:53:44
Huntsville 85	4	40N10	90w51	6:03:24
Hurlbut 54	29	40N01	89w32	5:58:08
Hurricane 26	4	39N11	89w11	5:56:44
Hurst 100	4	37N50	89w09	5:56:36
Hutchins Park 101	28	42N18	89w06	5:56:24
Hutsonville 17	4	39N07	87w40	5:50:40
Hutton 15	4	39N26	88w05	5:52:20
Hyde Park 16	1	41N48	87w36	5:50:24
Idaville Corner 38	132	40N34	87w54	5:51:36
Idlewild 49	27	42N21	88w01	5:52:04
Idlewood 41	4	38N18	88w55	5:55:40
Idylside 99	114	41N31	88w07	5:52:28
Iliana 92	54	40N12	87w32	5:50:08
Illiana Heights 46	82	41N10	87w40	5:50:40
Illini 58	57	39N55	89w05	5:56:20
Illinois City 81	4	41N24	90w54	6:03:36
Illinois Veterans Home 1	92	39N55	91w23	6:05:32
Illiopolis 84	29	39N51	89w15	5:57:00
Imbs 82	46	38N32	90w14	6:00:56
Imperial 49	42	42N16	87w56	5:51:44
Ina 41	4	38N09	88w54	5:55:36
Independence 75	4	39N36	90w43	6:02:52
Independence 83	4	37N39	88w32	5:54:08
Indian Creek 49	126	42N14	87w59	5:51:56
Indian Grove 53	72	40N43	88w31	5:54:04
Indian Head Park 16	1	41N47	87w54	5:51:36
Indian Hill 16	1	42N06	87w46	5:51:04
Indian Hill 22	12	41N47	88w09	5:52:36
Indian Hills 16	1	41N31	87w38	5:50:32
Indian Oaks 46	115	41N10	87w53	5:51:32
Indian Oaks 99	1	41N40	88w00	5:52:00
Indianola 92	72	39N56	87w44	5:50:56
Indian Point 48	4	40N46	90w23	6:01:32
Indian Point 49	6	42N28	88w07	5:52:28
Indian Prairie 96	4	38N31	88w32	5:54:08
Indian Ridge 56	15	42N23	88w26	5:53:44
Indiantown 6	55	41N17	89w34	5:58:16
Indian Trail Estates 49	6	42N10	87w53	5:51:32
Industry 55	4	40N20	90w36	6:02:24
Ingalls Park 99	114	41N31	88w03	5:52:12
Ingalton 22	54	41N52	88w11	5:52:44
Ingleside 49	27	42N23	88w09	5:52:36
Ingleside Shores 49	27	42N23	88w09	5:52:36
Ingraham 13	4	38N50	88w20	5:53:20
Ingram Hill 83	4	37N44	88w33	5:54:12
International Village 22	83	41N53	88w01	5:52:04
International Village 99	1	41N40	88w00	5:52:00
Inverness 16	6	42N08	88w06	5:52:24
Iola 13	4	38N50	88w38	5:54:32
Ipava 29	66	40N21	90w19	6:01:16
Irene 4	28	42N14	89w01	5:56:04
Irish Grove 65	4	40N05	89w37	5:58:28
Irishtown 14	55	38N42	89w20	5:57:20
Iroquois 38	56	40N50	87w35	5:50:20
Irving 68	7	39N12	89w24	5:57:36
Irving Park 16	2	41N57	87w45	5:51:00
Irvington 95	4	38N26	89w10	5:56:40
Irwin 46	60	41N03	87w59	5:51:56
Isabel 23	65	39N39	88w02	5:52:08
Isabel 29	4	40N19	90w10	6:00:40
Island Grove 40	4	39N08	88w28	5:53:52
Island Grove 84	55	39N46	89w55	5:59:40
Island Lake 49	1	42N16	88w12	5:52:48
Itasca 22	17	41N58	88w01	5:52:04
Itasca Ranchettes 22	17	41N58	88w01	5:52:04
Iuka 61	4	38N37	88w47	5:55:08
Ivanhoe 16	1	41N38	87w38	5:50:32
Ivanhoe 49	6	42N17	88w03	5:52:12
Ivanhoe 99	1	41N40	88w00	5:52:00
Ivesdale 10	57	39N57	88w28	5:53:52
Ivy Glen 45	7	41N47	88w20	5:53:20
Ivy Heights 60	29	38N53	90w05	6:00:20
Jackson Heights 60	7	38N57	90w11	6:00:44
Jackson Park 16	1	41N47	87w36	5:50:24
Jacksonville 69	113	39N44	90w14	6:00:56
Jacob 39	4	37N45	89w32	5:58:08
Jamaica 92	54	40N00	87w48	5:51:12
Jamesburg 92	38	40N16	87w45	5:51:00
Jamestown 14	63	38N52	89w33	5:58:12
Jamestown 73	63	38N02	89w34	5:58:16
Janesville 18	4	39N22	88w15	5:53:00
Jarvis 60	4	38N42	89w53	5:59:32
Jasper 96	4	38N26	88w19	5:53:16
Jefferson 16	2	41N58	87w45	5:51:00

ILLINOIS

Jeffries 100 65 37N49 88w56 5:55:44
Jeiseyville 11 26 39N35 89w24 5:57:36
Jenkins 20 8 40N09 88w57 5:55:48
Jerome 84 133 39N46 89w41 5:58:44
Jersey 42 25 39N09 90w18 6:01:12
Jerseyville 42 25 39N07 90w20 6:01:20
Jewett 18 54 39N13 88w15 5:53:00
Johannisburg 95 55 38N21 89w38 5:58:32
Johnsburg 56 27 42N21 88w14 5:52:56
Johnsonville 96 4 38N31 88w32 5:54:08
Johnston City 100 63 37N49 88w56 5:55:44
Johnstown 18 63 39N25 88w18 5:53:12
Joliet 99 114 41N32 88w05 5:52:20
Jonathan Creek 70 7 39N39 88w32 5:54:08
Jonesboro 91 4 37N27 89w16 5:57:04
Jones Ridge 39 50 37N50 89w41 5:58:44
Jonesville 50 117 41N18 89w03 5:56:12
Joppa 64 65 37N12 88w51 5:55:24
Jordan 98 4 41N53 89w41 5:58:44
Joshua 29 4 40N35 90w09 6:00:36
Joslin 81 4 41N34 90w13 6:00:52
Joy 66 4 41N12 90w53 6:03:32
Jubilee 72 58 40N51 89w49 5:59:16
Junction 30 4 37N43 88w14 5:52:56
Junction City 61 4 38N34 89w07 5:56:28
Junction City 72 98 40N45 89w37 5:58:28
Justice 16 1 41N45 87w51 5:51:24
Kampsville 7 63 39N18 90w37 6:02:28
Kane 31 55 39N11 90w21 6:01:24
Kaneville 45 55 41N50 88w31 5:54:04
Kangley 50 135 41N09 88w52 5:55:28
Kankakee 46 115 41N07 87w52 5:51:28
Kankakee Valley 46 26 41N01 87w43 5:50:52
Kansas 23 66 39N33 87w56 5:51:44
Kappa 102 41 40N41 89w01 5:56:04
Karbers Ridge 35 4 37N35 88w20 5:53:20
Karnak 77 4 37N18 88w58 5:55:52
Kasbeer 6 55 41N30 89w28 5:57:52
Kaskaskia 79 63 37N54 89w56 5:59:44
Kaufman 60 37 38N53 89w44 5:58:56
Kedron 30 4 37N44 88w21 5:53:24
Kedzie Grace 16 2 41N57 87w42 5:50:48
Keene 1 53 40N09 91w12 6:04:48
Keenes 96 4 38N20 88w38 5:54:32
Keeneyville 22 27 41N58 88w07 5:52:28
Keensburg 93 4 38N21 87w52 5:51:28
Keith 96 4 38N35 88w28 5:53:52
Keithsburg 66 66 41N06 90w56 6:03:44
Kell 61 4 38N30 88w54 5:55:36
Kellerville 1 63 40N02 90w57 6:03:48
Kelleyville 92 26 40N03 87w38 5:50:32
Kelly 94 4 41N01 90w30 6:02:00
Kemp 21 63 39N41 88w18 5:53:12
Kemper 42 55 39N13 90w10 6:00:40
Kempton 27 44 40N56 88w14 5:52:56
Kendall 47 7 41N36 88w25 5:53:40
Kendall Hills 60 29 38N53 90w05 6:00:20
Keneddy 101 4 42N29 89w02 5:56:08
Kenilwicke 16 6 42N06 88w02 5:52:08
Kenilworth 16 2 42N05 87w42 5:50:48
Kenney 20 55 40N06 89w05 5:56:20
Ken Rock 101 28 42N13 89w04 5:56:16
Kent 89 4 42N20 89w52 5:59:28
Keptown 25 4 39N04 88w45 5:55:00
Kernan 50 135 41N08 88w50 5:55:20
Kerr 10 54 40N21 87w58 5:51:52
Kerton 29 66 40N15 90w11 6:00:44
Kewanee 37 4 41N14 89w56 5:59:44
Keyesport 14 4 38N45 89w17 5:57:08
Key West 16 6 42N03 87w53 5:51:32
Kickapoo 72 4 40N45 89w42 5:58:48
Kidd 67 55 38N05 90w06 6:00:24
Kidley 23 7 39N48 87w41 5:50:44
Kilbourne 63 66 40N09 90w01 6:00:04
Kildeer 49 6 42N11 88w03 5:52:12
Kimberly Heights 16 6 41N35 87w46 5:51:04
Kincaid 11 26 39N35 89w25 5:57:40
Kinderhook 75 4 39N43 91w12 6:04:48
King 11 63 39N26 89w30 5:58:00
Kingdom 52 25 41N50 89w30 5:58:00
Kingman 87 63 39N16 88w38 5:54:32
Kings 71 6 42N00 89w06 5:56:24
Kings Cove 49 6 42N10 87w53 5:51:32
Kings Island 49 6 42N24 88w11 5:52:44
Kings Park 99 1 41N40 88w00 5:52:00
Kingston 1 66 39N42 91w03 6:04:12
Kingston 19 64 42N07 88w46 5:55:04
Kingston Mines 72 57 40N33 89w46 5:59:04
Kinkaid 39 4 37N49 89w32 5:58:08
Kinmundy 61 4 38N46 88w51 5:55:24
Kinsman 32 55 41N11 88w34 5:54:16
Kirkland 19 56 42N06 88w51 5:55:24
Kirksville 70 7 39N36 88w36 5:54:24
Kirkwood 94 4 40N52 90w45 6:03:00
Kishwaukee Glen 101 28 42N13 89w04 5:56:16
Klein Acres 10 29 40N19 88w08 5:52:32
Klondike 2 4 37N00 89w11 5:56:44
Klondike 49 6 42N26 88w09 5:52:36
Klondyke 51 4 38N43 87w52 5:51:28
Knapp's Noll 101 4 42N28 89w05 5:56:20
Knight Prairie 33 4 38N05 88w39 5:54:36
Knollcrest 16 2 41N35 87w40 5:50:40
Knollwood 49 27 42N17 87w53 5:51:32
Knollwood 84 133 39N49 89w37 5:58:28
Knottingham 22 12 41N48 88w01 5:52:04
Knox 48 4 40N56 90w16 6:01:04
Knoxville 48 74 40N55 90w17 6:01:08
Kortcamp 68 7 39N10 89w28 5:57:52
Kuhn 60 25 38N48 89w57 5:59:48
La Clede 26 4 38N53 88w43 5:54:52
Lacon 62 30 41N02 89w24 5:57:36
Ladd 6 134 41N23 89w13 5:56:52
Laenna 54 29 40N01 89w12 5:56:48
Lafayette 79 63 37N54 89w56 5:59:44
La Fayette 88 4 41N07 89w58 5:59:52
La Fontaine 16 1 42N04 87w48 5:51:12
Lafox 45 60 41N53 88w25 5:53:40
La Grange 5 65 39N53 90w39 6:02:36
La Grange 16 1 41N48 87w52 5:51:28
La Grange Highlands 16 1 41N47 87w53 5:51:32
La Grange Park 16 1 41N49 87w52 5:51:28
Laguna Woods 16 2 41N36 87w40 5:50:40
La Harpe 34 4 40N35 90w58 6:03:52
La Hogue 38 29 40N46 88w00 5:52:00
Lake 14 55 38N32 89w19 5:57:16
Lake Barrington 49 1 42N13 88w10 5:52:40
Lake Bluff 49 116 42N17 87w50 5:51:20
Lake Boulevard Addition 92 54 40N17 87w41 5:50:44
Lake Bracken 48 74 40N57 90w22 6:01:28
Lake Briarwood 16 27 42N04 87w59 5:51:56
Lake Camelot 72 98 40N34 89w44 5:58:56
Lake Carlinville 59 47 39N18 89w52 5:59:28
Lake Catherine 49 6 42N29 88w08 5:52:32
Lake Centralia 61 55 39N16 90w12 6:00:48
Lake Charleston 15 106 39N29 88w13 5:52:52
Lake Charlotte 45 95 41N54 88w19 5:53:16
Lake City 70 4 39N45 88w43 5:54:52
Lake Creek 100 4 37N49 88w53 5:55:32
Lakecrest 68 7 39N10 89w28 5:57:52
Lake Crest 100 4 37N37 88w50 5:55:20
Lake Estates 100 4 37N46 88w56 5:55:44
Lake Forest 49 116 42N15 87w50 5:51:20
Lake Forest Estates 82 25 38N32 90w00 6:00:00
Lake Fork 54 29 39N58 89w21 5:57:24
Lake Holiday 19 25 41N40 88w35 5:54:20
Lakehurst 49 140 42N23 87w52 5:51:28
Lake In The Hills 56 9 42N11 88w19 5:53:16
Lake in the Woods 22 12 41N48 88w01 5:52:04
Lake Iroquois 38 43 40N31 88w05 5:52:20
Lake Killarney 56 1 42N14 88w15 5:53:00
Lake Lancelot 72 98 40N34 89w44 5:58:56
Lakeland Hills 82 25 38N32 90w00 6:00:00
Lakeland Park 56 27 42N21 88w14 5:52:56
Lake Lawrence 51 4 38N45 87w31 5:50:04
Lake Lynwood 16 1 41N31 87w38 5:50:32
Lake Marie 49 6 42N28 88w07 5:52:28
Lake Marion 61 105 42N07 88w16 5:53:04
Lakemoor 56 18 42N20 88w12 5:52:48
Lake of the Winds 16 6 42N09 87w57 5:51:48
Lake of the Woods 72 57 40N52 89w41 5:58:44
Lake Pana 11 63 39N23 89w04 5:56:16
Lake Park Estates 16 6 42N06 88w02 5:52:08
Lake Park Forest 16 6 42N06 88w02 5:52:08
Lake Petersburg 65 29 40N01 89w51 5:59:24
Lake Piasa 42 37 39N02 90w09 6:00:36
Lakeside Knolls 68 7 39N10 89w28 5:57:52
Lakeside Villas 16 6 42N09 87w57 5:51:48
Lake Summerset 89 4 42N25 89w25 5:57:40
Lake Tacoma 100 4 37N43 89w14 5:56:56
Lake Thunderbird 78 4 41N11 89w24 5:57:36
Lakeview 16 1 41N57 87w40 5:50:40
Lakeview Acres 60 7 38N40 90w00 6:00:00
Lake View Estates 100 4 37N37 89w13 5:56:52
Lakeview Heights 96 4 38N23 88w22 5:53:28
Lake Villa 49 7 42N25 88w05 5:52:20
Lake Wildwood 62 56 41N07 89w12 5:56:48
Lakewood 16 29 41N29 87w43 5:50:52
Lakewood 22 54 41N52 88w11 5:52:44
Lakewood 56 56 39N20 88w54 5:55:36
Lakewood 60 7 38N57 90w11 6:00:44
Lakewood Park 100 4 37N43 89w14 5:56:56
Lakewood Shores 99 7 41N19 88w06 5:52:24
Lakewood Village 45 105 42N07 88w16 5:53:04
Lake Zurich 49 6 42N12 88w05 5:52:20
Lamard 96 4 38N26 88w25 5:53:40
Lamb 35 4 37N28 88w10 5:52:40
Lambert 16 1 41N40 88w00 5:52:00
La Moille 6 55 41N32 89w17 5:57:08
Lamoine 55 4 40N20 90w51 6:03:24
Lamotte 17 4 39N00 87w37 5:50:28
Lamplighter 57 104 40N34 88w54 5:55:36
Lanark 8 4 42N06 89w50 5:59:20
Lancaster 93 4 38N33 87w52 5:51:28
Landes 17 4 38N43 87w52 5:51:28
Lane 20 63 40N07 88w51 5:55:24
Lanesville 84 55 39N50 89w20 5:57:20
Langleyville 11 7 39N34 89w21 5:57:24
Lansdowne 82 25 38N38 90w04 6:00:16
Lansing 16 12 41N33 87w32 5:50:08
Laona 101 4 42N28 89w20 5:57:20
La Place 74 54 39N48 88w43 5:54:52
La Prairie 1 66 40N09 91w00 6:04:00
Laprairie Center 62 48 41N03 89w26 5:57:44
Larchland 94 4 40N55 90w38 6:02:32
Larkdale 49 6 42N16 88w08 5:52:32
Larkdale 58 26 39N50 88w56 5:55:44
Larkinsburg 13 4 38N52 88w38 5:54:32
La Rose 62 56 41N02 89w14 5:56:56
La Salle 50 117 41N20 89w06 5:56:24
Latham 54 56 39N58 89w10 5:56:40
Latham Park 101 4 42N22 89w04 5:56:16
Latona 40 4 39N03 88w19 5:53:16
Laura 72 58 40N55 89w55 5:59:40
La Vergne 16 1 41N51 87w48 5:51:12
Lawndale 54 36 40N13 89w17 5:57:08
Lawrence 56 7 42N27 88w39 5:54:36
Lawrenceville 51 4 38N44 87w41 5:50:44
Lawrencewood 16 1 42N02 87w49 5:51:16
Layton 85 65 40N07 90w34 6:02:16
Leaf River 71 55 42N09 89w24 5:57:36
Lebanon 82 7 38N37 89w46 5:59:04
Le Claire 60 25 38N48 89w57 5:59:48
Ledford 83 4 37N42 88w35 5:54:20
Lee 52 43 41N48 88w57 5:55:48
Lee Center 52 29 41N45 89w17 5:57:08
Leech 96 4 38N20 88w12 5:52:48
Leeds 50 29 41N04 89w03 5:56:12
Leef 60 63 38N52 89w40 5:58:40
Leepertown 6 41 41N18 89w22 5:57:28
Leesville 46 26 41N01 87w43 5:50:52
Lehigh 46 115 41N05 87w53 5:51:32
Leisure Village 49 6 42N24 88w11 5:52:44
Leland 50 26 41N37 88w48 5:55:12
Leland Grove 84 133 39N47 89w41 5:58:44
Lementon 82 29 38N26 89w54 5:59:36
Lemont 16 1 41N40 88w00 5:52:00
Lena 89 65 42N23 89w49 5:59:16
Lenox 94 4 40N51 90w37 6:02:28
Lenzburg 82 39 38N16 89w52 5:59:28
Leon Corners 98 4 41N40 89w56 5:59:44
Leonore 50 57 41N11 88w59 5:55:56
L'Erable 38 35 40N56 87w56 5:51:44
Lerna 15 63 39N25 88w17 5:53:08
Le Roy 57 81 40N21 88w46 5:55:04
Levan 39 4 37N49 89w26 5:57:44
Levee 75 66 39N44 91w18 6:05:12
Lewistown 29 7 40N24 90w09 6:00:36
Lewood 99 82 41N35 88w11 5:52:44
Lexington 57 7 40N39 88w47 5:55:08
Leyden 16 1 41N56 87w53 5:51:32
Liberty 1 66 39N53 91w06 6:04:24
Liberty 83 4 37N44 88w33 5:54:12
Liberty Acres 49 42 42N16 87w56 5:51:44
Liberty Lake 49 42 42N16 87w56 5:51:44
Liberty Park 22 19 41N47 87w59 5:51:56
Libertyville 49 42 42N18 87w57 5:51:48
Lick 84 30 39N41 89w42 5:58:48
Lick Creek 91 4 37N31 89w05 5:56:20
Licking 17 4 39N08 87w54 5:51:36
Lick Prairie 93 4 38N29 87w54 5:51:36
Lidice 99 114 41N33 88w07 5:52:28
Lightsville 71 4 42N11 89w24 5:57:36
Lilac Circle Homes 22 83 41N53 88w01 5:52:04
Lilly 90 4 40N32 89w21 5:57:24
Lily Cache 99 82 41N35 88w11 5:52:44
Lily Cache Acres 99 82 41N35 88w11 5:52:44
Lily Lake 45 84 41N52 88w35 5:54:20
Lilymoor 56 27 42N20 88w13 5:52:52
Lima 1 63 40N11 91w23 6:05:32
Limerick 6 55 41N33 89w28 5:57:52
Lincoln 54 29 40N09 89w22 5:57:28
Lincoln Addition 60 29 38N52 90w05 6:00:20
Lincoln Estates 99 4 41N30 87w49 5:51:16
Lincoln Gardens 60 7 38N54 90w10 6:00:40
Lincoln Hills 22 2 41N53 88w04 5:52:16
Lincoln Park 16 1 41N55 87w39 5:50:36
Lincolnshire 49 2 42N11 87w55 5:51:40
Lincolnshire 99 1 41N28 87w37 5:50:28
Lincoln's New Salem 65 29 39N59 89w49 5:59:16
Lincolnwood 16 1 42N02 87w44 5:50:56
Lincolnwood Hills 99 1 41N31 87w58 5:51:52
Lindenhurst 49 6 42N25 88w02 5:52:08
Lindenwood 71 57 42N03 89w02 5:56:08
Linder 31 55 39N18 90w19 6:01:16
Linn 93 4 38N32 87w43 5:50:52
Linn 102 4 40N53 89w13 5:56:52
Lintner 74 55 39N48 88w35 5:54:20
Lioncrest 16 29 41N29 87w43 5:50:52
Lis 40 4 38N59 88w10 5:52:40
Lisbon 47 55 41N29 88w29 5:53:56
Lisle 22 12 41N48 88w05 5:52:20
Litchfield 68 37 39N11 89w39 5:58:36
Literberry 69 63 39N51 90w12 6:00:48
Little America 29 7 40N24 90w09 6:00:36
Little Indian 9 63 39N58 90w13 6:00:52
Little Mackinaw 90 72 40N27 89w20 5:57:20
Little Rock 47 25 41N40 88w33 5:54:12
Littleton 85 4 40N14 90w37 6:02:28
Little York 94 4 41N01 90w45 6:03:00
Lively Grove 95 55 38N15 89w39 5:58:36
Liverpool 29 66 40N25 90w03 6:00:12
Livingston 12 55 39N23 87w42 5:50:48
Livingston 60 26 38N58 89w46 5:59:04
Loami 84 55 39N40 89w51 5:59:24
Loch Lomond 49 126 42N14 87w59 5:51:56
Lockhaven 42 7 38N57 90w11 6:00:44
Lockport 99 114 41N35 88w03 5:52:12
Locust 11 63 39N29 89w12 5:56:48

ILLINOIS

Loda 38	41	40N31	88w04	5:52:16
Lodge 74	55	40N07	88w34	5:54:16
Logan 23	7	39N48	87w41	5:50:44
Logan 28	4	37N57	88w50	5:55:20
Logan Square 16	1	41N55	87w42	5:50:48
Lomax 36	4	40N41	91w04	6:04:16
Lombard 22	83	41N53	88w01	5:52:04
Lombardville 88	4	41N11	89w39	5:58:36
London Mills 29	4	40N43	90w11	6:00:44
Lone Grove 26	4	38N53	88w52	5:55:28
Lone Tree 6	55	41N18	89w30	5:58:00
Long Branch 83	4	37N53	88w33	5:54:12
Long Creek 58	4	39N49	88w50	5:55:20
Long Grove 49	6	42N11	88w00	5:52:00
Long Lake 49	27	42N22	88w08	5:52:32
Long Meadow 22	12	41N48	88w01	5:52:04
Long Point 53	55	41N00	88w54	5:55:36
Longview 10	65	39N53	88w04	5:52:16
Longwood Farms 16	1	41N31	87w38	5:50:32
Longwood Manor 22	12	41N47	88w09	5:52:36
Loogootee 26	4	38N54	88w51	5:55:24
Looking Glass 14	55	38N31	89w39	5:58:36
Lookout Point 56	15	42N23	88w26	5:53:44
Loon Lake 49	6	42N27	88w05	5:52:20
Loraine 1	53	40N09	91w13	6:04:52
Loran 89	4	42N15	89w48	5:59:12
Lords' Park Manor 16	107	42N02	88w17	5:53:08
Lorenzo 99	7	41N19	88w06	5:52:24
Loretto 53	127	41N00	88w31	5:54:04
Lorraine Park 22	2	41N53	88w05	5:52:20
Lostant 50	43	41N09	89w04	5:56:16
Lost Nation 71	25	41N50	89w30	5:58:00
Lotus 10	54	40N22	88w26	5:53:44
Lotus Woods 49	6	42N26	88w11	5:52:44
Lou Del 67	8	38N20	90w09	6:00:36
Loudon 26	4	39N09	88w53	5:55:32
Louisville 13	4	38N46	88w30	5:54:00
Love 92	54	39N55	87w34	5:50:16
Lovejoy 38	80	40N32	87w43	5:50:52
Lovejoy 82	25	38N39	90w10	6:00:40
Loves Park 101	55	42N19	89w03	5:56:12
Lovington 70	61	39N43	88w38	5:54:32
Lowder 84	55	39N33	89w51	5:59:24
Lowe 70	55	39N44	88w32	5:54:08
Lowell 50	136	41N13	89w04	5:56:16
Lowpoint 102	32	40N52	89w19	5:57:16
Loxa 15	106	39N30	88w16	5:53:04
Lucas 25	4	38N57	88w25	5:53:40
Ludlow 10	30	40N23	88w08	5:52:32
Lukin 51	4	38N37	87w50	5:51:20
Lumaghi Heights 60	7	38N40	90w00	6:00:00
Luther 63	4	40N12	89w42	5:58:48
Lyman 27	30	40N38	88w11	5:52:44
Lynchburg 63	66	40N06	90w14	6:00:56
Lyndon 98	4	41N43	89w56	5:59:44
Lynn Center 37	4	41N18	90w22	6:01:28
Lynn Gardens 46	115	41N05	87w53	5:51:32
Lynnville 69	113	39N43	90w16	6:01:04
Lynnwood 47	4	41N41	88w21	5:53:24
Lynwood 16	12	41N31	87w32	5:50:08
Lyons 16	2	41N49	87w50	5:51:20
Macedonia 33	4	38N03	88w42	5:54:48
Mackinaw 90	118	40N32	89w21	5:57:24
Mackler Heights 16	1	41N31	87w38	5:50:32
Macomb 55	66	40N27	90w40	6:02:40
Macon 58	57	39N43	89w00	5:56:00
Macoupin 59	51	39N10	89w59	5:59:56
Madison 60	35	38N41	90w09	6:00:36
Madonnaville 67	8	38N20	90w09	6:00:36
Maeystown 67	63	38N13	90w14	6:00:56
Magnet 15	63	39N24	88w19	5:53:16
Magnolia 78	56	41N08	89w14	5:56:56
Mahomet 10	54	40N12	88w24	5:53:36
Makanda 39	4	37N37	89w13	5:56:52
Malden 6	55	41N25	89w22	5:57:28
Malone 90	29	40N22	89w40	5:58:40
Malta 19	40	41N56	88w52	5:55:28
Malvern 98	75	41N49	89w58	5:59:52
Manchester 86	63	39N33	90w20	6:01:20
Manhattan 99	82	41N26	87w59	5:51:56
Manito 63	7	40N26	89w47	5:59:08
Manlius 6	55	41N27	89w40	5:58:40
Mannheim 16	1	41N56	87w53	5:51:32
Mansfield 74	55	40N13	88w31	5:54:04
Manteno 46	26	41N15	87w50	5:51:20
Manville 53	55	41N03	88w46	5:55:04
Maplebrook 22	12	41N47	88w09	5:52:36
Maple Lane 98	26	41N48	89w43	5:58:52
Maple Park 45	84	41N52	88w35	5:54:20
Maple Point 18	4	39N15	88w10	5:52:40
Maples Mill 29	7	40N24	90w09	6:00:36
Mapleton 72	98	40N34	89w44	5:58:56
Maplewood 82	25	38N34	90w08	6:00:32
Maquon 48	4	40N48	90w10	6:00:40
Marblehead 1	92	39N55	91w23	6:05:32
Marcelline 1	53	40N04	91w22	6:05:28
Marcoe 41	4	38N18	88w55	5:55:40
Mardell Manor 72	98	40N40	89w40	5:58:40
Marengo 56	119	42N17	88w39	5:54:36
Marietta 29	63	40N30	90w23	6:01:32
Marina Terrace 47	4	41N41	88w21	5:53:24
Marina Village 47	4	41N41	88w21	5:53:24
Marine 60	55	38N47	89w47	5:59:08
Marion 100	63	37N44	88w56	5:55:44
Marion Circle 45	41	41N45	88w27	5:53:48
Marion Hills 22	54	41N46	87w57	5:51:48
Marissa 82	53	38N15	89w45	5:59:00
Mark 78	41	41N16	89w15	5:57:00
Market Place 10	21	40N07	88w15	5:53:00
Markham 16	1	41N36	87w42	5:50:48
Markham City 41	4	38N20	88w44	5:54:56
Marley 99	1	41N33	87w55	5:51:40
Marlow 41	4	38N16	88w47	5:55:08
Maroa 58	8	40N02	88w57	5:55:48
Marquette Heights 90	98	40N37	89w36	5:58:24
Marrowbone 70	55	39N38	88w45	5:55:00
Marseilles 50	120	41N20	88w43	5:54:52
Marshall 12	55	39N23	87w42	5:50:48
Marston 66	4	41N20	90w40	6:02:40
Martinsburg 75	4	39N32	90w52	6:03:28
Martinsville 12	55	39N20	87w53	5:51:32
Martinton 38	30	40N55	87w44	5:50:56
Marydale Manor 16	1	41N37	87w40	5:50:40
Maryland 71	63	42N09	89w31	5:58:04
Maryville 60	7	38N43	89w59	5:59:56
Mascoutah 82	55	38N29	89w48	5:59:12
Mason 25	4	38N57	88w38	5:54:32
Mason City 63	121	40N12	89w42	5:58:48
Massbach 43	4	42N19	90w13	6:00:52
Massilon 96	4	38N26	88w13	5:52:52
Matanzas Beach 63	55	40N18	90w04	6:00:16
Mathersville 66	4	41N16	90w36	6:02:24
Matteson 16	2	41N30	87w42	5:50:48
Mattoon 15	63	39N29	88w23	5:53:32
Maud 93	4	38N25	87w46	5:51:04
Maunie 97	4	38N02	88w03	5:52:12
Maxwell 84	55	39N39	89w55	5:59:40
Mayberry 33	4	37N59	88w25	5:53:40
Mayfair 90	98	40N37	89w29	5:57:56
Mayfield 19	36	42N01	88w46	5:55:04
Maynard Lake 10	21	40N07	88w15	5:53:00
Mayngaite 16	1	41N31	87w42	5:50:48
Maysville 75	4	39N42	90w41	6:02:44
Maytown 52	29	41N43	89w20	5:57:20
Mayview 10	138	40N06	88w12	5:52:48
Maywood 16	1	41N53	87w51	5:51:24
Mazon 32	122	41N14	88w25	5:53:40
McCall 34	4	40N25	91w09	6:04:36
McClellan 41	4	38N15	88w59	5:55:56
McClure 2	4	37N19	89w26	5:57:44
McClusky 42	25	39N05	90w22	6:01:28
McConnell 89	4	42N26	89w44	5:58:56
McCook 16	1	41N48	87w50	5:51:20
McCormick 76	4	37N37	88w42	5:54:48
McCullom Lake 56	62	42N22	88w18	5:53:12
McDowell 53	127	40N53	88w38	5:54:32
McFarlan 35	4	37N29	88w18	5:53:12
McGirr 19	60	41N46	88w46	5:55:04
McHenry 56	30	42N21	88w16	5:53:04
McHenry Shores 56	30	42N21	88w14	5:52:56
McKee 1	66	39N53	90w59	6:03:56
McKeen 12	55	39N23	87w42	5:50:48
McKendree 92	54	40N00	87w34	5:50:16
McLean 57	72	40N19	89w10	5:56:40
McLeansboro 33	4	38N06	88w32	5:54:08
McNabb 78	41	41N11	89w13	5:56:52
McQueen 22	54	41N52	88w11	5:52:44
McVey 59	29	39N27	89w47	5:59:08
Meacham 61	4	38N42	88w45	5:55:00
Meadowbrook 55	4	40N28	90w41	6:02:44
Meadowbrook 60	25	38N54	90w01	6:00:04
Meadowdale 45	105	42N07	88w16	5:53:04
Meadowdale Shopping Center 45	105	42N07	88w16	5:53:04
Meadow Heights 82	7	38N40	90w00	6:00:00
Meadow Mart 101	55	42N19	89w02	5:56:08
Meadows 57	35	40N45	88w43	5:54:52
Meadowview 46	115	41N05	87w53	5:51:32
Mechanicsburg 84	8	39N49	89w26	5:57:44
Medalist Park 16	6	42N06	88w02	5:52:08
Media 36	4	40N46	90w51	6:03:24
Medina 72	57	40N50	89w35	5:58:20
Medinah 22	27	41N59	88w03	5:52:12
Medinah on the Lake 22	27	41N58	88w05	5:52:20
Medora 59	55	39N11	90w09	6:00:36
Meeks 92	54	39N58	87w38	5:50:32
Meersman 81	87	41N30	90w26	6:01:44
Melrose 12	4	39N10	87w38	5:50:32
Melrose Park 16	1	41N54	87w52	5:51:28
Melville 60	7	38N57	90w11	6:00:44
Melvin 27	30	40N34	88w15	5:53:00
Mendon 1	53	40N05	91w18	6:05:12
Mendota 50	123	41N33	89w07	5:56:28
Menominee 43	4	42N29	90w32	6:02:08
Meppen 7	65	39N00	90w36	6:02:24
Mercer 66	4	41N12	90w43	6:02:52
Merchandise Mart 16	1	41N54	87w38	5:50:32
Meredosia 69	65	39N50	90w34	6:02:16
Meriden 50	56	41N35	88w59	5:55:56
Meridian 14	4	38N37	89w12	5:56:48
Meridian Heights 77	4	37N07	89w12	5:56:48
Mermet 64	4	37N19	88w56	5:55:44
Merna 57	68	40N31	88w50	5:55:20
Merriam 96	4	38N23	88w22	5:53:28
Merrimac 67	55	38N18	90w19	6:01:16
Merrionette Park 16	1	41N41	87w42	5:50:48
Merritt 86	4	39N44	90w25	6:01:40
Merry Oaks 81	87	41N30	90w26	6:01:44
Mesa Lake 93	4	38N33	87w52	5:51:28
Metamora 102	57	40N47	89w22	5:57:28
Metcalf 23	55	39N48	87w48	5:51:12
Metropolis 64	62	37N10	88w44	5:54:56
Mettawa 49	126	42N14	87w56	5:51:44
Meyer 1	66	40N22	91w34	6:06:16
Meyer 46	115	41N05	87w53	5:51:32
Meyers Bay 49	6	42N23	88w11	5:52:44
Michael 7	55	39N14	90w37	6:02:28
Middlebury 16	6	42N09	88w06	5:52:24
Middlefork 92	38	40N19	87w50	5:51:20
Middlegrove 29	4	40N42	90w06	6:00:24
Middleport 38	30	40N50	87w44	5:50:56
Middlesworth 87	7	39N24	88w48	5:55:12
Middletown 54	63	40N11	89w35	5:58:20
Midland City 20	55	40N09	89w08	5:56:32
Midland Hills 39	4	37N37	89w13	5:56:52
Midlothian 16	1	41N38	87w43	5:50:52
Midway 60	4	38N55	90w01	6:00:04
Midway 64	4	37N09	88w44	5:54:56
Midway 90	98	40N35	89w37	5:58:28
Midway 92	26	40N03	87w38	5:50:32
Mid-West 16	1	41N53	87w41	5:50:44
Milam 58	55	39N41	88w52	5:55:28
Milan 81	87	41N27	90w34	6:02:16
Mildred 84	133	39N46	89w38	5:58:32
Miles 59	37	39N02	90w09	6:00:36
Milford 38	7	40N38	87w42	5:50:48
Milks Grove 38	35	40N53	87w58	5:51:52
Millbrook 47	25	41N36	88w33	5:54:12
Millbrook 72	4	40N56	89w57	5:59:48
Millburn 49	6	42N26	88w00	5:52:00
Mill Creek 16	6	42N09	87w57	5:51:48
Millcreek 91	4	37N21	89w15	5:57:00
Milledgeville 8	63	41N58	89w46	5:59:04
Miller 50	55	41N25	88w39	5:54:36
Miller City 2	4	37N05	89w21	5:57:24
Miller Lake 41	4	38N18	88w55	5:55:40
Millersburg 66	4	41N12	90w50	6:03:20
Millersville 11	63	39N23	89w04	5:56:16
Miller Woods 16	1	41N31	87w38	5:50:32
Millhurst 47	25	41N40	88w32	5:54:08
Millington 47	7	41N34	88w36	5:54:24
Mills 3	55	38N48	89w25	5:57:40
Mill Shoals 97	4	38N15	88w21	5:53:24
Mill Spring 60	7	38N57	90w11	6:00:44
Millstadt 82	56	38N28	90w06	6:00:24
Milmine 74	54	39N54	88w39	5:54:36
Milo 6	4	41N11	89w35	5:58:20
Milton 75	4	39N34	90w39	6:02:36
Mineral 6	63	41N22	89w48	5:59:12
Mineral Springs 98	26	41N48	89w43	5:58:52
Minier 90	86	40N26	89w19	5:57:16
Minonk 102	124	40N54	89w02	5:56:08
Minooka 32	48	41N27	88w16	5:53:04
Misenheimer 91	4	37N23	89w18	5:57:12
Missal 53	135	41N08	88w50	5:55:20
Mission 50	55	41N30	88w38	5:54:32
Mission Hills 16	2	42N07	87w49	5:51:16
Mississippi 42	37	39N02	90w19	6:01:16
Missouri 5	76	40N04	90w45	6:03:00
Mitchell 60	4	38N46	90w05	6:00:20
Mitchellsville 83	4	37N41	88w38	5:54:32
Mitchie 67	63	38N12	90w16	6:01:04
Mobet Meadows 81	4	41N37	90w20	6:01:20
Moccasin 25	4	39N08	88w45	5:55:00
Mode 87	63	39N16	88w44	5:54:56
Modena 88	4	41N04	89w46	5:59:04
Modesto 59	63	39N29	89w59	5:59:56
Modoc 79	55	38N03	90w02	6:00:08
Moecherville 45	102	41N46	88w20	5:53:20
Mohawk 22	17	41N57	87w58	5:51:52
Mokena 99	3	41N32	87w53	5:51:32
Moline 81	87	41N30	90w31	6:02:04
Momence 46	82	41N10	87w40	5:50:40
Mona 27	44	40N54	88w11	5:52:44
Monee 99	26	41N25	87w44	5:50:56
Money Creek 57	7	40N38	88w52	5:55:28
Monica 72	55	40N56	89w45	5:59:00
Monmouth 94	23	40N55	90w39	6:02:36
Monroe Center 71	57	42N06	89w00	5:56:00
Monroe City 67	8	38N20	90w09	6:00:36
Mont 60	25	38N48	89w57	5:59:48
Montague Forest 45	107	42N02	88w17	5:53:08
Montebello 34	4	40N25	91w18	6:05:12
Monterey 29	4	40N32	89w58	5:59:52
Monterey Village 99	1	41N30	87w41	5:50:44
Montezuma 75	4	39N32	90w38	6:02:32
Montgomery 45	7	41N44	88w21	5:53:24
Monticello 74	30	40N01	88w34	5:54:16
Montmorency 98	4	41N43	89w41	5:58:44
Montrose 25	56	39N10	88w23	5:53:32
Moonshine 12	4	39N20	87w53	5:51:32
Moores Prairie 41	4	38N10	88w46	5:55:04
Mooseheart 45	2	41N49	88w20	5:53:20
Moredock 67	55	38N22	90w18	6:01:12
Morehaven 101	4	42N25	89w01	5:56:04
Morgan 15	65	39N36	88w06	5:52:24
Morgan Park 16	1	41N42	87w40	5:50:40
Moriah 12	4	39N18	87w59	5:51:56
Moro 60	4	38N58	89w59	5:59:56
Morris 32	125	41N22	88w26	5:53:44
Morris Hills 82	7	38N40	90w00	6:00:00
Morrison 98	75	41N49	89w58	5:59:52
Morrisonville 11	63	39N25	89w27	5:57:48
Morristown 37	4	41N21	90w17	6:01:08
Morristown 101	4	42N10	89w04	5:56:16
Morseville 43	4	42N21	90w01	6:00:04
Morton 90	98	40N37	89w28	5:57:52
Morton Grove 16	1	42N02	87w46	5:51:04
Morton Park 16	1	41N51	87w46	5:51:04
Moser Highlands 22	12	41N47	88w09	5:52:36
Mosquito 11	55	39N45	89w12	5:56:48
Mossville 72	4	40N49	89w34	5:58:16
Moulton 87	7	39N24	88w48	5:55:12
Mound City 77	4	37N05	89w10	5:56:40
Mounds 77	4	37N07	89w12	5:56:48
Mound Station 5	66	40N00	90w52	6:03:28
Mountain 83	4	37N40	88w26	5:53:44
Mountain Glen 91	4	37N32	89w15	5:57:00
Mount Auburn 11	63	39N44	89w19	5:57:16
Mount Carbon 39	4	37N46	89w21	5:57:24
Mount Carmel 93	59	38N25	87w46	5:51:04
Mount Carroll 8	4	42N06	89w59	5:59:56
Mount Clair 60	7	38N57	90w11	6:00:44

ILLINOIS

Mount Clare 59 55 39N06 89w50 5:59:20
Mount Erie 96 4 38N31 88w14 5:52:56
Mount Greenwood 16 1 41N42 87w42 5:50:48
Mount Hope 57 72 40N21 89w12 5:56:48
Mount Morris 71 28 42N03 89w26 5:57:44
Mount Olive 59 7 39N04 89w44 5:58:56
Mount Palatine 78 43 41N09 89w04 5:56:16
Mount Pleasant 91 4 37N28 88w58 5:55:52
Mount Pleasant 98 75 41N48 89w55 5:59:40
Mount Prospect 16 1 42N04 87w56 5:51:44
Mount Prospect Gardens 16 1 42N04 87w57 5:51:48
Mount Pulaski 54 29 40N01 89w17 5:57:08
Mount Sterling 5 76 39N59 90w45 6:03:00
Mount Vernon 41 4 38N19 88w55 5:55:40
Mount Zion 58 55 39N46 88w53 5:55:32
Moweaqua 87 57 39N38 89w01 5:56:04
Mozier 7 4 39N18 90w45 6:03:00
Muddy 83 4 37N46 88w31 5:54:04
Mulberry Grove 3 54 38N56 89w16 5:57:04
Mulkeytown 28 4 37N58 89w07 5:56:28
Muncie 92 43 40N07 87w51 5:51:24
Mundelein 49 126 42N16 88w00 5:52:00
Mundelein Ridge Estates 49 126 42N14 87w59 5:51:56
Munson 37 4 41N22 90w09 6:00:36
Munster 50 135 41N08 88w50 5:55:20
Murdock 21 65 39N49 88w05 5:52:20
Murphy Acres 99 114 41N33 88w07 5:52:28
Murphysboro 39 4 37N46 89w20 5:57:20
Murrayville 69 63 39N35 90w15 6:01:00
Mylith Park 49 6 42N21 88w14 5:52:56
Myrtle 71 4 42N11 89w24 5:57:36
Naausay 47 82 41N35 88w19 5:53:16
Nachusa 52 37 41N49 89w22 5:57:28
Nameoki 60 7 38N43 90w05 6:00:20
Naperville 22 12 41N46 88w09 5:52:36
Naplate 50 6 41N20 88w52 5:55:28
Naples 86 65 39N45 90w35 6:02:20
Nashua 71 28 41N58 89w19 5:57:16
Nashville 95 4 38N21 89w23 5:57:32
Nason 41 4 38N10 88w58 5:55:52
Natalie Estates 16 6 41N36 87w45 5:51:00
National Stock Yards 82 25 38N39 90w09 6:00:36
Natrona 63 29 40N18 89w36 5:58:24
Nauvoo 34 4 40N33 91w23 6:05:32
Navajo Hills 16 12 41N40 87w47 5:51:08
Naval Air Station 16 1 42N06 87w50 5:51:20
Neadmore 12 4 39N20 87w53 5:51:32
Nebo 75 4 39N27 90w47 6:03:08
Nebraska 53 55 40N53 88w52 5:55:28
Neelys 69 65 39N44 90w31 6:02:04
Nekoma 37 4 41N11 90w19 6:01:16
Nelson 52 86 41N47 89w34 5:58:16
Neoga 18 63 39N19 88w27 5:53:48
Neponset 6 63 41N17 89w48 5:59:12
Nettle Creek 32 55 41N25 88w32 5:54:08
Neunert 39 4 37N45 89w32 5:58:08
Nevada 53 127 41N04 88w32 5:54:08
Nevins 23 128 39N37 87w42 5:50:48
Newark 47 55 41N32 88w35 5:54:20
New Athens 82 35 38N19 89w53 5:59:32
New Baden 14 41 38N32 89w42 5:58:48
New Bedford 6 88 41N31 89w43 5:58:52
New Berlin 84 55 39N44 89w55 5:59:40
Newbern 42 4 38N56 90w21 6:01:24
New Blossom Hill 56 1 42N14 88w15 5:53:00
New Boston 66 4 41N10 91w00 6:04:00
Newburg 58 57 39N59 88w49 5:55:16
Newburg 75 4 39N37 90w44 6:02:56
New Burnside 44 4 37N35 88w46 5:55:04
New Camp 100 4 37N48 89w05 5:56:20
New Canton 75 4 39N38 91w06 6:04:24
Newcastle 83 4 37N37 88w42 5:54:48
New City 84 55 39N45 89w32 5:58:08
New Columbia 64 4 37N24 88w45 5:55:00
Newcomb 10 54 40N16 88w24 5:53:36
New Delhi 42 25 39N05 90w22 6:01:28
New Dennison 100 4 37N46 88w56 5:55:44
New Design 67 8 38N16 90w08 6:00:32
New Douglas 60 7 38N58 89w41 5:58:44
Newell 92 26 40N12 87w35 5:50:20
New Grand Chain 77 4 37N15 89w01 5:56:04
New Hanover 67 46 38N23 90w13 6:00:52
New Hartford 75 4 39N35 90w55 6:03:40
New Haven 30 4 37N55 88w08 5:52:32
New Hebron 17 4 39N00 87w44 5:50:56
New Holland 54 63 40N11 89w35 5:58:20
New La Grange 5 65 39N53 90w39 6:02:36
New Lebanon 19 29 42N05 88w28 5:53:52
New Lenox 99 1 41N31 87w58 5:51:52
New Liberty 76 4 37N08 88w38 5:54:32
Newman 21 55 39N48 87w59 5:51:56
Newmansville 9 29 40N00 90w01 6:00:04
New Memphis 14 55 38N29 89w41 5:58:44
New Milford 101 28 42N11 89w04 5:56:16
New Minden 95 4 38N26 89w22 5:57:28
New Palatine 79 63 38N05 89w51 5:59:24
New Philadelphia 55 63 40N30 90w23 6:01:32
Newport 49 17 42N28 87w56 5:51:44
Newport 60 25 38N41 90w07 6:00:28
New Salem 75 4 39N42 90w51 6:03:24
Newton 40 4 38N59 88w10 5:52:40
Newtown 53 55 41N04 88w45 5:55:00
Newtown 92 54 40N07 87w47 5:51:08
New Trier 16 1 42N05 87w45 5:51:00
New Virginia 100 4 37N49 88w56 5:55:44
New Windsor 66 4 41N12 90w27 6:01:48
Niantic 58 30 39N52 89w11 5:56:44
Nifa 45 103 41N50 88w19 5:53:16
Niles 16 2 42N02 87w48 5:51:12
Nilwood 59 53 39N24 89w46 5:59:04
Niota 34 4 40N37 91w15 6:05:00
Nippersink Terrace 49 6 42N26 88w14 5:52:56
Nixon 20 55 40N07 88w45 5:55:00
Nixon's Greenwood-Central 16 1 42N04 87w48 5:51:12
Noble 80 4 38N43 88w13 5:52:52
Nokomis 68 7 39N18 89w18 5:57:12
Nora 43 4 42N26 89w57 5:59:48
Nordic Park 22 17 41N58 88w01 5:52:04
Normal 57 104 40N31 88w59 5:55:56
Norman 32 4 41N18 88w31 5:54:04
Normandale 90 98 40N35 89w37 5:58:28
Normandy 6 29 41N34 89w39 5:58:36
Normandy Hill 16 2 42N07 87w49 5:51:16
Normandy Villa 16 1 41N31 87w38 5:50:32
Norpaul 16 1 41N56 87w53 5:51:32
Norridge 16 2 41N58 87w49 5:51:16
Norris 29 7 40N37 90w02 6:00:08
Norris City 97 4 37N59 88w20 5:53:20
North 16 1 42N03 87w42 5:50:48
North Alton 60 7 38N54 90w10 6:00:40
North Aurora 45 102 41N48 88w20 5:53:20
North Barrington 49 6 42N13 88w09 5:52:36
Northbelt Homesites 82 25 38N32 90w00 6:00:00
North Bluffs 86 65 39N46 90w31 6:02:04
Northbrook 16 1 42N08 87w50 5:51:20
Northbrook Knolls 16 2 42N07 87w49 5:51:16
Northbrook West 16 2 42N07 87w49 5:51:16
North Chicago 49 140 42N19 87w51 5:51:24
North City 28 4 38N00 89w04 5:56:16
North Dixon 52 25 41N50 89w30 5:58:00
North Dupo 82 46 38N33 90w12 6:00:48
Northeast 1 66 40N09 90w58 6:03:52
Northern 28 4 38N05 88w46 5:55:04
Northfield 16 1 42N06 87w46 5:51:04
Northfield Woods 16 6 42N05 87w53 5:51:32
North Fork 30 4 37N49 88w19 5:53:16
Northgate 16 27 41N58 88w06 5:52:24
North Glen Ellyn 22 2 41N53 88w04 5:52:16
North Hampton 72 51 40N55 89w30 5:58:00
North Harvey 16 2 41N36 87w40 5:50:40
North Henderson 66 4 41N07 90w29 6:01:56
North Hills 49 126 42N14 87w59 5:51:56
Northlake 16 2 41N54 87w54 5:51:36
North Libertyville Estates 49 42 42N16 87w56 5:51:44
North Litchfield 68 37 39N13 89w39 5:58:36
Northmore 60 7 38N57 90w11 6:00:44
Northmore Heights 25 4 39N07 88w33 5:54:12
North Mounds 77 4 37N07 89w12 5:56:48
North Muddy 40 4 39N01 88w19 5:53:16
North Okaw 15 65 39N36 88w24 5:53:36
North Ottawa 50 6 41N21 88w51 5:55:24
North Otter 59 4 39N29 89w53 5:59:32
North Palmyra 59 55 39N28 90w00 6:00:00
North Park 101 28 42N21 89w03 5:56:12
North Pekin 90 98 40N37 89w37 5:58:28
North Plato 45 29 42N05 88w28 5:53:52
North Riverside 16 1 41N51 87w49 5:51:16
North Shore 56 9 42N14 88w21 5:53:24
North Shoreland 100 4 37N46 88w56 5:55:44
North Town 16 1 42N00 87w42 5:50:48
North Utica 50 89 41N20 89w00 5:56:00
North Venice 60 25 38N41 90w10 6:00:40
Northville 50 7 41N35 88w39 5:54:36
North Winchester 86 63 39N39 90w29 6:01:56
Northwoods 19 110 42N06 88w42 5:54:48
North Woods 22 54 41N52 88w11 5:52:44
Northwoods Place 60 29 38N53 90w05 6:00:20
Norton 46 36 41N03 88w11 5:52:44
Nortonville 69 63 39N34 90w09 6:00:36
Norway 50 4 41N31 88w41 5:54:44
Norwood 66 4 41N04 90w33 6:02:12
Norwood 72 98 40N42 89w41 5:58:44
Norwood Park 16 1 41N59 87w50 5:51:20
Nottingham Park 16 1 41N47 87w46 5:51:04
Nottingham Woods 45 55 41N51 88w28 5:53:52
Novak Park 45 95 41N54 88w19 5:53:16
Nubbin Ridge 97 4 38N06 88w20 5:53:20
Nunda 56 6 42N17 88w15 5:53:00
Nutwood 42 55 39N06 90w30 6:02:00
Oak 76 4 37N35 88w26 5:53:44
Oak Brook 22 21 41N51 87w58 5:51:52
Oak Brook Shopping Center 22 2 41N48 87w56 5:51:44
Oakbrook Terrace 22 21 41N52 87w58 5:51:52
Oakdale 95 4 38N16 89w30 5:58:00
Oakdale Woods 22 17 41N57 87w58 5:51:52
Oakford 65 66 40N06 89w58 5:59:52
Oak Forest 16 1 41N37 87w44 5:50:56
Oakglen 16 19 41N34 87w34 5:50:16
Oak Grove 60 7 38N57 90w11 6:00:44
Oak Grove 81 4 41N25 90w34 6:02:16
Oak Hill 72 58 40N50 89w53 5:59:32
Oak Hills 82 7 38N38 89w59 5:59:56
Oak Hills Estates 4 28 42N16 89w00 5:56:00
Oakland 15 65 39N39 88w02 5:52:08
Oak Lawn 16 1 41N43 87w44 5:50:56
Oaklawn 92 54 40N17 87w41 5:50:44
Oakley 58 54 39N53 88w49 5:55:16
Oak Meadows 22 54 41N52 88w11 5:52:44
Oak Park 16 1 41N53 87w47 5:51:08
Oak Ridge 102 57 40N47 89w25 5:57:40
Oak Run 48 4 40N55 90w07 6:00:28
Oak Spring Woods 49 42 42N16 87w56 5:51:44
Oakton 16 1 42N01 87w54 5:51:36
Oakwood 22 19 41N47 87w59 5:51:56
Oakwood 72 98 40N41 89w37 5:58:28
Oakwood 92 56 40N08 87w50 5:51:20
Oakwood Heights 60 29 38N53 90w04 6:00:16
Oakwood Hills 56 1 42N14 88w15 5:53:00
Oakwood Knolls 49 6 42N28 88w07 5:52:28
Oakwood Shores 56 15 42N23 88w26 5:53:44
Oautoga Bluff 60 7 38N57 90w11 6:00:44
Obed 87 63 39N31 89w03 5:56:12
Oblong 17 4 39N00 87w55 5:51:40
Oconee 87 63 39N17 89w07 5:56:28
Ocoya 53 127 40N53 88w38 5:54:32
Odell 53 127 41N00 88w31 5:54:04
Odgen 93 4 38N25 87w46 5:51:04
Odin 61 4 38N34 89w04 5:56:16
O'Fallon 82 25 38N36 89w58 5:59:52
Ogden 10 54 40N09 87w58 5:51:52
Ogden Park 16 1 41N47 87w40 5:50:40
Oglesby 50 117 41N18 89w03 5:56:12
O'Hare Airport 16 1 41N59 87w52 5:51:28
Ohio 6 55 41N34 89w28 5:57:52
Ohio Grove 66 4 41N07 90w43 6:02:52
Ohlman 68 7 39N21 89w13 5:56:52
Oil Center 61 4 38N31 89w08 5:56:32
Oilfield 12 4 39N18 87w59 5:51:56
Okaw 87 7 39N29 88w45 5:55:00
Okawville 95 4 38N26 89w33 5:58:12
Old Camp 100 4 37N48 89w05 5:56:20
Old Du Quoin 73 4 38N01 89w14 5:56:56
Oldenburg 60 29 38N53 90w05 6:00:20
Olde Salem 16 27 41N58 88w06 5:52:24
Old Farm 22 12 41N47 88w09 5:52:36
Old Gilchrist 66 4 41N12 90w45 6:03:00
Old Kane 31 55 39N11 90w21 6:01:24
Old Marissa 82 55 38N15 89w45 5:59:00
Old Mill Creek 49 6 42N26 87w59 5:51:56
Old Mill Grove 49 6 42N12 88w03 5:52:12
Old Niota 34 4 40N37 91w15 6:05:00
Old Pearl 75 63 39N28 90w37 6:02:28
Old Ripley 3 63 38N53 89w33 5:58:12
Old Shawneetown 30 4 37N42 88w08 5:52:32
Old Stonington 11 4 39N38 89w11 5:56:44
Oldtown 57 79 40N26 88w52 5:55:28
Oldtown 83 4 37N37 88w42 5:54:48
Olena 36 4 40N45 90w54 6:03:36
Olio 102 71 40N43 89w14 5:56:56
Olive 60 26 38N58 89w45 5:59:00
Olive Branch 2 4 37N10 89w21 5:57:24
Oliver 23 56 39N29 87w41 5:50:44
Olivet 92 54 39N57 87w39 5:50:36
Olmstead 77 4 37N11 89w05 5:56:20
Olney 80 63 38N44 88w05 5:52:20
Olympia Fields 16 1 41N31 87w42 5:50:48
Olympia Gardens 16 1 41N31 87w38 5:50:32
Olympic Terrace 22 12 41N47 88w09 5:52:36
Olympic Village 16 1 41N31 87w38 5:50:32
Omaha 30 4 37N54 88w19 5:53:16
Omega 61 4 38N39 88w45 5:55:00
Omphghent 60 55 38N58 89w52 5:59:28
Onarga 38 29 40N43 88w01 5:52:04
Oneco 89 4 42N29 89w39 5:58:36
Oneida 48 4 41N04 90w13 6:00:52
Ontario 48 4 41N07 90w16 6:01:04
Ontarioville 22 27 41N58 88w06 5:52:24
Opdyke 41 4 38N16 88w47 5:55:08
Opheim 37 4 41N15 90w23 6:01:32
Ophir 50 56 41N30 88w59 5:55:56
Oquawka 36 4 40N56 90w57 6:03:48
Ora 39 4 37N55 89w26 5:57:44
Oran 54 55 40N11 89w12 5:56:48
Orange Prairie 72 98 40N45 89w37 5:58:28
Orangeville 89 65 42N28 89w39 5:58:36
Oraville 39 4 37N52 89w23 5:57:32
Orchard 96 4 38N35 88w38 5:54:32
Orchard Acres 56 9 42N14 88w21 5:53:24
Orchard Heights 80 4 38N44 88w05 5:52:20
Orchard Mines 72 98 40N40 89w40 5:58:40
Orchard Valley 49 140 42N22 87w53 5:51:32
Orchardville 96 4 38N38 88w38 5:54:32
Oreana 58 57 39N56 88w52 5:55:28
Oregon 71 28 42N01 89w20 5:57:20
Orel 96 4 38N18 88w34 5:54:16
Orient 28 4 37N55 88w59 5:55:56
Orion 37 4 41N21 90w23 6:01:32
Orland 16 1 41N36 87w52 5:51:28
Orland Hills 16 12 41N38 87w51 5:51:24
Orland Park 16 12 41N38 87w52 5:51:28
Orleans 69 4 39N43 90w02 6:00:08
Orleans Terrace 22 17 41N56 88w00 5:52:00
Orvil 54 29 40N16 89w26 5:57:44
Osage 28 4 37N53 89w07 5:56:28

Osage 50 4 41N04 88W59 5:55:56
Osbernville 11 55 39N42 89W07 5:56:28
Osborn 81 4 41N37 90W11 6:00:44
Osceola 88 4 41N11 89W42 5:58:48
Osco 37 4 41N22 90W16 6:01:04
Oskaloosa 13 4 38N47 88W38 5:54:32
Osman 57 55 40N18 88W28 5:53:52
Ospur 20 8 40N09 88W57 5:55:48
Ossami Lake 90 98 40N37 89W29 5:57:56
Oswego 47 43 41N41 88W21 5:53:24
Otego 26 4 38N58 88W58 5:55:52
Ottawa 50 6 41N21 88W51 5:55:24
Otterville 42 37 39N03 90W24 6:01:36
Otto 46 26 41N02 87W54 5:51:36
Ottoville 6 134 41N20 89W12 5:56:48
Owaneco 11 63 39N29 89W12 5:56:48
Owego 53 127 40N53 88W32 5:54:08
Owen 101 28 42N22 89W06 5:56:24
Oxford 37 4 41N12 90W23 6:01:32
Oxville 86 65 39N42 90W34 6:02:16
Ozark 44 4 37N33 88W46 5:55:04
Pacesetter Park 16
1 41N36 87W38 5:50:32
Paderborn 82 8 38N20 90W09 6:00:36
Padua 57 29 40N27 88W43 5:54:52
Paineville 100 4 37N48 89W02 5:56:08
Palatine 16 1 42N07 88W03 5:52:12
Palermo 23 96 39N55 87W50 5:51:20
Palestine 17 4 39N00 87W37 5:50:28
Palmer 11 63 39N27 89W24 5:57:36
Palmyra 59 55 39N26 90W00 6:00:00
Paloma 1 63 40N01 91W12 6:04:48
Palos Gardens 16 12 41N40 87W47 5:51:08
Palos Heights 16 12 41N40 87W48 5:51:12
Palos Hills 16 12 41N41 87W49 5:51:16
Palos Park 16 12 41N40 87W50 5:51:20
Palos Westgate 16
12 41N40 87W47 5:51:08
Palsgrove 8 4 42N06 89W58 5:59:52
Pam Anne Estates 16
1 42N04 87W48 5:51:12
Pana 11 63 39N23 89W05 5:56:20
Panama 68 63 39N01 89W32 5:58:08
Pankeyville 83 4 37N44 88W33 5:54:12
Panola 102 55 40N48 89W00 5:56:00
Panther Creek 9 29 40N00 90W07 6:00:28
Papineau 38 26 40N58 87W43 5:50:52
Paradise 15 63 39N24 88W19 5:53:16
Paris 23 128 39N36 87W42 5:50:48
Park City 49 140 42N21 87W53 5:51:32
Parker 12 4 39N24 87W57 5:51:48
Parker 44 4 37N37 88W50 5:55:20
Parkersburg 80 4 38N36 88W03 5:52:12
Parkfield Terrace 82
25 38N34 90W08 6:00:32
Park Forest 16 1 41N29 87W40 5:50:40
Park Forest South 16
1 41N30 87W41 5:50:44
Park Hills 25 4 39N07 88W33 5:54:12
Parkhome 16 1 41N51 87W46 5:51:04
Park Lane 46 26 41N01 87W43 5:50:52
Park Meadows 16 6 42N04 88W00 5:52:00
Park Ridge 16 1 42N02 87W51 5:51:24
Park Ridge Manor 16
1 42N02 87W51 5:51:24
Parkville 10 36 39N58 88W21 5:53:24
Parkwood 45 107 42N02 88W17 5:53:08
Parkwood Village 16
107 42N02 88W17 5:53:08
Parnell 20 63 40N14 88W43 5:54:52
Parrish 28 4 37N55 88W46 5:55:04
Parrish Addition 83
4 37N49 88W27 5:53:48
Partridge 102 51 40N52 89W26 5:57:44
Passport 80 4 38N42 88W13 5:52:52
Patoka 61 4 38N45 89W06 5:56:24
Patterson 31 63 39N29 90W31 6:02:04
Patterson Heights 60
7 38N57 90W11 6:00:44
Patton 93 4 38N29 87W45 5:51:00
Pattonsburg 62 54 41N03 89W08 5:56:32
Paulton 100 4 37N46 88W56 5:55:44
Pawnee 84 55 39N36 89W35 5:58:20
Pawpaw 52 56 41N41 88W59 5:55:56
Paxton 27 129 40N27 88W06 5:52:24
Paynes Point 71 4 41N59 89W13 5:56:52
Payson 1 85 39N49 91W15 6:05:00
Peach Orchard 27 30 40N34 88W16 5:53:04
Pea Ridge 5 66 40N04 90W51 6:03:24
Pearl 75 4 39N28 90W38 6:02:32
Pearl City 89 66 42N16 89W50 5:59:20
Pebble Beach 32 125 41N22 88W25 5:53:40
Pecatonica 101 30 42N19 89W22 5:57:28
Peerless 99 82 41N35 88W11 5:52:44
Pekin 90 98 40N35 89W40 5:58:40
Pekin Heights 90 98 40N35 89W37 5:58:28
Pella 27 57 40N48 88W11 5:52:44
Pembroke 46 82 41N04 87W35 5:50:20
Pendleton 41 4 38N15 88W46 5:55:04
Penfield 10 54 40N18 87W57 5:51:48
Pennsylvania 63 7 40N16 89W46 5:59:04
Penny Oaks 55 4 40N28 90W41 6:02:44
Penrose 98 26 41N48 89W43 5:58:52
Peoria 72 98 40N42 89W36 5:58:24
Peoria Heights 72
98 40N45 89W35 5:58:20
Peotone 99 30 41N20 87W48 5:51:12
Pepper Tree 16 6 42N06 88W02 5:52:08
Pequot 32 30 41N17 88W17 5:53:08
Percy 79 63 38N00 89W37 5:58:28
Perdueville 27 129 40N28 88W06 5:52:24
Perks 77 4 37N18 89W05 5:56:20
Perry 75 4 39N47 90W45 6:03:00
Perryton 66 4 41N17 90W44 6:02:56
Persifer 48 4 40N56 90W10 6:00:40
Peru 50 130 41N20 89W08 5:56:32
Pesotum 10 36 39N55 88W16 5:53:04
Peters 60 7 38N45 89W59 5:59:56
Petersburg 65 29 40N01 89W51 5:59:24
Peters Creek 35 4 37N29 88W14 5:52:56
Petite Lake 49 6 42N26 88W08 5:52:32
Petrolia 51 4 38N42 87W46 5:51:04
Petty 51 4 38N48 87W50 5:51:20
Pharoah's Gardens 100
4 37N55 89W15 5:57:00
Pheasant Creek 16 2 42N07 87W49 5:51:16
Pheasant Meadows 99
22 41N21 87W37 5:50:28
Pheasant Ridge 99 3 41N32 87W52 5:51:28
Phelps 82 46 38N32 90W14 6:00:56
Phenix 37 4 41N32 90W09 6:00:36
Philadelphia 9 63 39N55 90W07 6:00:28
Phillippe 16 6 42N04 88W00 5:52:00
Phillipstown 97 4 38N09 88W01 5:52:04
Philo 10 57 40N01 88W09 5:52:36
Phinney 10 138 40N06 88W12 5:52:48
Phoenix 16 26 41N37 87W38 5:50:32
Piasa 59 37 39N02 90W12 6:00:48
Piasa Hills 60 7 38N57 90W11 6:00:44
Picadilly Terrace 22
2 41N47 87W57 5:51:48
Pickaway 87 63 39N34 88W52 5:55:28
Pierce 19 43 41N51 88W39 5:54:36
Pierceburg 17 4 39N00 87W54 5:51:36
Pierron 3 90 38N47 89W36 5:58:24
Pierson 74 55 39N48 88W35 5:54:20
Piety Hill 50 117 41N18 89W03 5:56:12
Pigeon Grove 38 132 40N32 87W56 5:51:44
Pike 53 35 40N48 88W45 5:55:00
Pike 75 4 39N32 91W00 6:04:00
Pilot Knob 95 4 38N16 89W25 5:57:40
Pilsen 16 1 41N51 87W40 5:50:40
Pinckneyville 73 4 38N05 89W23 5:57:32
Pine Creek 71 4 41N59 89W27 5:57:48
Pinecrest 99 114 41N33 88W07 5:52:28
Pine Grove 32 125 41N22 88W25 5:53:40
Pinelands 22 95 41N54 88W19 5:53:16
Pine Meadow 99 1 41N40 88W00 5:52:00
Pine Rock 71 4 41N59 89W13 5:56:52
Pingree Grove 45 29 42N04 88W25 5:53:40
Pinkstaff 51 4 38N48 87W40 5:50:40
Pin Oak 60 25 38N47 89W53 5:59:32
Piopolis 33 4 38N06 88W32 5:54:08
Piper City 27 57 40N45 88W11 5:52:44
Pisgah 69 63 39N40 90W06 6:00:24
Pistakee 49 6 42N25 88W12 5:52:48
Pistakee Heights 49
6 42N21 88W14 5:52:56
Pistakee Highlands 56
27 42N21 88W14 5:52:56
Pistakee Hills 56
27 42N21 88W14 5:52:56
Pistaqua Heights 49
6 42N21 88W14 5:52:56
Pitman 68 63 39N24 89W39 5:58:36
Pittsburg 26 139 38N58 89W06 5:56:24
Pittsburg 100 4 37N47 88W51 5:55:24
Pittsfield 75 65 39N36 90W49 6:03:16
Pittwood 38 30 40N52 87W44 5:50:56
Pixley 13 4 38N48 88W18 5:53:12
Plainfield 99 82 41N37 88W12 5:52:48
Plainfield Acres 99
82 41N35 88W11 5:52:44
Plainview 59 53 39N10 89W59 5:59:56
Plainville 1 66 39N47 91W11 6:04:44
Plano 47 25 41N40 88W32 5:54:08
Plato 45 29 42N01 88W26 5:53:44
Plattville 47 25 41N39 88W27 5:53:48
Pleasant 29 66 40N19 90W17 6:01:08
Pleasant Dale 16 1 41N48 87W52 5:51:28
Pleasantdale Estates 22
1 41N40 88W00 5:52:00
Pleasant Grove 15
63 39N24 88W16 5:53:04
Pleasant Grove 44 4 37N28 88W58 5:55:52
Pleasant Hill 22 2 41N53 88W05 5:52:20
Pleasant Hill 57 7 40N39 88W47 5:55:08
Pleasant Hill 75 4 39N27 90W52 6:03:28
Pleasant Hills 16
27 41N58 88W04 5:52:16
Pleasant Mound 3 4 38N52 89W16 5:57:04
Pleasant Plains 84
29 39N52 89W55 5:59:40
Pleasant Ridge 53
72 40N48 88W24 5:53:36
Pleasant Ridge 60
63 38N02 89W34 5:58:16
Pleasant Run 16 6 42N09 87W57 5:51:48
Pleasant Vale 75 4 39N37 91W05 6:04:20
Pleasant Valley 43
4 42N15 90W02 6:00:08
Pleasant View 58 57 39N41 89W05 5:56:20
Pleasant View 85 65 40N07 90W34 6:02:16
Plumfield 28 4 37N54 88W55 5:55:40
Plum Grove Countryside 16
6 42N04 88W00 5:52:00
Plum Grove Estates 16
6 42N06 88W02 5:52:08
Plum Grove Hills 16
6 42N04 88W00 5:52:00
Plum Grove Village 16
6 42N04 88W00 5:52:00
Plum Grove Woods 16
6 42N06 88W02 5:52:08
Plum Hill 95 4 38N21 89W32 5:58:08
Plymouth 34 52 40N18 90W58 6:03:52
Poag 60 25 38N48 90W02 6:00:08
Pocahontas 3 55 38N50 89W33 5:58:12
Poe 67 93 38N10 90W00 6:00:00
Point Prec 7 65 38N55 90W35 6:02:20
Point West 22 83 41N53 88W01 5:52:04
Polo 71 7 41N59 89W35 5:58:20
Pomona 39 4 37N38 89W20 5:57:20
Pond 44 4 37N25 88W54 5:55:36
Pontiac 53 127 40N53 88W38 5:54:32
Pontiac 82 25 38N37 90W01 6:00:04
Pontoon Beach 60 7 38N44 90W04 6:00:16
Pontoosuc 34 4 40N35 91W13 6:04:52
Pope 26 4 38N47 89W11 5:56:44
Poplar City 63 63 40N14 89W51 5:59:24
Poplar Grove 4 91 42N22 88W49 5:55:16
Poplar Grove 81 87 41N30 90W26 6:01:44
Port Byron 81 4 41N38 90W20 6:01:20
Port Jackson 17 4 38N54 87W40 5:50:40
Portland 98 4 41N37 90W02 6:00:08
Portland Corners 98
4 41N40 89W56 5:59:44
Port Ridge 99 114 41N35 88W03 5:52:12
Posen 16 1 41N38 87W41 5:50:44
Posen 95 4 38N21 89W23 5:57:32
Posen Junction 16 1 41N39 87W42 5:50:48
Posey 14 55 38N37 89W22 5:57:28
Potomac 92 38 40N18 87W48 5:51:12
Pottawattamie Hills 16
2 41N35 87W40 5:50:40
Pottstown 72 98 40N45 89W37 5:58:28
Powder Creek 82 25 38N31 89W59 5:59:56
Powder Mill Woods 82
25 38N31 89W59 5:59:56
Powellton 34 4 40N37 91W15 6:05:00
Prairie 79 93 38N10 90W00 6:00:00
Prairie 87 63 39N17 88W38 5:54:32
Prairie Center 50 6 41N21 88W51 5:55:24
Prairie City 55 4 40N36 90W30 6:02:00
Prairie Creek 54 29 40N16 89W33 5:58:12
Prairie du Pont 82
46 38N32 90W14 6:00:56
Prairie Du Rocher 79
55 38N05 90W06 6:00:24
Prairie Green 22 2 41N53 88W05 5:52:20
Prairie Green 38 80 40N32 87W36 5:50:24
Prairie Grove 56 27 42N21 88W14 5:52:56
Prairie Home 87 55 39N39 88W44 5:54:56
Prairieton 11 57 39N37 89W04 5:56:16
Prairietown 60 8 38N56 89W50 5:59:20
Prairie View 49 26 42N12 87W57 5:51:48
Prairieville 52 25 41N50 89W30 5:58:00
Preemption 66 4 41N18 90W36 6:02:24
Prentice 69 4 39N50 90W02 6:00:08
Prestbury 45 102 41N46 88W20 5:53:20
Preston 79 63 38N05 89W56 5:59:44
Preston Heights 99
114 41N30 88W05 5:52:20
Prestwick 99 4 41N30 87W51 5:51:24
Prickett 60 25 38N48 89W57 5:59:48
Princeton 6 131 41N23 89W28 5:57:52
Princeville 72 55 40N56 89W46 5:59:04
Prophetstown 98 23 41N40 89W56 5:59:44
Prospect 10 29 40N19 88W08 5:52:32
Prospect Heights 16
6 42N06 87W56 5:51:44
Prospect Meadows 16
6 42N04 87W57 5:51:48
Prospect Park 82 25 38N38 90W04 6:00:16
Providence 6 55 41N18 89W30 5:58:00
Provincetown 16 6 41N35 87W46 5:51:04
Proving Ground 8 4 42N05 90W09 6:00:36
Prudential Plaza 16
1 41N53 87W37 5:50:28
Pruett 26 4 39N02 88W51 5:55:24
Pujol 79 63 37N54 89W56 5:59:44
Pulaski 77 4 37N13 89W12 5:56:48
Pulleys Mill 100 4 37N33 88W58 5:55:52
Putman 29 4 40N30 90W10 6:00:40
Putnam 78 8 41N11 89W24 5:57:36
Quarry 42 77 38N59 90W27 6:01:48
Quincy 1 92 39N56 91W23 6:05:32
Quiver 63 137 40N23 89W56 5:59:44
Quiver Beach 63 55 40N18 90W04 6:00:16
Raccoon 61 4 38N30 88W58 5:55:52
Raddle 39 4 37N45 89W32 5:58:08
Radford 11 57 39N38 89W01 5:56:04
Radnor 72 57 40N50 89W42 5:58:48
Radom 95 4 38N17 89W12 5:56:48
Rainbow Hill 45 95 41N54 88W19 5:53:16
Raleigh 83 4 37N49 88W32 5:54:08
Ramona Place 60 7 38N57 90W11 6:00:44
Ramsey 26 4 39N08 89W07 5:56:28
Randall Park 49 140 42N23 87W52 5:51:28
Randolph 57 35 40N20 88W58 5:55:52
Rankin 92 132 40N28 87W54 5:51:36
Ransom 50 56 41N09 88W39 5:54:36
Ransom Ridge Estates 16
1 42N02 87W51 5:51:24
Rantoul 10 29 40N19 88W09 5:52:36
Rapatee 48 4 40N43 90W16 6:01:04
Rapids City 81 4 41N35 90W22 6:01:28
Rardin 15 65 39N36 88W06 5:52:24
Raritan 36 4 40N41 90W51 6:03:24
Ravenswood 16 2 41N58 87W42 5:50:48
Ravinia 49 1 42N11 87W49 5:51:16
Rawalts 29 4 40N32 89W58 5:59:52
Rawlins 43 4 42N27 90W27 6:01:48
Ray 85 65 40N07 90W34 6:02:16
Raymond 68 62 39N19 89W34 5:58:16
Reading 53 55 41N04 88W52 5:55:28
Rector 83 4 37N53 88W26 5:53:44
Red Bud 79 93 38N13 90W00 6:00:00
Reddick 46 36 41N06 88W15 5:53:00
Redmon 23 67 39N39 87W52 5:51:28
Red Oak 89 4 42N18 89W38 5:58:32
Red Oak Terrace 49
1 42N11 87W49 5:51:16
Reed 99 37 41N15 88W13 5:52:52
Reeds Station 39 4 37N50 89W11 5:56:44
Rees 69 63 39N37 90W03 6:00:12
Reevesville 44 4 37N21 88W43 5:54:52
Regency Grove 22 12 41N48 88W01 5:52:04

ILLINOIS

Regency Terrace 22 27 41N58 88w05 5:52:20
Reilly 92 132 40N28 87w54 5:51:36
Reily Lake 79 63 38N01 89w54 5:59:36
Renault 67 55 38N09 90w08 6:00:32
Renchville 72 51 40N55 89w30 5:58:00
Rend City 28 4 38N00 88w56 5:55:44
Reno 3 63 38N59 89w31 5:58:04
Rentchler 82 25 38N32 90w00 6:00:00
Reseda 16 6 42N06 88w02 5:52:08
Resthaven 99 7 41N19 88w06 5:52:24
Reynolds 81 4 41N20 90w40 6:02:40
Reynoldsburg 44 4 37N32 88w50 5:55:20
Reynoldsville 91 4 37N27 89w16 5:57:04
Rice 43 4 42N20 90w23 6:01:32
Rice 73 4 38N21 89w23 5:57:32
Rich 16 6 41N31 87w45 5:51:00
Richardson 45 84 41N52 88w35 5:54:20
Richfield 1 66 39N48 91w05 6:04:20
Richland 87 63 39N23 88w38 5:54:32
Richland Grove 66 4 41N18 90w30 6:02:00
Richmond 56 48 42N29 88w18 5:53:12
Richton Hills 16 22 41N29 87w43 5:50:52
Richton Park 16 22 41N29 87w43 5:50:52
Richview 95 4 38N22 89w12 5:56:48
Richwood 42 55 39N08 90w33 6:02:12
Richwoods 72 98 40N47 89w37 5:58:28
Ricks 11 63 39N24 89w25 5:57:40
Ridge 87 63 39N29 88w52 5:55:28
Ridgecrest 32 125 41N22 88w25 5:53:40
Ridge Farm 92 54 39N54 87w39 5:50:36
Ridgefield 56 9 42N16 88w22 5:53:28
Ridgeland 38 29 40N43 88w05 5:52:20
Ridgemoor 22 2 41N48 87w56 5:51:44
Ridge Prairie Heights 82 25 38N36 89w58 5:59:52
Ridgeville 38 29 40N43 88w01 5:52:04
Ridgewood 16 114 41N32 88w03 5:52:12
Ridgway 30 4 37N48 88w16 5:53:04
Ridott 89 46 42N16 89w27 5:57:48
Riffel 13 4 38N46 88w30 5:54:00
Riggston 86 63 39N42 90w25 6:01:40
Riley 56 29 42N12 88w38 5:54:32
Riley Center 56 29 42N15 88w36 5:54:24
Rinard 96 4 38N34 88w28 5:53:52
Ringwood 56 45 42N24 88w18 5:53:12
Rio 48 4 41N07 90w24 6:01:36
Ripley 5 67 40N01 90w38 6:02:32
Rising Sun 97 4 38N06 88w09 5:52:36
Ritchie 99 7 41N19 88w06 5:52:24
Riverair 60 7 38N57 90w11 6:00:44
Riverdale 16 1 41N39 87w37 5:50:28
Riverdale 101 4 42N25 89w01 5:56:04
River Forest 16 1 41N54 87w49 5:51:16
River Glen 49 6 42N09 88w06 5:52:24
River Grove 16 1 41N56 87w50 5:51:20
River Heights 83 54 40N17 87w41 5:50:44
River Ridge 47 25 41N39 88w27 5:53:48
Riverside 16 1 41N50 87w49 5:51:16
Riverside Island 49 6 42N24 88w11 5:52:44
Riverside Lawns 16 1 41N51 87w50 5:51:20
Riverside Park 56 27 42N21 88w14 5:52:56
Riverton 84 29 39N51 89w33 5:58:12
Riverview 8 4 41N58 90w06 6:00:24
Riverview 98 26 41N46 89w41 5:58:44
Riverview Heights 47 4 41N41 88w21 5:53:24
Riverwoods 49 6 42N10 87w55 5:51:40
Rivoli 66 4 41N12 90w30 6:02:00
Roaches 41 4 38N20 89w02 5:56:08
Roachtown 82 55 38N28 90w06 6:00:24
Roanoke 102 21 40N48 89w12 5:56:48
Robbins 16 22 41N39 87w42 5:50:48
Robbs 76 4 37N28 88w42 5:54:48
Robein 90 98 40N39 89w34 5:58:16
Roberts 27 30 40N37 88w11 5:52:44
Roberts Park 16 1 41N43 87w45 5:51:00
Robin Hill 99 114 41N33 88w07 5:52:28
Robinson 17 32 39N00 87w44 5:50:56
Roby 11 8 39N48 89w24 5:57:36
Rochelle 71 6 41N56 89w04 5:56:16
Rochester 84 55 39N45 89w32 5:58:08
Rock 76 4 37N22 88w29 5:53:56
Rockbridge 31 55 39N16 90w12 6:00:48
Rock City 89 65 42N25 89w28 5:57:52
Rock Creek 35 4 37N28 88w10 5:52:40
Rockdale 99 114 41N31 88w07 5:52:28
Rock Falls 98 60 41N47 89w41 5:58:44
Rockford 101 28 42N16 89w06 5:56:24
Rockgate Estates 60 7 38N57 90w11 6:00:44
Rock Grove 89 4 42N28 89w29 5:57:56
Rock Island 81 87 41N30 90w34 6:02:16
Rockport 75 4 39N32 91w01 6:04:04
Rock Run 89 4 42N23 89w27 5:57:48
Rockton 101 65 42N27 89w04 5:56:16
Rockvale 71 28 42N04 89w19 5:57:16
Rockville 46 4 41N15 87w58 5:51:52
Rockwell 50 117 41N20 89w06 5:56:24
Rockwood 79 50 37N52 89w42 5:58:48
Rocky Run 34 63 40N15 91w24 6:05:36
Rodden 43 4 42N15 90w17 6:01:08
Rogers 27 38 40N58 88w11 5:52:44
Rogers Park 16 2 42N00 87w40 5:50:40
Rolling Acres 10 29 40N19 88w08 5:52:32
Rolling Acres 72 98 40N45 89w37 5:58:28
Rolling Meadows 16 6 42N05 88w01 5:52:04
Rolling Meadows 55 4 40N28 90w41 6:02:44
Rollo 19 28 41N35 88w56 5:55:44
Rome 72 51 40N53 89w30 5:58:00
Rome Heights 72 51 40N55 89w30 5:58:00
Romeoville 99 78 41N39 88w04 5:52:16
Romine 61 4 38N31 88w45 5:55:00
Rondout 49 27 42N17 87w54 5:51:36
Roodhouse 31 63 39N29 90w24 6:01:36
Rooks Creek 53 4 40N53 88w45 5:55:00
Rooney Heights 99 114 41N33 88w07 5:52:28
Roots 79 55 38N05 90w06 6:00:24
Root Spring 56 1 42N14 88w15 5:53:00
Ropers Landing 76 4 37N22 88w29 5:53:56
Rosamond 11 63 39N23 89w11 5:56:44
Roscoe 101 4 42N25 89w01 5:56:04
Rose 87 7 39N23 88w52 5:55:28
Rosebud 76 4 37N22 88w29 5:53:56
Rosecrans 49 17 42N26 87w57 5:51:48
Rosedale 42 65 39N03 90w32 6:02:08
Rosefield 72 58 40N46 89w49 5:59:16
Rose Hill 22 12 41N48 88w01 5:52:04
Rose Hill 40 59 39N06 88w09 5:52:36
Rose Lake 82 25 38N30 90w08 6:00:32
Roseland 16 1 41N42 87w37 5:50:28
Roselle 16 17 41N59 88w05 5:52:20
Rosemont 82 25 38N37 90w06 6:00:24
Roseville 94 4 40N44 90w40 6:02:40
Rosewood 60 29 38N53 90w05 6:00:20
Rosewood Heights 60 29 38N53 90w05 6:00:20
Rosiclare 35 4 37N26 88w20 5:53:20
Roslyn 18 4 39N13 88w30 5:54:00
Rossville 92 80 40N23 87w40 5:50:40
Round Grove 53 36 41N04 88w18 5:53:12
Round Grove 98 75 41N49 89w58 5:59:52
Round Knob 64 4 37N09 88w44 5:54:56
Round Lake 49 27 42N21 88w06 5:52:24
Round Lake Beach 49 27 42N22 88w05 5:52:20
Round Lake Heights 49 27 42N23 88w06 5:52:24
Round Lake Park 49 27 42N21 88w05 5:52:20
Round Prairie 96 4 38N31 88w26 5:53:44
Rountree 68 4 39N18 89w25 5:57:40
Rowe 53 127 40N53 88w38 5:54:32
Roxana 60 29 38N51 90w05 6:00:20
Royal 10 57 40N11 87w58 5:51:52
Royal Lake Resort 3 4 38N56 89w16 5:57:04
Royal Lake Resort 14 55 38N37 89w22 5:57:28
Royal Lakes Village 59 4 39N07 90w03 6:00:12
Royalton 28 94 37N53 89w07 5:56:28
Rozetta 36 4 40N56 90w51 6:03:24
Rubicon 31 55 39N23 90w12 6:00:48
Rudement 83 4 37N44 88w33 5:54:12
Ruma 79 55 38N07 90w00 6:00:00
Rush 43 4 42N25 90w02 6:00:08
Rushville 85 65 40N07 90w34 6:02:16
Russell 49 17 42N29 87w55 5:51:40
Russellville 51 4 38N49 87w32 5:50:08
Rutland 50 39 40N59 89w03 5:56:12
Rutledge 20 63 40N15 88w45 5:55:00
Ruyle 42 55 39N12 90w11 6:00:44
Sabina 57 30 40N27 88w38 5:54:32
Sacramento 97 4 38N06 88w20 5:53:20
Sadorus 10 36 39N58 88w21 5:53:24
Sag Bridge 16 1 41N40 88w00 5:52:00
Sailor Springs 13 4 38N46 88w22 5:53:28
Saint Albans 34 53 40N14 91w12 6:04:48
Saint Anne 46 26 41N01 87w43 5:50:52
Saint Anne Woods 46 26 41N01 87w43 5:50:52
Saint Augustine 48 4 40N43 90w25 6:01:40
Saint Charles 45 95 41N54 88w19 5:53:16
Saint Clair 82 25 38N32 89w59 5:59:56
Saint Clair Square 82 25 38N38 90w04 6:00:16
Saint David 29 7 40N30 90w03 6:00:12
Saint Elmo 26 56 39N02 88w51 5:55:24
Sainte Marie 40 4 38N56 88w01 5:52:04
Saint Francis 25 4 39N08 88w25 5:53:40
Saint Francisville 51 4 38N36 87w39 5:50:36
Saint George 46 115 41N10 87w53 5:51:32
Saint Jacob 60 7 38N42 89w46 5:59:04
Saint James 26 4 38N57 88w51 5:55:24
Saint James Estates 16 1 41N31 87w38 5:50:32
Saint Joe 67 8 38N20 90w09 6:00:36
Saint Johns 73 4 38N02 89w14 5:56:56
Saint Joseph 10 8 40N07 88w02 5:52:08
Saint Libory 82 55 38N22 89w43 5:58:52
Saint Mary 34 52 40N19 90w59 6:03:56
Saint Marys 25 4 39N07 88w33 5:54:12
Saint Paul 26 4 38N52 89w05 5:56:20
Saint Paul Junction 16 1 41N39 87w42 5:50:48
Saint Peter 26 4 38N52 88w51 5:55:24
Saint Regis 22 83 41N53 88w01 5:52:04
Saint Rose 14 55 38N41 89w33 5:58:12
Salem 61 4 38N38 88w57 5:55:48
Salina 46 39 41N10 88w04 5:52:16
Saline 60 63 38N47 89w39 5:58:36
Saline Mines 30 4 37N42 88w09 5:52:36
Salisbury 84 55 39N53 89w46 5:59:04
Salt Creek 63 63 40N10 89w46 5:59:04
Samoth 64 4 37N24 88w45 5:55:00
Samsville 24 4 38N31 88w00 5:52:00
Sand Barrens 51 4 38N35 87w39 5:50:36
Sandoval 61 4 38N37 89w07 5:56:28
Sandpebble Walk 16 6 42N09 87w57 5:51:48
Sand Prairie 90 21 40N26 89w40 5:58:40
Sandra Heights 16 1 41N31 87w38 5:50:32
Sand Ridge 39 4 37N43 89w29 5:57:56
Sandusky 2 4 37N14 89w16 5:57:04
Sandwich 19 25 41N39 88w37 5:54:28
Sandy 86 4 39N37 90w21 6:01:24
Sangamon 58 26 39N50 88w56 5:55:44
Sangamon 74 55 40N07 88w31 5:54:04
Sangamon Valley 9 63 40N01 90w13 6:00:52
San Jose 63 29 40N18 89w36 5:58:24
Santa Anna 20 57 40N15 88w39 5:54:36
Santa Fe 14 4 38N32 89w26 5:57:44
Santa Fe Park 16 2 41N48 87w56 5:51:44
Saratoga 91 4 37N28 89w15 5:57:00
Saratoga Center 62 30 41N06 89w22 5:57:28
Sargent 21 65 39N43 88w03 5:52:12
Sauget 82 25 38N36 90w10 6:00:40
Sauk 16 1 41N32 87w37 5:50:28
Sauk Village 16 6 41N29 87w34 5:50:16
Saunemin 53 36 40N54 88w24 5:53:36
Savanna 8 23 42N05 90w08 6:00:32
Savoy 10 25 40N03 88w15 5:53:00
Sawyerville 59 55 39N05 89w49 5:59:16
Say Brook 22 12 41N47 88w09 5:52:36
Saybrook 57 36 40N26 88w32 5:54:08
Scales Mound 43 4 42N29 90w15 6:01:00
Scarboro 52 56 41N47 89w02 5:56:08
Schaeferville 90 98 40N35 89w37 5:58:28
Schapville 43 4 42N19 90w13 6:00:52
Schaumburg 16 6 42N02 88w05 5:52:20
Scheller 41 4 38N11 89w06 5:56:24
Schiller Park 16 1 41N57 87w52 5:51:28
Schram City 68 7 39N10 89w27 5:57:48
Schrodt 93 4 38N25 87w46 5:51:04
Schuline 79 63 38N05 89w47 5:59:08
Schwer 38 7 40N38 87w42 5:50:48
Sciota 55 4 40N35 90w44 6:02:56
Scioto Mills 89 61 42N21 89w40 5:58:40
Scotland 23 7 39N48 87w41 5:50:44
Scotland 55 4 40N24 90w37 6:02:28
Scotsboro 100 6 37N46 88w56 5:55:44
Scott Air Force Base 82 6 38N32 89w52 5:59:28
Scottswood 10 138 40N06 88w12 5:52:48
Scottville 59 63 39N28 90w05 6:00:20
Seaton 66 4 41N06 90w48 6:03:12
Seatonville 6 134 41N22 89w16 5:57:04
Secor 102 55 40N45 89w08 5:56:32
Sefton 26 4 39N03 88w59 5:55:56
Selby 6 41 41N22 89w20 5:57:20
Selmaville 61 4 38N36 88w57 5:55:48
Seminary 26 4 38N52 89w12 5:56:48
Seminary 80 4 38N44 88w05 5:52:20
Senachwine 78 4 41N12 89w24 5:57:36
Seneca 50 46 41N19 88w37 5:54:28
Sepo 29 7 40N24 90w09 6:00:36
Serena 50 41 41N30 88w45 5:55:00
Sesser 28 4 38N05 89w03 5:56:12
Seven Hickory 15 106 39N35 88w11 5:52:44
Seven Hills 49 6 42N25 88w04 5:52:16
Seville 29 63 40N28 90w18 6:01:12
Seward 101 4 42N14 89w22 5:57:28
Sexson Corner 87 63 39N28 88w30 5:54:00
Seymour 10 54 40N06 88w26 5:53:44
Shabbona 19 60 41N45 88w53 5:55:32
Shabbona Grove 19 28 41N35 88w56 5:55:44
Shadetree 16 6 41N36 87w45 5:51:00
Shadow Lawn 46 82 41N10 87w40 5:50:40
Shady Grove 64 4 37N08 88w38 5:54:32
Shady Hill 49 6 42N09 88w06 5:52:24
Shafter 26 4 39N02 89w12 5:56:48
Shakerag 100 4 37N49 88w56 5:55:44
Shale City 66 4 41N12 90w45 6:03:00
Shanghai City 94 4 41N04 90w33 6:02:12
Shannon 8 66 42N09 89w44 5:58:56
Sharon 26 139 39N02 89w06 5:56:24
Sharpsburg 11 7 39N34 89w21 5:57:24
Shattuc 14 4 38N37 89w12 5:56:48
Shaw 49 6 42N23 88w07 5:52:28
Shawnee 30 4 37N44 88w08 5:52:32
Shawneetown 30 4 37N42 88w08 5:52:32
Shaws 52 29 41N43 89w20 5:57:20
Shaws Point 59 4 39N19 89w46 5:59:04
Sheffield 6 63 41N21 89w44 5:58:56
Sheffield Green 4 28 42N16 89w00 5:56:00
Shelby 24 4 38N30 88w06 5:52:24
Shelbyville 87 7 39N24 88w48 5:55:12
Sheldon 38 7 40N44 87w36 5:50:24
Sheldons Grove 85 66 40N08 90w22 6:01:28
Sherburnville 46 21 41N15 87w39 5:50:36
Sheridan 50 57 41N32 88w41 5:54:44
Sheridan Village 72 98 40N45 89w37 5:58:28
Sherman 84 53 39N54 89w36 5:58:24
Sherrard 66 4 41N19 90w31 6:02:04
Sherwood Forest 22 17 41N57 87w59 5:51:56
Shields 41 4 38N20 88w38 5:54:32
Shields 49 116 42N17 87w52 5:51:28
Shiloh 82 25 38N32 90w00 6:00:00
Shiloh Hill 79 63 37N56 89w33 5:58:12
Shiloh Valley 82 25 38N31 89w53 5:59:32
Shipman 59 53 39N07 90w03 6:00:12
Shirland 101 4 42N28 89w12 5:56:48
Shirley 57 37 40N24 89w04 5:56:16
Shoal Creek 3 63 38N58 89w33 5:58:12
Shobonier 26 4 38N52 89w05 5:56:20
Shokokon 36 4 40N44 91w04 6:04:16
Shore Acres 98 26 41N46 89w41 5:58:44
Shore Hills 56 15 42N23 88w26 5:53:44
Shorewood 46 26 41N01 87w43 5:50:52
Shorewood 99 82 41N31 88w12 5:52:48

ILLINOIS

Place		Lat	Long	Time
Shorewood Village 16	6	42N03	87W55	5:51:40
Shull's Urban Estates 10	29	40N19	88W08	5:52:32
Shumway 25	63	39N11	88W39	5:54:36
Sibley 27	55	40N35	88W23	5:53:32
Sicily 11	4	39N35	89W35	5:58:20
Sidell 92	96	39N55	87W49	5:51:16
Sidney 10	54	40N01	88W04	5:52:16
Sigel 87	1	39N14	88W30	5:54:00
Signal Hill 82	25	38N35	90W05	6:00:20
Silver Creek 89	4	42N15	89W34	5:58:16
Silver Lake 56	1	42N14	88W15	5:53:00
Silvis 81	87	41N30	90W25	6:01:40
Silvis Heights 81	87	41N30	90W24	6:01:36
Simpson 44	4	37N28	88W46	5:55:04
Simpson 97	4	38N09	88W02	5:52:08
Sims 96	4	38N22	88W32	5:54:08
Sinclair 69	63	39N49	90W07	6:00:28
Six Mile 28	4	37N55	89W04	5:56:16
Skokie 16	1	42N03	87W45	5:51:00
Slap Out 61	4	38N35	88W47	5:55:08
Sleepy Hollow 45	10	42N06	88W18	5:53:12
Smallwood 40	4	38N54	88W12	5:52:48
Smithboro 3	55	38N54	89W20	5:57:20
Smithfield 29	63	40N28	90W18	6:01:12
Smithshire 94	4	40N48	90W47	6:03:08
Smithton 82	25	38N26	89W59	5:59:56
Smithville 72	57	40N42	89W48	5:59:12
Snicarte 63	63	40N11	90W09	6:00:36
Snyder 12	4	39N13	87W40	5:50:40
Sollitt 46	22	41N21	87W37	5:50:28
Solon Mills 56	48	42N27	88W17	5:53:08
Somer 10	29	40N10	88W12	5:52:48
Somerset 22	2	41N48	87W56	5:51:44
Somerset 39	4	37N48	89W20	5:57:20
Somerset 56	9	42N14	88W21	5:53:24
Somerset 83	4	37N44	88W33	5:54:12
Somonauk 19	7	41N40	88W41	5:54:44
Songer 13	4	38N42	88W38	5:54:32
Sonora 34	4	40N30	91W18	6:05:12
Sorento 3	63	39N00	89W34	5:58:16
South 16	1	42N02	87W41	5:50:44
South Addison 22	21	41N53	87W58	5:51:52
South Barrington 16	6	42N05	88W08	5:52:32
South Beloit 101	65	42N29	89W02	5:56:08
South Bluffs 86	65	39N44	90W32	6:02:08
South Bridgeview 16	1	41N44	87W48	5:51:12
South Chicago 16	1	41N43	87W33	5:50:12
South Chicago Heights 16	1	41N29	87W38	5:50:32
South Clinton 20	8	40N09	88W57	5:55:48
South Crouch 33	4	38N09	88W31	5:54:04
South Danville 92	54	40N17	87W41	5:50:44
South Dixon 52	25	41N48	89W27	5:57:48
South Elgin 45	107	42N00	88W18	5:53:12
Southern 100	4	37N38	88W58	5:55:52
Southern View 84	133	39N45	89W39	5:58:36
South Fillmore 68	4	39N03	89W18	5:57:12
South Flannigan 33	4	37N56	88W39	5:54:36
South Fork 11	26	39N34	89W26	5:57:44
Southgate 16	6	42N04	88W00	5:52:00
South Grove 19	40	42N01	88W53	5:55:32
South Holland 16	19	41N36	87W36	5:50:24
South Homer 10	54	40N02	87W59	5:51:56
South Hurricane 26	4	39N07	89W12	5:56:48
South Jacksonville 69	113	39N43	90W14	6:00:56
South Litchfield 68	37	39N08	89W39	5:58:36
South Lockport 99	114	41N35	88W03	5:52:12
South Macon 58	57	39N42	88W59	5:55:56
South Moline 81	87	41N28	90W29	6:01:56
South Moline Gardens 81	87	41N30	90W30	6:02:00
Southmoor 60	7	38N57	90W11	6:00:44
South Mounds 77	4	37N44	88W33	5:54:12
South Muddy 40	4	38N54	88W19	5:53:16
South Oak Park 16	1	41N52	87W47	5:51:08
South Ottawa 50	6	41N18	88W52	5:55:28
South Otter 59	4	39N24	89W53	5:59:32
South Palmyra 59	63	39N24	89W59	5:59:56
South Pekin 90	98	40N30	89W39	5:58:36
Southport 72	58	40N50	89W53	5:59:32
South Rock Island 81	87	41N29	90W33	6:02:12
South Rome 72	51	40N55	89W30	5:58:00
South Ross 92	26	40N18	87W39	5:50:36
South Roxana 60	29	38N50	90W04	6:00:16
South Shore 16	1	41N46	87W34	5:50:16
South Standard 59	4	39N21	89W48	5:59:12
South Stickney 16	1	41N44	87W48	5:51:12
South Streator 53	135	41N06	88W50	5:55:20
South Twigg 33	4	37N56	88W32	5:54:08
South Waukegan 49	140	42N19	87W51	5:51:24
Southwest 17	4	38N52	87W52	5:51:28
South Wheatland 58	26	39N48	88W58	5:55:52
South Wilmington 32	36	41N10	88W17	5:53:08
South Winchester 86	63	39N36	90W30	6:02:00
Spanish Court 49	1	42N11	87W49	5:51:16
Sparks Hill 35	4	37N27	88W18	5:53:12
Sparland 62	48	41N02	89W26	5:57:44
Sparta 79	55	38N08	89W42	5:58:48
Spaulding 16	107	42N02	88W17	5:53:08
Spaulding 84	29	39N52	89W32	5:58:08
Speer 88	4	40N59	89W39	5:58:36
Spencer 99	1	41N31	87W58	5:51:52
Spencer Heights 77	4	37N07	89W12	5:56:48
Spillertown 100	4	37N46	88W55	5:55:40
Spin Lake 57	20	40N32	89W11	5:56:44
Sportsman Lake 61	4	38N36	88W57	5:55:48
Spring 4	26	42N12	88W46	5:55:04
Spring Bay 102	56	40N48	89W31	5:58:04
Spring Creek 75	4	39N27	90W44	6:02:56
Springerton 97	4	38N11	88W21	5:53:24
Springfield 84	133	39N48	89W39	5:58:36
Spring Garden 41	4	38N10	88W52	5:55:28
Spring Grove 56	6	42N27	88W14	5:52:56
Springhaven 60	7	38N57	90W11	6:00:44
Spring Hill 98	88	41N39	90W05	6:00:20
Spring Lake 10	54	40N12	88W24	5:53:36
Spring Lake 22	54	39N48	88W10	5:52:40
Spring Lake 90	55	40N29	89W47	5:59:08
Spring Point 18	4	39N13	88W24	5:53:36
Spring Valley 6	134	41N20	89W12	5:56:48
Squaw Grove 19	43	41N46	88W39	5:54:36
Stallings 60	7	38N44	90W04	6:00:16
Standard 78	57	41N15	89W11	5:56:44
Standard City 59	65	39N21	89W48	5:59:12
Stanford 57	36	40N26	89W13	5:56:52
Stanton 10	54	40N11	88W04	5:52:16
Stanton Point 49	27	42N23	88W09	5:52:36
Stark 88	55	40N56	89W45	5:59:00
Starks 45	29	42N05	88W28	5:53:52
Starnes 84	133	39N48	89W38	5:58:32
State Park Place 60	7	38N40	90W03	6:00:12
Staunton 59	26	39N01	89W47	5:59:08
Stavanger 50	46	41N19	88W36	5:54:24
Steel City 28	4	38N00	88W56	5:55:44
Steeleville 79	63	38N00	89W40	5:58:40
Steelton 98	26	41N48	89W43	5:58:52
Steeple Run 22	12	41N47	88W09	5:52:36
Steger 16	1	41N28	87W38	5:50:32
Stelle 46	38	41N00	88W12	5:52:48
Sterling 98	26	41N48	89W42	5:58:48
Sterling Place 82	25	38N37	90W01	6:00:04
Steuben 62	48	41N03	89W28	5:57:52
Stevenson 61	4	38N34	88W53	5:55:32
Steward 52	6	41N51	89W01	5:56:04
Stewardson 87	63	39N16	88W38	5:54:32
Stickney 16	1	41N47	87W46	5:51:04
Stillman Valley 71	56	42N06	89W11	5:56:44
Stillwell 34	4	40N15	91W11	6:04:44
Stiritz 100	4	37N54	88W55	5:55:40
Stockland 38	7	40N37	87W36	5:50:24
Stockton 43	66	42N21	90W01	6:00:04
Stock Yards 16	1	41N49	87W39	5:50:36
Stokes 91	4	37N27	89W06	5:56:24
Stolle 14	25	38N33	90W10	6:00:40
Stonebridge 16	2	41N35	87W40	5:50:40
Stone Church 35	4	37N28	88W22	5:53:28
Stone Church 95	55	38N24	89W39	5:58:36
Stonefort 83	4	37N37	88W42	5:54:48
Stonelake 56	11	42N19	88W27	5:53:48
Stone Park 16	2	41N54	87W53	5:51:32
Stoneyville 50	6	41N21	88W51	5:55:24
Stonington 11	55	39N44	89W12	5:56:48
Stookey 82	25	38N33	90W04	6:00:16
Storeyland 60	7	38N57	90W11	6:00:44
Storybrook 47	25	41N39	88W27	5:53:48
Stoy 17	4	39N00	87W50	5:51:20
Strasburg 87	63	39N21	88W37	5:54:28
Stratford 71	4	41N59	89W35	5:58:20
Stratford Hills 22	27	41N54	87W57	5:51:48
Strathmore Grove 16	6	42N09	87W57	5:51:48
Stratton 23	128	39N36	87W36	5:50:24
Stratton 41	4	38N20	88W38	5:54:32
Strawn 53	55	40N39	88W24	5:53:36
Streamwood 16	27	42N01	88W11	5:52:44
Streator 50	135	41N08	88W50	5:55:20
Streator Junction 102	71	40N43	89W17	5:57:08
Stringtown 80	4	38N44	88W05	5:52:20
Stronghurst 36	4	40N45	90W55	6:03:40
Sublette 52	57	41N39	89W14	5:56:56
Suburban Estates 22	12	41N48	88W01	5:52:04
Suburban Heights 95	4	38N31	89W08	5:56:32
Suez 66	4	41N07	90W36	6:02:24
Sugar Brook 99	1	41N40	88W00	5:52:00
Sugar Creek 14	55	38N37	89W39	5:58:36
Sugar Grove 45	41	41N45	88W27	5:53:48
Sugar Grove 66	4	41N12	90W45	6:03:00
Sugar Island 46	57	41N00	87W55	5:51:40
Sugar Loaf 82	46	38N31	90W11	6:00:44
Sullivan 70	7	39N36	88W37	5:54:28
Sullivant 27	55	40N34	88W23	5:53:32
Summerfield 82	7	38N36	89W45	5:59:00
Summerhill 16	2	42N07	87W49	5:51:16
Summer Hill 75	4	39N33	90W55	6:03:40
Summerlakes 22	26	41N49	88W11	5:52:44
Summersville 41	4	38N18	88W55	5:55:40
Summerville 59	4	39N10	90W08	6:00:32
Summit 16	1	41N48	87W48	5:51:12
Summit Heights 68	7	39N08	89W30	5:58:00
Summum 29	66	40N16	90W17	6:01:08
Sumner 51	4	38N43	87W52	5:51:28
Sumpter 18	4	39N17	88W16	5:53:04
Sunbeam 66	4	41N12	90W45	6:03:00
Sunbury 53	56	41N04	88W39	5:54:36
Sunfield 73	4	38N04	89W14	5:56:56
Sunny Crest 16	6	41N32	87W42	5:50:48
Sunny Hill 37	4	41N21	90W23	6:01:32
Sunny Hills Estates 22	12	41N48	88W01	5:52:04
Sunnyland 90	98	40N42	89W25	5:57:40
Sunny Land 99	114	41N33	88W07	5:52:28
Sunnyside 56	27	42N23	88W14	5:52:56
Sunnyside 100	4	37N48	89W02	5:56:08
Sunrise Ridge 56	15	42N23	88W26	5:53:44
Sunrise Ridge 99	114	41N35	88W03	5:52:12
Sunset Acres 49	42	42N16	87W56	5:51:44
Sunset Harbor 100	4	37N46	88W56	5:55:44
Sunset Hills 16	17	41N58	88W04	5:52:16
Sunset Lake 59	29	39N27	89W47	5:59:08
Sutter 34	4	40N17	91W21	6:05:24
Sutton 16	6	42N09	88W06	5:52:24
Sutton Point 16	2	42N07	87W49	5:51:16
Swan 94	4	40N40	90W37	6:02:28
Swan Creek 94	4	40N44	90W40	6:02:40
Swansea 82	25	38N32	89W59	5:59:56
Swanwick 73	4	38N10	89W32	5:58:08
Swedona 66	4	41N18	90W22	6:01:28
Sweet Water 65	4	40N03	89W42	5:58:48
Swiss Valley 99	1	41N28	87W37	5:50:28
Swissville 52	25	41N50	89W30	5:58:00
Swygert 53	127	40N53	88W38	5:54:32
Sycamore 19	6	41N59	88W41	5:54:44
Sylvan Hill 16	12	41N38	87W51	5:51:24
Sylvan Lake 49	6	42N16	88W03	5:52:12
Symerton 99	7	41N20	88W03	5:52:12
Symmes 23	128	39N32	87W42	5:50:48
Table Grove 29	66	40N22	90W25	6:01:40
Tabor 20	55	40N15	89W08	5:56:32
Taft 16	2	41N53	87W55	5:51:40
Talkington 84	55	39N34	89W52	5:59:28
Tall Trees 16	1	42N04	87W48	5:51:12
Tallula 65	29	39N56	89W56	5:59:44
Tamalco 3	4	38N47	89W18	5:57:12
Tamarac 16	1	41N32	87W41	5:50:44
Tamaroa 73	4	38N08	89W14	5:56:56
Tamms 2	4	37N14	89W16	5:57:04
Tamms Prec 2	4	37N15	89W17	5:57:08
Tampico 98	29	41N38	89W47	5:59:08
Tanglewood 16	27	41N58	88W06	5:52:24
Tate 83	4	37N53	88W39	5:54:36
Taylor 71	28	41N55	89W20	5:57:20
Taylor Ridge 81	4	41N23	90W40	6:02:40
Taylor Springs 68	7	39N08	89W30	5:58:00
Taylorville 11	7	39N33	89W18	5:57:12
Techny 16	2	42N07	87W49	5:51:16
Teheran 63	4	40N12	89W42	5:58:48
Temple Hill 76	4	37N22	88W29	5:53:56
Tennessee 55	4	40N24	90W52	6:03:28
Terminal Junction 81	87	41N29	90W34	6:02:16
Terra Cotta 56	9	42N14	88W21	5:53:24
Terre Haute 36	4	40N41	90W58	6:03:52
Teutopolis 25	56	39N08	88W29	5:53:56
Texas 20	8	40N06	88W59	5:55:56
Texas City 83	4	37N49	88W27	5:53:48
Texico 41	4	38N26	88W54	5:55:36
Thackeray 33	4	38N06	88W32	5:54:08
Thawville 38	30	40N41	88W07	5:52:28
Thayer 84	29	39N32	89W46	5:59:04
Thebes 2	4	37N13	89W28	5:57:52
The Burg 52	56	41N42	89W05	5:56:20
The Clusters 99	1	41N40	88W00	5:52:00
The Covered Bridges 22	2	41N53	88W05	5:52:20
The Fairway of Country Lakes 22	12	41N47	88W09	5:52:36
The Greens 16	6	42N03	87W53	5:51:32
The Greens of Woodgate 16	29	41N30	87W42	5:50:48
The Ledges 101	4	42N25	89W01	5:56:04
The Meadows 22	12	41N47	88W05	5:52:20
The Terrace 49	116	42N17	87W51	5:51:24
Third Lake 49	27	42N22	88W01	5:52:04
Thomas 6	29	41N38	89W47	5:59:08
Thomasboro 10	30	40N15	88W11	5:52:44
Thomasville 68	63	39N27	89W39	5:58:36
Thompson 43	4	42N25	90W10	6:00:40
Thompsonville 28	4	37N55	88W46	5:55:04
Thomson 8	4	41N58	90W06	6:00:24
Thornton 16	1	41N34	87W37	5:50:28
Thornwilde 22	26	41N49	88W11	5:52:44
Tierra Grande 16	6	41N35	87W46	5:51:04
Tilden 79	55	38N13	89W41	5:58:44
Tilton 92	26	40N06	87W38	5:50:32
Timber 72	55	40N35	89W50	5:59:20
Timber Lake 8	4	42N06	89W58	5:59:52
Timber Lake 49	6	42N09	88W06	5:52:24
Timberlake Estates 22	2	41N48	87W56	5:51:44
Timberlake Village 16	6	42N04	87W57	5:51:48
Timberline 99	114	41N33	88W07	5:52:28
Timber Ridge 16	1	41N44	87W50	5:51:20
Timber Ridge 22	54	41N52	88W11	5:52:44
Timber Trails 22	2	41N48	87W56	5:51:44
Time 75	4	39N34	90W44	6:02:56
Times Square 41	4	38N18	88W55	5:55:40
Timewell 5	66	40N00	90W52	6:03:28
Timothy 18	4	39N15	88W10	5:52:40
Tinley Park 16	1	41N35	87W47	5:51:08
Tinley Terrace 16	1	41N35	87W46	5:51:04
Tioga 34	53	40N05	91W17	6:05:08
Tipton 67	8	38N20	90W09	6:00:36
Tiskilwa 6	55	41N18	89W30	5:58:00
Todds Mill 73	4	38N21	89W23	5:57:32
Todds Point 87	63	39N33	88W46	5:55:04
Toledo 18	4	39N16	88W15	5:53:00
Tolono 10	36	39N59	88W16	5:53:04
Toluca 62	54	41N03	89W08	5:56:32
Tomahawk Bluff 50	117	41N20	89W06	5:56:24

ILLINOIS

Tompkins 94 4 40N51 90w43 6:02:52
Toms Prairie 96 4 38N23 88w22 5:53:28
Tonica 50 136 41N13 89w04 5:56:16
Tonti 61 4 38N39 88w59 5:55:56
Topeka 63 137 40N20 89w56 5:59:44
Toronto 84 133 39N48 89w38 5:58:32
Toulon 88 4 41N06 89w52 5:59:28
Tovey 11 26 39N35 89w27 5:57:48
Towanda 57 68 40N32 88w50 5:55:20
Tower Hill 87 63 39N23 88w58 5:55:52
Tower Lake 49 6 42N14 88w09 5:52:36
Towne Oaks 90 98 40N35 89w32 5:58:08
Trago Lake 13 4 38N40 88w28 5:53:52
Tremont 60 7 38N57 90w11 6:00:44
Tremont 90 98 40N28 89w29 5:57:56
Trenton 14 7 38N36 89w41 5:58:44
Triezenbers 16 12 41N40 87w47 5:51:08
Trilla 15 4 39N22 88w21 5:53:24
Trimble 17 4 39N04 87w41 5:50:44
Triple Lance Heights 100
4 37N43 89w14 5:56:56
Tri-state Village 22
2 41N48 87w56 5:51:44
Triumph 50 56 41N30 89w01 5:56:04
Triumvera 16 1 42N04 87w48 5:51:12
Trivoli 72 57 40N41 89w55 5:59:40
Trout Valley 56 1 42N14 88w15 5:53:00
Trowbridge 87 1 39N19 88w31 5:54:04
Troxel 45 84 41N52 88w35 5:54:20
Troy 60 90 38N44 89w53 5:59:32
Troy Grove 50 123 41N30 89w06 5:56:24
Tru Lock Acres 55 4 40N28 90w41 6:02:44
Truro 48 4 40N56 90w03 6:00:12
Tullamore 49 126 42N14 87w59 5:51:56
Tunbridge 20 55 40N06 89w05 5:56:20
Tunnel Hill 44 4 37N32 88w50 5:55:20
Turnberry 56 9 42N14 88w21 5:53:24
Tuscola 21 7 39N48 88w17 5:53:08
Twigg 33 4 38N00 88w33 5:54:12
Twilight Terrace 82
25 38N31 89w59 5:59:56
Twin City 10 138 40N06 88w12 5:52:48
Twin Lakes 60 4 38N44 89w53 5:59:32
Twin Oaks 16 6 42N03 87w55 5:51:40
Twin Oaks 99 114 41N33 88w07 5:52:28
Tyrone 28 4 37N59 89w06 5:56:24
Ulah 37 4 41N18 90w12 6:00:48
Ullin 77 4 37N17 89w11 5:56:44
Union 54 29 40N18 89w29 5:57:56
Union 56 29 42N14 88w33 5:54:12
Union Center 18 4 39N15 88w10 5:52:40
Union Grove 98 8 41N48 90w02 6:00:08
Union Hill 46 39 41N08 88w09 5:52:36
Union Hill 82 25 38N37 90w01 6:00:04
Uniontown 48 60 40N47 90w01 6:00:04
Unionville 64 4 37N08 88w38 5:54:32
Unionville 92 26 40N03 87w38 5:50:32
Unionville 98 75 41N49 89w58 5:59:52
Unity 2 4 37N09 89w16 5:57:04
Unity 74 55 39N50 88w32 5:54:08
University 10 138 40N06 88w12 5:52:48
University Heights 15
106 39N29 88w13 5:52:52
University Mall 39
57 39N59 88w49 5:55:16
Upper Alton 60 7 38N54 90w10 6:00:40
Uptown 16 1 41N58 87w40 5:50:40
Urbain 28 4 37N58 89w02 5:56:08
Urban 11 7 39N34 89w21 5:57:24
Urbana 10 138 40N07 88w12 5:52:48
Urbandale 2 4 37N00 89w11 5:56:44
Ursa 1 53 40N04 91w22 6:05:28
Ustick 98 55 41N53 90w02 6:00:08
Utica 50 8 41N21 88w59 5:55:56
Valier 28 4 38N01 89w03 5:56:12
Valley 88 4 41N01 89w42 5:58:48
Valley City 75 4 39N42 90w39 6:02:36
Valley Lo 16 1 42N04 87w48 5:51:12
Valley View 22 12 41N50 88w04 5:52:16
Valley View 45 95 41N54 88w19 5:53:16
Valley View 90 98 40N39 89w34 5:58:16
Valmeyer 67 55 38N18 90w19 6:01:16
Van Burensbrug 68 4 39N07 89w16 5:57:04
Vance 92 54 40N03 87w53 5:51:32
Vandalia 26 139 38N58 89w06 5:56:24
Van Orin 6 54 41N33 89w21 5:57:24
Varna 62 56 41N02 89w14 5:56:56
Venedy 95 55 38N24 89w39 5:58:36
Venetian Village 49
6 42N24 88w03 5:52:12
Venice 60 96 38N40 90w10 6:00:40
Venice Crossing 60
25 38N41 90w10 6:00:40
Vera 26 139 39N02 89w07 5:56:28
Vergennes 39 4 37N54 89w20 5:57:20
Vermilion 23 56 39N35 87w35 5:50:20
Vermilion Grove 92
54 39N54 87w39 5:50:36
Vermilion Heights 92
54 40N17 87w41 5:50:44
Vermilionville 50
136 41N13 89w04 5:56:16
Vermillion 50 136 41N13 89w00 5:56:00
Vermillion Estates 53
127 40N53 88w38 5:54:32
Vermont 29 66 40N18 90w26 6:01:44
Vernon 61 4 38N48 89w05 5:56:20
Vernon Hills 49 126 42N13 87w58 5:51:52
Verona 32 55 41N13 88w30 5:54:00
Versailles 5 65 39N53 90w39 6:02:36
Vets Row 72 51 40N55 89w30 5:58:00
Vicic 90 98 40N39 89w34 5:58:16
Victor 19 26 41N40 88w46 5:55:04
Victoria 48 4 41N02 90w06 6:00:24
Vienna 44 4 37N25 88w54 5:55:36
Vienna Woods 16 1 41N31 87w42 5:50:48

Village Square 22
12 41N48 88w01 5:52:04
Villa Grove 21 50 39N52 88w10 5:52:40
Villa Hills 82 25 38N32 90w05 6:00:20
Villa Marie 60 7 38N57 90w11 6:00:44
Villa Park 22 21 41N53 87w59 5:51:56
Villa Ridge 60 7 38N57 90w11 6:00:44
Villa Ridge 77 4 37N10 89w12 5:56:48
Villas Salceda 16 2 42N07 87w49 5:51:16
Villa Verde 16 6 42N09 87w57 5:51:48
Villa West 16 12 41N38 87w51 5:51:24
Villa Westbrook 55
4 40N28 90w41 6:02:44
Vinegar Hill 43 4 42N29 90w26 6:01:44
Viola 66 4 41N12 90w35 6:02:20
Virden 59 29 39N30 89w46 5:59:04
Virgil 45 84 41N57 88w32 5:54:08
Virginia 9 63 39N57 90w13 6:00:52
Volo 49 6 42N20 88w10 5:52:40
Vonachen Knolls 72
51 40N55 89w30 5:58:00
Voorhies 74 30 39N55 88w34 5:54:16
Vulcan 82 46 38N32 90w14 6:00:56
Wacker 8 4 42N06 89w58 5:59:52
Waddams 89 4 42N25 89w45 5:59:00
Waddams Grove 89 64 42N25 89w53 5:59:32
Wadsworth 49 17 42N26 87w56 5:51:44
Waggoner 68 63 39N23 89w39 5:58:36
Wakefield 80 4 38N59 88w10 5:52:40
Waldo 53 55 40N48 88w52 5:55:28
Walker 34 4 40N15 91w18 6:05:12
Walkerville 31 63 39N24 90w32 6:02:08
Wall 27 30 40N32 88w11 5:52:44
Wallace 50 6 41N25 88w53 5:55:32
Wallingford 99 82 41N25 87w59 5:51:56
Walnut 6 29 41N33 89w36 5:58:24
Walnut Grove 55 4 40N37 90w34 6:02:16
Walnut Hill 61 4 38N29 89w03 5:56:12
Walnut Prairie 12 4 39N13 87w40 5:50:40
Walpole 33 4 37N56 88w28 5:53:52
Walsh 79 63 38N05 89w51 5:59:24
Walshville 68 7 39N03 89w39 5:58:36
Waltham 50 56 41N25 88w59 5:55:56
Walton 52 25 41N50 89w30 5:58:00
Waltonville 41 4 38N13 89w02 5:56:08
Wamac 61 4 38N31 89w08 5:56:32
Wanda 60 25 38N48 89w57 5:59:48
Wanlock 66 4 41N12 90w45 6:03:00
Wapella 20 8 40N13 88w58 5:55:52
Wards Grove 43 4 42N20 89w57 5:59:48
Ware 91 4 37N27 89w24 5:57:36
Warner 37 4 41N21 90w23 6:01:32
Warren 43 65 42N30 90w00 6:00:00
Warrenhurst 22 26 41N49 88w11 5:52:44
Warren Park 16 1 41N51 87w46 5:51:04
Warrensburg 58 57 39N56 89w04 5:56:16
Warrenville 22 26 41N49 88w11 5:52:44
Warsaw 34 4 40N22 91w26 6:05:44
Wartburg 67 8 38N20 90w09 6:00:36
Wartrace 44 4 37N24 88w45 5:55:00
Wasco 45 29 41N56 88w24 5:53:36
Washburn 102 55 40N55 89w17 5:57:08
Washington 90 98 40N42 89w25 5:57:40
Washington Park 82
99 38N38 90w06 6:00:24
Wasson 83 4 37N47 88w29 5:53:56
Wataga 48 4 41N02 90w17 6:01:08
Waterford 29 7 40N21 90w07 6:00:28
Waterloo 67 8 38N20 90w09 6:00:36
Waterman 19 60 41N46 88w47 5:55:08
Watertown 81 87 41N30 90w26 6:01:44
Watervalley 91 4 37N32 89w15 5:57:00
Watseka 38 7 40N47 87w44 5:50:56
Watson 25 4 39N02 88w34 5:54:16
Wauconda 49 22 42N16 88w08 5:52:32
Waukegan 49 140 42N22 87w50 5:51:20
Wauponsee 32 125 41N20 88w25 5:53:40
Waverly 69 55 39N36 89w57 5:59:48
Waycinden Park 16 6 42N03 87w53 5:51:32
Wayne 22 26 41N57 88w15 5:53:00
Wayne City 96 4 38N21 88w35 5:54:20
Waynesville 20 55 40N15 89w08 5:56:32
Webber 41 23 38N21 88w45 5:55:00
Webster 34 4 40N25 91w09 6:04:36
Webster 76 4 37N23 88w40 5:54:40
Webster Park 6 134 41N20 89w12 5:56:48
Wedges Corner 49 6 42N23 88w00 5:52:00
Wedron 50 41 41N26 88w46 5:55:04
Wee-ma-tuk Hills 29
4 40N30 90w11 6:00:44
Weldon 20 55 40N07 88w45 5:55:00
Welge 79 63 37N57 89w43 5:58:52
Weller 37 4 41N12 90w09 6:00:36
Wellington 38 80 40N32 87w41 5:50:44
Wellington Heights 99
114 41N33 88w07 5:52:28
Wendelin 13 4 38N59 88w10 5:52:40
Wenona 62 29 41N03 89w03 5:56:12
Wenonah 68 7 39N19 89w17 5:57:08
Wesley 99 30 41N15 88w06 5:52:24
Westaway 45 102 41N46 88w20 5:53:20
Westbrook Estates 82
25 38N36 89w58 5:59:52
West Brooklyn 52 55 41N42 89w09 5:56:36
West Brook Village 55
4 40N28 90w41 6:02:44
Westbury 99 1 41N40 88w00 5:52:00
Westchester 16 1 41N51 87w53 5:51:32
West Chicago 22 1 41N53 88w12 5:52:48
West City 28 4 38N00 88w56 5:55:44
Westdale 16 1 41N54 87w52 5:51:28
Westdale Gardens 16
27 41N54 87w57 5:51:48
West Deerfield 49 2 42N11 87w52 5:51:28
West Dundee 45 10 42N06 88w17 5:53:08
West End 83 4 37N55 88w46 5:55:04

West End 101 28 42N16 89w09 5:56:36
Western 37 4 41N22 90w23 6:01:32
Western Mound 59 63 39N18 90w06 6:00:24
Western Springs 16
1 41N48 87w53 5:51:32
Westervelt 87 63 39N29 88w52 5:55:28
Westfield 12 4 39N27 88w00 5:52:00
Westfield 99 114 41N33 88w07 5:52:28
West Frankfort 28 4 37N54 88w55 5:55:40
West Frankfort Lake 28
4 37N54 88w55 5:55:40
West Galena 43 4 42N24 90w27 6:01:48
Westgate 100 4 37N46 88w56 5:55:44
West Glen 72 98 40N45 89w37 5:58:28
West Glenview 16 1 42N04 87w48 5:51:12
Westhaven 16 6 41N34 87w51 5:51:24
West Jersey 88 4 41N01 89w56 5:59:44
West Kankakee 46
115 41N05 87w53 5:51:32
West Lake 17 4 39N00 87w44 5:50:56
Westlake 22 2 41N53 88w04 5:52:16
West Lake Forest 49
2 42N14 87w53 5:51:32
West Liberty 40 4 38N51 88w05 5:52:20
West Lincoln 54 4 40N11 89w26 5:57:44
West Marion 100 4 37N44 88w58 5:55:52
West Meadowview 46
115 41N05 87w53 5:51:32
West Miltmore 49 6 42N25 88w04 5:52:16
West Monroe 35 4 37N33 88w23 5:53:32
Westmont 22 19 41N48 87w59 5:51:56
Westmore 22 83 41N53 88w01 5:52:04
Weston 57 35 40N45 88w43 5:54:52
West Peoria 72 98 40N43 89w42 5:58:48
West Point 34 4 40N15 91w11 6:04:44
Westport 51 4 38N45 87w31 5:50:04
Westridge 16 1 42N07 87w56 5:51:44
West Ridge 21 7 39N48 88w17 5:53:08
West Rosiclare 35 4 37N26 88w22 5:53:28
West Salem 24 4 38N31 88w01 5:52:04
West Union 12 4 39N13 87w40 5:50:40
Westview 25 38N32 90w06 6:00:24
Westville 92 96 40N02 87w38 5:50:32
Westwood 22 17 41N56 88w00 5:52:00
West York 17 4 39N10 87w39 5:50:36
Wetaug 77 4 37N19 89w09 5:56:36
Wethersfield 37 4 41N12 89w55 5:59:40
Wheatfield 14 4 38N42 89w26 5:57:44
Wheaton 22 2 41N52 88w06 5:52:24
Wheaton Center 22 2 41N53 88w05 5:52:20
Wheeler 40 4 39N03 88w19 5:53:16
Wheeling 16 21 42N08 87w55 5:51:40
Whiskey Corners 56
48 42N29 88w18 5:53:12
Whispering Hills 56
27 42N21 88w14 5:52:56
Whispering Oaks 49
2 42N14 87w53 5:51:32
Whitaker 46 21 41N15 87w39 5:50:36
Whiteash 100 4 37N47 88w56 5:55:44
White City 59 26 39N04 89w47 5:59:08
White Cliffs 60 7 38N57 90w11 6:00:44
Whitefield 62 48 41N06 89w28 5:57:52
Whitehall 16 6 42N04 87w57 5:51:48
White Hall 31 55 39N26 90w24 6:01:36
White Heath 74 30 40N05 88w31 5:54:04
White Oak 57 4 40N36 89w06 5:56:24
White Oaks Bay 56
15 42N23 88w26 5:53:44
White Pines 22 17 41N57 87w58 5:51:52
White Rock 71 6 42N01 89w07 5:56:28
Whites Addition 81
87 41N30 90w26 6:01:44
Whitford Place 60 7 38N57 90w11 6:00:44
Whitley 70 63 39N29 88w32 5:54:08
Whitmore 58 57 39N56 88w51 5:55:24
Whittington 28 4 38N05 88w54 5:55:36
Wichert 46 26 41N01 87w43 5:50:52
Wicker Park 16 1 41N54 87w40 5:50:40
Wickmore 60 7 38N57 90w11 6:00:44
Wilbern 62 56 40N58 89w18 5:57:12
Wilberton 26 4 38N52 88w57 5:55:48
Wilbur Heights 10
21 40N07 88w15 5:53:00
Wilcox 13 4 38N41 88w21 5:53:24
Wilcox 34 4 40N19 91w25 6:05:40
Wildrose 45 95 41N54 88w19 5:53:16
Wildwood 45 102 41N46 88w20 5:53:20
Wildwood 49 27 42N21 88w00 5:52:00
Will 99 30 41N20 87w43 5:50:52
Willard 2 4 37N05 89w21 5:57:24
Willard 82 25 38N36 89w58 5:59:52
Willeys 11 7 39N34 89w21 5:57:24
Williams 84 29 39N55 89w32 5:58:08
Williamsburg 70 55 39N43 88w38 5:54:32
Williamsfield 48 4 40N55 90w01 6:00:04
Williamson 60 26 38N59 89w46 5:59:04
Williams Park 49 1 42N15 88w11 5:52:44
Williams Place 60 7 38N57 90w11 6:00:44
Williamsville 84 29 39N57 89w33 5:58:12
Willisville 73 63 37N59 89w35 5:58:20
Willow 43 4 42N21 90w01 6:00:04
Willoway 22 12 41N47 88w09 5:52:36
Willow Branch 74 4 39N59 88w41 5:54:44
Willowbrook 22 2 41N47 87w57 5:51:48
Willow Brooke 101 4 42N29 89w02 5:56:08
Willow Creek 52 56 41N46 89w00 5:56:00
Willow Estates 19
110 42N06 88w42 5:54:48
Willow Estates 38
26 40N57 87w39 5:50:36
Willow Hill 40 4 38N59 88w00 5:52:00
Willow's East 16 1 42N04 87w48 5:51:12
Willow Springs 16 1 41N44 87w52 5:51:28
Willow Wood 16 6 42N06 88w02 5:52:08
Wilmette 16 1 42N05 87w42 5:50:48

Place		Lat.	Long.	Time
Wilmington 99	30	41N18	88W09	5:52:36
Wilson 49	34	42N21	87W55	5:51:40
Wilson Heights 60	7	38N40	90W00	6:00:00
Wilsonville 59	55	39N04	89W52	5:59:28
Wilton 99	4	41N21	87W57	5:51:48
Wilton Center 99	4	41N21	87W58	5:51:52
Winchester 86	63	39N38	90W27	6:01:48
Winden Oak 45	55	41N51	88W28	5:53:52
Windham Manor 16	2	42N07	87W49	5:51:16
Windsor 87	63	39N26	88W36	5:54:24
Windsor Park 10	138	40N06	88W12	5:52:48
Wine Hill 79	63	37N57	89W39	5:58:36
Winfield 22	30	41N52	88W10	5:52:40
Wing 53	141	40N45	88W24	5:53:36
Winkle 73	4	38N10	89W32	5:58:08
Winnebago 101	48	42N15	89W13	5:56:52
Winneshiek 89	4	42N18	89W38	5:58:32
Winnetka 16	2	42N06	87W44	5:50:56
Winslow 89	64	42N29	89W50	5:59:20
Winston Hills 22	12	41N48	88W01	5:52:04
Winston Park 16	6	42N06	88W02	5:52:08
Winston Village 99	1	41N40	88W00	5:52:00
Winston Woods 99	1	41N40	88W00	5:52:00
Winterrowd 25	4	39N04	88W23	5:53:32
Winthrop Harbor 49	142	42N29	87W50	5:51:20
Wireton 16	1	41N39	87W42	5:50:48
Witt 68	7	39N15	89W21	5:57:24
Woburn 3	55	38N54	89W24	5:57:36
Wolf Lake 91	4	37N30	89W26	5:57:44
Womac 59	47	39N18	89W52	5:59:28
Wonder Lake 56	15	42N22	88W32	5:54:08
Wonder View 56	15	42N23	88W26	5:53:44
Wonder Woods 56	15	42N23	88W26	5:53:44
Woodbine 43	4	42N20	90W09	6:00:36

Place		Lat.	Long.	Time
Woodborough 16	2	41N34	87W40	5:50:40
Woodburn 59	55	39N02	89W57	5:59:48
Woodbury 18	56	39N12	88W16	5:53:04
Wood Dale 22	17	41N58	87W59	5:51:56
Wooddale 72	98	40N40	89W40	5:58:40
Wooded Shores 56	15	42N23	88W26	5:53:44
Wood Hill 99	1	41N30	87W41	5:50:44
Woodhull 37	4	41N11	90W20	6:01:20
Woodland 38	29	40N43	87W44	5:50:56
Woodland Addition 50	6	41N21	88W51	5:55:24
Woodland Heights 16	27	41N58	88W06	5:52:24
Woodland Hills 45	2	41N52	88W19	5:53:16
Woodland Lake 92	54	40N04	87W42	5:50:48
Woodland Shores 52	25	41N50	89W30	5:58:00
Woodlawn 41	4	38N20	89W03	5:56:12
Woodlawn Heights 98	26	41N48	89W43	5:58:52
Woodmere 49	42	42N16	87W56	5:51:44
Woodridge 22	43	41N45	88W03	5:52:12
Wood River 60	29	38N52	90W05	6:00:20
Woodside 84	55	39N45	89W45	5:59:00
Woodside Estates 22	2	41N48	87W56	5:51:44
Woodson 69	63	39N38	90W14	6:00:56
Woodstock 56	11	42N19	88W27	5:53:48
Woodview Manor 16	1	42N07	87W56	5:51:44
Woodville 31	63	39N14	90W31	6:02:04
Woodworth 38	7	40N40	87W51	5:51:24
Woody 31	55	39N18	90W24	6:01:36
Woodyard 26	4	38N52	89W05	5:56:20
Wooster Lake 49	27	42N23	88W09	5:52:36
Woosung 71	4	41N55	89W34	5:58:16
Worden 60	8	38N56	89W50	5:59:20

Place		Lat.	Long.	Time
Worth 16	12	41N41	87W48	5:51:12
Wrights 31	4	39N23	90W19	6:01:16
Wrights Corner 26	4	39N11	88W47	5:55:08
Wyanet 6	55	41N22	89W34	5:58:16
Wynoose 80	4	38N42	88W13	5:52:52
Wyoming 88	4	41N04	89W46	5:59:04
Wysox 8	4	41N58	89W48	5:59:12
Wythe 34	4	40N20	91W36	6:06:24
Xenia 13	4	38N38	88W38	5:54:32
Yale 40	4	39N07	88W02	5:52:08
Yantisville 87	63	39N31	88W45	5:55:00
Yard Center 16	1	41N37	87W40	5:50:40
Yates 57	4	40N43	88W38	5:54:32
Yates City 48	60	40N47	90W01	6:00:04
Yatesville 69	4	39N53	90W01	6:00:04
Yellowhead 46	21	41N15	87W36	5:50:24
Yeoward Addition 98	26	41N46	89W41	5:58:44
York 12	4	39N13	87W40	5:50:40
York Center 22	21	41N52	87W59	5:51:56
Yorkfield 22	21	41N52	87W57	5:51:48
Yorkshire Woods 22	2	41N48	87W56	5:51:44
Yorktown 6	4	41N32	89W55	5:59:40
Yorkville 47	25	41N38	88W27	5:53:48
Young America 23	55	39N51	87W51	5:51:24
Young Hickory 29	4	40N40	90W15	6:01:00
Youngstown 94	4	40N44	90W40	6:02:40
Zanesville 68	4	39N18	89W39	5:58:36
Zearing 6	55	41N26	89W22	5:57:28
Zeigler 28	4	37N54	89W03	5:56:12
Zenith 96	4	38N38	88W38	5:54:32
Zif 96	4	38N35	88W19	5:53:16
Zion 8	4	42N05	90W09	6:00:36
Zion 49	142	42N27	87W50	5:51:20
Zuma 81	4	41N33	90W16	6:01:04

TIME TABLES

This state has a very complex time zone picture and not all of the time shifts are documented. Even newspaper reports present contradictory information. Time changes for smaller towns are not complete. In such instances, it is advisable to consider also the practice of nearby larger towns. As a general rule the CST portions of Indiana observe daylight time in the summer, while the EST portions do not observe daylight time. The exceptions are 1969 and 1970 when the entire state observed daylight time and the areas near Cincinnati and Louisville which observe EDT in the summer.

```
IN # 1
Before 11/18/1883  LMT
11/18/1883  12:00  IN#2
 6/13/1920  02:00  CDT
10/31/1920  02:00  CST
 3/27/1921  02:00  CDT
10/30/1921  02:00  CST
 4/30/1922  02:00  CDT
 9/24/1922  02:00  CST
 4/29/1923  02:00  CDT
 9/30/1923  02:00  CST
 4/27/1924  02:00  CDT
 9/28/1924  02:00  CST
 4/26/1925  02:00  CDT
 9/27/1925  02:00  CST
 4/25/1926  02:00  CDT
 9/26/1926  02:00  CST
 4/24/1927  02:00  CDT
 9/25/1927  02:00  CST
 4/29/1928  02:00  CDT
 9/30/1928  02:00  CST
 4/28/1929  02:00  CDT
 9/29/1929  02:00  CST
 4/27/1930  02:00  CDT
 9/28/1930  02:00  CST
 4/26/1931  02:00  CDT
 9/27/1931  02:00  CST
 4/24/1932  02:00  CDT
 9/25/1932  02:00  CST
 4/30/1933  02:00  CDT
 9/24/1933  02:00  CST
 4/29/1934  02:00  CDT
 9/30/1934  02:00  CST
 4/28/1935  02:00  CDT
 9/29/1935  02:00  CST
 4/26/1936  02:00  CDT
 9/27/1936  02:00  CST
 4/25/1937  02:00  CDT
 9/26/1937  02:00  CST
 4/24/1938  02:00  CDT
 9/25/1938  02:00  CST
 4/30/1939  02:00  CDT
 9/24/1939  02:00  CST
 4/28/1940  02:00  CDT
 9/29/1940  02:00  CST
 4/27/1941  02:00  CDT
 9/28/1941  02:00  CST
 2/09/1942  02:00  CWT
 9/30/1945  02:00  CST
 4/28/1946  02:00  CDT
 9/29/1946  02:00  CST
 4/27/1947  02:00  CDT
 9/28/1947  02:00  CST
 4/25/1948  02:00  CDT
 9/26/1948  02:00  CST
 4/24/1949  02:00  CDT
 9/25/1949  02:00  CST
 4/30/1950  02:00  CDT
 9/24/1950  02:00  CST
 4/29/1951  02:00  CDT
 9/30/1951  02:00  CST
 4/27/1952  02:00  CDT
 9/28/1952  02:00  CST
 4/26/1953  02:00  CDT
 9/27/1953  02:00  CST
 4/25/1954  02:00  CDT
 9/26/1954  02:00  CST
 4/24/1955  02:00  CDT
 9/25/1955  02:00  CST
 4/29/1956  02:00  CDT
 9/30/1956  02:00  CST
 4/28/1957  02:00  CDT
 9/29/1957  02:00  CST
 4/27/1958  02:00  CDT
 9/28/1958  02:00  CST
 4/26/1959  02:00  CDT
 9/27/1959  02:00  CST
 4/24/1960  02:00  CDT
 9/25/1960  02:00  CST
 4/30/1961  02:00  US#1
```

```
IN # 2
Before 11/18/1883  LMT
11/18/1883  12:00  CST
 3/31/1918  02:00  CWT
10/27/1918  02:00  CST
 3/30/1919  02:00  CWT
10/26/1919  02:00  CST
 2/09/1942  02:00  CWT
 9/30/1945  02:00  CST
 4/24/1955  02:00  CDT
10/30/1955  02:00  CST
 4/29/1956  02:00  CDT
10/28/1956  02:00  CST
 4/28/1957  02:00  US#2
```

```
IN # 3
Before 11/18/1883  LMT
11/18/1883  12:00  CST
 3/31/1918  02:00  CWT
10/27/1918  02:00  CST
 3/30/1919  02:00  CWT
10/26/1919  02:00  CST
 2/09/1942  02:00  CWT
 9/30/1945  02:00  CST
 4/28/1946  02:00  CDT
 9/29/1946  02:00  CST
 4/27/1947  02:00  CDT
 9/28/1947  02:00  CST
 4/25/1948  02:00  CDT
 9/26/1948  02:00  CST
 4/24/1949  02:00  CDT
 9/25/1949  02:00  CST
 4/24/1955  02:00  CDT
10/30/1955  02:00  CST
 4/29/1956  02:00  CDT
10/28/1956  02:00  CST
 4/28/1957  02:00  CDT
 9/29/1957  02:00  CST
 4/27/1958  02:00  CDT
 9/28/1958  02:00  CST
 4/26/1959  02:00  CDT
 9/27/1959  02:00  CST
 4/24/1960  02:00  CDT
 9/25/1960  02:00  CST
 4/30/1961  02:00  US#1
```

```
IN # 4
Before 11/18/1883  LMT
11/18/1883  12:00  CST
 3/31/1918  02:00  CWT
10/27/1918  02:00  CST
 3/30/1919  02:00  CWT
10/26/1919  02:00  CST
 4/28/1929  02:00  CDT
 9/29/1929  02:00  CST
 4/27/1930  02:00  CDT
 9/28/1930  02:00  CST
 4/26/1931  02:00  CDT
 9/27/1931  02:00  CST
 4/24/1932  02:00  CDT
 9/25/1932  02:00  CST
 4/30/1933  02:00  CDT
 9/24/1933  02:00  CST
 4/29/1934  02:00  CDT
 9/30/1934  02:00  CST
 4/28/1935  02:00  CDT
 9/29/1935  02:00  CST
 4/26/1936  02:00  CDT
 9/27/1936  02:00  CST
 4/25/1937  02:00  CDT
 9/26/1937  02:00  CST
 4/24/1938  02:00  CDT
 9/25/1938  02:00  CST
 4/30/1939  02:00  CDT
 9/24/1939  02:00  CST
 4/28/1940  02:00  CDT
 9/29/1940  02:00  CST
 4/27/1941  02:00  CDT
 9/28/1941  02:00  CST
 2/09/1942  02:00  CWT
 9/30/1945  02:00  CST
 4/28/1946  02:00  CDT
 9/29/1946  02:00  CST
 4/27/1947  02:00  CDT
 9/28/1947  02:00  CST
 4/25/1948  02:00  CDT
 9/26/1948  02:00  CST
 4/24/1949  02:00  CDT
 9/25/1949  02:00  CST
 4/30/1950  02:00  CDT
 9/24/1950  02:00  CST
 4/29/1951  02:00  CDT
 9/30/1951  02:00  CST
 4/27/1952  02:00  CDT
 9/28/1952  02:00  CST
 4/26/1953  02:00  CDT
 9/27/1953  02:00  CST
 4/25/1954  02:00  CDT
 9/26/1954  02:00  CST
 4/24/1955  02:00  CDT
10/30/1955  02:00  CST
 4/29/1956  02:00  CDT
10/28/1956  02:00  CST
 4/28/1957  02:00  CDT
 9/29/1957  02:00  CST
 4/27/1958  02:00  US#1
```

```
IN # 5
Before 11/18/1883  LMT
11/18/1883  12:00  IN#2
 4/26/1925  02:00  CDT
 9/27/1925  02:00  CST
 4/25/1926  02:00  CDT
 9/26/1926  02:00  CST
 4/24/1927  02:00  CDT
 9/25/1927  02:00  CST
 4/29/1928  02:00  CDT
 9/30/1928  02:00  CST
 4/28/1929  02:00  CDT
 9/29/1929  02:00  CST
 4/27/1930  02:00  CDT
 9/28/1930  02:00  CST
 4/26/1931  02:00  CDT
 9/27/1931  02:00  CST
 4/24/1932  02:00  CDT
 9/25/1932  02:00  CST
 4/30/1933  02:00  CDT
 9/24/1933  02:00  CST
 4/29/1934  02:00  CDT
 9/30/1934  02:00  CST
 4/28/1935  02:00  CDT
 9/29/1935  02:00  CST
 3/01/1936  02:00  CDT
11/15/1936  02:00  CST
 4/25/1937  02:00  CDT
 9/26/1937  02:00  CST
 4/24/1938  02:00  CDT
 9/25/1938  02:00  CST
 4/30/1939  02:00  CDT
 9/24/1939  02:00  CST
 4/28/1940  02:00  CDT
 9/29/1940  02:00  CST
 4/27/1941  02:00  CDT
 9/28/1941  02:00  CST
 2/09/1942  02:00  CWT
 9/30/1945  02:00  CST
 5/01/1946  02:00  CDT
10/01/1946  02:00  US#2
```

```
IN # 6
Before 11/18/1883  LMT
11/18/1883  12:00  CST
 3/31/1918  02:00  CWT
10/27/1918  02:00  CST
 3/30/1919  02:00  CWT
10/26/1919  02:00  CST
 6/13/1920  02:00  CDT
10/31/1920  02:00  CST
 3/27/1921  02:00  CDT
10/30/1921  02:00  CST
 4/30/1922  02:00  CDT
 9/24/1922  02:00  CST
 4/29/1923  02:00  CDT
 9/30/1923  02:00  CST
 4/27/1924  02:00  CDT
 9/28/1924  02:00  CST
 4/26/1925  02:00  CDT
 9/27/1925  02:00  CST
 4/25/1926  02:00  CDT
 9/26/1926  02:00  CST
 4/24/1927  02:00  CDT
 9/25/1927  02:00  CST
 4/29/1928  02:00  CDT
 9/30/1928  02:00  CST
 4/28/1929  02:00  CDT
 9/29/1929  02:00  CST
 4/27/1930  02:00  CDT
 9/28/1930  02:00  CST
 4/26/1931  02:00  CDT
 9/27/1931  02:00  CST
 4/24/1932  02:00  CDT
 9/25/1932  02:00  CST
 4/30/1933  02:00  CDT
 9/24/1933  02:00  CST
 4/29/1934  02:00  CDT
 9/30/1934  02:00  CST
 4/28/1935  02:00  CDT
 9/29/1935  02:00  CST
 3/01/1936  02:00  CDT
11/15/1936  02:00  CST
 4/25/1937  02:00  US#2
```

```
IN # 7
Before 11/18/1883  LMT
11/18/1883  12:00  IN#2
 5/01/1938  02:00  CDT
10/01/1938  02:00  CST
 2/09/1942  02:00  CWT
 9/30/1945  02:00  CST
 4/28/1946  02:00  CDT
 9/29/1946  02:00  CST
 4/27/1947  02:00  CDT
 9/28/1947  02:00  CST
 4/25/1948  02:00  CDT
 9/26/1948  02:00  CST
 4/24/1949  02:00  CDT
 9/25/1949  02:00  CST
 4/30/1950  02:00  CDT
 9/24/1950  02:00  CST
 4/29/1951  02:00  CDT
 9/30/1951  02:00  CST
 4/27/1952  02:00  CDT
 9/28/1952  02:00  CST
 4/26/1953  02:00  CDT
 9/27/1953  02:00  CST
 4/25/1954  02:00  CDT
 9/26/1954  02:00  CST
 4/24/1955  02:00  CDT
10/30/1955  02:00  CST
 4/29/1956  02:00  CDT
10/28/1956  02:00  CST
 4/28/1957  02:00  CDT
 9/29/1957  02:00  CST
 4/27/1958  02:00  US#1
```

```
IN # 8
Before 11/18/1883  LMT
11/18/1883  12:00  IN#2
 4/27/1930  00:01  CDT
 9/28/1930  00:01  CST
 4/26/1931  00:01  CDT
 9/27/1931  00:01  CST
 4/24/1932  00:01  CDT
 9/25/1932  00:01  CST
 4/30/1933  00:01  CDT
10/01/1933  00:01  CST
 4/29/1934  00:01  CDT
 9/30/1934  00:01  CST
 4/28/1935  00:01  CDT
 9/29/1935  00:01  CST
 4/26/1936  02:00  CDT
 9/27/1936  02:00  CST
 4/25/1937  02:00  CDT
 9/26/1937  02:00  CST
 4/24/1938  02:00  CDT
 9/25/1938  02:00  CST
 4/30/1939  02:00  CDT
 9/24/1939  02:00  CST
 4/28/1940  02:00  CDT
 9/29/1940  02:00  CST
 4/27/1941  02:00  CDT
 9/28/1941  02:00  CST
 2/09/1942  02:00  CWT
 9/30/1945  02:00  CST
 4/28/1946  02:00  US#3
```

```
IN # 9
Before 11/18/1883  LMT
11/18/1883  12:00  IN#2
 4/27/1930  02:00  CDT
 9/28/1930  02:00  CST
 4/26/1931  02:00  CDT
 9/27/1931  02:00  CST
 4/24/1932  02:00  CDT
 9/25/1932  02:00  CST
 4/30/1933  02:00  CDT
 9/24/1933  02:00  CST
 4/29/1934  02:00  CDT
 9/30/1934  02:00  CST
 4/28/1935  02:00  CDT
 9/29/1935  02:00  CST
 4/26/1936  02:00  CDT
 9/27/1936  02:00  CST
 4/25/1937  02:00  CDT
 9/26/1937  02:00  CST
 4/24/1938  02:00  CDT
 9/25/1938  02:00  CST
 4/30/1939  02:00  CDT
 9/24/1939  02:00  CST
 4/28/1940  02:00  CDT
 9/29/1940  02:00  CST
 4/27/1941  02:00  CDT
 9/28/1941  02:00  CST
 2/09/1942  02:00  CWT
 9/30/1945  02:00  CST
 4/28/1946  02:00  US#3
```

```
IN # 10
Before 11/18/1883  LMT
11/18/1883  12:00  IN#2
 4/27/1947  02:00  CDT
 9/28/1947  02:00  CST
 4/25/1948  02:00  CDT
 9/26/1948  02:00  CST
 4/24/1949  02:00  CDT
 9/25/1949  02:00  CST
 4/30/1950  02:00  CDT
 9/24/1950  02:00  CST
 4/29/1951  02:00  CDT
 9/30/1951  02:00  CST
 4/27/1952  02:00  CDT
 9/28/1952  02:00  CST
 4/26/1953  02:00  CDT
 9/27/1953  02:00  CST
 4/25/1954  02:00  CDT
 9/26/1954  02:00  CST
 4/24/1955  02:00  CDT
10/30/1955  02:00  CST
 4/29/1956  02:00  CDT
10/28/1956  02:00  CST
 4/28/1957  02:00  CDT
 9/29/1957  02:00  CST
 4/27/1958  02:00  CDT
 9/28/1958  02:00  CST
 4/26/1959  02:00  US#1
```

```
IN # 11
Before 11/18/1883  LMT
11/18/1883  12:00  CST
 3/31/1918  02:00  CWT
10/27/1918  02:00  CST
 3/30/1919  02:00  CWT
10/26/1919  02:00  CST
 4/28/1929  02:00  CDT
 9/29/1929  02:00  CST
 4/27/1930  02:00  CDT
 9/28/1930  02:00  CST
 4/26/1931  02:00  CDT
 9/27/1931  02:00  CST
 4/24/1932  02:00  CDT
 9/25/1932  02:00  CST
 4/30/1933  02:00  CDT
 9/24/1933  02:00  CST
 4/29/1934  02:00  CDT
 9/30/1934  02:00  CST
 4/28/1935  02:00  CDT
 9/29/1935  02:00  CST
 4/26/1936  02:00  CDT
 9/27/1936  02:00  CST
 4/25/1937  02:00  CDT
 9/26/1937  02:00  CST
 4/24/1938  02:00  CDT
 9/25/1938  02:00  CST
 4/30/1939  02:00  CDT
 9/24/1939  02:00  CST
 4/28/1940  02:00  CDT
 9/29/1940  02:00  CST
 4/27/1941  02:00  CDT
 9/28/1941  02:00  CST
 2/09/1942  02:00  CWT
 9/30/1945  02:00  CST
 4/28/1946  02:00  CDT
 9/29/1946  02:00  CST
 4/27/1947  02:00  CDT
 9/28/1947  02:00  CST
 4/25/1948  02:00  CDT
 9/26/1948  02:00  CST
 4/24/1949  02:00  CDT
 9/25/1949  02:00  CST
 4/30/1950  02:00  CDT
 9/24/1950  02:00  CST
 4/29/1951  02:00  CDT
 9/30/1951  02:00  CST
 4/27/1952  02:00  CDT
 9/28/1952  02:00  CST
 4/26/1953  02:00  CDT
 9/27/1953  02:00  CST
 4/25/1954  02:00  CDT
 9/26/1954  02:00  CST
 4/24/1955  02:00  CDT
10/30/1955  02:00  CST
 4/29/1956  02:00  CDT
10/28/1956  02:00  CST
 4/28/1957  02:00  CDT
 9/29/1957  02:00  CST
 4/27/1958  02:00  US#1
```

```
IN # 12
Before 11/18/1883  LMT
11/18/1883  12:00  IN#2
 5/13/1927  02:00  CDT
 9/25/1927  02:00  CST
 4/29/1928  02:00  CDT
 9/30/1928  02:00  CST
 4/28/1929  02:00  CDT
 9/29/1929  02:00  CST
 4/27/1930  02:00  CDT
 9/28/1930  02:00  CST
 4/26/1931  02:00  CDT
 9/27/1931  02:00  CST
 4/24/1932  02:00  CDT
 9/25/1932  02:00  CST
 4/30/1933  02:00  CDT
 9/24/1933  02:00  CST
 4/29/1934  02:00  CDT
 9/30/1934  02:00  CST
 4/28/1935  02:00  CDT
 9/29/1935  02:00  CST
 3/01/1936  02:00  CDT
11/15/1936  02:00  CST
 4/25/1937  02:00  CDT
 9/26/1937  02:00  CST
 4/24/1938  02:00  CDT
 9/25/1938  02:00  CST
 4/30/1939  02:00  CDT
 9/24/1939  02:00  CST
 4/28/1940  02:00  CDT
 9/29/1940  02:00  CST
 4/27/1941  02:00  CDT
 9/28/1941  02:00  CST
 2/09/1942  02:00  CWT
 9/30/1945  02:00  CST
 4/28/1946  02:00  CDT
 9/29/1946  02:00  CST
```

TIME TABLES

4/27/1947 02:00 CDT
9/28/1947 02:00 CST
4/25/1948 02:00 CDT
9/26/1948 02:00 CST
4/24/1949 02:00 CDT
9/25/1949 02:00 CST
4/30/1950 02:00 CDT
9/24/1950 02:00 CST
4/29/1951 02:00 CDT
9/30/1951 02:00 CST
4/27/1952 02:00 CDT
9/28/1952 02:00 CST
4/26/1953 02:00 CDT
9/27/1953 02:00 CST
4/25/1954 02:00 CDT
9/26/1954 02:00 CST
4/24/1955 02:00 CDT
10/30/1955 02:00 CST
4/29/1956 02:00 CDT
10/28/1956 02:00 CST
4/28/1957 02:00 CDT
9/29/1957 02:00 CST
4/27/1958 02:00 US#1

IN # 13
Before 11/18/1883 LMT
11/18/1883 12:00 IN#2
4/28/1946 02:00 CDT
9/29/1946 02:00 CST
4/27/1947 02:00 CDT
9/28/1947 02:00 CST
4/25/1948 02:00 CDT
9/26/1948 02:00 CST
4/24/1949 02:00 CDT
9/25/1949 02:00 CST
4/30/1950 02:00 CDT
9/24/1950 02:00 CST
4/29/1951 02:00 CDT
9/30/1951 02:00 CST
4/27/1952 02:00 CDT
9/28/1952 02:00 CST
4/26/1953 02:00 CDT
9/27/1953 02:00 CST
4/25/1954 02:00 CDT
9/26/1954 02:00 CST
4/24/1955 02:00 CDT
10/30/1955 02:00 CST
4/29/1956 02:00 CDT
10/28/1956 02:00 CST
4/28/1957 02:00 CDT
9/29/1957 02:00 CST
4/27/1958 02:00 US#1

IN # 14
Before 11/18/1883 LMT
11/18/1883 12:00 IN#2
4/30/1922 02:00 CDT
9/24/1922 02:00 CST
4/29/1923 02:00 CDT
9/30/1923 02:00 CST
4/27/1924 02:00 CDT
9/28/1924 02:00 CST
4/26/1925 02:00 CDT
9/27/1925 02:00 CST
4/25/1926 02:00 CDT
9/26/1926 02:00 CST
4/24/1927 02:00 CDT
9/25/1927 02:00 CST
4/29/1928 02:00 CDT
9/30/1928 02:00 CST
4/28/1929 02:00 CDT
9/29/1929 02:00 CST
4/27/1930 02:00 CDT
9/28/1930 02:00 CST
4/26/1931 02:00 CDT
9/27/1931 02:00 CST
4/24/1932 02:00 CDT
9/25/1932 02:00 CST
4/30/1933 02:00 CDT
9/24/1933 02:00 CST
4/29/1934 02:00 CDT
9/30/1934 02:00 CST
4/28/1935 02:00 CDT
9/29/1935 02:00 CST
3/01/1936 02:00 CDT
11/15/1936 02:00 CST
4/25/1937 02:00 US#2

IN # 15
Before 11/18/1883 LMT
11/18/1883 12:00 IN#2
4/24/1932 02:00 CDT
9/25/1932 02:00 CST
2/09/1942 02:00 CWT
9/30/1945 02:00 CST
4/25/1948 02:00 CDT
9/26/1948 02:00 CST
4/27/1952 02:00 CDT
9/28/1952 02:00 CST
4/26/1953 02:00 CDT
9/27/1953 02:00 CST
4/25/1954 02:00 CDT
9/26/1954 02:00 CST
4/24/1955 02:00 CDT
10/30/1955 02:00 CST
4/29/1956 02:00 CDT
10/28/1956 02:00 CST
4/28/1957 02:00 CDT
9/29/1957 02:00 CST
4/27/1958 02:00 US#1

IN # 16
Before 11/18/1883 LMT
11/18/1883 12:00 IN#2
4/26/1931 02:00 CDT
9/27/1931 02:00 CST
4/30/1939 02:00 CDT
9/24/1939 02:00 CST
4/28/1940 02:00 CDT
9/29/1940 02:00 CST
4/27/1941 02:00 CDT
9/28/1941 02:00 CST
2/09/1942 02:00 CWT
9/30/1945 02:00 CST
4/28/1946 02:00 CDT
9/29/1946 02:00 CST
4/25/1948 02:00 CDT
9/26/1948 02:00 CST
4/27/1952 02:00 CDT
9/28/1952 02:00 CST
4/26/1953 02:00 CDT
9/27/1953 02:00 CST
4/25/1954 02:00 CDT
9/26/1954 02:00 CST
4/24/1955 02:00 CDT
10/30/1955 02:00 CST
4/29/1956 02:00 CDT
10/28/1956 02:00 CST
4/28/1957 02:00 CDT
9/29/1957 02:00 CST
4/27/1958 02:00 US#1

IN # 17
Before 11/18/1883 LMT
11/18/1883 12:00 CST
3/31/1918 02:00 CWT
10/27/1918 02:00 CST
3/30/1919 02:00 CWT
10/26/1919 02:00 CST
6/13/1920 02:00 CDT
10/31/1920 02:00 CST
3/27/1921 02:00 CDT
10/30/1921 02:00 CST
4/30/1922 02:00 CDT
9/24/1922 02:00 CST
4/29/1923 02:00 CDT
9/30/1923 02:00 CST
4/27/1924 02:00 CDT
9/28/1924 02:00 CST
4/26/1925 02:00 CDT
9/27/1925 02:00 CST
4/25/1926 02:00 CDT
9/26/1926 02:00 CST
4/24/1927 02:00 CDT
9/25/1927 02:00 CST
4/29/1928 02:00 CDT
9/30/1928 02:00 CST
4/28/1929 02:00 CDT
9/29/1929 02:00 CST
4/27/1930 02:00 CDT
9/28/1930 02:00 CST
4/26/1931 02:00 CDT
9/27/1931 02:00 CST
5/01/1932 02:00 CDT
11/01/1932 01:00 CST
4/30/1933 02:00 CDT
9/24/1933 02:00 CST
4/29/1934 02:00 CDT
9/30/1934 02:00 CST
4/28/1935 02:00 CDT
9/29/1935 02:00 CST
3/01/1936 02:00 CDT
11/15/1936 02:00 CST
4/25/1937 02:00 CDT
9/26/1937 02:00 CST
4/24/1938 02:00 CDT
9/25/1938 02:00 CST
4/30/1939 02:00 CDT
9/24/1939 02:00 CST
4/28/1940 02:00 CDT
9/29/1940 02:00 CST
4/27/1941 02:00 CDT
10/27/1941 02:00 US#2

IN # 18
Before 11/18/1883 LMT
11/18/1883 12:00 IN#2
4/24/1938 02:00 CDT
9/25/1938 02:00 CST
4/30/1939 02:00 CDT
9/24/1939 02:00 CST
4/28/1940 02:00 CDT
9/29/1940 02:00 CST
4/27/1941 02:00 CDT
9/28/1941 02:00 CST
2/09/1942 02:00 CWT
9/30/1945 02:00 CST
4/26/1953 02:00 CDT
9/27/1953 02:00 CST
4/25/1954 02:00 CDT
9/26/1954 02:00 CST
4/24/1955 02:00 CDT
10/30/1955 02:00 CST
4/29/1956 02:00 CDT
10/28/1956 02:00 CST
4/28/1957 02:00 CDT
9/29/1957 02:00 CST
4/27/1958 02:00 US#1

IN # 19
Before 11/18/1883 LMT
11/18/1883 12:00 IN#2
4/28/1940 02:00 CDT
9/29/1940 02:00 CST
4/27/1941 02:00 CDT
9/28/1941 02:00 CST
2/09/1942 02:00 CWT
9/30/1945 02:00 CST
4/26/1953 02:00 CDT
9/27/1953 02:00 CST
4/25/1954 02:00 CDT
9/26/1954 02:00 CST
4/24/1955 02:00 CDT
10/30/1955 02:00 CST
4/29/1956 02:00 CDT
10/28/1956 02:00 CST
4/28/1957 02:00 CDT
9/29/1957 02:00 CST
4/27/1958 02:00 US#1

IN # 20
Before 11/18/1883 LMT
11/18/1883 12:00 CST
3/31/1918 02:00 CWT
10/27/1918 02:00 CST
3/30/1919 02:00 CWT
10/26/1919 02:00 CST
6/13/1920 02:00 CDT
10/31/1920 02:00 CST
3/27/1921 02:00 CDT
10/30/1921 02:00 CST
4/30/1922 02:00 CDT
9/24/1922 02:00 CST
4/29/1923 02:00 CDT
9/30/1923 02:00 CST
4/27/1924 02:00 CDT
9/28/1924 02:00 CST
4/26/1925 02:00 CDT
9/27/1925 02:00 CST
4/25/1926 02:00 CDT
9/26/1926 02:00 CST
4/24/1927 02:00 CDT
9/25/1927 02:00 CST
4/29/1928 02:00 CDT
9/30/1928 02:00 CST
4/28/1929 02:00 CDT
9/29/1929 02:00 CST
4/27/1930 02:00 CDT
9/28/1930 02:00 CST
4/26/1931 02:00 CDT
9/27/1931 02:00 CST
4/24/1932 02:00 CDT
9/25/1932 02:00 CST
4/30/1933 02:00 CDT
10/01/1933 02:00 CST
4/29/1934 02:00 CDT
9/30/1934 02:00 CST
4/28/1935 02:00 CDT
9/29/1935 02:00 CST
3/01/1936 02:00 CDT
11/15/1936 02:00 CST
4/25/1937 02:00 US#2

IN # 21
Before 11/18/1883 LMT
11/18/1883 12:00 IN#2
4/24/1938 02:00 CDT
9/25/1938 02:00 CST
4/30/1939 02:00 CDT
9/24/1939 02:00 CST
4/28/1940 02:00 CDT
9/29/1940 02:00 CST
4/27/1941 02:00 CDT
9/28/1941 02:00 CST
2/09/1942 02:00 CWT
9/30/1945 02:00 CST
4/28/1946 02:00 CDT
9/29/1946 02:00 CST
4/27/1947 02:00 CDT
9/28/1947 02:00 CST
4/25/1948 02:00 CDT
9/26/1948 02:00 CST
4/24/1949 02:00 CDT
9/25/1949 02:00 CST
4/30/1950 02:00 CDT
9/24/1950 02:00 CST
4/29/1951 02:00 CDT
9/30/1951 02:00 CST
4/27/1952 02:00 CDT
9/28/1952 02:00 CST
4/26/1953 02:00 CDT
9/27/1953 02:00 CST
4/25/1954 02:00 CDT
9/26/1954 02:00 CST
4/24/1955 02:00 CDT
10/30/1955 02:00 CST
4/29/1956 02:00 CDT
10/28/1956 02:00 CST
4/28/1957 02:00 CDT
9/29/1957 02:00 CST
4/27/1958 02:00 US#1

IN # 22
Before 11/18/1883 LMT
11/18/1883 12:00 IN#2
4/24/1938 02:00 CDT
9/25/1938 02:00 CST
4/30/1939 02:00 CDT
9/24/1939 02:00 CST
4/28/1940 02:00 CDT
9/29/1940 02:00 CST
4/27/1941 02:00 CDT
9/28/1941 02:00 CST
2/09/1942 02:00 CWT
9/30/1945 02:00 CST
4/28/1946 02:00 CDT
9/29/1946 02:00 CST
4/25/1948 02:00 CDT
9/26/1948 02:00 CST
4/24/1955 02:00 CDT
10/30/1955 02:00 CST
4/29/1956 02:00 CDT
10/28/1956 02:00 CST
4/28/1957 02:00 CDT
9/29/1957 02:00 CST
4/27/1958 02:00 US#1

IN # 23
Before 11/18/1883 LMT
11/18/1883 12:00 IN#2
4/26/1931 02:00 CDT
9/27/1931 02:00 CST
4/24/1932 02:00 CDT
9/25/1932 02:00 CST
4/30/1933 02:00 CDT
9/24/1933 02:00 CST
4/29/1934 02:00 CDT
9/30/1934 02:00 CST
4/28/1935 02:00 CDT
9/29/1935 02:00 CST
3/01/1936 02:00 CDT
11/15/1936 02:00 CST
4/25/1937 02:00 US#2

IN # 24
Before 11/18/1883 LMT
11/18/1883 12:00 IN#2
4/28/1946 02:00 CDT
9/29/1946 02:00 CST
4/27/1947 02:00 CDT
9/28/1947 02:00 CST
4/25/1948 02:00 CDT
9/26/1948 02:00 CST
4/24/1949 02:00 CDT
9/25/1949 02:00 CST
4/30/1950 02:00 CDT
9/24/1950 02:00 CST
4/29/1951 02:00 CDT
9/30/1951 02:00 CST
4/27/1952 02:00 CDT
9/28/1952 02:00 CST
4/26/1953 02:00 CDT
9/27/1953 02:00 CST
4/25/1954 02:00 CDT
9/26/1954 02:00 CST
4/24/1955 02:00 CDT
10/30/1955 02:00 CST
4/29/1956 02:00 CDT
10/28/1956 02:00 CST
4/28/1957 02:00 CDT
9/29/1957 02:00 CST
4/27/1958 02:00 US#1

IN # 25
Before 11/18/1883 LMT
11/18/1883 12:00 CST
3/31/1918 02:00 CWT
10/27/1918 02:00 CST
3/30/1919 02:00 CWT
10/26/1919 02:00 CST
2/09/1942 02:00 CWT
9/30/1945 02:00 CST
4/28/1946 02:00 CDT
9/29/1946 02:00 CST
4/27/1947 02:00 CDT
9/28/1947 02:00 CST
4/25/1948 02:00 CDT
9/26/1948 02:00 CST
4/24/1955 02:00 CDT
10/30/1955 02:00 CST
4/29/1956 02:00 CDT
10/28/1956 02:00 CST
4/28/1957 02:00 CDT
9/29/1957 02:00 CST
4/27/1958 02:00 CDT
9/28/1958 02:00 CST
4/26/1959 02:00 CDT
9/27/1959 02:00 CST
4/24/1960 02:00 CDT
9/25/1960 02:00 CST
4/30/1961 02:00 US#1

IN # 26
Before 11/18/1883 LMT
11/18/1883 12:00 CST
3/31/1918 02:00 CWT
10/27/1918 02:00 CST
3/30/1919 02:00 CWT
10/26/1919 02:00 CST
2/09/1942 02:00 CWT
9/30/1945 02:00 CST
4/27/1947 02:00 CDT
9/28/1947 02:00 CST
4/25/1948 02:00 CDT
9/26/1948 02:00 CST
4/24/1955 02:00 CDT
10/30/1955 02:00 CST
4/29/1956 02:00 CDT
10/28/1956 02:00 CST
4/28/1957 02:00 CDT
9/29/1957 02:00 CST
4/27/1958 02:00 CDT
9/28/1958 02:00 CST
4/26/1959 02:00 CDT
9/27/1959 02:00 CST
4/24/1960 02:00 CDT
9/25/1960 02:00 CST
4/30/1961 02:00 US#1

IN # 27
Before 11/18/1883 LMT
11/18/1883 12:00 IN#2
4/30/1950 02:00 CDT
9/24/1950 02:00 CST
4/29/1951 02:00 CDT
9/30/1951 02:00 CST
4/27/1952 02:00 CDT
9/28/1952 02:00 CST
4/26/1953 02:00 CDT
9/27/1953 02:00 CST
4/25/1954 02:00 CDT
9/26/1954 02:00 CST
4/24/1955 02:00 CDT
10/30/1955 02:00 CST
4/29/1956 02:00 CDT
10/28/1956 02:00 CST
4/28/1957 02:00 CDT
9/29/1957 02:00 CST
4/27/1958 02:00 CDT
9/28/1958 02:00 CST
4/26/1959 02:00 CDT
9/27/1959 02:00 CST
4/24/1960 02:00 CDT
9/25/1960 02:00 CST
4/30/1961 02:00 US#1

IN # 28
Before 11/18/1883 LMT
11/18/1883 12:00 IN#2
4/25/1954 02:00 CDT
9/26/1954 02:00 CST
4/24/1955 02:00 CDT
10/30/1955 02:00 CST
4/29/1956 02:00 CDT
10/28/1956 02:00 CST
4/28/1957 02:00 CDT
9/29/1957 02:00 CST
4/27/1958 02:00 CDT
9/28/1958 02:00 CST
4/26/1959 02:00 CDT
9/27/1959 02:00 CST
4/24/1960 02:00 CDT
9/25/1960 02:00 CST
4/30/1961 02:00 US#1

IN # 29
Before 11/18/1883 LMT
11/18/1883 12:00 IN#2
4/26/1953 02:00 CDT
9/27/1953 02:00 CST
4/25/1954 02:00 CDT
9/26/1954 02:00 CST
4/24/1955 02:00 CDT
10/30/1955 02:00 CST
4/29/1956 02:00 CDT
10/28/1956 02:00 CST
4/28/1957 02:00 CDT
9/29/1957 02:00 CST
4/27/1958 02:00 CDT
9/28/1958 02:00 CST
4/26/1959 02:00 CDT
9/27/1959 02:00 CST
4/24/1960 02:00 CDT
9/25/1960 02:00 CST
4/30/1961 02:00 US#1

IN # 30
Before 11/18/1883 LMT
11/18/1883 12:00 CST
3/31/1918 02:00 CWT
10/27/1918 02:00 CST
3/30/1919 02:00 CWT
10/26/1919 02:00 CST
2/09/1942 02:00 CWT
9/30/1945 02:00 CST
4/25/1954 02:00 EST
4/27/1969 02:00 EDT
10/26/1969 02:00 EST
4/26/1970 02:00 EDT
10/25/1970 02:00 EST

IN # 31
Before 11/18/1883 LMT
11/18/1883 12:00 CST
3/31/1918 02:00 CWT
10/27/1918 02:00 CST
3/30/1919 02:00 CWT
10/26/1919 02:00 CST
4/30/1933 02:00 CDT
9/24/1933 02:00 CST
5/05/1934 02:00 CDT
10/01/1934 02:00 CST
4/28/1935 02:00 CDT
9/01/1935 02:00 CST
4/26/1936 02:00 CDT
8/29/1936 02:00 CST
4/25/1937 02:00 CDT
8/28/1937 02:00 CST
4/24/1938 02:00 CDT
9/25/1938 02:00 CST
4/30/1939 02:00 CDT
10/01/1939 02:00 CST
4/28/1940 02:00 CDT
9/29/1940 02:00 CST
4/27/1941 02:00 CDT
9/28/1941 02:00 CST
2/09/1942 02:00 CWT
9/30/1945 02:00 CST
4/27/1947 02:00 CDT
9/28/1947 02:00 CST
4/25/1948 02:00 CDT
9/26/1948 02:00 CST
4/24/1949 02:00 CDT
9/25/1949 02:00 CST
4/30/1950 02:00 CDT
9/24/1950 02:00 CST
4/29/1951 02:00 CDT
9/30/1951 02:00 CST
4/27/1952 02:00 CDT
9/28/1952 02:00 CST

TIME TABLES

4/26/1953 02:00 CDT
9/27/1953 02:00 CST
4/25/1954 02:00 EST
4/27/1969 02:00 EDT
10/26/1969 02:00 EST
4/26/1970 02:00 EDT
10/25/1970 02:00 EST

IN # 32
Before 11/18/1883 LMT
11/18/1883 12:00 CST
3/31/1918 02:00 CWT
10/27/1918 02:00 CST
3/30/1919 02:00 CWT
10/26/1919 02:00 CST
4/27/1941 02:00 CDT
9/28/1941 02:00 CST
2/09/1942 02:00 CWT
9/30/1945 02:00 CST
4/25/1954 02:00 EST
4/27/1969 02:00 EDT
10/26/1969 02:00 EST
4/26/1970 02:00 EDT
10/25/1970 02:00 EST

IN # 33
Before 11/18/1883 LMT
11/18/1883 12:00 CST
3/31/1918 02:00 CWT
10/27/1918 02:00 CST
3/30/1919 02:00 CWT
10/26/1919 02:00 CST
2/09/1942 02:00 CWT
9/30/1945 02:00 CST
4/25/1954 02:00 EST
4/28/1968 02:00 US#1

IN # 34
Before 11/18/1883 LMT
11/18/1883 12:00 CST
3/31/1918 02:00 CWT
10/27/1918 02:00 CST
3/30/1919 02:00 CWT
10/26/1919 02:00 CST
4/28/1940 02:00 CDT
9/02/1940 02:00 CST
4/27/1941 02:00 CDT
9/28/1941 02:00 CST
2/09/1942 02:00 CWT
9/30/1945 02:00 CST
4/28/1946 02:00 CDT
9/29/1946 02:00 CST
4/27/1947 02:00 CDT
9/28/1947 02:00 CST
4/25/1948 02:00 CDT
9/26/1948 02:00 CST
4/24/1949 02:00 CDT
9/25/1949 02:00 CST
4/30/1950 02:00 CDT
9/24/1950 02:00 CST
4/29/1951 02:00 CDT
9/30/1951 02:00 CST
4/27/1952 02:00 CDT
9/28/1952 02:00 CST
4/26/1953 02:00 CDT
9/27/1953 02:00 CST
4/25/1954 02:00 EST
4/27/1969 02:00 EDT
10/26/1969 02:00 EST
4/26/1970 02:00 EDT
10/25/1970 02:00 EST

IN # 35
Before 11/18/1883 LMT
11/18/1883 12:00 CST
3/31/1918 02:00 CWT
10/27/1918 02:00 CST
3/30/1919 02:00 CWT
10/26/1919 02:00 CST
2/09/1942 02:00 CWT
9/30/1945 02:00 CST
4/25/1954 02:00 EST
4/27/1969 02:00 EDT
10/26/1969 02:00 EST
4/26/1970 02:00 EDT
10/25/1970 02:00 EST
4/25/1971 02:00 EDT
10/31/1971 02:00 EST
4/30/1972 02:00 EDT
10/29/1972 02:00 EST

IN # 36
Before 11/18/1883 LMT
11/18/1883 12:00 CST
3/31/1918 02:00 CWT
10/27/1918 02:00 CST
3/30/1919 02:00 CWT
10/26/1919 02:00 CST
2/09/1942 02:00 CWT
9/30/1945 02:00 CST
4/26/1953 02:00 CDT
9/27/1953 02:00 CST
4/25/1954 02:00 EST
4/27/1969 02:00 EDT
10/26/1969 02:00 EST
4/26/1970 02:00 EDT
10/25/1970 02:00 EST

IN # 37
Before 11/18/1883 LMT
11/18/1883 12:00 CST
3/31/1918 02:00 CWT
10/27/1918 02:00 CST
3/30/1919 02:00 CWT
10/26/1919 02:00 CST
2/09/1942 02:00 CWT
9/30/1945 02:00 CST
4/27/1947 02:00 CDT
9/28/1947 02:00 CST
4/25/1948 02:00 CDT
9/26/1948 02:00 CST
4/24/1949 02:00 CDT
9/25/1949 02:00 CST
4/30/1950 02:00 CDT
9/24/1950 02:00 CST
4/29/1951 02:00 CDT
9/30/1951 02:00 CST
4/27/1952 02:00 CDT
9/28/1952 02:00 CST
4/26/1953 02:00 CDT
9/27/1953 02:00 CST
4/25/1954 02:00 EST
4/30/1967 02:00 US#1

IN # 38
Before 11/18/1883 LMT
11/18/1883 12:00 CST
3/31/1918 02:00 CWT
10/27/1918 02:00 CST
3/30/1919 02:00 CWT
10/26/1919 02:00 CST
2/09/1942 02:00 CWT
9/30/1945 02:00 CST
4/24/1949 02:00 CDT
9/25/1949 02:00 CST
4/30/1950 02:00 CDT
9/24/1950 02:00 CST
4/29/1951 02:00 CDT
9/30/1951 02:00 CST
4/27/1952 02:00 CDT
9/28/1952 02:00 CST
4/26/1953 02:00 CDT
9/27/1953 02:00 CST
4/25/1954 02:00 EST
4/30/1967 02:00 US#1

IN # 39
Before 11/18/1883 LMT
11/18/1883 12:00 CST
3/31/1918 02:00 CWT
10/27/1918 02:00 CST
3/30/1919 02:00 CWT
10/26/1919 02:00 CST
4/30/1933 02:00 CDT
9/24/1933 02:00 CST
4/26/1936 02:00 CDT
9/27/1936 02:00 CST
5/02/1937 02:00 CDT
10/01/1937 02:00 CST
4/24/1938 02:00 CDT
9/25/1938 02:00 CST
4/30/1939 02:00 CDT
9/24/1939 02:00 CST
4/28/1940 02:00 CDT
9/29/1940 02:00 CST
2/09/1942 02:00 CWT
9/30/1945 02:00 CST
4/27/1947 02:00 CDT
9/28/1947 02:00 CST
4/25/1948 02:00 CDT
9/26/1948 02:00 CST
4/24/1949 02:00 CDT
9/25/1949 02:00 CST
4/30/1950 02:00 CDT
9/24/1950 02:00 CST
4/29/1951 02:00 CDT
9/30/1951 02:00 CST
4/27/1952 02:00 CDT
9/28/1952 02:00 CST
4/26/1953 02:00 CDT
9/27/1953 02:00 CST
4/25/1954 02:00 EST
4/27/1969 02:00 EDT
10/26/1969 02:00 EST
4/26/1970 02:00 EDT
10/25/1970 02:00 EST

IN # 40
Before 11/18/1883 LMT
11/18/1883 12:00 CST
3/31/1918 02:00 CWT
10/27/1918 02:00 CST
3/30/1919 02:00 CWT
10/26/1919 02:00 CST
4/26/1931 00:01 CDT
9/27/1931 00:01 CST
4/24/1932 00:01 CDT
9/25/1932 00:01 CST
4/30/1933 00:01 CDT
10/01/1933 00:01 CST
4/29/1934 00:01 CDT
9/30/1934 00:01 CST
4/28/1935 00:01 CDT
9/29/1935 00:01 CST
4/26/1936 02:00 CDT
9/27/1936 02:00 CST
4/25/1937 02:00 CDT
9/26/1937 02:00 CST
4/24/1938 02:00 CDT
9/25/1938 02:00 CST
4/30/1939 02:00 CDT
9/24/1939 02:00 CST
4/28/1940 02:00 CDT
9/29/1940 02:00 CST
4/27/1941 02:00 CDT
9/28/1941 02:00 CST
2/09/1942 02:00 CWT
9/30/1945 02:00 CST
4/28/1946 02:00 CDT
9/29/1946 02:00 CST
4/27/1947 02:00 CDT
9/28/1947 02:00 CST
4/25/1948 02:00 CDT
9/26/1948 02:00 CST
4/24/1949 02:00 CDT
9/25/1949 02:00 CST
4/30/1950 02:00 CDT
9/24/1950 02:00 CST
4/29/1951 02:00 CDT
9/30/1951 02:00 CST
4/27/1952 02:00 CDT
9/28/1952 02:00 CST
4/26/1953 02:00 CDT
9/27/1953 02:00 CST
4/25/1954 02:00 EST
4/27/1969 02:00 EDT
10/26/1969 02:00 EST
4/26/1970 02:00 EDT
10/25/1970 02:00 EST

IN # 41
Before 11/18/1883 LMT
11/18/1883 12:00 CST
3/31/1918 02:00 CWT
10/27/1918 02:00 CST
3/30/1919 02:00 CWT
10/26/1919 02:00 CST
4/28/1935 02:00 CDT
9/29/1935 02:00 CST
4/26/1936 02:00 CDT
9/27/1936 02:00 CST
4/25/1937 02:00 CDT
9/26/1937 02:00 CST
4/24/1938 02:00 CDT
9/11/1938 02:00 CST
5/01/1939 02:00 CDT
9/01/1939 02:00 CST
4/27/1941 02:00 CDT
11/23/1941 02:00 CST
2/09/1942 02:00 CWT
9/30/1945 02:00 CST
4/26/1953 02:00 CDT
9/27/1953 02:00 CST
4/25/1954 02:00 EST
4/27/1969 02:00 EDT
10/26/1969 02:00 EST
4/26/1970 02:00 EDT
10/25/1970 02:00 EST

IN # 42
Before 11/18/1883 LMT
11/18/1883 12:00 CST
3/31/1918 02:00 CWT
10/27/1918 02:00 CST
3/30/1919 02:00 CWT
10/26/1919 02:00 CST
4/28/1940 02:00 CDT
9/29/1940 02:00 CST
5/04/1941 00:01 CDT
9/01/1941 00:01 CST
2/09/1942 02:00 CWT
9/30/1945 02:00 CST
4/27/1947 02:00 CDT
9/28/1947 02:00 CST
4/25/1954 02:00 EST
4/27/1969 02:00 EDT
10/26/1969 02:00 EST
4/26/1970 02:00 EDT
10/25/1970 02:00 EST

IN # 43
Before 11/18/1883 LMT
11/18/1883 12:00 CST
3/31/1918 02:00 CWT
10/27/1918 02:00 CST
3/30/1919 02:00 CWT
10/26/1919 02:00 CST
4/24/1938 02:00 CDT
9/04/1938 02:00 CST
5/13/1939 02:00 CDT
10/01/1939 02:00 CST
4/27/1941 02:00 CDT
10/26/1941 02:00 CST
2/09/1942 02:00 CWT
9/30/1945 02:00 CST
4/28/1946 02:00 CDT
9/29/1946 02:00 CST
4/27/1947 02:00 CDT
9/28/1947 02:00 CST
4/25/1948 02:00 CDT
9/26/1948 02:00 CST
4/26/1953 02:00 CDT
9/27/1953 02:00 CST
4/25/1954 02:00 EST
4/27/1969 02:00 EDT
10/26/1969 02:00 EST
4/26/1970 02:00 EDT
10/25/1970 02:00 EST

IN # 44
Before 11/18/1883 LMT
11/18/1883 12:00 CST
3/31/1918 02:00 CWT
10/27/1918 02:00 CST
3/30/1919 02:00 CWT
10/26/1919 02:00 CST
4/29/1939 02:00 CDT
9/01/1939 02:00 CST
4/28/1940 02:00 CDT
9/02/1940 02:00 CST
4/27/1941 02:00 CDT
9/28/1941 02:00 CST
2/09/1942 02:00 CWT
9/30/1945 02:00 CST
4/28/1946 02:00 CDT
9/29/1946 02:00 CST
4/27/1947 02:00 CDT
9/28/1947 02:00 CST
4/25/1948 02:00 CDT
9/26/1948 02:00 CST
4/24/1949 02:00 CDT
9/25/1949 02:00 CST
4/30/1950 02:00 CDT
9/24/1950 02:00 CST
4/29/1951 02:00 CDT
9/30/1951 02:00 CST
4/27/1952 02:00 CDT
9/28/1952 02:00 CST
4/26/1953 02:00 CDT
9/27/1953 02:00 CST
4/25/1954 02:00 EST
4/27/1969 02:00 EDT
10/26/1969 02:00 EST
4/26/1970 02:00 EDT
10/25/1970 02:00 EST

IN # 45
Before 11/18/1883 LMT
11/18/1883 12:00 CST
3/31/1918 02:00 CWT
10/27/1918 02:00 CST
3/30/1919 02:00 CWT
10/26/1919 02:00 CST
4/28/1935 02:00 CDT
9/29/1935 02:00 CST
4/26/1936 02:00 CDT
9/27/1936 02:00 CST
4/25/1937 02:00 CDT
9/26/1937 02:00 CST
4/24/1938 02:00 CDT
9/25/1938 02:00 CST
4/30/1939 02:00 CDT
10/01/1939 02:00 CST
4/28/1940 02:00 CDT
9/29/1940 02:00 CST
4/27/1941 02:00 CDT
9/28/1941 02:00 CST
2/09/1942 02:00 CWT
9/30/1945 02:00 CST
4/25/1954 02:00 EST
4/27/1969 02:00 EDT
10/26/1969 02:00 EST
4/26/1970 02:00 EDT
10/25/1970 02:00 EST

IN # 46
Before 11/18/1883 LMT
11/18/1883 12:00 CST
3/31/1918 02:00 CWT
10/27/1918 02:00 CST
3/30/1919 02:00 CWT
10/26/1919 02:00 CST
4/25/1937 02:00 CDT
9/26/1937 02:00 CST
4/24/1938 02:00 CDT
9/25/1938 02:00 CST
4/30/1939 02:00 CDT
9/24/1939 02:00 CST
2/09/1942 02:00 CWT
9/30/1945 02:00 CST
4/28/1946 02:00 CDT
9/29/1946 02:00 CST
4/26/1953 02:00 CDT
9/27/1953 02:00 CST
4/25/1954 02:00 EST
4/27/1969 02:00 EDT
10/26/1969 02:00 EST
4/26/1970 02:00 EDT
10/25/1970 02:00 EST

IN # 47
Before 11/18/1883 LMT
11/18/1883 12:00 CST
3/31/1918 02:00 CWT
10/27/1918 02:00 CST
3/30/1919 02:00 CWT
10/26/1919 02:00 CST
4/28/1940 02:00 CDT
9/29/1940 02:00 CST
4/27/1941 02:00 CDT
9/28/1941 02:00 CST
2/09/1942 02:00 CWT
9/30/1945 02:00 CST
4/28/1946 02:00 CDT
9/29/1946 02:00 CST
4/27/1947 02:00 CDT
9/28/1947 02:00 CST
4/25/1948 02:00 CDT
9/26/1948 02:00 CST
4/24/1949 02:00 CDT
9/25/1949 02:00 CST
4/30/1950 02:00 CDT
9/24/1950 02:00 CST
4/29/1951 02:00 CDT
9/30/1951 02:00 CST
4/27/1952 02:00 CDT
9/28/1952 02:00 CST
4/26/1953 02:00 CDT
9/27/1953 02:00 CST
4/25/1954 02:00 EST
4/27/1969 02:00 EDT
10/26/1969 02:00 EST
4/26/1970 02:00 EDT
10/25/1970 02:00 EST

IN # 48
Before 11/18/1883 LMT
11/18/1883 12:00 CST
3/31/1918 02:00 CWT
10/27/1918 02:00 CST
3/30/1919 02:00 CWT
10/26/1919 02:00 CST
4/24/1938 02:00 CDT
9/25/1938 02:00 CST
4/30/1939 02:00 CDT
9/24/1939 02:00 CST
4/28/1940 02:00 CDT
9/29/1940 02:00 CST
4/27/1941 02:00 CDT
9/28/1941 02:00 CST
2/09/1942 02:00 CWT
9/30/1945 02:00 CST
4/27/1947 02:00 CDT
9/28/1947 02:00 CST
4/25/1948 02:00 CDT
9/26/1948 02:00 CST
4/26/1953 02:00 CDT
9/27/1953 02:00 CST
4/25/1954 02:00 EST
4/27/1969 02:00 EDT
10/26/1969 02:00 EST
4/26/1970 02:00 EDT
10/25/1970 02:00 EST

IN # 49
Before 11/18/1883 LMT
11/18/1883 12:00 CST
3/31/1918 02:00 CWT
10/27/1918 02:00 CST
3/30/1919 02:00 CWT
10/26/1919 02:00 CST
6/01/1937 02:00 CDT
9/01/1937 02:00 CST
5/15/1938 02:00 CDT
9/01/1938 02:00 CST
6/01/1939 02:00 CDT
9/01/1939 02:00 CST
4/28/1940 02:00 CDT
9/29/1940 02:00 CST
4/27/1941 02:00 CDT
9/28/1941 02:00 CST
2/09/1942 02:00 CWT
9/30/1945 02:00 CST
4/25/1954 02:00 EST
4/27/1969 02:00 EDT
10/26/1969 02:00 EST
4/26/1970 02:00 EDT
10/25/1970 02:00 EST

IN # 50
Before 11/18/1883 LMT
11/18/1883 12:00 CST
3/31/1918 02:00 CWT
10/27/1918 02:00 CST
3/30/1919 02:00 CWT
10/26/1919 02:00 CST
4/24/1938 02:00 CDT
9/25/1938 02:00 CST
4/30/1939 02:00 CDT
9/24/1939 02:00 CST
4/28/1940 02:00 CDT
9/29/1940 02:00 CST
4/27/1941 02:00 CDT
9/28/1941 02:00 CST
2/09/1942 02:00 CWT
9/30/1945 02:00 CST
4/25/1954 02:00 EST
4/27/1969 02:00 EDT
10/26/1969 02:00 EST
4/26/1970 02:00 EDT
10/25/1970 02:00 EST

IN # 51
Before 11/18/1883 LMT
11/18/1883 12:00 CST
3/31/1918 02:00 CWT
10/27/1918 02:00 CST
3/30/1919 02:00 CWT
10/26/1919 02:00 CST
2/09/1942 02:00 CWT
9/30/1945 02:00 CST
4/25/1954 02:00 EST
4/30/1967 02:00 US#1

IN # 52
Before 11/18/1883 LMT
11/18/1883 12:00 CST
3/31/1918 02:00 CWT
10/27/1918 02:00 CST
3/30/1919 02:00 CWT
10/26/1919 02:00 CST
2/09/1942 02:00 CWT
9/30/1945 02:00 CST
4/26/1953 02:00 CDT
9/27/1953 02:00 CST
4/25/1954 02:00 CDT
9/26/1954 02:00 CST
4/24/1955 02:00 CDT
9/25/1955 02:00 CST
4/29/1956 02:00 CDT
9/30/1956 02:00 CST
4/28/1957 02:00 CDT
9/29/1957 02:00 CST
4/27/1958 02:00 CDT
9/28/1958 02:00 CST

TIME TABLES

Date	Time	Zone
4/26/1959	02:00	CDT
9/27/1959	02:00	CST
4/24/1960	02:00	CDT
9/25/1960	02:00	CST
4/30/1961	02:00	CDT
10/29/1961	02:00	CST
4/29/1962	02:00	CDT
10/28/1962	02:00	CST
4/28/1963	02:00	CDT
10/27/1963	02:00	CST
4/26/1964	02:00	CDT
10/25/1964	02:00	CST
4/25/1965	02:00	EST
10/30/1966	02:00	CST
4/30/1967	02:00	US#1

IN # 53

Date	Time	Zone
Before 11/18/1883		LMT
11/18/1883	12:00	CST
3/31/1918	02:00	CWT
10/27/1918	02:00	CST
3/30/1919	02:00	CWT
10/26/1919	02:00	CST
2/09/1942	02:00	CWT
9/30/1945	02:00	CST
4/24/1955	02:00	CDT
9/25/1955	02:00	CST
4/29/1956	02:00	CDT
9/30/1956	02:00	CST
4/28/1957	02:00	CDT
9/29/1957	02:00	CST
4/27/1958	02:00	CDT
9/28/1958	02:00	CST
4/26/1959	02:00	CDT
9/27/1959	02:00	CST
4/24/1960	02:00	CDT
9/25/1960	02:00	CST
4/30/1961	02:00	CDT
10/29/1961	02:00	CST
4/29/1962	02:00	CDT
10/28/1962	02:00	CST
4/28/1963	02:00	CDT
10/27/1963	02:00	CST
4/26/1964	02:00	CDT
10/25/1964	02:00	CST
4/25/1965	02:00	EST
10/30/1966	02:00	CST
4/30/1967	02:00	US#1

IN # 54

Date	Time	Zone
Before 11/18/1883		LMT
11/18/1883	12:00	CST
3/31/1918	02:00	CWT
10/27/1918	02:00	CST
3/30/1919	02:00	CWT
10/26/1919	02:00	CST
2/09/1942	02:00	CWT
9/30/1945	02:00	CST
4/26/1953	02:00	CDT
9/27/1953	02:00	CST
4/25/1954	02:00	CDT
9/26/1954	02:00	CST
5/01/1955	00:00	CDT
9/04/1955	00:00	CST
4/29/1956	02:00	CDT
9/02/1956	02:00	CST
4/28/1957	02:00	CDT
9/29/1957	02:00	CST
4/27/1958	02:00	CDT
9/28/1958	02:00	CST
4/26/1959	02:00	CDT
9/27/1959	02:00	CST
4/24/1960	02:00	CDT
9/25/1960	02:00	CST
4/30/1961	02:00	CDT
10/29/1961	02:00	CST
4/29/1962	02:00	CDT
10/28/1962	02:00	CST
4/28/1963	02:00	CDT
10/27/1963	02:00	CST
4/26/1964	02:00	CDT
10/25/1964	02:00	CST
4/25/1965	02:00	EST
10/30/1966	02:00	CST
4/30/1967	02:00	US#1

IN # 55

Date	Time	Zone
Before 11/18/1883		LMT
11/18/1883	12:00	CST
3/31/1918	02:00	CWT
10/27/1918	02:00	CST
3/30/1919	02:00	CWT
10/26/1919	02:00	CST
2/09/1942	02:00	CWT
9/30/1945	02:00	CST
5/02/1948	02:00	CDT
10/26/1948	02:00	CST
4/29/1951	02:00	CDT
9/30/1951	02:00	CST
4/24/1955	02:00	CDT
9/25/1955	02:00	CST
4/29/1956	02:00	CDT
9/30/1956	02:00	CST
4/28/1957	02:00	CDT
9/29/1957	02:00	CST
4/27/1958	02:00	CDT
10/26/1958	02:00	CST
4/26/1959	02:00	CDT
9/27/1959	02:00	CST
4/24/1960	02:00	CDT
9/25/1960	02:00	CST
4/30/1961	02:00	CDT
9/24/1961	02:00	CST
4/29/1962	02:00	CDT
10/28/1962	02:00	CST
4/28/1963	02:00	CDT
10/27/1963	02:00	CST
4/26/1964	02:00	CDT
10/25/1964	02:00	CST
4/25/1965	02:00	EST
10/30/1966	02:00	CST
4/30/1967	02:00	US#1

IN # 56

Date	Time	Zone
Before 11/18/1883		LMT
11/18/1883	12:00	CST
3/31/1918	02:00	CWT
10/27/1918	02:00	CST
3/30/1919	02:00	CWT
10/26/1919	02:00	CST
2/09/1942	02:00	CWT
9/30/1945	02:00	CST
5/01/1955	00:00	CDT
9/25/1955	02:00	CST
4/29/1956	02:00	CDT
9/30/1956	02:00	CST
4/28/1957	02:00	CDT
9/29/1957	02:00	CST
4/27/1958	02:00	CDT
10/01/1958	02:00	CST
4/26/1959	02:00	CDT
9/27/1959	02:00	CST
4/24/1960	02:00	CDT
9/25/1960	02:00	CST
4/30/1961	02:00	CDT
10/29/1961	02:00	CST
4/29/1962	02:00	CDT
10/28/1962	02:00	CST
4/28/1963	02:00	CDT
10/27/1963	02:00	CST
4/26/1964	02:00	CDT
10/25/1964	02:00	CST
4/25/1965	02:00	EST
10/30/1966	02:00	CST
4/30/1967	02:00	US#1

IN # 57

Date	Time	Zone
Before 11/18/1883		LMT
11/18/1883	12:00	CST
3/31/1918	02:00	CWT
10/27/1918	02:00	CST
3/30/1919	02:00	CWT
10/26/1919	02:00	CST
2/09/1942	02:00	CWT
9/30/1945	02:00	CST
5/01/1955	02:00	CDT
9/25/1955	02:00	CST
5/01/1956	02:00	CDT
9/25/1956	02:00	CST
4/28/1957	02:00	CDT
9/29/1957	02:00	CST
4/27/1958	02:00	CDT
9/28/1958	02:00	CST
4/26/1959	02:00	CDT
9/27/1959	02:00	CST
4/24/1960	02:00	CDT
9/25/1960	02:00	CST
4/30/1961	02:00	CDT
10/29/1961	02:00	CST
4/29/1962	02:00	CDT
10/28/1962	02:00	CST
4/28/1963	02:00	CDT
10/27/1963	02:00	CST
4/26/1964	02:00	CDT
10/25/1964	02:00	CST
4/25/1965	02:00	EST
10/30/1966	02:00	CST
4/30/1967	02:00	US#1

IN # 58

Date	Time	Zone
Before 11/18/1883		LMT
11/18/1883	12:00	CST
3/31/1918	02:00	CWT
10/27/1918	02:00	CST
3/30/1919	02:00	CWT
10/26/1919	02:00	CST
2/09/1942	02:00	CWT
9/30/1945	02:00	CST
4/24/1955	02:00	CDT
9/25/1955	02:00	CST
4/29/1956	02:00	CDT
10/28/1956	02:00	CST
4/28/1957	02:00	CDT
9/29/1957	02:00	CST
4/27/1958	02:00	CDT
9/28/1958	02:00	CST
4/26/1959	02:00	CDT
9/27/1959	02:00	CST
4/24/1960	02:00	CDT
9/25/1960	02:00	CST
4/30/1961	02:00	CDT
10/29/1961	02:00	CST
4/29/1962	02:00	CDT
10/28/1962	02:00	CST
4/28/1963	02:00	CDT
10/27/1963	02:00	CST
4/26/1964	02:00	CDT
10/25/1964	02:00	CST
4/25/1965	02:00	EST
10/30/1966	02:00	CST
4/30/1967	02:00	US#1

IN # 59

Date	Time	Zone
Before 11/18/1883		LMT
11/18/1883	12:00	CST
3/31/1918	02:00	CWT
10/27/1918	02:00	CST
3/30/1919	02:00	CWT
10/26/1919	02:00	CST
2/09/1942	02:00	CWT
9/30/1945	02:00	CST
5/01/1955	00:00	CDT
9/25/1955	02:00	CST
4/29/1956	02:00	CDT
9/30/1956	02:00	CST
4/28/1957	02:00	CDT
9/29/1957	02:00	CST
4/27/1958	02:00	CDT
9/28/1958	02:00	CST
4/26/1959	02:00	CDT
9/27/1959	02:00	CST
4/24/1960	02:00	CDT
9/25/1960	02:00	CST
4/30/1961	02:00	CDT
10/29/1961	02:00	CST
4/29/1962	02:00	CDT
10/28/1962	02:00	CST
4/28/1963	02:00	CDT
10/27/1963	02:00	CST
4/26/1964	02:00	CDT
10/25/1964	02:00	CST
4/25/1965	02:00	EST
10/30/1966	02:00	CST
4/30/1967	02:00	US#1

IN # 60

Date	Time	Zone
Before 11/18/1883		LMT
11/18/1883	12:00	CST
3/31/1918	02:00	CWT
10/27/1918	02:00	CST
3/30/1919	02:00	CWT
10/26/1919	02:00	CST
2/09/1942	02:00	CWT
9/30/1945	02:00	CST
5/01/1955	00:00	CDT
9/25/1955	02:00	CST
4/29/1956	02:00	CDT
10/28/1956	02:00	CST
4/28/1957	02:00	CDT
9/29/1957	02:00	CST
4/27/1958	02:00	CDT
9/28/1958	02:00	CST
4/26/1959	02:00	CDT
9/27/1959	02:00	CST
4/24/1960	02:00	CDT
9/25/1960	02:00	CST
4/30/1961	02:00	CDT
10/29/1961	02:00	CST
4/29/1962	02:00	CDT
10/28/1962	02:00	CST
4/28/1963	02:00	CDT
10/27/1963	02:00	CST
4/26/1964	02:00	CDT
10/25/1964	02:00	CST
4/25/1965	02:00	EST
10/30/1966	02:00	CST
4/30/1967	02:00	US#1

IN # 61

Date	Time	Zone
Before 11/18/1883		LMT
11/18/1883	12:00	CST
3/31/1918	02:00	CWT
10/27/1918	02:00	CST
3/30/1919	02:00	CWT
10/26/1919	02:00	CST
2/09/1942	02:00	CWT
9/30/1945	02:00	CST
5/01/1955	00:00	CDT
8/28/1955	00:00	CST
4/29/1956	02:00	CDT
9/30/1956	02:00	CST
4/28/1957	02:00	CDT
9/29/1957	02:00	CST
4/27/1958	02:00	CDT
9/28/1958	02:00	CST
4/26/1959	02:00	CDT
9/27/1959	02:00	CST
4/24/1960	02:00	CDT
9/25/1960	02:00	CST
4/30/1961	02:00	CDT
10/29/1961	02:00	CST
4/29/1962	02:00	CDT
10/28/1962	02:00	CST
4/28/1963	02:00	CDT
10/27/1963	02:00	CST
4/26/1964	02:00	CDT
10/25/1964	02:00	CST
4/25/1965	02:00	EST
10/30/1966	02:00	CST
4/30/1967	02:00	US#1

IN # 62

Date	Time	Zone
Before 11/18/1883		LMT
11/18/1883	12:00	CST
3/31/1918	02:00	CWT
10/27/1918	02:00	CST
3/30/1919	02:00	CWT
10/26/1919	02:00	CST
2/09/1942	02:00	CWT
9/30/1945	02:00	CST
5/01/1955	00:00	CDT
8/29/1955	00:00	CST
4/29/1956	02:00	CDT
9/30/1956	02:00	CST
4/28/1957	02:00	CDT
9/29/1957	02:00	CST
4/27/1958	02:00	CDT
9/28/1958	02:00	CST
4/26/1959	02:00	CDT
9/27/1959	02:00	CST
4/24/1960	02:00	CDT
9/25/1960	02:00	CST
4/30/1961	02:00	CDT
10/29/1961	02:00	CST
4/29/1962	02:00	CDT
10/28/1962	02:00	CST
4/28/1963	02:00	CDT
10/27/1963	02:00	CST
4/26/1964	02:00	CDT
10/25/1964	02:00	CST
4/25/1965	02:00	EST
10/30/1966	02:00	CST
4/30/1967	02:00	US#1

IN # 63

Date	Time	Zone
Before 11/18/1883		LMT
11/18/1883	12:00	CST
3/31/1918	02:00	CWT
10/27/1918	02:00	CST
3/30/1919	02:00	CWT
10/26/1919	02:00	CST
2/09/1942	02:00	CWT
9/30/1945	02:00	CST
4/24/1955	02:00	CDT
9/25/1955	02:00	CST
4/29/1956	02:00	CDT
9/30/1956	02:00	CST
4/28/1957	02:00	CDT
9/29/1957	02:00	CST
4/27/1958	02:00	CDT
9/28/1958	02:00	CST
4/26/1959	02:00	CDT
9/27/1959	02:00	CST
4/24/1960	02:00	CDT
9/25/1960	02:00	CST
4/30/1961	02:00	CDT
10/29/1961	02:00	CST
4/29/1962	02:00	CDT
10/28/1962	02:00	CST
4/28/1963	02:00	CDT
10/27/1963	02:00	CST
4/26/1964	02:00	EST
10/30/1966	02:00	CST
4/30/1967	02:00	US#1

IN # 64

Date	Time	Zone
Before 11/18/1883		LMT
11/18/1883	12:00	CST
3/31/1918	02:00	CWT
10/27/1918	02:00	CST
3/30/1919	02:00	CWT
10/26/1919	02:00	CST
2/09/1942	02:00	CWT
9/30/1945	02:00	CST
5/01/1955	00:00	CDT
8/28/1955	00:00	CST
4/29/1956	02:00	CDT
9/30/1956	02:00	CST
4/28/1957	02:00	CDT
9/29/1957	02:00	CST
4/27/1958	02:00	CDT
9/28/1958	02:00	CST
4/26/1959	02:00	CDT
9/27/1959	02:00	CST
4/24/1960	02:00	CDT
9/25/1960	02:00	CST
4/30/1961	02:00	CDT
10/29/1961	02:00	CST
4/29/1962	02:00	CDT
10/28/1962	02:00	CST
4/28/1963	02:00	CDT
10/27/1963	02:00	CST
4/26/1964	02:00	EST
10/30/1966	02:00	CST
4/30/1967	02:00	US#1

IN # 65

Date	Time	Zone
Before 11/18/1883		LMT
11/18/1883	12:00	CST
3/31/1918	02:00	CWT
10/27/1918	02:00	CST
3/30/1919	02:00	CWT
10/26/1919	02:00	CST
2/09/1942	02:00	CWT
9/30/1945	02:00	CST
4/26/1953	02:00	CDT
9/27/1953	02:00	CST
4/25/1954	02:00	CDT
9/26/1954	02:00	CST
5/01/1955	00:00	CDT
8/28/1955	00:00	CST
4/29/1956	02:00	CDT
9/30/1956	02:00	CST
4/28/1957	02:00	CDT
9/29/1957	02:00	CST
4/27/1958	02:00	CDT
9/28/1958	02:00	CST
4/26/1959	02:00	CDT
9/27/1959	02:00	CST
4/24/1960	02:00	CDT
9/25/1960	02:00	CST
4/30/1961	02:00	CDT
10/29/1961	02:00	CST
4/29/1962	02:00	CDT
10/28/1962	02:00	CST
4/28/1963	02:00	CDT
10/27/1963	02:00	CST
4/26/1964	02:00	EST
10/30/1966	02:00	CST
4/30/1967	02:00	US#1

IN # 66

Date	Time	Zone
Before 11/18/1883		LMT
11/18/1883	12:00	CST
3/31/1918	02:00	CWT
10/27/1918	02:00	CST
3/30/1919	02:00	CWT
10/26/1919	02:00	CST
2/09/1942	02:00	CWT
9/30/1945	02:00	CST
4/29/1951	02:00	CDT
9/30/1951	02:00	CST
5/01/1955	00:00	CDT
9/04/1955	00:00	CST
4/29/1956	02:00	CDT
9/30/1956	02:00	CST
4/28/1957	02:00	CDT
9/29/1957	02:00	CST
4/27/1958	02:00	CDT
9/28/1958	02:00	CST
4/26/1959	02:00	CDT
9/27/1959	02:00	CST
4/24/1960	02:00	CDT
9/25/1960	02:00	CST
4/30/1961	02:00	CDT
10/29/1961	02:00	CST
4/29/1962	02:00	CDT
10/28/1962	02:00	CST
4/28/1963	02:00	CDT
10/27/1963	02:00	CST
4/26/1964	02:00	EST
10/30/1966	02:00	CST
4/30/1967	02:00	CDT
10/29/1967	02:00	CST
4/28/1968	02:00	CDT
10/27/1968	02:00	CST
4/27/1969	02:00	EDT
10/26/1969	02:00	EST
4/26/1970	02:00	EDT
10/25/1970	02:00	EST

IN # 67

Date	Time	Zone
Before 11/18/1883		LMT
11/18/1883	12:00	CST
3/31/1918	02:00	CWT
10/27/1918	02:00	CST
3/30/1919	02:00	CWT
10/26/1919	02:00	CST
2/09/1942	02:00	CWT
9/30/1945	02:00	CST
5/01/1955	00:00	CDT
9/04/1955	00:00	CST
4/29/1956	02:00	CDT
9/30/1956	02:00	CST
4/28/1957	02:00	CDT
9/29/1957	02:00	CST
4/27/1958	02:00	CDT
9/28/1958	02:00	CST
4/26/1959	02:00	CDT
9/27/1959	02:00	CST
4/24/1960	02:00	CDT
9/25/1960	02:00	CST
4/30/1961	02:00	CDT
10/29/1961	02:00	CST
4/29/1962	02:00	CDT
10/28/1962	02:00	CST
4/28/1963	02:00	CDT
10/27/1963	02:00	CST
4/26/1964	02:00	EST
10/30/1966	02:00	CST
4/30/1967	02:00	CDT
10/29/1967	02:00	CST
4/28/1968	02:00	CDT
10/27/1968	02:00	CST
4/27/1969	02:00	EDT
10/26/1969	02:00	EST
4/26/1970	02:00	EDT
10/25/1970	02:00	EST

IN # 68

Date	Time	Zone
Before 11/18/1883		LMT
11/18/1883	12:00	CST
3/31/1918	02:00	CWT
10/27/1918	02:00	CST
3/30/1919	02:00	CWT
10/26/1919	02:00	CST
2/09/1942	02:00	CWT
9/30/1945	02:00	CST
5/01/1955	02:00	CDT
9/25/1955	02:00	CST
4/29/1956	02:00	CDT
9/30/1956	02:00	CST
4/28/1957	02:00	CDT
9/29/1957	02:00	CST
4/27/1958	02:00	CDT
9/28/1958	02:00	CST
4/26/1959	02:00	CDT
9/27/1959	02:00	CST
4/24/1960	02:00	CDT
9/25/1960	02:00	CST
4/30/1961	02:00	CDT
10/29/1961	02:00	CST
4/29/1962	02:00	CDT
10/28/1962	02:00	CST
4/28/1963	02:00	CDT
10/27/1963	02:00	CST
4/26/1964	02:00	EST
10/29/1967	02:00	CST
4/28/1968	02:00	CDT
10/27/1968	02:00	CST
4/27/1969	02:00	EDT
10/26/1969	02:00	EST
4/26/1970	02:00	EDT
10/25/1970	02:00	EST

TIME TABLES

IN # 69

Date	Time	Zone
Before 11/18/1883		LMT
11/18/1883	12:00	CST
3/31/1918	02:00	CWT
10/27/1918	02:00	CST
3/30/1919	02:00	CWT
10/26/1919	02:00	CST
2/09/1942	02:00	CWT
9/30/1945	02:00	CST
5/01/1955	00:00	CDT
8/28/1955	00:00	CST
4/29/1956	02:00	CDT
9/30/1956	02:00	CST
4/28/1957	02:00	CDT
9/29/1957	02:00	CST
4/27/1958	02:00	CDT
9/28/1958	02:00	CST
4/26/1959	02:00	CDT
9/27/1959	02:00	CST
4/24/1960	02:00	CDT
9/25/1960	02:00	CST
4/30/1961	02:00	CDT
10/29/1961	02:00	CST
4/29/1962	02:00	CDT
10/28/1962	02:00	CST
4/28/1963	02:00	CDT
10/27/1963	02:00	CST
4/26/1964	02:00	EST
10/29/1967	02:00	CST
4/28/1968	02:00	CDT
10/27/1968	02:00	CST
4/27/1969	02:00	EDT
10/26/1969	02:00	EST
4/26/1970	02:00	EDT
10/25/1970	02:00	EST

IN # 70

Date	Time	Zone
Before 11/18/1883		LMT
11/18/1883	12:00	CST
3/31/1918	02:00	CWT
10/27/1918	02:00	CST
3/30/1919	02:00	CWT
10/26/1919	02:00	CST
2/09/1942	02:00	CWT
9/30/1945	02:00	CST
4/27/1952	02:00	CDT
9/28/1952	02:00	CST
4/24/1955	02:00	CDT
9/25/1955	02:00	CST
4/29/1956	02:00	CDT
9/30/1956	02:00	CST
4/28/1957	02:00	CDT
9/29/1957	02:00	CST
4/27/1958	02:00	CDT
9/28/1958	02:00	CST
4/26/1959	02:00	CDT
9/27/1959	02:00	CST
4/24/1960	02:00	CDT
9/25/1960	02:00	CST
4/30/1961	02:00	CDT
10/29/1961	02:00	CST
4/29/1962	02:00	CDT
10/28/1962	02:00	CST
4/28/1963	02:00	CDT
10/27/1963	02:00	CST
4/26/1964	02:00	EST
4/27/1969	02:00	EDT
10/26/1969	02:00	EST
4/26/1970	02:00	EDT
10/25/1970	02:00	EST

IN # 71

Date	Time	Zone
Before 11/18/1883		LMT
11/18/1883	12:00	CST
3/31/1918	02:00	CWT
10/27/1918	02:00	CST
3/30/1919	02:00	CWT
10/26/1919	02:00	CST
2/09/1942	02:00	CWT
9/30/1945	02:00	CST
4/30/1950	02:00	CDT
9/24/1950	02:00	CST
4/27/1952	02:00	CDT
9/28/1952	02:00	CST
4/26/1953	02:00	CDT
9/27/1953	02:00	CST
4/25/1954	02:00	CDT
9/26/1954	02:00	CST
4/24/1955	02:00	CDT
9/25/1955	02:00	CST
4/29/1956	02:00	CDT
10/28/1956	02:00	CST
4/28/1957	02:00	CDT
9/29/1957	02:00	CST
4/27/1958	02:00	CDT
10/26/1958	02:00	CST
4/26/1959	02:00	CDT
10/25/1959	02:00	CST
4/24/1960	02:00	CDT
10/30/1960	02:00	CST
4/30/1961	02:00	CDT
10/29/1961	02:00	CST
4/29/1962	02:00	CDT
10/28/1962	02:00	CST
4/28/1963	02:00	CDT
10/27/1963	02:00	CST
4/26/1964	02:00	EST
4/27/1969	02:00	EDT
10/26/1969	02:00	EST
4/26/1970	02:00	EDT
10/25/1970	02:00	EST

IN # 72

Date	Time	Zone
Before 11/18/1883		LMT
11/18/1883	12:00	CST
3/31/1918	02:00	CWT
10/27/1918	02:00	CST
3/30/1919	02:00	CWT
10/26/1919	02:00	CST
2/09/1942	02:00	CWT
9/30/1945	02:00	CST
4/26/1953	02:00	CDT
9/27/1953	02:00	CST
4/25/1954	02:00	CDT
9/26/1954	02:00	CST
4/24/1955	02:00	CDT
9/25/1955	02:00	CST
4/29/1956	02:00	CDT
9/30/1956	02:00	CST
4/28/1957	02:00	CDT
9/29/1957	02:00	CST
4/27/1958	02:00	CDT
9/28/1958	02:00	CST
4/26/1959	02:00	CDT
9/27/1959	02:00	CST
4/24/1960	02:00	CDT
9/25/1960	02:00	CST
4/30/1961	02:00	CDT
10/29/1961	02:00	CST
4/29/1962	02:00	CDT
10/28/1962	02:00	CST
4/28/1963	02:00	CDT
10/27/1963	02:00	CST
4/26/1964	02:00	EST
4/27/1969	02:00	EDT
10/26/1969	02:00	EST
4/26/1970	02:00	EDT
10/25/1970	02:00	EST

IN # 73

Date	Time	Zone
Before 11/18/1883		LMT
11/18/1883	12:00	CST
3/31/1918	02:00	CWT
10/27/1918	02:00	CST
3/30/1919	02:00	CWT
10/26/1919	02:00	CST
2/09/1942	02:00	CWT
9/30/1945	02:00	CST
4/24/1955	02:00	CDT
9/25/1955	02:00	CST
4/29/1956	02:00	CDT
9/30/1956	02:00	CST
4/28/1957	02:00	CDT
9/29/1957	02:00	CST
4/27/1958	02:00	CDT
9/28/1958	02:00	CST
4/26/1959	02:00	CDT
9/27/1959	02:00	CST
4/24/1960	02:00	CDT
9/25/1960	02:00	CST
4/30/1961	02:00	CDT
10/29/1961	02:00	CST
4/29/1962	02:00	CDT
10/28/1962	02:00	CST
4/28/1963	02:00	CDT
10/27/1963	02:00	CST
4/26/1964	02:00	EST
4/27/1969	02:00	EDT
10/26/1969	02:00	EST
4/26/1970	02:00	EDT
10/25/1970	02:00	EST

IN # 74

Date	Time	Zone
Before 11/18/1883		LMT
11/18/1883	12:00	CST
3/31/1918	02:00	CWT
10/27/1918	02:00	CST
3/30/1919	02:00	CWT
10/26/1919	02:00	CST
2/09/1942	02:00	CWT
9/30/1945	02:00	CST
4/26/1953	02:00	CDT
9/27/1953	02:00	CST
4/25/1954	02:00	CDT
9/26/1954	02:00	CST
5/01/1955	00:00	CDT
9/04/1955	00:00	CST
4/29/1956	02:00	CDT
9/02/1956	02:00	CST
4/28/1957	02:00	CDT
9/29/1957	02:00	CST
4/27/1958	02:00	CDT
9/28/1958	02:00	CST
4/26/1959	02:00	CDT
9/27/1959	02:00	CST
4/24/1960	02:00	CDT
9/25/1960	02:00	CST
4/30/1961	02:00	CDT
10/29/1961	02:00	CST
4/29/1962	02:00	CDT
10/28/1962	02:00	CST
4/28/1963	02:00	CDT
10/27/1963	02:00	CST
4/26/1964	02:00	EST
4/27/1969	02:00	EDT
10/26/1969	02:00	EST
4/26/1970	02:00	EDT
10/25/1970	02:00	EST

IN # 75

Date	Time	Zone
Before 11/18/1883		LMT
11/18/1883	12:00	CST
3/31/1918	02:00	CWT
10/27/1918	02:00	CST
3/30/1919	02:00	CWT
10/26/1919	02:00	CST
2/09/1942	02:00	CWT
9/30/1945	02:00	CST
5/01/1946	02:00	CDT
9/29/1946	02:00	CST
4/26/1953	02:00	CDT
9/27/1953	02:00	CST
4/25/1954	02:00	CDT
9/26/1954	02:00	CST
4/24/1955	02:00	CDT
9/25/1955	02:00	CST
4/29/1956	02:00	CDT
10/28/1956	02:00	CST
4/28/1957	02:00	CDT
9/29/1957	02:00	CST
4/27/1958	02:00	CDT
10/26/1958	02:00	CST
4/26/1959	02:00	CDT
10/25/1959	02:00	CST
4/24/1960	02:00	CDT
10/30/1960	02:00	CST
4/30/1961	02:00	CDT
10/29/1961	02:00	CST
4/29/1962	02:00	CDT
10/28/1962	02:00	CST
4/28/1963	02:00	CDT
10/27/1963	02:00	CST
4/26/1964	02:00	EST
4/27/1969	02:00	EDT
10/26/1969	02:00	EST
4/26/1970	02:00	EDT
10/25/1970	02:00	EST

IN # 76

Date	Time	Zone
Before 11/18/1883		LMT
11/18/1883	12:00	CST
3/31/1918	02:00	CWT
10/27/1918	02:00	CST
3/30/1919	02:00	CWT
10/26/1919	02:00	CST
2/09/1942	02:00	CWT
9/30/1945	02:00	CST
4/28/1946	02:00	CDT
9/29/1946	02:00	CST
4/30/1950	02:00	CDT
9/24/1950	02:00	CST
4/27/1952	02:00	CDT
9/28/1952	02:00	CST
4/26/1953	02:00	CDT
9/27/1953	02:00	CST
4/25/1954	02:00	CDT
9/26/1954	02:00	CST
4/24/1955	02:00	CDT
9/25/1955	02:00	CST
4/29/1956	02:00	CDT
10/28/1956	02:00	CST
4/28/1957	02:00	CDT
9/29/1957	02:00	CST
4/27/1958	02:00	CDT
10/26/1958	02:00	CST
4/26/1959	02:00	CDT
10/05/1959	00:01	CST
4/24/1960	02:00	CDT
9/25/1960	02:00	CST
4/30/1961	02:00	CDT
10/29/1961	02:00	CST
4/29/1962	02:00	CDT
10/28/1962	02:00	CST
4/28/1963	02:00	CDT
10/27/1963	02:00	CST
4/26/1964	02:00	EST
4/27/1969	02:00	EDT
10/26/1969	02:00	EST
4/26/1970	02:00	EDT
10/25/1970	02:00	EST

IN # 77

Date	Time	Zone
Before 11/18/1883		LMT
11/18/1883	12:00	CST
3/31/1918	02:00	CWT
10/27/1918	02:00	CST
3/30/1919	02:00	CWT
10/26/1919	02:00	CST
2/09/1942	02:00	CWT
9/30/1945	02:00	CST
4/28/1946	02:00	CDT
9/29/1946	02:00	CST
4/30/1950	02:00	CDT
9/24/1950	02:00	CST
4/29/1951	02:00	CDT
9/30/1951	02:00	CST
4/27/1952	02:00	CDT
9/28/1952	02:00	CST
4/26/1953	02:00	CDT
9/27/1953	02:00	CST
4/25/1954	02:00	CDT
9/26/1954	02:00	CST
4/24/1955	02:00	CDT
9/25/1955	02:00	CST
4/29/1956	02:00	CDT
10/28/1956	02:00	CST
4/28/1957	02:00	CDT
9/29/1957	02:00	CST
4/27/1958	02:00	CDT
10/26/1958	02:00	CST
4/26/1959	02:00	CDT
4/27/1959	02:00	[illegible]
9/27/1959	02:00	CST
4/24/1960	02:00	CDT
9/25/1960	02:00	CST
4/30/1961	02:00	CDT
10/29/1961	02:00	CST
4/29/1962	02:00	CDT
10/28/1962	02:00	CST
4/28/1963	02:00	CDT
10/27/1963	02:00	CST
4/26/1964	02:00	EST
4/27/1969	02:00	EDT
10/26/1969	02:00	EST
4/26/1970	02:00	EDT
10/25/1970	02:00	EST

IN # 78

Date	Time	Zone
Before 11/18/1883		LMT
11/18/1883	12:00	CST
3/31/1918	02:00	CWT
10/27/1918	02:00	CST
3/30/1919	02:00	CWT
10/26/1919	02:00	CST
2/09/1942	02:00	CWT
9/30/1945	02:00	CST
4/28/1946	02:00	CDT
9/29/1946	02:00	CST
4/26/1953	02:00	CDT
9/27/1953	02:00	CST
4/25/1954	02:00	CDT
9/26/1954	02:00	CST
5/01/1955	00:00	CDT
9/25/1955	02:00	CST
4/29/1956	02:00	CDT
9/30/1956	02:00	CST
4/28/1957	02:00	CDT
9/29/1957	02:00	CST
4/27/1958	02:00	CDT
9/28/1958	02:00	CST
4/26/1959	02:00	CDT
9/27/1959	02:00	CST
4/24/1960	02:00	CDT
10/30/1960	02:00	CST
4/30/1961	02:00	CDT
9/24/1961	02:00	CST
4/29/1962	02:00	CDT
10/28/1962	02:00	CST
4/28/1963	02:00	CDT
10/27/1963	02:00	CST
4/26/1964	02:00	EST
4/27/1969	02:00	EDT
10/26/1969	02:00	EST
4/26/1970	02:00	EDT
10/25/1970	02:00	EST

IN # 79

Date	Time	Zone
Before 11/18/1883		LMT
11/18/1883	12:00	CST
3/31/1918	02:00	CWT
10/27/1918	02:00	CST
3/30/1919	02:00	CWT
10/26/1919	02:00	CST
2/09/1942	02:00	CWT
9/30/1945	02:00	CST
4/30/1950	02:00	CDT
9/24/1950	02:00	CST
4/24/1955	02:00	CDT
9/25/1955	02:00	CST
4/29/1956	02:00	CDT
9/30/1956	02:00	CST
4/28/1957	02:00	CDT
9/29/1957	02:00	CST
4/27/1958	02:00	CDT
9/28/1958	02:00	CST
4/26/1959	02:00	CDT
9/27/1959	02:00	CST
4/24/1960	02:00	CDT
9/25/1960	02:00	CST
4/30/1961	02:00	CDT
10/29/1961	02:00	CST
4/29/1962	02:00	CDT
10/28/1962	02:00	CST
4/28/1963	02:00	CDT
10/27/1963	02:00	CST
4/26/1964	02:00	EST
4/27/1969	02:00	EDT
10/26/1969	02:00	EST
4/26/1970	02:00	EDT
10/25/1970	02:00	EST

IN # 80

Date	Time	Zone
Before 11/18/1883		LMT
11/18/1883	12:00	CST
3/31/1918	02:00	CWT
10/27/1918	02:00	CST
3/30/1919	02:00	CWT
10/26/1919	02:00	CST
2/09/1942	02:00	CWT
9/30/1945	02:00	CST
4/26/1953	02:00	CDT
9/27/1953	02:00	CST
4/25/1954	02:00	CDT
9/26/1954	02:00	CST
4/24/1955	02:00	CDT
9/25/1955	02:00	CST
4/29/1956	02:00	CDT
10/28/1956	02:00	CST
4/28/1957	02:00	CDT
9/29/1957	02:00	CST
4/27/1958	02:00	CDT
10/26/1958	02:00	CST
4/26/1959	02:00	CDT
10/25/1959	02:00	CST
4/24/1960	02:00	CDT
10/30/1960	02:00	CST
4/30/1961	02:00	CDT
10/29/1961	02:00	CST
4/29/1962	02:00	CDT
10/28/1962	02:00	CST
4/28/1963	02:00	CDT
10/27/1963	02:00	CST
4/26/1964	02:00	EST
4/27/1969	02:00	EDT
10/26/1969	02:00	EST
4/26/1970	02:00	EDT
10/25/1970	02:00	EST

IN # 81

Date	Time	Zone
Before 11/18/1883		LMT
11/18/1883	12:00	CST
3/31/1918	02:00	CWT
10/27/1918	02:00	CST
3/30/1919	02:00	CWT
10/26/1919	02:00	CST
2/09/1942	02:00	CWT
9/30/1945	02:00	CST
4/28/1946	02:00	CDT
9/29/1946	02:00	CST
4/30/1950	02:00	CDT
9/24/1950	02:00	CST
4/26/1953	02:00	CDT
9/27/1953	02:00	CST
4/25/1954	02:00	CDT
9/26/1954	02:00	CST
4/24/1955	02:00	CDT
9/25/1955	02:00	CST
4/29/1956	02:00	CDT
10/28/1956	02:00	CST
4/28/1957	02:00	CDT
9/29/1957	02:00	CST
4/27/1958	02:00	CDT
10/26/1958	02:00	CST
4/26/1959	02:00	CDT
10/25/1959	02:00	CST
4/24/1960	02:00	CDT
10/30/1960	02:00	CST
4/30/1961	02:00	CDT
10/29/1961	02:00	CST
4/29/1962	02:00	CDT
10/28/1962	02:00	CST
4/28/1963	02:00	CDT
10/27/1963	02:00	CST
4/26/1964	02:00	EST
4/27/1969	02:00	EDT
10/26/1969	02:00	EST
4/26/1970	02:00	EDT
10/25/1970	02:00	EST

IN # 82

Date	Time	Zone
Before 11/18/1883		LMT
11/18/1883	12:00	CST
3/31/1918	02:00	CWT
10/27/1918	02:00	CST
3/30/1919	02:00	CWT
10/26/1919	02:00	CST
2/09/1942	02:00	CWT
9/30/1945	02:00	CST
4/24/1955	02:00	CDT
9/25/1955	02:00	CST
4/29/1956	02:00	CDT
10/28/1956	02:00	CST
4/28/1957	02:00	CDT
9/29/1957	02:00	CST
4/27/1958	02:00	CDT
9/28/1958	02:00	CST
4/26/1959	02:00	CDT
9/27/1959	02:00	CST
4/24/1960	02:00	CDT
9/25/1960	02:00	CST
4/30/1961	02:00	CDT
10/29/1961	02:00	CST
4/29/1962	02:00	CDT
10/28/1962	02:00	CST
4/28/1963	02:00	CDT
10/27/1963	02:00	CST
4/26/1964	02:00	EST
4/27/1969	02:00	EDT
10/26/1969	02:00	EST
4/26/1970	02:00	EDT
10/25/1970	02:00	EST

IN # 83

Date	Time	Zone
Before 11/18/1883		LMT
11/18/1883	12:00	CST
3/31/1918	02:00	CWT
10/27/1918	02:00	CST
3/30/1919	02:00	CWT
10/26/1919	02:00	CST
2/09/1942	02:00	CWT
9/30/1945	02:00	CST
4/26/1953	02:00	CDT
9/27/1953	02:00	CST
4/25/1954	02:00	CDT
9/26/1954	02:00	CST
4/24/1955	02:00	CDT
9/25/1955	02:00	CST
4/29/1956	02:00	CDT
10/28/1956	02:00	CST
4/28/1957	02:00	CDT
9/29/1957	02:00	CST
4/27/1958	02:00	CDT
9/28/1958	02:00	CST
4/26/1959	02:00	CDT
9/27/1959	02:00	CST
4/24/1960	02:00	CDT
9/25/1960	02:00	CST
4/30/1961	02:00	CDT
10/29/1961	02:00	CST
4/29/1962	02:00	CDT
10/28/1962	02:00	CST
4/28/1963	02:00	CDT
10/27/1963	02:00	CST
4/26/1964	02:00	EST
4/27/1969	02:00	EDT

TIME TABLES

10/26/1969 02:00 EST
4/26/1970 02:00 EDT
10/25/1970 02:00 EST
....
IN # 84
Before 11/18/1883 LMT
11/18/1883 12:00 CST
3/31/1918 02:00 CWT
10/27/1918 02:00 CST
3/30/1919 02:00 CWT
10/26/1919 02:00 CST
2/09/1942 02:00 CWT
9/30/1945 02:00 CST
4/25/1954 02:00 CDT
9/26/1954 02:00 CST
4/24/1955 02:00 CDT
9/25/1955 02:00 CST
4/29/1956 02:00 CDT
10/01/1956 00:00 CST
4/28/1957 02:00 CDT
9/29/1957 02:00 CST
4/27/1958 02:00 CDT
9/28/1958 02:00 CST
4/26/1959 02:00 CDT
9/27/1959 02:00 CST
4/24/1960 02:00 CDT
9/25/1960 02:00 CST
4/30/1961 02:00 CDT
10/29/1961 02:00 CST
4/29/1962 02:00 CDT
10/28/1962 02:00 CST
4/28/1963 02:00 CDT
10/27/1963 02:00 CST
4/26/1964 02:00 EST
4/27/1969 02:00 EDT
10/26/1969 02:00 EST
4/26/1970 02:00 EDT
10/25/1970 02:00 EST
....
IN # 85
Before 11/18/1883 LMT
11/18/1883 12:00 CST
3/31/1918 02:00 CWT
10/27/1918 02:00 CST
3/30/1919 02:00 CWT
10/26/1919 02:00 CST
2/09/1942 02:00 CWT
9/30/1945 02:00 CST
5/01/1955 00:00 CDT
9/04/1955 00:00 CST
4/29/1956 02:00 CDT
9/30/1956 02:00 CST
4/28/1957 02:00 CDT
9/29/1957 02:00 CST
4/27/1958 02:00 CDT
9/28/1958 02:00 CST
4/26/1959 02:00 CDT
9/27/1959 02:00 CST
4/24/1960 02:00 CDT
9/25/1960 02:00 CST
4/30/1961 02:00 CDT
10/29/1961 02:00 CST
4/29/1962 02:00 CDT
10/28/1962 02:00 CST
4/28/1963 02:00 CDT
10/27/1963 02:00 CST
4/26/1964 02:00 EST
4/27/1969 02:00 EDT
10/26/1969 02:00 EST
4/26/1970 02:00 EDT
10/25/1970 02:00 EST
....
IN # 86
Before 11/18/1883 LMT
11/18/1883 12:00 CST
3/31/1918 02:00 CWT
10/27/1918 02:00 CST
3/30/1919 02:00 CWT
10/26/1919 02:00 CST
2/09/1942 02:00 CWT
9/30/1945 02:00 CST
5/01/1955 00:00 CDT
9/25/1955 02:00 CST
4/29/1956 02:00 CDT
9/30/1956 02:00 CST
4/28/1957 02:00 CDT
9/29/1957 02:00 CST
4/27/1958 02:00 CDT
9/28/1958 02:00 CST
4/26/1959 02:00 CDT
9/27/1959 02:00 CST
4/24/1960 02:00 CDT
9/25/1960 02:00 CST
4/30/1961 02:00 CDT
10/29/1961 02:00 CST
4/29/1962 02:00 CDT
10/28/1962 02:00 CST
4/28/1963 02:00 CDT
10/27/1963 02:00 CST
4/26/1964 02:00 EST
4/27/1969 02:00 EDT
10/26/1969 02:00 EST
4/26/1970 02:00 EDT
10/25/1970 02:00 EST
....
IN # 87
Before 11/18/1883 LMT
11/18/1883 12:00 CST
3/31/1918 02:00 CWT
10/27/1918 02:00 CST
3/30/1919 02:00 CWT
10/26/1919 02:00 CST
2/09/1942 02:00 CWT
9/30/1945 02:00 CST
4/26/1953 02:00 CDT
9/27/1953 02:00 CST
4/25/1954 02:00 CDT
9/26/1954 02:00 CST
5/01/1955 00:00 CDT
9/25/1955 02:00 CST
4/29/1956 02:00 CDT
9/30/1956 02:00 CST
4/28/1957 02:00 CDT
9/29/1957 02:00 CST
4/27/1958 02:00 CDT
9/28/1958 02:00 CST
4/26/1959 02:00 CDT
9/27/1959 02:00 CST
4/24/1960 02:00 CDT
9/25/1960 02:00 CST
4/30/1961 02:00 CDT
10/29/1961 02:00 CST
4/29/1962 02:00 CDT
10/28/1962 02:00 CST
4/28/1963 02:00 CDT
10/27/1963 02:00 CST
4/26/1964 02:00 EST
4/27/1969 02:00 EDT
10/26/1969 02:00 EST
4/26/1970 02:00 EDT
10/25/1970 02:00 EST
....
IN # 88
Before 11/18/1883 LMT
11/18/1883 12:00 CST
3/31/1918 02:00 CWT
10/27/1918 02:00 CST
3/30/1919 02:00 CWT
10/26/1919 02:00 CST
2/09/1942 02:00 CWT
9/30/1945 02:00 CST
4/26/1953 02:00 CDT
9/27/1953 02:00 CST
4/25/1954 02:00 CDT
9/26/1954 02:00 CST
4/24/1955 02:00 CDT
9/25/1955 02:00 CST
4/29/1956 02:00 CDT
9/30/1956 02:00 CST
4/28/1957 02:00 CDT
9/29/1957 02:00 CST
4/27/1958 02:00 CDT
9/28/1958 02:00 CST
4/26/1959 02:00 CDT
9/27/1959 02:00 CST
4/24/1960 02:00 CDT
9/25/1960 02:00 CST
4/30/1961 02:00 CDT
10/29/1961 02:00 CST
4/29/1962 02:00 CDT
10/28/1962 02:00 CST
4/28/1963 02:00 EST
4/27/1969 02:00 EDT
10/26/1969 02:00 EST
4/26/1970 02:00 EDT
10/25/1970 02:00 EST
....
IN # 89
Before 11/18/1883 LMT
11/18/1883 12:00 CST
3/31/1918 02:00 CWT
10/27/1918 02:00 CST
3/30/1919 02:00 CWT
10/26/1919 02:00 CST
2/09/1942 02:00 CWT
9/30/1945 02:00 CST
4/24/1955 02:00 CDT
9/25/1955 02:00 CST
4/29/1956 02:00 CDT
9/30/1956 02:00 CST
4/28/1957 02:00 CDT
9/29/1957 02:00 CST
4/27/1958 02:00 CDT
9/28/1958 02:00 CST
4/26/1959 02:00 CDT
9/27/1959 02:00 CST
4/24/1960 02:00 CDT
9/25/1960 02:00 CST
4/30/1961 02:00 CDT
10/29/1961 02:00 CST
4/29/1962 02:00 CDT
10/28/1962 02:00 CST
4/28/1963 02:00 EST
4/27/1969 02:00 EDT
10/26/1969 02:00 EST
4/26/1970 02:00 EDT
10/25/1970 02:00 EST
....
IN # 90
Before 11/18/1883 LMT
11/18/1883 12:00 CST
3/31/1918 02:00 CWT
10/27/1918 02:00 CST
3/30/1919 02:00 CWT
10/26/1919 02:00 CST
2/09/1942 02:00 CWT
9/30/1945 02:00 CST
4/28/1946 02:00 CDT
9/29/1946 02:00 CST
4/26/1953 02:00 CDT
9/27/1953 02:00 CST
4/25/1954 02:00 CDT
9/26/1954 02:00 CST
4/24/1955 02:00 CDT
9/25/1955 02:00 CST
4/29/1956 02:00 CDT
9/30/1956 02:00 CST
4/28/1957 02:00 CDT
9/29/1957 02:00 CST
4/27/1958 02:00 CDT
9/28/1958 02:00 CST
4/26/1959 02:00 CDT
9/27/1959 02:00 CST
4/24/1960 02:00 CDT
9/25/1960 02:00 CST
4/30/1961 02:00 CDT
10/29/1961 02:00 CST
4/29/1962 02:00 CDT
10/28/1962 02:00 CST
4/28/1963 02:00 EST
4/27/1969 02:00 EDT
10/26/1969 02:00 EST
4/26/1970 02:00 EDT
10/25/1970 02:00 EST
....
IN # 91
Before 11/18/1883 LMT
11/18/1883 12:00 CST
3/31/1918 02:00 CWT
10/27/1918 02:00 CST
3/30/1919 02:00 CWT
10/26/1919 02:00 CST
2/09/1942 02:00 CWT
9/30/1945 02:00 CST
5/01/1955 00:00 CDT
9/04/1955 00:00 CST
4/29/1956 02:00 CDT
9/30/1956 02:00 CST
4/28/1957 02:00 CDT
9/29/1957 02:00 CST
4/27/1958 02:00 CDT
9/28/1958 02:00 CST
4/26/1959 02:00 CDT
9/27/1959 02:00 CST
4/24/1960 02:00 CDT
9/25/1960 02:00 CST
4/30/1961 02:00 CDT
10/29/1961 02:00 CST
4/29/1962 02:00 CDT
10/28/1962 02:00 CST
4/28/1963 02:00 EST
4/27/1969 02:00 EDT
10/26/1969 02:00 EST
4/26/1970 02:00 EDT
10/25/1970 02:00 EST
....
IN # 92
Before 11/18/1883 LMT
11/18/1883 12:00 CST
3/31/1918 02:00 CWT
10/27/1918 02:00 CST
3/30/1919 02:00 CWT
10/26/1919 02:00 CST
2/09/1942 02:00 CWT
9/30/1945 02:00 CST
5/01/1955 00:00 CDT
9/01/1955 00:00 CST
4/29/1956 02:00 CDT
9/30/1956 02:00 CST
4/28/1957 02:00 CDT
9/29/1957 02:00 CST
4/27/1958 02:00 CDT
9/28/1958 02:00 CST
4/26/1959 02:00 CDT
10/25/1959 02:00 CST
4/24/1960 02:00 EST
10/29/1961 02:00 CST
4/29/1962 02:00 CDT
10/28/1962 02:00 CST
4/28/1963 02:00 CDT
10/27/1963 02:00 CST
4/26/1964 02:00 EST
4/27/1969 02:00 EDT
10/26/1969 02:00 EST
4/26/1970 02:00 EDT
10/25/1970 02:00 EST
....
IN # 93
Before 11/18/1883 LMT
11/18/1883 12:00 CST
3/31/1918 02:00 CWT
10/27/1918 02:00 CST
3/30/1919 02:00 CWT
10/26/1919 02:00 CST
2/09/1942 02:00 CWT
9/30/1945 02:00 CST
5/08/1955 02:00 CDT
9/04/1955 00:00 CST
4/29/1956 02:00 CDT
9/30/1956 02:00 CST
4/28/1957 02:00 CDT
9/29/1957 02:00 CST
4/27/1958 02:00 CDT
9/28/1958 02:00 CST
4/26/1959 02:00 CDT
9/27/1959 02:00 CST
4/24/1960 02:00 EST
10/29/1961 02:00 CST
4/29/1962 02:00 CDT
10/28/1962 02:00 CST
4/28/1963 02:00 CDT
10/27/1963 02:00 CST
4/26/1964 02:00 EST
4/27/1969 02:00 EDT
10/26/1969 02:00 EST
4/26/1970 02:00 EDT
10/25/1970 02:00 EST
....
IN # 94
Before 11/18/1883 LMT
11/18/1883 12:00 CST
3/31/1918 02:00 CWT
10/27/1918 02:00 CST
3/30/1919 02:00 CWT
10/26/1919 02:00 CST
2/09/1942 02:00 CWT
9/30/1945 02:00 CST
5/01/1955 00:00 CDT
9/01/1955 00:00 CST
4/29/1956 02:00 CDT
9/30/1956 02:00 CST
4/28/1957 02:00 CDT
9/29/1957 02:00 CST
4/27/1958 02:00 CDT
9/28/1958 02:00 CST
4/26/1959 02:00 CDT
9/27/1959 02:00 CST
4/24/1960 02:00 EST
10/29/1961 02:00 CST
4/29/1962 02:00 CDT
10/28/1962 02:00 CST
4/28/1963 02:00 CDT
10/27/1963 02:00 CST
4/26/1964 02:00 EST
4/27/1969 02:00 EDT
10/26/1969 02:00 EST
4/26/1970 02:00 EDT
10/25/1970 02:00 EST
....
IN # 95
Before 11/18/1883 LMT
11/18/1883 12:00 CST
3/31/1918 02:00 CWT
10/27/1918 02:00 CST
3/30/1919 02:00 CWT
10/26/1919 02:00 CST
2/09/1942 02:00 CWT
9/30/1945 02:00 CST
4/26/1953 02:00 CDT
9/27/1953 02:00 CST
4/25/1954 02:00 CDT
9/26/1954 02:00 CST
5/10/1955 02:00 CDT
9/04/1955 00:00 CST
4/29/1956 02:00 CDT
9/30/1956 02:00 CST
4/28/1957 02:00 CDT
9/29/1957 02:00 CST
4/27/1958 02:00 CDT
9/28/1958 02:00 CST
4/26/1959 02:00 CDT
9/27/1959 02:00 CST
4/24/1960 02:00 EST
10/29/1961 02:00 CST
4/29/1962 02:00 CDT
10/28/1962 02:00 CST
4/28/1963 02:00 CDT
10/27/1963 02:00 CST
4/26/1964 02:00 EST
4/27/1969 02:00 EDT
10/26/1969 02:00 EST
4/26/1970 02:00 EDT
10/25/1970 02:00 EST
....
IN # 96
Before 11/18/1883 LMT
11/18/1883 12:00 CST
3/31/1918 02:00 CWT
10/27/1918 02:00 CST
3/30/1919 02:00 CWT
10/26/1919 02:00 CST
2/09/1942 02:00 CWT
9/30/1945 02:00 CST
4/26/1953 02:00 CDT
9/27/1953 02:00 CST
4/25/1954 02:00 CDT
9/26/1954 02:00 CST
5/08/1955 00:00 CDT
9/04/1955 00:00 CST
4/29/1956 02:00 CDT
9/30/1956 02:00 CST
4/28/1957 02:00 CDT
9/29/1957 02:00 CST
4/27/1958 02:00 CDT
9/28/1958 02:00 CST
4/26/1959 02:00 CDT
9/27/1959 02:00 CST
4/24/1960 02:00 EST
10/29/1961 02:00 CST
4/29/1962 02:00 CDT
10/28/1962 02:00 CST
4/28/1963 02:00 CDT
10/27/1963 02:00 CST
4/26/1964 02:00 EST
4/27/1969 02:00 EDT
10/26/1969 02:00 EST
4/26/1970 02:00 EDT
10/25/1970 02:00 EST
....
IN # 97
Before 11/18/1883 LMT
11/18/1883 12:00 CST
3/31/1918 02:00 CWT
10/27/1918 02:00 CST
3/30/1919 02:00 CWT
10/26/1919 02:00 CST
2/09/1942 02:00 CWT
9/30/1945 02:00 CST
4/24/1955 02:00 EST
9/29/1957 02:00 CST
4/27/1958 02:00 EST
4/27/1969 02:00 EDT
10/26/1969 02:00 EST
4/26/1970 02:00 EDT
10/25/1970 02:00 EST
....
IN # 98
Before 11/18/1883 LMT
11/18/1883 12:00 CST
3/31/1918 02:00 CWT
10/27/1918 02:00 CST
3/30/1919 02:00 CWT
10/26/1919 02:00 CST
2/09/1942 02:00 CWT
9/30/1945 02:00 CST
4/26/1953 02:00 CDT
9/27/1953 02:00 CST
4/25/1954 02:00 CDT
9/26/1954 02:00 CST
4/24/1955 02:00 EST
9/29/1957 02:00 CST
4/27/1958 02:00 EST
4/27/1969 02:00 EDT
10/26/1969 02:00 EST
4/26/1970 02:00 EDT
10/25/1970 02:00 EST
....
IN # 99
Before 11/18/1883 LMT
11/18/1883 12:00 CST
3/31/1918 02:00 CWT
10/27/1918 02:00 CST
3/30/1919 02:00 CWT
10/26/1919 02:00 CST
2/09/1942 02:00 CWT
9/30/1945 02:00 CST
4/27/1947 02:00 CDT
9/06/1947 02:00 CST
4/25/1948 02:00 CDT
9/26/1948 02:00 CST
4/29/1951 02:00 CDT
9/30/1951 02:00 CST
4/24/1955 02:00 EST
9/29/1957 02:00 CST
4/27/1958 02:00 EST
4/27/1969 02:00 EDT
10/26/1969 02:00 EST
4/26/1970 02:00 EDT
10/25/1970 02:00 EST
....
IN # 100
Before 11/18/1883 LMT
11/18/1883 12:00 CST
3/31/1918 02:00 CWT
10/27/1918 02:00 CST
3/30/1919 02:00 CWT
10/26/1919 02:00 CST
6/22/1941 02:00 CDT
9/28/1941 02:00 CST
2/09/1942 02:00 CWT
9/30/1945 02:00 CST
4/28/1946 02:00 CDT
9/29/1946 02:00 CST
4/27/1947 02:00 CDT
9/28/1947 02:00 CST
4/25/1948 02:00 CDT
9/26/1948 02:00 CST
4/24/1949 02:00 CDT
9/25/1949 02:00 CST
4/30/1950 02:00 CDT
9/24/1950 02:00 CST
4/29/1951 02:00 CDT
9/30/1951 02:00 CST
4/27/1952 02:00 CDT
9/28/1952 02:00 CST
4/26/1953 02:00 CDT
9/27/1953 02:00 CST
4/25/1954 02:00 CDT
9/26/1954 02:00 CST
4/24/1955 02:00 EST
9/29/1957 02:00 CST
4/27/1958 02:00 EST
4/27/1969 02:00 EDT
10/26/1969 02:00 EST
4/26/1970 02:00 EDT
10/25/1970 02:00 EST
....
IN # 101
Before 11/18/1883 LMT
11/18/1883 12:00 CST
3/31/1918 02:00 CWT
10/27/1918 02:00 CST
3/30/1919 02:00 CWT
10/26/1919 02:00 CST
2/09/1942 02:00 CWT
9/30/1945 02:00 CST
4/24/1955 02:00 EST
9/29/1957 02:00 CST
4/27/1958 02:00 CDT
9/28/1958 02:00 CST
4/26/1959 02:00 EST
4/27/1969 02:00 EDT
10/26/1969 02:00 EST
4/26/1970 02:00 EDT
10/25/1970 02:00 EST
....
IN # 102
Before 11/18/1883 LMT
11/18/1883 12:00 CST
3/31/1918 02:00 CWT
10/27/1918 02:00 CST
3/30/1919 02:00 CWT
10/26/1919 02:00 CST
4/30/1933 02:00 CDT
9/24/1933 02:00 CST

TIME TABLES

4/29/1934 02:00 CDT
9/30/1934 02:00 CST
4/28/1935 02:00 CDT
9/29/1935 02:00 CST
4/26/1936 02:00 CDT
9/27/1936 02:00 CST
4/25/1937 02:00 CDT
9/26/1937 02:00 CST
4/24/1938 02:00 CDT
9/25/1938 02:00 CST
4/30/1939 02:00 CDT
9/24/1939 02:00 CST
4/28/1940 02:00 CDT
9/29/1940 02:00 CST
4/27/1941 02:00 CDT
9/28/1941 02:00 CST
2/09/1942 02:00 CWT
9/30/1945 02:00 CST
4/28/1946 02:00 CDT
9/29/1946 02:00 CST
4/27/1947 02:00 CDT
9/28/1947 02:00 CST
4/25/1948 02:00 CDT
9/26/1948 02:00 CST
4/24/1949 02:00 CDT
9/25/1949 02:00 CST
4/30/1950 02:00 CDT
9/24/1950 02:00 CST
4/29/1951 02:00 CDT
9/30/1951 02:00 CST
4/27/1952 02:00 CDT
9/28/1952 02:00 CST
4/26/1953 02:00 CDT
9/27/1953 02:00 CST
4/25/1954 02:00 CDT
9/26/1954 02:00 CST
4/24/1955 02:00 EST
9/29/1957 02:00 CST
4/27/1958 02:00 CDT
9/28/1958 02:00 CST
4/26/1959 02:00 EST
4/27/1969 02:00 EDT
10/26/1969 02:00 EST
4/26/1970 02:00 EDT
10/25/1970 02:00 EST

IN # 103
Before 11/18/1883 LMT
11/18/1883 12:00 CST
3/31/1918 02:00 CWT
10/27/1918 02:00 CST
3/30/1919 02:00 CWT
10/26/1919 02:00 CST
2/09/1942 02:00 CWT
9/30/1945 02:00 CST
4/28/1946 02:00 CDT
9/29/1946 02:00 CST
4/27/1947 02:00 CDT
9/28/1947 02:00 CST
4/25/1948 02:00 CDT
9/26/1948 02:00 CST
4/24/1949 02:00 CDT
9/25/1949 02:00 CST
4/30/1950 02:00 CDT
9/24/1950 02:00 CST
4/29/1951 02:00 CDT
9/30/1951 02:00 CST
4/27/1952 02:00 CDT
9/28/1952 02:00 CST
4/26/1953 02:00 CDT
9/27/1953 02:00 CST
4/25/1954 02:00 CDT
9/26/1954 02:00 CST
4/24/1955 02:00 EST
9/29/1957 02:00 CST
4/27/1958 02:00 CDT
9/28/1958 02:00 CST
4/26/1959 02:00 EST
4/27/1969 02:00 EDT
10/26/1969 02:00 EST
4/26/1970 02:00 EDT
10/25/1970 02:00 EST

IN # 104
Before 11/18/1883 LMT
11/18/1883 12:00 CST
3/31/1918 02:00 CWT
10/27/1918 02:00 CST
3/30/1919 02:00 CWT
10/26/1919 02:00 CST
2/09/1942 02:00 CWT
9/30/1945 02:00 CST
4/28/1946 02:00 CDT
9/29/1946 02:00 CST
4/27/1947 02:00 CDT
9/28/1947 02:00 CST
4/26/1953 02:00 CDT
9/27/1953 02:00 CST
4/25/1954 02:00 CDT
9/26/1954 02:00 CST
4/24/1955 02:00 EST
9/29/1957 02:00 CST
4/27/1958 02:00 CDT
9/28/1958 02:00 CST
4/26/1959 02:00 EST
4/27/1969 02:00 EDT
10/26/1969 02:00 EST
4/26/1970 02:00 EDT
10/25/1970 02:00 EST

IN # 105
Before 11/18/1883 LMT
11/18/1883 12:00 CST
3/31/1918 02:00 CWT
10/27/1918 02:00 CST
3/30/1919 02:00 CWT
10/26/1919 02:00 CST
2/09/1942 02:00 CWT
9/30/1945 02:00 CST
4/28/1946 02:00 CDT
9/29/1946 02:00 CST
4/27/1947 02:00 CDT
9/28/1947 02:00 CST
4/25/1948 02:00 CDT
9/26/1948 02:00 CST
4/27/1952 02:00 CDT
9/28/1952 02:00 CST
4/26/1953 02:00 CDT
9/27/1953 02:00 CST
4/25/1954 02:00 CDT
9/26/1954 02:00 CST
4/24/1955 02:00 EST
9/29/1957 02:00 CST
4/27/1958 02:00 CDT
9/28/1958 02:00 CST
4/26/1959 02:00 EST
4/27/1969 02:00 EDT
10/26/1969 02:00 EST
4/26/1970 02:00 EDT
10/25/1970 02:00 EST

IN # 106
Before 11/18/1883 LMT
11/18/1883 12:00 CST
3/31/1918 02:00 CWT
10/27/1918 02:00 CST
3/30/1919 02:00 CWT
10/26/1919 02:00 CST
2/09/1942 02:00 CWT
9/30/1945 02:00 CST
4/28/1946 02:00 CDT
9/29/1946 02:00 CST
4/29/1951 02:00 CDT
9/30/1951 02:00 CST
4/27/1952 02:00 CDT
9/28/1952 02:00 CST
4/26/1953 02:00 CDT
9/27/1953 02:00 CST
4/25/1954 02:00 CDT
9/26/1954 02:00 CST
4/24/1955 02:00 EST
9/29/1957 02:00 CST
4/27/1958 02:00 CDT
9/28/1958 02:00 CST
4/26/1959 02:00 EST
4/27/1969 02:00 EDT
10/26/1969 02:00 EST
4/26/1970 02:00 EDT
10/25/1970 02:00 EST

IN # 107
Before 11/18/1883 LMT
11/18/1883 12:00 CST
3/31/1918 02:00 CWT
10/27/1918 02:00 CST
3/30/1919 02:00 CWT
10/26/1919 02:00 CST
2/09/1942 02:00 CWT
9/30/1945 02:00 CST
4/27/1947 02:00 CDT
9/28/1947 02:00 CST
4/25/1948 02:00 CDT
9/26/1948 02:00 CST
4/26/1953 02:00 CDT
9/27/1953 02:00 CST
4/25/1954 02:00 CDT
9/26/1954 02:00 CST
4/24/1955 02:00 EST
9/29/1957 02:00 CST
4/27/1958 02:00 CDT
9/28/1958 02:00 CST
4/26/1959 02:00 EST
4/27/1969 02:00 EDT
10/26/1969 02:00 EST
4/26/1970 02:00 EDT
10/25/1970 02:00 EST

IN # 108
Before 11/18/1883 LMT
11/18/1883 12:00 CST
3/31/1918 02:00 CWT
10/27/1918 02:00 CST
3/30/1919 02:00 CWT
10/26/1919 02:00 CST
2/09/1942 02:00 CWT
9/30/1945 02:00 CST
4/26/1953 02:00 CDT
9/27/1953 02:00 CST
4/25/1954 02:00 CDT
9/26/1954 02:00 CST
4/24/1955 02:00 EST
9/29/1957 02:00 CST
4/27/1958 02:00 CDT
9/28/1958 02:00 CST
4/26/1959 02:00 EST
4/27/1969 02:00 EDT
10/26/1969 02:00 EST
4/26/1970 02:00 EDT
10/25/1970 02:00 EST

IN # 109
Before 11/18/1883 LMT
11/18/1883 12:00 CST
3/31/1918 02:00 CWT
10/27/1918 02:00 CST
3/30/1919 02:00 CWT
10/26/1919 02:00 CST
2/09/1942 02:00 CWT
9/30/1945 02:00 CST
4/25/1954 02:00 CDT
9/26/1954 02:00 CST
4/24/1955 02:00 EST
9/29/1957 02:00 CST
4/27/1958 02:00 CDT
9/28/1958 02:00 CST
4/26/1959 02:00 EST
4/27/1969 02:00 EDT
10/26/1969 02:00 EST
4/26/1970 02:00 EDT
10/25/1970 02:00 EST

IN # 110
Before 11/18/1883 LMT
11/18/1883 12:00 CST
3/31/1918 02:00 CWT
10/27/1918 02:00 CST
3/30/1919 02:00 CWT
10/26/1919 02:00 CST
2/09/1942 02:00 CWT
9/30/1945 02:00 CST
4/27/1947 02:00 CDT
10/01/1947 02:00 CST
4/25/1948 02:00 CDT
9/26/1948 02:00 CST
4/29/1951 02:00 CDT
9/30/1951 02:00 CST
4/24/1955 02:00 EST
9/29/1957 02:00 CST
4/27/1958 02:00 CDT
9/28/1958 02:00 CST
4/26/1959 02:00 EST
4/27/1969 02:00 EDT
10/26/1969 02:00 EST
4/26/1970 02:00 EDT
10/25/1970 02:00 EST

IN # 111
Before 11/18/1883 LMT
11/18/1883 12:00 CST
3/31/1918 02:00 CWT
10/27/1918 02:00 CST
3/30/1919 02:00 CWT
10/26/1919 02:00 CST
2/09/1942 02:00 CWT
9/30/1945 02:00 CST
4/28/1946 02:00 CDT
9/29/1946 02:00 CST
5/01/1947 02:00 CDT
10/01/1947 02:00 CST
4/29/1951 02:00 CDT
9/30/1951 02:00 CST
4/27/1952 02:00 CDT
9/28/1952 02:00 CST
4/26/1953 02:00 CDT
9/27/1953 02:00 CST
4/25/1954 02:00 CDT
9/26/1954 02:00 CST
4/24/1955 02:00 EST
9/29/1957 02:00 CST
4/27/1958 02:00 CDT
9/28/1958 02:00 CST
4/26/1959 02:00 EST
4/27/1969 02:00 EDT
10/26/1969 02:00 EST
4/26/1970 02:00 EDT
10/25/1970 02:00 EST

IN # 112
Before 11/18/1883 LMT
11/18/1883 12:00 CST
3/31/1918 02:00 CWT
10/27/1918 02:00 CST
3/30/1919 02:00 CWT
10/26/1919 02:00 CST
2/09/1942 02:00 CWT
9/30/1945 02:00 CST
4/30/1950 02:00 CDT
10/01/1950 02:00 CST
4/24/1955 02:00 EST
9/29/1957 02:00 CST
4/27/1958 02:00 CDT
9/28/1958 02:00 CST
4/26/1959 02:00 EST
4/27/1969 02:00 EDT
10/26/1969 02:00 EST
4/26/1970 02:00 EDT
10/25/1970 02:00 EST

IN # 113
Before 11/18/1883 LMT
11/18/1883 12:00 CST
3/31/1918 02:00 CWT
10/27/1918 02:00 CST
3/30/1919 02:00 CWT
10/26/1919 02:00 CST
2/09/1942 02:00 CWT
9/30/1945 02:00 CST
4/24/1955 02:00 EST
9/29/1957 02:00 CST
4/27/1958 02:00 CDT
9/28/1958 02:00 CST
4/26/1959 02:00 CDT
9/27/1959 02:00 CST
4/24/1960 02:00 EST
4/27/1969 02:00 EDT
10/26/1969 02:00 EST
4/26/1970 02:00 EDT
10/25/1970 02:00 EST

IN # 114
Before 11/18/1883 LMT
11/18/1883 12:00 CST
3/31/1918 02:00 CWT
10/27/1918 02:00 CST
3/30/1919 02:00 CWT
10/26/1919 02:00 CST
2/09/1942 02:00 CWT
9/30/1945 02:00 CST
4/26/1953 02:00 CDT
9/27/1953 02:00 CST
4/24/1955 02:00 EST
9/29/1957 02:00 CST
4/27/1958 02:00 CDT
9/28/1958 02:00 CST
4/26/1959 02:00 CDT
9/27/1959 02:00 CST
4/24/1960 02:00 EST
4/27/1969 02:00 EDT
10/26/1969 02:00 EST
4/26/1970 02:00 EDT
10/25/1970 02:00 EST

IN # 115
Before 11/18/1883 LMT
11/18/1883 12:00 CST
3/31/1918 02:00 CWT
10/27/1918 02:00 CST
3/30/1919 02:00 CWT
10/26/1919 02:00 CST
2/09/1942 02:00 CWT
9/30/1945 02:00 CST
4/26/1953 02:00 CDT
9/27/1953 02:00 CST
4/25/1954 02:00 CDT
9/26/1954 02:00 CST
4/24/1955 02:00 EST
9/29/1957 02:00 CST
4/27/1958 02:00 CDT
9/28/1958 02:00 CST
4/26/1959 02:00 CDT
9/27/1959 02:00 CST
4/24/1960 02:00 EST
4/27/1969 02:00 EDT
10/26/1969 02:00 EST
4/26/1970 02:00 EDT
10/25/1970 02:00 EST

IN # 116
Before 11/18/1883 LMT
11/18/1883 12:00 CST
3/31/1918 02:00 CWT
10/27/1918 02:00 CST
3/30/1919 02:00 CWT
10/26/1919 02:00 CST
2/09/1942 02:00 CWT
9/30/1945 02:00 CST
4/24/1955 02:00 EST
12/02/1956 02:00 CST
4/28/1957 02:00 CDT
9/29/1957 02:00 CST
4/27/1958 02:00 CDT
9/28/1958 02:00 CST
4/26/1959 02:00 EST
4/27/1969 02:00 EDT
10/26/1969 02:00 EST
4/26/1970 02:00 EDT
10/25/1970 02:00 EST

IN # 117
Before 11/18/1883 LMT
11/18/1883 12:00 CST
3/31/1918 02:00 CWT
10/27/1918 02:00 CST
3/30/1919 02:00 CWT
10/26/1919 02:00 CST
2/09/1942 02:00 CWT
9/30/1945 02:00 CST
4/30/1950 02:00 CDT
9/24/1950 02:00 CST
4/29/1951 02:00 CDT
9/30/1951 02:00 CST
4/27/1952 02:00 CDT
9/28/1952 02:00 CST
4/26/1953 02:00 CDT
9/27/1953 02:00 CST
4/25/1954 02:00 CDT
9/26/1954 02:00 CST
4/24/1955 02:00 EST
12/02/1956 02:00 CST
4/28/1957 02:00 CDT
9/29/1957 02:00 CST
4/27/1958 02:00 CDT
9/28/1958 02:00 CST
4/26/1959 02:00 EST
4/27/1969 02:00 EDT
10/26/1969 02:00 EST
4/26/1970 02:00 EDT
10/25/1970 02:00 EST

IN # 118
Before 11/18/1883 LMT
11/18/1883 12:00 CST
3/31/1918 02:00 CWT
10/27/1918 02:00 CST
3/30/1919 02:00 CWT
10/26/1919 02:00 CST
2/09/1942 02:00 CWT
9/30/1945 02:00 CST
4/25/1948 02:00 CDT
9/26/1948 02:00 CST
4/30/1950 02:00 CDT
9/24/1950 02:00 CST
4/29/1951 02:00 CDT
9/30/1951 02:00 CST
4/26/1953 02:00 CDT
9/27/1953 02:00 CST
4/24/1955 02:00 EST
12/02/1956 02:00 CST
4/28/1957 02:00 CDT
9/29/1957 02:00 CST
4/27/1958 02:00 CDT
9/28/1958 02:00 CST
4/26/1959 02:00 EST
4/27/1969 02:00 EDT
10/26/1969 02:00 EST
4/26/1970 02:00 EDT
10/25/1970 02:00 EST

IN # 119
Before 11/18/1883 LMT
11/18/1883 12:00 CST
3/31/1918 02:00 CWT
10/27/1918 02:00 CST
3/30/1919 02:00 CWT
10/26/1919 02:00 CST
2/09/1942 02:00 CWT
9/30/1945 02:00 CST
4/26/1953 02:00 CDT
9/27/1953 02:00 CST
4/25/1954 02:00 CDT
9/26/1954 02:00 CST
4/24/1955 02:00 EST
12/02/1956 02:00 CST
4/28/1957 02:00 CDT
9/29/1957 02:00 CST
4/27/1958 02:00 CDT
9/28/1958 02:00 CST
4/26/1959 02:00 EST
4/27/1969 02:00 EDT
10/26/1969 02:00 EST
4/26/1970 02:00 EDT
10/25/1970 02:00 EST

IN # 120
Before 11/18/1883 LMT
11/18/1883 12:00 CST
3/31/1918 02:00 CWT
10/27/1918 02:00 CST
3/30/1919 02:00 CWT
10/26/1919 02:00 CST
2/09/1942 02:00 CWT
9/30/1945 02:00 CST
4/29/1951 02:00 CDT
9/30/1951 02:00 CST
4/26/1953 02:00 CDT
9/27/1953 02:00 CST
4/24/1955 02:00 EST
12/02/1956 02:00 CST
4/28/1957 02:00 CDT
9/29/1957 02:00 CST
4/27/1958 02:00 CDT
9/28/1958 02:00 CST
4/26/1959 02:00 EST
4/27/1969 02:00 EDT
10/26/1969 02:00 EST
4/26/1970 02:00 EDT
10/25/1970 02:00 EST

IN # 121
Before 11/18/1883 LMT
11/18/1883 12:00 CST
3/31/1918 02:00 CWT
10/27/1918 02:00 CST
3/30/1919 02:00 CWT
10/26/1919 02:00 CST
2/09/1942 02:00 CWT
9/30/1945 02:00 CST
4/28/1946 02:00 CDT
9/29/1946 02:00 CST
4/27/1947 02:00 CDT
9/28/1947 02:00 CST
4/25/1948 02:00 CDT
9/26/1948 02:00 CST
4/24/1949 02:00 CDT
9/25/1949 02:00 CST
4/30/1950 02:00 CDT
10/01/1950 02:00 CST
4/29/1951 02:00 CDT
9/30/1951 02:00 CST
4/27/1952 02:00 CDT
9/28/1952 02:00 CST
4/26/1953 02:00 CDT
9/27/1953 02:00 CST
4/25/1954 02:00 CDT
9/26/1954 02:00 CST
4/24/1955 02:00 EST
12/02/1956 02:00 CST
4/28/1957 02:00 CDT
9/29/1957 02:00 CST
4/27/1958 02:00 CDT
9/28/1958 02:00 CST
4/26/1959 02:00 EST
4/27/1969 02:00 EDT
10/26/1969 02:00 EST
4/26/1970 02:00 EDT
10/25/1970 02:00 EST

IN # 122
Before 11/18/1883 LMT
11/18/1883 12:00 CST
3/31/1918 02:00 CWT
10/27/1918 02:00 CST
3/30/1919 02:00 CWT
10/26/1919 02:00 CST
2/09/1942 02:00 CWT

INDIANA

TIME TABLES

9/30/1945	02:00	CST
4/28/1946	02:00	CDT
9/29/1946	02:00	CST
4/27/1947	02:00	CDT
9/28/1947	02:00	CST
4/25/1948	02:00	CDT
9/26/1948	02:00	CST
4/24/1949	02:00	CDT
9/25/1949	02:00	CST
4/30/1950	02:00	CDT
9/24/1950	02:00	CST
4/29/1951	02:00	CDT
9/30/1951	02:00	CST
4/27/1952	02:00	CDT
9/28/1952	02:00	CST
4/26/1953	02:00	CDT
9/27/1953	02:00	CST
4/25/1954	02:00	CDT
9/26/1954	02:00	CST
4/24/1955	02:00	CDT
9/25/1955	02:00	CST
4/29/1956	02:00	CDT
9/30/1956	02:00	CST
4/28/1957	02:00	CDT
9/29/1957	02:00	CST
4/27/1958	02:00	CDT
9/28/1958	02:00	CST
4/26/1959	02:00	CDT
9/27/1959	02:00	CST
4/24/1960	02:00	EST
4/27/1969	02:00	EDT
10/26/1969	02:00	EST
4/26/1970	02:00	EDT
10/25/1970	02:00	EST

IN # 123

Before 11/18/1883		LMT
11/18/1883	12:00	CST
3/31/1918	02:00	CWT
10/27/1918	02:00	CST
3/30/1919	02:00	CWT
10/26/1919	02:00	CST
2/09/1942	02:00	CWT
9/30/1945	02:00	CST
4/27/1947	02:00	CDT
9/28/1947	02:00	CST
4/25/1948	02:00	CDT
9/26/1948	02:00	CST
4/30/1950	02:00	CDT
9/24/1950	02:00	CST
4/24/1955	02:00	CDT
10/30/1955	02:00	CST
4/29/1956	02:00	CDT
10/28/1956	02:00	CST
4/28/1957	02:00	CDT
9/29/1957	02:00	CST
4/27/1958	02:00	CDT
9/28/1958	02:00	CST
4/26/1959	02:00	CDT
9/27/1959	02:00	CST
4/24/1960	02:00	EST
4/27/1969	02:00	EDT
10/26/1969	02:00	EST
4/26/1970	02:00	EDT
10/25/1970	02:00	EST

IN # 124

Before 11/18/1883		LMT
11/18/1883	12:00	CST
3/31/1918	02:00	CWT
10/27/1918	02:00	CST
3/30/1919	02:00	CWT
10/26/1919	02:00	CST
2/09/1942	02:00	CWT
9/30/1945	02:00	CST
4/25/1948	02:00	CDT
10/01/1948	02:00	CST
4/24/1949	02:00	CDT
9/25/1949	02:00	CST
4/30/1950	02:00	CDT
9/24/1950	02:00	CST
4/24/1955	02:00	CDT
10/30/1955	02:00	CST
4/29/1956	02:00	CDT
10/28/1956	02:00	CST
4/28/1957	02:00	CDT
9/29/1957	02:00	CST
4/27/1958	02:00	CDT
9/28/1958	02:00	CST
4/26/1959	02:00	CDT
9/27/1959	02:00	CST
4/24/1960	02:00	EST
4/27/1969	02:00	EDT
10/26/1969	02:00	EST
4/26/1970	02:00	EDT
10/25/1970	02:00	EST

IN # 125

Before 11/18/1883		LMT
11/18/1883	12:00	CST
3/31/1918	02:00	CWT
10/27/1918	02:00	CST
3/30/1919	02:00	CWT
10/26/1919	02:00	CST
2/09/1942	02:00	CWT
9/30/1945	02:00	CST
4/27/1952	02:00	CDT
9/28/1952	02:00	CST
4/26/1953	02:00	CDT
9/27/1953	02:00	CST
4/25/1954	02:00	CDT
9/26/1954	02:00	CST
4/24/1955	02:00	CDT
9/25/1955	02:00	CST
4/29/1956	02:00	CDT
9/30/1956	02:00	CST
4/28/1957	02:00	CDT
9/29/1957	02:00	CST
4/27/1958	02:00	CDT
9/28/1958	02:00	CST
4/26/1959	02:00	CDT
9/27/1959	02:00	CST
4/24/1960	02:00	EST
4/27/1969	02:00	EDT
10/26/1969	02:00	EST
4/26/1970	02:00	EDT
10/25/1970	02:00	EST

IN # 126

Before 11/18/1883		LMT
11/18/1883	12:00	CST
3/31/1918	02:00	CWT
10/27/1918	02:00	CST
3/30/1919	02:00	CWT
10/26/1919	02:00	CST
2/09/1942	02:00	CWT
9/30/1945	02:00	CST
4/26/1953	02:00	CDT
9/27/1953	02:00	CST
4/25/1954	02:00	CDT
9/26/1954	02:00	CST
4/24/1955	02:00	CDT
9/25/1955	02:00	CST
4/29/1956	02:00	CDT
9/30/1956	02:00	CST
4/28/1957	02:00	CDT
9/29/1957	02:00	CST
4/27/1958	02:00	CDT
9/28/1958	02:00	CST
4/26/1959	02:00	CDT
9/27/1959	02:00	CST
4/24/1960	02:00	EST
4/27/1969	02:00	EDT
10/26/1969	02:00	EST
4/26/1970	02:00	EDT
10/25/1970	02:00	EST

IN # 127

Before 11/18/1883		LMT
11/18/1883	12:00	CST
3/31/1918	02:00	CWT
10/27/1918	02:00	CST
3/30/1919	02:00	CWT
10/26/1919	02:00	CST
2/09/1942	02:00	CWT
9/30/1945	02:00	CST
4/25/1954	02:00	CDT
9/26/1954	02:00	CST
4/24/1955	02:00	CDT
9/25/1955	02:00	CST
4/29/1956	02:00	CDT
9/30/1956	02:00	CST
4/28/1957	02:00	CDT
9/29/1957	02:00	CST
4/27/1958	02:00	CDT
9/28/1958	02:00	CST
4/26/1959	02:00	CDT
9/27/1959	02:00	CST
4/24/1960	02:00	EST
4/27/1969	02:00	EDT
10/26/1969	02:00	EST
4/26/1970	02:00	EDT
10/25/1970	02:00	EST

IN # 128

Before 11/18/1883		LMT
11/18/1883	12:00	CST
3/31/1918	02:00	CWT
10/27/1918	02:00	CST
3/30/1919	02:00	CWT
10/26/1919	02:00	CST
2/09/1942	02:00	CWT
9/30/1945	02:00	CST
4/24/1955	02:00	CDT
9/25/1955	02:00	CST
4/29/1956	02:00	CDT
9/30/1956	02:00	CST
4/28/1957	02:00	CDT
9/29/1957	02:00	CST
4/27/1958	02:00	CDT
9/28/1958	02:00	CST
4/26/1959	02:00	CDT
9/27/1959	02:00	CST
4/24/1960	02:00	EST
4/27/1969	02:00	EDT
10/26/1969	02:00	EST
4/26/1970	02:00	EDT
10/25/1970	02:00	EST

IN # 129

Before 11/18/1883		LMT
11/18/1883	12:00	CST
3/31/1918	02:00	CWT
10/27/1918	02:00	CST
3/30/1919	02:00	CWT
10/26/1919	02:00	CST
2/09/1942	02:00	CWT
9/30/1945	02:00	CST
4/27/1952	02:00	CDT
9/28/1952	02:00	CST
4/26/1953	02:00	CDT
9/27/1953	02:00	CST
4/24/1955	02:00	CDT
9/25/1955	02:00	CST
4/29/1956	02:00	CDT
10/01/1956	02:00	CST
4/28/1957	02:00	CDT
9/29/1957	02:00	CST
4/27/1958	02:00	CDT
9/28/1958	02:00	CST
4/26/1959	02:00	CDT
9/27/1959	02:00	CST
4/24/1960	02:00	EST
4/27/1969	02:00	EDT
10/26/1969	02:00	EST
4/26/1970	02:00	EDT
10/25/1970	02:00	EST

IN # 130

Before 11/18/1883		LMT
11/18/1883	12:00	CST
3/31/1918	02:00	CWT
10/27/1918	02:00	CST
3/30/1919	02:00	CWT
10/26/1919	02:00	CST
6/29/1941	02:00	CDT
10/26/1941	02:00	CST
2/09/1942	02:00	CWT
9/30/1945	02:00	CST
4/27/1947	02:00	CDT
9/28/1947	02:00	CST
4/26/1953	02:00	CDT
9/27/1953	02:00	CST
4/25/1954	02:00	CDT
9/26/1954	02:00	CST
4/24/1955	02:00	CDT
10/30/1955	02:00	CST
4/29/1956	02:00	CDT
11/19/1956	01:00	CST
4/28/1957	02:00	CDT
9/29/1957	02:00	CST
4/27/1958	02:00	CDT
10/26/1958	02:00	CST
4/26/1959	02:00	CDT
10/25/1959	02:00	CST
4/24/1960	02:00	EST
4/27/1969	02:00	EDT
10/26/1969	02:00	EST
4/26/1970	02:00	EDT
10/25/1970	02:00	EST

IN # 131

Before 11/18/1883		LMT
11/18/1883	12:00	CST
3/31/1918	02:00	CWT
10/27/1918	02:00	CST
3/30/1919	02:00	CWT
10/26/1919	02:00	CST
4/26/1936	02:00	CDT
9/27/1936	02:00	CST
4/24/1938	02:00	CDT
9/25/1938	02:00	CST
4/30/1939	02:00	CDT
9/24/1939	02:00	CST
4/28/1940	02:00	CDT
9/29/1940	02:00	CST
4/27/1941	02:00	CDT
9/28/1941	02:00	CST
2/09/1942	02:00	CWT
9/30/1945	02:00	CST
4/28/1946	02:00	CDT
9/29/1946	02:00	CST
4/25/1948	02:00	CDT
9/26/1948	02:00	CST
4/30/1950	02:00	CDT
9/24/1950	02:00	CST
4/29/1951	02:00	CDT
9/30/1951	02:00	CST
4/27/1952	02:00	CDT
9/28/1952	02:00	CST
4/26/1953	02:00	CDT
9/27/1953	02:00	CST
4/25/1954	02:00	CDT
9/26/1954	02:00	CST
4/24/1955	02:00	CDT
10/30/1955	02:00	CST
4/29/1956	02:00	CDT
9/29/1957	02:00	CST
4/27/1958	02:00	CDT
9/28/1958	02:00	CST
4/26/1959	02:00	CDT
9/27/1959	02:00	CST
4/24/1960	02:00	EST
4/27/1969	02:00	EDT
10/26/1969	02:00	EST
4/26/1970	02:00	EDT
10/25/1970	02:00	EST

IN # 132

Before 11/18/1883		LMT
11/18/1883	12:00	CST
3/31/1918	02:00	CWT
10/27/1918	02:00	CST
3/30/1919	02:00	CWT
10/26/1919	02:00	CST
2/09/1942	02:00	CWT
9/30/1945	02:00	CST
4/27/1947	02:00	CDT
9/28/1947	02:00	CST
4/24/1949	02:00	CDT
9/25/1949	02:00	CST
4/23/1950	02:00	CDT
9/09/1950	02:00	CST
4/28/1957	02:00	CDT
9/29/1957	02:00	CST
4/27/1958	02:00	CDT
9/28/1958	02:00	CST
4/26/1959	02:00	CDT
9/27/1959	02:00	CST
4/24/1960	02:00	EST
4/27/1969	02:00	EDT
10/26/1969	02:00	EST
4/26/1970	02:00	EDT
10/25/1970	02:00	EST

IN # 133

Before 11/18/1883		LMT
11/18/1883	12:00	CST
3/31/1918	02:00	CWT
10/27/1918	02:00	CST
3/30/1919	02:00	CWT
10/26/1919	02:00	CST
2/09/1942	02:00	CWT
9/30/1945	02:00	CST
4/27/1952	02:00	CDT
9/28/1952	02:00	CST
4/26/1953	02:00	CDT
9/27/1953	02:00	CST
4/25/1954	02:00	CDT
9/26/1954	02:00	CST
4/24/1955	02:00	CDT
9/25/1955	02:00	CST
4/29/1956	02:00	CDT
10/28/1956	02:00	CST
4/28/1957	02:00	CDT
9/29/1957	02:00	CST
4/27/1958	02:00	CDT
10/26/1958	02:00	CST
4/26/1959	02:00	CDT
10/25/1959	02:00	CST
4/24/1960	02:00	EST
4/27/1969	02:00	EDT
10/26/1969	02:00	EST
4/26/1970	02:00	EDT
10/25/1970	02:00	EST

IN # 134

Before 11/18/1883		LMT
11/18/1883	12:00	CST
3/31/1918	02:00	CWT
10/27/1918	02:00	CST
3/30/1919	02:00	CWT
10/26/1919	02:00	CST
6/29/1941	01:00	CDT
10/26/1941	01:00	CST
2/09/1942	02:00	CWT
9/30/1945	02:00	CST
5/04/1946	02:00	CDT
10/05/1946	02:00	CST
4/27/1947	02:00	CDT
9/28/1947	02:00	CST
4/25/1948	02:00	CDT
9/26/1948	02:00	CST
4/24/1949	02:00	CDT
9/25/1949	02:00	CST
4/23/1950	02:00	CDT
9/09/1950	02:00	CST
4/29/1951	02:00	CDT
9/30/1951	02:00	CST
4/27/1952	02:00	CDT
9/28/1952	02:00	CST
4/26/1953	02:00	CDT
9/27/1953	02:00	CST
4/25/1954	02:00	CDT
9/26/1954	02:00	CST
4/24/1955	02:00	CDT
10/30/1955	02:00	CST
4/29/1956	02:00	CDT
10/28/1956	01:00	CST
4/28/1957	02:00	CDT
9/29/1957	02:00	CST
4/27/1958	02:00	CDT
9/28/1958	02:00	CST
4/26/1959	02:00	CDT
9/27/1959	02:00	CST
4/24/1960	02:00	EST
4/27/1969	02:00	EDT
10/26/1969	02:00	EST
4/26/1970	02:00	EDT
10/25/1970	02:00	EST

IN # 135

Before 11/18/1883		LMT
11/18/1883	12:00	CST
3/31/1918	02:00	CWT
10/27/1918	02:00	CST
3/30/1919	02:00	CWT
10/26/1919	02:00	CST
4/27/1941	02:00	CDT
10/28/1941	02:00	CST
2/09/1942	02:00	CWT
9/30/1945	02:00	CST
4/25/1948	02:00	CDT
9/26/1948	02:00	CST
4/30/1950	02:00	CDT
9/24/1950	02:00	CST
4/24/1955	02:00	CDT
10/30/1955	02:00	CST
4/29/1956	02:00	CDT
10/28/1956	02:00	CST
4/28/1957	02:00	CDT
9/29/1957	02:00	CST
4/27/1958	02:00	CDT
9/28/1958	02:00	CST
4/26/1959	02:00	CDT
9/27/1959	02:00	CST
4/24/1960	02:00	EST
4/27/1969	02:00	EDT
10/26/1969	02:00	EST
4/26/1970	02:00	EDT
10/25/1970	02:00	EST

IN # 136

Before 11/18/1883		LMT
11/18/1883	12:00	CST
3/31/1918	02:00	CWT
10/27/1918	02:00	CST
3/30/1919	02:00	CWT
10/26/1919	02:00	CST
2/09/1942	02:00	CWT
9/30/1945	02:00	CST
4/26/1953	02:00	CDT
9/27/1953	02:00	CST
4/25/1954	02:00	CDT
9/26/1954	02:00	CST
4/24/1955	02:00	CDT
9/25/1955	02:00	CST
4/02/1956	02:00	CDT
9/29/1956	02:00	CST
4/28/1957	02:00	CDT
9/29/1957	02:00	CST
4/27/1958	02:00	CDT
9/28/1958	02:00	CST
4/26/1959	02:00	CDT
9/27/1959	02:00	CST
4/24/1960	02:00	EST
4/27/1969	02:00	EDT
10/26/1969	02:00	EST
4/26/1970	02:00	EDT
10/25/1970	02:00	EST

IN # 137

Before 11/18/1883		LMT
11/18/1883	12:00	CST
3/31/1918	02:00	CWT
10/27/1918	02:00	CST
3/30/1919	02:00	CWT
10/26/1919	02:00	CST
2/09/1942	02:00	CWT
9/30/1945	02:00	CST
5/01/1950	02:00	CDT
9/30/1950	02:00	CST
4/28/1957	02:00	CDT
9/29/1957	02:00	CST
4/27/1958	02:00	CDT
9/28/1958	02:00	CST
4/26/1959	02:00	CDT
9/27/1959	02:00	CST
4/24/1960	02:00	EST
4/27/1969	02:00	EDT
10/26/1969	02:00	EST
4/26/1970	02:00	EDT
10/25/1970	02:00	EST

IN # 138

Before 11/18/1883		LMT
11/18/1883	12:00	CST
3/31/1918	02:00	CWT
10/27/1918	02:00	CST
3/30/1919	02:00	CWT
10/26/1919	02:00	CST
6/29/1941	02:00	CDT
10/26/1941	02:00	CST
2/09/1942	02:00	CWT
9/30/1945	02:00	CST
4/30/1950	02:00	CDT
9/24/1950	02:00	CST
4/29/1951	02:00	CDT
9/30/1951	02:00	CST
4/27/1952	02:00	CDT
9/28/1952	02:00	CST
4/26/1953	02:00	CDT
9/27/1953	02:00	CST
4/25/1954	02:00	CDT
9/26/1954	02:00	CST
4/24/1955	02:00	CDT
10/30/1955	02:00	CST
4/29/1956	02:00	CDT
9/23/1956	00:01	CST
4/28/1957	02:00	CDT
9/29/1957	02:00	CST
4/27/1958	02:00	CDT
9/28/1958	02:00	CST
4/26/1959	02:00	CDT
9/27/1959	02:00	CST
4/24/1960	02:00	EST
4/27/1969	02:00	EDT
10/26/1969	02:00	EST
4/26/1970	02:00	EDT
10/25/1970	02:00	EST

IN # 139

Before 11/18/1883		LMT
11/18/1883	12:00	CST
3/31/1918	02:00	CWT
10/27/1918	02:00	CST
3/30/1919	02:00	CWT
10/26/1919	02:00	CST
2/09/1942	02:00	CWT
9/30/1945	02:00	CST
4/26/1953	02:00	CDT
9/27/1953	02:00	CST
4/25/1954	02:00	CDT
9/26/1954	02:00	CST
4/24/1955	02:00	CDT
10/30/1955	02:00	CST
4/29/1956	02:00	CDT
11/18/1956	02:00	CST
4/28/1957	02:00	CDT
9/29/1957	02:00	CST
4/27/1958	02:00	CDT
9/28/1958	02:00	CST
4/26/1959	02:00	CDT
9/27/1959	02:00	CST
4/24/1960	02:00	EST

TIME TABLES

4/27/1969	02:00	EDT
10/26/1969	02:00	EST
4/26/1970	02:00	EDT
10/25/1970	02:00	EST

IN # 140		
Before 11/18/1883		LMT
11/18/1883	12:00	CST
3/31/1918	02:00	CWT
10/27/1918	02:00	CST
3/30/1919	02:00	CWT
10/26/1919	02:00	CST
2/09/1942	02:00	CWT
9/30/1945	02:00	CST
5/05/1946	02:00	CDT
9/27/1946	02:00	CST
4/27/1947	02:00	CDT
9/28/1947	02:00	CST
4/25/1954	02:00	CDT
9/26/1954	02:00	CST
4/24/1955	02:00	CDT
9/25/1955	02:00	CST
4/29/1956	02:00	CDT
10/28/1956	02:00	CST
4/28/1957	02:00	CDT
9/29/1957	02:00	CST
4/27/1958	02:00	CDT
10/26/1958	02:00	CST
4/26/1959	02:00	CDT
10/25/1959	02:00	CST
4/24/1960	02:00	EST
4/27/1969	02:00	EDT
10/26/1969	02:00	EST
4/26/1970	02:00	EDT
10/25/1970	02:00	EST

IN # 141		
Before 11/18/1883		LMT
11/18/1883	12:00	CST
3/31/1918	02:00	CWT
10/27/1918	02:00	CST
3/30/1919	02:00	CWT
10/26/1919	02:00	CST
2/09/1942	02:00	CWT
9/30/1945	02:00	CST
4/24/1955	02:00	CDT
10/30/1955	02:00	CST
4/29/1956	02:00	CDT
11/18/1956	02:00	CST
4/28/1957	02:00	CDT
9/29/1957	02:00	CST
4/27/1958	02:00	CDT
9/28/1958	02:00	CST
4/26/1959	02:00	CDT
9/27/1959	02:00	CST
4/24/1960	02:00	EST
4/27/1969	02:00	EDT
10/26/1969	02:00	EST
4/26/1970	02:00	EDT
10/25/1970	02:00	EST

IN # 142		
Before 11/18/1883		LMT
11/18/1883	12:00	CST
3/31/1918	02:00	CWT
10/27/1918	02:00	CST
3/30/1919	02:00	CWT
10/26/1919	02:00	CST
2/09/1942	02:00	CWT
9/30/1945	02:00	CST
4/30/1950	02:00	CDT
9/24/1950	02:00	CST
4/25/1954	02:00	CDT
9/26/1954	02:00	CST
4/24/1955	02:00	CDT
9/25/1955	02:00	CST
4/29/1956	02:00	CDT
10/28/1956	02:00	CST
4/28/1957	02:00	CDT
9/29/1957	02:00	CST
4/27/1958	02:00	CDT
10/26/1958	02:00	CST
4/26/1959	02:00	CDT
10/25/1959	02:00	CST
4/24/1960	02:00	EST
4/27/1969	02:00	EDT
10/26/1969	02:00	EST
4/26/1970	02:00	EDT
10/25/1970	02:00	EST

IN # 143		
Before 11/18/1883		LMT
11/18/1883	12:00	CST
3/31/1918	02:00	CWT
10/27/1918	02:00	CST
3/30/1919	02:00	CWT
10/26/1919	02:00	CST
2/09/1942	02:00	CWT
9/30/1945	02:00	CST
4/25/1954	02:00	CDT
9/26/1954	02:00	CST
4/24/1955	02:00	CDT
9/25/1955	02:00	CST
4/29/1956	02:00	CDT
10/28/1956	02:00	CST
4/28/1957	02:00	CDT
9/29/1957	02:00	CST
4/27/1958	02:00	CDT
10/26/1958	02:00	CST
4/26/1959	02:00	CDT
10/25/1959	02:00	CST
4/24/1960	02:00	EST
4/27/1969	02:00	EDT
10/26/1969	02:00	EST
4/26/1970	02:00	EDT
10/25/1970	02:00	EST

IN # 144		
Before 11/18/1883		LMT
11/18/1883	12:00	CST
3/31/1918	02:00	CWT
10/27/1918	02:00	CST
3/30/1919	02:00	CWT
10/26/1919	02:00	CST
2/09/1942	02:00	CWT
9/30/1945	02:00	CST
4/26/1953	02:00	CDT
9/27/1953	02:00	CST
4/25/1954	02:00	CDT
9/26/1954	02:00	CST
4/24/1955	02:00	CDT
9/25/1955	02:00	CST
4/29/1956	02:00	CDT
10/28/1956	02:00	CST
4/28/1957	02:00	CDT
9/29/1957	02:00	CST
4/27/1958	02:00	CDT
10/26/1958	02:00	CST
4/26/1959	02:00	CDT
10/25/1959	02:00	CST
4/24/1960	02:00	EST
4/27/1969	02:00	EDT
10/26/1969	02:00	EST
4/26/1970	02:00	EDT
10/25/1970	02:00	EST

IN # 145		
Before 11/18/1883		LMT
11/18/1883	12:00	CST
3/31/1918	02:00	CWT
10/27/1918	02:00	CST
3/30/1919	02:00	CWT
10/26/1919	02:00	CST
2/09/1942	02:00	CWT
9/30/1945	02:00	CST
4/24/1955	02:00	CDT
10/30/1955	02:00	CST
4/29/1956	02:00	CDT
11/19/1956	01:00	CST
4/28/1957	02:00	CDT
9/29/1957	02:00	CST
4/27/1958	02:00	CDT
9/28/1958	02:00	CST
4/26/1959	02:00	CDT
9/27/1959	02:00	CST
4/24/1960	02:00	EST
4/27/1969	02:00	EDT
10/26/1969	02:00	EST
4/26/1970	02:00	EDT
10/25/1970	02:00	EST

IN # 146		
Before 11/18/1883		LMT
11/18/1883	12:00	CST
3/31/1918	02:00	CWT
10/27/1918	02:00	CST
3/30/1919	02:00	CWT
10/26/1919	02:00	CST
2/09/1942	02:00	CWT
9/30/1945	02:00	CST
4/24/1955	02:00	CDT
9/25/1955	02:00	CST
4/29/1956	02:00	CDT
10/28/1956	02:00	CST
4/28/1957	02:00	CDT
9/29/1957	02:00	CST
4/27/1958	02:00	CDT
9/28/1958	02:00	CST
4/26/1959	02:00	CDT
9/27/1959	02:00	CST
4/24/1960	02:00	EST
4/27/1969	02:00	EDT
10/26/1969	02:00	EST
4/26/1970	02:00	EDT
10/25/1970	02:00	EST

IN # 147		
Before 11/18/1883		LMT
11/18/1883	12:00	CST
3/31/1918	02:00	CWT
10/27/1918	02:00	CST
3/30/1919	02:00	CWT
10/26/1919	02:00	CST
2/09/1942	02:00	CWT
9/30/1945	02:00	CST
4/24/1955	02:00	CDT
10/30/1955	02:00	CST
4/29/1956	02:00	CDT
10/28/1956	02:00	CST
4/28/1957	02:00	CDT
9/29/1957	02:00	CST
4/27/1958	02:00	CDT
9/28/1958	02:00	CST
4/26/1959	02:00	CDT
9/27/1959	02:00	CST
4/24/1960	02:00	EST
4/27/1969	02:00	EDT
10/26/1969	02:00	EST
4/26/1970	02:00	EDT
10/25/1970	02:00	EST

IN # 148		
Before 11/18/1883		LMT
11/18/1883	12:00	CST
3/31/1918	02:00	CWT
10/27/1918	02:00	CST
3/30/1919	02:00	CWT
10/26/1919	02:00	CST
2/09/1942	02:00	CWT
9/30/1945	02:00	CST
4/25/1954	02:00	CDT
9/26/1954	02:00	CST
4/24/1955	02:00	CDT
10/30/1955	02:00	CST
4/29/1956	02:00	CDT
10/28/1956	02:00	CST
4/28/1957	02:00	CDT
9/29/1957	02:00	CST
4/27/1958	02:00	CDT
9/28/1958	02:00	CST
4/26/1959	02:00	CDT
9/27/1959	02:00	CST
4/24/1960	02:00	EST
4/27/1969	02:00	EDT
10/26/1969	02:00	EST
4/26/1970	02:00	EDT
10/25/1970	02:00	EST

IN # 149		
Before 11/18/1883		LMT
11/18/1883	12:00	CST
3/31/1918	02:00	CWT
10/27/1918	02:00	CST
3/30/1919	02:00	CWT
10/26/1919	02:00	CST
2/09/1942	02:00	CWT
9/30/1945	02:00	CST
4/26/1953	02:00	CDT
9/27/1953	02:00	CST
4/25/1954	02:00	CDT
9/26/1954	02:00	CST
4/24/1955	02:00	CDT
10/30/1955	02:00	CST
4/29/1956	02:00	CDT
10/28/1956	02:00	CST
4/28/1957	02:00	CDT
9/29/1957	02:00	CST
4/27/1958	02:00	CDT
9/28/1958	02:00	CST
4/26/1959	02:00	CDT
9/27/1959	02:00	CST
4/24/1960	02:00	EST
4/27/1969	02:00	EDT
10/26/1969	02:00	EST
4/26/1970	02:00	EDT
10/25/1970	02:00	EST

IN # 150		
Before 11/18/1883		LMT
11/18/1883	12:00	CST
3/31/1918	02:00	CWT
10/27/1918	02:00	CST
3/30/1919	02:00	CWT
10/26/1919	02:00	CST
2/09/1942	02:00	CWT
9/30/1945	02:00	CST
4/25/1948	02:00	CDT
9/26/1948	02:00	CST
4/24/1955	02:00	CDT
10/30/1955	02:00	CST
4/29/1956	02:00	CDT
10/28/1956	02:00	CST
4/28/1957	02:00	CDT
9/29/1957	02:00	CST
4/27/1958	02:00	CDT
9/28/1958	02:00	CST
4/26/1959	02:00	CDT
9/27/1959	02:00	CST
4/24/1960	02:00	EST
4/27/1969	02:00	EDT
10/26/1969	02:00	EST
4/26/1970	02:00	EDT
10/25/1970	02:00	EST

IN # 151		
Before 11/18/1883		LMT
11/18/1883	12:00	CST
3/31/1918	02:00	CWT
10/27/1918	02:00	CST
3/30/1919	02:00	CWT
10/26/1919	02:00	CST
2/09/1942	02:00	CWT
9/30/1945	02:00	CST
4/29/1951	02:00	CDT
9/30/1951	02:00	CST
4/28/1957	02:00	CDT
9/29/1957	02:00	CST
4/27/1958	02:00	CDT
9/28/1958	02:00	CST
4/26/1959	02:00	CDT
9/27/1959	02:00	CST
4/24/1960	02:00	EST
4/27/1969	02:00	EDT
10/26/1969	02:00	EST
4/26/1970	02:00	EDT
10/25/1970	02:00	EST

IN # 152		
Before 11/18/1883		LMT
11/18/1883	12:00	CST
3/31/1918	02:00	CWT
10/27/1918	02:00	CST
3/30/1919	02:00	CWT
10/26/1919	02:00	CST
2/09/1942	02:00	CWT
9/30/1945	02:00	CST
4/24/1955	02:00	CDT
10/30/1955	02:00	CST
4/29/1956	02:00	CDT
10/28/1956	02:00	CST
4/28/1957	02:00	CDT
9/29/1957	02:00	CST
4/27/1958	02:00	CDT
10/26/1958	02:00	CST
4/26/1959	02:00	CDT
10/25/1959	02:00	CST
4/24/1960	02:00	EST
4/27/1969	02:00	EDT
10/26/1969	02:00	EST
4/26/1970	02:00	EDT
10/25/1970	02:00	EST

IN # 153		
Before 11/18/1883		LMT
11/18/1883	12:00	CST
3/31/1918	02:00	CWT
10/27/1918	02:00	CST
3/30/1919	02:00	CWT
10/26/1919	02:00	CST
2/09/1942	02:00	CWT
9/30/1945	02:00	CST
4/27/1947	02:00	CDT
9/28/1947	02:00	CST
4/27/1952	02:00	CDT
9/28/1952	02:00	CST
4/26/1953	02:00	CDT
9/27/1953	02:00	CST
4/25/1954	02:00	CDT
9/26/1954	02:00	CST
4/24/1955	02:00	CDT
10/30/1955	02:00	CST
4/29/1956	02:00	CDT
10/28/1956	02:00	CST
4/28/1957	02:00	CDT
9/29/1957	02:00	CST
4/27/1958	02:00	CDT
9/28/1958	02:00	CST
4/26/1959	02:00	CDT
9/27/1959	02:00	CST
4/24/1960	02:00	EST
4/27/1969	02:00	EDT
10/26/1969	02:00	EST
4/26/1970	02:00	EDT
10/25/1970	02:00	EST

IN # 154		
Before 11/18/1883		LMT
11/18/1883	12:00	CST
3/31/1918	02:00	CWT
10/27/1918	02:00	CST
3/30/1919	02:00	CWT
10/26/1919	02:00	CST
2/09/1942	02:00	CWT
9/30/1945	02:00	CST
4/27/1952	02:00	CDT
9/28/1952	02:00	CST
4/26/1953	02:00	CDT
9/27/1953	02:00	CST
4/25/1954	02:00	CDT
9/26/1954	02:00	CST
4/24/1955	02:00	CDT
10/30/1955	02:00	CST
4/29/1956	02:00	CDT
10/28/1956	02:00	CST
4/28/1957	02:00	CDT
9/29/1957	02:00	CST
4/27/1958	02:00	CDT
9/28/1958	02:00	CST
4/26/1959	02:00	CDT
9/27/1959	02:00	CST
4/24/1960	02:00	EST
4/27/1969	02:00	EDT
10/26/1969	02:00	EST
4/26/1970	02:00	EDT
10/25/1970	02:00	EST

IN # 155		
Before 11/18/1883		LMT
11/18/1883	12:00	CST
3/31/1918	02:00	CWT
10/27/1918	02:00	CST
3/30/1919	02:00	CWT
10/26/1919	02:00	CST
2/09/1942	02:00	CWT
9/30/1945	02:00	CST
4/24/1955	02:00	CDT
10/30/1955	02:00	CST
4/29/1956	02:00	CDT
10/01/1956	00:00	CST
4/28/1957	02:00	CDT
9/29/1957	02:00	CST
4/27/1958	02:00	CDT
9/28/1958	02:00	CST
4/26/1959	02:00	CDT
9/27/1959	02:00	CST
4/24/1960	02:00	EST
4/27/1969	02:00	EDT
10/26/1969	02:00	EST
4/26/1970	02:00	EDT
10/25/1970	02:00	EST

IN # 156		
Before 11/18/1883		LMT
11/18/1883	12:00	CST
3/31/1918	02:00	CWT
10/27/1918	02:00	CST
3/30/1919	02:00	CWT
10/26/1919	02:00	CST
2/09/1942	02:00	CWT
9/30/1945	02:00	CST
4/24/1955	02:00	CDT
9/25/1955	02:00	CST
4/29/1956	02:00	CDT
10/01/1956	02:00	CST
4/28/1957	02:00	CDT
9/29/1957	02:00	CST
4/27/1958	02:00	CDT
9/28/1958	02:00	CST
4/26/1959	02:00	CDT
9/27/1959	02:00	CST
4/24/1960	02:00	EST
4/27/1969	02:00	EDT
10/26/1969	02:00	EST
4/26/1970	02:00	EDT
10/25/1970	02:00	EST

IN # 157		
Before 11/18/1883		LMT
11/18/1883	12:00	CST
3/31/1918	02:00	CWT
10/27/1918	02:00	CST
3/30/1919	02:00	CWT
10/26/1919	02:00	CST
2/09/1942	02:00	CWT
9/30/1945	02:00	CST
4/26/1953	02:00	CDT
9/27/1953	02:00	CST
4/25/1954	02:00	CDT
9/26/1954	02:00	CST
4/24/1955	02:00	CDT
9/25/1955	02:00	CST
4/29/1956	02:00	CDT
10/28/1956	02:00	CST
4/28/1957	02:00	CDT
9/29/1957	02:00	CST
4/27/1958	02:00	CDT
9/28/1958	02:00	CST
4/26/1959	02:00	CDT
9/27/1959	02:00	CST
4/24/1960	02:00	EST
4/27/1969	02:00	EDT
10/26/1969	02:00	EST
4/26/1970	02:00	EDT
10/25/1970	02:00	EST

IN # 158		
Before 11/18/1883		LMT
11/18/1883	12:00	CST
3/31/1918	02:00	CWT
10/27/1918	02:00	CST
3/30/1919	02:00	CWT
10/26/1919	02:00	CST
2/09/1942	02:00	CWT
9/30/1945	02:00	CST
4/26/1953	02:00	CDT
9/27/1953	02:00	CST
4/25/1954	02:00	CDT
9/26/1954	02:00	CST
4/24/1955	02:00	CDT
9/25/1955	02:00	CST
4/29/1956	02:00	CDT
10/01/1956	02:00	CST
4/28/1957	02:00	CDT
9/29/1957	02:00	CST
4/27/1958	02:00	CDT
9/28/1958	02:00	CST
4/26/1959	02:00	CDT
9/27/1959	02:00	CST
4/24/1960	02:00	EST
4/27/1969	02:00	EDT
10/26/1969	02:00	EST
4/26/1970	02:00	EDT
10/25/1970	02:00	EST

IN # 159		
Before 11/18/1883		LMT
11/18/1883	12:00	CST
3/31/1918	02:00	CWT
10/27/1918	02:00	CST
3/30/1919	02:00	CWT
10/26/1919	02:00	CST
2/09/1942	02:00	CWT
9/30/1945	02:00	CST
5/01/1955	00:00	CDT
9/04/1955	00:00	CST
4/29/1956	02:00	CDT
9/30/1956	02:00	CST
4/28/1957	02:00	CDT
9/29/1957	02:00	CST
4/27/1958	02:00	CDT
9/28/1958	02:00	CST
4/26/1959	02:00	CDT
9/27/1959	02:00	CST
4/24/1960	02:00	EST
4/27/1969	02:00	EDT
10/26/1969	02:00	EST
4/26/1970	02:00	EDT
10/25/1970	02:00	EST

IN # 160		
Before 11/18/1883		LMT
11/18/1883	12:00	CST
3/31/1918	02:00	CWT
10/27/1918	02:00	CST
3/30/1919	02:00	CWT
10/26/1919	02:00	CST
2/09/1942	02:00	CWT
9/30/1945	02:00	CST
4/24/1955	02:00	CDT
9/04/1955	00:00	CST
4/29/1956	02:00	CDT
9/30/1956	02:00	CST
4/28/1957	02:00	CDT
9/29/1957	02:00	CST
4/27/1958	02:00	CDT

TIME TABLES

9/28/1958	02:00	CST
4/26/1959	02:00	CDT
9/27/1959	02:00	CST
4/24/1960	02:00	EST
4/27/1969	02:00	EDT
10/26/1969	02:00	EST
4/26/1970	02:00	EDT
10/25/1970	02:00	EST

IN # 161

Before 11/18/1883		LMT
11/18/1883	12:00	CST
3/31/1918	02:00	CWT
10/27/1918	02:00	CST
3/30/1919	02:00	CWT
10/26/1919	02:00	CST
2/09/1942	02:00	CWT
9/30/1945	02:00	CST
4/26/1953	02:00	CDT
9/27/1953	02:00	CST
4/25/1954	02:00	CDT
9/26/1954	02:00	CST
4/24/1955	02:00	CDT
9/25/1955	02:00	CST
4/29/1956	02:00	CDT
9/30/1956	02:00	CST
4/28/1957	02:00	CDT
9/29/1957	02:00	CST
4/27/1958	02:00	CDT
9/28/1958	02:00	CST
4/26/1959	02:00	EST
4/27/1969	02:00	EDT
10/26/1969	02:00	EST
4/26/1970	02:00	EDT
10/25/1970	02:00	EST

IN # 162

Before 11/18/1883		LMT
11/18/1883	12:00	CST
3/31/1918	02:00	CWT
10/27/1918	02:00	CST
3/30/1919	02:00	CWT
10/26/1919	02:00	CST
2/09/1942	02:00	CWT
9/30/1945	02:00	CST
4/25/1948	02:00	CDT
9/26/1948	02:00	CST
4/27/1952	02:00	CDT
9/28/1952	02:00	CST
4/26/1953	02:00	CDT
9/27/1953	02:00	CST
4/25/1954	02:00	CDT
9/26/1954	02:00	CST
4/24/1955	02:00	CDT
9/25/1955	02:00	CST
4/29/1956	02:00	CDT
10/28/1956	02:00	CST
4/28/1957	02:00	CDT
9/29/1957	02:00	CST
4/27/1958	02:00	CDT
10/26/1958	02:00	CST
4/26/1959	02:00	CDT
10/25/1959	02:00	CST
4/24/1960	02:00	CDT
10/30/1960	02:00	CST
4/30/1961	02:00	EST
4/27/1969	02:00	EDT
10/26/1969	02:00	EST
4/26/1970	02:00	EDT
10/25/1970	02:00	EST

IN # 163

Before 11/18/1883		LMT
11/18/1883	12:00	CST
3/31/1918	02:00	CWT
10/27/1918	02:00	CST
3/30/1919	02:00	CWT
10/26/1919	02:00	CST
2/09/1942	02:00	CWT
9/30/1945	02:00	CST
4/25/1948	02:00	CDT
9/26/1948	02:00	CST
4/24/1955	02:00	CDT
9/25/1955	02:00	CST
4/29/1956	02:00	CDT
10/28/1956	02:00	CST
4/28/1957	02:00	CDT
9/29/1957	02:00	CST
4/27/1958	02:00	CDT
9/28/1958	02:00	CST
4/26/1959	02:00	CDT
9/27/1959	02:00	CST
4/24/1960	02:00	CDT
9/25/1960	02:00	CST
4/30/1961	02:00	EST
4/27/1969	02:00	EDT
10/26/1969	02:00	EST
4/26/1970	02:00	EDT
10/25/1970	02:00	EST

IN # 164

Before 11/18/1883		LMT
11/18/1883	12:00	CST
3/31/1918	02:00	CWT
10/27/1918	02:00	CST
3/30/1919	02:00	CWT
10/26/1919	02:00	CST
2/09/1942	02:00	CWT
9/30/1945	02:00	CST
4/26/1953	02:00	CDT
9/27/1953	02:00	CST
4/25/1954	02:00	CDT
9/26/1954	02:00	CST
4/24/1955	02:00	CDT
9/25/1955	02:00	CST
4/29/1956	02:00	CDT
9/30/1956	02:00	CST
4/28/1957	02:00	CDT
9/29/1957	02:00	CST
4/27/1958	02:00	CDT
9/28/1958	02:00	CST
4/26/1959	02:00	CDT
9/27/1959	02:00	CST
4/24/1960	02:00	CDT
9/25/1960	02:00	CST
4/30/1961	02:00	EST
4/27/1969	02:00	EDT
10/26/1969	02:00	EST
4/26/1970	02:00	EDT
10/25/1970	02:00	EST

IN # 165

Before 11/18/1883		LMT
11/18/1883	12:00	CST
3/31/1918	02:00	CWT
10/27/1918	02:00	CST
3/30/1919	02:00	CWT
10/26/1919	02:00	CST
2/09/1942	02:00	CWT
9/30/1945	02:00	CST
4/24/1955	02:00	CDT
9/25/1955	02:00	CST
4/29/1956	02:00	CDT
9/30/1956	02:00	CST
4/28/1957	02:00	CDT
9/29/1957	02:00	CST
4/27/1958	02:00	CDT
9/28/1958	02:00	CST
4/26/1959	02:00	CDT
9/27/1959	02:00	CST
4/24/1960	02:00	CDT
9/25/1960	02:00	CST
4/30/1961	02:00	EST
4/27/1969	02:00	EDT
10/26/1969	02:00	EST
4/26/1970	02:00	EDT
10/25/1970	02:00	EST

IN # 166

Before 11/18/1883		LMT
11/18/1883	12:00	CST
3/31/1918	02:00	CWT
10/27/1918	02:00	CST
3/30/1919	02:00	CWT
10/26/1919	02:00	CST
2/09/1942	02:00	CWT
9/30/1945	02:00	CST
4/24/1955	02:00	CDT
9/25/1955	02:00	CST
4/29/1956	02:00	CDT
9/30/1956	02:00	CST
4/28/1957	02:00	CDT
9/29/1957	02:00	CST
4/27/1958	02:00	CDT
9/28/1958	02:00	CST
4/26/1959	02:00	CDT
9/27/1959	02:00	CST
4/24/1960	02:00	CDT
9/25/1960	02:00	CST
4/30/1961	02:00	EST
4/27/1969	02:00	EDT
10/26/1969	02:00	EST
4/26/1970	02:00	EDT
10/25/1970	02:00	EST
4/25/1971	02:00	EDT
10/31/1971	02:00	EST
4/30/1972	02:00	EDT
10/29/1972	02:00	EST
4/29/1973	02:00	EDT
10/28/1973	02:00	EST
2/23/1975	02:00	US#1

IN # 167

Before 11/18/1883		LMT
11/18/1883	12:00	CST
3/31/1918	02:00	CWT
10/27/1918	02:00	CST
3/30/1919	02:00	CWT
10/26/1919	02:00	CST
4/27/1941	02:00	CDT
9/28/1941	02:00	CST
2/09/1942	02:00	CWT
9/30/1945	02:00	CST
4/27/1952	02:00	CDT
9/28/1952	02:00	CST
4/26/1953	02:00	CDT
9/27/1953	02:00	CST
4/25/1954	02:00	CDT
9/26/1954	02:00	CST
4/24/1955	02:00	CDT
9/25/1955	02:00	CST
4/29/1956	02:00	CDT
9/30/1956	02:00	CST
4/28/1957	02:00	CDT
9/29/1957	02:00	CST
4/27/1958	02:00	CDT
9/28/1958	02:00	CST
4/26/1959	02:00	CDT
10/25/1959	02:00	CST
4/24/1960	02:00	CDT
10/30/1960	02:00	CST
4/30/1961	02:00	EST
4/27/1969	02:00	EDT
10/26/1969	02:00	EST
4/26/1970	02:00	EDT
10/25/1970	02:00	EST
4/25/1971	02:00	EDT
10/31/1971	02:00	EST
4/30/1972	02:00	EDT
10/29/1972	02:00	EST
4/29/1973	02:00	EDT
10/28/1973	02:00	EST
2/23/1975	02:00	US#1

IN # 168

Before 11/18/1883		LMT
11/18/1883	12:00	CST
3/31/1918	02:00	CWT
10/27/1918	02:00	CST
3/30/1919	02:00	CWT
10/26/1919	02:00	CST
2/09/1942	02:00	CWT
9/30/1945	02:00	CST
4/25/1954	02:00	CDT
9/26/1954	02:00	CST
4/24/1955	02:00	CDT
9/25/1955	02:00	CST
4/29/1956	02:00	CDT
9/29/1957	02:00	CST
4/27/1958	02:00	CDT
10/26/1958	02:00	CST
4/26/1959	02:00	CDT
10/25/1959	02:00	CST
4/24/1960	02:00	CDT
10/30/1960	02:00	CST
4/30/1961	02:00	EST
4/27/1969	02:00	EDT
10/26/1969	02:00	EST
4/26/1970	02:00	EDT
10/25/1970	02:00	EST
4/25/1971	02:00	EDT
10/31/1971	02:00	EST
4/30/1972	02:00	EDT
10/29/1972	02:00	EST
4/29/1973	02:00	EDT
10/28/1973	02:00	EST
2/23/1975	02:00	US#1

IN # 169

Before 11/18/1883		LMT
11/18/1883	12:00	CST
3/31/1918	02:00	CWT
10/27/1918	02:00	CST
3/30/1919	02:00	CWT
10/26/1919	02:00	CST
2/09/1942	02:00	CWT
9/30/1945	02:00	CST
4/24/1955	02:00	CDT
9/25/1955	02:00	CST
4/29/1956	02:00	CDT
9/30/1956	02:00	CST
4/28/1957	02:00	CDT
9/29/1957	02:00	CST
4/27/1958	02:00	CDT
9/28/1958	02:00	CST
4/26/1959	02:00	CDT
9/27/1959	02:00	CST
4/24/1960	02:00	CDT
9/25/1960	02:00	CST
4/30/1961	02:00	EST
4/27/1969	02:00	EDT
10/26/1969	02:00	EST
4/26/1970	02:00	EDT
10/25/1970	02:00	EST
4/25/1971	02:00	EDT
10/31/1971	02:00	EST
4/30/1972	02:00	EDT
10/29/1972	02:00	EST
4/29/1973	02:00	EDT
10/28/1973	02:00	EST
2/23/1975	02:00	EDT
10/26/1975	02:00	EST

IN # 170

Before 11/18/1883		LMT
11/18/1883	12:00	CST
3/31/1918	02:00	CWT
10/27/1918	02:00	CST
3/30/1919	02:00	CWT
10/26/1919	02:00	CST
2/09/1942	02:00	CWT
9/30/1945	02:00	CST
4/26/1953	02:00	CDT
9/27/1953	02:00	CST
4/25/1954	02:00	CDT
9/26/1954	02:00	CST
4/24/1955	02:00	CDT
9/25/1955	02:00	CST
4/29/1956	02:00	CDT
11/04/1956	02:00	CST
4/28/1957	02:00	CDT
9/29/1957	02:00	CST
4/27/1958	02:00	CDT
9/28/1958	02:00	CST
4/26/1959	02:00	CDT
9/27/1959	02:00	CST
4/24/1960	02:00	CDT
9/25/1960	02:00	CST
4/30/1961	02:00	EST
4/27/1969	02:00	EDT
10/26/1969	02:00	EST
4/26/1970	02:00	EDT
10/25/1970	02:00	EST

IN # 171

Before 11/18/1883		LMT
11/18/1883	12:00	CST
3/31/1918	02:00	CWT
10/27/1918	02:00	CST
3/30/1919	02:00	CWT
10/26/1919	02:00	CST
4/27/1941	02:00	CDT
9/28/1941	02:00	CST
2/09/1942	02:00	CWT
9/30/1945	02:00	CST
4/28/1946	02:00	CDT
9/29/1946	02:00	CST
4/27/1947	02:00	CDT
9/28/1947	02:00	CST
4/25/1948	02:00	CDT
9/26/1948	02:00	CST
4/24/1949	02:00	CDT
9/10/1949	02:00	CST
4/30/1950	02:00	CDT
9/24/1950	02:00	CST
4/29/1951	02:00	CDT
9/30/1951	02:00	CST
4/27/1952	02:00	CDT
9/28/1952	02:00	CST
4/26/1953	02:00	CDT
9/27/1953	02:00	CST
4/25/1954	02:00	CDT
9/26/1954	02:00	CST
4/24/1955	02:00	CDT
10/30/1955	02:00	CST
4/02/1956	02:00	CDT
10/28/1956	02:00	CST
4/28/1957	02:00	CDT
9/29/1957	02:00	CST
4/27/1958	02:00	CDT
9/28/1958	02:00	CST
4/26/1959	02:00	CDT
9/27/1959	02:00	CST
4/24/1960	02:00	CDT
9/25/1960	02:00	CST
4/30/1961	02:00	EST
4/27/1969	02:00	EDT
10/26/1969	02:00	EST
4/26/1970	02:00	EDT
10/25/1970	02:00	EST

IN # 172

Before 11/18/1883		LMT
11/18/1883	12:00	CST
3/31/1918	02:00	CWT
10/27/1918	02:00	CST
3/30/1919	02:00	CWT
10/26/1919	02:00	CST
2/09/1942	02:00	CWT
9/30/1945	02:00	CST
5/29/1947	02:00	CDT
9/28/1947	02:00	CST
4/25/1948	02:00	CDT
9/26/1948	02:00	CST
4/29/1951	02:00	CDT
9/30/1951	02:00	CST
4/28/1957	02:00	CDT
9/29/1957	02:00	CST
4/27/1958	02:00	CDT
9/28/1958	02:00	CST
4/26/1959	02:00	CDT
9/27/1959	02:00	CST
4/24/1960	02:00	CDT
9/25/1960	02:00	CST
4/30/1961	02:00	EST
4/27/1969	02:00	EDT
10/26/1969	02:00	EST
4/26/1970	02:00	EDT
10/25/1970	02:00	EST

IN # 173

Before 11/18/1883		LMT
11/18/1883	12:00	CST
3/31/1918	02:00	CWT
10/27/1918	02:00	CST
3/30/1919	02:00	CWT
10/26/1919	02:00	CST
4/27/1941	02:00	CDT
9/28/1941	02:00	CST
2/09/1942	02:00	CWT
9/30/1945	02:00	CST
4/07/1946	02:00	CDT
9/01/1946	02:00	CST
4/27/1947	02:00	CDT
9/28/1947	02:00	CST
4/25/1948	02:00	CDT
9/26/1948	02:00	CST
4/24/1949	02:00	CDT
9/25/1949	02:00	CST
4/30/1950	02:00	CDT
9/24/1950	02:00	CST
4/29/1951	02:00	CDT
9/30/1951	02:00	CST
4/27/1952	02:00	CDT
9/28/1952	02:00	CST
4/26/1953	02:00	CDT
9/27/1953	02:00	CST
4/25/1954	02:00	CDT
9/26/1954	02:00	CST
4/24/1955	02:00	CDT
9/25/1955	02:00	CST
4/29/1956	02:00	CDT
11/04/1956	02:00	CST
4/28/1957	02:00	CDT
9/29/1957	02:00	CST
4/27/1958	02:00	CDT
9/28/1958	02:00	CST
4/26/1959	02:00	CDT
9/27/1959	02:00	CST
4/24/1960	02:00	CDT
9/25/1960	02:00	CST
4/30/1961	02:00	EST

IN # 174

Before 11/18/1883		LMT
11/18/1883	12:00	CST
3/31/1918	02:00	CWT
10/27/1918	02:00	CST
3/30/1919	02:00	CWT
10/26/1919	02:00	CST
2/09/1942	02:00	CWT
9/30/1945	02:00	CST
4/24/1955	02:00	CDT
9/25/1955	02:00	CST
4/29/1956	02:00	CDT
9/30/1956	02:00	CST
4/28/1957	02:00	CDT
9/29/1957	02:00	CST
4/27/1958	02:00	CDT
10/26/1958	02:00	CST
4/26/1959	02:00	CDT
9/27/1959	02:00	CST
4/24/1960	02:00	CDT
9/25/1960	02:00	CST
4/30/1961	02:00	EST
4/27/1969	02:00	EDT
10/26/1969	02:00	EST
4/26/1970	02:00	EDT
10/25/1970	02:00	EST

IN # 175

Before 11/18/1883		LMT
11/18/1883	12:00	CST
3/31/1918	02:00	CWT
10/27/1918	02:00	CST
3/30/1919	02:00	CWT
10/26/1919	02:00	CST
2/09/1942	02:00	CWT
9/30/1945	02:00	CST
4/27/1947	02:00	CDT
9/30/1947	02:00	CST
4/25/1948	02:00	CDT
9/26/1948	02:00	CST
4/24/1949	02:00	CDT
9/10/1949	02:00	CST
4/30/1950	02:00	CDT
9/24/1950	02:00	CST
4/24/1955	02:00	CDT
10/30/1955	02:00	CST
4/29/1956	02:00	CDT
10/28/1956	02:00	CST
4/28/1957	02:00	CDT
9/29/1957	02:00	CST
4/27/1958	02:00	CDT
9/28/1958	02:00	CST
4/26/1959	02:00	CDT
9/27/1959	02:00	CST
4/24/1960	02:00	CDT
9/25/1960	02:00	CST
4/30/1961	02:00	EST
4/27/1969	02:00	EDT
10/26/1969	02:00	EST
4/26/1970	02:00	EDT
10/25/1970	02:00	EST

IN # 176

Before 11/18/1883		LMT
11/18/1883	12:00	CST
3/31/1918	02:00	CWT
10/27/1918	02:00	CST
3/30/1919	02:00	CWT
10/26/1919	02:00	CST
4/27/1941	02:00	CDT
9/28/1941	02:00	CST
2/09/1942	02:00	CWT
9/30/1945	02:00	CST
4/28/1946	02:00	CDT
9/29/1946	02:00	CST
4/30/1950	02:00	CDT
9/24/1950	02:00	CST
4/29/1951	02:00	CDT
9/30/1951	02:00	CST
4/27/1952	02:00	CDT
9/28/1952	02:00	CST
4/26/1953	02:00	CDT
9/27/1953	02:00	CST
4/25/1954	02:00	CDT
9/26/1954	02:00	CST
4/24/1955	02:00	CDT
9/25/1955	02:00	CST
4/29/1956	02:00	CDT
10/28/1956	02:00	CST
4/28/1957	02:00	CDT
9/29/1957	02:00	CST
4/27/1958	02:00	CDT
10/26/1958	02:00	CST
4/26/1959	02:00	CDT
10/25/1959	02:00	CST
4/24/1960	02:00	CDT
10/30/1960	02:00	CST
4/30/1961	02:00	EST
4/28/1968	02:00	US#1

IN # 177

Before 11/18/1883		LMT
11/18/1883	12:00	CST
3/31/1918	02:00	CWT
10/27/1918	02:00	CST
3/30/1919	02:00	CWT
10/26/1919	02:00	CST
2/09/1942	02:00	CWT
9/30/1945	02:00	CST
4/29/1951	02:00	CDT
9/30/1951	02:00	CST
4/25/1954	02:00	CDT

TIME TABLES

9/26/1954 02:00 CST
4/24/1955 02:00 CDT
9/25/1955 02:00 CST
4/29/1956 02:00 CDT
9/30/1956 02:00 CST
4/28/1957 02:00 CDT
9/29/1957 02:00 CST
4/27/1958 02:00 CDT
9/28/1958 02:00 CST
4/26/1959 02:00 CDT
9/27/1959 02:00 CST
4/24/1960 02:00 CDT
9/25/1960 02:00 CST
4/30/1961 02:00 EST
4/27/1969 02:00 EDT
10/26/1969 02:00 EST
4/26/1970 02:00 EDT
10/25/1970 02:00 EST
4/25/1971 02:00 EDT
10/31/1971 02:00 EST
4/30/1972 02:00 EDT
10/29/1972 02:00 EST
4/29/1973 02:00 EDT
10/28/1973 02:00 EST
2/23/1975 02:00 EDT
10/26/1975 02:00 EST

IN # 178
Before 11/18/1883 LMT
11/18/1883 12:00 CST
3/31/1918 02:00 CWT
10/27/1918 02:00 CST
3/30/1919 02:00 CWT
10/26/1919 02:00 CST
2/09/1942 02:00 CWT
9/30/1945 02:00 CST
4/29/1951 02:00 CDT
9/30/1951 02:00 CST
4/27/1952 02:00 CDT
9/28/1952 02:00 CST
4/26/1953 02:00 CDT
9/27/1953 02:00 CST
4/25/1954 02:00 CDT
9/26/1954 02:00 CST
4/24/1955 02:00 CDT
9/25/1955 02:00 CST
4/29/1956 02:00 CDT
9/30/1956 02:00 CST
4/28/1957 02:00 CDT
9/29/1957 02:00 CST
4/27/1958 02:00 CDT
9/28/1958 02:00 CST
4/26/1959 02:00 CDT
9/27/1959 02:00 CST
4/24/1960 02:00 CDT
9/25/1960 02:00 CST
4/30/1961 02:00 EST
4/27/1969 02:00 EDT
10/26/1969 02:00 EST
4/26/1970 02:00 EDT
10/25/1970 02:00 EST
4/25/1971 02:00 EDT
10/31/1971 02:00 EST
4/30/1972 02:00 EDT
10/29/1972 02:00 EST
4/29/1973 02:00 EDT
10/28/1973 02:00 EST
2/23/1975 02:00 EDT
10/26/1975 02:00 EST

IN # 179
Before 11/18/1883 LMT
11/18/1883 12:00 CST
3/31/1918 02:00 CWT
10/27/1918 02:00 CST
3/30/1919 02:00 CWT
10/26/1919 02:00 CST
2/09/1942 02:00 CWT
9/30/1945 02:00 CST
4/26/1953 02:00 CDT
9/27/1953 02:00 CST
4/25/1954 02:00 CDT
9/26/1954 02:00 CST
4/24/1955 02:00 CDT
9/25/1955 02:00 CST
4/29/1956 02:00 CDT
9/30/1956 02:00 CST
4/28/1957 02:00 CDT
9/29/1957 02:00 CST
4/27/1958 02:00 CDT
9/28/1958 02:00 CST
4/26/1959 02:00 CDT
9/27/1959 02:00 CST
4/24/1960 02:00 CDT
9/25/1960 02:00 CST
4/30/1961 02:00 EST
4/27/1969 02:00 US#1

IN # 180
Before 11/18/1883 LMT
11/18/1883 12:00 CST
3/31/1918 02:00 CWT
10/27/1918 02:00 CST
3/30/1919 02:00 CWT
10/26/1919 02:00 CST
2/09/1942 02:00 CWT
9/30/1945 02:00 CST
4/24/1955 02:00 CDT
9/25/1955 02:00 CST
4/29/1956 02:00 CDT
9/30/1956 02:00 CST
4/28/1957 02:00 CDT
9/29/1957 02:00 CST
4/27/1958 02:00 CDT
9/28/1958 02:00 CST
4/26/1959 02:00 CDT
9/27/1959 02:00 CST
4/24/1960 02:00 CDT
10/30/1960 02:00 CST
4/30/1961 02:00 EST
4/27/1969 02:00 EDT
10/26/1969 02:00 EST
4/26/1970 02:00 EDT
10/25/1970 02:00 EST

IN # 181
Before 11/18/1883 LMT
11/18/1883 12:00 CST
3/31/1918 02:00 CWT
10/27/1918 02:00 CST
3/30/1919 02:00 CWT
10/26/1919 02:00 CST
2/09/1942 02:00 CWT
9/30/1945 02:00 CST
4/24/1955 02:00 CDT
10/30/1955 02:00 CST
4/29/1956 02:00 CDT
10/28/1956 02:00 CST
4/28/1957 02:00 CDT
9/29/1957 02:00 CST
4/27/1958 02:00 CDT
9/28/1958 02:00 CST
4/26/1959 02:00 CDT
9/27/1959 02:00 CST
4/24/1960 02:00 CDT
9/25/1960 02:00 CST
4/30/1961 02:00 EST
4/27/1969 02:00 EDT
10/26/1969 02:00 EST
4/26/1970 02:00 EDT
10/25/1970 02:00 EST

IN # 182
Before 11/18/1883 LMT
11/18/1883 12:00 CST
3/31/1918 02:00 CWT
10/27/1918 02:00 CST
3/30/1919 02:00 CWT
10/26/1919 02:00 CST
2/09/1942 02:00 CWT
9/30/1945 02:00 CST
4/25/1954 02:00 CDT
9/26/1954 02:00 CST
4/24/1955 02:00 CDT
10/30/1955 02:00 CST
4/29/1956 02:00 CDT
10/28/1956 02:00 CST
4/28/1957 02:00 CDT
9/29/1957 02:00 CST
4/27/1958 02:00 CDT
9/28/1958 02:00 CST
4/26/1959 02:00 CDT
9/27/1959 02:00 CST
4/24/1960 02:00 CDT
9/25/1960 02:00 CST
4/30/1961 02:00 EST
4/27/1969 02:00 EDT
10/26/1969 02:00 EST
4/26/1970 02:00 EDT
10/25/1970 02:00 EST

IN # 183
Before 11/18/1883 LMT
11/18/1883 12:00 CST
3/31/1918 02:00 CWT
10/27/1918 02:00 CST
3/30/1919 02:00 CWT
10/26/1919 02:00 CST
2/09/1942 02:00 CWT
9/30/1945 02:00 CST
4/26/1953 02:00 CDT
9/27/1953 02:00 CST
4/25/1954 02:00 CDT
9/26/1954 02:00 CST
4/24/1955 02:00 CDT
10/30/1955 02:00 CST
4/29/1956 02:00 CDT
10/28/1956 02:00 CST
4/28/1957 02:00 CDT
9/29/1957 02:00 CST
4/27/1958 02:00 CDT
9/28/1958 02:00 CST
4/26/1959 02:00 CDT
9/27/1959 02:00 CST
4/24/1960 02:00 CDT
9/25/1960 02:00 CST
4/30/1961 02:00 EST
4/27/1969 02:00 EDT
10/26/1969 02:00 EST
4/26/1970 02:00 EDT
10/25/1970 02:00 EST

IN # 184
Before 11/18/1883 LMT
11/18/1883 12:00 CST
3/31/1918 02:00 CWT
10/27/1918 02:00 CST
3/30/1919 02:00 CWT
10/26/1919 02:00 CST
2/09/1942 02:00 CWT
9/30/1945 02:00 CST
4/29/1951 02:00 CDT
9/30/1951 02:00 CST
4/28/1957 02:00 CDT
9/29/1957 02:00 CST
4/27/1958 02:00 CDT
9/28/1958 02:00 CST
4/26/1959 02:00 CDT
9/27/1959 02:00 CST
4/24/1960 02:00 CDT
9/25/1960 02:00 CST
4/30/1961 02:00 EST
4/27/1969 02:00 EDT
10/26/1969 02:00 EST
4/26/1970 02:00 EDT
10/25/1970 02:00 EST

IN # 185
Before 11/18/1883 LMT
11/18/1883 12:00 CST
3/31/1918 02:00 CWT
10/27/1918 02:00 CST
3/30/1919 02:00 CWT
10/26/1919 02:00 CST
2/09/1942 02:00 CWT
9/30/1945 02:00 CST
4/26/1953 02:00 CDT
9/27/1953 02:00 CST
4/25/1954 02:00 CDT
9/26/1954 02:00 CST
4/24/1955 02:00 CDT
9/25/1955 02:00 CST
4/29/1956 02:00 CDT
10/28/1956 02:00 CST
4/28/1957 02:00 CDT
9/29/1957 02:00 CST
4/27/1958 02:00 CDT
10/26/1958 02:00 CST
4/26/1959 02:00 CDT
10/25/1959 02:00 CST
4/24/1960 02:00 CDT
10/30/1960 02:00 CST
4/30/1961 02:00 EST
4/27/1969 02:00 US#1

IN # 186
Before 11/18/1883 LMT
11/18/1883 12:00 CST
3/31/1918 02:00 CWT
10/27/1918 02:00 CST
3/30/1919 02:00 CWT
10/26/1919 02:00 CST
2/09/1942 02:00 CWT
9/30/1945 02:00 CST
4/28/1946 02:00 CDT
9/29/1946 02:00 CST
4/27/1947 02:00 CDT
9/28/1947 02:00 CST
4/25/1948 02:00 CDT
9/26/1948 02:00 CST
4/24/1949 02:00 CDT
9/25/1949 02:00 CST
4/30/1950 02:00 CDT
9/24/1950 02:00 CST
4/29/1951 02:00 CDT
9/30/1951 02:00 CST
4/27/1952 02:00 CDT
9/28/1952 02:00 CST
4/26/1953 02:00 CDT
9/27/1953 02:00 CST
4/25/1954 02:00 CDT
9/26/1954 02:00 CST
4/24/1955 02:00 CDT
10/30/1955 02:00 CST
4/29/1956 02:00 CDT
10/28/1956 02:00 CST
4/28/1957 02:00 CDT
9/29/1957 02:00 CST
4/27/1958 02:00 CDT
9/28/1958 02:00 CST
4/26/1959 02:00 CDT
9/27/1959 02:00 CST
4/24/1960 02:00 CDT
9/25/1960 02:00 CST
4/30/1961 02:00 EST
4/27/1969 02:00 EDT
10/26/1969 02:00 EST
4/26/1970 02:00 EDT
10/25/1970 02:00 EST

IN # 187
Before 11/18/1883 LMT
11/18/1883 12:00 CST
3/31/1918 02:00 CWT
10/27/1918 02:00 CST
3/30/1919 02:00 CWT
10/26/1919 02:00 CST
2/09/1942 02:00 CWT
9/30/1945 02:00 CST
4/24/1955 02:00 CDT
9/25/1955 02:00 CST
4/29/1956 02:00 CDT
10/01/1956 02:00 CST
4/28/1957 02:00 CDT
9/29/1957 02:00 CST
4/27/1958 02:00 CDT
9/28/1958 02:00 CST
4/26/1959 02:00 CDT
9/27/1959 02:00 CST
4/24/1960 02:00 CDT
9/25/1960 02:00 CST
4/30/1961 02:00 EST
4/27/1969 02:00 EDT
10/26/1969 02:00 EST
4/26/1970 02:00 EDT
10/25/1970 02:00 EST

IN # 188
Before 11/18/1883 LMT
11/18/1883 12:00 CST
3/31/1918 02:00 CWT
10/27/1918 02:00 CST
3/30/1919 02:00 CWT
10/26/1919 02:00 CST
2/09/1942 02:00 CWT
9/30/1945 02:00 CST
4/24/1955 02:00 CDT
9/25/1955 02:00 CST
4/29/1956 02:00 CDT
10/28/1956 02:00 CST
4/28/1957 02:00 CDT
9/29/1957 02:00 CST
4/27/1958 02:00 CDT
9/28/1958 02:00 CST
4/26/1959 02:00 CDT
9/27/1959 02:00 CST
4/24/1960 02:00 CDT
9/25/1960 02:00 CST
4/30/1961 02:00 EST
4/27/1969 02:00 EDT
10/26/1969 02:00 EST
4/26/1970 02:00 EDT
10/25/1970 02:00 EST
4/25/1971 02:00 EDT
10/31/1971 02:00 EST
4/30/1972 02:00 EDT
10/29/1972 02:00 EST
4/29/1973 02:00 EDT
10/28/1973 02:00 EST
2/23/1975 02:00 US#1

IN # 189
Before 11/18/1883 LMT
11/18/1883 12:00 CST
3/31/1918 02:00 CWT
10/27/1918 02:00 CST
3/30/1919 02:00 CWT
10/26/1919 02:00 CST
2/09/1942 02:00 CWT
9/30/1945 02:00 CST
4/24/1955 02:00 CDT
9/25/1955 02:00 CST
4/05/1956 02:00 CDT
10/28/1956 02:00 CST
4/28/1957 02:00 CDT
9/29/1957 02:00 CST
4/27/1958 02:00 CDT
9/28/1958 02:00 CST
4/26/1959 02:00 CDT
9/27/1959 02:00 CST
4/24/1960 02:00 CDT
9/25/1960 02:00 CST
4/30/1961 02:00 EST
4/27/1969 02:00 EDT
10/26/1969 02:00 EST
4/26/1970 02:00 EDT
10/25/1970 02:00 EST
4/25/1971 02:00 EDT
10/31/1971 02:00 EST
4/30/1972 02:00 EDT
10/29/1972 02:00 EST
4/29/1973 02:00 EDT
10/28/1973 02:00 EST
2/23/1975 02:00 US#1

IN # 190
Before 11/18/1883 LMT
11/18/1883 12:00 CST
3/31/1918 02:00 CWT
10/27/1918 02:00 CST
3/30/1919 02:00 CWT
10/26/1919 02:00 CST
2/09/1942 02:00 CWT
9/30/1945 02:00 CST
4/24/1955 02:00 CDT
9/25/1955 02:00 CST
4/29/1956 02:00 CDT
10/01/1956 02:00 CST
4/28/1957 02:00 CDT
9/29/1957 02:00 CST
4/27/1958 02:00 CDT
10/26/1958 02:00 CST
4/26/1959 02:00 CDT
9/27/1959 02:00 CST
4/24/1960 02:00 CDT
9/25/1960 02:00 CST
4/30/1961 02:00 EST
4/27/1969 02:00 EDT
10/26/1969 02:00 EST
4/26/1970 02:00 EDT
10/25/1970 02:00 EST

IN # 191
Before 11/18/1883 LMT
11/18/1883 12:00 CST
3/31/1918 02:00 CWT
10/27/1918 02:00 CST
3/30/1919 02:00 CWT
10/26/1919 02:00 CST
2/09/1942 02:00 CWT
9/30/1945 02:00 CST
4/28/1957 02:00 CDT
9/29/1957 02:00 CST
4/27/1958 02:00 CDT
9/28/1958 02:00 CST
4/26/1959 02:00 CDT
9/27/1959 02:00 CST
4/24/1960 02:00 EST
10/29/1961 02:00 CST
4/29/1962 02:00 EST
4/27/1969 02:00 EDT
10/26/1969 02:00 EST
4/26/1970 02:00 EDT
10/25/1970 02:00 EST

IN # 192
Before 11/18/1883 LMT
11/18/1883 12:00 CST
3/31/1918 02:00 CWT
10/27/1918 02:00 CST
3/30/1919 02:00 CWT
10/26/1919 02:00 CST
2/09/1942 02:00 CWT
9/30/1945 02:00 CST
5/08/1955 00:00 CDT
9/04/1955 00:00 CST
4/29/1956 02:00 CDT
9/02/1956 02:00 CST
4/28/1957 02:00 CDT
9/29/1957 02:00 CST
4/27/1958 02:00 CDT
9/28/1958 02:00 CST
4/26/1959 02:00 CDT
9/27/1959 02:00 CST
4/24/1960 02:00 EST
10/29/1961 02:00 CST
4/29/1962 02:00 EST
4/27/1969 02:00 EDT
10/26/1969 02:00 EST
4/26/1970 02:00 EDT
10/25/1970 02:00 EST

IN # 193
Before 11/18/1883 LMT
11/18/1883 12:00 CST
3/31/1918 02:00 CWT
10/27/1918 02:00 CST
3/30/1919 02:00 CWT
10/26/1919 02:00 CST
2/09/1942 02:00 CWT
9/30/1945 02:00 CST
5/08/1955 02:00 CDT
9/04/1955 00:00 CST
4/29/1956 02:00 CDT
9/30/1956 02:00 CST
4/28/1957 02:00 CDT
9/29/1957 02:00 CST
4/27/1958 02:00 CDT
9/28/1958 02:00 CST
4/26/1959 02:00 CDT
9/27/1959 02:00 CST
4/24/1960 02:00 EST
10/29/1961 02:00 CST
4/29/1962 02:00 EST
4/27/1969 02:00 EDT
10/26/1969 02:00 EST
4/26/1970 02:00 EDT
10/25/1970 02:00 EST

IN # 194
Before 11/18/1883 LMT
11/18/1883 12:00 CST
3/31/1918 02:00 CWT
10/27/1918 02:00 CST
3/30/1919 02:00 CWT
10/26/1919 02:00 CST
2/09/1942 02:00 CWT
9/30/1945 02:00 CST
4/26/1953 02:00 CDT
9/27/1953 02:00 CST
4/25/1954 02:00 CDT
9/26/1954 02:00 CST
5/10/1955 02:00 CDT
9/04/1955 00:00 CST
4/29/1956 02:00 CDT
9/30/1956 02:00 CST
4/28/1957 02:00 CDT
9/29/1957 02:00 CST
4/27/1958 02:00 CDT
9/28/1958 02:00 CST
4/26/1959 02:00 CDT
9/27/1959 02:00 CST
4/24/1960 02:00 EST
10/29/1961 02:00 CST
4/29/1962 02:00 EST
4/27/1969 02:00 EDT
10/26/1969 02:00 EST
4/26/1970 02:00 EDT
10/25/1970 02:00 EST

IN # 195
Before 11/18/1883 LMT
11/18/1883 12:00 CST
3/31/1918 02:00 CWT
10/27/1918 02:00 CST
3/30/1919 02:00 CWT
10/26/1919 02:00 CST
2/09/1942 02:00 CWT
9/30/1945 02:00 CST
4/26/1953 02:00 CDT
9/27/1953 02:00 CST
4/25/1954 02:00 CDT
9/26/1954 02:00 CST
5/08/1955 00:00 CDT
9/04/1955 00:00 CST
4/29/1956 02:00 CDT
9/30/1956 02:00 CST
4/28/1957 02:00 CDT
9/29/1957 02:00 CST
4/27/1958 02:00 CDT
9/28/1958 02:00 CST
4/26/1959 02:00 CDT
9/27/1959 02:00 CST
4/24/1960 02:00 EST
10/29/1961 02:00 CST

TIME TABLES

4/29/1962 02:00 EST
4/27/1969 02:00 EDT
10/26/1969 02:00 EST
4/26/1970 02:00 EDT
10/25/1970 02:00 EST

IN # 196
Before 11/18/1883 LMT
11/18/1883 12:00 CST
3/31/1918 02:00 CWT
10/27/1918 02:00 CST
3/30/1919 02:00 CWT
10/26/1919 02:00 CST
2/09/1942 02:00 CWT
9/30/1945 02:00 CST
11/14/1954 02:00 EST
9/29/1957 02:00 CST
4/27/1958 02:00 CDT
9/28/1958 02:00 CST
4/26/1959 02:00 EST
4/27/1969 02:00 EDT
10/26/1969 02:00 EST
4/26/1970 02:00 EDT
10/25/1970 02:00 EST

IN # 197
Before 11/18/1883 LMT
11/18/1883 12:00 CST
3/31/1918 02:00 CWT
10/27/1918 02:00 CST
3/30/1919 02:00 CWT
10/26/1919 02:00 CST
2/09/1942 02:00 CWT
9/30/1945 02:00 CST
4/27/1947 02:00 CDT
9/28/1947 02:00 CST
4/27/1952 02:00 CDT
9/28/1952 02:00 CST
4/26/1953 02:00 CDT
9/27/1953 02:00 CST
4/25/1954 02:00 CDT
9/26/1954 02:00 CST
11/14/1954 02:00 EST
9/29/1957 02:00 CST
4/27/1958 02:00 CDT
9/28/1958 02:00 CST
4/26/1959 02:00 EST
4/27/1969 02:00 EDT
10/26/1969 02:00 EST
4/26/1970 02:00 EDT
10/25/1970 02:00 EST

IN # 198
Before 11/18/1883 LMT
11/18/1883 12:00 CST
3/31/1918 02:00 CWT
10/27/1918 02:00 CST
3/30/1919 02:00 CWT
10/26/1919 02:00 CST
2/09/1942 02:00 CWT
9/30/1945 02:00 CST
4/26/1953 02:00 CDT
9/27/1953 02:00 CST
4/25/1954 02:00 CDT
9/26/1954 02:00 CST
11/14/1954 02:00 EST
9/29/1957 02:00 CST
4/27/1958 02:00 CDT
9/28/1958 02:00 CST
4/26/1959 02:00 EST
4/27/1969 02:00 EDT
10/26/1969 02:00 EST
4/26/1970 02:00 EDT
10/25/1970 02:00 EST

IN # 199
Before 11/18/1883 LMT
11/18/1883 12:00 CST
3/31/1918 02:00 CWT
10/27/1918 02:00 CST
3/30/1919 02:00 CWT
10/26/1919 02:00 CST
2/09/1942 02:00 CWT
9/30/1945 02:00 CST
4/24/1955 02:00 CDT
9/25/1955 02:00 CST
4/29/1956 02:00 CDT
9/30/1956 02:00 CST
4/28/1957 02:00 CDT
9/29/1957 02:00 CST
4/27/1958 02:00 CDT
9/28/1958 02:00 CST
4/26/1959 02:00 CDT
9/27/1959 02:00 CST
4/24/1960 02:00 CDT
9/25/1960 02:00 CST
4/30/1961 02:00 CDT
10/29/1961 02:00 CST
4/29/1962 02:00 EST
4/27/1969 02:00 EDT
10/26/1969 02:00 EST
4/26/1970 02:00 EDT
10/25/1970 02:00 EST

IN # 200
Before 11/18/1883 LMT
11/18/1883 12:00 CST
3/31/1918 02:00 CWT
10/27/1918 02:00 CST
3/30/1919 02:00 CWT
10/26/1919 02:00 CST
2/09/1942 02:00 CWT
9/30/1945 02:00 CST
5/01/1955 00:00 CDT
9/04/1955 00:00 CST
4/29/1956 02:00 CDT
9/30/1956 02:00 CST
4/28/1957 02:00 CDT
9/29/1957 02:00 CST
4/27/1958 02:00 CDT
9/28/1958 02:00 CST
4/26/1959 02:00 CDT
9/27/1959 02:00 CST
4/24/1960 02:00 CDT
9/25/1960 02:00 CST
4/30/1961 02:00 CDT
10/29/1961 02:00 CST
4/29/1962 02:00 EST
4/27/1969 02:00 EDT
10/26/1969 02:00 EST
4/26/1970 02:00 EDT
10/25/1970 02:00 EST

IN # 201
Before 11/18/1883 LMT
11/18/1883 12:00 CST
3/31/1918 02:00 CWT
10/27/1918 02:00 CST
3/30/1919 02:00 CWT
10/26/1919 02:00 CST
4/30/1933 02:00 CDT
9/24/1933 02:00 CST
4/28/1935 02:00 CDT
9/29/1935 02:00 CST
4/26/1936 02:00 CDT
9/27/1936 02:00 CST
4/24/1938 02:00 CDT
9/25/1938 02:00 CST
4/30/1939 02:00 CDT
9/24/1939 02:00 CST
4/28/1940 02:00 CDT
9/29/1940 02:00 CST
4/27/1941 02:00 CDT
9/28/1941 02:00 CST
2/09/1942 02:00 CWT
9/30/1945 02:00 CST
4/28/1946 02:00 CDT
9/29/1946 02:00 CST
4/27/1947 02:00 CDT
9/28/1947 02:00 CST
4/25/1948 02:00 CDT
9/26/1948 02:00 CST
4/24/1949 02:00 CDT
9/25/1949 02:00 CST
4/30/1950 02:00 CDT
9/24/1950 02:00 CST
11/28/1954 02:00 EST
10/30/1955 02:00 CST
4/29/1956 02:00 CDT
9/30/1956 02:00 CST
4/28/1957 02:00 CDT
9/29/1957 02:00 CST
4/27/1958 02:00 CDT
9/28/1958 02:00 CST
4/26/1959 02:00 CDT
9/27/1959 02:00 CST
4/24/1960 02:00 CDT
9/25/1960 02:00 CST
4/30/1961 02:00 CDT
10/29/1961 02:00 CST
4/29/1962 02:00 EST
10/30/1966 02:00 CST
4/30/1967 02:00 CDT
10/29/1967 02:00 CST
4/28/1968 02:00 CDT
10/27/1968 02:00 CST
4/27/1969 02:00 EDT
10/26/1969 02:00 EST
4/26/1970 02:00 EDT
10/25/1970 02:00 EST

IN # 202
Before 11/18/1883 LMT
11/18/1883 12:00 CST
3/31/1918 02:00 CWT
10/27/1918 02:00 CST
3/30/1919 02:00 CWT
10/26/1919 02:00 CST
2/09/1942 02:00 CWT
9/30/1945 02:00 CST
4/28/1946 02:00 CDT
9/29/1946 02:00 CST
4/27/1947 02:00 CDT
9/28/1947 02:00 CST
4/25/1948 02:00 CDT
9/26/1948 02:00 CST
11/28/1954 02:00 EST
10/30/1955 02:00 CST
4/29/1956 02:00 CDT
9/30/1956 02:00 CST
4/28/1957 02:00 CDT
9/29/1957 02:00 CST
4/27/1958 02:00 CDT
9/28/1958 02:00 CST
4/26/1959 02:00 CDT
9/27/1959 02:00 CST
4/24/1960 02:00 CDT
9/25/1960 02:00 CST
4/30/1961 02:00 CDT
10/29/1961 02:00 CST
4/29/1962 02:00 EST
10/30/1966 02:00 CST
4/30/1967 02:00 CDT
10/29/1967 02:00 CST
4/28/1968 02:00 CDT
10/27/1968 02:00 CST
4/27/1969 02:00 EDT
10/26/1969 02:00 EST
4/26/1970 02:00 EDT
10/25/1970 02:00 EST

IN # 203
Before 11/18/1883 LMT
11/18/1883 12:00 CST
3/31/1918 02:00 CWT
10/27/1918 02:00 CST
3/30/1919 02:00 CWT
10/26/1919 02:00 CST
2/09/1942 02:00 CWT
9/30/1945 02:00 CST
4/26/1953 02:00 CDT
9/27/1953 02:00 CST
4/25/1954 02:00 CDT
9/26/1954 02:00 CST
11/28/1954 02:00 EST
10/30/1955 02:00 CST
4/29/1956 02:00 CDT
9/30/1956 02:00 CST
4/28/1957 02:00 CDT
9/29/1957 02:00 CST
4/27/1958 02:00 CDT
9/28/1958 02:00 CST
4/26/1959 02:00 CDT
9/27/1959 02:00 CST
4/24/1960 02:00 CDT
9/25/1960 02:00 CST
4/30/1961 02:00 CDT
10/29/1961 02:00 CST
4/29/1962 02:00 EST
10/30/1966 02:00 CST
4/30/1967 02:00 CDT
10/29/1967 02:00 CST
4/28/1968 02:00 CDT
10/27/1968 02:00 CST
4/27/1969 02:00 EDT
10/26/1969 02:00 EST
4/26/1970 02:00 EDT
10/25/1970 02:00 EST

IN # 204
Before 11/18/1883 LMT
11/18/1883 12:00 CST
3/31/1918 02:00 CWT
10/27/1918 02:00 CST
3/30/1919 02:00 CWT
10/26/1919 02:00 CST
2/09/1942 02:00 CWT
9/30/1945 02:00 CST
11/28/1954 02:00 EST
10/30/1955 02:00 CST
4/29/1956 02:00 CDT
9/30/1956 02:00 CST
4/28/1957 02:00 CDT
9/29/1957 02:00 CST
4/27/1958 02:00 CDT
9/28/1958 02:00 CST
4/26/1959 02:00 CDT
9/27/1959 02:00 CST
4/24/1960 02:00 CDT
9/25/1960 02:00 CST
4/30/1961 02:00 CDT
10/29/1961 02:00 CST
4/29/1962 02:00 EST
10/30/1966 02:00 CST
4/30/1967 02:00 CDT
10/29/1967 02:00 CST
4/28/1968 02:00 CDT
10/27/1968 02:00 CST
4/27/1969 02:00 EDT
10/26/1969 02:00 EST
4/26/1970 02:00 EDT
10/25/1970 02:00 EST

IN # 205
Before 11/18/1883 LMT
11/18/1883 12:00 CST
3/31/1918 02:00 CWT
10/27/1918 02:00 CST
3/30/1919 02:00 CWT
10/26/1919 02:00 CST
5/05/1940 02:00 CDT
10/01/1940 02:00 CST
5/01/1941 02:00 CDT
10/01/1941 02:00 CST
2/09/1942 02:00 CWT
9/30/1945 02:00 CST
5/01/1946 02:00 CDT
10/01/1946 02:00 CST
4/27/1947 02:00 CDT
9/28/1947 02:00 CST
4/25/1948 02:00 CDT
9/26/1948 02:00 CST
4/24/1949 02:00 CDT
9/25/1949 02:00 CST
4/30/1950 02:00 CDT
9/24/1950 02:00 CST
4/29/1951 02:00 CDT
9/30/1951 02:00 CST
4/27/1952 02:00 CDT
9/28/1952 02:00 CST
4/26/1953 02:00 CDT
9/27/1953 02:00 CST
4/25/1954 02:00 CDT
9/26/1954 02:00 CST
11/28/1954 02:00 EST
10/30/1955 02:00 CST
4/29/1956 02:00 CDT
10/28/1956 02:00 CST
4/28/1957 02:00 CDT
10/27/1957 02:00 CST
4/27/1958 02:00 CDT
10/26/1958 02:00 CST
4/26/1959 02:00 CDT
10/25/1959 02:00 CST
4/24/1960 02:00 CDT
10/30/1960 02:00 CST
4/30/1961 02:00 CDT
10/29/1961 02:00 CST
4/29/1962 02:00 EST
10/30/1966 02:00 CST
4/30/1967 02:00 CDT
10/29/1967 02:00 CST
4/28/1968 02:00 CDT
10/27/1968 02:00 CST
4/27/1969 02:00 EDT
10/26/1969 02:00 EST
4/26/1970 02:00 EDT
10/25/1970 02:00 EST

IN # 206
Before 11/18/1883 LMT
11/18/1883 12:00 CST
3/31/1918 02:00 CWT
10/27/1918 02:00 CST
3/30/1919 02:00 CWT
10/26/1919 02:00 CST
4/28/1940 02:00 CDT
9/29/1940 02:00 CST
4/27/1941 02:00 CDT
9/28/1941 02:00 CST
2/09/1942 02:00 CWT
9/30/1945 02:00 CST
4/28/1946 02:00 CDT
9/29/1946 02:00 CST
4/27/1947 02:00 CDT
9/28/1947 02:00 CST
4/25/1948 02:00 CDT
9/26/1948 02:00 CST
4/24/1949 02:00 CDT
9/25/1949 02:00 CST
4/30/1950 02:00 CDT
9/24/1950 02:00 CST
4/29/1951 02:00 CDT
9/30/1951 02:00 CST
4/27/1952 02:00 CDT
9/28/1952 02:00 CST
4/26/1953 02:00 CDT
9/27/1953 02:00 CST
4/25/1954 02:00 CDT
9/26/1954 02:00 CST
11/28/1954 02:00 EST
10/30/1955 02:00 CST
4/29/1956 02:00 CDT
10/28/1956 02:00 CST
4/28/1957 02:00 CDT
10/27/1957 02:00 CST
4/27/1958 02:00 CDT
10/26/1958 02:00 CST
4/26/1959 02:00 CDT
10/25/1959 02:00 CST
4/24/1960 02:00 CDT
10/30/1960 02:00 CST
4/30/1961 02:00 CDT
10/29/1961 02:00 CST
4/29/1962 02:00 EST
10/30/1966 02:00 CST
4/30/1967 02:00 CDT
10/29/1967 02:00 CST
4/28/1968 02:00 CDT
10/27/1968 02:00 CST
4/27/1969 02:00 EDT
10/26/1969 02:00 EST
4/26/1970 02:00 EDT
10/25/1970 02:00 EST

IN # 207
Before 11/18/1883 LMT
11/18/1883 12:00 CST
3/31/1918 02:00 CWT
10/27/1918 02:00 CST
3/30/1919 02:00 CWT
10/26/1919 02:00 CST
5/15/1929 02:00 CDT
9/30/1929 02:00 CST
5/10/1930 02:00 CDT
9/27/1930 02:00 CST
4/26/1931 02:00 CDT
9/28/1931 02:00 CST
4/24/1932 02:00 CDT
10/01/1932 02:00 CST
4/30/1933 02:00 CDT
9/24/1933 02:00 CST
4/29/1934 02:00 CDT
9/30/1934 02:00 CST
4/28/1935 02:00 CDT
9/29/1935 02:00 CST
4/26/1936 02:00 CDT
9/27/1936 02:00 CST
4/25/1937 02:00 CDT
9/26/1937 02:00 CST
4/24/1938 02:00 CDT
9/25/1938 02:00 CST
4/30/1939 02:00 CDT
9/24/1939 02:00 CST
4/28/1940 02:00 CDT
9/29/1940 02:00 CST
4/27/1941 02:00 CDT
9/28/1941 02:00 CST
2/09/1942 02:00 CWT
9/30/1945 02:00 CST
4/28/1946 02:00 CDT
9/29/1946 02:00 CST
4/27/1947 02:00 CDT
9/28/1947 02:00 CST
4/25/1948 02:00 CDT
9/26/1948 02:00 CST
4/24/1949 02:00 CDT
9/25/1949 02:00 CST
4/30/1950 02:00 CDT
9/24/1950 02:00 CST
4/29/1951 02:00 CDT
9/30/1951 02:00 CST
4/27/1952 02:00 CDT
9/28/1952 02:00 CST
4/26/1953 02:00 CDT
9/27/1953 02:00 CST
4/25/1954 02:00 CDT
9/26/1954 02:00 CST
11/28/1954 02:00 EST
10/30/1955 02:00 CST
4/29/1956 02:00 CDT
10/28/1956 02:00 CST
4/28/1957 02:00 CDT
9/29/1957 02:00 CST
4/27/1958 02:00 CDT
10/26/1958 02:00 CST
4/26/1959 02:00 CDT
10/25/1959 02:00 CST
4/24/1960 02:00 CDT
10/30/1960 02:00 CST
4/30/1961 02:00 CDT
10/29/1961 02:00 CST
4/29/1962 02:00 EST
10/30/1966 02:00 CST
4/30/1967 02:00 CDT
10/29/1967 02:00 CST
4/28/1968 02:00 CDT
10/27/1968 02:00 CST
4/27/1969 02:00 EDT
10/26/1969 02:00 EST
4/26/1970 02:00 EDT
10/25/1970 02:00 EST

IN # 208
Before 11/18/1883 LMT
11/18/1883 12:00 CST
3/31/1918 02:00 CWT
10/27/1918 02:00 CST
3/30/1919 02:00 CWT
10/26/1919 02:00 CST
4/26/1931 02:00 CDT
9/27/1931 02:00 CST
4/30/1932 00:01 CDT
10/02/1932 00:01 CST
4/30/1933 00:01 CDT
9/24/1933 00:01 CST
4/29/1934 02:00 CDT
9/30/1934 02:00 CST
4/28/1935 02:00 CDT
9/29/1935 02:00 CST
4/26/1936 02:00 CDT
9/27/1936 02:00 CST
4/25/1937 02:00 CDT
9/26/1937 02:00 CST
4/24/1938 02:00 CDT
9/25/1938 02:00 CST
4/30/1939 02:00 CDT
9/24/1939 02:00 CST
4/28/1940 02:00 CDT
9/29/1940 02:00 CST
4/27/1941 02:00 CDT
9/28/1941 02:00 CST
2/09/1942 02:00 CWT
9/30/1945 02:00 CST
4/28/1946 02:00 CDT
9/29/1946 02:00 CST
4/28/1947 02:00 CDT
9/29/1947 02:00 CST
4/25/1948 02:00 CDT
9/26/1948 02:00 CST
4/24/1949 02:00 CDT
9/25/1949 02:00 CST
4/30/1950 02:00 CDT
9/24/1950 02:00 CST
4/29/1951 02:00 CDT
9/30/1951 02:00 CST
4/27/1952 02:00 CDT
9/28/1952 02:00 CST
4/26/1953 02:00 CDT
9/27/1953 02:00 CST
4/25/1954 02:00 CDT
9/26/1954 02:00 CST
11/28/1954 02:00 EST
10/30/1955 02:00 CST
3/25/1956 02:00 CST
10/28/1956 02:00 CST
4/28/1957 02:00 CDT
10/27/1957 02:00 CST
4/27/1958 02:00 CDT
10/26/1958 02:00 CST
4/26/1959 02:00 CDT
10/25/1959 02:00 CST
4/24/1960 02:00 CDT
10/30/1960 02:00 CST
4/30/1961 02:00 CDT
10/29/1961 02:00 CST
4/29/1962 02:00 EST
10/30/1966 02:00 CST
4/30/1967 02:00 CDT
10/29/1967 02:00 CST
4/28/1968 02:00 CDT
10/27/1968 02:00 CST
4/27/1969 02:00 EDT
10/26/1969 02:00 EST
4/26/1970 02:00 EDT

TIME TABLES

Date	Time	Zone
10/25/1970	02:00	EST

IN # 209

Date	Time	Zone
Before 11/18/1883		LMT
11/18/1883	12:00	CST
3/31/1918	02:00	CWT
10/27/1918	02:00	CST
3/30/1919	02:00	CWT
10/26/1919	02:00	CST
4/28/1940	02:00	CDT
9/29/1940	02:00	CST
2/09/1942	02:00	CWT
9/30/1945	02:00	CST
4/25/1948	02:00	CDT
9/26/1948	02:00	CST
4/25/1954	02:00	CDT
9/26/1954	02:00	CST
11/28/1954	02:00	EST
10/30/1955	02:00	CST
4/29/1956	02:00	CDT
9/30/1956	02:00	CST
4/28/1957	02:00	CDT
9/29/1957	02:00	CST
4/27/1958	02:00	CDT
9/28/1958	02:00	CST
4/26/1959	02:00	CDT
9/27/1959	02:00	CST
4/24/1960	02:00	CDT
10/30/1960	02:00	CST
4/30/1961	02:00	CDT
10/29/1961	02:00	CST
4/29/1962	02:00	EST
10/30/1966	02:00	CST
4/30/1967	02:00	CDT
10/29/1967	02:00	CST
4/28/1968	02:00	CDT
10/27/1968	02:00	CST
4/27/1969	02:00	EDT
10/26/1969	02:00	EST
4/26/1970	02:00	EDT
10/25/1970	02:00	EST

IN # 210

Date	Time	Zone
Before 11/18/1883		LMT
11/18/1883	12:00	CST
3/31/1918	02:00	CWT
10/27/1918	02:00	CST
3/30/1919	02:00	CWT
10/26/1919	02:00	CST
4/27/1941	02:00	CDT
9/28/1941	02:00	CST
2/09/1942	02:00	CWT
9/30/1945	02:00	CST
4/27/1947	02:00	CDT
9/28/1947	02:00	CST
4/25/1948	02:00	CDT
9/26/1948	02:00	CST
4/24/1949	02:00	CDT
9/25/1949	02:00	CST
4/30/1950	02:00	CDT
9/24/1950	02:00	CST
4/29/1951	02:00	CDT
9/30/1951	02:00	CST
4/27/1952	02:00	CDT
9/28/1952	02:00	CST
4/26/1953	02:00	CDT
9/27/1953	02:00	CST
4/25/1954	02:00	CDT
9/26/1954	02:00	CST
11/28/1954	02:00	EST
10/30/1955	02:00	CST
4/29/1956	02:00	CDT
9/30/1956	02:00	CST
4/28/1957	02:00	CDT
9/29/1957	02:00	CST
4/27/1958	02:00	CDT
10/26/1958	02:00	CST
4/26/1959	02:00	CDT
10/25/1959	02:00	CST
4/24/1960	02:00	CDT
10/30/1960	02:00	CST
4/30/1961	02:00	CDT
10/29/1961	02:00	CST
4/29/1962	02:00	EST
10/30/1966	02:00	CST
4/30/1967	02:00	CDT
10/29/1967	02:00	CST
4/28/1968	02:00	CDT
10/27/1968	02:00	CST
4/27/1969	02:00	EDT
10/26/1969	02:00	EST
4/26/1970	02:00	EDT
10/25/1970	02:00	EST

IN # 211

Date	Time	Zone
Before 11/18/1883		LMT
11/18/1883	12:00	CST
3/31/1918	02:00	CWT
10/27/1918	02:00	CST
3/30/1919	02:00	CWT
10/26/1919	02:00	CST
2/09/1942	02:00	CWT
9/30/1945	02:00	CST
11/28/1954	02:00	EST
10/30/1955	02:00	CST
4/28/1957	02:00	CDT
9/29/1957	02:00	CST
4/27/1958	02:00	CDT
9/28/1958	02:00	CST
4/26/1959	02:00	CDT
9/27/1959	02:00	CST
4/24/1960	02:00	CDT
9/25/1960	02:00	CST
4/30/1961	02:00	EST
10/30/1966	02:00	CST
4/30/1967	02:00	EST
4/27/1969	02:00	EDT
10/26/1969	02:00	EST
4/26/1970	02:00	EDT
10/25/1970	02:00	EST

IN # 212

Date	Time	Zone
Before 11/18/1883		LMT
11/18/1883	12:00	CST
3/31/1918	02:00	CWT
10/27/1918	02:00	CST
3/30/1919	02:00	CWT
10/26/1919	02:00	CST
2/09/1942	02:00	CWT
9/30/1945	02:00	CST
4/28/1946	02:00	CDT
9/29/1946	02:00	CST
4/24/1949	02:00	CDT
9/25/1949	02:00	CST
11/28/1954	02:00	EST
10/30/1955	02:00	CST
4/28/1957	02:00	CDT
9/29/1957	02:00	CST
4/27/1958	02:00	CDT
9/28/1958	02:00	CST
4/26/1959	02:00	CDT
9/27/1959	02:00	CST
4/24/1960	02:00	CDT
9/25/1960	02:00	CST
4/30/1961	02:00	EST
10/30/1966	02:00	CST
4/30/1967	02:00	EST
4/27/1969	02:00	EDT
10/26/1969	02:00	EST
4/26/1970	02:00	EDT
10/25/1970	02:00	EST

IN # 213

Date	Time	Zone
Before 11/18/1883		LMT
11/18/1883	12:00	CST
3/31/1918	02:00	CWT
10/27/1918	02:00	CST
3/30/1919	02:00	CWT
10/26/1919	02:00	CST
2/09/1942	02:00	CWT
9/30/1945	02:00	CST
4/25/1948	02:00	CDT
10/01/1948	02:00	CST
4/24/1949	02:00	CDT
9/25/1949	02:00	CST
4/30/1950	02:00	CDT
9/24/1950	02:00	CST
11/28/1954	02:00	EST
10/30/1955	02:00	CST
4/29/1956	02:00	CDT
10/28/1956	02:00	CST
4/28/1957	02:00	CDT
9/29/1957	02:00	CST
4/27/1958	02:00	CDT
9/28/1958	02:00	CST
4/26/1959	02:00	CDT
9/27/1959	02:00	CST
4/24/1960	02:00	CDT
9/25/1960	02:00	CST
4/30/1961	02:00	EST
10/30/1966	02:00	CST
4/30/1967	02:00	EST
4/27/1969	02:00	EDT
10/26/1969	02:00	EST
4/26/1970	02:00	EDT
10/25/1970	02:00	EST

IN # 214

Date	Time	Zone
Before 11/18/1883		LMT
11/18/1883	12:00	CST
3/31/1918	02:00	CWT
10/27/1918	02:00	CST
3/30/1919	02:00	CWT
10/26/1919	02:00	CST
2/09/1942	02:00	CWT
9/30/1945	02:00	CST
4/26/1953	02:00	CDT
9/27/1953	02:00	CST
4/25/1954	02:00	CDT
9/26/1954	02:00	CST
11/28/1954	02:00	EST
10/30/1955	02:00	CST
4/29/1956	02:00	CDT
9/30/1956	02:00	CST
4/28/1957	02:00	CDT
9/29/1957	02:00	CST
4/27/1958	02:00	CDT
9/28/1958	02:00	CST
4/26/1959	02:00	CDT
9/27/1959	02:00	CST
4/24/1960	02:00	CDT
9/25/1960	02:00	CST
4/30/1961	02:00	EST
10/30/1966	02:00	CST
4/30/1967	02:00	EST
4/27/1969	02:00	EDT
10/26/1969	02:00	EST
4/26/1970	02:00	EDT
10/25/1970	02:00	EST

IN # 215

Date	Time	Zone
Before 11/18/1883		LMT
11/18/1883	12:00	CST
3/31/1918	02:00	CWT
10/27/1918	02:00	CST
3/30/1919	02:00	CWT
10/26/1919	02:00	CST
4/27/1941	02:00	CDT
9/28/1941	02:00	CST
2/09/1942	02:00	CWT
9/30/1945	02:00	CST
4/28/1946	02:00	CDT
9/29/1946	02:00	CST
4/27/1947	02:00	CDT
10/25/1947	02:00	CST
4/25/1948	02:00	CDT
9/26/1948	02:00	CST
4/24/1949	02:00	CDT
9/25/1949	02:00	CST
4/30/1950	02:00	CDT
9/24/1950	02:00	CST
4/29/1951	02:00	CDT
9/30/1951	02:00	CST
4/27/1952	02:00	CDT
9/28/1952	02:00	CST
4/26/1953	02:00	CDT
9/27/1953	02:00	CST
4/25/1954	02:00	CDT
9/26/1954	02:00	CST
11/28/1954	02:00	EST
10/30/1955	02:00	CST
4/29/1956	02:00	CDT
9/30/1956	02:00	CST
4/28/1957	02:00	CDT
9/29/1957	02:00	CST
4/27/1958	02:00	CDT
9/28/1958	02:00	CST
4/26/1959	02:00	CDT
9/27/1959	02:00	CST
4/24/1960	02:00	CDT
9/25/1960	02:00	CST
4/30/1961	02:00	EST
10/30/1966	02:00	CST
4/30/1967	02:00	EST
4/27/1969	02:00	EDT
10/26/1969	02:00	EST
4/26/1970	02:00	EDT
10/25/1970	02:00	EST

IN # 216

Date	Time	Zone
Before 11/18/1883		LMT
11/18/1883	12:00	CST
3/31/1918	02:00	CWT
10/27/1918	02:00	CST
3/30/1919	02:00	CWT
10/26/1919	02:00	CST
2/09/1942	02:00	CWT
9/30/1945	02:00	CST
4/28/1946	02:00	CDT
9/29/1946	02:00	CST
4/27/1947	02:00	CDT
10/25/1947	02:00	CST
4/25/1948	02:00	CDT
9/26/1948	02:00	CST
4/24/1949	02:00	CDT
9/25/1949	02:00	CST
4/30/1950	02:00	CDT
9/24/1950	02:00	CST
4/29/1951	02:00	CDT
9/30/1951	02:00	CST
4/27/1952	02:00	CDT
9/28/1952	02:00	CST
4/26/1953	02:00	CDT
9/27/1953	02:00	CST
4/25/1954	02:00	CDT
9/26/1954	02:00	CST
11/28/1954	02:00	EST
10/30/1955	02:00	CST
3/25/1956	02:00	CDT
10/27/1956	02:00	CST
4/28/1957	02:00	CDT
9/29/1957	02:00	CST
4/27/1958	02:00	CDT
9/28/1958	02:00	CST
4/26/1959	02:00	CDT
9/27/1959	02:00	CST
4/24/1960	02:00	CDT
9/25/1960	02:00	CST
4/30/1961	02:00	EST
10/30/1966	02:00	CST
4/30/1967	02:00	EST
4/27/1969	02:00	EDT
10/26/1969	02:00	EST
4/26/1970	02:00	EDT
10/25/1970	02:00	EST

IN # 217

Date	Time	Zone
Before 11/18/1883		LMT
11/18/1883	12:00	CST
3/31/1918	02:00	CWT
10/27/1918	02:00	CST
3/30/1919	02:00	CWT
10/26/1919	02:00	CST
4/28/1940	02:00	CDT
9/29/1940	02:00	CST
4/27/1941	02:00	CDT
9/28/1941	02:00	CST
2/09/1942	02:00	CWT
9/30/1945	02:00	CST
4/28/1946	02:00	CDT
9/29/1946	02:00	CST
4/27/1947	02:00	CDT
9/28/1947	02:00	CST
4/25/1948	02:00	CDT
9/26/1948	02:00	CST
4/24/1949	02:00	CDT
9/25/1949	02:00	CST
4/30/1950	02:00	CDT
9/24/1950	02:00	CST
4/29/1951	02:00	CDT
9/30/1951	02:00	CST
4/27/1952	02:00	CDT
9/28/1952	02:00	CST
4/26/1953	02:00	CDT
9/27/1953	02:00	CST
4/25/1954	02:00	CDT
9/26/1954	02:00	CST
11/28/1954	02:00	EST
10/30/1955	02:00	CST
4/29/1956	02:00	CDT
10/28/1956	02:00	CST
4/28/1957	02:00	CDT
10/27/1957	02:00	CST
4/27/1958	02:00	CDT
10/26/1958	02:00	CST
4/26/1959	02:00	CDT
10/25/1959	02:00	CST
4/24/1960	02:00	CDT
10/30/1960	02:00	CST
4/30/1961	02:00	EST
10/30/1966	02:00	CST
4/30/1967	02:00	EST
4/27/1969	02:00	EDT
10/26/1969	02:00	EST
4/26/1970	02:00	EDT
10/25/1970	02:00	EST

IN # 218

Date	Time	Zone
Before 11/18/1883		LMT
11/18/1883	12:00	CST
3/31/1918	02:00	CWT
10/27/1918	02:00	CST
3/30/1919	02:00	CWT
10/26/1919	02:00	CST
4/24/1938	02:00	CDT
9/25/1938	02:00	CST
4/30/1939	02:00	CDT
9/24/1939	02:00	CST
4/28/1940	02:00	CDT
9/29/1940	02:00	CST
4/27/1941	02:00	CDT
9/28/1941	02:00	CST
2/09/1942	02:00	CWT
9/30/1945	02:00	CST
4/28/1946	02:00	CDT
9/29/1946	02:00	CST
4/27/1947	02:00	CDT
9/28/1947	02:00	CST
4/25/1948	02:00	CDT
9/26/1948	02:00	CST
4/24/1949	02:00	CDT
9/25/1949	02:00	CST
4/30/1950	02:00	CDT
9/24/1950	02:00	CST
4/29/1951	02:00	CDT
9/30/1951	02:00	CST
4/27/1952	02:00	CDT
9/28/1952	02:00	CST
4/26/1953	02:00	CDT
9/27/1953	02:00	CST
4/25/1954	02:00	CDT
9/26/1954	02:00	CST
11/28/1954	02:00	EST
10/30/1955	02:00	CST
4/29/1956	02:00	CDT
10/28/1956	02:00	CST
4/28/1957	02:00	CDT
10/27/1957	02:00	CST
4/27/1958	02:00	CDT
10/26/1958	02:00	CST
4/26/1959	02:00	CDT
10/25/1959	02:00	CST
4/24/1960	02:00	CDT
10/30/1960	02:00	CST
4/30/1961	02:00	EST
10/30/1966	02:00	CST
4/30/1967	02:00	EST
4/27/1969	02:00	EDT
10/26/1969	02:00	EST
4/26/1970	02:00	EDT
10/25/1970	02:00	EST

IN # 219

Date	Time	Zone
Before 11/18/1883		LMT
11/18/1883	12:00	CST
3/31/1918	02:00	CWT
10/27/1918	02:00	CST
3/30/1919	02:00	CWT
10/26/1919	02:00	CST
4/24/1938	02:00	CDT
10/02/1938	02:00	CST
4/23/1939	02:00	CDT
10/01/1939	02:00	CST
4/28/1940	02:00	CDT
9/29/1940	02:00	CST
4/27/1941	02:00	CDT
9/28/1941	02:00	CST
2/09/1942	02:00	CWT
9/30/1945	02:00	CST
4/28/1946	02:00	CDT
9/29/1946	02:00	CST
4/27/1947	02:00	CDT
9/28/1947	02:00	CST
4/25/1948	02:00	CDT
9/26/1948	02:00	CST
4/24/1949	02:00	CDT
9/25/1949	02:00	CST
4/30/1950	02:00	CDT
9/24/1950	02:00	CST
4/29/1951	02:00	CDT
9/30/1951	02:00	CST
4/27/1952	02:00	CDT
9/28/1952	02:00	CST
4/26/1953	02:00	CDT
9/27/1953	02:00	CST
4/25/1954	02:00	CDT
9/26/1954	02:00	CST
11/28/1954	02:00	EST
10/30/1955	02:00	CST
4/29/1956	02:00	CDT
10/28/1956	02:00	CST
4/28/1957	02:00	CDT
9/29/1957	02:00	CST
4/27/1958	02:00	CDT
10/26/1958	02:00	CST
4/26/1959	02:00	CDT
10/25/1959	02:00	CST
4/24/1960	02:00	CDT
10/30/1960	02:00	CST
4/30/1961	02:00	EST
10/30/1966	02:00	CST
4/30/1967	02:00	EST
4/27/1969	02:00	EDT
10/26/1969	02:00	EST
4/26/1970	02:00	EDT
10/25/1970	02:00	EST

IN # 220

Date	Time	Zone
Before 11/18/1883		LMT
11/18/1883	12:00	CST
3/31/1918	02:00	CWT
10/27/1918	02:00	CST
3/30/1919	02:00	CWT
10/26/1919	02:00	CST
2/09/1942	02:00	CWT
9/30/1945	02:00	CST
4/27/1947	02:00	CDT
9/28/1947	02:00	CST
4/25/1948	02:00	CDT
9/26/1948	02:00	CST
4/24/1949	02:00	CDT
9/25/1949	02:00	CST
4/30/1950	02:00	CDT
9/24/1950	02:00	CST
4/29/1951	02:00	CDT
9/30/1951	02:00	CST
4/27/1952	02:00	CDT
9/28/1952	02:00	CST
4/26/1953	02:00	CDT
9/27/1953	02:00	CST
4/25/1954	02:00	CDT
9/26/1954	02:00	CST
4/24/1955	02:00	CDT
10/30/1955	02:00	CST
4/29/1956	02:00	CDT
10/28/1956	02:00	CST
4/28/1957	02:00	CDT
9/29/1957	02:00	CST
4/27/1958	02:00	CDT
9/28/1958	02:00	CST
4/26/1959	02:00	CDT
10/25/1959	02:00	CST
4/24/1960	02:00	CDT
10/30/1960	02:00	CST
4/30/1961	02:00	CDT
10/29/1961	02:00	CST
4/29/1962	02:00	EST
10/27/1963	02:00	CST
4/26/1964	02:00	US#1

IN # 221

Date	Time	Zone
Before 11/18/1883		LMT
11/18/1883	12:00	CST
3/31/1918	02:00	CWT
10/27/1918	02:00	CST
3/30/1919	02:00	CWT
10/26/1919	02:00	CST
2/09/1942	02:00	CWT
9/30/1945	02:00	CST
4/24/1955	02:00	CDT
10/30/1955	02:00	CST
4/29/1956	02:00	CDT
10/28/1956	02:00	CST
4/28/1957	02:00	CDT
9/29/1957	02:00	CST
4/27/1958	02:00	CDT
9/28/1958	02:00	CST
4/26/1959	02:00	CDT
9/27/1959	02:00	CST
4/24/1960	02:00	CDT
9/25/1960	02:00	CST
4/30/1961	02:00	CDT
10/29/1961	02:00	CST
4/29/1962	02:00	EST
10/27/1963	02:00	CST
4/26/1964	02:00	US#1

IN # 222

Date	Time	Zone
Before 11/18/1883		LMT
11/18/1883	12:00	CST
3/31/1918	02:00	CWT
10/27/1918	02:00	CST
3/30/1919	02:00	CWT
10/26/1919	02:00	CST
2/09/1942	02:00	CWT
9/30/1945	02:00	CST
4/25/1954	02:00	CDT
9/26/1954	02:00	CST
4/24/1955	02:00	CDT
10/30/1955	02:00	CST
4/29/1956	02:00	CDT
10/28/1956	02:00	CST
4/28/1957	02:00	CDT
9/29/1957	02:00	CST
4/27/1958	02:00	CDT

TIME TABLES

9/28/1958 02:00 CST
4/26/1959 02:00 CDT
9/27/1959 02:00 CST
4/24/1960 02:00 CDT
9/25/1960 02:00 CST
4/30/1961 02:00 CDT
10/29/1961 02:00 CST
4/29/1962 02:00 EST
10/27/1963 02:00 CST
4/26/1964 02:00 US#1
....
IN # 223
Before 11/18/1883 LMT
11/18/1883 12:00 CST
3/31/1918 02:00 CWT
10/27/1918 02:00 CST
3/30/1919 02:00 CWT
10/26/1919 02:00 CST
2/09/1942 02:00 CWT
9/30/1945 02:00 CST
4/26/1953 02:00 CDT
9/27/1953 02:00 CST
4/25/1954 02:00 CDT
9/26/1954 02:00 CST
4/24/1955 02:00 CDT
10/30/1955 02:00 CST
4/29/1956 02:00 CDT
10/28/1956 02:00 CST
4/28/1957 02:00 CDT
9/29/1957 02:00 CST
4/27/1958 02:00 CDT
9/28/1958 02:00 CST
4/26/1959 02:00 CDT
9/27/1959 02:00 CST
4/24/1960 02:00 CDT
9/25/1960 02:00 CST
4/30/1961 02:00 CDT
10/29/1961 02:00 CST
4/29/1962 02:00 EST
10/27/1963 02:00 CST
4/26/1964 02:00 US#1
....
IN # 224
Before 11/18/1883 LMT
11/18/1883 12:00 CST
3/31/1918 02:00 CWT
10/27/1918 02:00 CST
3/30/1919 02:00 CWT
10/26/1919 02:00 CST
2/09/1942 02:00 CWT
9/30/1945 02:00 CST
4/24/1955 02:00 CDT
10/30/1955 02:00 CST
4/29/1956 02:00 CDT
10/28/1956 02:00 CST
4/28/1957 02:00 CDT
9/29/1957 02:00 CST
4/27/1958 02:00 CDT
9/28/1958 02:00 CST
4/26/1959 02:00 CDT
9/27/1959 02:00 CST
4/24/1960 02:00 CDT
9/25/1960 02:00 CST
4/30/1961 02:00 EST
4/27/1969 02:00 EDT
10/26/1969 02:00 CST
4/26/1970 02:00 CDT
10/25/1970 02:00 CST
4/25/1971 02:00 US#1
....
IN # 225
Before 11/18/1883 LMT
11/18/1883 12:00 CST
3/31/1918 02:00 CWT
10/27/1918 02:00 CST
3/30/1919 02:00 CWT
10/26/1919 02:00 CST
2/09/1942 02:00 CWT
9/30/1945 02:00 CST
4/26/1953 02:00 CDT
9/27/1953 02:00 CST
4/25/1954 02:00 CDT
9/26/1954 02:00 CST
4/24/1955 02:00 CDT
10/30/1955 02:00 CST
4/29/1956 02:00 CDT
10/28/1956 02:00 CST
4/28/1957 02:00 CDT
9/29/1957 02:00 CST
4/27/1958 02:00 CDT
9/28/1958 02:00 CST
4/26/1959 02:00 CDT
9/27/1959 02:00 CST
4/24/1960 02:00 CDT
9/25/1960 02:00 CST
4/30/1961 02:00 EST
4/27/1969 02:00 EDT
10/26/1969 02:00 CST
4/26/1970 02:00 CDT
10/25/1970 02:00 CST
4/25/1971 02:00 US#1
....
IN # 226
Before 11/18/1883 LMT
11/18/1883 12:00 CST
3/31/1918 02:00 CWT
10/27/1918 02:00 CST
3/30/1919 02:00 CWT
10/26/1919 02:00 CST
2/09/1942 02:00 CWT
9/30/1945 02:00 CST
4/24/1955 02:00 CDT
10/30/1955 02:00 CST
4/29/1956 02:00 CDT
10/28/1956 02:00 CST
4/28/1957 02:00 CDT
9/29/1957 02:00 CST
4/27/1958 02:00 CDT
9/28/1958 02:00 CST
4/26/1959 02:00 CDT
9/27/1959 02:00 CST
4/24/1960 02:00 CDT
9/25/1960 02:00 CST
4/30/1961 02:00 EST
10/27/1963 02:00 CST
4/26/1964 02:00 CDT
10/25/1964 02:00 CST
4/25/1965 02:00 EST
10/30/1966 02:00 CST
4/30/1967 02:00 US#1
....
IN # 227
Before 11/18/1883 LMT
11/18/1883 12:00 CST
3/31/1918 02:00 CWT
10/27/1918 02:00 CST
3/30/1919 02:00 CWT
10/26/1919 02:00 CST
2/09/1942 02:00 CWT
9/30/1945 02:00 CST
4/26/1953 02:00 CDT
9/27/1953 02:00 CST
4/25/1954 02:00 CDT
9/26/1954 02:00 CST
4/24/1955 02:00 CDT
10/30/1955 02:00 CST
4/29/1956 02:00 CDT
10/28/1956 02:00 CST
4/28/1957 02:00 CDT
9/29/1957 02:00 CST
4/27/1958 02:00 CDT
9/28/1958 02:00 CST
4/26/1959 02:00 CDT
9/27/1959 02:00 CST
4/24/1960 02:00 CDT
9/25/1960 02:00 CST
4/30/1961 02:00 EST
10/27/1963 02:00 CST
4/26/1964 02:00 CDT
10/25/1964 02:00 CST
4/25/1965 02:00 EST
10/30/1966 02:00 CST
4/30/1967 02:00 US#1
....
IN # 228
Before 11/18/1883 LMT
11/18/1883 12:00 CST
3/31/1918 02:00 CWT
10/27/1918 02:00 CST
3/30/1919 02:00 CWT
10/26/1919 02:00 CST
2/09/1942 02:00 CWT
9/30/1945 02:00 CST
10/31/1954 00:01 EST
4/27/1969 02:00 EDT
10/26/1969 02:00 EST
4/26/1970 02:00 EDT
10/25/1970 02:00 EST
....
IN # 229
Before 11/18/1883 LMT
11/18/1883 12:00 CST
3/31/1918 02:00 CWT
10/27/1918 02:00 CST
3/30/1919 02:00 CWT
10/26/1919 02:00 CST
2/09/1942 02:00 CWT
9/30/1945 02:00 CST
10/31/1954 00:01 EST
4/28/1968 02:00 US#1
....
IN # 230
Before 11/18/1883 LMT
11/18/1883 12:00 CST
3/31/1918 02:00 CWT
10/27/1918 02:00 CST
3/30/1919 02:00 CWT
10/26/1919 02:00 CST
2/09/1942 02:00 CWT
9/30/1945 02:00 CST
4/26/1953 02:00 CDT
9/27/1953 02:00 CST
4/25/1954 02:00 CDT
9/26/1954 02:00 CST
10/31/1954 00:01 EST
4/27/1969 02:00 EDT
10/26/1969 02:00 EST
4/26/1970 02:00 EDT
10/25/1970 02:00 EST
....
IN # 231
Before 11/18/1883 LMT
11/18/1883 12:00 CST
3/31/1918 02:00 CWT
10/27/1918 02:00 CST
3/30/1919 02:00 CWT
10/26/1919 02:00 CST
2/09/1942 02:00 CWT
9/30/1945 02:00 CST
4/25/1954 02:00 CDT
9/26/1954 02:00 CST
10/31/1954 00:01 EST
4/27/1969 02:00 EDT
10/26/1969 02:00 EST
4/26/1970 02:00 EDT
10/25/1970 02:00 EST
....
IN # 232
Before 11/18/1883 LMT
11/18/1883 12:00 CST
3/31/1918 02:00 CWT
10/27/1918 02:00 CST
3/30/1919 02:00 CWT
10/26/1919 02:00 CST
4/26/1931 02:00 CDT
9/27/1931 02:00 CST
5/01/1932 00:01 CDT
9/25/1932 00:01 CST
4/30/1933 02:00 CDT
9/24/1933 02:00 CST
4/29/1934 02:00 CDT
9/30/1934 02:00 CST
4/28/1935 02:00 CDT
9/29/1935 02:00 CST
4/26/1936 02:00 CDT
9/27/1936 02:00 CST
4/25/1937 02:00 CDT
9/26/1937 02:00 CST
4/24/1938 02:00 CDT
9/25/1938 02:00 CST
4/30/1939 02:00 CDT
9/24/1939 02:00 CST
4/28/1940 02:00 CDT
9/29/1940 02:00 CST
4/27/1941 02:00 CDT
9/28/1941 02:00 CST
2/09/1942 02:00 CWT
9/30/1945 02:00 CST
4/28/1946 02:00 CDT
9/29/1946 02:00 CST
4/27/1947 02:00 CDT
9/28/1947 02:00 CST
4/25/1948 02:00 CDT
9/26/1948 02:00 CST
4/24/1949 02:00 CDT
9/25/1949 02:00 CST
4/30/1950 02:00 CDT
9/24/1950 02:00 CST
4/29/1951 02:00 CDT
9/30/1951 02:00 CST
4/27/1952 02:00 CDT
9/28/1952 02:00 CST
4/26/1953 02:00 CDT
9/27/1953 02:00 CST
4/25/1954 02:00 CDT
9/26/1954 02:00 CST
10/31/1954 00:01 EST
4/27/1969 02:00 EDT
10/26/1969 02:00 EST
4/26/1970 02:00 EDT
10/25/1970 02:00 EST
....
IN # 233
Before 11/18/1883 LMT
11/18/1883 12:00 CST
3/31/1918 02:00 CWT
10/27/1918 02:00 CST
3/30/1919 02:00 CWT
10/26/1919 02:00 CST
4/29/1928 00:01 CDT
9/30/1928 00:01 CST
4/28/1929 00:01 CDT
9/29/1929 00:01 CST
4/27/1930 00:01 CDT
9/28/1930 00:01 CST
4/26/1931 00:01 CDT
9/27/1931 00:01 CST
4/24/1932 00:01 CDT
9/25/1932 00:01 CST
4/30/1933 00:01 CDT
10/01/1933 00:01 CST
4/29/1934 00:01 CDT
9/30/1934 00:01 CST
4/28/1935 00:01 CDT
9/29/1935 00:01 CST
4/26/1936 02:00 CDT
9/27/1936 02:00 CST
4/25/1937 02:00 CDT
9/26/1937 02:00 CST
4/24/1938 02:00 CDT
9/25/1938 02:00 CST
4/30/1939 02:00 CDT
10/01/1939 02:00 CST
4/28/1940 02:00 CDT
9/29/1940 02:00 CST
4/27/1941 02:00 CDT
9/28/1941 02:00 CST
2/09/1942 02:00 CWT
9/30/1945 02:00 CST
4/28/1946 02:00 CDT
9/29/1946 02:00 CST
4/27/1947 02:00 CDT
9/28/1947 02:00 CST
4/25/1948 02:00 CDT
9/26/1948 02:00 CST
5/01/1949 02:00 CDT
9/25/1949 02:00 CST
4/30/1950 02:00 CDT
10/01/1950 02:00 CST
4/29/1951 02:00 CDT
9/30/1951 02:00 CST
4/27/1952 02:00 CDT
9/28/1952 02:00 CST
4/26/1953 02:00 CDT
9/27/1953 02:00 CST
4/25/1954 02:00 CDT
9/26/1954 02:00 CST
10/31/1954 00:01 EST
4/27/1969 02:00 EDT
10/26/1969 02:00 EST
4/26/1970 02:00 EDT
10/25/1970 02:00 EST
....
IN # 234
Before 11/18/1883 LMT
11/18/1883 12:00 CST
3/31/1918 02:00 CWT
10/27/1918 02:00 CST
3/30/1919 02:00 CWT
10/26/1919 02:00 CST
4/28/1929 02:00 CDT
9/29/1929 02:00 CST
4/27/1930 02:00 CDT
9/28/1930 02:00 CST
4/26/1931 02:00 CDT
9/27/1931 02:00 CST
4/24/1932 02:00 CDT
9/25/1932 02:00 CST
4/30/1933 02:00 CDT
10/01/1933 02:00 CST
4/29/1934 02:00 CDT
9/30/1934 02:00 CST
4/28/1935 02:00 CDT
9/29/1935 02:00 CST
4/26/1936 02:00 CDT
9/27/1936 02:00 CST
4/25/1937 02:00 CDT
9/26/1937 02:00 CST
4/24/1938 02:00 CDT
9/25/1938 02:00 CST
4/30/1939 02:00 CDT
9/24/1939 02:00 CST
4/28/1940 02:00 CDT
9/29/1940 02:00 CST
4/27/1941 02:00 CDT
9/28/1941 02:00 CST
2/09/1942 02:00 CWT
9/30/1945 02:00 CST
4/28/1946 02:00 CDT
9/29/1946 02:00 CST
4/27/1947 02:00 CDT
9/28/1947 02:00 CST
4/25/1948 02:00 CDT
9/26/1948 02:00 CST
4/24/1949 02:00 CDT
9/25/1949 02:00 CST
4/30/1950 02:00 CDT
9/24/1950 02:00 CST
4/29/1951 02:00 CDT
9/30/1951 02:00 CST
4/27/1952 02:00 CDT
9/28/1952 02:00 CST
4/26/1953 02:00 CDT
9/27/1953 02:00 CST
4/25/1954 02:00 CDT
9/26/1954 02:00 CST
10/31/1954 00:01 EST
4/27/1969 02:00 EDT
10/26/1969 02:00 EST
4/26/1970 02:00 EDT
10/25/1970 02:00 EST
....
IN # 235
Before 11/18/1883 LMT
11/18/1883 12:00 CST
3/31/1918 02:00 CWT
10/27/1918 02:00 CST
3/30/1919 02:00 CWT
10/26/1919 02:00 CST
5/01/1938 02:00 CDT
10/01/1938 02:00 CST
4/30/1939 02:00 CDT
9/30/1939 02:00 CST
4/27/1941 02:00 CDT
9/28/1941 02:00 CST
2/09/1942 02:00 CWT
9/30/1945 02:00 CST
4/26/1953 02:00 CDT
9/27/1953 02:00 CST
4/25/1954 02:00 CDT
9/26/1954 02:00 CST
10/31/1954 00:01 EST
4/27/1969 02:00 EDT
10/26/1969 02:00 EST
4/26/1970 02:00 EDT
10/25/1970 02:00 EST
....
IN # 236
Before 11/18/1883 LMT
11/18/1883 12:00 CST
3/31/1918 02:00 CWT
10/27/1918 02:00 CST
3/30/1919 02:00 CWT
10/26/1919 02:00 CST
4/28/1940 02:00 CDT
9/29/1940 02:00 CST
4/27/1941 02:00 CDT
9/28/1941 02:00 CST
2/09/1942 02:00 CWT
9/30/1945 02:00 CST
4/28/1946 02:00 CDT
9/29/1946 02:00 CST
4/27/1947 02:00 CDT
9/28/1947 02:00 CST
4/25/1948 02:00 CDT
9/26/1948 02:00 CST
4/24/1949 02:00 CDT
9/25/1949 02:00 CST
4/30/1950 02:00 CDT
9/24/1950 02:00 CST
4/29/1951 02:00 CDT
9/30/1951 02:00 CST
4/27/1952 02:00 CDT
9/28/1952 02:00 CST
4/26/1953 02:00 CDT
9/27/1953 02:00 CST
4/25/1954 02:00 CDT
9/26/1954 02:00 CST
10/31/1954 00:01 EST
4/27/1969 02:00 EDT
10/26/1969 02:00 EST
4/26/1970 02:00 EDT
10/25/1970 02:00 EST
....
IN # 237
Before 11/18/1883 LMT
11/18/1883 12:00 CST
3/31/1918 02:00 CWT
10/27/1918 02:00 CST
3/30/1919 02:00 CWT
10/26/1919 02:00 CST
5/01/1938 02:00 CDT
10/02/1938 02:00 CST
4/30/1939 02:00 CDT
10/01/1939 02:00 CST
4/28/1940 02:00 CDT
9/29/1940 02:00 CST
4/27/1941 02:00 CDT
9/28/1941 02:00 CST
2/09/1942 02:00 CWT
9/30/1945 02:00 CST
4/28/1946 02:00 CDT
9/29/1946 02:00 CST
4/27/1947 02:00 CDT
9/28/1947 02:00 CST
4/25/1948 02:00 CDT
9/26/1948 02:00 CST
4/24/1949 02:00 CDT
9/25/1949 02:00 CST
4/30/1950 02:00 CDT
9/24/1950 02:00 CST
4/29/1951 02:00 CDT
9/30/1951 02:00 CST
4/27/1952 02:00 CDT
9/28/1952 02:00 CST
4/26/1953 02:00 CDT
9/27/1953 02:00 CST
4/25/1954 02:00 CDT
9/26/1954 02:00 CST
10/31/1954 00:01 EST
4/27/1969 02:00 EDT
10/26/1969 02:00 EST
4/26/1970 02:00 EDT
10/25/1970 02:00 EST
....
IN # 238
Before 11/18/1883 LMT
11/18/1883 12:00 CST
3/31/1918 02:00 CWT
10/27/1918 02:00 CST
3/30/1919 02:00 CWT
10/26/1919 02:00 CST
6/13/1920 02:00 CDT
10/31/1920 02:00 CST
3/27/1921 02:00 CDT
10/30/1921 02:00 CST
4/30/1922 02:00 CDT
9/24/1922 02:00 CST
4/29/1923 02:00 CDT
9/30/1923 02:00 CST
4/27/1924 02:00 CDT
9/28/1924 02:00 CST
4/26/1925 02:00 CDT
9/27/1925 02:00 CST
4/25/1926 02:00 CDT
9/26/1926 02:00 CST
4/24/1927 02:00 CDT
9/25/1927 02:00 CST
4/29/1928 02:00 CDT
9/30/1928 02:00 CST
4/28/1929 02:00 CDT
9/29/1929 02:00 CST
4/27/1930 02:00 CDT
9/28/1930 02:00 CST
4/26/1931 02:00 CDT
9/27/1931 02:00 CST
4/30/1932 02:00 CDT
10/01/1932 02:00 CST
4/30/1933 02:00 CDT
10/01/1933 02:00 CST
4/29/1934 02:00 CDT
9/30/1934 02:00 CST
4/28/1935 02:00 CDT
9/29/1935 02:00 CST
4/26/1936 02:00 CDT
9/27/1936 02:00 CST
4/25/1937 02:00 CDT
9/26/1937 02:00 CST
4/24/1938 02:00 CDT
9/25/1938 02:00 CST
4/30/1939 02:00 CDT
9/24/1939 02:00 CST
4/28/1940 02:00 CDT
9/29/1940 02:00 CST
4/27/1941 02:00 CDT
9/28/1941 02:00 CST
2/09/1942 02:00 CWT
9/30/1945 02:00 CST
4/28/1946 02:00 CDT
9/29/1946 02:00 CST
4/27/1947 02:00 CDT
9/28/1947 02:00 CST
4/25/1948 02:00 CDT
9/26/1948 02:00 CST
4/24/1949 02:00 CDT

Date	Time	Zone
9/25/1949	02:00	CST
4/30/1950	02:00	CDT
9/24/1950	02:00	CST
4/29/1951	02:00	CDT
9/30/1951	02:00	CST
4/27/1952	02:00	CDT
9/28/1952	02:00	CST
4/26/1953	02:00	CDT
9/27/1953	02:00	CST
4/25/1954	02:00	CDT
9/26/1954	02:00	CST
10/31/1954	00:01	EST
4/27/1969	02:00	EDT
10/26/1969	02:00	EST
4/26/1970	02:00	EDT
10/25/1970	02:00	EST

IN # 239

Date	Time	Zone
Before 11/18/1883		LMT
11/18/1883	12:00	CST
3/31/1918	02:00	CWT
10/27/1918	02:00	CST
3/30/1919	02:00	CWT
10/26/1919	02:00	CST
4/25/1937	02:00	CDT
9/26/1937	02:00	CST
4/24/1938	02:00	CDT
9/25/1938	02:00	CST
4/30/1939	02:00	CDT
9/24/1939	02:00	CST
2/09/1942	02:00	CWT
9/30/1945	02:00	CST
4/27/1947	02:00	CDT
9/28/1947	02:00	CST
4/25/1948	02:00	CDT
9/26/1948	02:00	CST
4/26/1953	02:00	CDT
9/27/1953	02:00	CST
4/25/1954	02:00	CDT
9/26/1954	02:00	CST
10/31/1954	00:01	EST
4/27/1969	02:00	EDT
10/26/1969	02:00	EST
4/26/1970	02:00	EDT
10/25/1970	02:00	EST

IN # 240

Date	Time	Zone
Before 11/18/1883		LMT
11/18/1883	12:00	CST
3/31/1918	02:00	CWT
10/27/1918	02:00	CST
3/30/1919	02:00	CWT
10/26/1919	02:00	CST
2/09/1942	02:00	CWT
9/30/1945	02:00	CST
4/26/1953	02:00	CDT
9/27/1953	02:00	CST
4/25/1954	02:00	CDT
9/26/1954	02:00	CST
4/24/1955	02:00	CDT
10/30/1955	02:00	CST
4/29/1956	02:00	CDT
10/28/1956	02:00	CST
4/28/1957	02:00	CDT
9/29/1957	02:00	CST
4/27/1958	02:00	CDT
9/28/1958	02:00	CST
4/26/1959	02:00	CDT
9/27/1959	02:00	CST
4/24/1960	02:00	CDT
9/25/1960	02:00	CST
4/30/1961	02:00	EST
10/27/1963	02:00	CST
4/26/1964	02:00	EST
4/27/1969	02:00	EDT
10/26/1969	02:00	CST
4/26/1970	02:00	CDT
10/25/1970	02:00	CST
4/25/1971	02:00	US#1

IN # 241

Date	Time	Zone
Before 11/18/1883		LMT
11/18/1883	12:00	CST
3/31/1918	02:00	CWT
10/27/1918	02:00	CST
3/30/1919	02:00	CWT
10/26/1919	02:00	CST
2/09/1942	02:00	CWT
9/30/1945	02:00	CST
4/26/1953	02:00	CDT
9/27/1953	02:00	CST
4/25/1954	02:00	CDT
9/26/1954	02:00	CST
4/24/1955	02:00	CDT
10/30/1955	02:00	CST
4/29/1956	02:00	CDT
10/28/1956	02:00	CST
4/28/1957	02:00	CDT
9/29/1957	02:00	CST
4/27/1958	02:00	CDT
9/28/1958	02:00	CST
4/26/1959	02:00	CDT
9/27/1959	02:00	CST
4/24/1960	02:00	CDT
9/25/1960	02:00	CST
4/30/1961	02:00	EST
10/27/1963	02:00	CST
4/26/1964	02:00	CDT
10/25/1964	02:00	CST
4/25/1965	02:00	EST
4/27/1969	02:00	EDT
10/26/1969	02:00	CST
4/26/1970	02:00	CDT
10/25/1970	02:00	CST
4/25/1971	02:00	US#1

IN # 242

Date	Time	Zone
Before 11/18/1883		LMT
11/18/1883	12:00	CST
3/31/1918	02:00	CWT
10/27/1918	02:00	CST
3/30/1919	02:00	CWT
10/26/1919	02:00	CST
2/09/1942	02:00	CWT
9/30/1945	02:00	CST
4/25/1954	02:00	CDT
9/26/1954	02:00	CST
11/28/1954	02:00	EST
9/29/1957	02:00	CST
4/27/1958	02:00	CDT
9/28/1958	02:00	CST
4/26/1959	02:00	CDT
9/27/1959	02:00	CST
4/24/1960	02:00	CDT
9/25/1960	02:00	CST
4/30/1961	02:00	EST
4/27/1969	02:00	EDT
10/26/1969	02:00	EST
4/26/1970	02:00	EDT
10/25/1970	02:00	EST

IN # 243

Date	Time	Zone
Before 11/18/1883		LMT
11/18/1883	12:00	CST
3/31/1918	02:00	CWT
10/27/1918	02:00	CST
3/30/1919	02:00	CWT
10/26/1919	02:00	CST
2/09/1942	02:00	CWT
9/30/1945	02:00	CST
4/30/1950	02:00	CDT
9/01/1950	02:00	CST
11/07/1954	00:01	EST
9/29/1957	02:00	CST
4/27/1958	02:00	EST
9/27/1959	02:00	CST
4/24/1960	02:00	EST
4/27/1969	02:00	EDT
10/26/1969	02:00	EST
4/26/1970	02:00	EDT
10/25/1970	02:00	EST

IN # 244

Date	Time	Zone
Before 11/18/1883		LMT
11/18/1883	12:00	CST
3/31/1918	02:00	CWT
10/27/1918	02:00	CST
3/30/1919	02:00	CWT
10/26/1919	02:00	CST
2/09/1942	02:00	CWT
9/30/1945	02:00	CST
4/24/1955	02:00	EST
9/29/1957	02:00	CST
4/27/1958	02:00	CDT
9/28/1958	02:00	CST
10/01/1958	02:00	EST
4/27/1969	02:00	EDT
10/26/1969	02:00	EST
4/26/1970	02:00	EDT
10/25/1970	02:00	EST

IN # 245

Date	Time	Zone
Before 11/18/1883		LMT
11/18/1883	12:00	CST
3/31/1918	02:00	CWT
10/27/1918	02:00	CST
3/30/1919	02:00	CWT
10/26/1919	02:00	CST
2/09/1942	02:00	CWT
9/30/1945	02:00	CST
4/28/1946	02:00	CDT
9/29/1946	02:00	CST
4/26/1953	02:00	CDT
9/27/1953	02:00	CST
4/25/1954	02:00	CDT
9/26/1954	02:00	CST
4/24/1955	02:00	EST
9/29/1957	02:00	CST
4/27/1958	02:00	CDT
9/28/1958	02:00	CST
10/13/1958	02:00	EST
4/27/1969	02:00	EDT
10/26/1969	02:00	EST
4/26/1970	02:00	EDT
10/25/1970	02:00	EST

IN # 246

Date	Time	Zone
Before 11/18/1883		LMT
11/18/1883	12:00	CST
3/31/1918	02:00	CWT
10/27/1918	02:00	CST
3/30/1919	02:00	CWT
10/26/1919	02:00	CST
2/09/1942	02:00	CWT
9/30/1945	02:00	CST
4/27/1947	02:00	CDT
9/28/1947	02:00	CST
4/24/1955	02:00	CDT
9/25/1955	02:00	CST
4/29/1956	02:00	CDT
9/03/1956	02:00	CST
4/28/1957	02:00	CDT
9/29/1957	02:00	CST
4/27/1958	02:00	CDT
9/28/1958	02:00	CST
4/26/1959	02:00	CDT
9/27/1959	02:00	CST
4/24/1960	02:00	CDT
9/25/1960	02:00	CST
12/05/1960	02:00	EST
12/07/1960	00:00	CST
4/30/1961	02:00	CDT
10/29/1961	02:00	CST
4/29/1962	02:00	EST
4/27/1969	02:00	EDT
10/26/1969	02:00	EST
4/26/1970	02:00	EDT
10/25/1970	02:00	EST

IN # 247

Date	Time	Zone
Before 11/18/1883		LMT
11/18/1883	12:00	CST
3/31/1918	02:00	CWT
10/27/1918	02:00	CST
3/30/1919	02:00	CWT
10/26/1919	02:00	CST
2/09/1942	02:00	CWT
9/30/1945	02:00	CST
4/24/1955	02:00	EST
10/28/1956	02:00	CST
4/28/1957	02:00	CDT
9/29/1957	02:00	CST
4/27/1958	02:00	EST
4/27/1969	02:00	EDT
10/26/1969	02:00	EST
4/26/1970	02:00	EDT
10/25/1970	02:00	EST

IN # 248

Date	Time	Zone
Before 11/18/1883		LMT
11/18/1883	12:00	CST
3/31/1918	02:00	CWT
10/27/1918	02:00	CST
3/30/1919	02:00	CWT
10/26/1919	02:00	CST
2/09/1942	02:00	CWT
9/30/1945	02:00	CST
4/26/1953	02:00	CDT
9/27/1953	02:00	CST
4/25/1954	02:00	CDT
9/26/1954	02:00	CST
4/24/1955	02:00	EST
10/28/1956	02:00	CST
4/28/1957	02:00	CDT
9/29/1957	02:00	CST
4/27/1958	02:00	EST
4/27/1969	02:00	EDT
10/26/1969	02:00	EST
4/26/1970	02:00	EDT
10/25/1970	02:00	EST

IN # 249

Date	Time	Zone
Before 11/18/1883		LMT
11/18/1883	12:00	CST
3/31/1918	02:00	CWT
10/27/1918	02:00	CST
3/30/1919	02:00	CWT
10/26/1919	02:00	CST
6/22/1941	02:00	CDT
9/28/1941	02:00	CST
2/09/1942	02:00	CWT
9/30/1945	02:00	CST
4/28/1946	02:00	CDT
9/29/1946	02:00	CST
4/27/1947	02:00	CDT
9/28/1947	02:00	CST
4/25/1948	02:00	CDT
9/26/1948	02:00	CST
4/24/1949	02:00	CDT
9/25/1949	02:00	CST
4/30/1950	02:00	CDT
9/24/1950	02:00	CST
4/29/1951	02:00	CDT
9/30/1951	02:00	CST
4/27/1952	02:00	CDT
9/28/1952	02:00	CST
4/26/1953	02:00	CDT
9/27/1953	02:00	CST
4/25/1954	02:00	CDT
9/26/1954	02:00	CST
4/24/1955	02:00	EST
10/28/1956	02:00	CST
4/28/1957	02:00	CDT
9/29/1957	02:00	CST
4/27/1958	02:00	EST
4/27/1969	02:00	EDT
10/26/1969	02:00	EST
4/26/1970	02:00	EDT
10/25/1970	02:00	EST

IN # 250

Date	Time	Zone
Before 11/18/1883		LMT
11/18/1883	12:00	CST
3/31/1918	02:00	CWT
10/27/1918	02:00	CST
3/30/1919	02:00	CWT
10/26/1919	02:00	CST
2/09/1942	02:00	CWT
9/30/1945	02:00	CST
4/28/1946	02:00	CDT
9/29/1946	02:00	CST
4/27/1947	02:00	CDT
9/28/1947	02:00	CST
4/25/1948	02:00	CDT
9/26/1948	02:00	CST
4/24/1949	02:00	CDT
9/25/1949	02:00	CST
4/30/1950	02:00	CDT
9/24/1950	02:00	CST
4/29/1951	02:00	CDT
9/30/1951	02:00	CST
4/27/1952	02:00	CDT
9/28/1952	02:00	CST
4/26/1953	02:00	CDT
9/27/1953	02:00	CST
4/25/1954	02:00	CDT
9/26/1954	02:00	CST
4/24/1955	02:00	EST
10/28/1956	02:00	CST
4/28/1957	02:00	CDT
9/29/1957	02:00	CST
4/27/1958	02:00	EST
4/27/1969	02:00	EDT
10/26/1969	02:00	EST
4/26/1970	02:00	EDT
10/25/1970	02:00	EST

IN # 251

Date	Time	Zone
Before 11/18/1883		LMT
11/18/1883	12:00	CST
3/31/1918	02:00	CWT
10/27/1918	02:00	CST
3/30/1919	02:00	CWT
10/26/1919	02:00	CST
2/09/1942	02:00	CWT
9/30/1945	02:00	CST
4/24/1955	02:00	EST
10/28/1956	02:00	CST
4/28/1957	02:00	CDT
9/29/1957	02:00	CST
4/27/1958	02:00	CDT
9/28/1958	02:00	CST
4/26/1959	02:00	EST
4/27/1969	02:00	EDT
10/26/1969	02:00	EST
4/26/1970	02:00	EDT
10/25/1970	02:00	EST

IN # 252

Date	Time	Zone
Before 11/18/1883		LMT
11/18/1883	12:00	CST
3/31/1918	02:00	CWT
10/27/1918	02:00	CST
3/30/1919	02:00	CWT
10/26/1919	02:00	CST
2/09/1942	02:00	CWT
9/30/1945	02:00	CST
4/26/1953	02:00	CDT
9/27/1953	02:00	CST
4/25/1954	02:00	CDT
9/26/1954	02:00	CST
4/24/1955	02:00	EST
10/28/1956	02:00	CST
4/28/1957	02:00	CDT
9/29/1957	02:00	CST
4/27/1958	02:00	CDT
9/28/1958	02:00	CST
4/26/1959	02:00	EST
4/27/1969	02:00	EDT
10/26/1969	02:00	EST
4/26/1970	02:00	EDT
10/25/1970	02:00	EST

IN # 253

Date	Time	Zone
Before 11/18/1883		LMT
11/18/1883	12:00	CST
3/31/1918	02:00	CWT
10/27/1918	02:00	CST
3/30/1919	02:00	CWT
10/26/1919	02:00	CST
2/09/1942	02:00	CWT
9/30/1945	02:00	CST
12/12/1954	02:00	EST
9/29/1957	02:00	CST
4/27/1958	02:00	CDT
9/28/1958	02:00	CST
4/26/1959	02:00	EST
4/27/1969	02:00	EDT
10/26/1969	02:00	EST
4/26/1970	02:00	EDT
10/25/1970	02:00	EST

IN # 254

Date	Time	Zone
Before 11/18/1883		LMT
11/18/1883	12:00	CST
3/31/1918	02:00	CWT
10/27/1918	02:00	CST
3/30/1919	02:00	CWT
10/26/1919	02:00	CST
4/30/1939	02:00	CDT
9/24/1939	02:00	CST
4/28/1940	02:00	CDT
9/29/1940	02:00	CST
2/09/1942	02:00	CWT
9/30/1945	02:00	CST
4/28/1946	02:00	CDT
9/29/1946	02:00	CST
4/27/1947	02:00	CDT
9/28/1947	02:00	CST
4/25/1948	02:00	CDT
9/26/1948	02:00	CST
4/24/1949	02:00	CDT
9/25/1949	02:00	CST
4/30/1950	02:00	CDT
9/24/1950	02:00	CST
4/29/1951	02:00	CDT
9/30/1951	02:00	CST
4/27/1952	02:00	CDT
9/28/1952	02:00	CST
4/26/1953	02:00	CDT
9/27/1953	02:00	CST
4/25/1954	02:00	CDT
9/26/1954	02:00	CST
12/12/1954	02:00	EST
9/29/1957	02:00	CST
4/27/1958	02:00	CDT
9/28/1958	02:00	CST
4/26/1959	02:00	EST
4/27/1969	02:00	EDT
10/26/1969	02:00	EST
4/26/1970	02:00	EDT
10/25/1970	02:00	EST

IN # 255

Date	Time	Zone
Before 11/18/1883		LMT
11/18/1883	12:00	CST
3/31/1918	02:00	CWT
10/27/1918	02:00	CST
3/30/1919	02:00	CWT
10/26/1919	02:00	CST
2/09/1942	02:00	CWT
9/30/1945	02:00	CST
4/28/1946	02:00	CDT
9/29/1946	02:00	CST
4/27/1947	02:00	CDT
9/28/1947	02:00	CST
4/25/1948	02:00	CDT
9/26/1948	02:00	CST
4/24/1949	02:00	CDT
9/25/1949	02:00	CST
4/30/1950	02:00	CDT
9/24/1950	02:00	CST
4/29/1951	02:00	CDT
9/30/1951	02:00	CST
4/27/1952	02:00	CDT
9/28/1952	02:00	CST
4/26/1953	02:00	CDT
9/27/1953	02:00	CST
4/25/1954	02:00	CDT
9/26/1954	02:00	CST
12/12/1954	02:00	EST
9/29/1957	02:00	CST
4/27/1958	02:00	CDT
9/28/1958	02:00	CST
4/26/1959	02:00	EST
4/27/1969	02:00	EDT
10/26/1969	02:00	EST
4/26/1970	02:00	EDT
10/25/1970	02:00	EST

IN # 256

Date	Time	Zone
Before 11/18/1883		LMT
11/18/1883	12:00	CST
3/31/1918	02:00	CWT
10/27/1918	02:00	CST
3/30/1919	02:00	CWT
10/26/1919	02:00	CST
2/09/1942	02:00	CWT
9/30/1945	02:00	CST
4/27/1947	02:00	CDT
9/28/1947	02:00	CST
4/25/1948	02:00	CDT
9/26/1948	02:00	CST
4/24/1949	02:00	CDT
9/25/1949	02:00	CST
4/30/1950	02:00	CDT
9/24/1950	02:00	CST
4/29/1951	02:00	CDT
9/30/1951	02:00	CST
4/27/1952	02:00	CDT
9/28/1952	02:00	CST
4/26/1953	02:00	CDT
9/27/1953	02:00	CST
4/25/1954	02:00	CDT
9/26/1954	02:00	CST
12/12/1954	02:00	EST
9/29/1957	02:00	CST
4/27/1958	02:00	CDT
9/28/1958	02:00	CST
4/26/1959	02:00	EST
4/27/1969	02:00	EDT
10/26/1969	02:00	EST
4/26/1970	02:00	EDT
10/25/1970	02:00	EST

IN # 257

Date	Time	Zone
Before 11/18/1883		LMT
11/18/1883	12:00	CST
3/31/1918	02:00	CWT
10/27/1918	02:00	CST
3/30/1919	02:00	CWT
10/26/1919	02:00	CST
2/09/1942	02:00	CWT
9/30/1945	02:00	CST
4/26/1953	02:00	CDT
9/27/1953	02:00	CST
4/25/1954	02:00	CDT
9/26/1954	02:00	CST
12/12/1954	02:00	EST
9/29/1957	02:00	CST
4/27/1958	02:00	CDT
9/28/1958	02:00	CST
4/26/1959	02:00	EST
4/27/1969	02:00	EDT
10/26/1969	02:00	EST
4/26/1970	02:00	EDT
10/25/1970	02:00	EST

IN # 258

Date	Time	Zone
Before 11/18/1883		LMT
11/18/1883	12:00	CST
3/31/1918	02:00	CWT
10/27/1918	02:00	CST
3/30/1919	02:00	CWT
10/26/1919	02:00	CST

6/13/1920 02:00 CDT
10/31/1920 02:00 CST
3/27/1921 02:00 CDT
10/30/1921 02:00 CST
4/30/1922 02:00 CDT
9/24/1922 02:00 CST
4/29/1923 02:00 CDT
9/30/1923 02:00 CST
4/27/1924 02:00 CDT
9/28/1924 02:00 CST
4/26/1925 02:00 CDT
9/27/1925 02:00 CST
4/25/1926 02:00 CDT
9/26/1926 02:00 CST
4/24/1927 02:00 CDT
9/25/1927 02:00 CST
4/29/1928 02:00 CDT
9/30/1928 02:00 CST
4/28/1929 02:00 CDT
9/29/1929 02:00 CST
4/27/1930 02:00 CDT
9/28/1930 02:00 CST
4/26/1931 02:00 CDT
9/27/1931 02:00 CST
4/24/1932 02:00 CDT
9/25/1932 02:00 CST
4/30/1933 02:00 CDT
9/24/1933 02:00 CST
4/29/1934 02:00 CDT
9/30/1934 02:00 CST
4/28/1935 02:00 CDT
9/29/1935 02:00 CST
4/26/1936 02:00 CDT
9/27/1936 02:00 CST
4/25/1937 02:00 CDT
9/26/1937 02:00 CST
4/24/1938 02:00 CDT
9/25/1938 02:00 CST
4/30/1939 02:00 CDT
9/24/1939 02:00 CST
4/28/1940 02:00 CDT
9/29/1940 02:00 CST
4/27/1941 02:00 CDT
9/28/1941 02:00 CST
2/09/1942 02:00 CWT
9/30/1945 02:00 CST
4/28/1946 02:00 CDT
9/29/1946 02:00 CST
4/27/1947 02:00 CDT
9/28/1947 02:00 CST
4/25/1948 02:00 CDT
9/26/1948 02:00 CST
4/24/1949 02:00 CDT
9/25/1949 02:00 CST
4/30/1950 02:00 CDT
9/24/1950 02:00 CST
4/29/1951 02:00 CDT
9/30/1951 02:00 CST
4/27/1952 02:00 CDT
9/28/1952 02:00 CST
4/26/1953 02:00 CDT
9/27/1953 02:00 CST
4/25/1954 02:00 CDT
9/26/1954 02:00 CST
11/14/1954 02:00 EST
4/27/1969 02:00 EDT
10/26/1969 02:00 EST
4/26/1970 02:00 EDT
10/25/1970 02:00 EST

IN # 259

Before 11/18/1883 LMT
11/18/1883 12:00 CST
3/31/1918 02:00 CWT
10/27/1918 02:00 CST
3/30/1919 02:00 CWT
10/26/1919 02:00 CST
2/09/1942 02:00 CWT
9/30/1945 02:00 CST
11/14/1954 02:00 EST
4/27/1969 02:00 EDT
10/26/1969 02:00 EST
4/26/1970 02:00 EDT
10/25/1970 02:00 EST

IN # 260

Before 11/18/1883 LMT
11/18/1883 12:00 CST
3/31/1918 02:00 CWT
10/27/1918 02:00 CST
3/30/1919 02:00 CWT
10/26/1919 02:00 CST
4/30/1938 02:00 CDT
10/01/1938 02:00 CST
4/28/1940 02:00 CDT
9/29/1940 02:00 CST
4/27/1941 02:00 CDT
9/28/1941 02:00 CST
2/09/1942 02:00 CWT
9/30/1945 02:00 CST
4/28/1946 02:00 CDT
9/29/1946 02:00 CST
4/27/1947 02:00 CDT
9/28/1947 02:00 CST
11/14/1954 02:00 EST
4/27/1969 02:00 EDT
10/26/1969 02:00 EST
4/26/1970 02:00 EDT
10/25/1970 02:00 EST

IN # 261

Before 11/18/1883 LMT
11/18/1883 12:00 CST
3/31/1918 02:00 CWT
10/27/1918 02:00 CST
3/30/1919 02:00 CWT
10/26/1919 02:00 CST
4/27/1941 02:00 CDT
9/28/1941 02:00 CST
2/09/1942 02:00 CWT
9/30/1945 02:00 CST
11/14/1954 02:00 EST
4/27/1969 02:00 EDT
10/26/1969 02:00 EST
4/26/1970 02:00 EDT
10/25/1970 02:00 EST

IN # 262

Before 11/18/1883 LMT
11/18/1883 12:00 CST
3/31/1918 02:00 CWT
10/27/1918 02:00 CST
3/30/1919 02:00 CWT
10/26/1919 02:00 CST
4/26/1936 02:00 CDT
9/27/1936 02:00 CST
4/24/1938 02:00 CDT
9/25/1938 02:00 CST
4/30/1939 02:00 CDT
9/24/1939 02:00 CST
4/28/1940 02:00 CDT
9/29/1940 02:00 CST
4/27/1941 02:00 CDT
9/28/1941 02:00 CST
2/09/1942 02:00 CWT
9/30/1945 02:00 CST
4/28/1946 02:00 CDT
9/29/1946 02:00 CST
4/25/1948 02:00 CDT
9/26/1948 02:00 CST
11/14/1954 02:00 EST
4/27/1969 02:00 EDT
10/26/1969 02:00 EST
4/26/1970 02:00 EDT
10/25/1970 02:00 EST

IN # 263

Before 11/18/1883 LMT
11/18/1883 12:00 CST
3/31/1918 02:00 CWT
10/27/1918 02:00 CST
3/30/1919 02:00 CWT
10/26/1919 02:00 CST
4/26/1936 02:00 CDT
9/27/1936 02:00 CST
4/24/1938 02:00 CDT
9/25/1938 02:00 CST
4/30/1939 02:00 CDT
9/24/1939 02:00 CST
4/28/1940 02:00 CDT
9/29/1940 02:00 CST
4/27/1941 02:00 CDT
9/28/1941 02:00 CST
2/09/1942 02:00 CWT
9/30/1945 02:00 CST
11/14/1954 02:00 EST
4/27/1969 02:00 EDT
10/26/1969 02:00 EST
4/26/1970 02:00 EDT
10/25/1970 02:00 EST

IN # 264

Before 11/18/1883 LMT
11/18/1883 12:00 CST
3/31/1918 02:00 CWT
10/27/1918 02:00 CST
3/30/1919 02:00 CWT
10/26/1919 02:00 CST
2/09/1942 02:00 CWT
9/30/1945 02:00 CST
11/14/1954 02:00 EST
9/29/1957 02:00 CST
4/27/1958 02:00 EST
4/27/1969 02:00 EDT
10/26/1969 02:00 EST
4/26/1970 02:00 EDT
10/25/1970 02:00 EST

IN # 265

Before 11/18/1883 LMT
11/18/1883 12:00 CST
3/31/1918 02:00 CWT
10/27/1918 02:00 CST
3/30/1919 02:00 CWT
10/26/1919 02:00 CST
4/26/1936 02:00 CDT
9/27/1936 02:00 CST
4/24/1938 02:00 CDT
9/25/1938 02:00 CST
4/30/1939 02:00 CDT
9/24/1939 02:00 CST
4/28/1940 02:00 CDT
9/29/1940 02:00 CST
4/27/1941 02:00 CDT
9/28/1941 02:00 CST
2/09/1942 02:00 CWT
9/30/1945 02:00 CST
4/28/1946 02:00 CDT
9/29/1946 02:00 CST
4/27/1947 02:00 CDT
9/28/1947 02:00 CST
4/25/1948 02:00 CDT
9/26/1948 02:00 CST
4/24/1949 02:00 CDT
9/25/1949 02:00 CST
4/30/1950 02:00 CDT
9/24/1950 02:00 CST
4/29/1951 02:00 CDT
9/30/1951 02:00 CST
4/27/1952 02:00 CDT
9/28/1952 02:00 CST
4/26/1953 02:00 CDT
9/27/1953 02:00 CST
11/14/1954 02:00 EST
9/29/1957 02:00 CST
4/27/1958 02:00 EST
4/27/1969 02:00 EDT
10/26/1969 02:00 EST
4/26/1970 02:00 EDT
10/25/1970 02:00 EST

IN # 266

Before 11/18/1883 LMT
11/18/1883 12:00 CST
3/31/1918 02:00 CWT
10/27/1918 02:00 CST
3/30/1919 02:00 CWT
10/26/1919 02:00 CST
4/26/1936 02:00 CDT
9/27/1936 02:00 CST
4/24/1938 02:00 CDT
9/25/1938 02:00 CST
4/30/1939 02:00 CDT
9/24/1939 02:00 CST
4/28/1940 02:00 CDT
9/29/1940 02:00 CST
4/27/1941 02:00 CDT
9/28/1941 02:00 CST
2/09/1942 02:00 CWT
9/30/1945 02:00 CST
4/28/1946 02:00 CDT
9/29/1946 02:00 CST
4/25/1948 02:00 CDT
9/26/1948 02:00 CST
4/29/1951 02:00 CDT
9/30/1951 02:00 CST
4/27/1952 02:00 CDT
9/28/1952 02:00 CST
4/26/1953 02:00 CDT
9/27/1953 02:00 CST
4/25/1954 02:00 CDT
9/26/1954 02:00 CST
11/14/1954 02:00 EST
9/29/1957 02:00 CST
4/27/1958 02:00 EST
4/27/1969 02:00 EDT
10/26/1969 02:00 EST
4/26/1970 02:00 EDT
10/25/1970 02:00 EST

IN # 267

Before 11/18/1883 LMT
11/18/1883 12:00 CST
3/31/1918 02:00 CWT
10/27/1918 02:00 CST
3/30/1919 02:00 CWT
10/26/1919 02:00 CST
2/09/1942 02:00 CWT
9/30/1945 02:00 CST
4/27/1947 02:00 CDT
9/28/1947 02:00 CST
4/25/1948 02:00 CDT
9/26/1948 02:00 CST
4/30/1950 02:00 CDT
9/24/1950 02:00 CST
4/26/1953 02:00 CDT
9/27/1953 02:00 CST
4/25/1954 02:00 CDT
9/26/1954 02:00 CST
11/14/1954 02:00 EST
9/29/1957 02:00 CST
4/27/1958 02:00 EST
4/27/1969 02:00 EDT
10/26/1969 02:00 EST
4/26/1970 02:00 EDT
10/25/1970 02:00 EST

IN # 268

Before 11/18/1883 LMT
11/18/1883 12:00 CST
3/31/1918 02:00 CWT
10/27/1918 02:00 CST
3/30/1919 02:00 CWT
10/26/1919 02:00 CST
2/09/1942 02:00 CWT
9/30/1945 02:00 CST
4/25/1948 02:00 CDT
9/26/1948 02:00 CST
11/14/1954 02:00 EST
9/29/1957 02:00 CST
4/27/1958 02:00 EST
4/27/1969 02:00 EDT
10/26/1969 02:00 EST
4/26/1970 02:00 EDT
10/25/1970 02:00 EST

IN # 269

Before 11/18/1883 LMT
11/18/1883 12:00 CST
3/31/1918 02:00 CWT
10/27/1918 02:00 CST
3/30/1919 02:00 CWT
10/26/1919 02:00 CST
2/09/1942 02:00 CWT
9/30/1945 02:00 CST
4/26/1953 02:00 CDT
9/27/1953 02:00 CST
4/25/1954 02:00 CDT
9/26/1954 02:00 CST
11/14/1954 02:00 EST
9/29/1957 02:00 CST
4/27/1958 02:00 EST
4/27/1969 02:00 EDT
10/26/1969 02:00 EST
4/26/1970 02:00 EDT
10/25/1970 02:00 EST

IN # 270

Before 11/18/1883 LMT
11/18/1883 12:00 CST
3/31/1918 02:00 CWT
10/27/1918 02:00 CST
3/30/1919 02:00 CWT
10/26/1919 02:00 CST
2/09/1942 02:00 CWT
9/30/1945 02:00 CST
4/25/1954 02:00 CDT
9/26/1954 02:00 CST
11/14/1954 02:00 EST
9/29/1957 02:00 CST
4/27/1958 02:00 EST
4/27/1969 02:00 EDT
10/26/1969 02:00 EST
4/26/1970 02:00 EDT
10/25/1970 02:00 EST

IN # 271

Before 11/18/1883 LMT
11/18/1883 12:00 CST
3/31/1918 02:00 CWT
10/27/1918 02:00 CST
3/30/1919 02:00 CWT
10/26/1919 02:00 CST
5/08/1932 02:00 CDT
9/25/1932 02:00 CST
4/30/1933 02:00 CDT
9/24/1933 02:00 CST
4/29/1934 02:00 CDT
9/30/1934 02:00 CST
4/28/1935 02:00 CDT
9/29/1935 02:00 CST
4/26/1936 02:00 CDT
9/27/1936 02:00 CST
4/25/1937 02:00 CDT
9/26/1937 02:00 CST
4/24/1938 02:00 CDT
9/25/1938 02:00 CST
4/30/1939 02:00 CDT
9/24/1939 02:00 CST
4/28/1940 02:00 CDT
9/29/1940 02:00 CST
4/27/1941 02:00 CDT
9/28/1941 02:00 CST
2/09/1942 02:00 CWT
9/30/1945 02:00 CST
4/28/1946 02:00 CDT
9/29/1946 02:00 CST
4/27/1947 02:00 CDT
9/28/1947 02:00 CST
4/25/1948 02:00 CDT
9/26/1948 02:00 CST
4/24/1949 02:00 CDT
9/25/1949 02:00 CST
4/30/1950 02:00 CDT
9/24/1950 02:00 CST
4/29/1951 02:00 CDT
9/30/1951 02:00 CST
4/27/1952 02:00 CDT
9/28/1952 02:00 CST
4/26/1953 02:00 CDT
9/27/1953 02:00 CST
4/25/1954 02:00 CDT
9/26/1954 02:00 CST
11/14/1954 02:00 EST
9/29/1957 02:00 CST
4/27/1958 02:00 EST
4/27/1969 02:00 EDT
10/26/1969 02:00 EST
4/26/1970 02:00 EDT
10/25/1970 02:00 EST

IN # 272

Before 11/18/1883 LMT
11/18/1883 12:00 CST
3/31/1918 02:00 CWT
10/27/1918 02:00 CST
3/30/1919 02:00 CWT
10/26/1919 02:00 CST
2/09/1942 02:00 CWT
9/30/1945 02:00 CST
1/02/1955 00:01 EST
9/29/1957 02:00 CST
4/27/1958 02:00 EST
4/27/1969 02:00 EDT
10/26/1969 02:00 EST
4/26/1970 02:00 EDT
10/25/1970 02:00 EST

IN # 273

Before 11/18/1883 LMT
11/18/1883 12:00 CST
3/31/1918 02:00 CWT
10/27/1918 02:00 CST
3/30/1919 02:00 CWT
10/26/1919 02:00 CST
4/28/1935 02:00 CDT
9/29/1935 02:00 CST
4/26/1936 02:00 CDT
9/27/1936 02:00 CST
4/25/1937 02:00 CDT
10/03/1937 02:00 CST
4/30/1939 02:00 CDT
9/24/1939 02:00 CST
4/28/1940 02:00 CDT
9/29/1940 02:00 CST
4/27/1941 02:00 CDT
9/28/1941 02:00 CST
2/09/1942 02:00 CWT
9/30/1945 02:00 CST
4/30/1950 02:00 CDT
9/24/1950 02:00 CST
4/29/1951 02:00 CDT
9/30/1951 02:00 CST
4/27/1952 02:00 CDT
9/28/1952 02:00 CST
4/26/1953 02:00 CDT
9/27/1953 02:00 CST
4/25/1954 02:00 CDT
9/26/1954 02:00 CST
1/02/1955 00:01 EST
9/29/1957 02:00 CST
4/27/1958 02:00 EST
4/27/1969 02:00 EDT
10/26/1969 02:00 EST
4/26/1970 02:00 EDT
10/25/1970 02:00 EST

IN # 274

Before 11/18/1883 LMT
11/18/1883 12:00 CST
3/31/1918 02:00 CWT
10/27/1918 02:00 CST
3/30/1919 02:00 CWT
10/26/1919 02:00 CST
2/09/1942 02:00 CWT
9/30/1945 02:00 CST
1/02/1955 00:01 EST
9/29/1957 02:00 CST
4/27/1958 02:00 CDT
9/28/1958 02:00 CST
4/26/1959 02:00 EST
4/27/1969 02:00 EDT
10/26/1969 02:00 EST
4/26/1970 02:00 EDT
10/25/1970 02:00 EST

IN # 275

Before 11/18/1883 LMT
11/18/1883 12:00 CST
3/31/1918 02:00 CWT
10/27/1918 02:00 CST
3/30/1919 02:00 CWT
10/26/1919 02:00 CST
2/09/1942 02:00 CWT
9/30/1945 02:00 CST
4/25/1954 02:00 EST
9/29/1957 02:00 CST
4/27/1958 02:00 EST
4/27/1969 02:00 EDT
10/26/1969 02:00 EST
4/26/1970 02:00 EDT
10/25/1970 02:00 EST

IN # 276

Before 11/18/1883 LMT
11/18/1883 12:00 CST
3/31/1918 02:00 CWT
10/27/1918 02:00 CST
3/30/1919 02:00 CWT
10/26/1919 02:00 CST
2/09/1942 02:00 CWT
9/30/1945 02:00 CST
4/28/1946 02:00 CDT
9/29/1946 02:00 CST
4/27/1947 02:00 CDT
9/28/1947 02:00 CST
4/25/1948 02:00 CDT
9/26/1948 02:00 CST
4/24/1949 02:00 CDT
9/25/1949 02:00 CST
4/30/1950 02:00 CDT
9/24/1950 02:00 CST
4/29/1951 02:00 CDT
9/30/1951 02:00 CST
4/27/1952 02:00 CDT
9/28/1952 02:00 CST
4/26/1953 02:00 CDT
9/27/1953 02:00 CST
4/25/1954 02:00 CDT
9/29/1957 02:00 CST
4/27/1958 02:00 EST
4/27/1969 02:00 EDT
10/26/1969 02:00 EST
4/26/1970 02:00 EDT
10/25/1970 02:00 EST

IN # 277

Before 11/18/1883 LMT
11/18/1883 12:00 CST
3/31/1918 02:00 CWT
10/27/1918 02:00 CST
3/30/1919 02:00 CWT
10/26/1919 02:00 CST
2/09/1942 02:00 CWT
9/30/1945 02:00 CST
4/27/1947 02:00 CDT
9/28/1947 02:00 CST
4/25/1948 02:00 CDT
9/26/1948 02:00 CST
4/24/1949 02:00 CDT
9/25/1949 02:00 CST
4/30/1950 02:00 CDT
9/24/1950 02:00 CST
4/29/1951 02:00 CDT
9/30/1951 02:00 CST

TIME TABLES

4/27/1952 02:00 CDT
9/28/1952 02:00 CST
4/26/1953 02:00 CDT
9/27/1953 02:00 CST
4/25/1954 02:00 EST
9/29/1957 02:00 CST
4/27/1958 02:00 EST
4/27/1969 02:00 EDT
10/26/1969 02:00 EST
4/26/1970 02:00 EDT
10/25/1970 02:00 EST
....
IN # 278
Before 11/18/1883 LMT
11/18/1883 12:00 CST
3/31/1918 02:00 CWT
10/27/1918 02:00 CST
3/30/1919 02:00 CWT
10/26/1919 02:00 CST
2/09/1942 02:00 CWT
9/30/1945 02:00 CST
4/25/1948 02:00 CDT
9/26/1948 02:00 CST
4/25/1954 02:00 EST
9/29/1957 02:00 CST
4/27/1958 02:00 EST
4/27/1969 02:00 EDT
10/26/1969 02:00 EST
4/26/1970 02:00 EDT
10/25/1970 02:00 EST
....
IN # 279
Before 11/18/1883 LMT
11/18/1883 12:00 CST
3/31/1918 02:00 CWT
10/27/1918 02:00 CST
3/30/1919 02:00 CWT
10/26/1919 02:00 CST
2/09/1942 02:00 CWT
9/30/1945 02:00 CST
4/27/1947 02:00 CDT
9/28/1947 02:00 CST
4/26/1953 02:00 CDT
9/27/1953 02:00 CST
4/25/1954 02:00 EST
9/29/1957 02:00 CST
4/27/1958 02:00 EST
4/01/1960 02:00 EDT
10/01/1960 02:00 EST
4/30/1961 02:00 EDT
10/01/1961 02:00 E[illegible]T
10/29/1961 02:00 EST
4/27/1969 02:00 EDT
10/26/1969 02:00 EST
4/26/1970 02:00 EDT
10/25/1970 02:00 EST
....
IN # 280
Before 11/18/1883 LMT
11/18/1883 12:00 CST
3/31/1918 02:00 CWT
10/27/1918 02:00 CST
3/30/1919 02:00 CWT
10/26/1919 02:00 CST
2/09/1942 02:00 CWT
9/30/1945 02:00 CST
11/28/1954 02:00 EST
9/29/1957 02:00 CST
4/27/1958 02:00 CDT
9/28/1958 02:00 CST
4/26/1959 02:00 EST
4/27/1969 02:00 EDT
10/26/1969 02:00 EST
4/26/1970 02:00 EDT
10/25/1970 02:00 EST
....
IN # 281
Before 11/18/1883 LMT
11/18/1883 12:00 CST
3/31/1918 02:00 CWT
10/27/1918 02:00 CST
3/30/1919 02:00 CWT
10/26/1919 02:00 CST
2/09/1942 02:00 CWT
9/30/1945 02:00 CST
4/28/1946 02:00 CDT
9/29/1946 02:00 CST
4/27/1947 02:00 CDT
9/28/1947 02:00 CST
4/25/1948 02:00 CDT
9/26/1948 02:00 CST
4/24/1949 02:00 CDT
9/25/1949 02:00 CST
4/30/1950 02:00 CDT
9/24/1950 02:00 CST
4/29/1951 02:00 CDT
9/30/1951 02:00 CST
4/27/1952 02:00 CDT
9/28/1952 02:00 CST
4/26/1953 02:00 CDT
9/27/1953 02:00 CST
4/25/1954 02:00 CDT
9/26/1954 02:00 CST
11/28/1954 02:00 EST
9/29/1957 02:00 CST
4/27/1958 02:00 CDT
9/28/1958 02:00 CST
4/26/1959 02:00 EST
4/27/1969 02:00 EDT
10/26/1969 02:00 EST
4/26/1970 02:00 EDT
10/25/1970 02:00 EST
....
IN # 282
Before 11/18/1883 LMT
11/18/1883 12:00 CST
3/31/1918 02:00 CWT
10/27/1918 02:00 CST
3/30/1919 02:00 CWT
10/26/1919 02:00 CST
2/09/1942 02:00 CWT
9/30/1945 02:00 CST
4/25/1948 02:00 CDT
9/26/1948 02:00 CST
4/24/1949 02:00 CDT
9/25/1949 02:00 CST
4/30/1950 02:00 CDT
9/24/1950 02:00 CST
4/29/1951 02:00 CDT
9/30/1951 02:00 CST
4/27/1952 02:00 CDT
9/28/1952 02:00 CST
4/26/1953 02:00 CDT
9/27/1953 02:00 CST
4/25/1954 02:00 CDT
9/26/1954 02:00 CST
11/28/1954 02:00 EST
9/29/1957 02:00 CST
4/27/1958 02:00 CDT
9/28/1958 02:00 CST
4/26/1959 02:00 EST
4/27/1969 02:00 EDT
10/26/1969 02:00 EST
4/26/1970 02:00 EDT
10/25/1970 02:00 EST
....
IN # 283
Before 11/18/1883 LMT
11/18/1883 12:00 CST
3/31/1918 02:00 CWT
10/27/1918 02:00 CST
3/30/1919 02:00 CWT
10/26/1919 02:00 CST
2/09/1942 02:00 CWT
9/30/1945 02:00 CST
4/30/1950 02:00 CDT
9/24/1950 02:00 CST
4/29/1951 02:00 CDT
9/30/1951 02:00 CST
4/27/1952 02:00 CDT
9/28/1952 02:00 CST
4/26/1953 02:00 CDT
9/27/1953 02:00 CST
4/25/1954 02:00 CDT
9/26/1954 02:00 CST
11/28/1954 02:00 EST
9/29/1957 02:00 CST
4/27/1958 02:00 CDT
9/28/1958 02:00 CST
4/26/1959 02:00 EST
4/27/1969 02:00 EDT
10/26/1969 02:00 EST
4/26/1970 02:00 EDT
10/25/1970 02:00 EST
....
IN # 284
Before 11/18/1883 LMT
11/18/1883 12:00 CST
3/31/1918 02:00 CWT
10/27/1918 02:00 CST
3/30/1919 02:00 CWT
10/26/1919 02:00 CST
2/09/1942 02:00 CWT
9/30/1945 02:00 CST
4/26/1953 02:00 CDT
9/27/1953 02:00 CST
4/25/1954 02:00 CDT
9/26/1954 02:00 CST
11/28/1954 02:00 EST
9/29/1957 02:00 CST
4/27/1958 02:00 CDT
9/28/1958 02:00 CST
4/26/1959 02:00 EST
4/27/1969 02:00 EDT
10/26/1969 02:00 EST
4/26/1970 02:00 EDT
10/25/1970 02:00 EST
....
IN # 285
Before 11/18/1883 LMT
11/18/1883 12:00 CST
3/31/1918 02:00 CWT
10/27/1918 02:00 CST
3/30/1919 02:00 CWT
10/26/1919 02:00 CST
2/09/1942 02:00 CWT
9/30/1945 02:00 CST
11/28/1954 02:00 EST
4/29/1956 02:00 E[illegible]T
10/28/1956 02:00 EST
9/29/1957 02:00 CST
4/27/1958 02:00 CDT
9/28/1958 02:00 CST
4/26/1959 02:00 EST
4/27/1969 02:00 EDT
10/26/1969 02:00 EST
4/26/1970 02:00 EDT
10/25/1970 02:00 EST
....
IN # 286
Before 11/18/1883 LMT
11/18/1883 12:00 CST
3/31/1918 02:00 CWT
10/27/1918 02:00 CST
3/30/1919 02:00 CWT
10/26/1919 02:00 CST
2/09/1942 02:00 CWT
9/30/1945 02:00 CST
11/28/1954 02:00 EST
9/29/1957 02:00 CST
4/27/1958 02:00 CDT
9/28/1958 02:00 CST
4/26/1959 02:00 EST
4/27/1969 02:00 EDT
10/26/1969 02:00 EST
4/26/1970 02:00 EDT
10/25/1970 02:00 EST
....
IN # 287
Before 11/18/1883 LMT
11/18/1883 12:00 CST
3/31/1918 02:00 CWT
10/27/1918 02:00 CST
3/30/1919 02:00 CWT
10/26/1919 02:00 CST
2/09/1942 02:00 CWT
9/30/1945 02:00 CST
11/07/1954 00:01 EST
4/27/1969 02:00 EDT
10/26/1969 02:00 EST
4/26/1970 02:00 EDT
10/25/1970 02:00 EST
....
IN # 288
Before 11/18/1883 LMT
11/18/1883 12:00 CST
3/31/1918 02:00 CWT
10/27/1918 02:00 CST
3/30/1919 02:00 CWT
10/26/1919 02:00 CST
2/09/1942 02:00 CWT
9/30/1945 02:00 CST
4/26/1953 02:00 CDT
9/27/1953 02:00 CST
4/25/1954 02:00 CDT
9/26/1954 02:00 CST
11/07/1954 00:01 EST
4/27/1969 02:00 EDT
10/26/1969 02:00 EST
4/26/1970 02:00 EDT
10/25/1970 02:00 EST
....
IN # 289
Before 11/18/1883 LMT
11/18/1883 12:00 CST
3/31/1918 02:00 CWT
10/27/1918 02:00 CST
3/30/1919 02:00 CWT
10/26/1919 02:00 CST
2/09/1942 02:00 CWT
9/30/1945 02:00 CST
4/25/1954 02:00 CDT
9/26/1954 02:00 CST
11/07/1954 00:01 EST
4/27/1969 02:00 EDT
10/26/1969 02:00 EST
4/26/1970 02:00 EDT
10/25/1970 02:00 EST
....
IN # 290
Before 11/18/1883 LMT
11/18/1883 12:00 CST
3/31/1918 02:00 CWT
10/27/1918 02:00 CST
3/30/1919 02:00 CWT
10/26/1919 02:00 CST
5/01/1929 02:00 CDT
10/01/1929 02:00 CST
5/01/1930 02:00 CDT
10/01/1930 02:00 CST
4/28/1940 02:00 CDT
9/29/1940 02:00 CST
4/27/1941 02:00 CDT
9/28/1941 02:00 CST
2/09/1942 02:00 CWT
9/30/1945 02:00 CST
4/28/1946 02:00 CDT
9/29/1946 02:00 CST
4/27/1947 02:00 CDT
9/28/1947 02:00 CST
4/25/1948 02:00 CDT
9/26/1948 02:00 CST
4/24/1949 02:00 CDT
9/25/1949 02:00 CST
4/30/1950 02:00 CDT
9/29/1950 02:00 CST
4/29/1951 02:00 CDT
9/30/1951 02:00 CST
4/27/1952 02:00 CDT
9/28/1952 02:00 CST
4/26/1953 02:00 CDT
9/27/1953 02:00 CST
4/25/1954 02:00 CDT
9/26/1954 02:00 CST
11/07/1954 00:01 EST
4/27/1969 02:00 EDT
10/26/1969 02:00 EST
4/26/1970 02:00 EDT
10/25/1970 02:00 EST
....
IN # 291
Before 11/18/1883 LMT
11/18/1883 12:00 CST
3/31/1918 02:00 CWT
10/27/1918 02:00 CST
3/30/1919 02:00 CWT
10/26/1919 02:00 CST
2/09/1942 02:00 CWT
9/30/1945 02:00 CST
11/07/1954 00:01 EST
9/29/1957 02:00 CST
4/27/1958 02:00 EST
4/27/1969 02:00 EDT
10/26/1969 02:00 EST
4/26/1970 02:00 EDT
10/25/1970 02:00 EST
....
IN # 292
Before 11/18/1883 LMT
11/18/1883 12:00 CST
3/31/1918 02:00 CWT
10/27/1918 02:00 CST
3/30/1919 02:00 CWT
10/26/1919 02:00 CST
2/09/1942 02:00 CWT
9/30/1945 02:00 CST
4/27/1947 02:00 CDT
9/28/1947 02:00 CST
4/25/1948 02:00 CDT
9/26/1948 02:00 CST
4/24/1949 02:00 CDT
9/25/1949 02:00 CST
4/30/1950 02:00 CDT
9/24/1950 02:00 CST
4/29/1951 02:00 CDT
9/30/1951 02:00 CST
4/27/1952 02:00 CDT
9/28/1952 02:00 CST
4/26/1953 02:00 CDT
9/27/1953 02:00 CST
11/07/1954 00:01 EST
9/29/1957 02:00 CST
4/27/1958 02:00 EST
4/27/1969 02:00 EDT
10/26/1969 02:00 EST
4/26/1970 02:00 EDT
10/25/1970 02:00 EST
....
IN # 293
Before 11/18/1883 LMT
11/18/1883 12:00 CST
3/31/1918 02:00 CWT
10/27/1918 02:00 CST
3/30/1919 02:00 CWT
10/26/1919 02:00 CST
2/09/1942 02:00 CWT
9/30/1945 02:00 CST
4/27/1947 02:00 CDT
9/28/1947 02:00 CST
4/25/1948 02:00 CDT
9/26/1948 02:00 CST
4/27/1952 02:00 CDT
9/28/1952 02:00 CST
4/26/1953 02:00 CDT
9/27/1953 02:00 CST
11/07/1954 00:01 EST
9/29/1957 02:00 CST
4/27/1958 02:00 EST
4/27/1969 02:00 EDT
10/26/1969 02:00 EST
4/26/1970 02:00 EDT
10/25/1970 02:00 EST
....
IN # 294
Before 11/18/1883 LMT
11/18/1883 12:00 CST
3/31/1918 02:00 CWT
10/27/1918 02:00 CST
3/30/1919 02:00 CWT
10/26/1919 02:00 CST
2/09/1942 02:00 CWT
9/30/1945 02:00 CST
4/25/1948 02:00 CDT
9/26/1948 02:00 CST
11/07/1954 00:01 EST
9/29/1957 02:00 CST
4/27/1958 02:00 EST
4/27/1969 02:00 EDT
10/26/1969 02:00 EST
4/26/1970 02:00 EDT
10/25/1970 02:00 EST
....
IN # 295
Before 11/18/1883 LMT
11/18/1883 12:00 CST
3/31/1918 02:00 CWT
10/27/1918 02:00 CST
3/30/1919 02:00 CWT
10/26/1919 02:00 CST
2/09/1942 02:00 CWT
9/30/1945 02:00 CST
4/26/1953 02:00 CDT
9/27/1953 02:00 CST
4/25/1954 02:00 CDT
9/26/1954 02:00 CST
11/07/1954 00:01 EST
9/29/1957 02:00 CST
4/27/1958 02:00 EST
4/27/1969 02:00 EDT
10/26/1969 02:00 EST
4/26/1970 02:00 EDT
10/25/1970 02:00 EST
....
IN # 296
Before 11/18/1883 LMT
11/18/1883 02:00 CST
3/31/1918 02:00 CWT
10/27/1918 02:00 CST
3/30/1919 02:00 CWT
10/26/1919 02:00 CST
2/09/1942 02:00 CWT
9/30/1945 02:00 CST
5/01/1947 02:00 CDT
9/16/1947 02:00 CST
4/25/1948 02:00 CDT
9/26/1948 02:00 CST
4/24/1949 02:00 CDT
9/25/1949 02:00 CST
4/30/1950 02:00 CDT
9/24/1950 02:00 CST
4/26/1953 02:00 CDT
9/27/1953 02:00 CST
11/07/1954 00:01 EST
9/29/1957 02:00 CST
4/27/1958 02:00 EST
4/27/1969 02:00 EDT
10/26/1969 02:00 EST
4/26/1970 02:00 EDT
10/25/1970 02:00 EST
....
IN # 297
Before 11/18/1883 LMT
11/18/1883 12:00 CST
3/31/1918 02:00 CWT
10/27/1918 02:00 CST
3/30/1919 02:00 CWT
10/26/1919 02:00 CST
4/24/1938 02:00 CDT
10/01/1938 02:00 CST
4/28/1940 02:00 CDT
9/29/1940 02:00 CST
4/27/1941 02:00 CDT
9/28/1941 02:00 CST
2/09/1942 02:00 CWT
9/30/1945 02:00 CST
4/28/1946 02:00 CDT
9/29/1946 02:00 CST
4/27/1947 02:00 CDT
9/28/1947 02:00 CST
4/25/1948 02:00 CDT
9/26/1948 02:00 CST
4/24/1949 02:00 CDT
9/25/1949 02:00 CST
4/30/1950 02:00 CDT
9/24/1950 02:00 CST
4/29/1951 02:00 CDT
9/30/1951 02:00 CST
4/27/1952 02:00 CDT
9/28/1952 02:00 CST
4/26/1953 02:00 CDT
9/27/1953 02:00 CST
4/25/1954 02:00 CDT
9/26/1954 02:00 CST
11/07/1954 00:01 EST
9/29/1957 02:00 CST
4/27/1958 02:00 EST
4/26/1959 02:00 EDT
10/25/1959 02:00 EST
4/27/1969 02:00 EDT
10/26/1969 02:00 EST
4/26/1970 02:00 EDT
10/25/1970 02:00 EST
....
IN # 298
Before 11/18/1883 LMT
11/18/1883 12:00 CST
3/31/1918 02:00 CWT
10/27/1918 02:00 CST
3/30/1919 02:00 CWT
10/26/1919 02:00 CST
4/30/1939 02:00 CDT
10/01/1939 02:00 CST
4/28/1946 02:00 CDT
9/29/1946 02:00 CST
4/27/1947 02:00 CDT
9/28/1947 02:00 CST
4/25/1948 02:00 CDT
9/26/1948 02:00 CST
4/24/1949 02:00 CDT
9/25/1949 02:00 CST
4/30/1950 02:00 CDT
9/24/1950 02:00 CST
4/29/1951 02:00 CDT
9/30/1951 02:00 CST
4/27/1952 02:00 CDT
9/28/1952 02:00 CST
4/26/1953 02:00 CDT
9/27/1953 02:00 CST
4/25/1954 02:00 CDT
9/26/1954 02:00 CST
11/07/1954 00:01 EST
9/29/1957 02:00 CST
4/27/1958 02:00 EST
4/27/1969 02:00 EDT
10/26/1969 02:00 EST
4/26/1970 02:00 EDT
10/25/1970 02:00 EST
....
IN # 299
Before 11/18/1883 LMT
11/18/1883 12:00 CST
3/31/1918 02:00 CWT
10/27/1918 02:00 CST
3/30/1919 02:00 CWT
10/26/1919 02:00 CST
4/24/1938 02:00 CDT
9/25/1938 02:00 CST
4/30/1939 02:00 CDT
9/24/1939 02:00 CST
4/28/1940 02:00 CDT
9/02/1940 02:00 CST
2/09/1942 02:00 CWT
9/30/1945 02:00 CST
4/28/1946 02:00 CDT
9/29/1946 02:00 CST

TIME TABLES

4/27/1947 02:00 CDT
9/28/1947 02:00 CST
4/25/1948 02:00 CDT
9/26/1948 02:00 CST
4/24/1949 02:00 CDT
9/25/1949 02:00 CST
4/30/1950 02:00 CDT
9/24/1950 02:00 CST
4/29/1951 02:00 CDT
9/30/1951 02:00 CST
4/27/1952 02:00 CDT
9/28/1952 02:00 CST
4/26/1953 02:00 CDT
9/27/1953 02:00 CST
4/25/1954 02:00 CDT
9/26/1954 02:00 CST
11/07/1954 00:01 EST
9/29/1957 02:00 CST
4/27/1958 02:00 EST
4/27/1969 02:00 EDT
10/26/1969 02:00 EST
4/26/1970 02:00 EDT
10/25/1970 02:00 EST

....

IN # 300
Before 11/18/1883 LMT
11/18/1883 12:00 CST
3/31/1918 02:00 CWT
10/27/1918 02:00 CST
3/30/1919 02:00 CWT
10/26/1919 02:00 CST
2/09/1942 02:00 CWT
9/30/1945 02:00 CST
4/25/1948 02:00 CDT
9/26/1948 02:00 CST
4/24/1949 02:00 CDT
9/25/1949 02:00 CST
4/30/1950 02:00 CDT
9/24/1950 02:00 CST
4/29/1951 02:00 CDT
9/30/1951 02:00 CST
4/27/1952 02:00 CDT
9/28/1952 02:00 CST
4/26/1953 02:00 CDT
9/27/1953 02:00 CST
4/25/1954 02:00 CDT
9/26/1954 02:00 CST
11/07/1954 00:01 EST
9/29/1957 02:00 CST
4/27/1958 02:00 CDT
9/28/1958 02:00 CST
4/26/1959 02:00 EST
4/27/1969 02:00 EDT
10/26/1969 02:00 EST
4/26/1970 02:00 EDT
10/25/1970 02:00 EST

....

IN # 301
Before 11/18/1883 LMT
11/18/1883 12:00 CST
3/31/1918 02:00 CWT
10/27/1918 02:00 CST
3/30/1919 02:00 CWT
10/26/1919 02:00 CST
2/09/1942 02:00 CWT
9/30/1945 02:00 CST
4/25/1948 02:00 CDT
9/26/1948 02:00 CST
4/30/1950 02:00 CDT
9/24/1950 02:00 CST
4/29/1951 02:00 CDT
9/30/1951 02:00 CST
4/26/1953 02:00 CDT
9/27/1953 02:00 CST
4/25/1954 02:00 CDT
9/26/1954 02:00 CST
11/07/1954 00:01 EST
9/29/1957 02:00 CST
4/27/1958 02:00 CDT
9/28/1958 02:00 CST
4/26/1959 02:00 EST
4/27/1969 02:00 EDT
10/26/1969 02:00 EST
4/26/1970 02:00 EDT
10/25/1970 02:00 EST

....

IN # 302
Before 11/18/1883 LMT
11/18/1883 12:00 CST
3/31/1918 02:00 CWT
10/27/1918 02:00 CST
3/30/1919 02:00 CWT
10/26/1919 02:00 CST
2/09/1942 02:00 CWT
9/30/1945 02:00 CST
4/26/1953 02:00 CDT
9/27/1953 02:00 CST
4/25/1954 02:00 CDT
9/26/1954 02:00 CST
4/24/1955 02:00 EST
10/30/1955 00:01 CST
4/29/1956 02:00 EST
9/29/1957 02:00 CST
4/27/1958 02:00 CDT
9/28/1958 02:00 CST
4/26/1959 02:00 EST
4/27/1969 02:00 EDT
10/26/1969 02:00 EST
4/26/1970 02:00 EDT
10/25/1970 02:00 EST

....

IN # 303
Before 11/18/1883 LMT
11/18/1883 12:00 CST
3/31/1918 02:00 CWT
10/27/1918 02:00 CST
3/30/1919 02:00 CWT
10/26/1919 02:00 CST
2/09/1942 02:00 CWT
9/30/1945 02:00 CST
4/27/1952 02:00 EST
4/27/1969 02:00 EDT
10/26/1969 02:00 EST
4/26/1970 02:00 EDT
10/25/1970 02:00 EST

....

IN # 304
Before 11/18/1883 LMT
11/18/1883 12:00 CST
3/31/1918 02:00 CWT
10/27/1918 02:00 CST
3/30/1919 02:00 CWT
10/26/1919 02:00 CST
2/09/1942 02:00 CWT
9/30/1945 02:00 CST
4/27/1952 02:00 EST
4/25/1954 02:00 EDT
9/26/1954 02:00 EST
4/30/1967 02:00 EDT
10/29/1967 02:00 EST
4/28/1968 02:00 EDT
10/27/1968 02:00 EST
4/27/1969 02:00 EDT
10/26/1969 02:00 EST
4/26/1970 02:00 EDT
10/25/1970 02:00 EST

....

IN # 305
Before 11/18/1883 LMT
11/18/1883 12:00 CST
3/31/1918 02:00 CWT
10/27/1918 02:00 CST
3/30/1919 02:00 CWT
10/26/1919 02:00 CST
2/09/1942 02:00 CWT
9/30/1945 02:00 CST
11/28/1954 00:01 EST
9/29/1957 02:00 CST
4/27/1958 02:00 EST
4/27/1969 02:00 EDT
10/26/1969 02:00 EST
4/26/1970 02:00 EDT
10/25/1970 02:00 EST

....

IN # 306
Before 11/18/1883 LMT
11/18/1883 12:00 CST
3/31/1918 02:00 CWT
10/27/1918 02:00 CST
3/30/1919 02:00 CWT
10/26/1919 02:00 CST
2/09/1942 02:00 CWT
9/30/1945 02:00 CST
4/26/1953 02:00 CDT
9/27/1953 02:00 CST
4/25/1954 02:00 CDT
9/26/1954 02:00 CST
11/28/1954 00:01 EST
9/29/1957 02:00 CST
4/27/1958 02:00 EST
4/27/1969 02:00 EDT
10/26/1969 02:00 EST
4/26/1970 02:00 EDT
10/25/1970 02:00 EST

....

IN # 307
Before 11/18/1883 LMT
11/18/1883 12:00 CST
3/31/1918 02:00 CWT
10/27/1918 02:00 CST
3/30/1919 02:00 CWT
10/26/1919 02:00 CST
2/09/1942 02:00 CWT
9/30/1945 02:00 CST
11/28/1954 00:01 EST
9/29/1957 02:00 CST
4/27/1958 02:00 CDT
9/28/1958 02:00 CST
4/26/1959 02:00 EST
4/27/1969 02:00 EDT
10/26/1969 02:00 EST
4/26/1970 02:00 EDT
10/25/1970 02:00 EST

....

IN # 308
Before 11/18/1883 LMT
11/18/1883 12:00 CST
3/31/1918 02:00 CWT
10/27/1918 02:00 CST
3/30/1919 02:00 CWT
10/26/1919 02:00 CST
2/09/1942 02:00 CWT
9/30/1945 02:00 CST
4/28/1946 02:00 CDT
9/29/1946 02:00 CST
4/27/1947 02:00 CDT
9/28/1947 02:00 CST
4/25/1948 02:00 CDT
9/26/1948 02:00 CST
4/24/1949 02:00 CDT
9/25/1949 02:00 CST
4/30/1950 02:00 CDT
9/24/1950 02:00 CST
4/29/1951 02:00 CDT
9/30/1951 02:00 CST
4/27/1952 02:00 CDT
9/28/1952 02:00 CST
4/26/1953 02:00 CDT
9/27/1953 02:00 CST
4/25/1954 02:00 CDT
9/26/1954 02:00 CST
11/28/1954 00:01 EST
9/29/1957 02:00 CST
4/27/1958 02:00 CDT
9/28/1958 02:00 CST
4/26/1959 02:00 EST
4/27/1969 02:00 EDT
10/26/1969 02:00 EST
4/26/1970 02:00 EDT
10/25/1970 02:00 EST

....

IN # 309
Before 11/18/1883 LMT
11/18/1883 12:00 CST
3/31/1918 02:00 CWT
10/27/1918 02:00 CST
3/30/1919 02:00 CWT
10/26/1919 02:00 CST
2/09/1942 02:00 CWT
9/30/1945 02:00 CST
4/27/1947 02:00 CDT
9/28/1947 02:00 CST
4/30/1950 02:00 CDT
9/24/1950 02:00 CST
4/29/1951 02:00 CDT
9/30/1951 02:00 CST
4/27/1952 02:00 CDT
9/28/1952 02:00 CST
4/26/1953 02:00 CDT
9/27/1953 02:00 CST
4/25/1954 02:00 CDT
9/26/1954 02:00 CST
11/28/1954 00:01 EST
9/29/1957 02:00 CST
4/27/1958 02:00 CDT
9/28/1958 02:00 CST
4/26/1959 02:00 EST
4/27/1969 02:00 EDT
10/26/1969 02:00 EST
4/26/1970 02:00 EDT
10/25/1970 02:00 EST

....

IN # 310
Before 11/18/1883 LMT
11/18/1883 12:00 CST
3/31/1918 02:00 CWT
10/27/1918 02:00 CST
3/30/1919 02:00 CWT
10/26/1919 02:00 CST
2/09/1942 02:00 CWT
9/30/1945 02:00 CST
4/26/1953 02:00 CDT
9/27/1953 02:00 CST
4/25/1954 02:00 CDT
9/26/1954 02:00 CST
11/28/1954 00:01 EST
9/29/1957 02:00 CST
4/27/1958 02:00 CDT
9/28/1958 02:00 CST
4/26/1959 02:00 EST
4/27/1969 02:00 EDT
10/26/1969 02:00 EST
4/26/1970 02:00 EDT
10/25/1970 02:00 EST

....

IN # 311
Before 11/18/1883 LMT
11/18/1883 12:00 CST
3/31/1918 02:00 CWT
10/27/1918 02:00 CST
3/30/1919 02:00 CWT
10/26/1919 02:00 CST
2/09/1942 02:00 CWT
9/30/1945 02:00 CST
11/28/1954 00:01 EST
4/27/1969 02:00 EDT
10/26/1969 02:00 EST
4/26/1970 02:00 EDT
10/25/1970 02:00 EST

....

IN # 312
Before 11/18/1883 LMT
11/18/1883 12:00 CST
3/31/1918 02:00 CWT
10/27/1918 02:00 CST
3/30/1919 02:00 CWT
10/26/1919 02:00 CST
2/09/1942 02:00 CWT
9/30/1945 02:00 CST
4/26/1953 02:00 CDT
9/27/1953 02:00 CST
4/25/1954 02:00 CDT
9/26/1954 02:00 CST
11/21/1954 01:00 EST
9/29/1957 02:00 CST
4/27/1958 02:00 CDT
9/28/1958 02:00 CST
4/26/1959 02:00 EST
4/27/1969 02:00 EDT
10/26/1969 02:00 EST
4/26/1970 02:00 EDT
10/25/1970 02:00 EST

....

IN # 313
Before 11/18/1883 LMT
11/18/1883 12:00 CST
3/31/1918 02:00 CWT
10/27/1918 02:00 CST
3/30/1919 02:00 CWT
10/26/1919 02:00 CST
2/09/1942 02:00 CWT
9/30/1945 02:00 CST
11/28/1954 02:00 EST
9/29/1957 02:00 CST
4/27/1958 02:00 EST
4/27/1969 02:00 EDT
10/26/1969 02:00 EST
4/26/1970 02:00 EDT
10/25/1970 02:00 EST

....

IN # 314
Before 11/18/1883 LMT
11/18/1883 12:00 CST
3/31/1918 02:00 CWT
10/27/1918 02:00 CST
3/30/1919 02:00 CWT
10/26/1919 02:00 CST
2/09/1942 02:00 CWT
9/30/1945 02:00 CST
4/25/1948 02:00 CDT
9/26/1948 02:00 CST
4/30/1950 02:00 CDT
9/24/1950 02:00 CST
11/28/1954 02:00 EST
9/29/1957 02:00 CST
4/27/1958 02:00 EST
4/27/1969 02:00 EDT
10/26/1969 02:00 EST
4/26/1970 02:00 EDT
10/25/1970 02:00 EST

....

IN # 315
Before 11/18/1883 LMT
11/18/1883 12:00 CST
3/31/1918 02:00 CWT
10/27/1918 02:00 CST
3/30/1919 02:00 CWT
10/26/1919 02:00 CST
2/09/1942 02:00 CWT
9/30/1945 02:00 CST
4/25/1948 02:00 CDT
9/26/1948 02:00 CST
4/24/1949 02:00 CDT
9/25/1949 02:00 CST
4/30/1950 02:00 CDT
9/24/1950 02:00 CST
4/29/1951 02:00 CDT
9/30/1951 02:00 CST
4/27/1952 02:00 CDT
9/28/1952 02:00 CST
4/26/1953 02:00 CDT
9/27/1953 02:00 CST
4/25/1954 02:00 CDT
9/26/1954 02:00 CST
12/12/1954 00:01 EST
9/29/1957 02:00 CST
4/27/1958 02:00 CDT
9/28/1958 02:00 CST
4/26/1959 02:00 EST
4/27/1969 02:00 EDT
10/26/1969 02:00 EST
4/26/1970 02:00 EDT
10/25/1970 02:00 EST

....

IN # 316
Before 11/18/1883 LMT
11/18/1883 12:00 CST
3/31/1918 02:00 CWT
10/27/1918 02:00 CST
3/30/1919 02:00 CWT
10/26/1919 02:00 CST
2/09/1942 02:00 CWT
9/30/1945 02:00 CST
4/25/1948 02:00 CDT
9/26/1948 02:00 CST
4/24/1949 02:00 CDT
9/25/1949 02:00 CST
4/30/1950 02:00 CDT
9/24/1950 02:00 CST
4/29/1951 02:00 CDT
9/30/1951 02:00 CST
4/27/1952 02:00 CDT
9/28/1952 02:00 CST
4/26/1953 02:00 CDT
9/27/1953 02:00 CST
4/25/1954 02:00 CDT
9/26/1954 02:00 CST
11/28/1954 01:00 EST
9/29/1957 02:00 CST
4/27/1958 02:00 CDT
9/28/1958 02:00 CST
4/26/1959 02:00 EST
4/27/1969 02:00 EDT
10/26/1969 02:00 EST
4/26/1970 02:00 EDT
10/25/1970 02:00 EST

....

IN # 317
Before 11/18/1883 LMT
11/18/1883 12:00 CST
3/31/1918 02:00 CWT
10/27/1918 02:00 CST
3/30/1919 02:00 CWT
10/26/1919 02:00 CST
2/09/1942 02:00 CWT
9/30/1945 02:00 CST
4/25/1948 02:00 CDT
9/26/1948 02:00 CST
4/24/1949 02:00 CDT
9/25/1949 02:00 CST
4/30/1950 02:00 CDT
9/24/1950 02:00 CST
4/29/1951 02:00 CDT
9/30/1951 02:00 CST
4/27/1952 02:00 CDT
9/28/1952 02:00 CST
4/26/1953 02:00 CDT
9/27/1953 02:00 CST
4/25/1954 02:00 CDT
9/26/1954 02:00 CST
12/12/1954 01:00 EST
9/29/1957 02:00 CST
4/27/1958 02:00 CDT
9/28/1958 02:00 CST
4/26/1959 02:00 EST
4/27/1969 02:00 EDT
10/26/1969 02:00 EST
4/26/1970 02:00 EDT
10/25/1970 02:00 EST

....

IN # 318
Before 11/18/1883 LMT
11/18/1883 12:00 CST
3/31/1918 02:00 CWT
10/27/1918 02:00 CST
3/30/1919 02:00 CWT
10/26/1919 02:00 CST
6/01/1932 02:00 CDT
9/05/1932 02:00 CST
6/02/1933 02:00 CDT
9/04/1933 02:00 CST
6/03/1934 02:00 CDT
9/03/1934 02:00 CST
6/02/1935 02:00 CDT
9/02/1935 02:00 CST
4/30/1939 02:00 CDT
9/24/1939 02:00 CST
2/09/1942 02:00 CWT
9/30/1945 02:00 CST
4/28/1946 02:00 CDT
9/29/1946 02:00 CST
4/27/1947 02:00 CDT
9/28/1947 02:00 CST
4/25/1948 02:00 CDT
9/26/1948 02:00 CST
4/24/1949 02:00 CDT
9/25/1949 02:00 CST
4/30/1950 02:00 CDT
9/24/1950 02:00 CST
4/29/1951 02:00 CDT
9/30/1951 02:00 CST
4/27/1952 02:00 CDT
9/28/1952 02:00 CST
4/26/1953 02:00 CDT
9/27/1953 02:00 CST
4/25/1954 02:00 CDT
9/26/1954 02:00 CST
11/21/1954 02:00 EST
9/29/1957 02:00 CST
4/27/1958 02:00 CDT
9/28/1958 02:00 CST
4/26/1959 02:00 EST
4/27/1969 02:00 EDT
10/26/1969 02:00 EST
4/26/1970 02:00 EDT
10/25/1970 02:00 EST

....

IN # 319
Before 11/18/1883 LMT
11/18/1883 12:00 CST
3/31/1918 02:00 CWT
10/27/1918 02:00 CST
3/30/1919 02:00 CWT
10/26/1919 02:00 CST
2/09/1942 02:00 CWT
9/30/1945 02:00 CST
4/26/1953 02:00 CDT
9/27/1953 02:00 CST
4/25/1954 02:00 CDT
9/26/1954 02:00 CST
4/24/1955 02:00 CDT
9/25/1955 02:00 CST
4/29/1956 02:00 CDT
9/30/1956 02:00 CST
4/28/1957 02:00 CDT
9/29/1957 02:00 CST
4/27/1958 02:00 CDT
9/28/1958 02:00 CST
4/26/1959 02:00 CDT
9/27/1959 02:00 CST
4/24/1960 02:00 CDT
9/25/1960 02:00 CST
11/28/1960 00:00 EST
4/27/1969 02:00 EDT
10/26/1969 02:00 EST
4/26/1970 02:00 EDT
10/25/1970 02:00 EST

....

IN # 320
Before 11/18/1883 LMT
11/18/1883 12:00 CST
3/31/1918 02:00 CWT
10/27/1918 02:00 CST
3/30/1919 02:00 CWT
10/26/1919 02:00 CST
2/09/1942 02:00 CWT
9/30/1945 02:00 CST
4/24/1955 02:00 CDT
9/25/1955 02:00 CST
4/29/1956 02:00 CDT
9/30/1956 02:00 CST
4/28/1957 02:00 CDT
9/29/1957 02:00 CST
4/27/1958 02:00 CDT
9/28/1958 02:00 CST

TIME TABLES

4/26/1959	02:00	CDT
9/27/1959	02:00	CST
4/24/1960	02:00	CDT
9/25/1960	02:00	CST
11/28/1960	00:00	EST
4/27/1969	02:00	EDT
10/26/1969	02:00	EST
4/26/1970	02:00	EDT
10/25/1970	02:00	EST

IN # 321

Before 11/18/1883		LMT
11/18/1883	12:00	CST
3/31/1918	02:00	CWT
10/27/1918	02:00	CST
3/30/1919	02:00	CWT
10/26/1919	02:00	CST
2/09/1942	02:00	CWT
9/30/1945	02:00	CST
4/30/1950	02:00	CDT
9/24/1950	02:00	CST
4/26/1953	02:00	CDT
9/27/1953	02:00	CST
4/25/1954	02:00	CDT
9/26/1954	02:00	CST
4/24/1955	02:00	CDT
9/25/1955	02:00	CST
4/29/1956	02:00	CDT
10/08/1956	00:00	CST
4/28/1957	02:00	CDT
9/29/1957	02:00	CST
4/27/1958	02:00	CDT
9/28/1958	02:00	CST
4/26/1959	02:00	CDT
9/27/1959	02:00	CST
4/24/1960	02:00	CDT
9/25/1960	02:00	CST
11/28/1960	00:00	EST
4/27/1969	02:00	EDT
10/26/1969	02:00	EST
4/26/1970	02:00	EDT
10/25/1970	02:00	EST

IN # 322

Before 11/18/1883		LMT
11/18/1883	12:00	CST
3/31/1918	02:00	CWT
10/27/1918	02:00	CST
3/30/1919	02:00	CWT
10/26/1919	02:00	CST
2/09/1942	02:00	CWT
9/30/1945	02:00	CST
5/01/1955	00:00	CDT
9/04/1955	00:00	CST
4/29/1956	02:00	CDT
9/30/1956	02:00	CST
4/28/1957	02:00	CDT
9/29/1957	02:00	CST
4/27/1958	02:00	CDT
9/28/1958	02:00	CST
4/26/1959	02:00	CDT
9/27/1959	02:00	CST
4/24/1960	02:00	CDT
9/25/1960	02:00	CST
11/27/1960	02:00	EST
4/27/1969	02:00	EDT
10/26/1969	02:00	EST
4/26/1970	02:00	EDT
10/25/1970	02:00	EST

IN # 323

Before 11/18/1883		LMT
11/18/1883	12:00	CST
3/31/1918	02:00	CWT
10/27/1918	02:00	CST
3/30/1919	02:00	CWT
10/26/1919	02:00	CST
2/09/1942	02:00	CWT
9/30/1945	02:00	CST
5/08/1955	02:00	CDT
9/04/1955	00:00	CST
4/29/1956	02:00	CDT
9/30/1956	02:00	CST
4/28/1957	02:00	CDT
9/29/1957	02:00	CST
4/27/1958	02:00	CDT
9/28/1958	02:00	CST
4/26/1959	02:00	CDT
9/27/1959	02:00	CST
4/24/1960	02:00	CDT
9/25/1960	02:00	CST
11/27/1960	02:00	EST
10/29/1961	02:00	CST
4/29/1962	02:00	EST
4/27/1969	02:00	EDT
10/26/1969	02:00	EST
4/26/1970	02:00	EDT
10/25/1970	02:00	EST

IN # 324

Before 11/18/1883		LMT
11/18/1883	12:00	CST
3/31/1918	02:00	CWT
10/27/1918	02:00	CST
3/30/1919	02:00	CWT
10/26/1919	02:00	CST
2/09/1942	02:00	CWT
9/30/1945	02:00	CST
4/28/1946	02:00	CDT
9/29/1946	02:00	CST
4/27/1947	02:00	CDT
9/28/1947	02:00	CST
4/25/1948	02:00	CDT
9/26/1948	02:00	CST
4/24/1949	02:00	CDT
9/25/1949	02:00	CST
4/30/1950	02:00	CDT
9/24/1950	02:00	CST
4/29/1951	02:00	CDT
9/30/1951	02:00	CST
4/27/1952	02:00	CDT
9/28/1952	02:00	CST
4/26/1953	02:00	CDT
9/27/1953	02:00	CST
4/25/1954	02:00	CDT
9/26/1954	02:00	CST
11/28/1954	02:00	EST
10/30/1955	02:00	CST
4/29/1956	02:00	CDT
9/30/1956	02:00	CST
4/28/1957	02:00	CDT
9/29/1957	02:00	CST
4/27/1958	02:00	CDT
9/28/1958	02:00	CST
4/26/1959	02:00	CDT
9/27/1959	02:00	CST
4/24/1960	02:00	CDT
9/25/1960	02:00	CST
4/30/1961	02:00	EST
4/27/1969	02:00	EDT
10/26/1969	02:00	EST
4/26/1970	02:00	EDT
10/25/1970	02:00	EST

IN # 325

Before 11/18/1883		LMT
11/18/1883	12:00	CST
3/31/1918	02:00	CWT
10/27/1918	02:00	CST
3/30/1919	02:00	CWT
10/26/1919	02:00	CST
2/09/1942	02:00	CWT
9/30/1945	02:00	CST
4/25/1948	02:00	CDT
9/26/1948	02:00	CST
4/24/1949	02:00	CDT
9/25/1949	02:00	CST
4/30/1950	02:00	CDT
9/24/1950	02:00	CST
4/29/1951	02:00	CDT
9/30/1951	02:00	CST
4/27/1952	02:00	CDT
9/28/1952	02:00	CST
4/26/1953	02:00	CDT
9/27/1953	02:00	CST
4/25/1954	02:00	CDT
9/26/1954	02:00	CST
11/28/1954	02:00	EST
10/30/1955	02:00	CST
4/29/1956	02:00	CDT
9/30/1956	02:00	CST
4/28/1957	02:00	CDT
9/29/1957	02:00	CST
4/27/1958	02:00	CDT
9/28/1958	02:00	CST
4/26/1959	02:00	CDT
9/27/1959	02:00	CST
4/24/1960	02:00	CDT
9/25/1960	02:00	CST
4/30/1961	02:00	EST
4/27/1969	02:00	EDT
10/26/1969	02:00	EST
4/26/1970	02:00	EDT
10/25/1970	02:00	EST

IN # 326

Before 11/18/1883		LMT
11/18/1883	12:00	CST
3/31/1918	02:00	CWT
10/27/1918	02:00	CST
3/30/1919	02:00	CWT
10/26/1919	02:00	CST
4/27/1941	02:00	CDT
9/28/1941	02:00	CST
2/09/1942	02:00	CWT
9/30/1945	02:00	CST
4/25/1948	02:00	CDT
9/26/1948	02:00	CST
4/26/1953	02:00	CDT
9/27/1953	02:00	CST
4/25/1954	02:00	CDT
9/26/1954	02:00	CST
11/28/1954	02:00	EST
10/30/1955	02:00	CST
4/29/1956	02:00	CDT
10/28/1956	02:00	CST
4/28/1957	02:00	CDT
9/29/1957	02:00	CST
4/27/1958	02:00	CDT
10/26/1958	02:00	CST
4/26/1959	02:00	CDT
10/25/1959	02:00	CST
4/24/1960	02:00	CDT
10/30/1960	02:00	CST
4/30/1961	02:00	EST
4/27/1969	02:00	EDT
10/26/1969	02:00	EST
4/26/1970	02:00	EDT
10/25/1970	02:00	EST

IN # 327

Before 11/18/1883		LMT
11/18/1883	12:00	CST
3/31/1918	02:00	CWT
10/27/1918	02:00	CST
3/30/1919	02:00	CWT
10/26/1919	02:00	CST
2/09/1942	02:00	CWT
9/30/1945	02:00	CST
4/26/1953	02:00	CDT
9/27/1953	02:00	CST
4/25/1954	02:00	CDT
9/26/1954	02:00	CST
11/28/1954	02:00	EST
10/30/1955	02:00	CST
4/29/1956	02:00	CDT
9/30/1956	02:00	CST
4/28/1957	02:00	CDT
9/29/1957	02:00	CST
4/27/1958	02:00	CDT
9/28/1958	02:00	CST
4/26/1959	02:00	CDT
9/27/1959	02:00	CST
4/24/1960	02:00	CDT
9/25/1960	02:00	CST
4/30/1961	02:00	EST
4/27/1969	02:00	EDT
10/26/1969	02:00	EST
4/26/1970	02:00	EDT
10/25/1970	02:00	EST

IN # 328

Before 11/18/1883		LMT
11/18/1883	12:00	CST
3/31/1918	02:00	CWT
10/27/1918	02:00	CST
3/30/1919	02:00	CWT
10/26/1919	02:00	CST
2/09/1942	02:00	CWT
9/30/1945	02:00	CST
4/25/1954	02:00	CDT
9/26/1954	02:00	CST
11/28/1954	02:00	EST
10/30/1955	02:00	CST
4/29/1956	02:00	CDT
9/30/1956	02:00	CST
4/28/1957	02:00	CDT
9/29/1957	02:00	CST
4/27/1958	02:00	CDT
9/28/1958	02:00	CST
4/26/1959	02:00	CDT
9/27/1959	02:00	CST
4/24/1960	02:00	CDT
9/25/1960	02:00	CST
4/30/1961	02:00	EST
4/27/1969	02:00	EDT
10/26/1969	02:00	EST
4/26/1970	02:00	EDT
10/25/1970	02:00	EST

IN # 329

Before 11/18/1883		LMT
11/18/1883	12:00	CST
3/31/1918	02:00	CWT
10/27/1918	02:00	CST
3/30/1919	02:00	CWT
10/26/1919	02:00	CST
2/09/1942	02:00	CWT
9/30/1945	02:00	CST
4/28/1946	02:00	CDT
9/29/1946	02:00	CST
4/27/1947	02:00	CDT
9/28/1947	02:00	CST
4/25/1948	02:00	CDT
9/26/1948	02:00	CST
4/27/1952	02:00	CDT
9/28/1952	02:00	CST
4/26/1953	02:00	CDT
9/27/1953	02:00	CST
4/25/1954	02:00	CDT
9/26/1954	02:00	CST
11/28/1954	02:00	EST
10/30/1955	02:00	CST
4/02/1956	02:00	CDT
11/04/1956	02:00	CST
4/28/1957	02:00	CDT
9/29/1957	02:00	CST
4/27/1958	02:00	CDT
9/28/1958	02:00	CST
4/26/1959	02:00	CDT
10/25/1959	02:00	CST
4/24/1960	02:00	CDT
10/30/1960	02:00	CST
4/30/1961	02:00	EST
4/27/1969	02:00	EDT
10/26/1969	02:00	EST
4/26/1970	02:00	EDT
10/25/1970	02:00	EST

IN # 330

Before 11/18/1883		LMT
11/18/1883	12:00	CST
3/31/1918	02:00	CWT
10/27/1918	02:00	CST
3/30/1919	02:00	CWT
10/26/1919	02:00	CST
2/09/1942	02:00	CWT
9/30/1945	02:00	CST
4/26/1953	02:00	CDT
9/27/1953	02:00	CST
4/25/1954	02:00	CDT
9/26/1954	02:00	CST
1/02/1955	00:00	EST
2/13/1955	02:00	CST
4/24/1955	02:00	CDT
9/25/1955	02:00	CST
4/29/1956	02:00	CDT
9/30/1956	02:00	CST
4/28/1957	02:00	CDT
9/29/1957	02:00	CST
4/27/1958	02:00	CDT
9/28/1958	02:00	CST
4/26/1959	02:00	CDT
9/27/1959	02:00	CST
4/24/1960	02:00	CDT
9/25/1960	02:00	CST
4/30/1961	02:00	EST
4/27/1969	02:00	EDT
10/26/1969	02:00	EST
4/26/1970	02:00	EDT
10/25/1970	02:00	EST

IN # 331

Before 11/18/1883		LMT
11/18/1883	12:00	CST
3/31/1918	02:00	CWT
10/27/1918	02:00	CST
3/30/1919	02:00	CWT
10/26/1919	02:00	CST
2/09/1942	02:00	CWT
9/30/1945	02:00	CST
1/02/1955	00:00	EST
2/13/1955	02:00	CST
4/24/1955	02:00	CDT
9/25/1955	02:00	CST
4/29/1956	02:00	CDT
9/30/1956	02:00	CST
4/28/1957	02:00	CDT
9/29/1957	02:00	CST
4/27/1958	02:00	CDT
9/28/1958	02:00	CST
4/26/1959	02:00	CDT
9/27/1959	02:00	CST
4/24/1960	02:00	CDT
9/25/1960	02:00	CST
4/30/1961	02:00	EST
4/27/1969	02:00	EDT
10/26/1969	02:00	EST
4/26/1970	02:00	EDT
10/25/1970	02:00	EST

IN # 332

Before 11/18/1883		LMT
11/18/1883	12:00	CST
3/31/1918	02:00	CWT
10/27/1918	02:00	CST
3/30/1919	02:00	CWT
10/26/1919	02:00	CST
2/09/1942	02:00	CWT
9/30/1945	02:00	CST
4/28/1946	02:00	CDT
9/29/1946	02:00	CST
4/27/1947	02:00	CDT
9/28/1947	02:00	CST
4/25/1948	02:00	CDT
9/26/1948	02:00	CST
4/24/1949	02:00	CDT
9/25/1949	02:00	CST
4/30/1950	02:00	CDT
9/24/1950	02:00	CST
4/29/1951	02:00	CDT
9/30/1951	02:00	CST
4/27/1952	02:00	CDT
9/28/1952	02:00	CST
4/26/1953	02:00	CDT
9/27/1953	02:00	CST
4/25/1954	02:00	CDT
9/26/1954	02:00	CST
1/02/1955	00:00	EST
2/13/1955	02:00	CST
4/24/1955	02:00	CDT
9/25/1955	02:00	CST
4/29/1956	02:00	CDT
11/15/1956	02:00	CST
4/28/1957	02:00	CDT
9/29/1957	02:00	CST
4/27/1958	02:00	CDT
9/28/1958	02:00	CST
4/26/1959	02:00	CDT
9/27/1959	02:00	CST
4/24/1960	02:00	CDT
9/25/1960	02:00	CST
4/30/1961	02:00	EST
4/27/1969	02:00	EDT
10/26/1969	02:00	EST
4/26/1970	02:00	EDT
10/25/1970	02:00	EST

IN # 333

Before 11/18/1883		LMT
11/18/1883	12:00	CST
3/31/1918	02:00	CWT
10/27/1918	02:00	CST
3/30/1919	02:00	CWT
10/26/1919	02:00	CST
2/09/1942	02:00	CWT
9/30/1945	02:00	CST
4/27/1947	02:00	CDT
9/28/1947	02:00	CST
4/26/1953	02:00	CDT
9/27/1953	02:00	CST
4/25/1954	02:00	CDT
9/26/1954	02:00	CST
1/02/1955	00:00	EST
9/25/1955	02:00	CST
4/29/1956	02:00	CDT
9/30/1956	02:00	CST
4/28/1957	02:00	CDT
9/29/1957	02:00	CST
4/27/1958	02:00	CDT
9/28/1958	02:00	CST
4/26/1959	02:00	CDT
9/27/1959	02:00	CST
4/24/1960	02:00	CDT
9/25/1960	02:00	CST
4/30/1961	02:00	EST
4/27/1969	02:00	EDT
10/26/1969	02:00	EST
4/26/1970	02:00	EDT
10/25/1970	02:00	EST

IN # 334

Before 11/18/1883		LMT
11/18/1883	12:00	CST
3/31/1918	02:00	CWT
10/27/1918	02:00	CST
3/30/1919	02:00	CWT
10/26/1919	02:00	CST
2/09/1942	02:00	CWT
9/30/1945	02:00	CST
1/02/1955	00:00	EST
9/25/1955	02:00	CST
4/29/1956	02:00	CDT
9/30/1956	02:00	CST
4/28/1957	02:00	CDT
9/29/1957	02:00	CST
4/27/1958	02:00	CDT
9/28/1958	02:00	CST
4/26/1959	02:00	CDT
9/27/1959	02:00	CST
4/24/1960	02:00	CDT
9/25/1960	02:00	CST
4/30/1961	02:00	EST
4/27/1969	02:00	EDT
10/26/1969	02:00	EST
4/26/1970	02:00	EDT
10/25/1970	02:00	EST

IN # 335

Before 11/18/1883		LMT
11/18/1883	12:00	CST
3/31/1918	02:00	CWT
10/27/1918	02:00	CST
3/30/1919	02:00	CWT
10/26/1919	02:00	CST
2/09/1942	02:00	CWT
9/30/1945	02:00	CST
1/02/1955	00:00	EST
9/25/1955	02:00	CST
4/28/1957	02:00	CDT
9/29/1957	02:00	CST
4/27/1958	02:00	CDT
9/28/1958	02:00	CST
4/26/1959	02:00	CDT
9/27/1959	02:00	CST
4/24/1960	02:00	CDT
9/25/1960	02:00	CST
4/30/1961	02:00	EST
4/27/1969	02:00	EDT
10/26/1969	02:00	EST
4/26/1970	02:00	EDT
10/25/1970	02:00	EST

IN # 336

Before 11/18/1883		LMT
11/18/1883	12:00	CST
3/31/1918	02:00	CWT
10/27/1918	02:00	CST
3/30/1919	02:00	CWT
10/26/1919	02:00	CST
2/09/1942	02:00	CWT
9/30/1945	02:00	CST
4/28/1946	02:00	CDT
9/29/1946	02:00	CST
4/27/1947	02:00	CDT
9/28/1947	02:00	CST
4/25/1948	02:00	CDT
9/26/1948	02:00	CST
4/24/1949	02:00	CDT
9/25/1949	02:00	CST
4/30/1950	02:00	CDT
9/24/1950	02:00	CST
4/29/1951	02:00	CDT
9/30/1951	02:00	CST
4/27/1952	02:00	CDT
9/28/1952	02:00	CST
4/26/1953	02:00	CDT
9/27/1953	02:00	CST
4/25/1954	02:00	CDT
9/26/1954	02:00	CST
1/02/1955	00:00	EST
9/25/1955	02:00	CST
4/29/1956	02:00	CDT
9/30/1956	02:00	CST
4/28/1957	02:00	CDT
9/29/1957	02:00	CST
4/27/1958	02:00	CDT
9/28/1958	02:00	CST
4/26/1959	02:00	CDT
9/27/1959	02:00	CST
4/24/1960	02:00	CDT
9/25/1960	02:00	CST
4/30/1961	02:00	EST
4/27/1969	02:00	EDT
10/26/1969	02:00	EST
4/26/1970	02:00	EDT
10/25/1970	02:00	EST

IN # 337

Before 11/18/1883		LMT
11/18/1883	12:00	CST
3/31/1918	02:00	CWT
10/27/1918	02:00	CST
3/30/1919	02:00	CWT
10/26/1919	02:00	CST

TIME TABLES

2/09/1942 02:00 CWT
9/30/1945 02:00 CST
4/27/1947 02:00 CDT
9/28/1947 02:00 CST
4/26/1953 02:00 CDT
9/27/1953 02:00 CST
4/25/1954 02:00 CDT
9/26/1954 02:00 CST
1/02/1955 00:00 EST
9/25/1955 02:00 CST
4/29/1956 02:00 CDT
9/30/1956 02:00 CST
4/28/1957 02:00 CDT
9/29/1957 02:00 CST
4/27/1958 02:00 CDT
9/28/1958 02:00 CST
4/26/1959 02:00 CDT
9/27/1959 02:00 CST
4/24/1960 02:00 CDT
9/25/1960 02:00 CST
4/30/1961 02:00 EST
4/27/1969 02:00 EDT
10/26/1969 02:00 EST
4/26/1970 02:00 EDT
10/25/1970 02:00 EST
....

IN # 338

Before 11/18/1883 LMT
11/18/1883 12:00 CST
3/31/1918 02:00 CWT
10/27/1918 02:00 CST
3/30/1919 02:00 CWT
10/26/1919 02:00 CST
2/09/1942 02:00 CWT
9/30/1945 02:00 CST
4/26/1953 02:00 CDT
9/27/1953 02:00 CST
4/25/1954 02:00 CDT
9/26/1954 02:00 CST
1/02/1955 00:00 EST
9/25/1955 02:00 CST
4/29/1956 02:00 CDT
9/30/1956 02:00 CST
4/28/1957 02:00 CDT
9/29/1957 02:00 CST
4/27/1958 02:00 CDT
9/28/1958 02:00 CST
4/26/1959 02:00 CDT
9/27/1959 02:00 CST
4/24/1960 02:00 CDT
9/25/1960 02:00 CST
4/30/1961 02:00 EST
4/27/1969 02:00 EDT
10/26/1969 02:00 EST
4/26/1970 02:00 EDT
10/25/1970 02:00 EST
....

IN # 339

Before 11/18/1883 LMT
11/18/1883 12:00 CST
3/31/1918 02:00 CWT
10/27/1918 02:00 CST
3/30/1919 02:00 CWT
10/26/1919 02:00 CST
2/09/1942 02:00 CWT
9/30/1945 02:00 CST
4/28/1946 02:00 CDT
9/29/1946 02:00 CST
4/25/1948 02:00 CDT
9/26/1948 02:00 CST
4/24/1949 02:00 CDT
9/25/1949 02:00 CST
4/26/1953 02:00 CDT
9/27/1953 02:00 CST
4/25/1954 02:00 CDT
9/26/1954 02:00 CST
1/02/1955 00:00 EST
9/25/1955 02:00 CST
4/29/1956 02:00 CDT
11/04/1956 02:00 CST
4/28/1957 02:00 CDT
9/29/1957 02:00 CST
4/27/1958 02:00 CDT
10/26/1958 02:00 CST
4/26/1959 02:00 CDT
9/27/1959 02:00 CST
4/24/1960 02:00 CDT
9/25/1960 02:00 CST
4/30/1961 02:00 EST
4/27/1969 02:00 EDT
10/26/1969 02:00 EST
4/26/1970 02:00 EDT
10/25/1970 02:00 EST
....

IN # 340

Before 11/18/1883 LMT
11/18/1883 12:00 CST
3/31/1918 02:00 CWT
10/27/1918 02:00 CST
3/30/1919 02:00 CWT
10/26/1919 02:00 CST
4/26/1931 02:00 CDT
9/27/1931 02:00 CST
4/24/1932 02:00 CDT
9/25/1932 02:00 CST
2/09/1942 02:00 CWT
9/30/1945 02:00 CST
4/28/1946 02:00 CDT
9/29/1946 02:00 CST
4/30/1950 02:00 CDT
9/24/1950 02:00 CST
4/29/1951 02:00 CDT
9/30/1951 02:00 CST
4/27/1952 02:00 CDT
9/28/1952 02:00 CST
4/26/1953 02:00 CDT
9/27/1953 02:00 CST
4/25/1954 02:00 CDT
9/26/1954 02:00 CST
4/24/1955 02:00 CDT
9/25/1955 02:00 CST
4/29/1956 02:00 CDT
11/18/1956 00:00 CST
4/28/1957 02:00 CDT
9/29/1957 02:00 CST
4/27/1958 02:00 CDT
10/26/1958 02:00 CST
4/26/1959 02:00 CDT
10/25/1959 02:00 CST
4/24/1960 02:00 EST
11/13/1960 02:00 CST
4/30/1961 02:00 EST
4/27/1969 02:00 EDT
10/26/1969 02:00 EST
4/26/1970 02:00 EDT
10/25/1970 02:00 EST
....

IN # 341

Before 11/18/1883 LMT
11/18/1883 12:00 CST
3/31/1918 02:00 CWT
10/27/1918 02:00 CST
3/30/1919 02:00 CWT
10/26/1919 02:00 CST
2/09/1942 02:00 CWT
9/30/1945 02:00 CST
4/29/1951 02:00 CDT
9/30/1951 02:00 CST
4/27/1952 02:00 CDT
9/28/1952 02:00 CST
4/26/1953 02:00 CDT
9/27/1953 02:00 CST
4/25/1954 02:00 CDT
9/26/1954 02:00 CST
4/24/1955 02:00 CDT
9/25/1955 02:00 CST
4/29/1956 02:00 CDT
9/30/1956 02:00 CST
4/28/1957 02:00 CDT
9/29/1957 02:00 CST
4/27/1958 02:00 CDT
9/28/1958 02:00 CST
4/26/1959 02:00 CDT
9/27/1959 02:00 CST
4/24/1960 02:00 EST
11/13/1960 02:00 CST
4/30/1961 02:00 EST
4/27/1969 02:00 EDT
10/26/1969 02:00 EST
4/26/1970 02:00 EDT
10/25/1970 02:00 EST
....

IN # 342

Before 11/18/1883 LMT
11/18/1883 12:00 CST
3/31/1918 02:00 CWT
10/27/1918 02:00 CST
3/30/1919 02:00 CWT
10/26/1919 02:00 CST
2/09/1942 02:00 CWT
9/30/1945 02:00 CST
4/26/1953 02:00 CDT
9/27/1953 02:00 CST
4/25/1954 02:00 CDT
9/26/1954 02:00 CST
4/24/1955 02:00 CDT
9/25/1955 02:00 CST
4/29/1956 02:00 CDT
9/30/1956 02:00 CST
4/28/1957 02:00 CDT
9/29/1957 02:00 CST
4/27/1958 02:00 CDT
9/28/1958 02:00 CST
4/26/1959 02:00 CDT
9/27/1959 02:00 CST
4/24/1960 02:00 EST
11/13/1960 02:00 CST
4/30/1961 02:00 EST
4/27/1969 02:00 EDT
10/26/1969 02:00 EST
4/26/1970 02:00 EDT
10/25/1970 02:00 EST
....

IN # 343

Before 11/18/1883 LMT
11/18/1883 12:00 CST
3/31/1918 02:00 CWT
10/27/1918 02:00 CST
3/30/1919 02:00 CWT
10/26/1919 02:00 CST
2/09/1942 02:00 CWT
9/30/1945 02:00 CST
4/25/1954 02:00 CDT
9/26/1954 02:00 CST
4/24/1955 02:00 CDT
9/25/1955 02:00 CST
4/29/1956 02:00 CDT
9/30/1956 02:00 CST
4/28/1957 02:00 CDT
9/29/1957 02:00 CST
4/27/1958 02:00 CDT
9/28/1958 02:00 CST
4/26/1959 02:00 CDT
9/27/1959 02:00 CST
4/24/1960 02:00 EST
11/13/1960 02:00 CST
4/30/1961 02:00 EST
4/27/1969 02:00 EDT
10/26/1969 02:00 EST
4/26/1970 02:00 EDT
10/25/1970 02:00 EST
....

IN # 344

Before 11/18/1883 LMT
11/18/1883 12:00 CST
3/31/1918 02:00 CWT
10/27/1918 02:00 CST
3/30/1919 02:00 CWT
10/26/1919 02:00 CST
2/09/1942 02:00 CWT
9/30/1945 02:00 CST
4/24/1955 02:00 CDT
9/25/1955 02:00 CST
4/29/1956 02:00 CDT
9/30/1956 02:00 CST
4/28/1957 02:00 CDT
9/29/1957 02:00 CST
4/27/1958 02:00 CDT
9/28/1958 02:00 CST
4/26/1959 02:00 CDT
9/27/1959 02:00 CST
4/24/1960 02:00 EST
11/13/1960 02:00 CST
4/30/1961 02:00 EST
4/27/1969 02:00 EDT
10/26/1969 02:00 EST
4/26/1970 02:00 EDT
10/25/1970 02:00 EST
....

IN # 345

Before 11/18/1883 LMT
11/18/1883 12:00 CST
3/31/1918 02:00 CWT
10/27/1918 02:00 CST
3/30/1919 02:00 CWT
10/26/1919 02:00 CST
2/09/1942 02:00 CWT
9/30/1945 02:00 CST
4/27/1947 02:00 CDT
9/28/1947 02:00 CST
4/02/1948 02:00 CDT
9/26/1948 02:00 CST
4/30/1950 02:00 CDT
9/24/1950 02:00 CST
4/29/1951 02:00 CDT
9/30/1951 02:00 CST
4/27/1952 02:00 CDT
9/28/1952 02:00 CST
4/26/1953 02:00 CDT
9/27/1953 02:00 CST
4/25/1954 02:00 CDT
9/26/1954 02:00 CST
4/24/1955 02:00 CDT
9/25/1955 02:00 CST
4/29/1956 02:00 CDT
11/11/1956 02:00 CST
4/28/1957 02:00 CDT
9/29/1957 02:00 CST
4/27/1958 02:00 CDT
10/26/1958 02:00 CST
4/26/1959 02:00 CDT
10/25/1959 02:00 CST
4/24/1960 02:00 EST
11/13/1960 02:00 CST
4/30/1961 02:00 EST
4/27/1969 02:00 EDT
10/26/1969 02:00 EST
4/26/1970 02:00 EDT
10/25/1970 02:00 EST

COUNTIES

1 Adams
2 Allen
3 Bartholomew
4 Benton
5 Blackford
6 Boone
7 Brown
8 Carroll
9 Cass
10 Clark
11 Clay
12 Clinton
13 Crawford
14 Daviess
15 Dearborn
16 Decatur
17 De Kalb
18 Delaware
19 Dubois
20 Elkhart
21 Fayette
22 Floyd
23 Fountain
24 Franklin
25 Fulton
26 Gibson
27 Grant
28 Greene
29 Hamilton
30 Hancock
31 Harrison
32 Hendricks
33 Henry
34 Howard
35 Huntington
36 Jackson
37 Jasper
38 Jay
39 Jefferson
40 Jennings
41 Johnson
42 Knox
43 Kosciusko
44 La Grange
45 Lake
46 La Porte
47 Lawrence
48 Madison
49 Marion
50 Marshall
51 Martin
52 Miami
53 Monroe
54 Montgomery
55 Morgan
56 Newton
57 Noble
58 Ohio
59 Orange
60 Owen
61 Parke
62 Perry
63 Pike
64 Porter
65 Posey
66 Pulaski
67 Putnam
68 Randolph
69 Ripley
70 Rush
71 St Joseph
72 Scott
73 Shelby
74 Spencer
75 Starke
76 Steuben
77 Sullivan
78 Switzerland
79 Tippecanoe
80 Tipton
81 Union
82 Vanderburgh
83 Vermillion
84 Vigo
85 Wabash
86 Warren
87 Warrick
88 Washington
89 Wayne
90 Wells
91 White
92 Whitley

Abbey Dell 59	160	38N35	86w32	5:46:08
Abels Acres 3	147	39N13	85w54	5:43:36
Aberdeen 58	33	38N54	84w59	5:39:56
Abington 89	315	39N45	85w00	5:40:00
Aboite 2	228	41N00	85w19	5:41:16
Acme 36	147	38N58	85w58	5:43:52
Acton 49	100	39N40	85w59	5:43:56
Adams 16	108	39N23	85w34	5:42:16
Adams 55	101	39N25	86w25	5:45:40
Adamsboro 9	164	40N47	86w18	5:45:12
Adams Lake 44	30	41N32	85w22	5:41:28
Adams Mill 8	165	40N29	86w32	5:46:08
Addison 73	101	39N32	85w46	5:43:04
Addmore 10	166	38N18	85w45	5:43:00
Ade 56	2	40N52	87w22	5:49:28
Adel 60	344	39N17	86w46	5:47:04
Advance 6	251	40N00	86w37	5:46:28
Aetna 45	20	41N35	87w17	5:49:08
Ainsworth 45	6	41N29	87w16	5:49:04
Air Mail Field 49	100	39N45	86w14	5:44:56
Akron 25	242	41N02	86w01	5:44:04
Aladdin 48	101	40N16	85w41	5:42:44
Alamo 54	147	39N59	87w03	5:48:12
Albany 18	255	40N18	85w13	5:40:52
Albion 57	44	41N24	85w25	5:41:40
Aldine 75	28	41N13	86w46	5:47:04
Alert 16	101	39N11	85w34	5:42:16
Alexandria 48	105	40N16	85w41	5:42:44
Alfont 48	101	39N56	85w51	5:43:24
Alford 63	59	38N29	87w14	5:48:56
Alfordsville 14	85	38N34	86w57	5:47:48
Algiers 63	59	38N29	87w10	5:48:40
Alida 46	9	41N33	86w53	5:47:32
Allendale 84	77	39N26	87w24	5:49:36
Allens Acres 6	100	39N53	86w16	5:45:04
Allisonville 49	100	39N53	86w04	5:44:16
Allman 55	101	39N37	86w22	5:45:28
Alma Lake 61	89	39N31	87w08	5:48:32
Alpine 21	272	39N33	85w11	5:40:44
Alquina 21	272	39N37	85w03	5:40:12
Alta 83	73	39N47	87w23	5:49:32
Alto 34	331	40N29	86w08	5:44:32
Alton 13	169	38N08	86w25	5:45:40
Altona 17	228	41N21	85w09	5:40:36
Alvarado 76	30	41N32	84w55	5:39:40
Amber Valley 84	77	39N29	87w22	5:49:28
Ambia 4	150	40N29	87w31	5:50:04
Amboy 52	338	40N36	85w57	5:43:48
Americus 79	147	40N25	86w53	5:47:32
Ames 54	149	40N00	86w56	5:47:44
Amity 41	108	39N26	86w00	5:44:00
Amo 32	115	39N41	86w37	5:46:28
Anderson 48	102	40N10	85w41	5:42:44
Andersonville 24	275	39N30	85w17	5:41:08
Andrews 35	288	40N52	85w36	5:42:24
Andrews Manor 27	284	40N34	85w42	5:42:48
Angola 76	45	41N38	85w00	5:40:00
Annandale Estates 7	145	39N12	86w15	5:45:00
Annapolis 61	128	39N52	87w14	5:48:56
Anoka 9	164	40N43	86w18	5:45:12
Ansley Acres 2	233	41N04	85w10	5:40:40
Anthony 18	254	40N16	85w25	5:41:40

Place		Lat	Long	Time
Antioch 12	181	40n14	86w31	5:46:04
Antioch 28	93	39n10	87w12	5:48:48
Antioch 38	291	40n26	84w59	5:39:56
Antiville 38	291	40n26	84w59	5:39:56
Apache Acres 84	82	39n42	86w51	5:47:24
Arba 68	307	40n03	84w56	5:39:44
Arcadia 29	97	40n10	86w01	5:44:04
Arcana 27	284	40n34	85w42	5:42:48
Arcola 2	230	41n06	85w18	5:41:12
Arctic Springs 10	166	38n18	85w45	5:43:00
Argos 50	212	41n14	86w15	5:45:00
Ari 2	230	41n15	85w15	5:41:00
Ar'les Acres 29	97	40n03	86w01	5:44:04
Arlington 53	344	39n12	86w37	5:46:28
Arlington 70	101	39n39	85w35	5:42:20
Armiesburg 61	128	39n47	87w22	5:49:28
Armstrong 82	53	38n07	87w39	5:50:36
Armuth Acres 3	147	39n13	85w54	5:43:36
Arney 60	344	39n12	86w47	5:47:08
Aroma 29	97	40n13	86w02	5:44:08
Arrowhead Park 43	297	41n14	85w51	5:43:24
Art 11	89	39n31	87w08	5:48:32
Arthur 63	59	38n20	87w15	5:49:00
Artie 17	228	41n26	84w52	5:39:28
Ashboro 11	89	39n25	87w04	5:48:16
Asheboro 84	77	39n32	87w24	5:49:36
Asherville 11	89	39n31	87w08	5:48:32
Ash Grove 79	147	40n30	86w51	5:47:24
Ash Iron Springs 87	53	38n03	87w16	5:49:04
Ashland 33	253	39n56	85w26	5:41:44
Ashland 55	115	39n29	86w36	5:46:24
Ashley 76	30	41n32	85w04	5:40:16
Athens 25	328	41n03	86w07	5:44:28
Atherton 84	82	39n37	87w21	5:49:24
Atkinsonville 60	344	39n27	86w57	5:47:48
Atlanta 29	97	40n13	86w02	5:44:08
Attica 23	129	40n18	87w15	5:49:00
Atwood 43	295	41n16	85w59	5:43:56
Aubbeenaubbee 25	328	41n08	86w24	5:45:36
Auburn 17	234	41n22	85w04	5:40:16
Augusta 49	100	39n52	86w14	5:44:56
Augusta 63	59	38n23	87w13	5:48:52
Aultshire 18	254	40n13	85w21	5:41:24
Aurora 15	38	39n04	84w54	5:39:36
Austin 72	319	38n45	85w49	5:43:16
Avalon Hills 49	100	39n53	86w04	5:44:16
Avery 12	181	40n17	86w31	5:46:04
Avilla 57	46	41n22	85w14	5:40:56
Avoca 47	344	38n55	86w33	5:46:12
Avon 32	97	39n42	86w23	5:45:32
Avonburg 78	35	38n52	85w08	5:40:32
Avondale 27	284	40n34	85w42	5:42:48
Aylesworth 23	144	40n18	87w15	5:49:00
Ayr 50	218	41n27	86w05	5:44:20
Ayrshire 63	59	38n23	87w13	5:48:52
Azalia 3	147	39n05	85w51	5:43:24
Babcock 64	6	41n29	87w23	5:49:32
Baileys Corner 37	226	40n56	87w09	5:48:36
Bainbridge 67	128	39n46	86w49	5:47:16
Bainter Town 20	260	41n31	85w49	5:43:16
Ball State University 18	254	40n13	85w24	5:41:36
Baker 55	113	39n22	86w32	5:46:08
Bakers Corners 29	97	40n08	86w13	5:44:52
Bakertown 57	30	41n24	85w26	5:41:44
Balbee 38	291	40n30	85w09	5:40:36
Baldwin Heights 26	59	38n24	87w35	5:50:20
Bandon 62	69	38n10	86w35	5:46:20
Banquo 35	287	40n40	85w43	5:42:52
Banta 41	97	39n31	86w10	5:44:40
Bar-Barry Heights 79	147	40n26	86w56	5:47:44
Barbee 43	291	41n11	85w42	5:42:48
Bargersville 41	99	39n31	86w10	5:44:40
Barkley 37	2	41n02	87w04	5:48:16
Barnaby Acres 3	147	39n13	85w54	5:43:36
Barnard 67	128	39n51	86w42	5:46:48
Barnhart Town 84	77	39n28	87w26	5:49:44
Barr 14	85	38n41	87w01	5:48:04
Barrick Corner 11	89	39n17	87w07	5:48:28
Bartlettsville 47	344	38n51	86w30	5:46:00
Bartley 84	82	39n42	86w51	5:47:24
Barton 26	59	38n15	87w23	5:49:32
Bartonia 68	307	40n08	84w51	5:39:24
Bass Lake 75	222	41n13	86w36	5:46:24
Batesville 69	276	39n18	85w13	5:40:52
Bath 24	30	39n31	84w52	5:39:28
Battle Ground 79	147	40n30	86w51	5:47:24
Baugh City 87	53	38n03	87w22	5:49:28
Baugo 20	271	41n40	86w02	5:44:08
Beal 42	86	38n35	87w38	5:50:32
Bean Blossom 7	147	39n17	86w15	5:45:00
Bean Blossom 53	344	39n25	86w44	5:46:56
Bear Branch 58	33	39n01	85w04	5:40:16
Bearcreek 38	287	40n32	84w56	5:39:44
Beard 12	181	40n17	86w31	5:46:04
Beardstown 66	181	41n09	86w36	5:46:24
Bear Lake 57	30	41n24	85w26	5:41:44
Beatrice 64	2	41n19	87w12	5:48:48
Beattys Corner 46	9	41n43	86w53	5:47:32
Beatys Beach 44	30	41n41	85w35	5:42:20
Beaver City 56	2	40n52	87w22	5:49:28
Beaver Dam 43	291	41n04	86w00	5:44:00
Beck Grove 7	147	38n58	86w08	5:44:32
Becks Mill 88	165	38n36	86w06	5:44:24
Beckville 54	147	40n00	86w56	5:47:44
Bedford 47	345	38n52	86w29	5:45:56
Bedford Heights 47	345	38n51	86w30	5:46:00
Beecamp 39	97	38n45	85w19	5:41:16
Beech Brook 73	101	39n33	85w48	5:43:12
Beech Creek 28	193	39n07	86w45	5:47:00
Beech Grove 49	100	39n44	86w03	5:44:12
Beech Grove 55	101	39n25	86w25	5:45:40
Beechwood 13	169	38n12	86w21	5:45:24
Bee Ridge 11	89	39n31	87w08	5:48:32
Belknap 10	166	38n19	85w44	5:42:56
Bell Center 91	181	40n53	86w45	5:47:00
Bellefountain 38	291	40n26	84w52	5:39:28
Belle Union 67	128	39n31	86w48	5:47:12
Belleview 39	97	38n45	85w19	5:41:16
Belleville 32	247	39n42	86w31	5:46:04
Bellmore 61	128	39n46	87w06	5:48:24
Bell Rohr Park 43	291	41n20	85w51	5:43:24
Belmont 7	145	39n09	86w22	5:45:28
Belmont 33	253	39n56	85w26	5:41:44
Belshaw 45	26	41n14	87w26	5:49:44
Ben Davis 49	100	39n45	86w14	5:44:56
Bengal 73	101	39n28	85w55	5:43:40
Benham 69	275	39n04	85w15	5:41:00
Bennetts 52	335	40n29	86w08	5:44:32
Bennettsville 10	166	38n29	85w46	5:43:04
Bennington 78	35	38n52	85w08	5:40:32
Benton 20	261	41n35	85w50	5:43:20
Bentonville 21	274	39n45	85w15	5:41:00
Benwood 11	89	39n31	87w08	5:48:32
Berlien 76	30	41n38	85w00	5:40:00
Berne 1	230	40n39	84w57	5:39:48
Berwick Manor 73	101	39n33	85w48	5:43:12
Bethany 55	101	39n32	86w23	5:45:32
Bethel 18	253	40n10	85w30	5:42:00
Bethel 65	58	38n13	87w56	5:51:44
Bethel 89	315	40n00	84w50	5:39:20
Bethel Village 3	147	39n13	85w54	5:43:36
Bethlehem 10	166	38n32	85w25	5:41:40
Beverly Shores 64	9	41n41	86w59	5:47:56
Bicknell 42	74	38n47	87w19	5:49:16
Big Creek 91	147	40n41	86w52	5:47:28
Bigger 40	128	38n57	85w30	5:42:00
Big Lake 57	30	41n12	85w28	5:41:52
Big Springs 6	97	40n08	86w13	5:44:52
Billingsville 81	313	39n38	84w56	5:39:44
Billtown 11	89	39n31	87w08	5:48:32
Billville 11	89	39n31	87w08	5:48:32
Bippus 35	289	40n55	85w37	5:42:28
Birdseye 19	67	38n19	86w42	5:46:48
Birmingham 52	335	40n58	86w08	5:44:32
Black 65	58	37n58	87w54	5:51:36
Blackhawk 2	233	41n06	85w08	5:40:32
Blackhawk 84	82	39n19	87w23	5:49:32
Blackhawk Beach 64	6	41n30	87w06	5:48:24
Blackhawk Forest 2	233	41n06	85w08	5:40:32
Blackiston Heights 10	166	38n18	85w45	5:43:00
Blackiston Mill 10	166	38n18	85w45	5:43:00
Blackiston Village 10	166	38n18	85w45	5:43:00
Black Oak 45	6	41n34	87w25	5:49:40
Blaine 38	291	40n24	85w04	5:40:16
Blairsville 65	58	38n04	87w45	5:51:00
Blanford 83	73	39n40	87w31	5:50:04
Blocher 72	320	38n43	85w39	5:42:36
Bloomfield 28	192	39n01	86w57	5:47:48
Bloomfield 38	291	40n32	84w58	5:39:52
Bloomingdale 61	128	39n50	87w15	5:49:00
Blooming Grove 24	275	39n30	85w05	5:40:20
Bloomingport 68	307	40n01	84w59	5:39:56
Bloomington 53	340	39n10	86w32	5:46:08
Blountsville 33	253	40n03	85w15	5:41:00
Blue Creek 1	228	40n42	84w51	5:39:24
Blue Creek 24	30	39n14	85w06	5:40:24
Bluegrass 25	328	41n01	86w24	5:45:36
Blue Lake 92	228	41n14	85w19	5:41:16
Blue Lick 10	166	38n32	85w46	5:43:04
Blue Ridge 73	101	39n32	85w38	5:42:32
Blue River 88	165	38n36	86w06	5:44:24
Bluff Point 38	291	40n26	84w59	5:39:56
Bluffs 55	101	39n25	86w25	5:45:40
Bluffside 46	8	41n37	86w44	5:46:56
Bluffton 90	228	40n44	85w11	5:40:44
Bobtown 36	147	38n58	85w58	5:43:52
Bogard 14	85	38n47	87w04	5:48:16
Boggstown 73	101	39n34	85w55	5:43:40
Bogle Corner 11	89	39n10	87w12	5:48:48
Bolivar 4	148	40n31	87w09	5:48:36
Bonair 45	6	41n30	87w19	5:49:16
Bonnell 15	33	39n10	84w55	5:39:40
Bonnenburger 10	166	38n18	85w45	5:43:00
Bono 47	344	38n43	86w21	5:45:24
Bono 83	73	39n48	87w29	5:49:56
Boon 87	53	38n04	87w16	5:49:04
Boone Grove 64	28	41n21	87w08	5:48:32
Boonville 87	54	38n03	87w16	5:49:04
Borden 10	166	38n28	85w57	5:43:48
Boston 89	315	39n46	84w53	5:39:32
Boston Corner 2	228	40n58	84w52	5:39:28
Boswell 4	135	40n31	87w23	5:49:32
Boundary 38	291	40n20	84w55	5:39:40
Bourbon 50	326	41n18	86w07	5:44:28
Bowers 54	149	40n06	86w47	5:47:08
Bowerstown 35	287	40n49	85w32	5:42:08
Bowling Green 11	89	39n23	87w01	5:48:04
Bowman 63	59	38n29	87w21	5:49:24
Boxley 29	97	40n08	86w13	5:44:52
Boyleston 12	181	40n19	86w23	5:45:32
Bracken 35	287	40n49	85w32	5:42:08
Bradford 31	166	38n22	86w04	5:44:16
Bradford Park 18	254	40n11	85w26	5:41:44
Bradford Village 27	284	40n34	85w42	5:42:48
Bradley 74	61	38n01	87w02	5:48:08
Bramble 51	200	38n43	86w55	5:47:40
Branchville 62	69	38n10	86w35	5:46:20
Braxton 59	160	38n34	86w28	5:45:52
Braytown 78	35	38n45	85w04	5:40:16
Brazil 11	90	39n32	87w08	5:48:32
Breckenridge 31	166	38n13	86w07	5:44:28
Breezewood 27	284	40n34	85w42	5:42:48
Breezewood Park 18	254	40n11	85w23	5:41:32
Breezy Point 8	162	40n45	86w46	5:47:04
Bremen 50	218	41n27	86w09	5:44:36
Brems 75	221	41n21	86w42	5:46:48
Brendan Wood 6	247	40n04	86w28	5:45:52
Brendonwood 49	100	39n50	86w04	5:44:16
Brent Woods 73	101	39n33	85w48	5:43:12
Bretzville 19	67	38n18	86w57	5:47:48
Brewersville 40	128	39n00	85w38	5:42:32
Brewington Woods 18	254	40n11	85w23	5:41:32
Briarwood 55	101	39n35	86w29	5:45:56
Brice 38	291	40n26	84w59	5:39:56
Brick Chapel 67	128	39n39	86w52	5:47:28
Bridgeport 49	100	39n45	86w17	5:45:08
Bridgeton 61	89	39n39	87w11	5:48:44
Brierwood Hills 2	233	41n04	85w10	5:40:40
Bright 15	33	39n13	84w51	5:39:24
Brighton 44	30	41n43	85w25	5:41:40
Brightwood 49	100	39n48	86w06	5:44:24
Brimfield 57	32	41n27	85w24	5:41:36
Brinckley 68	307	40n15	85w10	5:40:40
Bringhurst 8	164	40n32	86w32	5:46:08
Brinker Heights 27	284	40n34	85w42	5:42:48
Bristol 20	263	41n43	85w49	5:43:16
Bristow 62	69	38n08	86w43	5:46:52
Broadmoor 49	100	39n49	86w11	5:44:44
Broad Ripple 49	100	39n52	86w07	5:44:28
Broadview 27	284	40n34	85w42	5:42:48
Broadview 47	344	38n51	86w30	5:46:00
Broadview Park Plaza 47	344	38n51	86w30	5:46:00
Bromer 59	160	38n40	86w27	5:45:48
Brook 56	226	40n52	87w22	5:49:28
Brookfield 73	101	39n35	85w52	5:43:28
Brook Haven 27	284	40n34	85w42	5:42:48
Brook Knoll 47	344	38n51	86w30	5:46:00
Brooklyn 55	108	39n32	86w22	5:45:28
Brookmoor 55	97	39n37	86w22	5:45:28
Brooks 29	97	40n03	86w01	5:44:04
Brooksburg 39	97	38n44	85w15	5:41:00
Brookside Estates 2	233	41n06	85w08	5:40:32
Brookside Estates 84	77	39n26	87w24	5:49:36
Brookston 91	147	40n36	86w52	5:47:28
Brook Trails 71	208	41n43	86w15	5:45:00
Brookville 24	30	39n25	85w01	5:40:04
Brookville Heights 30	97	39n43	85w53	5:43:32
Brookwood 43	297	41n14	85w51	5:43:24
Brookwood 45	6	41n30	87w19	5:49:16
Broom Hill 10	166	38n28	85w57	5:43:48
Brown Jug Corner 84	82	39n16	87w16	5:49:04
Brownsburg 32	97	39n50	86w24	5:45:36
Browns Crossing 55	101	39n25	86w25	5:45:40
Brownstown 13	169	38n20	86w28	5:45:52
Brownstown 36	141	38n53	86w03	5:44:12
Browns Valley 54	149	40n00	86w56	5:47:44
Brownsville 81	313	39n41	85w00	5:40:00
Bruce Lake 25	327	41n04	86w24	5:45:36
Bruceville 42	87	38n46	87w25	5:49:40
Brummitt Acres 64	4	41n37	87w06	5:48:24
Brunswick 45	2	41n23	87w29	5:49:56
Brushy Prairie 44	30	41n39	85w17	5:41:08
Bryant 38	288	40n32	84w58	5:39:52
Bryantsburg 39	97	38n45	85w19	5:41:16
Bryantsville 47	344	38n44	86w28	5:45:52
Buchanan Corner 11	89	39n10	87w12	5:48:48
Buck Creek 30	98	39n49	85w54	5:43:36
Buck Creek 79	152	40n29	86w46	5:47:04
Buckeye 35	287	40n41	85w25	5:41:40
Buckskin 26	59	38n20	87w29	5:49:56
Bucktown 77	80	39n00	87w16	5:49:04
Bud 41	97	39n29	86w03	5:44:12
Buddha 47	344	38n51	86w30	5:46:00
Buena Vista 24	275	39n26	85w16	5:41:04
Buffalo 91	181	40n53	86w45	5:47:00
Buffaloville 74	64	38n06	86w58	5:47:52
Buffington 45	6	41n35	87w24	5:49:36
Bufkin 65	58	37n56	87w54	5:51:36
Bugtown 65	58	38n10	87w47	5:51:08
Bullocktown 87	53	38n03	87w16	5:49:04
Bunker Hill 21	272	39n40	85w08	5:40:32
Bunker Hill 42	86	38n45	87w31	5:50:04
Bunker Hill 52	336	40n40	86w06	5:44:24
Bunker Hill 88	165	38n36	86w06	5:44:24
Burdick 64	4	41n37	87w06	5:48:24
Burglen Hills 62	69	37n57	86w46	5:47:04
Burket 43	296	41n09	85w58	5:43:52

Burlington 8 165 40N29 86w24 5:45:36
Burlington Beach 64 6 41N29 87w23 5:49:32
Burnett 84 82 39N32 87w18 5:49:12
Burnettsville 91 183 40N46 86w36 5:46:24
Burney 16 101 39N19 85w38 5:42:32
Burns City 51 323 38N48 86w53 5:47:32
Burns Harbor 64 4 41N36 87w07 5:48:28
Burnsville 3 147 39N13 85w54 5:43:36
Burr Oak 50 213 41N15 86w25 5:45:40
Burr Oak 57 30 41N24 85w26 5:41:44
Burrows 8 174 40N41 86w31 5:46:04
Busseron 42 86 38N50 87w27 5:49:48
Butler 17 235 41N26 84w52 5:39:28
Butlerville 40 128 39N02 85w31 5:42:04
Byrneville 31 166 38N18 85w58 5:43:52
Byron 46 2 41N40 86w37 5:46:28
Byron 61 128 39N52 87w03 5:48:12
Caborn 65 58 37N58 87w47 5:51:08
Cadiz 33 253 39N57 85w29 5:41:56
Caesar Creek 15 33 38N58 85w05 5:40:20
Cain 23 156 40N05 87w10 5:48:40
Cairo 79 147 40N26 86w56 5:47:44
Cale 51 159 38N49 86w45 5:47:00
California 75 221 41N13 86w39 5:46:36
Calumet 45 6 41N33 87w24 5:49:36
Calvertville 28 193 39N02 86w56 5:47:44
Cambria 12 181 40N23 86w33 5:46:12
Cambridge City 89 317 39N49 85w10 5:40:40
Camby 49 98 39N40 86w19 5:45:16
Camden 8 164 40N37 86w32 5:46:08
Cammack 18 253 40N12 85w30 5:42:00
Campbellsburg 88 164 38N39 86w16 5:45:04
Canaan 39 97 38N52 85w18 5:41:12
Candelglo Village 73 101 39N33 85w48 5:43:12
Candle Light Village 3 147 39N13 85w54 5:43:36
Cannelburg 14 85 38N40 87w00 5:48:00
Cannelton 62 68 37N55 86w45 5:47:00
Cannelton Heights 62 68 37N54 86w44 5:46:56
Canton 88 165 38N36 86w06 5:44:24
Capehart 14 85 38N40 87w11 5:48:44
Cape Sandy 13 169 38N12 86w21 5:45:24
Carbon 11 89 39N37 87w09 5:48:36
Carbondale 86 156 40N22 87w18 5:49:12
Cardonia 11 89 39N31 87w08 5:48:32
Carey 29 97 40N03 86w01 5:44:04
Carlisle 77 72 38N58 87w24 5:49:36
Carlos 68 307 40N01 85w01 5:40:04
Carlos City 68 307 40N01 85w01 5:40:04
Carmel 29 244 39N59 86w08 5:44:32
Carp 60 344 39N17 86w46 5:47:04
Carpenter 37 224 40N47 87w11 5:48:44
Carpentersville 67 128 39N49 86w48 5:47:12
Carriage Estates 3 147 39N13 85w54 5:43:36
Carriage Estates 30 97 39N43 85w53 5:43:32
Carrollton 8 165 40N34 86w26 5:45:44
Carter 74 65 38N10 86w57 5:47:48
Cartersburg 32 248 39N42 86w28 5:45:52
Carthage 70 101 39N44 85w34 5:42:16
Carwood 10 166 38N28 85w57 5:43:48
Cascade Heights 53 344 39N12 86w37 5:46:28
Cass 77 71 39N06 87w25 5:49:40
Cassville 34 331 40N29 86w08 5:44:32
Castleton 49 100 39N53 86w04 5:44:16
Cataract 60 344 39N26 86w49 5:47:16
Cates 23 156 40N00 87w20 5:49:20
Catlin 61 126 39N42 87w14 5:48:56
Cato 63 59 38N26 87w11 5:48:44
Cayuga 83 75 39N57 87w28 5:49:52
Cedar Creek 17 228 41N21 85w09 5:40:36
Cedar Grove 24 30 39N22 84w56 5:39:44
Cedar Lake 45 15 41N22 87w25 5:49:40
Cedar Point 91 162 40N45 86w46 5:47:04
Cedar Shores 2 228 41N14 84w58 5:39:52
Cedarville 2 228 41N14 84w58 5:39:52
Celestine 19 67 38N23 86w47 5:47:08
Cemar Estates 84 82 39N42 86w51 5:47:24
Cementville 10 166 38N18 85w45 5:43:00
Centenary 83 73 39N40 87w24 5:49:36
Centennial 23 156 39N58 87w17 5:49:08
Center 34 330 40N29 86w08 5:44:32
Center 38 291 40N26 84w59 5:39:56
Center 87 52 38N03 87w16 5:49:04
Centerpoint 11 89 39N25 87w04 5:48:16
Center Square 78 35 38N45 85w02 5:40:08
Centerton 55 108 39N31 86w24 5:45:36
Center Valley 32 97 39N37 86w22 5:45:28
Centerville 74 61 38N01 87w02 5:48:08
Centerville 89 316 39N49 85w00 5:40:00
Central 31 166 38N06 86w09 5:44:36
Central Barren 31 166 38N19 86w06 5:44:24
Ceylon 1 228 40N36 84w58 5:39:52
Chalmers 91 147 40N40 86w52 5:47:28
Chambersburg 59 160 38N31 86w24 5:45:36
Champion 84 77 39N28 87w26 5:49:44
Champlin Meadows 55 101 39N25 86w25 5:45:40
Chandler 87 53 38N03 87w22 5:49:28
Chapel Bluff 3 147 39N13 85w54 5:43:36
Chapel Hill 49 100 39N48 86w15 5:45:00
Chapelhill 53 344 38N56 86w23 5:45:32
Chapel Manor 45 6 41N30 87w19 5:49:16
Charlestown 10 167 38N27 85w40 5:42:40
Charle Sumac Estates 49 100 39N40 85w59 5:43:56
Charlottesville 30 108 39N47 85w37 5:42:28
Chase 4 147 40N31 87w23 5:49:32
Chelsea 39 113 38N39 85w37 5:42:28
Cherokee Terrace 10 166 38N18 85w45 5:43:00
Cherry Grove 54 147 40N00 86w56 5:47:44
Chester 89 318 39N52 84w52 5:39:28
Chesterfield 48 108 40N07 85w35 5:42:20
Chesterton 29 100 39N47 86w09 5:44:36
Chesterton 64 4 41N35 87w07 5:48:28
Chesterville 15 33 39N07 85w05 5:40:20
Chestnut Hill 64 4 41N37 87w06 5:48:24
Chestnut Ridge 36 147 38N58 85w58 5:43:52
Chicago Avenue 45 6 41N38 87w28 5:49:52
Chili 52 338 40N52 86w05 5:44:20
China 39 97 38N45 85w19 5:41:16
Chippewa 71 208 41N38 86w14 5:44:56
Chrisney 74 62 38N01 87w02 5:48:08
Christiansburg 7 147 39N13 85w54 5:43:36
Churubusco 92 230 41N14 85w19 5:41:16
Cicero 29 97 40N08 86w01 5:44:04
Cicero Heights 80 121 40N18 86w03 5:44:12
Cincinnati 28 193 39N02 86w44 5:46:56
Circle Park 76 30 41N32 84w55 5:39:40
Circleville 70 101 39N37 85w27 5:41:48
Clare 29 97 40N03 86w01 5:44:04
Clarksburg 16 101 39N26 85w21 5:41:24
Clarks Hill 79 147 40N15 86w43 5:46:52
Clarks Landing 76 30 41N32 84w55 5:39:40
Clarksville 10 176 38N18 85w46 5:43:04
Clarksville 29 97 40N03 86w01 5:44:04
Clay City 11 89 39N17 87w07 5:48:28
Clay City 74 64 38N04 86w54 5:47:36
Claypool 43 292 41N08 85w53 5:43:32
Claysville 88 165 38N37 86w17 5:45:08
Clayton 32 252 39N41 86w31 5:46:04
Clear Creek 53 343 39N07 86w32 5:46:08
Clear Lake 76 30 41N43 84w49 5:39:16
Clearspring 44 30 41N34 85w29 5:41:56
Clear Springs 36 147 38N53 86w05 5:44:20
Clermont 49 100 39N50 86w18 5:45:12
Clermont Heights 32 98 39N50 86w24 5:45:36
Clifford 3 149 39N17 85w52 5:43:28
Clifty 3 147 39N14 85w44 5:42:56
Clifty Village 3 147 39N13 85w54 5:43:36
Clinton 83 76 39N40 87w24 5:49:36
Clinton Falls 67 128 39N39 86w52 5:47:28
Cloud Crest Hills 7 145 39N12 86w15 5:45:00
Cloverdale 67 128 39N31 86w48 5:47:12
Cloverland 11 89 39N31 87w12 5:48:48
Clover Village 73 101 39N35 85w52 5:43:28
Clunette 43 291 41N19 85w55 5:43:40
Clymers 9 164 40N43 86w29 5:45:56
Coal Bluff 84 82 39N37 87w21 5:49:24
Coal City 60 199 39N14 87w03 5:48:12
Coal Creek 23 187 40N09 87w24 5:49:36
Coal Creek 54 147 40N07 87w04 5:48:16
Coalmont 11 89 39N12 87w14 5:48:56
Coatesville 32 115 39N41 86w40 5:46:40
Cochran 15 33 39N04 84w54 5:39:36
Coe 63 59 38N19 87w16 5:49:04
Coesse 92 228 41N07 85w24 5:41:36
Coffey Subdivision 7 145 39N12 86w15 5:45:00
Cofield Corner 58 33 38N57 84w51 5:39:24
Colburn 79 147 40N31 86w43 5:46:52
Colburn Acres 71 205 41N32 86w15 5:45:00
Cold Springs 15 33 39N07 85w05 5:40:20
Cold Springs 76 30 41N32 84w55 5:39:40
Colfax 12 183 40N12 86w40 5:46:40
Collamer 92 228 41N06 85w38 5:42:32
College Corner 38 291 40N26 84w59 5:39:56
College Corner 81 313 39N34 84w49 5:39:16
College Hill 9 165 40N46 86w22 5:45:28
College Meadows 29 100 39N54 86w08 5:44:32
Collegeville 37 226 40N56 87w09 5:48:36
Collett 38 295 40N23 84w59 5:39:56
Collins 92 230 41N13 85w24 5:41:36
Coloma 61 128 39N46 87w17 5:49:08
Colonial Hills 87 53 37N57 87w24 5:49:36
Colonial Park 84 77 39N26 87w24 5:49:36
Colonial Village 30 101 39N56 85w51 5:43:24
Columbia 21 272 39N40 85w08 5:40:32
Columbia City 92 236 41N10 85w29 5:41:56
Columbus 3 130 39N13 85w55 5:43:40
Commercial Place 67 128 39N39 86w52 5:47:28
Commiskey 40 128 38N52 85w39 5:42:36
Como 38 291 40N26 84w59 5:39:56
Concord 79 147 40N25 86w53 5:47:32
Connersville 21 273 39N39 85w08 5:40:32
Converse 52 337 40N35 85w54 5:43:36
Cook 45 16 41N22 87w26 5:49:44
Cool Spring 46 9 41N39 86w51 5:47:24
Coolwood Acres 64 6 41N29 87w23 5:49:32
Coppess Corner 1 228 40N45 84w57 5:39:48
Cordry Lake 7 147 39N21 86w07 5:44:28
Corn Brook 3 147 39N13 85w54 5:43:36
Cornettsville 14 85 38N45 87w07 5:48:28
Corning 14 85 38N40 87w03 5:48:12
Correct 69 275 39N04 85w15 5:41:00
Cortland 36 147 38N58 85w58 5:43:52
Corunna 17 237 41N26 85w09 5:40:36
Cory 11 89 39N23 87w12 5:48:48
Corydon 31 168 38N13 86w07 5:44:28
Cosperville 57 47 41N28 85w29 5:41:56
Cotton 78 35 38N52 85w01 5:40:04
Country Club Gardens 2 233 41N04 85w10 5:40:40
Country Club Heights 48 101 40N08 85w41 5:42:44
Countryside Estates 2 233 41N06 85w08 5:40:32
Country Terrace 18 254 40N11 85w23 5:41:32
Courter 52 335 40N42 86w07 5:44:28
Coveyville 47 344 38N51 86w30 5:46:00
Covington 23 163 40N09 87w24 5:49:36
Covington Dells 2 233 41N04 85w10 5:40:40
Cowan 18 253 40N06 85w24 5:41:36
Coxville 61 73 39N37 87w21 5:49:24
Craig 78 35 38N45 85w09 5:40:36
Craig Highlands 29 97 40N03 86w01 5:44:04
Craigville 90 228 40N47 85w06 5:40:24
Crandall 31 166 38N17 86w04 5:44:16
Crane 51 323 38N54 86w54 5:47:36
Crawford 47 344 38N51 86w30 5:46:00
Crawfordsville 54 131 40N02 86w54 5:47:36
Crawleyville 26 59 38N18 87w45 5:51:00
Cree Lake 57 30 41N26 85w16 5:41:04
Creston 45 2 41N20 87w24 5:49:36
Crestview 3 147 39N13 85w54 5:43:36
Crestview Heights 55 97 39N37 86w22 5:45:28
Crete 68 307 40N03 84w56 5:39:44
Crisman 64 23 41N29 87w28 5:49:52
Critchfield 41 100 39N40 86w09 5:44:36
Crocker 64 4 41N35 87w07 5:48:28
Crompton Hill 83 73 39N40 87w24 5:49:36
Cromwell 57 34 41N24 85w37 5:42:28
Crooked Lake 76 30 41N41 85w02 5:40:08
Cross Plains 69 275 38N57 85w12 5:40:48
Cross Roads 69 275 39N18 85w13 5:40:52
Crothersville 36 139 38N48 85w50 5:43:20
Crown Center 55 101 39N35 86w29 5:45:56
Crown Colony 2 233 41N04 85w09 5:40:36
Crown Point 45 5 41N25 87w22 5:49:28
Crows Nest 49 100 39N49 86w11 5:44:44
Crumley Crossing 5 196 40N23 85w13 5:40:52
Crump Estates 3 147 39N13 85w54 5:43:36
Crumstown 71 204 41N38 86w25 5:45:40
Crystal 19 67 38N27 86w48 5:47:12
Cuba 2 228 41N14 84w58 5:39:52
Cuba 3 302 39N21 85w58 5:43:52
Cuba 60 344 39N17 86w46 5:47:04
Culver 50 215 41N13 86w25 5:45:40
Cumberland 49 98 39N47 85w57 5:43:48
Cunot 60 344 39N31 86w48 5:47:12
Curby 13 169 38N20 86w28 5:45:52
Curry 77 80 39N13 87w24 5:49:36
Curryville 1 228 40N47 85w06 5:40:24
Curryville 77 80 39N11 87w24 5:49:36
Curtisville 80 119 40N21 85w44 5:42:56
Cutler 8 164 40N29 86w32 5:46:08
Cuzco 19 67 38N29 86w44 5:46:56
Cyclone 12 181 40N13 86w27 5:45:48
Cynthiana 65 58 38N11 87w43 5:50:52
Cypress 82 55 37N59 87w37 5:50:28
Dabney 69 275 39N04 85w23 5:41:32
Daggett 60 199 39N14 87w03 5:48:12
Daisy Hill 88 165 38N28 85w57 5:43:48
Dale 74 65 38N10 86w59 5:47:56
Daleville 18 253 40N07 85w33 5:42:12
Dallas 35 287 40N53 85w36 5:42:24
Dalton 89 317 39N58 85w10 5:40:40
Dana 83 82 39N48 87w30 5:50:00
Danville 32 250 39N46 86w32 5:46:08
Darlington 54 149 40N06 86w47 5:47:08
Darmstadt 82 55 38N00 87w33 5:50:12
Davis 46 9 41N43 86w53 5:47:32
Daylight 82 55 38N00 87w33 5:50:12
Dayton 79 132 40N23 86w46 5:47:04
Dayville 87 53 37N57 87w24 5:49:36
Deacon 9 165 40N39 86w18 5:45:12
Decatur 1 232 40N50 84w56 5:39:44
Decker 42 86 38N29 87w38 5:50:32
Deedsville 52 335 40N55 86w06 5:44:24
Deep River 45 6 41N33 87w17 5:49:08
Deer Creek 8 165 40N37 86w24 5:45:36
Deerfield 3 149 39N13 85w54 5:43:36
Deerfield 68 310 40N17 85w02 5:40:08
Deerfield 84 77 39N26 87w24 5:49:36
Deer Park 37 2 41N12 87w12 5:48:48
Deers Mills 54 147 39N52 87w03 5:48:12
De Fries Landing 43 291 41N21 85w49 5:43:16
De Gonia 87 53 38N03 87w11 5:48:44
Delaware 69 275 39N08 85w18 5:41:12
Delaware Trails 49 100 39N53 86w11 5:44:44
Delong 25 327 41N08 86w25 5:45:40
Delp 79 147 40N25 86w53 5:47:32
Delphi 8 133 40N36 86w41 5:46:44
Deming 29 97 40N08 86w01 5:44:04
Democrat 8 165 40N28 86w31 5:46:04
Demotte 37 2 41N12 87w12 5:48:48
Denham 66 183 41N09 86w43 5:46:52

INDIANA

INDIANA

Denmark 60	199	39N14	87w03	5:48:12
Denver 52	338	40N52	86w05	5:44:20
Depauw 31	166	38N20	86w13	5:44:52
Deputy 39	114	38N48	85w39	5:42:36
Derby 62	69	38N01	86w32	5:46:08
Desoto 18	253	40N16	85w18	5:41:12
Devonshire 49	100	39N50	86w04	5:44:16
Dewey 46	29	41N19	86w52	5:47:28
Dexter 62	69	38N01	86w32	5:46:08
Diamond 61	89	39N37	87w12	5:48:48
Diamond Lake 43	291	41N08	85w53	5:43:32
Diamond Lake 57	47	41N28	85w29	5:41:56
Dick Johnson 11	89	39N34	87w10	5:48:40
Dike 26	59	38N24	87w35	5:50:20
Dillman 90	196	40N36	85w27	5:41:48
Dillsboro 15	38	39N01	85w04	5:40:16
Disko 25	242	41N01	85w56	5:43:44
Dixon 2	228	40N58	84w52	5:39:28
Doans 28	193	39N02	86w56	5:47:44
Dodd 62	69	37N55	86w41	5:46:44
Dodds Bridge 77	80	39N13	87w31	5:50:04
Dogwood 31	166	38N06	86w05	5:44:20
Dolan 53	344	39N15	86w30	5:46:00
Domestic 90	228	40N36	85w05	5:40:20
Donaldson 50	214	41N22	86w27	5:45:48
Dongola 26	59	38N20	87w30	5:50:00
Doolittle Mills 62	69	38N15	86w35	5:46:20
Door Village 46	8	41N37	86w44	5:46:56
Douglas 26	59	38N24	87w35	5:50:20
Dover 6	247	40N04	86w28	5:45:52
Dover 15	33	39N10	84w55	5:39:40
Dover Hill 51	322	38N43	86w48	5:47:12
Dovers View 80	121	40N18	86w03	5:44:12
Dowden Acres 84	77	39N26	87w24	5:49:36
Downeyville 16	101	39N21	85w33	5:42:12
Dresden 28	193	38N56	86w44	5:46:56
Dresser 84	77	39N28	87w26	5:49:44
Drewersburg 24	30	39N21	84w50	5:39:20
Drexel Gardens 49	100	39N45	86w14	5:44:56
Driftwood 36	147	38N49	86w08	5:44:32
Dublin 89	317	39N49	85w12	5:40:48
Dubois 19	67	38N27	86w48	5:47:12
Duck Creek 48	101	40N21	85w49	5:43:16
Dudley 33	253	39N50	85w16	5:41:04
Dudleytown 36	147	38N58	85w58	5:43:52
Duff 19	67	38N18	86w57	5:47:48
Dugger 77	72	39N04	87w16	5:49:04
Dundee 48	101	40N16	85w41	5:42:44
Dune Acres 64	3	41N39	87w05	5:48:20
Duneland Beach 46	9	41N43	86w53	5:47:32
Dunfee 2	233	41N04	85w09	5:40:36
Dunkirk 9	165	40N46	86w22	5:45:28
Dunkirk 38	300	40N23	85w13	5:40:52
Dunlap 20	271	41N39	85w56	5:43:44
Dunlapsville 81	313	39N35	85w00	5:40:00
Dunn 4	147	40N37	87w19	5:49:16
Dunnington 4	147	40N34	87w29	5:49:56
Dunns Bridge 37	2	41N12	86w58	5:47:52
Dunreith 33	257	39N48	85w26	5:41:44
Dupont 39	161	38N53	85w31	5:42:04
Durbin 29	98	40N03	86w01	5:44:04
Dutch Town 17	228	41N21	85w09	5:40:36
Dyer 45	1	41N30	87w31	5:50:04
Eagle 6	97	39N58	86w17	5:45:08
Eagle Creek 45	2	41N17	87w17	5:49:08
Eagle Hollow 39	97	38N45	85w19	5:41:16
Eagletown 29	98	40N03	86w08	5:44:32
Eagle Village 6	100	39N53	86w16	5:45:04
Eaglewood Estates 6	100	39N53	86w16	5:45:04
Earle 82	55	38N00	87w33	5:50:12
Earlham 89	318	39N52	84w52	5:39:28
Earl Park 4	147	40N42	87w25	5:49:40
East Cedar Lake 45	15	41N22	87w24	5:49:36
East Chicago 45	6	41N38	87w29	5:49:56
East Clifford 3	147	39N13	85w54	5:43:36
East Columbus 3	130	39N13	85w54	5:43:36
East Connersville 21	273	39N40	85w08	5:40:32
East Enterprise 78	35	38N52	84w59	5:39:56
Eastern Heights 53	344	39N12	86w37	5:46:28
East Gary 45	6	41N35	87w14	5:48:56
Eastgate 3	147	39N13	85w54	5:43:36
Eastgate 10	166	38N18	85w45	5:43:00
East Gate 30	101	39N56	85w51	5:43:24
Eastgate 49	100	39N47	86w04	5:44:16
East Germantown 89	317	39N49	85w09	5:40:36
East Glenn 84	77	39N29	87w22	5:49:28
Eastland Gardens 2	233	41N04	85w09	5:40:36
East Monticello 91	162	40N45	86w46	5:47:04
East Mount Carmel 26	59	38N18	87w45	5:51:00
East Oolitic 47	344	38N51	86w30	5:46:00
Eastridge Manor 3	147	39N13	85w54	5:43:36
East Shelburn 77	80	39N11	87w24	5:49:36
East Shoals 51	322	38N40	86w47	5:47:08
East Union 29	97	40N13	86w02	5:44:08
Eastwich 79	147	40N25	86w53	5:47:32
Eaton 18	253	40N21	85w20	5:41:20
Echo Heights 18	254	40N11	85w23	5:41:32
Eckerty 13	169	38N19	86w37	5:46:28
Economy 89	315	39N59	85w05	5:40:20
Eden 44	30	41N34	85w36	5:42:24
Edgerton 2	228	41N07	84w51	5:39:24
Edgewater 64	6	41N29	87w23	5:49:32
Edgewood 3	147	39N13	85w54	5:43:36
Edgewood 46	9	41N43	86w53	5:47:32
Edgewood 47	344	38N51	86w30	5:46:00
Edgewood 49	100	39N41	86w08	5:44:32
Edgewood Park 2	233	41N04	85w09	5:40:36
Edinburg 41	302	39N21	85w58	5:43:52
Edison Park 71	208	41N41	86w12	5:44:48
Edna Mills 12	147	40N25	86w39	5:46:36
Edwardsport 42	87	38N49	87w15	5:49:00
Edwardsville 22	166	38N18	85w49	5:43:16
Eel 9	165	40N45	86w20	5:45:20
Effner 56	241	40N46	87w34	5:50:16
Ege 57	30	41N17	85w16	5:41:04
Ehrmandale 84	82	39N42	86w51	5:47:24
Ekin 29	97	40N13	86w02	5:44:08
Elberfeld 87	59	38N10	87w27	5:49:48
El Dorado 41	100	39N40	86w09	5:44:36
Elizabeth 31	166	38N07	85w58	5:43:52
Elizabethtown 3	149	39N08	85w49	5:43:16
Elizaville 6	251	40N08	86w23	5:45:32
Elkhart 20	271	41N41	85w58	5:43:52
Elkinsville 7	145	39N12	86w15	5:45:00
Ellettsville 53	344	39N14	86w38	5:46:32
Ellis 28	93	39N04	87w16	5:49:04
Elliston 28	193	39N02	86w56	5:47:44
Elmdale 54	147	40N00	86w56	5:47:44
Elmira 44	30	41N39	85w25	5:41:40
Elmore 14	85	38N52	87w04	5:48:16
Elmwood 52	335	40N42	86w07	5:44:28
Elnora 14	85	38N53	87w05	5:48:20
Elrod 69	275	39N01	85w04	5:40:16
Elston 79	147	40N25	86w53	5:47:32
Elwood 48	103	40N17	85w50	5:43:20
Elwren 53	344	39N07	86w40	5:46:40
Eminence 55	113	39N31	86w39	5:46:36
Emison 42	86	38N48	87w28	5:49:52
Emma 44	30	41N37	85w32	5:42:08
Emporia 48	101	39N59	85w37	5:42:28
Enchanted Hills 43	291	41N24	85w37	5:42:28
Englewood 47	344	38N51	86w30	5:46:00
English 13	169	38N20	86w28	5:45:52
English Lake 75	29	41N16	86w49	5:47:16
Enochsburg 16	101	39N21	85w33	5:42:12
Enos 56	2	40N57	87w27	5:49:48
Enos Corners 63	59	38N20	87w30	5:50:00
Enosville 63	59	38N18	87w16	5:49:04
Enterprise 74	61	37N53	87w03	5:48:12
Epsom 14	85	38N48	87w09	5:48:36
Epworth Forest 43	291	41N20	85w45	5:43:00
Erie 52	335	40N48	86w00	5:44:00
Ervin 34	165	40N31	86w18	5:45:12
Etna 43	291	41N18	86w02	5:44:08
Etna 92	228	41N16	85w34	5:42:16
Etna Green 43	295	41N17	86w03	5:44:12
Eugene 83	73	39N58	87w28	5:49:52
Eureka 74	61	37N53	87w03	5:48:12
Evanston 74	64	38N02	86w51	5:47:24
Evansville 82	55	37N58	87w35	5:50:20
Evergreen Acres 10	166	38N18	85w45	5:43:00
Everroad Park West 3	147	39N13	85w54	5:43:36
Everton 21	272	39N32	85w04	5:40:16
Fair Acres 88	165	38N36	86w06	5:44:24
Fairbanks 77	80	39N13	87w31	5:50:04
Fairfield 2	233	41N03	85w09	5:40:36
Fairfield Center 17	237	41N26	85w09	5:40:36
Fair Grounds 49	100	39N50	86w09	5:44:36
Fairland 73	101	39N35	85w52	5:43:28
Fairlawn 3	147	39N13	85w54	5:43:36
Fairmount 27	280	40N25	85w36	5:42:24
Fair Oaks 37	2	41N05	87w16	5:49:04
Fairplay 28	193	39N02	87w00	5:48:00
Fairview 21	272	39N42	85w17	5:41:08
Fairview 68	307	40N18	85w12	5:40:48
Fairview 78	35	38N52	85w08	5:40:32
Fairview Park 83	73	39N41	87w24	5:49:36
Fairwood Hills 49	100	39N53	86w03	5:44:12
Fall Creek Highlands 49	100	39N50	86w01	5:44:04
Falmouth 70	101	39N43	85w18	5:41:12
Farlen 14	91	38N51	86w59	5:47:56
Farmers 60	344	39N12	86w47	5:47:08
Farmersburg 77	80	39N15	87w23	5:49:32
Farmers Retreat 15	33	38N58	85w06	5:40:24
Farmersville 65	58	37N56	87w54	5:51:36
Farmland 68	307	40N11	85w08	5:40:32
Farrabee 88	165	38N36	86w06	5:44:24
Farrville 27	284	40N34	85w42	5:42:48
Fayette 6	247	40N04	86w28	5:45:52
Fayette 84	82	39N34	87w28	5:49:52
Fayetteville 47	344	38N51	86w30	5:46:00
Federal Hill 29	97	40N03	86w01	5:44:04
Fenn Haven 62	69	37N57	86w46	5:47:04
Fenns 73	108	39N33	85w48	5:43:12
Ferdinand 19	67	38N14	86w52	5:47:28
Ferguson Hill 84	77	39N29	87w27	5:49:48
Fern 67	128	39N39	86w52	5:47:28
Fewell Rhoades 55	101	39N25	86w25	5:45:40
Fiat 38	291	40N32	84w58	5:39:52
Fickle 45	17	41N35	87w21	5:49:24
Fieldcrest 29	97	40N13	86w02	5:44:08
Fields 55	97	39N37	86w22	5:45:28
Fillmore 67	126	39N40	86w45	5:47:00
Fincastle 67	128	39N51	86w48	5:47:12
Finley 72	320	38N41	85w51	5:43:24
Finly 30	97	39N42	85w49	5:43:16
Fishers 29	97	39N57	86w01	5:44:04
Fishersburg 48	101	40N04	85w50	5:43:20
Fisher's Woodland 29	97	40N03	86w01	5:44:04
Fish Lake 44	30	41N39	85w25	5:41:40
Fish Lake 46	2	41N33	86w33	5:46:12
Five Points 2	228	41N07	84w51	5:39:24
Five Points 42	86	38N37	87w21	5:49:24
Five Points 49	100	39N43	86w01	5:44:04
Five Points 55	97	39N37	86w22	5:45:28
Five Points 92	228	41N12	85w28	5:41:52
Five Points Corner 64	19	41N19	87w02	5:48:08
Flackville 49	100	39N47	86w13	5:44:52
Flat Rock 73	108	39N22	85w50	5:43:20
Flat Rock Park 3	147	39N13	85w54	5:43:36
Fleming 36	147	38N58	85w58	5:43:52
Fletcher Lake 25	328	41N01	86w24	5:45:36
Flint 76	30	41N39	85w08	5:40:32
Flintwood 3	147	39N13	85w54	5:43:36
Flora 8	170	40N33	86w31	5:46:04
Florence 78	35	38N47	84w55	5:39:40
Florida 48	101	40N07	85w42	5:42:48
Florida 61	72	39N38	87w25	5:49:40
Floyd 67	128	39N44	86w44	5:46:56
Floyds Knobs 22	166	38N19	85w52	5:43:28
Folsomville 87	53	38N08	87w10	5:48:40
Fontanet 84	82	39N34	87w15	5:49:00
Foraker 20	262	41N31	85w56	5:43:44
Foresman 56	226	40N52	87w22	5:49:28
Forest 12	181	40N22	86w19	5:45:16
Forest Hill 16	101	39N21	85w33	5:42:12
Forest Hills 29	97	40N03	86w01	5:44:04
Forest Hills 45	6	41N30	87w19	5:49:16
Forest Lake 32	97	39N42	86w23	5:45:32
Forest Manor 46	9	41N43	86w53	5:47:32
Forest Park 3	147	39N13	85w54	5:43:36
Forest Park Beach 76	30	41N32	84w55	5:39:40
Forest Park Heights 53	344	39N12	86w37	5:46:28
Forest Ridge 2	233	41N04	85w10	5:40:40
Forest Ridge 27	284	40N34	85w42	5:42:48
Forest Ridge Estates 2	233	41N04	85w10	5:40:40
Forrest Hills 48	101	40N21	85w44	5:42:56
Fort Benjamin Harrison 49	100	39N52	86w02	5:44:08
Fort Branch 26	56	38N15	87w35	5:50:20
Fort Ritner 47	344	38N47	86w17	5:45:08
Fortville 30	97	39N56	85w51	5:43:24
Fort Wayne 2	233	41N04	85w09	5:40:36
Foster 86	187	40N09	87w28	5:49:52
Fountain 23	129	40N18	87w15	5:49:00
Fountain City 89	282	39N57	84w55	5:39:40
Fountain Park 37	224	40N46	87w09	5:48:36
Fountain Park 76	30	41N32	84w55	5:39:40
Fountain Square 49	100	39N44	86w06	5:44:24
Fountaintown 73	101	39N42	85w47	5:43:08
Fowler 4	147	40N37	87w19	5:49:16
Fowlerton 27	280	40N25	85w34	5:42:16
Foxglen 29	97	40N03	86w01	5:44:04
Fox Hill 55	100	39N47	86w09	5:44:36
Fox Lake 76	30	41N38	85w00	5:40:00
Fox Ridge 67	128	39N39	86w52	5:47:28
Francesville 66	181	40N59	86w53	5:47:32
Francisco 26	59	38N20	87w27	5:49:48
Frankfort 12	171	40N17	86w31	5:46:04
Franklin 41	104	39N29	86w03	5:44:12
Franklin 89	317	39N54	85w10	5:40:40
Franklin Hills 62	69	37N57	86w46	5:47:04
Frankton 48	108	40N13	85w46	5:43:04
Fredericksburg 88	165	38N26	86w11	5:44:44
Fredonia 13	169	38N12	86w21	5:45:24
Freedom 60	108	39N12	86w47	5:47:08
Freeland Park 4	147	40N36	87w29	5:49:56
Freelandville 42	86	38N52	87w18	5:49:12
Freeman 60	344	39N17	86w46	5:47:04
Freeport 73	101	39N40	85w42	5:42:48
Freetown 36	147	38N59	86w08	5:44:32
Fremont 76	32	41N44	84w56	5:39:44
French 1	228	40N42	85w02	5:40:08
French 58	38	39N02	84w53	5:39:32
French Lake 84	77	39N26	87w24	5:49:36
French Lick 59	142	38N33	86w37	5:46:28
Frenchtown 31	166	38N20	86w13	5:44:52
Friendship 69	275	38N58	85w09	5:40:36
Friendswood 32	100	39N47	86w09	5:44:36
Fritchton 42	86	38N45	87w31	5:50:04
Fruitdale 7	147	39N22	86w15	5:45:00
Fugit 16	101	39N24	85w22	5:41:28
Fulda 74	64	38N07	86w50	5:47:20
Fulton 25	328	40N57	86w16	5:45:04
Furnessville 64	4	41N37	87w06	5:48:24
Gadsden 6	248	40N04	86w28	5:45:52
Galena 22	166	38N21	85w55	5:43:40
Galena 46	2	41N43	86w39	5:46:36
Galveston 9	164	40N35	86w11	5:44:44
Gambill 77	80	39N04	87w16	5:49:04
Gar Creek 2	233	41N04	85w03	5:40:12
Garden Acres 6	247	40N07	86w36	5:46:24
Garden Acres 53	344	39N12	86w37	5:46:28
Garden City 3	147	39N13	85w54	5:43:36
Garfield 49	100	39N44	86w06	5:44:24
Garrett 17	238	41N21	85w08	5:40:32
Gary 45	17	41N36	87w20	5:49:20
Gasburg 55	97	39N37	86w22	5:45:28
Gas City 27	282	40N29	85w37	5:42:28
Gaston 18	253	40N19	85w30	5:42:00
Gatchel 62	69	38N03	86w41	5:46:44
Geetingsville 12	181	40N17	86w31	5:46:04
Gem 30	97	40N53	81w35	5:26:20

INDIANA

Geneva 1 230 40N36 84w58 5:39:52
Geneva 73 101 39N22 85w50 5:43:20
Gentryville 74 64 38N07 87w02 5:48:08
Georgetown 2 228 41N14 84w58 5:39:52
Georgetown 9 165 40N44 86w31 5:46:04
Georgetown 22 166 38N18 85w57 5:43:48
Georgetown 68 307 40N15 85w10 5:40:40
Georgia 47 344 38N44 86w28 5:45:52
Georgia Heights 45 6 41N30 87w19 5:49:16
Germantown 16 108 39N26 85w38 5:42:32
Gessie 83 73 40N05 87w30 5:50:00
Giberson 47 344 38N51 86w30 5:46:00
Gibson 88 165 38N41 85w57 5:43:48
Gifford 37 2 41N11 87w03 5:48:12
Gilboa 4 147 40N42 87w09 5:48:36
Gilead 52 335 40N58 86w00 5:44:00
Gill 77 80 39N01 87w30 5:50:00
Gillam 37 226 41N04 86w58 5:47:52
Gilman 48 101 40N16 85w41 5:42:44
Gilmer Park 71 208 41N36 86w15 5:45:00
Gilmour 28 93 39N10 87w12 5:48:48
Gimco City 48 101 40N16 85w41 5:42:44
Gingrich 91 162 40N45 86w46 5:47:04
Gings 70 101 39N41 85w23 5:41:32
Giro 26 59 38N30 87w35 5:50:20
Glenayr 84 77 39N29 87w22 5:49:28
Glendale 14 85 38N34 87w05 5:48:20
Glendale 49 100 39N52 86w07 5:44:28
Glendale Lake 27 284 40N34 85w42 5:42:48
Glen Eden 76 30 41N38 85w00 5:40:00
Glenhall 79 147 40N21 87w03 5:48:12
Glenns Valley 49 100 39N40 86w09 5:44:36
Glen Park 45 6 41N32 87w22 5:49:28
Glenview 3 147 39N13 85w54 5:43:36
Glenwood 21 272 39N37 85w18 5:41:12
Glenwood Acres 65 58 37N56 87w54 5:51:36
Glenwood Park 2 233 41N06 85w08 5:40:32
Glezen 63 59 38N25 87w18 5:49:12
Gnaw Bone 7 145 39N12 86w15 5:45:00
Goblesville 35 287 40N59 85w31 5:42:04
Goff 27 284 40N34 85w42 5:42:48
Golden Hill 91 162 40N45 86w46 5:47:04
Golden Lake 76 50 41N35 85w01 5:40:04
Goldsmith 80 120 40N17 86w09 5:44:36
Golfview Estates 10 166 38N18 85w45 5:43:00
Goodland 56 240 40N46 87w18 5:49:12
Goose Lake 92 228 41N12 85w28 5:41:52
Goshen 20 258 41N35 85w50 5:43:20
Goshen 72 320 38N41 85w46 5:43:04
Gospel Grove 84 77 39N29 87w22 5:49:28
Gosport 60 342 39N21 86w40 5:46:40
Gowdy 70 101 39N37 85w27 5:41:48
Grabill 2 228 41N14 84w58 5:39:52
Graceland Heights 89 317 39N54 85w10 5:40:40
Grafton 65 58 37N56 87w54 5:51:36
Graham 39 114 38N47 85w38 5:42:32
Graham Valley 87 53 38N03 87w16 5:49:04
Graham Woods 64 4 41N37 87w06 5:48:24
Grammer 3 147 39N09 85w43 5:42:52
Grandview 49 100 39N49 86w11 5:44:44
Grandview 53 344 39N12 86w37 5:46:28
Grandview 74 61 37N56 86w59 5:47:56
Grandview Lake 3 147 39N13 85w54 5:43:36
Grandview Village 22 166 38N18 85w49 5:43:16
Granger 71 203 41N45 86w07 5:44:28
Grant City 33 253 39N53 85w35 5:42:20
Grantsburg 13 169 38N17 86w28 5:45:52
Granville 18 253 40N21 85w20 5:41:20
Grass 74 61 38N00 87w06 5:48:24
Grass Creek 25 327 40N57 86w24 5:45:36
Grasselli 45 6 41N38 87w28 5:49:52
Grassy Fork 36 147 38N48 86w01 5:44:04
Gravel Beach 44 30 41N32 85w05 5:40:20
Gravelton 20 259 41N25 85w51 5:43:24
Grayford 40 126 39N00 85w38 5:42:32
Graysville 77 80 39N07 87w33 5:50:12
Green Acres 45 6 41N29 87w18 5:49:12
Greenbriar 49 100 39N53 86w11 5:44:44
Greenbriar 67 128 39N39 86w52 5:47:28
Greenbrier 87 53 38N03 87w16 5:49:04
Greencastle 67 122 39N38 86w52 5:47:28
Green Center 57 30 41N24 85w26 5:41:44
Greendale 2 233 41N06 85w08 5:40:32
Greendale 15 37 39N07 84w52 5:39:28
Greenfield 30 98 39N47 85w46 5:43:04
Greenfield Estates 27 284 40N34 85w42 5:42:48
Greenhill 86 156 40N25 87w06 5:48:24
Greenleaf Manor 20 271 41N41 85w59 5:43:56
Green Meadows 73 101 39N35 85w52 5:43:28
Green Meadows 79 147 40N26 86w56 5:47:44
Greenoak 25 328 41N04 86w13 5:44:52
Greensboro 33 253 39N53 85w30 5:42:00
Greensburg 16 106 39N20 85w29 5:41:56
Greens Fork 89 315 39N53 85w02 5:40:08
Greentown 34 333 40N29 85w58 5:43:52
Greenvalley 29 97 40N03 86w01 5:44:04
Greenville 22 166 38N22 85w58 5:43:52
Greenwood 41 100 39N37 86w07 5:44:28
Greenwood 44 30 41N32 85w22 5:41:28
Greer 87 53 38N10 87w25 5:49:40
Gregg 55 101 39N31 86w31 5:46:04
Greybrook Lake 60 344 39N27 86w57 5:47:48
Griffin 65 58 38N12 87w55 5:51:40
Griffith 45 6 41N31 87w26 5:49:44
Groomsville 80 116 40N18 86w14 5:44:56
Grouseland 84 82 39N42 86w51 5:47:24
Groveland 67 128 39N46 86w49 5:47:16
Grovertown 75 223 41N22 86w30 5:46:00
Guilford 15 33 39N10 84w55 5:39:40
Guion 61 126 39N51 87w06 5:48:24
Guthrie 47 344 38N48 86w19 5:45:16
Guy 34 334 40N29 85w58 5:43:52
Gwynneville 73 101 39N40 85w39 5:42:36
Hacienda Village 2 233 41N06 85w08 5:40:32
Hackleman 27 280 40N25 85w44 5:42:56
Haddon 77 80 38N58 87w24 5:49:36
Hadley 32 115 39N41 86w40 5:46:40
Hagerstown 89 317 39N55 85w10 5:40:40
Halbert 51 322 38N40 86w44 5:46:56
Haleysbury 88 165 38N51 86w06 5:44:24
Hall 19 67 38N23 86w45 5:47:00
Hall 55 113 39N33 86w32 5:46:08
Hamblen 7 147 39N17 86w11 5:44:44
Hamburg 10 166 38N24 85w46 5:43:04
Hamburg 24 275 39N20 85w12 5:40:48
Hamilton 12 181 40N21 86w39 5:46:36
Hamilton 48 101 40N07 85w42 5:42:48
Hamilton 76 30 41N32 84w55 5:39:40
Hamilton Park 18 254 40N11 85w23 5:41:32
Hamlet 75 223 41N23 86w35 5:46:20
Hammond 45 6 41N38 87w30 5:50:00
Hamor Heights 3 147 39N13 85w54 5:43:36
Hancock 31 166 38N20 86w13 5:44:52
Handy 53 344 39N07 86w30 5:46:00
Hanfield 27 284 40N34 85w42 5:42:48
Hanging Grove 37 226 40N57 86w59 5:47:56
Hangman Crossing 36 147 38N58 85w58 5:43:52
Hanna 46 29 41N25 86w47 5:47:08
Hanover 39 101 38N43 85w28 5:41:52
Happy Hollow Heights 79 147 40N26 86w56 5:47:44
Harbison 19 67 38N30 86w52 5:47:28
Harbor 45 6 41N38 87w28 5:49:52
Hardinsburg 15 37 39N07 84w52 5:39:28
Hardinsburg 88 165 38N28 86w16 5:45:04
Hardscrabble 48 101 40N04 85w50 5:43:20
Harlan 2 228 41N12 84w55 5:39:40
Harmony 11 89 39N32 87w04 5:48:16
Harris 71 203 41N44 86w08 5:44:32
Harrisburg 21 272 39N42 85w10 5:40:40
Harris City 16 101 39N21 85w33 5:42:12
Harrison Hills 3 147 39N13 85w54 5:43:36
Harrison Lake 3 147 39N13 85w54 5:43:36
Harrisville 68 303 40N11 84w53 5:39:32
Harrodsburg 53 344 39N01 86w33 5:46:12
Hart 87 53 38N10 87w17 5:49:08
Hartford 1 228 40N37 85w03 5:40:12
Hartford 58 33 39N00 84w57 5:39:48
Hartford City 5 197 40N27 85w22 5:41:28
Hartford Place 3 147 39N13 85w54 5:43:36
Hartleyville 47 344 38N51 86w30 5:46:00
Hartsdale 45 6 41N29 87w27 5:49:48
Hartsville 3 147 39N16 85w42 5:42:48
Hartz Lake 75 221 41N09 86w29 5:45:56
Harveysburg 23 156 39N59 87w18 5:49:12
Hashtown 28 193 39N02 86w56 5:47:44
Haskells 46 2 41N29 86w54 5:47:36
Hastings 43 291 41N25 85w51 5:43:24
Hatfield 74 61 37N54 87w14 5:48:56
Haubstadt 26 59 38N12 87w34 5:50:16
Haw Creek 3 147 39N18 85w45 5:43:00
Hawthorne 47 344 38N51 86w30 5:46:00
Hayden 40 128 38N59 85w44 5:42:56
Haymond 24 275 39N18 85w13 5:40:52
Haysville 19 67 38N25 86w56 5:47:44
Hazelrigg 6 247 40N04 86w28 5:45:52
Hazelwood 2 233 41N06 85w08 5:40:32
Hazelwood 32 247 39N42 86w31 5:46:04
Hazelwood 73 101 39N33 85w48 5:43:12
Hazleton 26 59 38N29 87w33 5:50:12
Headlee 91 181 40N54 86w40 5:46:40
Heath 79 149 40N25 86w53 5:47:32
Heather Heights 3 147 39N13 85w54 5:43:36
Heaton Lake 20 271 41N41 85w59 5:43:56
Hebron 64 18 41N19 87w12 5:48:48
Hedrick 86 187 40N17 87w29 5:49:56
Heights Corner 60 344 39N17 86w46 5:47:04
Heilman 87 63 38N10 87w05 5:48:20
Helmcrest 30 101 39N56 85w51 5:43:24
Helmer 76 30 41N32 85w10 5:40:40
Helmsburg 7 151 39N17 86w18 5:45:12
Helt 83 73 39N45 87w28 5:49:52
Heltonville 47 344 38N56 86w23 5:45:32
Hemlock 34 330 40N25 86w03 5:44:12
Hemlock Lakes 23 187 39N58 87w17 5:49:08
Henderson 70 101 39N40 85w31 5:42:04
Hendricks 41 101 39N29 85w53 5:43:32
Hendricksville 28 193 39N09 86w42 5:46:48
Henryville 10 179 38N32 85w46 5:43:04
Hensley 41 101 39N23 86w11 5:44:44
Herbst 27 280 40N30 85w46 5:43:04
Herr 6 248 40N04 86w28 5:45:52
Hessen Cassel 2 233 41N03 85w08 5:40:32
Hesston 46 8 41N37 86w44 5:46:56
Hessville 45 6 41N35 87w28 5:49:52
Heth 31 166 38N04 86w10 5:44:40
Heusler 65 58 37N58 87w54 5:51:36
Hibbard 50 216 41N13 86w25 5:45:40
Hibernia 10 166 38N27 85w40 5:42:40
Hibernia Mills 54 147 40N00 86w56 5:47:44
Hickory Grove 4 147 40N32 87w29 5:49:56
Hickory Hills 27 284 40N34 85w42 5:42:48
Hideaway Lake 23 156 39N58 87w17 5:49:08
Highbanks 43 291 41N20 85w45 5:43:00
High Lake 57 30 41N24 85w26 5:41:44
Highland 45 6 41N33 87w28 5:49:52
Highland 82 55 38N00 87w35 5:50:20
Highland 83 73 39N47 87w23 5:49:32
Highland Center 24 30 39N25 84w56 5:39:44
Highland Meadows 27 284 40N34 85w42 5:42:48
Highland Village 53 344 39N12 86w37 5:46:28
Highwoods 49 100 39N47 86w13 5:44:52
Hiker Trace 3 147 39N13 85w54 5:43:36
Hildebrand Village 73 101 39N33 85w48 5:43:12
Hill And Dale 10 166 38N19 85w44 5:42:56
Hillcrest 3 147 39N13 85w54 5:43:36
Hillcrest 31 166 38N13 86w07 5:44:28
Hillcrest 64 6 41N30 87w06 5:48:24
Hillcrest Circle 47 344 38N51 86w30 5:46:00
Hillgrove 31 166 38N13 86w07 5:44:28
Hillham 19 67 38N33 86w37 5:46:28
Hillisburg 12 172 40N17 86w20 5:45:20
Hills And Dales 18 253 40N11 85w16 5:41:04
Hillsboro 23 129 40N07 87w10 5:48:40
Hillsboro 33 253 39N56 85w26 5:41:44
Hillsdale 83 73 39N47 87w23 5:49:32
Hilltown 40 128 38N50 85w39 5:42:36
Hillview Estates 3 147 39N13 85w54 5:43:36
Hindostan Falls 51 322 38N40 86w47 5:47:08
Hindustan 53 344 39N19 86w29 5:45:56
Hitchcock 88 165 38N36 86w06 5:44:24
Hi-View 71 208 41N40 86w14 5:44:56
Hoagland 2 230 40N57 85w00 5:40:00
Hobart 45 6 41N32 87w15 5:49:00
Hobbieville 28 193 39N01 86w43 5:46:52
Hobbs 80 117 40N17 85w57 5:43:48
Hoffman Lake 43 297 41N14 85w51 5:43:24
Hogan 15 33 39N04 84w58 5:39:52
Hogtown 13 169 38N22 86w21 5:45:24
Holida 49 100 39N53 86w11 5:44:44
Holiday 17 228 41N21 85w09 5:40:36
Holland 19 67 38N15 87w02 5:48:08
Hollandsburg 61 128 39N46 87w04 5:48:16
Hollybrook Lake 60 344 39N21 86w40 5:46:40
Holly Hills 84 77 39N26 87w24 5:49:36
Holton 69 275 39N05 85w23 5:41:32
Home Corner 27 284 40N34 85w42 5:42:48
Homecroft 49 100 39N41 86w07 5:44:28
Home Place 29 100 39N54 86w08 5:44:32
Homer 70 108 39N35 85w35 5:42:20
Homestead 15 33 39N08 84w51 5:39:24
Honduras 1 228 40N50 84w56 5:39:44
Honey Creek 33 108 40N06 85w32 5:42:08
Honeyville 44 32 41N32 85w42 5:42:48
Hoosier Acres 53 344 39N12 86w37 5:46:28
Hoosier Highlands 67 128 39N27 86w57 5:47:48
Hoosierville 11 89 39N31 87w08 5:48:32
Hoover 9 164 40N46 86w22 5:45:28
Hoover Crest 49 100 39N53 86w11 5:44:44
Hope 3 148 39N18 85w46 5:43:04
Hopewell 41 97 39N29 86w03 5:44:12
Horace 16 101 39N21 85w33 5:42:12
Horton 29 97 40N08 86w13 5:44:52
Houston 36 147 38N58 86w08 5:44:32
Hovey 65 58 37N56 87w54 5:51:36
Howard 61 128 39N55 87w19 5:49:16
Howe 44 39 41N43 85w25 5:41:40
Howell 82 55 37N59 87w37 5:50:28
Howesville 11 89 39N11 87w09 5:48:36
Hubbell 60 199 39N14 87w03 5:48:12
Hubbells Corner 15 33 39N14 85w06 5:40:24
Hudson 76 30 41N32 85w05 5:40:20
Hudson Lake 46 3 41N43 86w33 5:46:12
Hudsonville 14 85 38N40 87w03 5:48:12
Huff 74 64 38N02 86w51 5:47:24
Hull Addition 80 121 40N18 86w03 5:44:12
Hunter 49 100 39N43 86w01 5:44:04
Huntersville 24 275 39N18 85w13 5:40:52
Huntertown 2 239 41N14 85w10 5:40:40
Huntingburg 19 67 38N18 86w57 5:47:48
Huntington 35 290 40N53 85w30 5:42:00
Huntsville 48 101 40N00 85w45 5:43:00
Huntsville 68 307 40N03 85w08 5:40:32
Huron 47 344 38N43 86w40 5:46:40
Hurshtown 2 228 41N19 84w54 5:39:36
Hyde Park 18 254 40N12 85w19 5:41:16
Hymera 77 80 39N11 87w18 5:49:12
Idaho 84 77 39N26 87w24 5:49:36
Idaville 91 182 40N46 86w39 5:46:36
Ijamsville 85 264 41N00 85w46 5:43:04
Imperial Hills 41 100 39N41 86w07 5:44:28
Independence 86 129 40N18 87w15 5:49:00
Independence Hill 45 6 41N28 87w22 5:49:28
Indiana Beach 91 162 40N45 86w46 5:47:04

Indiana Girls School 49 100 39N48 86w15 5:45:00
Indiana Lake 20 259 41N43 85w49 5:43:16
Indiana Oaks 10 166 38N19 85w44 5:42:56
Indianapolis 49 100 39N46 86w09 5:44:36
Indian Creek Settlement 42 86 38N46 87w19 5:49:16
Indianhead Lake 32 247 39N46 86w31 5:46:04
Indian Heights 34 331 40N29 86w08 5:44:32
Indian Hills 3 147 39N13 85w54 5:43:36
Indian Lake 17 237 41N26 85w09 5:40:36
Indian Lake 49 100 39N50 86w01 5:44:04
Indianola 44 30 41N32 85w22 5:41:28
Indian Springs 51 159 38N48 86w46 5:47:04
Indian Village 57 30 41N24 85w37 5:42:28
Indian Village 71 208 41N43 86w14 5:44:56
Industry 18 254 40N11 85w23 5:41:32
Ingalls 48 101 39N58 85w48 5:43:12
Inglefield 82 53 38N07 87w34 5:50:16
Innisdale 48 101 40N16 85w41 5:42:44
Inwood 50 327 41N19 86w12 5:44:48
Iona 87 53 38N03 87w28 5:49:52
Ireland 19 67 38N25 87w00 5:48:00
Ironton 51 322 38N40 86w47 5:47:08
Iroquois 56 226 40N52 87w20 5:49:20
Irvington 49 100 39N47 86w04 5:44:16
Irvington Plaza Shopping Cen 49 100 39N47 86w04 5:44:16
Island City 28 93 39N02 87w10 5:48:40
Island Park 43 297 41N14 85w51 5:43:24
Island Park 76 30 41N32 84w55 5:39:40
Iva 63 59 38N27 87w06 5:48:24
Ivanhoe 49 100 39N47 86w04 5:44:16
Ivy Hills 49 100 39N52 86w07 5:44:28
Jacksonburg 89 317 39N49 85w11 5:40:44
Jackson Hill 77 80 39N11 87w24 5:49:36
Jackson Park 18 254 40N11 85w23 5:41:32
Jacksons 80 121 40N18 86w03 5:44:12
Jacksonville 83 73 39N40 87w24 5:49:36
Jalapa 27 284 40N34 85w42 5:42:48
Jamestown 6 251 39N56 86w38 5:46:32
Jamestown 76 32 41N44 84w53 5:39:32
Jasonville 28 94 39N10 87w12 5:48:48
Jasper 19 66 38N24 86w56 5:47:44
Jay City 38 291 40N32 84w58 5:39:52
Jefferson Proving Ground 39 97 38N45 85w19 5:41:16
Jeffersonville 10 176 38N17 85w44 5:42:56
Jerome 34 334 40N27 85w56 5:43:44
Jessups 61 72 39N39 87w15 5:49:00
Jewell Village 3 147 39N13 85w54 5:43:36
Jimtown 20 271 41N41 85w59 5:43:56
Jockey 87 53 38N05 87w07 5:48:28
Johnsburg 19 67 38N18 86w57 5:47:48
Johnson 26 59 38N18 87w45 5:51:00
Johnsonville 86 156 40N17 87w18 5:49:12
Johnstown 28 193 39N07 86w59 5:47:56
Johnstown 42 86 38N46 87w19 5:49:16
Jolietville 29 98 40N08 86w13 5:44:52
Jonesboro 27 284 40N29 85w38 5:42:32
Jonestown 83 73 39N40 87w24 5:49:36
Jonesville 3 149 39N04 85w53 5:43:32
Joppa 32 97 39N37 86w22 5:45:28
Jordan 60 344 39N27 86w57 5:47:48
Judah 47 344 38N51 86w30 5:46:00
Judson 34 330 40N29 86w08 5:44:32
Judson 61 128 39N49 87w09 5:48:36
Judyville 86 156 40N22 87w23 5:49:32
Julietta 49 100 39N43 86w01 5:44:04
Junction 52 335 40N42 86w07 5:44:28
Kalorama Park 43 291 41N20 85w51 5:43:24
Kasson 82 53 38N01 87w39 5:50:36
Keener 37 2 41N10 87w13 5:48:52
Kellerville 19 67 38N27 86w48 5:47:12
Kelso 15 33 39N15 84w58 5:39:52
Kempton 80 118 40N17 86w14 5:44:56
Kem Square 27 284 40N34 85w42 5:42:48
Kendallville 57 40 41N27 85w16 5:41:04
Kennard 33 253 39N54 85w31 5:42:04
Kennedy 74 64 38N04 86w54 5:47:36
Kent 39 97 38N45 85w19 5:41:16
Kent 86 187 40N12 87w29 5:49:56
Kentland 56 241 40N46 87w27 5:49:48
Kentwood 12 181 40N17 86w31 5:46:04
Kenwood 84 77 39N28 87w26 5:49:44
Kersey 37 2 41N12 87w12 5:48:48
Kewanna 25 325 41N01 86w25 5:45:40
Keyser 17 228 41N21 85w08 5:40:32
Keystone 90 196 40N36 85w16 5:41:04
Keytsville 61 128 39N33 86w58 5:47:52
Kilmore 12 181 40N21 86w31 5:46:04
Kimmell 57 30 41N24 85w33 5:42:12
Kinder 41 97 39N31 86w10 5:44:40
Kingman 23 146 39N58 87w17 5:49:08
Kingsbury 46 7 41N32 86w42 5:46:48
Kings Cave 31 166 38N13 86w07 5:44:28
Kingsford Heights 46 2 41N29 86w41 5:46:44
Kingsland 90 231 40N53 85w10 5:40:40
Kingston 16 101 39N21 85w33 5:42:12
Kingswood Terra 84 77 39N26 87w24 5:49:36
Kirkland 1 228 40N47 85w02 5:40:08
Kirklin 12 182 40N12 86w22 5:45:28
Kirkpatrick 54 148 40N09 86w58 5:47:52
Kirksville 53 344 39N03 86w36 5:46:24
Kirkville 26 59 38N20 87w30 5:50:00
Kitchel 97 39N41 84w52 5:39:28
Kitchell 81 313 39N41 84w54 5:39:36
Klaasville 45 2 41N22 87w26 5:49:44
Klemmes Corner 24 30 39N25 84w56 5:39:44
Klondike 79 147 40N26 86w56 5:47:44
Klondyke 61 73 39N47 87w22 5:49:28
Klondyke 83 73 39N40 87w24 5:49:36
Knapp Lake 57 30 41N24 85w37 5:42:28
Knight 82 55 37N58 87w28 5:49:52
Knighthood Village 73 101 39N33 85w48 5:43:12
Knightstown 33 108 39N48 85w31 5:42:04
Knightstown Lake 33 108 39N48 85w31 5:42:04
Knightsville 11 88 39N32 87w05 5:48:20
Kniman 37 2 41N09 87w08 5:48:32
Knob Hill 82 55 38N00 87w33 5:50:12
Knox 75 220 41N18 86w37 5:46:28
Kokomo 34 332 40N29 86w08 5:44:32
Koleen 28 193 38N58 86w50 5:47:20
Koontz Lake 75 221 41N28 86w29 5:45:56
Kossuth 88 165 38N36 86w06 5:44:24
Kouts 64 19 41N19 87w02 5:48:08
Kramer 86 129 40N18 87w15 5:49:00
Kreitsburg 45 6 41N31 87w28 5:49:52
Kriete Corners 36 147 38N58 85w58 5:43:52
Kurtz 36 147 38N58 86w12 5:44:48
Kyana 19 67 38N18 86w47 5:47:08
Kyle 15 33 39N04 84w54 5:39:36
Laconia 31 166 38N02 86w05 5:44:20
La Crosse 46 29 41N19 86w53 5:47:32
Ladoga 54 147 39N55 86w48 5:47:12
Lafayette 79 134 40N25 86w54 5:47:36
La Fontaine 85 268 40N40 85w43 5:42:52
Lagrange 44 31 41N39 85w25 5:41:40
Lagro 85 264 40N51 85w43 5:42:52
Lake Bodona 55 97 39N37 86w22 5:45:28
Lake Bruce 25 328 41N01 86w27 5:45:48
Lake Cicott 9 164 40N46 86w32 5:46:08
Lakecrest 29 97 40N03 86w01 5:44:04
Lake Dalecarlia 45 2 41N17 87w26 5:49:44
Lake Dilldear 15 33 39N01 85w04 5:40:16
Lake Edgewood 55 101 39N25 86w25 5:45:40
Lake Eliza 64 6 41N29 87w23 5:49:32
Lake Everett 2 233 41N05 85w10 5:40:40
Lake Front 45 6 41N39 87w30 5:50:00
Lake Geneva 78 35 38N45 85w04 5:40:16
Lake Hart 55 97 39N37 86w22 5:45:28
Lake Hills 45 23 41N28 87w27 5:49:48
Lake James 76 30 41N42 85w03 5:40:12
Lakeland 46 9 41N43 86w53 5:47:32
Lake Latonka 50 211 41N13 86w25 5:45:40
Lake Lincoln 74 64 38N07 87w00 5:48:00
Lake Manitou 25 328 41N03 86w11 5:44:44
Lake Maxine 55 113 39N27 86w43 5:46:52
Lake McCoy 16 101 39N21 85w33 5:42:12
Lake Mohee 5 196 40N27 85w22 5:41:28
Lake Noji 84 77 39N26 87w24 5:49:36
Lake of the Four Seasons 45 6 41N29 87w23 5:49:32
Lake of the Woods 50 211 41N27 86w09 5:44:36
Lake Park 46 3 41N43 86w32 5:46:08
Lake Primrose 55 101 39N25 86w25 5:45:40
Lake Shore 64 9 41N43 86w53 5:47:32
Lakeside 44 30 41N32 85w22 5:41:28
Lakeside Park 43 297 41N14 85w51 5:43:24
Lake Station 45 6 41N35 87w14 5:48:56
Lake Sullivan 77 71 39N06 87w25 5:49:40
Laketon 85 270 40N58 85w50 5:43:20
Lakeview 24 275 39N30 85w11 5:40:44
Lakeview 44 30 41N32 85w22 5:41:28
Lake View 64 6 41N29 87w23 5:49:32
Lakeview Estates 84 77 39N26 87w24 5:49:36
Lake Village 56 2 41N08 87w27 5:49:48
Lakeville 71 205 41N31 86w16 5:45:04
Lake Wood 27 284 40N34 85w42 5:42:48
Lakewood 84 77 39N26 87w24 5:49:36
Lakewood 91 162 40N45 86w46 5:47:04
Lakewood Hills 82 55 38N00 87w33 5:50:12
Lamar 74 64 38N04 86w54 5:47:36
Lamb 78 35 38N45 85w04 5:40:16
Lamb Lake 41 97 39N25 86w09 5:44:36
Lamong 29 97 40N08 86w13 5:44:52
Lamplighter 29 97 40N03 86w01 5:44:04
Lancaster 35 287 40N44 85w31 5:42:04
Lancaster 39 97 38N45 85w19 5:41:16
Lancaster Park 53 344 39N12 86w37 5:46:28
Landess 27 280 40N37 85w34 5:42:16
Lane 87 53 38N12 87w11 5:48:44
Lanesville 31 188 38N14 85w59 5:43:56
Langenbaum Lake 66 181 41N09 86w29 5:45:56
Lantana Estate 73 101 39N33 85w48 5:43:12
Lantern Hills 27 284 40N34 85w42 5:42:48
Lantern Park 18 254 40N11 85w23 5:41:32
Laotto 57 48 41N17 85w12 5:40:48
La Paz 50 217 41N28 86w18 5:45:12
Lapaz 50 217 41N28 86w18 5:45:12
Lapel 48 108 40N04 85w51 5:43:24
La Porte 46 8 41N36 86w43 5:46:52
Larimer Hill 84 77 39N28 87w26 5:49:44
Larwill 92 230 41N11 85w37 5:42:28
Laud 92 228 41N03 85w27 5:41:48
Laughery 69 275 39N15 85w15 5:41:00
Lauramie 79 147 40N16 86w48 5:47:12
Laurel 24 275 39N29 85w12 5:40:48
Lawrence 49 100 39N50 86w02 5:44:08
Lawrenceburg 15 37 39N06 84w52 5:39:28
Lawrenceport 47 344 38N44 86w28 5:45:52
Lawrenceville 15 33 39N14 85w06 5:40:24
Lawton 66 181 41N06 86w31 5:46:04
Leases Corner 9 165 40N52 86w22 5:45:28
Leavenworth 13 169 38N12 86w21 5:45:24
Lebanon 6 250 40N03 86w28 5:45:52
Lee 91 147 40N54 86w58 5:47:52
Leesburg 2 233 41N03 85w08 5:40:32
Leesburg 43 294 41N20 85w51 5:43:24
Leesville 47 344 38N51 86w30 5:46:00
Legendary Hills 49 100 39N53 86w16 5:45:04
Leininger Acres 80 121 40N18 86w03 5:44:12
Leipsic 59 160 38N41 86w21 5:45:24
Leisure 48 109 40N21 85w44 5:42:56
Leiters Ford 25 328 41N07 86w23 5:45:32
Lena 11 89 39N38 87w02 5:48:08
Leo 2 228 41N13 85w01 5:40:04
Leopold 62 69 38N06 86w35 5:46:20
Leota 72 320 38N41 85w46 5:43:04
Leroy 45 29 41N22 87w16 5:49:04
Letts 16 101 39N14 85w34 5:42:16
Lewis 84 83 39N16 87w16 5:49:04
Lewisburg 9 165 40N42 86w07 5:44:28
Lewis Creek 73 101 39N22 85w50 5:43:20
Lewisville 33 257 39N48 85w21 5:41:24
Lewisville 55 113 39N31 86w48 5:47:12
Lexington 8 165 40N29 86w32 5:46:08
Lexington 72 320 38N39 85w38 5:42:32
Liber 38 291 40N26 84w59 5:39:56
Liberty 81 314 39N38 84w56 5:39:44
Liberty Center 90 228 40N42 85w17 5:41:08
Liberty Hills 2 233 41N04 85w10 5:40:40
Liberty Mills 85 269 41N02 85w44 5:42:56
Liberty Park 45 5 41N26 87w22 5:49:28
Libertyville 84 82 39N36 87w31 5:50:04
Licking 5 196 40N26 85w23 5:41:32
Liggett 84 77 39N28 87w26 5:49:44
Ligonier 57 49 41N28 85w35 5:42:20
Lilly Dale 62 69 37N57 86w46 5:47:04
Lima 44 30 41N44 85w26 5:41:44
Limberlost Hills 84 77 39N29 87w22 5:49:28
Limedale 67 126 39N39 86w52 5:47:28
Lincoln 9 164 40N37 86w12 5:44:48
Lincoln City 74 64 38N07 87w00 5:48:00
Lincoln Heights 10 166 38N18 85w45 5:43:00
Lincoln Heights 48 101 40N16 85w41 5:42:44
Lincoln Hills 64 12 41N28 87w06 5:48:24
Lincoln Park 10 166 38N18 85w45 5:43:00
Lincolnshire 20 265 41N27 86w00 5:44:00
Lincolnshire 27 284 40N34 85w42 5:42:48
Lincoln Village 45 6 41N30 87w19 5:49:16
Lincolnville 85 264 40N44 85w41 5:42:44
Linden 54 153 40N11 86w54 5:47:36
Lindenwood 49 100 39N41 86w07 5:44:28
Linkville 50 211 41N20 86w19 5:45:16
Linn Grove 1 228 40N38 85w02 5:40:08
Linnsburg 54 147 40N00 86w56 5:47:44
Linton 28 92 39N02 87w10 5:48:40
Linwood 48 101 40N12 85w41 5:42:44
Linwood 49 100 39N47 86w07 5:44:28
Lippe 65 58 37N56 87w54 5:51:36
Lisbon 57 30 41N26 85w16 5:41:04
Little 63 59 38N29 87w17 5:49:08
Little Acres 36 147 38N58 85w58 5:43:52
Little Point 55 113 39N24 86w46 5:47:04
Little Saint Louis 31 166 38N20 86w13 5:44:52
Little York 88 165 38N42 85w54 5:43:36
Liverpool 45 17 41N33 87w18 5:49:12
Livonia 88 165 38N33 86w17 5:45:08
Lizton 32 247 39N53 86w32 5:46:08
Lochiel 4 147 40N37 87w19 5:49:16
Locke 20 264 41N29 86w01 5:44:04
Lockhart 63 59 38N17 87w09 5:48:36
Lockport 8 165 40N46 86w36 5:46:24
Lodi 61 128 39N57 87w24 5:49:36
Logan 15 33 39N15 84w52 5:39:28
Logansport 9 173 40N45 86w22 5:45:28
Lomax 75 28 41N12 86w53 5:47:32
London 73 101 39N35 85w52 5:43:28
London Heights 73 101 39N35 85w52 5:43:28
Lonetree 28 93 39N10 87w12 5:48:48
Long Acres 73 101 39N33 85w48 5:43:12
Long Beach 46 9 41N45 86w51 5:47:24
Long Lake 76 32 41N44 84w53 5:39:32
Long Lake 85 264 41N00 85w46 5:43:04
Long Lake Island 64 6 41N29 87w23 5:49:32
Longnecker 15 33 39N16 84w52 5:39:28
Longview Beach 10 166 38N18 85w45 5:43:00
Loogootee 51 246 38N41 86w55 5:47:40
Lookout 69 275 39N14 85w06 5:40:24
Loon Lake 57 30 41N12 85w28 5:41:52
Lorane 92 228 41N13 85w32 5:42:08
Loree 52 335 40N40 86w07 5:44:28
Losantville 68 307 40N02 85w11 5:40:44
Lost Creek 84 82 39N29 87w18 5:49:12
Lost River 51 322 38N34 86w46 5:47:04
Lottaville 45 6 41N30 87w22 5:49:28
Lotus 81 313 39N38 84w56 5:39:44
Lovett 40 128 38N55 85w38 5:42:32
Lowell 3 147 39N13 85w54 5:43:36
Lowell 45 27 41N17 87w24 5:49:36

INDIANA

Lower Sunset Park 8	162	40N45	86w46	5:47:04
Loyal 25	328	41N04	86w13	5:44:52
Luce 74	61	37N55	87w12	5:48:48
Lucerne 9	164	40N52	86w24	5:45:36
Lukens Lake 85	264	40N55	85w55	5:43:40
Luray 33	253	40N03	85w24	5:41:36
Luther 35	287	41N00	85w34	5:42:16
Lutheran Lake 3	147	38N58	85w58	5:43:52
Lydick 71	202	41N42	86w08	5:44:32
Lyford 61	73	39N40	87w21	5:49:24
Lynhurst 49	100	39N45	86w14	5:44:56
Lynn 68	312	40N03	84w56	5:39:44
Lynnville 87	53	38N12	87w18	5:49:12
Lyons 28	95	38N59	87w05	5:48:20
Lyonsville 21	272	39N40	85w08	5:40:32
Mace 54	147	39N58	86w50	5:47:20
Mac-Fair-Mar 9	165	40N46	86w22	5:45:28
Mackey 26	59	38N15	87w23	5:49:32
Macy 52	335	40N58	86w08	5:44:32
Madison 39	98	38N44	85w23	5:41:32
Magley 1	231	40N50	84w56	5:39:44
Magnet 62	69	38N06	86w28	5:45:52
Mahalasville 55	101	39N25	86w25	5:45:40
Mahon 35	287	40N49	85w32	5:42:08
Mahoning 45	6	41N38	87w28	5:49:52
Majenica 35	287	40N46	85w27	5:41:48
Malden 64	2	41N23	87w02	5:48:08
Malott Park 49	100	39N50	86w09	5:44:36
Maltersville 19	67	38N18	86w57	5:47:48
Manchester 15	33	39N09	85w01	5:40:04
Manhattan 67	128	39N36	86w52	5:47:28
Manilla 70	108	39N35	85w37	5:42:28
Manor Woods 2	233	41N04	85w10	5:40:40
Mansfield 61	128	39N41	87w06	5:48:24
Manson 12	183	40N14	86w35	5:46:20
Manville 39	97	38N45	85w19	5:41:16
Maple Lane 71	208	41N43	86w12	5:44:48
Maples 2	233	41N03	85w08	5:40:32
Mapleton 49	100	39N49	86w11	5:44:44
Maple Valley 33	253	39N47	85w37	5:42:28
Maplewood 32	247	39N46	86w31	5:46:04
Maplewood 84	77	39N28	87w26	5:49:44
Maplewood Park 2	233	41N06	85w08	5:40:32
Marco 28	194	38N59	87w05	5:48:20
Marengo 13	177	38N22	86w21	5:45:24
Mariah Hill 74	64	38N10	86w55	5:47:40
Marietta 73	101	39N33	85w48	5:43:12
Marineland Gardens 43	291	41N21	85w49	5:43:16
Marion 27	281	40N32	85w40	5:42:40
Marion Heights 84	77	39N28	87w27	5:49:48
Marion Manor 64	6	41N29	87w23	5:49:32
Markland 78	35	38N47	84w55	5:39:40
Markle 35	288	40N49	85w21	5:41:24
Markleville 48	101	39N59	85w37	5:42:28
Marlin Hills 53	344	39N12	86w37	5:46:28
Marquette Farm 84	82	39N42	86w51	5:47:24
Marrs 65	58	37N57	87w44	5:50:56
Marrs Center 65	58	37N56	87w54	5:51:36
Marshall 61	128	39N51	87w11	5:48:44
Marshfield 86	190	40N15	87w27	5:49:48
Mars Hill 49	100	39N45	86w14	5:44:56
Martin 82	55	37N59	87w37	5:50:28
Martin Heights 88	165	38N36	86w06	5:44:24
Martinsburg 88	165	38N30	86w01	5:44:04
Martinsville 55	108	39N26	86w25	5:45:40
Martz 11	89	39N17	87w07	5:48:28
Maryland 84	77	39N26	87w25	5:49:40
Marysville 10	166	38N35	85w39	5:42:36
Marysville 63	59	38N23	87w13	5:48:52
Marywood 84	77	39N26	87w25	5:49:40
Matlock Heights 53	344	39N12	86w37	5:46:28
Matthews 27	280	40N23	85w30	5:42:00
Mattix Corner 12	181	40N17	86w31	5:46:04
Mauckport 31	166	38N01	86w12	5:44:48
Maumee 2	228	41N08	84w51	5:39:24
Mauzy 70	101	39N37	85w27	5:41:48
Max 6	247	40N04	86w28	5:45:52
Maxinkuckee 50	211	41N13	86w25	5:45:40
Maxville 68	307	40N15	85w10	5:40:40
Maxwell 30	97	39N52	85w46	5:43:04
Maxwell 55	101	39N25	86w25	5:45:40
Mayfield 18	254	40N12	85w21	5:41:24
Maynard 45	6	41N33	87w30	5:50:00
May Ridge 3	147	39N18	85w46	5:43:04
Mays 70	101	39N45	85w26	5:41:44
Maysville 14	85	38N40	87w11	5:48:44
Maywood 49	100	39N45	86w14	5:44:56
McBride Heights 10	166	38N18	85w45	5:43:00
McCarthy Addition 48	101	40N16	85w41	5:42:44
McCarty 41	100	39N40	86w09	5:44:36
McClellan 56	2	41N02	87w27	5:49:48
McCol Place 88	165	38N36	86w06	5:44:24
McCool 64	23	41N29	87w28	5:49:52
McCordsville 30	97	39N54	85w55	5:43:40
McCoysburg 37	226	40N56	87w01	5:48:04
McCutchanville 82	55	38N00	87w33	5:50:12
McDaniel 55	101	39N25	86w25	5:45:40
McGrawsville 52	338	40N36	85w58	5:43:52
McKinley 88	165	38N37	86w17	5:45:08
McKinley Town and Country Sh 71	208	41N40	86w10	5:44:40
McNatts 90	196	40N33	85w17	5:41:08
Meadowbrook 2	233	41N04	85w03	5:40:12
Meadowbrook 79	147	40N25	86w53	5:47:32
Meadowdale 45	6	41N30	87w19	5:49:16

Meadowland Estates 45	6	41N30	87w19	5:49:16
Meadowland Manor 45	6	41N30	87w19	5:49:16
Meadowood 20	271	41N41	85w59	5:43:56
Meadowood 49	100	39N48	86w15	5:45:00
Meadowood Estates 48	101	40N21	85w44	5:42:56
Meadowview 9	165	40N46	86w22	5:45:28
Mead Village 3	147	39N13	85w54	5:43:36
Mecca 61	73	39N44	87w20	5:49:20
Mechanicsburg 6	251	40N12	86w21	5:45:24
Mechanicsburg 33	253	41N17	87w26	5:49:44
Medaryville 66	181	41N05	86w55	5:47:40
Medford 18	253	40N04	85w20	5:41:20
Medina 86	156	40N26	87w08	5:48:32
Medora 36	147	38N49	86w10	5:44:40
Mellott 23	136	40N10	87w09	5:48:36
Melody Acres 43	297	41N14	85w51	5:43:24
Melody Hill 82	55	38N00	87w33	5:50:12
Meltzer 73	101	39N33	85w48	5:43:12
Memphis 10	179	38N29	85w46	5:43:04
Mentone 43	243	41N10	86w02	5:44:08
Mentor 19	67	38N17	86w42	5:46:48
Meridian Hills 49	100	39N53	86w11	5:44:44
Merom 77	80	39N03	87w34	5:50:16
Merriam 57	30	41N18	85w26	5:41:44
Merrillville 45	6	41N29	87w20	5:49:20
Messick 33	253	39N56	85w26	5:41:44
Metamora 24	275	39N26	85w08	5:40:32
Metea 9	165	40N52	86w19	5:45:16
Metz 76	30	41N37	84w50	5:39:20
Mexico 52	338	40N49	86w07	5:44:28
Miami 52	335	40N37	86w08	5:44:32
Miami Bend 9	165	40N46	86w22	5:45:28
Miami Trails 71	208	41N38	86w14	5:44:56
Michaels 27	284	40N34	85w42	5:42:48
Michiana Shores 46	2	41N45	86w49	5:47:16
Michigan City 46	9	41N43	86w54	5:47:36
Michigantown 12	181	40N22	86w24	5:45:36
Mickleyville 49	100	39N45	86w14	5:44:56
Middle 32	247	39N51	86w28	5:45:52
Middleboro 89	318	39N52	84w52	5:39:28
Middlebury 20	259	41N41	85w42	5:42:48
Middlefork 12	181	40N25	86w24	5:45:36
Middlefork 39	161	38N53	85w31	5:42:04
Middletown 33	108	40N06	85w32	5:42:08
Middletown 73	108	39N27	85w40	5:42:40
Middletown Park 18	254	40N11	85w23	5:41:32
Midland 28	93	39N07	87w12	5:48:48
Midway 74	61	38N00	87w09	5:48:36
Mier 27	284	40N35	85w50	5:43:20
Mifflin 13	169	38N20	86w28	5:45:52
Milan 69	277	39N07	85w08	5:40:32
Milan Center 2	233	41N04	85w03	5:40:12
Milford 16	101	39N21	85w33	5:42:12
Milford 43	294	41N25	85w51	5:43:24
Mill 27	285	40N29	85w38	5:42:32
Mill Creek 23	156	40N01	87w16	5:49:04
Mill Creek 29	97	40N03	86w01	5:44:04
Mill Creek 46	2	41N35	86w32	5:46:08
Milledgeville 6	247	40N04	86w28	5:45:52
Miller 15	33	39N11	84w52	5:39:28
Miller 45	20	41N35	87w15	5:49:00
Millersburg 20	261	41N32	85w42	5:42:48
Millersburg 29	97	40N10	86w01	5:44:04
Millersburg 59	160	38N33	86w20	5:45:20
Millersburg 87	53	38N03	87w22	5:49:28
Millersville 49	100	39N50	86w04	5:44:16
Mill Grove 5	198	40N24	85w17	5:41:08
Millhousen 16	101	39N13	85w26	5:41:44
Milligan 61	128	39N51	87w03	5:48:12
Millport 88	165	38N51	86w06	5:44:24
Milltown 13	178	38N21	86w17	5:45:08
Millville 33	257	39N56	85w26	5:41:44
Milo 35	287	40N37	85w30	5:42:00
Milroy 70	101	39N30	85w28	5:41:52
Milton 58	33	38N59	85w00	5:40:00
Milton 89	317	39N47	85w09	5:40:36
Mineral 28	193	39N02	86w56	5:47:44
Mineral Springs 43	291	41N20	85w51	5:43:24
Mishawaka 71	207	41N40	86w11	5:44:44
Mitchell 47	341	38N44	86w28	5:45:52
Mitchellville 49	100	39N47	86w07	5:44:28
Mitcheltree 51	159	38N47	86w44	5:46:56
Mixersville 24	30	39N29	84w50	5:39:20
Moberly 31	166	38N20	86w13	5:44:52
Modesto 53	344	39N12	86w37	5:46:28
Modoc 68	307	40N03	85w08	5:40:32
Mongo 44	30	41N41	85w17	5:41:08
Monitor 79	147	40N25	86w53	5:47:32
Monmouth 1	228	40N50	84w56	5:39:44
Monon 91	154	40N52	86w53	5:47:32
Monoquet 43	297	41N14	85w51	5:43:24
Monroe 1	228	40N45	84w56	5:39:44
Monroe 79	147	40N25	86w53	5:47:32
Monroe City 42	86	38N37	87w21	5:49:24
Monroe Manor 46	8	41N37	86w44	5:46:56
Monroeville 2	230	40N59	84w52	5:39:28
Monrovia 55	101	39N35	86w29	5:45:56
Montclair 32	247	39N53	86w32	5:46:08
Monterey 66	182	41N09	86w29	5:45:56
Monterey Village 29	97	40N03	86w01	5:44:04
Montezuma 61	70	39N47	87w22	5:49:28
Montgomery 14	85	38N40	87w03	5:48:12
Monticello 91	162	40N45	86w46	5:47:04
Montmorenci 79	137	40N28	87w02	5:48:08
Montpelier 5	196	40N33	85w17	5:41:08
Moonville 48	101	40N16	85w41	5:42:44

Moore 17	230	41N26	84w52	5:39:28
Moorefield 49	100	39N47	86w13	5:44:52
Moorefield 78	35	38N45	85w19	5:41:16
Mooreland 33	253	40N00	85w16	5:41:04
Moores Hill 15	33	39N07	85w05	5:40:20
Mooresville 55	98	39N37	86w22	5:45:28
Moral 73	101	39N39	85w54	5:43:36
Moran 12	183	40N23	86w31	5:46:04
Morgan Park 64	4	41N37	87w06	5:48:24
Morgantown 55	110	39N22	86w16	5:45:04
Morningside 18	254	40N14	85w22	5:41:28
Morocco 56	2	40N57	87w27	5:49:48
Morris 69	278	39N17	85w11	5:40:44
Morristown 73	101	39N40	85w42	5:42:48
Morton 67	128	39N39	86w52	5:47:28
Moscow 70	101	39N30	85w34	5:42:16
Mott Station 31	166	38N19	86w06	5:44:24
Mound 86	187	40N09	87w28	5:49:52
Mount Auburn 73	101	39N24	85w54	5:43:36
Mount Auburn 89	317	39N49	85w11	5:40:44
Mount Ayr 56	2	40N57	87w18	5:49:12
Mount Carmel 24	30	39N24	84w53	5:39:32
Mount Carmel 88	165	38N37	86w17	5:45:08
Mount Etna 35	287	40N45	85w34	5:42:16
Mount Healthy 3	147	39N13	85w54	5:43:36
Mount Jackson 49	100	39N47	86w13	5:44:52
Mount Meridian 67	128	39N39	86w52	5:47:28
Mount Olympus 26	59	38N30	87w35	5:50:20
Mount Pisgah 44	30	41N39	85w25	5:41:40
Mount Pleasant 18	253	40N06	85w19	5:41:16
Mount Pleasant 41	97	39N29	86w03	5:44:12
Mount Pleasant 51	200	38N43	86w55	5:47:40
Mount Pleasant 62	69	38N07	86w31	5:46:04
Mounts 26	59	38N18	87w45	5:51:00
Mount Sinai 15	33	39N07	85w05	5:40:20
Mount Sterling 78	35	38N47	85w04	5:40:16
Mount Summit 33	253	40N00	85w23	5:41:32
Mount Vernon 65	58	37N56	87w54	5:51:36
Mount Zion 90	228	40N38	85w20	5:41:20
Mulberry 12	175	40N21	86w39	5:46:36
Mull 68	307	40N10	84w59	5:39:56
Muncie 18	254	40N12	85w23	5:41:32
Munster 45	24	41N34	87w31	5:50:04
Muren 63	59	38N23	87w13	5:48:52
Murray 90	228	40N43	85w07	5:40:28
Nabb 10	166	38N36	85w38	5:42:32
Napoleon 69	275	39N12	85w20	5:41:20
Nappanee 20	265	41N27	86w00	5:44:00
Nashville 7	145	39N12	86w15	5:45:00
Navilleton 22	166	38N19	85w52	5:43:28
Nead 52	335	40N42	86w07	5:44:28
Nebraska 40	128	39N04	85w28	5:41:52
Needham 41	101	39N29	86w00	5:44:00
Needmore 7	145	39N14	86w20	5:45:20
Needmore 47	344	38N51	86w30	5:46:00
Negangards Corner 69	275	39N07	85w08	5:40:32
Nevada 80	119	40N23	86w05	5:44:20
Nevada Mills 76	30	41N44	85w05	5:40:20
Nevins 84	82	39N34	87w15	5:49:00
New Albany 22	176	38N18	85w49	5:43:16
New Alsace 15	33	39N13	85w00	5:40:00
New Amsterdam 31	166	38N06	86w16	5:45:04
Newark 28	193	39N08	86w48	5:47:12
Newark Village 29	97	39N58	86w07	5:44:28
New Augusta 49	100	39N53	86w14	5:44:56
New Bellsville 7	147	39N13	85w54	5:43:36
Newbern 3	147	39N13	85w54	5:43:36
Newberry 28	191	38N55	87w01	5:48:04
New Boston 31	166	38N03	85w48	5:43:12
New Boston 74	64	38N02	86w51	5:47:24
New Brunswick 6	247	40N04	86w28	5:45:52
Newburgh 87	53	37N57	87w24	5:49:36
New Burlington 18	254	40N11	85w23	5:41:32
New Carlisle 71	201	41N42	86w31	5:46:04
New Castle 33	256	39N55	85w22	5:41:28
New Chicago 45	6	41N33	87w16	5:49:04
New Columbus 48	101	40N07	85w42	5:42:48
New Corydon 38	287	40N32	84w58	5:39:52
New Durham 46	21	41N34	86w53	5:47:32
New Elizabethtown 36	147	38N58	85w58	5:43:52
New Elliott 45	6	41N30	87w25	5:49:40
New Fairfield 24	30	39N25	84w56	5:39:44
New Farmington 36	147	38N58	85w58	5:43:52
New Frankfort 72	320	38N41	85w46	5:43:04
New Garden 89	282	39N58	84w55	5:39:40
New Goshen 84	82	39N35	87w28	5:49:52
New Harmony 65	58	38N08	87w56	5:51:44
New Haven 2	233	41N04	85w01	5:40:04
New Haven Heights 2	233	41N04	85w03	5:40:12
New Hope 60	344	39N17	86w46	5:47:04
New Hope 87	53	38N03	87w16	5:49:04
New Lancaster 80	116	40N21	85w44	5:42:56
Newland 37	226	40N56	87w09	5:48:36
New Lebanon 77	80	39N02	87w28	5:49:52
New Lisbon 33	253	39N52	85w16	5:41:04
New Lisbon 68	311	40N12	84w48	5:39:12
New London 34	165	40N26	86w11	5:44:44
New Marion 69	275	39N04	85w23	5:41:32
New Market 54	149	39N57	86w55	5:47:40

New Maysville 67 128 39N48 86w43 5:46:52
New Middletown 31 189 38N10 86w03 5:44:12
New Mount Pleasant 38 291 40N21 85w04 5:40:16
New Palestine 30 101 39N43 85w53 5:43:32
New Paris 20 260 41N30 85w50 5:43:20
New Pekin 88 165 38N30 86w01 5:44:04
New Philadelphia 88 165 38N36 86w06 5:44:24
New Pittsburg 68 311 40N17 84w55 5:39:40
New Point 16 101 39N19 85w20 5:41:20
Newport 83 79 39N53 87w25 5:49:40
New Providence 10 166 38N28 85w57 5:43:48
New Richmond 54 147 40N11 86w59 5:47:56
New Ross 54 147 39N58 86w43 5:46:52
New Salem 70 101 39N33 85w21 5:41:24
New Salisbury 31 166 38N19 86w06 5:44:24
New Santa Fe 52 335 40N42 86w07 5:44:28
Newton 37 227 40N58 87w14 5:48:56
Newtonville 74 64 38N00 86w57 5:47:48
Newtown 23 156 40N13 87w09 5:48:36
New Trenton 24 30 39N19 84w54 5:39:36
New Unionville 53 344 39N13 86w28 5:45:52
Newville 17 228 41N21 84w51 5:39:24
New Washington 10 166 38N34 85w33 5:42:12
New Waverly 9 174 40N46 86w12 5:44:48
New Whiteland 41 97 39N34 86w06 5:44:24
New Winchester 32 113 39N46 86w31 5:46:04
Nibbyville 20 259 41N43 85w49 5:43:16
Niles 18 253 40N21 85w16 5:41:04
Nine Mile Place 2 233 41N01 85w10 5:40:40
Nineveh 41 101 39N23 86w06 5:44:24
Noblesville 29 245 40N03 86w01 5:44:04
Noblitt Falls 3 147 39N13 85w54 5:43:36
Nora 49 100 39N54 86w08 5:44:32
Nora Plaza 49 100 39N54 86w08 5:44:32
Norland Park 17 234 41N22 85w04 5:40:16
Normal 27 280 40N30 85w49 5:43:16
Norman 36 147 38N57 86w16 5:45:04
Normanda 80 121 40N18 86w03 5:44:12
Normandy Addition 18 254 40N11 85w23 5:41:32
Norris 88 165 38N36 86w06 5:44:24
Norristown 73 101 39N22 85w50 5:43:20
North 50 211 41N26 86w17 5:45:08
Northaven 10 166 38N18 85w45 5:43:00
North Bend 75 221 41N13 86w32 5:46:08
Northcliff 3 147 39N13 85w54 5:43:36
North Columbus 3 130 39N13 85w54 5:43:36
North Crows Nest 49 100 39N49 86w11 5:44:44
North Delphi 8 133 40N35 86w40 5:46:40
Northeast 59 160 38N38 86w21 5:45:24
Northern Meadows 6 100 39N53 86w16 5:45:04
Northfield 6 249 39N53 86w16 5:45:04
Northfield Village 6 247 40N04 86w28 5:45:52
North Gate 3 147 39N13 85w54 5:43:36
Northgate Village 27 284 40N34 85w42 5:42:48
North Grove 52 338 40N37 85w59 5:43:56
North Harbor 29 97 40N03 86w01 5:44:04
North Hayden 45 26 41N17 87w26 5:49:44
North Judson 75 10 41N13 86w46 5:47:04
North Liberty 71 210 41N32 86w26 5:45:44
North Madison 39 98 38N45 85w19 5:41:16
North Manchester 85 269 41N00 85w46 5:43:04
North Oaks 90 228 40N43 85w07 5:40:28
North Ogilville 3 147 39N13 85w54 5:43:36
Northpine Estates 84 82 39N37 87w21 5:49:24
North Ridge Village 29 100 39N54 86w08 5:44:32
North Salem 32 251 39N52 86w39 5:46:36
North Terre Haute 84 77 39N31 87w24 5:49:36
North Vernon 40 126 39N00 85w38 5:42:32
North Webster 43 291 41N20 85w45 5:43:00
Northwest 59 160 38N39 86w38 5:46:32
Northwood 20 265 41N27 86w00 5:44:00
Northwood 27 284 40N34 85w42 5:42:48
Northwood 67 128 39N39 86w52 5:47:28
Northwood 84 82 39N42 86w51 5:47:24
Northwood Hills 29 97 39N58 86w07 5:44:28
North Wood Park 64 6 41N29 87w23 5:49:32
Norton 19 67 38N33 86w37 5:46:28
Nortonsburg 3 147 39N13 85w54 5:43:36
Norway 91 181 40N47 86w46 5:47:04
Notre Dame 71 208 41N42 86w14 5:44:56
Nottingham 90 228 40N37 85w09 5:40:36
Nulltown 21 272 39N34 85w10 5:40:40
Numa 61 73 39N38 87w21 5:49:24
Nyesville 61 128 39N46 87w17 5:49:08
Nyona Lake 25 328 40N58 86w08 5:44:32
Oakcrest 3 147 39N13 85w54 5:43:36
Oakdale 52 335 40N42 86w07 5:44:28
Oakford 34 331 40N25 86w06 5:44:24
Oak Forest 24 30 39N25 84w56 5:39:44
Oak Grove 4 147 40N32 87w17 5:49:08
Oak Grove 75 221 41N13 86w25 5:45:40
Oak Grove 84 77 39N26 87w24 5:49:36
Oak Hills 3 147 39N18 85w46 5:43:04
Oakland City 26 59 38N20 87w21 5:49:24
Oaklandon 49 100 39N50 86w01 5:44:04
Oaklawn Terrace 10 166 38N18 85w45 5:43:00
Oak Park 10 176 38N19 85w41 5:42:44
Oaktown 42 86 38N52 87w27 5:49:48
Oakville 18 253 40N05 85w23 5:41:32
Oakwood 76 30 41N32 84w55 5:39:40
Oakwood Commons 27 284 40N34 85w42 5:42:48
Oakwood Manor 46 9 41N43 86w53 5:47:32
Oakwood Park 43 291 41N21 85w49 5:43:16
Oakwood Shores 76 30 41N32 84w55 5:39:40
Oatsville 26 59 38N29 87w17 5:49:08
Ober 75 221 41N16 86w31 5:46:04
Occident 70 101 39N44 85w34 5:42:16
Ockley 8 128 40N29 86w38 5:46:32
Odell 79 147 40N17 87w05 5:48:20
Odon 14 91 38N51 86w59 5:47:56
Ogden 33 108 39N48 85w31 5:42:04
Ogden Dunes 64 6 41N38 87w11 5:48:44
Ogilville 3 147 39N13 85w54 5:43:36
Ohio Falls 10 166 38N18 85w45 5:43:00
Oil 62 69 38N11 86w35 5:46:20
Old Bargersville 41 97 39N31 86w10 5:44:40
Old Bath 24 30 39N25 84w56 5:39:44
Oldenburg 24 275 39N21 85w12 5:40:48
Old Milan 69 275 39N07 85w08 5:40:32
Old Otto 10 166 38N34 85w33 5:42:12
Old Pekin 88 165 38N30 86w01 5:44:04
Old Saint Louis 3 147 39N18 85w46 5:43:04
Old Stone 87 53 37N57 87w24 5:49:36
Old Tip Town 50 328 41N12 86w07 5:44:28
Oldtown 15 37 39N07 84w52 5:39:28
Old Watson 10 166 38N18 85w45 5:43:00
Olean 69 275 39N04 85w15 5:41:00
Oliver 65 58 37N56 87w54 5:51:36
Omega 29 97 40N10 86w01 5:44:04
Ontario 44 30 41N43 85w25 5:41:40
Onward 9 164 40N42 86w12 5:44:48
Oolitic 47 344 38N54 86w32 5:46:08
Ora 75 222 41N10 86w33 5:46:12
Orange 21 272 39N34 85w17 5:41:08
Orangeville 59 160 38N38 86w33 5:46:12
Orchard Heights 71 208 41N40 86w14 5:44:56
Orchard Park 29 100 39N47 86w09 5:44:36
Oregon Heights 45 17 41N34 87w17 5:49:08
Orestes 48 112 40N17 85w44 5:42:56
Oriole 62 69 38N06 86w35 5:46:20
Orland 76 30 41N44 85w10 5:40:40
Orleans 59 125 38N40 86w27 5:45:48
Ormas 57 30 41N18 85w33 5:42:12
Osborn Landing 43 297 41N14 85w51 5:43:24
Osceola 71 204 41N40 86w05 5:44:20
Osgood 69 279 39N08 85w18 5:41:12
Osolo 20 271 41N43 85w57 5:43:48
Ossian 90 228 40N53 85w10 5:40:40
Oswego 43 291 41N19 85w48 5:43:12
Otis 46 21 41N36 86w54 5:47:36
Otisco 10 166 38N33 85w40 5:42:40
Otsego 76 30 41N34 84w55 5:39:40
Otterbein 4 124 40N29 87w06 5:48:24
Otter Lake 76 30 41N38 85w00 5:40:00
Otter Village 69 275 39N04 85w23 5:41:32
Otto 10 166 38N34 85w33 5:42:12
Otwell 63 59 38N27 87w06 5:48:24
Owasco 8 128 40N27 86w37 5:46:28
Owensburg 28 193 38N56 86w44 5:46:56
Owensville 26 59 38N16 87w41 5:50:44
Oxford 4 123 40N31 87w15 5:49:00
Packertown 43 291 41N07 85w46 5:43:04
Paint Mill Lake 84 77 39N26 87w24 5:49:36
Palestine 24 30 39N25 84w56 5:39:44
Palestine 43 291 41N10 85w58 5:43:52
Palmer 45 6 41N29 87w23 5:49:32
Palmyra 31 166 38N24 86w07 5:44:28
Paoli 59 143 38N33 86w28 5:45:52
Papakeechie Lake 43 291 41N21 85w49 5:43:16
Paradise 87 53 37N57 87w24 5:49:36
Paradise Lakes 55 101 39N25 86w25 5:45:40
Paragon 55 115 39N24 86w34 5:46:16
Paris Crossing 40 128 38N50 85w39 5:42:36
Parish Grove 4 147 40N36 87w28 5:49:52
Park 28 193 39N02 86w56 5:47:44
Parker City 68 307 40N11 85w12 5:40:48
Parkersburg 54 147 39N55 86w48 5:47:12
Parkers Settlement 65 58 38N06 87w47 5:51:08
Park Fletcher 49 100 39N45 86w14 5:44:56
Park Forest Estates 3 147 39N13 85w54 5:43:36
Parkmor 20 271 41N41 85w59 5:43:56
Park Ridge 53 344 39N12 86w37 5:46:28
Parkside 3 147 39N13 85w54 5:43:36
Park View Heights 52 335 40N42 86w07 5:44:28
Parkway Hills 2 233 41N04 85w10 5:40:40
Parkwood 10 166 38N18 85w45 5:43:00
Parr 37 2 41N02 87w12 5:48:48
Pate 58 33 38N57 84w51 5:39:24
Patricksburg 60 344 39N19 86w57 5:47:48
Patriot 78 35 38N50 84w50 5:39:20
Patronville 74 61 37N53 87w03 5:48:12
Patton 8 162 40N45 86w46 5:47:04
Patton Hill 47 344 38N51 86w30 5:46:00
Patton Lake 55 101 39N25 86w25 5:45:40
Paw Paw 85 264 40N55 85w52 5:43:28
Paxton 77 80 39N01 87w24 5:49:36
Paynesville 39 101 38N43 85w28 5:41:52
Peabody 92 228 41N04 85w31 5:42:04
Pearsontown 59 160 38N22 86w21 5:45:24
Pecksburg 32 251 39N42 86w31 5:46:04
Peerless 47 344 38N51 86w30 5:46:00
Pekin 88 165 38N30 86w00 5:44:00
Pelzer 87 53 37N59 87w15 5:49:00
Pence 86 187 40N22 87w31 5:50:04
Pendleton 48 101 40N00 85w45 5:43:00
Penn Park 76 30 41N32 84w55 5:39:40
Penntown 69 275 39N14 85w06 5:40:24
Pennville 38 291 40N30 85w09 5:40:36
Pennville 89 317 39N49 85w11 5:40:44
Peoga 7 147 39N25 86w09 5:44:36
Peoria 52 335 40N42 86w07 5:44:28
Peppertown 24 275 39N27 85w08 5:40:32
Perkinsville 48 101 40N07 85w42 5:42:48
Perry Manor 49 100 39N41 86w07 5:44:28
Perrysburg 52 335 40N58 86w08 5:44:32
Perrysville 83 84 40N03 87w26 5:49:44
Pershing 36 139 39N00 86w09 5:44:36
Pershing 89 317 39N49 85w09 5:40:36
Perth 11 89 39N35 87w12 5:48:48
Peru 52 339 40N45 86w04 5:44:16
Petersburg 63 59 38N30 87w17 5:49:08
Peterson 1 228 40N50 84w56 5:39:44
Petersville 3 147 39N13 85w54 5:43:36
Petroleum 90 228 40N37 85w09 5:40:36
Pettit 79 147 40N25 86w53 5:47:32
Pheasant Run 2 233 41N04 85w09 5:40:36
Philomath 81 313 39N44 85w00 5:40:00
Phlox 34 334 40N24 85w56 5:43:44
Pickard 12 181 40N12 86w21 5:45:24
Pickwick Park 43 291 41N21 85w49 5:43:16
Pierce 88 165 38N31 86w04 5:44:16
Pierceton 43 295 41N12 85w42 5:42:48
Pierceville 69 275 39N07 85w08 5:40:32
Pierson 84 82 39N19 87w18 5:49:12
Pike 6 248 40N04 86w28 5:45:52
Pikes Peak 7 147 39N13 85w54 5:43:36
Pilot Knob 13 169 38N20 86w16 5:45:04
Pimento 84 82 39N19 87w23 5:49:32
Pine Lake 46 8 41N38 86w46 5:47:04
Pine Ridge 84 77 39N28 87w26 5:49:44
Pine Valley 59 160 38N34 86w28 5:45:52
Pine Village 86 143 40N27 87w15 5:49:00
Pinhook 46 8 41N34 86w50 5:47:20
Pinhook 47 344 38N51 86w30 5:46:00
Pinola 46 8 41N35 86w47 5:47:08
Pittsboro 32 247 39N52 86w28 5:45:52
Pittsburg 8 128 40N35 86w40 5:46:40
Plain 43 291 41N18 85w49 5:43:16
Plainfield 32 98 39N42 86w24 5:45:36
Plainville 14 85 38N48 87w09 5:48:36
Plano 55 101 39N25 86w25 5:45:40
Plato 44 30 41N39 85w21 5:41:24
Plattsburg 88 165 38N51 86w06 5:44:24
Pleasant 78 35 38N52 85w25 5:41:40
Pleasant Gardens 67 128 39N33 86w58 5:47:52
Pleasant Lake 76 50 41N35 85w01 5:40:04
Pleasant Mills 1 228 40N47 84w51 5:39:24
Pleasant Plain 35 287 40N41 85w25 5:41:40
Pleasant Run 47 344 38N57 86w23 5:45:32
Pleasant Valley 71 208 41N40 86w10 5:44:40
Pleasant View 73 101 39N40 85w57 5:43:48
Pleasant View Village 3 302 39N21 85w58 5:43:52
Pleasantville 77 80 38N58 87w25 5:49:40
Pleasure Valley 73 101 39N27 85w40 5:42:40
Plevna 34 331 40N29 86w08 5:44:32
Plummer 28 193 39N02 86w56 5:47:44
Plum Tree 35 287 40N41 85w25 5:41:40
Plymouth 50 219 41N21 86w19 5:45:16
Poe 2 233 41N04 85w09 5:40:36
Point 65 58 37N51 87w59 5:51:56
Point Commerce 28 193 39N07 86w59 5:47:56
Point Isabel 27 280 40N25 85w50 5:43:20
Poland 11 89 39N27 86w57 5:47:48
Poling 38 287 40N32 84w58 5:39:52
Poneto 90 228 40N39 85w13 5:40:52
Pontiac 11 89 39N36 87w06 5:48:24
Popcorn 47 344 38N56 86w37 5:46:28
Portage 64 6 41N34 87w11 5:48:44
Porter 64 11 41N24 87w08 5:48:32
Portersville 19 67 38N25 86w56 5:47:44
Port Fulton 10 166 38N18 85w45 5:43:00
Portland 38 298 40N26 84w59 5:39:56
Portland Mills 61 128 39N39 86w52 5:47:28
Poseyville 65 58 38N10 87w47 5:51:08
Pottawattamie Park 46 9 41N43 86w52 5:47:28
Pottersville 60 344 39N17 86w46 5:47:04
Powers 38 295 40N26 84w59 5:39:56
Prairie City 11 89 39N28 87w07 5:48:28
Prairie Creek 84 82 39N18 87w31 5:50:04
Prairieton 84 82 39N22 87w29 5:49:56
Prairie Village 84 77 39N26 87w24 5:49:36
Prather 10 166 38N27 85w40 5:42:40

Prather 55 101 39N25 86W25 5:45:40
Preble 1 231 40N53 85W02 5:40:08
Prescott 73 101 39N33 85W48 5:43:12
Presidential Village 2 233 41N04 85W09 5:40:36
Pretty Lake 44 30 41N32 85W22 5:41:28
Prince Hall Plaza 27 284 40N34 85W42 5:42:48
Prince's Lakes 41 101 39N21 86W07 5:44:28
Princeton 26 60 38N21 87W34 5:50:16
Progress 18 253 40N07 85W27 5:41:48
Progress Acres 84 82 39N42 86W51 5:47:24
Prospect 59 160 38N36 86W37 5:46:28
Providence 41 97 39N31 86W10 5:44:40
Prowsville 88 165 38N37 86W17 5:45:08
Publico 22 166 38N18 85W49 5:43:16
Puckett 27 284 40N34 85W42 5:42:48
Pulaski 66 181 40N58 86W40 5:46:40
Pumpkin Center 59 160 38N40 86W27 5:45:48
Pumpkin Center 88 165 38N41 85W46 5:43:04
Purdue University 79 147 40N26 86W56 5:47:44
Putnamville 67 128 39N34 86W52 5:47:28
Pyrmont 8 128 40N35 86W40 5:46:40
Quail Meadows Estates 24 275 39N18 85W13 5:40:52
Quaker 83 73 39N48 87W29 5:49:56
Queensville 40 126 39N00 85W38 5:42:32
Quercus Grove 78 35 38N52 84W55 5:39:40
Quincy 60 344 39N27 86W43 5:46:52
Raber 92 228 41N12 85W28 5:41:52
Raccoon 67 128 39N51 86W53 5:47:32
Radioville 66 181 41N05 86W54 5:47:36
Radley 27 284 40N29 85W38 5:42:32
Radnor 8 128 40N30 86W38 5:46:32
Raglesville 14 91 38N49 86W58 5:47:52
Ragsdale 42 86 38N45 87W20 5:49:20
Railroad 75 2 41N13 86W52 5:47:28
Rainbow 49 100 39N47 86W13 5:44:52
Rainbow Highlands 49 100 39N50 86W01 5:44:04
Rainbow Ridge 49 100 39N47 86W13 5:44:52
Rainsville 86 129 40N25 87W15 5:49:00
Raleigh 70 101 39N45 85W22 5:41:28
Ramsey 31 166 38N19 86W09 5:44:36
Ranburn Woods 45 6 41N32 87W22 5:49:28
Randolph 68 307 40N17 85W02 5:40:08
Raub 4 147 40N44 87W29 5:49:56
Ravenswood 49 100 39N54 86W08 5:44:32
Ravinamy 79 147 40N26 86W56 5:47:44
Ray 76 32 41N44 84W53 5:39:32
Raymond 24 30 39N28 84W51 5:39:24
Raysville 33 108 39N48 85W31 5:42:04
Red Bridge 85 264 40N36 85W58 5:43:52
Red Bush 87 53 37N57 87W24 5:49:36
Redding 36 147 39N01 85W56 5:43:44
Reddington 36 147 38N58 85W58 5:43:52
Redkey 38 301 40N21 85W09 5:40:36
Redmond Park 43 291 41N21 85W49 5:43:16
Reed Station 18 254 40N11 85W23 5:41:32
Reelsville 67 126 39N33 86W58 5:47:52
Reeve 14 85 38N33 86W59 5:47:56
Rego 59 160 38N28 86W16 5:45:04
Reiffsburg 90 228 40N39 85W09 5:40:36
Remington 37 225 40N46 87W09 5:48:36
Reno 32 113 39N41 86W40 5:46:40
Rensselaer 37 227 40N57 87W09 5:48:36
Reo 74 61 37N53 87W03 5:48:12
Republican 39 101 38N43 85W33 5:42:12
Reserve 61 73 39N49 87W25 5:49:40
Retreat 36 147 38N48 85W55 5:43:40
Rexville 45 6 41N30 87W19 5:49:16
Rexville 69 275 38N57 85W20 5:41:20
Reynolds 91 149 40N45 86W52 5:47:28
Riceville 13 169 38N17 86W42 5:46:48
Richey Park 91 162 40N45 86W46 5:47:04
Rich Grove 66 181 41N07 86W45 5:47:00
Richland 70 101 39N30 85W24 5:41:36
Richland 74 61 37N57 87W10 5:48:40
Richmond 89 318 39N50 84W54 5:39:36
Richvalley 85 264 40N47 85W54 5:43:36
Riddle 13 169 38N20 86W28 5:45:52
Ridgemede 53 344 39N12 86W37 5:46:28
Ridgeport 28 193 39N02 86W56 5:47:44
Ridgeview 52 335 40N42 86W07 5:44:28
Ridgeview Heights 2 233 41N03 85W08 5:40:32
Ridgeville 68 309 40N18 85W02 5:40:08
Ridgeway 2 233 41N01 85W10 5:40:40
Ridinger Lake 43 291 41N11 85W42 5:42:48
Rigdon 27 280 40N21 85W44 5:42:56
Riley 84 82 39N23 87W18 5:49:12
Rileysburg 83 73 40N09 87W24 5:49:36
Riley Village 73 101 39N33 85W48 5:43:12
Ringwald 39 97 38N45 85W19 5:41:16
Ripley 66 183 41N03 86W36 5:46:24
Rising Sun 58 51 38N57 84W51 5:39:24
Rivare 1 231 40N50 84W56 5:39:44
River Forest 48 101 40N06 85W43 5:42:52
Riverhaven 2 233 41N04 85W08 5:40:32
River Ridge 10 166 38N27 85W40 5:42:40
Riverside 10 166 38N18 85W45 5:43:00
Riverside 23 129 40N18 87W15 5:49:00
Riverside 46 2 41N12 86W53 5:47:32
Riverton 77 80 39N03 87W34 5:50:16
River Vale 47 344 38N44 86W28 5:45:52
Riverview 77 80 39N13 87W31 5:50:04
Riverview Acres 3 147 39N13 85W54 5:43:36
Riverwood 29 97 40N03 86W01 5:44:04
Roachdale 67 128 39N51 86W48 5:47:12
Roann 85 269 40N55 85W55 5:43:40
Roanoke 35 287 40N57 85W22 5:41:28
Robb 65 58 38N10 87W49 5:51:16
Roberts 23 129 40N18 87W15 5:49:00
Robertsdale 45 6 41N39 87W30 5:50:00
Robinson 65 58 38N03 87W45 5:51:00
Robinwood 84 77 39N29 87W22 5:49:28
Roble Woods 64 6 41N29 87W23 5:49:32
Rob Roy 23 129 40N18 87W15 5:49:00
Rochester 25 329 41N04 86W13 5:44:52
Rockcreek 35 287 40N49 85W32 5:42:08
Rockdale 24 30 39N19 84W51 5:39:24
Rockfield 8 174 40N39 86W34 5:46:16
Rockford 36 139 38N58 85W58 5:43:52
Rockford 90 230 40N43 85W07 5:40:28
Rock Island 49 100 39N52 86W14 5:44:56
Rock Lake 25 242 41N02 86W02 5:44:08
Rocklane 41 100 39N40 86W09 5:44:36
Rockport 74 57 37N53 87W03 5:48:12
Rockville 61 157 39N46 87W14 5:48:56
Rocky Fork Lake 61 89 39N31 87W08 5:48:32
Rocky Ripple 49 100 39N51 86W09 5:44:36
Roland 59 160 38N34 86W37 5:46:28
Roll 5 196 40N33 85W24 5:41:36
Rolling Acres 87 53 38N03 87W16 5:49:04
Rolling Hill Estates 45 6 41N30 87W19 5:49:16
Rolling Hills 2 233 41N04 85W10 5:40:40
Rolling Hills 10 166 38N27 85W40 5:42:40
Rolling Hills 27 284 40N34 85W42 5:42:48
Rolling Prairie 46 22 41N41 86W37 5:46:28
Rolling Ridge 73 101 39N33 85W48 5:43:12
Rollins 51 322 38N40 86W47 5:47:08
Rome 62 69 37N55 86W32 5:46:08
Rome City 57 41 41N30 85W23 5:41:32
Romney 79 147 40N15 86W54 5:47:36
Romona 60 342 39N17 86W46 5:47:04
Root 1 228 40N53 84W56 5:39:44
Roseburg 27 284 40N34 85W42 5:42:48
Roseburg 81 313 39N32 84W57 5:39:48
Rosedale 61 72 39N37 87W16 5:49:04
Rosedale Hills 49 100 39N41 86W07 5:44:28
Rose Hill Gardens 84 82 39N42 86W51 5:47:24
Roseland 71 208 41N43 86W15 5:45:00
Roselawn 56 2 41N09 87W19 5:49:16
Rosewood 31 166 38N07 85W58 5:43:52
Ross 45 6 41N32 87W23 5:49:32
Rosston 6 100 39N53 86W16 5:45:04
Rosstown 3 147 39N13 85W54 5:43:36
Rossville 12 147 40N25 86W36 5:46:24
Roth Park 8 162 40N45 86W46 5:47:04
Round Grove 91 147 40N36 87W02 5:48:08
Round Lake 57 30 41N26 85W16 5:41:04
Royal Center 9 170 40N52 86W30 5:46:00
Royalton 6 97 39N50 86W24 5:45:36
Royal View 3 147 39N13 85W54 5:43:36
Royer Lake 44 30 41N39 85W25 5:41:40
Royerton 18 254 40N15 85W21 5:41:24
Rugby 3 147 39N18 85W46 5:43:04
Rural 68 307 40N10 84W59 5:39:56
Rushville 70 107 39N37 85W27 5:41:48
Russell 67 128 39N50 86W58 5:47:52
Russell Lake 6 100 39N53 86W16 5:45:04
Russellville 67 128 39N52 86W59 5:47:56
Russels Point 76 30 41N32 84W55 5:39:40
Russiaville 34 165 40N25 86W16 5:45:04
Rustic Hills 87 53 37N57 87W24 5:49:36
Rutherford 51 200 38N34 86W53 5:47:32
Rutland 50 211 41N20 86W19 5:45:16
Ryan Place 65 58 37N56 87W54 5:51:36
Rykers Ridge 39 97 38N45 85W19 5:41:16
Saddle Lake 1 228 40N50 84W56 5:39:44
Sagers Lake 64 6 41N29 87W23 5:49:32
Sagunay Lake 46 2 41N40 86W37 5:46:28
Saint Anthony 19 67 38N19 86W50 5:47:20
Saint Bernice 83 73 39N43 87W31 5:50:04
Saint Croix 62 69 38N13 86W35 5:46:20
Saint Henry 19 67 38N12 86W52 5:47:28
Saint James 26 59 38N15 87W35 5:50:20
Saint Joe 17 228 41N19 84W54 5:39:36
Saint John 45 23 41N27 87W28 5:49:52
Saint John 87 53 38N10 87W27 5:49:48
Saint Johns 17 228 41N21 85W09 5:40:36
Saint Joseph 2 233 41N08 85W04 5:40:16
Saint Joseph 82 55 38N04 87W39 5:50:36
Saint Joseph Hill 10 166 38N19 85W44 5:42:56
Saint Leon 15 33 39N17 84W58 5:39:52
Saint Louis Crossing 3 149 39N13 85W54 5:43:36
Saint Marks 19 67 38N19 86W50 5:47:20
Saint Marks 62 69 37N57 86W46 5:47:04
Saint Mary-of-the-Woods 84 77 39N30 87W30 5:50:00
Saint Marys 1 228 40N48 84W51 5:39:24
Saint Marys 22 166 38N19 85W52 5:43:28
Saint Marys 71 208 41N42 86W14 5:44:56
Saint Maurice 16 101 39N21 85W33 5:42:12
Saint Meinrad 74 64 38N10 86W49 5:47:16
Saint Omer 16 101 39N26 85W38 5:42:32
Saint Paul 16 101 39N26 85W38 5:42:32
Saint Peter 24 30 39N19 85W02 5:40:08
Saint Philip 65 58 37N56 87W54 5:51:36
Saint Thomas 42 86 38N45 87W31 5:50:04
Saint Wendells 65 58 38N07 87W40 5:50:40

INDIANA

Salamonia 38 287 40N23 84W52 5:39:28
Salamonie 35 287 40N42 85W23 5:41:32
Salem 38 287 40N18 84W50 5:39:20
Salem 81 313 39N38 84W56 5:39:44
Salem 88 180 38N36 86W06 5:44:24
Salem Center 76 30 41N32 85W05 5:40:20
Salem Heights 46 8 41N37 86W44 5:46:56
Saline City 11 89 39N22 87W06 5:48:24
Salt Creek Commons 64 6 41N29 87W23 5:49:32
Saltillo 88 165 38N40 86W18 5:45:12
Saluda 39 101 38N38 85W30 5:42:00
Samaria 41 97 39N25 86W09 5:44:36
Sandborn 42 86 38N54 87W11 5:48:44
Sandcut 84 82 39N42 86W51 5:47:24
Sanders 53 344 39N12 86W37 5:46:28
Sandford 84 82 39N33 87W31 5:50:04
Sand Ridge 74 61 37N53 87W03 5:48:12
Sandusky 16 101 39N21 85W33 5:42:12
Sandy Beach 8 162 40N45 86W46 5:47:04
Sandy Hook 3 147 39N13 85W54 5:43:36
Sandytown 83 73 39N40 87W24 5:49:36
San Jacinto 40 128 39N02 85W31 5:42:04
San Pierre 75 2 41N12 86W53 5:47:32
Santa Claus 74 64 38N07 86W55 5:47:40
Santa Fe 52 335 40N42 86W07 5:44:28
Saratoga 68 306 40N14 84W55 5:39:40
Sardinia 16 101 39N09 85W38 5:42:32
Savah 65 58 37N56 87W54 5:51:36
Scenic Heights 62 69 37N57 86W46 5:47:04
Scenic Hill 51 200 38N43 86W55 5:47:40
Schaefer Lake 3 147 39N18 85W46 5:43:04
Schererville 45 6 41N30 87W27 5:49:48
Schneider 45 2 41N11 87W27 5:49:48
Schnellville 19 67 38N20 86W45 5:47:00
Scipio 24 30 39N21 84W46 5:39:04
Scipio 40 126 39N05 85W43 5:42:52
Scircleville 12 184 40N17 86W18 5:45:12
Scotland 28 193 38N55 86W54 5:47:36
Scott 44 30 41N43 85W35 5:42:20
Scott City 77 80 39N11 87W24 5:49:36
Scottsburg 63 59 38N20 87W30 5:50:00
Scottsburg 72 321 38N41 85W47 5:43:08
Scottsville 22 166 38N28 85W57 5:43:48
Seafield 91 149 40N46 87W02 5:48:08
Sedalia 12 183 40N25 86W31 5:46:04
Sedan 17 237 41N26 85W05 5:40:20
Seelyville 84 83 39N30 87W16 5:49:04
Sellersburg 10 179 38N24 85W45 5:43:00
Sellers Lake 43 291 41N11 85W42 5:42:48
Selma 18 253 40N11 85W16 5:41:04
Selvin 87 53 38N12 87W06 5:48:24
Servia 85 270 40N57 85W44 5:42:56
Sevastopol 43 291 41N08 86W01 5:44:04
Seventeenth Avenue 45 17 41N35 87W20 5:49:20
Seward 43 291 41N06 85W57 5:43:48
Sexton 70 101 39N43 85W27 5:41:48
Seymour 36 138 38N58 85W53 5:43:32
Shadeland 27 284 40N34 85W42 5:42:48
Shadeland 79 147 40N25 86W53 5:47:32
Shady Hills 27 284 40N34 85W42 5:42:48
Shady Hills Estates 27 284 40N34 85W42 5:42:48
Shady Lawn 45 6 41N29 87W23 5:49:32
Shady Nook 44 30 41N32 85W22 5:41:28
Shady Side 64 4 41N37 87W06 5:48:24
Shamrock Lakes 5 196 40N24 85W26 5:41:44
Shannondale 54 147 40N00 86W56 5:47:44
Sharon 8 170 40N33 86W31 5:46:04
Sharpsville 80 119 40N23 86W05 5:44:20
Shawnee 23 156 40N14 87W16 5:49:04
Shawswick 47 344 38N51 86W27 5:45:48
Shawville 84 82 39N42 86W51 5:47:24
Sheffield 79 147 40N21 86W46 5:47:04
Shelburn 77 81 39N11 87W24 5:49:36
Shelburne 55 101 39N25 86W25 5:45:40
Shelby 45 28 41N12 87W21 5:49:24
Shelbyville 73 111 39N31 85W47 5:43:08
Shepardsville 84 82 39N36 87W25 5:49:40
Sheridan 29 108 40N08 86W13 5:44:52
Sheridan 46 9 41N43 86W53 5:47:32
Sherwood Forest 49 100 39N54 86W08 5:44:32
Shideler 18 253 40N19 85W21 5:41:24
Shields 36 147 38N58 85W58 5:43:52
Shiloh Village 3 147 39N13 85W54 5:43:36
Shipshewana 44 30 41N40 85W35 5:42:20
Shirkleville 84 77 39N28 87W26 5:49:44
Shirley 33 97 39N53 85W35 5:42:20
Shoals 51 322 38N40 86W47 5:47:08
Shoe Lake 43 291 41N20 85W51 5:43:24
Shooters Hill 49 100 39N49 86W11 5:44:44
Shoreland Hills 46 9 41N43 86W53 5:47:32
Shores Acres 49 100 39N52 86W07 5:44:28
Siberia 62 69 38N14 86W44 5:46:56
Sidney 43 293 41N06 85W44 5:42:56
Silver Creek 10 166 38N23 85W45 5:43:00
Silverdale 74 61 37N53 87W03 5:48:12
Silver Grove 22 166 38N18 85W49 5:43:16
Silver Hills 22 166 38N18 85W49 5:43:16
Silver Lake 43 291 41N04 85W54 5:43:36
Silver Lakes Estates 10 166 38N18 85W45 5:43:00
Silverville 47 344 38N48 86W39 5:46:36
Silverwood 23 156 39N58 87W24 5:49:36
Simonton Lake 20 271 41N41 85W59 5:43:56
Simpson 35 289 40N49 85W32 5:42:08
Sims 3 147 39N13 85W54 5:43:36
Sims 27 280 40N32 85W49 5:43:16

Sitka 91 181 40N50 86W45 5:47:00
Skelton 26 59 38N18 87W45 5:51:00
Skelton 87 53 38N05 87W09 5:48:36
Skinner Lake 57 30 41N24 85W26 5:41:44
Sleepy Hollow 73 101 39N27 85W40 5:42:40
Sleeth 8 128 40N35 86W40 5:46:40
Sloan 86 156 40N17 87W18 5:49:12
Smartsburg 54 147 40N00 86W56 5:47:44
Smedley 88 165 38N37 86W17 5:45:08
Smithfield 17 237 41N29 85W01 5:40:04
Smithfield 18 253 40N09 85W16 5:41:04
Smithland 73 101 39N33 85W48 5:43:12
Smithson 91 147 40N45 86W52 5:47:28
Smith Valley 41 97 39N36 86W12 5:44:48
Smithville 53 344 39N04 86W30 5:46:00
Smockville 61 89 39N36 87W06 5:48:24
Smyrna 39 101 38N48 85W30 5:42:00
Snacks 49 100 39N50 86W15 5:45:00
Snow Hill 68 310 40N10 84W59 5:39:56
Solitude 65 58 38N01 87W54 5:51:36
Solsberry 28 193 39N05 86W45 5:47:00
Somerset 85 264 40N40 85W51 5:43:24
Somerville 26 59 38N17 87W23 5:49:32
South Bend 71 208 41N41 86W15 5:45:00
South Bethany 3 147 39N13 85W54 5:43:36
South Boston 88 165 38N36 86W06 5:44:24
South Center 46 2 41N23 86W35 5:46:20
Southeast 59 160 38N27 86W23 5:45:32
Southeast Grove 45 2 41N19 87W12 5:48:48
Southeast Manor 73 101 39N35 85W52 5:43:28
South Edgewood 48 101 40N07 85W42 5:42:48
South Gate 24 30 39N19 84W58 5:39:52
Southgate 46 9 41N43 86W53 5:47:32
South Harbor 29 97 40N03 86W01 5:44:04
South Haven 64 6 41N32 87W10 5:48:40
South Hunt 49 100 39N45 86W14 5:44:56
South Kokomo 34 332 40N29 86W08 5:44:32
South Lake 84 77 39N28 87W26 5:49:44
South Marion 27 284 40N34 85W42 5:42:48
South Milford 44 30 41N32 85W16 5:41:04
Southmoor 45 6 41N30 87W19 5:49:16
South Mud Lake 25 328 40N58 86W08 5:44:32
South Park 43 291 41N21 85W49 5:43:16
South Peru 52 335 40N42 86W07 5:44:28
Southport 49 100 39N40 86W07 5:44:28
South Raub 79 147 40N25 86W53 5:47:32
South Salem 68 287 40N16 84W50 5:39:20
South Wanatah 46 2 41N26 86W54 5:47:36
South Washington 14 85 38N40 87W11 5:48:44
South West 20 259 41N32 85W56 5:43:44
South Whitley 92 229 41N05 85W38 5:42:32
Southwick Village 2 233 41N04 85W09 5:40:36
Southwood 46 9 41N43 86W53 5:47:32
Southwood 84 77 39N26 87W25 5:49:40
Spades 69 275 39N14 85W06 5:40:24
Sparksville 36 147 38N47 86W14 5:44:56
Sparta 15 33 39N07 85W05 5:40:20
Spartanburg 68 307 40N04 84W51 5:39:24
Spearsville 7 147 39N25 86W09 5:44:36
Speed 10 185 38N25 85W45 5:43:00
Speedway 49 100 39N47 86W15 5:45:00
Speicher 85 264 40N51 85W48 5:43:12
Speicherville 85 264 40N51 85W48 5:43:12
Spelterville 84 82 39N31 87W25 5:49:40
Spencer 60 342 39N17 86W46 5:47:04
Spencerville 17 228 41N19 84W54 5:39:36
Spiceland 33 253 39N50 85W26 5:41:44
Spice Valley 47 344 38N46 86W37 5:46:28
Spraytown 36 147 38N58 85W58 5:43:52
Springersville 21 272 39N40 85W00 5:40:00
Springfield 65 58 37N56 87W54 5:51:36
Spring Grove 89 318 39N51 84W53 5:39:32
Spring Grove Heights 89 318 39N52 84W52 5:39:28
Spring Hill Estates 84 77 39N26 87W24 5:49:36
Spring Hills 49 100 39N49 86W11 5:44:44
Spring Hollow 49 100 39N53 86W11 5:44:44
Spring Lake Park 30 97 39N46 85W51 5:43:24
Spring Mill Estates 49 100 39N53 86W11 5:44:44
Springport 33 253 40N03 85W24 5:41:36
Springtown 32 247 39N46 86W31 5:46:04
Spring Valley Estates 84 77 39N26 87W24 5:49:36
Springville 46 8 41N37 86W44 5:46:56
Springville 47 344 38N56 86W37 5:46:28
Springwood 84 82 39N42 86W51 5:47:24
Spurgeon 63 59 38N15 87W16 5:49:04
Spurgeons Corner 7 147 38N58 86W08 5:44:32
Stampers Creek 59 160 38N32 86W21 5:45:24
Stanford 53 344 39N05 86W40 5:46:40
Star City 66 183 40N58 86W33 5:46:12
Stardust Village 29 97 40N03 86W01 5:44:04
Starlight 10 166 38N28 85W57 5:43:48
Starve Hollow Lake 36 147 38N51 86W06 5:44:24
State Line 45 6 41N39 87W30 5:50:00
State Line 84 77 39N28 87W26 5:49:44
State Line 86 187 40N12 87W32 5:50:08
State Line City 86 187 40N12 87W32 5:50:08
Staunton 11 88 39N29 87W11 5:48:44
Stavetown 24 30 39N25 84W56 5:39:44
Stearleyville 11 89 39N31 87W08 5:48:32
Steele 1 228 40N45 84W57 5:39:48
Steele 14 85 38N46 87W10 5:48:40
Steen 42 86 38N39 87W18 5:49:12
Steinmeir Estates 49 100 39N53 86W04 5:44:16
Stendal 63 59 38N16 87W09 5:48:36
Sterling 13 169 38N21 86W28 5:45:52
Sterling 23 156 40N07 87W16 5:49:04
Steubenville 76 30 41N32 85W04 5:40:16
Stevenson 87 53 38N01 87W26 5:49:44
Stewart 86 156 40N17 87W18 5:49:12
Stewartsville 65 58 38N11 87W50 5:51:20
Stilesville 32 113 39N38 86W38 5:46:32
Stillwell 46 2 41N33 86W36 5:46:24
Stinesville 53 344 39N24 86W46 5:47:04
Stockdale 52 335 40N55 85W55 5:43:40
Stockton 28 93 39N03 87W11 5:48:44
Stockwell 79 147 40N17 86W46 5:47:04
Stone 68 310 40N10 84W59 5:39:56
Stonebluff 23 156 40N07 87W16 5:49:04
Stoneburner Landing 43 297 41N14 85W51 5:43:24
Stonecrest 27 284 40N34 85W42 5:42:48
Stonegate Square 87 53 37N57 87W24 5:49:36
Stone Head 7 145 39N12 86W15 5:45:00
Stones Crossing 41 100 39N40 86W09 5:44:36
Stoney Creek 68 307 40N09 85W10 5:40:40
Stonington 47 344 38N44 86W28 5:45:52
Stony Lonesome 3 147 39N13 85W54 5:43:36
Stony Ridge 43 291 41N20 85W51 5:43:24
Story 7 145 39N03 86W14 5:44:56
Straughn 33 257 39N48 85W18 5:41:12
Strawtown 29 97 40N03 86W01 5:44:04
Stringtown 6 247 40N04 86W28 5:45:52
Stringtown 30 101 40N53 81W35 5:26:20
Stringtown 69 275 39N07 85W08 5:40:32
Stroh 44 30 41N35 85W12 5:40:48
Suburban Gardens 45 6 41N31 87W28 5:49:52
Sugar Creek 73 101 39N35 85W52 5:43:28
Sugar Ridge 11 89 39N22 87W06 5:48:24
Sullivan 77 71 39N06 87W24 5:49:36
Sulphur 13 169 38N14 86W28 5:45:52
Sulphur Springs 33 257 40N00 85W27 5:41:48
Sumava Resorts 56 2 41N10 87W26 5:49:44
Summit Grove 83 73 39N40 87W24 5:49:36
Summit Ridge 2 233 41N06 85W08 5:40:32
Summitville 48 101 40N21 85W39 5:42:36
Sundown Manor 55 97 39N37 86W22 5:45:28
Sunman 69 278 39N14 85W06 5:40:24
Sunnybrook Acres 2 233 41N06 85W08 5:40:32
Sunnycrest 27 284 40N34 85W42 5:42:48
Sunnymede 2 233 41N04 85W09 5:40:36
Sunnymede 85 264 40N48 85W49 5:43:16
Sunnymede Woods 2 233 41N04 85W09 5:40:36
Sunrise Beach 43 291 41N21 85W49 5:43:16
Sunset Parkway 36 147 38N58 85W58 5:43:52
Sunset Village 10 166 38N27 85W40 5:42:40
Sunshine Gardens 49 100 39N40 86W09 5:44:36
Sunview 48 101 39N56 85W51 5:43:24
Surprise 36 147 38N58 85W58 5:43:52
Sussex Woods 45 6 41N33 87W17 5:49:08
Swan 57 30 41N19 85W13 5:40:52
Swanington 4 147 40N37 87W19 5:49:16
Swayzee 27 284 40N30 85W50 5:43:20
Sweetser 27 284 40N34 85W46 5:43:04
Sweetwater Lake 7 147 39N21 86W07 5:44:28
Switz City 28 96 39N02 87W03 5:48:12
Sycamore 34 334 40N29 85W56 5:43:44
Sycamore Hills 48 101 40N21 85W44 5:42:56
Sycamore Knolls 84 77 39N26 87W24 5:49:36
Sycamore Park 84 77 39N29 87W27 5:49:48
Sylvan Hills 27 284 40N34 85W42 5:42:48
Sylvania 61 128 39N55 87W19 5:49:16
Sylvan Manor 64 6 41N29 87W23 5:49:32
Syndicate 83 73 39N40 87W24 5:49:36
Syracuse 43 299 41N26 85W47 5:43:08
Syria 59 160 38N40 86W27 5:45:48
Tab 86 156 40N24 87W28 5:49:52
Tabertown 84 82 39N30 87W16 5:49:04
Talbot 4 147 40N31 87W27 5:49:48
Tall Timbers 27 284 40N34 85W42 5:42:48
Talma 25 328 41N00 86W07 5:44:28
Tamarack 64 9 41N41 86W59 5:47:56
Tampico 36 147 38N53 86W05 5:44:20
Tangier 61 128 39N55 87W19 5:49:16
Tanglewood 2 233 41N04 85W03 5:40:12
Taswell 13 169 38N20 86W34 5:46:16
Taylorsville 3 149 39N18 85W57 5:43:48
Tecumseh 84 77 39N28 87W26 5:49:44
Teegarden 50 211 41N28 86W29 5:45:56
Tee Lake 46 8 41N37 86W44 5:46:56
Tefft 37 25 41N12 86W58 5:47:52
Tell City 62 68 37N57 86W46 5:47:04
Temple 13 169 38N20 86W28 5:45:52
Templeton 4 147 40N30 87W12 5:48:48
Tennyson 87 53 38N05 87W07 5:48:28
Tera North 84 82 39N42 86W51 5:47:24

INDIANA

Terhune 6 108 40N08 86W13 5:44:52
Terrace Bay 8 162 40N45 86W46 5:47:04
Terrace Lake 3 147 39N13 85W54 5:43:36
Terre Haute 84 77 39N28 87W25 5:49:40
Tetersburg 80 116 40N17 86W07 5:44:28
Texas 15 33 39N04 84W54 5:39:36
Thayer 56 2 41N10 87W20 5:49:20
Thomas Lake 67 128 39N39 86W52 5:47:28
Thomaston 46 2 41N26 86W54 5:47:36
Thorncreek 92 228 41N13 85W29 5:41:56
Thornhope 66 181 40N55 86W32 5:46:08
Thorntown 6 251 40N08 86W36 5:46:24
Thurman 2 233 41N04 85W03 5:40:12
Tilden 32 247 39N46 86W31 5:46:04
Tillman 2 228 40N58 84W52 5:39:28
Timbercrest 2 233 41N04 85W10 5:40:40
Timbercrest 9 165 40N46 86W22 5:45:28
Timberhurst 44 30 41N32 85W22 5:41:28
Tiosa 25 328 41N09 86W11 5:44:44
Tippecanoe 50 324 41N12 86W07 5:44:28
Tipton 80 121 40N17 86W02 5:44:08
Tipton Park 3 147 39N13 85W54 5:43:36
Toad Hop 84 77 39N27 87W28 5:49:52
Tobin 62 69 37N57 86W35 5:46:20
Tobinsport 62 69 37N50 86W40 5:46:40
Tocsin 90 231 40N50 85W07 5:40:28
Toledo 35 287 40N49 85W32 5:42:08
Tolleston 45 17 41N35 87W22 5:49:28
Toll Gate Heights 90 228 40N43 85W07 5:40:28
Tomahawk Village 49 100 39N48 86W15 5:45:00
Topeka 44 42 41N32 85W32 5:42:08
Toto 75 221 41N16 86W42 5:46:48
Tower 13 169 38N20 86W28 5:45:52
Townley 2 228 40N58 84W52 5:39:28
Town of Pines 64 9 41N41 86W57 5:47:48
Tracy 46 2 41N30 86W41 5:46:44
Traders Point 49 100 39N53 86W16 5:45:04
Trafalgar 41 101 39N25 86W09 5:44:36
Trail Creek 46 9 41N41 86W51 5:47:24
Travisville 90 228 40N43 85W07 5:40:28
Treaty 85 264 40N42 85W48 5:43:12
Tremont 64 4 41N37 87W06 5:48:24
Trenton 5 196 40N27 85W22 5:41:28
Trevlac 7 147 39N16 86W20 5:45:20
Trier Ridge Park 2 233 41N03 85W08 5:40:32
Tri Lakes 92 228 41N14 85W26 5:41:44
Trilobi Hills 49 100 39N50 86W01 5:44:04
Trinity 38 287 40N32 84W58 5:39:52
Trinity Springs 51 159 38N45 86W46 5:47:04
Troy 62 69 38N00 86W48 5:47:12
Tudor 3 147 39N13 85W54 5:43:36
Tulip 28 193 39N02 86W56 5:47:44
Tunker 92 228 41N03 85W32 5:42:08
Tunnelton 47 344 38N46 86W21 5:45:24
Turkey Creek 43 291 41N24 85W43 5:42:52
Turkey Creek Meadows 45 6 41N30 87W20 5:49:20
Turman 77 80 39N08 87W33 5:50:12
Turner 11 88 39N31 87W10 5:48:40
Turpin 87 53 38N03 87W16 5:49:04
Turtle Creek 27 284 40N34 85W42 5:42:48
Twelve Mile 9 165 40N52 86W13 5:44:52
Twelve Points 84 77 39N29 87W24 5:49:36
Twin Branch 71 208 41N40 86W10 5:44:40
Twin Brooks 49 100 39N41 86W07 5:44:28
Twin Crest 3 147 39N13 85W54 5:43:36
Twin Lakes 50 211 41N20 86W19 5:45:16
Twin Oaks Lake 55 97 39N22 86W15 5:45:00
Tyner 50 211 41N25 86W24 5:45:36
Ulen 6 247 40N04 86W28 5:45:52
Underwood 10 179 38N36 85W47 5:43:08
Underwood Meadows 48 101 40N21 85W44 5:42:56
Union 63 59 38N30 87W35 5:50:20
Union City 68 304 40N12 84W49 5:39:16
Uniondale 90 231 40N50 85W15 5:41:00
Union Mills 46 2 41N30 86W47 5:47:08
Unionport 68 307 40N15 85W10 5:40:40
Uniontown 36 147 38N48 85W55 5:43:40
Uniontown 62 69 38N08 86W43 5:46:52
Unionville 53 344 39N14 86W25 5:45:40
Universal 83 73 39N37 87W27 5:49:48
University Heights 49 100 39N41 86W07 5:44:28
Upland 27 283 40N28 85W29 5:41:56
Upper Long Lake 57 30 41N24 85W26 5:41:44
Upper Sunset Park 8 162 40N45 86W46 5:47:04
Upton 65 58 37N56 87W54 5:51:36
Uptown 49 100 39N50 86W09 5:44:36
Urbana 85 264 40N54 85W48 5:43:12
Urmeyville 41 97 39N29 86W03 5:44:12
Utah 15 33 39N04 84W54 5:39:36
Utica 10 166 38N21 85W40 5:42:40
Valeene 59 160 38N26 86W24 5:45:36
Valentine 44 36 41N39 85W25 5:41:40
Valley Acres 27 284 40N34 85W42 5:42:48
Valley Brook 85 264 40N48 85W49 5:43:16
Valley City 31 166 38N06 86W13 5:44:52
Valley View Hills 20 271 41N41 85W59 5:43:56
Vallonia 36 147 38N51 86W06 5:44:24
Vallyd Acres 2 233 41N04 85W09 5:40:36
Valparaiso 64 12 41N28 87W04 5:48:16
Van 9 165 40N46 86W22 5:45:28
Vanada Camps 87 53 37N57 87W24 5:49:36
Van Bibber Lake 67 128 39N39 86W52 5:47:28

Van Buren 27 286 40N37 85W30 5:42:00
Van Buren Park 53
344 39N12 86W37 5:46:28
Vandalia 60 344 39N17 86W46 5:47:04
Vanmeter Park 66
181 41N03 86W36 5:46:24
Vawter Park 43 291 41N21 85W49 5:43:16
Veale 14 85 38N35 87W10 5:48:40
Veedersburg 23 140 40N07 87W16 5:49:04
Velpen 63 59 38N21 87W06 5:48:24
Vera Cruz 90 228 40N42 85W05 5:40:20
Vermillion 83 73 39N53 87W27 5:49:48
Vermillion Acres 84
77 39N28 87W26 5:49:44
Vermont 34 331 40N29 86W08 5:44:32
Verne 42 86 38N45 87W31 5:50:04
Vernon 40 126 38N59 85W36 5:42:24
Versailles 69 275 39N04 85W15 5:41:00
Vesta 10 166 38N27 85W40 5:42:40
Vevay 78 35 38N45 85W04 5:40:16
Vicksburg 28 93 39N02 87W10 5:48:40
Victor 53 344 39N12 86W37 5:46:28
Victoria 28 93 39N02 87W10 5:48:40
Vienna 72 319 38N39 85W47 5:43:08
Vigo 42 86 38N48 87W15 5:49:00
Vigo 84 82 39N22 87W28 5:49:52
Vilas 60 344 39N17 86W46 5:47:04
Villa North 90 228 40N43 85W07 5:40:28
Vincennes 42 78 38N41 87W32 5:50:08
Vistula 20 259 41N43 85W49 5:43:16
Volga 39 97 38N45 85W19 5:41:16
Wabash 85 267 40N48 85W49 5:43:16
Wabash Shores 79
147 40N26 86W56 5:47:44
Wadena 4 147 40N37 87W19 5:49:16
Wadesville 65 58 38N06 87W47 5:51:08
Wakarusa 20 266 41N32 86W01 5:44:04
Wakefield Village 57
30 41N26 85W16 5:41:04
Wakeland 55 113 39N24 86W34 5:46:16
Wake Robin Fields 64
4 41N37 87W06 5:48:24
Walden 2 233 41N06 85W08 5:40:32
Waldron 73 101 39N27 85W40 5:42:40
Waldron Lake 57 47 41N28 85W29 5:41:56
Walesboro 3 149 39N13 85W54 5:43:36
Walford Manor 10
166 38N18 85W45 5:43:00
Walker Park 43 291 41N20 85W51 5:43:24
Walkerton 71 206 41N28 86W29 5:45:56
Walkerville 73 101 39N33 85W48 5:43:12
Wallace 23 156 39N59 87W09 5:48:36
Wallen 2 233 41N03 85W08 5:40:32
Wall Lake 44 30 41N44 85W10 5:40:40
Walnut 50 211 41N14 86W15 5:45:00
Walnut Gardens 8
162 40N45 86W46 5:47:04
Walnut Grove 29 97 40N10 86W01 5:44:04
Walnut Heights 47
344 38N51 86W30 5:46:00
Walnut Level 89 315 39N53 85W02 5:40:08
Walnut Ridge 10 166 38N18 85W45 5:43:00
Walnut Ridge 40 128 39N00 85W38 5:42:32
Walton 9 164 40N40 86W15 5:45:00
Waltz 85 264 40N42 85W51 5:43:24
Wanamaker 49 100 39N43 86W01 5:44:04
Wanatah 46 2 41N26 86W54 5:47:36
Wanda Lake 84 77 39N28 87W26 5:49:44
Ward 68 305 40N16 84W58 5:39:52
Warren 35 287 40N41 85W26 5:41:44
Warren Hills 49 100 39N47 86W01 5:44:04
Warren Park 49 100 39N47 86W04 5:44:16
Warrenton 26 59 38N15 87W35 5:50:20
Warrington 30 101 39N53 85W36 5:42:24
Warsaw 43 297 41N14 85W51 5:43:24
Washington 14 85 38N40 87W10 5:48:40
Washington Center 92
228 41N12 85W28 5:41:52
Washington Place 49
100 39N47 86W04 5:44:16
Waterford 46 9 41N40 86W51 5:47:24
Waterford Mills 20
259 41N33 85W50 5:43:20
Waterloo 17 237 41N26 85W01 5:40:04
Waterloo 21 272 39N46 85W05 5:40:20
Wathen Heights 10
166 38N18 85W45 5:43:00
Watson 10 166 38N22 85W42 5:42:48
Waugh 6 97 40N00 86W21 5:45:24
Wauhob Lake 64 6 41N29 87W23 5:49:32
Waveland 54 149 39N53 87W03 5:48:12
Waverly 55 101 39N25 86W25 5:45:40
Waverly Woods 55
101 39N25 86W25 5:45:40
Wawaka 57 47 41N28 85W29 5:41:56
Wawpecong 52 335 40N29 86W08 5:44:32
Waymansville 3 147 39N13 85W54 5:43:36
Wayne Center 57 30 41N26 85W16 5:41:04
Waynedale 2 233 41N01 85W10 5:40:40
Waynesburg 16 101 39N16 85W42 5:42:48
Waynesville 3 149 39N13 85W54 5:43:36
Waynetown 54 155 40N05 87W04 5:48:16
Wea 79 147 40N22 86W53 5:47:32
Webster 89 315 39N54 84W57 5:39:48
Wegan 36 147 38N53 86W05 5:44:20
Weisburg 15 33 39N14 85W06 5:40:24

Wellington Heights 73
101 39N33 85W48 5:43:12
Wells 52 335 40N42 86W07 5:44:28
Wellsboro 46 13 41N30 86W46 5:47:04
Wenmeir 3 147 39N13 85W54 5:43:36
Wesley 54 147 40N03 87W07 5:48:28
West 50 211 41N20 86W24 5:45:36
Westacres 18 254 40N11 85W23 5:41:32
West Atherton 61 73 39N37 87W21 5:49:24
West Baden Springs 59
127 38N35 86W37 5:46:28
West Brook Acres 24
275 39N18 85W13 5:40:52
West Brook Downs 53
344 39N12 86W37 5:46:28
Westchester 38 291 40N26 84W59 5:39:56
Westchester 64 4 41N38 87W03 5:48:12
West College Corner 81
313 39N34 84W49 5:39:16
West Creek 45 2 41N16 87W28 5:49:52
West Elwood 80 116 40N21 85W44 5:42:56
Western Acres 64 4 41N37 87W06 5:48:24
Western Hills 65 58 37N56 87W54 5:51:36
Westfield 29 98 40N02 86W08 5:44:32
West Fork 13 169 38N14 86W32 5:46:08
West Franklin 65 58 37N56 87W54 5:51:36
West Glen Park 45 6 41N32 87W22 5:49:28
West Harrison 15 33 39N16 84W49 5:39:16
West Haven 43 297 41N14 85W51 5:43:24
West Hill 64 6 41N29 87W23 5:49:32
West Indianapolis 49
100 39N45 86W11 5:44:44
West Lafayette 79
134 40N27 86W55 5:47:40
Westland 30 101 40N53 81W35 5:26:20
Westlawn 2 233 41N04 85W10 5:40:40
Westlea 27 284 40N34 85W42 5:42:48
West Lebanon 86 146 40N16 87W23 5:49:32
West Liberty 34 334 40N29 85W58 5:43:52
West Liberty 38 287 40N32 84W58 5:39:52
West Linton 28 92 39N02 87W10 5:48:40
West Middleton 34
165 40N26 86W13 5:44:52
Westmoor 2 233 41N04 85W10 5:40:40
West Muncie 18 253 40N10 85W30 5:42:00
West Newton 49 100 39N47 86W09 5:44:36
West Noblesville 29
97 40N03 86W01 5:44:04
West Peru 52 335 40N42 86W07 5:44:28
West Petersburg 63
59 38N29 87W17 5:49:08
Westphalia 42 87 38N52 87W14 5:48:56
Westpoint 79 152 40N21 87W03 5:48:12
West Point 91 152 40N42 87W00 5:48:00
Westport 16 101 39N11 85W34 5:42:16
Westport Addition 18
254 40N11 85W23 5:41:32
Westside 15 33 39N04 84W54 5:39:36
West Terre Haute 84
77 39N28 87W27 5:49:48
West Union 61 128 39N47 87W22 5:49:28
Westville 46 9 41N33 86W53 5:47:32
Westwood 33 253 39N56 85W26 5:41:44
Wey Lake 84 82 39N31 87W14 5:48:56
Wheatfield 37 26 41N14 87W06 5:48:24
Wheatland 42 86 38N40 87W19 5:49:16
Wheatonville 87 53 38N10 87W27 5:49:48
Wheeler 64 23 41N31 87W11 5:48:44
Wheeling 8 170 40N33 86W24 5:45:36
Wheeling 18 253 40N22 85W28 5:41:52
Whiskey Run 13 169 38N21 86W18 5:45:12
Whitaker 55 115 39N24 86W34 5:46:16
Whitcomb 24 30 39N25 84W56 5:39:44
Whitcomb Heights 84
77 39N28 87W27 5:49:48
White Cloud 31 166 38N13 86W07 5:44:28
Whitehall 60 344 39N11 86W41 5:46:44
Whiteland 41 98 39N33 86W05 5:44:20
Whiteoak 63 59 38N23 87W13 5:48:52
White Post 66 181 41N02 86W52 5:47:28
White Ridge 27 284 40N34 85W42 5:42:48
White River Bluffs 47
344 38N51 86W30 5:46:00
Whites Crossing 28
93 39N02 87W10 5:48:40
Whitestown 6 97 40N00 86W21 5:45:24
Whitesville 54 147 39N58 86W50 5:47:20
Whitewater 89 318 39N52 84W52 5:39:28
Whitfield 51 200 38N38 86W55 5:47:40
Whiting 45 14 41N41 87W30 5:50:00
Wickliffe 13 169 38N19 86W37 5:46:28
Widner 42 86 38N51 87W20 5:49:20
Wilbur 55 101 39N25 86W25 5:45:40
Wildcat 80 116 40N22 85W55 5:43:40
Wilders 46 28 41N19 86W53 5:47:32
Wildwood 27 284 40N34 85W42 5:42:48
Wildwood Lake 59
160 38N34 86W28 5:45:52
Wildwood Landing 76
30 41N35 85W12 5:40:48
Wilfred 77 80 39N11 87W24 5:49:36
Wilkinson 30 97 39N53 85W36 5:42:24
Williams 1 228 40N50 84W56 5:39:44
Williams 47 342 38N48 86W39 5:46:36
Williamsburg 89 315 39N57 85W00 5:40:00

Williams Creek 49
100 39N54 86W08 5:44:32
Williamsport 86 158 40N17 87W17 5:49:08
Williamstown 16 101 39N21 85W33 5:42:12
Willisville 63 59 38N29 87W17 5:49:08
Willow Branch 30
101 39N53 85W41 5:42:44
Willowbrook Estates 55
101 39N25 86W25 5:45:40
Willow Creek 64 23 41N29 87W28 5:49:52
Willow Valley 51
322 38N40 86W47 5:47:08
Wills 46 2 41N39 86W34 5:46:16
Wilmington 15 38 39N04 84W56 5:39:44
Wilmington 17 228 41N24 84W55 5:39:40
Wilmot 57 30 41N11 85W42 5:42:48
Wilshire 12 181 40N17 86W31 5:46:04
Wilson 10 166 38N28 85W57 5:43:48
Wilson 64 23 41N29 87W28 5:49:52
Wilson 73 101 39N33 85W48 5:43:12
Wilson Lake 92 228 41N12 85W28 5:41:52
Winamac 66 186 41N03 86W36 5:46:24
Winchester 68 308 40N10 84W59 5:39:56
Windemere Lake 84
77 39N28 87W26 5:49:44
Windfall 80 119 40N22 85W57 5:43:48
Windom 51 322 38N40 86W47 5:47:08
Windsor 68 307 40N07 85W12 5:40:48
Windsor Village 49
100 39N47 86W04 5:44:16
Winfield 45 29 41N23 87W16 5:49:04
Wingate 54 147 39N58 87W07 5:48:28
Winona 75 221 41N13 86W35 5:46:20
Winona Lake 43 297 41N14 85W49 5:43:16
Winslow 63 59 38N23 87W13 5:48:52
Winthrop 86 129 40N18 87W15 5:49:00
Witmer Manor 44 30 41N32 85W22 5:41:28
Witts 81 313 39N38 84W56 5:39:44
Wolcott 91 149 40N46 87W03 5:48:12
Wolcottville 44 43 41N32 85W22 5:41:28
Wolff 55 101 39N25 86W25 5:45:40
Wolflake 57 30 41N20 85W30 5:42:00
Wonder Lake 84 77 39N26 87W24 5:49:36
Wood 10 166 38N27 85W56 5:43:44
Woodburn 2 228 41N08 84W51 5:39:24
Woodbury 30 101 39N54 85W55 5:43:40
Woodcrest 55 101 39N25 86W25 5:45:40
Woodgate 84 77 39N26 87W24 5:49:36
Woodland 71 208 41N41 86W18 5:45:12
Woodland Heights 27
284 40N34 85W42 5:42:48
Woodland Lake 7 147 39N22 86W15 5:45:00
Woodland Park 18
254 40N12 85W19 5:41:16
Woodland Park 44 30 41N32 85W22 5:41:28
Woodland Trace 29
97 39N58 86W07 5:44:28
Woodlawn Heights 48
101 40N07 85W42 5:42:48
Woodridge 84 77 39N29 87W22 5:49:28
Woodruff 44 30 41N32 85W22 5:41:28
Woodruff Place 49
100 39N47 86W07 5:44:28
Woodstock 36 147 38N58 85W58 5:43:52
Woodstock 49 100 39N49 86W11 5:44:44
Woodville 64 4 41N37 87W06 5:48:24
Woodville Hills 53
344 39N12 86W37 5:46:28
Wooster 43 291 41N11 85W42 5:42:48
Worth 6 97 40N00 86W21 5:45:24
Worthington 28 195 39N07 86W59 5:47:56
Wright 28 93 39N07 87W11 5:48:44
Wright Manor 45 6 41N30 87W19 5:49:16
Wrights Corners 15
33 39N04 84W54 5:39:36
Wyatt 71 209 41N32 86W10 5:44:40
Wynnedale 49 100 39N49 86W11 5:44:44
Yankeetown 87 53 37N55 87W18 5:49:12
Yeddo 23 156 40N01 87W16 5:49:04
Yellowbanks 43 291 41N20 85W45 5:43:00
Yellow Creek Lake 43
291 41N08 85W53 5:43:32
Yeoman 8 165 40N40 86W44 5:46:56
Yockey 47 344 38N44 86W28 5:45:52
Yoder 2 228 40N56 85W11 5:40:44
York 76 30 41N38 85W00 5:40:00
Yorktown 18 257 40N10 85W30 5:42:00
Yorkville 15 33 39N10 84W55 5:39:40
Young 55 101 39N37 86W22 5:45:28
Young America 9 165 40N34 86W21 5:45:24
Youngs Corner 24 30 39N25 84W56 5:39:44
Youngs Creek 59 160 38N28 86W30 5:46:00
Youngstown 84 77 39N26 87W24 5:49:36
Youngstown Acres 84
77 39N26 87W24 5:49:36
Youngstown Meadows 84
77 39N26 87W24 5:49:36
Yountsville 54 147 40N00 86W58 5:47:52
Yule Estates 48 101 40N16 85W41 5:42:44
Zanesville 2 228 40N55 85W17 5:41:08
Zelma 47 344 38N57 86W16 5:45:04
Zenas 40 128 39N02 85W31 5:42:04
Zionsville 6 97 39N57 86W16 5:45:04
Zoar 19 67 38N16 87W09 5:48:36
Zulu 2 228 40N58 84W52 5:39:28

TIME TABLES

Dates of daylight time observance are not completely reliable because of wide-spread local diversity, including varied observances within cities.

IA # 1

Before 11/18/1883		LMT
11/18/1883	12:00	CST
3/31/1918	02:00	CWT
10/27/1918	02:00	CST
3/30/1919	02:00	CWT
10/26/1919	02:00	CST
2/09/1942	02:00	CWT
9/30/1945	02:00	CST
4/26/1964	02:00	CDT
10/25/1964	02:00	CST
5/30/1965	02:00	CDT
9/06/1965	02:00	CST
4/24/1966	02:00	US#1

IA # 2

Before 11/18/1883		LMT
11/18/1883	12:00	CST
3/31/1918	02:00	CWT
10/27/1918	02:00	CST
3/30/1919	02:00	CWT
10/26/1919	02:00	CST
2/09/1942	02:00	CWT
9/30/1945	02:00	CST
5/30/1965	02:00	CDT
9/06/1965	02:00	CST
4/24/1966	02:00	US#1

IA # 3

Before 11/18/1883		LMT
11/18/1883	12:00	CST
3/31/1918	02:00	CWT
10/27/1918	02:00	CST
3/30/1919	02:00	CWT
10/26/1919	02:00	CST
2/09/1942	02:00	CWT
9/30/1945	02:00	CST
4/24/1960	02:00	CDT
10/30/1960	02:00	CST
4/26/1964	02:00	CDT
10/25/1964	02:00	CST
5/30/1965	02:00	CDT
9/06/1965	02:00	CST
4/24/1966	02:00	US#1

IA # 4

Before 11/18/1883		LMT
11/18/1883	12:00	CST
3/31/1918	02:00	CWT
10/27/1918	02:00	CST
3/30/1919	02:00	CWT
10/26/1919	02:00	CST
2/09/1942	02:00	CWT
9/30/1945	02:00	CST
4/24/1960	02:00	CDT
10/30/1960	02:00	CST
5/30/1965	02:00	CDT
9/06/1965	02:00	CST
4/24/1966	02:00	US#1

IA # 5

Before 11/18/1883		LMT
11/18/1883	12:00	CST
3/31/1918	02:00	CWT
10/27/1918	02:00	CST
3/30/1919	02:00	CWT
10/26/1919	02:00	CST
2/09/1942	02:00	CWT
9/30/1945	02:00	CST
4/28/1963	02:00	CDT
10/27/1963	02:00	CST
4/26/1964	02:00	CDT
10/25/1964	02:00	CST
5/30/1965	02:00	CDT
9/06/1965	02:00	CST
4/24/1966	02:00	US#1

IA # 6

Before 11/18/1883		LMT
11/18/1883	12:00	CST
3/31/1918	02:00	CWT
10/27/1918	02:00	CST
3/30/1919	02:00	CWT
10/26/1919	02:00	CST
2/09/1942	02:00	CWT
9/30/1945	02:00	CST
6/03/1963	02:00	CDT
8/26/1963	02:00	CST
4/26/1964	02:00	CDT
10/25/1964	02:00	CST
5/30/1965	02:00	CDT
9/06/1965	02:00	CST
4/24/1966	02:00	US#1

IA # 7

Before 11/18/1883		LMT
11/18/1883	12:00	CST
3/31/1918	02:00	CWT
10/27/1918	02:00	CST
3/30/1919	02:00	CWT
10/26/1919	02:00	CST
2/09/1942	02:00	CWT
9/30/1945	02:00	CST
4/26/1959	02:00	CDT
9/28/1959	02:00	CST
4/24/1960	02:00	CDT
10/30/1960	02:00	CST
4/30/1961	02:00	CDT
10/29/1961	02:00	CST
4/29/1962	02:00	CDT
10/28/1962	02:00	CST
4/28/1963	02:00	CDT
10/27/1963	02:00	CST
4/26/1964	02:00	CDT
10/25/1964	02:00	CST
5/30/1965	02:00	CDT
9/06/1965	02:00	CST
4/24/1966	02:00	US#1

IA # 8

Before 11/18/1883		LMT
11/18/1883	12:00	CST
3/31/1918	02:00	CWT
10/27/1918	02:00	CST
3/30/1919	02:00	CWT
10/26/1919	02:00	CST
2/09/1942	02:00	CWT
9/30/1945	02:00	CST
4/25/1954	02:00	CDT
9/26/1954	02:00	CST
4/24/1960	02:00	CDT
10/30/1960	02:00	CST
4/30/1961	02:00	CDT
10/29/1961	02:00	CST
4/29/1962	02:00	CDT
10/28/1962	02:00	CST
4/28/1963	02:00	CDT
10/27/1963	02:00	CST
4/26/1964	02:00	CDT
10/25/1964	02:00	CST
5/30/1965	02:00	CDT
9/06/1965	02:00	CST
4/24/1966	02:00	US#1

IA # 9

Before 11/18/1883		LMT
11/18/1883	12:00	CST
3/31/1918	02:00	CWT
10/27/1918	02:00	CST
3/30/1919	02:00	CWT
10/26/1919	02:00	CST
2/09/1942	02:00	CWT
9/30/1945	02:00	CST
4/28/1963	02:00	CDT
9/01/1963	02:00	CST
4/26/1964	02:00	CDT
10/25/1964	02:00	CST
5/30/1965	02:00	CDT
9/06/1965	02:00	CST
4/24/1966	02:00	US#1

IA # 10

Before 11/18/1883		LMT
11/18/1883	12:00	CST
3/31/1918	02:00	CWT
10/27/1918	02:00	CST
3/30/1919	02:00	CWT
10/26/1919	02:00	CST
2/09/1942	02:00	CWT
9/30/1945	02:00	CST
4/28/1946	02:00	CDT
9/29/1946	02:00	CST
4/27/1947	02:00	CDT
9/28/1947	02:00	CST
4/24/1960	02:00	CDT
10/23/1960	02:00	CST
4/30/1961	02:00	CDT
10/29/1961	02:00	CST
4/29/1962	02:00	CDT
9/15/1962	02:00	CST
4/28/1963	02:00	CDT
9/01/1963	02:00	CST
4/26/1964	02:00	CDT
9/27/1964	02:00	CST
5/30/1965	02:00	CDT
9/06/1965	02:00	CST
4/24/1966	02:00	US#1

IA # 11

Before 11/18/1883		LMT
11/18/1883	12:00	CST
3/31/1918	02:00	CWT
10/27/1918	02:00	CST
3/30/1919	02:00	CWT
10/26/1919	02:00	CST
2/09/1942	02:00	CWT
9/30/1945	02:00	CST
4/24/1960	02:00	CDT
10/30/1960	02:00	CST
4/30/1961	02:00	CDT
9/03/1961	02:00	CST
4/28/1963	02:00	CDT
8/25/1963	02:00	CST
4/26/1964	02:00	CDT
10/31/1964	02:00	CST
5/30/1965	02:00	CDT
9/06/1965	02:00	CST
4/24/1966	02:00	US#1

IA # 12

Before 11/18/1883		LMT
11/18/1883	12:00	CST
3/31/1918	02:00	CWT
10/27/1918	02:00	CST
3/30/1919	02:00	CWT
10/26/1919	02:00	CST
4/27/1941	02:00	CDT
9/28/1941	02:00	CST
2/09/1942	02:00	CWT
9/30/1945	02:00	CST
4/28/1957	02:00	CDT
10/29/1957	02:00	CST
4/27/1958	02:00	CDT
10/28/1958	02:00	CST
4/26/1959	02:00	CDT
10/27/1959	02:00	CST
4/24/1960	02:00	CDT
10/30/1960	02:00	CST
4/30/1961	02:00	CDT
10/29/1961	02:00	CST
4/29/1962	02:00	CDT
10/28/1962	02:00	CST
4/28/1963	02:00	CDT
10/27/1963	02:00	CST
4/26/1964	02:00	CDT
10/25/1964	02:00	CST
5/30/1965	02:00	CDT
9/06/1965	02:00	CST
4/24/1966	02:00	US#1

IA # 13

Before 11/18/1883		LMT
11/18/1883	12:00	CST
3/31/1918	02:00	CWT
10/27/1918	02:00	CST
3/30/1919	02:00	CWT
10/26/1919	02:00	CST
2/09/1942	02:00	CWT
9/30/1945	02:00	CST
6/01/1963	02:00	CDT
9/01/1963	02:00	CST
4/26/1964	02:00	CDT
10/25/1964	02:00	CST
5/30/1965	02:00	CDT
9/06/1965	02:00	CST
4/24/1966	02:00	US#1

IA # 14

Before 11/18/1883		LMT
11/18/1883	12:00	CST
3/31/1918	02:00	CWT
10/27/1918	02:00	CST
3/30/1919	02:00	CWT
10/26/1919	02:00	CST
2/09/1942	02:00	CWT
9/30/1945	02:00	CST
6/03/1962	02:00	CDT
8/26/1962	02:00	CST
4/26/1964	02:00	CDT
10/25/1964	02:00	CST
5/30/1965	02:00	CDT
9/06/1965	02:00	CST
4/24/1966	02:00	US#1

IA # 15

Before 11/18/1883		LMT
11/18/1883	12:00	CST
3/31/1918	02:00	CWT
10/27/1918	02:00	CST
3/30/1919	02:00	CWT
10/26/1919	02:00	CST
2/09/1942	02:00	CWT
9/30/1945	02:00	CST
4/28/1946	02:00	CDT
9/29/1946	02:00	CST
4/28/1957	02:00	CDT
9/29/1957	02:00	CST
4/29/1962	02:00	CDT
10/28/1962	02:00	CST
6/02/1963	02:00	CDT
9/01/1963	02:00	CST
4/26/1964	02:00	CDT
10/25/1964	02:00	CST
5/30/1965	02:00	CDT
9/06/1965	02:00	CST
4/24/1966	02:00	US#1

IA # 16

Before 11/18/1883		LMT
11/18/1883	12:00	CST
3/31/1918	02:00	CWT
10/27/1918	02:00	CST
3/30/1919	02:00	CWT
10/26/1919	02:00	CST
2/09/1942	02:00	CWT
9/30/1945	02:00	CST
4/24/1960	02:00	CDT
10/30/1960	02:00	CST
4/30/1961	02:00	CDT
10/29/1961	02:00	CST
4/29/1962	02:00	CDT
9/16/1962	02:00	CST
4/28/1963	02:00	CDT
9/29/1963	02:00	CST
4/26/1964	02:00	CDT
9/27/1964	02:00	CST
5/30/1965	02:00	CDT
9/06/1965	02:00	CST
4/24/1966	02:00	US#1

IA # 17

Before 11/18/1883		LMT
11/18/1883	12:00	CST
3/31/1918	02:00	CWT
10/27/1918	02:00	CST
3/30/1919	02:00	CWT
10/26/1919	02:00	CST
2/09/1942	02:00	CWT
9/30/1945	02:00	CST
4/24/1960	02:00	CDT
10/30/1960	02:00	CST
4/30/1961	02:00	CDT
10/29/1961	02:00	CST
4/29/1962	02:00	CDT
9/02/1962	02:00	CST
4/28/1963	02:00	CDT
9/01/1963	02:00	CST
4/26/1964	02:00	CDT
9/06/1964	02:00	CST
5/30/1965	02:00	CDT
9/06/1965	02:00	CST
4/24/1966	02:00	US#1

IA # 18

Before 11/18/1883		LMT
11/18/1883	12:00	CST
3/31/1918	02:00	CWT
10/27/1918	02:00	CST
3/30/1919	02:00	CWT
10/26/1919	02:00	CST
2/09/1942	02:00	CWT
9/30/1945	02:00	CST
4/24/1960	02:00	CDT
10/30/1960	02:00	CST
4/28/1963	02:00	CDT
10/27/1963	02:00	CST
4/26/1964	02:00	CDT
10/25/1964	02:00	CST
5/30/1965	02:00	CDT
9/06/1965	02:00	CST
4/24/1966	02:00	US#1

IA # 19

Before 11/18/1883		LMT
11/18/1883	12:00	CST
3/31/1918	02:00	CWT
10/27/1918	02:00	CST
3/30/1919	02:00	CWT
10/26/1919	02:00	CST
2/09/1942	02:00	CWT
9/30/1945	02:00	CST
5/26/1963	02:00	CDT
9/01/1963	02:00	CST
4/26/1964	02:00	CDT
10/25/1964	02:00	CST
5/30/1965	02:00	CDT
9/06/1965	02:00	CST
4/24/1966	02:00	US#1

IA # 20

Before 11/18/1883		LMT
11/18/1883	12:00	CST
3/31/1918	02:00	CWT
10/27/1918	02:00	CST
3/30/1919	02:00	CWT
10/26/1919	02:00	CST
2/09/1942	02:00	CWT
9/30/1945	02:00	CST
4/30/1961	02:00	CDT
10/29/1961	02:00	CST
4/29/1962	02:00	CDT
9/02/1962	02:00	CST
4/28/1963	02:00	CDT
9/01/1963	02:00	CST
4/26/1964	02:00	CDT
10/31/1964	02:00	CST
5/30/1965	02:00	CDT
9/06/1965	02:00	CST
4/24/1966	02:00	US#1

IA # 21

Before 11/18/1883		LMT
11/18/1883	12:00	CST
3/31/1918	02:00	CWT
10/27/1918	02:00	CST
3/30/1919	02:00	CWT
10/26/1919	02:00	CST
2/09/1942	02:00	CWT
9/30/1945	02:00	CST
4/24/1960	02:00	CDT
10/30/1960	02:00	CST
4/30/1961	02:00	CDT
9/03/1961	02:00	CST
4/29/1962	02:00	CDT
9/15/1962	02:00	CST
4/28/1963	02:00	CDT
9/29/1963	02:00	CST
4/26/1964	02:00	CDT
10/31/1964	02:00	CST
5/30/1965	02:00	CDT
9/06/1965	02:00	CST
4/24/1966	02:00	US#1

IA # 22

Before 11/18/1883		LMT
11/18/1883	12:00	CST
3/31/1918	02:00	CWT
10/27/1918	02:00	CST
3/30/1919	02:00	CWT
10/26/1919	02:00	CST
2/09/1942	02:00	CWT
9/30/1945	02:00	CST
4/24/1960	02:00	CDT
10/30/1960	02:00	CST
4/30/1961	02:00	CDT
9/03/1961	02:00	CST
4/26/1964	02:00	CDT
10/25/1964	02:00	CST
5/30/1965	02:00	CDT
9/06/1965	02:00	CST
4/24/1966	02:00	US#1

IA # 23

Before 11/18/1883		LMT
11/18/1883	12:00	CST
3/31/1918	02:00	CWT
10/27/1918	02:00	CST
3/30/1919	02:00	CWT
10/26/1919	02:00	CST
2/09/1942	02:00	CWT
9/30/1945	02:00	CST
5/26/1963	02:00	CDT
8/26/1963	02:00	CST
4/26/1964	02:00	CDT
10/25/1964	02:00	CST
5/30/1965	02:00	CDT
9/06/1965	02:00	CST
4/24/1966	02:00	US#1

IA # 24

Before 11/18/1883		LMT
11/18/1883	12:00	CST
3/31/1918	02:00	CWT
10/27/1918	02:00	CST
3/30/1919	02:00	CWT
10/26/1919	02:00	CST
2/09/1942	02:00	CWT
9/30/1945	02:00	CST
4/24/1960	02:00	CDT
10/30/1960	02:00	CST
4/29/1962	02:00	CDT
9/16/1962	02:00	CST
4/28/1963	02:00	CDT
9/15/1963	02:00	CST
4/26/1964	02:00	CDT
10/25/1964	02:00	CST
5/30/1965	02:00	CDT
9/06/1965	02:00	CST
4/24/1966	02:00	US#1

IA # 25

Before 11/18/1883		LMT
11/18/1883	12:00	CST
3/31/1918	02:00	CWT
10/27/1918	02:00	CST
3/30/1919	02:00	CWT
10/26/1919	02:00	CST
2/09/1942	02:00	CWT
9/30/1945	02:00	CST
4/29/1962	02:00	CDT
9/15/1962	02:00	CST
4/28/1963	02:00	CDT
9/29/1963	02:00	CST
4/26/1964	02:00	CDT
10/25/1964	02:00	CST
5/30/1965	02:00	CDT
9/06/1965	02:00	CST
4/24/1966	02:00	US#1

COUNTIES

1 Adair
2 Adams
3 Allamakee
4 Appanoose
5 Audubon
6 Benton
7 Black Hawk
8 Boone
9 Bremer
10 Buchanan
11 Buena Vista
12 Butler
13 Calhoun
14 Carroll
15 Cass
16 Cedar
17 Cerro Gordo
18 Cherokee
19 Chickasaw
20 Clarke
21 Clay
22 Clayton
23 Clinton
24 Crawford
25 Dallas
26 Davis
27 Decatur
28 Delaware
29 Des Moines
30 Dickinson
31 Dubuque
32 Emmet
33 Fayette
34 Floyd
35 Franklin
36 Fremont
37 Greene
38 Grundy
39 Guthrie
40 Hamilton
41 Hancock
42 Hardin
43 Harrison
44 Henry
45 Howard
46 Humboldt
47 Ida
48 Iowa
49 Jackson
50 Jasper
51 Jefferson
52 Johnson
53 Jones
54 Keokuk
55 Kossuth
56 Lee
57 Linn
58 Louisa
59 Lucas
60 Lyon
61 Madison
62 Mahaska
63 Marion
64 Marshall
65 Mills
66 Mitchell
67 Monona
68 Monroe
69 Montgomery
70 Muscatine
71 O'Brien
72 Osceola
73 Page
74 Palo Alto
75 Plymouth
76 Pocahontas
77 Polk
78 Pottawattamie
79 Poweshiek
80 Ringgold
81 Sac
82 Scott
83 Shelby
84 Sioux
85 Story
86 Tama
87 Taylor
88 Union
89 Van Buren
90 Wapello
91 Warren
92 Washington
93 Wayne
94 Webster
95 Winnebago
96 Winneshiek
97 Woodbury
98 Worth
99 Wright

Place		Lat	Long	Time
Abingdon 51	2	41N05	92w08	6:08:32
Ackley 42	2	42N33	93w03	6:12:12
Ackworth 91	2	41N22	93w28	6:13:52
Adair 1	2	41N30	94w39	6:18:36
Adaza 37	2	42N09	94w29	6:17:56
Adel 25	2	41N37	94w01	6:16:04
Afton 88	2	41N02	94w12	6:16:48
Agency 90	4	41N00	92w19	6:09:16
Ainsworth 92	1	41N17	91w33	6:06:12
Akron 75	2	42N50	96w33	6:26:12
Albert City 11	2	42N47	94w57	6:19:48
Albia 68	2	41N02	92w48	6:11:12
Albion 64	2	42N07	92w59	6:11:56
Alburnett 57	1	42N09	91w37	6:06:28
Alden 42	2	42N31	93w23	6:13:32
Alexander 35	2	42N48	93w29	6:13:56
Algona 55	2	43N04	94w14	6:16:56
Alleman 77	2	41N49	93w37	6:14:28
Allendorf 72	2	43N25	95w39	6:22:36
Allens Grove 82	1	41N43	90w45	6:03:00
Allerton 93	2	40N42	93w22	6:13:28
Allison 12	2	42N45	92w48	6:11:12
Alpha 33	2	43N00	92w03	6:08:12
Alta 11	2	42N40	95w18	6:21:12
Alta Vista 19	2	43N12	92w25	6:09:40
Alton 84	2	42N59	96w01	6:24:04
Altoona 77	2	41N39	93w28	6:13:52
Alvord 60	2	43N21	96w18	6:25:12
Amana 48	1	41N48	91w52	6:07:28
Amaqua 8	2	42N04	94w06	6:16:24
Amber 53	1	42N08	91w11	6:04:44
Amboy 50	2	41N42	93w04	6:12:16
America 75	2	42N46	96w09	6:24:36
Ames 85	2	42N02	93w37	6:14:28
Amherst 18	2	42N47	95w48	6:23:12
Amity 73	2	40N37	95w05	6:20:20
Amsterdam 41	2	42N57	93w48	6:15:12
Anamosa 53	1	42N07	91w17	6:05:08
Anderson 36	2	40N48	95w36	6:22:24
Andover 23	1	42N00	90w15	6:01:00
Andrew 49	1	42N09	90w36	6:02:24
Anita 15	2	41N27	94w46	6:19:04
Ankeny 77	2	41N44	93w36	6:14:24
Anthon 97	2	42N23	95w52	6:23:28
Aplington 12	2	42N35	92w53	6:11:32
Arbor Hill 1	2	41N22	94w19	6:17:16
Arcadia 14	2	42N05	95w03	6:20:12
Archer 71	2	43N07	95w45	6:23:00
Aredale 12	2	42N50	93w00	6:12:00
Argyle 56	1	40N32	91w34	6:06:16
Arion 24	2	41N57	95w27	6:21:48
Arispe 88	2	40N57	94w13	6:16:52
Arlington 33	1	42N45	91w40	6:06:40
Armstrong 32	2	43N24	94w29	6:17:56
Armstrong Grove 32	2	43N23	94w30	6:18:00
Arnolds Park 30	2	43N21	95w08	6:20:32
Artesian 9	2	42N44	92w29	6:09:56
Arthur 47	2	42N20	95w21	6:21:24
Asbury 31	1	42N31	90w46	6:03:04
Ashton 72	2	43N19	95w47	6:23:08
Aspinwall 24	2	41N54	95w08	6:20:32
Atalissa 70	1	41N34	91w10	6:04:40
Athelstan 87	2	40N35	94w33	6:18:12
Athens 80	2	40N43	94w06	6:16:24
Atkins 6	1	42N00	91w51	6:07:24
Atlantic 15	2	41N24	95w01	6:20:04
Attica 63	2	41N14	93w01	6:12:04
Auburn 81	2	42N15	94w53	6:19:32
Audubon 5	2	41N43	94w56	6:19:44
Augusta 29	8	40N49	91w13	6:04:52
Aurelia 18	2	42N43	95w26	6:21:44
Aureola 34	2	42N58	92w52	6:11:28
Aurora 10	1	42N37	91w44	6:06:56
Austinville 12	2	42N35	92w57	6:11:48
Avery 68	2	41N04	92w43	6:10:52
Avoca 78	2	41N29	95w20	6:21:20
Avon 77	2	41N33	93w32	6:14:08
Avon Lake 77	2	41N33	93w32	6:14:08
Ayrshire 74	2	43N02	94w50	6:19:20
Badger 94	2	42N37	94w09	6:16:36
Bagley 39	2	41N51	94w26	6:17:44
Baldwin 49	1	42N04	90w50	6:03:20
Balltown 31	1	42N38	90w51	6:03:24
Baltimore 44	22	40N53	91w26	6:05:44
Bancroft 55	2	43N18	94w13	6:16:52
Bangor 64	2	42N10	93w05	6:12:20
Banks 33	2	42N51	92w01	6:08:04
Bankston 31	1	42N30	90w58	6:03:52
Banner 97	2	42N31	96w09	6:24:36
Barclay 7	2	42N31	92w08	6:08:32
Barnes 11	2	42N52	95w13	6:20:52
Barnes City 62	2	41N31	92w27	6:09:48
Barney 61	2	41N08	94w04	6:16:16
Barnum 94	2	42N31	94w21	6:17:24
Barrett Superette 1	2	41N33	94w24	6:17:36
Bartlett 36	2	40N53	95w47	6:23:08
Barton 98	2	43N23	93w05	6:12:20
Bassett 19	2	43N04	92w31	6:10:04
Batavia 51	4	41N00	92w10	6:08:40
Bath 17	2	43N03	93w12	6:12:48
Battle 47	2	42N26	95w36	6:22:24
Battle Creek 47	2	42N19	95w36	6:22:24
Baxter 50	2	41N49	93w09	6:12:36
Bayard 39	2	41N51	94w33	6:18:12
Beacon 62	2	41N17	92w41	6:10:44
Beaconsfield 80	2	40N48	94w03	6:16:12
Beaman 38	2	42N13	92w49	6:11:16
Bear Creek 79	2	41N44	92w29	6:09:56
Beaver 8	2	42N02	94w08	6:16:32
Beaverdale 77	2	41N36	93w40	6:14:40
Beaverdale Heights 29	8	40N49	91w10	6:04:40
Beckwith 51	1	41N00	91w57	6:07:48
Bedford 87	2	40N40	94w44	6:18:56
Beebeetown 43	2	41N39	95w48	6:23:12
Beech 91	2	41N23	93w16	6:13:04
Bel Air Beach 11	2	42N38	95w11	6:20:44
Belknap 26	2	40N49	92w26	6:09:44
Bellair 4	2	40N44	92w56	6:11:44
Belle Plaine 6	2	41N54	92w17	6:09:08
Bellevue 49	6	42N16	90w26	6:01:44
Bellville 76	2	42N37	94w38	6:18:32
Belmond 99	2	42N51	93w37	6:14:28
Belmont 91	2	41N17	93w23	6:13:32
Beloit 60	2	43N18	96w36	6:26:24
Belvidere 67	2	42N01	95w58	6:23:52
Bennett 16	1	41N45	90w59	6:03:56
Bennezette 12	2	42N52	92w58	6:11:52
Bennington 7	2	42N36	92w16	6:09:04
Bentley	2	41N23	95w37	6:22:28
Benton 80	2	40N42	94w22	6:17:28
Bentonsport 89	1	40N44	91w58	6:07:52
Berea 1	2	41N27	94w47	6:19:08
Berkley 8	2	41N57	94w07	6:16:28
Bernard 31	1	42N18	90w50	6:03:20
Berne 24	2	42N04	95w43	6:22:52
Bertram 57	1	41N57	91w32	6:06:08
Berwick 77	2	41N40	93w33	6:14:12
Bethel 33	2	42N57	92w01	6:08:04
Bethesda 73	2	40N47	95w02	6:20:08
Bethlehem 93	2	40N59	93w12	6:12:48
Bettendorf 82	7	41N32	90w30	6:02:00
Bevington 61	2	41N22	93w47	6:15:08
Big Creek 7	2	42N19	92w13	6:08:52
Big Rock 82	1	41N46	90w50	6:03:20
Bingham 73	2	40N44	95w18	6:21:12
Birmingham 89	1	40N53	91w57	6:07:48
Black Oak 62	2	41N23	92w49	6:11:16
Bladensburg 90	2	41N02	92w25	6:09:40
Blairsburg 40	2	42N29	93w39	6:14:36
Blairstown 6	2	41N55	92w05	6:08:20
Blakesburg 90	2	40N58	92w38	6:10:32
Blanchard 73	2	40N35	95w13	6:20:52
Blencoe 67	2	41N56	96w05	6:24:20
Blockton 87	2	40N37	94w29	6:17:56
Bloomfield 26	2	40N45	92w25	6:09:40
Blue Grass 82	5	41N33	90w42	6:02:48
Bluff Creek 68	2	41N07	92w48	6:11:12
Bluff Park 56	20	40N31	91w25	6:05:40
Bluffton 96	1	43N24	91w55	6:07:40
Boardman 22	1	42N52	91w26	6:05:44
Bode 46	2	42N52	94w17	6:17:08
Bolan 98	2	43N21	93w13	6:12:52
Bonair 45	2	43N27	92w17	6:09:08
Bonaparte 89	1	40N42	91w48	6:07:12
Bondurant 77	2	41N42	93w28	6:13:52
Boomer 78	2	41N28	95w46	6:23:04
Boone 8	2	42N04	93w53	6:15:32
Booneville 25	2	41N32	93w53	6:15:32
Booth 74	2	42N56	94w51	6:19:24
Botna 83	2	41N51	95w08	6:20:32
Boulder 57	1	42N15	91w26	6:05:44
Bouton 25	2	41N51	94w01	6:16:04
Boxholm 8	2	42N10	94w06	6:16:24
Boyd 19	2	43N04	92w20	6:09:20
Boyden 84	2	43N12	96w00	6:24:00
Boyer 24	2	42N11	95w14	6:20:56
Boyer Valley 81	2	42N26	95w09	6:20:36
Braddyville 73	2	40N35	95w02	6:20:08
Bradford 19	2	42N57	92w32	6:10:08
Bradford 35	2	42N38	93w15	6:13:00
Bradgate 46	2	42N48	94w25	6:17:40
Brainard 33	1	42N58	91w38	6:06:32
Brandon 10	1	42N19	92w00	6:08:00
Brayton 5	2	41N33	94w56	6:19:44
Brazil 4	2	40N47	92w57	6:11:48
Breda 14	2	42N11	94w59	6:19:56
Bremen 28	1	42N31	91w12	6:04:48
Bremer 9	2	42N46	92w24	6:09:36
Bridgewater 1	2	41N15	94w40	6:18:40
Brighton 92	1	41N10	91w49	6:07:16
Bristow 12	2	42N46	92w55	6:11:40
Britt 41	2	43N06	93w48	6:15:12
Bronson 97	2	42N25	96w13	6:24:52
Brooke 11	2	42N52	95w21	6:21:24
Brooklyn 79	2	41N44	92w27	6:09:48
Brooks 2	2	40N58	94w48	6:19:12
Brookside 7	2	42N32	92w26	6:09:44
Brown 57	1	42N05	91w25	6:05:40
Bruce 6	2	42N15	92w14	6:08:56
Brunsville 75	2	42N49	96w16	6:25:04
Brushy 94	2	42N28	94w01	6:16:04
Bryant 23	1	41N58	90w20	6:01:20
Buchanan 16	7	41N32	90w31	6:02:04
Buckcreek 9	2	42N51	92w07	6:08:28
Buckeye 42	2	42N25	93w23	6:13:32
Buck Grove 24	2	41N55	95w23	6:21:32
Buckingham 86	2	42N16	92w27	6:09:48
Buffalo 82	5	41N27	90w44	6:02:56
Buffalo Center 95	2	43N23	93w57	6:15:48
Buffalo Heights 82	1	41N31	90w44	6:02:56
Buncombe 84	2	43N02	96w28	6:25:52
Burchinal 17	2	43N04	93w17	6:13:08
Burdette 35	2	42N32	93w23	6:13:32
Burlington 29	8	40N49	91w14	6:04:56
Burnside 94	2	42N20	94w07	6:16:28
Burrell 27	2	40N42	93w50	6:15:20
Burr Oak 96	1	43N27	91w52	6:07:28
Burt 55	2	43N12	94w13	6:16:52
Bussey 63	2	41N12	92w53	6:11:32
Byron 10	1	42N31	91w47	6:07:08
Cairo 58	1	41N17	91w21	6:05:24
Calamus 23	1	41N50	90w46	6:03:04
Caldwell 4	2	40N38	92w48	6:11:12
Caledonia 71	2	42N58	95w48	6:23:12
Calhoun 43	2	41N33	95w55	6:23:40
California Junction 43	2	41N33	95w55	6:23:40
Callender 94	2	42N22	94w17	6:17:08
Call Terminal 97	2	42N30	96w23	6:25:32
Calmar 96	1	43N11	91w52	6:07:28
Calumet 71	2	42N57	95w33	6:22:12
Camanche 23	9	41N47	90w15	6:01:00
Cambria 93	2	40N50	93w24	6:13:36
Cambridge 85	2	41N54	93w32	6:14:08
Cameron 5	2	41N49	94w55	6:19:40
Camp 77	2	41N33	93w23	6:13:32
Camp Dodge 77	2	41N40	93w47	6:15:08
Canaan 44	1	41N03	91w26	6:05:44
Canby 1	2	41N31	94w32	6:18:08
Canoe 96	1	43N24	91w48	6:07:12
Canton 49	1	42N10	90w54	6:03:36
Cantril 89	2	40N39	92w04	6:08:16
Capel 84	2	43N07	96w03	6:24:12
Capitol Heights 77	2	41N36	93w34	6:14:16
Carbon 2	2	41N03	94w50	6:19:20
Carbondale 77	2	41N36	93w34	6:14:16
Carl 2	2	41N07	94w40	6:18:40

IOWA

Place	Zone	Lat.	Long.	Time
Carlisle 91	2	41N30	93w29	6:13:56
Carlton 86	2	42N05	92w42	6:10:48
Carmel 84	2	43N08	96w14	6:24:56
Carnarvon 81	2	42N15	95w01	6:20:04
Carnes 84	2	42N59	96w01	6:24:04
Carney 77	2	41N39	93w37	6:14:28
Carnforth 79	2	41N45	92w15	6:09:00
Carpenter 66	2	43N25	93w01	6:12:04
Carroll 14	2	42N04	94w52	6:19:28
Carson 78	2	41N14	95w25	6:21:40
Carter Lake 78	2	41N17	95w55	6:23:40
Cartersville 17	2	42N59	93w10	6:12:40
Cascade 31	1	42N18	91w01	6:04:04
Casey 39	2	41N30	94w32	6:18:08
Casino Beach 11	2	42N38	95w11	6:20:44
Castalia 96	1	43N07	91w41	6:06:44
Castana 67	2	42N04	95w55	6:23:40
Castle Grove 53	1	42N15	91w18	6:05:12
Cedar 62	2	41N13	92w31	6:10:04
Cedar Bluff 16	7	41N32	90w31	6:02:04
Cedar City 7	2	42N32	92w26	6:09:44
Cedar Falls 7	2	42N32	92w27	6:09:48
Cedar Rapids 57	1	41N59	91w40	6:06:40
Cedar Valley 16	1	41N37	91w10	6:04:40
Cedar View 34	2	43N04	92w41	6:10:44
Centennial 60	2	43N24	96w30	6:26:00
Centerdale 16	1	41N34	91w16	6:05:04
Center Grove 30	2	43N23	95w05	6:20:20
Center Grove 31	15	42N30	90w42	6:02:48
Center Junction 53	1	42N07	91w05	6:04:20
Center Point 57	1	42N12	91w46	6:07:04
Centerville 4	2	40N44	92w52	6:11:28
Centerville 8	2	42N05	93w56	6:15:44
Central City 57	1	42N12	91w32	6:06:08
Central College 63	2	41N24	92w55	6:11:40
Central Heights 17	2	43N09	93w13	6:12:52
Centralia 31	1	42N29	90w50	6:03:20
Chapin 35	2	42N50	93w13	6:12:52
Chariton 59	2	41N01	93w19	6:13:16
Charles City 34	2	43N04	92w41	6:10:44
Charleston 56	1	40N36	91w32	6:06:08
Charlotte 23	1	41N58	90w28	6:01:52
Charter Oak 24	2	42N04	95w36	6:22:24
Chatsworth 84	2	42N55	96w31	6:26:04
Chelsea 86	2	41N55	92w24	6:09:36
Chequest 89	2	40N47	92w08	6:08:32
Cherokee 18	2	42N45	95w33	6:22:12
Chester 45	2	43N29	92w22	6:09:28
Chickasaw 19	2	43N02	92w29	6:09:56
Chillicothe 90	2	41N05	92w32	6:10:08
Church 3	1	43N22	91w13	6:04:52
Churchville 91	2	41N30	93w37	6:14:28
Churdan 37	2	42N09	94w29	6:17:56
Cincinnati 4	2	40N38	92w56	6:11:44
Clare 94	2	42N35	94w21	6:17:24
Clarence 16	1	41N53	91w04	6:04:16
Clarinda 73	2	40N44	95w02	6:20:08
Clarion 99	2	42N44	93w44	6:14:56
Clark 86	2	42N10	92w23	6:09:32
Clarkdale 4	2	40N44	92w52	6:11:28
Clarksville 12	2	42N47	92w40	6:10:40
Clayton 22	1	42N54	91w09	6:04:36
Clayton Center 22	1	42N51	91w24	6:05:36
Clayworks 94	2	42N30	94w11	6:16:44
Clearfield 87	2	40N48	94w29	6:17:56
Clear Lake 17	2	43N08	93w23	6:13:32
Cleghorn 18	2	42N49	95w43	6:22:52
Clemons 64	2	42N07	93w10	6:12:40
Cleona 82	5	41N38	90w51	6:03:24
Clermont 33	1	43N00	91w39	6:06:36
Cleves 42	2	42N33	93w02	6:12:08
Cliffland 90	2	41N02	92w25	6:09:40
Climbing Hill 97	2	42N21	96w05	6:24:20
Clinton 23	10	41N51	90w12	6:00:48
Clio 93	2	40N38	93w27	6:13:48
Clive 77	2	41N36	93w44	6:14:56
Cloverdale 72	2	43N24	95w45	6:23:00
Cloverhills 77	2	41N35	93w44	6:14:56
Clutier 86	2	42N04	92w24	6:09:36
Clyde 50	2	41N55	93w18	6:13:12
Coal Creek 54	2	41N24	92w21	6:09:24
Coalville 94	2	42N30	94w11	6:16:44
Coburg 69	2	40N55	95w16	6:21:04
Coffins Grove 28	1	42N29	91w21	6:05:24
Coggon 57	1	42N17	91w32	6:06:08
Coin 73	2	40N40	95w14	6:20:56
Coldwater 12	2	42N52	92w51	6:11:24
Colesburg 28	1	42N38	91w12	6:04:48
Colfax 50	2	41N41	93w14	6:12:56
College 57	1	41N54	91w39	6:06:36
College Springs 73	2	40N37	95w07	6:20:28
Collins 85	2	41N54	93w18	6:13:12
Colo 85	2	42N01	93w19	6:13:16
Colonial Village 77	2	41N35	93w44	6:14:56
Columbia 63	2	41N10	93w09	6:12:36
Columbus City 58	1	41N15	91w23	6:05:32
Columbus Junction 58	1	41N17	91w22	6:05:28
Colwell 34	2	43N09	92w36	6:10:24
Commerce 77	2	41N35	93w44	6:14:56
Communia 22	1	42N51	91w24	6:05:36
Competine 90	2	41N08	92w14	6:08:56
Concordia 29	1	40N45	91w07	6:04:28
Conesville 70	1	41N23	91w21	6:05:24
Confidence 93	2	40N59	93w03	6:12:12
Conger 91	2	41N18	93w47	6:15:08
Cono 10	1	42N20	91w47	6:07:08
Conover 96	1	43N12	91w53	6:07:32
Conrad 38	2	42N14	92w52	6:11:28
Conroy 48	1	41N44	92w00	6:08:00
Conway 87	2	40N45	94w37	6:18:28
Cook 81	2	42N26	95w16	6:21:04
Cool 91	1	41N37	90w34	6:02:16
Coon 11	2	42N42	94w57	6:19:48
Coon Rapids 14	2	41N53	94w41	6:18:44
Coon Valley 81	2	42N21	94w57	6:19:48
Cooper 37	2	41N55	94w20	6:17:20
Coppock 44	1	41N10	91w42	6:06:48
Coralville 52	1	41N43	91w37	6:06:28
Corinth 46	2	42N41	94w16	6:17:04
Corley 83	2	41N39	95w20	6:21:20
Cornelia 99	2	42N47	93w41	6:14:44
Cornell 21	2	42N53	95w09	6:20:36
Corning 2	2	40N59	94w44	6:18:56
Correctionville 97	2	42N29	95w47	6:23:08
Corwin 47	2	42N20	95w30	6:22:00
Corwith 41	2	42N59	93w57	6:15:48
Corydon 93	2	40N46	93w19	6:13:16
Cosgrove 52	1	41N44	91w48	6:07:12
Cotter 58	1	41N18	91w25	6:05:40
Cou Falls 52	1	41N51	91w42	6:06:48
Coulter 35	2	42N44	93w22	6:13:28
Council Bluffs 78	2	41N16	95w52	6:23:28
Covington 57	1	41N59	91w44	6:06:56
Cox Creek 22	1	42N47	91w26	6:05:44
Craig 75	2	42N54	96w19	6:25:16
Crandalls Lodge 30	2	43N26	95w06	6:20:24
Cranston 70	1	41N23	91w16	6:05:04
Crawfordsville 92	1	41N12	91w32	6:06:08
Crescent 78	2	41N22	95w53	6:23:32
Cresco 45	2	43N22	92w07	6:08:28
Creston 88	2	41N04	94w22	6:17:28
Crestwood 77	2	41N36	93w41	6:14:44
Crocker 77	2	41N43	93w38	6:14:32
Cromwell 88	2	41N02	94w28	6:17:52
Crossroads Center 7	2	42N31	92w20	6:09:20
Crossroads Center 94	2	42N30	94w11	6:16:44
Croton 56	1	40N35	91w41	6:06:44
Crystal Lake 41	2	43N13	93w47	6:15:08
Culver 70	1	41N26	91w03	6:04:12
Cumberland 15	2	41N16	94w52	6:19:28
Cumberland Square 82	7	41N33	90w30	6:02:00
Cumming 91	2	41N29	93w46	6:15:04
Cummins 76	2	42N52	94w44	6:18:56
Curlew 74	2	42N59	94w44	6:18:56
Cushing 97	2	42N28	95w42	6:22:48
Cylinder 74	2	43N05	94w33	6:18:12
Dahlonega 90	2	41N04	92w21	6:09:24
Dakota City 46	2	42N43	94w12	6:16:48
Dalby 3	1	43N13	91w18	6:05:12
Dale 39	2	41N31	94w25	6:17:40
Dallas 63	2	41N14	93w15	6:13:00
Dallas Center 25	2	41N41	93w58	6:15:52
Dana 37	2	42N06	94w14	6:16:56
Danbury 97	2	42N14	95w43	6:22:52
Danville 29	11	40N52	91w19	6:05:16
Darbyville 4	2	40N44	92w52	6:11:28
Davenport 82	12	41N32	90w35	6:02:20
Davis City 27	2	40N38	93w49	6:15:16
Dawson 25	2	41N50	94w13	6:16:52
Dayton 94	2	42N16	94w05	6:16:20
Daytonville 92	1	41N28	91w50	6:07:20
Dean 4	2	40N41	92w41	6:10:44
Decatur City 27	2	40N45	93w50	6:15:20
Decorah 96	1	43N18	91w48	6:07:12
Dedham 14	2	41N55	94w49	6:19:16
Deep Creek 23	1	42N00	90w22	6:01:28
Deep River 79	2	41N35	92w22	6:09:28
Deerfield 19	2	43N08	92w30	6:10:00
Defiance 83	2	41N49	95w20	6:21:20
Delana 46	2	42N52	94w16	6:17:04
Delaware 28	1	42N29	91w21	6:05:24
Delhi 28	1	42N26	91w20	6:05:20
Delmar 23	1	42N00	90w37	6:02:28
Deloit 24	2	42N06	95w19	6:21:16
Delphos 80	2	40N40	94w20	6:17:20
Delta 54	2	41N19	92w20	6:09:20
Denhart 41	2	42N56	93w48	6:15:12
Denison 24	2	42N01	95w21	6:21:24
Denmark 56	1	40N44	91w20	6:05:20
Denver 9	2	42N40	92w20	6:09:20
Depew 74	2	43N05	94w34	6:18:16
Derby 59	2	40N56	93w27	6:13:48
Des Moines 77	2	41N35	93w37	6:14:28
De Soto 25	2	41N32	94w01	6:16:04
Dewar 7	2	42N31	92w13	6:08:52
De Witt 23	13	41N49	90w33	6:02:12
Dexter 25	2	41N31	94w14	6:16:56
Diagonal 80	2	40N49	94w20	6:17:20
Diamond 18	2	42N36	95w27	6:21:48
Diamond Center 18	2	42N43	95w26	6:21:44
Diamond Lake 30	2	43N28	95w13	6:20:52
Dickens 21	2	43N08	95w01	6:20:04
Dike 38	2	42N28	92w38	6:10:32
Dillon 64	2	42N02	92w54	6:11:36
Dinsdale 86	2	42N19	92w36	6:10:24
Dixon 82	5	41N45	90w47	6:03:08
Dodge Park 78	2	41N16	95w51	6:23:24
Dodgeville 29	1	40N57	91w09	6:04:36
Dolliver 32	2	43N28	94w37	6:18:28
Donahue 82	1	41N42	90w41	6:02:44
Donnan 33	1	42N54	91w53	6:07:32
Donnellson 56	14	40N38	91w34	6:06:16
Doon 60	2	43N17	96w14	6:24:56
Dorchester 3	1	43N28	91w31	6:06:04
Doris 10	1	42N29	91w53	6:07:32
Douds 89	2	40N50	92w05	6:08:20
Dougherty 17	2	42N55	93w03	6:12:12
Dow City 24	2	41N56	95w29	6:21:56
Downey 16	1	41N37	91w21	6:05:24
Dows 99	2	42N39	93w30	6:14:00
Doyle 20	2	40N57	93w56	6:15:44
Drakesville 26	2	40N48	92w29	6:09:56
Dresden 19	2	42N57	92w16	6:09:04
Dubuque 31	15	42N30	90w41	6:02:44
Dudley 90	2	41N02	92w25	6:09:40
Dumont 12	2	42N45	92w58	6:11:52
Dunbar 64	2	41N56	92w47	6:11:08
Duncan 41	2	43N06	93w48	6:15:12
Duncombe 94	2	42N28	94w00	6:16:00
Dundee 28	1	42N35	91w33	6:06:12
Dunkerton 7	2	42N34	92w10	6:08:40
Dunlap 43	2	41N51	95w36	6:22:24
Durango 31	1	42N34	90w47	6:03:08
Durant 16	13	41N36	90w54	6:03:36
Durham 63	2	41N19	92w55	6:11:40
Dutch Creek 92	1	41N17	91w53	6:07:32
Dutchtown 28	1	42N31	91w25	6:05:40
Dyersville 31	1	42N29	91w08	6:04:32
Dysart 86	2	42N10	92w18	6:09:12
Eagle Center 7	2	42N29	92w23	6:09:32
Eagle Grove 99	2	42N40	93w54	6:15:36
Eagle Point 31	15	42N30	90w42	6:02:48
Earlham 61	2	41N30	94w07	6:16:28
Earling 83	2	41N47	95w25	6:21:40
Earlville 28	1	42N29	91w17	6:05:08
Early 81	2	42N28	95w09	6:20:36
East 69	2	40N56	95w00	6:20:00
East Amana 48	1	41N49	91w51	6:07:24
East Boyer 24	2	41N59	95w16	6:21:04
East Des Moines 77	2	41N35	93w37	6:14:28
East Lancaster 54	2	41N16	92w07	6:08:28
East Lincoln 66	2	43N14	92w38	6:10:32
East Lucas 52	1	41N38	91w32	6:06:08
East Orange 84	2	42N57	95w57	6:23:48
East Peru 61	2	41N14	93w56	6:15:44
East Pleasant Plain 51	1	41N11	91w49	6:07:16
East River 73	2	40N41	94w59	6:19:56
East Waterloo 7	2	42N32	92w17	6:09:08
Eddyville 90	2	41N09	92w38	6:10:32
Edgewood 22	1	42N39	91w24	6:05:36
Edgewood Park 82	7	41N33	90w30	6:02:00
Edison 78	2	41N16	95w51	6:23:24
Edna 60	2	43N23	96w06	6:24:24
Egan 3	1	43N13	91w09	6:04:36
Egralharve 30	2	43N26	95w06	6:20:24
Elberon 86	2	42N00	92w19	6:09:16
Eldon 90	2	40N55	92w13	6:08:52
Eldora 42	2	42N22	93w05	6:12:20
Eldorado 33	1	43N03	91w50	6:07:20
Eldridge 82	5	41N39	90w35	6:02:20
Elgin 33	1	42N57	91w38	6:06:32
Eliot 58	1	41N06	91w00	6:04:00
Elkader 22	1	42N51	91w24	6:05:36
Elk Creek 50	2	41N33	92w56	6:11:44
Elkhart 77	2	41N48	93w31	6:14:04
Elk Horn 83	2	41N36	95w03	6:20:12
Elkport 22	1	42N44	91w17	6:05:08
Elk River 23	1	42N01	90w14	6:00:56
Elk Run Heights 7	2	42N28	92w16	6:09:04
Ell 41	2	43N02	93w34	6:14:16
Elliott 69	2	41N09	95w10	6:20:40
Ellis 42	2	42N26	93w18	6:13:12
Ellston 80	2	40N51	94w07	6:16:28
Ellsworth 40	2	42N18	93w34	6:14:16
Elma 45	2	43N15	92w26	6:09:44
Elon 3	1	43N13	91w18	6:05:12
Elrick 58	23	41N11	91w11	6:04:44
Elvira 23	10	41N52	90w12	6:00:48
Elwood 23	1	41N59	90w45	6:03:00
Ely 57	1	41N52	91w35	6:06:20
Emeline 49	1	42N04	90w50	6:03:20
Emerson 65	2	41N01	95w27	6:21:48
Emery 17	2	43N09	93w13	6:12:52
Emmet 32	2	43N28	94w49	6:19:16
Emmetsburg 74	2	43N07	94w41	6:18:44
Enterprise 77	2	41N48	93w31	6:14:04
Epworth 31	1	42N27	90w56	6:03:44
Ericson 8	2	42N05	93w56	6:15:44
Erin 41	2	43N02	93w48	6:15:12
Essex 73	2	40N50	95w18	6:21:12
Estherville 32	2	43N24	94w50	6:19:20
Etna 42	2	42N31	93w04	6:12:16
Evans 62	2	41N18	92w44	6:10:56
Evansdale 7	2	42N30	92w17	6:09:08
Evans Junction 62	2	41N16	92w41	6:10:44
Evanston 94	2	42N28	94w01	6:16:04
Evergreen 82	12	41N32	90w36	6:02:24
Everly 21	2	43N10	95w19	6:21:16
Ewart 79	2	41N39	92w37	6:10:28
Ewoldt 14	2	41N54	95w02	6:20:08
Excelsior 30	2	43N23	95w20	6:21:20
Exira 5	2	41N35	94w52	6:19:28
Exline 4	2	40N39	92w50	6:11:20
Fabius 26	2	40N39	92w35	6:10:20
Fairbank 10	2	42N38	92w03	6:08:12
Fairfax 57	1	41N55	91w47	6:07:08
Fairfield 51	3	41N01	91w57	6:07:48
Fair Ground 31	15	42N30	90w42	6:02:48
Fairmount Park 78	2	41N16	95w51	6:23:24
Fairport 70	1	41N26	90w54	6:03:36
Fairview 53	1	42N07	91w17	6:05:08
Falls 17	2	43N13	93w05	6:12:20
Fanslers 39	2	41N41	94w30	6:18:00
Farley 31	1	42N27	91w00	6:04:00
Farlin 37	2	42N04	94w27	6:17:48
Farmersburg 22	1	42N58	91w18	6:05:12
Farmers Creek 49	1	42N10	90w43	6:02:52
Farmington 89	1	40N38	91w44	6:06:56
Farnhamville 13	2	42N17	94w25	6:17:40
Farragut 36	2	40N43	95w29	6:21:56
Farrar 77	2	41N54	93w23	6:13:32
Farson 90	2	41N10	92w18	6:09:12
Faulkner 35	2	42N37	93w05	6:12:20
Fayette 33	1	42N51	91w48	6:07:12
Felix 38	2	42N15	92w57	6:11:48

IOWA

Fenton 55 2 43N13 94W26 6:17:44
Ferguson 64 2 41N56 92W52 6:11:28
Fern 38 2 42N35 92W48 6:11:12
Fernald 85 2 42N04 93W24 6:13:36
Fern Valley 74 2 43N01 94W31 6:18:04
Fertile 98 2 43N16 93W25 6:13:40
Festina 96 1 43N07 91W52 6:07:28
Fillmore 31 1 42N18 91W01 6:04:04
Fillmore 48 1 41N34 92W00 6:08:00
Finchford 7 2 42N38 92W33 6:10:12
First Street 57 1 41N59 91W40 6:06:40
Fiscus 5 2 41N43 94W56 6:19:44
Fisher 36 2 40N42 95W26 6:21:44
Five Points 31 1 42N33 90W50 6:03:20
Flagler 63 2 41N19 93W06 6:12:24
Flint River 29 8 40N52 91W12 6:04:48
Florence 6 1 41N54 91W53 6:07:32
Florenceville 45 2 43N22 92W08 6:08:32
Floris 26 2 40N52 92W20 6:09:20
Floyd 34 2 43N08 92W44 6:10:56
Folletts 23 1 41N45 90W21 6:01:24
Fonda 76 2 42N35 94W51 6:19:24
Fontanelle 1 2 41N17 94W34 6:18:16
Forbush 4 2 40N44 92W52 6:11:28
Forest City 95 2 43N16 93W39 6:14:36
Fort Atkinson 96 1 43N09 91W56 6:07:44
Fort Dodge 94 2 42N30 94W11 6:16:44
Fort Madison 56 16 40N38 91W27 6:05:48
Fostoria 21 2 43N15 95W09 6:20:36
Four Corners 51 1 41N00 91W44 6:06:56
Four Mile 77 2 41N34 93W28 6:13:52
Fox 7 2 42N25 92W07 6:08:28
Fox River 26 2 40N47 92W35 6:10:20
Frankfort 69 2 41N02 95W06 6:20:24
Franklin 56 1 40N38 91W34 6:06:16
Franklin 78 2 41N16 95W51 6:23:24
Frankville 96 1 43N11 91W37 6:06:28
Fraser 8 2 42N08 93W58 6:15:52
Fredericksburg 19 2 42N58 92W12 6:08:48
Frederika 9 2 42N53 92W19 6:09:16
Fredonia 58 1 41N17 91W21 6:05:24
Freeman 17 2 43N09 93W13 6:12:52
Freeman 21 2 43N08 94W58 6:19:52
Freeport 96 1 43N19 91W48 6:07:12
Fremont 62 2 41N13 92W26 6:09:44
French Creek 3 1 43N24 91W26 6:05:44
Froelich 22 1 42N58 91W22 6:05:28
Fruitland 70 1 41N21 91W08 6:04:32
Fulton 49 1 42N09 90W41 6:02:44
Galbraith 55 2 43N15 94W07 6:16:28
Galesburg 50 2 41N35 93W02 6:12:08
Galland 56 20 40N31 91W25 6:05:40
Galt 99 2 42N42 93W36 6:14:24
Galva 47 2 42N30 95W25 6:21:40
Gambrill 82 1 41N45 90W32 6:02:08
Garber 22 1 42N45 91W16 6:05:04
Garden 8 2 41N54 93W45 6:15:00
Garden City 42 2 42N15 93W24 6:13:36
Garden Grove 27 2 40N50 93W36 6:14:24
Gardiner 25 2 41N51 94W01 6:16:04
Garfield 4 2 40N47 92W57 6:11:48
Garnavillo 22 1 42N52 91W14 6:04:56
Garner 41 2 43N06 93W36 6:14:24
Garrison 6 2 42N09 92W08 6:08:32
Garwin 86 2 42N06 92W41 6:10:44
Gay 87 2 40N41 94W32 6:18:08
Gaza 71 2 43N01 95W35 6:22:20
Geneva 35 2 42N41 93W08 6:12:32
Genoa Bluff 48 2 41N47 92W04 6:08:16
George 60 2 43N20 96W00 6:24:00
Georgetown 68 2 41N02 92W48 6:11:12
Germantown 71 2 42N57 95W47 6:23:08
German Valley 55 2 43N13 94W09 6:16:36
Germanville 51 1 41N11 91W49 6:07:16
Giard 22 1 43N02 91W19 6:05:16
Gibson 54 2 41N29 92W24 6:09:36
Gifford 42 2 42N17 93W05 6:12:20
Gilbert 85 2 42N07 93W39 6:14:36
Gilbertville 7 2 42N25 92W13 6:08:52
Gillett Grove 21 2 43N01 95W02 6:20:08
Gilliatt 2 41N18 95W45 6:23:00
Gilman 64 2 41N53 92W47 6:11:08
Gilmore City 76 2 42N44 94W27 6:17:48
Gladbrook 86 2 42N11 92W43 6:10:52
Glasgow 51 1 40N56 91W47 6:07:08
Glendale Acres 78 2 41N16 95W51 6:23:24
Glendon 39 2 41N33 94W24 6:17:36
Glenwood 65 2 41N03 95W45 6:23:00
Glidden 14 2 42N04 94W44 6:18:56
Goddard 50 2 41N41 93W16 6:13:04
Goewey 72 2 43N18 95W41 6:22:44
Goldfield 99 2 42N44 93W55 6:15:40
Goodell 41 2 42N55 93W37 6:14:28
Goodrich 24 2 42N05 95W22 6:21:28
Goose Lake 23 1 41N58 90W23 6:01:32
Goshen 70 1 41N33 91W11 6:04:44
Gower 16 1 41N43 91W17 6:05:08
Gowrie 94 2 42N17 94W17 6:17:08
Grace Hill 92 1 41N18 91W41 6:06:44
Graettinger 74 2 43N14 94W45 6:19:00
Graf 31 1 42N29 90W53 6:03:32
Grafton 98 2 43N20 93W04 6:12:16
Graham 52 1 41N44 91W25 6:05:40
Grand 77 2 41N35 93W37 6:14:28
Grand Junction 37 2 42N02 94W14 6:16:56
Grand Mound 23 1 41N50 90W39 6:02:36
Grand River 27 2 40N49 93W58 6:15:52
Grandview 58 1 41N16 91W11 6:04:44
Grange 97 2 42N21 96W11 6:24:44
Granger 25 2 41N46 93W49 6:15:16
Granger Homesteads 25
2 41N46 93W50 6:15:20
Granite 60 2 43N27 96W27 6:25:48
Grant 69 2 41N09 94W59 6:19:56
Grant Center 67 2 42N10 96W00 6:24:00
Grant City 81 2 42N17 94W53 6:19:32
Grant Wood 82 7 41N33 90W30 6:02:00
Granville 84 2 42N59 95W54 6:23:36
Gravity 87 2 40N46 94W45 6:19:00
Gray 5 2 41N51 94W59 6:19:56
Great Oak 74 2 43N01 94W44 6:18:56
Greeley 28 1 42N35 91W21 6:05:24
Greenbrier 37 2 41N53 94W27 6:17:48
Green Castle 50 2 41N41 93W16 6:13:04
Greencastle 64 2 41N54 92W48 6:11:12
Greene 12 2 42N54 92W48 6:11:12
Greenfield 1 2 41N18 94W28 6:17:52
Greenfield Plaza 91
2 41N33 93W37 6:14:28
Green Island 49 1 42N09 90W20 6:01:20
Green Mountain 64 2 42N06 92W49 6:11:16
Greenville 21 2 43N01 95W09 6:20:36
Greenwood 55 2 43N18 94W16 6:17:04
Griggs 47 2 42N31 95W33 6:22:12
Grimes 77 2 41N41 93W47 6:15:08
Grinnell 79 2 41N45 92W43 6:10:52
Griswold 15 2 41N14 95W08 6:20:32
Grundy Center 38 2 42N22 92W47 6:11:08
Gruver 32 2 43N24 94W42 6:18:48
Guernsey 79 2 41N39 92W21 6:09:24
Guilford 68 2 41N01 92W56 6:11:44
Gunder 22 1 42N58 91W31 6:06:04
Guss 87 2 40N56 94W54 6:19:36
Guthrie Center 39 2 41N41 94W30 6:18:00
Guttenberg 22 1 42N47 91W06 6:04:24
Halbur 14 2 42N00 94W58 6:19:52
Hale 53 1 42N01 91W04 6:04:16
Halfa 2 43N21 94W33 6:18:12
Hamburg 36 2 40N36 95W39 6:22:36
Hamill 56 9 40N38 91W34 6:06:16
Hamilton 63 2 41N11 92W56 6:11:44
Hamlin 5 2 41N40 94W54 6:19:36
Hampshire 23 1 41N56 90W15 6:01:00
Hampton 35 2 42N45 93W13 6:12:52
Hancock 78 2 41N24 95W21 6:21:24
Hanford 17 2 43N09 93W13 6:12:52
Hanley 61 2 41N18 93W47 6:15:08
Hanlontown 98 2 43N17 93W23 6:13:32
Hanna 55 2 43N15 94W07 6:16:28
Hanover 3 1 43N17 91W29 6:05:56
Hanover 11 2 42N40 95W19 6:21:16
Hansell 35 2 42N46 93W06 6:12:24
Harcourt 94 2 42N16 94W11 6:16:44
Hardy 46 2 42N49 94W03 6:16:12
Harlan 83 2 41N39 95W19 6:21:16
Harper 54 2 41N22 92W03 6:08:12
Harpers Ferry 3 1 43N12 91W09 6:04:36
Harris 72 2 43N27 95W27 6:21:48
Harrisburg 89 1 40N47 91W47 6:07:08
Hartford 91 2 41N28 93W24 6:13:36
Hartland 98 2 43N28 93W19 6:13:16
Hartley 71 2 43N11 95W29 6:21:56
Hartwick 79 2 41N47 92W21 6:09:24
Harvard 93 2 40N42 93W22 6:13:28
Harvey 63 2 41N19 92W55 6:11:40
Haskins 92 1 41N18 91W34 6:06:16
Hastie 77 2 41N36 93W34 6:14:16
Hastings 65 2 41N01 95W30 6:22:00
Hauntown 23 10 41N52 90W12 6:00:48
Havelock 76 2 42N50 94W42 6:18:48
Haven 86 2 41N58 92W35 6:10:20
Haverhill 64 2 41N57 92W58 6:11:52
Hawarden 84 2 43N00 96W29 6:25:56
Hawkeye 33 1 42N56 91W57 6:07:48
Hawleyville 73 2 40N47 95W02 6:20:08
Hawthorne 69 2 40N57 95W14 6:20:56
Hayesville 54 2 41N16 92W15 6:09:00
Hayfield 41 2 43N11 93W42 6:14:48
Hazel Dell 78 2 41N24 95W46 6:23:04
Hazel Green 28 1 42N20 91W25 6:05:40
Hazleton 10 1 42N37 91W54 6:07:36
Hebron 1 2 41N13 94W25 6:17:40
Hebron 55 2 43N28 94W03 6:16:12
Hedrick 54 2 41N11 92W19 6:09:16
Henderson 65 2 41N08 95W26 6:21:44
Hepburn 73 2 40N51 95W01 6:20:04
Herdland 21 2 42N57 95W05 6:20:20
Herndon 39 2 41N57 92W58 6:11:52
Herrold 77 2 41N40 93W47 6:15:08
Hesper 96 1 43N28 91W48 6:07:12
Hiawatha 57 1 42N02 91W41 6:06:44
High 48 1 41N48 91W52 6:07:28
High Lake 32 2 43N18 94W43 6:18:52
Highland Center 90
2 41N08 92W21 6:09:24
Highland Park 77 2 41N36 93W39 6:14:36
Highlandville 96 1 43N27 91W40 6:06:40
High Point 27 2 40N47 93W36 6:14:24
Highview 40 2 42N28 93W49 6:15:16
Hills 52 1 41N33 91W32 6:06:08
Hillsboro 44 1 40N52 91W42 6:06:48
Hilton 48 1 41N44 92W00 6:08:00
Hinton 75 2 42N38 96W18 6:25:12
Hiteman 68 2 41N04 92W54 6:11:36
Hobarton 55 2 43N04 94W14 6:16:56
Holbrook 48 1 41N35 92W00 6:08:00
Holiday Lake 79 2 41N44 92W27 6:09:48
Holland 38 2 42N24 92W48 6:11:12
Holly Springs 97 2 42N14 96W06 6:24:24
Holman 72 2 43N24 95W44 6:22:56
Holmes 99 2 42N44 93W44 6:14:56
Holstein 47 2 42N29 95W33 6:22:12
Holt 87 2 40N51 94W45 6:19:00
Holy Cross 31 1 42N36 91W00 6:04:00
Homer 40 2 42N28 93W49 6:15:16
Homestead 48 1 41N45 91W53 6:07:32
Honey Creek 78 2 41N27 95W52 6:23:28
Hopeville 20 2 41N03 93W56 6:15:44
Hopkinton 28 1 42N21 91W15 6:05:00
Hornick 97 2 42N14 96W06 6:24:24
Horton 9 2 42N44 92W29 6:09:56
Horton 72 2 43N28 95W34 6:22:16
Hospers 84 2 43N04 95W54 6:23:36
Houghton 56 9 40N47 91W37 6:06:28
Howard Center 45 2 43N23 92W15 6:09:00
Howe 1 2 41N31 94W25 6:17:40
Hubbard 42 2 42N18 93W18 6:13:12
Hudson 7 2 42N24 92W28 6:09:52
Hull 84 2 43N11 96W09 6:24:36
Humboldt 46 2 42N44 94W13 6:16:52
Humeston 93 2 40N52 93W30 6:14:00
Hungerford 75 2 42N36 96W16 6:25:04
Huntington 32 2 43N30 94W48 6:19:12
Huron 29 1 41N02 91W02 6:04:08
Hurstville 49 1 42N06 90W41 6:02:44
Hutchins 41 2 43N06 93W48 6:15:12
Huxley 85 2 41N54 93W36 6:14:24
Iconium 4 2 40N54 92W57 6:11:48
Ida Grove 47 2 42N21 95W28 6:21:52
Illyria 33 1 42N52 91W40 6:06:40
Imogene 36 2 40N53 95W29 6:21:56
Independence 10 1 42N28 91W54 6:07:36
Indiana 63 2 41N13 93W02 6:12:08
Indianapolis 62 2 41N24 92W21 6:09:24
Indian Creek 57 1 42N01 91W36 6:06:24
Indian Creek 78 2 41N16 95W51 6:23:24
Indianola 91 2 41N22 93W34 6:14:16
Indian Village 86 2 41N59 92W42 6:10:48
Industry 94 2 42N35 94W51 6:19:24
Ingham 35 2 42N47 93W04 6:12:16
Ingraham 65 2 41N07 95W35 6:22:20
Inland 16 1 41N43 90W58 6:03:52
Inwood 60 2 43N19 96W26 6:25:44
Ionia 19 2 43N02 92W27 6:09:48
Iowa Army Ammunition Plant 29
1 40N49 91W06 6:04:24
Iowa Center 85 2 41N54 93W23 6:13:32
Iowa City 52 1 41N40 91W32 6:06:08
Iowa Falls 42 2 42N31 93W16 6:13:04
Iowa Lake 32 2 43N28 94W30 6:18:00
Iowa State University Sta 85
2 42N03 93W35 6:14:20
Ira 50 2 41N47 93W12 6:12:48
Ireton 84 2 42N58 96W19 6:25:16
Ironhills 49 1 42N04 90W40 6:02:40
Irving 6 2 41N54 92W16 6:09:04
Irvington 55 2 43N00 94W12 6:16:48
Irwin 83 2 41N47 95W12 6:20:48
Ivy 77 2 41N39 93W28 6:13:52
Jack Creek 32 2 43N18 94W37 6:18:28
Jackson Junction 96
2 43N07 92W02 6:08:08
Jacksonville 19 2 43N09 92W17 6:09:08
Jacksonville 83 2 41N39 95W20 6:21:20
Jamaica 39 2 41N51 94W18 6:17:12
James 75 2 42N32 96W24 6:25:36
James 78 2 41N23 95W26 6:21:44
Jamestown 45 2 43N23 92W30 6:10:00
Jamison 20 2 41N07 93W44 6:14:56
Janesville 9 2 42N39 92W28 6:09:52
Jefferson 37 2 42N01 94W23 6:17:32
Jenkins 66 2 43N23 92W37 6:10:28
Jerico 19 2 43N11 92W15 6:09:00
Jerome 4 2 40N44 92W52 6:11:28
Jesup 10 2 42N29 92W04 6:08:16
Jewell 40 2 42N20 93W39 6:14:36
Joetown 52 1 41N29 91W42 6:06:48
Johns 4 2 40N47 93W02 6:12:08
Johnston 77 2 41N43 93W43 6:14:52
Joice 98 2 43N22 93W27 6:13:48
Jolley 13 2 42N29 94W43 6:18:52
Jones 88 2 41N02 94W04 6:16:16
Jordan 8 2 42N03 93W47 6:15:08
Julien 31 15 42N30 90W42 6:02:48
Junction 37 2 42N04 94W14 6:16:56
Juniata 11 2 42N38 95W11 6:20:44
Kalo 94 2 42N25 94W10 6:16:40
Kalona 92 1 41N29 91W43 6:06:52
Kamrar 40 2 42N24 93W44 6:14:56
Kanawha 41 2 42N56 93W48 6:15:12
Kedron 97 2 42N26 95W50 6:23:20
Keg Creek 78 2 41N12 95W41 6:22:44
Kellerton 80 2 40N43 94W03 6:16:12
Kelley 85 2 41N57 93W40 6:14:40
Kellogg 50 2 41N44 92W55 6:11:40
Kendallville 96 2 43N22 92W08 6:08:32
Kendrick 37 2 42N05 94W34 6:18:16
Kennebec 67 2 42N06 95W58 6:23:52
Kensett 98 2 43N21 93W13 6:12:52
Kent 88 2 40N57 94W28 6:17:52
Kenwood 24 2 41N55 95W27 6:21:48
Keokuk 56 17 40N24 91W24 6:05:36
Keomah 62 2 41N17 92W38 6:10:32
Keosauqua 89 1 40N44 91W58 6:07:52
Keota 54 1 41N22 91W57 6:07:48
Kesley 12 2 42N40 92W55 6:11:40
Keswick 54 2 41N27 92W14 6:08:56
Keystone 6 2 42N00 92W12 6:08:48
Key West 31 15 42N27 90W41 6:02:44
Kilbourn 89 1 40N54 91W57 6:07:48
Killduff 50 2 41N36 92W54 6:11:36
Kimballton 5 2 41N38 95W04 6:20:16
King 1 42N24 90W25 6:01:40
Kingsley 75 2 42N35 95W58 6:23:52
Kingston 29 1 41N01 91W09 6:04:36
Kinross 54 1 41N28 91W59 6:07:56
Kirkman 83 2 41N44 95W16 6:21:04
Kirkville 90 2 41N10 92W30 6:10:00
Kiron 24 2 42N12 95W20 6:21:20
Klemme 41 2 43N01 93W36 6:14:24
Klinger 9 2 42N42 92W14 6:08:56
Knierim 13 2 42N27 94W27 6:17:48
Kniest 14 2 42N10 94W56 6:19:44
Knittel 9 2 42N42 92W14 6:08:56
Knoke 13 2 42N31 94W46 6:19:04
Knoxville 63 2 41N19 93W06 6:12:24
Konigsmark 57 1 41N59 91W40 6:06:40
Kossuth 29 1 41N01 91W09 6:04:36

 IOWA

Place	Zone	Lat	Long	Time
Koszta 48	2	41N50	92W12	6:08:48
Lacelle 20	2	41N02	93W46	6:15:04
Lacey 62	2	41N24	92W38	6:10:32
Lacona 91	2	41N12	93W23	6:13:32
Ladora 48	2	41N45	92W11	6:08:44
La Fayette 57	1	42N09	91W37	6:06:28
La Grange 43	2	41N33	95W46	6:23:04
Lake Canyada 82	12	41N32	90W36	6:02:24
Lake City 13	2	42N16	94W44	6:18:56
Lake Creek 13	2	42N21	94W42	6:18:48
Lake Mills 95	2	43N25	93W32	6:14:08
Lake Park 30	2	43N27	95W19	6:21:16
Lakeport 97	2	42N16	96W17	6:25:08
Lake Prairie 63	2	41N26	92W55	6:11:40
Lakeside 11	2	42N37	95W10	6:20:40
Lake View 81	2	42N18	95W03	6:20:12
Lakeville 30	2	43N24	95W13	6:20:52
Lakewood 91	2	41N30	93W37	6:14:28
Lakota 55	2	43N23	94W06	6:16:24
Lambs Grove 50	2	41N42	93W05	6:12:20
La Moille 64	2	42N02	92W54	6:11:36
Lamoni 27	2	40N37	93W56	6:15:44
Lamont 10	1	42N36	91W38	6:06:32
La Motte 49	1	42N18	90W37	6:02:28
Lanesboro 14	2	42N11	94W41	6:18:44
Langdon 21	2	43N13	95W05	6:20:20
Langworthy 53	1	42N11	91W14	6:04:56
Lansing 3	1	43N22	91W13	6:04:52
Lanyon 94	2	42N13	94W12	6:16:48
La Porte City 7	2	42N19	92W12	6:08:48
Larchwood 60	2	43N27	96W26	6:25:44
Larrabee 18	2	42N52	95W33	6:22:12
Last Chance 59	2	40N56	93W27	6:13:48
Latimer 35	2	42N46	93W22	6:13:28
Latty 29	1	40N49	91W06	6:04:24
Laurel 64	2	41N53	92W55	6:11:40
Laurens 76	2	42N51	94W52	6:19:28
Lavinia 13	2	42N44	93W34	6:14:16
Lawler 19	2	43N04	92W09	6:08:36
Lawn Hill 42	2	42N16	93W10	6:12:40
Lawton 97	2	42N29	96W11	6:24:44
Layton 78	2	41N28	95W11	6:20:44
Leando 89	2	40N50	92W05	6:08:20
Lebanon 84	2	43N05	96W11	6:24:44
Lebanon 89	1	40N44	91W58	6:07:52
Le Claire 82	18	41N36	90W21	6:01:24
Ledyard 55	2	43N25	94W10	6:16:40
Leeds 97	2	42N32	96W24	6:25:36
Le Grand 64	2	42N00	92W47	6:11:08
Lehigh 94	2	42N22	94W03	6:16:12
Leighton 62	2	41N20	92W47	6:11:08
Leland 95	2	43N20	93W38	6:14:32
Le Mars 75	2	42N47	96W10	6:24:40
Lenox 87	2	40N53	94W34	6:18:16
Leon 27	2	40N44	93W45	6:15:00
Le Roy 27	2	40N53	93W32	6:14:08
Lester 60	2	43N27	96W20	6:25:20
Letts 58	1	41N20	91W14	6:04:56
Levey 81	2	42N15	95W10	6:20:40
Lewis 15	2	41N18	95W05	6:20:20
Liberal 60	2	43N24	96W02	6:24:08
Liberty 20	2	41N11	93W44	6:14:56
Liberty Center 91	2	41N12	93W30	6:14:00
Libertyville 51	2	40N57	92W03	6:08:12
Lidderdale 14	2	42N08	94W47	6:19:08
Lime City 16	1	41N35	91W01	6:04:04
Lime Springs 45	2	43N27	92W17	6:09:08
Linby 51	2	41N09	92W09	6:08:36
Lincoln 86	2	42N16	92W42	6:10:48
Linden 25	2	41N39	94W16	6:17:04
Lineville 93	2	40N35	93W32	6:14:08
Linn Grove 11	2	42N53	95W15	6:21:00
Linn Junction 57	1	41N59	91W40	6:06:40
Linton 3	1	43N09	91W18	6:05:12
Linwood 82	12	41N32	90W35	6:02:20
Lisbon 57	1	41N55	91W23	6:05:32
Liscomb 64	2	42N11	93W00	6:12:00
Liston 97	2	42N15	95W45	6:23:00
Little Cedar 66	2	43N23	92W44	6:10:56
Littleport 22	1	42N45	91W23	6:05:32
Little Rock 60	2	43N27	95W50	6:23:20
Little Sioux 43	2	41N48	96W04	6:24:16
Littleton 10	2	42N29	92W04	6:08:16
Little Turkey 19	2	43N04	92W11	6:08:44
Livermore 46	2	42N52	94W11	6:16:44
Livingston 4	2	40N38	92W55	6:11:40
Lizard 76	2	42N36	94W30	6:18:00
Lloyd 30	2	43N18	94W59	6:19:56
Lockridge 51	3	40N59	91W45	6:07:00
Locust 96	1	43N19	91W48	6:07:12
Lodomillo 22	1	42N42	91W26	6:05:44
Logan 43	2	41N39	95W47	6:23:08
Logansport 8	2	42N05	93W56	6:15:44
Lohrville 13	2	42N17	94W33	6:18:12
Lone Rock 55	2	43N13	94W19	6:17:16
Lone Tree 52	1	41N30	91W27	6:05:48
Long Creek 27	2	40N52	93W50	6:15:20
Longfellow 78	2	41N16	95W51	6:23:24
Long Grove 82	1	41N42	90W35	6:02:20
Lorah 15	2	41N24	95W01	6:20:04
Lorimor 88	2	41N08	94W03	6:16:12
Lost Grove 94	2	42N16	94W14	6:16:56
Lost Island 74	2	43N13	94W51	6:19:24
Lost Island Lake 21	2	43N07	94W53	6:19:32
Lost Nation 23	1	41N58	90W49	6:03:16
Lotts Creek 55	2	43N13	94W19	6:17:16
Lourdes 45	2	43N16	92W18	6:09:12
Loveland 78	2	41N33	95W55	6:23:40
Lovell 53	1	42N16	91W11	6:04:44
Lovilia 68	2	41N08	92W55	6:11:40
Lovington 77	2	41N37	93W43	6:14:52
Lowden 16	1	41N52	90W56	6:03:44
Lowell 44	1	40N50	91W26	6:05:44
Low Moor 23	1	41N49	90W21	6:01:24
Luana 22	1	43N03	91W27	6:05:48
Lucas 59	2	41N02	93W27	6:13:48
Ludlow 3	1	43N13	91W33	6:06:12
Lundstrom Heights 77	2	41N39	93W37	6:14:28
Luther 8	2	41N58	93W49	6:15:16
Luton 97	2	42N20	96W14	6:24:56
Luverne 46	2	42N55	94W05	6:16:20
Lu Verne 55	2	43N15	94W07	6:16:28
Luxemburg 31	1	42N36	91W05	6:04:20
Luzerne 6	2	41N54	92W11	6:08:44
Lyman 15	2	41N14	94W59	6:19:56
Lynn 84	2	43N08	95W55	6:23:40
Lynn Grove 50	2	41N33	92W49	6:11:16
Lynnville 50	2	41N35	92W50	6:11:20
Lyons 23	10	41N52	90W12	6:00:48
Lyons 57	1	42N01	91W36	6:06:24
Lyons 65	2	40N57	95W44	6:22:56
Lytton 81	2	42N25	94W51	6:19:24
Macedonia 78	2	41N12	95W25	6:21:40
Mackey 8	2	42N05	93W56	6:15:44
Macksburg 61	2	41N13	94W11	6:16:44
Macy 42	2	42N33	93W02	6:12:08
Madison 78	2	41N16	95W51	6:23:24
Madrid 8	2	41N53	93W49	6:15:16
Magnolia 43	2	41N42	95W52	6:23:28
Magor 41	2	42N57	93W55	6:15:40
Maine 57	1	42N11	91W32	6:06:08
Makee 3	1	43N18	91W26	6:05:44
Malaka 50	2	41N49	93W04	6:12:16
Malcom 79	2	41N43	92W33	6:10:12
Mallard 74	2	42N56	94W41	6:18:44
Mallory 22	1	42N42	91W12	6:04:48
Malone 23	13	41N50	90W32	6:02:08
Maloy 80	2	40N40	94W25	6:17:40
Malvern 65	2	41N00	95W35	6:22:20
Manawa 78	2	41N16	95W51	6:23:24
Manchester 28	1	42N29	91W27	6:05:48
Manilla 24	2	41N53	95W14	6:20:56
Manly 98	2	43N17	93W12	6:12:48
Manning 14	2	41N55	95W04	6:20:16
Manson 13	2	42N32	94W32	6:18:08
Mantua 68	2	41N02	92W42	6:10:48
Maple Heights 34	2	43N04	92W41	6:10:44
Maple Hill 32	2	43N23	94W35	6:18:20
Maple River 14	2	42N05	94W56	6:19:44
Mapleton 67	2	42N10	95W47	6:23:08
Maple Valley 11	2	42N36	95W21	6:21:24
Maquoketa 49	5	42N05	90W36	6:02:24
Marathon 11	2	42N52	94W59	6:19:56
Marble Rock 34	2	42N58	92W52	6:11:28
Marcus 18	2	42N50	95W48	6:23:12
Marcy 8	2	41N59	93W59	6:15:56
Marengo 48	2	41N48	92W04	6:08:16
Marietta 64	2	42N04	93W03	6:12:12
Marion 57	1	42N02	91W36	6:06:24
Mariposa 50	2	41N49	92W56	6:11:44
Mark 26	2	40N40	92W31	6:10:04
Marne 15	2	41N27	95W06	6:20:24
Marquette 22	1	43N03	91W11	6:04:44
Marquisville 77	2	41N38	93W36	6:14:24
Marshall 58	1	41N10	91W19	6:05:16
Marshalltown 64	2	42N03	92W55	6:11:40
Martelle 53	1	42N01	91W22	6:05:28
Martensdale 91	2	41N23	93W45	6:15:00
Martinsburg 54	2	41N11	92W15	6:09:00
Martinstown 4	2	40N41	92W59	6:11:56
Marysville 63	2	41N11	92W57	6:11:48
Maryville 33	1	42N44	91W40	6:06:40
Mason City 17	2	43N09	93W12	6:12:48
Masonville 28	1	42N29	91W36	6:06:24
Massena 15	2	41N15	94W46	6:19:04
Massey 31	15	42N30	90W42	6:02:48
Massillon 16	1	41N55	90W55	6:03:40
Matlock 84	2	43N15	95W56	6:23:44
Maurice 84	2	42N58	96W11	6:24:44
Maxfield 9	2	42N41	92W16	6:09:04
Maxwell 85	2	41N54	93W23	6:13:32
May City 72	2	43N19	95W29	6:21:56
Maynard 33	1	42N47	91W53	6:07:32
Maysville 82	1	41N39	90W43	6:02:52
McCallsburg 85	2	42N10	93W23	6:13:32
McCausland 82	5	41N44	90W27	6:01:48
McClelland 78	2	41N20	95W41	6:22:44
McGregor 22	1	43N01	91W11	6:04:44
McIntire 66	2	43N26	92W36	6:10:24
McNally 84	2	42N58	96W19	6:25:16
Mechanicsville 16	1	41N54	91W16	6:05:04
Mederville 22	1	42N51	91W24	6:05:36
Mediapolis 29	19	41N00	91W10	6:04:40
Medora 91	1	41N37	90W34	6:02:16
Melbourne 64	2	41N57	93W06	6:12:24
Melcher 63	2	41N14	93W15	6:13:00
Melrose 68	2	40N59	93W03	6:12:12
Meltonville 98	2	43N23	92W55	6:11:40
Melville 5	2	41N44	94W48	6:19:12
Melvin 72	2	43N17	95W37	6:22:28
Mendon 22	1	43N01	91W13	6:04:52
Menlo 39	2	41N31	94W24	6:17:36
Mercer 2	2	40N57	94W38	6:18:32
Meriden 18	2	42N48	95W38	6:22:32
Meroa 66	2	43N17	92W49	6:11:16
Merrill 75	2	42N43	96W15	6:25:00
Meservey 17	2	42N55	93W29	6:13:56
Methodist Camp 30	2	43N26	95W06	6:20:24
Meyer 66	2	43N26	92W35	6:10:20
Middle 48	1	41N59	91W39	6:06:36
Middleburg 84	2	43N00	96W04	6:24:16
Middlefield 10	1	42N26	91W39	6:06:36
Middle Fork 80	2	40N36	94W18	6:17:12
Middletown 29	8	40N50	91W15	6:05:00
Midland 60	2	43N28	96W01	6:24:04
Midvale 85	2	41N55	93W35	6:14:20
Midway 34	2	43N04	92W41	6:10:44
Midway 57	1	42N01	91W36	6:06:24
Midway Beach 70	1	41N26	91W03	6:04:12
Miles 49	1	42N03	90W19	6:01:16
Milford 30	2	43N20	95W09	6:20:36
Military 96	1	43N09	91W48	6:07:12
Miller 41	2	43N11	93W36	6:14:24
Millersburg 48	2	41N34	92W10	6:08:40
Millerton 93	2	40N51	93W18	6:13:12
Millnerville 75	2	42N46	96W36	6:26:24
Millville 22	1	42N42	91W05	6:04:20
Milo 91	2	41N17	93W27	6:13:48
Milton 89	2	40N41	92W10	6:08:40
Minburn 25	2	41N45	94W02	6:16:08
Minden 78	2	41N28	95W32	6:22:08
Mineola 65	2	41N08	95W42	6:22:48
Mineral Ridge 8	2	42N05	93W56	6:15:44
Minerva 64	2	42N05	93W11	6:12:44
Mingo 50	2	41N46	93W18	6:13:12
Missouri Valley 43	2	41N34	95W53	6:23:32
Mitchell 66	2	43N19	92W53	6:11:32
Mitchellville 77	2	41N40	93W22	6:13:28
Modale 43	2	41N37	96W03	6:24:12
Moingona 8	2	42N01	93W56	6:15:44
Mona 66	2	43N33	92W38	6:10:32
Mondamin 43	2	41N42	96W01	6:24:04
Moneta 71	2	43N13	95W24	6:21:36
Monmouth 49	1	42N05	90W50	6:03:20
Monona 22	1	43N02	91W26	6:05:44
Monroe 50	2	41N31	93W06	6:12:24
Monteith 39	2	41N38	94W26	6:17:44
Monterey 26	2	40N45	92W25	6:09:40
Montezuma 79	2	41N35	92W32	6:10:08
Montgomery 30	2	43N26	95W11	6:20:44
Monti 10	1	42N17	91W32	6:06:08
Monticello 53	1	42N15	91W12	6:04:48
Montour 86	2	41N59	92W43	6:10:52
Montpelier 70	5	41N29	90W50	6:03:20
Montrose 56	20	40N30	91W26	6:05:44
Mooar 56	17	40N25	91W24	6:05:36
Moorhead 67	2	41N56	95W51	6:23:24
Moorland 94	2	42N26	94W18	6:17:12
Moran 25	2	41N51	93W56	6:15:44
Moravia 4	2	40N53	92W49	6:11:16
Morley 53	1	42N01	91W15	6:05:00
Morningside 97	2	42N28	96W22	6:25:28
Morning Sun 58	1	41N05	91W15	6:05:00
Morrison 38	2	42N20	92W41	6:10:44
Morse 52	1	41N45	91W26	6:05:44
Morton 73	2	40N41	95W19	6:21:16
Morton Mills 69	2	41N05	94W59	6:19:56
Mosalem 31	1	42N25	90W36	6:02:24
Moscow 70	1	41N34	91W05	6:04:20
Mott 35	2	42N47	93W12	6:12:48
Moulton 4	2	40N41	92W41	6:10:44
Mound Prairie 50	2	41N39	93W11	6:12:44
Mount Auburn 6	2	42N15	92W06	6:08:24
Mount Ayr 80	2	40N43	94W14	6:16:56
Mount Carmel 14	2	42N01	94W51	6:19:24
Mount Etna 2	2	41N07	94W44	6:18:56
Mount Hamill	1	40N45	91W37	6:06:28
Mount Joy 82	12	41N32	90W36	6:02:24
Mount Pleasant 44	21	40N58	91W33	6:06:12
Mount Sterling 89	1	40N37	91W56	6:07:44
Mount Union 44	1	41N03	91W23	6:05:32
Mount Valley 95	2	43N17	93W33	6:14:12
Mount Vernon 57	1	41N55	91W23	6:05:32
Mount Zion 89	1	40N47	91W56	6:07:44
Moville 97	2	42N29	96W04	6:24:16
Munterville 90	2	40N58	92W39	6:10:36
Murphy 9	2	42N44	92W29	6:09:56
Murray 20	2	41N03	93W57	6:15:48
Muscatine 70	5	41N25	91W03	6:04:12
Mystic 4	2	40N47	92W57	6:11:48
Napier 8	2	42N03	93W35	6:14:20
Nashua 19	2	42N57	92W32	6:10:08
Nashville 49	1	42N04	90W40	6:02:40
Nassau 84	2	42N57	96W03	6:24:12
National 22	1	42N57	91W17	6:05:08
Nebraska 73	2	40N46	94W57	6:19:48
Neils 95	2	43N20	93W38	6:14:32
Nemaha 81	2	42N31	95W06	6:20:24
Neola 78	2	41N27	95W37	6:22:28
Nevada 85	2	42N01	93W27	6:13:48
Nevinville 2	2	41N09	94W30	6:18:00
New Albany 85	2	42N01	93W16	6:13:04
New Albin 3	1	43N30	91W17	6:05:08
Newark 94	2	42N36	94W03	6:16:12
Newbern 59	2	41N11	93W23	6:13:32
New Boston 56	1	40N32	91W34	6:06:16
New Buda 27	2	40N37	93W50	6:15:20
Newburg 50	2	41N45	92W39	6:10:36
Newburg 66	2	43N24	92W58	6:11:52
Newell 11	2	42N36	95W00	6:20:00
New Era 70	1	41N26	91W03	6:04:12
Newhall 6	1	42N00	91W58	6:07:52
New Hampton 19	2	43N03	92W19	6:09:16
New Hartford 12	2	42N34	92W37	6:10:28
New Haven 66	2	43N17	92W39	6:10:36
New Hope 88	2	41N07	94W04	6:16:16
Newkirk 84	2	43N04	95W55	6:23:40
New Liberty 82	1	41N43	90W53	6:03:32
New London 44	22	40N55	91W24	6:05:36
New Market 87	2	40N44	94W54	6:19:36
New Oregon 45	2	43N17	92W08	6:08:32
Newport 52	1	41N45	91W30	6:06:00
New Providence 42	2	42N16	93W10	6:12:40
New Sharon 62	2	41N28	92W39	6:10:36
Newton 50	2	41N42	93W03	6:12:12
New Vienna 31	1	42N33	91W07	6:04:28
New Virginia 91	2	41N11	93W44	6:14:56
New Wine 31	1	42N31	91W04	6:04:16
New York 93	2	40N59	93W12	6:12:48
Nichols 70	1	41N29	91W19	6:05:16
Niles 34	2	43N08	92W37	6:10:28
Nishnabotny 24	2	41N54	95W16	6:21:04
Noble 15	2	41N12	94W59	6:19:56
Noble 92	21	40N59	91W33	6:06:12

Nodaway 2	2	40n56	94w54	6:19:36
Nokomis 11	2	42n42	95w20	6:21:20
Nora Springs 34	2	43n09	93w01	6:12:04
Nordness 96	1	43n19	91w48	6:07:12
Northboro 73	2	40n37	95w17	6:21:08
North Branch 39	2	41n31	94w39	6:18:36
North Buena Vista 22	1	42n41	90w58	6:03:52
North Cedar 7	2	42n32	92w26	6:09:44
North English 48	2	41n31	92w05	6:08:20
Northfield 29	1	41n01	91w09	6:04:36
North Fork 28	1	42n26	91w12	6:04:48
North Liberty 52	1	41n45	91w36	6:06:24
North Side 97	2	42n31	96w24	6:25:36
North Washington 19	2	43n07	92w25	6:09:40
North Welton 23	1	42n00	90w37	6:02:28
Northwest 82	12	41n32	90w36	6:02:24
Northwood 98	2	43n27	93w13	6:12:52
Norwalk 91	2	41n29	93w41	6:14:44
Norway 6	1	41n54	91w55	6:07:40
Norwich 73	2	40n46	95w23	6:21:32
Norwood 59	2	41n07	93w29	6:13:56
Norwoodville 77	2	41n36	93w34	6:14:16
Numa 4	2	40n41	92w59	6:11:56
Nyman 73	2	40n57	95w14	6:20:56
Oak 65	2	41n07	95w42	6:22:48
Oak Dale 45	2	43n28	92w30	6:10:00
Oakdale 52	1	41n42	91w36	6:06:24
Oakfield 5	2	41n34	94w59	6:19:56
Oakland 78	2	41n19	95w23	6:21:32
Oakland Acres 50	2	41n45	92w39	6:10:36
Oakland Mills 44	21	40n59	91w33	6:06:12
Oakley 59	2	41n01	93w18	6:13:12
Oakville 58	1	41n06	91w03	6:04:12
Oakwood 34	2	42n58	92w52	6:11:28
Oasis 52	1	41n37	91w10	6:04:40
Ocheyedan 72	2	43n25	95w32	6:22:08
Odebolt 81	2	42n19	95w15	6:21:00
Oelwein 33	1	42n41	91w55	6:07:40
Ogden 8	2	42n02	94w02	6:16:08
Ohio 61	2	41n15	93w55	6:15:40
Okoboji 30	2	43n23	95w08	6:20:32
Old Balltown 31	1	42n38	90w50	6:03:20
Olds 44	1	41n08	91w33	6:06:12
Old Town 30	2	43n18	95w09	6:20:36
Olin 53	1	42n00	91w08	6:04:32
Olive 23	1	41n49	90w44	6:02:56
Olivet 62	2	41n20	92w47	6:11:08
Ollie 54	2	41n12	92w06	6:08:24
Omega 71	2	43n07	95w27	6:21:48
Onawa 67	2	42n02	96w06	6:24:24
Oneida 28	1	42n33	91w21	6:05:24
Onslow 53	1	42n06	91w01	6:04:04
Ontario 85	2	42n03	93w35	6:14:20
Oralabor 77	2	41n39	93w37	6:14:28
Oran 33	2	42n40	92w02	6:08:08
Orange 7	2	42n29	92w23	6:09:32
Orange City 84	2	43n00	96w04	6:24:16
Orchard 66	2	43n14	92w47	6:11:08
Oregon 92	1	41n18	91w32	6:06:08
Orient 1	2	41n12	94w25	6:17:40
Orillia 91	2	41n29	93w46	6:15:04
Orleans 30	2	43n26	95w06	6:20:24
Orono 70	1	41n23	91w20	6:05:20
Orthel 41	2	43n07	93w54	6:15:36
Osage 66	2	43n17	92w49	6:11:16
Osborne 22	1	42n51	91w24	6:05:36
Osceola 20	2	41n02	93w46	6:15:04
Osgood 74	2	43n06	94w41	6:18:44
Oskaloosa 62	2	41n18	92w39	6:10:36
Ossian 96	1	43n09	91w46	6:07:04
Osterdock 22	1	42n44	91w10	6:04:40
Otho 94	2	42n25	94w09	6:16:36
Otley 63	2	41n28	93w02	6:12:08
Oto 97	2	42n17	95w54	6:23:36
Otranto 66	2	43n28	92w59	6:11:56
Otter 91	2	41n17	93w30	6:14:00
Otter Creek 49	1	42n14	90w41	6:02:44
Otterville 10	1	42n29	91w53	6:07:32
Ottosen 46	2	42n54	94w23	6:17:32
Ottumwa 90	4	41n01	92w25	6:09:40
Ottumwa Junction 90	2	41n02	92w25	6:09:40
Owasa 42	2	42n26	93w12	6:12:48
Owen 17	2	43n03	93w05	6:12:20
Oxford 52	1	41n43	91w47	6:07:08
Oxford Junction 53	1	41n59	90w57	6:03:48
Oxford Mills 53	1	41n59	90w57	6:03:48
Oyens 75	2	42n49	96w03	6:24:12
Pacific Junction 65	2	41n01	95w45	6:23:00
Packard 12	2	42n51	92w44	6:10:56
Packwood 51	2	41n08	92w05	6:08:20
Paint Creek 3	1	43n14	91w18	6:05:12
Painted Rocks 63	2	41n28	93w02	6:12:08
Palermo 38	2	42n20	92w50	6:11:20
Palestine 85	2	41n56	93w37	6:14:28
Palmer 76	2	42n38	94w36	6:18:24
Palm Grove 94	2	42n30	94w11	6:16:44
Palmyra 91	2	41n25	93w27	6:13:48
Palo 57	1	42n04	91w48	6:07:12
Palo Alto 50	2	41n39	93w03	6:12:12
Panama 83	2	41n44	95w28	6:21:52
Panora 39	2	41n42	94w22	6:17:28
Panorama Park 82	7	41n33	90w27	6:01:48
Paradise 24	2	41n59	95w30	6:22:00
Paralta 57	1	42n04	91w26	6:05:44
Paris 26	2	40n48	92w29	6:09:56
Paris 57	1	42n14	91w35	6:06:20
Parkersburg 12	2	42n35	92w47	6:11:08
Park Hills 63	2	41n28	93w02	6:12:08
Parkview 82	1	41n39	90w35	6:02:20
Parnell 48	1	41n35	92w00	6:08:00
Paton 37	2	42n10	94w16	6:17:04
Patterson 61	2	41n21	93w52	6:15:28
Paullina 71	2	42n59	95w41	6:22:44
Payne 36	2	40n36	95w39	6:22:36
Pekin 51	2	41n08	92w05	6:08:20
Pella 63	2	41n25	92w55	6:11:40
Peoples 8	2	41n54	93w59	6:15:56
Peoria 62	2	41n24	92w55	6:11:40
Peosta 31	1	42n27	90w51	6:03:24
Percival 36	2	40n45	95w49	6:23:16
Perkins 84	2	43n11	96w09	6:24:36
Perlee 51	1	41n00	91w57	6:07:48
Perry 25	2	41n51	94w06	6:16:24
Pershing 63	2	41n16	93w01	6:12:04
Persia 43	2	41n35	95w33	6:22:12
Peru 31	1	42n36	90w44	6:02:56
Peru 61	2	41n15	93w55	6:15:40
Petersburg 28	1	42n29	91w08	6:04:32
Peterson 21	2	42n55	95w21	6:21:24
Petersville 23	1	41n58	90w28	6:01:52
Pierce 73	2	40n51	95w20	6:21:20
Pierson 97	2	42n33	95w52	6:23:28
Pike 70	1	41n29	91w17	6:05:08
Pilot Grove 56	1	40n46	91w32	6:06:08
Pilot Grove 69	2	41n06	95w06	6:20:24
Pilot Mound 8	2	42n10	94w01	6:16:04
Pinehurst 78	2	41n16	95w51	6:23:24
Pioneer 46	2	42n39	94w23	6:17:32
Piper 13	2	42n44	93w34	6:14:16
Pisgah 43	2	41n50	95w55	6:23:40
Pitcher 18	2	42n42	95w27	6:21:48
Pittsburg 89	1	40n44	91w58	6:07:52
Pittsford 12	2	42n46	92w58	6:11:52
Pitzer 61	2	41n30	94w07	6:16:28
Plainfield 9	2	42n51	92w32	6:10:08
Plain View 82	1	41n40	90w48	6:03:12
Plank 54	2	41n21	92w07	6:08:28
Plano 4	2	40n45	93w03	6:12:12
Plato 84	2	43n07	96w16	6:25:04
Platteville 87	2	40n40	94w43	6:18:52
Plattville 65	2	41n02	95w47	6:23:08
Plaza Hills 77	2	41n36	93w41	6:14:44
Pleasantgrove 29	22	40n57	91w24	6:05:36
Pleasant Hill 77	2	41n35	93w31	6:14:04
Pleasanton 27	2	40n35	93w45	6:15:00
Pleasant Plain 51	1	41n09	91w51	6:07:24
Pleasant Prairie 70	1	41n26	91w03	6:04:12
Pleasant Ridge 56	24	40n46	91w26	6:05:44
Pleasant Valley 82	1	41n34	90w25	6:01:40
Pleasantville 63	2	41n23	93w18	6:13:12
Plover 76	2	42n53	94w38	6:18:32
Plum Creek 55	2	43n08	94w09	6:16:36
Plymouth 17	2	43n15	93w07	6:12:28
Pocahontas 76	2	42n44	94w40	6:18:40
Poe 80	2	40n41	94w11	6:16:44
Poland 11	2	42n53	94w58	6:19:52
Polk City 77	2	41n46	93w43	6:14:52
Pomeroy 13	2	42n33	94w41	6:18:44
Popejoy 35	2	42n36	93w26	6:13:44
Portland 17	2	43n09	93w13	6:12:52
Port Louisa 58	1	41n14	91w08	6:04:32
Portsmouth 83	2	41n39	95w31	6:22:04
Pospect Park 78	2	41n16	95w51	6:23:24
Post 3	1	43n09	91w33	6:06:12
Postville 3	1	43n05	91w34	6:06:16
Powersville 34	2	42n54	92w48	6:11:12
Poweshiek 50	2	41n45	93w17	6:13:08
Powhatan 76	2	42n52	94w37	6:18:28
Poyner 7	2	42n31	92w13	6:08:52
Prairie 36	2	40n47	95w33	6:22:12
Prairieburg 57	1	42n14	91w25	6:05:40
Prairie City 50	2	41n36	93w14	6:12:56
Prairie Creek 31	1	42n20	90w51	6:03:24
Prairie Grove 29	8	40n49	91w10	6:04:40
Prairie Springs 49	1	42n20	90w37	6:02:28
Prescott 2	2	41n01	94w37	6:18:28
Preston 49	1	42n03	90w24	6:01:36
Primghar 71	2	43n05	95w38	6:22:32
Primrose 56	1	40n38	91w34	6:06:16
Princeton 82	5	41n40	90w20	6:01:20
Prole 91	2	41n24	93w44	6:14:56
Promise City 93	2	40n45	93w09	6:12:36
Prospect Hill 29	1	40n49	91w06	6:04:24
Prospect Park 78	2	41n16	95w51	6:23:24
Protivin 45	2	43n13	92w06	6:08:24
Prussia 1	2	41n23	94w32	6:18:08
Pulaski 26	2	40n42	92w16	6:09:04
Pymosa 15	2	41n27	94w59	6:19:56
Quandahl 3	1	43n19	91w48	6:07:12
Quarry 64	2	42n02	92w54	6:11:36
Quasqueton 10	1	42n24	91w45	6:07:00
Quimby 18	2	42n38	95w38	6:22:32
Quincy 2	2	41n02	94w46	6:19:04
Radcliffe 42	2	42n19	93w27	6:13:48
Raglan 43	2	41n44	95w58	6:23:52
Rake 95	2	43n29	93w55	6:15:40
Ralston 14	2	42n03	94w39	6:18:36
Ramsey 55	2	43n18	94w09	6:16:36
Randalia 33	1	42n52	91w53	6:07:32
Randall 40	2	42n14	93w35	6:14:20
Randolph 36	2	40n52	95w34	6:22:16
Rands 13	2	42n20	94w35	6:18:20
Rathbun 4	2	40n48	92w53	6:11:32
Rawles 65	2	40n57	95w38	6:22:32
Raymar 7	2	42n29	92w23	6:09:32
Raymond 7	2	42n28	92w13	6:08:52
Read 22	1	42n51	91w20	6:05:20
Readlyn 9	2	42n42	92w14	6:08:56
Reasnor 50	2	41n35	93w01	6:12:04
Redding 80	2	40n36	94w23	6:17:32
Redfield 25	2	41n35	94w12	6:16:48
Red Line 83	2	41n44	95w16	6:21:04
Red Oak 69	2	41n01	95w14	6:20:56
Red Rock 63	2	41n26	93w07	6:12:28
Reeve 35	2	42n41	93w12	6:12:48
Reinbeck 38	2	42n19	92w36	6:10:24
Rembrandt 11	2	42n50	95w10	6:20:40
Remsen 75	2	42n49	95w58	6:23:52
Renwick 46	2	42n50	93w59	6:15:56
Rhodes 64	2	41n56	93w11	6:12:44
Rice 80	2	40n40	94w20	6:17:20
Riceville 66	2	43n22	92w33	6:10:12
Richards 13	2	42n44	93w34	6:14:16
Richland 54	1	41n11	92w00	6:08:00
Richman 93	2	40n51	93w30	6:14:00
Richmond 92	1	41n29	91w42	6:06:48
Rickardsville 31	1	42n35	90w52	6:03:28
Ricketts 24	2	42n08	95w35	6:22:20
Ridgeport 8	2	42n05	93w56	6:15:44
Ridgeway 96	1	43n18	91w59	6:07:56
Riley 80	2	40n37	94w05	6:16:20
Rinard 13	2	42n20	94w29	6:17:56
Ringsted 32	2	43n18	94w31	6:18:04
Ripley 12	2	42n42	92w51	6:11:24
Rippey 37	2	41n56	94w12	6:16:48
Risingsun 77	2	41n36	93w34	6:14:16
Ritter 71	2	43n10	95w50	6:23:20
Riverdale 82	7	41n33	90w30	6:02:00
River Junction 52	1	41n30	91w27	6:05:48
Riverside 92	1	41n29	91w35	6:06:20
River Sioux 43	2	41n48	96w03	6:24:12
Riverton 36	2	40n41	95w34	6:22:16
Roberts 94	2	42n25	94w10	6:16:40
Robertson 42	2	42n33	93w02	6:12:08
Roberts Park 78	2	41n16	95w51	6:23:24
Robins 57	1	42n04	91w39	6:06:36
Robinson 28	1	42n20	91w35	6:06:20
Rochester 16	1	41n40	91w07	6:04:28
Rock Creek 50	2	41n44	92w49	6:11:16
Rock Creek 66	2	43n17	92w49	6:11:16
Rockdale 31	15	42n30	90w42	6:02:48
Rock Falls 17	2	43n13	93w05	6:12:20
Rockford 34	2	43n03	92w57	6:11:48
Rock Grove 34	2	43n10	92w58	6:11:52
Rock Rapids 60	2	43n26	96w10	6:24:40
Rock Valley 84	2	43n12	96w18	6:25:12
Rockwell 17	2	42n59	93w11	6:12:44
Rockwell City 13	2	42n24	94w38	6:18:32
Rodman 74	2	43n02	94w32	6:18:08
Rodney 67	2	42n12	95w57	6:23:48
Roelyn 94	2	42n26	94w17	6:17:08
Roland 85	2	42n10	93w30	6:14:00
Rolfe 76	2	42n49	94w31	6:18:04
Rome 44	4	40n59	91w41	6:06:44
Roosevelt 76	2	42n47	94w37	6:18:28
Roosevelt 78	2	41n16	95w51	6:23:24
Roscoe 26	2	40n39	92w15	6:09:00
Rose Grove 40	2	42n25	93w31	6:14:04
Rose Hill 62	2	41n19	92w28	6:09:52
Roselle 14	2	42n00	94w55	6:19:40
Ross 5	2	41n46	94w55	6:19:40
Rossie 21	2	43n01	95w11	6:20:44
Rossville 3	1	43n11	91w23	6:05:32
Round Prairie 51	1	40n57	91w47	6:07:08
Rowan 99	2	42n45	93w33	6:14:12
Rowley 10	1	42n22	91w51	6:07:24
Royal 21	2	43n04	95w17	6:21:08
Rubio 92	1	41n13	91w56	6:07:44
Rudd 34	2	43n10	92w52	6:11:28
Runnells 77	2	41n31	93w21	6:13:24
Rush Lake 74	2	42n56	94w44	6:18:56
Russell 59	2	40n59	93w12	6:12:48
Ruthven 74	2	43n08	94w54	6:19:36
Rutland 46	2	42n46	94w18	6:17:12
Rutledge 90	2	41n02	92w25	6:09:40
Ryan 28	1	42n21	91w29	6:05:56
Sabula 49	19	42n05	90w11	6:00:44
Sac 81	2	42n15	94w57	6:19:48
Sac City 81	2	42n25	95w00	6:20:00
Sageville 31	1	42n36	90w43	6:02:52
Saint Ansgar 66	2	43n23	92w55	6:11:40
Saint Anthony 64	2	42n07	93w12	6:12:48
Saint Benedict 55	2	43n04	94w14	6:16:56
Saint Catherines 31	15	42n30	90w42	6:02:48
Saint Charles 61	2	41n17	93w49	6:15:16
Saint Donatus 49	1	42n22	90w33	6:02:12
Saint Johns 43	2	41n33	95w54	6:23:36
Saint Joseph 55	2	42n52	94w17	6:17:08
Saint Lucas 33	1	43n05	91w56	6:07:44
Saint Marys 91	2	41n19	93w44	6:14:56
Saint Olaf 22	1	42n56	91w23	6:05:32
Saint Paul 56	1	40n46	91w31	6:06:04
Salem 44	1	40n51	91w38	6:06:32
Salina 51	1	41n03	91w55	6:07:40
Salix 97	2	42n19	96w17	6:25:08
Sanborn 71	2	43n11	95w40	6:22:40
Sand Creek 88	2	40n57	94w12	6:16:48
Sand Prairie 56	1	40n32	91w34	6:06:16
Sand Springs 28	1	42n19	91w11	6:04:44
Sandusky 56	17	40n25	91w24	6:05:36
Sandyville 91	2	41n22	93w23	6:13:32
Santiago 77	2	41n40	93w22	6:13:28
Saratoga 45	2	43n22	92w25	6:09:40
Sattre 96	1	43n19	91w48	6:07:12
Saude 19	2	43n04	92w11	6:08:44
Savannah 26	2	40n45	92w25	6:09:40
Sawyer 56	1	40n37	91w22	6:05:28
Saydel 77	2	41n38	93w36	6:14:24
Saylor 77	2	41n39	93w37	6:14:28
Saylorville 77	2	41n38	93w36	6:14:24
Scarville 95	2	43n28	93w37	6:14:28
Schaller 81	2	42n30	95w18	6:21:12
Schleswig 24	2	42n10	95w26	6:21:44
Schley 45	2	43n18	92w13	6:08:52
Scotch Grove 53	1	42n10	91w04	6:04:16
Scotch Ridge 91	2	41n33	93w32	6:14:08
Scranton 37	2	42n01	94w33	6:18:12
Searsboro 79	2	41n35	92w42	6:10:48

IOWA

Place	Zone	Lat	Long	Time
Sedan 4	2	40N44	92w52	6:11:28
Seely 39	2	41N44	94w35	6:18:20
Selma 89	2	40N52	92w09	6:08:36
Seneca 55	2	43N18	94w22	6:17:28
Seney 75	2	42N51	96w08	6:24:32
Sergeant Bluff 97	2	42N24	96w22	6:25:28
Settlers 84	2	43N14	96w29	6:25:56
Sewal 93	2	40N39	93w16	6:13:04
Sexton 55	2	43N06	94w01	6:16:04
Seymour 93	2	40N45	93w07	6:12:28
Shady Grove 10	2	42N29	92w04	6:08:16
Shaffton 23	10	41N49	90w15	6:01:00
Shambaugh 73	2	40N42	95w03	6:20:12
Shannon City 88	2	40N53	94w16	6:17:04
Sharon Center 52	1	41N41	91w34	6:06:16
Sharpsburg 87	2	40N48	94w38	6:18:32
Shawondasse 31	15	42N30	90w42	6:02:48
Sheffield 35	2	42N54	93w13	6:12:52
Shelby 83	2	41N31	95w27	6:21:48
Sheldahl 77	2	41N52	93w42	6:14:48
Sheldon 71	2	43N11	95w51	6:23:24
Shell Rock 12	2	42N43	92w35	6:10:20
Shellsburg 6	1	42N06	91w52	6:07:28
Shenandoah 73	2	40N46	95w22	6:21:28
Sheridan 79	2	41N43	92w34	6:10:16
Sherrill 31	1	42N37	90w47	6:03:08
Sherwood 13	2	42N22	94w44	6:18:56
Shiloh 38	2	42N26	92w57	6:11:48
Shipley 85	2	41N59	93w31	6:14:04
Shueyville 52	1	41N58	91w42	6:06:48
Siam 87	2	40N38	94w53	6:19:32
Sibley 72	2	43N24	95w45	6:23:00
Sidney 36	2	40N45	95w39	6:22:36
Sigourney 54	2	41N20	92w12	6:08:48
Silver 18	2	42N36	95w33	6:22:12
Silver City 65	2	41N07	95w39	6:22:36
Silver Creek 47	2	42N26	95w23	6:21:32
Silver Lake 98	2	43N27	93w13	6:12:52
Sinclair 12	2	42N35	92w48	6:11:12
Sioux Center 84	2	43N05	96w11	6:24:44
Sioux City 97	2	42N30	96w24	6:25:36
Sioux Rapids 11	2	42N53	95w09	6:20:36
Six Mile 23	10	41N52	90w12	6:00:48
Slater 85	2	41N54	93w39	6:14:36
Slifer 94	2	42N19	94w18	6:17:12
Sloan 97	2	42N14	96w14	6:24:56
Smithfield 33	1	42N46	91w47	6:07:08
Smithland 97	2	42N14	95w56	6:23:44
Soap Creek 26	2	40N51	92w28	6:09:52
Soldier 67	2	42N00	95w47	6:23:08
Solon 52	1	41N48	91w30	6:06:00
Somers 13	2	42N23	94w26	6:17:44
South 61	2	41N18	93w50	6:15:20
South Amana 48	1	41N46	91w58	6:07:52
South Des Moines 77	2	41N33	93w37	6:14:28
South English 54	2	41N27	92w05	6:08:20
South Muscatine 70	1	41N26	91w03	6:04:12
South Ottumwa 90	2	41N02	92w25	6:09:40
Spaulding 88	2	41N07	94w25	6:17:40
Spencer 21	2	43N09	95w09	6:20:36
Sperry 29	1	40N57	91w09	6:04:36
Spillville 96	1	43N13	91w59	6:07:56
Spirit Lake 30	2	43N26	95w06	6:20:24
Spragueville 49	1	42N04	90w26	6:01:44
Spring 18	2	42N52	95w27	6:21:48
Springbrook 49	1	42N10	90w29	6:01:56
Spring Creek 7	2	42N21	92w07	6:08:28
Springdale 16	1	41N38	91w17	6:05:08
Spring Grove 57	5	42N15	91w40	6:06:40
Spring Hill 91	2	41N25	93w39	6:14:36
Spring Rock 23	1	41N49	90w51	6:03:24
Springville 57	1	42N03	91w27	6:05:48
Squaw 91	2	41N12	93w36	6:14:24
Stacyville 66	2	43N26	92w47	6:11:08
Stanhope 40	2	42N17	93w48	6:15:12
Stanley 10	1	42N39	91w49	6:07:16
Stanton 69	2	40N59	95w06	6:20:24
Stanwood 16	1	41N53	91w08	6:04:32
Stanzel 1	2	41N19	94w28	6:17:52
Stapleton 19	2	43N02	92w10	6:08:40
State Center 64	2	42N01	93w10	6:12:40
Steady Run 54	2	41N12	92w14	6:08:56
Steamboat Rock 42	2	42N25	93w04	6:12:16
Stennett 69	2	41N05	95w12	6:20:48
Stiles 26	2	40N38	92w21	6:09:24
Stilson 41	2	43N02	93w53	6:15:32
Stockholm 24	2	42N10	95w16	6:21:04
Stockport 89	1	40N51	91w50	6:07:20
Stockton 70	5	41N36	90w51	6:03:24
Stock Yards 97	2	42N30	96w22	6:25:28
Stone City 53	1	42N07	91w17	6:05:08
Storm Lake 11	2	42N39	95w13	6:20:52
Story City 85	2	42N11	93w36	6:14:24
Stout 38	2	42N32	92w43	6:10:52
Strahan 65	2	40N57	95w30	6:22:00
Stratford 40	2	42N16	93w56	6:15:44
Strawberry Point 22	1	42N41	91w32	6:06:08
Stringtown 2	2	40N53	94w34	6:18:16
Struble 75	2	42N53	96w12	6:24:48
Stuart 39	2	41N30	94w19	6:17:16
Sugar Grove 25	2	41N44	94w00	6:16:00
Sully 50	2	41N35	92w51	6:11:24
Sulphur Springs 11	2	42N38	95w11	6:20:44
Summerset 1	2	41N18	94w32	6:18:08
Summerset 91	1	41N37	90w34	6:02:16
Summitville 56	20	40N28	91w27	6:05:48
Sumner 9	2	42N51	92w06	6:08:24
Sumner No 2 9	2	42N52	92w09	6:08:36
Sunbury 16	1	41N40	90w56	6:03:44
Sunshine 4	2	40N44	92w52	6:11:28
Superior 30	2	43N26	94w57	6:19:48
Sutherland 71	2	42N58	95w29	6:21:56
Sutliff 52	1	41N55	91w23	6:05:32
Swaledale 17	2	42N59	93w19	6:13:16
Swan 63	2	41N28	93w19	6:13:16
Swea City 55	2	43N23	94w19	6:17:16
Swedesburg 44	1	41N06	91w33	6:06:12
Sweetland 70	1	41N29	90w57	6:03:48
Sweetland Center 70	1	41N26	91w03	6:04:12
Swisher 52	1	41N50	91w42	6:06:48
Table Mound 31	1	42N26	90w43	6:02:52
Tabor 36	2	40N54	95w40	6:22:40
Taintor 62	2	41N30	92w44	6:10:56
Talleyrand 54	1	41N22	91w57	6:07:48
Talmage 88	2	41N02	94w03	6:16:12
Tama 86	2	41N58	92w35	6:10:20
Tara 94	2	42N30	94w18	6:17:12
Tarkio 73	2	40N46	95w12	6:20:48
Teeds Grove 23	1	42N01	90w15	6:01:00
Templar Park 30	2	43N26	95w06	6:20:24
Templeton 14	2	41N55	94w57	6:19:48
Ten Mile 23	1	41N58	90w20	6:01:20
Tennant 83	2	41N35	95w26	6:21:44
Tenville Junction 69	2	40N56	94w59	6:19:56
Terril 30	2	43N18	94w58	6:19:52
Tete Des Morts 49	1	42N20	90w30	6:02:00
Thayer 88	2	41N02	94w03	6:16:12
Thirty 4	2	40N44	92w52	6:11:28
Thompson 95	2	43N22	93w46	6:15:04
Thor 46	2	42N41	94w03	6:16:12
Thornburg 54	2	41N27	92w20	6:09:20
Thornton 17	2	42N57	93w23	6:13:32
Thorpe 28	1	42N31	91w25	6:05:40
Thurman 36	2	40N49	95w45	6:23:00
Ticonic 67	2	42N05	95w54	6:23:36
Tiffin 52	1	41N42	91w40	6:06:40
Tilden 18	2	42N42	95w48	6:23:12
Timber Creek 64	2	41N59	92w56	6:11:44
Timberland Heights 85	2	42N03	93w35	6:14:20
Tingley 80	2	40N51	94w12	6:16:48
Tinley 78	2	41N16	95w51	6:23:24
Tippecanoe 44	1	40N58	91w38	6:06:32
Tipton 16	1	41N46	91w08	6:04:32
Titonka 55	2	43N14	94w03	6:16:12
Toddville 57	1	42N06	91w43	6:06:52
Toeterville 66	2	43N27	92w53	6:11:32
Toledo 86	2	42N00	92w35	6:10:20
Toolesboro 58	23	41N11	91w11	6:04:44
Toronto 23	1	41N54	90w52	6:03:28
Tracy 63	2	41N17	92w53	6:11:32
Traer 86	2	42N12	92w28	6:09:52
Trenton 44	1	41N04	91w39	6:06:36
Treynor 78	2	41N14	95w36	6:22:24
Triboji Beach 30	2	43N26	95w06	6:20:24
Tripoli 9	2	42N49	92w16	6:09:04
Troy 26	2	40N45	92w12	6:08:48
Troy Mills 57	1	42N18	91w41	6:06:44
Truax 62	2	41N10	92w38	6:10:32
Truesdale 11	2	42N44	95w11	6:20:44
Truro 61	2	41N14	93w50	6:15:20
Turin 67	2	42N01	95w58	6:23:52
Turkey River 22	1	42N45	91w06	6:04:24
Tuskeego 27	2	40N43	94w03	6:16:12
Twelve Mile Lake 32	2	43N18	94w50	6:19:20
Twin City Plaza Addition 78	2	41N16	95w51	6:23:24
Twin Lake 41	2	42N57	93w41	6:14:44
Twin Lakes 13	2	42N26	94w42	6:18:48
Twin View Heights 52	1	41N49	91w31	6:06:04
Udell 4	2	40N47	92w45	6:11:00
Ulmer 81	2	42N16	94w58	6:19:52
Ulster 34	2	43N04	92w51	6:11:24
Underwood 78	2	41N24	95w40	6:22:40
Union 42	2	42N15	93w04	6:12:16
Union Center 75	2	42N47	96w10	6:24:40
Union City 3	1	43N28	91w27	6:05:48
Union Mills 62	2	41N28	92w39	6:10:36
Union Prairie 3	1	43N18	91w33	6:06:12
Unionville 4	2	40N49	92w42	6:10:48
University Heights 52	1	41N40	91w34	6:06:16
University Park 62	2	41N17	92w37	6:10:28
Urbana 6	1	42N13	91w52	6:07:28
Urbandale 77	2	41N38	93w43	6:14:52
Ute 67	2	42N03	95w42	6:22:48
Utica 19	2	43N09	92w10	6:08:40
Vail 24	2	42N04	95w12	6:20:48
Valeria 50	2	41N44	93w20	6:13:20
Van Cleve 64	2	41N56	93w06	6:12:24
Vandalia 50	2	41N38	93w15	6:13:00
Van Horne 6	2	42N01	92w05	6:08:20
Van Meter 25	2	41N32	93w57	6:15:48
Van Wert 27	2	40N52	93w48	6:15:12
Varina 76	2	42N40	94w54	6:19:36
Ventura 17	2	43N08	93w27	6:13:48
Veo 51	1	41N11	92w00	6:08:00
Vermilion 4	2	40N43	92w52	6:11:28
Vernon 89	1	40N44	91w58	6:07:52
Vernon Springs 45	2	43N23	92w09	6:08:36
Vernon View 57	1	41N59	91w40	6:06:40
Victor 48	2	41N45	92w15	6:09:00
Victoria 15	2	41N12	94w47	6:19:08
Victory 39	2	41N44	94w27	6:17:48
Vienna 64	2	42N10	92w50	6:11:20
Village 89	2	40N53	92w08	6:08:32
Village Creek 3	1	43N22	91w13	6:04:52
Villisca 69	2	40N56	94w59	6:19:56
Vincent 94	2	42N36	94w01	6:16:04
Vining 86	2	41N59	92w25	6:09:40
Vinton 6	2	42N10	92w01	6:08:04
Viola 57	1	42N06	91w23	6:05:32
Virginia 91	2	41N12	93w43	6:14:52
Volga 22	1	42N48	91w33	6:06:12
Volney 3	1	43N03	91w24	6:05:36
Voorhies 7	2	42N20	92w29	6:09:56
Wacousta 46	2	42N52	94w23	6:17:32
Wadena 33	1	42N50	91w39	6:06:36
Wagner 22	1	42N58	91w26	6:05:44
Wahpeton 30	2	43N23	95w11	6:20:44
Walcott 82	5	41N35	90w47	6:03:08
Wales 69	2	41N01	95w27	6:21:48
Walford 6	1	41N53	91w50	6:07:20
Walker 57	1	42N17	91w47	6:07:08
Wallingford 32	2	43N19	94w48	6:19:12
Wall Lake 81	2	42N16	95w05	6:20:20
Walnut 78	2	41N29	95w13	6:20:52
Walnut City 4	2	40N47	92w57	6:11:48
Wapello 58	23	41N11	91w11	6:04:44
Wapsinonoc 70	1	41N33	91w17	6:05:08
Ward 20	2	41N02	93w51	6:15:24
Ware 76	2	42N47	94w46	6:19:04
Washburn 7	2	42N25	92w16	6:09:04
Washington 92	1	41N18	91w42	6:06:48
Washta 18	2	42N35	95w43	6:22:52
Waterloo 7	2	42N30	92w21	6:09:24
Waterman 71	2	42N58	95w26	6:21:44
Waterville 3	1	43N13	91w18	6:05:12
Watkins 6	1	41N53	91w59	6:07:56
Watson 22	1	43N03	91w24	6:05:36
Waubeek 57	1	42N13	91w31	6:06:04
Waubonsie 80	2	40N43	94w22	6:17:28
Waucoma 33	2	43N03	92w02	6:08:08
Waukee 25	2	41N37	93w53	6:15:32
Waukon 3	1	43N16	91w29	6:05:56
Waukon Junction 3	1	43N09	91w11	6:04:44
Waupeton 31	1	42N38	90w50	6:03:20
Waveland 78	2	41N12	95w12	6:20:48
Waverly 9	2	42N44	92w29	6:09:56
Wayland 44	1	41N08	91w40	6:06:40
Weaver 46	2	42N41	94w23	6:17:32
Webb 21	2	42N57	95w01	6:20:04
Webster 54	2	41N26	92w10	6:08:40
Webster 61	2	41N21	94w00	6:16:00
Webster City 40	2	42N28	93w49	6:15:16
Welcome 84	2	43N07	96w09	6:24:36
Weldon 27	2	40N54	93w44	6:14:56
Weller 68	2	41N08	92w54	6:11:36
Wellman 92	1	41N28	91w50	6:07:20
Wells 4	2	40N38	92w42	6:10:48
Wellsburg 38	2	42N26	92w56	6:11:44
Welton 23	1	41N55	90w36	6:02:24
Wesley 55	2	43N05	94w00	6:16:00
West 48	1	41N48	91w58	6:07:52
West 69	2	40N57	95w19	6:21:16
West Bend 55	2	42N57	94w27	6:17:48
West Bend 74	2	43N27	94w27	6:17:48
West Branch 16	1	41N40	91w20	6:05:20
West Broadway 78	2	41N16	95w51	6:23:24
Westburg 10	2	42N25	92w01	6:08:04
West Burlington 29	18	40N50	91w09	6:04:36
West Chester 92	1	41N20	91w49	6:07:16
West Des Moines 77	2	41N35	93w43	6:14:52
Western College 57	1	41N58	91w42	6:06:48
Westerville 27	2	40N50	93w56	6:15:44
Westfield 75	2	42N45	96w36	6:26:24
West Fort Dodge 94	2	42N30	94w11	6:16:44
Westgate 33	1	42N46	92w00	6:08:00
West Grove 26	2	40N43	92w34	6:10:16
West Lancaster 54	2	41N16	92w14	6:08:56
West Le Mars 75	2	42N47	96w10	6:24:40
West Liberty 70	1	41N34	91w16	6:05:04
West Lincoln 66	2	43N14	92w45	6:11:00
West Lucas 52	1	41N38	91w34	6:06:16
West Mitchell 66	2	43N19	92w52	6:11:28
West Okoboji 30	2	43N21	95w09	6:20:36
Weston 78	2	41N20	95w44	6:22:56
Westphalia 83	2	41N44	95w23	6:21:32
West Point 56	24	40N43	91w27	6:05:48
Westport 30	2	43N18	95w20	6:21:20
West Side 24	2	42N04	95w09	6:20:36
Westside 24	2	42N05	95w07	6:20:28
West Storm Lake 11	2	42N38	95w11	6:20:44
West Union 33	1	42N57	91w49	6:07:16
Wever 56	25	40N43	91w13	6:04:52
What Cheer 54	2	41N24	92w21	6:09:24
Wheatland 23	1	41N50	90w51	6:03:24
White Cloud 65	2	40N54	95w38	6:22:32
White Elm 26	2	40N52	92w09	6:08:36
White Oak 77	2	41N48	93w31	6:14:04
White Pigeon 54	2	41N31	92w04	6:08:16
Whitewater 31	1	42N20	90w58	6:03:52
Whiting 67	2	42N08	96w09	6:24:36
Whittemore 55	2	43N04	94w26	6:17:44
Whitten 42	2	42N16	93w00	6:12:00
Whittier 57	1	42N06	91w28	6:05:52
Wichita 39	2	41N41	94w30	6:18:00
Wick 91	2	41N18	93w47	6:15:08
Wieston 13	2	42N32	94w32	6:18:08
Wildwood Camp 82	1	41N42	90w35	6:02:20
Willey 14	2	41N59	94w49	6:19:16
William Penn College 62	2	41N17	92w38	6:10:32
Williams 40	2	42N29	93w33	6:14:12
Williamsburg 48	2	41N40	92w01	6:08:04
Williamson 2	2	41N01	94w37	6:18:28
Williamson 59	2	41N05	93w15	6:13:00
Williamstown 52	1	41N29	91w42	6:06:48
Wilson 72	2	43N28	95w41	6:22:44
Wilton 70	5	41N34	90w58	6:03:52
Windham 52	1	41N44	91w48	6:07:12
Windsor 33	1	42N57	91w54	6:07:36
Windsor Heights 77	2	41N36	93w43	6:14:52

IOWA

Place		Lat.	Long.	Time
Winfield 44	1	41N07	91w26	6:05:44
Winnebago Heights 17	2	43N09	93w13	6:12:52
Winterset 61	2	41N20	94w01	6:16:04
Winthrop 10	1	42N28	91w44	6:06:56
Wiota 15	2	41N24	94w54	6:19:36
Wiscotta 25	2	41N35	94w12	6:16:48
Wisner 35	2	42N52	93w26	6:13:44
Woden 41	2	43N14	93w55	6:15:40
Wolf Creek 97	2	42N26	95w57	6:23:48
Wood 22	1	42N39	91w24	6:05:36
Woodbine 43	2	41N44	95w43	6:22:52
Woodburn 20	2	41N01	93w36	6:14:24
Woodbury 97	2	42N26	96w18	6:25:12
Woodland 27	2	40N42	93w36	6:14:24
Woodward 25	2	41N51	93w55	6:15:40
Woolstock 99	2	42N34	93w51	6:15:24
Worth 8	2	42N00	93w51	6:15:24
Worthington 31	1	42N24	91w07	6:04:28
Wright 62	2	41N15	92w32	6:10:08
Wyacondah 26	2	40N40	92w28	6:09:52
Wyman 58	1	41N11	91w28	6:05:52
Wyoming 53	1	42N05	90w58	6:03:52
Yale 39	2	41N47	94w21	6:17:24
Yarmouth 29	1	41N01	91w19	6:05:16
Yellow Springs 29	1	41N02	91w11	6:04:44
Yetter 13	2	42N19	94w51	6:19:24
Yorktown 73	2	40N44	95w09	6:20:36
Zaneta 38	2	42N25	92w27	6:09:48
Zearing 85	2	42N10	93w17	6:13:08
Zion 1	2	41N13	94w25	6:17:40
Zook Spur 25	2	41N52	93w49	6:15:16
Zwingle 31	1	42N18	90w41	6:02:44

TIME TABLES

The time tables for western Kansas reflect the observed CST, rather than the MST mandated by the Interstate Commerce Commission. Zone shifts in the extreme western part of the state are sometimes estimated from incomplete information.

KS # 1

Before 11/18/1883		LMT
11/18/1883	12:00	CST
3/31/1918	02:00	CWT
10/27/1918	02:00	CST
3/30/1919	02:00	CWT
10/26/1919	02:00	CST
2/09/1942	02:00	CWT
9/30/1945	02:00	CST
4/30/1967	02:00	US#1

KS # 2

Before 11/18/1883		LMT
11/18/1883	12:00	MST
3/31/1918	02:00	MWT
10/27/1918	02:00	MST
3/30/1919	02:00	MWT
10/26/1919	02:00	MST
2/09/1942	02:00	MWT
9/30/1945	02:00	MST
4/24/1966	02:00	US#1

KS # 3

Before 11/18/1883		LMT
11/18/1883	12:00	MST
3/31/1918	02:00	MWT
10/27/1918	02:00	MST
3/30/1919	02:00	MWT
10/26/1919	02:00	MST
8/07/1927	02:00	CST
2/09/1942	02:00	CWT
9/30/1945	02:00	CST
4/30/1967	02:00	US#1

KS # 4

Before 11/18/1883		LMT
11/18/1883	12:00	MST
3/31/1918	02:00	MWT
10/27/1918	02:00	MST
3/30/1919	02:00	MWT
10/26/1919	02:00	MST
2/09/1942	02:00	MWT
9/30/1945	02:00	CST
4/30/1967	02:00	US#1

KS # 5

Before 11/18/1883		LMT
11/18/1883	12:00	MST
3/31/1918	02:00	MWT
10/27/1918	02:00	MST
3/30/1919	02:00	MWT
10/26/1919	02:00	MST
2/09/1942	02:00	MWT
9/30/1945	02:00	MST
4/28/1963	02:00	CST
4/30/1967	02:00	US#1

COUNTIES

1 Allen
2 Anderson
3 Atchison
4 Barber
5 Barton
6 Bourbon
7 Brown
8 Butler
9 Chase
10 Chautauqua
11 Cherokee
12 Cheyenne
13 Clark
14 Clay
15 Cloud
16 Coffey
17 Comanche
18 Cowley
19 Crawford
20 Decatur
21 Dickinson
22 Doniphan
23 Douglas
24 Edwards
25 Elk
26 Ellis
27 Ellsworth
28 Finney
29 Ford
30 Franklin
31 Geary
32 Gove
33 Graham
34 Grant
35 Gray
36 Greeley
37 Greenwood
38 Hamilton
39 Harper
40 Harvey
41 Haskell
42 Hodgeman
43 Jackson
44 Jefferson
45 Jewell
46 Johnson
47 Kearny
48 Kingman
49 Kiowa
50 Labette
51 Lane
52 Leavenworth
53 Lincoln
54 Linn
55 Logan
56 Lyon
57 McPherson
58 Marion
59 Marshall
60 Meade
61 Miami
62 Mitchell
63 Montgomery
64 Morris
65 Morton
66 Nemaha
67 Neosho
68 Ness
69 Norton
70 Osage
71 Osborne
72 Ottawa
73 Pawnee
74 Phillips
75 Pottawatomie
76 Pratt
77 Rawlins
78 Reno
79 Republic
80 Rice
81 Riley
82 Rooks
83 Rush
84 Russell
85 Saline
86 Scott
87 Sedgwick
88 Seward
89 Shawnee
90 Sheridan
91 Sherman
92 Smith
93 Stafford
94 Stanton
95 Stevens
96 Sumner
97 Thomas
98 Trego
99 Wabaunsee
100 Wallace
101 Washington
102 Wichita
103 Wilson
104 Woodson
105 Wyandotte

Abbyville 78	1	37N58	98w12	6:32:48
Abilene 21	1	38N55	97w13	6:28:52
Achilles 77	1	39N42	100w49	6:43:16
Ada 72	1	39N09	97w53	6:31:32
Adams 48	1	37N27	98w05	6:32:20
Adams 66	1	39N47	95w57	6:23:48
Adell 90	1	39N31	100w14	6:40:56
Admire 56	1	38N39	96w06	6:24:24
Adrian 43	1	39N21	95w59	6:23:56
Aetna 4	1	37N05	98w58	6:35:52
Afton 87	1	37N36	97w38	6:30:32
Agency 70	1	38N34	95w33	6:22:12
Agenda 79	1	39N43	97w26	6:29:44
Agnes City 56	1	38N41	96w14	6:24:56
Agra 74	1	39N46	99w07	6:36:28
Agricola 16	1	38N25	95w32	6:22:08
Airbase Spur 5	1	38N22	98w46	6:35:04
Akron 18	1	37N21	97w01	6:28:04
Alameda 48	1	37N39	98w07	6:32:28
Alamota 51	1	38N28	100w19	6:41:16
Albano 93	1	37N53	98w52	6:35:28
Albert 5	1	38N27	99w01	6:36:04
Alcona 82	1	39N26	99w33	6:38:12
Alden 80	1	38N15	98w19	6:33:16
Aldine 69	1	39N57	99w54	6:39:36
Aleppo 87	1	37N40	97w41	6:30:44
Alexander 83	1	38N28	99w33	6:38:12
Alexandria 52	1	39N16	95w07	6:20:28
Aliceville 16	1	38N09	95w33	6:22:12
Allen 56	1	38N39	96w10	6:24:40
Allison 20	1	39N37	100w14	6:40:56
Allodium 33	1	39N30	100w06	6:40:24
Alma 99	1	39N01	96w17	6:25:08
Almelo 69	1	39N36	100w07	6:40:28
Almena 69	1	39N54	99w43	6:38:52
Alta 40	1	38N08	97w39	6:30:36
Altamont 50	1	37N12	95w18	6:21:12
Alta Vista 99	1	38N52	96w29	6:25:56
Alton 71	1	39N28	98w57	6:35:48
Altoona 103	1	37N32	95w40	6:22:40
Altory 20	1	39N47	100w21	6:41:24
Americus 56	1	38N30	96w16	6:25:04
Ames 15	1	39N34	97w27	6:29:48
Amy 51	1	38N29	100w36	6:42:24
Andale 87	1	37N48	97w38	6:30:32
Andover 8	1	37N43	97w07	6:28:28
Angelus 90	1	39N11	100w41	6:42:44
Angola 50	1	37N06	95w27	6:21:48
Anna 6	1	37N42	94w47	6:19:08
Anness 87	1	37N26	97w46	6:31:04
Anson 96	1	37N22	97w32	6:30:08
Antelope 58	1	38N26	96w59	6:27:56
Anthony 39	1	37N09	98w02	6:32:08
Antioch 61	1	38N45	94w50	6:19:20
Antonino 26	1	38N47	99w24	6:37:36
Appanoose 30	1	38N42	95w28	6:21:52
Appleton 13	1	37N24	100w05	6:40:20
Arbor 77	1	39N42	101w01	6:44:04
Arcade 74	1	39N47	99w14	6:36:56
Arcadia 19	1	37N38	94w37	6:18:28
Argentine 105	1	39N04	94w41	6:18:44
Argonia 96	1	37N16	97w46	6:31:04
Arion 15	1	39N29	97w46	6:31:04
Arkansas City 18	1	37N04	97w02	6:28:08
Arlington 78	1	37N54	98w11	6:32:44
Arma 19	1	37N33	94w42	6:18:48
Arnold 68	1	38N38	100w03	6:40:12
Arrington 3	1	39N28	95w32	6:22:08
Arthur Heights 87	1	37N44	97w17	6:29:08
Arvonia 70	1	38N29	95w52	6:23:28
Ash Creek 27	1	38N39	98w12	6:32:48
Asherville 62	1	39N24	97w59	6:31:56
Ash Grove 53	1	39N10	98w22	6:33:28
Ashland 13	1	37N11	99w46	6:39:04
Ashland 81	1	39N12	96w33	6:26:12
Ash Rock 82	1	39N31	99w06	6:36:24
Ashton 96	1	37N05	97w14	6:28:56
Ash Valley 73	1	38N18	99w12	6:36:48
Assaria 85	1	38N41	97w36	6:30:24
Atchison 3	1	39N34	95w07	6:20:28
Athelstane 14	1	39N11	97w12	6:28:48
Athens 45	1	39N37	98w20	6:33:20
Athol 92	1	39N46	98w55	6:35:40
Atlanta 18	1	37N26	96w46	6:27:04
Attica 39	1	37N15	98w13	6:32:52
Atwood 77	1	39N48	101w03	6:44:12
Aubry 46	1	38N47	94w41	6:18:44
Auburn 89	1	38N54	95w49	6:23:16
Augusta 8	1	37N41	96w59	6:27:56
Augustine 55	4	38N45	101w22	6:45:28
Aulne 58	1	38N17	97w05	6:28:20
Aurora 15	1	39N27	97w32	6:30:08
Aurora Park 87	1	37N44	97w17	6:29:08
Avilla 17	1	37N05	99w18	6:37:12
Axtell 59	1	39N52	96w15	6:25:00
Bachelor 37	1	37N50	96w11	6:24:44
Badger 11	1	37N05	94w38	6:18:32
Baileyville 66	1	39N51	96w11	6:24:44
Baker 7	1	39N51	95w32	6:22:08
Bala 81	1	39N19	96w57	6:27:48
Balderson 59	1	39N57	96w31	6:26:04
Baldwin City 23	1	38N47	95w11	6:20:44
Bancroft 66	1	39N40	95w56	6:23:44
Barclay 70	1	38N35	95w53	6:23:32
Barnard 53	1	39N11	98w03	6:32:12
Barnes 101	1	39N43	96w52	6:27:28
Barnesville 6	1	38N00	94w43	6:18:52
Barrett 97	1	39N31	101w17	6:45:08
Bartlett 50	1	37N03	95w13	6:20:52
Basehor 52	1	39N08	94w56	6:19:44
Bassett 1	1	37N54	95w24	6:21:36
Bassettville 20	1	39N42	100w41	6:42:44
Batesville 104	1	37N48	95w57	6:23:48
Battle Creek 53	1	39N11	98w13	6:32:52
Battle Hill 57	1	38N29	97w25	6:29:40
Bavaria 85	1	38N48	97w45	6:31:00
Baxter Springs 11	1	37N02	94w44	6:18:56
Bayard 1	1	38N05	95w12	6:20:48
Bazaar 9	1	38N16	96w32	6:26:08
Bazine 68	1	38N27	99w42	6:38:48
Beagle 61	1	38N25	94w57	6:19:48
Bear Creek 38	2	37N50	101w55	6:47:40
Beardsley 77	1	39N49	101w14	6:44:56
Beattie 59	1	39N52	96w25	6:25:40
Beaumont 8	1	37N39	96w32	6:26:08
Beaver 5	1	38N38	98w40	6:34:40
Beeler 68	1	38N26	100w12	6:40:48
Beeson 29	1	37N45	100w01	6:40:04
Bellaire 87	1	37N44	97w17	6:29:08
Bellaire 92	1	39N48	98w40	6:34:40
Bellefont 29	1	37N53	99w40	6:38:40
Belle Plain 69	1	39N47	99w48	6:39:12
Belle Plaine 96	1	37N24	97w17	6:29:08
Belle Prairie 83	1	38N25	99w32	6:38:08
Belleville 79	1	39N50	97w38	6:30:32
Belmont 48	1	37N32	98w00	6:32:00
Beloit 62	1	39N28	98w06	6:32:24
Belpre 24	1	37N57	99w06	6:36:24
Belvidere 49	1	37N27	99w05	6:36:20
Belvue 75	1	39N13	96w11	6:24:44
Bendena 22	1	39N44	95w12	6:20:48
Benedict 103	1	37N38	95w45	6:23:00
Benkelman 12	4	39N40	101w55	6:47:40
Bennett 48	1	37N26	97w52	6:31:28
Bennington 72	1	39N02	97w36	6:30:24
Bentley 87	1	37N54	97w31	6:30:04
Benton 8	1	37N47	97w06	6:28:24
Berlin 39	1	37N10	97w57	6:31:48
Bern 66	1	39N58	95w58	6:23:52
Berryton 89	1	38N56	95w38	6:22:32
Berwick 66	1	39N57	95w51	6:23:24
Bethany 71	1	39N31	98w39	6:34:36
Bethel 105	1	39N09	94w46	6:19:04
Beulah 19	1	37N26	94w50	6:19:20
Beverly 53	1	39N01	97w58	6:31:52
Beverly Hills 53	1	39N10	94w45	6:19:00
Big Bend 79	1	39N57	97w52	6:31:28
Big Bow 94	3	37N34	101w34	6:46:16
Bigelow 59	1	39N37	96w31	6:26:04
Big Springs 23	1	39N01	95w29	6:21:56
Big Timber 83	1	38N38	99w19	6:37:16
Bird City 12	4	39N45	101w32	6:46:08
Birmingham 43	1	39N25	95w41	6:22:44
Bismarck Grove 23	1	38N58	95w15	6:21:00
Bison 83	1	38N31	99w12	6:36:48
Black Jack 23	1	38N47	95w11	6:20:44
Black Wolf 27	1	38N45	98w19	6:33:16
Blaine 75	1	39N30	96w24	6:25:36
Blair 22	1	39N46	94w57	6:19:48
Blakely 31	1	38N55	96w46	6:27:04
Blakeman 77	1	39N49	101w07	6:44:28
Bloom 29	1	37N29	99w54	6:39:36
Bloomington 8	1	37N41	96w59	6:27:56

KANSAS

Bloomington 71	1	39N27	98w47	6:35:08
Blue 75	1	39N11	96w33	6:26:12
Blue Hill 62	1	39N16	98w19	6:33:16
Blue Mound 54	1	38N05	95w00	6:20:00
Blue Rapids 59	1	39N41	96w39	6:26:36
Blue Valley 75	1	39N27	96w38	6:26:32
Bluff 96	1	37N04	97w45	6:31:00
Bluff City 39	1	37N05	97w53	6:31:32
Bodaville 81	1	39N43	96w52	6:27:28
Bogue 33	1	39N22	99w41	6:38:44
Boicourt 54	1	38N16	94w43	6:18:52
Bolton 18	1	37N02	97w02	6:28:08
Bolton 63	1	37N14	95w43	6:22:52
Bonaville 57	1	38N33	97w32	6:30:08
Bonita 46	1	38N53	94w49	6:19:16
Bonner Springs 105	1	39N03	94w53	6:19:32
Bonnie Ridge 85	1	38N50	97w36	6:30:24
Boyle 44	1	39N21	95w28	6:21:52
Brainerd 8	1	37N58	97w09	6:28:36
Brantford 101	1	39N42	97w19	6:29:16
Brazilton 19	1	37N34	94w58	6:19:52
Bremen 59	1	39N54	96w47	6:27:08
Brenham 49	1	37N36	99w10	6:36:40
Breton 97	1	39N28	100w45	6:43:00
Brewster 97	1	39N22	101w23	6:45:32
Bridgeport 85	1	38N38	97w37	6:30:28
Bronson 6	1	37N54	95w04	6:20:16
Brookdale 83	1	38N32	99w25	6:37:40
Brookhaven Estates 87	1	37N41	97w18	6:29:12
Brookridge 46	1	38N58	94w41	6:18:44
Brookville 85	1	38N46	97w52	6:31:28
Broughton 14	1	39N19	97w03	6:28:12
Brown 13	1	37N23	99w48	6:39:12
Brownell 68	1	38N38	99w45	6:39:00
Browns Creek 45	1	39N37	98w13	6:32:52
Browns Grove 73	1	38N13	99w31	6:38:04
Browns Spur 48	1	37N39	98w07	6:32:28
Brownville 97	1	39N22	101w22	6:45:28
Bruno 8	1	37N41	97w06	6:28:24
Bryant 33	1	39N12	100w04	6:40:16
Buckeye 21	1	38N55	97w13	6:28:52
Bucklin 29	1	37N33	99w38	6:38:32
Bucyrus 61	1	38N44	94w44	6:18:56
Buffalo 103	1	37N42	95w42	6:22:48
Buhler 78	1	38N08	97w46	6:31:04
Bunker Hill 84	1	38N53	98w42	6:34:48
Burden 18	1	37N19	96w45	6:27:00
Burdett 73	1	38N12	99w32	6:38:08
Burdick 64	1	38N34	96w51	6:27:24
Burlingame 70	1	38N45	95w50	6:23:20
Burlington 16	1	38N12	95w45	6:23:00
Burns 58	1	38N05	96w53	6:27:32
Burntwood 77	1	39N56	101w16	6:45:04
Burr Oak 45	1	39N52	98w18	6:33:12
Burrton 40	1	38N02	97w41	6:30:44
Busby 25	1	37N28	96w16	6:25:04
Bush City 2	1	38N13	95w09	6:20:36
Bushong 56	1	38N39	96w16	6:25:04
Bushton 80	1	38N31	98w24	6:33:36
Butler 49	1	37N41	99w24	6:37:36
Buttermilk 17	1	37N16	99w20	6:37:20
Buxton 103	1	37N27	95w55	6:23:40
Byers 76	1	37N48	98w52	6:35:28
Byron 93	1	38N13	98w38	6:34:32
Cadmus 54	1	38N26	94w50	6:19:20
Cairo 76	1	37N39	98w34	6:34:16
Caldwell 96	1	37N02	97w37	6:30:28
Calhoun 12	4	39N56	101w41	6:46:44
California 16	1	38N18	95w53	6:23:32
Calista 48	1	37N39	98w17	6:33:08
Callahan 87	1	37N41	97w25	6:29:40
Calvert 69	1	39N53	99w43	6:38:52
Calvin 45	1	39N42	98w13	6:32:52
Cambria 85	1	38N55	97w33	6:30:12
Cambridge 18	1	37N19	96w40	6:26:40
Camp Forsyth 31	1	39N11	96w52	6:27:28
Camp Funston 81	1	39N06	96w44	6:26:56
Camp Naish 105	1	39N05	94w45	6:19:00
Campus 32	1	39N08	100w52	6:43:28
Camp Whiteside 31	1	39N06	96w47	6:27:08
Canada 50	1	37N07	95w27	6:21:48
Canada 58	1	38N21	97w01	6:28:04
Caney 63	1	37N01	95w56	6:23:44
Caneyville 10	1	37N15	96w27	6:25:48
Canton 57	1	38N23	97w26	6:29:44
Canville 67	1	37N37	95w27	6:21:48
Capaldo 19	1	37N26	94w42	6:18:48
Capioma 66	1	39N47	95w51	6:23:24
Carbondale 70	1	38N49	95w41	6:22:44
Carlton 21	1	38N41	97w18	6:29:12
Carlyle 1	1	38N00	95w23	6:21:32
Carmi 76	1	37N47	98w38	6:34:32
Carneiro 27	1	38N44	98w02	6:32:08
Carona 11	1	37N16	94w52	6:19:28
Carr Creek 62	1	39N26	98w26	6:33:44
Cassoday 8	1	38N03	96w38	6:26:32
Castle 57	1	38N23	97w52	6:31:28
Castleton 78	1	37N52	97w58	6:31:52
Catharine 26	1	38N56	99w13	6:36:52
Catlin 58	1	38N13	97w06	6:28:24
Cato 19	1	37N39	94w38	6:18:32
Cave 95	3	37N19	101w12	6:44:48
Cawker City 62	1	39N31	98w26	6:33:44
Cedar 46	1	38N59	94w58	6:19:52
Cedar 92	1	39N39	98w56	6:35:44
Cedar Bluffs 20	1	39N59	100w34	6:42:16
Cedar Point 9	1	38N16	96w49	6:27:16
Cedar Vale 10	1	37N06	96w30	6:26:00
Cedron 53	1	39N11	98w26	6:33:44
Celia 77	1	39N48	101w18	6:45:12
Centerview 24	1	37N56	99w15	6:37:00
Centerville 54	1	38N13	95w01	6:20:04
Centralia 66	1	39N44	96w08	6:24:32

Centropolis 30	1	38N43	95w21	6:21:24
Chanute 67	1	37N41	95w27	6:21:48
Chapman 21	1	38N58	97w01	6:28:04
Charleston 35	4	37N52	100w34	6:42:16
Chase 80	1	38N21	98w21	6:33:24
Chautauqua 10	1	37N01	96w11	6:24:44
Cheever 21	1	39N05	97w12	6:28:48
Chelsea 8	1	37N56	96w43	6:26:52
Cheney 87	1	37N38	97w47	6:31:08
Cherokee 19	1	37N21	94w49	6:19:16
Cherry 63	1	37N19	95w33	6:22:12
Cherry Creek 12	4	39N47	101w57	6:47:48
Cherryvale 63	1	37N16	95w33	6:22:12
Chetopa 50	1	37N02	95w05	6:20:20
Chicaskia 39	1	37N21	97w52	6:31:28
Chicopee 19	1	37N23	94w45	6:19:00
Child's Acres 87	1	37N46	97w28	6:29:52
Chiles 61	1	38N41	94w46	6:19:04
Chisholm 87	1	37N38	97w21	6:29:24
Cicero 96	1	37N20	97w21	6:29:24
Cimarron 35	4	37N48	100w21	6:41:24
Circleville 43	1	39N31	95w52	6:23:28
Civic Center 105	1	39N06	94w40	6:18:40
Claflin 5	1	38N31	98w32	6:34:08
Clare 46	1	38N50	94w52	6:19:28
Clarence 5	1	38N24	98w59	6:35:56
Clark 58	1	38N29	97w06	6:28:24
Clarks Creek 64	1	38N44	96w53	6:27:32
Claudell 92	1	39N40	99w02	6:36:08
Clay Center 14	1	39N23	97w08	6:28:32
Clayton 69	1	39N44	100w11	6:40:44
Clearfield 23	1	38N47	95w11	6:20:44
Clear Fork 59	1	39N37	96w24	6:25:36
Clearview City 46	1	38N57	95w00	6:20:00
Clearwater 87	1	37N30	97w30	6:30:00
Clements 9	1	38N18	96w44	6:26:56
Cleveland 48	1	37N33	98w08	6:32:32
Cleveland Run 12	4	39N55	101w48	6:47:12
Clifford 8	1	38N03	96w59	6:27:56
Clifton 101	1	39N34	97w17	6:29:08
Climax 37	1	37N43	96w13	6:24:52
Clinton 23	1	38N55	95w23	6:21:32
Clonmel 87	1	37N29	97w39	6:30:36
Cloverdale 78	1	38N04	97w57	6:31:48
Cloverdale 85	1	38N50	97w36	6:30:24
Clyde 15	1	39N36	97w24	6:29:36
Coalvale 19	1	37N39	94w38	6:18:32
Coats 76	1	37N31	98w50	6:35:20
Cockerill 19	1	37N33	94w37	6:18:28
Codell 82	1	39N12	99w11	6:36:44
Coffeyville 63	1	37N02	95w37	6:22:28
Colby 97	1	39N24	101w03	6:44:12
Coldwater 17	1	37N16	99w20	6:37:20
Coleman 101	1	39N47	97w12	6:28:48
College 19	1	37N26	94w42	6:18:48
Collyer 98	1	39N02	100w07	6:40:28
Colony 2	1	38N04	95w22	6:21:28
Colorado 53	1	39N00	97w59	6:31:56
Columbia 27	1	38N49	98w19	6:33:16
Columbus 11	1	37N10	94w50	6:19:20
Colwich 87	1	37N47	97w32	6:30:08
Comanche 5	1	38N18	98w35	6:34:20
Concordia 15	1	39N34	97w40	6:30:40
Conkling 73	1	38N19	99w19	6:37:16
Connell 87	1	37N38	97w18	6:29:12
Conway 57	1	38N22	97w47	6:31:08
Conway Springs 96	1	37N24	97w39	6:30:36
Cook 20	1	39N37	100w41	6:42:44
Coolidge 38	2	38N03	102w01	6:48:04
Copeland 35	3	37N33	100w38	6:42:32
Cora 92	1	39N53	98w40	6:34:40
Corbin 63	1	37N16	95w33	6:22:12
Corbin 96	1	37N08	97w33	6:30:12
Corinth 71	1	39N26	98w33	6:34:12
Corinth Square Center 46	1	39N00	94w37	6:18:28
Corning 66	1	39N39	96w02	6:24:08
Corwin 39	1	37N05	98w18	6:33:12
Cottage Grove 1	1	37N45	95w20	6:21:20
Cottage Hill 59	1	39N37	96w45	6:27:00
Cottonwood 9	1	38N17	96w44	6:26:56
Cottonwood Falls 9	1	38N22	96w32	6:26:08
Council Grove 64	1	38N40	96w29	6:25:56
Countryside 46	1	39N01	94w39	6:18:36
Courtland 79	1	39N47	97w54	6:31:36
Covert 71	1	39N17	98w49	6:35:16
Coyville 103	1	37N41	95w54	6:23:36
Craig 46	1	38N58	94w44	6:18:56
Crandall 16	1	38N05	95w38	6:22:32
Crawford 80	1	38N31	98w13	6:32:52
Creek 96	1	37N21	97w45	6:31:00
Crestline 11	1	37N10	94w42	6:18:48
Creswell 18	1	37N05	97w01	6:28:04
Croft 76	1	37N30	99w00	6:36:00
Crooked Creek 60	1	37N24	100w20	6:41:20
Croweburg 19	1	37N33	94w37	6:18:28
Cruppers Corner 78	1	38N04	97w57	6:31:48
Crystal Plains 92	1	39N42	98w40	6:34:40
Crystal Springs 39	1	37N16	98w08	6:32:32
Cuba 79	1	39N48	97w27	6:29:48
Cullison 76	1	37N38	98w54	6:35:36
Culver 72	1	38N58	97w46	6:31:04
Cummings 3	1	39N28	95w15	6:21:00
Cunningham 48	1	37N39	98w26	6:33:44
Cunningham Highlands 46	1	39N00	94w41	6:18:44
Curranville 19	1	37N33	94w37	6:18:28
Cutler 30	1	38N31	95w07	6:20:28
Dale 48	1	37N36	97w58	6:31:52
Dalton 96	1	37N16	97w24	6:29:36

Damar 82	1	39N19	99w35	6:38:20
Danville 39	1	37N17	97w54	6:31:36
Darlington 40	1	37N58	97w19	6:29:16
Dartmouth 5	1	38N22	98w46	6:35:04
Dearing 63	1	37N03	95w42	6:22:48
Deerfield 47	5	37N59	101w08	6:44:32
Deerhead 4	1	37N14	98w56	6:35:44
De Graff 8	1	38N06	96w53	6:27:32
Delano 87	1	37N41	97w27	6:29:48
Delavan 64	1	38N40	96w49	6:27:16
Delhi 71	1	39N11	98w33	6:34:12
Delia 43	1	39N15	95w59	6:23:56
Dellvale 69	1	39N46	100w02	6:40:08
Delmore 57	1	38N29	97w32	6:30:08
Delphos 72	1	39N17	97w46	6:31:04
Denison 43	1	39N24	95w38	6:22:32
Denmark 53	1	39N05	98w17	6:33:08
Dennis 50	1	37N21	95w25	6:21:40
Densmore 69	1	39N38	99w44	6:38:56
Dent 12	4	39N42	101w45	6:47:00
Denton 22	1	39N44	95w16	6:21:04
Denton-McWorter Addition 87	1	37N46	97w28	6:29:52
Derby 87	1	37N33	97w16	6:29:04
Dermot 65	3	37N07	101w38	6:46:32
De Soto 46	1	38N59	94w58	6:19:52
Detroit 21	1	38N55	97w13	6:28:52
Devon 6	1	37N55	94w49	6:19:16
Dexter 18	1	37N11	96w43	6:26:52
Diamond Creek 9	1	38N26	96w42	6:26:48
Diamond Springs 64	1	38N34	96w51	6:27:24
Diamond Valley 64	1	38N34	96w45	6:27:00
Dighton 51	1	38N29	100w28	6:41:52
Dillwyn 93	1	37N58	98w58	6:35:52
Dispatch 92	1	39N31	98w26	6:33:44
Dixon 96	1	37N15	97w45	6:31:00
Dodge City 29	1	37N45	100w01	6:40:04
Doniphan 22	1	39N38	95w05	6:20:20
Dor 92	1	39N37	99w01	6:36:04
Dorrance 84	1	38N51	98w35	6:34:20
Douglass 8	1	37N31	97w01	6:28:04
Dover 89	1	38N58	95w56	6:23:44
Downs 71	1	39N30	98w33	6:34:12
Doyle 58	1	38N14	96w53	6:27:32
Dragoon 70	1	38N43	95w50	6:23:20
Dresden 20	1	39N37	100w25	6:41:40
Driftwood 77	1	39N57	101w04	6:44:16
Drum Creek 63	1	37N14	95w36	6:22:24
Drury 96	1	37N02	97w36	6:30:24
Drywood 6	1	37N43	94w41	6:18:44
Dubuque 5	1	38N51	98w35	6:34:20
Duck Creek 103	1	37N26	95w54	6:23:36
Dudley 41	3	37N34	101w01	6:44:04
Duluth 75	1	39N32	96w13	6:24:52
Dunavant 44	1	39N18	95w20	6:21:20
Dundee 5	1	38N19	98w54	6:35:36
Dunkirk 19	1	37N26	94w42	6:18:48
Dunlap 64	1	38N35	96w22	6:25:28
Dunlay 54	1	38N20	94w59	6:19:56
Duquoin 39	1	37N23	98w05	6:32:20
Durham 58	1	38N29	97w13	6:28:52
Durham Park 58	1	38N29	97w12	6:28:48
Dwight 64	1	38N51	96w36	6:26:24
Earlton 67	1	37N55	95w28	6:21:52
Eastborough 87	1	37N41	97w15	6:29:00
East Branch 58	1	38N13	97w12	6:28:48
East Cooper 93	1	38N03	98w32	6:34:08
East El Dorado 8	1	37N49	96w51	6:27:24
East Forbes 89	1	39N02	95w41	6:22:44
East Hale 97	1	39N23	101w13	6:44:52
East Hamilton 26	1	39N04	99w27	6:37:48
East Hess 35	3	37N36	100w16	6:41:04
East Hibbard 47	2	38N10	101w13	6:44:52
East Hutchinson 78	1	38N04	97w57	6:31:48
Easton 52	1	39N21	95w07	6:20:28
East Saline 90	1	39N14	100w13	6:40:52
Eastshore 58	1	38N21	97w01	6:28:04
East Washington 80	1	38N13	97w58	6:31:52
Edgerton 46	1	38N46	95w01	6:20:04
Edison 19	1	37N31	94w51	6:19:24
Edmond 69	1	39N37	99w50	6:39:20
Edna 50	1	37N04	95w22	6:21:28
Edson 91	2	39N20	101w33	6:46:12
Edwards 102	4	38N37	101w14	6:44:56
Edwardsville 105	1	39N04	94w49	6:19:16
Effingham 3	1	39N31	95w24	6:21:36
Elbing 8	1	38N03	97w08	6:28:32
El Dorado 8	1	37N49	96w52	6:27:28
Elgin 10	1	37N00	96w17	6:25:08
Elkader 55	4	38N53	100w53	6:43:32
Elk City 63	1	37N18	95w55	6:23:40
Elk Creek 79	1	39N42	97w25	6:29:40
Elk Falls 25	1	37N22	96w11	6:24:44
Elkhart 65	3	37N00	101w54	6:47:36
Elkhorn 53	1	39N00	98w06	6:32:24
Ellinwood 5	1	38N21	98w35	6:34:20
Ellis 26	1	38N56	99w34	6:38:16
Ellsworth 27	1	38N44	98w14	6:32:56
Elmdale 9	1	38N22	96w39	6:26:36
Elmer 78	1	38N04	97w57	6:31:48
Elmerdaro 56	1	38N15	96w03	6:24:12
Elm Grove 50	1	37N04	95w19	6:21:16
Elmhurst 46	1	39N00	94w41	6:18:44
Elm Mills 4	1	37N26	98w40	6:34:40
Elmo 21	1	38N41	97w14	6:28:56
Elmont 89	1	39N10	95w42	6:22:48
Elsmore 1	1	37N48	95w09	6:20:36
Elwood 22	1	39N45	94w52	6:19:28
Elyria 57	1	38N17	97w38	6:30:32
Eminence 104	1	37N47	95w41	6:22:44
Emma 40	1	38N08	97w25	6:29:40
Emmeram 26	1	38N51	99w09	6:36:36

KANSAS

Place		Lat.	Long.	Time
Emmett 75	1	39N19	96w03	6:24:12
Empire City 11	1	37N05	94w38	6:18:32
Empire Junction 11	1	37N05	94w38	6:18:32
Emporia 56	1	38N25	96w11	6:24:44
Englevale 19	1	37N36	94w44	6:18:56
Englewood 13	1	37N02	99w59	6:39:56
Ensign 35	3	37N39	100w14	6:40:56
Enterprise 21	1	38N54	97w07	6:28:28
Erie 67	1	37N34	95w15	6:21:00
Erving 45	1	39N37	98w27	6:33:48
Esbon 45	1	39N49	98w26	6:33:44
Eskridge 99	1	38N52	96w06	6:24:24
Eudora 23	1	38N57	95w06	6:20:24
Eureka 37	1	37N49	96w17	6:25:08
Evan 48	1	37N41	97w52	6:31:28
Everest 7	1	39N41	95w26	6:21:44
Everett 104	1	37N59	95w39	6:22:36
Evergreen 12	4	39N52	101w28	6:45:52
Exeter 14	1	39N16	97w12	6:28:48
Fairfax 70	1	38N43	95w40	6:22:40
Fairfax 105	1	39N08	94w37	6:18:28
Fairfield 84	1	38N44	98w46	6:35:04
Fairmont Addition 81	1	39N12	96w33	6:26:12
Fairmount 52	1	39N11	94w56	6:19:44
Fairplay 58	1	38N14	96w59	6:27:56
Fairport 84	1	39N03	99w02	6:36:08
Fairview 7	1	39N50	95w44	6:22:56
Fairway 46	1	39N02	94w38	6:18:32
Fall Leaf 52	1	39N00	95w02	6:20:08
Fall River 37	1	37N36	96w02	6:24:08
Falun 85	1	38N40	97w46	6:31:04
Fancy Creek 81	1	39N25	96w53	6:27:32
Fanning 22	1	39N47	95w05	6:20:20
Fargo 88	1	37N09	100w45	6:43:00
Farlington 19	1	37N37	94w49	6:19:16
Farlinville 54	1	38N13	95w01	6:20:04
Farmington 3	1	39N31	95w24	6:21:36
Farmington 78	1	38N04	97w57	6:31:48
Faulkner 11	1	37N06	95w01	6:20:04
Fawn Creek 63	1	37N03	95w43	6:22:52
Fellsburg 24	1	37N49	99w11	6:36:44
Finley 20	1	39N58	100w41	6:42:44
Five Creeks 14	1	39N21	97w19	6:29:16
Fleming 19	1	37N26	94w42	6:18:48
Flora 21	1	39N05	97w18	6:29:12
Floral 18	1	37N21	96w56	6:27:44
Florence 58	1	38N15	96w56	6:27:44
Flush 75	1	39N11	96w25	6:25:40
Fontana 61	1	38N25	94w51	6:19:24
Foote 35	4	37N56	100w20	6:41:20
Ford 29	1	37N38	99w45	6:39:00
Formoso 45	1	39N47	97w59	6:31:56
Forrester 68	1	38N31	99w59	6:39:56
Fort Dodge 29	1	37N44	99w56	6:39:44
Fort Larned 73	1	38N11	99w06	6:36:24
Fort Leavenworth 52	1	39N22	94w55	6:19:40
Fort Riley 31	1	39N04	96w47	6:27:08
Fort Scott 6	1	37N50	94w42	6:18:48
Fostoria 75	1	39N26	96w30	6:26:00
Fountain 72	1	39N11	97w52	6:31:28
Four Corners 70	1	38N47	95w44	6:22:56
Four Mile 64	1	38N35	96w31	6:26:04
Fowler 60	1	37N23	100w12	6:40:48
Fox Town 19	1	37N33	94w37	6:18:28
Fragrant Hill 21	1	39N05	97w01	6:28:04
Frankfort 59	1	39N42	96w25	6:25:40
Franklin 19	1	37N32	94w42	6:18:48
Frederick 80	1	38N31	98w16	6:33:04
Fredonia 103	1	37N32	95w49	6:23:16
Freemount 57	1	38N35	97w41	6:30:44
Freeport 39	1	37N12	97w51	6:31:24
Fremont 56	1	38N30	96w09	6:24:36
Friend 28	4	38N16	100w55	6:43:40
Frizell 73	1	38N11	99w06	6:36:24
Frontenac 19	1	37N27	94w42	6:18:48
Fruitland 63	1	37N14	95w43	6:22:52
Fulton 6	1	38N01	94w43	6:18:52
Furley 87	1	37N53	97w13	6:28:52
Gaeland 32	1	38N56	100w44	6:42:56
Galatia 5	1	38N38	98w58	6:35:52
Gale 58	1	38N24	97w06	6:28:24
Galena 11	1	37N04	94w38	6:18:32
Galesburg 67	1	37N28	95w21	6:21:24
Galt 80	1	38N29	98w05	6:32:20
Galva 57	1	38N23	97w32	6:30:08
Garden City 28	4	37N58	100w53	6:43:32
Garden Plain 87	1	37N40	97w41	6:30:44
Gardner 46	1	38N49	94w56	6:19:44
Gardner Lake 46	1	38N49	94w55	6:19:40
Garfield 73	1	38N05	99w14	6:36:56
Garfield Center 14	1	39N23	97w08	6:28:32
Garland 6	1	37N44	94w37	6:18:28
Garnett 2	1	38N17	95w14	6:20:56
Gas 1	1	37N55	95w21	6:21:24
Gaylord 92	1	39N39	98w51	6:35:24
Geary 22	1	39N46	94w57	6:19:48
Gem 97	1	39N26	100w54	6:43:36
Geneseo 80	1	38N31	98w10	6:32:40
Geneva 1	1	38N00	95w28	6:21:52
German 92	1	39N58	99w01	6:36:04
Gettysburg 33	1	39N24	100w02	6:40:08
Geuda Springs 96	1	37N07	97w09	6:28:36
Gill 14	1	39N11	97w07	6:28:28
Gilman 66	1	39N52	95w57	6:23:48
Girard 19	1	37N31	94w51	6:19:24
Glade 74	1	39N41	99w19	6:37:16
Glasco 15	1	39N22	97w50	6:31:20
Glendale 85	1	38N54	97w52	6:31:28
Glen Elder 62	1	39N30	98w18	6:33:12
Glenlock 2	1	38N17	95w15	6:21:00
Glenwood 74	1	39N58	99w14	6:36:56
Glick 49	1	37N28	99w05	6:36:20
Goddard 87	1	37N39	97w34	6:30:16
Goessel 58	1	38N15	97w21	6:29:24
Goff 66	1	39N40	95w56	6:23:44
Golden Belt 53	1	38N55	98w19	6:33:16
Golden Belt Spur 85	1	38N50	97w36	6:30:24
Goodland 91	2	39N21	101w43	6:46:52
Goodman 46	1	39N01	94w42	6:18:48
Goodrich 54	1	38N17	95w00	6:20:00
Gordon 8	1	37N35	96w59	6:27:56
Gore 96	1	37N25	97w11	6:28:44
Gorham 84	1	38N53	99w01	6:36:04
Goshen 14	1	39N31	97w01	6:28:04
Gove 32	1	38N58	100w29	6:41:56
Grafton 10	1	37N04	96w14	6:24:56
Graham 33	1	39N30	99w48	6:39:12
Grainfield 32	1	39N07	100w28	6:41:52
Granada 66	1	39N42	95w51	6:23:24
Grand River 87	1	37N41	97w46	6:31:04
Grand Summit 18	1	37N19	96w40	6:26:40
Grandview 105	1	39N04	94w53	6:19:32
Grandview Plaza 31	1	39N02	96w48	6:27:12
Granite 74	1	39N58	99w28	6:37:52
Grantville 44	1	39N05	95w34	6:22:16
Grasshopper 3	1	39N37	95w29	6:21:56
Great Bend 5	1	38N22	98w46	6:35:04
Greeley 2	1	38N22	95w08	6:20:32
Green 14	1	39N26	97w00	6:28:00
Greenbush 19	1	37N31	94w51	6:19:24
Green Garden 27	1	38N34	98w19	6:33:16
Greenleaf 101	1	39N44	96w59	6:27:56
Greensburg 49	1	37N36	99w18	6:37:12
Greenwich 87	1	37N47	97w12	6:28:48
Greenwich Heights 87	1	37N39	97w13	6:28:52
Grenola 25	1	37N21	96w27	6:25:48
Gretna 74	1	39N43	99w22	6:37:28
Gridley 16	1	38N06	95w53	6:23:32
Grigston 86	4	38N29	100w43	6:42:52
Grinnell 32	1	39N08	100w38	6:42:32
Grinter Heights 105	1	39N05	94w45	6:19:00
Gross 19	1	37N39	94w38	6:18:32
Grove 89	1	39N10	95w52	6:23:28
Grove Center 105	1	39N05	94w45	6:19:00
Groveland 57	1	38N18	97w45	6:31:00
Guelph 96	1	37N04	97w18	6:29:12
Guilford 103	1	37N36	95w43	6:22:52
Guittard 59	1	39N52	96w24	6:25:36
Gypsum 85	1	38N42	97w26	6:29:44
Gypsum Creek 57	1	38N34	97w26	6:29:44
Hackberry 50	1	37N04	95w13	6:20:52
Hackney 18	1	37N10	97w02	6:28:08
Haddam 101	1	39N52	97w18	6:29:12
Haggard 35	4	37N48	100w21	6:41:24
Half Mound 44	1	39N21	95w28	6:21:52
Halford 97	1	39N24	101w03	6:44:12
Hallet 42	1	38N05	100w04	6:40:16
Hallowell 11	1	37N11	95w00	6:20:00
Halls Summit 16	1	38N21	95w41	6:22:44
Halstead 40	1	38N00	97w31	6:30:04
Hamilton 37	1	37N59	96w10	6:24:40
Hamlin 7	1	39N57	95w37	6:22:28
Hammond 6	1	37N56	94w42	6:18:48
Hampden 16	1	38N12	95w42	6:22:48
Hampton 83	1	38N38	99w32	6:38:08
Hancock 71	1	39N21	98w40	6:34:40
Hanover 101	1	39N54	96w53	6:27:32
Hanston 42	1	38N07	99w43	6:38:52
Happy 33	1	39N12	99w53	6:39:32
Harding 6	1	38N01	94w53	6:19:32
Hardtner 4	1	37N01	98w39	6:34:36
Hargrave 83	1	38N35	99w34	6:38:16
Harlan 92	1	39N36	98w46	6:35:04
Harmon 96	1	37N21	97w19	6:29:16
Harmony 95	3	37N19	101w27	6:45:48
Harper 39	1	37N17	98w01	6:32:04
Harris 2	1	38N19	95w26	6:21:44
Hartford 56	1	38N18	95w57	6:23:48
Hartland 47	2	37N59	101w26	6:45:44
Harveyville 99	1	38N47	95w58	6:23:52
Haskell 23	1	38N58	95w15	6:21:00
Haskell 41	3	37N33	100w51	6:43:24
Hatton 38	2	37N59	101w45	6:47:00
Havana 63	1	37N06	95w57	6:23:48
Haven 78	1	37N54	97w47	6:31:08
Havensville 75	1	39N31	96w05	6:24:20
Haverhill 8	1	37N41	96w59	6:27:56
Haviland 49	1	37N37	99w06	6:36:24
Hawkeye 71	1	39N32	98w53	6:35:32
Haynesville 76	1	37N46	98w31	6:34:04
Hays 26	1	38N53	99w20	6:37:20
Haysville 87	1	37N34	97w21	6:29:24
Hazelton 4	1	37N05	98w24	6:33:36
Healy 51	1	38N36	100w37	6:42:28
Hedville 85	1	38N52	97w46	6:31:04
Heizer 5	1	38N25	98w53	6:35:32
Hendricks 10	1	37N03	96w18	6:25:12
Henry 72	1	39N05	97w52	6:31:28
Hepler 19	1	37N40	94w58	6:19:52
Herington 21	1	38N40	96w57	6:27:48
Herkimer 59	1	39N54	96w43	6:26:52
Herndon 77	1	39N55	100w47	6:43:08
Herzog 26	1	38N54	99w09	6:36:36
Hesper 23	1	38N56	95w06	6:20:24
Hessdale 99	1	39N01	96w17	6:25:08
Hesston 40	1	38N08	97w26	6:29:44
Hewins 10	1	37N03	96w25	6:25:40
Hiattville 6	1	37N43	94w52	6:19:28
Hiawatha 7	1	39N51	95w32	6:22:08
Hickok 34	3	37N34	101w14	6:44:56
Hickory 8	1	37N36	96w38	6:26:32
Hidden Lakes 87	1	37N42	97w25	6:29:40
Highland 22	1	39N52	95w16	6:21:04
Highpoint 68	1	38N20	99w42	6:38:48
High Prairie 52	1	39N15	95w00	6:20:00
Hill City 33	1	39N22	99w51	6:39:24
Hillcrest 78	1	38N04	97w57	6:31:48
Hillsboro 58	1	38N21	97w12	6:28:48
Hillsdale 61	1	38N40	94w51	6:19:24
Hilltop 37	1	38N03	96w03	6:24:12
Hitschmann 5	1	38N38	98w05	6:32:20
Hobart 60	1	37N16	100w35	6:42:20
Hobart 82	1	39N21	99w19	6:37:16
Hocker Grove 46	1	39N01	94w42	6:18:48
Hoge 52	1	39N06	95w05	6:20:20
Hoisington 5	1	38N31	98w47	6:35:08
Holcomb 28	4	37N59	100w59	6:43:56
Holland 21	1	38N40	97w19	6:29:16
Hollenberg 101	1	39N59	97w00	6:28:00
Holliday 46	1	39N02	94w49	6:19:16
Hollis 15	1	39N38	97w33	6:30:12
Holmdel Gardens 78	1	38N04	97w58	6:31:52
Holmwood 45	1	39N52	98w13	6:32:52
Holton 43	1	39N28	95w44	6:22:56
Holyrood 27	1	38N35	98w25	6:33:40
Home 59	1	39N51	96w31	6:26:04
Homestead 9	1	38N10	96w41	6:26:44
Homewood 30	1	38N31	95w23	6:21:32
Hoosier 48	1	37N41	98w12	6:32:48
Hope 21	1	38N41	97w05	6:28:20
Hopewell 76	1	37N48	99w00	6:36:00
Horace 36	2	38N29	101w47	6:47:08
Horton 7	1	39N40	95w32	6:22:08
Houston 92	1	39N37	98w53	6:35:32
Howard 25	1	37N28	96w16	6:25:04
Hoxie 90	1	39N21	100w26	6:41:44
Hoyt 43	1	39N15	95w43	6:22:52
Hudson 93	1	38N06	98w40	6:34:40
Hugoton 95	3	37N11	101w21	6:45:24
Humboldt 1	1	37N49	95w26	6:21:44
Hunnewell 96	1	37N01	97w25	6:29:40
Hunter 62	1	39N14	98w24	6:33:36
Huntsville 78	1	38N03	98w19	6:33:16
Huron 3	1	39N38	95w21	6:21:24
Huscher 15	1	39N32	97w35	6:30:20
Hutchinson 78	1	38N05	97w56	6:31:44
Hymer 9	1	38N29	96w41	6:26:44
Idana 14	1	39N22	97w16	6:29:04
Imes 30	1	38N33	95w06	6:20:24
Independence 63	1	37N14	95w42	6:22:48
Independent 5	1	38N34	98w32	6:34:08
Indian Creek 2	1	38N06	95w28	6:21:52
Indian Creek 46	1	38N58	94w38	6:18:32
Indian Valley 89	1	39N05	95w40	6:22:40
Indian Village 63	1	37N05	95w38	6:22:32
Industry 14	1	39N08	97w10	6:28:40
Ingalls 35	4	37N50	100w27	6:41:48
Inman 57	1	38N14	97w47	6:31:08
Iola 1	1	37N55	95w24	6:21:36
Ionia 45	1	39N40	98w21	6:33:24
Iowa Point 22	1	39N57	95w15	6:21:00
Irving 7	1	39N56	95w24	6:21:36
Isabel 4	1	37N28	98w33	6:34:12
Isbel 86	4	38N29	101w02	6:44:08
Itasca 91	2	39N19	101w40	6:46:40
Iuka 76	1	37N44	98w44	6:34:56
Ivanhoe 28	4	37N48	100w50	6:43:20
Ivy 56	1	38N38	96w05	6:24:20
Jacobs Creek Landing 16	1	38N18	95w57	6:23:48
Jamestown 15	1	39N36	97w52	6:31:28
Janesville 37	1	37N59	96w11	6:24:44
Jaqua 12	4	39N40	102w01	6:48:04
Jarbalo 52	1	39N19	94w55	6:19:40
Jarrett 11	1	37N01	94w44	6:18:56
Jayhawk 23	1	38N58	95w15	6:21:00
Jefferson 63	1	37N07	95w46	6:23:04
Jennings 20	1	39N41	100w18	6:41:12
Jerome 32	1	38N47	100w29	6:41:56
Jetmore 42	1	38N04	99w54	6:39:36
Jewell 45	1	39N40	98w10	6:32:40
Jingo 61	1	38N24	94w42	6:18:48
Johnson 68	1	38N20	100w08	6:40:32
Johnson 94	3	37N34	101w45	6:47:00
Jones 65	3	37N04	101w59	6:47:56
Joy 49	1	37N36	99w18	6:37:12
Junction 70	1	38N41	95w34	6:22:16
Junction City 31	1	39N02	96w50	6:27:20
Juniata 53	1	39N01	97w58	6:31:52
Kackley 79	1	39N42	97w51	6:31:24
Kalloch 63	1	37N02	95w37	6:22:28
Kalvesta 28	4	38N04	100w18	6:41:12
Kanona 20	1	39N50	100w31	6:42:04
Kanopolis 27	1	38N43	98w09	6:32:36
Kanorado 91	2	39N20	102w02	6:48:08
Kansas City 105	1	39N07	94w38	6:18:32
Kanwaka 23	1	38N58	95w25	6:21:40
Kapioma 3	1	39N29	95w31	6:22:04
Keats 81	1	39N14	96w43	6:26:52
Kechi 87	1	37N47	97w19	6:29:16
Keene 99	1	38N51	96w06	6:24:24
Kellogg 18	1	37N14	96w59	6:27:56
Kelly 66	1	39N44	96w00	6:24:00
Kendall 38	2	37N56	101w33	6:46:12
Kennekuk 3	1	39N40	95w32	6:22:08
Kenneth 46	1	38N51	94w37	6:18:28
Kensington 92	1	39N46	99w02	6:36:08
Kentucky 44	1	39N07	95w25	6:21:40
Keystone 86	4	38N29	100w52	6:43:28
Keysville 73	1	38N08	99w24	6:37:36
Key West 16	1	38N23	95w45	6:23:00
Kickapoo 52	1	39N21	94w58	6:19:52
Kickapoo Indian Res 7	1	39N40	95w32	6:22:08
Kill Creek 71	1	39N21	98w53	6:35:32
Kimball 67	1	37N41	95w10	6:20:40
Kimeo 101	1	39N37	96w59	6:27:56
Kincaid 2	1	38N05	95w09	6:20:36

KANSAS

King City 57	1	38N18	97w39	6:30:36
Kingery 97	1	39N13	101w17	6:45:08
Kingman 48	1	37N39	98w07	6:32:28
Kingsdown 29	1	37N32	99w46	6:39:04
Kings Gardens 78	1	38N04	97w57	6:31:48
Kinsley 24	1	37N55	99w25	6:37:40
Kiowa 4	1	37N01	98w29	6:33:56
Kipp 85	1	38N47	97w27	6:29:48
Kirkwood 19	1	37N26	94w42	6:18:48
Kiro 89	1	39N06	95w52	6:23:28
Kirwin 74	1	39N40	99w07	6:36:28
Kismet 88	1	37N12	100w42	6:42:48
Kniveton 19	1	37N26	94w42	6:18:48
Labette 50	1	37N14	95w11	6:20:44
Lacey 97	1	39N27	100w53	6:43:32
Lackmans 46	1	38N56	94w46	6:19:04
La Crosse 83	1	38N32	99w18	6:37:12
La Cygne 54	1	38N21	94w46	6:19:04
Ladore 67	1	37N26	95w18	6:21:12
Ladysmith 14	1	39N23	97w08	6:28:32
Lafayette 10	1	37N15	96w09	6:24:36
Lafontaine 103	1	37N24	95w51	6:23:24
La Harpe 1	1	37N55	95w18	6:21:12
Laing 77	1	39N47	100w47	6:43:08
Lake City 4	1	37N21	98w49	6:35:16
Lake Kohola 9	1	38N35	96w22	6:25:28
Lake of the Forest 105	1	39N05	94w51	6:19:24
Lake Quivira 46	1	39N04	94w41	6:18:44
Lake Shore 27	1	38N43	98w09	6:32:36
Lakeshore 89	1	39N01	95w40	6:22:40
Lakeside Acres Addition 87	1	37N42	97w17	6:29:08
Lake Wabaunsee 99	1	39N01	96w17	6:25:08
Lakin 47	2	37N57	101w15	6:45:00
Lamar 72	1	39N21	97w27	6:29:48
Lamont 37	1	38N07	96w02	6:24:08
Lanark 82	1	39N31	99w13	6:36:52
Lancaster 3	1	39N34	95w18	6:21:12
Lane 30	1	38N26	95w05	6:20:20
Langdon 78	1	37N51	98w19	6:33:16
Langley 27	1	38N33	97w58	6:31:52
Lansing 52	1	39N15	94w54	6:19:36
Larkinburg 43	1	39N28	95w44	6:22:56
Larned 73	1	38N11	99w06	6:36:24
Larrabee 32	1	38N47	100w16	6:41:04
Latham 8	1	37N32	96w38	6:26:32
Latimer 64	1	38N44	96w51	6:27:24
Lawn 39	1	37N15	98w18	6:33:12
Lawn Ridge 12	4	39N37	101w45	6:47:00
Lawrence 23	1	38N58	95w14	6:20:56
Lawton 11	1	37N13	94w38	6:18:32
Leavenworth 52	1	39N19	94w55	6:19:40
Leawood 46	1	38N58	94w37	6:18:28
Lebanon 92	1	39N49	98w33	6:34:12
Lebo 16	1	38N25	95w51	6:23:24
Lecompton 23	1	39N01	95w26	6:21:44
Lees 55	4	38N44	100w55	6:43:40
Lehigh 58	1	38N22	97w18	6:29:12
Lehunt 63	1	37N14	95w43	6:22:52
Leloup 30	1	38N42	95w10	6:20:40
LeLoup 30	1	38N10	95w18	6:21:12
Lenape 52	1	39N00	95w02	6:20:08
Lenexa 46	1	38N58	94w45	6:19:00
Lenora 69	1	39N37	100w00	6:40:00
Leon 8	1	37N42	96w46	6:27:04
Leona 22	1	39N47	95w19	6:21:16
Leonardville 81	1	39N22	96w51	6:27:24
Leota 69	1	39N47	100w01	6:40:04
Leoti 102	4	38N29	101w21	6:45:24
Leoville 20	1	39N35	100w28	6:41:52
Lerado 78	1	37N43	98w19	6:33:16
Le Roy 16	1	38N05	95w38	6:22:32
Levant 97	1	39N23	101w12	6:44:48
Lewis 24	1	37N56	99w15	6:37:00
Liberal 88	3	37N03	100w55	6:43:40
Liberty 63	1	37N09	95w36	6:22:24
Liebenthal 83	1	38N39	99w19	6:37:16
Lillis 59	1	39N43	96w16	6:25:04
Limestone 45	1	39N47	98w19	6:33:16
Lincoln 53	1	39N03	98w09	6:32:36
Lincoln Center 53	1	39N03	98w09	6:32:36
Lincolnville 58	1	38N30	96w58	6:27:52
Linda 77	1	39N48	101w02	6:44:08
Lindsborg 57	1	38N35	97w40	6:30:40
Linn 101	1	39N41	97w05	6:28:20
Linwood 52	1	39N00	95w02	6:20:08
Little Blue 101	1	39N47	96w52	6:27:28
Little Caney 10	1	37N04	96w01	6:24:04
Little River 80	1	38N24	98w01	6:32:04
Little Valley 57	1	38N13	97w52	6:31:28
Little Walnut 8	1	37N41	96w46	6:27:04
Llanos 91	2	39N28	101w27	6:45:48
Lockport 41	3	37N35	100w43	6:42:52
Loda 78	1	37N47	98w11	6:32:44
Logan 74	1	39N40	99w34	6:38:16
Logansport 55	4	38N53	101w03	6:44:12
Lola 11	1	37N10	95w01	6:20:04
London 96	1	37N26	97w25	6:29:40
Lone Elm 2	1	38N06	95w14	6:20:56
Lone Star 23	1	38N52	95w21	6:21:24
Longford 14	1	39N10	97w20	6:29:20
Long Island 74	1	39N57	99w32	6:38:08
Longton 25	1	37N23	96w05	6:24:20
Lookout 26	1	38N45	99w22	6:37:28
Loretta 83	1	38N39	99w12	6:36:48
Loring 105	1	39N04	94w53	6:19:32
Lorraine 27	1	38N34	98w19	6:33:16
Lost Springs 58	1	38N34	96w58	6:27:52
Louisburg 61	1	38N37	94w41	6:18:44
Louisville 75	1	39N15	96w18	6:25:12
Lovewell 45	1	39N52	97w59	6:31:56
Lowe 101	1	39N57	97w12	6:28:48
Lowell 11	1	37N01	94w44	6:18:56
Lowemont 52	1	39N23	95w04	6:20:16
Lucas 84	1	39N04	98w32	6:34:08
Ludell 77	1	39N52	100w58	6:43:52
Lulu 62	1	39N31	97w59	6:31:56
Luray 84	1	39N03	98w39	6:34:36
Lydia 102	4	38N29	101w21	6:45:24
Lyle 20	1	39N50	100w11	6:40:44
Lyndon 70	1	38N37	95w41	6:22:44
Lyons 80	1	38N21	98w12	6:32:48
Mackie 19	1	37N08	94w51	6:19:24
Macksville 93	1	37N58	98w58	6:35:52
Macon 40	1	38N03	97w26	6:29:44
Madison 37	1	38N08	96w08	6:24:32
Mahaska 101	1	39N59	97w20	6:29:20
Maize 87	1	37N46	97w28	6:29:52
Manchester 21	1	39N06	97w19	6:29:16
Manhattan 81	1	39N11	96w35	6:26:20
Mankato 45	1	39N47	98w13	6:32:52
Manning 86	4	38N29	100w57	6:43:48
Manter 94	4	37N31	101w53	6:47:32
Mantey 54	1	38N04	94w42	6:18:48
Maple 18	1	37N26	97w06	6:28:24
Maple City 18	1	37N03	96w46	6:27:04
Maple Hill 99	1	39N05	96w02	6:24:08
Mapleton 6	1	38N01	94w53	6:19:32
Marena 42	1	38N10	99w41	6:38:44
Marienthal 102	4	38N29	101w13	6:44:52
Marietta 59	1	39N58	96w36	6:26:24
Marion 58	1	38N21	97w01	6:28:04
Marion County Lake 58	1	38N21	97w01	6:28:04
Marketplace at Georgetown 46	1	39N00	94w41	6:18:44
Marmaton 6	1	37N50	94w42	6:18:48
Marquette 57	1	38N33	97w50	6:31:20
Marysville 59	1	39N51	96w39	6:26:36
Matfield 9	1	38N09	96w31	6:26:04
Matfield Green 9	1	38N09	96w31	6:26:04
May Day 81	1	39N32	96w53	6:27:32
Mayetta 43	1	39N20	95w43	6:22:52
Mayfield 96	1	37N16	97w33	6:30:12
Mayline 38	2	37N59	101w45	6:47:00
McAdoo 4	1	37N26	98w49	6:35:16
McAllaster 55	4	39N03	101w24	6:45:36
McCamish 46	1	38N49	95w01	6:20:04
McClellan 76	1	37N41	98w57	6:35:48
McConnell Air Force Base 87	1	37N38	97w16	6:29:04
McCracken 83	1	38N36	99w33	6:38:12
McCune 19	1	37N21	95w01	6:20:04
McDonald 77	1	39N47	101w22	6:45:28
McFarland 99	1	39N03	96w14	6:24:56
McLouth 44	1	39N12	95w13	6:20:52
McPherson 57	1	38N22	97w40	6:30:40
Meade 60	1	37N17	100w20	6:41:20
Meade Center 60	1	37N16	100w21	6:41:24
Mecca Acres 8	1	37N41	97w18	6:29:12
Medford 78	1	38N07	98w12	6:32:48
Medicine 82	1	39N21	99w07	6:36:28
Medicine Lodge 4	1	37N17	98w35	6:34:20
Medina 44	1	39N04	95w24	6:21:36
Medora 78	1	38N09	97w51	6:31:24
Medway 38	2	38N02	101w52	6:47:28
Melrose 11	1	37N02	94w58	6:19:52
Melvern 70	1	38N30	95w38	6:22:32
Menlo 97	1	39N21	100w43	6:42:52
Menno 58	1	38N18	97w19	6:29:16
Menoken 89	1	39N08	95w46	6:23:04
Mentor 85	1	38N45	97w36	6:30:24
Mercier 7	1	39N40	95w32	6:22:08
Meredith 15	1	39N21	97w39	6:30:36
Meriden 44	1	39N11	95w34	6:22:16
Meridian 57	1	38N13	97w26	6:29:44
Merriam 46	1	39N01	94w41	6:18:44
Mertilla 60	3	37N23	100w29	6:41:56
Michigan 70	1	38N35	95w32	6:22:08
Michigan 86	4	38N38	100w54	6:43:36
Middle Creek 61	1	38N34	94w42	6:18:48
Midland 87	1	37N38	97w18	6:29:12
Midland Park 87	1	37N35	97w20	6:29:20
Midway 48	1	37N40	97w56	6:31:44
Midway 77	1	39N54	100w47	6:43:08
Mikesell 77	1	39N42	101w08	6:44:32
Milan 96	1	37N15	97w41	6:30:44
Milberger 84	1	38N53	98w51	6:35:24
Mildred 1	1	38N01	95w10	6:20:40
Milford 31	1	39N10	96w55	6:27:40
Millbrook 33	1	39N18	99w53	6:39:32
Millbrook 87	1	37N42	97w25	6:29:40
Miller 56	1	38N38	95w59	6:23:56
Millerton 96	1	37N23	97w39	6:30:36
Millwood 52	1	39N21	95w07	6:20:28
Milo 53	1	39N11	98w03	6:32:12
Milton 96	1	37N26	97w46	6:31:04
Miltonvale 15	1	39N21	97w27	6:29:48
Mineral 11	1	37N16	94w48	6:19:12
Mingo 97	1	39N24	101w03	6:44:12
Mingona 4	1	37N18	98w41	6:34:44
Minneapolis 72	1	39N08	97w42	6:30:48
Minneha 87	1	37N41	97w12	6:28:48
Minneola 13	1	37N26	100w01	6:40:04
Mirage 77	1	39N39	101w14	6:44:56
Mission 46	1	39N02	94w38	6:18:32
Mission Creek 99	1	38N56	96w02	6:24:08
Mission Highlands 46	1	39N02	94w38	6:18:32
Mission Hills 46	1	39N01	94w37	6:18:28
Mission Woods 46	1	39N02	94w37	6:18:28
Missler 60	1	37N17	100w20	6:41:20
Mitchell 80	1	38N23	98w06	6:32:24
Modell 69	1	39N37	99w55	6:39:40
Modoc 86	4	38N29	101w05	6:44:20
Moline 25	1	37N22	96w18	6:25:12
Monett 10	1	37N04	96w14	6:24:56
Monmouth 19	1	37N21	95w01	6:20:04
Monmouth 89	1	38N56	95w34	6:22:16
Monroe 2	1	38N18	95w12	6:20:48
Monrovia 3	1	39N31	95w24	6:21:36
Monrovia 46	1	39N01	94w42	6:18:48
Montana 50	1	37N17	95w06	6:20:24
Montezuma 35	3	37N36	100w27	6:41:48
Monticello 46	1	39N00	94w51	6:19:24
Mont Ida 2	1	38N13	95w22	6:21:28
Montrose 45	1	39N47	98w05	6:32:20
Monument 55	4	39N06	101w01	6:44:04
Moran 1	1	37N55	95w10	6:20:40
Moray 22	1	39N47	95w05	6:20:20
Morehead 50	1	37N23	95w31	6:22:04
Morgan 97	1	39N22	101w04	6:44:16
Morganville 14	1	39N28	97w12	6:28:48
Morlan 33	1	39N13	99w41	6:38:44
Morland 33	1	39N21	100w05	6:40:20
Morrill 7	1	39N56	95w42	6:22:48
Morrison Ridge 46	1	39N01	94w39	6:18:36
Morrowville 101	1	39N51	97w10	6:28:40
Morse 46	1	38N53	94w49	6:19:16
Moscow 95	3	37N20	101w12	6:44:48
Mound City 54	1	38N08	94w49	6:19:16
Moundridge 57	1	38N12	97w31	6:30:04
Mound Valley 50	1	37N12	95w24	6:21:36
Mount Ayr 71	1	39N21	98w59	6:35:56
Mount Hope 87	1	37N52	97w40	6:30:40
Mount Vernon 48	1	37N38	97w47	6:31:08
Mulberry 19	1	37N33	94w37	6:18:28
Mullinville 49	1	37N35	99w29	6:37:56
Mulvane 96	1	37N29	97w15	6:29:00
Muncie 105	1	39N05	94w45	6:19:00
Munden 79	1	39N55	97w32	6:30:08
Munger 87	1	37N42	97w17	6:29:08
Munjor 26	1	38N49	99w16	6:37:04
Murdock 48	1	37N37	97w56	6:31:44
Murray 59	1	39N52	96w17	6:25:08
Muscotah 3	1	39N33	95w31	6:22:04
Narka 79	1	39N58	97w25	6:29:40
Naron 76	1	37N47	98w57	6:35:48
Nashville 48	1	37N27	98w25	6:33:40
Natoma 71	1	39N11	99w02	6:36:08
Natrona 76	1	37N43	98w40	6:34:40
Navarre 21	1	38N48	97w06	6:28:24
Neal 37	1	37N50	96w05	6:24:20
Nekoma 83	1	38N28	99w27	6:37:48
Nelson 15	1	39N31	97w32	6:30:08
Nemaha 66	1	39N57	96w04	6:24:16
Neodesha 103	1	37N25	95w41	6:22:44
Neola 93	1	37N48	98w26	6:33:44
Neosho Falls 104	1	38N00	95w33	6:22:12
Neosho Rapids 56	1	38N22	95w59	6:23:56
Nescatunga 17	1	37N14	99w13	6:36:52
Ness City 68	1	38N27	99w54	6:39:36
Netawaka 43	1	39N36	95w43	6:22:52
Neuchatel 66	1	39N37	96w11	6:24:44
Neutral 11	1	37N06	94w48	6:19:12
Nevada 68	1	38N38	99w55	6:39:40
New Albany 103	1	37N34	95w56	6:23:44
New Almelo 69	1	39N36	100w07	6:40:28
Newark 103	1	37N25	95w35	6:22:20
Newbern 21	1	38N50	97w12	6:28:48
Newbury 99	1	39N04	96w10	6:24:40
New Cambria 85	1	38N53	97w30	6:30:00
New Gottland 57	1	38N29	97w39	6:30:36
New Lancaster 61	1	38N28	94w44	6:18:56
Newman 44	1	39N04	95w24	6:21:36
New Salem 18	1	37N14	96w59	6:27:56
Newton 40	1	38N03	97w21	6:29:24
Nickerson 78	1	38N08	98w05	6:32:20
Nicodemus 33	1	39N24	99w37	6:38:28
Niles 72	1	38N58	97w28	6:29:52
Niotaze 10	1	37N04	96w01	6:24:04
Nippawalla 4	1	37N10	98w33	6:34:12
Norcatur 20	1	39N50	100w11	6:40:44
Northampton 82	1	39N15	99w33	6:38:12
North Branch 45	1	39N59	98w22	6:33:28
Northbranch 45	1	39N52	98w18	6:33:12
North Brown 24	1	37N52	99w19	6:37:16
Northern Hills 89	1	39N05	95w40	6:22:40
North Fort Riley 31	1	39N05	96w49	6:27:16
North Hayes 78	1	38N07	98w26	6:33:44
North Homestead 5	1	38N34	98w45	6:35:00
North Newton 40	1	38N04	97w21	6:29:24
North Osage City 70	1	38N38	95w49	6:23:16
North Randall 97	1	39N20	100w53	6:43:32
North Rich 2	1	38N08	95w08	6:20:32
North Roscoe 42	1	38N12	100w09	6:40:36
North Seward 93	1	38N13	98w45	6:35:00
North Topeka 89	1	39N05	95w40	6:22:40
North Wichita 87	1	37N42	97w19	6:29:16
Norton 69	1	39N50	99w53	6:39:32
Nortonville 44	1	39N25	95w20	6:21:20
Norway 79	1	39N42	97w47	6:31:08
Norwich 48	1	37N27	97w51	6:31:24
Nutty Combe 12	4	39N58	101w57	6:47:48
Oak 92	1	39N48	98w33	6:34:12
Oakhill 14	1	39N15	97w21	6:29:24
Oaklawn 87	1	37N38	97w18	6:29:12
Oakley 55	4	39N08	100w51	6:43:24
Oak Valley 25	1	37N20	96w01	6:24:04
Obeeville 78	1	38N04	97w57	6:31:48
Oberlin 20	1	39N49	100w32	6:42:08
Ocheltree 46	1	38N45	94w50	6:19:20
Odee 60	1	37N05	100w21	6:41:24
Odell 39	1	37N15	97w51	6:31:24
Odin 5	1	38N34	98w37	6:34:28
Offerle 24	1	37N54	99w33	6:38:12
Ogallah 98	1	38N59	99w44	6:38:56
Ogden 81	1	39N07	96w43	6:26:52
Oketo 59	1	39N58	96w36	6:26:24
Olathe 46	1	38N53	94w49	6:19:16

KANSAS

Place	Zone	Lat.	Long.	Time
Olcott 78	1	37N48	98w26	6:33:44
Olive 20	1	39N53	100w28	6:41:52
Olivet 70	1	38N29	95w45	6:23:00
Olmitz 5	1	38N31	98w56	6:35:44
Olpe 56	1	38N16	96w10	6:24:40
Olsburg 75	1	39N26	96w37	6:26:28
Omnia 18	1	37N26	96w47	6:27:08
Onaga 75	1	39N29	96w10	6:24:40
Oneida 66	1	39N52	95w56	6:23:44
Opolis 19	1	37N21	94w37	6:18:28
Orchard Park 50	1	37N20	95w16	6:21:04
Orlando 12	4	39N47	101w42	6:46:48
Osage City 70	1	38N38	95w50	6:23:20
Osawatomie 61	1	38N31	94w57	6:19:48
Osborn 96	1	37N16	97w32	6:30:08
Osborne 71	1	39N26	98w42	6:34:48
Oskaloosa 44	1	39N13	95w19	6:21:16
Ost 78	1	37N52	97w40	6:30:40
Oswego 50	1	37N10	95w06	6:20:24
Otego 45	1	39N52	98w18	6:33:12
Otis 83	1	38N32	99w03	6:36:12
Ottawa 30	1	38N37	95w16	6:21:04
Otter 18	1	37N10	96w33	6:26:12
Otter Creek 37	1	37N40	96w23	6:25:32
Ottumwa 16	1	38N17	95w48	6:23:12
Overbrook 70	1	38N47	95w33	6:22:12
Overland 64	1	38N49	96w51	6:27:24
Overland Park 46	1	38N58	94w40	6:18:40
Owl Creek 104	1	37N52	95w35	6:22:20
Oxford 96	1	37N17	97w10	6:28:40
Ozark 2	1	38N05	95w21	6:21:24
Ozawkie 44	1	39N16	95w26	6:21:44
Packers 105	1	39N06	94w40	6:18:40
Padonia 7	1	39N56	95w34	6:22:16
Page City 55	4	39N05	101w09	6:44:36
Painterhood 25	1	37N29	96w03	6:24:12
Palacky 27	1	38N39	98w26	6:33:44
Palco 82	1	39N15	99w34	6:38:16
Palermo 22	1	39N46	94w57	6:19:48
Palestine 96	1	37N21	97w13	6:28:52
Palmer 101	1	39N38	97w08	6:28:32
Palmyra 23	1	38N49	95w10	6:20:40
Paola 61	1	38N35	94w53	6:19:32
Paradise 84	1	39N07	98w55	6:35:40
Paris 54	1	38N13	94w49	6:19:16
Park 32	1	39N07	100w22	6:41:28
Park City 87	1	37N48	97w19	6:29:16
Park East 87	1	37N42	97w17	6:29:08
Parker 54	1	38N20	95w00	6:20:00
Parkerville 64	1	38N46	96w40	6:26:40
Parnell 90	1	39N26	100w30	6:42:00
Parsons 50	1	37N20	95w16	6:21:04
Partridge 78	1	37N58	98w05	6:32:20
Patterson 40	1	37N57	97w39	6:30:36
Pauline 89	1	38N58	95w41	6:22:44
Pawnee Rock 5	1	38N16	99w01	6:36:04
Paw Paw 25	1	37N34	96w14	6:24:56
Paxico 99	1	39N04	96w10	6:24:40
Paxon 76	1	37N31	98w38	6:34:32
Paxton 55	4	38N45	101w09	6:44:36
Peabody 58	1	38N10	97w07	6:28:28
Pearl 21	1	38N58	97w01	6:28:04
Peck 96	1	37N29	97w22	6:29:28
Peck Addition 89	1	39N01	95w40	6:22:40
Penalosa 48	1	37N43	98w19	6:33:16
Pence 86	4	38N29	100w57	6:43:48
Pendennis 51	1	38N38	100w20	6:41:20
Pen Dennis 51	1	38N37	100w27	6:41:48
Penn 71	1	39N26	98w41	6:34:44
Penokee 33	1	39N21	99w58	6:39:52
Peoria 30	1	38N35	95w09	6:20:36
Perry 44	1	39N05	95w24	6:21:36
Perth 96	1	37N11	97w31	6:30:04
Peru 10	1	37N05	96w06	6:24:24
Peters 48	1	37N31	98w18	6:33:12
Petrolia 1	1	37N45	95w29	6:21:56
Pfeifer 26	1	38N43	99w10	6:36:40
Phillipsburg 74	1	39N45	99w19	6:37:16
Pickrell Corner 8	1	37N41	96w59	6:27:56
Piedmont 37	1	37N37	96w22	6:25:28
Pierceville 28	4	37N53	100w40	6:42:40
Pike 56	1	38N23	96w17	6:25:08
Pilot Knob 39	1	37N15	97w58	6:31:52
Pilsen 58	1	38N21	97w01	6:28:04
Piper 105	1	39N08	94w52	6:19:28
Piqua 104	1	37N56	95w32	6:22:08
Pittsburg 19	1	37N25	94w42	6:18:48
Plains 60	1	37N16	100w35	6:42:20
Plainview 74	1	39N37	99w28	6:37:52
Plainville 82	1	39N14	99w18	6:37:12
Pleasantdale 83	1	38N38	99w05	6:36:20
Pleasant Grove 23	1	38N51	95w16	6:21:04
Pleasant Hill 26	1	38N52	99w27	6:37:48
Pleasanton 54	1	38N11	94w43	6:18:52
Pleasant Ridge 73	1	38N08	99w18	6:37:12
Pleasant View 11	1	37N17	94w40	6:18:40
Pleasant View 46	1	38N53	94w49	6:19:16
Plevna 78	1	37N59	98w19	6:33:16
Plum 74	1	39N47	99w07	6:36:28
Plumb 99	1	38N48	96w00	6:24:00
Plum Creek 62	1	39N31	98w06	6:32:24
Plum Grove 8	1	37N57	96w59	6:27:56
Plymell 28	4	37N58	100w50	6:43:20
Plymouth 56	1	38N25	96w20	6:25:20
Polk 19	1	37N31	94w51	6:19:24
Pollard 80	1	38N21	98w12	6:32:48
Pomona 30	1	38N36	95w27	6:21:48
Porter 12	4	39N56	101w33	6:46:12
Porterville 6	1	37N36	95w05	6:20:20
Portis 71	1	39N34	98w41	6:34:44
Portland 96	1	37N05	97w19	6:29:16
Potawatomi Indian Res 43	1	39N40	95w32	6:22:08
Potosi 54	1	38N11	94w41	6:18:44
Potter 3	1	39N26	95w09	6:20:36
Potwin 8	1	37N56	97w01	6:28:04
Powell 17	1	37N20	99w07	6:36:28
Powhattan 7	1	39N46	95w38	6:22:32
Prairie 45	1	39N37	98w06	6:32:24
Prairie View 74	1	39N50	99w34	6:38:16
Prairie Village 46	1	39N00	94w38	6:18:32
Pratt 76	1	37N39	98w44	6:34:56
Prescott 54	1	38N04	94w42	6:18:48
Preston 76	1	37N46	98w33	6:34:12
Pretty Prairie 78	1	37N47	98w01	6:32:04
Princeton 30	1	38N29	95w16	6:21:04
Prospect 8	1	37N50	96w45	6:27:00
Prospect Park 87	1	37N38	97w25	6:29:40
Protection 17	1	37N12	99w29	6:37:56
Province Village 46	1	38N53	94w49	6:19:16
Punkin Center 78	1	38N04	97w57	6:31:48
Purcell 22	1	39N38	95w21	6:21:24
Quenemo 70	1	38N35	95w32	6:22:08
Quincy 37	1	37N53	96w00	6:24:00
Quindaro 105	1	39N09	94w45	6:19:00
Quinter 32	1	39N04	100w14	6:40:56
Radium 93	1	38N11	98w54	6:35:36
Radley 19	1	37N29	94w46	6:19:04
Rago 48	1	37N27	98w05	6:32:20
Ramona 58	1	38N36	97w04	6:28:16
Randall 45	1	39N38	98w03	6:32:12
Randolph 81	1	39N26	96w46	6:27:04
Ransom 68	1	38N38	99w56	6:39:44
Rantoul 30	1	38N33	95w06	6:20:24
Raymond 80	1	38N17	98w25	6:33:40
Reading 56	1	38N33	96w02	6:24:08
Reager 69	1	39N50	100w06	6:40:24
Reamsville 92	1	39N47	98w47	6:35:08
Redel 46	1	38N46	94w40	6:18:40
Redfield 6	1	37N50	94w53	6:19:32
Red Vermillion 66	1	39N37	96w04	6:24:16
Redwing 5	1	38N31	98w47	6:35:08
Reece 37	1	37N48	96w27	6:25:48
Reilly 66	1	39N36	95w57	6:23:48
Renco 52	1	39N06	95w05	6:20:20
Reno 52	1	39N03	95w07	6:20:28
Republic 79	1	39N55	97w49	6:31:16
Republican 14	1	39N11	97w01	6:28:04
Reserve 7	1	39N59	95w34	6:22:16
Rexford 97	1	39N28	100w45	6:43:00
Rice 15	1	39N34	97w33	6:30:12
Rich 2	1	38N05	95w08	6:20:32
Richfield 65	3	37N16	101w47	6:47:08
Richland 89	1	38N53	95w32	6:22:08
Richmond 30	1	38N24	95w15	6:21:00
Richter 30	1	38N37	95w16	6:21:04
Ridgeway 70	1	38N49	95w40	6:22:40
Riley 81	1	39N18	96w50	6:27:20
Rinehart 21	1	38N55	96w59	6:27:56
Ringer 87	1	37N42	97w25	6:29:40
Ringo 19	1	37N31	94w51	6:19:24
Risley 58	1	38N23	97w12	6:28:48
River 73	1	38N13	98w58	6:35:52
Riverdale 96	1	37N22	97w23	6:29:32
Riverton 11	1	37N05	94w42	6:18:48
Riverview 26	1	39N05	99w19	6:37:16
Riverview 87	1	37N45	97w22	6:29:28
Robert L. Roberts 105	1	39N08	94w41	6:18:44
Robinson 7	1	39N49	95w25	6:21:40
Rochester 48	1	37N26	98w18	6:33:12
Rock 18	1	37N27	97w00	6:28:00
Rock Branch 69	1	39N58	100w01	6:40:04
Rock Creek 44	1	39N15	95w32	6:22:08
Rockford 87	1	37N32	97w14	6:28:56
Rockville 80	1	38N19	97w59	6:31:56
Rockwell 69	1	39N52	100w08	6:40:32
Rocky Ford 81	1	39N12	96w33	6:26:12
Roeland Park 46	1	39N02	94w39	6:18:36
Rolla 65	3	37N07	101w38	6:46:32
Rolling Prairie 64	1	38N50	96w46	6:27:04
Rome 96	1	37N10	97w23	6:29:32
Roosevelt 20	1	39N53	100w21	6:41:24
Roper 103	1	37N40	95w44	6:22:56
Rosalia 8	1	37N49	96w37	6:26:28
Roscoe 78	1	37N47	98w05	6:32:20
Rose 104	1	37N53	95w44	6:22:56
Rose Creek 79	1	39N57	97w32	6:30:08
Rosedale 105	1	39N04	94w38	6:18:32
Rose Hill 8	1	37N34	97w07	6:28:28
Roseland 11	1	37N17	94w51	6:19:24
Rose Valley 93	1	37N53	98w45	6:35:00
Rosewood 50	1	37N20	95w16	6:21:04
Rossville 89	1	39N08	95w57	6:23:48
Rotate 77	1	39N39	101w21	6:45:24
Round Mound 71	1	39N16	99w00	6:36:00
Round Springs 62	1	39N15	98w12	6:32:48
Rovohl 97	1	39N31	101w03	6:44:12
Roxbury 57	1	38N33	97w26	6:29:44
Royal 29	1	37N52	100w07	6:40:28
Rozel 73	1	38N12	99w24	6:37:36
Ruella 39	1	37N14	98w11	6:32:44
Ruleton 91	2	39N21	101w43	6:46:52
Rush 82	1	39N21	99w26	6:37:44
Rush Center 83	1	38N28	99w19	6:37:16
Rushville 74	1	39N37	99w21	6:37:24
Russell 84	1	38N54	98w52	6:35:28
Russell Springs 55	4	38N55	101w11	6:44:44
Rutland 63	1	37N12	95w53	6:23:32
Ryan 96	1	37N16	97w38	6:30:32
Rydal 79	1	39N48	97w47	6:31:08
Sabetha 66	1	39N54	95w48	6:23:12
Saffordville 9	1	38N24	96w32	6:26:08
Saint Benedict 66	1	39N53	96w06	6:24:24
Saint Bridget 59	1	39N57	96w17	6:25:08
Saint Clere 75	1	39N22	96w05	6:24:20
Saint Francis 12	4	39N47	101w48	6:47:12
Saint George 75	1	39N12	96w25	6:25:40
Saint John 93	1	38N00	98w46	6:35:04
Saint Joseph 15	1	39N31	97w24	6:29:36
Saint Leo 48	1	37N32	98w25	6:33:40
Saint Mark 87	1	37N44	97w34	6:30:16
Saint Marys 75	1	39N12	96w04	6:24:16
Saint Mary's College 52	1	39N19	94w55	6:19:40
Saint Pats 3	1	39N34	95w08	6:20:32
Saint Paul 67	1	37N31	95w10	6:20:40
Saint Peter 33	1	39N11	100w06	6:40:24
Saint Theresa 102	4	38N29	101w21	6:45:24
Salamanca 11	1	37N10	94w53	6:19:32
Salina 85	1	38N50	97w37	6:30:28
Saline 26	1	39N04	99w07	6:36:28
Sallyards 37	1	37N50	96w30	6:26:00
Salt Springs 37	1	37N39	96w02	6:24:08
Sanford 73	1	38N11	99w19	6:37:16
Santa Fe 73	1	38N08	99w11	6:36:44
Sappa 20	1	39N47	100w41	6:42:44
Saratoga 76	1	37N38	98w42	6:34:48
Sarcoxie 52	1	39N06	95w14	6:20:56
Satanta 41	3	37N26	100w59	6:43:56
Saunders 94	3	37N31	101w53	6:47:32
Savonburg 1	1	37N45	95w09	6:20:36
Sawlog 42	1	37N58	99w54	6:39:36
Sawmill 73	1	38N08	99w31	6:38:04
Sawyer 76	1	37N30	98w41	6:34:44
Saxman 80	1	38N17	98w08	6:32:32
Scammon 11	1	37N17	94w49	6:19:16
Scandia 79	1	39N48	97w47	6:31:08
Schoenchen 26	1	38N43	99w20	6:37:20
Schulte 87	1	37N38	97w28	6:29:52
Scipio 2	1	38N17	95w15	6:21:00
Scott City 86	4	38N29	100w54	6:43:36
Scottsville 62	1	39N32	97w57	6:31:48
Scranton 70	1	38N47	95w44	6:22:56
Sedan 10	1	37N08	96w11	6:24:44
Sedgwick 40	1	37N55	97w26	6:29:44
Seguin 90	1	39N20	100w36	6:42:24
Selden 90	1	39N33	100w34	6:42:16
Selkirk 102	4	38N29	101w32	6:46:08
Selma 2	1	38N08	95w08	6:20:32
Seneca 66	1	39N50	96w04	6:24:16
Severance 22	1	39N46	95w15	6:21:00
Severy 37	1	37N37	96w14	6:24:56
Seward 93	1	38N11	98w48	6:35:12
Shady Bend 53	1	39N03	98w09	6:32:36
Shady Brook 21	1	38N42	96w54	6:27:36
Shaffer 83	1	38N27	99w01	6:36:04
Shallow Water 86	4	38N23	100w55	6:43:40
Sharon 4	1	37N15	98w25	6:33:40
Sharon Springs 100	2	38N54	101w45	6:47:00
Sharpe 16	1	38N17	95w41	6:22:44
Shaw 67	1	37N36	95w19	6:21:16
Shawnee 46	1	39N01	94w43	6:18:52
Shawnee Mission 46	1	39N02	94w39	6:18:36
Shell Rock 37	1	38N07	96w01	6:24:04
Sherlock 28	4	38N00	101w02	6:44:08
Sherman 11	1	37N16	95w04	6:20:16
Shermanville 91	2	39N29	101w34	6:46:16
Sherwin 11	1	37N11	94w57	6:19:48
Sherwood Estates 89	1	39N02	95w43	6:22:52
Shields 51	1	38N37	100w27	6:41:48
Shiley 73	1	38N18	99w32	6:38:08
Shiloh 67	1	37N26	95w28	6:21:52
Shimer 17	1	37N05	99w09	6:36:36
Shirley 15	1	39N32	97w25	6:29:40
Sibley 15	1	39N37	97w40	6:30:40
Silica 80	1	38N21	98w35	6:34:20
Silverdale 18	1	37N03	96w54	6:27:36
Silver Lake 89	1	39N06	95w52	6:23:28
Simpson 62	1	39N23	97w56	6:31:44
Sinclair 45	1	39N52	97w59	6:31:56
Sitka 13	1	37N11	99w39	6:38:36
Skellyville 48	1	37N39	98w26	6:33:44
Skiddy 64	1	38N52	96w47	6:27:08
Skidmore 11	1	37N17	94w50	6:19:20
Smileyville 8	1	37N30	97w01	6:28:04
Smith 97	1	39N27	100w47	6:43:08
Smith Center 92	1	39N47	98w47	6:35:08
Smoky 91	2	39N12	101w43	6:46:52
Smoky View 85	1	38N39	97w39	6:30:36
Smolan 85	1	38N44	97w41	6:30:44
Sodville 29	1	37N31	99w45	6:39:00
Soldier 43	1	39N32	95w58	6:23:52
Solomon 21	1	38N55	97w22	6:29:28
Solomon Rapids 62	1	39N31	98w13	6:32:52
Somerset 61	1	38N34	94w53	6:19:32
South Basehor 52	1	39N09	94w56	6:19:44
South Bend 5	1	38N18	98w45	6:35:00
South Brown 24	1	37N47	99w20	6:37:20
South Dodge 29	1	37N45	100w01	6:40:04
Southeast 87	1	37N41	97w17	6:29:08
South Haven 96	1	37N03	97w24	6:29:36
South Hoisington 5	1	38N31	98w47	6:35:08
South Homestead 5	1	38N29	98w46	6:35:04
South Hutchinson 78	1	38N02	97w56	6:31:44
South Mound 67	1	37N26	95w14	6:20:56
South Park 46	1	39N01	94w42	6:18:48
South Radley 19	1	37N26	94w42	6:18:48
South Randall 97	1	39N11	100w50	6:43:20
South Roscoe 42	1	37N58	100w07	6:40:28

South Salem 37	1	37N54	96w25	6:25:40
South Seward 93	1	38N08	98w45	6:35:00
South Sharps Creek 57	1	38N28	97w52	6:31:28
Southside 47	5	37N53	101w12	6:44:48
Southwest Gardens 46	1	39N01	94w42	6:18:48
Sparks 22	1	39N52	95w16	6:21:04
Spearville 29	1	37N51	99w45	6:39:00
Speed 74	1	39N41	99w25	6:37:40
Spivey 48	1	37N27	98w10	6:32:40
Spring Brook 90	1	39N13	100w28	6:41:52
Springdale 52	1	39N21	95w07	6:20:28
Springdale 87	1	37N21	97w38	6:30:32
Spring Grove 11	1	37N05	94w38	6:18:32
Spring Hill 46	1	38N45	94w50	6:19:20
Springvale 76	1	37N31	98w57	6:35:48
Stafford 93	1	37N58	98w36	6:34:24
Stanley 46	1	38N51	94w40	6:18:40
Stanton 61	1	38N30	94w57	6:19:48
Star 16	1	38N13	95w36	6:22:24
Stark 67	1	37N42	95w09	6:20:36
Starr 15	1	39N21	97w25	6:29:40
State House 89	1	39N03	95w41	6:22:44
State Line 91	2	39N19	102w00	6:48:00
Sterling 80	1	38N13	98w12	6:32:48
Stilwell 46	1	38N46	94w39	6:18:36
Stippville 11	1	37N13	94w50	6:19:20
Stockton 82	1	39N26	99w16	6:37:04
Stohrville 39	1	37N04	97w52	6:31:28
Straight Creek 43	1	39N31	95w38	6:22:32
Stranger 52	1	39N08	95w01	6:20:04
Strauss 50	1	37N21	95w01	6:20:04
Strawberry 101	1	39N42	97w12	6:28:48
Strawn 16	1	38N12	95w45	6:23:00
Strong 9	1	38N27	96w31	6:26:04
Strong City 9	1	38N24	96w32	6:26:08
Studley 90	1	39N21	100w10	6:40:40
Stull 23	1	39N03	95w24	6:21:36
Stuttgart 74	1	39N48	99w28	6:37:52
Sublette 41	3	37N29	100w51	6:43:24
Suburban Heights 63	1	37N14	95w43	6:22:52
Sugar Creek 61	1	38N27	94w40	6:18:40
Sugar Loaf 82	1	39N31	99w27	6:37:48
Sullivan 34	3	37N26	101w19	6:45:16
Sullivans Track 34	3	37N35	101w22	6:45:28
Summerfield 59	1	40N00	96w21	6:25:24
Summers 97	1	39N14	101w03	6:44:12
Sun City 4	1	37N23	98w55	6:35:40
Sunflower 46	1	38N57	95w00	6:20:00
Sunnydale 87	1	37N50	97w22	6:29:28
Sunset Park 87	1	37N38	97w21	6:29:24
Susank 5	1	38N38	98w46	6:35:04
Sutton 51	1	38N20	100w37	6:42:28
Swan 92	1	39N52	99w01	6:36:04
Swede Creek 81	1	39N32	96w43	6:26:52
Sycamore 63	1	37N20	95w43	6:22:52
Sylvan Grove 53	1	39N01	98w24	6:33:36
Sylvia 78	1	37N57	98w25	6:33:40
Syracuse 38	2	37N59	101w45	6:47:00
Talleyrand 103	1	37N25	95w48	6:23:12
Talmage 21	1	39N02	97w16	6:29:04
Talmo 79	1	39N49	97w38	6:30:32
Taloga 65	3	37N04	101w53	6:47:32
Tampa 58	1	38N33	97w09	6:28:36
Tasco 90	1	39N21	100w18	6:41:12
Tecumseh 89	1	39N03	95w35	6:22:20
Ten Mile 61	1	38N41	94w45	6:19:00
Tennis 28	4	37N58	100w50	6:43:20
Terra Heights 89	1	38N59	95w41	6:22:44
Terry 28	4	38N11	100w58	6:43:52
Tescott 72	1	39N01	97w53	6:31:32
Teterville 37	1	38N03	96w26	6:25:44
Thayer 67	1	37N29	95w28	6:21:52
The Dell 87	1	37N41	97w25	6:29:40
Thomas 27	1	38N34	98w12	6:32:48
Thompsonville 44	1	39N04	95w24	6:21:36
Thornburg 92	1	39N47	98w47	6:35:08
Thrall 37	1	37N49	96w17	6:25:08
Tilden 71	1	39N27	98w49	6:35:16
Timberhill 6	1	37N59	94w53	6:19:32
Timken 83	1	38N29	99w11	6:36:44
Tioga 67	1	37N41	95w28	6:21:52
Tipton 62	1	39N21	98w28	6:33:52
Tisdale 18	1	37N15	96w52	6:27:28
Toledo 9	1	38N25	96w25	6:25:40
Tonganoxie 52	1	39N07	95w05	6:20:20
Tonovay 37	1	37N49	96w17	6:25:08
Topeka 89	1	39N03	95w40	6:22:40
Toronto 104	1	37N48	95w57	6:23:48
Towanda 8	1	37N48	97w00	6:28:00
Tower Grove 46	1	39N00	94w41	6:18:44
Trading Post 54	1	38N11	94w43	6:18:52
Traer 20	1	39N56	100w40	6:42:40
Travel Air 87	1	37N44	97w16	6:29:04
Treece 11	1	37N00	94w51	6:19:24
Trego Center 98	1	39N02	99w53	6:39:32
Trenton 24	1	37N51	99w31	6:38:04
Trenton 85	1	38N50	97w36	6:30:24
Tribune 36	2	38N28	101w45	6:47:00
Trivoli 27	1	38N35	98w06	6:32:24
Trousdale 24	1	37N49	99w05	6:36:20
Troy 22	1	39N47	95w05	6:20:20
Turck 11	1	37N08	94w51	6:19:24
Turkville 26	1	39N14	99w18	6:37:12
Turon 78	1	37N48	98w26	6:33:44
Twin Grove 37	1	37N38	96w14	6:24:56
Twin Mound 82	1	39N16	99w13	6:36:52
Tyro 63	1	37N02	95w49	6:23:16
Udall 18	1	37N23	97w07	6:28:28
Ulysses 34	3	37N35	101w22	6:45:28
Union Center 25	1	37N32	96w25	6:25:40
Uniontown 6	1	37N51	94w59	6:19:56
University 23	1	38N58	95w15	6:21:00
Upland 21	1	39N05	97w01	6:28:04
Urbana 67	1	37N34	95w24	6:21:36
Ursula 49	1	37N31	99w16	6:37:04
Utica 68	1	38N39	100w10	6:40:40
V.A. Hospital 89	1	39N02	95w41	6:22:44
Valeda 50	1	37N02	95w37	6:22:28
Valencia 89	1	39N02	95w43	6:22:52
Valley Brook 70	1	38N37	95w40	6:22:40
Valley Center 87	1	37N50	97w22	6:29:28
Valley Falls 44	1	39N21	95w28	6:21:52
Valverde 96	1	37N11	97w12	6:28:48
Varner 48	1	37N43	98w02	6:32:08
Vassar 70	1	38N42	95w37	6:22:28
Verdi 72	1	38N59	97w30	6:30:00
Verdigris 103	1	37N41	95w55	6:23:40
Vermillion 59	1	39N43	96w16	6:25:04
Vernon 18	1	37N15	97w06	6:28:24
Vernon 104	1	37N53	95w44	6:22:56
Vesper 53	1	39N02	98w17	6:33:08
Vesta 13	1	37N12	99w59	6:39:56
Vicksburg 45	1	39N42	97w59	6:31:56
Victor 71	1	39N16	98w53	6:35:32
Victoria 26	1	38N52	99w09	6:36:36
Vienna 75	1	39N26	96w10	6:24:40
Vilas 103	1	37N40	95w35	6:22:20
Vine Creek 72	1	39N10	97w20	6:29:20
Vining 14	1	39N34	97w18	6:29:12
Vinita 48	1	37N36	97w52	6:31:28
Vinland 23	1	38N50	95w11	6:20:44
Viola 87	1	37N29	97w39	6:30:36
Virgil 37	1	37N59	96w01	6:24:04
Vliets 59	1	39N43	96w20	6:25:20
Voda 98	1	39N02	100w07	6:40:28
Volland 99	1	38N57	96w25	6:25:40
Voltaire 91	2	39N29	101w43	6:46:52
Voorhees 95	3	37N04	101w25	6:45:40
Wabaunsee 99	1	39N09	96w21	6:25:24
Waco 87	1	37N37	97w25	6:29:40
Wagon Wheel Ranch 8	1	37N41	96w59	6:27:56
Wagstaff 61	1	38N40	94w48	6:19:12
Wakarusa 89	1	38N53	95w42	6:22:48
WaKeeney 98	1	38N59	99w52	6:39:28
Wakefield 14	1	39N13	97w01	6:28:04
Waldo 84	1	39N07	98w49	6:35:16
Waldron 39	1	37N00	98w11	6:32:44
Walker 26	1	38N52	99w05	6:36:20
Wallace 100	2	38N58	101w36	6:46:24
Walnut 19	1	37N36	95w05	6:20:20
Walnut Creek 62	1	39N26	98w19	6:33:16
Walnut Grove 67	1	37N36	95w10	6:20:40
Walton 40	1	38N07	97w15	6:29:00
Wamego 75	1	39N12	96w18	6:25:12
Wano 12	4	39N47	101w48	6:47:12
Waring 68	1	38N37	99w42	6:38:48
Warren 64	1	38N45	96w25	6:25:40
Warwick 79	1	39N55	97w49	6:31:16
Washburn University 89	1	39N02	95w41	6:22:44
Washington 101	1	39N49	97w03	6:28:12
Washington Street 87	1	37N41	97w20	6:29:20
Waterloo 48	1	37N37	97w56	6:31:44
Waterloo 56	1	38N42	96w01	6:24:04
Waterville 59	1	39N42	96w45	6:27:00
Wathena 22	1	39N46	94w57	6:19:48
Wauneta 10	1	37N07	96w23	6:25:32
Waverly 16	1	38N23	95w36	6:22:24
Wayne 79	1	39N43	97w33	6:30:12
Wayside 63	1	37N07	95w52	6:23:28
Wea 61	1	38N39	94w40	6:18:40
Webber 45	1	39N56	98w02	6:32:08
Wego-Waco 87	1	37N38	97w18	6:29:12
Weir 11	1	37N19	94w46	6:19:04
Welda 2	1	38N10	95w18	6:21:12
Wellington 96	1	37N16	97w24	6:29:36
Wells 72	1	39N08	97w33	6:30:12
Wellsford 49	1	37N37	99w02	6:36:08
Wellsville 30	1	38N43	95w05	6:20:20
Wendell 97	1	39N31	100w49	6:43:16
Weskan 100	2	38N52	101w57	6:47:48
Wesleyan 85	1	38N50	97w36	6:30:24
West Branch 58	1	38N13	97w19	6:29:16
West Center 95	3	37N11	101w27	6:45:48
West Cherry 63	1	37N19	95w38	6:22:32
West Coffeyville 63	1	37N02	95w37	6:22:28
West Cooper 93	1	38N03	98w38	6:34:32
Western 55	4	38N53	101w24	6:45:36
Westfall 53	1	38N56	98w00	6:32:00
West Hale 97	1	39N22	101w20	6:45:20
West Hamilton 26	1	39N04	99w32	6:38:08
West Hess 35	3	37N37	100w23	6:41:32
West Hibbard 47	2	38N10	101w26	6:45:44
Westland 49	1	37N31	99w30	6:38:00
West Mineral 11	1	37N17	94w55	6:19:40
Westminster 78	1	37N57	98w12	6:32:48
Westmoreland 75	1	39N24	96w25	6:25:40
Westola 65	3	37N15	101w58	6:47:52
Westphalia 2	1	38N13	95w27	6:21:48
West Plains 60	1	37N15	100w32	6:42:08
West Saline 90	1	39N14	100w20	6:41:20
West Union 69	1	39N37	99w42	6:38:48
West Washington 80	1	38N13	98w05	6:32:20
Westwood 46	1	39N02	94w37	6:18:28
Westwood Hills 46	1	39N02	94w38	6:18:32
Wetmore 66	1	39N38	95w49	6:23:16
Wheaton 75	1	39N30	96w19	6:25:16
Wheatridge Addition 87	1	37N42	97w25	6:29:40
Wheeler 12	4	39N46	101w43	6:46:52
White 48	1	37N41	98w05	6:32:20
White City 64	1	38N48	96w44	6:26:56
White Cloud 22	1	39N59	95w18	6:21:12
White Mound 45	1	39N52	98w27	6:33:48
Whitewater 8	1	37N58	97w09	6:28:36
Whitewoman 102	4	38N21	101w21	6:45:24
Whiting 43	1	39N37	95w37	6:22:28
Wichita 87	1	37N42	97w20	6:29:20
Wichita Heights 87	1	37N42	97w19	6:29:16
Wilburn 29	1	37N31	100w06	6:40:24
Wilburton 65	3	37N00	101w54	6:47:36
Wilder 46	1	38N59	94w58	6:19:52
Wild Horse 33	1	39N19	99w41	6:38:44
Willard 89	1	39N06	95w57	6:23:48
Willcox 98	1	38N47	99w52	6:39:28
Williamsburg 30	1	38N29	95w28	6:21:52
Williamsport 89	1	38N56	95w42	6:22:48
Williamstown 44	1	39N04	95w20	6:21:20
Willis 7	1	39N43	95w31	6:22:04
Willowbrook 78	1	38N06	98w00	6:32:00
Willowdale 48	1	37N31	98w18	6:33:12
Willow Springs 23	1	38N49	95w18	6:21:12
Wilmington 99	1	38N49	96w06	6:24:24
Wilmore 17	1	37N20	99w13	6:36:52
Wilmot 18	1	37N22	96w53	6:27:32
Wilroads Gardens 29	1	37N45	100w01	6:40:04
Wilsey 64	1	38N38	96w41	6:26:44
Wilson 27	1	38N50	98w29	6:33:56
Winchester 44	1	39N19	95w16	6:21:04
Windhorst 29	1	37N47	99w38	6:38:32
Windom 57	1	38N23	97w55	6:31:40
Windsor 18	1	37N19	96w38	6:26:32
Windsor Park 87	1	37N43	97w16	6:29:04
Windthorst 29	1	37N51	99w45	6:39:00
Winfield 18	1	37N14	96w59	6:27:56
Wingfield 31	1	39N01	96w39	6:26:36
Winifred 59	1	39N46	96w29	6:25:56
Winona 55	4	39N04	101w15	6:45:00
Winterset 84	1	38N45	98w59	6:35:56
Winway 50	1	37N20	95w16	6:21:04
Wolcott 105	1	39N11	94w49	6:19:16
Wolf River 22	1	39N47	95w15	6:21:00
Womer 92	1	39N48	98w40	6:34:40
Wonsevu 9	1	38N06	96w53	6:27:32
Woodbine 21	1	38N48	96w57	6:27:48
Woodlawn 66	1	39N54	95w48	6:23:12
Woodruff 74	1	40N00	99w26	6:37:44
Woods 95	3	37N11	101w21	6:45:24
Woodston 82	1	39N27	99w06	6:36:24
Worden 23	1	38N47	95w11	6:20:44
Wright 29	1	37N47	99w54	6:39:36
Wyandotte 105	1	39N05	94w46	6:19:04
Xenia 6	1	38N00	94w59	6:19:56
Yaggy 78	1	38N04	97w57	6:31:48
Yale 19	1	37N29	94w39	6:18:36
Yates Center 104	1	37N53	95w44	6:22:56
Yocemento 26	1	38N55	99w25	6:37:40
Yoder 78	1	37N57	97w52	6:31:28
York 93	1	37N52	98w32	6:34:08
Zarah 46	1	39N01	94w49	6:19:16
Zeandale 81	1	39N08	96w27	6:25:48
Zenda 48	1	37N27	98w17	6:33:08
Zenith 93	1	37N58	98w36	6:34:24
Zook 73	1	38N11	99w06	6:36:24
Zurich 82	1	39N14	99w26	6:37:44

KANSAS

TIME TABLES

Eastern Kentucky shows a gradual shift from Central to Eastern time. In order to comply with mandated CST, there was wide-spread observance of daylight time in central Kentucky during the late 1950's, including continuous observance of CDT in many cities after 1957. Since there was frequent local variation in starting and ending dates of daylight savings periods, caution must be advised.

KY # 1

Before 11/18/1883		LMT
11/18/1883	12:00	CST
3/31/1918	02:00	CWT
10/27/1918	02:00	CST
3/30/1919	02:00	CWT
10/26/1919	02:00	CST
2/09/1942	02:00	CWT
9/30/1945	02:00	CST
4/28/1968	02:00	US#1

KY # 2

Before 11/18/1883		LMT
11/18/1883	12:00	CST
3/31/1918	02:00	CWT
10/27/1918	02:00	CST
3/30/1919	02:00	CWT
10/26/1919	02:00	CST
2/09/1942	02:00	CWT
9/30/1945	02:00	CST
4/26/1953	02:00	CDT
9/27/1953	02:00	CST
4/28/1968	02:00	US#1

KY # 3

Before 11/18/1883		LMT
11/18/1883	12:00	CST
3/31/1918	02:00	CWT
10/27/1918	02:00	CST
3/30/1919	02:00	CWT
10/26/1919	02:00	CST
2/09/1942	02:00	CWT
9/30/1945	02:00	CST
4/29/1956	02:00	CDT
9/30/1956	02:00	CST
4/28/1968	02:00	US#1

KY # 4

Before 11/18/1883		LMT
11/18/1883	12:00	CST
3/31/1918	02:00	CWT
10/27/1918	02:00	CST
3/30/1919	02:00	CWT
10/26/1919	02:00	CST
2/09/1942	02:00	CWT
9/30/1945	02:00	CST
4/26/1964	02:00	CDT
10/25/1964	02:00	CST
4/28/1968	02:00	US#1

KY # 5

Before 11/18/1883		LMT
11/18/1883	12:00	CST
3/31/1918	02:00	CWT
10/27/1918	02:00	CST
3/30/1919	02:00	CWT
10/26/1919	02:00	CST
2/09/1942	02:00	CWT
9/30/1945	02:00	CST
4/26/1964	02:00	CDT
10/25/1964	02:00	CST
4/24/1966	02:00	US#1

KY # 6

Before 11/18/1883		LMT
11/18/1883	12:00	CST
3/31/1918	02:00	CWT
10/27/1918	02:00	CST
3/30/1919	02:00	CWT
10/26/1919	02:00	CST
4/27/1941	02:00	CDT
9/28/1941	02:00	CST
2/09/1942	02:00	CWT
9/30/1945	02:00	CST
4/28/1968	02:00	US#1

KY # 7

Before 11/18/1883		LMT
11/18/1883	12:00	CST
3/31/1918	02:00	CWT
10/27/1918	02:00	CST
3/30/1919	02:00	CWT
10/26/1919	02:00	CST
4/27/1941	02:00	CDT
9/28/1941	02:00	CST
2/09/1942	02:00	CWT
9/30/1945	02:00	CST
4/29/1956	02:00	CDT
9/30/1956	02:00	CST
4/28/1968	02:00	US#1

KY # 8

Before 11/18/1883		LMT
11/18/1883	12:00	CST
3/31/1918	02:00	CWT
10/27/1918	02:00	CST
3/30/1919	02:00	CWT
10/26/1919	02:00	CST
2/09/1942	02:00	CWT
9/30/1945	02:00	CST
4/24/1955	02:00	CDT
9/25/1955	02:00	CST
4/28/1957	02:00	CDT
9/29/1957	02:00	CST
4/28/1968	02:00	US#1

KY # 9

Before 11/18/1883		LMT
11/18/1883	12:00	CST
3/31/1918	02:00	CWT
10/27/1918	02:00	CST
3/30/1919	02:00	CWT
10/26/1919	02:00	CST
2/09/1942	02:00	CWT
9/30/1945	02:00	CST
4/29/1956	02:00	CDT
9/30/1956	02:00	CST
4/28/1957	02:00	CDT
9/29/1957	02:00	CST
4/28/1968	02:00	US#1

KY # 10

Before 11/18/1883		LMT
11/18/1883	12:00	CST
3/31/1918	02:00	CWT
10/27/1918	02:00	CST
3/30/1919	02:00	CWT
10/26/1919	02:00	CST
4/03/1927	02:00	EST
2/09/1942	02:00	EWT
9/30/1945	02:00	EST
4/28/1968	02:00	US#1

KY # 11

Before 11/18/1883		LMT
11/18/1883	12:00	CST
3/31/1918	02:00	CWT
10/27/1918	02:00	CST
3/30/1919	02:00	CWT
10/26/1919	02:00	CST
4/03/1927	02:00	EST
2/09/1942	02:00	EWT
9/30/1945	02:00	EST
4/26/1953	02:00	EDT
9/27/1953	02:00	EST
4/28/1968	02:00	US#1

KY # 12

Before 11/18/1883		LMT
11/18/1883	12:00	CST
3/31/1918	02:00	CWT
10/27/1918	02:00	CST
3/30/1919	02:00	CWT
10/26/1919	02:00	CST
4/03/1927	02:00	EST
2/09/1942	02:00	EWT
9/30/1945	02:00	EST
4/26/1953	02:00	EDT
9/27/1953	02:00	EST
4/25/1954	02:00	EDT
9/06/1954	02:00	EST
4/28/1968	02:00	US#1

KY # 13

Before 11/18/1883		LMT
11/18/1883	12:00	CST
3/31/1918	02:00	CWT
10/27/1918	02:00	CST
3/30/1919	02:00	CWT
10/26/1919	02:00	CST
4/03/1927	02:00	EST
4/27/1941	02:00	EDT
9/28/1941	02:00	EST
2/09/1942	02:00	EWT
9/30/1945	02:00	EST
4/25/1954	02:00	EDT
9/26/1954	02:00	EST
4/28/1968	02:00	US#1

KY # 14

Before 11/18/1883		LMT
11/18/1883	12:00	CST
3/31/1918	02:00	CWT
10/27/1918	02:00	CST
3/30/1919	02:00	CWT
10/26/1919	02:00	CST
2/09/1942	02:00	CWT
9/30/1945	02:00	CST
9/28/1947	02:00	EST
4/28/1968	02:00	US#1

KY # 15

Before 11/18/1883		LMT
11/18/1883	12:00	CST
3/31/1918	02:00	CWT
10/27/1918	02:00	CST
3/30/1919	02:00	CWT
10/26/1919	02:00	CST
2/09/1942	02:00	CWT
9/30/1945	02:00	CST
4/03/1960	02:00	EST
4/28/1968	02:00	US#1

KY # 16

Before 11/18/1883		LMT
11/18/1883	12:00	CST
3/31/1918	02:00	CWT
10/27/1918	02:00	CST
3/30/1919	02:00	CWT
10/26/1919	02:00	CST
2/09/1942	02:00	CWT
9/30/1945	02:00	CST
4/29/1956	02:00	CDT
9/30/1956	02:00	CST
4/03/1960	02:00	EST
4/28/1968	02:00	US#1

KY # 17

Before 11/18/1883		LMT
11/18/1883	12:00	CST
3/31/1918	02:00	CWT
10/27/1918	02:00	CST
3/30/1919	02:00	CWT
10/26/1919	02:00	CST
2/09/1942	02:00	CWT
9/30/1945	02:00	CST
4/28/1957	02:00	CDT
9/29/1957	02:00	CST
4/03/1960	02:00	EST
4/28/1968	02:00	US#1

KY # 18

Before 11/18/1883		LMT
11/18/1883	12:00	CST
3/31/1918	02:00	CWT
10/27/1918	02:00	CST
3/30/1919	02:00	CWT
10/26/1919	02:00	CST
2/09/1942	02:00	CWT
9/30/1945	02:00	CST
4/30/1956	00:00	CDT
9/03/1956	00:00	CST
4/26/1959	02:00	CDT
4/03/1960	02:00	EST
4/28/1968	02:00	US#1

KY # 19

Before 11/18/1883		LMT
11/18/1883	12:00	CST
3/31/1918	02:00	CWT
10/27/1918	02:00	CST
3/30/1919	02:00	CWT
10/26/1919	02:00	CST
4/27/1941	02:00	CDT
9/28/1941	02:00	CST
2/09/1942	02:00	CWT
9/30/1945	02:00	CST
4/28/1946	02:00	CDT
9/29/1946	02:00	CST
4/30/1950	02:00	CDT
9/24/1950	02:00	CST
4/29/1951	02:00	CDT
9/30/1951	02:00	CST
4/25/1954	02:00	CDT
9/26/1954	02:00	CST
4/24/1955	02:00	CDT
9/25/1955	02:00	CST
4/29/1956	02:00	CDT
9/30/1956	02:00	CST
4/28/1957	02:00	CDT
4/03/1960	02:00	EST
4/28/1968	02:00	US#1

KY # 20

Before 11/18/1883		LMT
11/18/1883	12:00	CST
3/31/1918	02:00	CWT
10/27/1918	02:00	CST
3/30/1919	02:00	CWT
10/26/1919	02:00	CST
4/27/1941	02:00	CDT
9/28/1941	02:00	CST
2/09/1942	02:00	CWT
9/30/1945	02:00	CST
4/28/1946	02:00	CDT
9/29/1946	02:00	CST
4/26/1953	02:00	CDT
9/27/1953	02:00	CST
4/25/1954	02:00	CDT
9/26/1954	02:00	CST
4/24/1955	02:00	CDT
9/25/1955	02:00	CST
4/29/1956	02:00	CDT
9/30/1956	02:00	CST
4/28/1957	02:00	CDT
4/03/1960	02:00	EST
4/28/1968	02:00	US#1

KY # 21

Before 11/18/1883		LMT
11/18/1883	12:00	CST
3/31/1918	02:00	CWT
10/27/1918	02:00	CST
3/30/1919	02:00	CWT
10/26/1919	02:00	CST
2/09/1942	02:00	CWT
9/30/1945	02:00	CST
4/25/1954	02:00	CDT
9/26/1954	02:00	CST
4/24/1955	02:00	CDT
9/25/1955	02:00	CST
4/29/1956	02:00	CDT
9/30/1956	02:00	CST
4/28/1957	02:00	CDT
9/29/1957	02:00	CST
4/27/1958	02:00	CDT
10/26/1958	02:00	CST
4/26/1959	02:00	CDT
10/25/1959	02:00	CST
4/03/1960	02:00	EST
4/28/1968	02:00	US#1

KY # 22

Before 11/18/1883		LMT
11/18/1883	12:00	CST
3/31/1918	02:00	CWT
10/27/1918	02:00	CST
3/30/1919	02:00	CWT
10/26/1919	02:00	CST
2/09/1942	02:00	CWT
9/30/1945	02:00	CST
4/25/1954	02:00	CDT
9/26/1954	02:00	CST
4/24/1955	02:00	CDT
9/04/1955	02:00	CST
4/29/1956	02:00	CDT
9/30/1956	02:00	CST
4/28/1957	02:00	CDT
4/03/1960	02:00	EST
4/28/1968	02:00	US#1

KY # 23

Before 11/18/1883		LMT
11/18/1883	12:00	CST
3/31/1918	02:00	CWT
10/27/1918	02:00	CST
3/30/1919	02:00	CWT
10/26/1919	02:00	CST
4/27/1941	02:00	CDT
9/01/1941	02:00	CST
2/09/1942	02:00	CWT
9/30/1945	02:00	CST
4/03/1960	02:00	EST
4/28/1968	02:00	US#1

KY # 24

Before 11/18/1883		LMT
11/18/1883	12:00	CST
3/31/1918	02:00	CWT
10/27/1918	02:00	CST
3/30/1919	02:00	CWT
10/26/1919	02:00	CST
2/09/1942	02:00	CWT
9/30/1945	02:00	CST
4/30/1950	02:00	CDT
9/24/1950	02:00	CST
4/25/1954	02:00	CDT
9/06/1954	02:00	CST
4/24/1955	02:00	CDT
9/04/1955	02:00	CST
4/29/1956	02:00	CDT
9/04/1956	02:00	CST
4/28/1957	02:00	CDT
10/31/1959	02:00	CST
4/03/1960	02:00	EST
4/28/1968	02:00	US#1

KY # 25

Before 11/18/1883		LMT
11/18/1883	12:00	CST
3/31/1918	02:00	CWT
10/27/1918	02:00	CST
3/30/1919	02:00	CWT
10/26/1919	02:00	CST
2/09/1942	02:00	CWT
9/30/1945	02:00	CST
4/30/1950	02:00	CDT
9/30/1956	02:00	CST
4/28/1957	02:00	CDT
4/03/1960	02:00	EST
4/28/1968	02:00	US#1

KY # 26

Before 11/18/1883		LMT
11/18/1883	12:00	CST
3/31/1918	02:00	CWT
10/27/1918	02:00	CST
3/30/1919	02:00	CWT
10/26/1919	02:00	CST
4/27/1941	02:00	CDT
9/13/1941	02:00	CST
2/09/1942	02:00	CWT
9/30/1945	02:00	CST
4/28/1957	02:00	CDT
9/29/1957	02:00	CST
4/27/1958	02:00	CDT
10/26/1958	02:00	CST
4/03/1960	02:00	EST
4/28/1968	02:00	US#1

KY # 27

Before 11/18/1883		LMT
11/18/1883	12:00	CST
3/31/1918	02:00	CWT
10/27/1918	02:00	CST
3/30/1919	02:00	CWT
10/26/1919	02:00	CST
4/27/1941	02:00	CDT
10/01/1941	02:00	CST
2/09/1942	02:00	CWT
9/30/1945	02:00	CST
4/28/1946	02:00	CDT
9/29/1946	02:00	CST
4/30/1950	02:00	CDT
9/24/1950	02:00	CST
4/29/1951	02:00	CDT
9/30/1951	02:00	CST
4/27/1952	02:00	CDT
6/18/1952	02:00	CST
4/26/1953	02:00	CDT
9/27/1953	02:00	CST
4/25/1954	02:00	CDT
9/05/1954	02:00	CST
4/24/1955	02:00	CDT
9/05/1955	02:00	CST
4/29/1956	02:00	CDT
9/30/1956	02:00	CST
4/28/1957	02:00	CDT
4/03/1960	02:00	EST
4/28/1968	02:00	US#1

KY # 28

Before 11/18/1883		LMT
11/18/1883	12:00	CST
3/31/1918	02:00	CWT
10/27/1918	02:00	CST
3/30/1919	02:00	CWT
10/26/1919	02:00	CST
2/09/1942	02:00	CWT
9/30/1945	02:00	CST
4/25/1954	02:00	CDT
9/05/1954	02:00	CST
4/24/1955	02:00	CDT
9/05/1955	02:00	CST
4/29/1956	02:00	CDT
9/04/1956	02:00	CST
4/28/1957	02:00	CDT
4/03/1960	02:00	EST
4/28/1968	02:00	US#1

KY # 29

Before 11/18/1883		LMT
11/18/1883	12:00	CST
3/31/1918	02:00	CWT
10/27/1918	02:00	CST
3/30/1919	02:00	CWT
10/26/1919	02:00	CST
4/27/1941	02:00	CDT
10/01/1941	02:00	CST
2/09/1942	02:00	CWT
9/30/1945	02:00	CST
4/28/1946	02:00	CDT
9/29/1946	02:00	CST
4/30/1950	02:00	CDT
9/24/1950	02:00	CST
4/29/1951	02:00	CDT
9/30/1951	02:00	CST
4/26/1953	02:00	CDT
9/27/1953	02:00	CST
4/25/1954	02:00	CDT
9/05/1954	02:00	CST
4/24/1955	02:00	CDT
9/25/1955	02:00	CST
4/29/1956	02:00	CDT
9/30/1956	02:00	CST
4/28/1957	02:00	CDT
4/03/1960	02:00	EST
4/28/1968	02:00	US#1

KY # 30

Before 11/18/1883		LMT
11/18/1883	12:00	CST
3/31/1918	02:00	CWT
10/27/1918	02:00	CST
3/30/1919	02:00	CWT
10/26/1919	02:00	CST
4/27/1941	02:00	CDT
9/28/1941	02:00	CST
2/09/1942	02:00	CWT
9/30/1945	02:00	CST
4/28/1946	02:00	CDT
9/29/1946	02:00	CST
4/25/1954	02:00	CDT
9/26/1954	02:00	CST
4/24/1955	02:00	CDT
9/25/1955	02:00	CST
4/29/1956	02:00	CDT
9/03/1956	02:00	CST
4/28/1957	02:00	CDT
4/03/1960	02:00	EST

4/28/1968 02:00 US#1

KY # 31
Before 11/18/1883 LMT
11/18/1883 12:00 CST
3/31/1918 02:00 CWT
10/27/1918 02:00 CST
3/30/1919 02:00 CWT
10/26/1919 02:00 CST
2/09/1942 02:00 CWT
9/30/1945 02:00 CST
4/30/1956 00:00 CDT
9/03/1956 00:00 CST
5/29/1957 02:00 CDT
9/02/1957 02:00 CST
6/23/1958 00:00 CDT
9/02/1958 00:00 CST
4/26/1959 02:00 CDT
4/03/1960 02:00 EST
4/28/1968 02:00 US#1

KY # 32
Before 11/18/1883 LMT
11/18/1883 12:00 CST
3/31/1918 02:00 CWT
10/27/1918 02:00 CST
3/30/1919 02:00 CWT
10/26/1919 02:00 CST
4/27/1941 02:00 CDT
10/01/1941 02:00 CST
2/09/1942 02:00 CWT
9/30/1945 02:00 CST
4/28/1946 02:00 CDT
9/29/1946 02:00 CST
4/30/1950 02:00 CDT
9/24/1950 02:00 CST
4/26/1953 02:00 CDT
9/27/1953 02:00 CST
4/25/1954 02:00 CDT
9/06/1954 02:00 CST
4/24/1955 02:00 CDT
9/25/1955 02:00 CST
4/29/1956 02:00 CDT
9/01/1956 02:00 CST
4/28/1957 02:00 CDT
4/03/1960 02:00 EST
4/28/1968 02:00 US#1

KY # 33
Before 11/18/1883 LMT
11/18/1883 12:00 CST
3/31/1918 02:00 CWT
10/27/1918 02:00 CST
3/30/1919 02:00 CWT
10/26/1919 02:00 CST
2/09/1942 02:00 CWT
9/30/1945 02:00 CST
4/27/1958 02:00 CDT
10/26/1958 02:00 CST
4/03/1960 02:00 EST
4/28/1968 02:00 US#1

KY # 34
Before 11/18/1883 LMT
11/18/1883 12:00 CST
3/31/1918 02:00 CWT
10/27/1918 02:00 CST
3/30/1919 02:00 CWT
10/26/1919 02:00 CST
2/09/1942 02:00 CWT
9/30/1945 02:00 CST
4/29/1956 02:00 CDT
9/02/1956 00:00 CST
4/28/1957 02:00 CDT
4/03/1960 02:00 EST
4/28/1968 02:00 US#1

KY # 35
Before 11/18/1883 LMT
11/18/1883 12:00 CST
3/31/1918 02:00 CWT
10/27/1918 02:00 CST
3/30/1919 02:00 CWT
10/26/1919 02:00 CST
4/27/1941 02:00 CDT
9/28/1941 02:00 CST
2/09/1942 02:00 CWT
9/30/1945 02:00 CST
4/03/1960 02:00 EST
4/28/1968 02:00 US#1

KY # 36
Before 11/18/1883 LMT
11/18/1883 12:00 CST
3/31/1918 02:00 CWT
10/27/1918 02:00 CST
3/30/1919 02:00 CWT
10/26/1919 02:00 CST
4/27/1941 02:00 CDT
9/28/1941 02:00 CST
2/09/1942 02:00 CWT
9/30/1945 02:00 CST
4/29/1956 02:00 CDT
9/30/1956 02:00 CST
4/03/1960 02:00 EST
4/28/1968 02:00 US#1

KY # 37
Before 11/18/1883 LMT
11/18/1883 12:00 CST
3/31/1918 02:00 CWT
10/27/1918 02:00 CST
3/30/1919 02:00 CWT
10/26/1919 02:00 CST
4/27/1941 02:00 CDT
9/28/1941 02:00 CST
2/09/1942 02:00 CWT
9/30/1945 02:00 CST
4/25/1954 02:00 CDT
9/26/1954 02:00 CST
4/29/1956 02:00 CDT
9/30/1956 02:00 CST
4/28/1957 02:00 CDT
4/03/1960 02:00 EST
4/28/1968 02:00 US#1

KY # 38
Before 11/18/1883 LMT
11/18/1883 12:00 CST
3/31/1918 02:00 CWT
10/27/1918 02:00 CST
3/30/1919 02:00 CWT
10/26/1919 02:00 CST
2/09/1942 02:00 CWT
9/30/1945 02:00 CST
4/26/1953 02:00 CDT
9/27/1953 02:00 CST
4/25/1954 02:00 CDT
9/26/1954 02:00 CST
4/27/1958 02:00 CDT
10/26/1958 02:00 CST
4/03/1960 02:00 EST
4/28/1968 02:00 US#1

KY # 39
Before 11/18/1883 LMT
11/18/1883 12:00 CST
3/31/1918 02:00 CWT
10/27/1918 02:00 CST
3/30/1919 02:00 CWT
10/26/1919 02:00 CST
2/09/1942 02:00 CWT
9/30/1945 02:00 CST
4/25/1954 02:00 CDT
9/26/1954 02:00 CST
4/03/1960 02:00 EST
4/28/1968 02:00 US#1

KY # 40
Before 11/18/1883 LMT
11/18/1883 12:00 CST
3/31/1918 02:00 CWT
10/27/1918 02:00 CST
3/30/1919 02:00 CWT
10/26/1919 02:00 CST
2/09/1942 02:00 CWT
9/30/1945 02:00 CST
4/29/1956 02:00 CDT
9/30/1956 02:00 CST
4/28/1957 02:00 CDT
9/29/1957 02:00 CST
4/27/1958 02:00 CDT
10/26/1958 02:00 CST
4/26/1959 02:00 CDT
10/25/1959 02:00 CST
4/03/1960 02:00 EST
4/28/1968 02:00 US#1

KY # 41
Before 11/18/1883 LMT
11/18/1883 12:00 CST
3/31/1918 02:00 CWT
10/27/1918 02:00 CST
3/30/1919 02:00 CWT
10/26/1919 02:00 CST
2/09/1942 02:00 CWT
9/30/1945 02:00 CST
4/29/1956 02:00 CDT
9/30/1956 02:00 CST
4/28/1957 02:00 CDT
4/03/1960 02:00 EST
4/28/1968 02:00 US#1

KY # 42
Before 11/18/1883 LMT
11/18/1883 12:00 CST
3/31/1918 02:00 CWT
10/27/1918 02:00 CST
3/30/1919 02:00 CWT
10/26/1919 02:00 CST
4/27/1941 02:00 CDT
9/28/1941 02:00 CST
2/09/1942 02:00 CWT
9/30/1945 02:00 CST
4/24/1955 02:00 CDT
9/25/1955 02:00 CST
4/29/1956 02:00 CDT
9/30/1956 02:00 CST
4/28/1957 02:00 CDT
9/01/1957 02:00 CST
4/27/1958 02:00 CDT
10/26/1958 02:00 CST
4/26/1959 02:00 CDT
10/25/1959 02:00 CST
4/03/1960 02:00 EST
4/28/1968 02:00 US#1

KY # 43
Before 11/18/1883 LMT
11/18/1883 12:00 CST
3/31/1918 02:00 CWT
10/27/1918 02:00 CST
3/30/1919 02:00 CWT
10/26/1919 02:00 CST
2/09/1942 02:00 CWT
9/30/1945 02:00 CST
4/29/1951 02:00 CDT
9/30/1951 02:00 CST
4/25/1954 02:00 CDT
9/26/1954 02:00 CST
4/24/1955 02:00 CDT
9/25/1955 02:00 CST
4/29/1956 02:00 CDT
9/30/1956 02:00 CST
4/28/1957 02:00 CDT
4/03/1960 02:00 EST
4/28/1968 02:00 US#1

KY # 44
Before 11/18/1883 LMT
11/18/1883 12:00 CST
3/31/1918 02:00 CWT
10/27/1918 02:00 CST
3/30/1919 02:00 CWT
10/26/1919 02:00 CST
2/09/1942 02:00 CWT
9/30/1945 02:00 CST
4/30/1950 02:00 CDT
9/24/1950 02:00 CST
4/29/1951 02:00 CDT
9/30/1951 02:00 CST
4/25/1954 02:00 CDT
9/26/1954 02:00 CST
4/24/1955 02:00 CDT
9/25/1955 02:00 CST
4/29/1956 02:00 CDT
9/30/1956 02:00 CST
4/28/1957 02:00 CDT
4/03/1960 02:00 EST
4/28/1968 02:00 US#1

KY # 45
Before 11/18/1883 LMT
11/18/1883 12:00 CST
3/31/1918 02:00 CWT
10/27/1918 02:00 CST
3/30/1919 02:00 CWT
10/26/1919 02:00 CST
2/09/1942 02:00 CWT
9/30/1945 02:00 CST
4/28/1957 02:00 CDT
9/22/1957 02:00 CST
4/03/1960 02:00 EST
4/28/1968 02:00 US#1

KY # 46
Before 11/18/1883 LMT
11/18/1883 12:00 CST
3/31/1918 02:00 CWT
10/27/1918 02:00 CST
3/30/1919 02:00 CWT
10/26/1919 02:00 CST
2/09/1942 02:00 CWT
9/30/1945 02:00 CST
4/29/1957 02:00 CDT
9/29/1957 02:00 CST
4/27/1958 02:00 CDT
10/26/1958 02:00 CST
4/03/1960 02:00 EST
4/28/1968 02:00 US#1

KY # 47
Before 11/18/1883 LMT
11/18/1883 12:00 CST
3/31/1918 02:00 CWT
10/27/1918 02:00 CST
3/30/1919 02:00 CWT
10/26/1919 02:00 CST
4/27/1941 02:00 CDT
10/01/1941 02:00 CST
2/09/1942 02:00 CWT
9/30/1945 02:00 CST
4/28/1957 02:00 CDT
9/29/1957 02:00 CST
4/03/1960 02:00 EST
4/28/1968 02:00 US#1

KY # 48
Before 11/18/1883 LMT
11/18/1883 12:00 CST
3/31/1918 02:00 CWT
10/27/1918 02:00 CST
3/30/1919 02:00 CWT
10/26/1919 02:00 CST
2/09/1942 02:00 CWT
9/30/1945 02:00 CST
7/23/1961 02:00 EST
4/28/1968 02:00 US#1

KY # 49
Before 11/18/1883 LMT
11/18/1883 12:00 CST
3/31/1918 02:00 CWT
10/27/1918 02:00 CST
3/30/1919 02:00 CWT
10/26/1919 02:00 CST
2/09/1942 02:00 CWT
9/30/1945 02:00 CST
4/26/1953 02:00 CDT
9/27/1953 02:00 CST
4/24/1955 02:00 CDT
9/25/1955 02:00 CST
4/29/1956 02:00 CDT
9/30/1956 02:00 CST
4/28/1957 02:00 CDT
9/29/1957 02:00 CST
4/27/1958 02:00 CDT
10/26/1958 02:00 CST
4/26/1959 02:00 CDT
10/25/1959 02:00 CST
4/24/1960 02:00 CDT
10/30/1960 02:00 CST
4/30/1961 02:00 CDT
7/23/1961 02:00 EST
4/28/1968 02:00 US#1

KY # 50
Before 11/18/1883 LMT
11/18/1883 12:00 CST
3/31/1918 02:00 CWT
10/27/1918 02:00 CST
3/30/1919 02:00 CWT
10/26/1919 02:00 CST
4/27/1941 02:00 CDT
9/28/1941 02:00 CST
2/09/1942 02:00 CWT
9/30/1945 02:00 CST
4/26/1953 02:00 CDT
9/27/1953 02:00 CST
4/25/1954 02:00 CDT
9/26/1954 02:00 CST
4/24/1955 02:00 CDT
9/25/1955 02:00 CST
4/29/1956 02:00 CDT
9/30/1956 02:00 CST
4/27/1958 02:00 CDT
10/26/1958 02:00 CST
7/23/1961 02:00 EST
4/28/1968 02:00 US#1

KY # 51
Before 11/18/1883 LMT
11/18/1883 12:00 CST
3/31/1918 02:00 CWT
10/27/1918 02:00 CST
3/30/1919 02:00 CWT
10/26/1919 02:00 CST
2/09/1942 02:00 CWT
9/30/1945 02:00 CST
4/25/1954 02:00 CDT
9/26/1954 02:00 CST
4/24/1955 02:00 CDT
9/25/1955 02:00 CST
4/29/1956 02:00 CDT
9/30/1956 02:00 CST
4/28/1957 02:00 CDT
9/29/1957 02:00 CST
4/27/1958 02:00 CDT
10/26/1958 02:00 CST
4/26/1959 02:00 CDT
10/25/1959 02:00 CST
4/24/1960 02:00 CDT
10/30/1960 02:00 CST
4/30/1961 02:00 CDT
7/23/1961 02:00 EST
4/28/1968 02:00 US#1

KY # 52
Before 11/18/1883 LMT
11/18/1883 12:00 CST
3/31/1918 02:00 CWT
10/27/1918 02:00 CST
3/30/1919 02:00 CWT
10/26/1919 02:00 CST
4/27/1941 02:00 CDT
8/31/1941 02:00 CST
2/09/1942 02:00 CWT
9/30/1945 02:00 CST
4/28/1957 02:00 CDT
9/29/1957 02:00 CST
7/23/1961 02:00 EST
4/28/1968 02:00 US#1

KY # 53
Before 11/18/1883 LMT
11/18/1883 12:00 CST
3/31/1918 02:00 CWT
10/27/1918 02:00 CST
3/30/1919 02:00 CWT
10/26/1919 02:00 CST
2/09/1942 02:00 CWT
9/30/1945 02:00 CST
4/26/1953 02:00 CDT
9/27/1953 02:00 CST
4/27/1958 02:00 CDT
10/26/1958 02:00 CST
7/23/1961 02:00 EST
4/28/1968 02:00 US#1

KY # 54
Before 11/18/1883 LMT
11/18/1883 12:00 CST
3/31/1918 02:00 CWT
10/27/1918 02:00 CST
3/30/1919 02:00 CWT
10/26/1919 02:00 CST
2/09/1942 02:00 CWT
9/30/1945 02:00 CST
4/27/1958 02:00 CDT
10/26/1958 02:00 CST
7/23/1961 02:00 EST
4/28/1968 02:00 US#1

KY # 55
Before 11/18/1883 LMT
11/18/1883 12:00 CST
3/31/1918 02:00 CWT
10/27/1918 02:00 CST
3/30/1919 02:00 CWT
10/26/1919 02:00 CST
2/09/1942 02:00 CWT
9/30/1945 02:00 CST
4/26/1953 02:00 CDT
9/27/1953 02:00 CST
4/25/1954 02:00 CDT
9/26/1954 02:00 CST
7/23/1961 02:00 EST
4/28/1968 02:00 US#1

KY # 56
Before 11/18/1883 LMT
11/18/1883 12:00 CST
3/31/1918 02:00 CWT
10/27/1918 02:00 CST
3/30/1919 02:00 CWT
10/26/1919 02:00 CST
4/27/1941 02:00 CDT
9/28/1941 02:00 CST
2/09/1942 02:00 CWT
9/30/1945 02:00 CST
7/23/1961 02:00 EST
4/28/1968 02:00 US#1

KY # 57
Before 11/18/1883 LMT
11/18/1883 12:00 CST
3/31/1918 02:00 CWT
10/27/1918 02:00 CST
3/30/1919 02:00 CWT
10/26/1919 02:00 CST
4/27/1941 02:00 CDT
9/28/1941 02:00 CST
2/09/1942 02:00 CWT
9/30/1945 02:00 CST
4/26/1953 02:00 CDT
9/27/1953 02:00 CST
4/24/1955 02:00 CDT
9/25/1955 02:00 CST
4/29/1956 02:00 CDT
9/30/1956 02:00 CST
4/28/1957 02:00 CDT
9/29/1957 02:00 CST
4/27/1958 02:00 CDT
10/26/1958 02:00 CST
4/26/1959 02:00 CDT
10/25/1959 02:00 CST
4/24/1960 02:00 CDT
10/30/1960 02:00 CST
4/30/1961 02:00 CDT
7/23/1961 02:00 EST
4/28/1968 00:02 US#1

KY # 58
Before 11/18/1883 LMT
11/18/1883 12:00 CST
3/31/1918 02:00 CWT
10/27/1918 02:00 CST
3/30/1919 02:00 CWT
10/26/1919 02:00 CST
4/27/1941 02:00 CDT
9/28/1941 02:00 CST
2/09/1942 02:00 CWT
9/30/1945 02:00 CST
4/25/1954 02:00 CDT
9/26/1954 02:00 CST
4/24/1955 02:00 CDT
9/25/1955 02:00 CST
4/29/1956 02:00 CDT
9/30/1956 02:00 CST
4/28/1957 02:00 CDT
9/29/1957 02:00 CST
4/27/1958 02:00 CDT
10/26/1958 02:00 CST
4/26/1959 02:00 CDT
10/25/1959 02:00 CST
4/24/1960 02:00 CDT
10/30/1960 02:00 CST
4/30/1961 02:00 CDT
7/23/1961 02:00 EST
4/28/1968 02:00 US#1

KY # 59
Before 11/18/1883 LMT
11/18/1883 12:00 CST
3/31/1918 02:00 CWT
10/27/1918 02:00 CST
3/30/1919 02:00 CWT
10/26/1919 02:00 CST
4/27/1941 02:00 CDT
9/28/1941 02:00 CST
2/09/1942 02:00 CWT
9/30/1945 02:00 CST
4/26/1953 02:00 CDT
9/27/1953 02:00 CST
4/25/1954 02:00 CDT
9/06/1954 02:00 CST
4/24/1955 02:00 CDT
9/25/1955 02:00 CST
4/29/1956 02:00 CDT
9/30/1956 02:00 CST
4/28/1957 02:00 CDT
9/29/1957 02:00 CST
4/27/1958 02:00 CDT
10/26/1958 02:00 CST
4/26/1959 02:00 CDT
10/25/1959 02:00 CST
4/24/1960 02:00 CDT
10/30/1960 02:00 CST
4/30/1961 02:00 CDT
7/23/1961 02:00 EST
4/28/1968 02:00 US#1

KY # 60
Before 11/18/1883 LMT
11/18/1883 12:00 CST

 KENTUCKY

TIME TABLES

3/31/1918 02:00 CWT
10/27/1918 02:00 CST
3/30/1919 02:00 CWT
10/26/1919 02:00 CST
2/09/1942 02:00 CWT
9/30/1945 02:00 CST
4/24/1955 02:00 CDT
9/25/1955 02:00 CST
4/29/1956 02:00 CDT
9/30/1956 02:00 CST
4/28/1957 02:00 CDT
9/29/1957 02:00 CST
4/27/1958 02:00 CDT
10/26/1958 02:00 CST
4/26/1959 02:00 CDT
10/25/1959 02:00 CST
4/24/1960 02:00 CDT
10/30/1960 02:00 CST
4/30/1961 02:00 CDT
7/23/1961 02:00 EST
4/28/1968 02:00 US#1

....

KY # 61

Before 11/18/1883 LMT
11/18/1883 12:00 CST
3/31/1918 02:00 CWT
10/27/1918 02:00 CST
3/30/1919 02:00 CWT
10/26/1919 02:00 CST
4/27/1941 02:00 CDT
9/28/1941 02:00 CST
2/09/1942 02:00 CWT
9/30/1945 02:00 CST
4/26/1953 02:00 CDT
9/27/1953 02:00 CST
4/27/1958 02:00 CDT
10/26/1958 02:00 CST
7/23/1961 02:00 EST
4/28/1968 02:00 US#1

....

KY # 62

Before 11/18/1883 LMT
11/18/1883 12:00 CST
3/31/1918 02:00 CWT
10/27/1918 02:00 CST
3/30/1919 02:00 CWT
10/26/1919 02:00 CST
2/09/1942 02:00 CWT
9/30/1945 02:00 CST
4/29/1956 02:00 CDT
9/30/1956 02:00 CST
4/28/1957 02:00 CDT
9/29/1957 02:00 CST
4/27/1958 02:00 CDT
10/26/1958 02:00 CST
4/26/1959 02:00 CDT
10/25/1959 02:00 CST
4/24/1960 02:00 CDT
10/30/1960 02:00 CST
4/30/1961 02:00 CDT
7/23/1961 02:00 EST
4/28/1968 02:00 US#1

....

KY # 63

Before 11/18/1883 LMT
11/18/1883 12:00 CST
3/31/1918 02:00 CWT
10/27/1918 02:00 CST
3/30/1919 02:00 CWT
10/26/1919 02:00 CST
4/27/1941 02:00 CDT
9/28/1941 02:00 CST
2/09/1942 02:00 CWT
9/30/1945 02:00 CST
5/02/1954 02:00 CDT
9/05/1954 02:00 CST
6/03/1956 02:00 CDT
9/02/1956 02:00 CST
4/28/1957 02:00 CDT
9/29/1957 02:00 CST
4/27/1958 02:00 CDT
10/26/1958 02:00 CST
4/26/1959 02:00 CDT
10/25/1959 02:00 CST
4/24/1960 02:00 CDT
10/30/1960 02:00 CST
4/30/1961 02:00 CDT
7/23/1961 02:00 EST
4/28/1968 02:00 US#1

....

KY # 64

Before 11/18/1883 LMT
11/18/1883 12:00 CST
3/31/1918 02:00 CWT
10/27/1918 02:00 CST
3/30/1919 02:00 CWT
10/26/1919 02:00 CST
2/09/1942 02:00 CWT
9/30/1945 02:00 CST
4/28/1957 02:00 CDT
9/29/1957 02:00 CST
4/27/1958 02:00 CDT
10/26/1958 02:00 CST
7/23/1961 02:00 EST
4/28/1968 02:00 US#1

....

KY # 65

Before 11/18/1883 LMT
11/18/1883 12:00 CST
3/31/1918 02:00 CWT
10/27/1918 02:00 CST
3/30/1919 02:00 CWT
10/26/1919 02:00 CST
2/09/1942 02:00 CWT
9/30/1945 02:00 CST
4/30/1950 02:00 CDT
9/24/1950 02:00 CST
4/29/1951 02:00 CDT
9/30/1951 02:00 CST
4/27/1952 02:00 CDT
9/28/1952 02:00 CST
4/26/1953 02:00 CDT
9/27/1953 02:00 CST
4/25/1954 02:00 CDT
9/26/1954 02:00 CST
4/24/1955 02:00 CDT
9/25/1955 02:00 CST
4/29/1956 02:00 CDT
10/28/1956 02:00 CST
4/28/1957 02:00 CDT
10/25/1959 02:00 CST
4/30/1960 02:00 CDT
10/29/1960 02:00 CST
4/30/1961 02:00 CDT
7/23/1961 02:00 EST
4/28/1968 02:00 EDT
10/27/1968 02:00 EST
4/27/1969 02:00 EDT
10/26/1969 02:00 EST
4/26/1970 02:00 EDT
10/25/1970 02:00 EST
4/25/1971 02:00 EDT
10/31/1971 02:00 EST
4/30/1972 02:00 EDT
10/29/1972 02:00 EST
4/29/1973 02:00 EDT
10/28/1973 02:00 EST
1/06/1974 02:00 CDT
10/27/1974 02:00 EST
10/27/1974 02:00 US#1

....

KY # 66

Before 11/18/1883 LMT
11/18/1883 12:00 CST
3/31/1918 02:00 CWT
10/27/1918 02:00 CST
3/30/1919 02:00 CWT
10/26/1919 02:00 CST
5/01/1921 02:00 CDT
9/01/1921 02:00 CST
4/27/1941 02:00 CDT
9/28/1941 02:00 CST
2/09/1942 02:00 CWT
9/30/1945 02:00 CST
4/28/1946 02:00 CDT
9/29/1946 02:00 CST
4/30/1950 02:00 CDT
9/24/1950 02:00 CST
4/29/1951 02:00 CDT
9/30/1951 02:00 CST
4/27/1952 02:00 CDT
9/28/1952 02:00 CST
4/26/1953 02:00 CDT
9/27/1953 02:00 CST
4/25/1954 02:00 CDT
9/26/1954 02:00 CST
4/24/1955 02:00 CDT
9/25/1955 02:00 CST
4/29/1956 02:00 CDT
10/28/1956 02:00 CST
4/28/1957 02:00 CDT
10/25/1959 02:00 CST
4/30/1960 02:00 CDT
10/29/1960 02:00 CST
4/30/1961 02:00 CDT
7/23/1961 02:00 EST
4/28/1968 02:00 EDT
10/27/1968 02:00 EST
4/27/1969 02:00 EDT
10/26/1969 02:00 EST
4/26/1970 02:00 EDT
10/25/1970 02:00 EST
4/25/1971 02:00 EDT
10/31/1971 02:00 EST
4/30/1972 02:00 EDT
10/29/1972 02:00 EST
4/29/1973 02:00 EDT
10/28/1973 02:00 EST
1/06/1974 02:00 CDT
10/27/1974 02:00 EST
10/27/1974 02:00 US#1

....

KY # 67

Before 11/18/1883 LMT
11/18/1883 12:00 CST
3/31/1918 02:00 CWT
10/27/1918 02:00 CST
3/30/1919 02:00 CWT
10/26/1919 02:00 CST
4/27/1941 02:00 CDT
9/28/1941 02:00 CST
2/09/1942 02:00 CWT
9/30/1945 02:00 CST
4/30/1950 02:00 CDT
9/24/1950 02:00 CST
4/29/1951 02:00 CDT
9/30/1951 02:00 CST
4/27/1952 02:00 CDT
9/28/1952 02:00 CST
4/26/1953 02:00 CDT
9/27/1953 02:00 CST
4/25/1954 02:00 CDT
9/26/1954 02:00 CST
4/24/1955 02:00 CDT
9/25/1955 02:00 CST
4/29/1956 02:00 CDT
10/28/1956 02:00 CST
4/28/1957 02:00 CDT
10/25/1959 02:00 CST
4/30/1960 02:00 CDT
10/29/1960 02:00 CST
4/30/1961 02:00 CDT
7/23/1961 02:00 EST
4/28/1968 02:00 EDT
10/27/1968 02:00 EST
4/27/1969 02:00 EDT
10/26/1969 02:00 EST
4/26/1970 02:00 EDT
10/25/1970 02:00 EST
4/25/1971 02:00 EDT
10/31/1971 02:00 EST
4/30/1972 02:00 EDT
10/29/1972 02:00 EST
4/29/1973 02:00 EDT
10/28/1973 02:00 EST
1/06/1974 02:00 CDT
10/27/1974 02:00 EST
10/27/1974 02:00 US#1

....

KY # 68

Before 11/18/1883 LMT
11/18/1883 12:00 CST
3/31/1918 02:00 CWT
10/27/1918 02:00 CST
3/30/1919 02:00 CWT
10/26/1919 02:00 CST
3/28/1920 02:00 CDT
10/31/1920 02:00 CST
4/02/1921 02:00 CDT
9/25/1921 02:00 CST
4/30/1922 02:00 CDT
9/24/1922 02:00 CST
4/29/1923 02:00 CDT
9/30/1923 02:00 CST
4/27/1924 02:00 CDT
9/28/1924 02:00 CST
4/26/1925 02:00 CDT
9/27/1925 02:00 CST
4/25/1926 02:00 CDT
8/05/1926 02:00 EST
9/26/1943 02:00 CST
4/30/1944 02:00 EST
9/24/1944 02:00 CST
9/30/1945 02:00 EST
4/30/1967 02:00 US#1

COUNTIES

1 Adair
2 Allen
3 Anderson
4 Ballard
5 Barren
6 Bath
7 Bell
8 Boone
9 Bourbon
10 Boyd
11 Boyle
12 Bracken
13 Breathitt
14 Breckinridge
15 Bullitt
16 Butler
17 Caldwell
18 Calloway
19 Campbell
20 Carlisle
21 Carroll
22 Carter
23 Casey
24 Christian
25 Clark
26 Clay
27 Clinton
28 Crittenden
29 Cumberland
30 Daviess
31 Edmonson
32 Elliott
33 Estill
34 Fayette
35 Fleming
36 Floyd
37 Franklin
38 Fulton
39 Gallatin
40 Garrard
41 Grant
42 Graves
43 Grayson
44 Green
45 Greenup
46 Hancock
47 Hardin
48 Harlan
49 Harrison
50 Hart
51 Henderson
52 Henry
53 Hickman
54 Hopkins
55 Jackson
56 Jefferson
57 Jessamine
58 Johnson
59 Kenton
60 Knott
61 Knox
62 Larue
63 Laurel
64 Lawrence
65 Lee
66 Leslie
67 Letcher
68 Lewis
69 Lincoln
70 Livingston
71 Logan
72 Lyon
73 McCracken
74 McCreary
75 McLean
76 Madison
77 Magoffin
78 Marion
79 Marshall
80 Martin
81 Mason
82 Meade
83 Menifee
84 Mercer
85 Metcalfe
86 Monroe
87 Montgomery
88 Morgan
89 Muhlenberg
90 Nelson
91 Nicholas
92 Ohio
93 Oldham
94 Owen
95 Owsley
96 Pendleton
97 Perry
98 Pike
99 Powell
100 Pulaski
101 Robertson
102 Rockcastle
103 Rowan
104 Russell
105 Scott
106 Shelby
107 Simpson
108 Spencer
109 Taylor
110 Todd
111 Trigg
112 Trimble
113 Union
114 Warren
115 Washington
116 Wayne
117 Webster
118 Whitley
119 Wolfe
120 Woodford

Aaron 27	1	36N49	85w11	5:40:44
Abbott 112	48	38N36	85w19	5:41:16
Abegall 101	10	38N39	83w58	5:35:52
Aberdeen 16	1	37N15	86w41	5:46:44
Absher 1	1	37N06	85w18	5:41:12
Acorn 100	18	37N08	84w22	5:37:28
Acton 109	48	37N21	85w21	5:41:24
Acup 97	45	37N12	83w08	5:32:32
Adaburg 92	1	37N27	86w54	5:47:36
Adairville 71	1	36N40	86w51	5:47:24
Adams 64	10	38N03	82w43	5:30:52
Adamson 67	15	37N11	82w38	5:30:32
Add 80	10	37N52	82w32	5:30:08
Addison 14	1	37N47	86w28	5:45:52
Adeline 64	10	38N25	82w36	5:30:24
Aden 22	15	38N17	83w05	5:32:20
Adolphus 2	1	36N39	86w16	5:45:04
Advance 45	10	38N31	82w43	5:30:52
Aetnaville 92	1	37N40	86w46	5:47:04
Aflex 98	10	37N40	82w14	5:28:56
Ages 48	14	36N52	83w15	5:33:00
Airport Gardens 97	45	37N15	83w11	5:32:44
Ajax 97	45	37N18	83w10	5:32:40
Akers 48	14	36N59	82w59	5:31:56
Akersville 86	1	36N43	85w58	5:43:52
Albany 27	1	36N42	85w08	5:40:32
Alberta 49	15	38N23	84w32	5:38:08
Albia 100	18	37N17	84w40	5:38:40
Albright 69	15	37N28	84w30	5:38:00
Alcalde 100	18	37N03	84w33	5:38:12
Alcorn 55	15	37N26	84w00	5:36:00
Alexandria 19	10	38N58	84w23	5:37:32
Alger 26	15	37N09	83w46	5:35:04
Alhambra 101	10	38N31	83w50	5:35:20
Aliceton 11	15	37N35	85w03	5:40:12
Allais 97	45	37N15	83w11	5:32:44
Allegre 110	1	36N56	87w12	5:48:48
Allen 36	10	37N37	82w43	5:30:52
Allendale 44	1	37N20	85w33	5:42:12
Allen Springs 2	1	36N53	86w21	5:45:24
Allensville 110	1	36N43	87w04	5:48:16
Allock 97	45	37N13	83w04	5:32:16
Almo 18	1	36N42	88w16	5:53:04
Almo Heights 18	1	36N42	88w16	5:53:04
Alonzo 2	1	36N39	86w16	5:45:04
Alpha 27	1	36N46	85w01	5:40:04
Alpine 100	18	36N55	84w31	5:38:04
Alta 92	1	37N34	86w44	5:46:56
Alton 3	43	38N05	84w56	5:39:44
Altro 13	15	37N23	83w23	5:33:32
Alumbaugh 33	26	37N42	83w58	5:35:52
Alum Springs 11	15	37N35	84w48	5:39:12
Alva 48	14	36N44	83w25	5:33:40
Alvaton 114	1	36N53	86w21	5:45:24
Amandaville 29	1	36N51	85w20	5:41:20
Amba 36	10	37N32	82w38	5:30:32

Amburgey 60 15 37N15 83w00 5:32:00
Ammie 26 15 37N09 83w46 5:35:04
Ammons 14 1 37N55 86w31 5:46:04
Amos 2 1 36N42 86w04 5:44:16
Anchorage 56 67 38N16 85w34 5:42:16
Anco 60 15 37N15 83w03 5:32:12
Anderson 71 1 37N05 86w51 5:47:24
Andyville 82 48 37N59 86w19 5:45:16
Anna 114 1 37N06 86w28 5:45:52
Anneta 43 1 37N22 86w15 5:45:00
Annville 55 15 37N19 83w58 5:35:52
Ano 100 18 37N08 84w22 5:37:28
Ansel 100 18 37N11 84w38 5:38:32
Antepast 26 15 37N16 83w39 5:34:36
Anthoston 51 1 37N46 87w32 5:50:08
Antioch Mills 49 35 38N31 84w23 5:37:32
Anton 54 1 37N21 87w24 5:49:36
Apex 24 1 37N11 87w23 5:49:32
Apex 67 15 37N10 82w47 5:31:08
Appliance Park 56
65 38N10 85w39 5:42:36
Arch 47 48 37N42 86w08 5:44:32
Argentum 45 10 38N33 82w58 5:31:52
Argillite 45 10 38N29 82w50 5:31:20
Argo 98 10 37N29 82w04 5:28:16
Argyle 23 48 37N14 84w45 5:39:00
Arjay 7 14 36N49 83w37 5:34:28
Ark 7 14 36N44 83w48 5:35:12
Arkansas Creek 36
10 37N34 82w45 5:31:00
Arkle 61 14 36N57 84w00 5:36:00
Arlington 20 1 36N49 88w54 5:55:36
Arlington 76 30 37N45 84w18 5:37:12
Arlington Heights 37
19 38N12 84w52 5:39:28
Arnett 95 15 37N29 83w40 5:34:40
Arnold 92 1 37N27 86w41 5:46:44
Arrington Corner 46
1 37N54 86w45 5:47:00
Arrowood 13 15 37N27 83w27 5:33:48
Artemus 61 14 36N50 83w51 5:35:24
Arthur 31 1 37N11 86w19 5:45:16
Arthurmable 77 10 37N37 82w58 5:31:52
Artville 83 15 37N57 83w29 5:33:56
Arvel 65 15 37N26 84w00 5:36:00
Ary 97 45 37N23 83w09 5:32:36
Ashbyburg 54 1 37N29 87w30 5:50:00
Ashcamp 98 10 37N15 82w28 5:29:52
Asher 66 15 37N03 83w24 5:33:36
Ashers Fork 26 15 37N01 83w38 5:34:32
Ashland 10 10 38N28 82w38 5:30:32
Ashlock 29 1 36N33 85w30 5:42:00
Ashville 56 65 38N10 85w36 5:42:24
Askin 14 1 37N38 86w43 5:46:52
Asphalt 31 1 37N11 86w19 5:45:16
Atchison 109 48 37N21 85w21 5:41:24
Athens 34 27 37N57 84w22 5:37:28
Athertonville 62 56 37N38 85w36 5:42:24
Athol 65 15 37N33 83w34 5:34:16
Atkinstown 55 15 37N24 83w56 5:35:44
Atlanta 63 36 37N08 84w05 5:36:20
Atoka 11 24 37N39 84w46 5:39:04
Atwood 59 10 38N58 84w34 5:38:16
Auburn 71 1 36N52 86w43 5:46:52
Audubon Park 56 66 38N12 85w44 5:42:56
Augusta 12 10 38N47 84w00 5:36:00
Ault 32 15 38N18 83w11 5:32:44
Aurora 79 1 36N47 88w09 5:52:36
Austerlitz 9 29 38N13 84w15 5:37:00
Austin 5 1 36N50 86w01 5:44:04
Auxier 36 10 37N44 82w46 5:31:04
Avawam 97 45 37N13 83w17 5:33:08
Avena 49 20 38N23 84w17 5:37:08
Avoca 56 67 38N15 85w34 5:42:16
Avondale 73 1 37N03 88w37 5:54:28
Avondale Heights 73
1 37N03 88w37 5:54:28
Axtel 14 1 37N39 86w28 5:45:52
Ayers 118 14 36N44 84w10 5:36:40
Backusburg 18 1 36N42 88w24 5:53:36
Bagdad 106 48 38N16 85w03 5:40:12
Bailey Creek 48 14 36N52 83w12 5:32:48
Bailey Mine 10 10 38N20 82w46 5:31:04
Baileys Branch 86 1 36N39 85w38 5:42:32
Baileys Switch 61
14 36N54 83w53 5:35:32
Bainbridge 24 1 36N58 87w42 5:50:48
Baizetown 92 1 37N27 86w41 5:46:44
Baker Branch 58 10 37N51 82w46 5:31:04
Bakerton 29 1 36N51 85w20 5:41:20
Bald Eagle 6 15 38N12 83w56 5:35:44
Bald Hill 35 15 38N25 83w47 5:35:08
Bald Knob 37 15 38N16 84w56 5:39:44
Baldrock 63 36 37N08 84w05 5:36:20
Baldwin 76 30 37N45 84w18 5:37:12
Balkan 7 14 36N46 83w33 5:34:12
Ballardsville 93 57 38N19 85w28 5:41:52
Balltown 90 48 37N44 85w30 5:42:00
Baltimore 42 1 36N44 88w38 5:54:32
Bancroft 56 67 38N17 85w35 5:42:20
Bancroft 89 1 37N11 87w23 5:49:32
Bandana 4 1 37N09 88w56 5:55:44
Bandy 100 18 37N17 84w40 5:38:40
Bangor 103 15 38N11 83w26 5:33:44
Bank Lick 59 13 38N52 84w37 5:38:28
Banner 36 10 37N36 82w42 5:30:48
Banock 16 1 37N27 86w41 5:46:44
Baptist 119 15 37N45 83w33 5:34:12
Barbourmeade 56 65 38N18 85w37 5:42:28
Barbourville 61 14 36N52 83w53 5:35:32
Barcreek 26 15 37N16 83w39 5:34:36
Bardo 48 14 36N45 83w22 5:33:28
Bardstown 90 62 37N49 85w28 5:41:52
Bardstown Junction 15
50 38N00 85w43 5:42:52
Bardwell 20 1 36N52 89w01 5:56:04

Bardwell West 20 1 36N51 89w03 5:56:12
Bark Camp 118 14 36N57 84w06 5:36:24
Barlow 4 1 37N03 89w03 5:56:12
Barnesburg 100 18 37N06 84w36 5:38:24
Barnes Store 17 1 37N07 87w53 5:51:32
Barnett Creek 1 1 37N16 85w03 5:40:12
Barnetts Creek 58
10 37N50 82w53 5:31:32
Barnrock 58 10 37N56 82w53 5:31:32
Barnsley 54 1 37N20 87w30 5:50:00
Barnyard 61 14 36N50 83w46 5:35:04
Barrallton 15 50 38N00 85w43 5:42:52
Barren River 114 7 37N00 86w25 5:45:40
Barridge 97 45 37N12 83w02 5:32:08
Barrier 116 1 36N50 84w51 5:39:24
Barterville 91 37 38N19 84w02 5:36:08
Barwick 13 15 37N23 83w23 5:33:32
Bascom 32 15 38N05 83w08 5:32:32
Basil 1 1 37N04 85w25 5:41:40
Basin Springs 14 1 37N53 86w17 5:45:08
Baskett 51 1 37N52 87w28 5:49:52
Bass 23 48 37N17 85w06 5:40:24
Bath 60 15 37N18 82w55 5:31:40
Battle Run 35 15 38N26 83w52 5:35:28
Battletown 82 48 38N04 86w18 5:45:12
Baughman 61 14 36N52 83w48 5:35:12
Baughman Heights 11
24 37N39 84w46 5:39:04
Baxter 48 14 36N52 83w20 5:33:20
Bayfork 114 1 36N53 86w21 5:45:24
Bays 13 15 37N39 83w15 5:33:00
Bays Branch 36 10 37N47 82w48 5:31:12
Bealers Knob 75 1 37N32 87w16 5:49:04
Beals 51 1 37N51 87w21 5:49:24
Bear Branch 66 15 37N10 83w33 5:34:12
Beartown 32 15 38N10 83w08 5:32:32
Bearville 60 15 37N22 83w04 5:32:16
Bear Wallow 5 6 37N08 85w58 5:43:52
Beattyville 65 15 37N35 83w42 5:34:48
Beaumont 85 1 36N53 85w39 5:42:36
Beauty 80 10 37N50 82w26 5:29:44
Beaver 36 10 37N21 82w48 5:31:12
Beaver Bottom 98 10 37N19 82w21 5:29:24
Beaver Dam 92 1 37N24 86w52 5:47:28
Beaver Junction 36
10 37N37 82w43 5:30:52
Beaverlick 8 10 38N53 84w42 5:38:48
Beckamridge 104 1 37N04 85w06 5:40:24
Becknerville 25 32 38N00 84w11 5:36:44
Becks Store 29 1 36N58 85w26 5:41:44
Beckton 5 6 37N00 85w55 5:43:40
Beda 92 1 37N31 86w57 5:47:48
Bedford 112 54 38N36 85w19 5:41:16
Bee 50 1 37N18 86w04 5:44:16
Beech 13 15 37N23 83w23 5:33:32
Beech 48 14 36N47 83w20 5:33:20
Beechburg 35 15 38N27 83w38 5:34:32
Beech Creek 89 1 37N11 87w03 5:48:12
Beech Grove 15 48 37N50 85w44 5:42:56
Beech Grove 75 1 37N37 87w24 5:49:36
Beechland 71 1 36N59 86w57 5:47:48
Beechmont 89 1 37N10 87w20 5:49:20
Beechville 85 1 36N59 85w37 5:42:28
Beechwood 94 15 38N25 84w45 5:39:00
Beechwood Village 56
65 38N15 85w38 5:42:32
Beechy 45 10 38N43 82w58 5:31:52
Beelerton 53 1 36N30 88w53 5:55:32
Bee Lick 100 18 37N28 84w30 5:38:00
Bee Spring 31 1 37N17 86w17 5:45:08
Beetle 22 15 38N20 82w57 5:31:48
Bel-air 25 32 38N00 84w11 5:36:44
Belcher 98 10 37N21 82w22 5:29:28
Belcourt 117 1 37N29 87w30 5:50:00
Belfry 98 10 37N37 82w16 5:29:04
Belknap 119 15 37N44 83w20 5:33:20
Belknap Beach 98 49 38N21 85w37 5:42:28
Bell City 32 15 38N05 83w08 5:32:32
Bell City 42 1 36N31 88w30 5:54:00
Bellefonte 45 10 38N30 82w41 5:30:44
Bellemeade 56 65 38N15 85w36 5:42:24
Bellepoint 37 19 38N12 84w52 5:39:28
Belleview 8 10 39N02 84w44 5:38:56
Bellevue 19 68 39N07 84w29 5:37:56
Bellewood 56 65 38N16 85w40 5:42:40
Bell Farm 74 15 36N42 84w29 5:37:56
Bells Run 92 1 37N41 86w52 5:47:28
Bellview 37 19 38N12 84w52 5:39:28
Bellwood 90 48 37N48 85w28 5:41:52
Belmont 15 48 37N54 85w43 5:42:52
Belmont 49 20 38N23 84w17 5:37:08
Belton 89 1 37N10 87w02 5:48:08
Bengal 109 48 37N21 85w21 5:41:24
Benham 48 14 36N58 82w57 5:31:48
Benito 48 14 36N54 83w12 5:32:48
Bennettstown 24 1 36N44 87w34 5:50:16
Benson 37 19 38N12 84w52 5:39:28
Bent 100 18 37N06 84w36 5:38:24
Benton 79 3 36N52 88w21 5:53:24
Berea 76 42 37N34 84w17 5:37:08
Berkeley 20 1 36N47 89w01 5:56:04
Berlin 12 10 38N48 84w13 5:36:52
Bernice 26 15 37N13 83w47 5:35:08
Bernstadt 63 15 37N09 84w12 5:36:48
Berry 49 35 38N31 84w23 5:37:32
Berrys Lick 16 1 37N04 86w45 5:47:00
Berrytown 56 67 38N15 85w34 5:42:16
Berry West 49 35 38N28 84w26 5:37:44
Bertha 61 14 36N57 84w00 5:36:00
Bethanna 77 10 37N47 83w11 5:32:44
Bethany 119 15 37N39 83w28 5:33:52
Bethel 6 15 38N15 83w52 5:35:28
Bethel 57 28 37N53 84w34 5:38:16
Bethelridge 23 48 37N14 84w45 5:39:00
Bethesda 116 1 36N50 84w51 5:39:24
Bethlehem 52 48 38N24 85w04 5:40:16

Betsey 116 1 36N54 84w45 5:39:00
Betsy Layne 36 10 37N34 82w38 5:30:32
Beulah 53 1 36N48 88w47 5:55:08
Beulah 54 1 37N16 87w41 5:50:44
Beulah Heights 74
15 36N48 84w26 5:37:44
Beverly 7 14 36N56 83w32 5:34:08
Beverly Hills 11 24 37N39 84w46 5:39:04
Bevier 89 1 37N13 87w03 5:48:12
Bevinsville 36 10 37N22 82w43 5:30:52
Bewleyville 14 1 37N50 86w15 5:45:00
Biddle 105 25 38N13 84w33 5:38:12
Big Bear Creek 79 1 37N10 87w02 5:48:08
Big Bone 8 10 38N57 84w41 5:38:44
Big Branch 98 10 37N19 82w21 5:29:24
Big Clifty 43 1 37N33 86w09 5:44:36
Big Creek 26 15 37N10 83w34 5:34:16
Big Fork 66 15 37N04 83w13 5:32:52
Biggs 98 10 37N25 82w16 5:29:04
Bighill 76 15 37N33 84w13 5:36:52
Big Laurel 48 14 36N59 83w13 5:32:52
Big Ready 31 1 37N14 86w26 5:45:44
Big Rock 66 15 37N03 83w12 5:32:48
Big Sandy Junction 10
10 38N25 82w36 5:30:24
Big Shoal 98 10 37N29 82w31 5:30:04
Big Spring 14 48 37N48 86w09 5:44:36
Bigstone 32 15 38N05 83w08 5:32:32
Big Woods 83 15 37N55 83w31 5:34:04
Billows 102 15 37N06 84w36 5:38:24
Bilvia 67 15 37N08 82w46 5:31:04
Bimble 61 14 36N53 83w50 5:35:20
Birdie 3 43 38N02 84w54 5:39:36
Birdsville 70 1 37N13 88w27 5:53:48
Birk City 30 1 37N45 87w07 5:48:28
Birmingham 79 1 37N10 87w02 5:48:08
Biscayne 67 15 37N14 82w46 5:31:04
Black Bottom 48 14 36N55 83w06 5:32:24
Black Diamond 89 1 37N13 87w03 5:48:12
Blackey 67 15 37N08 82w58 5:31:52
Blackford 117 1 37N27 87w56 5:51:44
Black Gnat 109 48 37N21 85w21 5:41:24
Black Gold 31 1 37N15 86w17 5:45:08
Black Jack 107 1 36N43 86w35 5:46:20
Blackjoe 48 14 36N51 83w19 5:33:16
Black Mountain 48
14 36N51 83w10 5:32:40
Black Rock 43 1 36N40 87w26 5:49:44
Blacks Ferry 14 36N42 84w29 5:37:56
Black Snake 7 14 36N44 83w25 5:33:40
Blackwater 63 15 37N05 83w56 5:35:44
Blackwell 52 48 38N20 85w03 5:40:12
Bladeston 12 10 38N41 84w04 5:36:16
Blaine 64 10 38N02 82w55 5:31:40
Blairs Mills 88 15 38N05 83w18 5:33:12
Blake 95 15 37N29 83w40 5:34:40
Blanche 7 14 36N48 83w39 5:34:36
Blanchet 41 10 38N30 84w34 5:38:16
Blandville 4 1 36N57 88w58 5:55:52
Blaze 88 15 38N01 83w20 5:33:20
Bledsoe 48 14 36N55 83w21 5:33:24
Blevins 64 10 38N02 82w50 5:31:20
Blincoe 115 56 37N38 85w24 5:41:36
Bliss 1 1 37N06 85w18 5:41:12
Bloomfield 90 56 37N55 85w19 5:41:16
Bloomingdale 25 32 38N00 84w11 5:36:44
Bloomington 43 1 37N29 86w18 5:45:12
Bloomington 77 10 37N49 83w10 5:32:40
Bloss 102 35 37N21 84w20 5:37:20
Blowing Spring 44 6 37N16 85w30 5:42:00
Blowing Springs 50
1 37N18 86w04 5:44:16
Blue Bank 35 15 38N25 83w47 5:35:08
Blue Diamond 97 45 37N17 83w13 5:32:52
Bluehole 26 15 37N06 83w45 5:35:00
Blue John 100 18 36N55 84w31 5:38:04
Blue Level 114 1 36N55 86w34 5:46:16
Blue Lick Springs 91
37 38N19 84w02 5:36:08
Blue Moon 36 10 37N32 82w45 5:31:00
Blue Ridge Manor 56
67 38N15 85w34 5:42:16
Blue River 36 10 37N37 82w51 5:31:24
Blue Spring 111 1 36N52 87w50 5:51:20
Bluestone 103 15 38N11 83w26 5:33:44
Blue Water Estates 111
1 36N52 87w50 5:51:20
Bluff Boom 44 6 37N16 85w30 5:42:00
Bluff City 51 8 37N49 87w37 5:50:28
Blythe 86 1 36N39 85w38 5:42:32
Board Tree 98 10 37N34 82w09 5:28:36
Boat 97 45 37N15 83w11 5:32:44
Boaz 42 1 36N53 88w38 5:54:32
Bobbs 58 10 37N49 82w46 5:31:04
Bobs Creek 48 14 36N47 83w14 5:32:56
Bobtown 76 42 37N35 84w17 5:37:08
Bohon 84 15 37N49 84w55 5:39:40
Boiling Spring 114
7 37N00 86w25 5:45:40
Boldman 98 10 37N29 82w31 5:30:04
Boles 86 1 36N42 85w42 5:42:48
Boltsfork 10 10 38N20 82w46 5:31:04
Bolyn 60 15 37N29 82w50 5:31:20
Bon 118 14 36N44 84w10 5:36:40
Bon Air Hills 37 19 38N12 84w52 5:39:28
Bonanza 36 10 37N41 82w46 5:31:04
Bonayer 5 6 37N06 86w03 5:44:12
Bond 55 15 37N19 83w59 5:35:56
Bondurant 38 1 36N31 89w19 5:57:16
Bondville 84 15 37N55 84w52 5:39:28
Boneyville 69 15 37N32 84w40 5:38:40
Bon Haven 25 32 38N00 84w11 5:36:44
Bonnieville 50 1 37N23 85w54 5:43:36
Bonny 88 15 37N52 83w21 5:33:24
Bonnyman 97 45 37N18 83w13 5:32:52
Booker 115 48 37N41 85w13 5:40:52

KENTUCKY

Boone 102 15 37n31 84w19 5:37:16
Boone Heights 61 14 36n52 83w53 5:35:32
Boonesboro 25 15 37n56 84w16 5:37:04
Booneville 95 15 37n29 83w41 5:34:44
Boons Camp 58 10 37n50 82w42 5:30:48
Bordley 113 1 37n29 87w50 5:51:20
Boreing 63 15 37n02 84w17 5:37:08
Boston 16 1 37n05 86w51 5:47:24
Boston 90 48 37n47 85w40 5:42:40
Boston 96 10 38n47 84w22 5:37:28
Botland 90 48 37n48 85w28 5:41:52
Botto 26 15 37n05 83w42 5:34:48
Bourbon 100 18 37n06 84w36 5:38:24
Bourne 40 15 37n43 84w37 5:38:28
Bouty 118 14 36n44 84w10 5:36:40
Bow 29 1 36n46 85w21 5:41:24
Bowen 99 15 37n51 83w46 5:35:04
Bowling Green 114 7 36n59 86w27 5:45:48
Boyce 114 1 36n53 86w21 5:45:24
Boyd 49 35 38n31 84w23 5:37:32
Boyds Crossing 44 1 37n20 85w33 5:42:12
Boydsville 42 1 36n38 88w36 5:54:24
Bracht 59 10 38n47 84w36 5:38:24
Bradford 12 10 38n48 84w13 5:36:52
Bradfordsville 78 48 37n30 85w09 5:40:36
Bradley 77 10 37n45 83w04 5:32:16
Bradshaw 55 15 37n24 83w56 5:35:44
Brady 103 15 38n11 83w26 5:33:44
Brainard 36 10 37n45 83w04 5:32:16
Bramlett 44 6 37n16 85w30 5:42:00
Brandenburg 82 64 38n00 86w10 5:44:40
Brandy Keg 36 10 37n41 82w46 5:31:04
Brassfield 76 15 37n44 84w07 5:36:28
Bratton 101 10 38n32 84w02 5:36:08
Braxton 84 43 37n46 84w51 5:39:24
Brazil 55 15 37n26 84w00 5:36:00
Breckinridge 49 20 38n23 84w17 5:37:08
Breeding 1 1 36n58 85w26 5:41:44
Bremen 89 1 37n22 87w13 5:48:52
Brent 19 68 39n05 84w27 5:37:48
Brentsville 9 29 38n13 84w15 5:37:00
Brentwood 54 1 37n20 87w30 5:50:00
Brewers 79 1 36n51 88w21 5:53:24
Briartown 115 48 37n41 85w13 5:40:52
Briarwood 56 67 38n17 85w35 5:42:20
Briarwood Manor 114 7 37n00 86w25 5:45:40
Bridgeport 37 15 38n09 84w55 5:39:40
Bridge Street 73 1 37n03 88w37 5:54:28
Briensburg 79 1 36n54 88w19 5:53:16
Brightshade 26 15 37n09 83w46 5:35:04
Brinegar 22 15 38n18 83w11 5:32:44
Brinkley 60 15 37n19 82w57 5:31:48
Bristow 114 1 37n03 86w22 5:45:28
Britmark 110 1 36n48 87w09 5:48:36
Broad Bottom 98 10 37n32 82w36 5:30:24
Broadfields 56 65 38n14 85w39 5:42:36
Broad Ford 43 1 37n30 86w13 5:44:52
Broadwell 49 20 38n23 84w17 5:37:08
Brock 63 36 37n08 84w05 5:36:20
Brodhead 102 23 37n24 84w25 5:37:40
Bromley 59 68 39n04 84w35 5:38:20
Bromley 94 15 38n40 84w54 5:39:36
Bromo 102 35 37n21 84w20 5:37:20
Bronston 100 18 36n59 84w37 5:38:28
Brooklyn 16 1 37n18 86w35 5:46:20
Brooks 15 48 38n04 85w43 5:42:52
Brookside 48 14 36n52 83w15 5:33:00
Brooksville 12 10 38n41 84w04 5:36:16
Broughtentown 69 15 37n28 84w30 5:38:00
Browder 89 1 37n12 87w02 5:48:08
Brownies Creek 7 14 36n46 83w35 5:34:20
Browning 114 1 36n55 86w34 5:46:16
Brownings Corner 96 10 38n40 84w20 5:37:20
Browningtown 15 50 38n00 85w43 5:42:52
Brownsboro 98 49 38n16 85w40 5:42:40
Brownsboro Farm 56 65 38n18 85w36 5:42:24
Brownsboro Village 56 65 38n15 85w39 5:42:36
Browns Crossroads 27 1 36n41 85w08 5:40:32
Browns Ford 2 1 36n43 85w58 5:43:52
Browns Fork 97 45 37n14 83w14 5:32:56
Browns Grove 18 1 36n36 88w19 5:53:16
Browns Valley 30 1 37n36 87w07 5:48:28
Brownsville 31 1 37n12 86w16 5:45:04
Brownsville 38 1 36n34 89w11 5:56:44
Brownwood Manor 30 1 37n45 87w07 5:48:28
Bruin 32 15 38n11 83w01 5:32:04
Brutus 26 15 37n15 83w35 5:34:20
Bryan 104 1 36n57 85w09 5:40:36
Bryants 61 14 36n47 83w56 5:35:44
Bryantsville 40 15 37n44 84w39 5:38:36
Buchanan 64 10 38n15 82w37 5:30:28
Buck Creek 95 15 37n29 83w40 5:34:40
Buckettown 76 42 37n35 84w17 5:37:08
Buckeye 40 15 37n37 84w35 5:38:20
Buck Grove 82 48 37n56 86w11 5:44:44
Buckhorn 97 45 37n21 83w28 5:33:52
Buckingham 36 10 37n22 82w44 5:30:56
Buckner 98 59 38n23 85w26 5:41:44
Buechel 56 65 38n12 85w39 5:42:36
Buel 75 1 37n32 87w16 5:49:04
Buena Vista 40 15 37n37 84w35 5:38:20
Buena Vista 49 20 38n23 84w17 5:37:08
Buena Vista 68 10 38n36 83w19 5:33:16
Buena Vista 79 1 37n01 88w18 5:53:12
Buffalo 62 48 37n31 85w42 5:42:48
Buffalo 111 1 36n53 87w40 5:50:40
Buford 92 1 37n36 87w07 5:48:28
Bug 27 1 36n41 85w08 5:40:32
Bugtussle 86 1 36n38 85w48 5:43:12
Bulan 97 45 37n18 83w09 5:32:36
Bullittsville 8 10 39n05 84w44 5:38:56
Bummer 102 15 37n22 84w16 5:37:04
Buras 14 1 37n44 86w15 5:45:00
Burdick 109 48 37n21 85w21 5:41:24
Burdine 67 15 37n11 82w38 5:30:32
Burfield 116 1 36n46 84w46 5:39:04
Burg 88 15 37n46 83w18 5:33:12
Burgin 84 16 37n45 84w46 5:39:04
Burke 32 15 38n06 83w03 5:32:12
Burkes Spring 78 56 37n38 85w24 5:41:36
Burkesville 29 1 36n48 85w22 5:41:28
Burkhart 119 15 37n42 83w16 5:33:04
Burk Hollow 118 14 36n35 84w08 5:36:32
Burlington 8 10 39n02 84w43 5:38:52
Burna 70 1 37n15 88w22 5:53:28
Burnaugh 10 10 38n25 82w36 5:30:24
Burnetta 100 18 37n04 84w45 5:39:00
Burning Fork 77 10 37n44 83w01 5:32:04
Burning Springs 26 15 37n15 83w49 5:35:16
Burnside 100 31 36n59 84w36 5:38:24
Burnwell 98 10 37n38 82w13 5:28:52
Burr 102 35 37n21 84w20 5:37:20
Burton 36 10 37n22 82w43 5:30:52
Burtonville 68 10 38n46 83w45 5:35:00
Bush 63 15 37n06 83w58 5:35:52
Bushong 86 1 36n42 85w42 5:42:48
Bushtown 84 43 37n46 84w51 5:39:24
Buskirk 88 15 37n49 83w26 5:33:44
Buskirk 98 10 37n37 82w10 5:28:40
Busy 97 45 37n17 83w17 5:33:08
Butchertown 23 48 37n19 84w56 5:39:44
Butler 37 10 38n47 84w22 5:37:28
Butler 96 10 38n47 84w22 5:37:28
Buttenberry 75 1 37n26 87w09 5:48:36
Butterfly 97 45 37n17 83w16 5:33:04
Buttimer Hill 37 19 38n12 84w52 5:39:28
Bybee 76 15 37n44 84w07 5:36:28
Bypro 36 10 37n22 82w42 5:30:48
Cabell 116 1 36n50 84w51 5:39:24
Caddo 96 10 38n40 84w20 5:37:20
Cadiz 111 1 36n52 87w50 5:51:20
Cains Store 100 18 37n08 84w50 5:39:20
Cairo 51 1 37n42 87w39 5:50:36
Caldwell Manor 11 24 37n39 84w46 5:39:04
Caleast 76 30 37n45 84w18 5:37:12
Caledonia 111 1 36n53 87w40 5:50:40
Calf Creek 80 10 37n52 82w32 5:30:08
Calhoun 75 4 37n32 87w16 5:49:04
California 19 10 38n54 84w18 5:37:12
Callaboose 119 15 37n45 83w33 5:34:12
Callaway 7 14 36n47 83w34 5:34:16
Calvary 78 63 37n31 85w16 5:41:04
Calvert City 79 1 37n02 88w21 5:53:24
Calvin 7 14 36n44 83w38 5:34:32
Camargo 87 15 37n58 83w52 5:35:28
Cambridge 56 65 38n13 85w37 5:42:28
Cambridge Shores 79 1 37n01 88w18 5:53:12
Cambridge Village 56 65 38n13 85w37 5:42:28
Camelia 73 1 37n05 88w45 5:55:00
Camelot 56 67 38n17 85w35 5:42:20
Campbellsburg 52 54 38n33 85w07 5:40:28
Campbellsville 109 48 37n21 85w20 5:41:20
Camp Dick Robinson 40 15 37n37 84w35 5:38:20
Camp Dix 68 10 38n29 83w17 5:33:08
Camp Ground 63 15 37n02 83w58 5:35:52
Camp Kennedy 40 15 37n37 84w35 5:38:20
Camp Nelson 40 15 37n37 84w35 5:38:20
Camp Pleasant 37 15 38n16 84w41 5:38:44
Campsprings 19 10 39n00 84w22 5:37:28
Camp Taylor 56 66 38n11 85w43 5:42:52
Campton 119 15 37n44 83w33 5:34:12
Canada 98 10 37n37 82w20 5:29:20
Canby 94 15 38n30 84w34 5:38:16
Cane Creek 13 15 37n33 83w22 5:33:28
Cane Creek 63 15 37n05 83w56 5:35:44
Cane Valley 1 1 37n11 85w19 5:41:16
Caney 88 15 38n04 83w21 5:33:24
Caneyville 43 1 37n26 86w29 5:45:56
Canmer 50 1 37n17 85w46 5:43:04
Cannel City 88 15 37n47 83w17 5:33:08
Cannon 61 14 36n55 83w51 5:35:24
Cannonsburg 10 10 38n23 82w42 5:30:48
Canoe 13 15 37n25 83w29 5:33:56
Canton 111 1 36n48 87w58 5:51:52
Canton Heights Estates 111 1 36n48 87w58 5:51:52
Canyon Falls 65 15 37n35 83w43 5:34:52
Capital Heights 37 19 38n12 84w52 5:39:28
Capito 7 14 36n37 83w44 5:34:56
Carbondale 54 1 37n10 87w41 5:50:44
Carbon Glow 67 15 37n09 82w58 5:31:52
Carcassonne 67 15 37n10 82w59 5:31:56
Carden 5 6 37n00 85w55 5:43:40
Cardinal 7 14 36n47 83w31 5:34:04
Cardwell 115 48 37n49 85w02 5:40:08
Carl 24 1 36n48 87w09 5:48:36
Carlisle 91 37 38n19 84w01 5:36:04
Carntown 96 10 38n50 84w15 5:37:00
Carpenter 118 14 36n52 83w53 5:35:32
Carr Creek 60 15 37n13 82w57 5:31:48
Carr Fork 60 15 37n15 82w58 5:31:52
Carrie 60 15 37n20 83w02 5:32:08
Carrollton 21 38 38n41 85w11 5:40:44
Carrs 68 10 38n36 83w19 5:33:16
Carrsville 70 1 37n24 88w22 5:53:28
Carter 22 15 38n26 83w08 5:32:32
Carthage 19 10 38n56 84w18 5:37:12
Cartwright 27 1 36n41 85w08 5:40:32
Carver 77 10 37n39 83w03 5:32:12
Cary 7 14 36n46 83w42 5:34:48
Casey 16 1 37n14 86w41 5:46:44
Casey Creek 1 1 37n14 85w09 5:40:36
Caseyville 113 1 37n33 87w59 5:51:56
Cash 50 1 37n28 85w54 5:43:36
Casky 24 1 36n49 87w26 5:49:44
Cassaday 114 7 37n00 86w25 5:45:40
Catalpa 64 10 38n25 82w36 5:30:24
Catawba 96 10 38n40 84w20 5:37:20
Catherine 104 1 37n08 84w55 5:39:40
Catlettsburg 10 10 38n25 82w36 5:30:24
Catron Creek 48 14 36n48 83w20 5:33:20
Caudell 67 15 37n07 82w49 5:31:16
Causey 66 15 37n11 83w18 5:33:12
Cave City 5 6 37n08 85w58 5:43:52
Cavehill 114 1 36n55 86w34 5:46:16
Cavelawn 37 19 38n12 84w52 5:39:28
Cave Ridge 85 1 36n59 85w37 5:42:28
Cave Spring 71 1 36n51 86w53 5:47:32
Cawood 48 14 36n47 83w14 5:32:56
Cayce 38 1 36n30 88w53 5:55:32
Cecil 73 1 37n03 88w37 5:54:28
Cecilia 47 48 37n40 85w57 5:43:48
Cedar Bluff 17 1 37n05 87w51 5:51:24
Cedarcrest 116 1 36n59 84w54 5:39:36
Cedar Flat 85 1 36n59 85w37 5:42:28
Cedar Grove 100 18 37n06 84w36 5:38:24
Cedar Grove 110 1 36n55 87w06 5:48:24
Cedar Spring 31 6 37n06 86w03 5:44:12
Cedar Springs 2 6 36n45 86w11 5:44:44
Cedarville 98 10 37n19 82w21 5:29:24
Center 85 1 37n06 85w41 5:42:44
Centerfield 93 57 38n19 85w28 5:41:52
Center Point 86 1 36n42 85w42 5:42:48
Centertown 92 1 37n25 87w01 5:48:04
Centerview 14 1 37n39 86w17 5:45:08
Central City 89 1 37n18 87w07 5:48:28
Centreville 9 25 38n13 84w33 5:38:12
Ceralvo 92 1 37n20 87w00 5:48:00
Cerulean 111 1 36n58 87w43 5:50:52
Cerulean Springs 111 1 36n56 87w48 5:51:12
Chad 48 14 36n59 82w59 5:31:56
Chalybeate 31 1 37n03 86w13 5:44:52
Chambers 46 1 37n54 86w45 5:47:00
Chance 1 1 37n06 85w18 5:41:12
Chandlers Chapel 71 1 36n52 86w43 5:46:52
Chandlerville 58 10 37n53 82w48 5:31:12
Chapel Hill 2 1 36n43 86w18 5:45:12
Chaplin 90 48 37n54 85w13 5:40:52
Chapman 64 10 38n07 82w36 5:30:24
Chappell 66 15 37n01 83w21 5:33:24
Charleston 54 1 37n10 87w41 5:50:44
Charley 64 10 38n07 82w36 5:30:24
Charters 68 10 38n34 83w26 5:33:44
Chatham 12 10 38n46 84w00 5:36:00
Chavies 97 45 37n21 83w21 5:33:24
Chenoa 7 14 36n41 83w51 5:35:24
Chenowee 13 15 37n33 83w22 5:33:28
Cherokee 56 66 38n13 85w41 5:42:44
Cherokee 64 10 38n05 82w50 5:31:20
Cherry 18 1 36n36 88w19 5:53:16
Cherrywood 56 65 38n16 85w39 5:42:36
Cherrywood Village 56 65 38n15 85w39 5:42:36
Chesnutburg 26 15 37n17 83w48 5:35:12
Chestnut Gap 95 15 37n29 83w40 5:34:40
Chestnut Grove 106 51 38n13 85w14 5:40:56
Chevrolet 48 14 36n49 83w16 5:33:04
Chicken Bristle 69 15 37n32 84w40 5:38:40
Chilton 48 37n28 84w59 5:39:56
Chloe 98 10 37n29 82w31 5:30:04
Choatville 37 19 38n12 84w52 5:39:28
Christianburg 106 48 38n17 85w04 5:40:16
Christine 1 1 37n06 85w18 5:41:12
Christopher 97 45 37n15 83w11 5:32:44
Christy 103 15 38n11 83w26 5:33:44
Church 43 1 37n29 86w18 5:45:12
Church Hill 24 1 36n51 87w30 5:50:00
Cinda 66 15 37n06 83w18 5:33:12
Cisco 77 10 37n50 83w07 5:32:28
Cisselville 115 48 37n41 85w13 5:40:52
Clare 2 1 36n43 86w35 5:46:20
Clarence 100 18 37n17 84w40 5:38:40
Clark 56 65 38n11 85w28 5:41:52
Clark Hill 22 15 38n18 83w11 5:32:44
Clarksburg 68 10 38n36 83w19 5:33:16
Clarkson 43 1 37n30 86w13 5:44:52
Claryville 19 10 38n55 84w24 5:37:36
Claxton 17 1 37n10 87w41 5:50:44
Clay 117 1 37n29 87w51 5:51:24
Clay City 99 15 37n52 83w55 5:35:40
Clayhole 13 15 37n28 83w17 5:33:08
Claymour 110 1 36n48 87w09 5:48:36
Claypool 114 7 37n00 86w25 5:45:40
Claysville 49 15 38n32 84w02 5:36:08
Clay Village 106 48 38n12 85w07 5:40:28
Claywell 29 1 36n48 85w22 5:41:28
Clear Creek 7 14 36n46 83w42 5:34:48
Clear Creek Springs 7 14 36n46 83w42 5:34:48
Clearfield 103 15 38n07 83w27 5:33:48
Clear Run 92 1 37n27 86w54 5:47:36
Cleaton 89 1 37n15 87w06 5:48:24
Clementsville 23 48 37n20 85w03 5:40:12
Clemons 97 45 37n18 83w13 5:32:52
Cleopatra 75 1 37n32 87w16 5:49:04
Clermont 15 48 37n56 85w39 5:42:36
Cliff 36 10 37n41 82w46 5:31:04
Clifford 64 10 37n59 82w36 5:30:24
Clifton 11 24 37n39 84w46 5:39:04

Clifton 120	44	38N03	84w44	5:38:56
Clifton Mills 14	1	37N53	86w17	5:45:08
Clifty 110	1	37N00	87w09	5:48:36
Climax 102	15	37N28	84w13	5:36:52
Clinton 53	1	36N40	89w00	5:56:00
Clintonville 9	15	38N08	84w17	5:37:08
Clio 118	14	36N44	84w10	5:36:40
Closplint 48	14	36N54	83w04	5:32:16
Clover 48	14	36N51	83w15	5:33:00
Clover Bottom 55	15	37N30	84w09	5:36:36
Cloverdale 37	19	38N12	84w52	5:39:28
Cloverport 14	1	37N50	86w38	5:46:32
Clovertown 48	14	36N51	83w19	5:33:16
Cloyds Landing 29	1	36N42	85w22	5:41:28
Club House Heights 37	19	38N12	84w52	5:39:28
Clutts 48	14	36N58	82w57	5:31:48
Clyffeside 10	10	38N28	82w39	5:30:36
Coakley 44	1	37N20	85w33	5:42:12
Coalgood 48	14	36N49	83w15	5:33:00
Coal Run 98	10	37N32	82w33	5:30:12
Coalton 10	10	38N20	82w46	5:31:04
Cobb 17	1	36N59	87w47	5:51:08
Cobblers Knob 14	1	37N47	86w28	5:45:52
Cobhill 33	15	37N43	83w50	5:35:20
Coburg 1	6	37N16	85w30	5:42:00
Codyville 14	1	37N47	86w28	5:45:52
Coe 86	1	36N42	85w42	5:42:48
Cofer 85	1	36N59	85w37	5:42:28
Cogswell 103	15	38N11	83w26	5:33:44
Coiltown 54	1	37N23	87w39	5:50:36
Colby Hills 25	32	38N00	84w11	5:36:44
Coldiron 48	14	36N50	83w27	5:33:48
Cold Spring 19	10	39N01	84w26	5:37:44
Coldwater 18	1	36N36	88w19	5:53:16
Coleman 98	10	37N31	82w09	5:28:36
Colemansville 49	35	38N31	84w23	5:37:32
Coles Bend 5	1	37N03	86w13	5:44:52
Colesburg 47	48	37N47	85w47	5:43:08
Coletown 34	27	37N56	84w27	5:37:48
Colfax 35	15	38N13	83w38	5:34:32
College 76	42	37N35	84w17	5:37:08
College Campus 18	1	36N36	88w19	5:53:16
College Heights 114	7	37N00	86w25	5:45:40
College Hill 76	15	37N47	84w07	5:36:28
Collista 58	10	37N47	82w48	5:31:12
Colly 67	15	37N07	82w47	5:31:08
Colmar 7	14	36N40	83w39	5:34:36
Colo 100	18	37N06	84w36	5:38:24
Colonial Terrace 56	67	38N17	85w35	5:42:20
Colony 63	15	37N08	84w11	5:36:44
Colson 67	15	37N14	82w51	5:31:24
Columbia 1	1	37N06	85w18	5:41:12
Columbus 53	1	36N46	89w06	5:56:24
Colville 49	20	38N23	84w17	5:37:08
Combs 97	45	37N16	83w13	5:32:52
Comer 75	1	37N32	87w16	5:49:04
Concord 35	15	37N12	82w42	5:30:48
Concord 68	10	38N41	83w30	5:34:00
Concordia 82	48	38N04	86w26	5:45:44
Confederate 72	1	37N05	88w05	5:52:20
Confluence 66	15	37N16	83w23	5:33:32
Congleton 65	15	37N35	83w43	5:34:52
Conkling 95	15	37N29	83w40	5:34:40
Conley 77	10	37N45	82w59	5:31:56
Connersville 49	20	38N23	84w17	5:37:08
Conrard 100	18	37N06	84w36	5:38:24
Constantine 14	1	37N41	86w14	5:44:56
Conway 102	15	37N29	84w20	5:37:20
Cooktown 5	1	36N50	86w01	5:44:04
Cool Springs 92	1	37N18	86w53	5:47:32
Coon 98	10	37N29	82w31	5:30:04
Cooper 116	1	36N46	84w52	5:39:28
Co-Operative 74	15	36N42	84w37	5:38:28
Cooperstown 71	1	36N51	86w53	5:47:32
Coopersville 116	1	36N44	84w47	5:39:08
Copebranch 13	15	37N33	83w22	5:33:28
Coral Hill 5	6	37N00	85w55	5:43:40
Coral Ridge 56	65	38N06	85w45	5:43:00
Corbin 118	14	36N57	84w06	5:36:24
Cordell 64	10	38N02	82w50	5:31:20
Cordia 60	15	37N15	83w11	5:32:44
Cordova 41	10	38N30	84w34	5:38:16
Corinth 41	10	38N30	84w34	5:38:16
Corinth 71	1	36N51	86w53	5:47:32
Cork 85	1	36N59	85w37	5:42:28
Corn Creek 112	48	38N36	85w19	5:41:16
Corners 14	1	37N53	86w17	5:45:08
Cornette 63	36	37N08	84w05	5:36:20
Cornettsville 97	45	37N08	83w05	5:32:20
Cornishville 84	15	37N48	84w59	5:39:56
Cornwell 83	15	37N57	83w38	5:34:32
Corydon 51	1	37N44	87w43	5:50:52
Cote 48	14	36N52	83w12	5:32:48
Cottageville 68	10	38N36	83w19	5:33:16
Cottle 88	15	37N53	83w12	5:32:48
Cottonburg 76	30	37N45	84w18	5:37:12
Country Club Heights 81	10	38N35	83w52	5:35:28
Counts Cross Roads 22	15	38N18	83w11	5:32:44
Covedale 68	10	38N36	83w19	5:33:16
Covington 59	68	39N05	84w31	5:38:04
Cowan 35	15	38N24	83w54	5:35:36
Cow Creek 33	26	37N41	83w57	5:35:48
Cowcreek 95	15	37N24	83w36	5:34:24
Coxs Creek 90	48	37N55	85w29	5:41:56
Coxton 48	14	36N51	83w19	5:33:16
Crab Orchard 69	15	37N28	84w30	5:38:00
Cracker 36	10	37N34	82w45	5:31:00
Crailhope 44	1	37N09	85w42	5:42:48
Craintown 35	15	38N25	83w47	5:35:08
Crane Nest 61	14	36N59	83w53	5:35:32
Craney 103	15	38N11	83w26	5:33:44
Cranks 48	14	36N46	83w10	5:32:40
Cranston 103	15	38N16	83w26	5:33:44
Cravens 90	48	37N48	85w28	5:41:52
Crawford 63	36	37N08	84w05	5:36:20
Crawford 97	45	37N18	83w13	5:32:52
Craycraft 1	1	37N06	85w18	5:41:12
Crayne 28	1	37N16	88w05	5:52:20
Craynor 36	10	37N26	82w40	5:30:40
Creal 44	1	37N27	85w40	5:42:40
Creekmore 74	15	36N38	84w26	5:37:44
Creekville 26	15	37N07	83w33	5:34:12
Creelsboro 104	1	36N54	85w11	5:40:44
Crescent Hill 56	66	38N15	85w42	5:42:48
Crescent Park 59	68	39N03	84w35	5:38:20
Crescent Springs 59	68	39N03	84w35	5:38:20
Crestmoor 114	7	37N00	86w25	5:45:40
Creston 23	48	37N16	85w03	5:40:12
Crestview 19	10	39N01	84w25	5:37:40
Crestview Hills 59	10	39N01	84w35	5:38:20
Crestwood 37	19	38N12	84w52	5:39:28
Crestwood 93	57	38N19	85w28	5:41:52
Creswell 17	1	37N12	88w04	5:52:16
Crider 17	1	37N10	87w58	5:51:52
Crittenden 41	10	38N47	84w36	5:38:24
Croakes 115	48	37N41	85w13	5:40:52
Crockett 88	15	37N59	83w05	5:32:20
Crocus 1	1	37N01	85w15	5:41:00
Crofton 24	1	37N03	87w29	5:49:56
Croley 53	1	36N40	89w00	5:56:00
Cromona 67	15	37N11	82w41	5:30:44
Cromwell 92	1	37N20	86w47	5:47:08
Cropper 106	48	38N19	85w07	5:40:28
Crossgate 56	67	38N17	85w35	5:42:20
Crossland 18	1	36N30	88w19	5:53:16
Cross Roads 71	1	36N59	86w57	5:47:48
Crown 67	15	37N09	82w50	5:31:20
Crowtown 17	1	37N07	87w53	5:51:32
Cruise 63	15	37N11	84w07	5:36:28
Crummies 48	14	36N47	83w12	5:32:48
Crutchfield 38	1	36N35	88w56	5:55:44
Crystal 33	15	37N40	83w50	5:35:20
Crystal Lake 93	59	38N24	85w23	5:41:32
Cuba 42	1	36N44	88w38	5:54:32
Cubage 7	14	36N42	83w31	5:34:04
Cub Run 50	1	37N18	86w04	5:44:16
Culbertson 10	10	38N25	82w36	5:30:24
Cullen 113	1	37N41	87w55	5:51:40
Culver 32	15	38N05	82w59	5:31:56
Culvertown 90	56	37N40	85w35	5:42:20
Cumberland 48	14	36N59	82w59	5:31:56
Cumberland City 27	1	36N48	85w04	5:40:16
Cumberland College 118	14	36N44	84w10	5:36:40
Cumberland Falls 118	14	36N50	84w14	5:36:56
Cumminsville 12	10	38N41	84w04	5:36:16
Cundiff 1	1	36N57	85w15	5:41:00
Cunningham 20	1	36N54	88w53	5:55:32
Cupio 15	61	38N00	85w57	5:43:48
Curdsville 30	1	37N44	87w20	5:49:20
Curt 13	15	37N33	83w22	5:33:28
Custer 14	1	37N44	86w15	5:45:00
Cutshin 66	15	37N06	83w16	5:33:04
Cutuno 77	10	37N43	83w14	5:32:56
Cuzick 76	30	37N45	84w18	5:37:12
Cyclone 86	1	36N53	85w42	5:42:48
Cynthiana 49	20	38N23	84w18	5:37:12
Cyrus 77	10	37N48	83w05	5:32:20
Dabney 100	18	37N06	84w36	5:38:24
Dabolt 55	15	37N20	84w01	5:36:04
Dahl 100	18	37N06	84w36	5:38:24
Daisy 97	45	37N04	83w06	5:32:24
Dal 118	14	36N44	84w10	5:36:40
Dale 77	10	37N43	83w14	5:32:56
Dalesburg 13	15	37N29	83w40	5:34:40
Dalesburg 35	15	38N25	83w47	5:35:08
Daley 66	15	37N08	83w17	5:33:08
Dallams Creek 71	1	36N59	86w57	5:47:48
Dalton 54	1	37N18	87w46	5:51:04
Dan 83	15	37N57	83w29	5:33:56
Dan 92	1	37N27	86w41	5:46:44
Dana 36	10	37N33	82w41	5:30:44
Danby 71	1	36N51	86w53	5:47:32
Daniels Creek 58	10	37N46	82w45	5:31:00
Danleytown 45	10	38N34	82w50	5:31:20
Dants 78	56	37N38	85w24	5:41:36
Danville 11	24	37N39	84w46	5:39:04
Darbyton 48	14	36N52	83w12	5:32:48
Darfork 97	45	37N15	83w11	5:32:44
Dartmont 48	14	36N52	83w12	5:32:48
Datha 55	15	37N19	83w58	5:35:52
Davella 80	10	37N48	82w35	5:30:20
David 36	10	37N36	82w54	5:31:36
Davidson 92	1	37N32	86w41	5:46:44
Davis 105	15	38N23	84w32	5:38:08
Davis Branch 10	10	38N25	82w36	5:30:24
Davisburg 7	14	36N46	83w42	5:34:48
Davis Cross Roads 16	1	37N04	86w45	5:47:00
Davisport 80	10	37N50	82w36	5:30:24
Davistown 40	15	37N37	84w35	5:38:20
Davistown 120	47	38N09	84w41	5:38:44
Davisville 64	10	37N57	82w51	5:31:24
Dawson Springs 54	1	37N10	87w41	5:50:44
Day 67	15	37N07	82w49	5:31:16
Dayhoit 48	14	36N50	83w22	5:33:28
Daylight 54	1	37N10	87w41	5:50:44
Daysboro 119	15	37N48	83w25	5:33:40
Daysville 110	1	36N48	87w04	5:48:16
Dayton 19	68	39N07	84w28	5:37:52
Deane 67	15	37N14	82w46	5:31:04
Deatsville 90	48	37N54	85w34	5:42:16
Debord 80	10	37N50	82w33	5:30:12
Decker 16	1	37N25	86w29	5:45:56
DeCoursey 59	68	39N01	84w29	5:37:56
Decoy 60	15	37N30	83w05	5:32:20
Dee Acres 30	1	37N44	86w59	5:47:56
Deese 55	15	37N20	84w01	5:36:04
Defiance 97	45	37N12	83w05	5:32:20
Defoe 52	48	38N20	85w03	5:40:12
Defries 50	1	37N17	85w46	5:43:04
Dehart 88	39	37N55	83w16	5:33:04
De Koven 113	1	37N35	88w04	5:52:16
Delafield 114	7	37N00	86w25	5:45:40
Delaplain 105	25	38N13	84w33	5:38:12
Delaware 30	1	37N42	87w20	5:49:20
Delia 41	10	38N39	84w34	5:38:16
Dellville 52	48	38N31	85w12	5:40:48
Delmer 100	18	37N04	84w45	5:39:00
Delphia 97	45	37N02	83w05	5:32:20
Delta 116	1	36N52	84w39	5:38:36
Dema 60	15	37N18	82w45	5:31:00
Demlytown 93	57	38N19	85w28	5:41:52
Democrat 67	15	37N14	82w48	5:31:12
Demond 88	15	37N49	83w26	5:33:44
De Mossville 96	10	38N48	84w25	5:37:40
Demunbruns Store 31	1	37N11	86w06	5:44:24
Denison 50	1	37N18	86w04	5:44:16
Denmark 104	1	36N59	85w04	5:40:16
Denney 116	1	36N49	84w39	5:38:36
Dennis 71	1	36N51	86w53	5:47:32
Denniston 83	15	37N55	83w32	5:34:08
Denton 22	15	38N16	82w52	5:31:28
Denver 58	10	37N47	82w51	5:31:24
Depoy 89	1	37N13	87w14	5:48:56
Derby 117	1	37N29	87w50	5:51:20
Dermont 30	1	37N45	87w07	5:48:28
Devon 8	10	38N58	84w37	5:38:28
Devondale 56	65	38N16	85w37	5:42:28
Dewdrop 32	15	38N05	83w08	5:32:32
Dewitt 61	14	36N55	83w42	5:34:48
Dexter 18	1	36N44	88w17	5:53:08
Dexterville 16	1	37N14	86w41	5:46:44
Diablock 97	45	37N15	83w11	5:32:44
Diamond 117	1	37N29	87w50	5:51:20
Diamond Springs 71	1	36N59	86w57	5:47:48
Dice 97	45	37N21	83w11	5:32:44
Dimple 16	1	37N14	86w41	5:46:44
Dingus 88	15	37N55	83w06	5:32:24
Dinwood 36	10	37N29	82w45	5:31:00
Dione 48	14	36N59	82w59	5:31:56
Dirigo 1	1	36N58	85w26	5:41:44
Dishman Springs 61	14	36N54	84w05	5:36:20
Disputanta 102	15	37N29	84w15	5:37:00
Dix Fork 98	10	37N37	82w21	5:29:24
Dixie 48	14	36N54	83w12	5:32:48
Dixie 51	1	36N39	88w04	5:52:16
Dixie Heights 59	68	39N01	84w34	5:38:16
Dixon 117	1	37N31	87w41	5:50:44
Dixville 84	43	37N46	84w51	5:39:24
Dizney 48	14	36N51	83w07	5:32:28
Dobbins 32	15	38N11	82w52	5:31:28
Dock 36	10	37N41	82w46	5:31:04
Doddy 2	6	36N45	86w11	5:44:44
Doe Creek 33	26	37N42	83w58	5:35:52
Doe Valley Estates 82	48	38N00	86w10	5:44:40
Dogcreek 50	1	37N18	86w04	5:44:16
Dogtown 79	1	36N51	88w21	5:53:24
Dog Walk 69	15	37N28	84w30	5:38:00
Dogwalk 92	1	37N24	86w36	5:46:24
Dogwood 42	1	36N49	88w38	5:54:32
Donaldson 111	1	36N52	87w50	5:51:20
Donansburg 44	1	37N12	85w37	5:42:28
Donerail 34	27	38N05	84w29	5:37:56
Dongola 67	15	37N06	82w51	5:31:24
Dony 36	10	37N27	82w43	5:30:52
Dortha 63	15	36N57	84w06	5:36:24
Dorton 98	10	37N17	82w35	5:30:20
Dorton Branch 7	14	36N46	83w42	5:34:48
Do Stop 43	1	37N25	86w29	5:45:56
Dot 71	1	36N40	86w51	5:47:24
Dougan Town 29	1	36N48	85w22	5:41:28
Douglas 98	10	37N23	82w33	5:30:12
Douglass Hills 56	65	38N15	85w32	5:42:08
Dover 81	10	38N45	83w53	5:35:32
Doylesville 76	30	37N45	84w18	5:37:12
Dozier Heights 54	1	37N20	87w30	5:50:00
Draffenville 79	1	36N51	88w21	5:53:24
Draffin 98	10	37N21	82w24	5:29:36
Drake 114	1	36N50	86w25	5:45:40
Drakesboro 89	1	37N12	87w02	5:48:08
Dressen 48	14	36N51	83w19	5:33:16
Dreyfus 76	15	37N37	84w11	5:36:44
Drift 36	10	37N31	82w45	5:31:00
Dripping Spring 31	1	37N03	86w13	5:44:52
Drip Rock 33	15	37N35	83w58	5:35:52
Druid Hills 56	65	38N16	85w40	5:42:40
Drum 100	18	37N06	84w36	5:38:24
Dry Creek 60	15	37N17	82w45	5:31:00
Dryfork 5	1	36N50	85w54	5:43:36
Dry Fork 98	10	37N20	82w27	5:29:48
Dryhill 66	15	37N10	83w22	5:33:28
Dry Ridge 41	12	38N41	84w35	5:38:20
Dublin 42	1	36N44	88w48	5:55:12
Dubre 29	1	36N50	85w34	5:42:16
Duckers 120	47	38N09	84w41	5:38:44
Duckrun 118	14	36N44	84w10	5:36:40
Duco 77	10	37N36	83w02	5:32:08
Duff 43	1	36N50	85w30	5:42:00
Dukedom 42	1	36N34	88w49	5:55:16
Dukes 46	1	37N54	86w45	5:47:00
Dulaney 17	1	37N07	87w53	5:51:32
Duluth 76	42	37N35	84w17	5:37:08

KENTUCKY

Dulworth 1	1	37N06	85W18	5:41:12
Dunbar 16	1	37N11	86W45	5:47:00
Duncan 23	48	37N22	84W41	5:38:44
Duncan 84	43	37N46	84W51	5:39:24
Duncannon 76	30	37N45	84W18	5:37:12
Dundee 92	1	37N34	86W46	5:47:04
Dunham 67	15	37N11	82W38	5:30:32
Dunlap 98	10	37N25	82W16	5:29:04
Dunleary 98	10	37N19	82W21	5:29:24
Dunmor 89	1	37N05	87W00	5:48:00
Dunnville 23	48	37N12	85W01	5:40:04
Dunraven 97	45	37N19	83W19	5:33:16
Durbin 10	10	38N25	82W36	5:30:24
Durbintown 49	35	38N31	84W23	5:37:32
Dwale 36	10	37N37	82W43	5:30:52
Dwarf 97	45	37N20	83W08	5:32:32
Dycusburg 28	1	37N10	88W11	5:52:44
Dyer 14	1	37N42	86W13	5:44:52
Dykes 100	18	37N06	84W36	5:38:24
Eadsville 116	1	36N50	84W51	5:39:24
Eagle Station 21	15	38N39	84W57	5:39:48
Earlington 54	1	37N16	87W30	5:50:00
Earnestville 65	15	37N29	83W40	5:34:40
East Bernstadt 63	15	37N11	84W07	5:36:28
Easterday 21	38	38N41	85W11	5:40:44
Eastern 36	10	37N31	82W48	5:31:12
East Fayette 34	27	38N02	84W23	5:37:32
East Fork 85	1	36N59	85W37	5:42:28
East Frankfort 37	19	38N12	84W52	5:39:28
East Hickman 67	15	37N53	84W34	5:38:16
East Jenkins 67	15	37N11	82W38	5:30:32
Eastland 81	10	38N35	83W52	5:35:28
Eastland Park 114	7	37N00	86W25	5:45:40
East McDowell 36	10	37N27	82W43	5:30:52
Easton 46	1	37N38	86W43	5:46:52
East Pineville 7	14	36N46	83W42	5:34:48
East Point 58	10	37N45	82W47	5:31:08
East Somerset 100	31	37N06	84W36	5:38:24
East Union 91	37	38N19	84W02	5:36:08
Eastview 47	48	37N35	86W03	5:44:12
Eastwood 56	65	38N10	85W36	5:42:24
Ebenezer 84	15	37N55	84W51	5:39:24
Ebenezer 86	1	36N42	85W42	5:42:48
Ebenezer 89	1	37N13	87W03	5:48:12
Eberle 55	15	37N18	84W05	5:36:20
Echo 85	1	37N05	85W42	5:42:48
Echols 92	1	37N20	86W58	5:47:52
Eddyville 72	1	37N03	88W04	5:52:16
Edenton 76	30	37N45	84W18	5:37:12
Edgewater 98	10	37N17	82W28	5:29:52
Edgewood 7	14	36N37	83W44	5:34:56
Edgewood 59	10	39N01	84W35	5:38:20
Edmonton 85	1	36N59	85W37	5:42:28
Edna 77	10	37N48	83W09	5:32:36
Edsel 32	15	38N11	82W52	5:31:28
Edwards 71	1	36N59	86W57	5:47:48
Eglon 55	15	37N26	84W00	5:36:00
Egypt 55	15	37N19	83W54	5:35:36
Eighty Eight 5	1	36N55	85W47	5:43:08
Ekron 82	48	37N56	86W11	5:44:44
Elamton 88	15	37N56	83W09	5:32:36
Elba 75	1	37N42	87W20	5:49:20
Elcomb 48	14	36N51	83W19	5:33:16
Eldridge 32	15	38N04	83W03	5:32:12
Elfie 16	1	37N24	86W36	5:46:24
Eli 104	1	37N02	84W57	5:39:48
Elias 55	15	37N23	83W50	5:35:20
Elihu 100	18	37N03	84W36	5:38:24
Elizabeth 9	29	38N13	84W15	5:37:00
Elizabethtown 47	58	37N42	85W52	5:43:28
Elizaville 35	15	38N25	83W49	5:35:16
Elkatawa 13	15	37N34	83W25	5:33:40
Elk Creek 108	48	38N06	85W22	5:41:28
Elkfork 88	15	37N58	83W08	5:32:32
Elk Horn 109	48	37N19	85W17	5:41:08
Elkhorn City 98	10	37N18	82W21	5:29:24
Elkton 110	1	36N49	87W09	5:48:36
Ella 1	1	37N06	85W18	5:41:12
Ellen 64	10	38N07	82W36	5:30:24
Eller 104	1	37N04	85W06	5:40:24
Ellington 29	1	36N42	85W22	5:41:28
Elliottville 103	15	38N11	83W16	5:33:04
Ellisburg 23	48	37N28	84W49	5:39:16
Elliston 41	10	38N44	84W45	5:39:00
Elliston 76	30	37N45	84W18	5:37:12
Ellisville 91	37	38N19	84W02	5:36:08
Ellmitch 92	1	37N38	86W43	5:46:52
Elmburg 106	48	38N21	85W07	5:40:28
Elmrock 60	15	37N27	83W01	5:32:04
Elmville 37	15	38N16	84W41	5:38:44
Elna 88	15	37N55	82W58	5:31:52
Elrod 100	18	37N12	84W28	5:37:52
Elsie 77	10	37N47	83W08	5:32:32
Elsinore 37	19	38N12	84W52	5:39:28
Elsmere 59	10	39N01	84W36	5:38:24
Elva 79	1	36N55	88W31	5:54:04
Elys 61	14	36N47	83W44	5:34:56
Emanuel 61	14	36N57	84W00	5:36:00
Emberton 86	1	36N42	85W42	5:42:48
Emerson 68	10	38N21	83W15	5:33:00
Eminence 52	60	38N22	85W11	5:40:44
Emlyn 118	14	36N42	84W08	5:36:32
Emma 36	10	37N31	82W45	5:31:00
Emmalena 60	15	37N21	83W04	5:32:16
Empire 24	1	37N11	87W27	5:49:48
Endee 95	15	37N29	83W40	5:34:40
Endicott 36	10	37N40	82W38	5:30:32
Engle 97	45	37N23	83W15	5:33:00
English 21	38	38N41	85W11	5:40:44
Ennis 89	1	37N13	87W03	5:48:12
Enon 17	1	37N12	88W04	5:52:16
Ensor 30	1	37N47	86W59	5:47:56
Enterprise 22	15	38N18	83W11	5:32:44
Eolia 67	15	37N03	82W47	5:31:08
Epleys 71	1	36N56	86W56	5:47:44
Epperson 73	1	37N03	88W37	5:54:28
Epson 77	10	37N45	83W14	5:32:56
Epworth 68	10	38N46	83W45	5:35:00
Eriline 26	15	37N11	83W36	5:34:24
Erlanger 59	10	39N01	84W36	5:38:24
Ermine 67	15	37N07	82W47	5:31:08
Erose 61	14	36N56	83W37	5:34:28
Esco 98	10	37N29	82W31	5:30:04
Essie 66	15	37N04	83W27	5:33:48
Estesburg 100	18	37N20	84W40	5:38:40
Estill 36	10	37N27	82W49	5:31:16
Esto 104	1	37N04	85W06	5:40:24
Estrado 76	30	37N45	84W18	5:37:12
Ethridge 39	11	38N47	84W54	5:39:36
Etna 100	18	37N17	84W40	5:38:40
Etoile 5	1	36N50	85W54	5:43:36
Etty 98	10	37N15	82W40	5:30:40
Eubank 100	31	37N17	84W40	5:38:40
Eunice 1	1	37N06	85W18	5:41:12
Evanston 13	15	37N34	83W08	5:32:32
Evarts 48	14	36N51	83W09	5:32:36
Eveleigh 43	1	37N29	86W18	5:45:12
Evelyn 65	26	37N42	83W58	5:35:52
Ever 77	10	37N51	83W03	5:32:12
Everett 110	1	36N55	87W06	5:48:24
Evergreen 37	19	38N12	84W52	5:39:28
Evergreen 64	10	38N07	82W36	5:30:24
Eversole 95	15	37N29	83W40	5:34:40
Ewing 35	15	38N26	83W52	5:35:28
Ewingford 112	48	38N36	85W19	5:41:16
Ewington 87	21	38N03	83W57	5:35:48
Exie 44	6	37N16	85W30	5:42:00
Ezel 88	15	37N54	83W27	5:33:48
Faber 118	14	36N57	84W06	5:36:24
Fagan 83	15	37N57	83W38	5:34:32
Fairbanks 42	1	36N38	88W36	5:54:24
Fairbanks 94	15	38N32	84W50	5:39:20
Fairdale 56	65	38N06	85W46	5:43:04
Fairdealing 79	1	36N50	88W14	5:52:56
Fairfield 14	1	37N44	86W21	5:45:24
Fairfield 90	56	37N56	85W23	5:41:32
Fair Grounds 81	10	38N35	83W52	5:35:28
Fairland 27	1	36N41	85W08	5:40:32
Fairmeade 56	65	38N15	85W38	5:42:32
Fairmont 56	65	38N10	85W36	5:42:24
Fairmont 117	1	37N29	87W50	5:51:20
Fairplay 1	1	37N01	85W18	5:41:12
Fairview 24	1	36N51	87W18	5:49:12
Fairview 31	1	37N11	86W19	5:45:16
Fairview 35	15	38N28	83W56	5:35:44
Fairview 59	68	39N03	84W32	5:38:08
Fairview 72	1	37N05	88W05	5:52:20
Fairview 118	14	36N44	84W10	5:36:40
Fairview Heights 37	19	38N12	84W52	5:39:28
Fairview Hill 22	15	38N17	82W55	5:31:40
Falcon 77	10	37N47	83W00	5:32:00
Fall Rock 26	15	37N13	83W47	5:35:08
Fallsburg 64	10	38N11	82W40	5:30:40
Falls of Rough 43	1	37N35	86W33	5:46:12
Falmouth 96	10	38N41	84W20	5:37:20
Fancy Farm 42	1	36N48	88W47	5:55:08
Fannin 32	15	38N05	83W08	5:32:32
Fariston 63	36	37N08	84W05	5:36:20
Farler 97	45	37N09	83W11	5:32:44
Farmers 103	15	38N09	83W33	5:34:12
Farmers Mill 48	14	36N49	83W16	5:33:04
Farmersville 17	1	37N07	87W53	5:51:32
Farmington 42	1	36N42	88W32	5:54:08
Farraday 67	15	37N10	82W47	5:31:08
Farristown 76	15	37N37	84W18	5:37:12
Faubush 100	18	37N04	84W50	5:39:20
Faulconer 11	24	37N39	84W46	5:39:04
Faxon 18	1	36N36	88W19	5:53:16
Faye 32	15	38N04	83W11	5:32:44
Faywood 120	44	38N03	84W44	5:38:56
Fearisville 68	10	38N38	83W36	5:34:24
Fearsville 24	1	36N51	87W30	5:50:00
Feathersburg 1	1	37N16	85W09	5:40:36
Fedscreek 98	10	37N25	82W16	5:29:04
Fee 7	14	36N45	83W28	5:33:52
Feliciana 42	1	36N34	88W49	5:55:16
Felty 26	15	37N09	83W46	5:35:04
Fentress McMahon 43	1	37N35	86W33	5:46:12
Fenwick 115	48	37N41	85W13	5:40:52
Ferguson 100	18	37N04	84W36	5:38:24
Ferguson Creek 98	10	37N29	82W31	5:30:04
Fern Creek 56	65	38N09	85W36	5:42:24
Ferndale 7	14	36N46	83W42	5:34:48
Fernleaf 81	10	38N45	83W53	5:35:32
Fern View 56	65	38N10	85W36	5:42:24
Ferrells Creek 98	10	37N21	82W22	5:29:28
Field 7	14	36N54	83W36	5:34:24
Fielden 32	15	38N08	82W58	5:31:52
Figg 106	51	38N13	85W14	5:40:56
Fillmore 65	15	37N36	83W33	5:34:12
Fincastle 56	67	38N17	85W35	5:42:20
Finchville 106	48	38N09	85W19	5:41:16
Finley 109	48	37N28	85W20	5:41:20
Finney 5	6	37N00	85W55	5:43:40
Firebrick 68	10	38N41	83W03	5:32:12
Firmantown 120	44	38N03	84W44	5:38:56
Fisher 14	1	37N29	86W18	5:45:12
Fisherville 56	65	38N26	85W29	5:41:56
Fishtrap 98	10	37N26	82W23	5:29:32
Fiskburg 59	10	38N48	84W25	5:37:40
Fisty 60	15	37N20	83W06	5:32:24
Fitch 22	15	38N18	83W11	5:32:44
Fitchburg 33	26	37N41	83W57	5:35:48
Five Forks 64	10	38N07	82W36	5:30:24
Five Mile 13	15	37N35	83W25	5:33:40
Fixer 65	15	37N41	83W41	5:34:44
Flag Spring 19	10	38N55	84W16	5:37:04
Flaherty 82	48	37N50	86W04	5:44:16
Flanary 98	10	37N23	82W15	5:29:00
Flat 119	15	37N39	83W33	5:34:12
Flat Fork 77	10	37N50	83W02	5:32:08
Flatgap 58	10	37N56	82W53	5:31:32
Flat Lick 61	14	36N50	83W46	5:35:04
Flat Rock 16	1	37N14	86W41	5:46:44
Flat Rock 17	1	37N12	88W04	5:52:16
Flat Rock 74	15	36N44	84W28	5:37:52
Flatwoods 45	10	38N31	82W43	5:30:52
Fleet 2	1	36N38	85W48	5:43:12
Fleming 67	15	37N12	82W42	5:30:48
Flemingsburg 35	34	38N25	83W45	5:35:00
Flemingsburg Junction 35	15	38N25	83W47	5:35:08
Flener 16	1	37N14	86W41	5:46:44
Fletcher 63	36	37N08	84W05	5:36:20
Flingsville 41	10	38N47	84W36	5:38:24
Flippin 86	1	36N43	85W52	5:43:28
Flora 46	1	37N54	86W45	5:47:00
Florence 8	10	39N00	84W38	5:38:32
Flosie 116	1	36N52	84W39	5:38:36
Flournoy 113	1	37N41	87W55	5:51:40
Floyd 100	18	37N17	84W40	5:38:40
Floydsburg 93	57	38N19	85W28	5:41:52
Fogertown 26	15	37N13	83W54	5:35:36
Folsom 41	10	38N44	84W45	5:39:00
Folsomdale 42	1	36N49	88W38	5:54:32
Fonde 7	14	36N36	83W53	5:35:32
Fonthill 104	1	37N04	85W06	5:40:24
Foraker 77	10	37N40	83W08	5:32:32
Ford 25	15	37N53	84W16	5:37:04
Fords Branch 98	10	37N26	82W31	5:30:04
Fordsville 92	1	37N38	86W43	5:46:52
Forest Cottage 29	1	36N48	85W22	5:41:28
Forest Grove 25	32	38N00	84W11	5:36:44
Forest Hill 73	1	37N03	88W37	5:54:28
Forest Hills 59	68	39N02	84W31	5:38:04
Forest Hills 98	10	37N37	82W14	5:28:56
Forks 33	15	37N46	83W59	5:35:56
Forks Of Elkhorn 37	19	38N12	84W49	5:39:16
Forkton 86	1	36N42	85W42	5:42:48
Forrestdale 73	1	37N05	88W53	5:55:32
Forrest Park 25	32	38N00	84W11	5:36:44
Fort Campbell 24	1	36N39	87W33	5:50:12
Fort Campbell North 24	1	36N38	87W28	5:49:52
Fort Knox 47	48	37N54	85W57	5:43:48
Fort Mitchell 59	68	39N02	84W34	5:38:16
Fort Thomas 19	68	39N05	84W27	5:37:48
Fort Wright 59	68	39N04	84W33	5:38:12
Foster 12	10	38N48	84W13	5:36:52
Fount 61	14	36N59	83W50	5:35:20
Fountain Run 86	1	36N43	85W57	5:43:48
Fourmile 7	14	36N46	83W46	5:35:04
Four Oaks 96	10	38N40	84W20	5:37:20
Fourseam 97	45	37N15	83W11	5:32:44
Fox 33	26	37N42	83W58	5:35:52
Foxboro 56	67	38N15	85W34	5:42:16
Fox Creek 3	43	37N59	84W58	5:39:52
Foxport 35	15	38N24	83W37	5:34:28
Foxtown 55	15	37N30	84W00	5:36:00
Frakes 7	14	36N38	83W56	5:35:44
Frances 28	1	37N13	88W09	5:52:36
Francisville 8	10	39N06	84W44	5:38:56
Frankfort 37	19	38N12	84W52	5:39:28
Franklin 107	2	36N43	86W35	5:46:20
Franklin Acres 37	19	38N12	84W52	5:39:28
Franklin Cross Roads 47	48	37N35	86W00	5:44:00
Franklin Heights 37	19	38N12	84W52	5:39:28
Franklin Mines 28	1	37N20	88W04	5:52:16
Franklinton 52	48	38N21	85W07	5:40:28
Frazer 116	1	36N57	84W42	5:38:48
Frazertown 93	57	38N19	85W28	5:41:52
Fredericktown 115	48	37N41	85W13	5:40:52
Fredonia 17	1	37N12	88W04	5:52:16
Fredville 77	10	37N37	82W58	5:31:52
Freeburn 98	10	37N34	82W09	5:28:36
Freedom 5	1	36N48	85W49	5:43:16
Freedom 104	1	36N59	85W04	5:40:16
Freetown 86	1	36N38	85W48	5:43:12
Free Union 117	1	37N31	87W41	5:50:44
Fremont 73	1	36N58	88W37	5:54:28
Frenchburg 83	15	37N57	83W38	5:34:32
Fresh Meadows 48	14	36N50	83W22	5:33:28
Frew 66	15	37N11	83W15	5:33:00
Friendly Hills 56	65	38N09	85W42	5:42:48
Frisby 116	1	36N50	84W51	5:39:24
Fritz 77	10	37N42	83W09	5:32:36
Frogtown 34	44	38N03	84W44	5:38:56
Frogue 29	1	36N46	85W21	5:41:24
Frozen Creek 13	15	37N35	83W25	5:33:40
Fruithill 24	1	37N03	87W29	5:49:56
Fry 44	6	37N16	85W30	5:42:00
Fuget 58	10	37N53	82W55	5:31:40
Fulgham 53	1	36N40	89W00	5:56:00
Fullerton 45	10	38N43	82W58	5:31:52
Fulton 38	1	36N30	88W53	5:55:32
Fultz 22	15	38N17	83W01	5:32:04
Funston 74	15	36N50	84W29	5:37:56
Furnace 33	15	37N46	83W50	5:35:20
Fusonia 97	45	37N11	83W09	5:32:36
Future City 73	1	37N05	88W53	5:55:32
Gabbard 95	15	37N23	83W37	5:34:28
Gabe 44	6	37N16	85W30	5:42:00
Gadberry 1	1	37N01	85W18	5:41:12
Gage 4	1	37N05	88W58	5:55:52
Gainesville 2	6	36N45	86W11	5:44:44

KENTUCKY

Galdia 77	10	37N45	83w04	5:32:16
Gallup 64	10	38N07	82w36	5:30:24
Galveston 36	10	37N26	82w38	5:30:32
Gamaliel 86	1	36N38	85w48	5:43:12
Gapcreek 116	1	36N46	85w01	5:40:04
Gap in Knob 15	50	38N00	85w43	5:42:52
Gapville 77	10	37N38	82w58	5:31:52
Gardenside 34	27	38N02	84w32	5:38:08
Garden Village 98	10	37N29	82w31	5:30:04
Gardnersville 96	10	38N48	84w25	5:37:40
Garfield 14	1	37N47	86w21	5:45:24
Garlin 1	1	37N07	85w15	5:41:00
Garner 10	10	38N20	82w46	5:31:04
Garner 60	15	37N21	82w56	5:31:44
Garrard 26	15	37N07	83w45	5:35:00
Garrett 36	10	37N29	82w50	5:31:20
Garrett 82	48	37N56	86w11	5:44:44
Garrettsburg 24	1	36N44	87w34	5:50:16
Garrison 68	10	38N36	83w10	5:32:40
Garvin Ridge 22	15	38N18	83w11	5:32:44
Gascon 85	1	36N59	85w37	5:42:28
Gaskill 67	15	37N11	82w38	5:30:32
Gasper 71	1	36N57	86w44	5:46:56
Gasper River 114	1	37N00	86w33	5:46:12
Gassaway 5	6	37N00	85w55	5:43:40
Gates 103	15	38N11	83w26	5:33:44
Gatewood 30	1	37N54	86w45	5:47:00
Gatliff 118	14	36N41	84w01	5:36:04
Gatun 48	14	36N52	83w20	5:33:20
Gausdale 118	14	36N52	83w53	5:35:32
Gaybourn 120	44	38N03	84w44	5:38:56
Gays Creek 97	45	37N19	83w26	5:33:44
Gee 3	43	38N02	84w54	5:39:36
Geneva 51	1	37N44	87w42	5:50:48
Geneva 69	15	37N28	84w49	5:39:16
Gentrys Mill 1	1	37N06	85w18	5:41:12
Georges Creek 64	10	38N07	82w36	5:30:24
Georgetown 105	25	38N13	84w33	5:38:12
Germantown 12	10	38N39	83w58	5:35:52
Gertrude 12	10	38N41	84w04	5:36:16
Gesling 22	15	38N26	83w08	5:32:32
Gest 52	48	38N21	85w07	5:40:28
Gethsemane 90	56	37N40	85w35	5:42:20
Ghent 21	15	38N44	85w04	5:40:16
Gibbs 61	14	36N52	83w53	5:35:32
Gifford 77	10	37N46	83w07	5:32:28
Gilbertsville 79	1	37N01	88w18	5:53:12
Gillem Branch 58	10	37N57	82w57	5:31:48
Gilley 67	15	36N59	83w07	5:32:28
Gillmore 119	15	37N44	83w22	5:33:28
Gilpin 23	48	37N15	84w53	5:39:32
Gilreath 74	15	36N39	84w26	5:37:44
Gilstrap 16	1	37N27	86w41	5:46:44
Gimlet 32	15	38N18	83w11	5:32:44
Ginseng 62	48	38N10	85w36	5:42:24
Girdler 61	14	36N59	83w50	5:35:20
Girkin 114	7	37N00	86w25	5:45:40
Gishton 89	1	37N22	87w13	5:48:52
Glasgow 5	6	37N00	85w55	5:43:40
Gleanings 62	48	37N38	85w31	5:42:04
Glenarm 93	57	38N19	85w28	5:41:52
Glencoe 39	11	38N43	84w49	5:39:16
Glendale 47	48	37N36	85w54	5:43:36
Glen Dean 14	1	37N39	86w32	5:46:08
Glengary 56	65	38N06	85w45	5:43:00
Glenmore 114	1	37N06	86w28	5:45:52
Glensboro 3	43	38N02	84w54	5:39:36
Glens Fork 1	1	37N00	85w15	5:41:00
Glen Springs 68	10	38N36	83w19	5:33:16
Glenview 56	65	38N17	85w38	5:42:32
Glenview Acres 56	67	38N17	85w35	5:42:20
Glenview Heights 56	67	38N17	85w35	5:42:20
Glenview Hills 56	67	38N17	85w35	5:42:20
Glenview Manor 56	67	38N17	85w35	5:42:20
Glenville 75	1	37N36	87w12	5:48:48
Globe 22	15	38N18	83w11	5:32:44
Glomawr 97	45	37N15	83w11	5:32:44
Goddard 35	15	38N24	83w37	5:34:28
Goering 46	1	37N54	86w45	5:47:00
Goffs Corner 25	32	38N00	84w11	5:36:44
Goforth 96	10	38N40	84w20	5:37:20
Goins 118	14	36N42	83w58	5:35:52
Goldbug 118	14	36N44	84w10	5:36:40
Gold City 107	1	36N43	86w35	5:46:20
Golden Ash 48	14	36N51	83w18	5:33:12
Golden Pond 111	1	36N48	88w02	5:52:08
Golo 42	1	36N42	88w24	5:53:36
Goochtown 100	18	37N17	84w40	5:38:40
Goodluck 85	1	36N59	85w37	5:42:28
Goodnight 5	6	37N08	85w58	5:43:52
Goody 98	10	37N40	82w16	5:29:04
Goose Creek 56	67	38N17	85w35	5:42:20
Gooserock 26	15	37N05	83w42	5:34:48
Gordon 67	15	37N00	83w01	5:32:04
Gordon Ford 88	15	37N53	83w12	5:32:48
Gordonsville 71	1	36N51	86w53	5:47:32
Goshen 93	49	38N24	85w34	5:42:16
Gott 114	7	37N00	86w25	5:45:40
Grab 44	6	37N16	85w30	5:42:00
Grace 26	15	37N12	83w52	5:35:28
Gracey 24	1	36N53	87w40	5:50:40
Gradyville 1	1	37N04	85w25	5:41:40
Graefenburg 106	19	38N12	84w52	5:39:28
Graham 89	1	37N15	87w17	5:49:08
Graham Hill 51	8	37N49	87w37	5:50:28
Grahamville 73	1	37N05	88w45	5:55:00
Grahn 22	15	38N17	83w04	5:32:16
Grancer 16	1	37N21	86w34	5:46:16
Grand Rivers 70	1	37N00	88w14	5:52:56
Grandview 86	1	36N42	85w42	5:42:48
Grandview Heights 37	19	38N12	84w52	5:39:28
Grange City 35	15	38N18	83w40	5:34:40
Grangertown 113	1	37N33	87w59	5:51:56
Grant	10	38N59	84w50	5:39:20
Grants Lick 19	10	38N52	84w24	5:37:36
Grapevine 54	1	37N20	87w30	5:50:00
Grassland 31	1	37N11	86w19	5:45:16
Grassy Creek 88	15	37N52	83w21	5:33:24
Grassy Lick 87	21	38N03	83w57	5:35:48
Gratz 94	17	38N28	84w57	5:39:48
Gravel Switch 78	48	37N34	85w05	5:40:20
Gray 61	14	36N57	84w00	5:36:00
Grayfox 77	10	37N45	83w04	5:32:16
Gray Hawk 55	15	37N24	83w56	5:35:44
Graymoor 56	65	38N17	85w37	5:42:28
Grays Branch 45	10	38N39	82w53	5:31:32
Grays Knob 48	14	36N49	83w18	5:33:12
Grayson 22	46	38N20	82w57	5:31:48
Grayson Springs 43	1	37N30	86w13	5:44:52
Graysville 14	1	37N53	86w17	5:45:08
Greasy Creek 98	10	37N26	82w30	5:30:00
Great Crossing 105	25	38N13	84w33	5:38:12
Greear 88	39	37N55	83w16	5:33:04
Green 32	15	38N18	83w11	5:32:44
Green Acres 11	24	37N39	84w46	5:39:04
Greenbriar 30	1	37N45	87w07	5:48:28
Greenbrier 69	15	37N20	84w40	5:38:40
Greencastle 114	1	37N07	86w30	5:46:00
Greendale 34	27	38N07	84w32	5:38:08
Green Grove 29	1	36N46	85w21	5:41:24
Green Hall 95	15	37N24	83w50	5:35:20
Green Hill 55	15	37N19	83w58	5:35:52
Greenhill 114	7	37N00	86w25	5:45:40
Greenmount 63	36	37N08	84w05	5:36:20
Greenough 98	10	37N17	82w28	5:29:52
Green Road 61	14	36N58	83w50	5:35:20
Greensburg 44	6	37N16	85w30	5:42:00
Green Spring 56	67	38N17	85w35	5:42:20
Greenup 45	10	38N35	82w50	5:31:20
Greenville 89	1	37N12	87w11	5:48:44
Greenwood 74	15	36N53	84w30	5:38:00
Greenwood 114	7	37N00	86w25	5:45:40
Grefco 22	15	38N18	83w11	5:32:44
Gregory 116	1	36N50	84w41	5:38:44
Gregoryville 22	15	38N20	82w57	5:31:48
Gresham 44	1	37N11	85w28	5:41:52
Grethel 36	10	37N29	82w39	5:30:36
Grider 29	1	36N48	85w22	5:41:28
Griderville 5	6	37N08	85w58	5:43:52
Griffin 116	1	36N53	84w30	5:38:00
Grove Center 113	1	37N39	88w01	5:52:04
Grundy 100	18	37N06	84w36	5:38:24
Guage 13	15	37N36	83w12	5:32:48
Gubser Mill 19	10	38N55	84w16	5:37:04
Guerrant 13	15	37N31	83w30	5:34:00
Guffey 48	14	36N52	83w12	5:32:48
Guffie 75	1	37N32	87w16	5:49:04
Gulfco 10	10	38N28	82w39	5:30:36
Gullett 77	10	37N43	83w07	5:32:28
Gulnare 98	10	37N38	82w33	5:30:12
Gulston 48	14	36N46	83w20	5:33:20
Gum Sulphur 102	15	37N28	84w30	5:38:00
Gum Tree 86	1	36N42	85w42	5:42:48
Gunlock 77	10	37N33	82w55	5:31:40
Gunns Chapel 40	15	37N37	84w35	5:38:20
Gus 89	1	37N07	87w00	5:48:00
Guston 82	48	37N53	86w14	5:44:56
Guthrie 110	1	36N39	87w10	5:48:40
Guthrie's Ridge 29	1	36N42	85w22	5:41:28
Guy 114	7	37N00	86w25	5:45:40
Gwinn Island 11	24	37N39	84w46	5:39:04
Gypsy 77	10	37N39	82w59	5:31:56
Habit 30	1	37N44	86w59	5:47:56
Hackley 40	15	37N37	84w35	5:38:20
Haddix 13	15	37N26	83w23	5:33:32
Hadensville 110	1	36N39	87w10	5:48:40
Hadley 114	1	37N04	86w36	5:46:24
Hager 77	10	37N45	83w14	5:32:56
Hagerhill 58	10	37N47	82w48	5:31:12
Hail 100	18	37N06	84w36	5:38:24
Halcom 32	15	38N05	83w08	5:32:32
Haldeman 103	15	38N15	83w19	5:33:16
Haleys Mill 24	1	37N03	87w29	5:49:56
Halfway 2	1	36N48	86w18	5:45:12
Halifax 2	6	36N45	86w11	5:44:44
Hall 57	28	37N47	84w37	5:38:28
Hall 60	15	37N11	82w43	5:30:52
Hallie 67	15	37N06	83w01	5:32:04
Halls Gap 69	15	37N28	84w38	5:38:32
Halls Store 71	1	36N45	86w53	5:47:32
Halo 36	10	37N19	82w41	5:30:44
Hamby 54	1	37N11	87w33	5:50:12
Hamilton 8	10	38N57	84w41	5:38:44
Hamlin 18	1	36N39	88w04	5:52:16
Hammackville 110	1	36N43	87w16	5:49:04
Hammond 58	10	37N52	82w42	5:30:48
Hammond 61	14	36N53	83w46	5:35:04
Hammonville 50	1	37N22	85w45	5:43:00
Hampton 70	1	37N17	88w22	5:53:28
Hampton Manor 25	32	38N00	84w11	5:36:44
Handshoe 60	15	37N29	82w54	5:31:36
Hanly 57	28	37N53	84w34	5:38:16
Hannah 64	10	38N02	82w50	5:31:20
Hansbrough 47	48	37N35	86w00	5:44:00
Hansbrough 106	51	38N13	85w14	5:40:56
Hansford 102	35	37N21	84w20	5:37:20
Hanson 54	1	37N25	87w29	5:49:56
Happy 97	45	37N12	83w06	5:32:24
Happy Acre 104	1	37N04	85w06	5:40:24
Happy Landing 76	42	37N35	84w17	5:37:08
Harcrow 48	14	36N52	83w12	5:32:48
Hardburly 97	45	37N18	83w07	5:32:28
Hardin 79	1	36N46	88w18	5:53:12
Hardinsburg 14	1	37N47	86w28	5:45:52
Hardin Springs 47	48	37N33	86w09	5:44:36
Hardshell 13	15	37N27	83w16	5:33:04
Hardwick 116	1	36N57	84w42	5:38:48
Hardy 98	10	37N37	82w15	5:29:00
Hardyville 50	1	37N14	85w45	5:43:00
Hare 63	15	37N11	84w07	5:36:28
Hargett 33	26	37N42	83w58	5:35:52
Hargis 100	18	36N57	84w29	5:37:56
Harlan 48	14	36N51	83w19	5:33:16
Harlan Crossroads 86	1	36N42	85w42	5:42:48
Harlan Gas 48	14	36N51	83w18	5:33:12
Harmony 94	15	38N32	84w50	5:39:20
Harmony Village 93	49	38N21	85w37	5:42:28
Harned 14	1	37N45	86w25	5:45:40
Harold 36	10	37N32	82w38	5:30:32
Harper 77	10	37N48	83w12	5:32:48
Harpers Ferry 52	48	38N20	85w03	5:40:12
Harreldsville 16	1	36N59	86w57	5:47:48
Harris 68	10	38N36	83w19	5:33:16
Harris Grove 18	1	36N36	88w19	5:53:16
Harrisonville 106	48	38N09	85w05	5:40:20
Harrodsburg 84	43	37N46	84w51	5:39:24
Harrods Creek 56	65	38N20	85w38	5:42:32
Hart 63	36	37N08	84w05	5:36:20
Hartford 92	1	37N27	86w55	5:47:40
Hartley 98	10	37N20	82w35	5:30:20
Harveyton 97	45	37N19	83w12	5:32:48
Harvy 79	1	36N51	88w21	5:53:24
Haskingsville 44	6	37N16	85w30	5:42:00
Hatcher 109	48	37N21	85w21	5:41:24
Hatfield 98	10	37N37	82w16	5:29:04
Hatton 106	48	38N14	85w00	5:40:00
Hawesville 46	1	37N54	86w45	5:47:00
Hawkins 24	1	36N58	87w42	5:50:48
Haynesville 92	1	37N40	86w46	5:47:04
Hays 114	1	37N03	86w13	5:44:52
Hays Crossing 103	15	38N11	83w26	5:33:44
Haysville 82	48	37N53	86w14	5:44:56
Hayward 22	15	38N16	83w18	5:33:12
Haywood 5	6	37N00	85w55	5:43:40
Hazard 97	45	37N15	83w12	5:32:48
Hazel 18	1	36N30	88w20	5:53:20
Hazel Green 119	15	37N47	83w24	5:33:36
Hazel Patch 63	15	37N11	84w07	5:36:28
Head of Cedar 105	15	38N16	84w41	5:38:44
Head of Grassy 68	10	38N24	83w16	5:33:04
Head Quarters 91	15	38N23	84w02	5:36:08
Hearin 117	1	37N29	87w50	5:51:20
Heath 73	1	37N05	88w47	5:55:08
Hebbardsville 51	1	37N47	87w23	5:49:32
Hebron 8	10	39N04	84w42	5:38:48
Hecla 54	1	37N17	87w31	5:50:04
Hector 26	15	37N09	83w39	5:34:36
Hedgeville 11	15	37N37	84w35	5:38:20
Heekin 41	10	38N39	84w34	5:38:16
Heenon 98	10	37N39	82w35	5:30:20
Heflin 92	1	37N27	86w54	5:47:36
Hegira 29	1	36N48	85w22	5:41:28
Heidelberg 65	15	37N33	83w47	5:35:08
Heidrick 61	14	36N52	83w54	5:35:36
Heiner 97	45	37N18	83w10	5:32:40
Helechawa 119	15	37N46	83w20	5:33:20
Helena 81	10	38N30	83w47	5:35:08
Hellier 98	10	37N19	82w28	5:29:52
Helton 66	15	36N58	83w24	5:33:36
Henderson 51	8	37N50	87w35	5:50:20
Hendricks 77	10	37N43	83w07	5:32:28
Hendron 73	1	37N03	88w37	5:54:28
Henrietta 58	10	37N52	82w42	5:30:48
Henry Clay 34	27	38N02	84w29	5:37:56
Henry Clay 98	10	37N19	82w28	5:29:52
Henryville 91	37	38N19	84w02	5:36:08
Henshaw 113	1	37N37	88w03	5:52:12
Hensley 14	1	37N53	86w17	5:45:08
Hensley 26	15	37N09	83w46	5:35:04
Hensleytown 24	1	36N40	87w26	5:49:44
Herbert 92	1	37N40	86w46	5:47:04
Herd 55	15	37N22	83w52	5:35:28
Herman 110	1	36N39	87w10	5:48:40
Herndon 24	1	36N44	87w34	5:50:16
Heselton 68	10	38N36	83w19	5:33:16
Hesler 94	15	38N28	84w47	5:39:08
Hestand 86	1	36N39	85w38	5:42:32
Hiatt 102	15	37N24	84w25	5:37:40
Hickman 38	1	36N34	89w11	5:56:44
Hickory 42	1	36N49	88w38	5:54:32
Hickory Flat 107	1	36N43	86w35	5:46:20
Hickory Grove 3	43	38N02	84w54	5:39:36
Hickory Grove 29	1	36N42	85w22	5:41:28
Hickory Grove 42	1	36N50	88w42	5:54:48
Hidalgo 116	1	36N50	84w51	5:39:24
Higdon 43	1	37N30	86w13	5:44:52
High Bridge 57	28	37N49	84w43	5:38:52
High Falls 119	15	37N45	83w33	5:34:12
Highgrove 90	48	37N54	85w29	5:41:56
High Knob 55	15	37N19	83w58	5:35:52
Highland 69	15	37N20	84w40	5:38:40
Highland Heights 19	68	39N02	84w27	5:37:48
Highland Spring 5	6	37N08	85w58	5:43:52
Highplains 14	1	37N48	86w09	5:44:36
High Point 73	1	37N05	88w45	5:55:00
Highsplint 48	14	36N52	83w12	5:32:48
High Top 63	36	37N08	84w05	5:36:20
Highview 56	65	38N11	85w39	5:42:36
Highway 27	1	36N41	85w08	5:40:32
Hi Hat 36	10	37N23	82w44	5:30:56

KENTUCKY

Hikes Point 56	65	38N13	85w37	5:42:28
Hilda 103	15	38N11	83w26	5:33:44
Hillcrest 76	30	37N45	84w18	5:37:12
Hillsboro 35	15	38N18	83w40	5:34:40
Hillsdale 107	1	36N43	86w35	5:46:20
Hillside 89	1	37N18	87w08	5:48:32
Hilltop 35	15	38N23	83w55	5:35:40
Hilltop 41	10	38N39	84w34	5:38:16
Hill Top 74	15	36N43	84w32	5:38:08
Hillview 15	48	38N06	85w42	5:42:48
Hilton 97	45	37N15	83w11	5:32:44
Hima 26	15	37N07	83w47	5:35:08
Himyar 61	14	36N50	83w48	5:35:12
Hindman 60	15	37N20	82w59	5:31:56
Hinkle 61	14	36N54	83w49	5:35:16
Hinkleville 4	1	37N05	88w58	5:55:52
Hinton 49	15	38N29	84w32	5:38:08
Hippo 36	10	37N32	82w52	5:31:28
Hiram 48	14	36N59	82w59	5:31:56
Hisel 55	15	37N33	84w05	5:36:20
Hiseville 5	1	37N06	85w49	5:43:16
Hislope 100	18	37N04	84w45	5:39:00
Hitchins 22	15	38N17	82w55	5:31:40
Hite 36	10	37N33	82w45	5:31:00
Hitesville 113	1	37N41	87w55	5:51:40
Hobart 27	1	36N46	85w21	5:41:24
Hobson 109	48	37N25	85w22	5:41:28
Hode 80	10	37N53	82w25	5:29:40
Hodgenville 62	48	37N34	85w44	5:42:56
Hogue 100	18	37N10	84w43	5:38:52
Holbrook 41	10	38N39	84w34	5:38:16
Holifield 42	1	36N39	88w44	5:54:56
Holland 2	1	36N41	86w03	5:44:12
Holliday 88	15	37N52	83w12	5:32:48
Hollonville 119	15	37N45	83w33	5:34:12
Hollow Bill 71	1	36N59	86w57	5:47:48
Hollow Creek 56	65	38N11	85w39	5:42:36
Hollybush 60	15	37N20	82w51	5:31:24
Hollyhill 74	15	36N40	84w20	5:37:20
Hollyvilla 56	65	38N06	85w45	5:43:00
Holmes Mill 48	14	36N52	83w00	5:32:00
Holt 14	1	37N47	86w28	5:45:52
Holt 89	1	37N15	87w06	5:48:24
Holy Cross 78	56	37N38	85w24	5:41:36
Homer 71	1	36N51	86w53	5:47:32
Honaker 36	10	37N31	82w40	5:30:40
Honeybee 74	15	36N51	84w23	5:37:32
Hooktown 91	20	38N23	84w17	5:37:08
Hootentown 25	32	38N00	84w11	5:36:44
Hope 87	15	38N01	83w46	5:35:04
Hopeful Heights 8	10	39N00	84w39	5:38:36
Hopewell 44	15	38N20	82w57	5:31:48
Hopewell 56	65	38N13	85w35	5:42:20
Hopkinsville 24	1	36N52	87w29	5:49:56
Hopkinsville West 24	1	36N54	87w33	5:50:12
Hopson 17	1	37N07	87w53	5:51:32
Horntown 43	1	37N30	86w13	5:44:52
Horntown 104	1	37N04	85w06	5:40:24
Horse Branch 92	1	37N28	86w41	5:46:44
Horse Cave 50	6	37N11	85w54	5:43:36
Horse Creek Junction 26	15	37N09	83w46	5:35:04
Horton 92	1	37N24	86w53	5:47:32
Hoskinston 66	15	37N05	83w24	5:33:36
Hosman 7	14	36N47	83w46	5:35:04
Houston 13	15	37N27	83w31	5:34:04
Houston Acres 56	65	38N13	85w37	5:42:28
Hovious 1	1	37N16	85w09	5:40:36
Howard 47	61	38N00	85w57	5:43:48
Howard Mills 87	21	38N03	83w57	5:35:48
Howards Creek 13	15	37N29	83w21	5:33:24
Howardstown 90	48	37N34	85w36	5:42:24
Howel 24	1	36N40	87w26	5:49:44
Howe Valley 47	48	37N35	86w00	5:44:00
Hubble 69	15	37N37	84w35	5:38:20
Hubbs 61	14	36N47	83w55	5:35:40
Huddy 98	10	37N36	82w17	5:29:08
Hudgins 44	1	37N20	85w33	5:42:12
Hudson 14	1	37N39	86w17	5:45:08
Hudsonville 14	1	37N43	86w17	5:45:08
Hueys Corner 8	10	38N57	84w41	5:38:44
Hueysville 36	10	37N32	82w50	5:31:20
Huff 31	1	37N15	86w24	5:45:36
Hughey 72	1	37N04	88w08	5:52:32
Hulen 7	14	36N47	83w31	5:34:04
Humble 104	1	37N07	85w03	5:40:12
Hummel 102	15	37N25	84w18	5:37:12
Hunnewell 45	10	38N29	82w50	5:31:20
Hunt 25	32	38N00	84w11	5:36:44
Hunter 36	10	37N30	82w45	5:31:00
Hunters 90	48	37N48	85w28	5:41:52
Hunterton 120	44	38N03	84w44	5:38:56
Huntsville 16	1	37N10	86w53	5:47:32
Hurley 55	15	37N26	84w00	5:36:00
Hurricane Hills 90	48	37N47	85w40	5:42:40
Hurst 13	15	37N40	83w31	5:34:04
Hurstbourne Acres 56	65	38N13	85w36	5:42:24
Hustonville 69	15	37N29	84w47	5:39:08
Hutch 7	14	36N37	83w44	5:34:56
Hutchison 9	29	38N13	84w15	5:37:00
Hyattsville 40	15	37N37	84w35	5:38:20
Hyden 66	15	37N10	83w22	5:33:28
Hydro 114	1	37N03	86w13	5:44:52
Hylton 98	10	37N13	82w34	5:30:16
Iberia 43	1	37N30	86w13	5:44:52
Ibex 32	15	38N18	83w11	5:32:44
Ice 67	15	37N07	82w49	5:31:16
Ida 27	1	36N41	85w08	5:40:32
Idamay 65	15	37N31	83w46	5:35:04
Idlewild 8	10	39N02	84w44	5:38:56
Ilsley 54	1	37N10	87w41	5:50:44
Independence 59	10	38N57	84w33	5:38:12
Index 88	39	37N54	83w17	5:33:08
Indiancreek 61	14	36N57	84w00	5:36:00
Indian Fields 25	15	37N56	84w00	5:36:00
Indian Hills 11	24	37N39	84w46	5:39:04
Indian Hills 21	38	38N41	85w11	5:40:44
Indian Hills 37	19	38N12	84w52	5:39:28
Indian Hills 56	65	38N18	85w39	5:42:36
Indian Hills 104	1	37N04	85w06	5:40:24
Indian Hills 114	7	37N00	86w25	5:45:40
Indian Hills Cherokee Sect 56	65	38N17	85w40	5:42:40
Indian Lake 46	1	37N54	86w45	5:47:00
Indian Old Field 25	32	38N00	84w11	5:36:44
Inez 80	10	37N52	82w32	5:30:08
Ingle 100	18	37N06	84w52	5:39:28
Ingleside 4	1	37N05	88w53	5:55:32
Ingram 7	14	36N44	83w48	5:35:12
Insco 71	1	36N51	86w53	5:47:32
Insko 88	15	37N46	83w18	5:33:12
Iron Hill 22	15	38N24	83w03	5:32:12
Ironville 10	10	38N28	82w39	5:30:36
Iroquois 56	66	38N10	85w47	5:43:08
Irvine 33	26	37N42	83w58	5:35:52
Irvington 14	1	37N53	86w17	5:45:08
Irvins Store 104	1	37N04	85w06	5:40:24
Island 75	1	37N27	87w09	5:48:36
Island City 95	15	37N22	83w46	5:35:04
Isom 67	15	37N11	82w54	5:31:36
Isonville 32	15	38N05	83w02	5:32:08
Iuka 70	1	37N05	88w14	5:52:56
Ivel 36	10	37N35	82w39	5:30:36
Iverdale 7	14	36N46	83w42	5:34:48
Ivis 60	15	37N20	82w59	5:31:56
Ivor 96	10	38N55	84w16	5:37:04
Ivy Grove 7	14	36N47	83w44	5:34:56
Ivyton 77	10	37N43	82w58	5:31:52
Jabez 104	1	36N59	84w54	5:39:36
Jackhorn 67	15	37N13	82w42	5:30:48
Jacks Creek 26	15	37N11	83w36	5:34:24
Jackson 13	15	37N33	83w23	5:33:32
Jacksonville 9	29	38N13	84w15	5:37:00
Jacksonville 106	48	38N16	85w03	5:40:12
Jackstown 9	15	38N15	84w04	5:36:16
Jacktown 23	48	37N30	85w09	5:40:36
Jacobs 22	15	38N14	83w16	5:33:04
Jamboree 98	10	37N30	82w08	5:28:32
Jamestown 104	1	36N59	85w04	5:40:16
Jarvis 61	14	36N52	83w53	5:35:32
Jason 66	15	37N10	83w33	5:34:12
Jason Ridge 110	1	36N59	87w09	5:48:36
Jayem 7	14	36N46	83w42	5:34:48
Jeff 97	45	37N12	83w08	5:32:32
Jeffersontown 56	65	38N08	85w38	5:42:32
Jeffersonville 87	15	37N59	83w51	5:35:24
Jeffrey 86	1	36N48	85w49	5:43:16
Jellico 118	14	36N35	84w08	5:36:32
Jellicocreek 118	14	36N44	84w10	5:36:40
Jenkins 67	15	37N10	82w38	5:30:32
Jensenton 115	48	37N41	85w13	5:40:52
Jenson 7	14	36N47	83w38	5:34:32
Jeptha 88	39	37N55	83w16	5:33:04
Jeremiah 67	15	37N10	82w56	5:31:44
Jericho 41	10	38N44	84w45	5:39:00
Jericho 52	48	38N23	85w15	5:41:00
Jericho 62	48	37N34	85w44	5:42:56
Jerico 71	1	36N59	86w57	5:47:48
Jeriel 22	15	38N20	82w57	5:31:48
Jessietown 78	48	37N29	85w20	5:41:20
Jetson 16	1	37N15	86w32	5:46:08
Jett 37	19	38N12	84w52	5:39:28
Jetts Creek 13	15	37N29	83w31	5:34:04
Jewell City 54	1	37N29	87w30	5:50:00
Jimtown 115	48	37N41	85w13	5:40:52
Jinks 33	15	37N37	84w02	5:36:08
Job 80	10	37N56	82w32	5:30:08
Jock 31	1	37N17	86w17	5:45:08
Johnetta 102	15	37N25	84w12	5:36:48
Johns Creek 58	10	37N46	82w45	5:31:00
Johnson Bottom 98	10	37N34	82w09	5:28:36
Johns Run 22	15	38N14	82w55	5:31:40
Johnsville 12	10	38N48	84w13	5:36:52
Jonancy 98	10	37N19	82w35	5:30:20
Jonestown 34	27	37N59	84w30	5:38:00
Jonesville 41	10	38N38	84w46	5:39:04
Jonican 98	10	37N26	82w23	5:29:32
Joppa 1	1	37N06	85w18	5:41:12
Josephine 105	15	38N23	84w32	5:38:08
Joy 70	1	37N17	88w22	5:53:28
Joyes 106	51	38N13	85w14	5:40:56
Juan 13	15	37N33	83w22	5:33:28
Judio 29	1	36N42	85w22	5:41:28
Judson 40	15	37N37	84w35	5:38:20
Judy 87	21	38N03	83w57	5:35:48
Judyville 9	37	38N19	84w02	5:36:08
Julien 24	1	36N53	87w40	5:50:40
Julip 118	14	36N45	84w04	5:36:16
Jumbo 69	15	37N32	84w40	5:38:40
Junction City 11	41	37N35	84w48	5:39:12
Justell 36	10	37N33	82w38	5:30:32
Justice 71	1	36N59	86w57	5:47:48
Justiceville 98	10	37N29	82w31	5:30:04
Kaler 42	1	36N49	88w38	5:54:32
Kaliopi 66	15	37N14	83w25	5:33:40
Kansas 42	1	36N57	88w43	5:54:52
Karlus 104	1	36N59	85w04	5:40:16
Kavanaugh 10	10	38N25	82w36	5:30:24
Kavito 104	1	37N04	84w50	5:39:20
Kayjay 61	14	36N52	83w53	5:35:32
Keaton 58	10	37N59	82w58	5:31:52
Keavy 63	15	37N00	84w10	5:36:40
Keefer 41	10	38N30	84w34	5:38:16
Keene 57	27	37N57	84w38	5:38:32
Keeneland 56	67	38N17	85w34	5:42:16
Kehoe 45	10	38N36	83w10	5:32:40
Keith 48	14	36N51	83w22	5:33:28
Kelat 49	35	38N31	84w23	5:37:32
Kellacey 88	39	37N55	83w16	5:33:04
Kelly 24	1	36N58	87w29	5:49:56
Kellyville 1	1	37N06	85w18	5:41:12
Keltner 1	1	37N07	85w24	5:41:36
Kemp 1	1	37N07	85w24	5:41:36
Kenmont 97	45	37N12	83w08	5:32:32
Kennedy 24	1	36N40	87w26	5:49:44
Keno 100	18	36N58	84w35	5:38:20
Kensee 118	14	36N35	84w08	5:36:32
Kenton 59	10	38N52	84w27	5:37:48
Kentontown 101	10	38N32	84w02	5:36:08
Kenton Vale 59	68	39N03	84w31	5:38:04
Kentucky Ridge 7	14	36N42	83w45	5:35:00
Kenvir 48	14	36N51	83w10	5:32:40
Kerby Knob 55	15	37N31	84w07	5:36:28
Kern Orchard 113	1	37N33	87w59	5:51:56
Kerz 58	10	37N53	82w51	5:31:24
Kessinger 50	1	37N16	85w53	5:43:32
Keswick 118	14	36N35	84w08	5:36:32
Kettle 29	1	36N42	85w22	5:41:28
Kettle Island 7	14	36N48	83w36	5:34:24
Kevil 4	1	37N05	88w53	5:55:32
Kewanee 98	10	37N26	82w31	5:30:04
Keysburg 71	1	36N43	87w04	5:48:16
Kidder 116	1	36N59	84w37	5:38:28
Kidds Crossing 116	1	36N46	84w44	5:38:56
Kidds Store 23	48	37N28	84w49	5:39:16
Kiddville 25	21	38N03	83w57	5:35:48
Kildav 48	14	36N52	83w12	5:32:48
Kilgore 22	15	38N20	82w46	5:31:04
Kimbrell 33	26	37N42	83w58	5:35:52
Kimper 98	10	37N30	82w21	5:29:24
Kinchloes Bluff 89	1	37N18	87w08	5:48:32
Kingbee 100	18	37N09	84w44	5:38:56
Kings Creek 67	15	37N03	82w55	5:31:40
Kingsley 56	66	38N13	85w41	5:42:44
Kings Mountain 69	15	37N22	84w41	5:38:44
Kingston 76	15	37N39	84w15	5:37:00
Kingswood 14	1	37N45	86w25	5:45:40
Kinniconick 68	10	38N36	83w19	5:33:16
Kino 5	6	37N00	85w55	5:43:40
Kirbyton 20	1	36N52	89w01	5:56:04
Kirk 14	1	37N47	86w28	5:45:52
Kirkland 115	43	37N46	84w51	5:39:24
Kirkmansville 110	1	37N01	87w15	5:49:00
Kirksey 18	1	36N41	88w22	5:53:28
Kirksville 76	30	37N45	84w18	5:37:12
Kirkwood 84	15	37N55	84w55	5:39:40
Kirkwood Springs 54	1	37N10	87w41	5:50:44
Kiserton 9	29	38N13	84w15	5:37:00
Kite 60	15	37N19	82w48	5:31:12
Kitts 48	14	36N51	83w18	5:33:12
Knifley 1	1	37N14	85w11	5:40:44
Knob Lick 85	1	37N05	85w42	5:42:48
Knottsville 30	1	37N44	86w59	5:47:56
Knowlton 99	15	37N51	83w52	5:35:28
Knoxville 96	10	38N39	84w34	5:38:16
Kodak 97	45	37N13	83w03	5:32:12
Kona 67	15	37N10	82w44	5:30:56
Koon 72	1	37N04	88w08	5:52:32
Korea 83	15	37N57	83w29	5:33:56
Kosmosdale 56	65	38N07	85w51	5:43:24
Kragon 13	15	37N33	83w22	5:33:28
Krebs 73	1	37N03	88w37	5:54:28
Kronos 92	1	37N25	87w00	5:48:00
Krypton 97	45	37N20	83w19	5:33:16
Kuttawa 72	1	37N04	88w07	5:52:28
Kuttawa Springs 72	1	37N04	88w08	5:52:32
Kyrock 31	1	37N15	86w17	5:45:08
Labascus 23	48	37N19	84w56	5:39:44
La Center 4	1	37N04	88w58	5:55:52
Lacey 77	10	37N51	83w03	5:32:12
Lackey 36	10	37N28	82w50	5:31:20
Lacon 43	1	37N33	86w09	5:44:36
Laden 48	14	36N55	83w14	5:32:56
La Fayette 24	1	36N40	87w40	5:50:40
La Grange 93	59	38N25	85w23	5:41:32
Lair 49	20	38N20	84w18	5:37:12
Lake 63	15	37N05	83w53	5:35:32
Lake City 70	1	37N00	88w14	5:52:56
Lake Dreamland 56	66	38N11	85w49	5:43:16
Lake Louisvilla 56	65	38N19	85w31	5:42:04
Lakeside Park 59	68	39N02	84w34	5:38:16
Lakeview 59	68	39N02	84w33	5:38:12
Lakeville 77	10	37N45	83w04	5:32:16
Lamasco 72	1	36N59	87w56	5:51:44
Lamb 86	1	36N46	85w54	5:43:36
Lambert 36	10	37N23	82w44	5:30:56
Lambric 13	15	37N34	83w08	5:32:32
Lamero 102	15	37N18	84w11	5:36:44
Lamont 73	1	37N05	88w48	5:55:12
Lamont 97	45	37N15	83w11	5:32:44
Lancaster 40	34	37N37	84w35	5:38:20
Lancer 36	10	37N40	82w46	5:31:04
Landsaw 119	15	37N45	83w33	5:34:12
Langley 36	10	37N32	82w47	5:31:08
Langnau 63	36	37N08	84w05	5:36:20
Larkslane 60	15	37N23	82w53	5:31:32
Larue 26	15	37N09	83w46	5:35:04
Latonia 59	68	39N03	84w32	5:38:08
Latonia Lakes 59	10	38N59	84w30	5:38:00
Laura 80	10	37N43	82w26	5:29:44
Laurel Creek 26	15	37N09	83w46	5:35:04
Laurel Fork 7	14	36N38	83w56	5:35:44
Laurel Gap 10	10	38N25	82w36	5:30:24
Lawhorn Hill 23	48	37N19	84w56	5:39:44

Lawrenceburg 3 43 38N02 84w54 5:39:36
Lawrenceville 41 10 38N39 84w34 5:38:16
Lawson 13 15 37N33 83w22 5:33:28
Lawton 22 15 38N21 83w13 5:32:52
Layman 48 14 36N50 83w27 5:33:48
Laynesville 36 10 37N32 82w38 5:30:32
Leach 10 10 36N38 83w56 5:35:44
Leafdale 62 48 37N34 85w44 5:42:56
Leander 58 10 37N46 82w52 5:31:28
Leatha 77 10 37N47 83w00 5:32:00
Leatherwood 97 45 37N02 83w11 5:32:44
Lebanon 78 63 37N34 85w15 5:41:00
Lebanon Junction 15
53 37N50 85w44 5:42:56
Leburn 60 15 37N21 82w57 5:31:48
Leckieville 98 10 37N40 82w16 5:29:04
Lecta 5 6 37N00 85w55 5:43:40
Ledbetter 70 1 37N03 88w28 5:53:52
Ledocio 64 10 38N07 82w36 5:30:24
Lee City 119 15 37N44 83w20 5:33:20
Leeco 65 15 37N43 83w42 5:34:48
Leesburg 49 15 38N18 84w25 5:37:40
Lees Lick 49 20 38N23 84w17 5:37:08
Leestown 37 19 38N12 84w52 5:39:28
Leestown Terrace 37
19 38N12 84w52 5:39:28
Leetown 16 1 37N11 86w45 5:47:00
Legrand 50 6 37N11 85w54 5:43:36
Leighton 33 26 37N42 83w58 5:35:52
Leisure 88 39 37N55 83w16 5:33:04
Leitchfield 43 1 37N29 86w18 5:45:12
Leitchfield Crossing 50
1 37N23 85w54 5:43:36
Lejunior 48 14 36N54 83w12 5:32:48
Lenarue 48 14 36N49 83w15 5:33:00
Lennut 97 45 37N16 83w13 5:32:52
Lenore 90 48 37N54 85w29 5:41:56
Lenox 88 15 37N58 83w12 5:32:48
Lenoxburg 12 10 38N45 84w13 5:36:52
Leon 22 15 38N20 82w57 5:31:48
Lerose 95 15 37N29 83w37 5:34:28
Lesbas 63 36 37N08 84w05 5:36:20
Leslie 29 1 36N48 85w22 5:41:28
Letcher 67 15 37N09 82w58 5:31:52
Letitia 45 10 38N43 82w58 5:31:52
Levee 87 15 37N59 83w51 5:35:24
Level Green 102 35 37N21 84w20 5:37:20
Levi 95 15 37N29 83w40 5:34:40
Levias 28 1 37N20 88w04 5:52:16
Lewis 48 14 36N52 83w12 5:32:48
Lewisburg 71 15 38N33 83w46 5:35:04
Lewisburg 81 10 38N35 83w52 5:35:28
Lewis Creek 66 15 37N00 83w18 5:33:12
Lewisport 46 1 37N56 86w54 5:47:36
Lexie 119 15 37N45 83w33 5:34:12
Lexington 34 27 38N03 84w30 5:38:00
Lexington-Blue Grass Army De 9
27 38N04 84w29 5:37:56
Liberty 23 48 37N19 84w56 5:39:44
Liberty 110 1 36N48 87w09 5:48:36
Liberty 117 1 37N31 87w41 5:50:44
Liberty Road 88 39 37N55 83w16 5:33:04
Lick Branch 88 39 37N55 83w16 5:33:04
Lickburg 77 10 37N48 83w05 5:32:20
Lick Creek 98 10 37N24 82w18 5:29:12
Licking River 88 39 37N55 83w16 5:33:04
Lick Skillet 71 1 36N45 87w01 5:48:04
Lida 63 15 37N05 83w56 5:35:44
Liggett 48 14 36N51 83w19 5:33:16
Ligon 36 10 37N22 82w41 5:30:44
Liletown 44 6 37N16 85w30 5:42:00
Lily 63 15 37N02 84w17 5:37:08
Limaburg 8 10 39N02 84w44 5:38:56
Limestone 22 15 38N16 83w12 5:32:48
Limestone Springs 15
50 38N00 85w43 5:42:52
Limeville 45 10 38N43 82w58 5:31:52
Limp 47 48 37N35 86w03 5:44:12
Lincoln 26 15 37N09 83w46 5:35:04
Lincoln 31 1 37N16 86w15 5:45:00
Lincoln Ridge 106
48 38N13 85w21 5:41:24
Lincolnshire 56 65 38N13 85w37 5:42:28
Lindseyville 31 1 37N14 86w17 5:45:08
Linefork 67 15 37N01 82w57 5:31:48
Linton 111 1 36N41 87w55 5:51:40
Linwood 50 1 37N27 85w45 5:43:00
Lionilli 98 10 37N11 82w38 5:30:32
Lisletown 25 32 38N00 84w11 5:36:44
Lisman 117 1 37N28 87w44 5:50:56
Littcarr 60 15 37N15 82w57 5:31:48
Little 13 15 37N26 83w22 5:33:28
Little Barren 44 6 37N16 85w30 5:42:00
Little Bear Creek 79
1 37N01 88w18 5:53:12
Little Creek 7 14 36N48 83w39 5:34:36
Little Cypress 79 1 37N01 88w21 5:53:24
Little Dixie 98 10 37N29 82w31 5:30:04
Little Hickman 57
28 37N53 84w34 5:38:16
Little Mount 108 48 38N02 85w21 5:41:24
Little Muddy 16 1 37N14 86w41 5:46:44
Little Needmore 11
24 37N39 84w46 5:39:04
Little Rock 9 15 38N12 84w03 5:36:12
Little Sandy 32 15 38N04 83w11 5:32:44
Little Tar Springs 46
1 37N54 86w45 5:47:00
Littleton 26 15 37N09 83w46 5:35:04
Littrell 29 1 36N42 85w22 5:41:28
Livermore 75 1 37N29 87w08 5:48:32
Livia 30 1 37N32 87w16 5:49:04
Livingston 102 15 37N17 84w13 5:36:52
Lloyd 45 10 38N37 82w52 5:31:28
Load 45 10 38N33 82w58 5:31:52

Lockards Creek 26
15 37N07 83w45 5:35:00
Lockport 52 48 38N26 84w58 5:39:52
Lockwood 10 10 38N25 82w36 5:30:24
Locust 21 55 38N43 85w22 5:41:28
Locust Grove 25 32 38N00 84w11 5:36:44
Locust Grove 96 10 38N40 84w20 5:37:20
Locust Hill 14 1 37N44 86w21 5:45:24
Lodiburg 14 1 37N53 86w17 5:45:08
Logana 57 28 37N53 84w34 5:38:16
Logansport 16 1 37N16 86w45 5:47:00
Logantown 69 15 37N32 84w40 5:38:40
Loglick 25 32 38N00 84w11 5:36:44
Logmont 7 14 36N37 83w44 5:34:56
Log Mountain 7 14 36N46 83w42 5:34:48
Logville 77 10 37N52 83w07 5:32:28
Lola 70 1 37N19 88w18 5:53:12
Lombard 99 15 37N51 83w52 5:35:28
London 63 36 37N08 84w05 5:36:20
Lone 65 15 37N32 83w36 5:34:24
Lone Oak 73 1 37N02 88w40 5:54:40
Lone Star 50 1 37N23 85w54 5:43:36
Long Fork 98 10 37N18 82w39 5:30:36
Longlick 105 15 38N16 84w41 5:38:44
Long Ridge 94 15 38N32 84w50 5:39:20
Longstreet 104 1 37N04 85w06 5:40:24
Long View 47 58 37N42 85w52 5:43:28
Lookout 98 10 37N19 82w28 5:29:52
Loretto 78 56 37N39 85w24 5:41:36
Lost Creek 13 15 37N29 83w19 5:33:16
Lost River 114 7 37N00 86w25 5:45:40
Lot 118 14 36N35 84w08 5:36:32
Lothair 97 45 37N14 83w10 5:32:40
Lotus 15 48 37N54 85w34 5:42:16
Louden 118 14 36N45 84w04 5:36:16
Louellen 48 14 36N55 83w06 5:32:24
Louisa 64 10 38N07 82w36 5:30:24
Louisville 56 66 38N15 85w46 5:43:04
Lovelaceville 4 1 37N00 88w50 5:55:20
Lovely 80 10 37N50 82w24 5:29:36
Loving 114 1 37N02 86w15 5:45:00
Lowell 40 15 37N37 84w24 5:37:36
Lower Gillmore 119
15 37N44 83w22 5:33:28
Lower Kings Addition 45
10 38N43 82w58 5:31:52
Lower Pompey 98 10 37N29 82w31 5:30:04
Lowes 42 1 36N53 88w46 5:55:04
Lowgap 1 1 36N58 85w26 5:41:44
Lowmansville 64 10 37N55 82w44 5:30:56
Loyall 48 14 36N52 83w22 5:33:28
Lucas 5 1 36N53 86w02 5:44:08
Lucile 32 15 38N05 83w08 5:32:32
Lucky Fork 95 15 37N23 83w37 5:34:28
Lucky Stop 87 15 37N59 83w51 5:35:24
Ludlow 59 68 39N05 84w33 5:38:12
Lunah 13 15 37N36 83w12 5:32:48
Luner 102 35 37N21 84w20 5:37:20
Lupton 48 14 36N52 83w12 5:32:48
Lusby's Mill 94 15 38N32 84w50 5:39:20
Luzon 117 1 37N31 87w41 5:50:44
Lykins 77 10 37N47 83w11 5:32:44
Lynch 48 14 36N58 82w54 5:31:36
Lyndon 56 65 38N15 85w36 5:42:24
Lynn 45 10 38N34 82w50 5:31:20
Lynncamp 63 15 36N57 84w06 5:36:24
Lynn City 89 1 37N25 87w16 5:49:04
Lynn Grove 18 1 36N35 88w26 5:53:44
Lynnview 56 66 38N11 85w43 5:42:52
Lynnville 42 1 36N34 88w34 5:54:16
Lyons 62 56 37N40 85w35 5:42:20
Lytten 32 15 38N05 83w13 5:32:52
Mac 109 48 37N21 85w21 5:41:24
Macedonia 13 15 37N26 83w28 5:33:52
Macedonia 24 1 37N03 87w29 5:49:56
Macedonia 55 15 37N26 84w00 5:36:00
Maceo 30 1 37N52 87w00 5:48:00
Mackville 48 37N44 85w04 5:40:16
Macon 50 1 37N16 85w53 5:43:32
Madisonville 54 4 37N20 87w30 5:50:00
Magan 92 1 37N38 86w43 5:46:52
Maggard 77 10 37N49 83w07 5:32:28
Maggie 111 1 36N52 87w50 5:51:20
Magnolia 62 48 37N27 85w45 5:43:00
Main Street 98 10 37N29 82w31 5:30:04
Majestic 98 10 37N32 83w06 5:32:24
Major 95 15 37N29 83w40 5:34:40
Malaga 119 15 37N43 83w27 5:33:48
Mallie 60 15 37N18 82w55 5:31:40
Malone 88 39 37N52 83w16 5:33:04
Maloneton 45 10 38N41 82w55 5:31:40
Mammoth Cave 31 1 37N11 86w06 5:44:24
Manchester 26 15 37N09 83w46 5:35:04
Manco 98 10 37N17 82w28 5:29:52
Manda 92 1 37N20 86w47 5:47:08
Mangum 100 18 37N10 84w46 5:39:04
Manila 58 10 37N51 82w54 5:31:36
Manitou 54 1 37N22 87w35 5:50:20
Mannington 24 1 37N08 87w28 5:49:52
Mannsville 109 48 37N22 85w12 5:40:48
Manor Creek 56 67 38N17 85w35 5:42:20
Manton 36 10 37N33 82w47 5:31:08
Manton 115 56 37N38 85w24 5:41:36
Manuel 97 45 37N15 83w11 5:32:44
Maple Grove 111 1 36N52 87w50 5:51:20
Maple Mount 30 1 37N42 87w26 5:49:44
Maplesville 63 36 37N08 84w05 5:36:20
Marcellus 40 15 37N37 84w35 5:38:20
Marcum 26 15 37N07 83w33 5:34:12
Mare Creek 36 10 37N35 82w39 5:30:36
Maretburg 102 35 37N21 84w20 5:37:20
Mariba 83 15 37N55 83w35 5:34:20
Marion 28 1 37N20 88w05 5:52:20
Mark 100 18 37N06 84w36 5:38:24
Marksbury 40 15 37N37 84w35 5:38:20
Marlowe 67 15 37N07 82w49 5:31:16

Marne No.Ø2 48 14 36N52 83w12 5:32:48
Marrowbone 29 1 36N50 85w30 5:42:00
Marshall 81 10 38N35 83w52 5:35:28
Marshallville 77 10 37N41 82w59 5:31:56
Marshes Siding 74
15 36N45 84w29 5:37:56
Martha 64 10 38N01 82w55 5:31:40
Martha Mills 35 15 38N25 83w47 5:35:08
Martin 36 10 37N34 82w45 5:31:00
Martinsville 114 1 37N02 86w15 5:45:00
Martwick 89 1 37N18 87w08 5:48:32
Mary 119 15 37N40 83w31 5:34:04
Mary Alice 48 14 36N47 83w20 5:33:20
Marydell 63 15 37N07 83w55 5:35:40
Maryhill Estates 56
65 38N16 85w39 5:42:36
Mashfork 77 10 37N46 83w01 5:32:04
Mason 41 10 38N35 84w35 5:38:20
Mason 77 10 37N45 83w04 5:32:16
Masonic Home 56 66 38N13 85w45 5:43:00
Masonville 24 1 36N51 87w30 5:50:00
Masonville 30 1 37N36 87w07 5:48:28
Massac 73 1 37N03 88w37 5:54:28
Matanzas 92 1 37N25 87w00 5:48:00
Matlock 114 7 37N00 86w25 5:45:40
Matthew 88 15 37N51 83w10 5:32:40
Mattingly 14 1 37N50 86w38 5:46:32
Mattoon 28 1 37N20 88w04 5:52:16
Mattoxtown 34 27 38N08 84w27 5:37:48
Maud 115 48 37N49 85w18 5:41:12
Maulden 55 15 37N21 83w52 5:35:28
Maurice 59 68 39N01 84w32 5:38:08
Mavity 10 10 38N25 82w36 5:30:24
Maxie 118 14 36N35 84w08 5:36:32
Maxine 62 48 37N32 85w54 5:43:36
Maxville 8 10 39N02 84w44 5:38:56
Maxwell 30 1 37N36 87w07 5:48:28
May 60 15 37N16 82w53 5:31:32
Mayfield 42 1 36N44 88w38 5:54:32
Mayflower 98 10 37N37 82w29 5:29:56
Mayhew 10 10 38N20 82w46 5:31:04
Mayking 67 15 37N08 82w46 5:31:04
Maynard 2 6 36N45 86w11 5:44:44
Mayo 84 15 37N52 84w56 5:39:44
Mays Lick 81 10 38N31 83w50 5:35:20
Maysville 81 11 38N39 83w46 5:35:04
Maytown 88 15 37N51 83w28 5:33:52
Maywood 69 15 37N32 84w40 5:38:40
Mazie 64 10 38N02 82w58 5:31:52
McAfee 84 43 37N46 84w51 5:39:24
McAndrews 98 10 37N33 82w16 5:29:04
McBrayer 3 43 38N02 84w54 5:39:36
McCarr 98 10 37N34 82w12 5:28:48
McClure 80 10 37N48 82w25 5:29:40
McCombs 98 10 37N39 82w35 5:30:20
McCreary 40 15 37N37 84w35 5:38:20
McCreight 26 15 37N01 83w49 5:35:16
McDaniels 14 1 37N36 86w26 5:45:44
McDavid 22 15 38N20 82w57 5:31:48
McDowell 36 10 37N27 82w44 5:30:56
McGaha 1 1 37N06 85w18 5:41:12
McGlone 22 15 38N17 83w05 5:32:20
McGowan 17 1 37N07 87w53 5:51:32
McHenry 92 1 37N23 86w55 5:47:40
McKee 55 15 37N26 84w00 5:36:00
McKinney 69 15 37N27 84w46 5:39:04
McKinneysburg 96 10 38N40 84w20 5:37:20
McQuady 14 1 37N42 86w31 5:46:04
McRoberts 67 15 37N12 82w40 5:30:40
McVeigh 98 10 37N32 82w15 5:29:00
McVille 8 10 39N02 84w44 5:38:56
McWhorter 63 36 37N08 84w05 5:36:20
Meador 2 6 36N45 86w11 5:44:44
Meadow Branch 119
15 37N45 83w33 5:34:12
Meadowbrook 25 32 38N00 84w11 5:36:44
Meadow Creek 118 14 36N50 84w07 5:36:28
Meadow Vale 56 67 38N17 85w35 5:42:20
Meadowview 76 30 37N45 84w18 5:37:12
Meadowview Estates 56
65 38N13 85w38 5:42:32
Meally 58 10 37N48 82w44 5:30:56
Means 83 15 37N57 83w46 5:35:04
Meece 100 18 37N03 84w33 5:38:12
Meeting Creek 47 48 37N35 86w03 5:44:12
Melber 73 1 36N57 88w43 5:54:52
Melbourne 19 10 39N02 84w22 5:37:28
Meldrum 7 14 36N40 83w42 5:34:48
Mell 44 6 37N16 85w30 5:42:00
Melvin 36 10 37N21 82w42 5:30:48
Memphis Junction 114
7 36N57 86w29 5:45:56
Mendola Village 58
10 37N47 82w48 5:31:12
Mentor 19 10 38N53 84w15 5:37:00
Meredith 43 1 37N29 86w18 5:45:12
Merrimac 109 48 37N25 85w08 5:40:32
Merry Oaks 5 1 37N03 86w13 5:44:52
Mershons 63 15 37N11 84w07 5:36:28
Meshack 86 1 36N42 85w42 5:42:48
Meta 98 10 37N29 82w31 5:30:04
Mexico 28 1 37N20 88w04 5:52:16
Midas 36 10 37N32 82w50 5:31:20
Middleburg 23 48 37N18 84w47 5:39:08
Middle Creek 62 48 37N34 85w44 5:42:56
Middlefork 55 15 37N26 84w00 5:36:00
Middlesboro 7 14 36N36 83w43 5:34:52
Middlesborough 7 14 36N37 83w44 5:34:56
Middleton 107 1 36N45 86w44 5:46:56
Middleton Heights 106
51 38N13 85w14 5:40:56
Middletown 56 65 38N15 85w32 5:42:08
Middletown 76 42 37N35 84w17 5:37:08
Middletown 104 1 36N59 85w04 5:40:16
Midland 6 15 38N07 83w37 5:34:28
Midland 89 1 37N22 87w13 5:48:52

KENTUCKY

Midway 18	1	36N33	88W20	5:53:20
Midway 28	1	37N20	88W04	5:52:16
Midway 82	48	37N53	86W14	5:44:56
Midway 120	47	38N09	84W41	5:38:44
Milburn 20	1	36N48	88W54	5:55:36
Mildred 55	15	37N26	84W00	5:36:00
Milford 12	10	38N35	84W09	5:36:36
Millard 98	10	37N24	82W27	5:29:48
Mill Creek 81	10	38N31	83W50	5:35:20
Milledgeville 69	15	37N30	84W49	5:39:16
Miller 38	1	36N34	89W11	5:56:44
Millersburg 9	29	38N17	84W12	5:36:48
Millers Creek 33	15	37N40	83W54	5:35:36
Millerstown 43	1	37N25	86W08	5:44:32
Million 76	30	37N45	84W18	5:37:12
Mill Pond 26	15	37N09	83W46	5:35:04
Millport 89	1	37N25	87W16	5:49:04
Mills 61	14	36N55	83W39	5:34:36
Millseat 10	10	38N28	82W39	5:30:36
Mill Springs 116	1	36N54	84W50	5:39:20
Millstone 67	15	37N10	82W45	5:31:00
Milltown 1	1	37N07	85W24	5:41:36
Milltown 91	15	38N16	83W56	5:35:44
Millville 120	15	38N08	84W49	5:39:16
Millwood 43	1	37N27	86W23	5:45:32
Milner 120	44	38N03	84W44	5:38:56
Milo 80	10	37N55	82W35	5:30:20
Milton 112	55	38N43	85W22	5:41:28
Mima 88	15	37N55	83W02	5:32:08
Minerva 81	10	38N42	83W55	5:35:40
Miniard 97	45	37N05	83W06	5:32:24
Minnie 36	10	37N28	82W45	5:31:00
Minor Lane Heights 56	65	38N07	85W43	5:42:52
Minorsville 105	15	38N16	84W41	5:38:44
Mintonville 23	48	37N11	84W49	5:39:16
Miracle 7	14	36N46	83W35	5:34:20
Mistletoe 95	15	37N19	83W35	5:34:20
Mitchellsburg 11	15	37N36	84W57	5:39:48
Mize 88	15	37N52	83W23	5:33:32
Moberly 76	30	37N45	84W18	5:37:12
Mockingbird Valley 56	66	38N16	85W41	5:42:44
Moct 13	15	37N38	83W25	5:33:40
Modoc 29	1	36N46	85W21	5:41:24
Molus 48	14	36N50	83W27	5:33:48
Monford 16	1	37N15	86W32	5:46:08
Monica 65	15	37N35	83W43	5:34:52
Monitor 112	48	38N36	85W19	5:41:16
Monroe 50	1	37N15	85W47	5:43:08
Montclair 106	51	38N13	85W14	5:40:56
Monterey 94	17	38N25	84W52	5:39:28
Montgomery 111	1	36N52	87W50	5:51:20
Montgomerys Mill 44	6	37N16	85W30	5:42:00
Monticello 116	1	36N50	84W51	5:39:24
Montpelier 1	1	37N01	85W11	5:40:44
Montrose Park 37	19	38N12	84W52	5:39:28
Mooleyville 14	1	38N01	86W28	5:45:52
Moon 88	15	37N59	83W03	5:32:12
Moorefield 91	15	38N16	83W56	5:35:44
Moores Creek 55	15	37N17	84W00	5:36:00
Moores Ferry 6	15	38N07	83W37	5:34:28
Moores Mill 86	1	36N42	85W42	5:42:48
Mooresville 115	48	37N41	85W13	5:40:52
Moorland 56	67	38N16	85W35	5:42:20
Moorman 89	1	37N23	87W09	5:48:36
Moranburg 81	10	38N35	83W52	5:35:28
Morcoal 98	10	37N34	82W15	5:29:00
Moree 80	10	37N48	82W25	5:29:40
Morehead 103	17	38N11	83W26	5:33:44
Moreland 69	15	37N28	84W49	5:39:16
Morgan 96	10	38N36	84W24	5:37:36
Morganfield 113	1	37N41	87W55	5:51:40
Morgantown 16	1	37N14	86W41	5:46:44
Morningglory 91	20	38N23	84W17	5:37:08
Morning View 59	10	38N58	84W34	5:38:16
Morrill 55	15	37N31	84W12	5:36:48
Morris Fork 13	15	37N20	83W25	5:33:40
Mortiner Station 71	1	36N40	86W51	5:47:24
Mortons Gap 54	1	37N14	87W28	5:49:52
Mortonsville 120	15	37N58	84W45	5:39:00
Moscow 53	1	36N37	89W02	5:56:08
Moseleyville 30	1	37N45	87W07	5:48:28
Mosley Bend 66	15	37N15	83W24	5:33:36
Mossy Bottom 98	10	37N29	82W31	5:30:04
Motley 114	7	37N00	86W25	5:45:40
Mount Aerial 2	1	36N50	86W25	5:45:40
Mountain Ash 118	14	36N44	84W10	5:36:40
Mountain Valley 13	15	37N40	83W15	5:33:00
Mount Auburn 96	10	38N47	84W22	5:37:28
Mount Beulah 50	1	37N16	85W53	5:43:32
Mount Carmel 35	15	38N25	83W47	5:35:08
Mount Eden 108	48	38N03	85W09	5:40:36
Mount Gilead 44	6	37N16	85W30	5:42:00
Mount Gilead 86	1	36N42	85W42	5:42:48
Mount Herman 86	1	36N47	85W45	5:43:00
Mount Lebanon 57	28	37N53	84W34	5:38:16
Mount Olive 23	48	37N21	84W50	5:39:20
Mount Olive 65	15	37N35	83W43	5:34:52
Mount Olivet 101	10	38N32	84W02	5:36:08
Mount Pisgah 116	1	36N50	84W51	5:39:24
Mount Pleasant 112	48	38N36	85W19	5:41:16
Mount Salem 69	15	37N28	84W49	5:39:16
Mount Sherman 62	48	37N27	85W40	5:42:40
Mount Sterling 87	21	38N04	83W56	5:35:44
Mount Tabor 62	48	37N31	85W42	5:42:48
Mount Tabor 110	1	36N48	87W09	5:48:36
Mount Union 2	1	36N39	86W16	5:45:04
Mount Vernon 102	35	37N21	84W21	5:37:24
Mount Victor 114	7	37N00	86W25	5:45:40
Mount Victory 100	18	37N02	84W25	5:37:40
Mount Washington 15	48	38N03	85W33	5:42:12
Mount Zion 2	6	36N45	86W11	5:44:44
Mount Zion 41	10	38N44	84W45	5:39:00
Mount Zion 100	18	37N11	84W38	5:38:32
Mousie 60	15	37N25	82W53	5:31:32
Mouthcard 98	10	37N23	82W15	5:29:00
Moxley 94	15	38N33	85W00	5:40:00
Mozelle 66	15	37N00	83W24	5:33:36
Mud Camp 29	1	36N48	85W22	5:41:28
Mud Creek 36	10	37N29	82W39	5:30:36
Muddy Ford 105	15	38N18	84W30	5:38:00
Mud Lick 86	1	36N42	85W42	5:42:48
Mulberry 106	51	38N13	85W14	5:40:56
Muldraugh 82	61	37N56	85W59	5:43:56
Mulfordtown 113	1	37N33	87W59	5:51:56
Mullins 102	35	37N21	84W20	5:37:20
Mullins Addition 98	10	37N29	82W31	5:30:04
Mummie 55	15	37N21	83W54	5:35:36
Munfordville 50	1	37N16	85W54	5:43:36
Murl 116	1	36N50	84W51	5:39:24
Murphyfork 88	15	37N48	83W25	5:33:40
Murphysville 81	10	38N35	83W52	5:35:28
Murray 18	1	36N37	88W19	5:53:16
Muses Mills 35	15	38N21	83W32	5:34:08
Music 22	15	38N20	82W46	5:31:04
Myers 91	15	38N21	83W57	5:35:48
Myra 98	10	37N17	82W35	5:30:20
Mystic 14	1	37N53	86W17	5:45:08
Nampa 98	10	37N37	82W10	5:28:40
Nancy 100	18	37N04	84W45	5:39:00
Naomi 100	18	37N04	84W45	5:39:00
Napfor 97	45	37N19	83W19	5:33:16
Napier 66	15	37N00	83W18	5:33:12
Naples 45	10	38N28	82W39	5:30:36
Napoleon 39	11	38N43	84W49	5:39:16
Narrows 92	1	37N34	86W44	5:46:56
Narvel 27	1	36N46	85W01	5:40:04
Nathanton 55	15	37N21	83W54	5:35:36
Natural Bridge 99	15	37N48	83W42	5:34:48
Nazareth 90	48	37N51	85W28	5:41:52
Neafus 43	1	37N24	86W36	5:46:24
Neave 12	10	38N40	84W20	5:37:20
Nebo 54	1	37N23	87W39	5:50:36
Ned 13	15	37N25	83W16	5:33:04
Needmore 4	1	37N05	88W53	5:55:32
Needmore 11	24	37N39	84W46	5:39:04
Needmore 17	1	37N07	87W53	5:51:32
Needmore 81	10	38N31	83W50	5:35:20
Needmore 106	48	38N09	85W19	5:41:16
Nelse 98	10	37N24	82W25	5:29:40
Nelson 89	1	37N18	87W08	5:48:32
Nelsonville 90	48	37N47	85W40	5:42:40
Neon 67	15	37N11	82W43	5:30:52
Neosheo 107	1	36N43	86W35	5:46:20
Nepton 35	15	38N26	83W52	5:35:28
Nerinx 78	56	37N40	85W23	5:41:32
Nero 58	10	37N46	82W45	5:31:00
Netty 77	10	37N45	83W14	5:32:56
Neubert 48	14	36N51	83W18	5:33:12
Nevada 84	15	37N42	84W55	5:39:40
Nevin 3	43	38N02	84W54	5:39:36
Nevisdale 118	14	36N41	84W03	5:36:12
New 94	15	38N32	84W50	5:39:20
New Allen 36	10	37N37	82W43	5:30:52
Newburg 56	65	38N12	85W39	5:42:36
Newby 76	30	37N45	84W18	5:37:12
New Camp 98	10	37N41	82W16	5:29:04
New Castle 52	54	38N26	85W10	5:40:40
New Columbus 94	15	38N30	84W34	5:38:16
Newcombe 32	15	38N04	83W03	5:32:12
New Concord 18	1	36N33	88W09	5:52:36
New Cypress 53	1	36N40	89W00	5:56:00
New Cypress 89	1	37N22	87W13	5:48:52
Newfound 26	15	37N16	83W39	5:34:36
Newfoundland 32	15	38N08	83W06	5:32:24
Newgarden 47	48	37N53	85W59	5:43:56
New Haven 90	56	37N40	85W36	5:42:24
New Hope 90	48	37N38	85W31	5:42:04
New Liberty 94	15	38N37	84W53	5:39:32
Newman 30	1	37N45	87W07	5:48:28
New Market 78	48	37N29	85W20	5:41:20
Newport 19	68	39N05	84W30	5:38:00
New Providence 18	1	36N30	88W19	5:53:16
New Roe 2	1	36N39	86W16	5:45:04
New Salem 28	1	37N20	88W04	5:52:16
New Salem 69	15	37N28	84W49	5:39:16
Newstead 24	1	36N51	87W30	5:50:00
New Stithton 47	48	37N53	85W59	5:43:56
Newt 44	6	37N16	85W30	5:42:00
Newtown 105	15	38N13	84W28	5:37:52
New Zion 55	15	37N29	83W54	5:35:36
New Zion 105	27	38N05	84W29	5:37:56
Niagara 51	1	37N43	87W29	5:49:56
Nicholasville 57	28	37N53	84W34	5:38:16
Nichols 15	61	38N00	85W57	5:43:48
Nichols 53	1	36N40	89W00	5:56:00
Nicholson 59	10	38N58	84W34	5:38:16
Nickell 88	15	37N52	83W21	5:33:24
Nickolson 111	1	36N58	87W42	5:50:48
Nina 40	15	37N40	84W28	5:37:52
Nineteen 92	1	37N24	86W53	5:47:32
Ninevah 3	43	38N02	84W54	5:39:36
Nippa 58	10	37N54	82W47	5:31:08
Noble 13	15	37N28	83W17	5:33:08
Nobob 5	1	36N53	85W42	5:42:48
Nocreek 92	1	37N27	86W54	5:47:36
Noctor 13	15	37N34	83W20	5:33:20
Node 85	1	37N09	85W42	5:42:48
Noetown 7	14	36N37	83W44	5:34:56
Noland 33	26	37N42	83W58	5:35:52
Nolansburg 48	14	36N57	83W07	5:32:28
Nolin 47	48	37N32	85W54	5:43:36
Nonesuch 120	44	38N03	84W44	5:38:56
Nonnel 89	1	37N13	87W03	5:48:12
Nora 27	1	36N41	85W08	5:40:32
Norbourne Estates 56	65	38N15	85W39	5:42:36
Norfleet 100	18	37N04	84W45	5:39:00
Noris 64	10	38N03	82W43	5:30:52
Normal 10	10	38N28	82W39	5:30:36
Normal Heights 37	19	38N12	84W52	5:39:28
Normandy 108	48	38N02	85W21	5:41:24
North 34	27	38N05	84W29	5:37:56
North Corbin 63	15	37N00	84W04	5:36:16
North Fayette 34	27	38N08	84W28	5:37:52
Northfield 56	65	38N18	85W38	5:42:32
North Hazard 97	45	37N15	83W11	5:32:44
North Irvine 33	26	37N42	83W58	5:35:52
North Lebanon 78	63	37N36	85W13	5:40:52
North Lyon 72	1	37N06	88W08	5:52:32
North Middletown 9	17	38N09	84W07	5:36:28
North Oldham 93	49	38N27	85W30	5:42:00
North Pleasureville 52	48	38N21	85W07	5:40:28
Northtown 50	6	37N11	85W54	5:43:36
Norton Branch 22	15	38N20	82W46	5:31:04
Nortonville 54	1	37N12	88W27	5:53:48
Norwood 56	67	38N17	85W35	5:42:20
Norwood 100	18	37N11	84W38	5:38:32
Nuckols 75	1	37N29	87W08	5:48:32
Nugent Cross Roads 120	44	38N03	84W44	5:38:56
Nugym 7	14	36N48	83W39	5:34:36
Number One 116	1	36N50	84W51	5:39:24
Oakdale 13	15	37N33	83W28	5:33:52
Oakdale 73	1	37N03	88W37	5:54:28
Oak Forest 2	6	36N45	86W11	5:44:44
Oak Grove 24	1	36N40	87W26	5:49:44
Oak Hill 54	1	37N11	87W27	5:49:48
Oak Hill 100	18	37N06	84W36	5:38:24
Oakland 114	1	37N02	86W15	5:45:00
Oakland Mills 91	37	38N19	84W02	5:36:08
Oak Level 79	1	36N52	88W28	5:53:52
Oakley 63	15	37N11	84W07	5:36:28
Oak Ridge 30	1	37N45	87W07	5:48:28
Oak Ridge 59	68	39N03	84W32	5:38:08
Oaks 7	14	36N43	83W38	5:34:32
Oaks 73	1	37N03	88W37	5:54:28
Oaks 92	1	37N38	86W43	5:46:52
Oakton 53	1	36N40	89W04	5:56:16
Oakville 71	1	36N45	86W53	5:47:32
Oddville 49	20	38N23	84W17	5:37:08
Offutt 58	10	37N51	82W44	5:30:56
Ogle 26	15	37N02	83W43	5:34:52
Oil City 5	6	37N00	85W55	5:43:40
Oil Springs 58	10	37N49	82W57	5:31:48
Oil Valley 116	1	36N50	84W51	5:39:24
O. K. 100	18	37N17	84W40	5:38:40
Oklahoma 30	1	37N41	86W52	5:47:28
Okolona 56	65	38N08	85W41	5:42:44
Olaton 92	1	37N32	86W42	5:46:48
Old Allen 36	10	37N37	82W43	5:30:52
Old Christianburg 106	48	38N16	85W03	5:40:12
Old Flat Lick 61	14	36N50	83W46	5:35:04
Oldham Acres 93	49	38N21	85W37	5:42:28
Old Landing 65	15	37N38	83W48	5:35:12
Old Olga 104	1	36N59	85W04	5:40:16
Old Orchard 65	15	37N29	83W54	5:35:36
Oldtown 45	10	38N26	82W54	5:31:36
Old Volney 71	1	36N45	87W01	5:48:04
Olga 104	1	36N59	85W04	5:40:16
Olin 55	15	37N26	84W00	5:36:00
Olive 79	1	36N46	88W18	5:53:12
Olive Branch 106	51	38N13	85W14	5:40:56
Olive Hill 22	33	38N18	83W13	5:32:52
Oliver 45	10	38N37	82W52	5:31:28
Ollie 31	1	37N17	86W11	5:44:44
Olmstead 71	1	36N45	87W01	5:48:04
Olney 54	1	37N10	87W41	5:50:44
Olympia 6	15	38N04	83W40	5:34:40
Olympia Springs 6	15	38N04	83W40	5:34:40
Omaha 60	15	37N17	82W51	5:31:24
Oneida 26	15	37N16	83W40	5:34:40
Oneonta 19	10	38N59	84W18	5:37:12
Ono 104	1	37N04	85W06	5:40:24
Onton 117	1	37N36	87W32	5:50:08
Ophir 88	15	37N54	82W59	5:31:56
Oppy 80	10	37N50	82W24	5:29:36
Orangeburg 81	10	38N35	83W39	5:34:36
Oregon 84	15	37N55	84W51	5:39:24
Orell 56	65	38N07	85W51	5:43:24
Orinoco 98	10	37N37	82W16	5:29:04
Orkney 36	10	37N26	82W44	5:30:56
Orlando 102	15	37N22	84W16	5:37:04
Orr 64	10	38N11	82W52	5:31:28
Ortiz 117	1	37N36	87W32	5:50:08
Orville 52	48	38N21	85W07	5:40:28
Osborn 36	10	37N32	82W38	5:30:32
Oscaloosa 67	15	37N06	82W53	5:31:32
Oscar 4	1	37N05	88W58	5:55:52
Otas 118	14	36N57	84W06	5:36:24
Ote 44	6	37N16	85W30	5:42:00
Otia 86	1	36N42	85W42	5:42:48
Ottawa 102	15	37N24	84W25	5:37:40
Ottenheim 69	15	37N20	84W40	5:38:40
Otter Pond 17	1	37N07	87W53	5:51:32
Ova 77	10	37N44	83W10	5:32:40
Oven Fork 67	15	37N04	82W48	5:31:12
Overlook 72	1	37N05	88W05	5:52:20
Owensboro 30	5	37N46	87W07	5:48:28
Owensby 104	1	36N59	85W04	5:40:16
Owenton 94	40	38N32	84W50	5:39:20
Owingsville 6	15	38N09	83W46	5:35:04

Place		Lat.	Long.	Time
Owsley 98	10	37N29	82W31	5:30:04
Oxford 105	15	38N16	84W30	5:38:00
Ozark 1	1	37N06	85W18	5:41:12
Pactolus 22	15	38N20	82W57	5:31:48
Paducah 73	9	37N05	88W37	5:54:28
Paint Cliff 74	15	36N42	84W37	5:38:28
Paint Creek 88	15	37N56	83W05	5:32:20
Paint Lick 40	15	37N37	84W24	5:37:36
Paintsville 58	10	37N49	82W48	5:31:12
Palma 79	1	36N51	88W21	5:53:24
Palmer 33	26	37N42	83W58	5:35:52
Panama 88	39	37N55	83W16	5:33:04
Panarama City 18	1	36N36	88W19	5:53:16
Panco 26	15	37N15	83W35	5:34:20
Panola 76	15	37N44	84W07	5:36:28
Panther 30	1	37N38	87W14	5:48:56
Paris 9	29	38N13	84W15	5:37:00
Park 5	6	37N11	85W54	5:43:36
Park City 5	6	37N06	86W03	5:44:12
Parkers Lake 74	15	36N51	84W29	5:37:56
Park Hills 59	68	39N04	84W33	5:38:12
Parksville 11	15	37N36	84W54	5:39:36
Parkway Village 56	66	38N13	85W44	5:42:56
Parmleysville 116	1	36N44	84W44	5:38:56
Parnell 116	1	36N50	84W51	5:39:24
Parrot 55	15	37N19	84W03	5:36:12
Partridge 67	15	37N00	82W54	5:31:36
Parvin 33	26	37N42	83W58	5:35:52
Pascal 50	1	37N15	85W47	5:43:08
Patesville 46	1	37N47	86W43	5:46:52
Pathfork 48	14	36N45	83W28	5:33:52
Patsey 33	15	37N43	83W47	5:35:08
Pauley 98	10	37N29	82W31	5:30:04
Paw Paw 98	10	37N26	82W07	5:28:28
Paxton 13	15	37N38	83W25	5:33:40
Payne Gap 67	15	37N09	82W39	5:30:36
Paynes 105	27	38N05	84W29	5:37:56
Payneville 82	48	37N59	86W19	5:45:16
Payton 88	15	37N48	83W25	5:33:40
Peabody 26	15	37N08	83W35	5:34:20
Peachgrove 96	10	38N47	84W22	5:37:28
Peaks Mill 37	15	38N18	84W49	5:39:16
Pea Ridge 105	15	38N16	84W41	5:38:44
Pea Ridge 110	1	36N48	87W09	5:48:36
Pearl 118	14	36N36	83W58	5:35:52
Pearman 43	1	37N30	86W13	5:44:52
Pebworth 95	15	37N30	83W44	5:34:56
Pecksridge 35	15	38N25	83W47	5:35:08
Peedee 24	1	36N44	87W34	5:50:16
Pellville 46	1	37N45	86W49	5:47:16
Pellyton 1	1	37N06	85W18	5:41:12
Pembroke 24	1	36N47	87W21	5:49:24
Pence 119	15	37N39	83W28	5:33:52
Penchem 110	1	36N43	87W16	5:49:04
Pendleton 52	48	38N28	85W18	5:41:12
Penile 56	65	38N07	85W51	5:43:24
Penny 18	1	36N36	88W19	5:53:16
Pennyrile Mall 24	1	36N51	87W30	5:50:00
Penrod 89	1	37N08	87W00	5:48:00
Peonia 43	1	37N30	86W13	5:44:52
Peoples 55	15	37N17	84W03	5:36:12
Permon 61	14	36N50	84W07	5:36:28
Perry Park 94	15	38N33	85W00	5:40:00
Perrytown 2	6	36N45	86W11	5:44:44
Perryville 11	41	37N39	84W57	5:39:48
Persimmon Grove 19	10	38N55	84W16	5:37:04
Persimon 86	1	36N42	85W42	5:42:48
Petersburg 8	10	39N04	84W52	5:39:28
Petersburg 56	65	38N12	85W39	5:42:36
Petersville 68	10	38N27	83W30	5:34:00
Petra 12	10	38N41	84W04	5:36:16
Petrie 46	1	37N54	86W45	5:47:00
Petroleum 2	1	36N39	86W16	5:45:04
Petros 114	1	36N55	86W34	5:46:16
Pettit 30	1	37N45	87W07	5:48:28
Pewee Valley 93	57	38N19	85W29	5:41:56
Peytona 106	51	38N13	85W14	5:40:56
Peyton Creek 98	10	37N29	82W31	5:30:04
Peytonsburg 29	1	36N38	85W24	5:41:36
Peytons Store 23	48	37N28	84W49	5:39:16
Peytontown 76	30	37N45	84W18	5:37:12
Phelps 98	10	37N31	82W09	5:28:36
Phillipsburg 78	48	37N27	85W16	5:41:04
Philpot 30	1	37N44	86W59	5:47:56
Phyllis 98	10	37N26	82W21	5:29:24
Pickett 1	1	37N07	85W24	5:41:36
Picnic 1	1	36N58	85W26	5:41:44
Pierce 44	1	37N11	85W36	5:42:24
Pigeon 98	10	37N29	82W31	5:30:04
Pigeonroost 26	15	37N09	83W46	5:35:04
Pike View 50	1	37N22	85W45	5:43:00
Pikeville 98	10	37N29	82W31	5:30:04
Pilgrim 80	10	37N48	82W25	5:29:40
Pilot 33	15	37N51	83W52	5:35:28
Pilot Oak 42	1	36N34	88W49	5:55:16
Pilotview 25	32	38N00	84W11	5:36:44
Pinchem 25	32	38N00	84W11	5:36:44
Pinckard 120	44	38N03	84W44	5:38:56
Pinckneyville 70	1	37N16	88W15	5:53:00
Pine Grove 23	48	37N21	84W50	5:39:20
Pine Grove 25	15	38N02	84W16	5:37:04
Pine Grove 63	15	37N02	84W17	5:37:08
Pine Hill 102	35	37N21	84W20	5:37:20
Pine Knob 43	1	37N25	86W29	5:45:56
Pine Knot 74	15	36N39	84W26	5:37:44
Pine Mountain 48	14	36N55	83W18	5:33:12
Piner 59	10	38N58	84W34	5:38:16
Pine Ridge 119	15	37N46	83W37	5:34:28
Pine Top 60	15	37N16	82W53	5:31:32
Pineville 7	14	36N46	83W42	5:34:48
Piney Fork 28	1	37N20	88W04	5:52:16
Pink 57	28	37N53	84W34	5:38:16
Pinsonfork 98	10	37N33	82W15	5:29:00
Pioneer Village 15	50	38N00	85W43	5:42:52
Pippa Passes 60	15	37N20	82W53	5:31:32
Piqua 101	10	38N32	84W02	5:36:08
Pisgah 120	44	38N03	84W44	5:38:56
Piso 98	10	37N35	82W16	5:29:04
Pitts 33	26	37N41	83W57	5:35:48
Pittsburg 63	15	37N10	84W07	5:36:28
Plank 26	15	37N05	83W39	5:34:36
Plano 114	7	37N00	86W25	5:45:40
Plantation 56	65	38N18	85W36	5:42:24
Plato 100	18	37N06	84W36	5:38:24
Pleasant Hill 16	1	37N13	86W53	5:47:32
Pleasant Hill 18	1	36N42	88W16	5:53:04
Pleasant Hill 96	10	38N47	84W22	5:37:28
Pleasant Home 94	15	38N32	84W50	5:39:20
Pleasant Ridge 30	1	37N36	87W07	5:48:28
Pleasant Valley 91	15	38N26	83W52	5:35:28
Pleasant Valley 98	10	37N28	82W31	5:30:04
Pleasant View 118	14	36N44	84W10	5:36:40
Pleasure Ridge Park 56	65	38N09	85W49	5:43:16
Pleasureville 35	15	38N24	83W37	5:34:28
Pleasureville 52	48	38N21	85W07	5:40:28
Plummers Landing 35	15	38N19	83W33	5:34:12
Plummers Mill 35	15	38N19	83W33	5:34:12
Plum Springs 114	1	37N02	86W22	5:45:28
Plumville 81	10	38N35	83W52	5:35:28
Plutarch 77	10	37N49	83W07	5:32:28
Plymouth Village 56	65	38N14	85W39	5:42:36
Poindexter 49	20	38N26	84W19	5:37:16
Pointer 100	18	37N08	84W46	5:39:04
Point Leavell 40	15	37N37	84W35	5:38:20
Polksville 6	15	38N07	83W37	5:34:28
Polkville 114	1	37N02	86W15	5:45:00
Polly 67	15	37N13	82W51	5:31:24
Pomeroyton 83	15	37N53	83W32	5:34:08
Pomp 88	39	37N55	83W16	5:33:04
Pond Creek 55	15	37N19	83W58	5:35:52
Pondsville 114	1	37N03	86W13	5:44:52
Poole 117	1	37N38	87W39	5:50:36
Poor Fork 48	14	36N55	83W12	5:32:48
Poortown 57	28	37N53	84W34	5:38:16
Pope 2	1	36N50	86W25	5:45:40
Poplar 22	15	38N26	83W08	5:32:32
Poplar Flat 68	10	38N46	83W45	5:35:00
Poplar Grove 75	1	37N25	87W16	5:49:04
Poplar Grove 94	15	38N43	84W49	5:39:16
Poplar Highlands 45	10	38N32	82W43	5:30:52
Poplar Plains 35	15	38N22	83W41	5:34:44
Poplarville 100	18	37N01	84W26	5:37:44
Porter 105	15	38N23	84W32	5:38:08
Portersburg 26	15	37N08	83W51	5:35:24
Portland 1	1	37N07	85W24	5:41:36
Portland 96	10	38N48	84W25	5:37:40
Port Royal 52	48	38N33	85W05	5:40:20
Portsmouth 13	15	37N33	83W22	5:33:28
Possum Trot 79	1	37N01	88W21	5:53:24
Post 43	1	37N25	86W29	5:45:56
Potters 64	10	38N07	82W36	5:30:24
Potters Fork 67	15	37N11	82W38	5:30:32
Pottsville 42	1	36N49	88W38	5:54:32
Pottsville 115	48	37N41	85W13	5:40:52
Poverty 75	1	37N32	87W16	5:49:04
Powderly 89	1	37N14	87W10	5:48:40
Powell 33	26	37N42	83W58	5:35:52
Powell Valley 99	15	37N52	83W55	5:35:40
Powersburg 116	1	36N50	84W51	5:39:24
Powersville 12	10	38N41	84W04	5:36:16
Prater 22	15	38N18	83W11	5:32:44
Pratt 117	1	37N36	87W32	5:50:08
Preachersville 69	15	37N28	84W30	5:38:00
Preece 80	10	37N52	82W32	5:30:08
Premium 67	15	37N04	82W58	5:31:52
Prentiss 92	1	37N24	86W53	5:47:32
Press 13	15	37N32	83W19	5:33:16
Preston 6	15	38N05	83W45	5:35:00
Prestonsburg 36	10	37N40	82W47	5:31:08
Prestonville 21	38	38N41	85W12	5:40:48
Prewitt 87	21	38N03	83W57	5:35:48
Price 36	10	37N24	82W44	5:30:56
Prices Mill 107	1	36N40	86W51	5:47:24
Pricetown 23	48	37N19	84W56	5:39:44
Priceville 50	1	37N16	85W53	5:43:32
Pride 113	1	37N34	87W53	5:51:32
Primrose 65	15	37N36	83W37	5:34:28
Princess 10	10	38N28	82W39	5:30:36
Princeton 17	1	37N07	87W53	5:51:32
Printer 36	10	37N32	82W45	5:31:00
Pritchardsville 5	6	37N00	85W55	5:43:40
Privett 55	15	37N21	83W54	5:35:36
Proctor 65	15	37N35	83W43	5:34:52
Produce Place 56	65	38N12	85W39	5:42:36
Prospect 56	65	38N21	85W37	5:42:28
Prosperity 31	1	37N17	86W17	5:45:08
Providence 57	27	38N01	84W32	5:38:08
Providence 61	14	36N52	83W53	5:35:32
Providence 107	1	36N43	86W35	5:46:20
Providence 112	48	38N31	85W12	5:40:48
Providence 117	1	37N24	87W46	5:51:04
Provo 16	1	37N14	86W50	5:47:20
Pruden 7	14	36N35	83W54	5:35:36
Pryorsburg	1	36N41	88W43	5:54:52
Pryors Chapel 42	1	36N44	88W38	5:54:32
Pryse 33	15	37N40	83W53	5:35:32
Public 100	18	36N49	84W42	5:38:48
Pueblo 116	1	36N49	84W42	5:38:48
Pulaski 100	18	37N13	84W38	5:38:32
Pulliam 115	48	37N49	85W07	5:40:28
Pumpkin Center 17	1	37N07	87W53	5:51:32
Puncheon 60	15	37N18	82W47	5:31:08
Purdy 1	1	37N06	85W18	5:41:12
Putney 48	14	36N55	83W14	5:32:56
Pyramid 36	10	37N34	82W54	5:31:36
Pyrus 1	1	37N04	85W25	5:41:40
Quail 102	15	37N24	84W25	5:37:40
Quality 16	1	37N05	86W51	5:47:24
Queens 68	10	38N36	83W19	5:33:16
Quicksand 13	15	37N32	83W21	5:33:24
Quincy 68	10	38N37	83W08	5:32:32
Quinton 100	18	36N59	84W37	5:38:28
Rabbit Hash 8	10	38N56	84W51	5:39:24
Rabbit Ridge 54	1	37N23	87W39	5:50:36
Raccoon 98	10	37N32	82W21	5:29:24
Raceland 45	10	38N32	82W44	5:30:56
Radcliff 47	48	37N51	85W57	5:43:48
Ragland 73	1	37N05	88W53	5:55:32
Railton 5	6	37N06	86W03	5:44:12
Rain 118	14	36N43	83W58	5:35:52
Ralph 92	1	37N41	86W52	5:47:28
Randolph 85	1	36N59	85W37	5:42:28
Ransom 98	10	37N34	82W11	5:28:44
Rapids 107	1	36N43	86W35	5:46:20
Raven 60	15	37N17	82W45	5:31:00
Ravenna 33	26	37N41	83W57	5:35:48
Raymond 14	1	37N53	86W20	5:45:20
Raywick 78	48	37N32	85W26	5:41:44
Ready 43	1	37N25	86W29	5:45:56
Rectorville 81	10	38N35	83W39	5:34:36
Red Bird 7	14	36N56	83W32	5:34:08
Redbird 118	14	36N44	84W10	5:36:40
Redbud 48	14	36N52	83W12	5:32:48
Redbush 58	10	37N57	82W57	5:31:48
Red Cross 5	6	37N06	86W03	5:44:12
Redfox 60	15	37N13	82W57	5:31:48
Red Hill 2	1	36N50	86W25	5:45:40
Red Hill 30	1	37N36	87W07	5:48:28
Red Hill 47	48	37N49	85W58	5:43:52
Redhouse 76	30	37N45	84W18	5:37:12
Red Lick 33	15	37N41	84W02	5:36:08
Redlick 76	42	37N35	84W17	5:37:08
Redlick 85	1	36N59	85W37	5:42:28
Red River 71	1	36N40	86W51	5:47:24
Redwine 88	15	38N01	83W14	5:32:56
Reed 51	1	37N51	87W21	5:49:24
Reeds Crossing 76	30	37N45	84W18	5:37:12
Reedville 22	15	38N20	82W57	5:31:48
Reedyville 16	1	37N14	86W26	5:45:44
Regina 98	10	37N22	82W24	5:29:36
Region 16	1	37N14	86W26	5:45:44
Reidland 73	1	37N01	88W32	5:54:08
Reid Village 87	21	38N03	83W57	5:35:48
Relief 88	15	37N57	83W00	5:32:00
Rella 7	14	36N48	83W39	5:34:36
Renaker 49	35	38N31	84W23	5:37:32
Render 92	1	37N24	86W53	5:47:32
Renfro Valley 102	35	37N23	84W20	5:37:20
Renfrow 92	1	37N27	86W41	5:46:44
Repton 28	1	37N23	88W01	5:52:04
Revelo 74	15	36N41	84W28	5:37:52
Rex 50	1	37N15	85W47	5:43:08
Reynolds Station 92	1	37N40	86W46	5:47:04
Reynoldsville 6	15	38N12	83W56	5:35:44
Rhea 48	14	36N52	83W20	5:33:20
Rheber 23	48	37N12	85W00	5:40:00
Rhoda 31	1	37N11	86W19	5:45:16
Rhodelia 82	48	38N00	86W25	5:45:40
Ribbon 104	1	36N59	85W04	5:40:16
Ribolt 68	10	38N46	83W45	5:35:00
Rice Station 33	26	37N42	83W58	5:35:52
Ricetown 95	15	37N23	83W37	5:34:28
Riceville 38	1	36N30	88W53	5:55:32
Riceville 58	10	37N44	82W55	5:31:40
Richam 98	10	37N29	82W31	5:30:04
Richardson 64	10	37N57	82W39	5:30:36
Richardsville 114	1	37N06	86W28	5:45:52
Richelieu 71	1	37N00	86W41	5:46:44
Richland 54	1	37N20	87W30	5:50:00
Richlawn 56	65	38N15	85W38	5:42:32
Richmond 76	30	37N45	84W18	5:37:12
Rich Pond 114	1	36N54	86W31	5:46:04
Richwood 8	13	38N55	84W38	5:38:32
Ridgeview Heights 59	10	38N59	84W35	5:38:20
Ridgeway 48	14	36N52	83W12	5:32:48
Riley 78	48	37N34	85W06	5:40:24
Rineyville 47	48	37N45	85W58	5:43:52
Ringgold 100	18	37N06	84W36	5:38:24
Ringos Mills 35	15	38N18	83W40	5:34:40
Rio Vista 48	14	36N51	83W21	5:33:24
Risner 36	10	37N35	82W50	5:31:20
Ritchie 60	15	37N19	83W05	5:32:20
Ritner 116	1	36N48	84W38	5:38:32
Rivals 108	48	38N02	85W21	5:41:24
River 58	10	37N52	82W44	5:30:56
Riverfront 56	66	38N14	85W49	5:43:16
River Ridge 48	14	36N52	83W12	5:32:48
Riverside 56	65	38N11	85W52	5:43:28
Riverside 114	1	37N10	86W33	5:46:12
Riverside Gardens 56	66	38N11	85W49	5:43:16
Riverton 45	10	38N34	82W50	5:31:20
Riverview 45	10	38N28	82W39	5:30:36
Riverview Estates 84	43	37N46	84W51	5:39:24
Riverwood 56	67	38N17	85W35	5:42:20
Road Creek Junction 98	10	37N19	82W21	5:29:24
Roaring Spring 111	1	36N52	87W50	5:51:20
Roark 66	15	37N02	83W31	5:34:04
Robards 51	1	37N41	87W33	5:50:12

KENTUCKY

Robinson 49	35	38N29	84w21	5:37:24
Robinson Creek 98	10	37N22	82w33	5:30:12
Robinsville 76	30	37N45	84w18	5:37:12
Robinswood 56	65	38N15	85w39	5:42:36
Robridge 92	1	37N25	87w00	5:48:00
Rochester 16	1	37N13	86w53	5:47:32
Rockbridge 86	1	36N42	85w42	5:42:48
Rockcastle 111	1	36N52	87w50	5:51:20
Rock Creek 43	1	37N30	86w13	5:44:52
Rockdale 10	10	38N28	82w39	5:30:36
Rockdale 94	15	38N32	84w50	5:39:20
Rockfield 114	1	36N55	86w34	5:46:16
Rock Haven 82	48	37N49	85w58	5:43:52
Rockholds 118	14	36N50	84w07	5:36:28
Rockhouse 98	10	37N20	82w27	5:29:48
Rockland 114	7	37N00	86w25	5:45:40
Rockport 92	1	37N20	86w59	5:47:56
Rock Springs 51	1	37N44	87w42	5:50:48
Rockvale 14	1	37N39	86w37	5:46:28
Rockybranch 116	1	36N44	84w44	5:38:56
Rocky Hill 5	1	36N58	86w05	5:44:20
Rocky Hill 31	1	37N04	86w08	5:44:32
Rodburn 103	15	38N11	83w26	5:33:44
Roff 14	1	37N42	86w25	5:45:40
Rogers 119	15	37N45	83w38	5:34:32
Rogers Gap 105	25	38N13	84w33	5:38:12
Rogersville 47	58	37N42	85w52	5:43:28
Rolling Acres 56	65	38N15	85w39	5:42:36
Rollingburg 44	6	37N16	85w30	5:42:00
Rolling Fields 56	65	38N16	85w40	5:42:40
Rolling Hills 56	67	38N17	85w35	5:42:20
Rollington 93	57	38N19	85w29	5:41:56
Rome 30	1	37N43	87w11	5:48:44
Romine 109	48	37N21	85w21	5:41:24
Roscoe 32	15	38N05	83w08	5:32:32
Roseburg 50	1	37N18	86w04	5:44:16
Rose Crossroads 104	1	36N59	85w04	5:40:16
Rosefork 119	15	37N45	83w33	5:34:12
Rose Hill 84	43	37N46	84w51	5:39:24
Rose Terrace 47	48	37N53	85w59	5:43:56
Rosetta 14	1	37N53	86w17	5:45:08
Roseville 5	6	37N00	85w55	5:43:40
Roseville 46	1	37N40	86w46	5:47:04
Rosewood 89	1	37N07	87w10	5:48:40
Rosine 92	1	37N27	86w44	5:46:56
Ross 19	10	39N02	84w22	5:37:28
Rossington 73	1	37N05	88w53	5:55:32
Rossland 61	14	36N57	84w00	5:36:00
Rosslyn 99	15	37N51	83w49	5:35:16
Rosspoint 48	14	36N52	83w20	5:33:20
Rothwell 83	15	37N57	83w38	5:34:32
Roundhill 31	1	37N14	86w26	5:45:44
Round Hill 76	30	37N45	84w18	5:37:12
Roundstone 102	35	37N21	84w20	5:37:20
Rouse 59	68	39N04	84w31	5:38:04
Rousseau 13	15	37N34	83w13	5:32:52
Routt 56	65	38N13	85w35	5:42:20
Rowdy 97	45	37N24	83w12	5:32:48
Rowena 104	1	36N59	85w04	5:40:16
Rowland 69	15	37N32	84w40	5:38:40
Rowland 73	1	37N03	88w37	5:54:28
Rowlandtown 73	1	37N03	88w37	5:54:28
Rowletts 50	6	37N14	85w54	5:43:36
Roxana 67	15	37N07	82w57	5:31:48
Royal 43	1	37N30	86w13	5:44:52
Royalton 77	10	37N36	82w58	5:31:52
Royrader 55	15	37N19	83w58	5:35:52
Royville 104	1	37N04	85w08	5:40:32
Ruckerville 25	32	38N00	84w11	5:36:44
Ruddels Mills 9	20	38N23	84w17	5:37:08
Ruin 32	15	38N05	83w08	5:32:32
Rumsey 75	1	37N32	87w16	5:49:04
Rural 98	10	37N45	82w19	5:29:16
Rush 10	10	38N20	82w46	5:31:04
Russell 45	10	38N31	82w43	5:30:52
Russell Heights 45	10	38N32	82w43	5:30:52
Russell Springs 104	1	37N03	85w05	5:40:20
Russellville 71	1	36N51	86w53	5:47:32
Ruth 100	18	37N04	84w31	5:38:04
Rutherford 48	14	36N52	83w00	5:32:00
Rutland 49	20	38N23	84w17	5:37:08
Ryland 59	10	38N56	84w28	5:37:52
Ryland Heights 59	68	39N03	84w32	5:38:08
Sackett 67	15	37N13	82w51	5:31:24
Sacramento 75	1	37N25	87w16	5:49:04
Sadieville 105	16	38N23	84w32	5:38:08
Sadler 43	1	37N22	86w20	5:45:20
Saint Catharine 115	48	37N43	85w16	5:41:04
Saint Charles 54	1	37N11	87w36	5:50:24
Saint Dennis 56	66	38N11	85w49	5:43:16
Saint Elmo 24	1	36N47	87w22	5:49:28
Saint Francis 78	56	37N38	85w26	5:41:44
Saint Helens 65	15	37N35	83w36	5:34:24
Saint John 47	48	37N42	85w58	5:43:52
Saint Johns 73	1	37N03	88w37	5:54:28
Saint Joseph 30	1	37N42	87w20	5:49:20
Saint Joseph 78	48	37N34	85w26	5:41:44
Saint Mary 78	56	37N35	85w20	5:41:20
Saint Matthews 56	65	38N15	85w39	5:42:36
Saint Paul 43	1	37N29	86w18	5:45:12
Saint Paul 68	10	38N40	83w05	5:32:20
Saint Regis Park 56	65	38N14	85w37	5:42:28
Saint Vincent 113	1	37N41	87w55	5:51:40
Saldee 13	15	37N27	83w22	5:33:28
Salem 70	1	37N16	88w15	5:53:00
Salem 104	1	37N04	85w06	5:40:24
Salmon 107	1	36N43	86w35	5:46:20
Saloma 109	48	37N25	85w25	5:41:40
Salt Gum 61	14	36N57	83w42	5:34:48
Salt Lick 6	15	38N07	83w37	5:34:28
Salt River 15	50	38N00	85w43	5:42:52
Saltwell 91	37	38N19	84w02	5:36:08
Salvisa 84	15	37N55	84w51	5:39:24
Salyersville 77	10	37N45	83w04	5:32:16
Sample 14	1	37N54	86w29	5:45:56
Samuels 90	48	37N53	85w32	5:42:08
Sandclift 116	1	36N40	84w59	5:39:56
Sanders 21	15	38N39	84w57	5:39:48
Sandgap 55	15	37N29	84w06	5:36:24
Sand Hill 33	26	37N42	83w58	5:35:52
Sand Hill 48	14	36N59	82w59	5:31:56
Sand Hill 114	7	37N00	86w25	5:45:40
Sand Springs 55	15	37N26	84w00	5:36:00
Sand Springs 102	35	37N21	84w20	5:37:20
Sandy City 10	10	38N25	82w36	5:30:24
Sandy Hook 32	33	38N05	83w08	5:32:32
Sanfordtown 59	68	39N02	84w34	5:38:16
Sano 104	1	37N06	85w18	5:41:12
Sarah 32	15	38N05	83w08	5:32:32
Saratoga 72	1	37N07	87w53	5:51:32
Sardis 81	10	38N32	83w57	5:35:48
Sassafras 60	15	37N13	83w03	5:32:12
Sasser 63	15	37N05	83w53	5:35:32
Saul 97	45	37N16	83w30	5:34:00
Savage 27	1	36N41	85w08	5:40:32
Savage Branch 10	10	38N25	82w36	5:30:24
Savoy 118	14	36N44	84w10	5:36:40
Savoyard 85	6	37N11	85w54	5:43:36
Sawyer 74	15	36N54	84w21	5:37:24
Saxton 118	14	36N38	84w07	5:36:28
Saylor 66	15	36N58	83w24	5:33:36
Scale 79	1	36N51	88w21	5:53:24
Scalf 61	14	36N55	83w42	5:34:48
Schochoh 71	1	36N40	86w51	5:47:24
Schoolville 25	21	38N03	83w57	5:35:48
Schultztown 92	1	37N24	86w53	5:47:32
Science Hill 100	31	37N11	84w38	5:38:32
Scot 48	14	36N59	82w59	5:31:56
Scott 59	68	39N02	84w34	5:38:16
Scottown 92	1	37N20	86w58	5:47:52
Scottsburg 17	1	37N07	87w53	5:51:32
Scotts Ferry 29	1	36N48	85w22	5:41:28
Scotts Station 106	51	38N13	85w14	5:40:56
Scottsville 2	6	36N45	86w11	5:44:44
Scoville 95	15	37N29	83w40	5:34:40
Scranton 83	15	37N59	83w31	5:34:04
Scuddy 97	45	37N12	83w05	5:32:20
Seaville 115	43	37N46	84w51	5:39:24
Sebastians Branch 13	15	37N26	83w28	5:33:52
Sebree 117	1	37N36	87w32	5:50:08
Seco 67	15	37N10	82w44	5:30:56
Sedalia 42	1	36N35	88w35	5:54:20
Segal 31	1	37N11	86w19	5:45:16
Seitz 77	10	37N42	83w10	5:32:40
Select 92	1	37N20	86w47	5:47:08
Sellars 88	15	37N46	83w20	5:33:20
Seminary 27	1	36N41	85w08	5:40:32
Semiway 75	1	37N32	87w16	5:49:04
Seneca Gardens 56	66	38N14	85w41	5:42:44
Senterville 98	10	37N19	82w21	5:29:24
Se Ree 14	1	37N41	86w23	5:45:32
Sergent 67	15	37N09	82w46	5:31:04
Settle 2	1	36N51	86w09	5:44:36
Seventy Six 27	1	36N41	85w08	5:40:32
Sewell 13	15	37N38	83w25	5:33:40
Sewellton 104	1	36N59	85w04	5:40:16
Sextons Creek 26	15	37N19	83w47	5:35:08
Seymour 50	6	37N11	85w54	5:43:36
Shady Grove 28	1	37N20	87w53	5:51:32
Shady Grove 73	1	37N03	88w37	5:54:28
Shady Grove 85	1	37N09	85w42	5:42:48
Shadynook 49	20	38N23	84w17	5:37:08
Shafter 100	18	37N06	84w36	5:38:24
Shannon 81	10	38N31	83w50	5:35:20
Sharer 16	1	37N04	86w36	5:46:24
Sharkey 35	15	38N18	83w40	5:34:40
Sharon 12	10	38N46	84w00	5:36:00
Sharondale 98	10	37N37	82w16	5:29:04
Sharon Grove 110	1	36N55	87w06	5:48:24
Sharpe 79	1	36N58	88w28	5:53:52
Sharpsburg 6	15	38N13	83w52	5:35:28
Sharpsville 115	43	37N46	84w51	5:39:24
Shawhan 9	29	38N18	84w16	5:37:04
Shawnee Estates 114	7	37N00	86w25	5:45:40
Shearer Valley 116	1	36N50	84w51	5:39:24
Shelbiana 98	10	37N26	82w30	5:30:00
Shelby 56	66	38N13	85w44	5:42:56
Shelby City 11	24	37N39	84w46	5:39:04
Shelby Gap 98	10	37N13	82w34	5:30:16
Shelbyville 106	51	38N13	85w14	5:40:56
Shelbyville Road Plaza 56	65	38N15	85w39	5:42:36
Shepherdsville 15	50	37N59	85w43	5:42:52
Shepola 100	18	37N04	84w45	5:39:00
Sherburne 35	15	38N25	83w47	5:35:08
Sheridan 28	1	37N21	88w12	5:52:48
Sherman 41	10	38N44	84w36	5:38:24
Sherwood Shores 79	1	37N01	88w18	5:53:12
Shetland 120	44	38N03	84w44	5:38:56
Shiloh 18	1	36N41	88w12	5:52:48
Shipley 27	1	36N40	85w13	5:40:52
Shively 56	66	38N12	85w49	5:43:16
Shoal 66	15	37N16	83w26	5:33:44
Shop Branch 55	15	37N26	84w00	5:36:00
Shopville 100	18	37N09	84w29	5:37:56
Shore Acres 120	19	38N12	84w52	5:39:28
Short Creek 43	1	37N32	86w29	5:45:56
Short Town 48	14	36N52	83w12	5:32:48
Shoulderblade 13	15	37N33	83w22	5:33:28
Shreve 92	1	37N38	86w43	5:46:52
Shrewsbury 43	1	37N25	86w29	5:45:56
Sibert 26	15	37N09	83w46	5:35:04
Sidell 26	15	37N09	83w46	5:35:04
Sideview 87	21	38N03	83w57	5:35:48
Sideway 32	15	38N12	83w13	5:32:52
Sidney 98	10	37N37	82w20	5:29:20
Siler 61	14	36N57	84w00	5:36:00
Siler 118	14	36N41	84w00	5:36:00
Silerville 74	15	36N38	84w26	5:37:44
Siloam 45	10	38N43	82w58	5:31:52
Silver City 16	1	37N14	86w41	5:46:44
Silver Grove 19	10	39N02	84w24	5:37:36
Silverhill 88	15	37N53	83w03	5:32:12
Simmons 92	1	37N23	86w55	5:47:40
Simpson 13	15	37N45	83w33	5:34:12
Simpsonville 106	48	38N13	85w21	5:41:24
Sims Fork 7	14	36N48	83w39	5:34:36
Sinai 3	43	38N02	84w54	5:39:36
Sip 58	10	37N53	82w51	5:31:24
Sirocco 82	48	38N00	86w10	5:44:40
Sitka 58	10	37N53	82w51	5:31:24
Sizerock 66	15	37N13	83w30	5:34:00
Skaggs 64	10	38N01	82w55	5:31:40
Skate 63	36	37N08	84w05	5:36:20
Skibo 89	1	37N13	87w11	5:48:44
Skillman 46	1	37N54	86w45	5:47:00
Skinnersburg 105	15	38N16	84w41	5:38:44
Skullbuster 105	15	38N16	84w41	5:38:44
Skylight 93	49	38N21	85w37	5:42:28
Skyline 67	15	37N05	82w59	5:31:56
Slade 99	15	37N48	83w42	5:34:48
Slat 116	1	36N50	84w51	5:39:24
Slate Lick 76	42	37N35	84w17	5:37:08
Slater 4	1	36N58	89w05	5:56:20
Slate Valley 6	15	38N09	83w46	5:35:04
Slaughters 117	1	37N29	87w30	5:50:00
Slaughtersville 117	1	37N29	87w30	5:50:00
Slavans 74	15	36N45	84w40	5:38:40
Slemp 97	45	37N05	83w06	5:32:24
Slickford 116	1	36N50	84w51	5:39:24
Slick Rock 5	6	37N00	85w55	5:43:40
Sligo 52	48	38N28	85w18	5:41:12
Sloan 36	10	37N38	82w45	5:31:00
Sloans Valley 100	18	36N56	84w32	5:38:08
Smilax 66	15	37N08	83w17	5:33:08
Smile 103	15	38N11	83w26	5:33:44
Smith 48	14	36N44	83w15	5:33:00
Smithfield 52	48	38N23	85w15	5:41:00
Smithland 70	1	37N09	88w24	5:53:36
Smith Mills 51	1	37N48	87w46	5:51:04
Smithsboro 60	15	37N13	83w03	5:32:12
Smiths Creek 22	15	38N28	83w11	5:32:44
Smiths Grove 114	1	37N03	86w12	5:44:48
Smith Town 74	15	36N42	84w31	5:38:04
Smithview 43	1	37N25	86w29	5:45:56
Smoky Valley 22	15	38N18	83w11	5:32:44
Smyrna 56	65	38N09	85w42	5:42:48
Snap 43	1	37N30	86w13	5:44:52
Snell 100	18	37N05	84w26	5:37:44
Snow 27	1	36N41	85w08	5:40:32
Snow Hill 106	51	38N13	85w14	5:40:56
Soft Shell 60	15	37N24	82w57	5:31:48
Soldier 22	15	38N16	83w18	5:33:12
Solway 47	48	37N33	86w09	5:44:36
Somerset 100	31	37N05	84w36	5:38:24
Sonora 47	48	37N32	85w54	5:43:36
Sorgho 30	1	37N45	87w07	5:48:28
South 43	1	37N20	86w22	5:45:28
South 75	1	37N27	87w14	5:48:56
South Buffalo 62	48	37N31	85w42	5:42:48
South Carrollton 89	1	37N20	87w09	5:48:36
South Corbin 118	14	36N57	84w06	5:36:24
Southdown 67	15	37N07	82w47	5:31:08
South Fayette 34	27	37N57	84w27	5:37:48
South Fork 13	15	37N33	83w22	5:33:28
South Fork 69	15	37N25	84w44	5:38:56
Southfork 95	15	37N29	83w40	5:34:40
Southgate 19	68	39N04	84w29	5:37:56
South Hill 16	1	37N14	86w41	5:46:44
South Irvine 33	26	37N42	83w58	5:35:52
Southland 34	27	38N01	84w32	5:38:08
South Lebanon 78	63	37N32	85w15	5:41:00
South Oldham 93	57	38N20	85w28	5:41:52
South Park 56	65	38N06	85w45	5:43:00
South Park View 56	65	38N07	85w43	5:42:52
South Portsmouth 45	10	38N44	83w00	5:32:00
South River 65	15	37N32	83w46	5:35:04
South Shore 45	10	38N43	82w58	5:31:52
South Union 71	1	36N53	86w39	5:46:36
Southville 106	51	38N13	85w14	5:40:56
South Williamson 98	10	37N40	82w17	5:29:08
Southwire 46	1	37N54	86w45	5:47:00
Spa 71	1	36N59	86w57	5:47:48
Spanglin 32	15	38N05	83w13	5:32:52
Spann 116	1	36N50	84w51	5:39:24
Sparksville 1	1	37N20	86w22	5:45:28
Sparta 39	11	38N41	84w54	5:39:36
Spears 57	27	38N02	84w29	5:37:56
Speck 1	1	37N16	85w09	5:40:36
Speedwell 76	30	37N45	84w18	5:37:12
Speight 98	10	37N17	82w41	5:30:44
Spence 19	68	39N05	84w29	5:37:56
Spencer 87	21	38N03	83w57	5:35:48
Spencer Ridge 65	15	37N35	83w43	5:34:52
Spider 60	15	37N18	82w55	5:31:40
Spiro 102	35	37N21	84w20	5:37:20

KENTUCKY

Spottsville 51 1 37N50 87w27 5:49:48
Spring Bayou 73 1 37N05 88w53 5:55:32
Spring Creek 26 15 37N07 83w33 5:34:12
Springdale 56 67 38N17 85w35 5:42:20
Springdale 81 10 38N35 83w52 5:35:28
Springfield 115 48 37N41 85w13 5:40:52
Spring Grove 113 1 37N41 87w55 5:51:40
Springhill 53 1 36N40 89w00 5:56:00
Springhill 114 7 37N00 86w25 5:45:40
Spring Lake 59 10 39N00 84w28 5:37:52
Springlake 59 10 39N00 84w28 5:37:52
Spring Lee 56 65 38N15 85w39 5:42:36
Springlee 56 65 38N15 85w39 5:42:36
Spring Lick 43 1 37N27 86w33 5:46:12
Spring Station 120 47 38N09 84w41 5:38:44
Sprout 91 15 38N16 83w53 5:35:32
Spruce Pine 66 15 36N58 83w24 5:33:36
Sprule 61 14 37N01 83w51 5:35:24
Spurlington 109 48 37N21 85w21 5:41:24
Spurlock 26 15 37N13 83w38 5:34:32
Squib 100 18 37N06 84w36 5:38:24
Squiresville 94 15 38N32 84w50 5:39:20
Stab 100 18 37N09 84w26 5:37:44
Stacy 15 37N24 83w13 5:32:52
Stacy Fork 88 15 37N50 83w16 5:33:04
Staffordsville 58 10 37N51 82w50 5:31:20
Stambaugh 58 10 37N53 82w48 5:31:12
Stamping Ground 105 16 38N16 84w41 5:38:44
Standing Rock 65 15 37N43 83w42 5:34:48
Stanfill 48 14 36N51 83w19 5:33:16
Stanford 69 40 37N32 84w40 5:38:40
Stanley 30 1 37N50 87w15 5:49:00
Stanton 99 16 37N54 83w52 5:35:28
Stanville 36 10 37N41 82w44 5:30:56
Stark 32 15 38N10 83w08 5:32:32
Star Mills 47 48 37N36 85w54 5:43:36
State Line 38 1 36N34 89w11 5:56:44
Static 27 1 36N41 85w08 5:40:32
Station Camp 33 15 37N38 83w56 5:35:44
Stay 95 15 37N35 83w43 5:34:52
Stearns 74 15 36N42 84w29 5:37:56
Steele 98 10 37N24 82w12 5:28:48
Steff 43 1 37N26 86w36 5:46:24
Stella 18 1 36N38 88w24 5:53:36
Stella 77 10 37N44 83w10 5:32:40
Stephens 32 15 38N08 82w58 5:31:52
Stephensburg 47 48 37N37 86w01 5:44:04
Stephensport 14 1 37N55 86w31 5:46:04
Stepstone 87 15 38N09 83w46 5:35:04
Steubenville 116 1 36N53 84w48 5:39:12
Stewart 84 43 37N46 84w51 5:39:24
Stewartsville 41 10 38N39 84w34 5:38:16
Stiles 90 48 38N10 85w36 5:42:24
Stillwater 119 15 37N45 83w33 5:34:12
Stinnett 66 15 37N05 83w24 5:33:36
Stinnettsville 14 1 37N53 86w17 5:45:08
Stinson 22 10 38N20 82w57 5:31:48
Stites 15 61 38N00 85w57 5:43:48
Stockholm 31 1 37N14 86w17 5:45:08
Stone 98 10 37N35 82w16 5:29:04
Stonewall 12 10 38N41 84w04 5:36:16
Stonewall 105 15 38N23 84w32 5:38:08
Stoney Fork 7 14 36N50 83w32 5:34:08
Stoney Fork Junction 7 14 36N37 83w44 5:34:56
Stoops 87 21 38N03 83w57 5:35:48
Stop 116 1 36N50 84w51 5:39:24
Stopover 98 10 37N31 82w06 5:28:24
Stormking 97 45 37N15 83w11 5:32:44
Stovall 5 6 37N06 86w03 5:44:12
Straight Creek 7 14 36N46 83w40 5:34:40
Strait Creek 22 15 38N19 83w20 5:33:20
Strathmoor Gardens 56 65 38N13 85w40 5:42:40
Strathmoor Manor 56 66 38N13 85w41 5:42:44
Strathmoor Village 56 66 38N13 85w41 5:42:44
Stricklett 68 10 38N36 83w19 5:33:16
Stringtown 3 43 38N02 84w54 5:39:36
Stringtown 8 10 39N05 84w39 5:38:36
Stringtown 41 35 38N31 84w23 5:37:32
Stringtown 76 30 37N45 84w18 5:37:12
Stringtown 77 10 37N45 83w04 5:32:16
Stringtown 84 43 37N46 84w51 5:39:24
Stringtown 89 1 37N25 87w16 5:49:04
Strunk 74 15 36N38 84w26 5:37:44
Sturgeon 95 15 37N25 83w45 5:35:00
Sturgis 113 1 37N33 87w59 5:51:56
Sublett 77 10 37N41 83w03 5:32:12
Sublimity City 63 36 37N08 84w05 5:36:20
Subtle 85 1 36N59 85w37 5:42:28
Sudith 83 15 38N01 83w38 5:34:32
Sugar Bay 39 11 38N47 84w54 5:39:36
Sugar Grove 16 1 37N05 86w40 5:46:40
Sugar Hill 100 18 37N06 84w36 5:38:24
Sugartit 8 10 39N00 84w38 5:38:32
Sullivan 113 1 37N30 87w57 5:51:48
Sulphur 52 48 38N30 85w17 5:41:08
Sulphur Lick 86 1 36N42 85w42 5:42:48
Sulphur Springs 92 1 37N34 86w44 5:46:56
Sulphur Well 57 28 37N53 84w34 5:38:16
Sulphur Well 85 1 36N59 85w37 5:42:28
Summer Shade 85 1 36N55 85w41 5:42:44
Summersville 44 1 37N20 85w33 5:42:12
Summit 10 10 38N28 82w39 5:30:36
Summit 47 48 37N34 86w05 5:44:20
Sumpter 116 1 36N46 84w52 5:39:28
Sunfish 31 1 37N16 86w25 5:45:40
Sunny Acres 59 68 39N01 84w30 5:38:00
Sunnybrook 116 1 36N40 84w59 5:39:56
Sunny Corner 46 1 37N54 86w45 5:47:00
Sunnydale 92 1 37N34 86w44 5:46:56
Sunnyside 114 7 37N00 86w25 5:45:40
Sunrise 49 15 38N33 84w14 5:36:56
Sunshine 45 10 38N43 82w58 5:31:52
Sunshine 48 14 36N51 83w19 5:33:16
Susie 116 1 36N50 84w51 5:39:24
Suterville 105 15 38N16 84w41 5:38:44
Sutherland 30 1 37N40 87w07 5:48:28
Sutton 35 15 38N25 83w47 5:35:08
Sutton 98 10 37N26 82w30 5:30:00
Suwanee 72 1 37N04 88w08 5:52:32
Swain 74 15 36N39 84w26 5:37:44
Swallowfield 37 19 38N12 84w52 5:39:28
Swamp Branch 58 10 37N44 82w55 5:31:40
Swampton 77 10 37N39 83w00 5:32:00
Swan Lake 61 14 36N52 83w53 5:35:32
Swanpond 61 14 36N52 83w53 5:35:32
Sweeden 31 1 37N15 86w17 5:45:08
Sweeneyville 109 48 37N21 85w21 5:41:24
Switzer 37 15 38N16 84w41 5:38:44
Sycamore Estates 120 44 38N03 84w44 5:38:56
Sylvandell 49 20 38N23 84w17 5:37:08
Sylvania 56 65 38N08 85w51 5:43:24
Symbol 63 15 37N16 84w08 5:36:32
Symsonia 42 1 36N55 88w31 5:54:04
Tabernacle 110 1 36N48 87w09 5:48:36
Tablow 84 43 37N46 84w51 5:39:24
Taffy 92 1 37N27 86w54 5:47:36
Taft 95 15 37N29 83w40 5:34:40
Talbert 13 15 37N25 83w28 5:33:52
Talcum 60 15 37N23 83w05 5:32:20
Tallega 65 15 37N34 83w36 5:34:24
Talley 62 48 37N28 85w54 5:43:36
Talmage 84 43 37N46 84w51 5:39:24
Tanglewood 37 19 38N12 84w52 5:39:28
Tanksley 26 15 37N13 83w42 5:34:48
Tanner 62 48 37N34 85w44 5:42:56
Tannery 68 10 38N36 83w19 5:33:16
Tar Fork 14 1 37N50 86w38 5:46:32
Tar Hill 43 1 37N29 86w18 5:45:12
Tarkiln 64 10 38N02 82w50 5:31:20
Tateville 100 18 36N58 84w35 5:38:20
Tatumsville 79 1 37N01 88w18 5:53:12
Taulbee 13 15 37N38 83w22 5:33:28
Taylor Mill 59 10 39N00 84w30 5:38:00
Taylor Mines 92 1 37N24 86w53 5:47:32
Taylorsport 8 10 39N06 84w42 5:38:48
Taylors Store 18 1 36N30 88w19 5:53:16
Taylorsville 108 52 38N02 85w21 5:41:24
Teaberry 36 10 37N26 82w39 5:30:36
Tedders 61 14 37N02 83w50 5:35:20
Teddy 23 48 37N19 84w56 5:39:44
Teetersville 48 14 36N51 83w19 5:33:16
Teges 26 15 37N18 83w40 5:34:40
Tejay 7 14 36N46 83w33 5:34:12
Temperance 107 1 36N43 86w35 5:46:20
Temple Hill 5 1 36N53 85w51 5:43:24
Teresita 94 15 38N32 84w50 5:39:20
Terrapin 84 43 37N46 84w51 5:39:24
Terrill 76 30 37N45 84w18 5:37:12
Terry Manor 56 65 38N08 85w51 5:43:24
Terryville 64 10 38N01 82w55 5:31:40
Texas 115 48 37N39 85w07 5:40:28
Thealka 58 10 37N49 82w47 5:31:08
Thelma 58 10 37N49 82w46 5:31:04
The Moors Camp 79 1 37N01 88w18 5:53:12
The Ridge 32 15 38N05 83w08 5:32:32
Thistleton Subdivision 37 19 38N12 84w52 5:39:28
Thomas 36 10 37N40 82w38 5:30:32
Thompson 25 21 38N03 83w57 5:35:48
Thompsonville 115 48 37N41 85w13 5:40:52
Thorn Hill 37 19 38N12 84w52 5:39:28
Thorn Hill Heights 37 19 38N12 84w52 5:39:28
Thornton 67 15 37N11 82w47 5:31:08
Thoroughbred Acres 56 67 38N17 85w35 5:42:20
Thousandsticks 66 15 37N11 83w26 5:33:44
Threeforks 80 10 37N45 82w26 5:29:44
Threeforks 114 1 37N02 86w15 5:45:00
Threelinks 55 35 37N21 84w20 5:37:20
Three Point 48 14 36N47 83w14 5:32:56
Three Springs 50 1 37N15 85w47 5:43:08
Three Springs 114 7 37N00 86w25 5:45:40
Thruston 30 1 37N45 87w07 5:48:28
Thurlow 44 6 37N16 85w30 5:42:00
Tidalwave 118 14 36N50 84w07 5:36:28
Tilden 117 1 37N36 87w43 5:50:52
Tilford 16 1 37N25 86w29 5:45:56
Tilford 97 45 37N02 83w05 5:32:20
Tiline 70 1 37N11 88w14 5:52:56
Tilton 35 15 38N25 83w47 5:35:08
Tina 60 15 37N22 83w01 5:32:04
Tinsley 7 14 36N47 83w46 5:35:04
Tiny Town 110 1 36N39 87w10 5:48:40
Tip Top 77 10 37N39 83w03 5:32:12
Toddspoint 106 51 38N13 85w14 5:40:56
Toler 98 10 37N38 82w15 5:29:00
Toliver 119 15 37N48 83w25 5:33:40
Tollesboro 68 10 38N35 83w34 5:34:16
Tolliver Town 67 15 37N11 82w41 5:30:44
Tolu 28 1 37N26 88w15 5:53:00
Tomahawk 80 10 37N52 82w36 5:30:24
Tompkinsville 86 1 36N42 85w41 5:42:44
Tonieville 62 48 37N34 85w44 5:42:56
Tooley Hill 89 1 37N13 87w11 5:48:44
Toonerville 98 10 37N23 82w15 5:29:00
Topmost 60 15 37N22 82w47 5:31:08
Topton 63 36 37N08 84w05 5:36:20
Toria 1 1 36N58 85w26 5:41:44
Torrent 119 15 37N42 83w41 5:34:44
Totz 48 14 36N57 83w07 5:32:28
Toulouse 66 15 37N17 83w17 5:33:08
Touristville 116 1 36N56 84w46 5:39:04
Tousey 43 1 37N35 86w33 5:46:12
Towers Chapel 75 1 37N25 87w16 5:49:04
Trace 68 10 38N36 83w19 5:33:16
Tracy 5 1 36N48 85w59 5:43:56
Tram 36 10 37N34 82w39 5:30:36
Trammel 2 6 36N45 86w11 5:44:44
Trapp 25 32 38N00 84w11 5:36:44
Trappist 90 48 37N40 85w32 5:42:08
Travellers Rest 95 15 37N29 83w40 5:34:40
Tremont 48 14 36N51 83w24 5:33:36
Trent 119 15 37N46 83w28 5:33:52
Trenton 110 1 36N43 87w16 5:49:04
Tress Shop 110 1 36N48 87w09 5:48:36
Tribbey 97 45 37N18 83w08 5:32:32
Tribune 28 1 37N20 88w04 5:52:16
Tri City 42 1 36N40 88w32 5:54:08
Trigg Furnace 111 1 36N52 87w50 5:51:20
Trimble 100 18 37N00 84w45 5:39:00
Trinity 68 10 38N36 83w19 5:33:16
Trisler 92 1 37N38 86w43 5:46:52
Tri-State 10 10 38N25 82w36 5:30:24
Trosper 61 14 36N47 83w50 5:35:20
Troy 120 44 38N03 84w44 5:38:56
Tucker 56 65 38N06 85w42 5:42:48
Tuckertown 114 1 37N02 86w15 5:45:00
Tuggleville 7 14 36N44 83w25 5:33:40
Turin 95 15 37N29 83w40 5:34:40
Turkey 13 15 37N29 83w31 5:34:04
Turkey Creek 98 10 37N40 82w18 5:29:12
Turkey Foot 105 15 38N23 84w32 5:38:08
Turkeytown 69 15 37N28 84w30 5:38:00
Turnersville 69 15 37N32 84w40 5:38:40
Turnertown 16 1 37N04 86w45 5:47:00
Tutor Key 58 10 37N51 82w46 5:31:04
Tuttle 63 15 37N01 83w56 5:35:44
Tway 48 14 36N51 83w19 5:33:16
Twentysix 88 39 37N55 83w16 5:33:04
Twila 48 14 36N50 83w25 5:33:40
Tyewhoppety 110 1 36N59 87w09 5:48:36
Tygarts 45 10 38N36 83w00 5:32:00
Tyler 73 1 37N03 88w37 5:54:28
Tyner 55 15 37N21 83w54 5:35:36
Typo 97 45 37N17 83w15 5:33:00
Tyrone 3 43 38N02 84w54 5:39:36
Ula 100 18 37N06 84w36 5:38:24
Ulvah 67 15 37N08 83w03 5:32:12
Ulysses 64 10 37N57 82w40 5:30:40
Union 8 10 38N57 84w41 5:38:44
Union City 76 15 37N48 84w12 5:36:48
Union Hall 33 26 37N41 83w57 5:35:48
Union Mills 57 28 37N53 84w34 5:38:16
Union Ridge 89 1 37N07 87w00 5:48:00
Union Star 14 1 37N56 86w27 5:45:48
Uniontown 113 1 37N47 87w56 5:51:44
Unity 10 10 38N28 82w39 5:30:36
University 34 27 38N02 84w30 5:38:00
Uno 50 6 37N11 85w54 5:43:36
Upchurch 27 1 36N41 85w08 5:40:32
Upper Clover 48 14 36N53 83w04 5:32:16
Upper Elk 98 10 37N29 82w04 5:28:16
Upper Kings Addition 45 10 38N43 82w58 5:31:52
Upper Tygarts 22 15 38N16 83w16 5:33:04
Upton 47 48 37N28 85w54 5:43:36
Urban 26 15 37N08 83w51 5:35:24
Utica 30 1 37N38 87w05 5:48:20
Utility 46 1 37N54 86w45 5:47:00
Uz 67 15 37N07 82w49 5:31:16
Vada 65 15 37N37 83w35 5:34:20
Valeria 119 15 37N49 83w31 5:34:04
Valley Hill 115 48 37N41 85w13 5:40:52
Valley Oak 100 18 37N06 84w36 5:38:24
Valley Station 56 65 38N07 85w50 5:43:20
Valley View 76 15 37N51 84w26 5:37:44
Van 67 15 37N09 82w51 5:31:24
Vanarsdell 84 43 37N46 84w51 5:39:24
Van Buren 3 17 37N59 85w10 5:40:40
Vanceburg 68 10 38N36 83w19 5:33:16
Vancleve 13 15 37N38 83w25 5:33:40
Van Cleve 18 1 36N36 88w19 5:53:16
Vanderburg 117 1 37N31 87w41 5:50:44
Vandetta 54 1 37N25 87w29 5:49:56
Vanhook 100 18 37N06 84w36 5:38:24
Van Lear 58 10 37N47 82w44 5:30:56
Vanzant 14 1 37N39 86w37 5:46:28
Varilla 7 14 36N43 83w38 5:34:32
Varney 98 10 37N38 82w25 5:29:40
Vaughns Mill 99 15 37N49 83w55 5:35:40
Veachland 106 51 38N13 85w14 5:40:56
Veechdale 106 48 38N13 85w21 5:41:24
Venters 98 10 37N19 82w21 5:29:24
Vento 47 48 37N28 85w54 5:43:36
Venus 49 20 38N23 84w17 5:37:08
Verne 118 14 36N44 84w10 5:36:40
Vernon 86 1 36N38 85w31 5:42:04
Verona 8 10 38N49 84w40 5:38:40
Versailles 120 44 38N03 84w44 5:38:56
Vertrees 47 48 37N42 86w08 5:44:32
Vest 60 15 37N24 83w00 5:32:00
Vester 1 1 37N06 85w18 5:41:12
Vicco 97 45 37N13 83w04 5:32:16
Victoria 54 1 37N20 87w30 5:50:00
Victory 63 15 37N15 84w06 5:36:24
Villa Hills 59 68 39N03 84w35 5:38:20
Vincent 95 15 37N28 83w47 5:35:08
Vine Grove 47 48 37N49 85w59 5:43:56
Vine Grove Junction 47 48 37N50 85w56 5:43:44
Vineyard 57 28 37N53 84w34 5:38:16
Vinnie 104 1 37N04 84w50 5:39:20
Viola 42 1 36N51 88w38 5:54:32

KENTUCKY

Viper 97 45 37N11 83w09 5:32:36
Virden 99 15 37N52 83w55 5:35:40
Virgie 98 10 37N20 82w35 5:30:20
Visalia 59 10 38N55 84w27 5:37:48
Volga 58 10 37N52 82w52 5:31:28
Vortex 119 15 37N42 83w31 5:34:04
Vox 63 15 37N02 84w17 5:37:08
Wabaco 97 45 37N15 83w11 5:32:44
Wabd 102 35 37N21 84w20 5:37:20
Waco 76 15 37N45 84w09 5:36:36
Waddy 106 48 38N08 85w04 5:40:16
Wadesboro 18 1 36N46 88w18 5:53:12
Wagersville 33 26 37N42 83w58 5:35:52
Wagner 103 15 38N11 83w16 5:33:04
Waite 116 1 36N46 85w01 5:40:04
Wakefield 108 48 38N02 85w21 5:41:24
Walden 118 14 36N51 84w10 5:36:40
Waldo 77 10 37N35 82w59 5:31:56
Wales 98 10 37N20 82w35 5:30:20
Walker 61 14 36N53 83w43 5:34:52
Walkertown 97 45 37N15 83w11 5:32:44
Wallaceton 76 15 37N37 84w24 5:37:36
Wallingford 35 15 38N24 83w37 5:34:28
Wallins Creek 48 14 36N49 83w26 5:33:44
Wallonia 111 1 36N59 87w47 5:51:08
Wallsend 7 14 36N46 83w42 5:34:48
Walltown 23 48 37N20 84w40 5:38:40
Walnut Grove 2 1 36N39 86w16 5:45:04
Walnut Grove 100 18 37N16 84w27 5:37:48
Walnut Hill 2 6 36N45 86w11 5:44:44
Waltersville 99 15 37N52 83w55 5:35:40
Walton 8 13 38N52 84w37 5:38:28
Waltz 103 15 38N11 83w26 5:33:44
Wanamaker 117 1 37N36 87w32 5:50:08
Waneta 55 15 37N29 84w02 5:36:08
Warbranch 66 15 36N58 83w26 5:33:44
Warco 36 10 37N32 82w47 5:31:08
War Creek 13 15 37N33 83w22 5:33:28
Warfield 80 10 37N50 82w27 5:29:48
Warnock 45 10 38N34 82w50 5:31:20
Warsaw 39 11 38N47 84w54 5:39:36
Washington 81 10 38N37 83w49 5:35:16
Wasioto 7 14 36N46 83w42 5:34:48
Watauga 27 1 36N41 85w08 5:40:32
Waterford 108 48 38N02 85w21 5:41:24
Watergap 36 10 37N38 82w45 5:31:00
Water Valley 42 1 36N34 88w49 5:55:16
Waterview 29 1 36N49 85w28 5:41:52
Watkinsville 105 15 38N16 84w41 5:38:44
Watterfern Hills 56 65 38N10 85w36 5:42:24
Watts 13 15 37N29 83w19 5:33:16
Watts Creek 118 14 36N44 84w10 5:36:40
Waverly 113 1 37N43 87w48 5:51:12
Waverly Hills 56 65 38N08 85w51 5:43:24
Wax 43 1 37N21 86w07 5:44:28
Wayland 36 10 37N27 82w48 5:31:12
Waynesburg 69 15 37N22 84w40 5:38:40
Weaverton 51 8 37N49 87w37 5:50:28
Webb Mills 47 48 37N33 86w02 5:44:08
Webbs 44 6 37N16 85w30 5:42:00
Webbs Cross Roads 104 1 37N07 85w03 5:40:12
Webbville 64 10 38N11 82w52 5:31:28
Weberstown 46 1 37N45 86w49 5:47:16
Webster 14 1 37N53 86w20 5:45:20
Wedonia 81 10 38N31 83w50 5:35:20
Weeksbury 36 10 37N20 82w42 5:30:48
Weir 89 1 37N07 87w13 5:48:52
Welborn 100 18 37N06 84w36 5:38:24
Welchburg 55 15 37N21 83w54 5:35:36
Welchs Creek 16 1 37N19 86w38 5:46:32
Weldon 82 48 38N00 86w10 5:44:40
Wellhope 102 35 37N21 84w20 5:37:20
Wellington 56 65 38N13 85w40 5:42:40
Wellington 83 15 37N55 83w31 5:34:04
Wells 88 39 37N52 83w16 5:33:04
Wells 89 1 37N18 87w08 5:48:32
Wellsburg 12 10 38N48 84w13 5:36:52
Wells Landing 11 24 37N39 84w46 5:39:04
Wendover 66 15 37N08 83w16 5:33:04
Wentz 97 45 37N08 83w05 5:32:20
Wesco 54 1 37N20 87w30 5:50:00
Wesleyan Park 25 32 38N00 84w11 5:36:44
Wesleyville 22 15 38N18 83w11 5:32:44
Westbend 99 15 37N54 83w58 5:35:52
West Buechel 56 65 38N12 85w40 5:42:40
West Clifty 43 1 37N29 86w18 5:45:12
West Danville 11 24 37N39 84w46 5:39:04
Western 38 1 36N33 89w20 5:57:20
West Fairview 10 10 38N28 82w39 5:30:36
West Fayette 34 27 38N02 84w34 5:38:16
Westfork 2 6 36N45 86w11 5:44:44
West Frankfort 37 19 38N12 84w52 5:39:28
West Garrett 36 10 37N29 82w50 5:31:20
West Irvine 33 26 37N43 84w00 5:36:00
West Liberty 88 39 37N55 83w16 5:33:04
West Louisville 30 1 37N42 87w17 5:49:08
West Paducah 73 1 37N05 88w45 5:55:00
West Paris 9 29 38N13 84w15 5:37:00
West Point 47 61 37N59 85w57 5:43:48
Westport 93 49 38N29 85w29 5:41:56
West Prestonsburg 36 10 37N41 82w46 5:31:04
West Royalton 77 10 37N41 83w02 5:32:08
West Russell 45 10 38N32 82w43 5:30:52
West Van Lear 58 10 37N47 82w47 5:31:08
Westview 14 1 37N42 86w25 5:45:40
West Viola 42 1 36N49 88w38 5:54:32
West Wheatcroft 117 1 37N29 87w52 5:51:28
West Wind Park 56 65 38N08 85w51 5:43:24
Westwood 10 10 38N28 82w39 5:30:36
Westwood 56 65 38N13 85w37 5:42:28
Weymouth 42 1 36N30 88w53 5:55:32
Wheatcroft 117 1 37N30 87w52 5:51:28
Wheatley 94 15 38N37 84w59 5:39:56
Wheeler 61 14 36N44 83w51 5:35:24
Wheelersburg 77 10 37N50 83w01 5:32:04
Wheelwright 36 10 37N20 82w43 5:30:52
Whick 13 15 37N26 83w22 5:33:28
Whickerville 50 1 37N15 85w47 5:43:08
Whipple 7 14 36N46 83w33 5:34:12
Whippoorwill 71 1 36N51 86w53 5:47:32
Whipps Millgate 56 67 38N15 85w34 5:42:16
Whipps Mill Village 56 67 38N17 85w35 5:42:20
Whispering Hills 56 65 38N09 85w42 5:42:48
Whitaker 36 10 37N15 82w47 5:31:08
Whitaker 67 15 37N10 82w44 5:30:56
Whitco 67 15 37N07 82w49 5:31:16
White City 54 1 37N11 87w23 5:49:32
White City 62 48 37N35 85w40 5:42:40
White Hall 76 30 37N45 84w18 5:37:12
Whitehouse 58 10 37N52 82w42 5:30:48
White Lily 100 18 37N04 84w31 5:38:04
White Mills 47 48 37N33 86w02 5:44:08
White Oak 40 15 37N37 84w35 5:38:20
White Oak 88 15 37N52 83w12 5:32:48
White Oak Junction 74 15 36N42 84w37 5:38:28
White Plains 2 6 36N45 86w11 5:44:44
White Plains 54 1 37N11 87w23 5:49:32
White Run 92 1 37N27 86w41 5:46:44
Whites 76 42 37N35 84w17 5:37:08
Whitesburg 67 15 37N07 82w49 5:31:16
White Sulphur 17 1 37N12 88w04 5:52:16
White Sulphur 105 25 38N13 84w33 5:38:12
Whitesville 30 1 37N41 86w52 5:47:28
White Tower 59 10 38N56 84w31 5:38:04
White Villa 59 10 38N58 84w34 5:38:16
Whitewood 44 6 37N16 85w30 5:42:00
Whitfield 15 48 38N02 85w21 5:41:24
Whitley City 74 15 36N44 84w28 5:37:52
Whittle 104 1 37N04 85w06 5:40:24
Wiborg 74 15 36N49 84w29 5:37:56
Wickliffe 4 1 36N58 89w05 5:56:20
Wicks Well 54 1 37N20 87w30 5:50:00
Widecreek 13 15 37N37 83w32 5:34:08
Wilbur 64 10 38N02 82w50 5:31:20
Wild Cat 26 15 37N14 83w41 5:34:44
Wilder 19 68 39N02 84w27 5:37:48
Wilders 19 68 39N03 84w29 5:37:56
Wildie 102 15 37N25 84w18 5:37:12
Wildwood 56 67 38N15 85w34 5:42:16
Wilhurst 13 15 37N38 83w25 5:33:40
Willailla 102 15 37N24 84w25 5:37:40
Willard 22 15 38N13 82w54 5:31:36
Williams 88 15 37N52 83w12 5:32:48
Williams 92 1 37N23 86w55 5:47:40
Williamsburg 118 14 36N42 84w14 5:36:56
Williamsport 58 10 37N49 82w44 5:30:56
Williams Station 117 1 37N29 87w50 5:51:20
Williams Store 71 1 36N45 86w53 5:47:32
Williamstown 41 10 38N38 84w34 5:38:16
Willisburg 115 48 37N50 85w08 5:40:32
Willow 12 10 38N41 84w04 5:36:16
Willow Crest 37 19 38N12 84w52 5:39:28
Willow Grove 12 10 38N48 84w13 5:36:52
Willow Shade 85 1 36N51 85w37 5:42:28
Willow Tree 33 26 37N41 83w57 5:35:48
Wilmore 57 22 37N52 84w40 5:38:40
Wilson 51 1 37N44 87w42 5:50:48
Wilsonville 11 24 37N39 84w46 5:39:04
Wilsonville 108 48 38N11 85w28 5:41:52
Wilstacy 13 15 37N33 83w22 5:33:28
Wilton 61 14 36N54 84w05 5:36:20
Win 58 10 37N53 82w58 5:31:52
Winchester 25 32 38N00 84w11 5:36:44
Wind Cave 55 15 37N31 83w56 5:35:44
Winding Way 37 19 38N12 84w52 5:39:28
Windsor 23 48 37N08 84w55 5:39:40
Windy 116 1 36N45 84w59 5:39:56
Windy Hill 92 1 37N27 86w41 5:46:44
Windy Hills 56 65 38N16 85w38 5:42:32
Windyville 31 1 37N11 86w19 5:45:16
Wingo 42 1 36N39 88w44 5:54:56
Winifred 58 10 37N56 82w53 5:31:32
Winslow Park 28 1 37N20 88w04 5:52:16
Winston 33 15 37N42 84w05 5:36:20
Winston Park 59 68 39N02 84w31 5:38:04
Wiscoal 60 15 37N15 83w03 5:32:12
Wisconsin 60 15 37N15 83w03 5:32:12
Wisdom 85 1 36N59 85w37 5:42:28
Wisemantown 33 26 37N42 83w58 5:35:52
Wises Landing 112 48 38N36 85w19 5:41:16
Wiswell 18 1 36N36 88w19 5:53:16
Wittensville 58 10 37N52 82w48 5:31:12
Witt Springs 33 26 37N42 83w58 5:35:52
Wofford 118 14 36N47 84w08 5:36:32
Wolf 22 15 38N24 83w07 5:32:28
Wolf Coal 13 15 37N24 83w23 5:33:32
Wolf Creek 82 48 38N04 86w18 5:45:12
Wolf Lick 71 1 36N59 86w57 5:47:48
Wolfpit 98 10 37N19 82w21 5:29:24
Wollingtown 43 1 37N22 86w15 5:45:00
Wonder 36 10 37N40 82w38 5:30:32
Wonnie 77 10 37N49 83w10 5:32:40
Woodbine 118 14 36N54 84w05 5:36:20
Woodburn 114 1 36N50 86w32 5:46:08
Woodbury 16 1 37N11 86w38 5:46:32
Woodhill 56 65 38N09 85w42 5:42:48
Woodlake 37 19 38N12 84w52 5:39:28
Woodland Hills 56 67 38N16 85w32 5:42:08
Woodland Park 97 45 37N15 83w11 5:32:44
Woodlawn 19 68 39N02 84w27 5:37:48
Woodlawn 73 1 37N03 88w37 5:54:28
Woodlawn 90 48 37N48 85w28 5:41:52
Woodlawn Park 56 65 38N16 85w38 5:42:32
Woodman 98 10 37N31 82w03 5:28:12
Woodrow 14 1 37N47 86w21 5:45:24
Woods 36 10 37N41 82w46 5:31:04
Woods 48 14 36N52 83w12 5:32:48
Woodsbend 88 39 37N55 83w16 5:33:04
Woodside 56 67 38N17 85w35 5:42:20
Woodsonville 50 6 37N11 85w54 5:43:36
Woodstock 100 18 37N06 84w36 5:38:24
Woodville 73 1 37N05 88w53 5:55:32
Woolcott 12 10 38N41 84w04 5:36:16
Woollum 61 14 37N01 83w49 5:35:16
Wooton 66 15 37N11 83w18 5:33:12
Worthington 45 10 38N33 82w44 5:30:56
Worthington 56 67 38N17 85w35 5:42:20
Worthville 21 16 38N37 85w04 5:40:16
Wray Gap 116 1 36N50 84w51 5:39:24
Wrights 109 48 37N21 85w21 5:41:24
Wrightsburg 75 1 37N32 87w16 5:49:04
Wrigley 88 15 38N01 83w16 5:33:04
Wurtland 45 10 38N30 82w47 5:31:08
Wynns 24 1 37N11 87w23 5:49:32
Yaden 118 14 36N43 84w03 5:36:12
Yancey 48 14 36N51 83w19 5:33:16
Yeaddiss 66 15 37N04 83w13 5:32:52
Yeager 61 14 36N52 83w48 5:35:12
Yeager 98 10 37N29 82w31 5:30:04
Yeaman 43 1 37N31 86w35 5:46:20
Yellow Rock 65 15 37N35 83w47 5:35:08
Yelvington 30 1 37N52 87w00 5:48:00
Yerkes 97 45 37N17 83w18 5:33:12
Yesse 2 6 36N45 86w11 5:44:44
Yocum 88 15 37N59 83w20 5:33:20
Yocum Creek 48 14 36N52 83w12 5:32:48
York 45 10 38N34 83w03 5:32:12
Yorktown 98 10 37N28 82w31 5:30:04
Yosemite 23 48 37N21 84w50 5:39:20
Younger Creek 47 58 37N42 85w52 5:43:28
Youngs Creek 118 14 36N50 84w07 5:36:28
Youngtown 16 1 37N14 86w41 5:46:44
Yuma 109 48 37N16 85w18 5:41:12
Zachariah 65 15 37N42 83w41 5:34:44
Zag 88 39 37N55 83w16 5:33:04
Zebulon 98 10 37N32 82w28 5:29:52
Zion 41 10 38N44 84w45 5:39:00
Zion 51 1 37N49 87w29 5:49:56
Zion 110 1 36N39 87w10 5:48:40
Zion Hill 120 47 38N09 84w41 5:38:44
Zoe 65 15 37N41 83w41 5:34:44
Zoneton 15 50 38N00 85w43 5:42:52
Zula 116 1 36N46 85w01 5:40:04

TIME TABLES

LA # 1			LA # 2		
Before 11/18/1883		LMT	Before 11/18/1883		LMT
11/18/1883	12:00	CST	11/18/1883	12:00	CST
3/31/1918	02:00	CWT	3/31/1918	02:00	CWT
10/27/1918	02:00	CST	10/27/1918	02:00	CST
3/30/1919	02:00	CWT	3/30/1919	02:00	CWT
10/26/1919	02:00	CST	10/26/1919	02:00	CST
2/09/1942	02:00	CWT	2/09/1942	02:00	CWT
9/30/1945	02:00	CST	9/30/1945	02:00	CST
4/30/1967	02:00	US#1	4/29/1946	02:00	CDT
....			9/29/1946	02:00	CST
			4/30/1967	02:00	US#1

COUNTIES

1 Acadia
2 Allen
3 Ascension
4 Assumption
5 Avoyelles
6 Beauregard
7 Bienville
8 Bossier
9 Caddo
10 Calcasieu
11 Caldwell
12 Cameron
13 Catahoula
14 Claiborne
15 Concordia
16 De Soto
17 East Baton Rouge
18 East Carroll
19 East Feliciana
20 Evangeline
21 Franklin
22 Grant
23 Iberia
24 Iberville
25 Jackson
26 Jefferson
27 Jefferson Davis
28 Lafayette
29 Lafourche
30 La Salle
31 Lincoln
32 Livingston
33 Madison
34 Morehouse
35 Natchitoches
36 Orleans
37 Ouachita
38 Plaquemines
39 Pointe Coupee
40 Rapides
41 Red River
42 Richland
43 Sabine
44 St Bernard
45 St Charles
46 St Helena
47 St James
48 St John the Baptist
49 St Landry
50 St Martin
51 St Mary
52 St Tammany
53 Tangipahoa
54 Tensas
55 Terrebonne
56 Union
57 Vermilion
58 Vernon
59 Washington
60 Webster
61 West Baton Rouge
62 West Carroll
63 West Feliciana
64 Winn

Abbeville 57	1	29N58	92w08	6:08:32
Abby Plantation 29	1	29N47	90w50	6:03:20
Aben 3	1	30N06	91w00	6:04:00
Abington 41	1	32N01	93w43	6:14:52
Abita Springs 52	1	30N29	90w02	6:00:08
Acadia Academy 1	1	30N29	92w25	6:09:40
Acme 15	1	31N17	91w49	6:07:16
Acy 3	1	30N13	90w49	6:03:16
Ada 7	1	32N33	93w09	6:12:36
Addis 61	1	30N21	91w16	6:05:04
Adeline 51	1	29N55	91w40	6:06:40
Adner 8	1	32N32	93w30	6:14:00
Advance 25	1	32N17	92w43	6:10:52
Afton 33	1	32N25	91w11	6:04:44
Aimwell 13	1	31N47	91w59	6:07:56
Airview Terrace 40	1	31N17	92w29	6:09:56
Ajax 35	1	31N44	93w24	6:13:36
Akers 53	1	30N17	90w24	6:01:36
Albania 51	1	29N55	91w40	6:06:40
Albany 32	1	30N30	90w35	6:02:20
Alco 58	1	31N20	93w08	6:12:32
Alden Bridge 8	1	32N47	93w43	6:14:52
Alexandria 40	1	31N18	92w27	6:09:48
Alfalfa 40	1	31N24	92w40	6:10:40
Alice 63	1	30N50	91w12	6:04:48
Allemand 55	1	29N36	90w43	6:02:52
Allemands 29	1	29N49	90w29	6:01:56
Allen 35	1	31N50	93w17	6:13:08
Allendale 61	1	30N30	91w16	6:05:04
Alluvial City 44	2	29N50	89w52	5:59:28
Aloha 22	1	31N35	92w46	6:11:04
Aloysia 24	1	30N10	91w09	6:04:36
Alsatia	1	32N37	91w11	6:04:44
Alsen 17	1	30N34	91w13	6:04:52
Alto 42	1	32N22	91w52	6:07:28
Alton 52	1	30N20	89w46	5:59:04
Alvin Callender 38	2	29N45	90w00	6:00:00
Ama 45	2	29N57	90w18	6:01:12
Amelia 51	1	29N40	91w06	6:04:24
Amite 53	1	30N44	90w30	6:02:00
Anacoco 58	1	31N15	93w21	6:13:24
Anandale 40	1	31N16	92w27	6:09:48
Andrepont 49	1	30N32	92w05	6:08:20
Andrew 57	1	30N05	92w15	6:09:00
Andrew Guillot Subdivision 29	1	29N47	90w50	6:03:20
Angelina 48	1	30N03	90w38	6:02:32
Angie 59	1	30N58	89w49	5:59:16
Annadale 24	1	30N10	91w09	6:04:36
Ansley 25	1	32N24	92w42	6:10:48
Antioch 14	1	32N47	93w03	6:12:12
Antioch 31	1	32N32	92w47	6:11:08
Antonia 22	1	31N34	92w25	6:09:40
Antrim 8	1	32N53	93w42	6:14:48
Arabi 44	2	29N57	90w00	6:00:00
Ararat 10	1	30N13	93w12	6:12:48
Arboth 61	1	30N34	91w21	6:05:24
Arcadia 7	1	32N33	92w55	6:11:40
Archibald 42	1	32N21	91w47	6:07:08
Archie 13	1	31N37	91w49	6:07:16
Arcola 53	1	30N46	90w31	6:02:04
Ardoyne 55	1	29N36	90w43	6:02:52
Argo 13	1	31N22	91w54	6:07:36
Arizona 14	1	32N47	93w03	6:12:12
Arlington 17	1	30N23	91w10	6:04:40
Armistead 41	1	32N02	93w20	6:13:20
Arnaudville 49	1	30N24	91w56	6:07:44
Ashland 35	1	32N09	93w06	6:12:24
Ashland 55	1	29N36	90w43	6:02:52
Ashley 33	1	32N25	91w11	6:04:44
Athens 14	1	32N39	93w01	6:12:04
Atkins 8	1	32N19	93w32	6:14:08
Atlanta 64	1	31N48	92w45	6:11:00
Audubon 17	1	30N27	91w08	6:04:32
Audubon Terrace 17	1	30N25	91w09	6:04:36
Augusta 24	1	30N10	91w09	6:04:36
Augusta 38	2	29N45	90w00	6:00:00
Avalon 51	1	29N42	91w18	6:05:12
Avandale 54	1	31N55	91w14	6:04:56
Avery Island 23	1	29N55	91w54	6:07:36
Avondale 26	2	29N55	90w11	6:00:44
Aycock 14	1	32N47	93w03	6:12:12
Azucena 54	1	31N48	91w23	6:05:32
Bagdad 22	1	31N31	92w42	6:10:48
Bains 63	1	30N50	91w23	6:05:32
Baker 17	1	30N35	91w10	6:04:40
Baldwin 51	1	29N50	91w33	6:06:12
Ball 40	1	31N25	92w25	6:09:40
Bancroft 6	1	30N34	93w41	6:14:44
Bankers 50	1	30N10	91w50	6:07:20
Banks 17	1	30N33	91w10	6:04:40
Banks Springs 11	1	32N06	92w05	6:08:20
Baptist 53	1	30N31	90w27	6:01:48
Barataria 26	2	29N44	90w08	6:00:32
Barksdale Air Force Base 8	1	32N30	93w38	6:14:32
Barnet Springs 31	1	32N32	92w38	6:10:32
Barron 40	1	31N21	92w10	6:08:40
Barton 3	1	30N06	91w00	6:04:00
Basile 20	1	30N29	92w36	6:10:24
Baskin 21	1	32N16	91w45	6:07:00
Baskinton 21	1	32N15	91w45	6:07:00
Bastrop 34	1	32N47	91w55	6:07:40
Batchelor	1	30N51	91w40	6:06:40
Bates 1	1	30N29	92w25	6:09:40
Baton Rouge 17	1	30N27	91w11	6:04:44
Batree 47	1	30N00	90w44	6:02:56
Bawcomville 37	1	32N31	92w09	6:08:36
Bayou Barbary 32	1	30N30	90w45	6:03:00
Bayou Blue 29	1	29N36	90w43	6:02:52
Bayou Cane 55	1	29N38	90w45	6:03:00
Bayou Chicot 20	1	30N49	92w21	6:09:24
Bayou Current 49	1	30N42	91w45	6:07:00
Bayou Gauche 45	1	29N49	90w29	6:01:56
Bayou Goula 24	1	30N13	91w10	6:04:40
Bayou Pigeon 24	1	30N17	91w14	6:04:56
Bayou Sale 51	1	29N48	91w30	6:06:00
Bayou Sorrel 24	1	30N10	91w20	6:05:20
Bayou Vista 51	1	29N41	91w16	6:05:04
Baywood 17	1	30N35	91w00	6:04:00
Beachview 26	2	29N59	90w15	6:01:00
Bear Creek 7	1	32N21	92w59	6:11:56
Beaver 20	1	30N49	92w40	6:10:40
Bee Bayou 42	1	32N28	91w45	6:07:00
Beekman 34	1	32N47	91w55	6:07:40
Beggs 49	1	30N57	92w11	6:08:44
Bel 2	1	30N15	93w15	6:13:00
Belair 38	2	29N52	89w57	5:59:48
Belair Cove 20	1	30N41	92w17	6:09:08
Belcher 9	1	32N45	93w50	6:15:20
Bell City 10	1	30N07	92w58	6:11:52
Belle Amie 29	1	29N33	90w20	6:01:20
Belle Chasse 38	2	29N51	89w59	5:59:56
Belle Point 48	1	30N04	90w33	6:02:12
Belle River 4	1	29N42	91w14	6:04:56
Belle Rose 4	1	30N03	91w03	6:04:12
Belle Terre 4	1	30N04	91w01	6:04:04
Belleview 49	1	30N32	92w05	6:08:20
Bellevue 8	1	32N32	93w30	6:14:00
Bellfontaine 17	1	30N27	91w04	6:04:16
Bell Helene 3	1	30N12	91w01	6:04:04
Bellview 11	1	32N06	92w05	6:08:20
Bellview 26	2	29N54	90w03	6:00:12
Bellview 51	1	29N48	91w30	6:06:00
Bellwood 35	1	31N32	93w12	6:12:48
Belmont 39	1	30N29	91w32	6:06:08
Belmont 43	1	31N43	93w31	6:14:04
Belmont 47	1	30N01	90w46	6:03:04
Benson 16	1	31N52	93w42	6:14:48
Bentley 22	1	31N31	92w30	6:10:00
Benton 8	1	32N42	93w44	6:14:56
Bermuda 35	1	31N40	93w03	6:12:12
Bernice 56	1	32N49	92w39	6:10:36
Bertrandville 38	2	29N47	90w01	6:00:04
Berwick 51	1	29N41	91w13	6:04:52
Bethany 9	1	32N22	94w03	6:16:12
Bienville 7	1	32N22	92w59	6:11:56
Big Bend 5	1	31N05	91w48	6:07:12
Big Cane 49	1	30N50	92w05	6:08:20
Big Creek 21	1	32N15	91w45	6:07:00
Big Island 40	1	31N21	92w10	6:08:40
Big Ridge 11	1	32N06	92w05	6:08:20
Billeaud 28	1	30N09	91w58	6:07:52
Bivens 6	1	30N45	93w32	6:14:08
Blackburn 14	1	32N58	93w08	6:12:32
Black Hawk 15	1	31N35	91w26	6:05:44
Blade 30	1	31N41	92w07	6:08:28
Blairstown 19	1	30N52	91w01	6:04:04
Blanchard 9	1	32N31	93w43	6:14:52
Blanche 40	1	30N59	92w34	6:10:16
Blanks 39	1	30N33	91w36	6:06:24
Blankston 11	1	32N06	92w05	6:08:20
Blond 52	1	30N29	90w06	6:00:24
Bluff Creek	1	30N46	90w53	6:03:32
Bob Acres 23	1	29N57	91w59	6:07:56
Bodcau 8	1	32N32	93w30	6:14:00
Bogalusa 59	1	30N47	89w52	5:59:28
Bohemia 38	1	29N35	89w48	5:59:12
Boleyn 43	1	31N44	93w24	6:13:36
Bolinger 8	1	32N57	93w41	6:14:44
Bolivar 53	1	30N56	90w31	6:02:04
Bonaire 17	1	30N25	91w09	6:04:36
Bond 2	1	30N49	92w40	6:10:40
Bonfouca 52	1	30N17	89w46	5:59:04
Bonita 34	1	32N55	91w40	6:06:40
Bon Secour 47	1	29N59	90w50	6:03:20
Book 13	1	31N37	91w49	6:07:16
Boothville 38	1	29N20	89w25	5:57:40
Bordelonville 5	1	31N06	91w55	6:07:40
Borgne Mouth 44	2	29N54	89w54	5:59:36
Borodino 5	1	31N02	91w59	6:07:56
Bosco 37	1	32N17	92w05	6:08:20
Boscoville 49	1	30N32	92w05	6:08:20
Bossier City 8	1	32N31	93w44	6:14:56
Boston 57	1	29N57	92w02	6:08:08
Boudreaux 55	1	29N25	90w42	6:02:48
Boudreaux Canal 55	1	29N27	90w36	6:02:24
Bougere 15	1	31N35	91w26	6:05:44
Bourg 55	1	29N34	90w36	6:02:24
Boutte 45	1	29N54	90w23	6:01:32
Boyce 40	1	31N23	92w40	6:10:40
Braithwaite 38	2	29N52	89w57	5:59:48
Branch 1	1	30N21	92w16	6:09:04
Breaux Bridge 50	1	30N16	91w54	6:07:36
Breezy Hill 22	1	31N31	92w24	6:09:36
Bridge City 26	2	29N56	90w10	6:00:40
Brignac 3	1	30N14	90w55	6:03:40
Brimstone 10	1	30N13	93w21	6:13:24
Bristol 49	1	30N23	92w05	6:08:20
Brittany 3	1	30N13	90w53	6:03:32
Broadmoor 36	2	29N57	90w06	6:00:24
Broadmoor 55	1	29N36	90w43	6:02:52
Brooks 39	1	30N42	91w26	6:05:44
Brouillette 5	1	31N08	92w04	6:08:16
Broussard 28	1	30N09	91w58	6:07:52
Brown 7	1	32N15	93w10	6:12:40
Brownfields 17	1	30N33	91w10	6:04:40
Brown Heights 17	1	30N35	91w10	6:04:40
Brownlee 8	1	32N35	93w44	6:14:56
Brownsville 37	1	32N29	92w09	6:08:36
Brownville 11	1	32N06	92w05	6:08:20
Brule 4	1	29N50	90w57	6:03:48
Brule Guillot 29	1	29N47	90w50	6:03:20
Brule Labadie 4	1	29N50	90w57	6:03:48
Bruly La Croix 24	1	30N10	91w09	6:04:36

Bruly Saint Martin 4 1 30N03 91w03 6:04:12
Brusle Saint Vincent 4 1 29N56 91w02 6:04:08
Brusly 61 1 30N23 91w14 6:04:56
Bryceland 7 1 32N27 92w59 6:11:56
Buckeye 40 1 31N21 92w13 6:08:52
Buckner 42 1 32N28 91w45 6:07:00
Bueche 61 1 30N34 91w21 6:05:24
Buhler 10 1 30N20 93w22 6:13:28
Bunkie 5 1 30N57 92w11 6:08:44
Buras 38 1 29N22 89w32 5:58:08
Burkplace 7 1 32N15 93w10 6:12:40
Burr Ferry 58 1 31N04 93w30 6:14:00
Burroughs 11 1 32N06 92w05 6:08:20
Burrwood 38 1 29N17 89w21 5:57:24
Burton Lane 47 1 30N00 90w44 6:02:56
Bush 52 1 30N36 89w54 5:59:36
Bushes 21 1 32N10 91w43 6:06:52
Butte La Rose 50 1 30N17 91w41 6:06:44
Bywaters 36 2 29N58 90w04 6:00:16
Caddo 9 1 32N45 93w59 6:15:56
Cade 50 1 30N05 91w54 6:07:36
Cadeville 37 1 32N24 92w25 6:09:40
Caernovan 44 2 29N52 89w54 5:59:36
Caffery 51 1 29N48 91w30 6:06:00
Caire Spur 47 1 29N59 90w50 6:03:20
Calcasieu 40 1 30N59 92w34 6:10:16
Calhoun 37 1 32N31 92w22 6:09:28
Calumet 51 1 29N42 91w18 6:05:12
Calvin 64 1 31N58 92w47 6:11:08
Camelia Gardens 40 1 31N17 92w29 6:09:56
Cameron 12 1 29N48 93w20 6:13:20
Camperdown 51 1 29N48 91w30 6:06:00
Campti 35 1 31N54 93w07 6:12:28
Canebrake 15 1 31N42 91w28 6:05:52
Caney 58 1 31N08 93w16 6:13:04
Cankton 49 1 30N21 92w07 6:08:28
Cannonburg 24 1 30N10 91w09 6:04:36
Capitan 28 1 30N06 92w00 6:08:00
Capitol 17 1 30N28 91w11 6:04:44
Caplis 8 1 32N24 93w37 6:14:28
Carencro 28 1 30N19 92w03 6:08:12
Carlisle 38 1 29N41 89w58 5:59:52
Carlton 37 1 32N31 92w22 6:09:28
Carlyss 10 1 30N11 93w23 6:13:32
Carmel 16 1 32N05 93w37 6:14:28
Carrollton 36 2 29N57 90w07 6:00:28
Carterville 8 1 32N54 93w42 6:14:48
Cartwright 25 1 32N32 92w31 6:10:04
Carville 24 1 30N13 91w06 6:04:24
Caspiana 9 1 32N17 93w33 6:14:12
Castle Village 40 1 31N17 92w29 6:09:56
Castor 7 1 32N15 93w10 6:12:40
Castor Plunge 40 1 31N17 92w29 6:09:56
Catahoula 50 1 30N12 91w44 6:06:56
Catherine 24 1 30N13 91w10 6:04:40
Cat Island 11 1 32N06 92w05 6:08:20
Catuna 16 1 32N01 93w43 6:14:52
Cavett 9 1 32N45 93w50 6:15:20
Cecile 9 1 32N28 93w43 6:14:52
Cecilia 50 1 30N20 91w51 6:07:24
Cedar Crest 17 1 30N26 91w04 6:04:16
Cedar Glen 17 1 30N31 91w09 6:04:36
Cedar Grove 4 1 29N50 90w57 6:03:48
Cedar Grove 9 1 32N26 93w45 6:15:00
Cedar Grove 38 2 29N45 90w00 6:00:00
Cedarton 31 1 32N32 92w31 6:10:04
Centenary 9 1 32N29 93w44 6:14:56
Center Point 5 1 31N15 92w13 6:08:52
Centerville 20 1 30N51 92w15 6:09:00
Centerville 51 1 29N46 91w26 6:05:44
Central 17 1 30N29 91w09 6:04:36
Central 47 1 30N06 90w50 6:03:20
Central 55 1 29N36 90w43 6:02:52
Chacahoula 55 1 29N45 90w49 6:03:16
Chackbay 29 1 29N47 90w50 6:03:20
Chalmette 44 2 29N56 89w58 5:59:52
Chalmette Vista 44 2 29N57 90w01 6:00:04
Chamberlin 61 1 30N28 91w13 6:04:52
Chambers 40 1 31N11 92w25 6:09:40
Chandler Park 40 1 31N17 92w29 6:09:56
Charenton 51 1 29N53 91w32 6:06:08
Charles Park 40 1 31N17 92w29 6:09:56
Charlieville 42 1 32N28 91w45 6:07:00
Chase 21 1 32N06 91w42 6:06:48
Chataignier 20 1 30N34 92w19 6:09:16
Chatham 25 1 32N18 92w27 6:09:48
Chauvin 55 1 29N26 90w36 6:02:24
Chef Menteur 36 2 30N01 90w03 6:00:12
Chenal 1 30N37 91w23 6:05:32
Cheneyville 40 1 31N01 92w17 6:09:08
Cheniere 37 1 32N31 92w09 6:08:36
Cherokee Court 26 2 29N58 90w13 6:00:52
Cherokee Village 40 1 31N17 92w29 6:09:56
Chesbrough 53 1 30N56 90w31 6:02:04
Chestnut 35 1 32N03 93w01 6:12:04
Chickama 40 1 31N05 92w24 6:09:36
Chickasaw 62 1 32N52 91w23 6:05:32
Chinchuba 52 1 30N22 90w04 6:00:16
Chipola 46 1 30N50 90w40 6:02:40
Chloe 10 1 30N13 93w12 6:12:48
Choctaw 24 1 30N28 91w13 6:04:52
Choctaw 29 1 29N47 90w50 6:03:20
Chopin 35 1 31N30 92w52 6:11:28
Chopique 20 1 30N34 92w19 6:09:16
Choudrant 31 1 32N32 92w31 6:10:04
Choupique 29 1 29N47 90w50 6:03:20
Choupique 51 1 29N48 91w30 6:06:00
Chula 4 1 29N50 90w57 6:03:48
Church Point 1 1 30N24 92w13 6:08:52
Cinclare 61 1 30N28 91w13 6:04:52
Cindy Park 44 2 29N57 89w56 5:59:44
Claiborne 37 1 32N31 92w09 6:08:36
Claiborne 52 1 30N29 90w06 6:00:24
Claibourne Gardens 26 2 29N54 90w09 6:00:36
Clare 43 1 31N20 93w37 6:14:28
Clarence 35 1 31N49 93w02 6:12:08
Clarks 11 1 32N02 92w08 6:08:32
Clay 25 1 32N26 92w41 6:10:44
Clayton 15 1 31N43 91w33 6:06:12
Clearwater 20 1 31N01 92w17 6:09:08
Clifton 59 1 30N56 90w11 6:00:44
Clinton 19 1 30N52 91w01 6:04:04
Clio 32 1 30N26 90w33 6:02:12
Clotilda 29 1 29N43 90w36 6:02:24
Cloutierville 35 1 31N33 92w55 6:11:40
Clovelly Farms 29 1 29N33 90w20 6:01:20
Cocke 55 1 29N45 90w49 6:03:16
Cocodrie 55 1 29N15 90w40 6:02:40
Cocoville 5 1 31N04 92w03 6:08:12
Colfax 22 1 31N31 92w42 6:10:48
Colgrade 64 1 31N55 92w38 6:10:32
College 53 1 30N31 90w27 6:01:48
Collinsburg 8 1 32N54 93w42 6:14:48
Collinston 34 1 32N41 91w52 6:07:28
Colonial Heights 9 1 32N28 93w49 6:15:16
Colony Park 26 2 29N59 90w15 6:01:00
Colquitt 14 1 32N57 92w58 6:11:52
Columbia 11 1 32N06 92w05 6:08:20
Columbia 48 1 30N03 90w34 6:02:16
Columbia Heights 11 1 32N06 92w05 6:08:20
Comite 17 1 30N31 91w07 6:04:28
Como 21 1 32N10 91w43 6:06:52
Concession 38 2 29N50 90w00 6:00:00
Concord 62 1 32N52 91w23 6:05:32
Consuella 54 1 31N48 91w23 6:05:32
Contreras 44 2 29N50 89w52 5:59:28
Convent 47 1 30N01 90w50 6:03:20
Converse 43 1 31N47 93w42 6:14:48
Conway 56 1 32N54 92w15 6:09:00
Coon 39 1 30N51 91w40 6:06:40
Cooper Road 9 1 32N33 93w49 6:15:16
Coopers 58 1 31N08 93w16 6:13:04
Cooters Point 54 1 31N48 91w23 6:05:32
Copenhagen 11 1 32N06 92w05 6:08:20
Cora 58 1 31N10 92w55 6:11:40
Corbin 32 1 30N30 90w51 6:03:24
Corey 11 1 32N30 92w05 6:08:20
Corinth 31 1 32N42 92w39 6:10:36
Cornerview 3 1 30N14 90w55 6:03:40
Cornor 63 1 31N06 91w18 6:05:12
Cortableau 49 1 30N33 91w58 6:07:52
Coteau 55 1 29N36 90w43 6:02:52
Coteau Holmes 50 1 30N08 91w44 6:06:56
Coteau Rodaire 50 1 30N24 91w56 6:07:44
Cotile 40 1 31N22 92w45 6:11:00
Cotton Plant 11 1 32N03 92w07 6:08:28
Cottonport 5 1 30N59 92w03 6:08:12
Cotton Valley 60 1 32N49 93w25 6:13:40
Couchwood 60 1 32N46 93w23 6:13:32
Coulon Plantation 29 1 29N47 90w50 6:03:20
Country Club Subdivision 29 1 29N47 90w50 6:03:20
Coushatta 41 1 32N01 93w21 6:13:24
Covington 52 1 30N29 90w06 6:00:24
Covington Country Club Estat 52 1 30N29 90w06 6:00:24
Cow Island 12 1 29N50 92w46 6:11:04
Cow Island 57 1 29N58 92w07 6:08:28
Cravens 58 1 30N56 92w56 6:11:44
Creedmoor 44 2 29N50 89w52 5:59:28
Creole 12 1 29N49 93w07 6:12:28
Crescent 24 1 30N15 91w17 6:05:08
Crescent 55 1 29N36 90w43 6:02:52
Creston 35 1 31N59 93w03 6:12:12
Crew Lake 42 1 32N28 91w45 6:07:00
Crews 64 1 31N40 92w53 6:11:32
Crichton 41 1 32N02 93w20 6:13:20
Cross-road 11 1 32N03 92w07 6:08:28
Cross Roads 41 1 32N02 93w20 6:13:20
Crowley 1 1 30N13 92w22 6:09:28
Crown Point 26 2 29N46 90w05 6:00:20
Crowville 21 1 32N15 91w35 6:06:20
Crozier 55 1 29N36 90w43 6:02:52
Cullen 60 1 32N58 93w27 6:13:48
Curry 64 1 31N55 92w38 6:10:32
Curtis 8 1 32N32 93w42 6:14:48
Custom House 36 2 29N58 90w04 6:00:16
Cut Off 29 1 29N33 90w20 6:01:20
Cypremort 51 1 29N48 91w30 6:06:00
Cypress 35 1 31N36 93w02 6:12:08
Cypress 37 1 32N31 92w09 6:08:36
Cypress Gardens 44 2 29N57 89w56 5:59:44
Cypress Gardens 55 1 29N36 90w43 6:02:52
Cypress Island 50 1 30N10 91w50 6:07:20
Daigleville 55 1 29N36 90w43 6:02:52
Dalcour 38 2 29N52 89w57 5:59:48
Danville 7 1 32N14 92w51 6:11:24
Darbonne 56 1 32N32 92w31 6:10:04
Darlington 46 1 30N53 90w47 6:03:08
Darnell 62 1 32N41 91w27 6:05:48
Darrow 3 1 30N07 90w59 6:03:56
Daspit 23 1 30N00 91w49 6:07:16
Davant 38 1 29N37 89w51 5:59:24
Dayson 60 1 32N49 93w25 6:13:40
Dean 56 1 32N54 92w15 6:09:00
Dean Chapel 37 1 32N31 92w09 6:08:36
Deerford 17 1 30N35 91w11 6:04:44
Deer Park 15 1 31N35 91w26 6:05:44
Deer Range 1 29N37 89w54 5:59:36
Dehlco 42 1 32N28 91w45 6:07:00
Delacroix 44 2 29N50 89w52 5:59:28
Delacroix 50 1 30N10 91w50 6:07:20
Del Bueno Park 44 2 29N57 89w56 5:59:44
Delcambre 57 1 29N57 91w58 6:07:52
Delhi 42 1 32N28 91w30 6:06:00
Delta 33 1 32N20 90w56 6:03:44
Delta Farms 29 1 29N39 90w32 6:02:08
Denham Springs 32 1 30N29 90w57 6:03:48
Dennis Mills 46 1 30N25 90w54 6:03:36
Denson 32 1 30N26 90w33 6:02:12
Dent Terrace 17 1 30N25 91w09 6:04:36
De Quincy 10 1 30N27 93w26 6:13:44
De Ridder 6 1 30N51 93w17 6:13:08
Derry 35 1 31N32 92w57 6:11:48
Des Allemands 45 1 29N49 90w28 6:01:52
De Selle 40 1 31N17 92w29 6:09:56
Deshotels 49 1 30N37 92w04 6:08:16
Destrehan 45 1 29N57 90w22 6:01:28
Devall 61 1 30N28 91w13 6:04:52
Deville 40 1 31N22 92w10 6:08:40
Dewdrop 34 1 32N47 91w55 6:07:40
Diamond 1 29N32 89w46 5:59:04
Dixie 9 1 32N42 93w50 6:15:20
Dixie Acres 37 1 32N42 92w04 6:08:16
Dixie Gardens 9 1 32N28 93w43 6:14:52
Dixie Inn 60 1 32N36 93w20 6:13:20
Dodson 64 1 32N05 92w39 6:10:36
Dona 16 1 32N05 93w49 6:15:16
Donaldsonville 3 1 30N06 90w59 6:03:56
Donner 55 1 29N42 90w58 6:03:52
Dora 5 1 30N59 92w03 6:08:12
Dorcyville 24 1 30N10 91w09 6:04:36
Douglas 31 1 32N32 92w31 6:10:04
Downsville 56 1 31N54 92w15 6:09:00
Downtown 37 1 32N30 92w05 6:08:20
Downtown 51 1 29N42 91w14 6:04:56
Doyle 32 1 30N30 90w45 6:03:00
Doyline 60 1 32N35 93w22 6:13:28
Drew 10 1 30N13 93w12 6:12:48
Drew 37 1 32N31 92w09 6:08:36
Dry Creek 6 1 30N40 93w03 6:12:12
Dry Prong 22 1 31N35 92w32 6:10:08
Dubach 31 1 32N42 92w39 6:10:36
Dubberly 60 1 32N33 93w14 6:12:56
Dufresne 45 1 29N55 90w22 6:01:28
Dulac 55 1 29N23 90w43 6:02:52
Dunbarton 15 1 31N44 91w40 6:06:40
Dunn 42 1 32N28 91w35 6:06:20
Duplessis 3 1 30N16 90w57 6:03:48
Dupont 5 1 30N56 91w57 6:07:48
Dupont 24 1 30N17 91w14 6:04:56
Dupont 39 1 30N40 91w28 6:05:52
Duson 28 1 30N14 92w11 6:08:44
Dutch Bayou 48 1 30N04 90w33 6:02:12
Dutch Town 3 1 30N12 91w01 6:04:04
Dykesville 14 1 32N58 93w08 6:12:32
East Hodge 25 1 32N17 92w43 6:10:52
East Krotz Springs 49 1 30N32 91w45 6:07:00
Easton 20 1 30N45 92w26 6:09:44
East Point 41 1 32N10 93w26 6:13:44
Eastside Columbia 11 1 32N06 92w05 6:08:20
Echo 40 1 31N07 92w15 6:09:00
Eden 30 1 31N41 92w07 6:08:28
Edgard 48 1 30N03 90w34 6:02:16
Edgefield 41 1 32N03 93w20 6:13:20
Edgerly 10 1 30N14 93w30 6:14:00
Edna 27 1 30N25 92w53 6:11:32
Effie 5 1 31N13 92w09 6:08:36
Egan 1 1 30N14 92w30 6:10:00
Elam 21 1 31N59 91w39 6:06:36
Elba 49 1 30N45 91w46 6:07:04
Eliza 61 1 30N17 91w14 6:04:56
Elizabeth 2 1 30N52 92w48 6:11:12
Ellendale 55 1 29N38 90w49 6:03:16
Ellsworth 55 1 29N41 90w49 6:03:16
Elmer 29 1 29N47 90w50 6:03:20
Elmer 40 1 31N08 92w41 6:10:44
Elmfield 4 1 29N56 91w02 6:04:08
Elm Grove 8 1 32N21 93w33 6:14:12
Elm Hall 4 1 29N56 91w02 6:04:08
Elm Park 63 1 30N47 91w23 6:05:32
Elmwood 58 1 31N08 93w16 6:13:04
Elton 27 1 30N29 92w42 6:10:48
Empire 38 1 29N23 89w36 5:58:24
Encalade 38 1 29N28 89w42 5:58:48
England 40 1 31N20 92w33 6:10:12
England Air Force Base 40 1 31N17 92w29 6:09:56
Englewood 33 1 32N25 91w11 6:04:44
Englewood 51 1 29N42 91w14 6:04:56
English Turn 38 2 29N53 89w58 5:59:52
Enterprise 1 31N54 91w53 6:07:32
Enterprise 13 1 31N09 92w46 6:11:04
Enterprise 23 1 29N55 91w40 6:06:40
Eola 5 1 30N55 92w13 6:08:52
Epps 62 1 32N36 91w29 6:05:56
Erath 57 1 29N58 92w02 6:08:08
Eros 25 1 32N24 92w25 6:09:40
Erwinville 61 1 30N32 91w24 6:05:36
Essen Heights 17 1 30N25 91w09 6:04:36
Estelle 26 2 29N51 90w06 6:00:24
Esther 57 1 29N58 92w07 6:08:28
Estherwood 1 1 30N11 92w28 6:09:52
Ethel 19 1 30N47 91w08 6:04:32
Eunice 49 1 30N30 92w25 6:09:40
Eureka 37 1 31N54 92w15 6:09:00
Eva 15 1 31N26 91w47 6:07:08
Evangeline 1 1 30N16 92w34 6:10:16
Evans 58 1 30N59 93w30 6:14:00
Evelyn 16 1 31N59 93w27 6:13:48
Evergreen 5 1 30N57 92w07 6:08:28
Extension 21 1 31N58 91w49 6:07:16

Fairbanks 37 1 32N39 92w02 6:08:08
Fairfax 51 1 29N48 91w30 6:06:00
Fair Grounds 9 1 32N28 93w49 6:15:16
Fairlane 55 1 29N36 90w43 6:02:52
Fairmont 22 1 31N31 92w42 6:10:48
Fairview 15 1 31N35 91w26 6:05:44
Falgoust 47 1 29N59 90w50 6:03:20
Farmerville 56 1 32N47 92w24 6:09:36
Fazendeville 44 2 29N57 90w01 6:00:04
Felixville 19 1 30N57 90w53 6:03:32
Fellowship 30 1 31N42 92w11 6:08:44
Fenton 27 1 30N22 92w55 6:11:40
Ferriday 15 1 31N38 91w33 6:06:12
Ferry Lake 9 1 32N45 93w59 6:15:56
Fields 6 1 30N32 93w35 6:14:20
Fifth Ward 5 1 31N08 92w04 6:08:16
Fillmore 8 1 32N32 93w30 6:14:00
Fisher 43 1 31N30 93w28 6:13:52
Fishville 22 1 31N31 92w24 6:09:36
Flat Creek 64 1 31N49 92w20 6:09:20
Flatwoods 40 1 31N24 92w52 6:11:28
Flora 35 1 31N37 93w06 6:12:24
Florence 51 1 29N48 91w30 6:06:00
Florien 43 1 31N27 93w28 6:13:52
Florrissant 44 2 29N50 89w52 5:59:28
Flournoy 9 1 32N28 93w49 6:15:16
Floyd 62 1 32N44 91w26 6:05:44
Fluker 53 1 30N49 90w31 6:02:04
Flynn 49 1 30N32 92w05 6:08:20
Foley 2 1 30N37 92w46 6:11:04
Foley 4 1 29N56 91w02 6:04:08
Folsom 52 1 30N38 90w11 6:00:44
Fondale 37 1 32N30 92w05 6:08:20
Forbing 9 1 32N24 93w44 6:14:56
Fordoche 39 1 30N36 91w37 6:06:28
Foreman 17 1 30N27 91w04 6:04:16
Forest 62 1 32N47 91w25 6:05:40
Forest Glen 52 1 30N19 89w56 5:59:44
Forest Hill 40 1 31N03 92w32 6:10:08
Forest Oaks 17 1 30N27 91w04 6:04:16
Forest Park 37 1 32N31 92w09 6:08:36
Forked Island 57 1 29N50 92w18 6:09:12
Forksville 37 1 32N31 92w22 6:09:28
Fort De Russy 5 1 31N08 92w04 6:08:16
Fortier Heights 26
2 29N54 90w09 6:00:36
Fort Jesup 43 1 31N37 93w24 6:13:36
Fort Necessity 21 1 32N03 91w49 6:07:16
Fort Polk 58 1 31N04 93w11 6:12:44
Fort Saint Leon 38
2 29N45 90w00 6:00:00
Fosters 8 1 32N32 93w42 6:14:48
Fosters Canal 38 1 29N28 89w42 5:58:48
Foules 13 1 31N45 91w32 6:06:08
Fountain Place 17 1 30N31 91w09 6:04:36
Fourborge 20 1 30N41 92w17 6:09:08
Four Forks 9 1 32N11 93w55 6:15:40
Fowler 37 1 32N39 92w02 6:08:08
Francis Place 44 2 29N57 89w56 5:59:44
Franklin 51 1 29N48 91w30 6:06:00
Franklinton 59 1 30N51 90w09 6:00:36
Fred 17 1 30N39 91w06 6:04:24
Freetown 4 1 29N56 91w02 6:04:08
Freetown 51 1 29N48 91w30 6:06:00
French Settlement 32
1 30N04 90w50 6:03:20
Frenier 48 1 30N06 90w26 6:01:44
Friendship 7 1 32N21 92w59 6:11:56
Frierson 16 1 32N15 93w42 6:14:48
Frisco 39 1 30N33 91w33 6:06:12
Frogmore 15 1 31N36 91w40 6:06:40
Frost 32 1 30N30 90w45 6:03:00
Frost Town 37 1 31N54 92w15 6:09:00
Fryeburg 7 1 32N25 93w14 6:12:56
Fullerton 58 1 31N00 92w59 6:11:56
Funston 16 1 32N03 93w58 6:15:52
Gaars Mill 64 1 32N05 92w40 6:10:40
Gahagan 41 1 32N02 93w20 6:13:20
Galbraith 35 1 31N30 92w49 6:11:16
Galion 34 1 32N52 91w45 6:07:00
Galliano 29 1 29N26 90w18 6:01:12
Galvez 3 1 30N18 90w58 6:03:52
Gandy Spur 43 1 31N27 93w27 6:13:48
Gansville 64 1 32N05 92w40 6:10:40
Garden City 51 1 29N46 91w28 6:05:52
Gardner 40 1 31N16 92w42 6:10:48
Garyville 48 1 30N03 90w37 6:02:28
Gassoway 18 1 32N59 91w13 6:04:52
Gayles 9 1 32N28 93w43 6:14:52
Ged 10 1 30N12 93w35 6:14:20
Geismar 3 1 30N12 91w01 6:04:04
Gentilly 36 2 30N00 90w05 6:00:20
Georgetown 22 1 31N46 92w23 6:09:32
Georgeville 46 1 30N38 90w30 6:02:00
Georgia 4 1 29N56 91w02 6:04:08
Gheens 29 1 29N41 90w28 6:01:52
Gibbstown 12 1 29N49 93w07 6:12:28
Gibsland 7 1 32N33 93w03 6:12:12
Gibson 55 1 29N41 90w59 6:03:56
Gilark 60 1 32N38 93w19 6:13:16
Gilbert 21 1 32N03 91w40 6:06:40
Gilliam 9 1 32N50 93w51 6:15:24
Gillis 10 1 30N22 93w12 6:12:48
Girard 42 1 32N29 91w48 6:07:12
Glencoe 51 1 29N48 91w30 6:06:00
Glen Dale 48 1 30N03 90w31 6:02:04
Glenmora 40 1 30N59 92w35 6:10:20
Glenwild 51 1 29N41 91w13 6:04:52
Glenwood 4 1 29N56 91w02 6:04:08
Gloria 38 2 29N45 90w00 6:00:00
Gloster 16 1 32N12 93w49 6:15:16
Glynn 39 1 30N38 91w21 6:05:24
Godchaux 29 1 29N43 90w36 6:02:24
Godchaux Community 48
1 30N04 90w29 6:01:56

Gold Dust 5 1 30N57 92w11 6:08:44
Golden Meadow 29 1 29N24 90w16 6:01:04
Golden Star Plantation 48
1 30N00 90w44 6:02:56
Goldman 54 1 31N50 91w23 6:05:32
Goldonna 35 1 32N01 92w54 6:11:36
Goldridge 24 1 30N10 91w09 6:04:36
Gonzales 3 1 30N14 90w55 6:03:40
Good Hope 45 1 30N00 90w25 6:01:40
Good Pine 30 1 31N41 92w07 6:08:28
Goodwill 62 1 32N52 91w23 6:05:32
Goodwood 49 1 30N42 91w45 6:07:00
Goosport 10 1 30N14 93w11 6:12:44
Gordon 14 1 32N58 93w08 6:12:32
Gorhamtown 64 1 31N56 92w36 6:10:24
Gorum 35 1 31N26 92w56 6:11:44
Goudeau 5 1 30N52 92w01 6:08:04
Gouldsboro 26 2 29N54 90w03 6:00:12
Gradney Island 49 1 30N32 92w05 6:08:20
Grambling 31 1 32N31 92w43 6:10:52
Gramercy 47 1 30N03 90w41 6:02:44
Grand Bayou 41 1 32N01 93w43 6:14:52
Grandbois 29 1 29N34 90w36 6:02:24
Grand Caillou 55 1 29N36 90w43 6:02:52
Grand Cane 16 1 32N05 93w49 6:15:16
Grand Chenier 12 1 29N48 92w57 6:11:48
Grand Coteau 49 1 30N25 92w03 6:08:12
Grand Ecore 35 1 31N49 93w05 6:12:20
Grand Isle 26 1 29N14 90w00 6:00:00
Grand Lake 12 1 30N13 93w12 6:12:48
Grand Point 47 1 30N02 90w43 6:02:52
Grand Prairie 49 1 30N37 92w04 6:08:16
Grand River 24 1 30N17 91w14 6:04:56
Grangeville 46 1 30N42 90w35 6:02:20
Grant 2 1 30N47 92w57 6:11:48
Gray 55 1 29N42 90w47 6:03:08
Gray Point 20 1 30N41 92w17 6:09:08
Grayson 11 1 32N03 92w06 6:08:24
Greenacres 8 1 32N32 93w42 6:14:48
Green Acres 15 1 31N35 91w26 6:05:44
Green Acres 17 1 30N31 91w09 6:04:36
Green Gables 40 1 31N19 92w25 6:09:40
Greenlaw 53 1 30N56 90w31 6:02:04
Green Lawn 26 2 29N59 90w15 6:01:00
Green Lawn Terrace 26
2 29N59 90w15 6:01:00
Greensburg 46 1 30N50 90w40 6:02:40
Greenwell Springs 17
1 30N35 91w00 6:04:00
Greenwich Village 10
1 30N13 93w12 6:12:48
Greenwood 9 1 32N27 93w58 6:15:52
Greenwood 55 1 29N41 90w59 6:03:56
Greenwood Park 9 1 32N27 93w47 6:15:08
Greinwich Terrace 10
1 30N13 93w12 6:12:48
Greinwich Village 10
1 30N13 93w12 6:12:48
Gretna 26 2 29N55 90w04 6:00:16
Grosse Tete 24 1 30N25 91w26 6:05:44
Gueydan 57 1 30N02 92w31 6:10:04
Gullett 1 30N43 90w30 6:02:00
Gum Ridge 34 1 32N38 91w46 6:07:04
Gurley 19 1 30N52 91w08 6:04:32
Guy 2 1 30N37 92w46 6:11:04
Haaswood 52 1 30N21 89w46 5:59:04
Hackberry 12 1 30N00 93w21 6:13:24
Hackley 59 1 30N51 90w09 6:00:36
Hagewood 35 1 31N43 93w13 6:12:52
Hahnville 45 1 29N59 90w25 6:01:40
Haile 56 1 32N50 92w09 6:08:36
Haire 57 1 30N00 92w17 6:09:08
Half Way 4 1 30N06 91w00 6:04:00
Hall Summit 41 1 32N11 93w18 6:13:12
Hamburg 5 1 31N02 91w56 6:07:44
Hammet 15 1 31N35 91w26 6:05:44
Hammond 53 1 30N30 90w28 6:01:52
Hanna 41 1 31N58 93w21 6:13:24
Happy Jack 38 1 29N31 89w44 5:58:56
Harahan 26 2 29N56 90w11 6:00:44
Hardwood 63 1 30N48 91w23 6:05:32
Hargis 22 1 31N40 92w53 6:11:32
Harlem 38 1 29N37 89w51 5:59:24
Harlem 57 1 29N58 92w07 6:08:28
Harmon 41 1 32N04 93w26 6:13:44
Harold Park 26 2 29N59 90w15 6:01:00
Harrisonburg 13 1 31N46 91w49 6:07:16
Harvey 26 2 29N54 90w03 6:00:12
Hatches 43 1 31N47 93w42 6:14:48
Hathaway 27 1 30N21 92w40 6:10:40
Haughton 8 1 32N32 93w30 6:14:00
Hawthorne 58 1 31N08 93w16 6:13:04
Hayes 10 1 30N07 92w55 6:11:40
Haynesville 14 1 32N58 93w08 6:12:32
Hazelwood 49 1 30N33 91w58 6:07:52
Hearn Island 11 1 32N06 92w05 6:08:20
Hebert 11 1 32N11 91w59 6:07:56
Hecker 10 1 30N15 93w01 6:12:04
Heflin 60 1 32N27 93w16 6:13:04
Helena 54 1 31N48 91w23 6:05:32
Henderson 50 1 30N19 91w48 6:07:12
Henfer Park 26 2 29N58 90w13 6:00:52
Henry 57 1 29N53 92w05 6:08:20
Hermitage 39 1 30N38 91w28 6:05:52
Hessmer 5 1 31N03 92w08 6:08:32
Hester 47 1 30N01 90w46 6:03:04
Hewes 39 1 30N37 91w28 6:05:52
Hickory 5 1 30N59 92w03 6:08:12
Hickory 52 1 30N22 89w45 5:59:00
Hickory Grove 40 1 31N21 92w10 6:08:40
Hickory Valley 64 1 32N05 92w29 6:09:56
Hicks 58 1 31N11 93w01 6:12:04
Hico 31 1 32N45 92w43 6:10:52
Higginbotham 1 1 30N24 92w13 6:08:52
Highland 54 1 31N48 91w23 6:05:32

Highland Acres 26 2 29N58 90w13 6:00:52
Highland Park 37 1 32N30 92w05 6:08:20
Highland Park 55 1 29N36 90w43 6:02:52
Highland Park Heights 17
1 30N25 91w09 6:04:36
High Mount 10 1 30N13 93w12 6:12:48
Highway Park 26 2 29N59 90w15 6:01:00
Hi-Land 44 2 29N54 89w54 5:59:36
Hillaryville 3 1 30N07 90w59 6:03:56
Hillsdale 46 1 30N42 90w35 6:02:20
Hilly 31 1 32N42 92w39 6:10:36
Hineston 40 1 31N09 92w46 6:11:04
Hinkle 8 1 32N32 93w42 6:14:48
Hodge 25 1 32N17 92w43 6:10:52
Hohen Solms 3 1 30N10 91w09 6:04:36
Holden 32 1 30N30 90w40 6:02:40
Hollingsworth 41 1 32N02 93w20 6:13:20
Holloway 40 1 31N21 92w10 6:08:40
Holly 16 1 32N05 93w49 6:15:16
Holly Beach 12 1 29N46 93w28 6:13:52
Hollybrook 18 1 32N48 91w11 6:04:44
Holly Grove 21 1 31N59 91w39 6:06:36
Hollyridge 1 32N28 91w38 6:06:32
Holly Ridge 42 1 32N28 91w38 6:06:32
Holly Ridge 54 1 31N48 91w23 6:05:32
Hollywood 10 1 30N13 93w20 6:13:20
Hollywood 55 1 29N36 90w43 6:02:52
Hollywood 63 1 30N47 91w23 6:05:32
Holmwood 10 1 30N15 93w01 6:12:04
Holsey 14 1 32N48 92w52 6:11:28
Holum 11 1 32N03 92w07 6:08:28
Home Place 38 1 29N28 89w42 5:58:48
Homer 14 1 32N48 93w04 6:12:16
Hood 14 1 32N33 92w55 6:11:40
Hood Camp 40 1 31N23 92w57 6:11:48
Hopedale 44 1 29N49 89w39 5:58:36
Hope Villa 3 1 30N25 91w09 6:04:36
Hornbeck 58 1 31N20 93w24 6:13:36
Hosston 9 1 32N53 93w53 6:15:32
Hotwells 40 1 31N24 92w40 6:10:40
Houltonville 52 1 30N24 90w10 6:00:40
Houma 55 1 29N36 90w43 6:02:52
Houston River 10 1 30N15 93w15 6:13:00
Howard 41 1 32N28 93w43 6:14:52
Hubertville 23 1 29N55 91w40 6:06:40
Hudson 64 1 32N02 92w35 6:10:20
Hughes 8 1 32N41 93w44 6:14:56
Humphreys 55 1 29N41 90w59 6:03:56
Hunter 16 1 32N01 93w43 6:14:52
Huron 50 1 30N24 91w56 6:07:44
Hurricane 14 1 32N39 93w01 6:12:04
Husser 53 1 30N41 90w20 6:01:20
Hutton 58 1 31N20 93w02 6:12:08
Hyde 5 1 30N59 91w49 6:07:16
Hydropolis 5 1 31N04 92w03 6:08:12
Hymel 47 1 30N00 90w44 6:02:56
Iberville 24 1 30N18 91w07 6:04:28
Ida 9 1 33N00 93w54 6:15:36
Idlewild 51 1 29N42 91w18 6:05:12
Idlewild 55 1 29N36 90w43 6:02:52
Ikes 6 1 30N51 93w17 6:13:08
Independence 53 1 30N38 90w30 6:02:00
Indian Bayou 57 1 30N14 92w16 6:09:04
Indian Mound 17 1 30N35 91w00 6:04:00
Indian Village 2 1 30N27 92w59 6:11:56
Indian Village 37 1 32N31 92w22 6:09:28
Industrial 9 1 32N33 93w47 6:15:08
Innis 39 1 30N53 91w41 6:06:44
Inniswold 17 1 30N25 91w06 6:04:24
Intracoastal City 57
1 29N47 92w09 6:08:36
Iota 1 1 30N20 92w30 6:10:00
Iowa 10 1 30N14 93w01 6:12:04
Irish Bend 51 1 29N48 91w30 6:06:00
Irma 35 1 31N46 93w06 6:12:24
Ironton 38 1 29N28 89w42 5:58:48
Isabel 59 1 30N47 89w51 5:59:24
Isle Labbe 50 1 30N10 91w50 6:07:20
Istrouma 17 1 30N29 91w09 6:04:36
Ivan 8 1 32N41 93w44 6:14:56
Jackson 19 1 30N50 91w13 6:04:52
Jacoby 39 1 30N56 91w42 6:06:48
Jamestown 7 1 32N21 93w13 6:12:52
Janie 35 1 31N30 92w51 6:11:24
Jarreau 39 1 30N38 91w28 6:05:52
Jay 29 1 29N36 90w28 6:01:52
Jeanerette 23 1 29N55 91w40 6:06:40
Jean Lafitte 26 1 29N41 90w06 6:00:24
Jefferson 26 2 29N58 90w10 6:00:40
Jefferson Heights 26
2 29N58 90w10 6:00:40
Jefferson Island 23
1 29N59 91w58 6:07:52
Jefferson Terrace 17
1 30N25 91w09 6:04:36
Jena 30 1 31N41 92w08 6:08:32
Jennings 27 1 30N13 92w40 6:10:40
Jesuit Bend 38 2 29N45 90w00 6:00:00
Jewella 9 1 32N28 93w49 6:15:16
Jigger 21 1 32N02 91w45 6:07:00
Johnson 48 1 30N03 90w34 6:02:16
Johnson Ridge 55 1 29N47 90w50 6:03:20
Johnson's Bayou 12
1 29N48 93w37 6:14:28
Jones 34 1 32N58 91w39 6:06:36
Jonesboro 25 1 32N15 92w43 6:10:52
Jonesburg 42 1 32N32 91w46 6:07:04
Jones Park 26 2 29N59 90w15 6:01:00
Jonesville 13 1 31N38 91w49 6:07:16
Jordon Hill 64 1 31N55 92w38 6:10:32
Joyce 64 1 31N56 92w35 6:10:20
Juanita 1 30N37 93w26 6:13:44
Junction 6 1 30N45 93w32 6:14:08
Junction City 14 1 33N01 92w44 6:10:56
Kadesh 22 1 31N40 92w53 6:11:32

LOUISIANA

Kaplan 57	1	30N00	92w17	6:09:08
Keatchie 16	1	32N11	93w54	6:15:36
Kedron 46	1	30N42	90w35	6:02:20
Keithville 9	1	32N20	93w50	6:15:20
Kelly 11	1	31N59	92w11	6:08:44
Kellys 25	1	32N32	92w38	6:10:32
Kendale 26	2	29N59	90w15	6:01:00
Kendricks Ferry 21	1	32N03	91w39	6:06:36
Kenilworth 44	2	29N50	89w52	5:59:28
Kenmore 39	1	30N29	91w32	6:06:08
Kennedy Heights 26	2	29N54	90w09	6:00:36
Kenner 26	2	29N59	90w15	6:01:00
Kentwood 53	1	30N56	90w31	6:02:04
Kickapoo 16	1	32N12	93w49	6:15:16
Kilbourne 62	1	33N00	91w19	6:05:16
Killian 32	1	30N26	90w33	6:02:12
Killona 45	1	30N00	90w29	6:01:56
Kinder 2	1	30N29	92w51	6:11:24
King Hill 35	1	32N02	93w20	6:13:20
Kingston 16	1	32N11	93w43	6:14:52
Kingsville 40	1	31N19	92w25	6:09:40
Kiroli Woods 37	1	32N31	92w09	6:08:36
Kisatchie 35	1	31N25	93w10	6:12:40
Kleinpeter 17	1	30N25	91w09	6:04:36
Klondyke 55	1	29N34	90w36	6:02:24
Klotzville 4	1	30N01	91w03	6:04:12
Knight	1	30N55	93w27	6:13:48
Kolin 40	1	31N17	92w19	6:09:16
Kolter 16	1	32N11	93w55	6:15:40
Koran 8	1	32N32	93w30	6:14:00
Kraemer 29	1	29N52	90w42	6:02:48
Krotz Springs 49	1	30N32	91w45	6:07:00
Kurthwood 58	1	31N20	93w10	6:12:40
Laark 34	1	32N58	91w39	6:06:36
Labadieville 4	1	29N50	90w57	6:03:48
Labarre 39	1	30N43	91w33	6:06:12
Lacamp 58	1	31N10	92w55	6:11:40
Lacassine 27	1	30N14	92w55	6:11:40
La Chute 9	1	32N30	93w45	6:15:00
Lacombe 52	1	30N19	89w56	5:59:44
Lacour 39	1	30N51	91w40	6:06:40
Lafayette 28	1	30N14	92w01	6:08:04
Lafayette Square 36	2	29N56	90w05	6:00:20
Lafitte 26	1	29N41	90w06	6:00:24
Lafourche 29	1	29N46	90w46	6:03:04
Lagan 47	1	29N59	90w50	6:03:20
Lake Arthur 27	1	30N05	92w41	6:10:44
Lake Bruin 54	1	31N55	91w14	6:04:56
Lake Charles 10	1	30N14	93w13	6:12:52
Lake End 41	1	31N55	93w18	6:13:12
Lake Judge Perez 38	1	29N28	89w42	5:58:48
Lakeland 39	1	30N36	91w24	6:05:36
Lake Providence 18	1	32N48	91w10	6:04:40
Lakeshore 37	1	32N30	92w05	6:08:20
Lakeside 12	1	30N05	92w40	6:10:40
Lakeside 40	1	31N19	92w25	6:09:40
Lakeview 9	1	32N33	93w47	6:15:08
Lakeview 35	1	31N40	93w03	6:12:12
Lakeview 36	2	30N00	90w06	6:00:24
Lamar 21	1	32N28	91w29	6:05:56
Lamourie 40	1	31N08	92w25	6:09:40
Lampman 57	1	29N58	92w07	6:08:28
Landay Gautreaux Subdivision 55	1	29N47	90w50	6:03:20
Lapine 37	1	32N31	92w09	6:08:36
La Place 48	1	30N04	90w29	6:01:56
La Reusitte 38	2	29N45	90w00	6:00:00
Larose 29	1	29N34	90w23	6:01:32
Larto 13	1	31N22	91w54	6:07:36
Latanier 40	1	31N05	92w24	6:09:36
Laurel Grove 29	1	29N49	90w53	6:03:32
Laurel Hill 63	1	31N06	91w18	6:05:12
Laurel Lea 17	1	30N25	91w09	6:04:36
Laurel Ridge 24	1	30N10	91w09	6:04:36
Laurel Valley Plantation 29	1	29N47	90w50	6:03:20
Lawhon 7	1	32N20	93w17	6:13:08
Lawtell 49	1	30N31	92w11	6:08:44
Lazy Acres 55	1	29N36	90w43	6:02:52
Leander 58	1	31N09	92w51	6:11:24
Lebeau 49	1	30N44	91w59	6:07:56
Le Blanc 2	1	30N31	92w57	6:11:48
Lecompte 40	1	31N06	92w24	6:09:36
Ledoux	1	30N38	92w12	6:08:48
Lee Bayou	1	31N46	91w34	6:06:16
Lee Heights 40	1	31N19	92w25	6:09:40
Lees Creek 59	1	30N47	89w51	5:59:24
Lees Landing 53	1	30N26	90w26	6:01:44
Leesville 58	1	31N09	93w16	6:13:04
Leeville 29	1	29N15	90w12	6:00:48
Lefleurs 20	1	30N38	92w25	6:09:40
Legonier 39	1	30N56	91w42	6:06:48
Leighton 29	1	29N47	90w50	6:03:20
Leland 13	1	31N51	91w40	6:06:40
Lemannville 3	1	30N06	91w00	6:04:00
Le Moyen 49	1	30N48	92w04	6:08:16
Lena 40	1	31N28	92w46	6:11:04
Leonville 49	1	30N29	91w59	6:07:56
Leroy 57	1	30N06	92w07	6:08:28
Leton 60	1	32N56	93w18	6:13:12
Lettsworth 39	1	30N56	91w42	6:06:48
Levert 50	1	30N10	91w50	6:07:20
Levins 15	1	31N38	91w32	6:06:08
Lewisburg 49	1	30N27	92w10	6:08:40
Lewisburg 52	1	30N22	90w04	6:00:16
Lewiston 53	1	30N56	90w31	6:02:04
Lewistown 29	1	29N43	90w36	6:02:24
Liberty 41	1	32N02	93w20	6:13:20
Liberty Hill 7	1	32N20	92w53	6:11:32
Libuse 40	1	31N21	92w20	6:09:20
Liddieville 21	1	32N08	91w51	6:07:24
Lillie 56	1	32N56	92w39	6:10:36
Linda Lee 32	1	30N25	90w54	6:03:36
Lindsay 19	1	30N43	91w13	6:04:52
Link 1	1	30N21	92w16	6:09:04
Linton 8	1	32N41	93w44	6:14:56
Linville 56	1	32N51	92w11	6:08:44
Lions 48	1	30N04	90w33	6:02:12
Lisbon 14	1	32N48	92w52	6:11:28
Lismore 15	1	31N37	91w49	6:07:16
Litroe 56	1	33N00	92w12	6:08:48
Little Caillou 55	1	29N27	90w36	6:02:24
Little Creek 30	1	31N43	92w18	6:09:12
Little Farms 26	2	29N58	90w13	6:00:52
Little Texas 4	1	29N56	91w02	6:04:08
Live Oak 38	2	29N45	90w00	6:00:00
Live Oak Manor 26	2	29N54	90w09	6:00:36
Livingston 32	1	30N30	90w45	6:03:00
Livonia 39	1	30N34	91w33	6:06:12
Lobdell 61	1	30N28	91w13	6:04:52
Lockhart 56	1	32N56	92w36	6:10:24
Lockport 29	1	29N39	90w33	6:02:12
Lockport Heights 29	1	29N39	90w32	6:02:08
Locust Ridge 54	1	31N55	91w14	6:04:56
Logansport 16	1	31N58	94w00	6:16:00
Log Cabin 34	1	32N47	91w55	6:07:40
Loggy Bayou 41	1	32N19	93w32	6:14:08
Logtown 37	1	32N30	92w05	6:08:20
Lonepine 20	1	30N51	92w15	6:09:00
Lone Star 24	1	30N10	91w09	6:04:36
Longbridge 5	1	31N01	92w01	6:08:04
Longlake 11	1	32N06	92w05	6:08:20
Longleaf 40	1	31N00	92w34	6:10:16
Long Straw 25	1	32N32	92w31	6:10:04
Longstreet 16	1	32N06	93w57	6:15:48
Longview 21	1	32N10	91w43	6:06:52
Longville 6	1	30N36	93w14	6:12:56
Longwood 9	1	32N41	93w58	6:15:52
Longwood 17	1	30N17	91w08	6:04:32
Loranger 53	1	30N38	90w24	6:01:36
Loreauville 23	1	30N03	91w44	6:06:56
Lorelein 21	1	32N03	91w39	6:06:36
Lottie 39	1	30N33	91w39	6:06:36
Louisiana and Arkansas Junct 64	1	31N55	92w38	6:10:32
Louisiana Junction 8	1	32N32	93w42	6:14:48
Louisville 37	1	32N30	92w05	6:08:20
Lower Bonne Idee 34	1	32N38	91w46	6:07:04
Lower Vacherie 47	1	30N00	90w44	6:02:56
Loyds Bridge 40	1	31N01	92w17	6:09:08
Lozes 23	1	30N00	91w49	6:07:16
Lucas 9	1	32N28	93w43	6:14:52
Lucerne 15	1	31N35	91w26	6:05:44
Lucknow 42	1	32N28	91w45	6:07:00
Lucky 7	1	32N21	92w59	6:11:56
Lucy 48	1	30N03	90w34	6:02:16
Ludington 6	1	30N53	93w17	6:13:08
Ludivine Plantation	1	29N35	90w25	6:01:40
Ludvine 29	1	29N39	90w32	6:02:08
Lukeville 61	1	30N28	91w13	6:04:52
Lula 16	1	31N52	93w42	6:14:48
Luling 45	1	29N56	90w22	6:01:28
Luna 37	1	32N31	92w09	6:08:36
Lunita 10	1	30N19	93w40	6:14:40
Lutcher 47	1	30N02	90w42	6:02:48
Lydia 23	1	30N00	91w49	6:07:16
Lyons Point 1	1	30N13	92w22	6:09:28
Madewood 4	1	29N56	91w02	6:04:08
Madison Park 9	1	32N28	93w43	6:14:52
Madisonville 52	1	30N24	90w10	6:00:40
Magnolia 4	1	30N03	91w03	6:04:12
Magnolia 17	1	30N35	91w00	6:04:00
Magnolia 32	1	30N30	90w40	6:02:40
Magnolia 35	1	31N40	93w03	6:12:12
Magnolia 38	1	29N28	89w42	5:58:48
Magnolia 55	1	29N36	90w43	6:02:52
Magnolia Woods 17	1	30N25	91w09	6:04:36
Mallard Junction 10	1	30N13	93w12	6:12:48
Mamou 20	1	30N38	92w25	6:09:40
Manchester 10	1	30N15	93w01	6:12:04
Mandalay 55	1	29N36	90w43	6:02:52
Mandeville 52	1	30N22	90w04	6:00:16
Mangham 42	1	32N19	91w47	6:07:08
Manifest 13	1	31N43	91w58	6:07:52
Mansfield 16	1	32N02	93w43	6:14:52
Mansura 5	1	31N04	92w03	6:08:12
Many 43	1	31N34	93w29	6:13:56
Maplewood 10	1	30N13	93w21	6:13:24
Marco 35	1	31N31	92w46	6:11:04
Maringouin 24	1	30N29	91w31	6:06:04
Marion 56	1	32N54	92w15	6:09:00
Marksville 5	1	31N08	92w04	6:08:16
Marrero 26	2	29N54	90w06	6:00:24
Marsalis 14	1	32N39	93w01	6:12:04
Mars Hill 64	1	31N48	92w45	6:11:00
Marthaville 35	1	31N44	93w24	6:13:36
Martin 41	1	32N05	93w13	6:12:52
Martin Junction 60	1	32N28	93w16	6:13:04
Martin Park 40	1	31N17	92w29	6:09:56
Maryland 51	1	29N48	91w30	6:06:00
Mason 21	1	32N10	91w43	6:06:52
Mathews 29	1	29N42	90w33	6:02:12
Maurepas 32	1	30N18	90w40	6:02:40
Maurice 57	1	30N07	92w08	6:08:32
Maxie 1	1	30N20	92w25	6:09:40
Mayfair 17	1	30N25	91w09	6:04:36
Mayna 13	1	31N25	91w51	6:07:24
McCall 3	1	30N06	91w00	6:04:00
McClendon 59	1	30N51	90w09	6:00:36
McCrea 39	1	30N51	91w40	6:06:40
McDade 8	1	32N19	93w32	6:14:08
McDonoghville 26	2	29N54	90w03	6:00:12
McGinty 34	1	32N58	91w39	6:06:36
McIlhenny 23	1	29N55	91w55	6:07:40
McIntyre 60	1	32N36	93w19	6:13:16
McKneeley 39	1	30N36	91w37	6:06:28
McLeod 29	1	29N39	90w32	6:02:08
McManus 19	1	30N50	91w08	6:04:32
McNary 40	1	31N00	92w34	6:10:16
McNeely 22	1	31N31	92w42	6:10:48
McNutt 40	1	31N24	92w40	6:10:40
McVeigh 50	1	30N24	91w56	6:07:44
Meadowbrook 26	2	29N54	90w03	6:00:12
Meadow Park Heights 9	1	32N27	93w47	6:15:08
Meadowview Park 8	1	32N32	93w42	6:14:48
Meaux 57	1	30N01	92w11	6:08:44
Mechanicsville 55	1	29N36	90w43	6:02:52
Meeker 40	1	31N04	92w23	6:09:32
Melder 40	1	31N06	92w38	6:10:32
Melrose 35	1	31N30	91w59	6:07:56
Melville 49	1	30N42	91w45	6:07:00
Meraux 44	2	29N56	89w56	5:59:44
Mermentau 1	1	30N11	92w35	6:10:20
Mer Rouge 34	1	32N47	91w48	6:07:12
Merryville 6	1	30N45	93w33	6:14:12
Messick 35	1	32N02	93w20	6:13:20
Metairie 26	2	29N58	90w10	6:00:40
Methvin 41	1	32N02	93w20	6:13:20
Michoud 36	2	30N04	89w52	5:59:28
Mid City 36	2	29N59	90w05	6:00:20
Mid-city Annex 9	1	32N30	93w46	6:15:04
Midland 1	1	30N11	92w30	6:10:00
Midway 8	1	32N41	93w44	6:14:56
Midway 40	1	31N03	92w32	6:10:08
Midway 60	1	32N54	93w27	6:13:48
Mill Creek 64	1	31N55	92w38	6:10:32
Milldale 17	1	30N35	91w11	6:04:44
Millerton 14	1	32N58	93w08	6:12:32
Millerville 1	1	30N16	92w34	6:10:16
Millerville 17	1	30N27	91w04	6:04:16
Millikin 18	1	32N58	91w14	6:04:56
Milly Plantation 24	1	30N17	91w14	6:04:56
Milton 28	1	30N06	92w05	6:08:20
Mimosa Park 45	1	29N54	90w21	6:01:24
Minden 60	1	32N37	93w17	6:13:08
Mineral Springs 31	1	32N42	92w39	6:10:36
Minerva 55	1	29N36	90w43	6:02:52
Minorca 15	1	31N38	91w32	6:06:08
Mira 9	1	32N57	93w53	6:15:32
Mire 1	1	30N14	92w16	6:09:04
Missionary 9	1	32N57	93w53	6:15:32
Mitchell 43	1	31N47	93w38	6:14:32
Mittie 2	1	30N42	92w54	6:11:36
Mix 39	1	30N42	91w26	6:05:44
Modeste 3	1	30N11	91w01	6:04:04
Moncla 5	1	31N08	92w04	6:08:16
Monette Ferry 35	1	31N28	92w46	6:11:04
Monroe 37	1	32N30	92w07	6:08:28
Montcalm 7	1	32N32	92w47	6:11:08
Montecello 54	1	31N48	91w23	6:05:32
Montegut 55	1	29N28	90w33	6:02:12
Monterey 15	1	31N27	91w43	6:06:52
Montgomery 22	1	31N40	92w53	6:11:32
Monticello 18	1	32N48	91w11	6:04:44
Montpelier 46	1	30N41	90w39	6:02:36
Montrose 35	1	31N46	93w06	6:12:24
Montz 45	1	30N04	90w29	6:01:56
Mooringsport 9	1	32N41	93w58	6:15:52
Mora 35	1	31N23	92w57	6:11:48
Morbihan 23	1	30N00	91w49	6:07:16
Moreauville 5	1	31N02	91w58	6:07:52
Moreland 40	1	31N17	92w29	6:09:56
Morgan City 51	1	29N42	91w12	6:04:48
Morganza 39	1	30N44	91w36	6:06:24
Morningside 9	1	32N27	93w47	6:15:08
Morrisonville 24	1	30N17	91w14	6:04:56
Morrow 49	1	30N50	92w05	6:08:20
Morse 1	1	30N08	92w30	6:10:00
Morvant 29	1	29N47	90w50	6:03:20
Morville 15	1	31N35	91w26	6:05:44
Moss Bluff 10	1	30N18	93w11	6:12:44
Moss Lake 10	1	30N13	93w21	6:13:24
Mossville 10	1	30N15	93w15	6:13:00
Mot 8	1	32N54	93w42	6:14:48
Mound 33	1	32N21	91w01	6:04:04
Mount Airy 48	1	30N03	90w38	6:02:32
Mount Carmel 43	1	31N27	93w27	6:13:48
Mount Hermon 59	1	30N58	90w18	6:01:12
Mount Lawrence 4	1	29N51	91w00	6:04:00
Mount Lebanon 7	1	32N30	93w03	6:12:12
Mount Olive 7	1	32N21	92w43	6:10:52
Mount Sinai 14	1	32N58	93w08	6:12:32
Mount Union 56	1	32N56	92w36	6:10:24
Mount Zion 41	1	32N02	93w20	6:13:20
Mount Zion 64	1	31N40	92w53	6:11:32
Mowata 1	1	30N21	92w16	6:09:04
Mudville 22	1	31N46	92w23	6:09:32
Mulberry 55	1	29N36	90w43	6:02:52
Myrtle Grove 38	1	29N28	89w42	5:58:48
Naborton 16	1	32N03	93w35	6:14:20
Nairn	1	29N26	89w37	5:58:28
Naomi 38	2	29N45	90w00	6:00:00
Napoleonville 4	1	29N56	91w02	6:04:08
Napoleonville Junction 29	1	29N47	90w50	6:03:20
Naquin 29	1	29N47	90w50	6:03:20
Natalbany 53	1	30N33	90w29	6:01:56
Natchez 35	1	31N41	93w03	6:12:12
Natchitoches 35	1	31N46	93w05	6:12:20
Nebo 30	1	31N35	92w09	6:08:36
Negreet 43	1	31N28	93w35	6:14:20

LOUISIANA

Nesser 17	1	30N27	91w04	6:04:16
New Belledeau 5	1	31N03	92w07	6:08:28
Newellton 54	1	32N04	91w14	6:04:56
New Era 15	1	31N22	91w49	6:07:16
New Iberia 23	1	30N01	91w49	6:07:16
New Light 42	1	32N18	91w47	6:07:08
Newllano 58	1	31N07	93w16	6:13:04
New Orleans 36	2	29N58	90w04	6:00:16
New Roads 39	1	30N42	91w26	6:05:44
New Sarpy 45	1	29N59	90w23	6:01:32
Newton 10	1	30N13	93w12	6:12:48
Nibletts Bluff 10	1	30N12	93w35	6:14:20
Nicholls University 29	1	29N47	90w50	6:03:20
Noble 43	1	31N41	93w41	6:14:44
Noles Landing 60	1	32N33	93w18	6:13:12
Norah 29	1	29N39	90w32	6:02:08
Norco 45	1	30N00	90w25	6:01:40
Normandy Park 26	2	29N54	90w09	6:00:36
North Bend 51	1	29N48	91w30	6:06:00
Northeast 37	1	32N30	92w05	6:08:20
North Fort Polk 58	1	31N07	93w10	6:12:40
North Highlands	1	32N35	93w48	6:15:12
North Hodge 25	1	32N17	92w43	6:10:52
North Merrydale 17	1	30N29	91w09	6:04:36
North Monroe 37	1	32N30	92w05	6:08:20
North Shore 52	1	30N17	89w46	5:59:04
North Shreveport	1	32N33	93w48	6:15:12
North Slidell 52	1	30N17	89w46	5:59:04
Norton Shop 14	1	32N56	93w18	6:13:12
Norwood 19	1	30N58	91w06	6:04:24
Notleyville 49	1	30N33	91w58	6:07:52
Notnac 54	1	32N04	91w14	6:04:56
Nunez 57	1	29N58	92w07	6:08:28
Oakbluff 51	1	29N48	91w30	6:06:00
Oakdale 2	1	30N49	92w40	6:10:40
Oakdale 26	2	29N53	90w05	6:00:20
Oak Forest 55	1	29N41	90w59	6:03:56
Oak Grove 12	1	29N49	93w07	6:12:28
Oak Grove 22	1	31N35	92w32	6:10:08
Oak Grove 31	1	32N32	92w47	6:11:08
Oak Grove 43	1	31N47	93w42	6:14:48
Oak Grove 62	1	32N52	91w23	6:05:32
Oak Hills Place 17	1	30N25	91w09	6:04:36
Oakland 39	1	30N36	91w24	6:05:36
Oakland 56	1	33N00	92w21	6:09:24
Oaklawn 52	1	30N19	89w56	5:59:44
Oakley 4	1	29N56	91w02	6:04:08
Oak Manor 17	1	30N27	91w04	6:04:16
Oaknolia 19	1	30N43	91w09	6:04:36
Oak Point 38	2	29N45	90w00	6:00:00
Oak Ridge 34	1	32N38	91w47	6:07:08
Oaks 14	1	32N58	93w08	6:12:32
Oakshire Manor 55	1	29N36	90w43	6:02:52
Oakville 38	2	29N47	90w02	6:00:08
Oberlin 2	1	30N37	92w46	6:11:04
Odenburg 5	1	30N59	91w49	6:07:16
Oil Center 28	1	30N13	92w02	6:08:08
Oil City 9	1	32N45	93w58	6:15:52
Okaloosa 37	1	32N24	92w25	6:09:40
Old Athens 14	1	32N39	93w01	6:12:04
Oldfield 32	1	30N30	90w51	6:03:24
Old Lafitte 26	1	29N41	90w06	6:00:24
Old Shongaloo 60	1	32N56	93w18	6:13:12
Olga 38	1	29N20	89w25	5:57:40
Olivier 23	1	30N00	91w49	6:07:16
Olla 30	1	31N54	92w14	6:08:56
Ollie 38	2	29N45	90w00	6:00:00
Omega 33	1	32N33	91w11	6:04:44
Opelousas 49	1	30N32	92w05	6:08:20
Orange Grove Plantation 29	1	29N47	90w50	6:03:20
Oretta 6	1	30N32	93w26	6:13:44
Ormond 45	1	29N57	90w22	6:01:28
Oscar 39	1	30N37	91w28	6:05:52
Osceola 53	1	30N38	90w24	6:01:36
Ossun 28	1	30N14	92w06	6:08:24
Ostrica 38	1	29N21	89w32	5:58:08
Otis 40	1	31N13	92w44	6:10:56
Ouachita 56	1	32N42	92w04	6:08:16
Oubre 23	1	30N04	91w44	6:06:56
Oxford 16	1	31N56	93w38	6:14:32
Oxford 51	1	29N48	91w30	6:06:00
Pace 60	1	32N36	93w19	6:13:16
Packton 64	1	31N55	92w38	6:10:32
Paincourtville 4	1	29N59	91w03	6:04:12
Palmetto 49	1	30N43	91w55	6:07:40
Palo Alto 3	1	30N06	91w00	6:04:00
Panchoville 27	1	30N29	92w42	6:10:48
Panola 15	1	31N38	91w32	6:06:08
Paradis 45	1	29N53	90w26	6:01:44
Paradise 40	1	31N19	92w25	6:09:40
Paradise Manor 26	2	29N58	90w13	6:00:52
Parhams 13	1	31N28	91w45	6:07:00
Park Manor 26	2	30N00	90w13	6:00:52
Parks 50	1	30N13	91w50	6:07:20
Parkside Manor 26	2	29N58	90w13	6:00:52
Patoutville 23	1	29N55	91w40	6:06:40
Patterson 51	1	29N42	91w18	6:05:12
Paulina 47	1	30N02	90w43	6:02:52
Pearl River 52	1	30N23	89w45	5:59:00
Peason 43	1	31N27	93w27	6:13:48
Pecan Grove 26	2	29N54	90w09	6:00:36
Pecaniere 49	1	30N24	91w56	6:07:44
Pecan Place 24	1	30N17	91w14	6:04:56
Peck 13	1	31N51	91w40	6:06:40
Pelican 16	1	31N53	93w35	6:14:20
Perkins 10	1	30N24	93w25	6:13:40
Perry 57	1	29N57	92w10	6:08:40
Perryville 37	1	32N42	92w00	6:08:00
Pertuits Store 47	1	29N59	90w50	6:03:20
Phoenix 38	1	29N39	89w56	5:59:44
Pickering 58	1	31N08	93w16	6:13:04
Pierre Part 4	1	30N00	91w20	6:05:20
Pigeon 4	1	30N04	91w17	6:05:08
Pilottown 38	1	29N11	89w15	5:57:00
Pine 59	1	30N51	90w09	6:00:36
Pine Coupee 40	1	31N24	92w52	6:11:28
Pine Grove 37	1	32N30	92w05	6:08:20
Pine Grove 46	1	30N43	90w45	6:03:00
Pine Island 26	1	30N29	92w42	6:10:48
Pine Oak Terrace 9	1	32N27	93w47	6:15:08
Pine Prairie 20	1	30N47	92w25	6:09:40
Pineville 40	1	31N19	92w26	6:09:44
Pioneer 62	1	32N44	91w26	6:05:44
Pitkin 58	1	30N56	92w56	6:11:44
Pitreville 1	1	30N24	92w13	6:08:52
Plain Dealing 8	1	32N54	93w42	6:14:48
Plains 17	1	30N35	91w11	6:04:44
Plainview 59	1	30N47	89w51	5:59:24
Plaisance 49	1	30N32	92w05	6:08:20
Plantation Acres 40	1	31N17	92w29	6:09:56
Plantation Park 8	1	32N32	93w42	6:14:48
Plaquemine 24	1	30N17	91w14	6:04:56
Plattenville 4	1	30N00	91w01	6:04:04
Plaucheville 5	1	30N58	91w59	6:07:56
Pleasant Hill 7	1	32N31	93w03	6:12:12
Pleasant Hill 43	1	31N49	93w31	6:14:04
Pleasant Hills 17	1	30N31	91w09	6:04:36
Pleasant Ridge 30	1	31N54	92w14	6:08:56
Plettenberg 63	1	30N53	91w29	6:05:56
Point	1	32N40	92w17	6:09:08
Point 56	1	31N54	92w15	6:09:00
Point Au Chien 55	1	29N29	90w33	6:02:12
Point Blue 20	1	30N38	92w18	6:09:12
Pointe a la Hache 38	1	29N35	89w48	5:59:12
Poland 40	1	31N17	92w29	6:09:56
Pollock 22	1	31N32	92w25	6:09:40
Ponchatoula 53	1	30N26	90w26	6:01:44
Ponchatoula Beach 53	1	30N26	90w26	6:01:44
Poole 8	1	32N19	93w32	6:14:08
Poplar Grove 61	1	30N28	91w13	6:04:52
Port Allen 61	1	30N27	91w12	6:04:48
Port Barre 49	1	30N34	91w57	6:07:48
Port Barrow 3	1	30N06	91w00	6:04:00
Port Eads 38	1	29N17	89w21	5:57:24
Porterville 60	1	32N54	93w27	6:13:48
Port Hudson 17	1	30N41	91w16	6:05:04
Port Sulphur 38	1	29N29	89w42	5:58:48
Port Vincent 32	1	30N20	90w51	6:03:24
Post Trailer Park 58	1	31N08	93w16	6:13:04
Potash 38	1	29N28	89w42	5:58:48
Pot Cove 49	1	30N31	92w11	6:08:44
Powhatan 35	1	31N52	93w12	6:12:48
Poydras 44	2	29N52	89w54	5:59:36
Prairie Ronde 49	1	30N32	92w05	6:08:20
Prairieville 3	1	30N18	90w58	6:03:52
Pratt 7	1	32N31	93w03	6:12:12
Pricetown 26	2	29N54	90w09	6:00:36
Pride 17	1	30N42	90w59	6:03:56
Princeton 8	1	32N35	93w31	6:14:04
Provencal 35	1	31N39	93w12	6:12:48
Providence 26	2	29N59	90w15	6:01:00
Puckett 17	1	30N35	91w11	6:04:44
Pumpkin Center 53	1	30N31	90w27	6:01:48
Quaid 13	1	31N37	91w49	6:07:16
Quarantine	1	29N12	89w16	5:57:04
Quimby 33	1	32N25	91w11	6:04:44
Quitman 25	1	32N21	92w43	6:10:52
Raceland 29	1	29N44	90w36	6:02:24
Ragley 6	1	30N31	93w14	6:12:56
Ramah 24	1	30N29	91w32	6:06:08
Rambin 16	1	31N53	93w35	6:14:20
Randall 49	1	30N32	92w05	6:08:20
Rapides 40	1	31N19	92w32	6:10:08
Rattan 43	1	31N27	93w27	6:13:48
Ravenwood	1	30N40	91w42	6:06:48
Rayne 1	1	30N14	92w16	6:09:04
Rayville 42	1	32N29	91w46	6:07:04
Readhimer 35	1	32N03	93w01	6:12:04
Rebecca 55	1	29N36	90w43	6:02:52
Red Chute 8	1	32N32	93w30	6:14:00
Reddell 20	1	30N40	92w25	6:09:40
Red Fish 5	1	30N59	91w49	6:07:16
Red Gum 15	1	31N45	91w32	6:06:08
Redland 8	1	32N54	93w42	6:14:48
Red Oak 17	1	30N28	91w05	6:04:20
Reedton 20	1	30N38	92w25	6:09:40
Reeves 2	1	30N31	93w03	6:12:12
Reggio 44	1	29N50	89w46	5:59:04
Reids 2	1	30N56	92w56	6:11:44
Remy 47	1	30N02	90w43	6:02:52
Reserve 48	1	30N03	90w33	6:02:12
Retreat 63	1	30N59	91w29	6:05:56
Rhinehart 13	1	31N38	92w00	6:08:00
Rhymes Store 42	1	32N28	91w45	6:07:00
Riceville 57	1	30N02	92w30	6:10:00
Richard 1	1	30N24	92w13	6:08:52
Richmond 33	1	32N25	91w11	6:04:44
Richohoc 51	1	29N48	91w30	6:06:00
Richwood 37	1	32N30	92w05	6:08:20
Ridge 28	1	30N14	92w16	6:09:04
Ridgecrest 15	1	31N36	91w32	6:06:08
Ridgewood 17	1	30N35	91w00	6:04:00
Rienzi Plantation 29	1	29N47	90w50	6:03:20
Rigolette 40	1	31N23	92w24	6:09:36
Ringgold 7	1	32N20	93w17	6:13:08
Rio 59	1	30N47	89w51	5:59:24
Risinger Woods 9	1	32N33	93w47	6:15:08
Riverlands 48	1	30N04	90w29	6:01:56
River Ridge 26	2	29N58	90w13	6:00:52
Riverton 11	1	32N10	92w06	6:08:24
Riverwood 52	1	30N29	90w06	6:00:24
Roanoke 27	1	30N14	92w45	6:11:00
Robeline 35	1	31N41	93w18	6:13:12
Robert 53	1	30N30	90w21	6:01:24
Robson 9	1	32N28	93w43	6:14:52
Rock 40	1	31N28	92w46	6:11:04
Rock Hill 22	1	31N35	92w32	6:10:08
Rocky Branch 56	1	32N46	92w24	6:09:36
Rocky Mount 8	1	32N54	93w42	6:14:48
Rodessa 9	1	32N58	94w00	6:16:00
Rogers 30	1	31N32	92w14	6:08:56
Romeville 47	1	30N04	90w51	6:03:24
Roosevelt 18	1	32N33	91w11	6:04:44
Rork 1	1	30N29	92w25	6:09:40
Rosa 49	1	30N45	92w00	6:08:00
Rosedale 4	1	29N56	91w02	6:04:08
Rosedale 24	1	30N26	91w27	6:05:48
Rosefield 30	1	32N03	92w07	6:08:28
Roseland 53	1	30N46	90w31	6:02:04
Rosepine 58	1	30N55	93w17	6:13:08
Rougon 39	1	30N36	91w22	6:05:28
Rousseau 29	1	29N47	90w50	6:03:20
Routon 30	1	31N41	92w07	6:08:28
Roy 7	1	32N14	93w09	6:12:36
Ruby 40	1	31N11	92w15	6:09:00
Ruple 14	1	32N58	93w08	6:12:32
Rural Park 26	2	29N58	90w13	6:00:52
Ruston 31	1	32N32	92w38	6:10:32
Ruth 50	1	30N16	91w54	6:07:36
Sadie 56	1	32N54	92w15	6:09:00
Sadou 28	1	30N14	92w11	6:08:44
Sailes 7	1	32N31	93w03	6:12:12
Saint Amant 3	1	30N13	90w51	6:03:24
Saint Benedict	1	30N31	90w07	6:00:28
Saint Bernard 44	2	29N50	89w52	5:59:28
Saint Bernard Grove 44	2	29N57	89w56	5:59:44
Saint Charles 29	1	29N43	90w36	6:02:24
Saint Clair 38	2	29N52	89w57	5:59:48
Saint Claude Heights 44	2	29N57	90w00	6:00:00
Saint Delphine 61	1	30N22	91w16	6:05:04
Saint Elmo 3	1	30N07	90w59	6:03:56
Saint Francisville 63	1	30N47	91w23	6:05:32
Saint Gabriel 24	1	30N16	91w06	6:04:24
Saint Genevieve 15	1	31N35	91w26	6:05:44
Saint James 47	1	29N59	90w50	6:03:20
Saint Joe 52	1	30N21	89w45	5:59:00
Saint John 29	1	29N47	90w50	6:03:20
Saint Joseph 54	1	31N55	91w14	6:04:56
Saint Landry 20	1	30N51	92w15	6:09:00
Saint Martinville 50	1	30N07	91w50	6:07:20
Saint Maurice 64	1	31N45	92w58	6:11:52
Saint Rosalie 38	2	29N45	90w00	6:00:00
Saint Rose 45	1	29N57	90w19	6:01:16
Saint Tammany 52	1	30N19	89w56	5:59:44
Saint Thomas 4	1	29N56	91w02	6:04:08
Saline 7	1	32N10	92w59	6:11:56
Samstown 24	1	30N10	91w09	6:04:36
Samtown 40	1	31N16	92w26	6:09:44
Sandy Hill 58	1	31N08	93w16	6:13:04
San Francisco Plantation 48	1	30N04	90w33	6:02:12
Sardis 43	1	31N47	93w42	6:14:48
Sarepta 60	1	32N54	93w27	6:13:48
Satsuma 32	1	30N30	90w45	6:03:00
Scarsdale 38	2	29N52	89w57	5:59:48
Schriever 55	1	29N45	90w49	6:03:16
Scotlandville 17	1	30N31	91w11	6:04:44
Scott 28	1	30N14	92w06	6:08:24
Searcy 30	1	31N42	92w14	6:08:56
Sebastapol 44	2	29N50	89w52	5:59:28
Sellers 45	1	30N00	90w25	6:01:40
Selma 22	1	31N46	92w23	6:09:32
Sentell 9	1	32N33	93w47	6:15:08
Serena	1	31N26	91w52	6:07:28
Seymourville 24	1	30N17	91w13	6:04:52
Shadyside 51	1	29N48	91w30	6:06:00
Shamrock 35	1	31N41	93w18	6:13:12
Sharon 14	1	32N48	92w52	6:11:28
Sharon Hills 17	1	30N31	91w09	6:04:36
Sharp 40	1	31N28	92w46	6:11:04
Shaw 15	1	31N35	91w26	6:05:44
Shelburn 18	1	32N53	91w14	6:04:56
Shell Beach 44	1	29N52	89w41	5:58:44
Shelton 34	1	32N49	91w54	6:07:36
Sherburne 39	1	30N31	91w43	6:06:52
Sheridan 59	1	30N51	90w09	6:00:36
Shiloh 53	1	30N42	90w35	6:02:20
Shiloh 56	1	32N50	92w39	6:10:36
Shongaloo 60	1	32N56	93w18	6:13:12
Shops 37	1	32N30	92w05	6:08:20
Shreve Island 9	1	32N28	93w43	6:14:52
Shreveport 9	1	32N31	93w45	6:15:00
Shrewsbury 26	2	29N58	90w10	6:00:40
Shuteston 49	1	30N32	92w05	6:08:20
Sibley 31	1	32N32	92w31	6:10:04
Sibley 60	1	32N33	93w18	6:13:12
Sicard 37	1	32N32	92w02	6:08:08
Sicily Island 13	1	31N51	91w40	6:06:40
Siegle 37	1	32N31	92w09	6:08:36
Sieper 40	1	31N13	92w49	6:11:16
Sikes 64	1	32N05	92w29	6:09:56
Sikes Ferry 60	1	32N54	93w27	6:13:48
Silverwood 27	1	30N11	92w35	6:10:20
Simmesport 5	1	30N59	91w49	6:07:16
Simms 22	1	31N31	92w24	6:09:36
Simpson 58	1	31N16	93w01	6:12:04
Simsboro 31	1	32N32	92w47	6:11:08
Singer 6	1	30N39	93w25	6:13:40
Slacks 24	1	30N29	91w32	6:06:08

LOUISIANA

Slagle 58	1	31N12	93w08	6:12:32
Slaughter 19	1	30N43	91w09	6:04:36
Slidell 52	1	30N17	89w47	5:59:08
Sligo 8	1	32N27	93w35	6:14:20
Smithfield 61	1	30N28	91w13	6:04:52
Smith Ridge 55	1	29N36	90w43	6:02:52
Smoke Bend 3	1	30N07	91w01	6:04:04
Socola 38	1	29N28	89w42	5:58:48
Somerset 54	1	32N04	91w14	6:04:56
Sondheimer 18	1	32N33	91w11	6:04:44
Soniat 24	1	30N10	91w09	6:04:36
Sorrell 51	1	29N53	91w37	6:06:28
Sorrento 3	1	30N11	90w51	6:03:24
South Acres 10	1	30N13	93w21	6:13:24
South Bend 51	1	29N48	91w30	6:06:00
South Coast 51	1	29N48	91w30	6:06:00
Southdown 55	1	29N35	90w44	6:02:56
Southdown Plantation 47	1	30N00	90w44	6:02:56
Southeast 17	1	30N25	91w09	6:04:36
Southern 17	1	30N30	91w11	6:04:44
Southfield 9	1	32N28	93w43	6:14:52
South Fort Polk 58	1	31N03	93w12	6:12:48
South Kenner 26	2	29N54	90w09	6:00:36
South Lafourche 29	1	29N47	90w50	6:03:20
South Mansfield 16	1	32N01	93w43	6:14:52
South Park 40	1	31N17	92w29	6:09:56
South Park Trailer Court 58	1	31N08	93w16	6:13:04
South Pass 38	1	29N17	89w21	5:57:24
Southport 26	2	29N58	90w10	6:00:40
Southwestern 28	1	30N13	92w02	6:08:08
Spearsville 56	1	32N56	92w36	6:10:24
Spencer 56	1	32N45	92w08	6:08:32
Spillman 63	1	30N50	91w12	6:04:48
Splane Place 37	1	32N31	92w09	6:08:36
Spokane 15	1	31N42	91w28	6:05:52
Springcreek 53	1	30N56	90w31	6:02:04
Springfield 32	1	30N26	90w33	6:02:12
Springhill 59	1	30N51	90w09	6:00:36
Springhill 60	1	33N00	93w28	6:13:52
Springridge 9	1	32N20	93w50	6:15:20
Spring Ridge 43	1	31N49	93w31	6:14:04
Springville 32	1	30N26	90w41	6:02:44
Springville 41	1	32N02	93w20	6:13:20
Standard 30	1	31N55	92w13	6:08:52
Stanley 16	1	31N58	93w54	6:15:36
Star 38	2	29N45	90w00	6:00:00
Starhill 63	1	30N50	91w12	6:04:48
Starks 10	1	30N19	93w40	6:14:40
Start 42	1	32N29	91w52	6:07:28
State Line 59	1	30N51	90w09	6:00:36
Stella 38	2	29N52	89w57	5:59:48
Sterlington 37	1	32N42	92w05	6:08:20
Stevensdale 17	1	30N27	91w04	6:04:16
Stille 58	1	31N08	93w16	6:13:04
Stonewall 16	1	32N17	93w50	6:15:20
Stoney Point 59	1	30N51	90w09	6:00:36
Stonypoint 17	1	30N35	91w00	6:04:00
Sugar Creek 14	1	32N40	92w53	6:11:32
Sugartown 6	1	30N50	93w01	6:12:04
Sulphur 10	1	30N14	93w23	6:13:32
Summerfield 14	1	32N55	92w50	6:11:20
Summer Grove 9	1	32N27	93w47	6:15:08
Summerville 30	1	31N45	92w10	6:08:40
Sun 52	1	30N39	89w54	5:59:36
Sunnybrook 17	1	30N31	91w07	6:04:28
Sunrise 61	1	30N28	91w13	6:04:52
Sunset 49	1	30N25	92w04	6:08:16
Sunshine 24	1	30N17	91w08	6:04:32
Sun Spur 42	1	32N28	91w29	6:05:56
Supreme 4	1	29N51	91w00	6:04:00
Susan Park 26	2	29N59	90w15	6:01:00
Swampers 21	1	32N10	91w43	6:06:52
Swartz 37	1	32N35	91w59	6:07:56
Sweet Lake 12	1	30N07	92w58	6:11:52
Swords 49	1	30N24	92w13	6:08:52
Taconey 15	1	31N35	91w26	6:05:44
Taft 45	1	29N58	90w25	6:01:40
Talisheek 52	1	30N32	89w52	5:59:28
Talla Bena 33	1	32N33	91w11	6:04:44
Tallulah 33	1	32N25	91w11	6:04:44
Tangipahoa 53	1	30N53	90w31	6:02:04
Tanglewood 40	1	31N17	92w29	6:09:56
Tannehill 64	1	32N00	92w39	6:10:36
Tate Cove 20	1	30N41	92w17	6:09:08
Taylor 7	1	32N33	93w07	6:12:28
Taylor Hill 40	1	31N28	92w46	6:11:04
Taylortown 8	1	32N19	93w32	6:14:08
Tech 31	1	32N32	92w38	6:10:32
Teddy 19	1	30N58	91w06	6:04:24
Temple 58	1	31N17	92w58	6:11:52
Tendal 33	1	32N26	91w22	6:05:28
Terry 62	1	32N56	91w21	6:05:24
Terrytown 26	2	29N54	90w03	6:00:12
Theriot 55	1	29N28	90w45	6:03:00
The Y 20	1	30N41	92w17	6:09:08
Thibodaux 29	1	29N48	90w49	6:03:16
Thistlewaite 49	1	30N37	92w04	6:08:16
Thomas 59	1	30N51	90w09	6:00:36
Thomastown 33	1	32N25	91w11	6:04:44
Three Oaks 44	2	29N57	90w00	6:00:00
Thronwell 27	1	30N05	92w40	6:10:40
Tickfaw 53	1	30N35	90w29	6:01:56
Tigerville 48	1	30N03	90w34	6:02:16
Timberlane 26	2	29N54	90w03	6:00:12
Timber Trails 40	1	31N17	92w29	6:09:56
Tioga 40	1	31N23	92w26	6:09:44
Toca 44	1	29N52	89w50	5:59:20
Toomey 10	1	30N12	93w35	6:14:20
Topsy 27	1	30N13	93w12	6:12:48
Torbert 39	1	30N33	91w29	6:05:56
Toro 43	1	31N17	93w33	6:14:12
Torras 39	1	30N56	91w42	6:06:48
Tower Park 58	1	31N08	93w16	6:13:04
Town and Country 37	1	32N30	92w05	6:08:20
Transylvania 18	1	32N41	91w11	6:04:44
Trees 9	1	32N47	94w02	6:16:08
Tremont 31	1	32N32	92w31	6:10:04
Trinity 13	1	31N37	91w49	6:07:16
Trinity 24	1	30N26	91w27	6:05:48
Triumph 38	1	29N20	89w30	5:58:00
Trout 30	1	31N42	92w11	6:08:44
Troy 19	1	30N58	91w06	6:04:24
Truxno 56	1	32N54	92w15	6:09:00
Tullos 30	1	31N49	92w19	6:09:16
Tunica 63	1	30N56	91w33	6:06:12
Turkey Creek 20	1	30N53	92w25	6:09:40
Turnerville 24	1	30N17	91w14	6:04:56
Turtle Lake 15	1	31N38	91w32	6:06:08
Twin Oaks 34	1	32N55	91w40	6:06:40
Uncle Sam 47	1	30N35	91w11	6:04:44
Union 47	1	30N05	90w54	6:03:36
Union Church 7	1	32N21	92w43	6:10:52
Union Hill 40	1	30N59	92w34	6:10:16
Union Springs 43	1	31N47	93w42	6:14:48
Unionville 31	1	32N42	92w39	6:10:36
University 17	1	30N25	91w11	6:04:44
Upland 34	1	32N47	91w55	6:07:40
Upstream 26	2	29N58	90w13	6:00:52
Urania 30	1	31N52	92w18	6:09:12
Utility 13	1	31N37	91w49	6:07:16
Vacherie 47	1	30N00	90w44	6:02:56
Valmar 44	2	29N57	89w56	5:59:44
Valverda 39	1	30N29	91w32	6:06:08
Vanceville 8	1	32N41	93w44	6:14:56
Varnado 59	1	30N54	89w50	5:59:20
Vatican 28	1	30N19	92w03	6:08:12
Velma 53	1	30N42	90w35	6:02:20
Venice 38	1	29N17	89w22	5:57:28
Ventress 39	1	30N41	91w25	6:05:40
Verda 22	1	31N42	92w46	6:11:04
Verdun 32	1	30N30	90w45	6:03:00
Verdunville 51	1	29N48	91w30	6:06:00
Vernon 25	1	32N23	92w34	6:10:16
Verret 44	1	29N52	89w47	5:59:08
Veterans Administration Hosp 9	1	32N30	93w45	6:15:00
Vick 5	1	31N14	92w06	6:08:24
Vidalia 15	1	31N34	91w26	6:05:44
Vidrine 20	1	30N42	92w24	6:09:36
Vienna 31	1	32N36	92w39	6:10:36
Vieux Carre 36	2	29N58	90w05	6:00:20
Village St. George 17	1	30N25	91w09	6:04:36
Ville Platte 20	1	30N41	92w17	6:09:08
Vincent 10	1	30N13	93w21	6:13:24
Vincent Park 44	2	29N57	89w56	5:59:44
Vinton 10	1	30N11	93w35	6:14:20
Violet 44	2	29N54	89w54	5:59:36
Vivian 9	1	32N53	93w59	6:15:56
Vixen 11	1	32N06	92w05	6:08:20
Voorhies 5	1	31N02	91w59	6:07:56
Vowells Mill 35	1	31N41	93w18	6:13:12
Wadely Landing 30	1	31N41	92w07	6:08:28
Wadesboro 53	1	30N26	90w26	6:01:44
Waggaman 26	2	29N55	90w13	6:00:52
Wakefield 63	1	30N54	91w21	6:05:24
Waldheim 52	1	30N29	90w06	6:00:24
Walker 32	1	32N11	92w35	6:10:20
Wallace 48	1	30N03	90w34	6:02:16
Wallace Ridge 13	1	31N37	91w49	6:07:16
Wall Lake 37	1	32N31	92w09	6:08:36
Walnut Hill 58	1	31N12	93w08	6:12:32
Walters 13	1	31N33	92w00	6:08:00
Ward 2	1	30N49	92w40	6:10:40
Warden 42	1	32N32	91w30	6:06:00
Wardview 8	1	32N54	93w42	6:14:48
Wardville 34	1	32N47	91w55	6:07:40
Wardville 40	1	31N18	92w24	6:09:36
Warnerton 59	1	30N59	90w11	6:00:44
Washburn 16	1	32N11	93w55	6:15:40
Washington 49	1	30N37	92w04	6:08:16
Waterford Spur 45	1	30N00	90w29	6:01:56
Waterproof 54	1	31N48	91w23	6:05:32
Waterproof 55	1	29N36	90w43	6:02:52
Watson 32	1	30N35	90w57	6:03:48
Waverly 33	1	32N27	91w25	6:05:40
Waxia 49	1	30N37	92w04	6:08:16
Webre Steib Plantation 47	1	30N00	90w44	6:02:56
Weeks	1	29N48	91w49	6:07:16
Weil 40	1	31N17	92w29	6:09:56
Welcome 47	1	30N03	90w53	6:03:32
Weldon 14	1	32N52	92w44	6:10:56
Welsh 27	1	30N14	92w49	6:11:16
Wemple 16	1	32N01	93w43	6:14:52
Westdale 41	1	32N10	93w29	6:13:56
Westfield 4	1	29N56	91w02	6:04:08
Westlake 10	1	30N15	93w15	6:13:00
Westminster 17	1	30N25	91w06	6:04:24
West Monroe 37	1	32N31	92w09	6:08:36
Weston 25	1	32N15	92w36	6:10:24
Westover 61	1	30N28	91w13	6:04:52
Westport 40	1	30N56	92w56	6:11:44
Westwego 26	2	29N54	90w08	6:00:32
Weyanoke 63	1	30N56	91w27	6:05:48
Whatley Landing 30	1	31N42	92w11	6:08:44
Wheeling 64	1	31N45	92w50	6:11:20
White 29	1	29N47	90w50	6:03:20
White Castle 24	1	30N10	91w09	6:04:36
Whitehall 30	1	31N37	92w03	6:08:12
Whitehall 32	1	30N26	90w33	6:02:12
White Hall 47	1	30N06	90w50	6:03:20
White Hills 17	1	30N35	91w10	6:04:40
White Sulphur Springs 30	1	31N42	92w11	6:08:44
Whiteville 49	1	30N47	92w09	6:08:36
Whittington 40	1	31N17	92w29	6:09:56
Wickland Terrace 17	1	30N27	91w04	6:04:16
Wickliffe 39	1	30N40	91w28	6:05:52
Wilda 40	1	31N24	92w40	6:10:40
Wildsville 15	1	31N37	91w47	6:07:08
Wildwood 17	1	30N25	91w09	6:04:36
Wilhite 56	1	31N54	92w15	6:09:00
Williams 41	1	32N28	93w43	6:14:52
Williana 22	1	31N35	92w32	6:10:08
Willow Glen 40	1	31N15	92w26	6:09:44
Wills Point 38	2	29N52	89w57	5:59:48
Wilmer 53	1	30N49	90w22	6:01:28
Wilshire Park 40	1	31N17	92w29	6:09:56
Wilson 19	1	30N55	91w07	6:04:28
Wilsona 54	1	31N55	91w14	6:04:56
Wilson Point 40	1	31N17	92w29	6:09:56
Wilton Subdivision 9	1	32N33	93w47	6:15:08
Winnfield 64	1	31N56	92w38	6:10:32
Winnsboro 21	1	32N10	91w43	6:06:52
Wisner 21	1	31N59	91w39	6:06:36
Womack 25	1	32N19	92w27	6:09:48
Womack 41	1	32N02	93w20	6:13:20
Woodardville 7	1	32N16	93w17	6:13:08
Woodhaven 53	1	30N35	90w29	6:01:56
Woodland 19	1	30N52	91w01	6:04:04
Woodland 38	1	29N28	89w42	5:58:48
Woodlawn 4	1	29N56	91w02	6:04:08
Woodlawn 27	1	30N18	92w58	6:11:52
Woodlawn 38	2	29N52	89w57	5:59:48
Woodlawn 55	1	29N36	90w43	6:02:52
Woodside 5	1	30N51	91w50	6:07:20
Woodside 40	1	31N17	92w29	6:09:56
Woodville 31	1	32N32	92w38	6:10:32
Woodworth 40	1	31N09	92w30	6:10:00
Wyandotte 51	1	29N42	91w14	6:04:56
Wyatt 25	1	32N09	92w42	6:10:48
Yellow Pine 60	1	32N33	93w18	6:13:12
Youngsville 28	1	30N06	92w00	6:08:00
Yscloskey	1	29N50	89w41	5:58:44
Zachary 17	1	30N39	91w09	6:04:36
Zebedee 42	1	32N28	91w45	6:07:00
Zenoria 30	1	31N42	92w11	6:08:44
Zimmerman	1	31N25	92w42	6:10:48
Zion 22	1	31N46	92w23	6:09:32
Zion City 17	1	30N31	91w09	6:04:36
Zona	1	30N44	90w05	6:00:20
Zwolle 43	1	31N38	93w39	6:14:36
Zylks 9	1	32N58	94w00	6:16:00

TIME TABLES

ME # 1
Before 1/01/1887 LMT
1/01/1887 12:00 EST
3/31/1918 02:00 EWT
10/27/1918 02:00 EST
3/30/1919 02:00 EWT
10/26/1919 02:00 EST
2/09/1942 02:00 EWT
9/30/1945 02:00 EST
4/24/1955 02:00 US#2

ME # 2
Before 1/01/1887 LMT
1/01/1887 12:00 ME#1
4/27/1941 02:00 US#2

ME # 3
Before 1/01/1887 LMT
1/01/1887 12:00 ME#1
4/24/1938 02:00 EDT
10/01/1938 02:00 EST
4/30/1939 02:00 EDT
9/24/1939 02:00 EST
4/28/1940 02:00 EDT
9/29/1940 02:00 EST
4/27/1941 02:00 EDT
9/28/1941 02:00 EST
2/09/1942 02:00 EWT
9/30/1945 02:00 EST
4/24/1955 02:00 US#2

ME # 4
Before 1/01/1887 LMT
1/01/1887 12:00 ME#1
4/24/1938 02:00 EDT
10/01/1938 02:00 EST
4/30/1939 02:00 US#2

ME # 5
Before 1/01/1887 LMT
1/01/1887 12:00 ME#1
4/24/1938 02:00 EDT
10/01/1938 02:00 EST
4/30/1939 02:00 EDT
9/24/1939 02:00 EST
4/28/1940 02:00 EDT
9/29/1940 02:00 EST
4/27/1941 02:00 EDT
9/28/1941 02:00 EST
2/09/1942 02:00 EWT
9/30/1945 02:00 EST
4/27/1947 02:00 US#2

ME # 6
Before 1/01/1887 LMT
1/01/1887 12:00 ME#1
4/24/1932 02:00 US#2

ME # 7
Before 1/01/1887 LMT
1/01/1887 12:00 ME#1
4/29/1934 02:00 EDT
9/30/1934 02:00 EST
4/28/1935 02:00 EDT
9/29/1935 02:00 EST
4/26/1936 02:00 EDT
9/27/1936 02:00 EST
4/25/1937 02:00 EDT
9/26/1937 02:00 EST
4/24/1938 02:00 EDT
10/01/1938 02:00 EST
4/30/1939 02:00 EDT
9/24/1939 02:00 EST
4/28/1940 02:00 EDT
9/24/1940 02:00 EST
4/27/1941 02:00 US#2

ME # 8
Before 1/01/1887 LMT
1/01/1887 12:00 ME#1
4/30/1933 02:00 US#2

ME # 9
Before 1/01/1887 LMT
1/01/1887 12:00 ME#1
4/24/1938 02:00 EDT
10/01/1938 02:00 EST
4/30/1939 02:00 EDT
9/24/1939 02:00 EST
2/09/1942 02:00 EWT
9/30/1945 02:00 EST
4/24/1955 02:00 US#2

ME # 10
Before 1/01/1887 LMT
1/01/1887 12:00 ME#1
4/24/1938 02:00 EDT
10/01/1938 02:00 EST
4/30/1939 02:00 EDT
9/24/1939 02:00 EST
2/09/1942 02:00 EWT
9/30/1945 02:00 EST
4/28/1946 02:00 US#2

ME # 11
Before 1/01/1887 LMT
1/01/1887 12:00 ME#1
4/24/1938 02:00 EDT
10/01/1938 02:00 EST
4/30/1939 02:00 EDT
9/24/1939 02:00 EST
2/09/1942 02:00 EWT
9/30/1945 02:00 EST
4/24/1949 02:00 US#2

ME # 12
Before 1/01/1887 LMT
1/01/1887 12:00 ME#1
4/29/1923 02:00 EDT
9/30/1923 02:00 EST
4/27/1924 02:00 EDT
9/28/1924 02:00 EST
4/26/1925 02:00 EDT
9/27/1925 02:00 EST
4/25/1926 02:00 EDT
9/26/1926 02:00 EST
4/24/1927 02:00 EDT
9/25/1927 02:00 EST
4/29/1928 02:00 EDT
9/30/1928 02:00 EST
4/28/1929 02:00 EDT
9/29/1929 02:00 EST
4/27/1930 02:00 EDT
9/28/1930 02:00 EST
4/26/1931 02:00 EDT
9/27/1931 02:00 EST
4/24/1932 02:00 EDT
9/25/1932 02:00 EST
4/30/1933 02:00 EDT
9/24/1933 02:00 EST
4/29/1934 02:00 EDT
9/30/1934 02:00 EST
4/28/1935 02:00 EDT
9/29/1935 02:00 EST
4/26/1936 02:00 EDT
9/27/1936 02:00 EST
4/25/1937 02:00 EDT
9/26/1937 02:00 EST
4/24/1938 02:00 EDT
10/01/1938 02:00 EST
4/30/1939 02:00 EDT
9/24/1939 02:00 EST
4/28/1940 02:00 EDT
9/29/1940 02:00 EST
4/27/1941 02:00 EDT
9/28/1941 02:00 EST
2/09/1942 02:00 EWT
9/30/1945 02:00 EST
4/24/1955 02:00 US#2

ME # 13
Before 1/01/1887 LMT
1/01/1887 12:00 ME#1
6/15/1923 02:00 EDT
9/15/1923 02:00 EST
6/15/1924 02:00 EDT
9/15/1924 02:00 EST
6/15/1925 02:00 EDT
9/15/1925 02:00 EST
6/15/1926 02:00 EDT
9/15/1926 02:00 EST
6/15/1927 02:00 EDT
9/15/1927 02:00 EST
6/15/1928 02:00 EDT
9/15/1928 02:00 EST
6/15/1929 02:00 EDT
9/15/1929 02:00 EST
6/15/1930 02:00 EDT
9/15/1930 02:00 EST
6/15/1931 02:00 EDT
9/15/1931 02:00 EST
6/15/1932 02:00 EDT
9/15/1932 02:00 EST
6/15/1933 02:00 EDT
9/15/1933 02:00 EST
6/15/1934 02:00 EDT
9/15/1934 02:00 EST
6/15/1935 02:00 EDT
9/15/1935 02:00 EST
4/26/1936 02:00 EDT
9/27/1936 02:00 EST
4/25/1937 02:00 EDT
9/26/1937 02:00 EST
4/24/1938 02:00 EDT
10/01/1938 02:00 EST
4/30/1939 02:00 EDT
9/24/1939 02:00 EST
4/28/1940 02:00 EDT
9/29/1940 02:00 EST
4/27/1941 02:00 EDT
9/28/1941 02:00 EST
2/09/1942 02:00 US#2

ME # 14
Before 1/01/1887 LMT
1/01/1887 12:00 ME#1
4/14/1920 02:00 EDT
9/26/1920 02:00 EST
4/03/1921 02:00 EDT
9/25/1921 02:00 EST
4/02/1922 02:00 EDT
9/24/1922 02:00 EST
4/29/1923 02:00 EDT
9/30/1923 02:00 EST
4/27/1924 02:00 EDT
9/28/1924 02:00 EST
4/26/1925 02:00 EDT
9/27/1925 02:00 EST
4/25/1926 02:00 EDT
9/26/1926 02:00 EST
4/24/1927 02:00 EDT
9/25/1927 02:00 EST
4/29/1928 02:00 EDT
9/30/1928 02:00 EST
4/28/1929 02:00 EDT
9/29/1929 02:00 EST
4/27/1930 02:00 EDT
9/28/1930 02:00 EST
4/26/1931 02:00 EDT
9/27/1931 02:00 EST
4/24/1932 02:00 EDT
9/25/1932 02:00 EST
4/30/1933 02:00 EDT
9/24/1933 02:00 EST
4/29/1934 02:00 EDT
9/30/1934 02:00 EST
4/28/1935 02:00 EDT
9/29/1935 02:00 EST
4/26/1936 02:00 EDT
9/27/1936 02:00 EST
4/25/1937 02:00 EDT
9/26/1937 02:00 EST
4/24/1938 02:00 EDT
10/01/1938 02:00 EST
4/30/1939 02:00 EDT
10/15/1939 02:00 EST
4/28/1940 02:00 US#2

ME # 15
Before 1/01/1887 LMT
1/01/1887 12:00 ME#1
4/26/1931 02:00 EDT
9/27/1931 02:00 EST
4/24/1932 02:00 EDT
9/25/1932 02:00 EST
4/30/1933 02:00 EDT
9/24/1933 02:00 EST
4/29/1934 02:00 EDT
10/30/1934 02:00 EST
4/28/1935 02:00 EDT
9/29/1935 02:00 EST
4/26/1936 02:00 EDT
9/27/1936 02:00 EST
4/25/1937 02:00 EDT
9/26/1937 02:00 EST
4/30/1938 02:00 EDT
9/25/1938 02:00 EST
4/30/1939 02:00 US#2

ME # 16
Before 1/01/1887 LMT
1/01/1887 12:00 ME#1
4/14/1920 02:00 EDT
9/26/1920 02:00 EST
4/03/1921 02:00 EDT
9/25/1921 02:00 EST
4/02/1922 02:00 EDT
9/24/1922 02:00 EST
4/29/1923 02:00 EDT
9/30/1923 02:00 EST
4/27/1924 02:00 EDT
9/28/1924 02:00 EST
4/26/1925 02:00 EDT
9/27/1925 02:00 EST
4/25/1926 02:00 EDT
9/26/1926 02:00 EST
4/24/1927 02:00 EDT
9/25/1927 02:00 EST
4/29/1928 02:00 EDT
9/30/1928 02:00 EST
4/28/1929 02:00 EDT
9/29/1929 02:00 EST
4/27/1930 02:00 EDT
9/28/1930 02:00 EST
4/26/1931 02:00 EDT
9/27/1931 02:00 EST
4/24/1932 02:00 EDT
9/25/1932 02:00 EST
4/30/1933 02:00 EDT
9/24/1933 02:00 EST
4/29/1934 02:00 EDT
9/30/1934 02:00 EST
4/28/1935 02:00 EDT
9/29/1935 02:00 EST
4/26/1936 02:00 EDT
9/27/1936 02:00 EST
4/25/1937 02:00 EDT
9/26/1937 02:00 EST
4/28/1938 02:00 EDT
10/01/1938 02:00 EST
4/30/1939 02:00 EDT
10/15/1939 02:00 EST
4/28/1940 02:00 US#2

ME # 17
Before 1/01/1887 LMT
1/01/1887 12:00 ME#1
4/29/1934 02:00 EDT
9/30/1934 02:00 EST
4/28/1935 02:00 EDT
9/29/1935 02:00 EST
4/26/1936 02:00 EDT
9/27/1936 02:00 EST
4/25/1937 02:00 EDT
9/26/1937 02:00 EST
6/01/1939 02:00 EDT
10/15/1939 02:00 EST
6/01/1940 02:00 EDT
10/15/1940 02:00 EST
6/01/1941 02:00 EDT
10/15/1941 02:00 EST
2/09/1942 02:00 US#2

ME # 18
Before 1/01/1887 LMT
1/01/1887 12:00 ME#1
4/24/1938 02:00 EDT
10/01/1938 02:00 EST
4/30/1939 02:00 EDT
10/15/1939 02:00 EST
4/28/1940 02:00 US#2

ME # 19
Before 1/01/1887 LMT
1/01/1887 12:00 ME#1
4/24/1938 02:00 EDT
10/01/1938 02:00 EST
4/30/1939 02:00 EDT
9/24/1939 02:00 EST
4/28/1940 02:00 EDT
9/29/1940 02:00 EST
4/27/1941 02:00 EDT
9/08/1941 02:00 EST
2/09/1942 02:00 EWT
9/30/1945 02:00 EST
4/24/1949 02:00 US#2

ME # 20
Before 1/01/1887 LMT
1/01/1887 12:00 ME#1
4/24/1932 02:00 EDT
9/25/1932 02:00 EST
4/29/1934 02:00 EDT
9/30/1934 02:00 EST
4/28/1935 02:00 EDT
9/29/1935 02:00 EST
4/26/1936 02:00 EDT
9/27/1936 02:00 EST
4/25/1937 02:00 EDT
9/26/1937 02:00 EST
4/24/1938 02:00 EDT
10/01/1938 02:00 EST
4/30/1939 02:00 EDT
10/01/1939 02:00 EST
4/28/1940 02:00 US#2

ME # 21
Before 1/01/1887 LMT
1/01/1887 12:00 ME#1
4/24/1938 02:00 EDT
10/01/1938 02:00 EST
4/30/1939 02:00 EDT
10/15/1939 02:00 EST
4/28/1940 02:00 EDT
9/29/1940 02:00 EST
2/09/1942 02:00 EWT
9/30/1945 02:00 EST
4/24/1949 02:00 US#2

ME # 22
Before 1/01/1887 LMT
1/01/1887 12:00 ME#1
4/27/1941 02:00 EDT
10/28/1941 02:00 EST
2/09/1942 02:00 US#2

ME # 23
Before 1/01/1887 LMT
1/01/1887 12:00 ME#1
4/24/1938 02:00 EDT
10/01/1938 02:00 EST
4/30/1939 02:00 EDT
9/24/1939 02:00 EST
4/28/1940 02:00 EDT
9/29/1940 02:00 EST
4/27/1941 02:00 EDT
9/07/1941 02:00 EST
2/09/1942 02:00 EWT
9/30/1945 02:00 EST
4/24/1955 02:00 US#2

ME # 24
Before 1/01/1887 LMT
1/01/1887 12:00 ME#1
4/25/1937 02:00 EDT
9/26/1937 02:00 EST
4/24/1938 02:00 EDT
10/01/1938 02:00 EST
4/30/1939 02:00 EDT
9/24/1939 02:00 EST
4/28/1940 02:00 EDT
9/29/1940 02:00 EST
4/27/1941 02:00 EDT
9/28/1941 02:00 EST
2/09/1942 02:00 EWT
9/30/1945 02:00 EST
4/27/1947 02:00 US#2

ME # 25
Before 1/01/1887 LMT
1/01/1887 12:00 ME#1
5/03/1936 02:00 EDT
9/27/1936 02:00 EST
4/25/1937 02:00 EDT
9/26/1937 02:00 EST
4/24/1938 02:00 EDT
10/01/1938 02:00 EST
4/30/1939 02:00 US#2

ME # 26
Before 1/01/1887 LMT
1/01/1887 12:00 ME#1
4/28/1935 02:00 EDT
9/29/1935 02:00 EST
4/26/1936 02:00 EDT
9/27/1936 02:00 EST
4/25/1937 02:00 EDT
9/26/1937 02:00 EST
4/24/1938 02:00 EDT
10/01/1938 02:00 EST
4/30/1939 02:00 EDT
9/24/1939 02:00 EST
4/28/1940 02:00 EDT
9/29/1940 02:00 EST
4/27/1941 02:00 EDT
9/28/1941 02:00 EST
2/09/1942 02:00 EWT
9/30/1945 02:00 EST
4/27/1947 02:00 US#2

ME # 27
Before 1/01/1887 LMT
1/01/1887 12:00 ME#1
4/26/1931 02:00 EDT
9/27/1931 02:00 EST
4/28/1935 02:00 EDT
9/29/1935 02:00 EST
4/26/1936 02:00 EDT
9/27/1936 02:00 EST
4/25/1937 02:00 EDT
9/26/1937 02:00 EST
4/24/1938 02:00 EDT
10/01/1938 02:00 EST
4/30/1939 02:00 US#2

ME # 28
Before 1/01/1887 LMT
1/01/1887 12:00 ME#1
4/29/1934 02:00 EDT
9/30/1934 02:00 EST
4/24/1938 02:00 EDT
10/01/1938 02:00 EST
4/30/1939 02:00 US#2

ME # 29
Before 1/01/1887 LMT
1/01/1887 12:00 ME#1
4/26/1931 02:00 EDT
9/27/1931 02:00 EST
4/24/1932 02:00 EDT
9/25/1932 02:00 EST
4/30/1933 02:00 EDT
9/24/1933 02:00 EST
4/29/1934 02:00 EDT
9/30/1934 02:00 EST
4/28/1935 02:00 EDT
9/29/1935 02:00 EST
4/26/1936 02:00 EDT
9/27/1936 02:00 EST
4/25/1937 02:00 EDT
9/26/1937 02:00 EST
4/24/1938 02:00 EDT
10/01/1938 02:00 EST
4/30/1939 02:00 EDT
9/24/1939 02:00 EST
4/28/1940 02:00 EDT
9/29/1940 02:00 EST
4/27/1941 02:00 EDT
9/28/1941 02:00 EST
2/09/1942 02:00 EWT
9/30/1945 02:00 EST
4/24/1955 02:00 US#2

ME # 30
Before 1/01/1887 LMT
1/01/1887 12:00 ME#1
4/26/1931 02:00 EDT
9/27/1931 02:00 EST
4/24/1932 02:00 EDT
9/25/1932 02:00 EST
4/30/1933 02:00 EDT
9/24/1933 02:00 EST
4/29/1934 02:00 EDT
9/30/1934 02:00 EST
4/28/1935 02:00 EDT
9/29/1935 02:00 EST
4/26/1936 02:00 EDT
9/27/1936 02:00 EST
4/25/1937 02:00 EDT
9/26/1937 02:00 EST
4/24/1938 02:00 EDT
10/01/1938 02:00 EST
4/30/1939 02:00 EDT
9/24/1939 02:00 EST
4/28/1940 02:00 EDT
9/29/1940 02:00 EST
4/27/1941 02:00 EDT
10/26/1941 02:00 EST
2/09/1942 02:00 US#2

ME # 31
Before 1/01/1887 LMT
1/01/1887 12:00 ME#1
4/29/1934 02:00 US#2

ME # 32
Before 1/01/1887 LMT
1/01/1887 12:00 ME#1
4/28/1935 02:00 US#2

ME # 33
Before 1/01/1887 LMT
1/01/1887 12:00 ME#1
4/26/1936 02:00 US#2

ME # 34
Before 1/01/1887 LMT
1/01/1887 12:00 ME#1
4/25/1937 02:00 US#2

ME # 35
Before 1/01/1887 LMT
1/01/1887 12:00 ME#1
4/28/1940 02:00 US#2

ME # 36
Before 1/01/1887 LMT
1/01/1887 12:00 ME#1
4/30/1933 02:00 EDT
9/24/1933 02:00 EST

TIME TABLES

4/24/1938 02:00 EDT
10/01/1938 02:00 EST
4/30/1939 02:00 US#2
....
ME # 37
Before 1/01/1887 LMT
1/01/1887 12:00 ME#1
4/30/1933 02:00 EDT
9/24/1933 02:00 EST
2/09/1942 02:00 US#2
....
ME # 38
Before 1/01/1887 LMT
1/01/1887 12:00 ME#1
4/24/1932 02:00 EDT
9/25/1932 02:00 EST
4/30/1933 02:00 EDT
9/24/1933 02:00 EST
4/28/1935 02:00 EDT
9/29/1935 02:00 EST
4/26/1936 02:00 EDT
9/27/1936 02:00 EST
4/25/1937 02:00 EDT
9/26/1937 02:00 EST
4/24/1938 02:00 EDT
10/01/1938 02:00 EST
4/30/1939 02:00 US#2
....
ME # 39
Before 1/01/1887 LMT
1/01/1887 12:00 ME#1
4/26/1931 02:00 EDT
9/27/1931 02:00 EST
4/24/1932 02:00 EDT
9/25/1932 02:00 EST
4/29/1934 02:00 EDT
9/30/1934 02:00 EST
4/28/1935 02:00 EDT
9/29/1935 02:00 EST
4/26/1936 02:00 EDT
9/27/1936 02:00 EST
4/25/1937 02:00 EDT
9/26/1937 02:00 EST
4/24/1938 02:00 EDT
10/01/1938 02:00 EST
4/30/1939 02:00 EDT
9/24/1939 02:00 EST
4/28/1940 02:00 EDT
9/29/1940 02:00 EST
4/27/1941 02:00 EDT
9/28/1941 02:00 EST
2/09/1942 02:00 EWT
9/30/1945 02:00 EST
4/24/1949 02:00 US#2
....
ME # 40
Before 1/01/1887 LMT
1/01/1887 12:00 ME#1
4/26/1931 02:00 EDT
9/27/1931 02:00 EST
4/24/1932 02:00 EDT
9/25/1932 02:00 EST
4/30/1933 02:00 EDT
9/24/1933 02:00 EST
4/26/1936 02:00 EDT
9/27/1936 02:00 EST
4/25/1937 02:00 EDT
9/26/1937 02:00 EST
4/24/1938 02:00 EDT
10/01/1938 02:00 EST
4/30/1939 02:00 US#2
....
ME # 41
Before 1/01/1887 LMT
1/01/1887 12:00 ME#1
4/24/1932 02:00 EDT
9/25/1932 02:00 EST
4/25/1937 02:00 EDT
9/26/1937 02:00 EST
4/24/1938 02:00 EDT
10/01/1938 02:00 EST
4/30/1939 02:00 US#2
....
ME # 42
Before 1/01/1887 LMT
1/01/1887 12:00 ME#1
4/30/1933 02:00 EDT
9/24/1933 02:00 EST
2/09/1942 02:00 EWT
9/30/1945 02:00 EST
4/24/1955 02:00 US#2
....
ME # 43
Before 1/01/1887 LMT
1/01/1887 12:00 ME#1
4/28/1946 02:00 EDT
9/29/1946 02:00 EST
4/25/1948 02:00 US#2
....
ME # 44
Before 1/01/1887 LMT
1/01/1887 12:00 ME#1
4/26/1931 02:00 US#2
....
ME # 45
Before 1/01/1887 LMT
1/01/1887 12:00 ME#1
4/28/1946 02:00 US#2
....
ME # 46
Before 1/01/1887 LMT
1/01/1887 12:00 ME#1
4/28/1940 02:00 EDT
9/29/1940 02:00 EST
4/27/1941 02:00 EDT
9/28/1941 02:00 EST
2/09/1942 02:00 EWT
9/30/1945 02:00 EST
4/27/1947 02:00 US#2
....
ME # 47
Before 1/01/1887 LMT
1/01/1887 12:00 ME#1
4/24/1949 02:00 US#2
....
ME # 48
Before 1/01/1887 LMT
1/01/1887 12:00 ME#1
4/26/1931 02:00 EDT
9/08/1931 02:00 EST
4/24/1932 02:00 EDT
9/25/1932 02:00 EST
4/30/1933 02:00 EDT
9/24/1933 02:00 EST
4/29/1934 02:00 EDT
9/30/1934 02:00 EST
4/28/1935 02:00 EDT
9/29/1935 02:00 EST
4/26/1936 02:00 EDT
9/27/1936 02:00 EST
4/25/1937 02:00 EDT
9/26/1937 02:00 EST
4/24/1938 02:00 EDT
10/01/1938 02:00 EST
4/30/1939 02:00 US#2
....
ME # 49
Before 1/01/1887 LMT
1/01/1887 12:00 ME#1
4/30/1939 02:00 EDT
9/24/1939 02:00 EST
4/28/1940 02:00 EDT
9/29/1940 02:00 EST
4/27/1941 02:00 EDT
9/28/1941 02:00 EST
2/09/1942 02:00 EWT
9/30/1945 02:00 EST
4/24/1955 02:00 US#2

COUNTIES

1 Androscoggin
2 Aroostook
3 Cumberland
4 Franklin
5 Hancock
6 Kennebec
7 Knox
8 Lincoln
9 Oxford
10 Penobscot
11 Piscataquis
12 Sagadahoc
13 Somerset
14 Waldo
15 Washington
16 York

Abbot 11 1 45N12 69w28 4:37:52
Abbotts Mill 9 44 44N33 70w33 4:42:12
Acadia Terrace 2 11 47N09 67w56 4:31:44
Acton 16 1 43N31 70w55 4:43:40
Addison 15 1 44N34 67w43 4:30:52
Admiralty Village 16 4 43N05 70w45 4:43:00
Albion 6 1 44N32 69w27 4:37:48
Alexander 15 1 45N05 67w28 4:29:52
Alfred 16 14 43N29 70w43 4:42:52
Alfred Mills 16 14 43N29 70w43 4:42:52
Allagash Plantation 2 1 47N06 69w04 4:36:16
Allens Mills 4 8 44N40 70w09 4:40:36
Alna 8 1 44N05 69w37 4:38:28
Alton 10 47 45N02 68w44 4:34:56
Amherst 5 45 44N50 68w22 4:33:28
Amity 2 1 45N55 67w50 4:31:20
Andover 9 1 44N38 70w45 4:43:00
Anson 13 4 44N50 69w55 4:39:40
Appleton 7 1 44N18 69w15 4:37:00
Aroostook Farm 2 39 46N42 68w00 4:32:00
Arrowsic 12 1 43N52 69w47 4:39:08
Arundel 16 14 43N26 70w32 4:42:08
Ashdale 12 1 43N46 69w52 4:39:28
Ashland 2 47 46N38 68w24 4:33:36
Ashville 5 1 44N29 68w07 4:32:28
Athens 13 31 44N57 69w40 4:38:40
Atkinson 11 1 45N10 69w04 4:36:16
Atkinson Corner 11 34 45N11 69w13 4:36:52
Atlantic 5 1 44N11 68w25 4:33:40
Auburn 1 13 44N06 70w14 4:40:56
Augusta 6 44 44N19 69w47 4:39:08
Aurora 5 45 44N52 68w17 4:33:08
Avon 4 1 44N46 70w19 4:41:16
Back Narrows 8 1 43N53 69w38 4:38:32
Bailey Island 3 1 43N44 70w00 4:40:00
Baileyville 15 29 45N08 67w24 4:29:36
Baker Corner 3 31 43N44 70w26 4:41:44
Balch Pond 16 1 43N37 71w01 4:44:04
Bald Head Cliff 16 6 43N15 70w36 4:42:24
Baldwin 3 34 43N50 70w42 4:42:48
Bancroft 2 45 45N43 67w58 4:31:52
Bangor 10 14 44N48 68w46 4:35:04
Bar Harbor 5 12 44N23 68w13 4:32:52
Baring 15 1 45N08 67w19 4:29:16
Bar Mills 16 6 43N37 70w36 4:42:24
Barnard Plantation 11 1 45N19 69w09 4:36:36
Barrett 2 1 46N52 68w01 4:32:04
Bartlett Mills 16 48 43N23 70w33 4:42:12
Basin 15 35 44N37 67w45 4:31:00
Basin Mills 10 31 44N53 68w40 4:34:40
Bass Harbor 5 1 44N14 68w21 4:33:24
Bath 12 15 43N55 69w49 4:39:16
Bauneg Beg 16 14 43N26 70w46 4:43:04
Bay Point 12 1 43N48 69w45 4:39:00
Bayside 14 36 44N26 69w01 4:36:04
Bayview 16 44 43N31 70w27 4:41:48
Bayville 8 1 43N51 69w37 4:38:28
Beals 15 1 44N29 67w36 4:30:24
Beans Corner 4 6 44N35 70w13 4:40:52
Beaver Dam 16 44 43N16 70w52 4:43:28
Beddington 15 45 44N48 68w03 4:32:12
Beech Ridge 16 4 43N09 70w39 4:42:36
Belfast 14 36 44N26 69w01 4:36:04
Belgrade 6 35 44N27 69w50 4:39:20
Belgrade Lakes 6 35 44N32 69w53 4:39:32
Belmont 14 1 44N23 69w07 4:36:28
Belmont Corner 14 36 44N26 69w01 4:36:04
Benedicta 2 1 45N48 68w24 4:33:36
Benton 6 8 44N36 69w32 4:38:08
Benton Falls 6 8 44N33 69w39 4:38:36
Benton Station 6 8 44N35 69w36 4:38:24
Bernard 5 1 44N14 68w22 4:33:28
Bernier 16 14 43N26 70w46 4:43:04
Berwick 16 44 43N16 70w52 4:43:28
Bethel 9 37 44N25 70w47 4:43:08
Biddeford 16 16 43N30 70w28 4:41:52
Biddeford Pool 16 16 43N29 70w27 4:41:48
Bingham 13 38 45N03 69w53 4:39:32
Birch Harbor 5 1 44N23 68w03 4:32:12
Birch Island 3 1 43N55 69w58 4:39:52
Blackinton Corners 7 7 44N08 69w09 4:36:36
Black Point 3 5 43N35 70w21 4:41:24
Blackstrap 3 44 43N42 70w15 4:41:00
Blackwell 13 20 44N48 69w53 4:39:32
Blaine 2 1 46N29 67w51 4:31:24
Blaisdell Corners 16 45 43N25 70w52 4:43:28
Blake Corner 1 8 44N00 70w03 4:40:12
Blanchard 11 1 45N11 69w27 4:37:48
Blanchard Plantation 11 1 45N15 69w37 4:38:28
Blue Hill 5 3 44N25 68w35 4:34:20
Blue Point 3 5 43N35 70w21 4:41:24
Bolsters Mills 3 1 44N07 70w41 4:42:44
Bonny Eagle 16 1 43N40 70w36 4:42:24
Boothbay 8 3 43N53 69w37 4:38:28
Boothbay Harbor 8 3 43N51 69w38 4:38:32
Boothbay Park 16 44 43N31 70w27 4:41:48
Bowdoin 12 31 44N03 69w58 4:39:52
Bowdoinham 12 31 44N02 69w52 4:39:28
Bowerbank 11 1 45N19 69w15 4:37:00
Bradford 10 1 45N05 68w55 4:35:40
Bradford Center 10 1 45N04 69w04 4:36:16
Bradley 10 6 44N54 68w38 4:34:32
Brannen 2 39 46N41 68w10 4:32:40
Bremen 8 1 44N00 69w26 4:37:44
Brentwood Acres 3 44 43N38 70w16 4:41:04
Brewer 10 14 44N48 68w46 4:35:04
Brewer Lake 10 4 44N44 68w50 4:35:20
Bridgewater 2 47 46N25 67w51 4:31:24
Bridgton 3 3 44N03 70w42 4:42:48
Brighton 13 1 44N56 69w40 4:38:40
Brighton Plantation 13 1 45N03 69w42 4:38:48
Bristol 8 9 43N55 69w30 4:38:00
Brixham 16 4 43N09 70w39 4:42:36
Brixham Upper Corners 16 4 43N09 70w39 4:42:36
Broad Cove 3 44 43N38 70w16 4:41:04
Broad Cove 8 26 44N06 69w23 4:37:32
Brooklin 5 1 44N17 68w35 4:34:20
Brooks 14 1 44N33 69w08 4:36:32
Brooksville 5 1 44N21 68w45 4:35:00
Brookton 15 1 45N32 67w46 4:31:04
Brownfield 9 1 43N56 70w55 4:43:40
Browning 16 14 43N26 70w46 4:43:04
Brownville 11 47 45N18 69w02 4:36:08
Brownville Junction 11 47 45N21 69w03 4:36:12
Brunswick 3 14 43N55 69w58 4:39:52
Brunswick Naval Air Station 3 1 43N54 69w56 4:39:44
Bryant Pond 9 44 44N23 70w39 4:42:36
Buckfield 9 32 44N17 70w22 4:41:28
Bucks Harbor 15 41 44N39 67w23 4:29:32
Bucksport 5 44 44N34 68w47 4:35:08
Buggy Meetinghouse 3 5 43N35 70w21 4:41:24
Bunganuc Landing 3 1 43N55 69w58 4:39:52
Bunker Hill 8 35 44N02 69w33 4:38:12
Bunkers Harbor 5 1 44N23 68w03 4:32:12
Burkettville 7 1 44N18 69w19 4:37:16
Burlington 10 1 45N12 68w25 4:33:40
Burnham 14 45 44N42 69w26 4:37:44
Burnt Meadow Ponp 9 1 43N56 70w55 4:43:40
Bustins Island 3 8 43N48 70w05 4:40:20
Buxton 16 45 43N39 70w33 4:42:12
Byron 9 45 44N43 70w38 4:42:32
Calais 15 6 45N11 67w17 4:29:08
Cambridge 13 1 45N03 69w25 4:37:40
Camden 7 9 44N13 69w04 4:36:16
Campbell 2 39 46N42 68w00 4:32:00
Campbells 15 47 45N10 67w16 4:29:04
Camp Ellis 16 44 43N31 70w27 4:41:48
Canaan 13 1 44N45 69w35 4:38:20
Canton 9 44 44N27 70w18 4:41:12
Canton Point 9 44 44N28 70w19 4:41:16
Cape Cottage 3 44 43N38 70w16 4:41:04
Cape Cottage Woods 3 44 43N38 70w16 4:41:04
Cape Elizabeth 3 44 43N36 70w14 4:40:56
Cape Junction 14 1 44N29 68w59 4:35:56
Cape Neddick 16 4 43N10 70w36 4:42:24
Cape Porpoise 16 44 43N22 70w26 4:41:44
Capitol Island 8 1 43N51 69w38 4:38:32
Caratunk 13 1 45N14 70w00 4:40:00
Caratunk Plantation 13 1 45N12 69w54 4:39:36
Cardville 10 1 45N03 68w36 4:34:24
Caribou 2 11 46N52 68w01 4:32:04
Carmel 10 45 44N48 69w02 4:36:08
Carrabassett 1 45N05 70w13 4:40:52
Carrabassett Valley 4 1 44N57 70w09 4:40:36
Carroll 10 1 45N24 68w08 4:32:32
Carroll Plantation 10 1 45N25 68w02 4:32:08
Carson 2 47 46N47 68w09 4:32:36
Carthage 4 45 44N37 70w25 4:41:40
Cary 2 1 45N57 67w50 4:31:20
Cary Plantation 2 1 45N59 67w51 4:31:24
Casco 3 1 44N00 70w31 4:42:04
Cash Corner 3 44 43N38 70w16 4:41:04
Castine 5 9 44N25 68w48 4:35:12
Castle Hill 2 1 46N42 68w13 4:32:52
Caswell Plantation 2 1 47N00 67w50 4:31:20
Cathance 12 45 44N01 69w54 4:39:36
Cedar Grove 8 8 44N06 69w44 4:38:56
Center Lebanon 16 45 43N25 70w52 4:43:28
Center Lovell 9 1 44N11 70w53 4:43:32
Center Minot 1 13 44N06 70w14 4:40:56
Center Montville 14 1 44N32 69w18 4:37:12
Center Vassalboro 6 45 44N28 69w41 4:38:44

Centerville 15 1 44N43 67w40 4:30:40
Central District 15 46 44N39 67w44 4:30:56
Chamberlain 8 1 43N53 69w29 4:37:56
Chapman 2 1 46N38 68w07 4:32:28
Charleston 10 1 45N04 69w03 4:36:12
Charlotte 15 1 45N01 67w16 4:29:04
Chase's Mill 1 32 44N17 70w22 4:41:28
Chases Pond 16 4 43N09 70w39 4:42:36
Chebeague Island 3 1 43N44 70w07 4:40:28
Chelsea 6 6 44N16 69w44 4:38:56
Cherryfield 15 35 44N36 67w56 4:31:44
Chester 10 1 45N25 68w31 4:34:04
Chesterville 4 1 44N33 70w06 4:40:24
Chesuncook 11 1 45N28 69w36 4:38:24
Chicopee 16 44 43N41 70w27 4:41:48
China 6 1 44N25 69w33 4:38:12
Chisholm 4 44 44N29 70w12 4:40:48
Christmas Cove 8 1 43N52 69w34 4:38:16
Cider Hill 16 4 43N09 70w39 4:42:36
Clapboard Island 3 44 43N42 70w15 4:41:00
Clark Island 7 1 44N01 69w08 4:36:32
Clarks Mill 16 6 43N36 70w35 4:42:20
Clay Hill 16 4 43N10 70w36 4:42:24
Clayton Lake 2 1 46N37 69w31 4:38:04
Cliff Island 3 44 43N40 70w17 4:41:08
Clifton 10 4 44N48 68w32 4:34:08
Clinton 6 32 44N38 69w30 4:38:00
Coburn Gore 4 1 45N13 70w30 4:42:00
Codyville Plantation 15 1 45N27 67w40 4:30:40
Colby 2 1 46N52 68w01 4:32:04
Coles Corner 14 4 44N38 68w51 4:35:24
Columbia 15 46 44N39 67w48 4:31:12
Columbia Falls 15 46 44N39 67w44 4:30:56
Concordville 16 4 43N11 70w37 4:42:28
Convene 3 2 43N50 70w47 4:43:08
Cooks Corner 3 1 43N55 69w58 4:39:52
Cooks Corner 14 1 44N40 69w14 4:36:56
Cooks Mills 3 1 44N00 70w32 4:42:08
Cooper 15 1 44N59 67w25 4:29:40
Coopers Corner 16 44 43N22 70w29 4:41:56
Coopers Mills 8 1 44N16 69w33 4:38:12
Coplin Plantation 4 1 45N06 70w28 4:41:52
Corea 5 1 44N24 67w58 4:31:52
Corinna 10 6 44N55 69w16 4:37:04
Corinth 10 6 44N59 69w01 4:36:04
Cornish 16 5 43N46 70w49 4:43:16
Cornville 13 1 44N52 69w40 4:38:40
Costigan 10 1 45N01 68w38 4:34:32
Costons Corner 13 1 44N53 69w27 4:37:48
Cousins Island 3 8 43N48 70w12 4:40:48
Cranberry Isles 5 1 44N16 68w15 4:33:00
Crawford 15 1 45N02 67w34 4:30:16
Crescent Beach 3 44 43N38 70w16 4:41:04
Crescent Lake 3 1 44N00 70w32 4:42:08
Criehaven 7 1 43N52 68w53 4:35:32
Crockett Corner 3 1 43N54 70w14 4:40:56
Crocketts Neck 16 4 43N05 70w41 4:42:44
Crossman Corner 1 8 44N00 70w03 4:40:12
Crouseville 2 1 46N45 68w06 4:32:24
Crystal 2 47 46N01 68w22 4:33:28
Cumberland 3 44 43N47 70w13 4:40:52
Cumberland Mills 3 44 43N41 70w21 4:41:24
Cundys Harbor 3 1 43N55 69w58 4:39:52
Cupsuptic 9 45 44N58 70w47 4:43:08
Curtis Corner 1 46 44N21 70w08 4:40:32
Cushing 7 1 44N00 69w16 4:37:04
Cutler 15 41 44N40 67w12 4:28:48
Cutts Island 16 4 43N05 70w41 4:42:44
Cyr Plantation 2 1 47N06 67w58 4:31:52
Daggett 2 39 46N42 68w00 4:32:00
Dallas Plantation 4 1 44N59 70w35 4:42:20
Damariscotta 8 4 44N02 69w29 4:37:56
Damariscotta Mills 8 4 44N02 69w33 4:38:12
Damascus 10 1 44N48 69w03 4:36:12
Danforth 15 4 45N40 67w52 4:31:28
Danville 1 13 44N06 70w14 4:40:56
Davenport Cove 2 4 45N40 67w52 4:31:28
Davis Island 8 27 43N59 69w39 4:38:36
Days Ferry 12 15 43N55 69w48 4:39:12
Dayton 16 45 43N33 70w35 4:42:20
Deblois 15 45 44N44 68w01 4:32:04
Dedham 5 45 44N41 68w36 4:34:24
Deering 2 39 46N42 68w00 4:32:00
Deer Isle 5 1 44N14 68w41 4:34:44
Delano Park 3 44 43N38 70w16 4:41:04
Denmark 9 2 43N58 70w47 4:43:08
Dennistown Plantation 13 1 45N40 70w20 4:41:20
Dennysville 15 24 44N55 67w14 4:28:56
Derby 11 4 45N14 68w59 4:35:56
Detroit 13 6 44N48 69w20 4:37:20
Dexter 10 40 45N01 69w18 4:37:12
Dickey 2 11 47N10 68w53 4:35:32
Dickvale 9 17 44N32 70w27 4:41:48
Dixfield 9 17 44N32 70w28 4:41:52
Dixmont 10 1 44N41 69w10 4:36:40
Dog Island Corner 14 36 44N26 69w01 4:36:04
Dorman 15 35 44N37 67w49 4:31:16
Douglas Hill 3 34 43N48 70w40 4:42:40
Dover-Foxcroft 11 34 45N10 69w11 4:36:44
Dover South Mills 11 34 45N11 69w13 4:36:52
Dow Airport 10 14 44N49 68w45 4:35:00
Drake Corner 14 1 44N18 69w07 4:36:28
Drakes Island 16 33 43N19 70w35 4:42:20
Dresden 8 8 44N05 69w44 4:38:56
Drew Plantation 10 1 45N36 68w04 4:32:16
Dryden 4 6 44N35 70w13 4:40:52
Dry Mills 3 1 43N53 70w20 4:41:20
Ducktrap 14 1 44N18 69w07 4:36:28
Dunkertown 3 1 44N08 70w30 4:42:00
Dunns 3 8 43N48 70w16 4:41:04
Dunns Corner 6 31 44N23 69w58 4:39:52
Durgintown 9 1 43N48 70w48 4:43:12
Durham 1 1 43N58 70w07 4:40:28
Dyer Brook 2 47 46N05 68w12 4:32:48
Eagle Island 5 1 44N12 68w42 4:34:48
Eagle Lake 2 11 47N03 68w36 4:34:24
East Andover 9 1 44N37 70w43 4:42:52
East Auburn 1 13 44N06 70w14 4:40:56
East Baldwin 3 34 43N48 70w40 4:42:40
East Benton 6 8 44N31 69w27 4:37:48
East Bethel 9 37 44N25 70w48 4:43:12
East Blue Hill 5 3 44N25 68w31 4:34:04
East Boothbay 8 3 43N52 69w35 4:38:20
Eastbrook 5 45 44N41 68w14 4:32:56
East Buckfield 9 32 44N17 70w22 4:41:28
East Corinth 10 6 45N00 69w01 4:36:04
East Denmark 9 2 43N53 70w48 4:43:12
East Dixfield 4 6 44N35 70w18 4:41:12
East Dixmont 10 1 44N41 69w10 4:36:40
East Dover 11 34 45N11 69w13 4:36:52
East Eddington 10 4 44N48 68w34 4:34:16
East Edgecomb 8 27 43N59 69w39 4:38:36
East Exeter 10 6 45N00 69w01 4:36:04
East Franklin 5 33 44N32 68w09 4:32:36
East Friendship 7 1 43N59 69w20 4:37:20
East Fryeburg 9 45 43N56 70w55 4:43:40
East Hampden 10 14 44N49 68w45 4:35:00
East Harpswell 3 1 43N55 69w58 4:39:52
East Hiram 9 2 43N53 70w49 4:43:16
East Holden 10 4 44N44 68w38 4:34:32
East Knox 14 1 44N35 69w17 4:37:08
East Lamoine 5 32 44N33 68w27 4:33:48
East Lebanon 16 45 43N25 70w52 4:43:28
East Limington 16 34 43N48 70w39 4:42:36
East Livermore 1 44 44N25 70w07 4:40:28
East Lowell 10 45 44N49 69w07 4:36:28
East Machias 15 41 44N45 67w24 4:29:36
East Madison 13 20 44N46 69w43 4:38:52
East Millinocket 10 9 45N38 68w35 4:34:20
East Monmouth 6 31 44N18 69w59 4:39:56
East Newport 10 6 44N49 69w13 4:36:52
East New Portland 13 44 44N53 70w06 4:40:24
East Northport 14 36 44N26 69w01 4:36:04
Easton 2 9 46N39 67w52 4:31:28
East Orland 5 44 44N34 68w43 4:34:52
East Orrington 10 4 44N44 68w50 4:35:20
East Otisfield 3 1 44N08 70w30 4:42:00
East Palermo 14 1 44N25 69w28 4:37:52
East Parsonfield 16 2 43N44 70w51 4:43:24
East Peru 9 17 44N29 70w23 4:41:32
East Pittston 6 6 44N14 69w47 4:39:08
East Poland 1 44 44N04 70w20 4:41:20
Eastport 15 44 44N54 67w00 4:28:00
East Sebago 3 35 43N51 70w39 4:42:36
East Stoneham 9 1 44N21 70w49 4:43:16
East Sullivan 5 33 44N29 68w08 4:32:32
East Sumner 9 32 44N17 70w22 4:41:28
East Surry 5 32 44N33 68w27 4:33:48
East Thorndike 14 1 44N35 69w17 4:37:08
East Troy 14 1 44N40 69w14 4:36:56
East Union 7 7 44N13 69w17 4:37:08
East Vassalboro 6 45 44N27 69w36 4:38:24
East Waterboro 16 45 43N34 70w41 4:42:44
East Waterford 9 4 44N12 70w41 4:42:44
East Wilton 4 6 44N37 70w12 4:40:48
East Windham 3 31 43N44 70w26 4:41:44
East Winn 10 32 45N22 68w17 4:33:08
East Winthrop 6 6 44N19 69w54 4:39:36
Eaton 15 4 45N40 67w52 4:31:28
Eddington 10 4 44N49 68w39 4:34:36
Eden 5 1 44N26 68w17 4:33:08
Edes Falls 3 1 43N58 70w37 4:42:28
Edgecomb 8 27 43N58 69w38 4:38:32
Edinburg 10 1 45N11 68w40 4:34:40
Edmunds 15 24 44N54 67w14 4:28:56
Eggemoggin 5 1 44N17 68w42 4:34:48
Egypt 5 32 44N33 68w27 4:33:48
Eliot 16 4 43N07 70w47 4:43:08
Elizabeth Park 3 44 43N38 70w16 4:41:04
Ellingswood Corner 14 4 44N38 68w51 4:35:24
Elliottsville Plantation 11 1 45N24 69w26 4:37:44
Ellis Pond 9 45 44N37 70w35 4:42:20
Ellsworth 5 32 44N33 68w25 4:33:40
Ellsworth Falls 5 32 44N33 68w27 4:33:48
Embden 13 1 44N54 69w56 4:39:44
Emery Mills 16 1 43N30 70w51 4:43:24
Emerys Bridge 16 44 43N14 70w49 4:43:16
Emerys Corner 16 1 43N41 70w48 4:43:12
Enfield 10 34 45N15 68w36 4:34:24
English 2 39 46N42 68w00 4:32:00
E Plantation 2 1 46N29 67w56 4:31:44
Estabrook Settlement 2 1 45N57 67w50 4:31:20
Estcourt Station 2 1 46N40 67w55 4:31:40
Estes Lake 16 14 43N26 70w46 4:43:04
Etna 10 45 44N49 69w07 4:36:28
Eustis 4 1 45N13 70w29 4:41:56
Exeter 10 6 44N58 69w09 4:36:36
Exeter Mills 10 6 45N00 69w01 4:36:04
Fairbanks 4 8 44N40 70w09 4:40:36
Fairfield 13 8 44N37 69w40 4:38:40
Fairmount 2 18 46N46 67w50 4:31:20
Falmouth 3 44 43N44 70w14 4:40:56
Farmingdale 6 6 44N16 69w50 4:39:20
Farmington 4 8 44N40 70w09 4:40:36
Farmington Falls 4 8 44N37 70w05 4:40:20
Farwells Corner 14 1 44N40 69w14 4:36:56
Fayette 6 44 44N27 70w04 4:40:16
Felch Corner 16 1 43N41 70w48 4:43:12
Ferry Beach 16 44 43N31 70w27 4:41:48
Five Corners 13 1 44N55 69w25 4:37:40
Five Corners 16 44 43N18 70w44 4:42:56
Five Islands 12 1 43N49 69w43 4:38:52
Five Points 16 16 43N29 70w27 4:41:48
Fletchers Landing 5 32 44N33 68w27 4:33:48
Foggs Corner 1 1 44N11 70w08 4:40:32
Forest City 15 1 45N32 67w46 4:31:04
Fort Fairfield 2 18 46N46 67w50 4:31:20
Fort Hill 16 16 43N29 70w27 4:41:48
Fort Kent 2 11 47N15 68w36 4:34:24
Fort Kent Mills 2 11 47N14 68w35 4:34:20
Fort Kent Village 2 11 47N15 68w36 4:34:24
Fortunes Rocks 16 16 43N29 70w27 4:41:48
Fort Williams 3 44 43N38 70w16 4:41:04
Fosters Corner 14 1 44N33 69w07 4:36:28
Fosters Corners 3 31 43N44 70w26 4:41:44
Four Corners 16 48 43N23 70w33 4:42:12
Frankfort 14 4 44N37 68w53 4:35:32
Franklin 5 33 44N35 68w14 4:32:56
Freedom 14 9 44N29 69w20 4:37:20
Freeport 3 8 43N52 70w06 4:40:24
Frenchboro 5 1 44N07 68w22 4:33:28
Frenchville 2 11 47N17 68w23 4:33:32
Friendship 7 1 43N59 69w20 4:37:20
Frye 9 45 44N37 70w35 4:42:20
Fryeburg 9 45 44N01 70w59 4:43:56
Fryeburg Harbor 9 45 44N01 70w59 4:43:56
Gardiner 6 6 44N14 69w47 4:39:08
Garfield Plantation 2 1 46N37 68w28 4:33:52
Garland 10 40 45N02 69w10 4:36:40
Georges River 7 7 44N07 69w15 4:37:00
Georgetown 12 1 43N48 69w44 4:38:56
Gerrishville 5 1 44N24 68w05 4:32:20
Gerry 10 6 44N56 68w40 4:34:40
Gilead 9 45 44N24 70w59 4:43:56
Glenburn 10 45 44N54 68w50 4:35:20
Glenburn Center 10 14 44N49 68w45 4:35:00
Glen Cove 7 7 44N08 69w06 4:36:24
Glendon 8 26 44N06 69w23 4:37:32
Glenmere 7 1 43N58 69w12 4:36:48
Glenwood Plantation 2 1 45N48 68w06 4:32:24
Goodings 2 39 46N42 68w00 4:32:00
Good Will Farm 13 1 44N41 69w38 4:38:32
Goodwins Mills 16 14 43N29 70w43 4:42:52
Goose Rocks Beach 16 44 43N22 70w29 4:41:56
Gorham 3 44 43N42 70w27 4:41:48
Gotts Island 5 1 44N16 68w19 4:33:16
Gould Landing 10 14 44N49 68w45 4:35:00
Gouldsboro 5 1 44N27 68w02 4:32:08
Grand Beach 16 44 43N31 70w23 4:41:32
Grand Falls Plantation 10 1 45N10 68w20 4:33:20
Grand Isle 2 9 47N16 68w08 4:32:32
Grand Lake Stream 15 1 45N11 67w46 4:31:04
Grand Lake Stream Plantati 15 1 45N13 67w44 4:30:56
Granite Hill 6 6 44N16 69w47 4:39:08
Gray 3 1 43N53 70w20 4:41:20
Great Diamond Island 3 45 44N51 68w20 4:33:20
Great Pond 5 45 44N51 68w20 4:33:20
Great Works 10 6 44N56 68w40 4:34:40
Greeley Landing 11 34 45N11 69w13 4:36:52
Greenbush 10 45 45N04 68w35 4:34:20
Greene 1 45 44N12 70w08 4:40:32
Greenfield 10 1 45N03 68w29 4:33:56
Green Lake 5 45 44N40 68w33 4:34:12
Greens Corner 14 1 44N40 69w14 4:36:56
Greenville 11 19 45N28 69w35 4:38:20
Greenwood 9 1 44N20 70w40 4:42:40
Grimes Mill 2 47 46N52 68w01 4:32:04
Grindstone 10 1 45N37 68w35 4:34:20
Grindstone Neck 5 1 44N24 68w05 4:32:20
Grove 15 1 45N00 67w26 4:29:44
Groveville 16 44 43N41 70w27 4:41:48
Guerette 2 1 47N03 68w08 4:32:32
Guilford 11 3 45N10 69w23 4:37:32
Guillemette 16 14 43N26 70w46 4:43:04
Guinea Corner 16 16 43N29 70w27 4:41:48
Guiou 2 39 46N42 68w00 4:32:00
Hacketts Mills 1 1 44N05 70w19 4:41:16
Haines Corner 1 44 44N25 70w07 4:40:28
Halldale 14 1 44N35 69w17 4:37:08
Hallowell 6 6 44N17 69w48 4:39:12

MAINE

Hall Quarry 5 2 44N22 68W20 4:33:20
Hamlin 2 11 47N09 67W56 4:31:44
Hamlin Plantation 2 1 47N05 67W53 4:31:32
Hammond Plantation 2 1 46N13 67W57 4:31:48
Hampden 10 4 44N44 68W53 4:35:32
Hampden Compact 10 14 44N45 68W50 4:35:20
Hampden Highlands 10 14 44N44 68W51 4:35:24
Hancock 5 33 44N32 68W17 4:33:08
Hancock Point 5 33 44N32 68W15 4:33:00
Hanover 9 1 44N30 70W43 4:42:52
Harborside 5 1 44N21 68W49 4:35:16
Harmon Beach 3 1 43N46 70W32 4:42:08
Harmons Corner 1 13 44N06 70W14 4:40:56
Harmony 13 31 44N58 69W33 4:38:12
Harpswell 3 1 43N47 69W58 4:39:52
Harrimans Point 8 27 44N00 69W40 4:38:40
Harrington 15 35 44N37 67W49 4:31:16
Harrison 3 49 44N06 70W39 4:42:36
Hartford 9 45 44N23 70W20 4:41:20
Hartland 13 45 44N53 69W27 4:37:48
Harts Neck 7 1 43N58 69W12 4:36:48
Haskell Corner 1 13 44N06 70W14 4:40:56
Hatch's Corner 8 8 44N06 69W44 4:38:56
Hayford Corner 14 36 44N26 69W01 4:36:04
Haynesville 2 1 45N50 67W59 4:31:56
Head Of Tide 14 36 44N26 69W01 4:36:04
Head Tide 8 1 44N06 69W36 4:38:24
Hebron 9 45 44N12 70W23 4:41:32
Hendricks Harbor 8 1 43N49 69W41 4:38:44
Hermon 10 4 44N49 68W55 4:35:40
Hermon Center 10 14 44N49 68W45 4:35:00
Heron Island 8 1 43N52 69W34 4:38:16
Hersey 2 1 46N04 68W23 4:33:32
Higgins Beach 3 5 43N35 70W21 4:41:24
Higginsville 10 45 44N55 68W56 4:35:44
Highland 7 7 44N07 69W15 4:37:00
Highland Lake 3 44 43N41 70W21 4:41:24
Highland Lake Vista 3 31 43N44 70W26 4:41:44
Highland Plantation 13 1 45N03 70W05 4:40:20
Highpine 16 33 43N19 70W35 4:42:20
Hills Beach 16 16 43N29 70W27 4:41:48
Hillside 3 45 43N48 70W40 4:42:40
Hinckley 13 45 44N41 69W38 4:38:32
Hiram 9 2 43N52 70W50 4:43:20
Hodgdon 2 1 46N03 67W52 4:31:28
Holden 10 4 44N45 68W39 4:34:36
Hollandville 16 1 43N41 70W48 4:43:12
Hollis 16 6 43N37 70W37 4:42:28
Holmes Mill 14 36 44N26 69W01 4:36:04
Hope 7 1 44N15 69W11 4:36:44
Houghton 9 45 44N40 70W36 4:42:24
Houlton 2 11 46N08 67W51 4:31:24
Howes Corners 1 1 44N15 70W22 4:41:28
Howes Corners 10 1 44N46 69W13 4:36:52
Howland 10 45 45N14 68W40 4:34:40
Hoytown 15 41 44N43 67W28 4:29:52
Hudson 10 45 45N00 68W53 4:35:32
Hulls Cove 5 1 44N25 68W15 4:33:00
Hunnewell Hill 3 5 43N35 70W21 4:41:24
Hunts Corner 9 37 44N25 70W48 4:43:12
Hutchins Corner 11 1 45N02 69W36 4:38:24
Indian Island 10 6 44N56 68W40 4:34:40
Indian Point 5 2 44N22 68W20 4:33:20
Indian Point 15 47 45N10 67W16 4:29:04
Indian River 15 35 44N37 67W45 4:31:00
Indian Township Passamaquodd 15 1 45N13 67W34 4:30:16
Industrial 2 39 46N42 68W00 4:32:00
Industry 4 1 44N45 70W03 4:40:12
Ingall's Hill 3 1 44N03 70W43 4:42:52
Intervale 3 1 43N57 70W16 4:41:04
Irish Settlement 15 4 45N40 67W52 4:31:28
Island Falls 2 45 46N01 68W16 4:33:04
Isle au Haut 7 1 44N04 68W38 4:34:32
Isle of Springs 8 1 43N51 69W38 4:38:32
Islesboro 14 1 44N18 68W54 4:35:36
Islesford 5 1 44N16 68W14 4:32:56
Jackman 13 4 45N37 70W14 4:40:56
Jackson 14 1 44N37 69W09 4:36:36
Jackson Corners 14 1 44N33 69W07 4:36:28
Jacksonville 15 45 44N46 67W24 4:29:36
Jay 4 44 44N30 70W13 4:40:52
Jefferson 8 1 44N13 69W27 4:37:48
Jemtland 2 11 47N03 68W08 4:32:32
Jonesboro 15 1 44N40 67W35 4:30:20
Jones Corner 14 1 44N25 69W28 4:37:52
Jonesport 15 1 44N32 67W37 4:30:28
Jonesport Center 15 1 44N32 67W37 4:30:28
Kalers Corner 8 26 44N06 69W23 4:37:32
Keegan 2 9 47N09 67W56 4:31:44
Kenduskeag 10 45 44N55 68W56 4:35:44
Kennebago Lake 4 1 44N58 70W39 4:42:36
Kennebec 15 41 44N43 67W28 4:29:52
Kennebunk 16 48 43N23 70W33 4:42:12
Kennebunk Beach 16 48 43N23 70W33 4:42:12
Kennebunk Landing 16 48 43N23 70W33 4:42:12
Kennebunk Lower Village 16 44 43N22 70W29 4:41:56
Kennebunkport 16 44 43N23 70W27 4:41:48
Kennedy Terrace 2 11 47N09 67W56 4:31:44
Kents Hill 6 1 44N24 70W00 4:40:00
Kezar Falls 16 1 43N48 70W53 4:43:32
Kingfield 4 1 44N58 70W09 4:40:36
Kingman 10 35 45N33 68W12 4:32:48
Kingsbury Plantation 11 1 45N10 69W36 4:38:24
Kings Grant 3 44 43N38 70W16 4:41:04
Kinney Cove 15 4 45N40 67W52 4:31:28
Kinney Shores 16 44 43N31 70W27 4:41:48
Kittery 16 4 43N05 70W45 4:43:00
Kittery Point 16 4 43N05 70W42 4:42:48
Knights Landing 11 1 45N18 69W02 4:36:08
Knightville 3 44 43N38 70W16 4:41:04
Knowles Corner 2 47 46N08 68W10 4:32:40
Knox 14 1 44N31 69W14 4:36:56
Kokadjo 11 1 45N28 69W36 4:38:24
La Grange 10 45 45N10 68W50 4:35:20
Lake City 7 1 44N12 69W04 4:36:16
Lake Moxie 13 45 45N20 69W58 4:39:52
Lake Parlin 1 45N27 70W07 4:40:28
Lake View Plantation 11 1 45N22 68W53 4:35:32
Lakeville Plantation 10 1 45N21 68W04 4:32:16
Lakewood 13 6 44N46 69W43 4:38:52
Lambert Lake 15 1 45N33 67W32 4:30:08
Lamoine 5 1 44N29 68W18 4:33:12
Lamoine Beach 5 32 44N33 68W27 4:33:48
Larone 13 8 44N35 69W36 4:38:24
Larrabee 15 41 44N42 67W24 4:29:36
Lawry 7 1 43N59 69W20 4:37:20
Lebanon 16 45 43N24 70W55 4:43:40
Lee 10 32 45N22 68W17 4:33:08
Leeds 1 46 44N18 70W07 4:40:28
Leeds Center 1 46 44N21 70W08 4:40:32
Levant 10 45 44N52 68W58 4:35:52
Lewiston 1 14 44N06 70W13 4:40:52
Libby Hill 6 6 44N14 69W47 4:39:08
Liberty 14 1 44N24 69W18 4:37:12
Lille 2 11 47N17 68W07 4:32:28
Limerick 16 1 43N41 70W48 4:43:12
Limerick Mills 16 1 43N41 70W48 4:43:12
Limestone 2 11 46N55 67W50 4:31:20
Limington 16 34 43N45 70W42 4:42:48
Lincoln 10 6 45N22 68W30 4:34:00
Lincoln Compact 10 6 45N22 68W30 4:34:00
Lincoln Plantation 9 1 44N56 71W02 4:44:08
Lincolns Mills 10 6 44N55 69W16 4:37:04
Lincolnville 14 1 44N17 69W01 4:36:04
Linekin 8 1 43N52 69W35 4:38:20
Linneus 2 1 46N03 67W52 4:31:28
Lisbon 1 8 44N02 70W06 4:40:24
Lisbon Falls 1 8 44N00 70W04 4:40:16
Litchfield 6 6 44N10 69W57 4:39:48
Little Deer Isle 5 1 44N17 68W42 4:34:48
Little Falls 3 31 43N44 70W26 4:41:44
Littlefield 1 13 44N06 70W14 4:40:56
Little Machias 15 41 44N40 67W12 4:28:48
Littleton 2 47 46N14 67W51 4:31:24
Livermore 1 44 44N25 70W13 4:40:52
Livermore Falls 1 44 44N29 70W11 4:40:44
Locke Mills 9 37 44N24 70W42 4:42:48
Long Beach 3 1 43N46 70W32 4:42:08
Long Beach 16 4 43N11 70W37 4:42:28
Longcove 7 1 44N01 69W12 4:36:48
Long Island 3 44 43N40 70W17 4:41:08
Long Island Plantation 5 1 44N11 68W21 4:33:24
Long Pond 47 45N37 70W05 4:40:20
Lookout 7 1 44N05 68W38 4:34:32
Loring Air Force Base 2 1 46N55 67W50 4:31:20
Lovell 9 1 44N07 70W54 4:43:36
Lowell 10 1 45N12 68W28 4:33:52
Lowelltown 4 45N31 70W39 4:42:36
Lower Dennysville 15 24 44N54 67W14 4:28:56
Lubec 15 42 44N52 66W59 4:27:56
Lucerne 5 45 44N44 68W38 4:34:32
Ludlow 2 47 46N10 67W58 4:31:52
Lyman 16 1 43N29 70W38 4:42:32
Lynchville 9 1 44N21 70W49 4:43:16
Machias 15 41 44N43 67W28 4:29:52
Machiasport 15 41 44N40 67W23 4:29:32
Mackworth Point 3 44 43N42 70W15 4:41:00
MacMahan 12 1 43N55 69W50 4:39:20
Macwahoc 2 1 45N38 68W16 4:33:04
Macwahoc Plantation 2 1 45N38 68W16 4:33:04
Madawaska 2 11 47N21 68W20 4:33:20
Madawaska Lake 2 1 47N03 68W08 4:32:32
Madison 13 20 44N48 69W53 4:39:32
Madrid 4 1 44N55 70W26 4:41:44
Magalloway Plantation 9 1 44N52 71W01 4:44:04
Maine Coast Mall 5 32 44N33 68W27 4:33:48
Maine Mall 3 44 43N38 70W16 4:41:04
Mainstream 13 31 44N58 69W33 4:38:12
Mallison Falls 3 31 43N44 70W26 4:41:44
Manchester 6 4 44N20 69W52 4:39:28
Manset 5 1 44N16 68W19 4:33:16
Maple Grove 2 18 46N46 67W50 4:31:20
Mapleton 2 39 46N42 68W07 4:32:28
Maplewood 16 1 43N40 70W55 4:43:40
Margison 2 1 46N56 68W07 4:32:28
Mariaville 5 45 44N45 68W24 4:33:36
Marion 15 45 44N53 67W19 4:29:16
Marlboro 5 32 44N33 68W27 4:33:48
Marrtown 12 1 43N48 69W45 4:39:00
Marshfield 15 41 44N44 67W29 4:29:56
Mars Hill 2 11 46N31 67W52 4:31:28
Marshville 15 35 44N37 67W49 4:31:16
Marston Corner 1 13 44N06 70W14 4:40:56
Martin 7 1 43N59 69W20 4:37:20
Martinsville 7 1 43N58 69W12 4:36:48
Masardis 2 47 46N30 68W22 4:33:28
Mason Bay 15 1 44N32 67W37 4:30:28
Mast Landing 3 8 43N52 70W06 4:40:24
Matinicus 7 1 43N52 68W53 4:35:32
Matinicus Isle Plantation 7 1 43N52 68W54 4:35:36
Mattawamkeag 10 32 45N32 68W21 4:33:24
Maxfield 10 1 45N17 68W45 4:35:00
Mayberry Hill 3 1 44N00 70W32 4:42:08
Mayville 9 37 44N25 70W48 4:43:12
McFarlands Corner 14 1 44N32 69W18 4:37:12
Mechanic Falls 1 6 44N06 70W25 4:41:40
Meddybemps 15 1 45N02 67W21 4:29:24
Medford 11 47 45N17 68W51 4:35:24
Medomak 8 1 44N00 69W25 4:37:40
Medway 10 1 45N35 68W31 4:34:04
Melvin Heights 7 1 44N12 69W04 4:36:16
Mercer 13 31 44N41 69W56 4:39:44
Merepoint 3 8 43N50 70W01 4:40:04
Merrill 2 1 46N10 68W15 4:33:00
Mexico 9 44 44N34 70W33 4:42:12
Middledam 9 1 44N38 70W45 4:43:00
Middle Intervale 9 37 44N25 70W48 4:43:12
Milbridge 15 1 44N32 67W53 4:31:32
Milford 10 6 44N57 68W39 4:34:36
Milliken Mills 16 44 43N31 70W23 4:41:32
Millinocket 10 10 45N39 68W43 4:34:52
Milltown 15 47 45N10 67W16 4:29:04
Milo 11 4 45N15 68W59 4:35:56
Milton 9 44 44N23 70W39 4:42:36
Minot 1 34 44N08 70W20 4:41:20
Minturn 5 1 44N09 68W26 4:33:44
Molunkus 2 35 45N33 68W12 4:32:48
Monarda 2 47 45N52 68W23 4:33:32
Monhegan 8 1 43N46 69W19 4:37:16
Monmouth 6 31 44N14 70W02 4:40:08
Monroe 14 1 44N36 69W01 4:36:04
Monson 11 19 45N17 69W30 4:38:00
Monticello 2 47 46N19 67W51 4:31:24
Montsweag 12 27 44N00 69W40 4:38:40
Montville 14 36 44N27 69W16 4:37:04
Moody 16 6 43N16 70W36 4:42:24
Moody Beach 16 6 43N16 70W36 4:42:24
Moody Mountain 14 1 44N13 69W17 4:37:08
Moosehead 11 1 45N28 69W37 4:38:28
Moose River 13 4 45N39 70W16 4:41:04
Moro Plantation 2 1 46N10 68W21 4:33:24
Morrill 14 36 44N26 69W09 4:36:36
Morse Corners 10 6 44N55 69W16 4:37:04
Moscow 13 38 45N05 69W52 4:39:28
Mount Chase Plantation 10 1 46N03 68W28 4:33:52
Mount Desert 5 2 44N22 68W20 4:33:20
Mount Pisgah 8 1 43N51 69W38 4:38:32
Mount Vernon 6 4 44N28 69W58 4:39:52
Mousam Lake 16 1 43N32 70W55 4:43:40
Murphy Corner 12 27 44N00 69W40 4:38:40
Muscongus 8 1 44N00 69W25 4:37:40
Muscongus Bay 8 26 44N05 69W29 4:37:56
Naples 3 1 43N58 70W37 4:42:28
Nashville Plantation 2 1 46N42 68W29 4:33:56
Naskeag 5 1 44N16 68W34 4:34:16
Naval Base 16 4 43N04 70W47 4:43:08
Neadeauville 10 32 45N31 68W21 4:33:24
Nequasset 12 15 43N55 69W48 4:39:12
Newagen 8 1 43N47 69W39 4:38:36
New Auburn 1 13 44N06 70W14 4:40:56
Newburgh 10 1 44N43 69W01 4:36:04
New Canada Plantation 2 1 47N11 68W32 4:34:08
Newcastle 8 35 44N02 69W32 4:38:08
Newfield 16 1 43N38 70W54 4:43:36
New Gloucester 3 31 43N49 70W21 4:41:24
Newhall 3 31 43N44 70W26 4:41:44
New Harbor 8 1 43N52 69W30 4:38:00
New Limerick 2 47 46N07 67W58 4:31:52
New Meadows 12 1 43N55 69W50 4:39:20
Newport 10 6 44N50 69W17 4:37:08
New Portland 13 44 44N55 70W01 4:40:04
Newry 9 1 44N31 70W50 4:43:20
New Sharon 4 31 44N39 70W01 4:40:04
New Sweden 2 10 46N59 68W07 4:32:28
Newtown 16 16 43N29 70W27 4:41:48
New Vineyard 4 1 44N48 70W07 4:40:28
Nicolin 5 32 44N33 68W27 4:33:48
Nobleboro 8 26 44N05 69W29 4:37:56
Nobleborough 8 26 44N06 69W29 4:37:56
Norcross 45 45N38 68W48 4:35:12
Norridgewock 13 31 44N42 69W51 4:39:24
North Alfred 16 14 43N29 70W43 4:42:52
North Amity 2 1 45N57 67W50 4:31:20
North Anson 13 4 44N51 69W54 4:39:36
North Auburn 1 13 44N06 70W14 4:40:56
North Baldwin 3 34 43N48 70W40 4:42:40
North Bangor 10 14 44N49 68W45 4:35:00
North Bath 12 15 43N55 69W50 4:39:20
North Belgrade 6 35 44N27 69W50 4:39:20
North Berwick 16 44 43N18 70W44 4:42:56
North Bethel 9 37 44N25 70W48 4:43:12
North Blue Hill 5 3 44N25 68W36 4:34:24
North Bradford 10 1 45N04 69W04 4:36:16

North Brewer 10 14 44N47 68w46 4:35:04
North Bridgton 3 3 44N06 70w50 4:43:20
North Brooklin 5 1 44N18 68w34 4:34:16
North Brooksville 5 1 44N21 68w45 4:35:00
North Buckfield 9 32 44N17 70w22 4:41:28
North Carmel 10 45 44N48 69w03 4:36:12
North Castine 5 44 44N34 68w44 4:34:56
North Cutler 15 41 44N44 67w24 4:29:36
North Dixmont 10 1 44N41 69w10 4:36:40
North East Carry 11 1 45N41 69w44 4:38:56
Northeast Harbor 5 1 44N18 68w17 4:33:08
North Edgecomb 8 27 43N59 69w39 4:38:36
North Ellsworth 5 32 44N33 68w27 4:33:48
North Fairfield 13 8 44N35 69w36 4:38:24
North Falmouth 3 44 43N42 70w15 4:41:00
Northfield 15 1 44N50 67w35 4:30:20
North Fryeburg 9 45 44N07 70w58 4:43:52
North Gorham 3 44 43N46 70w32 4:42:08
North Gray 3 1 43N53 70w20 4:41:20
North Guilford 11 3 45N10 69w24 4:37:36
North Harpswell 3 1 43N45 70w01 4:40:04
North Haven 7 1 44N08 68w53 4:35:32
North Hill 9 32 44N17 70w22 4:41:28
North Jay 4 8 44N33 70w14 4:40:56
North Lebanon 16 45 43N25 70w52 4:43:28
North Leeds 1 46 44N21 70w08 4:40:32
North Limington 16 34 43N48 70w39 4:42:36
North Litchfield 6 6 44N13 69w56 4:39:44
North Livermore 1 44 44N28 70w11 4:40:44
North Lovell 9 1 44N21 70w49 4:43:16
North Lubec 15 42 44N52 67w01 4:28:04
North Lyndon 2 1 46N52 68w01 4:32:04
North Monmouth 6 31 44N17 70w02 4:40:08
North Monroe 14 1 44N37 69w01 4:36:04
North Newcastle 8 35 44N02 69w33 4:38:12
North Newport 10 6 44N55 69w16 4:37:04
North New Portland 13 44 44N53 70w06 4:40:24
North Nobleboro 8 26 44N06 69w23 4:37:32
North Norway 9 25 44N13 70w32 4:42:08
North Orland 5 44 44N44 68w38 4:34:32
North Orrington 10 4 44N44 68w50 4:35:20
North Palermo 14 1 44N25 69w28 4:37:52
North Paris 9 30 44N20 70w35 4:42:20
North Parsonfield 16 2 43N49 70w53 4:43:32
North Penobscot 5 1 44N28 68w43 4:34:52
North Perry 15 44 44N58 67w05 4:28:20
North Pittston 6 6 44N14 69w47 4:39:08
Northport 14 36 44N21 68w59 4:35:56
North Pownal 3 1 43N54 70w14 4:40:56
North Raymond 3 1 44N02 70w22 4:41:28
North Scarborough 3 5 43N35 70w21 4:41:24
North Searsmont 14 36 44N26 69w01 4:36:04
North Searsport 14 45 44N28 68w55 4:35:40
North Sebago 3 35 43N51 70w39 4:42:36
North Sedgwick 5 1 44N18 68w37 4:34:28
North Shapleigh 16 1 43N36 70w53 4:43:32
North Sullivan 5 33 44N32 68w15 4:33:00
North Turner 1 1 44N20 70w15 4:41:00
North Vassalboro 6 45 44N29 69w37 4:38:28
North Wade 2 47 46N47 68w09 4:32:36
North Waldoboro 8 26 44N06 69w23 4:37:32
North Warren 7 7 44N07 69w15 4:37:00
North Waterboro 16 45 43N37 70w44 4:42:56
North Waterford 9 4 44N14 70w46 4:43:04
North Wayne 6 46 44N21 70w04 4:40:16
Northwest Bethel 9 37 44N25 70w48 4:43:12
North Whitefield 8 1 44N13 69w35 4:38:20
North Windham 3 31 43N50 70w26 4:41:44
North Windsor 6 1 44N22 69w33 4:38:12
North Woodstock 9 44 44N23 70w39 4:42:36
North Yarmouth 3 8 43N50 70w15 4:41:00
Norumbega 5 1 44N21 68w45 4:35:00
Norway 9 25 44N13 70w32 4:42:08
Norway Lake 9 25 44N13 70w32 4:42:08
Number Four 9 1 44N08 70w53 4:43:32
Oakfield 2 47 46N05 68w08 4:32:32
Oak Hill 1 45 44N02 70w22 4:41:28
Oak Hill 3 5 43N35 70w21 4:41:24
Oakland 6 6 44N33 69w43 4:38:52
Oak Ridge 16 16 43N29 70w27 4:41:48
Oak Terrace 16 4 43N05 70w45 4:43:00
Ocean Park 16 44 43N30 70w23 4:41:32
Ocean Point 8 1 43N49 69w36 4:38:24
Oceanside 16 4 43N11 70w37 4:42:28
Oceanview Harbor 3 5 43N35 70w21 4:41:24
Oceanville 5 1 44N09 68w40 4:34:40
Ogontz 13 1 45N41 69w44 4:38:56
Ogunquit 16 6 43N15 70w36 4:42:24
Olamon 10 45 45N07 68w37 4:34:28
Olde Mill Brook 3 5 43N35 70w21 4:41:24

Old Orchard Beach 16 44 43N31 70w23 4:41:32
Old Town 10 6 44N56 68w39 4:34:36
Onawa 11 19 45N17 69w30 4:38:00
Oquossoc 4 45 44N58 70w46 4:43:04
Orffs Corner 8 26 44N06 69w23 4:37:32
Orient 2 1 45N49 67w50 4:31:20
Orland 5 44 44N33 68w42 4:34:48
Orono 10 31 44N53 68w40 4:34:40
Orrington 10 4 44N44 68w47 4:35:08
Orrington Center 10 4 44N44 68w50 4:35:20
Orrs Island 3 1 43N46 69w59 4:39:56
Osborn Plantation 5 45 44N47 68w16 4:33:04
Otis 5 45 44N42 68w28 4:33:52
Otisfield 3 1 44N05 70w33 4:42:12
Otter Creek 5 1 44N19 68w12 4:32:48
Owls Head 7 7 44N05 69w04 4:36:16
Oxbow 2 1 46N25 68w28 4:33:52
Oxbow Plantation 2 1 46N25 68w30 4:34:00
Oxford 9 1 44N08 70w30 4:42:00
Palermo 14 1 44N23 69w27 4:37:48
Palmyra 13 1 44N51 69w22 4:37:28
Paris 9 30 44N16 70w30 4:42:00
Parker Head 12 1 43N49 69w49 4:39:16
Parkhurst 2 39 46N42 68w00 4:32:00
Parkman 11 1 45N07 69w26 4:37:44
Parsonfield 16 2 43N46 70w54 4:43:36
Passadumkeag 10 45 45N11 68w37 4:34:28
Patten 10 47 46N00 68w27 4:33:48
Peabbles Cove 3 44 43N38 70w16 4:41:04
Peaks Island 3 44 43N40 70w11 4:40:44
Pea Ridge 10 1 45N23 68w30 4:34:00
Pejepscot 12 1 43N58 70w01 4:40:04
Pemaquid 8 1 43N54 69w31 4:38:04
Pemaquid Beach 8 1 43N52 69w31 4:38:04
Pemaquid Harbor 8 1 43N53 69w31 4:38:04
Pembroke 15 24 44N57 67w11 4:28:44
Penley Corners 1 13 44N06 70w14 4:40:56
Penobscot 5 1 44N28 68w43 4:34:52
Penobscot Indian Reservation 10 1 46N21 68w34 4:34:16
Perham 2 47 46N53 68w14 4:32:56
Perry 2 39 46N42 68w00 4:32:00
Perry 15 44 44N58 67w05 4:28:20
Perrys Corner 16 1 43N41 70w48 4:43:12
Peru 9 17 44N30 70w27 4:41:48
Peter Dana Point 15 1 45N13 67w34 4:30:16
Phair 2 39 46N42 68w00 4:32:00
Phillips 4 1 44N49 70w21 4:41:24
Phippsburg 12 1 43N46 69w50 4:39:20
Pigeon Hill 15 1 44N32 67w53 4:31:32
Pike Corner 3 1 44N00 70w32 4:42:08
Pine Cliff 8 1 43N51 69w38 4:38:32
Pine Hill 16 4 43N10 70w36 4:42:24
Pine Park 16 44 43N31 70w23 4:41:32
Pine Point 3 5 43N35 70w21 4:41:24
Pittsfield 13 6 44N47 69w23 4:37:32
Pittston 6 6 44N11 69w42 4:38:48
Pittston Farm 13 6 45N54 69w58 4:39:52
Plaisted 2 47 47N06 68w35 4:34:20
Plantation No 14 15 24 44N55 67w20 4:29:20
Plantation No 21 15 1 45N09 67w37 4:30:28
Plantation No 33 5 45 44N58 68w18 4:33:12
Pleasant Beach 7 1 44N00 69w07 4:36:28
Pleasantdale 3 44 43N38 70w16 4:41:04
Pleasant Hill 3 44 43N42 70w15 4:41:00
Pleasant Lake 15 1 45N08 67w19 4:29:16
Pleasant Point 7 1 43N59 69w17 4:37:08
Pleasant Point Indian Res 15 44 44N58 67w05 4:28:20
Pleasant Pond 13 1 45N14 70w00 4:40:00
Pleasant Ridge Plantation 13 38 45N05 69w59 4:39:56
Pleasantville 7 7 44N07 69w15 4:37:00
Plummer Island 3 5 43N35 70w21 4:41:24
Plymouth 10 1 44N47 69w13 4:36:52
Poland 1 44 44N03 70w23 4:41:32
Pond Cove 3 44 43N38 70w16 4:41:04
Poors Mills 14 36 44N26 69w01 4:36:04
Popham Beach 12 1 43N49 69w49 4:39:16
Portage 2 47 46N46 68w29 4:33:56
Port Clyde 7 1 43N56 69w16 4:37:04
Porter 9 2 43N49 70w55 4:43:40
Porterfield 9 2 43N49 70w53 4:43:32
Porter Landing 3 8 43N52 70w06 4:40:24
Portland 3 44 43N39 70w16 4:41:04
Pownal 3 1 43N53 70w11 4:40:44
Pownal Center 3 1 43N54 70w14 4:40:56
Prentiss 10 1 45N24 68w08 4:32:32
Prentiss Plantation 10 1 45N30 68w07 4:32:28
Presque Isle 2 21 46N41 68w01 4:32:04
Prides Corner 3 44 43N41 70w21 4:41:24
Princeton 15 1 45N13 67w34 4:30:16
Promenade Mall 1 14 44N06 70w12 4:40:48
Promised Land 1 6 44N06 70w23 4:41:32
Prospect 14 4 44N33 68w52 4:35:28
Prospect Ferry 14 1 44N29 68w59 4:35:56
Prospect Harbor 5 1 44N24 68w02 4:32:08
Prouts Neck 3 5 43N35 70w21 4:41:24
Pulpit Harbor 7 1 44N08 68w53 4:35:32
Pumpkin Valley 3 1 44N03 70w43 4:42:52
Quimby 2 47 46N58 68w36 4:34:24
Randolph 6 6 44N14 69w46 4:39:04
Rangeley 4 3 44N58 70w39 4:42:36
Rangeley Plantation 4 1 44N53 70w41 4:42:44
Raymond 3 1 43N55 70w28 4:41:52

MAINE

Rayville 3 1 44N08 70w30 4:42:00
Razorville 7 1 44N16 69w22 4:37:28
Reach 5 1 44N13 68w41 4:34:44
Readfield 6 31 44N23 69w57 4:39:48
Redbank Village 3 44 43N38 70w16 4:41:04
Red Beach 15 47 45N10 67w16 4:29:04
Redding 9 1 44N22 70w27 4:41:48
Reed Plantation 2 2 45N40 68w06 4:32:24
Reeds 4 1 44N49 70w21 4:41:24
Remick Corners 16 4 43N05 70w45 4:43:00
Richmond 12 8 44N05 69w48 4:39:12
Richmond Mill 6 46 44N21 70w04 4:40:16
Richville 3 1 43N46 70w32 4:42:08
Ridlonville 9 44 44N34 70w33 4:42:12
Rileys 4 44 44N30 70w13 4:40:52
Ripley 13 40 45N00 69w24 4:37:36
Ripley 15 35 44N37 67w49 4:31:16
Riverview 2 39 46N42 68w00 4:32:00
Robbinston 15 1 45N04 67w09 4:28:36
Robinson 2 11 46N31 67w52 4:31:28
Robinson Corner 1 14 44N06 70w12 4:40:48
Robyville 10 45 44N55 68w56 4:35:44
Rockland 7 7 44N06 69w07 4:36:28
Rockport 7 44 44N11 69w06 4:36:24
Rockville 7 7 44N08 69w09 4:36:36
Rockwood 13 1 45N41 69w45 4:39:00
Rogers Corners 14 1 44N40 69w14 4:36:56
Rome 6 1 44N34 69w53 4:39:32
Roque Bluffs 15 1 44N37 67w28 4:29:52
Ross Corner 16 1 43N32 70w43 4:42:52
Round Pond 8 1 43N57 69w28 4:37:52
Rowe Corners 1 13 44N06 70w14 4:40:56
Roxbury 9 45 44N38 70w37 4:42:28
Rumford 9 44 44N33 70w33 4:42:12
Rumford Corner 9 44 44N23 70w39 4:42:36
Rumford Junction 1 13 44N06 70w14 4:40:56
Rumford Point 9 44 44N30 70w40 4:42:40
Sabattus 1 45 44N07 70w04 4:40:16
Sabbathday Lake 3 1 44N02 70w22 4:41:28
Saco 16 14 43N30 70w27 4:41:48
Saint Agatha 2 1 47N14 68w20 4:33:20
Saint Albans 13 1 44N56 69w24 4:37:36
Saint Croix Junction 15 47 45N10 67w16 4:29:04
Saint David 2 11 47N20 68w14 4:32:56
Saint Francis 2 11 47N10 68w54 4:35:36
Saint Francis College 16 16 43N29 70w27 4:41:48
Saint Francis Plantation 2 1 47N09 68w53 4:35:32
Saint George 7 1 43N58 69w13 4:36:52
Saint John 2 1 47N15 68w36 4:34:24
Saint John Plantation 2 1 47N13 68w46 4:35:04
Saint Josephs College 3 31 43N50 70w26 4:41:44
Salem 4 1 44N54 70w17 4:41:08
Salmon Falls 15 47 45N10 67w16 4:29:04
Salmon Falls 16 6 43N37 70w36 4:42:24
Salsbury Cove 5 1 44N26 68w17 4:33:08
Sandhill Corner 8 1 44N16 69w33 4:38:12
Sandy Beach 10 14 44N49 68w45 4:35:00
Sandy Creek 3 1 44N03 70w43 4:42:52
Sandy Point 14 1 44N31 68w49 4:35:16
Sandy River Beach 15 1 44N32 67w37 4:30:28
Sandy River Plantation 4 1 44N55 70w33 4:42:12
Sanford 16 14 43N27 70w47 4:43:08
Sangerville 11 22 45N08 69w19 4:37:16
Sargentville 5 1 44N18 68w40 4:34:40
Saunders 2 39 46N42 68w00 4:32:00
Scarborough 3 5 43N35 70w21 4:41:24
Scituate 16 4 43N09 70w39 4:42:36
Scotland 16 4 43N09 70w39 4:42:36
Scott 2 39 46N42 68w00 4:32:00
Scribners Mills 3 1 44N07 70w41 4:42:44
Seabury 16 4 43N09 70w39 4:42:36
Seal Cove 5 1 44N18 68w24 4:33:36
Seal Harbor 5 1 44N18 68w14 4:32:56
Searsmont 14 1 44N22 69w11 4:36:44
Searsport 14 45 44N28 68w56 4:35:44
Seawall 5 1 44N16 68w19 4:33:16
Sebago 3 35 43N53 70w40 4:42:40
Sebago Lake 3 35 43N46 70w32 4:42:08
Sebasco Estates 12 1 43N46 69w52 4:39:28
Sebec 11 22 45N15 69w07 4:36:28
Sebec Corners 11 34 45N11 69w13 4:36:52
Sebec Lake 11 1 45N18 69w21 4:37:24
Seboeis 10 1 45N22 68w43 4:34:52
Seboomook 13 1 45N41 69w44 4:38:56
Sedgwick 5 1 44N18 68w37 4:34:28
Shady Nook 16 1 43N37 71w01 4:44:04
Shaker Village 3 1 44N02 70w22 4:41:28
Shapleigh 16 1 43N33 70w51 4:43:24
Shaw Mills 3 1 43N46 70w32 4:42:08
Shawmut 13 32 44N38 69w35 4:38:20
Sheepscott 8 27 44N00 69w40 4:38:40
Shepherds Hill 16 4 43N05 70w45 4:43:00
Sheridan 2 47 46N39 68w24 4:33:36
Sherman 2 47 45N54 68w23 4:33:32
Sherman Mills 2 47 45N52 68w23 4:33:32
Shermans Corner 14 36 44N26 69w01 4:36:04
Sherman Station 2 47 45N54 68w26 4:33:44
Sherwood Acres 3 44 43N38 70w16 4:41:04
Shin Pond 10 1 45N57 68w30 4:34:00
Shirley 11 19 45N22 69w37 4:38:28
Shirley Mills 11 19 45N22 69w37 4:38:28
Shore Acres 3 44 43N38 70w16 4:41:04

Place		Lat	Long	Time
Sidney 6	35	44N27	69w45	4:39:00
Silver Ridge 2	47	45N52	68w23	4:33:32
Simonton Corners 7	1	44N12	69w04	4:36:16
Simpson Corners 10	1	44N41	69w10	4:36:40
Sinclair 2	1	47N10	68w16	4:33:04
Skillings Corner 1	13	44N06	70w14	4:40:56
Skowhegan 13	6	44N46	69w43	4:38:52
Slab City 9	1	44N21	70w49	4:43:16
Slab City 14	1	44N18	69w07	4:36:28
Small Point 12	1	43N44	69w50	4:39:20
Smithfield 13	1	44N36	69w48	4:39:12
Smiths Mills 3	1	43N46	70w32	4:42:08
Smithville 15	1	44N31	67w58	4:31:52
Smyrna 2	47	46N09	68w06	4:32:24
Smyrna Mills 2	47	46N08	68w10	4:32:40
Soldier Pond 2	11	47N09	68w35	4:34:20
Solon 13	23	44N57	69w52	4:39:28
Somerville 8	1	44N16	69w33	4:38:12
Somerville Plantation 8	1	44N18	69w28	4:37:52
Somesville	2	44N22	68w20	4:33:20
Songo Lock 3	1	43N58	70w37	4:42:28
Sorrento 5	1	44N29	68w11	4:32:44
Sound 5	2	44N22	68w20	4:33:20
South Action 16	45	43N25	70w52	4:43:28
South Addison 15	35	44N37	67w45	4:31:00
South Andover 9	1	44N38	70w45	4:43:00
South Arm 9	1	44N38	70w45	4:43:00
South Bancroft 2	4	45N40	67w52	4:31:28
South Berwick 16	44	43N14	70w45	4:43:00
South Blue Hill 5	3	44N23	68w34	4:34:16
South Brewer 10	14	44N47	68w46	4:35:04
South Bridgton 3	3	44N03	70w43	4:42:52
South Bristol 8	1	43N54	69w34	4:38:16
South Buxton 16	44	43N41	70w27	4:41:48
South Casco 3	1	43N55	70w31	4:42:04
South China 6	1	44N24	69w34	4:38:16
South Deer Isle 5	1	44N09	68w40	4:34:40
South Dover 11	34	45N11	69w13	4:36:52
South Durham 1	8	43N52	70w06	4:40:24
South Eliot 16	4	43N06	70w47	4:43:08
South Etna 10	45	44N49	69w07	4:36:28
South Exeter 10	6	44N55	69w16	4:37:04
South Freeport 3	8	43N49	70w07	4:40:28
South Gardiner 6	6	44N13	69w47	4:39:08
South Gorham 3	44	43N41	70w27	4:41:48
South Gouldsboro 5	1	44N26	68w07	4:32:28
South Gray 3	1	43N53	70w20	4:41:20
South Harpswell 3	1	43N45	70w01	4:40:04
South Hiram 9	2	43N49	70w53	4:43:32
South Hollis 16	6	43N36	70w35	4:42:20
South Hope 7	1	44N13	69w17	4:37:08
South Jefferson 8	35	44N02	69w33	4:38:12
South Lagrange 10	47	45N07	68w49	4:35:16
South Lebanon 16	45	43N25	70w52	4:43:28
South Levant 10	45	44N52	68w56	4:35:44
South Lewiston 1	14	44N06	70w12	4:40:48
South Liberty 14	36	44N26	69w01	4:36:04
South Limington 16	34	43N41	70w48	4:43:12
South Lincoln 10	6	45N22	68w30	4:34:00
South Livermore 1	44	44N28	70w11	4:40:44
South Lubec 15	42	44N52	66w59	4:27:56
South Monmouth 6	31	44N14	70w02	4:40:08
South Montville 14	36	44N26	69w01	4:36:04
South Newcastle 8	27	43N59	69w39	4:38:36
South Orland 5	44	44N34	68w44	4:34:56
South Orrington 10	4	44N44	68w50	4:35:20
South Paris 9	30	44N14	70w31	4:42:04
South Parsonsfield 16	1	43N41	70w48	4:43:12
South Penobscot 5	1	44N28	68w43	4:34:52
Southport 8	9	43N49	69w40	4:38:40
South Portland 3	44	43N38	70w15	4:41:00
South Portland Gardens 3	44	43N38	70w16	4:41:04
South Portland Heights 3	44	43N38	70w16	4:41:04
South Princeton 15	1	45N13	67w34	4:30:16
South Rangeley 4	45	44N58	70w47	4:43:08
South Sanford 16	14	43N26	70w46	4:43:04
South Sebec 11	34	45N11	69w13	4:36:52
South Side 16	4	43N09	70w39	4:42:36
South Standish 3	1	43N40	70w36	4:42:24
South Surry 5	32	44N30	68w31	4:34:04
South Thomaston 7	44	44N03	69w08	4:36:32
South Union 7	7	44N07	69w15	4:37:00
South Waldoboro 8	26	44N06	69w23	4:37:32
South Waterford 9	4	44N10	70w43	4:42:52
Southwest Harbor 5	1	44N17	68w20	4:33:20
South Windham 3	31	43N44	70w26	4:41:44
South Windsor 6	1	44N19	69w35	4:38:20
South Woodstock 9	44	44N20	70w35	4:42:20
South Woodville 10	1	45N23	68w30	4:34:00
Spears Corner 6	6	44N14	69w47	4:39:08
Spragueville 2	39	46N42	68w00	4:32:00
Springfield 10	1	45N24	68w08	4:32:32
Springvale 16	14	43N28	70w48	4:43:12
Spruce Head 7	1	44N01	69w08	4:36:32
Spruce Point 8	1	43N51	69w38	4:38:32
Spruce Shores 8	1	43N52	69w35	4:38:20
Squa Pan 2	47	46N38	68w24	4:33:36
Squirrel Island 8	1	43N48	69w38	4:38:32
Stacyville 10	47	45N52	68w28	4:33:52
Standish 3	1	43N46	70w33	4:42:12
Starboard 15	41	44N39	67w23	4:29:32
Starks 13	1	44N44	69w58	4:39:52
State Road 2	39	46N42	68w00	4:32:00
Stebbins 2	18	46N46	67w50	4:31:20
Steep Falls 3	34	43N48	70w39	4:42:36
Stetson 10	1	44N53	69w08	4:36:32
Steuben 15	1	44N30	67w57	4:31:48
Stevens Corner 16	1	43N37	71w01	4:44:04
Stickney Corner 7	1	44N16	69w22	4:37:28
Stillwater 10	6	44N56	68w40	4:34:40
Stockholm 2	11	47N03	68w08	4:32:32
Stockton Springs 14	1	44N30	68w51	4:35:24
Stoneham 9	1	44N16	70w51	4:43:24
Stonington 5	1	44N09	68w40	4:34:40
Stow 9	1	44N10	70w59	4:43:56
Stratton 4	9	45N08	70w26	4:41:44
Stricklands 1	46	44N21	70w08	4:40:32
Strong 4	1	44N48	70w13	4:40:52
Sullivan 5	33	44N32	68w09	4:32:36
Sumner 9	32	44N23	70w26	4:41:44
Sunset 5	1	44N12	68w42	4:34:48
Sunshine 5	1	44N13	68w41	4:34:44
Surry 5	32	44N29	68w31	4:34:04
Sutton Island 5	1	44N18	68w17	4:33:08
Swans Island 5	1	44N10	68w27	4:33:48
Swanville 14	1	44N31	69w01	4:36:04
Sweden 2	10	46N57	68w08	4:32:32
Tacoma 6	6	44N13	69w56	4:39:44
Tallwood 6	31	44N23	69w58	4:39:52
Talmadge 15	1	45N20	67w44	4:30:56
Tatnic 16	44	43N18	70w44	4:42:56
Temple 4	1	44N42	70w17	4:41:08
Temple Heights 14	36	44N26	69w01	4:36:04
Tenants Harbor 7	1	43N58	69w12	4:36:48
The Forks Plantation 13	1	45N18	69w55	4:39:40
The Ledges 3	8	43N48	70w12	4:40:48
The Ridge 3	1	44N03	70w43	4:42:52
Thomaston 7	7	44N05	69w11	4:36:44
Thompson's Point 3	1	43N58	70w37	4:42:28
Thorndike 14	1	44N35	69w15	4:37:00
Thorndike Center 14	1	44N35	69w17	4:37:08
Thornton Heights 3	44	43N38	70w16	4:41:04
Tibbettstown 15	46	44N39	67w44	4:30:56
Topsfield 15	1	45N25	67w44	4:30:56
Topsham 12	1	43N58	69w57	4:39:48
Tory Hill 16	6	43N37	70w36	4:42:24
Town Farm Hill 3	1	44N07	70w41	4:42:44
Town House Corners 16	44	43N22	70w29	4:41:56
Tracy Corners 15	35	44N37	67w45	4:31:00
Trafton 2	47	46N38	68w24	4:33:36
Trainor Corner 8	6	44N14	69w47	4:39:08
Trap Corner 9	30	44N20	70w35	4:42:20
Tremont 5	1	44N16	68w23	4:33:32
Trenton 5	1	44N27	68w22	4:33:28
Trevett 8	15	43N53	69w40	4:38:40
Troutdale 13	45	45N20	69w58	4:39:52
Troy 14	1	44N41	69w15	4:37:00
Troy Center 14	1	44N40	69w14	4:36:56
Turbats Creek 16	44	43N22	70w29	4:41:56
Turner 1	1	44N16	70w15	4:41:00
Turner Center 1	1	44N16	70w13	4:40:52
Twelve Corners 6	44	44N28	70w11	4:40:44
Two Lights 3	44	43N38	70w16	4:41:04
Union 7	7	44N13	69w17	4:37:08
Unionville 15	35	44N36	67w56	4:31:44
Unity 14	45	44N37	69w20	4:37:20
Unity College 14	45	44N40	69w14	4:36:56
Unity Plantation 6	6	44N32	69w43	4:38:52
Upper Abbot 11	1	45N11	69w27	4:37:48
Upper Frenchville 2	11	47N17	68w26	4:33:44
Upper Gloucester 3	1	43N57	70w16	4:41:04
Upton 9	1	44N42	71w01	4:44:04
Van Buren 2	11	47N10	67w57	4:31:48
Vanceboro 15	43	45N34	67w26	4:29:44
Vassalboro 6	45	44N28	69w41	4:38:44
Veazie 10	14	44N51	68w43	4:34:52
Verona 5	33	44N32	68w47	4:35:08
Vienna 6	1	44N33	70w02	4:40:08
Viking Village 9	37	44N25	70w48	4:43:12
Vinalhaven 7	1	44N03	68w50	4:35:20
Violette 2	11	47N09	67w56	4:31:44
Wade 2	1	46N48	68w13	4:32:52
Waite 15	1	45N20	67w42	4:30:48
Waites Landing 3	44	43N42	70w15	4:41:00
Waldo 14	1	44N31	69w05	4:36:20
Waldoboro 8	26	44N06	69w23	4:37:32
Wales 1	1	44N10	70w03	4:40:12
Walkers Mill 9	37	44N25	70w48	4:43:12
Wallagrass 2	47	47N09	68w35	4:34:20
Walnut Hill 3	45	43N48	70w16	4:41:04
Walpole 8	1	43N57	69w32	4:38:08
Waltham 5	45	44N43	68w20	4:33:20
Wards Cove 3	1	43N46	70w32	4:42:08
Wardtown 3	8	43N52	70w06	4:40:24
Warren 7	7	44N08	69w15	4:37:00
Washburn 2	47	46N47	68w09	4:32:36
Washington 7	1	44N16	69w22	4:37:28
Waterboro 16	45	43N35	70w43	4:42:52
Waterford 9	4	44N11	70w43	4:42:52
Waterman Beach 7	1	44N00	69w07	4:36:28
Waterville 6	14	44N33	69w38	4:38:32
Waverly 13	6	44N47	69w23	4:37:32
Wayne 6	46	44N21	70w03	4:40:12
Webster 1	1	44N07	70w06	4:40:24
Webster 10	31	44N53	68w40	4:34:40
Webster Corner 1	8	44N02	70w06	4:40:24
Webster Plantation 10	1	45N28	68w09	4:32:36
Weeks Mills 4	31	44N38	70w02	4:40:08
Weeks Mills 6	1	44N22	69w33	4:38:12
Weld 4	1	44N42	70w25	4:41:40
Wellington 11	1	45N02	69w36	4:38:24
Wells 16	33	43N18	70w37	4:42:28
Wesley 15	1	44N57	67w40	4:30:40
West Appleton 7	36	44N26	69w01	4:36:04
West Athens 13	1	44N56	69w40	4:38:40
West Auburn 1	13	44N06	70w14	4:40:56
West Baldwin 3	34	43N50	70w47	4:43:08
West Bath 12	15	43N53	69w51	4:39:24
West Bethel 9	37	44N24	70w52	4:43:28
West Boothbay Harbor 8	3	43N51	69w38	4:38:32
West Bowdoin 12	31	44N03	70w01	4:40:04
West Bridgton 3	3	44N03	70w43	4:42:52
Westbrook 3	44	43N41	70w22	4:41:28
West Brooksville 5	1	44N21	68w45	4:35:00
West Buxton 16	1	43N40	70w36	4:42:24
West Charleston 10	1	45N05	69w03	4:36:12
West Corinth 10	6	45N00	69w01	4:36:04
West Cumberland 3	44	43N48	70w16	4:41:04
West Denmark 9	2	43N56	70w55	4:43:40
West Dresden 8	8	44N06	69w44	4:38:56
West Durham 1	8	43N52	70w06	4:40:24
West Ellsworth 5	32	44N33	68w27	4:33:48
West End 3	44	43N40	70w17	4:41:08
West Enfield 10	34	45N14	68w39	4:34:36
West Falmouth 3	44	43N42	70w15	4:41:00
West Farmington 4	8	44N40	70w10	4:40:40
Westfield 2	47	46N34	67w55	4:31:40
West Forks 13	1	45N20	69w58	4:39:52
West Forks Plantation 13	1	45N23	70w01	4:40:04
West Franklin 5	33	44N32	68w09	4:32:36
West Fryeburg 9	45	44N01	70w59	4:43:56
West Gardiner 6	6	44N13	69w52	4:39:28
West Georgetown 12	1	43N48	69w45	4:39:00
West Gorham 3	44	43N41	70w27	4:41:48
West Gouldsboro 5	1	44N29	68w08	4:32:32
West Gray 3	1	43N53	70w20	4:41:20
West Harpswell 3	1	43N45	70w01	4:40:04
West Harrington 15	35	44N37	67w49	4:31:16
West Hollis 16	6	43N36	70w35	4:42:20
West Jonesport 15	1	44N32	67w37	4:30:28
West Kennebunk 16	48	43N24	70w34	4:42:16
West Lebanon 16	45	43N25	70w52	4:43:28
West Leeds 1	46	44N21	70w08	4:40:32
West Levant 10	45	44N52	68w56	4:35:44
West Lovell 9	1	44N08	70w53	4:43:32
West Lubec 15	42	44N52	66w59	4:27:56
West Mills 4	8	44N40	70w09	4:40:36
West Minot 1	34	44N10	70w22	4:41:28
West Mount Vernon 6	4	44N30	69w59	4:39:56
West Newfield 16	1	43N39	70w56	4:43:44
West Old Town 10	6	44N56	68w40	4:34:40
Weston 2	1	45N44	67w52	4:31:28
West Paris 9	30	44N19	70w33	4:42:12
West Penobscot 5	1	44N28	68w43	4:34:52
West Peru 9	17	44N32	70w27	4:41:48
Westpoint 12	1	43N46	69w52	4:39:28
West Poland 1	44	44N02	70w26	4:41:44
Westport 8	27	44N00	69w40	4:38:40
Westport Island 8	15	43N56	69w42	4:38:48
West Princeton 15	1	45N13	67w34	4:30:16
West Rockport 7	1	44N11	69w08	4:36:32
West Scarborough 3	5	43N35	70w21	4:41:24
West Sebago 3	35	43N48	70w40	4:42:40
West Seboeis 10	47	45N32	68w53	4:35:32
West Southport 8	1	43N49	69w41	4:38:44
West Stonington 5	1	44N09	68w40	4:34:40
West Sullivan 5	33	44N32	68w14	4:32:56
West Sumner 9	32	44N22	70w27	4:41:48
West Tremont 5	1	44N16	68w24	4:33:36
West Waldoboro 8	26	44N06	69w23	4:37:32
West Washington 7	1	44N16	69w33	4:38:12
West Winterport 14	4	44N38	68w51	4:35:24
Whitefield 8	1	44N10	69w38	4:38:32
White Rock 3	44	43N41	70w27	4:41:48
Whites Corner 3	1	43N57	70w16	4:41:04
Whiting 15	41	44N45	67w16	4:29:04
Whitneyville 15	45	44N44	67w31	4:30:04
Wildes District 16	44	43N22	70w29	4:41:56
Wildwood Park 3	1	43N45	70w18	4:41:12
Wiley Corner 7	1	44N01	69w12	4:36:48
Willard 3	44	43N38	70w16	4:41:04
Williamsburg 11	1	45N18	69w02	4:36:08
Willimantic 11	1	45N18	69w23	4:37:32
Wilson Corner 5	32	44N33	68w27	4:33:48
Wilsons Mills 9	1	44N57	71w02	4:44:08
Wilton 4	6	44N36	70w14	4:40:56
Windemere 14	1	44N40	69w14	4:36:56
Windham 3	31	43N48	70w24	4:41:36
Windsor 6	1	44N19	69w35	4:38:20
Wings Mills 6	35	44N27	69w50	4:39:20

MAINE

Place		Lat.	Long.	Time
Winkumpaugh Corners 5	32	44N33	68w27	4:33:48
Winn 10	32	45N27	68w20	4:33:20
Winnecook 14	1	44N42	69w26	4:37:44
Winnegance 12	1	43N55	69w50	4:39:20
Winslow 6	14	44N33	69w37	4:38:28
Winslows Mills 8	26	44N06	69w23	4:37:32
Winter Harbor 5	1	44N24	68w05	4:32:20
Winterport 14	4	44N39	68w53	4:35:32
Winterville 2	47	46N58	68w34	4:34:16
Winthrop 6	6	44N18	69w58	4:39:52
Wiscasset 8	27	44N00	69w40	4:38:40
Wonsqueak Harbor 5	1	44N23	68w03	4:32:12
Woodfords 3	44	43N40	70w16	4:41:04
Woodland 15	29	45N09	67w25	4:29:40
Woodmans Mills 14	1	44N22	69w12	4:36:48
Woodstock 9	44	44N23	70w35	4:42:20
Woodville 10	32	45N30	68w28	4:33:52
Woolwich 12	15	43N57	69w47	4:39:08
Worthley Pond 9	17	44N29	70w23	4:41:32
Wrightville 2	47	46N39	68w24	4:33:36
Wyman 15	1	44N32	67w53	4:31:32
Wytopitlock 2	2	45N39	68w05	4:32:20
Yarmouth 3	8	43N48	70w11	4:40:44
York 16	28	43N10	70w40	4:42:40
York Beach 16	28	43N11	70w37	4:42:28
York Center 16	28	43N09	70w38	4:42:32
York Cliffs 16	28	43N10	70w36	4:42:24
York Corner 16	28	43N09	70w39	4:42:36
York Harbor 16	28	43N08	70w38	4:42:32
York Heights 16	28	43N09	70w39	4:42:36
Youngs Corner 1	13	44N06	70w14	4:40:56
Youngtown 14	1	44N18	69w07	4:36:28

TIME TABLES

Daylight time was unofficially observed in the greater Baltimore area various years during the 20's and 30's. Our tables reflect this informal usage of daylight time; however, caution must be advised during this period.

MD # 1
Before 11/18/1883 LMT
11/18/1883 12:00 EST
3/31/1918 02:00 EWT
10/27/1918 02:00 EST
3/30/1919 02:00 EWT
10/26/1919 02:00 EST
3/28/1920 02:00 EDT
10/31/1920 02:00 EST
4/30/1922 02:00 EDT
9/24/1922 02:00 EST
4/27/1924 02:00 EDT
9/28/1924 02:00 EST
4/26/1925 02:00 EDT
9/27/1925 02:00 EST
4/25/1926 02:00 EDT
9/26/1926 02:00 EST
4/27/1930 02:00 EDT
9/28/1930 02:00 EST
2/09/1942 02:00 EWT
9/30/1945 02:00 EST
4/27/1947 02:00 EDT
9/28/1947 02:00 EST
4/25/1948 02:00 EDT
9/26/1948 02:00 EST
4/24/1949 02:00 EDT
9/25/1949 02:00 EST
4/30/1950 02:00 EDT
9/24/1950 02:00 EST
4/29/1951 02:00 EDT
9/30/1951 02:00 EST
4/27/1952 02:00 EDT
9/28/1952 02:00 EST
4/26/1953 02:00 EDT
9/27/1953 02:00 EST
4/25/1954 02:00 EDT
9/26/1954 02:00 EST
4/24/1955 02:00 EDT
9/25/1955 02:00 EST
4/29/1956 02:00 EDT
9/29/1956 02:00 EST
4/28/1957 02:00 US#4

MD # 2
Before 11/18/1883 LMT
11/18/1883 12:00 EST
3/31/1918 02:00 EWT
10/27/1918 02:00 EST
3/30/1919 02:00 EWT
10/26/1919 02:00 EST
2/09/1942 02:00 EWT
9/30/1945 02:00 EST
4/24/1955 02:00 EDT
9/25/1955 02:00 EST
4/29/1956 02:00 EDT
9/30/1956 02:00 EST
4/30/1967 02:00 US#2

MD # 3
Before 11/18/1883 LMT
11/18/1883 12:00 EST
3/31/1918 02:00 EWT
10/27/1918 02:00 EST
3/30/1919 02:00 EWT
10/26/1919 02:00 EST
2/09/1942 02:00 EWT
9/30/1945 02:00 EST
4/27/1947 02:00 US#4

MD # 4
Before 11/18/1883 LMT
11/18/1883 12:00 EST
3/31/1918 02:00 EWT
10/27/1918 02:00 EST
3/30/1919 02:00 EWT
10/26/1919 02:00 EST
2/09/1942 02:00 EWT
9/30/1945 02:00 EST
5/19/1947 00:00 US#4

MD # 5
Before 11/18/1883 LMT
11/18/1883 12:00 EST
3/31/1918 02:00 EWT
10/27/1918 02:00 EST
3/30/1919 02:00 EWT
10/26/1919 02:00 EST
2/09/1942 02:00 EWT
9/30/1945 02:00 EST
5/19/1947 02:00 EDT
9/02/1947 00:00 EST
4/25/1948 02:00 US#4

MD # 6
Before 11/18/1883 LMT
11/18/1883 12:00 EST
3/31/1918 02:00 EWT
10/27/1918 02:00 EST
3/30/1919 02:00 EWT
10/26/1919 02:00 EST
2/09/1942 02:00 EWT
9/30/1945 02:00 EST
5/18/1947 02:00 EDT
9/28/1947 02:00 EST
5/02/1948 02:00 EDT
9/26/1948 02:00 US#4

MD # 7
Before 11/18/1883 LMT
11/18/1883 12:00 EST
3/31/1918 02:00 EWT
10/27/1918 02:00 EST
3/30/1919 02:00 EWT
10/26/1919 02:00 EST
2/09/1942 02:00 EWT
9/30/1945 02:00 EST
4/25/1948 02:00 EDT
9/26/1948 02:00 EST
4/30/1950 02:00 US#4

MD # 8
Before 11/18/1883 LMT
11/18/1883 12:00 EST
3/31/1918 02:00 EWT
10/27/1918 02:00 EST
3/30/1919 02:00 EWT
10/26/1919 02:00 EST
2/09/1942 02:00 EWT
9/30/1945 02:00 EST
4/25/1948 02:00 US#4

MD # 9
Before 11/18/1883 LMT
11/18/1883 12:00 EST
3/31/1918 02:00 EWT
10/27/1918 02:00 EST
3/30/1919 02:00 EWT
10/26/1919 02:00 EST
2/09/1942 02:00 EWT
9/30/1945 02:00 EST
5/18/1947 02:00 US#4

MD # 10
Before 11/18/1883 LMT
11/18/1883 12:00 EST
3/31/1918 02:00 EWT
10/27/1918 02:00 EST
3/30/1919 02:00 EWT
10/26/1919 02:00 EST
2/09/1942 02:00 EWT
9/30/1945 02:00 EST
5/11/1947 02:00 EDT
9/29/1947 02:00 US#4

MD # 11
Before 11/18/1883 LMT
11/18/1883 12:00 EST
3/31/1918 02:00 EWT
10/27/1918 02:00 EST
3/30/1919 02:00 EWT
10/26/1919 02:00 EST
2/09/1942 02:00 EWT
9/30/1945 02:00 EST
5/19/1947 02:00 US#4

MD # 12
Before 11/18/1883 LMT
11/18/1883 12:00 EST
3/31/1918 02:00 EWT
10/27/1918 02:00 EST
3/30/1919 02:00 EWT
10/26/1919 02:00 EST
2/09/1942 02:00 EWT
9/30/1945 02:00 EST
5/19/1947 02:00 EDT
9/02/1947 02:00 EST
4/25/1948 02:00 EDT
9/26/1948 02:00 EST
4/30/1950 02:00 US#4

MD # 13
Before 11/18/1883 LMT
11/18/1883 12:00 EST
3/31/1918 02:00 EWT
10/27/1918 02:00 EST
3/30/1919 02:00 EWT
10/26/1919 02:00 EST
2/09/1942 02:00 EWT
9/30/1945 02:00 EST
4/29/1951 02:00 US#4

MD # 14
Before 11/18/1883 LMT
11/18/1883 12:00 EST
3/31/1918 02:00 EWT
10/27/1918 02:00 EST
3/30/1919 02:00 EWT
10/26/1919 02:00 EST
2/09/1942 02:00 EWT
9/30/1945 02:00 EST
4/27/1947 02:00 EDT
9/28/1947 02:00 EST
5/11/1953 02:00 US#5

MD # 15
Before 11/18/1883 LMT
11/18/1883 12:00 EST
3/31/1918 02:00 EWT
10/27/1918 02:00 EST
3/30/1919 02:00 EWT
10/26/1919 02:00 EST
2/09/1942 02:00 EWT
9/30/1945 02:00 EST
4/30/1950 02:00 US#4

MD # 16
Before 11/18/1883 LMT
11/18/1883 12:00 EST
3/31/1918 02:00 EWT
10/27/1918 02:00 EST
3/30/1919 02:00 EWT
10/26/1919 02:00 EST
2/09/1942 02:00 EWT
9/30/1945 02:00 EST
5/11/1947 02:00 EDT
9/28/1947 02:00 EST
5/02/1948 02:00 EDT
9/26/1948 02:00 EST
4/24/1949 02:00 EDT
9/25/1949 02:00 EST
5/04/1950 02:00 EDT
9/24/1950 02:00 EST
4/29/1951 02:00 EDT
9/30/1951 02:00 EST
4/27/1952 02:00 EDT
9/28/1952 02:00 EST
4/30/1953 02:00 EDT
9/27/1953 02:00 EST
4/25/1954 02:00 US#3

MD # 17
Before 11/18/1883 LMT
11/18/1883 12:00 EST
3/31/1918 02:00 EWT
10/27/1918 02:00 EST
3/30/1919 02:00 EWT
10/26/1919 02:00 EST
2/09/1942 02:00 EWT
9/30/1945 02:00 EST
4/25/1954 02:00 US#4

MD # 18
Before 11/18/1883 LMT
11/18/1883 12:00 EST
3/31/1918 02:00 EWT
10/27/1918 02:00 EST
3/30/1919 02:00 EWT
10/26/1919 02:00 EST
2/09/1942 02:00 EWT
9/30/1945 02:00 EST
4/28/1957 02:00 US#4

MD # 19
Before 11/18/1883 LMT
11/18/1883 12:00 EST
3/31/1918 02:00 EWT
10/27/1918 02:00 EST
3/30/1919 02:00 EWT
10/26/1919 02:00 EST
2/09/1942 02:00 EWT
9/30/1945 02:00 EST
4/25/1948 02:00 EDT
9/26/1948 02:00 EST
4/30/1950 02:00 US#5

MD # 20
Before 11/18/1883 LMT
11/18/1883 12:00 EST
3/31/1918 02:00 EWT
10/27/1918 02:00 EST
3/30/1919 02:00 EWT
10/26/1919 02:00 EST
2/09/1942 02:00 EWT
9/30/1945 02:00 EST
4/27/1947 02:00 EDT
9/28/1947 02:00 EST
4/25/1948 02:00 EDT
9/26/1948 02:00 EST
4/24/1949 02:00 EDT
9/25/1949 02:00 EST
4/30/1950 02:00 EDT
9/24/1950 02:00 EST
4/29/1951 02:00 EDT
9/30/1951 02:00 EST
4/27/1952 02:00 EDT
9/28/1952 02:00 EST
4/26/1953 02:00 EDT
9/27/1953 02:00 EST
4/25/1954 02:00 EDT
9/26/1954 02:00 EST
4/24/1955 02:00 EDT
9/25/1955 02:00 EST
4/29/1956 02:00 EDT
9/29/1956 00:00 EST
4/28/1957 02:00 US#4

MD # 21
Before 11/18/1883 LMT
11/18/1883 12:00 EST
3/31/1918 02:00 EWT
10/27/1918 02:00 EST
3/30/1919 02:00 EWT
10/26/1919 02:00 EST
2/09/1942 02:00 EWT
9/30/1945 02:00 EST
5/11/1947 02:00 EDT
9/28/1947 02:00 US#4

MD # 22
Before 11/18/1883 LMT
11/18/1883 12:00 EST
3/31/1918 02:00 EWT
10/27/1918 02:00 EST
3/30/1919 02:00 EWT
10/26/1919 02:00 EST
2/09/1942 02:00 EWT
9/30/1945 02:00 EST
5/11/1947 02:00 EDT
9/02/1947 02:00 EST
4/25/1948 02:00 US#4

MD # 23
Before 11/18/1883 LMT
11/18/1883 12:00 EST
3/31/1918 02:00 EWT
10/27/1918 02:00 EST
3/30/1919 02:00 EWT
10/26/1919 02:00 EST
2/09/1942 02:00 EWT
9/30/1945 02:00 EST
4/25/1948 02:00 US#5

MD # 24
Before 11/18/1883 LMT
11/18/1883 12:00 EST
3/31/1918 02:00 EWT
10/27/1918 02:00 EST
3/30/1919 02:00 EWT
10/26/1919 02:00 EST
2/09/1942 02:00 EWT
9/30/1945 02:00 EST
4/27/1947 02:00 US#5

MD # 25
Before 11/18/1893 LMT
11/18/1893 12:00 EST
3/31/1918 02:00 EWT
10/27/1918 02:00 EST
3/30/1919 02:00 EWT
10/26/1919 02:00 EST
2/09/1942 02:00 EWT
9/30/1945 02:00 EST
4/28/1946 02:00 US#4

MD # 26
Before 11/18/1883 LMT
11/18/1883 12:00 EST
3/31/1918 02:00 EWT
10/27/1918 02:00 EST
3/30/1919 02:00 EWT
10/26/1919 02:00 EST
2/09/1942 02:00 EWT
9/30/1945 02:00 EST
5/19/1947 02:00 EDT
9/02/1947 02:00 EST
4/25/1948 02:00 US#5

MD # 27
Before 11/18/1883 LMT
11/18/1883 12:00 EST
3/31/1918 02:00 EWT
10/27/1918 02:00 EST
3/30/1919 02:00 EWT
10/26/1919 02:00 EST
2/09/1942 02:00 EWT
9/30/1945 02:00 EST
5/19/1947 02:00 EDT
9/02/1947 02:00 EST
4/25/1948 02:00 US#4

MD # 28
Before 11/18/1883 LMT
11/18/1883 12:00 EST
3/31/1918 02:00 EWT
10/27/1918 02:00 EST
3/30/1919 02:00 EWT
10/26/1919 02:00 EST
2/09/1942 02:00 EWT
9/30/1945 02:00 EST
5/19/1947 02:00 EDT
9/02/1947 02:00 EST
4/25/1948 02:00 EDT
9/26/1948 02:00 EST
4/30/1950 02:00 US#5

COUNTIES

1 Allegany
2 Anne Arundel
3 Baltimore
4 Calvert
5 Caroline
6 Carroll
7 Cecil
8 Charles
9 Dorchester
10 Frederick
11 Garrett
12 Harford
13 Howard
14 Kent
15 Montgomery
16 Prince Georges
17 Queen Annes
18 St Marys
19 Somerset
20 Talbot
21 Washington
22 Wicomico
23 Worcester
24 Baltimore City

Place	Table	Lat	Long	Time
Abell 18	4	38N15	76w45	5:07:00
Aberdeen 12	8	39N31	76w10	5:04:40
Aberdeen Proving Ground 12	8	39N28	76w08	5:04:32
Abingdon 12	8	39N28	76w17	5:05:08
Accident 11	2	39N38	79w19	5:17:16
Accokeek 16	16	38N40	77w02	5:08:08
Accokeek Acres 16	16	38N40	77w02	5:08:08
Accokeek Groves 16	16	38N40	77w02	5:08:08
Acco Park 16	16	38N40	77w02	5:08:08
Adamstown 10	7	39N19	77w28	5:09:52
Adelina 4	9	38N33	76w35	5:06:20
Adelphi 16	16	38N59	76w58	5:07:52
Adelphi Manor 16	16	38N59	76w58	5:07:52
Ady 12	8	39N40	76w23	5:05:32
Aero Acres 3	3	39N20	76w27	5:05:48
Aikin 7	25	39N34	76w04	5:04:16
Airey 9	8	38N34	76w05	5:04:20
Albantown 3	3	39N36	76w51	5:07:24
Albeth Heights 13	3	39N20	76w52	5:07:28
Aldino 12	8	39N31	76w10	5:04:40
Alesia 6	8	39N40	76w51	5:07:24
Allanwood 15	16	39N04	77w04	5:08:16
Allegany 1	24	39N39	78w55	5:15:40
Allegany Grove 1	3	39N38	78w48	5:15:12
Allen 22	7	38N17	75w41	5:02:44
Allenford 13	3	39N16	76w49	5:07:16
Allens Fresh 8	6	38N27	76w55	5:07:40
Allenwood 22	7	38N22	75w36	5:02:24
Allview 13	3	39N12	76w52	5:07:28

MARYLAND

Allview Estates 13
3 39N16 76w49 5:07:16
Alpha 13 3 39N21 76w54 5:07:36
Alpine Beach 2 20 39N09 76w33 5:06:12
Alta Vista 15 16 39N01 77w08 5:08:32
Alta Vista Gardens 15
16 39N01 77w08 5:08:32
Alta Vista Terrace 15
16 39N01 77w08 5:08:32
Amber Meadows 16 16 38N30 75w52 5:03:28
American Corner 5
15 38N47 75w49 5:03:16
American Square 16
16 38N47 76w58 5:07:52
Ammendale 16 16 39N02 76w55 5:07:40
Anchorage 2 20 39N03 76w30 5:06:00
Ancient Oak Estates 15
16 39N08 77w12 5:08:48
Ancient Oak North 15
16 39N08 77w12 5:08:48
Andersontown 5 15 38N53 75w50 5:03:20
Andover Estates 18
4 38N12 76w31 5:06:04
Andrews 9 8 38N19 76w08 5:04:32
Andrews 16 16 38N48 76w54 5:07:36
Andrews Air Force Base 16
16 38N48 76w52 5:07:28
Andrews Air Force Hospital 16
16 38N49 76w51 5:07:24
Andrews Estates 16
16 38N50 76w55 5:07:40
Andrews Hill 16 16 38N49 76w56 5:07:44
Andrews Manor 16 16 38N49 76w56 5:07:44
Annapolis 2 20 38N59 76w30 5:06:00
Annapolis Junction 13
3 39N08 76w47 5:07:08
Annapolis Rock 13 3 39N22 77w04 5:08:16
Anneslie 3 3 39N24 76w36 5:06:24
Antietam 21 8 39N25 77w45 5:11:00
Apple Grove 16 16 38N47 76w58 5:07:52
Appleton Acres 7 7 39N37 75w50 5:03:20
Appletown 21 7 39N31 77w39 5:10:36
Appolds 10 7 39N36 77w19 5:09:16
Aquasco 16 16 38N35 76w43 5:06:52
Arden on the Severn 2
20 39N02 76w36 5:06:24
Ardmore 16 16 38N58 76w51 5:07:24
Ardwick 16 16 38N56 76w53 5:07:32
Argonne Hills 2 20 39N06 76w45 5:07:00
Arlington 24 1 39N21 76w41 5:06:44
Armagh 3 3 39N24 76w36 5:06:24
Armiger 2 20 39N09 76w33 5:06:12
Arnold 2 20 39N02 76w30 5:06:00
Arnold Heights 16
16 38N50 76w55 5:07:40
Arnoldtown 10 7 39N24 77w38 5:10:32
Arrowhead 13 3 39N16 76w49 5:07:16
Arrowood 15 16 39N00 77w08 5:08:32
Arundel Gardens 2
20 39N14 76w37 5:06:28
Arundel on the Bay 2
20 38N57 76w29 5:05:56
Arundel Plaza 2 20 39N05 76w34 5:06:16
Arundel View 2 20 39N04 76w40 5:06:40
Arundel Village 2
20 39N13 76w36 5:06:24
Asbury 19 19 37N57 75w52 5:03:28
Ashburton 15 16 39N01 77w08 5:08:32
Asher Glade 11 2 39N39 79w24 5:17:36
Ashland 3 3 39N29 76w39 5:06:36
Ashton 15 16 39N09 77w07 5:08:28
Ashton Pond 15 16 39N09 77w01 5:08:04
Asleigh 15 16 39N00 77w08 5:08:32
Aspen Hill 15 16 39N05 77w06 5:08:24
Aspen Hill Park 15
16 39N05 77w07 5:08:28
Aspen Knolls 15 16 39N05 77w07 5:08:28
Athel 22 7 38N28 75w46 5:03:04
Atholton 13 3 39N16 76w49 5:07:16
Atholton Manor 13 3 39N16 76w49 5:07:16
Atkinsons 23 19 38N12 75w30 5:02:00
Augusta 21 7 39N20 77w37 5:10:28
Aure Hill 15 16 39N00 77w08 5:08:32
Auth Village 16 16 38N49 76w56 5:07:44
Autumn Hill 13 3 39N16 76w49 5:07:16
Avalon Shores 2 20 38N50 76w30 5:06:00
Avenel 16 16 38N59 76w58 5:07:52
Avenel-Hillandale 15
16 39N01 76w59 5:07:56
Avenue 18 4 38N16 76w46 5:07:04
Avilton 11 2 39N39 79w03 5:16:12
Avondale 16 16 38N57 76w56 5:07:44
Ayrlawn 15 16 39N01 77w08 5:08:32
Azundel Gardens 2
20 39N14 76w37 5:06:28
Back River Highlands 3
3 39N19 76w28 5:05:52
Baden 16 16 38N42 76w51 5:07:24
Bainbridge Center 7
7 39N37 76w06 5:04:24
Bakersville 21 7 39N31 77w39 5:10:36
Bald Eagle 16 16 38N42 76w51 5:07:24
Baldwin 3 3 39N30 76w28 5:05:52
Ballard 16 16 38N47 76w53 5:07:32
Ballard Gardens 3 3 39N20 76w27 5:05:48
Ballenger 10 7 39N23 77w29 5:09:56
Baltimore 24 1 39N17 76w37 5:06:28
Baltimore Corner 5
15 39N05 75w46 5:03:04
Baltimore Highlands 3
3 39N14 76w39 5:06:36
Banks O'Dee 8 6 38N23 76w57 5:07:48
Bannockburn 15 16 39N01 77w08 5:08:32
Bannockburn Estates 15
16 39N01 77w08 5:08:32
Bannockburn Heights 15
16 39N01 77w08 5:08:32
Barber 20 13 38N39 76w01 5:04:04
Barclay 17 15 39N09 75w52 5:03:28
Bar Harbor 2 20 39N09 76w33 5:06:12
Bark Hill 6 8 39N34 77w11 5:08:44
Barnaby Manor Oaks 16
16 38N47 76w58 5:07:52
Barnaby Village 16
16 38N47 76w58 5:07:52
Bar Neck 20 13 38N43 76w20 5:05:20
Barnes Corner 7 7 39N40 76w06 5:04:24
Barnesville 15 16 39N13 77w23 5:09:32
Barrelville 1 24 39N42 78w53 5:15:32
Barren Creek 22 7 38N28 75w46 5:03:04
Barrett 6 8 39N24 76w56 5:07:44
Barstow 4 9 38N32 76w37 5:06:28
Bartholow 10 7 39N22 77w09 5:08:36
Barton 1 3 39N32 79w01 5:16:04
Bartonsville 10 7 39N26 77w27 5:09:48
Battery Park 15 16 39N01 77w08 5:08:32
Battle Grove 3 3 39N14 76w31 5:06:04
Bay 18 4 38N17 76w28 5:05:52
Bayberry 2 20 39N03 76w30 5:06:00
Bay City 17 15 38N59 76w19 5:05:16
Bay Hundred 20 13 38N45 76w19 5:05:16
Baynesville 3 3 39N24 76w36 5:06:24
Bay Ridge 2 20 38N56 76w28 5:05:52
Bayside Beach 2 20 39N08 76w27 5:05:48
Bay View 7 7 39N39 75w58 5:03:52
Bay View Estates 7
7 39N25 75w55 5:03:40
Beachville 18 4 38N09 76w25 5:05:40
Beachwood Forest 2
20 39N09 76w33 5:06:12
Beachwood Grove 2
20 39N09 76w33 5:06:12
Beacon Heights 16
16 38N58 76w55 5:07:40
Beacon Hill 2 20 39N03 76w30 5:06:00
Beallsville 15 16 39N11 77w25 5:09:40
Beantown 8 6 38N38 76w53 5:07:32
Beaufort Park 13 3 39N10 76w54 5:07:36
Beaverbrook 13 3 39N16 76w49 5:07:16
Beaver Creek 21 7 39N34 77w38 5:10:32
Beaver Dam 23 19 38N04 75w34 5:02:16
Beaverdam Estates 16
16 38N56 76w53 5:07:32
Beaver Heights 16
16 38N54 76w54 5:07:36
Beckleysville 3 3 39N36 76w51 5:07:24
Bedfordshire Estates 15
16 39N03 77w10 5:08:40
Beechwood on the Burley 2
20 39N03 76w30 5:06:00
Bel Air 1 3 39N38 78w48 5:15:12
Bel Air 12 9 39N32 76w21 5:05:24
Belair 16 16 38N57 76w47 5:07:08
Bel Air Acres 8 6 38N38 76w53 5:07:32
Bel Air Acres 12 8 39N32 76w21 5:05:24
Belair Buckingham 16
16 38N57 76w47 5:07:08
Belair Chapel Forge 16
16 38N57 76w47 5:07:08
Belair Foxhill 16
16 38N57 76w47 5:07:08
Belair Heather Hills 16
16 38N57 76w47 5:07:08
Belair Idlewild 16
16 38N57 76w47 5:07:08
Belair Kenilworth 16
16 38N57 76w47 5:07:08
Belair Longridge 16
16 38N57 76w47 5:07:08
Belair Overbrook 16
16 38N57 76w47 5:07:08
Belair Rockledge 16
16 38N57 76w47 5:07:08
Belair Somerset 16
16 38N57 76w47 5:07:08
Belair Tulip Grove 16
16 38N57 76w47 5:07:08
Belair White Hall 16
16 38N57 76w47 5:07:08
Belair Yorktown 16
16 38N57 76w47 5:07:08
Bel Alton 8 6 38N28 76w59 5:07:56
Belcamp 12 8 39N28 76w14 5:04:56
Belle Farm Estates 3
3 39N22 76w43 5:06:52
Bellefonte 16 16 38N47 76w53 5:07:32
Belle Grove 1 3 39N38 78w23 5:13:32
Bellemead 16 16 38N58 76w53 5:07:32
Bellevue 20 13 38N42 76w11 5:04:44
Bellevue Estates 16
16 38N40 77w02 5:08:08
Bellhaven Beach 2
20 39N09 76w33 5:06:12
Bellwood Park 8 6 38N38 76w53 5:07:32
Belmar 3 3 39N21 76w32 5:06:08
Bel Pre Woods 15 16 39N05 77w07 5:08:28
Beltsville 16 16 39N02 76w54 5:07:36
Beltsville Heights 16
16 39N02 76w55 5:07:40
Belvedere Heights 2
20 39N03 76w30 5:06:00
Bembe Beach 2 20 38N57 76w29 5:05:56
Benedict 8 6 38N31 76w41 5:06:44
Benevola 21 7 39N31 77w39 5:10:36
Ben Oaks 2 20 39N05 76w34 5:06:16
Benson 12 8 39N31 76w25 5:05:40
Bentley Springs 3 3 39N40 76w41 5:06:44
Bentons Pleasure 17
15 38N58 76w17 5:05:08
Benville 8 6 38N38 76w53 5:07:32
Berkley 12 8 39N38 76w12 5:04:48
Berkshire 16 16 38N51 76w54 5:07:36
Berlin 23 27 38N20 75w13 5:00:52
Berrett 6 8 39N25 77w01 5:08:04
Berry 8 6 38N38 76w53 5:07:32
Berwyn 16 16 38N59 76w54 5:07:36
Berwyn Heights 16
16 39N00 76w55 5:07:40
Bestgate 2 20 39N03 76w30 5:06:00
Bethany Manor 13 3 39N16 76w49 5:07:16
Bethel 6 8 39N30 76w53 5:07:32
Bethel 7 7 39N32 75w49 5:03:16
Bethel 10 7 39N26 77w27 5:09:48
Bethesda 15 16 38N59 77w06 5:08:24
Bethgate 13 3 39N16 76w49 5:07:16
Bethlehem 5 15 38N45 75w57 5:03:48
Betterton 14 8 39N22 76w04 5:04:16
Beulah 9 8 38N38 75w52 5:03:28
Beverly Beach 2 20 38N54 76w30 5:06:00
Beverly Farms 15 16 39N03 77w10 5:08:40
Big Pines 15 16 39N05 77w10 5:08:40
Big Pool 21 7 39N08 78w01 5:12:04
Big Spring 21 7 39N40 77w57 5:11:48
Bigwoods 14 15 39N17 76w06 5:04:24
Birchwood City 16
16 38N49 76w59 5:07:56
Bird River Beach 3
3 39N20 76w27 5:05:48
Birdsville 2 20 38N54 76w36 5:06:24
Birmingham Estates 16
16 39N02 76w55 5:07:40
Bishop 23 23 38N27 75w11 5:00:44
Bishops Head 9 8 38N16 76w04 5:04:16
Bishopville 23 23 38N27 75w11 5:00:44
Bittinger 11 2 39N35 79w13 5:16:52
Bivalve 22 7 38N18 75w53 5:03:32
Black Bay Beach 2
20 38N51 76w36 5:06:24
Black Horse 12 8 39N37 76w38 5:06:32
Black Rock Estates 15
16 39N10 77w16 5:09:04
Blacks Corner 6 8 39N34 76w59 5:07:56
Blackwater 9 8 38N30 76w09 5:04:36
Bladensburg 16 16 38N56 76w56 5:07:44
Bladenwoods 16 16 38N57 76w56 5:07:44
Blair 15 16 39N00 77w02 5:08:08
Blenheim 3 3 39N31 76w37 5:06:28
Bloomfield 10 7 39N26 77w27 5:09:48
Blooming Rose Settlement 11
2 39N39 79w24 5:17:36
Bloomington 11 17 39N30 79w07 5:16:28
Bloomsbury 3 3 39N17 76w43 5:06:52
Blueball 7 7 39N37 75w50 5:03:20
Blueberry Hills 15
16 39N06 77w11 5:08:44
Blue Hill 21 8 39N42 78w11 5:12:44
Blue Mount 3 3 39N35 76w37 5:06:28
Blue Mountain 10 7 39N38 77w25 5:09:40
Blue Ridge Manor 15
16 39N03 77w03 5:08:12
Blue Ridge View 6 8 39N34 76w59 5:07:56
Blythedale 7 25 39N34 76w04 5:04:16
Bolivar 10 7 39N26 77w33 5:10:12
Bolton 8 6 38N38 76w53 5:07:32
Bond Mill Woods 16
16 39N05 76w58 5:07:52
Bonds 16 16 38N40 77w02 5:08:08
Bon Haven 2 20 39N03 76w30 5:06:00
Bonnie Acres 13 3 39N16 76w49 5:07:16
Bonnie Brae 6 8 39N24 76w56 5:07:44
Bonnie Knob 10 7 39N32 77w19 5:09:16
Booker Heights 16
16 38N54 76w54 5:07:36
Boonsboro 21 7 39N30 77w39 5:10:36
Borden Shaft 1 24 39N39 78w55 5:15:40
Borden Yard 1 24 39N39 78w55 5:15:40
Boring 3 3 39N32 76w49 5:07:16
Boulevard Heights 16
16 38N54 76w54 5:07:36
Bowens 4 9 38N33 76w35 5:06:20
Bowie 16 16 39N00 76w47 5:07:08
Bowleys Quarters 3
3 39N20 76w27 5:05:48
Bowling Alley 8 6 38N29 76w47 5:07:08
Bowling Green 1 3 39N38 78w48 5:15:12
Boxiron 23 23 38N06 75w24 5:01:36
Boxwood Village 16
16 39N00 76w53 5:07:32
Boyds 15 16 39N11 77w19 5:09:16
Bozman 20 13 38N46 76w16 5:05:04
Bradbury Heights 16
16 38N54 76w54 5:07:36
Bradbury Park 16 16 38N50 76w55 5:07:40
Braddock 10 7 39N25 77w30 5:10:00
Braddock Estates 1
24 39N39 78w55 5:15:40
Braddock Heights 10
7 39N25 77w30 5:10:00
Bradley Farms 15 16 39N03 77w10 5:08:40
Bradley Hills 15 16 39N01 77w08 5:08:32
Bradley Hills Grove 15
16 39N01 77w08 5:08:32
Bradley Woods 15 16 39N01 77w08 5:08:32
Bramble Hills 6 8 39N34 76w59 5:07:56
Branchville 16 16 39N00 76w55 5:07:40
Brandywine 16 16 38N42 76w51 5:07:24
Brandywine Heights 16
16 38N42 76w51 5:07:24
Brandywine Woods 16
16 38N47 76w52 5:07:28
Breathedsville 21 7 39N39 77w44 5:10:56
Breezewood Farms 13
3 39N20 76w52 5:07:28
Breezy Point 4 9 38N42 76w32 5:06:08
Brentwood 16 16 38N57 76w57 5:07:48
Breton Beach 18 4 38N18 76w39 5:06:36

MARYLAND

Briarcrest Heights 10 7 39N22 77w32 5:10:08
Briarwood 16 16 39N05 76w58 5:07:52
Briddletown 23 27 38N19 75w13 5:00:52
Bridgeport 10 7 39N40 77w10 5:08:40
Bridgeport 21 7 39N39 77w44 5:10:56
Bridgetown 5 15 39N02 75w53 5:03:32
Brighton 3 3 39N20 76w43 5:06:52
Brighton 15 16 39N12 77w02 5:08:08
Brightwood Acres 21 7 39N39 77w44 5:10:56
Brinkleigh 13 3 39N16 76w49 5:07:16
Brinkleigh Manor 13 3 39N16 76w49 5:07:16
Brinkley Manor 16 16 38N49 76w56 5:07:44
Brinkleys 19 23 38N02 75w43 5:02:52
Brinklow 15 16 39N10 77w01 5:08:04
Bristol 2 20 38N47 76w40 5:06:40
Broad Creek 12 8 39N43 76w21 5:05:24
Broadmoor 3 3 39N29 76w39 5:06:36
Broad Run 10 7 39N24 77w38 5:10:32
Broadview 16 16 38N49 76w56 5:07:44
Broadview Acres 10 7 39N26 77w27 5:09:48
Broadwater 2 20 38N48 76w32 5:06:08
Broadwater Estates 16 16 38N47 76w58 5:07:52
Broadwood Manor 15 16 39N05 77w07 5:08:28
Brock Bridge 16 16 39N05 76w58 5:07:52
Brock Hall 16 16 38N47 76w52 5:07:28
Brookdale 15 16 38N59 77w05 5:08:20
Brooke Manor 16 16 38N48 76w59 5:07:56
Brookeville 15 16 39N11 77w04 5:08:16
Brookhaven 15 16 39N05 77w07 5:08:28
Brook Hill 10 7 39N26 77w27 5:09:48
Brooklandville 3 3 39N25 76w40 5:06:40
Brooklyn 2 20 39N13 76w37 5:06:28
Brooklyn-Curtis Bay 2 20 39N14 76w37 5:06:28
Brooklyn Park 2 20 39N14 76w37 5:06:28
Brookmont 15 16 38N57 77w06 5:08:24
Brookside Manor 16 16 38N58 76w58 5:07:52
Brookview 9 8 38N34 75w48 5:03:12
Brookville Knolls 15 16 39N11 77w03 5:08:12
Brookwood 16 16 38N47 76w52 5:07:28
Broomes Island 4 9 38N25 76w33 5:06:12
Browningsville 15 16 39N22 77w16 5:09:04
Browns Corner 17 15 39N03 76w04 5:04:16
Brownstown 15 16 39N10 77w16 5:09:04
Brownsville 17 15 39N03 76w04 5:04:16
Brownsville 21 7 39N23 77w40 5:10:40
Browns Woods 2 20 39N03 76w30 5:06:00
Bruceville 6 8 39N36 77w14 5:08:56
Bruceville 20 13 38N40 75w59 5:03:56
Brunswick 10 18 39N19 77w37 5:10:28
Bryantown 8 6 38N34 76w51 5:07:24
Bryantown 17 15 38N59 76w10 5:04:40
Buckeystown 10 7 39N18 77w28 5:09:52
Buckingham View 6 8 39N34 76w59 5:07:56
Buck Lodge 16 16 38N59 76w58 5:07:52
Bucktown 9 8 38N29 76w02 5:04:08
Budds Creek 18 4 38N26 76w44 5:06:56
Buffalo Run 11 2 39N39 79w24 5:17:36
Burgundy Estates 15 16 39N05 77w07 5:08:28
Burgundy Knolls 15 16 39N05 77w10 5:08:40
Burgundy Village 15 16 39N05 77w10 5:08:40
Burkittsville 10 7 39N23 77w38 5:10:32
Burnbrae 3 3 39N24 76w36 5:06:24
Burning Tree Estates 15 16 39N00 77w08 5:08:32
Burning Tree Manor 15 16 39N00 77w08 5:08:32
Burns Corner 12 8 39N31 76w10 5:04:40
Burnt Hill 15 16 39N14 77w17 5:09:08
Burnt Mills 15 16 39N01 77w00 5:08:00
Burnt Mills Hills 15 16 39N01 77w00 5:08:00
Burnt Mills Knolls 15 16 39N01 77w00 5:08:00
Burnt Mills Manor 15 16 39N01 77w00 5:08:00
Burnt Mills Village 15 16 39N01 77w00 5:08:00
Burrisville 17 15 39N03 76w04 5:04:16
Burrsville 5 15 38N53 75w50 5:03:20
Burtner 21 7 39N31 77w39 5:10:36
Burtonsville 15 16 39N07 76w56 5:07:44
Bush 12 8 39N28 76w17 5:05:08
Bushs Corner 12 8 39N41 76w22 5:05:28
Bushwood 18 4 38N18 76w47 5:07:08
Butler 3 3 39N32 76w44 5:06:56
Butlertown 14 15 39N17 76w06 5:04:24
Byforde 15 16 39N02 77w06 5:08:24
Bynum 12 8 39N35 76w23 5:05:32
Bynum Ridge 12 8 39N35 76w23 5:05:32
Byrdtown 19 28 37N59 75w51 5:03:24
Cabin Creek 9 8 38N38 75w52 5:03:28
Cabin John 15 16 38N59 77w10 5:08:40
Cactus Hill 16 16 38N40 77w02 5:08:08
California 18 4 38N18 76w31 5:06:04
Callaway 18 4 38N14 76w31 5:06:04
Caltor Manor 16 16 38N47 76w58 5:07:52
Calvary 12 8 39N34 76w15 5:05:00
Calvert 7 7 39N42 75w59 5:03:56
Calvert 24 1 39N18 76w36 5:06:24
Calvert Beach 4 9 38N28 76w30 5:06:00
Calvert Manor 16 16 38N40 77w02 5:08:08
Calverton 15 16 39N04 76w57 5:07:48
Cambria 3 3 39N31 76w37 5:06:28
Cambridge 9 10 38N34 76w05 5:04:20
Camden 22 7 38N19 75w36 5:02:24
Camelback Village 15 16 39N09 77w05 5:08:20
Camelot 16 16 38N59 76w49 5:07:16
Camotop 15 16 39N03 77w10 5:08:40
Campbelltown 23 23 38N27 75w11 5:00:44
Camp Springs 16 16 38N48 76w55 5:07:40
Campus Hills 3 3 39N24 76w36 5:06:24
Canada Hill 10 7 39N30 77w34 5:10:16
Canal 7 7 39N36 76w07 5:04:28
Candlewood Park 15 16 39N06 77w11 5:08:44
Cape Anne 2 20 38N48 76w32 5:06:08
Cape Arthur 2 20 39N05 76w34 5:06:16
Cape Isle Of Wight 23 19 38N23 75w05 5:00:20
Cape Loch Haven 2 20 38N56 76w33 5:06:12
Cape May Beach 3 3 39N19 76w28 5:05:52
Cape Saint John 2 20 39N03 76w30 5:06:00
Capital Estates 8 6 38N36 76w57 5:07:48
Capitol Heights 16 16 38N53 76w55 5:07:40
Capitol Plaza 16 16 38N58 76w53 5:07:32
Capitol View Park 15 16 39N00 77w02 5:08:08
Captain Saint Claire 2 20 39N03 76w30 5:06:00
Captains Cove 16 16 38N47 76w58 5:07:52
Captains Hill 23 19 38N23 75w05 5:00:20
Carderock Springs 15 16 39N00 77w08 5:08:32
Cardiff 12 8 39N43 76w20 5:05:20
Carea 12 8 39N44 76w28 5:05:52
Carlos 1 24 39N39 78w55 5:15:40
Carlos Junction 1 24 39N39 78w55 5:15:40
Carmichael 17 15 38N56 76w08 5:04:32
Carmody Hills 16 16 38N54 76w54 5:07:36
Carney 3 3 39N23 76w33 5:06:12
Carney Grove 3 3 39N23 76w33 5:06:12
Carney Heights 3 3 39N23 76w33 5:06:12
Carole Acres 15 16 39N04 76w59 5:07:56
Carole Highlands 16 16 38N59 76w58 5:07:52
Carpenter Point 7 25 39N34 76w04 5:04:16
Carroll 24 1 39N17 76w41 5:06:44
Carroll Heights 21 7 39N39 77w44 5:10:56
Carroll Highlands 6 8 39N24 76w56 5:07:44
Carroll Island 3 3 39N20 76w27 5:05:48
Carroll Manor 15 16 38N59 77w01 5:08:04
Carrollton 6 8 39N33 76w55 5:07:40
Carrollton Manor 2 20 39N05 76w35 5:06:20
Carrollwood 3 3 39N20 76w27 5:05:48
Carsins 12 8 39N32 76w13 5:04:52
Carsondale 16 16 38N58 76w51 5:07:24
Carter Hill 15 16 39N05 77w10 5:08:40
Carvel Beach 2 20 39N14 76w35 5:06:20
Carver Heights 18 4 38N15 76w27 5:05:48
Cascade 21 7 39N42 77w30 5:10:00
Casselman 11 2 39N42 79w10 5:16:40
Castle Marina 17 15 38N58 76w17 5:05:08
Castleton 12 8 39N38 76w12 5:04:48
Catchpenny 22 7 38N23 75w44 5:02:56
Catoctin 10 7 39N34 77w33 5:10:12
Catoctin Furnace 10 7 39N38 77w25 5:09:40
Catoctin View 10 7 39N22 77w09 5:08:36
Catonsville 3 3 39N17 76w44 5:06:56
Catonsville Heights 3 3 39N17 76w43 5:06:52
Catonsville Manor 3 3 39N20 76w43 5:06:52
Cavetown 21 7 39N39 77w35 5:10:20
Cayots 7 7 39N32 75w49 5:03:16
Cearfoss 21 7 39N39 77w44 5:10:56
Cecilton 7 7 39N24 75w52 5:03:28
Cedar Acres 13 3 39N16 76w49 5:07:16
Cedar Beach 3 3 39N19 76w28 5:05:52
Cedar Grove 15 16 39N15 77w14 5:08:56
Cedar Grove Beach 9 8 38N36 75w55 5:03:40
Cedar Hall 23 19 38N04 75w34 5:02:16
Cedar Haven 16 16 38N34 76w41 5:06:44
Cedar Heights 16 16 38N54 76w54 5:07:36
Cedarhurst 6 8 39N30 76w53 5:07:32
Cedarhurst-on-the-Bay 2 20 38N50 76w30 5:06:00
Cedar Lawn 21 7 39N39 77w46 5:11:04
Cedarmere 3 3 39N26 76w48 5:07:12
Cedar Park 2 20 39N03 76w30 5:06:00
Cedartown 23 27 38N10 75w24 5:01:36
Cedarville 16 16 38N42 76w51 5:07:24
Centennial 13 3 39N16 76w49 5:07:16
Centennial Estates 13 3 39N16 76w49 5:07:16
Center Court 15 16 39N08 77w12 5:08:48
Centerville 10 7 39N22 77w19 5:09:16
Centreville 17 11 39N03 76w04 5:04:16
Ceresville 10 7 39N26 77w27 5:09:48
Chadwick Manor 3 3 39N20 76w43 5:06:52
Chalk Point 2 20 38N51 76w36 5:06:24
Champ 19 26 38N12 75w41 5:02:44
Chance 19 26 38N11 75w43 5:02:52
Chaney 4 9 38N43 76w40 5:06:40
Chaneyville 4 9 38N43 76w36 5:06:24
Chapel 20 13 38N51 76w01 5:04:04
Chapel Hill 16 16 38N47 76w58 5:07:52
Chapel Oaks 16 16 38N54 76w54 5:07:36
Chapel Oaks-Cedar Heights 16 16 38N54 76w54 5:07:36
Chapel View 13 3 39N16 76w49 5:07:16
Chaptico 18 4 38N22 76w46 5:07:04
Charles Manor 12 8 39N31 76w25 5:05:40
Charlesmont 3 3 39N14 76w31 5:06:04
Charlestown 1 3 39N34 78w59 5:15:56
Charlestown 7 7 39N35 75w59 5:03:56
Charlestown Manor Beach 7 7 39N36 75w56 5:03:44
Charlesville 10 7 39N26 77w27 5:09:48
Charlotte Hall 18 4 38N29 76w47 5:07:08
Charlton 21 7 39N40 77w57 5:11:48
Charred Oak Estates 15 16 39N00 77w08 5:08:32
Chartley 3 3 39N27 76w49 5:07:16
Chase 3 3 39N22 76w22 5:05:28
Chatham 16 16 38N59 76w58 5:07:52
Chattolanee 3 3 39N26 76w48 5:07:12
Chelsea Beach 2 20 39N09 76w33 5:06:12
Chelsea Woods 16 16 39N00 76w53 5:07:32
Cheltenham 16 16 38N42 76w50 5:07:20
Cheltenham Forest 16 16 38N47 76w53 5:07:32
Cherry Hill 7 7 39N40 75w51 5:03:24
Cherry Hill 16 16 39N00 76w55 5:07:40
Cherrywalk 22 7 38N25 75w41 5:02:44
Chesaco Park 3 3 39N20 76w31 5:06:04
Chesapeake Beach 4 9 38N41 76w32 5:06:08
Chesapeake City 7 7 39N32 75w49 5:03:16
Chesapeake Estates 17 15 38N59 76w19 5:05:16
Chesapeake Heights 22 7 38N22 75w36 5:02:24
Chesapeake Landing 14 15 39N13 76w04 5:04:16
Chesapeake Ranch Estates 4 9 38N25 76w27 5:05:48
Chesapeake Terrace 3 3 39N14 76w31 5:06:04
Cheshaven 7 7 39N25 75w55 5:03:40
Chester 17 15 38N58 76w17 5:05:08
Chesterfield 2 20 39N02 76w36 5:06:24
Chester Harbor 17 15 39N13 76w04 5:04:16
Chester River Beach 17 15 38N58 76w13 5:04:52
Chestertown 14 21 39N13 76w04 5:04:16
Chesterville 14 15 39N17 75w55 5:03:40
Chesterville Forest 14 15 39N15 75w50 5:03:20
Chestnut Grove 10 7 39N26 77w27 5:09:48
Chestnut Grove 21 7 39N29 77w42 5:10:48
Chestnut Hill 3 3 39N24 76w36 5:06:24
Chestnut Hill 12 8 39N35 76w23 5:05:32
Chestnut Hill 13 3 39N16 76w49 5:07:16
Chestnut Hill Estates 13 3 39N16 76w49 5:07:16
Chestnut Hills 16 16 39N02 76w55 5:07:40
Chestnut Ridge 3 3 39N27 76w49 5:07:16
Cheverly 16 16 38N56 76w55 5:07:40
Cheverly Manor 16 16 38N56 76w53 5:07:32
Chevy Chase 15 16 38N59 77w05 5:08:20
Chevy Chase Gardens 15 16 38N59 77w05 5:08:20
Chevy Chase Lake 15 16 38N59 77w05 5:08:20
Chevy Chase Manor 15 16 38N59 77w05 5:08:20
Chevy Chase Terrace 15 16 38N59 77w05 5:08:20
Chevy Chase View 15 16 39N02 77w06 5:08:24
Chewsville 21 8 39N38 77w40 5:10:40
Chicamuxen 8 6 38N36 77w10 5:08:40
Childs 7 7 39N39 75w52 5:03:28
Chillum 16 16 38N58 77w00 5:08:00
Chillum Gardens 16 16 38N59 76w58 5:07:52
Chillum Heights 16 16 38N58 76w58 5:07:52
Chillum Manor 16 16 38N58 76w58 5:07:52
Choptank 5 15 38N41 75w57 5:03:48
Christs Rock 9 8 38N34 76w05 5:04:20
Church Creek 9 8 38N30 76w09 5:04:36
Church Hill 10 7 39N30 77w34 5:10:16
Church Hill 17 15 39N09 75w59 5:03:56
Churchill 15 16 39N10 77w16 5:09:04
Churchton 2 20 38N48 76w32 5:06:08
Churchville 12 8 39N34 76w15 5:05:00
Cissel Farms 13 3 39N11 76w57 5:07:48
Claggettsville 15 16 39N17 77w12 5:08:48
Claiborne 20 13 38N50 76w17 5:05:08
Clarksburg 15 16 39N14 77w17 5:09:08
Clarks Landing 18 4 38N21 76w34 5:06:16
Clarksville 13 3 39N12 76w57 5:07:48
Clarksville Ridge 13 3 39N12 76w57 5:07:48
Clarysville 1 24 39N39 78w55 5:15:40
Clayton Manor 12 8 39N25 76w22 5:05:28
Clearfield 6 8 39N34 76w59 5:07:56
Clear Spring 21 7 39N39 77w56 5:11:44
Clearview 12 8 39N23 76w15 5:05:00
Clearview Village 2 20 39N09 76w33 5:06:12
Clearwater Beach 2 20 39N14 76w35 5:06:20
Clements 18 4 38N20 76w43 5:06:52
Cliffs City 14 15 39N13 76w04 5:04:16
Clifton 8 6 38N23 76w57 5:07:48
Clifton 10 7 39N26 77w27 5:09:48
Clifton 24 1 39N19 76w35 5:06:20

Clinton 16 16 38N46 76w54 5:07:36
Clinton Acres 16 16 38N42 76w51 5:07:24
Clinton Estates 16 16 38N47 76w53 5:07:32
Clinton Gardens 16 16 38N47 76w53 5:07:32
Clinton Vista 16 16 38N47 76w53 5:07:32
Clopper 15 16 39N08 77w12 5:08:48
Cloverfields 17 15 38N59 76w19 5:05:16
Clover Hill 10 7 39N26 77w27 5:09:48
Cloverlea 2 20 38N54 76w30 5:06:00
Cloverly 15 16 39N04 76w59 5:07:56
Club Hill 15 16 39N08 77w12 5:08:48
Cobb Island 8 6 38N16 76w51 5:07:24
Cobbler's Woods 16 16 38N58 76w51 5:07:24
Cockeysville 3 3 39N29 76w39 5:06:36
Cohasset 15 16 39N01 77w08 5:08:32
Cohill 21 8 39N42 78w11 5:12:44
Cokesburg 19 19 38N04 75w34 5:02:16
Cokesbury 7 7 39N36 76w07 5:04:28
Coleman 14 15 39N21 76w05 5:04:20
Colesville 15 16 39N05 77w00 5:08:00
Colesville Manor 15 16 39N04 76w59 5:07:56
Colesville Park 15 16 39N04 76w59 5:07:56
College 6 8 39N34 76w59 5:07:56
College Estates 10 7 39N26 77w27 5:09:48
College Gardens 15 16 39N05 77w10 5:08:40
College Heights Estates 16 16 38N58 76w58 5:07:52
College Park 16 16 38N59 76w56 5:07:44
College Park Woods 16 16 39N00 76w55 5:07:40
College View 15 16 39N03 77w03 5:08:12
Colmar Manor 16 16 38N56 76w57 5:07:48
Colonial Acres 7 7 39N37 75w50 5:03:20
Colonial Acres 12 8 39N32 76w21 5:05:24
Colonial Gardens 3 3 39N17 76w43 5:06:52
Colonial Heights 1 3 39N38 78w48 5:15:12
Colonial Park 3 3 39N20 76w43 5:06:52
Colonial Park 21 7 39N39 77w44 5:10:56
Colonial Village 3 3 39N22 76w43 5:06:52
Colora 7 7 39N40 76w06 5:04:24
Coltons Point 18 4 38N14 76w45 5:07:00
Columbia 13 3 39N14 76w50 5:07:20
Columbia Beach 2 20 38N50 76w30 5:06:00
Columbia Hills 13 3 39N16 76w49 5:07:16
Columbia Park 16 16 38N56 76w53 5:07:32
Colvilla 6 8 39N34 76w59 5:07:56
Compton 18 4 38N17 76w42 5:06:48
Comus 15 16 39N15 77w21 5:09:24
Concord 5 15 38N26 75w53 5:03:32
Concord 7 7 39N32 75w49 5:03:16
Congressional Forest Estates 15 16 39N00 77w08 5:08:32
Connecticut Avenue Estates 15 16 39N03 77w03 5:08:12
Connecticut Avenue Hills 15 16 39N03 77w03 5:08:12
Connecticut Avenue Park 15 16 39N04 77w04 5:08:16
Connecticut Gardens 15 16 39N03 77w03 5:08:12
Conowingo 7 7 39N40 76w10 5:04:40
Conowingo Village 12 8 39N40 76w10 5:04:40
Constant Friendship 12 8 39N28 76w17 5:05:08
Contee 16 16 39N05 76w58 5:07:52
Cooksville 13 3 39N19 77w01 5:08:04
Coopersville 3 3 39N32 76w44 5:06:56
Coopstown 12 8 39N35 76w23 5:05:32
Copenhaver 15 16 39N03 77w10 5:08:40
Copperville 6 8 39N40 77w10 5:08:40
Copperville 20 13 38N46 76w04 5:04:16
Coral Hills 16 16 38N52 76w56 5:07:44
Corbett 3 3 39N35 76w37 5:06:28
Corbett 21 7 39N39 77w44 5:10:56
Cordova 20 8 38N53 76w00 5:04:00
Cornersville 9 8 38N34 76w05 5:04:20
Cornfield Harbor 18 4 38N05 76w21 5:05:24
Corriganville 1 3 39N42 78w47 5:15:08
Costen 19 19 38N04 75w34 5:02:16
Costens 23 19 38N02 75w32 5:02:08
Cottage City 16 16 38N56 76w57 5:07:48
Country Club Acres 11 14 39N24 79w23 5:17:32
Country Club Park 3 3 39N26 76w37 5:06:28
Country Club Village 15 16 39N01 77w08 5:08:32
Courthouse 15 16 39N05 77w10 5:08:40
Courtleigh 3 3 39N22 76w45 5:07:00
Cove 11 2 39N37 79w19 5:17:16
Coventry 3 3 39N23 76w33 5:06:12
Cove Point 4 9 38N25 76w27 5:05:48
Cowentown 7 7 39N37 75w50 5:03:20
Coxs Corner 22 7 38N20 75w52 5:03:28
Craigtown 7 7 39N36 76w05 5:04:20
Cranberry 6 8 39N34 76w59 5:07:56
Crapo 9 8 38N19 76w08 5:04:32
Creagerstown 10 7 39N35 77w21 5:09:24
Crellin 11 14 39N23 79w28 5:17:52
Cresaptown 1 3 39N36 78w50 5:15:20
Crescendo 20 13 38N48 76w18 5:05:12
Crest Haven 15 16 39N01 76w59 5:07:56
Crest Leigh 13 3 39N16 76w49 5:07:16
Crestview 15 16 39N01 77w08 5:08:32

Crestview Manor 16 16 38N47 76w53 5:07:32
Crestwood 2 20 39N12 76w39 5:06:36
Crestwood 22 7 38N22 75w36 5:02:24
Crestwood Acres 12 8 39N23 76w15 5:05:00
Creswell 12 8 39N32 76w21 5:05:24
Crisfield 19 28 37N59 75w51 5:03:24
Criswood Manor 13 3 39N12 76w57 5:07:48
Crocheron 9 8 38N15 76w03 5:04:12
Crofton 2 20 39N00 76w41 5:06:44
Cromwood 3 3 39N23 76w33 5:06:12
Croom 16 16 38N45 76w46 5:07:04
Crosby 14 15 39N07 76w12 5:04:48
Crosier Gardens 16 16 38N50 76w55 5:07:40
Crowder 13 3 39N16 76w49 5:07:16
Crownsville 2 20 39N02 76w36 5:06:24
Crumpton 17 15 39N13 75w56 5:03:44
Crystal Beach 2 20 39N26 75w59 5:03:56
Crystal Beach Manor 7 7 39N25 75w55 5:03:40
Crystal Springs 16 16 39N00 76w55 5:07:40
Cub Hill 3 3 39N23 76w33 5:06:12
Cuckhold Creek 8 6 38N23 76w57 5:07:48
Cumberland 1 24 39N39 78w46 5:15:04
Cumberlandrive 1 3 39N38 78w48 5:15:12
Dailsville 9 8 38N34 76w05 5:04:20
Daisy 13 3 39N22 77w04 5:08:16
Dalton 13 3 39N16 76w49 5:07:16
Damascus 15 16 39N17 77w12 5:08:48
Dameron 18 4 38N09 76w22 5:05:28
Dames Quarter 19 19 38N10 75w52 5:03:28
Dam No. Ø4 21 7 39N27 77w45 5:11:00
Daniel 6 8 39N22 77w04 5:08:16
Daniels Park 16 16 39N00 76w55 5:07:40
Danville 1 3 39N32 78w53 5:15:32
Darcy Estates 16 16 38N49 76w56 5:07:44
Dares Beach 4 9 38N33 76w35 5:06:20
Dargan 21 7 39N19 77w44 5:10:56
Darleigh Manor 3 3 39N23 76w30 5:06:00
Darlington 12 8 39N38 76w12 5:04:48
Darnestown 15 16 39N06 77w18 5:09:12
Darryl Gardens 3 3 39N23 76w26 5:05:44
Daugherty Town 19 28 37N59 75w51 5:03:24
Davidsonville 2 20 38N55 76w38 5:06:32
Dawson 1 3 39N26 78w59 5:15:56
Dawsonville 15 16 39N08 77w21 5:09:24
Day 6 8 39N22 77w04 5:08:16
Daysville 10 7 39N29 77w21 5:09:24
Dayton 13 3 39N14 76w59 5:07:56
Deale 2 20 38N47 76w33 5:06:12
Deale Beach 2 20 38N47 76w33 5:06:12
Deal Island 19 19 38N08 75w57 5:03:48
Deanwood Park 16 16 38N54 76w54 5:07:36
Decatur Heights 16 16 38N57 76w56 5:07:44
Deep Creek 2 20 39N03 76w30 5:06:00
Deerfield 12 8 39N38 76w12 5:04:48
Deerfield 15 16 39N00 77w08 5:08:32
Deer Park 11 14 39N25 79w20 5:17:20
Deer Park 15 16 39N08 77w12 5:08:48
Deer Park 16 16 38N49 76w56 5:07:44
Deer Park Heights 16 16 38N49 76w56 5:07:44
Deer Park Plaza 3 3 39N22 76w45 5:07:00
Deers Head 22 7 38N22 75w36 5:02:24
Defense Heights 3 3 39N14 76w31 5:06:04
Defense Heights 16 16 38N57 76w54 5:07:36
Delight 3 3 39N26 76w48 5:07:12
Delmar 22 7 38N27 75w35 5:02:20
Delmont 2 20 39N09 76w40 5:06:40
Den Lee Acres 16 16 38N47 76w53 5:07:32
Dennings 6 8 39N33 77w06 5:08:24
Dennis 22 7 38N19 75w24 5:01:36
Dennis Grove Apartments 16 16 38N48 76w59 5:07:56
Denton 5 11 38N53 75w50 5:03:20
Derwood 15 16 39N06 77w11 5:08:44
Detmold 1 3 39N34 78w59 5:15:56
Detour 6 8 39N36 77w16 5:09:04
Devonshire Forest 3 3 39N26 76w37 5:06:28
Dickerson 15 16 39N13 77w26 5:09:44
Discovery 10 7 39N29 77w21 5:09:24
District Heights 16 16 38N51 76w54 5:07:36
Dixon 17 15 39N10 75w50 5:03:20
Dodge Park 16 16 38N56 76w53 5:07:32
Dogwood Flats 1 3 39N32 79w01 5:16:04
Dogwood Hills 3 3 39N24 76w36 5:06:24
Dominion 17 15 38N57 76w17 5:05:08
Doncaster 8 6 38N36 77w10 5:08:40
Donleigh 13 3 39N11 76w52 5:07:28
Donnybrook 3 3 39N24 76w36 5:06:24
Dorceytown 6 8 39N22 77w09 5:08:36
Dorchester Estates 16 16 38N47 76w53 5:07:32
Dorsey 2 20 39N15 76w41 5:06:44
Doubs 10 7 39N19 77w28 5:09:52
Dowell 4 9 38N21 76w28 5:05:52
Downsville 21 7 39N33 77w49 5:11:16
Drawbridge 9 8 38N26 75w53 5:03:32
Drayden 18 4 38N11 76w29 5:05:56
Dresden Green 16 16 38N58 76w51 5:07:24
Druid 24 1 39N19 76w38 5:06:32
Drumcliff 18 4 38N21 76w34 5:06:16
Drum Point 4 9 38N25 76w27 5:05:48
Drury 2 20 38N51 76w36 5:06:24
Drybranch 12 8 39N37 76w38 5:06:32
Dry Run 21 7 39N39 77w56 5:11:44
Dublin 12 8 39N39 76w16 5:05:04
Dulaney Village 3 3 39N26 76w37 5:06:28

Dulls Corner 2 20 39N03 76w30 5:06:00
Dumbarton 3 3 39N22 76w43 5:06:52
Dumbarton Heights 3 3 39N22 76w43 5:06:52
Dunbrook 2 20 39N09 76w33 5:06:12
Dundalk 3 3 39N16 76w32 5:06:08
Dundee Village 3 3 39N20 76w27 5:05:48
Dunkirk 4 9 38N43 76w40 5:06:40
Dunlaney Village 3 3 39N26 76w37 5:06:28
Dunloggin 13 3 39N16 76w49 5:07:16
Dunwood 12 8 39N25 76w22 5:05:28
Dupont Heights 16 16 38N50 76w55 5:07:40
Dynard 18 4 38N22 76w47 5:07:08
Eagle Harbor 16 16 38N34 76w41 5:06:44
Eagle Hill 2 20 39N09 76w33 5:06:12
Eakles Mill 21 7 39N29 77w42 5:10:48
Earleigh Heights 2 20 39N05 76w34 5:06:16
Earleville 7 7 39N25 75w55 5:03:40
Earlton 12 8 39N33 76w06 5:04:24
East Columbia Park 16 16 38N56 76w53 5:07:32
East End 24 1 39N18 76w35 5:06:20
Eastfield 3 3 39N14 76w31 5:06:04
East Meadow 16 16 38N48 76w59 5:07:56
East New Market 9 8 38N36 75w55 5:03:40
East Oakland 11 14 39N26 79w22 5:17:28
Easton 20 11 38N47 76w05 5:04:20
Easton Point 20 13 38N46 76w04 5:04:16
East Pines 16 16 38N58 76w55 5:07:40
Eastpoint 3 3 39N14 76w31 5:06:04
Eastport 2 20 38N57 76w29 5:05:56
East Princess Anne 20 26 38N13 75w38 5:02:32
East Riverdale 16 16 38N58 76w55 5:07:40
East Springbrook 15 16 39N04 76w59 5:07:56
Eastview 6 8 39N30 76w53 5:07:32
Eastview 10 7 39N26 77w27 5:09:48
Eckhart 1 24 39N39 78w53 5:15:32
Eden 19 19 38N17 75w39 5:02:36
Eden Terrace 3 3 39N17 76w43 5:06:52
Edesville 14 15 39N09 76w13 5:04:52
Edgemere 3 3 39N14 76w27 5:05:48
Edgemont 10 7 39N26 77w27 5:09:48
Edgemont 21 7 39N39 77w34 5:10:16
Edgemoor 15 16 39N01 77w08 5:08:32
Edgewater 2 20 38N56 76w33 5:06:12
Edgewater Beach 2 20 38N56 76w33 5:06:12
Edgewood 10 7 39N26 77w27 5:09:48
Edgewood 12 8 39N25 76w18 5:05:12
Edgewood 15 16 39N01 77w08 5:08:32
Edgewood Arsenal 12 8 39N28 76w08 5:04:32
Edgewood Meadows 12 8 39N23 76w15 5:05:00
Edgewood Park 3 3 39N23 76w33 5:06:12
Editors Park 16 16 38N58 76w58 5:07:52
Edmondson Heights 3 3 39N20 76w43 5:06:52
Edmondson Ridge 3 3 39N17 76w43 5:06:52
Edmonston 16 16 38N57 76w56 5:07:44
Ednor 15 16 39N04 76w59 5:07:56
Ednor Acres 15 16 39N04 76w59 5:07:56
Egg Hill 7 7 39N37 75w50 5:03:20
Elder Hill 11 2 39N39 79w24 5:17:36
Eldersburg 6 8 39N24 76w56 5:07:44
Eldorado 9 8 38N35 75w47 5:03:08
Elk Mills 7 7 39N40 75w50 5:03:20
Elkmore 7 7 39N37 75w50 5:03:20
Elkneck 7 7 39N36 75w56 5:03:44
Elk Ranch Park 7 7 39N37 75w50 5:03:20
Elkridge 13 3 39N13 76w43 5:06:52
Elkton 7 8 39N36 75w50 5:03:20
Elkton Heights 7 7 39N37 75w50 5:03:20
Elktonia 2 20 39N03 76w30 5:06:00
Elkton Landing 7 7 39N37 75w50 5:03:20
Elkwood Estates 7 7 39N37 75w50 5:03:20
Ellerslie 1 3 39N42 78w47 5:15:08
Ellerton 10 7 39N30 77w34 5:10:16
Ellicott City 13 3 39N16 76w48 5:07:12
Elliott 9 8 38N19 76w00 5:04:00
Elmwood 3 3 39N21 76w32 5:06:08
Elvaton Acres 2 20 39N09 76w40 5:06:40
Elwood 9 8 38N38 75w52 5:03:28
Emmitsburg 10 3 39N42 77w20 5:09:20
Emmorton 12 8 39N30 76w20 5:05:20
Emory Church 6 8 39N34 76w50 5:07:20
Emory Grove 3 24 39N42 76w41 5:06:44
Emory Grove 15 16 39N08 77w12 5:08:48
Engles Mill 11 2 39N37 79w19 5:17:16
Englewood 16 16 38N56 76w53 5:07:32
English Consul 3 3 39N14 76w37 5:06:28
English Manor 15 16 39N05 77w07 5:08:28
English Village 15 16 39N01 77w08 5:08:32
Enterprise Estates 16 16 38N30 75w52 5:03:28
Epping Forest 2 20 39N03 76w30 5:06:00
Ernstville 21 7 39N08 78w01 5:12:04
Escena 16 16 38N47 76w58 5:07:52
Essex 3 3 39N19 76w29 5:05:56
Etchison 15 16 39N08 77w12 5:08:48
Etzler Estates 10 7 39N26 77w27 5:09:48
Evergreen Heights 12 8 39N32 76w21 5:05:24
Evergreen Park 3 3 39N19 76w28 5:05:52
Evergreen Valley Estates 13 3 39N16 76w49 5:07:16
Ewell 19 19 38N00 76w02 5:04:08
Ewingville 17 15 39N13 76w04 5:04:16
Fairbank 20 13 38N41 76w20 5:05:20

MARYLAND

Fairfield 6	8	39N34	76w59	5:07:56
Fairfield 22	7	38N22	75w36	5:02:24
Fairfield Knolls 16	16	38N51	76w54	5:07:36
Fairgreen Acres 21	7	39N39	77w44	5:10:56
Fair Haven 2	20	38N43	76w40	5:06:40
Fair Hill 7	7	39N42	75w52	5:03:28
Fairidge 15	16	39N08	77w12	5:08:48
Fairknoll 15	16	39N04	76w59	5:07:56
Fairland 15	16	39N04	76w59	5:07:56
Fairland Acres 15	16	39N07	76w56	5:07:44
Fairland Heights 15	16	39N04	76w59	5:07:56
Fairlee 14	15	39N13	76w10	5:04:40
Fairmont 12	8	39N32	76w21	5:05:24
Fairmount 19	23	38N06	75w49	5:03:16
Fairmount Heights 16	16	38N54	76w55	5:07:40
Fair Play 21	7	39N33	77w44	5:10:56
Fairview 2	20	39N09	76w33	5:06:12
Fairview 21	7	39N39	77w56	5:11:44
Fairview Estates 15	16	39N04	76w59	5:07:56
Fairway 12	8	39N32	76w21	5:05:24
Fairway Hills 15	16	39N01	77w08	5:08:32
Fallston 12	8	39N31	76w25	5:05:40
Farmington 7	7	39N42	76w04	5:04:16
Farmington 15	16	38N59	77w05	5:08:20
Faulkner 8	6	38N26	76w59	5:07:56
Faulkner Ridge 13	3	39N16	76w49	5:07:16
Fawsett Farms 15	16	39N03	77w10	5:08:40
Feagaville 10	7	39N26	77w27	5:09:48
Federalsburg 5	8	38N42	75w47	5:03:08
Feesersburg 6	8	39N34	77w11	5:08:44
Felicity Cove 2	20	38N50	76w30	5:06:00
Fellowship Forest 3	3	39N24	76w36	5:06:24
Fenwick 8	6	38N38	77w04	5:08:16
Ferndale 2	20	39N11	76w39	5:06:36
Fernglen Manor 2	20	39N10	76w37	5:06:28
Fernwood 15	16	39N01	77w08	5:08:32
Fiddlersburg 21	7	39N39	77w44	5:10:56
Figgs Landing 23	27	38N10	75w24	5:01:36
Finksburg 6	8	39N30	76w53	5:07:32
Finzel 11	2	39N39	78w55	5:15:40
Fishing Creek 9	8	38N20	76w14	5:04:56
Fleishman Village 16	16	38N50	76w55	5:07:40
Flickersville 21	7	39N29	77w42	5:10:48
Flint Hill 10	7	39N19	77w28	5:09:52
Flintstone 1	3	39N42	78w34	5:14:16
Flohrville 6	8	39N24	76w56	5:07:44
Florence 13	3	39N22	77w04	5:08:16
Flower Avenue Park 15	16	38N59	77w01	5:08:04
Flower Valley Estates 15	16	39N05	77w07	5:08:28
Font Hill 13	3	39N16	76w49	5:07:16
Font Hill Manor 13	3	39N16	76w49	5:07:16
Forest Greens 12	8	39N31	76w10	5:04:40
Forest Heights 16	16	38N49	77w00	5:08:00
Forest Hill 12	8	39N35	76w23	5:05:32
Forest Knolls 15	16	39N01	77w00	5:08:00
Forest Knolls 16	16	38N47	76w58	5:07:52
Forest Lake 12	8	39N35	76w23	5:05:32
Forest Manor 16	16	38N51	76w54	5:07:36
Foreston 3	3	39N34	76w50	5:07:20
Forest Spring Park 3	3	39N17	76w43	5:06:52
Forestville 16	16	38N51	76w52	5:07:28
Forestville Estates 16	16	38N51	76w54	5:07:36
Forestville Phelps Addition 16	16	38N51	76w54	5:07:36
Forge Acres 3	3	39N23	76w26	5:05:44
Forge Heights 3	3	39N24	76w29	5:05:56
Fork 3	3	39N28	76w27	5:05:48
Forrest Hall 18	4	38N26	76w44	5:06:56
Fort Detrick 10	7	39N26	77w27	5:09:48
Fort Foote Estates 16	16	38N51	76w54	5:07:36
Fort Foote Village 16	16	38N47	76w58	5:07:52
Fort George Meade 2	20	39N05	76w50	5:07:20
Fort Howard 3	3	39N12	76w27	5:05:48
Fort Meade 2	20	39N06	76w45	5:07:00
Fort Ritchie 21	7	39N42	77w30	5:10:00
Fort Sumner 15	16	38N57	77w06	5:08:24
Fort Washington Estates 16	16	38N47	76w58	5:07:52
Fort Washington Forest 16	16	38N47	76w58	5:07:52
Foundry Siding 1	24	39N29	79w03	5:16:12
Fountaindale 10	7	39N26	77w33	5:10:12
Fountain Green 12	8	39N32	76w21	5:05:24
Fountain Green Heights 12	8	39N32	76w21	5:05:24
Fountain Head 21	8	39N42	77w43	5:10:52
Fountain Mills 10	7	39N22	77w19	5:09:16
Fountain Rock 10	7	39N29	77w21	5:09:24
Fountain Valley 6	8	39N34	76w59	5:07:56
Four Locks 21	7	39N40	77w57	5:11:48
Four Winds 3	3	39N24	76w36	5:06:24
Fowblesburg 3	3	39N34	76w50	5:07:20
Fox Chapel 15	16	39N10	77w16	5:09:04
Foxhall 15	16	39N04	77w04	5:08:16
Fox Hills 15	16	39N03	77w10	5:08:40
Foxley Manor 14	15	39N13	76w04	5:04:16
Fox Rest Woods 16	16	39N05	76w58	5:07:52
Fox Trailer Village 3	3	39N20	76w27	5:05:48
Foxville 10	7	39N41	77w27	5:09:48
Franklin 6	8	39N28	77w04	5:08:16
Franklin 24	1	39N17	76w39	5:06:36
Franklin Manor 2	20	38N48	76w32	5:06:08
Franklin Park 15	16	39N04	77w09	5:08:36
Franklinville 3	3	39N29	76w23	5:05:32
Franklinville 10	7	39N38	77w25	5:09:40
Frederick 10	3	39N25	77w25	5:09:40
Freedom 6	8	39N23	76w56	5:07:44
Freeland 3	24	39N42	76w41	5:06:44
Frenchtown 7	25	39N34	76w04	5:04:16
Friendly 16	16	38N47	76w58	5:07:52
Friendly Farms 16	16	38N47	76w58	5:07:52
Friends Creek 10	7	39N42	77w20	5:09:20
Friendship 2	20	38N44	76w35	5:06:20
Friendship Heights 15	16	38N59	77w05	5:08:20
Friendship Park 21	7	39N39	77w44	5:10:56
Friendsville 11	2	39N40	79w24	5:17:36
Frizzelburg 6	8	39N34	76w59	5:07:56
Frostburg 1	24	39N39	78w56	5:15:44
Frostown 10	7	39N26	77w33	5:10:12
Fruitland 22	7	38N19	75w37	5:02:28
Fullerton 3	3	39N21	76w32	5:06:08
Fulton 13	3	39N09	76w55	5:07:40
Funkstown 21	7	39N36	77w42	5:10:48
Furnace Branch 2	20	39N10	76w37	5:06:28
Gaither 6	8	39N22	76w59	5:07:56
Gaithersburg 15	16	39N08	77w12	5:08:48
Galena 14	15	39N21	75w53	5:03:32
Galestown 9	8	38N34	75w43	5:02:52
Galesville 2	20	38N51	76w33	5:06:12
Gallant Green 8	6	38N38	76w53	5:07:32
Gamber 6	8	39N30	76w53	5:07:32
Gambrills 2	20	39N04	76w40	5:06:40
Gannon 1	24	39N29	79w03	5:16:12
Gapland 21	7	39N24	77w40	5:10:40
Garfield 10	7	39N39	77w34	5:10:16
Garland 2	20	39N10	76w37	5:06:28
Garrett Forest 15	16	39N04	77w04	5:08:16
Garrett Park 15	16	39N02	77w06	5:08:24
Garrett Park Estates 15	16	39N02	77w06	5:08:24
Garretts Mill 21	7	39N20	77w37	5:10:28
Garrison 3	3	39N24	76w45	5:07:00
Gatts Corner 2	20	38N54	76w30	5:06:00
Gayfields 15	16	39N04	77w04	5:08:16
Gaywood 16	16	38N58	76w51	5:07:24
Georgetown 2	20	39N09	76w47	5:07:08
Georgetown 14	15	39N13	76w04	5:04:16
Georgetown Village 15	16	39N01	77w08	5:08:32
Georgian Forest 15	16	39N03	77w03	5:08:12
Germantown 15	16	39N11	77w16	5:09:04
Germantown 23	27	38N19	75w13	5:00:52
Germantown Estates 15	16	39N10	77w16	5:09:04
Gibson Island 2	20	39N05	76w26	5:05:44
Gibson Manor 12	8	39N32	76w21	5:05:24
Gilmore 1	3	39N34	78w56	5:15:44
Gilpintown 1	3	39N42	78w34	5:14:16
Gingerville-Wilenor Estates 2	20	38N56	76w33	5:06:12
Girdletree 23	23	38N06	75w24	5:01:36
Gist 6	8	39N24	76w56	5:07:44
Glade Town 10	7	39N29	77w21	5:09:24
Gladstone Acres 12	8	39N38	76w12	5:04:48
Glassmanor 16	16	38N48	76w59	5:07:56
Glazewood Manor 16	16	38N59	77w01	5:08:04
Glebe Heights 2	20	38N56	76w33	5:06:12
Glenallen 15	16	39N03	77w03	5:08:12
Glenarden 16	16	38N56	76w52	5:07:28
Glen Arm 3	3	39N27	76w30	5:06:00
Glen Brook 13	3	39N16	76w49	5:07:16
Glenbrook Knoll 15	16	39N01	77w08	5:08:32
Glenbrook Village 15	16	39N01	77w08	5:08:32
Glen Burnie 2	20	39N10	76w37	5:06:28
Glencoe 3	3	39N32	76w39	5:06:36
Glencoe 14	8	39N18	76w00	5:04:00
Glen Cove 15	16	39N01	77w08	5:08:32
Glendale 3	3	39N24	76w36	5:06:24
Glendale 22	7	38N22	75w36	5:02:24
Glendale Heights 16	16	38N59	76w49	5:07:16
Glen Echo 15	16	38N58	77w08	5:08:32
Glen Echo Heights 15	16	38N57	77w06	5:08:24
Glenelg 13	3	39N16	77w00	5:08:00
Glen Farms 7	7	39N41	75w43	5:02:52
Glen Gardens 2	20	39N10	76w37	5:06:28
Glen Hills 15	16	39N05	77w10	5:08:40
Glen Isle 2	20	39N03	76w30	5:06:00
Glen Kyle 7	7	39N41	75w43	5:02:52
Glenmar 13	3	39N16	76w49	5:07:16
Glen Mar Park 15	16	39N01	77w08	5:08:32
Glen Mary Heights 7	7	39N37	75w50	5:03:20
Glenmont 3	3	39N24	76w36	5:06:24
Glenmont 15	16	39N04	77w04	5:08:16
Glenmont Forest 15	16	39N04	77w04	5:08:16
Glenmont Heights 15	16	39N04	77w04	5:08:16
Glenmore 2	20	39N10	76w37	5:06:28
Glen Morris 3	3	39N27	76w49	5:07:16
Glenn Dale 16	16	38N59	76w49	5:07:16
Glenn Heights 12	8	39N33	76w06	5:04:24
Glen Oaks 15	16	39N03	77w10	5:08:40
Glenora Hills 15	16	39N05	77w10	5:08:40
Glenside Park 3	3	39N23	76w33	5:06:12
Glenville 12	8	39N38	76w12	5:04:48
Glenwaye Gardens 15	16	39N04	77w04	5:08:16
Glen Westover 7	7	39N41	75w43	5:02:52
Glenwood 12	8	39N32	76w21	5:05:24
Glenwood 13	3	39N17	77w02	5:08:08
Glenwood Park 16	16	38N58	76w51	5:07:24
Glover Acres 6	8	39N34	76w59	5:07:56
Gluckheim 9	8	38N36	75w55	5:03:40
Glymont 8	6	38N36	77w10	5:08:40
Glyndon 3	3	39N29	76w48	5:07:12
Glyn Mar 16	16	38N40	77w02	5:08:08
Golden Beach 18	4	38N26	76w44	5:06:56
Golden Hill 9	8	38N30	76w09	5:04:36
Golden Ring Mall 3	3	39N20	76w31	5:06:04
Goldsboro 5	8	39N02	75w47	5:03:08
Golf Club Shores 23	27	38N19	75w13	5:00:52
Golts 14	15	39N20	75w47	5:03:08
Good Acres 21	7	39N39	77w44	5:10:56
Good Hope 15	16	39N04	76w59	5:07:56
Good Luck 16	16	39N00	76w48	5:07:12
Goodwill 23	19	38N04	75w34	5:02:16
Gorman 11	2	39N18	79w21	5:17:24
Gortner 11	14	39N24	79w23	5:17:32
Goshen 15	16	39N08	77w12	5:08:48
Goshen Estates 15	16	39N08	77w12	5:08:48
Gotts 2	20	39N02	76w36	5:06:24
Govans 24	1	39N22	76w36	5:06:24
Governors Run 4	9	38N30	76w32	5:06:08
Graceham 10	7	39N38	77w25	5:09:40
Graceland Park 3	3	39N14	76w31	5:06:04
Grahamtown 1	24	39N39	78w55	5:15:40
Granby Woods 15	16	39N06	77w11	5:08:44
Grand Bel Manor 15	16	39N03	77w03	5:08:12
Granite 3	3	39N21	76w51	5:07:24
Grantsville 11	17	39N40	79w10	5:16:40
Grasonville 17	15	38N57	76w13	5:04:52
Gratitude 14	15	39N08	76w14	5:04:56
Gray Haven 3	3	39N14	76w31	5:06:04
Gray Manor 3	3	39N14	76w31	5:06:04
Gray Rock 13	3	39N16	76w49	5:07:16
Grays Corner 23	27	38N19	75w13	5:00:52
Grayton 8	6	38N27	77w13	5:08:52
Great Mills 18	4	38N14	76w30	5:06:00
Green Acres 15	16	39N01	77w08	5:08:32
Greenbelt 16	16	39N00	76w53	5:07:32
Greenberry Hills 21	7	39N39	77w44	5:10:56
Greenbriar 21	7	39N31	77w39	5:10:36
Greenbrier 3	3	39N24	76w36	5:06:24
Greenbrier 16	16	39N00	76w53	5:07:32
Greenfield 16	16	38N47	76w53	5:07:32
Greenfield Mills 10	7	39N19	77w28	5:09:52
Green Glade 11	2	39N27	79w14	5:16:56
Green Haven 2	20	39N08	76w33	5:06:12
Green Hill 22	7	38N23	75w44	5:02:56
Greenhill Acres 21	7	39N39	77w44	5:10:56
Green Meadows 8	6	38N36	77w10	5:08:40
Green Meadows 16	16	38N58	76w58	5:07:52
Greenmount 6	8	39N36	76w51	5:07:24
Green Ridge 1	3	39N38	78w23	5:13:32
Green Ridge 3	3	39N26	76w37	5:06:28
Greenridge 12	8	39N32	76w21	5:05:24
Greensboro 5	11	38N58	75w48	5:03:12
Greensburg 21	7	39N39	77w34	5:10:16
Green Spring Hills 12	8	39N25	76w22	5:05:28
Greentop Manor 3	3	39N29	76w39	5:06:36
Greentree 15	16	39N08	77w12	5:08:48
Greentree Manor 15	16	39N01	77w08	5:08:32
Greenvale Village 21	7	39N39	77w34	5:10:16
Greenville 6	8	39N40	77w10	5:08:40
Greenwich Forest 15	16	39N01	77w08	5:08:32
Greenwood Acres 2	20	39N03	76w30	5:06:00
Greenwood Farms 13	3	39N11	76w57	5:07:48
Greenwood Forest 16	16	38N58	76w51	5:07:24
Green Wood Knolls 15	16	39N04	77w04	5:08:16
Greystone Manor 21	7	39N39	77w44	5:10:56
Grimesville 3	24	39N42	76w41	5:06:44
Gross 1	3	39N41	78w40	5:14:40
Grosstown 8	6	38N32	76w47	5:07:08
Grove 5	15	38N43	75w55	5:03:40
Grove Hill 10	7	39N26	77w27	5:09:48
Guilford 13	3	39N16	76w49	5:07:16
Guilford Downs 13	3	39N16	76w49	5:07:16
Gunpowder Estates 3	3	39N24	76w29	5:05:56
Gwynn Acres 13	3	39N16	76w49	5:07:16
Gwynnbrook 3	3	39N26	76w48	5:07:12
Gwynn Oak 24	1	39N20	76w43	5:06:52
Hack Point 7	7	39N25	75w55	5:03:40
Hacks Point Acre 7	7	39N25	75w55	5:03:40
Hagerstown 21	25	39N39	77w43	5:10:52
Halethorpe 3	3	39N15	76w42	5:06:48
Halfway 21	7	39N37	77w46	5:11:04
Hall 16	16	38N54	76w44	5:06:56

Hallett Heights 23 27 38N10 75w24 5:01:36
Halley Estates 8 6 38N36 76w57 5:07:48
Hall's Crossroad 12 8 39N32 76w10 5:04:40
Halpine 15 16 39N04 77w07 5:08:28
Halpine View 15 16 39N05 77w07 5:08:28
Halpine Village 15 16 39N04 77w09 5:08:36
Hambleton Estates 2 20 39N03 76w30 5:06:00
Hamilton 24 1 39N21 76w34 5:06:16
Hamilton Park 21 7 39N39 77w44 5:10:56
Hammond Park 13 3 39N05 76w58 5:07:52
Hammond Wood 15 16 39N03 77w03 5:08:12
Hampden 24 1 39N20 76w38 5:06:32
Hampshire Knolls 16 16 38N59 76w58 5:07:52
Hampstead 6 8 39N37 76w51 5:07:24
Hampton 3 3 39N24 76w36 5:06:24
Hampton Garden 3 3 39N24 76w36 5:06:24
Hance Point 7 7 39N36 75w56 5:03:44
Hancock 21 8 39N42 78w11 5:12:44
Hanesville 14 15 39N17 76w06 5:04:24
Hanover 2 20 39N12 76w43 5:06:52
Hansonville 10 7 39N26 77w27 5:09:48
Harbor View 2 20 38N56 76w33 5:06:12
Harborview 3 3 39N14 76w31 5:06:04
Harborview 17 15 38N58 76w17 5:05:08
Harewood Park 3 3 39N20 76w27 5:05:48
Harford Estates 12 8 39N35 76w23 5:05:32
Harford Farms 3 3 39N23 76w33 5:06:12
Harford Furnace 12 8 39N32 76w21 5:05:24
Harford Hills 3 3 39N23 76w33 5:06:12
Harford Park 3 3 39N23 76w33 5:06:12
Harmans 2 20 39N10 76w42 5:06:48
Harmony 5 15 38N47 75w53 5:03:32
Harmony 10 7 39N26 77w33 5:10:12
Harmony Grove 10 7 39N26 77w27 5:09:48
Harmony Hall 16 16 38N47 76w58 5:07:52
Harmony Hills 15 16 39N04 77w04 5:08:16
Harney 6 8 39N40 77w10 5:08:40
Harper's Choice 13 3 39N16 76w49 5:07:16
Harpers Corner 18 4 38N26 76w44 5:06:56
Harrison Ferry 9 8 38N38 75w52 5:03:28
Harrisonville 3 3 39N23 76w50 5:07:20
Harristown 3 3 39N17 76w43 5:06:52
Harrisville 6 8 39N22 77w09 5:08:36
Harrisville 7 7 39N40 76w06 5:04:24
Harundale 2 20 39N10 76w37 5:06:28
Harwood 2 20 38N52 76w37 5:06:28
Har-Wood 13 3 39N15 76w41 5:06:44
Harwood Park 13 3 39N15 76w41 5:06:44
Hauvers 10 7 39N40 77w28 5:09:52
Havenwood 3 3 39N26 76w37 5:06:28
Havenwood Hills 21 7 39N39 77w34 5:10:16
Havre de Grace 12 8 39N33 76w06 5:04:24
Havre de Grace Heights 12 8 39N33 76w06 5:04:24
Hawbottom 10 7 39N26 77w33 5:10:12
Hawkeye 9 8 38N36 75w55 5:03:40
Hawthorne 3 3 39N20 76w27 5:05:48
Hazelhurst 11 2 39N27 79w14 5:16:56
Hazelmoor 7 7 39N25 75w55 5:03:40
Head of the Creek 22 7 38N23 75w44 5:02:56
Heather Hill Apartments 16 16 38N49 76w56 5:07:44
Hebbville 3 3 39N20 76w46 5:07:04
Hebron 22 7 38N25 75w41 5:02:44
Helen 18 4 38N23 76w43 5:06:52
Henderson 5 15 39N05 75w47 5:03:08
Hendry Estates 15 16 39N01 77w08 5:08:32
Herald Harbor 2 20 39N02 76w36 5:06:24
Hereford 3 3 39N35 76w40 5:06:40
Heritage Farm 15 16 39N03 77w10 5:08:40
Heritage Harbor 2 20 39N03 76w30 5:06:00
Hermitage Park 15 16 39N04 77w04 5:08:16
Hernwood Heights 3 3 39N22 76w45 5:07:00
Hickman 5 15 38N53 75w50 5:03:20
Hickory 12 8 39N35 76w21 5:05:24
Hickory Hills 12 8 39N32 76w21 5:05:24
Hicksburg 9 8 38N36 75w55 5:03:40
Hidden Point 2 20 39N03 76w30 5:06:00
High Bridge 16 16 38N57 76w47 5:07:08
High Bridge Estates 16 16 38N57 76w47 5:07:08
Highfield 15 16 39N08 77w12 5:08:48
Highland 10 7 39N30 77w34 5:10:16
Highland 13 3 39N11 76w57 5:07:48
Highland Beach 2 20 38N56 76w28 5:05:52
Highland Park 16 16 38N54 76w54 5:07:36
Highlands 15 16 39N09 77w05 5:08:20
Highland Stone 15 16 39N03 77w10 5:08:40
Highlandtown 24 1 39N15 76w33 5:06:12
High Meadows 10 7 39N22 77w16 5:09:04
High Point 2 20 39N09 76w33 5:06:12
High Point 15 16 39N01 77w08 5:08:32
High Point Estates 15 16 39N02 76w55 5:07:40
High Ridge 13 3 39N05 76w58 5:07:52
High Ridge Park 13 3 39N05 76w58 5:07:52
Highview Estates 13 3 39N16 76w49 5:07:16
Highview on the Bay 2 20 38N47 76w36 5:06:24
Hillandale 15 16 39N01 76w59 5:07:56
Hillandale Forest 15 16 39N01 77w02 5:08:08
Hillandale Heights 15 16 39N01 76w59 5:07:56
Hill Crest 15 16 38N59 77w01 5:08:04
Hillcrest Heights 16 16 38N50 76w57 5:07:48
Hillmead 15 16 39N01 77w08 5:08:32
Hillmeade 16 16 38N59 76w49 5:07:16
Hillmeade Manor 16 16 38N59 76w49 5:07:16
Hillsboro 5 15 38N53 75w54 5:03:36
Hillsborough Estates 16 16 39N05 76w58 5:07:52
Hillside 6 8 39N34 76w59 5:07:56
Hillside 16 16 38N54 76w54 5:07:36
Hillsmere Shores 2 20 38N57 76w29 5:05:56
Hills Point 9 8 38N34 76w05 5:04:20
Hill Top 8 6 38N29 77w07 5:08:28
Hobbs 5 15 38N53 75w50 5:03:20
Hoffman 1 24 39N39 78w55 5:15:40
Holbrook 3 3 39N22 76w45 5:07:00
Holiday Acres 21 7 39N39 77w34 5:10:16
Holiday Beach 4 9 38N42 76w32 5:06:08
Holiday Park 15 16 39N04 77w04 5:08:16
Holland Cliff Shores 4 9 38N37 76w37 5:06:28
Hollingsworth Manor 7 7 39N37 75w50 5:03:20
Holloway Estates 16 16 38N47 76w52 5:07:28
Holly Beach 3 3 39N19 76w28 5:05:52
Holly Hill 15 16 39N00 77w08 5:08:32
Holly Hill Harbor 2 20 38N56 76w33 5:06:12
Holly Spring 16 16 38N51 76w54 5:07:36
Hollywood 16 16 39N00 76w55 5:07:40
Hollywood 18 4 38N21 76w34 5:06:16
Hollywood Beach 7 7 39N32 75w49 5:03:16
Hollywood Estates 16 16 39N00 76w55 5:07:40
Hollywood Park 15 16 38N21 76w34 5:06:16
Hollywood Shores 18 4 38N21 76w34 5:06:16
Homecrest 3 3 39N21 76w32 5:06:08
Homecrest 15 16 39N04 77w04 5:08:16
Homestead Estates 15 16 39N04 76w59 5:07:56
Homewood 1 3 39N38 78w48 5:15:12
Homewood 15 16 39N02 77w06 5:08:24
Honga 9 8 38N30 76w09 5:04:36
Hood College 10 7 39N26 77w27 5:09:48
Hood's Mill 6 8 39N19 77w01 5:08:04
Hoopers Island 9 8 38N19 76w14 5:04:56
Hoopersville 9 8 38N16 76w11 5:04:44
Hope Hill 10 7 39N26 77w27 5:09:48
Hopeland 10 7 39N26 77w27 5:09:48
Hopewell 19 28 37N59 75w51 5:03:24
Hopkins Corner 12 8 39N33 76w06 5:04:24
Hopkins Mead 13 3 39N12 76w57 5:07:48
Horizon Run 15 16 39N08 77w12 5:08:48
Houcksville 6 8 39N36 76w51 5:07:24
Howard Heights 13 3 39N16 76w49 5:07:16
Howardville 3 3 39N22 76w43 5:06:52
Hoyes 11 2 39N39 79w24 5:17:36
Hudson 9 8 38N36 76w15 5:05:00
Hughesville 8 6 38N32 76w47 5:07:08
Hunt Club Estates 13 3 39N15 76w41 5:06:44
Hunters Hill 3 3 39N26 76w37 5:06:28
Huntersville 18 4 38N26 76w44 5:06:56
Hunting Hill 15 16 39N05 77w10 5:08:40
Hunting Hills 4 9 38N37 76w37 5:06:28
Hunting Lodge 3 3 39N23 76w33 5:06:12
Hunting Park 22 7 38N22 75w36 5:02:24
Hunting Ridge Estates 12 8 39N30 76w28 5:05:52
Huntington Terrace 15 16 39N01 77w08 5:08:32
Huntingtown 4 9 38N37 76w37 5:06:28
Huntsmoor 3 3 39N15 76w41 5:06:44
Huntsville 16 16 38N56 76w53 5:07:32
Hunt Valley 3 3 39N29 76w39 5:06:36
Hurlock 9 8 38N38 75w52 5:03:28
Hurry 18 4 38N22 76w47 5:07:08
Hutton 11 14 39N24 79w23 5:17:32
Huyett 21 7 39N39 77w44 5:10:56
Hyattstown 15 16 39N14 77w17 5:09:08
Hyattsville 16 16 38N57 76w56 5:07:44
Hyde Park 3 3 39N19 76w28 5:05:52
Hydes 3 3 39N29 76w30 5:06:00
Hynesboro 16 16 38N58 76w51 5:07:24
Hynson 5 15 38N26 75w53 5:03:32
Idlewild 2 20 38N50 76w30 5:06:00
Idlewylde 3 3 39N24 76w36 5:06:24
Ijamsville 10 7 39N22 77w19 5:09:16
Ilchester 13 3 39N15 76w46 5:07:04
Indian Head 8 6 38N36 77w10 5:08:40
Indian Head Manor 8 6 38N38 77w04 5:08:16
Indian Head Plant 8 6 38N35 77w12 5:08:48
Indian Queen East 16 16 38N47 76w58 5:07:52
Indian Queen Estates 16 16 38N47 76w58 5:07:52
Indian Spring 21 7 39N40 78w01 5:12:04
Indian Springs 10 7 39N26 77w27 5:09:48
Indian Springs 21 7 39N08 78w01 5:12:04
Indiantown 23 27 38N10 75w24 5:01:36
Ingleside 17 15 39N06 75w53 5:03:32
Inverness 3 3 39N14 76w31 5:06:04

Inverness Forest 15 16 39N03 77w10 5:08:40
Inverness Village 15 16 39N03 77w10 5:08:40
Ironshire 23 27 38N19 75w13 5:00:52
Ironsides 8 6 38N30 77w10 5:08:40
Island Creek 4 9 38N28 76w30 5:06:00
Island View Beach 3 3 39N19 76w28 5:05:52
Issue 8 6 38N17 76w53 5:07:32
Ivy Hills 13 3 39N16 76w49 5:07:16
Ivytown 20 13 38N46 76w04 5:04:16
Jackson 10 7 39N31 77w33 5:10:12
Jacksonville 3 3 39N31 76w34 5:06:16
Jacksonville 19 28 37N59 75w51 5:03:24
Jacktown 9 8 38N34 76w05 5:04:20
Jacobsville 2 20 39N07 76w31 5:06:04
Jarrettsville 12 8 39N36 76w29 5:05:56
Jefferson 10 7 39N23 77w32 5:10:08
Jefferson Heights 10 7 39N22 77w32 5:10:08
Jefferson Heights 16 16 38N54 76w54 5:07:36
Jefferson Heights 21 7 39N39 77w44 5:10:56
Jennings 11 2 39N42 79w10 5:16:40
Jerusalem 3 3 39N29 76w23 5:05:32
Jerusalem 10 7 39N30 77w34 5:10:16
Jerusalem 15 16 39N09 77w25 5:09:40
Jessup 2 20 39N09 76w47 5:07:08
Jesterville 22 7 38N18 75w53 5:03:32
Jewell 2 20 38N43 76w40 5:06:40
Johnsons 11 2 39N42 78w59 5:15:56
Johnsontown 14 15 39N13 76w04 5:04:16
Johnstown 4 9 38N19 76w27 5:05:48
Johnsville 6 8 39N24 76w56 5:07:44
Johnsville 10 7 39N33 77w13 5:08:52
Jones 2 20 39N05 76w34 5:06:16
Jonestown 5 15 38N43 75w55 5:03:40
Joppa 12 8 39N26 76w22 5:05:28
Joppa Heights 3 3 39N23 76w33 5:06:12
Joppa Manor 3 3 39N23 76w33 5:06:12
Joppa Springs 3 3 39N23 76w33 5:06:12
Joppatowne 12 8 39N25 76w21 5:05:24
Josenhans 3 3 39N19 76w28 5:05:52
Joyce Lane 2 20 39N03 76w30 5:06:00
Kalmia 12 8 39N32 76w21 5:05:24
Kalten Acres 6 8 39N34 76w59 5:07:56
Kastle Acres 16 16 38N47 76w53 5:07:32
Kaywood Gardens 16 16 38N57 76w58 5:07:52
Keedysville 21 7 39N29 77w42 5:10:48
Keeler Glade 11 2 39N39 79w24 5:17:36
Keifer 1 3 39N32 78w28 5:13:52
Kemp Mill 15 16 39N02 77w01 5:08:04
Kemp Mill Estates 15 16 39N04 76w59 5:07:56
Kempton 11 2 39N09 79w30 5:18:00
Kemptown 10 7 39N22 77w16 5:09:04
Ken Gar 15 16 39N02 77w06 5:08:24
Kenmore 16 16 38N56 76w53 5:07:32
Kennedyville 14 8 39N18 76w00 5:04:00
Kensington 15 16 39N02 77w05 5:08:20
Kensington Estates 15 16 39N02 77w06 5:08:24
Kensington Heights 15 16 39N02 77w06 5:08:24
Kensington View 15 16 39N02 77w06 5:08:24
Kent 16 16 38N55 76w51 5:07:24
Kent Island 17 15 38N57 76w19 5:05:16
Kent Island Estates 17 15 38N59 76w19 5:05:16
Kentland 16 16 38N55 76w53 5:07:32
Kentmore Park 14 15 39N22 75w58 5:03:52
Kentmorr 17 15 38N59 76w19 5:05:16
Kent Village 16 16 38N56 76w53 5:07:32
Kenwood 3 3 39N21 76w32 5:06:08
Kenwood 15 16 38N59 77w05 5:08:20
Kenwood Beach 4 9 38N30 76w32 5:06:08
Kerby Hills 16 16 38N48 76w59 5:07:56
Kettering 16 16 38N47 76w52 5:07:28
Keymar 6 8 39N36 77w14 5:08:56
Keysers Ridge 11 2 39N42 79w10 5:16:40
Keysville 6 8 39N40 77w10 5:08:40
Kidmore Lane 16 16 38N58 76w51 5:07:24
Kifer 1 3 39N34 78w29 5:13:56
Kilmarock 15 16 38N59 77w01 5:08:04
Kings County 3 3 39N29 76w23 5:05:32
Kings Grove 1 3 39N43 78w44 5:14:56
Kings Manor 8 6 38N36 76w57 5:07:48
Kings Ridge 3 3 39N23 76w33 5:06:12
Kingston 19 23 38N05 75w44 5:02:56
Kingstown 17 15 39N12 76w03 5:04:12
Kingsville 3 3 39N27 76w25 5:05:40
Kirkham 20 13 38N46 76w04 5:04:16
Kirkwood 16 16 38N57 76w56 5:07:44
Kitzmiller 11 2 39N23 79w12 5:16:48
Kitzmillerville 11 2 39N23 79w12 5:16:48
Klej Grange 23 19 38N04 75w34 5:02:16
Knapps Meadow 1 3 39N34 78w59 5:15:56
Knettishall 3 3 39N24 76w36 5:06:24
Knoebels Corner 3 3 39N27 76w30 5:06:00
Knollview 13 3 39N16 76w49 5:07:16
Knollwood 3 3 39N24 76w36 5:06:24
Knollwood 16 16 38N59 76w58 5:07:52
Knoxville 10 7 39N20 77w37 5:10:28
Kump Station 6 8 39N40 77w10 5:08:40
Ladiesburg 10 7 39N35 77w16 5:09:04
Lakeland 2 20 39N05 76w34 5:06:16
Lakeland 16 16 39N00 76w55 5:07:40
Lake Linganore 10 7 39N26 77w27 5:09:48
Lake Normandy Estates 15 16 39N03 77w10 5:08:40
Lake Roland 3 3 39N24 76w36 5:06:24

Lakes 9 8 38N22 76w08 5:04:32
Lake Shore 2 20 39N07 76w29 5:05:56
Lakeside Manor 15
16 39N05 77w07 5:08:28
Lakeside Vista 12 8 39N25 76w22 5:05:28
Lakeview 13 3 39N05 76w58 5:07:52
Lakeview 15 16 39N00 77w08 5:08:32
Lake Village 16 16 38N57 76w47 5:07:08
Lakewood 22 7 38N22 75w36 5:02:24
Lakewood Estates 4
9 38N43 76w40 5:06:40
Lakewood Estates 15
16 39N05 77w10 5:08:40
Landon Woods 15 16 39N01 77w08 5:08:32
Landover 16 16 38N56 76w54 5:07:36
Landover Estates 16
16 38N58 76w53 5:07:32
Landover Hills 16
16 38N57 76w53 5:07:32
Landover Knolls 16
16 38N56 76w53 5:07:32
Landover Park 16 16 38N56 76w53 5:07:32
Lane Beach 18 4 38N18 76w39 5:06:36
Langley Park 16 16 38N59 76w59 5:07:56
Lanham 16 16 38N58 76w52 5:07:28
Lanham Acres 16 16 38N58 76w51 5:07:24
Lanham Heights 16
16 38N58 76w51 5:07:24
Lansdowne 3 3 39N15 76w40 5:06:40
Lantz 10 7 39N41 77w27 5:09:48
Lapidum 12 8 39N33 76w06 5:04:24
La Plata 8 6 38N32 76w59 5:07:56
Lappans 21 7 39N32 77w45 5:11:00
Larchmont Knolls 15
16 39N02 77w06 5:08:24
Largo 16 16 38N54 76w50 5:07:20
La-Rox Heights 6 8 39N34 76w59 5:07:56
Laurel 16 16 39N06 76w51 5:07:24
Laurel Acres 2 20 39N09 76w33 5:06:12
Laurel Brook 12 8 39N31 76w25 5:05:40
Laureldale 3 3 39N23 76w33 5:06:12
Laurel Grove 18 4 38N26 76w44 5:06:56
Laurel Shopping Center 16
16 39N05 76w58 5:07:52
Laurel Walk 16 16 39N05 76w58 5:07:52
La Vale 1 24 39N39 78w50 5:15:20
Lawsonia 19 28 37N59 75w51 5:03:24
Lawsons 19 19 38N00 75w48 5:03:12
Lawyer Heights 10 7 39N38 77w25 5:09:40
Layhill 15 16 39N04 77w04 5:08:16
Layhill Gardens 15
16 39N04 77w04 5:08:16
Layhill Village 15
16 39N04 77w04 5:08:16
Laytonia 15 16 39N08 77w12 5:08:48
Laytonsville 15 16 39N13 77w09 5:08:36
Lees Woods 12 8 39N32 76w21 5:05:24
Le Gore 10 7 39N33 77w19 5:09:16
Leisure World 15 16 39N04 77w04 5:08:16
Leitersburg 21 7 39N41 77w38 5:10:32
Leon 2 20 38N51 76w36 5:06:24
Leonardtown 18 4 38N17 76w38 5:06:32
Leslie 7 7 39N36 75w56 5:03:44
Level 12 8 39N35 76w12 5:04:48
Lewisdale 16 16 38N59 76w58 5:07:52
Lewis Heights 16 16 38N59 76w58 5:07:52
Lewis Spring Manor 16
16 38N47 76w53 5:07:32
Lewistown 10 7 39N32 77w26 5:09:44
Lewistown 20 8 38N53 76w00 5:04:00
Lexington Park 18 4 38N16 76w27 5:05:48
Liberty 10 7 39N29 77w15 5:09:00
Liberty Grove 7 7 39N39 76w07 5:04:28
Liberty Manor 3 3 39N20 76w43 5:06:52
Libertytown 10 7 39N29 77w14 5:08:56
Libertytown 23 27 38N19 75w13 5:00:52
Lime Kiln 10 7 39N26 77w27 5:09:48
Linchester 5 15 38N43 75w55 5:03:40
Lincoln Avenue 21 7 39N39 77w44 5:10:56
Lincoln Heights 22
7 38N22 75w36 5:02:24
Lincoln Park 15 16 39N05 77w10 5:08:40
Linden Heights 3 3 39N23 76w33 5:06:12
Lineboro 6 8 39N43 76w51 5:07:24
Linganore 10 7 39N29 77w10 5:08:40
Linhigh 3 3 39N21 76w32 5:06:08
Linkwood 9 8 38N34 75w59 5:03:56
Linstead-on-the-Severn 2
20 39N05 76w34 5:06:16
Linthicum 2 20 39N12 76w39 5:06:36
Linthicum Heights 2
20 39N12 76w39 5:06:36
Linwood 6 8 39N34 77w09 5:08:36
Linwood 13 3 39N16 76w49 5:07:16
Lipins Corner 2 20 39N09 76w33 5:06:12
Lisbon 13 3 39N19 77w04 5:08:16
Little Orleans 1 3 39N38 78w23 5:13:32
Livingston Grove 16
16 38N40 77w02 5:08:08
Livingston Park 16
16 38N48 76w59 5:07:56
Llandaff 20 13 38N46 76w04 5:04:16
Lloyds 9 8 38N34 76w05 5:04:20
Loartown 1 24 39N39 78w55 5:15:40
Lochearn 3 3 39N20 76w43 5:06:52
Loch Glen 3 3 39N24 76w36 5:06:24
Loch Hill 3 3 39N22 76w36 5:06:24
Loch Lynn Heights 11
14 39N23 79w23 5:17:32
Loch Raven 3 3 39N24 76w36 5:06:24
Loch Raven Heights 3
3 39N24 76w36 5:06:24
Loch Raven Village 3
3 39N24 76w36 5:06:24
Locust Grove 1 3 39N38 78w48 5:15:12
Locust Grove 14 8 39N18 76w00 5:04:00
Locust Grove 21 7 39N26 77w40 5:10:40
Locust Grove Beach 4
9 38N42 76w32 5:06:08
Locust Hill Estates 15
16 39N01 77w08 5:08:32
Locust Valley 10 7 39N26 77w33 5:10:12
Lodgecliffe 9 8 38N34 76w05 5:04:20
Lodge Forest 3 3 39N14 76w31 5:06:04
Lonaconing 1 24 39N34 79w00 5:16:00
Londontowne 2 20 38N56 76w33 5:06:12
Lone Oak 15 16 39N01 77w08 5:08:32
Long 1 3 39N38 78w48 5:15:12
Long Bar Harbor 12
8 39N28 76w17 5:05:08
Long Beach 4 9 38N28 76w30 5:06:00
Long Corner 13 3 39N22 77w09 5:08:36
Longfellow 13 3 39N16 76w49 5:07:16
Longford 3 3 39N26 76w37 5:06:28
Long Green 3 3 39N28 76w31 5:06:04
Long Green Station 3
3 39N27 76w30 5:06:00
Long Meadow 6 8 39N24 76w56 5:07:44
Long Meadow Estates 15
16 39N01 77w08 5:08:32
Longview Beach 18 4 38N18 76w47 5:07:08
Longwood 15 16 39N01 77w08 5:08:32
Longwoods 20 8 38N52 76w05 5:04:20
Lord 1 24 39N39 78w55 5:15:40
Loreley 3 3 39N23 76w26 5:05:44
Loretta Heights 2
20 39N03 76w30 5:06:00
Lothian 2 20 38N50 76w37 5:06:28
Louisville 6 8 39N30 76w53 5:07:32
Lou Mar Estates 12
8 39N28 76w17 5:05:08
Love Point 17 15 39N02 76w19 5:05:16
Loveville 18 4 38N21 76w41 5:06:44
Lower Magothy Beach 2
20 39N05 76w34 5:06:16
Lower Marlboro 4 9 38N39 76w41 5:06:44
Loyola 24 1 39N21 76w38 5:06:32
Luke 1 24 39N29 79w04 5:16:16
Lusby 4 9 38N25 76w27 5:05:48
Lusby Crossroads 2
20 39N03 76w30 5:06:00
Lute 15 16 39N04 77w04 5:08:16
Lutherville 3 3 39N26 76w37 5:06:28
Lutherville-Timonium 3
3 39N25 76w38 5:06:32
Lutz Hill 3 3 39N20 76w31 5:06:04
Luxmanor 15 16 39N04 77w09 5:08:36
Lynbrook 15 16 39N01 77w08 5:08:32
Lynch 14 8 39N18 76w04 5:04:16
Lynch Point 3 3 39N14 76w31 5:06:04
Lynne Acres 3 3 39N20 76w43 5:06:52
Lyons Creek 2 20 38N51 76w36 5:06:24
Lyons Creek 4 9 38N43 76w40 5:06:40
Lyons Homes 3 3 39N14 76w31 5:06:04
Lystra Farms 3 3 39N25 76w43 5:06:52
Maceys Corner 2 20 39N05 76w34 5:06:16
Maddox 18 4 38N22 76w47 5:07:08
Madison 9 8 38N30 76w13 5:04:52
Madonna 12 8 39N36 76w29 5:05:56
Magnolia 12 8 39N24 76w19 5:05:16
Magothy Beach 2 20 39N09 76w33 5:06:12
Magothy Park Beach 2
20 39N09 76w33 5:06:12
Mago Vista 2 20 39N03 76w30 5:06:00
Main Street 22 7 38N22 75w36 5:02:24
Malcolm 8 6 38N38 76w53 5:07:32
Malvern 3 3 39N24 76w36 5:06:24
Manchester 6 3 39N40 76w53 5:07:32
Manchester Estates 16
16 38N47 76w58 5:07:52
Manhattan Beach 2
20 39N05 76w34 5:06:16
Manokin 19 23 38N07 75w46 5:03:04
Manokin 22 7 38N22 75w36 5:02:24
Manor 3 3 39N35 76w37 5:06:28
Manor by the Lake 15
16 39N05 77w07 5:08:28
Manor Park 15 16 39N05 77w07 5:08:28
Manor View 3 3 39N27 76w30 5:06:00
Manor Woods 15 16 39N05 77w07 5:08:28
Maple Crest 3 3 39N20 76w27 5:05:48
Maplecrest 6 8 39N34 76w59 5:07:56
Maple Plains 22 7 38N22 75w36 5:02:24
Mapleside 1 3 39N38 78w48 5:15:12
Maple View 6 8 39N34 76w59 5:07:56
Mapleville 10 7 39N22 77w09 5:08:36
Mapleville 21 7 39N31 77w39 5:10:36
Maplewood 13 3 39N16 76w49 5:07:16
Maplewood 15 16 39N01 77w08 5:08:32
Maplewood 16 16 38N48 76w59 5:07:56
Marbury 8 6 38N33 77w09 5:08:36
Mardela Springs 22
7 38N28 75w46 5:03:04
Margate 2 20 39N10 76w37 5:06:28
Mariners 19 28 37N59 75w51 5:03:24
Marion Station 19
23 38N02 75w46 5:03:04
Marlboro 16 16 38N50 76w44 5:06:56
Marley 2 20 39N10 76w37 5:06:28
Marling Farms 17 15 38N58 76w17 5:05:08
Marlow Heights 16
16 38N49 76w56 5:07:44
Marlton 16 16 38N47 76w52 5:07:28
Marlywood 3 3 39N24 76w36 5:06:24
Marriottsville 13 3 39N21 76w54 5:07:36
Mars Estates 3 3 39N19 76w28 5:05:52
Marshall 12 8 39N37 76w29 5:05:56
Marshall Hall 8 6 38N41 77w06 5:08:24
Marshalls Corner 8
6 38N32 76w59 5:07:56
Marston 6 8 39N33 77w06 5:08:24
Martin Manor 6 8 39N34 76w59 5:07:56

MARYLAND

Martinsburg 15 16 39N13 77w26 5:09:44
Martins Woods 16 16 38N58 76w51 5:07:24
Marydel 5 15 39N07 75w45 5:03:00
Maryland City 2 20 39N06 76w49 5:07:16
Maryland Line 3 3 39N43 76w40 5:06:40
Maryland Park 16 16 38N54 76w54 5:07:36
Maryland Point 8 6 38N27 77w13 5:08:52
Marymount 15 16 39N01 77w08 5:08:32
Masons Beach 2 20 38N47 76w33 5:06:12
Mason Springs 8 6 38N36 77w10 5:08:40
Massey 14 15 39N19 75w49 5:03:16
Masseys 14 15 39N19 75w50 5:03:20
Mattapex 17 15 38N59 76w19 5:05:16
Mattapony 16 16 38N57 76w56 5:07:44
Matthews 20 13 38N49 75w57 5:03:48
Matthewstown 2 20 39N12 76w43 5:06:52
Maugansville 21 8 39N42 77w47 5:11:08
Mayberry 6 8 39N34 76w59 5:07:56
Mayberry Wells 16
16 39N05 76w58 5:07:52
Mayfield 2 20 39N02 76w41 5:06:44
Mayfield 13 3 39N16 76w49 5:07:16
Mayo 2 20 38N53 76w31 5:06:04
McAlpine 13 3 39N16 76w49 5:07:16
McCahill Estates 16
16 39N05 76w58 5:07:52
McCanns Corner 12 8 39N40 76w23 5:05:32
McComas Beach 11 14 39N24 79w23 5:17:32
McCoole 1 3 39N29 78w59 5:15:56
McDaniel 20 13 38N49 76w17 5:05:08
McDonogh 3 3 39N22 76w43 5:06:52
McHenry 11 2 39N33 79w21 5:17:24
McKaig 10 7 39N22 77w09 5:08:36
McKay Beach 18 4 38N18 76w39 5:06:36
McKendree 16 16 38N42 76w51 5:07:24
McKinleyville 14 15 39N08 76w14 5:04:56
McKinstrys Mills 6
8 39N34 77w11 5:08:44
Meadowbrook 16 16 38N57 76w47 5:07:08
Meadowbrook Estates 15
16 39N10 77w16 5:09:04
Meadowcliff 3 3 39N27 76w30 5:06:00
Meadowood 15 16 39N04 76w59 5:07:56
Meadowvale Manor 12
8 39N33 76w06 5:04:24
Meadowview 7 7 39N37 75w50 5:03:20
Meadowview Park 7 7 39N37 75w50 5:03:20
Mechanicsville 12 8 39N32 76w21 5:05:24
Mechanicsville 18 4 38N26 76w44 5:06:56
Medford 6 8 39N33 77w06 5:08:24
Melitota 14 15 39N13 76w04 5:04:16
Mellwood 16 16 38N48 76w48 5:07:12
Melrose 6 8 39N39 76w53 5:07:32
Melson 22 7 38N27 75w35 5:02:20
Merchants 24 1 39N18 76w38 5:06:32
Merrimack Park 15
16 39N01 77w08 5:08:32
Merritt Heights 22
7 38N22 75w36 5:02:24
Merrymount 3 3 39N20 76w43 5:06:52
Meyer Manor 6 8 39N34 76w59 5:07:56
Michigan Park Hills 16
16 38N59 76w58 5:07:52
Middleborough 3 3 39N19 76w28 5:05:52
Middlebrook 15 16 39N10 77w16 5:09:04
Middle Brooke 6 8 39N34 76w59 5:07:56
Middleburg 6 8 39N37 77w14 5:08:56
Middlepoint 10 7 39N30 77w34 5:10:16
Middle River 3 3 39N20 76w27 5:05:48
Middlesex 3 3 39N19 76w28 5:05:52
Middleton Farm 16
16 38N49 76w56 5:07:44
Middletown 3 24 39N42 76w41 5:06:44
Middletown 10 7 39N27 77w33 5:10:12
Middletown Heights 10
7 39N26 77w33 5:10:12
Midland 1 3 39N36 78w57 5:15:48
Midlothian 1 3 39N38 78w57 5:15:48
Milestown 18 4 38N16 76w46 5:07:04
Milford 3 3 39N21 76w44 5:06:56
Milford Ridge 3 3 39N20 76w43 5:06:52
Millbrook 16 16 39N05 76w58 5:07:52
Mill Creek Towne 15
16 39N05 76w58 5:07:52
Miller 1 24 39N39 78w55 5:15:40
Millers 6 8 39N40 76w51 5:07:24
Millers Island 3 3 39N13 76w28 5:05:52
Millersville 2 20 39N04 76w39 5:06:36
Mill Green 12 8 39N40 76w23 5:05:32
Millington 14 15 39N16 75w50 5:03:20
Mill Run 1 24 39N29 79w03 5:16:12
Millwood 16 16 38N54 76w54 5:07:36
Mimosa Cove 2 20 38N47 76w33 5:06:12
Mitchell Manor 11 2 39N11 76w52 5:07:28
Mitchellville 16 16 38N30 75w52 5:03:28
Monie 19 26 38N12 75w41 5:02:44
Monkton 3 3 39N35 76w37 5:06:28
Monrovia 10 7 39N22 77w16 5:09:04
Montevideo 13 3 39N09 76w47 5:07:08
Montgomery Knolls 13
3 39N16 76w49 5:07:16
Montgomery Square 15
16 39N03 77w10 5:08:40
Montgomery Village 15
16 39N08 77w12 5:08:48
Montgomery White Oak 15
16 39N04 76w59 5:07:56
Montrose 15 16 39N03 77w08 5:08:32
Monumental 3 3 39N15 76w41 5:06:44
Mooresfield 13 3 39N10 76w54 5:07:36
Morgan 6 8 39N22 77w04 5:08:16
Morgantown 1 24 39N39 78w55 5:15:40
Morgantown 8 6 38N23 76w57 5:07:48
Morganza 18 4 38N23 76w42 5:06:48
Morningside 16 16 38N50 76w54 5:07:36
Moscow 1 3 39N32 79w01 5:16:04

Motters 10 7 39N36 77w19 5:09:16
Mount Aetna 21 7 39N39 77w44 5:10:56
Mountaindale 10 7 39N38 77w25 5:09:40
Mountain Lake Park 11
14 39N24 79w23 5:17:32
Mountain Lake View 6
8 39N34 76w59 5:07:56
Mountain View Estates 15
16 39N08 77w12 5:08:48
Mount Airy 6 8 39N22 77w10 5:08:40
Mount Airy Estates 10
7 39N22 77w09 5:08:36
Mount Briar 21 7 39N29 77w42 5:10:48
Mount Carmel 2 20 39N09 76w33 5:06:12
Mount De Sales 3 3 39N17 76w43 5:06:52
Mount Harmony 4 9 38N43 76w36 5:06:24
Mount Hebron 13 3 39N16 76w49 5:07:16
Mount Hermon 22 7 38N22 75w36 5:02:24
Mount Lena 21 7 39N31 77w39 5:10:36
Mount Olive 6 8 39N22 77w09 5:08:36
Mount Pleasant 10 7 39N27 77w20 5:09:20
Mount Pleasant 22 7 38N24 75w21 5:01:24
Mount Pleasant Beach 2
20 39N09 76w33 5:06:12
Mount Rainier 16 16 38N56 76w58 5:07:52
Mount Savage 1 24 39N42 78w53 5:15:32
Mount Vernon 19 19 38N15 75w47 5:03:08
Mount Victoria 8 6 38N21 76w54 5:07:36
Mountview 13 3 39N21 76w54 5:07:36
Mount View Gardens 21
7 39N39 77w44 5:10:56
Mountville 10 7 39N26 77w27 5:09:48
Mount Washington 24
1 39N22 76w40 5:06:40
Mount Westley 23 27 38N10 75w24 5:01:36
Mount Zion 5 15 39N07 75w45 5:03:00
Mount Zion 10 7 39N26 77w27 5:09:48
Mount Zoar 7 7 39N40 76w10 5:04:40
Mousetown 21 7 39N31 77w39 5:10:36
Muirkirk 16 16 39N02 76w55 5:07:40
Murray Hills 16 16 38N48 76w59 5:07:56
Myers 6 8 39N41 77w02 5:08:08
Myersdale 21 8 39N42 78w11 5:12:44
Myersville 10 7 39N30 77w34 5:10:16
Nanjemoy 8 6 38N27 77w13 5:08:52
Nanticoke 22 7 38N16 75w54 5:03:36
Narrows 17 15 38N58 76w13 5:04:52
Narrows Park 1 3 39N38 78w48 5:15:12
National Naval Medical Cente 15
16 39N01 77w08 5:08:32
Naval Academy 2 20 38N58 76w30 5:06:00
Naval Air Facility 16
16 38N52 77w00 5:08:00
Neavitt 20 13 38N44 76w17 5:05:08
Neck 9 8 38N35 76w15 5:05:00
Needwood Estates 15
16 39N06 77w11 5:08:44
Neeld Estates 4 9 38N37 76w37 5:06:28
Neelsville 15 16 39N10 77w16 5:09:04
Neilwood 15 16 39N04 77w09 5:08:36
New Addition 10 7 39N20 77w37 5:10:28
Newark 23 19 38N15 75w17 5:01:08
New Birmingham Manor 15
16 39N07 76w56 5:07:44
Newburg 8 6 38N23 76w57 5:07:48
New Carrollton 16
16 38N58 76w53 5:07:32
Newcomb 20 13 38N45 76w11 5:04:44
New Germany 11 2 39N42 79w10 5:16:40
New Hampshire Estates 15
16 39N01 76w59 5:07:56
New Hampshire Gardens 16
16 38N59 77w01 5:08:04
Newhope 22 7 38N24 75w21 5:01:24
New London 10 7 39N22 77w09 5:08:36
New Market 10 7 39N23 77w17 5:09:08
New Market 18 4 38N29 76w47 5:07:08
New Midway 10 7 39N34 77w18 5:09:12
Newport 8 6 38N29 76w47 5:07:08
Newport Hills 15 16 39N02 77w06 5:08:24
Newton 5 15 38N43 75w55 5:03:40
Newton Village 16
16 38N57 76w56 5:07:44
Newtown 14 15 39N18 76w09 5:04:36
Newtown 20 8 38N53 76w00 5:04:00
New Valley 7 7 39N40 76w10 5:04:40
New Windsor 6 8 39N32 77w05 5:08:20
Nikep 1 24 39N33 79w00 5:16:00
Nob Hill 13 3 39N16 76w49 5:07:16
Norbeck 15 16 39N04 77w04 5:08:16
Normandy Heights 13
3 39N16 76w49 5:07:16
Normans 17 15 38N59 76w19 5:05:16
Normira 7 7 39N37 75w50 5:03:20
Norris Corner 12 8 39N28 76w17 5:05:08
Norrisville 12 8 39N37 76w38 5:06:32
Northampton 3 3 39N26 76w37 5:06:28
Northampton 16 16 38N47 76w52 5:07:28
North Barnaby 16 16 38N48 76w59 5:07:56
North Beach 4 9 38N43 76w32 5:06:08
North Beach Park 2
20 38N42 76w32 5:06:08
North Branch 1 3 39N36 78w45 5:15:00
North Brentwood 16
16 38N57 76w57 5:07:48
North Chevy Chase 15
16 38N59 77w05 5:08:20
North Deale 2 20 38N47 76w33 5:06:12
North East 7 7 39N35 75w58 5:03:52
Northeast Heights 7
7 39N36 75w56 5:03:44
North Englewood 16
16 38N56 76w53 5:07:32
Northern 21 7 39N39 77w44 5:10:56
North Forestville 16
16 38N51 76w54 5:07:36
North Glade 11 2 39N27 79w14 5:16:56
North Hampton 16 16 38N47 76w52 5:07:28
North Indian Head Estates 8
6 38N38 77w04 5:08:16
North Junction 21 7 39N39 77w44 5:10:56
North Laurel 13 3 39N05 76w58 5:07:52
North Laurel Park 13
3 39N05 76w58 5:07:52
North Linthicum 2
20 39N12 76w39 5:06:36
North Ocean City 23
19 38N23 75w05 5:00:20
North Point 3 3 39N14 76w31 5:06:04
North Point Village 3
3 39N14 76w31 5:06:04
North Potomac 15 16 39N03 77w10 5:08:40
Northridge Manor 21
7 39N39 77w44 5:10:56
North Sherwood Forest 15
16 39N04 76w59 5:07:56
Northshire 3 3 39N14 76w31 5:06:04
North Shore 2 20 39N09 76w33 5:06:12
North Springbrook 15
16 39N04 76w59 5:07:56
North Takoma Park 15
16 39N00 77w00 5:08:00
North Wellham 2 20 39N10 76w37 5:06:28
Northwest Park 15
16 39N01 76w59 5:07:56
Northwood 24 1 39N19 76w37 5:06:28
Northwood Park 15
16 39N01 77w00 5:08:00
Northwood Village 15
16 39N03 77w03 5:08:12
Norwood 15 16 39N08 77w02 5:08:08
Norwood Estates 15
16 39N04 76w59 5:07:56
Notch Cliff 3 3 39N27 76w30 5:06:00
Nottingham 3 3 39N20 76w31 5:06:04
Nottingham 16 16 38N43 76w44 5:06:56
Nutters 22 7 38N19 75w33 5:02:12
Oak Acres 10 7 39N26 77w27 5:09:48
Oak Court 2 20 39N03 76w30 5:06:00
Oak Crest 16 16 39N05 76w58 5:07:52
Oakcrest Towers 16
16 38N51 76w54 5:07:36
Oakdale 15 16 39N03 77w03 5:08:12
Oak Forest 3 3 39N17 76w43 5:06:52
Oakington 12 8 39N33 76w06 5:04:24
Oakland 3 3 39N42 76w41 5:06:44
Oakland 6 8 39N24 76w56 5:07:44
Oakland 11 14 39N25 79w24 5:17:36
Oakland 16 16 38N51 76w54 5:07:36
Oakland Park 3 3 39N22 76w45 5:07:00
Oakland Terrace 15
16 39N02 77w06 5:08:24
Oaklawn 16 16 38N48 76w59 5:07:56
Oakleigh 3 3 39N23 76w33 5:06:12
Oakleigh Forest 2
20 39N05 76w34 5:06:16
Oakleigh Manor 3 3 39N24 76w36 5:06:24
Oaklyn Manor 12 8 39N25 76w22 5:05:28
Oakmont 15 16 39N01 77w08 5:08:32
Oak Orchard 16 16 38N47 76w53 5:07:32
Oak Park 3 3 39N15 76w41 5:06:44
Oak Park 11 14 39N24 79w23 5:17:32
Oak Ridge 21 7 39N39 77w44 5:10:56
Oak Summit 3 3 39N23 76w33 5:06:12
Oak View 15 16 39N01 76w59 5:07:56
Oakville 18 4 38N26 76w44 5:06:56
Oakville 19 26 38N12 75w41 5:02:44
Oakwood 7 7 39N41 76w10 5:04:40
Oakwood Knolls 15
16 39N01 77w08 5:08:32
Ocean City 23 12 38N20 75w05 5:00:20
Ocean City Harbor 23
19 38N23 75w05 5:00:20
Ocean Pines 23 27 38N19 75w13 5:00:52
Odenton 2 20 39N05 76w42 5:06:48
Odenton Gardens 2
20 39N02 76w41 5:06:44
Oella 3 3 39N16 76w49 5:07:16
Old Bay Trail 16 16 38N47 76w52 5:07:28
Olde Colonial Woods 15
16 39N09 77w05 5:08:20
Olde Fort Village 16
16 38N47 76w58 5:07:52
Olde Towne Village 16
16 38N51 76w54 5:07:36
Old Farm 15 16 39N04 77w09 5:08:36
Old Field 9 8 38N30 76w09 5:04:36
Oldfield 10 7 39N34 77w11 5:08:44
Old Field 15 16 39N03 77w10 5:08:40
Old Salem Village 15
16 39N04 76w59 5:07:56
Oldtown 1 3 39N33 78w37 5:14:28
Olive 10 7 39N20 77w37 5:10:28
Oliver Beach 3 3 39N20 76w27 5:05:48
Olivet 4 9 38N25 76w27 5:05:48
Olivet Hill 14 15 39N20 75w47 5:03:08
Olney 15 16 39N09 77w04 5:08:16
Olney Mills 15 16 39N09 77w05 5:08:20
Olney Square 15 16 39N09 77w05 5:08:20
One Spot 13 3 39N09 76w47 5:07:08
Oraville 18 4 38N26 76w44 5:06:56
Orchard Beach 2 20 39N10 76w32 5:06:08
Orchard Hills 3 3 39N26 76w37 5:06:28
Orchard Hills 21 7 39N39 77w44 5:10:56
Oregon 3 3 39N29 76w39 5:06:36
Oriole 19 19 38N10 75w49 5:03:16
Orleans 1 3 39N40 78w25 5:13:40
Otter Point 12 8 39N28 76w17 5:05:08
Overlea 3 3 39N22 76w32 5:06:08
Owings 4 9 38N43 76w36 5:06:24
Owings Beach 2 20 38N47 76w33 5:06:12
Owings Mills 3 3 39N25 76w47 5:07:08
Oxford 20 11 38N41 76w11 5:04:44
Oxon Hill 16 16 38N48 76w59 5:07:56
Oxon Run Hills 16
16 38N49 76w56 5:07:44
Oyster Harbor 2 20 39N03 76w30 5:06:00
Padonia 3 3 39N29 76w39 5:06:36
Paint Branch Estates 15
16 39N04 76w59 5:07:56
Paint Branch Farm 15
16 39N04 76w59 5:07:56
Palmer Park 16 16 38N55 76w52 5:07:28
Palmers Corner 16
16 38N47 76w58 5:07:52
Palmetto 19 26 38N12 75w41 5:02:44
Paradise 3 3 39N17 76w43 5:06:52
Paradise Beach 2 20 39N09 76w33 5:06:12
Paramount 21 7 39N39 77w44 5:10:56
Paramount Manor 21
7 39N39 77w44 5:10:56
Paris 4 9 38N43 76w36 5:06:24
Parkertown 23 27 38N19 75w13 5:00:52
Parker Wharf 4 9 38N28 76w30 5:06:00
Park Hall 18 4 38N13 76w26 5:05:44
Park Hall 21 7 39N31 77w39 5:10:36
Parkhead 21 7 39N08 78w01 5:12:04
Parkland 16 16 38N51 76w54 5:07:36
Parkland Apartments 16
16 38N51 76w54 5:07:36
Parkland Terrace 16
16 38N50 76w55 5:07:40
Park Mills 10 7 39N19 77w28 5:09:52
Park Overlook 15 16 39N06 77w11 5:08:44
Park Ridge 15 16 39N08 77w12 5:08:48
Parkside 15 16 39N01 77w08 5:08:32
Parkside Estates 15
16 39N06 77w11 5:08:44
Parkton 3 3 39N39 76w40 5:06:40
Parktowne 3 3 39N23 76w33 5:06:12
Parkview 16 16 38N47 76w53 5:07:32
Parkview Gardens 16
16 38N58 76w55 5:07:40
Parkville 3 3 39N23 76w33 5:06:12
Parkwood 15 16 39N01 77w08 5:08:32
Parrsville 6 8 39N22 77w09 5:08:36
Parsons 22 7 38N23 75w33 5:02:12
Parsonsburg 22 7 38N23 75w28 5:01:52
Partridge Place 15
16 39N08 77w12 5:08:48
Pasadena 2 20 39N07 76w35 5:06:20
Patapsco 6 8 39N32 76w54 5:07:36
Patterson 24 1 39N17 76w35 5:06:20
Patuxent 2 20 39N02 76w41 5:06:44
Patuxent 18 4 38N22 76w35 5:06:20
Patuxent Beach 18 4 38N18 76w31 5:06:04
Patuxent Park 18 4 38N15 76w27 5:05:48
Patuxent River 18 4 38N18 76w26 5:05:44
Peach Orchard Heights 15
16 39N07 76w56 5:07:44
Peachwood 15 16 39N04 76w59 5:07:56
Peacock Corners 14
15 39N15 75w50 5:03:20
Pearl 10 7 39N26 77w27 5:09:48
Pectonville 21 7 39N08 78w01 5:12:04
Pekin 1 3 39N32 79w00 5:16:00
Pendennis Mount 2
20 39N03 76w30 5:06:00
Pen Mar 21 7 39N42 77w30 5:10:00
Pepper Mill Village 16
16 38N54 76w54 5:07:36
Perry Hall 3 3 39N25 76w28 5:05:52
Perry Hall Estates 3
3 39N23 76w30 5:06:00
Perry Hall Manor 3
3 39N24 76w29 5:05:56
Perryman 12 8 39N27 76w12 5:04:48
Perry Point 7 7 39N33 76w04 5:04:16
Perrys Corner 17 15 38N58 76w13 5:04:52
Perryville 7 8 39N34 76w04 5:04:16
Perrywood Estates 15
16 39N07 76w56 5:07:44
Petersburg 9 8 38N38 75w52 5:03:28
Petersville 10 7 39N20 77w38 5:10:32
Petuxent Palisades 4
9 38N43 76w40 5:06:40
Pfeiffer Corners 13
3 39N16 76w49 5:07:16
Phoenix 3 3 39N31 76w37 5:06:28
Picketts Corner 6 8 39N22 77w04 5:08:16
Pike 15 16 39N04 77w09 5:08:36
Pikesville 3 3 39N23 76w43 5:06:52
Pilot 7 7 39N40 76w10 5:04:40
Pimlico Race Track 24
1 39N22 76w41 5:06:44
Pine Cliff 10 7 39N26 77w27 5:09:48
Pinecrest 16 16 38N59 77w01 5:08:04
Pinefield 8 6 38N38 76w53 5:07:32
Pine Grove Village 2
20 39N09 76w33 5:06:12
Pinehurst 2 20 39N07 76w26 5:05:44
Pinehurst Estates 16
16 38N48 76w59 5:07:56
Pine Knoll 6 8 39N34 76w59 5:07:56
Pine Orchard 13 3 39N17 76w52 5:07:28
Pinesburg 21 7 39N36 77w49 5:11:16
Pines on Severn 2
20 39N03 76w30 5:06:00
Pine Valley 3 3 39N26 76w37 5:06:28
Pine Whiff Beach 2
20 38N56 76w33 5:06:12
Pinewood Hill 16 16 38N47 76w58 5:07:52
Piney Glen Farms 15
16 39N03 77w10 5:08:40
Piney Grove 1 3 39N38 78w23 5:13:32
Piney Point 18 4 38N09 76w31 5:06:04
Pinto 1 3 39N34 78w50 5:15:20
Pioneer City 2 20 39N09 76w40 5:06:40

MARYLAND

Piscataway 16	16	38N42	76w58	5:07:52
Piscataway Hills 16	16	38N47	76w58	5:07:52
Pisgah 8	6	38N32	77w08	5:08:32
Pittsburg 22	7	38N24	75w25	5:01:40
Pittsville 22	7	38N24	75w25	5:01:40
Plainfield 22	7	38N22	75w36	5:02:24
Plane Number Four 10	7	39N22	77w09	5:08:36
Pleasant Grove 3	3	39N27	76w49	5:07:16
Pleasant Hill 3	3	39N26	76w48	5:07:12
Pleasant Hill 7	7	39N37	75w50	5:03:20
Pleasant Hills 12	8	39N29	76w23	5:05:32
Pleasant Springs 16	16	38N42	76w51	5:07:24
Pleasant Valley 6	8	39N34	76w59	5:07:56
Pleasant Valley 21	7	39N39	77w34	5:10:16
Pleasant View 10	7	39N19	77w28	5:09:52
Pleasant View 13	3	39N16	76w49	5:07:16
Pleasantville 2	20	39N10	76w37	5:06:28
Pleasantville 21	7	39N19	77w44	5:10:56
Pleasant Walk 10	7	39N30	77w34	5:10:16
Plum Point 4	9	38N37	76w37	5:06:28
Pocomoke 23	5	38N05	75w34	5:02:16
Pointer Ridge 16	16	38N30	75w52	5:03:28
Point Lookout 18	4	38N05	76w21	5:05:24
Point of Rocks 10	7	39N17	77w32	5:10:08
Point of Rocks Estates 10	7	39N17	77w32	5:10:08
Point Pleasant 2	20	39N10	76w37	5:06:28
Pomfret 8	6	38N35	77w02	5:08:08
Pomona 14	15	39N10	76w07	5:04:28
Pomonkey 8	6	38N37	77w05	5:08:20
Ponder Cove 2	20	38N56	76w33	5:06:12
Pondsville 21	7	39N39	77w34	5:10:16
Pooks Hill 15	16	39N01	77w08	5:08:32
Poole 12	8	39N38	76w12	5:04:48
Poolesville 15	16	39N09	77w25	5:09:40
Popes Creek 8	6	38N24	77w00	5:08:00
Poplar Grove 12	8	39N40	76w23	5:05:32
Poplar Hill Estates 16	16	38N47	76w53	5:07:32
Poplar Knob 10	7	39N38	77w25	5:09:40
Poplar Springs 13	3	39N22	77w09	5:08:36
Port Deposit 7	7	39N37	76w05	5:04:20
Porters Park 3	3	39N19	76w28	5:05:52
Porterstown 21	7	39N29	77w42	5:10:48
Port Herman 7	7	39N32	75w49	5:03:16
Port Republic 4	9	38N30	76w32	5:06:08
Port Tobacco 8	6	38N31	77w01	5:08:04
Port Tobacco Riviera 8	6	38N31	77w01	5:08:04
Potomac 15	16	39N01	77w13	5:08:52
Potomac Falls 15	16	39N03	77w10	5:08:40
Potomac Green 15	16	39N03	77w10	5:08:40
Potomac Heights 8	6	38N36	77w09	5:08:36
Potomac Heights 21	7	39N39	77w44	5:10:56
Potomac Park 1	3	39N38	78w48	5:15:12
Potomac Ranch 15	16	39N03	77w10	5:08:40
Potomac Shores 8	6	38N31	77w01	5:08:04
Potomac Shores 18	4	38N18	76w39	5:06:36
Potomac Valley 15	16	38N58	77w08	5:08:32
Potomac View 8	6	38N23	76w57	5:07:48
Pot Spring 3	3	39N26	76w37	5:06:28
Powder Mill Estates 16	16	38N59	76w58	5:07:52
Powder Mill Village 16	16	39N02	76w55	5:07:40
Powellville 22	7	38N20	75w22	5:01:28
Powhatan Beach 2	20	39N09	76w33	5:06:12
Powhattan Mill 3	3	39N20	76w43	5:06:52
Prathertown 15	16	39N08	77w12	5:08:48
Preston 5	15	38N43	75w55	5:03:40
Preston Manor 12	8	39N28	76w17	5:05:08
Price 17	15	39N06	75w58	5:03:52
Priceville 3	3	39N32	76w39	5:06:36
Prince Frederick 4	9	38N33	76w35	5:06:20
Prince Georges Plaza 16	16	38N57	76w57	5:07:48
Princess Anne 19	26	38N12	75w42	5:02:48
Princeton 16	16	38N49	76w56	5:07:44
Principio Furnace 7	25	39N34	76w04	5:04:16
Prospect Knolls 16	16	38N57	76w47	5:07:08
Providence 3	3	39N24	76w36	5:06:24
Providence 7	7	39N41	75w53	5:03:32
Public Landing 23	27	38N10	75w24	5:01:36
Pumphrey 2	20	39N13	76w39	5:06:36
Purdum 15	16	39N22	77w16	5:09:04
Putnam 12	8	39N34	76w28	5:05:52
Putty Hill 3	3	39N23	76w33	5:06:12
Pylesville 12	8	39N41	76w22	5:05:28
Quail Run 15	16	39N08	77w12	5:08:48
Quaint Acres 15	16	39N04	76w59	5:07:56
Quaker Ridge 16	16	38N47	76w52	5:07:28
Quantico 22	7	38N22	75w45	5:03:00
Queen Anne 20	13	38N55	75w57	5:03:48
Queen Anne Colony 17	15	38N59	76w19	5:05:16
Queens Chapel 16	16	38N58	76w58	5:07:52
Queenstown 16	16	38N57	76w58	5:07:52
Queenstown 17	15	38N59	76w10	5:04:40
Quince Orchard 15	16	39N08	77w12	5:08:48
Quincy Manor 16	16	38N58	76w53	5:07:32
Rabbit Town 9	8	38N29	75w50	5:03:20
Radiant Valley 16	16	38N58	76w53	5:07:32
Ramblewood Village 16	16	38N47	76w53	5:07:32
Ramgate 16	16	38N47	76w58	5:07:52
Ranchleigh 3	3	39N22	76w40	5:06:40
Randalia 7	7	39N32	75w49	5:03:16
Randallstown 3	3	39N22	76w48	5:07:12
Randle Cliff Beach 4	9	38N40	76w32	5:06:08
Randolph 15	16	39N02	77w06	5:08:24
Randolph Farms 15	16	39N05	77w07	5:08:28
Randolph Hills 15	16	39N03	77w07	5:08:28
Random View 6	8	39N34	76w59	5:07:56
Raspeburg 24	1	39N21	76w32	5:06:08
Rawlings 1	3	39N33	78w54	5:15:36
Rawlings Heights 1	3	39N32	78w53	5:15:32
Raynor Heights 2	20	39N12	76w39	5:06:36
Rayville 3	3	39N39	76w40	5:06:40
Reddings Corner 14	15	39N17	76w06	5:04:24
Redford Estates 16	16	38N47	76w58	5:07:52
Redhouse 11	14	39N24	79w23	5:17:32
Red Point 7	7	39N36	75w56	5:03:44
Reeder Development 10	7	39N26	77w27	5:09:48
Reese 6	8	39N34	76w59	5:07:56
Regal Estates 4	9	38N43	76w40	5:06:40
Regency Estates 15	16	39N04	77w09	5:08:36
Regent Park 15	16	39N03	77w10	5:08:40
Regent Square 15	16	39N05	77w10	5:08:40
Rehobeth 19	19	38N02	75w40	5:02:40
Reid 21	8	39N39	77w44	5:10:56
Reids Grove 9	8	38N35	75w47	5:03:08
Reisterstown 3	3	39N27	76w49	5:07:16
Relay 3	3	39N15	76w41	5:06:44
Reliance 9	8	38N37	75w39	5:02:36
Remsburg Heights 10	7	39N26	77w27	5:09:48
Rest Haven 2	20	38N47	76w33	5:06:12
Revell 2	20	39N03	76w30	5:06:00
Reynolds 1	24	39N29	79w03	5:16:12
Rhodesdale 9	8	38N35	75w47	5:03:08
Rhodes Point 19	19	37N58	76w03	5:04:12
Richards Oak 7	7	39N40	76w06	5:04:24
Riderwood 3	3	39N23	76w38	5:06:32
Riderwood Hills 3	3	39N23	76w38	5:06:32
Ridge 18	4	38N07	76w22	5:05:28
Ridgelake 13	3	39N16	76w49	5:07:16
Ridgeleigh 3	3	39N24	76w36	5:06:24
Ridgely 5	15	38N57	75w53	5:03:32
Ridgeview 2	20	39N09	76w42	5:06:48
Ridgeville 10	7	39N22	77w09	5:08:36
Ridgeway 2	20	39N09	76w40	5:06:40
Ridgley Park 6	8	39N24	76w56	5:07:44
Riggins Corner 9	8	38N30	76w09	5:04:36
Ringgold 21	7	39N42	77w31	5:10:04
Rio Vista 20	13	38N47	76w13	5:04:52
Ripley 8	6	38N32	76w59	5:07:56
Rippling Estates 2	20	39N10	76w37	5:06:28
Rippling Ridge 2	20	39N10	76w37	5:06:28
Rising Sun 7	7	39N42	76w04	5:04:16
Rison 8	6	38N33	77w11	5:08:44
Ritchie 16	16	38N51	76w54	5:07:36
Ritchie Heights 16	16	38N51	76w54	5:07:36
Ritchie Manor 16	16	38N51	76w54	5:07:36
Riva 2	20	38N57	76w35	5:06:20
River Bend 16	16	38N47	76w58	5:07:52
River Bend Estates 16	16	38N51	76w54	5:07:36
River Club Estates 2	20	38N56	76w33	5:06:12
Riverdale 2	20	39N05	76w34	5:06:16
Riverdale 16	16	38N58	76w56	5:07:44
Riverdale Heights 16	16	38N58	76w55	5:07:40
Riverdale Hills 16	16	38N58	76w55	5:07:40
River Falls 15	16	39N03	77w10	5:08:40
River Forest 16	16	38N47	76w58	5:07:52
River Meadows 13	3	39N16	76w49	5:07:16
River Ridge Estates 16	16	38N48	76w59	5:07:56
Riverside 8	6	38N27	77w13	5:08:52
River Springs 18	4	38N16	76w46	5:07:04
Riverton 22	7	38N28	75w46	5:03:04
Riverview Village 8	6	38N36	77w10	5:08:40
Riviera Beach 2	20	39N10	76w31	5:06:04
Robbins 9	8	38N19	76w08	5:04:32
Roberts 17	15	39N08	75w59	5:03:56
Roberts Glen 15	16	39N03	77w10	5:08:40
Robinson 2	20	39N05	76w34	5:06:16
Robinwood 21	7	39N39	77w44	5:10:56
Rockaway Beach 3	3	39N19	76w28	5:05:52
Rock Creek Forest 15	16	38N59	77w05	5:08:20
Rock Creek Hills 15	16	39N02	77w06	5:08:24
Rock Creek Manor 15	16	39N05	77w07	5:08:28
Rock Creek Palisades 15	16	39N02	77w06	5:08:24
Rock Creek Village 15	16	39N05	77w07	5:08:28
Rockdale 3	3	39N22	76w46	5:07:04
Rock Hall 10	7	39N15	77w29	5:09:56
Rock Hall 14	15	39N08	76w14	5:04:56
Rock Hill Beach 2	20	39N09	76w33	5:06:12
Rockland 13	3	39N16	76w49	5:07:16
Rock Point 8	6	38N16	76w50	5:07:20
Rock Run 12	8	39N33	76w06	5:04:24
Rocks 12	8	39N38	76w25	5:05:40
Rockview Beach 2	20	39N09	76w33	5:06:12
Rockville 15	16	39N05	77w09	5:08:36
Rockwell 3	3	39N17	76w43	5:06:52
Rocky Acres 10	7	39N38	77w25	5:09:40
Rocky Gorge Estates 16	16	39N05	76w58	5:07:52
Rocky Ridge 10	8	39N36	77w19	5:09:16
Rocky Springs 10	7	39N26	77w27	5:09:48
Rodgers Forge 3	3	39N24	76w36	5:06:24
Rogers Heights 16	16	38N57	76w56	5:07:44
Rohrersville 21	7	39N26	77w40	5:10:40
Roland Park 24	1	39N21	76w38	5:06:32
Rolling Acres 6	8	39N34	76w59	5:07:56
Rolling Acres 13	3	39N16	76w49	5:07:16
Rolling Acres 16	16	38N47	76w52	5:07:28
Rolling Ridge 16	16	38N54	76w54	5:07:36
Rolling Terrace 15	16	38N59	77w01	5:08:04
Rollingwood 15	16	38N59	77w05	5:08:20
Rolphs 17	15	39N13	76w04	5:04:16
Romancoke on the Bay 17	15	38N59	76w19	5:05:16
Rosaryville Estates 16	16	38N47	76w52	5:07:28
Rosecroft Gardens 16	16	38N47	76w58	5:07:52
Rosecroft Park 16	16	38N47	76w58	5:07:52
Rosedale 3	3	39N19	76w31	5:06:04
Rosedale Estates 16	16	38N47	76w58	5:07:52
Rosedale Park 15	16	38N59	77w05	5:08:20
Rose Haven 2	20	38N44	76w32	5:06:08
Rose Hill Estates 15	16	39N01	77w08	5:08:32
Rosemont 3	3	39N14	76w37	5:06:28
Rosemont 10	7	39N20	77w37	5:10:28
Rosemont 15	16	39N08	77w12	5:08:48
Rose Valley Estates 16	16	38N47	76w58	5:07:52
Rossville 3	3	39N19	76w28	5:05:52
Round Bay 2	20	39N05	76w34	5:06:16
Round Hill 10	7	39N26	77w27	5:09:48
Roundtop 21	8	39N42	78w11	5:12:44
Rowlandsville 7	7	39N40	76w10	5:04:40
Royal Beach 2	20	39N09	76w33	5:06:12
Royal Oak 20	13	38N45	76w11	5:04:44
Royal Oak 22	7	38N23	75w44	5:02:56
Royal View 15	16	39N05	77w07	5:08:28
Rugby Hall 2	20	39N03	76w30	5:06:00
Ruhl 3	24	39N42	76w41	5:06:44
Rumbley 19	23	38N07	75w42	5:02:48
Ruthsburg 17	15	39N00	75w58	5:03:52
Rutledge 12	8	39N31	76w25	5:05:40
Ruxton 3	3	39N24	76w36	5:06:24
Ryans Glade 11	2	39N18	79w26	5:17:44
Rycerville 8	6	38N26	76w44	5:06:56
Sabillasville 10	7	39N42	77w27	5:09:48
Sackertown 19	28	37N59	75w51	5:03:24
Saint Andrews Estates 18	4	38N18	76w31	5:06:04
Saint Anthony 10	7	39N42	77w20	5:09:20
Saint Aubins Heights 20	13	38N46	76w04	5:04:16
Saint Augustine 7	7	39N32	75w49	5:03:16
Saint Charles 8	6	38N38	76w53	5:07:32
Saint Clement Shores 18	4	38N18	76w39	5:06:36
Saint Denis 3	3	39N15	76w41	5:06:44
Saint George Island 18	4	38N06	76w28	5:05:52
Saint Georges 3	3	39N29	76w49	5:07:16
Saint Georges Park 18	4	38N10	76w32	5:06:08
Saint Helena Baltimore 3	3	39N14	76w31	5:06:04
Saint Inigoes 18	4	38N09	76w23	5:05:32
Saint James 21	7	39N34	77w45	5:11:00
Saint James 23	19	38N04	75w34	5:02:16
Saint Jeromes 18	4	38N09	76w22	5:05:28
Saint Johns Manor 13	3	39N16	76w49	5:07:16
Saint Johns Village 13	3	39N16	76w49	5:07:16
Saint Leonard 4	9	38N28	76w30	5:06:00
Saint Margarets 2	20	39N03	76w30	5:06:00
Saint Mark's 10	7	39N20	77w37	5:10:28
Saint Martin 23	23	38N26	75w12	5:00:48
Saint Marys City 18	4	38N11	76w26	5:05:44
Saint Michaels 20	11	38N47	76w14	5:04:56
Saint Peters 19	19	38N11	75w49	5:03:16
Saint Stephen 19	26	38N12	75w41	5:02:44
Salem 9	8	38N29	75w55	5:03:40
Salisbury 22	22	38N22	75w36	5:02:24
Samples Manor 21	7	39N19	77w44	5:10:56
Sams Creek 6	8	39N33	77w06	5:08:24
Sanders Park 2	20	39N09	76w33	5:06:12
Sandgates 18	4	38N26	76w44	5:06:56
Sand Spring 11	2	39N39	79w24	5:17:36
Sandy Acres 9	8	38N34	76w05	5:04:20
Sandy Bottom 14	15	39N12	76w11	5:04:44
Sandy Hook 21	7	39N22	77w43	5:10:52
Sandy Spring 15	16	39N09	77w02	5:08:08
Sandyville 6	8	39N30	76w53	5:07:32
Sang Run 11	2	39N33	79w22	5:17:28
Sanmar 21	7	39N31	77w39	5:10:36
Sansbury Park 16	16	38N51	76w54	5:07:36
Santo Domingo 22	7	38N28	75w46	5:03:04
Sassafras 14	15	39N20	75w47	5:03:08
Satyr Hill 3	3	39N23	76w33	5:06:12
Savage 13	3	39N08	76w50	5:07:20

MARYLAND

Place	Zone	Lat.	Long.	Time
Scaggsville 13	3	39N09	76w54	5:07:36
Scarboro 12	8	39N40	76w23	5:05:32
Scarboro 23	27	38N10	75w24	5:01:36
Schultz 16	16	38N47	76w53	5:07:32
Scientists Cliffs 4	9	38N30	76w32	5:06:08
Scotland 15	16	39N03	77w10	5:08:40
Scotland 18	4	38N05	76w22	5:05:28
Scotland Beach 18	4	38N05	76w21	5:05:24
Scrabbletown 2	20	38N54	76w30	5:06:00
Seabrook 16	16	38N58	76w51	5:07:24
Seabrook Acres 16	16	38N58	76w51	5:07:24
Seabrook Park Estates 16	16	38N58	76w51	5:07:24
Seat Pleasant 16	16	38N54	76w55	5:07:40
Sebring 13	3	39N16	76w49	5:07:16
Secretary 9	8	38N37	75w57	5:03:48
Security 21	8	39N39	77w44	5:10:56
Selby-on-the-Bay 2	20	38N55	76w31	5:06:04
Selbysport 11	2	39N39	79w24	5:17:36
Sellman 15	16	39N13	77w26	5:09:44
Seneca 15	16	39N05	77w20	5:09:20
Severn 2	20	39N08	76w42	5:06:48
Severna Forest 2	20	39N05	76w34	5:06:16
Severna Park 2	20	39N04	76w33	5:06:12
Severn Grove 2	20	39N03	76w30	5:06:00
Severn Heights 2	20	39N05	76w34	5:06:16
Severnside 2	20	39N03	76w30	5:06:00
Shad Point 22	7	38N22	75w36	5:02:24
Shady Oaks 2	20	38N51	76w36	5:06:24
Shady Side 2	20	38N50	76w31	5:06:04
Shaft 1	3	39N38	78w57	5:15:48
Shallmar 11	2	39N23	79w12	5:16:48
Shane 3	3	39N37	76w38	5:06:32
Sharewood Acres 13	3	39N09	76w47	5:07:08
Sharonville 2	20	39N09	76w33	5:06:12
Sharperville 16	16	38N38	76w53	5:07:32
Sharpsburg 21	7	39N28	77w45	5:11:00
Sharpstown 14	15	39N08	76w14	5:04:56
Sharptown 22	7	38N31	75w43	5:02:52
Shavox 22	7	38N22	75w36	5:02:24
Shawsville 12	8	39N38	76w33	5:06:12
Shawsville Acres 12	8	39N37	76w38	5:06:32
Shelltown 19	23	38N02	75w46	5:03:04
Shervettes Corner 6	8	39N24	76w56	5:07:44
Sherwood 20	13	38N46	76w19	5:05:16
Sherwood Forest 15	16	39N04	76w59	5:07:56
Sherwood Forest 16	16	38N47	76w52	5:07:28
Sherwood Manor 16	16	38N30	75w52	5:03:28
Sherwood Manor 22	7	38N22	75w36	5:02:24
Shetland Hills 3	3	39N26	76w37	5:06:28
Shiloh 8	6	38N23	76w57	5:07:48
Shiloh 9	8	38N38	75w52	5:03:28
Shipley 2	20	39N12	76w39	5:06:36
Shookstown 10	7	39N26	77w27	5:09:48
Shore Acres 2	20	39N03	76w30	5:06:00
Shoreham Beach 2	20	38N56	76w33	5:06:12
Shorewood Gardens 14	15	39N21	75w53	5:03:32
Shorewood Gardens Estates 14	15	39N20	75w47	5:03:08
Showell 23	19	38N24	75w13	5:00:52
Silesia 16	16	38N44	77w00	5:08:00
Siloam 22	7	38N17	75w39	5:02:36
Silver Grove 21	7	39N39	77w44	5:10:56
Silver Hill 16	16	38N50	76w55	5:07:40
Silver Hill Park 16	16	38N50	76w55	5:07:40
Silver Run 6	8	39N34	76w59	5:07:56
Silver Spring 15	16	39N01	77w02	5:08:08
Silver Spring Heights 12	8	39N32	76w21	5:05:24
Simpsonville 13	3	39N11	76w52	5:07:28
Sinepuxent 23	27	38N19	75w13	5:00:52
Skidmore 2	20	39N01	76w25	5:05:40
Skipton 20	8	38N53	76w00	5:04:00
Skyline 16	16	38N50	76w55	5:07:40
Skyline Estates 10	7	39N26	77w27	5:09:48
Slabtown 1	24	39N42	78w53	5:15:32
Smallwood 6	8	39N34	76w59	5:07:56
Smith Island 19	19	38N02	76w00	5:04:00
Smithsburg 21	8	39N39	77w35	5:10:20
Smithville 5	15	38N26	75w53	5:03:32
Smithville 9	8	38N28	76w18	5:05:12
Smoketown 21	7	39N31	77w39	5:10:36
Snowden Manor 6	8	39N34	76w59	5:07:56
Snow Hill 23	27	38N11	75w24	5:01:36
Snow Hill Manor 16	16	39N05	76w58	5:07:52
Snug Harbor 2	20	38N50	76w30	5:06:00
Snug Harbor 23	27	38N19	75w13	5:00:52
Snydersburg 6	8	39N36	76w51	5:07:24
Society Hill 18	4	38N18	76w39	5:06:36
Sollers Homes 3	3	39N14	76w31	5:06:04
Sollers Point 3	3	39N14	76w31	5:06:04
Solley 2	20	39N10	76w37	5:06:28
Solomons 4	9	38N19	76w27	5:05:48
Solomons Island 4	9	38N25	76w29	5:05:56
Somerset 15	16	38N58	77w06	5:08:24
Sonoma 15	16	39N01	77w08	5:08:32
South 24	1	39N16	76w38	5:06:32
South Cheverly Forest 16	16	38N58	76w53	5:07:32
South Down Shores 2	20	38N56	76w33	5:06:12
Southern Garden Apartments 16	16	38N50	77w00	5:08:00
South Gate 2	20	39N08	76w37	5:06:28
South Haven 2	20	39N03	76w30	5:06:00
South Kensington 15	16	39N01	77w05	5:08:20
Southland Hills 3	3	39N24	76w36	5:06:24
South Laurel 16	16	39N04	76w51	5:07:24
Southlawn 16	16	38N48	76w59	5:07:56
South Layhill 15	16	39N04	77w04	5:08:16
South Piscataway 16	16	38N40	77w02	5:08:08
South River Park 2	20	38N56	76w33	5:06:12
South Salisbury 22	7	38N22	75w36	5:02:24
Southview Apartments 16	16	38N48	76w59	5:07:56
South Woodside Park 15	16	39N00	77w02	5:08:08
Sparks 3	3	39N32	76w39	5:06:36
Sparks Glencoe 3	3	39N32	76w39	5:06:36
Sparrows Point 3	3	39N13	76w28	5:05:52
Spaulding Heights 16	16	38N51	76w54	5:07:36
Spauldings 16	16	38N50	76w55	5:07:40
Spence 23	27	38N10	75w24	5:01:36
Spencerville 15	16	39N07	76w58	5:07:52
Spielman 21	7	39N32	77w45	5:11:00
Spoolsville 10	7	39N26	77w33	5:10:12
Springbrook 15	16	39N04	76w59	5:07:56
Springbrook Forest 15	16	39N03	77w03	5:08:12
Springbrook Manor 15	16	39N04	76w59	5:07:56
Springbrook Terrace 16	16	38N58	76w55	5:07:40
Springbrook Village 15	16	39N04	76w59	5:07:56
Springfield 15	16	39N01	77w08	5:08:32
Spring Gap 1	3	39N34	78w43	5:14:52
Spring Garden Estates 10	7	39N29	77w21	5:09:24
Spring Grove 22	7	38N28	75w46	5:03:04
Spring Hill 22	7	38N25	75w41	5:02:44
Springhill Acres 22	7	38N22	75w36	5:02:24
Springhill Lake 16	16	39N00	76w53	5:07:32
Springlake 15	16	39N00	77w08	5:08:32
Springs Mill 6	8	39N34	76w59	5:07:56
Spring Valley 21	7	39N39	77w44	5:10:56
Stablersville 3	3	39N37	76w38	5:06:32
Stafford 12	8	39N38	76w12	5:04:48
Stanbrook 3	3	39N14	76w31	5:06:04
Stansbury Manor 3	3	39N20	76w27	5:05:48
Starkeys Corner 17	15	39N08	75w59	5:03:56
Starr 17	15	39N03	76w04	5:04:16
Stemmer's Run 3	3	39N20	76w27	5:05:48
Stepney 12	8	39N31	76w10	5:04:40
Steuart Level 2	20	38N56	76w33	5:06:12
Stevenson 3	3	39N25	76w43	5:06:52
Stevensville 17	15	38N59	76w19	5:05:16
Stewart Town 15	16	39N08	77w12	5:08:48
Stillmeadows 2	20	39N09	76w40	5:06:40
Still Pond 14	8	39N20	76w03	5:04:12
Stockton 23	19	38N03	75w25	5:01:40
Stonecrest 13	3	39N16	76w49	5:07:16
Stonegate 15	16	39N04	76w59	5:07:56
Stoneleigh 3	3	39N24	76w36	5:06:24
Stoneybrook Estates 15	16	39N04	77w04	5:08:16
Stony Beach 2	20	39N14	76w35	5:06:20
Stony Run 2	20	39N12	76w43	5:06:52
Straits 9	8	38N16	76w04	5:04:16
Stratford 3	3	39N26	76w37	5:06:28
Strathmore At Bel Pre 15	16	39N04	77w04	5:08:16
Stratton Woods 15	16	39N01	77w08	5:08:32
Strawberry Hills Estates 8	6	38N38	77w04	5:08:16
Strawleigh 10	7	39N26	77w27	5:09:48
Street 12	8	39N40	76w23	5:05:32
Stronghold 10	7	39N13	77w26	5:09:44
Sudbrook Park 3	3	39N22	76w43	5:06:52
Sudlersville 17	15	39N11	75w52	5:03:28
Sugarland 15	16	39N09	77w25	5:09:40
Suitland 16	16	38N51	76w56	5:07:44
Suitland Manor 16	16	38N50	76w55	5:07:40
Sullivan Heights 6	8	39N34	76w59	5:07:56
Summerfield Farms 15	16	39N27	76w30	5:06:00
Summerhill 15	16	39N09	77w25	5:09:40
Summit Farms 3	3	39N20	76w31	5:06:04
Sumner 15	16	39N01	77w08	5:08:32
Sunderland 4	9	38N40	76w36	5:06:24
Sunny Acres 16	16	38N51	76w54	5:07:36
Sunnybrook 3	3	39N30	76w35	5:06:20
Sunnybrook Hills 3	3	39N31	76w37	5:06:28
Sunny Isle of Kent 17	15	38N59	76w19	5:05:16
Sunrise 6	8	39N34	76w59	5:07:56
Sunset Acres 21	7	39N39	77w44	5:10:56
Sunset Beach 2	20	39N09	76w33	5:06:12
Sunset Hills 10	7	39N26	77w27	5:09:48
Sunset Knoll 2	20	39N09	76w33	5:06:12
Sunset View 6	8	39N34	76w59	5:07:56
Sunshine 15	16	39N13	77w04	5:08:16
Sunyar 22	7	38N22	75w36	5:02:24
Surratts 16	16	38N46	76w53	5:07:32
Surratts Gardens 16	16	38N47	76w53	5:07:32
Susquehanna Hills 12	8	39N33	76w06	5:04:24
Sutton Acres 8	6	38N31	77w01	5:08:04
Swan Creek 12	8	39N31	76w10	5:04:40
Swanton 11	2	39N28	79w14	5:16:56
Sweet Air 3	3	39N31	76w32	5:06:08
Sycamore Acres 15	16	39N05	77w07	5:08:28
Sykesville 6	8	39N22	76w58	5:07:52
Sylmar 7	7	39N42	76w04	5:04:16
Sylvan View 2	20	39N09	76w33	5:06:12
Table Rock 11	2	39N18	79w21	5:17:24
Takoma Park 15	16	38N59	77w00	5:08:00
Tall Timbers 18	4	38N10	76w32	5:06:08
Tammany Manor 21	7	39N36	77w49	5:11:16
Taneytown 6	8	39N40	77w11	5:08:44
Tangier 19	19	38N09	75w55	5:03:40
Tanglewood 2	20	39N03	76w30	5:06:00
Tantallon 16	16	38N47	76w58	5:07:52
Tanterra 15	16	39N11	77w03	5:08:12
Tanyard 5	15	38N43	75w55	5:03:40
Taylors Island 9	8	38N28	76w18	5:05:12
Taylorville 23	27	38N19	75w13	5:00:52
Temple Heights 16	16	38N49	76w56	5:07:44
Temple Hills 16	16	38N49	76w56	5:07:44
Temple Hills Park 16	16	38N49	76w56	5:07:44
Templeton Knolls 16	16	38N58	76w55	5:07:40
Templeton Manor 16	16	38N58	76w55	5:07:40
Templeville 17	15	39N08	75w46	5:03:04
Temple Woods 16	16	38N49	76w56	5:07:44
Terrace Gardens 2	20	39N03	76w30	5:06:00
Texas 3	3	39N29	76w39	5:06:36
The Downs 2	20	39N03	76w30	5:06:00
The Elbow 11	2	39N35	79w03	5:16:12
The Glen 15	16	39N03	77w10	5:08:40
The Hamlet 15	16	38N59	77w05	5:08:20
The Oaks 13	3	39N16	76w49	5:07:16
Theodore 7	7	39N42	76w04	5:04:16
The Orchards 13	3	39N16	76w49	5:07:16
The Pines 16	16	38N47	76w52	5:07:28
Thomas Choice 15	16	39N08	77w12	5:08:48
Thomas Run 12	8	39N32	76w21	5:05:24
Thomas Town 5	15	38N53	75w50	5:03:20
Thompkinsville 8	6	38N19	76w53	5:07:32
Thompson Corner 18	4	38N26	76w44	5:06:56
Thompsons Corner 15	16	39N14	77w17	5:09:08
Thompsontown 9	8	38N36	75w55	5:03:40
Thomson Estates 7	7	39N37	75w50	5:03:20
Thornleigh 3	3	39N23	76w38	5:06:32
Thorwood Park 3	3	39N23	76w33	5:06:12
Thurmont 10	8	39N37	77w25	5:09:40
Thurston 10	7	39N13	77w26	5:09:44
Tilden Woods 15	16	39N04	77w09	5:08:36
Tilghman 20	13	38N43	76w20	5:05:20
Tilghmanton 21	7	39N31	77w39	5:10:36
Timber Grove 3	3	39N26	76w48	5:07:12
Timber Ridge 2	20	39N12	76w43	5:06:52
Timber Ridge 6	8	39N34	76w59	5:07:56
Timberview 13	3	39N15	76w41	5:06:44
Timonium 3	3	39N28	76w40	5:06:40
Tobytown 15	16	39N08	77w12	5:08:48
Toddville 9	8	38N18	76w04	5:04:16
Tolchester Beach 14	15	39N13	76w14	5:04:56
Tollgate 3	3	39N26	76w48	5:07:12
Tompkinsville 8	6	38N23	76w57	5:07:48
Tonytank 22	7	38N22	75w36	5:02:24
Tower Acres 13	3	39N05	76w58	5:07:52
Tower Garden on the Bay 17	15	38N59	76w19	5:05:16
Town Creek 1	3	39N32	78w28	5:13:52
Town Creek Manor 18	4	38N15	76w27	5:05:48
Town Point 7	7	39N32	75w49	5:03:16
Townsend 17	15	38N47	76w53	5:07:32
Towson 3	3	39N24	76w36	5:06:24
Tracys Landing 2	20	38N47	76w36	5:06:24
Trappe 18	4	38N09	76w22	5:05:28
Trappe 20	11	38N40	76w04	5:04:16
Trappe 23	27	38N19	75w13	5:00:52
Trappe Station 20	13	38N41	76w10	5:04:40
Travilah 15	16	39N08	77w12	5:08:48
Treasure Cove 16	16	38N47	76w58	5:07:52
Trent Hall 18	4	38N26	76w44	5:06:56
Trenton 3	3	39N34	76w50	5:07:20
Troutville 10	7	39N32	77w19	5:09:16
Tulip Hill 10	7	39N26	77w27	5:09:48
Tulip Hill 15	16	38N57	77w06	5:08:24
Tunis Mills 20	13	38N49	76w10	5:04:40
Turkey Point 2	20	38N56	76w33	5:06:12
Turner 3	3	39N14	76w31	5:06:04
Tuscarora 10	7	39N28	77w27	5:09:48
Tuxedo 16	16	38N56	76w53	5:07:32
Tuxedo Colony 16	16	38N56	76w53	5:07:32
Twinbrook 15	16	39N05	77w07	5:08:28
Twinkling Acres 16	16	38N47	76w53	5:07:32
Twin River Beach 3	3	39N20	76w27	5:05:48
Tyaskin 22	7	38N19	75w50	5:03:20
Tydings on the Bay 2	20	39N03	76w30	5:06:00
Tylerton 19	19	37N58	76w01	5:04:04
Tyrone 6	8	39N34	76w59	5:07:56
Union Bridge 6	8	39N34	77w11	5:08:44
Union Corner 5	8	39N02	75w47	5:03:08
Union Mills 6	8	39N34	76w59	5:07:56
Union Street 1	24	39N39	78w43	5:14:52

MARYLAND

Uniontown 6 8 39N37 77w07 5:08:28
Unionville 3 3 39N28 76w31 5:06:04
Unionville 10 7 39N28 77w11 5:08:44
Unionville 20 13 38N49 76w08 5:04:32
Unionville 23 19 38N04 75w34 5:02:16
Unity 15 16 39N11 77w03 5:08:12
University Gardens 16 16 38N59 76w58 5:07:52
University Hills 16 16 38N59 76w58 5:07:52
University Park 16 16 38N58 76w57 5:07:48
Upperco 3 3 39N34 76w50 5:07:20
Upper Crossroads 12 8 39N33 76w29 5:05:56
Upper Fairmount 19 23 38N06 75w47 5:03:08
Upper Falls 3 3 39N26 76w24 5:05:36
Upper Ferry Estates 22 7 38N22 75w36 5:02:24
Upper Hill 19 23 38N07 75w47 5:03:08
Upper Homewood 1 3 39N38 78w48 5:15:12
Upper Marlboro 16 16 38N49 76w45 5:07:00
Urbana 10 7 39N19 77w22 5:09:28
Utica 10 7 39N38 77w25 5:09:40
Utica Mills Estates 10 7 39N38 77w25 5:09:40
Vale 12 8 39N32 76w21 5:05:24
Vale Summit 1 3 39N37 78w55 5:15:40
Valley Crest 3 3 39N26 76w37 5:06:28
Valley Lee 18 4 38N11 76w32 5:06:08
Valley Mede 13 3 39N16 76w49 5:07:16
Valley Stream Estates 15 16 39N07 76w56 5:07:44
Valley View 13 3 39N16 76w49 5:07:16
Valley View 16 16 38N47 76w58 5:07:52
Valleywood 22 7 38N22 75w36 5:02:24
Van Bibber 12 8 39N23 76w15 5:05:00
Van Bibber Manor 12 8 39N23 76w15 5:05:00
Van Lear Manor 21 7 39N36 77w49 5:11:16
Vansville 16 16 39N03 76w56 5:07:44
Venice on the Bay 2 20 39N09 76w33 5:06:12
Venton 19 26 38N12 75w41 5:02:44
Vernon 3 3 39N37 76w38 5:06:32
Victory Villa 3 3 39N20 76w27 5:05:48
Vienna 9 8 38N29 75w50 5:03:20
Viers Mill Village 15 16 39N04 77w04 5:08:16
View More Acres 10 7 39N26 77w27 5:09:48
Villa Cresta 3 3 39N23 76w33 5:06:12
Village Square North 16 16 39N05 76w58 5:07:52
Villa Heights 16 16 39N34 77w45 5:11:00
Villa Maria 3 3 39N15 76w41 5:06:44
Villa Monticello 13 3 39N19 77w01 5:08:04
Villa Nova 3 3 39N20 76w43 5:06:52
Waggaman Heights 16 16 38N49 76w56 5:07:44
Wagner Park 6 8 39N34 76w59 5:07:56
Wakefield 3 3 39N26 76w37 5:06:28
Wakefield 6 8 39N33 77w06 5:08:24
Wakefield Meadows 12 8 39N32 76w21 5:05:24
Walbrook 24 1 39N19 76w40 5:06:40
Waldon Woods 16 16 38N47 76w53 5:07:32
Waldorf 8 6 38N38 76w55 5:07:40
Walker Mill 16 16 38N52 76w55 5:07:40
Walkersville 10 7 39N29 77w21 5:09:24
Wallville 4 9 38N28 76w30 5:06:00
Walnut Hill 15 16 39N08 77w12 5:08:48
Walnut Ridge 6 8 39N34 76w59 5:07:56
Walnut Woods 15 16 39N04 77w09 5:08:36
Walston 22 7 38N23 75w28 5:01:52
Walter Heights 16 16 38N49 76w56 5:07:44
Wango 22 7 38N22 75w36 5:02:24
Wards Chapel 3 3 39N22 76w45 5:07:00
Warfieldburg 6 8 39N34 76w59 5:07:56
Warington Hills 8 6 38N36 77w10 5:08:40
Warlinda 8 6 38N32 76w59 5:07:56
Warren 3 3 39N29 76w39 5:06:36
Warwick 7 7 39N25 75w47 5:03:08
Washington Grove 15 16 39N08 77w11 5:08:44
Waterbury 2 20 39N02 76w36 5:06:24
Waterford 16 16 38N51 76w54 5:07:36
Waterloo 13 3 39N10 76w47 5:07:08
Wateroak Point 2 20 39N09 76w33 5:06:12
Watersville 6 8 39N22 77w09 5:08:36
Waterview 22 7 38N17 75w54 5:03:36
Watkins Glen 15 16 39N03 77w10 5:08:40
Waverly 24 1 39N20 76w36 5:06:24
Wayside 8 6 38N23 76w57 5:07:48
Webster 12 8 39N34 76w10 5:04:40
Webster Village 12 8 39N33 76w06 5:04:24
Weems Creek 2 20 39N03 76w30 5:06:00
Weisburg 3 3 39N37 76w38 5:06:32
Welcome 8 6 38N29 77w06 5:08:24
Welhams 2 20 39N10 76w37 5:06:28
Wellington Estates 13 3 39N05 76w58 5:07:52
Wellwood 3 3 39N22 76w43 5:06:52
Wenona 19 19 38N08 75w57 5:03:48
Wesley 9 8 38N19 76w08 5:04:32
Wesmond 15 16 39N09 77w25 5:09:40
West 19 26 38N12 75w41 5:02:44
West Annapolis 2 20 39N03 76w30 5:06:00
West Beach 4 9 38N42 76w32 5:06:08
West Bethesda 15 16 39N00 77w08 5:08:32
Westboro 15 16 39N01 77w08 5:08:32
West Bowie 16 16 38N57 76w47 5:07:08
Westchester 15 16 39N03 77w03 5:08:12
Westchester Estates 16 16 38N49 76w56 5:07:44
Westchester Park 16 16 39N00 76w55 5:07:40
West Denton 5 15 38N53 75w50 5:03:20
West Edmondale 3 3 39N17 76w41 5:06:44
West Elkridge 13 3 39N15 76w41 5:06:44
West End 2 20 39N03 76w30 5:06:00
Westernport 1 24 39N29 79w03 5:16:12
Western Shores Estates 4 9 38N30 76w32 5:06:08
West Friendship 13 3 39N18 76w57 5:07:48
Westgate 15 16 39N01 77w08 5:08:32
West Gate Woods 16 16 38N58 76w51 5:07:24
West Hills 3 3 39N17 76w43 5:06:52
West Hills 10 7 39N26 77w27 5:09:48
West Hyattsville 16 16 38N58 76w58 5:07:52
Westlake 22 7 38N22 75w36 5:02:24
West Lanham Hills 16 16 38N58 76w53 5:07:32
West Laurel 16 16 39N07 76w53 5:07:32
West Laurel Acres 16 16 39N05 76w58 5:07:52
West Liberty 3 3 39N37 76w38 5:06:32
Westminster 6 3 39N35 77w00 5:08:00
Westmoreland Hills 15 16 39N01 77w08 5:08:32
West Nottingham 7 7 39N40 76w06 5:04:24
West Oakland 11 14 39N25 79w27 5:17:48
West Ocean City 23 19 38N23 75w05 5:00:20
Westover 19 23 38N07 75w43 5:02:52
Westowne 3 3 39N17 76w41 5:06:44
Westphalia Estates 16 16 38N47 76w52 5:07:28
Westphalia Woods 16 16 38N47 76w52 5:07:28
West Princess Anne 19 26 38N12 75w43 5:02:52
West River 2 20 38N51 76w36 5:06:24
West Severna Park 2 20 39N05 76w34 5:06:16
West Shadyside 2 20 38N50 76w30 5:06:00
West Springbrook 15 16 39N03 77w03 5:08:12
West Twin River Beach 3 3 39N20 76w27 5:05:48
Westview Park 3 3 39N17 76w43 5:06:52
West View Shores 7 7 39N25 75w55 5:03:40
West Vindex 11 2 39N23 79w12 5:16:48
Westwood 16 16 38N39 76w44 5:06:56
Westwood Estates 16 16 38N47 76w52 5:07:28
Wetipquin 22 7 38N23 75w44 5:02:56
Weverton 21 7 39N20 77w37 5:10:28
Wexford 2 20 39N03 76w30 5:06:00
Whaleysville 23 19 38N24 75w18 5:01:12
Wheaton 15 16 39N03 77w03 5:08:12
Wheatoncrest 15 16 39N03 77w03 5:08:12
Wheaton Hills 15 16 39N03 77w03 5:08:12
Wheaton View 15 16 39N03 77w03 5:08:12
Wheaton Woods 15 16 39N05 77w07 5:08:28
Whiskey Bottom 13 3 39N05 76w58 5:07:52
Whiteburg 23 27 38N10 75w24 5:01:36
White Crystal Beach 7 7 39N25 75w55 5:03:40
Whitefield Knolls 16 16 38N58 76w51 5:07:24
Whitefield Woods 16 16 38N58 76w51 5:07:24
Whiteford 12 8 39N43 76w21 5:05:24
White Hall 3 3 39N37 76w38 5:06:32
Whitehall 16 16 38N40 77w02 5:08:08
Whitehall Manor 15 16 39N01 77w08 5:08:32
Whitehaven 22 7 38N16 75w47 5:03:08
Whitehouse 3 3 39N34 76w50 5:07:20
Whiteleysburg 5 15 38N58 75w48 5:03:12
White Marsh 3 3 39N23 76w26 5:05:44
White Oak 15 16 39N03 76w59 5:07:56
White Oak Manor 16 16 39N04 76w59 5:07:56
White Oak Shopping Center 15 16 39N04 76w59 5:07:56
White Plains 8 6 38N36 76w57 5:07:48
White Point Beach 18 4 38N18 76w39 5:06:36
White Rock 10 7 39N26 77w27 5:09:48
White Sands 4 9 38N25 76w27 5:05:48
Whiton 22 27 38N10 75w24 5:01:36
Whittemore Park 3 3 39N15 76w41 5:06:44
Wickford 15 16 39N04 77w09 5:08:36
Wicomico 8 6 38N29 76w47 5:07:08
Wicomico Beach 8 6 38N23 76w57 5:07:48
Widgeon 19 26 38N12 75w41 5:02:44
Wilburn Estates 16 16 38N54 76w54 5:07:36
Wilde Lake 13 3 39N16 76w49 5:07:16
Wildercroft 16 16 38N58 76w55 5:07:40
Wild Rose Shores 2 20 38N57 76w29 5:05:56
Wild Wood Beach 3 3 39N19 76w28 5:05:52
Wildwood Estates 16 16 38N47 76w53 5:07:32
Wildwood Hills 15 16 39N00 77w08 5:08:32
Wildwood Manor 15 16 39N01 77w08 5:08:32
Wilelinor Estates 2 20 38N56 76w33 5:06:12
Willards 22 7 38N24 75w21 5:01:24
Willerburn Acres 15 16 39N03 77w10 5:08:40
Williamsburg 9 8 38N40 75w50 5:03:20
Williamsburg Estates 16 16 38N47 76w52 5:07:28
Williamsburg Village 15 16 39N09 77w05 5:08:20
Williamsport 21 8 39N36 77w49 5:11:16
Williams Wharf 4 9 38N28 76w30 5:06:00
Williston 5 15 38N53 75w50 5:03:20
Willoughby Beach 12 8 39N23 76w15 5:05:00
Willow Beach Colony 4 9 38N42 76w32 5:06:08
Willowbrook 15 16 39N03 77w10 5:08:40
Willows 4 9 38N38 76w32 5:06:08
Willows of Riverbend 16 16 38N47 76w58 5:07:52
Wills Creek 1 3 39N42 78w44 5:14:56
Wilson 21 7 39N39 77w56 5:11:44
Wilson Hills 15 16 39N04 77w04 5:08:16
Wilson Point 3 3 39N20 76w27 5:05:48
Wilsons 21 7 39N39 77w52 5:11:28
Wiltondale 3 3 39N24 76w36 5:06:24
Wilton Farm Acres 13 3 39N16 76w49 5:07:16
Winchester on the Severn 2 20 39N03 76w30 5:06:00
Winchester Park 6 8 39N34 76w59 5:07:56
Windbrook 16 16 38N47 76w53 5:07:32
Windermere 15 16 39N04 77w09 5:08:36
Windham Manor 15 16 39N04 76w59 5:07:56
Winding Brook Village 7 7 39N37 75w50 5:03:20
Windmere Acres 13 3 39N08 76w49 5:07:16
Windsor Heights 6 8 39N34 76w59 5:07:56
Winfield 6 8 39N34 76w59 5:07:56
Wingate 9 8 38N18 76w06 5:04:24
Wingates Point 9 8 38N18 76w06 5:04:24
Wiseburg 3 3 39N37 76w38 5:06:32
Wittman 20 13 38N48 76w18 5:05:12
Wolfsville 10 7 39N30 77w34 5:10:16
Wood Acres 15 16 39N01 77w08 5:08:32
Woodberry Forest 16 16 38N49 76w56 5:07:44
Woodbine 6 8 39N22 77w04 5:08:16
Woodbrook 3 3 39N24 76w36 5:06:24
Woodburn 15 16 39N01 77w08 5:08:32
Woodcroft 3 3 39N23 76w33 5:06:12
Woodensburg 3 3 39N27 76w49 5:07:16
Woodfield 15 16 39N15 77w11 5:08:44
Woodhaven 15 16 39N01 77w08 5:08:32
Woodhaven Park 8 6 38N32 76w59 5:07:56
Woodland 1 24 39N39 78w55 5:15:40
Woodland Acres 18 4 38N25 76w33 5:06:12
Woodland Beach 2 20 38N56 76w33 5:06:12
Woodland Point 8 6 38N23 76w57 5:07:48
Woodland Village 8 6 38N36 77w10 5:08:40
Wood Lane 16 16 38N58 76w51 5:07:24
Woodlark 16 16 38N58 76w51 5:07:24
Woodlawn 3 3 39N19 76w44 5:06:56
Woodlawn 7 7 39N36 76w07 5:04:28
Woodlawn 16 16 38N58 76w53 5:07:32
Woodlawn Heights 2 20 39N10 76w37 5:06:28
Woodlawn-Woodmoor 3 3 39N19 76w43 5:06:52
Woodmont 15 16 38N59 77w05 5:08:20
Woodmoor 3 3 39N20 76w43 5:06:52
Woodmoor 15 16 39N01 77w00 5:08:00
Wood Point 21 7 39N39 77w44 5:10:56
Woodsboro 10 7 39N33 77w19 5:09:16
Woodstock 13 3 39N20 76w52 5:07:28
Woodville 10 7 39N24 77w11 5:08:44
Woolerys 6 8 39N31 76w56 5:07:44
Woolford 9 8 38N30 76w11 5:04:44
Worthington 13 3 39N16 76w49 5:07:16
Worthington Valley 3 3 39N29 76w49 5:07:16
Worton 14 15 39N17 76w06 5:04:24
Wrights Crossing 1 24 39N39 78w55 5:15:40
Wye Mills 20 13 38N56 76w05 5:04:20
Wyngate 15 16 39N01 77w08 5:08:32
Wynnewood 3 3 39N15 76w41 5:06:44
Yarrowsburg 21 7 39N20 77w37 5:10:28
Yellow Springs 10 7 39N26 77w27 5:09:48
Yorkshire Knolls 16 16 38N54 76w54 5:07:36
Yorktown Village 15 16 39N01 77w08 5:08:32
Zion 7 7 39N41 75w58 5:03:52
Zittlestown 21 7 39N31 77w39 5:10:36

TIME TABLES

MA # 1

Before 11/18/1883		LMT
11/18/1883	12:00	EST
3/31/1918	02:00	EWT
10/27/1918	02:00	EST
3/30/1919	02:00	EWT
10/26/1919	02:00	EST
4/25/1920	02:00	EDT
10/31/1920	02:00	EST
4/24/1921	02:00	EDT
9/25/1921	02:00	EST
4/30/1922	02:00	EDT
9/24/1922	02:00	EST
4/29/1923	02:00	EDT
9/30/1923	02:00	EST
4/27/1924	02:00	EDT
9/28/1924	02:00	EST
4/26/1925	02:00	EDT
9/27/1925	02:00	EST
4/25/1926	02:00	EDT
9/26/1926	02:00	EST
4/24/1927	02:00	EDT
9/25/1927	02:00	EST
4/29/1928	02:00	EDT
9/30/1928	02:00	EST
4/28/1929	02:00	EDT
9/29/1929	02:00	EST
4/27/1930	02:00	EDT
9/28/1930	02:00	EST
4/26/1931	02:00	EDT
9/27/1931	02:00	EST
4/24/1932	02:00	EDT
9/25/1932	02:00	EST
4/30/1933	02:00	EDT
9/24/1933	02:00	EST
4/29/1934	02:00	EDT
9/30/1934	02:00	EST
4/28/1935	02:00	EDT
9/29/1935	02:00	EST
4/26/1936	02:00	EDT
9/27/1936	02:00	EST
4/25/1937	02:00	EDT
9/26/1937	02:00	EST
4/24/1938	02:00	EDT
10/01/1938	02:00	EST
4/30/1939	02:00	EDT
9/24/1939	02:00	EST
4/28/1940	02:00	EDT
9/29/1940	02:00	EST
4/27/1941	02:00	EDT
9/28/1941	02:00	EST
2/09/1942	02:00	EWT
9/30/1945	02:00	EST
4/28/1946	02:00	EDT
9/29/1946	02:00	EST
4/27/1947	02:00	EDT
9/28/1947	02:00	EST
4/25/1948	02:00	EDT
9/26/1948	02:00	EST
4/24/1949	02:00	EDT
9/25/1949	02:00	EST
4/30/1950	02:00	EDT
9/24/1950	02:00	EST
4/29/1951	02:00	EDT
9/30/1951	02:00	EST
4/27/1952	02:00	EDT
9/28/1952	02:00	EST
4/26/1953	02:00	EDT
9/27/1953	02:00	EST
4/25/1954	02:00	EDT
10/31/1954	02:00	EST
4/24/1955	02:00	EDT
10/30/1955	02:00	EST
4/29/1956	02:00	EDT
10/28/1956	02:00	EST
4/28/1957	02:00	EDT
10/27/1957	02:00	EST
4/27/1958	02:00	EDT
10/26/1958	02:00	EST
4/26/1959	02:00	EDT
10/25/1959	02:00	EST
4/24/1960	02:00	EDT
10/30/1960	02:00	EST
4/30/1961	02:00	EDT
10/29/1961	02:00	EST
4/29/1962	02:00	EDT
10/28/1962	02:00	EST
4/28/1963	02:00	EDT
10/27/1963	02:00	EST
4/26/1964	02:00	EDT
10/25/1964	02:00	EST
4/25/1965	02:00	EDT
10/31/1965	02:00	EST
4/24/1966	02:00	EDT
10/30/1966	02:00	EST
4/30/1967	02:00	US#1

MA # 2

Before 11/18/1883		LMT
11/18/1883	12:00	EST
3/31/1918	02:00	EWT
10/27/1918	02:00	EST
3/30/1919	02:00	EWT
10/26/1919	02:00	EST
4/30/1922	02:00	EDT
9/24/1922	02:00	EST
4/29/1923	02:00	US#1

COUNTIES

1 Barnstable
2 Berkshire
3 Bristol
4 Dukes
5 Essex
6 Franklin
7 Hampden
8 Hampshire
9 Middlesex
10 Nantucket
11 Norfolk
12 Plymouth
13 Suffolk
14 Worcester

Place	Table	Lat.	Long.	Time
Abington 12	1	42N06	70w57	4:43:48
Acapesket 1	1	41N46	70w30	4:42:00
Accord 12	1	42N11	70w53	4:43:32
Acoaxet 3	1	41N30	71w06	4:44:24
Acton 9	1	42N29	71w26	4:45:44
Acushnet 3	1	41N41	70w55	4:43:40
Adams 2	1	42N38	73w07	4:52:28
Adamsdale 3	1	41N58	71w20	4:45:20
Adams Shore 11	1	42N15	71w00	4:44:00
Adamsville 6	1	42N40	72w42	4:50:48
Agawam 7	1	42N04	72w39	4:50:36
Agawam Beach 12	1	41N46	70w43	4:42:52
Alford 2	1	42N14	73w25	4:53:40
Allendale 2	1	42N27	73w15	4:53:00
Allerton 12	1	42N17	70w53	4:43:32
Allston 13	1	42N21	71w08	4:44:32
Amesbury 5	1	42N51	70w56	4:43:44
Amherst 8	1	42N23	72w31	4:50:04
Amrita 1	1	41N40	70w37	4:42:28
Andover 5	1	42N40	71w08	4:44:32
Annisquam 5	1	42N39	70w41	4:42:44
Antassawamock Beach 12	1	41N40	70w49	4:43:16
Apponagansett Village 3	1	41N37	70w58	4:43:52
Arlington 9	1	42N25	71w09	4:44:36
Arlington Heights 9	1	42N26	71w10	4:44:40
Ashburnham 14	1	42N39	71w54	4:47:36
Ashby 9	1	42N40	71w48	4:47:12
Ashcroft 11	1	42N14	71w10	4:44:40
Ashdod 12	1	42N02	70w40	4:42:40
Ashfield 6	2	42N31	72w48	4:51:12
Ashland 9	1	42N16	71w28	4:45:52
Ashley Falls 2	1	42N03	73w20	4:53:20
Ashley Heights 3	1	41N46	70w58	4:43:52
Assinippi 12	1	42N10	70w51	4:43:24
Assonet 3	1	41N48	71w04	4:44:16
Assonet Bay Shores 3	1	41N48	71w04	4:44:16
Assumption College 14	1	42N16	71w49	4:47:16
Astor 13	1	42N19	71w05	4:44:20
Athol 14	1	42N36	72w14	4:48:56
Atlantic 11	1	42N15	71w00	4:44:00
Attitash 5	1	42N51	70w56	4:43:44
Attleboro 3	1	41N57	71w17	4:45:08
Attleboro Falls 3	1	41N58	71w20	4:45:20
Auburn 14	1	42N12	71w50	4:47:20
Auburndale 9	1	42N21	71w22	4:45:28
Auburnville 12	1	42N05	70w56	4:43:44
Avon 11	1	42N08	71w03	4:44:12
Ayer 9	1	42N34	71w35	4:46:20
Ayer Center 9	1	42N33	71w35	4:46:20
Ayers Village 5	1	42N47	71w05	4:44:20
Babson Park 11	1	42N18	71w23	4:45:32
Back Bay Annex 13	1	42N19	71w05	4:44:20
Baileys Corners 12	1	42N02	70w40	4:42:40
Bakers Grove 14	1	42N33	71w55	4:47:40
Bakers Island 5	1	42N31	70w54	4:43:36
Baldwinville 14	1	42N37	72w05	4:48:20
Ballardvale 5	1	42N38	71w10	4:44:40
Baptist Corner 6	1	42N36	72w44	4:50:56
Baptist Village 7	1	42N04	72w30	4:50:00
Barkerville 2	1	42N27	73w15	4:53:00
Barnstable 1	1	41N42	70w18	4:41:12
Barre 14	1	42N25	72w06	4:48:24
Barre Plains 14	1	42N23	72w07	4:48:28
Barrowsville 3	1	41N58	71w11	4:44:44
Bass Point 5	1	42N26	70w56	4:43:44
Bass River 1	1	41N40	70w10	4:40:40
Bass Rocks 5	1	42N37	70w40	4:42:40
Bayside 12	1	42N17	70w53	4:43:32
Bay State 8	1	42N20	72w40	4:50:40
Bayview 3	1	41N37	70w58	4:43:52
Bayview 5	1	42N37	70w40	4:42:40
Beach 13	1	42N25	71w00	4:44:00
Beachmont 13	1	42N25	71w00	4:44:00
Beach Point 1	1	42N02	70w06	4:40:24
Beachwood 2	1	42N17	73w19	4:53:16
Beaver Brook 9	1	42N23	71w14	4:44:56
Becket 2	1	42N17	73w05	4:52:20
Becket Center 2	1	42N17	72w59	4:51:56
Bedford 9	1	42N29	71w17	4:45:08
Bedford Springs 9	1	42N29	71w17	4:45:08
Beechwood 11	1	42N13	70w49	4:43:16
Belcher Square 2	1	42N12	73w22	4:53:28
Belchertown 8	1	42N17	72w24	4:49:36
Bellingham 11	1	42N04	71w29	4:45:56
Bell Rock 9	1	42N26	71w04	4:44:16
Belmont 9	1	42N24	71w11	4:44:44
Bennetts Corner 12	1	42N01	71w00	4:44:00
Berkley 3	1	41N50	71w05	4:44:20
Berkshire 2	1	42N31	73w12	4:52:48
Berkshire Christian College 2	1	42N21	73w17	4:53:08
Berkshire Heights 2	1	42N12	73w22	4:53:28
Berlin 14	1	42N23	71w38	4:46:32
Bernardston 6	1	42N40	72w32	4:50:08
Beverly 5	1	42N33	70w53	4:43:32
Beverly Cove 5	1	42N34	70w53	4:43:32
Beverly Farms 5	1	42N34	70w53	4:43:32
Beverly Junction 5	1	42N34	70w53	4:43:32
Big Pond 2	1	42N10	73w02	4:52:08
Billerica 9	1	42N34	71w16	4:45:04
Birds Hill 11	1	42N17	71w14	4:44:56
Blackinton 2	1	42N42	73w06	4:52:24
Black Rock 11	1	42N15	70w50	4:43:20
Blackstone 14	1	42N02	71w33	4:46:12
Blandford 7	1	42N12	72w57	4:51:48
Bleachery 9	1	42N23	71w14	4:44:56
Blissville 6	1	42N35	72w19	4:49:16
Blue Hills 11	1	42N15	71w05	4:44:20
Blush Hollow 8	1	42N21	73w01	4:52:04
Bolton 14	1	42N26	71w37	4:46:28
Bondsville 7	1	42N12	72w21	4:49:24
Boston 13	1	42N22	71w04	4:44:16
Boston College 9	1	42N19	71w10	4:44:40
Boston University 13	1	42N21	71w06	4:44:24
Bourne 1	1	41N43	70w36	4:42:24
Bourne Center 1	1	41N44	70w36	4:42:24
Bournedale 1	1	41N45	70w36	4:42:24
Boxborough 9	1	42N29	71w31	4:46:04
Boxford 5	1	42N41	71w02	4:44:08
Boxford Center 5	1	42N41	70w59	4:43:56
Boylston 14	1	42N21	71w44	4:46:56
Bradford 5	1	42N47	71w05	4:44:20
Bradstreet 8	2	42N22	72w36	4:50:24
Braintree 11	1	42N13	71w00	4:44:00
Braintree Highlands 11	1	42N13	70w59	4:43:56
Braleys 3	1	41N46	70w58	4:43:52
Bramanville 14	1	42N12	71w46	4:47:04
Brant Rock 12	1	42N05	70w39	4:42:36
Brayton Point 3	1	41N45	71w09	4:44:36
Braytonville 2	1	42N42	73w06	4:52:24
Brewster 1	1	41N45	70w03	4:40:12
Briarwood Beach 12	1	41N46	70w43	4:42:52
Bridgewater 12	1	42N00	70w59	4:43:56
Brier 2	1	42N37	73w07	4:52:28
Brier Neck 5	1	42N37	70w40	4:42:40
Brigadoon Village 5	1	42N36	71w01	4:44:04
Briggs Corner 3	1	41N56	71w18	4:45:12
Briggsville 2	1	42N42	73w06	4:52:24
Brighton 13	1	42N21	71w08	4:44:32
Brightside 7	1	42N12	72w37	4:50:28
Brightwood 7	1	42N07	72w36	4:50:24
Brimfield 7	1	42N07	72w13	4:48:52
Broadway 9	1	42N26	71w04	4:44:16
Brockton 12	1	42N05	71w01	4:44:04
Brookfield 14	1	42N11	72w06	4:48:24
Brookline 11	1	42N20	71w07	4:44:28
Brookline Hill 11	1	42N20	71w08	4:44:32
Brooks Place 12	1	42N01	71w00	4:44:00
Brooks Village 14	1	42N33	72w04	4:48:16
Brookville 11	1	42N08	71w01	4:44:04
Brushwood 11	1	42N05	71w24	4:45:36
Bryantsville Acres 12	1	42N03	70w51	4:43:24
Bryantville 12	1	42N03	70w51	4:43:24
Buckland 6	1	42N35	72w47	4:51:08
Buena Vista Shores 12	1	41N51	70w56	4:43:44
Buffington Corner 3	1	41N45	71w09	4:44:36
Buffumville 14	1	42N07	71w52	4:47:28
Bullardville 14	1	42N41	72w03	4:48:12
Burkville 6	1	42N31	72w42	4:50:48
Burlington 9	1	42N30	71w12	4:44:48
Burrage 12	1	42N05	70w53	4:43:32
Buzzards Bay 1	1	41N45	70w36	4:42:24
Byfield 5	1	42N46	70w57	4:43:48
Cabot 9	1	42N21	71w12	4:44:48
Cahoon Hollow 1	1	41N56	70w02	4:40:08
Cambridge 9	1	42N22	71w06	4:44:24
Cambridgeport 9	1	42N23	71w08	4:44:32
Campello 12	1	42N05	71w01	4:44:04
Campground Landing 1	1	41N52	69w59	4:39:56
Camp Grounds 14	1	42N24	71w46	4:47:04
Canterbury Estates 1	1	41N46	70w30	4:42:00
Canton 11	1	42N09	71w09	4:44:36
Cape Cod Mall 1	1	41N39	70w17	4:41:08
Carletonville 5	1	42N31	70w54	4:43:36
Carlisle 9	1	42N32	71w21	4:45:24
Carver 12	1	41N52	70w46	4:43:04
Caryville	1	42N08	71w27	4:45:48
Castle Hill 5	1	42N31	70w54	4:43:36
Castleton Mall 11	1	42N08	71w06	4:44:24
Cataumet 1	1	41N40	70w37	4:42:28
Cathedral 13	1	42N20	71w04	4:44:16
Cedar Bushes 12	1	41N55	70w34	4:42:16
Cedar Hill 11	1	42N10	70w53	4:43:32
Cedarville 12	1	41N45	70w36	4:42:24
Center 9	1	42N29	71w09	4:44:36
Centerville 1	1	41N39	70w21	4:41:24
Centerville 5	1	42N34	70w53	4:43:32
Central Square 9	1	42N29	71w09	4:44:36
Central Village 3	1	41N37	71w04	4:44:16
Chaffin 14	1	42N21	71w51	4:47:24
Chapel Hill Estates 12	1	42N04	70w49	4:43:16
Chappaquiddick Island 4	1	41N23	70w31	4:42:04
Chappaquoit 1	1	41N36	70w38	4:42:32
Charlemont 6	1	42N38	72w51	4:51:24
Charles River 11	1	42N17	71w14	4:44:56
Charles River Grove 11	1	42N05	71w28	4:45:52
Charlestown 13	1	42N23	71w04	4:44:16
Charlton 14	1	42N08	71w58	4:47:52
Charlton Depot 14	1	42N10	71w59	4:47:56
Chartley 3	1	41N57	71w14	4:44:56
Chaseville 14	1	42N03	71w54	4:47:36
Chatham 1	1	41N41	69w58	4:39:52
Chelmsford 9	1	42N36	71w21	4:45:24
Chelsea 13	1	42N23	71w02	4:44:08
Cherry Brook 9	1	42N22	71w18	4:45:12
Cherry Valley 14	1	42N13	71w53	4:47:32
Cheshire 2	1	42N34	73w08	4:52:32
Cheshire Harbor 2	1	42N37	73w07	4:52:28
Chester 7	1	42N18	72w56	4:51:44
Chesterfield 8	1	42N23	72w50	4:51:20
Chestnut Hill 9	1	42N19	71w10	4:44:40
Chicopee 7	1	42N09	72w37	4:50:28
Chilmark 4	1	41N21	70w45	4:43:00
Chiltonville 12	1	41N58	70w40	4:42:40
Churchill Shores 12	1	41N51	70w56	4:43:44

MASSACHUSETTS

City Mills 11	1	42N07	71w19	4:45:16
Clarksburg 2	1	42N43	73w05	4:52:20
Clayton 2	1	42N02	73w20	4:53:20
Cleghorn 14	1	42N35	71w48	4:47:12
Clematis Brook 9	1	42N23	71w14	4:44:56
Clevelandtown 4	1	41N23	70w31	4:42:04
Clicquot 11	1	42N10	71w22	4:45:28
Clifton 5	1	42N30	70w52	4:43:28
Cliftondale 5	1	42N28	71w01	4:44:04
Clinton 14	1	42N25	71w41	4:46:44
Cobbs Village 1	1	41N42	70w18	4:41:12
Cochesett 12	1	42N01	71w00	4:44:00
Cochituate 9	1	42N19	71w22	4:45:28
Cohasset 11	1	42N14	70w48	4:43:12
Cold Spring 2	1	42N12	73w06	4:52:24
Collinsville 9	1	42N41	71w19	4:45:16
Colonial Acres 1	1	41N39	70w15	4:41:00
Colonial Park 14	1	42N03	71w54	4:47:36
Colrain 6	1	42N40	72w44	4:50:56
Coltsville 2	1	42N27	73w15	4:53:00
Cominsville 14	1	42N13	71w53	4:47:32
Concord 9	1	42N28	71w21	4:45:24
Congamond 7	1	42N04	72w46	4:51:04
Conomo 5	1	42N38	70w47	4:43:08
Conway 6	1	42N31	72w42	4:50:48
Cook Street 9	1	42N21	71w12	4:44:48
Cooleyville 6	1	42N30	72w20	4:49:20
Cordaville 14	1	42N16	71w32	4:46:08
Cotley 3	1	41N54	71w06	4:44:24
Cottage Hill 13	1	42N22	70w59	4:43:56
Cottage Park 13	1	42N22	70w59	4:43:56
Cotuit 1	1	41N37	70w26	4:41:44
Court Park 13	1	42N22	70w59	4:43:56
Coury Heights 3	1	41N41	70w55	4:43:40
Cow Yard 3	1	41N37	70w58	4:43:52
Craigville 1	1	41N38	70w20	4:41:20
Craigville Beach 1	1	41N38	70w20	4:41:20
Crescent Beach 12	1	41N40	70w49	4:43:16
Crescent Beach 13	1	42N25	71w00	4:44:00
Crescent Mills 7	1	42N14	72w53	4:51:32
Crooks Corner 11	1	42N05	71w28	4:45:52
Crownridge Estates 11	1	42N11	71w18	4:45:12
Cummaquid 1	1	41N42	70w16	4:41:04
Cummington 8	1	42N28	72w55	4:51:40
Cushman 8	1	42N23	72w31	4:50:04
Cuttyhunk 4	1	41N25	70w56	4:43:44
Daley Corner 3	1	42N04	71w06	4:44:24
Dalton 2	1	42N28	73w11	4:52:44
Danvers 5	1	42N34	70w56	4:43:44
Danversport 5	1	42N34	70w57	4:43:48
Dartmouth 3	1	41N37	70w58	4:43:52
Davisville 1	1	41N46	70w30	4:42:00
Dedham 11	1	42N15	71w10	4:44:40
Deerfield 6	2	42N32	72w36	4:50:24
Dennis 1	1	41N43	70w10	4:40:40
Dennis Port 1	1	41N40	70w07	4:40:28
Devereux 5	1	42N30	70w52	4:43:28
Dighton 3	1	41N49	71w09	4:44:36
Division Street 3	1	41N37	70w55	4:43:40
Dodge 14	1	42N08	71w58	4:47:52
Dodgeville 3	1	41N56	71w18	4:45:12
Dorchester 13	1	42N17	71w04	4:44:16
Dorothy Manor 14	1	42N12	71w46	4:47:04
Dorothy Pond 14	1	42N12	71w46	4:47:04
Douglas 14	1	42N03	71w45	4:47:00
Dover 11	1	42N15	71w17	4:45:08
Dracut 9	1	42N40	71w18	4:45:12
Drury 2	1	42N39	73w00	4:52:00
Drury Square 14	1	42N12	71w50	4:47:20
Dry Pond 11	1	42N08	71w06	4:44:24
Dudley 14	1	42N03	71w56	4:47:44
Dudley Hill 14	1	42N03	71w54	4:47:36
Dunstable 9	1	42N41	71w29	4:45:56
Duxbury 12	1	42N03	70w40	4:42:40
Dwight 8	1	42N23	72w31	4:50:04
Eagle Hill	1	42N42	70w49	4:43:16
Eagleville 14	1	42N35	72w19	4:49:16
East Acton 9	1	42N29	71w25	4:45:40
East Arlington 9	1	42N25	71w10	4:44:40
East Billerica 9	1	42N35	71w14	4:44:56
East Blackstone 14	1	42N01	71w30	4:46:00
East Boston 13	1	42N23	71w02	4:44:08
East Boxford 5	1	42N41	70w59	4:43:56
East Braintree 11	1	42N13	70w59	4:43:56
East Brewster 1	1	41N46	70w05	4:40:20
East Bridgewater 12	1	42N02	70w57	4:43:48
East Brimfield 7	1	42N07	72w12	4:48:48
East Brookfield 14	1	42N12	72w02	4:48:08
East Cambridge 9	1	42N23	71w08	4:44:32
East Carver 12	1	41N55	70w48	4:43:12
East Charlemont 6	1	42N36	72w44	4:50:56
East Chelmsford 9	1	42N37	71w22	4:45:28
East Dedham 11	1	42N14	71w10	4:44:40
East Deerfield 6	1	42N33	72w36	4:50:24
East Dennis 1	1	41N45	70w10	4:40:40
East Douglas 14	1	42N04	71w43	4:46:52
East Everett 9	1	42N25	71w03	4:44:12
East Fairhaven 3	1	41N39	70w53	4:43:32
East Falmouth 1	1	41N33	70w33	4:42:12
East Fitchburg 14	1	42N35	71w48	4:47:12
East Foxboro 11	1	42N04	71w16	4:45:04
East Freetown 3	1	41N46	70w58	4:43:52
East Gardner 14	1	42N34	72w00	4:48:00
East Gloucester 5	1	42N37	70w40	4:42:40
East Greenfield 6	1	42N36	72w36	4:50:24
Eastham 1	1	41N50	69w59	4:39:56
Easthampton 8	1	42N16	72w40	4:50:40
East Harwich 1	1	41N41	70w01	4:40:04
East Haverhill 5	1	42N47	71w05	4:44:20
East Holliston 9	1	42N12	71w26	4:45:44
East Junction 3	1	41N56	71w18	4:45:12
East Lee 2	1	42N19	73w15	4:53:00
East Leverett 6	2	42N27	72w30	4:50:00
East Lexington 9	1	42N26	71w14	4:44:56
East Longmeadow 7	1	42N04	72w31	4:50:04
East Lynn 5	1	42N29	70w58	4:43:52
East Mansfield 3	1	42N01	71w11	4:44:44
East Marion 12	1	41N42	70w46	4:43:04
East Middleboro 12	1	41N51	70w56	4:43:44
East Millbury 14	1	42N12	71w46	4:47:04
East Milton 11	1	42N15	71w05	4:44:20
East Northfield 6	1	42N41	72w27	4:49:48
East Norton 3	1	41N58	71w11	4:44:44
Easton 3	1	42N03	71w06	4:44:24
Eastondale 3	1	42N03	71w05	4:44:20
East Orleans 1	1	41N47	69w58	4:39:52
East Otis 2	1	42N10	73w02	4:52:08
East Pembroke 12	1	42N04	70w49	4:43:16
East Pepperell 9	1	42N40	71w34	4:46:16
East Princeton 14	1	42N28	71w50	4:47:20
East Sandwich 1	1	41N45	70w27	4:41:48
East Somerville 9	1	42N23	71w06	4:44:24
East Sudbury 9	1	42N23	71w25	4:45:40
East Swansea 3	1	41N45	71w13	4:44:52
East Taunton 3	1	41N54	71w06	4:44:24
East Templeton 14	1	42N34	71w58	4:47:52
Eastview Park 9	1	42N23	71w14	4:44:56
East Village 14	1	42N03	71w54	4:47:36
Eastville 4	1	41N27	70w34	4:42:16
East Walpole 11	1	42N10	71w13	4:44:52
East Wareham 12	1	41N46	70w40	4:42:40
East Watertown 9	1	42N22	71w11	4:44:44
East Weymouth 11	1	42N13	70w57	4:43:48
East Windsor 2	1	42N31	73w04	4:52:16
East Woburn 9	1	42N29	71w09	4:44:36
Eddyville 12	1	41N51	70w56	4:43:44
Edgartown 4	1	41N23	70w31	4:42:04
Edgemere 14	1	42N17	71w43	4:46:52
Edgewater Estates 12	1	42N04	70w49	4:43:16
Edgeworth 9	1	42N26	71w04	4:44:16
Egremont 2	1	42N10	73w27	4:53:48
Egypt 12	1	42N13	70w46	4:43:04
Ellisville 12	1	41N45	70w36	4:42:24
Elmdale 14	1	42N05	71w38	4:46:32
Elm Grove 6	1	42N40	72w42	4:50:48
Elm Square 12	1	42N01	71w00	4:44:00
Elmwood 7	1	42N12	72w37	4:50:28
Elmwood 12	1	42N01	70w58	4:43:52
Endicott 11	1	42N14	71w10	4:44:40
Englewood 1	1	41N39	70w15	4:41:00
Erving 6	1	42N36	72w25	4:49:40
Essex 5	1	42N38	70w47	4:43:08
Essex 13	1	42N19	71w05	4:44:20
Essex Falls 5	1	42N38	70w48	4:43:12
Everett 9	1	42N24	71w04	4:44:16
Everett Junction 9	1	42N25	71w03	4:44:12
Factory Hollow 6	1	42N36	72w36	4:50:24
Fairhaven 3	1	41N39	70w55	4:43:40
Fall River 3	1	41N43	71w10	4:44:40
Falls Mall Shopping Center 8	1	42N15	72w35	4:50:20
Falmouth 1	1	41N33	70w37	4:42:28
Farley 6	1	42N36	72w24	4:49:36
Farmersville 1	1	41N46	70w30	4:42:00
Farm Hill 9	1	42N29	71w06	4:44:24
Farnams 2	1	42N33	73w09	4:52:36
Farnumsville 14	1	42N15	71w41	4:46:44
Faulkner 9	1	42N26	71w04	4:44:16
Fayville 14	1	42N18	71w30	4:46:00
Feeding Hills 7	1	42N04	72w41	4:50:44
Felchville 9	1	42N17	71w21	4:45:24
Fells 9	1	42N28	71w04	4:44:16
Fellsway 9	1	42N25	71w07	4:44:28
Fieldston 12	1	42N06	70w39	4:42:36
Findlen 11	1	42N14	71w10	4:44:40
Fireworks 12	1	42N07	70w49	4:43:16
First Cliff 12	1	42N12	70w44	4:42:56
First Encounter 1	1	41N50	69w58	4:39:52
Fiskdale 14	1	42N07	72w06	4:48:24
Fitchburg 14	1	42N35	71w48	4:47:12
Five Corners 3	1	42N04	71w06	4:44:24
Five Corners 12	1	41N47	70w46	4:43:04
Flint 3	1	41N42	71w08	4:44:32
Florence 8	1	42N20	72w40	4:50:40
Florida 2	1	42N40	73w01	4:52:04
Fore River 11	1	42N15	71w00	4:44:00
Forestdale 1	1	41N41	70w01	4:40:04
Forestdale Estates 12	1	42N04	70w49	4:43:16
Forest Lake 7	1	42N09	72w20	4:49:20
Forest Park 7	1	42N05	72w34	4:50:16
Forest Park 11	1	42N05	71w28	4:45:52
Forest River 5	1	42N31	70w54	4:43:36
Forge Village 9	1	42N35	71w29	4:45:56
Fort Bellingham 11	1	42N05	71w28	4:45:52
Fort Devens 9	1	42N33	71w36	4:46:24
Fort Duvall 12	1	42N17	70w53	4:43:32
Fort Heath 13	1	42N22	70w59	4:43:56
Fort Revere 12	1	42N17	70w53	4:43:32
Foundry Village 6	1	42N40	72w42	4:50:48
Foxboro 11	1	42N04	71w16	4:45:04
Foxvale 11	1	42N04	71w16	4:45:04
Framingham 9	1	42N17	71w25	4:45:40
Franklin 11	1	42N05	71w24	4:45:36
Franklin Park 13	1	42N25	71w00	4:44:00
Freetown 3	1	41N46	70w58	4:43:52
Fresh Pond 9	1	42N23	71w08	4:44:32
Freshwater Cove 5	1	42N37	70w40	4:42:40
Fuller Shores 12	1	41N51	70w56	4:43:44
Furnace Pond Colony 12	1	42N04	70w49	4:43:16
Furnace Village 3	1	42N02	71w06	4:44:24
Gardner 14	1	42N34	71w59	4:47:56
Gay Head 4	1	41N20	70w48	4:43:12
Georgetown 5	1	42N44	70w59	4:43:56
Germantown 11	1	42N15	71w00	4:44:00
Gilbertville 14	1	42N18	72w12	4:48:48
Gill 6	2	42N38	72w30	4:50:00
Gillett Corner 7	1	42N04	72w46	4:51:04
Gleasondale 9	1	42N24	71w32	4:46:08
Glendale 2	1	42N17	73w21	4:53:24
Glen Echo 11	1	42N08	71w06	4:44:24
Glen Grove 14	1	42N09	71w58	4:47:52
Glenridge 11	1	42N15	71w19	4:45:16
Glenwood 9	1	42N25	71w07	4:44:28
Globe Village 14	1	42N05	72w02	4:48:08
Gloucester 5	1	42N37	70w40	4:42:40
Goshen 8	1	42N26	72w48	4:51:12
Gosnold 4	1	41N27	70w48	4:43:12
Goss Heights 8	1	42N14	72w53	4:51:32
Grafton 14	1	42N14	71w42	4:46:48
Granby 8	1	42N15	72w31	4:50:04
Graniteville 9	1	42N36	71w28	4:45:52
Granville 7	1	42N04	72w54	4:51:36
Gray Gables 1	1	41N45	70w36	4:42:24
Great Barrington 2	1	42N12	73w22	4:53:28
Greenbush 12	1	42N11	70w45	4:43:00
Greendale 14	1	42N19	71w47	4:47:08
Greenfield 6	1	42N35	72w36	4:50:24
Green Harbor 12	1	42N05	70w39	4:42:36
Greenlodge 11	1	42N14	71w10	4:44:40
Green Ridge Park 2	1	42N29	73w10	4:52:40
Greenville 14	1	42N13	71w53	4:47:32
Greenwood 9	1	42N30	71w04	4:44:16
Greenwood Manor Estates 12	1	42N04	70w49	4:43:16
Greylock 2	1	42N42	73w06	4:52:24
Griswoldville 6	1	42N39	72w43	4:50:52
Groton 9	1	42N37	71w34	4:46:16
Grove Hall 13	1	42N18	71w05	4:44:20
Groveland 5	1	42N45	71w01	4:44:04
Hadley 8	1	42N21	72w34	4:50:16
Halfway Pond 12	1	41N45	70w36	4:42:24
Halifax 12	1	42N00	70w51	4:43:24
Hamilton 5	1	42N37	70w51	4:43:24
Hamilton Beach 12	1	41N46	70w43	4:42:52
Hampden 7	1	42N04	72w26	4:49:44
Hampton Mills 8	1	42N16	72w39	4:50:36
Hancock 2	1	42N33	73w19	4:53:16
Hancock Village 11	1	42N20	71w08	4:44:32
Hanover 12	1	42N07	70w49	4:43:16
Hanscom Air Force Base 9	1	42N29	71w17	4:45:08
Hanson 12	1	42N03	70w52	4:43:28
Happy Hills 11	1	42N05	71w28	4:45:52
Harbor Beach 12	1	41N40	70w49	4:43:16
Harding 11	1	42N11	71w18	4:45:12
Harding Estates 11	1	42N11	71w18	4:45:12
Hardwick 14	1	42N21	72w12	4:48:48
Harthaven 4	1	41N27	70w34	4:42:16
Hartsville 2	1	42N12	73w22	4:53:28
Harvard 14	1	42N30	71w35	4:46:20
Harwich 1	1	41N42	70w03	4:40:12
Harwich Port 1	1	41N40	70w05	4:40:20
Harwood 9	1	42N32	71w31	4:46:04
Hastings 9	1	42N22	71w18	4:45:12
Hatchville 1	1	41N46	70w30	4:42:00
Hatfield 8	2	42N23	72w37	4:50:28
Hathorne 5	1	42N35	70w58	4:43:52
Haverhill 5	1	42N47	71w05	4:44:20
Hawley 6	1	42N35	72w54	4:51:36
Hayden Row	1	42N12	71w31	4:46:04
Haydenville 8	1	42N22	72w42	4:50:48
Head of Westport 3	1	41N37	71w04	4:44:16
Heath 6	1	42N41	72w48	4:51:12
Heaven Heights 3	1	41N46	70w58	4:43:52
Hemlocks 12	1	41N51	70w56	4:43:44
Heywood 14	1	42N34	72w00	4:48:00
Hicksville 3	1	41N37	70w58	4:43:52
Highland 7	1	42N07	72w33	4:50:12
Highland Lake 11	1	42N08	71w19	4:45:16
Highland Park 7	1	42N12	72w37	4:50:28
Highlands 7	1	42N12	72w37	4:50:28
Highlands 9	1	42N38	71w20	4:45:20
Hillcrest Acres 3	1	41N37	71w04	4:44:16
Hilltop Acres 12	1	41N51	70w56	4:43:44
Hingham 12	1	42N15	70w53	4:43:32
Hinsdale 2	1	42N26	73w07	4:52:28
Hinsdale Estates 11	1	42N05	71w28	4:45:52
Hodges Village 14	1	42N07	71w52	4:47:28
Holbrook 11	1	42N09	71w01	4:44:04
Holbrook Grove 11	1	42N09	71w01	4:44:04
Holden 14	1	42N21	71w52	4:47:28
Holland 7	1	42N03	72w10	4:48:40
Holliston 9	1	42N12	71w26	4:45:44
Holly Woods 12	1	41N40	70w49	4:43:16
Holyoke 7	1	42N12	72w37	4:50:28
Hoosac Tunnel 2	1	42N40	72w00	4:48:00
Hopedale 14	1	42N07	71w31	4:46:04
Hopkinton 9	1	42N14	71w31	4:46:04
Horseneck Beach 3	1	41N37	71w04	4:44:16
Hortonville 3	1	41N45	71w13	4:44:52
Houghs Neck 11	1	42N15	71w00	4:44:00
Houghtonville 2	1	42N42	73w06	4:52:24
Housatonic 2	1	42N16	73w22	4:53:28
Hovey's Corner 9	1	42N39	71w35	4:46:20
Howe 5	1	42N36	71w01	4:44:04
Hubbardston 14	1	42N29	72w00	4:48:00
Huckleberry Corner 12	1	41N47	70w46	4:43:04
Huckleyberry Shores 12	1	41N51	70w56	4:43:44
Hudson 9	1	42N23	71w34	4:46:16

Place		Lat.	Long.	Time
Hull 12	1	42N18	70w55	4:43:40
Humarock 12	1	42N08	70w41	4:42:44
Huntington 8	1	42N17	72w51	4:51:24
Hyannis 1	1	41N39	70w17	4:41:08
Hyannis Park 1	1	41N39	70w17	4:41:08
Hyannis Port 1	1	41N38	70w18	4:41:12
Hyde Park 13	1	42N15	71w08	4:44:32
Idlewell 11	1	42N12	70w57	4:43:48
Idlewood 3	1	41N37	70w58	4:43:52
Indian Mound Beach 12	1	41N45	70w36	4:42:24
Indian Shore 12	1	41N51	70w56	4:43:44
Indleside 7	1	42N12	72w37	4:50:28
Inman Square 9	1	42N22	71w06	4:44:24
Interlaken 2	1	42N17	73w19	4:53:16
Ipswich 5	1	42N41	70w50	4:43:20
Island Creek 12	1	42N02	70w40	4:42:40
Islington 11	1	42N14	71w11	4:44:44
Jamaica Plain	1	42N19	71w06	4:44:24
Jefferson 14	1	42N22	71w53	4:47:32
Jefferson Shores 12	1	41N45	70w36	4:42:24
John Fitzgerald Kennedy 13	1	42N19	71w05	4:44:20
Joppa 5	1	42N49	70w52	4:43:28
Katama 4	1	41N23	70w31	4:42:04
Kearney Square 9	1	42N38	71w18	4:45:12
Kempton Croft 3	1	41N37	70w58	4:43:52
Kenberma 12	1	42N17	70w53	4:43:32
Kendal Green 9	1	42N22	71w18	4:45:12
Kendall Square 9	1	42N22	71w05	4:44:20
Kenmore 13	1	42N21	71w06	4:44:24
Kent Park	1	42N07	70w41	4:42:44
Kenwood 9	1	42N41	71w19	4:45:16
Kingsbury Beach 1	1	41N50	69w58	4:39:52
Kings Forest 5	1	42N41	70w59	4:43:56
Kingston 12	1	42N00	70w44	4:42:56
Kingston Plaza 12	1	41N58	70w40	4:42:40
Kingston Shores 12	1	41N58	70w40	4:42:40
Knightville 8	1	42N14	72w53	4:51:32
Knollmere 3	1	41N39	70w53	4:43:32
Konkapot 2	1	42N07	73w16	4:53:04
Lagoon Heights 4	1	41N27	70w34	4:42:16
Lake Forest Park 9	1	42N17	71w21	4:45:24
Lake Hiawatha 11	1	42N05	71w28	4:45:52
Lake Mattawa 6	1	42N35	72w19	4:49:16
Lake Pearl 11	1	42N04	71w20	4:45:20
Lake Pleasant 6	1	42N33	72w31	4:50:04
Lakeside 12	1	41N51	70w56	4:43:44
Lake Street 9	1	42N25	71w10	4:44:40
Lakeview 9	1	42N23	71w14	4:44:56
Lakeview Terrace 2	1	42N27	73w15	4:53:00
Lakeville 12	1	41N49	71w00	4:44:00
Lakeville Center 12	1	41N51	70w56	4:43:44
Lakewood 2	1	42N27	73w15	4:53:00
Lakewood Hills 1	1	41N45	70w27	4:41:48
Lakewood Park 14	1	42N33	71w55	4:47:40
Lambs Grove 14	1	42N15	72w00	4:48:00
Lancaster 14	1	42N28	71w41	4:46:44
Lands End 5	1	42N39	70w37	4:42:28
Lanesborough 2	1	42N31	73w14	4:52:56
Lanesville 5	1	42N37	70w40	4:42:40
Lane Village 14	1	42N38	71w54	4:47:36
Larrywaug 2	1	42N17	73w19	4:53:16
Laurel Park 8	1	42N20	72w40	4:50:40
Lawrence 5	1	42N43	71w10	4:44:40
Le Count Hollow 1	1	41N55	70w00	4:40:00
Lee 2	1	42N19	73w15	4:53:00
Leeds 8	1	42N19	72w39	4:50:36
Leicester 14	1	42N14	71w54	4:47:36
Leino Park 14	1	42N33	71w55	4:47:40
Lenox 2	1	42N22	73w17	4:53:08
Lenox Dale 2	1	42N20	73w15	4:53:00
Leominster 14	1	42N32	71w46	4:47:04
Leverett 6	2	42N28	72w29	4:49:56
Lexington 9	1	42N27	71w14	4:44:56
Leyden 6	1	42N41	72w37	4:50:28
Liberty Plain 12	1	42N11	70w53	4:43:32
Lincoln 9	1	42N26	71w18	4:45:12
Linden 9	1	42N26	71w04	4:44:16
Lindenwood 9	1	42N29	71w06	4:44:24
Linwood 14	1	42N06	71w39	4:46:36
Lithia 8	1	42N27	72w50	4:51:20
Little Acres 12	1	42N03	70w51	4:43:24
Little Harbor Beach 12	1	41N46	70w43	4:42:52
Little Nahant 5	1	42N26	70w56	4:43:44
Little Neck 3	1	41N45	71w13	4:44:52
Little Neck 5	1	42N41	70w50	4:43:20
Little River 7	1	42N08	72w45	4:51:00
Littleton 9	1	42N32	71w31	4:46:04
Littleton Common 9	1	42N33	71w28	4:45:52
Lobsterville 4	1	41N21	70w45	4:43:00
Lockerville 9	1	42N17	71w21	4:45:24
Locks Village 6	1	42N27	72w25	4:49:40
Long Beach 5	1	42N37	70w40	4:42:40
Long Hill Acres 12	1	42N06	70w48	4:43:12
Long Island 13	1	42N15	71w00	4:44:00
Longmeadow 7	1	42N03	72w34	4:50:16
Long Plain 3	1	41N41	70w55	4:43:40
Long Pond Village 12	1	41N45	70w36	4:42:24
Longwood 11	1	42N20	71w08	4:44:32
Loudville 8	1	42N16	72w39	4:50:36
Lovell Corners 11	1	42N12	70w57	4:43:48
Lowell 9	1	42N38	71w19	4:45:16
Lower Village 9	1	42N26	71w30	4:46:00
Lower Wire Village 14	1	42N15	72w00	4:48:00
Ludlow 7	1	42N10	72w28	4:49:52
Lunds Corner 3	1	41N41	70w56	4:43:44
Lunenburg 14	1	42N35	71w46	4:47:04
Luther Corner 3	1	41N52	71w19	4:45:16
Lynn 5	1	42N28	70w57	4:43:48
Lynnfield 5	1	42N32	71w03	4:44:12
Lynnhurst 5	1	42N28	71w01	4:44:04
Lyonsville 6	1	42N40	72w42	4:50:48
Madaket 10	1	41N17	70w06	4:40:24
Magnolia 5	1	42N37	70w40	4:42:40
Mahkeenac Heights 2	1	42N21	73w17	4:53:08
Malden 9	1	42N26	71w04	4:44:16
Manchaug 14	1	42N06	71w45	4:47:00
Manchester 5	1	42N35	70w46	4:43:04
Manleys Corner 12	1	42N01	71w00	4:44:00
Manomet 12	1	41N55	70w34	4:42:16
Manomet Beach 12	1	41N55	70w34	4:42:16
Manomet Bluffs 12	1	41N55	70w34	4:42:16
Manomet Heights 12	1	41N55	70w34	4:42:16
Mansfield 3	1	42N02	71w13	4:44:52
Maple Grove 2	1	42N37	73w07	4:52:28
Maplewood 9	1	42N26	71w04	4:44:16
Maplewood 14	1	42N14	71w42	4:46:48
Mara Vista 1	1	41N46	70w30	4:42:00
Marblehead 5	1	42N30	70w51	4:43:24
Marblehead Neck 5	1	42N30	70w52	4:43:28
Marion 12	1	41N42	70w45	4:43:00
Marlboro 5	1	42N47	71w05	4:44:20
Marlborough 9	1	42N21	71w33	4:46:12
Marsh Corner 5	1	42N44	71w11	4:44:44
Marshfield 12	1	42N06	70w42	4:42:48
Marstons Mills 1	1	41N39	70w25	4:41:40
Martha's Vineyard 4	1	41N25	70w40	4:42:40
Mashpee 1	1	41N36	70w29	4:41:56
Masons Corner 3	1	41N46	70w58	4:43:52
Matfield 12	1	42N01	71w00	4:44:00
Mattapan 13	1	42N16	71w06	4:44:24
Mattapoisett 12	1	41N40	70w49	4:43:16
Maushop Village 1	1	41N35	70w27	4:41:48
Mayflower Grove 12	1	42N03	70w51	4:43:24
Mayflower Heights 1	1	42N03	70w11	4:40:44
Maynard 9	1	42N26	71w27	4:45:48
Mayo Beach 1	1	41N56	70w02	4:40:08
Medfield 11	1	42N11	71w18	4:45:12
Medford 9	1	42N25	71w07	4:44:28
Medford Hillside 9	1	42N25	71w07	4:44:28
Medway 11	1	42N08	71w24	4:45:36
Megansett 1	1	41N39	70w37	4:42:28
Melrose 9	1	42N27	71w04	4:44:16
Melrose Highlands 9	1	42N27	71w04	4:44:16
Menauhant 1	1	41N46	70w30	4:42:00
Mendon 14	1	42N07	71w33	4:46:12
Menemsha 4	1	41N21	70w46	4:43:04
Merino Village 14	1	42N03	71w54	4:47:36
Merrick 7	1	42N07	72w38	4:50:32
Merrimac 5	1	42N50	71w00	4:44:00
Merrimack College 5	1	42N42	71w08	4:44:32
Merrimacport 5	1	42N50	71w00	4:44:00
Merrimac Terrace 5	1	42N47	71w05	4:44:20
Merrymount 11	1	42N15	71w00	4:44:00
Metcalfs 9	1	42N12	71w26	4:45:44
Methuen 5	1	42N44	71w11	4:44:44
Middleboro 12	1	41N54	70w55	4:43:40
Middlefield 8	1	42N21	73w01	4:52:04
Middleton 5	1	42N36	71w01	4:44:04
Milford 14	1	42N08	71w31	4:46:04
Millbrook 12	1	42N02	70w40	4:42:40
Millbury 14	1	42N12	71w46	4:47:04
Millers Falls 6	1	42N35	72w30	4:50:00
Millerville 14	1	42N01	71w30	4:46:00
Millis 11	1	42N10	71w22	4:45:28
Mill River 2	1	42N07	73w16	4:53:04
Millville 14	1	42N03	71w35	4:46:20
Milton 11	1	42N15	71w05	4:44:20
Minot 12	1	42N14	70w46	4:43:04
Mishaum Point 3	1	41N37	70w58	4:43:52
M.I.T. 9	1	42N22	71w06	4:44:24
Monomoy 10	1	41N17	70w06	4:40:24
Monponsett 12	1	42N01	70w51	4:43:24
Monroe 6	1	42N43	72w59	4:51:56
Monroe Bridge 6	1	42N43	72w57	4:51:48
Monson 7	1	42N06	72w20	4:49:20
Montague 6	1	42N33	72w32	4:50:08
Montague City 6	1	42N35	72w35	4:50:20
Montclair 11	1	42N15	71w00	4:44:00
Montello 12	1	42N05	71w01	4:44:04
Monterey 2	1	42N11	73w14	4:52:56
Montgomery 7	1	42N12	72w49	4:51:16
Montserrat 5	1	42N34	70w53	4:43:32
Montvale 9	1	42N29	71w09	4:44:36
Montville 2	1	42N07	73w08	4:52:32
Monument Beach 1	1	41N43	70w37	4:42:28
Moores Corner 6	2	42N27	72w30	4:50:00
Morningdale 14	1	42N19	71w41	4:46:44
Morrills 11	1	42N11	71w12	4:44:48
Morseville 9	1	42N17	71w21	4:45:24
Morseville 14	1	42N09	71w58	4:47:52
Mountain Farms Mall 8	1	42N21	72w35	4:50:20
Mount Auburn 9	1	42N22	71w11	4:44:44
Mount Hermon 6	1	42N40	72w29	4:49:56
Mount Saint James 14	1	42N15	71w49	4:47:16
Mount Tom 8	1	42N17	72w37	4:50:28
Mount Washington 2	1	42N06	73w28	4:53:52
Mundale 7	1	42N08	72w45	4:51:00
Munroe 9	1	42N26	71w14	4:44:56
Myricks 3	1	41N54	71w06	4:44:24
Mystic Grove 14	1	42N08	71w58	4:47:52
Mystic Junction 9	1	42N23	71w06	4:44:24
Nabnasset 9	1	42N37	71w25	4:45:40
Nahant 5	1	42N26	70w55	4:43:40
Nameloc Heights 12	1	41N45	70w36	4:42:24
Namskaket 1	1	41N47	70w00	4:40:00
Nantasket Beach 12	1	42N17	70w53	4:43:32
Nantucket 10	1	41N17	70w06	4:40:24
Nashaquitsa 4	1	41N21	70w45	4:43:00
Natick 9	1	42N17	71w21	4:45:24
Natick Laboratories 9	1	42N17	71w21	4:45:24
Nauset Heights 1	1	41N47	69w58	4:39:52
Needham 11	1	42N17	71w14	4:44:56
Needham Heights 11	1	42N18	71w14	4:44:56
Needham Junction 11	1	42N17	71w14	4:44:56
Nelsons Grove 12	1	41N51	70w56	4:43:44
Nelsons Shores 12	1	41N51	70w56	4:43:44
New Ashford 2	1	42N36	73w14	4:52:56
New Bedford 3	1	41N38	70w56	4:43:44
New Boston 2	1	42N07	73w08	4:52:32
New Braintree 14	1	42N19	72w07	4:48:28
Newbury 5	1	42N46	70w53	4:43:32
Newbury Old Town 5	1	42N49	70w52	4:43:28
Newburyport 5	1	42N49	70w53	4:43:32
New Lenox 2	1	42N21	73w17	4:53:08
New Marlboro 2	1	42N12	73w22	4:53:28
New Marlborough 2	1	42N06	73w15	4:53:00
New Salem 6	1	42N30	72w20	4:49:20
Newton 9	1	42N21	71w12	4:44:48
Newton Highlands 9	1	42N19	71w12	4:44:48
Newton Lower Falls 9	1	42N20	71w14	4:44:56
Newton Upper Falls 9	1	42N19	71w13	4:44:52
Newtonville 9	1	42N21	71w12	4:44:48
Newtown 1	1	41N39	70w25	4:41:40
New Village 14	1	42N07	71w40	4:46:40
Nipmuck Pond 14	1	42N06	71w33	4:46:12
Nobska Beach 12	1	41N46	70w43	4:42:52
Nonantum 9	1	42N20	71w12	4:44:48
Nonquitt 3	1	41N37	70w58	4:43:52
Noquochoke 3	1	41N37	71w04	4:44:16
Norfolk 11	1	42N07	71w20	4:45:20
Norfolk Downs 11	1	42N15	71w00	4:44:00
North 3	1	41N40	70w56	4:43:44
North Abington 12	1	42N08	70w57	4:43:48
North Acton 9	1	42N29	71w26	4:45:44
North Adams 2	1	42N42	73w07	4:52:28
North Adams Junction 2	1	42N27	73w15	4:53:00
North Amherst 8	1	42N24	72w32	4:50:08
Northampton 8	1	42N19	72w38	4:50:32
North Andover 5	1	42N42	71w08	4:44:32
North Ashburnham 14	1	42N38	71w54	4:47:36
North Attleboro 3	1	41N59	71w20	4:45:20
North Bellingham 11	1	42N07	71w27	4:45:48
North Beverly 5	1	42N34	70w53	4:43:32
North Billerica 9	1	42N35	71w17	4:45:08
North Blandford 7	1	42N11	72w56	4:51:44
Northborough 14	1	42N19	71w39	4:46:36
Northbridge 14	1	42N08	71w39	4:46:36
North Brookfield 14	1	42N16	72w03	4:48:12
North Cambridge 9	1	42N23	71w08	4:44:32
North Carver 12	1	41N55	70w48	4:43:12
North Chatham 1	1	41N42	69w57	4:39:48
North Chelmsford 9	1	42N38	71w23	4:45:32
North Chester 7	1	42N14	72w53	4:51:32
North Cohasset 11	1	42N16	70w51	4:43:24
North Dartmouth 3	1	41N37	70w58	4:43:52
North Dighton 3	1	41N52	71w08	4:44:32
North Duxbury 12	1	42N02	70w40	4:42:40
North Eastham 1	1	41N52	69w59	4:39:56
North Easton 3	1	42N04	71w06	4:44:24
North Egremont 2	1	42N12	73w26	4:53:44
Northey Point 5	1	42N31	70w54	4:43:36
North Falmouth 1	1	41N39	70w37	4:42:28
North Farms 8	1	42N20	72w40	4:50:40
Northfield 6	1	42N42	72w27	4:49:48
North Foxboro 11	1	42N04	71w16	4:45:04
North Grafton 14	1	42N14	71w42	4:46:48
North Hadley 8	1	42N21	72w35	4:50:20
North Hancock 2	1	42N43	73w12	4:52:48
North Hanover 12	1	42N09	70w52	4:43:28
North Harwich 1	1	41N41	70w01	4:40:04
North Hatfield 8	2	42N25	72w37	4:50:28
North Lakeville 12	1	41N51	70w56	4:43:44
North Lancaster 14	1	42N28	71w41	4:46:44
North Leominster 14	1	42N32	71w46	4:47:04
North Leverett 6	2	42N27	72w30	4:50:00
North Lexington 9	1	42N26	71w14	4:44:56
North Littleton 9	1	42N32	71w31	4:46:04
North Marshfield 12	1	42N09	70w46	4:43:04
North Middleboro 12	1	41N51	70w56	4:43:44
North Milford 14	1	42N08	71w32	4:46:08
North Natick 9	1	42N17	71w21	4:45:24
North New Salem 6	1	42N35	72w19	4:49:16
North Orange 6	1	42N35	72w19	4:49:16
North Otis 2	1	42N12	73w06	4:52:24
North Oxford 14	1	42N09	71w52	4:47:28

MASSACHUSETTS

MASSACHUSETTS

North Pembroke 12 1 42N06 70w47 4:43:08
North Pepperell 9 1 42N39 71w35 4:46:20
North Plymouth 12 1 41N58 70w41 4:42:44
North Plympton 12 1 41N58 70w40 4:42:40
North Quincy 11 1 42N17 71w01 4:44:04
North Randolph 11 1 42N10 71w03 4:44:12
North Reading 9 1 42N35 71w05 4:44:20
North Rehoboth 3 1 41N50 71w16 4:45:04
North Rutland 14 1 42N22 71w57 4:47:48
North Salem 5 1 42N31 70w54 4:43:36
North Saugus 5 1 42N28 71w01 4:44:04
North Scituate 12 1 42N13 70w47 4:43:08
North Seekonk 3 1 41N52 71w19 4:45:16
Northside 14 1 42N09 71w58 4:47:52
North Sommerville 9 1 42N23 71w06 4:44:24
North Stoughton 11 1 42N08 71w06 4:44:24
North Sudbury 9 1 42N25 71w24 4:45:36
North Swansea 3 1 41N45 71w13 4:44:52
North Tewksbury 9 1 42N39 71w15 4:45:00
North Tisbury 4 1 41N27 70w36 4:42:24
North Truro 1 1 42N02 70w05 4:40:20
North Uxbridge 14 1 42N07 71w38 4:46:32
North Waltham 9 1 42N23 71w14 4:44:56
North Weymouth 11 1 42N15 70w57 4:43:48
North Wilmington 9 1 42N34 71w09 4:44:36
North Woburn 9 1 42N29 71w09 4:44:36
Norton 3 1 41N58 71w11 4:44:44
Norton Grove 3 1 41N58 71w11 4:44:44
Norwell 12 1 42N10 70w48 4:43:12
Norwood 11 1 42N12 71w12 4:44:48
Nutting Lake 9 1 42N32 71w16 4:45:04
Oak Bluffs 4 1 41N27 70w34 4:42:16
Oakdale 7 1 42N12 72w37 4:50:28
Oakdale 11 1 42N14 71w10 4:44:40
Oakdale 14 1 42N23 71w48 4:47:12
Oakdale Village 12 1 41N46 70w43 4:42:52
Oak Grove 9 1 42N26 71w04 4:44:16
Oakham 14 1 42N21 72w02 4:48:08
Oak Island 13 1 42N25 71w00 4:44:00
Oakland 9 1 42N29 71w09 4:44:36
Oakland Vale 5 1 42N28 71w01 4:44:04
Ocean Bluff 12 1 42N06 70w39 4:42:36
Ocean Grove 3 1 41N45 71w13 4:44:52
Ocean Heights 4 1 41N23 70w31 4:42:04
Ocean Spray 13 1 42N22 70w59 4:43:56
Old City 9 1 42N41 71w44 4:46:56
Old Furnace 14 1 42N18 72w12 4:48:48
Oldham Pines 12 1 42N04 70w49 4:43:16
Oldham Village 12 1 42N04 70w49 4:43:16
Old Silver Beach 1 1 41N39 70w37 4:42:28
Onset 12 1 41N45 70w39 4:42:36
Orange 6 1 42N36 72w19 4:49:16
Ordway 9 1 42N24 71w35 4:46:20
Orleans 1 1 41N47 70w00 4:40:00
Osceola 2 1 42N23 73w22 4:53:28
Osterville 1 1 41N37 70w22 4:41:28
Otis 2 1 42N12 73w06 4:52:24
Otis Air Force Base 1 1 41N39 70w33 4:42:12
Otter River 14 1 42N36 72w04 4:48:16
Overbrook 11 1 42N18 71w17 4:45:08
Oxford 14 1 42N09 71w52 4:47:28
Oxford Center 14 1 42N07 71w52 4:47:28
Oyster Harbors 1 1 41N38 70w23 4:41:32
Packard Heights 6 1 42N36 72w14 4:48:56
Padanaram Village 3 1 41N37 70w58 4:43:52
Pages Beach 14 1 42N38 71w54 4:47:36
Pakachoag 14 1 42N12 71w50 4:47:20
Palmer 7 1 42N11 72w19 4:49:16
Park Street 9 1 42N25 71w07 4:44:28
Parkwood Beach 12 1 41N46 70w43 4:42:52
Pattenville 9 1 42N33 71w16 4:45:04
Patuisset 1 1 41N41 70w37 4:42:28
Paxton 14 1 42N18 71w55 4:47:40
Payson Park 9 1 42N22 71w11 4:44:44
Peabody 5 1 42N31 70w56 4:43:44
Pelham 8 1 42N23 72w26 4:49:44
Pembroke 12 1 42N03 70w49 4:43:16
Pembroke Heights 12 1 42N06 70w48 4:43:12
Pembroke Pines 12 1 42N03 70w51 4:43:24
Pepperell 9 1 42N40 71w35 4:46:20
Perryville 3 1 41N50 71w16 4:45:04
Peru 2 1 42N26 73w02 4:52:08
Petersham 14 1 42N29 72w12 4:48:48
Phelps Mills 5 1 42N32 70w57 4:43:48
Phillipston 14 1 42N33 72w08 4:48:32
Phillipston Four Corners 14 1 42N36 72w14 4:48:56
Pierces Bridge 9 1 42N26 71w14 4:44:56
Pierceville 12 1 41N47 70w46 4:43:04
Piety Corner 9 1 42N23 71w14 4:44:56
Pigeon Cove 5 1 42N41 70w38 4:42:32
Pilgrim Heights 1 1 42N02 70w06 4:40:24
Pilgrim Pines Estates 12 1 42N03 70w51 4:43:24
Pilgrim Village 11 1 42N05 71w28 4:45:52
Pine Bluffs 12 1 41N51 70w56 4:43:44
Pinefield 5 1 42N41 70w50 4:43:20
Pine Grove 8 1 42N20 72w40 4:50:40
Pine Grove 9 1 42N21 71w12 4:44:48
Pinehurst 9 1 42N32 71w14 4:44:56
Pinehurst Beach 12 1 41N46 70w43 4:42:52
Pine Island Lake 8 1 42N20 72w40 4:50:40
Pine Lake 9 1 42N24 71w28 4:45:52
Pine Rest 9 1 42N23 71w26 4:45:44
Pingryville 9 1 42N32 71w31 4:46:04

Pitcherville 14 1 42N29 72w01 4:48:04
Pittsfield 2 1 42N27 73w15 4:53:00
Plainfield 8 1 42N31 72w55 4:51:40
Plainville 11 1 42N01 71w20 4:45:20
Pleasant Lake 1 1 41N41 70w01 4:40:04
Plimptonville 11 1 42N08 71w15 4:45:00
Plum Island 5 1 42N49 70w52 4:43:28
Plummer Corner 14 1 42N07 71w40 4:46:40
Plymouth 1 41N57 70w40 4:42:40
Plympton 12 1 41N58 70w49 4:43:16
Pocasset 1 1 41N41 70w37 4:42:28
Pocomo 10 1 41N17 70w06 4:40:24
Podunk 14 1 42N14 72w03 4:48:12
Point Allerton 12 1 42N17 70w53 4:43:32
Point Independence 12 1 41N45 70w36 4:42:24
Point Of Pines 13 1 42N25 71w00 4:44:00
Point Pleasant 14 1 42N03 71w54 4:47:36
Point Shirley 13 1 42N22 70w59 4:43:56
Polpis 10 1 41N17 70w06 4:40:24
Ponakin Mill 14 1 42N28 71w41 4:46:44
Pond Village 1 1 42N02 70w06 4:40:24
Pondville 11 1 42N04 71w20 4:45:20
Pondville 12 1 41N45 70w36 4:42:24
Pondville 14 1 42N12 71w50 4:47:20
Pontoosuc Gardens 2 1 42N27 73w15 4:53:00
Pope Beach 3 1 41N39 70w53 4:43:32
Popponesset Beach 1 1 41N35 70w27 4:41:48
Post Island 11 1 42N15 71w00 4:44:00
Precinct 12 1 41N51 70w56 4:43:44
Prentice Gardens 14 1 42N07 71w40 4:46:40
Prides Crossing 5 1 42N34 70w53 4:43:32
Princeton 14 1 42N28 71w53 4:47:32
Princeton Station 14 1 42N29 72w01 4:48:04
Priscilla Beach 12 1 41N56 70w34 4:42:16
Provincetown 1 1 42N03 70w11 4:40:44
Prudential Center 13 1 42N19 71w05 4:44:20
Quaise 10 1 41N17 70w06 4:40:24
Quidnet 10 1 41N17 70w06 4:40:24
Quincy 11 1 42N15 71w00 4:44:00
Quissett 1 1 41N34 70w38 4:42:32
Rakeville 11 1 42N05 71w28 4:45:52
Randolph 11 1 42N10 71w02 4:44:08
Raynham 3 1 41N56 71w03 4:44:12
Reading 9 1 42N32 71w07 4:44:28
Reading Highlands 9 1 42N31 71w07 4:44:28
Readville 13 1 42N19 71w05 4:44:20
Readyville Manor 11 1 42N14 71w10 4:44:40
Redstone Shopping Center 9 1 42N29 71w06 4:44:24
Rehoboth 3 1 41N51 71w15 4:45:00
Renfrew 2 1 42N37 73w07 4:52:28
Reservoir 11 1 42N20 71w08 4:44:32
Revere 13 1 42N25 71w01 4:44:04
Revere Beach 13 1 42N25 71w00 4:44:00
Rexhame 1 42N07 70w40 4:42:40
Richardson Corners 14 1 42N09 71w58 4:47:52
Richmond 2 1 42N22 73w21 4:53:24
Richmond Furnace 2 1 42N23 73w22 4:53:28
Rings Island 5 1 42N49 70w52 4:43:28
Rio Vista 9 1 42N35 71w17 4:45:08
Risingdale 2 1 42N12 73w22 4:53:28
Riverdale 5 1 42N37 70w40 4:42:40
Riverdale 11 1 42N14 71w10 4:44:40
Riverdale 14 1 42N09 71w39 4:46:36
Rivermoor 12 1 42N12 70w44 4:42:56
River Pines 9 1 42N34 71w17 4:45:08
Riverside 2 1 42N43 73w12 4:52:48
Riverside 5 1 42N47 71w05 4:44:20
Riverside 6 1 42N36 72w33 4:50:12
Riverside 7 1 42N12 72w37 4:50:28
Riverside 9 1 42N21 71w12 4:44:48
Riverside 12 1 41N45 70w39 4:42:36
Riverview 5 1 42N37 70w40 4:42:40
Riverview 9 1 42N23 71w14 4:44:56
Roberts 9 1 42N23 71w14 4:44:56
Rochdale 14 1 42N12 71w54 4:47:36
Rochester 12 1 41N45 70w51 4:43:24
Rock 12 1 41N51 70w56 4:43:44
Rockdale 2 1 42N16 73w22 4:53:28
Rock Harbor 1 1 41N47 70w00 4:40:00
Rock Island 11 1 42N15 71w00 4:44:00
Rockland 12 1 42N08 70w55 4:43:40
Rockport 5 1 42N39 70w37 4:42:28
Rocks Village 5 1 42N47 71w05 4:44:20
Rock Valley 7 1 42N12 72w37 4:50:28
Rockville 11 1 42N08 71w22 4:45:28
Rocky Hill 14 1 42N08 71w32 4:46:08
Rocky Nook 12 1 41N58 70w40 4:42:40
Rocky Nook Point 12 1 41N58 70w40 4:42:40
Rolling Acres Estates 9 1 42N37 71w25 4:45:40
Roosterville 2 1 42N07 73w08 4:52:32
Rosemont 5 1 42N47 71w05 4:44:20
Roslindale 13 1 42N18 71w07 4:44:28
Rowe 6 2 42N42 72w54 4:51:36
Rowley 5 1 42N43 70w53 4:43:32
Roxbury 13 1 42N20 71w06 4:44:24
Roxbury Crossing 13 1 42N20 71w06 4:44:24
Royalston 14 1 42N40 72w11 4:48:44
Russell 7 1 42N10 72w50 4:51:20
Russells Mills 3 1 41N37 70w58 4:43:52
Russellville 8 1 42N08 72w45 4:51:00
Rust Craft 11 1 42N14 71w10 4:44:40

Rutland 14 1 42N23 71w58 4:47:52
Saconesset Hills 1 1 41N34 70w38 4:42:32
Sagamore 1 1 41N47 70w32 4:42:08
Sagamore Beach 1 1 41N48 70w32 4:42:08
Sagamore Highlands 1 1 41N45 70w33 4:42:12
Saint Hyacinth College Semin 8 1 42N16 72w31 4:50:04
Salem 5 1 42N31 70w53 4:43:32
Salem Neck 5 1 42N31 70w54 4:43:36
Salem State College 5 1 42N31 70w54 4:43:36
Salisbury 5 1 42N51 70w53 4:43:32
Salisbury Point 5 1 42N51 70w56 4:43:44
Salters Point 3 1 41N37 70w58 4:43:52
Sampsons Corner 12 1 41N51 70w56 4:43:44
Sandersdale 14 1 42N05 72w02 4:48:08
Sand Hill 12 1 42N12 70w44 4:42:56
Sandisfield 2 1 42N06 73w07 4:52:28
Sandwich 1 1 41N46 70w30 4:42:00
Sandy Beach 11 1 42N14 70w48 4:43:12
Sandy Beach 14 1 42N22 71w57 4:47:48
Santuit 1 1 41N37 70w26 4:41:44
Saugus 5 1 42N28 71w01 4:44:04
Saundersville 14 1 42N15 71w41 4:46:44
Savoy 2 1 42N35 73w01 4:52:04
Saxonville 9 1 42N18 71w25 4:45:40
Scituate 12 1 42N12 70w44 4:42:56
Scorton Shores 1 1 41N45 70w27 4:41:48
Scott Hill Acres 11 1 42N05 71w28 4:45:52
Searstown 14 1 42N32 71w46 4:47:04
Searsville 8 1 42N23 72w44 4:50:56
Sea View 1 42N08 70w43 4:42:52
Second Cliff 12 1 42N12 70w44 4:42:56
Seekonk 3 1 41N51 71w19 4:45:16
Segreganset 3 1 41N50 71w07 4:44:28
Shaker Village 14 1 42N30 71w35 4:46:20
Sharon 11 1 42N07 71w11 4:44:44
Shattuckville 6 1 42N38 72w44 4:50:56
Shawkemo 10 1 41N17 70w06 4:40:24
Shawsheen Heights 5 1 42N39 71w08 4:44:32
Shawsheen Village 5 1 42N39 71w08 4:44:32
Sheffield 2 1 42N06 73w22 4:53:28
Shelburne 6 1 42N36 72w40 4:50:40
Shelburne Falls 6 1 42N36 72w45 4:51:00
Sheldonville 11 1 42N02 71w23 4:45:32
Shell Beach 12 1 41N40 70w49 4:43:16
Shepardville 11 1 41N58 71w20 4:45:20
Sherborn 9 1 42N14 71w22 4:45:28
Sherwood Forest 2 1 42N20 73w05 4:52:20
Sherwood Forest 3 1 41N41 70w55 4:43:40
Sherwood Plaza 9 1 42N17 71w21 4:45:24
Shimmo 10 1 41N17 70w06 4:40:24
Shirley 9 1 42N34 71w38 4:46:32
Shoppers' World 9 1 42N18 71w25 4:45:40
Shore Acres 3 1 41N37 70w58 4:43:52
Shore Acres 12 1 42N13 70w44 4:42:56
Shrewsbury 14 1 42N18 71w43 4:46:52
Shutesbury 6 1 42N27 72w24 4:49:36
Siasconset 10 1 41N16 69w58 4:39:52
Silver Beach 1 1 41N38 70w38 4:42:32
Silver Hill 9 1 42N22 71w18 4:45:12
Silver Lake 9 1 42N34 71w11 4:44:44
Silver Lake 12 1 41N58 70w40 4:42:40
Silver Shell Beach 3 1 41N39 70w53 4:43:32
Silver Spring Beach 1 1 41N52 69w59 4:39:56
Sippewisset 1 1 41N34 70w38 4:42:32
Smiths Ferry 7 1 42N12 72w37 4:50:28
Snug Harbor 12 1 42N02 70w40 4:42:40
Soldiers Field 13 1 42N22 71w08 4:44:32
Somerset 3 1 41N47 71w08 4:44:32
Somerville 9 1 42N23 71w06 4:44:24
South 3 1 41N41 71w10 4:44:40
South Acton 9 1 42N28 71w27 4:45:48
South Amherst 8 1 42N23 72w31 4:50:04
Southampton 8 2 42N14 72w43 4:50:52
South Ashburnham 14 1 42N36 71w55 4:47:40
South Ashfield 6 2 42N32 72w48 4:51:12
South Athol 14 1 42N32 72w16 4:49:04
South Attleboro 3 1 41N56 71w18 4:45:12
South Barre 14 1 42N23 72w06 4:48:24
South Bellingham 11 1 42N05 71w28 4:45:52
South Berlin 14 1 42N22 71w38 4:46:32
South Billerica 9 1 42N29 71w17 4:45:08
South Bolton 14 1 42N26 71w36 4:46:24
Southborough 14 1 42N18 71w32 4:46:08
South Boston 13 1 42N20 71w03 4:44:12
South Braintree 11 1 42N13 70w59 4:43:56
Southbridge 14 1 42N02 72w02 4:48:08
South Byfield 5 1 42N46 70w57 4:43:48
South Carver 12 1 41N51 70w45 4:43:00
South Charlton 14 1 42N08 71w58 4:47:52
South Chatham 1 1 41N41 70w01 4:40:04
South Chelmsford 9 1 42N34 71w23 4:45:32
South Dartmouth 3 1 41N37 70w58 4:43:52
South Deerfield 6 1 42N29 72w37 4:50:28
South Dennis 1 1 41N41 70w09 4:40:36
South Duxbury 12 1 42N01 70w41 4:42:44
South Easton 3 1 42N03 71w05 4:44:20
South Egremont 2 1 42N10 73w25 4:53:40
South Essex 5 1 42N38 70w46 4:43:04
Southfield 2 1 42N06 73w14 4:52:56
South Fitchburg 14 1 42N35 71w48 4:47:12
South Foxboro 11 1 42N04 71w16 4:45:04

MASSACHUSETTS

South Framingham 9	1	42N18	71w25	4:45:40
South Gardner 14	1	42N34	72w00	4:48:00
South Georgetown 5	1	42N47	71w05	4:44:20
South Grafton 14	1	42N15	71w41	4:46:44
South Hadley 8	1	42N14	72w35	4:50:20
South Hadley Falls 8	1	42N15	72w35	4:50:20
South Hamilton 5	1	42N37	70w53	4:43:32
South Hanover 12	1	42N07	70w49	4:43:16
South Harwich 1	1	41N41	70w03	4:40:12
South Hingham 12	1	42N14	70w54	4:43:36
South Hyannis 1	1	41N39	70w17	4:41:08
South Lakeville 12	1	41N51	70w56	4:43:44
South Lancaster 14	1	42N26	71w41	4:46:44
South Lawrence 5	1	42N42	71w10	4:44:40
South Lee 2	1	42N17	73w17	4:53:08
South Lincoln 9	1	42N25	71w20	4:45:20
South Lowell 9	1	42N36	71w13	4:44:52
South Lynnfield 5	1	42N32	71w02	4:44:08
South Mashpee 1	1	41N39	70w29	4:41:56
South Middleboro 12	1	41N51	70w56	4:43:44
South Milford 14	1	42N08	71w33	4:46:12
South Monson 7	1	42N06	72w19	4:49:16
South Natick 9	1	42N17	71w21	4:45:24
South Orleans 1	1	41N47	69w59	4:39:56
South Peabody 5	1	42N32	70w57	4:43:48
South Quincy 11	1	42N15	71w00	4:44:00
South Royalston 14	1	42N38	72w09	4:48:36
South Salem 5	1	42N31	70w54	4:43:36
South Sandisfield 2	1	42N07	73w08	4:52:32
South Sandwich 1	1	41N46	70w30	4:42:00
South Spencer 14	1	42N15	72w00	4:48:00
South Stoughton 11	1	42N08	71w06	4:44:24
South Sutton 14	1	42N04	71w43	4:46:52
South Swansea 3	1	41N45	71w13	4:44:52
South Truro 1	1	41N59	70w03	4:40:12
South Uxbridge 14	1	42N05	71w38	4:46:32
South Village 9	1	42N41	71w49	4:47:16
Southville 14	1	42N16	71w32	4:46:08
South Walpole 11	1	42N06	71w16	4:45:04
South Waltham 9	1	42N23	71w14	4:44:56
South Wareham 12	1	41N46	70w43	4:42:52
South Wellfleet 1	1	41N55	70w00	4:40:00
South Westport 3	1	41N34	71w03	4:44:12
South Weymouth 11	1	42N10	70w57	4:43:48
Southwick 7	1	42N03	72w46	4:51:04
South Williamstown 2	1	42N43	73w12	4:52:48
South Wilmington 9	1	42N29	71w09	4:44:36
South Worthington 8	1	42N14	72w53	4:51:32
South Yarmouth 1	1	41N40	70w17	4:41:08
Spencer 14	1	42N15	72w00	4:48:00
Spindleville 14	1	42N08	71w33	4:46:12
Springdale 7	1	42N12	72w37	4:50:28
Springfield 7	1	42N06	72w35	4:50:20
Squantum 11	1	42N17	71w01	4:44:04
Standish 3	1	42N07	70w46	4:43:04
Staples Shore 12	1	41N51	70w56	4:43:44
State House 13	1	42N19	71w05	4:44:20
State Line 2	1	42N17	73w19	4:53:16
Sterling 14	1	42N26	71w46	4:47:04
Sterling Junction 14	1	42N24	71w46	4:47:04
Stetson Road 12	1	42N04	70w49	4:43:16
Stevens Corner 2	1	42N27	73w15	4:53:00
Still River 14	1	42N30	71w37	4:46:28
Stockbridge 2	1	42N18	73w20	4:53:20
Stoneham 9	1	42N29	71w06	4:44:24
Stone Haven 11	1	42N14	71w10	4:44:40
Stoneville 6	1	42N36	72w24	4:49:36
Stoneville 14	1	42N12	71w50	4:47:20
Stony Beach 12	1	42N17	70w53	4:43:32
Stony Brook 9	1	42N22	71w18	4:45:12
Stoughton 11	1	42N08	71w06	4:44:24
Stow 9	1	42N26	71w30	4:46:00
Straits Pond 12	1	42N17	70w53	4:43:32
Sturbridge 14	1	42N06	72w05	4:48:20
Sudbury 9	1	42N23	71w25	4:45:40
Sunderland 6	2	42N27	72w34	4:50:16
Sunnyside 14	1	42N03	71w54	4:47:36
Surfside 10	1	41N17	70w06	4:40:24
Surfside 12	1	42N17	70w53	4:43:32
Sutton 14	1	42N08	71w45	4:47:00
Swampscott 5	1	42N28	70w55	4:43:40
Swansea 3	1	41N45	71w13	4:44:52
Sweets Corner 2	1	42N43	73w12	4:52:48
Swift River 8	1	42N27	72w54	4:51:36
Swifts Beach 12	1	41N46	70w43	4:42:52
Symmes Corner 9	1	42N27	71w09	4:44:36
Tafts Corner 14	1	42N15	72w00	4:48:00
Tahanto Beach 1	1	41N41	70w37	4:42:28
Tapley Street Annex 7	1	42N07	72w33	4:50:12
Tapleyville 5	1	42N34	70w57	4:43:48
Taunton 3	1	41N54	71w06	4:44:24
Teaticket 1	1	41N46	70w30	4:42:00
Templeton 14	1	42N34	72w04	4:48:16
Ten Hills 9	1	42N23	71w06	4:44:24
Tennyville 7	1	42N09	72w20	4:49:20
Tewksbury 9	1	42N37	71w14	4:44:56
Texas 14	1	42N09	71w52	4:47:28
The Green 12	1	41N51	70w56	4:43:44
The Pines 9	1	42N32	71w14	4:44:56
Thomastown 12	1	41N51	70w56	4:43:44
Thorndike 7	1	42N11	72w20	4:49:20
Three Rivers 7	1	42N10	72w22	4:49:28
Thumpertown Beach 1	1	41N52	69w59	4:39:56
Tihonet 12	1	41N46	70w43	4:42:52
Tinkertown 12	1	42N02	70w40	4:42:40
Tinkhamtown 12	1	41N40	70w49	4:43:16
Tisbury 4	1	41N27	70w37	4:42:28
Tobeys Island 1	1	41N43	70w37	4:42:28
Tolland 7	1	42N05	73w01	4:52:04
Tonset 1	1	41N47	70w00	4:40:00
Topsfield 5	1	42N38	70w57	4:43:48
Touisset 3	1	41N45	71w13	4:44:52
Town Crest Village 2	1	42N33	73w09	4:52:36
Townsend 9	1	42N40	71w42	4:46:48
Tremont 13	1	42N21	71w04	4:44:16
Truro 1	1	42N01	70w04	4:40:16
Tufts University 9	1	42N25	71w07	4:44:28
Tully 6	1	42N36	72w14	4:48:56
Turkey Hill Shores 14	1	42N22	71w57	4:47:48
Turners Falls 6	1	42N35	72w33	4:50:12
Turnpike 14	1	42N17	71w43	4:46:52
Tyngsboro 9	1	42N41	71w26	4:45:44
Tyringham 2	1	42N15	73w12	4:52:48
Union Market 9	1	42N22	71w11	4:44:44
Union Point 14	1	42N03	71w54	4:47:36
Unionville 11	1	42N05	71w24	4:45:36
Uphams Corner 13	1	42N19	71w04	4:44:16
Upper Four Corners 12	1	41N51	70w56	4:43:44
Upper Wire Village 14	1	42N15	72w00	4:48:00
Upton 14	1	42N11	71w37	4:46:28
Uxbridge 14	1	42N04	71w38	4:46:32
Vallersville 12	1	41N45	70w36	4:42:24
Valley View 11	1	42N05	71w28	4:45:52
Van Deusenville 2	1	42N16	73w22	4:53:28
Varnumtown 9	1	42N41	71w19	4:45:16
Veterans Administration Hosp 13	1	42N19	71w07	4:44:28
Victory Hill 2	1	42N27	73w15	4:53:00
Village 11	1	42N08	71w24	4:45:36
Vineyard Haven 4	1	41N27	70w36	4:42:24
Vineyard Highlands 4	1	41N27	70w34	4:42:16
Waban 9	1	42N20	71w14	4:44:56
Wachusett 14	1	42N35	71w48	4:47:12
Waites Corner 14	1	42N35	71w48	4:47:12
Wakeby 1	1	41N46	70w30	4:42:00
Wakefield 9	1	42N30	71w04	4:44:16
Walden Pond 5	1	42N28	71w00	4:44:00
Walden Pond 9	1	42N26	71w20	4:45:20
Wales 7	1	42N03	72w14	4:48:56
Walnut Hill 9	1	42N29	71w09	4:44:36
Walpole 11	1	42N09	71w15	4:45:00
Walpole Heights 11	1	42N10	71w13	4:44:52
Waltham 9	1	42N23	71w14	4:44:56
Waltham Highlands 9	1	42N23	71w14	4:44:56
Wamesit 9	1	42N37	71w16	4:45:04
Wapping 6	1	42N33	72w36	4:50:24
Waquoit 1	1	41N46	70w30	4:42:00
Ward Hill 5	1	42N47	71w05	4:44:20
Ware 8	1	42N16	72w14	4:48:56
Wareham 12	1	41N46	70w43	4:42:52
Warren 14	1	42N12	72w12	4:48:48
Warren Terrace 12	1	42N04	70w49	4:43:16
Warrentown 12	1	41N51	70w56	4:43:44
Warwick 6	1	42N40	72w20	4:49:20
Washington 2	1	42N21	73w08	4:52:32
Watertown 9	1	42N22	71w11	4:44:44
Waterville 12	1	41N51	70w56	4:43:44
Waterville 14	1	42N41	72w03	4:48:12
Wauwinet 10	1	41N17	70w06	4:40:24
Waveland 12	1	42N17	70w53	4:43:32
Waverley 9	1	42N23	71w11	4:44:44
Wawela Park 14	1	42N03	71w54	4:47:36
Wayland 9	1	42N22	71w22	4:45:28
Wayside Inn 9	1	42N23	71w25	4:45:40
Webster 14	1	42N03	71w53	4:47:32
Webster Junction 14	1	42N12	71w50	4:47:20
Webster Square 14	1	42N15	71w50	4:47:20
Wedgemere 9	1	42N27	71w09	4:44:36
Weeset 1	1	41N47	70w00	4:40:00
Weir Village 3	1	41N54	71w06	4:44:24
Wellesley 11	1	42N18	71w18	4:45:12
Wellesley Fells 11	1	42N18	71w17	4:45:08
Wellesley Hills 11	1	42N18	71w17	4:45:08
Wellfleet 1	1	41N55	70w01	4:40:04
Wellington 9	1	42N25	71w07	4:44:28
Wellville 14	1	42N38	71w54	4:47:36
Wendell 6	1	42N33	72w24	4:49:36
Wendell Depot 6	1	42N36	72w22	4:49:28
Wenham 5	1	42N36	70w53	4:43:32
West Abington 12	1	42N07	70w57	4:43:48
West Acton 9	1	42N29	71w29	4:45:56
West Andover 5	1	42N40	71w10	4:44:40
West Auburn 14	1	42N12	71w50	4:47:20
West Barnstable 1	1	41N42	70w23	4:41:32
West Becket 2	1	42N19	73w15	4:53:00
West Bedford 9	1	42N29	71w17	4:45:08
West Berlin 14	1	42N23	71w38	4:46:32
West Billerica 9	1	42N35	71w17	4:45:08
Westborough 14	1	42N16	71w37	4:46:28
West Boxford 5	1	42N43	71w04	4:44:16
West Boylston 14	1	42N22	71w47	4:47:08
West Brewster 1	1	41N46	70w05	4:40:20
West Bridgewater 12	1	42N02	71w01	4:44:04
West Brimfield 7	1	42N09	72w20	4:49:20
West Brookfield 14	1	42N16	72w09	4:48:36
West Cambridge 9	1	42N23	71w08	4:44:32
West Chatham 1	1	41N41	70w00	4:40:00
West Chelmsford 9	1	42N37	71w22	4:45:28
West Chesterfield 8	1	42N24	72w59	4:51:56
West Chop 4	1	41N27	70w36	4:42:24
West Concord 9	1	42N28	71w23	4:45:32
West Cummington 8	1	42N30	72w58	4:51:52
Westdale 12	1	42N02	70w58	4:43:52
West Deerfield 6	1	42N33	72w36	4:50:24
West Dennis 1	1	41N39	70w10	4:40:40
West Dudley 14	1	42N05	72w02	4:48:08
West Duxbury 12	1	42N02	70w40	4:42:40
West Everett 9	1	42N25	71w03	4:44:12
West Falmouth 1	1	41N36	70w38	4:42:32
West Farms 8	1	42N20	72w40	4:50:40
Westfield 7	1	42N07	72w45	4:51:00
West Fitchburg 14	1	42N35	71w48	4:47:12
Westford 9	1	42N35	71w26	4:45:44
West Foxboro 11	1	42N04	71w16	4:45:04
West Gloucester 5	1	42N37	70w40	4:42:40
West Granville 7	1	42N04	72w52	4:51:28
West Groton 9	1	42N36	71w34	4:46:16
Westhampton 8	1	42N19	72w46	4:51:04
West Hanover 12	1	42N07	70w53	4:43:32
West Harwich 1	1	41N40	70w07	4:40:28
West Hatfield 8	2	42N22	72w38	4:50:32
West Hawley 6	1	42N38	72w52	4:51:28
West Hingham 12	1	42N14	70w54	4:43:36
West Hyannisport 1	1	41N39	70w17	4:41:08
Westlands 9	1	42N37	71w22	4:45:28
West Leominster 14	1	42N32	71w46	4:47:04
West Leyden 6	1	42N40	72w33	4:50:12
West Lynn 5	1	42N28	70w59	4:43:56
West Manchester 5	1	42N34	70w46	4:43:04
West Mansfield 3	1	42N02	71w13	4:44:52
West Medford 9	1	42N25	71w08	4:44:32
West Medway 11	1	42N09	71w26	4:45:44
West Millbury 14	1	42N10	71w48	4:47:12
Westminster 14	1	42N33	71w54	4:47:36
West Natick 9	1	42N17	71w21	4:45:24
West New Boston 2	1	42N07	73w08	4:52:32
West Newbury 5	1	42N47	70w58	4:43:52
West Newton 9	1	42N21	71w13	4:44:52
Weston 9	1	42N22	71w18	4:45:12
West Otis 2	1	42N11	73w13	4:52:52
Westover Air Force Base 7	1	42N11	72w34	4:50:16
West Peabody 5	1	42N32	70w57	4:43:48
West Pelham 8	1	42N23	72w31	4:50:04
West Pittsfield 2	1	42N27	73w15	4:53:00
Westport 3	1	41N38	71w05	4:44:20
Westport Factory 3	1	41N37	71w04	4:44:16
Westport Point 3	1	41N31	71w05	4:44:20
West Quincy 11	1	42N15	71w00	4:44:00
West Roxbury 13	1	42N17	71w09	4:44:36
West Royalston 14	1	42N36	72w14	4:48:56
West Side 14	1	42N16	71w50	4:47:20
West Somerville 9	1	42N24	71w07	4:44:28
West Springfield 7	1	42N06	72w38	4:50:32
West Sterling 14	1	42N24	71w46	4:47:04
West Stockbridge 2	1	42N19	73w22	4:53:28
West Stoughton 11	1	42N08	71w06	4:44:24
West Summit 2	1	42N42	73w06	4:52:24
West Sutton 14	1	42N12	71w46	4:47:04
West Tisbury 4	1	41N24	70w39	4:42:36
West Townsend 9	1	42N41	71w44	4:46:56
West Upton 14	1	42N10	71w37	4:46:28
Westville 3	1	41N54	71w06	4:44:24
West Walpole 11	1	42N08	71w15	4:45:00
West Wareham 12	1	41N47	70w46	4:43:04
West Warren 14	1	42N13	72w14	4:48:56
West Watertown 9	1	42N22	71w11	4:44:44
West Whately 6	1	42N22	72w42	4:50:48
West Wind Shores 12	1	41N45	70w36	4:42:24
West Woburn 9	1	42N29	71w09	4:44:36
Westwood 11	1	42N13	71w14	4:44:56
West Worthington 8	1	42N24	72w56	4:51:44
West Wrentham 11	1	42N02	71w23	4:45:32
West Yarmouth 1	1	41N38	70w18	4:41:12
Wethersfield 11	1	42N05	71w28	4:45:52
Weymouth 11	1	42N13	70w58	4:43:52
Weymouth Heights 11	1	42N12	70w57	4:43:48
Weymouth Landing 11	1	42N12	70w57	4:43:48
Whalom 14	1	42N35	71w48	4:47:12
Whately 6	2	42N26	72w38	4:50:32
Wheelwright 14	1	42N21	72w08	4:48:32
White City 14	1	42N08	71w33	4:46:12
White City Shopping Center 14	1	42N17	71w43	4:46:52
Whitehead 12	1	42N17	70w53	4:43:32
White Horse Beach 12	1	41N56	70w34	4:42:16
White Island Shores 12	1	41N46	70w40	4:42:40
White Oaks 2	1	42N43	73w12	4:52:48
Whitinsville 14	1	42N07	71w40	4:46:40
Whitman 12	1	42N05	70w56	4:43:44
Whittenton 3	1	41N54	71w06	4:44:24
Wianno 1	1	41N38	70w23	4:41:32
Wilbraham 7	1	42N07	72w27	4:49:48
Wilkinsonville 14	1	42N11	71w43	4:46:52
Williamsburg 8	1	42N23	72w43	4:50:52
Williamstown 2	1	42N43	73w12	4:52:48
Williamsville 2	1	42N16	73w22	4:53:28

MASSACHUSETTS

Place		Lat	Long	Time
Williamsville 14	1	42N29	72W01	4:48:04
Wilmington 9	1	42N33	71W10	4:44:40
Wilson 5	1	42N37	70W40	4:42:40
Wimbledon 1	1	41N39	70W15	4:41:00
Winchendon 14	1	42N41	72W03	4:48:12
Winchendon Springs 14	1	42N42	72W01	4:48:04
Winchester 9	1	42N27	71W08	4:44:32
Winchester Highlands 9	1	42N27	71W09	4:44:36
Windmere 12	1	42N17	70W53	4:43:32
Windsor 2	1	42N31	73W02	4:52:08
Winmere 9	1	42N30	71W12	4:44:48
Winnecunnet 3	1	41N58	71W11	4:44:44
Winslows 11	1	42N11	71W12	4:44:48
Winter Hill 9	1	42N24	71W06	4:44:24
Winthrop 13	1	42N23	70W59	4:43:56
Winthrop Highlands 13	1	42N22	70W59	4:43:56
Woburn 9	1	42N29	71W09	4:44:36
Wollaston 11	1	42N16	71W01	4:44:04
Woodland Park 14	1	42N12	71W50	4:47:20
Woodlawn 8	1	42N15	72W35	4:50:20
Woods Hole 1	1	41N31	70W40	4:42:40
Woodside 14	1	42N19	71W39	4:46:36
Woodville 9	1	42N14	71W34	4:46:16
Worcester 14	1	42N16	71W48	4:47:12
Woronoco 7	1	42N10	72W50	4:51:20
Woronoco Heights 7	1	42N10	72W50	4:51:20
Worthington 8	1	42N23	72W56	4:51:44
Wrentham 11	1	42N04	71W20	4:45:20
Wyben 7	1	42N08	72W45	4:51:00
Wyoming 9	1	42N28	71W04	4:44:16
Yankee Orchards 2	1	42N27	73W15	4:53:00
Yarmouth 1	1	41N42	70W17	4:41:08
Yarmouth Port 1	1	41N42	70W14	4:40:56
Zoar 6	1	42N40	72W56	4:51:44
Zylonite 2	1	42N37	73W07	4:52:28

TIME TABLES

Not all zone shifts have been documented: neither the lower peninsula shifts to Eastern time during the 20's and 30's, nor the upper peninsula shifts back and forth. Many dates for zone shifts given here are generalizations based on fragmentary information. The Eastern time zone portions of Michigan went on Daylight time in 1975 on April 27, rather than February 23 with the rest of the country. Most of the tables for the lower peninsula reflect a return to Central time beginning on February 15, 1943, for the duration of World War II, returning to Eastern time at the end of the War. The more industrial areas remained on EWT.

MI # 1
Before 9/18/1885 LMT
9/18/1885 12:00 CST
3/31/1918 02:00 CWT
10/27/1918 02:00 CST
3/30/1919 02:00 CWT
10/26/1919 02:00 CST
4/26/1931 02:00 EST
2/09/1942 02:00 EWT
2/15/1943 02:00 CWT
9/30/1945 02:00 EST
6/14/1967 00:01 EDT
10/29/1967 00:01 EST
4/29/1973 02:00 EDT
10/28/1973 02:00 EST
1/06/1974 02:00 EDT
10/27/1974 02:00 EST
4/27/1975 02:00 EDT
10/26/1975 02:00 US#1

MI # 2
Before 9/18/1885 LMT
9/18/1885 12:00 CST
5/15/1915 02:00 EST
2/09/1942 02:00 EWT
9/30/1945 02:00 EST
4/25/1948 02:00 EDT
9/26/1948 02:00 EST
6/14/1967 00:01 EDT
10/29/1967 00:01 EST
4/29/1973 02:00 EDT
10/28/1973 02:00 EST
1/06/1974 02:00 EDT
10/27/1974 02:00 EST
4/27/1975 02:00 EDT
10/26/1975 02:00 US#1

MI # 3
Before 9/18/1885 LMT
9/18/1885 12:00 CST
3/31/1918 02:00 CWT
10/27/1918 02:00 CST
3/30/1919 02:00 CWT
10/26/1919 02:00 CST
6/13/1920 02:00 CDT
10/31/1920 02:00 CST
3/27/1921 02:00 CDT
10/31/1921 02:00 CST
4/30/1922 02:00 CDT
9/24/1922 02:00 CST
4/29/1923 02:00 CDT
9/30/1923 02:00 CST
4/27/1924 02:00 CDT
9/28/1924 02:00 CST
4/26/1925 02:00 CDT
9/27/1925 02:00 CST
4/25/1926 02:00 CDT
9/26/1926 02:00 CST
4/24/1927 02:00 CDT
9/25/1927 02:00 CST
4/29/1928 02:00 CDT
9/30/1928 02:00 CST
4/28/1929 02:00 CDT
9/29/1929 02:00 CST
4/27/1930 02:00 CDT
9/28/1930 02:00 CST
4/26/1931 02:00 EST
2/09/1942 02:00 EWT
2/15/1943 02:00 CWT
9/30/1945 02:00 EST
6/14/1967 00:01 EDT
10/29/1967 00:01 EST
4/29/1973 02:00 EDT
10/28/1973 02:00 EST
1/06/1974 02:00 EDT
10/27/1974 02:00 EST
4/27/1975 02:00 EDT
10/26/1975 02:00 US#1

MI # 4
Before 9/18/1885 LMT
9/18/1885 12:00 CST
3/31/1918 02:00 CWT
10/27/1918 02:00 CST
3/30/1919 02:00 CWT
10/26/1919 02:00 CST
3/27/1921 02:00 CDT
10/31/1921 02:00 CST
4/30/1922 02:00 CDT
9/24/1922 02:00 CST
4/29/1923 02:00 CDT
9/30/1923 02:00 CST
4/27/1924 02:00 CDT
9/28/1924 02:00 CST
4/26/1925 02:00 CDT
9/27/1925 02:00 CST
4/25/1926 02:00 CDT
9/26/1926 02:00 CST
4/24/1927 02:00 CDT
9/25/1927 02:00 CST
4/29/1928 02:00 CDT
9/30/1928 02:00 CST
4/28/1929 02:00 CDT
9/29/1929 02:00 CST
4/27/1930 02:00 CDT
9/28/1930 02:00 CST
4/26/1931 02:00 EST
2/09/1942 02:00 EWT
2/15/1943 02:00 CWT
9/30/1945 02:00 EST
6/14/1967 00:01 EDT
10/29/1967 00:01 EST
4/29/1973 02:00 EDT
10/28/1973 02:00 EST
1/06/1974 02:00 EDT
10/27/1974 02:00 EST
4/27/1975 02:00 EDT
10/26/1975 02:00 US#1

MI # 5
Before 9/18/1885 LMT
9/18/1885 12:00 CST
3/31/1918 02:00 CWT
10/27/1918 02:00 CST
3/30/1919 02:00 CWT
10/26/1919 02:00 CST
3/27/1921 02:00 CDT
10/31/1921 02:00 CST
4/30/1922 02:00 CDT
9/24/1922 02:00 CST
4/29/1923 02:00 CDT
9/30/1923 02:00 CST
4/27/1924 02:00 CDT
9/28/1924 02:00 CST
4/26/1925 02:00 CDT
9/27/1925 02:00 CST
4/25/1926 02:00 CDT
9/26/1926 02:00 CST
4/24/1927 02:00 CDT
9/25/1927 02:00 CST
4/29/1928 02:00 CDT
9/30/1928 02:00 CST
4/28/1929 02:00 CDT
9/29/1929 02:00 CST
4/27/1930 02:00 CDT
9/28/1930 02:00 CST
4/26/1931 02:00 EST
2/09/1942 02:00 EWT
2/15/1943 02:00 CWT
9/30/1945 02:00 EST
4/25/1948 02:00 EDT
9/26/1948 02:00 EST
6/14/1967 00:01 EDT
10/29/1967 00:01 EST
4/29/1973 02:00 EDT
10/28/1973 02:00 EST
1/06/1974 02:00 EDT
10/27/1974 02:00 EST
4/27/1975 02:00 EDT
10/26/1975 02:00 US#1

MI # 6
Before 9/18/1885 LMT
9/18/1885 12:00 CST
3/31/1918 02:00 CWT
10/27/1918 02:00 CST
3/30/1919 02:00 CWT
10/26/1919 02:00 CST
4/26/1931 02:00 EST
2/09/1942 02:00 EWT
2/15/1943 02:00 CWT
9/30/1945 02:00 EST
4/28/1946 02:00 EDT
9/29/1946 02:00 EST
6/14/1967 00:01 EDT
10/29/1967 00:01 EST
4/29/1973 02:00 EDT
10/28/1973 02:00 EST
1/06/1974 02:00 EDT
10/27/1974 02:00 EST
4/27/1975 02:00 EDT
10/26/1975 02:00 US#1

MI # 7
Before 9/18/1885 LMT
9/18/1885 12:00 CST
3/31/1918 02:00 CWT
10/27/1918 02:00 CST
3/30/1919 02:00 CWT
10/26/1919 02:00 CST
4/26/1931 02:00 EST
2/09/1942 02:00 EWT
2/15/1943 02:00 CWT
9/30/1945 02:00 EST
4/25/1948 02:00 EDT
9/26/1948 02:00 EST
6/14/1967 00:01 EDT
10/29/1967 00:01 EST
4/29/1973 02:00 EDT
10/28/1973 02:00 EST
1/06/1974 02:00 EDT
10/27/1974 02:00 EST
4/27/1975 02:00 EDT
10/26/1975 02:00 US#1

MI # 8
Before 9/18/1885 LMT
9/18/1885 12:00 CST
3/31/1918 02:00 CWT
10/27/1918 02:00 CST
3/30/1919 02:00 CWT
10/26/1919 02:00 CST
4/10/1920 02:00 CDT
9/18/1920 02:00 CST
5/01/1921 02:00 CDT
10/02/1921 02:00 CST
5/01/1926 02:00 CDT
9/04/1926 02:00 CST
4/30/1927 02:00 CDT
9/03/1927 02:00 CST
4/29/1928 02:00 CDT
9/30/1928 02:00 CST
4/28/1929 02:00 CDT
9/29/1929 02:00 CST
4/27/1930 02:00 CDT
9/28/1930 02:00 CST
4/26/1931 02:00 EST
2/09/1942 02:00 EWT
2/15/1943 02:00 CWT
9/30/1945 02:00 EST
6/14/1967 00:01 EDT
10/29/1967 00:01 EST
4/29/1973 02:00 EDT
10/28/1973 02:00 EST
1/06/1974 02:00 EDT
10/27/1974 02:00 EST
4/27/1975 02:00 EDT
10/26/1975 02:00 US#1

MI # 9
Before 9/18/1885 LMT
9/18/1885 12:00 CST
3/31/1918 02:00 CWT
10/27/1918 02:00 CST
3/30/1919 02:00 CWT
10/26/1919 02:00 CST
3/27/1921 02:00 CDT
10/31/1921 02:00 CST
4/30/1922 02:00 CDT
9/24/1922 02:00 CST
4/29/1923 02:00 CDT
9/30/1923 02:00 CST
4/27/1924 02:00 CDT
9/28/1924 02:00 CST
4/26/1925 02:00 CDT
9/27/1925 02:00 CST
4/25/1926 02:00 CDT
9/26/1926 02:00 CST
3/02/1927 02:00 CDT
11/05/1927 02:00 CST
4/26/1931 02:00 EST
2/09/1942 02:00 EWT
2/15/1943 02:00 CWT
9/30/1945 02:00 EST
6/14/1967 00:01 EDT
10/29/1967 00:01 EST
4/29/1973 02:00 EDT
10/28/1973 02:00 EST
1/06/1974 02:00 EDT
10/27/1974 02:00 EST
4/27/1975 02:00 EDT
10/26/1975 02:00 US#1

MI # 10
Before 9/18/1885 LMT
9/18/1885 12:00 CST
3/31/1918 02:00 CWT
10/27/1918 02:00 CST
3/30/1919 02:00 CWT
10/26/1919 02:00 CST
4/26/1931 02:00 EST
2/09/1942 02:00 EWT
2/15/1943 02:00 CWT
9/30/1945 02:00 EST
4/25/1948 02:00 EDT
9/26/1948 02:00 EST
4/29/1973 02:00 EDT
10/28/1973 02:00 EST
1/06/1974 02:00 EDT
10/27/1974 02:00 EST
4/27/1975 02:00 EDT
10/26/1975 02:00 US#1

MI # 11
Before 9/18/1885 LMT
9/18/1885 12:00 CST
3/31/1918 02:00 CWT
10/27/1918 02:00 CST
3/30/1919 02:00 CWT
10/26/1919 02:00 CST
2/09/1942 02:00 CWT
9/30/1945 02:00 EST
4/28/1946 02:00 EDT
9/29/1946 02:00 EST
4/25/1948 02:00 EDT
9/26/1948 02:00 EST
4/29/1973 02:00 EDT
10/28/1973 02:00 EST
1/06/1974 02:00 EDT
10/27/1974 02:00 EST
4/27/1975 02:00 EDT
10/26/1975 02:00 US#1

MI # 12
Before 9/18/1885 LMT
9/18/1885 12:00 CST
3/31/1918 02:00 CWT
10/27/1918 02:00 CST
3/30/1919 02:00 CWT
10/26/1919 02:00 CST
2/09/1942 02:00 CWT
9/30/1945 02:00 EST
6/14/1967 00:01 EDT
10/29/1967 00:01 EST
4/29/1973 02:00 EDT
10/28/1973 02:00 EST
1/06/1974 02:00 EDT
10/27/1974 02:00 EST
4/27/1975 02:00 EDT
10/26/1975 02:00 US#1

MI # 13
Before 9/18/1885 LMT
9/18/1885 12:00 CST
3/31/1918 02:00 CWT
10/27/1918 02:00 CST
3/30/1919 02:00 CWT
10/26/1919 02:00 CST
4/28/1929 02:00 CDT
9/29/1929 02:00 CST
4/27/1930 02:00 CDT
9/28/1930 02:00 CST
4/26/1931 02:00 CDT
9/27/1931 02:00 CST
4/24/1932 02:00 CDT
9/25/1932 02:00 CST
4/30/1933 02:00 CDT
9/24/1933 02:00 CST
4/29/1934 02:00 CDT
9/30/1934 02:00 CST
4/28/1935 02:00 CDT
9/29/1935 02:00 CST
4/26/1936 02:00 CDT
9/27/1936 02:00 CST
4/25/1937 02:00 CDT
9/26/1937 02:00 CST
4/24/1938 02:00 CDT
9/25/1938 02:00 CST
4/30/1939 02:00 CDT
9/24/1939 02:00 CST
4/28/1940 02:00 CDT
9/29/1940 02:00 CST
4/27/1941 02:00 CDT
10/26/1941 02:00 CST
2/09/1942 02:00 CWT
9/30/1945 02:00 EST
4/27/1947 02:00 EDT
9/28/1947 02:00 EST
4/25/1948 02:00 EDT
9/26/1948 02:00 EST
4/29/1973 02:00 EDT
10/28/1973 02:00 EST
1/06/1974 02:00 EDT
10/27/1974 02:00 EST
4/27/1975 02:00 EDT
10/26/1975 02:00 US#1

MI # 14
Before 9/18/1885 LMT
9/18/1885 12:00 CST
3/31/1918 02:00 CWT
10/27/1918 02:00 CST
3/30/1919 02:00 CWT
10/26/1919 02:00 CST
4/26/1931 02:00 CDT
9/27/1931 02:00 CST
4/24/1932 02:00 CDT
9/25/1932 02:00 CST
4/30/1933 02:00 CDT
9/24/1933 02:00 CST
4/29/1934 02:00 CDT
9/30/1934 02:00 CST
4/28/1935 02:00 CDT
9/29/1935 02:00 CST
4/26/1936 02:00 CDT
9/27/1936 02:00 CST
4/25/1937 02:00 CDT
9/26/1937 02:00 CST
4/24/1938 02:00 CDT
9/25/1938 02:00 CST
4/30/1939 02:00 CDT
9/24/1939 02:00 CST
4/28/1940 02:00 CDT
9/29/1940 02:00 CST
4/27/1941 02:00 CDT
10/26/1941 02:00 CST
2/09/1942 02:00 CWT
9/30/1945 02:00 EST
4/25/1948 02:00 EDT
9/26/1948 02:00 EST
4/29/1973 02:00 EDT
10/28/1973 02:00 EST
1/06/1974 02:00 EDT
10/27/1974 02:00 EST
4/27/1975 02:00 EDT
10/26/1975 02:00 US#1

MI # 15
Before 9/18/1885 LMT
9/18/1885 12:00 CST
3/31/1918 02:00 CWT
10/27/1918 02:00 CST
3/30/1919 02:00 CWT
10/26/1919 02:00 CST
2/09/1942 02:00 CWT
9/30/1945 02:00 EST
4/27/1947 02:00 EDT
9/28/1947 02:00 EST
4/25/1948 02:00 EDT
9/26/1948 02:00 EST
4/29/1973 02:00 EDT
10/28/1973 02:00 EST
1/06/1974 02:00 EDT
10/27/1974 02:00 EST
4/27/1975 02:00 EDT
10/26/1975 02:00 US#1

MI # 16
Before 9/18/1885 LMT
9/18/1885 12:00 CST
3/31/1918 02:00 CWT
10/27/1918 02:00 CST
3/30/1919 02:00 CWT
10/26/1919 02:00 CST
4/27/1941 02:00 CDT
10/26/1941 02:00 CST
2/09/1942 02:00 CWT
9/30/1945 02:00 EST
4/28/1946 02:00 EDT
9/29/1946 02:00 EST
4/25/1948 02:00 EDT
9/26/1948 02:00 EST
4/29/1973 02:00 EDT
10/28/1973 02:00 EST
1/06/1974 02:00 EDT
10/27/1974 02:00 EST
4/27/1975 02:00 EDT
10/26/1975 02:00 US#1

MI # 17
Before 9/18/1885 LMT
9/18/1885 12:00 CST
3/31/1918 02:00 CWT
10/27/1918 02:00 CST
3/30/1919 02:00 CWT
10/26/1919 02:00 CST
2/09/1942 02:00 CWT
9/30/1945 02:00 EST
4/28/1946 02:00 EDT
9/29/1946 02:00 EST
4/27/1947 02:00 EDT
9/28/1947 02:00 EST
4/25/1948 02:00 EDT
9/26/1948 02:00 EST
4/29/1973 02:00 EDT
10/28/1973 02:00 EST
1/06/1974 02:00 EDT
10/27/1974 02:00 EST
4/27/1975 02:00 EDT
10/26/1975 02:00 US#1

MI # 18
Before 9/18/1885 LMT
9/18/1885 12:00 CST
3/31/1918 02:00 CWT
10/27/1918 02:00 CST
3/30/1919 02:00 CWT
10/26/1919 02:00 CST
2/09/1942 02:00 CWT
9/30/1945 02:00 EST

TIME TABLES

4/25/1948 02:00 EDT
9/26/1948 02:00 EST
4/24/1949 02:00 EDT
9/25/1949 02:00 EST
4/29/1973 02:00 EDT
10/28/1973 02:00 EST
1/06/1974 02:00 EDT
10/27/1974 02:00 EST
4/27/1975 02:00 EDT
10/26/1975 02:00 US#1

MI # 19

Before 9/18/1885 LMT
9/18/1885 12:00 CST
3/31/1918 02:00 CWT
10/27/1918 02:00 CST
3/30/1919 02:00 CWT
10/26/1919 02:00 CST
4/29/1928 00:01 CDT
9/28/1928 00:01 CST
4/27/1930 00:01 CDT
9/28/1930 00:01 CST
4/26/1931 00:01 CDT
9/27/1931 00:01 CST
4/24/1932 00:01 CDT
9/25/1932 00:01 CST
4/30/1933 00:01 CDT
9/24/1933 00:01 CST
5/15/1934 00:01 CDT
10/01/1934 00:01 CST
4/28/1935 00:01 CDT
9/29/1935 00:01 CST
4/26/1936 00:01 CDT
9/27/1936 00:01 CST
4/25/1937 00:01 CDT
9/26/1937 00:01 CST
4/24/1938 00:01 CDT
9/25/1938 00:01 CST
4/30/1939 00:01 CDT
9/24/1939 00:01 CST
4/28/1940 00:01 CDT
9/29/1940 00:01 CST
4/27/1941 00:01 CDT
10/26/1941 00:01 CST
2/09/1942 02:00 CWT
9/30/1945 02:00 EST
4/28/1946 02:00 EDT
9/29/1946 02:00 EST
4/27/1947 02:00 EDT
9/28/1947 02:00 EST
4/25/1948 02:00 EDT
9/26/1948 02:00 EST
4/29/1973 02:00 EDT
10/28/1973 02:00 EST
1/06/1974 02:00 EDT
10/27/1974 02:00 EST
4/27/1975 02:00 EDT
10/26/1975 02:00 US#1

MI # 20

Before 9/18/1885 LMT
9/18/1885 12:00 CST
3/31/1918 02:00 CWT
10/27/1918 02:00 CST
3/30/1919 02:00 CWT
10/26/1919 02:00 CST
5/01/1932 02:00 CDT
10/02/1932 02:00 CST
4/30/1933 02:00 CDT
10/01/1933 02:00 CST
4/29/1934 02:00 CDT
9/30/1934 02:00 CST
5/01/1935 02:00 CDT
10/01/1935 02:00 CST
4/26/1936 02:00 CDT
9/27/1936 02:00 CST
4/25/1937 02:00 CDT
9/26/1937 02:00 CST
4/24/1938 02:00 CDT
9/25/1938 02:00 CST
4/30/1939 02:00 CDT
9/24/1939 02:00 CST
4/28/1940 02:00 CDT
9/29/1940 02:00 CST
4/27/1941 02:00 CDT
10/26/1941 02:00 CST
2/09/1942 02:00 CWT
9/30/1945 02:00 EST
4/28/1946 02:00 EDT
9/29/1946 02:00 EST
4/27/1947 02:00 EDT
9/28/1947 02:00 EST
4/25/1948 02:00 EDT
9/26/1948 02:00 EST
4/24/1949 02:00 EDT
9/25/1949 02:00 EST
4/29/1973 02:00 EDT
10/28/1973 02:00 EST
1/06/1974 02:00 EDT
10/27/1974 02:00 EST
4/27/1975 02:00 EDT
10/26/1975 02:00 US#1

MI # 21

Before 9/18/1885 LMT
9/18/1885 12:00 CST
3/31/1918 02:00 CWT
10/27/1918 02:00 CST
3/30/1919 02:00 CWT
10/26/1919 02:00 CST
5/04/1930 02:00 CDT
9/28/1930 02:00 CST
5/03/1931 02:00 CDT
9/27/1931 02:00 CST
6/01/1933 02:00 CDT
9/03/1933 02:00 CST
6/01/1934 02:00 CDT
9/02/1934 02:00 CST
5/01/1935 02:00 CDT
10/01/1935 02:00 CST
4/26/1936 02:00 CDT
9/27/1936 02:00 CST
4/25/1937 02:00 CDT
9/26/1937 02:00 CST
4/24/1938 02:00 CDT
9/25/1938 02:00 CST
4/30/1939 02:00 CDT
9/24/1939 02:00 CST
4/28/1940 02:00 CDT
9/29/1940 02:00 CST
4/27/1941 02:00 CDT
10/26/1941 02:00 CST
2/09/1942 02:00 CWT
9/30/1945 02:00 EST
4/28/1946 02:00 EDT
9/29/1946 02:00 EST
4/27/1947 02:00 EDT
9/28/1947 02:00 EST
4/25/1948 02:00 EDT
9/26/1948 02:00 EST
4/24/1949 02:00 EDT
9/25/1949 02:00 EST
4/29/1973 02:00 EDT
10/28/1973 02:00 EST
1/06/1974 02:00 EDT
10/27/1974 02:00 EST
4/27/1975 02:00 EDT
10/26/1975 02:00 US#1

MI # 22

Before 9/18/1885 LMT
9/18/1885 12:00 CST
3/31/1918 02:00 CWT
10/27/1918 02:00 CST
3/30/1919 02:00 CWT
10/26/1919 02:00 CST
5/04/1930 00:01 CDT
9/28/1930 00:01 CST
5/03/1931 00:01 CDT
9/27/1931 00:01 CST
5/01/1932 00:01 CDT
9/25/1932 00:01 CST
5/07/1933 00:01 CDT
10/01/1933 00:01 CST
5/06/1934 00:01 CDT
9/30/1934 00:01 CST
5/05/1935 00:01 CDT
9/29/1935 00:01 CST
4/26/1936 02:00 CDT
9/27/1936 02:00 CST
5/01/1937 02:00 CDT
10/01/1937 02:00 CST
4/24/1938 02:00 CDT
9/25/1938 02:00 CST
4/30/1939 02:00 CDT
9/24/1939 02:00 CST
5/05/1940 02:00 CDT
9/29/1940 02:00 CST
5/04/1941 02:00 CDT
9/28/1941 02:00 CST
2/09/1942 02:00 CWT
9/30/1945 02:00 EST
4/25/1948 02:00 EDT
9/26/1948 02:00 EST
4/29/1973 02:00 EDT
10/28/1973 02:00 EST
1/06/1974 02:00 EDT
10/27/1974 02:00 EST
4/27/1975 02:00 EDT
10/26/1975 02:00 US#1

MI # 23

Before 9/18/1885 LMT
9/18/1885 12:00 CST
3/31/1918 02:00 CWT
10/27/1918 02:00 CST
3/30/1919 02:00 CWT
10/26/1919 02:00 CST
5/04/1930 02:00 CDT
9/28/1930 02:00 CST
5/03/1931 02:00 CDT
9/27/1931 02:00 CST
5/01/1932 02:00 CDT
9/25/1932 02:00 CST
6/01/1933 02:00 CDT
9/03/1933 02:00 CST
6/01/1934 02:00 CDT
9/02/1934 02:00 CST
5/01/1935 02:00 CDT
10/01/1935 02:00 CST
4/26/1936 02:00 CDT
9/27/1936 02:00 CST
4/25/1937 02:00 CDT
9/26/1937 02:00 CST
4/24/1938 02:00 CDT
9/25/1938 02:00 CST
4/30/1939 02:00 CDT
9/24/1939 02:00 CST
4/28/1940 02:00 CDT
9/29/1940 02:00 CST
4/27/1941 02:00 CDT
10/26/1941 02:00 CST
2/09/1942 02:00 CWT
9/30/1945 02:00 EST
4/25/1948 02:00 EDT
9/26/1948 02:00 EST
4/24/1949 02:00 EDT
9/25/1949 02:00 EST
4/29/1973 02:00 EDT
10/28/1973 02:00 EST
1/06/1974 02:00 EDT
10/27/1974 02:00 EST
4/27/1975 02:00 EDT
10/26/1975 02:00 US#1

MI # 24

Before 9/18/1885 LMT
9/18/1885 12:00 CST
3/31/1918 02:00 CWT
10/27/1918 02:00 CST
3/30/1919 02:00 CWT
10/26/1919 02:00 CST
6/01/1928 02:00 CDT
10/01/1928 02:00 CST
6/01/1929 02:00 CDT
10/01/1929 02:00 CST
6/01/1930 02:00 CDT
10/01/1930 02:00 CST
2/09/1942 02:00 CWT
9/30/1945 02:00 EST
4/25/1948 02:00 EDT
9/26/1948 02:00 EST
4/29/1973 02:00 EDT
10/28/1973 02:00 EST
1/06/1974 02:00 EDT
10/27/1974 02:00 EST
4/27/1975 02:00 EDT
10/26/1975 02:00 US#1

MI # 25

Before 9/18/1885 LMT
9/18/1885 12:00 CST
3/31/1918 02:00 CWT
10/27/1918 02:00 CST
3/30/1919 02:00 CWT
10/26/1919 02:00 CST
2/09/1942 02:00 CWT
9/30/1945 02:00 EST
4/25/1948 02:00 EDT
9/26/1948 02:00 EST
4/29/1973 02:00 EDT
10/28/1973 02:00 EST
1/06/1974 02:00 EDT
10/27/1974 02:00 EST
4/27/1975 02:00 EDT
10/26/1975 02:00 US#1

MI # 26

Before 9/18/1885 LMT
9/18/1885 12:00 CST
3/31/1918 02:00 CWT
10/27/1918 02:00 CST
3/30/1919 02:00 CWT
10/26/1919 02:00 CST
5/01/1932 02:00 CDT
10/31/1932 02:00 CST
4/30/1933 02:00 CDT
9/24/1933 02:00 CST
4/29/1934 02:00 CDT
9/30/1934 02:00 CST
5/01/1935 02:00 CDT
10/01/1935 02:00 CST
5/01/1936 02:00 CDT
10/01/1936 02:00 CST
4/25/1937 02:00 CDT
9/26/1937 02:00 CST
2/09/1942 02:00 CWT
9/30/1945 02:00 EST
4/28/1946 02:00 EDT
9/29/1946 02:00 EST
4/25/1948 02:00 EDT
9/26/1948 02:00 EST
4/24/1949 02:00 EDT
9/25/1949 02:00 EST
6/14/1967 00:01 EDT
10/29/1967 00:01 EST
4/29/1973 02:00 EDT
10/28/1973 02:00 EST
1/06/1974 02:00 EDT
10/27/1974 02:00 EST
4/27/1975 02:00 EDT
10/26/1975 02:00 US#1

MI # 27

Before 9/18/1885 LMT
9/18/1885 12:00 CST
3/31/1918 02:00 CWT
10/27/1918 02:00 CST
3/30/1919 02:00 CWT
10/26/1919 02:00 CST
5/01/1932 02:00 CDT
10/31/1932 02:00 CST
2/09/1942 02:00 CWT
9/30/1945 02:00 EST
4/25/1948 02:00 EDT
9/26/1948 02:00 EST
4/29/1973 02:00 EDT
10/28/1973 02:00 EST
1/06/1974 02:00 EDT
10/27/1974 02:00 EST
4/27/1975 02:00 EDT
10/26/1975 02:00 US#1

MI # 28

Before 9/18/1885 LMT
9/18/1885 12:00 CST
3/31/1918 02:00 CWT
10/27/1918 02:00 CST
3/30/1919 02:00 CWT
10/26/1919 02:00 CST
5/01/1935 02:00 CDT
10/01/1935 02:00 CST
5/01/1937 02:00 CDT
9/01/1937 02:00 CST
2/09/1942 02:00 CWT
9/30/1945 02:00 EST
4/25/1948 02:00 EDT
9/26/1948 02:00 EST
4/24/1949 02:00 EDT
9/25/1949 02:00 EST
4/29/1973 02:00 EDT
10/28/1973 02:00 EST
1/06/1974 02:00 EDT
10/27/1974 02:00 EST
4/27/1975 02:00 EDT
10/26/1975 02:00 US#1

MI # 29

Before 9/18/1885 LMT
9/18/1885 12:00 CST
3/31/1918 02:00 CWT
10/27/1918 02:00 CST
3/30/1919 02:00 CWT
10/26/1919 02:00 CST
5/01/1935 02:00 CDT
10/01/1935 02:00 CST
2/09/1942 02:00 CWT
9/30/1945 02:00 EST
4/25/1948 02:00 EDT
9/26/1948 02:00 EST
4/24/1949 02:00 EDT
9/25/1949 02:00 EST
4/29/1973 02:00 EDT
10/28/1973 02:00 EST
1/06/1974 02:00 EDT
10/27/1974 02:00 EST
4/27/1975 02:00 EDT
10/26/1975 02:00 US#1

MI # 30

Before 9/18/1885 LMT
9/18/1885 12:00 CST
3/31/1918 02:00 CWT
10/27/1918 02:00 CST
3/30/1919 02:00 CWT
10/26/1919 02:00 CST
5/01/1935 02:00 CDT
10/01/1935 02:00 CST
5/01/1936 02:00 CDT
9/05/1936 02:00 CST
4/25/1937 02:00 CDT
9/26/1937 02:00 CST
2/09/1942 02:00 CWT
9/30/1945 02:00 EST
4/27/1947 02:00 EDT
9/28/1947 02:00 EST
4/25/1948 02:00 EDT
9/26/1948 02:00 EST
4/29/1973 02:00 EDT
10/28/1973 02:00 EST
1/06/1974 02:00 EDT
10/27/1974 02:00 EST
4/27/1975 02:00 EDT
10/26/1975 02:00 US#1

MI # 31

Before 9/18/1885 LMT
9/18/1885 12:00 CST
3/31/1918 02:00 CWT
10/27/1918 02:00 CST
3/30/1919 02:00 CWT
10/26/1919 02:00 CST
5/01/1937 02:00 CDT
10/01/1937 02:00 CST
2/09/1942 02:00 CWT
9/30/1945 02:00 EST
4/25/1948 02:00 EDT
9/26/1948 02:00 EST
4/29/1973 02:00 EDT
10/28/1973 02:00 EST
1/06/1974 02:00 EDT
10/27/1974 02:00 EST
4/27/1975 02:00 EDT
10/26/1975 02:00 US#1

MI # 32

Before 9/18/1885 LMT
9/18/1885 12:00 CST
3/31/1918 02:00 CWT
10/27/1918 02:00 CST
3/30/1919 02:00 CWT
10/26/1919 02:00 CST
5/01/1935 02:00 CDT
10/01/1935 02:00 CST
2/09/1942 02:00 CWT
9/30/1945 02:00 EST
4/25/1948 02:00 EDT
9/26/1948 02:00 EST
4/29/1973 02:00 EDT
10/28/1973 02:00 EST
1/06/1974 02:00 EDT
10/27/1974 02:00 EST
4/27/1975 02:00 EDT
10/26/1975 02:00 US#1

MI # 33

Before 9/18/1885 LMT
9/18/1885 12:00 CST
3/31/1918 02:00 CWT
10/27/1918 02:00 CST
3/30/1919 02:00 CWT
10/26/1919 02:00 CST
4/01/1937 02:00 CDT
10/11/1937 02:00 CST
2/09/1942 02:00 CWT
9/30/1945 02:00 EST
4/25/1948 02:00 EDT
9/26/1948 02:00 EST
4/29/1973 02:00 EDT
10/28/1973 02:00 EST
1/06/1974 02:00 EDT
10/27/1974 02:00 EST
4/27/1975 02:00 EDT
10/26/1975 02:00 US#1

MI # 34

Before 9/18/1885 LMT
9/18/1885 12:00 CST
3/31/1918 02:00 CWT
10/27/1918 02:00 CST
3/30/1919 02:00 CWT
10/26/1919 02:00 CST
5/01/1932 02:00 CDT
9/30/1932 02:00 CST
4/30/1933 02:00 CDT
9/24/1933 02:00 CST
4/29/1934 02:00 CDT
9/30/1934 02:00 CST
5/01/1935 02:00 CDT
10/01/1935 02:00 CST
5/01/1936 02:00 CDT
10/01/1936 02:00 CST
5/01/1937 02:00 CDT
10/01/1937 02:00 CST
2/09/1942 02:00 CWT
9/30/1945 02:00 EST
4/25/1948 02:00 EDT
9/26/1948 02:00 EST
4/29/1973 02:00 EDT
10/28/1973 02:00 EST
1/06/1974 02:00 EDT
10/27/1974 02:00 EST
4/27/1975 02:00 EDT
10/26/1975 02:00 US#1

MI # 35

Before 9/18/1885 LMT
9/18/1885 12:00 CST
3/31/1918 02:00 CWT
10/27/1918 02:00 CST
3/30/1919 02:00 CWT
10/26/1919 02:00 CST
5/01/1937 02:00 CDT
10/01/1937 02:00 CST
4/24/1938 02:00 CDT
9/25/1938 02:00 CST
4/30/1939 02:00 CDT
9/24/1939 02:00 CST
4/28/1940 02:00 CDT
9/29/1940 02:00 CST
4/27/1941 02:00 CDT
10/26/1941 02:00 CST
2/09/1942 02:00 CWT
9/30/1945 02:00 EST
4/27/1947 02:00 EDT
9/28/1947 02:00 EST
4/25/1948 02:00 EDT
9/26/1948 02:00 EST
4/29/1973 02:00 EDT
10/28/1973 02:00 EST
1/06/1974 02:00 EDT
10/27/1974 02:00 EST
4/27/1975 02:00 EDT
10/26/1975 02:00 US#1

MI # 36

Before 9/18/1885 LMT
9/18/1885 12:00 CST
3/31/1918 02:00 CWT
10/27/1918 02:00 CST
3/30/1919 02:00 CWT
10/26/1919 02:00 CST
4/15/1920 02:00 EST
2/09/1942 02:00 EWT
9/30/1945 02:00 EST
6/14/1967 00:01 EDT
10/29/1967 00:01 EST
4/29/1973 02:00 EDT
10/28/1973 02:00 EST
1/06/1974 02:00 EDT
10/27/1974 02:00 EST
4/27/1975 02:00 EDT
10/26/1975 02:00 US#1

MI # 37

Before 9/18/1885 LMT
9/18/1885 12:00 CST
3/31/1918 02:00 CWT
10/27/1918 02:00 CST
3/30/1919 02:00 CWT
10/26/1919 02:00 CST
4/15/1920 02:00 EST
2/09/1942 02:00 EWT
9/30/1945 02:00 EST
4/25/1948 02:00 EDT
9/26/1948 02:00 EST
6/14/1967 00:01 EDT
10/29/1967 00:01 EST
4/29/1973 02:00 EDT
10/28/1973 02:00 EST
1/06/1974 02:00 EDT
10/27/1974 02:00 EST
4/27/1975 02:00 EDT
10/26/1975 02:00 US#1

TIME TABLES

MI # 38

Before 9/18/1885		LMT
9/18/1885	12:00	CST
3/31/1918	02:00	CWT
10/27/1918	02:00	CST
3/30/1919	02:00	CWT
10/26/1919	02:00	CST
11/24/1921	02:00	EST
2/09/1942	02:00	EWT
9/30/1945	02:00	EST
6/14/1967	00:01	EDT
10/29/1967	00:01	EST
4/29/1973	02:00	EDT
10/28/1973	02:00	EST
1/06/1974	02:00	EDT
10/27/1974	02:00	EST
4/27/1975	02:00	EDT
10/26/1975	02:00	US#1

MI # 39

Before 9/18/1885		LMT
9/18/1885	12:00	CST
3/31/1918	02:00	CWT
10/27/1918	02:00	CST
3/30/1919	02:00	CWT
10/26/1919	02:00	CST
11/14/1922	02:00	EST
2/09/1942	02:00	EWT
9/30/1945	02:00	EST
6/14/1967	00:01	EDT
10/29/1967	00:01	EST
4/29/1973	02:00	EDT
10/28/1973	02:00	EST
1/06/1974	02:00	EDT
10/27/1974	02:00	EST
4/27/1975	02:00	EDT
10/26/1975	02:00	US#1

MI # 40

Before 9/18/1885		LMT
9/18/1885	12:00	CST
3/31/1918	02:00	CWT
10/27/1918	02:00	CST
3/30/1919	02:00	CWT
10/26/1919	02:00	CST
3/27/1921	02:00	CDT
10/31/1921	02:00	CST
4/30/1922	02:00	CDT
9/24/1922	02:00	CST
4/29/1923	02:00	CDT
9/30/1923	02:00	CST
4/01/1924	02:00	EST
2/09/1942	02:00	EWT
2/15/1943	02:00	CWT
9/30/1945	02:00	EST
6/14/1967	00:01	EDT
10/29/1967	00:01	EST
4/29/1973	02:00	EDT
10/28/1973	02:00	EST
1/06/1974	02:00	EDT
10/27/1974	02:00	EST
4/27/1975	02:00	EDT
10/26/1975	02:00	US#1

MI # 41

Before 9/18/1885		LMT
9/18/1885	12:00	CST
3/31/1918	02:00	CWT
10/27/1918	02:00	CST
3/30/1919	02:00	CWT
10/26/1919	02:00	CST
5/01/1923	02:00	CDT
5/01/1924	00:01	EST
2/09/1942	02:00	EWT
2/15/1943	02:00	CWT
9/30/1945	02:00	EST
6/14/1967	00:01	EDT
10/29/1967	00:01	EST
4/29/1973	02:00	EDT
10/28/1973	02:00	EST
1/06/1974	02:00	EDT
10/27/1974	02:00	EST
4/27/1975	02:00	EDT
10/26/1975	02:00	US#1

MI # 42

Before 9/18/1885		LMT
9/18/1885	12:00	CST
3/31/1918	02:00	CWT
10/27/1918	02:00	CST
3/30/1919	02:00	CWT
10/26/1919	02:00	CST
5/04/1925	02:00	EST
2/09/1942	02:00	EWT
2/15/1943	02:00	CWT
9/30/1945	02:00	EST
6/14/1967	00:01	EDT
10/29/1967	00:01	EST
4/29/1973	02:00	EDT
10/28/1973	02:00	EST
1/06/1974	02:00	EDT
10/27/1974	02:00	EST
4/27/1975	02:00	EDT
10/26/1975	02:00	US#1

MI # 43

Before 9/18/1885		LMT
9/18/1885	12:00	CST
3/31/1918	02:00	CWT
10/27/1918	02:00	CST
3/30/1919	02:00	CWT
10/26/1919	02:00	CST
3/27/1921	02:00	CDT
10/31/1921	02:00	CST
4/30/1922	02:00	CDT
9/24/1922	02:00	CST
4/29/1923	02:00	CDT
9/30/1923	02:00	CST
4/27/1924	02:00	CDT
9/28/1924	02:00	CST
4/26/1925	02:00	CDT
9/27/1925	02:00	CST
4/25/1926	02:00	CDT
9/26/1926	02:00	CST
4/01/1927	02:00	EST
2/09/1942	02:00	EWT
2/15/1943	02:00	CWT
9/30/1945	02:00	EST
6/14/1967	00:01	EDT
10/29/1967	00:01	EST
4/29/1973	02:00	EDT
10/28/1973	02:00	EST
1/06/1974	02:00	EDT
10/27/1974	02:00	EST
4/27/1975	02:00	EDT
10/26/1975	02:00	US#1

MI # 44

Before 9/18/1885		LMT
9/18/1885	12:00	CST
3/31/1918	02:00	CWT
10/27/1918	02:00	CST
3/30/1919	02:00	CWT
10/26/1919	02:00	CST
12/23/1928	02:00	EST
2/09/1942	02:00	EWT
2/15/1943	02:00	CWT
9/30/1945	02:00	EST
6/14/1967	00:01	EDT
10/29/1967	00:01	EST
4/29/1973	02:00	EDT
10/28/1973	02:00	EST
1/06/1974	02:00	EDT
10/27/1974	02:00	EST
4/27/1975	02:00	EDT
10/26/1975	02:00	US#1

MI # 45

Before 9/18/1885		LMT
9/18/1885	12:00	CST
3/31/1918	02:00	CWT
10/27/1918	02:00	CST
3/30/1919	02:00	CWT
10/26/1919	02:00	CST
12/23/1928	02:00	EST
2/09/1942	02:00	EWT
2/15/1943	02:00	CWT
9/30/1945	02:00	EST
5/15/1946	02:00	EDT
9/29/1946	02:00	EST
6/14/1967	00:01	EDT
10/29/1967	00:01	EST
4/29/1973	02:00	EDT
10/28/1973	02:00	EST
1/06/1974	02:00	EDT
10/27/1974	02:00	EST
4/27/1975	02:00	EDT
10/26/1975	02:00	US#1

MI # 46

Before 9/18/1885		LMT
9/18/1885	12:00	CST
3/31/1918	02:00	CWT
10/27/1918	02:00	CST
3/30/1919	02:00	CWT
10/26/1919	02:00	CST
2/28/1931	02:00	EST
2/09/1942	02:00	EWT
2/15/1943	02:00	CWT
9/30/1945	02:00	EST
6/14/1967	00:01	EDT
10/29/1967	00:01	EST
4/29/1973	02:00	EDT
10/28/1973	02:00	EST
1/06/1974	02:00	EDT
10/27/1974	02:00	EST
4/27/1975	02:00	EDT
10/26/1975	02:00	US#1

MI # 47

Before 9/18/1885		LMT
9/18/1885	12:00	CST
3/31/1918	02:00	CWT
10/27/1918	02:00	CST
3/30/1919	02:00	CWT
10/26/1919	02:00	CST
4/11/1920	02:00	CDT
10/10/1920	02:00	CST
4/17/1921	02:00	CDT
10/09/1921	02:00	CST
4/30/1922	02:00	CDT
10/01/1922	02:00	CST
4/15/1923	02:00	CDT
10/07/1923	02:00	CST
4/13/1924	02:00	CDT
10/05/1924	02:00	CST
4/12/1925	02:00	CDT
11/14/1926	02:00	CST
3/27/1927	00:01	CDT
10/31/1927	00:01	CST
3/18/1928	00:01	CDT
11/11/1928	00:01	CST
3/17/1929	00:01	CDT
11/10/1929	00:01	CST
3/16/1930	00:01	CDT
11/09/1930	00:01	CST
2/28/1931	02:00	EST
2/09/1942	02:00	EWT
2/15/1943	02:00	CWT
9/30/1945	02:00	EST
6/14/1967	00:01	EDT
10/29/1967	00:01	EST
4/29/1973	02:00	EDT
10/28/1973	02:00	EST
1/06/1974	02:00	EDT
10/27/1974	02:00	EST
4/27/1975	02:00	EDT
10/26/1975	02:00	US#1

MI # 48

Before 9/18/1885		LMT
9/18/1885	12:00	CST
3/31/1918	02:00	CWT
10/27/1918	02:00	CST
3/30/1919	02:00	CWT
10/26/1919	02:00	CST
3/29/1931	02:00	EST
2/09/1942	02:00	EWT
2/15/1943	02:00	CWT
9/30/1945	02:00	EST
6/14/1967	00:01	EDT
10/29/1967	00:01	EST
4/29/1973	02:00	EDT
10/28/1973	02:00	EST
1/06/1974	02:00	EDT
10/27/1974	02:00	EST
4/27/1975	02:00	EDT
10/26/1975	02:00	US#1

MI # 49

Before 9/18/1885		LMT
9/18/1885	12:00	CST
3/31/1918	02:00	CWT
10/27/1918	02:00	CST
3/30/1919	02:00	CWT
10/26/1919	02:00	CST
4/09/1922	00:01	CDT
9/24/1922	00:01	CST
4/08/1923	00:01	CDT
9/30/1923	00:01	CST
4/12/1924	00:01	CDT
9/28/1924	00:01	CST
4/12/1925	00:01	CDT
9/27/1925	00:01	CST
4/11/1926	00:01	CDT
9/26/1926	00:01	CST
4/10/1927	00:01	CDT
9/25/1927	00:01	CST
4/08/1928	00:01	CDT
9/30/1928	00:01	CST
4/14/1929	00:01	CDT
9/29/1929	00:01	CST
4/13/1930	00:01	CDT
9/28/1930	00:01	CST
4/11/1931	02:00	EST
2/09/1942	02:00	EWT
2/15/1943	02:00	CWT
9/30/1945	02:00	EST
6/14/1967	00:01	EDT
10/29/1967	00:01	EST
4/29/1973	02:00	EDT
10/28/1973	02:00	EST
1/06/1974	02:00	EDT
10/27/1974	02:00	EST
4/27/1975	02:00	EDT
10/26/1975	02:00	US#1

MI # 50

Before 9/18/1885		LMT
9/18/1885	12:00	CST
3/31/1918	02:00	CWT
10/27/1918	02:00	CST
3/30/1919	02:00	CWT
10/26/1919	02:00	CST
6/01/1928	02:00	CDT
10/01/1928	02:00	CST
6/01/1929	02:00	CDT
10/01/1929	02:00	CST
6/01/1930	02:00	CDT
10/01/1930	02:00	CST
6/01/1931	02:00	EST
2/09/1942	02:00	EWT
2/15/1943	02:00	CWT
9/30/1945	02:00	EST
4/25/1948	02:00	EDT
9/26/1948	02:00	EST
4/29/1973	02:00	EDT
10/28/1973	02:00	EST
1/06/1974	02:00	EDT
10/27/1974	02:00	EST
4/27/1975	02:00	EDT
10/26/1975	02:00	US#1

MI # 51

Before 9/18/1885		LMT
9/18/1885	12:00	CST
3/31/1918	02:00	CWT
10/27/1918	02:00	CST
3/30/1919	02:00	CWT
10/26/1919	02:00	CST
3/10/1932	02:00	EST
2/09/1942	02:00	EWT
2/15/1943	02:00	CWT
9/30/1945	02:00	EST
6/14/1967	00:01	EDT
10/29/1967	00:01	EST
4/29/1973	02:00	EDT
10/28/1973	02:00	EST
1/06/1974	02:00	EDT
10/27/1974	02:00	EST
4/27/1975	02:00	EDT
10/26/1975	02:00	US#1

MI # 52

Before 9/18/1885		LMT
9/18/1885	12:00	CST
3/31/1918	02:00	CWT
10/27/1918	02:00	CST
3/30/1919	02:00	CWT
10/26/1919	02:00	CST
3/10/1932	02:00	EST
2/09/1942	02:00	EWT
2/15/1943	02:00	CWT
9/30/1945	02:00	EST
4/28/1946	02:00	EDT
9/29/1946	02:00	EST
6/14/1967	00:01	EDT
10/29/1967	00:01	EST
4/29/1973	02:00	EDT
10/28/1973	02:00	EST
1/06/1974	02:00	EDT
10/27/1974	02:00	EST
4/27/1975	02:00	EDT
10/26/1975	02:00	US#1

MI # 53

Before 9/18/1885		LMT
9/18/1885	12:00	CST
3/31/1918	02:00	CWT
10/27/1918	02:00	CST
3/30/1919	02:00	CWT
10/26/1919	02:00	CST
3/17/1920	00:01	CDT
10/02/1920	00:01	CST
4/17/1921	00:01	CDT
10/02/1921	00:01	CST
4/16/1922	00:01	CDT
10/02/1922	00:01	CST
4/15/1923	00:01	CDT
9/03/1923	00:01	CST
5/04/1924	00:01	CDT
10/04/1924	00:01	CST
4/11/1925	00:01	CDT
10/11/1925	00:01	CST
4/10/1926	00:01	CDT
9/26/1926	00:01	CST
4/09/1927	00:01	CDT
9/25/1927	00:01	CST
3/21/1928	00:01	CDT
9/30/1928	00:01	CST
3/20/1929	00:01	CDT
9/29/1929	00:01	CST
4/12/1930	00:01	CDT
9/28/1930	00:01	CST
4/11/1931	00:01	CDT
9/27/1931	00:01	CST
3/10/1932	02:00	EST
2/09/1942	02:00	EWT
2/15/1943	02:00	CWT
9/30/1945	02:00	EST
6/14/1967	00:01	EDT
10/29/1967	00:01	EST
4/29/1973	02:00	EDT
10/28/1973	02:00	EST
1/06/1974	02:00	EDT
10/27/1974	02:00	EST
4/27/1975	02:00	EDT
10/26/1975	02:00	US#1

MI # 54

Before 9/18/1885		LMT
9/18/1885	12:00	CST
3/31/1918	02:00	CWT
10/27/1918	02:00	CST
3/30/1919	02:00	CWT
10/26/1919	02:00	CST
4/26/1931	02:00	CDT
9/27/1931	02:00	CST
3/10/1932	02:00	EST
2/09/1942	02:00	EWT
2/15/1943	02:00	CWT
9/30/1945	02:00	EST
6/14/1967	00:01	EDT
10/29/1967	00:01	EST
4/29/1973	02:00	EDT
10/28/1973	02:00	EST
1/06/1974	02:00	EDT
10/27/1974	02:00	EST
4/27/1975	02:00	EDT
10/26/1975	02:00	US#1

MI # 55

Before 9/18/1885		LMT
9/18/1885	12:00	CST
3/31/1918	02:00	CWT
10/27/1918	02:00	CST
3/30/1919	02:00	CWT
10/26/1919	02:00	CST
4/12/1931	02:00	CDT
10/11/1931	02:00	CST
3/10/1932	02:00	EST
2/09/1942	02:00	EWT
2/15/1943	02:00	CWT
9/30/1945	02:00	EST
6/14/1967	00:01	EDT
10/29/1967	00:01	EST
4/29/1973	02:00	EDT
10/28/1973	02:00	EST
1/06/1974	02:00	EDT
10/27/1974	02:00	EST
4/27/1975	02:00	EDT
10/26/1975	02:00	US#1

MI # 56

Before 9/18/1885		LMT
9/18/1885	12:00	CST
3/31/1918	02:00	CWT
10/27/1918	02:00	CST
3/30/1919	02:00	CWT
10/26/1919	02:00	CST
4/01/1931	02:00	CDT
10/01/1931	02:00	CST
3/10/1932	02:00	EST
2/09/1942	02:00	EWT
2/15/1943	02:00	CWT
9/30/1945	02:00	EST
6/14/1967	00:01	EDT
10/29/1967	00:01	EST
4/29/1973	02:00	EDT
10/28/1973	02:00	EST
1/06/1974	02:00	EDT
10/27/1974	02:00	EST
4/27/1975	02:00	EDT
10/26/1975	02:00	US#1

MI # 57

Before 9/18/1885		LMT
9/18/1885	12:00	CST
3/31/1918	02:00	CWT
10/27/1918	02:00	CST
3/30/1919	02:00	CWT
10/26/1919	02:00	CST
4/04/1932	02:00	EST
2/09/1942	02:00	EWT
2/15/1943	02:00	CWT
9/30/1945	02:00	EST
6/14/1967	00:01	EDT
10/29/1967	00:01	EST
4/29/1973	02:00	EDT
10/28/1973	02:00	EST
1/06/1974	02:00	EDT
10/27/1974	02:00	EST
4/27/1975	02:00	EDT
10/26/1975	02:00	US#1

MI # 58

Before 9/18/1885		LMT
9/18/1885	12:00	CST
3/31/1918	02:00	CWT
10/27/1918	02:00	CST
3/30/1919	02:00	CWT
10/26/1919	02:00	CST
3/27/1921	02:00	CDT
10/31/1921	02:00	CST
4/30/1922	02:00	CDT
9/24/1922	02:00	CST
4/29/1923	02:00	CDT
9/30/1923	02:00	CST
4/27/1924	02:00	CDT
9/28/1924	02:00	CST
4/26/1925	02:00	CDT
9/27/1925	02:00	CST
4/25/1926	02:00	CDT
9/26/1926	02:00	CST
4/24/1927	02:00	CDT
9/25/1927	02:00	CST
4/29/1928	02:00	CDT
9/30/1928	02:00	CST
4/28/1929	02:00	CDT
9/29/1929	02:00	CST
4/27/1930	02:00	CDT
9/28/1930	02:00	CST
4/26/1931	02:00	CDT
9/27/1931	02:00	CST
4/04/1932	02:00	EST
2/09/1942	02:00	EWT
2/15/1943	02:00	CWT
9/30/1945	02:00	EST
6/14/1967	00:01	EDT
10/29/1967	00:01	EST
4/29/1973	02:00	EDT
10/28/1973	02:00	EST
1/06/1974	02:00	EDT
10/27/1974	02:00	EST
4/27/1975	02:00	EDT
10/26/1975	02:00	US#1

MI # 59

Before 9/18/1885		LMT
9/18/1885	12:00	CST
3/31/1918	02:00	CWT
10/27/1918	02:00	CST
3/30/1919	02:00	CWT
10/26/1919	02:00	CST
4/04/1932	02:00	EST
2/09/1942	02:00	EWT
2/15/1943	02:00	CWT
9/30/1945	02:00	EST
4/28/1946	02:00	EDT
9/29/1946	02:00	EST
6/14/1967	00:01	EDT
10/29/1967	00:01	EST
4/29/1973	02:00	EDT
10/28/1973	02:00	EST
1/06/1974	02:00	EDT
10/27/1974	02:00	EST
4/27/1975	02:00	EDT
10/26/1975	02:00	US#1

MI # 60

Before 9/18/1885		LMT
9/18/1885	12:00	CST
3/31/1918	02:00	CWT
10/27/1918	02:00	CST
3/30/1919	02:00	CWT

TIME TABLES

10/26/1919 02:00 CST
4/04/1932 02:00 EST
2/09/1942 02:00 EWT
2/15/1943 02:00 CWT
9/30/1945 02:00 EST
4/25/1948 02:00 EDT
9/26/1948 02:00 EST
6/14/1967 00:01 EDT
10/29/1967 00:01 EST
4/29/1973 02:00 EDT
10/28/1973 02:00 EST
1/06/1974 02:00 EDT
10/27/1974 02:00 EST
4/27/1975 02:00 EDT
10/26/1975 02:00 US#1
....
MI # 61
Before 9/18/1885 LMT
9/18/1885 12:00 CST
3/31/1918 02:00 CWT
10/27/1918 02:00 CST
3/30/1919 02:00 CWT
10/26/1919 02:00 CST
4/04/1920 02:00 CDT
9/26/1920 02:00 CST
4/03/1921 02:00 CDT
9/25/1921 02:00 CST
4/02/1922 02:00 CDT
9/24/1922 02:00 CST
4/01/1923 02:00 CDT
9/30/1923 02:00 CST
4/06/1924 02:00 CDT
9/28/1924 02:00 CST
4/05/1925 02:00 CDT
9/27/1925 02:00 CST
4/04/1926 02:00 CDT
9/26/1926 02:00 CST
4/03/1927 02:00 CDT
9/25/1927 02:00 CST
4/01/1928 02:00 CDT
9/30/1928 02:00 CST
4/07/1929 02:00 CDT
9/29/1929 02:00 CST
4/06/1930 02:00 CDT
9/28/1930 02:00 CST
4/05/1931 02:00 CDT
9/27/1931 02:00 CST
4/04/1932 02:00 EST
2/09/1942 02:00 EWT
2/15/1943 02:00 CWT
9/30/1945 02:00 EST
4/28/1946 02:00 EDT
9/29/1946 02:00 EST
6/14/1967 00:01 EDT
10/29/1967 00:01 EST
4/29/1973 02:00 EDT
10/28/1973 02:00 EST
1/06/1974 02:00 EDT
10/27/1974 02:00 EST
4/27/1975 02:00 EDT
10/26/1975 02:00 US#1
....
MI # 62
Before 9/18/1885 LMT
9/18/1885 12:00 CST
3/31/1918 02:00 CWT
10/27/1918 02:00 CST
3/30/1919 02:00 CWT
10/26/1919 02:00 CST
4/12/1931 02:00 CDT
9/27/1931 02:00 CST
4/04/1932 02:00 EST
2/09/1942 02:00 EWT
2/15/1943 02:00 CWT
9/30/1945 02:00 EST
6/14/1967 00:01 EDT
10/29/1967 00:01 EST
4/29/1973 02:00 EDT
10/28/1973 02:00 EST
1/06/1974 02:00 EDT
10/27/1974 02:00 EST
4/27/1975 02:00 EDT
10/26/1975 02:00 US#1
....
MI # 63
Before 9/18/1885 LMT
9/18/1885 12:00 CST
3/31/1918 02:00 CWT
10/27/1918 02:00 CST
3/30/1919 02:00 CWT
10/26/1919 02:00 CST
5/01/1927 02:00 CDT
9/25/1927 02:00 CST
4/05/1931 02:00 CDT
10/04/1931 02:00 CST
4/04/1932 02:00 EST
2/09/1942 02:00 EWT
2/15/1943 02:00 CWT
9/30/1945 02:00 EST
6/14/1967 00:01 EDT
10/29/1967 00:01 EST
4/29/1973 02:00 EDT
10/28/1973 02:00 EST
1/06/1974 02:00 EDT
10/27/1974 02:00 EST
4/27/1975 02:00 EDT
10/26/1975 02:00 US#1
....
MI # 64
Before 9/18/1885 LMT
9/18/1885 12:00 CST
3/31/1918 02:00 CWT
10/27/1918 02:00 CST
3/30/1919 02:00 CWT
10/26/1919 02:00 CST
4/26/1931 02:00 CDT
9/27/1931 02:00 CST
4/04/1932 02:00 EST
2/09/1942 02:00 EWT
2/15/1943 02:00 CWT
9/30/1945 02:00 EST
6/14/1967 00:01 EDT
10/29/1967 00:01 EST
4/29/1973 02:00 EDT
10/28/1973 02:00 EST
1/06/1974 02:00 EDT
10/27/1974 02:00 EST
4/27/1975 02:00 EDT
10/26/1975 02:00 US#1
....
MI # 65
Before 9/18/1885 LMT
9/18/1885 12:00 CST
3/31/1918 02:00 CWT
10/27/1918 02:00 CST
3/30/1919 02:00 CWT
10/26/1919 02:00 CST
4/01/1931 02:00 CDT
11/01/1931 02:00 CST
4/04/1932 02:00 EST
2/09/1942 02:00 EWT
2/15/1943 02:00 CWT
9/30/1945 02:00 EST
6/14/1967 00:01 EDT
10/29/1967 00:01 EST
4/29/1973 02:00 EDT
10/28/1973 02:00 EST
1/06/1974 02:00 EDT
10/27/1974 02:00 EST
4/27/1975 02:00 EDT
10/26/1975 02:00 US#1
....
MI # 66
Before 9/18/1885 LMT
9/18/1885 12:00 CST
3/31/1918 02:00 CWT
10/27/1918 02:00 CST
3/30/1919 02:00 CWT
10/26/1919 02:00 CST
4/12/1931 02:00 CDT
9/12/1931 02:00 CST
4/04/1932 02:00 EST
2/09/1942 02:00 EWT
2/15/1943 02:00 CWT
9/30/1945 02:00 EST
6/14/1967 00:01 EDT
10/29/1967 00:01 EST
4/29/1973 02:00 EDT
10/28/1973 02:00 EST
1/06/1974 02:00 EDT
10/27/1974 02:00 EST
4/27/1975 02:00 EDT
10/26/1975 02:00 US#1
....
MI # 67
Before 9/18/1885 LMT
9/18/1885 12:00 CST
3/31/1918 02:00 CWT
10/27/1918 02:00 CST
3/30/1919 02:00 CWT
10/26/1919 02:00 CST
4/17/1932 02:00 EST
2/09/1942 02:00 EWT
2/15/1943 02:00 CWT
9/30/1945 02:00 EST
6/14/1967 00:01 EDT
10/29/1967 00:01 EST
4/29/1973 02:00 EDT
10/28/1973 02:00 EST
1/06/1974 02:00 EDT
10/27/1974 02:00 EST
4/27/1975 02:00 EDT
10/26/1975 02:00 US#1
....
MI # 68
Before 9/18/1885 LMT
9/18/1885 12:00 CST
3/31/1918 02:00 CWT
10/27/1918 02:00 CST
3/30/1919 02:00 CWT
10/26/1919 02:00 CST
4/12/1925 02:00 CDT
9/27/1925 02:00 CST
4/11/1926 02:00 CDT
9/26/1926 02:00 CST
4/10/1927 02:00 CDT
9/25/1927 02:00 CST
4/08/1928 02:00 CDT
9/30/1928 02:00 CST
4/14/1929 02:00 CDT
9/29/1929 02:00 CST
4/13/1930 02:00 CDT
9/28/1930 02:00 CST
4/12/1931 02:00 CDT
9/27/1931 02:00 CST
4/10/1932 02:00 CDT
9/25/1932 02:00 CST
11/10/1932 02:00 EST
2/09/1942 02:00 EWT
2/15/1943 02:00 CWT
9/30/1945 02:00 EST
6/14/1967 00:01 EDT
10/29/1967 00:01 EST
4/29/1973 02:00 EDT
10/28/1973 02:00 EST
1/06/1974 02:00 EDT
10/27/1974 02:00 EST
4/27/1975 02:00 EDT
10/26/1975 02:00 US#1
....
MI # 69
Before 9/18/1885 LMT
9/18/1885 12:00 CST
3/31/1918 02:00 CWT
10/27/1918 02:00 CST
3/30/1919 02:00 CWT
10/26/1919 02:00 CST
5/02/1932 02:00 CDT
11/22/1932 02:00 CST
4/30/1933 02:00 EST
2/09/1942 02:00 EWT
2/15/1943 02:00 CWT
9/30/1945 02:00 EST
4/25/1948 02:00 EDT
9/26/1948 02:00 EST
4/29/1973 02:00 EDT
10/28/1973 02:00 EST
1/06/1974 02:00 EDT
10/27/1974 02:00 EST
4/27/1975 02:00 EDT
10/26/1975 02:00 US#1
....
MI # 70
Before 9/18/1885 LMT
9/18/1885 12:00 CST
3/31/1918 02:00 CWT
10/27/1918 02:00 CST
3/30/1919 02:00 CWT
10/26/1919 02:00 CST
6/01/1931 02:00 CDT
9/01/1931 02:00 CST
6/01/1932 02:00 CDT
9/01/1932 02:00 CST
4/30/1933 02:00 EST
2/09/1942 02:00 EWT
2/15/1943 02:00 CWT
9/30/1945 02:00 EST
6/14/1967 00:01 EDT
10/29/1967 00:01 EST
4/29/1973 02:00 EDT
10/28/1973 02:00 EST
1/06/1974 02:00 EDT
10/27/1974 02:00 EST
4/27/1975 02:00 EDT
10/26/1975 02:00 US#1
....
MI # 71
Before 9/18/1885 LMT
9/18/1885 12:00 CST
3/31/1918 02:00 CWT
10/27/1918 02:00 CST
3/30/1919 02:00 CWT
10/26/1919 02:00 CST
4/02/1932 00:01 CDT
10/02/1932 00:01 CST
4/02/1933 00:01 CDT
10/02/1933 00:01 CST
4/02/1934 00:01 CDT
10/02/1934 00:01 CST
4/02/1935 00:01 EST
2/09/1942 02:00 EWT
2/15/1943 02:00 CWT
9/30/1945 02:00 EST
6/14/1967 00:01 EDT
10/29/1967 00:01 EST
4/29/1973 02:00 EDT
10/28/1973 02:00 EST
1/06/1974 02:00 EDT
10/27/1974 02:00 EST
4/27/1975 02:00 EDT
10/26/1975 02:00 US#1
....
MI # 72
Before 9/18/1885 LMT
9/18/1885 12:00 CST
3/31/1918 02:00 CWT
10/27/1918 02:00 CST
3/30/1919 02:00 CWT
10/26/1919 02:00 CST
4/07/1935 02:00 EST
2/09/1942 02:00 EWT
2/15/1943 02:00 CWT
9/30/1945 02:00 EST
6/14/1967 00:01 EDT
10/29/1967 00:01 EST
4/29/1973 02:00 EDT
10/28/1973 02:00 EST
1/06/1974 02:00 EDT
10/27/1974 02:00 EST
4/27/1975 02:00 EDT
10/26/1975 02:00 US#1
....
MI # 73
Before 9/18/1885 LMT
9/18/1885 12:00 CST
3/31/1918 02:00 CWT
10/27/1918 02:00 CST
3/30/1919 02:00 CWT
10/26/1919 02:00 CST
4/02/1933 02:00 CDT
10/15/1933 02:00 CST
4/08/1934 02:00 CDT
9/30/1934 02:00 CST
4/07/1935 02:00 EST
2/09/1942 02:00 EWT
2/15/1943 02:00 CWT
9/30/1945 02:00 EST
6/14/1967 00:01 EDT
10/29/1967 00:01 EST
4/29/1973 02:00 EDT
10/28/1973 02:00 EST
1/06/1974 02:00 EDT
10/27/1974 02:00 EST
4/27/1975 02:00 EDT
10/26/1975 02:00 US#1
....
MI # 74
Before 9/18/1885 LMT
9/18/1885 12:00 CST
3/31/1918 02:00 CWT
10/27/1918 02:00 CST
3/30/1919 02:00 CWT
10/26/1919 02:00 CST
4/26/1931 02:00 CDT
9/27/1931 02:00 CST
4/24/1932 02:00 CDT
9/25/1932 02:00 CST
4/30/1933 02:00 CDT
9/24/1933 02:00 CST
4/29/1934 02:00 CDT
9/30/1934 02:00 CST
4/07/1935 02:00 EST
2/09/1942 02:00 EWT
2/15/1943 02:00 CWT
9/30/1945 02:00 EST
6/14/1967 00:01 EDT
10/29/1967 00:01 EST
4/29/1973 02:00 EDT
10/28/1973 02:00 EST
1/06/1974 02:00 EDT
10/27/1974 02:00 EST
4/27/1975 02:00 EDT
10/26/1975 02:00 US#1
....
MI # 75
Before 9/18/1885 LMT
9/18/1885 12:00 CST
3/31/1918 02:00 CWT
10/27/1918 02:00 CST
3/30/1919 02:00 CWT
10/26/1919 02:00 CST
4/30/1933 02:00 CDT
9/24/1933 02:00 CST
4/29/1934 02:00 CDT
9/30/1934 02:00 CST
4/07/1935 02:00 EST
2/09/1942 02:00 EWT
2/15/1943 02:00 CWT
9/30/1945 02:00 EST
6/14/1967 00:01 EDT
10/29/1967 00:01 EST
4/29/1973 02:00 EDT
10/28/1973 02:00 EST
1/06/1974 02:00 EDT
10/27/1974 02:00 EST
4/27/1975 02:00 EDT
10/26/1975 02:00 US#1
....
MI # 76
Before 9/18/1885 LMT
9/18/1885 12:00 CST
3/31/1918 02:00 CWT
10/27/1918 02:00 CST
3/30/1919 02:00 CWT
10/26/1919 02:00 CST
4/03/1933 02:00 CDT
10/01/1933 02:00 CST
4/08/1934 02:00 CDT
10/01/1934 02:00 CST
4/07/1935 02:00 EST
2/09/1942 02:00 EWT
2/15/1943 02:00 CWT
9/30/1945 02:00 EST
6/14/1967 00:01 EDT
10/29/1967 00:01 EST
4/29/1973 02:00 EDT
10/28/1973 02:00 EST
1/06/1974 02:00 EDT
10/27/1974 02:00 EST
4/27/1975 02:00 EDT
10/26/1975 02:00 US#1
....
MI # 77
Before 9/18/1885 LMT
9/18/1885 12:00 CST
3/31/1918 02:00 CWT
10/27/1918 02:00 CST
3/30/1919 02:00 CWT
10/26/1919 02:00 CST
3/27/1921 02:00 CDT
10/31/1921 02:00 CST
4/30/1922 02:00 CDT
9/24/1922 02:00 CST
4/29/1923 02:00 CDT
9/30/1923 02:00 CST
4/27/1924 02:00 CDT
9/28/1924 02:00 CST
4/26/1925 02:00 CDT
9/27/1925 02:00 CST
4/25/1926 02:00 CDT
9/26/1926 02:00 CST
4/24/1927 02:00 CDT
9/25/1927 02:00 CST
4/29/1928 02:00 CDT
9/30/1928 02:00 CST
4/28/1929 02:00 CDT
9/29/1929 02:00 CST
4/27/1930 02:00 CDT
9/28/1930 02:00 CST
4/26/1931 02:00 CDT
9/27/1931 02:00 CST
4/24/1932 02:00 CDT
9/25/1932 02:00 CST
4/30/1933 02:00 CDT
9/24/1933 02:00 CST
4/29/1934 02:00 CDT
9/30/1934 02:00 CST
4/28/1935 02:00 EST
2/09/1942 02:00 EWT
2/15/1943 02:00 CWT
9/30/1945 02:00 EST
6/14/1967 00:01 EDT
10/29/1967 00:01 EST
4/29/1973 02:00 EDT
10/28/1973 02:00 EST
1/06/1974 02:00 EDT
10/27/1974 02:00 EST
4/27/1975 02:00 EDT
10/26/1975 02:00 US#1
....
MI # 78
Before 9/18/1885 LMT
9/18/1885 12:00 CST
3/31/1918 02:00 CWT
10/27/1918 02:00 CST
3/30/1919 02:00 CWT
10/26/1919 02:00 CST
4/28/1935 02:00 EST
2/09/1942 02:00 EWT
2/15/1943 02:00 CWT
9/30/1945 02:00 EST
4/25/1948 02:00 EDT
9/26/1948 02:00 EST
4/29/1973 02:00 EDT
10/28/1973 02:00 EST
1/06/1974 02:00 EDT
10/27/1974 02:00 EST
4/27/1975 02:00 EDT
10/26/1975 02:00 US#1
....
MI # 79
Before 9/18/1885 LMT
9/18/1885 12:00 CST
3/31/1918 02:00 CWT
10/27/1918 02:00 CST
3/30/1919 02:00 CWT
10/26/1919 02:00 CST
4/29/1925 02:00 CDT
9/30/1925 02:00 CST
4/24/1932 02:00 CDT
10/31/1932 02:00 CST
4/30/1933 02:00 CDT
9/24/1933 02:00 CST
4/29/1934 02:00 CDT
9/30/1934 02:00 CST
5/01/1935 02:00 CDT
10/01/1935 02:00 CST
5/01/1936 02:00 CDT
9/01/1936 02:00 CST
9/27/1936 02:00 EST
2/09/1942 02:00 EWT
2/15/1943 02:00 CWT
9/30/1945 02:00 EST
4/25/1948 02:00 EDT
9/26/1948 02:00 EST
4/24/1949 02:00 EDT
9/25/1949 02:00 EST
4/29/1973 02:00 EDT
10/28/1973 02:00 EST
1/06/1974 02:00 EDT
10/27/1974 02:00 EST
4/27/1975 02:00 EDT
10/26/1975 02:00 US#1
....
MI # 80
Before 9/18/1885 LMT
9/18/1885 12:00 CST
3/31/1918 02:00 CWT
10/27/1918 02:00 CST
3/30/1919 02:00 CWT
10/26/1919 02:00 CST
2/09/1942 02:00 CWT
9/30/1945 02:00 CST
4/25/1948 02:00 CDT
9/26/1948 02:00 CST
12/10/1967 02:00 EST
4/29/1973 02:00 EDT
10/28/1973 02:00 EST
1/06/1974 02:00 EDT
10/27/1974 02:00 EST
4/27/1975 02:00 EDT
10/26/1975 02:00 US#1
....
MI # 81
Before 9/18/1885 LMT
9/18/1885 12:00 CST
3/31/1918 02:00 CWT
10/27/1918 02:00 CST
3/30/1919 02:00 CWT
10/26/1919 02:00 CST
2/09/1942 02:00 CWT
9/30/1945 02:00 CST
4/24/1966 02:00 CDT
10/30/1966 02:00 CST
4/27/1969 02:00 EST
4/29/1973 02:00 CST
4/29/1973 02:00 US#1
....
MI # 82
Before 9/18/1885 LMT
9/18/1885 12:00 CST
3/31/1918 02:00 CWT
10/27/1918 02:00 CST
3/30/1919 02:00 CWT
10/26/1919 02:00 CST

TIME TABLES

5/15/1935 02:00 CDT
8/31/1935 02:00 CST
2/09/1942 02:00 CWT
9/30/1945 02:00 CST
4/28/1946 02:00 CDT
9/29/1946 02:00 CST
5/01/1950 02:00 CDT
10/01/1950 02:00 CST
4/27/1952 02:00 CDT
9/28/1952 02:00 CST
4/24/1966 02:00 CDT
10/30/1966 02:00 CST
4/27/1969 02:00 EST
4/29/1973 02:00 CST
4/29/1973 02:00 US#1
....
MI # 83
Before 9/18/1885 LMT
9/18/1885 12:00 CST
3/31/1918 02:00 CWT
10/27/1918 02:00 CST
3/30/1919 02:00 CWT
10/26/1919 02:00 CST
2/09/1942 02:00 CWT
9/30/1945 02:00 CST
5/05/1946 02:00 CDT
9/29/1946 02:00 CST
4/30/1950 02:00 CDT
9/24/1950 02:00 CST
4/24/1960 02:00 CDT
10/30/1960 02:00 CST
4/30/1961 02:00 CDT
9/24/1961 02:00 CST
4/29/1962 02:00 CDT
9/30/1962 02:00 CST
4/28/1963 02:00 CDT
9/29/1963 02:00 CST
4/26/1964 02:00 CDT
10/25/1964 02:00 CST
4/25/1965 02:00 CDT
10/31/1965 02:00 CST
4/24/1966 02:00 CDT
10/30/1966 02:00 CST
4/27/1969 02:00 EST
4/29/1973 02:00 CST
4/29/1973 02:00 US#1
....
MI # 84
Before 9/18/1885 LMT
9/18/1885 12:00 CST
3/31/1918 02:00 CWT
10/27/1918 02:00 CST
3/30/1919 02:00 CWT
10/26/1919 02:00 CST
5/15/1935 02:00 CDT
9/01/1935 02:00 CST
2/09/1942 02:00 CWT
9/30/1945 02:00 CST
5/01/1946 02:00 CDT
9/29/1946 02:00 CST
4/27/1947 02:00 CDT
9/28/1947 02:00 CST
5/01/1950 02:00 CDT
10/01/1950 02:00 CST
4/27/1952 02:00 CDT
9/28/1952 02:00 CST
4/24/1966 02:00 CDT
10/30/1966 02:00 CST
4/27/1969 02:00 EST
4/29/1973 02:00 CST
4/29/1973 02:00 US#1
....
MI # 85
Before 9/18/1885 LMT
9/18/1885 12:00 CST
3/31/1918 02:00 CWT
10/27/1918 02:00 CST
3/30/1919 02:00 CWT
10/26/1919 02:00 CST
2/09/1942 02:00 CWT
9/30/1945 02:00 CST
4/28/1946 02:00 CDT
9/29/1946 02:00 CST
4/27/1947 02:00 CDT
9/28/1947 02:00 CST
4/30/1961 02:00 CDT
9/24/1961 02:00 CST
4/29/1962 02:00 CDT
9/30/1962 02:00 CST
4/28/1963 02:00 CDT
9/29/1963 02:00 CST
4/26/1964 02:00 CDT
9/27/1964 02:00 CST
4/25/1965 02:00 CDT
10/31/1965 02:00 CST
4/24/1966 02:00 CDT
10/30/1966 02:00 CST
4/27/1969 02:00 EST
4/29/1973 02:00 CST
4/29/1973 02:00 US#1
....
MI # 86
Before 9/18/1885 LMT
9/18/1885 12:00 CST
3/31/1918 02:00 CWT
10/27/1918 02:00 CST
3/30/1919 02:00 CWT
10/26/1919 02:00 CST
2/09/1942 02:00 CWT
9/30/1945 02:00 CST
4/28/1946 02:00 CDT
9/29/1946 02:00 CST
4/24/1966 02:00 CDT
10/30/1966 02:00 CST
4/27/1969 02:00 EST
4/29/1973 02:00 CST
4/29/1973 02:00 US#1
....
MI # 87
Before 9/18/1885 LMT
9/18/1885 12:00 CST
3/31/1918 02:00 CWT
10/27/1918 02:00 CST
3/30/1919 02:00 CWT
10/26/1919 02:00 CST
2/09/1942 02:00 CWT
9/30/1945 02:00 CST
4/28/1946 02:00 CDT
9/29/1946 02:00 CST
4/25/1948 02:00 CDT
9/26/1948 02:00 CST
4/24/1960 02:00 CDT
10/30/1960 02:00 CST
4/30/1961 02:00 CDT
9/24/1961 02:00 CST
4/29/1962 02:00 CDT
9/30/1962 02:00 CST
4/28/1963 02:00 CDT
9/29/1963 02:00 CST
4/26/1964 02:00 CDT
10/25/1964 02:00 CST
4/25/1965 02:00 CDT
10/31/1965 02:00 CST
4/24/1966 02:00 CDT
10/30/1966 02:00 CST
4/27/1969 02:00 EST
4/29/1973 02:00 CST
4/29/1973 02:00 US#1
....
MI # 88
Before 9/18/1885 LMT
9/18/1885 12:00 CST
3/31/1918 02:00 CWT
10/27/1918 02:00 CST
3/30/1919 02:00 CWT
10/26/1919 02:00 CST
4/26/1931 02:00 EST
2/09/1942 02:00 EWT
9/30/1945 02:00 EST
6/14/1967 00:01 EDT
10/29/1967 00:01 EST
4/29/1973 02:00 EDT
10/28/1973 02:00 EST
1/06/1974 02:00 EDT
10/27/1974 02:00 EST
4/27/1975 02:00 EDT
10/26/1975 02:00 US#1
....
MI # 89
Before 9/18/1885 LMT
9/18/1885 12:00 CST
3/31/1918 02:00 CWT
10/27/1918 02:00 CST
3/30/1919 02:00 CWT
10/26/1919 02:00 CST
4/26/1931 02:00 EST
2/09/1942 02:00 EWT
9/30/1945 02:00 EST
4/25/1948 02:00 EDT
9/26/1948 02:00 EST
6/14/1967 00:01 EDT
10/29/1967 00:01 EST
4/29/1973 02:00 EDT
10/28/1973 02:00 EST
1/06/1974 02:00 EDT
10/27/1974 02:00 EST
4/27/1975 02:00 EDT
10/26/1975 02:00 US#1
....
MI # 90
Before 9/18/1885 LMT
9/18/1885 12:00 CST
3/31/1918 02:00 CWT
10/27/1918 02:00 CST
3/30/1919 02:00 CWT
10/26/1919 02:00 CST
12/01/1923 00:01 EST
2/09/1942 02:00 EWT
9/30/1945 02:00 EST
6/14/1967 00:01 EDT
10/29/1967 00:01 EST
4/29/1973 02:00 EDT
10/28/1973 02:00 EST
1/06/1974 02:00 EDT
10/27/1974 02:00 EST
4/27/1975 02:00 EDT
10/26/1975 02:00 US#1
....
MI # 91
Before 9/18/1885 LMT
9/18/1885 12:00 CST
3/31/1918 02:00 CWT
10/27/1918 02:00 CST
3/30/1919 02:00 CWT
10/26/1919 02:00 CST
11/14/1922 02:00 EST
2/09/1942 02:00 EWT
2/15/1943 02:00 CWT
9/30/1945 02:00 EST
6/14/1967 00:01 EDT
10/29/1967 00:01 EST
4/29/1973 02:00 EDT
10/28/1973 02:00 EST
1/06/1974 02:00 EDT
10/27/1974 02:00 EST
4/27/1975 02:00 EDT
10/26/1975 02:00 US#1
....
MI # 92
Before 9/18/1885 LMT
9/18/1885 12:00 CST
3/31/1918 02:00 CWT
10/27/1918 02:00 CST
3/30/1919 02:00 CWT
10/26/1919 02:00 CST
4/24/1932 02:00 EST
2/09/1942 02:00 EWT
2/15/1943 02:00 CWT
9/30/1945 02:00 EST
6/14/1967 00:01 EDT
10/29/1967 00:01 EST
4/29/1973 02:00 EDT
10/28/1973 02:00 EST
1/06/1974 02:00 EDT
10/27/1974 02:00 EST
4/27/1975 02:00 EDT
10/26/1975 02:00 US#1
....
MI # 93
Before 9/18/1885 LMT
9/18/1885 12:00 CST
3/31/1918 02:00 CWT
10/27/1918 02:00 CST
3/30/1919 02:00 CWT
10/26/1919 02:00 CST
6/13/1920 02:00 CDT
10/31/1920 02:00 CST
3/27/1921 02:00 CDT
10/31/1921 02:00 CST
4/30/1922 02:00 CDT
9/24/1922 02:00 CST
4/29/1923 02:00 CDT
9/30/1923 02:00 CST
4/27/1924 02:00 CDT
9/28/1924 02:00 CST
4/26/1925 02:00 CDT
9/27/1925 02:00 CST
4/25/1926 02:00 CDT
9/26/1926 02:00 CST
4/24/1927 02:00 CDT
9/25/1927 02:00 CST
4/29/1928 02:00 CDT
9/30/1928 02:00 CST
4/28/1929 02:00 CDT
9/29/1929 02:00 CST
4/27/1930 02:00 CDT
9/28/1930 02:00 CST
5/10/1931 02:00 CDT
9/19/1931 02:00 CST
4/24/1932 02:00 EST
2/09/1942 02:00 EWT
2/15/1943 02:00 CWT
9/30/1945 02:00 EST
6/14/1967 00:01 EDT
10/29/1967 00:01 EST
4/29/1973 02:00 EDT
10/28/1973 02:00 EST
1/06/1974 02:00 EDT
10/27/1974 02:00 EST
4/27/1975 02:00 EDT
10/26/1975 02:00 US#1
....
MI # 94
Before 9/18/1885 LMT
9/18/1885 12:00 CST
3/31/1918 02:00 CWT
10/27/1918 02:00 CST
3/30/1919 02:00 CWT
10/26/1919 02:00 CST
4/24/1932 02:00 EST
2/09/1942 02:00 EWT
2/15/1943 02:00 CWT
9/30/1945 02:00 EST
4/28/1946 02:00 EDT
9/29/1946 02:00 EST
6/14/1967 00:01 EDT
10/29/1967 00:01 EST
4/29/1973 02:00 EDT
10/28/1973 02:00 EST
1/06/1974 02:00 EDT
10/27/1974 02:00 EST
4/27/1975 02:00 EDT
10/26/1975 02:00 US#1
....
MI # 95
Before 9/18/1885 LMT
9/18/1885 12:00 CST
3/31/1918 02:00 CWT
10/27/1918 02:00 CST
3/30/1919 02:00 CWT
10/26/1919 02:00 CST
5/01/1931 00:00 CDT
10/01/1931 00:00 CST
4/24/1932 02:00 EST
2/09/1942 02:00 EWT
2/15/1943 02:00 CWT
9/30/1945 02:00 EST
4/25/1948 02:00 EDT
9/26/1948 02:00 EST
4/29/1973 02:00 EDT
10/28/1973 02:00 EST
1/06/1974 02:00 EDT
10/27/1974 02:00 EST
4/27/1975 02:00 EDT
10/26/1975 02:00 US#1
....
MI # 96
Before 9/18/1885 LMT
9/18/1885 12:00 CST
3/31/1918 02:00 CWT
10/27/1918 02:00 CST
3/30/1919 02:00 CWT
10/26/1919 02:00 CST
4/24/1932 02:00 EST
2/09/1942 02:00 EWT
2/15/1943 02:00 CWT
9/30/1945 02:00 EST
4/25/1948 02:00 EDT
9/26/1948 02:00 EST
4/29/1973 02:00 EDT
10/28/1973 02:00 EST
1/06/1974 02:00 EDT
10/27/1974 02:00 EST
4/27/1975 02:00 EDT
10/26/1975 02:00 US#1
....
MI # 97
Before 9/18/1885 LMT
9/18/1885 12:00 CST
3/31/1918 02:00 CWT
10/27/1918 02:00 CST
3/30/1919 02:00 CWT
10/26/1919 02:00 CST
4/26/1931 02:00 CDT
9/27/1931 02:00 CST
4/24/1932 02:00 EST
2/09/1942 02:00 EWT
2/15/1943 02:00 CWT
9/30/1945 02:00 EST
6/14/1967 00:01 EDT
10/29/1967 00:01 EST
4/29/1973 02:00 EDT
10/28/1973 02:00 EST
1/06/1974 02:00 EDT
10/27/1974 02:00 EST
4/27/1975 02:00 EDT
10/26/1975 02:00 US#1
....
MI # 98
Before 9/18/1885 LMT
9/18/1885 12:00 CST
3/31/1918 02:00 CWT
10/27/1918 02:00 CST
3/30/1919 02:00 CWT
10/26/1919 02:00 CST
6/01/1931 02:00 CDT
10/01/1931 02:00 CST
4/24/1932 02:00 EST
2/09/1942 02:00 EWT
2/15/1943 02:00 CWT
9/30/1945 02:00 EST
4/25/1948 02:00 EDT
9/26/1948 02:00 EST
4/29/1973 02:00 EDT
10/28/1973 02:00 EST
1/06/1974 02:00 EDT
10/27/1974 02:00 EST
4/27/1975 02:00 EDT
10/26/1975 02:00 US#1
....
MI # 99
Before 9/18/1885 LMT
9/18/1885 12:00 CST
3/31/1918 02:00 CWT
10/27/1918 02:00 CST
3/30/1919 02:00 CWT
10/26/1919 02:00 CST
3/29/1931 02:00 CDT
11/01/1931 02:00 CST
4/24/1932 02:00 EST
2/09/1942 02:00 EWT
2/15/1943 02:00 CWT
9/30/1945 02:00 EST
6/14/1967 00:01 EDT
10/29/1967 00:01 EST
4/29/1973 02:00 EDT
10/28/1973 02:00 EST
1/06/1974 02:00 EDT
10/27/1974 02:00 EST
4/27/1975 02:00 EDT
10/26/1975 02:00 US#1
....
MI # 100
Before 9/18/1885 LMT
9/18/1885 12:00 CST
3/31/1918 02:00 CWT
10/27/1918 02:00 CST
3/30/1919 02:00 CWT
10/26/1919 02:00 CST
2/29/1931 02:00 CDT
11/01/1931 02:00 CST
4/24/1932 02:00 EST
2/09/1942 02:00 EWT
2/15/1943 02:00 CWT
9/30/1945 02:00 EST
6/14/1967 00:01 EDT
10/29/1967 00:01 EST
4/29/1973 02:00 EDT
10/28/1973 02:00 EST
1/06/1974 02:00 EDT
10/27/1974 02:00 EST
4/27/1975 02:00 EDT
10/26/1975 02:00 US#1
....
MI # 101
Before 9/18/1885 LMT
9/18/1885 12:00 CST
3/31/1918 02:00 CWT
10/27/1918 02:00 CST
3/30/1919 02:00 CWT
10/26/1919 02:00 CST
3/08/1931 02:00 CDT
11/01/1931 02:00 CST
4/24/1932 02:00 EST
2/09/1942 02:00 EWT
2/15/1943 02:00 CWT
9/30/1945 02:00 EST
6/14/1967 00:01 EDT
10/29/1967 00:01 EST
4/29/1973 02:00 EDT
10/28/1973 02:00 EST
1/06/1974 02:00 EDT
10/27/1974 02:00 EST
4/27/1975 02:00 EDT
10/26/1975 02:00 US#1
....
MI # 102
Before 9/18/1885 LMT
9/18/1885 12:00 CST
3/31/1918 02:00 CWT
10/27/1918 02:00 CST
3/30/1919 02:00 CWT
10/26/1919 02:00 CST
3/01/1931 02:00 CDT
11/01/1931 02:00 CST
4/24/1932 02:00 EST
2/09/1942 02:00 EWT
2/15/1943 02:00 CWT
9/30/1945 02:00 EST
6/14/1967 00:01 EDT
10/29/1967 00:01 EST
4/29/1973 02:00 EDT
10/28/1973 02:00 EST
1/06/1974 02:00 EDT
10/27/1974 02:00 EST
4/27/1975 02:00 EDT
10/26/1975 02:00 US#1
....
MI # 103
Before 9/18/1885 LMT
9/18/1885 12:00 CST
3/31/1918 02:00 CWT
10/27/1918 02:00 CST
3/30/1919 02:00 CWT
10/26/1919 02:00 CST
4/27/1931 02:00 CDT
10/04/1931 02:00 CST
4/24/1932 02:00 EST
2/09/1942 02:00 EWT
2/15/1943 02:00 CWT
9/30/1945 02:00 EST
6/14/1967 00:01 EDT
10/29/1967 00:01 EST
4/29/1973 02:00 EDT
10/28/1973 02:00 EST
1/06/1974 02:00 EDT
10/27/1974 02:00 EST
4/27/1975 02:00 EDT
10/26/1975 02:00 US#1
....
MI # 104
Before 9/18/1885 LMT
9/18/1885 12:00 CST
3/31/1918 02:00 CWT
10/27/1918 02:00 CST
3/30/1919 02:00 CWT
10/26/1919 02:00 CST
4/01/1932 02:00 CDT
9/01/1932 02:00 CST
4/01/1933 02:00 EST
2/09/1942 02:00 EWT
2/15/1943 02:00 CWT
9/30/1945 02:00 EST
6/14/1967 00:01 EDT
10/29/1967 00:01 EST
4/29/1973 02:00 EDT
10/28/1973 02:00 EST
1/06/1974 02:00 EDT
10/27/1974 02:00 EST
4/27/1975 02:00 EDT
10/26/1975 02:00 US#1
....
MI # 105
Before 9/18/1885 LMT
9/18/1885 12:00 CST
3/31/1918 02:00 CWT
10/27/1918 02:00 CST
3/30/1919 02:00 CWT
10/26/1919 02:00 CST
4/30/1932 00:01 CDT
10/02/1932 00:01 CST
4/30/1933 01:00 CDT
9/24/1933 01:00 CST
4/29/1934 02:00 CDT
9/30/1934 02:00 CST
4/28/1935 02:00 CDT
9/29/1935 02:00 CST
3/01/1936 02:00 CDT
10/01/1936 02:00 CST
4/25/1937 02:00 EST
2/09/1942 02:00 EWT
2/15/1943 02:00 CWT
9/30/1945 02:00 EST
6/14/1967 00:01 EDT
10/29/1967 00:01 EST
4/29/1973 02:00 EDT
10/28/1973 02:00 EST
1/06/1974 02:00 EDT
10/27/1974 02:00 EST
4/27/1975 02:00 EDT
10/26/1975 02:00 US#1
....
MI # 106
Before 9/18/1885 LMT
9/18/1885 12:00 CST

MICHIGAN

TIME TABLES

Date	Time	Zone
3/31/1918	02:00	CWT
10/27/1918	02:00	CST
3/30/1919	02:00	CWT
10/26/1919	02:00	CST
4/30/1933	02:00	CDT
9/24/1933	02:00	CST
5/01/1934	02:00	CDT
10/01/1934	02:00	CST
5/01/1935	02:00	CDT
10/01/1935	02:00	CST
4/26/1936	02:00	CDT
9/27/1936	02:00	CST
4/25/1937	02:00	EST
2/09/1942	02:00	EWT
2/15/1943	02:00	CWT
9/30/1945	02:00	EST
6/14/1967	00:01	EDT
10/29/1967	00:01	EST
4/29/1973	02:00	EDT
10/28/1973	02:00	EST
1/06/1974	02:00	EDT
10/27/1974	02:00	EST
4/27/1975	02:00	EDT
10/26/1975	02:00	US#1

MI # 107

Date	Time	Zone
Before 9/18/1885		LMT
9/18/1885	12:00	CST
3/31/1918	02:00	CWT
10/27/1918	02:00	CST
3/30/1919	02:00	CWT
10/26/1919	02:00	CST
5/01/1932	02:00	CDT
10/01/1932	02:00	CST
4/30/1933	02:00	CDT
9/24/1933	02:00	CST
4/29/1934	02:00	CDT
9/30/1934	02:00	CST
4/28/1935	02:00	CDT
9/29/1935	02:00	CST
4/26/1936	02:00	CDT
9/27/1936	02:00	CST
4/25/1937	02:00	EST
2/09/1942	02:00	EWT
2/15/1943	02:00	CWT
9/30/1945	02:00	EST
6/14/1967	00:01	EDT
10/29/1967	00:01	EST
4/29/1973	02:00	EDT
10/28/1973	02:00	EST
1/06/1974	02:00	EDT
10/27/1974	02:00	EST
4/27/1975	02:00	EDT
10/26/1975	02:00	US#1

MI # 108

Date	Time	Zone
Before 9/18/1885		LMT
9/18/1885	12:00	CST
3/31/1918	02:00	CWT
10/27/1918	02:00	CST
3/30/1919	02:00	CWT
10/26/1919	02:00	CST
4/28/1935	02:00	CDT
9/29/1935	02:00	CST
5/01/1936	02:00	CDT
10/01/1936	02:00	CST
4/25/1937	02:00	EST
2/09/1942	02:00	EWT
2/15/1943	02:00	CWT
9/30/1945	02:00	EST
6/14/1967	00:01	EDT
10/29/1967	00:01	EST
4/29/1973	02:00	EDT
10/28/1973	02:00	EST
1/06/1974	02:00	EDT
10/27/1974	02:00	EST
4/27/1975	02:00	EDT
10/26/1975	02:00	US#1

MI # 109

Date	Time	Zone
Before 9/18/1885		LMT
9/18/1885	12:00	CST
3/31/1918	02:00	CWT
10/27/1918	02:00	CST
3/30/1919	02:00	CWT
10/26/1919	02:00	CST
4/27/1930	02:00	CDT
9/28/1930	02:00	CST
4/26/1931	02:00	CDT
9/27/1931	02:00	CST
4/24/1932	02:00	CDT
9/25/1932	02:00	CST
4/30/1933	02:00	CDT
9/24/1933	02:00	CST
4/29/1934	02:00	CDT
9/30/1934	02:00	CST
4/28/1935	02:00	CDT
9/29/1935	02:00	CST
3/01/1936	02:00	CDT
10/31/1936	02:00	CST
4/25/1937	02:00	CDT
9/26/1937	02:00	CST
4/24/1938	02:00	CDT
9/25/1938	02:00	CST
4/30/1939	02:00	CDT
9/24/1939	02:00	CST
4/28/1940	02:00	CDT
9/29/1940	02:00	CST
4/27/1941	02:00	CDT
10/26/1941	02:00	CST
2/09/1942	02:00	CWT
9/30/1945	02:00	EST
6/14/1967	00:01	EDT
10/29/1967	00:01	EST
4/29/1973	02:00	EDT
10/28/1973	02:00	EST
1/06/1974	02:00	EDT
10/27/1974	02:00	EST
4/27/1975	02:00	EDT
10/26/1975	02:00	US#1

MI # 110

Date	Time	Zone
Before 9/18/1885		LMT
9/18/1885	12:00	CST
3/31/1918	02:00	CWT
10/27/1918	02:00	CST
3/30/1919	02:00	CWT
10/26/1919	02:00	CST
4/26/1936	02:00	EST
2/09/1942	02:00	EWT
2/15/1943	02:00	CWT
9/30/1945	02:00	EST
6/14/1967	00:01	EDT
10/29/1967	00:01	EST
4/29/1973	02:00	EDT
10/28/1973	02:00	EST
1/06/1974	02:00	EDT
10/27/1974	02:00	EST
4/27/1975	02:00	EDT
10/26/1975	02:00	US#1

MI # 111

Date	Time	Zone
Before 9/18/1885		LMT
9/18/1885	12:00	CST
3/31/1918	02:00	CWT
10/27/1918	02:00	CST
3/30/1919	02:00	CWT
10/26/1919	02:00	CST
4/26/1931	02:00	CDT
9/27/1931	02:00	CST
10/06/1931	02:00	EST
2/09/1942	02:00	EWT
2/15/1943	02:00	CWT
9/30/1945	02:00	EST
6/14/1967	00:01	EDT
10/29/1967	00:01	EST
4/29/1973	02:00	EDT
10/28/1973	02:00	EST
1/06/1974	02:00	EDT
10/27/1974	02:00	EST
4/27/1975	02:00	EDT
10/26/1975	02:00	US#1

COUNTIES

1 Alcona
2 Alger
3 Allegan
4 Alpena
5 Antrim
6 Arenac
7 Baraga
8 Barry
9 Bay
10 Benzie
11 Berrien
12 Branch
13 Calhoun
14 Cass
15 Charlevoix
16 Cheboygan
17 Chippewa
18 Clare
19 Clinton
20 Crawford
21 Delta
22 Dickinson
23 Eaton
24 Emmet
25 Genesee
26 Gladwin
27 Gogebic
28 Grand Traverse
29 Gratiot
30 Hillsdale
31 Houghton
32 Huron
33 Ingham
34 Ionia
35 Iosco
36 Iron
37 Isabella
38 Jackson
39 Kalamazoo
40 Kalkaska
41 Kent
42 Keweenaw
43 Lake
44 Lapeer
45 Leelanau
46 Lenawee
47 Livingston
48 Luce
49 Mackinac
50 Macomb
51 Manistee
52 Marquette
53 Mason
54 Mecosta
55 Menominee
56 Midland
57 Missaukee
58 Monroe
59 Montcalm
60 Montmorency
61 Muskegon
62 Newaygo
63 Oakland
64 Oceana
65 Ogemaw
66 Ontonagon
67 Osceola
68 Oscoda
69 Otsego
70 Ottawa
71 Presque Isle
72 Roscommon
73 Saginaw
74 St Clair
75 St Joseph
76 Sanilac
77 Schoolcraft
78 Shiawassee
79 Tuscola
80 Van Buren
81 Washtenaw
82 Wayne
83 Wexford

Place		Lat	Long	Time
Abscota 13	1	42N06	85w05	5:40:20
Ackerson Lake 38	90	42N15	84w24	5:37:36
Acme 28	1	44N47	85w28	5:41:52
Ada 41	64	42N59	85w30	5:42:00
Adair 74	1	42N49	82w45	5:31:00
Adams Park 39	100	42N07	85w32	5:42:08
Adamsville 14	72	41N47	86w02	5:44:08
Addison 46	1	41N59	84w21	5:37:24
Adrian 46	5	41N54	84w02	5:36:08
Advance 15	1	45N13	85w01	5:40:04
Aetna 62	57	43N28	85w56	5:43:44
Afton 16	1	45N22	84w30	5:38:00
Agate 66	25	46N28	89w01	5:56:04
Agnew 70	51	42N55	86w09	5:44:36
Ahmeek 42	96	47N18	88w24	5:53:36
Akron 79	1	43N38	83w32	5:34:08
Alabaster 35	1	44N12	83w33	5:34:12
Alaiedon 33	1	42N38	84w25	5:37:40
Alamo 39	92	42N22	85w43	5:42:52
Alanson 24	67	45N27	84w47	5:39:08
Alaska 41	57	42N51	85w30	5:42:00
Alba 5	1	44N59	84w58	5:39:52
Albee 73	1	43N16	83w59	5:35:56
Albert 60	1	44N53	84w17	5:37:08
Alberta 7	25	46N46	88w27	5:53:48
Albion 13	40	42N15	84w45	5:39:00
Albion 31	96	47N15	88w27	5:53:48
Alcona 1	1	44N48	83w25	5:33:40
Alden 5	1	44N53	85w17	5:41:08
Alembic 37	1	43N36	84w46	5:39:04
Algansee 12	1	41N51	84w53	5:39:32
Alger 6	1	44N08	84w07	5:36:28
Algoma 41	57	43N10	85w37	5:42:28
Algonac 74	1	42N37	82w32	5:30:08
Algonquin Lake 8	62	42N39	85w17	5:41:08
Allegan 3	42	42N32	85w51	5:43:24
Allen 30	1	41N57	84w46	5:39:04
Allendale 70	51	42N58	85w57	5:43:48
Allen Park 82	2	42N16	83w13	5:32:52
Allens Cove 58	1	41N48	83w27	5:33:48
Allenton 14	108	41N48	86w05	5:44:20
Allenton 74	1	42N55	82w57	5:31:48
Allenville 49	25	46N00	84w50	5:39:20
Allis 71	1	45N17	84w12	5:36:48
Allouez 42	96	47N19	88w22	5:53:28
Alma 29	44	43N23	84w39	5:38:36
Almeda Beach 72	1	44N30	84w36	5:38:24
Almena 80	72	42N17	85w49	5:43:16
Almer 79	1	43N31	83w24	5:33:36
Almira 10	1	44N44	85w53	5:43:32
Almont 44	1	42N55	83w03	5:32:12
Aloha 16	1	45N30	84w26	5:37:44
Alpena 4	1	45N04	83w27	5:33:48
Alpha 36	86	46N03	88w23	5:53:32
Alpine 41	61	43N04	85w44	5:42:56
Alston 31	25	46N49	88w38	5:54:32
Alto 41	64	42N51	85w23	5:41:32
Altona 54	1	43N33	85w19	5:41:16
Alverno 16	1	44N48	82w55	5:31:40
Amador 76	1	43N16	82w37	5:30:28
Amasa 36	81	46N14	88w27	5:53:48
Amber 53	57	43N58	86w21	5:45:24
Amble 59	57	43N26	85w23	5:41:32
Amboy 30	1	41N43	84w36	5:38:24
Amelith 9	36	43N36	83w54	5:35:36
Anchor Bay Gardens 50	88	42N39	82w48	5:31:12
Anchorville 74	1	42N42	82w41	5:30:44
Anderson 47	1	42N27	83w57	5:35:48
Anderson 56	1	43N37	84w12	5:36:48
Andersonville 63	88	42N45	83w33	5:34:12
Andrews 11	72	41N57	86w20	5:45:20
Ann Arbor 81	38	42N17	83w45	5:35:00
Antioch 83	1	44N23	85w38	5:42:32
Antoine 22	87	45N48	88w04	5:52:16
Antrim 5	1	44N55	85w04	5:40:16
Antrim 78	1	42N49	84w06	5:36:24
Antwerp 80	46	42N12	85w50	5:43:20
Anvil 27	81	46N29	90w03	6:00:12
Applegate 76	1	43N21	82w38	5:30:32
Arbela 79	1	43N15	83w38	5:34:32
Arbutus Beach 69	1	45N02	84w41	5:38:44
Arcada 29	1	43N20	84w40	5:38:40
Arcadia 51	1	44N30	86w14	5:44:56
Arden 11	72	41N57	86w20	5:45:20
Arenac 6	1	44N02	83w52	5:35:28
Argenta 3	102	42N27	85w39	5:42:36
Argentine 25	1	42N48	83w51	5:35:24
Argyle 76	1	43N34	82w56	5:31:44
Arlene 57	1	44N25	85w24	5:41:36
Arlington 80	74	42N18	86w03	5:44:12
Armada 50	1	42N51	82w53	5:31:32
Armstrong Corners 80	46	42N13	85w53	5:43:32
Arnheim 7	25	46N49	88w38	5:54:32
Arnold 52	25	45N54	87w13	5:48:52
Arthur 18	1	43N57	84w40	5:38:40
Arvon 7	25	46N50	88w12	5:52:48
Ash 58	1	42N03	83w21	5:33:24
Ashland 62	64	43N21	85w51	5:43:24
Ashley 29	1	43N11	84w29	5:37:56
Ashmore 79	1	43N39	83w28	5:33:52
Ashton 67	97	43N52	85w31	5:42:04
Askel 31	25	46N49	88w38	5:54:32
Assinins 7	25	46N47	88w30	5:54:00
Assyria 8	57	42N28	85w08	5:40:32
Athens 13	1	42N05	85w14	5:40:56
Atlanta 60	1	45N00	84w09	5:36:36
Atlantic Mine 31	96	47N05	88w38	5:54:32
Atlas 25	1	42N55	83w31	5:34:04
Attica 44	1	43N01	83w10	5:32:40
Atwood 5	1	45N10	85w15	5:41:00
Auburn 9	1	43N36	84w04	5:36:16
Auburn Heights 63	88	42N39	83w14	5:32:56
Au Gres 6	1	44N03	83w42	5:34:48
Augusta 39	92	42N20	85w21	5:41:24
Aura 7	25	46N52	88w19	5:53:16
Aurelius 33	1	42N33	84w32	5:38:08
Aurora 27	81	46N27	90w09	6:00:36
Au Sable 35	1	44N25	83w20	5:33:20
Austin 30	1	41N45	84w45	5:39:00
Austin 52	25	46N17	87w29	5:49:56
Austin Lake 39	47	42N13	85w35	5:42:20
Au Train 2	25	46N26	86w50	5:47:20
Auvinen Corner 27	81	46N27	90w09	6:00:36
Avalon Beach 58	36	41N55	83w23	5:33:32
Avalon Lake 60	1	45N04	83w54	5:35:36
Averill 56	1	43N37	84w12	5:36:48
Avery 11	74	41N48	86w37	5:46:28
Avery 60	1	44N59	84w05	5:36:20
Avoca 74	1	43N04	82w42	5:30:48
Avon 63	88	42N40	83w09	5:32:36
Avondale 61	49	43N12	86w14	5:44:56
Avondale 67	1	43N54	85w16	5:41:04
Azalia 58	1	42N01	83w40	5:34:40
Bach 32	1	43N41	83w21	5:33:24
Backus 72	1	44N18	84w33	5:38:12
Bad Axe 32	1	43N48	83w00	5:32:00
Bagley 55	81	45N28	87w37	5:50:28
Bagley 69	6	44N59	84w41	5:38:44
Baie de Wasai 17	12	46N27	84w15	5:37:00
Bailey 61	64	43N17	85w49	5:43:16
Bainbridge 11	74	42N07	86w17	5:45:08
Bainbridge Center 11	74	42N07	86w17	5:45:08
Bakertown 11	77	41N50	86w22	5:45:28
Baldwin 43	92	43N54	85w51	5:43:24
Ballards 41	64	43N10	85w42	5:42:48
Baltic 31	96	47N05	88w38	5:54:32
Baltimore 8	57	42N33	85w15	5:41:00
Baltimore 66	25	46N31	89w11	5:56:44

Banat 55 81 45N28 87w37 5:50:28
Bancroft 78 1 42N53 84w04 5:36:16
Banfield 8 57 42N27 85w16 5:41:04
Bangor 80 74 42N18 86w07 5:44:28
Bankers 30 1 41N55 84w38 5:38:32
Banks 5 1 45N10 85w18 5:41:12
Banksons Lake 80 46 42N10 85w51 5:43:24
Bannister 29 1 43N08 84w25 5:37:40
Baraga 7 26 46N47 88w30 5:54:00
Barbeau 17 12 46N17 84w17 5:37:08
Barker Creek 40 1 44N46 85w24 5:41:36
Bark River 21 17 45N44 87w18 5:49:12
Bar Lake 51 111 44N19 86w18 5:45:12
Barnard 15 1 45N19 85w15 5:41:00
Barnum 52 25 46N30 87w40 5:50:40
Baroda 11 74 41N57 86w29 5:45:56
Barron Lake 14 105 41N51 86w12 5:44:48
Barry 8 57 42N28 85w23 5:41:32
Barryton 54 1 43N45 85w09 5:40:36
Barton 62 57 43N46 85w37 5:42:28
Barton City 1 1 44N41 83w36 5:34:24
Barton Hills 81 38 42N17 83w42 5:34:48
Barton Lake 39 100 42N05 85w34 5:42:16
Base Line Lake 3 92 42N22 85w53 5:43:32
Bass Lake 53 57 43N51 86w25 5:45:40
Batavia 12 1 41N57 85w06 5:40:24
Batavia Center 12 1 41N57 85w00 5:40:00
Bates 28 1 44N46 85w24 5:41:36
Bates 36 81 46N09 88w36 5:54:24
Bath 19 41 42N49 84w27 5:37:48
Battle Creek 13 43 42N19 85w11 5:40:44
Bauer 70 54 42N52 85w51 5:43:24
Baw Beese Lake 30 1 41N55 84w38 5:38:32
Bay 15 1 45N18 85w03 5:40:12
Bay City 9 36 43N36 83w54 5:35:36
Bay De Noc 21 25 45N45 86w56 5:47:44
Bay Mills 17 110 46N27 84w39 5:38:36
Bay Park 79 1 43N39 83w28 5:33:52
Bay Port 32 1 43N51 83w23 5:33:32
Bayport Park 25 1 42N49 83w43 5:34:52
Bayshore 15 1 45N22 85w06 5:40:24
Bay View 5 1 45N04 85w16 5:41:04
Bay View 24 67 45N22 84w57 5:39:48
Beachwood 65 1 44N25 84w07 5:36:28
Beacon 52 25 46N31 87w58 5:51:52
Beacon Hill 31 25 46N19 87w03 5:48:12
Beadle Lake 13 43 42N16 85w12 5:40:48
Bear Creek 24 67 45N22 84w54 5:39:36
Bearinger 71 1 45N31 84w11 5:36:44
Bearinger Corners 58 1 41N46 83w45 5:35:00
Bear Lake 51 1 44N25 86w09 5:44:36
Beaugrand 16 1 45N40 84w33 5:38:12
Beaver 9 1 43N39 83w57 5:35:48
Beaver 21 25 46N04 87w10 5:48:40
Beaver Creek 20 1 44N33 84w43 5:38:52
Beaverdam 70 54 42N49 86w01 5:44:04
Beaver Grove 52 25 46N33 87w24 5:49:36
Beaver Island 15 1 45N40 85w33 5:42:12
Beaverton 26 1 43N53 84w29 5:37:56
Bedford 13 43 42N23 85w14 5:40:56
Bedore 74 1 42N35 82w34 5:30:16
Beebe 29 1 43N18 84w36 5:38:24
Beech 82 36 42N23 83w17 5:33:08
Beecher 25 1 43N04 83w42 5:34:48
Beechwood 36 81 46N09 88w46 5:55:04
Beechwood 70 52 42N48 86w07 5:44:28
Belding 34 92 43N06 85w14 5:40:56
Belknap 71 1 45N20 83w49 5:35:16
Bellaire 5 1 44N59 85w13 5:40:52
Belle Isle 82 2 42N21 82w58 5:31:52
Belleville 82 36 42N12 83w29 5:33:56
Bellevue 23 1 42N27 85w01 5:40:04
Bell Oak 33 1 42N40 84w10 5:36:40
Belmont 41 61 43N05 85w37 5:42:28
Belsay 25 1 43N01 83w41 5:34:44
Belvedere 15 1 45N19 85w15 5:41:00
Belvidere 59 57 43N25 85w09 5:40:36
Bendon 10 1 44N39 85w46 5:43:04
Bengal 19 1 42N59 84w40 5:38:40
Bennington 78 1 42N54 84w13 5:36:52
Benona 64 57 43N34 86w30 5:46:00
Bentheim 3 97 42N41 86w00 5:44:00
Bentley 9 1 43N57 84w08 5:36:32
Bently Corners 13 1 42N09 84w48 5:39:12
Benton 81 38 42N10 83w47 5:35:08
Benton Central 11 4 42N07 86w25 5:45:40
Benton Harbor 11 4 42N06 86w27 5:45:48
Benton Heights 11 4 42N06 86w27 5:45:48
Benzonia 10 1 44N38 86w05 5:44:20
Bergland 66 25 46N36 89w34 5:58:16
Berkley 63 2 42N30 83w11 5:32:44
Berlamont 80 72 42N23 85w57 5:43:48
Berlin Center 34 92 42N59 85w04 5:40:16
Berrien 11 72 41N56 86w18 5:45:12
Berrien Springs 11 72 41N57 86w20 5:45:20
Bertrand 11 105 41N47 86w16 5:45:04
Berville 74 1 42N55 82w53 5:31:32
Bessemer 27 86 46N29 90w03 6:00:12
Bete Grise 42 96 47N18 88w26 5:53:44
Bethany 29 1 43N25 84w33 5:38:12
Bethany Beach 11 74 41N53 86w37 5:46:28
Bethel 12 1 41N51 85w06 5:40:24
Betzer 30 1 41N47 84w24 5:37:36
Beulah 10 1 44N38 86w06 5:44:24
Beverly 41 61 42N55 85w42 5:42:48
Beverly Hills 52 25 46N30 87w36 5:50:24
Beverly Hills 63 88 42N31 83w16 5:33:04
Big Bay 52 25 46N49 87w44 5:50:56
Big Beaver 63 88 42N34 83w09 5:32:36
Big Creek 68 1 44N38 84w13 5:36:52
Biggs Settlement 68 1 44N39 84w08 5:36:32
Big Prairie 62 57 43N31 85w38 5:42:32
Big Rapids 54 1 43N42 85w29 5:41:56
Big Rock 60 1 45N00 84w09 5:36:36
Billings 26 1 43N52 84w19 5:37:16
Bingham Farms 63 88 42N31 83w17 5:33:08
Birch Beach 76 1 43N16 82w32 5:30:08
Birch Creek 55 81 45N07 87w37 5:50:28
Birch Hill Park 82 36 42N18 83w23 5:33:32
Birch Run 73 1 43N15 83w48 5:35:12
Birchwood 11 74 41N52 86w38 5:46:32
Birchwood 16 1 44N48 82w55 5:31:40
Birmingham 63 89 42N33 83w13 5:32:52
Birmingham Farms 63 88 43N15 83w48 5:35:12
Bishop 62 64 43N25 85w47 5:43:08
Bismarck 71 1 45N18 83w57 5:35:48
Bitely 62 57 43N45 85w52 5:43:28
Black Lake Bluffs 71 1 45N21 84w13 5:36:52
Blackman 38 90 42N17 84w25 5:37:40
Blackmar 73 1 43N15 83w48 5:35:12
Black River 1 1 44N49 83w19 5:33:16
Black River Harbor 27 81 46N27 90w09 6:00:36
Blaine 10 1 44N33 86w11 5:44:44
Blaine 74 1 43N09 82w35 5:30:20
Blair 28 1 44N38 85w39 5:42:36
Blanchard 37 57 43N31 85w05 5:40:20
Blaney Park 77 25 46N00 86w01 5:44:04
Blendon 70 51 42N54 85w58 5:43:52
Bliss 24 67 45N41 84w54 5:39:36
Blissfield 46 1 41N50 83w52 5:35:28
Bloomer 59 57 43N10 84w53 5:39:32
Bloomfield 63 88 42N34 83w16 5:33:04
Bloomfield Glens 63 88 42N32 83w17 5:33:08
Bloomfield Highlands 63 88 42N38 83w19 5:33:16
Bloomfield Hills 63 88 42N35 83w15 5:33:00
Bloomfield Village 63 88 42N33 83w12 5:32:48
Bloomingdale 80 72 42N23 85w56 5:43:44
Blue Creek 11 4 42N06 86w27 5:45:48
Blue Jacket 31 96 47N15 88w27 5:53:48
Blue Water Beach 76 1 43N16 82w32 5:30:08
Blumfield 73 1 43N26 83w45 5:35:00
Blumfield Corners 73 1 43N27 83w42 5:34:48
Boardman 40 1 44N39 85w17 5:41:08
Bohemia 66 25 46N52 88w58 5:55:52
Boichott Acres 19 41 42N45 84w34 5:38:16
Bois Blanc 49 1 45N46 84w28 5:37:52
Bolles Harbor 58 36 41N55 83w23 5:33:32
Bombay 56 1 43N37 84w12 5:36:48
Boon 83 1 44N17 85w36 5:42:24
Bootjack 31 96 47N12 88w24 5:53:36
Borculo 70 54 42N49 86w01 5:44:04
Borland 54 1 43N35 85w27 5:41:48
Boston 31 95 47N08 88w36 5:54:24
Boston 34 92 42N54 85w15 5:41:00
Bostwick Lake 41 65 43N07 85w34 5:42:16
Bourret 26 1 44N08 84w14 5:36:56
Bowens Mills 8 57 42N43 85w28 5:41:52
Bowne 41 64 42N49 85w22 5:41:28
Boyne City 15 1 45N13 85w01 5:40:04
Boyne Falls 15 1 45N10 84w55 5:39:40
Bradley 3 92 42N38 85w39 5:42:36
Bradleyville 79 1 43N34 83w31 5:34:04
Brampton 21 17 45N55 87w03 5:48:12
Branch 53 57 43N57 86w07 5:44:28
Brandon 63 88 42N50 83w23 5:33:32
Brandywine Lake 80 72 42N22 85w53 5:43:32
Brant 73 1 43N16 84w14 5:36:56
Brassar 17 45 46N29 84w21 5:37:24
Bravo 3 92 42N31 86w06 5:44:24
Breckenridge 29 1 43N24 84w29 5:37:56
Breedsville 80 74 42N21 86w04 5:44:16
Breen 22 87 45N59 87w42 5:50:48
Breitung 22 87 45N51 88w00 5:52:00
Brent Creek 25 1 43N04 83w47 5:35:08
Brentwood 61 49 43N12 86w16 5:45:04
Brest 58 1 41N58 83w15 5:33:00
Brethren 51 1 44N18 86w01 5:44:04
Bretton Woods 23 41 42N44 84w36 5:38:24
Brevort 49 25 46N01 85w02 5:40:08
Brice 29 1 43N11 84w43 5:38:52
Bridgehampton 76 1 43N28 82w42 5:30:48
Bridgeport 73 91 43N22 83w53 5:35:32
Bridgeton 62 57 43N21 85w59 5:43:56
Bridgeville 29 1 43N00 84w33 5:38:12
Bridgewater 81 1 42N10 83w54 5:35:36
Bridgman 11 74 41N57 86w33 5:46:12
Brightmoor 82 2 42N24 83w14 5:32:56
Brighton 47 1 42N32 83w47 5:35:08
Briley 60 1 45N00 84w10 5:36:40
Brimley 17 110 46N24 84w34 5:38:16
Brinton 37 1 43N45 85w00 5:40:00
Bristol 41 61 42N59 85w42 5:42:48
Bristol 43 1 44N06 85w28 5:41:52
Britton 46 1 41N59 83w50 5:35:20
Broadway Manor 61 49 43N12 86w14 5:44:56
Brockway 74 1 43N07 82w49 5:31:16
Brohman 62 57 43N41 85w49 5:43:16
Bronson 12 1 41N52 85w12 5:40:48
Brookfield 23 1 42N34 84w50 5:39:20
Brooklands 63 88 42N39 83w09 5:32:36
Brooklyn 38 1 42N07 84w15 5:37:00
Brook Park 61 49 43N12 86w16 5:45:04
Brooks 9 36 43N36 83w54 5:35:36
Brooks 62 64 43N25 85w45 5:43:00
Brookside 61 49 43N12 86w16 5:45:04
Brookside 62 57 43N28 85w56 5:43:44
Brookwood 61 49 43N12 86w16 5:45:04
Broomfield 37 1 43N36 85w01 5:40:04
Brown 51 1 44N19 86w08 5:44:32
Brown City 76 1 43N13 82w59 5:31:56
Brownlee Park 13 43 42N19 85w08 5:40:32
Brownstown 82 36 42N07 83w15 5:33:00
Brownsville 14 73 41N55 86w01 5:44:04
Brownwood Lake 80 46 42N13 85w53 5:43:32
Bruce Crossing 66 32 46N31 89w11 5:56:44
Brunswick 62 57 43N26 86w02 5:44:08
Brutus 24 67 45N30 84w47 5:39:08
Buchanan 11 77 41N50 86w22 5:45:28
Buckeye 26 1 43N57 84w26 5:37:44
Buckhorn 11 72 41N57 86w20 5:45:20
Buckley 83 1 44N30 85w41 5:42:44
Buckroe 52 25 46N33 87w24 5:49:36
Bucks Corners 64 64 43N47 86w26 5:45:44
Buel 76 1 43N18 82w43 5:30:52
Buena Vista 73 91 43N25 83w54 5:35:36
Bullock Creek 56 1 43N37 84w12 5:36:48
Bumbletown 42 96 47N17 88w25 5:53:40
Bunker Hill 33 1 42N28 84w18 5:37:12
Bunny Run 63 88 42N47 83w13 5:32:52
Burdell 67 1 44N07 85w30 5:42:00
Burdickville 45 1 44N51 85w51 5:43:24
Burgess 15 1 45N19 85w15 5:41:00
Burleigh 35 1 44N12 83w49 5:35:16
Burley Corner 13 43 42N20 85w10 5:40:40
Burlingame 41 61 42N55 85w42 5:42:48
Burlington 13 1 42N06 85w05 5:40:20
Burnips 3 92 42N44 85w50 5:43:20
Burns 78 1 42N49 83w59 5:35:56
Burnside 44 1 43N13 83w03 5:32:12
Burr Oak 75 1 41N51 85w19 5:41:16
Burt 73 1 43N14 83w54 5:35:36
Burtchville 74 1 43N07 82w30 5:30:00
Burt Lake 16 1 45N27 84w43 5:38:52
Burton 25 1 43N00 83w39 5:34:36
Burton 78 1 43N00 84w11 5:36:44
Bushnell 59 57 43N10 85w01 5:40:04
Butler 12 1 42N02 84w53 5:39:32
Butman 26 1 44N08 84w21 5:37:24
Butterfield 57 1 44N18 84w55 5:39:40
Butternut 59 57 43N11 84w51 5:39:24
Byron 78 1 42N49 83w57 5:35:48
Byron Center 41 57 42N49 85w42 5:42:48
Cableton 80 93 42N24 86w16 5:45:04
Cadillac 83 8 44N15 85w24 5:41:36
Cadmus 46 1 41N52 84w10 5:36:40
Cady 50 88 42N35 82w54 5:31:36
Calcite 71 1 45N25 83w49 5:35:16
Calderwood 66 25 46N28 89w01 5:56:04
Caldwell 57 1 44N23 85w17 5:41:08
Caledonia 41 57 42N47 85w31 5:42:04
California 12 1 41N48 84w53 5:39:32
Calumet 31 10 47N14 88w27 5:53:48
Calvin 14 72 41N51 85w56 5:43:44
Calvin Center 14 72 41N50 85w56 5:43:44
Cambria 30 1 41N51 84w39 5:38:36
Cambridge 46 1 42N02 84w11 5:36:44
Cambridge Junction 46 1 42N06 84w15 5:37:00
Camden 30 1 41N45 84w46 5:39:04
Campau 74 1 42N58 82w29 5:29:56
Campbell 21 25 46N04 87w10 5:48:40
Campbell 34 94 42N49 85w15 5:41:00
Campbells Corners 65 1 44N17 84w14 5:36:56
Camp Lake 41 64 43N10 85w42 5:42:48
Canada Corners 61 64 43N14 85w47 5:43:08
Canada Creek Ranch 60 1 45N00 84w09 5:36:36
Canada Shores 12 1 41N57 85w00 5:40:00
Canal 17 45 46N29 84w21 5:37:24
Canandaigua 46 1 41N52 84w14 5:36:56
Canfield Beach 71 1 45N21 84w13 5:36:52
Cannon 41 57 43N04 85w30 5:42:00
Cannonsburg 41 57 43N03 85w28 5:41:52
Canton 82 36 42N19 83w28 5:33:52
Capac 74 1 43N01 82w56 5:31:44
Carbondale 55 86 45N20 87w37 5:50:28
Caribou Lake 17 12 46N00 83w54 5:35:36
Carland 78 1 43N03 84w17 5:37:08
Carleton 58 7 42N04 83w24 5:33:36
Carlisle 23 1 42N34 84w50 5:39:20
Carlisle 41 61 42N54 85w38 5:42:32
Carlshend 52 25 46N19 87w13 5:48:52
Carlson 7 25 46N47 88w30 5:54:00
Carlton 8 60 42N43 85w15 5:41:00
Carlton Center 8 60 42N43 85w15 5:41:00
Carmel 23 1 42N33 84w54 5:39:36
Carney 55 86 45N35 87w34 5:50:16
Caro 79 1 43N29 83w24 5:33:36
Carpenter Lake 30 1 41N50 84w45 5:39:00
Carp Lake 24 67 45N42 84w47 5:39:08
Carrollton 73 91 43N28 83w57 5:35:48
Carrs 43 92 43N56 86w02 5:44:08
Carson City 59 57 43N11 84w51 5:39:24
Carsonville 76 1 43N26 82w40 5:30:40
Cascade 41 59 42N54 85w29 5:41:56
Case 71 1 45N17 84w04 5:36:16
Caseville 32 1 43N56 83w16 5:33:04
Cash 76 1 43N25 82w50 5:31:20
Casnovia 61 64 43N14 85w48 5:43:12
Caspian 36 86 46N04 88w38 5:54:32
Cass City 79 1 43N36 83w11 5:32:44
Cassopolis 14 73 41N55 86w01 5:44:04
Castle 73 91 43N25 83w57 5:35:48
Castle Park 3 92 42N47 86w07 5:44:28
Castleton 8 57 42N38 85w08 5:40:32
Cathro 4 1 45N04 83w27 5:33:48
Cato 59 57 43N26 85w16 5:41:04
Cedar 45 1 44N51 85w48 5:43:12

Place		Lat.	Long.	Time
Cedar 67	1	43N57	85w23	5:41:32
Cedar Bend 33	41	42N44	84w26	5:37:44
Cedarcreek 8	57	42N30	85w24	5:41:36
Cedar Lake 59	57	43N24	84w58	5:39:52
Cedar Lake 80	72	42N01	85w49	5:43:16
Cedar River 55	81	45N25	87w22	5:49:28
Cedar Springs 41	64	43N13	85w33	5:42:12
Cedarville 49	25	46N00	84w22	5:37:28
Cedarville 55	81	45N29	87w23	5:49:32
Cement City 46	1	42N04	84w20	5:37:20
Centennial Heights 31	96	47N15	88w27	5:53:48
Center 24	67	45N36	84w54	5:39:36
Center Line 50	2	42N29	83w02	5:32:08
Centerville 45	1	44N54	85w45	5:43:00
Central 42	96	47N18	88w26	5:53:44
Central Lake 5	1	45N04	85w16	5:41:04
Central Park 70	51	42N47	86w07	5:44:28
Centreville 75	103	41N55	85w32	5:42:08
Ceresco 13	43	42N16	85w04	5:40:16
Chamberlains 75	1	42N01	85w49	5:43:16
Champion 52	29	46N31	87w58	5:51:52
Channing 22	87	46N09	88w05	5:52:20
Chapin 73	1	43N10	84w20	5:37:20
Charing Cross Estates 63	88	42N34	83w16	5:33:04
Charleston 39	92	42N18	85w21	5:41:24
Charleston 76	1	43N40	82w47	5:31:08
Charlesworth 23	1	42N31	84w39	5:38:36
Charlevoix 15	1	45N19	85w16	5:41:04
Charlotte 23	1	42N34	84w50	5:39:20
Charlton 69	1	44N59	84w26	5:37:44
Chase 43	1	43N53	85w38	5:42:32
Chassell 31	98	47N01	88w32	5:54:08
Chatham 2	25	46N21	86w56	5:47:44
Chatham Corners 2	25	46N21	86w56	5:47:44
Chauncey 41	61	43N05	85w37	5:42:28
Cheboygan 16	9	45N39	84w29	5:37:56
Chelsea 81	1	42N19	84w01	5:36:04
Cherry Bend 45	1	44N45	85w37	5:42:28
Cherry Grove 83	1	44N13	85w31	5:42:04
Cherry Hill 82	36	42N22	83w29	5:33:56
Cherry Valley 43	92	43N57	85w45	5:43:00
Chesaning 73	1	43N11	84w07	5:36:28
Cheshire 3	92	42N28	85w57	5:43:48
Cheshire Center 3	42	42N32	85w51	5:43:24
Chester 23	1	42N34	84w50	5:39:20
Chesterfield 50	88	42N40	82w49	5:31:16
Chestonia 5	1	44N59	85w01	5:40:04
Chicagon Lake 36	81	46N06	88w20	5:53:20
Chicora 3	42	42N32	85w51	5:43:24
Chief Lake 51	1	44N22	86w01	5:44:04
Chikaming 11	74	41N51	86w38	5:46:32
Chilson 47	1	42N32	83w52	5:35:28
China 74	1	42N47	82w32	5:30:08
Chippewa Lake 54	1	43N45	85w18	5:41:12
Choate 66	11	46N32	89w17	5:57:08
Chocolay 52	25	46N28	87w18	5:49:12
Christie Lake 80	72	42N07	85w58	5:43:52
Christmas 2	22	46N26	86w43	5:46:52
Churchill 61	49	43N12	86w16	5:45:04
Churchill 65	1	44N18	84w04	5:36:16
Church Street 25	1	43N01	83w42	5:34:48
Circle Pine Center 8	57	42N30	85w24	5:41:36
Cisco Lake 27	81	46N13	89w11	5:56:44
Clair Haven 50	88	42N36	82w49	5:31:16
Clam Lake 83	1	44N12	85w24	5:41:36
Clam River 5	1	44N59	85w13	5:40:52
Clam Union 57	1	44N13	85w02	5:40:08
Clare 18	1	43N49	84w46	5:39:04
Claremont 61	49	43N12	86w16	5:45:04
Clarence 13	1	42N23	84w46	5:39:04
Clarenceville 63	88	42N27	83w19	5:33:16
Clarendon 13	1	42N07	84w53	5:39:32
Clarion 15	1	45N10	84w55	5:39:40
Clark 49	25	46N01	84w22	5:37:28
Clarklake 38	1	42N07	84w21	5:37:24
Clarkston 63	88	42N44	83w25	5:33:40
Clarksville 34	92	42N50	85w15	5:41:00
Clawson 63	2	42N32	83w09	5:32:36
Clay 74	1	42N38	82w35	5:30:20
Claybanks 64	57	43N31	86w26	5:45:44
Clays Landing 74	1	42N35	82w34	5:30:16
Clayton 46	1	41N52	84w14	5:36:56
Clear Lake 65	1	44N17	84w14	5:36:56
Clear Lake 75	97	41N57	85w38	5:42:32
Clearwater 40	1	44N49	85w16	5:41:04
Clement 26	1	44N08	84w20	5:37:20
Cleon 51	1	44N28	85w52	5:43:28
Cleveland 45	1	44N55	85w52	5:43:28
Clifford 44	1	43N19	83w11	5:32:44
Climax 39	101	42N14	85w20	5:41:20
Clinton 46	1	42N04	83w58	5:35:52
Clinton River Meadows 50	88	42N34	83w02	5:32:08
Clinton Village 33	41	42N47	84w31	5:38:04
Clintonville 63	88	42N41	83w20	5:33:20
Clio 25	1	43N11	83w44	5:34:56
Cloverdale 8	57	42N32	85w23	5:41:32
Cloverville 61	49	43N12	86w14	5:44:56
Clyde 63	88	42N41	83w37	5:34:28
Coal Dock 52	25	46N33	87w24	5:49:36
Coats Grove 8	57	42N41	85w11	5:40:44
Coddes Beach 71	1	45N21	84w13	5:36:52
Cody 25	1	43N00	83w39	5:34:36
Coe 37	1	43N31	84w40	5:38:40
Cohoctah 47	1	42N46	83w57	5:35:48
Cohoctah Center 47	1	42N39	84w04	5:36:16
Colberry Park 63	88	42N34	83w16	5:33:04
Cold Springs 40	1	44N49	85w02	5:40:08
Coldwater 12	4	41N57	85w00	5:40:00
Coleman 56	1	43N46	84w35	5:38:20
College Park 82	2	42N25	83w09	5:32:36
College Town 9	36	43N36	83w54	5:35:36
Colling 79	1	43N39	83w28	5:33:52
Collins 34	92	42N59	84w57	5:39:48
Coloma 11	74	42N11	86w19	5:45:16
Colon 75	1	41N57	85w19	5:41:16
Colonville 18	1	43N50	84w46	5:39:04
Columbia 38	1	42N07	84w18	5:37:12
Columbiaville 44	1	43N09	83w25	5:33:40
Columbus Grove 58	1	41N48	83w27	5:33:48
Colwood 79	1	43N39	83w28	5:33:52
Comins 68	1	44N44	84w02	5:36:08
Commerce 63	88	42N36	83w29	5:33:56
Comstock 39	47	42N18	85w29	5:41:56
Comstock Park 41	61	43N02	85w40	5:42:40
Concord 38	1	42N11	84w38	5:38:32
Cone 58	1	42N00	83w32	5:34:08
Conklin 70	51	43N08	85w52	5:43:28
Connorville 27	86	46N29	89w56	5:59:44
Constantine 75	92	41N50	85w40	5:42:40
Convis 13	1	42N23	85w00	5:40:00
Conway 24	67	45N25	84w52	5:39:28
Conway 47	1	42N44	84w06	5:36:24
Cooks 77	33	45N55	86w30	5:46:00
Cooks Corners 34	92	43N06	85w14	5:40:56
Cooper 39	92	42N22	85w34	5:42:16
Cooper Center 39	92	42N22	85w34	5:42:16
Coopersville 70	55	43N04	85w57	5:43:48
Copemish 51	1	44N29	85w55	5:43:40
Copenhagen 77	14	45N58	86w15	5:45:00
Copper City 31	96	47N17	88w23	5:53:32
Copper Harbor 42	96	47N28	87w53	5:51:32
Coral 59	64	43N22	85w24	5:41:36
Corey 14	97	41N57	85w38	5:42:32
Corey Lake 75	97	41N57	85w38	5:42:32
Corinne 49	25	46N06	85w42	5:42:48
Corinth 41	57	42N49	85w42	5:42:48
Cornell 21	25	45N55	87w14	5:48:56
Corunna 78	1	42N59	84w07	5:36:28
Corwith 69	1	45N09	84w39	5:38:36
Coryell Islands 49	25	46N00	84w22	5:37:28
Cottage Grove 72	1	44N30	84w36	5:38:24
Cottage Park 17	12	46N22	84w26	5:37:44
Cottrellville 74	1	42N42	82w34	5:30:16
Court 39	47	42N17	85w35	5:42:20
Courtland 41	57	43N10	85w30	5:42:00
Covert 80	74	42N17	86w16	5:45:04
Covington 7	18	46N33	88w32	5:54:08
Cranbrook 63	88	42N34	83w16	5:33:04
Crapo 54	97	43N51	85w27	5:41:48
Crawford 37	1	43N36	84w46	5:39:04
Creighton 77	25	46N21	86w18	5:45:12
Crescent Lake Estates 63	88	42N39	83w24	5:33:36
Cressey 8	57	42N27	85w22	5:41:28
Creswell 5	1	44N56	85w22	5:41:28
Crisp 70	51	42N47	86w07	5:44:28
Crockery 70	97	43N05	86w05	5:44:20
Crofton 40	1	44N38	85w17	5:41:08
Crooked Lake 8	57	42N30	85w24	5:41:36
Crooked Lake 47	1	42N32	83w47	5:35:08
Cross Village 24	67	45N39	85w00	5:40:00
Croswell 76	1	43N16	82w37	5:30:28
Crotch Lake 75	1	41N48	85w25	5:41:40
Croton 62	57	43N25	85w37	5:42:28
Croton Heights 62	64	43N25	85w47	5:43:08
Crump 9	1	43N44	83w58	5:35:52
Crystal 59	57	43N16	84w55	5:39:40
Crystal Beach 12	1	41N57	85w00	5:40:00
Crystal Falls 36	82	46N05	88w20	5:53:20
Crystalia 10	1	44N38	86w14	5:44:56
Crystal Lake 10	1	44N38	86w12	5:44:48
Crystall Falls 36	82	46N05	88w20	5:53:20
Crystal Valley 64	64	43N42	86w22	5:45:28
Cumber 76	1	43N42	82w56	5:31:44
Cumming 65	1	44N23	84w04	5:36:16
Cunard 55	81	45N42	87w37	5:50:28
Curran 1	1	44N43	83w48	5:35:12
Curtis 1	1	44N33	83w43	5:34:52
Curtis 49	25	46N12	85w45	5:43:00
Curtis 56	1	43N46	84w35	5:38:20
Curtisville 1	1	44N28	83w53	5:35:32
Custer 53	64	43N57	86w13	5:44:52
Cutlerville 41	61	42N50	85w40	5:42:40
Dafter 17	12	46N22	84w26	5:37:44
Daggett 55	86	45N28	87w37	5:50:28
Dailey 14	73	41N55	86w01	5:44:04
Dallas 19	1	42N59	84w47	5:39:08
Dalton 61	57	43N20	86w13	5:44:52
Damon 65	1	44N25	84w07	5:36:28
Danak 9	36	43N36	83w54	5:35:36
Danby 34	92	42N49	84w54	5:39:36
Danish Landing 20	1	44N40	84w43	5:38:52
Dansville 33	1	42N34	84w19	5:37:16
Darragh 40	1	44N44	85w11	5:40:44
Daugherty Corners 39	47	42N17	85w34	5:42:16
Davis 50	88	42N04	85w08	5:40:32
Davisburg 63	88	42N45	83w33	5:34:12
Davison 25	1	43N02	83w31	5:34:04
Day 59	57	43N20	85w02	5:40:08
Dayton 11	106	41N48	86w30	5:46:00
Daytona 79	1	43N29	83w24	5:33:36
Dayton Center 62	57	43N28	85w56	5:43:44
Dealno 6	1	44N03	83w41	5:34:44
Dearborn 82	2	42N19	83w11	5:32:44
Dearborn Heights 82	2	42N20	83w18	5:33:12
Decatur 80	72	42N07	85w58	5:43:52
Decker 76	1	43N28	83w03	5:32:12
Deckerville 76	1	43N32	82w44	5:30:56
Deep River 6	1	44N02	83w59	5:35:56
Deerfield 46	1	41N53	83w47	5:35:08
Deerfield Center 37	1	43N36	84w46	5:39:04
Deerfield Center 47	1	42N49	83w47	5:35:08
Deer Park 48	25	46N41	85w34	5:42:16
Deerton 2	25	46N29	87w03	5:48:12
Deford 79	1	43N31	83w11	5:32:44
Delaware 76	1	43N39	82w41	5:30:44
Delaware Mine 42	96	47N18	88w26	5:53:44
Delhi 33	41	42N38	84w32	5:38:08
Delhi 81	38	42N17	83w45	5:35:00
Delray 82	2	42N18	83w08	5:32:32
Delta 23	41	42N44	84w38	5:38:32
Delta Mills 23	41	42N45	84w34	5:38:16
Delton 8	57	42N30	85w24	5:41:36
Delwin 37	1	43N36	84w46	5:39:04
Denmark 79	1	43N26	83w39	5:34:36
Denton 82	36	42N16	83w32	5:34:08
Derby 11	74	42N01	86w31	5:46:04
De Tour Village 17	12	46N00	83w54	5:35:36
Detroit 82	2	42N20	83w03	5:32:12
Detroit Beach 58	1	41N56	83w19	5:33:16
Detroit River 82	2	42N22	83w04	5:32:16
Devereaux 38	1	42N20	84w43	5:38:52
Devils Lake 46	1	41N59	84w17	5:37:08
De Witt 19	41	42N51	84w34	5:38:16
Dexter 81	1	42N20	83w53	5:35:32
Diamond Lake 62	64	43N33	85w46	5:43:04
Diamond Shores 14	73	41N55	86w01	5:44:04
Diamond Springs 3	97	42N41	86w00	5:44:00
Dice 73	1	43N32	84w07	5:36:28
Dice Corners 56	1	43N37	84w12	5:36:48
Dickson 51	1	44N18	85w56	5:43:44
Diffin 2	25	46N14	87w00	5:48:00
Dighton 67	1	44N06	85w28	5:41:52
Dimondale 23	41	42N39	84w39	5:38:36
Diorite 52	11	46N32	87w48	5:51:12
Disco 50	88	42N37	83w02	5:32:08
Dixboro 81	38	42N19	83w40	5:34:40
Dixon 2	25	46N20	86w51	5:47:24
Dodgeville 31	95	47N05	88w35	5:54:20
Dollar Bay 31	96	47N07	88w30	5:54:00
Dollarville 48	24	46N21	85w32	5:42:08
Dolph 57	1	44N15	85w05	5:40:20
Dominican 46	1	41N54	84w02	5:36:08
Donaldson 17	45	46N29	84w21	5:37:24
Donken 31	25	46N56	88w49	5:55:16
Dorr 3	92	42N44	85w43	5:42:52
Dorrance 12	1	41N57	85w00	5:40:00
Doster 3	92	42N29	85w33	5:42:12
Douglas 3	92	42N39	86w12	5:44:48
Douglass 59	57	43N20	85w09	5:40:36
Dover 18	1	43N50	84w46	5:39:04
Dover 81	1	42N20	83w53	5:35:32
Dowagiac 14	71	41N59	86w07	5:44:28
Dowling 8	57	42N31	85w15	5:41:00
Downington 76	1	43N31	82w44	5:30:56
Doyle 77	25	46N10	86w03	5:44:12
Drayton Plains 63	88	42N42	83w23	5:33:32
Drenthe 70	54	42N49	86w01	5:44:04
Dresden Village 50	88	42N34	83w02	5:32:08
Drummond 17	12	45N59	83w43	5:34:52
Drummond Island 17	12	46N01	83w44	5:34:56
Dryburg 17	12	46N12	84w44	5:38:56
Dryden 44	1	42N56	83w09	5:32:36
Dublin 51	1	44N13	85w58	5:43:52
Duck Lake 3	92	42N22	85w53	5:43:32
Duck Lake 13	1	42N25	84w46	5:39:04
Duel 9	1	43N37	84w12	5:36:48
Duffield 25	1	42N59	83w47	5:35:08
Dukes 52	25	46N23	87w15	5:49:00
Dumont Lake 3	42	42N32	85w51	5:43:24
Duncan 16	1	44N48	82w55	5:31:40
Duncan 31	25	46N31	88w50	5:55:20
Dundee 58	1	41N57	83w40	5:34:40
Dunham 27	86	46N23	89w41	5:58:44
Dunningville 3	42	42N32	85w51	5:43:24
Duplain 19	1	43N04	84w26	5:37:44
Durand 78	70	42N55	83w59	5:35:56
Dwight 32	1	43N59	82w57	5:31:48
Eagle 19	1	42N49	84w47	5:39:08
Eagle Harbor 42	96	47N24	88w10	5:52:40
Eagle Lake 14	108	41N48	86w04	5:44:16
Eagle Lake 80	46	42N13	85w53	5:43:32
Eagle Point 14	73	41N55	86w01	5:44:04
Eagle River 42	10	47N25	88w18	5:53:12
Eames 63	88	42N41	83w20	5:33:20
East Bay 28	1	44N43	85w32	5:42:08
East China 74	1	42N46	82w29	5:29:56
East Comstock 39	92	42N18	85w31	5:42:04
East Cooper 39	92	42N22	85w33	5:42:12
East Dayton 79	1	43N29	83w24	5:33:36
East Detroit 50	2	42N28	82w57	5:31:48
Eastern Heights 41	61	42N54	85w38	5:42:32
East Gilead 12	1	41N52	85w12	5:40:48
East Grand Rapids 41	61	42N57	85w37	5:42:28
East Houghton 31	25	46N19	87w03	5:48:12
East Jordan 15	1	45N10	85w07	5:40:28
East Kingsford 22	87	45N47	88w04	5:52:16
Eastlake 51	111	44N15	86w18	5:45:12
Eastland Center 82	2	42N25	82w54	5:31:36
East Lansing 33	41	42N44	84w29	5:37:56
Eastlawn 81	36	42N14	83w36	5:34:24
East Leroy 13	1	42N10	85w13	5:40:52

Eastmanville 70	55	43N04	85w59	5:43:56
East Melvindale 82	2	42N17	83w11	5:32:44
Easton 34	92	43N00	85w07	5:40:28
Easton 78	1	43N00	84w11	5:36:44
Eastover Farms 63	88	42N34	83w16	5:33:04
East Paris 41	61	42N54	85w38	5:42:32
Eastport 5	1	45N07	85w21	5:41:24
East Rockwood 82	36	42N03	83w13	5:32:52
East Saugatuck 3	74	42N41	86w06	5:44:24
East Sebwa 34	97	42N46	85w00	5:40:00
East Side 25	1	43N02	83w42	5:34:48
East Tawas 35	1	44N17	83w29	5:33:56
East Thetford 25	1	43N08	83w44	5:34:56
Eastview 50	1	42N48	83w01	5:32:04
Eastwood 39	47	42N19	85w32	5:42:08
Eaton 23	1	42N33	84w46	5:39:04
Eaton Rapids 23	1	42N31	84w39	5:38:36
Eau Claire 11	72	41N59	86w18	5:45:12
Eben Junction 2	25	46N21	86w58	5:47:52
Echo 5	1	45N04	85w09	5:40:36
Eckerman 17	12	46N22	85w02	5:40:08
Eckford 13	1	42N12	84w53	5:39:32
Ecorse 82	2	42N15	83w09	5:32:36
Eden 33	1	42N35	84w27	5:37:48
Edenville 56	1	43N46	84w25	5:37:40
Edgemont Park 33	41	42N44	84w36	5:38:24
Edgerton 41	65	43N07	85w34	5:42:16
Edgewater 11	1	42N05	86w30	5:46:00
Edgewater Heights 82	36	42N12	83w31	5:34:04
Edgewood 29	1	43N18	84w36	5:38:24
Edgewood 61	49	43N12	86w14	5:44:56
Edmore 59	57	43N25	85w03	5:40:12
Edwards 65	1	44N13	84w18	5:37:12
Edwardsburg 14	108	41N48	86w06	5:44:24
Edwards Corners 75	1	42N01	85w49	5:43:16
Egelston 61	57	43N14	86w06	5:44:24
Eight Point Lake 18	1	43N51	85w00	5:40:00
Elba 44	1	43N03	83w19	5:33:16
Elberta 10	1	44N37	86w14	5:44:56
Elbridge 64	57	43N41	86w13	5:44:52
Elbridge Center 64	64	43N42	86w22	5:45:28
Elizabeth Lake Estates 63	88	42N39	83w24	5:33:36
Elkland 79	1	43N38	83w11	5:32:44
Elk Rapids 5	1	44N54	85w25	5:41:40
Elkton 32	1	43N49	83w11	5:32:44
Ellington 79	1	43N32	83w17	5:33:08
Ellis 16	1	45N20	84w33	5:38:12
Ellsworth 5	1	45N10	85w15	5:41:00
Elmdale 41	57	42N51	85w15	5:41:00
Elmer 76	1	43N25	82w50	5:31:20
Elm Grove 18	1	43N50	84w46	5:39:04
Elm Hall 29	1	43N22	84w50	5:39:20
Elmira 69	1	45N04	84w51	5:39:24
Elm River 31	25	46N54	88w51	5:55:24
Elo 31	25	46N49	88w38	5:54:32
Eloise 82	36	42N19	83w22	5:33:28
Elsie 19	1	43N05	84w23	5:37:32
Elwell 29	1	43N23	84w45	5:39:00
Ely 52	25	46N27	87w48	5:51:12
Emerald 54	1	43N54	85w16	5:41:04
Emerson 17	12	46N22	85w02	5:40:08
Emerson 29	1	43N20	84w33	5:38:12
Emerson Highlands 61	49	43N12	86w14	5:44:56
Emmett 74	1	42N59	82w46	5:31:04
Empire 45	1	44N49	86w04	5:44:16
Engadine 49	25	46N08	85w34	5:42:16
Englishville 41	64	43N10	85w42	5:42:48
Ensign 21	25	45N54	86w53	5:47:32
Ensley 62	57	43N20	85w37	5:42:28
Ensley Center 62	57	43N17	85w31	5:42:04
Enterprise 57	1	44N23	84w55	5:39:40
Entrican 59	57	43N18	85w05	5:40:20
Epsilon 24	67	45N22	84w57	5:39:48
Erie 58	1	41N46	83w30	5:34:00
Erwin 27	81	46N23	90w05	6:00:20
Escanaba 21	19	45N45	87w04	5:48:16
Essex 19	1	43N05	84w40	5:38:40
Essexville 9	1	43N37	83w50	5:35:20
Estey 26	1	43N54	84w11	5:36:44
Estral Beach 58	1	41N59	83w14	5:32:56
Euclid Center 11	4	42N06	86w27	5:45:48
Eureka 19	1	43N06	84w31	5:38:04
Eureka 59	57	43N10	85w16	5:41:04
Evangeline 15	1	45N15	85w01	5:40:04
Evans 41	64	43N13	85w33	5:42:12
Evans Lake 46	1	42N01	84w04	5:36:16
Evart 67	1	43N54	85w15	5:41:00
Eveline 15	1	45N14	85w09	5:40:36
Everett 62	64	43N31	85w45	5:43:00
Evergreen Acres 58	36	41N55	83w23	5:33:32
Evergreen Park 70	68	43N04	86w11	5:44:44
Evergreen Shores 49	25	45N55	84w44	5:38:56
Ewen 66	25	46N32	89w17	5:57:08
Ewing 52	25	46N05	87w18	5:49:12
Excelsior 40	1	44N44	85w02	5:40:08
Exeter 58	1	42N03	83w28	5:33:52
Eyedywild Beach 69	1	45N02	84w41	5:38:44
Fabius 75	97	41N57	85w42	5:42:48
Factoryville 75	1	42N01	85w21	5:41:24
Fairbanks 21	25	45N40	86w40	5:46:40
Fairfax 75	1	41N57	85w19	5:41:16
Fairfield 46	1	41N54	84w02	5:36:08
Fairfield Addition 61	49	43N12	86w14	5:44:56
Fairgrove 79	1	43N32	83w33	5:34:12
Fairhaven 32	1	43N48	83w24	5:33:36
Fair Haven 74	1	42N41	82w39	5:30:36
Fair Plain 11	4	42N05	86w27	5:45:48
Fairport 21	25	45N38	86w40	5:46:40
Fairview 68	1	44N44	84w03	5:36:12
Faithorn 55	81	45N39	87w45	5:51:00
Falmouth 57	1	44N15	85w05	5:40:20
Fargo 74	1	43N04	82w42	5:30:48
Farmers Creek 44	1	42N56	83w17	5:33:08
Farmington 63	88	42N28	83w23	5:33:32
Farmington Acres 63	88	42N29	83w21	5:33:24
Farmington Hills 63	88	42N28	83w23	5:33:32
Farmwood 61	49	43N12	86w16	5:45:04
Farrandville 25	1	43N08	83w44	5:34:56
Farwell 18	1	43N50	84w52	5:39:28
Fawn River 75	1	41N48	85w21	5:41:24
Fayette 21	25	45N43	86w40	5:46:40
Fayette 30	1	41N58	84w40	5:38:40
Federal Station 63	88	42N38	83w17	5:33:08
Felch 22	87	46N00	87w50	5:51:20
Felch Mountain 22	87	46N01	87w50	5:51:20
Fenkell 82	2	42N24	83w08	5:32:32
Fenmore 73	1	43N08	84w25	5:37:40
Fennville 3	74	42N36	86w06	5:44:24
Fenton 25	1	42N48	83w42	5:34:48
Fenwick 59	57	43N09	85w05	5:40:20
Fern 53	64	43N57	86w13	5:44:52
Ferndale 61	49	43N12	86w14	5:44:56
Ferndale 63	2	42N28	83w08	5:32:32
Ferris 59	57	43N20	84w54	5:39:36
Ferry 64	57	43N36	86w13	5:44:52
Ferrysburg 70	68	43N05	86w13	5:44:52
Fibre 17	12	46N12	84w44	5:38:56
Fife Lake 28	1	44N35	85w21	5:41:24
Filer 51	111	44N13	86w18	5:45:12
Filer City 51	111	44N13	86w18	5:45:12
Filion 32	1	43N54	83w00	5:32:00
Fillmore 3	74	42N43	86w04	5:44:16
Findley 75	1	41N51	85w19	5:41:16
Fisher 41	61	42N55	85w42	5:42:48
Fisher Building 82	2	42N22	83w04	5:32:16
Fishers Lake 75	97	41N57	85w38	5:42:32
Fisherville 9	1	43N36	84w05	5:36:20
Fish Lake 75	1	41N48	85w25	5:41:40
Fitchburg 33	1	42N27	84w11	5:36:44
Five Lakes 44	1	43N03	83w19	5:33:16
Five Points 82	36	42N23	83w17	5:33:08
Flat Rock 21	25	45N51	87w01	5:48:04
Flat Rock 82	37	42N06	83w17	5:33:08
Flint 25	39	43N01	83w41	5:34:44
Florence 75	94	41N52	85w36	5:42:24
Florida 31	96	47N15	88w27	5:53:48
Flowerfield 75	92	42N02	85w43	5:42:52
Flushing 25	1	43N04	83w51	5:35:24
Flynn 76	1	43N17	82w55	5:31:40
Foote Site Village 35	1	44N25	83w20	5:33:20
Forbes 36	81	46N06	88w39	5:54:36
Ford Lake 53	57	44N03	86w11	5:44:44
Ford River 21	11	45N43	87w10	5:48:40
Forest Beach 24	67	45N26	84w59	5:39:56
Forester 76	1	43N31	82w36	5:30:24
Forest Grove 70	54	42N52	85w51	5:43:24
Forest Grove Station 70	54	42N52	85w51	5:43:24
Forest Hills 41	61	42N56	85w35	5:42:20
Forest Home 5	1	44N59	85w15	5:41:00
Forest Lake 2	25	46N20	86w51	5:47:24
Forestville 76	1	43N40	82w37	5:30:28
Fork 54	1	43N46	85w09	5:40:36
Forsyth 52	11	46N17	87w24	5:49:36
Fort Dearborn 82	2	42N18	83w15	5:33:00
Fort Gratiot 74	1	43N02	82w28	5:29:52
Fort Shelby 82	2	42N22	83w04	5:32:16
Fortune Lake 36	81	46N06	88w20	5:53:20
Fort Wayne Junction 30	1	41N59	84w40	5:38:40
Foster 65	1	44N23	84w18	5:37:12
Foster City 22	87	45N58	87w45	5:51:00
Fosters 73	1	43N15	83w48	5:35:12
Fostoria 79	1	43N15	83w22	5:33:28
Fountain 53	57	44N03	86w11	5:44:44
Fountain Park 30	1	41N53	84w33	5:38:12
Four Mile Corner 48	25	46N21	85w30	5:42:00
Four Mile Lake 81	1	42N20	83w53	5:35:32
Four Towns 63	88	42N39	83w24	5:33:36
Fowler 19	1	43N00	84w44	5:38:56
Fowlerville 47	1	42N39	84w04	5:36:16
Fox 55	81	45N25	87w22	5:49:28
Francisco 38	1	42N15	84w12	5:36:48
Frandor 33	41	42N44	84w31	5:38:04
Frankenlust 9	1	43N33	83w59	5:35:56
Frankenmuth 73	1	43N20	83w44	5:34:56
Frankentrost 73	91	43N25	83w55	5:35:40
Frankfort 10	1	44N38	86w14	5:44:56
Franklin 63	88	42N32	83w18	5:33:12
Franklin Knolls 63	88	42N32	83w17	5:33:08
Franklin Mine 31	95	47N08	88w36	5:54:24
Fraser 50	88	42N32	82w57	5:31:48
Freda 31	96	47N08	88w49	5:55:16
Freda 31	25	46N19	87w03	5:48:12
Frederic 20	1	44N47	84w45	5:39:00
Fredonia 13	1	42N12	85w00	5:40:00
Freedom 81	1	42N13	83w57	5:35:48
Freeland 73	1	43N32	84w07	5:36:28
Freeman 18	1	43N57	85w01	5:40:04
Freeport 8	64	42N46	85w19	5:41:16
Free Soil 53	57	44N07	86w14	5:44:56
Freiburgers 76	1	43N42	82w56	5:31:44
Fremont 62	58	43N28	85w57	5:43:48
French Landing 82	36	42N13	83w22	5:33:28
Frenchtown 58	36	41N57	83w22	5:33:28
French Town 64	64	43N47	86w26	5:45:44
Friendship 24	67	45N31	85w02	5:40:08
Frontier 30	1	41N47	84w36	5:38:24
Frost 18	1	44N06	84w47	5:39:08
Frost 73	1	43N32	84w07	5:36:28
Frost Corners 34	92	42N52	84w54	5:39:36
Fruitland 61	64	43N21	86w20	5:45:20
Fruitport 61	97	43N07	86w09	5:44:36
Fuller 27	81	46N13	89w11	5:56:44
Fulton 29	1	43N10	84w40	5:38:40
Fulton 39	92	42N06	85w22	5:41:28
Fulton 42	96	47N18	88w26	5:53:44
Fulton Center 29	1	43N11	84w41	5:38:44
Gaastra 36	86	46N03	88w36	5:54:24
Gagetown 79	1	43N39	83w15	5:33:00
Gaines 25	1	42N52	83w55	5:35:40
Galesburg 39	92	42N17	85w26	5:41:44
Galewood 41	61	42N55	85w42	5:42:48
Galien 11	106	41N47	86w31	5:46:04
Ganges 3	92	42N33	86w12	5:44:48
Garden 21	25	45N47	86w34	5:46:16
Garden City 82	36	42N20	83w21	5:33:24
Garden Corners 21	33	45N54	86w32	5:46:08
Gardendale 74	1	42N58	82w29	5:29:56
Gardenville 17	45	46N29	84w21	5:37:24
Gardner 55	81	45N28	87w37	5:50:28
Garth 21	25	45N56	86w58	5:47:52
Gay 42	96	47N14	88w10	5:52:40
Gaylord 69	1	45N02	84w41	5:38:44
Geddes 81	38	42N17	83w42	5:34:48
General Post Office 82	2	42N22	83w04	5:32:16
Genesee 25	1	43N07	83w37	5:34:28
Genoa 47	1	42N34	83w50	5:35:20
Georgetown 70	54	42N54	85w50	5:43:20
Gera 73	1	43N20	83w44	5:34:56
Germfask 77	25	46N15	85w56	5:43:44
Gerrish 72	1	44N28	84w41	5:38:44
Gibbs City 36	86	46N06	88w39	5:54:36
Gibbs Corners 67	1	43N54	85w11	5:40:44
Gibraltar 82	36	42N05	83w11	5:32:44
Gibson 9	1	43N57	84w06	5:36:24
Gidding 7	25	46N49	88w38	5:54:32
Gilchrist 49	25	46N06	85w27	5:41:48
Gilead 12	1	41N47	85w07	5:40:28
Gilford 79	1	43N31	83w38	5:34:32
Gingell 63	88	42N41	83w20	5:33:20
Girard 12	1	42N02	85w00	5:40:00
Gladstone 21	13	45N51	87w01	5:48:04
Gladwin 26	1	43N59	84w29	5:37:56
Glen Arbor 45	1	44N54	85w59	5:43:56
Glendale 80	72	42N19	85w57	5:43:48
Glendora 11	74	41N53	86w29	5:45:56
Glengary 63	88	42N32	83w27	5:33:48
Glen Haven 45	1	44N51	85w48	5:43:12
Glenn 3	92	42N31	86w14	5:44:56
Glennie 1	1	44N34	83w43	5:34:52
Glenwood 14	71	41N59	86w07	5:44:28
Glenwood Forest 41	61	42N54	85w38	5:42:32
Gobles 80	72	42N22	85w53	5:43:32
Goddyne 9	36	43N37	83w51	5:35:24
Godwin 41	61	42N55	85w42	5:42:48
Godwin Heights 41	61	42N55	85w42	5:42:48
Goetzville 17	12	46N03	84w05	5:36:20
Gogebic 27	86	46N23	89w41	5:58:44
Golden 64	64	43N41	86w27	5:45:48
Golfcrest 58	36	41N55	83w23	5:33:32
Golfside 81	38	42N16	83w43	5:34:52
Goodar 65	1	44N28	83w57	5:35:48
Goodells 74	1	42N59	82w40	5:30:40
Good Hart 24	67	45N34	85w07	5:40:28
Gooding 41	64	43N10	85w42	5:42:48
Goodison 63	88	42N39	83w09	5:32:36
Goodland 44	1	43N07	83w03	5:32:12
Goodrich 25	1	42N55	83w31	5:34:04
Goodwell 62	57	43N36	85w37	5:42:28
Gordon Beach 11	75	41N50	86w42	5:46:48
Gordonville 56	1	43N37	84w12	5:36:48
Gore 32	1	43N58	82w45	5:31:00
Gormer 67	1	44N06	85w09	5:40:36
Gotts 32	1	43N56	83w16	5:33:04
Gould City 49	25	46N06	85w42	5:42:48
Gourley 55	81	45N36	87w23	5:49:32
Gowen 59	57	43N15	85w18	5:41:12
Graafschap 3	92	42N47	86w07	5:44:28
Graham Lake 13	43	42N20	85w11	5:40:44
Grandale Gardens 82	36	42N23	83w17	5:33:08
Grand Beach 11	109	41N46	86w47	5:47:08
Grand Blanc 25	1	42N56	83w38	5:34:32
Grand Circus Park 82	2	42N20	83w03	5:32:12
Grand Haven 70	68	43N04	86w13	5:44:52
Grand Island 2	25	46N30	86w40	5:46:40
Grand Junction 80	72	42N24	86w04	5:44:16
Grand Ledge 23	1	42N45	84w45	5:39:00
Grand Marais 2	80	46N40	85w59	5:43:56
Grand Rapids 41	61	42N58	85w40	5:42:40
Grand River 82	2	42N21	83w06	5:32:24
Grand Valley 70	51	42N58	85w52	5:43:28
Grand Valley State College 70	51	42N58	85w57	5:43:48
Grand View 16	1	45N25	84w37	5:38:28
Grand View Beach 16	1	45N25	84w37	5:38:28
Grandview Beach 58	1	41N52	83w27	5:33:48

Grandville 41 61 42N54 85W46 5:43:04
Granite Bluff 22 87 45N48 88W04 5:52:16
Grant 62 64 43N20 85W51 5:43:24
Grant Center 54 1 43N42 85W29 5:41:56
Grape 58 36 41N55 83W23 5:33:32
Grass Lake 38 1 42N15 84W13 5:36:52
Gratiot 82 2 42N21 83W01 5:32:04
Grattan 41 57 43N04 85W23 5:41:32
Gravel Lake 80 46 42N10 85W51 5:43:24
Grawn 28 1 44N40 85W42 5:42:48
Grayling 20 1 44N40 84W43 5:38:52
Great Lake Beach 76
1 43N16 82W32 5:30:08
Great Western 36 81 46N06 88W20 5:53:20
Greeley 4 1 45N05 83W43 5:34:52
Green 66 25 46N52 89W18 5:57:12
Greenbush 1 1 44N35 83W19 5:33:16
Greendale 56 1 43N36 84W32 5:38:08
Greenfield Park 13
43 42N20 85W11 5:40:44
Greenfield Village 82
2 42N18 83W15 5:33:00
Green Garden 52 25 46N33 87W24 5:49:36
Green Lake 3 92 42N47 85W31 5:42:04
Green Lake 28 1 44N39 85W45 5:43:00
Greenland 66 25 46N47 89W06 5:56:24
Greenleaf 76 1 43N38 83W04 5:32:16
Green Oak 47 1 42N29 83W44 5:34:56
Green River 5 1 44N55 85W04 5:40:16
Greenville 59 57 43N11 85W15 5:41:00
Greenwood 65 1 44N08 84W07 5:36:28
Gregory 47 1 42N28 84W05 5:36:20
Greilickville 45 1 44N45 85W37 5:42:28
Gresham 23 1 42N34 84W50 5:39:20
Grim 26 1 44N00 84W14 5:36:56
Grind Stone City 32
1 44N03 82W54 5:31:36
Groos 21 25 45N51 87W01 5:48:04
Gros Cap 49 25 45N53 84W49 5:39:16
Grosse Ile 82 2 42N08 83W08 5:32:32
Grosse Pointe 82 2 42N24 82W55 5:31:40
Grosse Pointe Farms 82
2 42N24 82W54 5:31:36
Grosse Pointe Park 82
2 42N23 82W56 5:31:44
Grosse Pointe Shores 82
2 42N26 82W53 5:31:32
Grosse Pointe Woods 82
2 42N27 82W54 5:31:36
Grosvenor 46 1 41N50 83W52 5:35:28
Grout 26 1 43N57 84W33 5:38:12
Groveland 63 88 42N50 83W31 5:34:04
Gulliver 77 25 46N00 86W01 5:44:04
Gull Lake 39 92 42N23 85W27 5:41:48
Gun Lake 53 57 44N06 86W13 5:44:52
Gunplain 3 102 42N27 85W36 5:42:24
Gustin 1 1 44N39 83W27 5:33:48
Gwinn 52 16 46N17 87W27 5:49:48
Haakwood 16 1 45N16 84W36 5:38:24
Hadley 44 1 42N56 83W23 5:33:32
Hagar 11 74 42N11 86W23 5:45:32
Hagar Shores 11 74 42N12 86W20 5:45:20
Hagensville 71 1 45N25 83W49 5:35:16
Hagerman Lake 36 81 46N06 88W39 5:54:36
Haight 66 25 46N24 89W11 5:56:44
Hale 35 1 44N23 83W48 5:35:12
Halls Corner 54 1 43N37 85W14 5:40:56
Hamar 7 25 46N47 88W30 5:54:00
Hamburg 47 1 42N28 83W50 5:35:20
Hamilton 3 97 42N41 86W00 5:44:00
Hammond Bay 71 1 45N24 84W05 5:36:20
Hampton 9 1 43N36 83W49 5:35:16
Hamtramck 82 2 42N24 83W03 5:32:12
Hancock 31 95 47N08 88W35 5:54:20
Handy 47 1 42N38 84W06 5:36:24
Hannah 28 1 44N35 85W32 5:42:08
Hanover 38 1 42N06 84W33 5:38:12
Harbert 11 74 41N52 86W38 5:46:32
Harbor Beach 32 88 43N51 82W39 5:30:36
Harbor Haven 61 49 43N12 86W16 5:45:04
Harbor Hills 61 49 43N12 86W16 5:45:04
Harbor Park 61 49 43N12 86W16 5:45:04
Harbor Point 24 67 45N26 84W59 5:39:56
Harbor Springs 24
67 45N26 85W00 5:40:00
Hardwood 22 87 45N58 87W42 5:50:48
Haring 83 1 44N19 85W24 5:41:36
Harlan 51 1 44N29 85W55 5:43:40
Harlem 70 51 42N47 86W07 5:44:28
Harper 82 2 42N24 83W00 5:32:00
Harper Woods 82 2 42N27 82W56 5:31:44
Harrietta 83 1 44N19 85W42 5:42:48
Harris 55 86 45N47 87W23 5:49:32
Harrisburg 70 66 43N12 85W57 5:43:48
Harrison 18 1 44N01 84W48 5:39:12
Harrisville 1 1 44N39 83W17 5:33:08
Harsens Island 74 1 42N35 82W34 5:30:16
Hart 64 64 43N42 86W22 5:45:28
Hartford 80 74 42N13 86W10 5:44:40
Hartland 47 1 42N39 83W44 5:34:56
Hartwick 67 1 44N02 85W14 5:40:56
Harvey 52 25 46N29 87W22 5:49:28
Harwood 22 87 45N57 87W42 5:50:48
Haslett 33 1 42N45 84W24 5:37:36
Hastings 8 62 42N39 85W17 5:41:08
Hatton 18 1 43N57 84W47 5:39:08
Hautala Corner 27
81 46N27 90W09 6:00:36
Havana 73 1 43N08 84W10 5:36:40
Hawes 1 1 44N44 83W30 5:34:00
Hawk Head 3 93 42N24 86W16 5:45:04
Hawkins 62 97 43N52 85W31 5:42:04
Hawks 71 1 45N18 83W53 5:35:32
Hay 26 1 43N58 84W19 5:37:16
Haynes 1 1 44N44 83W20 5:33:20

Hazelhurst Camp 11
74 41N52 86W38 5:46:32
Hazel Park 63 2 42N28 83W06 5:32:24
Hazelton 78 1 43N05 83W59 5:35:56
Heath 3 97 42N39 85W57 5:43:48
Hebron 16 1 45N41 84W40 5:38:40
Helena 5 1 44N54 85W15 5:41:00
Hell 47 1 42N27 83W57 5:35:48
Helps 55 86 45N48 87W22 5:49:28
Hemans 76 1 43N28 83W03 5:32:12
Hematite 36 86 46N18 88W29 5:53:56
Hemlock 73 1 43N25 84W14 5:36:56
Henderson 78 1 43N05 84W12 5:36:48
Henderson 83 1 44N12 85W38 5:42:32
Hendricks 49 25 46N09 85W11 5:40:44
Henrietta 38 1 42N23 84W18 5:37:12
Henry Street 61 49 43N12 86W16 5:45:04
Herman 7 25 46N40 88W22 5:53:28
Hermansville 55 86 45N42 87W36 5:50:24
Herrington 70 51 43N02 85W50 5:43:20
Herron 4 1 45N01 83W39 5:34:36
Hersey 67 97 43N51 85W27 5:41:48
Hesperia 64 57 43N34 86W03 5:44:12
Hessel 49 25 46N00 84W26 5:37:44
Hetherton 60 1 44N59 84W27 5:37:48
Hiawatha 36 81 46N06 88W39 5:54:36
Hiawatha 77 25 46N06 86W18 5:45:12
Hickory Corners 8
57 42N27 85W22 5:41:28
Hickory Heights 63
88 42N34 83W16 5:33:04
Hickory Island 82 2 42N08 83W09 5:32:36
Higgins 72 1 44N26 84W33 5:38:12
Higgins Lake 72 1 44N26 84W42 5:38:48
High Island 15 1 45N44 85W41 5:42:44
Highland 63 88 42N38 83W37 5:34:28
Highland Park 39 92 42N23 85W27 5:41:48
Highland Park 82 2 42N24 83W06 5:32:24
Highland View 61 49 43N12 86W16 5:45:04
Highway 31 96 47N15 88W27 5:53:48
Higman Park 11 4 42N06 86W27 5:45:48
Hill 65 1 44N23 83W57 5:35:48
Hillcrest 27 81 46N27 90W09 6:00:36
Hillcrest Orchard 58
1 41N52 83W27 5:33:48
Hilliards 3 92 42N37 85W46 5:43:04
Hillman 60 1 45N04 83W54 5:35:36
Hills and Dales 41
61 43N00 85W38 5:42:32
Hills Corners 11 74 41N57 86W29 5:45:56
Hillsdale 30 1 41N56 84W38 5:38:32
Hillside Gardens 38
90 42N15 84W24 5:37:36
Hinchman 11 72 41N57 86W20 5:45:20
Hinton 54 1 43N31 85W16 5:41:04
Hockaday 26 1 43N59 84W29 5:37:56
Hodunk 12 1 42N37 83W26 5:33:44
Holland 70 53 42N47 86W07 5:44:28
Holloway 46 1 41N59 83W50 5:35:20
Holly 63 88 42N48 83W38 5:34:32
Hollywood 11 1 42N05 86W30 5:46:00
Holmes 55 81 45N32 87W44 5:50:56
Holt 33 41 42N39 84W31 5:38:04
Holton 61 57 43N25 86W05 5:44:20
Home Acres 41 61 42N54 85W38 5:42:32
Home Acres 61 49 43N12 86W14 5:44:56
Homer 13 1 42N09 84W49 5:39:16
Homer 36 81 46N06 88W39 5:54:36
Homestead 10 1 44N39 85W59 5:43:56
Homestead 17 45 46N29 84W21 5:37:24
Hongore Bay 16 1 45N21 84W13 5:36:52
Honor 10 1 44N40 86W01 5:44:04
Hooper 3 102 42N27 85W39 5:42:36
Hope 56 1 43N46 84W20 5:37:20
Hopkins 3 92 42N37 85W46 5:43:04
Hopkinsburg 3 92 42N37 85W46 5:43:04
Hopwood Acres 33 41 42N44 84W31 5:38:04
Horr 37 1 43N41 84W58 5:39:52
Horton 38 1 42N09 84W31 5:38:04
Horton 65 1 44N12 84W11 5:36:44
Horton Bay 15 1 45N13 85W01 5:40:04
Houghton 31 95 47N07 88W34 5:54:16
Houghton Lake 72 1 44N18 84W45 5:39:00
Houghton Lake Heights 72
1 44N19 84W46 5:39:04
Houghton Point 72 1 44N18 84W45 5:39:00
Houserville 29 1 43N23 84W39 5:38:36
Howard 14 105 41N51 86W11 5:44:44
Howard City 59 64 43N24 85W28 5:41:52
Howardsville 75 1 42N01 85W49 5:43:16
Howell 47 1 42N36 83W56 5:35:44
Howlandsburg 39 92 42N17 85W25 5:41:40
Hoxeyville 83 1 44N11 85W43 5:42:52
Hoytville 23 92 42N46 84W54 5:39:36
Hubbard Lake 4 1 44N52 83W35 5:34:20
Hubbardston 34 92 43N06 84W50 5:39:20
Hubbell 31 96 47N11 88W26 5:53:44
Hudson 46 1 41N51 84W21 5:37:24
Hudson Mills 81 1 42N20 83W53 5:35:32
Hudsonville 70 54 42N52 85W52 5:43:28
Hulbert 17 12 46N21 85W09 5:40:36
Hulbert Corners 17
12 46N21 85W09 5:40:36
Humboldt 52 25 46N24 87W54 5:51:36
Hume 32 1 43N58 83W03 5:32:12
Hunters Creek 44 1 43N03 83W19 5:33:16
Huntington Woods 63
2 42N29 83W09 5:32:36
Huron Beach 71 1 45N30 84W06 5:36:24
Huron Gardens 63 88 42N39 83W24 5:33:36
Huronia Heights 76
1 43N16 82W32 5:30:08
Huron Mountain 52
25 46N49 87W44 5:50:56
Hurontown 31 25 46N19 87W03 5:48:12
Hutula 7 25 46N32 88W36 5:54:24

Hylas 22 87 45N58 87W42 5:50:48
Ida 58 1 41N55 83W34 5:34:16
Idlewild 43 92 43N54 85W46 5:43:04
Imlay 44 1 43N02 83W04 5:32:16
Imperial Heights 7
25 46N34 88W16 5:53:04
Ina 67 1 44N06 85W28 5:41:52
Independence 63 88 42N44 83W23 5:33:32
Indianfield 39 47 42N13 85W35 5:42:20
Indianfields 79 1 43N28 83W24 5:33:36
Indian Lake 14 72 41N59 86W12 5:44:48
Indian River 16 1 45N25 84W37 5:38:28
Indiantown 73 91 43N25 83W55 5:35:40
Indian Village 61
49 43N12 86W16 5:45:04
Industrial Home 46
1 41N54 84W02 5:36:08
Ingalls 55 86 45N23 87W37 5:50:28
Ingallston 55 81 45N18 87W29 5:49:56
Ingersoll 56 1 43N31 84W14 5:36:56
Ingham 33 1 42N33 84W17 5:37:08
Ingleside 16 1 45N38 84W47 5:39:08
Inkster 82 2 42N18 83W19 5:33:16
Inland 10 1 44N39 85W53 5:43:32
Inland Corners 10 1 44N39 85W46 5:43:04
Interior 66 25 46N26 89W03 5:56:12
Interlaken 61 49 43N16 86W16 5:45:04
Interlochen 28 1 44N39 85W46 5:43:04
Inverness 16 1 45N35 84W31 5:38:04
Inwood 77 25 46N03 86W27 5:45:48
Ionia 34 92 42N59 85W04 5:40:16
Iosco 47 1 42N33 84W05 5:36:20
Ira 74 1 42N42 82W40 5:30:40
Iron Mountain 22 83 45N49 88W04 5:52:16
Iron River 36 84 46N06 88W39 5:54:36
Irons 43 1 44N08 85W55 5:43:40
Ironton 15 1 45N19 85W15 5:41:00
Ironwood 27 85 46N27 90W09 6:00:36
Irving 8 64 42N44 85W22 5:41:28
Isabella 21 25 45N56 86W58 5:47:52
Isabella 37 1 43N41 84W47 5:39:08
Isadore 45 1 44N51 85W48 5:43:12
Ishpeming 52 20 46N29 87W40 5:50:40
Island Lake 47 1 41N59 83W50 5:35:20
Island Park 39 92 42N23 85W27 5:41:48
Island View 21 25 45N43 87W18 5:49:12
Isle Royale 42 25 48N00 88W54 5:55:36
Isle Royale National Pk 42
25 48N00 88W54 5:55:36
Ithaca 29 1 43N18 84W36 5:38:24
Iva 73 1 43N25 84W14 5:36:56
Ivanrest 41 61 42N54 85W44 5:42:56
Jackson 38 90 42N15 84W24 5:37:36
Jacobsville 31 96 47N12 88W24 5:53:36
Jam 56 1 43N25 84W20 5:37:20
James 73 1 43N22 84W03 5:36:12
Jamestown 70 54 42N50 85W51 5:43:24
Jasper 46 1 41N48 84W02 5:36:08
Jeddo 74 1 43N09 82W35 5:30:20
Jefferson 38 1 42N06 84W15 5:37:00
Jefferson 82 2 42N22 82W59 5:31:56
Jenison 70 54 42N54 85W49 5:43:16
Jenison Park 70 51 42N47 86W07 5:44:28
Jennings 57 1 44N20 85W12 5:40:48
Jerome 30 1 42N01 84W28 5:37:52
Jerome 56 1 43N41 84W25 5:37:40
Jessieville 27 81 46N27 90W09 6:00:36
Johannesburg 69 1 44N59 84W27 5:37:48
Johnsons Landing 55
81 45N07 87W37 5:50:28
Johnstown 8 57 42N28 85W15 5:41:00
Jones 14 72 41N54 85W48 5:43:12
Jonesfield 73 1 43N26 84W20 5:37:20
Jonesville 30 1 41N59 84W40 5:38:40
Joppa 13 1 42N10 85W13 5:40:52
Jordan 5 1 45N05 85W02 5:40:08
Jossman Acres 63 88 42N43 83W25 5:33:40
Joyfield 10 1 44N33 86W06 5:44:24
Joyfield 82 2 42N18 83W13 5:32:52
Juddville 78 1 42N59 84W07 5:36:28
Jugville 62 64 43N33 85W46 5:43:04
Juhl 76 1 43N20 83W05 5:32:20
Juniata 79 1 43N26 83W31 5:34:04
Kalamazoo 39 47 42N17 85W35 5:42:20
Kalamo 23 1 42N33 85W01 5:40:04
Kaleva 51 1 44N22 86W01 5:44:04
Kalkaska 40 1 44N44 85W11 5:40:44
Karlin 28 1 44N35 85W47 5:43:08
Kasson 45 1 44N49 85W53 5:43:32
Kawkawlin 9 1 43N39 83W57 5:35:48
Kearney 5 1 45N00 85W08 5:40:32
Kearsarge 31 25 46N27 90W09 6:00:36
Keego Harbor 63 88 42N37 83W21 5:33:24
Keeler 80 72 42N06 86W11 5:44:44
Keene 34 92 42N59 85W15 5:41:00
Keewahdin Beach 74
1 42N58 82W29 5:29:56
Kegomic 24 67 45N22 84W57 5:39:48
Kellogg 3 92 42N33 85W46 5:43:04
Kelloggsville 41 62 42N39 85W17 5:41:08
Kellys Corners 61
66 43N12 85W57 5:43:48
Kendall 80 72 42N22 85W49 5:43:16
Kenockee 74 1 43N02 82W41 5:30:44
Kensington 82 2 42N24 82W56 5:31:44
Kent City 41 64 43N12 85W45 5:43:00
Kenton 31 25 46N28 88W54 5:55:36
Kentwood 41 61 42N53 85W36 5:42:24
Kerby 78 1 42N59 84W07 5:36:28
Kercheval 82 2 42N23 82W57 5:31:48
Kerns Corner 40 1 44N44 85W11 5:40:44
Kerr Hill 44 1 42N55 83W31 5:34:04
Kessington 14 108 41N48 86W05 5:44:20
Kewadin 5 1 44N56 85W22 5:41:28
Keweenaw Bay 7 27 46N52 88W29 5:53:56
Keystone 28 1 44N45 85W37 5:42:28

Kibbie 80	93	42N24	86w16	5:45:04
Killmaster 1	1	44N39	83w18	5:33:12
Kilmanagh 32	1	43N44	83w27	5:33:48
Kimball 74	1	42N57	82w33	5:30:12
Kincheloe 17	12	46N16	84w29	5:37:56
Kincheloe Air Force Base 17	12	46N14	84w28	5:37:52
Kinde 32	1	43N56	83w00	5:32:00
Kinderhook 12	1	41N47	85w00	5:40:00
Kingsford 22	87	45N48	88w04	5:52:16
Kings Landing 11	105	41N57	86w18	5:45:12
Kingsley 28	1	44N35	85w32	5:42:08
Kings Mill 44	1	43N14	83w12	5:32:48
Kingston 79	1	43N25	83w11	5:32:44
Kinneville 33	1	42N31	84w39	5:38:36
Kinney 41	61	42N59	85w42	5:42:48
Kinross 17	12	46N17	84w31	5:38:04
Kipling 21	13	45N52	87w01	5:48:04
K I Sawyer Air Force Base 52	25	46N20	87w22	5:49:28
Kissipee 60	1	44N59	84w27	5:37:48
Kisslers Corner 53	66	43N12	85w57	5:43:48
Kiva 2	25	46N16	87w02	5:48:08
Klacking 65	1	44N23	84w11	5:36:44
Klinger Lake 75	1	41N48	85w25	5:41:40
Klingville 31	96	47N01	88w32	5:54:08
Kloman 55	81	45N41	87w32	5:50:08
Klondike 64	57	43N34	86w02	5:44:08
Kneeland 68	1	44N39	84w08	5:36:32
Knollwood Park 38	90	42N14	84w24	5:37:36
Kochville 73	91	43N28	83w59	5:35:56
Koehler 16	1	45N25	84w31	5:38:04
Koss 55	81	45N25	87w37	5:50:28
Koylton 79	1	43N22	83w10	5:32:40
Krakow 71	1	45N17	83w35	5:34:20
Kurtz 1	1	44N34	83w43	5:34:52
Kyro 7	25	46N49	88w38	5:54:32
La Branch 55	86	45N48	87w22	5:49:28
Lacey 8	57	42N27	85w01	5:40:04
Lachine 4	1	45N05	83w43	5:34:52
Lac La Belle 42	96	47N18	88w26	5:53:44
Lacota 80	72	42N24	86w08	5:44:32
Ladoga 2	25	46N12	86w58	5:47:52
Lafayette 29	1	43N20	84w26	5:37:44
La Grange 14	73	41N57	86w02	5:44:08
La Grange Park 43	92	43N54	85w51	5:43:24
Laing 76	1	43N28	82w58	5:31:52
Laingsburg 78	1	42N54	84w21	5:37:24
Laird 31	25	46N42	88w48	5:55:12
Lake 18	1	43N51	85w00	5:40:00
Lake Angeline 52	25	46N30	87w40	5:50:40
Lake Angelus 63	88	42N42	83w19	5:33:16
Lake Ann 10	1	44N44	85w50	5:43:20
Lake City 57	1	44N20	85w13	5:40:52
Lake Fenton 25	1	42N49	83w43	5:34:52
Lake George 18	1	43N58	84w57	5:39:48
Lake Gerald 31	25	46N56	88w49	5:55:16
Lake Harbor 61	49	43N12	86w16	5:45:04
Lake Harbor Estates 61	49	43N12	86w16	5:45:04
Lake Harbor Hills 61	49	43N12	86w16	5:45:04
Lake Harbor Point 61	49	43N12	86w16	5:45:04
Lakeland 47	1	42N28	83w51	5:35:24
Lake Lansing 33	1	42N45	84w24	5:37:36
Lake Leelanau 45	1	44N59	85w43	5:42:52
Lake Linden 31	96	47N11	88w24	5:53:36
Lake Margrethe 20	1	44N40	84w43	5:38:52
Lake Michigan Beach 11	74	42N13	86w22	5:45:28
Lake Michigan Estates 61	49	43N12	86w16	5:45:04
Lake Nepessing 44	1	43N03	83w19	5:33:16
Lake Odessa 34	92	42N47	85w08	5:40:32
Lake of the Woods 12	1	41N57	85w00	5:40:00
Lake Orion 63	88	42N47	83w14	5:32:56
Lake Orion Heights 63	88	42N46	83w16	5:33:04
Lake Pleasant 44	1	43N02	83w10	5:32:40
Lakeport 74	1	43N07	82w30	5:30:00
Lake Roland 31	25	46N19	87w03	5:48:12
Lake Sherwood 63	88	42N36	83w29	5:33:56
Lake Shore 3	92	42N39	86w12	5:44:48
Lakeside 11	75	41N51	86w40	5:46:40
Lakeside 32	1	44N03	83w00	5:32:00
Laketon 61	49	43N16	86w18	5:45:12
Laketown 3	92	42N44	86w10	5:44:40
Lakeview 11	75	41N50	86w42	5:46:48
Lakeview 13	43	42N17	85w12	5:40:48
Lakeview 59	57	43N26	85w17	5:41:08
Lakeville 63	88	42N49	83w09	5:32:36
Lakewood 39	47	42N14	85w35	5:42:20
Lakewood 52	25	46N33	87w24	5:49:36
Lakewood 58	1	41N48	83w27	5:33:48
Lakewood Club 61	57	43N22	86w15	5:45:00
Lakewood Point 11	74	42N11	86w19	5:45:16
Lamar 41	61	42N55	85w42	5:42:48
Lamb 74	1	42N59	82w40	5:30:40
Lambertville 58	7	41N46	83w38	5:34:32
Lamont 70	97	43N01	86w09	5:44:36
Lamotte 76	1	43N28	83w02	5:32:08
Langport 29	1	43N25	84w20	5:37:20
Langston 59	57	43N18	85w05	5:40:20
L'Anse 7	79	46N43	88w19	5:53:16
Lansing 33	41	42N44	84w33	5:38:12
Lapeer 44	1	43N03	83w19	5:33:16
Lapeer Heights 25	1	43N00	83w35	5:34:20
Lapeer Junction 44	1	43N03	83w19	5:33:16
Laporte 56	1	43N32	84w07	5:36:28
Larkin 56	1	43N42	84w14	5:36:56
Larson Beach 1	1	44N51	83w28	5:33:52
La Salle 58	1	41N51	83w28	5:33:52
La Salle Gardens 63	88	42N39	83w24	5:33:36
Lathrop 21	11	46N04	87w10	5:48:40
Lathrup Village 63	2	42N30	83w12	5:32:48
Laurel 76	1	43N25	82w50	5:31:20
Laurium 31	96	47N14	88w27	5:53:48
Lawndale 39	47	42N17	85w34	5:42:16
Lawndale 73	91	43N27	83w57	5:35:48
Lawnel Subdivision 61	49	43N12	86w16	5:45:04
Lawrence 80	72	42N13	86w03	5:44:12
Lawson 52	25	46N23	87w15	5:49:00
Lawton 80	104	42N10	85w50	5:43:20
Layton Corners 73	1	42N19	84w01	5:36:04
Leaton 37	1	43N36	84w46	5:39:04
Leavitt 64	57	43N41	86w06	5:44:24
Lebanon 19	1	43N04	84w47	5:39:08
Lee Center 13	1	42N27	84w55	5:39:40
Leedys Gardens 58	36	41N55	83w23	5:33:32
Leelanau 45	1	45N06	85w38	5:42:32
Leetsville 40	1	44N55	85w04	5:40:16
LeGraph 82	2	42N17	83w17	5:33:08
Leighton 3	92	42N44	85w36	5:42:24
Leisure 3	93	42N24	86w16	5:45:04
Leland 45	1	45N01	85w45	5:43:00
Lemon Park 39	100	42N07	85w32	5:42:08
Lenawee Junction 46	1	41N52	83w56	5:35:44
Lennon 78	1	42N59	83w56	5:35:44
Lenox 50	88	42N46	82w48	5:31:12
Leo 7	18	46N32	88w32	5:54:08
Leonard 63	88	42N52	83w08	5:32:32
Leoni 38	90	42N15	84w19	5:37:16
Leonidas 75	1	42N02	85w21	5:41:24
Le Roy 67	1	44N02	85w27	5:41:48
Les Cheneaux Club 49	25	45N59	84w22	5:37:28
Leslie 33	1	42N27	84w26	5:37:44
Level Park 13	43	42N20	85w11	5:40:44
Levering 24	67	45N38	84w47	5:39:08
Lewiston 60	1	44N53	84w18	5:37:12
Lexington 76	1	43N16	82w32	5:30:08
Lexington Heights 76	1	43N16	82w32	5:30:08
Liberty 38	1	42N04	84w21	5:37:24
Lidke's Corners 53	57	43N57	86w17	5:45:08
Lilley 62	57	43N46	85w51	5:43:24
Lima 81	1	42N18	83w57	5:35:48
Lime Island 17	12	46N03	84w05	5:36:20
Limestone 2	25	46N15	87w02	5:48:08
Lincoln 1	1	44N41	83w25	5:33:40
Lincoln Estates 61	49	43N12	86w16	5:45:04
Lincoln Meadows 61	49	43N12	86w16	5:45:04
Lincoln Park 61	49	43N12	86w16	5:45:04
Lincoln Park 82	2	42N15	83w11	5:32:44
Linden 25	1	42N49	83w47	5:35:08
Lindland's Subdivision 61	49	43N12	86w16	5:45:04
Linwood 9	1	43N44	83w58	5:35:52
Linwood 82	2	42N23	83w07	5:32:28
Lisbon 41	57	43N08	85w52	5:43:28
Liske 71	1	45N18	83w53	5:35:32
Litchfield 30	1	42N03	84w46	5:39:04
Littlefield 24	67	45N26	84w48	5:39:12
Little Lake 52	17	46N17	87w20	5:49:20
Little Point Sable 64	64	43N37	86w22	5:45:28
Little Summer Island 21	25	45N37	86w41	5:46:44
Little Traverse 24	67	45N26	84w55	5:39:40
Little Venice 23	92	42N46	84w54	5:39:36
Livernois 82	2	42N20	83w08	5:32:32
Livingston 69	1	45N04	84w41	5:38:44
Livonia 82	36	42N23	83w23	5:33:32
Loch Alpine 81	38	42N17	83w45	5:35:00
Locke 33	1	42N44	84w12	5:36:48
Lockport 75	97	41N57	85w36	5:42:24
Locust Corners 30	1	41N51	84w21	5:37:24
Lodi 40	1	44N44	85w11	5:40:44
Lodi 81	38	42N13	83w50	5:35:20
London 58	1	42N02	83w36	5:34:24
Long Beach 61	49	43N12	86w16	5:45:04
Long Lake 18	1	44N01	84w48	5:39:12
Long Lake 28	1	44N44	85w45	5:43:00
Long Lake 30	1	41N50	84w45	5:39:00
Long Lake 34	92	43N04	85w08	5:40:32
Long Lake 35	1	44N25	83w52	5:35:28
Long Point 16	1	44N48	82w55	5:31:40
Long Rapids 4	1	45N09	83w42	5:34:48
Longrie 55	81	45N25	87w37	5:50:28
Loomis 37	1	43N50	84w46	5:39:04
Loon Lake 63	88	42N33	83w30	5:34:00
Loretto 22	87	45N47	87w49	5:51:16
Lottivue 50	88	42N40	82w47	5:31:08
Loud 60	1	44N54	84w04	5:36:16
Lovells 20	1	44N48	84w29	5:37:56
Lowell 41	57	42N56	85w20	5:41:20
Lower Pewabic 31	95	47N08	88w36	5:54:24
Lucas 57	1	44N12	85w13	5:40:52
Luce 73	1	42N19	84w01	5:36:04
Ludington 53	63	43N57	86w27	5:45:48
Lulu 58	1	41N55	83w34	5:34:16
Lum 44	1	43N06	83w09	5:32:36
Luna Pier 58	1	41N48	83w27	5:33:48
Lupton 65	1	44N26	84w01	5:36:04
Luther 43	1	44N02	85w41	5:42:44
Luzerne 68	1	44N37	84w16	5:37:04
Lyndon 81	1	42N23	84w04	5:36:16
Lynn 74	1	43N07	82w56	5:31:44
Lyon Lake 13	1	42N16	84w58	5:39:52
Lyon Manor 72	1	44N28	84w44	5:38:56
Lyons 34	92	42N59	84w58	5:39:52
Mable 28	1	44N46	85w24	5:41:36
Macatawa 70	51	42N46	86w13	5:44:52
Mackinac Island 49	25	45N51	84w37	5:38:28
Mackinaw 16	1	45N45	84w41	5:38:44
Mackinaw City 16	1	45N47	84w44	5:38:56
Macomb 50	88	42N40	82w54	5:31:36
Macon 46	1	42N03	83w50	5:35:20
Madison 46	1	41N52	84w03	5:36:12
Madison Heights 63	2	42N30	83w06	5:32:24
Mancelona 5	1	44N54	85w04	5:40:16
Manchester 81	1	42N09	84w02	5:36:08
Mangum 52	25	46N33	87w24	5:49:36
Manistee 51	111	44N15	86w19	5:45:16
Manistique 77	14	45N57	86w15	5:45:00
Manitou Beach 46	1	41N58	84w19	5:37:16
Manitou Beach 71	1	45N25	83w49	5:35:16
Manlius 3	74	42N38	86w05	5:44:20
Mansfield 36	86	46N07	88w11	5:52:44
Manton 83	1	44N25	85w24	5:41:36
Maple 82	2	42N19	83w10	5:32:40
Maple City 45	1	44N51	85w51	5:43:24
Maple Forest 20	1	44N49	84w39	5:38:36
Maple Grove 52	25	46N23	87w15	5:49:00
Maple Grove 61	64	43N25	86w22	5:45:28
Maple Grove Downs 61	49	43N12	86w16	5:45:04
Maple Hill 59	57	43N19	85w30	5:42:00
Maplehurst 13	43	42N20	85w11	5:40:44
Maplehurst 61	49	43N12	86w16	5:45:04
Maple Lake 80	46	42N13	85w53	5:43:32
Maple Leaf 74	1	42N35	82w34	5:30:16
Maple Rapids 19	1	43N06	84w42	5:38:48
Maple Ridge 6	1	44N07	83w48	5:35:12
Maple River 24	67	45N31	84w47	5:39:08
Mapleton 28	1	44N45	85w37	5:42:28
Mapleton 56	1	43N37	84w12	5:36:48
Maple Valley 72	1	44N23	84w25	5:37:40
Maplewood 3	92	42N47	86w07	5:44:28
Marathon 44	1	43N12	83w24	5:33:36
Marble Lake 12	1	41N57	84w53	5:39:32
Marcellus 14	72	42N02	85w49	5:43:16
Marengo 13	1	42N18	84w53	5:39:32
Marenisco 27	86	46N23	89w45	5:59:00
Marilla 51	1	44N22	85w54	5:43:36
Marine City 74	1	42N43	82w30	5:30:00
Marion 67	1	44N06	85w09	5:40:36
Marion Springs 73	1	43N16	84w14	5:36:56
Markey 72	1	44N23	84w40	5:38:40
Marlborough 43	92	43N54	85w51	5:43:24
Marlette 76	1	43N20	83w05	5:32:20
Marne 70	51	43N02	85w50	5:43:20
Marquette 52	21	46N33	87w24	5:49:36
Marshall 13	1	42N16	84w58	5:39:52
Martin 3	92	42N32	85w39	5:42:36
Martinsville 82	36	42N14	83w29	5:33:56
Martiny 54	1	43N41	85w16	5:41:04
Marysville 74	1	42N54	82w29	5:29:56
Mason 31	96	47N10	88w26	5:53:44
Mason 33	1	42N35	84w27	5:37:48
Masonville 21	35	45N55	86w59	5:47:56
Mass 66	25	46N45	89w05	5:56:20
Mastodon 36	86	46N01	88w19	5:53:16
Matchwood 66	25	46N36	89w27	5:57:48
Matherton 34	92	43N06	84w50	5:39:20
Mathias 2	25	46N12	86w54	5:47:36
Mattawan 80	72	42N13	85w47	5:43:08
Matteson 12	1	41N56	85w13	5:40:52
Matteson Lake 12	1	41N52	85w12	5:40:48
Maybee 58	7	42N00	83w31	5:34:04
Mayfield 28	1	44N38	85w32	5:42:08
Mayflower 31	96	47N15	88w27	5:53:48
Mayville 79	1	43N20	83w21	5:33:24
Maywood 21	25	45N56	86w58	5:47:52
Maywood 50	88	42N34	83w02	5:32:08
McBain 57	1	44N12	85w13	5:40:52
McBrides 59	57	43N21	85w02	5:40:08
McClean 62	57	43N28	85w56	5:43:44
McClures 73	91	43N27	83w57	5:35:48
McCords 41	64	42N51	85w23	5:41:32
McDonald 80	74	42N19	86w07	5:44:28
McDonough 73	1	43N18	84w09	5:36:36
McFarland 52	11	46N04	87w10	5:48:40
McGregor 76	1	43N31	82w44	5:30:56
McIntyre Landing 20	1	44N40	84w43	5:38:52
McIvor 35	1	44N14	83w43	5:34:52
McKain Corners 39	97	42N11	85w25	5:41:40
McKinley 68	1	44N39	84w08	5:36:32
McLeods Corner 48	25	46N17	85w23	5:41:32
McMillan 48	25	46N20	85w41	5:42:44
Meade 50	88	42N44	82w48	5:31:12
Meadowbrook 61	49	43N12	86w16	5:45:04
Meadow Lake Farms 63	88	43N15	83w48	5:35:12
Meads Landing 72	1	44N18	84w45	5:39:00
Mears 64	64	43N41	86w25	5:45:40
Meauwataka 83	1	44N15	85w24	5:41:36
Mecosta 54	1	43N37	85w14	5:40:56
Medina 46	1	41N46	84w18	5:37:12
Melita 6	1	44N02	84w01	5:36:04
Mellen 55	81	45N21	87w37	5:50:28
Melrose 15	1	45N15	84w55	5:39:40
Melstrand 2	25	46N28	86w25	5:45:40
Melvin 76	1	43N11	82w52	5:31:28
Melvindale 82	2	42N17	83w11	5:32:44
Memphis 74	1	42N54	82w46	5:31:04

MICHIGAN

Mendon 75	92	42N00	85w27	5:41:48
Menominee 55	86	45N06	87w37	5:50:28
Menonaqua Beach 24	67	45N26	84w59	5:39:56
Mentha 80	72	42N22	85w53	5:43:32
Meridian 33	41	42N44	84w26	5:37:44
Merrill 73	1	43N25	84w20	5:37:20
Merriman 22	87	45N48	88w04	5:52:16
Merritt 9	1	43N31	83w45	5:35:00
Merritt 57	1	44N20	84w57	5:39:48
Merriweather 66	25	46N34	89w39	5:58:36
Merson 3	42	42N32	85w51	5:43:24
Mesick 83	1	44N24	85w43	5:42:52
Metamora 44	1	42N57	83w17	5:33:08
Metropolitan 22	87	45N48	88w04	5:52:16
Metz 71	1	45N15	83w49	5:35:16
Meyer 55	81	45N44	87w38	5:50:32
Miami Park Beach 3	93	42N24	86w16	5:45:04
Michiana 11	109	41N46	86w48	5:47:12
Michigamme 52	34	46N32	88w07	5:52:28
Michigan Center 38	90	42N14	84w20	5:37:20
Michigan State University 33	41	42N44	84w28	5:37:52
Middlebelt 82	36	42N13	83w22	5:33:28
Middle Branch 67	1	44N02	85w09	5:40:36
Middlebury 78	1	43N00	84w20	5:37:20
Middle Island Point 52	25	46N33	87w24	5:49:36
Middleton 29	1	43N11	84w43	5:38:52
Middle Village 24	67	45N34	85w07	5:40:28
Middleville 8	57	42N43	85w28	5:41:52
Midland 56	88	43N37	84w14	5:36:56
Midland Park 39	92	42N23	85w23	5:41:32
Midway Gardens 58	1	41N47	83w34	5:34:16
Mikado 1	1	44N35	83w25	5:33:40
Milan 81	7	42N05	83w41	5:34:44
Milburg 11	4	42N06	86w27	5:45:48
Milford 63	88	42N35	83w36	5:34:24
Milham 39	47	42N15	85w34	5:42:16
Millbrook 54	57	43N30	85w09	5:40:36
Millecoquins Lake 49	25	46N07	85w34	5:42:16
Millen 1	1	44N38	83w37	5:34:28
Millersburg 71	1	45N20	84w04	5:36:16
Millers Park 5	1	44N54	85w25	5:41:40
Millett 23	41	42N44	84w36	5:38:24
Milleville Beach 82	36	42N03	83w11	5:32:44
Mill Grove 3	42	42N32	85w51	5:43:24
Millington 79	1	43N17	83w32	5:34:08
Milliron Park 61	49	43N14	86w13	5:44:52
Mill Lake 80	72	42N22	85w53	5:43:32
Mills 31	96	47N10	88w26	5:53:44
Mills 76	1	43N31	82w44	5:30:56
Millville 33	1	42N27	84w11	5:36:44
Millville 44	1	43N03	83w19	5:33:16
Milnes 30	1	41N59	84w40	5:38:40
Milwaukee Junction 82	2	42N23	83w02	5:32:08
Minard 38	1	42N15	84w36	5:38:24
Minden 76	1	43N39	82w48	5:31:12
Minden City 76	1	43N40	82w47	5:31:08
Mineral Hills 36	81	46N07	88w39	5:54:36
Miner Lake 3	42	42N32	85w51	5:43:24
Miners Spur 21	25	45N56	86w58	5:47:52
Minor Beach 77	14	45N58	86w15	5:45:00
Mio 68	1	44N39	84w08	5:36:32
Missaukee Park 57	1	44N20	85w12	5:40:48
Mitchell 1	1	44N44	83w48	5:35:12
Moddersville 57	1	43N51	85w00	5:40:00
Moffatt 6	1	44N08	84w07	5:36:28
Mohawk 42	96	47N18	88w21	5:53:24
Moline 3	92	42N44	85w40	5:42:40
Moltke 71	1	45N25	83w57	5:35:48
Mona Beach 61	49	43N12	86w14	5:44:56
Mona Shores 61	49	43N12	86w16	5:45:04
Mona View 61	49	43N12	86w14	5:44:56
Mona Vista 61	49	43N12	86w14	5:44:56
Monitor 9	36	43N36	83w58	5:35:52
Monongahela 36	81	46N06	88w20	5:53:20
Monroe 58	36	41N55	83w24	5:33:36
Monroe Center 28	1	44N40	85w42	5:42:48
Montague 61	64	43N25	86w22	5:45:28
Montcalm 59	57	43N15	85w16	5:41:04
Montello Park 70	51	42N47	86w07	5:44:28
Monterey 3	92	42N38	85w50	5:43:20
Montgomery 30	1	41N47	84w48	5:39:12
Montmorency 60	1	45N09	84w02	5:36:08
Montrose 25	1	43N11	83w54	5:35:36
Moore 76	1	43N28	82w57	5:31:48
Moore Park 75	97	41N57	85w38	5:42:32
Moorestown 57	1	44N20	85w12	5:40:48
Mooreville 81	1	42N00	83w32	5:34:08
Moorland 61	66	43N15	85w58	5:43:52
Moran 49	25	46N00	84w50	5:39:20
Morenci 46	1	41N43	84w13	5:36:52
Morgan Corners 13	43	42N20	85w11	5:40:44
Morley 54	1	43N29	85w27	5:41:48
Morrice 78	1	42N50	84w11	5:36:44
Morseville 73	1	43N15	83w48	5:35:12
Morton 54	1	43N36	85w16	5:41:04
Moscow 30	1	42N02	84w31	5:38:04
Mosherville 30	1	42N04	84w39	5:38:36
Motley 31	25	46N45	88w48	5:55:12
Mott Park 25	1	43N02	83w44	5:34:56
Mottville 75	1	41N47	85w44	5:42:56
Mountain Beach 70	51	42N55	86w09	5:44:36
Mount Clemens 50	88	42N35	82w53	5:31:32
Mount Elliott 82	2	42N26	83w03	5:32:12
Mount Forest 9	1	43N52	84w06	5:36:24
Mount Haley 56	1	43N32	84w20	5:37:20
Mount Morris 25	1	43N07	83w42	5:34:48
Mount Pleasant 3	93	42N24	86w16	5:45:04
Mount Pleasant 37	1	43N36	84w46	5:39:04
Mount Vernon 50	88	42N39	83w09	5:32:36
Mueller 77	25	46N04	85w55	5:43:40
Muir 34	92	43N00	84w56	5:39:44
Mullet 16	1	45N30	84w35	5:38:20
Mullet Lake 16	1	45N34	84w32	5:38:08
Mulliken 23	92	42N46	84w54	5:39:36
Mundy 25	1	42N56	83w41	5:34:44
Munger 9	1	43N31	83w46	5:35:04
Munising 2	22	46N25	86w40	5:46:40
Munith 38	1	42N23	84w16	5:37:04
Munro 16	1	45N36	84w39	5:38:36
Munson 46	1	41N43	84w13	5:36:52
Muskegon 61	49	43N14	86w16	5:45:04
Muskegon Heights 61	49	43N12	86w15	5:45:00
Mussey 74	1	43N02	82w56	5:31:44
Muttonville 50	1	42N49	82w45	5:31:00
Nadeau 55	86	45N34	87w34	5:50:16
Nagel Corner 71	1	45N18	83w53	5:35:32
Nahma 21	25	45N50	86w40	5:46:40
Nankin Mills 82	36	42N19	83w22	5:33:28
Naomi 11	72	41N59	86w18	5:45:12
Napier 11	74	42N12	86w16	5:45:04
Napoleon 38	1	42N11	84w17	5:37:08
Nashville 8	57	42N36	85w05	5:40:20
Nathan 55	81	45N28	87w37	5:50:28
National City 35	1	44N14	83w43	5:34:52
National Mine 52	25	46N28	87w41	5:50:44
Naubinway 49	25	46N06	85w27	5:41:48
Nazareth 39	47	42N19	85w33	5:42:12
Neebish Island 17	12	46N16	84w09	5:36:36
Needmore 23	1	42N34	84w50	5:39:20
Neeley 3	102	42N27	85w39	5:42:36
Negaunee 52	23	46N30	87w36	5:50:24
Nelson 41	57	43N15	85w30	5:42:00
Nelson 73	1	43N25	84w14	5:36:56
Nessen City 10	1	44N31	85w52	5:43:28
Nester 72	1	44N12	84w29	5:37:56
Nestoria 7	25	46N34	88w16	5:53:04
New Allouez 42	96	47N18	88w24	5:53:36
Newark 29	1	43N15	84w40	5:38:40
Newark 63	88	42N47	83w37	5:34:28
Newaygo 62	64	43N25	85w48	5:43:12
New Baltimore 50	88	42N41	82w44	5:30:56
Newberg 14	72	41N56	85w49	5:43:16
Newberry 48	50	46N21	85w30	5:42:00
New Boston 82	36	42N10	83w24	5:33:36
New Bradford 50	88	42N34	83w02	5:32:08
New Bristol 36	81	46N06	88w20	5:53:20
New Buffalo 11	109	41N47	86w45	5:47:00
Newburg 46	1	42N00	83w57	5:35:48
New Era 64	64	43N34	86w21	5:45:24
Newfield 64	57	43N35	86w06	5:44:24
New Greenleaf 76	1	43N36	83w10	5:32:40
New Groningen 70	51	42N47	86w07	5:44:28
New Haven 50	88	42N44	82w48	5:31:12
New Haven Center 29	1	43N11	84w43	5:38:52
New Holland 70	51	42N47	86w07	5:44:28
New Hudson 63	88	42N31	83w37	5:34:28
Newkirk 43	1	44N04	85w44	5:42:56
Newland 51	111	44N15	86w19	5:45:16
New Lothrop 78	1	43N07	83w58	5:35:52
Newport 58	1	41N58	83w15	5:33:00
New Richmond 3	74	42N39	86w06	5:44:24
New Salem 3	92	42N49	83w57	5:35:48
New Swanzy 52	25	46N17	87w26	5:49:44
New Troy 11	74	41N53	86w33	5:46:12
Nicholson 78	1	42N50	84w13	5:36:52
Nicholsville 14	72	42N01	85w49	5:43:16
Nickel Plate 34	92	42N59	85w04	5:40:16
Niles 11	105	41N50	86w15	5:45:00
Nine Mile 9	1	43N51	83w58	5:35:52
Nirvana 43	1	43N53	85w38	5:42:32
Nisula 31	25	46N45	88w48	5:55:12
Noble 12	1	41N47	85w14	5:40:56
Noordeloos 70	51	42N47	86w07	5:44:28
Norman 51	1	44N13	85w57	5:43:48
North Adams 30	1	41N58	84w32	5:38:08
North Allis 71	1	45N24	84w12	5:36:48
North Arms 5	1	44N59	85w13	5:40:52
North Aurelius 33	1	42N35	84w27	5:37:48
North Bell 34	92	42N51	85w15	5:41:00
North Blendon 70	54	42N52	85w51	5:43:24
North Bradley 56	1	43N43	84w29	5:37:56
North Branch 44	1	43N14	83w12	5:32:48
North Dorr 3	92	42N43	85w43	5:42:52
Northeastern 82	2	42N20	83w11	5:32:44
North End 82	2	42N21	83w03	5:32:12
North Epworth 53	57	43N57	86w27	5:45:48
North Escanaba 21	19	45N45	87w04	5:48:16
North Farmington 63	88	42N29	83w21	5:33:24
Northfield 58	36	41N55	83w23	5:33:32
Northfield 81	38	42N23	83w44	5:34:56
Northfield Hills 63	88	42N34	83w09	5:32:36
North Fox Island 45	1	45N29	85w47	5:43:08
Northgate 41	61	43N00	85w38	5:42:32
North Lake 44	1	43N13	83w28	5:33:52
North Lake 52	25	46N31	87w45	5:51:00
North Lake 80	72	42N22	85w53	5:43:32
North Lakeport 74	1	42N58	82w29	5:29:56
Northland 52	25	46N04	87w36	5:50:24
Northland Center 63	2	42N28	83w14	5:32:56
North Lansing 33	41	42N44	84w35	5:38:20
North Manitou 45	1	45N07	85w59	5:43:56
North Morenci 46	1	41N43	84w13	5:36:52
North Muskegon 61	49	43N15	86w17	5:45:08
North Niles 11	105	41N52	86w15	5:45:00
North Paynesville 66	25	46N30	89w07	5:56:28
North Plains 34	92	43N05	84w54	5:39:36
Northport 45	1	45N08	85w37	5:42:28
North Shade 29	1	43N10	84w47	5:39:08
North Shores 58	1	41N52	83w27	5:33:48
North Side 25	1	43N04	83w42	5:34:48
North Star 29	1	43N15	84w32	5:38:08
North Street 74	1	43N03	82w32	5:30:08
North Unity 45	1	44N51	85w51	5:43:24
Northville 41	61	43N00	85w38	5:42:32
Northville 82	36	42N26	83w29	5:33:56
Northwestern 82	2	42N22	83w08	5:32:32
North Wheeler 29	1	43N25	84w26	5:37:44
Northwood 39	47	42N18	85w37	5:42:28
Nortondale 61	49	43N12	86w16	5:45:04
Norton Oaks 61	49	43N12	86w16	5:45:04
Norton Shores 61	49	43N11	86w16	5:45:04
Norvell 38	1	42N07	84w10	5:36:40
Norwalk 51	1	44N20	86w11	5:44:44
Norway 22	87	45N47	87w55	5:51:40
Norwayne 82	36	42N18	83w23	5:33:32
Norwood 15	1	45N15	85w21	5:41:24
Nottawa 75	1	41N55	85w27	5:41:48
Novesta 79	1	43N33	83w10	5:32:40
Novi 63	88	42N29	83w29	5:33:56
Nowesco 17	12	46N12	84w44	5:38:56
Nunda 16	1	45N15	84w29	5:37:56
Nunica 70	51	43N10	86w04	5:44:16
Oakdale 61	49	43N12	86w14	5:44:56
Oakfield 41	57	43N10	85w22	5:41:28
Oakfield Center 41	57	43N11	85w15	5:41:00
Oak Grove 47	1	42N42	83w56	5:35:44
Oak Grove 62	64	43N25	85w47	5:43:08
Oak Grove 63	88	42N39	83w14	5:32:56
Oak Grove 69	1	45N02	84w41	5:38:44
Oak Grove 72	1	44N30	84w36	5:38:24
Oak Hill 51	111	44N14	86w19	5:45:16
Oakhurst 79	1	43N34	83w31	5:34:04
Oak Island 63	88	42N32	83w27	5:33:48
Oakland 3	97	42N41	86w00	5:44:00
Oakland 63	88	42N45	83w09	5:32:36
Oaklawn 70	51	42N47	86w07	5:44:28
Oakley 73	1	43N09	84w10	5:36:40
Oakley Park 63	88	42N34	83w30	5:34:00
Oak Park 13	43	42N20	85w11	5:40:44
Oak Park 63	2	42N28	83w11	5:32:44
Oak Ridge 63	2	42N31	83w09	5:32:36
Oak Shade Park 46	1	42N06	84w15	5:37:00
Oakville 58	1	42N05	83w35	5:34:20
Oakwood 63	88	42N49	83w16	5:33:04
Oakwood 75	1	41N48	85w38	5:42:32
Oakwood 82	2	42N17	83w11	5:32:44
Oakwood Junction 82	2	42N15	83w13	5:32:52
Oceola 47	1	42N39	83w51	5:35:24
Ocqueoc 71	1	45N26	84w04	5:36:16
Oden 24	67	45N25	84w50	5:39:20
Odessa 34	92	42N49	85w08	5:40:32
Odessac 71	1	45N26	84w04	5:36:16
Odgers 36	1	41N59	84w21	5:37:24
Ogden 46	1	41N46	83w56	5:35:44
Ogden Center 46	1	41N50	83w52	5:35:28
Ogemaw 65	1	44N18	84w18	5:37:12
Oil City 56	1	43N31	84w41	5:38:44
Okemos 33	41	42N43	84w26	5:37:44
Ola 29	1	43N11	84w29	5:37:56
Old Mill Gardens 13	43	42N16	85w12	5:40:48
Old Mission 28	1	44N57	85w29	5:41:56
Oldport 58	1	41N58	83w15	5:33:00
Olive Center 70	51	42N47	86w07	5:44:28
Olive Hills 70	51	42N55	86w09	5:44:36
Olivet 23	1	42N27	84w56	5:39:44
Olson 56	1	43N37	84w12	5:36:48
Omena 45	1	45N03	85w35	5:42:20
Omer 6	1	44N03	83w51	5:35:24
Onaway 71	3	45N21	84w14	5:36:56
Oneida 23	1	42N44	84w46	5:39:04
O'neil 40	1	44N44	85w11	5:40:44
Onekama 51	1	44N22	86w12	5:44:48
Onondaga 33	1	42N28	84w32	5:38:08
Onota 2	25	46N28	87w01	5:48:04
Onsted 46	1	42N00	84w11	5:36:44
Ontonagon 66	25	46N52	89w19	5:57:16
Ontwa 14	108	41N47	86w03	5:44:12
Orangeville 8	57	42N33	85w29	5:41:56
Orchard Beach 16	1	44N48	82w55	5:31:40
Orchard Lake 63	88	42N35	83w25	5:33:40
Orchard Lake Village 63	88	42N35	83w22	5:33:28
Oregon 44	1	43N06	83w24	5:33:36
Orient 67	1	43N52	85w09	5:40:36
Orion 63	88	42N44	83w17	5:33:08
Orlando Park 41	61	43N00	85w38	5:42:32
Orleans 34	92	43N05	85w08	5:40:32
Oronoko 11	72	41N57	86w23	5:45:32
Orr 73	1	43N25	84w14	5:36:56
Ortonville 63	88	42N51	83w27	5:33:48
Osceola 31	96	47N15	88w27	5:53:48
Oscoda 35	1	44N26	83w20	5:33:20
Oshtemo 39	92	42N17	85w42	5:42:48
Osier 21	25	45N56	86w58	5:47:52
Oskar 31	25	46N19	87w03	5:48:12
Ossawinamakee Beach 77	14	45N58	86w15	5:45:00
Osseo 30	1	41N53	84w33	5:38:12
Ossineke 4	1	44N55	83w26	5:33:44
Osterhout Lake 3	92	42N24	86w04	5:44:16
Otisco 34	92	43N04	85w16	5:41:04
Otisville 25	1	43N10	83w31	5:34:04
Otsego 3	102	42N27	85w42	5:42:48

MICHIGAN

Otsego Lake 69	1	44N54	84W40	5:38:40
Ottawa Beach 70	51	42N47	86W07	5:44:28
Ottawa Lake 58	1	41N46	83W45	5:35:00
Otterburn 25	1	42N59	83W47	5:35:08
Otter Lake 44	1	43N13	83W28	5:33:52
Otto 64	57	43N31	86W13	5:44:52
Overisel 3	97	42N44	85W58	5:43:52
Ovid 19	1	43N01	84W22	5:37:28
Owasippe 61	57	43N22	86W10	5:44:40
Owendale 32	1	43N43	83W16	5:33:04
Owosso 78	1	43N00	84W11	5:36:44
Oxbow 63	88	42N39	83W24	5:33:36
Oxford 63	88	42N49	83W16	5:33:04
Ozark 49	25	46N00	84W50	5:39:20
Paavola 31	95	47N08	88W36	5:54:24
Painesdale 31	96	47N03	88W40	5:54:40
Palatka 36	81	46N04	88W38	5:54:32
Palisades Park 80	74	42N17	86W16	5:45:04
Palmer 52	11	46N27	87W35	5:50:20
Palms 76	1	43N37	82W46	5:31:04
Palmyra 46	1	41N52	83W57	5:35:48
Palo 34	92	43N07	84W59	5:39:56
Papin 7	25	46N49	88W38	5:54:32
Paradise 17	12	46N38	85W02	5:40:08
Parchment 39	47	42N20	85W34	5:42:16
Paris 32	1	43N44	82W49	5:31:16
Paris 54	1	43N46	85W30	5:42:00
Parisville 32	1	43N43	82W44	5:30:56
Park 41	61	42N59	85W42	5:42:48
Parkdale 51	111	44N17	86W19	5:45:16
Parkers Corners 47	1	42N39	84W04	5:36:16
Park Grove 82	2	42N26	82W59	5:31:56
Park Lake 19	41	42N49	84W27	5:37:48
Park Lake Corner 67	1	44N06	85W09	5:40:36
Park Plaza 82	2	42N14	83W11	5:32:44
Parks 62	57	43N46	85W30	5:42:00
Park Shore Resort 14	73	41N55	86W00	5:44:00
Parkview Terrace 61	49	43N12	86W14	5:44:56
Parkville 75	97	41N57	85W38	5:42:32
Parma 38	1	42N16	84W36	5:38:24
Parnell 41	64	42N57	85W29	5:41:56
Parshallville 47	1	42N49	83W43	5:34:52
Partello 13	1	42N27	84W55	5:39:40
Patterson Gardens 58	36	41N54	83W26	5:33:44
Patterson Lake 47	1	42N27	83W57	5:35:48
Paulding 66	11	46N24	89W10	5:56:40
Pavilion 39	92	42N12	85W29	5:41:56
Paw Paw 80	46	42N13	85W53	5:43:32
Paw Paw Lake 11	74	42N13	86W16	5:45:04
Payment 17	12	46N29	84W12	5:36:48
Paynesville 66	25	46N30	89W07	5:56:28
Peacock 43	92	44N02	85W52	5:43:28
Peaine 15	1	45N40	85W32	5:42:08
Pearl 3	74	42N33	86W06	5:44:24
Pearl Beach 12	1	41N57	85W00	5:40:00
Pearl Beach 74	1	42N38	82W36	5:30:24
Pearl Grange 11	4	42N06	86W27	5:45:48
Pearline 70	51	42N58	85W57	5:43:48
Peck 76	1	43N16	82W49	5:31:16
Pelkie 7	25	46N49	88W38	5:54:32
Pellston 24	67	45N33	84W47	5:39:08
Penford 82	2	42N14	83W16	5:33:04
Peninsula 28	1	44N52	85W32	5:42:08
Penn 14	76	41N56	85W56	5:43:44
Pennellwood 11	72	41N57	86W20	5:45:20
Pennfield 13	43	42N22	85W08	5:40:32
Penobscot 82	2	42N20	83W03	5:32:12
Pentland 48	25	46N18	85W28	5:41:52
Pentoga 36	81	46N06	88W20	5:53:20
Pentwater 64	64	43N47	86W26	5:45:44
Pequaming 7	25	46N46	88W27	5:53:48
Pere Marquette 53	57	43N57	86W25	5:45:40
Perkins 21	25	45N59	87W04	5:48:16
Perrinton 29	1	43N11	84W41	5:38:44
Perronville 55	81	45N48	87W22	5:49:28
Perry 78	1	42N50	84W13	5:36:52
Perry Lake Heights 63	88	42N51	83W27	5:33:48
Peshawbestown 45	1	45N02	85W36	5:42:24
Peters 74	1	42N43	82W30	5:30:00
Petersburg 58	7	41N54	83W43	5:34:52
Petoskey 24	67	45N22	84W57	5:39:48
Petrieville 23	1	42N31	84W39	5:38:36
Pettysville 47	1	42N27	83W57	5:35:48
Pewabic 31	95	47N08	88W36	5:54:24
Pewamo 34	92	43N00	84W51	5:39:24
Phillipsville 31	25	46N27	90W09	6:00:36
Phoenix 42	96	47N18	88W26	5:53:44
Pickford 17	12	46N10	84W22	5:37:28
Pierport 51	1	44N25	86W13	5:44:52
Pierson 59	57	43N20	85W30	5:42:00
Pigeon 32	1	43N50	83W16	5:33:04
Pike Lake 49	25	46N06	85W42	5:42:48
Pilgrim 10	1	44N38	86W14	5:44:56
Pinckney 47	1	42N27	83W57	5:35:48
Pinconning 9	1	43N51	83W58	5:35:52
Pine 59	57	43N20	85W16	5:41:04
Pine Bluffs 72	1	44N30	84W36	5:38:24
Pine Creek 13	1	42N10	85W13	5:40:52
Pine Grove 80	72	42N23	85W50	5:43:20
Pine Grove Beach 43	92	43N54	85W51	5:43:24
Pine River 6	1	43N59	83W58	5:35:52
Pine River 29	1	43N25	84W40	5:38:40
Pine Run 25	1	43N08	83W44	5:34:56
Pine Stump Junction 48	25	46N21	85W30	5:42:00
Pinnebog 32	1	43N56	83W00	5:32:00
Pinora 43	1	43N57	85W37	5:42:28

Pioneer 57	1	44N28	85W09	5:40:36
Pipestone 11	72	42N02	86W17	5:45:08
Pisgah Heights 67	1	44N06	85W09	5:40:36
Pittsburg 78	1	43N00	84W11	5:36:44
Pittsfield 81	38	42N14	83W42	5:34:48
Pittsford 30	1	41N51	84W25	5:37:40
Plainfield 47	1	42N28	84W05	5:36:20
Plainfield Heights 41	61	43N00	85W38	5:42:32
Plainwell 3	102	42N27	85W38	5:42:32
Platte 10	1	44N44	86W01	5:44:04
Plaza 13	43	42N16	85W12	5:40:48
Pleasant Lake 30	1	41N53	84W33	5:38:12
Pleasant Lake 38	1	42N23	84W16	5:37:04
Pleasant Lake 81	1	42N09	84W02	5:36:08
Pleasanton 51	1	44N28	86W08	5:44:32
Pleasant Plains 43	92	43N52	85W51	5:43:24
Pleasant Ridge 63	2	42N29	83W09	5:32:36
Pleasant Valley 5	1	45N09	85W08	5:40:32
Pleasant Valley 56	1	43N24	84W37	5:38:28
Pleasant View 24	67	45N30	84W55	5:39:40
Plumbrook Estates 50	88	42N34	83W02	5:32:08
Plumbrook Farms 50	88	42N34	83W02	5:32:08
Plumbrook Village 50	88	42N34	83W02	5:32:08
Plymouth 27	81	46N29	89W56	5:59:44
Plymouth 82	36	42N22	83W28	5:33:52
Podunk 81	1	42N09	84W02	5:36:08
Pogy 54	97	43N51	85W27	5:41:48
Point Au Gres 6	1	44N03	83W41	5:34:44
Pointe Aux Barques 32	1	44N04	82W57	5:31:48
Pointe aux Chenes 74	1	42N37	82W32	5:30:08
Pointe aux Peaux Farms 58	1	41N58	83W15	5:33:00
Pointe Aux Pins 49	1	45N44	84W29	5:37:56
Point Nipigon 16	1	44N48	82W55	5:31:40
Pokagon 14	72	41N56	86W10	5:44:40
Polkton 70	55	43N04	85W59	5:43:56
Pomona 51	1	44N29	85W55	5:43:40
Pompeii 29	1	43N11	84W36	5:38:24
Ponshewaing 24	67	45N27	84W47	5:39:08
Pontiac 63	37	42N38	83W18	5:33:12
Pontiac Lake 63	88	42N39	83W24	5:33:36
Poplar Beach 8	57	42N27	85W14	5:40:56
Portage 39	92	42N12	85W35	5:42:20
Portage Entry 31	96	47N01	88W32	5:54:08
Portage Lake 75	92	42N00	85W27	5:41:48
Portage Point 51	1	44N22	86W14	5:44:56
Port Austin 32	1	44N03	83W00	5:32:00
Port Gypsum 35	1	44N16	83W31	5:34:04
Port Hope 32	1	43N57	82W43	5:30:52
Port Huron 74	39	42N58	82W26	5:29:44
Portland 34	92	42N52	84W54	5:39:36
Port Sanilac 76	88	43N26	82W33	5:30:12
Port Sheldon 70	51	42N54	86W10	5:44:40
Portsmouth 9	36	43N34	83W51	5:35:24
Posen 71	1	45N16	83W42	5:34:48
Poseyville 56	1	43N37	84W12	5:36:48
Potters Corners 34	92	42N56	85W13	5:40:52
Potters Lake 44	1	43N03	83W19	5:33:16
Potterville 23	1	42N38	84W45	5:39:00
Poverty Island 21	25	45N32	86W40	5:46:40
Powell 52	25	46N47	87W41	5:50:44
Powers 55	86	45N41	87W32	5:50:08
Prairie Creek 34	92	42N59	85W04	5:40:16
Prairie Farm 73	1	43N18	84W09	5:36:36
Prairie Ronde 39	92	42N07	85W43	5:42:52
Prairie View 13	43	42N16	85W12	5:40:48
Prairieville 8	57	42N28	85W30	5:42:00
Prattville 30	1	41N47	84W24	5:37:36
Prescott 65	1	44N11	83W56	5:35:44
Presque Isle 71	1	45N18	83W29	5:33:56
Princeton 52	11	46N17	87W29	5:49:56
Prosper 57	1	44N15	85W05	5:40:20
Prudenville 72	1	44N18	84W39	5:38:36
Pulaski 38	1	42N07	84W39	5:38:36
Pulawski 71	1	45N20	83W43	5:34:52
Pullman 3	92	42N29	86W05	5:44:20
Pullman Corners 14	108	41N48	86W05	5:44:20
Putnam 47	1	42N28	83W58	5:35:52
Quakertown 63	88	42N29	83W23	5:33:32
Quanicassee 79	1	43N32	83W33	5:34:12
Quarry 32	1	43N51	83W23	5:33:32
Quincy 12	1	41N57	84W53	5:39:32
Quincy Mine 31	95	47N08	88W36	5:54:24
Quinnesec 22	87	45N48	87W59	5:51:56
Raber 17	12	46N05	84W09	5:36:36
Raco 17	12	46N22	84W43	5:38:52
Rainy Beach 71	1	45N21	84W13	5:36:52
Raisin 46	1	41N57	83W58	5:35:52
Raisinville 58	1	41N58	83W31	5:34:04
Ralph 22	87	46N06	87W47	5:51:08
Rambaultown 31	96	47N15	88W27	5:53:48
Ramona 62	64	43N33	85W46	5:43:04
Ramsay 27	81	46N28	90W00	6:00:00
Ranch Acres 70	68	43N04	86W11	5:44:44
Randall Beach 63	88	42N38	83W14	5:32:56
Randall Lake 12	1	41N57	85W00	5:40:00
Randville 22	87	45N48	88W04	5:52:16
Rankin 25	1	42N59	83W47	5:35:08
Ransom 30	1	41N47	84W32	5:38:08
Rapid City 40	1	44N50	85W17	5:41:08
Rapid River 21	35	45N56	86W58	5:47:52
Rapson 32	1	43N48	83W00	5:32:00
Rathbone 29	1	43N24	84W28	5:37:52
Rattle Run 74	1	42N50	82W29	5:29:56

Ravenna 61	66	43N11	85W56	5:43:44
Ravenswood 33	41	42N44	84W36	5:38:24
Ravenswood Heights 39	47	42N17	85W34	5:42:16
Ravenwood 58	36	41N55	83W23	5:33:32
Rawsonville 81	36	42N13	83W34	5:34:16
Ray 12	1	41N44	84W53	5:39:32
Ray 50	88	42N45	82W55	5:31:40
Ray Center 50	88	42N44	82W48	5:31:12
Raymond Corners 43	1	44N02	85W41	5:42:44
Rea 58	1	41N57	83W40	5:34:40
Reading 30	1	41N50	84W45	5:39:00
Readmond 24	67	45N36	85W02	5:40:08
Recreation Park 39	47	42N14	85W35	5:42:20
Recreation Park 61	49	43N12	86W14	5:44:56
Redding 18	1	44N02	85W02	5:40:08
Redford 82	36	42N23	83W18	5:33:12
Redman 32	1	43N56	82W43	5:30:52
Red Oak 68	1	44N53	84W18	5:37:12
Red Park 51	111	44N15	86W19	5:45:16
Redridge 31	25	46N19	87W03	5:48:12
Reed City 67	97	43N53	85W31	5:42:04
Reeder 57	1	44N18	85W10	5:40:40
Reeds Lake 41	61	42N56	85W37	5:42:28
Reeman 62	57	43N28	85W56	5:43:44
Reese 79	1	43N27	83W42	5:34:48
Remus 54	57	43N36	85W09	5:40:36
Reno 35	1	44N18	83W49	5:35:16
Republic 52	25	46N25	87W59	5:51:56
Rescue 32	1	43N39	83W15	5:33:00
Resort 24	67	45N20	85W01	5:40:04
Rexton 49	25	46N10	85W14	5:40:56
Reynolds 59	64	43N26	85W30	5:42:00
Rhodes 26	1	43N54	84W11	5:36:44
Rich 44	1	43N17	83W17	5:33:08
Richfield Center 25	1	43N05	83W34	5:34:16
Richland 39	92	42N22	85W27	5:41:48
Richmond 50	1	42N49	82W45	5:31:00
Richmondville 76	1	43N31	82W44	5:30:56
Richville 79	1	43N25	83W41	5:34:44
Ridgeway 46	1	41N58	83W50	5:35:20
Riga 46	1	41N47	83W49	5:35:16
Riley Center 74	1	42N59	82W46	5:31:04
Ripley 31	95	47N08	88W36	5:54:24
Ritter Hills 61	49	43N12	86W16	5:45:04
River Bluff 11	105	41N50	86W15	5:45:00
Riverdale 29	1	43N23	84W50	5:39:20
Riverland 21	19	45N45	87W04	5:48:16
River Rouge 82	2	42N16	83W08	5:32:32
Riverside 11	74	42N11	86W23	5:45:32
Riverside 38	90	42N15	84W24	5:37:36
Riverside 57	1	44N13	85W09	5:40:36
Riverside 74	1	42N35	82W34	5:30:16
Riverton 53	57	43N52	86W20	5:45:20
Riverview 82	2	42N11	83W11	5:32:44
Rives 38	1	42N23	84W25	5:37:40
Roberts Corners 48	25	46N21	85W30	5:42:00
Roberts Landing 74	1	42N37	82W32	5:30:08
Robinson 70	97	43N00	86W05	5:44:20
Rochester 63	88	42N41	83W08	5:32:32
Rock 21	15	46N04	87W10	5:48:40
Rockford 41	65	43N07	85W34	5:42:16
Rockland 66	25	46N44	89W11	5:56:44
Rockport 4	1	45N12	83W23	5:33:32
Rock River 2	25	46N21	87W00	5:48:00
Rockwood 82	36	42N04	83W15	5:33:00
Rodney 54	1	43N40	85W19	5:41:16
Rogers 36	81	46N06	88W39	5:54:36
Rogers 71	1	45N27	83W52	5:35:28
Rogers City 71	1	45N25	83W49	5:35:16
Rogers Heights 41	61	42N55	85W42	5:42:48
Rolland 37	1	43N31	85W02	5:40:08
Rollin 46	1	41N57	84W19	5:37:16
Rome 46	1	41N57	84W11	5:36:44
Rome Center 46	1	41N54	84W02	5:36:08
Romeo 50	1	42N48	83W01	5:32:04
Romulus 82	37	42N13	83W24	5:33:36
Ronald 34	92	43N05	85W01	5:40:04
Rondo 16	1	45N16	84W36	5:38:24
Roodmont 61	49	43N12	86W16	5:45:04
Roosevelt 73	1	43N25	84W14	5:36:56
Roosevelt Park 61	49	43N12	86W16	5:45:04
Roscommon 72	88	44N30	84W35	5:38:20
Roseburg 76	1	43N08	82W48	5:31:12
Rosebush 37	1	43N42	84W46	5:39:04
Rose Center 63	88	42N47	83W37	5:34:28
Rose City 65	1	44N25	84W07	5:36:28
Rosedale 17	12	46N23	84W21	5:37:24
Rose Lake 67	1	44N01	85W24	5:41:36
Roseville 50	2	42N30	82W56	5:31:44
Ross 39	92	42N23	85W22	5:41:28
Rothbury 64	64	43N30	86W21	5:45:24
Roulo 82	36	42N11	83W29	5:33:56
Round Lake 46	1	41N59	84W17	5:37:08
Round Lake 53	57	44N03	86W11	5:44:44
Rousseau 66	25	46N45	89W05	5:56:20
Roxand 23	92	42N43	84W54	5:39:36
Royal Oak 63	2	42N30	83W09	5:32:36
Royalton 11	1	42N01	86W26	5:45:44
Royalton Heights 11	1	42N05	86W30	5:46:00
Rubicon 32	1	43N54	82W43	5:30:52
Ruby 74	1	42N59	82W40	5:30:40
Rudyard 17	12	46N14	84W36	5:38:24
Rumely 2	25	46N21	86W58	5:47:52
Rush 78	1	43N05	84W14	5:36:56
Rushton 47	1	42N28	83W39	5:34:36
Rusk 70	54	42N49	86W01	5:44:04

Russell Island 74 1 42N37 82W32 5:30:08
Russellville 25 1 43N05 83W34 5:34:16
Rust 60 1 44N57 83W57 5:35:48
Ruth 32 1 43N43 82W44 5:30:56
Rutland 8 57 42N39 85W22 5:41:28
Ryan 73 1 43N25 84W20 5:37:20
Sac Bay 21 25 45N43 86W40 5:46:40
Saddle Lake 80 72 42N24 86W04 5:44:16
Sage 26 1 44N01 84W33 5:38:12
Saginaw 73 91 43N25 83W57 5:35:48
Sagola 22 87 46N08 88W02 5:52:08
Saint Anthony 58 7 41N47 83W34 5:34:16
Saint Charles 73 1 43N18 84W09 5:36:36
Saint Clair 74 1 42N50 82W30 5:30:00
Saint Clair Flats 74
1 42N35 82W34 5:30:16
Saint Clair Haven 50
88 42N35 82W54 5:31:36
Saint Clair Shores 50
2 42N30 82W54 5:31:36
Saint Elmo 56 1 43N37 84W12 5:36:48
Saint Helen 72 1 44N23 84W25 5:37:40
Saint Ignace 49 69 45N52 84W44 5:38:56
Saint Jacques 21 25 45N56 86W58 5:47:52
Saint James 15 1 45N45 85W31 5:42:04
Saint Johns 19 1 43N00 84W33 5:38:12
Saint Joseph 11 4 42N06 86W29 5:45:56
Saint Louis 29 1 43N25 84W36 5:38:24
Saint Martin Island 21
25 45N30 86W46 5:47:04
Saint Marys Junction 31
95 47N08 88W36 5:54:24
Saint Marys Lake 13
43 42N20 85W11 5:40:44
Saint Nicholas 21
25 46N04 87W10 5:48:40
Salem 81 1 42N24 83W35 5:34:20
Saline 81 38 42N10 83W47 5:35:08
Salisbury 52 25 46N30 87W40 5:50:40
Salzburg 9 36 43N36 83W54 5:35:36
Samaria 58 1 41N48 83W35 5:34:20
Sanborn 4 1 44N55 83W27 5:33:48
Sand Beach 32 1 43N49 82W41 5:30:44
Sand Creek 46 1 41N50 84W06 5:36:24
Sand Hill 73 91 43N26 84W00 5:36:00
Sand Lake 35 1 44N14 83W43 5:34:52
Sand Lake 41 57 43N18 85W31 5:42:04
Sand Lake Corners 46
1 42N00 84W11 5:36:44
Sand River 52 25 46N29 87W03 5:48:12
Sands 52 11 46N25 87W26 5:49:44
Sandstone 38 1 42N18 84W32 5:38:08
Sandusky 76 1 43N25 82W50 5:31:20
Sanford 56 1 43N40 84W23 5:37:32
Sanilac 76 1 43N24 82W35 5:30:20
San Souci Beach 12
1 41N57 85W00 5:40:00
Santiago 6 1 44N09 83W47 5:35:08
Saranac 34 92 42N56 85W13 5:40:52
Sauble 43 92 44N02 85W59 5:43:56
Saugatuck 3 92 42N38 86W10 5:44:40
Sault Sainte Marie 17
45 46N30 84W21 5:37:24
Sawyer 11 74 41N53 86W35 5:46:20
Sawyer Air Force Base 52
25 46N20 87W22 5:49:28
Sawyer Lake 22 87 46N09 88W05 5:52:20
Schaffer 21 11 45N46 87W18 5:49:12
Schmidt Corner 31
25 46N19 87W03 5:48:12
Schoolcraft 39 99 42N07 85W38 5:42:32
Schultz 8 62 42N39 85W17 5:41:08
Scio 81 38 42N18 83W49 5:35:16
Sciota 78 1 42N54 84W19 5:37:16
Scipio 30 1 42N02 84W39 5:38:36
Scottdale 11 1 42N05 86W30 5:46:00
Scott Lake 36 86 46N03 88W36 5:54:24
Scotts 39 97 42N11 85W25 5:41:40
Scottville 53 57 43N58 86W17 5:45:08
Sears 67 1 43N54 85W11 5:40:44
Sebewa 34 97 42N49 85W01 5:40:04
Sebewa Center 34 92 42N52 84W54 5:39:36
Sebewaing 32 1 43N44 83W27 5:33:48
Sebille Manor 50 88 42N38 82W50 5:31:20
Secord 26 1 44N02 84W20 5:37:20
Seidler Corners 9 1 43N36 84W05 5:36:20
Selfridge Air Force Base 50
88 42N37 82W49 5:31:16
Selkirk 65 1 44N17 84W14 5:36:56
Selma 83 1 44N17 85W32 5:42:08
Seminole Park 61 49 43N12 86W16 5:45:04
Seneca 46 1 41N46 84W11 5:36:44
Seneca Location 42
96 47N18 88W26 5:53:44
Seney 77 78 46N21 85W56 5:43:44
Senter 31 96 47N07 88W31 5:54:04
Seven Harbors 63 88 42N38 83W37 5:34:28
Seven Oaks 82 2 42N26 83W12 5:32:48
Seville 29 1 43N25 84W47 5:39:08
Seymour Square 41
61 42N58 85W40 5:42:40
Shabbona 76 1 43N28 83W03 5:32:12
Shadyside 30 1 41N53 84W33 5:38:12
Shafer Location 36
81 46N06 88W20 5:53:20
Shaftsburg 78 1 42N48 84W18 5:37:12
Shanghai Corners 11
72 41N59 86W18 5:45:12
Sharon 81 1 42N12 84W04 5:36:16
Sharon Hollow 81 1 42N09 84W02 5:36:08
Shattuckville 73 91 43N26 84W00 5:36:00
Shelby 64 64 43N37 86W22 5:45:28
Shelby Village 50
88 42N37 83W02 5:32:08
Shelbyville 3 92 42N35 85W38 5:42:32
Sheldon 82 36 42N16 83W29 5:33:56
Shepardsville 19 1 43N00 84W22 5:37:28
Shepherd 37 1 43N32 84W41 5:38:44
Sheridan 59 57 43N13 85W06 5:40:24
Sherman 83 1 44N24 85W43 5:42:52
Sherman City 37 1 43N44 85W06 5:40:24
Sherman Lake 39 92 42N20 85W21 5:41:24
Sherman Manor 61 49 43N12 86W16 5:45:04
Sherman Woods 74 1 42N58 82W29 5:29:56
Sherwood 12 1 42N02 85W14 5:40:56
Sherwood Corners 68
1 44N39 84W08 5:36:32
Sherwood Park 39 47 42N17 85W34 5:42:16
Shiawassee 78 1 42N55 84W06 5:36:24
Shiawassetown 78 1 42N55 84W06 5:36:24
Shields 73 1 43N25 84W04 5:36:16
Shiloh 34 92 43N04 85W08 5:40:32
Shingleton 2 30 46N21 86W28 5:45:52
Shorecrest 3 92 41N57 85W19 5:41:16
Shoreham 11 74 42N04 86W31 5:46:04
Shore Line Junction 31
95 47N08 88W36 5:54:24
Shorewood Hills 11
74 41N53 86W37 5:46:28
Shorewood Hills-Flower Hills 11
74 41N52 86W38 5:46:32
Sibley 82 36 42N08 83W13 5:32:52
Sickles 29 1 43N18 84W36 5:38:24
Sidnaw 31 25 46N30 88W43 5:54:52
Sidney 59 57 43N15 85W08 5:40:32
Sigel 32 1 43N49 82W49 5:31:16
Silver City 66 25 46N52 89W18 5:57:12
Silver Creek 3 102 42N27 85W39 5:42:36
Silver Creek 14 72 42N02 86W10 5:44:40
Silver Lake 41 65 43N07 85W34 5:42:16
Silverwood 79 1 43N19 83W15 5:33:00
Simar 66 25 46N45 89W05 5:56:20
Sims 6 1 44N04 83W38 5:34:32
Sister Lakes 80 72 42N05 86W12 5:44:48
Sitka 62 57 43N28 85W56 5:43:44
Six Lakes 59 57 43N26 85W09 5:40:36
Skandia 52 25 46N21 87W11 5:48:44
Skanee 7 25 46N53 88W13 5:52:52
Skeels 26 1 43N59 84W29 5:37:56
Skidmore 22 87 45N48 88W04 5:52:16
Skidway Lake 65 1 44N12 83W56 5:35:44
Slagle 83 1 44N18 85W46 5:43:04
Slapneck 2 25 46N21 86W56 5:47:44
Slocum 61 66 43N12 85W57 5:43:48
Sly Farms 63 88 42N32 83W17 5:33:08
Smith Corners 64 64 43N42 86W22 5:45:28
Smiths Creek 74 1 42N55 82W36 5:30:24
Smyrna 34 92 43N04 85W16 5:41:04
Snover 76 1 43N28 82W58 5:31:52
Snyderville 74 1 42N49 82W45 5:31:00
Sodus 11 1 42N02 86W23 5:45:32
Solon 45 1 44N51 85W48 5:43:12
Somerset 30 1 42N02 84W25 5:37:40
Sonoma 13 43 42N20 85W11 5:40:44
Soo 17 45 46N30 84W21 5:37:24
Soo Corner 48 25 46N19 85W15 5:41:00
South Arm 15 1 45N10 85W10 5:40:40
South Blendon 70 54 42N52 85W51 5:43:24
South Boardman 40 1 44N38 85W17 5:41:08
South Branch 65 1 44N28 83W53 5:35:32
South Butler 12 1 41N57 84W53 5:39:32
South Camden 30 1 41N47 84W48 5:39:12
Southfield 63 88 42N29 83W17 5:33:08
South Fox Island 45
1 45N25 85W51 5:43:24
Southgate 82 2 42N12 83W12 5:32:48
South Haven 80 93 42N24 86W16 5:45:04
South Ionia 34 92 42N58 85W04 5:40:16
Southkent 41 61 42N54 85W38 5:42:32
Southland 38 90 42N14 84W24 5:37:36
South Lyon 63 88 42N28 83W39 5:34:36
South Manitou 45 1 45N01 85W45 5:43:00
South Monroe 58 36 41N54 83W25 5:33:40
South Monterey 3 92 42N36 85W50 5:43:20
South Park 74 1 42N58 82W29 5:29:56
South Range 31 96 47N04 88W38 5:54:32
South Riley 19 41 42N51 84W34 5:38:16
South Rockwood 58 1 42N04 83W16 5:33:04
South Whitehall 61
64 43N24 86W20 5:45:20
Spalding 55 81 45N47 87W30 5:50:00
Sparlingville 74 1 42N58 82W32 5:30:08
Sparr 69 1 45N02 84W41 5:38:44
Sparta 41 64 43N10 85W42 5:42:48
Spaulding 73 6 43N22 83W58 5:35:52
Speaker 76 1 43N12 82W49 5:31:16
Spencer 40 1 44N44 85W11 5:40:44
Spencer 41 57 43N15 85W22 5:41:28
Spinks Corners 11 4 42N06 86W27 5:45:48
Spratt 4 1 45N05 83W43 5:34:52
Spring Arbor 38 1 42N12 84W33 5:38:12
Spring Beach 14 73 41N55 86W01 5:44:04
Springdale 51 1 44N29 86W00 5:44:00
Springfield 13 43 42N16 85W12 5:40:48
Springfield 63 88 42N43 83W25 5:33:40
Springfield Place 13
43 42N18 85W13 5:40:52
Spring Grove 3 74 42N36 86W06 5:44:24
Spring Lake 70 56 43N05 86W11 5:44:44
Springport 38 1 42N22 84W42 5:38:48
Springvale 24 67 45N21 84W48 5:39:12
Springville 46 1 42N00 84W11 5:36:44
Springville 83 1 44N23 85W46 5:43:04
Springwells 82 2 42N19 83W07 5:32:28
Spruce 1 1 44N51 83W28 5:33:52
Spurr 7 25 46N33 88W12 5:52:48
Stalwart 17 12 46N06 84W14 5:36:56
Stambaugh 36 86 46N05 88W38 5:54:32
Standale 41 61 42N59 85W42 5:42:48
Standish 6 1 43N59 83W57 5:35:48
Stanley 13 43 42N16 85W04 5:40:16
Stannard 66 25 46N36 89W10 5:56:40
Stanton 59 57 43N18 85W05 5:40:20
Stanwood 54 1 43N35 85W27 5:41:48
Star 5 1 45N00 84W55 5:39:40
Star Corners 51 1 44N13 85W58 5:43:52
Steamburg 30 1 41N55 84W38 5:38:32
Steiner 58 36 41N55 83W23 5:33:32
Stephenson 55 86 45N25 87W36 5:50:24
Sterling 6 1 44N02 84W02 5:36:08
Sterling Heights 50
88 42N35 83W01 5:32:04
Steuben 77 25 46N11 86W27 5:45:48
Stevensville 11 74 42N01 86W31 5:46:04
Stittsville 57 1 44N20 85W12 5:40:48
Stockbridge 33 1 42N27 84W11 5:36:44
Stoney Corners 57 1 44N12 85W13 5:40:52
Stonington 21 25 45N43 86W58 5:47:52
Stony Creek 58 36 41N55 83W23 5:33:32
Stony Creek 63 88 42N39 83W09 5:32:36
Stony Creek 81 1 42N00 83W32 5:34:08
Stony Lake 64 64 43N37 86W22 5:45:28
Stony Point 58 1 41N57 83W16 5:33:04
Strasburg 58 36 41N55 83W23 5:33:32
Strathmoor 82 2 42N23 83W11 5:32:44
Strawberry Point 70
68 43N04 86W11 5:44:44
Strickland 37 1 43N23 84W50 5:39:20
Stronach 51 111 44N13 86W17 5:45:08
Strongs 17 12 46N22 84W58 5:39:52
Stuart Lake 13 1 42N16 84W58 5:39:52
Sturgeon Point 1 1 44N39 83W18 5:33:12
Sturgeon River 21
25 45N56 86W58 5:47:52
Sturgis 75 48 41N48 85W25 5:41:40
Sugargrove 53 57 43N57 86W17 5:45:08
Sugar Island 17 12 46N28 84W12 5:36:48
Sugar Rapids 26 1 43N59 84W29 5:37:56
Sullivan 61 57 43N11 86W05 5:44:20
Summer Haven 61 49 43N12 86W16 5:45:04
Summer Island 21 25 45N34 86W39 5:46:36
Summit City 28 1 44N35 85W32 5:42:08
Summit Heights 72 1 44N18 84W45 5:39:00
Sumner 29 1 43N20 84W47 5:39:08
Sumnerville 14 72 41N56 86W12 5:44:48
Sumpter 82 36 42N09 83W29 5:33:56
Sun 62 64 43N20 85W49 5:43:16
Sunfield 23 97 42N46 85W00 5:40:00
Sunnyside 74 1 42N59 82W40 5:30:40
Sunrise Heights 13
43 42N18 85W10 5:40:40
Sunset Beach 38 1 42N06 84W15 5:37:00
Sunset Beach 77 14 45N58 86W15 5:45:00
Surrey 18 1 43N52 84W54 5:39:36
Suttons Bay 45 1 44N59 85W39 5:42:36
Swains Lake 38 1 42N10 84W39 5:38:36
Swan Creek 73 1 43N21 84W08 5:36:32
Swartz Creek 25 1 42N58 83W50 5:35:20
Swedetown 31 96 47N15 88W27 5:53:48
Sweetwater 43 92 43N57 85W59 5:43:56
Sylvan 81 1 42N19 84W01 5:36:04
Sylvan Lake 63 88 42N37 83W20 5:33:20
Sylvester 54 1 43N37 85W14 5:40:56
Tacoma Park 50 88 42N34 83W02 5:32:08
Talbot 55 86 45N28 87W37 5:50:28
Tallmadge 70 51 42N59 85W49 5:43:16
Tallman 53 57 44N03 86W11 5:44:44
Tamarack 31 96 47N15 88W27 5:53:48
Tamarack Lake 27 81 46N09 88W46 5:55:04
Tapiola 31 96 46N54 88W37 5:54:28
Tarryton 50 88 42N34 83W02 5:32:08
Tawas 35 1 44N17 83W34 5:34:16
Tawas Centre 35 1 44N17 83W29 5:33:56
Tawas City 35 1 44N16 83W31 5:34:04
Taylor 82 2 42N14 83W16 5:33:04
Taylor Park 39 47 42N18 85W37 5:42:28
Taylor Park 82 2 42N14 83W16 5:33:04
Taymouth 73 1 43N16 83W52 5:35:28
Tecumseh 46 1 42N00 83W57 5:35:48
Tekonsha 13 1 42N05 85W00 5:40:00
Teleford 82 2 42N19 83W16 5:33:04
Telreka 82 2 42N14 83W16 5:33:04
Temperance 58 1 41N47 83W34 5:34:16
Temple 18 1 44N01 84W48 5:39:12
Tesch 21 25 45N43 87W18 5:49:12
Texas 39 92 42N12 85W42 5:42:48
Texas Corners 39 47 42N17 85W34 5:42:16
The Finger Board Corner 16
1 45N22 84W30 5:38:00
The Heights 38 1 42N06 84W15 5:37:00
The Mission 17 110 46N24 84W34 5:38:16
Theodore 22 87 45N48 88W04 5:52:16
Thetford 25 1 43N10 83W38 5:34:32
Thetford Center 25
1 43N08 83W44 5:34:56
Thomas 63 88 42N49 83W16 5:33:04
Thomas 73 1 43N25 84W05 5:36:20
Thomaston 27 81 46N31 89W56 5:59:44
Thompson 77 25 45N54 86W21 5:45:24
Thompsonville 10 1 44N31 85W56 5:43:44
Thornapple 8 57 42N43 85W29 5:41:56
Thornton 74 1 42N55 82W36 5:30:24
Thornville 44 1 42N56 83W17 5:33:08
Three Lakes 7 25 46N33 88W13 5:52:52
Three Mile Lake 80
46 42N13 85W53 5:43:32
Three Oaks 11 107 41N48 86W36 5:46:24
Three Rivers 75 97 41N57 85W38 5:42:32
Tilden 52 25 46N24 87W40 5:50:40
Tipton 46 1 42N01 84W04 5:36:16
Tittabawassee 73 1 43N31 84W07 5:36:28
Tobacco 26 1 43N51 84W26 5:37:44
Tobin Location 36
81 46N06 88W20 5:53:20
Toivola 31 96 47N00 88W47 5:55:08
Tompkins 38 1 42N23 84W32 5:38:08
Tonquish 82 36 42N18 83W23 5:33:32
Topaz 66 25 46N32 89W17 5:57:08

MICHIGAN

Topinabee 16 1 45N29 84w36 5:38:24
Toquin 80 74 42N12 86w10 5:44:40
Torch Lake Village 5 1 45N07 85w21 5:41:24
Torch River 5 1 44N50 85w17 5:41:08
Towar Gardens 33 41 42N44 84w28 5:37:52
Tower 16 1 45N21 84w18 5:37:12
Tower Hill 11 74 41N53 86w37 5:46:28
Town Corners 64 64 43N33 86w21 5:45:24
Traunik 2 25 46N16 86w58 5:47:52
Traverse Bay 31 96 47N12 88w24 5:53:36
Traverse City 28 1 44N46 85w38 5:42:32
Tremaine Corners 34 92 42N59 85w04 5:40:16
Trenary 2 31 46N12 86w58 5:47:52
Trent 61 64 43N17 85w49 5:43:16
Trenton 82 37 42N08 83w11 5:32:44
Triangle Park 72 1 44N30 84w36 5:38:24
Trimountain 31 96 47N03 88w40 5:54:40
Trips Subdivision 63 88 42N37 83w26 5:33:44
Trist 38 1 42N15 84w12 5:36:48
Trombly 21 25 46N04 87w10 5:48:40
Trout Creek 66 28 46N29 89w01 5:56:04
Trout Lake 17 92 46N12 85w01 5:40:04
Trowbridge 3 92 42N28 85w50 5:43:20
Trowbridge 33 41 42N44 84w28 5:37:52
Trowbridge Park 52 25 46N33 87w24 5:49:36
Troy 63 88 42N37 83w09 5:32:36
Trufant 59 57 43N19 85w21 5:41:24
Turin 52 11 46N12 87w15 5:49:00
Turk Lake 59 57 43N11 85w15 5:41:00
Turner 6 1 44N09 83w47 5:35:08
Tuscarora 16 1 45N25 84w38 5:38:32
Tuscola 79 1 43N21 83w38 5:34:32
Tustin 67 1 44N06 85w28 5:41:52
Twelve Corners 11 4 42N06 86w27 5:45:48
Twin Beach 63 88 42N32 83w27 5:33:48
Twining 6 1 44N07 83w49 5:35:16
Twin Lake 61 57 43N22 86w10 5:44:40
Twin Lakes 14 71 41N59 86w07 5:44:28
Twin Lakes 31 25 46N52 88w55 5:55:40
Two Rivers 37 1 43N36 84w46 5:39:04
Tyre 76 1 43N42 82w56 5:31:44
Tyrone Lake 47 1 42N49 83w43 5:34:52
Ubly 32 1 43N43 82w56 5:31:44
Unadilla 47 1 42N28 84w05 5:36:20
Union 14 72 41N48 85w54 5:43:36
Union City 12 1 42N04 85w08 5:40:32
Union Lake 63 88 42N37 83w27 5:33:48
Union Pier 11 75 41N50 86w42 5:46:48
Unionville 79 1 43N39 83w28 5:33:52
University of Michigan 81 38 42N17 83w44 5:34:56
Upjohn 39 47 42N13 85w35 5:42:20
Urbandale 13 43 42N20 85w10 5:40:40
Urbandale 33 41 42N41 84w33 5:38:12
Utica 50 88 42N38 83w02 5:32:08
Valley 3 92 42N33 85w58 5:43:52
Valley Center 76 1 43N11 82w52 5:31:28
Valley Farms 33 41 42N46 84w32 5:38:08
Van 24 67 45N38 84w47 5:39:08
Van Buren 82 36 42N13 83w29 5:33:56
Vandalia 14 76 41N55 85w55 5:43:40
Vanderbilt 69 1 45N09 84w40 5:38:40
Vandercook Lake 38 90 42N14 84w24 5:37:36
Van Dyke 50 2 42N28 83w00 5:32:00
Van Etten Lake 35 1 44N25 83w20 5:33:20
Van Meer 2 25 46N21 86w28 5:45:52
Van Pelham 82 2 42N17 83w17 5:33:08
Vassar 79 1 43N22 83w35 5:34:20
Venice 78 1 43N00 83w59 5:35:56
Ventnor Manor 50 88 42N34 83w02 5:32:08
Vergennes 41 57 42N59 85w22 5:41:28
Vermontville 23 92 42N39 85w01 5:40:04
Vernon 78 70 42N56 84w02 5:36:08
Vernon City 37 1 43N50 84w46 5:39:04
Verona 27 81 46N29 89w56 5:59:44
Verona 32 6 43N48 82w56 5:31:44
Verona Park 13 43 42N21 85w09 5:40:36
Vestaburg 59 57 43N24 84w54 5:39:36
Veterans Administration Hosp 22 87 45N48 88w04 5:52:16
Vevay 33 1 42N33 84w25 5:37:40
Vickery Landing 8 57 42N31 85w15 5:41:00
Vickeryville 59 57 43N13 85w04 5:40:16
Vicksburg 39 100 42N07 85w32 5:42:08
Victor 19 1 42N54 84w25 5:37:40
Victoria 66 25 46N41 89w11 5:56:44
Victory 53 57 44N02 86w21 5:45:24
Vineland 11 1 42N05 86w30 5:46:00
Virginia Park 70 51 42N47 86w07 5:44:28
Vogel Center 57 1 44N12 85w13 5:40:52
Volinia 14 72 42N02 85w56 5:43:44
Volney 62 57 43N45 85w52 5:43:28
Vriesland 70 54 42N49 86w01 5:44:04
Vulcan 22 87 45N47 87w53 5:51:32
Wabaningo 61 64 43N24 86w20 5:45:20
Wacousta 19 1 42N45 84w45 5:39:00
Wadhams 74 1 42N58 82w29 5:29:56
Wagarville 26 1 43N59 84w29 5:37:56
Wainola 66 25 46N45 89w05 5:56:20
Wakefield 27 86 46N29 89w56 5:59:44
Wakelee 14 72 42N01 85w49 5:43:16
Wakeshma 39 92 42N07 85w21 5:41:24
Waldenburg 50 88 42N35 82w54 5:31:36
Waldron 30 1 41N44 84w25 5:37:40
Wales 74 1 42N57 82w41 5:30:44
Walhalla 53 57 43N57 86w07 5:44:28
Walker 41 61 42N59 85w46 5:43:04
Walkers Point 49 1 44N48 82w55 5:31:40
Walkerville 64 57 43N43 86w08 5:44:32
Wallace 55 81 45N20 87w37 5:50:28
Walled Lake 63 88 42N32 83w29 5:33:56
Wallin 10 1 44N31 85w56 5:43:44
Wall Lake 8 57 42N30 85w24 5:41:36
Walloon Lake 15 1 45N16 84w56 5:39:44
Walnut Lake 63 88 42N32 83w17 5:33:08
Walton 23 1 42N28 84w54 5:39:36
Waltz 82 36 42N06 83w23 5:33:32
Wardcliff 33 41 42N44 84w28 5:37:52
Warner 5 1 45N04 84w54 5:39:36
Warren 50 2 42N31 83w02 5:32:08
Wasepi 75 103 41N56 85w32 5:42:08
Washington 50 88 42N41 83w03 5:32:12
Waterford 63 88 42N39 83w23 5:33:32
Waterloo 38 1 42N22 84w11 5:36:44
Watermill Lake 43 92 43N54 85w46 5:43:04
Waters 69 1 44N53 84w42 5:38:48
Watersmeet 27 86 46N16 89w11 5:56:44
Watertown 76 1 43N25 82w50 5:31:20
Watervale 10 1 44N30 86w14 5:44:56
Watervliet 11 74 42N12 86w16 5:45:04
Watrousville 79 1 43N22 83w35 5:34:20
Watson 3 92 42N33 85w44 5:42:56
Wattles Park 13 43 42N20 85w11 5:40:44
Watton 7 25 46N32 88w36 5:54:24
Waucedah 22 87 45N49 87w45 5:51:00
Waukuzoo 70 51 42N47 86w07 5:44:28
Waverly 23 41 42N44 84w36 5:38:24
Wawatam Beach 16 1 45N47 84w44 5:38:56
Wayland 3 92 42N40 85w39 5:42:36
Wayne 82 36 42N17 83w23 5:33:32
Weadlock 16 1 45N38 84w47 5:39:08
Weale 32 1 43N51 83w23 5:33:32
Weare 64 57 43N47 86w20 5:45:20
Webber 43 92 43N57 85w51 5:43:24
Webberville 33 1 42N40 84w10 5:36:40
Webster 81 1 42N23 83w51 5:35:24
Weesaw 11 74 41N52 86w32 5:46:08
Weidman 37 1 43N41 84w58 5:39:52
Weldon 10 1 44N33 86w00 5:44:00
Wellington 4 6 45N09 83w49 5:35:16
Wells 21 19 45N47 87w05 5:48:20
Wellston 51 1 44N13 85w58 5:43:52
Wellsville 46 1 41N50 83w52 5:35:28
Wequetonsing 24 67 45N26 84w59 5:39:56
West Acres 63 1 42N36 83w26 5:33:44
West Bloomfield 63 88 42N34 83w22 5:33:28
West Branch 65 1 44N17 84w14 5:36:56
Westchester Village 63 88 43N15 83w48 5:35:12
Westgate 41 61 43N03 85w41 5:42:44
West Highland 63 88 42N38 83w37 5:34:28
West Ishpeming 52 25 46N30 87w40 5:50:40
West Kinderhook 12 1 41N57 85w00 5:40:00
Westland 82 36 42N18 83w23 5:33:32
West Leroy 13 1 42N10 85w13 5:40:52
West Millbrook 54 57 43N31 85w05 5:40:20
West Novi 63 88 42N33 83w30 5:34:00
West Olive 70 51 42N55 86w09 5:44:36
Weston 46 1 41N46 84w06 5:36:24
Westphalia 19 1 42N56 84w48 5:39:12
West Plains 61 49 43N12 86w16 5:45:04
West Roodmont 61 49 43N12 86w16 5:45:04
West Sebewa 34 92 42N52 84w54 5:39:36
West Traverse 24 67 45N27 85w01 5:40:04
Westville 59 57 43N18 85w05 5:40:20
West Willow 81 36 42N15 83w37 5:34:28
West Windsor 23 1 42N34 84w50 5:39:20
Westwood 39 47 42N18 85w38 5:42:32
Westwood 40 1 44N55 85w04 5:40:16
Westwood 61 49 43N12 86w16 5:45:04
Wetmore 2 22 46N23 86w37 5:46:28
Wetzel 5 1 44N55 85w04 5:40:16
Wexford 83 1 44N28 85w46 5:43:04
Wheatfield 33 1 42N39 84w18 5:37:12
Wheeler 29 1 43N25 84w26 5:37:44
White 31 25 46N45 88w48 5:55:12
White City 27 81 46N23 89w41 5:58:44
White Cloud 62 64 43N33 85w46 5:43:04
Whitefish 17 12 46N35 85w07 5:40:28
Whitefish Point 17 12 46N45 84w59 5:39:56
Whiteford 58 1 41N46 83w42 5:34:48
Whiteford Center 58 1 41N46 83w45 5:35:00
Whitehall 61 64 43N24 86w21 5:45:24
White Lake 63 88 42N39 83w29 5:33:56
White Lake Center 63 88 42N37 83w26 5:33:44
White Oak 33 1 42N33 84w12 5:36:48
White Pigeon 75 1 41N48 85w39 5:42:36
White Pine 66 25 46N45 89w35 5:58:20
White River 61 57 43N26 86w25 5:45:40
White Rock 35 1 44N14 83w43 5:34:52
Whites Beach 6 1 43N59 83w58 5:35:52
Whitewater 28 1 44N47 85w23 5:41:32
Whitmore Lake 81 1 42N27 83w45 5:35:00
Whitney 6 6 44N07 83w37 5:34:28
Whitney 55 81 45N43 87w22 5:49:28
Whittaker 81 1 42N08 83w36 5:34:24
Whittemore 35 1 44N14 83w48 5:35:12
Wickware 76 1 43N36 83w10 5:32:40
Wilber 35 1 44N23 83w31 5:34:04
Wilcox 62 64 43N36 85w45 5:43:00
Wildwood 15 1 45N13 85w01 5:40:04
Wildwood 24 67 45N27 84w47 5:39:08
Wildwood 51 1 44N25 86w11 5:44:44
Wildwood 61 49 43N12 86w16 5:45:04
Wiley 53 57 43N57 86w17 5:45:08
Willard 9 1 43N36 84w05 5:36:20
Williams 9 1 43N37 84w08 5:36:32
Williamsburg 28 1 44N46 85w24 5:41:36
Williamston 33 1 42N41 84w17 5:37:08
Williamsville 14 76 41N55 85w55 5:43:40
Williamsville 47 1 42N28 84w05 5:36:20
Willis 81 36 42N09 83w34 5:34:16
Willow 82 36 42N07 83w24 5:33:36
Willow Run 81 36 42N16 83w35 5:34:20
Willwalk 17 45 46N29 84w21 5:37:24
Wilmot 16 1 45N15 84w40 5:38:40
Wilmot 79 1 43N31 83w11 5:32:44
Wilson 55 81 45N42 87w27 5:49:48
Winchester Village 25 1 42N59 83w47 5:35:08
Windemere 33 41 42N44 84w36 5:38:24
Windiate 63 88 42N42 83w24 5:33:36
Windmill Island 70 51 42N47 86w07 5:44:28
Windsor 23 1 42N38 84w40 5:38:40
Winegars 26 1 43N59 84w29 5:37:56
Winfield 59 57 43N25 85w23 5:41:32
Wing Lake Shores 63 88 42N32 83w17 5:33:08
Winn 37 1 43N32 84w54 5:39:36
Winona 31 25 46N53 88w55 5:55:40
Winsor 32 1 43N48 83w18 5:33:12
Winterfield 18 1 44N07 85w02 5:40:08
Winters 2 25 46N10 86w58 5:47:52
Winthrop Junction 52 25 46N30 87w40 5:50:40
Wise 37 1 43N47 84w40 5:38:40
Wisner 79 1 43N36 83w38 5:34:32
Witch Lake 52 25 46N16 87w59 5:51:56
Wixom 63 88 42N32 83w32 5:34:08
Wojciechowski 9 36 43N36 83w54 5:35:36
Wolf Lake 38 90 42N15 84w24 5:37:36
Wolf Lake 43 92 43N54 85w51 5:43:24
Wolf Lake 61 57 43N15 86w07 5:44:28
Wolverine 16 1 45N17 84w36 5:38:24
Wolverine Lake 63 88 42N33 83w29 5:33:56
Woodard Lake 34 92 43N09 85w05 5:40:20
Woodbridge 30 1 41N47 84w39 5:38:36
Woodbury 8 57 42N45 85w04 5:40:16
Wood Creek Farms 63 88 42N31 83w20 5:33:20
Wooden Shoe Village 26 1 43N59 84w29 5:37:56
Woodhaven 82 36 42N08 83w14 5:32:56
Woodhull 78 1 42N49 84w19 5:37:16
Woodland 8 57 42N44 85w08 5:40:32
Woodland Beach 58 1 41N56 83w19 5:33:16
Woodland Park 62 57 43N42 85w52 5:43:28
Woods Corner 37 1 43N50 84w52 5:39:28
Woodside 31 96 47N07 88w31 5:54:04
Wood Spur 66 25 46N52 89w18 5:57:12
Woodstock 46 1 42N02 84w18 5:37:12
Woodville 9 1 43N51 83w58 5:35:52
Woodville 38 90 42N15 84w24 5:37:36
Woodville 62 64 43N33 85w46 5:43:04
Wooster 62 57 43N28 85w56 5:43:44
Worth 6 1 43N51 83w58 5:35:52
Worth 76 1 43N13 82w33 5:30:12
Wright 70 51 43N08 85w52 5:43:28
Wrights Corners 13 1 42N16 84w58 5:39:52
Wurtsmith Air Force Base 35 1 44N27 83w24 5:33:36
Wyandotte 82 2 42N12 83w09 5:32:36
Wyman 59 57 43N31 85w05 5:40:20
Wyoming 41 61 42N54 85w42 5:42:48
Wyoming Park 41 61 42N55 85w42 5:42:48
Yale 27 81 46N29 90w03 6:00:12
Yale 74 1 43N08 82w48 5:31:12
Yankee Springs 8 57 42N39 85w30 5:42:00
Yates 43 92 43N52 85w47 5:43:08
Yellow Jacket 31 96 47N15 88w27 5:53:48
York 81 1 42N08 83w43 5:34:52
Yorkville 39 92 42N23 85w27 5:41:48
Ypsilanti 81 36 42N14 83w37 5:34:28
Yuba 28 1 44N46 85w24 5:41:36
Yuma 83 1 44N24 85w43 5:42:52
Zeba 7 25 46N46 88w27 5:53:48
Zeeland 70 54 42N49 86w01 5:44:04
Zenith Heights 15 1 45N13 85w01 5:40:04
Zilwaukee 73 91 43N29 83w55 5:35:40
Zutphen 70 54 42N52 85w51 5:43:24

TIME TABLES

MN # 1

Date	Time	Zone
Before 2/26/1901		LMT
2/26/1901	12:00	CST
3/31/1918	02:00	CWT
10/27/1918	02:00	CST
3/30/1919	02:00	CWT
10/26/1919	02:00	CST
2/09/1942	02:00	CWT
9/30/1945	02:00	CST
4/28/1957	02:00	CDT
9/29/1957	02:00	CST
4/27/1958	02:00	CDT
9/02/1958	02:00	CST
5/24/1959	02:00	CDT
9/08/1959	02:00	CST
5/22/1960	02:00	CDT
9/06/1960	02:00	CST
5/28/1961	02:00	CDT
9/05/1961	02:00	CST
5/27/1962	02:00	CDT
9/04/1962	02:00	CST
5/26/1963	02:00	CDT
9/03/1963	02:00	CST
5/24/1964	02:00	CDT
9/08/1964	02:00	CST
5/23/1965	02:00	CDT
9/07/1965	02:00	CST
4/24/1966	02:00	US#1

MN # 2

Date	Time	Zone
Before 2/26/1901		LMT
2/26/1901	12:00	CST
3/31/1918	02:00	CWT
10/27/1918	02:00	CST
3/30/1919	02:00	CWT
10/26/1919	02:00	CST
4/24/1932	02:00	CDT
9/06/1932	02:00	CST
4/28/1946	02:00	CDT
9/29/1946	02:00	CST
4/28/1957	02:00	CDT
9/29/1957	02:00	CST
4/27/1958	02:00	CDT
9/02/1958	02:00	CST
4/26/1959	02:00	CDT
9/27/1959	02:00	CST
5/22/1960	02:00	CDT
9/06/1960	02:00	CST
5/28/1961	02:00	CDT
9/05/1961	02:00	CST
5/27/1962	02:00	CDT
9/04/1962	02:00	CST
5/26/1963	02:00	CDT
9/03/1963	02:00	CST
5/24/1964	02:00	CDT
9/08/1964	02:00	CST
4/25/1965	02:00	CDT
10/31/1965	02:00	CST
4/24/1966	02:00	US#1

MN # 3

Date	Time	Zone
Before 2/26/1901		LMT
2/26/1901	12:00	CST
3/31/1918	02:00	CWT
10/27/1918	02:00	CST
3/30/1919	02:00	CWT
10/26/1919	02:00	CST
2/09/1942	02:00	CWT
9/30/1945	02:00	CST
4/28/1957	02:00	CDT
9/29/1957	02:00	CST
4/27/1958	02:00	CDT
9/02/1958	02:00	CST
4/26/1959	02:00	CDT
9/27/1959	02:00	CST
5/22/1960	02:00	CDT
9/06/1960	02:00	CST
5/28/1961	02:00	CDT
9/05/1961	02:00	CST
5/27/1962	02:00	CDT
9/04/1962	02:00	CST
5/26/1963	02:00	CDT
9/03/1963	02:00	CST
5/24/1964	02:00	CDT
9/08/1964	02:00	CST
5/23/1965	02:00	CDT
9/07/1965	02:00	CST
4/24/1966	02:00	US#1

MN # 4

Date	Time	Zone
Before 2/26/1901		LMT
2/26/1901	12:00	CST
3/31/1918	02:00	CWT
10/27/1918	02:00	CST
3/30/1919	02:00	CWT
10/26/1919	02:00	CST
2/09/1942	02:00	CWT
9/30/1945	02:00	CST
4/28/1957	02:00	CDT
9/29/1957	02:00	CST
4/27/1958	02:00	CDT
9/02/1958	02:00	CST
4/26/1959	02:00	CDT
10/25/1959	02:00	CST
5/22/1960	02:00	CDT
9/06/1960	02:00	CST
5/28/1961	02:00	CDT
9/05/1961	02:00	CST
5/27/1962	02:00	CDT
9/04/1962	02:00	CST
5/26/1963	02:00	CDT
9/03/1963	02:00	CST
5/24/1964	02:00	CDT
9/08/1964	02:00	CST
5/23/1965	02:00	CDT
9/07/1965	02:00	CST
4/24/1966	02:00	US#1

MN # 5

Date	Time	Zone
Before 2/26/1901		LMT
2/26/1901	12:00	CST
3/31/1918	02:00	CWT
10/27/1918	02:00	CST
3/30/1919	02:00	CWT
10/26/1919	02:00	CST
2/09/1942	02:00	CWT
9/30/1945	02:00	CST
4/28/1957	02:00	CDT
9/29/1957	02:00	CST
4/27/1958	02:00	CDT
9/02/1958	02:00	CST
5/24/1959	02:00	CDT
9/08/1959	02:00	CST
5/22/1960	02:00	CDT
9/06/1960	02:00	CST
5/28/1961	02:00	CDT
9/05/1961	02:00	CST
5/27/1962	02:00	CDT
9/04/1962	02:00	CST
5/26/1963	02:00	CDT
9/03/1963	02:00	CST
5/24/1964	02:00	CDT
9/08/1964	02:00	CST
5/09/1965	02:00	CDT
10/31/1965	02:00	CST
4/24/1966	02:00	US#1

MN # 6

Date	Time	Zone
Before 2/26/1901		LMT
2/26/1901	12:00	CST
3/31/1918	02:00	CWT
10/27/1918	02:00	CST
3/30/1919	02:00	CWT
10/26/1919	02:00	CST
2/09/1942	02:00	CWT
9/30/1945	02:00	CST
4/28/1957	02:00	CDT
9/29/1957	02:00	CST
4/27/1958	02:00	CDT
9/02/1958	02:00	CST
5/24/1959	02:00	CDT
9/08/1959	02:00	CST
5/22/1960	02:00	CDT
9/06/1960	02:00	CST
5/28/1961	02:00	CDT
9/05/1961	02:00	CST
5/27/1962	02:00	CDT
9/04/1962	02:00	CST
5/26/1963	02:00	CDT
9/03/1963	02:00	CST
5/24/1964	02:00	CDT
9/08/1964	02:00	CST
4/25/1965	02:00	CDT
10/31/1965	02:00	CST
4/24/1966	02:00	US#1

MN # 7

Date	Time	Zone
Before 2/26/1901		LMT
2/26/1901	12:00	CST
3/31/1918	02:00	CWT
10/27/1918	02:00	CST
3/30/1919	02:00	CWT
10/26/1919	02:00	CST
2/09/1942	02:00	CWT
9/30/1945	02:00	CST
4/28/1957	02:00	CDT
9/29/1957	02:00	CST
4/27/1958	02:00	CDT
9/02/1958	02:00	CST
4/26/1959	02:00	CDT
9/27/1959	02:00	CST
5/22/1960	02:00	CDT
9/06/1960	02:00	CST
5/28/1961	02:00	CDT
9/05/1961	02:00	CST
5/27/1962	02:00	CDT
9/04/1962	02:00	CST
5/26/1963	02:00	CDT
9/03/1963	02:00	CST
5/24/1964	02:00	CDT
9/08/1964	02:00	CST
4/25/1965	02:00	CDT
10/31/1965	02:00	CST
4/24/1966	02:00	US#1

COUNTIES

1 Aitkin
2 Anoka
3 Becker
4 Beltrami
5 Benton
6 Big Stone
7 Blue Earth
8 Brown
9 Carlton
10 Carver
11 Cass
12 Chippewa
13 Chisago
14 Clay
15 Clearwater
16 Cook
17 Cottonwood
18 Crow Wing
19 Dakota
20 Dodge
21 Douglas
22 Faribault
23 Fillmore
24 Freeborn
25 Goodhue
26 Grant
27 Hennepin
28 Houston
29 Hubbard
30 Isanti
31 Itasca
32 Jackson
33 Kanabec
34 Kandiyohi
35 Kittson
36 Koochiching
37 Lac Qui Parle
38 Lake
39 Lake of the Woods
40 Le Sueur
41 Lincoln
42 Lyon
43 McLeod
44 Mahnomen
45 Marshall
46 Martin
47 Meeker
48 Mille Lacs
49 Morrison
50 Mower
51 Murray
52 Nicollet
53 Nobles
54 Norman
55 Olmsted
56 Otter Tail
57 Pennington
58 Pine
59 Pipestone
60 Polk
61 Pope
62 Ramsey
63 Red Lake
64 Redwood
65 Renville
66 Rice
67 Rock
68 Roseau
69 St Louis
70 Scott
71 Sherburne
72 Sibley
73 Stearns
74 Steele
75 Stevens
76 Swift
77 Todd
78 Traverse
79 Wabasha
80 Wadena
81 Waseca
82 Washington
83 Watonwan
84 Wilkin
85 Winona
86 Wright
87 Yellow Medicine

Place	TT	Lat	Long	Time
Aastad 56	1	46N09	96w05	6:24:20
Acoma 43	1	44N56	94w26	6:17:44
Acton 47	1	45N07	94w41	6:18:44
Ada 54	1	47N18	96w31	6:26:04
Adams 50	1	43N34	92w43	6:10:52
Adolph 69	1	46N46	92w17	6:09:08
Adrian 53	1	43N38	95w56	6:23:44
Aetna 59	1	44N09	96w07	6:24:28
Afton 82	1	44N55	92w49	6:11:16
Agassiz 37	1	45N12	96w17	6:25:08
Agder 45	1	48N13	96w03	6:24:12
Agram 49	1	45N57	94w10	6:16:40
Aitkin 1	1	46N32	93w42	6:14:48
Akeley 29	1	47N00	94w44	6:18:56
Alango 69	1	47N46	92w45	6:11:00
Alaska 4	1	47N47	95w04	6:20:16
Alba 32	1	43N43	95w24	6:21:36
Albany 73	1	45N38	94w34	6:18:16
Alberta 75	1	45N35	96w03	6:24:12
Albert Lea 24	1	43N39	93w22	6:13:28
Albertville 86	1	45N14	93w39	6:14:36
Albin 8	1	44N09	94w41	6:18:44
Albion 86	1	45N12	94w04	6:16:16
Albion Center 86	1	45N16	94w08	6:16:32
Alborn 69	1	46N58	92w34	6:10:16
Alden 24	1	43N40	93w34	6:14:16
Aldrich 80	1	46N25	94w58	6:19:52
Alexandria 21	1	45N53	95w22	6:21:28
Alfsborg 72	1	44N30	94w19	6:17:16
Alida 15	1	47N32	95w15	6:21:00
Allen Junction 69	1	47N31	92w09	6:08:36
Alliance 14	1	46N41	96w36	6:26:24
Alma 45	1	48N20	96w42	6:26:48
Alma City 81	1	44N07	93w42	6:14:48
Almelund 13	1	45N29	92w47	6:11:08
Almond 6	1	45N28	96w25	6:25:40
Almora 56	1	46N19	95w26	6:21:44
Alpha 32	1	43N38	94w52	6:19:28
Alta Vista 41	1	44N35	96w09	6:24:36
Alton 81	1	44N04	93w42	6:14:48
Altona 59	1	44N09	96w23	6:25:32
Altura 85	1	44N04	91w56	6:07:44
Alvarado 45	1	48N12	97w00	6:28:00
Alvwood 31	1	47N44	94w16	6:17:04
Amador 13	1	45N31	92w46	6:11:04
Amboy 7	1	43N53	94w10	6:16:40
Amherst 23	1	43N38	91w53	6:07:32
Amiret 42	1	44N19	95w42	6:22:48
Amo 17	1	43N59	95w16	6:21:04
Amor 56	1	46N26	95w43	6:22:52
Andover 2	3	45N10	93w19	6:13:16
Andover 60	1	47N44	96w41	6:26:44
Andrea 84	1	46N20	96w21	6:25:24
Andyville 50	1	43N41	92w58	6:11:52
Angle Inlet 39	1	49N21	95w04	6:20:16
Angora 69	1	47N47	92w38	6:10:32
Angus 60	1	48N05	96w42	6:26:48
Ann 17	1	44N09	95w24	6:21:36
Annandale 86	1	45N16	94w08	6:16:32
Ann Lake 33	1	45N56	93w26	6:13:44
Anoka 2	1	45N12	93w23	6:13:32
Ansel 11	1	46N38	94w42	6:18:48
Anthony 54	1	47N22	96w39	6:26:36
Antlers Park 19	1	44N41	93w15	6:13:00
Antrim 83	1	43N53	94w26	6:17:44
Appleton 76	1	45N12	96w01	6:24:04
Apple Valley 19	1	44N45	93w13	6:12:52
Arago 29	1	47N01	95w06	6:20:24
Arbo 31	1	47N20	93w31	6:14:04
Arco 41	1	44N23	96w11	6:24:44
Arctander 34	1	45N17	95w12	6:20:48
Arcturus 31	1	47N19	93w24	6:13:36
Arden Hills 62	3	45N03	93w10	6:12:40
Ardenhurst 31	1	47N48	94w13	6:16:52
Arena 37	1	45N01	96w17	6:25:08
Arendahl 23	1	43N48	91w53	6:07:32
Argonne 19	1	44N41	93w15	6:13:00
Argyle 45	1	48N20	96w49	6:27:16
Arlington 72	1	44N36	94w05	6:16:20
Arlone 58	1	45N56	92w45	6:11:00
Armstrong 24	1	43N40	93w35	6:14:20
Arna 58	1	46N06	92w19	6:09:16
Arnesen 39	1	48N48	95w06	6:20:24
Arnold 69	1	46N53	92w05	6:08:20
Arrowhead 69	1	46N51	92w44	6:10:56
Arthyde 1	1	46N15	93w16	6:13:04
Artichoke 6	1	45N17	96w19	6:25:16
Artichoke Lake 6	1	45N14	96w10	6:24:40
Arveson 35	1	48N35	96w27	6:25:48
Ashby 26	1	46N06	95w49	6:23:16
Ashcreek 67	1	43N31	96w16	6:25:04
Ash Lake 41	1	44N25	96w16	6:25:04
Ash Lake 69	1	48N03	92w50	6:11:20
Ashland 20	1	43N59	92w52	6:11:28
Ashley 73	1	45N43	95w05	6:20:20
Askov 58	1	46N12	92w47	6:11:08
Aspelund 25	1	44N16	92w59	6:11:56
Assumption 10	1	44N41	94w01	6:16:04
Athens 30	1	45N27	93w18	6:13:12
Atherton 84	1	46N35	96w28	6:25:52
Atkinson 9	1	46N37	92w37	6:10:28
Atlanta 3	1	47N01	96w08	6:24:32
Atwater 34	1	45N08	94w47	6:19:08
Atwood 27	3	44N55	93w20	6:13:20
Audubon 3	1	46N52	95w59	6:23:56
Augsburg 45	1	48N30	96w43	6:26:52
Augusta 10	1	44N48	93w37	6:14:28
Augusta 37	1	45N01	96w24	6:25:36
Ault 69	1	47N15	91w54	6:07:36
Aurdal 56	1	46N20	95w58	6:23:52
Aure 4	1	47N36	95w08	6:20:32
Aurora 69	1	47N32	92w14	6:08:56
Austin 50	1	43N40	92w58	6:11:52
Austin Junction 50	1	43N41	92w58	6:11:52
Auto Club 27	3	44N50	93w16	6:13:04
Automba 9	1	46N33	92w58	6:11:52
Averill 14	1	46N58	96w33	6:26:12
Avoca 51	1	43N57	95w39	6:22:36
Avon 73	1	45N38	94w27	6:17:48
Babbitt 69	1	47N41	91w54	6:07:36
Backus 11	1	46N49	94w31	6:18:04
Badger 68	1	48N47	96w01	6:24:04
Badoura 29	1	46N51	94w43	6:18:52
Bagley 15	1	47N32	95w24	6:21:36
Baker 14	1	46N43	96w33	6:26:12
Balaton 42	1	44N14	95w52	6:23:28
Bald Eagle 62	1	45N06	93w01	6:12:04
Baldwin 71	1	45N31	93w35	6:14:20

MINNESOTA

Balkan 69	1	47N32	92w52	6:11:28
Ball Bluff 1	1	46N59	93w14	6:12:56
Ball Club 31	1	47N19	93w56	6:15:44
Balmoral 56	1	46N17	95w43	6:22:52
Bancroft 24	1	43N43	93w21	6:13:24
Bandon 65	1	44N35	94w48	6:19:12
Bangor 61	1	45N33	95w11	6:20:44
Barber 22	1	43N43	93w57	6:15:48
Barclay 11	1	46N46	94w22	6:17:28
Barden 70	1	44N48	93w32	6:14:08
Barnesville 14	1	46N39	96w25	6:25:40
Barnett 68	1	48N40	96w04	6:24:16
Barnum 9	1	46N30	92w42	6:10:48
Barr 25	1	44N18	92w40	6:10:40
Barrett 26	1	45N55	95w53	6:23:32
Barrows 18	1	46N48	94w15	6:17:00
Barry 6	1	45N34	96w34	6:26:16
Barsness 61	1	45N32	95w26	6:21:44
Bartlett 77	1	46N19	94w58	6:19:52
Barto 68	1	48N46	96w13	6:24:52
Bashaw 8	1	44N10	94w56	6:19:44
Bass Brook 31	1	47N14	93w39	6:14:36
Bassett 69	1	47N28	91w54	6:07:36
Basswood 56	1	46N30	95w38	6:22:32
Basswood Grove 82	1	44N40	92w50	6:11:20
Bath 24	1	43N49	93w21	6:13:24
Battle 4	1	47N59	94w42	6:18:48
Battle Lake 56	1	46N17	95w43	6:22:52
Battle Plain 67	1	43N48	96w07	6:24:28
Battle River 4	1	47N46	94w29	6:17:56
Baudette 39	1	48N43	94w36	6:18:24
Baxter 18	1	46N21	94w17	6:17:08
Bay Lake 18	1	46N23	93w52	6:15:28
Bayport 82	5	45N01	92w47	6:11:08
Baytown 82	1	45N01	92w48	6:11:12
Bayview 48	1	46N04	93w40	6:14:40
Bear Creek 15	1	47N22	95w14	6:20:56
Beardsley 6	1	45N33	96w43	6:26:52
Bear Park 54	1	47N27	96w08	6:24:32
Bear River 31	1	47N51	92w41	6:10:44
Bear Valley 79	1	44N27	92w16	6:09:04
Bearville 31	1	47N44	93w09	6:12:36
Beatty 69	1	47N59	92w38	6:10:32
Beauford 7	1	44N00	93w56	6:15:44
Beaulieu 44	1	47N20	95w48	6:23:12
Beaver 85	1	44N12	91w52	6:07:28
Beaver Bay 38	1	47N16	91w18	6:05:12
Beaver Creek 67	1	43N37	96w22	6:25:28
Beaver Falls 65	1	44N36	95w03	6:20:12
Bechyn 65	1	44N39	95w05	6:20:20
Becida 29	1	47N21	95w05	6:20:20
Becker 71	1	45N24	93w53	6:15:32
Bejou 44	1	47N26	95w58	6:23:52
Belfast 51	1	43N54	95w31	6:22:04
Belgium 60	1	47N59	96w33	6:26:12
Belgrade 73	1	45N27	95w00	6:20:00
Bellaire 62	3	45N04	93w00	6:12:00
Bellechester 25	1	44N22	92w31	6:10:04
Belle Creek 25	1	44N25	92w44	6:10:56
Belle Plaine 70	1	44N37	93w46	6:15:04
Belle Prairie 49	1	46N02	94w16	6:17:04
Belleriver 21	1	45N58	95w14	6:20:56
Bellevue 49	1	45N52	94w17	6:17:08
Bellingham 37	1	45N08	96w17	6:25:08
Belmont 32	1	43N43	95w05	6:20:20
Beltrami 60	1	47N33	96w32	6:26:08
Belvidere 25	1	44N25	92w28	6:09:52
Belview 64	1	44N36	95w20	6:21:20
Bemidji 4	1	47N28	94w53	6:19:32
Bena 11	1	47N21	94w12	6:16:48
Benedict 29	1	47N10	94w41	6:18:44
Bennettville 1	1	46N32	93w42	6:14:48
Bennington 50	1	43N38	92w30	6:10:00
Benson 76	1	45N19	95w36	6:22:24
Benton 10	1	44N46	93w49	6:15:16
Benville 4	1	48N19	95w33	6:22:12
Ben Wade 61	1	45N45	95w37	6:22:28
Bergen 32	1	43N47	95w00	6:20:00
Bergville 31	1	48N19	93w41	6:14:44
Berlin 74	1	43N54	93w21	6:13:24
Bernadotte 52	1	44N26	94w19	6:17:16
Berne 20	1	44N09	92w54	6:11:36
Berner 15	1	47N44	95w31	6:22:04
Beroun 58	1	45N55	92w58	6:11:52
Bertha 77	1	46N16	95w04	6:20:16
Beseman 9	1	46N43	93w00	6:12:00
Bethany 85	1	44N05	91w59	6:07:56
Bethel 2	1	45N24	93w16	6:13:04
Beulah 11	1	46N50	93w52	6:15:28
Big Bend 12	1	45N08	95w47	6:23:08
Big Bend City 12	1	45N09	95w46	6:23:04
Bigelow 53	1	43N30	95w42	6:22:48
Big Falls 36	1	48N12	93w48	6:15:12
Bigfork 31	1	47N45	93w39	6:14:36
Big Island 27	1	44N54	93w34	6:14:16
Big Lake 71	1	45N20	93w45	6:15:00
Big Stone 6	1	45N23	96w26	6:25:44
Big Stone City 6	1	45N17	96w26	6:25:44
Big Woods 45	1	48N20	97w04	6:28:16
Bingham Lake 17	1	43N54	95w03	6:20:12
Birch 4	1	47N38	94w29	6:17:56
Birch Beach 39	1	48N46	94w57	6:19:48
Birch Cooley 65	1	44N35	94w56	6:19:44
Birch Creek 58	1	46N23	92w59	6:11:56
Birchdale 36	1	48N37	94w06	6:16:24
Birchdale 77	1	45N48	94w50	6:19:20
Birch Lake 11	1	46N56	94w29	6:17:56
Birchwood 82	3	45N03	92w58	6:11:52
Bird Island 65	1	44N46	94w54	6:19:36
Biscay 43	1	44N50	94w16	6:17:04
Bismarck 72	1	44N35	94w26	6:17:44
Biwabik 69	1	47N32	92w21	6:09:24
Bixby 74	1	43N57	93w06	6:12:24
Blackberry 31	1	47N09	93w24	6:13:36
Blackduck 4	1	47N44	94w33	6:18:12
Black Hammer 28	1	43N38	91w40	6:06:40
Blackhoof 9	1	46N33	92w36	6:10:24
Black River 36	1	48N31	93w48	6:15:12
Black River 57	1	48N00	96w17	6:25:08
Blaine 2	3	45N10	93w13	6:12:52
Blakeley 70	1	44N36	93w51	6:15:24
Blind Lake 11	1	46N51	94w18	6:17:12
Blomford 30	1	45N30	93w15	6:13:00
Blomkest 34	1	44N57	95w01	6:20:04
Bloom 53	1	43N48	95w45	6:23:00
Bloom Dale 27	3	44N50	93w19	6:13:16
Bloomer 45	1	48N19	96w57	6:27:48
Bloomfield 23	1	43N38	92w23	6:09:32
Blooming Grove 81	1	44N09	93w29	6:13:56
Blooming Prairie 74	1	43N54	93w06	6:12:24
Bloomington 27	3	44N50	93w17	6:13:08
Blooming Valley 68	1	48N57	96w21	6:25:24
Blowers 56	1	46N35	95w13	6:20:52
Blueberry 80	1	46N46	95w06	6:20:24
Blue Earth 22	1	43N38	94w06	6:16:24
Blue Grass 80	1	46N33	95w01	6:20:04
Blue Hill 71	1	45N31	93w42	6:14:48
Blue Mounds 61	1	45N33	95w34	6:22:16
Bluffton 56	1	46N28	95w14	6:20:56
Bock 48	1	45N47	93w33	6:14:12
Bodum 30	1	45N30	93w15	6:13:00
Bogus Brook 48	1	45N41	93w34	6:14:16
Bois Fort 36	1	48N03	92w50	6:11:20
Bombay 25	1	44N16	92w59	6:11:56
Bonanza Grove 6	1	45N33	96w44	6:26:56
Bondin 51	1	43N53	95w38	6:22:32
Bongards 10	1	44N46	93w56	6:15:44
Bonnie Glen 13	1	45N22	92w53	6:11:32
Boon Lake 65	1	44N51	94w33	6:18:12
Border 36	1	48N43	94w36	6:18:24
Borgholm 48	1	45N46	93w35	6:14:20
Borup 54	1	47N11	96w30	6:26:00
Bovey 31	1	47N17	93w25	6:13:40
Bowlus 49	1	45N49	94w24	6:17:36
Bowstring 31	1	47N33	93w52	6:15:28
Boxville 45	1	48N11	96w49	6:27:16
Boyd 37	1	44N51	95w54	6:23:36
Boy Lake 11	1	47N07	94w16	6:17:04
Boy River 11	1	47N10	94w07	6:16:28
Bradbury 48	1	46N02	93w45	6:15:00
Bradford 30	1	45N30	93w15	6:13:00
Braham 30	1	45N44	93w10	6:12:40
Brainerd 18	1	46N22	94w12	6:16:48
Branch 13	1	45N31	92w58	6:11:52
Brandon 21	1	45N58	95w36	6:22:24
Brandrup 84	1	46N09	96w29	6:25:56
Brandsvold 60	1	47N38	95w45	6:23:00
Brandt 60	1	48N04	96w35	6:26:20
Bratsberg 23	1	43N48	91w49	6:07:16
Bray 57	1	48N04	96w26	6:25:44
Breckenridge 84	1	46N16	96w35	6:26:20
Breezy Point 18	1	46N36	94w11	6:16:44
Breitung 69	1	47N49	92w14	6:08:56
Bremen 58	1	46N17	92w58	6:11:52
Bremen 79	1	44N15	92w17	6:09:08
Brennyville 5	1	45N40	93w55	6:15:40
Brevator 69	1	46N48	92w27	6:09:48
Brevik 11	1	47N00	94w16	6:17:04
Brewster 53	1	43N42	95w28	6:21:52
Bricelyn 22	1	43N34	93w49	6:15:16
Bridgewater 66	1	44N25	93w13	6:12:52
Brighton 52	1	44N21	94w19	6:17:16
Brimson 69	1	47N17	91w52	6:07:28
Brislet 60	1	48N08	96w42	6:26:48
Bristol 23	1	43N33	92w08	6:08:32
Britt 69	1	47N39	92w32	6:10:08
Brockway 73	1	45N43	94w20	6:17:20
Brookfield 65	1	44N51	94w42	6:18:48
Brooklyn 69	5	47N25	92w55	6:11:40
Brooklyn Center 27	3	45N05	93w20	6:13:20
Brooklyn Park 27	3	45N06	93w23	6:13:32
Brook Park 58	1	45N57	93w04	6:12:16
Brooks 63	1	47N49	96w00	6:24:00
Brookston 69	1	46N52	92w36	6:10:24
Brookville 64	1	44N20	94w55	6:19:40
Brooten 73	1	45N30	95w08	6:20:32
Browerville 77	1	46N05	94w52	6:19:28
Browns Creek 63	1	47N57	96w17	6:25:08
Brownsdale 50	1	43N45	92w52	6:11:28
Browns Valley 78	1	45N36	96w50	6:27:20
Brownsville 28	1	43N42	91w17	6:05:08
Brownton 43	1	44N44	94w21	6:17:24
Bruce 77	1	45N58	94w43	6:18:52
Bruno 58	1	46N17	92w40	6:10:40
Brunswick 33	1	45N46	93w19	6:13:16
Brush Creek 22	1	43N38	93w53	6:15:32
Brushvale 84	1	46N22	96w39	6:26:36
Buckman 49	1	45N54	94w06	6:16:24
Buffalo 86	1	45N10	93w53	6:15:32
Buffalo Lake 65	1	44N44	94w37	6:18:28
Buh 49	1	46N02	94w08	6:16:32
Buhl 69	1	47N30	92w47	6:11:08
Bullard 80	1	46N30	94w50	6:19:20
Bull Moose 11	1	46N46	94w36	6:18:24
Bunde 12	1	44N57	95w22	6:21:28
Bungo 11	1	46N40	94w33	6:18:12
Burbank 34	1	45N22	94w57	6:19:48
Burchard 42	1	44N15	96w00	6:24:00
Burke 59	1	43N59	96w07	6:24:28
Burleene 77	1	46N04	95w05	6:20:20
Burlington 3	1	46N46	95w44	6:22:56
Burnett 69	1	46N54	92w32	6:10:08
Burnhamville 77	1	45N53	94w42	6:18:48
Burns 2	1	45N21	93w27	6:13:48
Burnside 25	1	44N35	92w37	6:10:28
Burnstown 8	1	44N14	94w56	6:19:44
Burnsville 19	1	44N47	93w17	6:13:08
Burr 87	1	44N45	96w21	6:25:24
Burschville 27	1	45N03	93w38	6:14:32
Burton 87	1	44N40	96w02	6:24:08
Burtrum 77	1	45N52	94w41	6:18:44
Buse 56	1	46N15	96w04	6:24:16
Butler 56	1	46N40	95w21	6:21:24
Butterfield 83	1	43N58	94w48	6:19:12
Butternut 7	1	44N06	94w13	6:16:52
Butternut Valley 7	1	44N09	94w18	6:17:12
Buyck 69	1	48N07	92w32	6:10:08
Buzzle 4	1	47N38	95w07	6:20:28
Bygland 60	1	47N49	96w56	6:27:44
Byron 55	1	44N02	92w39	6:10:36
Cable 71	1	45N32	94w13	6:16:52
Cairo 65	1	44N30	94w41	6:18:44
Caledonia 28	6	43N38	91w30	6:06:00
Callaway 3	1	46N59	95w54	6:23:36
Calumet 31	1	47N19	93w17	6:13:08
Cambria 7	1	44N13	94w18	6:17:12
Cambridge 30	1	45N34	93w13	6:12:52
Camden 10	1	44N51	93w57	6:15:48
Camden 27	3	45N01	93w18	6:13:12
Cameron 51	1	44N04	96w00	6:24:00
Camp 65	1	44N31	94w48	6:19:12
Campbell 84	1	46N06	96w24	6:25:36
Camp Lake 76	1	45N22	95w27	6:21:48
Camp Release 37	1	44N56	95w49	6:23:16
Camp Ripley 49	1	45N57	94w25	6:17:40
Canby 87	1	44N43	96w16	6:25:04
Candor 56	1	46N40	95w51	6:23:24
Canisteo 20	1	43N59	92w44	6:10:56
Cannon 35	1	48N51	96w36	6:26:24
Cannon City 66	1	44N20	93w13	6:12:52
Cannon Falls 25	1	44N31	92w54	6:11:36
Cannon Lake 66	1	44N17	93w16	6:13:04
Canosia 69	1	46N54	92w14	6:08:56
Canton 23	1	43N32	91w56	6:07:44
Canyon 69	1	47N02	92w28	6:09:52
Cardigan Junction 62	3	45N04	93w10	6:12:40
Caribou 35	1	48N56	96w28	6:25:52
Carimona 23	1	43N38	92w08	6:08:32
Carlisle 56	1	46N22	96w11	6:24:44
Carlos 21	1	45N58	95w18	6:21:12
Carlston 24	1	43N43	93w35	6:14:20
Carlton 9	1	46N40	92w25	6:09:40
Carp 39	1	48N43	94w36	6:18:24
Carpenter 31	1	47N51	93w16	6:13:04
Carrolton 23	1	43N43	92w01	6:08:04
Carson 17	1	43N59	95w03	6:20:12
Carsonville 3	1	46N56	95w21	6:21:24
Carver 10	1	44N46	93w38	6:14:32
Cascade 55	5	44N04	92w28	6:09:52
Cashel 76	1	45N12	95w32	6:22:08
Cass Lake 11	1	47N23	94w37	6:18:28
Castle Danger 38	1	47N02	91w41	6:06:44
Castle Rock 19	1	44N35	93w07	6:12:28
Cedar 2	1	45N19	93w17	6:13:08
Cedar Beach 55	1	44N10	92w32	6:10:08
Cedarbend 68	1	48N50	95w23	6:21:32
Cedar Grove 19	3	44N54	93w14	6:12:56
Cedar Lake 70	1	44N36	93w28	6:13:52
Cedar Mills 47	1	44N57	94w31	6:18:04
Cedar Valley 69	1	47N07	93w00	6:12:00
Celina 69	1	47N49	93w10	6:12:40
Center 18	1	46N30	94w09	6:16:36
Center City 13	1	45N24	92w49	6:11:16
Center Creek 46	1	43N43	94w18	6:17:12
Centerville 2	1	45N10	93w03	6:12:12
Centerville 85	7	44N03	91w40	6:06:40
Central Lakes 69	1	47N28	92w33	6:10:12
Central Point 25	1	44N28	92w17	6:09:08
Ceresco 7	1	43N59	94w18	6:17:12
Cerro GordØ 37	1	45N02	96w03	6:24:12
Ceylon 46	1	43N32	94w38	6:18:32
Champion 84	1	46N04	96w20	6:25:20
Champlin 27	1	45N11	93w24	6:13:36
Chanarambie 51	1	43N59	96w00	6:24:00
Chandler 51	1	43N56	95w57	6:23:48
Chanhassen 10	1	44N52	93w32	6:14:08
Charlestown 64	1	44N14	95w09	6:20:36
Charlesville 26	1	46N01	96w19	6:25:16
Chaska 10	1	44N47	93w35	6:14:20
Chatfield 23	1	43N51	92w11	6:08:44
Chatham 86	1	45N10	93w57	6:15:48
Chemolite 82	1	44N50	92w56	6:11:44
Chengwatana 58	1	45N52	92w52	6:11:28
Cherry 69	1	47N25	92w45	6:11:00
Cherry Grove 23	1	43N41	92w23	6:09:32
Cherry Grove 25	1	44N14	92w52	6:11:28
Chester 55	5	44N02	92w28	6:09:52
Chicago Bay 16	1	47N50	89w58	5:59:52
Chicago Lake 27	3	44N56	93w15	6:13:00
Chickamaw Beach 11	1	46N45	94w23	6:17:32
Chief 44	1	47N22	95w52	6:23:28
Chippewa Falls 61	1	45N32	95w20	6:21:20
Chisago City 13	1	45N22	92w53	6:11:32
Chisago Lake 13	1	45N22	92w51	6:11:24
Chisholm 69	1	47N29	92w53	6:11:32
Choice 23	1	43N31	91w46	6:07:04
Chokio 75	1	45N34	96w10	6:24:40
Chowens Corner 27	1	44N58	93w30	6:14:00
Christiania 32	1	43N48	95w05	6:20:20
Circle Pines 2	1	45N09	93w09	6:12:36
City 55	5	44N02	92w28	6:09:52
Civic Center 69	2	46N47	92w06	6:08:24
Clara City 12	1	44N57	95w22	6:21:28
Claremont 20	1	44N04	92w59	6:11:56
Clarissa 77	1	46N08	94w57	6:19:48
Clarkfield 87	1	44N48	95w48	6:23:12
Clarks Grove 24	1	43N46	93w20	6:13:20
Clayton 50	1	43N38	92w38	6:10:32
Clearbrook 15	1	47N42	95w26	6:21:44

Clear Lake 71 1 45N27 94W00 6:16:00
Clearwater 86 1 45N25 94W03 6:16:12
Clements 64 1 44N23 95W00 6:20:12
Clementson 39 1 48N42 94W26 6:17:44
Cleveland 40 1 44N19 93W50 6:15:20
Cliff 19 3 44N55 93W07 6:12:28
Climax 60 1 47N37 96W49 6:27:16
Clinton 6 1 45N28 96W26 6:25:44
Clinton Falls 74 1 44N08 93W13 6:12:52
Clitherall 56 1 46N14 95W42 6:22:48
Clontarf 76 1 45N23 95W40 6:22:40
Cloquet 9 1 46N43 92W28 6:09:52
Clotho 77 1 45N59 94W51 6:19:24
Clough 49 1 46N09 94W30 6:18:00
Cloverdale 58 1 46N01 92W56 6:11:44
Clover Leaf 57 1 48N08 95W55 6:23:40
Cloverton 58 1 46N10 92W19 6:09:16
Clow 35 1 48N56 97W00 6:28:00
Clyde 85 1 43N59 91W57 6:07:48
Coates 19 1 44N43 93W02 6:12:08
Cobden 8 1 44N17 94W51 6:19:24
Cohasset 31 1 47N16 93W37 6:14:28
Cokato 86 1 45N05 94W11 6:16:44
Colby 69 1 47N31 92W09 6:08:36
Cold Spring 73 1 45N27 94W26 6:17:44
Coleraine 31 1 47N17 93W27 6:13:48
Colfax 34 1 45N22 95W04 6:20:16
Collegeville 73 1 45N36 94W22 6:17:28
Collins 43 1 44N46 94W26 6:17:44
Collinwood 47 1 45N02 94W18 6:17:12
Collis 78 1 45N39 96W26 6:25:44
Cologne 10 1 44N46 93W47 6:15:08
Columbia 60 1 47N33 95W37 6:22:28
Columbia Heights 2 3 45N03 93W15 6:13:00
Columbus 2 1 45N16 93W05 6:12:20
Colvin 69 1 47N20 92W13 6:08:52
Comfort 33 1 45N52 93W12 6:12:48
Comfrey 8 1 44N07 94W54 6:19:36
Commerce 27 3 44N58 93W16 6:13:04
Como 45 1 48N30 96W04 6:24:16
Como 62 3 45N00 93W11 6:12:44
Compton 56 1 46N25 95W13 6:20:52
Comstock 14 1 46N40 96W45 6:27:00
Conception 79 1 44N19 92W00 6:08:00
Concord 20 1 44N09 92W52 6:11:28
Conger 24 1 43N37 93W32 6:14:08
Connelly 84 1 46N20 96W34 6:26:16
Constance 2 3 45N10 93W19 6:13:16
Cook 69 1 47N51 92W41 6:10:44
Cooley 31 1 47N22 93W14 6:12:56
Coon Creek 42 1 44N19 96W01 6:24:04
Coon Lake Beach 2 1 45N20 93W00 6:12:00
Coon Rapids 2 3 45N09 93W19 6:13:16
Copas 82 1 45N15 92W48 6:11:12
Copley 15 1 47N33 95W23 6:21:32
Corcoran 27 1 45N06 93W33 6:14:12
Cordova 40 1 44N19 93W42 6:14:48
Corinna 86 1 45N17 94W05 6:16:20
Cormant 4 1 47N52 94W37 6:18:28
Cormorant 3 1 46N44 96W04 6:24:16
Corning 50 1 43N41 92W58 6:11:52
Correll 6 1 45N14 96W10 6:24:40
Corvuso 47 1 44N56 94W40 6:18:40
Cosmos 47 1 44N57 94W40 6:18:40
Cottage Grove 82 1 44N50 92W56 6:11:44
Cottage Wood 27 1 44N54 93W34 6:14:16
Cotton 69 1 47N10 92W28 6:09:52
Cottonwood 42 1 44N37 95W41 6:22:44
Courtland 52 1 44N16 94W20 6:17:20
Cove 48 1 46N04 93W40 6:14:40
Craigville 36 1 47N54 93W37 6:14:28
Crane Lake 69 1 48N16 92W29 6:09:56
Crate 12 1 45N00 95W26 6:21:44
Credit River 70 1 44N40 93W22 6:13:28
Croftville 16 1 47N45 90W20 6:01:20
Croke 78 1 45N43 96W26 6:25:44
Cromwell 9 1 46N41 92W53 6:11:32
Crooked Creek 28 1 43N36 91W20 6:05:20
Crooked Lake 11 1 46N50 94W00 6:16:00
Crooks 65 1 44N51 95W11 6:20:44
Crookston 60 1 47N47 96W37 6:26:28
Crosby 18 1 46N29 93W58 6:15:52
Crosby Beach 18 1 46N30 93W55 6:15:40
Crosslake 18 1 46N40 94W07 6:16:28
Crow Lake 73 1 45N27 95W04 6:20:16
Crown 30 1 45N27 93W28 6:13:52
Crow River 47 1 45N14 94W43 6:18:52
Crow Wing 18 1 46N17 94W15 6:17:00
Crow Wing Lake 29 1 46N51 94W52 6:19:28
Crystal 27 3 45N03 93W22 6:13:28
Crystal Bay 27 1 44N58 93W36 6:14:24
Crystal Bay 38 1 47N37 91W13 6:04:52
Cuba 3 1 46N56 96W07 6:24:28
Culdrum 49 1 45N59 94W34 6:18:16
Culver 69 1 46N56 92W33 6:10:12
Cummingsville 55 1 43N51 92W11 6:08:44
Currie 51 1 44N03 95W40 6:22:40
Cushing 49 1 46N09 94W35 6:18:20
Cusson 69 1 48N06 92W51 6:11:24
Custer 42 1 44N14 95W47 6:23:08
Cuyuna 18 1 46N31 93W56 6:15:44
Cyrus 61 1 45N37 95W44 6:22:56
Dagget Brook 18 1 46N13 94W07 6:16:28
Dahlgren 10 1 44N45 93W42 6:14:48
Dailey 48 1 45N57 93W41 6:14:44
Dakota 85 6 43N55 91W22 6:05:28
Dalbo 30 1 45N40 93W25 6:13:40
Dale 14 1 46N47 96W19 6:25:16
Dale 17 1 43N59 95W09 6:20:36
Dalton 56 1 46N10 95W55 6:23:40
Dane Prairie 56 1 46N14 95W57 6:23:48
Danforth 58 1 46N08 92W38 6:10:32
Danielson 47 1 45N01 94W41 6:18:44
Danube 65 1 44N48 95W06 6:20:24
Danvers 76 1 45N17 95W45 6:23:00
Danville 7 1 43N54 93W50 6:15:20
Darfur 83 1 44N03 94W50 6:19:20
Darling 49 1 46N04 94W26 6:17:44
Darnen 75 1 45N33 95W56 6:23:44
Darwin 47 1 45N07 94W26 6:17:44
Dassel 47 1 45N05 94W19 6:17:16
Davis 35 1 48N35 96W50 6:27:20
Dawson 37 1 44N56 96W03 6:24:12
Day 30 1 45N43 93W23 6:13:32
Dayton 27 1 45N15 93W31 6:14:04
Daytons Bluff 62 3 44N58 93W04 6:12:16
Dead Lake 56 1 46N30 95W43 6:22:52
Dean Lake 18 1 46N36 93W48 6:15:12
Debs 4 1 47N36 95W08 6:20:32
Decoria 7 1 44N04 93W56 6:15:44
Deephaven 27 1 44N56 93W31 6:14:04
Deer 68 1 48N35 96W12 6:24:48
Deer Creek 56 1 46N24 95W19 6:21:16
Deerfield 74 1 44N10 93W15 6:13:00
Deerhorn 84 1 46N35 96W36 6:26:24
Deer Park 57 1 48N00 95W47 6:23:08
Deer River 31 1 47N20 93W48 6:15:12
Deerwood 18 1 46N29 93W54 6:15:36
De Graff 76 1 45N16 95W28 6:21:52
Delafield 32 1 43N49 95W12 6:20:48
Delano 86 1 45N02 93W47 6:15:08
Delavan 22 1 43N48 94W04 6:16:16
Delaware 26 1 45N53 96W04 6:24:16
Delft 17 1 43N59 95W05 6:20:20
Delhi 64 1 44N35 95W11 6:20:44
Dell 22 1 43N38 94W06 6:16:24
Dell Grove 58 1 46N12 92W55 6:11:40
Dellwood 82 1 45N06 92W59 6:11:56
Delton 17 1 44N04 95W02 6:20:08
Denham 58 1 46N22 92W57 6:11:48
Denmark 82 1 44N45 92W51 6:11:24
Dennison 25 1 44N25 93W02 6:12:08
Dent 56 1 46N33 95W43 6:22:52
Denver 67 1 43N48 96W14 6:24:56
Derrynane 40 1 44N30 93W42 6:14:48
Des Moines 32 1 43N38 95W05 6:20:20
Des Moines River 51 1 43N59 95W31 6:22:04
Detroit 3 1 46N50 95W51 6:23:24
Detroit Lakes 3 1 46N49 95W51 6:23:24
Dewald 53 1 43N38 95W45 6:23:00
Dewey 68 1 48N41 96W18 6:25:12
Dexter 50 1 43N43 92W42 6:10:48
Diamond Lake 27 3 44N54 93W18 6:13:12
Diamond Lake 41 1 44N20 96W16 6:25:04
Dieter 68 1 48N56 95W58 6:23:52
Dilworth 14 1 46N53 96W42 6:26:48
Dodge Center 20 1 44N02 92W52 6:11:28
Dollymount 78 1 45N43 96W20 6:25:20
Donaldson 35 1 48N35 96W53 6:27:32
Donnelly 75 1 45N42 96W01 6:24:04
Dora 56 1 46N35 95W51 6:23:24
Dora Lake 31 1 48N19 93W41 6:14:44
Doran 84 1 46N11 96W29 6:25:56
Dorothy 63 1 47N56 96W28 6:25:52
Dorset 29 1 46N55 95W04 6:20:16
Douglas 55 1 44N07 92W34 6:10:16
Dover 55 1 43N59 92W08 6:08:32
Dovray 51 1 44N04 95W31 6:22:04
Dovre 34 1 45N12 95W04 6:20:16
Downer 14 1 46N45 96W29 6:25:56
Drammen 41 1 44N20 96W23 6:25:32
Dresbach 85 1 43N54 91W21 6:05:24
Dryden 72 1 44N36 94W11 6:16:44
Dublin 76 1 45N12 95W26 6:21:44
Dudley 15 1 47N38 95W14 6:20:56
Duelm 5 1 45N34 93W56 6:15:44
Duluth 69 2 46N47 92W07 6:08:28
Dumfries 79 1 44N23 92W02 6:08:08
Dumont 78 1 45N43 96W26 6:25:44
Dunbar 22 1 43N48 93W46 6:15:04
Dundas 66 1 44N26 93W12 6:12:48
Dundee 53 1 43N51 95W28 6:21:52
Dunn 56 1 46N33 96W00 6:24:00
Dunnell 46 1 43N34 94W47 6:19:08
Duquette 58 1 46N22 92W33 6:10:12
Durand 4 1 47N41 94W53 6:19:32
Duxbury 58 1 46N05 92W19 6:09:16
Eagan 19 3 44N49 93W11 6:12:44
Eagle Bend 77 1 46N10 95W02 6:20:08
Eagle Creek 70 1 44N46 93W28 6:13:52
Eagle Lake 7 1 44N10 93W53 6:15:32
Eagle Point 45 1 48N30 97W07 6:28:28
Eagle Valley 77 1 46N09 94W57 6:19:48
East Beaver Bay 38 1 47N16 91W18 6:05:12
East Bethel 2 1 45N20 93W11 6:12:44
East Chain 46 1 43N34 94W22 6:17:28
East Cottage Grove 82 1 44N50 92W56 6:11:44
East End 69 2 46N47 92W06 6:08:24
Eastern 56 1 46N09 95W12 6:20:48
Eastern Heights 62 3 44N58 93W01 6:12:04
East Grand Forks 60 1 47N56 97W01 6:28:04
East Gull Lake 11 1 46N25 94W21 6:17:24
East Hastings 19 1 44N40 92W50 6:11:20
East Lake 1 1 46N32 93W17 6:13:08
East Lake Francis Shores 30 1 45N30 93W15 6:13:00
East Lake Lillian 34 1 44N56 94W49 6:19:16
Easton 22 1 43N46 93W54 6:15:36
East Park 45 1 48N30 96W19 6:25:16
East Prairieville 66 1 44N17 93W16 6:13:04
East Side 48 1 46N13 93W29 6:13:56
East Union 10 1 44N46 93W38 6:14:32
East Valley 45 1 48N20 96W05 6:24:20
Ebro 15 1 47N30 95W31 6:22:04
Echo 87 1 44N37 95W25 6:21:40
Echols 83 1 43N59 94W38 6:18:32
Eckles 4 1 47N33 94W59 6:19:56
Eckvoll 45 1 48N19 95W47 6:23:08
Eddsville 65 1 44N46 94W53 6:19:32
Eddy 15 1 47N38 95W30 6:22:00
Eden 20 1 44N02 92W51 6:11:24
Eden Lake 73 1 45N22 94W35 6:18:20
Eden Prairie 27 1 44N51 93W29 6:13:56
Eden Valley 47 1 45N19 94W33 6:18:12
Edgerton 59 1 43N53 96W08 6:24:32
Edgewood 30 1 45N34 93W13 6:12:52
Edina 27 3 44N53 93W21 6:13:24
Edison 76 1 45N11 95W54 6:23:36
Edna 56 1 46N35 95W44 6:22:56
Edwards 34 1 45N01 95W11 6:20:44
Effie 31 1 47N50 93W38 6:14:32
Effington 56 1 46N14 95W27 6:21:48
Eglon 14 1 46N51 96W15 6:25:00
Eidsvold 42 1 44N35 96W02 6:24:08
Eidswold 70 1 44N34 93W19 6:13:16
Eitzen 28 1 43N30 91W28 6:05:52
Elba 85 1 44N05 92W01 6:08:04
Elbow Lake 26 1 46N00 95W58 6:23:52
Eldorado 75 1 45N43 96W11 6:24:44
Eldred 60 1 47N41 96W47 6:27:08
Elgin 79 1 44N08 92W15 6:09:00
Elizabeth 56 1 46N23 96W08 6:24:32
Elk 53 1 43N43 95W38 6:22:32
Elk Lake 26 1 45N53 95W49 6:23:16
Elkland 66 1 44N17 93W16 6:13:04
Elko 70 1 44N34 93W19 6:13:16
Elk River 71 1 45N18 93W35 6:14:20
Elkton 50 1 43N40 92W42 6:10:48
Ellendale 74 1 43N52 93W18 6:13:12
Ellington 20 1 44N09 92W59 6:11:56
Ellsborough 51 1 44N09 96W00 6:24:00
Ellsburg 69 1 47N15 92W25 6:09:40
Ellsworth 53 1 43N31 96W01 6:24:04
Elm Creek 46 1 43N43 94W48 6:19:12
Elmdale 49 1 45N49 94W33 6:18:12
Elmer 69 1 47N06 92W46 6:11:04
Elmira 55 1 43N53 92W08 6:08:32
Elmo 56 1 46N14 95W20 6:21:20
Elmore 22 1 43N30 94W05 6:16:20
Elmwood 14 1 46N40 96W36 6:26:24
Elmwood 27 3 44N57 93W21 6:13:24
Elrosa 73 1 45N34 94W57 6:19:48
Elway 62 3 44N55 93W10 6:12:40
Ely 69 1 47N55 91W51 6:07:24
Elysian 40 1 44N15 93W42 6:14:48
Emardville 63 1 47N53 96W02 6:24:08
Embarrass 69 1 47N40 92W12 6:08:48
Emco 69 1 47N31 92W09 6:08:36
Emerald 22 1 43N38 93W57 6:15:48
Emily 18 1 46N44 93W58 6:15:52
Emmet 65 1 44N45 95W10 6:20:40
Emmons 24 1 43N30 93W29 6:13:56
Empire 19 1 44N37 93W01 6:12:04
Enfield 86 1 45N18 93W47 6:15:08
Englund 45 1 48N29 96W27 6:25:48
Enstrom 68 1 48N51 95W33 6:22:12
Enterprise 32 1 43N43 94W55 6:19:40
Equality 63 1 47N54 95W47 6:23:08
Erdahl 26 1 45N58 95W50 6:23:20
Erhard 56 1 46N29 96W06 6:24:24
Erhards Grove 56 1 46N30 96W06 6:24:24
Ericksonville 48 1 46N04 93W40 6:14:40
Ericsburg 36 1 48N29 93W20 6:13:20
Ericson 65 1 44N51 95W18 6:21:12
Erie 3 1 46N51 95W43 6:22:52
Erie 57 1 48N09 95W48 6:23:12
Erin 66 1 44N25 93W27 6:13:48
Erskine 60 1 47N40 96W00 6:24:00
Esko 9 1 46N42 92W22 6:09:28
Espelie 45 1 48N14 95W39 6:22:36
Essig 8 1 44N20 94W36 6:18:24
Estes Brook 48 1 45N42 93W49 6:15:16
Esther 60 1 48N04 97W03 6:28:12
Etna 23 1 43N41 92W23 6:09:32
Etter 19 1 44N34 92W44 6:10:56
Euclid 60 1 47N58 96W39 6:26:36
Eureka 19 1 44N35 93W13 6:12:52
Evan 8 1 44N21 94W50 6:19:20
Evansville 21 1 46N00 95W41 6:22:44
Eveleth 69 1 47N28 92W32 6:10:08
Everdell 84 1 46N16 96W35 6:26:20
Everglade 75 1 45N38 96W11 6:24:44
Evergreen 3 1 46N45 95W29 6:21:56
Everts 56 1 46N20 95W43 6:22:52
Ewington 32 1 43N38 95W24 6:21:36
Excel 45 1 48N13 96W10 6:24:40
Excelsior 27 3 44N54 93W34 6:14:16
Eyota 55 1 43N59 92W14 6:08:56
Fahlun 34 1 45N01 94W56 6:19:44
Fairbanks 69 1 47N20 91W54 6:07:36
Fairfax 65 1 44N32 94W43 6:18:52
Fairhaven 73 1 45N22 94W11 6:16:44
Fairmont 46 1 43N39 94W28 6:17:52
Faith 54 1 47N16 96W15 6:25:00
Falcon Heights 62 3 45N01 93W10 6:12:40
Falk 15 1 47N27 95W29 6:21:56
Fall Lake 38 1 48N00 91W39 6:06:36
Falun 68 1 48N45 95W33 6:22:12
Fanny 60 1 47N54 96W40 6:26:40
Farden 29 1 47N22 94W45 6:19:00
Faribault 66 1 44N18 93W16 6:13:04
Farley 60 1 48N08 96W50 6:27:20
Farming 73 1 45N33 94W34 6:18:16
Farmington 19 1 44N38 93W08 6:12:32
Farm Island 1 1 46N28 93W44 6:14:56
Farris 29 1 47N23 94W36 6:18:24
Farwell 61 1 45N45 95W37 6:22:28

MINNESOTA

Fawn Lake 77 1 46N14 94W43 6:18:52
Faxon 72 1 44N39 93W50 6:15:20
Fayal 69 1 47N26 92W29 6:09:56
Featherstone 25 1 44N30 92W36 6:10:24
Federal Dam 11 1 47N15 94W14 6:16:56
Feeley 31 1 47N10 93W17 6:13:08
Felton 14 1 47N05 96W30 6:26:00
Fenton 51 1 43N54 95W53 6:23:32
Fergus Falls 56 1 46N17 96W04 6:24:16
Fern 29 1 47N22 95W07 6:20:28
Fernando 43 1 44N39 94W28 6:17:52
Fertile 60 1 47N32 96W17 6:25:08
Field 69 1 47N51 92W45 6:11:00
Fieldon 83 1 43N59 94W26 6:17:44
Fifty Lakes 18 1 46N45 94W04 6:16:16
Fillmore 23 1 43N43 92W15 6:09:00
Fine Lakes 69 1 46N48 92W53 6:11:32
Finland 38 1 47N25 91W15 6:05:00
Finlayson 58 1 46N12 92W55 6:11:40
Fisher 60 1 47N48 96W48 6:27:12
Fish Lake 13 1 45N35 93W05 6:12:20
Fitzen 1 43N31 91W28 6:05:52
Flensburg 49 1 45N57 94W32 6:18:08
Fletcher 27 1 45N10 93W32 6:14:08
Flom 54 1 47N10 96W08 6:24:32
Floodwood 69 1 46N55 92W56 6:11:44
Flora 65 1 44N40 95W10 6:20:40
Florence 42 1 44N14 96W03 6:24:12
Florenton 69 1 47N31 92W32 6:10:08
Florian 45 1 48N29 96W27 6:25:48
Florida 87 1 44N46 96W23 6:25:32
Flowing 14 1 47N01 96W31 6:26:04
Foldahl 45 1 48N20 96W34 6:26:16
Folden 56 1 46N21 95W26 6:21:44
Foley 5 1 45N40 93W55 6:15:40
Folsom 78 1 46N04 95W05 6:20:20
Fond Du Lac Indian Reservati 9
1 47N32 94W49 6:19:16
Forada 21 1 45N48 95W21 6:21:24
Forbes 69 1 47N22 92W36 6:10:24
Ford 33 1 46N07 93W14 6:12:56
Fordson 19 3 44N55 93W14 6:12:56
Forest 66 1 44N25 93W20 6:13:20
Forest City 47 1 45N13 94W28 6:17:52
Forest Grove 36 1 48N22 93W37 6:14:28
Forest Lake 82 1 45N17 92W59 6:11:56
Forest Mills 25 1 44N18 92W40 6:10:40
Foreston 48 1 45N44 93W43 6:14:52
Forest Prairie 47 1 45N17 94W27 6:17:48
Forestville 23 1 43N38 92W16 6:09:04
Fork 45 1 48N25 97W06 6:28:24
Fortier 87 1 44N41 96W24 6:25:36
Fort Ripley 18 1 46N10 94W22 6:17:28
Fort Snelling 27 3 44N54 93W14 6:12:56
Fosston 60 1 47N35 95W45 6:23:00
Fossum 54 1 47N15 96W11 6:24:44
Foster 6 1 45N28 96W27 6:25:48
Fountain 23 1 43N45 92W08 6:08:32
Fountain Prairie 59
1 44N09 96W15 6:25:00
Four Corners 69 2 46N48 92W08 6:08:32
Four Town 45 1 48N18 95W37 6:22:28
Fox 1 48N50 95W54 6:23:36
Foxhome 84 1 46N17 96W19 6:25:16
Fox Lake 46 1 43N43 94W41 6:18:44
Framnas 75 1 45N37 95W49 6:23:16
Franconia 13 1 45N21 92W40 6:10:40
Frankford 50 1 43N44 92W31 6:10:04
Frankfort 86 1 45N13 93W41 6:14:44
Franklin 65 1 47N32 92W32 6:10:08
Franklin Avenue 27
3 44N58 93W16 6:13:04
Frazee 3 1 46N44 95W42 6:22:48
Fredenberg 69 1 46N58 92W14 6:08:56
Freeborn 24 1 43N48 93W34 6:14:16
Freeburg 28 6 43N38 91W29 6:05:56
Freedhem 49 1 46N04 94W13 6:16:52
Freedom 81 1 43N59 93W42 6:14:48
Freeland 37 1 44N51 96W16 6:25:04
Freeman 24 1 43N33 93W21 6:13:24
Freeport 73 1 45N40 94W41 6:18:44
Fremont 85 1 43N54 91W54 6:07:36
French 69 1 47N40 93W01 6:12:04
French Lake 86 1 45N12 94W12 6:16:48
French River 69 1 46N54 91W54 6:07:36
Friberg 56 1 46N25 95W58 6:23:52
Fridley 2 3 45N05 93W16 6:13:04
Friendship 87 1 44N46 95W48 6:23:12
Friesland 58 1 46N01 92W56 6:11:44
Frohn 4 1 47N27 94W44 6:18:56
Frontenac 25 1 44N31 92W21 6:09:24
Frost 22 1 43N35 93W56 6:15:44
Fulda 51 1 43N53 95W36 6:22:24
Funkley 4 1 47N47 94W26 6:17:44
Gail Lake 18 1 46N47 94W12 6:16:48
Galena 46 1 43N48 94W41 6:18:44
Gales 64 1 44N20 95W32 6:22:08
Garden 60 1 47N33 96W08 6:24:32
Garden City 7 1 44N03 94W10 6:16:40
Garfield 21 1 45N56 95W30 6:22:00
Garnes 63 1 47N55 95W53 6:23:32
Garrison 18 1 46N18 93W50 6:15:20
Garvin 42 1 44N13 95W46 6:23:04
Gary 54 1 47N22 96W16 6:25:04
Gatzke 45 1 48N25 95W47 6:23:08
Gaylord 72 1 44N33 94W13 6:16:52
Gem Lake 62 3 45N04 93W01 6:12:04
Gemmell 36 1 47N59 94W07 6:16:28
Geneva 24 1 43N49 93W16 6:13:04
Gennessee 34 1 45N07 94W49 6:19:16
Genoa 55 1 44N02 92W39 6:10:36
Genoa 69 1 47N28 92W33 6:10:12
Genola 49 1 45N58 94W07 6:16:28
Gentilly 60 1 47N48 96W26 6:25:44
Georgetown 14 1 47N05 96W48 6:27:12
Georgeville 73 1 45N27 95W00 6:20:00
Germania 77 1 46N14 94W57 6:19:48
Germantown 17 1 44N09 95W10 6:20:40
Gervais 63 1 47N53 96W10 6:24:40
Getty 73 1 45N38 94W57 6:19:48
Gheen 69 1 47N58 92W49 6:11:16
Ghent 42 1 44N31 95W54 6:23:36
Gibbon 72 1 44N32 94W31 6:18:04
Giese 1 1 46N12 92W59 6:11:56
Gilbert 69 1 47N29 92W28 6:09:52
Gilchrist 61 1 45N27 95W19 6:21:16
Gilfillan 64 1 44N32 95W07 6:20:28
Gillford 79 1 44N20 92W22 6:09:28
Gilman 5 1 45N44 93W57 6:15:48
Gilmanton 5 1 45N42 93W58 6:15:52
Girard 56 1 46N22 95W35 6:22:20
Gladstone 62 3 45N01 93W02 6:12:08
Glasgow 79 1 44N20 92W08 6:08:32
Glen 1 1 46N25 93W31 6:14:04
Glencoe 43 1 44N46 94W09 6:16:36
Glendale 69 1 48N03 92W50 6:11:20
Glendorado 5 1 45N36 93W49 6:15:16
Glen Lake 27 3 44N56 93W25 6:13:40
Glenville 24 1 43N34 93W17 6:13:08
Glenwood 61 1 45N39 95W23 6:21:32
Glenwood Junction 27
3 45N01 93W24 6:13:36
Glory 1 1 46N32 93W42 6:14:48
Gloster 62 3 45N01 93W02 6:12:08
Gluek 12 1 44N59 95W29 6:21:56
Glyndon 14 1 46N50 96W37 6:26:28
Gnesen 69 1 47N00 92W07 6:08:28
Godahl 8 1 43N59 94W38 6:18:32
Godfrey 60 1 47N38 96W14 6:24:56
Golden Hill 55 5 44N02 92W28 6:09:52
Golden Hills 27 3 44N57 93W21 6:13:24
Golden Valley 27 3 44N59 93W23 6:13:32
Gonvick 15 1 47N44 95W31 6:22:04
Goodhue 25 1 44N24 92W37 6:10:28
Goodland 31 1 47N10 93W09 6:12:36
Goodridge 57 1 48N09 95W48 6:23:12
Good Thunder 7 1 44N00 94W04 6:16:16
Goodview 85 6 44N04 91W42 6:06:48
Goose Prairie 14 1 47N01 96W16 6:25:04
Gordon 77 1 45N53 95W04 6:20:16
Gordonsville 24 1 43N31 93W15 6:13:00
Gorman 56 1 46N40 95W36 6:22:24
Gorton 26 1 45N53 96W11 6:24:44
Gotha 10 1 44N46 93W47 6:15:08
Gould 11 1 47N11 94W12 6:16:48
Gowan 1 46N51 92W51 6:11:24
Grace 12 1 45N07 95W33 6:22:12
Graceton 1 48N45 94W50 6:19:20
Graceville 6 1 45N34 96W26 6:25:44
Grafton 72 1 44N40 94W34 6:18:16
Graham 5 1 45N46 94W05 6:16:20
Graham Lakes 53 1 43N42 95W28 6:21:52
Granada 46 1 43N42 94W21 6:17:24
Granby 52 1 44N21 94W12 6:16:48
Grand Falls 36 1 48N12 93W48 6:15:12
Grand Forks 60 1 47N59 97W02 6:28:08
Grand Lake 69 1 46N54 92W22 6:09:28
Grand Marais 16 1 47N45 90W20 6:01:20
Grand Meadow 50 1 43N42 92W34 6:10:16
Grand Plain 45 1 48N13 95W55 6:23:40
Grand Portage 16 1 47N58 89W41 5:58:44
Grand Portage Indian Res 16
1 47N32 94W49 6:19:16
Grand Prairie 53 1 43N33 96W00 6:24:00
Grand Rapids 31 1 47N14 93W31 6:14:04
Grandview 42 1 44N30 95W55 6:23:40
Grand View Heights 56
1 46N36 95W34 6:22:16
Grandy 30 1 45N38 93W27 6:13:48
Grange 59 1 44N04 96W15 6:25:00
Granger 23 1 43N30 92W08 6:08:32
Granite 49 1 46N02 94W01 6:16:04
Granite Falls 87 1 44N49 95W33 6:22:12
Granite Ledge 5 1 45N46 93W49 6:15:16
Granite Rock 64 1 44N25 95W25 6:21:40
Grant 82 1 45N05 92W54 6:11:36
Grant Valley 4 1 47N27 94W59 6:19:56
Granville 35 1 48N51 96W52 6:27:28
Grass Lake 33 1 45N46 93W14 6:12:56
Grasston 33 1 45N48 93W09 6:12:36
Grattan 31 1 47N48 94W06 6:16:24
Gray 59 1 43N59 96W14 6:24:56
Greaney 69 1 47N58 92W49 6:11:16
Great Bend 17 1 43N54 95W09 6:20:36
Greater Leech Lake Indian Re 4
1 47N32 94W49 6:19:16
Great Scott 69 1 47N32 92W44 6:10:56
Greenbush 68 1 48N42 96W11 6:24:44
Greenfield 27 1 45N03 93W38 6:14:32
Green Isle 72 1 44N41 94W01 6:16:04
Green Lake 34 1 45N12 94W57 6:19:48
Greenleaf 47 1 45N01 94W33 6:18:12
Greenleafton 23 1 43N35 92W13 6:08:52
Green Meadow 54 1 47N22 96W23 6:25:32
Green Prairie 49 1 46N03 94W22 6:17:28
Greenvale 19 1 44N30 93W13 6:12:52
Green Valley 42 1 44N32 95W45 6:23:00
Greenwald 73 1 45N36 94W52 6:19:28
Greenway 31 1 47N19 93W17 6:13:08
Greenwood 27 1 44N54 93W34 6:14:16
Gregory 44 1 47N27 95W52 6:23:28
Grey Cloud Island 82
1 44N48 93W00 6:12:00
Grey Eagle 77 1 45N50 94W45 6:19:00
Grimstad 68 1 48N41 95W47 6:23:08
Grogan 83 1 43N59 94W38 6:18:32
Groningen 58 1 46N08 92W52 6:11:28
Grove 73 1 45N38 94W50 6:19:20
Grove City 47 1 45N09 94W41 6:18:44
Grove Lake 1 45N37 95W09 6:20:36
Grove Park 60 1 47N42 96W10 6:24:40
Grow 2 1 45N15 93W20 6:13:20
Grygla 45 1 48N18 95W37 6:22:28
Guckeen 22 1 43N38 94W06 6:16:24
Gully 60 1 47N48 95W40 6:22:40
Gutches Grove 77 1 45N59 94W51 6:19:24
Guthrie 29 1 47N18 94W48 6:19:12
Hackensack 11 1 46N56 94W31 6:18:04
Hackett 39 1 48N43 94W36 6:18:24
Hader 25 1 44N18 92W40 6:10:40
Hadley 51 1 44N00 95W51 6:23:24
Hagali 4 1 47N43 94W44 6:18:56
Hagan 12 1 45N07 95W55 6:23:40
Hagen 14 1 47N06 96W22 6:25:28
Halden 69 1 46N54 92W59 6:11:56
Hale 43 1 44N56 94W12 6:16:48
Hallock 35 1 48N47 96W57 6:27:48
Halma 35 1 48N40 96W36 6:26:24
Halstad 54 1 47N21 96W50 6:27:20
Hamburg 10 3 44N44 93W58 6:15:52
Hamden 3 1 46N56 95W59 6:23:56
Hamel 27 1 45N02 93W31 6:14:04
Hamilton 23 1 43N41 92W23 6:09:32
Ham Lake 2 1 45N15 93W13 6:12:52
Hamlin 37 1 44N56 96W10 6:24:40
Hammer 87 1 44N46 96W17 6:25:08
Hammond 79 1 44N13 92W23 6:09:32
Hampden 35 1 48N51 97W00 6:28:00
Hampton 19 1 44N37 93W00 6:12:00
Hamre 4 1 48N15 95W25 6:21:40
Hancock 75 1 45N30 95W48 6:23:12
Hangaard 15 1 47N53 95W32 6:22:08
Hanley Falls 87 1 44N42 95W37 6:22:28
Hanover 86 1 45N10 93W40 6:14:40
Hanska 8 1 44N09 94W30 6:18:00
Hansonville 41 1 44N35 96W23 6:25:32
Hantho 37 1 45N07 96W04 6:24:16
Happyland 36 1 48N24 93W34 6:14:16
Harding 49 1 46N07 94W03 6:16:12
Hardwick 67 1 43N47 96W12 6:24:48
Harmony 23 1 43N33 92W01 6:08:04
Harnell Park 69 1 46N52 92W29 6:09:56
Harris 13 1 45N35 92W58 6:11:52
Harrison 34 1 45N12 94W49 6:19:16
Hart 85 1 43N54 91W47 6:07:08
Hartford 77 1 46N04 94W50 6:19:20
Hart Lake 29 1 47N17 94W45 6:19:00
Hartland 24 1 43N48 93W29 6:13:56
Harvey 47 1 45N12 94W34 6:18:16
Hassan 27 1 45N11 93W35 6:14:20
Hassan Valley 43 1 44N51 94W18 6:17:12
Hassman 1 1 46N36 93W37 6:14:28
Hastings 19 1 44N44 92W51 6:11:24
Hasty 86 1 45N22 93W59 6:15:56
Hatfield 59 1 43N58 96W12 6:24:48
Haugen 1 1 46N43 93W07 6:12:28
Havana 74 1 44N04 93W06 6:12:24
Havelock 12 1 45N01 95W33 6:22:12
Haven 71 1 45N31 94W04 6:16:16
Hawick 34 1 45N21 94W50 6:19:20
Hawk Creek 65 1 44N46 95W25 6:21:40
Hawley 14 1 46N53 96W19 6:25:16
Hay Brook 33 1 46N07 93W22 6:13:28
Hay Creek 25 1 44N29 92W33 6:10:12
Haydenville 37 1 45N01 96W11 6:24:44
Hayes 76 1 45N18 95W24 6:21:36
Hayfield 20 1 43N53 92W51 6:11:24
Hayland 48 1 45N51 93W35 6:14:20
Haypoint 1 1 46N59 93W36 6:14:24
Hayward 24 1 43N39 93W15 6:13:00
Hazel Run 87 1 44N45 95W43 6:22:52
Hazelwood 66 1 44N27 93W10 6:12:40
Hector 65 1 44N45 94W43 6:18:52
Hegbert 76 1 45N22 96W04 6:24:16
Hegne 54 1 47N17 96W37 6:26:28
Heiberg 54 1 47N16 96W15 6:25:00
Heidelberg 40 1 44N30 93W38 6:14:32
Heier 44 1 47N27 95W44 6:22:56
Height Of Land 3 1 46N52 95W36 6:22:24
Heinola 56 1 46N35 95W20 6:21:20
Helen 43 1 44N46 94W04 6:16:16
Helena 70 1 44N35 93W35 6:14:20
Helga 29 1 47N22 94W51 6:19:24
Helgeland 60 1 48N08 96W35 6:26:20
Henderson 72 1 44N31 93W55 6:15:40
Hendricks 41 1 44N30 96W25 6:25:40
Hendrickson 29 1 47N17 94W51 6:19:24
Hendrum 54 1 47N16 96W49 6:27:16
Henning 56 1 46N20 95W28 6:21:52
Henrietta 29 1 46N56 94W59 6:19:56
Henriette 58 1 45N53 93W07 6:12:28
Henrytown 23 1 43N33 92W00 6:08:00
Henryville 65 1 44N40 95W03 6:20:12
Hereim 68 1 48N41 96W12 6:24:48
Herman 26 1 45N49 96W09 6:24:36
Hermantown 69 2 46N48 92W08 6:08:32
Heron Lake 32 1 43N48 95W19 6:21:16
Hersey 53 1 43N43 95W31 6:22:04
Hewitt 77 1 46N20 95W05 6:20:20
Hiawatha Spur 19 3 44N54 93W14 6:12:56
Hibbing 69 5 47N25 92W55 6:11:40
Hickory 57 1 47N59 95W39 6:22:36
Hidden Valley 82 1 45N16 92W59 6:11:56
Higdem 60 1 48N08 97W06 6:28:24
High Forest 55 1 43N53 92W31 6:10:04
Highland 23 1 43N41 91W52 6:07:28
Highland 27 3 45N00 93W18 6:13:12
Highland 38 1 47N02 91W41 6:06:44
Highland Grove 14 1 46N55 96W14 6:24:56
High Landing 57 1 48N04 95W47 6:23:08
Highland Park 62 3 44N55 93W10 6:12:40
Highwater 17 1 44N09 95W16 6:21:04
Hill 35 1 48N51 97W07 6:28:28
Hill City 1 1 46N59 93W36 6:14:24
Hill Lake 1 1 46N59 93W37 6:14:28

Hillman 49	1	46N00	93w53	6:15:32
Hill River 60	1	47N43	95w46	6:23:04
Hills 67	1	43N32	96w21	6:25:24
Hillsdale 85	1	44N03	91w47	6:07:08
Hillside 69	2	46N48	92w06	6:08:24
Hilltop 2	3	45N04	93w15	6:13:00
Hillview	1	46N41	95w16	6:21:04
Hillview 56	1	46N30	94w56	6:19:44
Hinckley 58	1	46N01	92w56	6:11:44
Hines 4	1	47N41	94w38	6:18:32
Hiram 11	1	46N57	94w34	6:18:16
Hitterdal 14	1	46N59	96w16	6:25:04
Hobart 56	1	46N09	95w50	6:23:20
Hodges 75	1	45N33	95w48	6:23:12
Hoff 61	1	45N33	95w41	6:22:44
Hoffman 26	1	45N50	95w48	6:23:12
Hoffmans Corners 62	3	45N04	93w01	6:12:04
Hokah 28	6	43N46	91w21	6:05:24
Holden 25	1	44N20	92w59	6:11:56
Holding 73	1	45N43	94w27	6:17:48
Holdingford 73	1	45N44	94w28	6:17:52
Holland 59	1	44N06	96w11	6:24:44
Hollandale 24	1	43N46	93w12	6:12:48
Holloway 76	1	45N15	95w55	6:23:40
Holly 51	1	44N09	95w31	6:22:04
Hollywood 10	1	44N56	93w57	6:15:48
Holman 31	1	47N19	93w24	6:13:36
Holmes City 21	1	45N50	95w32	6:22:08
Holmesville 3	1	46N56	95w44	6:22:56
Holst 15	1	47N38	95w30	6:22:00
Holt 45	1	48N18	96w11	6:24:44
Holy Cross 14	1	46N40	96w43	6:26:52
Holyoke 9	1	46N28	92w23	6:09:32
Home 8	1	44N21	94w42	6:18:48
Home Brook 11	1	46N28	94w27	6:17:48
Home Lake 54	1	47N11	96w15	6:25:00
Homer 85	1	43N59	91w33	6:06:12
Homestead 56	1	46N35	95w20	6:21:20
Honner 64	1	44N33	95w04	6:20:16
Hoot Lake 56	1	46N18	96w06	6:24:24
Hope 74	1	43N58	93w16	6:13:04
Hopkins 27	3	44N56	93w24	6:13:36
Hornet 4	1	47N48	94w30	6:18:00
Horton 75	1	45N29	95w56	6:23:44
Houston 28	6	43N46	91w34	6:06:16
Hovland 16	1	47N51	89w58	5:59:52
Howard Lake 86	1	45N04	94w04	6:16:16
Hoyt Lakes 69	1	47N31	92w09	6:08:36
Hubbard 29	1	46N50	95w01	6:20:04
Hudson 21	1	45N49	95w20	6:21:20
Hugo 82	1	45N10	93w00	6:12:00
Humboldt 35	1	48N56	97w06	6:28:24
Hunter 32	1	43N38	95w12	6:20:48
Huntersville 80	1	46N45	94w51	6:19:24
Huntley 22	1	43N44	94w14	6:16:56
Huntly 45	1	48N30	96w12	6:24:48
Huntsville 60	1	47N53	96w57	6:27:48
Husby Spur 62	3	45N04	93w10	6:12:40
Huss 68	1	48N35	96w04	6:24:16
Hutchinson 43	1	44N54	94w22	6:17:28
Hyde Park 79	1	44N16	92w21	6:09:24
Ida 21	1	45N59	95w28	6:21:52
Ideal 18	1	46N40	94w09	6:16:36
Ideal Corners 18	1	46N36	94w11	6:16:44
Idington 69	1	47N47	92w38	6:10:32
Idun 1	1	46N13	93w22	6:13:28
Ihlen 59	1	43N55	96w22	6:25:28
Imogene 46	1	43N42	94w22	6:17:28
Independence 27	1	45N02	93w42	6:14:48
Independence 69	1	46N56	92w33	6:10:12
Indian Lake 53	1	43N33	95w31	6:22:04
Indus 36	1	48N37	93w50	6:15:20
Industrial 62	3	44N57	93w10	6:12:40
Industrial 69	1	46N53	92w29	6:09:56
Inger 31	1	47N33	93w59	6:15:56
Inguadona 11	1	46N59	94w08	6:16:32
Inman 56	1	46N20	95w19	6:21:16
Interlachen 27	3	44N56	93w25	6:13:40
International Falls 36	1	48N36	93w25	6:13:40
Inver Grove Heights 19	3	44N51	93w01	6:12:04
Iona 51	1	43N55	95w47	6:23:08
Iosco 81	1	44N09	93w36	6:14:24
Iron 69	1	47N25	92w36	6:10:24
Irondale 18	1	46N28	94w01	6:16:04
Ironhub 18	1	46N32	93w42	6:14:48
Iron Range 31	1	47N21	93w24	6:13:36
Ironton 18	1	46N28	93w59	6:15:56
Irving 34	1	45N17	94w49	6:19:16
Isabella 38	1	47N37	91w21	6:05:24
Isanti 30	1	45N29	93w15	6:13:00
Island Lake 4	1	47N41	94w54	6:19:36
Island Park 27	1	44N56	93w40	6:14:40
Island View 36	1	48N37	93w11	6:12:44
Isle 48	1	46N08	93w28	6:13:52
Isle Harbor 48	1	46N06	93w30	6:14:00
Itasca 15	1	47N17	95w14	6:20:56
Ivanhoe 41	1	44N28	96w15	6:25:00
Iverson 9	1	46N39	92w25	6:09:40
Jackson 32	1	43N37	95w00	6:20:00
Jacobson 1	1	47N00	93w16	6:13:04
Jacobs Prairie 73	1	45N27	94w25	6:17:40
Jadis 68	1	48N52	95w48	6:23:12
Jakeville 5	1	45N40	93w55	6:15:40
Jameson 36	1	48N36	93w18	6:13:12
Jamestown 7	1	44N13	93w50	6:15:20
Janesville 81	1	44N07	93w42	6:14:48
Jarretts 79	1	44N15	92w17	6:09:08
Jasper 59	1	43N51	96w24	6:25:36
Jay 46	1	43N38	94w48	6:19:12
Jeffers 17	1	44N03	95w12	6:20:48
Jefferson 28	1	43N32	91w20	6:05:20
Jenkins 18	1	46N39	94w20	6:17:20
Jennie 47	1	45N05	94w18	6:17:12
Jessenland 72	1	44N36	93w57	6:15:48
Jessie Lake 31	1	47N21	94w09	6:16:36
Jevne 1	1	46N37	93w22	6:13:28
Jo Daviess 22	1	43N38	94w11	6:16:44
Johnsburg 50	1	43N34	92w43	6:10:52
Johnson 6	1	45N34	96w18	6:25:12
Johnsonville 64	1	44N20	95w25	6:21:40
Johnsville 2	3	45N10	93w16	6:13:04
Jonathan 10	1	44N48	93w37	6:14:28
Jones 4	1	47N28	95w07	6:20:28
Jordan 70	1	44N40	93w38	6:14:32
Judson 7	1	44N12	94w12	6:16:48
Jupiter 35	1	48N40	96w43	6:26:52
Kabetogama 69	1	48N25	93w13	6:12:52
Kalevala 9	1	46N33	92w53	6:11:32
Kalmar 55	1	44N04	92w37	6:10:28
Kanabec 33	1	45N52	93w26	6:13:44
Kanaranzi 67	1	43N35	96w06	6:24:24
Kandiyohi 34	1	45N07	94w56	6:19:44
Kandota 77	1	45N49	94w58	6:19:52
Karlstad 35	1	48N35	96w31	6:26:04
Kasota 40	1	44N17	93w58	6:15:52
Kasson 20	1	44N02	92w45	6:11:00
Kathio 48	1	46N09	93w47	6:15:08
Keene 14	1	46N56	96w21	6:25:24
Keewatin 31	1	47N24	93w05	6:12:20
Kego 11	1	47N01	94w15	6:17:00
Kelliher 4	1	47N57	94w27	6:17:48
Kellogg 79	1	44N19	92w00	6:08:00
Kelly Lake 69	1	47N25	93w01	6:12:04
Kelsey 69	1	47N09	92w36	6:10:24
Kelso 72	1	44N30	94w04	6:16:16
Kennedy 35	1	48N39	96w54	6:27:36
Kenneth 67	1	43N45	96w04	6:24:16
Kensington 21	1	45N47	95w42	6:22:48
Kent 84	1	46N26	96w41	6:26:44
Kenyon 25	1	44N16	92w59	6:11:56
Kerkhoven 76	1	45N12	95w19	6:21:16
Kerrick 58	1	46N20	92w35	6:10:20
Kertsonville 60	1	47N43	96w25	6:25:40
Kettle River 9	1	46N29	92w53	6:11:32
Keystone 60	1	47N59	96w49	6:27:16
Kiester 22	1	43N32	93w43	6:14:52
Kildare 76	1	45N17	95w27	6:21:48
Kilkenny 40	1	44N19	93w34	6:14:16
Kimball 32	1	43N48	94w58	6:19:52
Kimball 73	1	45N19	94w18	6:17:12
Kimball Prairie 73	1	45N19	94w18	6:17:12
Kimberly 1	1	46N34	93w28	6:13:52
Kinbrae 53	1	43N49	95w29	6:21:56
King 60	1	47N37	95w53	6:23:32
Kinghurst 31	1	47N43	94w06	6:16:24
Kingman 65	1	44N51	94w57	6:19:48
Kingsdale 58	1	46N14	92w18	6:09:12
Kings Park 55	1	44N10	92w32	6:10:08
Kingston 47	1	45N12	94w19	6:17:16
Kinmount 69	1	48N03	92w50	6:11:20
Kinney 69	1	47N31	92w44	6:10:56
Kintire 64	1	44N35	95w18	6:21:12
Kitzville 69	5	47N25	92w55	6:11:40
Klossner 52	1	44N22	94w26	6:17:44
Knapp 86	1	45N05	94w11	6:16:44
Knife Falls 9	1	46N43	92w30	6:10:00
Knife Lake 33	1	45N56	93w19	6:13:16
Knife River 38	1	46N57	91w47	6:07:08
Knute 60	1	47N38	96w00	6:24:00
Komensky 43	1	44N53	94w22	6:17:28
Kragero 12	1	45N06	95w55	6:23:40
Kragnes 14	1	46N59	96w45	6:27:00
Krain 73	1	45N44	94w34	6:18:16
Kratka 57	1	48N04	95w55	6:23:40
Kroschel 33	1	46N06	93w06	6:12:24
Kugler 69	1	47N45	92w15	6:09:00
Kurtz 14	1	46N45	96w44	6:26:56
Lac qui Parle 37	1	45N01	95w55	6:23:40
La Crescent 28	6	43N50	91w18	6:05:12
La Crosse 32	1	43N48	95w24	6:21:36
Lafayette 52	1	44N27	94w24	6:17:36
La Garde 44	1	47N16	95w44	6:22:56
Lagoona Beach 6	1	45N17	96w26	6:25:44
La Grand 21	1	45N54	95w26	6:21:44
Lake Alice 29	1	47N12	95w06	6:20:24
Lake Andrew 34	1	45N18	95w04	6:20:16
Lake Belt 46	1	43N33	94w40	6:18:40
Lake Benton 41	1	44N16	96w17	6:25:08
Lake Bronson 35	1	48N44	96w40	6:26:40
Lake Center 3	1	46N52	95w59	6:23:56
Lake City 79	1	44N27	92w16	6:09:04
Lake Crystal 7	1	44N06	94w13	6:16:52
Lake Edwards 18	1	46N30	94w12	6:16:48
Lake Elizabeth 34	1	45N01	94w49	6:19:16
Lake Emma 29	1	47N01	94w59	6:19:56
Lake Eunice 3	1	46N46	95w59	6:23:56
Lakefield 32	1	43N41	95w10	6:20:40
Lake Fremont 46	1	43N33	94w49	6:19:16
Lake George 29	1	47N12	94w59	6:19:56
Lake Grove 44	1	47N11	95w52	6:23:28
Lake Hanska 8	1	44N09	94w33	6:18:12
Lake Hattie 29	1	47N17	95w06	6:20:24
Lake Henry 73	1	45N27	94w49	6:19:16
Lake Hubert 18	1	46N30	94w15	6:17:00
Lake Ida 54	1	47N17	96w22	6:25:28
Lake Itasca 15	1	47N15	95w13	6:20:52
Lake Jessie 31	1	47N38	93w51	6:15:24
Lake Johanna 61	1	45N28	95w10	6:20:40
Lakeland 82	1	44N58	92w46	6:11:04
Lakeland Shores 82	1	44N57	92w46	6:11:04
Lake Lillian 34	1	44N57	94w53	6:19:32
Lake Marshall 42	1	44N25	95w47	6:23:08
Lake Mary 21	1	45N48	95w27	6:21:48
Lake Netta 2	3	45N10	93w19	6:13:16
Lake Nichols 69	1	47N02	92w28	6:09:52
Lake Park 3	1	46N53	96w06	6:24:24
Lake Pleasant 63	1	47N48	96w17	6:25:08
Lakeport 29	1	47N12	94w44	6:18:56
Lake Prairie 52	1	44N25	94w04	6:16:16
Lake Sarah 27	1	45N03	93w38	6:14:32
Lake Sarah 51	1	44N08	95w46	6:23:04
Lake Shore 11	1	46N24	94w18	6:17:12
Lake Shore Park 62	3	45N04	93w01	6:12:04
Lakeside 65	1	44N44	94w37	6:18:28
Lakeside 69	2	46N50	92w04	6:08:16
Lake Stay 41	1	44N25	96w08	6:24:32
Lake St. Croix Beach 82	1	44N55	92w46	6:11:04
Laketown 10	1	44N51	93w42	6:14:48
Lake Valley 78	1	45N48	96w28	6:25:52
Lakeville 19	1	44N39	93w14	6:12:56
Lake Wilson 51	1	44N00	95w57	6:23:48
Lakewood 69	1	46N54	92w00	6:08:00
Lakin 49	1	45N52	93w51	6:15:24
Lambert 63	1	47N48	95w54	6:23:36
Lamberton 64	1	44N14	95w17	6:21:08
Lammers 4	1	47N33	95w07	6:20:28
Lamoille 85	1	44N00	91w28	6:05:52
Lamson 47	1	45N05	94w18	6:17:12
Lancaster 35	1	48N52	96w48	6:27:12
Land 26	1	45N48	95w49	6:23:16
Landfall 82	3	44N57	92w59	6:11:56
Lanesboro 23	1	43N43	91w58	6:07:52
Lanesburgh 40	1	44N30	93w34	6:14:16
Langdon 82	1	44N50	92w56	6:11:44
Langhei 61	1	45N27	95w34	6:22:16
Langola 5	1	45N47	94w12	6:16:48
Langor 4	1	47N48	94w35	6:18:20
Lansing 50	1	43N43	93w00	6:12:00
Laona 68	1	48N51	95w10	6:20:40
Laporte 29	1	47N13	94w45	6:19:00
La Prairie 31	1	47N14	93w30	6:14:00
Larkin 53	1	43N43	95w52	6:23:28
Larsmont 38	1	46N59	91w45	6:07:00
La Salle 83	1	44N04	94w33	6:18:12
Lastrup 49	1	46N02	94w04	6:16:16
Lauderdale 62	3	45N01	93w12	6:12:48
Lavell 69	1	47N16	92w49	6:11:16
Lavinia	1	47N31	94w49	6:19:16
Lavinia 69	5	47N25	92w55	6:11:40
Lawler 1	1	46N32	93w10	6:12:40
Lawndale 84	1	46N33	96w21	6:25:24
Lax Lake 38	1	47N18	91w17	6:05:08
Leader 11	1	46N32	94w39	6:18:36
Leaf Lake 56	1	46N25	95w28	6:21:52
Leaf Mountain 56	1	46N09	95w35	6:22:20
Leaf River 80	1	46N30	95w06	6:20:24
Leaf Valley 21	1	46N03	95w27	6:21:48
Leavenworth 8	1	44N15	94w48	6:19:12
Le Center 40	1	44N23	93w44	6:14:56
Leech Lake 11	1	47N11	94w36	6:18:24
Leeds 51	1	43N59	95w53	6:23:32
Leenthrop 12	1	44N56	95w33	6:22:12
Leetonia 69	5	47N25	92w55	6:11:40
Le Hillier 7	1	44N10	94w01	6:16:04
Leiding 69	1	48N02	92w50	6:11:20
Leigh 49	1	46N02	93w54	6:15:36
Lemond 74	1	43N59	93w21	6:13:24
Lengby 60	1	47N31	95w38	6:22:32
Lenora 23	1	43N32	91w55	6:07:40
Lent 13	1	45N31	92w57	6:11:48
Leonard 15	1	47N39	95w16	6:21:04
Leonardsville 78	1	45N37	96w19	6:25:16
Leonidas 69	1	47N27	92w34	6:10:16
Leota 53	1	43N50	96w01	6:24:04
Le Ray 7	1	44N12	93w49	6:15:16
Le Roy 50	1	43N31	92w30	6:10:00
Le Sauk 73	1	45N38	94w14	6:16:56
Leslie 77	1	45N58	95w04	6:20:16
Lessor 60	1	47N43	95w54	6:23:36
Lester Prairie 43	1	44N53	94w02	6:16:08
Le Sueur 40	1	44N28	93w55	6:15:40
Leven 61	1	45N43	95w20	6:21:20
Lewis 48	1	46N01	93w30	6:14:00
Lewiston 85	1	43N59	91w52	6:07:28
Lewisville 83	1	43N55	94w26	6:17:44
Lexington 2	3	45N08	93w10	6:12:40
Lexington 40	1	44N23	93w43	6:14:52
Libby 1	1	46N48	93w22	6:13:28
Lien 26	1	45N53	95w56	6:23:44
Lilydale 19	3	44N54	93w08	6:12:32
Lima 11	1	47N02	93w56	6:15:44
Lime 7	1	44N13	93w57	6:15:48
Lime Creek 51	1	43N53	95w34	6:22:16
Lime Lake 51	1	43N59	95w38	6:22:32
Limestone 41	1	44N30	96w08	6:24:32
Lincoln 49	1	46N13	94w39	6:18:36
Lind 68	1	48N35	96w20	6:25:20
Linden 8	1	44N10	94w26	6:17:44
Linden Grove 69	1	47N52	92w52	6:11:28
Linden Hills 27	3	44N55	93w19	6:13:16
Lindford 36	1	48N24	93w34	6:14:16
Lindstrom 13	1	45N23	92w51	6:11:24
Lino Lakes 2	1	45N12	93w06	6:12:24
Linsell 45	1	48N31	95w40	6:22:40
Linwood 2	1	45N23	93w04	6:12:16
Lisbon 87	1	44N51	95w48	6:23:12
Lismore 53	1	43N45	95w57	6:23:48
Litchfield 47	1	45N08	94w32	6:18:08
Litomysl 74	1	44N05	93w13	6:12:52
Little Canada 62	3	45N01	93w06	6:12:24
Little Chicago 66	1	44N27	93w10	6:12:40
Little Elk 77	1	46N04	94w43	6:18:52
Little Falls 49	1	45N59	94w22	6:17:28
Littlefork 36	1	48N24	93w34	6:14:16
Little Marais 38	1	47N25	91w07	6:04:28
Little Pine 18	1	46N45	93w50	6:15:20
Little Rock 49	1	45N50	94w17	6:17:08
Little Rock 53	1	43N33	95w52	6:23:28

MINNESOTA

Little Sauk 77	1	45N52	94w55	6:19:40
Little Swan 69	5	47N25	92w55	6:11:40
Livonia 71	1	45N26	93w34	6:14:16
Lockhart 54	1	47N26	96w33	6:26:12
Lodi 50	1	43N33	92w38	6:10:32
Loman 36	1	48N31	93w49	6:15:16
London 24	1	43N32	93w04	6:12:16
Lone Pine 31	1	47N19	93w08	6:12:32
Lone Tree 12	1	45N01	95w18	6:21:12
Long Beach 61	1	45N39	95w27	6:21:48
Long Lake 27	1	44N59	93w34	6:14:16
Long Point 39	1	48N46	94w57	6:19:48
Long Prairie 77	1	45N59	94w52	6:19:28
Long Siding 48	1	45N34	93w35	6:14:20
Longville 11	1	46N59	94w13	6:16:52
Lonsdale 66	1	44N29	93w26	6:13:44
Loon Lake 11	1	46N34	94w21	6:17:24
Loop 27	3	44N59	93w16	6:13:04
Lorain 53	1	43N38	95w31	6:22:04
Loretto 27	1	45N03	93w38	6:14:32
Loring 27	3	44N58	93w17	6:13:08
Loring Park 27	3	44N58	93w18	6:13:12
Louisburg 37	1	45N10	96w10	6:24:40
Louriston 12	1	45N06	95w26	6:21:44
Lowell 60	1	47N48	96w48	6:27:12
Lower Sioux Indian Res 64	1	47N32	94w49	6:19:16
Lowry 61	1	45N42	95w31	6:22:04
Lowry Hill 27	3	44N58	93w18	6:13:12
Lowville 51	1	44N04	95w53	6:23:32
Lucan 64	1	44N25	95w25	6:21:40
Lucas 42	1	44N35	95w40	6:22:40
Luce	1	46N40	95w39	6:22:36
Lude 39	1	48N46	94w57	6:19:48
Lund 21	1	46N03	95w41	6:22:44
Lura 22	1	43N48	93w57	6:15:48
Lutsen 16	1	47N39	90w41	6:02:44
Luverne 67	1	43N39	96w13	6:24:52
Luxemburg 73	1	45N22	94w26	6:17:44
Lydia 70	1	44N40	93w38	6:14:32
Lyle 50	1	43N30	92w57	6:11:48
Lynd 42	1	44N23	95w54	6:23:36
Lyndale 27	1	45N01	93w41	6:14:44
Lynden 73	1	45N24	94w05	6:16:20
Lynn 43	1	44N51	94w26	6:17:44
Lynwood 69	5	47N25	92w55	6:11:40
Lyra 7	1	43N59	94w04	6:16:16
Mabel 23	1	43N32	91w46	6:07:04
Macsville 26	1	45N49	96w04	6:24:16
Macville 1	1	46N54	93w38	6:14:32
Madelia 83	1	44N03	94w25	6:17:40
Madison 37	1	45N01	96w11	6:24:44
Madison Lake 7	1	44N12	93w49	6:15:16
Magnolia 67	1	43N38	96w07	6:24:28
Mahkonce 44	1	47N19	95w58	6:23:52
Mahnomen 44	1	47N19	95w58	6:23:52
Mahtomedi 82	3	45N04	92w57	6:11:48
Mahtowa 9	1	46N34	92w38	6:10:32
Maine 56	1	46N25	95w51	6:23:24
Maine Prairie 73	1	45N22	94w19	6:17:16
Makinen 69	1	47N21	92w22	6:09:28
Malmo 1	1	46N20	93w01	6:12:04
Malta 6	1	45N27	96w18	6:25:12
Malung 68	1	48N46	95w41	6:22:44
Mamre 34	1	45N12	95w11	6:20:44
Manannah 47	1	45N15	94w37	6:18:28
Manchester 24	1	43N43	93w27	6:13:48
Mandt 12	1	45N06	95w41	6:22:44
Manfred 37	1	44N51	96w24	6:25:36
Manhattan Beach 18	1	46N44	94w08	6:16:32
Manitou 27	1	44N54	93w34	6:14:16
Manitou 36	1	48N38	94w00	6:16:00
Mankato 7	1	44N10	94w00	6:16:00
Mansfield 24	1	43N33	93w35	6:14:20
Manston 84	1	46N30	96w28	6:25:52
Mantorville 20	1	44N05	92w45	6:11:00
Mantrap 29	1	47N01	94w51	6:19:24
Manyaska 46	1	43N38	94w40	6:18:40
Maple 11	1	46N35	94w26	6:17:44
Maple Bay 60	1	47N38	96w13	6:24:52
Maple Grove 27	1	45N09	93w29	6:13:56
Maple Hill 16	1	47N45	90w20	6:01:20
Maple Island 24	1	43N46	93w11	6:12:44
Maple Lake 86	1	45N14	94w00	6:16:00
Maple Plain 27	1	45N00	93w40	6:14:40
Mapleton 7	1	43N56	93w57	6:15:48
Mapleview 50	1	43N42	92w58	6:11:52
Maplewood 62	3	45N00	93w03	6:12:12
Marble 31	1	47N20	93w19	6:13:16
Marcell 31	1	47N36	93w42	6:14:48
Margie 36	1	48N06	93w57	6:15:48
Marietta 37	1	45N01	96w25	6:25:40
Marine On St. Croix 82	1	45N12	92w46	6:11:04
Marion 55	1	43N59	92w24	6:09:36
Markham 69	1	47N21	92w22	6:09:28
Markville 58	1	46N05	92w19	6:09:16
Marshall 42	1	44N27	95w47	6:23:08
Marshan 19	1	44N40	92w51	6:11:24
Marsh Creek 44	1	47N22	95w59	6:23:56
Marshfield 41	1	44N20	96w08	6:24:32
Marsh Grove 45	1	48N20	96w26	6:25:44
Martin 67	1	43N33	96w24	6:25:36
Martin Lake 2	1	45N24	92w59	6:11:56
Martinsburg 65	1	44N40	94w41	6:18:44
Mary 54	1	47N12	96w37	6:26:28
Marysburg 7	1	44N12	93w49	6:15:16
Marysland 76	1	45N17	95w49	6:23:16
Marystown 70	1	44N48	93w32	6:14:08
Marysville 86	1	45N06	93w57	6:15:48
Mason 51	1	44N04	95w46	6:23:04
Matawan 81	1	43N52	93w38	6:14:32
Mattson 35	1	48N46	96w56	6:27:44
Max 31	1	47N37	94w04	6:16:16
Maxwell 37	1	44N51	96w02	6:24:08
Mayer 10	1	44N53	93w53	6:15:32
Mayfield 57	1	48N00	95w54	6:23:36
Mayhew 5	1	45N35	94w10	6:16:40
Mayhew Lake 5	1	45N41	94w04	6:16:16
Maynard 12	1	44N55	95w28	6:21:52
Mayville 28	1	43N38	91w26	6:05:44
Mayville 50	1	43N41	92w58	6:11:52
Maywood 5	1	45N42	93w49	6:15:16
Mazeppa 79	1	44N19	92w29	6:09:56
McCauleyville 84	1	46N25	96w40	6:26:40
McCrea 45	1	48N14	96w42	6:26:48
McDavitt 69	1	47N19	92w37	6:10:28
McDonaldsville 54	1	47N17	96w30	6:26:00
McGrath 1	1	46N15	93w17	6:13:08
McGregor 1	1	46N37	93w19	6:13:16
McIntosh 60	1	47N38	95w53	6:23:32
McKee 19	3	44N55	93w14	6:12:56
McKinley 69	1	47N31	92w25	6:09:40
McPherson 7	1	44N04	93w50	6:15:20
Meadow 80	1	46N41	94w58	6:19:52
Meadow Brook 11	1	46N29	94w38	6:18:32
Meadowlands 69	1	47N04	92w44	6:10:56
Meadows 84	1	46N25	96w28	6:25:52
Medford 74	1	44N11	93w15	6:13:00
Medicine Lake 27	3	45N00	93w25	6:13:40
Medina 27	1	45N02	93w35	6:14:20
Medo 7	1	43N59	93w50	6:15:20
Mehurin 37	1	44N56	96w24	6:25:36
Meire Grove 73	1	45N38	94w52	6:19:28
Melby 21	1	46N04	95w44	6:22:56
Melrose 73	1	45N40	94w49	6:19:16
Melrude 69	1	47N15	92w25	6:09:40
Melville 65	1	44N46	94w49	6:19:16
Menahga 80	1	46N45	95w06	6:20:24
Mendota 19	3	44N53	93w10	6:12:40
Mendota Heights 19	3	44N53	93w08	6:12:32
Mentor 60	1	47N42	96w09	6:24:36
Meriden 74	1	44N04	93w21	6:13:24
Merrifield 18	1	46N28	94w10	6:16:40
Merton 74	1	44N09	93w06	6:12:24
Mesaba 69	1	47N31	92w09	6:08:36
Meyhew Lake 5	1	45N35	94w10	6:16:40
Mickinock 68	1	48N40	95w41	6:22:44
Middle River 45	1	48N26	96w10	6:24:40
Middletown 32	1	43N33	95w05	6:20:20
Middleville 86	1	45N07	94w04	6:16:16
Midway 3	1	46N45	95w06	6:20:24
Midway 62	3	44N57	93w10	6:12:40
Midway 69	1	47N31	92w32	6:10:08
Miesville 19	1	44N36	92w49	6:11:16
Milaca 48	1	45N45	93w39	6:14:36
Milan 12	1	45N07	95w55	6:23:40
Milford 8	1	44N20	94w53	6:19:32
Mille Lacs Indian Reservatio 58	1	47N32	94w49	6:19:16
Millersburg 66	1	44N17	93w16	6:13:04
Millerville 21	1	46N03	95w35	6:22:20
Millville 79	1	44N15	92w17	6:09:08
Millwood 73	1	45N43	94w42	6:18:48
Milo 48	1	45N41	93w42	6:14:48
Milroy 64	1	44N25	95w33	6:22:12
Milton 20	1	44N09	92w44	6:10:56
Miltona 21	1	46N03	95w18	6:21:12
Minden 5	1	45N36	94w05	6:16:20
Minerva 15	1	47N22	95w23	6:21:32
Minneapolis 27	3	44N59	93w16	6:13:04
Minnehaha 27	3	44N57	93w14	6:12:56
Minneiska 79	6	44N12	91w52	6:07:28
Minneola 25	1	44N19	92w44	6:10:56
Minneota 42	1	44N34	95w59	6:23:56
Minnesota City 85	1	44N06	91w46	6:07:04
Minnesota Falls 87	1	44N46	95w32	6:22:08
Minnesota Lake 22	1	43N51	93w50	6:15:20
Minnesota Transfer 62	3	44N57	93w11	6:12:44
Minnetonka 27	3	44N56	93w27	6:13:48
Minnetonka Beach 27	1	44N56	93w35	6:14:20
Minnetonka Mills 27	3	44N56	93w25	6:13:40
Minnetrista 27	1	44N56	93w42	6:14:48
Minnewana 1	1	46N36	93w19	6:13:16
Minnewaska 61	1	45N39	95w29	6:21:56
Minnie 4	1	48N19	95w16	6:21:04
Missabe Mountain 69	1	47N30	92w29	6:09:56
Mission 18	1	46N35	94w08	6:16:32
Mission Creek 58	1	45N56	92w58	6:11:52
Mitchell 84	1	46N30	96w35	6:26:20
Mizpah 36	1	47N55	94w12	6:16:48
Moe 21	1	45N53	95w35	6:22:20
Moland 14	1	46N56	96w37	6:26:28
Moland 66	1	44N16	92w59	6:11:56
Moltke 72	1	44N35	94w34	6:18:16
Money Creek 28	1	43N49	91w37	6:06:28
Monroe 42	1	44N14	95w40	6:22:40
Monson 78	1	45N53	96w30	6:26:00
Monterey 46	1	43N45	94w43	6:18:52
Montevideo 12	1	44N57	95w43	6:22:52
Montgomery 40	1	44N26	93w35	6:14:20
Monticello 86	1	45N18	93w48	6:15:12
Montrose 86	1	45N04	93w55	6:15:40
Moonshine 6	1	45N32	96w18	6:25:12
Moore 75	1	45N28	95w48	6:23:12
Moorhead 14	1	46N53	96w45	6:27:00
Moose 68	1	48N51	96w04	6:24:16
Moose Creek 15	1	47N28	95w14	6:20:56
Moose Lake 9	1	46N27	92w46	6:11:04
Moose Park 31	1	47N43	94w21	6:17:24
Moose River 45	1	48N30	95w49	6:23:16
Mora 33	1	45N53	93w18	6:13:12
Moran 77	1	46N14	94w50	6:19:20
Moranville 68	1	48N51	95w18	6:21:12
Morcom 69	1	47N46	93w01	6:12:04
Morgan 64	1	44N25	94w56	6:19:44
Morgan Park 69	1	46N41	92w13	6:08:52
Morken 14	1	47N01	96w38	6:26:32
Morningside 27	3	44N55	93w20	6:13:20
Morrill 49	1	45N50	93w58	6:15:52
Morris 75	1	45N35	95w55	6:23:40
Morrison 1	1	46N37	93w37	6:14:28
Morristown 66	1	44N14	93w27	6:13:48
Morton 65	1	44N33	94w59	6:19:56
Moscow 24	1	43N43	93w05	6:12:20
Motley 49	1	46N20	94w38	6:18:32
Moulton 51	1	43N54	95w59	6:23:56
Mound 27	1	44N56	93w40	6:14:40
Mound Prairie 28	1	43N47	91w26	6:05:44
Mounds View 62	3	45N07	93w13	6:12:52
Mountain Iron 69	1	47N32	92w37	6:10:28
Mountain Lake 17	1	43N57	94w56	6:19:44
Mount Morris 49	1	45N57	93w52	6:15:28
Mount Pleasant 79	1	44N25	92w22	6:09:28
Mount Royal 69	2	46N50	92w06	6:08:24
Mount Vernon 85	1	44N09	91w54	6:07:36
Moyer 76	1	45N17	95w55	6:23:40
Moylan 45	1	48N14	95w47	6:23:08
Mudgett 48	1	45N56	93w35	6:14:20
Mulligan 8	1	44N10	94w48	6:19:12
Munch 58	1	45N56	92w50	6:11:20
Munger 69	2	46N47	92w08	6:08:32
Munson 73	1	45N27	94w35	6:18:20
Murdock 76	1	45N13	95w24	6:21:36
Murphy City 38	1	47N31	91w20	6:05:20
Murray 51	1	44N04	95w39	6:22:36
Myrtle 24	1	43N34	93w08	6:12:32
Nashua 84	1	46N02	96w19	6:25:16
Nashville 46	1	43N48	94w18	6:17:12
Nashwauk 31	1	47N23	93w10	6:12:40
Nassau 37	1	45N04	96w26	6:25:44
Navarre 27	1	44N58	93w36	6:14:24
Naytahwaush 44	1	47N16	95w38	6:22:32
Nebish 4	1	47N46	94w52	6:19:28
Nelson 21	1	46N00	95w15	6:21:00
Nelson Park 45	1	48N30	96w35	6:26:20
Nereson 68	1	48N41	95w57	6:23:48
Nerstrand 66	1	44N20	93w04	6:12:16
Nesbit 60	1	47N53	96w48	6:27:12
Ness 69	1	46N59	92w45	6:11:00
Nessel 13	1	45N41	93w04	6:12:16
Nett Lake 69	1	48N07	93w06	6:12:24
Nett Lake Indian Reservation 36	1	47N32	94w49	6:19:16
Nett River 36	1	48N12	93w22	6:13:28
Nevada 50	1	43N33	92w52	6:11:28
Nevis 29	1	46N58	94w51	6:19:24
New Auburn 72	1	44N40	94w14	6:16:56
New Avon 64	1	44N25	95w10	6:20:40
New Brighton 62	3	45N04	93w12	6:12:48
Newburg 23	1	43N32	91w46	6:07:04
New Dosey 58	1	46N11	92w22	6:09:28
Newfolden 45	1	48N21	96w20	6:25:20
New Germany 10	1	44N53	93w58	6:15:52
New Hartford 85	1	43N54	91w25	6:05:40
New Haven 55	1	44N09	92w37	6:10:28
New Hope 27	3	45N02	93w23	6:13:32
Newhouse 28	1	43N31	91w46	6:07:04
New Independence 69	1	46N58	92w29	6:09:56
New London 34	1	45N18	94w56	6:19:44
New Maine 45	1	48N25	96w19	6:25:16
New Market 70	1	44N35	93w19	6:13:16
New Munich 73	1	45N38	94w45	6:19:00
Newport 82	3	44N52	93w00	6:12:00
New Prague 40	1	44N32	93w35	6:14:20
New Prairie 61	1	45N38	95w42	6:22:48
New Richland 81	1	43N54	93w30	6:14:00
New Rome 72	1	44N37	94w05	6:16:20
Newry 24	1	43N48	93w05	6:12:20
New Scandia 82	1	45N15	92w50	6:11:20
New Solum 45	1	48N14	96w18	6:25:12
New Sweden 52	1	44N16	94w20	6:17:20
Newton 56	1	46N30	95w20	6:21:20
New Trier 19	1	44N36	92w56	6:11:44
New Ulm 8	1	44N19	94w28	6:17:52
New York Mills 56	1	46N31	95w22	6:21:28
Nichols 69	1	47N30	92w36	6:10:24
Nickerson 58	1	46N22	92w27	6:09:48
Nicollet 52	1	44N17	94w11	6:16:44
Nicols 19	3	44N55	93w14	6:12:56
Nidaros 56	1	46N14	95w35	6:22:20
Nielsville 60	1	47N32	96w49	6:27:16
Nilsen 84	1	46N20	96w28	6:25:52
Nimrod 80	1	46N38	94w53	6:19:32
Nininger 19	1	44N45	92w56	6:11:44
Nisswa 18	1	46N31	94w17	6:17:08
Nodine 85	1	43N55	91w21	6:05:24
Nokay Lake 18	1	46N23	94w00	6:16:00
Nokomis 27	3	44N54	93w15	6:13:00
Nopeming 69	1	46N42	92w16	6:09:04
Norcross 26	1	45N52	96w12	6:24:48
Norden 57	1	48N08	96w18	6:25:12
Nordick 84	1	46N25	96w35	6:26:20
Nore 31	1	47N49	94w21	6:17:24
Norfolk 65	1	44N40	94w55	6:19:40
Normandale 27	3	44N53	93w21	6:13:24
Normania 87	1	44N41	95w48	6:23:12
Normanna 69	1	47N01	91w59	6:07:56
Norseland 52	1	44N25	94w07	6:16:28
North 57	1	48N08	96w10	6:24:40
North Benton 5	1	45N40	93w55	6:15:40
North Branch 13	1	45N31	92w59	6:11:56
Northcote 35	1	48N51	97w00	6:28:00
North Cross Lake 18	1	46N41	94w08	6:16:32
Northdale 2	3	45N10	93w16	6:13:04
North Douglas 27	3	45N01	93w21	6:13:24

Northern 4	1	47N33	94w51	6:19:24
Northfield 66	1	44N27	93w09	6:12:36
North Fork 73	1	45N33	95w04	6:20:16
North Germany 80	1	46N35	94w58	6:19:52
North Hero 64	1	44N14	95w25	6:21:40
North Hibbing 69	5	47N25	92w55	6:11:40
North Mankato 52	1	44N10	94w01	6:16:04
North Oaks 62	3	45N06	93w04	6:12:16
Northome 36	1	47N52	94w17	6:17:08
North Ottawa 26	1	45N59	96w12	6:24:48
North Prairie 49	1	45N50	94w28	6:17:52
North Red River 35	1	48N46	97w06	6:28:24
North Redwood 64	1	44N34	95w06	6:20:24
Northrop 46	1	43N44	94w26	6:17:44
North Saint Paul 62	3	45N01	92w59	6:11:56
Northside 24	1	43N39	93w22	6:13:28
North Star 8	1	44N14	95w03	6:20:12
Northwest Terminal 27	3	45N01	93w15	6:13:00
Norton 85	1	44N04	91w54	6:07:36
Norway Lake 34	1	45N22	95w12	6:20:48
Norwegian Grove 56	1	46N35	96w13	6:24:52
Norwood 10	3	44N46	93w55	6:15:40
Nowthen 2	3	45N10	93w19	6:13:16
Noyes 35	1	49N00	97w12	6:28:48
Numedal 57	1	48N09	96w26	6:25:44
Nunda 24	1	43N33	93w29	6:13:56
Nymore 4	1	47N32	94w49	6:19:16
Oak 73	1	45N38	94w42	6:18:48
Oak Center 79	1	44N27	92w16	6:09:04
Oakdale 82	3	44N59	92w58	6:11:52
Oak Grove 2	1	45N20	93w20	6:13:20
Oakhill 77	1	45N59	94w51	6:19:24
Oak Island 39	1	49N19	94w51	6:19:24
Oak Knoll 27	3	44N56	93w25	6:13:40
Oakland 24	1	43N41	93w05	6:12:20
Oak Lawn 18	1	46N22	93w20	6:13:20
Oak Park 2	3	45N10	93w16	6:13:04
Oak Park 5	1	45N42	93w49	6:15:16
Oak Park Heights 82	1	45N02	92w48	6:11:12
Oakport 14	1	46N56	96w45	6:27:00
Oak Ridge 85	1	44N12	91w52	6:07:28
Oak Street 27	3	44N59	93w14	6:12:56
Oak Valley 56	1	46N20	95w13	6:20:52
Oakwood 79	1	44N14	92w15	6:09:00
O'brien 4	1	47N48	94w43	6:18:52
Odessa 6	1	45N16	96w20	6:25:20
Odin 83	1	43N54	94w48	6:19:12
Ogema 3	1	47N06	95w56	6:23:44
Ogilvie 33	1	45N50	93w26	6:13:44
Okabena 32	1	43N44	95w19	6:21:16
Oklee 63	1	47N50	95w51	6:23:24
Old Frontenac 25	1	44N27	92w16	6:09:04
Olga 60	1	47N46	95w37	6:22:28
Olivia 65	1	44N47	94w59	6:19:56
Olney 53	1	43N38	95w52	6:23:28
Omro 87	1	44N46	96w02	6:24:08
Onamia 48	1	46N04	93w40	6:14:40
Oneka 82	1	45N10	92w57	6:11:48
Onigum 11	1	47N06	94w35	6:18:20
Onstad 60	1	47N38	96w23	6:25:32
Opole 73	1	45N44	94w28	6:17:52
Orange 21	1	45N48	95w12	6:20:48
Orchard Lake 19	1	44N41	93w15	6:13:00
Orion 55	1	43N53	92w15	6:09:00
Orleans 35	1	48N56	96w56	6:27:44
Ormsby 83	1	43N51	94w42	6:18:48
Orono 27	1	44N58	93w33	6:14:12
Oronoco 55	1	44N10	92w32	6:10:08
Orr 69	1	48N03	92w50	6:11:20
Orrock 71	1	45N26	93w43	6:14:52
Orton 80	1	46N40	94w51	6:19:24
Ortonville 6	1	45N19	96w27	6:25:48
Orwell 56	1	46N14	96w12	6:24:48
Osage 3	1	46N55	95w16	6:21:04
Osakis 21	1	45N52	95w09	6:20:36
Osborne 59	1	43N53	96w07	6:24:28
Oscar 56	1	46N25	96w13	6:24:52
Osceola 65	1	44N51	94w49	6:19:16
Oshawa 52	1	44N18	94w03	6:16:12
Oshkosh 87	1	44N46	96w09	6:24:36
Oslo 20	1	43N53	92w51	6:11:24
Oslo 45	1	48N12	97w08	6:28:32
Oslund 31	1	47N39	93w52	6:15:28
Osseo 27	3	45N07	93w24	6:13:36
Ostrander 23	1	43N37	92w26	6:09:44
Oteneagen 31	1	47N28	94w07	6:16:28
Otisco 81	1	43N59	93w30	6:14:00
Otisville 82	1	45N15	92w48	6:11:12
Otrey 6	1	45N22	96w18	6:25:12
Otsego 86	1	45N16	93w37	6:14:28
Ottawa 40	1	44N23	93w57	6:15:48
Ottertail 56	1	46N26	95w33	6:22:12
Otto 56	1	46N30	95w28	6:21:52
Outing 11	1	46N49	93w57	6:15:48
Owatonna 74	1	44N05	93w14	6:12:56
Owens 69	1	47N50	92w37	6:10:28
Oxford 30	1	45N27	93w10	6:12:40
Oxlip 30	1	45N30	93w15	6:13:00
Oylen 80	1	46N35	94w48	6:19:12
Paddock 56	1	46N40	95w13	6:20:52
Padua 73	1	45N45	94w57	6:19:48
Page 48	1	45N52	93w41	6:14:44
Palisade 1	1	46N43	93w29	6:13:56
Palmdale 13	1	45N25	92w39	6:10:36
Palmer 71	1	45N31	93w56	6:15:44
Palmers 69	2	46N50	92w04	6:08:16
Palmville 68	1	48N36	95w46	6:23:04
Palmyra 65	1	44N40	94w48	6:19:12
Palo 69	1	47N32	92w14	6:08:56
Parent 5	1	45N40	93w55	6:15:40
Park 58	1	46N18	92w29	6:09:56
Parke 14	1	46N46	96w15	6:25:00
Parkers Prairie 56	1	46N09	95w20	6:21:20
Park Rapids 29	1	46N55	95w04	6:20:16
Park Rapids Junction 73	1	45N45	94w57	6:19:48
Parkville 69	1	47N32	92w35	6:10:20
Partridge 58	1	46N12	92w44	6:10:56
Paxton 64	1	44N30	95w03	6:20:12
Payne 69	1	47N06	92w36	6:10:24
Paynesville 73	1	45N23	94w43	6:18:52
Peace 33	1	46N01	93w15	6:13:00
Pearl Lake 73	1	45N19	94w18	6:17:12
Pease 48	1	45N42	93w39	6:14:36
Pelan 35	1	48N40	96w27	6:25:48
Pelican Lake 26	1	46N05	95w51	6:23:24
Pelican Lakes 18	1	46N37	94w12	6:16:48
Pelican Rapids 56	1	46N34	96w05	6:24:20
Pelland 36	1	48N36	93w18	6:13:12
Pemberton 7	1	44N01	93w47	6:15:08
Pembina 44	1	47N17	96w00	6:24:00
Pencer 68	1	48N42	95w38	6:22:32
Pengilly 31	1	47N20	93w12	6:12:48
Penn 43	1	44N40	94w19	6:17:16
Pennington 4	1	47N29	94w29	6:17:56
Pennock 34	1	45N09	95w10	6:20:40
Pepin 79	1	44N23	92w08	6:08:32
Pepperton 75	1	45N38	96w04	6:24:16
Pequaywan Lake 69	2	46N50	92w06	6:08:24
Pequot Lakes 18	1	46N36	94w19	6:17:16
Percy 35	1	48N46	96w36	6:26:24
Perham 56	1	46N36	95w34	6:22:16
Perley 54	1	47N11	96w48	6:27:12
Perry 37	1	45N07	96w17	6:25:08
Perry Lake 18	1	46N35	93w58	6:15:52
Petersburg 32	1	43N32	94w55	6:19:40
Peterson 23	1	43N47	91w50	6:07:20
Petran 24	1	43N39	93w13	6:12:52
Phelps 56	1	46N17	95w52	6:23:28
Philbrook 77	1	46N20	94w38	6:18:32
Pickerel Lake 24	1	43N38	93w29	6:13:56
Pickwick 85	7	44N03	91w40	6:06:40
Pierz 49	1	45N59	94w06	6:16:24
Pigeon River 16	1	48N01	89w42	5:58:48
Pike 69	1	47N40	92w22	6:09:28
Pike Bay 11	1	47N22	94w37	6:18:28
Pike Creek 49	1	45N59	94w27	6:17:48
Pike Lake 69	2	46N48	92w08	6:08:32
Pillager 11	1	46N20	94w28	6:17:52
Pillsbury 76	1	45N12	95w18	6:21:12
Pillsbury 77	1	45N59	94w34	6:18:16
Pilot Grove 22	1	43N33	94w11	6:16:44
Pilotmound 23	1	43N49	92w01	6:08:04
Pine Bend 44	1	47N31	95w38	6:22:32
Pine Center 18	1	46N13	93w55	6:15:40
Pine City 58	1	45N50	92w59	6:11:56
Pinecreek 68	1	48N59	95w56	6:23:44
Pine Island 25	1	44N12	92w39	6:10:36
Pine Point 3	1	47N01	95w22	6:21:28
Pine River 11	1	46N43	94w24	6:17:36
Pine Springs 82	1	45N02	92w57	6:11:48
Pineville 69	1	47N32	92w14	6:08:56
Pinewood 4	1	47N36	95w08	6:20:32
Pioneer 62	3	44N58	93w05	6:12:20
Pipestone 59	1	44N00	96w19	6:25:16
Pitt 39	1	48N43	94w43	6:18:52
Plainview 79	1	44N10	92w10	6:08:40
Plato 43	1	44N46	94w01	6:16:04
Platte 49	1	46N07	94w07	6:16:28
Platte Lake 18	1	46N13	94w00	6:16:00
Pleasant Grove 55	1	43N54	92w23	6:09:32
Pleasant Hill 85	1	43N54	91w32	6:06:08
Pleasant Lake 73	1	45N30	94w17	6:17:08
Pleasant Mound 7	1	43N53	94w18	6:17:12
Pleasant Prairie 46	1	43N38	94w18	6:17:12
Pleasant Valley 50	1	43N48	92w38	6:10:32
Pleasant View 54	1	47N22	96w32	6:26:08
Pliny 1	1	46N17	93w15	6:13:00
Plummer 63	1	47N55	96w03	6:24:12
Plymouth 27	3	45N02	93w27	6:13:48
Pohlitz 68	1	48N56	96w04	6:24:16
Point Douglas 82	1	44N40	92w50	6:11:20
Pokegama 58	1	45N52	93w02	6:12:08
Polk Centre 57	1	48N00	96w25	6:25:40
Polonia 68	1	48N46	96w19	6:25:16
Pomme De Terre 26	1	46N04	95w57	6:23:48
Ponemah 4	1	48N01	94w56	6:19:44
Ponsford 3	1	46N58	95w23	6:21:32
Ponto Lake 11	1	46N50	94w21	6:17:24
Poplar 11	1	46N35	94w42	6:18:48
Poplar Grove 68	1	48N35	95w56	6:23:44
Poplar River 63	1	47N48	96w02	6:24:08
Popple 15	1	47N33	95w30	6:22:00
Popple Creek 5	1	45N35	94w10	6:16:40
Popple Grove 44	1	47N12	96w00	6:24:00
Poppleton 35	1	48N51	96w44	6:26:56
Portage 69	1	48N08	92w35	6:10:20
Port Cargill 70	1	44N47	93w15	6:13:00
Porter 87	1	44N38	96w10	6:24:40
Port Hope 4	1	47N38	94w45	6:19:00
Posen 87	1	44N35	95w32	6:22:08
Post Town 55	1	44N02	92w39	6:10:36
Potsdam 55	1	44N08	92w15	6:09:00
Powderhorn 27	3	44N56	93w15	6:13:00
Powers 11	1	46N50	94w28	6:17:52
Prairie Island Indian Reserv 25	1	47N32	94w49	6:19:16
Prairie Lake 69	1	46N48	92w58	6:11:52
Prairie View 84	1	46N35	96w21	6:25:24
Prairieville 8	1	44N20	94w48	6:19:12
Prairieville 66	1	44N17	93w16	6:13:04
Pratt 74	1	44N05	93w13	6:12:52
Preble 23	1	43N38	91w47	6:07:08
Predmore 55	1	43N59	92w15	6:09:00
Prescott 22	1	43N43	94w04	6:16:16
Preston 23	1	43N40	92w05	6:08:20
Preston Lake 65	1	44N45	94w34	6:18:16
Priam 34	1	45N01	95w14	6:20:56
Princeton 48	1	45N34	93w35	6:14:20
Prinsburg 34	1	44N56	95w11	6:20:44
Prior 6	1	45N27	96w33	6:26:12
Prior Lake 70	1	44N43	93w25	6:13:40
Prior Lake Indian Res 27	1	47N32	94w49	6:19:16
Proctor 69	1	46N45	92w14	6:08:56
Prosit 69	1	47N00	92w37	6:10:28
Prosper 23	1	43N31	91w57	6:07:48
Providence 37	1	44N51	96w09	6:24:36
Pulaski 49	1	46N07	94w00	6:16:00
Puposky 4	1	47N41	94w54	6:19:36
Quamba 33	1	45N55	93w11	6:12:44
Queen 60	1	47N38	95w37	6:22:28
Quincy 55	1	44N03	92w08	6:08:32
Quiring 4	1	47N52	95w23	6:21:32
Rabbit Lake 18	1	46N32	93w51	6:15:24
Racine 50	1	43N47	92w29	6:09:56
Radium 45	1	48N14	96w37	6:26:28
Rail Prairie 49	1	46N16	94w24	6:17:36
Rainy Junction 69	1	47N31	92w32	6:10:08
Ramey 49	1	45N40	93w55	6:15:40
Ramsey 2	1	45N16	93w26	6:13:44
Ramsey 50	1	43N41	92w58	6:11:52
Randall 49	1	46N05	94w30	6:18:00
Randolph 19	1	44N32	93w01	6:12:04
Ranier 36	1	48N36	93w22	6:13:28
Ransom 53	1	43N33	95w45	6:23:00
Rapidan 7	1	44N04	94w04	6:16:16
Rasset 86	1	45N11	93w52	6:15:28
Rauch 36	1	47N58	92w49	6:11:16
Ravenna 19	1	44N41	92w45	6:11:00
Ray 36	1	48N25	93w13	6:12:52
Raymond 34	1	45N02	95w14	6:20:56
Reading 53	1	43N42	95w42	6:22:48
Reads Landing 79	1	44N21	92w04	6:08:16
Redby 4	1	47N53	94w55	6:19:40
Red Eye 80	1	46N41	95w06	6:20:24
Redlake 4	1	47N53	95w01	6:20:04
Red Lake Falls 63	1	47N53	96w16	6:25:04
Red Lake Indian Reservation 4	1	47N53	95w01	6:20:04
Redpath 78	1	45N54	96w19	6:25:16
Red Rock 16	1	47N58	89w41	5:58:44
Red Rock 50	1	43N43	92w52	6:11:28
Red Wing 25	1	44N34	92w31	6:10:04
Redwood Falls 64	1	44N32	95w07	6:20:28
Reformatory 71	1	45N32	94w13	6:16:52
Regal 34	1	45N25	94w51	6:19:24
Reine 68	1	48N34	95w32	6:22:08
Reiner 57	1	48N08	95w40	6:22:40
Reis 60	1	47N33	96w31	6:26:04
Remer 11	1	47N04	93w55	6:15:40
Rendsville 75	1	45N43	95w56	6:23:44
Reno 28	1	43N36	91w17	6:05:08
Renville 65	1	44N48	95w13	6:20:52
Revere 64	1	44N13	95w22	6:21:28
Reynolds 77	1	45N59	94w58	6:19:52
Rheiderland 12	1	44N56	95w18	6:21:12
Rhinehart 60	1	47N54	97w01	6:28:04
Rice 5	1	45N45	94w13	6:16:52
Riceford 28	1	43N31	91w46	6:07:04
Rice Junction 73	1	45N32	94w13	6:16:52
Rice Lake 69	2	46N52	92w07	6:08:28
Riceland 24	1	43N43	93w12	6:12:48
Rice River 1	1	46N29	93w14	6:12:56
Riceville 3	1	47N01	96w00	6:24:00
Richardson 49	1	46N07	93w53	6:15:32
Richardville 35	1	48N56	96w52	6:27:28
Richfield 27	3	44N53	93w17	6:13:08
Richland 66	1	44N14	93w06	6:12:24
Richmond 73	1	45N27	94w31	6:18:04
Rich Valley 19	3	44N53	93w03	6:12:12
Rich Valley 43	1	44N51	94w11	6:16:44
Richville 56	1	46N31	95w38	6:22:32
Richwood 3	1	46N58	95w49	6:23:16
Ridgely 52	1	44N26	94w40	6:18:40
Ridgeway 85	6	43N46	91w33	6:06:12
Rindal 54	1	47N32	96w17	6:25:08
River 63	1	47N57	96w10	6:24:40
Riverdale 83	1	44N04	94w34	6:18:16
River Falls 57	1	48N00	96w09	6:24:36
Riverside 27	3	44N58	93w16	6:13:04
Riverside 37	1	44N56	96w02	6:24:08
Riverside Heights 22	1	43N38	94w06	6:16:24
Riverton 18	1	46N28	94w01	6:16:04
Riverview 62	3	44N55	93w05	6:12:20
Robbin 35	1	48N34	97w08	6:28:32
Robbinsdale 27	3	45N02	93w21	6:13:24
Roberts 84	1	46N30	96w41	6:26:44
Robinson 69	1	47N54	91w51	6:07:24
Rochert 3	1	46N51	95w41	6:22:44
Rochester 55	5	44N01	92w28	6:09:52
Rock 59	1	44N04	96w07	6:24:28
Rock Creek 58	1	45N45	92w57	6:11:48
Rock Dell 55	1	43N54	92w37	6:10:28
Rockford 86	1	45N05	93w44	6:14:56
Rock Lake 42	1	44N14	95w54	6:23:36
Rocksbury 57	1	48N04	96w09	6:24:36
Rockville 73	1	45N27	94w19	6:17:16
Rockwell 54	1	47N11	96w23	6:25:32
Rogers 27	1	45N11	93w33	6:14:12
Rollag 14	1	46N47	96w19	6:25:16
Rolling Forks 61	1	45N27	95w26	6:21:44
Rolling Green 46	1	43N38	94w33	6:18:12
Rollingstone 85	6	44N06	91w47	6:07:08
Rollins	1	47N16	91w52	6:07:28
Rollis 45	1	48N25	95w48	6:23:12

MINNESOTA

Rome 22	1	43n33	93w56	6:15:44
Ronneby 5	1	45n41	93w52	6:15:28
Roome 60	1	47n42	96w48	6:27:12
Roosevelt 68	1	48n48	95w06	6:20:24
Roscoe 25	1	44n18	92w48	6:11:12
Roscoe 73	1	45n26	94w38	6:18:32
Roseau 68	1	48n51	95w46	6:23:04
Rosebud 60	1	47n33	95w44	6:22:56
Rose City 21	1	46n06	95w10	6:20:40
Rose Creek 50	1	43n36	92w50	6:11:20
Rosedale 44	1	47n19	95w58	6:23:52
Rose Dell 67	1	43n48	96w22	6:25:28
Rose Hill 17	1	43n58	95w24	6:21:36
Roseland 34	1	44n56	95w04	6:20:16
Rosemount 19	1	44n45	93w08	6:12:32
Rosen 37	1	45n09	96w24	6:25:36
Rosendale 47	1	45n02	94w43	6:18:52
Roseville 62	3	45n01	93w10	6:12:40
Rosewood 45	1	48n12	96w17	6:25:08
Rosing 49	1	46n18	94w26	6:17:44
Ross 68	1	48n55	95w55	6:23:40
Rossburg 1	1	46n32	93w42	6:14:48
Ross Lake 18	1	46n40	93w51	6:15:24
Rost 32	1	43n38	95w19	6:21:16
Rothsay 84	1	46n28	96w17	6:25:08
Round Grove 43	1	44n41	94w26	6:17:44
Round Lake 53	1	43n32	95w28	6:21:52
Round Prairie 77	1	45n54	94w53	6:19:32
Rowena 64	1	44n24	95w16	6:21:04
Royal 41	1	44n30	96w15	6:25:00
Royalton 49	1	45n50	94w18	6:17:12
Roy Lake 15	1	47n19	95w58	6:23:52
Ruby Junction 69	5	47n25	92w55	6:11:40
Runeberg 3	1	46n46	95w13	6:20:52
Rush City 13	1	45n41	92w58	6:11:52
Rushford 23	1	43n49	91w46	6:07:04
Rushford Village 23	1	43n47	91w52	6:07:28
Rush Lake 56	1	46n31	95w37	6:22:28
Rushmore 53	1	43n37	95w48	6:23:12
Rush River 72	1	44n28	93w54	6:15:36
Rushseba 13	1	45n41	92w56	6:11:44
Ruskin 66	1	44n17	93w16	6:13:04
Russell 42	1	44n19	95w57	6:23:48
Russia 60	1	47n38	96w31	6:26:04
Rustad 14	1	46n44	96w45	6:27:00
Ruthton 59	1	44n11	96w06	6:24:24
Rutland 46	1	43n43	94w25	6:17:40
Rutledge 58	1	46n16	92w52	6:11:28
Sabin 14	1	46n47	96w39	6:26:36
Sacred Heart 65	1	44n45	95w17	6:21:08
Saginaw 69	1	46n52	92w27	6:09:48
Sago 31	1	47n04	93w17	6:13:08
Saint Anna 73	1	45n37	94w27	6:17:48
Saint Anthony 27	3	45n01	93w13	6:12:52
Saint Anthony 73	1	45n40	94w35	6:18:20
Saint Anthony Falls 27	3	44n59	93w14	6:12:56
Saint Augusta 73	1	45n29	94w10	6:16:40
Saint Bonifacius 27	1	44n54	93w45	6:15:00
Saint Charles 85	1	43n58	92w04	6:08:16
Saint Clair 7	1	44n05	93w51	6:15:24
Saint Clair 62	3	44n56	93w10	6:12:40
Saint Cloud 73	1	45n34	94w10	6:16:40
Saint Croix Junction 82	1	44n40	92w50	6:11:20
Saint Francis 2	1	45n23	93w22	6:13:28
Saint Francis 73	1	45n42	94w42	6:18:48
Saint George 52	1	44n23	94w32	6:18:08
Saint Hilaire 57	1	48n01	96w14	6:24:56
Saint James 83	1	43n59	94w38	6:18:32
Saint Johns 34	1	45n07	95w11	6:20:44
Saint Joseph 73	1	45n34	94w19	6:17:16
Saint Killian 53	1	43n46	95w50	6:23:20
Saint Lawrence 70	1	44n39	93w41	6:14:44
Saint Leo 87	1	44n43	96w03	6:24:12
Saint Louis Park 27	3	44n57	93w21	6:13:24
Saint Martin 73	1	45n30	94w40	6:18:40
Saint Mary 81	1	44n04	93w34	6:14:16
Saint Mary's Point 82	1	44n55	92w46	6:11:04
Saint Mathias 18	1	46n12	94w15	6:17:00
Saint Michael 86	1	45n13	93w40	6:14:40
Saint Nicholas 73	1	45n23	94w23	6:17:32
Saint Olaf 56	1	46n14	95w50	6:23:20
Saint Patrick 70	1	44n31	93w36	6:14:24
Saint Paul 62	3	44n57	93w06	6:12:24
Saint Paul Park 82	3	44n50	93w00	6:12:00
Saint Peter 52	1	44n20	93w57	6:15:48
Saint Rosa 73	1	45n44	94w43	6:18:52
Saint Stephen 73	1	45n42	94w16	6:17:04
Saint Stephens 73	1	45n42	94w16	6:17:04
Saint Thomas 40	1	44n28	93w54	6:15:36
Saint Vincent 35	1	48n58	97w14	6:28:56
Saint Wendel 73	1	45n37	94w19	6:17:16
Salem Corners 55	1	44n02	92w39	6:10:36
Salo 1	1	46n33	93w07	6:12:28
Salol 68	1	48n52	95w34	6:22:16
Sanborn 64	1	44n13	95w08	6:20:32
Sand Creek 70	1	44n41	93w35	6:14:20
Sanders 57	1	48n04	96w18	6:25:12
Sand Lake 31	1	47n38	93w58	6:15:52
Sandnes 87	1	44n40	95w39	6:22:36
Sandstone 58	1	46n08	92w52	6:11:28
Sandsville 60	1	48n08	96w57	6:27:48
Sandy 69	1	47n40	92w30	6:10:00
Sanford 26	1	45n58	95w57	6:23:48
San Francisco 10	1	44n42	93w43	6:14:52
Santiago 71	1	45n32	93w49	6:15:16
Saratoga 85	1	43n54	92w01	6:08:04
Sargeant 50	1	43n48	92w48	6:11:12
Sartell 73	1	45n37	94w12	6:16:48
Sauk Centre 73	1	45n44	94w57	6:19:48
Sauk Rapids 5	1	45n35	94w10	6:16:40
Saum 4	1	47n59	94w41	6:18:44
Savage 70	1	44n47	93w20	6:13:20
Savannah 3	1	47n06	95w14	6:20:56
Savannah 31	1	47n19	93w24	6:13:36
Sawyer 9	1	46n40	92w38	6:10:32
Scambler 56	1	46n40	96w07	6:24:28
Scandia 60	1	47n32	96w38	6:26:32
Scandia 82	1	45n15	92w48	6:11:12
Scandia Valley 49	1	46n15	94w34	6:18:16
Scanlon 9	1	46n42	92w26	6:09:44
Schley 11	1	47n22	94w23	6:17:32
Schoolcraft 29	1	47n17	94w59	6:19:56
Schroeder 16	1	47n32	90w54	6:03:36
Sciota 19	1	44n31	93w04	6:12:16
Scott 75	1	45n33	96w03	6:24:12
Seaforth 64	1	44n29	95w20	6:21:20
Searles 8	1	44n14	94w26	6:17:44
Seavey 1	1	46n17	93w22	6:13:28
Sebeka 80	1	46n38	95w05	6:20:20
Section Thirty 38	1	47n54	91w51	6:07:24
Sedan 61	1	45n35	95w15	6:21:00
Seely 22	1	43n33	93w53	6:15:32
Selma 17	1	44n04	94w55	6:19:40
Severance 72	1	44n30	94w33	6:18:12
Seward 53	1	43n49	95w39	6:22:36
Shafer 13	1	45n26	92w44	6:10:56
Shakopee 70	1	44n48	93w32	6:14:08
Shamrock 1	1	46n43	93w13	6:12:52
Shaokatan 41	1	44n25	96w23	6:25:32
Sharon 40	1	44n25	93w49	6:15:16
Shaw 69	1	47n07	92w21	6:09:24
Sheffield Mill 66	1	44n17	93w16	6:13:04
Shelburne 42	1	44n15	96w02	6:24:08
Shelby 7	1	43n53	94w11	6:16:44
Sheldon 28	1	43n41	91w36	6:06:24
Shell Lake 3	1	46n56	95w29	6:21:56
Shell River 80	1	46n46	94w59	6:19:56
Shell Rock 24	1	43n33	93w13	6:12:52
Shelly 54	1	47n28	96w49	6:27:16
Sherack 60	1	48n01	96w46	6:27:04
Sherburn 46	1	43n39	94w43	6:18:52
Sheridan 64	1	44n30	95w17	6:21:08
Sherman 64	1	44n29	94w56	6:19:44
Sheshebee 1	1	46n42	93w15	6:13:00
Shetek 51	1	44n10	95w38	6:22:32
Shevlin 15	1	47n32	95w15	6:21:00
Shible 76	1	45n17	96w03	6:24:12
Shieldsville 66	1	44n20	93w28	6:13:52
Shingobee 11	1	47n03	94w36	6:18:24
Shooks 4	1	47n52	94w27	6:17:48
Shoreham 3	1	46n49	95w51	6:23:24
Shoreview 62	3	45n05	93w07	6:12:28
Shorewood 27	1	44n54	93w35	6:14:20
Shotley 4	1	48n04	94w38	6:18:32
Shovel Lake 1	1	46n53	93w41	6:14:44
Side Lake 69	1	47n40	93w02	6:12:08
Sigel 8	1	44n15	94w33	6:18:12
Silica 69	5	47n25	92w55	6:11:40
Silo 85	1	43n59	91w52	6:07:28
Silver 9	1	46n27	92w52	6:11:28
Silver Bay 38	1	47n18	91w16	6:05:04
Silver Brook 9	1	46n37	92w26	6:09:44
Silver Creek 38	1	47n02	91w41	6:06:44
Silver Creek 86	1	45n19	93w59	6:15:56
Silverdale 36	1	47n58	92w49	6:11:16
Silver Lake 43	1	44n54	94w12	6:16:48
Silver Leaf 3	1	46n45	95w36	6:22:24
Silverton 57	1	48n08	96w03	6:24:12
Simpson 55	1	43n56	92w25	6:09:40
Sinclair 15	1	47n43	95w16	6:21:04
Sinnott 45	1	48n30	96w51	6:27:24
Sioux Agency 87	1	44n41	95w25	6:21:40
Sioux Valley 32	1	43n33	95w19	6:21:16
Six Mile Grove 76	1	45n17	95w41	6:22:44
Skagen 68	1	48n45	96w05	6:24:20
Skandia 51	1	44n09	95w53	6:23:32
Skane 35	1	48n40	96w58	6:27:52
Skelton 9	1	46n32	92w43	6:10:52
Skibo 69	1	47n31	92w09	6:08:36
Skree 14	1	46n45	96w20	6:25:20
Skyburg 25	1	44n16	92w59	6:11:56
Skyline 7	1	44n09	94w02	6:16:08
Slater 11	1	47n05	93w59	6:15:56
Slayton 51	1	43n59	95w45	6:23:00
Sleepy Eye 8	1	44n18	94w43	6:18:52
Sletten 60	1	47n32	95w53	6:23:32
Smiley 57	1	48n04	96w03	6:24:12
Smiths Mill 7	1	44n07	93w42	6:14:48
Smoky Hollow 11	1	46n57	93w49	6:15:16
Snellman 3	1	46n55	95w15	6:21:00
Sobieski 49	1	45n55	94w29	6:17:56
Soderville 2	1	45n17	93w14	6:12:56
Sodus 42	1	44n20	95w47	6:23:08
Sogn 25	1	44n25	93w02	6:12:08
Solem 21	1	45n48	95w42	6:22:48
Soler 68	1	48n50	96w11	6:24:44
Solway 4	1	47n32	95w08	6:20:32
Somerset 74	1	43n59	93w14	6:12:56
Soudan 69	1	47n49	92w14	6:08:56
South Bend 7	1	44n08	94w05	6:16:20
South Branch 83	1	43n53	94w33	6:18:12
Southbrook 17	1	43n54	95w24	6:21:36
Southdale 27	3	44n53	93w21	6:13:24
South Fork 33	1	45n47	93w28	6:13:52
South Grove 19	3	44n53	93w03	6:12:12
South Harbor 48	1	46n06	93w38	6:14:32
South Haven 86	1	45n18	94w13	6:16:52
South International Falls 36	1	48n35	93w24	6:13:36
South Red River 35	1	48n40	97w04	6:28:16
South Rushford 23	1	43n48	91w49	6:07:16
Southside 86	1	45n17	94w12	6:16:48
South St. Paul 19	3	44n53	93w02	6:12:08
Spafford 32	1	43n37	95w36	6:22:24
Spalding 1	1	46n33	93w15	6:13:00
Spang 31	1	47n04	93w39	6:14:36
Sparta 12	1	44n57	95w42	6:22:48
Spectacle Lake 30	1	45n34	93w13	6:12:52
Spencer 1	1	46n32	93w38	6:14:32
Spencer Brook 30	1	45n31	93w26	6:13:44
Spicer 34	1	45n14	94w56	6:19:44
Split Rock 9	1	46n28	92w59	6:11:56
Spooner 39	1	48n43	94w36	6:18:24
Spring Brook 35	1	48n35	96w43	6:26:52
Springdale 64	1	44n15	95w32	6:22:08
Springfield 8	1	44n14	94w59	6:19:56
Spring Grove 28	1	43n34	91w38	6:06:32
Spring Hill 73	1	45n32	94w50	6:19:20
Spring Lake 31	1	47n39	93w52	6:15:28
Spring Lake 70	1	44n40	93w28	6:13:52
Spring Lake Park 2	3	45n07	93w15	6:13:00
Spring Park 27	1	44n56	93w38	6:14:32
Spring Prairie 14	1	46n50	96w30	6:26:00
Springsteel Island 68	1	48n54	95w19	6:21:16
Springvale 30	1	45n36	93w20	6:13:20
Spring Valley 23	1	43n43	92w23	6:09:32
Springwater 67	1	43n43	96w22	6:25:28
Spruce 68	1	48n50	95w41	6:22:44
Spruce Center 21	1	46n03	95w18	6:21:12
Spruce Hill 21	1	46n04	95w14	6:20:56
Spruce Valley 45	1	48n25	96w11	6:24:44
Squaw Lake 31	1	47n38	94w08	6:16:32
Stacy 13	1	45n24	93w00	6:12:00
Stafford 68	1	48n46	95w49	6:23:16
Stanchfield 30	1	45n41	93w12	6:12:48
Stanford 30	1	45n26	93w24	6:13:36
Stanley 42	1	44n30	95w40	6:22:40
Stanton 25	1	44n29	93w01	6:12:04
Staples 77	1	46n21	94w48	6:19:12
Star 57	1	48n04	95w40	6:22:40
Starbuck 61	1	45n37	95w32	6:22:08
Stark 8	1	44n15	94w42	6:18:48
Stark 13	1	45n35	92w59	6:11:56
Star Lake 56	1	46n35	95w51	6:23:24
Stately 8	1	44n09	95w02	6:20:08
Steele Center 74	1	44n05	93w13	6:12:52
Steen 67	1	43n31	96w16	6:25:04
Steenerson 4	1	48n14	95w17	6:21:08
Stephen 45	1	48n27	96w53	6:27:32
Sterling 7	1	43n54	94w03	6:16:12
Sterling Center 7	1	43n53	94w10	6:16:40
Stevens 75	1	45n28	96w11	6:24:44
Stewart 38	1	47n02	91w41	6:06:44
Stewart 43	1	44n43	94w29	6:17:56
Stewartville 55	1,	43n51	92w29	6:09:56
Stillwater 82	5	45n03	92w49	6:11:16
Stockholm 86	1	45n06	94w12	6:16:48
Stockton 85	1	44n02	91w46	6:07:04
Stoneham 12	1	44n56	95w26	6:21:44
Stoney Brook 69	1	46n49	92w36	6:10:24
Stony Brook 26	1	46n04	96w05	6:24:20
Stony Run 87	1	44n51	95w39	6:22:36
Storden 17	1	44n04	95w17	6:21:08
Stowe Prairie 77	1	46n18	95w05	6:20:20
Straight River 29	1	46n51	95w06	6:20:24
Strand 54	1	47n22	96w15	6:25:00
Strandquist 45	1	48n29	96w27	6:25:48
Strathcona 68	1	48n33	96w10	6:24:40
Strout 47	1	45n08	94w31	6:18:04
Stubbs Bay 27	1	45n03	93w38	6:14:32
Stuntz 69	5	47n24	92w57	6:11:48
Sturgeon 69	1	47n46	92w53	6:11:32
Sturgeon Lake 58	1	46n23	92w49	6:11:16
Sugar Loaf 85	7	44n03	91w40	6:06:40
Sullivan 60	1	47n59	96w56	6:27:44
Summit 74	1	43n52	93w03	6:12:12
Summit Lake 53	1	43n43	95w44	6:22:56
Sumner 23	1	43n48	92w23	6:09:32
Sumter 43	1	44n46	94w19	6:17:16
Sunburg 34	1	45n21	95w14	6:20:56
Sundal 54	1	47n28	96w15	6:25:00
Sundown 64	1	44n20	95w03	6:20:12
Sunfish Lake 19	3	44n53	93w05	6:12:20
Sunnyside 84	1	46n14	96w27	6:25:48
Sunrise 13	1	45n33	92w51	6:11:24
Svea 34	1	45n00	95w01	6:20:04
Sveadahl 83	1	43n59	94w38	6:18:32
Sverdrup 56	1	46n20	95w50	6:23:20
Swanburg 18	1	46n44	94w24	6:17:36
Swan Lake 75	1	45n43	95w49	6:23:16
Swan River 31	1	47n05	93w12	6:12:48
Swanville 49	1	45n55	94w38	6:18:32
Swatara 1	1	46n54	93w40	6:14:40
Swede Grove 47	1	45n12	94w42	6:18:48
Swede Prairie 87	1	44n40	95w55	6:23:40
Swedes Forest 64	1	44n39	95w19	6:21:16
Sweet 59	1	43n59	96w22	6:25:28
Swenoda 76	1	45n12	95w41	6:22:44
Swift 68	1	48n52	95w13	6:20:52
Swift Falls 76	1	45n19	95w36	6:22:24
Sylvan 11	1	46n20	94w23	6:17:32
Synnes 75	1	45n28	96w03	6:24:12
Syre 54	1	47n16	96w15	6:25:00
Tabor 60	1	48n05	96w52	6:27:28
Taconite 31	1	47n19	93w24	6:13:36
Taconite Harbor 16	1	47n32	90w55	6:03:40
Talmoon 31	1	47n21	94w09	6:16:36
Tamarac 45	1	48n25	96w50	6:27:20
Tamarack 1	1	46n39	93w08	6:12:32
Tanberg 84	1	46n30	96w21	6:25:24
Tansem 14	1	46n40	96w14	6:24:56
Taopi 50	1	43n34	92w38	6:10:32
Taunton 42	1	44n36	96w04	6:24:16
Tawney 23	1	43n31	91w46	6:07:04

MINNESOTA

Place		Lat.	Long.	Time
Taylor 78	1	45N59	96w30	6:26:00
Taylors Falls 13	1	45N25	92w39	6:10:36
Tegner 35	1	48N40	96w51	6:27:24
Teien 35	1	48N35	97w05	6:28:20
Tenhassen 46	1	43N33	94w32	6:18:08
Ten Lake 4	1	47N27	94w37	6:18:28
Ten Mile Lake 37	1	44N51	95w54	6:23:36
Tenney 84	1	46N03	96w27	6:25:48
Tenstrike 4	1	47N39	94w41	6:18:44
Terrace 61	1	45N31	95w19	6:21:16
Terrebonne 63	1	47N50	96w08	6:24:32
The Arches 85	1	43N59	91w52	6:07:28
Theilman 79	1	44N17	92w12	6:08:48
Thief Lake 45	1	48N30	95w57	6:23:48
Thief River Falls 57	1	48N07	96w10	6:24:40
Third Crow Wing Lake 29	1	46N58	94w51	6:19:24
Third River 31	1	47N38	94w21	6:17:24
Thomastown 80	1	46N25	94w51	6:19:24
Thompson 35	1	48N46	96w52	6:27:28
Thompson Grove 82	1	44N50	92w56	6:11:44
Thompson Heights 2	3	45N10	93w16	6:13:04
Thompson Park 2	3	45N10	93w16	6:13:04
Thompson Riverview Terrace 2	3	45N10	93w16	6:13:04
Thomson 9	1	46N43	92w25	6:09:40
Thor 1	1	46N32	93w42	6:14:48
Thorpe 29	1	47N06	94w52	6:19:28
Three Lakes 64	1	44N24	95w03	6:20:12
Thunder Lake 11	1	46N56	94w01	6:16:04
Tilden 60	1	47N33	96w23	6:25:32
Timothy 18	1	46N44	94w07	6:16:28
Tintah 78	1	46N01	96w19	6:25:16
Toad Lake 3	1	46N51	95w28	6:21:52
Tobique	1	47N07	94w03	6:16:12
Todd 29	1	46N57	95w06	6:20:24
Tofte 16	1	47N35	90w50	6:03:20
Togo 31	1	47N49	93w10	6:12:40
Toimi 69	1	47N17	91w52	6:07:28
Toivola 69	1	47N10	92w49	6:11:16
Tonka Bay 27	1	44N55	93w35	6:14:20
Toqua 6	1	45N33	96w33	6:26:12
Tordenskjold 56	1	46N14	95w50	6:23:20
Torning 76	1	45N18	95w34	6:22:16
Torrey 11	1	47N11	93w51	6:15:24
Tower 69	1	47N48	92w17	6:09:08
Tracy 42	1	44N14	95w37	6:22:28
Traffic 27	3	44N58	93w17	6:13:08
Trail 60	1	47N47	95w42	6:22:48
Trails End 16	1	47N45	90w20	6:01:20
Transit 72	1	44N35	94w19	6:17:16
Traverse 52	1	44N21	94w01	6:16:04
Trelipe 11	1	46N58	94w07	6:16:28
Trimont 46	1	43N46	94w43	6:18:52
Triumph 46	1	43N45	94w43	6:18:52
Trommald 18	1	46N30	94w02	6:16:08
Trondhjem 56	1	46N30	96w13	6:24:52
Trosky 59	1	43N53	96w15	6:25:00
Trout Brook 25	1	44N33	92w32	6:10:08
Trout Lake 31	1	47N14	93w24	6:13:36
Troy 85	1	43N58	92w04	6:08:16
Truman 46	1	43N50	94w26	6:17:44
Tumuli 56	1	46N09	95w57	6:23:48
Tunsberg 12	1	45N02	95w47	6:23:08
Turner 1	1	46N48	93w15	6:13:00
Turtle Creek 77	1	46N09	94w43	6:18:52
Turtle River 4	1	47N35	94w46	6:19:04
Twig 69	1	46N52	92w21	6:09:24
Twin Cities 27	3	44N54	93w14	6:12:56
Twin Lakes 24	1	43N34	93w25	6:13:40
Twin Valley 54	1	47N16	96w16	6:25:04
Two Harbors 38	6	47N02	91w40	6:06:40
Two Inlets 3	1	47N03	95w13	6:20:52
Two Rivers 49	1	45N49	94w23	6:17:32
Tyler 41	1	44N17	96w08	6:24:32
Tynsid 60	1	47N43	96w54	6:27:36
Tyro 87	1	44N46	95w55	6:23:40
Tyrone 40	1	44N30	93w49	6:15:16
Udolpho 50	1	43N48	92w59	6:11:56
Ulen 14	1	47N05	96w16	6:25:04
Underwood 56	1	46N17	95w52	6:23:28
Union 28	1	43N42	91w25	6:05:40
Union Grove 47	1	45N17	94w42	6:18:48
Union Hill 40	1	44N31	93w36	6:14:24
University 27	3	44N59	93w14	6:12:56
Upper Nicollet 27	3	44N58	93w17	6:13:08
Upper Sioux Indian Res 65	1	47N32	94w49	6:19:16
Upsala 49	1	45N49	94w34	6:18:16
Uptown 27	3	44N57	93w17	6:13:08
Uptown 62	3	44N56	93w07	6:12:28
Urbank 56	1	46N08	95w31	6:22:04
Urness 21	1	45N53	95w42	6:22:48
Utica 85	1	43N59	91w54	6:07:36
Vadnais Heights 62	3	45N03	93w04	6:12:16
Vail 64	1	44N25	95w17	6:21:08
Vallers 42	1	44N35	95w47	6:23:08
Valley 45	1	48N19	95w40	6:22:40
Valley Ridge 19	1	44N47	93w15	6:13:00
Van Buren 69	1	46N58	92w53	6:11:32
Vasa 25	1	44N30	92w44	6:10:56
Vega 45	1	48N14	96w57	6:27:48
Veldt 45	1	48N25	95w41	6:22:44
Verdi 41	1	44N13	96w21	6:25:24
Verdon 1	1	46N54	93w22	6:13:28
Vergas 56	1	46N40	95w48	6:23:12
Vermilion Lake 69	1	47N45	92w22	6:09:28
Vermillion 19	1	44N40	92w59	6:11:56
Vermillion Dam 69	1	48N03	92w50	6:11:20
Vermillion Lake Indian Res 69	1	47N32	94w49	6:19:16
Verndale 80	1	46N24	95w01	6:20:04
Vernon 20	1	43N54	92w44	6:10:56
Vernon Center 7	1	43N58	94w10	6:16:40
Verona 22	1	43N43	94w11	6:16:44
Veseli 66	1	44N31	93w27	6:13:48
Vesta 64	1	44N31	95w25	6:21:40
Victor 86	1	45N01	94w04	6:16:16
Victoria 10	3	44N52	93w38	6:14:32
Viding 14	1	47N06	96w38	6:26:32
Vienna 67	1	43N43	96w07	6:24:28
Viking 45	1	48N13	96w24	6:25:36
Villard 61	1	45N43	95w16	6:21:04
Vineland 48	1	46N04	93w40	6:14:40
Vineland 60	1	47N38	96w49	6:27:16
Vining 56	1	46N16	95w32	6:22:08
Viola 55	1	44N04	92w16	6:09:04
Virginia 69	1	47N31	92w32	6:10:08
Vista 81	1	43N59	93w30	6:14:00
Vivian 81	1	43N53	93w40	6:14:40
Waasa 69	1	47N40	92w07	6:08:28
Wabana 31	1	47N24	93w31	6:14:04
Wabasha 79	1	44N23	92w02	6:08:08
Wabasso 64	1	44N24	95w15	6:21:00
Wabedo 11	1	46N57	94w16	6:17:04
Waconia 10	3	44N51	93w47	6:15:08
Wacouta 25	1	44N33	92w26	6:09:44
Wadena 80	1	46N26	95w08	6:20:32
Wagner 1	1	46N13	93w06	6:12:24
Wahkon 48	1	46N07	93w31	6:14:04
Wahnena 11	1	47N15	93w54	6:15:36
Waite Park 73	1	45N33	94w14	6:16:56
Wakefield 73	1	45N28	94w27	6:17:48
Walbo 30	1	45N34	93w13	6:12:52
Walcott 66	1	44N15	93w13	6:12:52
Waldo 38	1	47N02	91w41	6:06:44
Waldorf 81	1	43N56	93w42	6:14:48
Wales 38	1	47N02	91w41	6:06:44
Walker 11	1	47N06	94w35	6:18:20
Walls 78	1	45N43	96w34	6:26:16
Walnut Grove 64	1	44N13	95w28	6:21:52
Walnut Lake 22	1	43N43	93w53	6:15:32
Walter 37	1	45N07	96w24	6:25:36
Walters 22	1	43N36	93w40	6:14:40
Waltham 50	1	43N49	92w53	6:11:32
Walworth 3	1	47N06	96w08	6:24:32
Wanamingo 25	1	44N18	92w47	6:11:08
Wanda 64	1	44N19	95w13	6:20:52
Wang 65	1	44N51	95w25	6:21:40
Wanger 45	1	48N25	96w43	6:26:52
Wannaska 68	1	48N40	95w44	6:22:56
Warba 31	1	47N08	93w17	6:13:08
Ward 77	1	46N09	94w50	6:19:20
Ward Springs 77	1	45N48	94w48	6:19:12
Warman 33	1	46N04	93w17	6:13:08
Warren 45	1	48N12	96w46	6:27:04
Warrenton 45	1	48N14	96w49	6:27:16
Warroad 68	1	48N54	95w19	6:21:16
Warsaw 66	1	44N15	93w24	6:13:36
Waseca 81	1	44N05	93w30	6:14:00
Washington 23	1	43N41	92w23	6:09:32
Washington 40	1	44N15	93w48	6:15:12
Washington Lake 72	1	44N40	93w57	6:15:48
Wasioja 20	1	44N04	92w52	6:11:28
Waskish 4	1	48N10	94w31	6:18:04
Wastedo 25	1	44N31	92w54	6:11:36
Watab 5	1	45N41	94w11	6:16:44
Waterbury 64	1	44N20	95w17	6:21:08
Waterford 19	1	44N30	93w08	6:12:32
Watertown 10	1	44N56	93w50	6:15:20
Waterville 40	1	44N13	93w34	6:14:16
Watkins 47	1	45N19	94w24	6:17:36
Watopa 79	1	44N14	92w00	6:08:00
Watson 12	1	45N01	95w48	6:23:12
Waubun 44	1	47N11	95w57	6:23:48
Waukenabo 1	1	46N43	93w38	6:14:32
Waukon 54	1	47N23	96w07	6:24:28
Waverly 86	1	45N04	93w58	6:15:52
Wawina 31	1	47N03	93w07	6:12:28
Wayzata 27	4	44N58	93w30	6:14:00
Wealthwood 1	1	46N24	93w39	6:14:36
Weaver 79	1	44N12	91w52	6:07:28
Weber 30	1	45N31	92w58	6:11:52
Webster 66	1	44N30	93w21	6:13:24
Wegdahl 12	1	44N53	95w39	6:22:36
Weimer 32	1	43N49	95w16	6:21:04
Welch 25	1	44N36	92w44	6:10:56
Welcome 46	1	43N40	94w37	6:18:28
Wellington 65	1	44N35	94w41	6:18:44
Wells 22	1	43N45	93w44	6:14:56
Wendell 26	1	46N02	96w06	6:24:24
Wergeland 87	1	44N41	96w09	6:24:36
West Albany 79	1	44N19	92w16	6:09:04
West Albion 86	1	45N16	94w08	6:16:32
West Bank 76	1	45N12	95w48	6:23:12
Westbrook 17	1	44N03	95w26	6:21:44
Westbury 3	1	46N49	95w51	6:23:24
West Concord 20	1	44N09	92w54	6:11:36
West Duluth 69	2	46N45	92w10	6:08:40
West End 62	3	44N56	93w07	6:12:28
Westerheim 42	1	44N35	95w55	6:23:40
Western 56	1	46N14	96w12	6:24:48
Westfield 20	1	43N54	92w59	6:11:56
Westford 46	1	43N48	94w26	6:17:44
West Heron Lake 32	1	43N43	95w19	6:21:16
West Lake Francis Shores 30	1	45N30	93w15	6:13:00
West Lakeland 82	1	44N58	92w49	6:11:16
Westline 64	1	44N25	95w32	6:22:08
West Newton 52	1	44N25	94w33	6:18:12
West Newton 79	1	44N19	92w00	6:08:00
Weston	1	45N11	92w59	6:11:56
West Point 30	1	45N34	93w13	6:12:52
Westport 61	1	45N43	95w10	6:20:40
West Red Wing 25	1	44N33	92w32	6:10:08
West Rock 58	1	45N50	92w58	6:11:52
West Saint Paul 19	3	44N54	93w05	6:12:20
Westside 53	1	43N38	96w00	6:24:00
West Union 77	1	45N48	95w05	6:20:20
West Valley 45	1	48N25	96w27	6:25:48
West Virginia 69	1	47N31	92w32	6:10:08
Whalan 23	1	43N44	91w55	6:07:40
Wheatland 66	1	44N30	93w28	6:13:52
Wheaton 78	1	45N48	96w30	6:26:00
Wheeling 66	1	44N20	93w06	6:12:24
Whipholt 11	1	47N03	94w22	6:17:28
White 69	1	47N28	92w15	6:09:00
White Bear 62	3	45N05	93w01	6:12:04
White Bear Beach 62	1	45N06	92w59	6:11:56
White Bear Lake 62	3	45N05	93w01	6:12:04
Whited 33	1	45N56	93w12	6:12:48
White Earth 3	1	47N06	95w50	6:23:20
White Earth Indian Res 3	1	47N32	94w49	6:19:16
Whiteface 69	1	47N14	92w24	6:09:36
Whitefield 34	1	45N08	95w02	6:20:08
Whiteford 45	1	48N25	95w54	6:23:36
White Oak 29	1	46N56	94w43	6:18:52
White Pine 1	1	46N22	93w15	6:13:00
White Rock 25	1	44N27	92w46	6:11:04
Whitewater 85	1	44N09	92w01	6:08:04
Whyte 38	1	47N02	91w41	6:06:44
Wig Wam Bay 48	1	46N04	93w40	6:14:40
Wilbert 46	1	43N32	94w38	6:18:32
Wilder 32	1	43N50	95w12	6:20:48
Wild Rice 54	1	47N17	96w15	6:25:00
Wildwood 36	1	48N19	93w41	6:14:44
Wilkinson 11	1	47N15	94w38	6:18:32
Willernie 82	3	45N03	92w58	6:11:52
Williams 39	1	48N45	94w54	6:19:36
Willmar 34	1	45N07	95w03	6:20:12
Willow Creek 7	1	43N53	94w10	6:16:40
Willow Lake 64	1	44N20	95w10	6:20:40
Willow River 58	1	46N19	92w51	6:11:24
Willow Valley 69	1	47N56	92w53	6:11:32
Wilma 58	1	46N08	92w28	6:09:52
Wilmington 28	1	43N33	91w32	6:06:08
Wilmont 53	1	43N46	95w50	6:23:20
Wilno 41	1	44N30	96w14	6:24:56
Wilpen 69	5	47N25	92w55	6:11:40
Wilson	1	43N41	91w41	6:06:44
Wilson 85	7	44N03	91w40	6:06:40
Wilton 4	1	47N30	95w00	6:20:00
Wilton 81	1	44N05	93w30	6:14:00
Winchester 54	1	47N12	96w30	6:26:00
Windemere 58	1	46N23	92w44	6:10:56
Windom 17	1	43N52	95w07	6:20:28
Windsor 78	1	45N41	96w41	6:26:44
Winfield 65	1	44N51	95w03	6:20:12
Winger 60	1	47N32	95w59	6:23:56
Wing River 80	1	46N30	94w58	6:19:52
Winnebago 22	1	43N46	94w10	6:16:40
Winnebago 28	6	43N38	91w29	6:05:56
Winnebago City 22	1	43N48	94w11	6:16:44
Winona 85	7	44N03	91w39	6:06:36
Winsor 15	1	47N48	95w30	6:22:00
Winsted 43	1	44N58	94w03	6:16:12
Winthrop 72	1	44N32	94w22	6:17:28
Winton 69	1	47N56	91w48	6:07:12
Wirock 51	1	43N55	95w47	6:23:08
Wirt 31	1	47N44	93w58	6:15:52
Wisconsin 32	1	43N38	94w55	6:19:40
Wiscoy 85	1	43N54	91w39	6:06:36
Withrow 82	1	44N59	92w47	6:11:08
Witoka 85	1	43N43	91w37	6:06:28
Wolf 69	1	47N25	92w36	6:10:24
Wolf Lake 3	1	46N48	95w21	6:21:24
Wolford 18	1	46N32	94w01	6:16:04
Wolverton 84	1	46N34	96w44	6:26:56
Woodbury 82	3	44N55	92w57	6:11:48
Wood Lake 87	1	44N39	95w32	6:22:08
Woodland 27	1	44N57	93w31	6:14:04
Woodland 33	1	46N09	93w28	6:13:52
Woodland 69	2	46N50	92w06	6:08:24
Woodland Park 56	1	46N19	95w26	6:21:44
Woods 12	1	45N06	95w18	6:21:12
Woodstock 59	1	44N01	96w06	6:24:24
Woodville 81	1	44N04	93w28	6:13:52
Workman 1	1	46N43	93w23	6:13:32
Worthington 53	1	43N37	95w36	6:22:24
Wouri 69	1	47N36	92w29	6:09:56
Wrenshall 9	1	46N37	92w23	6:09:32
Wright 9	1	46N40	93w00	6:12:00
Wrightstown 56	1	46N17	95w11	6:20:44
Wyandotte 57	1	48N00	96w03	6:24:12
Wyanett 30	1	45N36	93w27	6:13:48
Wyattville 85	1	43N41	91w47	6:07:08
Wykeham 77	1	46N09	95w05	6:20:20
Wykoff 23	1	43N42	92w16	6:09:04
Wylie 63	1	47N57	96w25	6:25:40
Wyman 69	1	47N31	92w09	6:08:36
Wyoming 13	1	45N20	92w57	6:11:48
Yellow Bank 37	1	45N12	96w24	6:25:36
York 23	1	43N33	92w16	6:09:04
Yorktown 27	3	44N53	93w21	6:13:24
Young America 10	3	44N45	93w57	6:15:48
Yucatan 28	1	43N44	91w41	6:06:44
Zemple 31	1	47N20	94w07	6:16:28
Zerkel 15	1	47N31	95w24	6:21:36
Zim 69	1	47N18	92w36	6:10:24
Zimmerman 71	1	45N27	93w35	6:14:20
Zion 73	1	45N27	94w42	6:18:48
Zumbra Heights 10	1	44N54	93w34	6:14:16
Zumbro 79	1	44N14	92w24	6:09:36
Zumbro Falls 79	1	44N17	92w26	6:09:44
Zumbrota 25	1	44N17	92w40	6:10:40

MISSISSIPPI

TIME TABLES

MS # 1

Date	Time	Zone
Before 11/18/1883		LMT
11/18/1883	12:00	CST
3/31/1918	02:00	CWT
10/27/1918	02:00	CST
3/30/1919	02:00	CWT
10/26/1919	02:00	CST
2/09/1942	02:00	CWT
9/30/1945	02:00	CST
4/30/1967	02:00	US#1

....

MS # 2

Date	Time	Zone
Before 11/18/1883		LMT
11/18/1883	12:00	CST
3/31/1918	02:00	CWT
10/27/1918	02:00	CST
3/30/1919	02:00	CWT
10/26/1919	02:00	CST
4/28/1935	02:00	CDT
9/29/1935	02:00	CST
2/09/1942	02:00	CWT
9/30/1945	02:00	CST
4/30/1967	02:00	US#1

COUNTIES

1 Adams
2 Alcorn
3 Amite
4 Attala
5 Benton
6 Bolivar
7 Calhoun
8 Carroll
9 Chickasaw
10 Choctaw
11 Claiborne
12 Clarke
13 Clay
14 Coahoma
15 Copiah
16 Covington
17 De Soto
18 Forrest
19 Franklin
20 George
21 Greene
22 Grenada
23 Hancock
24 Harrison
25 Hinds
26 Holmes
27 Humphreys
28 Issaquena
29 Itawamba
30 Jackson
31 Jasper
32 Jefferson
33 Jefferson Davis
34 Jones
35 Kemper
36 Lafayette
37 Lamar
38 Lauderdale
39 Lawrence
40 Leake
41 Lee
42 Leflore
43 Lincoln
44 Lowndes
45 Madison
46 Marion
47 Marshall
48 Monroe
49 Montgomery
50 Neshoba
51 Newton
52 Noxubee
53 Oktibbeha
54 Panola
55 Pearl River
56 Perry
57 Pike
58 Pontotoc
59 Prentiss
60 Quitman
61 Rankin
62 Scott
63 Sharkey
64 Simpson
65 Smith
66 Stone
67 Sunflower
68 Tallahatchie
69 Tate
70 Tippah
71 Tishomingo
72 Tunica
73 Union
74 Walthall
75 Warren
76 Washington
77 Wayne
78 Webster
79 Wilkinson
80 Winston
81 Yalobusha
82 Yazoo

Abbeville 36	1	34N30	89W30	5:58:00
Abbott 13	1	33N36	88W39	5:54:36
Aberdeen 48	1	33N49	88W33	5:54:12
Ackerman 10	1	33N19	89W11	5:56:44
Acona 26	1	33N07	90W03	6:00:12
Adams 25	1	32N10	90W34	6:02:16
Adaton 53	1	33N28	88W49	5:55:16
Agricola 20	1	30N48	88W31	5:54:04
Airey 24	1	30N38	89W08	5:56:32
Albin 68	1	33N55	90W20	6:01:20
Alcorn	1	31N53	91W08	6:04:32
Alcorn State University 11	1	31N49	91W03	6:04:12
Alesville 36	1	34N22	89W31	5:58:04
Algoma 58	1	34N11	89W02	5:56:08
Allen 15	1	31N52	90W24	6:01:36
Alligator 6	1	34N06	90W43	6:02:52
Alma 41	1	34N26	88W40	5:54:40
Alpine 73	1	34N24	88W52	5:55:28
Altitude 59	1	34N40	88W34	5:54:16
Alva 49	1	33N38	89W43	5:58:52
Amistead 14	1	34N22	90W38	6:02:32
Amory 48	1	33N59	88W29	5:53:56
Anchor 9	1	33N47	89W03	5:56:12
Anchorage 27	1	32N51	90W24	6:01:36
Anding 82	1	32N41	90W24	6:01:36
Anguilla 63	1	32N59	90W50	6:03:20
Anse 61	1	32N09	90W08	6:00:32
Ansley 23	1	30N14	89W29	5:57:56
Antioch 31	1	32N05	89W15	5:57:00
Antioch 34	1	31N42	89W08	5:56:32
Anvil 70	1	34N54	88W54	5:55:36
Apple Ridge 25	2	32N19	90W11	6:00:44
Arbo 16	1	31N45	89W39	5:58:36
Arcola 76	1	33N16	90W53	6:03:32
Ariel 3	1	31N12	91W01	6:04:04
Arkabutla 69	1	34N42	90W07	6:00:28
Arlington 43	1	31N26	90W27	6:01:48
Arm 39	1	31N30	90W01	6:00:04
Arnold Line 37	1	31N18	89W18	5:57:12
Artesia 44	1	33N25	88W39	5:54:36
Ashland 5	1	34N50	89W11	5:56:44
Ashwood 79	1	31N06	91W18	6:05:12
Askew 54	1	34N32	90W11	6:00:44
Atlanta 9	1	33N47	89W03	5:56:12
Auburn 43	1	31N22	90W37	6:02:28
Austin 72	1	34N42	90W23	6:01:32
Avalon 8	1	33N39	90W05	6:00:20
Avent 21	1	31N02	88W48	5:55:12
Avon 76	1	33N14	91W03	6:04:12
Bacots 57	1	31N14	90W28	6:01:52
Bailey 38	1	32N28	88W43	5:54:52
Baird 67	1	33N26	90W35	6:02:20
Baker 73	1	34N29	89W01	5:56:04
Baldwyn 59	1	34N31	88W38	5:54:32
Ballard 45	1	32N37	90W02	6:00:08
Ballardsville 29	1	34N15	88W43	5:54:52
Ballentine 54	1	34N30	90W12	6:00:48
Ballground 75	1	32N29	90W48	6:03:12
Baltzer 67	1	34N12	90W34	6:02:16
Banks 72	1	34N50	90W14	6:00:56
Bankston 10	1	33N16	89W17	5:57:08
Banner 7	1	34N06	89W23	5:57:32
Barlow 15	1	31N52	90W24	6:01:36
Barnes 40	1	32N44	89W32	5:58:08
Barnett 12	1	31N59	88W54	5:55:36
Barr 69	1	34N38	89W47	5:59:08
Barrontown 18	1	31N18	89W18	5:57:12
Bartahatchie 48	1	33N41	88W19	5:53:16
Barth 55	1	30N50	89W32	5:58:08
Barto 57	1	31N14	90W28	6:01:52
Basic 12	1	32N13	88W46	5:55:04
Basin 20	1	30N55	88W35	5:54:20
Bassfield 33	1	31N30	89W45	5:59:00
Batesville 54	1	34N19	89W57	5:59:48
Batson 18	1	31N18	89W18	5:57:12
Battlefield 25	2	32N19	90W11	6:00:44
Battle Field 51	1	32N30	88W51	5:55:24
Battlefield Village Regional 75	1	32N20	90W52	6:03:28
Battles 77	1	31N30	88W31	5:54:04
Baugh 14	1	34N13	90W43	6:02:52
Baxter 31	1	32N08	89W14	5:56:56
Baxterville 37	1	31N05	89W36	5:58:24
Bay Saint Louis 23	1	30N19	89W20	5:57:20
Bayside Park 23	1	30N19	89W20	5:57:20
Bay Springs 31	1	31N59	89W17	5:57:08
Bay St Louis 23	1	30N19	89W20	5:57:20
Bay View Plaza 24	1	30N25	88W55	5:55:40
Beacon Hill 73	1	34N29	89W01	5:56:04
Beans Ferry 29	1	34N16	88W25	5:53:40
Bear Garden 76	1	33N11	90W51	6:03:24
Bear Town 57	1	31N14	90W28	6:01:52
Beasley 13	1	33N35	88W57	5:55:48
Beatrice 12	1	32N10	88W50	5:55:20
Beatty 8	1	33N16	89W44	5:58:56
Beaumont 56	1	31N10	88W55	5:55:40
Beauregard 15	1	31N43	90W23	6:01:32
Beauvoir 24	1	30N25	88W55	5:55:40
Becker 48	1	33N56	88W29	5:53:56
Beechwood 3	1	31N10	90W48	6:03:12
Beelake 26	1	33N11	90W13	6:00:52
Belden 41	1	34N19	88W47	5:55:08
Belen 60	1	34N16	90W21	6:01:24
Bellefontaine 78	1	33N39	89W19	5:57:16
Belle Isle 23	1	30N15	89W37	5:58:28
Belleville 56	1	31N13	89W01	5:56:04
Bellewood 27	1	33N16	90W35	6:02:20
Bells School 53	1	33N28	88W49	5:55:16
Belmont 71	1	34N31	88W13	5:52:52
Belzoni 27	1	33N11	90W29	6:01:56
Benndale 20	1	30N52	88W48	5:55:12
Benoit 6	1	33N39	91W01	6:04:04
Bentley 7	1	33N44	89W04	5:56:16
Benton 82	1	32N50	90W16	6:01:04
Bentonia 82	1	32N38	90W22	6:01:28
Benwood 81	1	33N59	89W41	5:58:44
Berclair 42	1	33N30	90W20	6:01:20
Berryville 82	1	32N50	90W15	6:01:00
Bertice 40	1	32N36	89W35	5:58:20
Berwick 3	1	31N10	90W48	6:03:12
Bet 69	1	34N41	89W59	5:59:56
Bethany 41	1	34N30	88W38	5:54:32
Betheden 80	1	33N07	89W03	5:56:12
Bethel 51	1	32N19	89W10	5:56:40
Bethlehem 47	1	34N39	89W18	5:57:12
Beulah 6	1	33N47	90W59	6:03:56
Bewelcome 3	1	31N12	91W01	6:04:04
Bexley 20	1	30N55	88W35	5:54:20
Bigbee 48	1	34N01	88W31	5:54:04
Bigbee Valley 52	1	33N15	88W21	5:53:24
Big Creek 7	1	33N51	89W25	5:57:40
Biggersville 2	1	34N50	88W34	5:54:16
Big Level 66	1	30N47	89W08	5:56:32
Big Point 30	1	30N35	88W29	5:53:56
Biloxi 24	1	30N24	88W53	5:55:32
Binford 48	1	33N50	88W33	5:54:12
Binnsville 35	1	32N50	88W29	5:53:56
Birdie 60	1	34N22	90W31	6:02:04
Bissell 41	1	34N15	88W47	5:55:08
Black Hawk 8	1	33N20	90W01	6:00:04
Blackjack 53	1	33N28	88W49	5:55:16
Blackland 59	1	34N40	88W34	5:54:16
Blackmonton 8	1	33N20	89W45	5:59:00
Blackwater 35	1	32N34	88W41	5:54:44
Blackwater 36	1	34N39	89W27	5:57:48
Blaine 67	1	33N37	90W31	6:02:04
Blair 41	1	34N26	88W40	5:54:40
Blakely 75	1	32N20	90W52	6:03:28
Blanton 63	1	32N54	90W53	6:03:32
Blodgett 34	1	31N29	89W02	5:56:08
Bloody Springs 71	1	34N31	88W13	5:52:52
Blue Hills 11	1	31N53	90W53	6:03:32
Blue Lake 68	1	33N49	90W32	6:02:08
Blue Mountain 70	1	34N40	89W02	5:56:08
Blue Springs 73	1	34N24	88W52	5:55:28
Bluff 70	1	34N40	89W01	5:56:04
Bluff Springs 35	1	32N46	88W39	5:54:36
Bobo 14	1	34N08	90W41	6:02:44
Bobo 60	1	34N19	89W57	5:59:48
Boggan Bend 41	1	34N26	88W40	5:54:40
Bogue Chitto 43	1	31N26	90W27	6:01:48
Boice 77	1	31N41	88W39	5:54:36
Bolatushu 40	1	33N01	89W46	5:59:04
Bolivar 6	1	33N40	91W03	6:04:12
Bolton 25	1	32N21	90W28	6:01:52
Bond 50	1	32N46	89W07	5:56:28
Bond 66	1	30N54	89W10	5:56:40
Bon Homme 18	1	31N18	89W19	5:57:16
Bonita 38	1	32N28	88W40	5:54:40
Boone 14	1	34N12	90W34	6:02:16
Booneville 59	1	34N40	88W34	5:54:16
Bounds Crossroads 29	1	34N27	88W08	5:52:32
Bourbon 76	1	33N20	90W48	6:03:12
Bovina 75	1	32N20	90W52	6:03:28
Bowdre 72	1	34N49	90W19	6:01:16
Bowling Green 26	1	33N05	89W51	5:59:24
Bowman 69	1	34N41	89W59	5:59:56
Boyer 67	1	33N27	90W39	6:02:36
Boyette 4	1	33N01	89W46	5:59:04
Boyle 6	1	33N42	90W44	6:02:56
Bradley 53	1	33N28	88W49	5:55:16
Branch 62	1	32N28	89W44	5:58:56
Brandon 61	1	32N16	89W59	5:59:56
Branyan 73	1	34N24	88W52	5:55:28
Brasfield 32	1	31N49	91W03	6:04:12
Braxton 64	1	32N01	89W58	5:59:52
Brazil 68	1	33N58	90W17	6:01:08
Brewer 12	1	32N03	88W43	5:54:52
Brewer 41	1	34N07	88W43	5:54:52
Brewer 56	1	31N21	88W56	5:55:44
Bright 17	1	34N50	89W59	5:59:56
Bristers Store 39	1	31N22	90W12	6:00:48
Brookhaven 43	1	31N35	90W26	6:01:44
Brook Hollow 25	2	32N19	90W11	6:00:44
Brooklyn 18	1	31N03	89W11	5:56:44
Brooks 67	1	33N49	90W32	6:02:08
Brooksville 52	1	33N14	88W35	5:54:20
Brownfield 70	1	34N57	88W54	5:55:36
Brownsville 25	1	32N27	90W26	6:01:44
Brozville 26	1	33N07	90W03	6:00:12
Bruce 7	1	33N59	89W21	5:57:24
Brunswick 75	1	32N20	90W52	6:03:28
Bryant 81	1	33N59	89W41	5:58:44
Buckatunna 77	1	31N32	88W32	5:54:08
Buckhorn 58	1	34N11	89W10	5:56:40
Bude 19	1	31N28	90W51	6:03:24
Buelah Hubbard 51	1	32N26	89W01	5:56:04
Buena Vista 9	1	33N56	89W00	5:56:00
Buena Vista 70	1	34N44	88W57	5:55:48
Bunker Hill 46	1	31N18	89W50	5:59:20
Bunkley 19	1	31N28	90W54	6:03:36
Burgess 36	1	34N22	89W31	5:58:04
Burns 65	1	32N08	89W33	5:58:12

Place		Lat.	Long.	Time
Burnside 50	1	32N51	89w06	5:56:24
Burnsville 71	1	34N51	88w19	5:53:16
Burrow 2	1	34N54	88w54	5:55:36
Burtons 59	1	34N40	88w34	5:54:16
Bush 64	1	31N47	90w04	6:00:16
Busy Corner 3	1	31N10	90w48	6:03:12
Buxton 54	1	34N34	90w13	6:00:52
Byhalia 47	1	34N52	89w41	5:58:44
Byram 25	1	32N11	90w15	6:01:00
Cadamy 29	1	34N14	88w16	5:53:04
Cadaretta 78	1	33N45	89w37	5:58:28
Caesar 55	1	30N32	89w40	5:58:40
Caile 67	1	33N16	90w35	6:02:20
Caledonia 44	1	33N41	88w20	5:53:20
Calhoun 34	1	31N42	89w08	5:56:32
Calhoun 51	1	32N19	89w10	5:56:40
Calhoun City 7	1	33N51	89w19	5:57:16
Cambridge 36	1	34N25	89w37	5:58:28
Camden 45	1	32N47	89w50	5:59:20
Cameron 45	1	32N53	89w58	5:59:52
Cameta 63	1	32N54	90w53	6:03:32
Campbell 70	1	34N44	88w57	5:55:48
Camphill 70	1	34N57	88w54	5:55:36
Canaan 5	1	34N56	89w08	5:56:32
Candlestick 25	2	32N19	90w11	6:00:44
Canton 45	1	32N37	90w02	6:00:08
Cardsville 29	1	34N05	88w37	5:54:28
Carlisle 11	1	32N00	90w47	6:03:08
Carmack 4	1	33N20	89w45	5:59:00
Carmichael 12	1	31N53	88w41	5:54:44
Carmichael 25	1	32N06	90w37	6:02:28
Carmichael 56	1	31N10	88w55	5:55:40
Carnes 18	1	31N00	89w27	5:57:48
Carolina 29	1	34N05	88w37	5:54:28
Carpenter 15	1	32N02	90w41	6:02:44
Carriere 55	1	30N37	89w39	5:58:36
Carrollton 8	1	33N30	89w55	5:59:40
Carson 33	1	31N32	89w48	5:59:12
Carter 82	1	32N59	90w27	6:01:48
Carterville 18	1	31N18	89w18	5:57:12
Carthage 40	1	32N44	89w32	5:58:08
Cary 63	1	32N49	90w56	6:03:44
Cascilla 68	1	33N51	90w00	6:00:00
Caseyville 43	1	31N46	90w22	6:01:28
Cassels 3	1	31N12	91w01	6:04:04
Cayuga 25	1	32N06	90w37	6:02:28
Cecil 4	1	33N12	89w47	5:59:08
Cedarbluff 13	1	33N35	88w50	5:55:20
Cedar Hill 45	1	32N33	90w18	6:01:12
Cedar Hill 49	1	33N38	89w43	5:58:52
Cedar Lake 24	1	30N25	88w55	5:55:40
Cedars 75	1	32N20	90w52	6:03:28
Cedarview 17	1	34N57	89w49	5:59:16
Center 4	1	33N03	89w35	5:58:20
Center 50	1	32N46	89w07	5:56:28
Center 73	1	34N24	88w52	5:55:28
Center Ridge 65	1	31N50	89w26	5:57:44
Centerville 29	1	34N26	88w40	5:54:40
Centralgrove 48	1	33N50	88w33	5:54:12
Centreville 79	1	31N05	91w04	6:04:16
Chalybeate 70	1	34N56	88w52	5:55:28
Champion Hill 25	1	32N20	90w36	6:02:24
Chapel Hill 25	1	32N06	90w37	6:02:28
Charleston 68	1	34N01	90w04	6:00:16
Charlton 45	1	32N37	90w02	6:00:08
Chatawa 57	1	31N04	90w28	6:01:52
Chatham 76	1	33N06	91w06	6:04:24
Cheraw 46	1	31N10	89w50	5:59:20
Cherrycreek 58	1	34N24	88w52	5:55:28
Chester 10	1	33N19	89w10	5:56:40
Chesterville 41	1	34N15	88w43	5:54:52
Chicora 77	1	31N34	88w34	5:54:16
Chipwood 24	1	30N25	88w55	5:55:40
Chiwapa 58	1	34N15	89w01	5:56:04
Choctaw 6	1	33N38	90w46	6:03:04
Choctaw 34	1	31N42	89w08	5:56:32
Choctaw Indian Reservation 50	1	32N46	89w07	5:56:28
Chulahoma 47	1	34N46	89w27	5:57:48
Chunky 51	1	32N20	88w56	5:55:44
Church Hill 32	1	31N43	91w14	6:04:56
Clack 72	1	34N49	90w19	6:01:16
Clara 77	1	31N35	88w42	5:54:48
Clark 32	1	31N53	90w53	6:03:32
Clarksburg 61	1	32N21	89w39	5:58:36
Clarksdale 14	1	34N12	90w35	6:02:20
Clarkson 78	1	33N38	89w09	5:56:36
Clarmont 14	1	34N12	90w34	6:02:16
Clay 29	1	34N16	88w25	5:53:40
Clayton 72	1	34N32	90w27	6:01:48
Clayton Village 53	1	33N28	88w49	5:55:16
Claytown 80	1	33N07	89w03	5:56:12
Cleo 34	1	31N42	89w08	5:56:32
Clermont Harbor 23	1	30N16	89w25	5:57:40
Cleveland 6	1	33N45	90w43	6:02:52
Clifton 62	1	32N22	89w28	5:57:52
Cliftonville 52	1	33N14	88w35	5:54:20
Clinton 25	1	32N20	90w20	6:01:20
Clove Hill 14	1	34N13	90w32	6:02:08
Cloverdale 1	1	31N34	91w22	6:05:28
Coahoma 14	1	34N22	90w31	6:02:04
Cobbs 43	1	31N35	90w27	6:01:48
Cockrum 17	1	34N48	89w49	5:59:16
Coffeeville 81	1	33N59	89w41	5:58:44
Cohay 65	1	32N01	89w27	5:57:48
Coila 8	1	33N24	89w58	5:59:52
Colby 82	1	32N49	90w42	6:02:48
Coldwater 69	1	34N41	89w59	5:59:56
Coles 3	1	31N17	91w02	6:04:08
Coles Creek 7	1	33N51	89w25	5:57:40
College 44	1	33N34	88w25	5:53:40
College Hill 36	1	34N22	89w31	5:58:04
Collins 16	1	31N39	89w33	5:58:12
Collinsville 38	1	32N30	88w51	5:55:24
Colonial 25	2	32N19	90w11	6:00:44
Colony Town 42	1	33N30	90w20	6:01:20
Colsub 48	1	33N59	88w29	5:53:56
Columbia 46	1	31N15	89w50	5:59:20
Columbus 44	1	33N30	88w25	5:53:40
Columbus Air Force Base 44	1	33N39	88w27	5:53:48
Commerce 72	1	34N49	90w19	6:01:16
Como 54	1	34N31	89w56	5:59:44
Conehatta 51	1	32N27	89w17	5:57:08
Conway 40	1	32N44	89w32	5:58:08
Cooksville 52	1	33N07	88w34	5:54:16
Coosa 40	1	32N44	89w32	5:58:08
Corinth 2	1	34N56	88w31	5:54:04
Cornersville 47	1	34N39	89w18	5:57:12
Corrona 41	1	34N26	88w40	5:54:40
Cotton Plant 70	1	34N40	89w01	5:56:04
Cottonville 69	1	34N41	89w59	5:59:56
Counts 14	1	34N12	90w34	6:02:16
County Line 21	1	31N26	88w28	5:53:52
Courtland 54	1	34N14	89w57	5:59:48
Cowart 68	1	34N00	90w03	6:00:12
Coxburg 26	1	33N07	90w03	6:00:12
Coxs Ferry 25	1	32N21	90w28	6:01:52
Coy 35	1	32N53	88w50	5:55:20
Craig Springs 53	1	33N21	89w03	5:56:12
Crandall 12	1	31N58	88w32	5:54:08
Crane Creek 23	1	30N47	89w08	5:56:32
Cranfield 1	1	31N30	91w04	6:04:16
Crawford 44	1	33N18	88w37	5:54:28
Crenshaw 54	1	34N30	90w12	6:00:48
Crockett 69	1	34N37	89w58	5:59:52
Crosby 3	1	31N17	91w04	6:04:16
Crossroad 40	1	32N44	89w32	5:58:08
Crossroads 50	1	32N46	89w07	5:56:28
Crossroads 55	1	30N50	89w32	5:58:08
Cross Roads 61	1	32N19	89w47	5:59:08
Crossroads 76	1	33N25	91w00	6:04:00
Crotts 34	1	31N36	89w12	5:56:48
Crowder 60	1	34N11	90w08	6:00:32
Cruger 26	1	33N19	90w14	6:00:56
Crupp 82	1	32N51	90w24	6:01:36
Crystal Springs 15	1	31N59	90w21	6:01:24
Cub Lake 17	1	34N50	89w59	5:59:56
Cuevas 24	1	30N19	89w14	5:56:56
Cumberland 78	1	33N33	89w05	5:56:20
Curtis Station 54	1	34N19	89w57	5:59:48
Cybur 55	1	30N32	89w40	5:58:40
Cynthia 25	2	32N19	90w11	6:00:44
Dahomey 6	1	33N39	91w01	6:04:04
Daisy-Vestry 30	1	30N47	89w08	5:56:32
Daleville 38	1	32N34	88w41	5:54:44
Damascus 35	1	32N46	88w39	5:54:36
Dancy 78	1	33N44	89w04	5:56:16
Daniel 65	1	32N05	89w47	5:59:08
Darbun 74	1	31N17	90w03	6:00:12
Darden 73	1	34N33	89w07	5:56:28
Darling 60	1	34N22	90w23	6:01:32
Darlove 76	1	33N14	90w47	6:03:08
Darracott 48	1	33N50	88w33	5:54:12
Darrington 79	1	31N17	91w04	6:04:16
Davenport 14	1	34N12	90w34	6:02:16
Davis 45	1	32N37	90w02	6:00:08
Days 17	1	34N54	90w13	6:00:52
Deasonville 82	1	32N48	90w03	6:00:12
Decatur 51	1	32N26	89w07	5:56:28
Deemer 50	1	32N45	89w07	5:56:28
Deerbrook 52	1	33N14	88w35	5:54:20
Deeson 6	1	34N01	90w52	6:03:28
De Kalb 35	1	32N46	88w39	5:54:36
De Lay 36	1	34N22	89w31	5:58:04
De Lisle 24	1	30N23	89w16	5:57:04
Delta 54	1	34N30	90w12	6:00:48
Delta Drive 25	2	32N19	90w11	6:00:44
Delta State College 6	1	33N44	90w43	6:02:52
Denham 77	1	31N39	88w32	5:54:08
Denmark 36	1	34N19	89w21	5:57:24
Dennis 71	1	34N34	88w14	5:52:56
Dennis Landing 6	1	33N57	90w56	6:03:44
Dentontown 7	1	33N45	89w22	5:57:28
Dentville 15	1	32N02	90w41	6:02:44
Deovolente 27	1	33N11	90w29	6:01:56
Derby 55	1	30N50	89w32	5:58:08
Derma 7	1	33N51	89w17	5:57:08
De Soto 12	1	31N58	88w43	5:54:52
Deweese 50	1	32N43	88w56	5:55:44
Dexter 74	1	31N07	90w09	6:00:36
Diamondhead 23	1	30N19	89w20	5:57:20
D'Iberville 24	1	30N26	88w53	5:55:32
Dixie 18	1	31N18	89w18	5:57:12
Dixie Pine 18	1	31N18	89w18	5:57:12
Dixon 50	1	32N46	89w07	5:56:28
D'Lo 64	1	31N59	89w54	5:59:36
Doddsville 67	1	33N40	90w32	6:02:08
Dogtown 36	1	34N22	89w31	5:58:04
Doloroso 79	1	31N06	91w18	6:05:12
Domascus 35	1	32N46	88w39	5:54:36
Donegal 79	1	31N06	91w18	6:05:12
Doolittle 51	1	32N19	89w10	5:56:40
Dorsey 29	1	34N16	88w25	5:53:40
Doskie 71	1	34N50	88w19	5:53:16
Dossville 40	1	32N56	89w33	5:58:12
Dover 50	1	32N34	89w07	5:56:28
Dover 82	1	32N39	90w22	6:01:28
Dowdville 50	1	32N46	89w07	5:56:28
Dowell 40	1	32N44	89w32	5:58:08
Drew 67	1	33N49	90w32	6:02:08
Dry Creek 16	1	31N38	89w33	5:58:12
Dubard 22	1	33N47	89w48	5:59:12
Dubbs 72	1	34N34	90w23	6:01:32
Dublin 14	1	34N04	90w30	6:02:00
Duck Hill 49	1	33N38	89w43	5:58:52
Duffee 51	1	32N29	88w56	5:55:44
Dumas 70	1	34N38	88w50	5:55:20
Duncan 6	1	34N03	90w45	6:03:00
Dundee 72	1	34N32	90w27	6:01:48
Dunleith 76	1	33N24	90w54	6:03:36
Durant 26	1	33N05	89w51	5:59:24
Dwiggins 67	1	33N49	90w32	6:02:08
Dwyer 67	1	33N33	90w32	6:02:08
Eagle Lake 75	1	32N20	90w52	6:03:28
Earlygrove 47	1	34N55	89w19	5:57:16
East Aberdeen 48	1	33N50	88w33	5:54:12
Eastabuchie 34	1	31N26	89w17	5:57:08
Eastfork 3	1	31N20	90w41	6:02:44
Eastlawn 30	1	30N23	88w32	5:54:08
East Lincoln 43	1	31N35	90w27	6:01:48
East Moss Point 30	1	30N24	88w31	5:54:04
Eastport 71	1	34N53	88w06	5:52:24
Eastside 30	1	30N24	88w31	5:54:04
East Side 56	1	31N21	88w56	5:55:44
East Tupelo 41	1	34N15	88w43	5:54:52
Eatonville 18	1	31N18	89w18	5:57:12
Ebenezer 26	1	32N58	90w06	6:00:24
Ecru 58	1	34N21	89w02	5:56:08
Eddiceton 19	1	31N30	90w48	6:03:12
Eden 82	1	32N59	90w20	6:01:20
Edinburg 40	1	32N48	89w20	5:57:20
Edwards 25	1	32N20	90w36	6:02:24
Effie 68	1	34N00	90w03	6:00:12
Eggville 41	1	34N23	88w41	5:54:44
Egremont 63	1	32N54	90w53	6:03:32
Egypt 9	1	33N54	88w44	5:54:56
Eldorado 75	1	32N29	90w48	6:03:12
Electric Mills 35	1	32N46	88w28	5:53:52
Elizabeth 76	1	33N20	90w53	6:03:32
Ellard 7	1	34N00	89w21	5:57:24
Elliott 22	1	33N41	89w45	5:59:00
Ellistown 73	1	34N34	88w14	5:52:56
Ellisville 34	1	31N36	89w12	5:56:48
Elsie 7	1	33N53	89w11	5:56:44
Elwood 12	1	32N03	88w43	5:54:52
Eminence 16	1	31N34	89w30	5:58:00
Emory 26	1	33N07	90w03	6:00:12
Endville 58	1	34N24	88w52	5:55:28
Energy 12	1	32N28	88w40	5:54:40
Enid 68	1	34N07	89w56	5:59:44
Enon 74	1	31N22	90w12	6:00:48
Enondale 35	1	32N41	88w28	5:53:52
Enterprise 3	1	31N10	90w48	6:03:12
Enterprise 12	1	32N10	88w49	5:55:16
Enterprise 43	1	31N26	90w27	6:01:48
Enterprise 73	1	34N33	89w07	5:56:28
Enzor 38	1	32N28	88w40	5:54:40
Eret 77	1	31N26	88w28	5:53:52
Errata 34	1	31N42	89w08	5:56:32
Erwin 76	1	33N06	91w06	6:04:24
Escatawpa 30	1	30N26	88w33	5:54:12
Eset 77	1	31N26	88w28	5:53:52
Eskridge 49	1	33N29	89w44	5:58:56
Estes 80	1	33N07	89w03	5:56:12
Estesmill 40	1	32N44	89w32	5:58:08
Estill 76	1	33N13	90w53	6:03:32
Ethel 4	1	33N07	89w28	5:57:52
Etta 73	1	34N28	89w14	5:56:56
Eucutta 77	1	31N53	88w41	5:54:44
Eudora 17	1	34N50	89w59	5:59:56
Eunice 3	1	31N12	91w01	6:04:04
Eupora 78	1	33N32	89w16	5:57:04
Eureka Springs 54	1	34N15	89w56	5:59:44
Eutaw 6	1	33N39	91w01	6:04:04
Evansville 69	1	34N41	89w59	5:59:56
Evansville 72	1	34N38	90w23	6:01:32
Everett 64	1	31N57	89w53	5:59:32
Evergreen 24	1	30N24	89w05	5:56:20
Evergreen 29	1	34N16	88w25	5:53:40
Expose 46	1	31N18	89w50	5:59:20
Fairfield 73	1	34N24	88w52	5:55:28
Fairground 50	1	32N46	89w07	5:56:28
Fairhaven 17	1	34N57	89w49	5:59:16
Fairhill 52	1	32N59	88w34	5:54:16
Fair Oaks Springs 43	1	31N35	90w27	6:01:48
Fair River 43	1	31N35	90w27	6:01:48
Fairview 29	1	34N29	88w11	5:52:44
Fairview 67	1	33N27	90w39	6:02:36
Falcon	1	34N24	90w16	6:01:04
Falcon 60	1	34N28	89w14	5:56:56
Falkner 70	1	34N51	88w56	5:55:44
Fame 78	1	33N33	89w16	5:57:04
Fannin 61	1	32N16	89w59	5:59:56
Farmhaven 45	1	32N37	90w02	6:00:08
Farmington 2	1	34N54	88w34	5:54:16
Farrell 14	1	34N16	90w40	6:02:40
Fayette 32	1	31N43	91w04	6:04:16
Fenton 23	1	30N19	89w14	5:56:56
Fentress 10	1	33N19	89w10	5:56:40
Fenwick 1	1	31N34	91w22	6:05:28
Fernwood 57	1	31N11	90w27	6:01:48
Fitler 28	1	32N44	91w02	6:04:08
Fitzhugh 67	1	33N49	90w32	6:02:08
Flora 45	1	32N33	90w19	6:01:16
Florence 61	1	32N09	90w08	6:00:32
Flowerdale 41	1	34N15	88w43	5:54:52
Floweree 75	1	32N29	90w48	6:03:12
Flowood 61	2	32N22	90w09	6:00:36
Floyd 5	1	34N50	89w11	5:56:44
Fondren 25	2	32N19	90w11	6:00:44
Fontainebleau 30	1	30N26	88w49	5:55:16
Foote 76	1	33N11	90w51	6:03:24
Fords Creek 55	1	30N50	89w32	5:58:08
Forest 62	1	32N22	89w29	5:57:56
Forest Hill 25	2	32N19	90w11	6:00:44
Forkville 62	1	32N28	89w40	5:58:40
Fort Adams 79	1	31N05	91w33	6:06:12
Fort Stephens 35	1	32N28	88w43	5:54:52

MISSISSIPPI

Four Corners 4 1 33N03 89w35 5:58:20
Four Mile 27 1 33N11 90w29 6:01:56
Foxworth 46 1 31N14 89w52 5:59:28
Francis 6 1 34N03 90w45 6:03:00
Freeny 40 1 32N42 89w29 5:57:56
Freerun 82 1 32N51 90w24 6:01:36
Freetrade 40 1 32N44 89w32 5:58:08
Freeze Corner 17 1 34N50 89w59 5:59:56
French Camp 10 1 33N18 89w24 5:57:36
Friars Point 14 1 34N22 90w38 6:02:32
Friendship 43 1 31N35 90w27 6:01:48
Friendship 58 1 34N21 89w01 5:56:04
Frostbridge 77 1 31N41 88w39 5:54:36
Fruitland Park 18 1 30N55 89w10 5:56:40
Fugate 82 1 32N50 90w15 6:01:00
Fulton 29 1 34N16 88w25 5:53:40
Furrs 58 1 34N15 89w01 5:56:04
Futheyville 22 1 33N47 89w48 5:59:12
Gallman 15 1 31N56 90w23 6:01:32
Gandsi 16 1 31N34 89w30 5:58:00
Garden City 19 1 31N22 91w08 6:04:32
Garlandville 31 1 32N19 89w10 5:56:40
Gatesville 15 1 32N00 90w15 6:01:00
Gatewood 81 1 33N59 89w41 5:58:44
Gattman 48 1 33N53 88w14 5:52:56
Gautier 30 1 30N23 88w37 5:54:28
Geeslin Corner 22 1 33N47 89w48 5:59:12
Geeville 59 1 34N35 88w42 5:54:48
Georgetown 15 1 31N52 90w10 6:00:40
Germania 82 1 32N40 90w33 6:02:12
Gholson 52 1 32N56 88w44 5:54:56
Gibbons 63 1 32N48 90w56 6:03:44
Gibson 48 1 33N50 88w33 5:54:12
Giles 35 1 32N50 88w29 5:53:56
Gill 40 1 32N44 89w32 5:58:08
Gillsburg 3 1 31N00 90w28 6:01:52
Gilmer 16 1 31N50 89w26 5:57:44
Gitano 34 1 31N50 89w26 5:57:44
Glade 34 1 31N42 89w08 5:56:32
Glancy 15 1 31N49 90w30 6:02:00
Glen 2 1 34N52 88w31 5:54:04
Glen Allan 76 1 33N02 91w02 6:04:08
Glendale 18 1 31N18 89w18 5:57:12
Glendora 68 1 33N50 90w18 6:01:12
Glenfield 73 1 34N29 89w01 5:56:04
Gloster 3 1 31N12 91w01 6:04:04
Glover 17 1 34N58 90w16 6:01:04
Gluckstadt 45 1 32N28 90w07 6:00:28
Golden 71 1 34N29 88w11 5:52:44
Goldfield 67 1 33N49 90w32 6:02:08
Gooden Lake 27 1 33N11 90w29 6:01:56
Goodfood 58 1 34N15 89w01 5:56:04
Good Hope 40 1 32N36 89w35 5:58:20
Good Hope 56 1 31N21 88w56 5:55:44
Goodman 26 1 32N58 89w55 5:59:40
Goodwater 12 1 31N56 88w56 5:55:44
Goodyear 55 1 30N32 89w40 5:58:40
Gore Springs 22 1 33N45 89w37 5:58:28
Goshen Springs 61 1 32N16 89w59 5:59:56
Goss 46 1 31N21 89w53 5:59:32
Grace 28 1 33N00 90w58 6:03:52
Grady 78 1 33N33 89w16 5:57:04
Graham 73 1 34N30 88w38 5:54:32
Grand Gulf 11 1 32N02 91w03 6:04:12
Grange 39 1 31N44 89w59 5:59:56
Grange Hall 75 1 32N20 90w52 6:03:28
Grapeland 6 1 33N39 91w01 6:04:04
Gravel Siding 71 1 34N49 88w11 5:52:44
Gravestown 70 1 34N44 88w57 5:55:48
Gray 40 1 32N44 89w32 5:58:08
Greenbrier Park 55 1 30N32 89w40 5:58:40
Greenfield 51 1 32N27 89w17 5:57:08
Greenfield 61 1 32N16 89w59 5:59:56
Greenfield Addition 76 1 33N25 91w00 6:04:00
Greenville 76 1 33N24 91w04 6:04:16
Greenwood 29 1 34N16 88w25 5:53:40
Greenwood 42 1 33N31 90w11 6:00:44
Greenwood Springs 48 1 33N48 88w18 5:53:12
Grenada 22 1 33N47 89w49 5:59:16
Griffith 13 1 33N35 88w50 5:55:20
Gulde 61 1 32N16 89w59 5:59:56
Gulf Hills Country Club 30 1 30N26 88w49 5:55:16
Gulf Park Estates 30 1 30N26 88w49 5:55:16
Gulfport 24 1 30N22 89w06 5:56:24
Gums 81 1 33N59 89w41 5:58:44
Gum Springs 62 1 32N22 89w28 5:57:52
Gunn 65 1 32N04 89w41 5:58:44
Gunnison 6 1 33N57 90w57 6:03:48
Guntown 41 1 34N27 88w40 5:54:40
Gwin 26 1 33N11 90w13 6:00:52
Gwinville 33 1 31N44 89w59 5:59:56
Hale 12 1 31N53 88w41 5:54:44
Halltown 73 1 34N29 89w01 5:56:04
Hamburg 19 1 31N30 91w04 6:04:16
Hamilton 48 1 33N44 88w27 5:53:48
Hampton 76 1 33N02 91w02 6:04:08
Hand 35 1 32N28 88w43 5:54:52
Handle 80 1 33N07 89w03 5:56:12
Handsboro 24 1 30N24 89w05 5:56:20
Hard Cash 27 1 33N11 90w29 6:01:56
Hardy 22 1 33N47 89w48 5:59:12
Harleston 30 1 30N55 88w35 5:54:20
Harmontown 36 1 34N31 89w56 5:59:44
Harmony 12 1 32N03 88w43 5:54:52
Harperville 62 1 32N30 89w29 5:57:56
Harriston 32 1 31N44 91w02 6:04:08
Harrisville 64 1 31N58 90w05 6:00:20
Harvey 18 1 31N21 89w15 5:57:00
Hathorn 46 1 31N18 89w50 5:59:20
Hatley 48 1 33N59 88w29 5:53:56
Hattiesburg 18 1 31N20 89w17 5:57:08
Haynes Bluff 75 1 32N29 90w48 6:03:12
Hays 62 1 32N27 89w17 5:57:08
Hazlehurst 15 1 31N52 90w24 6:01:36
Heads 76 1 33N28 90w51 6:03:24
Heathman 67 1 33N27 90w39 6:02:36
Hebron 33 1 31N44 89w59 5:59:56
Hebron 34 1 31N50 89w26 5:57:44
Heidelberg 31 1 31N53 88w59 5:55:56
Helena 30 1 30N23 88w32 5:54:08
Helm 76 1 33N24 90w54 6:03:36
Henderson's Point 24 1 30N19 89w14 5:56:56
Hendrix 49 1 33N26 89w34 5:58:16
Henley 35 1 32N50 88w29 5:53:56
Henleyfield 55 1 30N32 89w39 5:58:36
Herbert Springs 50 1 32N30 88w51 5:55:24
Hermanville 11 1 31N58 90w50 6:03:20
Hernando 17 1 34N49 90w00 6:00:00
Hero 31 1 32N19 89w10 5:56:40
Hesterville 4 1 33N12 89w47 5:59:08
Heucks 43 1 31N35 90w27 6:01:48
Hickory 51 1 32N19 89w01 5:56:04
Hickory Flat 5 1 34N37 89w11 5:56:44
Hickory Grove 53 1 33N28 88w49 5:55:16
Hicks 32 1 31N43 91w04 6:04:16
Higgins 37 1 31N25 89w33 5:58:12
High Hill 40 1 32N46 89w07 5:56:28
Highlandale 42 1 33N45 90w24 6:01:36
Highpoint 1 33N11 89w09 5:56:36
High Point 80 1 33N07 89w03 5:56:12
Hightown 2 1 34N54 88w34 5:54:16
Highway Village 79 1 31N06 91w18 6:05:12
Hillhouse 14 1 34N07 90w49 6:03:16
Hillman 21 1 31N09 88w34 5:54:16
Hillsboro 62 1 32N27 89w31 5:58:04
Hillsdale 55 1 30N50 89w32 5:58:08
Hinchcliff 60 1 34N19 90w17 6:01:08
Hinkle 2 1 34N46 88w32 5:54:08
Hintonville 56 1 31N13 89w01 5:56:04
Hinze 80 1 33N12 89w20 5:57:20
Hiwannee 77 1 31N49 88w41 5:54:44
Hobo Station 59 1 34N40 88w34 5:54:16
Hohenlinden 78 1 33N44 89w04 5:56:16
Holcomb 22 1 33N46 89w59 5:59:56
Holcut 71 1 34N44 88w19 5:53:16
Hollandale 76 1 33N10 90w51 6:03:24
Hollis 7 1 33N53 89w11 5:56:44
Holly Bluff 82 1 32N49 90w42 6:02:48
Holly Grove 8 1 33N24 90w12 6:00:48
Holly Ridge 67 1 33N27 90w45 6:03:00
Holly Springs 47 1 34N46 89w27 5:57:48
Hollywood 72 1 34N45 90w22 6:01:28
Holmesville 57 1 31N12 90w19 6:01:16
Holts 71 1 34N50 88w19 5:53:16
Homewood 62 1 32N16 89w36 5:58:24
Homochitto 3 1 31N12 91w01 6:04:04
Honey Island 27 1 33N11 90w13 6:00:52
Hoover Lake and Park 61 1 32N09 90w08 6:00:32
Hope 50 1 32N46 89w07 5:56:28
Hopewell 5 1 35N03 89w05 5:56:20
Hopoca 40 1 32N44 89w32 5:58:08
Horn Lake 17 1 34N58 90w02 6:00:08
Horseshoe 26 1 33N11 90w13 6:00:52
Hot Coffee 16 1 31N44 89w27 5:57:48
Houlka 9 1 34N02 89w01 5:56:04
House 50 1 32N34 89w07 5:56:28
Houston 9 1 33N54 89w00 5:56:00
Howard 26 1 33N08 90w11 6:00:44
Howison 24 1 30N40 89w08 5:56:32
Hoy 34 1 31N42 89w08 5:56:32
Hub 46 1 31N18 89w50 5:59:20
Hubbard 25 1 32N20 90w36 6:02:24
Hudsonville 47 1 34N52 89w23 5:57:32
Humber 14 1 34N12 90w34 6:02:16
Hurley 30 1 30N40 88w30 5:54:00
Hurricane 58 1 34N18 89w11 5:56:44
Hurricane Creek 38 1 32N28 88w40 5:54:40
Hushpuckena 6 1 34N01 90w45 6:03:00
Improve 46 1 31N18 89w50 5:59:20
Increase 38 1 32N28 88w40 5:54:40
Inda 66 1 30N47 89w08 5:56:32
Independence 62 1 32N21 89w39 5:58:36
Independence 69 1 34N42 89w49 5:59:16
Indianola 67 1 33N27 90w39 6:02:36
Indian Springs 2 1 34N52 88w31 5:54:04
Indian Springs 56 1 31N18 89w18 5:57:12
Industrial 55 1 30N32 89w40 5:58:40
Ingomar 73 1 34N25 89w02 5:56:08
Ingrams Mill 17 1 34N52 89w41 5:58:44
Inverness 67 1 33N21 90w35 6:02:20
Iowana 30 1 30N24 88w38 5:54:32
Ireland 79 1 31N06 91w18 6:05:12
Irene 57 1 31N17 90w28 6:01:52
Isola 27 1 33N16 90w35 6:02:20
Itta Bena 42 1 33N30 90w20 6:01:20
Iuka 71 1 34N49 88w12 5:52:48
Jacinto 2 1 34N46 88w32 5:54:08
Jack 15 1 32N06 90w37 6:02:28
Jackson 25 2 32N18 90w12 6:00:48
Jago 17 1 34N58 90w02 6:00:08
Jaketown 27 1 33N11 90w29 6:01:56
James 76 1 33N12 91w04 6:04:16
Jamestown 46 1 31N10 89w50 5:59:20
Jayess 39 1 31N22 90w12 6:00:48
Jeff Davis 75 1 32N20 90w52 6:03:28
Jefferson 8 1 33N30 89w55 5:59:40
Jeffries 14 1 34N32 90w27 6:01:48
Jennings 57 1 31N09 90w27 6:01:48
Jericho 73 1 34N30 88w38 5:54:32
Johns 61 1 32N08 89w50 5:59:20
Johnson 34 1 31N36 89w12 5:56:48
Johnstons Station 43 1 31N21 90w27 6:01:48
Jonathan 21 1 31N09 88w34 5:54:16
Jonestown 14 1 34N19 90w27 6:01:48
Jonestown 82 1 32N51 90w24 6:01:36
Joseph 4 1 33N01 89w46 5:59:04
Jug Fork 41 1 34N24 88w52 5:55:28
Jumpertown 59 1 34N40 88w34 5:54:16
Kalem 62 1 32N21 89w39 5:58:36
Katzenmeyer 75 1 32N29 90w48 6:03:12
Keesler Air Force Base 24 1 30N25 88w55 5:55:40
Kellis Store 35 1 32N56 88w44 5:54:56
Kelona 31 1 31N56 88w56 5:55:44
Kendrick 2 1 34N54 88w34 5:54:16
Keownville 73 1 34N29 89w01 5:56:04
Kerin 26 1 33N19 90w14 6:00:56
Kewanee 38 1 32N25 88w30 5:54:00
Key Field 38 1 32N28 88w40 5:54:40
Kienstra 1 1 31N05 91w33 6:06:12
Kilmichael 49 1 33N27 89w34 5:58:16
Kiln 23 1 30N25 89w25 5:57:40
King and Anderson 14 1 34N12 90w34 6:02:16
Kings 75 1 32N20 90w52 6:03:28
Kinlock 67 1 33N27 90w39 6:02:36
Kirby 19 1 31N31 90w59 6:03:56
Kirkville 29 1 34N30 88w38 5:54:32
Klondike 35 1 32N28 88w43 5:54:52
Knobtown 21 1 31N26 88w28 5:53:52
Knoxo 74 1 31N07 90w09 6:00:36
Knoxville 19 1 31N30 91w04 6:04:16
Kokomo 46 1 31N12 90w00 6:00:00
Kola 16 1 31N38 89w33 5:58:12
Kolola Springs 44 1 33N39 88w25 5:53:40
Kosciusko 4 1 33N04 89w35 5:58:20
Kossuth 2 1 34N52 88w39 5:54:36
Kreole 30 1 30N24 88w30 5:54:00
Lackey 48 1 33N50 88w33 5:54:12
Lafayette Springs 36 1 34N19 89w16 5:57:04
Lake 62 1 32N21 89w20 5:57:20
Lake City 82 1 32N51 90w24 6:01:36
Lake Cormorant 17 1 34N54 90w13 6:00:52
Lakeland 61 2 32N19 90w11 6:00:44
Lake of Hills 17 1 34N50 89w59 5:59:56
Lakeshore 23 1 30N15 89w26 5:57:44
Lake View 17 1 34N58 90w16 6:01:04
Lamar 5 1 34N55 89w19 5:57:16
Lamar Park 37 1 31N18 89w18 5:57:12
Lambert 60 1 34N12 90w17 6:01:08
Lamkin 27 1 33N06 90w30 6:02:00
Lamont 6 1 33N32 91w05 6:04:20
Lampton 46 1 31N18 89w50 5:59:20
Landon 24 1 30N24 89w05 5:56:20
Laneheart 79 1 31N06 91w18 6:05:12
Langford 61 1 32N16 89w59 5:59:56
Langsdale 12 1 31N53 88w41 5:54:44
Lantrip 7 1 34N00 89w21 5:57:24
Larue 30 1 30N26 88w49 5:55:16
Latimer 30 1 30N26 88w49 5:55:16
Latonia 20 1 30N55 88w35 5:54:20
Lauderdale 38 1 32N31 88w31 5:54:04
Laurel 34 1 31N41 89w08 5:56:32
Laurelhill 50 1 32N46 89w07 5:56:28
Lawrence 51 1 32N19 89w14 5:56:56
Laws Hill 47 1 34N39 89w27 5:57:48
Leaf 21 1 31N02 88w48 5:55:12
Leakesville 21 1 31N09 88w33 5:54:12
Learned 25 1 32N12 90w33 6:02:12
Leavell Woods 25 2 32N19 90w11 6:00:44
Lebanon 25 1 32N15 90w25 6:01:40
Lebanon 47 1 34N39 89w18 5:57:12
Leedy 71 1 34N48 88w22 5:53:28
Leesburg 61 1 32N21 89w39 5:58:36
Leesdale 1 1 31N30 91w04 6:04:16
Leeville 18 1 31N18 89w18 5:57:12
Le Flore 22 1 33N42 90w04 6:00:16
Leland 76 1 33N24 90w54 6:03:36
Lemon 65 1 32N22 89w28 5:57:52
Lena 40 1 32N36 89w36 5:58:24
Lessley 79 1 31N10 91w25 6:05:40
Le Tourneau 75 1 32N20 90w52 6:03:28
Leverett 68 1 33N51 90w00 6:00:00
Lewisburg 17 1 34N57 89w49 5:59:16
Lexie 74 1 31N05 90w10 6:00:40
Lexington 26 1 33N07 90w03 6:00:12
Liberty 3 1 31N10 90w49 6:03:16
Liberty 35 1 32N46 88w39 5:54:36
Lightsey 77 1 31N42 89w08 5:56:32
Lillian 62 1 32N22 89w28 5:57:52
Limbert 34 1 31N42 89w08 5:56:32
Lines 80 1 32N56 88w44 5:54:56
Linn 67 1 33N40 90w31 6:02:04
Linwood 50 1 32N37 89w08 5:56:32
Linwood 82 1 32N48 90w03 6:00:12
Little Creek 56 1 31N10 88w55 5:55:40
Little Rock 51 1 32N32 89w02 5:56:08
Little Texas 72 1 34N42 90w23 6:01:32
Little Yazoo 82 1 32N39 90w22 6:01:28
Litton 6 1 33N38 90w46 6:03:04
Lizana 24 1 30N24 89w05 5:56:20
Lobdell 6 1 33N47 90w59 6:03:56
Lobutcha 80 1 33N12 89w20 5:57:20
Loch Leven 79 1 31N05 91w33 6:06:12
Locke Station 54 1 34N19 89w57 5:59:48
Lockhart 38 1 32N31 88w31 5:54:04
Locum 73 1 34N38 88w50 5:55:20
Lodi 49 1 33N27 89w26 5:57:44
Lombardy 67 1 33N57 90w46 6:03:04
Long 76 1 33N24 90w54 6:03:36
Long Beach 24 1 30N21 89w09 5:56:36
Longino 50 1 32N46 89w07 5:56:28
Long Lake 14 1 34N22 90w31 6:02:04

Long Lake 75 1 32N20 90w52 6:03:28
Longshot 6 1 33N39 91w01 6:04:04
Longtown 54 1 34N34 90w13 6:00:52
Longview 53 1 33N24 88w55 5:55:40
Longview 58 1 34N19 88w47 5:55:08
Looxahoma 69 1 34N37 89w58 5:59:52
Lorenzen 63 1 32N54 90w53 6:03:32
Lorman 32 1 31N49 91w03 6:04:12
Louin 31 1 32N04 89w16 5:57:04
Louise 27 1 32N59 90w35 6:02:20
Louisville 80 1 33N07 89w03 5:56:12
Love 17 1 34N50 89w59 5:59:56
Loyd 7 1 33N53 89w11 5:56:44
Lucas 33 1 31N36 89w52 5:59:28
Lucedale 20 1 30N56 88w35 5:54:20
Lucien 19 1 31N35 90w27 6:01:48
Luckney 61 2 32N19 90w09 6:00:36
Ludlow 62 1 32N34 89w43 5:58:52
Lula 14 1 34N27 90w29 6:01:56
Lumberton 37 1 31N00 89w27 5:57:48
Lurand 14 1 34N12 90w34 6:02:16
Luther 40 1 32N44 89w32 5:58:08
Lux 16 1 31N18 89w18 5:57:12
Lyman 24 1 30N30 89w07 5:56:28
Lynn Creek 52 1 33N14 88w35 5:54:20
Lynville 35 1 32N53 88w50 5:55:20
Lyon 14 1 34N13 90w33 6:02:12
Maben 53 1 33N33 89w05 5:56:20
Macedonia 18 1 31N18 89w18 5:57:12
Macedonia 41 1 34N15 88w43 5:54:52
Macedonia 73 1 34N33 89w07 5:56:28
Macel 68 1 33N45 90w12 6:00:48
Mack 47 1 34N46 89w27 5:57:48
Macon 52 1 33N07 88w34 5:54:16
Madden 40 1 32N41 89w21 5:57:24
Madison 45 1 32N28 90w07 6:00:28
Madisonville 45 1 32N37 90w02 6:00:08
Magee 64 1 31N52 89w44 5:58:56
Magenta 76 1 33N24 90w54 6:03:36
Magnolia 57 1 31N09 90w28 6:01:52
Mahned 56 1 31N13 89w01 5:56:04
Malvina 6 1 33N51 91w02 6:04:08
Mannassa 12 1 32N03 88w43 5:54:52
Mantachie 29 1 34N19 88w30 5:54:00
Mantee 78 1 33N44 89w03 5:56:12
Marcella 26 1 33N11 90w13 6:00:52
Marianna 47 1 34N46 89w27 5:57:48
Marie 67 1 33N27 90w39 6:02:36
Marietta 59 1 34N30 88w28 5:53:52
Marion 38 1 32N25 88w39 5:54:36
Maris Town 45 1 32N37 90w02 6:00:08
Marks 60 1 34N16 90w16 6:01:04
Mars Hill 3 1 31N17 90w28 6:01:52
Martin 38 1 32N30 88w51 5:55:24
Martinsville 15 1 31N48 90w25 6:01:40
Martinville 64 1 31N57 89w53 5:59:32
Marydell 40 1 32N44 89w32 5:58:08
Mashulaville 52 1 33N07 88w34 5:54:16
Matherville 77 1 31N52 88w34 5:54:16
Mathiston 78 1 33N32 89w07 5:56:28
Mattson 14 1 34N06 90w31 6:02:04
Maxie 18 1 30N59 89w12 5:56:48
Maybank 18 1 31N18 89w18 5:57:12
Maybell 34 1 31N36 89w12 5:56:48
Mayersville 28 1 32N54 91w03 6:04:12
Mayhew 44 1 33N29 88w38 5:54:32
Mayton 61 1 32N16 89w59 5:59:56
Maywood 17 1 34N57 89w49 5:59:16
McAdams 4 1 33N01 89w41 5:58:44
McAfee 40 1 32N44 89w32 5:58:08
McBride 32 1 31N53 90w53 6:03:32
McCall Creek 19 1 31N31 90w42 6:02:48
McCallum 18 1 31N14 89w13 5:56:52
McCarley 8 1 33N31 89w50 5:59:20
McComb 57 1 31N15 90w27 6:01:48
McCondy 9 1 33N49 88w51 5:55:24
McCool 4 1 33N12 89w21 5:57:24
McCrary 44 1 33N34 88w25 5:53:40
McCutcheon 76 1 33N21 90w56 6:03:44
McDonald 50 1 32N40 89w08 5:56:32
McElveen 3 1 31N17 90w28 6:01:52
McHenry 66 1 30N43 89w08 5:56:32
McLain 21 1 31N07 88w50 5:55:20
McLaurin 18 1 31N10 89w13 5:56:52
McLaurin Heights 61 2 32N19 90w09 6:00:36
McLeod 52 1 33N07 88w34 5:54:16
McMillan 80 1 33N10 89w07 5:56:28
McNair 32 1 31N38 91w03 6:04:12
McNeal 31 1 32N05 89w15 5:57:00
McNeill 55 1 30N40 89w38 5:58:32
McRaney 16 1 31N38 89w33 5:58:12
McSwain 56 1 31N21 88w56 5:55:44
McVille 4 1 32N56 89w37 5:58:28
McWillie 4 2 32N19 90w11 6:00:44
Meadville 19 1 31N28 90w54 6:03:36
Mechanicsburg 82 1 32N39 90w22 6:01:28
Meehan 38 1 32N28 88w40 5:54:40
Melba 37 1 31N25 89w33 5:58:12
Meltonville 45 1 32N37 90w02 6:00:08
Mendenhall 64 1 31N58 89w52 5:59:28
Meridian 38 1 32N22 88w42 5:54:48
Merigold 6 1 33N50 90w43 6:02:52
Merit 64 1 31N57 89w53 5:59:32
Merrill 20 1 30N59 88w43 5:54:52
Mesa 74 1 31N07 90w09 6:00:36
Metcalfe 76 1 33N27 91w00 6:04:00
Meyers 18 1 31N18 89w18 5:57:12
Michigan City 5 1 34N59 89w15 5:57:00
Midnight 27 1 33N03 90w35 6:02:20
Midway 25 2 32N15 90w14 6:00:56
Midway 40 1 32N44 89w32 5:58:08
Midway 62 1 32N22 89w28 5:57:52
Midway 71 1 34N49 88w11 5:52:44
Mile Branch 19 1 31N28 90w54 6:03:36
Mileston 26 1 33N11 90w13 6:00:52
Mill Creek 34 1 31N42 89w08 5:56:32
Mill Creek 55 1 30N32 89w39 5:58:36
Millcreek 80 1 33N07 89w03 5:56:12
Mill Creek Cabin Area 71 1 34N49 88w11 5:52:44
Miller 17 1 34N55 89w46 5:59:04
Millington 35 1 32N50 88w29 5:53:56
Mill Town 45 1 32N37 90w02 6:00:08
Mimms 54 1 34N19 89w57 5:59:48
Mineral Wells 17 1 34N59 89w52 5:59:28
Mingo 71 1 34N38 88w14 5:52:56
Minter City 42 1 33N45 90w18 6:01:12
Missionary 31 1 32N09 89w00 5:56:00
Mississippi City 24 1 30N23 89w02 5:56:08
Mississippi College 25 1 32N51 89w36 5:58:24
Mississippi Valley State Col 42 1 33N30 90w20 6:01:20
Mitchell 70 1 34N44 88w57 5:55:48
Mize 65 1 31N52 89w33 5:58:12
Mocarter 72 1 34N49 90w19 6:01:16
Money 42 1 33N39 90w13 6:00:52
Monroe 19 1 31N28 90w54 6:03:36
Monterey 61 1 32N09 90w08 6:00:32
Monte Vista 78 1 33N36 89w16 5:57:04
Montgomery 43 1 31N46 90w22 6:01:28
Monticello 39 1 31N33 90w07 6:00:28
Montpelier 13 1 33N43 88w57 5:55:48
Montrose 31 1 32N08 89w14 5:56:56
Moores Mill 71 1 34N34 88w14 5:52:56
Mooreville 41 1 34N16 88w35 5:54:20
Moorhead 67 1 33N27 90w30 6:02:00
Morgan City 42 1 33N23 90w21 6:01:24
Morgans 25 2 32N15 90w14 6:00:56
Morgantown 46 1 31N19 89w55 5:59:40
Morgantown 53 1 33N21 89w03 5:56:12
Morning Star 25 1 32N20 90w36 6:02:24
Morriston 18 1 31N18 89w18 5:57:12
Morton 62 1 32N21 89w39 5:58:36
Moscow 35 1 32N46 88w39 5:54:36
Moselle 34 1 31N30 89w17 5:57:08
Moss 31 1 31N49 89w11 5:56:44
Moss Point 30 1 30N25 88w30 5:54:00
Mound Bayou 6 1 33N53 90w44 6:02:56
Mound City 6 1 33N47 90w59 6:03:56
Mound City 73 1 34N24 88w52 5:55:28
Mount Carmel 33 1 31N39 89w47 5:59:08
Mount Olive 3 1 31N20 90w41 6:02:44
Mount Olive 16 1 31N46 89w39 5:58:36
Mount Olive 19 1 31N28 90w54 6:03:36
Mount Pleasant 29 1 34N14 88w16 5:53:04
Mount Pleasant 47 1 34N57 89w31 5:58:04
Mount Vernon 41 1 34N15 88w43 5:54:52
Mount Zion 64 1 31N52 89w44 5:58:56
Movella 20 1 30N55 88w35 5:54:20
Mulberry 77 1 31N41 88w39 5:54:36
Muldon 48 1 33N50 88w33 5:54:12
Muldrow 53 1 33N28 88w49 5:55:16
Mullins Store 36 1 34N22 89w31 5:58:04
Murdock Crossing 42 1 33N30 90w20 6:01:20
Murphreesboro 68 1 33N59 89w54 5:59:36
Murphy 76 1 33N11 90w51 6:03:24
Murry 70 1 34N44 88w57 5:55:48
Myrick 34 1 31N40 89w00 5:56:00
Myrleville 82 1 32N39 90w22 6:01:28
Myrtle 73 1 34N34 89w07 5:56:28
Nancy 12 1 31N56 88w56 5:55:44
Nason 22 1 33N46 89w58 5:59:52
Natchez 1 1 31N34 91w24 6:05:36
National Cemetery 75 1 32N20 90w52 6:03:28
Naval Air Station 38 1 32N28 88w40 5:54:40
Necaise 23 1 30N47 89w08 5:56:32
Neely 21 1 31N10 88w45 5:55:00
Negro Crossroads 25 1 31N59 90w22 6:01:28
Nellieburg 38 1 32N24 88w47 5:55:08
Nesbit 17 1 34N53 90w01 6:00:04
Neshoba 50 1 32N37 89w08 5:56:32
Nettleton 41 1 34N05 88w37 5:54:28
Nevada 25 1 32N21 90w28 6:01:52
New Albany 73 1 34N29 89w00 5:56:00
New Augusta 56 1 31N12 89w02 5:56:08
New Byram 25 2 32N19 90w11 6:00:44
New Fitler 28 1 32N37 91w01 6:04:04
New Harmony 73 1 34N24 88w52 5:55:28
Newhebron 39 1 31N44 89w59 5:59:56
New Hope 44 1 33N34 88w25 5:53:40
Newman 25 1 32N20 90w36 6:02:24
Newmans 75 1 32N20 90w52 6:03:28
Newmans Grove 75 1 32N12 90w33 6:02:12
Newport 4 1 33N01 89w46 5:59:04
New Salem 29 1 34N16 88w25 5:53:40
New Sight 43 1 31N35 90w27 6:01:48
New Site 59 1 34N33 88w31 5:54:04
Newton 51 1 32N19 89w10 5:56:40
New Town 69 1 34N37 89w58 5:59:52
New Wren 48 1 33N50 88w33 5:54:12
Nicholson 55 1 30N29 89w43 5:58:52
Nida 26 1 33N05 90w26 6:01:44
Niles 6 1 33N51 91w02 6:04:08
Nitta Yuma 63 1 33N02 90w51 6:03:24
Nixon 27 1 33N03 90w34 6:02:16
Nixon 58 1 34N15 89w01 5:56:04
Nod 82 1 32N50 90w15 6:01:00
Nola 39 1 31N39 90w12 6:00:48
Norfield 43 1 31N26 90w27 6:01:48
Norris 62 1 32N22 89w28 5:57:52
North 25 2 32N19 90w11 6:00:44
North 38 1 32N28 88w40 5:54:40
North Bend 50 1 32N46 89w07 5:56:28
North Carrollton 8 1 33N31 89w55 5:59:40
North Crossroads 71 1 34N49 88w11 5:52:44
North Gulfport 24 1 30N24 89w05 5:56:20
North Haven 73 1 34N29 89w01 5:56:04
North Tunica 72 1 34N42 90w23 6:01:32
Northwest Junior College 69 1 34N37 89w58 5:59:52
Northwood Hills 24 1 30N24 89w05 5:56:20
Noxapater 80 1 33N00 89w04 5:56:16
Oak Bowery 34 1 31N36 89w12 5:56:48
Oak Grove 26 1 33N11 90w13 6:00:52
Oak Grove 34 1 31N30 89w17 5:57:08
Oak Grove 37 1 31N18 89w18 5:57:12
Oakland 29 1 34N16 88w25 5:53:40
Oakland 57 1 31N17 90w28 6:01:52
Oakland 81 1 34N03 89w55 5:59:40
Oakley 25 1 32N13 90w30 6:02:00
Oak Ridge 75 1 32N20 90w52 6:03:28
Oaks 45 1 32N42 89w50 5:59:20
Oak Vale 39 1 31N26 89w58 5:59:52
Obadiah 38 1 32N28 88w43 5:54:52
Ocean Springs 30 1 30N25 88w50 5:55:20
Ocobla 50 1 32N46 89w07 5:56:28
Ofahoma 40 1 32N43 89w42 5:58:48
Oil City 82 1 32N39 90w22 6:01:28
Okolona 9 1 34N00 88w45 5:55:00
Oktibbeha 53 1 33N33 89w05 5:56:20
Oktoc 53 1 33N28 88w49 5:55:16
Old Cairo 59 1 34N40 88w34 5:54:16
Oldenburg 19 1 31N30 91w04 6:04:16
Oldham 71 1 34N49 88w11 5:52:44
Old Hamilton 48 1 33N44 88w27 5:53:48
Old Houlka 9 1 34N07 89w01 5:56:04
Old Union 41 1 34N07 88w43 5:54:52
Olive Branch 17 1 34N58 89w50 5:59:20
Oloh 37 1 31N25 89w33 5:58:12
Oma 39 1 31N44 90w09 6:00:36
Omega 26 1 33N11 90w13 6:00:52
Onward 1 32N44 90w56 6:03:44
Ora 16 1 31N38 89w33 5:58:12
Orange 12 1 32N03 88w53 5:55:32
Orange Grove 24 1 30N24 89w05 5:56:20
Orange Grove 30 1 30N23 88w32 5:54:08
Orange Hill 25 1 32N21 90w28 6:01:52
O'reilly 6 1 33N42 90w43 6:02:52
Orwood 36 1 34N22 89w31 5:58:04
Osborn 53 1 33N28 88w49 5:55:16
Osborne Creek 59 1 34N40 88w34 5:54:16
Osyka 57 1 31N00 90w28 6:01:52
Ovett 34 1 31N29 89w02 5:56:08
Owens Wells 26 1 33N07 90w03 6:00:12
Oxberry 22 1 33N46 89w58 5:59:52
Oxford 3 1 31N12 91w01 6:04:04
Oxford 36 1 34N22 89w31 5:58:04
Ozona 55 1 30N35 89w40 5:58:40
Pace 6 1 33N48 90w52 6:03:28
Pachuta 12 1 32N02 88w53 5:55:32
Paden 71 1 34N40 88w16 5:53:04
Palmers Crossing 18 1 31N18 89w18 5:57:12
Palmetto 41 1 34N15 88w43 5:54:52
Panther Burn 63 1 33N03 90w52 6:03:28
Parham 48 1 33N48 88w18 5:53:12
Paris 36 1 34N11 89w28 5:57:52
Parkplace 54 1 34N31 89w56 5:59:44
Pascagoula 30 1 30N21 88w33 5:54:12
Pass Christian 24 1 30N19 89w15 5:57:00
Patosi 82 1 32N51 90w24 6:01:36
Patrick 53 1 33N28 88w49 5:55:16
Patterson 4 1 33N03 89w35 5:58:20
Pattison 11 1 31N53 90w53 6:03:32
Paul 68 1 33N51 90w00 6:00:00
Paulding 31 1 32N02 89w02 5:56:08
Paulette 52 1 33N00 88w26 5:53:44
Paynes 68 1 33N55 90w04 6:00:16
Pearl 61 2 32N17 90w07 6:00:28
Pearl 64 1 32N09 90w08 6:00:32
Pearl City 61 2 32N19 90w09 6:00:36
Pearlhaven 43 1 31N35 90w27 6:01:48
Pearlington 23 1 30N15 89w37 5:58:28
Pearson 61 2 32N19 90w09 6:00:36
Pecan 30 1 30N23 88w32 5:54:08
Pecan Grove 34 1 31N36 89w12 5:56:48
Peck 73 1 34N29 89w01 5:56:04
Peetsville 15 1 31N46 90w22 6:01:28
Pelahatchie 61 1 32N19 89w48 5:59:12
Penantly 31 1 32N09 89w00 5:56:00
Pendorff 34 1 31N42 89w08 5:56:32
Penns 44 1 33N18 88w37 5:54:28
Pentecost 67 1 33N37 90w38 6:02:32
Penton 17 1 34N52 90w17 6:01:08
Peoples 70 1 34N44 88w57 5:55:48
Peoria 3 1 31N08 90w41 6:02:44
Percy 76 1 33N07 90w53 6:03:32
Perdue 51 1 32N26 89w01 5:56:04
Perkinston 66 1 30N47 89w08 5:56:32
Perrytown 79 1 31N17 91w04 6:04:16
Perth 32 1 31N43 91w04 6:04:16
Perthshire 6 1 33N57 90w56 6:03:44
Petal 18 1 31N21 89w16 5:57:04
Peyton 11 1 31N54 90w56 6:03:44
Pheba 13 1 33N35 88w57 5:55:48
Philadelphia 50 1 32N46 89w07 5:56:28
Philipp 68 1 33N45 90w12 6:00:48
Phillipstown 42 1 33N24 90w12 6:00:48
Phoenix 82 1 32N35 90w34 6:02:16
Piave 21 1 31N21 88w56 5:55:44
Picayune 55 1 30N32 89w41 5:58:44
Pickens 26 1 32N53 89w58 5:59:52
Pickwick 46 1 31N10 89w50 5:59:20
Pierce Crossroads 82 1 32N51 90w24 6:01:36

MISSISSIPPI

Place		Lat.	Long.	Time
Piggtown 40	1	32N36	89w35	5:58:20
Pinckneyville 79	1	31N01	91w29	6:05:56
Pinebluff 13	1	33N44	89w04	5:56:16
Pinebur 46	1	31N18	89w50	5:59:20
Pinedale 73	1	34N28	89w14	5:56:56
Pine Flat 36	1	34N09	89w38	5:58:32
Pinegrove 5	1	34N37	89w11	5:56:44
Pine Grove 18	1	31N18	89w18	5:57:12
Pine Grove 41	1	34N07	88w43	5:54:52
Pine Grove 70	1	34N40	88w34	5:54:16
Pine Ridge 1	1	31N34	91w22	6:05:28
Pine Ridge 37	1	31N09	89w24	5:57:36
Pine Valley 81	1	34N09	89w38	5:58:32
Pineview 34	1	31N42	89w08	5:56:32
Pineville 65	1	32N22	89w28	5:57:52
Piney Woods 61	1	32N04	90w00	6:00:00
Pinola 64	1	31N53	89w58	5:59:52
Pisgah 59	1	34N46	88w32	5:54:08
Pisgah 61	1	32N16	89w59	5:59:56
Pistol Ridge 18	1	31N00	89w27	5:57:48
Pittman 46	1	31N10	89w50	5:59:20
Pittsboro 7	1	33N56	89w20	5:57:20
Plain 61	2	32N19	90w11	6:00:44
Plantersville 41	1	34N12	88w40	5:54:40
Plattsburgh 80	1	32N46	89w07	5:56:28
Pleasant Hill 15	1	31N41	90w47	6:03:08
Pleasant Hill 17	1	34N53	90w01	6:00:04
Pleasant Hill 73	1	34N29	89w01	5:56:04
Pleasant Ridge 73	1	34N38	88w50	5:55:20
Pluto 26	1	33N11	90w13	6:00:52
Plymouth 58	1	34N15	89w01	5:56:04
Poagville 69	1	34N41	89w59	5:59:56
Pocahontas 25	1	32N28	90w17	6:01:08
Pokal 64	1	31N44	89w59	5:59:56
Polfry 30	1	30N26	88w49	5:55:16
Polkville	1	32N11	89w42	5:58:48
Pollock 67	1	33N27	90w39	6:02:36
Pontotoc 58	1	34N15	89w00	5:56:00
Poolville 73	1	34N33	89w07	5:56:28
Pope 54	1	34N13	89w57	5:59:48
Poplar Corners 17	1	34N58	90w16	6:01:04
Poplar Creek 49	1	33N21	89w34	5:58:16
Poplar Springs 26	1	33N05	89w51	5:59:24
Poplar Springs 49	1	33N26	89w34	5:58:16
Poplar Springs 51	1	32N19	89w10	5:56:40
Poplarville 55	1	30N51	89w32	5:58:08
Porterville 35	1	32N41	88w28	5:53:52
Port Gibson 11	1	31N58	90w59	6:03:56
Possumneck 4	1	33N12	89w47	5:59:08
Possum Trot 58	1	34N15	89w01	5:56:04
Post 38	1	32N30	88w51	5:55:24
Potts Camp 47	1	34N39	89w18	5:57:12
Powell 14	1	34N32	90w27	6:01:48
Powers 34	1	31N42	89w08	5:56:32
Prairie 48	1	33N48	88w40	5:54:40
Prairie Point 52	1	33N09	88w24	5:53:36
Prentiss 33	1	31N36	89w52	5:59:28
Presidential Hills 25	2	32N19	90w11	6:00:44
Preston 35	1	32N53	88w50	5:55:20
Pricedale 57	1	31N17	90w18	6:01:12
Prichard 72	1	34N42	90w14	6:00:56
Prince Chapel 35	1	32N53	88w50	5:55:20
Priscilla 76	1	33N25	91w00	6:04:00
Prismatic 35	1	32N36	88w44	5:54:56
Progress 57	1	31N14	90w28	6:01:52
Prospect 51	1	32N27	89w17	5:57:08
Puckett 61	1	32N05	89w47	5:59:08
Pulaski 62	1	32N16	89w36	5:58:24
Pumpkin Center 73	1	34N29	89w01	5:56:04
Purvis 37	1	31N09	89w25	5:57:40
Pyland 9	1	33N56	89w00	5:56:00
Quentin 19	1	31N30	90w45	6:03:00
Quincy 48	1	33N55	88w22	5:53:28
Quitman 12	1	32N02	88w44	5:54:56
Quito 42	1	33N27	90w18	6:01:12
Rainey 34	1	31N30	89w17	5:57:08
Raleigh 65	1	32N02	89w32	5:58:08
Randolph 58	1	34N11	89w10	5:56:40
Rankin 61	1	32N16	89w59	5:59:56
Ras 31	1	32N05	89w15	5:57:00
Ratliff 29	1	34N26	88w40	5:54:40
Rawls Springs 18	1	31N18	89w18	5:57:12
Raworth 62	1	32N21	89w39	5:58:36
Raymond 25	1	32N16	90w25	6:01:40
Raytown 45	1	32N37	90w02	6:00:08
Red Banks 47	1	34N50	89w34	5:58:16
Reddoch 16	1	31N50	89w26	5:57:44
Red Lick 32	1	31N48	90w59	6:03:56
Redstar 43	1	31N35	90w27	6:01:48
Redwater 40	1	32N44	89w32	5:58:08
Redwood 75	1	32N29	90w48	6:03:12
Reedtown 25	1	32N06	90w37	6:02:28
Reform 10	1	33N26	89w09	5:56:36
Refuge 27	1	33N11	90w13	6:00:52
Refuge 76	1	33N25	91w00	6:04:00
Reganton	1	32N09	90w45	6:03:00
Reid 7	1	33N53	89w11	5:56:44
Remus 40	1	32N44	89w32	5:58:08
Rena Lara 14	1	34N09	90w47	6:03:08
Renfroe 40	1	32N52	89w27	5:57:48
Revive 45	1	32N42	89w50	5:59:20
Rexburg 76	1	33N24	90w54	6:03:36
Rexford 64	1	32N09	90w08	6:00:32
Rhodes 56	1	31N21	88w56	5:55:44
Riceville 24	1	30N47	89w08	5:56:32
Rich 14	1	34N25	90w27	6:01:48
Richardson 55	1	30N32	89w40	5:58:40
Richey 63	1	32N54	90w53	6:03:32
Richland 26	1	32N58	89w55	5:59:40
Richland 27	1	33N06	90w30	6:02:00
Richmond 41	1	34N12	88w40	5:54:40
Richton 56	1	31N16	88w56	5:55:44
Ridgeland 45	1	32N26	90w08	6:00:32
Rienzi 2	1	34N46	88w32	5:54:08
Ripley 70	1	34N44	88w57	5:55:48
Rising Sun 42	1	33N24	90w12	6:00:48
River Oakes 1	1	31N34	91w22	6:05:28
Riverton 14	1	34N12	90w34	6:02:16
Robbs 58	1	34N07	89w17	5:57:08
Roberts 51	1	32N14	89w14	5:56:56
Robinsonville 72	1	34N49	90w19	6:01:16
Robinwood 39	1	31N33	90w06	6:00:24
Rochdale 6	1	34N03	90w45	6:03:00
Rock Hill 2	1	34N54	88w34	5:54:16
Rock Hill 18	1	31N09	89w24	5:57:36
Rock Hill 61	1	32N16	89w59	5:59:56
Rockport 15	1	31N48	90w09	6:00:36
Rocky Hill 53	1	33N28	88w49	5:55:16
Rocky Springs 11	1	32N00	90w47	6:03:08
Rodney 32	1	31N52	91w12	6:04:48
Roebuck 42	1	33N24	90w12	6:00:48
Rogerslacy 31	1	31N47	89w02	5:56:08
Rolling Fork 63	1	32N55	90w53	6:03:32
Rome 67	1	33N58	90w29	6:01:56
Roseacres 14	1	34N22	90w31	6:02:04
Rosebloom 68	1	33N51	90w00	6:00:00
Rosedale 6	1	33N51	91w02	6:04:08
Rose Hill 31	1	32N09	89w00	5:56:00
Rosella 39	1	31N33	90w06	6:00:24
Rosemary 25	2	32N15	90w14	6:00:56
Rosetta 79	1	31N19	91w06	6:04:24
Rough Edge 58	1	34N15	89w01	5:56:04
Roundaway 14	1	34N12	90w34	6:02:16
Roundlake 6	1	34N03	90w45	6:03:00
Roxie 19	1	31N30	91w04	6:04:16
Rudyard 14	1	34N22	90w31	6:02:04
Ruleville 67	1	33N44	90w33	6:02:12
Runnelstown 56	1	31N18	89w18	5:57:12
Rural Hill 80	1	33N12	89w20	5:57:20
Russell 38	1	32N28	88w40	5:54:40
Russellville 82	1	32N20	90w52	6:03:28
Russum 11	1	31N49	91w03	6:04:12
Ruth 43	1	31N23	90w19	6:01:16
Sabino 60	1	34N15	90w17	6:01:08
Sabougla 7	1	33N45	89w22	5:57:28
Saint Ann 40	1	32N44	89w32	5:58:08
Saint Martin 30	1	30N26	88w54	5:55:36
Saints Rest 67	1	33N27	90w39	6:02:36
Salem 74	1	31N07	90w09	6:00:36
Sallis 4	1	33N01	89w46	5:59:04
Saltillo 41	1	34N23	88w41	5:54:44
Sanatorium 64	1	31N52	89w44	5:58:56
Sandersville 34	1	31N47	89w02	5:56:08
Sand Hill 15	1	31N46	90w22	6:01:28
Sand Hill 21	1	31N21	88w56	5:55:44
Sand Hill 34	1	31N36	89w12	5:56:48
Sandhill 61	1	32N29	89w53	5:59:32
Sandpoint 65	1	32N01	89w27	5:57:48
Sandtown 50	1	32N46	89w07	5:56:28
Sandy Hook 46	1	31N02	89w49	5:59:16
Sandy Springs 29	1	34N16	88w25	5:53:40
Sanford 16	1	31N29	89w26	5:57:44
Santa Rosa	1	30N26	89w39	5:58:36
Sapa 78	1	33N33	89w16	5:57:04
Sarah 69	1	34N34	90w13	6:00:52
Saratoga 64	1	31N52	89w44	5:58:56
Sardis 15	1	31N52	90w24	6:01:36
Sardis 54	1	34N26	89w55	5:59:40
Sarepta 7	1	34N07	89w17	5:57:08
Sartinsville 74	1	31N22	90w12	6:00:48
Satartia 82	1	32N40	90w33	6:02:12
Saucier 24	1	30N39	89w08	5:56:32
Saukum 79	1	31N17	91w04	6:04:16
Sauls 39	1	31N23	90w19	6:01:16
Savage 69	1	34N38	90w14	6:00:56
Savannah 55	1	30N50	89w32	5:58:08
Savoy 38	1	32N28	88w40	5:54:40
Schamberville 38	1	32N30	88w51	5:55:24
Schlater 42	1	33N39	90w21	6:01:24
Scobey 81	1	33N56	89w52	5:59:28
Scooba 35	1	32N50	88w29	5:53:56
Scotland Forks 82	1	32N39	90w22	6:01:28
Scott 6	1	33N36	91w05	6:04:20
Sebastopol 62	1	32N34	89w20	5:57:20
Sellers 23	1	30N47	89w08	5:56:32
Seminary 16	1	31N34	89w30	5:58:00
Senatobia 69	1	34N37	89w58	5:59:52
Seneca 37	1	31N00	89w27	5:57:48
Sessums 53	1	33N25	88w49	5:55:16
Seven Springs 25	1	32N15	90w25	6:01:40
Shackleford 26	1	33N11	90w13	6:00:52
Shady Grove 15	1	31N52	90w24	6:01:36
Shady Grove 34	1	31N42	89w08	5:56:32
Shannon 41	1	34N07	88w43	5:54:52
Sharkey 68	1	34N00	90w03	6:00:12
Sharon 34	1	31N42	89w08	5:56:32
Sharon 45	1	32N40	89w56	5:59:44
Sharpsburg 45	1	32N53	89w58	5:59:52
Shaw 6	1	33N36	90w47	6:03:08
Shelby 6	1	33N57	90w46	6:03:04
Shellmound 42	1	33N31	90w12	6:00:48
Shepherd 7	1	34N00	89w21	5:57:24
Sherard 14	1	34N13	90w43	6:02:52
Sherman 58	1	34N22	88w50	5:55:20
Sherwood 10	1	33N32	89w08	5:56:32
Sherwood Forest 61	1	32N16	89w59	5:59:56
Shiloh 61	1	32N19	89w47	5:59:08
Shipman 20	1	30N55	88w35	5:54:20
Shivers 64	1	31N48	89w59	5:59:56
Shrock 4	1	32N58	89w55	5:59:40
Shubuta 12	1	31N52	88w42	5:54:48
Shuford 54	1	34N15	89w56	5:59:44
Shuqualak 52	1	32N59	88w34	5:54:16
Sibleton 49	1	33N26	89w34	5:58:16
Sibley 1	1	31N23	91w24	6:05:36
Sidon 42	1	33N25	90w12	6:00:48
Signal 75	1	32N20	90w52	6:03:28
Silver City 27	1	33N06	90w30	6:02:00
Silver Creek 39	1	31N36	90w00	6:00:00
Silver Run 55	1	30N47	89w08	5:56:32
Singleton 40	1	32N44	89w32	5:58:08
Siwell 25	2	32N19	90w11	6:00:44
Skene 6	1	33N42	90w47	6:03:08
Skuna 7	1	34N00	89w21	5:57:24
Slate Spring 7	1	33N44	89w22	5:57:28
Slayden 47	1	34N57	89w27	5:57:48
Sledge 60	1	34N26	90w13	6:00:52
Sloan 45	1	32N37	90w02	6:00:08
Smedes 63	1	32N54	90w53	6:03:32
Smith 16	1	31N38	89w33	5:58:12
Smith 38	1	32N25	88w30	5:54:00
Smithdale 3	1	31N20	90w41	6:02:44
Smiths 25	1	32N20	90w36	6:02:24
Smithville 48	1	34N04	88w23	5:53:32
Smyrna 4	1	33N03	89w35	5:58:20
Smyrna 15	1	31N52	90w24	6:01:36
Snave 28	1	32N37	91w01	6:04:04
Snell 12	1	32N11	88w30	5:54:00
Snow Lake Shores 5	1	34N50	89w11	5:56:44
Society Hill 33	1	31N26	89w57	5:59:48
Somerville 42	1	33N45	90w24	6:01:36
Sonora 9	1	33N56	89w00	5:56:00
Sontag 39	1	31N39	90w12	6:00:48
Soso 34	1	31N45	89w17	5:57:08
South Amory 48	1	33N59	88w29	5:53:56
Southaven 17	1	34N59	90w01	6:00:04
Southern 18	1	31N18	89w18	5:57:12
South McComb 57	1	31N14	90w28	6:01:52
Spanish Fort 63	1	32N49	90w42	6:02:48
Sparta 9	1	33N47	89w03	5:56:12
Spay 10	1	33N12	89w20	5:57:20
Splunge 48	1	33N48	88w18	5:53:12
Spring Cottage 46	1	31N18	89w50	5:59:20
Spring Creek 50	1	32N46	89w07	5:56:28
Springdale 36	1	34N09	89w38	5:58:32
Spring Hill 5	1	34N59	89w15	5:57:00
Spring Hill 36	1	34N15	89w14	5:56:56
Springville 58	1	34N14	89w06	5:56:24
Stafford Springs 31	1	31N54	88w56	5:55:44
Stallo 50	1	32N55	89w06	5:56:24
Stampley 32	1	31N38	91w08	6:04:32
Standing Pine 40	1	32N44	89w32	5:58:08
Stanton 1	1	31N47	91w14	6:04:56
Star 61	1	32N06	90w03	6:00:12
Starkville 53	1	33N28	88w49	5:55:16
State College 53	1	33N27	88w47	5:55:08
State Line 21	1	31N26	88w28	5:53:52
Steel 62	1	32N22	89w28	5:57:52
Steens 44	1	33N34	88w19	5:53:16
Steiner 67	1	33N38	90w46	6:03:04
Stewart 49	1	33N27	89w26	5:57:44
Stokes 45	1	32N37	90w02	6:00:08
Stoneville 76	1	33N31	90w55	6:03:40
Stonewall 12	1	32N08	88w47	5:55:08
Stonewall 17	1	34N52	89w41	5:58:44
Stovall 14	1	34N18	90w39	6:02:36
Stover	1	34N03	90w17	6:01:08
Straight Bayou 63	1	32N58	90w50	6:03:20
Stratton 51	1	32N34	89w07	5:56:28
Strayhorn 69	1	34N34	90w13	6:00:52
Strengthford 77	1	31N42	89w08	5:56:32
Strickland 2	1	34N54	88w34	5:54:16
Stringer 31	1	31N52	89w16	5:57:04
Stringtown 6	1	33N34	90w59	6:03:56
Stronghope 15	1	31N46	90w22	6:01:28
Strongs 48	1	33N50	88w33	5:54:12
Sturgis 53	1	33N21	89w03	5:56:12
Sucarnochee 35	1	32N41	88w28	5:53:52
Success 24	1	30N38	89w08	5:56:32
Summerland 65	1	31N48	89w22	5:57:28
Summit 57	1	31N17	90w28	6:01:52
Sumner 68	1	33N58	90w22	6:01:28
Sumrall 37	1	31N25	89w33	5:58:12
Sunflower 67	1	33N33	90w32	6:02:08
Sunnycrest 22	1	33N47	89w48	5:59:12
Sunnyside 42	1	33N45	90w24	6:01:36
Sunrise 18	1	31N18	89w18	5:57:12
Sunrise 40	1	32N44	89w32	5:58:08
Suqualena 38	1	32N27	88w50	5:55:20
Swan Lake 68	1	33N53	90w17	6:01:08
Sweatman 49	1	33N38	89w35	5:58:20
Swiftown 42	1	33N18	90w25	6:01:40
Swiftwater 76	1	33N25	91w00	6:04:00
Sylvarena 65	1	32N01	89w23	5:57:32
Symonds 6	1	33N51	91w02	6:04:08
Tallula 28	1	32N54	90w53	6:03:32
Talowah 37	1	31N04	89w26	5:57:44
Tamola	1	32N35	88w29	5:53:56
Taska 47	1	34N50	89w34	5:58:16
Tatum 3	1	31N12	91w01	6:04:04
Taylor 36	1	34N16	89w35	5:58:20
Taylorsville 65	1	31N50	89w26	5:57:44
Tchula 26	1	33N11	90w13	6:00:52
Teasdale 68	1	34N07	89w56	5:59:44
Ted 65	1	32N05	89w15	5:57:00
Ten Mile 66	1	30N47	89w08	5:56:32
Terrell 33	1	31N36	89w52	5:59:28
Terry 25	1	32N06	90w18	6:01:12
Terza 54	1	34N19	89w57	5:59:48
Thaxton 58	1	34N18	89w11	5:56:44
Theadville 12	1	32N03	88w43	5:54:52
The Mall 75	1	32N20	90w52	6:03:28
Thomastown 40	1	32N52	89w40	5:58:40
Thomasville 61	1	32N09	90w08	6:00:32
Thompson 3	1	31N15	90w38	6:02:32
Thompsonville 25	1	31N59	90w22	6:01:28
Thorn 9	1	33N57	89w06	5:56:24
Thornton 26	1	33N05	90w19	6:01:16
Thrashers 59	1	34N43	88w32	5:54:08
Three Rivers 30	1	30N23	88w32	5:54:08
Thyatira 69	1	34N37	89w58	5:59:52

MISSISSIPPI

Tibbee 13 1 33N36 88w39 5:54:36
Tibbs 72 1 34N26 90w13 6:00:52
Tie Plant 22 1 33N44 89w47 5:59:08
Tilden 29 1 34N11 88w21 5:53:24
Tillatoba 81 1 33N59 89w54 5:59:36
Tillman 11 1 31N51 90w55 6:03:40
Tilton 39 1 31N33 90w06 6:00:24
Tinsley 82 1 32N44 90w28 6:01:52
Tiplersville 70 1 34N54 88w55 5:55:40
Tippah 5 1 34N50 89w11 5:56:44
Tippo 68 1 33N55 90w17 6:01:08
Tishomingo 71 1 34N38 88w14 5:52:56
Toccopola 58 1 34N15 89w14 5:56:56
Tocowa 54 1 34N15 89w56 5:59:44
Tomnolen 78 1 33N29 89w22 5:57:28
Toomsuba 38 1 32N25 88w31 5:54:04
Topeka 39 1 31N22 90w12 6:00:48
Topisaw 57 1 31N17 90w28 6:01:52
Topton 38 1 32N28 88w40 5:54:40
Touchstone 64 1 32N02 89w58 5:59:52
Tougaloo 25 1 32N24 90w09 6:00:36
Townsend 35 1 32N41 88w28 5:53:52
Trapp 50 1 32N46 89w07 5:56:28
Traxler 65 1 31N52 89w44 5:58:56
Trebloc 9 1 33N50 88w50 5:55:20
Tremont 29 1 34N14 88w16 5:53:04
Triangle-Hospital 24
1 30N26 88w54 5:55:36
Tribbett 76 1 33N21 90w48 6:03:12
Trinity 44 1 33N18 88w37 5:54:28
Troy 58 1 34N07 88w53 5:55:32
Truitt 45 1 32N53 89w58 5:59:52
Tucker 34 1 31N38 89w06 5:56:24
Tula 36 1 34N14 89w22 5:57:28
Tunica 72 1 34N41 90w23 6:01:32
Tupelo 41 1 34N16 88w43 5:54:52
Turnbull 79 1 31N06 91w18 6:05:12
Turnerville 1 32N01 89w12 5:56:48
Turon 29 1 34N04 88w24 5:53:36
Tuscola 40 1 32N37 89w32 5:58:08
Tutwiler 68 1 34N01 90w26 6:01:44
Twin 46 1 30N58 89w49 5:59:16
Tylertown 74 1 31N07 90w09 6:00:36
Tyro 69 1 34N35 89w42 5:58:48
Tyson 81 1 33N59 89w41 5:58:44
Union 34 1 31N36 89w12 5:56:48
Union 41 1 34N12 88w40 5:54:40
Union 51 1 32N34 89w07 5:56:28
Union 64 1 31N47 90w04 6:00:16
Union Church 32 1 31N41 90w47 6:03:08
Union Hall 43 1 31N35 90w27 6:01:48
University Of Mississippi 36
1 34N21 89w32 5:58:08
U.S. Naval Construction Batt 24
1 30N24 89w05 5:56:20
Usrytown 62 1 32N22 89w28 5:57:52
Utica 25 1 32N07 90w37 6:02:28
Utica Junior College 15
1 32N06 90w37 6:02:28
Vaiden 8 1 33N20 89w45 5:59:00
Valewood 28 1 33N02 91w02 6:04:08
Valley 82 1 32N51 90w24 6:01:36
Valley Hill 8 1 33N30 89w55 5:59:40
Valley Park 28 1 32N38 90w52 6:03:28

Value 61 1 32N17 90w00 6:00:00
Van Buren 29 1 34N05 88w37 5:54:28
Vance 60 1 34N04 90w21 6:01:24
Vancleave 30 1 30N32 88w42 5:54:48
Van Vleet 9 1 33N59 88w54 5:55:36
Van Winkle 25 2 32N19 90w11 6:00:44
Vardaman 7 1 33N53 89w11 5:56:44
Vaughan 82 1 32N48 90w03 6:00:12
Vaughn 43 1 31N35 90w27 6:01:48
Velma 81 1 34N04 89w39 5:58:36
Vernal 21 1 30N55 88w35 5:54:20
Vernon 80 1 33N07 89w03 5:56:12
Verona 41 1 34N12 88w43 5:54:52
Vestry 1 30N44 88w47 5:55:08
Vicksburg 75 1 32N21 90w53 6:03:32
Victoria 47 1 34N51 89w44 5:58:56
Vidalia 23 1 30N19 89w14 5:56:56
Villa Ridge 55 1 31N00 89w27 5:57:48
Vimville 38 1 32N28 88w40 5:54:40
Virlilia 45 1 32N37 90w02 6:00:08
Vossburg 31 1 31N56 88w56 5:55:44
Waco 67 1 33N21 90w35 6:02:20
Waddell 13 1 33N35 88w50 5:55:20
Wade 30 1 30N39 88w34 5:54:16
Wade 67 1 33N49 90w32 6:02:08
Wahalak 35 1 32N50 88w29 5:53:56
Wakefield 69 1 34N41 89w59 5:59:56
Waldrup 31 1 31N58 89w17 5:57:08
Wallerville 73 1 34N27 88w57 5:55:48
Wallhill 47 1 34N41 89w59 5:59:56
Walls 17 1 34N58 90w09 6:00:36
Walnut 60 1 34N04 90w21 6:01:24
Walnut 70 1 34N57 88w54 5:55:36
Walnut Grove 40 1 32N36 89w28 5:57:52
Walters 34 1 31N36 89w12 5:56:48
Waltersville 75 1 32N22 90w52 6:03:28
Walthall 78 1 33N37 89w17 5:57:08
Wanilla 39 1 31N39 90w08 6:00:32
Wardwell 7 1 33N53 89w11 5:56:44
Warsaw 47 1 34N52 89w41 5:58:44
Washington 1 1 31N35 91w18 6:05:12
Waterford 47 1 34N39 89w28 5:57:52
Water Oak 77 1 31N41 88w39 5:54:36
Water Valley 81 1 34N10 89w38 5:58:32
Watson 47 1 34N52 89w41 5:58:44
Wautubbee 12 1 32N10 88w50 5:55:20
Waveland 23 1 30N17 89w23 5:57:32
Waxhaw 6 1 33N57 90w56 6:03:44
Way 45 1 32N45 90w02 6:00:08
Waynesboro 77 1 31N40 88w39 5:54:36
Wayside 76 1 33N16 91w02 6:04:08
Weathersby 64 1 31N56 89w50 5:59:20
Webb 68 1 33N57 90w21 6:01:24
Weir 10 1 33N16 89w18 5:57:12
Wells Town 39 1 31N00 89w27 5:57:48
Wenasoga 2 1 34N59 88w36 5:54:24
Wesson 15 1 31N42 90w24 6:01:36
West 26 1 33N12 89w47 5:59:08
West 38 1 32N28 88w40 5:54:40
West Biloxi 24 1 30N25 88w55 5:55:40
West Days 17 1 34N54 90w13 6:00:52
West Gulfport 24 1 30N24 89w05 5:56:20
West Jackson 25 2 32N19 90w11 6:00:44
Westland 25 2 32N19 90w11 6:00:44

West Lincoln 43 1 31N35 90w27 6:01:48
West Point 13 1 33N36 88w39 5:54:36
West Poplarville 55
1 30N50 89w32 5:58:08
Westside 11 1 31N58 90w59 6:03:56
West Union 73 1 34N33 89w07 5:56:28
Wheeler 59 1 34N35 88w37 5:54:28
Whistle 77 1 31N41 88w39 5:54:36
White Apple 19 1 31N27 91w04 6:04:16
Whitebluff 46 1 31N10 89w50 5:59:20
White Cap 3 1 31N12 91w01 6:04:04
Whitehead 68 1 33N50 90w18 6:01:12
Whites 13 1 33N36 88w39 5:54:36
Whites 61 1 32N09 90w08 6:00:32
Whitesand 33 1 31N44 89w59 5:59:56
White Sand 55 1 33N41 88w19 5:53:16
Whites Crossing 66
1 30N51 89w08 5:56:32
Whitfield 34 1 31N29 89w02 5:56:08
Whitney 67 1 33N49 90w32 6:02:08
Whynot 38 1 32N28 88w40 5:54:40
Wickware 51 1 32N19 89w10 5:56:40
Wiggins 40 1 32N44 89w32 5:58:08
Wiggins 66 1 30N51 89w08 5:56:32
Wilkinson 79 1 31N13 91w14 6:04:56
Willet 76 1 33N11 90w51 6:03:24
Williamsburg 16 1 31N37 89w37 5:58:28
Williamsville 4 1 33N03 89w35 5:58:20
Williamsville 50 1 32N46 89w07 5:56:28
Willis Heights 41 1 34N15 88w43 5:54:52
Willowood 25 2 32N19 90w11 6:00:44
Willows 11 1 31N58 90w59 6:03:56
Wiltshire 8 1 33N20 89w45 5:59:00
Winborn 5 1 34N38 89w16 5:57:04
Winchester 77 1 31N37 88w35 5:54:20
Windsor Park 30 1 30N26 88w49 5:55:16
Wingate 56 1 31N13 89w01 5:56:04
Winona 49 1 33N29 89w44 5:58:56
Winstonville 6 1 33N55 90w45 6:03:00
Winterville 76 1 33N30 91w04 6:04:16
Wolf Springs 38 1 32N28 88w40 5:54:40
Woodburn 67 1 33N27 90w39 6:02:36
Woodland 9 1 33N47 89w03 5:56:12
Woodland 58 1 34N15 89w01 5:56:04
Woodland Lake 17 1 34N50 89w59 5:59:56
Woodville 79 1 31N06 91w18 6:05:12
Woodwards 77 1 31N41 88w39 5:54:36
Wool Market 24 1 30N29 89w01 5:56:04
Wortham 24 1 30N38 89w08 5:56:32
Wren 48 1 33N50 88w33 5:54:12
Wright 6 1 33N51 91w02 6:04:08
Wyatte 69 1 34N39 89w41 5:58:44
Yazoo City 82 1 32N51 90w25 6:01:40
Yocona 36 1 34N22 89w31 5:58:04
Yokena 75 1 32N20 90w52 6:03:28
Youngs 22 1 33N59 89w41 5:58:44
Zama 4 1 32N59 89w23 5:57:32
Zemuly 4 1 33N01 89w46 5:59:04
Zero 38 1 32N28 88w40 5:54:40
Zetus 43 1 31N35 90w27 6:01:48
Zieglerville 82 1 32N50 90w15 6:01:00
Zion 58 1 34N15 89w01 5:56:04
Zumbro 6 1 33N44 90w43 6:02:52

TIME TABLES

MO # 1

Before 11/18/1883		LMT
11/18/1883	12:00	CST
3/31/1918	02:00	CWT
10/27/1918	02:00	CST
3/30/1919	02:00	CWT
10/26/1919	02:00	CST
2/09/1942	02:00	CWT
9/30/1945	02:00	CST
4/28/1946	02:00	CDT
9/29/1946	02:00	CST
4/27/1947	02:00	CDT
9/28/1947	02:00	CST
4/25/1948	02:00	CDT
9/26/1948	02:00	CST
4/24/1949	02:00	CDT
9/25/1949	02:00	CST
4/30/1950	02:00	CDT
9/24/1950	02:00	CST
4/29/1951	02:00	CDT
9/30/1951	02:00	CST
4/27/1952	02:00	CDT
9/28/1952	02:00	CST
4/26/1953	02:00	CDT
9/27/1953	02:00	CST
4/25/1954	02:00	CDT
9/26/1954	02:00	CST
4/24/1955	02:00	CDT
9/25/1955	02:00	CST
4/29/1956	02:00	CDT
10/28/1956	02:00	CST
4/28/1957	02:00	CDT
10/27/1957	02:00	CST
4/27/1958	02:00	CDT
10/26/1958	02:00	CST
4/26/1959	02:00	CDT
10/25/1959	02:00	CST
4/24/1960	02:00	CDT
10/30/1960	02:00	CST
4/30/1961	02:00	CDT
10/29/1961	02:00	CST
4/29/1962	02:00	CDT
10/28/1962	02:00	CST
4/28/1963	02:00	CDT
10/27/1963	02:00	CST
4/26/1964	02:00	CDT
10/25/1964	02:00	CST
4/25/1965	02:00	CDT
10/31/1965	02:00	CST
4/24/1966	02:00	CDT
10/30/1966	02:00	CST
4/30/1967	02:00	US#1

MO # 2

Before 11/18/1883		LMT
11/18/1883	12:00	CST
3/31/1918	02:00	CWT
10/27/1918	02:00	CST
3/30/1919	02:00	CWT
10/26/1919	02:00	CST
2/09/1942	02:00	CWT
9/30/1945	02:00	CST
4/27/1947	02:00	CDT
9/28/1947	02:00	CST
4/25/1948	02:00	CDT
9/26/1948	02:00	CST
4/24/1949	02:00	CDT
9/25/1949	02:00	CST
4/30/1950	02:00	CDT
9/24/1950	02:00	CST
4/29/1951	02:00	CDT
9/30/1951	02:00	CST
4/27/1952	02:00	CDT
9/28/1952	02:00	CST
4/26/1953	02:00	CDT
9/27/1953	02:00	CST
4/25/1954	02:00	CDT
9/26/1954	02:00	CST
4/24/1955	02:00	CDT
9/25/1955	02:00	CST
4/29/1956	02:00	CDT
9/30/1956	02:00	CST
4/28/1957	02:00	MO#1
4/30/1967	02:00	US#1

MO # 3

Before 11/18/1883		LMT
11/18/1883	12:00	CST
3/31/1918	02:00	CWT
10/27/1918	02:00	CST
3/30/1919	02:00	CWT
10/26/1919	02:00	CST
2/09/1942	02:00	CWT
9/30/1945	02:00	CST
4/30/1967	02:00	US#1

MO # 4

Before 11/18/1883		LMT
11/18/1883	12:00	CST
3/31/1918	02:00	CWT
10/27/1918	02:00	CST
3/30/1919	02:00	CWT
10/26/1919	02:00	CST
2/09/1942	02:00	CWT
9/30/1945	02:00	CST
4/24/1949	02:00	CDT
9/25/1949	02:00	CST
4/26/1953	02:00	CDT
9/27/1953	02:00	CST
4/27/1958	02:00	CDT
10/26/1958	02:00	CST
4/29/1962	02:00	MO#1
4/30/1967	02:00	US#1

MO # 5

Before 11/18/1883		LMT
11/18/1883	12:00	CST
3/31/1918	02:00	CWT
10/27/1918	02:00	CST
3/30/1919	02:00	CWT
10/26/1919	02:00	CST
2/09/1942	02:00	CWT
9/30/1945	02:00	CST
4/25/1954	02:00	CDT
9/26/1954	02:00	CST
4/24/1955	02:00	CDT
9/25/1955	02:00	CST
4/29/1956	02:00	CDT
9/30/1956	02:00	CST
4/28/1957	02:00	CDT
10/27/1957	02:00	CST
4/27/1958	02:00	CDT
10/26/1958	02:00	CST
4/26/1959	02:00	CDT
10/25/1959	02:00	CST
4/30/1967	02:00	US#1

MO # 6

Before 11/18/1883		LMT
11/18/1883	12:00	CST
3/31/1918	02:00	CWT
10/27/1918	02:00	CST
3/30/1919	02:00	CWT
10/26/1919	02:00	CST
2/09/1942	02:00	CWT
9/30/1945	02:00	CST
4/25/1954	02:00	CDT
9/26/1954	02:00	CST
4/29/1956	02:00	MO#1
4/30/1967	02:00	US#1

MO # 7

Before 11/18/1883		LMT
11/18/1883	12:00	CST
3/31/1918	02:00	CWT
10/27/1918	02:00	CST
3/30/1919	02:00	CWT
10/26/1919	02:00	CST
2/09/1942	02:00	CWT
9/30/1945	02:00	CST
4/25/1954	02:00	CDT
9/26/1954	02:00	CST
4/26/1964	02:00	MO#1
4/30/1967	02:00	US#1

MO # 8

Before 11/18/1883		LMT
11/18/1883	12:00	CST
3/31/1918	02:00	CWT
10/27/1918	02:00	CST
3/30/1919	02:00	CWT
10/26/1919	02:00	CST
2/09/1942	02:00	CWT
9/30/1945	02:00	CST
4/24/1955	02:00	MO#2
4/30/1967	02:00	US#1

MO # 9

Before 11/18/1883		LMT
11/18/1883	12:00	CST
3/31/1918	02:00	CWT
10/27/1918	02:00	CST
3/30/1919	02:00	CWT
10/26/1919	02:00	CST
2/09/1942	02:00	CWT
9/30/1945	02:00	CST
4/29/1956	02:00	CDT
9/30/1956	02:00	CST
4/30/1967	02:00	US#1

MO # 10

Before 11/18/1883		LMT
11/18/1883	12:00	CST
3/31/1918	02:00	CWT
10/27/1918	02:00	CST
3/30/1919	02:00	CWT
10/26/1919	02:00	CST
2/09/1942	02:00	CWT
9/30/1945	02:00	CST
4/29/1956	02:00	CDT
9/30/1956	02:00	CST
4/28/1957	02:00	CDT
10/27/1957	02:00	CST
4/24/1966	02:00	CDT
10/30/1966	02:00	CST
4/30/1967	02:00	US#1

MO # 11

Before 11/18/1883		LMT
11/18/1883	12:00	CST
3/31/1918	02:00	CWT
10/27/1918	02:00	CST
3/30/1919	02:00	CWT
10/26/1919	02:00	CST
2/09/1942	02:00	CWT
9/30/1945	02:00	CST
4/29/1956	02:00	CDT
9/30/1956	02:00	CST
4/27/1958	02:00	CDT
10/26/1958	02:00	CST
4/30/1967	02:00	US#1

MO # 12

Before 11/18/1883		LMT
11/18/1883	12:00	CST
3/31/1918	02:00	CWT
10/27/1918	02:00	CST
3/30/1919	02:00	CWT
10/26/1919	02:00	CST
2/09/1942	02:00	CWT
9/30/1945	02:00	CST
4/29/1956	02:00	MO#2
4/30/1967	02:00	US#1

MO # 13

Before 11/18/1883		LMT
11/18/1883	12:00	CST
3/31/1918	02:00	CWT
10/27/1918	02:00	CST
3/30/1919	02:00	CWT
10/26/1919	02:00	CST
2/09/1942	02:00	CWT
9/30/1945	02:00	CST
4/27/1958	02:00	CDT
10/26/1958	02:00	CST
4/30/1967	02:00	US#1

MO # 14

Before 11/18/1883		LMT
11/18/1883	12:00	CST
3/31/1918	02:00	CWT
10/27/1918	02:00	CST
3/30/1919	02:00	CWT
10/26/1919	02:00	CST
2/09/1942	02:00	CWT
9/30/1945	02:00	CST
4/26/1959	02:00	CDT
10/25/1959	02:00	CST
4/24/1960	02:00	CDT
10/30/1960	02:00	CST
4/29/1962	02:00	CDT
10/28/1962	02:00	CST
4/28/1963	02:00	CDT
10/27/1963	02:00	CST
4/26/1964	02:00	CDT
10/25/1964	02:00	CST
4/24/1966	02:00	US#1

MO # 15

Before 11/18/1883		LMT
11/18/1883	12:00	CST
3/31/1918	02:00	CWT
10/27/1918	02:00	CST
3/30/1919	02:00	CWT
10/26/1919	02:00	CST
2/09/1942	02:00	CWT
9/30/1945	02:00	CST
4/26/1959	02:00	CDT
10/25/1959	02:00	CST
4/28/1963	02:00	MO#1
4/30/1967	02:00	US#1

MO # 16

Before 11/18/1883		LMT
11/18/1883	12:00	CST
3/31/1918	02:00	CWT
10/27/1918	02:00	CST
3/30/1919	02:00	CWT
10/26/1919	02:00	CST
2/09/1942	02:00	CWT
9/30/1945	02:00	CST
4/26/1959	02:00	MO#1
4/30/1967	02:00	US#1

MO # 17

Before 11/18/1883		LMT
11/18/1883	12:00	CST
3/31/1918	02:00	CWT
10/27/1918	02:00	CST
3/30/1919	02:00	CWT
10/26/1919	02:00	CST
2/09/1942	02:00	CWT
9/30/1945	02:00	CST
4/24/1960	02:00	MO#1
4/30/1967	02:00	US#1

MO # 18

Before 11/18/1883		LMT
11/18/1883	12:00	CST
3/31/1918	02:00	CWT
10/27/1918	02:00	CST
3/30/1919	02:00	CWT
10/26/1919	02:00	CST
2/09/1942	02:00	CWT
9/30/1945	02:00	CST
4/24/1960	02:00	CDT
10/30/1960	02:00	CST
4/28/1963	02:00	CDT
10/27/1963	02:00	CST
4/30/1967	02:00	US#1

MO # 19

Before 11/18/1883		LMT
11/18/1883	12:00	CST
3/31/1918	02:00	CWT
10/27/1918	02:00	CST
3/30/1919	02:00	CWT
10/26/1919	02:00	CST
2/09/1942	02:00	CWT
9/30/1945	02:00	CST
4/25/1965	02:00	CDT
10/31/1965	02:00	CST
4/30/1967	02:00	US#1

MO # 20

Before 11/18/1883		LMT
11/18/1883	12:00	CST
3/31/1918	02:00	CWT
10/27/1918	02:00	CST
3/30/1919	02:00	CWT
10/26/1919	02:00	CST
2/09/1942	02:00	CWT
9/30/1945	02:00	CST
4/25/1965	02:00	CDT
9/05/1965	02:00	CST
4/24/1966	02:00	US#1

MO # 21

Before 11/18/1883		LMT
11/18/1883	12:00	CST
3/31/1918	02:00	CWT
10/27/1918	02:00	CST
3/30/1919	02:00	CWT
10/26/1919	02:00	CST
2/09/1942	02:00	CWT
9/30/1945	02:00	CST
4/29/1962	02:00	CDT
9/30/1962	02:00	CST
4/28/1963	02:00	CDT
9/08/1963	02:00	CST
4/26/1964	02:00	CDT
9/06/1964	02:00	CST
4/25/1965	02:00	CDT
10/03/1965	02:00	CST
4/24/1966	02:00	US#1

MO # 22

Before 11/18/1883		LMT
11/18/1883	12:00	CST
3/31/1918	02:00	CWT
10/27/1918	02:00	CST
3/30/1919	02:00	CWT
10/26/1919	02:00	CST
2/09/1942	02:00	CWT
9/30/1945	02:00	CST
4/28/1963	02:00	CDT
9/08/1963	02:00	CST
4/26/1964	02:00	CDT
9/28/1964	02:00	CST
4/30/1967	02:00	US#1

MO # 23

Before 11/18/1883		LMT
11/18/1883	12:00	CST
3/31/1918	02:00	CWT
10/27/1918	02:00	CST
3/30/1919	02:00	CWT
10/26/1919	02:00	CST
2/09/1942	02:00	CWT
9/30/1945	02:00	CST
4/30/1961	02:00	CDT
10/29/1961	02:00	CST
4/29/1962	02:00	CDT
10/28/1962	02:00	CST
4/28/1963	02:00	CDT
8/31/1963	02:00	CST
4/26/1964	02:00	CDT
8/29/1964	02:00	CST
4/30/1967	02:00	US#1

MO # 24

Before 11/18/1883		LMT
11/18/1883	12:00	CST
3/31/1918	02:00	CWT
10/27/1918	02:00	CST
3/30/1919	02:00	CWT
10/26/1919	02:00	CST
2/09/1942	02:00	CWT
9/30/1945	02:00	CST
4/24/1960	02:00	CDT
10/30/1960	02:00	CST
4/29/1962	02:00	CDT
9/30/1962	02:00	CST
4/28/1963	02:00	CDT
9/08/1963	02:00	CST
4/26/1964	02:00	CDT
9/06/1964	02:00	CST
4/25/1965	02:00	CDT
10/03/1965	02:00	CST
4/24/1966	02:00	US#1

MO # 25

Before 11/18/1883		LMT
11/18/1883	12:00	CST
3/31/1918	02:00	CWT
10/27/1918	02:00	CST
3/30/1919	02:00	CWT
10/26/1919	02:00	CST
2/09/1942	02:00	CWT
9/30/1945	02:00	CST
4/24/1960	02:00	CDT
10/30/1960	02:00	CST
4/29/1962	02:00	CDT
9/30/1962	02:00	CST
4/28/1963	02:00	CDT
10/26/1963	02:00	CST
4/26/1964	02:00	MO#1
4/30/1967	02:00	US#1

MO # 26

Before 11/18/1883		LMT
11/18/1883	12:00	CST
3/31/1918	02:00	CWT
10/27/1918	02:00	CST
3/30/1919	02:00	CWT
10/26/1919	02:00	CST
2/09/1942	02:00	CWT
9/30/1945	02:00	CST
4/28/1963	02:00	CDT
9/01/1963	02:00	CST
5/01/1964	02:00	CDT
9/01/1964	02:00	CST
5/07/1965	02:00	CDT
9/05/1965	02:00	CST
4/24/1966	02:00	US#1

MO # 27

Before 11/18/1883		LMT
11/18/1883	12:00	CST
3/31/1918	02:00	CWT
10/27/1918	02:00	CST
3/30/1919	02:00	CWT
10/26/1919	02:00	CST
2/09/1942	02:00	CWT
9/30/1945	02:00	CST
4/24/1960	02:00	CDT
10/30/1960	02:00	CST
4/30/1961	02:00	CDT
9/10/1961	02:00	CST
4/29/1962	02:00	CDT
9/09/1962	02:00	CST
4/28/1963	02:00	CDT
9/08/1963	02:00	CST
4/26/1964	02:00	CDT
9/13/1964	02:00	CST
4/25/1965	02:00	CDT
9/12/1965	02:00	CST
4/24/1966	02:00	CDT
9/11/1966	02:00	CST
4/30/1967	02:00	US#1

MO # 28

Before 11/18/1883		LMT
11/18/1883	12:00	CST
3/31/1918	02:00	CWT
10/27/1918	02:00	CST
3/30/1919	02:00	CWT
10/26/1919	02:00	CST
2/09/1942	02:00	CWT
9/30/1945	02:00	CST
4/26/1964	02:00	CDT
10/31/1964	02:00	CST
4/25/1965	02:00	MO#1
4/30/1967	02:00	US#1

MO # 29

Before 11/18/1883		LMT
11/18/1883	12:00	CST
3/31/1918	02:00	CWT
10/27/1918	02:00	CST
3/30/1919	02:00	CWT
10/26/1919	02:00	CST
2/09/1942	02:00	CWT
9/30/1945	02:00	CST
4/26/1964	02:00	CDT
9/06/1964	02:00	CST
4/30/1967	02:00	US#1

MO # 30

Before 11/18/1883		LMT
11/18/1883	12:00	CST
3/31/1918	02:00	CWT
10/27/1918	02:00	CST
3/30/1919	02:00	CWT
10/26/1919	02:00	CST
2/09/1942	02:00	CWT
9/30/1945	02:00	CST
4/30/1961	02:00	CDT
10/29/1961	02:00	CST
5/20/1962	02:00	CDT
8/25/1962	02:00	CST
5/19/1963	02:00	CDT
8/25/1963	02:00	CST
5/17/1964	02:00	CDT
9/01/1964	02:00	CST
5/23/1965	02:00	CDT
9/04/1965	02:00	CST
4/24/1966	02:00	US#1

MO # 31

Before 11/18/1883		LMT
11/18/1883	12:00	CST
3/31/1918	02:00	CWT
10/27/1918	02:00	CST
3/30/1919	02:00	CWT
10/26/1919	02:00	CST
2/09/1942	02:00	CWT
9/30/1945	02:00	CST
4/25/1954	02:00	CDT
9/26/1954	02:00	CST
4/28/1963	02:00	MO#1
4/30/1967	02:00	US#1

MO # 32

Before 11/18/1883		LMT
11/18/1883	12:00	CST
3/31/1918	02:00	CWT
10/27/1918	02:00	CST
3/30/1919	02:00	CWT
10/26/1919	02:00	CST
2/09/1942	02:00	CWT
9/30/1945	02:00	CST
5/17/1964	02:00	CDT
9/01/1964	02:00	CST
5/23/1965	02:00	CDT
8/22/1965	02:00	CST
5/22/1966	02:00	CDT
8/27/1966	02:00	CST
4/30/1967	02:00	US#1

MO # 33

Before 11/18/1883		LMT
11/18/1883	12:00	CST
3/31/1918	02:00	CWT
10/27/1918	02:00	CST
3/30/1919	02:00	CWT
10/26/1919	02:00	CST
2/09/1942	02:00	CWT
9/30/1945	02:00	CST
4/29/1962	02:00	CDT

TIME TABLES

9/09/1962 02:00 CST
4/28/1963 02:00 CDT
9/29/1963 02:00 CST
5/17/1964 02:00 CDT
9/01/1964 02:00 CST
4/25/1965 02:00 CDT
10/31/1965 02:00 CST
4/24/1966 02:00 CDT
9/24/1966 02:00 CST
4/30/1967 02:00 US#1

....

MO # 34
Before 11/18/1883 LMT
11/18/1883 12:00 CST
3/31/1918 02:00 CWT
10/27/1918 02:00 CST
3/30/1919 02:00 CWT
10/26/1919 02:00 CST
2/09/1942 02:00 CWT
9/30/1945 02:00 CST
4/28/1963 02:00 CDT
10/27/1963 02:00 CST
5/18/1964 02:00 CDT
9/01/1964 02:00 CST
5/22/1965 02:00 CDT
8/28/1965 02:00 CST
4/24/1966 02:00 CDT
10/30/1966 02:00 CST
4/30/1967 02:00 US#1

....

MO # 35
Before 11/18/1883 LMT
11/18/1883 12:00 CST
3/31/1918 02:00 CWT
10/27/1918 02:00 CST
3/30/1919 02:00 CWT
10/26/1919 02:00 CST
2/09/1942 02:00 CWT
9/30/1945 02:00 CST
4/30/1961 02:00 CDT
9/09/1961 02:00 CST
4/29/1962 02:00 CDT
9/30/1962 02:00 CST
4/28/1963 02:00 CDT
9/08/1963 02:00 CST
4/26/1964 02:00 CDT
9/28/1964 02:00 CST
4/25/1965 02:00 MO#1
4/30/1967 02:00 US#1

....

MO # 36
Before 11/18/1883 LMT
11/18/1883 12:00 CST
3/31/1918 02:00 CWT
10/27/1918 02:00 CST
3/30/1919 02:00 CWT
10/26/1919 02:00 CST
2/09/1942 02:00 CWT
9/30/1945 02:00 CST
4/25/1965 02:00 CDT
9/05/1965 02:00 CST
4/24/1966 02:00 CDT
10/30/1966 02:00 CST
4/30/1967 02:00 US#1

....

MO # 37
Before 11/18/1883 LMT
11/18/1883 12:00 CST
3/31/1918 02:00 CWT
10/27/1918 02:00 CST
3/30/1919 02:00 CWT
10/26/1919 02:00 CST
2/09/1942 02:00 CWT
9/30/1945 02:00 CST
4/24/1960 02:00 CDT
10/30/1960 02:00 CST
4/29/1962 02:00 CDT
9/02/1962 02:00 CST
4/26/1964 02:00 CDT
9/06/1964 02:00 CST
4/25/1965 02:00 CDT
9/05/1965 02:00 CST
4/24/1966 02:00 CDT
9/04/1966 02:00 CST
4/30/1967 02:00 US#1

....

MO # 38
Before 11/18/1883 LMT
11/18/1883 12:00 CST
3/31/1918 02:00 CWT
10/27/1918 02:00 CST
3/30/1919 02:00 CWT
10/26/1919 02:00 CST
2/09/1942 02:00 CWT
9/30/1945 02:00 CST
4/28/1963 02:00 CDT
9/29/1963 02:00 CST
4/26/1964 02:00 CDT
9/27/1964 02:00 CST
4/30/1965 02:00 CDT
10/31/1965 02:00 CST
4/24/1966 02:00 US#1

....

MO # 39
Before 11/18/1883 LMT
11/18/1883 12:00 CST
3/31/1918 02:00 CWT
10/27/1918 02:00 CST
3/30/1919 02:00 CWT
10/26/1919 02:00 CST
2/09/1942 02:00 CWT
9/30/1945 02:00 CST
4/24/1960 02:00 CDT
10/30/1960 02:00 CST
4/29/1962 02:00 CDT
9/09/1962 02:00 CST
4/28/1963 02:00 CDT
9/08/1963 02:00 CST
4/26/1964 02:00 CDT
9/13/1964 02:00 CST
4/25/1965 02:00 CDT
9/05/1965 02:00 CST
4/24/1966 02:00 CDT
9/11/1966 02:00 CST
4/30/1967 02:00 US#1

....

MO # 40
Before 11/18/1883 LMT
11/18/1883 12:00 CST
3/31/1918 02:00 CWT
10/27/1918 02:00 CST
3/30/1919 02:00 CWT
10/26/1919 02:00 CST
2/09/1942 02:00 CWT
9/30/1945 02:00 CST
4/28/1963 02:00 MO#1
4/30/1967 02:00 US#1

....

MO # 41
Before 11/18/1883 LMT
11/18/1883 12:00 CST
3/31/1918 02:00 CWT
10/27/1918 02:00 CST
3/30/1919 02:00 CWT
10/26/1919 02:00 CST
2/09/1942 02:00 CWT
9/30/1945 02:00 CST
4/28/1963 02:00 CDT
9/08/1963 02:00 CST
4/26/1964 02:00 CDT
9/13/1964 02:00 CST
4/30/1967 02:00 US#1

....

MO # 42
Before 11/18/1883 LMT
11/18/1883 12:00 CST
3/31/1918 02:00 CWT
10/27/1918 02:00 CST
3/30/1919 02:00 CWT
10/26/1919 02:00 CST
2/09/1942 02:00 CWT
9/30/1945 02:00 CST
4/28/1963 02:00 CDT
9/29/1963 02:00 CST
4/30/1965 02:00 CDT
10/31/1965 02:00 CST
4/24/1966 02:00 US#1

....

MO # 43
Before 11/18/1883 LMT
11/18/1883 12:00 CST
3/31/1918 02:00 CWT
10/27/1918 02:00 CST
3/30/1919 02:00 CWT
10/26/1919 02:00 CST
2/09/1942 02:00 CWT
9/30/1945 02:00 CST
5/20/1962 02:00 CDT
8/25/1962 02:00 CST
5/15/1964 02:00 CDT
9/01/1964 02:00 CST
4/25/1965 02:00 CDT
9/05/1965 02:00 CST
4/24/1966 02:00 US#1

....

MO # 44
Before 11/18/1883 LMT
11/18/1883 12:00 CST
3/31/1918 02:00 CWT
10/27/1918 02:00 CST
3/30/1919 02:00 CWT
10/26/1919 02:00 CST
2/09/1942 02:00 CWT
9/30/1945 02:00 CST
4/24/1966 02:00 US#1

....

MO # 45
Before 11/18/1883 LMT
11/18/1883 12:00 CST
3/31/1918 02:00 CWT
10/27/1918 02:00 CST
3/30/1919 02:00 CWT
10/26/1919 02:00 CST
2/09/1942 02:00 CWT
9/30/1945 02:00 CST
4/24/1966 02:00 CDT
9/05/1966 02:00 CST
4/30/1967 02:00 US#1

....

MO # 46
Before 11/18/1883 LMT
11/18/1883 12:00 CST
3/31/1918 02:00 CWT
10/27/1918 02:00 CST
3/30/1919 02:00 CWT
10/26/1919 02:00 CST
2/09/1942 02:00 CWT
9/30/1945 02:00 CST
4/26/1965 02:00 MO#1
4/30/1967 02:00 US#1

....

MO # 47
Before 11/18/1883 LMT
11/18/1883 12:00 CST
3/31/1918 02:00 CWT
10/27/1918 02:00 CST
3/30/1919 02:00 CWT
10/26/1919 02:00 CST
2/09/1942 02:00 CWT
9/30/1945 02:00 CST
4/29/1956 02:00 CDT
9/30/1956 02:00 CST
4/24/1966 02:00 US#1

....

MO # 48
Before 11/18/1883 LMT
11/18/1883 12:00 CST
3/31/1918 02:00 CWT
10/27/1918 02:00 CST
3/30/1919 02:00 CWT
10/26/1919 02:00 CST
2/09/1942 02:00 CWT
9/30/1945 02:00 CST
5/08/1956 02:00 CDT
9/30/1956 02:00 CST
4/30/1967 02:00 US#1

....

MO # 49
Before 11/18/1883 LMT
11/18/1883 12:00 CST
3/31/1918 02:00 CWT
10/27/1918 02:00 CST
3/30/1919 02:00 CWT
10/26/1919 02:00 CST
2/09/1942 02:00 CWT
9/30/1945 02:00 CST
4/26/1964 02:00 CDT
10/25/1964 02:00 CST
4/30/1967 02:00 US#1

COUNTIES

1 Adair
2 Andrew
3 Atchison
4 Audrain
5 Barry
6 Barton
7 Bates
8 Benton
9 Bollinger
10 Boone
11 Buchanan
12 Butler
13 Caldwell
14 Callaway
15 Camden
16 Cape Girardeau
17 Carroll
18 Carter
19 Cass
20 Cedar
21 Chariton
22 Christian
23 Clark
24 Clay
25 Clinton
26 Cole
27 Cooper
28 Crawford
29 Dade
30 Dallas
31 Daviess
32 Dekalb
33 Dent
34 Douglas
35 Dunklin
36 Franklin
37 Gasconade
38 Gentry
39 Greene
40 Grundy
41 Harrison
42 Henry
43 Hickory
44 Holt
45 Howard
46 Howell
47 Iron
48 Jackson
49 Jasper
50 Jefferson
51 Johnson
52 Knox
53 Laclede
54 Lafayette
55 Lawrence
56 Lewis
57 Lincoln
58 Linn
59 Livingston
60 McDonald
61 Macon
62 Madison
63 Maries
64 Marion
65 Mercer
66 Miller
67 Mississippi
68 Moniteau
69 Monroe
70 Montgomery
71 Morgan
72 New Madrid
73 Newton
74 Nodaway
75 Oregon
76 Osage
77 Ozark
78 Pemiscot
79 Perry
80 Pettis
81 Phelps
82 Pike
83 Platte
84 Polk
85 Pulaski
86 Putnam
87 Ralls
88 Randolph
89 Ray
90 Reynolds
91 Ripley
92 St Charles
93 St Clair
94 St Francois
95 St Louis
96 Ste Genevieve
97 Saline
98 Schuyler
99 Scotland
100 Scott
101 Shannon
102 Shelby
103 Stoddard
104 Stone
105 Sullivan
106 Taney
107 Texas
108 Vernon
109 Warren
110 Washington
111 Wayne
112 Webster
113 Worth
114 Wright
115 St Louis City

Abesville 104	3	36N48	93W28	6:13:52
Abo 53	47	37N41	92W40	6:10:40
Acorn Corner 78	3	36N05	89W52	5:59:28
Acornridge 103	3	36N57	90W10	6:00:40
Adair 1	3	40N09	92W23	6:09:32
Adair 15	3	38N09	92W59	6:11:56
Adrian 7	3	38N24	94W21	6:17:24
Advance 103	3	37N06	89W55	5:59:40
Affton 95	40	38N33	90W20	6:01:20
Agency 11	3	39N40	94W45	6:19:00
Agnes 53	47	37N41	92W40	6:10:40
Aid 103	3	36N53	89W56	5:59:44
Airline Acres 67	3	36N47	89W23	5:57:32
Airport 95	40	38N46	90W24	6:01:36
Alanthus 38	3	40N13	94W32	6:18:08
Alba 49	3	37N14	94W25	6:17:40
Albany 38	3	40N15	94W20	6:17:20
Albany 89	3	39N12	94W05	6:16:20
Aldrich 84	3	37N33	93W33	6:14:12
Alexander 8	3	38N08	93W26	6:13:44
Alexandria 23	20	40N27	91W28	6:05:52
Alfalfa Center 67	3	36N56	89W20	5:57:20
Algonquin 95	40	38N36	90W20	6:01:20
Allbright 62	3	37N26	90W10	6:00:40
Allen 113	3	40N26	94W17	6:17:08
Allendale 113	3	40N29	94W17	6:17:08
Allenton 95	40	38N30	90W41	6:02:44
Allenville 16	3	37N11	89W39	5:58:36
All Saints Village 92	2	38N48	90W37	6:02:28
Alma 54	3	39N06	93W33	6:14:12
Almartha 77	3	36N48	92W35	6:10:20
Almon 43	3	37N57	93W13	6:12:52
Alpha 40	3	40N02	93W22	6:13:28
Alpine 104	3	36N38	93W33	6:14:12
Altamont 31	3	39N53	94W05	6:16:20
Altenburg 79	3	37N38	89W35	5:58:20
Alton 75	3	36N42	91W24	6:05:36
Amazonia 2	3	39N53	94W54	6:19:36
Americus 70	3	38N47	91W34	6:06:16
Amity 32	3	39N52	94W26	6:17:44
Amoret 7	3	38N15	94W35	6:18:20
Amsterdam 7	3	38N21	94W35	6:18:20
Amy 46	3	36N48	92W00	6:08:00
Anabel 61	45	39N45	92W20	6:09:20
Anaconda 36	17	38N20	90W58	6:03:52
Ancell 100	3	37N13	89W31	5:58:04
Anderson 60	3	36N39	94W27	6:17:48
Annada 82	21	39N16	90W50	6:03:20
Annapolis 47	3	37N22	90W42	6:02:48
Anniston 67	3	36N50	89W20	5:57:20
Anson 23	3	40N38	91W45	6:07:00
Anthonies Mill 110	46	38N09	91W15	6:05:00
Antioch 23	30	40N25	91W43	6:06:52
Antioch 24	3	39N12	94W32	6:18:08
Antonia 50	3	38N22	90W23	6:01:32
Anutt 33	3	37N47	91W44	6:06:56
Apache Flats 26	3	38N32	92W10	6:08:40
Apple Creek 16	3	37N32	89W46	5:59:04
Applecreek 79	3	37N45	89W49	5:59:16
Appleton City 93	3	38N11	94W02	6:16:08
Aquilla 103	3	36N53	89W56	5:59:44
Arab 9	3	37N06	90W05	6:00:20
Arbela 99	3	40N28	92W01	6:08:04
Arbor 16	3	37N11	89W39	5:58:36
Arbor Terrace 95	40	38N42	90W17	6:01:08
Arbyrd 35	3	36N03	90W15	6:01:00
Arcadia 47	3	37N35	90W38	6:02:32
Archie 19	3	38N29	94W21	6:17:24
Arcola 29	3	37N33	93W53	6:15:32
Ardeola 103	3	37N06	89W55	5:59:40
Arditta 46	3	36N48	92W00	6:08:00
Ardmore 61	3	39N38	92W29	6:09:56
Argentville 57	16	39N00	90W44	6:02:56

Argo 28 46 38N09 91W15 6:05:00
Argyle 76 3 38N18 92W02 6:08:08
Arkmo 35 3 36N03 90W15 6:01:00
Arkoe 74 3 40N16 94W50 6:19:20
Arley 24 3 39N22 94W22 6:17:28
Arlington 81 3 37N56 91W57 6:07:48
Armstrong 45 3 39N16 92W42 6:10:48
Arnold 50 3 38N26 90W23 6:01:32
Aroma 73 44 36N55 94W15 6:17:00
Arroll 107 3 37N11 91W39 6:06:36
Arrowhead Beach 66
3 38N11 92W38 6:10:32
Arrow Rock 97 3 39N04 92W57 6:11:48
Arthur 108 3 38N06 94W22 6:17:28
Asbury 49 3 37N16 94W36 6:18:24
Ash 5 3 36N33 94W02 6:16:08
Ash 69 3 39N27 92W14 6:08:56
Ashburn 82 22 39N33 91W10 6:04:40
Asherville 103 3 36N57 90W10 6:00:40
Ash Grove 39 3 37N19 93W35 6:14:20
Ash Hill 12 3 36N42 90W14 6:00:56
Ashland 10 3 38N47 92W16 6:09:04
Ashley 82 3 39N15 91W13 6:04:52
Ashton 23 3 40N27 91W53 6:07:32
Aspenhoff 109 3 38N38 91W03 6:04:12
Athens 23 3 40N30 91W40 6:06:40
Athens 38 3 40N14 94W18 6:17:12
Atherton 48 3 39N06 94W26 6:17:44
Atlanta 61 3 39N54 92W29 6:09:56
Atlas 49 3 37N06 94W23 6:17:32
Auburn 57 25 39N10 90W47 6:03:08
Augusta 92 3 38N34 90W53 6:03:32
Aullville 54 3 39N01 93W41 6:14:44
Aurora 55 3 36N58 93W43 6:14:52
Aurora Springs 66 3 38N16 92W36 6:10:24
Austin 19 3 38N31 94W19 6:17:16
Auxvasse 14 3 39N01 91W54 6:07:36
Ava 34 3 36N57 92W40 6:10:40
Avalon 59 3 39N40 93W27 6:13:48
Avenue City 2 3 39N47 94W48 6:19:12
Avert 103 3 36N53 89W56 5:59:44
Avilla 49 3 37N08 94W08 6:16:32
Avon 96 3 37N47 90W25 6:01:40
Avondale 24 3 39N09 94W34 6:18:16
Azen 99 3 40N28 92W01 6:08:04
Babbtown 76 3 38N26 92W00 6:08:00
Bacon 68 3 38N48 92W28 6:09:52
Bacon 108 3 37N59 94W07 6:16:28
Baden 115 1 38N41 90W14 6:00:56
Baderville 72 3 36N36 89W37 5:58:28
Badger 108 3 37N48 94W14 6:16:56
Bado 107 3 37N08 92W06 6:08:24
Bagnell 66 3 38N14 92W36 6:10:24
Bahner 80 3 38N41 93W05 6:12:20
Baker 103 3 36N48 89W49 5:59:16
Bakersfield 77 3 36N31 92W09 6:08:36
Bakersville 78 3 36N16 89W55 5:59:40
Baldwin Lake 19 3 38N48 94W16 6:17:04
Baldwin Park 19 3 38N48 94W16 6:17:04
Ballard 7 3 38N22 94W09 6:16:36
Ballwin 95 40 38N36 90W32 6:02:08
Bancroft 31 3 40N09 93W52 6:15:28
Banner 47 3 37N41 90W44 6:02:56
Bannister 15 3 37N58 92W58 6:11:52
Bardley 75 3 36N37 90W49 6:03:16
Baring 52 3 40N15 92W12 6:08:48
Barnard 74 3 40N10 94W50 6:19:20
Barnesville 61 3 39N54 92W29 6:09:56
Barnett 71 3 38N23 92W41 6:10:44
Barnhart 50 3 38N21 90W24 6:01:36
Barren Fork 77 3 36N44 92W30 6:10:00
Barretts 95 40 38N34 90W28 6:01:52
Barry 24 3 39N16 94W33 6:18:12
Bartlett 101 3 36N59 91W25 6:05:40
Barton City 6 3 37N36 94W26 6:17:44
Barwick 13 3 39N47 94W06 6:16:24
Bates City 54 3 39N00 94W04 6:16:16
Battlefield 39 3 37N10 93W25 6:13:40
Baxter 104 3 36N34 93W30 6:14:00
Bay 37 3 38N42 91W26 6:05:44
Bayou 77 3 36N34 92W11 6:08:44
Bayshore 50 3 38N26 90W23 6:01:32
Beaman 80 3 38N41 93W05 6:12:20
Bean Lake 83 3 39N35 95W01 6:20:04
Bearcreek 20 3 37N38 93W35 6:14:20
Beaufort 36 3 38N25 91W11 6:04:44
Beauvais 96 3 37N51 90W04 6:00:16
Beaver 106 3 36N44 92W53 6:11:32
Beaver Dam 12 3 36N42 90W32 6:02:08
Beck 50 3 38N26 90W23 6:01:32
Beckville 111 3 37N09 90W42 6:02:48
Bedford 57 3 39N00 91W00 6:04:00
Bedford 59 3 39N37 93W21 6:13:24
Bedison 74 3 40N16 94W41 6:18:44
Bee Branch 21 3 39N39 92W47 6:11:08
Bee Ridge 52 3 40N05 92W07 6:08:28
Belews Creek 50 3 38N14 90W34 6:02:16
Belfast 73 44 36N52 94W22 6:17:28
Belgique 79 3 37N50 89W47 5:59:08
Belgrade 110 3 37N47 90W51 6:03:24
Bellair 27 3 38N47 92W48 6:11:12
Bella Villa 95 1 38N34 90W17 6:01:08
Bell City 103 3 37N01 89W49 5:59:16
Belle 63 3 38N17 91W43 6:06:52
Belle Center 49 3 37N04 94W30 6:18:00
Bellefontaine 95 40 38N37 90W35 6:02:20
Bellefontaine 110 3 37N59 90W41 6:02:44
Bellefontaine Neighbors 95
40 38N45 90W14 6:00:56
Bellerive 95 40 38N43 90W19 6:01:16
Bellerive Estates 95
40 38N40 90W26 6:01:44
Belleview 47 3 37N41 90W44 6:02:56
Belleville 49 3 37N04 94W30 6:18:00
Bellflower 70 3 39N00 91W21 6:05:24

Bel-Nor 95 40 38N42 90W19 6:01:16
Bel-Ridge 95 40 38N43 90W20 6:01:20
Belton 19 3 38N49 94W32 6:18:08
Belvidere 48 3 38N54 94W32 6:18:08
Bem 37 3 38N21 91W30 6:06:00
Ben Avis 95 1 38N41 90W16 6:01:04
Benbow 64 3 40N00 91W40 6:06:40
Bendavis 107 3 37N18 92W12 6:08:48
Benjamin 56 23 40N08 91W30 6:06:00
Bennett 91 3 36N39 90W58 6:03:52
Benton 100 3 37N06 89W34 5:58:16
Benton City 4 3 39N08 91W46 6:07:04
Benton Park 115 1 38N38 90W15 6:01:00
Berdell Hills 95 40 38N43 90W18 6:01:12
Berger 36 3 38N41 91W20 6:05:20
Berkeley 95 40 38N45 90W20 6:01:20
Berlin 38 3 40N05 94W30 6:18:00
Bernheimer 109 3 38N38 91W03 6:04:12
Bernie 103 3 36N40 89W58 5:59:52
Berryman 28 3 37N55 91W06 6:04:24
Bertrand 67 3 36N55 89W27 5:57:48
Berwick 73 3 36N54 94W06 6:16:24
Bessville 9 3 37N18 89W59 5:59:56
Bethany 41 3 40N16 94W02 6:16:08
Bethel 102 3 39N54 92W02 6:08:08
Bethlehem 42 3 38N19 93W41 6:14:44
Bethlehem 60 3 36N45 94W05 6:16:20
Bethpage 60 3 36N46 94W11 6:16:44
Beulah 62 3 37N17 90W38 6:02:32
Beulah 81 3 37N37 91W55 6:07:40
Beverly 83 3 39N22 94W52 6:19:28
Beverly Hills 95 40 38N42 90W17 6:01:08
Bevier 61 44 39N45 92W34 6:10:16
Biblegrove 99 3 40N15 92W13 6:08:52
Biehle 79 3 37N45 89W49 5:59:16
Big Apple 75 3 36N37 91W37 6:06:28
Bigelow 44 3 40N06 95W19 6:21:16
Big Piney 85 3 37N55 91W54 6:07:36
Big Prairie 72 3 36N46 89W33 5:58:12
Big Ridge 72 3 36N46 89W35 5:58:20
Big Spring 70 3 38N48 91W29 6:05:56
Billings 22 3 37N04 93W33 6:14:12
Billingsville 27 3 38N58 92W45 6:11:00
Billmore 75 3 36N34 91W13 6:04:52
Birch Tree 101 3 37N00 91W30 6:06:00
Birds Corners 103 3 36N48 89W49 5:59:16
Bird Springs 77 3 36N47 92W13 6:08:52
Birdtown 77 3 36N47 92W13 6:08:52
Birmingham 24 3 39N09 94W27 6:17:48
Bismarck 94 3 37N46 90W38 6:02:32
Bixby 47 3 37N40 91W07 6:04:28
Black 90 3 37N32 90W56 6:03:44
Blackburn 97 3 39N06 93W29 6:13:56
Black Creek 102 3 39N49 92W04 6:08:16
Blackjack 93 3 37N42 93W48 6:15:12
Black Jack 95 40 38N48 90W16 6:01:04
Black Pond 75 3 36N51 91W33 6:06:12
Black Walnut 92 18 38N53 90W22 6:01:28
Blackwater 27 3 38N59 92W59 6:11:56
Blackwell 94 3 38N03 90W37 6:02:28
Blairstown 42 49 38N34 93W58 6:15:52
Bland 37 3 38N18 91W38 6:06:32
Blendville 49 3 37N04 94W30 6:18:00
Bliss 110 3 38N03 90W37 6:02:28
Blodgett 100 3 37N00 89W32 5:58:08
Blomeyer 16 3 37N11 89W39 5:58:36
Bloomfield 103 3 36N53 89W56 5:59:44
Blooming Rose 81 3 37N37 91W55 6:07:40
Bloomington 11 3 39N35 94W36 6:19:44
Bloomington 61 44 39N45 92W34 6:10:16
Bloomsdale 96 3 38N01 90W13 6:00:52
Blue Branch 8 3 38N15 93W23 6:13:32
Blue Eye 104 3 36N30 93W24 6:13:36
Blue Mound 59 3 39N40 93W38 6:14:32
Blue Ridge 41 3 40N16 94W02 6:16:08
Blue Springs 48 3 39N01 94W17 6:17:08
Blue Summit 48 3 39N05 94W29 6:17:56
Blue Vue 48 3 39N00 94W28 6:17:52
Bluffton 70 3 38N43 91W31 6:06:04
Blythedale 41 3 40N29 93W56 6:15:44
Boaz 22 3 37N02 93W28 6:13:52
Boekerton 72 3 36N26 89W42 5:58:48
Bogard 17 3 39N27 93W32 6:14:08
Bogle 38 3 40N21 94W24 6:17:36
Bois Brule 79 3 37N49 89W47 5:59:08
Bois D'Arc 39 3 37N16 93W30 6:14:00
Bolckow 2 3 40N07 94W50 6:19:20
Boles 36 3 38N30 90W49 6:03:16
Bolivar 84 3 37N37 93W25 6:13:40
Bona 29 3 37N33 93W33 6:14:12
Bonanza 13 3 39N35 93W55 6:15:40
Bonham 55 3 36N58 93W43 6:14:52
Bonhomme 95 40 38N38 90W30 6:02:00
Bonne Femme 45 3 39N13 92W31 6:10:04
Bonne Terre 94 3 37N55 90W33 6:02:12
Bonnots Mill 76 3 38N35 91W58 6:07:52
Boonesboro 45 3 39N01 92W45 6:11:00
Boons Lick 45 3 39N04 92W52 6:11:28
Boonville 27 3 38N58 92W44 6:10:56
Boschertown 92 2 38N50 90W28 6:01:52
Bosky Dell 60 3 36N39 94W27 6:17:48
Boss 33 3 37N39 91W12 6:04:48
Boston 6 3 37N30 94W17 6:17:08
Bosworth 17 3 39N28 93W20 6:13:20
Boulder City 73 44 36N55 94W15 6:17:00
Boulware 37 3 38N30 91W33 6:06:12
Bourbois 37 3 38N12 91W35 6:06:20
Bourbon 28 46 38N09 91W15 6:05:00
Bowen 51 3 38N32 93W31 6:14:04
Bowers Mill 55 3 37N08 94W03 6:16:12
Bowlan 101 3 37N10 91W08 6:04:32
Bowling Green 82 3 39N21 91W12 6:04:48
Bowman 105 3 40N10 93W16 6:13:04
Box 20 3 37N49 94W00 6:16:00
Boydsville 14 3 38N51 91W57 6:07:48

Boynton 105 3 40N12 93W07 6:12:28
Boys Ranch 84 3 37N28 93W21 6:13:24
Boys Town 81 10 38N00 91W37 6:06:28
Bradfield 104 3 37N00 93W38 6:14:32
Bradleyville 106 3 36N47 92W55 6:11:40
Braggadocio 78 3 36N11 89W50 5:59:20
Bragg City 78 3 36N16 89W55 5:59:40
Braley 25 3 39N34 94W27 6:17:48
Branch 15 3 37N58 92W58 6:11:52
Brandon 8 3 38N32 93W31 6:14:04
Brandsville 46 3 36N39 91W42 6:06:48
Branson 106 3 36N39 93W13 6:12:52
Brashear 1 3 40N09 92W23 6:09:32
Brasher 78 3 36N04 89W42 5:58:48
Braymer 13 3 39N35 93W48 6:15:12
Brays 66 3 38N05 92W17 6:09:08
Brazeau 79 3 37N39 89W35 5:58:20
Brazito 26 3 38N32 92W10 6:08:40
Breckenridge 13 3 39N46 93W48 6:15:12
Breckenridge Hills 95
40 38N43 90W22 6:01:28
Breen Acres 83 3 39N13 94W40 6:18:40
Bremen 115 1 38N38 90W15 6:01:00
Brentwood 95 40 38N37 90W21 6:01:24
Breton 110 3 37N55 90W45 6:03:00
Brewer 79 3 37N45 89W49 5:59:16
Briar 91 3 36N39 90W58 6:03:52
Bridgeport 109 3 38N46 91W21 6:05:24
Bridges 77 3 36N36 92W26 6:09:44
Bridgeton 95 40 38N45 90W23 6:01:32
Bridgeton Terrace 95
40 38N45 90W23 6:01:32
Brighton 84 3 37N28 93W21 6:13:24
Brimson 40 3 40N09 93W44 6:14:56
Brinktown 63 3 38N08 92W05 6:08:20
Briscoe 57 3 38N59 90W59 6:03:56
Brixey 77 3 36N45 92W24 6:09:36
Broadway 115 1 38N41 90W14 6:00:56
Bronaugh 108 3 37N41 94W28 6:17:52
Brookdale 95 40 38N40 90W26 6:01:44
Brookfield 58 44 39N47 93W04 6:12:16
Brookline 39 3 37N09 93W25 6:13:40
Brooklyn 41 3 40N23 93W56 6:15:44
Brooklyn Heights 49
3 37N10 94W23 6:17:32
Broseley 12 3 36N40 90W15 6:01:00
Brown 34 3 36N52 92W29 6:09:56
Brownbranch 106 3 36N48 92W50 6:11:20
Brownfield 53 3 37N52 92W24 6:09:36
Browning 58 3 40N02 93W10 6:12:40
Brownington 42 3 38N15 93W43 6:14:52
Browns 10 3 38N58 92W13 6:08:52
Browns Spring 104 3 37N04 93W33 6:14:12
Brownwood 103 3 37N05 89W57 5:59:48
Brumley 66 3 38N05 92W29 6:09:56
Bruner 22 3 37N01 92W58 6:11:52
Brunot 111 3 37N17 90W38 6:02:32
Brunswick 21 3 39N26 93W08 6:12:32
Brushcreek 53 47 37N41 92W40 6:10:40
Brushyknob 34 3 36N58 92W40 6:10:40
Bryan 34 3 36N56 92W15 6:09:00
Bryson 80 3 38N37 93W25 6:13:40
Buck Donic 35 3 36N03 90W18 6:01:12
Buckeye 101 3 37N07 91W15 6:05:00
Buckhart 34 3 36N56 92W19 6:09:16
Buckhorn 62 3 37N26 90W10 6:00:40
Buckhorn 85 3 37N49 92W12 6:08:48
Bucklin 58 3 39N47 92W53 6:11:32
Buckner 48 3 39N08 94W12 6:16:48
Buck Prairie 55 3 37N00 93W39 6:14:36
Bucoda 35 3 36N08 90W10 6:00:40
Bucyrus 107 3 37N21 92W01 6:08:04
Buell 70 3 39N02 91W26 6:05:44
Buffalo 30 3 37N39 93W06 6:12:24
Buffington 103 3 36N48 89W49 5:59:16
Bunceton 27 3 38N47 92W48 6:11:12
Bunker 90 3 37N27 91W13 6:04:52
Bunker Hill 45 3 39N18 92W31 6:10:04
Burbank 111 3 37N08 90W27 6:01:48
Burdett 7 3 38N24 94W21 6:17:24
Burdine 107 3 37N07 92W05 6:08:20
Burfordville 16 3 37N22 89W48 5:59:12
Burgess 6 3 37N33 94W37 6:18:28
Burke City 95 1 38N41 90W16 6:01:04
Burlington Junction 74
3 40N27 95W04 6:20:16
Burnham 46 3 37N00 91W58 6:07:52
Burns 84 3 37N37 93W25 6:13:40
Burr 91 3 36N29 91W03 6:04:12
Burris Fork 68 3 38N30 92W31 6:10:04
Burr Oak 57 3 39N04 90W46 6:03:04
Burton 45 3 39N15 92W36 6:10:24
Burtville 51 3 38N46 93W33 6:14:12
Butcher 43 3 37N53 93W33 6:14:12
Butler 7 3 38N16 94W20 6:17:20
Butler Hill Estates 95
40 38N31 90W22 6:01:28
Butterfield 5 3 36N45 93W54 6:15:36
Butts 28 46 38N09 91W15 6:05:00
Bynumville 21 3 39N25 92W48 6:11:12
Byrd 16 3 37N23 89W41 5:58:44
Byron 76 3 38N17 91W43 6:06:52
Cabanne 115 1 38N38 90W15 6:01:00
Cabool 107 3 37N07 92W06 6:08:24
Cadet 110 3 37N59 90W41 6:02:44
Cainsville 41 3 40N26 93W46 6:15:04
Cairo 88 3 39N31 92W27 6:09:48
Caldwell 14 3 38N43 92W00 6:08:00
Caledonia 110 3 37N46 90W46 6:03:04
Calhoun 42 3 38N28 93W38 6:14:32
California 68 3 38N38 92W34 6:10:16
Callao 61 44 39N44 92W40 6:10:40
Callaway 92 3 38N45 90W52 6:03:28
Calm 75 3 36N35 91W05 6:04:20
Calumet 82 24 39N19 90W54 6:03:36

MISSOURI

Calverton Park 95 40 38N46 90w19 6:01:16
Calvey 36 3 38N24 90w47 6:03:08
Calwood 14 3 38N54 91w50 6:07:20
Cambridge 97 3 39N16 93w02 6:12:08
Camden 89 3 39N12 94w01 6:16:04
Camden Point 83 3 39N27 94w45 6:19:00
Camdenton 15 3 38N01 92w45 6:11:00
Cameron 25 3 39N44 94w14 6:16:56
Campbell 35 3 36N30 90w04 6:00:16
Campbellton 36 3 38N36 91w13 6:04:52
Camp Clark 108 3 37N51 94w21 6:17:24
Canaan 37 3 38N22 91w26 6:05:44
Canalou 72 3 36N46 89w41 5:58:44
Cane Creek 12 3 36N53 90w35 6:02:20
Cane Hill 20 3 37N29 93w41 6:14:44
Caney Creek 100 3 37N05 89w39 5:58:36
Cannon Mines 110 3 37N59 90w41 6:02:44
Canton 56 23 40N08 91w32 6:06:08
Cantwell 94 3 37N52 90w31 6:02:04
Cap Au Gris 57 16 39N00 90w44 6:02:56
Cape Fair 104 3 36N44 93w31 6:14:04
Cape Girardeau 16 3 37N19 89w32 5:58:08
Caplinger Mills 20 3 37N48 93w48 6:15:12
Cappeln 92 17 38N49 90w58 6:03:52
Capps 66 3 38N14 92w28 6:09:52
Capps Creek 5 44 36N54 94w01 6:16:04
Cardwell 35 3 36N03 90w17 6:01:08
Carl Junction 49 3 37N11 94w34 6:18:16
Carlow 31 3 39N59 93w48 6:15:12
Carmack 38 3 40N15 94w20 6:17:20
Carola 12 3 36N36 90w15 6:01:00
Carondelet 115 1 38N34 90w15 6:01:00
Carr 95 40 38N48 90w20 6:01:20
Carrington 14 3 38N51 91w57 6:07:48
Carr Lane 104 3 36N22 93w34 6:14:16
Carrollton 17 3 39N22 93w30 6:14:00
Carsonville 95 40 38N43 90w18 6:01:12
Carter 18 3 36N59 91w01 6:04:04
Carterville 49 3 37N09 94w26 6:17:44
Carthage 49 3 37N11 94w19 6:17:16
Caruth 35 3 36N14 90w03 6:00:12
Caruthersville 78 3 36N11 89w39 5:58:36
Carytown 49 3 37N08 94w20 6:17:20
Cascade 111 3 37N18 90w16 6:01:04
Case 109 3 38N42 91w26 6:05:44
Cash 61 44 39N46 92w37 6:10:28
Cassidy 22 3 37N02 93w17 6:13:08
Cassville 5 3 36N41 93w52 6:15:28
Castle Point 95 40 38N44 90w15 6:01:00
Castle Rock 49 3 37N04 94w30 6:18:00
Castlewood 95 40 38N36 90w30 6:02:00
Catawissa 36 3 38N25 90w47 6:03:08
Catherine 62 3 37N33 90w17 6:01:08
Cato 5 3 36N47 93w41 6:14:44
Catron 72 3 36N37 89w42 5:58:48
Caulfield 46 3 36N37 92w06 6:08:24
Caverna 60 3 36N26 94w20 6:17:20
Cave Spring 39 3 37N25 93w33 6:14:12
Cawood 2 3 40N07 94w49 6:19:16
Cedar Bluff 75 3 36N33 91w09 6:04:36
Cedar City 14 3 38N36 92w11 6:08:44
Cedarcreek 106 3 36N35 93w00 6:12:00
Cedar Gap 114 3 37N09 92w46 6:11:04
Cedar Hill 50 3 38N21 90w39 6:02:36
Cedar Hill Lakes 50 3 38N21 90w39 6:02:36
Cedar Ridge 30 3 37N36 92w59 6:11:56
Cedar Springs 20 3 37N52 93w54 6:15:36
Cedarville 29 3 37N37 94w01 6:16:04
Celt 30 3 37N51 93w02 6:12:08
Center 87 3 39N30 91w32 6:06:08
Centertown 26 3 38N38 92w25 6:09:40
Centerview 51 3 38N45 93w51 6:15:24
Centerville 90 3 37N26 90w58 6:03:52
Central 48 3 39N03 94w31 6:18:04
Central 115 1 38N38 90w15 6:01:00
Central City 49 3 37N04 94w30 6:18:00
Centralia 10 3 39N13 92w08 6:08:32
Centropolis 48 3 39N01 94w31 6:18:04
Chadwick 22 3 36N56 93w03 6:12:12
Chaffee 100 3 37N11 89w40 5:58:40
Chain Of Rocks 57 14 38N56 90w45 6:03:00
Chalk Level 93 3 38N09 93w48 6:15:12
Chambersburg 23 30 40N25 91w43 6:06:52
Chamois 76 3 38N41 91w46 6:07:04
Champ 95 2 38N44 90w27 6:01:48
Champion 34 3 36N56 92w22 6:09:28
Champion City 36 3 38N25 91w14 6:04:56
Chandler 24 3 39N22 94w22 6:17:28
Chapel 46 3 36N56 91w43 6:06:52
Chapel Hill 54 3 39N00 94w04 6:16:16
Chariton 86 3 40N29 93w01 6:12:04
Charity 30 3 37N31 93w01 6:12:04
Charlack 95 40 38N42 90w21 6:01:24
Charles Nagel 115 1 38N40 90w15 6:01:00
Charleston 67 3 36N55 89w21 5:57:24
Charlotte 7 3 38N16 94w28 6:17:52
Charrette 109 3 38N39 91w05 6:04:20
Charteroak 103 3 36N37 89w42 5:58:48
Cherokee Pass 62 3 37N32 90w19 6:01:16
Cherry Box 102 3 39N54 92w11 6:08:44
Cherry Valley 17 3 39N15 93w43 6:14:52
Cherry Valley Estates 39 44 37N11 93w17 6:13:08
Cherryville 28 3 37N51 91w17 6:05:08
Chesapeake 55 3 37N07 93w41 6:14:44
Chesterfield 95 40 38N40 90w35 6:02:20
Chestnutridge 22 3 36N51 93w11 6:12:44
Chicopee 18 3 37N00 91w01 6:04:04
Chilhowee 51 3 38N36 93w51 6:15:24
Chillicothe 59 3 39N48 93w33 6:14:12
Chitwood 49 3 37N04 94w30 6:18:00
Chloe 93 3 38N08 93w44 6:14:56
Chouteau 24 3 39N12 94w28 6:17:52
Chouteau 115 1 38N37 90w16 6:01:04
Christian Bechtold 115 1 38N36 90w14 6:00:56
Christopher 73 44 36N52 94w22 6:17:28
Chula 59 3 39N55 93w29 6:13:56
Cinque Hommes 79 3 37N39 89w51 5:59:24
Circle City 103 3 36N48 89w49 5:59:16
Civic Center 48 3 39N06 94w34 6:18:16
Civil Bend 31 3 40N03 94w08 6:16:32
Clapper 69 37 39N39 91w44 6:06:56
Clara 107 3 37N19 91w58 6:07:52
Clarence 102 45 39N45 92w16 6:09:04
Clark 88 3 39N17 92w21 6:09:24
Clark City 23 30 40N25 91w43 6:06:52
Clark Fork 27 3 38N51 92w42 6:10:48
Clarksburg 68 3 38N40 92w40 6:10:40
Clarksdale 32 3 39N49 94w33 6:18:12
Clarkson Valley 95 40 38N37 90w35 6:02:20
Clarksville 82 24 39N22 90w54 6:03:36
Clarkton 35 3 36N27 89w58 5:59:52
Claryville 79 3 37N45 89w49 5:59:16
Claycomo 24 3 39N12 94w30 6:18:00
Clayton 95 40 38N39 90w20 6:01:20
Clear Creek 27 3 38N50 92w56 6:11:44
Clearmont 74 3 40N31 95w02 6:20:08
Clear Spring 18 3 37N00 91w01 6:04:04
Clear Springs 107 3 37N00 91w58 6:07:52
Clearwater 96 3 37N46 90w08 6:00:32
Cleavesville 37 3 38N18 91w38 6:06:32
Cleveland 19 3 38N41 94w36 6:18:24
Clever 22 3 37N02 93w28 6:13:52
Cliff Village 73 3 37N02 94w31 6:18:04
Clifton 88 3 39N28 92w40 6:10:40
Clifton City 27 3 38N46 93w03 6:12:12
Clifton Hill 88 3 39N26 92w40 6:10:40
Climax Springs 15 3 38N06 93w03 6:12:12
Clines Island 103 3 36N48 89w49 5:59:16
Clinton 42 3 38N22 93w46 6:15:04
Cliquot 84 3 37N42 93w29 6:13:56
Clover Bottom 36 49 38N33 91w01 6:04:04
Cloverdale 30 3 37N36 92w59 6:11:56
Clubb 111 3 37N18 90w24 6:01:36
Clyde 74 3 40N16 94w40 6:18:40
Coal 42 3 38N20 93w37 6:14:28
Coatsville 98 3 40N35 92w39 6:10:36
Cobalt City 62 3 37N32 90w17 6:01:08
Cockrell 21 3 39N34 92w49 6:11:16
Cody 39 3 37N07 93w04 6:12:16
Coffey 31 3 40N06 94w00 6:16:00
Coffeyton 28 46 38N09 91w15 6:05:00
Coffman 96 3 37N47 90w12 6:00:48
Coldspring 34 3 37N06 92w25 6:09:40
Cold Spring 81 3 37N50 91w45 6:07:00
Cold Springs 8 3 38N15 93w23 6:13:32
Coldwater 111 3 37N18 90w24 6:01:36
Cole 8 3 38N19 93w12 6:12:48
Cole Camp 8 3 38N28 93w12 6:12:48
College Mound 61 3 39N38 92w29 6:09:56
Collins 93 3 37N54 93w37 6:14:28
Coloma 17 3 39N28 93w31 6:14:04
Colony 52 3 40N15 92w00 6:08:00
Columbia 10 3 38N57 92w20 6:09:20
Columbus 51 3 38N52 93w53 6:15:32
Combs 17 3 39N24 93w22 6:13:28
Commerce 100 3 37N09 89w27 5:57:48
Commerce Tower 48 3 39N03 94w31 6:18:04
Commercial 39 44 37N14 93w18 6:13:12
Como 72 3 36N35 89w50 5:59:20
Competition 53 3 37N29 92w26 6:09:44
Conception 74 3 40N13 94w41 6:18:44
Conception Junction 74 3 40N16 94w42 6:18:48
Conclay 95 40 38N38 90w22 6:01:28
Concord 14 3 39N01 91w54 6:07:36
Concord 78 3 36N14 89w45 5:59:00
Concord 95 40 38N31 90w22 6:01:28
Concord Hill 109 3 38N38 91w03 6:04:12
Concordia 54 3 38N59 93w34 6:14:16
Connelsville 1 3 40N14 92w43 6:10:52
Conran 72 3 36N29 89w39 5:58:36
Converse 25 3 39N33 94w20 6:17:20
Conway 53 3 37N30 92w49 6:11:16
Cook Station 28 3 37N49 91w26 6:05:44
Cool Valley 95 40 38N44 90w18 6:01:12
Coon Island 12 3 36N33 90w24 6:01:36
Cooper 38 3 40N13 94w31 6:18:04
Cooper Hill 76 3 38N18 91w38 6:06:32
Cooter 78 3 36N03 89w49 5:59:16
Cora 105 3 40N12 93w07 6:12:28
Corbin 93 3 38N00 93w38 6:14:32
Corder 54 3 39N06 93w38 6:14:32
Cornelia 51 3 38N45 93w44 6:14:56
Corning 44 3 40N15 95w27 6:21:48
Cornwall 62 3 37N33 90w17 6:01:08
Corridon 90 3 37N26 90w58 6:03:52
Corry 29 3 37N29 93w41 6:14:44
Corsicana 5 3 36N48 93w59 6:15:56
Corso 57 3 39N08 91w11 6:04:44
Corticelli 68 3 38N31 92w26 6:09:44
Cosby 2 3 39N52 94w41 6:18:44
Cossville 49 3 37N15 94w27 6:17:48
Cote Sans Dessein 14 3 38N38 91w59 6:07:56
Cottage Farm 50 3 38N14 90w34 6:02:16
Cottleville 92 2 38N45 90w39 6:02:36
Cotton Hill 35 3 36N34 90w00 6:00:00
Cotton Plant 35 3 36N02 90w07 6:00:28
Cottonwood Point 78 3 36N11 89w40 5:58:40
Couch 75 3 36N36 91w22 6:05:28
Coulstone 107 3 37N30 91w52 6:07:28
Country Club 48 3 39N01 94w35 6:18:20
Country Club Hills 95 40 38N43 90w17 6:01:08
Country Club Village 2 44 39N50 94w49 6:19:16
Country Life Acres 95 40 38N37 90w27 6:01:48
Courtney 48 3 39N10 94w23 6:17:32
Courtois 110 3 37N56 91w14 6:04:56
Cowan 111 3 37N12 90w19 6:01:16
Cowgill 13 3 39N34 93w55 6:15:40
Coy 60 3 36N39 94w27 6:17:48
Crabbs 112 3 37N09 92w46 6:11:04
Craig 44 3 40N12 95w23 6:21:32
Crane 104 3 36N54 93w34 6:14:16
Crane Creek 5 3 36N52 93w39 6:14:36
Cream Ridge 59 3 39N55 93w30 6:14:00
Creighton 19 3 38N30 94w04 6:16:16
Crescent 95 40 38N31 90w39 6:02:36
Crescent Lake 24 3 39N20 94w13 6:16:52
Crestwood 95 40 38N34 90w23 6:01:32
Cretcher 97 3 38N58 93w25 6:13:40
Creve Coeur 95 40 38N40 90w27 6:01:48
Crites Corner 18 3 36N56 90w45 6:03:00
Crocker 85 47 37N57 92w16 6:09:04
Crook 76 3 38N29 91w51 6:07:24
Crooked Creek 9 3 37N25 90w04 6:00:16
Crooked River 89 3 39N17 93w50 6:15:20
Crosno 67 3 36N56 89w20 5:57:20
Cross Keys 95 40 38N49 90w18 6:01:12
Cross Roads 34 3 36N58 92w40 6:10:40
Cross Roads 77 3 36N47 92w13 6:08:52
Cross Timbers 43 3 38N01 93w14 6:12:56
Crosstown 79 3 37N45 89w44 5:58:56
Crowder 100 3 36N58 89w41 5:58:44
Cruise Mill 110 3 38N03 90w37 6:02:28
Crump 16 3 37N14 89w48 5:59:12
Crystal City 50 12 38N14 90w23 6:01:32
Crystal Lake Park 95 40 38N37 90w26 6:01:44
Cuba 28 3 38N04 91w24 6:05:36
Cullen 85 3 37N50 92w09 6:08:36
Cunningham 21 3 39N40 93w13 6:12:52
Curdton 103 3 36N57 90w10 6:00:40
Cureall 46 3 36N54 92w01 6:08:04
Current River 91 3 36N32 90w50 6:03:20
Currentview 91 3 36N37 90w49 6:03:16
Curryville 82 3 39N21 91w21 6:05:24
Cyclone 60 3 36N37 94w16 6:17:04
Cypress 41 3 40N10 94w03 6:16:12
Cyrene 82 3 39N17 91w06 6:04:24
Dadeville 29 3 37N29 93w41 6:14:44
Daisy 16 3 37N31 89w48 5:59:12
Dale 3 3 40N20 95w16 6:21:04
Dalton 21 3 39N24 92w59 6:11:56
Damascus 93 3 38N00 93w38 6:14:32
Dameron 57 25 39N10 90w47 6:03:08
Danby 50 3 38N01 90w13 6:00:52
Danville 70 3 38N55 91w31 6:06:04
Dardenne 92 2 38N47 90w41 6:02:44
Darien 33 3 37N39 91w32 6:06:08
Daris Crossing 94 3 37N52 90w31 6:02:04
Darksville 88 3 39N26 92w33 6:10:12
Darlington 38 3 40N12 94w24 6:17:36
Date 107 3 37N06 91w43 6:06:52
Daugherty 19 3 38N40 94w21 6:17:24
Davis 57 3 38N59 90w59 6:03:56
Davis Store 12 3 36N40 90w15 6:01:00
Davisville 28 3 37N49 91w11 6:04:44
Dawn 59 3 39N40 93w38 6:14:32
Dawson 114 3 37N15 92w18 6:09:12
Dawt 77 3 36N36 92w16 6:09:04
Dayton 19 3 38N34 94w11 6:16:44
Dearborn 83 3 39N32 94w46 6:19:04
Decaturville 15 3 37N55 92w42 6:10:48
Dederick 108 3 37N52 94w01 6:16:04
Deepwater 42 3 38N15 93w46 6:15:04
Deerfield 108 3 37N50 94w30 6:18:00
Deering 78 3 36N12 89w53 5:59:32
Deer Land 35 3 36N14 90w03 6:00:12
Deer Park 10 3 38N58 92w13 6:08:52
Deer Ridge 56 34 40N07 91w50 6:07:20
Defiance 92 3 38N38 90w47 6:03:08
Deicke 95 40 38N31 90w39 6:02:36
De Kalb 11 3 39N35 94w55 6:19:40
De Lassus 94 3 37N47 90w25 6:01:40
Delaware 101 3 37N05 91w25 6:05:40
Dellwood 95 40 38N45 90w17 6:01:08
Delmar 42 3 38N23 93w46 6:15:04
Delmo 72 3 36N53 89w34 5:58:16
Delta 16 3 37N12 89w44 5:58:56
Dennis Acres 73 3 37N03 94w30 6:18:00
Dent 47 3 37N40 91w04 6:04:16
Denton 78 3 36N05 89w53 5:59:32
Denver 113 3 40N24 94w19 6:17:16
Des Arc 47 3 37N17 90w38 6:02:32
Desloge 94 3 37N53 90w32 6:02:08
Des Moines 23 43 40N25 91w33 6:06:12
De Soto 50 4 38N08 90w34 6:02:16
Des Peres 95 40 38N36 90w27 6:01:48
Dessa 73 44 36N52 94w22 6:17:28
Detmold 36 3 38N36 91w13 6:04:52
Devils Elbow 85 3 37N51 92w04 6:08:16
De Witt 17 3 39N24 93w15 6:13:00
Dexter 103 3 36N48 89w57 5:59:48
Diamond 73 3 37N00 94w19 6:17:16
Dickerson 56 26 40N06 91w39 6:06:36
Diehlstadt 100 3 36N58 89w26 5:57:44
Diggins 112 3 37N10 92w51 6:11:24
Dillard 28 3 37N44 91w13 6:04:52
Dillon 81 10 37N57 91w48 6:07:12
Dissen 36 3 38N36 91w13 6:04:52
Dittmer 50 3 38N20 90w41 6:02:44
Dixie 14 3 38N43 92w05 6:08:20
Dixon 85 47 38N00 92w06 6:08:24
Dockery 89 3 39N17 93w58 6:15:52

MISSOURI

Doe Run 94 3 37N45 90w30 6:02:00
Dogwood 34 3 37N09 92w46 6:11:04
Dogwood 67 3 36N47 89w23 5:57:32
Dolan 19 3 38N37 94w30 6:18:00
Dongola 9 3 37N06 89w55 5:59:40
Doniphan 91 3 36N37 90w50 6:03:20
Doolittle 81 3 37N56 91w53 6:07:32
Dora 77 3 36N47 92w13 6:08:52
Dorena 67 3 36N47 89w23 5:57:32
Doss 33 3 37N39 91w32 6:06:08
Dove 53 47 37N41 92w40 6:10:40
Dover 54 3 39N12 93w41 6:14:44
Dover 56 3 40N03 91w29 6:05:56
Downing 98 44 40N29 92w22 6:09:28
Doyal 93 3 37N58 93w41 6:14:44
Doylesport 6 3 37N36 94w13 6:16:52
Drake 37 3 38N28 91w28 6:05:52
Dresden 80 3 38N45 93w20 6:13:20
Drew 53 47 37N41 92w40 6:10:40
Drexel 19 3 38N29 94w37 6:18:28
Dripping Spring 10 3 38N58 92w13 6:08:52
Drury 34 3 36N56 92w19 6:09:16
Drynob 53 3 37N38 92w27 6:09:48
Drywood 108 3 37N42 94w20 6:17:20
Duck Creek 103 3 36N53 90w09 6:00:36
Dudenville 29 3 37N23 94w06 6:16:24
Dudley 103 3 36N47 90w06 6:00:24
Duenweg 49 3 37N05 94w25 6:17:40
Dugginsville 77 3 36N30 92w42 6:10:48
Duke 81 3 37N40 92w01 6:08:04
Duncan 105 3 40N05 93w11 6:12:44
Duncans Bridge 69 45 39N45 92w15 6:09:00
Dundee 36 49 38N33 91w01 6:04:04
Dunksburg 51 3 38N58 93w25 6:13:40
Dunlap 40 3 40N07 93w25 6:13:40
Dunn 107 3 37N08 92w16 6:09:04
Dunnegan 84 3 37N43 93w35 6:14:20
Duquesne 49 3 37N05 94w28 6:17:52
Durham 56 26 40N04 91w40 6:06:40
Durnell 103 3 37N01 89w49 5:59:16
Dutchtown 16 3 37N15 89w39 5:58:36
Dutzow 109 49 38N36 91w00 6:04:00
Duval 49 3 37N18 94w27 6:17:48
Dye 83 3 39N25 94w54 6:19:36
Eagle 61 3 39N49 92w27 6:09:48
Eagle Rock 5 3 36N33 93w46 6:15:04
Eagleville 41 3 40N28 93w59 6:15:56
Easley 10 3 38N58 92w13 6:08:52
Easley 61 3 40N00 92w41 6:10:44
East Benton 22 3 37N04 92w57 6:11:48
East Bonne Terre 94 3 37N55 90w33 6:02:12
East Boone 7 3 38N26 94w27 6:17:48
East Dallas 112 3 37N12 92w54 6:11:36
East Fulton 14 3 38N50 91w54 6:07:36
East James 104 3 36N37 93w22 6:13:28
East Kansas City 24 3 39N10 94w30 6:18:00
East Kirkwood 95 40 38N37 90w21 6:01:24
East Leavenworth 83 3 39N19 94w51 6:19:24
East Lynne 19 3 38N40 94w14 6:16:56
East Mexico 4 3 39N10 91w52 6:07:28
Easton 11 3 39N43 94w39 6:18:36
East Prairie 67 19 36N47 89w23 5:57:32
East Purdy 5 3 36N49 93w55 6:15:40
East Trenton Lake 40 3 40N07 93w35 6:14:20
Eastwood 18 3 37N00 91w01 6:04:04
Ebenezer 39 44 37N14 93w18 6:13:12
Eccles 21 3 39N26 92w56 6:11:44
Economy 61 3 39N54 92w29 6:09:56
Ectonville 24 3 39N23 94w35 6:18:20
Edgar Springs 81 3 37N42 91w52 6:07:28
Edgehill 90 3 37N32 90w56 6:03:44
Edgerton 83 3 39N30 94w38 6:18:32
Edgerton Junction 83 3 39N31 94w46 6:19:04
Edgewater Beach 106 3 36N41 93w07 6:12:28
Edgewood 82 3 39N17 91w06 6:04:24
Edina 52 3 40N10 92w11 6:08:44
Edinburg 40 3 40N07 93w35 6:14:20
Edmonson 8 3 38N23 93w20 6:13:20
Edmundson 95 40 38N44 90w22 6:01:28
Edwards 8 3 38N08 93w10 6:12:40
Egypt 17 3 39N18 93w42 6:14:48
Egypt Mills 16 3 37N19 89w32 5:58:08
Eldon 66 3 38N21 92w35 6:10:20
El Dorado Springs 20 3 37N52 94w01 6:16:04
Eldridge 53 3 37N50 92w45 6:11:00
Elijah 77 3 36N37 92w06 6:08:24
Elk 103 3 36N42 89w49 5:59:16
Elk Creek 107 3 37N11 92w00 6:08:00
Elk Creek 114 3 37N25 92w28 6:09:52
Elk Fork 80 3 38N41 93w27 6:13:48
Elkhart 7 3 38N21 94w27 6:17:48
Elkhead 22 3 37N00 93w05 6:12:20
Elkhorn 89 3 39N12 94w05 6:16:20
Elkhurst 10 3 38N58 92w13 6:08:52
Elkland 112 3 37N27 93w02 6:12:08
Elk River 60 3 36N33 94w30 6:18:00
Elk Springs 60 3 36N35 94w27 6:17:48
Elkton 43 3 37N51 93w25 6:13:40
Ellington 90 3 37N14 90w58 6:03:52
Ellis Prairie 107 3 37N25 92w02 6:08:08
Ellisville 95 40 38N36 90w33 6:02:12
Ellsinore 18 3 36N56 90w45 6:03:00
Elm 51 3 38N45 94w04 6:16:16
Elm 86 3 40N25 92w46 6:11:04
Elmdale Village 95 40 38N42 90w22 6:01:28
Elmer 61 3 39N57 92w39 6:10:36
Elmira 89 3 39N30 94w09 6:16:36
Elmo 74 3 40N31 95w07 6:20:28
Elmont 36 44 38N13 91w09 6:04:36
Elm Point 92 2 38N49 90w30 6:02:00
Elmwood 97 3 39N05 93w24 6:13:36
Elsberry 57 25 39N10 90w47 6:03:08
Elsey 104 3 36N51 93w32 6:14:08
Elston 26 3 38N32 92w10 6:08:40
Elvins 94 3 37N50 90w32 6:02:08
Elwood 39 44 37N13 93w18 6:13:12
Ely 64 39 39N48 91w31 6:06:04
Emden 102 3 39N48 91w52 6:07:28
Emerson 64 3 39N57 91w36 6:06:24
Eminence 101 3 37N09 91w21 6:05:24
Emma 97 3 38N58 93w27 6:13:48
Empire 2 3 40N00 94w41 6:18:44
Empire Prairie 2 3 40N05 94w30 6:18:00
Englewood 10 3 38N46 92w15 6:09:00
Englewood 48 3 39N04 94w26 6:17:44
Enon 68 3 38N31 92w26 6:09:44
Enterprise 58 3 40N00 93w04 6:12:16
Enyart 38 3 40N20 94w25 6:17:40
Eolia 82 3 39N14 91w01 6:04:04
Epps 12 3 36N49 90w33 6:02:12
Epworth 102 3 39N48 92w02 6:08:08
Equality 66 3 38N15 92w30 6:10:00
Erie 60 3 36N43 94w21 6:17:24
Ernest 29 3 37N29 93w56 6:15:44
Ernestville 54 3 38N59 93w34 6:14:16
Essex 103 3 36N49 89w52 5:59:28
Estes 82 3 39N08 91w25 6:05:40
Esther 94 3 37N51 90w30 6:02:00
Estill 45 3 39N01 92w44 6:10:56
Ethel 61 3 39N54 92w45 6:11:00
Ethlyn 57 14 38N56 90w45 6:03:00
Etlah 36 3 38N41 91w20 6:05:20
Etterville 66 3 38N22 92w28 6:09:52
Eudora 84 3 37N29 93w33 6:14:12
Eugene 26 3 38N21 92w24 6:09:36
Eunice 107 3 37N15 91w47 6:07:08
Eureka 95 40 38N30 90w38 6:02:32
Evans 34 3 36N58 92w40 6:10:40
Evansville 11 3 39N45 94w48 6:19:12
Evansville 69 3 39N25 92w25 6:09:40
Eve 108 3 37N50 94w30 6:18:00
Everett 19 3 38N31 94w27 6:17:48
Eversonville 58 3 39N47 93w23 6:13:32
Everton 29 3 37N21 93w42 6:14:48
Ewing 56 26 40N06 91w43 6:06:52
Excello 61 3 39N38 92w29 6:09:56
Excelsior 71 3 38N26 92w51 6:11:24
Excelsior Springs 24 3 39N20 94w13 6:16:52
Excelsior Springs Junction 24 3 39N12 94w05 6:16:20
Exeter 5 3 36N40 93w56 6:15:44
Fagus 12 3 36N31 90w16 6:01:04
Fairdealing 91 3 36N40 90w37 6:02:28
Fairfax 3 3 40N20 95w24 6:21:36
Fairfield 8 3 38N09 93w24 6:13:36
Fair Grounds 115 1 38N40 90w13 6:00:52
Fair Grove 39 3 37N23 93w09 6:12:36
Fair Haven 108 3 37N57 94w09 6:16:36
Fairleigh 11 3 39N47 94w48 6:19:12
Fairmont 23 3 40N23 91w56 6:07:44
Fair Play 84 3 37N38 93w35 6:14:20
Fairport 32 3 39N59 94w21 6:17:24
Fairview 73 3 36N49 94w05 6:16:20
Fairview 95 40 38N44 90w15 6:01:00
Fairview Acres 94 3 37N51 90w32 6:02:08
Falcon 53 3 37N36 92w23 6:09:32
Falling Spring 75 3 36N51 91w17 6:05:08
Fanchon 46 3 36N55 91w50 6:07:20
Fanning 28 3 38N04 91w24 6:05:36
Farber 4 3 39N16 91w34 6:06:16
Farley 83 3 39N17 94w50 6:19:20
Farmer 82 3 39N21 91w20 6:05:20
Farmersville 59 3 40N07 93w35 6:14:20
Farmington 94 3 37N47 90w25 6:01:40
Farrar 79 3 37N42 89w41 5:58:44
Farrenberg 72 3 36N35 89w34 5:58:16
Faucett 11 3 39N36 94w48 6:19:12
Fayette 45 3 39N09 92w41 6:10:44
Fayetteville 51 3 38N53 93w45 6:15:00
Federal Reserve 48 3 39N03 94w31 6:18:04
Femme Osage 92 3 38N37 90w52 6:03:28
Fenton 95 40 38N31 90w26 6:01:44
Ferguson 95 40 38N45 90w18 6:01:12
Fernview Estates 95 40 38N40 90w26 6:01:44
Ferrelview 83 3 39N19 94w40 6:18:40
Fertile 110 3 37N59 90w41 6:02:44
Festus 50 12 38N13 90w24 6:01:36
Fidelity 49 3 37N05 94w18 6:17:12
Field 115 1 38N38 90w15 6:01:00
Fields Creek 42 3 38N25 93w47 6:15:08
Filley 20 3 37N52 94w01 6:16:04
Fillmore 2 3 40N02 94w58 6:19:52
Findley 34 3 37N01 92w41 6:10:44
Fishertown 101 3 37N00 91w20 6:05:20
Fisk 12 3 36N47 90w12 6:00:48
Five Mile 73 3 36N58 94w33 6:18:12
Flag Springs 2 3 39N59 94w36 6:18:24
Flag Springs 81 10 38N00 91w37 6:06:28
Flat 81 3 37N55 91w54 6:07:36
Flat River 94 3 37N51 90w31 6:02:04
Flatwood 101 3 37N09 91w21 6:05:24
Flatwoods 91 3 36N40 90w42 6:02:48
Fleming 89 3 39N12 94w03 6:16:12
Flemington 84 3 37N46 93w30 6:14:00
Fletchall 113 3 40N31 94w24 6:17:36
Fletcher 50 3 38N09 90w44 6:02:56
Flinthill 92 3 38N53 90w52 6:03:28
Flordell Hills 95 40 38N43 90w16 6:01:04
Florence 71 3 38N35 92w59 6:11:56
Florida 69 3 39N33 91w51 6:07:24
Florissant 95 40 38N48 90w20 6:01:20
Floyd 89 3 39N12 94w05 6:16:20
Flucom 50 4 38N08 90w33 6:02:12
Foil 77 3 36N51 92w37 6:10:28
Foley 57 16 39N03 90w45 6:03:00
Folk 76 3 38N26 92w00 6:08:00
Folker 23 3 40N32 91w53 6:07:32
Foose 30 3 37N39 93w06 6:12:24
Forbes 44 3 39N55 95w03 6:20:12
Ford City 38 3 40N07 94w28 6:17:52
Fordland 112 3 37N09 92w57 6:11:48
Forest City 44 3 39N59 95w12 6:20:48
Forest Green 21 3 39N19 92w50 6:11:20
Forest Park 55 3 36N56 93w55 6:15:40
Foristell 92 17 38N49 90w58 6:03:52
Forker 58 3 39N47 93w10 6:12:40
Fornfelt 100 3 37N13 89w31 5:58:04
Forrest Mill 49 3 37N07 94w10 6:16:40
Forsyth 106 3 36N41 93w06 6:12:24
Fort Bellefontaine 95 40 38N50 90w14 6:00:56
Fortescue 44 3 40N03 95w19 6:21:16
Fort Henry 88 3 39N26 92w33 6:10:12
Fort Leonard Wood 85 11 37N50 92w12 6:08:48
Fort Osage 48 3 39N09 94w14 6:16:56
Fortuna 68 3 38N34 92w48 6:11:12
Fort Wyman Heights 81 10 37N57 91w48 6:07:12
Fort Zumwalt 92 2 38N49 90w42 6:02:48
Foster 7 3 38N10 94w30 6:18:00
Fountain Grove 58 3 39N47 93w18 6:13:12
Fox Creek 41 3 40N15 93w49 6:15:16
Foxcreek 95 6 38N29 90w44 6:02:56
Frailie 72 3 36N27 89w55 5:59:40
Frankclay 94 3 37N52 90w37 6:02:28
Frankenstein 76 3 38N35 91w58 6:07:52
Frankford 82 3 39N29 91w19 6:05:16
Franklin 45 3 39N01 92w45 6:11:00
Franks 85 47 38N00 92w06 6:08:24
Frazier 11 3 39N39 94w44 6:18:56
Fredericksburg 37 3 38N40 91w38 6:06:32
Fredericktown 62 3 37N34 90w18 6:01:12
Fredville 73 44 36N52 94w22 6:17:28
Freeborn 35 3 36N26 89w59 5:59:56
Freeburg 76 3 38N19 91w56 6:07:44
Freedom 54 3 38N59 93w37 6:14:28
Freedom 76 3 38N40 91w46 6:07:04
Freeman 19 3 38N37 94w30 6:18:00
Freistatt 55 3 37N01 93w54 6:15:36
Fremont 18 3 36N57 91w10 6:04:40
French Mills 62 3 37N35 90w38 6:02:32
French Village 94 3 37N58 90w24 6:01:36
Friedheim 16 3 37N34 89w49 5:59:16
Frisbee 35 3 36N24 90w01 6:00:04
Frisco 103 3 36N48 89w49 5:59:16
Fristoe 8 3 38N07 93w17 6:13:08
Frohna 79 3 37N38 89w37 5:58:28
Frontenac 95 40 38N38 90w25 6:01:40
Fruitland 16 3 37N27 89w38 5:58:32
Fruitland 39 3 37N23 93w09 6:12:36
Frumet 50 4 38N08 90w33 6:02:12
Fulton 14 3 38N52 91w57 6:07:48
Gaines 42 3 38N23 93w46 6:15:04
Gainesville 77 3 36N36 92w26 6:09:44
Galena 104 3 36N48 93w28 6:13:52
Galesburg 49 3 37N11 94w28 6:17:52
Gallatin 31 3 39N55 93w58 6:15:52
Galloway 39 44 37N08 93w14 6:12:56
Galmey 43 3 37N57 93w24 6:13:36
Galt 40 3 40N08 93w23 6:13:32
Gamburg 91 3 36N36 90w41 6:02:44
Game 78 3 36N11 89w40 5:58:40
Gamma 70 3 39N00 91w21 6:05:24
Garden City 19 3 38N34 94w12 6:16:48
Gardenview 95 40 38N48 90w20 6:01:20
Garland 42 3 38N23 93w46 6:15:04
Garrison 22 3 36N50 93w01 6:12:04
Garwood 90 3 37N09 90w42 6:02:48
Gasconade 37 3 38N40 91w34 6:06:16
Gashland 24 3 39N12 94w34 6:18:16
Gateway Drive 73 3 37N04 94w30 6:18:00
Gatewood 91 3 36N35 91w05 6:04:20
Gaynor 74 3 40N26 94w37 6:18:28
Gazette 82 3 39N08 91w25 6:05:40
Gentry 38 3 40N20 94w25 6:17:40
Gentryville 34 3 36N58 92w40 6:10:40
Gentryville 38 3 40N15 94w20 6:17:20
Georgetown 80 3 38N43 93w23 6:13:32
Georgeville 89 3 39N35 93w55 6:15:40
Gerald 36 3 38N24 91w20 6:05:20
Germantown 42 3 38N16 93w59 6:15:56
Gerster 93 3 37N57 93w35 6:14:20
Gibbs 1 3 40N06 92w25 6:09:40
Gibson 35 3 36N27 90w02 6:00:08
Gideon 72 3 36N27 89w55 5:59:40
Gilbert 35 3 36N02 90w07 6:00:28
Gilliam 97 3 39N14 93w00 6:12:00
Gillis Bluff 12 3 36N33 90w17 6:01:08
Gilman 41 3 40N09 93w52 6:15:28
Gilman City 41 3 40N08 93w53 6:15:32
Gilmore 92 8 38N49 90w51 6:03:24
Ginger Blue 60 3 36N33 94w30 6:18:00
Gipsy 9 3 37N09 90w11 6:00:44
Girdner 34 3 36N58 92w40 6:10:40
Gladden 33 3 37N30 91w28 6:05:52
Gladstone 24 3 39N13 94w35 6:18:20
Glasgow 45 3 39N14 92w51 6:11:24
Glasgow Village 95 40 38N44 90w14 6:00:56
Glaze 66 3 38N06 92w31 6:10:04

MISSOURI

Glenaire 24	3	39N14	94w27	6:17:48
Glenallen 9	3	37N19	90w02	6:00:08
Glencoe 95	40	38N33	90w36	6:02:24
Glendale 86	3	40N30	92w42	6:10:48
Glendale 95	40	38N36	90w23	6:01:32
Glen Echo 95	40	38N43	90w18	6:01:12
Glen Echo Park 95	40	38N42	90w18	6:01:12
Glenn 91	3	36N34	90w36	6:02:24
Glennon 9	3	37N18	89w59	5:59:56
Glennonville 35	3	36N30	90w04	6:00:16
Glen Park 50	12	38N17	90w24	6:01:36
Glensted 71	3	38N26	92w51	6:11:24
Glenstone 39	44	37N11	93w17	6:13:08
Glenwood 98	44	40N31	92w35	6:10:20
Glidewell 39	44	37N14	93w18	6:13:12
Glover 47	3	37N29	90w42	6:02:48
Gobler 78	3	36N09	89w57	5:59:48
Godair 78	3	36N22	89w43	5:58:52
Goebel 75	3	36N43	91w18	6:05:12
Golden 5	3	36N31	93w39	6:14:36
Golden City 6	3	37N24	94w05	6:16:20
Goldman 50	3	38N14	90w34	6:02:16
Goldsberry 46	3	37N00	91w43	6:06:52
Goldsberry 61	3	39N54	92w44	6:10:56
Gomer 13	3	39N45	93w56	6:15:44
Gooch Mill 27	3	38N49	92w35	6:10:20
Goodfellow Terrace 95	40	38N42	90w16	6:01:04
Goodhope 34	3	36N58	92w40	6:10:40
Goodland 47	3	37N41	90w44	6:02:56
Goodman 60	3	36N44	94w25	6:17:40
Goodman Heights 60	3	36N44	94w23	6:17:32
Goodson 84	3	37N42	93w15	6:13:00
Gordonville 16	3	37N19	89w41	5:58:44
Gorin 99	3	40N22	92w01	6:08:04
Goshen 65	5	40N24	93w35	6:14:20
Gospel Ridge 85	3	37N49	92w12	6:08:48
Gower 25	3	39N37	94w36	6:18:24
Graff 114	3	37N19	92w17	6:09:08
Graham 74	3	40N12	95w03	6:20:12
Grain Valley 48	3	39N01	94w12	6:16:48
Granby 73	44	36N55	94w15	6:17:00
Grand Center 88	44	39N46	92w37	6:10:28
Grand Falls 73	3	37N04	94w30	6:18:00
Grandin 18	3	36N50	90w50	6:03:20
Grand Pass 97	3	39N12	93w23	6:13:32
Grandview 48	3	38N53	94w32	6:18:08
Granger 99	3	40N28	91w58	6:07:52
Graniteville 47	3	37N29	90w40	6:02:40
Grant 95	40	38N34	90w20	6:01:20
Grant City 113	3	40N29	94w25	6:17:40
Grantsville 58	3	39N56	93w04	6:12:16
Grantwood 95	40	38N35	90w21	6:01:24
Granville 69	3	39N29	92w00	6:08:00
Grape Grove 89	3	39N26	93w51	6:15:24
Grassy 9	3	37N16	90w08	6:00:32
Gravelhill 16	3	37N22	89w48	5:59:12
Gravelton 111	3	37N26	90w10	6:00:40
Gravois 115	1	38N35	90w19	6:01:16
Gravois Mills 71	3	38N19	92w49	6:11:16
Grayridge 103	3	36N50	89w47	5:59:08
Grayson 25	3	39N32	94w34	6:18:16
Grays Point 55	3	37N13	93w50	6:15:20
Gray Summit 36	6	38N29	90w49	6:03:16
Graysville 86	3	40N30	92w42	6:10:48
Green Bay Terrace 15	3	38N10	92w47	6:11:08
Greenbrier 9	3	37N06	89w55	5:59:40
Green Castle 105	3	40N17	92w52	6:11:28
Green City 105	3	40N16	92w57	6:11:48
Greendale 95	40	38N42	90w19	6:01:16
Greenfield 29	3	37N25	93w51	6:15:24
Green Forest 12	3	36N46	90w24	6:01:36
Green Lawn 87	3	39N26	91w40	6:06:40
Green Mound Ridge 22	3	36N56	93w17	6:13:08
Green Mountain 114	3	37N08	92w16	6:09:04
Green Oaks 103	3	36N47	90w06	6:00:24
Green Ridge 80	3	38N37	93w25	6:13:40
Greensburg 52	3	40N16	92w16	6:09:04
Greenstreet 36	3	38N25	91w11	6:04:44
Greentop 98	3	40N21	92w34	6:10:16
Greenville 24	3	39N22	94w22	6:17:28
Greenville 111	3	37N08	90w27	6:01:48
Greenwood 48	3	38N51	94w20	6:17:20
Greer 75	3	36N46	91w21	6:05:24
Gregory 23	23	40N08	91w30	6:06:00
Gretna 106	3	36N39	93w13	6:12:52
Grimmet 46	3	36N44	91w52	6:07:28
Grisham 9	3	37N18	89w59	5:59:56
Grover 51	3	38N52	93w33	6:14:12
Grover 95	40	38N34	90w38	6:02:32
Grovespring 114	3	37N24	92w37	6:10:28
Grubville 50	3	38N17	90w45	6:03:00
Guilford 74	3	40N10	94w44	6:18:56
Gumbo 94	3	37N52	90w31	6:02:04
Gunn City 19	3	38N40	94w10	6:16:40
Guthrie 14	3	38N46	92w06	6:08:24
Hadley 95	40	38N39	90w19	6:01:16
Hagers Grove 102	45	39N45	92w15	6:09:00
Hahatonka 15	3	38N00	92w44	6:10:56
Hahn 9	3	37N18	89w59	5:59:56
Hailey 5	3	36N47	93w41	6:14:44
Hale 17	3	39N36	93w20	6:13:20
Half Rock 65	3	40N15	93w33	6:14:12
Half Way 84	3	37N37	93w15	6:13:00
Halls 11	3	39N43	94w51	6:19:24
Hallsville 10	3	39N07	92w13	6:08:52
Halltown 55	3	37N12	93w38	6:14:32
Hamilton 13	3	39N45	94w00	6:16:00
Hamlin Farm 78	3	36N14	89w45	5:59:00
Hammond 77	3	36N42	92w40	6:10:40
Hams Prairie 14	3	38N51	91w57	6:07:48
Hancock 85	47	37N57	92w16	6:09:04
Handy 91	3	36N57	91w10	6:04:40
Hanley Hills 95	40	38N41	90w20	6:01:20
Hannibal 64	27	39N42	91w22	6:05:28
Hannon 6	3	37N33	94w31	6:18:04
Happy Hollow 110	3	37N59	90w41	6:02:44
Hardeman 97	3	39N03	93w05	6:12:20
Hardenville 77	3	36N35	92w19	6:09:16
Hardin 89	3	39N16	93w50	6:15:20
Harg 10	3	38N58	92w13	6:08:52
Harmony 110	3	37N49	91w00	6:04:00
Harper 93	3	38N00	93w38	6:14:32
Harris 105	3	40N18	93w21	6:13:24
Harrisburg 10	3	39N09	92w28	6:09:52
Harrisonville 19	3	38N39	94w21	6:17:24
Harry S Truman 48	3	39N04	94w25	6:17:40
Hart 61	44	36N50	94w37	6:18:28
Hart 114	3	37N12	92w28	6:09:52
Hartford 82	3	39N11	91w17	6:05:08
Hartford 86	3	40N29	93w01	6:12:04
Hartsburg 10	3	38N42	92w19	6:09:16
Hartshorn 107	3	37N16	91w40	6:06:40
Hartville 114	3	37N15	92w31	6:10:04
Hartwell 42	3	38N28	94w00	6:16:00
Hartzell 72	3	36N27	89w55	5:59:40
Harvester 92	2	38N47	90w30	6:02:00
Harviell 12	3	36N40	90w28	6:01:52
Harwood 108	3	37N57	94w09	6:16:36
Haseltine 39	44	37N13	93w18	6:13:12
Hassard 87	37	39N39	91w44	6:06:56
Hastain 8	3	38N08	93w10	6:12:40
Hatfield 41	3	40N32	94w09	6:16:36
Hatton 14	3	39N01	91w54	6:07:36
Havenhurst 60	3	36N36	94w23	6:17:32
Haw Creek 71	3	38N27	92w58	6:11:52
Hawkeye 85	47	37N57	92w16	6:09:04
Hawk Point 57	28	38N58	91w08	6:04:32
Hayden 63	47	38N00	92w06	6:08:24
Hayes Park 48	3	39N11	94w12	6:16:48
Hayti 78	3	36N14	89w44	5:58:56
Hayti Heights 78	3	36N14	89w45	5:59:00
Hayward 78	3	36N26	89w42	5:58:48
Haywood City 100	3	37N02	89w38	5:58:32
Hazelgreen 53	3	37N52	92w24	6:09:36
Hazel Hill 51	3	38N53	93w47	6:15:08
Hazel Run 94	3	37N55	90w33	6:02:12
Hazelwood 95	40	38N47	90w22	6:01:28
Heaths Creek 80	3	38N52	93w07	6:12:28
Heatonville 55	3	37N13	93w50	6:15:20
Hebron 34	3	36N44	91w52	6:07:28
Hecla 58	3	39N53	93w11	6:12:44
Hedge City 52	3	40N01	92w12	6:08:48
Helena 2	3	39N55	94w39	6:18:36
Helm 85	47	38N00	92w06	6:08:24
Heman Park 95	40	38N40	90w18	6:01:12
Hematite 50	3	38N12	90w29	6:01:56
Hemple 25	3	39N45	94w30	6:18:00
Henderson 112	3	37N07	93w04	6:12:16
Henderson Mound 72	3	36N46	89w35	5:58:20
Hendrickson 12	3	36N54	90w28	6:01:52
Henley 26	3	38N21	92w19	6:09:16
Henrietta 89	3	39N14	93w56	6:15:44
Henry 108	3	38N00	94w33	6:18:12
Henson 67	3	36N56	89w20	5:57:20
Herculaneum 50	12	38N16	90w23	6:01:32
Hercules 106	3	36N47	92w55	6:11:40
Hermann 37	19	38N42	91w27	6:05:48
Hermitage 43	3	37N56	93w19	6:13:16
Hermondale 78	3	36N05	89w52	5:59:28
Hickman Mills 48	3	38N55	94w07	6:16:28
Hickory 44	3	40N05	95w06	6:20:24
Hickory Creek 40	3	40N07	93w35	6:14:20
Hickory Grove 109	17	38N48	91w00	6:04:00
Hickory Hill 26	3	38N21	92w19	6:09:16
Higbee 88	3	39N19	92w31	6:10:04
Higdon 62	3	37N33	90w17	6:01:08
Higginsville 54	3	39N04	93w43	6:14:52
High Gate 63	10	38N00	91w37	6:06:28
High Hill 70	3	38N53	91w23	6:05:32
Highland 79	3	37N45	89w49	5:59:16
Highlandville 22	3	36N56	93w17	6:13:08
Highley Heights 94	3	37N53	90w31	6:02:04
High Point 68	3	38N29	92w35	6:10:20
High Prairie 112	3	37N18	92w45	6:11:00
High Ridge 50	3	38N29	90w32	6:02:08
Hilda 106	3	36N40	92w59	6:11:56
Hill 17	3	39N34	93w35	6:14:20
Hillhouse Addition 15	3	37N52	92w24	6:09:36
Hilliard 12	3	36N46	90w24	6:01:36
Hillsboro 50	3	38N14	90w34	6:02:16
Hillsdale 95	40	38N41	90w17	6:01:08
Hill Top 91	3	36N37	90w49	6:03:16
Himmel 103	3	37N01	89w49	5:59:16
Hinch 28	46	38N09	91w15	6:05:00
Hinton 10	3	38N58	92w13	6:08:52
Hiram 111	3	37N11	90w19	6:01:16
Hoberg 55	3	37N04	93w51	6:15:24
Hobson 33	3	37N39	91w32	6:06:08
Hocomo 46	3	36N48	92w00	6:08:00
Hodge 54	3	39N12	93w31	6:14:04
Hoene Spring 50	3	38N30	90w37	6:02:28
Holcomb 35	3	36N24	90w02	6:00:08
Holden 51	3	38N43	94w00	6:16:00
Holland 78	3	36N03	89w52	5:59:28
Holliday 69	3	39N30	92w08	6:08:32
Holliday Landing 111	3	37N08	90w27	6:01:48
Hollister 106	3	36N38	93w12	6:12:48
Hollow 95	6	38N29	90w44	6:02:56
Hollywood 35	3	36N03	90w11	6:00:44
Holstein 109	3	38N38	91w03	6:04:12
Holt 24	3	39N27	94w21	6:17:24
Holts Summit 14	3	38N39	92w07	6:08:28
Homer 7	3	38N16	94w34	6:18:16
Homestead Village 89	3	39N20	94w13	6:16:52
Homestown 78	3	36N20	89w49	5:59:16
Honey Creek 26	3	38N32	92w10	6:08:40
Honey Creek 42	3	38N26	93w51	6:15:24
Hooker 53	3	37N46	92w46	6:11:04
Hooker 85	3	37N55	91w54	6:07:36
Hoover 83	3	39N13	94w39	6:18:36
Hope 76	3	38N40	91w38	6:06:32
Hopewell 109	3	38N38	91w03	6:04:12
Hopewell 110	3	37N57	90w43	6:02:52
Hopkins 74	3	40N33	94w49	6:19:16
Horine 50	12	38N17	90w24	6:01:36
Hornersville 35	3	36N02	90w07	6:00:28
Hornet 73	44	36N50	94w37	6:18:28
Hortense 42	3	38N23	93w46	6:15:04
Horton 108	3	37N59	94w22	6:17:28
Hough 72	3	36N44	89w28	5:57:52
House Creek 18	3	37N00	91w01	6:04:04
House Springs 50	3	38N25	90w34	6:02:16
Houston 107	3	37N22	91w58	6:07:52
Houstonia 80	3	38N54	93w22	6:13:28
Houston Lake 83	3	39N12	94w37	6:18:28
Howards Ridge 77	3	36N38	93w13	6:12:52
Howardville 72	3	36N34	89w36	5:58:24
Howell 46	3	36N43	91w50	6:07:20
Howes Mill 33	3	37N38	91w16	6:05:04
H. S. Jewell 39	44	37N12	93w18	6:13:12
Hubble 16	3	37N17	89w43	5:58:52
Huckaby 84	3	37N42	93w15	6:13:00
Hudson 7	3	38N11	94w02	6:16:08
Huggins 38	3	40N16	94w26	6:17:44
Huggins 107	3	37N19	92w12	6:08:48
Hughes 74	3	40N12	95w00	6:20:00
Hughesville 80	3	38N50	93w18	6:13:12
Hugo 15	3	38N03	92w43	6:10:52
Humansville 84	3	37N48	93w35	6:14:20
Hume 7	3	38N06	94w35	6:18:20
Humphreys 105	3	40N08	93w18	6:13:12
Hunnewell 102	29	39N40	91w52	6:07:28
Hunter 18	3	36N54	90w51	6:03:24
Hunterville 103	3	36N48	89w49	5:59:16
Huntingdale 42	3	38N23	93w46	6:15:04
Huntleigh 95	40	38N37	90w25	6:01:40
Huntsdale 10	3	38N58	92w13	6:08:52
Huntsville 88	3	39N26	92w33	6:10:12
Hurdland 52	3	40N09	92w18	6:09:12
Hurley 104	3	36N56	93w30	6:14:00
Hurlingen 11	3	39N43	94w38	6:18:32
Huron 84	3	37N37	93w25	6:13:40
Hurricane 9	3	37N18	89w59	5:59:56
Hurricane Deck 15	3	38N08	92w48	6:11:12
Hurryville 94	3	37N47	90w25	6:01:40
Hutton Valley 46	3	36N57	91w50	6:07:20
Iantha 6	3	37N31	94w24	6:17:36
Iatan 83	3	39N25	94w54	6:19:36
Iberia 66	3	38N05	92w18	6:09:12
Iconium 93	3	38N00	93w38	6:14:32
Idalia 103	3	36N53	89w56	5:59:44
Ike 106	3	36N45	93w23	6:13:32
Ilasco 87	3	39N41	91w28	6:05:52
Illmo 100	19	37N13	89w30	5:58:00
Imperial 50	3	38N22	90w23	6:01:32
Independence 48	3	39N06	94w25	6:17:40
Index 19	3	38N37	94w09	6:16:36
Indian 82	3	39N16	91w21	6:05:24
Indian Creek 69	3	39N35	91w48	6:07:12
Indian Grove 21	3	39N26	93w08	6:12:32
Indian Lake 28	3	38N04	91w24	6:05:36
Ink 101	3	37N09	91w21	6:05:24
Inza 11	3	39N43	94w52	6:19:28
Ionia 8	3	38N30	93w19	6:13:16
Irena 113	3	40N29	94w25	6:17:40
Irondale 110	3	37N50	90w41	6:02:44
Iron Gates 49	3	37N04	94w33	6:18:12
Iron Mountain 94	3	37N42	90w39	6:02:36
Iron Mountain Lake 94	3	37N46	90w37	6:02:28
Ironton 47	3	37N36	90w38	6:02:32
Irwin 6	3	37N35	94w17	6:17:08
Isabella 77	3	36N35	92w37	6:10:28
Isadora 113	3	40N29	94w25	6:17:40
Ives 103	3	36N47	90w06	6:00:24
J & G Junction 49	3	37N04	94w30	6:18:00
Jackson 16	3	37N23	89w40	5:58:40
Jacksonville 88	3	39N35	92w28	6:09:52
Jadwin 33	3	37N29	91w35	6:06:20
James 104	3	36N38	93w25	6:13:40
James Bayou 67	3	36N38	89w16	5:57:04
James Crews 48	3	39N05	94w33	6:18:12
Jameson 31	3	40N00	93w59	6:15:56
Jamesport 31	3	39N58	93w48	6:15:12
Jamestown 68	3	38N46	92w29	6:09:56
Jamesville 104	3	37N02	93w28	6:13:52
Jane 60	3	36N33	94w18	6:17:12
Japan 36	44	38N13	91w09	6:04:36
Jarvis 50	3	38N14	90w34	6:02:16
Jasper 49	3	37N20	94w18	6:17:12
Jaudon 19	3	38N51	94w24	6:17:36
Jaywye 72	3	36N26	89w42	5:58:48
Jeddo 52	3	40N05	92w00	6:08:00
Jeff 75	3	36N32	91w23	6:05:32
Jefferson 2	44	39N51	94w50	6:19:20
Jefferson City 26	3	38N34	92w10	6:08:40
Jefferson Memorial 95	1	38N38	90w12	6:00:48
Jenkins 5	3	36N47	93w41	6:14:44
Jennings 95	40	38N43	90w16	6:01:04
Jerico 114	3	37N09	92w46	6:11:04
Jerico Springs 20	3	37N37	94w01	6:16:04
Jerk Tail 114	3	37N15	92w31	6:10:04

MISSOURI

Jerome 81	3	37N56	91w59	6:07:56
Jesse M. Donaldson 83	3	38N45	92w26	6:09:44
Jewett 62	3	37N22	90w42	6:02:48
Jim Henry 66	3	38N18	92w18	6:09:12
Joachim 50	12	38N15	90w26	6:01:44
Jobe 75	3	36N35	91w16	6:05:04
Johnson City 93	3	38N11	94w02	6:16:08
Johnston 61	3	40N00	92w22	6:09:28
Johnstown 7	3	38N16	93w59	6:15:56
Johnstown 49	3	37N09	94w26	6:17:44
Jonesburg 70	3	38N51	91w18	6:05:12
Joplin 49	3	37N06	94w31	6:18:04
Jordan 43	3	38N01	93w14	6:12:56
Jordan W Chambers 95	1	38N39	90w12	6:00:48
Josephville 92	8	38N49	90w51	6:03:24
Judge 76	3	38N29	91w51	6:07:24
Junction City 62	3	37N34	90w17	6:01:08
Junland 12	3	36N46	90w24	6:01:36
Kahoka 23	30	40N25	91w44	6:06:56
Kaiser 66	3	38N08	92w35	6:10:20
Kampville 92	2	38N47	90w30	6:02:00
Kampville Beach 92	2	38N47	90w30	6:02:00
Kampville Court 92	2	38N47	90w30	6:02:00
Kansas City 48	3	39N06	94w35	6:18:20
Kaolin 47	3	37N40	90w53	6:03:32
Kaseyville 61	44	39N46	92w37	6:10:28
Kearney 24	3	39N22	94w22	6:17:28
Keethtown 66	3	38N05	92w17	6:09:08
Kellerville 102	3	39N48	92w02	6:08:08
Kelley 91	3	36N46	90w58	6:03:52
Kelso 100	3	37N11	89w33	5:58:12
Keltner 22	3	36N59	93w02	6:12:08
Kendricktown 49	3	37N08	94w20	6:17:20
Kennett 35	3	36N14	90w03	6:00:12
Kenoma 6	3	37N30	94w17	6:17:08
Keota 61	44	39N45	92w34	6:10:16
Kerr 13	3	39N45	94w14	6:16:56
Kersey Coates 48	3	39N03	94w34	6:18:16
Kewanee 72	3	36N40	89w34	5:58:16
Keyes Summit 95	40	38N34	90w28	6:01:52
Keysville 28	3	37N53	91w23	6:05:32
Keytesville 21	3	39N26	92w56	6:11:44
Kidder 13	3	39N47	94w06	6:16:24
Kiddoo 73	44	36N52	94w22	6:17:28
Kiel 36	3	38N36	91w13	6:04:52
Killarney Shores 47	3	37N29	90w40	6:02:40
Kimberling City 104	3	36N45	93w23	6:13:32
Kimberling Hills 104	3	36N45	93w23	6:13:32
Kime 111	3	37N08	90w27	6:01:48
Kimmswick 50	3	38N22	90w22	6:01:28
Kinder 16	3	37N22	89w49	5:59:16
Kinder 103	3	37N01	90w05	6:00:20
Kinfolk Ridge 78	3	36N11	89w40	5:58:40
King 75	3	36N47	91w12	6:04:48
King City 38	3	40N03	94w31	6:18:04
Kingdom City 14	3	38N57	91w56	6:07:44
King Prairie 5	3	36N53	93w52	6:15:28
Kings Point 29	3	37N23	93w57	6:15:48
Kingston 13	3	39N39	94w02	6:16:08
Kingsville 51	3	38N45	94w04	6:16:16
Kinloch 95	40	38N45	90w19	6:01:16
Kinsey 96	3	38N01	90w13	6:00:52
Kirbyville 106	3	36N37	93w10	6:12:40
Kirksville 1	3	40N12	92w35	6:10:20
Kirkwood 95	31	38N35	90w24	6:01:36
Kissee Mills 106	3	36N40	93w01	6:12:04
Kliever 68	3	38N38	92w34	6:10:16
Knob Lick 94	3	37N41	90w22	6:01:28
Knob Noster 51	3	38N46	93w33	6:14:12
Knobview 28	3	38N04	91w29	6:05:56
Knox City 52	3	40N09	92w01	6:08:04
Knoxville 89	3	39N26	94w01	6:16:04
Kodiak 2	3	39N56	94w50	6:19:20
Koeltztown 76	3	38N19	92w02	6:08:08
Koshkonong 75	3	36N36	91w39	6:06:36
Krakow 36	49	38N33	91w01	6:04:04
Kurreville 16	3	37N26	89w48	5:59:12
Labadie 36	3	38N32	90w49	6:03:16
La Belle 56	32	40N07	91w55	6:07:40
Laclede 58	3	39N47	93w10	6:12:40
Laddonia 4	3	39N15	91w39	6:06:36
Ladue 42	3	38N23	93w46	6:15:04
Ladue 95	40	38N38	90w22	6:01:28
Lafayette 25	3	39N42	94w32	6:18:08
Laflin 9	3	37N15	89w56	5:59:44
La Font 72	3	36N30	89w39	5:58:36
La Forge 72	3	36N35	89w34	5:58:16
Lagonda 21	3	39N46	92w45	6:11:00
La Grange 56	33	40N03	91w35	6:06:20
Laguna Beach 15	3	38N09	92w38	6:10:32
Lake Adelle 50	3	38N21	90w39	6:02:36
Lake Arrowhead 36	3	38N18	90w50	6:03:20
Lake City 48	3	39N08	94w12	6:16:48
Lake City Arsenal 48	3	39N06	94w26	6:17:44
Lake Contrary 11	3	39N46	94w51	6:19:24
Lake Creek 80	3	38N35	93w07	6:12:28
Lake Junction 95	40	38N36	90w20	6:01:20
Lakeland 66	3	38N11	92w38	6:10:32
Lake Lotawana 48	3	38N56	94w16	6:17:04
Lakenan 102	3	39N41	92w02	6:08:08
Lake-of-the-Woods 40	3	40N07	93w35	6:14:20
Lake Ozark 66	3	38N12	92w39	6:10:36
Lake Sherwood 109	3	38N38	91w03	6:04:12
Lakeshire 95	40	38N35	90w20	6:01:20
Lakeside 49	3	37N04	94w30	6:18:00
Lakeside 50	3	38N26	90w23	6:01:32
Lakeside 66	3	38N13	92w36	6:10:24
Lake Spring 33	3	37N47	91w41	6:06:44
Lake Tapawingo 48	3	39N01	94w19	6:17:16
Lake Tekakwitha 50	6	38N29	90w44	6:02:56
Lakeview 66	3	38N16	92w36	6:10:24
Lakeview 104	3	36N45	93w23	6:13:32
Lakeview Heights 8	3	38N23	93w20	6:13:20
Lake Viking 31	3	39N55	93w58	6:15:52
Lake Waukomis 83	3	39N14	94w38	6:18:32
Lake Winnebago 19	3	38N49	94w22	6:17:28
Lake Wittona 40	3	40N07	93w35	6:14:20
Lamar 6	3	37N30	94w16	6:17:04
Lamar Heights 6	3	37N30	94w18	6:17:12
Lambert 100	3	37N06	89w33	5:58:12
Lamine 27	3	38N57	92w53	6:11:32
La Monte 80	3	38N46	93w26	6:13:44
Lampe 104	3	36N34	93w30	6:14:00
Lanagan 60	3	36N37	94w27	6:17:48
Lancaster 98	44	40N31	92w32	6:10:08
Langdon 3	3	40N05	94w30	6:18:00
Lanton 46	3	36N31	91w48	6:07:12
La Plata 61	3	40N02	92w29	6:09:56
Laquey 85	3	37N46	92w18	6:09:12
Laredo 40	3	40N02	93w27	6:13:48
Larimore 95	40	38N46	90w12	6:00:48
La Russell 49	3	37N09	94w04	6:16:16
Latham 68	3	38N34	92w41	6:10:44
Lathrop 25	3	39N33	94w20	6:17:20
Latour 51	3	38N38	94w06	6:16:24
Laurel Heights 48	3	39N00	94w28	6:17:52
Laurie 71	3	38N12	92w50	6:11:20
La Valle 103	3	36N37	89w42	5:58:48
Lawrenceburg 55	3	37N21	93w42	6:14:48
Lawrenceton 96	3	38N01	90w13	6:00:52
Lawson 89	3	39N26	94w12	6:16:48
Lead Hill 22	3	36N56	92w56	6:11:44
Leadington 94	3	37N50	90w29	6:01:56
Lead Mine 30	3	37N51	93w02	6:12:08
Leadwood 94	3	37N52	90w33	6:02:12
Leann 5	3	36N58	93w43	6:14:52
Leasburg 28	3	38N05	91w18	6:05:12
Leawood 73	3	37N02	94w30	6:18:00
Lebanon 53	47	37N41	92w40	6:10:40
Lebo 46	3	36N44	91w52	6:07:28
Lecoma 33	3	37N47	91w44	6:06:56
Lee 83	3	39N19	94w51	6:19:24
Leeds 48	3	39N03	94w30	6:18:00
Leemon 16	3	37N23	89w40	5:58:40
Leeper 111	3	37N04	90w42	6:02:48
Lees Summit 48	3	38N56	94w22	6:17:28
Leesville 42	3	38N19	93w34	6:14:16
Leeton 51	3	38N35	93w42	6:14:48
Lemay 95	40	38N32	90w16	6:01:04
Lemons 86	3	40N29	93w01	6:12:04
Lenox 33	3	37N39	91w46	6:07:04
Lentner 102	3	39N43	92w09	6:08:36
Leonard 102	3	39N54	92w11	6:08:44
Leopold 9	3	37N15	89w56	5:59:44
Leora 103	3	36N53	89w56	5:59:44
Leota 46	3	36N48	92w00	6:08:00
Leroy 6	3	37N36	94w33	6:18:12
Le Sieur 72	3	36N26	89w37	5:58:28
Leslie 36	3	38N25	91w14	6:04:56
Lesterville 90	3	37N27	90w51	6:03:24
Levasy 48	3	39N09	94w09	6:16:36
Lewis 42	3	38N23	93w46	6:15:04
Lewis And Clark Village 11	3	39N35	95w01	6:20:04
Lewistown 56	34	40N05	91w49	6:07:16
Lexington 54	3	39N11	93w52	6:15:28
Liberal 6	3	37N34	94w31	6:18:04
Liberty 14	3	38N43	92w05	6:08:20
Liberty 24	3	39N15	94w25	6:17:40
Libertyville 94	3	37N42	90w17	6:01:08
Lick 27	3	38N58	92w45	6:11:00
Lick Creek 77	3	36N32	92w20	6:09:20
Licking 107	3	37N30	91w52	6:07:28
Liege 70	3	39N00	91w21	6:05:24
Light 63	10	38N00	91w37	6:06:28
Liguori 50	3	38N21	90w24	6:01:36
Lilbourn 72	3	36N36	89w37	5:58:28
Lilly 25	3	39N34	94w27	6:17:48
Lincoln 8	3	38N23	93w20	6:13:20
Lindbergh 14	3	38N58	92w13	6:08:52
Linden 22	3	37N04	93w07	6:12:28
Lindenlure Lake 22	3	37N07	93w04	6:12:16
Lindley 40	3	40N02	93w22	6:13:28
Lindley 65	3	40N31	93w42	6:14:48
Lindsey 8	3	38N19	93w24	6:13:36
Lingo 61	3	39N45	92w47	6:11:08
Linkville 83	3	39N14	94w38	6:18:32
Linn 76	3	38N29	91w51	6:07:24
Linn Creek 15	3	38N02	92w43	6:10:52
Linneus 58	3	39N53	93w11	6:12:44
Lisbon 45	3	39N14	92w50	6:11:20
Lisle 19	3	38N29	94w36	6:18:24
Lithium 79	3	37N50	89w53	5:59:32
Little Prairie 78	3	36N09	89w43	5:58:52
Little River 78	3	36N21	89w50	5:59:20
Livonia 86	3	40N30	92w42	6:10:48
Lock Springs 31	3	39N51	93w47	6:15:08
Lockwood 29	3	37N23	93w57	6:15:48
Locust Creek 58	3	39N53	93w10	6:12:40
Locust Hill 52	3	40N01	92w12	6:08:48
Lodi 111	3	37N15	90w27	6:01:48
Logan 55	3	37N00	93w38	6:14:32
Log Cabin Station 89	3	39N18	93w41	6:14:44
Lohman 26	3	38N33	92w22	6:09:28
Lonedell 36	3	38N19	90w50	6:03:20
Lone Elm 27	3	38N47	92w48	6:11:12
Lone Elm 49	3	37N04	94w30	6:18:00
Lone Hill 12	3	36N46	90w24	6:01:36
Lone Jack 48	3	38N52	94w10	6:16:40
Lone Oak 7	3	38N12	94w19	6:17:16
Lone Star 72	3	36N36	89w37	5:58:28
Lone Tree 19	3	38N40	94w21	6:17:24
Long Lane 30	3	37N36	92w59	6:11:56
Long Prairie 67	3	36N52	89w27	5:57:48
Longrun 77	3	36N39	92w43	6:10:52
Longtown 79	3	37N40	89w47	5:59:08
Longview 48	3	38N58	94w29	6:17:56
Longview 60	3	36N45	94w05	6:16:20
Longwood 80	3	38N53	93w12	6:12:48
Looney 84	3	37N28	93w23	6:13:32
Loose Creek 76	3	38N31	91w57	6:07:48
Lorance 9	3	37N18	89w59	5:59:56
Lost Creek 111	3	37N02	90w17	6:01:08
Louisburg 30	3	37N46	93w08	6:12:32
Louisiana 82	35	39N27	91w03	6:04:12
Louisville 57	3	39N17	91w06	6:04:24
Lowground 86	3	40N14	92w43	6:10:52
Lowndes 111	3	37N09	90w16	6:01:04
Lowry City 93	3	38N08	93w44	6:14:56
Low Wassie 101	3	37N00	91w20	6:05:20
Lucas 42	3	38N28	94w00	6:16:00
Lucas and Hunt Village 95	40	38N43	90w18	6:01:12
Lucerne 86	3	40N28	93w18	6:13:12
Ludlow 59	3	39N39	93w42	6:14:48
Luebbering 36	3	38N16	90w49	6:03:16
Lulu 75	3	36N42	91w24	6:05:36
Luna 77	3	36N36	92w26	6:09:44
Lupus 68	3	38N51	92w27	6:09:48
Luray 23	3	40N27	91w53	6:07:32
Lusk 100	3	36N56	89w20	5:57:20
Lutesville 9	3	37N18	89w59	5:59:56
Luystown 76	3	38N35	91w58	6:07:52
Lyda 61	3	39N55	92w27	6:09:48
Lynch 107	3	37N26	92w01	6:08:04
Lynchburg 53	3	37N30	92w18	6:09:12
Lyon 36	3	38N36	91w13	6:04:52
Macedonia 81	10	37N57	91w48	6:07:12
Machens 92	18	38N56	90w21	6:01:24
Mackenzie 95	40	38N35	90w19	6:01:16
Macks Creek 15	3	37N58	92w58	6:11:52
Macomb 114	3	37N06	92w30	6:10:00
Macon 61	44	39N44	92w28	6:09:52
Madison 69	3	39N28	92w13	6:08:52
Madisonville 87	3	39N31	91w32	6:06:08
Madry 5	3	36N58	93w43	6:14:52
Magnolia 51	3	38N43	93w59	6:15:56
Main City 19	3	38N29	94w36	6:18:24
Maitland 44	3	40N12	95w05	6:20:20
Malden 35	3	36N34	89w57	5:59:48
Malta Bend 97	3	39N12	93w22	6:13:28
Mammoth 77	3	36N36	92w26	6:09:44
Manchester 95	40	38N36	90w31	6:02:04
Mandeville 17	3	39N28	93w31	6:14:04
Manes 114	3	37N23	92w22	6:09:28
Manila 80	3	38N37	93w25	6:13:40
Mansfield 114	3	37N06	92w35	6:10:20
Many Springs 75	3	36N42	91w24	6:05:36
Mapaville 50	3	38N15	90w28	6:01:52
Maplegrove 49	3	37N23	94w06	6:16:24
Maples 107	3	37N30	91w52	6:07:28
Maplewood 95	31	38N37	90w19	6:01:16
Marble Hill 9	3	37N18	89w58	5:59:52
Marceline 58	3	39N43	92w57	6:11:48
March 30	3	37N27	93w02	6:12:08
Margona Village 95	40	38N42	90w20	6:01:20
Marion 26	3	38N41	92w22	6:09:28
Marionville 55	3	37N00	93w38	6:14:32
Marlborough 95	40	38N34	90w20	6:01:20
Marling 70	3	39N08	91w25	6:05:40
Marquand 62	3	37N26	90w10	6:00:40
Marshall 97	3	39N07	93w12	6:12:48
Marshfield 112	3	37N15	92w54	6:11:36
Marston 72	3	36N31	89w37	5:58:28
Marthasville 109	3	38N38	91w04	6:04:16
Martinsburg 4	3	39N06	91w39	6:06:36
Martinstown 86	3	40N29	93w01	6:12:04
Martinsville 41	3	40N20	94w10	6:16:40
Marvin Terrace 95	40	38N42	90w22	6:01:28
Maryden 110	3	37N46	90w37	6:02:28
Maryknoll 57	14	38N56	90w45	6:03:00
Maryland Heights 95	40	38N43	90w26	6:01:44
Mary Ridge 95	40	38N43	90w23	6:01:32
Marys Home 66	3	38N18	92w21	6:09:24
Maryville 74	3	40N21	94w52	6:19:28
Mason 64	27	39N44	91w24	6:05:36
Masters 20	3	37N38	93w35	6:14:20
Matson 92	3	38N38	90w47	6:03:08
Mattese 95	40	38N29	90w21	6:01:24
Matthews 72	3	36N46	89w35	5:58:20
Maud 102	45	39N45	92w15	6:09:00
Maupin 36	3	38N16	90w49	6:03:16
Maxville 50	3	38N26	90w23	6:01:32
May 60	3	36N44	94w24	6:17:36
May 83	3	39N15	94w41	6:18:44
Mayesburg 7	3	38N28	94w00	6:16:00
Mayfield 9	3	37N30	90w00	6:00:00
Mayfield 53	3	37N49	92w28	6:09:52
Maysville 32	3	39N53	94w22	6:17:28
Mayview 54	3	39N03	93w50	6:15:20
Maywood 56	3	39N58	91w36	6:06:24
McBaine 10	3	38N53	92w27	6:09:48
McBride 79	3	37N50	89w50	5:59:20
McCarty 78	3	36N11	89w40	5:58:40
McClurg 106	3	36N47	92w47	6:11:08
McCracken 22	3	37N01	93w09	6:12:36
McCredie 14	3	38N57	91w58	6:07:52
McDowell 5	3	36N49	93w48	6:15:12
McElhany 73	3	36N44	94w24	6:17:36

McFall 38 3 40N07 94w13 6:16:52
McGee 111 3 37N05 90w12 6:00:48
McGirk 68 3 38N37 92w29 6:09:56
McKinley 55 3 37N00 93w38 6:14:32
McKittrick 70 3 38N44 91w27 6:05:48
McMillen 60 3 36N40 94w33 6:18:12
McMullin 100 3 36N53 89w34 5:58:16
McMurtrey 34 3 36N56 92w28 6:09:52
McNatt 60 3 36N46 94w11 6:16:44
Meacham Park 95 40 38N37 90w21 6:01:24
Meadowbrook Downs 95
40 38N42 90w22 6:01:28
Meadville 58 3 39N47 93w18 6:13:12
Mecca 25 3 39N30 94w34 6:18:16
Medford 51 3 38N43 93w59 6:15:56
Medill 23 30 40N26 91w47 6:07:08
Medoc 49 3 37N11 94w28 6:17:52
Mehlville 95 40 38N31 90w20 6:01:20
Meinert 29 3 37N23 93w57 6:15:48
Melbourne 41 3 40N09 93w44 6:14:56
Melzo 50 4 38N08 90w33 6:02:12
Memphis 99 36 40N28 92w10 6:08:40
Mendon 21 3 39N36 93w08 6:12:32
Menfro 79 3 37N47 89w43 5:58:52
Mentor 39 3 37N07 93w04 6:12:16
Mercer 65 3 40N31 93w32 6:14:08
Mercyville 61 3 39N57 92w39 6:10:36
Merritt 34 3 36N59 93w02 6:12:08
Merwin 7 3 38N24 94w35 6:18:20
Mesler 103 3 37N05 89w48 5:59:12
Meta 76 3 38N19 92w10 6:08:40
Metz 108 3 38N00 94w27 6:17:48
Mexico 4 3 39N10 91w53 6:07:32
Miami 97 3 39N19 93w14 6:12:56
Michelles Corner 107
3 37N21 92w01 6:08:04
Micola 78 3 36N05 89w52 5:59:28
Middle Brook 47 3 37N40 90w39 6:02:36
Middle Grove 69 3 39N24 92w16 6:09:04
Middleton 54 3 39N09 93w33 6:14:12
Middletown 70 3 39N08 91w25 6:05:40
Midland 95 40 38N43 90w24 6:01:36
Midvale 107 3 37N11 91w39 6:06:36
Midway 10 3 38N58 92w13 6:08:52
Midway 73 3 37N03 94w30 6:18:00
Mike 21 3 39N43 92w57 6:11:48
Milan 105 3 40N12 93w07 6:12:28
Mildred 106 3 36N37 93w10 6:12:40
Milford 6 3 37N35 94w09 6:16:36
Millard 1 3 40N07 92w33 6:10:12
Millcreek 62 3 37N32 90w19 6:01:16
Mill Creek 71 3 38N36 92w53 6:11:32
Miller 55 3 37N13 93w50 6:15:20
Millersburg 14 3 38N54 92w07 6:08:28
Millersville 16 3 37N26 89w48 5:59:12
Mill Grove 65 3 40N19 93w36 6:14:24
Mill Spring 111 3 37N03 90w40 6:02:40
Millville 89 3 39N17 93w58 6:15:52
Millwood 57 3 39N05 91w05 6:04:20
Milo 108 3 37N45 94w18 6:17:12
Milton 3 3 40N20 95w23 6:21:32
Milton 88 3 39N25 92w25 6:09:40
Minaville 24 3 39N11 94w28 6:17:52
Mincy 106 3 36N37 93w10 6:12:40
Mindenmines 6 3 37N29 94w35 6:18:20
Mine La Motte 62 3 37N37 90w17 6:01:08
Mineola 70 3 38N54 91w34 6:06:16
Miner 100 3 36N53 89w33 5:58:12
Mineral Point 110 3 37N57 90w44 6:02:56
Mineral Spring 5 3 36N41 93w52 6:15:28
Mingo 7 3 38N25 94w07 6:16:28
Mingo 103 3 36N57 90w10 6:00:40
Minimum 47 3 37N22 90w42 6:02:48
Minnith 96 3 37N54 89w56 5:59:44
Mint Hill 76 3 38N40 91w46 6:07:04
Minton 44 3 40N03 95w19 6:21:16
Mirabile 13 3 39N40 94w09 6:16:36
Missionary Acres 111
3 37N08 90w27 6:01:48
Mississippi 67 3 36N49 89w13 5:56:52
Missouri City 24 3 39N14 94w18 6:17:12
Mitchell 94 3 37N52 90w31 6:02:04
Moberly 88 3 39N25 92w26 6:09:44
Modena 65 3 40N18 93w41 6:14:44
Mokane 14 3 38N41 91w53 6:07:32
Moline Acres 95 40 38N45 90w15 6:01:00
Molino 4 3 39N10 91w52 6:07:28
Monark Springs 73
44 36N52 94w22 6:17:28
Monegaw 93 3 38N09 93w53 6:15:32
Monegaw Springs 93
3 38N00 93w38 6:14:32
Monett 5 3 36N55 93w55 6:15:40
Monkey Run 87 3 39N41 91w28 6:05:52
Monroe City 69 37 39N39 91w44 6:06:56
Montague 22 3 36N56 93w17 6:13:08
Montevallo 108 3 37N44 94w07 6:16:28
Montgomery 114 3 37N25 92w20 6:09:20
Montgomery City 70
3 38N59 91w30 6:06:00
Monticello 56 3 40N07 91w43 6:06:52
Montier 101 3 37N00 91w36 6:06:24
Montreal 15 3 37N59 92w30 6:10:00
Montrose 42 3 38N16 93w59 6:15:56
Montserrat 51 3 38N46 93w38 6:14:32
Moody 46 3 36N32 91w59 6:07:56
Mooney 84 3 37N29 93w15 6:13:00
Mooresville 59 3 39N44 93w42 6:14:48
Mora 8 3 38N32 93w11 6:12:44
Morehouse 72 3 36N51 89w41 5:58:44
Moreland 100 3 37N07 89w33 5:58:12
Morgan 53 3 37N31 92w41 6:10:44
Morgan Heights 49 3 37N08 94w20 6:17:20
Morley 100 3 37N03 89w37 5:58:28
Morrison 37 3 38N40 91w38 6:06:32
Morrisville 84 3 37N29 93w25 6:13:40
Morse Mill 50 3 38N17 90w40 6:02:40
Morton 89 3 39N17 93w58 6:15:52
Mosby 24 3 39N19 94w18 6:17:12
Moscow Mills 57 38 38N57 90w55 6:03:40
Moselle 36 3 38N27 91w01 6:04:04
Moss Creek 17 3 39N19 93w35 6:14:20
Mound 7 3 38N21 94w22 6:17:28
Mound City 44 3 40N07 95w14 6:20:56
Moundville 108 3 37N46 94w27 6:17:48
Mountain Grove 114
3 37N08 92w16 6:09:04
Mountain View 46 3 37N00 91w42 6:06:48
Mount Airy 88 3 39N26 92w33 6:10:12
Mount Hope 36 17 38N20 90w58 6:03:52
Mount Hulda 8 3 38N28 93w12 6:12:48
Mount Leonard 97 3 39N08 93w24 6:13:36
Mount Moriah 41 3 40N20 93w48 6:15:12
Mount Shira 60 3 36N33 94w30 6:18:00
Mount Sterling 37 3 38N28 91w38 6:06:32
Mount Vernon 55 3 37N06 93w49 6:15:16
Mount Zion 34 3 36N58 92w40 6:10:40
Mount Zion 42 3 38N15 93w46 6:15:04
Muffittville 12 3 36N36 90w15 6:01:00
Muirfield 95 40 38N40 90w26 6:01:44
Mulberry 6 3 37N33 94w37 6:18:28
Mulberry 7 3 38N15 94w35 6:18:20
Munsell 101 3 37N00 91w20 6:05:20
Murphy 50 40 38N29 90w29 6:01:56
Murray 39 3 37N19 93w28 6:13:52
Murry 10 3 39N07 92w13 6:08:52
Musicks Ferry 95 40 38N52 90w20 6:01:20
Musselfork 21 3 39N34 92w55 6:11:40
Myatt 46 3 36N33 91w44 6:06:56
Myers 40 3 40N14 93w21 6:13:24
Myrtle 75 3 36N31 91w16 6:05:04
Mystic 105 3 40N16 92w57 6:11:48
Nadine 87 3 39N18 91w29 6:05:56
Napier 44 3 39N59 95w12 6:20:48
Napoleon 54 3 39N08 94w05 6:16:20
Napton 97 3 39N03 93w05 6:12:20
Narrows 61 3 39N39 92w28 6:09:52
Nashua 24 3 39N16 94w33 6:18:12
Nashville 6 3 37N23 94w30 6:18:00
Naylor 91 3 36N34 90w36 6:02:24
Nebo 53 3 37N36 92w23 6:09:32
Neck City 49 3 37N16 94w27 6:17:48
Neely 12 3 36N34 90w32 6:02:08
Neelys Landing 16 3 37N30 89w30 5:58:00
Neelyville 12 3 36N34 90w30 6:02:00
Neeper 23 30 40N25 91w43 6:06:52
Neier 36 3 38N27 91w01 6:04:04
Nelson 97 3 39N00 93w02 6:12:08
Nelsonville 64 3 40N00 91w40 6:06:40
Nemo 43 3 37N50 93w18 6:13:12
Neola 29 3 37N25 93w51 6:15:24
Neosho 73 44 36N52 94w22 6:17:28
Netherlands 78 3 36N14 89w45 5:59:00
Nettleton 13 3 39N46 93w54 6:15:36
Nevada 108 3 37N51 94w22 6:17:28
Newark 52 3 40N00 91w58 6:07:52
New Bloomfield 14 3 38N43 92w05 6:08:20
New Boston 58 3 39N57 92w51 6:11:24
Newburg 81 48 37N55 91w54 6:07:36
New Cambria 61 3 39N46 92w45 6:11:00
New Court Village 56
26 40N06 91w45 6:07:00
New Florence 70 3 38N55 91w27 6:05:48
New Frankfort 97 3 39N13 93w04 6:12:16
New Franklin 45 3 39N01 92w44 6:10:56
New Hamburg 100 3 37N08 89w35 5:58:20
New Hampton 41 3 40N16 94w12 6:16:48
New Harmony 82 3 39N21 91w20 6:05:20
New Hartford 82 3 39N12 91w16 6:05:04
New Haven 36 3 38N37 91w13 6:04:52
New Home 7 3 38N10 94w28 6:17:52
Newhope 57 25 39N10 90w47 6:03:08
New Lebanon 27 3 38N47 92w48 6:11:12
New Liberty 75 3 37N00 91w20 6:05:20
New Lisbon 103 3 36N58 90w01 6:00:04
New London 87 3 39N35 91w24 6:05:36
New Madrid 72 3 36N36 89w32 5:58:08
New Market 83 3 39N31 94w46 6:19:04
New Melle 92 3 38N43 90w53 6:03:32
New Offenburg 96 3 37N54 90w12 6:00:48
New Piper 42 3 38N28 94w00 6:16:00
New Point 44 3 40N03 95w05 6:20:20
Newport 6 3 37N31 94w07 6:16:28
Newton 101 3 37N21 91w25 6:05:40
Newtonia 73 3 36N53 94w11 6:16:44
Newtown 105 3 40N22 93w20 6:13:20
New Truxton 109 3 39N00 91w14 6:04:56
New Wells 16 3 37N34 89w38 5:58:32
New York 13 3 39N40 93w55 6:15:40
Niangua 112 3 37N23 92w50 6:11:20
Nichols 39 44 37N13 93w18 6:13:12
Nind 1 3 40N11 92w35 6:10:20
Nine Mile Prairie 14
3 38N55 91w43 6:06:52
Ninnescah 93 3 38N15 93w46 6:15:04
Nishnabotna 3 3 40N26 95w38 6:22:32
Nixa 22 3 37N03 93w18 6:13:12
Noble 77 3 36N46 92w35 6:10:20
Nodaway 2 3 39N53 94w54 6:19:36
Noel 60 3 36N33 94w29 6:17:56
Norborne 17 3 39N18 93w40 6:14:40
Norman 33 3 37N45 91w35 6:06:20
Normandy 95 40 38N42 90w18 6:01:12
Norris 42 49 38N33 93w58 6:15:52
North 29 3 37N31 93w53 6:15:32
North Benton 30 3 37N41 93w06 6:12:24
North Boonville 45
3 39N01 92w44 6:10:56
North Campbell 39
44 37N15 93w18 6:13:12
North County 95 40 38N46 90w12 6:00:48
Northeast 48 3 39N07 94w31 6:18:04
Northern Heights 83
3 39N13 94w38 6:18:32
North Fork 6 3 37N25 94w21 6:17:24
North Galloway 22 3 36N56 93w17 6:13:08
North Kansas City 24
3 39N09 94w35 6:18:20
Northland Shopping Center 95
40 38N44 90w15 6:01:00
North Lilbourn 72 3 36N36 89w37 5:58:28
North Moniteau 27 3 38N45 92w39 6:10:36
Northmoor 83 3 39N10 94w36 6:18:24
North Morgan 29 3 37N33 93w40 6:14:40
North Noel 60 3 36N33 94w30 6:18:00
North Patton 9 3 37N30 90w00 6:00:00
North River 102 3 39N48 91w52 6:07:28
North Salem 58 3 40N00 92w56 6:11:44
North Sugar Creek 88
3 39N27 92w28 6:09:52
Northview 112 3 37N17 93w00 6:12:00
North Wardell 78 3 36N21 89w49 5:59:16
Northwood Acres 83
3 39N13 94w40 6:18:40
Northwoods 95 40 38N42 90w17 6:01:08
Northwye 81 10 37N59 91w46 6:07:04
Norwood 114 3 37N07 92w24 6:09:36
Norwood Court 95 40 38N43 90w18 6:01:12
Nottinghill 77 3 36N40 92w34 6:10:16
Novelty 52 3 40N01 92w12 6:08:48
Novinger 1 3 40N14 92w43 6:10:52
Number Eight 61 44 39N45 92w34 6:10:16
Nyhart 7 3 38N16 94w20 6:17:20
Oak 32 3 39N52 94w26 6:17:44
Oak Grove 48 3 39N00 94w08 6:16:32
Oak Grove Heights 39
44 37N12 93w18 6:13:12
Oakhill 5 3 36N24 93w44 6:14:56
Oak Hill 28 44 38N12 91w10 6:04:40
Oakland 49 3 37N09 94w28 6:17:52
Oakland 53 47 37N41 92w40 6:10:40
Oakland 95 40 38N36 90w23 6:01:32
Oakland Park 49 3 37N07 94w28 6:17:52
Oak Ridge 16 3 37N30 89w44 5:58:56
Oaks 24 3 39N12 94w35 6:18:20
Oakside 101 3 37N00 91w42 6:06:48
Oakton 6 3 37N30 94w17 6:17:08
Oakview 24 3 39N13 94w35 6:18:20
Oakville 95 40 38N28 90w18 6:01:12
Oakwood 24 3 39N12 94w34 6:18:16
Oakwood 64 3 39N41 91w28 6:05:52
Oakwood Manor 24 3 39N12 94w34 6:18:16
Oakwood Park 24 3 39N12 94w35 6:18:20
Oasis 57 16 39N03 90w45 6:03:00
Oates 90 3 37N32 90w56 6:03:44
Ocie 77 3 36N33 92w45 6:11:00
Octa 35 3 36N08 90w10 6:00:40
Odessa 54 3 39N00 93w57 6:15:48
Odin 114 3 37N15 92w31 6:10:04
O'Fallon 92 2 38N49 90w42 6:02:48
Ogborn 94 3 37N47 90w25 6:01:40
Oglesville 12 3 36N36 90w15 6:01:00
Ohio 67 3 36N56 89w11 5:56:44
Ohio 93 3 38N08 93w44 6:14:56
Okete 57 3 38N59 90w59 6:03:56
Olathia 34 3 37N06 92w35 6:10:20
Old Appleton 16 3 37N36 89w43 5:58:52
Old Bland 37 3 38N18 91w38 6:06:32
Old Chilhowee 51 3 38N35 93w51 6:15:24
Old Farm Estates 95
40 38N40 90w26 6:01:44
Oldfield 22 3 36N58 93w02 6:12:08
Old Fredonia 8 3 38N15 93w23 6:13:32
Oldham 10 3 38N46 92w15 6:09:00
Old Merritt 34 3 36N59 93w02 6:12:08
Old Mines 110 3 38N01 90w45 6:03:00
Old Monroe 57 14 38N56 90w45 6:03:00
Old Orchard 95 40 38N36 90w20 6:01:20
Old Success 107 3 37N27 92w05 6:08:20
Old Van Cleve 63 3 38N19 92w10 6:08:40
Old Woollam 37 3 38N21 91w30 6:06:00
Olean 66 3 38N25 92w32 6:10:08
Olga 22 3 37N10 92w56 6:11:44
Olive 30 3 37N23 93w09 6:12:36
Olive 95 1 38N38 90w12 6:00:48
Oliver 106 3 36N36 93w13 6:12:52
Olivette 95 40 38N40 90w21 6:01:24
Olney 57 3 39N05 91w15 6:05:00
Olympia Village 50
3 36N50 89w20 5:57:20
Omaha 86 3 40N29 93w01 6:12:04
Ongo 34 3 37N00 93w05 6:12:20
Oran 100 3 37N05 89w39 5:58:36
Orange 55 3 36N58 93w43 6:14:52
Orchard Farm 92 15 38N53 90w27 6:01:48
Orchard Lakes 95 40 38N40 90w26 6:01:44
Orearville 97 3 39N13 93w04 6:12:16
Oregon 44 3 39N59 95w09 6:20:36
Origanna 53 3 37N36 92w23 6:09:32
Oriole 16 3 37N19 89w32 5:58:08
Orla 53 47 37N41 92w40 6:10:40
Oronogo 49 3 37N11 94w28 6:17:52
Orrick 89 3 39N13 94w07 6:16:28
Orrsburg 74 3 40N26 94w37 6:18:28
Osage 26 3 38N32 92w10 6:08:40
Osage Beach 15 3 38N09 92w38 6:10:32
Osage Bend 26 3 38N32 92w10 6:08:40
Osage Bluff 26 3 38N32 92w10 6:08:40
Osage City 26 3 38N33 92w02 6:08:08
Osage Heights 93 3 37N59 93w49 6:15:16
Osage Hill 95 40 38N37 90w21 6:01:24
Osborn 32 3 39N45 94w21 6:17:24
Oscar 107 3 37N30 91w52 6:07:28
Osceola 93 3 38N03 93w42 6:14:48
Osgood 105 3 40N12 93w20 6:13:20

Osiris 20 3 37N37 94W01 6:16:04
Oskaloosa 6 3 37N38 94W35 6:18:20
Otterville 27 3 38N42 93W00 6:12:00
Otto 50 3 38N22 90W23 6:01:32
Ottoville 50 3 38N25 90W34 6:02:16
Overland 95 40 38N41 90W22 6:01:28
Overton 27 3 38N58 92W45 6:11:00
Owens 114 3 37N06 92W25 6:09:40
Owensville 37 3 38N21 91W30 6:06:00
Owsley 51 3 38N37 93W25 6:13:40
Oxford 113 3 40N26 94W37 6:18:28
Oxly 91 3 36N36 90W41 6:02:44
Oyer 93 3 37N52 94W01 6:16:04
Ozark 22 3 37N01 93W12 6:12:48
Ozark Beach 106 3 36N41 93W07 6:12:28
Ozark Springs 85 3 37N49 92W12 6:08:48
Ozora 96 3 37N54 89W56 5:59:44
Pacific 36 6 38N29 90W45 6:03:00
Pack 60 3 36N33 94W30 6:18:00
Pagedale 95 40 38N41 90W19 6:01:16
Painton 103 3 37N05 89W48 5:59:12
Palestine 27 3 38N51 92W50 6:11:20
Palisades 95 40 38N32 90W35 6:02:20
Palmyra 64 39 39N48 91W32 6:06:08
Palopinto 8 3 38N23 93W20 6:13:20
Papin 50 4 38N08 90W33 6:02:12
Papinsville 7 3 38N04 94W05 6:16:20
Paradise 24 3 39N23 94W35 6:18:20
Paris 69 3 39N29 92W00 6:08:00
Paris Springs 55 3 37N21 93W42 6:14:48
Parkdale 50 3 38N29 90W32 6:02:08
Parker Lake 79 3 37N45 89W49 5:59:16
Parkville 83 3 39N12 94W41 6:18:44
Parkway 36 17 38N20 90W58 6:03:52
Parkway 48 3 39N01 94W32 6:18:08
Parma 72 3 36N37 89W48 5:59:12
Parnell 74 3 40N26 94W37 6:18:28
Parson Creek 58 3 39N46 93W18 6:13:12
Pasadena Hills 95
40 38N42 90W18 6:01:12
Pasadena Park 95 40 38N43 90W18 6:01:12
Pascola 78 3 36N17 89W52 5:59:28
Passaic 7 3 38N19 94W21 6:17:24
Passo 8 3 38N15 93W23 6:13:32
Patterson 111 3 37N11 90W33 6:02:12
Patton 9 3 37N30 90W01 6:00:04
Pattonsburg 31 3 40N03 94W08 6:16:32
Paulding 35 3 36N03 90W15 6:01:00
Paulina Hills 50 3 38N26 90W23 6:01:32
Paynesville 82 21 39N16 90W54 6:03:36
Peace Valley 46 3 36N55 91W50 6:07:20
Peach Orchard 78 3 36N22 89W56 5:59:44
Peaksville 23 3 40N30 91W40 6:06:40
Pea Ridge 110 44 38N13 91W09 6:04:36
Pebble Acres 95 40 38N40 90W26 6:01:44
Peculiar 19 3 38N43 94W28 6:17:52
Peerless Park 95 40 38N32 90W29 6:01:56
Peers 109 3 38N38 91W03 6:04:12
Pemiscot 78 3 36N04 89W44 5:58:56
Pendleton 94 3 37N44 90W29 6:01:56
Pendleton 109 17 38N49 91W09 6:04:36
Penermon 103 3 36N48 89W49 5:59:16
Penn 105 3 40N16 92W57 6:11:48
Pennsboro 29 3 37N23 93W50 6:15:20
Pennville 105 3 40N16 92W57 6:11:48
Peno 82 3 39N29 91W17 6:05:08
Peoria 110 3 37N47 90W51 6:03:24
Pepsin 73 44 36N55 94W15 6:17:00
Perche 10 3 39N06 92W25 6:09:40
Perkins 100 3 37N06 89W46 5:59:04
Perrin 25 3 39N34 94W27 6:17:48
Perry 87 3 39N26 91W40 6:06:40
Perryville 79 3 37N43 89W52 5:59:28
Pershing 37 3 38N40 91W38 6:06:32
Peru 7 3 38N16 94W20 6:17:20
Peruque 92 2 38N47 90W30 6:02:00
Petersburg 45 3 39N01 92W45 6:11:00
Petersville 36 3 38N32 90W49 6:03:16
Pevely 50 12 38N17 90W24 6:01:36
Phelps 55 3 37N08 94W03 6:16:12
Phelps City 3 3 40N23 95W36 6:22:24
Philadelphia 64 3 39N50 91W45 6:07:00
Phillipsburg 53 3 37N33 92W47 6:11:08
Pickering 74 3 40N27 94W49 6:19:16
Piedmont 111 3 37N09 90W42 6:02:48
Pierce City 55 44 36N57 94W00 6:16:00
Pierre Laclede 115
1 38N38 90W15 6:01:00
Pilgrim 29 3 37N22 93W46 6:15:04
Pilot Grove 27 3 38N53 92W55 6:11:40
Pilot Knob 47 3 37N37 90W38 6:02:32
Pinckney 109 3 38N42 91W14 6:04:56
Pine 91 3 36N37 90W49 6:03:16
Pine Creek 77 3 36N41 92W19 6:09:16
Pine Crest 107 3 37N11 91W39 6:06:36
Pine Lawn 95 40 38N41 90W17 6:01:08
Pineville 60 3 36N36 94W22 6:17:28
Piney Park 36 17 38N18 90W57 6:03:48
Pinhook 67 3 36N47 89W23 5:57:32
Pioneer 5 3 36N50 94W03 6:16:12
Piper 42 3 38N16 93W59 6:15:56
Pisgah 27 3 38N47 92W48 6:11:12
Pittsburg 43 3 37N50 93W18 6:13:12
Pittsville 51 3 38N51 94W00 6:16:00
Plad 30 3 37N51 93W02 6:12:08
Plato 107 3 37N30 92W13 6:08:52
Platte City 83 3 39N22 94W47 6:19:08
Platte Woods 83 3 39N14 94W39 6:18:36
Plattin 50 3 38N08 90W24 6:01:36
Plattsburg 25 3 39N34 94W27 6:17:48
Plaza 48 3 39N03 94W36 6:18:24
Plaza 115 1 38N38 90W15 6:01:00
Pleasant Gap 7 3 38N10 94W14 6:16:56
Pleasant Green 27 3 38N48 92W58 6:11:52
Pleasant Grove 27 3 38N49 92W35 6:10:20

Pleasant Hill 19 3 38N47 94W16 6:17:04
Pleasant Hope 84 3 37N28 93W16 6:13:04
Pleasant Ridge 5 3 36N54 93W47 6:15:08
Pleasant Ridge 7 3 38N11 94W02 6:16:08
Pleasant Valley 24
3 39N13 94W29 6:17:56
Pleasant Valley 49
3 37N08 94W20 6:17:20
Plevna 52 3 39N58 92W05 6:08:20
Plew 55 3 37N08 94W03 6:16:12
Plymouth 17 3 39N36 93W48 6:15:12
Pocahontas 16 3 37N30 89W38 5:58:32
Point Lookout 106 3 36N37 93W14 6:12:56
Point Pleasant 72 3 36N26 89W42 5:58:48
Pollock 105 3 40N21 93W05 6:12:20
Polo 13 3 39N33 94W03 6:16:12
Pomona 46 3 36N52 91W55 6:07:40
Pom-o-sa Heights 8
3 38N15 93W23 6:13:32
Ponce de Leon 104 3 36N53 93W22 6:13:28
Pond 95 40 38N33 90W36 6:02:24
Pond Creek 39 3 37N08 93W34 6:14:16
Pondfork 77 3 36N42 92W40 6:10:40
Pontiac 77 3 36N31 92W35 6:10:20
Poplar Bluff 12 13 36N46 90W24 6:01:36
Portage 72 3 36N27 89W47 5:59:08
Portage Des Sioux 92
18 38N56 90W21 6:01:24
Portageville 72 3 36N26 89W42 5:58:48
Porter 22 3 37N03 93W19 6:13:16
Port Hudson 36 3 38N36 91W13 6:04:52
Portland 14 3 38N43 91W43 6:06:52
Possumwalk 74 3 40N27 95W04 6:20:16
Post Oak 51 3 38N34 93W45 6:15:00
Potosi 110 3 37N56 90W47 6:03:08
Pottersville 46 3 36N54 92W01 6:08:04
Powe 103 3 36N40 89W58 5:59:52
Powell 60 3 36N37 94W11 6:16:44
Powersite 106 3 36N39 93W07 6:12:28
Powersville 86 3 40N33 93W15 6:13:00
Poynor 91 3 36N31 90W55 6:03:40
Prairie City 7 3 38N04 94W05 6:16:20
Prairie Hill 21 3 39N31 92W44 6:10:56
Prairie Home 27 3 38N49 92W35 6:10:20
Prairieville 82 3 39N16 91W00 6:04:00
Prathersville 10 3 38N58 92W13 6:08:52
Prathersville 24 3 39N19 94W16 6:17:04
Pratt 91 3 36N37 90W49 6:03:16
Prescott 107 3 37N19 91W58 6:07:52
Preston 43 3 37N57 93W13 6:12:52
Preston 49 3 37N08 94W20 6:17:20
Princeton 65 5 40N24 93W35 6:14:20
Principia 95 40 38N37 90W26 6:01:44
Progress 115 1 38N38 90W15 6:01:00
Prospect 112 3 37N23 92W50 6:11:20
Prospect Hill 95 40 38N44 90W14 6:00:56
Prosperity 49 3 37N04 94W30 6:18:00
Protem 106 3 36N32 92W51 6:11:24
Pulaski 91 3 36N37 90W49 6:03:16
Pulaskifield 5 3 36N56 93W55 6:15:40
Pumpkin Center 74 3 40N10 94W49 6:19:16
Purcell 49 3 37N15 94W26 6:17:44
Purdin 58 3 39N57 93W10 6:12:40
Purdy 5 3 36N49 93W55 6:15:40
Pure Air 1 3 40N14 92W43 6:10:52
Purina Farm 36 6 38N29 90W49 6:03:16
Purman 91 3 36N37 90W49 6:03:16
Purvis 15 3 38N10 92W47 6:11:08
Puxico 103 3 36N57 90W10 6:00:40
Pyletown 103 3 36N48 89W58 5:59:52
Pyrmont 71 3 38N27 93W00 6:12:00
Quarles 42 3 38N23 93W46 6:15:04
Queen City 98 3 40N25 92W34 6:10:16
Quick City 93 3 38N05 94W02 6:16:08
Quincy 43 19 38N01 93W28 6:13:52
Quitman 74 3 40N22 95W05 6:20:20
Qulin 12 3 36N36 90W15 6:01:00
Racine 73 3 36N54 94W32 6:18:08
Racket 8 3 38N23 93W46 6:15:04
Racola 110 3 37N59 90W41 6:02:44
Radar 63 3 38N11 91W57 6:07:48
Rader 112 3 37N23 92W50 6:11:20
Ralls 87 3 39N41 91W28 6:05:52
Randles 16 3 37N11 89W39 5:58:36
Randol 16 3 37N24 89W32 5:58:08
Ravanna 65 3 40N25 93W26 6:13:44
Ravena 24 3 39N13 94W28 6:17:52
Ravena Gardens 24 3 39N13 94W28 6:17:52
Ravenwood 74 3 40N22 94W41 6:18:44
Raymondville 107 3 37N20 91W50 6:07:20
Raymore 19 3 38N48 94W29 6:17:56
Raytown 48 3 39N01 94W28 6:17:52
Rayville 89 3 39N21 94W04 6:16:16
Rea 2 3 40N04 94W46 6:19:04
Readsville 14 3 38N48 91W43 6:06:52
Rector 101 3 37N39 91W32 6:06:08
Red Bird 37 3 38N18 91W38 6:06:32
Reddish 56 3 40N14 91W46 6:07:04
Redford 90 3 37N19 90W54 6:03:36
Redings Mill 73 3 37N01 94W31 6:18:04
Redman 61 45 39N45 92W20 6:09:20
Red Oak 55 3 37N13 94W00 6:16:00
Reeds 49 3 37N07 94W10 6:16:40
Reeds Spring 104 3 36N45 93W23 6:13:32
Regal 89 3 39N36 93W48 6:15:12
Reger 105 3 40N09 93W11 6:12:44
Renick 88 3 39N21 92W25 6:09:40
Rensselaer 87 3 39N40 91W33 6:06:12
Republic 39 3 37N07 93W29 6:13:56
Rescue 55 3 37N08 94W03 6:16:12
Revere 23 3 40N35 91W41 6:06:44
Reynolds 90 3 37N24 91W04 6:04:16
Rhineland 70 3 38N43 91W31 6:06:04
Rhyse 33 3 37N39 91W32 6:06:08
Richards 108 3 37N55 94W33 6:18:12

Richards-Gebaur Air Force Ba 48
3 38N54 94W32 6:18:08
Rich Fountain 76 3 38N24 91W53 6:07:32
Rich Hill 7 3 38N06 94W22 6:17:28
Richland 85 9 37N51 92W26 6:09:44
Richmond 89 3 39N17 93W58 6:15:52
Richmond Heights 95
40 38N38 90W19 6:01:16
Richville 34 3 36N47 92W13 6:08:52
Richville 44 3 39N59 95W09 6:20:36
Richwood 60 3 36N42 94W07 6:16:28
Richwoods 110 3 38N10 90W50 6:03:20
Ridge 17 3 39N29 93W22 6:13:28
Ridgedale 106 3 36N32 93W15 6:13:00
Ridgeley 83 3 39N30 94W38 6:18:32
Ridgeway 41 3 40N23 93W57 6:15:48
Ridgley 5 3 36N40 93W56 6:15:44
Riggs 10 3 39N14 92W17 6:09:08
Rimby 84 3 37N42 93W15 6:13:00
Risco 72 3 36N33 89W49 5:59:16
Ritchey 73 3 36N57 94W11 6:16:44
River Aux Vases 96
3 37N59 90W03 6:00:12
River Bend Estates 95
40 38N37 90W35 6:02:20
Rivermines 94 3 37N51 90W32 6:02:08
Riverside 35 3 36N03 90W18 6:01:12
Riverside 83 3 39N10 94W36 6:18:24
Riverton 75 3 36N42 91W24 6:05:36
Riverview 95 40 38N45 90W13 6:00:52
Rives 35 3 36N06 90W01 6:00:04
Roach 15 3 38N00 92W55 6:11:40
Roads 17 3 39N18 93W41 6:14:44
Roanoke 45 3 39N19 92W41 6:10:44
Roaring River 5 3 36N33 93W45 6:15:00
Roark 37 3 38N39 91W28 6:05:52
Robberson 39 3 37N21 93W20 6:13:20
Robertson 95 40 38N46 90W22 6:01:28
Robertsville 36 3 38N25 90W49 6:03:16
Roby 107 3 37N31 92W08 6:08:32
Rocheport 10 3 38N59 92W34 6:10:16
Rochester 2 3 39N55 94W41 6:18:44
Rock 50 3 38N26 90W25 6:01:40
Rockaway Beach 106
3 36N42 93W10 6:12:40
Rockbridge 77 3 36N47 92W25 6:09:40
Rock Hill 95 40 38N37 90W22 6:01:28
Rockingham 89 3 39N16 93W50 6:15:20
Rock Port 3 3 40N25 95W31 6:22:04
Rock Prairie 29 3 37N20 93W41 6:14:44
Rock Springs 94 3 37N52 90W31 6:02:04
Rockview 100 3 37N11 89W39 5:58:36
Rockville 7 3 38N04 94W05 6:16:20
Rocky Comfort 60 3 36N45 94W05 6:16:20
Rocky Fork 10 3 39N05 92W15 6:09:00
Rocky Mount 71 3 38N18 92W42 6:10:48
Rocky Ridge 96 3 37N53 90W13 6:00:52
Rogersville 112 3 37N07 93W03 6:12:12
Rolla 81 10 37N57 91W46 6:07:04
Romance 77 3 36N48 92W35 6:10:20
Rombauer 12 3 36N51 90W17 6:01:08
Rome 34 3 36N50 92W46 6:11:04
Rondo 84 3 37N48 93W30 6:14:00
Roosterville 24 3 39N13 94W28 6:17:52
Rosati 81 10 38N00 91W37 6:06:28
Roscoe 93 3 37N57 93W49 6:15:16
Rosebud 37 3 38N23 91W25 6:05:40
Rose Hill 51 3 38N38 94W02 6:16:08
Roseland 42 3 38N28 93W37 6:14:28
Roselle 62 3 37N36 90W32 6:02:08
Rosendale 2 3 40N03 94W49 6:19:16
Rothville 21 3 39N39 93W04 6:12:16
Roubidoux 107 3 37N21 92W01 6:08:04
Round Grove 55 3 37N13 93W50 6:15:20
Round Prairie 14 3 38N49 92W05 6:08:20
Round Spring 101 3 37N05 91W30 6:06:00
Rover 75 3 36N43 91W37 6:06:28
Rowena 4 3 39N13 92W17 6:09:08
Royal 81 10 38N00 91W37 6:06:28
Royal Heights 49 3 37N04 94W30 6:18:00
Ruble 90 3 37N14 90W58 6:03:52
Rucker 10 3 39N17 92W20 6:09:20
Rueter 106 3 36N36 92W52 6:11:28
Rush 11 3 39N34 95W02 6:20:08
Rush Hill 4 3 39N13 91W43 6:06:52
Rush Tower 50 12 38N13 90W24 6:01:36
Rushville 11 3 39N35 95W01 6:20:04
Russ 53 47 37N41 92W40 6:10:40
Russellville 26 3 38N31 92W26 6:09:44
Russellville 89 3 39N16 93W50 6:15:20
Ruth 104 3 36N45 93W22 6:13:28
Rutledge 99 3 40N19 92W05 6:08:20
Sabula 47 3 37N27 90W42 6:02:48
Sac 29 3 37N31 93W46 6:15:04
Saco 62 3 37N22 90W26 6:01:44
Sac-o-Sage Heights 93
3 37N59 93W49 6:15:16
Safe 63 10 38N00 91W37 6:06:28
Sage Hill 55 3 36N58 93W43 6:14:52
Saginaw 73 3 37N02 94W28 6:17:52
Sagrada 15 3 38N08 93W10 6:12:40
Saint Albans 36 3 38N35 90W46 6:03:04
Saint Ann 95 40 38N44 90W23 6:01:32
Saint Anthony 66 3 38N05 92W17 6:09:08
Saint Aubert 14 3 38N44 91W54 6:07:36
Saint Catharine 58
3 39N48 93W00 6:12:00
Saint Charles 92 2 38N47 90W29 6:01:56
Saint Clair 36 17 38N21 90W59 6:03:56
Saint Clement 82 3 39N21 91W11 6:04:44
Saint Cloud 28 46 38N09 91W15 6:05:00
Sainte Genevieve 96
3 37N59 90W03 6:00:12
Saint Elizabeth 66
3 38N15 92W16 6:09:04

MISSOURI

Saint Ferdinand 95 40 38N45 90w14 6:00:56
Saint Francisville 23 3 40N22 91w27 6:05:48
Saint Francois 94 3 37N52 90w31 6:02:04
Saint George 95 40 38N32 90w20 6:01:20
Saint George 114 3 37N15 92w31 6:10:04
Saint James 81 10 38N00 91w37 6:06:28
Saint Johns 95 40 38N43 90w21 6:01:24
Saint Joseph 11 3 39N46 94w50 6:19:20
Saint Jude Acres 96 3 37N58 90w03 6:00:12
Saint Louis 115 1 38N37 90w12 6:00:48
Saint Martins 26 3 38N32 92w10 6:08:40
Saint Marys 96 3 37N53 89w57 5:59:48
Saint Michael 62 3 37N33 90w17 6:01:08
Saint Patrick 23 3 40N16 91w38 6:06:32
Saint Paul 92 2 38N49 90w42 6:02:48
Saint Peters 92 2 38N48 90w38 6:02:32
Saint Robert 85 3 37N49 92w11 6:08:44
Saint Thomas 26 3 38N23 92w13 6:08:52
Salcedo 100 3 36N53 89w34 5:58:16
Salem 33 3 37N39 91w32 6:06:08
Saline 65 3 40N26 93w46 6:15:04
Saline City 97 3 39N13 93w04 6:12:16
Saling 4 3 39N18 92w12 6:08:48
Salisbury 21 3 39N25 92w48 6:11:12
Salt Creek 21 3 39N34 93w02 6:12:08
Salt Fork 97 3 39N01 93w09 6:12:36
Salt Pond 97 3 39N00 93w26 6:13:44
Salt Spring 88 3 39N26 92w33 6:10:12
Samford 78 3 36N05 89w52 5:59:28
Samos 67 3 36N56 89w20 5:57:20
Sampsell 59 3 39N50 93w42 6:14:48
Sampson 112 3 37N23 92w50 6:11:20
San Antonio 11 3 39N43 94w38 6:18:32
Sand Hill 99 3 40N21 92w07 6:08:28
Sandy Hook 68 3 38N45 92w25 6:09:40
Sandywoods 100 3 36N59 89w31 5:58:04
Santa Fe 69 3 39N22 91w49 6:07:16
Santa Rosa 32 3 40N03 94w08 6:16:32
Sapp 10 3 38N58 92w13 6:08:52
Sappington 95 40 38N32 90w23 6:01:32
Saratoga 60 3 36N33 94w30 6:18:00
Sarcoxie 49 3 37N03 94w07 6:16:28
Sargent 107 3 37N06 91w59 6:07:56
Savannah 2 3 39N56 94w50 6:19:20
Saverton 87 41 39N38 91w19 6:05:16
Saxton 11 3 39N44 94w49 6:19:16
Schell City 108 3 38N01 94w07 6:16:28
Schlatitz 9 3 37N06 89w55 5:59:40
Schluersburg 92 3 38N35 90w53 6:03:32
Schofield 84 3 37N37 93w15 6:13:00
Scholten 5 3 36N47 93w41 6:14:44
Schubert 26 3 38N32 92w10 6:08:40
Schuermann Heights 95 40 38N43 90w22 6:01:28
Scobeville 35 3 36N14 90w03 6:00:12
Scopus 9 3 37N26 89w56 5:59:44
Scotland 49 3 37N08 94w20 6:17:20
Scott 106 3 36N33 93w06 6:12:24
Scott City 100 3 37N13 89w31 5:58:04
Scotts Corner 4 3 39N14 91w39 6:06:36
Scrivner 26 3 38N31 92w26 6:09:44
Seaton 81 3 37N39 91w32 6:06:08
Sedalia 80 3 38N42 93w14 6:12:56
Sedgewickville 9 3 37N31 89w54 5:59:36
Seligman 5 3 36N31 93w56 6:15:44
Sellers 56 26 40N07 91w40 6:06:40
Selma 50 12 38N13 90w24 6:01:36
Selmore 22 3 37N01 93w12 6:12:48
Senate Grove 36 3 38N36 91w13 6:04:52
Senath 35 3 36N08 90w10 6:00:40
Seneca 73 44 36N51 94w37 6:18:28
Sereno 79 3 37N45 89w49 5:59:16
Seven Pines 95 40 38N40 90w26 6:01:44
Seymour 112 3 37N09 92w46 6:11:04
Shackelford 97 3 39N07 93w12 6:12:48
Shade 78 3 36N14 89w45 5:59:00
Shady Dell 12 3 36N46 90w24 6:01:36
Shady Dell 103 3 37N01 89w49 5:59:16
Shady Grove 22 3 37N00 93w05 6:12:20
Shady Grove 85 3 37N49 92w12 6:08:48
Shamrock 14 3 39N00 91w42 6:06:48
Shannondale 101 3 37N39 91w32 6:06:08
Sharon 97 3 39N13 93w04 6:12:16
Shaw 10 3 38N58 92w13 6:08:52
Shawan 103 3 37N01 89w49 5:59:16
Shawnee Mound 42 3 38N35 93w51 6:15:24
Shawneetown 16 3 37N33 89w39 5:58:36
Shearwood 59 3 39N59 93w48 6:15:12
Shelbina 102 3 39N47 92w02 6:08:08
Shelbyville 102 3 39N48 92w02 6:08:08
Sheldon 108 3 37N40 94w18 6:17:12
Shell Knob 5 3 36N38 93w38 6:14:32
Shelton 52 3 40N05 92w16 6:09:04
Sheridan 113 3 40N31 94w37 6:18:28
Sherley 91 3 36N38 90w56 6:03:44
Sherman 95 40 38N32 90w35 6:02:20
Sherrill 107 3 37N31 91w50 6:07:20
Shibboleth 110 3 37N59 90w41 6:02:44
Shibleys Point 1 3 40N14 92w43 6:10:52
Shirley 110 3 37N55 90w55 6:03:40
Shoal 25 3 39N42 94w16 6:17:04
Shoal Creek 73 3 37N01 94w30 6:18:00
Shoal Creek Drive 73 3 37N02 94w31 6:18:04
Shook 111 3 37N03 90w19 6:01:16
Short Bend 33 3 37N45 91w26 6:05:44
Shoveltown 95 40 38N49 90w17 6:01:08
Shrewsbury 95 40 38N35 90w20 6:01:20
Sibley 48 3 39N11 94w12 6:16:48
Sidney 86 3 40N17 92w52 6:11:28
Sigsbee 102 3 39N53 92w01 6:08:04
Sikeston 100 3 36N53 89w35 5:58:20
Silex 57 3 39N08 91w04 6:04:16
Siloam Springs 46 3 36N48 92w05 6:08:20
Silva 111 3 37N11 90w28 6:01:52
Silver Creek 73 3 37N04 94w30 6:18:00
Silver Dollar City 104 3 36N39 93w13 6:12:52
Silver Lake 79 3 38N00 89w41 5:58:44
Silver Mine 62 3 37N33 90w17 6:01:08
Simcoe 60 3 36N45 94w05 6:16:20
Simmons 107 3 37N14 92w01 6:08:04
Simpson 51 3 38N53 93w40 6:14:40
Sinking 33 3 37N28 91w17 6:05:08
Sisson 46 3 36N51 91w46 6:07:04
Sitze Store 9 3 37N16 90w07 6:00:28
Six Flags Over Mid-America 115 1 38N30 90w37 6:02:28
Skidmore 74 3 40N17 95w05 6:20:20
Slagle 84 3 37N37 93w25 6:13:40
Slater 97 3 39N13 93w04 6:12:16
Sleeper 53 3 37N46 92w36 6:10:24
Sligo 33 3 37N39 91w32 6:06:08
Smallett 34 3 36N58 92w40 6:10:40
Smithfield 49 3 37N10 94w33 6:18:12
Smithton 80 3 38N41 93w05 6:12:20
Smithville 24 3 39N23 94w35 6:18:20
Sni Mills 48 3 38N59 94w10 6:16:40
Snow Hill 57 3 39N03 90w53 6:03:32
Snow Hollow Lake 47 3 37N40 90w39 6:02:36
Snyder 21 3 39N30 93w12 6:12:48
Solo 107 3 37N14 91w57 6:07:48
Somerset 65 3 40N31 93w26 6:13:44
Souder 77 3 36N47 92w28 6:09:52
Soulard 115 1 38N38 90w15 6:01:00
South 29 3 37N19 93w47 6:15:08
South Benton 30 3 37N37 93w06 6:12:24
South Cedar City 14 3 38N36 92w10 6:08:40
Southeast 48 3 38N58 94w32 6:18:08
Southern Aire 50 3 38N26 90w23 6:01:32
South Fork 46 3 36N38 91w58 6:07:52
South Galloway 22 3 36N52 93w17 6:13:08
South Gifford 61 3 40N02 92w41 6:10:44
South Gorin 99 3 40N22 92w01 6:08:04
South Greenfield 29 3 37N23 93w50 6:15:20
South Liberty 24 3 39N13 94w28 6:17:52
South Lineville 65 3 40N35 93w32 6:14:08
South Moniteau 27 3 38N43 92w40 6:10:40
South Morgan 29 3 37N29 93w40 6:14:40
South Point 36 49 38N33 91w01 6:04:04
South River 64 41 39N43 91w34 6:06:16
South Shore 92 15 38N53 90w31 6:02:04
South Side 39 44 37N12 93w18 6:13:12
South Sugar Creek 88 3 39N25 92w24 6:09:36
South Troost 48 3 38N58 94w35 6:18:20
South Troy 57 3 38N59 90w59 6:03:56
South Van Buren 18 3 37N00 91w01 6:04:04
South West 6 3 37N25 94w33 6:18:12
Southwest 115 1 38N36 90w17 6:01:08
South West City 60 3 36N32 94w36 6:18:24
Spalding 87 3 39N41 91w28 6:05:52
Spanish Lake 95 40 38N48 90w13 6:00:52
Sparta 22 3 37N00 93w05 6:12:20
Speed 27 3 38N58 92w45 6:11:00
Speedwell 93 3 37N57 93w58 6:15:52
Spencerburg 82 3 39N30 91w19 6:05:16
Sperry 1 3 40N11 92w35 6:10:20
Spickard 40 3 40N14 93w36 6:14:24
Spickardsville 40 3 40N15 93w33 6:14:12
Spokane 22 3 36N52 93w18 6:13:12
Sprague 7 3 38N06 94w22 6:17:28
Spring Bluff 36 44 38N13 91w09 6:04:36
Spring Branch 48 3 39N06 94w26 6:17:44
Spring City 73 3 37N04 94w30 6:18:00
Spring Creek 81 3 37N40 92w01 6:08:04
Springfield 39 44 37N13 93w17 6:13:08
Spring Garden 66 3 38N21 92w24 6:09:36
Springhill 59 3 39N48 93w33 6:14:12
Spring Hollow 53 3 37N40 92w48 6:11:12
Spring River 55 3 36N58 93w49 6:15:16
Springtown 110 3 37N57 90w43 6:02:52
Spring Valley 60 3 36N33 94w30 6:18:00
Sprott 96 3 37N53 90w13 6:00:52
Spruce 7 3 38N21 94w08 6:16:32
Spurgeon 73 44 36N52 94w22 6:17:28
Squires 34 3 36N51 92w37 6:10:28
Stahl 1 3 40N14 92w43 6:10:52
Stanberry 38 3 40N13 94w35 6:18:20
Stanhope 97 3 39N10 93w23 6:13:32
Stanley 78 3 36N14 89w45 5:59:00
Stanton 36 3 38N17 91w06 6:04:24
Star City 5 3 36N49 93w55 6:15:40
Stark 43 3 37N56 93w10 6:12:40
Stark 82 35 39N27 91w03 6:04:12
Stark City 73 3 36N52 94w11 6:16:44
Starkenburg 70 3 38N43 91w31 6:06:04
Steedman 14 3 38N42 91w49 6:07:16
Steele 78 3 36N05 89w50 5:59:20
Steelville 28 3 37N58 91w22 6:05:28
Steffenville 56 3 39N58 91w53 6:07:32
Steinmetz 45 3 39N14 92w50 6:11:20
Stella 73 3 36N46 94w12 6:16:48
Stephens 10 3 38N58 92w13 6:08:52
Stet 17 3 39N26 93w45 6:15:00
Stewartsville 32 3 39N45 94w30 6:18:00
Stillhouse Springs 85 3 37N52 92w24 6:09:36
Stillings 83 3 39N19 94w53 6:19:32
Stinson 55 3 37N13 93w50 6:15:20
Stockton 20 3 37N42 93w48 6:15:12
Stockyards 11 3 39N43 94w51 6:19:24
Stockyards 48 3 39N06 94w36 6:18:24
Stokes Mound 17 3 39N34 93w29 6:13:56
Stokley 80 3 38N46 93w26 6:13:44
Stones Corner 49 3 37N04 94w30 6:18:00
Stony Hill 37 3 38N36 91w13 6:04:52
Stotesbury 108 3 37N59 94w34 6:18:16
Stotts City 55 3 37N06 93w57 6:15:48
Stoutland 15 3 37N49 92w31 6:10:04
Stoutsville 69 3 39N33 91w51 6:07:24
Stover 71 3 38N27 92w59 6:11:56
Strafford 39 3 37N16 93w07 6:12:28
Strain 36 44 38N13 91w09 6:04:36
Strasburg 19 3 38N46 94w10 6:16:40
Stringtown 12 3 36N46 90w24 6:01:36
Stringtown 26 3 38N33 92w22 6:09:28
Stringtown 49 3 37N10 94w33 6:18:12
Stults 104 3 36N45 93w23 6:13:32
Sturdivant 9 3 37N03 90w01 6:00:04
Sturgeon 10 3 39N14 92w17 6:09:08
Sturges 59 3 39N48 93w33 6:14:12
Sublette 1 3 40N21 92w34 6:10:16
Success 107 3 37N27 92w05 6:08:20
Sugar Creek 48 3 39N07 94w27 6:17:48
Sugar Lake 11 3 39N35 95w01 6:20:04
Sugartree 17 3 39N15 93w33 6:14:12
Sullivan 36 44 38N13 91w10 6:04:40
Sulphur Springs 50 3 38N20 90w23 6:01:32
Sumach 35 3 36N24 90w01 6:00:04
Summerfield 63 3 38N17 91w43 6:06:52
Summersville 107 3 37N11 91w40 6:06:40
Summit 110 3 37N57 90w43 6:02:52
Summit City 77 3 36N48 92w35 6:10:20
Sumner 21 3 39N39 93w15 6:13:00
Sunland Hills 95 40 38N48 90w20 6:01:20
Sunlight 110 3 37N47 90w51 6:03:24
Sunny Slope 48 3 39N02 94w34 6:18:16
Sunnyvale 73 3 37N03 94w30 6:18:00
Sunrise 35 3 36N02 90w07 6:00:28
Sunrise Beach 15 3 38N11 92w47 6:11:08
Sunset Hills 95 40 38N33 90w25 6:01:40
Sutherland 51 3 38N32 93w31 6:14:04
Swan 106 3 36N42 93w05 6:12:20
Swedeborg 85 3 37N55 92w20 6:09:20
Sweden 34 3 36N58 92w40 6:10:40
Sweet Home 23 3 40N31 91w40 6:06:40
Sweet Springs 97 3 38N58 93w25 6:13:40
Sweetwater 73 44 36N52 94w22 6:17:28
Sweetwater 90 3 37N41 90w12 6:00:48
Swift 78 3 36N14 89w45 5:59:00
Swinton 103 3 37N06 89w55 5:59:40
Swiss 37 3 38N42 91w26 6:05:44
Sycamore 77 3 36N42 92w17 6:09:08
Sycamore Hills 95 40 38N42 90w21 6:01:24
Syenite 94 3 37N41 90w22 6:01:28
Sylvania 29 3 37N23 93w57 6:15:48
Sylvania 100 3 37N06 89w42 5:58:48
Syracuse 71 3 38N40 92w53 6:11:32
Taber 93 3 38N03 94w00 6:16:00
Taberville 93 3 38N03 94w00 6:16:00
Table Rock Townsite 106 3 36N39 93w13 6:12:52
Taitsville 89 3 39N33 94w02 6:16:08
Tallapoosa 72 3 36N31 89w48 5:59:12
Taneyville 106 3 36N44 93w02 6:12:08
Tanner 100 3 36N53 89w34 5:58:16
Tanyard 73 3 37N04 94w30 6:18:00
Taos 11 3 39N36 94w48 6:19:12
Taos 26 3 38N32 92w10 6:08:40
Tara 95 40 38N34 90w20 6:01:20
Tarkio 3 3 40N27 95w23 6:21:32
Tarrants 82 3 39N22 91w11 6:04:44
Tarrant Village 82 3 39N21 91w11 6:04:44
Tarsney Lakes 48 3 38N57 94w12 6:16:48
Tauria 104 3 36N45 93w23 6:13:32
Tavern 85 47 37N57 92w16 6:09:04
Taylor 64 3 39N56 91w32 6:06:08
Tea 37 3 38N23 91w24 6:05:36
Tebbetts 14 3 38N37 91w58 6:07:52
Tebo 42 3 38N30 93w40 6:14:40
Tecumseh 77 3 36N35 92w17 6:09:08
Templeton 3 3 40N23 95w37 6:22:28
Tempo 95 40 38N40 90w26 6:01:44
Ten Brook 50 3 38N26 90w23 6:01:32
Tenmile 61 3 39N49 92w21 6:09:24
Teresita 101 3 36N59 91w38 6:06:32
Terre DuLac 94 3 37N55 90w33 6:02:12
Texas 33 3 37N34 91w41 6:06:44
Thayer 75 3 36N31 91w33 6:06:12
Theodosia 77 3 36N35 92w39 6:10:36
Theodosia Hills 77 3 36N35 92w40 6:10:40
Third Creek 37 3 38N24 91w34 6:06:16
Thirty Four Corner 67 3 36N56 89w20 5:57:20
Thomas 91 3 36N33 90w38 6:02:32
Thomas Hill 88 3 39N26 92w40 6:10:40
Thomasville 75 3 36N47 91w32 6:06:08
Thompson 4 3 39N11 91w59 6:07:56
Thomson 99 3 40N28 92w01 6:08:04
Thornfield 77 3 36N42 92w40 6:10:40
Thrush 42 3 38N23 93w46 6:15:04
Tiff 110 3 38N01 90w39 6:02:36
Tiff City 60 3 36N41 94w17 6:17:08
Tiffin 93 3 37N57 93w56 6:15:44
Tiger Fork 102 3 39N53 91w54 6:07:36
Tightwad 42 3 38N23 93w46 6:15:04
Tillman 103 3 37N06 89w55 5:59:40
Tilsit 16 3 37N23 89w40 5:58:40
Timber 101 3 37N39 91w32 6:06:08
Times Beach 95 40 38N31 90w36 6:02:24
Tina 17 3 39N32 93w27 6:13:48

MISSOURI

Tindall 40 3 40N10 93w36 6:14:24
Tinkerville 35 3 36N14 90w03 6:00:12
Tin Town 84 3 37N39 93w06 6:12:24
Tipperary 1 3 40N14 92w43 6:10:52
Tipton 68 3 38N39 92w47 6:11:08
Tip Top 47 3 37N35 90w38 6:02:32
Tobin 99 3 40N21 92w12 6:08:48
Toga 103 3 37N06 89w55 5:59:40
Toldeo 77 3 36N51 92w37 6:10:28
Tolona 56 34 40N05 91w45 6:07:00
Tom 8 3 38N15 93w26 6:13:44
Toppertown 103 3 37N01 89w49 5:59:16
Tower Grove 115 1 38N38 90w15 6:01:00
Town and Country 95 40 38N38 90w27 6:01:48
Town N Four Village 95 40 38N40 90w26 6:01:44
Tracy 83 3 39N23 94w48 6:19:12
Trail Creek 41 3 40N20 93w49 6:15:16
Trask 46 3 37N00 91w42 6:06:48
Treloar 109 3 38N39 91w10 6:04:40
Tremont 11 3 39N40 94w39 6:18:36
Trenton 40 3 40N05 93w37 6:14:28
Trimble 25 3 39N28 94w34 6:18:16
Triplett 21 3 39N30 93w12 6:12:48
Trotter 17 3 39N24 93w35 6:14:20
Troutt 110 3 37N56 90w47 6:03:08
Troy 57 42 38N59 90w59 6:03:56
Truesdale 109 17 38N49 91w08 6:04:32
Truman Corners 48 3 38N54 94w32 6:18:08
Truxton 57 3 39N00 91w14 6:04:56
Tuckahoe 49 3 37N04 94w30 6:18:00
Tucker 91 3 36N35 91w05 6:04:20
Tuckers Corner 49 3 37N15 94w27 6:17:48
Tunas 30 3 37N51 93w02 6:12:08
Turnback 55 3 37N07 93w39 6:14:36
Turners 39 3 37N11 93w09 6:12:36
Turnerville 46 3 37N00 91w42 6:06:48
Turney 25 3 39N38 94w19 6:17:16
Tuscumbia 66 3 38N14 92w28 6:09:52
Tuxedo Park 95 40 38N36 90w20 6:01:20
Twelve Mile 62 3 37N22 90w25 6:01:40
Twin Groves 49 3 37N13 94w34 6:18:16
Twin Oaks 95 40 38N34 90w30 6:02:00
Twin Springs 36 3 38N16 91w06 6:04:24
Tyler 43 3 37N51 93w25 6:13:40
Tyler 78 3 36N05 89w52 5:59:28
Tyrone 107 3 37N19 91w58 6:07:52
Udall 77 3 36N32 92w16 6:09:04
Ulman 66 3 38N09 92w27 6:09:48
Umber 20 3 37N42 93w48 6:15:12
Union 36 3 38N27 91w00 6:04:00
Union 89 3 39N26 94w10 6:16:40
Union City 104 3 37N04 93w33 6:14:12
Union Star 32 3 39N59 94w36 6:18:24
Uniontown 79 3 37N37 89w43 5:58:52
Unionville 86 3 40N29 93w01 6:12:04
Unity Village 48 3 38N57 94w24 6:17:36
University City 95 40 38N40 90w20 6:01:20
Uplands Park 95 40 38N41 90w17 6:01:08
Upper Loutre 70 3 39N06 91w32 6:06:08
Upton 107 3 37N25 92w09 6:08:36
Urbana 30 3 37N51 93w10 6:12:40
Urbandale 88 3 39N25 92w25 6:09:40
Urich 42 3 38N28 94w02 6:16:08
Utica 59 3 39N45 93w38 6:14:32
Valle 50 4 38N06 90w33 6:02:12
Valles Mines 50 3 38N02 90w30 6:02:00
Valley 61 3 39N50 92w41 6:10:44
Valley City 51 3 38N46 93w33 6:14:12
Valley Park 95 40 38N33 90w29 6:01:56
Valley Plaza 12 3 36N46 90w24 6:01:36
Valley View 8 3 38N15 93w23 6:13:32
Valley View 96 3 38N01 90w13 6:00:52
Valley Water Mills 39 44 37N14 93w18 6:13:12
Van 84 3 37N37 93w25 6:13:40
Van Buren 18 3 37N00 91w01 6:04:04
Vance 112 3 37N23 92w50 6:11:20
Vancleve 63 3 38N19 92w10 6:08:40
Vandalia 4 3 39N19 91w29 6:05:56
Vandiver 4 3 39N10 91w51 6:07:24
Vanduser 100 3 37N00 89w41 5:58:44
Van Horn 17 3 39N29 93w28 6:13:52
Vanzant 34 3 36N58 92w18 6:09:12
Varner 91 3 36N36 90w41 6:02:44
Velda 95 40 38N42 90w18 6:01:12
Vera 82 3 39N21 91w11 6:04:44
Verdella 6 3 37N33 94w31 6:18:04
Vernon 23 3 40N21 91w29 6:05:56
Verona 55 3 36N58 93w48 6:15:12
Versailles 71 3 38N26 92w51 6:11:24
Vest 99 3 40N28 92w17 6:09:08
Veterans Hospital 24 3 39N04 94w33 6:18:12
Vibbard 89 3 39N23 94w09 6:16:36
Viburnum 47 3 37N43 91w08 6:04:32
Vichy 63 3 38N06 91w46 6:07:04
Victoria 50 4 38N08 90w33 6:02:12
Vida 81 3 37N51 91w48 6:07:12
Vienna 63 3 38N11 91w57 6:07:48
Vigus 95 2 38N44 90w28 6:01:52
Village of Charlack 95 40 38N42 90w22 6:01:28
Villa Heights 49 3 37N04 94w30 6:18:00
Villa Ridge 36 3 38N28 90w53 6:03:32
Vineland 50 4 38N08 90w33 6:02:12
Vineyard 55 3 37N07 93w59 6:15:56
Vinita Park 95 40 38N42 90w20 6:01:20
Vinita Terrace 95 40 38N41 90w20 6:01:20
Vinson 103 3 36N48 89w58 5:59:52
Viola 5 3 36N38 93w38 6:14:32
Virgil 108 3 37N48 94w08 6:16:32
Virgil City 20 3 37N52 94w01 6:16:04
Virginia 7 3 38N16 94w20 6:17:20
Virginia 78 3 36N06 89w54 5:59:36
Vista 93 3 37N58 93w40 6:14:40
Vulcan 47 3 37N19 90w40 6:02:40
Waco 49 3 37N15 94w36 6:18:24
Wagoner 20 3 37N42 93w48 6:15:12
Wainwright 14 3 38N39 92w07 6:08:28
Wakenda 17 3 39N19 93w22 6:13:28
Waldron 83 3 39N14 94w48 6:19:12
Walker 108 3 37N54 94w14 6:16:56
Wallace 11 3 39N31 94w46 6:19:04
Walls 34 3 36N51 92w35 6:10:20
Wall Street 30 3 37N36 92w59 6:11:56
Walnut Creek 61 3 39N55 92w41 6:10:44
Walnut Grove 39 3 37N25 93w33 6:14:12
Walnut Shade 106 3 36N44 93w12 6:12:48
Wanamaker 97 3 39N07 93w12 6:12:48
Wanda 73 3 36N52 94w11 6:16:44
Wappapello 111 3 36N56 90w16 6:01:04
Wardell 78 3 36N21 89w49 5:59:16
Wardsville 26 3 38N29 92w11 6:08:44
Ware 50 3 38N14 90w34 6:02:16
Warren 64 37 39N39 91w44 6:06:56
Warrensburg 51 3 38N46 93w44 6:14:56
Warrenton 109 17 38N49 91w09 6:04:36
Warsaw 8 3 38N15 93w23 6:13:32
Warson Woods 95 40 38N37 90w23 6:01:32
Washburn 5 3 36N35 93w58 6:15:52
Washington 36 49 38N33 91w01 6:04:04
Washington Center 41 3 40N20 94w10 6:16:40
Wasola 77 3 36N48 92w35 6:10:20
Waterloo 54 3 39N08 93w59 6:15:56
Watkins 33 3 37N43 91w44 6:06:56
Watson 3 3 40N29 95w40 6:22:40
Waverly 54 3 39N13 93w31 6:14:04
Wayland 23 43 40N24 91w35 6:06:20
Wayne 5 3 36N35 93w58 6:15:52
Waynesville 85 9 37N50 92w12 6:08:48
Weatherby 32 3 39N55 94w14 6:16:56
Weatherby Lake 83 3 39N15 94w42 6:18:48
Weaubleau 43 3 37N54 93w32 6:14:08
Webb 90 3 37N10 90w49 6:03:16
Webb City 49 3 37N09 94w28 6:17:52
Weber Hill 50 3 38N25 90w34 6:02:16
Webster Groves 95 31 38N35 90w22 6:01:28
Webster Park 95 40 38N36 90w20 6:01:20
Wedgewood 95 40 38N48 90w20 6:01:20
Wedgewood Green 95 40 38N48 90w20 6:01:20
Weingarten 96 3 37N53 90w13 6:00:52
Wela 73 44 36N50 94w37 6:18:28
Welch 16 3 37N11 89w46 5:59:04
Weldon Spring 92 2 38N47 90w30 6:02:00
Weldon Springs Heights 92 2 38N47 90w30 6:02:00
Wellington 54 3 39N08 93w59 6:15:56
Wellston 95 40 38N40 90w18 6:01:12
Wellsville 70 3 39N04 91w34 6:06:16
Wentworth 73 3 36N59 94w04 6:16:16
Wentzville 92 8 38N49 90w51 6:03:24
Wesco 28 3 37N51 91w26 6:05:44
West 72 3 36N48 89w39 5:58:36
West Alton 92 7 38N52 90w13 6:00:52
West Aurora 66 3 38N16 92w36 6:10:24
West Boone 7 3 38N26 94w34 6:18:16
Westboro 3 3 40N32 95w19 6:21:16
West County 95 40 38N40 90w26 6:01:44
West County Center 115 1 38N37 90w26 6:01:44
West Dallas 112 3 37N12 93w00 6:12:00
West Dolan 19 3 38N37 94w35 6:18:20
West Doniphan 91 3 36N36 90w52 6:03:28
West Ely 64 3 39N41 91w28 6:05:52
West Eminence 101 3 37N09 91w21 6:05:24
West Fulton 14 3 38N50 92w00 6:08:00
Westland Estates 95 40 38N40 90w26 6:01:44
West Line 19 3 38N38 94w35 6:18:20
Weston 83 3 39N25 94w54 6:19:36
West Peculiar 19 3 38N43 94w28 6:17:52
Westphalia 76 3 38N26 92w00 6:08:00
West Plains 46 3 36N44 91w51 6:07:24
West Point 7 3 38N21 94w33 6:18:12
Westport 48 3 39N03 94w35 6:18:20
West Quincy 64 3 39N56 91w32 6:06:08
Westview 73 44 36N52 94w22 6:17:28
Westville 21 3 39N43 92w57 6:11:48
Westwood 95 40 38N38 90w26 6:01:44
Wet Glaize 15 3 37N49 92w31 6:10:04
Wheatland 43 3 37N57 93w24 6:13:36
Wheaton 5 3 36N47 94w02 6:16:08
Wheelerville 5 3 36N47 93w41 6:14:44
Wheeling 59 3 39N49 93w23 6:13:32
Whispering Hills 95 40 38N40 90w26 6:01:44
Whitakerville 8 3 38N15 93w23 6:13:32
White Branch 8 3 38N15 93w23 6:13:32
White Church 46 3 36N51 91w47 6:07:08
White City 15 3 38N00 92w44 6:10:56
White Cloud 74 3 40N12 94w53 6:19:32
Whitecorn 92 18 38N56 90w21 6:01:24
White Hall Fields 24 3 39N13 94w28 6:17:52
Whiteman 51 3 38N44 93w33 6:14:12
Whiteman Air Force Base 51 3 38N43 93w23 6:13:32
Whiteoak 35 3 36N20 90w02 6:00:08
White River 5 3 36N32 93w38 6:14:32
White Rock 60 3 36N32 94w16 6:17:04
Whiteside 57 3 39N11 91w01 6:04:04
Whitesville 2 3 40N04 94w46 6:19:04
Whitewater 16 3 37N14 89w48 5:59:12
Whiting 67 3 36N47 89w23 5:57:32
Wien 21 3 39N46 92w45 6:11:00
Wilbur Park 95 40 38N35 90w18 6:01:12
Wilcox 74 3 40N18 94w51 6:19:24
Wilderness 28 3 37N47 91w12 6:04:48
Wildwood 41 3 40N16 94w02 6:16:08
Wildwood Estates 39 44 37N11 93w17 6:13:08
Wildwood Lake 48 3 39N00 94w28 6:17:52
Wilhelmina 35 3 36N30 90w04 6:00:16
Willard 39 3 37N18 93w26 6:13:44
Willhoit 77 3 36N41 92w30 6:10:00
William M Chick 48 3 39N06 94w32 6:18:08
Williamsburg 14 3 38N55 91w42 6:06:48
Williamstown 56 3 40N14 91w48 6:07:12
Williamsville 111 3 36N58 90w33 6:02:12
Willmathsville 1 3 40N21 92w34 6:10:16
Willow Fork 68 3 38N37 92w47 6:11:08
Willow Springs 46 3 37N00 91w58 6:07:52
Wilson City 67 3 36N55 89w13 5:56:52
Wilton 10 3 38N42 92w19 6:09:16
Winchester 23 23 40N08 91w30 6:06:00
Winchester 95 40 38N35 90w31 6:02:04
Winchester Gap 53 47 37N41 92w40 6:10:40
Windsor 42 3 38N32 93w31 6:14:04
Windsor Springs 95 40 38N37 90w21 6:01:24
Windyville 30 3 37N43 92w56 6:11:44
Winfield 57 16 39N00 90w44 6:02:56
Winigan 105 3 40N03 92w54 6:11:36
Winona 101 3 37N01 91w20 6:05:20
Winston 33 3 39N52 94w08 6:16:32
Winthrop 11 3 39N35 95w01 6:20:04
Wishart 84 3 37N31 93w28 6:13:52
Withers Mill 64 3 39N41 91w28 6:05:52
Wittenberg 79 3 37N39 89w31 5:58:04
Wolf Island 67 3 36N44 89w16 5:57:04
Womack 96 3 37N33 90w17 6:01:08
Woodbine Heights 95 40 38N37 90w21 6:01:24
Woodcliffe 39 44 37N11 93w17 6:13:08
Woodland 64 39 39N48 91w31 6:06:04
Woodland Park 66 3 38N16 92w36 6:10:24
Woodlandville 10 3 38N59 92w34 6:10:16
Woodlawn 69 3 39N35 92w13 6:08:52
Woodridge 95 40 38N48 90w20 6:01:20
Woodruff 83 3 39N25 94w54 6:19:36
Woods Heights 89 3 39N20 94w10 6:16:40
Woodside 75 3 36N45 91w23 6:05:32
Woodson Terrace 95 40 38N44 90w22 6:01:28
Woodville 61 3 39N38 92w29 6:09:56
Woolam 37 3 38N18 91w38 6:06:32
Woolridge 27 3 38N55 92w32 6:10:08
Worland 7 3 38N11 94w36 6:18:24
Wornall 48 3 38N58 94w16 6:17:04
Worth 113 3 40N24 94w27 6:17:48
Wortham 94 3 37N52 90w31 6:02:04
Worthington 86 3 40N25 92w41 6:10:44
Wright City 109 17 38N50 91w01 6:04:04
Wyaconda 23 3 40N24 91w55 6:07:40
Wyatt 67 3 36N55 89w13 5:56:52
Wyatt Park 11 3 39N45 94w48 6:19:12
Wyeth 2 3 40N03 94w49 6:19:16
Yarrow 1 3 40N11 92w35 6:10:20
Yates 88 3 39N18 92w31 6:10:04
Yonkerville 55 44 36N57 94w00 6:16:00
York 86 3 40N32 93w17 6:13:08
Youngstown 1 3 40N14 92w43 6:10:52
Yount 79 3 37N45 89w49 5:59:16
Yukon 107 3 37N16 91w51 6:07:24
Zalma 9 3 37N09 90w05 6:00:20
Zanoni 77 3 36N41 92w20 6:09:20
Zell 96 3 37N59 90w03 6:00:12
Zion 62 3 37N33 90w17 6:01:08
Zion Hill 81 10 38N00 91w37 6:06:28
Zora 8 3 38N27 93w00 6:12:00

TIME TABLES

MT # 1		
Before 11/18/1883		LMT
11/18/1883	12:00	MST
3/31/1918	02:00	MWT
10/27/1918	02:00	MST
3/30/1919	02:00	MWT
10/26/1919	02:00	MST
2/09/1942	02:00	MWT
9/30/1945	02:00	MST
4/30/1967	02:00	US#1

MT # 2		
Before 11/18/1883		LMT
11/18/1883	12:00	MST
3/31/1918	02:00	MWT
10/27/1918	02:00	MST
3/30/1919	02:00	MWT
10/26/1919	02:00	MST
2/09/1942	02:00	MWT
9/30/1945	02:00	MST
5/15/1946	02:00	MDT
9/28/1946	02:00	MST
5/31/1947	02:00	MDT
8/31/1947	02:00	MST
5/02/1948	02:00	MDT
9/06/1948	02:00	MST
5/01/1949	02:00	MDT
9/04/1949	02:00	MST
4/30/1950	02:00	MDT
9/04/1950	02:00	MST
5/06/1951	02:00	MDT
9/30/1951	02:00	MST
4/25/1954	02:00	MDT
9/07/1954	02:00	MST
4/24/1955	02:00	MDT
9/04/1955	02:00	MST
5/06/1956	02:00	MDT
9/03/1956	02:00	MST
4/28/1957	02:00	MDT
9/29/1957	02:00	MST
4/27/1958	02:00	MDT
9/28/1958	02:00	MST
5/31/1959	02:00	MDT
9/13/1959	02:00	MST
5/29/1960	02:00	MDT
9/06/1960	02:00	MST
5/30/1961	02:00	MDT
9/04/1961	02:00	MST
5/30/1962	02:00	MDT
9/05/1962	02:00	MST
5/30/1963	02:00	MDT
9/02/1963	02:00	MST
5/30/1964	02:00	MDT
9/08/1964	02:00	MST
5/30/1965	02:00	MDT
9/06/1965	02:00	MST
4/24/1966	02:00	US#1

MT # 3		
Before 11/18/1883		LMT
11/18/1883	12:00	MST
3/31/1918	02:00	MWT
10/27/1918	02:00	MST
3/30/1919	02:00	MWT
10/26/1919	02:00	MST
4/28/1935	02:00	MDT
9/29/1935	02:00	MST
4/26/1936	02:00	MDT
9/27/1936	02:00	MST
5/30/1963	02:00	MDT
9/02/1963	02:00	MST
4/30/1967	02:00	US#1

MT # 4		
Before 11/18/1883		LMT
11/18/1883	12:00	MST
3/31/1918	02:00	MWT
10/27/1918	02:00	MST
3/30/1919	02:00	MWT
10/26/1919	02:00	MST
2/09/1942	02:00	MWT
9/30/1945	02:00	MST
5/30/1964	02:00	MDT
9/08/1964	02:00	MST
4/30/1967	02:00	US#1

MT # 5		
Before 11/18/1883		LMT
11/18/1883	12:00	MST
3/31/1918	02:00	MWT
10/27/1918	02:00	MST
3/30/1919	02:00	MWT
10/26/1919	02:00	MST
2/09/1942	02:00	MWT
9/30/1945	02:00	MST
5/15/1946	02:00	MDT
9/28/1946	02:00	MST
5/12/1947	02:00	MDT
8/31/1947	02:00	MST
5/02/1948	02:00	MDT
9/06/1948	02:00	MST
4/24/1949	02:00	MDT
9/05/1949	02:00	MST
5/01/1950	02:00	MDT
9/04/1950	02:00	MST
5/06/1951	02:00	MDT
9/03/1951	02:00	MST
4/27/1952	02:00	MDT
9/01/1952	02:00	MST
4/26/1953	02:00	MDT
9/07/1953	02:00	MST
4/25/1954	02:00	MDT
9/06/1954	02:00	MST
4/24/1955	02:00	MDT
9/04/1955	02:00	MST
5/06/1956	02:00	MDT
9/03/1956	02:00	MST
4/28/1957	02:00	MDT
9/29/1957	02:00	MST
4/27/1958	02:00	MDT
9/28/1958	02:00	MST
5/31/1959	02:00	MDT
9/13/1959	02:00	MST
5/29/1960	02:00	MDT
9/06/1960	02:00	MST
5/30/1961	02:00	MDT
9/04/1961	02:00	MST
5/30/1962	02:00	MDT
9/05/1962	02:00	MST
5/30/1963	02:00	MDT
9/02/1963	02:00	MST
5/30/1964	02:00	MDT
9/08/1964	02:00	MST
5/30/1965	02:00	MDT
9/06/1965	02:00	MST
4/24/1966	02:00	US#1

MT # 6		
Before 11/18/1883		LMT
11/18/1883	12:00	MST
3/31/1918	02:00	MWT
10/27/1918	02:00	MST
3/30/1919	02:00	MWT
10/26/1919	02:00	MST
2/09/1942	02:00	MWT
9/30/1945	02:00	MST
4/25/1955	02:00	MDT
9/25/1955	02:00	MST
4/29/1956	02:00	MDT
9/03/1956	02:00	MST
4/30/1967	02:00	US#1

MT # 7		
Before 11/18/1883		LMT
11/18/1883	12:00	MST
3/31/1918	02:00	MWT
10/27/1918	02:00	MST
3/30/1919	02:00	MWT
10/26/1919	02:00	MST
2/09/1942	02:00	MWT
9/30/1945	02:00	MST
5/01/1949	02:00	MDT
9/05/1949	02:00	MST
5/31/1953	02:00	MDT
9/06/1953	02:00	MST
4/25/1954	02:00	MDT
9/07/1954	02:00	MST
4/30/1967	02:00	US#1

MT # 8		
Before 11/18/1883		LMT
11/18/1883	12:00	MST
3/31/1918	02:00	MWT
10/27/1918	02:00	MST
3/30/1919	02:00	MWT
10/26/1919	02:00	MST
2/09/1942	02:00	MWT
9/30/1945	02:00	MST
4/27/1952	02:00	MDT
9/28/1952	02:00	MST
4/30/1967	02:00	US#1

MT # 9		
Before 11/18/1883		LMT
11/18/1883	12:00	PST
1/01/1895	00:00	MST
3/31/1918	02:00	MWT
10/27/1918	02:00	MST
3/30/1919	02:00	MWT
10/26/1919	02:00	MST
2/09/1942	02:00	MWT
9/30/1945	02:00	MST
4/30/1967	02:00	US#1

MT # 10		
Before 11/18/1883		LMT
11/18/1883	12:00	PST
1/01/1895	00:00	MST
3/31/1918	02:00	MWT
10/27/1918	02:00	MST
3/30/1919	02:00	MWT
10/26/1919	02:00	MST
2/09/1942	02:00	MWT
9/30/1945	02:00	MST
5/15/1946	02:00	MDT
9/28/1946	02:00	MST
5/31/1947	02:00	MDT
8/31/1947	02:00	MST
5/02/1948	02:00	MDT
9/06/1948	02:00	MST
4/26/1953	02:00	MDT
9/07/1953	02:00	MST
4/30/1967	02:00	US#1

COUNTIES

1 Beaverhead
2 Big Horn
3 Blaine
4 Broadwater
5 Carbon
6 Carter
7 Cascade
8 Chouteau
9 Custer
10 Daniels
11 Dawson
12 Deer Lodge
13 Fallon
14 Fergus
15 Flathead
16 Gallatin
17 Garfield
18 Glacier
19 Golden Valley
20 Granite
21 Hill
22 Jefferson
23 Judith Basin
24 Lake
25 Lewis and Clark
26 Liberty
27 Lincoln
28 McCone
29 Madison
30 Meagher
31 Mineral
32 Missoula
33 Musselshell
34 Park
35 Petroleum
36 Phillips
37 Pondera
38 Powder River
39 Powell
40 Prairie
41 Ravalli
42 Richland
43 Roosevelt
44 Rosebud
45 Sanders
46 Sheridan
47 Silver Bow
48 Stillwater
49 Sweet Grass
50 Teton
51 Toole
52 Treasure
53 Valley
54 Wheatland
55 Wibaux
56 Yellowstone

Absarokee 48	1	45N31	109w27	7:17:48
Acton 56	1	45N56	108w41	7:14:44
Adel 7	1	47N16	111w42	7:26:48
Agency 45	9	47N19	114w19	7:37:16
Alberton 31	9	47N01	114w37	7:38:28
Albion 6	1	45N01	104w25	6:57:40
Alder 29	1	45N19	112w06	7:28:24
Alhambra 22	1	46N28	111w59	7:27:56
Alpine 5	1	45N21	109w30	7:18:00
Alzada 6	1	45N02	104w25	6:57:40
Amazon 22	1	46N14	112w07	7:28:28
Amsterdam 16	1	45N45	111w19	7:25:16
Anaconda 12	2	46N08	112w57	7:31:48
Anceney 16	1	45N39	111w21	7:25:24
Andes 42	1	48N09	104w31	6:58:04
Angela 44	1	46N44	106w12	7:04:48
Antelope 46	1	48N42	104w27	6:57:48
Apgar 15	9	48N30	113w59	7:35:56
Argenta 1	9	45N13	112w38	7:30:32
Arlee 24	9	47N10	114w05	7:36:20
Armington 7	1	47N22	110w54	7:23:36
Arrow Creek 23	1	47N21	110w10	7:20:40
Ashland 44	1	45N36	106w16	7:05:04
Ashuelot 7	1	47N30	111w49	7:27:16
Augusta 25	1	47N30	112w24	7:29:36
Austin 25	1	46N39	112w15	7:29:00
Avon 39	9	46N36	112w36	7:30:24
Babb 18	9	48N51	113w27	7:33:48
Bainville 43	1	48N08	104w13	6:56:52
Baker 13	1	46N22	104w17	6:57:08
Ballantine 56	1	45N57	108w09	7:12:36
Bannack 1	9	45N10	113w00	7:32:00
Barber 19	1	46N19	109w23	7:17:32
Basin 22	1	46N16	112w16	7:29:04
Bearcreek 5	1	45N10	109w09	7:16:36
Bearmouth 20	9	46N48	113w20	7:33:20
Bear Spring 14	1	47N19	109w57	7:19:48
Beaverton 53	1	48N26	107w15	7:09:00
Beehive 48	1	46N15	107w20	7:09:20
Belfry 5	1	45N09	109w01	7:16:04
Belgrade 16	1	45N47	111w11	7:24:44
Belknap 45	9	47N40	115w25	7:41:40
Belle Creek 38	1	45N27	105w24	7:01:36
Belmont 19	1	46N18	108w56	7:15:44
Belt 7	1	47N23	110w55	7:23:40
Benchland 23	1	47N05	110w01	7:20:04
Biddle 38	1	45N06	105w20	7:01:20
Biem 43	1	48N09	104w55	6:59:40
Big Arm 24	9	47N48	114w18	7:37:12
Bigfork 15	9	48N04	114w04	7:36:16
Bighorn 52	1	46N10	107w27	7:09:48
Big Sandy 8	1	48N11	110w07	7:20:28
Big Sky 16	4	45N41	111w03	7:24:12
Big Timber 49	1	45N50	109w57	7:19:48
Billings 56	3	45N47	108w30	7:14:00
Billings Heights 56	3	45N47	108w30	7:14:00
Birney 44	1	45N19	106w31	7:06:04
Black Eagle 7	1	47N32	111w17	7:25:08
Blackfeet Indian Reservation 18	9	48N33	113w01	7:32:04
Blackfoot 18	9	48N34	112w53	7:31:32
Bloomfield 11	1	47N25	104w55	6:59:40
Blossburg 39	1	46N38	112w19	7:29:16
Bonner 32	9	46N52	113w52	7:35:28
Boulder 22	1	46N14	112w07	7:28:28
Box Elder 21	1	48N19	110w01	7:20:04
Boyd 5	1	45N28	109w04	7:16:16
Boyes 6	1	45N16	105w02	7:00:08
Bozeman 16	4	45N41	111w02	7:24:08
Bozeman Hot Springs 16	4	45N41	111w03	7:24:12
Brady 37	1	48N02	111w51	7:27:24
Brandenberg 44	1	46N24	105w50	7:03:20
Brandon 29	1	45N28	112w12	7:28:48
Bridger 5	1	45N18	108w55	7:15:40
Broadus 38	1	45N27	105w25	7:01:40
Broadview 56	1	46N06	108w53	7:15:32
Broadwater 25	1	46N36	112w05	7:28:20
Brock Creek 39	9	46N31	112w57	7:31:48
Brockton 43	1	48N09	104w55	6:59:40
Brockway 28	1	47N18	105w45	7:03:00
Brown Addition 7	1	47N24	111w10	7:24:40
Browning 18	9	48N34	113w01	7:32:04
Brusett 17	1	47N25	107w16	7:09:04
Buffalo 14	1	46N49	109w50	7:19:20
Buffalo Creek 56	1	46N13	107w51	7:11:24
Busby 2	1	45N32	106w58	7:07:52
Butte 47	5	46N00	112w32	7:30:08
Bynum 50	1	47N59	112w19	7:29:16
Camas 45	9	47N37	114w40	7:38:40
Camas Prairie 45	9	47N22	114w35	7:38:20
Cameron 29	1	45N13	111w41	7:26:44
Canyon Creek 25	1	46N49	112w16	7:29:04
Canyon Ferry 25	1	46N35	112w02	7:28:08
Capitol 6	1	45N26	104w04	6:56:16
Cardwell 22	1	45N52	111w57	7:27:48
Carlyle 55	1	46N40	104w04	6:56:16
Carter 8	1	47N47	110w57	7:23:48
Carterville 44	1	46N16	106w27	7:05:48
Cascade 7	1	47N16	111w42	7:26:48
Castle Rock 44	1	46N16	106w41	7:06:44
Castner Falls 7	1	47N16	111w42	7:26:48
Cat Creek 35	1	47N04	108w00	7:12:00
Centerville 7	1	47N24	111w10	7:24:40
Centerville 47	5	46N00	112w31	7:30:04
Central Park 16	1	45N47	111w11	7:24:44
Chapman 36	1	48N47	107w52	7:11:28
Charlo 24	9	47N26	114w10	7:36:40
Charlos Heights 41	9	46N15	114w10	7:36:40
Checkerboard 30	1	46N38	110w19	7:21:16
Chester 26	1	48N31	110w58	7:23:52
Chico Hot Springs 34	1	45N19	110w42	7:22:48
Chinook 3	1	48N35	109w14	7:16:56
Choteau 50	1	47N49	112w11	7:28:44
Christina 14	1	47N23	109w19	7:17:16
Church Hill 16	1	45N51	111w20	7:25:20
Circle 28	1	47N25	105w35	7:02:20
Clancy 22	1	46N28	111w59	7:27:56
Clinton 32	9	46N46	113w43	7:34:52
Clyde Park 34	1	45N53	110w36	7:22:24
Coalridge 46	1	48N42	104w11	6:56:44
Coalwood 38	1	45N44	105w35	7:02:20
Cobden 31	9	47N12	114w53	7:39:32
Coffee Creek 14	1	47N21	110w05	7:20:20
Cohagen 17	1	47N03	106w37	7:06:28
Collins 50	1	47N56	111w49	7:27:16
Colorado Gulch 25	1	46N35	112w02	7:28:08
Colstrip 44	1	45N53	106w38	7:06:32
Columbia Falls 15	9	48N23	114w11	7:36:44
Columbia Gardens 47	5	46N00	112w31	7:30:04
Columbia Heights 15	9	48N22	114w11	7:36:44
Columbus 48	1	45N38	109w15	7:17:00
Comanche 56	1	46N00	108w46	7:15:04
Condon 32	9	47N34	113w45	7:35:00
Conner 41	9	45N56	114w07	7:36:28
Conrad 37	1	48N10	111w57	7:27:48
Cooke City 34	1	45N01	109w56	7:19:44
Coram 15	9	48N25	114w03	7:36:12
Corbin 22	1	46N23	112w04	7:28:16
Corvallis 41	9	46N19	114w07	7:36:28

Place		Lat.	Long.	Time
Corwin Springs 34	1	45N07	110w47	7:23:08
Cottonwood 39	6	46N23	112w40	7:30:40
Crackerville 12	9	46N04	112w48	7:31:12
Craig 25	1	47N05	111w58	7:27:52
Crane 42	1	47N35	104w16	6:57:04
Creston 15	9	48N11	114w08	7:36:32
Crow Agency 2	1	45N36	107w28	7:09:52
Crow Indian Reservation 2	1	45N36	107w27	7:09:48
Crow Rock 40	1	46N24	105w50	7:03:20
Culbertson 43	1	48N09	104w31	6:58:04
Cushman 19	1	46N17	109w02	7:16:08
Custer 56	1	46N08	107w33	7:10:12
Cut Bank 18	1	48N38	112w20	7:29:20
Dagmar 46	1	48N35	104w12	6:56:48
Danvers 14	1	47N14	109w43	7:18:52
Darby 41	9	46N01	114w11	7:36:44
Dayton 24	9	47N52	114w17	7:37:08
Dearborn 25	1	47N00	112w04	7:28:16
De Borgia 31	9	47N23	115w21	7:41:24
Decker 2	1	45N01	106w52	7:07:28
Deer Lodge 39	6	46N24	112w44	7:30:56
Deer Lodge Valley 12	9	46N09	112w50	7:31:20
Del Bonita 18	1	48N38	112w20	7:29:20
Dell 1	9	44N44	112w42	7:30:48
Delphia 33	1	46N30	108w13	7:12:52
Delpine 30	1	46N38	110w19	7:21:16
Dempsey 39	6	46N24	112w44	7:30:56
Denton 14	1	47N19	109w57	7:19:48
Dentons Point 12	2	46N08	112w57	7:31:48
Devon 51	1	48N28	111w29	7:25:56
Dewey 1	9	45N47	112w51	7:31:24
Dillon 1	9	45N13	112w38	7:30:32
Divide 47	10	45N45	112w45	7:31:00
Dixon 45	9	47N19	114w19	7:37:16
Dodson 36	1	48N24	108w15	7:13:00
Dover 23	1	47N09	110w13	7:20:52
Dovetail 35	1	47N00	108w21	7:13:24
Drummond 20	9	46N40	113w09	7:32:36
Dublin Gulch 47	5	46N00	112w31	7:30:04
Dunkirk 51	1	48N29	111w40	7:26:40
Dupuyer 37	1	48N12	112w30	7:30:00
Dutton 50	1	47N51	111w43	7:26:52
Eagleton 8	1	48N11	110w06	7:20:24
East Butte 47	5	46N00	112w31	7:30:04
East Glacier Park 18	9	48N27	113w13	7:32:52
East Helena 25	1	46N35	111w56	7:27:44
East Missoula 32	9	46N51	114w01	7:36:04
East Powder River 38	1	45N20	105w16	7:01:04
Edgar 5	1	45N28	108w51	7:15:24
Ekalaka 6	1	45N53	104w33	6:58:12
Elkhorn Hot Springs 1	9	45N18	113w07	7:32:28
Elliston 39	1	46N33	112w26	7:29:44
Elmdale 42	1	48N09	104w55	6:59:40
Elmo 24	9	47N50	114w21	7:37:24
Emigrant 34	1	45N23	110w44	7:22:56
Enid 42	1	47N42	104w47	6:59:08
Ennis 29	1	45N21	111w44	7:26:56
Epsie 38	1	45N30	105w39	7:02:36
Eskay 8	1	48N11	110w06	7:20:24
Essex 15	9	48N17	113w37	7:34:28
Ethridge 51	1	48N34	112w08	7:28:32
Eureka 27	9	48N53	115w03	7:40:12
Eustis 22	1	45N59	111w58	7:27:52
Evaro 32	9	46N51	114w01	7:36:04
Evergreen 15	9	48N12	114w19	7:37:16
Everson 14	1	47N19	109w57	7:19:48
Fairfield 50	1	47N37	111w59	7:27:56
Fairview 42	1	47N51	104w03	6:56:12
Fallon 40	1	46N50	105w08	7:00:32
Farmington 50	1	47N53	112w10	7:28:40
Feely 47	10	45N45	112w45	7:31:00
Ferdig 51	1	48N45	111w46	7:27:04
Fergus 14	1	47N20	109w04	7:16:16
Fife 7	1	47N27	111w01	7:24:04
Findon 30	1	46N38	110w19	7:21:16
First Creek 36	1	47N56	107w59	7:11:56
Fishtail 48	1	45N27	109w30	7:18:00
Five Mile Creek 5	1	45N22	108w49	7:15:16
Flathead Indian Reservation 15	9	47N32	114w06	7:36:24
Flat Willow 35	1	46N50	108w24	7:13:36
Flaxville 10	1	48N48	105w11	7:00:44
Floral Park 47	5	45N59	112w29	7:29:56
Florence 41	9	46N38	114w05	7:36:20
Floweree 8	1	47N44	111w02	7:24:08
Forestgrove 14	1	47N00	109w05	7:16:20
Forest Park 11	1	47N06	104w42	6:58:48
Forsyth 44	1	46N16	106w41	7:06:44
Fort Belknap 3	1	48N14	108w38	7:14:32
Fort Belknap Indian Res 3	1	48N32	108w47	7:15:08
Fort Benton 8	1	47N49	110w40	7:22:40
Fortine 27	9	48N46	114w54	7:39:36
Fort Keogh 9	1	46N24	105w50	7:03:20
Fort Kipp 43	1	48N09	104w55	6:59:40
Fort Peck 53	1	48N01	106w27	7:05:48
Fort Peck Indian Reservation 10	1	48N07	105w12	7:00:48
Fort Shaw 7	1	47N30	111w49	7:27:16
Four Buttes 10	1	48N49	105w36	7:02:24
Fourchette 36	1	47N56	107w59	7:11:56
Four Corners 51	1	48N44	111w51	7:27:24
Francis 16	1	46N09	111w05	7:24:20
Frazer 53	1	48N03	106w02	7:04:08
Frenchtown 32	9	47N01	114w14	7:36:56
Froid 43	1	48N20	104w30	6:58:00
Fromberg 5	1	45N24	108w54	7:15:36
Galata 51	1	48N28	111w21	7:25:24
Gallatin Gateway 16	1	45N35	111w12	7:24:48
Gardiner 34	1	45N02	110w42	7:22:48
Garland 9	1	46N24	105w50	7:03:20
Garneill 14	1	46N45	109w45	7:19:00
Garrison 39	9	46N31	112w49	7:31:16
Garryowen 2	1	45N32	107w25	7:09:40
Georgetown 12	2	46N08	112w57	7:31:48
Geraldine 8	1	47N36	110w16	7:21:04
Geyser 23	1	47N16	110w30	7:22:00
Gibson Flats 7	1	47N30	111w17	7:25:08
Gildford 21	1	48N34	110w18	7:21:12
Gilman 25	1	47N31	112w21	7:29:24
Gilt Edge 14	1	47N04	109w26	7:17:44
Glacier 15	9	48N43	113w57	7:35:48
Glacier Colony 18	1	48N38	112w20	7:29:20
Glacier National Park 18	9	48N45	113w37	7:34:28
Glasgow 53	1	48N12	106w38	7:06:32
Glasgow Air Base 53	1	48N12	106w38	7:06:32
Gleason Resort 50	1	47N49	112w11	7:28:44
Glen 1	9	45N28	112w43	7:30:52
Glendive 11	1	47N07	104w43	6:58:52
Glentana 53	1	48N51	106w15	7:05:00
Goldcreek 39	9	46N35	112w55	7:31:40
Golden Ridge 50	1	47N37	111w59	7:27:56
Goldstone 21	1	48N34	110w33	7:22:12
Grant 1	9	45N01	113w04	7:32:16
Grantsdale 41	9	46N12	114w09	7:36:36
Grassrange 14	1	47N02	108w48	7:15:12
Grayling 16	1	44N48	111w12	7:24:48
Great Falls 7	1	47N30	111w17	7:25:08
Greenfield 50	1	47N37	111w59	7:27:56
Greenough 32	9	46N55	113w25	7:33:40
Gregson 47	10	46N01	112w42	7:30:48
Greycliff 49	1	45N46	109w47	7:19:08
Half Moon 15	9	48N22	114w11	7:36:44
Hall 20	9	46N35	113w12	7:32:48
Hamilton 41	9	46N15	114w10	7:36:40
Hammond 6	1	45N14	104w56	6:59:44
Hammond Valley 44	1	46N16	106w41	7:06:44
Hanover 14	1	47N07	109w33	7:18:12
Happy Valley 15	9	48N24	114w20	7:37:20
Hardin 2	1	45N44	107w37	7:10:28
Hardy 7	1	47N16	111w42	7:26:48
Harlem 3	1	48N32	108w47	7:15:08
Harlowton 54	1	46N26	109w50	7:19:20
Harrison 29	1	45N42	111w47	7:27:08
Hathaway 44	1	46N17	106w12	7:04:48
Haugan 31	9	47N23	115w24	7:41:36
Havre 21	1	48N33	109w41	7:18:44
Hays 3	1	47N59	108w41	7:14:44
Heart Butte 37	9	48N17	112w50	7:31:20
Heath 14	1	47N04	109w26	7:17:44
Hedgesville 54	1	46N28	109w30	7:18:00
Helena 25	1	46N36	112w02	7:28:08
Hellgate 32	9	46N51	114w01	7:36:04
Helmville 39	9	46N52	112w58	7:31:52
Heron 45	9	48N03	115w57	7:43:48
Herron Park 21	1	48N33	109w41	7:18:44
Hesper 56	3	45N47	108w34	7:14:16
Highwood 8	1	47N35	110w47	7:23:08
Hilger 14	1	47N15	109w22	7:17:28
Hingham 21	1	48N33	110w25	7:21:40
Hinsdale 53	1	48N24	107w05	7:08:20
Hobson 23	1	47N00	109w52	7:19:28
Hodges 11	1	46N59	104w23	6:57:32
Hogeland 3	1	48N51	108w40	7:14:40
Holt 15	9	48N05	114w06	7:36:24
Holter Dam 25	1	47N00	112w04	7:28:16
Homestead 46	1	48N25	104w32	6:58:08
Hopp 8	1	48N11	110w06	7:20:24
Hot Springs 45	9	47N37	114w40	7:38:40
Howard 44	1	46N16	106w41	7:06:44
Hughesville 23	1	47N04	110w38	7:22:32
Hungry Horse 15	9	48N23	114w04	7:36:16
Huntley 56	1	45N54	108w19	7:13:16
Huson 32	9	47N02	114w20	7:37:20
Hysham 52	1	46N18	107w14	7:08:56
Iliad 8	1	48N11	110w06	7:20:24
Ingomar 44	1	46N35	107w23	7:09:32
Intake 11	1	47N18	104w31	6:58:04
Inverness 21	1	48N33	110w41	7:22:44
Ismay 9	1	46N30	104w48	6:59:12
Jackson 1	9	45N22	113w25	7:33:40
Janney 47	5	45N55	112w30	7:30:00
Jardine 34	1	45N02	110w42	7:22:48
Jeffers 29	1	45N21	111w42	7:26:48
Jefferson City 22	1	46N24	112w02	7:28:08
Jefferson Island 29	1	45N52	111w55	7:27:40
Jellison Place 54	1	46N26	110w04	7:20:16
Joliet 5	1	45N29	108w58	7:15:52
Joplin 26	1	48N34	110w46	7:23:04
Jordan 17	1	47N19	106w55	7:07:40
Judith Gap 54	1	46N41	109w45	7:19:00
Kalispell 15	9	48N12	114w19	7:37:16
Kenilworth 8	1	48N11	110w06	7:20:24
Kevin 51	1	48N45	111w58	7:27:52
Kila 15	9	48N07	114w27	7:37:48
Kinsey 9	1	46N34	105w40	7:02:40
Kirby 2	1	45N20	106w59	7:07:56
Klein 33	1	46N24	108w33	7:14:12
Kolin 23	1	47N07	109w46	7:19:04
Kremlin 21	1	48N34	110w05	7:20:20
Kuehn 2	1	46N17	107w14	7:08:56
Lake McDonald 15	9	48N37	113w53	7:35:32
Lakeside 15	9	48N01	114w13	7:36:52
Lakeview 1	1	44N36	111w49	7:27:16
Lambert 42	1	47N41	104w37	6:58:28
Lame Deer 44	1	45N37	106w40	7:06:40
Landusky 36	1	47N54	108w37	7:14:28
Larchwood 45	9	47N50	115w36	7:42:24
Laredo 21	1	48N26	109w53	7:19:32
Larslan 53	1	48N35	106w12	7:04:48
Lasalle 15	9	48N22	114w11	7:36:44
Laurel 56	1	45N40	108w46	7:15:04
Laurin 29	1	45N28	112w12	7:28:48
Lavina 19	1	46N18	108w56	7:15:44
Lavon 29	9	45N28	112w43	7:30:52
Lebo 30	1	46N38	110w19	7:21:16
Ledger 37	1	48N16	111w49	7:27:16
Lennep 30	1	46N25	110w33	7:22:12
Lewistown 14	1	47N04	109w26	7:17:44
Libby 27	9	48N23	115w33	7:42:12
Lima 1	9	44N38	112w36	7:30:24
Limestone 48	1	46N15	107w20	7:09:20
Lincoln 25	9	46N58	112w41	7:30:44
Lindsay 11	1	47N13	105w09	7:00:36
Little Missouri 6	1	45N21	104w36	6:58:24
Livingston 34	4	45N40	110w34	7:22:16
Lloyd 3	1	48N18	109w22	7:17:28
Locate 9	1	46N26	105w18	7:01:12
Lockwood 56	3	45N47	108w30	7:14:00
Lodge Grass 2	1	45N19	107w22	7:09:28
Lodgepole 3	1	48N02	108w32	7:14:08
Logan 16	1	45N53	111w26	7:25:44
Lohman 3	1	48N35	109w24	7:17:36
Lolo 32	9	46N45	114w05	7:36:20
Lolo Hot Springs 32	9	46N45	114w05	7:36:20
Loma 8	1	47N56	110w30	7:22:00
Lonepine 45	9	47N42	114w38	7:38:32
Loring 36	1	48N47	107w52	7:11:28
Lost Creek 12	2	46N08	112w57	7:31:48
Lothair 26	1	48N28	111w14	7:24:56
Lower Sun River 7	1	47N30	111w17	7:25:08
Lozeau 31	9	47N07	114w47	7:39:08
Lustre 53	1	48N24	105w53	7:03:32
Luther 5	1	45N17	109w26	7:17:44
Madison Valley 29	1	45N16	111w40	7:26:40
Madoc 10	1	48N49	105w17	7:01:08
Maiden 14	1	47N04	109w26	7:17:44
Maiden Rock 47	10	45N41	112w44	7:30:56
Malmstrom 7	1	47N31	111w12	7:24:48
Malmstrom Air Force Base 7	1	47N31	111w12	7:24:48
Malta 36	1	48N21	107w52	7:11:28
Manhattan 16	1	45N51	111w20	7:25:20
Many Glacier Hotel 18	9	48N51	113w26	7:33:44
Marion 15	9	48N06	114w40	7:38:40
Marsh 11	1	46N53	104w56	6:59:44
Martin City 15	9	48N24	114w02	7:36:08
Martinsdale 30	1	46N28	110w19	7:21:16
Marysville 25	1	46N45	112w18	7:29:12
Maudlow 16	1	46N06	111w10	7:24:40
Maxville 20	9	46N28	113w14	7:32:56
McAllister 29	1	45N27	111w44	7:26:56
McCabe 43	1	48N15	104w23	6:57:32
McClellans Creek 25	1	46N36	111w55	7:27:40
McGlone Heights 47	5	46N00	112w31	7:30:04
McLeod 49	1	45N40	110w06	7:20:24
McQueen 47	5	46N00	112w31	7:30:04
Medicine Lake 46	1	48N30	104w30	6:58:00
Medicine Springs 41	9	45N56	114w07	7:36:28
Melrose 47	10	45N38	112w41	7:30:44
Melstone 33	1	46N36	107w52	7:11:28
Melville 49	1	46N06	109w57	7:19:48
Mildred 40	1	46N41	104w58	6:59:52
Miles City 9	1	46N25	105w51	7:03:24
Milford Colony 25	1	47N00	112w04	7:28:16
Mill Creek 12	2	46N08	112w57	7:31:48
Miller Colony 50	1	47N49	112w11	7:28:44
Mill Iron 6	1	45N51	104w13	6:56:52
Milltown 32	9	46N53	113w54	7:35:36
Miner 34	1	45N12	110w54	7:23:36
Missoula 32	9	46N52	114w01	7:36:04
Missoula West 32	9	46N51	114w04	7:36:16
Mizpah 9	1	46N24	105w50	7:03:20
Moccasin 23	1	47N03	109w55	7:19:40
Moffit Canyon 16	4	45N41	111w03	7:24:12
Moiese 24	9	47N22	114w16	7:37:04
Molt 48	1	45N52	108w56	7:15:44
Mona 42	1	48N09	104w55	6:59:40
Monarch 7	1	47N06	110w50	7:23:20
Monida 1	1	44N34	112w19	7:29:16
Montague 8	1	47N41	110w27	7:21:48
Montana City 22	1	46N32	111w57	7:27:48
Montanapolis Springs 34	1	45N25	110w38	7:22:32
Moon Creek 9	1	46N09	105w59	7:03:56
Moore 14	1	46N59	109w42	7:18:48
Morgan 36	1	49N00	107w50	7:11:20
Mosby 17	1	47N00	107w53	7:11:32
Mount Ellis 16	4	45N41	111w03	7:24:12
Musselshell 33	1	46N31	108w06	7:12:24
Myers 52	1	46N15	107w20	7:09:20
Nashua 53	1	48N08	106w22	7:05:28
Navajo 10	1	48N48	105w10	7:00:40
Neihart 7	1	46N56	110w44	7:22:56
New Chicago 20	9	46N40	113w09	7:32:36
New Rockport Colony 50	1	47N49	112w11	7:28:44
Niarada 45	9	47N49	114w36	7:38:24
Nibbe 56	1	45N58	108w10	7:12:40
Nickwall 28	1	48N06	105w39	7:02:36

MONTANA

Nine Mile 32 9 47N02 114w20 7:37:20
Nissler 47 5 46N00 112w31 7:30:04
Norris 29 1 45N34 111w41 7:26:44
North Country 19 1 46N34 109w12 7:16:48
North Custer 9 1 46N38 105w49 7:03:16
Northern Cheyenne Indian Res 2 1 45N37 106w40 7:06:40
North Garfield 17 1 47N25 107w13 7:08:52
North Havre 21 1 48N33 109w41 7:18:44
North Of The Yellowstone 49 1 46N02 109w54 7:19:36
Northridge Heights 15 9 48N12 114w19 7:37:16
North Treasure 52 1 46N17 107w19 7:09:16
Noxon 45 9 48N02 115w47 7:43:08
Nye 48 1 46N15 107w20 7:09:20
Oilmont 51 1 48N44 111w51 7:27:24
Olive 38 1 45N32 105w32 7:02:08
Ollie 13 1 46N22 104w16 6:57:04
Olney 15 9 48N33 114w35 7:38:20
Opheim 53 1 48N51 106w24 7:05:36
Opportunity 12 9 46N06 112w50 7:31:20
Orchard Homes 32 9 46N51 114w01 7:36:04
Ossette 10 1 48N35 106w12 7:04:48
Oswego 53 1 48N03 105w53 7:03:32
Otter 38 1 45N12 106w12 7:04:48
Outlook 46 1 48N53 104w47 6:59:08
Ovando 39 9 47N01 113w08 7:32:32
Pablo 24 9 47N36 114w07 7:36:28
Paradise 45 9 47N23 114w48 7:39:12
Park City 48 1 45N38 108w53 7:15:32
Park Grove 53 1 48N03 106w26 7:05:44
Peerless 10 1 48N47 105w50 7:03:20
Pendroy 50 1 48N04 112w18 7:29:12
Perma 45 9 47N22 114w35 7:38:20
Petrolia 35 1 47N00 108w21 7:13:24
Philipsburg 20 7 46N20 113w18 7:33:12
Piltzville 32 9 46N52 113w52 7:35:28
Pine Creek 34 1 45N40 110w34 7:22:16
Pinegrove 32 9 46N51 114w01 7:36:04
Pinnacle 15 9 48N21 113w39 7:34:36
Pioneer 56 3 45N47 108w34 7:14:16
Plains 45 9 47N28 114w53 7:39:32
Pleasant Valley 15 9 48N06 114w40 7:38:40
Plentywood 46 1 48N47 104w34 6:58:16
Plevna 13 1 46N25 104w31 6:58:04
Plum Creek 14 1 47N14 109w43 7:18:52
Polaris 1 9 45N22 113w07 7:32:28
Polebridge 15 9 48N46 114w17 7:37:08
Polson 24 9 47N41 114w09 7:36:36
Pompeys Pillar 56 1 45N59 107w57 7:11:48
Pony 29 1 45N40 111w54 7:27:36
Poplar 43 1 48N07 105w12 7:00:48
Portage 7 1 47N39 111w07 7:24:28
Post Creek 24 9 47N23 114w06 7:36:24
Potomac 32 9 46N53 113w35 7:34:20
Powderville 38 1 45N45 105w06 7:00:24
Power 50 1 47N43 111w41 7:26:44
Pray 34 1 45N23 110w41 7:22:44
Proctor 24 9 47N54 114w18 7:37:12
Pryor 2 1 45N26 108w32 7:14:08
Racetrack 39 6 46N24 112w44 7:30:56
Radersburg 4 1 46N12 111w38 7:26:32
Ramsay 47 10 46N01 112w42 7:30:48
Rapelje 48 1 45N58 109w16 7:17:04
Rattlesnake 32 9 46N53 113w58 7:35:52
Ravalli 24 9 47N17 114w11 7:36:44
Ravenna 20 9 46N46 113w43 7:34:52
Raymond 46 1 48N53 104w35 6:58:20
Raynesford 23 1 47N16 110w44 7:22:56
Red Bluff 29 1 45N34 111w41 7:26:44
Red Lodge 5 1 45N11 109w15 7:17:00
Red Rock 1 9 44N55 112w50 7:31:20
Redstone 46 1 48N49 104w57 6:59:48
Reedpoint 48 1 45N43 109w33 7:18:12
Regina 36 1 47N56 107w59 7:11:56
Reserve 46 1 48N36 104w28 6:57:52
Rexford 27 9 48N53 115w13 7:40:52
Richey 11 1 47N39 105w04 7:00:16
Richland 53 1 48N49 106w03 7:04:12
Ridgway 6 1 45N14 104w55 6:59:40
Rimini 25 1 46N35 112w02 7:28:08
Ringling 30 1 46N16 110w49 7:23:16
Rising Sun 18 9 48N27 113w13 7:32:52
Riverside 41 9 46N15 114w10 7:36:40
Rivulet 31 9 47N00 114w29 7:37:56
Roberts 5 1 45N22 109w10 7:16:40
Rocker 47 5 46N00 112w31 7:30:04
Rock Springs 44 1 46N49 106w15 7:05:00
Rockvale 5 1 45N33 108w51 7:15:24
Rocky Boys Indian Res 8 1 48N19 110w01 7:20:04
Rollins 24 9 47N55 114w12 7:36:48
Ronan 24 9 47N32 114w06 7:36:24
Roosville 27 9 48N53 115w03 7:40:12
Roscoe 5 1 45N21 109w30 7:18:00
Rosebud 44 1 46N16 106w27 7:05:48
Ross Fork 14 1 47N05 109w42 7:18:48
Roundup 33 1 46N27 108w33 7:14:12
Roy 14 1 47N20 108w58 7:15:52
Ruby 29 1 45N19 112w06 7:28:24
Rudyard 21 1 48N34 110w33 7:22:12
Ryegate 19 1 46N18 109w15 7:17:00
Saco 36 1 48N28 107w21 7:09:24
Saint Ignatius 24 9 47N19 114w06 7:36:24
Saint Labre Mission 44 1 45N27 106w05 7:04:20
Saint Mary 18 9 48N45 113w26 7:33:44
Saint Peter 7 1 47N16 111w42 7:26:48
Saint Regis 31 9 47N18 115w06 7:40:24
Saint Xavier 2 1 45N28 107w43 7:10:52
Salmon Prairie 24 9 48N04 114w04 7:36:16
Saltese 31 9 47N25 115w31 7:42:04
Sand Coulee 7 1 47N24 111w10 7:24:40
Sand Creek 28 1 48N06 105w39 7:02:36
Sanders 52 1 46N18 107w06 7:08:24
Sand Springs 17 1 47N06 107w30 7:10:00
Santa Rita 18 1 48N42 112w19 7:29:16
Sapphire Village 23 1 47N00 109w52 7:19:28
Sappington 16 1 45N48 111w46 7:27:04
Sarpy 2 1 45N48 107w17 7:09:08
Savage 42 1 47N27 104w21 6:57:24
Savoy 3 1 48N32 108w47 7:15:08
Scobey 10 1 48N47 105w25 7:01:40
Seaver Park 25 1 46N35 112w02 7:28:08
Sedan 16 1 46N00 110w40 7:22:40
Seeley Lake 32 9 47N11 113w29 7:33:56
Shawmut 54 1 46N21 109w31 7:18:04
Shelby 51 1 48N30 111w51 7:27:24
Shepherd 56 1 45N57 108w21 7:13:24
Sheridan 29 1 45N27 112w12 7:28:48
Shields Valley 34 1 45N55 110w39 7:22:36
Shirley 9 1 46N30 105w36 7:02:24
Shonkin 8 1 47N38 110w34 7:22:16
Sidney 42 1 47N43 104w09 6:56:36
Silesia 5 1 45N33 108w51 7:15:24
Silverbow 47 10 46N01 112w40 7:30:40
Silver Bow Park 47 5 46N00 112w30 7:30:00
Silver Gate 34 1 45N00 109w59 7:19:56
Silver Star 29 1 45N41 112w17 7:29:08
Simms 7 1 47N30 111w56 7:27:44
Simpson 21 1 48N56 110w12 7:20:48
Sinclair 39 6 46N24 112w44 7:30:56
Smelter Hill 7 1 47N32 111w17 7:25:08
Snider 45 9 47N36 115w13 7:40:52
Somers 15 9 48N05 114w13 7:36:52
Sonnette 38 1 45N25 105w50 7:03:20
South Butte 47 5 45N56 112w29 7:29:56
Southern Cross 12 2 46N08 112w57 7:31:48
South Fork 15 9 48N23 114w00 7:36:00
South Garfield 17 1 47N04 106w45 7:07:00
South Of The Yellowstone 49 1 45N40 110w02 7:20:08
South Toole 51 1 48N30 111w45 7:27:00
South Treasure 52 1 46N05 107w09 7:08:36
South Yellowstone 56 1 45N43 108w29 7:13:56
Spring Creek Colony 14 1 47N04 109w26 7:17:44
Springdale 34 1 45N44 110w13 7:20:52
Springdale Colony 30 1 46N33 110w54 7:23:36
Square Butte 8 1 47N31 110w12 7:20:48
Stacey 38 1 45N38 106w01 7:04:04
Stanford 23 1 47N09 110w13 7:20:52
Stark 32 9 47N02 114w20 7:37:20
Starr School 18 9 48N33 113w01 7:32:04
State Capitol 25 1 46N35 112w02 7:28:08
Stemple 25 1 46N49 112w16 7:29:04
Stevensville 41 9 46N30 114w05 7:36:20
Stockett 7 1 47N21 111w10 7:24:40
Stone 20 9 46N35 113w12 7:32:48
Straw 14 1 46N49 109w50 7:19:20
Stryker 27 9 48N41 114w46 7:39:04
Suffolk 14 1 47N28 109w21 7:17:24
Sula 41 9 45N50 113w58 7:35:52
Sumatra 44 1 46N37 107w33 7:10:12
Summit 15 9 48N27 113w13 7:32:52
Summit Valley 29 1 45N52 111w55 7:27:40
Sunburst 51 1 48N53 111w55 7:27:40
Sunnyside 12 2 46N08 112w57 7:31:48
Sun Prairie 36 1 48N21 107w52 7:11:28
Sun River 7 1 47N32 111w43 7:26:52
Superior 31 9 47N12 114w53 7:39:32
Swan Lake 24 9 47N56 113w51 7:35:24
Sweetgrass 51 1 49N00 111w57 7:27:48
Swiftcurrent 18 9 48N51 113w26 7:33:44
Tampico 53 1 48N18 106w50 7:07:20
Tarkio 31 9 47N01 114w44 7:38:56
Teigen 35 1 47N02 108w36 7:14:24
Terminal Annex 56 3 45N47 108w30 7:14:00
Terry 40 1 46N47 105w19 7:01:16
The Pines 45 9 47N28 114w53 7:39:32
Thompson Falls 45 9 47N36 115w21 7:41:24
Three Forks 16 1 45N54 111w33 7:26:12
Toston 4 1 46N11 111w26 7:25:44
Townsend 4 1 46N19 111w31 7:26:04
Tracy 7 1 47N25 111w09 7:24:36
Trego 27 9 48N42 114w52 7:39:28
Trident 16 1 45N57 111w28 7:25:52
Trout Creek 45 9 47N50 115w36 7:42:24
Troy 27 9 48N28 115w53 7:43:32
Turah 32 9 46N46 113w43 7:34:52
Turner 3 1 48N51 108w24 7:13:36
Twin Bridges 29 1 45N33 112w20 7:29:20
Twin Creeks 32 9 46N52 113w52 7:35:28
Twodot 54 1 46N26 110w04 7:20:16
Ulm 7 1 47N26 111w30 7:26:00
Unionville 25 1 46N33 112w05 7:28:20
Upper Yellowstone Valley 34 1 45N31 110w36 7:22:24
Utica 23 1 46N58 110w05 7:20:20
Valier 37 1 48N18 112w16 7:29:04
Vananda 44 1 46N24 107w00 7:08:00
Vandalia 53 1 48N21 106w55 7:07:40
Van Norman 17 1 47N21 106w23 7:05:32
Varney 29 1 45N20 111w44 7:26:56
Vaughn 7 1 47N34 111w33 7:26:12
Victor 41 9 46N25 114w09 7:36:36
Vida 28 1 47N50 105w29 7:01:56
Virginia City 29 1 45N18 111w56 7:27:44
Volborg 9 1 45N51 105w41 7:02:44
Volt 43 1 48N06 105w39 7:02:36
Wagner 36 1 48N22 108w05 7:12:20
Walkerville 47 5 46N02 112w32 7:30:08
Waltham 8 1 47N34 110w53 7:23:32
Wan-i-gan 34 1 45N25 110w38 7:22:32
Ware 14 1 47N14 109w43 7:18:52
Warland 27 9 48N30 115w17 7:41:08
Warm Spring Creek 36 1 48N08 108w12 7:12:48
Warm Springs 12 8 46N11 112w48 7:31:12
Warren 5 1 45N03 108w39 7:14:36
Warrick 8 1 48N11 110w06 7:20:24
Washoe 5 1 45N10 109w12 7:16:48
Waterloo 29 1 45N43 112w12 7:28:48
Wayne 7 1 47N23 110w55 7:23:40
Webster 13 1 46N22 104w16 6:57:04
Weldon 28 1 47N25 105w35 7:02:20
Westby 46 1 48N52 104w03 6:56:12
West End 31 9 47N19 115w10 7:40:40
West Glacier 15 9 48N30 113w59 7:35:56
West Lewistown 14 1 47N04 109w26 7:17:44
West Park Plaza 56 3 45N47 108w34 7:14:16
West Riverside 32 9 46N51 114w01 7:36:04
West Shore 24 9 47N51 114w21 7:37:24
West Valley 12 9 46N09 113w02 7:32:08
West Yellowstone 16 1 44N40 111w06 7:24:24
Wheeler 53 1 48N01 106w30 7:06:00
Whitefish 15 9 48N25 114w20 7:37:20
Whitefish Lake 15 9 48N24 114w25 7:37:40
Whitehall 22 1 45N52 112w06 7:28:24
Whitepine 45 9 47N50 115w36 7:42:24
White Sulphur Springs 30 1 46N38 111w09 7:24:36
Whitetail 10 1 48N54 105w10 7:00:40
Whitewater 36 1 48N46 107w38 7:10:32
Whitlash 26 1 48N55 111w15 7:25:00
Wibaux 55 1 46N59 104w11 6:56:44
Wickes 22 1 46N24 112w02 7:28:08
Willard 13 1 46N12 104w22 6:57:28
Williamsburg 47 5 46N00 112w31 7:30:04
Willow Creek 16 1 45N49 111w39 7:26:36
Wilsall 34 1 46N00 110w40 7:22:40
Windham 23 1 47N05 110w08 7:20:32
Winifred 14 1 47N34 109w23 7:17:32
Winnett 35 1 47N00 108w21 7:13:24
Winston 4 1 46N29 111w39 7:26:36
Wisdom 1 9 45N37 113w27 7:33:48
Wise River 1 9 45N48 112w57 7:31:48
Wolf Creek 25 1 47N00 112w04 7:28:16
Wolf Point 43 1 48N05 105w39 7:02:36
Woods Bay 24 9 48N04 114w04 7:36:16
Woodside 41 9 46N19 114w09 7:36:36
Woodworth 39 9 46N55 113w25 7:33:40
Worden 56 1 45N58 108w10 7:12:40
Wyola 2 1 45N08 107w24 7:09:36
Yaak 27 9 48N50 115w43 7:42:52
Yellowtail 2 1 45N44 107w37 7:10:28
York 25 1 46N35 112w02 7:28:08
Zortman 36 1 47N55 108w32 7:14:08
Zurich 3 1 48N35 109w02 7:16:08

TIME TABLES

NE # 1
Before 11/18/1883 LMT
11/18/1883 12:00 CST
3/31/1918 02:00 CWT
10/27/1918 02:00 CST
3/30/1919 02:00 CWT
10/26/1919 02:00 CST
2/09/1942 02:00 CWT
9/30/1945 02:00 CST
4/30/1967 02:00 US#1
....

NE # 2
Before 11/18/1883 LMT
11/18/1883 12:00 MST
3/31/1918 02:00 MWT
10/27/1918 02:00 MST
3/30/1919 02:00 MWT
10/26/1919 02:00 MST
2/09/1942 02:00 MWT
9/30/1945 02:00 MST
4/30/1967 02:00 US#1
....

NE # 3
Before 11/18/1883 LMT
11/18/1883 12:00 MST
3/31/1918 02:00 MWT
10/27/1918 02:00 MST
3/30/1919 02:00 MWT
10/26/1919 02:00 MST
2/09/1942 02:00 MWT
9/30/1945 02:00 MST
4/30/1967 02:00 MDT
10/29/1967 02:00 MST
1/01/1968 02:00 CST
4/28/1968 02:00 CDT
4/28/1968 02:00 US#1
....

NE # 4
Before 11/18/1883 LMT
11/18/1883 12:00 MST
3/31/1918 02:00 MWT
10/27/1918 02:00 MST
3/30/1919 02:00 MWT
10/26/1919 02:00 MST
2/09/1942 02:00 MWT
9/30/1945 02:00 MST
1/01/1955 00:00 MDT
12/31/1955 24:00 MST
4/29/1956 02:00 MDT
9/29/1956 02:00 MST
4/30/1967 02:00 MDT
10/29/1967 02:00 MST
1/01/1968 02:00 CST
4/28/1968 02:00 CDT
4/28/1968 02:00 US#1
....

NE # 5
Before 11/18/1883 LMT
11/18/1883 12:00 MST
3/31/1918 02:00 MWT
10/27/1918 02:00 MST
3/30/1919 02:00 MWT
10/26/1919 02:00 MST
2/09/1942 02:00 MWT
9/30/1945 02:00 MST
4/30/1967 02:00 MDT
10/29/1967 02:00 MST
4/28/1968 02:00 MDT
10/27/1968 02:00 MST
4/27/1969 02:00 MDT
6/29/1969 02:00 CDT
10/26/1969 02:00 CST
10/26/1969 02:00 US#1
....

NE # 6
Before 11/18/1883 LMT
11/18/1883 12:00 MST
3/31/1918 02:00 MWT
10/27/1918 02:00 MST
3/30/1919 02:00 MWT
10/26/1919 02:00 MST
2/09/1942 02:00 MWT
9/30/1945 02:00 MST
1/01/1955 00:00 MDT
12/31/1955 24:00 MST
4/29/1956 02:00 MDT
9/29/1956 02:00 MST
4/30/1967 02:00 MDT
10/29/1967 02:00 MST
4/28/1968 02:00 MDT
10/27/1968 02:00 MST
4/27/1969 02:00 MDT
6/29/1969 02:00 CDT
10/26/1969 02:00 CST
10/26/1969 02:00 US#1

COUNTIES

1 Adams
2 Antelope
3 Arthur
4 Banner
5 Blaine
6 Boone
7 Box Butte
8 Boyd
9 Brown
10 Buffalo
11 Burt
12 Butler
13 Cass
14 Cedar
15 Chase
16 Cherry
17 Cheyenne
18 Clay
19 Colfax
20 Cuming
21 Custer
22 Dakota
23 Dawes
24 Dawson
25 Deuel
26 Dixon
27 Dodge
28 Douglas
29 Dundy
30 Fillmore
31 Franklin
32 Frontier
33 Furnas
34 Gage
35 Garden
36 Garfield
37 Gosper
38 Grant
39 Greeley
40 Hall
41 Hamilton
42 Harlan
43 Hayes
44 Hitchcock
45 Holt
46 Hooker
47 Howard
48 Jefferson
49 Johnson
50 Kearney
51 Keith
52 Keya Paha
53 Kimball
54 Knox
55 Lancaster
56 Lincoln
57 Logan
58 Loup
59 McPherson
60 Madison
61 Merrick
62 Morrill
63 Nance
64 Nemaha
65 Nuckolls
66 Otoe
67 Pawnee
68 Perkins
69 Phelps
70 Pierce
71 Platte
72 Polk
73 Red Willow
74 Richardson
75 Rock
76 Saline
77 Sarpy
78 Saunders
79 Scotts Bluff
80 Seward
81 Sheridan
82 Sherman
83 Sioux
84 Stanton
85 Thayer
86 Thomas
87 Thurston
88 Valley
89 Washington
90 Wayne
91 Webster
92 Wheeler
93 York

Abby 46	2	41N52	101w16	6:45:04
Abie 12	1	41N20	96w57	6:27:48
Adams 34	1	40N28	96w31	6:26:04
Addison 54	1	42N45	97w40	6:30:40
Agate	2	42N25	103w48	6:55:12
Agnew 55	1	41N01	96w49	6:27:16
Ainsworth 9	4	42N33	99w52	6:39:28
Air Park West 55	1	40N51	96w47	6:27:08
Akron 6	1	41N41	98w00	6:32:00
Alban 65	1	40N08	98w13	6:32:52
Albany 42	1	40N18	99w28	6:37:52
Albion 6	1	41N42	98w00	6:32:00
Alda 40	1	40N52	98w28	6:33:52
Alexandria 85	1	40N15	97w23	6:29:32
Alexis 12	1	41N21	97w19	6:29:16
Algernon 21	1	41N14	99w19	6:37:16
Alkali 35	2	41N51	102w22	6:49:28
Allen 26	1	42N25	96w51	6:27:24
Alliance 7	2	42N06	102w52	6:51:28
Allston 29	2	40N11	101w43	6:46:52
Alma 42	1	40N06	99w22	6:37:28
Almeria 58	1	41N50	99w31	6:38:04
Aloys 20	1	41N50	96w43	6:26:52
Altona 90	1	42N14	97w01	6:28:04
Alvo 13	1	40N52	96w23	6:25:32
Amelia 45	1	42N14	98w55	6:35:40
Ames 27	1	41N27	96w38	6:26:32
Amherst 10	1	40N50	99w16	6:37:04
Andrews 83	2	42N36	103w43	6:54:52
Angora 62	2	41N51	103w08	6:52:32
Angus 65	1	40N17	97w59	6:31:56
Anoka 8	1	42N57	98w50	6:35:20
Anselmo 21	3	41N37	99w52	6:39:28
Ansley 21	1	41N18	99w23	6:37:32
Antioch 81	2	42N04	102w35	6:50:20
Arabia 16	5	42N38	100w14	6:40:56
Arago 74	1	40N08	95w30	6:22:00
Arapahoe 33	1	40N18	99w54	6:39:36
Arborville 93	1	41N00	97w46	6:31:04
Arcadia 88	1	41N25	99w08	6:36:32
Archer 61	1	41N10	98w08	6:32:32
Arizona 11	1	41N46	96w09	6:24:36
Arlington 89	1	41N27	96w21	6:25:24
Armada 10	1	40N55	99w22	6:37:28
Arnold 21	1	41N26	100w12	6:40:48
Arthur 3	2	41N35	101w41	6:46:44
Ashby 38	2	42N01	101w56	6:47:44
Ash Grove 31	1	40N14	99w07	6:36:28
Ashland 78	1	41N03	96w23	6:25:32
Ashton 82	1	41N15	98w48	6:35:12
Assumption 1	1	40N31	98w34	6:34:16
Aten 14	1	42N44	97w30	6:30:00
Atkinson 45	1	42N32	98w59	6:35:56
Atlanta 69	1	40N22	99w28	6:37:52
Auburn 64	1	40N23	95w51	6:23:24
Aurora 41	1	40N52	98w00	6:32:00
Autumn Hills 28	1	41N18	96w02	6:24:08
Avoca 13	1	40N48	96w07	6:24:28
Axtell 50	1	40N29	99w08	6:36:32
Ayr 1	1	40N26	98w26	6:33:44
Baker 93	1	40N50	97w39	6:30:36
Bancroft 20	1	42N01	96w34	6:26:16
Barada 74	1	40N13	95w35	6:22:20
Barley 16	2	42N41	101w22	6:45:28
Bartlett 92	1	41N53	98w33	6:34:12
Bartley 73	1	40N15	100w18	6:41:12
Basin 8	1	42N57	99w08	6:36:32
Bassett 75	1	42N35	99w32	6:38:08
Batin 91	1	40N13	98w33	6:34:12
Battle Creek 60	1	42N00	97w36	6:30:24
Bayard 62	2	41N45	103w20	6:53:20
Bazile 2	1	42N24	97w54	6:31:36
Bazile Mills 54	1	42N31	97w53	6:31:32
Beatrice 34	1	40N16	96w45	6:27:00
Beaver City 33	3	40N08	99w50	6:39:20
Beaver Creek 91	1	40N08	98w20	6:33:20
Beaver Crossing 80	1	40N47	97w17	6:29:08
Bedford 64	1	40N19	95w51	6:23:24
Bee 80	1	41N00	97w04	6:28:16
Beechwood 28	1	41N19	95w55	6:23:40
Beemer 20	1	41N56	96w48	6:27:12
Belden 14	1	42N25	97w13	6:28:52
Belgrade 63	1	41N28	98w04	6:32:16
Bell Creek 11	1	41N52	96w24	6:25:36
Belle 45	1	42N39	98w50	6:35:20
Belle Prairie 30	1	40N24	97w32	6:30:08
Bellevue 77	1	41N09	95w54	6:23:36
Bellwood 12	1	41N21	97w14	6:28:56
Belmont 23	2	42N41	103w25	6:53:40
Belmont 66	1	40N39	95w57	6:23:48
Belvidere 85	1	40N15	97w33	6:30:12
Benedict 93	1	41N00	97w36	6:30:24
Benkelman 29	2	40N03	101w32	6:46:08
Bennet 55	1	40N41	96w30	6:26:00
Bennett 30	1	40N34	97w47	6:31:08
Bennington 28	1	41N22	96w09	6:24:36
Benson 28	1	41N18	96w01	6:24:04
Benton 64	1	40N18	95w59	6:23:56
Berea 7	2	42N13	102w59	6:51:56
Berlin 66	1	40N45	96w04	6:24:16
Bertrand 69	1	40N32	99w38	6:38:32
Berwyn 21	1	41N21	99w30	6:38:00
Beverly 44	3	40N19	101w03	6:44:12
Big Blue 76	1	40N34	96w58	6:27:52
Bignell 56	1	41N04	100w31	6:42:04
Big Springs 25	2	41N04	102w05	6:48:20
Bingham 81	2	42N01	102w05	6:48:20
Birdwood 56	3	41N17	101w04	6:44:16
Bismarck 20	1	41N52	96w57	6:27:48
Bismark 71	1	41N31	97w18	6:29:12
Bixby 30	1	40N36	97w51	6:31:24
Blackbird 87	1	42N08	96w22	6:25:28
Bladen 91	1	40N19	98w36	6:34:24
Blair 89	1	41N33	96w08	6:24:32
Blakely 34	1	40N18	96w52	6:27:28
Bloomfield 54	1	42N36	97w39	6:30:36
Bloomington 31	1	40N08	99w00	6:36:00
Blue Creek 35	2	41N32	102w06	6:48:24
Blue Hill 91	1	40N20	98w27	6:33:48
Blue River Lodge 76	1	40N37	96w57	6:27:48
Blue Springs 34	1	40N09	96w40	6:26:40
Bluff 41	1	41N05	97w53	6:31:32
Boelus 47	1	41N05	98w43	6:34:52
Bonanza 6	1	41N45	98w14	6:32:56
Bondville 73	3	40N08	100w29	6:41:56
Bone Creek 12	1	41N21	97w05	6:28:20
Bonner 62	2	41N57	103w01	6:52:04
Boone 6	1	41N38	97w55	6:31:40
Bostwick 65	1	40N03	98w11	6:32:44
Bowen 83	2	42N39	103w57	6:55:48
Bow Valley 14	1	42N43	97w15	6:29:00
Box Butte 7	2	42N16	102w51	6:51:24
Box Elder 56	1	40N54	100w36	6:42:24
Boys Town 28	1	41N16	96w08	6:24:32
Brace 37	1	40N39	99w55	6:39:40
Braden 3	2	41N30	101w52	6:47:28
Bradshaw 93	1	40N53	97w45	6:31:00
Brady 56	1	41N01	100w22	6:41:28
Brainard 12	1	41N11	97w00	6:28:00
Brandon	2	40N48	101w55	6:47:40
Brandon 68	2	41N08	100w46	6:43:04
Brayton 39	1	41N24	98w23	6:33:32
Brenna 90	1	42N08	97w04	6:28:16
Breslau 70	1	42N22	97w36	6:30:24
Brewster 5	3	41N56	99w52	6:39:28
Bridgeport 62	2	41N40	103w06	6:52:24
Briggs 28	1	41N19	96w02	6:24:08
Brinkerhoff 75	1	42N41	99w38	6:38:32
Bristol 82	1	41N05	98w52	6:35:28
Bristow 8	1	42N51	98w35	6:34:20
Broadwater 62	2	41N36	102w51	6:51:24
Brock 64	1	40N29	95w58	6:23:52
Broken Bow 21	1	41N24	99w38	6:38:32
Brown 93	1	40N50	97w46	6:31:04
Brownlee 16	5	42N17	100w37	6:42:28
Brownson 17	2	41N11	103w07	6:52:28
Brownville 64	1	40N24	95w40	6:22:40
Brule 51	2	41N06	101w53	6:47:32
Bruning 85	1	40N19	97w33	6:30:12
Bruno 12	1	41N17	96w58	6:27:52
Brunswick 2	1	42N20	97w58	6:31:52
Brush Creek 76	1	40N29	97w05	6:28:20
Bryant 30	1	40N24	97w46	6:31:04
Buchanan 56	1	40N45	100w37	6:42:28
Buckley 48	1	40N04	97w18	6:29:12
Bucktail	3	41N34	101w26	6:45:44
Buda 55	1	40N34	96w45	6:27:00
Bunker Hill 17	2	41N17	103w07	6:52:28
Burchard 67	1	40N09	96w21	6:25:24
Burnett 2	1	42N03	97w53	6:31:32
Burr 66	1	40N33	96w19	6:25:16
Burress 30	1	40N38	97w35	6:30:20
Burrows 71	1	41N37	97w32	6:30:08
Burt 57	3	41N39	100w20	6:41:20
Burton 52	1	42N55	99w35	6:38:20
Burtons Bend 33	1	40N19	100w01	6:40:04
Burwell 36	1	41N47	99w08	6:36:32
Bush 8	1	42N51	98w23	6:33:32
Bushnell 53	2	41N14	103w54	6:55:36
Bussell 15	2	40N27	101w51	6:47:24
Butler 71	1	41N23	97w28	6:29:52
Butte 8	1	42N58	98w51	6:35:24
Butterfly 84	1	41N52	97w12	6:28:48
Byron 85	1	40N00	97w46	6:31:04

Place	Zone	Latitude	Longitude	Time
Cadams 65	1	40N01	98w04	6:32:16
Cairo 40	1	41N00	98w36	6:34:24
Calamus 9	3	42N11	99w45	6:39:00
Caldwell 92	1	41N57	98w22	6:33:28
Calf Creek 16	2	42N11	101w22	6:45:28
Callaway 21	1	41N18	99w56	6:39:44
Calvert 29	2	40N18	101w23	6:45:32
Cambridge 33	1	40N17	100w10	6:40:40
Cameron 40	1	40N55	98w40	6:34:40
Campbell 31	1	40N18	98w44	6:34:56
Camp Clark 62	2	41N42	103w05	6:52:20
Canada 72	1	41N13	97w26	6:29:44
Canby 15	2	40N35	101w44	6:46:56
Carleton 85	1	40N18	97w41	6:30:44
Carroll 90	1	42N17	97w12	6:28:48
Castle Rock 79	2	41N45	103w29	6:53:56
Catherton 91	1	40N13	98w40	6:34:40
Cedar Bluffs 78	1	41N24	96w37	6:26:28
Cedar Creek 13	1	41N02	96w06	6:24:24
Cedar Rapids 6	1	41N34	98w09	6:32:36
Center 54	1	42N37	97w53	6:31:32
Centerville 55	1	40N39	96w44	6:26:56
Central City 61	1	41N07	98w00	6:32:00
Ceresco 78	1	41N03	96w39	6:26:36
Chadron 23	2	42N50	103w00	6:52:00
Chalco 77	1	41N08	96w15	6:25:00
Chambers 45	1	42N12	98w45	6:35:00
Champion 15	2	40N27	101w45	6:47:00
Chapin 90	1	42N13	97w12	6:28:48
Chapman 61	1	41N02	98w10	6:32:40
Chappell 25	2	41N06	102w28	6:49:52
Chase	2	40N34	101w49	6:47:16
Chelsea 30	1	40N29	97w32	6:30:08
Cheney	1	40N44	96w35	6:26:20
Cherry Creek 10	1	41N00	98w47	6:35:08
Chester 85	1	40N01	97w37	6:30:28
Chicago 28	1	41N15	96w14	6:24:56
Clark 26	1	42N29	96w57	6:27:48
Clarks 61	1	41N13	97w50	6:31:20
Clarkson 19	1	41N43	97w07	6:28:28
Clatonia 34	1	40N28	96w51	6:27:24
Clay Center 18	1	40N32	98w03	6:32:12
Clearwater 2	1	42N10	98w11	6:32:44
Cliff 21	3	41N30	99w59	6:39:56
Clinton 81	2	42N46	102w21	6:49:24
Clover Valley 70	1	42N13	97w40	6:30:40
Cody 16	2	42N56	101w15	6:45:00
Cody Lake 57	3	41N39	100w29	6:41:56
Coleman 45	1	42N45	98w44	6:34:56
Coleridge 14	1	42N30	97w13	6:28:52
Colfax 19	1	41N32	96w58	6:27:52
College View 55	1	40N47	96w39	6:26:36
Collins 10	1	40N41	99w08	6:36:32
Colon 78	1	41N18	96w37	6:26:28
Colton 17	2	41N10	102w48	6:51:12
Columbia 54	1	42N29	97w40	6:30:40
Columbus 71	1	41N26	97w22	6:29:28
Comstock 21	1	41N34	99w14	6:36:56
Concord 26	1	42N23	96w59	6:27:56
Conley 45	1	42N08	98w45	6:35:00
Constance 14	1	42N44	97w30	6:30:00
Cook 49	1	40N31	96w10	6:24:40
Copenhagen 2	1	42N21	97w47	6:31:08
Cordova 80	1	40N43	97w21	6:29:24
Cornell 44	3	40N03	100w56	6:43:44
Corner 21	1	41N42	99w17	6:37:08
Cornlea 71	1	41N41	97w34	6:30:16
Cortland 34	1	40N30	96w42	6:26:48
Cosmo 50	1	40N24	98w53	6:35:32
Cotesfield 47	1	41N22	98w38	6:34:32
Cotterell 27	1	41N31	96w44	6:26:56
Council Creek 63	1	41N26	97w53	6:31:32
Court House Rock 62	2	41N36	103w01	6:52:04
Covington 22	1	42N28	96w28	6:25:52
Cowles 91	1	40N10	98w27	6:33:48
Cox 56	1	41N14	100w29	6:41:56
Coyote 24	1	40N52	99w51	6:39:24
Cozad 24	1	40N52	99w59	6:39:56
Crab Orchard 49	1	40N20	96w25	6:25:40
Craig 11	1	41N47	96w22	6:25:28
Crawford 23	2	42N41	103w25	6:53:40
Creighton 54	1	42N28	97w54	6:31:36
Creston 71	1	41N42	97w19	6:29:16
Crete 76	1	40N38	96w58	6:27:52
Crofton 54	1	42N44	97w30	6:30:00
Crookston 16	5	42N56	100w45	6:43:00
Crowell 27	1	41N40	96w40	6:26:40
Crown Point 28	1	41N19	96w02	6:24:08
Cub Creek 48	1	40N13	97w05	6:28:20
Culbertson 44	3	40N14	100w50	6:43:20
Cuming City 89	1	41N36	96w09	6:24:36
Curtis 32	1	40N38	100w31	6:42:04
Cushing 47	1	41N18	98w22	6:33:28
Daily 26	1	42N34	96w57	6:27:48
Dakota City 22	1	42N25	96w25	6:25:40
Dalton 17	2	41N25	102w58	6:51:52
Danbury 73	3	40N03	100w25	6:41:40
Dannebrog 47	1	41N07	98w33	6:34:12
Dannevirke 47	1	41N19	98w42	6:34:48
Darr 24	1	40N49	99w53	6:39:32
Davenport 85	1	40N19	97w49	6:31:16
Davey 55	1	40N59	96w40	6:26:40
David City 12	1	41N15	97w08	6:28:32
Davis Creek 88	1	41N27	98w55	6:35:40
Davison 17	2	41N23	103w07	6:52:28
Dawes 87	1	42N04	96w28	6:25:52
Dawson 74	1	40N08	95w50	6:23:20
Daykin 48	1	40N21	97w18	6:29:12
Debolt 28	1	41N19	96w00	6:24:00
Decatur 11	1	42N00	96w15	6:25:00
Deep Well 41	1	40N50	98w14	6:32:56
Deerfield 43	3	40N39	101w17	6:45:08
Delaware 66	1	40N39	96w04	6:24:16
Delight 21	1	41N16	99w58	6:39:52

Place	Zone	Latitude	Longitude	Time
Deloit 45	1	42N08	98w22	6:33:28
Denman 10	1	40N37	98w39	6:34:36
Denton 55	1	40N44	96w51	6:27:24
Denver 1	1	40N34	98w26	6:33:44
Deshler 85	1	40N09	97w44	6:30:56
De Soto 89	1	41N30	96w05	6:24:20
Deweese 18	1	40N21	98w08	6:32:32
De Witt 76	1	40N24	96w55	6:27:40
Dickens 56	3	40N50	101w00	6:44:00
Diller 48	1	40N07	96w56	6:27:44
Dimick 84	1	41N47	97w19	6:29:16
Dix 53	2	41N14	103w29	6:53:56
Dixon 26	1	42N25	97w00	6:28:00
Dodge 27	1	41N43	96w53	6:27:32
Dolphin 54	1	42N39	97w33	6:30:12
Doniphan 40	1	40N46	98w22	6:33:28
Dorchester 76	1	40N39	97w07	6:28:28
Dorp 57	3	41N29	100w40	6:42:40
Dorsey 7	2	42N22	103w05	6:52:20
Dorsey 45	1	42N50	98w28	6:33:52
Douglas 66	1	40N36	96w23	6:25:32
Douglas Grove 21	1	41N33	99w21	6:37:24
Dowling 54	1	42N34	97w32	6:30:08
Downtown 28	1	41N17	95w57	6:23:48
Driftwood 44	3	40N03	100w49	6:43:16
Dry Cedar 36	1	41N47	98w52	6:35:28
Dublin 6	1	41N39	98w14	6:32:56
Du Bois 67	1	40N02	96w04	6:24:16
Dumas 36	1	42N12	98w45	6:35:00
Dunbar 66	1	40N40	96w02	6:24:08
Duncan 71	1	41N23	97w30	6:30:00
Dunning 5	3	41N54	100w16	6:41:04
Dustin 45	1	42N50	98w59	6:35:56
Dwight 12	1	41N05	97w01	6:28:04
Eagle 13	1	40N49	96w26	6:25:44
Earl 32	1	40N29	100w09	6:40:36
East Chadron 23	2	42N51	102w53	6:51:32
East Custer 21	1	41N16	99w38	6:38:32
East Gordon 81	2	42N44	102w08	6:48:32
East Hinman 56	1	41N08	100w44	6:42:56
East Mirage 81	2	42N30	102w36	6:50:24
East Newman 63	1	41N21	97w53	6:31:32
East Ogallala 51	2	41N06	101w40	6:46:40
East Rock Bluffs 13	1	40N55	95w51	6:23:24
East Valley 73	1	40N13	100w16	6:41:04
East Winters Creek 79	2	41N53	103w37	6:54:28
Eastwood 62	2	41N38	102w43	6:50:52
Eaton 50	1	40N34	98w48	6:35:12
Eckery 68	2	40N56	101w45	6:47:00
Eddyville 24	1	41N01	99w38	6:38:32
Edgar 18	1	40N22	97w58	6:31:52
Edison 33	1	40N17	99w47	6:39:08
Edward 3	2	41N38	101w52	6:47:28
Eight Mile Grove 13	1	41N01	96w04	6:24:16
Elba 47	1	41N17	98w34	6:34:16
Eldorado	1	40N41	98w00	6:32:00
Elgin 2	1	41N59	98w05	6:32:20
Eli 16	2	42N57	101w29	6:45:56
Elim 21	1	41N15	100w08	6:40:32
Elk City 28	1	41N22	96w16	6:25:04
Elk Creek 49	1	40N17	96w08	6:24:32
Elkhorn 28	1	41N17	96w14	6:24:56
Ellis 34	1	40N13	96w53	6:27:32
Ellsworth 81	2	42N04	102w17	6:49:08
Elm Creek 10	1	40N43	99w22	6:37:28
Elmwood 13	1	40N50	96w18	6:25:12
Elmwood Park 28	1	41N15	96w00	6:24:00
Elsie 68	2	40N51	101w23	6:45:32
Elsmere 16	5	42N10	100w11	6:40:44
Elwood 37	1	40N36	99w52	6:39:28
Elyria 88	1	41N41	99w00	6:36:00
Emerald 55	1	40N47	96w42	6:26:48
Emerick 60	1	41N52	97w46	6:31:04
Emerson 22	1	42N17	96w44	6:26:56
Emmet 45	1	42N29	98w49	6:35:16
Enders 15	2	40N27	101w32	6:46:08
Endicott 48	1	40N05	97w06	6:28:24
Enola 60	1	41N54	97w28	6:29:52
Epworth 4	2	41N29	104w00	6:56:00
Ericson 92	1	41N47	98w41	6:34:44
Erina 36	1	42N02	98w53	6:35:32
Eustis 32	1	40N40	100w02	6:40:08
Evergreen 23	2	42N34	103w22	6:53:28
Ewing 45	1	42N16	98w21	6:33:24
Exeter 30	1	40N39	97w27	6:29:48
Extension 81	2	42N57	102w33	6:50:12
Fairbury 48	1	40N08	97w11	6:28:44
Fairfield 18	1	40N26	98w06	6:32:24
Fairmont 30	1	40N38	97w35	6:30:20
Falls City 74	1	40N03	95w36	6:22:24
Fanning 79	2	41N58	103w45	6:55:00
Farmers 31	1	40N08	99w08	6:36:32
Farmers Valley 41	1	40N45	97w53	6:31:32
Farnam 24	1	40N42	100w13	6:40:52
Farwell 47	1	41N13	98w38	6:34:32
Ferry 22	1	42N28	96w24	6:25:36
Filley 34	1	40N18	96w31	6:26:04
First Lafayette 64	1	40N28	96w01	6:24:04
Firth 55	1	40N33	96w37	6:26:28
Flats	3	41N34	101w21	6:45:24
Florence 28	1	41N21	95w59	6:23:56
Flournoy 87	1	42N12	96w43	6:26:52
Flowerfield 4	2	41N29	103w53	6:55:32
Fontanelle 89	1	41N33	96w20	6:25:20
Ford 79	2	41N59	103w55	6:55:40
Fordyce 14	1	42N42	97w22	6:29:28
Fort Calhoun 89	1	41N27	96w02	6:24:08
Fort Robinson 23	2	42N40	103w28	6:53:52
Foster 70	1	42N16	97w40	6:30:40
Four Mile 66	1	40N39	95w51	6:23:24

NEBRASKA

Place	Zone	Latitude	Longitude	Time
Fox Creek 56	1	40N47	100w30	6:42:00
Frankfort 54	1	42N49	97w32	6:30:08
Franklin 31	1	40N06	98w57	6:35:48
Freedom 44	3	40N03	101w10	6:44:40
Fremont 27	1	41N26	96w30	6:26:00
Frenchtown 2	1	42N14	98w14	6:32:56
Friend 76	1	40N38	97w17	6:29:08
Fritsch 73	1	40N18	100w28	6:41:52
Fullerton 63	1	41N22	97w58	6:31:52
Funk 69	1	40N28	99w15	6:37:00
Funston 79	2	41N57	103w38	6:54:32
Gage Valley 47	1	41N12	98w20	6:33:20
Galena 26	1	42N29	96w50	6:27:20
Gandy 57	3	41N29	100w27	6:41:48
Gardner 10	1	40N55	98w47	6:35:08
Garland 80	1	40N57	96w59	6:27:56
Garrison 12	1	41N11	97w10	6:28:40
Gaslin 56	1	40N58	100w23	6:41:32
Geneva 30	1	40N32	97w36	6:30:24
Genoa 63	1	41N27	97w44	6:30:56
Georgia 16	2	42N53	100w58	6:43:52
Geranium 88	1	41N37	99w09	6:36:36
Gering 79	2	41N50	103w40	6:54:40
Germanville 43	3	40N34	100w50	6:43:20
Gibbon 10	1	40N45	98w51	6:35:24
Gibson 48	1	40N18	97w05	6:28:20
Gilchrist 62	2	41N56	102w49	6:51:16
Gilead 85	1	40N09	97w25	6:29:40
Gillan 24	1	40N56	99w57	6:39:48
Gillaspie 16	2	42N32	101w23	6:45:32
Gilmore 77	1	41N11	95w57	6:23:48
Giltner 41	1	40N47	98w09	6:32:36
Gladstone 48	1	40N10	97w19	6:29:16
Glen 83	2	42N41	103w25	6:53:40
Glengary 30	1	40N29	97w25	6:29:40
Glenover 34	1	40N16	96w44	6:26:56
Glenrock 64	1	40N29	95w51	6:23:24
Glenville 18	1	40N30	98w15	6:33:00
Glenwood Park 10	1	40N42	99w05	6:36:20
Goehner 80	1	40N50	97w13	6:28:52
Golden 45	1	42N19	98w23	6:33:32
Good Luck 77	1	41N11	95w58	6:23:52
Good Samaritan Village 1	1	40N35	98w24	6:33:36
Good Streak 62	2	41N58	103w16	6:53:04
Goose Creek 16	5	42N20	100w18	6:41:12
Gordon 81	2	42N48	102w12	6:48:48
Gothenburg 24	1	40N56	100w10	6:40:40
Government 43	3	40N34	101w00	6:44:00
Grace 68	2	40N47	102w00	6:48:00
Gracy 75	1	42N09	99w21	6:37:24
Graf 49	1	40N22	96w11	6:24:44
Grafton 30	1	40N39	97w46	6:31:04
Grainton 68	3	40N49	101w17	6:45:08
Grand Island 40	1	40N55	98w21	6:33:24
Grand Praire 71	1	41N37	97w25	6:29:40
Grant 68	2	40N50	101w43	6:46:52
Granville 71	1	41N42	97w33	6:30:12
Grattan 45	1	42N29	98w39	6:34:36
Greeley 39	1	41N33	98w32	6:34:08
Green 78	1	41N06	96w31	6:26:04
Green Garden 60	1	41N47	97w32	6:30:08
Green Meadows 28	1	41N18	96w05	6:24:20
Green Valley 45	1	42N26	99w07	6:36:28
Greenwood 13	1	40N58	96w27	6:25:48
Gresham 93	1	41N02	97w24	6:29:36
Gretna 77	1	41N08	96w15	6:25:00
Gross 8	1	42N57	98w34	6:34:16
Grove 60	1	41N57	97w46	6:31:04
Grover 80	1	40N46	97w03	6:28:12
Guide Rock 91	1	40N04	98w20	6:33:20
Gurley 17	2	41N19	102w58	6:51:52
Hackberry 72	1	41N06	97w26	6:29:44
Hadar 70	1	42N06	97w27	6:29:48
Haig 79	2	41N53	103w45	6:55:00
Haigler 29	2	40N01	101w56	6:47:44
Hallam 55	1	40N32	96w47	6:27:08
Halsey 86	3	41N54	100w16	6:41:04
Hamlet 43	3	40N23	101w14	6:44:56
Hammond 65	1	40N19	97w53	6:31:32
Hampton 41	1	40N53	97w53	6:31:32
Hancock 90	1	42N08	97w12	6:28:48
Hansen 1	1	40N42	98w22	6:33:28
Harbine 48	1	40N11	96w58	6:27:52
Hardy 65	1	40N01	97w56	6:31:44
Harmony 91	1	40N19	98w40	6:34:40
Harrisburg 4	2	41N33	103w44	6:54:56
Harrison 83	2	42N41	103w53	6:55:32
Hartington 14	1	42N37	97w16	6:29:04
Harvard 18	1	40N37	98w06	6:32:24
Hastings 1	1	40N35	98w23	6:33:32
Hat Creek 83	2	42N48	103w44	6:54:56
Havelock 55	1	40N49	96w40	6:26:40
Havens 61	1	41N13	97w50	6:31:20
Hawley 5	3	42N00	100w02	6:40:08
Hayes Center 43	3	40N31	101w01	6:44:04
Hayland 1	1	40N35	98w30	6:34:00
Haymow 84	1	41N53	97w04	6:28:16
Haynes 62	2	41N51	103w08	6:52:32
Hays 93	1	40N45	97w39	6:30:36
Hay Springs 81	2	42N41	102w41	6:50:44
Hazard 82	1	41N06	99w09	6:36:36
Heartwell 50	1	40N34	98w47	6:35:08
Hebron 85	1	40N10	97w35	6:30:20
Helena 49	1	40N27	96w17	6:25:08
Hemingford 7	2	42N19	103w04	6:52:16
Henderson 93	1	40N47	97w49	6:31:16
Hendley 33	3	40N08	99w58	6:39:52
Hendricks 66	1	40N34	96w24	6:25:36
Henry 79	2	42N00	104w03	6:56:12
Herman 89	1	41N40	96w13	6:24:52
Herrick 54	1	42N49	97w40	6:30:40
Hershey 56	3	41N10	101w00	6:44:00
Hickman 55	1	40N37	96w38	6:26:32
High Ridge 43	3	40N34	101w11	6:44:44

NEBRASKA

Hildreth 31	1	40N20	99w03	6:36:12
Hill 54	1	42N44	97w47	6:31:08
Hillerage 79	2	41N52	103w40	6:54:40
Hillside 24	1	40N55	99w44	6:38:56
Hinman 56	1	41N09	100w50	6:43:20
Hoag 34	1	40N16	96w44	6:26:56
Holbrook 33	1	40N18	100w01	6:40:04
Holdrege 69	1	40N26	99w22	6:37:28
Holland 55	1	40N36	96w35	6:26:20
Hollinger 33	1	40N15	99w38	6:38:32
Holmes 24	1	40N44	100w03	6:40:12
Holmesville 34	1	40N12	96w40	6:26:40
Holstein 1	1	40N28	98w39	6:34:36
Holt 34	1	40N24	96w45	6:27:00
Holt Creek 45	1	42N20	99w10	6:36:40
Homer 22	1	42N19	96w29	6:25:56
Hooper 27	1	41N37	96w33	6:26:12
Hoover 29	2	40N13	101w36	6:46:24
Hopewell 43	3	40N24	101w04	6:44:16
Horace 39	1	41N28	98w42	6:34:48
Hordville 41	1	41N05	97w53	6:31:32
Horrell 32	1	40N34	100w16	6:41:04
Hoskins 90	1	42N07	97w18	6:29:12
Howard City 47	1	41N04	98w43	6:34:52
Howe 64	1	40N19	95w49	6:23:16
Howells 19	1	41N43	97w00	6:28:00
Hubbard 22	1	42N23	96w36	6:26:24
Hubbell 85	1	40N01	97w29	6:29:56
Hull 4	2	41N38	103w57	6:55:48
Humboldt 74	1	40N10	95w57	6:23:48
Humphrey 71	1	41N42	97w29	6:29:56
Hunter 90	1	42N13	96w57	6:27:48
Huntley 42	1	40N13	99w18	6:37:12
Huntsman 17	2	41N14	102w57	6:51:48
Huskerville	1	40N52	96w47	6:27:08
Hyannis 38	2	42N00	101w46	6:47:04
Imperial 15	2	40N31	101w39	6:46:36
Inavale 91	1	40N08	98w40	6:34:40
Independent 88	1	41N27	98w48	6:35:12
Indian Creek 29	2	40N08	101w30	6:46:00
Indianola 73	1	40N14	100w25	6:41:40
Industry 69	1	40N24	99w29	6:37:56
Inglewood 27	1	41N25	96w30	6:26:00
Inland 18	1	40N36	98w13	6:32:52
Inman 45	1	42N23	98w32	6:34:08
Inovale	1	40N08	98w40	6:34:40
Iowa 45	1	42N28	98w22	6:33:28
Irvington 28	1	41N19	96w03	6:24:12
Irwin 16	2	42N53	101w59	6:47:56
Island Grove 34	1	40N08	96w31	6:26:04
Ithaca 78	1	41N10	96w33	6:26:12
Jacinto 53	2	41N14	103w29	6:53:56
Jackson 22	1	42N27	96w34	6:26:16
Jamison 52	1	42N36	99w19	6:37:16
Jansen 48	1	40N11	97w05	6:28:20
Jeffrey 56	1	40N52	100w23	6:41:32
Johnson 64	1	40N24	96w01	6:24:04
Johnson Lake 37	1	40N35	99w52	6:39:28
Johnstown 9	3	42N34	100w03	6:40:12
Joliet 71	1	41N37	97w39	6:30:36
Josie 45	1	42N08	99w11	6:36:44
Julian 64	1	40N31	95w52	6:23:28
Juniata 1	1	40N36	98w30	6:34:00
Kalamazoo 60	1	41N47	97w40	6:30:40
Kearney 10	1	40N42	99w05	6:36:20
Keene 50	1	40N26	99w04	6:36:16
Kelso 47	1	41N10	98w40	6:34:40
Kem 56	1	40N54	100w50	6:43:20
Kenesaw 1	1	40N37	98w39	6:34:36
Kennard 89	1	41N28	96w12	6:24:48
Kennebec 24	1	41N01	99w40	6:38:40
Kennedy	2	42N33	100w49	6:43:16
Kent 58	1	41N48	99w17	6:37:08
Kewanee 16	5	42N55	100w22	6:41:28
Keystone 51	2	41N13	101w35	6:46:20
Kilfoil 21	3	41N29	99w48	6:39:12
Kilgore 16	2	42N56	100w57	6:43:48
Kimball 53	2	41N14	103w40	6:54:40
Kincaid 35	2	41N55	102w09	6:48:36
King Lake 28	1	41N19	96w21	6:25:24
Kingsburg 84	1	41N57	97w04	6:28:16
Kiowa 79	2	41N52	103w58	6:55:52
Kirkwood 75	1	42N43	99w19	6:37:16
Knievels Corner 45	1	42N16	98w21	6:33:24
Knowles 32	1	40N24	100w23	6:41:32
Kowanda 35	2	41N24	102w21	6:49:24
Kramer 55	1	40N35	96w52	6:27:28
Kronborg 41	1	40N59	97w58	6:31:52
Kuesters Lake 40	1	40N56	98w21	6:33:24
Lackey 16	2	42N22	101w32	6:46:08
Lake Forest Estates 28	1	41N18	96w02	6:24:08
Lakeland 9	3	42N17	100w04	6:40:16
Lake Platte View 28	1	41N17	96w17	6:25:08
Lakeside 81	2	42N03	102w26	6:49:44
Lamar 15	2	40N34	101w59	6:47:56
Lancaster 55	1	40N50	96w36	6:26:24
Lanham 34	1	40N00	96w52	6:27:28
La Platte 77	1	41N05	95w56	6:23:44
Laurel 14	1	42N26	97w06	6:28:24
Lavaca 16	2	42N42	101w58	6:47:52
La Vista 77	1	41N11	96w02	6:24:08
Lawn 7	2	42N18	103w19	6:53:16
Lawrence 65	1	40N18	98w16	6:33:04
Laws 32	1	40N34	100w37	6:42:28
Lay 75	1	42N29	99w20	6:37:20
Lebanon 73	3	40N03	100w17	6:41:08
Lee Valley 28	1	41N18	96w02	6:24:08
Leicester 18	1	40N39	98w13	6:32:52
Leigh 19	1	41N42	97w14	6:28:56
Lemley 59	3	41N30	100w49	6:43:16
Lemon 56	1	41N17	100w45	6:43:00
Lemoyne 51	2	41N17	101w49	6:47:16

Lena 3	2	41N39	101w30	6:46:00
Leonard 23	2	42N29	103w18	6:53:12
Leroy 93	1	40N50	97w33	6:30:12
Leshara 78	1	41N20	96w27	6:25:48
Leslie 90	1	42N08	96w52	6:27:28
Lewellen 35	2	41N20	102w09	6:48:36
Lewis 18	1	40N34	97w59	6:31:56
Lewiston 67	1	40N14	96w25	6:25:40
Lexington 24	1	40N47	99w45	6:39:00
Liberty 34	1	40N05	96w29	6:25:56
Lillian 21	1	41N36	99w33	6:38:12
Lincoln 55	1	40N49	96w41	6:26:44
Lindsay 71	1	41N42	97w42	6:30:48
Lindy 54	1	42N44	97w44	6:30:56
Line 91	1	40N02	98w33	6:34:12
Linwood 12	1	41N25	96w56	6:27:44
Lisbon 68	2	40N48	101w54	6:47:36
Lisco 35	2	41N30	102w37	6:50:28
Litchfield 82	1	41N10	99w09	6:36:36
Little Blue 1	1	40N24	98w20	6:33:20
Little Salt 55	1	41N00	96w44	6:26:56
Little York 58	1	41N59	99w21	6:37:24
Lockridge 93	1	40N55	97w39	6:30:36
Lodgepole 17	2	41N09	102w38	6:50:32
Loma 12	1	41N08	96w57	6:27:48
Lone Pine 4	2	41N29	103w29	6:53:56
Lonergan 51	2	41N19	101w54	6:47:36
Lone Valley 57	3	41N39	100w38	6:42:32
Long Pine 9	1	42N32	99w42	6:38:48
Long Springs 4	2	41N32	103w43	6:54:52
Loomis 69	1	40N29	99w31	6:38:04
Lorenzo 17	2	41N03	103w04	6:52:16
Loretto 6	1	41N46	98w05	6:32:20
Lorton 66	1	40N35	96w01	6:24:04
Louisville 13	1	41N00	96w10	6:24:40
Loup City 82	1	41N17	98w58	6:35:52
Loup Ferry 63	1	41N21	98w07	6:32:28
Loup Fork 47	1	41N05	98w41	6:34:44
Lowell 50	1	40N39	98w51	6:35:24
Lushton 93	1	40N43	97w44	6:30:56
Lutz 29	2	40N18	101w39	6:46:36
Lyman 79	2	41N55	104w02	6:56:08
Lynch 8	1	42N50	98w28	6:33:52
Lynden 33	3	40N07	100w02	6:40:08
Lynn 18	1	40N35	98w04	6:32:16
Lyons 11	1	41N56	96w28	6:25:52
Macedonia 15	2	40N36	101w51	6:47:24
Macon 31	1	40N13	98w57	6:35:48
Macy 87	1	42N07	96w21	6:25:24
Madison 60	1	41N50	97w27	6:29:48
Madison Square 58	1	41N46	99w33	6:38:12
Madrid 68	2	40N51	101w33	6:46:12
Magnet 14	1	42N27	97w28	6:29:52
Malcolm 55	1	40N54	96w52	6:27:28
Malmo 78	1	41N16	96w43	6:26:52
Manchester 6	1	41N42	98w00	6:32:00
Manley 13	1	40N55	96w10	6:24:40
Maple 27	1	41N31	96w37	6:26:28
Maple Grove 49	1	40N18	96w17	6:25:08
Maple Hill 28	1	41N18	96w02	6:24:08
Marble 78	1	41N11	96w23	6:25:32
Marietta 78	1	41N16	96w31	6:26:04
Marion 73	3	40N01	100w29	6:41:56
Mariposa 78	1	41N16	96w44	6:26:56
Marquette 41	1	41N00	98w01	6:32:04
Marshall 18	1	40N29	97w59	6:31:56
Marsland 23	2	42N27	103w18	6:53:12
Martell 55	1	40N38	96w45	6:27:00
Martin 40	1	40N43	98w34	6:34:16
Martinsburg 26	1	42N30	96w50	6:27:20
Marvin 68	2	40N47	101w17	6:45:08
Mascot 42	1	40N16	99w33	6:38:12
Maskell 26	1	42N41	96w59	6:27:56
Mason City 21	1	41N13	99w18	6:37:12
Max 29	2	40N07	101w24	6:45:36
Maxwell 56	1	41N05	100w31	6:42:04
May 50	1	40N29	98w47	6:35:08
Mayfield 40	1	41N00	98w33	6:34:12
Maywood 32	1	40N39	100w37	6:42:28
McArdle 28	1	41N17	96w05	6:24:20
McClure 45	1	42N13	98w34	6:34:16
McCook 73	1	40N12	100w38	6:42:32
McCool Junction 93	1	40N45	97w36	6:30:24
McCulley 8	1	42N57	98w57	6:35:48
McFadden 93	1	40N45	97w32	6:30:08
McGrew 79	2	41N45	103w25	6:53:40
McLean 70	1	42N23	97w28	6:29:52
Mead 78	1	41N14	96w29	6:25:56
Meadow Grove 60	1	42N02	97w44	6:30:56
Medicine 56	1	40N46	100w45	6:43:00
Melbeta 79	2	41N47	103w31	6:54:04
Memphis 78	1	41N06	96w26	6:25:44
Menominee 14	1	42N47	97w23	6:29:32
Mercer 28	1	41N19	96w21	6:25:24
Meridian 48	1	40N13	97w18	6:29:12
Merna 21	3	41N29	99w46	6:39:04
Merriman 16	2	42N55	101w42	6:46:48
Merry 87	1	42N13	96w35	6:26:20
Michigan 88	1	41N37	99w03	6:36:12
Middle Creek 55	1	40N49	96w52	6:27:28
Midvale 36	1	41N47	98w59	6:35:56
Milan 81	2	42N52	102w25	6:49:40
Milburn 21	3	41N43	99w44	6:38:56
Miles 67	1	40N08	96w17	6:25:08
Milford 80	1	40N47	97w03	6:28:12
Mill 55	1	41N00	96w31	6:26:04
Millard 28	1	41N13	96w07	6:24:28
Miller 10	1	40N56	99w23	6:37:32
Milligan 30	1	40N30	97w23	6:29:32
Mills 52	1	42N57	99w27	6:37:48
Milton 21	1	40N56	99w24	6:37:36
Minatare 79	2	41N49	103w30	6:54:00
Minden 50	1	40N30	98w57	6:35:48

Minnetonka 81	2	42N32	102w25	6:49:40
Mirage 50	1	40N29	99w06	6:36:24
Mission Creek 67	1	40N03	96w24	6:25:36
Mitchell 79	2	41N57	103w49	6:55:16
Momence 30	1	40N29	97w46	6:31:04
Monowi 8	1	42N50	98w20	6:33:20
Monroe 71	1	41N28	97w36	6:30:24
Monterey 20	1	41N47	96w51	6:27:24
Montrose 83	2	42N56	103w45	6:55:00
Moomaw Corner 62	2	41N45	103w19	6:53:16
Moon Lake 9	3	42N24	100w05	6:40:20
Moorefield 32	1	40N41	100w24	6:41:36
Morrill 79	2	41N58	103w56	6:55:44
Morse Bluff 78	1	41N26	96w46	6:27:04
Mother Lake 16	2	42N11	101w48	6:47:12
Mount Clare 65	1	40N17	98w16	6:33:04
Mount Pleasant 13	1	40N55	96w03	6:24:12
Mud Creek 92	1	41N47	98w23	6:33:32
Mullally 42	1	40N08	99w14	6:36:56
Mullen 46	2	42N03	101w01	6:44:04
Murdock 13	1	40N55	96w17	6:25:08
Murphy 41	1	40N54	98w13	6:32:52
Murray 13	1	40N55	95w56	6:23:44
Mynard 13	1	40N58	95w56	6:23:44
Naper 8	1	42N58	99w06	6:36:24
Naponee 31	1	40N05	99w09	6:36:36
Nashville 89	1	41N19	95w57	6:23:48
Natick 86	3	41N55	100w21	6:41:24
Nebraska City 66	1	40N41	95w52	6:23:28
Nehawka 13	1	40N50	95w59	6:23:56
Neligh 2	1	42N08	98w02	6:32:08
Nelson 65	1	40N12	98w04	6:32:16
Nemaha 64	1	40N20	95w41	6:22:44
Nenzel 16	2	42N56	101w06	6:44:24
Newark 50	1	40N38	99w00	6:36:00
Newcastle 26	1	42N39	96w53	6:27:32
New Era 33	1	40N18	99w41	6:38:44
New Helena 21	3	41N37	99w52	6:39:28
Newman 78	1	41N11	96w51	6:27:24
Newman Grove 60	1	41N45	97w47	6:31:08
Newport 75	1	42N36	99w20	6:37:20
Newton 48	1	40N03	96w58	6:27:52
New York 93	1	40N55	97w32	6:30:08
Nickerson 27	1	41N32	96w28	6:25:52
Niobrara 54	1	42N45	98w02	6:32:08
Noble 88	1	41N42	98w51	6:35:24
Nonpareil 7	2	42N14	103w05	6:52:20
Nora 65	1	40N10	97w58	6:31:52
Norden	1	42N52	100w05	6:40:20
Norfolk 60	1	42N02	97w25	6:29:40
Norman 50	1	40N29	98w48	6:35:12
North Auburn 64	1	40N23	95w51	6:23:24
North Bend 27	1	41N28	96w47	6:27:08
North Bluff 55	1	40N55	96w37	6:26:28
North Cedar 78	1	41N25	96w37	6:26:28
North Crawford 23	2	42N47	103w26	6:53:44
North Deer Creek 60	1	42N04	97w39	6:30:36
North Dry Creek 70	1	42N24	97w47	6:31:08
North Fork 76	1	40N29	97w12	6:28:48
North Franklin 31	1	40N18	98w47	6:35:08
North Loup 88	1	41N30	98w46	6:35:04
North Mc Williams 66	1	40N35	96w04	6:24:16
North Oaks 28	1	41N19	96w02	6:24:08
North Omaha 28	1	41N19	95w57	6:23:48
North Palmyra 66	1	40N44	96w24	6:25:36
North Platte 56	1	41N08	100w46	6:43:04
Northport 62	2	41N41	103w05	6:52:20
North Rosedale 56	3	41N20	100w55	6:43:40
North Russell 66	1	40N44	96w17	6:25:08
North Shore 22	1	42N28	96w24	6:25:36
North Star 32	1	40N29	100w30	6:42:00
North Syracuse 66	1	40N40	96w11	6:24:44
North Valley 73	1	40N18	100w14	6:40:56
Northwest 28	1	41N18	96w02	6:24:08
Nowell 56	3	41N05	100w59	6:43:56
Nysted 47	1	41N07	98w33	6:34:12
Oak 65	1	40N14	97w54	6:31:36
Oakdale 2	1	42N04	97w58	6:31:52
Oak Grove 31	1	40N03	99w01	6:36:04
Oakland 11	1	41N50	96w28	6:25:52
Obert 14	1	42N41	97w02	6:28:08
Oconee 71	1	41N28	97w35	6:30:20
Oconto 21	1	41N09	99w46	6:39:04
Octavia 12	1	41N21	97w04	6:28:16
Odell 34	1	40N03	96w48	6:27:12
Odessa 10	1	40N42	99w15	6:37:00
Offutt Air Force Base 77	1	41N09	95w57	6:23:48
Ogallala 51	2	41N08	101w43	6:46:52
Ohio 74	1	40N08	95w37	6:22:28
Ohiowa 30	1	40N25	97w27	6:29:48
Old Mill 28	1	41N18	96w02	6:24:08
Olean 19	1	41N43	96w53	6:27:32
Olive Branch 55	1	40N34	96w51	6:27:24
Omadi 22	1	42N24	96w29	6:25:56
Omaha 28	1	41N17	96w01	6:24:04
Omaha Indian Reservation 87	1	42N14	96w28	6:25:52
Oneida 50	1	40N24	99w06	6:36:24
O'neill 45	1	42N27	98w39	6:34:36
Ong 18	1	40N24	97w50	6:31:20
Orafino 32	1	40N30	100w15	6:41:00
Orange 23	2	42N39	103w23	6:53:32
Orchard 2	1	42N20	98w15	6:33:00
Ord 88	1	41N36	98w56	6:35:44
Ordville 17	2	41N15	103w03	6:52:12
Orleans 42	1	40N08	99w27	6:37:48

NEBRASKA

Orum 89 1 41N33 96w09 6:24:36
Orville 41 1 40N44 98w00 6:32:00
Osage 66 1 40N34 96w11 6:24:44
Osborn 32 1 40N24 100w44 6:42:56
Osceola 72 1 41N11 97w33 6:30:12
Osgood 56 1 41N05 100w46 6:43:04
Oshkosh 35 2 41N24 102w21 6:49:24
Osmond 70 1 42N22 97w36 6:30:24
Otis 41 1 41N00 97w53 6:31:32
Otoe 66 1 40N43 96w07 6:24:28
Otter Creek 26 1 42N27 96w45 6:27:00
Ough 29 2 40N18 101w30 6:46:00
Overton 24 1 40N44 99w32 6:38:08
Oxford 33 1 40N15 99w38 6:38:32
Palisade 44 3 40N21 101w07 6:44:28
Palmer 61 1 41N13 98w15 6:33:00
Palmyra 66 1 40N42 96w23 6:25:32
Panama 55 1 40N36 96w31 6:26:04
Panhandle 83 2 42N26 103w57 6:55:48
Papillion 77 1 41N09 96w03 6:24:12
Park 35 2 41N17 102w09 6:48:36
Parks 29 2 40N03 101w44 6:46:56
Parkview 40 1 40N54 98w21 6:33:24
Paul 66 1 40N36 95w54 6:23:36
Pauline 1 1 40N25 98w21 6:33:24
Pawnee City 67 1 40N07 96w09 6:24:36
Paxton 51 2 41N07 101w21 6:45:24
Payne 56 1 41N03 100w36 6:42:24
Pearl 15 2 40N40 101w38 6:46:32
Pebble 27 1 41N42 96w44 6:26:56
Peckham 56 1 40N56 100w17 6:41:08
Pender 87 1 42N07 96w43 6:26:52
Penn 35 2 41N24 102w21 6:49:24
Peoria 54 1 42N39 97w40 6:30:40
Pershing 11 1 41N47 96w30 6:26:00
Peru 64 1 40N29 95w44 6:22:56
Petersburg 6 1 41N51 98w05 6:32:20
Pewaukee 75 1 42N11 99w34 6:38:16
Phillips 41 1 40N54 98w13 6:32:52
Pickrell 34 1 40N23 96w44 6:26:56
Pierce 70 1 42N12 97w32 6:30:08
Pigeon Creek 22 1 42N24 96w41 6:26:44
Pilger 84 1 42N00 97w03 6:28:12
Pine 9 3 42N33 99w42 6:38:48
Pine Creek 81 2 42N20 102w24 6:49:36
Pine Glen 9 3 42N41 99w45 6:39:00
Plainview 70 1 42N21 97w47 6:31:08
Plant 56 1 41N00 100w41 6:42:44
Platte Center 71 1 41N32 97w29 6:29:56
Platte Valley 28 1 41N21 96w21 6:25:24
Plattsmouth 13 1 41N01 95w53 6:23:32
Pleasant 48 1 40N08 96w58 6:27:52
Pleasant Dale 80 1 40N48 96w56 6:27:44
Pleasanthill 76 1 40N39 97w07 6:28:28
Pleasant Home 72 1 41N06 97w45 6:31:00
Pleasanton 10 1 40N58 99w05 6:36:20
Pleasant Valley 27
1 41N37 96w51 6:27:24
Plum Grove 70 1 42N24 97w33 6:30:12
Plymouth 48 1 40N18 97w00 6:28:00
Pohocco 78 1 41N22 96w31 6:26:04
Polk 72 1 41N05 97w46 6:31:04
Ponca 26 1 42N34 96w43 6:26:52
Ponce Indian Reservation 54
1 42N14 96w28 6:25:52
Poole 10 1 40N59 98w58 6:35:52
Porter 74 1 40N13 95w51 6:23:24
Posen 47 1 41N13 98w40 6:34:40
Potsdam 91 1 40N18 98w27 6:33:48
Potter 17 2 41N13 103w19 6:53:16
Powell 48 1 40N13 97w17 6:29:08
Prague 78 1 41N19 96w49 6:27:16
Prairie 69 1 40N24 99w22 6:37:28
Prairie Center 10
1 40N47 99w10 6:36:40
Prairie Dog 42 3 40N02 99w22 6:37:28
Prairie Home 55 1 40N49 96w40 6:26:40
Prairie Island 61
1 41N09 97w52 6:31:28
Precept 33 3 40N08 99w36 6:38:24
Preston 74 1 40N02 95w31 6:22:04
Primrose 6 1 41N38 98w14 6:32:56
Princeton 55 1 40N35 96w42 6:26:48
Prosser 1 1 40N41 98w34 6:34:16
Purdum 5 3 42N04 100w16 6:41:04
Quinnebaugh 11 1 41N57 96w12 6:24:48
Raeville 6 1 41N54 98w03 6:32:12
Ragan 42 1 40N19 99w17 6:37:08
Ralston 28 1 41N12 96w03 6:24:12
Ramshorn 84 1 41N47 97w12 6:28:48
Randolph 14 1 42N23 97w22 6:29:28
Ravenna 10 1 41N02 98w55 6:35:40
Raymond 55 1 40N57 96w47 6:27:08
Read 12 1 41N05 97w19 6:29:16
Reading 12 1 41N11 97w19 6:29:16
Redbird 45 1 42N50 98w28 6:33:52
Red Cloud 91 1 40N05 98w32 6:34:08
Redington 62 2 41N35 103w16 6:53:04
Red Willow 73 3 40N13 100w29 6:41:56
Regency 28 1 41N16 96w03 6:24:12
Regency 28 1 41N16 96w03 6:24:12
Reno 81 2 42N10 102w37 6:50:28
Republican City 42
1 40N06 99w13 6:36:52
Reuben 42 1 40N13 99w28 6:37:52
Reynolds 48 1 40N04 97w20 6:29:20
Richardson 12 1 41N05 96w58 6:27:52
Richfield 77 1 41N06 96w05 6:24:20
Richland 19 1 41N26 97w13 6:28:52
Richmond 33 3 40N03 99w48 6:39:12
Ridgeley 27 1 41N37 96w44 6:26:56
Ridnour 44 3 40N13 101w02 6:44:08
Ringgold 59 3 41N31 100w47 6:43:08
Rising City 12 1 41N12 97w18 6:29:12
Riverdale 10 1 40N47 99w10 6:36:40
Riverside Lakes 28
1 41N17 96w17 6:25:08
Riverside Park 61
1 41N07 98w00 6:32:00
Riverton 31 1 40N05 98w46 6:35:04
Roanoke 28 1 41N18 96w02 6:24:08
Robb 37 1 40N40 99w42 6:38:48
Roca 55 1 40N39 96w40 6:26:40
Rockford 34 1 40N15 96w36 6:26:24
Rockton 33 3 40N03 100w01 6:40:04
Rockville 82 1 41N07 98w50 6:35:20
Rogers 19 1 41N28 96w55 6:27:40
Rohrs 64 1 40N23 95w51 6:23:24
Rokeby 55 1 40N47 96w42 6:26:48
Rosalie 87 1 42N03 96w31 6:26:04
Roscoe 51 2 41N08 101w35 6:46:20
Rose 75 1 42N09 99w28 6:37:52
Rosedale 56 3 41N14 100w54 6:43:36
Roseland 1 1 40N28 98w34 6:34:16
Roselma 6 1 41N40 98w07 6:32:28
Rosemont 91 1 40N17 98w22 6:33:28
Rosenburg 71 1 41N42 97w41 6:30:44
Roubadeau 79 2 41N47 103w46 6:55:04
Royal 2 1 42N19 98w08 6:32:32
Ruby 1 40N50 97w05 6:28:20
Rulo 74 1 40N03 95w26 6:21:44
Running Water 83 2 42N25 103w47 6:55:08
Rusco 10 1 40N55 99w07 6:36:28
Rush Creek 35 2 41N18 102w29 6:49:56
Rushville 81 2 42N43 102w28 6:49:52
Ruskin 65 1 40N09 97w52 6:31:28
Ryno 21 1 41N21 99w48 6:39:12
Saint Bernard 71 1 41N43 97w38 6:30:32
Saint Charles 20 1 41N49 96w45 6:27:00
Saint Columbans 77
1 41N05 95w52 6:23:28
Saint Edward 6 1 41N34 97w52 6:31:28
Saint Helena 14 1 42N49 97w15 6:29:00
Saint James 14 1 42N44 97w10 6:28:40
Saint Johns 22 1 42N28 96w35 6:26:20
Saint Libory 47 1 41N05 98w21 6:33:24
Saint Mary 49 1 40N25 96w18 6:25:12
Saint Michael 10 1 41N02 98w55 6:35:40
Saint Paul 47 1 41N13 98w27 6:33:48
Saint Stephens 65
1 40N15 98w16 6:33:04
Salem 74 1 40N05 95w43 6:22:52
Salt Creek 13 1 40N59 96w24 6:25:36
Saltillo 55 1 40N39 96w38 6:26:32
Sand Creek 45 1 42N43 98w59 6:35:56
Santee 54 1 42N51 97w50 6:31:20
Santee Indian Reservation 54
1 42N14 96w28 6:25:52
Sappa 42 3 40N08 99w34 6:38:16
Saratoga 45 1 42N45 98w50 6:35:20
Sarben 51 2 41N10 101w18 6:45:12
Sargent 21 1 41N39 99w22 6:37:28
Saronville 18 1 40N36 97w56 6:31:44
Sartoria 10 1 41N00 99w15 6:37:00
Savannah 12 1 41N21 97w12 6:28:48
Scandinavia 42 1 40N19 99w20 6:37:20
Schaupps 82 1 41N15 98w48 6:35:12
Schneider 10 1 40N55 98w53 6:35:32
Schoolcraft 60 1 41N52 97w39 6:30:36
School Creek 18 1 40N39 97w53 6:31:32
Schuyler 19 1 41N27 97w04 6:28:16
Scotia 39 1 41N28 98w42 6:34:48
Scottsbluff 79 2 41N52 103w40 6:54:40
Scovill 41 1 40N45 98w13 6:32:52
Scribner 27 1 41N40 96w40 6:26:40
Second Lafayette 64
1 40N29 95w56 6:23:44
Sedan 65 1 40N22 97w58 6:31:52
Selden 75 1 42N20 99w34 6:38:16
Sellers 56 3 41N00 100w50 6:43:20
Seneca 86 3 42N03 100w50 6:43:20
Seward 80 1 40N55 97w06 6:28:24
Seymour Park 28 1 41N13 96w03 6:24:12
Shamrock 45 1 42N18 98w44 6:34:56
Sharon 10 1 40N50 98w47 6:35:08
Sheep Creek 83 2 42N12 103w51 6:55:24
Shelby 72 1 41N12 97w26 6:29:44
Shelton 10 1 40N47 98w44 6:34:56
Shickley 30 1 40N25 97w43 6:30:52
Shields 45 1 42N34 98w39 6:34:36
Sholes 90 1 42N20 97w18 6:29:12
Shubert 74 1 40N14 95w41 6:22:44
Sicily 34 1 40N08 96w45 6:27:00
Sidney 17 2 41N08 102w59 6:51:56
Silver Creek 61 1 41N19 97w40 6:30:40
Silver Lake 1 1 40N23 98w33 6:34:12
Skull Creek 12 1 41N16 96w58 6:27:52
Slough 70 1 42N13 97w25 6:29:40
Smith 9 3 42N21 99w45 6:39:00
Smithfield 37 1 40N34 99w45 6:39:00
Snake Creek 83 2 42N15 103w36 6:54:24
Snyder 27 1 41N43 96w47 6:27:08
Somerset 56 3 40N47 100w50 6:43:20
South 53 2 41N03 103w40 6:54:40
South Bend 13 1 41N00 96w15 6:25:00
South Cedar 78 1 41N21 96w37 6:26:28
South Crawford 23
2 42N39 103w23 6:53:32
South Deer Creek 60
1 42N01 97w39 6:30:36
South Dry Creek 70
1 42N19 97w46 6:31:04
South Loup 40 1 41N00 98w39 6:34:36
South Mc Williams 66
1 40N33 96w04 6:24:16
South Minden 50 1 40N30 98w57 6:35:48
South Omaha 28 1 41N13 95w58 6:23:52
South Palmyra 66 1 40N40 96w24 6:25:36
South Pass 55 1 40N34 96w38 6:26:32
South Russell 66 1 40N39 96w18 6:25:12
South Sioux City 22
1 42N28 96w24 6:25:36
South Syracuse 66
1 40N38 96w11 6:24:44
South Yankton 14 1 42N53 97w23 6:29:32
Spade 54 1 42N39 97w54 6:31:36
Spalding 39 1 41N42 98w22 6:33:28
Sparks 16 5 42N55 100w15 6:41:00
Sparta 54 1 42N39 98w01 6:32:04
Speiser 74 1 40N03 95w57 6:23:48
Spencer 8 1 42N53 98w42 6:34:48
Spencer Park 1 1 40N35 98w24 6:33:36
Spotted Horse 3 2 41N28 101w34 6:46:16
Spotted Tail 83 2 42N02 103w45 6:55:00
Sprague 55 1 40N38 96w45 6:27:00
Spring Bank 26 1 42N24 96w50 6:27:20
Spring Branch 84 1 42N03 97w19 6:29:16
Spring Creek 21 1 41N28 99w17 6:37:08
Springfield 77 1 41N05 96w08 6:24:32
Spring Green 33 3 40N03 99w55 6:39:40
Spring Grove 42 1 40N19 99w34 6:38:16
Spring Ranch 18 1 40N24 98w13 6:32:52
Springview 52 1 42N50 99w45 6:39:00
Stamford 42 3 40N08 99w36 6:38:24
Stanton 84 1 41N57 97w14 6:28:56
Staplehurst 80 1 40N58 97w10 6:28:40
Stapleton 57 1 41N29 100w31 6:42:04
Starkey 44 3 40N13 101w09 6:44:36
State House 55 1 40N49 96w40 6:26:40
Steel Creek 45 1 42N41 98w21 6:33:24
Steele City 48 1 40N02 97w02 6:28:08
Stegall 79 2 41N58 103w56 6:55:44
Steinauer 67 1 40N12 96w14 6:24:56
Stella 74 1 40N14 95w46 6:23:04
Sterling 49 1 40N28 96w23 6:25:32
Stevens Creek 55 1 40N50 96w31 6:26:04
Stewart 93 1 41N00 97w26 6:29:44
Still Meadow 28 1 41N19 96w02 6:24:08
Stillwater 91 1 40N13 98w20 6:33:20
Stockham 41 1 40N43 97w56 6:31:44
Stocking 78 1 41N11 96w37 6:26:28
Stockton 55 1 40N44 96w31 6:26:04
Stockville 32 1 40N32 100w23 6:41:32
Stock Yards 28 1 41N13 95w58 6:23:52
Storm Lake 62 2 41N48 102w44 6:50:56
Stove Creek 13 1 40N49 96w18 6:25:12
Strahan 90 1 42N13 97w05 6:28:20
Strang 30 1 40N25 97w35 6:30:20
Stratton 44 3 40N09 101w14 6:44:56
Strohl 58 1 41N50 99w31 6:38:04
Stromsburg 72 1 41N07 97w36 6:30:24
Stuart 45 1 42N36 99w08 6:36:32
Sugar Loaf 83 2 42N54 103w35 6:54:20
Sughrue 35 2 41N17 102w20 6:49:20
Sumner 24 1 40N57 99w31 6:38:04
Sunnyslope 28 1 41N18 96w02 6:24:08
Sunol 17 2 41N09 102w46 6:51:04
Sunshine 56 3 41N04 101w12 6:44:48
Superior 65 1 40N01 98w04 6:32:16
Surprise 12 1 41N06 97w19 6:29:16
Survey 16 2 42N01 101w56 6:47:44
Sutherland 56 3 41N10 101w08 6:44:32
Sutton 18 1 40N36 97w52 6:31:28
Swan Creek 76 1 40N23 97w05 6:28:20
Swan Lake 43 3 40N29 101w10 6:44:40
Swanton 76 1 40N23 97w05 6:28:20
Swedeburg 78 1 41N08 96w37 6:26:28
Swedehome 72 1 41N07 97w36 6:30:24
Sweetwater 1 41N03 99w01 6:36:04
Syracuse 66 1 40N39 96w11 6:24:44
Table Rock 67 1 40N11 96w06 6:24:24
Tabor 79 2 41N50 103w31 6:54:04
Talmage 66 1 40N32 96w01 6:24:04
Tamora 80 1 40N54 97w14 6:28:56
Tarnov 71 1 41N37 97w30 6:30:00
Taylor 58 1 41N46 99w23 6:37:32
Tecumseh 49 1 40N22 96w11 6:24:44
Tekamah 11 1 41N47 96w13 6:24:52
Telbasta 89 1 41N27 96w21 6:25:24
Terrytown 79 2 41N51 103w40 6:54:40
Thayer 93 1 40N58 97w30 6:30:00
Thedford 86 3 41N59 100w35 6:42:20
The Mall 56 1 41N08 100w46 6:43:04
Thompson 48 1 40N08 97w11 6:28:44
Thompson 70 1 42N23 97w39 6:30:36
Thornburg 43 3 40N29 100w50 6:43:20
Thornton 10 1 40N50 99w00 6:36:00
Thune 3 2 41N29 101w27 6:45:48
Thurman 75 1 42N29 99w32 6:38:08
Thurston 87 1 42N11 96w42 6:26:48
Tilden 60 1 42N03 97w50 6:31:20
Timber Creek 63 1 41N26 98w07 6:32:28
Tipton 13 1 40N50 96w24 6:25:36
Tobias 76 1 40N25 97w20 6:29:20
Todd Creek 49 1 40N19 96w08 6:24:32
Touhy 78 1 41N08 96w50 6:27:20
Townsend 83 2 42N05 104w01 6:56:04
Trenton 44 3 40N11 101w01 6:44:04
Triumph 21 1 41N23 100w00 6:40:00
Trognitz 17 2 41N22 103w18 6:53:12
Trumbull 18 1 40N41 98w16 6:33:04
Tryon 59 3 41N33 100w57 6:43:48
Tyrone 73 3 40N08 100w15 6:41:00
Uehling 27 1 41N44 96w30 6:26:00
Ulysses 12 1 41N04 97w12 6:28:48
Unadilla 66 1 40N41 96w16 6:25:04
Union 13 1 40N49 95w55 6:23:40
Union Creek 84 1 41N52 97w18 6:29:12
Union Valley 17 2 41N24 102w54 6:51:36
University Place 55
1 40N51 96w39 6:26:36
Upland 31 1 40N19 98w54 6:35:36
Upper Driftwood 44
3 40N03 101w03 6:44:12
Utica 80 1 40N54 97w21 6:29:24

Place		Lat	Long	Time
Valentine 16	6	42N52	100w33	6:42:12
Valley 28	1	41N19	96w21	6:25:24
Valley Grange 73	3	40N09	100w36	6:42:24
Valparaiso 78	1	41N05	96w50	6:27:20
Venango 68	2	40N46	102w02	6:48:08
Venice 28	1	41N17	96w17	6:25:08
Venus 54	1	42N20	98w14	6:32:56
Verdel 54	1	42N49	98w12	6:32:48
Verdigre 54	1	42N36	98w02	6:32:08
Verdon 74	1	40N09	95w43	6:22:52
Verona 1	1	40N39	98w33	6:34:12
Vesta 49	1	40N21	96w20	6:25:20
Veterans' Administration Hos 28	1	41N15	95w58	6:23:52
Victor 65	1	40N18	98w13	6:32:52
Victoria 21	3	41N37	99w48	6:39:12
Vieregg 61	1	40N57	98w15	6:33:00
Vincent 33	3	40N13	100w01	6:40:04
Vinton 88	1	41N31	99w02	6:36:08
Virginia 34	1	40N15	96w30	6:26:00
Vroman 56	1	41N01	100w16	6:41:04
Wabash 13	1	40N55	96w17	6:25:08
Waco 93	1	40N54	97w28	6:29:52
Wagners Lake 71	1	41N26	97w21	6:29:24
Wahoo 78	1	41N13	96w37	6:26:28
Wakefield 26	1	42N16	96w52	6:27:28
Wallace 56	3	40N50	101w10	6:44:40
Walnut Creek 91	1	40N03	98w40	6:34:40
Walnut Grove 54	1	42N31	98w15	6:33:00
Walthill 87	1	42N09	96w30	6:26:00
Walton 55	1	40N48	96w34	6:26:16
Wanda 1	1	40N34	98w40	6:34:40
Wann 78	1	41N09	96w21	6:25:24
Warbonnet 83	2	42N49	103w55	6:55:40
Ware 8	1	42N59	98w46	6:35:04
Warnerville 60	1	41N57	97w26	6:29:44
Warsaw 47	1	41N12	98w34	6:34:16
Washington 89	1	41N24	96w13	6:24:52
Waterbury 26	1	42N27	96w44	6:26:56
Waterloo 28	1	41N15	96w19	6:25:16
Wauneta 15	2	40N25	101w23	6:45:32
Wausa 54	1	42N30	97w32	6:30:08
Waverly 55	1	40N55	96w32	6:26:08
Wayne 90	1	42N14	97w01	6:28:04
Wayside 23	2	42N57	103w20	6:53:20
Weeping Water 13	1	40N52	96w08	6:24:32
Weissert 21	1	41N28	99w27	6:37:48
Weitzel 6	1	41N42	97w53	6:31:32
Well 56	1	40N53	100w42	6:42:48
Wellfleet 56	1	40N45	100w44	6:42:56
Wells 16	2	42N17	101w02	6:44:08
West Branch 67	1	40N03	96w17	6:25:08
West Chadron 23	2	42N51	103w04	6:52:16
West Dodge 28	1	41N16	95w58	6:23:52
Western 76	1	40N24	97w12	6:28:48
Westerville 21	1	41N24	99w23	6:37:32
West Gordon 81	2	42N49	102w16	6:49:04
West Lincoln 55	1	40N50	96w44	6:26:56
Westmark 69	1	40N34	99w28	6:37:52
West Mirage 81	2	42N27	102w42	6:50:48
West Newman 63	1	41N18	98w02	6:32:08
West Oak 55	1	41N00	96w51	6:27:24
West Ogallala 51	2	41N07	101w47	6:47:08
West Omaha 28	1	41N16	96w03	6:24:12
Weston 78	1	41N12	96w45	6:27:00
West Point 20	1	41N51	96w43	6:26:52
West Rock Bluffs 13	1	40N55	95w57	6:23:48
Westside 69	1	40N38	99w35	6:38:20
West Union 21	1	41N41	99w30	6:38:00
West Winters Creek 79	2	41N53	103w42	6:54:48
Weyerts 17	2	41N09	102w38	6:50:32
Whistle Creek 83	2	42N25	103w34	6:54:16
Whiteclay 81	2	43N00	102w33	6:50:12
White River 83	2	42N37	103w32	6:54:08
Whitetail 51	2	41N16	101w36	6:46:24
Whitewater 59	3	41N39	101w17	6:45:08
Whitman 38	2	42N03	101w31	6:46:04
Whitney 23	2	42N47	103w15	6:53:00
Whittier 56	1	41N22	100w31	6:42:04
Wilber 76	1	40N29	96w58	6:27:52
Wilbur 90	1	42N18	97w05	6:28:20
Wilcox 50	1	40N22	99w10	6:36:40
Williamsburg 69	1	40N39	99w27	6:37:48
Willis 22	1	42N27	96w34	6:26:16
Willow Creek 70	1	42N14	97w46	6:31:04
Willowdale 45	1	42N34	98w25	6:33:40
Willow Grove 73	3	40N14	100w35	6:42:20
Willow Island 24	1	40N53	100w04	6:40:16
Willow Springs 36	1	41N51	99w05	6:36:20
Wilsonville 33	3	40N07	100w07	6:40:28
Winnebago 87	1	42N14	96w28	6:25:52
Winnebago Indian Reservation 87	1	42N14	96w28	6:25:52
Winnetoon 54	1	42N31	97w58	6:31:52
Winside 90	1	42N11	97w10	6:28:40
Winslow 27	1	41N37	96w30	6:26:00
Wisner 20	1	41N59	96w55	6:27:40
Wolbach 39	1	41N24	98w24	6:33:36
Wood Lake 16	5	42N38	100w14	6:40:56
Wood River 40	1	40N49	98w36	6:34:24
Woodson 68	2	40N57	101w22	6:45:28
Woodville 71	1	41N34	97w46	6:31:04
Worden 59	3	41N39	101w04	6:44:16
Worms 61	1	41N05	98w21	6:33:24
Wounded Knee 81	2	42N57	102w14	6:48:56
Wright 7	2	42N06	103w03	6:52:12
Wrights 4	2	41N37	103w29	6:53:56
Wymore 34	1	40N07	96w40	6:26:40
Wynot 14	1	42N45	97w10	6:28:40
Wyoming 66	1	40N41	95w52	6:23:28
Yale 88	1	41N26	99w02	6:36:08
Yankee 68	2	40N47	101w24	6:45:36
Yankee Hill 55	1	40N46	96w44	6:26:56
Yockey 62	2	41N45	103w11	6:52:44
York 93	1	40N52	97w36	6:30:24
Yossem's Paradise Valley 28	1	41N18	96w02	6:24:08
Yutan 78	1	41N15	96w24	6:25:36
Zero 1	1	40N24	98w27	6:33:48
Zimmer 32	1	40N29	100w43	6:42:52

TIME TABLES

There is uncertainty about the time zone boundary in the sparsely populated eastern part of the state. Changes from Mountain time to Pacific time or the reverse in rural areas are undocumented.

NV # 1

Before 11/18/1883		LMT
11/18/1883	12:00	PST
3/31/1918	02:00	PWT
10/27/1918	02:00	PST
3/30/1919	02:00	PWT
10/26/1919	02:00	PST
2/09/1942	02:00	PWT
9/30/1945	02:00	PST
3/14/1948	02:00	PDT
1/01/1949	02:00	PST
4/30/1950	02:00	PDT
9/24/1950	02:00	PST
4/29/1951	02:00	PDT
9/30/1951	02:00	PST
4/27/1952	02:00	PDT
9/28/1952	02:00	PST
4/26/1953	02:00	PDT
9/27/1953	02:00	PST
4/25/1954	02:00	PDT
9/26/1954	02:00	PST
4/24/1955	02:00	PDT
9/25/1955	02:00	PST
4/29/1956	02:00	PDT
9/30/1956	02:00	PST
4/28/1957	02:00	PDT
9/29/1957	02:00	PST
4/27/1958	02:00	PDT
9/28/1958	02:00	PST
4/26/1959	02:00	PDT
9/27/1959	02:00	PST
4/24/1960	02:00	PDT
9/25/1960	02:00	PST
4/30/1961	02:00	PDT
9/24/1961	02:00	PST
4/29/1962	02:00	PDT
10/28/1962	02:00	PST
4/28/1963	02:00	PDT
10/27/1963	02:00	PST
4/26/1964	02:00	PDT
10/25/1964	02:00	PST
4/25/1965	02:00	PDT
10/31/1965	02:00	PST
4/24/1966	02:00	PDT
10/30/1966	02:00	PST
4/30/1967	02:00	US#1

NV # 2

Before 11/18/1883		LMT
11/18/1883	12:00	PST
3/31/1918	02:00	PWT
10/27/1918	02:00	PST
3/30/1919	02:00	PWT
10/26/1919	02:00	PST
1/01/1930	00:00	MST
2/09/1942	02:00	MWT
9/30/1945	02:00	MST
4/30/1967	02:00	US#1

NV # 3

Before 11/18/1883		LMT
11/18/1883	12:00	MST
3/31/1918	02:00	MWT
10/27/1918	02:00	MST
3/30/1919	02:00	MWT
10/26/1919	02:00	MST
2/09/1942	02:00	MWT
9/30/1945	02:00	MST
9/24/1965	00:00	PST
4/24/1966	02:00	US#1

NV # 4

Before 11/18/1883		LMT
11/18/1883	12:00	PST
3/31/1918	02:00	PWT
10/27/1918	02:00	PST
3/30/1919	02:00	PWT
10/26/1919	02:00	PST
1/01/1930	00:00	MST
2/09/1942	02:00	MWT
9/30/1945	02:00	MST
9/24/1965	00:00	PST
4/24/1966	02:00	US#1

COUNTIES

1 Churchill
2 Clark
3 Douglas
4 Elko
5 Esmeralda
6 Eureka
7 Humboldt
8 Lander
9 Lincoln
10 Lyon
11 Mineral
12 Nye
13 Pershing
14 Storey
15 Washoe
16 White Pine
17 Carson City

Acoma 9	3	37N33	114W10	7:36:40
Alamo 9	3	37N22	115W10	7:40:40
Alunite 2	1	35N59	114W55	7:39:40
Arden 2	1	36N01	115W14	7:40:56
Argenta 8	1	40N32	116W59	7:47:56
Arthur 4	1	41N06	114W58	7:39:52
Ash Springs 9	3	37N32	115W14	7:40:56
Austin 8	1	39N30	117W04	7:48:16
Babbitt 11	1	38N32	118W39	7:54:36
Baker 16	2	39N06	114W13	7:36:52
Bald Mountain 15	1	41N44	119W41	7:58:44
Basalt 11	1	37N48	118W32	7:54:08
Battle Mountain 8	1	40N38	116W56	7:47:44
Beatty 12	1	36N54	116W46	7:47:04
Beowawe 6	1	40N35	116W29	7:45:56.
Black Springs 15	1	39N37	119W51	7:59:24
Blue Diamond 2	1	36N03	115W24	7:41:36
Bonanza 2	1	36N12	115W10	7:40:40
Boulder City 2	1	35N59	114W50	7:39:20
Bradys Hot Springs 1	1	39N47	119W02	7:56:08
Bunkerville 2	1	36N46	114W08	7:36:32
Cactus Springs 2	1	37N44	118W05	7:52:20
Caliente 9	3	37N37	114W31	7:38:04
Canal 10	1	39N35	119W15	7:57:00
Carlin 4	1	40N43	116W07	7:44:28
Carlton Square 2	1	36N12	115W08	7:40:32
Carp 9	3	37N07	114W29	7:37:56
Carroll Station 8	1	39N27	118W45	7:55:00
Carson City 17	1	39N10	119W46	7:59:04
Carson Meadows 17	1	39N09	119W47	7:59:08
Carver Park 2	1	36N03	114W59	7:39:56
Carvers 12	1	38N43	117W04	7:48:16
Caselton 9	3	37N55	114W29	7:37:56
Centerville 3	1	38N49	119W41	7:58:44
Charleston 4	2	40N50	115W46	7:43:04
Charleston Park 2	1	36N12	115W14	7:40:56
Cherry Creek 16	2	39N54	114W53	7:39:32
Cibola Park 2	1	36N12	115W08	7:40:32
Coaldale 5	1	38N04	117W14	7:48:56
Cobre 4	2	41N07	114W24	7:37:36
Cold Spring 1	1	39N27	118W45	7:55:00
Contact 4	2	41N46	114W45	7:39:00
Copperfield 15	1	39N38	119W57	7:59:48
Cordero 7	2	41N59	117W46	7:51:04
Cosgrave 13	1	40N48	118W01	7:52:04
Cottonwood Cove 2	1	35N28	114W55	7:39:40
Cover City 4	1	41N06	114W58	7:39:52
Crescent Valley 6	1	40N35	116W29	7:45:56
Crestline 9	3	37N40	114W08	7:36:32
Crystal Bay 15	1	39N15	120W00	8:00:00
Currie 4	2	40N16	114W45	7:39:00
Dayton 10	1	39N14	119W36	7:58:24
Deeth 4	1	41N04	115W17	7:41:08
Denio 7	1	41N59	118W38	7:54:32
Desert Inn Country Club 2	1	36N07	115W08	7:40:32
Dixie Valley 1	1	39N27	118W45	7:55:00
Downtown 2	1	36N11	115W07	7:40:28
Dresslerville 3	1	38N49	119W41	7:58:44
Dry Lake 2	1	37N44	118W05	7:52:20
Duck Valley 4	1	41N57	116W06	7:44:24
Duckwater 12	1	38N54	115W41	7:42:44
Duckwater Indian Reservation 12	1	38N54	115W41	7:42:44
Dunphy 6	1	40N43	116W32	7:46:08
Dyer 5	1	37N41	118W05	7:52:20
East Ely 16	4	39N15	114W53	7:39:32
East Fork 3	1	38N58	119W45	7:59:00
Eastgate 1	1	39N19	117W53	7:51:32
East Las Vegas 2	1	36N06	115W04	7:40:16
East Line 4	2	40N31	114W17	7:37:08
Echo Bay 2	1	36N33	114W27	7:37:48
Elburz 4	1	40N57	115W27	7:41:48
Elgin 9	3	37N21	114W32	7:38:08
Elko 4	1	40N50	115W46	7:43:04
Elks Point 3	1	39N00	119W57	7:59:48
Ely 16	4	39N15	114W54	7:39:36
Empire 15	1	40N35	119W21	7:57:24
Esmeralda 5	1	38N51	117W07	7:48:28
Eureka 6	4	39N31	115W58	7:43:52
Fallon 1	1	39N28	118W47	7:55:08
Fallon Indian Reservation 1	1	39N32	118W37	7:54:28
Fallon Station 1	1	39N26	118W43	7:54:52
Federal 2	1	36N11	115W07	7:40:28
Fernley 10	1	39N36	119W15	7:57:00
Fort McDermitt Indian Reserv 7	2	42N00	117W43	7:50:52
Frenchman 1	1	39N17	118W16	7:53:04
Gabbs 12	1	38N52	117W55	7:51:40
Galena 15	1	39N31	119W49	7:59:16
Gardnerville 3	1	38N56	119W45	7:59:00
Gardnerville Ranchos 3	1	38N49	119W41	7:58:44
Garside 2	1	36N10	115W12	7:40:48
Genoa 3	1	39N00	119W51	7:59:24
Gerlach 15	1	40N39	119W21	7:57:24
Glenbrook 3	1	39N05	119W56	7:59:44
Glendale 15	1	39N36	119W45	7:59:00
Golconda 7	1	40N58	117W30	7:50:00
Gold Acres 8	1	40N16	116W44	7:46:56
Goldfield 5	1	37N42	117W14	7:48:56
Gold Hill 14	1	39N19	119W39	7:58:36
Gold Point 5	1	37N21	117W22	7:49:28
Gold Run 7	1	41N03	117W15	7:49:00
Goodsprings 2	1	35N47	115W20	7:41:20
Goshute Indian Reservation 16	2	39N53	114W00	7:36:00
Greenbrae 15	1	39N36	119W45	7:59:00
Halleck 4	1	40N57	115W27	7:41:48
Harney 6	1	40N35	116W20	7:45:20
Hawthorne 11	1	38N32	118W38	7:54:32
Hazen 1	1	39N34	119W03	7:56:12
Henderson 2	1	36N02	114W59	7:39:56
Henry 4	2	41N42	114W49	7:39:16
Hidden Valley 15	1	39N31	119W48	7:59:12
Hiko 9	3	37N32	115W14	7:40:56
Huffakers 15	1	39N31	119W48	7:59:12
Humboldt 13	1	40N36	118W15	7:53:00
Huntridge 2	1	36N09	115W08	7:40:32
Imlay 13	1	40N40	118W09	7:52:36
Incline Village 15	1	39N00	119W57	7:59:48
Indian Springs 2	1	36N35	115W40	7:42:40
Ione 12	1	38N57	117W35	7:50:20
Islen 9	3	37N32	114W19	7:37:16
Jackpot 4	2	41N59	114W40	7:38:40
Jarbidge 4	2	41N53	115W26	7:41:44
Jean 2	1	35N47	115W20	7:41:20
Jiggs 4	1	40N26	115W40	7:42:40
Kingston 8	1	39N30	117W04	7:48:16
Lake 13	1	40N24	118W20	7:53:20
Lake Mead Base 2	1	36N12	115W05	7:40:20
Lakeridge 3	1	39N00	119W57	7:59:48
Lake Tahoe 3	1	39N01	119W57	7:59:48
Lamoille 4	1	40N44	115W29	7:41:56
Lane 16	4	39N16	114W57	7:39:48
Las Vegas 2	1	36N10	115W09	7:40:36
Las Vegas Highlands 2	1	36N12	115W08	7:40:32
Lathrop Wells 12	1	36N39	116W24	7:45:36
Laughlin 2	1	35N28	114W35	7:38:20
Lee 4	1	40N34	115W36	7:42:24
Lemmon Valley 15	1	39N31	119W49	7:59:16
Lida 5	1	37N28	117W30	7:50:00
Lincoln Park 3	1	39N05	119W56	7:59:44
Logan 2	1	36N37	114W26	7:37:44
Logandale 2	1	36N36	114W29	7:37:56
Longacres Park 2	1	36N11	115W07	7:40:28
Lovelock 13	1	40N11	118W28	7:53:52
Lund 16	4	38N52	115W00	7:40:00
Luning 11	1	38N30	118W11	7:52:44
Manhattan 12	1	38N32	117W04	7:48:16
Mason 10	1	38N59	119W10	7:56:40
Mason Valley 10	1	38N59	119W08	7:56:32
McDermitt 7	2	42N00	117W43	7:50:52
McGill 16	4	39N23	114W47	7:39:08
Mercury 12	1	36N40	116W00	7:44:00
Mesquite 2	1	36N45	114W19	7:37:16
Metropolis 4	1	41N06	114W58	7:39:52
Midas 4	1	41N18	116W45	7:47:00
Mill City 13	1	40N41	118W04	7:52:16
Mina 11	1	38N24	118W07	7:52:28
Minden 3	1	38N57	119W46	7:59:04
Moapa 2	1	36N40	114W37	7:38:28
Moapa River 2	1	39N09	119W47	7:59:08
Mogul 15	1	39N31	119W48	7:59:12
Montello 4	2	41N16	114W12	7:36:48
Mountain City 4	2	41N50	115W58	7:43:52
Mount Montgomery 11	1	38N00	118W18	7:53:12
Nellis 2	1	36N14	115W03	7:40:12
Nellis Air Force Base 2	1	36N12	115W05	7:40:20
Nelson 2	1	35N43	114W50	7:39:20
New Empire 17	1	39N09	119W47	7:59:08
New River 1	1	39N30	118W46	7:55:04
New Washoe City 15	1	39N09	119W47	7:59:08
Nixon 15	1	39N50	119W21	7:57:24
North Battle Mountain 8	1	40N43	116W54	7:47:36
North Fork 4	1	40N50	115W46	7:43:04
North Las Vegas 2	1	36N12	115W07	7:40:28
Oasis 4	2	41N02	114W29	7:37:56
Oreana 13	1	40N20	118W19	7:53:16
Orovada 7	1	41N34	117W47	7:51:08
Overton 2	1	36N33	114W27	7:37:48
Owyhee 4	2	41N57	116W06	7:44:24
Pahrump 12	1	36N12	115W59	7:43:56
Palisade 6	1	40N37	116W12	7:44:48
Panaca 9	3	37N47	114W23	7:37:32
Paradise 2	1	36N07	115W08	7:40:32
Paradise Hill 7	1	40N59	117W44	7:50:56
Paradise Palms 2	1	36N07	115W08	7:40:32
Paradise Valley 2	1	36N07	115W08	7:40:32
Paradise Valley 7	1	41N30	117W32	7:50:08
Park Terrace 17	1	39N09	119W47	7:59:08
Parran 1	1	39N48	118W46	7:55:04
Patrick 15	1	39N33	119W34	7:58:16
Patsville 4	2	41N49	115W57	7:43:48
Peavine 15	1	39N31	119W48	7:59:12
Pequop 4	2	41N13	114W36	7:38:24
Pioche 9	3	37N56	114W27	7:37:48
Pittman 2	1	36N03	114W59	7:39:56
Pleasant Valley 15	1	39N31	119W48	7:59:12
Preston 16	4	39N15	114W53	7:39:32
Prince 9	3	37N54	114W28	7:37:52
Proctor 4	2	40N54	114W17	7:37:08
Pyramid Lake Indian Res 15	1	39N50	119W21	7:57:24
Reese River 12	1	39N30	117W04	7:48:16
Reipetown 16	4	39N17	114W59	7:39:56
Reno 15	1	39N31	119W48	7:59:12
Rixie 6	1	40N39	116W36	7:46:24
Round Mountain 12	1	38N43	117W04	7:48:16
Rox 9	3	36N53	114W40	7:38:40
Ruby Valley 4	2	40N30	115W21	7:41:24
Ruth 16	4	39N17	114W59	7:39:56
Rye Patch 13	1	40N38	118W18	7:53:12
Salt Wells 1	1	39N23	118W35	7:54:20
San Jacinto 4	2	41N53	114W47	7:39:08

Place	Zone	Lat	Long	Time
Schurz 11	1	38N57	118w49	7:55:16
Searchlight 2	1	35N28	114w55	7:39:40
Shafter 4	2	40N52	114w26	7:37:44
Shantytown 4	2	40N30	115w21	7:41:24
Sheridan 3	1	38N49	119w41	7:58:44
Sierra 15	1	39N36	119w54	7:59:36
Silver City 10	1	39N16	119w38	7:58:32
Silverpeak 5	1	37N45	117w38	7:50:32
Silver Springs 10	1	39N25	119w14	7:56:56
Skyland 3	1	39N00	119w57	7:59:48
Sloan 2	1	35N57	115w13	7:40:52
Smith 10	1	38N48	119w20	7:57:20
Smith Valley 10	1	38N46	119w17	7:57:08
Smoke Creek 15	1	40N28	119w40	7:58:40
Sparks 15	1	39N36	119w43	7:58:52
Stagecoach 10	1	39N25	119w14	7:56:56
Stateline 2	1	35N47	115w20	7:41:20
Stateline 3	1	39N01	119w57	7:59:48
Steamboat 15	1	39N23	119w44	7:58:56
Steptoe 16	4	39N32	114w55	7:39:40
Stewart 17	1	39N07	119w45	7:59:00
Stewarts Point 2	1	36N33	114w27	7:37:48
Stillwater 1	1	39N31	118w33	7:54:12
Summit Lake 7	1	41N35	119w05	7:56:20
Sunrise Manor 2	1	36N11	115w03	7:40:12
Sun Valley 15	1	39N36	119w47	7:59:08
Sutcliffe 15	1	39N57	119w36	7:58:24
Tahoe 3	1	39N01	119w57	7:59:48
Tecoma 4	2	41N20	114w15	7:37:00
Tempiute 9	3	37N39	115w38	7:42:32
Thorne 11	1	38N36	118w35	7:54:20
Thousand Springs 4	1	41N06	114w58	7:39:52
Tippett 16	2	39N52	114w21	7:37:24
Tonopah 12	1	38N04	117w14	7:48:56
Topaz Lake 3	1	38N49	119w41	7:58:44
Topaz Ranch Estates 3	1	38N45	119w23	7:57:32
Toulon 13	1	40N04	118w39	7:54:36
Toy 13	1	40N01	118w40	7:54:40
Tracy-Clark 15	1	39N36	119w45	7:59:00
Tuscarora 4	1	41N19	116w14	7:44:56
Union 7	1	41N04	117w53	7:51:32
Unionville 13	1	40N39	118w09	7:52:36
University 15	1	39N33	119w50	7:59:20
Ursine 9	3	37N59	114w13	7:36:52
Valmy 7	1	40N48	117w08	7:48:32
Vegas Creek 2	1	36N09	115w05	7:40:20
Vegas View 2	1	36N12	115w08	7:40:32
Verdi 15	1	39N31	119w59	7:59:56
Victory Village 2	1	36N03	114w59	7:39:56
Virginia City 14	1	39N19	119w39	7:58:36
Vista 15	1	39N36	119w45	7:59:00
Wabuska 10	1	39N09	119w11	7:56:44
Wadsworth 15	1	39N38	119w17	7:57:08
Walker River Indian Reservat 1	1	38N57	118w49	7:55:16
Warm Springs 12	1	38N12	116w07	7:44:28
Washington 15	1	39N32	119w50	7:59:20
Washoe City 15	1	39N19	119w49	7:59:16
Washoe-Dresslerville Indian 3	1	38N56	118w45	7:55:00
Weed Heights 10	1	38N59	119w13	7:56:52
Wellington 10	1	38N45	119w23	7:57:32
Wells 4	1	41N07	114w58	7:39:52
Wendover 4	2	40N44	114w02	7:36:08
Whitney 2	1	36N06	115w03	7:40:12
Wilkins 4	2	41N27	114w50	7:39:20
Willow Beach 2	1	35N58	114w50	7:39:20
Winchester 2	1	36N08	115w07	7:40:28
Winnemucca 7	1	40N58	117w44	7:50:56
Woolsey 13	1	40N17	118w22	7:53:28
Yerington 10	1	38N59	119w10	7:56:40
Yerington Indian Reservation 10	1	38N59	119w10	7:56:40
Yomba Indian Reservation 12	1	39N08	117w25	7:49:40
Zephyr Cove 3	1	39N00	119w57	7:59:48

TIME TABLES

NH # 1
Before 11/18/1883 LMT
11/18/1883 12:00 EST
3/31/1918 02:00 EWT
10/27/1918 02:00 EST
3/30/1919 02:00 EWT
10/26/1919 02:00 EST
5/11/1937 02:00 EDT
9/26/1937 02:00 EST
4/24/1938 02:00 EDT
10/02/1938 02:00 EST
4/30/1939 02:00 EDT
9/24/1939 02:00 EST
4/28/1940 02:00 EDT
9/29/1940 02:00 EST
4/27/1941 02:00 EDT
9/28/1941 02:00 EST
2/09/1942 02:00 EWT
9/30/1945 02:00 EST
4/28/1946 02:00 EDT
9/29/1946 02:00 EST
4/27/1947 02:00 EDT
9/28/1947 02:00 EST
4/25/1948 02:00 EDT
9/26/1948 02:00 EST
4/24/1949 02:00 EDT
9/25/1949 02:00 EST
4/30/1950 02:00 EDT
9/24/1950 02:00 EST
4/29/1951 02:00 EDT
9/30/1951 02:00 EST
4/27/1952 02:00 EDT
9/28/1952 02:00 EST
4/26/1953 02:00 EDT
9/27/1953 02:00 EST
4/25/1954 02:00 EDT
10/27/1954 02:00 EST
4/24/1955 02:00 US#2
....
NH # 2
Before 11/18/1883 LMT
11/18/1883 12:00 EST
3/31/1918 02:00 EWT
10/27/1918 02:00 EST
3/30/1919 02:00 EWT
10/26/1919 02:00 EST
4/26/1931 02:00 EDT
9/27/1931 02:00 EST
4/24/1932 02:00 EDT
9/25/1932 02:00 EST
4/30/1933 02:00 EDT
9/24/1933 02:00 EST
4/29/1934 02:00 EDT
9/30/1934 02:00 EST
4/28/1935 02:00 EDT
9/29/1935 02:00 EST
4/26/1936 02:00 EDT
9/27/1936 02:00 EST
4/25/1937 02:00 EDT
9/26/1937 02:00 EST
4/24/1938 02:00 NH#1
4/24/1955 02:00 US#1
....
NH # 3
Before 11/18/1883 LMT
11/18/1883 12:00 EST
3/31/1918 02:00 EWT
10/27/1918 02:00 EST
3/30/1919 02:00 EWT
10/26/1919 02:00 EST
4/24/1932 02:00 EDT
9/25/1932 02:00 EST
4/30/1933 02:00 EDT
9/24/1933 02:00 EST
4/29/1934 02:00 EDT
9/30/1934 02:00 EST
4/28/1935 02:00 EDT
9/29/1935 02:00 EST
4/26/1936 02:00 EDT
9/27/1936 02:00 EST
4/25/1937 02:00 EDT
9/26/1937 02:00 EST
4/24/1938 02:00 NH#1
4/24/1955 02:00 US#1
....
NH # 4
Before 11/18/1883 LMT
11/18/1883 12:00 EST
3/31/1918 02:00 EWT
10/27/1918 02:00 EST
3/30/1919 02:00 EWT
10/26/1919 02:00 EST
4/30/1933 02:00 EDT
9/24/1933 02:00 EST
4/29/1934 02:00 EDT
9/30/1934 02:00 EST
4/28/1935 02:00 EDT
9/29/1935 02:00 EST
4/26/1936 02:00 EDT
9/27/1936 02:00 EST
4/25/1937 02:00 EDT
9/26/1937 02:00 EST
4/24/1938 02:00 NH#1
4/24/1955 02:00 US#1
....
NH # 5
Before 11/18/1883 LMT
11/18/1883 12:00 EST
3/31/1918 02:00 EWT
10/27/1918 02:00 EST
3/30/1919 02:00 EWT
10/26/1919 02:00 EST
4/29/1934 02:00 EDT
9/30/1934 02:00 EST
4/28/1935 02:00 EDT
9/29/1935 02:00 EST
4/26/1936 02:00 EDT
9/27/1936 02:00 EST
4/25/1937 02:00 EDT
9/26/1937 02:00 EST
4/24/1938 02:00 NH#1
4/24/1955 02:00 US#1
....
NH # 6
Before 11/18/1883 LMT
11/18/1883 12:00 EST
3/31/1918 02:00 EWT
10/27/1918 02:00 EST
3/30/1919 02:00 EWT
10/26/1919 02:00 EST
4/28/1935 02:00 EDT
9/29/1935 02:00 EST
4/26/1936 02:00 EDT
9/27/1936 02:00 EST
4/25/1937 02:00 EDT
9/26/1937 02:00 EST
4/24/1938 02:00 NH#1
4/24/1955 02:00 US#1
....
NH # 7
Before 11/18/1883 LMT
11/18/1883 12:00 EST
3/31/1918 02:00 EWT
10/27/1918 02:00 EST
3/30/1919 02:00 EWT
10/26/1919 02:00 EST
4/26/1936 02:00 EDT
9/27/1936 02:00 EST
5/11/1937 02:00 NH#1
4/24/1955 02:00 US#1
....
NH # 8
Before 11/18/1883 LMT
11/18/1883 12:00 EST
3/31/1918 02:00 EWT
10/27/1918 02:00 EST
3/30/1919 02:00 EWT
10/26/1919 02:00 EST
4/24/1932 02:00 EDT
9/25/1932 02:00 EST
4/30/1933 02:00 EDT
9/24/1933 02:00 EST
5/11/1937 02:00 NH#1
4/24/1955 02:00 US#1
....
NH # 9
Before 11/18/1883 LMT
11/18/1883 12:00 EST
3/31/1918 02:00 EWT
10/27/1918 02:00 EST
3/30/1919 02:00 EWT
10/26/1919 02:00 EST
4/30/1933 02:00 EDT
9/24/1933 02:00 EST
4/28/1935 02:00 EDT
9/29/1935 02:00 EST
5/11/1937 02:00 NH#1
4/24/1955 02:00 US#1
....
NH # 10
Before 11/18/1883 LMT
11/18/1883 12:00 EST
3/31/1918 02:00 EWT
10/27/1918 02:00 EST
3/30/1919 02:00 EWT
10/26/1919 02:00 EST
4/24/1932 02:00 EDT
9/25/1932 02:00 EST
4/30/1933 02:00 EDT
9/24/1933 02:00 EST
4/29/1934 02:00 EDT
9/30/1934 02:00 EST
5/11/1937 02:00 NH#1
4/24/1955 02:00 US#1
....
NH # 11
Before 11/18/1883 LMT
11/18/1883 12:00 EST
3/31/1918 02:00 EWT
10/27/1918 02:00 EST
3/30/1919 02:00 EWT
10/26/1919 02:00 EST
4/26/1931 02:00 EDT
9/27/1931 02:00 EST
4/28/1935 02:00 EDT
9/29/1935 02:00 EST
4/26/1936 02:00 EDT
9/27/1936 02:00 EST
4/25/1937 02:00 EDT
9/26/1937 02:00 EST
4/24/1938 02:00 NH#1
4/24/1955 02:00 US#1
....
NH # 12
Before 11/18/1883 LMT
11/18/1883 12:00 EST
3/31/1918 02:00 EWT
10/27/1918 02:00 EST
3/30/1919 02:00 EWT
10/26/1919 02:00 EST
4/30/1933 02:00 EDT
9/24/1933 02:00 EST
4/29/1934 02:00 EDT
9/30/1934 02:00 EST
5/11/1937 02:00 NH#1
4/24/1955 02:00 US#1
....
NH # 13
Before 11/18/1883 LMT
11/18/1883 12:00 EST
3/31/1918 02:00 EWT
10/27/1918 02:00 EST
3/30/1919 02:00 EWT
10/26/1919 02:00 EST
4/29/1934 02:00 EDT
9/30/1934 02:00 EST
5/11/1937 02:00 NH#1
4/24/1955 02:00 US#1
....
NH # 14
Before 11/18/1883 LMT
11/18/1883 12:00 EST
3/31/1918 02:00 EWT
10/27/1918 02:00 EST
3/30/1919 02:00 EWT
10/26/1919 02:00 EST
4/26/1931 02:00 EDT
9/27/1931 02:00 EST
5/11/1937 02:00 NH#1
4/24/1955 02:00 US#1
....
NH # 15
Before 11/18/1883 LMT
11/18/1883 12:00 EST
3/31/1918 02:00 EWT
10/27/1918 02:00 EST
3/30/1919 02:00 EWT
10/26/1919 02:00 EST
4/26/1931 02:00 EDT
9/27/1931 02:00 EST
4/29/1934 02:00 EDT
9/30/1934 02:00 EST
4/26/1936 02:00 EDT
9/27/1936 02:00 EST
5/11/1937 02:00 NH#1
4/24/1955 02:00 US#1
....
NH # 16
Before 11/18/1883 LMT
11/18/1883 12:00 EST
3/31/1918 02:00 EWT
10/27/1918 02:00 EST
3/30/1919 02:00 EWT
10/26/1919 02:00 EST
4/29/1934 02:00 EDT
9/30/1934 02:00 EST
4/28/1935 02:00 EDT
9/29/1935 02:00 EST
5/11/1937 02:00 NH#1
4/24/1955 02:00 US#1
....
NH # 17
Before 11/18/1883 LMT
11/18/1883 12:00 EST
3/31/1918 02:00 EWT
10/27/1918 02:00 EST
3/30/1919 02:00 EWT
10/26/1919 02:00 EST
4/30/1933 02:00 EDT
9/24/1933 02:00 EST
5/11/1937 02:00 NH#1
4/24/1955 02:00 US#1
....
NH # 18
Before 11/18/1883 LMT
11/18/1883 12:00 EST
3/31/1918 02:00 EWT
10/27/1918 02:00 EST
3/30/1919 02:00 EWT
10/26/1919 02:00 EST
4/29/1934 02:00 EDT
9/30/1934 02:00 EST
5/11/1937 02:00 NH#1
4/24/1955 02:00 US#1

COUNTIES

1 Belknap
2 Carroll
3 Cheshire
4 Coos
5 Grafton
6 Hillsborough
7 Merrimack
8 Rockingham
9 Strafford
10 Sullivan

Ackerman's Trailer Park 8
2 42N47 71w12 4:44:48
Acworth 10 1 43N12 72w17 4:49:08
Albany 2 1 43N58 71w13 4:44:52
Alexandria 5 1 43N38 71w50 4:47:20
Allenstown 7 1 43N09 71w23 4:45:32
Alstead 3 1 43N08 72w19 4:49:16
Alton 1 1 43N27 71w13 4:44:52
Amherst 6 14 42N51 71w37 4:46:28
Andover 7 1 43N26 71w49 4:47:16
Antrim 6 1 43N03 71w58 4:47:52
Arlington Park 8 2 42N50 71w13 4:44:52
Ashland 5 1 43N42 71w38 4:46:32
Ashuelot 3 7 42N47 72w26 4:49:44
Atkinson 8 2 42N50 71w09 4:44:36
Atkinson Heights 8
2 42N51 71w10 4:44:40
Auburn 8 1 43N00 71w20 4:45:20
Baboosic Lake 6 14 42N52 71w38 4:46:32
Bagley 7 6 43N17 71w49 4:47:16
Bank Village 6 1 42N42 71w51 4:47:24
Barnstead 1 1 43N21 71w15 4:45:00
Barrington 9 1 43N13 71w02 4:44:08
Barryvilla 9 17 43N18 70w59 4:43:56
Bartlett 2 8 44N06 71w12 4:44:48
Base 4 1 44N16 71w33 4:46:12
Bath 5 1 44N11 71w59 4:47:56
Bayside 8 2 43N02 70w50 4:43:20
Beans Island 8 3 43N02 71w11 4:44:44
Beaver Lake 8 2 42N54 71w19 4:45:16
Bedford 6 7 42N57 71w30 4:46:00
Beebe River 5 9 43N50 71w39 4:46:36
Belmont 1 1 43N27 71w29 4:45:56
Bennington 6 1 43N00 71w55 4:47:40
Benton 5 1 44N03 71w54 4:47:36
Berlin 4 10 44N28 71w11 4:44:44
Bethlehem 5 1 44N17 71w41 4:46:44
Bethlehem Junction 5
1 44N23 71w37 4:46:28
Birch Hill 9 1 43N27 71w13 4:44:52
Blair 5 16 43N45 71w41 4:46:44
Blais Park 4 10 44N27 71w11 4:44:44
Blodgett Landing 7
1 43N19 72w02 4:48:08
Bonds Corner 3 1 42N52 71w58 4:47:52
Boscawen 7 1 43N19 71w37 4:46:28
Bow 7 2 43N08 71w32 4:46:08
Bowkerville 3 1 42N50 72w11 4:48:44
Bradford 7 4 43N14 71w57 4:47:48
Brentwood 8 1 42N59 71w03 4:44:12
Bretton Woods 4 1 44N15 71w26 4:45:44
Bridgewater 5 1 43N40 71w42 4:46:48
Bristol 5 1 43N36 71w44 4:46:56
Brookfield 2 1 43N34 71w05 4:44:20
Brookline 6 1 42N44 71w40 4:46:40
Bungy 4 1 44N54 71w30 4:46:00
Burkehaven 10 1 43N23 72w05 4:48:20
Cambridge 4 1 44N40 71w08 4:44:32
Camp Hedding 8 1 43N02 71w04 4:44:16
Campton 5 9 43N50 71w39 4:46:36
Campton Hollow 5 16 43N45 71w41 4:46:44
Campton Lower Village 5
9 43N52 71w38 4:46:32
Canaan 5 1 43N40 72w03 4:48:12
Candia 8 1 43N04 71w18 4:45:12
Candia Village 8 2 42N48 71w15 4:45:00
Canobie Lake 8 2 42N47 71w12 4:44:48
Canterbury 7 1 43N20 71w34 4:46:16
Carroll 4 1 44N17 71w30 4:46:00
Cascade 4 10 44N24 71w11 4:44:44
Cedre Pond 4 1 44N34 71w11 4:44:44
Center Barnstead 1
1 43N21 71w16 4:45:04
Center Conway 2 1 44N00 71w04 4:44:16
Center Effingham 2
1 43N42 70w59 4:43:56
Center Harbor 1 1 43N42 71w30 4:46:00
Center Haverhill 5
1 44N05 72w02 4:48:08
Center Ossipee 2 1 43N45 71w09 4:44:36
Center Sandwich 2 1 43N48 71w26 4:45:44
Center Strafford 9
1 43N16 71w08 4:44:32
Center Tuftonboro 2
1 43N42 71w13 4:44:52
Central Park 9 7 43N15 70w52 4:43:28
Charlestown 10 1 43N14 72w25 4:49:40
Chase Village 6 1 43N04 71w38 4:46:32
Chateau Richelieu 6
2 42N45 71w29 4:45:56
Chatham 2 1 44N10 71w01 4:44:04
Cheever 5 1 43N48 71w49 4:47:16
Chesham 3 1 42N54 72w13 4:48:52
Chester 8 1 42N58 71w15 4:45:00
Chesterfield 3 1 42N54 72w28 4:49:52
Chichester 7 1 43N15 71w23 4:45:32
Chocorua 2 1 43N53 71w13 4:44:52
Christian Hollow 3
1 43N05 72w26 4:49:44
Cilleyville 7 1 43N26 71w51 4:47:24
Claremont 10 7 43N23 72w20 4:49:20
Clarks Landing 2 1 43N43 71w28 4:45:52
Clarksville 4 1 45N01 71w21 4:45:24
Clinton 6 1 43N02 71w56 4:47:44
Clinton Grove 6 1 43N04 71w38 4:46:32
Clovelly 6 2 42N45 71w29 4:45:56
Coburn Woods 6 2 42N45 71w29 4:45:56
Cold River 3 1 43N05 72w26 4:49:44
Colebrook 4 1 44N54 71w30 4:46:00
Columbia 4 1 44N50 71w29 4:45:56
Columbia Valley 4 1 44N54 71w30 4:46:00
Concord 7 2 43N12 71w32 4:46:08
Cones 4 1 44N45 71w37 4:46:28
Contoocook 7 1 43N13 71w43 4:46:52
Converseville 3 5 42N46 72w02 4:48:08
Conway 2 1 43N59 71w07 4:44:28
Cornish 10 1 43N28 72w19 4:49:16
Cornish Flat 10 1 43N30 72w17 4:49:08
Cotoocook Lake 3 5 42N49 72w01 4:48:04
Crawford Notch 4 1 44N16 71w33 4:46:12
Cricket Corner 6 14 42N52 71w38 4:46:32
Croydon 10 15 43N22 72w10 4:48:40
Crystal 4 10 44N27 71w11 4:44:44
Cushman 4 1 44N23 71w37 4:46:28
Dalton 4 1 44N24 71w40 4:46:40

Danbury 7	1	43N32	71w52	4:47:28
Danville 8	1	42N55	71w07	4:44:28
Davisville 7	1	43N13	71w43	4:46:52
Deerfield 8	1	43N08	71w15	4:45:00
Deering 6	1	43N05	71w51	4:47:24
Derry 8	2	42N53	71w19	4:45:16
Dixville 4	1	44N53	71w16	4:45:04
Dixville Notch 4	1	44N54	71w30	4:46:00
Dorchester 5	1	43N47	71w58	4:47:52
Dover 9	7	43N12	70w53	4:43:32
Dover Point 9	7	43N12	70w53	4:43:32
Drewsville 3	1	43N08	72w24	4:49:36
Dublin 3	1	42N54	72w03	4:48:12
Dummer 4	1	44N40	71w15	4:45:00
Dunbarton 7	1	43N06	71w37	4:46:28
Durham 9	1	43N08	70w56	4:43:44
East Alstead 3	1	43N09	72w22	4:49:28
East Alton 1	1	43N27	71w13	4:44:52
East Andover 7	1	43N27	71w45	4:47:00
East Candia 8	1	43N03	71w15	4:45:00
East Concord 7	2	43N13	71w33	4:46:12
East Conway 2	1	44N01	70w59	4:43:56
East Deering 6	1	43N07	71w54	4:47:36
East Derry 8	2	42N54	71w19	4:45:16
East Dummer 4	1	44N34	71w11	4:44:44
East Grafton 5	1	43N33	71w57	4:47:48
East Grantham 10	1	43N29	72w08	4:48:32
East Hampstead 8	2	42N53	71w08	4:44:32
East Haverhill 5	1	44N02	71w58	4:47:52
East Hebron 5	1	43N42	71w46	4:47:04
East Holderness 5	1	43N42	71w38	4:46:32
East Kingston 8	1	42N55	71w00	4:44:00
East Lempster 10	1	43N14	72w11	4:48:44
Eastman 10	1	43N29	72w08	4:48:32
East Milford 6	14	42N50	71w39	4:46:36
Easton 5	1	44N08	71w47	4:47:08
East Plainfield 10	1	43N39	72w15	4:49:00
East Ridge 3	5	42N46	72w02	4:48:08
East Rochester 9	17	43N18	70w59	4:43:56
East Sandwich 2	1	43N43	71w28	4:45:52
East Sullivan 3	1	43N00	72w12	4:48:48
East Sutton 7	6	43N17	71w49	4:47:16
East Swanzey 3	1	42N51	72w15	4:49:00
East Tilton 1	1	43N28	71w32	4:46:08
East Unity 10	15	43N22	72w10	4:48:40
Eastview 3	1	42N56	72w05	4:48:20
East Wakefield 2	1	43N37	71w01	4:44:04
East Washington 10	1	43N07	71w54	4:47:36
East Wilder 5	1	43N39	72w15	4:49:00
East Wolfeboro 2	1	43N35	71w13	4:44:52
Eaton 2	1	43N55	71w04	4:44:16
Effingham 2	1	43N45	71w03	4:44:12
Effingham Falls 2	1	43N45	71w10	4:44:40
Elkins 7	1	43N25	71w56	4:47:44
Ellsworth 5	1	43N53	71w47	4:47:08
Elmwood 7	1	43N31	71w52	4:47:28
Enfield 5	1	43N39	72w09	4:48:36
Epping 8	1	43N02	71w04	4:44:16
Epsom 7	1	43N12	71w22	4:45:28
Errol 4	1	44N47	71w08	4:44:32
Etna 5	1	43N42	72w14	4:48:56
Exeter 8	5	42N59	70w57	4:43:48
Fabyan 4	1	44N16	71w33	4:46:12
Farmington 9	1	43N22	71w04	4:44:16
Fitzwilliam 3	1	42N46	72w09	4:48:36
Forest Lake 3	1	42N46	72w23	4:49:32
Forest Ridge 6	2	42N45	71w29	4:45:56
Foundry 9	7	43N15	70w52	4:43:28
Foyes Corner 8	1	43N01	70w46	4:43:04
Francestown 6	1	42N59	71w49	4:47:16
Franconia 5	1	44N12	71w43	4:46:52
Franklin 7	11	43N27	71w39	4:46:36
Franklin Pierce College 3	5	42N46	72w02	4:48:08
Freedom 2	1	43N49	71w03	4:44:12
Fremont 8	1	42N59	71w07	4:44:28
Gardners Grove 1	1	43N28	71w32	4:46:08
Gates Corner 9	7	43N12	70w53	4:43:32
Gaza 1	6	43N29	71w35	4:46:20
Georges Mills 10	1	43N26	72w04	4:48:16
Gilford 1	3	43N33	71w26	4:45:44
Gilmanton 1	1	43N25	71w21	4:45:24
Gilsum 3	1	43N03	72w16	4:49:04
Glen 2	8	44N07	71w11	4:44:44
Glencliff 5	1	43N59	71w54	4:47:36
Glendale 1	3	43N33	71w29	4:45:56
Glenmere 9	5	43N05	70w56	4:43:44
Goffstown 6	1	43N01	71w36	4:46:24
Gonic 9	17	43N18	70w59	4:43:56
Goodrich Falls 2	8	44N09	71w11	4:44:44
Gorham 4	12	44N23	71w10	4:44:40
Goshen 10	1	43N17	72w08	4:48:32
Gosport 8	2	43N04	70w47	4:43:08
Gossville 7	1	43N13	71w20	4:45:20
Grafton 5	1	43N34	71w57	4:47:48
Grange 4	1	44N29	71w34	4:46:16
Granite 2	1	43N41	71w07	4:44:28
Grantham 10	1	43N29	72w08	4:48:32
Grasmere 6	7	43N00	71w31	4:46:04
Great Boars Head 8	2	42N56	70w50	4:43:20
Greenfield 6	1	42N57	71w52	4:47:28
Greenland 8	2	43N02	70w50	4:43:20
Greenville 6	1	42N46	71w49	4:47:16
Groton 5	1	43N44	71w51	4:47:24
Groveton 4	1	44N36	71w31	4:46:04
Guild 10	15	43N22	72w10	4:48:40
Hampstead 8	2	42N53	71w10	4:44:40
Hampton 8	2	42N57	70w50	4:43:20
Hampton Falls 8	2	42N56	70w53	4:43:32
Hancock 6	1	42N58	71w59	4:47:56
Hanover 5	1	43N42	72w17	4:49:08
Happy Corner 4	1	45N03	71w21	4:45:24
Happy Valley 6	1	42N52	71w58	4:47:52
Harrisville 3	1	42N56	72w06	4:48:24
Harts Location 2	1	44N08	71w22	4:45:28
Hastings 7	1	43N25	71w58	4:47:52
Haven Hill 9	17	43N18	70w59	4:43:56
Haverhill 5	1	44N05	72w00	4:48:00
Hayes 9	17	43N18	70w59	4:43:56
Hays 8	5	42N59	70w57	4:43:48
Hebron 5	1	43N42	71w48	4:47:12
Hedding 8	1	43N02	71w04	4:44:16
Hemlock Center 10	1	43N14	72w25	4:49:40
Henniker 7	1	43N11	71w50	4:47:20
High Bridge 6	1	42N42	71w51	4:47:24
Hill 7	1	43N32	71w42	4:46:48
Hillsboro 6	1	43N07	71w54	4:47:36
Hillsborough 6	1	43N08	71w57	4:47:48
Hinsdale 3	7	42N47	72w29	4:49:56
Holderness 5	1	43N45	71w36	4:46:24
Hollis 6	1	42N45	71w34	4:46:16
Hooksett 7	3	43N03	71w26	4:45:44
Hopkinton 7	1	43N13	71w42	4:46:48
Horses Corner 7	1	43N15	71w23	4:45:32
Hoyts Corner 7	4	43N16	71w57	4:47:48
Hudson 6	2	42N46	71w26	4:45:44
Intervale 2	1	44N05	71w08	4:44:32
Jackson 2	8	44N09	71w11	4:44:44
Jady Hill 8	5	42N59	70w57	4:43:48
Jaffrey 3	5	42N49	72w02	4:48:08
Jaffrey Compact 3	5	42N49	72w01	4:48:04
Jefferson 4	1	44N24	71w28	4:45:52
Jenness Beach 8	2	42N59	70w46	4:43:04
Kearsarge 2	1	44N04	71w07	4:44:28
Keene 3	1	42N56	72w17	4:49:08
Kelleys Corner 7	1	43N18	71w20	4:45:20
Kellyville 10	1	43N19	72w21	4:49:24
Kelwyn Park 9	7	43N15	70w52	4:43:28
Kensington 8	5	42N56	70w57	4:43:48
Kidderville 4	1	44N54	71w30	4:46:00
Kingston 8	2	42N56	71w03	4:44:12
Laconia 1	3	43N32	71w28	4:45:52
Lakeport 1	3	43N33	71w29	4:45:56
Lancaster 4	1	44N29	71w34	4:46:16
Landaff 5	1	44N10	71w53	4:47:32
Langdon 10	1	43N10	72w23	4:49:32
Langs Corner 8	1	43N01	70w46	4:43:04
Laskey Corner 9	1	43N29	71w02	4:44:08
Laurel Lake 3	1	42N47	72w09	4:48:36
Leavitts Hill 8	2	42N48	71w15	4:45:00
Lebanon 5	1	43N39	72w15	4:49:00
Lee 9	1	43N07	71w00	4:44:00
Lee's 8	5	42N59	70w57	4:43:48
Lempster 10	1	43N13	72w11	4:48:44
Lincoln 5	3	44N03	71w40	4:46:40
Lisbon 5	1	44N13	71w55	4:47:40
Litchfield 6	1	42N55	71w26	4:45:44
Little Boars Head 8	2	42N54	70w50	4:43:20
Little Island Pond 6	1	42N44	71w19	4:45:16
Littleton 5	13	44N18	71w46	4:47:04
Livermore Falls 5	16	43N45	71w41	4:46:44
Lochmere 1	1	43N28	71w32	4:46:08
Lockehaven 5	1	43N39	72w09	4:48:36
Londonderry 8	2	42N53	71w23	4:45:32
Loudon 7	1	43N18	71w27	4:45:48
Louisburg Square 6	2	42N45	71w29	4:45:56
Lower Bartlett 2	1	44N05	71w08	4:44:32
Lower Gilmanton 1	1	43N18	71w20	4:45:20
Lower Village 3	1	43N03	72w16	4:49:04
Lower Village 7	6	43N17	71w49	4:47:16
Lyman 5	1	44N16	71w56	4:47:44
Lyme 5	1	43N49	72w09	4:48:36
Lyndeborough 6	3	42N54	71w46	4:47:04
Madbury 9	1	43N10	70w57	4:43:48
Madison 2	1	43N53	71w10	4:44:40
Manchester 6	7	43N00	71w28	4:45:52
Maplewood 6	1	43N04	71w38	4:46:32
Marlborough 3	1	42N54	72w13	4:48:52
Marlow 3	1	43N07	72w12	4:48:48
Marshall Corner 8	5	42N59	70w57	4:43:48
Martin 7	3	43N03	71w27	4:45:48
Mason 6	1	42N45	71w45	4:47:00
Meadows 4	1	44N22	71w28	4:45:52
Melrose Corner 9	17	43N18	70w59	4:43:56
Melvin Mills 7	6	43N17	71w49	4:47:16
Melvin Village 2	1	43N42	71w18	4:45:12
Meredith 1	1	43N39	71w30	4:46:00
Meriden 10	1	43N33	72w15	4:49:00
Merrimack 6	1	42N52	71w30	4:46:00
Middleton 9	1	43N29	71w03	4:44:12
Milan 4	1	44N34	71w13	4:44:52
Milford 6	14	42N50	71w39	4:46:36
Mill Hollow 3	1	43N09	72w22	4:49:28
Millsfield 4	1	44N47	71w15	4:45:00
Mill Village 3	1	43N05	72w07	4:48:28
Millville Lake 8	2	42N47	71w12	4:44:48
Milton 9	1	43N25	70w59	4:43:56
Mirror Lake 2	1	43N36	71w17	4:45:08
Monroe 5	1	44N17	72w01	4:48:04
Mont Vernon 6	1	42N54	71w41	4:46:44
Moultonboro 2	1	43N45	71w24	4:45:36
Moultonville 2	1	43N45	71w10	4:44:40
Mountain View Estates 6	2	42N45	71w29	4:45:56
Mount Saint Mary College 7	3	43N03	71w27	4:45:48
Mount Sunapee 7	1	43N21	72w04	4:48:16
Mount Washington 4	1	44N16	71w18	4:45:12
Munsonville 3	1	43N01	72w09	4:48:36
Nashua 6	2	42N45	71w28	4:45:52
Nelson 3	1	43N00	72w08	4:48:32
New Boston 6	1	42N59	71w41	4:46:44

NEW HAMPSHIRE

Newbury 7	1	43N19	72w02	4:48:08
New Castle 8	2	43N04	70w43	4:42:52
New Durham 9	1	43N26	71w09	4:44:36
Newfields 8	5	43N02	70w58	4:43:52
New Hampton 1	1	43N36	71w39	4:46:36
Newington 8	1	43N06	70w50	4:43:20
New Ipswich 6	1	42N42	71w54	4:47:36
New London 7	1	43N25	71w57	4:47:48
Newmarket 8	5	43N05	70w56	4:43:44
Newport 10	15	43N22	72w10	4:48:40
New Rye 7	1	43N08	71w27	4:45:48
Newton 8	2	42N52	71w03	4:44:12
Noone 6	1	42N52	71w58	4:47:52
North Barnstead 1	1	43N21	71w16	4:45:04
North Beach 8	2	42N56	70w50	4:43:20
North Branch 6	1	43N02	71w56	4:47:44
North Brookline 6	14	42N50	71w39	4:46:36
North Charlestown 10	1	43N14	72w25	4:49:40
North Chatham 2	1	44N07	70w58	4:43:52
North Chichester 7	1	43N15	71w23	4:45:32
North Conway 2	1	44N03	71w08	4:44:32
North Danville 8	3	43N00	71w08	4:44:32
Northfield 7	6	43N26	71w36	4:46:24
North Grantham 10	1	43N39	72w15	4:49:00
North Groton 5	1	43N48	71w49	4:47:16
North Hampton 8	2	42N59	70w50	4:43:20
North Haverhill 5	1	44N05	72w02	4:48:08
North Holderness 5	16	43N45	71w41	4:46:44
North Londonderry 8	2	42N51	71w22	4:45:28
North Newport 10	15	43N22	72w10	4:48:40
North Pelham 6	1	42N44	71w19	4:45:16
North Richmond 3	1	42N46	72w23	4:49:32
North Salem 8	2	42N50	71w13	4:44:52
North Sanbornton 1	6	43N29	71w35	4:46:20
North Sandwich 2	1	43N50	71w24	4:45:36
North Stratford 4	1	44N45	71w38	4:46:32
North Sutton 7	1	43N22	71w56	4:47:44
North Swanzey 3	1	42N56	72w17	4:49:08
Northumberland 4	1	44N35	71w31	4:46:04
North Village 6	1	42N52	71w58	4:47:52
North Walpole 3	1	43N08	72w27	4:49:48
North Wilmot 7	1	43N31	71w52	4:47:28
North Wolfeboro 2	1	43N35	71w13	4:44:52
Northwood 8	1	43N12	71w09	4:44:36
North Woodstock 5	3	44N02	71w41	4:46:44
Nottingham 8	1	43N08	71w07	4:44:28
Noyes Terrace 8	2	42N47	71w12	4:44:48
Nuttings Beach 5	1	43N36	71w44	4:46:56
Odell 4	1	44N44	71w23	4:45:32
Old Millstream Estates 8	5	42N59	70w57	4:43:48
Old Northwood 8	1	43N12	71w06	4:44:24
Onway Lake 8	3	43N02	71w11	4:44:44
Orange 5	1	43N39	71w58	4:47:52
Orford 5	1	43N54	72w04	4:48:16
Ossipee 2	1	43N41	71w07	4:44:28
Pannaway Manor 8	2	43N04	70w47	4:43:08
Parker Hill 5	1	44N14	71w54	4:47:36
Partridge Lake 5	13	44N18	71w46	4:47:04
Passaconaway 2	1	43N59	71w07	4:44:28
Pease Air Force Base 8	2	43N04	70w47	4:43:08
Pelham 6	1	42N44	71w19	4:45:16
Pembroke 7	1	43N11	71w28	4:45:52
Pendleton Beach 1	3	43N33	71w29	4:45:56
Pequaket 2	1	43N53	71w11	4:44:44
Percy 4	1	44N36	71w31	4:46:04
Peterborough 6	1	42N53	71w57	4:47:48
Pickering 9	17	43N18	70w59	4:43:56
Pickpocket Woods 8	5	42N59	70w57	4:43:48
Piermont 5	1	43N59	72w02	4:48:08
Pike 5	1	44N02	71w58	4:47:52
Pinardville 6	7	42N59	71w28	4:45:52
Pine Brook Estates 8	5	42N59	70w57	4:43:48
Pinecrest 8	5	42N59	70w57	4:43:48
Pine Valley 6	3	42N51	71w44	4:46:56
Pinkhams Grant 4	1	44N16	71w15	4:45:00
Pittsburg 4	1	45N03	71w24	4:45:36
Pittsfield 7	1	43N18	71w20	4:45:20
Plaice Cove 8	2	42N56	70w50	4:43:20
Plainfield 10	1	43N32	72w21	4:49:24
Plaistow 8	2	42N50	71w06	4:44:24
Plymouth 5	16	43N46	71w41	4:46:44
Ponemah 6	14	42N50	71w39	4:46:36
Portsmouth 8	2	43N05	70w45	4:43:00
Potter Place 7	1	43N26	71w51	4:47:24
Puckershire 10	1	43N19	72w21	4:49:24
Quaker City 10	1	43N14	72w25	4:49:40
Quincy 5	1	43N48	71w49	4:47:16
Randolph 4	1	44N24	71w19	4:45:16
Raymond 8	3	43N02	71w11	4:44:44
Redstone 2	1	44N00	71w04	4:44:16
Reeds Ferry 6	1	42N52	71w30	4:46:00
Richardson 6	14	42N50	71w39	4:46:36
Richmond 3	1	42N46	72w16	4:49:04
Rindge 3	5	42N45	72w00	4:48:00
Riverdale 6	7	43N00	71w31	4:46:04
Riverside 8	2	42N53	70w52	4:43:28
Robinson Corner 5	1	43N33	71w57	4:47:48
Roby 7	6	43N17	71w49	4:47:16
Rochester 9	17	43N18	70w59	4:43:56
Rollinsford 9	1	43N14	70w49	4:43:16
Roxbury 3	1	42N57	72w13	4:48:52
Royal Crest Estates 6	2	42N45	71w29	4:45:56
Rumney 5	1	43N50	71w49	4:47:16
Rye 8	1	43N01	70w46	4:43:04

NEW HAMPSHIRE

Rye North Beach 8	1	43N01	70w46	4:43:04
Sachem Village 5	1	43N39	72w15	4:49:00
Salem 8	2	42N47	71w13	4:44:52
Salisbury 7	1	43N24	71w45	4:47:00
Salisbury Heights 7	1	43N23	71w43	4:46:52
Sanbornton 1	1	43N31	71w35	4:46:20
Sanbornville 2	1	43N33	71w02	4:44:08
Sandown 8	1	42N56	71w11	4:44:44
Sandwich 2	1	43N50	71w25	4:45:40
Sawyers 9	7	43N12	70w53	4:43:32
Scotland 3	1	42N46	72w23	4:49:32
Seabrook 8	2	42N53	70w52	4:43:28
Seacrest Village 8	2	43N04	70w47	4:43:08
Severance 8	7	43N00	71w28	4:45:52
Sharon 6	5	42N47	71w57	4:47:48
Shelburne 4	1	44N24	71w06	4:44:24
Sherwood Forest 8	5	42N59	70w57	4:43:48
Shirley Hill 6	7	43N00	71w31	4:46:04
Short Falls 7	1	43N13	71w20	4:45:20
Silver Lake 2	1	43N53	71w11	4:44:44
Smiths Point 1	3	43N33	71w29	4:45:56
Smithtown 8	2	42N53	70w52	4:43:28
Smithville 6	1	42N45	71w51	4:47:24
Snowville 2	1	43N54	71w09	4:44:36
Snumshire 10	1	43N14	72w25	4:49:40
Somersworth 9	7	43N15	70w52	4:43:28
Soo Nipi 7	1	43N25	71w58	4:47:52
South Acworth 10	1	43N11	72w17	4:49:08
South Alexandria 5	1	43N36	71w44	4:46:56
South Barnstead 1	1	43N21	71w16	4:45:04
South Brookline 6	1	42N44	71w40	4:46:40
South Charlestown 10	1	43N14	72w25	4:49:40
South Chatham 2	1	44N01	70w59	4:43:56
South Conway 2	1	44N00	71w04	4:44:16
South Cornish 10	1	43N29	72w23	4:49:32
South Danville 8	1	42N55	71w07	4:44:28
South Deerfield 8	1	43N09	71w13	4:44:52
South Effingham 2	1	43N42	70w59	4:43:56
South Hampton 8	1	42N53	70w58	4:43:52
South Hooksett 7	3	43N03	71w27	4:45:48
South Keene 3	1	42N56	72w17	4:49:08
South Kingston 8	2	42N56	71w03	4:44:12
South Lee 9	5	43N05	70w56	4:43:44
South Lyndeboro 6	3	42N53	71w47	4:47:08
South Merrimack 6	2	42N45	71w29	4:45:56
South Milford 6	14	42N50	71w39	4:46:36
South Newbury 7	1	43N18	72w00	4:48:00
South Pittsfield 7	1	43N18	71w20	4:45:20
South Stoddard 3	1	43N05	72w07	4:48:28
South Sutton 7	1	43N19	71w56	4:47:44
South Tamworth 2	1	43N50	71w18	4:45:12
South Weare 6	1	43N04	71w38	4:46:32
South Wolfeboro 2	1	43N35	71w13	4:44:52
Spofford 3	18	42N54	72w21	4:49:24
Springfield 10	1	43N29	72w03	4:48:12
Squantum 3	5	42N49	72w01	4:48:04
Stark 4	1	44N36	71w24	4:45:36
Stewartstown 4	1	44N58	71w25	4:45:40
Stinson Lake 5	1	43N52	71w49	4:47:16
Stoddard 3	1	43N05	72w07	4:48:28
Strafford 9	1	43N16	71w09	4:44:36
Stratford 4	1	44N43	71w33	4:46:12
Stratham 8	5	43N01	70w55	4:43:40
Strawberry Banke 8	2	43N04	70w47	4:43:08
Success 4	1	44N32	71w05	4:44:20
Sugar Hill 5	1	44N13	71w47	4:47:08
Sullivan 3	1	43N01	72w13	4:48:52
Sunapee 10	1	43N17	72w06	4:48:24
Suncook 7	1	43N08	71w27	4:45:48
Surry 3	1	43N01	72w20	4:49:20
Sutton 7	1	43N20	71w56	4:47:44
Swanzey 3	18	42N52	72w18	4:49:12
Swiftwater 5	1	44N09	72w02	4:48:08
Tamworth 2	1	43N52	71w16	4:45:04
Temple 6	1	42N46	71w53	4:47:32
The Glen 4	1	45N03	71w21	4:45:24
Thornton 5	1	43N56	71w39	4:46:36
Tilton 1	6	43N27	71w36	4:46:24
Tinkerville 5	1	44N14	71w54	4:47:36
Trapshire 10	1	43N14	72w25	4:49:40
Troy 3	1	42N49	72w11	4:48:44
Tuftonboro 2	1	43N40	71w16	4:45:04
Twin Mountain 4	1	44N16	71w32	4:46:08
Union 2	1	43N30	71w02	4:44:08
Unity 10	1	43N16	72w16	4:49:04
Upper Kidderville 4	1	44N54	71w30	4:46:00
Wakefield 2	1	43N34	71w01	4:44:04
Wallis Sands 8	1	43N01	70w46	4:43:04
Walpole 3	1	43N05	72w26	4:49:44
Warner 7	6	43N17	71w48	4:47:12
Warren 5	1	43N56	71w54	4:47:36
Washington 10	1	43N11	72w06	4:48:24
Waterloo 7	6	43N17	71w49	4:47:16
Water Village 2	1	43N41	71w07	4:44:28
Waterville Estates 5	9	43N52	71w38	4:46:32
Waterville Valley 5	1	43N56	71w30	4:46:00
Wawbeek 2	1	43N36	71w17	4:45:08
Weare 6	1	43N06	71w44	4:46:56
Webster 7	1	43N20	71w43	4:46:52
Webster Lake 7	11	43N27	71w39	4:46:36
Weirs Beach 1	3	43N33	71w29	4:45:56
Wendell 10	15	43N23	72w08	4:48:32
Wentworth 5	1	43N52	71w55	4:47:40
Wentworth By The Sea 8	2	43N04	70w43	4:42:52
Wentworths Location 4	1	44N51	71w07	4:44:28
West Alton 1	3	43N33	71w29	4:45:56
West Brentwood 8	2	42N56	71w03	4:44:12
West Campton 5	9	43N52	71w38	4:46:32
West Canaan 5	1	43N36	72w01	4:48:04
West Center Harbor 1	1	43N42	71w38	4:46:32
West Chesterfield 3	1	42N54	72w31	4:50:04
West Claremont 10	1	43N19	72w21	4:49:24
West Deering 6	1	43N02	71w56	4:47:44
West Drummer 4	10	44N27	71w11	4:44:44
West Epping 8	1	43N02	71w04	4:44:16
West Franklin 7	11	43N27	71w39	4:46:36
West Gonic 9	17	43N18	70w59	4:43:56
West Hampstead 8	2	42N53	71w11	4:44:44
West Henniker 7	1	43N11	71w49	4:47:16
West Hopkinton 7	1	43N13	71w43	4:46:52
West Lebanon 5	1	43N39	72w15	4:49:00
West Milan 4	10	44N27	71w11	4:44:44
Westmoreland 3	1	42N58	72w26	4:49:44
West Nottingham 8	1	43N05	71w03	4:44:12
West Ossipee 2	1	43N49	71w12	4:44:48
West Peterborough 6	1	42N52	71w58	4:47:52
West Plymouth 5	16	43N45	71w41	4:46:44
Westport 3	1	42N46	72w23	4:49:32
West Rindge 3	5	42N46	72w02	4:48:08
West Rumney 5	1	43N48	71w49	4:47:16
West Rye 8	1	43N01	70w46	4:43:04
West Salisbury 7	1	43N26	71w49	4:47:16
West Springfield 10	1	43N30	72w03	4:48:12
West Stewartstown 4	1	45N00	71w32	4:46:08
West Swanzey 3	18	42N52	72w20	4:49:20
West Thornton 5	9	43N52	71w38	4:46:32
West Unity 10	1	43N19	72w21	4:49:24
Westville 8	2	42N49	71w07	4:44:28
West Wilton 6	3	42N51	71w44	4:46:56
West Windham 8	3	42N48	71w18	4:45:12
Whiteface 2	1	43N50	71w24	4:45:36
Whitefield 4	1	44N23	71w37	4:46:28
Whittier 2	1	43N49	71w12	4:44:48
Willey House 2	1	44N05	71w17	4:45:08
Wilmot 7	1	43N25	71w54	4:47:36
Wilton 6	3	42N51	71w44	4:46:56
Winchester 3	1	42N46	72w23	4:49:32
Windham 8	3	42N48	71w17	4:45:08
Windsor 6	1	43N08	72w01	4:48:04
Winnipesaukee 2	1	43N43	71w28	4:45:52
Winnisquam 1	1	43N28	71w32	4:46:08
Winona 1	1	43N40	71w34	4:46:16
Wolfeboro 2	1	43N35	71w13	4:44:52
Wonalancet 2	1	43N54	71w21	4:45:24
Woodman 2	1	43N37	71w01	4:44:04
Woodmere 3	5	42N49	72w01	4:48:04
Woodstock 5	3	44N00	71w42	4:46:48
Woodsville 5	1	44N09	72w02	4:48:08

TIME TABLES

NJ # 1		
Before 11/18/1883		LMT
11/18/1883	12:00	EST
3/31/1918	02:00	EWT
10/27/1918	02:00	EST
3/30/1919	02:00	EWT
10/26/1919	02:00	EST
3/28/1920	02:00	EDT
10/31/1920	02:00	EST
4/24/1921	02:00	EDT
9/25/1921	02:00	EST
4/30/1922	02:00	EDT
9/24/1922	02:00	EST
4/29/1923	02:00	EDT
9/30/1923	02:00	EST
4/27/1924	02:00	EDT
9/28/1924	02:00	EST
4/26/1925	02:00	EDT
9/27/1925	02:00	EST
4/25/1926	02:00	EDT
9/26/1926	02:00	EST
4/24/1927	02:00	EDT
9/25/1927	02:00	EST
4/29/1928	02:00	EDT
9/30/1928	02:00	EST
4/28/1929	02:00	EDT
9/29/1929	02:00	EST
4/27/1930	02:00	EDT
9/28/1930	02:00	EST
4/26/1931	02:00	EDT
9/27/1931	02:00	EST
4/24/1932	02:00	EDT
9/25/1932	02:00	EST
4/30/1933	02:00	EDT
9/24/1933	02:00	EST
4/29/1934	02:00	EDT
9/30/1934	02:00	EST
4/28/1935	02:00	EDT
9/29/1935	02:00	EST
4/26/1936	02:00	EDT
9/27/1936	02:00	EST
4/25/1937	02:00	EDT
9/26/1937	02:00	EST
4/24/1938	02:00	EDT
9/25/1938	02:00	EST
4/30/1939	02:00	EDT
9/24/1939	02:00	EST
4/28/1940	02:00	EDT
9/29/1940	02:00	EST
4/27/1941	02:00	EDT
9/28/1941	02:00	EST
2/09/1942	02:00	EWT
9/30/1945	02:00	EST
4/28/1946	02:00	EDT
9/29/1946	02:00	EST
4/27/1947	02:00	EDT
9/28/1947	02:00	EST
4/25/1948	02:00	EDT
9/26/1948	02:00	EST
4/24/1949	02:00	EDT
9/25/1949	02:00	EST
4/30/1950	02:00	EDT
9/24/1950	02:00	EST
4/29/1951	02:00	EDT
9/30/1951	02:00	EST
4/27/1952	02:00	EDT
9/28/1952	02:00	EST
4/26/1953	02:00	EDT
9/27/1953	02:00	EST
4/25/1954	02:00	EDT
9/26/1954	02:00	EST
4/24/1955	02:00	EDT
10/30/1955	02:00	EST
4/29/1956	02:00	EDT
10/28/1956	02:00	EST
4/28/1957	02:00	EDT
10/27/1957	02:00	EST
4/27/1958	02:00	EDT
10/26/1958	02:00	EST
4/26/1959	02:00	EDT
10/25/1959	02:00	EST
4/24/1960	02:00	EDT
10/30/1960	02:00	EST
4/30/1961	02:00	EDT
10/29/1961	02:00	EST
4/29/1962	02:00	EDT
10/28/1962	02:00	EST
4/28/1963	02:00	EDT
10/27/1963	02:00	EST
4/26/1964	02:00	EDT
10/25/1964	02:00	EST
4/25/1965	02:00	EDT
10/31/1965	02:00	EST
4/24/1966	02:00	EDT
10/30/1966	02:00	EST
4/30/1967	02:00	US#1

NJ # 2		
Before 11/18/1883		LMT
11/18/1883	12:00	EST
3/31/1918	02:00	EWT
10/27/1918	02:00	EST
3/30/1919	02:00	EWT
10/26/1919	02:00	EST
4/24/1921	02:00	US#2

NJ # 3		
Before 11/18/1883		LMT
11/18/1883	12:00	EST
3/31/1918	02:00	EWT
10/27/1918	02:00	EST
3/30/1919	02:00	EWT
10/26/1919	02:00	EST
4/30/1922	02:00	US#2

NJ # 4		
Before 11/18/1883		LMT
11/18/1883	12:00	EST
3/31/1918	02:00	EWT
10/27/1918	02:00	EST
3/30/1919	02:00	EWT
10/26/1919	02:00	EST
4/29/1928	02:00	US#2

NJ # 5		
Before 11/18/1883		LMT
11/18/1883	12:00	EST
3/31/1918	02:00	EWT
10/27/1918	02:00	EST
3/30/1919	02:00	EWT
10/26/1919	02:00	EST
4/27/1930	02:00	US#2

NJ # 6		
Before 11/18/1883		LMT
11/18/1883	12:00	EST
3/31/1918	02:00	EWT
10/27/1918	02:00	EST
3/30/1919	02:00	EWT
10/26/1919	02:00	EST
3/28/1920	02:00	EDT
10/31/1920	02:00	EST
4/24/1921	02:00	EDT
9/25/1921	02:00	EST
4/30/1922	02:00	EDT
9/24/1922	02:00	EST
4/29/1923	02:00	EDT
9/30/1923	02:00	EST
4/27/1924	02:00	EDT
9/28/1924	02:00	EST
4/26/1925	02:00	EDT
9/27/1925	02:00	EST
4/25/1926	02:00	EDT
9/26/1926	02:00	EST
4/24/1927	02:00	EDT
9/25/1927	02:00	EST
4/29/1928	02:00	EDT
9/30/1928	02:00	EST
4/28/1929	02:00	EDT
9/29/1929	02:00	EST
4/27/1930	02:00	EDT
9/28/1930	02:00	EST
4/26/1931	02:00	EDT
9/27/1931	02:00	EST
4/24/1932	02:00	EDT
9/25/1932	02:00	EST
4/30/1933	02:00	EDT
9/24/1933	02:00	EST
4/29/1934	02:00	EDT
9/30/1934	02:00	EST
4/28/1935	02:00	EDT
9/29/1935	02:00	EST
4/26/1936	02:00	EDT
9/27/1936	02:00	EST
4/25/1937	00:01	EDT
9/26/1937	00:01	EST
4/24/1938	00:01	EDT
9/25/1938	00:01	EST
4/30/1939	00:01	EDT
9/24/1939	00:01	EST
4/28/1940	00:01	EDT
9/29/1940	00:01	EST
4/27/1941	00:01	EDT
9/28/1941	00:01	EST
2/09/1942	02:00	EWT
9/30/1945	02:00	EST
4/28/1946	00:01	EDT
9/29/1946	00:01	EST
4/27/1947	00:01	EDT
9/28/1947	00:01	EST
4/25/1948	00:01	EDT
9/26/1948	00:01	EST
4/24/1949	00:01	EDT
9/25/1949	00:01	EST
4/30/1950	00:01	EDT
9/24/1950	00:01	EST
4/29/1951	00:01	EDT
9/30/1951	00:01	EST
4/27/1952	00:01	EDT
9/28/1952	00:01	EST
4/26/1953	00:01	EDT
9/27/1953	00:01	EST
4/25/1954	00:01	EDT
9/26/1954	00:01	EST
4/24/1955	00:01	EDT
10/30/1955	00:01	EST
4/29/1956	00:01	EDT
10/28/1956	00:01	EST
4/28/1957	00:01	EDT
10/27/1957	00:01	EST
4/27/1958	00:01	EDT
10/26/1958	00:01	EST
4/26/1959	00:01	EDT
10/25/1959	00:01	EST
4/24/1960	00:01	EDT
10/30/1960	00:01	EST
4/30/1961	00:01	EDT
10/29/1961	00:01	EST
4/29/1962	00:01	EDT
10/28/1962	00:01	EST
4/28/1963	00:01	EDT
10/27/1963	00:01	EST
4/26/1964	00:01	EDT
10/25/1964	00:01	EST
4/25/1965	00:01	EDT
10/31/1965	00:01	EST
4/24/1966	00:01	EDT
10/30/1966	00:01	EST
4/30/1967	02:00	US#1

NJ # 7		
Before 11/18/1883		LMT
11/18/1883	12:00	EST
3/31/1918	02:00	EWT
10/27/1918	02:00	EST
3/30/1919	02:00	EWT
10/26/1919	02:00	EST
6/05/1921	02:00	EDT
9/25/1921	02:00	EST
4/30/1922	02:00	US#2

NJ # 8		
Before 11/18/1883		LMT
11/18/1883	12:00	EST
3/31/1918	02:00	EWT
10/27/1918	02:00	EST
3/30/1919	02:00	EWT
10/26/1919	02:00	EST
6/05/1921	02:00	EDT
9/25/1921	02:00	EST
6/04/1922	02:00	EDT
9/24/1922	02:00	EST
6/03/1923	02:00	EDT
9/23/1923	02:00	EST
6/01/1924	02:00	EDT
9/28/1924	02:00	EST
4/26/1925	02:00	EDT
9/27/1925	02:00	EST
4/25/1926	02:00	EDT
9/26/1926	02:00	EST
4/24/1927	02:00	EDT
9/25/1927	02:00	EST
4/29/1928	02:00	EDT
9/30/1928	02:00	EST
4/28/1929	02:00	EDT
9/29/1929	02:00	EST
4/27/1930	02:00	EDT
9/28/1930	02:00	EST
4/26/1931	02:00	EDT
9/27/1931	02:00	EST
6/26/1932	02:00	EDT
9/25/1932	02:00	EST
4/30/1933	02:00	US#2

NJ # 9		
Before 11/18/1883		LMT
11/18/1883	12:00	EST
3/31/1918	02:00	EWT
10/27/1918	02:00	EST
3/30/1919	02:00	EWT
10/26/1919	02:00	EST
4/18/1920	02:00	EDT
10/31/1920	02:00	US#2

NJ # 10		
Before 4/02/1902		LMT
4/02/1902	12:00	EST
3/31/1918	02:00	EWT
10/27/1918	02:00	EST
3/30/1919	02:00	EWT
10/26/1919	02:00	EST
6/10/1922	02:00	EDT
9/24/1922	02:00	EST
6/03/1923	02:00	EDT
9/30/1923	02:00	EST
6/01/1924	02:00	EDT
9/28/1924	02:00	EST
6/07/1925	02:00	EDT
9/27/1925	02:00	EST
6/06/1926	02:00	EDT
9/26/1926	02:00	EST
6/05/1927	02:00	EDT
9/25/1927	02:00	EST
6/03/1928	02:00	EDT
9/30/1928	02:00	EST
6/02/1929	02:00	EDT
9/29/1929	02:00	EST
6/01/1930	02:00	EDT
9/28/1930	02:00	EST
6/06/1931	02:00	EDT
9/26/1931	02:00	EST
6/03/1932	02:00	EDT
9/25/1932	02:00	EST
6/04/1933	02:00	EDT
9/24/1933	02:00	EST
6/05/1934	02:00	EDT
9/30/1934	02:00	EST
6/06/1935	02:00	EDT
9/29/1935	02:00	EST
4/26/1936	02:00	US#2

NJ # 11		
Before 11/18/1883		LMT
11/18/1883	12:00	EST
3/31/1918	02:00	EWT
10/27/1918	02:00	EST
3/30/1919	02:00	EWT
10/26/1919	02:00	EST
3/28/1920	00:01	EDT
10/31/1920	00:01	EST
4/24/1921	00:01	EDT
9/25/1921	00:01	EST
4/30/1922	00:01	EDT
9/24/1922	00:01	EST
4/29/1923	00:01	EDT
9/30/1923	00:01	EST
4/27/1924	00:01	EDT
9/28/1924	00:01	EST
4/26/1925	00:01	EDT
9/27/1925	00:01	EST
4/25/1926	00:01	EDT
9/26/1926	00:01	EST
4/24/1927	00:01	EDT
9/25/1927	00:01	EST
4/29/1928	00:01	EDT
9/30/1928	00:01	EST
4/28/1929	00:01	EDT
9/29/1929	00:01	EST
4/27/1930	00:01	EDT
9/28/1930	00:01	EST
4/26/1931	00:01	EDT
9/27/1931	00:01	EST
4/24/1932	00:01	EDT
9/25/1932	00:01	EST
4/30/1933	00:01	EDT
9/24/1933	00:01	EST
4/29/1934	00:01	EDT
9/30/1934	00:01	EST
4/28/1935	00:01	EDT
9/29/1935	00:01	EST
4/26/1936	00:01	EDT
9/27/1936	00:01	EST
4/25/1937	00:01	EDT
9/26/1937	00:01	EST
4/24/1938	00:01	EDT
9/25/1938	00:01	EST
4/30/1939	00:01	EDT
9/24/1939	00:01	EST
4/28/1940	00:01	EDT
9/29/1940	00:01	EST
4/27/1941	00:01	EDT
9/28/1941	00:01	EST
2/09/1942	02:00	EWT
9/30/1945	02:00	EST
4/28/1946	00:01	EDT
9/29/1946	00:01	EST
4/27/1947	00:01	EDT
9/28/1947	00:01	EST
4/25/1948	00:01	EDT
9/26/1948	00:01	EST
4/24/1949	00:01	EDT
9/25/1949	00:01	EST
4/30/1950	00:01	EDT
9/24/1950	00:01	EST
4/29/1951	00:01	EDT
9/30/1951	00:01	EST
4/27/1952	00:01	EDT
9/28/1952	00:01	EST
4/26/1953	00:01	EDT
9/27/1953	00:01	EST
4/25/1954	00:01	EDT
9/26/1954	00:01	EST
4/24/1955	00:01	EDT
10/30/1955	00:01	EST
4/29/1956	00:01	EDT
10/28/1956	00:01	EST
4/28/1957	00:01	EDT
10/27/1957	00:01	EST
4/27/1958	00:01	EDT
10/26/1958	00:01	EST
4/26/1959	00:01	EDT
10/25/1959	00:01	EST
4/24/1960	00:01	EDT
10/30/1960	00:01	EST
4/30/1961	00:01	EDT
10/29/1961	00:01	EST
4/29/1962	00:01	EDT
10/28/1962	00:01	EST
4/28/1963	00:01	EDT
10/27/1963	00:01	EST
4/26/1964	00:01	EDT
10/25/1964	00:01	EST
4/25/1965	00:01	EDT
10/31/1965	00:01	EST
4/24/1966	00:01	EDT
10/30/1966	00:01	EST
4/30/1967	02:00	US#1

NJ # 12		
Before 11/18/1883		LMT
11/18/1883	12:00	EST
3/31/1918	02:00	EWT
10/27/1918	02:00	EST
3/30/1919	02:00	EWT
10/26/1919	02:00	EST
4/25/1937	02:00	US#2

NJ # 13		
Before 11/18/1883		LMT
11/18/1883	12:00	EST
3/31/1918	02:00	EWT
10/27/1918	02:00	EST
3/30/1919	02:00	EWT
10/26/1919	02:00	EST
4/26/1931	02:00	EDT
9/27/1931	02:00	EST
4/25/1937	02:00	US#2

NJ # 14		
Before 11/18/1883		LMT
11/18/1883	12:00	EST
3/31/1918	02:00	EWT
10/27/1918	02:00	EST
3/30/1919	02:00	EWT
10/26/1919	02:00	EST
4/24/1932	02:00	US#2

NJ # 15		
Before 11/18/1883		LMT
11/18/1883	12:00	EST
3/31/1918	02:00	EWT
10/27/1918	02:00	EST
3/30/1919	02:00	EWT
10/26/1919	02:00	EST
4/30/1933	02:00	US#2

NJ # 16		
Before 11/18/1883		LMT
11/18/1883	12:00	EST
3/31/1918	02:00	EWT
10/27/1918	02:00	EST
3/30/1919	02:00	EWT
10/26/1919	02:00	EST
4/29/1934	02:00	US#2

NJ # 17		
Before 11/18/1883		LMT
11/18/1883	12:00	EST
3/31/1918	02:00	EWT
10/27/1918	02:00	EST
3/30/1919	02:00	EWT
10/26/1919	02:00	EST
4/26/1931	02:00	US#2

NJ # 18		
Before 11/18/1883		LMT
11/18/1883	12:00	EST
3/31/1918	02:00	EWT
10/27/1918	02:00	EST
3/30/1919	02:00	EWT
10/26/1919	02:00	EST
4/26/1936	02:00	US#2

COUNTIES

1 Atlantic
2 Bergen
3 Burlington
4 Camden
5 Cape May
6 Cumberland
7 Essex
8 Gloucester
9 Hudson
10 Hunterdon
11 Mercer
12 Middlesex
13 Monmouth
14 Morris
15 Ocean
16 Passaic
17 Salem
18 Somerset
19 Sussex
20 Union
21 Warren

Place	Table	Lat	Long	Time
Absecon 1	2	39N26	74w30	4:58:00
Academy 7	1	40N44	74w11	4:56:44
Academy Estates 14	1	40N49	74w25	4:57:40
Adams 12	1	40N29	74w27	4:57:48
Adamston 15	12	40N02	74w07	4:56:28
Adelphia 13	1	40N13	74w15	4:57:00
Agasote 11	1	40N14	74w47	4:59:08

NEW JERSEY

Ajax Park 11 1 40N14 74w47 4:59:08
Albion 4 17 39N47 74w57 4:59:48
Albion Place 16 1 40N52 74w10 4:56:40
Aldene 20 1 40N39 74w16 4:57:04
Aldine 17 1 39N36 75w10 5:00:40
Aldrich Estates 13 12 40N14 74w13 4:56:52
Alexandria 10 13 40N36 75w01 5:00:04
Allaire 13 12 40N14 74w13 4:56:52
Allamuchy 21 15 40N55 74w50 4:59:20
Allendale 2 2 41N02 74w08 4:56:32
Allenhurst 13 1 40N14 74w00 4:56:00
Allentown 13 12 40N11 74w35 4:58:20
Allenwood 13 1 40N09 74w06 4:56:24
Allerton 10 13 40N38 74w50 4:59:20
Alloway 17 17 39N34 75w22 5:01:28
Allwood 16 1 40N51 74w09 4:56:36
Almolind 8 1 39N49 75w08 5:00:32
Almonesson 8 1 39N49 75w08 5:00:32
Alpha 21 17 40N40 75w10 5:00:40
Alphano 21 12 40N52 74w55 4:59:40
Alpine 2 1 40N59 73w55 4:55:40
Amber Terrace 4 1 39N48 75w00 5:00:00
Amon Heights 4 2 39N58 75w03 5:00:12
Ampere 7 1 40N46 74w12 4:56:48
Ancora 4 2 39N56 75w02 5:00:08
Anderson 21 13 40N45 74w59 4:59:56
Andover 19 12 40N59 74w45 4:59:00
Andrews 4 1 39N43 74w58 4:59:52
Anglesea 5 11 39N00 74w49 4:59:16
Annandale 10 13 40N39 74w53 4:59:32
Anthony 10 13 40N42 74w57 4:59:48
Applegarth 12 1 40N19 74w31 4:58:04
Apple Hill 4 2 39N54 75w00 5:00:00
Apshawa 16 16 41N01 74w22 4:57:28
Arbor 12 1 40N34 74w27 4:57:48
Arbors 12 12 40N24 74w21 4:57:24
Ardena 13 1 40N15 74w17 4:57:08
Arlington 9 1 40N46 74w09 4:56:36
Arneytown 3 12 40N11 74w35 4:58:20
Arrowhead Park 15 12 40N02 74w07 4:56:28
Arrowhead Village 15 12 40N02 74w07 4:56:28
Asbury 21 13 40N42 75w01 5:00:04
Asbury Gardens 13 1 40N12 74w02 4:56:08
Asbury Park 13 6 40N13 74w01 4:56:04
Ashland 4 2 39N52 75w01 5:00:04
Atco 4 17 39N46 74w53 4:59:32
Atlantic City 1 7 39N22 74w26 4:57:44
Atlantic Highlands 13 1 40N25 74w03 4:56:12
Atsion 3 12 39N56 74w45 4:59:00
Auburn 17 10 39N43 75w22 5:01:28
Audubon 4 2 39N53 75w04 5:00:16
Augusta 19 17 41N08 74w44 4:58:56
Aura 8 1 39N42 75w07 5:00:28
Avalon 5 2 39N06 74w44 4:58:56
Avenel 12 2 40N35 74w17 4:57:08
Avis Mills 17 17 39N39 75w20 5:01:20
Avon by the Sea 13 1 40N12 74w01 4:56:04
Avondale 7 1 40N49 74w10 4:56:40
Awosting 16 12 41N10 74w20 4:57:20
Babbitt 9 1 40N47 74w01 4:56:04
Bacons Neck 6 1 39N28 75w15 5:01:00
Bakersville 1 2 39N22 74w34 4:58:16
Bakersville 11 1 40N17 74w42 4:58:48
Baleville 19 12 41N03 74w45 4:59:00
Baltusrol 20 1 40N42 74w19 4:57:16
Bamber Lake 15 14 39N50 74w11 4:56:44
Baptistown 10 12 40N31 75w00 5:00:00
Barbertown 10 12 40N32 75w03 5:00:12
Barclay Farm 4 2 39N49 75w06 5:00:24
Bargaintown 1 1 39N21 74w35 4:58:20
Barkers Corner 21 12 40N52 74w55 4:59:40
Barley Sheaf 10 1 40N31 74w52 4:59:28
Barlow 4 2 39N49 75w06 5:00:24
Barnegat 15 1 39N45 74w14 4:56:56
Barnegat Beach 15 1 39N47 74w12 4:56:48
Barnegat Light 15 12 39N45 74w07 4:56:28
Barnegat Pier 15 12 39N56 74w08 4:56:32
Barnegat Pines 15 14 39N50 74w11 4:56:44
Barnsboro 8 2 39N46 75w10 5:00:40
Barrington 4 2 39N52 75w03 5:00:12
Barrington Manor 4 2 39N54 75w02 5:00:08
Bartley 14 12 40N47 74w42 4:58:48
Basking Ridge 18 1 40N42 74w33 4:58:12
Bass River 3 17 39N36 74w27 4:57:48
Batesville 4 2 39N49 75w06 5:00:24
Batsto 3 2 39N56 75w02 5:00:08
Battentown 8 10 39N45 75w19 5:01:16
Bay Harbor Estates 15 12 40N02 74w07 4:56:28
Bay Head 15 2 40N04 74w03 4:56:12
Bayonne 9 1 40N40 74w07 4:56:28
Bay Shore 15 1 39N56 74w13 4:56:52
Bay Shore West 5 1 38N56 74w55 4:59:40
Bay Side 15 1 39N42 74w15 4:57:00
Bayview Shores 15 2 40N03 74w03 4:56:12
Bayville 15 12 39N55 74w09 4:56:36
Bayway 20 1 40N39 74w13 4:56:52
Baywood 15 12 40N02 74w07 4:56:28
Beach Creek 5 11 39N00 74w49 4:59:16
Beach Glen 14 12 40N56 74w29 4:57:56
Beach Haven 15 17 39N34 74w14 4:56:56
Beach Haven Crest 15 17 39N37 74w12 4:56:48
Beach Haven Gardens 15 17 39N37 74w12 4:56:48
Beach Haven Heights 15 17 39N37 74w12 4:56:48
Beach Haven Terrace 15 17 39N37 74w12 4:56:48
Beach View 15 1 39N45 74w13 4:56:52
Beachwood 15 1 39N56 74w12 4:56:48
Bear Tavern 11 12 40N23 74w46 4:59:04
Beatyestown 21 1 40N52 74w50 4:59:20
Beaufort 7 1 40N49 74w18 4:57:12
Beaver Dam 17 12 39N39 75w31 5:02:04
Beaver Lake 19 17 41N06 74w35 4:58:20
Beckerville 15 1 40N01 74w19 4:57:16
Bedminster 18 12 40N41 74w39 4:58:36
Beechwood Heights 14 14 40N52 74w38 4:58:32
Beemerville 19 1 41N13 74w36 4:58:24
Beesleys Point 5 17 39N16 74w39 4:58:36
Belcoville 1 17 39N27 74w44 4:58:56
Belford 13 2 40N25 74w05 4:56:20
Belle Mead 18 2 40N28 74w40 4:58:40
Belleplain 5 12 39N16 74w47 4:59:08
Belleville 7 1 40N47 74w09 4:56:36
Bellmawr 4 2 39N52 75w05 5:00:20
Bells Crossing 10 13 40N42 74w57 4:59:48
Bells Lake 8 2 39N48 75w03 5:00:12
Bellview 3 2 40N00 75w00 5:00:00
Bellwood Park 4 2 39N53 75w06 5:00:24
Belmar 13 1 40N11 74w02 4:56:08
Belvidere 21 17 40N50 75w05 5:00:20
Belwood Park 7 1 40N48 74w10 4:56:40
Bennett 5 1 38N56 74w55 4:59:40
Bennetts Mills 15 1 40N08 74w16 4:57:04
Berdines Corner 12 1 40N29 74w27 4:57:48
Bergen 9 1 40N43 74w04 4:56:16
Bergenfield 2 1 40N56 74w00 4:56:00
Bergenline 9 1 40N46 74w02 4:56:08
Bergen Point 9 1 40N40 74w07 4:56:28
Berkeley 15 1 39N55 74w10 4:56:40
Berkeley Heights 20 17 40N41 74w27 4:57:48
Berkeley Shore Estates 15 12 39N55 74w09 4:56:36
Berlin 4 17 39N48 74w56 4:59:44
Berlin Heights 4 17 39N49 74w58 4:59:52
Bernards 18 1 40N41 74w34 4:58:16
Bernardsville 18 1 40N43 74w34 4:58:16
Bertrand Island 14 1 40N55 74w38 4:58:32
Bethlehem 10 13 40N40 75w01 5:00:04
Betsytown 20 1 40N40 74w12 4:56:48
Beverly 3 1 40N04 74w55 4:59:40
Billingsport 8 2 39N51 75w12 5:00:48
Birch Hills 14 1 40N49 74w25 4:57:40
Birchwood Lakes 3 17 39N53 74w49 4:59:16
Birchwood Park 15 12 40N02 74w07 4:56:28
Birmingham 3 12 39N59 74w43 4:58:52
Bishops 4 17 39N49 74w58 4:59:52
Bivalve 6 12 39N15 75w02 5:00:08
Black Horse 12 1 40N29 74w27 4:57:48
Black Horse Pike 4 2 39N53 75w04 5:00:16
Blackwood 4 2 39N48 75w04 5:00:16
Blackwood Terrace 8 1 39N49 75w08 5:00:32
Blairstown 21 14 40N59 75w00 5:00:00
Blawenburg 18 12 40N25 74w42 4:58:48
Blenheim 4 2 39N48 75w03 5:00:12
Bloomfield 7 1 40N48 74w12 4:56:48
Bloomfield Terrace 12 12 40N24 74w21 4:57:24
Bloomingdale 16 16 41N00 74w20 4:57:20
Bloomsbury 10 13 40N39 75w05 5:00:20
Blue Anchor 4 17 39N41 74w53 4:59:32
Blue Bell 8 17 39N33 75w01 5:00:04
Blue Star 18 2 40N37 74w25 4:57:40
Bogota 2 1 40N52 74w02 4:56:08
Bon Air 4 2 39N58 75w03 5:00:12
Bonhamptown 12 17 40N32 74w22 4:57:28
Boonton 14 1 40N54 74w25 4:57:40
Bordentown 3 1 40N09 74w43 4:58:52
Bossert Estates 3 1 40N09 74w42 4:58:48
Bound Brook 4 2 39N49 75w06 5:00:24
Bound Brook 18 17 40N34 74w32 4:58:08
Bound Brook Heights 12 1 40N34 74w27 4:57:48
Bowman Manor 5 12 39N02 74w56 4:59:44
Braddock 4 17 39N42 74w53 4:59:32
Bradevelt 13 1 40N19 74w15 4:57:00
Bradley Beach 13 1 40N12 74w01 4:56:04
Bradley Gardens 18 2 40N34 74w40 4:58:40
Bradley Park 13 1 40N12 74w02 4:56:08
Braeburn Heights 11 1 40N16 74w46 4:59:04
Braeburn Park 11 1 40N16 74w46 4:59:04
Brainards 21 17 40N41 75w10 5:00:40
Brainy Boro 12 17 40N32 74w22 4:57:28
Branchburg 18 2 40N34 74w42 4:58:48
Branchport 13 1 40N18 74w00 4:56:00
Branchville 19 17 41N09 74w45 4:59:00
Brant Beach 15 17 39N37 74w12 4:56:48
Brass Castle 21 13 40N45 74w59 4:59:56
Breton Woods 15 12 40N02 74w07 4:56:28
Brick 15 12 40N04 74w07 4:56:28
Brick Church 7 1 40N45 74w13 4:56:52
Bricksboro 6 2 39N26 75w01 5:00:04
Brick Town 15 12 40N02 74w07 4:56:28
Bridgeboro 3 17 40N02 74w57 4:59:48
Bridgeport 8 10 39N48 75w21 5:01:24
Bridgeton 6 1 39N26 75w14 5:00:56
Bridgeville 21 17 40N50 75w05 5:00:20
Bridgewater 18 2 40N36 74w37 4:58:28
Brielle 13 2 40N06 74w04 4:56:16
Brigadoon 8 1 39N49 75w08 5:00:32
Brigantine 1 17 39N24 74w23 4:57:32
Brighton Beach 15 17 39N37 74w12 4:56:48
Brights 12 2 40N28 74w20 4:57:20
Broadway 21 13 40N44 75w03 5:00:12
Bromley Place 11 1 40N13 74w44 4:58:56
Brookdale 4 2 39N49 75w06 5:00:24
Brookdale 7 1 40N48 74w11 4:56:44
Brookfields 4 2 39N49 75w06 5:00:24
Brooklawn 4 2 39N53 75w07 5:00:28
Brooklawn 4 2 39N53 75w07 5:00:28
Brookside 14 12 40N48 74w34 4:58:16
Brook Valley 14 16 41N00 74w21 4:57:24
Brookville 15 1 39N45 74w13 4:56:52
Brookwood 15 12 40N08 74w20 4:57:20
Brotmanville 17 1 39N28 75w15 5:01:00
Browns Mills 3 3 39N58 74w35 4:58:20
Browntown 12 12 40N24 74w21 4:57:24
Brunswick 12 1 40N29 74w27 4:57:48
Brunswick Gardens 12 12 40N23 74w20 4:57:20
Buckingham Village 8 17 39N45 75w04 5:00:16
Buckshutem 6 2 39N26 75w01 5:00:04
Budd Lake 14 1 40N52 74w44 4:58:56
Buddtown 3 12 39N56 74w42 4:58:48
Buena 1 17 39N31 74w57 4:59:48
Buena Vista 1 17 39N31 74w54 4:59:36
Bulltown 3 8 39N33 74w37 4:58:28
Bunker Hill 8 17 39N45 75w04 5:00:16
Bunnvale 10 12 40N43 74w50 4:59:20
Burcliff Farms 11 1 40N16 74w46 4:59:04
Burleigh 5 13 39N05 74w50 4:59:20
Burlington 3 1 40N04 74w51 4:59:24
Bustleton 3 1 40N05 74w51 4:59:24
Butler 14 16 41N00 74w20 4:57:20
Butlers Park 10 13 40N45 74w59 4:59:56
Buttzville 21 17 40N50 75w00 5:00:00
Byram 10 1 40N24 74w59 4:59:56
Byram 19 1 40N57 74w43 4:58:52
Byram Cove 19 1 40N56 74w40 4:58:40
Caldwell 7 1 40N50 74w17 4:57:08
Califon 10 12 40N43 74w50 4:59:20
Callahans 14 1 40N55 74w39 4:58:36
Cambridge 3 17 40N02 74w57 4:59:48
Camden 4 2 39N56 75w07 5:00:28
Camp Tecumseh 10 13 40N35 74w58 4:59:52
Candlewood 13 1 40N09 74w13 4:56:52
Canton 17 17 39N34 75w28 5:01:52
Cape Breton 15 12 40N02 74w07 4:56:28
Cape May 5 1 38N56 74w56 4:59:44
Cape May Court House 5 13 39N05 74w50 4:59:20
Cape May Point 5 1 38N56 74w58 4:59:52
Capitol Hill 3 17 40N03 74w56 4:59:44
Cardiff 1 2 39N23 74w33 4:58:12
Carlls Corner 6 1 39N28 75w15 5:01:00
Carlstadt 2 1 40N50 74w06 4:56:24
Carlton Hill 2 1 40N50 74w06 4:56:24
Carmel 6 2 39N26 75w01 5:00:04
Carmerville 13 1 40N11 74w02 4:56:08
Carneys Point 17 1 39N43 75w28 5:01:52
Carpenterville 21 17 40N41 75w10 5:00:40
Carrs Corner 13 12 40N18 74w22 4:57:28
Carteret 12 1 40N34 74w13 4:56:52
Cassville 12 40N06 74w23 4:57:32
Castle Point 9 1 40N45 74w02 4:56:08
Cecil 8 1 39N41 75w00 5:00:00
Cedar Beach 13 17 40N26 74w07 4:56:28
Cedar Beach 15 12 39N55 74w09 4:56:36
Cedar Bonnet Island 15 1 39N42 74w15 4:57:00
Cedar Bridge Manor 15 12 40N02 74w07 4:56:28
Cedar Brook 4 17 39N43 74w54 4:59:36
Cedar Crest Manor 17 1 39N44 75w28 5:01:52
Cedar Croft 15 12 40N02 74w07 4:56:28
Cedar Glen Lakes 15 12 39N57 74w23 4:57:32
Cedar Grove 5 13 39N05 74w50 4:59:20
Cedar Grove 7 1 40N51 74w14 4:56:56
Cedar Heights 10 13 40N39 74w53 4:59:32
Cedar Knolls 14 1 40N49 74w27 4:57:48
Cedar Lake 14 12 40N53 74w29 4:57:56
Cedar Run 15 2 39N38 74w18 4:57:12
Cedarville 6 13 39N20 75w12 5:00:48
Cedarville 17 17 39N39 75w20 5:01:20
Cedarwood Park 15 12 40N02 74w07 4:56:28
Centennial Lake 3 17 39N54 74w55 4:59:40
Center 11 1 40N13 74w46 4:59:04
Center Square 8 10 39N45 75w19 5:01:16
Centerton 3 17 39N59 74w52 4:59:28
Centerton 17 1 39N36 75w10 5:00:40
Central 7 1 40N45 74w13 4:56:52
Central Park 12 1 40N29 74w17 4:57:08
Central Park 17 12 39N39 75w31 5:02:04
Centre City 8 2 39N46 75w10 5:00:40
Centre Grove 6 2 39N26 75w01 5:00:04
Ceramics 12 17 40N32 74w22 4:57:28
Chadwick Beach 15 12 40N00 74w04 4:56:16
Chairville 3 17 39N53 74w49 4:59:16
Chambersburg 11 1 40N13 74w45 4:59:00
Chambers Corner 3 1 40N00 74w47 4:59:08
Changewater 21 12 40N44 74w57 4:59:48
Chapel Heights 8 17 39N45 75w04 5:00:16
Charleston Springs 13 1 40N15 74w17 4:57:08

Charlotteburg 16 12 40N54 74w31 4:58:04
Chatham 14 1 40N44 74w23 4:57:32
Chatsworth 3 14 39N49 74w32 4:58:08
Cheesequake 12 12 40N24 74w21 4:57:24
Cherry Hill 4 2 39N56 75w02 5:00:08
Cherry Hill Estates 4
2 39N49 75w06 5:00:24
Cherry Quay 15 12 40N02 74w07 4:56:28
Cherry Ridge 4 2 39N49 75w06 5:00:24
Cherry Valley 4 2 39N49 75w06 5:00:24
Cherryville 10 1 40N31 74w52 4:59:28
Chesilhurst 4 17 39N44 74w52 4:59:28
Chester 14 12 40N47 74w42 4:58:48
Chesterfield 3 12 40N08 74w39 4:58:36
Chestnut 20 1 40N42 74w16 4:57:04
Chewalla Park 11 1 40N14 74w42 4:58:48
Chews Landing 4 2 39N48 75w03 5:00:12
Chrome 12 12 40N27 74w23 4:57:32
Churchtown 17 12 39N39 75w31 5:02:04
Cinnaminson 3 2 40N00 74w59 4:59:56
Clara Barton 12 17 40N32 74w22 4:57:28
Clark 20 1 40N38 74w18 4:57:12
Clarksboro 8 2 39N48 75w14 5:00:56
Clarksburg 13 2 40N12 74w27 4:57:48
Clarks Landing 15 2 40N05 74w03 4:56:12
Clarksville 2 40N18 74w41 4:58:44
Clarktown 1 17 39N27 74w44 4:58:56
Clayton 8 1 39N40 75w06 5:00:24
Clayville 6 1 39N29 75w01 5:00:04
Clementon 4 1 39N49 75w00 5:00:00
Clermont 3 1 40N00 74w47 4:59:08
Clermont 5 13 39N05 74w50 4:59:20
Cliffdale Park 14
12 40N47 74w55 4:59:40
Cliffside Park 2 1 40N49 73w59 4:55:56
Cliffwood 13 2 40N27 74w14 4:56:56
Cliffwood Beach 13
2 40N26 74w11 4:56:44
Cliffwood Lake 19
17 41N05 74w31 4:58:04
Clifton 16 3 40N52 74w09 4:56:36
Clinton 10 13 40N38 74w55 4:59:40
Clinton Hill 7 1 40N43 74w12 4:56:48
Closter 2 1 40N58 73w58 4:55:52
Closter Plaza 2 1 40N58 73w58 4:55:52
Cloverdale 4 2 39N53 75w06 5:00:24
Cloverdale 6 2 39N26 75w01 5:00:04
Cloverhill 10 1 40N31 74w52 4:59:28
Clover Leaf Lakes 1
17 39N27 74w44 4:58:56
Cohansey 6 1 39N28 75w15 5:01:00
Cokesbury 10 13 40N38 74w50 4:59:20
Cold Indian Springs 13
1 40N14 74w01 4:56:04
Cold Spring 5 1 38N56 74w55 4:59:40
Colesville 19 12 41N17 74w39 4:58:36
College Town 8 1 39N42 75w07 5:00:28
Collings Lakes 1 1 39N41 75w00 5:00:00
Collingswood 4 1 39N55 75w04 5:00:16
Collingwood Park 13
12 40N14 74w09 4:56:36
Collinsville 14 17 40N48 74w29 4:57:56
Cologne 1 8 39N30 74w37 4:58:28
Colonia 12 2 40N35 74w19 4:57:16
Colonial Gardens 12
1 40N29 74w27 4:57:48
Colonial Terrace 13
1 40N14 74w01 4:56:04
Colts Neck 13 12 40N17 74w11 4:56:44
Columbia 21 12 40N56 75w06 5:00:24
Columbia Lakes 4 2 39N49 75w06 5:00:24
Columbus 3 1 40N05 74w43 4:58:52
Colwick 4 2 39N49 75w06 5:00:24
Commercial 6 12 39N17 75w02 5:00:08
Congressional Estates 4
2 39N49 75w06 5:00:24
Conklintown 16 1 41N02 74w18 4:57:12
Conovertown 1 2 39N26 74w30 4:58:00
Constable Hook 9 1 40N40 74w07 4:56:28
Convent Station 14
1 40N47 74w27 4:57:48
Cookstown 3 3 40N03 74w34 4:58:16
Coontown 18 2 40N37 74w25 4:57:40
Cooper Park Village 4
2 39N49 75w06 5:00:24
Cooper Village 8 1 39N49 75w08 5:00:32
Copper Hill 10 12 40N26 74w52 4:59:28
Corbin City 1 12 39N19 74w46 4:59:04
Cornish 21 17 40N50 75w05 5:00:20
Country Lake Estates 3
12 39N58 74w34 4:58:16
Coxes Corner 13 12 40N11 74w35 4:58:20
Coytesville 2 1 40N51 73w58 4:55:52
Cozy Lake 14 12 41N03 74w29 4:57:56
Cragmere Park 2 12 41N06 74w09 4:56:36
Cranberry Lake 19 1 40N57 74w44 4:58:56
Cranbury 12 1 40N19 74w31 4:58:04
Crandon Lakes 19 12 41N03 74w45 4:59:00
Cranford 20 1 40N40 74w18 4:57:12
Creamridge 13 12 40N08 74w32 4:58:08
Crescent Heights 3
3 39N58 74w41 4:58:44
Crescent Park 4 2 39N53 75w06 5:00:24
Cresskill 2 1 40N57 73w58 4:55:52
Crestmoor 14 12 40N47 74w46 4:59:04
Creston 11 1 40N14 74w42 4:58:48
Crestwood Village 15
12 39N57 74w23 4:57:32
Cropwell 3 17 39N54 74w55 4:59:40
Cross Keys 8 1 39N43 75w02 5:00:08
Crossmans 12 1 40N29 74w17 4:57:08
Crossroads 3 17 39N53 74w49 4:59:16
Crosswicks 3 1 40N09 74w39 4:58:36
Croton 10 1 40N31 74w52 4:59:28
Crow Foot 3 17 39N46 74w59 4:59:56

Crystal Lake 2 17 41N02 74w14 4:56:56
Crystal Lake 15 12 39N55 74w09 4:56:36
Culvers Lake 19 17 41N09 74w45 4:59:00
Cumberland 6 2 39N26 75w01 5:00:04
Cuthbert Manor 4 1 39N55 75w04 5:00:16
Cyn-Wyd 3 1 40N05 74w51 4:59:24
Da Costa 1 2 39N56 75w02 5:00:08
Danceys Corner 17 1 39N44 75w28 5:01:52
Daretown 17 1 39N36 75w10 5:00:40
Darlington 12 41N05 74w11 4:56:44
Darlington Heights 3
12 39N56 74w45 4:59:00
Darts Mills 10 1 40N31 74w52 4:59:28
Davis 13 12 40N08 74w32 4:58:08
Davis Bridge 14 12 40N40 74w31 4:58:04
Dayton 12 1 40N23 74w31 4:58:04
Deal 13 1 40N15 74w00 4:56:00
Deans 12 12 40N25 74w31 4:58:04
Deauville Beach 15
12 40N00 74w04 4:56:16
De Cou Village 11 1 40N12 74w44 4:58:56
Deepwater 17 1 39N41 75w29 5:01:56
Deerfield 6 12 39N28 75w08 5:00:32
Deerfield Street 6
12 39N31 75w14 5:00:56
Deer Park 4 2 39N49 75w06 5:00:24
Deer Trail Lake 19
17 41N05 74w31 4:58:04
Delair 4 2 39N58 75w03 5:00:12
Delanco 3 17 40N03 74w57 4:59:48
Delawanna 16 1 40N50 74w09 4:56:36
Delaware 10 12 40N27 74w57 4:59:48
Delaware 21 15 40N53 75w04 5:00:16
Delaware Gardens 4
2 39N58 75w03 5:00:12
Delaware Park 21 17 40N41 75w10 5:00:40
Delcrest 3 17 40N02 74w57 4:59:48
Del Haven 5 12 39N02 74w56 4:59:44
Delmont 6 12 39N13 74w57 4:59:48
Delran 3 2 40N01 74w58 4:59:52
Delwood 4 2 39N49 75w06 5:00:24
Demarest 2 1 40N57 73w58 4:55:52
Dennis 5 12 39N11 74w48 4:59:12
Dennisville 5 12 39N12 74w49 4:59:16
Denville 14 12 40N53 74w29 4:57:56
Deptford 8 1 39N49 75w08 5:00:32
Devonshire 1 8 39N33 74w37 4:58:28
Dias Creek 5 13 39N05 74w50 4:59:20
Dilts Corner 10 1 40N24 74w59 4:59:56
Dividing Creek 6 12 39N16 75w06 5:00:24
Doddtown 7 1 40N46 74w12 4:56:48
Dolphin 1 2 39N22 74w34 4:58:16
Dorchester 6 17 39N17 74w58 4:59:52
Dorothy 1 12 39N24 74w50 4:59:20
Dover 14 1 40N53 74w35 4:58:20
Dover Hills 14 1 40N53 74w34 4:58:16
Dover Shores 15 1 39N56 74w13 4:56:52
Downe 6 12 39N16 75w07 5:00:28
Downer 8 1 39N41 75w00 5:00:00
Downs Farms 4 2 39N49 75w06 5:00:24
Drakestown 14 1 40N52 74w50 4:59:20
Drew University 14
1 40N45 74w25 4:57:40
Dumont 2 1 40N56 74w00 4:56:00
Dunbarton 4 17 39N46 74w59 4:59:56
Dundee 16 1 40N52 74w08 4:56:32
Dunellen 12 2 40N35 74w28 4:57:52
Dunham's Corner 12
12 40N25 74w23 4:57:32
Dunham Siding 2 1 40N47 74w01 4:56:04
Durham 12 17 40N32 74w22 4:57:28
Durham Park 12 1 40N34 74w27 4:57:48
Dutch Neck 11 12 40N17 74w37 4:58:28
Eagleswood 15 2 39N39 74w18 4:57:12
Earle 13 12 40N17 74w11 4:56:44
East 16 4 40N55 74w09 4:56:36
Eastampton 3 1 40N00 74w45 4:59:00
East Amwell 10 12 40N26 74w49 4:59:16
East Berlin 4 17 39N49 74w58 4:59:52
East Bound Brook 12
17 40N35 74w30 4:58:00
East Bridgeton 6 1 39N28 75w15 5:01:00
East Brunswick 12
12 40N26 74w25 4:57:40
East Burlington 3 1 40N05 74w51 4:59:24
East Camden 4 2 39N57 75w05 5:00:20
East Freehold 13 1 40N15 74w17 4:57:08
East Greenwich 8 2 39N48 75w14 5:00:56
East Hanover 14 17 40N49 74w21 4:57:24
East Keansburg 13
17 40N27 74w07 4:56:28
East Long Branch 13
1 40N18 74w00 4:56:00
East Millstone 18
12 40N30 74w35 4:58:20
East Newark 9 1 40N45 74w09 4:56:36
East Orange 7 1 40N46 74w13 4:56:52
East Paterson 2 1 40N54 74w08 4:56:32
East Pennsauken 4 2 39N58 75w03 5:00:12
East Riverton 3 2 40N00 75w00 5:00:00
East Rutherford 2 1 40N50 74w06 4:56:24
East Side 6 1 39N28 75w15 5:01:00
East Spotswood 12
12 40N24 74w21 4:57:24
East Trenton Heights 11
1 40N16 74w46 4:59:04
East Vineland 1 1 39N29 75w01 5:00:04
East Wenonah 8 2 39N48 75w08 5:00:32
East Windsor 11 1 40N16 74w33 4:58:12
East Woodbury 8 1 39N49 75w08 5:00:32
Eatontown 13 1 40N19 74w04 4:56:16
Eayrestown 3 1 40N00 74w47 4:59:08
Echelon 4 2 39N50 75w01 5:00:04
Echo Lake 16 12 40N54 74w31 4:58:04
Edgebrook 12 1 40N29 74w27 4:57:48

Edgewater 2 1 40N50 73w59 4:55:56
Edgewater Park 3 1 40N04 74w54 4:59:36
Edgewater Park Estates 3
1 40N05 74w51 4:59:24
Edgewood 5 13 39N05 74w50 4:59:20
Edgewood Park 15 12 40N08 74w20 4:57:20
Edinburg 11 12 40N16 74w37 4:58:28
Edison 12 1 40N31 74w25 4:57:40
Egg Harbor City 1 8 39N32 74w39 4:58:36
Eilers Corners 11 1 40N16 74w32 4:58:08
Elberon 13 1 40N18 74w00 4:56:00
Eldora 5 12 39N16 74w47 4:59:08
Eldridge Park 11 1 40N16 74w46 4:59:04
Eldridges Hill 17
17 39N39 75w20 5:01:20
Elizabeth 20 1 40N40 74w13 4:56:52
Elizabethport 20 1 40N39 74w12 4:56:48
Elk 8 1 39N40 75w08 5:00:32
Elks Terrace 17 17 39N34 75w28 5:01:52
Ellisburg 4 2 39N49 75w06 5:00:24
Ellisdale 3 12 40N11 74w35 4:58:20
Elm 4 2 39N56 75w02 5:00:08
Elmer 17 1 39N36 75w10 5:00:40
Elmora 20 1 40N39 74w13 4:56:52
Elmwood Park 2 1 40N55 74w07 4:56:28
Elsinboro 17 17 39N33 75w29 5:01:56
Elsmere 8 1 39N42 75w07 5:00:28
Elwood 1 12 39N35 74w43 4:58:52
Emerson 2 1 40N59 74w02 4:56:08
Englewood 2 9 40N54 73w59 4:55:56
Englewood Cliffs 2
1 40N53 73w57 4:55:48
English Creek 1 17 39N27 74w44 4:58:56
Englishtown 13 12 40N18 74w22 4:57:28
Erial 4 1 39N43 74w58 4:59:52
Erlton 4 2 39N49 75w06 5:00:24
Erma 5 1 38N56 74w55 4:59:40
Ernston 12 2 40N28 74w20 4:57:20
Erskine 16 12 41N06 74w16 4:57:04
Esponong 14 12 40N57 74w37 4:58:28
Essex Fells 7 1 40N50 74w17 4:57:08
Estell Manor 1 12 39N22 74w47 4:59:08
Estelville 1 12 39N22 74w47 4:59:08
Estling Lake 14 12 40N53 74w29 4:57:56
Etra 11 1 40N15 74w30 4:58:00
Everett 13 12 40N22 74w09 4:56:36
Everittstown 10 13 40N35 74w58 4:59:52
Evesboro 3 17 39N55 74w55 4:59:40
Evesham 3 17 39N51 74w53 4:59:32
Ewan 8 1 39N42 75w11 5:00:44
Ewansville 3 1 39N59 74w44 4:58:56
Ewing 11 1 40N16 74w47 4:59:08
Ewingville 11 1 40N16 74w46 4:59:04
Extonville 11 12 40N11 74w35 4:58:20
Fairfield 7 1 40N53 74w17 4:57:08
Fairfield 13 1 40N15 74w17 4:57:08
Fair Haven 13 1 40N22 74w02 4:56:08
Fair Lawn 2 2 40N56 74w08 4:56:32
Fairmount 10 12 40N43 74w50 4:59:20
Fairton 6 1 39N23 75w13 5:00:52
Fairview 2 1 40N48 73w59 4:55:56
Fairview 3 17 39N53 74w49 4:59:16
Fairview 8 17 39N45 75w04 5:00:16
Fairview 13 2 40N23 74w05 4:56:20
Fairview Knolls 12
12 40N25 74w23 4:57:32
Falcon Courts North 3
3 40N01 74w38 4:58:32
Fanwood 20 2 40N39 74w23 4:57:32
Far Hills 18 12 40N41 74w38 4:58:32
Farmersville 10 12 40N43 74w50 4:59:20
Farmingdale 13 12 40N12 74w10 4:56:40
Farmington 1 2 39N23 74w33 4:58:12
Farrington Lake Heights 12
1 40N27 74w26 4:57:44
Fayson Lakes 14 16 41N00 74w21 4:57:24
Fellowship 3 17 39N58 74w56 4:59:44
Fenwick 17 17 39N37 75w20 5:01:20
Fernwood Terrace 11
1 40N14 74w47 4:59:08
Ferrell 8 1 39N38 75w10 5:00:40
Ferry Road Manor 11
1 40N15 74w48 4:59:12
Fieldsboro 3 1 40N08 74w44 4:58:56
Fieldstone 18 1 40N42 74w33 4:58:12
Finderne 18 2 40N34 74w35 4:58:20
Finesville 21 17 40N41 75w10 5:00:40
Firthtown 21 17 40N41 75w10 5:00:40
Fish House 4 2 39N58 75w03 5:00:12
Fishing Creek 5 1 38N56 74w55 4:59:40
Five Corners 9 1 40N43 74w04 4:56:16
Five Points 17 17 39N46 75w24 5:01:36
Five Points 19 12 41N03 74w45 4:59:00
Flagtown 18 2 40N31 74w41 4:58:44
Flanders 14 1 40N51 74w42 4:58:48
Flatbrookville 19
12 40N56 75w06 5:00:24
Flemington 10 1 40N31 74w52 4:59:28
Florence 3 1 40N07 74w49 4:59:16
Florence 4 17 39N49 74w58 4:59:52
Florham Park 14 1 40N47 74w23 4:57:32
Folsom 1 12 39N36 74w51 4:59:24
Ford Estates 8 1 39N49 75w08 5:00:32
Ford Landing 3 2 40N00 75w01 5:00:04
Fords 12 1 40N32 74w19 4:57:16
Forest Grove 8 1 39N29 75w01 5:00:04
Forest Hill 4 2 39N49 75w06 5:00:24
Forest Hill 15 12 39N55 74w09 4:56:36
Forked River 15 14 39N50 74w12 4:56:48
Forrest Lake Estates 8
17 39N34 75w02 5:00:08
Fort Dix 3 3 40N00 74w35 4:58:20
Fort Elfsborg 17 17 39N34 75w28 5:01:52
Fortescue 6 12 39N14 75w10 5:00:40
Fort Hancock 13 1 40N24 73w59 4:55:56

NEW JERSEY

Fort Lee 2	1	40N51	73w58	4:55:52
Fort Mercer 8	1	39N51	75w10	5:00:40
Fort Monmouth 13	1	40N19	74w02	4:56:08
Fort Mott 17	17	39N34	75w28	5:01:52
Fort Plains 13	1	40N15	74w17	4:57:08
Foster Village 2	1	40N55	74w04	4:56:16
Foul Rift 21	17	40N50	75w05	5:00:20
Fox Hills 14	1	40N53	74w26	4:57:44
Fox Hollow Woods 4	2	39N49	75w06	5:00:24
Francis Mills 15	12	40N08	74w20	4:57:20
Frankford 19	17	41N10	74w44	4:58:56
Franklin 19	17	41N07	74w35	4:58:20
Franklin Lakes 2	17	41N01	74w12	4:56:48
Franklin Park 18	12	40N26	74w33	4:58:12
Franklinville 8	12	39N37	75w05	5:00:20
Frazier Park 15	17	39N37	74w12	4:56:48
Fredon 19	15	41N02	74w49	4:59:16
Free Acres 20	17	40N41	74w27	4:57:48
Freehold 13	1	40N16	74w17	4:57:08
Freewood Acres 13	12	40N10	74w14	4:56:56
Frelinghuysen 21	18	40N58	74w53	4:59:32
Frenchtown 10	12	40N32	75w04	5:00:16
Freneau 13	2	40N25	74w14	4:56:56
Friendship 17	1	39N38	75w10	5:00:40
Fries Mill 8	1	39N39	75w03	5:00:12
Galilee 13	1	40N20	73w59	4:55:56
Galloping Hill 18	1	40N42	74w33	4:58:12
Galloway 1	2	39N29	74w32	4:58:08
Gandys Beach 6	12	39N18	75w11	5:00:44
Garden City 8	1	39N49	75w08	5:00:32
Garden Lake 4	1	39N48	75w00	5:00:00
Gardens 5	1	39N16	74w35	4:58:20
Garden State 2	1	40N57	74w04	4:56:16
Gardenville Center 8	1	39N49	75w08	5:00:32
Garfield 2	1	40N52	74w06	4:56:24
Garwood 20	1	40N39	74w19	4:57:16
General Lafayette 9	1	40N43	74w04	4:56:16
Genoa 12	2	40N25	74w14	4:56:56
Georgetown 3	12	40N04	74w43	4:58:52
Georgetowne 3	17	39N54	74w55	4:59:40
Georgia 13	1	40N15	74w17	4:57:08
Germania 1	8	39N33	74w37	4:58:28
Gibbsboro 4	17	39N50	74w58	4:59:52
Gibbstown 8	2	39N50	75w18	5:01:12
Gilford Park 15	12	39N57	74w08	4:56:32
Gillespie 12	2	40N28	74w20	4:57:20
Gillette 14	17	40N41	74w28	4:57:52
Gilman Lake 8	1	39N38	75w10	5:00:40
Glacier Hills 14	17	40N50	74w29	4:57:56
Gladstone 18	12	40N43	74w40	4:58:40
Glassboro 8	1	39N42	75w07	5:00:28
Glasser 19	1	40N56	74w40	4:58:40
Glen Cove 15	12	39N55	74w09	4:56:36
Glendale 4	2	39N50	75w01	5:00:04
Glendale 11	1	40N14	74w47	4:59:08
Glendola 13	1	40N11	74w02	4:56:08
Glendora 4	2	39N50	75w04	5:00:16
Glen Gardner 10	13	40N42	74w57	4:59:48
Glen Ridge 7	2	40N48	74w12	4:56:48
Glen Rock 2	4	40N57	74w09	4:56:36
Glenside 17	12	39N40	75w30	5:02:00
Glenview 4	2	39N49	75w06	5:00:24
Glenwood 19	12	41N15	74w29	4:57:56
Gloucester 4	1	39N49	75w03	5:00:12
Gloucester City 4	2	39N54	75w08	5:00:32
Godfrey Manor 15	12	40N02	74w07	4:56:28
Golf Hill 14	14	40N52	74w38	4:58:32
Golf Manor 17	1	39N44	75w28	5:01:52
Golf View 17	1	39N42	75w28	5:01:52
Gordon Lakes 16	16	41N00	74w21	4:57:24
Goshen 5	13	39N08	74w51	4:59:24
Gouldtown 6	1	39N28	75w15	5:01:00
Grandin 10	13	40N39	74w53	4:59:32
Grand Spruce 8	10	39N45	75w19	5:01:16
Granton Junction 9	1	40N47	74w01	4:56:04
Grantwood 2	1	40N49	74w00	4:56:00
Grasselli 20	1	40N38	74w15	4:57:00
Grassy Sound 5	11	39N00	74w49	4:59:16
Gravel Hill 12	12	40N18	74w22	4:57:28
Great Eastern Mills 16	4	40N54	74w12	4:56:48
Great Meadows 21	12	40N52	74w55	4:59:40
Great Notch 16	4	40N54	74w12	4:56:48
Green 19	15	40N59	74w48	4:59:12
Green Acres 11	1	40N14	74w47	4:59:08
Green Bank 3	8	39N33	74w37	4:58:28
Green Brook 18	17	40N36	74w29	4:57:56
Green Creek 5	12	39N03	74w54	4:59:36
Green Curve Heights 11	1	40N16	74w46	4:59:04
Greendell 19	15	40N58	74w49	4:59:16
Greenfield 5	2	39N10	74w44	4:58:56
Greenfield Heights 8	1	39N49	75w08	5:00:32
Green Grove 13	12	40N14	74w05	4:56:20
Green Haven 4	2	39N49	75w06	5:00:24
Green Hut Park 14	1	40N53	74w34	4:58:16
Green Knoll 18	2	40N34	74w36	4:58:24
Greenland 4	2	39N51	75w02	5:00:08
Green Pond 14	12	41N01	74w29	4:57:56
Greensand 12	17	40N32	74w22	4:57:28
Greens Bridge 21	17	40N41	75w10	5:00:40
Green Village 14	1	40N44	74w27	4:57:48
Greenville 9	1	40N42	74w05	4:56:20
Greenville 15	1	40N06	74w13	4:56:52
Greenville 17	1	39N36	75w10	5:00:40
Greenwich 6	12	39N24	75w21	5:01:24
Greenwood Village 11	1	40N13	74w44	4:58:56
Grenloch 8	2	39N47	75w04	5:00:16
Griggstown 18	12	40N26	74w37	4:58:28
Grove 7	1	40N48	74w11	4:56:44
Grove Chapel 6	17	39N33	75w01	5:00:04
Grovers Mills 11	2	40N19	74w37	4:58:28
Groveville 11	1	40N10	74w40	4:58:40
Guttenberg 9	1	40N48	74w00	4:56:00
Hackensack 2	1	40N53	74w03	4:56:12
Hackettstown 21	1	40N51	74w50	4:59:20
Haddon 4	1	39N54	75w04	5:00:16
Haddonfield 4	2	39N54	75w02	5:00:08
Haddon Heights 4	2	39N53	75w04	5:00:16
Haddon Hills 4	2	39N54	75w02	5:00:08
Haddon Leigh 4	2	39N54	75w02	5:00:08
Haddontowne 4	2	39N49	75w06	5:00:24
Hainesburg 21	12	40N56	75w06	5:00:24
Haines Corner 11	12	40N12	74w40	4:58:40
Hainesport 3	1	39N59	74w50	4:59:20
Hainesville 19	17	41N09	74w45	4:59:00
Haledon 16	4	40N56	74w11	4:56:44
Haledon-North Haledon 16	4	40N56	74w11	4:56:44
Haleyville 6	12	39N15	75w02	5:00:08
Halls Corners 12	12	40N25	74w23	4:57:32
Halsey 19	12	41N03	74w45	4:59:00
Hamburg 19	17	41N09	74w34	4:58:16
Hamden 10	13	40N39	74w53	4:59:32
Hamilton 13	1	40N12	74w05	4:56:20
Hamilton Square 11	1	40N14	74w40	4:58:40
Hammond Heights 8	2	39N48	75w08	5:00:32
Hammonton 1	2	39N39	74w48	4:59:12
Hampton 10	13	40N42	74w58	4:59:52
Hancocks Bridge 17	17	39N31	75w28	5:01:52
Hanover 14	1	40N48	74w22	4:57:28
Hanover Neck 14	17	40N49	74w22	4:57:28
Harbourton 11	12	40N23	74w51	4:59:24
Harding 14	12	40N45	74w30	4:58:00
Harding Lakes 1	17	39N27	74w44	4:58:56
Hardingville 8	1	39N38	75w10	5:00:40
Hardistonville 19	17	41N09	74w35	4:58:20
Hardwick 21	16	41N01	74w56	4:59:44
Hardyston 19	17	41N07	74w34	4:58:16
Harfield 15	12	40N08	74w20	4:57:20
Harker Village 8	1	39N49	75w08	5:00:32
Harlingen 18	2	40N28	74w40	4:58:40
Harmersville 17	17	39N34	75w28	5:01:52
Harmony 13	2	40N24	74w07	4:56:28
Harmony 15	12	40N08	74w20	4:57:20
Harmony 21	17	40N45	75w08	5:00:32
Harmony Park 13	2	40N26	74w13	4:56:52
Harrington Park 2	1	40N59	73w59	4:55:56
Harrison 9	1	40N45	74w09	4:56:36
Harrison Mountain Lake 16	12	41N06	74w16	4:57:04
Harrisonville 8	12	39N41	75w16	5:01:04
Hartford 3	17	39N58	74w56	4:59:44
Harvey Cedars 15	12	39N42	74w08	4:56:32
Hasbrouck Heights 2	1	40N52	74w05	4:56:20
Haskell 16	1	41N02	74w18	4:57:12
Haven Beach 15	17	39N37	74w12	4:56:48
Haven Homes 12	17	40N32	74w22	4:57:28
Haworth 2	1	40N58	73w59	4:55:56
Hawthorne 16	1	40N57	74w10	4:56:40
Hazen 21	17	40N50	75w05	5:00:20
Hazlet 13	2	40N25	74w12	4:56:48
Head Of River 1	12	39N16	74w47	4:59:08
Heatherwood 12	12	40N24	74w21	4:57:24
Hedding 3	1	40N09	74w42	4:58:48
Heislerville 6	12	39N15	75w07	5:00:28
Helmetta 12	12	40N23	74w26	4:57:44
Hensfoot 10	13	40N42	74w57	4:59:48
Herberts Corner 12	12	40N25	74w23	4:57:32
Herbertsville 15	12	40N02	74w07	4:56:28
Heritage Village 3	17	39N54	74w55	4:59:40
Herman 3	8	39N33	74w37	4:58:28
Herwood 4	2	39N49	75w06	5:00:24
Hesstown 6	2	39N26	75w01	5:00:04
Hewitt 16	12	41N09	74w19	4:57:16
Hibernia 14	12	40N57	74w30	4:58:00
Hickstown 4	2	39N48	75w03	5:00:12
Higbee Town 1	2	39N26	74w30	4:58:00
High Bridge 10	13	40N40	74w54	4:59:36
Highland Beach 13	1	40N22	73w59	4:55:56
Highland Lakes 19	12	41N11	74w28	4:57:52
Highland Park 4	2	39N53	75w06	5:00:24
Highland Park 12	1	40N30	74w26	4:57:44
Highlands 13	1	40N24	73w59	4:55:56
High Point Manor 12	12	40N24	74w21	4:57:24
Highs Beach 5	13	39N05	74w50	4:59:20
Hightstown 11	1	40N16	74w31	4:58:04
Highview Park 13	1	40N07	74w03	4:56:12
Hillcrest 4	2	39N57	75w03	5:00:12
Hillcrest 16	4	40N55	74w12	4:56:48
Hillcrest 21	17	40N41	75w10	5:00:40
Hilliard 15	1	39N42	74w15	4:57:00
Hillsborough 18	2	40N30	74w39	4:58:36
Hillsdale 2	1	41N00	74w03	4:56:12
Hillside 20	1	40N42	74w13	4:56:52
Hilltop 4	2	39N48	75w03	5:00:12
Hilltop Terrace 12	12	40N25	74w23	4:57:32
Hilltown 14	1	40N54	74w35	4:58:20
Hillwood Lakes 11	1	40N16	74w46	4:59:04
Hilton 13	1	40N25	74w02	4:56:08
Hinchman 4	2	39N49	75w06	5:00:24
Hi-Nella 4	2	39N50	75w01	5:00:04
Hoboken 9	1	40N44	74w02	4:56:08
Hoffmans 10	12	40N43	74w50	4:59:20
Ho-Ho-Kus 2	2	41N00	74w07	4:56:28
Holgate 15	17	39N37	74w12	4:56:48
Holiday City 15	1	39N56	74w13	4:56:52
Holland 10	13	40N36	75w07	5:00:28
Holly Brook 3	1	40N00	74w47	4:59:08
Holly Crest 15	12	40N02	74w07	4:56:28
Holly Park 15	12	39N55	74w09	4:56:36
Holmansville 15	12	40N08	74w20	4:57:20
Holmdel 13	12	40N21	74w11	4:56:44
Holmdel Village 13	12	40N21	74w11	4:56:44
Holmeson 13	2	40N10	74w31	4:58:04
Homestead 9	1	40N47	74w01	4:56:04
Homestead Park 14	17	40N41	74w27	4:57:48
Homestead Village 18	1	40N42	74w33	4:58:12
Hootens Hollow 4	2	39N49	75w06	5:00:24
Hoot Owl Estates 3	17	39N53	74w49	4:59:16
Hoover Village 6	1	39N28	75w15	5:01:00
Hopatcong 19	1	40N55	74w40	4:58:40
Hope 21	12	40N54	74w59	4:59:56
Hopelawn 12	1	40N31	74w17	4:57:08
Hopewell 11	12	40N23	74w46	4:59:04
Hornerstown 13	12	40N07	74w31	4:58:04
Howell 13	12	40N10	74w12	4:56:48
Hudson City 9	1	40N45	74w04	4:56:16
Hudson Heights 9	1	40N47	74w01	4:56:04
Hughesville 10	12	40N34	75w06	5:00:24
Huntington 21	17	40N41	75w10	5:00:40
Huntsburg 19	12	41N03	74w45	4:59:00
Hunt Tract 4	2	39N49	75w06	5:00:24
Hurdtown 14	12	40N58	74w36	4:58:24
Hurffville 8	17	39N45	75w04	5:00:16
Hutchinson 21	17	40N41	75w10	5:00:40
Hutchinson Mills 11	1	40N14	74w42	4:58:48
Hyson 15	12	40N08	74w20	4:57:20
Ideal Beach 13	17	40N27	74w08	4:56:32
Idell 10	12	40N32	75w03	5:00:12
Imlaystown 13	12	40N09	74w31	4:58:04
Imperial Manor 4	2	39N49	75w06	5:00:24
Independence 21	1	40N53	74w53	4:59:32
Independence Corner 19	1	41N13	74w36	4:58:24
Indian Cabin 1	8	39N33	74w37	4:58:28
Indian Lake 14	12	40N53	74w29	4:57:56
Indian Mills 3	12	39N56	74w45	4:59:00
Industrial-Hillside 20	1	40N42	74w13	4:56:52
Interlaken 13	1	40N14	74w01	4:56:04
Iona 8	12	39N37	75w05	5:00:20
Ironbound 7	1	40N43	74w10	4:56:40
Ironia 14	14	40N50	74w38	4:58:32
Iron Rock 4	2	39N57	75w03	5:00:12
Irven Heights 11	1	40N16	74w46	4:59:04
Irvington 7	2	40N44	74w14	4:56:56
Iselin 12	2	40N35	74w19	4:57:16
Island Beach 15	12	39N56	74w05	4:56:20
Island Heights 15	1	39N57	74w09	4:56:36
Ivystone Farms 4	17	39N46	74w59	4:59:56
Ivywood 3	2	40N00	75w00	5:00:00
Jackson 15	12	40N06	74w19	4:57:16
Jacksonburg 21	16	40N59	74w57	4:59:48
Jacksons Mills 15	12	40N08	74w20	4:57:20
Jacksonville 3	1	40N09	74w42	4:58:48
Jacksonville 14	17	40N56	74w18	4:57:12
Jacobstown 3	3	40N01	74w38	4:58:32
Jamesburg 12	12	40N21	74w27	4:57:48
Janvier 8	12	39N37	75w05	5:00:20
Jefferson 8	17	39N45	75w13	5:00:52
Jeffrey Lane Estates 15	12	39N55	74w09	4:56:36
Jenkins 3	14	39N46	74w33	4:58:12
Jericho 8	1	39N49	75w08	5:00:32
Jersey City 9	1	40N44	74w04	4:56:16
Jerseyville 13	1	40N14	74w14	4:56:56
Jobstown 3	3	40N02	74w41	4:58:44
Johnsonburg 21	18	40N58	74w53	4:59:32
Jones Island 6	12	39N20	75w12	5:00:48
Jordantown 4	2	39N57	75w03	5:00:12
Journal Square 9	1	40N44	74w04	4:56:16
Juliustown 3	3	40N01	74w40	4:58:40
Jutland 10	13	40N38	74w55	4:59:40
Kampfe Lake 16	16	41N01	74w20	4:57:20
Kay Gardens 17	17	39N46	75w24	5:01:36
Keansburg 13	17	40N27	74w08	4:56:32
Kearny 9	2	40N46	74w09	4:56:36
Keasbey 12	1	40N31	74w19	4:57:16
Kendall Park 12	12	40N25	74w34	4:58:16
Kenilworth 20	1	40N41	74w18	4:57:12
Kenvil 14	14	40N53	74w37	4:58:28
Kenwood 4	2	39N49	75w06	5:00:24
Keswick Grove 15	12	39N57	74w23	4:57:32
Keyport 13	2	40N26	74w12	4:56:48
Kingfisher Cove 15	12	40N02	74w07	4:56:28
Kings Hill 4	2	39N49	75w06	5:00:24
Kingsland 2	1	40N49	74w07	4:56:28
Kingston 18	2	40N23	74w37	4:58:28
Kingston Estates 4	2	39N49	75w06	5:00:24
Kingsway Village 4	2	39N49	75w06	5:00:24
Kingswood 4	2	39N49	75w06	5:00:24
Kingwood 10	12	40N29	75w01	5:00:04
Kinkora 3	1	40N09	74w42	4:58:48
Kinnelon 14	16	41N00	74w22	4:57:28
Kirbys Mill 3	17	39N53	74w49	4:59:16
Kirkwood 4	2	39N50	75w01	5:00:04
Kittatinny Lake 19	17	41N09	74w45	4:59:00
Klinesville 10	1	40N31	74w52	4:59:28

Knollwood 4 2 39N49 75w06 5:00:24
Knowlton 21 15 40N55 75w04 5:00:16
Kresson 4 17 39N54 74w55 4:59:40
Lafayette 19 17 41N06 74w41 4:58:44
Lahiere 12 17 40N32 74w22 4:57:28
Lake 8 17 39N33 75w01 5:00:04
Lake Arrowhead 14 12 40N53 74w29 4:57:56
Lake Como 13 1 40N09 74w02 4:56:08
Lake Denmark 14 1 40N53 74w34 4:58:16
Lake Forest 14 1 40N55 74w39 4:58:36
Lake Grinnell 19 17 41N06 74w38 4:58:32
Lake Hiawatha 14 1 40N53 74w23 4:57:32
Lake Hopatcong 14 12 40N57 74w37 4:58:28
Lakehurst 15 1 40N01 74w19 4:57:16
Lakehurst Naval Air Station 15 1 40N01 74w19 4:57:16
Lake Iliff 19 12 41N03 74w45 4:59:00
Lake Intervale 14 1 40N54 74w25 4:57:40
Lake Lackawanna 19 1 40N55 74w42 4:58:48
Lake Lenape 19 12 41N00 74w44 4:58:56
Lake Lookover 16 12 41N08 74w18 4:57:12
Lake Mohawk 19 12 41N01 74w39 4:58:36
Lake Nelson 12 1 40N34 74w27 4:57:48
Lake Owassa 19 12 41N03 74w45 4:59:00
Lake Parsippany 14 1 40N51 74w26 4:57:44
Lake Pine 3 17 39N52 74w51 4:59:24
Lake Ridge 12 2 40N25 74w14 4:56:56
Lake Riviera 15 12 40N02 74w07 4:56:28
Lake Shawnee 14 1 40N54 74w35 4:58:20
Lakeside 16 12 41N11 74w20 4:57:20
Lakeside Park 11 1 40N12 74w44 4:58:56
Lake Stockholm 14 17 41N04 74w32 4:58:08
Lake Swannanoa 14 12 41N03 74w29 4:57:56
Lake Tamarack 19 17 41N05 74w31 4:58:04
Lake Telemark 14 12 40N57 74w30 4:58:00
Lakeview 13 12 40N11 74w35 4:58:20
Lake Villa Estates 4 17 39N49 74w58 4:59:52
Lakewood 15 1 40N06 74w13 4:56:52
Lambertville 10 1 40N22 74w57 4:59:48
Lambs Terrace 4 1 39N43 74w58 4:59:52
Lamington 18 12 40N40 74w44 4:58:56
Landing 14 1 40N54 74w40 4:58:40
Landisville 1 17 39N31 74w57 4:59:48
Land of Pines 13 1 40N09 74w14 4:56:56
Landsdown 10 13 40N39 74w53 4:59:32
Lanes Mills 15 1 40N06 74w13 4:56:52
Lanoka Harbor 15 14 39N52 74w10 4:56:40
Larison's Corner 10 12 40N26 74w52 4:59:28
Larrabees 13 1 40N06 74w13 4:56:52
Laurel Acres 15 12 40N02 74w07 4:56:28
Laureldale 1 17 39N27 74w44 4:58:56
Laurel Harbor 15 14 39N52 74w10 4:56:40
Laurel Homes 12 1 40N31 74w17 4:57:08
Laurelhurst 15 12 40N02 74w07 4:56:28
Laurel Lake 6 2 39N26 75w01 5:00:04
Laurel Manor 4 1 39N48 75w00 5:00:00
Laurel Manor 15 12 40N02 74w07 4:56:28
Laurel Springs 4 1 39N49 75w00 5:00:00
Laurelton Acres 15 12 40N02 74w07 4:56:28
Laurelton Heights 15 12 40N02 74w07 4:56:28
Laurelton Park 15 12 40N02 74w07 4:56:28
Laurence Harbor 12 2 40N27 74w15 4:57:00
Lavallette 15 12 39N58 74w04 4:56:16
Lawnside 4 2 39N52 75w02 5:00:08
Lawrence Brook 12 12 40N25 74w23 4:57:32
Lawrenceville 11 1 40N18 74w44 4:58:56
Layton 19 12 41N13 74w50 4:59:20
Lebanon 10 13 40N38 74w50 4:59:20
Lebanon Lakes 3 12 39N58 74w34 4:58:16
Lebanon Park 3 12 39N56 74w45 4:59:00
Ledgewood 14 14 40N53 74w39 4:58:36
Leeds Point 1 17 39N30 74w26 4:57:44
Leektown 3 8 39N33 74w37 4:58:28
Leesburg 6 17 39N15 74w59 4:59:56
Leisure Village 15 1 40N06 74w13 4:56:52
Leisure World 12 12 40N21 74w26 4:57:44
Lenola 3 17 39N58 74w56 4:59:44
Leonardo 13 1 40N25 74w04 4:56:16
Leonia 2 1 40N52 73w59 4:55:56
Levittown 1 40N03 74w53 4:59:32
Lewisville 11 1 40N16 74w46 4:59:04
Liberty 21 12 40N52 74w57 4:59:48
Liberty Corner 18 1 40N40 74w35 4:58:20
Libertyville 19 1 41N13 74w36 4:58:24
Lincoln 8 17 39N44 75w13 5:00:52
Lincoln Park 14 17 40N55 74w18 4:57:12
Lincroft 13 1 40N20 74w07 4:56:28
Linden 20 1 40N38 74w15 4:57:00
Lindeneau 12 17 40N32 74w22 4:57:28
Lindenwold 4 1 39N49 74w59 4:59:56
Lindy Lake 16 16 41N00 74w21 4:57:24
Linvale 10 12 40N26 74w52 4:59:28
Linwood 1 1 39N21 74w35 4:58:20
Little Egg Harbor 15 2 39N37 74w21 4:57:24
Little Falls 16 17 40N53 74w14 4:56:56
Little Ferry 2 1 40N51 74w02 4:56:08
Little Silver 13 1 40N19 74w02 4:56:08
Littleton 14 17 40N50 74w29 4:57:56
Little York 10 13 40N37 75w05 5:00:20
Livingston 7 1 40N48 74w19 4:57:16
Livingston Park 12 1 40N29 74w27 4:57:48
Loch Arbour 13 1 40N14 74w00 4:56:00
Locktown 10 1 40N31 74w52 4:59:28
Locust 13 2 40N23 74w02 4:56:08
Lodi 2 1 40N53 74w05 4:56:20
Logan 8 10 39N48 75w21 5:01:24
Lommasons Glen 21 17 40N50 75w05 5:00:20
Long Beach 15 12 39N38 74w12 4:56:48
Long Branch 13 1 40N18 74w00 4:56:00
Long Bridge 21 12 40N52 74w55 4:59:40
Longport 1 7 39N19 74w31 4:58:04
Long Valley 14 12 40N47 74w46 4:59:04
Longwood Lake 14 12 41N03 74w29 4:57:56
Lopatcong 21 17 40N42 75w10 5:00:40
Lorillard Beach 13 2 40N26 74w11 4:56:44
Lorraine 20 1 40N40 74w16 4:57:04
Loveladies 15 17 39N37 74w12 4:56:48
Lower 5 1 38N59 74w55 4:59:40
Lower Alloways Creek 17 12 39N29 75w25 5:01:40
Lower Bank 3 8 39N33 74w37 4:58:28
Lower Berkshire Valley 14 1 40N54 74w35 4:58:20
Lower Harmony 21 17 40N41 75w10 5:00:40
Lower Montville 14 1 40N52 74w22 4:57:28
Lower Squankum 13 12 40N10 74w10 4:56:40
Lower Valley 10 12 40N43 74w50 4:59:20
Low Moor 13 1 40N22 73w59 4:55:56
Lows Hollow 21 13 40N42 75w07 5:00:28
Lozier Park 2 1 40N57 74w02 4:56:08
Lucaston 4 17 39N49 74w58 4:59:52
Lumberton 3 1 39N58 74w48 4:59:12
Lyndhurst 2 1 40N48 74w07 4:56:28
Lyndhurst 2 1 40N48 74w07 4:56:28
Lynn Oaks 12 2 40N35 74w19 4:57:16
Lyons 18 1 40N41 74w33 4:58:12
Lyonsville 14 1 40N54 74w25 4:57:40
Macopin 16 16 41N00 74w21 4:57:24
Madison 14 1 40N46 74w25 4:57:40
Madisonville 18 1 40N42 74w33 4:58:12
Magnolia 3 3 39N58 74w41 4:58:44
Magnolia 4 2 39N51 75w02 5:00:08
Mahoneyville 17 12 39N39 75w31 5:02:04
Mahwah 2 12 41N05 74w09 4:56:36
Malaga 8 17 39N34 75w02 5:00:08
Malapardis 14 1 40N49 74w25 4:57:40
Mall 7 1 40N44 74w19 4:57:16
Manahawkin 15 1 39N42 74w15 4:57:00
Manalapan 13 12 40N16 74w24 4:57:36
Manasquan 13 1 40N08 74w03 4:56:12
Manasquan Shores 13 1 40N07 74w03 4:56:12
Manchester 15 12 39N57 74w24 4:57:36
Mandalay 15 12 40N02 74w07 4:56:28
Mannington 17 12 39N37 75w25 5:01:40
Manor Park 15 12 40N02 74w07 4:56:28
Mansfield Square 3 12 40N04 74w43 4:58:52
Mantoloking 15 2 40N03 74w03 4:56:12
Mantua 8 2 39N48 75w11 5:00:44
Mantua Grove 8 2 39N49 75w13 5:00:52
Mantua Heights 8 2 39N46 75w10 5:00:40
Manunka Chunk 21 12 40N56 75w06 5:00:24
Manville 18 2 40N33 74w35 4:58:20
Maplecrest 7 1 40N44 74w16 4:57:04
Maple Meade 12 1 40N29 74w27 4:57:48
Maple Shade 3 2 39N57 75w00 5:00:00
Maple Shade 3 2 39N57 75w00 5:00:00
Maplewood 7 1 40N44 74w16 4:57:04
Marcella 14 12 41N00 74w28 4:57:52
Margate City 1 7 39N20 74w30 4:58:00
Marksboro 21 16 40N59 74w57 4:59:48
Marlboro 6 1 39N28 75w15 5:01:00
Marlboro 13 1 40N19 74w15 4:57:00
Marlton 3 17 39N54 74w55 4:59:40
Marlton Heights 17 17 39N39 75w20 5:01:20
Marlton Hills 3 17 39N54 74w55 4:59:40
Marlton Lakes 3 17 39N46 74w59 4:59:56
Marlyn Manor 5 1 39N01 74w53 4:59:32
Marmora 5 17 39N16 74w39 4:58:36
Marshalls Corner 11 12 40N23 74w46 4:59:04
Marshalltown 17 12 39N38 75w27 5:01:48
Martins Beach 3 1 40N02 74w53 4:59:32
Martinsville 18 17 40N36 74w34 4:58:16
Maryland 15 12 40N08 74w20 4:57:20
Masonville 3 17 39N59 74w52 4:59:28
Matawan 13 2 40N25 74w14 4:56:56
Maurice River 6 17 39N17 74w56 4:59:44
Mauricetown 6 17 39N17 74w58 4:59:52
Maxim 13 1 40N06 74w13 4:56:52
Mayetta 15 2 39N38 74w18 4:57:12
Mayfair At Marlton 3 17 39N54 74w55 4:59:40
Mayfair Gardens 8 17 39N45 75w04 5:00:16
Mays Landing 1 17 39N27 74w44 4:58:56
Mayville 5 13 39N05 74w50 4:59:20
Maywood 2 1 40N54 74w04 4:56:16
McAfee 19 17 41N11 74w32 4:58:08
McCoys Corner 19 1 41N13 74w36 4:58:24
McDonoughs 12 1 40N29 74w17 4:57:08
McGuire 3 3 40N02 74w35 4:58:20
McGuire Air Force Base 3 3 40N01 74w36 4:58:24
McKee City 1 2 39N26 74w37 4:58:28
Meadowbrook 4 2 39N57 75w03 5:00:12
Meadowbrook Village 15 12 40N08 74w20 4:57:20

NEW JERSEY

Meadowview 9 1 40N47 74w01 4:56:04
Meadow Village 7 1 40N51 74w14 4:56:56
Mechanicsville 12 1 40N29 74w17 4:57:08
Medford 3 17 39N54 74w50 4:59:20
Medford Farms 3 12 39N52 74w45 4:59:00
Medford Lakes 3 17 39N52 74w48 4:59:12
Melrose 3 17 39N53 74w49 4:59:16
Melrose 12 1 40N29 74w17 4:57:08
Menantico 6 2 39N26 75w01 5:00:04
Mendham 14 14 40N47 74w36 4:58:24
Menlo Park 12 17 40N32 74w22 4:57:28
Menlo Park Mall 12 17 40N32 74w22 4:57:28
Menlo Park Terrace 12 17 40N32 74w22 4:57:28
Mercerville 11 1 40N14 74w41 4:58:44
Merchantville 4 2 39N57 75w03 5:00:12
Meriden 14 1 40N54 74w25 4:57:40
Metedeconk 15 12 40N02 74w07 4:56:28
Metedeconk Park 15 12 40N02 74w07 4:56:28
Metedeconk Pines 15 12 40N02 74w07 4:56:28
Metuchen 12 17 40N32 74w22 4:57:28
Meyersville 14 17 40N41 74w28 4:57:52
Miami Beach 5 12 39N02 74w56 4:59:44
Mickleton 8 2 39N48 75w14 5:00:56
Middle 5 13 39N04 74w51 4:59:24
Middlebush 18 1 40N29 74w29 4:57:56
Middlesex 12 17 40N35 74w30 4:58:00
Middletown 5 12 39N16 74w47 4:59:08
Middletown 13 12 40N24 74w08 4:56:32
Middletown 14 1 40N54 74w35 4:58:20
Middle Valley 14 12 40N47 74w46 4:59:04
Middleville 19 12 41N03 74w52 4:59:28
Midland Park 2 2 41N00 74w09 4:56:36
Midstreams 15 12 40N02 74w07 4:56:28
Midtown 7 1 40N44 74w11 4:56:44
Midvale 16 1 41N02 74w18 4:57:12
Milford 10 12 40N34 75w06 5:00:24
Military Ocean Terminal 9 1 40N40 74w07 4:56:28
Millbrook 14 1 40N52 74w34 4:58:16
Millbrook 21 12 40N56 75w06 5:00:24
Millburn 7 1 40N43 74w19 4:57:16
Millhurst 13 12 40N15 74w21 4:57:24
Millington 14 12 40N40 74w31 4:58:04
Millside Heights 3 17 40N02 74w57 4:59:48
Millstone 18 12 40N30 74w35 4:58:20
Milltown 12 1 40N27 74w27 4:57:48
Milltown 20 1 40N42 74w19 4:57:16
Millville 6 2 39N24 75w02 5:00:08
Milmay 1 12 39N26 74w52 4:59:28
Milton 14 12 41N03 74w29 4:57:56
Mimosa Lake 3 17 39N54 74w55 4:59:40
Mine Brook 18 12 40N41 74w38 4:58:32
Mine Hill 14 14 40N53 74w36 4:58:24
Minotola 1 17 39N31 74w57 4:59:48
Miramar 5 17 39N16 74w39 4:58:36
Mizpah 1 12 39N29 74w50 4:59:20
Money Island 15 1 39N56 74w13 4:56:52
Monitor 9 1 40N47 74w01 4:56:04
Monksville 16 1 41N02 74w18 4:57:12
Monmouth 13 1 40N19 74w04 4:56:16
Monmouth Beach 13 2 40N20 73w59 4:55:56
Monmouth Hills 13 1 40N24 73w59 4:55:56
Monmouth Junction 12 12 40N23 74w33 4:58:12
Monmouth Park 13 1 40N19 74w01 4:56:04
Monroe 14 1 40N49 74w25 4:57:40
Monroe 19 17 41N07 74w38 4:58:32
Monroeville 17 1 39N38 75w10 5:00:40
Montague 19 12 41N17 74w44 4:58:56
Montana 21 17 40N41 75w10 5:00:40
Montclair 7 1 40N49 74w13 4:56:52
Montgomery 18 12 40N26 74w40 4:58:40
Montvale 2 1 41N03 74w02 4:56:08
Montville 14 1 40N55 74w23 4:57:32
Moonachie 2 1 40N51 74w04 4:56:16
Moores Corner 17 17 39N34 75w28 5:01:52
Moores Meadows 3 12 39N56 74w45 4:59:00
Moorestown 3 17 39N58 74w57 4:59:48
Morehousetown 7 1 40N47 74w19 4:57:16
Morgan 12 1 40N29 74w17 4:57:08
Morganville 13 2 40N23 74w14 4:56:56
Morris 4 2 39N58 75w03 5:00:12
Morris 14 17 40N48 74w29 4:57:56
Morris Beach 1 17 39N27 74w44 4:58:56
Morris Park 21 17 40N41 75w10 5:00:40
Morris Plains 14 17 40N50 74w29 4:57:56
Morristown 12 2 40N25 74w14 4:56:56
Morristown 14 17 40N48 74w29 4:57:56
Morrisville 4 2 39N58 75w03 5:00:12
Morsemere 2 1 40N50 74w00 4:56:00
Morses Creek 20 1 40N38 74w15 4:57:00
Mountain Lake 21 17 40N50 75w05 5:00:20
Mountain Lakes 14 1 40N54 74w26 4:57:44
Mountainside 20 1 40N41 74w21 4:57:24
Mountain Spring 16 16 41N02 74w23 4:57:32
Mountain Spring Lakes 16 16 41N00 74w21 4:57:24
Mountain Station 7 2 40N45 74w16 4:57:04
Mountain View 16 17 40N57 74w15 4:57:00
Mountainville 10 13 40N38 74w50 4:59:20
Mount Airy 10 12 40N23 74w51 4:59:24
Mount Arlington 14 12 40N56 74w38 4:58:32
Mount Bethel 12 40N38 74w31 4:58:04
Mount Ephraim 4 2 39N53 75w05 5:00:20
Mount Fern 14 14 40N52 74w35 4:58:20
Mount Freedom 14 14 40N50 74w34 4:58:16
Mount Hermon 21 16 40N59 74w57 4:59:48

NEW JERSEY

Mount Holly 3 1 40N00 74W47 4:59:08
Mount Hope 14 1 40N56 74W33 4:58:12
Mount Hope Mineral Junction 14
1 40N54 74W35 4:58:20
Mount Laurel 3 17 39N58 74W53 4:59:32
Mount Olive 14 1 40N51 74W44 4:58:56
Mount Pleasant 5 12 39N16 74W47 4:59:08
Mount Pleasant 10
12 40N34 75W06 5:00:24
Mount Rose 11 12 40N23 74W46 4:59:04
Mount Royal 8 2 39N49 75W13 5:00:52
Mount Salem 19 1 41N13 74W36 4:58:24
Mount Tabor 14 12 40N53 74W29 4:57:56
Muhlenberg 20 2 40N37 74W25 4:57:40
Mullica 1 12 39N36 74W42 4:58:48
Mullica Hill 8 17 39N44 75W14 5:00:56
Murray Hill 20 1 40N42 74W24 4:57:36
Myrtle Grove 19 12 41N03 74W45 4:59:00
Mystic Islands 15 2 39N36 74W20 4:57:20
Natco 13 2 40N26 74W11 4:56:44
National Park 8 2 39N52 75W11 5:00:44
Naughright 14 12 40N47 74W46 4:59:04
Navesink 13 1 40N24 74W02 4:56:08
Navesink Beach 13 1 40N22 73W59 4:55:56
Nejecho Beach 15 12 40N02 74W07 4:56:28
Neptune 13 1 40N13 74W02 4:56:08
Nesco 1 2 39N56 75W02 5:00:08
Neshanic 18 2 40N31 74W44 4:58:56
Netcong 14 1 40N54 74W42 4:58:48
Netherwood 20 2 40N38 74W24 4:57:36
New Albany 3 2 40N00 75W00 5:00:00
Newark 7 1 40N44 74W10 4:56:40
Newark Heights 7 1 40N44 74W16 4:57:04
Newbakers Corners 21
16 40N59 74W57 4:59:48
New Bedford 13 1 40N11 74W02 4:56:08
Newbolds Corner 3 1 40N00 74W47 4:59:08
New Bridge 2 1 40N56 74W01 4:56:04
New Brooklyn 4 1 39N43 74W58 4:59:52
New Brunswick 12 1 40N30 74W27 4:57:48
New Brunswick Heights 12
1 40N34 74W27 4:57:48
New Canton 11 12 40N11 74W35 4:58:20
New Durham 9 1 40N47 74W01 4:56:04
New Durham 12 1 40N34 74W27 4:57:48
New Egypt 15 12 40N04 74W32 4:58:08
Newfield 8 17 39N33 75W01 5:00:04
Newfoundland 14 12 41N03 74W26 4:57:44
New Gretna 3 17 39N35 74W28 4:57:52
New Hampton 10 13 40N42 74W57 4:59:48
New Hanover 3 3 40N03 74W34 4:58:16
New Italy 6 1 39N29 75W01 5:00:04
New Jersey & New York Jct 2
1 40N50 74W06 4:56:24
New Lisbon 3 3 39N58 74W38 4:58:32
New Milford 2 1 40N57 74W01 4:56:04
New Monmouth 13 1 40N25 74W06 4:56:24
Newport 6 12 39N18 75W11 5:00:44
Newport 10 13 40N42 74W57 4:59:48
New Providence 20 1 40N43 74W22 4:57:28
New Sharon 12 40N12 74W33 4:58:12
New Sharon 8 17 39N45 75W04 5:00:16
New Shrewsbury 13 1 40N17 74W06 4:56:24
Newton 19 12 41N03 74W45 4:59:00
Newton Heights 12
12 40N25 74W23 4:57:32
Newtonville 1 17 39N34 74W52 4:59:28
New Vernon 14 12 40N45 74W30 4:58:00
New Village 21 13 40N42 75W07 5:00:28
New York & Greenwood Lake Ju 9
1 40N46 74W09 4:56:36
Nixon 12 17 40N32 74W22 4:57:28
Norma 17 1 39N29 75W05 5:00:20
Normandie 13 1 40N22 73W59 4:55:56
Normandy Beach 15
12 40N00 74W04 4:56:16
Normandy Harbor 15
12 40N00 74W04 4:56:16
North 7 1 40N46 74W10 4:56:40
North Arlington 2 1 40N48 74W08 4:56:32
North Asbury Park 13
1 40N14 74W01 4:56:04
North Beach 15 17 39N37 74W12 4:56:48
North Beach Haven 15
17 39N37 74W12 4:56:48
North Bergen 9 1 40N48 74W01 4:56:04
North Branch 18 2 40N36 74W41 4:58:44
North Brunswick 12
1 40N29 74W27 4:57:48
North Caldwell 7 1 40N52 74W16 4:57:04
North Cape May 5 1 38N59 74W57 4:59:48
North Cedarville 6
12 39N20 75W12 5:00:48
North Center 7 1 40N48 74W11 4:56:44
North Church 19 17 41N06 74W35 4:58:20
North Church Estates 19
17 41N09 74W35 4:58:20
North Crosswicks 11
1 40N09 74W39 4:58:36
North Dennis 5 12 39N12 74W49 4:59:16
North Edison 12 17 40N32 74W22 4:57:28
North Elizabeth 20
1 40N40 74W13 4:56:52
Northfield 1 2 39N22 74W33 4:58:12
Northfield 7 1 40N47 74W19 4:57:16
North Hackensack 2
1 40N56 74W02 4:56:08
North Haledon 16 4 40N58 74W11 4:56:44
North Hanover 3 12 40N04 74W24 4:57:36
North Hawthorne 16
4 40N55 74W10 4:56:40
North Highlands Beach 5
12 39N02 74W56 4:59:44
North Long Branch 13
1 40N18 74W00 4:56:00

North Merchantville 4
2 39N57 75W03 5:00:12
Northmont 4 2 39N53 75W05 5:00:20
North Plainfield 18
2 40N38 74W26 4:57:44
North Port Norris 6
12 39N15 75W02 5:00:08
North Stelton 12 1 40N34 74W27 4:57:48
Northvale 2 12 41N01 73W57 4:55:48
North Vineland 6 1 39N29 75W01 5:00:04
North Wildwood 5 1 39N00 74W48 4:59:12
Norton 10 13 40N42 74W57 4:59:48
Nortonville 8 10 39N45 75W19 5:01:16
Norwood 2 17 41N00 73W58 4:55:52
Nottingham 11 1 40N14 74W42 4:58:48
Nutley 7 5 40N49 74W09 4:56:36
Oakdale 3 1 40N00 74W47 4:59:08
Oak Glen 13 12 40N14 74W13 4:56:52
Oak Hill 13 2 40N24 74W07 4:56:28
Oakhurst 13 1 40N16 74W01 4:56:04
Oakland 2 17 41N02 74W14 4:56:56
Oaklyn 4 2 39N54 75W05 5:00:20
Oak Ridge 16 12 41N03 74W29 4:57:56
Oak Ridge Lake 14
12 41N03 74W29 4:57:56
Oak Shades 13 2 40N25 74W14 4:56:56
Oak Tree 12 17 40N32 74W22 4:57:28
Oak Valley 8 2 39N48 75W08 5:00:32
Oakwood 3 17 39N53 74W49 4:59:16
Oakwood Beach 17 17 39N34 75W28 5:01:52
Oakwood Park 20 1 40N42 74W24 4:57:36
Ocean 13 1 40N14 74W01 4:56:04
Ocean Beach 15 12 39N58 74W04 4:56:16
Ocean City 5 1 39N17 74W35 4:58:20
Ocean Gate 15 12 39N56 74W08 4:56:32
Ocean Grove 13 1 40N13 74W01 4:56:04
Ocean Heights 1 1 39N21 74W35 4:58:20
Oceanport 13 1 40N19 74W03 4:56:12
Ocean View 5 2 39N10 74W44 4:58:56
Oceanville 1 2 39N28 74W28 4:57:52
Ogdensburg 19 17 41N05 74W36 4:58:24
Old Bridge 12 12 40N25 74W22 4:57:28
Old Charleston Woods 4
2 39N49 75W06 5:00:24
Old Forge Village 14
17 40N48 74W29 4:57:56
Old Manor 13 2 40N26 74W13 4:56:52
Oldmans 17 1 39N45 75W25 5:01:40
Old Orchard 4 2 39N49 75W06 5:00:24
Old Tappan 2 1 41N01 73W59 4:55:56
Oldwick 10 12 40N40 74W45 4:59:00
Olivet 17 1 39N36 75W10 5:00:40
Oradell 2 1 40N57 74W02 4:56:08
Orange 7 1 40N46 74W14 4:56:56
Orchard Center 6 1 39N28 75W15 5:01:00
Orchard Heights 12
12 40N25 74W23 4:57:32
Orchard View 3 1 40N05 74W51 4:59:24
Orston 4 2 39N53 75W04 5:00:16
Ortley Beach 15 12 39N57 74W05 4:56:20
Osage 4 2 39N50 75W01 5:00:04
Osbornsville 15 12 40N02 74W07 4:56:28
Othello 6 1 39N28 75W15 5:01:00
Outcalt 12 12 40N21 74W26 4:57:44
Outwater 2 1 40N53 74W06 4:56:24
Overbrook 4 1 39N48 75W00 5:00:00
Overbrook 7 1 40N51 74W14 4:56:56
Owens 19 1 41N13 74W36 4:58:24
Oxford 21 17 40N49 75W00 5:00:00
Oyster Creek 1 17 39N30 74W26 4:57:44
Packanack Lake 16
17 40N57 74W15 4:57:00
Pahaquarry 21 16 41N02 75W02 5:00:08
Palatine 17 1 39N36 75W10 5:00:40
Palermo 5 17 39N16 74W39 4:58:36
Palisade 2 1 40N51 73W58 4:55:52
Palisades Park 2 1 40N50 74W00 4:56:00
Palmyra 3 2 40N01 75W01 5:00:04
Pamrapo 9 1 40N40 74W07 4:56:28
Pancoast 1 17 39N31 74W57 4:59:48
Panther Lake 19 12 40N59 74W45 4:59:00
Paradise Lakes 17
17 39N34 75W22 5:01:28
Paramus 2 1 40N55 74W04 4:56:16
Park 16 4 40N55 74W09 4:56:36
Parker 14 12 40N47 74W46 4:59:04
Parkertown 15 2 39N36 74W20 4:57:20
Park Ridge 2 1 41N02 74W02 4:56:08
Park Ridge Farms 3
1 40N09 74W42 4:58:48
Parkside 21 17 40N41 75W10 5:00:40
Park Village 20 1 40N39 74W18 4:57:12
Parkway Pines 13 1 40N06 74W13 4:56:52
Parkway Village 11
1 40N15 74W48 4:59:12
Parlin 12 2 40N28 74W20 4:57:20
Parry 3 2 40N00 75W00 5:00:00
Parsippany 14 1 40N52 74W26 4:57:44
Pasadena 15 12 39N57 74W23 4:57:32
Passaic 16 1 40N51 74W07 4:56:28
Passaic Junction 2
1 40N54 74W05 4:56:20
Passaic Park 16 1 40N52 74W08 4:56:32
Paterson 16 4 40N55 74W11 4:56:44
Patricks Corner 12
12 40N25 74W23 4:57:32
Pattenburg 10 13 40N42 75W01 5:00:04
Paulina 21 16 40N59 74W57 4:59:48
Paulins Kill 19 12 41N03 74W45 4:59:00
Paulsboro 8 2 39N50 75W15 5:01:00
Peahala Park 15 17 39N37 74W12 4:56:48
Peapack 18 12 40N43 74W40 4:58:40
Pedricktown 17 17 39N46 75W24 5:01:36
Peermont 5 2 39N06 74W44 4:58:56

Pelican Island 15
12 39N57 74W05 4:56:20
Pellettown 19 17 41N08 74W44 4:58:56
Pemberton 3 3 39N58 74W41 4:58:44
Pemberton Heights 3
3 39N58 74W41 4:58:44
Penbryn 4 17 39N49 74W58 4:59:52
Pennington 11 12 40N20 74W47 4:59:08
Pennsauken 4 2 39N57 75W03 5:00:12
Pennsauken 4 2 39N57 75W03 5:00:12
Penns Beach 17 12 39N39 75W31 5:02:04
Penns Grove 17 1 39N44 75W28 5:01:52
Penns Neck 2 40N20 74W38 4:58:32
Pennsville 17 12 39N39 75W31 5:02:04
Penny Pot 1 2 39N56 75W02 5:00:08
Penton 17 17 39N34 75W28 5:01:52
Penwell 10 12 40N47 74W55 4:59:40
Peppermill Farms 4
2 39N49 75W06 5:00:24
Pequannock 14 17 40N56 74W17 4:57:08
Perrineville 13 2 40N14 74W27 4:57:48
Perth Amboy 12 1 40N31 74W16 4:57:04
Petersburg 5 17 41N01 74W32 4:58:08
Pettys Island 4 2 39N58 75W03 5:00:12
Phalanx 13 12 40N17 74W11 4:56:44
Phillipsburg 21 17 40N42 75W12 5:00:48
Phoenix 12 17 40N32 74W22 4:57:28
Picatinny 14 1 40N53 74W34 4:58:16
Pierces Point 5 13 39N05 74W50 4:59:20
Piersonville 3 12 40N12 74W40 4:58:40
Pilesgrove 17 17 39N39 75W19 5:01:16
Pine Acres 8 2 39N48 75W08 5:00:32
Pine Beach 15 1 39N56 74W10 4:56:40
Pine Brook 13 1 40N19 74W04 4:56:16
Pine Brook 14 1 40N52 74W20 4:57:20
Pine Cliff Lake 16
12 41N08 74W22 4:57:28
Pine Grove 3 17 39N54 74W55 4:59:40
Pine Hill 4 17 39N47 74W59 4:59:56
Pinehurst 1 2 39N26 74W30 4:58:00
Pine Lake Park 15 1 39N56 74W13 4:56:52
Pines Lake 16 17 40N57 74W15 4:57:00
Pine Terrace 15 1 39N56 74W13 4:56:52
Pine Valley 4 1 39N47 75W00 5:00:00
Pinewald 15 12 39N55 74W09 4:56:36
Piscataway 12 17 40N34 74W28 4:57:52
Pitman 8 2 39N44 75W08 5:00:32
Pittsgrove 17 12 39N32 75W08 5:00:32
Pittstown 10 13 40N35 74W58 4:59:52
Plainfield 20 2 40N37 74W25 4:57:40
Plainsboro 12 2 40N20 74W36 4:58:24
Plauderville 2 1 40N53 74W06 4:56:24
Plaza Park 3 1 40N05 74W51 4:59:24
Pleasant Grove 14
12 40N47 74W46 4:59:04
Pleasant Grove 15
12 40N08 74W20 4:57:20
Pleasant Mills 1 2 39N56 75W02 5:00:08
Pleasant Plains 15
1 39N56 74W13 4:56:52
Pleasant Run 3 2 40N00 75W00 5:00:00
Pleasant Run 10 1 40N31 74W52 4:59:28
Pleasant Terrace 6
12 39N13 74W57 4:59:48
Pleasant Valley 21
13 40N45 74W59 4:59:56
Pleasantville 1 2 39N24 74W32 4:58:08
Pleasantville 6 1 39N29 75W01 5:00:04
Pleasure Bay 13 1 40N18 74W00 4:56:00
Pluckemin 18 12 40N39 74W38 4:58:32
Plumbsock 19 1 41N13 74W36 4:58:24
Plumsted 15 12 40N05 74W30 4:58:00
Pohatcong 21 17 40N40 75W10 5:00:40
Pointers 17 17 39N34 75W28 5:01:52
Point Pleasant 15 2 40N05 74W03 4:56:12
Point Pleasant Beach 15
2 40N05 74W03 4:56:12
Polkville 21 12 40N56 75W06 5:00:24
Pomona 1 17 39N29 74W35 4:58:20
Pompton Junction 16
1 41N00 74W17 4:57:08
Pompton Lakes 16 1 41N00 74W17 4:57:08
Pompton Plains 14 1 40N58 74W18 4:57:12
Porchtown 8 17 39N33 75W01 5:00:04
Port-au-Peck 13 1 40N19 74W01 4:56:04
Port Colden 21 13 40N45 74W59 4:59:56
Port Elizabeth 6 17 39N19 74W59 4:59:56
Portertown 17 17 39N39 75W20 5:01:20
Port Johnson 9 1 40N40 74W07 4:56:28
Port Monmouth 13 17 40N26 74W07 4:56:28
Port Morris 14 1 40N54 74W40 4:58:40
Port Murray 21 12 40N47 74W55 4:59:40
Port Norris 6 12 39N15 75W02 5:00:08
Port Reading 12 1 40N34 74W16 4:57:04
Port Reading Junction 18
2 40N32 74W36 4:58:24
Port Republic 1 2 39N27 74W28 4:57:52
Port Warren 21 13 40N42 75W07 5:00:28
Possumtown 12 1 40N34 74W27 4:57:48
Potter 12 17 40N32 74W22 4:57:28
Potterstown 10 13 40N38 74W50 4:59:20
Pottersville 18 12 40N43 74W44 4:58:56
Powerville 14 1 40N54 74W25 4:57:40
Preakness 16 17 40N57 74W15 4:57:00
Presidential Lakes 3
12 39N58 74W34 4:58:16
Princeton 11 2 40N21 74W39 4:58:36
Princeton Junction 11
2 40N19 74W37 4:58:28
Prospect Heights 11
1 40N16 74W46 4:59:04
Prospect Highlands 11
1 40N16 74W46 4:59:04
Prospect Park 11 1 40N16 74W46 4:59:04
Prospect Park 16 4 40N56 74W10 4:56:40

Prospect Plains 12
1 40N19 74w29 4:57:56
Prospect Point 14 1 40N54 74w35 4:58:20
Prospertown 13 12 40N08 74w32 4:58:08
Pullentown 13 12 40N10 74w33 4:58:12
Quaker Gardens 11 1 40N14 74w42 4:58:48
Quakertown 10 13 40N34 74w57 4:59:48
Quarryville 19 1 41N13 74w36 4:58:24
Quinton 17 17 39N31 75w22 5:01:28
Radburn 2 1 40N56 74w07 4:56:28
Rahway 20 2 40N37 74w16 4:57:04
Rainbow Lakes 14 12 40N53 74w29 4:57:56
Raines Corner 17 1 39N44 75w28 5:01:52
Ralston 14 14 40N47 74w36 4:58:24
Ramblewood 3 17 39N56 74w57 4:59:48
Ramsey 2 12 41N04 74w09 4:56:36
Ramseysburg 21 12 40N56 75w06 5:00:24
Rancocas 3 1 40N01 74w52 4:59:28
Rancocas Heights 3
1 40N00 74w47 4:59:08
Rancocas Woods 3 1 40N00 74w47 4:59:08
Randolph 14 14 40N51 74w35 4:58:20
Raritan 18 2 40N34 74w38 4:58:32
Raritan Manor 12 17 40N32 74w22 4:57:28
Raritan River RR Junction 12
1 40N29 74w17 4:57:08
Raven Rock 10 1 40N24 74w59 4:59:56
Readington 10 12 40N34 74w44 4:58:56
Reaville 10 1 40N31 74w52 4:59:28
Rebel Hill 18 1 40N42 74w33 4:58:12
Red Bank 13 2 40N21 74w05 4:56:20
Red Lion 3 12 39N56 74w45 4:59:00
Red Lion 12 1 40N29 74w27 4:57:48
Reed Crossing 4 17 39N49 74w58 4:59:52
Reeds Beach 5 13 39N05 74w50 4:59:20
Reevytown 13 1 40N12 74w02 4:56:08
Repaupo 8 10 39N48 75w18 5:01:12
Retreat 3 12 39N56 74w45 4:59:00
Richland 1 17 39N30 74w52 4:59:28
Richwood 8 1 39N43 75w10 5:00:40
Ridge Acres 18 1 40N42 74w33 4:58:12
Ridgefield 2 1 40N50 74w01 4:56:04
Ridgefield Park 2 1 40N51 74w02 4:56:08
Ridgeway 15 1 40N01 74w19 4:57:16
Ridgewood 2 2 40N59 74w07 4:56:28
Riegelsville 21 12 40N34 75w06 5:00:24
Ringoes 10 12 40N26 74w52 4:59:28
Ringwood 16 12 41N07 74w15 4:57:00
Rio Grande 5 1 39N01 74w53 4:59:32
Ritz 2 1 40N53 74w06 4:56:24
River Bank 15 1 39N56 74w10 4:56:40
Riverdale 14 1 41N00 74w18 4:57:12
River Edge 2 1 40N55 74w02 4:56:08
River Edge Manor 2
1 40N56 74w01 4:56:04
Riverside 3 2 40N02 74w58 4:59:52
Riverside Park 3 2 40N02 74w59 4:59:56
Riverton 3 2 40N01 75w01 5:00:04
River Vale 2 1 41N01 74w01 4:56:04
Riverview Manor 12
1 40N34 74w27 4:57:48
Riviera Beach 15 1 40N06 74w06 4:56:24
Roadstown 6 1 39N28 75w15 5:01:00
Robbinsville 11 12 40N13 74w37 4:58:28
Robert Barry Apartments 8
1 39N50 75w09 5:00:36
Robertsville 13 12 40N21 74w17 4:57:08
Robin Estates 15 12 40N08 74w20 4:57:20
Robin Hood Homes 3
17 40N03 74w56 4:59:44
Rochelle Park 2 1 40N54 74w05 4:56:20
Rochelle Park 2 1 40N54 74w05 4:56:20
Rockaway 14 12 40N54 74w31 4:58:04
Rockaway Neck 14 1 40N52 74w25 4:57:40
Rockaway Valley 14
1 40N54 74w25 4:57:40
Rockleigh 2 12 41N00 73w56 4:55:44
Rockport 21 1 40N52 74w50 4:59:20
Rock Ridge Lake 14
12 40N53 74w29 4:57:56
Rocktown 10 12 40N26 74w52 4:59:28
Rocky Hill 18 2 40N24 74w38 4:58:32
Roebling 3 12 40N07 74w47 4:59:08
Roosevelt 13 2 40N13 74w29 4:57:56
Roosevelt City 15
12 39N57 74w23 4:57:32
Roosevelt Park 6 2 39N26 75w01 5:00:04
Rosedale 1 2 39N56 75w02 5:00:08
Rose Hill Heights 21
17 40N41 75w10 5:00:40
Roseland 7 1 40N49 74w18 4:57:12
Roselle 20 1 40N40 74w15 4:57:00
Rosemont 10 12 40N26 74w59 4:59:56
Rosemont 11 1 40N14 74w42 4:58:48
Rosenhayn 6 12 39N29 75w08 5:00:32
Roseville 7 1 40N45 74w11 4:56:44
Roseville 19 12 40N59 74w45 4:59:00
Ross Corner 19 17 41N08 74w44 4:58:56
Rowe Street 7 1 40N48 74w11 4:56:44
Roxburg 21 17 40N41 75w10 5:00:40
Roxbury 14 14 40N52 74w39 4:58:36
Royal Estates 12 12 40N25 74w23 4:57:32
Rudeville 19 17 41N09 74w33 4:58:12
Rumson 13 1 40N23 74w00 4:56:00
Runnemede 4 2 39N51 75w05 5:00:20
Russia 14 12 41N03 74w29 4:57:56
Rutherford 2 2 40N50 74w06 4:56:24
Saddle Brook 2 1 40N54 74w06 4:56:24
Saddle River 2 1 41N02 74w06 4:56:24
Saint Cloud 7 1 40N47 74w15 4:57:00
Saint Josephs Village 2
1 41N00 73w57 4:55:48
Salem 17 17 39N34 75w28 5:01:52
Salem Hills 13 1 40N06 74w13 4:56:52
Sand Brook 10 1 40N24 74w59 4:59:56
Sands Point 13 1 40N19 74w01 4:56:04
Sandy Point 15 12 40N02 74w07 4:56:28
Sandyston 19 12 41N13 74w49 4:59:16
Saxton Falls 21 1 40N55 74w42 4:58:48
Sayres Neck 6 12 39N20 75w12 5:00:48
Sayreville 12 17 40N28 74w22 4:57:28
Sayreville Junction 12
2 40N28 74w20 4:57:20
Sayre Woods 12 2 40N28 74w20 4:57:20
Schellengers Landing 5
1 38N56 74w55 4:59:40
Schooleys Mountian 14
1 40N48 74w49 4:59:16
Scobeyville 13 12 40N18 74w08 4:56:32
Scotch Bonnet 5 13 39N05 74w50 4:59:20
Scotch Plains 20 2 40N39 74w24 4:57:36
Scudders Falls 11 1 40N15 74w48 4:59:12
Scullville 1 17 39N27 74w44 4:58:56
Seaboard 9 1 40N46 74w09 4:56:36
Sea Breeze 6 1 39N28 75w15 5:01:00
Sea Bright 13 2 40N22 73w59 4:55:56
Seabrook 6 1 39N28 75w15 5:01:00
Seabrook Farms 6 12 39N30 75w13 5:00:52
Sea Girt 13 1 40N08 74w02 4:56:08
Sea Isle City 5 2 39N09 74w42 4:58:48
Seaside Heights 15
12 39N56 74w05 4:56:20
Seaside Park 15 12 39N55 74w05 4:56:20
Seaview Park 1 2 39N26 74w30 4:58:00
Seaville 5 2 39N10 74w44 4:58:56
Secaucus 9 2 40N47 74w04 4:56:16
Sedgefield 14 17 40N50 74w29 4:57:56
Sergeantsville 10
12 40N27 74w57 4:59:48
Serviss Acres 12 12 40N25 74w23 4:57:32
Seven Stars 15 1 40N06 74w13 4:56:52
Sewaren 12 1 40N33 74w16 4:57:04
Sewell 8 2 39N46 75w09 5:00:36
Shafto Corners 13
12 40N14 74w13 4:56:52
Shamong 3 12 39N47 74w45 4:59:00
Shark River Hills 13
1 40N11 74w03 4:56:12
Sharptown 17 17 39N40 75w22 5:01:28
Shaw Crest 5 11 39N00 74w49 4:59:16
Shelter Cove 15 1 39N56 74w13 4:56:52
Sherwood Green 8 1 39N49 75w08 5:00:32
Shiloh 6 12 39N28 75w18 5:01:12
Shiloh Crossing 6 1 39N28 75w15 5:01:00
Shimer Manor 21 17 40N41 75w10 5:00:40
Ship Bottom 15 12 39N39 74w11 4:56:44
Shippenport 14 1 40N54 74w40 4:58:40
Shirley 17 1 39N36 75w10 5:00:40
Shongum 14 14 40N50 74w34 4:58:16
Shore Acres 15 12 40N02 74w07 4:56:28
Shore Crest 12 2 40N35 74w19 4:57:16
Shore Hills 14 1 40N55 74w39 4:58:36
Short Hills 7 1 40N43 74w18 4:57:12
Shrewsbury 13 1 40N19 74w04 4:56:16
Shrewsbury Township 13
1 40N19 74w04 4:56:16
Sicklerville 4 1 39N44 74w58 4:59:52
Sidney 10 13 40N35 74w58 4:59:52
Siloam 13 1 40N15 74w17 4:57:08
Silver Bay 15 1 39N56 74w13 4:56:52
Silver Lake 7 1 40N48 74w10 4:56:40
Silver Lake 21 16 40N59 74w57 4:59:48
Silver Springs 14 1 40N54 74w40 4:58:40
Silverton 15 1 39N56 74w13 4:56:52
Sim Place 3 1 39N45 74w13 4:56:52
Singac 16 4 40N54 74w12 4:56:48
Sinnickson Landing 17
17 39N34 75w28 5:01:52
Six Points 17 1 39N28 75w15 5:01:00
Skillman 18 12 40N25 74w43 4:58:52
Skylands 16 12 41N06 74w16 4:57:04
Sky Line Lake 16 1 41N02 74w18 4:57:12
Slackwood 11 1 40N15 74w44 4:58:56
Sloop Creek Estates 15
12 39N55 74w09 4:56:36
Sloping Hills 18 1 40N42 74w33 4:58:12
Smalleytown 18 17 40N39 74w29 4:57:56
Smithburg 13 12 40N13 74w21 4:57:24
Smiths Mills 16 16 41N00 74w21 4:57:24
Smith Tract 15 17 39N37 74w12 4:56:48
Smithville 1 2 39N26 74w30 4:58:00
Smithville 3 1 40N00 74w47 4:59:08
Smoke Rise 14 16 41N00 74w21 4:57:24
Snow Hill 4 2 39N52 75w02 5:00:08
Soho 7 1 40N48 74w10 4:56:40
Somerdale 4 2 39N51 75w01 5:00:04
Somerset 18 1 40N29 74w28 4:57:52
Somers Point 1 1 39N19 74w36 4:58:24
Somerville 18 3 40N03 74w38 4:58:32
South 7 1 40N43 74w11 4:56:44
South Amboy 12 2 40N29 74w18 4:57:12
Southampton 3 12 39N55 74w43 4:58:52
Southard 13 1 40N09 74w14 4:56:56
South Belmar 13 1 40N10 74w02 4:56:08
South Bound Brook 12
17 40N34 74w32 4:58:08
South Branch 18 2 40N32 74w42 4:58:48
South Brunswick 12
12 40N23 74w32 4:58:08
South Camden 4 2 39N55 75w06 5:00:24
South Dennis 5 12 39N11 74w49 4:59:16
South Egg Harbor 1
8 39N33 74w37 4:58:28
South Glassboro 8 1 39N42 75w07 5:00:28
South Hackensack 2
1 40N52 74w03 4:56:12
South Harrison 8 12 39N42 75w16 5:01:04
South Kearny 9 1 40N46 74w09 4:56:36
South Lakewood 15 1 40N06 74w13 4:56:52

NEW JERSEY

South Livingston 7
1 40N47 74w19 4:57:16
South Mantoloking 15
2 40N03 74w03 4:56:12
South Merchantville 4
2 39N57 75w03 5:00:12
South Ogdensburg 19
17 41N05 74w36 4:58:24
South Old Bridge 12
12 40N24 74w21 4:57:24
South Orange 7 1 40N45 74w15 4:57:00
South Paterson 16 1 40N54 74w09 4:56:36
South Pemberton 3 3 39N58 74w41 4:58:44
South Plainfield 12
2 40N34 74w25 4:57:40
South River 12 12 40N27 74w23 4:57:32
South Seaside Park 15
12 39N56 74w05 4:56:20
South Seaville 5 12 39N11 74w46 4:59:04
South Toms River 15
1 39N56 74w12 4:56:48
South Vineland 6 1 39N29 75w01 5:00:04
South Westville 8 1 39N50 75w09 5:00:36
Southwest Vineland 6
1 39N29 75w01 5:00:04
South Woodstown 17
17 39N39 75w20 5:01:20
Sparta 19 17 41N02 74w38 4:58:32
Sparta Lake 19 17 41N03 74w34 4:58:16
Sperry Springs 19 1 40N56 74w40 4:58:40
Spotswood 12 12 40N23 74w23 4:57:32
Spray Beach 15 17 39N37 74w12 4:56:48
Springdale 17 40N36 74w31 4:58:04
Springdale 4 2 39N49 75w06 5:00:24
Springdale 19 12 41N03 74w45 4:59:00
Springfield 20 1 40N43 74w19 4:57:16
Spring Gardens 11 1 40N14 74w47 4:59:08
Spring Lake 13 1 40N09 74w02 4:56:08
Spring Lake Heights 13
1 40N09 74w03 4:56:12
Spring Side 1 40N04 74w51 4:59:24
Springside 3 1 40N04 74w51 4:59:24
Springtown 6 1 39N28 75w15 5:01:00
Springtown 21 17 40N41 75w10 5:00:40
Springville 3 17 39N58 74w56 4:59:44
Stafford 15 12 39N41 74w16 4:57:04
Staffordville 15 2 39N38 74w18 4:57:12
Stanhope 19 1 40N54 74w42 4:58:48
Stanton 10 13 40N35 74w50 4:59:20
Stanton Station 10
1 40N31 74w52 4:59:28
Stanwick 3 17 39N58 74w56 4:59:44
Stanwick Glen 3 17 39N58 74w56 4:59:44
Star Cross 8 1 39N38 75w01 5:00:04
State Hospital 11 1 40N13 74w46 4:59:04
Staten Island Junction 20
1 40N39 74w18 4:57:12
Steelmantown 5 12 39N16 74w47 4:59:08
Steelmanville 1 1 39N21 74w35 4:58:20
Stelton 12 17 40N32 74w22 4:57:28
Stephensburg 14 12 40N47 74w55 4:59:40
Stephenville 12 17 40N32 74w22 4:57:28
Stevens 3 1 40N05 74w51 4:59:24
Stewartsville 21 13 40N42 75w07 5:00:28
Still Valley 21 17 40N41 75w10 5:00:40
Stillwater 19 12 41N04 74w52 4:59:28
Stirling 14 12 40N41 74w30 4:58:00
Stockholm 19 17 41N05 74w31 4:58:04
Stockton 10 1 40N24 74w59 4:59:56
Stone Harbor 5 17 39N03 74w45 4:59:00
Stone Tavern 13 12 40N08 74w32 4:58:08
Stonetown 16 1 41N02 74w18 4:57:12
Stoney Brook Estates 8
1 39N49 75w08 5:00:32
Stony Hill 20 17 40N41 74w27 4:57:48
Stow Creek 6 12 39N27 75w21 5:01:24
Stow Creek Landing 6
1 39N28 75w15 5:01:00
Stratford 4 2 39N50 75w01 5:00:04
Strathmere 5 17 39N12 74w39 4:58:36
Strathmore 13 2 40N24 74w13 4:56:52
Styertowne 16 1 40N51 74w09 4:56:36
Suburban 13 1 40N21 74w03 4:56:12
Succasunna 14 14 40N52 74w38 4:58:32
Summerfield 21 17 40N50 75w05 5:00:20
Summit 20 1 40N43 74w22 4:57:28
Summit Avenue 9 1 40N46 74w02 4:56:08
Sunbury 3 3 39N58 74w41 4:58:44
Sunnyside 10 13 40N39 74w53 4:59:32
Sunrise Beach 15 14 39N50 74w11 4:56:44
Sunrise Park 14 14 40N52 74w38 4:58:32
Sunset Hill 18 2 40N21 74w39 4:58:36
Surf City 15 12 39N40 74w10 4:56:40
Sussex 19 1 41N13 74w37 4:58:28
Sutton Park 14 1 40N51 74w42 4:58:48
Swainton 5 13 39N05 74w50 4:59:20
Swartswood 19 12 41N05 74w50 4:59:20
Swartswood Lake 19
12 41N03 74w45 4:59:00
Swedesboro 8 10 39N45 75w19 5:01:16
Sweetwater 1 2 39N56 75w02 5:00:08
Swinesburg 10 12 40N34 75w06 5:00:24
Sykesville 3 3 40N01 74w38 4:58:32
Sylvan Glen 3 1 40N09 74w42 4:58:48
Sylvan Lake 3 1 40N05 74w51 4:59:24
Tabernacle 3 12 39N51 74w43 4:58:52
Tabor 14 12 40N52 74w29 4:57:56
Tanners Corner 12
12 40N25 74w23 4:57:32
Tansboro 4 17 39N46 74w55 4:59:40
Taunton Lake 17 39N51 74w52 4:59:28
Taunton Lakes 3 17 39N54 74w55 4:59:40
Taurus 9 1 40N47 74w01 4:56:04
Tavistock 4 2 39N53 75w02 5:00:08
Taylor Mills 13 12 40N18 74w22 4:57:28

Taylortown 14 1 40N56 74w24 4:57:36
Teabo 14 1 40N54 74w35 4:58:20
Teaneck 2 1 40N53 74w01 4:56:04
Tenafly 2 1 40N55 73w58 4:55:52
Tennent 13 1 40N17 74w20 4:57:20
Teterboro 2 1 40N52 74w03 4:56:12
Tewksbury 10 12 40N42 74w47 4:59:08
The Acres 8 1 39N42 75w07 5:00:28
The Dunes 15 17 39N37 74w12 4:56:48
The Orchards 11 1 40N14 74w42 4:58:48
Thompson Beach 6 12 39N15 75w07 5:00:28
Thorofare 8 2 39N51 75w12 5:00:48
Three Bridges 10 1 40N31 74w48 4:59:12
Timber Lakes 8 1 39N41 75w00 5:00:00
Timbuctoo 3 1 40N00 74w47 4:59:08
Tinton Falls 13 1 40N19 74w04 4:56:16
Titusville 11 12 40N18 74w53 4:59:32
Toms River 15 1 39N58 74w12 4:56:48
Totowa 16 4 40N54 74w13 4:56:52
Towaco 14 16 40N56 74w20 4:57:20
Town Bank 5 1 38N56 74w55 4:59:40
Town Brook 13 2 40N24 74w07 4:56:28
Town Center 7 1 40N47 74w15 4:57:00
Town Estates 3 1 40N05 74w51 4:59:24
Townley 20 1 40N42 74w16 4:57:04
Townsbury 21 17 40N48 75w00 5:00:00
Townsends Inlet 5 2 39N09 74w42 4:58:48
Tracy 12 12 40N18 74w22 4:57:28
Tranquility 19 15 40N57 74w49 4:59:16
Tremley 20 1 40N38 74w15 4:57:00
Tremley Point 20 1 40N38 74w15 4:57:00
Trenton 11 1 40N14 74w46 4:59:04
Trenton East 11 1 40N13 74w45 4:59:00
Trenton Gardens 11
1 40N12 74w44 4:58:56
Trenton Highlands 11
1 40N14 74w42 4:58:48
Trenton Naval Air Propulsion 11
1 40N15 74w48 4:59:12
Troy Hills 14 1 40N51 74w24 4:57:36
Tuckahoe 5 12 39N17 74w45 4:59:00
Tuckerton 15 2 39N36 74w20 4:57:20
Turkey Point Corner 6
12 39N15 75w02 5:00:08
Turnersville 8 1 39N47 75w03 5:00:12
Tuttles Corner 19
17 41N09 74w45 4:59:00
Twin Rivers 11 1 40N16 74w32 4:58:08
Tyler Park 9 1 40N47 74w01 4:56:04
Undercliff 2 1 40N50 73w59 4:55:56
Union 20 1 40N42 74w17 4:57:08
Union Beach 13 2 40N27 74w12 4:56:48
Union Center 20 1 40N42 74w16 4:57:04
Union City 9 1 40N45 74w02 4:56:08
Union Hill 14 1 40N53 74w34 4:58:16
Union Square 20 1 40N40 74w12 4:56:48
Uniontown 21 17 40N41 75w10 5:00:40
Union Valley 12 1 40N19 74w31 4:58:04
Unionville 3 1 40N00 74w46 4:59:04
Upper 5 17 39N15 74w41 4:58:44
Upper Berkshire Valley 14
1 40N54 74w35 4:58:20
Upper Deerfield 6 1 39N29 75w12 5:00:48
Upper Freehold 13 1 40N12 74w31 4:58:04
Upper Greenwood Lake 16
12 41N11 74w23 4:57:32
Upper Harmony 21 17 40N41 75w10 5:00:40
Upper Mohawk 19 17 41N02 74w38 4:58:32
Upper Montclair 7 1 40N50 74w12 4:56:48
Upper Montvale 2 1 41N03 74w02 4:56:08
Upper Penns Neck 17
1 39N43 75w28 5:01:52
Upper Pittsgrove 17
1 39N37 75w12 5:00:48
Upper Saddle River 2
12 41N04 74w06 4:56:24
Uptown 9 1 40N45 74w02 4:56:08
V.A. Hospital 7 1 40N45 74w13 4:56:52
Vail Homes 13 1 40N19 74w04 4:56:16
Vails 21 12 40N56 75w06 5:00:24
Vailsburg 7 1 40N45 74w14 4:56:56
Valentines 12 17 40N32 74w22 4:57:28
Valley 12 17 40N32 74w22 4:57:28
Valley 16 17 40N57 74w15 4:57:00
Vanada Woods 15 12 40N02 74w07 4:56:28
Vanderburg 13 12 40N17 74w11 4:56:44
Van Hiseville 15 12 40N07 74w21 4:57:24
Van Marters Corner 13
2 40N26 74w13 4:56:52
Vasa Home 14 1 40N52 74w50 4:59:20
Vauxhall 20 1 40N43 74w17 4:57:08
Ventnor City 1 7 39N20 74w29 4:57:56
Ventnor Heights 1 7 39N20 74w29 4:57:56
Verga 8 1 39N50 75w09 5:00:36
Vernon 19 12 41N12 74w29 4:57:56
Vernoy 10 12 40N43 74w50 4:59:20
Verona 7 1 40N50 74w15 4:57:00
Victoria 8 17 39N33 75w01 5:00:04
Victory Gardens 14
1 40N53 74w33 4:58:12
Victory Lakes 8 1 39N41 75w00 5:00:00
Vienna 21 12 40N52 74w54 4:59:36
Vienna Gardens 1 8 39N30 74w37 4:58:28
Villas 5 12 39N02 74w56 4:59:44
Vincentown 3 12 39N56 74w45 4:59:00
Vineland 6 1 39N29 75w02 5:00:08
Vineyard Homes 12
17 40N32 74w22 4:57:28
Voken Tract 4 2 39N49 75w06 5:00:24
Voorhees 4 17 39N51 74w59 4:59:56
Voorhees Corner 10
1 40N31 74w52 4:59:28
Vulcanite 21 17 40N41 75w10 5:00:40
Wading River 3 8 39N33 74w37 4:58:28
Waldwick 2 2 41N01 74w07 4:56:28
Wall 13 1 40N10 74w05 4:56:20
Wallington 2 1 40N51 74w07 4:56:28
Wallkill Lake 19 1 41N13 74w36 4:58:24
Wallpack Center 19
12 41N08 74w54 4:59:36
Wallworth Park 4 2 39N49 75w06 5:00:24
Walnut Valley 21 12 40N56 75w06 5:00:24
Walt Whitman Homes 8
2 39N51 75w12 5:00:48
Wanamassa 13 12 41N14 74w02 4:56:08
Wanaque 16 1 41N02 74w18 4:57:12
Wantage 19 1 41N14 74w37 4:58:28
Waretown 15 1 39N47 74w12 4:56:48
Warners 20 1 40N38 74w15 4:57:00
Warner Village 11 1 40N13 74w45 4:59:00
Warren 18 12 40N38 74w30 4:58:00
Warren Glen 21 13 40N42 75w07 5:00:28
Warren Grove 15 1 39N45 74w13 4:56:52
Warren Point 2 1 40N56 74w07 4:56:28
Warrington 21 12 40N56 75w06 5:00:24
Washington 21 12 40N46 74w59 4:59:56
Washington Crossing 11
12 40N23 74w46 4:59:04
Washington Heights 12
12 40N25 74w23 4:57:32
Washington Park 7 1 40N44 74w11 4:56:44
Washington Park 12
17 40N32 74w22 4:57:28
Washington Valley 14
17 40N48 74w29 4:57:56
Washingtonville 18
2 40N37 74w25 4:57:40
Watchung 18 2 40N38 74w27 4:57:48
Waterford 4 17 39N46 74w51 4:59:24
Waterford Works 4
17 39N43 74w51 4:59:24
Waterloo 19 1 40N55 74w42 4:58:48
Watsessing 7 1 40N48 74w11 4:56:44
Watsontown 4 1 39N48 75w00 5:00:00
Wayne 16 17 40N57 74w15 4:57:00
Wayside 13 1 40N14 74w01 4:56:04
Weehawken 9 1 40N46 74w00 4:56:00
Weekstown 1 8 39N33 74w37 4:58:28
Weequahic 7 1 40N43 74w12 4:56:48
Wellington Park 3 2 40N00 75w00 5:00:00
Wellwood 4 2 39N57 75w03 5:00:12
Wenonah 8 1 39N48 75w09 5:00:36
West 7 1 40N44 74w12 4:56:48
West Allenhurst 13
1 40N14 74w00 4:56:00
Westampton 3 1 40N01 74w50 4:59:20
West Amwell 10 12 40N23 74w53 4:59:32
West Arlington 9 1 40N46 74w09 4:56:36
West Atco 4 17 39N46 74w59 4:59:56
West Atlantic City 1
2 39N23 74w33 4:58:12
West Belmar 13 1 40N11 74w02 4:56:08
West Berlin 4 17 39N49 74w57 4:59:48
Westboro 13 1 40N21 74w03 4:56:12
West Brunswick 18 1 40N29 74w29 4:57:56
West Caldwell 7 1 40N51 74w18 4:57:12
West Cape May 5 1 38N57 74w56 4:59:44
West Carteret 12 12 40N27 74w23 4:57:32
West Collingswood 4
2 39N54 75w05 5:00:20
West Collingswood Heights 4
2 39N53 75w05 5:00:20
West Creek 15 2 39N38 74w18 4:57:12
West Deal 13 1 40N14 74w01 4:56:04
West Deptford 8 1 39N50 75w10 5:00:40
West End 8 1 39N49 75w08 5:00:32
West End 13 1 40N18 74w00 4:56:00
West Englewood 2 1 40N54 74w01 4:56:04
West Essex 7 1 40N51 74w16 4:57:04
West Farms 13 12 40N14 74w13 4:56:52
Westfield 20 1 40N39 74w21 4:57:24
West Fort Lee 2 1 40N51 73w58 4:55:52
West Freehold 13 1 40N15 74w18 4:57:12
West Grove 13 1 40N12 74w02 4:56:08
West Haddonfield 4
2 39N54 75w02 5:00:08
West Hoboken 9 1 40N46 74w02 4:56:08
West Hudson 9 1 40N46 74w09 4:56:36
West Keansburg 13
17 40N27 74w08 4:56:32
West Long Branch 13
1 40N17 74w01 4:56:04
West Mahwah 2 12 41N06 74w09 4:56:36
West Mantoloking 15
12 40N02 74w07 4:56:28
West Merchantville 4
2 39N57 75w03 5:00:12
West Milford 16 12 41N08 74w23 4:57:32
Westmont 4 2 39N54 75w03 5:00:12
West Moorestown 3
17 39N58 74w56 4:59:44
West New York 9 1 40N47 74w01 4:56:04
West Norwood 2 17 41N00 73w58 4:55:52
West Ocean City 5
17 39N16 74w39 4:58:36
West Ocean Grove 13
1 40N12 74w02 4:56:08
Weston-Manville 18
2 40N32 74w36 4:58:24
West Orange 7 1 40N47 74w14 4:56:56
West Paterson 16 4 40N54 74w12 4:56:48
West Point Island 15
12 39N58 74w04 4:56:16
West Point Pleasant 15
2 40N05 74w03 4:56:12
West Portal 10 13 40N42 75w01 5:00:04
West Side 9 1 40N45 74w02 4:56:08
West Trenton 11 1 40N15 74w48 4:59:12
West Tuckerton 15 2 39N36 74w20 4:57:20
West View 2 1 40N51 74w01 4:56:04
West Village 6 1 39N28 75w15 5:01:00
Westville 8 2 39N52 75w08 5:00:32
Westville Grove 8 1 39N50 75w09 5:00:36
Westville Oaks 8 1 39N50 75w09 5:00:36
West Wildwood 5 11 39N00 74w49 4:59:16
West Windsor 11 2 40N18 74w37 4:58:28
Westwood 2 1 41N00 74w02 4:56:08
Weymouth 1 17 39N19 74w41 4:58:44
Whale Beach 5 17 39N12 74w39 4:58:36
Wharton 14 1 40N54 74w35 4:58:20
Wheat Road 1 17 39N31 74w57 4:59:48
Whiglane 17 1 39N38 75w10 5:00:40
Whippany 14 1 40N50 74w25 4:57:40
White 21 17 40N49 75w03 5:00:12
White Horse 11 1 40N11 74w42 4:58:48
Whitehouse 10 12 40N37 74w46 4:59:04
White House Station 10
12 40N37 74w46 4:59:04
White Meadow Lake 14
12 40N55 74w31 4:58:04
Whiteoak Ridge 7 1 40N44 74w19 4:57:16
Whitesbog 3 12 39N58 74w34 4:58:16
Whitesboro 5 13 39N03 74w51 4:59:24
Whitesville 13 1 40N12 74w02 4:56:08
Whitesville 15 13 40N42 74w57 4:59:48
Whitings 15 12 39N57 74w23 4:57:32
Whitman Square 8 1 39N45 75w03 5:00:12
Wickatunk 13 12 40N21 74w15 4:57:00
Wilburtha 11 1 40N15 74w48 4:59:12
Wilburtha Manor 11
1 40N15 74w48 4:59:12
Wilderness Acres 4
2 39N49 75w06 5:00:24
Wildwood 5 11 38N59 74w50 4:59:20
Wildwood Crest 5 11 38N58 74w50 4:59:20
Wildwood Gables 5
11 39N00 74w49 4:59:16
Wildwood Highlands Beach 5
12 39N02 74w56 4:59:44
Williamstown 8 1 39N41 75w00 5:00:00
Williamstown Junction 4
17 39N49 74w58 4:59:52
Willingboro 3 1 40N03 74w54 4:59:36
Willowdale 4 2 39N49 75w06 5:00:24
Willow Grove 17 17 39N33 75w01 5:00:04
Windsor 11 12 40N14 74w35 4:58:20
Winfield 20 1 40N38 74w17 4:57:08
Winslow 4 2 39N39 74w52 4:59:28
Winston Park 13 12 40N14 74w13 4:56:52
Wood Acres 12 17 40N32 74w22 4:57:28
Wood Acres 13 12 40N14 74w13 4:56:52
Woodbine 5 12 39N15 74w49 4:59:16
Woodbine Junction 5
12 39N16 74w47 4:59:08
Woodbridge 12 1 40N34 74w17 4:57:08
Woodbridge Oaks 12
1 40N34 74w19 4:57:16
Woodbury 8 1 39N50 75w09 5:00:36
Woodbury Gardens 8
1 39N49 75w08 5:00:32
Woodbury Heights 8
1 39N49 75w09 5:00:36
Woodcliff 9 1 40N47 74w01 4:56:04
Woodcliff Lake 2 1 41N01 74w03 4:56:12
Woodcrest 4 2 39N52 75w01 5:00:04
Woodglen 10 13 40N42 74w57 4:59:48
Woodland 3 14 39N50 74w32 4:58:08
Woodlynne 4 2 39N55 75w06 5:00:24
Woodmere 17 17 39N34 75w28 5:01:52
Woodport 14 12 40N59 74w37 4:58:28
Wood-Ridge 2 1 40N51 74w05 4:56:20
Woodruffs 6 1 39N28 75w15 5:01:00
Woods Tavern 18 2 40N30 74w39 4:58:36
Woodstock 12 41N00 74w32 4:58:08
Woodstown 17 17 39N39 75w20 5:01:20
Woodstream 3 17 39N54 74w55 4:59:40
Woodsville 11 12 40N23 74w46 4:59:04
Woolwich 8 10 39N45 75w19 5:01:16
Wortendyke 2 2 41N00 74w08 4:56:32
Wrights 12 1 40N27 74w25 4:57:40
Wrights Mill 8 1 39N38 75w10 5:00:40
Wrightstown 3 1 40N01 74w38 4:58:32
Wrightsville 3 2 40N00 75w00 5:00:00
Wrightsville 13 2 40N10 74w31 4:58:04
Wyckoff 2 17 41N01 74w11 4:56:44
Wyckoff Mills 13 1 40N15 74w17 4:57:08
Wynnewood 12 1 40N34 74w27 4:57:48
Yardville 11 1 40N11 74w40 4:58:40
Yellow Frame 19 12 41N03 74w45 4:59:00
York Estates 11 1 40N16 74w32 4:58:08
Yorktown 17 17 39N39 75w20 5:01:20
Zarephath 18 17 40N32 74w34 4:58:16
Zion 18 12 40N25 74w43 4:58:52

NEW MEXICO

TIME TABLES

NM # 1
Before 11/18/1883 LMT
11/18/1883 12:00 MST
3/31/1918 02:00 MWT
10/27/1918 02:00 MST
3/30/1919 02:00 MWT
10/26/1919 02:00 MST
2/09/1942 02:00 MWT
9/30/1945 02:00 MST
4/30/1967 02:00 US#1
....

NM # 2
Before 11/18/1883 LMT
11/18/1883 12:00 MST
3/31/1918 02:00 MWT
10/27/1918 02:00 MST
3/30/1919 02:00 MWT
10/26/1919 02:00 MST
2/09/1942 02:00 MWT
9/30/1945 02:00 MST
4/24/1966 02:00 US#1
....

NM # 3
Before 11/18/1883 LMT
11/18/1883 12:00 MST
3/31/1918 02:00 MWT
10/27/1918 02:00 MST
3/30/1919 02:00 MWT
10/26/1919 02:00 MST
2/09/1942 02:00 MWT
9/30/1945 02:00 MST
4/26/1953 02:00 MDT
9/27/1953 02:00 MST
4/25/1954 02:00 MDT
9/26/1954 02:00 MST
4/24/1955 02:00 MDT
9/25/1955 02:00 MST
4/29/1956 02:00 MDT
9/30/1956 02:00 MST
4/28/1957 02:00 MDT
9/29/1957 02:00 MST
4/27/1958 02:00 MDT
9/28/1958 02:00 MST
4/26/1959 02:00 MDT
9/27/1959 02:00 MST
4/24/1960 02:00 MDT
9/25/1960 02:00 MST
4/30/1961 02:00 MDT
9/24/1961 02:00 MST
4/29/1962 02:00 MDT
9/30/1962 02:00 MST
4/28/1963 02:00 MDT
9/29/1963 02:00 MST
4/26/1964 02:00 MDT
9/27/1964 02:00 MST
4/25/1965 02:00 MDT
9/26/1965 02:00 MST
4/24/1966 02:00 US#1
....

NM # 4
Before 11/18/1883 LMT
11/18/1883 12:00 MST
3/31/1918 02:00 MWT
10/27/1918 02:00 MST
3/30/1919 02:00 MWT
10/26/1919 02:00 MST
2/09/1942 02:00 MWT
9/30/1945 02:00 MST
4/24/1955 02:00 MDT
5/08/1955 02:00 MST
4/30/1967 02:00 US#1

COUNTIES

1 Bernalillo
2 Catron
3 Chaves
4 Colfax
5 Curry
6 De Baca
7 Dona Ana
8 Eddy
9 Grant
10 Guadalupe
11 Harding
12 Hidalgo
13 Lea
14 Lincoln
15 Los Alamos
16 Luna
17 McKinley
18 Mora
19 Otero
20 Quay
21 Rio Arriba
22 Roosevelt
23 Sandoval
24 San Juan
25 San Miguel
26 Santa Fe
27 Sierra
28 Socorro
29 Taos
30 Torrance
31 Union
32 Valencia

Abbott 4	1	36N18	104w16	6:57:04
Abeytas 28	1	34N34	106w47	7:07:08
Abiquiu 21	1	36N13	106w19	7:05:16
Abo 30	1	34N28	106w19	7:05:16
Abuelo 18	1	35N58	105w20	7:01:20
Acoma 32	1	35N05	107w36	7:10:24
Acoma Indian Reservation 32	1	35N05	106w39	7:06:36
Acomita 32	1	35N03	107w34	7:10:16
Adelino 32	1	34N49	106w44	7:06:56
Adobe Acres 1	1	35N04	106w41	7:06:44
Agua Fria 26	1	35N40	105w57	7:03:48
Alameda 1	1	35N11	106w37	7:06:28
Alamillo 28	1	34N15	106w54	7:07:36
Alamo 28	1	34N07	107w14	7:08:56
Alamogordo 19	1	32N54	105w57	7:03:48
Albert 11	1	35N46	103w57	6:55:48
Albuquerque 1	1	35N05	106w39	7:06:36
Alcade	1	36N05	106w03	7:04:12
Alcalde 21	1	36N03	106w02	7:04:08
Algodones 23	1	35N23	106w29	7:05:56
Alire 21	1	36N32	106w29	7:05:56
Allison 17	1	35N32	108w47	7:15:08
Alma 2	1	33N19	108w53	7:15:32
Alpine Village 14	1	33N20	105w40	7:02:40
Alto 14	1	33N23	105w41	7:02:44
Alto Crest 14	1	33N20	105w40	7:02:40
Amalia 29	1	36N57	105w27	7:01:48
Ambrosia Lake 17	1	35N10	107w52	7:11:28
Amistad 31	1	35N55	103w09	6:52:36
Anaconda 32	1	35N10	107w52	7:11:28
Anapra 7	1	31N49	106w33	7:06:12
Ancho 14	1	33N56	105w45	7:03:00
Angel Fire 4	1	36N33	105w16	7:01:04
Angostura 29	1	36N11	105w40	7:02:40
Animas 12	1	31N57	108w48	7:15:12
Anthony 7	1	32N00	106w36	7:06:24
Anton Chico 10	1	35N12	105w09	7:00:36
Apache Creek 2	1	33N43	108w45	7:15:00
Apache Park 14	1	33N20	105w40	7:02:40
Apodaca 21	1	36N12	105w53	7:03:32
Arabela 14	1	33N22	105w14	7:00:56
Aragon 2	1	33N53	108w32	7:14:08
Arch 22	1	34N11	103w20	6:53:20
Arenas Valley 9	1	32N48	108w11	7:12:44
Arkansas Junction 13	1	32N42	103w09	6:52:36
Armijo 1	1	35N04	106w39	7:06:36
Arrey 27	1	32N48	107w19	7:09:16
Arroyo del Agua 21	1	36N10	106w37	7:06:28
Arroyo Hondo 29	1	36N32	105w40	7:02:40
Arroyo Seco 29	1	36N31	105w34	7:02:16
Artesia 8	1	32N51	104w24	6:57:36
Artesia Camp 19	1	32N48	105w34	7:02:16
Atoka 8	1	32N50	104w25	6:57:40
Aurora 18	1	36N10	105w03	7:00:12
Aurora 25	1	35N18	105w22	7:01:28
Aztec 24	1	36N49	108w00	7:12:00
Bacaville 32	1	34N40	106w46	7:07:04
Bard 20	2	35N08	103w15	6:53:00
Barranca 21	1	36N12	106w19	7:05:16
Bayard 9	1	32N46	108w08	7:12:32
Becenti 17	1	35N41	108w09	7:12:36
Belen 32	1	34N40	106w46	7:07:04
Bell Ranch 25	1	35N32	104w06	6:56:24
Bellview 5	1	34N49	103w07	6:52:28
Bennett 13	1	32N04	103w12	6:52:48
Bent 19	1	33N09	105w51	7:03:24
Berino 7	1	32N04	106w37	7:06:28
Bernalillo 23	1	35N18	106w33	7:06:12
Bernardo 28	1	34N34	106w47	7:07:08
Beulah 25	1	35N46	105w15	7:01:00
Biklabito 24	1	36N50	109w01	7:16:04
Bingham 28	1	33N55	106w21	7:05:24
Bisti 24	1	36N46	108w10	7:12:40
Black Forest 14	1	33N20	105w40	7:02:40
Black Lake 4	1	36N10	105w03	7:00:12
Black River Village 8	1	32N25	104w14	6:56:56
Black Rock 17	1	35N05	108w47	7:15:08
Blanco 24	1	36N43	107w50	7:11:20
Bloomfield 24	1	36N43	107w59	7:11:56
Bluewater	1	35N15	107w59	7:11:56
Boles 19	1	32N55	105w57	7:03:48
Bosque 32	1	34N34	106w47	7:07:08
Bosque Farms 32	1	35N04	106w41	7:06:44
Boys Ranch 28	1	34N40	106w46	7:07:04
Brazos 21	1	36N44	106w34	7:06:16
Bread Springs 17	1	35N31	108w44	7:14:56
Brimhall 17	1	35N47	108w37	7:14:28
Broadmoor 3	1	33N23	104w32	6:58:08
Broadmoor Shopping Center 13	1	32N42	103w09	6:52:36
Broadview 5	1	34N49	103w13	6:52:52
Broadview Acres 32	1	35N10	107w52	7:11:28
Buckeye 13	1	32N57	103w21	6:53:24
Buckhorn 9	1	33N02	108w42	7:14:48
Buena Vista 18	1	35N55	105w15	7:01:00
Bueyeros 11	1	35N59	103w41	6:54:44
Burnham 24	1	36N46	108w10	7:12:40
Butterfield Park 7	1	32N20	106w43	7:06:52
Caballo 27	1	32N58	107w19	7:09:16
Cameron 20	2	34N49	103w19	6:53:16
Campus 28	1	34N03	106w54	7:07:36
Canada de los Alamos 26	1	35N40	105w57	7:03:48
Canjilon 21	1	36N29	106w26	7:05:44
Cannon 5	1	34N25	103w19	6:53:16
Cannon Air Force Base 5	1	34N24	103w16	6:53:04
Canoncito 1	1	35N02	107w23	7:09:32
Canoncito 21	1	36N12	105w53	7:03:32
Canoncito 25	1	35N46	105w15	7:01:00
Canoncito 26	1	35N40	105w57	7:03:48
Canoncito Indian Reservation 1	1	35N05	106w39	7:06:36
Canones 21	1	36N11	106w26	7:05:44
Canon Plaza	1	36N33	106w09	7:04:36
Canova 21	1	36N10	105w58	7:03:52
Canyon 23	1	35N37	106w44	7:06:56
Canyoncito 26	1	35N35	105w46	7:03:04
Capitan 14	1	33N35	105w35	7:02:20
Caprock 13	1	33N24	103w43	6:54:52
Capulin 31	1	36N45	104w00	6:56:00
Carlsbad 8	1	32N25	104w14	6:56:56
Carnuel 1	1	35N05	106w32	7:06:08
Carrizozo 14	1	33N38	105w53	7:03:32
Carson 29	1	36N22	105w46	7:03:04
Casa Blanca 32	1	35N03	107w28	7:09:52
Causey 22	1	33N53	103w08	6:52:32
Cebolla 21	1	36N32	106w29	7:05:56
Cedar Creek 14	1	33N20	105w40	7:02:40
Cedar Crest 1	1	35N04	106w31	7:06:04
Cedar Grove 26	1	35N09	105w59	7:03:56
Cedar Hill 24	1	36N50	108w00	7:12:00
Cedarvale 30	1	34N22	105w42	7:02:48
Cedro Village 1	1	35N05	106w23	7:05:32
Central 9	1	32N47	108w09	7:12:36
Cerrillos 26	1	35N26	106w08	7:04:32
Cerritos 25	1	35N18	105w22	7:01:28
Cerro 29	1	36N45	105w36	7:02:24
Chacon 18	1	36N09	105w22	7:01:28
Chama 21	1	36N54	106w35	7:06:20
Chamberino 7	1	32N03	106w41	7:06:44
Chamisal 29	1	36N10	105w44	7:02:56
Chamita 21	1	36N03	106w04	7:04:16
Chaparral 19	1	32N00	106w36	7:06:24
Chapelle 25	1	35N24	105w19	7:01:16
Chaperito 25	1	35N36	105w13	7:00:52
Chical 32	1	34N49	106w44	7:06:56
Chi-Ch'il-Tah 17	1	35N16	108w45	7:15:00
Chili 21	1	36N04	106w07	7:04:28
Chilili 1	1	34N53	106w14	7:04:56
Chimayo 21	1	36N00	105w56	7:03:44
Chippeway Park 19	1	32N57	105w45	7:03:00
Chloride 27	1	33N20	107w41	7:10:44
Chupadero 26	1	35N40	105w57	7:03:48
Church Rock 17	1	35N46	108w35	7:14:20
Cimarron 4	1	36N31	104w55	6:59:40
Clapham 31	1	36N28	103w11	6:52:44
Claunch 28	1	34N09	106w00	7:04:00
Clayton 31	1	36N27	103w11	6:52:44
Cleveland 18	1	36N00	105w22	7:01:28
Cliff 9	1	32N58	108w37	7:14:28
Clines Corners 30	1	35N01	105w40	7:02:40
Cloud Country Estates 19	1	32N57	105w45	7:03:00
Cloudcroft 19	1	32N58	105w45	7:03:00
Cloverdale 12	1	31N57	108w48	7:15:12
Clovis 5	1	34N24	103w12	6:52:48
Cochiti 23	1	35N37	106w21	7:05:24
Cochiti Indian Reservation 23	1	35N05	106w39	7:06:36
Cochiti Lake 23	1	35N34	106w20	7:05:20
Colmor	1	36N13	104w39	6:58:36
Colonias 10	1	34N56	104w41	6:58:44
Columbine 29	1	36N42	105w36	7:02:24
Columbus 16	1	31N50	107w38	7:10:32
Community Center 15	3	35N51	106w16	7:05:04
Conchas	1	35N22	104w11	6:56:44
Conchas Dam 25	1	35N28	104w05	6:56:20
Continental Divide 17	1	35N25	108w19	7:13:16
Contreras 28	1	34N21	106w51	7:07:24
Coolidge 17	1	35N25	108w19	7:13:16
Corazon 25	1	35N36	105w13	7:00:52
Cordova 21	1	36N01	105w52	7:03:28
Corona 14	1	34N15	105w36	7:02:24
Coronado 26	1	35N40	105w57	7:03:48
Corrales 23	1	35N22	106w44	7:06:56
Coruco 25	1	35N22	105w27	7:01:48
Costilla 29	1	36N59	105w32	7:02:08
Cotton City 12	1	31N57	108w48	7:15:12
Counselor 23	1	36N14	106w51	7:07:24
Country Club Estates 1	1	35N10	106w39	7:06:36
Country Club Heights 14	1	33N20	105w40	7:02:40
Cowles 25	1	35N49	105w40	7:02:40
Coyote 21	1	36N10	106w37	7:06:28
Crossroads 13	1	33N31	103w20	6:53:20
Crownpoint 17	1	35N41	108w09	7:12:36
Cruzville 2	1	33N43	108w45	7:15:00
Crystal 24	1	35N04	108w51	7:15:24
Cuba 23	1	35N43	107w07	7:08:28
Cubero 32	1	35N05	107w31	7:10:04
Cuchillo 27	1	33N14	107w22	7:09:28
Cuervo 10	1	35N02	104w25	6:57:40
Cundiyo 26	1	36N00	105w56	7:03:44
Cuyamunque	1	35N52	106w00	7:04:00
Dahlia 10	1	35N12	105w09	7:00:36
Dalies 32	1	34N49	106w44	7:06:56
Dalton Pass 17	1	35N41	108w09	7:12:36
Datil 2	1	34N09	107w51	7:11:24
Del Norte 14	1	33N20	105w40	7:02:40
Deming 16	1	32N16	107w46	7:11:04
Derry 27	1	32N47	107w17	7:09:08
Des Moines 31	1	36N46	103w50	6:55:20
De Vargas Shopping Center 26	1	35N40	105w57	7:03:48
Dexter 3	1	33N12	104w22	6:57:28
Dilia 10	1	35N12	105w04	7:00:16
Dixon 21	1	36N12	105w53	7:03:32
Dog Canyon Estates 19	1	32N55	105w57	7:03:48
Domingo 23	1	35N31	106w19	7:05:16
Dona Ana 7	1	32N23	106w49	7:07:16
Dora 22	1	33N50	103w15	6:53:00
Downtown 1	1	35N05	106w39	7:06:36
Dulce 21	1	36N56	107w00	7:08:00
Dunken 3	1	32N37	105w24	7:01:36
Duran 30	1	34N28	105w24	7:01:36
Dusty 28	1	33N38	107w39	7:10:36
Eagle Nest 4	1	36N33	105w16	7:01:04
East De Baca 6	1	34N21	104w10	6:56:40
East Grand Plains 3	1	33N23	104w32	6:58:08
East Pecos 25	1	35N34	105w40	7:02:40
East Vaughn 10	1	34N36	105w13	7:00:52
Edgewood 26	1	35N04	106w11	7:04:44
El Ancon 25	1	35N22	105w27	7:01:48
El Cerrito 25	1	35N18	105w22	7:01:28

El Cerro 32 1 34N49 106w44 7:06:56
El Duende 21 1 36N04 106w07 7:04:28
Elephant Butte 27
1 33N09 107w11 7:08:44
El Gauche 21 1 36N00 106w05 7:04:20
El Guique 21 1 36N03 106w04 7:04:16
El Huerfano 24 1 36N43 107w59 7:11:56
Elida 22 1 33N57 103w39 6:54:36
Elk 3 1 32N53 105w29 7:01:56
Elkins 3 1 33N42 104w04 6:56:16
El Llanito 23 1 35N18 106w33 7:06:12
El Llano 21 1 36N00 106w05 7:04:20
El Llano 25 1 35N36 105w13 7:00:52
El Portero 26 1 36N00 105w56 7:03:44
El Porvenir 25 1 35N43 105w25 7:01:40
El Prado 29 1 36N26 105w35 7:02:20
El Pueblo 25 1 35N22 105w27 7:01:48
El Rancho 26 1 36N00 106w05 7:04:20
El Rancho Loma Linda 29
1 36N11 105w40 7:02:40
El Renz-O-Ranch 4
1 36N33 105w16 7:01:04
El Rincon de los Trujillos 21
1 36N00 105w56 7:03:44
El Rito 21 1 36N21 106w11 7:04:44
El Turquillo 18 1 36N08 105w14 7:00:56
El Vado 21 1 36N36 106w44 7:06:56
El Valle 29 1 36N14 105w40 7:02:40
Embudo 21 1 36N13 105w56 7:03:44
Enchanted Hills 14
1 33N20 105w40 7:02:40
Encinal 32 1 35N05 107w31 7:10:04
Encino 30 1 34N39 105w28 7:01:52
Engle 1 33N04 107w02 7:08:08
Ensenada 21 1 36N44 106w32 7:06:08
Escabosa 1 1 34N56 106w17 7:05:08
Escondida 28 1 34N06 106w54 7:07:36
Espanola 21 1 35N59 106w05 7:04:20
Estaca 21 1 36N03 106w04 7:04:16
Estancia 30 1 34N46 106w04 7:04:16
Eunice 13 1 32N26 103w10 6:52:40
Fairacres 7 1 32N20 106w56 7:07:44
Fairview 21 1 36N00 106w05 7:04:20
Farley 4 1 36N18 103w58 6:55:52
Farmington 24 1 36N44 108w12 7:12:48
Faywood 9 1 32N30 108w00 7:12:00
Faywood Hot Springs 9
1 32N30 108w03 7:12:12
Fence Lake 32 1 34N39 108w41 7:14:44
Field 5 1 34N25 103w38 6:54:32
Fierro 9 1 32N51 108w05 7:12:20
Five Points 1 1 35N04 106w41 7:06:44
Flora Vista 24 1 36N48 108w03 7:12:12
Florida 28 1 34N03 106w54 7:07:36
Floyd 22 1 34N13 103w35 6:54:20
Flume Canyon 14 1 33N20 105w40 7:02:40
Flying H 3 1 33N02 105w08 7:00:32
Folsom 31 1 36N51 103w55 6:55:40
Forest Heights 14
1 33N20 105w40 7:02:40
Forest Park 1 1 35N04 106w31 7:06:04
Forrest 20 2 34N48 103w36 6:54:24
Fort Stanton 14 1 33N30 105w31 7:02:04
Fort Sumner 6 1 34N28 104w15 6:57:00
Fort Wingate 17 1 35N28 108w33 7:14:12
Fort Wingate Army Depot 17
1 35N31 108w44 7:14:56
French Corners 4 1 36N22 104w35 6:58:20
Fruitland 24 1 36N44 108w24 7:13:36
Gabaldon 25 1 35N30 105w19 7:01:16
Gage 1 32N14 108w05 7:12:20
Galisteo 26 1 35N40 105w57 7:03:48
Gallegos 11 1 35N22 103w25 6:53:40
Gallina 21 1 36N14 106w51 7:07:24
Gallinas 25 1 35N39 105w17 7:01:08
Gallup 17 1 35N32 108w45 7:15:00
Gamerco 17 1 35N34 108w46 7:15:04
Garanbuio 25 1 35N18 105w24 7:01:36
Garfield 7 1 32N46 107w16 7:09:04
Garita 25 1 35N16 104w29 6:57:56
Garrison 22 1 33N59 103w14 6:52:56
Gascon 18 1 35N53 105w27 7:01:48
Gavilan 21 1 36N18 107w03 7:08:12
Gila 9 1 32N58 108w38 7:14:32
Gila Hot Springs 9
1 32N46 108w16 7:13:04
Gladstone 31 1 36N18 103w58 6:55:52
Glencoe 14 1 33N24 105w28 7:01:52
Glen Grove 14 1 33N20 105w40 7:02:40
Glenrio 20 2 35N11 103w03 6:52:12
Glenwood 2 1 33N19 108w53 7:15:32
Glorieta 26 1 35N35 105w46 7:03:04
Gobernador 21 1 36N43 107w50 7:11:20
Golden 26 1 35N16 106w13 7:04:52
Golondrinas 18 1 35N55 105w15 7:01:00
Gonzales Ranch 25
1 35N28 104w38 6:58:32
Grady 5 1 34N49 103w19 6:53:16
Gran Quivira 30 1 34N31 106w14 7:04:56
Grants 32 1 35N09 107w52 7:11:28
Greenfield 3 1 33N11 104w22 6:57:28
Green Meadows 14 1 33N20 105w40 7:02:40
Green Tree 1 33N20 105w35 7:02:20
Grenville 31 1 36N36 103w37 6:54:28
Grier 5 1 34N24 103w16 6:53:04
Guachupangue 21 1 36N00 106w05 7:04:20
Guadalupita 18 1 36N08 105w14 7:00:56
Guagolotes 25 1 35N18 105w22 7:01:28
Guique 21 1 36N03 106w04 7:04:16
Hachita 9 1 31N55 108w19 7:13:16
Hacienda Acres 7 1 32N20 106w43 7:06:52
Hagerman 3 1 33N07 104w20 6:57:20
Hamilton Terrace 14
1 33N20 105w40 7:02:40
Hanover 9 1 32N48 108w06 7:12:24

Happy Valley 8 1 32N25 104w14 6:56:56
Hatch 7 1 32N40 107w09 7:08:36
Hayden 31 1 35N59 103w16 6:53:04
Hernandez 21 1 36N04 106w07 7:04:28
High Rolls 1 32N57 105w50 7:03:20
Hillburn City 13 1 32N57 103w21 6:53:24
Hillsboro 27 1 32N55 107w34 7:10:16
Hobbies 1 1 35N05 106w23 7:05:32
Hobbs 13 1 32N42 103w08 6:52:32
Holiday Acres 14 1 33N20 105w40 7:02:40
Hollene 5 1 34N24 103w16 6:53:04
Holloman 19 1 32N52 106w06 7:04:24
Holloman Air Force Base 19
1 32N52 106w06 7:04:24
Hollywood 14 1 33N19 105w37 7:02:28
Holman 18 1 36N02 105w23 7:01:32
Hondo 14 1 33N24 105w16 7:01:04
Hooverville 25 1 35N22 104w11 6:56:44
Hope 8 1 32N49 104w44 6:58:56
Horse Springs 2 1 34N09 107w51 7:11:24
Hospah 17 1 35N41 108w09 7:12:36
Hot Springs Landing 27
1 33N09 107w11 7:08:44
House 20 2 34N39 103w54 6:55:36
Humble City 13 1 32N48 103w13 6:52:52
Hurley 9 1 32N42 108w08 7:12:32
Hyde Park Estates 26
1 35N40 105w57 7:03:48
Idlewild 4 1 36N33 105w16 7:01:04
Ilfeld 25 1 35N25 105w34 7:02:16
Indian Hills 14 1 33N20 105w40 7:02:40
Isleta 1 1 34N55 106w42 7:06:48
Isleta Indian Reservation 32
1 35N05 106w39 7:06:36
Isleta Pueblo 1 1 34N56 106w40 7:06:40
Jacona 26 1 35N40 105w57 7:03:48
Jal 13 1 32N07 103w12 6:52:48
Jarales 32 1 34N37 106w46 7:07:04
Jemez 23 1 35N43 106w43 7:06:52
Jemez Indian Reservation 23
1 35N05 106w39 7:06:36
Jemez Pueblo 23 1 35N37 106w44 7:06:56
Jemez Springs 23 1 35N46 106w41 7:06:44
Jicarilla 21 1 36N49 107w10 7:08:40
Jicarilla Indian Reservation 21
1 36N56 107w00 7:08:00
Junta 21 1 36N13 105w56 7:03:44
Kenna 22 1 33N51 103w46 6:55:04
Kinebeto 24 1 36N46 108w10 7:12:40
Kingston 27 1 32N55 107w42 7:10:48
Kingswood 14 1 33N20 105w40 7:02:40
Kirtland 24 1 36N48 108w23 7:13:32
Kirtland Air Force Base
1 35N02 106w37 7:06:28
Knowles 13 1 32N42 103w09 6:52:36
La Bolsa 21 1 36N13 105w56 7:03:44
La Cienega 26 1 35N40 105w57 7:03:48
La Constancia 32 1 34N40 106w46 7:07:04
La Cueva 18 1 35N57 105w15 7:01:00
La Cueva 26 1 35N35 105w46 7:03:04
La Fraqua 25 1 35N18 105w24 7:01:36
Laguna 32 1 34N57 107w25 7:09:40
Laguna Indian Reservation 32
1 35N05 106w39 7:06:36
Lagunita 25 1 35N22 105w27 7:01:48
La Huerta 8 1 32N25 104w14 6:56:56
La Jara 23 1 36N05 106w58 7:07:52
La Joya 26 1 35N35 105w46 7:03:04
Lajoya 28 1 34N21 106w51 7:07:24
La Junta 21 1 36N13 105w56 7:03:44
Lake Arthur 3 1 33N00 104w22 6:57:28
Lake Valley 24 1 35N41 108w09 7:12:36
Lake View Pines 4
1 36N33 105w16 7:01:04
Lakewood 8 1 32N38 104w23 6:57:32
La Ladera 32 1 34N49 106w44 7:06:56
La Loma 10 1 35N11 105w07 7:00:28
La Luz 19 1 32N59 105w57 7:03:48
Lama 29 1 36N42 105w36 7:02:24
La Madera 21 1 36N23 106w02 7:04:08
La Madera 23 1 35N10 106w22 7:05:28
La Manga 25 1 35N36 105w13 7:00:52
La Mesa 7 1 32N07 106w42 7:06:48
La Mesilla 7 1 32N18 106w47 7:07:08
La Mesilla 21 1 36N00 106w05 7:04:20
Lamy 26 1 35N29 105w53 7:03:32
La Plata 24 1 36N56 108w12 7:12:48
La Puebla 26 1 36N00 106w05 7:04:20
La Puente 21 1 36N42 106w36 7:06:24
Las Cruces 7 1 32N19 106w47 7:07:08
Las Nutrias 28 1 34N31 106w46 7:07:04
Las Palomas 27 1 33N03 107w17 7:09:08
Las Placitas 21 1 36N21 106w11 7:04:44
Las Tablas 21 1 36N33 106w02 7:04:08
Las Tusas 25 1 35N46 105w15 7:01:00
Las Vegas 25 1 35N36 105w13 7:00:52
La Union 7 1 31N57 106w40 7:06:40
La Villita 21 1 36N05 106w03 7:04:12
Lea North Central 13
1 32N57 103w22 6:53:28
Lea South Central 13
1 32N44 103w14 6:52:56
Ledoux 18 1 35N56 105w22 7:01:28
Lemitar 28 1 34N10 106w55 7:07:40
Levy 18 1 36N05 104w41 6:58:44
Leyba 25 1 35N13 105w34 7:02:16
Lincoln 14 1 33N30 105w23 7:01:32
Linda Vista 3 1 33N23 104w32 6:58:08
Lindrith 21 1 36N18 107w03 7:08:12
Lingo 22 1 33N47 103w07 6:52:28
Little Walnut Village 9
1 32N46 108w16 7:13:04
Little Water 24 1 36N47 108w41 7:14:44
Llano 29 1 36N08 105w41 7:02:44

Llano Del Medio 10
1 35N11 105w07 7:00:28
Llano Largo 29 1 36N09 105w40 7:02:40
Llano Quemado 29 1 36N22 105w37 7:02:28
Llaves 21 1 36N24 106w46 7:07:04
Loco Hills 8 1 32N47 104w10 6:56:40
Logan 20 2 35N22 103w25 6:53:40
Lordsburg 12 1 32N21 108w43 7:14:52
Los Alamos 15 3 35N53 106w19 7:05:16
Los Alamos 25 1 35N46 105w15 7:01:00
Los Chavez 32 1 34N40 106w46 7:07:04
Los Febres 18 1 36N10 105w03 7:00:12
Los Hueros 18 1 36N10 105w03 7:00:12
Los Lentes 32 1 34N49 106w44 7:06:56
Los Luceros 21 1 36N05 106w03 7:04:12
Los Lunas 32 1 34N48 106w44 7:06:56
Los Montoyas 25 1 35N36 105w13 7:00:52
Los Ojos 21 1 36N44 106w34 7:06:16
Los Pachecos 21 1 35N34 105w40 7:02:40
Los Padillas 1 1 35N04 106w41 7:06:44
Los Pinos 21 1 36N59 106w03 7:04:12
Los Ranchos 1 1 35N05 106w39 7:06:36
Los Ranchos de Albuquerque 1
1 35N10 106w39 7:06:36
Lost Lodge 19 1 32N57 105w45 7:03:00
Los Trujillos 32 1 34N40 106w46 7:07:04
Los Vigiles 25 1 35N36 105w13 7:00:52
Lourdes 25 1 35N36 105w13 7:00:52
Lovato 25 1 35N18 105w24 7:01:36
Loving 8 1 32N17 104w06 6:56:24
Lovington 13 1 32N57 103w21 6:53:24
Lower Laposada 25
1 35N34 105w40 7:02:40
Lower Nutria 17 1 35N04 108w51 7:15:24
Lower Pueblo 25 1 35N18 105w24 7:01:36
Lower Ranchito 29
1 36N30 106w01 7:04:04
Lower Rociada 25 1 35N51 105w26 7:01:44
Lower San Francisco Plaza 2
1 33N43 108w45 7:15:00
Lucero 18 1 36N00 105w12 7:00:48
Lucy 30 1 34N36 106w02 7:04:08
Luis Lopez 28 1 33N59 106w53 7:07:32
Lumberton 21 1 36N56 106w56 7:07:44
Luna 2 1 33N49 108w57 7:15:48
Lyden 21 1 36N10 105w58 7:03:52
MacImiliano 25 1 35N36 105w13 7:00:52
Madrid 26 1 35N26 106w08 7:04:32
Maes 25 1 35N36 105w13 7:00:52
Magdalena 28 1 34N07 107w15 7:09:00
Malaga 8 1 32N14 104w04 6:56:16
Maljamar 13 1 32N51 103w46 6:55:04
Mangas Springs 9 1 32N46 108w16 7:13:04
Manuelitas 25 1 35N46 105w15 7:01:00
Manuelito 17 1 35N25 109w00 7:16:00
Manzano 30 1 34N31 106w14 7:04:56
Mariano Lake 17 1 35N31 108w44 7:14:56
Maxwell 4 1 36N32 104w33 6:58:12
Mayhill 19 1 32N53 105w29 7:01:56
McAlister 20 2 34N42 103w47 6:55:08
McCartys 11 1 35N37 103w06 6:52:24
McCartys 32 1 35N04 107w41 7:10:44
McDonald 13 1 33N09 103w19 6:53:16
McGaffey 17 1 35N28 108w33 7:14:12
McIntosh 30 1 34N52 106w03 7:04:12
Meadow Lake 32 1 34N49 106w44 7:06:56
Meadow Vista 7 1 31N48 106w35 7:06:20
Medanales 1 36N11 106w11 7:04:44
Melrose 5 1 34N26 103w38 6:54:32
Mentmore 17 1 35N31 108w51 7:15:24
Mesa Poleo 21 1 36N10 106w37 7:06:28
Mescalero 19 1 33N09 105w46 7:03:04
Mescalero Indian Reservation 19
1 33N09 105w46 7:03:04
Mesilla 7 1 32N16 106w48 7:07:12
Mesilla Park 7 1 32N21 106w44 7:06:56
Mesita 32 1 35N02 107w23 7:09:32
Mesquite 7 1 32N10 106w42 7:06:48
Mexican Springs 17
1 35N47 108w50 7:15:20
Miami 4 1 36N21 104w48 6:59:12
Midway 3 1 33N23 104w32 6:58:08
Milagro 10 1 34N39 105w27 7:01:48
Milan 32 1 35N11 107w54 7:11:36
Mills 11 1 36N05 104w15 6:57:00
Milnesand 22 1 33N39 103w20 6:53:20
Mimbres 9 1 32N51 107w59 7:11:56
Mineral Hill 25 1 35N36 105w13 7:00:52
Mission Park 32 1 34N49 106w44 7:06:56
Mogollon 2 1 33N19 108w53 7:15:32
Monero 21 1 36N55 106w52 7:07:28
Monte Aplanado 18
1 35N58 105w20 7:01:20
Monte Verde 4 1 36N33 105w16 7:01:04
Montezuma 25 1 35N39 105w17 7:01:08
Monticello 27 1 33N24 107w27 7:09:48
Montoya 20 2 35N06 104w04 6:56:16
Monument 13 1 32N37 103w16 6:53:04
Mora 18 1 35N58 105w20 7:01:20
Moriarty 30 1 34N59 106w03 7:04:12
Moses 31 1 36N38 103w08 6:52:32
Mosquero 11 1 35N47 103w58 6:55:52
Mountainair 30 1 34N31 106w15 7:05:00
Mountain View 1 1 35N04 106w41 7:06:44
Mountain View 3 1 33N23 104w32 6:58:08
Mount Dora 31 1 36N31 103w29 6:53:56
Mule Creek 9 1 33N07 108w57 7:15:48
Nadine 13 1 32N42 103w09 6:52:36
Nageezi 24 1 36N16 107w45 7:11:00
Nambe 26 1 35N40 105w57 7:03:48
Nambe Indian Reservation 26
1 35N05 106w39 7:06:36
Nambe Pueblo 26 1 35N40 105w57 7:03:48
Nara Visa 20 2 35N37 103w06 6:52:24
Naschitti 24 1 35N52 108w47 7:15:08

Navajo 14 1 33N20 105w40 7:02:40
Navajo 17 1 35N04 108w51 7:15:24
Navajo Dam 24 1 36N56 107w56 7:11:44
Navajo Indian Reservation 17
1 35N41 109w03 7:16:12
Navajo Wingate Village 17
1 35N46 108w35 7:14:20
Newcomb 24 1 36N17 108w42 7:14:48
Newkirk 10 1 35N04 104w16 6:57:04
New Laguna 32 1 35N02 107w25 7:09:40
New York 32 1 35N05 107w31 7:10:04
Nogal 14 1 33N33 105w42 7:02:48
North Carmen 18 1 35N58 105w20 7:01:20
North Harding 11 1 36N01 104w04 6:56:16
North Hidalgo 12 1 32N18 108w53 7:15:32
North Hurley 9 1 32N42 108w08 7:12:32
North San Ysidro 25
1 35N40 105w57 7:03:48
North Valley 1 1 35N10 106w38 7:06:32
Nutrias 21 1 36N42 106w33 7:06:12
Ocate 18 1 36N11 105w03 7:00:12
Oil Center 13 1 32N30 103w16 6:53:04
Ojito 21 1 36N18 107w03 7:08:12
Ojito 29 1 36N14 105w40 7:02:40
Ojo Caliente 29 1 36N18 106w03 7:04:12
Ojo Caliente 32 1 35N04 108w51 7:15:24
Ojo Feliz 18 1 36N04 105w07 7:00:28
Ojo Sarco 21 1 36N07 105w47 7:03:08
Old Albuquerque 1
1 35N06 106w40 7:06:40
Old Moses 31 1 36N38 103w08 6:52:32
Old Picacho 7 1 32N18 106w50 7:07:20
Omega 2 1 34N20 108w30 7:14:00
Organ 7 1 32N26 106w36 7:06:24
Orogrande 19 1 32N24 106w05 7:04:20
Oscura 14 1 33N29 106w03 7:04:12
Otis 8 1 32N25 104w14 6:56:56
Paguate 32 1 35N08 107w23 7:09:32
Pajarito 1 1 34N59 106w42 7:06:48
Pajarito 26 1 36N00 106w05 7:04:20
Pajarito Acres 15
3 35N51 106w16 7:05:04
Palmer Plaza 24 1 36N46 108w10 7:12:40
Paradise Hills 1 1 35N10 106w39 7:06:36
Paraje 32 1 35N03 107w28 7:09:52
Park Springs 25 1 35N36 105w13 7:00:52
Park View 1 36N44 106w34 7:06:16
Pastura 10 1 34N47 104w57 6:59:48
Pecos 25 1 35N35 105w41 7:02:44
Penablanca 23 1 35N34 106w20 7:05:20
Penasco 29 1 36N10 105w41 7:02:44
Penasco Blanco 25
1 35N51 105w26 7:01:44
Pendaries 25 1 35N51 105w26 7:01:44
Pep 22 1 33N50 103w20 6:53:20
Peralta 32 1 34N50 106w41 7:06:44
Perea 17 1 35N28 108w33 7:14:12
Pescado 17 1 35N04 108w51 7:15:24
Petaca 21 1 36N30 106w01 7:04:04
Philadelphia 32 1 35N05 107w31 7:10:04
Philmont 4 1 36N31 104w55 6:59:40
Picacho 14 1 33N21 105w09 7:00:36
Picuris 29 1 36N11 105w43 7:02:52
Picuris Indian Reservation 29
1 35N05 106w39 7:06:36
Pie Town 2 1 34N18 108w09 7:12:36
Pilar 29 1 36N16 105w48 7:03:12
Pine 25 1 35N34 105w40 7:02:40
Pinedale 17 1 35N31 108w44 7:14:56
Pine View 29 1 36N11 105w40 7:02:40
Pineywoods Estates 19
1 32N57 105w45 7:03:00
Pinon 19 1 32N37 105w24 7:01:36
Pinos Altos 9 1 32N52 108w13 7:12:52
Pinoswells 30 1 34N22 105w42 7:02:48
Pintada 10 1 34N56 104w41 6:58:44
Placita 29 1 36N11 105w40 7:02:40
Placitas 21 1 36N29 106w26 7:05:44
Placitas 23 1 35N18 106w25 7:05:40
Placitas 27 1 33N24 107w27 7:09:48
Plaza Blanca 21 1 36N43 106w37 7:06:28
Pleasant Hill 5 1 34N31 103w04 6:52:16
Pleasanton 2 1 33N17 108w53 7:15:32
Pojoaque 26 1 35N54 106w01 7:04:04
Pojoaque Indian Reservation 26
1 35N05 106w39 7:06:36
Pojoaque Valley 26
1 35N40 105w57 7:03:48
Polvadera 28 1 34N12 106w55 7:07:40
Ponderosa 23 1 35N40 106w40 7:06:40
Ponderosa Heights 14
1 33N20 105w40 7:02:40
Ponderosa Pines 1
1 35N05 106w23 7:05:32
Portales 22 1 34N11 103w20 6:53:20
Porter 20 2 35N06 103w19 6:53:16
Pot Creek 29 1 36N25 105w34 7:02:16
Prairieview 13 1 32N57 103w21 6:53:24
Prewitt 17 1 35N22 108w03 7:12:12
Progresso 30 1 34N36 106w02 7:04:08
Pueblito 21 1 36N03 106w04 7:04:16
Pueblitos 32 1 34N40 106w46 7:07:04
Pueblo Pintado 17
1 36N01 107w04 7:08:16
Puertocito Indian Reservatio 28
1 35N05 106w39 7:06:36
Puerto De Luna 10
1 34N50 104w37 6:58:28
Punta de Agua 30 1 34N31 106w14 7:04:56
Quarris Acres 19 1 32N57 105w45 7:03:00
Quarteles 26 1 36N00 106w05 7:04:20
Quay 20 2 34N56 103w46 6:55:04
Queen 8 1 32N25 104w14 6:56:56
Quemado 2 1 34N20 108w30 7:14:00
Querinda Park 29 1 36N42 105w24 7:01:36
Questa 29 1 36N42 105w36 7:02:24
Radium Springs 7 1 32N30 106w56 7:07:44
Rainsville 18 1 36N00 105w12 7:00:48
Ramah 17 1 35N08 108w30 7:14:00
Ramah Indian Reservation 17
1 35N04 108w51 7:15:24
Ramon 14 1 34N26 104w37 6:58:28
Ranches of Taos 29
1 36N22 105w37 7:02:28
Ranchito 29 1 36N24 105w36 7:02:24
Ranchitos 21 1 35N18 106w33 7:06:12
Ranchos De Taos 1 36N22 105w37 7:02:28
Ranchos Lake Conchas 25
1 35N22 104w11 6:56:44
Ranchvale 5 1 34N24 103w16 6:53:04
Raton 4 1 36N54 104w24 6:57:36
Red Hill 2 1 34N20 108w30 7:14:00
Red River 29 1 36N42 105w24 7:01:36
Redrock 9 1 32N41 108w44 7:14:56
Regina 23 1 36N11 106w57 7:07:48
Rehoboth 17 1 35N32 108w39 7:14:36
Rencona 25 1 35N30 105w40 7:02:40
Reservation 17 1 35N49 108w44 7:14:56
Reserve 2 1 33N43 108w45 7:15:00
Ribera 25 1 35N23 105w27 7:01:48
Rincon 7 1 32N40 107w04 7:08:16
Rinconado 21 1 36N13 105w56 7:03:44
Rincon Montoso 25
1 35N46 105w15 7:01:00
Rio Chama 21 1 36N13 106w13 7:04:52
Rio Chiquito 26 1 36N00 105w56 7:03:44
Rio Grande 28 1 34N09 106w52 7:07:28
Rio Grande Estates 32
1 34N40 106w46 7:07:04
Rio Lucio 29 1 36N10 105w41 7:02:44
Rio Rancho 23 1 35N20 106w35 7:06:20
Rito de las Sillas 21
1 36N11 106w34 7:06:16
Riverside 8 1 32N50 104w25 6:57:40
Riverside 14 1 33N23 104w32 6:58:08
Riverside 21 1 36N00 106w05 7:04:20
Robin Hood Park 19
1 32N57 105w45 7:03:00
Rociada 25 1 35N51 105w26 7:01:44
Rock Canyon 27 1 33N09 107w11 7:08:44
Rock Springs 17 1 35N31 108w44 7:14:56
Rodarte 29 1 36N09 105w40 7:02:40
Rodeo 12 1 31N50 109w02 7:16:08
Rodey 7 1 32N40 107w09 7:08:36
Rogers 22 1 33N59 103w14 6:52:56
Romeroville 25 1 35N36 105w13 7:00:52
Rosebud 11 1 35N55 103w09 6:52:36
Roswell 3 1 33N24 104w32 6:58:08
Rowe 25 1 35N30 105w41 7:02:44
Roy 11 1 35N57 104w12 6:56:48
Ruidoso 14 1 33N20 105w41 7:02:44
Ruidoso Downs 14 1 33N20 105w35 7:02:20
Rutheron 21 1 36N43 106w37 7:06:28
Sabinal 28 1 34N34 106w47 7:07:08
Sabinoso 25 1 35N42 104w24 6:57:36
Sacramento 19 1 32N48 105w34 7:02:16
Saint Vrain 5 1 34N25 103w29 6:53:56
Salem 7 1 32N43 107w13 7:08:52
San Acacia 28 1 34N15 106w54 7:07:36
San Antonio 1 1 35N04 106w31 7:06:04
San Antonio 25 1 35N36 105w13 7:00:52
San Antonio 28 1 33N55 106w52 7:07:28
San Antonio de Padua del Ran 26
1 35N40 105w57 7:03:48
San Antonito 1 1 35N10 106w22 7:05:28
San Antonito 28 1 33N55 106w52 7:07:28
Sanchez 25 1 35N51 104w04 6:56:16
San Cristobal 29 1 36N36 105w39 7:02:36
San Cristoval 26 1 35N16 106w01 7:04:04
Sanctuario 26 1 36N00 105w56 7:03:44
Sandia 1 1 35N03 106w33 7:06:12
Sandia Indian Reservation 23
1 35N05 106w39 7:06:36
Sandia Knoll 1 1 35N10 106w22 7:05:28
Sandia Park 1 1 35N10 106w22 7:05:28
Sandia Pueblo 23 1 35N18 106w33 7:06:12
San Felipe Indian Res 23
1 35N05 106w39 7:06:36
San Felipe Pueblo 23
1 35N26 106w27 7:05:48
San Fidel 32 1 35N05 107w36 7:10:24
San Francisco 28 1 34N34 106w47 7:07:08
San Francisco Plaza 2
1 33N43 108w45 7:15:00
San Geronimo 25 1 35N36 105w13 7:00:52
San Ignacio 25 1 35N46 105w21 7:01:24
San Ildefonso 26 1 35N53 106w07 7:04:28
San Ildefonso Indian Res 23
1 35N05 106w39 7:06:36
San Ildefonso Pueblo 26
1 35N40 105w57 7:03:48
San Jon 20 2 35N06 103w20 6:53:20
San Jose 21 1 36N04 106w07 7:04:28
San Jose 25 1 35N24 105w29 7:01:56
San Juan 25 1 35N24 105w29 7:01:56
San Juan Indian Reservation 21
1 35N05 106w39 7:06:36
San Juan Pueblo 21
1 36N03 106w04 7:04:16
San Lorenzo 1 32N49 107w55 7:11:40
San Mateo 32 1 35N20 107w39 7:10:36
San Mateo Springs 32
1 35N20 107w39 7:10:36
San Miguel 7 1 32N09 106w44 7:06:56
San Miguel 25 1 35N22 105w27 7:01:48
Sanostee 24 1 36N47 108w41 7:14:44
San Pablo 25 1 35N36 105w13 7:00:52
San Patricio 14 1 33N25 105w20 7:01:20
San Pedro 21 1 36N00 106w05 7:04:20
San Rafael 25 1 35N28 104w25 6:57:40

San Rafael 32 1 35N07 107w53 7:11:32
San Sebastian 26 1 35N35 105w59 7:03:56
Santa Ana Indian Reservation 23
1 35N05 106w39 7:06:36
Santa Ana Pueblo 23
1 35N26 106w37 7:06:28
Santa Clara Indian Res 21
1 35N05 106w39 7:06:36
Santa Clara Pueblo 21
1 36N00 106w05 7:04:20
Santa Cruz 26 1 35N59 105w55 7:03:40
Santa Fe 26 4 35N41 105w57 7:03:48
Santa Rita 1 32N48 108w04 7:12:16
Santa Rosa 10 1 34N57 104w41 6:58:44
Santo Domingo 23 1 35N34 106w26 7:05:44
Santo Domingo Indian Res 23
1 35N05 106w39 7:06:36
Santo Domingo Pueblo 23
1 35N31 106w22 7:05:28
Santo Nino 26 1 35N59 106w03 7:04:12
Santo Tomas 7 1 32N07 106w40 7:06:40
San Ysidro 23 1 35N34 106w46 7:07:04
Sapello 25 1 35N47 105w15 7:01:00
Seama 32 1 35N05 107w31 7:10:04
Seboyeta 32 1 35N12 107w23 7:09:32
Seboyetita 32 1 35N12 107w23 7:09:32
Sedan 31 1 36N09 103w08 6:52:32
Sedillo Hill 1 1 35N05 106w23 7:05:32
Sena 25 1 35N18 105w24 7:01:36
Seneca 31 1 36N38 103w08 6:52:32
Separ 9 1 32N21 108w42 7:14:48
Serafina 25 1 35N24 105w19 7:01:16
Servilleta Plaza 21
1 36N23 106w02 7:04:08
Seton Village 26 1 35N40 105w57 7:03:48
Seven Lakes 17 1 35N41 108w09 7:12:36
Seven Rivers 8 1 32N38 104w23 6:57:32
Seven Springs 23 1 35N46 106w41 7:06:44
Sheep Springs 17 1 35N52 108w47 7:15:08
Sherman 9 1 32N45 107w51 7:11:24
Shiprock 24 1 36N47 108w41 7:14:44
Sierra Vista 14 1 33N23 105w41 7:02:44
Sierra Vista Estates 1
1 35N04 106w31 7:06:04
Sile 23 1 35N34 106w20 7:05:20
Silver City 9 1 32N46 108w17 7:13:08
Smiths Lake 17 1 35N24 108w13 7:12:52
Socorro 28 1 34N04 106w54 7:07:36
Sofia 31 1 36N35 103w37 6:54:28
Soham 25 1 35N24 105w29 7:01:56
Solano 11 1 35N51 104w04 6:56:16
Sombrillo 26 1 36N00 106w05 7:04:20
South Carmen 18 1 35N56 105w22 7:01:28
South Harding 11 1 35N45 103w34 6:54:16
South Hidalgo 12 1 31N41 108w43 7:14:52
South San Ysidro 25
1 35N24 105w29 7:01:56
South Springs Acres 3
1 33N23 104w32 6:58:08
South Valley 1 1 35N03 106w40 7:06:40
Spindle 14 1 33N33 105w34 7:02:16
Springer 4 1 36N22 104w36 6:58:24
Springstead 17 1 35N46 108w35 7:14:20
Standing Rock 17 1 35N48 108w22 7:13:28
Stanley 26 1 35N09 105w59 7:03:56
Star Lake 17 1 36N01 107w04 7:08:16
Stead 31 1 36N06 103w12 6:52:48
Sunland Park 7 1 31N48 106w35 7:06:20
Sunshine 16 1 32N15 107w45 7:11:00
Sunspot 19 1 32N39 105w42 7:02:48
Sun Valley 14 1 33N23 105w41 7:02:44
Taiban 6 1 34N26 104w01 6:56:04
Tajique 30 1 34N45 106w17 7:05:08
Talpa 29 1 36N22 105w37 7:02:28
Taos 29 1 36N24 105w35 7:02:20
Taos Indian Reservation 29
1 35N05 106w39 7:06:36
Taos Pueblo 29 1 36N26 105w31 7:02:04
Taos Ski Valley 29
1 36N25 105w34 7:02:16
Tatum 13 1 33N16 103w19 6:53:16
Taylor Springs 4 1 36N22 104w35 6:58:20
Tecolote 25 1 35N36 105w13 7:00:52
Tecolotito 25 1 35N12 105w09 7:00:36
Tererro 25 1 35N46 105w40 7:02:40
Tesuque 26 1 35N46 105w56 7:03:44
Tesuque Indian Reservation 26
1 35N05 106w39 7:06:36
Tesuque Pueblo 26
1 35N40 105w57 7:03:48
Texico 5 1 34N24 103w03 6:52:12
Thomas 31 1 36N28 103w11 6:52:44
Thoreau 17 1 35N24 108w13 7:12:52
Three Rivers 19 1 33N19 106w05 7:04:20
Tierra Amarilla 21
1 36N42 106w33 7:06:12
Tierra Monte 25 1 35N51 105w26 7:01:44
Tijeras 1 1 35N05 106w23 7:05:32
Timberon 19 1 32N37 105w24 7:01:36
Tinaja 32 1 35N08 108w30 7:14:00
Tinian 17 1 36N46 108w10 7:12:40
Tinnie 14 1 33N22 105w14 7:00:56
Tiptonville 18 1 35N48 104w59 6:59:56
Toadlena 24 1 36N14 108w53 7:15:32
Tocito 24 1 36N17 108w42 7:14:48
Tohatchi 17 1 35N52 108w47 7:15:08
Tohlakai 17 1 35N31 108w44 7:14:56
Tolar 22 1 34N27 103w56 6:55:44
Tome 32 1 34N44 106w44 7:06:56
T-o Ranch 4 1 36N54 104w26 6:57:44
Torreon 23 1 36N01 107w04 7:08:16
Torreon 30 1 34N45 106w17 7:05:08
Tortugas 7 1 32N21 106w44 7:06:56
Totavi 26 1 35N51 106w16 7:05:04
Trampas 29 1 36N08 105w45 7:03:00

Place		Lat	Long	Time
Trechado 32	1	34N39	108w41	7:14:44
Trementina 25	1	35N28	104w25	6:57:40
Tres Piedras 29	1	36N39	105w58	7:03:52
Tres Ritos 29	1	36N11	105w40	7:02:40
Truchas 21	1	36N03	105w49	7:03:16
Trujillo 25	1	35N32	104w42	6:58:48
Truth or Consequences 27	1	33N08	107w15	7:09:00
Tucumcari 20	2	35N10	103w44	6:54:56
Tularosa 19	1	33N05	106w01	7:04:04
Turley 24	1	36N43	107w50	7:11:20
Turn 32	1	34N40	106w46	7:07:04
Turquillo 18	1	36N08	105w14	7:00:56
Twin Forks Estates 19	1	32N57	105w45	7:03:00
Twin Lakes 17	1	35N31	108w44	7:14:56
Two Gray Hills 24	1	35N52	108w47	7:15:08
Tyrone 9	1	32N40	108w22	7:13:28
University 22	1	34N11	103w20	6:53:20
Upper Anton Chico 10	1	35N12	105w09	7:00:36
Upper Dilia 10	1	35N11	105w07	7:00:28
Upper Pueblo 25	1	35N18	105w24	7:01:36
Upper Rociada 25	1	35N51	105w26	7:01:44
Ute Mountain Indian Res 24	1	37N12	108w44	7:14:56
Ute Park 4	1	36N34	105w06	7:00:24
Vadito 29	1	36N11	105w40	7:02:40
Vado 7	1	32N07	106w40	7:06:40
Valdez 29	1	36N32	105w35	7:02:20
Valencia 32	1	34N49	106w44	7:06:56
Vallecitas 21	1	36N35	106w05	7:04:20
Vallecitos de los Indios 23	1	35N46	106w41	7:06:44
Valle Escondido 29	1	36N25	105w34	7:02:16
Valmora 18	1	35N49	104w55	6:59:40
Val Verde 4	1	36N33	105w16	7:01:04
Vanadium 9	1	32N47	108w07	7:12:28
Vanderwagen 17	1	35N16	108w45	7:15:00
Vaughn 10	1	34N36	105w13	7:00:52
Veguita 28	1	34N31	106w46	7:07:04
Velarde 21	1	36N10	105w58	7:03:52
Ventero 29	1	36N57	105w27	7:01:48
Vermejo Park 4	1	36N54	104w26	6:57:44
Villanueva 25	1	35N16	105w22	7:01:28
Virden 12	1	32N41	109w00	7:16:00
Volcano Cliffs 1	1	35N11	106w42	7:06:48
Wagon Mound 18	1	36N01	104w42	6:58:48
Walker 3	1	33N23	104w32	6:58:08
Water Canyon	1	34N05	107w05	7:08:20
Waterfall 19	1	32N57	105w45	7:03:00
Waterflow 24	1	36N45	108w27	7:13:48
Watrous 18	1	35N48	104w59	6:59:56
Weed 19	1	32N48	105w31	7:02:04
West Carlsbad 8	1	32N25	104w14	6:56:56
West De Baca 6	1	34N26	104w36	6:58:24
West Las Vegas 25	1	35N36	105w13	7:00:52
White Horse 17	1	36N01	107w04	7:08:16
White Lakes 26	1	35N09	105w59	7:03:56
White Oaks 14	1	33N38	105w52	7:03:28
White Rock 15	1	35N49	106w13	7:04:52
White Rock 24	1	35N41	108w09	7:12:36
Whites 8	1	32N11	104w22	6:57:28
White Sands	1	32N23	106w28	7:05:52
White Sands Missile Range 7	1	32N22	106w37	7:06:28
Willard 30	1	34N36	106w02	7:04:08
Williams Acres 17	1	35N31	108w44	7:14:56
Williamsburg 27	1	33N07	107w18	7:09:12
Window Rock Junction 17	1	35N31	108w44	7:14:56
Winston 27	1	33N20	107w39	7:10:36
Yeso 6	1	34N26	104w37	6:58:28
Youngsville 21	1	36N11	106w34	7:06:16
Zamora 1	1	35N05	106w23	7:05:32
Zia Indian Reservation 23	1	35N05	106w39	7:06:36
Zia Pueblo 23	1	35N30	106w43	7:06:52
Zuni 17	1	35N04	108w51	7:15:24
Zuni Indian Reservation 17	1	35N04	108w51	7:15:24
Zuni Pueblo 17	1	35N04	108w51	7:15:24

NEW YORK

TIME TABLES

NY # 1		
Before 11/18/1883		LMT
11/18/1883	12:00	EST
3/31/1918	02:00	EWT
10/27/1918	02:00	EST
3/30/1919	02:00	EWT
10/26/1919	02:00	EST
3/28/1920	02:00	EDT
10/31/1920	02:00	EST
4/24/1921	02:00	EDT
9/25/1921	02:00	EST
4/30/1922	02:00	EDT
9/24/1922	02:00	EST
4/29/1923	02:00	EDT
9/30/1923	02:00	EST
4/27/1924	02:00	EDT
9/28/1924	02:00	EST
4/26/1925	02:00	EDT
9/27/1925	02:00	EST
4/25/1926	02:00	EDT
9/26/1926	02:00	EST
4/24/1927	02:00	EDT
9/25/1927	02:00	EST
4/29/1928	02:00	EDT
9/30/1928	02:00	EST
4/28/1929	02:00	EDT
9/29/1929	02:00	EST
4/27/1930	02:00	EDT
9/28/1930	02:00	EST
4/26/1931	02:00	EDT
9/27/1931	02:00	EST
4/24/1932	02:00	EDT
9/25/1932	02:00	EST
4/30/1933	02:00	EDT
9/24/1933	02:00	EST
4/29/1934	02:00	EDT
9/30/1934	02:00	EST
4/28/1935	02:00	EDT
9/29/1935	02:00	EST
4/26/1936	02:00	EDT
9/27/1936	02:00	EST
4/25/1937	02:00	EDT
9/26/1937	02:00	EST
4/24/1938	02:00	EDT
9/25/1938	02:00	EST
4/30/1939	02:00	EDT
9/24/1939	02:00	EST
4/28/1940	02:00	EDT
9/29/1940	02:00	EST
4/27/1941	02:00	EDT
9/28/1941	02:00	EST
2/09/1942	02:00	EWT
9/30/1945	02:00	EST
4/28/1946	02:00	EDT
9/29/1946	02:00	EST
4/27/1947	02:00	EDT
9/28/1947	02:00	EST
4/25/1948	02:00	EDT
9/26/1948	02:00	EST
4/24/1949	02:00	EDT
9/25/1949	02:00	EST
4/30/1950	02:00	EDT
9/24/1950	02:00	EST
4/29/1951	02:00	EDT
9/30/1951	02:00	EST
4/27/1952	02:00	EDT
9/28/1952	02:00	EST
4/26/1953	02:00	EDT
9/27/1953	02:00	EST
4/25/1954	02:00	EDT
9/26/1954	02:00	EST
4/24/1955	02:00	EDT
10/30/1955	02:00	EST
4/29/1956	02:00	EDT
10/28/1956	02:00	EST
4/28/1957	02:00	EDT
10/27/1957	02:00	EST
4/27/1958	02:00	EDT
10/26/1958	02:00	EST
4/26/1959	02:00	EDT
10/25/1959	02:00	EST
4/24/1960	02:00	EDT
10/30/1960	02:00	EST
4/30/1961	02:00	EDT
10/29/1961	02:00	EST
4/29/1962	02:00	EDT
10/28/1962	02:00	EST
4/28/1963	02:00	EDT
10/27/1963	02:00	EST
4/26/1964	02:00	EDT
10/25/1964	02:00	EST
4/25/1965	02:00	EDT
10/31/1965	02:00	EST
4/24/1966	02:00	EDT
10/30/1966	02:00	EST
4/30/1967	02:00	US#1

NY # 2		
Before 11/18/1883		LMT
11/18/1883	12:00	EST
3/31/1918	02:00	EWT
10/27/1918	02:00	EST
3/30/1919	02:00	EWT
10/26/1919	02:00	EST
3/28/1920	02:00	EDT
10/31/1920	02:00	EST
4/24/1921	02:00	EDT
9/25/1921	02:00	EST
4/30/1922	02:00	EDT
9/24/1922	02:00	EST
4/29/1923	02:00	EDT
9/30/1923	02:00	EST
4/27/1924	02:00	EDT
9/28/1924	02:00	EST
4/26/1925	02:00	EDT
9/27/1925	02:00	EST
4/25/1926	02:00	EDT
9/26/1926	02:00	EST
4/24/1927	02:00	EDT
9/25/1927	02:00	EST
4/29/1928	02:00	EDT
9/30/1928	02:00	EST
4/28/1929	02:00	EDT
9/29/1929	02:00	EST
4/27/1930	02:00	EDT
9/28/1930	02:00	EST
4/26/1931	02:00	EDT
9/27/1931	02:00	EST
4/24/1932	02:00	EDT
9/25/1932	02:00	EST
4/30/1933	02:00	EDT
9/24/1933	02:00	EST
4/29/1934	02:00	EDT
9/30/1934	02:00	EST
4/28/1935	02:00	EDT
9/29/1935	02:00	EST
4/26/1936	02:00	EDT
9/27/1936	02:00	EST
4/25/1937	02:00	EDT
9/26/1937	02:00	EST
4/24/1938	02:00	EDT
9/25/1938	02:00	EST
4/30/1939	02:00	EDT
9/24/1939	02:00	EST
4/28/1940	02:00	EDT
9/29/1940	02:00	EST
4/27/1941	02:00	EDT
9/28/1941	02:00	EST
2/09/1942	02:00	EWT
9/30/1945	02:00	EST
4/24/1955	02:00	US#2

NY # 3		
Before 11/18/1883		LMT
11/18/1883	12:00	EST
3/31/1918	02:00	EWT
10/27/1918	02:00	EST
3/30/1919	02:00	EWT
10/26/1919	02:00	EST
3/28/1920	02:00	EDT
10/31/1920	02:00	EST
4/29/1928	02:00	EDT
9/30/1928	02:00	EST
4/28/1929	02:00	EDT
9/29/1929	02:00	EST
4/27/1930	02:00	EDT
9/28/1930	02:00	EST
4/26/1931	02:00	EDT
9/27/1931	02:00	EST
4/24/1932	02:00	EDT
9/25/1932	02:00	EST
4/30/1933	02:00	EDT
9/24/1933	02:00	EST
4/29/1934	02:00	EDT
9/30/1934	02:00	EST
4/28/1935	02:00	EDT
9/29/1935	02:00	EST
4/26/1936	02:00	EDT
9/27/1936	02:00	EST
4/25/1937	02:00	EDT
9/26/1937	02:00	EST
4/24/1938	02:00	EDT
9/25/1938	02:00	EST
4/30/1939	02:00	EDT
9/24/1939	02:00	EST
4/28/1940	02:00	EDT
9/29/1940	02:00	EST
4/27/1941	02:00	EDT
9/28/1941	02:00	EST
2/09/1942	02:00	EWT
9/30/1945	02:00	EST
4/24/1955	02:00	US#2

NY # 4		
Before 11/18/1883		LMT
11/18/1883	12:00	EST
3/31/1918	02:00	EWT
10/27/1918	02:00	EST
3/30/1919	02:00	EWT
10/26/1919	02:00	EST
3/28/1920	02:00	EDT
10/31/1920	02:00	EST
2/09/1942	02:00	US#2

NY # 5		
Before 11/18/1883		LMT
11/18/1883	12:00	EST
3/31/1918	02:00	EWT
10/27/1918	02:00	EST
3/30/1919	02:00	EWT
10/26/1919	02:00	EST
3/28/1920	02:00	EDT
10/31/1920	02:00	EST
4/24/1938	02:00	EDT
9/25/1938	02:00	EST
4/30/1939	02:00	EDT
9/24/1939	02:00	EST
2/09/1942	02:00	EWT
9/30/1945	02:00	EST
4/24/1955	02:00	US#2

NY # 6		
Before 11/18/1883		LMT
11/18/1883	12:00	EST
3/31/1918	02:00	EWT
10/27/1918	02:00	EST
3/30/1919	02:00	EWT
10/26/1919	02:00	EST
3/28/1920	02:00	EDT
10/31/1920	02:00	EST
4/29/1923	02:00	US#2

NY # 7		
Before 11/18/1883		LMT
11/18/1883	12:00	EST
3/31/1918	02:00	EWT
10/27/1918	02:00	EST
3/30/1919	02:00	EWT
10/26/1919	02:00	EST
3/28/1920	02:00	EDT
10/31/1920	02:00	EST
4/26/1925	02:00	US#2

NY # 8		
Before 11/18/1883		LMT
11/18/1883	12:00	NY#4
4/29/1928	02:00	NY#1
4/30/1967	02:00	US#1

NY # 9		
Before 11/18/1883		LMT
11/18/1883	12:00	NY#4
4/28/1929	02:00	NY#1
4/30/1967	02:00	US#1

NY # 10		
Before 11/18/1883		LMT
11/18/1883	12:00	NY#4
4/27/1930	02:00	NY#1
4/30/1967	02:00	US#1

NY # 11		
Before 11/18/1883		LMT
11/18/1883	12:00	NY#4
4/26/1931	02:00	NY#1
4/30/1967	02:00	US#1

NY # 12		
Before 11/18/1883		LMT
11/18/1883	12:00	NY#4
4/24/1938	02:00	NY#1
4/30/1967	02:00	US#1

NY # 13		
Before 11/18/1883		LMT
11/18/1883	12:00	NY#4
4/30/1939	02:00	NY#1
4/30/1967	02:00	US#1

NY # 14		
Before 11/18/1883		LMT
11/18/1883	12:00	NY#4
4/28/1940	02:00	NY#1
4/30/1967	02:00	US#1

NY # 15		
Before 11/18/1883		LMT
11/18/1883	12:00	NY#4
4/27/1941	02:00	NY#1
4/30/1967	02:00	US#1

NY # 16		
Before 11/18/1883		LMT
11/18/1883	12:00	EST
3/31/1918	02:00	EWT
10/27/1918	02:00	EST
3/30/1919	02:00	EWT
10/26/1919	02:00	EST
3/28/1920	02:00	EDT
10/31/1920	02:00	EST
2/09/1942	02:00	EWT
9/30/1945	02:00	EST
4/27/1947	02:00	NY#1
4/30/1967	02:00	US#1

NY # 17		
Before 11/18/1883		LMT
11/18/1883	12:00	EST
3/31/1918	02:00	EWT
10/27/1918	02:00	EST
3/30/1919	02:00	EWT
10/26/1919	02:00	EST
3/28/1920	02:00	EDT
10/31/1920	02:00	EST
2/09/1942	02:00	EWT
9/30/1945	02:00	EST
4/25/1948	02:00	NY#1
4/30/1967	02:00	US#1

NY # 18		
Before 11/18/1883		LMT
11/18/1883	12:00	EST
3/31/1918	02:00	EWT
10/27/1918	02:00	EST
3/30/1919	02:00	EWT
10/26/1919	02:00	EST
3/28/1920	02:00	EDT
10/31/1920	02:00	EST
2/09/1942	02:00	EWT
9/30/1945	02:00	EST
4/24/1949	02:00	NY#1
4/30/1967	02:00	US#1

NY # 19		
Before 11/18/1883		LMT
11/18/1883	12:00	EST
3/31/1918	02:00	EWT
10/27/1918	02:00	EST
3/30/1919	02:00	EWT
10/26/1919	02:00	EST
3/28/1920	02:00	EDT
10/31/1920	02:00	EST
2/09/1942	02:00	EWT
9/30/1945	02:00	EST
4/30/1950	02:00	NY#1
4/30/1967	02:00	US#1

NY # 20		
Before 11/18/1883		LMT
11/18/1883	12:00	EST
3/31/1918	02:00	EWT
10/27/1918	02:00	EST
3/30/1919	02:00	EWT
10/26/1919	02:00	EST
3/28/1920	02:00	EDT
10/31/1920	02:00	EST
2/09/1942	02:00	EWT
9/30/1945	02:00	EST
4/29/1951	02:00	NY#1
4/30/1967	02:00	US#1

NY # 21		
Before 11/18/1883		LMT
11/18/1883	12:00	NY#4
4/30/1933	02:00	NY#1
4/30/1967	02:00	US#1

NY # 22		
Before 11/18/1883		LMT
11/18/1883	12:00	EST
3/31/1918	02:00	EWT
10/27/1918	02:00	EST
3/30/1919	02:00	EWT
10/26/1919	02:00	EST
3/28/1920	02:00	EDT
10/31/1920	02:00	EST
2/09/1942	02:00	EWT
9/30/1945	02:00	EST
4/26/1953	02:00	NY#1
4/30/1967	02:00	US#1

NY # 23		
Before 11/18/1883		LMT
11/18/1883	12:00	NY#4
4/26/1931	02:00	NY#2
4/24/1955	02:00	US#2

NY # 24		
Before 11/18/1883		LMT
11/18/1883	12:00	NY#4
4/28/1940	02:00	NY#2
4/24/1955	02:00	US#2

NY # 25		
Before 11/18/1883		LMT
11/18/1883	12:00	EST
3/31/1918	02:00	EWT
10/27/1918	02:00	EST
3/30/1919	02:00	EWT
10/26/1919	02:00	EST
3/28/1920	02:00	EDT
10/31/1920	02:00	EST
4/27/1941	02:00	EDT
9/28/1941	02:00	EST
2/09/1942	02:00	EWT
9/30/1945	02:00	EST
4/24/1955	02:00	NY#1
4/30/1967	02:00	US#1

NY # 26		
Before 11/18/1883		LMT
11/18/1883	12:00	EST
3/31/1918	02:00	EWT
10/27/1918	02:00	EST
3/30/1919	02:00	EWT
10/26/1919	02:00	EST
3/28/1920	02:00	EDT
10/31/1920	02:00	EST
4/28/1940	02:00	EDT
9/29/1940	02:00	EST
2/09/1942	02:00	EWT
9/30/1945	02:00	EST
4/24/1955	02:00	NY#1
4/30/1967	02:00	US#1

NY # 27		
Before 11/18/1883		LMT
11/18/1883	12:00	NY#4
9/29/1946	02:00	EST
4/24/1955	02:00	NY#1
4/30/1967	02:00	US#1

NY # 28		
Before 11/18/1883		LMT
11/18/1883	12:00	EST
3/31/1918	02:00	EWT
10/27/1918	02:00	EST
3/30/1919	02:00	EWT
10/26/1919	02:00	EST
3/28/1920	02:00	EDT
10/31/1920	02:00	EST
2/09/1942	02:00	EWT
9/30/1945	02:00	EST
4/27/1947	02:00	EDT
9/28/1947	02:00	EST
4/24/1955	02:00	NY#1
4/30/1967	02:00	US#1

NY # 29		
Before 11/18/1883		LMT
11/18/1883	12:00	EST
3/31/1918	02:00	EWT
10/27/1918	02:00	EST
3/30/1919	02:00	EWT
10/26/1919	02:00	EST
3/28/1920	02:00	EDT
10/31/1920	02:00	EST
2/09/1942	02:00	EWT
9/30/1945	02:00	EST
4/25/1948	02:00	EDT
9/26/1948	02:00	EST
4/24/1955	02:00	NY#1
4/30/1967	02:00	US#1

NY # 30		
Before 11/18/1883		LMT
11/18/1883	12:00	EST
3/31/1918	02:00	EWT
10/27/1918	02:00	EST
3/30/1919	02:00	EWT
10/26/1919	02:00	EST
3/28/1920	02:00	EDT
10/31/1920	02:00	EST
2/09/1942	02:00	EWT
9/30/1945	02:00	EST
4/24/1949	02:00	EDT
9/25/1949	02:00	EST
4/24/1955	02:00	NY#1
4/30/1967	02:00	US#1

NY # 31		
Before 11/18/1883		LMT
11/18/1883	12:00	EST
3/31/1918	02:00	EWT
10/27/1918	02:00	EST
3/30/1919	02:00	EWT
10/26/1919	02:00	EST
3/28/1920	02:00	EDT
10/31/1920	02:00	EST
2/09/1942	02:00	EWT
9/30/1945	02:00	EST
4/29/1951	02:00	EDT
9/30/1951	02:00	EST
4/24/1955	02:00	NY#1
4/30/1967	02:00	US#1

NY # 32		
Before 11/18/1883		LMT
11/18/1883	12:00	EST
3/31/1918	02:00	EWT
10/27/1918	02:00	EST
3/30/1919	02:00	EWT
10/26/1919	02:00	EST
3/28/1920	02:00	EDT
10/31/1920	02:00	EST
2/09/1942	02:00	EWT
9/30/1945	02:00	EST
4/26/1953	02:00	EDT
9/27/1953	02:00	EST
4/24/1955	02:00	NY#1
4/30/1967	02:00	US#1

NY # 33		
Before 11/18/1883		LMT
11/18/1883	12:00	EST
3/31/1918	02:00	EWT
10/27/1918	02:00	EST
3/30/1919	02:00	EWT
10/26/1919	02:00	EST
3/28/1920	02:00	EDT
10/31/1920	02:00	EST
2/09/1942	02:00	EWT
9/30/1945	02:00	EST
4/27/1947	02:00	EDT
9/28/1947	02:00	EST
4/25/1948	02:00	EDT
9/26/1948	02:00	EST
4/24/1955	02:00	NY#1
4/30/1967	02:00	US#1

NY # 34		
Before 11/18/1883		LMT
11/18/1883	12:00	EST
3/31/1918	02:00	EWT
10/27/1918	02:00	EST
3/30/1919	02:00	EWT
10/26/1919	02:00	EST
3/28/1920	02:00	EDT
10/31/1920	02:00	EST
2/09/1942	02:00	EWT
9/30/1945	02:00	EST
4/25/1948	02:00	EDT
9/26/1948	02:00	EST
4/24/1949	02:00	EDT
9/25/1949	02:00	EST
4/24/1955	02:00	NY#1
4/30/1967	02:00	US#1

NY # 35		
Before 11/18/1883		LMT
11/18/1883	12:00	EST
3/31/1918	02:00	EWT
10/27/1918	02:00	EST
3/30/1919	02:00	EWT
10/26/1919	02:00	EST
3/28/1920	02:00	EDT
10/31/1920	02:00	EST
2/09/1942	02:00	EWT
9/30/1945	02:00	EST
4/25/1948	02:00	EDT
9/26/1948	02:00	EST
4/24/1949	02:00	EDT
9/25/1949	02:00	EST
4/30/1950	02:00	EDT
9/24/1950	02:00	EST
4/24/1955	02:00	NY#1
4/30/1967	02:00	US#1

NY # 36		
Before 11/18/1883		LMT

TIME TABLES

11/18/1883 12:00 EST
3/31/1918 02:00 EWT
10/27/1918 02:00 EST
3/30/1919 02:00 EWT
10/26/1919 02:00 EST
3/28/1920 02:00 EDT
10/31/1920 02:00 EST
2/09/1942 02:00 EWT
9/30/1945 02:00 EST
4/27/1947 02:00 EDT
9/28/1947 02:00 EST
4/25/1948 02:00 EDT
9/26/1948 02:00 EST
4/24/1949 02:00 EDT
9/25/1949 02:00 EST
4/30/1950 02:00 EDT
9/24/1950 02:00 EST
4/24/1955 02:00 NY#1
4/30/1967 02:00 US#1
....
NY # 37
Before 11/18/1883 LMT
11/18/1883 12:00 NY#4
4/28/1935 02:00 NY#1
4/30/1967 02:00 US#1
....
NY # 38
Before 11/18/1883 LMT
11/18/1883 12:00 NY#1
9/29/1946 02:00 EST
4/24/1955 02:00 NY#1
4/30/1967 02:00 US#1
....
NY # 39
Before 11/18/1883 LMT
11/18/1883 12:00 NY#2
4/25/1948 02:00 EDT
9/26/1948 02:00 EST
4/24/1955 02:00 NY#1
4/30/1967 02:00 US#1
....
NY # 40
Before 11/18/1883 LMT
11/18/1883 12:00 NY#4
4/29/1934 02:00 NY#1
4/30/1967 02:00 US#1
....
NY # 41
Before 11/18/1883 LMT
11/18/1883 12:00 NY#1
9/25/1921 02:00 EST
4/30/1939 02:00 NY#1
4/30/1967 02:00 US#1
....
NY # 42
Before 11/18/1883 LMT
11/18/1883 12:00 NY#4
4/24/1932 02:00 NY#1
4/30/1967 02:00 US#1
....
NY # 43
Before 11/18/1883 LMT
11/18/1883 12:00 NY#2
4/29/1951 02:00 NY#1
4/30/1967 02:00 US#1
....
NY # 44
Before 11/18/1883 LMT
11/18/1883 12:00 EST
3/31/1918 02:00 EWT
10/27/1918 02:00 EST
3/30/1919 02:00 EWT
10/26/1919 02:00 EST
3/28/1920 02:00 EDT
10/31/1920 02:00 EST
4/28/1940 02:00 EDT
9/29/1940 02:00 EST
4/27/1941 02:00 EDT
9/28/1941 02:00 EST
2/09/1942 02:00 EWT
9/30/1945 02:00 EST
4/28/1946 02:00 EDT
9/29/1946 02:00 EST
4/24/1955 02:00 NY#1
4/30/1967 02:00 US#1
....
NY # 45
Before 11/18/1883 LMT
11/18/1883 12:00 EST
3/31/1918 02:00 EWT
10/27/1918 02:00 EST
3/30/1919 02:00 EWT
10/26/1919 02:00 EST
3/28/1920 02:00 EDT
10/31/1920 02:00 EST
4/24/1921 02:00 EDT
9/25/1921 02:00 EST
4/25/1937 02:00 NY#1
4/30/1967 02:00 US#1
....
NY # 46
Before 11/18/1883 LMT
11/18/1883 12:00 NY#2
4/29/1951 02:00 EDT
9/30/1951 02:00 EST
4/26/1953 02:00 NY#1
4/30/1967 02:00 US#1
....
NY # 47
Before 11/18/1883 LMT
11/18/1883 12:00 NY#4
4/25/1937 02:00 EDT
9/26/1937 02:00 EST
2/09/1942 02:00 EWT
9/30/1945 02:00 EST
4/24/1955 02:00 NY#1
4/30/1967 02:00 US#1
....
NY # 48
Before 11/18/1883 LMT
11/18/1883 12:00 EST
3/31/1918 02:00 EWT
10/27/1918 02:00 EST
3/30/1919 02:00 EWT
10/26/1919 02:00 EST
3/28/1920 02:00 EDT
10/31/1920 02:00 EST
4/29/1923 02:00 EDT
9/30/1923 02:00 EST
4/27/1924 02:00 EDT
9/28/1924 02:00 EST
4/26/1925 02:00 EDT
9/27/1925 02:00 EST
4/25/1926 02:00 EDT
9/26/1926 02:00 EST
4/24/1927 02:00 EDT
9/25/1927 02:00 EST
4/29/1928 02:00 EDT
9/30/1928 02:00 EST
4/28/1929 02:00 EDT
9/29/1929 02:00 EST
4/27/1930 02:00 EDT
9/28/1930 02:00 EST
4/26/1931 02:00 EDT
9/27/1931 02:00 EST
4/24/1932 02:00 EDT
9/25/1932 02:00 EST
4/30/1933 02:00 EDT
9/24/1933 02:00 EST
4/29/1934 02:00 EDT
9/30/1934 02:00 EST
4/28/1935 02:00 EDT
9/29/1935 02:00 EST
4/26/1936 02:00 EDT
9/27/1936 02:00 EST
4/25/1937 02:00 EDT
9/26/1937 02:00 EST
4/24/1938 02:00 EDT
9/25/1938 02:00 EST
4/30/1939 02:00 EDT
9/24/1939 02:00 EST
4/28/1940 02:00 EDT
9/29/1940 02:00 EST
4/27/1941 02:00 EDT
9/28/1941 02:00 EST
2/09/1942 02:00 EWT
9/30/1945 02:00 EST
4/25/1948 02:00 EDT
9/26/1948 02:00 EST
4/24/1955 02:00 NY#1
4/30/1967 02:00 US#1
....
NY # 49
Before 11/18/1883 LMT
11/18/1883 12:00 NY#4
4/25/1937 02:00 NY#1
4/30/1967 02:00 US#1
....
NY # 50
Before 11/18/1883 LMT
11/18/1883 12:00 NY#4
4/28/1935 02:00 EDT
9/29/1935 02:00 EST
4/26/1936 02:00 EDT
9/27/1936 02:00 EST
4/25/1937 02:00 EDT
9/26/1937 02:00 EST
4/24/1938 02:00 EDT
9/25/1938 02:00 EST
4/30/1939 02:00 EDT
9/24/1939 02:00 EST
2/09/1942 02:00 EWT
9/30/1945 02:00 EST
4/24/1955 02:00 NY#1
4/30/1967 02:00 US#1
....
NY # 51
Before 11/18/1883 LMT
11/18/1883 12:00 NY#1
4/30/1939 02:00 EDT
10/01/1939 02:00 NY#1
4/30/1967 02:00 US#1
....
NY # 52
Before 11/18/1883 LMT
11/18/1883 12:00 EST
3/31/1918 02:00 EWT
10/27/1918 02:00 EST
3/30/1919 02:00 EWT
10/26/1919 02:00 EST
3/28/1920 02:00 EDT
10/31/1920 02:00 EST
4/24/1932 02:00 EDT
9/25/1932 02:00 EST
4/30/1933 02:00 EDT
9/24/1933 02:00 EST
4/29/1934 02:00 EDT
9/30/1934 02:00 EST
4/28/1935 02:00 EDT
9/29/1935 02:00 EST
4/26/1936 02:00 EDT
9/27/1936 02:00 EST
4/25/1937 02:00 EDT
9/26/1937 02:00 EST
4/24/1938 02:00 EDT
9/25/1938 02:00 EST
4/30/1939 02:00 EDT
9/24/1939 02:00 EST
4/28/1940 02:00 EDT
9/29/1940 02:00 EST
4/27/1941 02:00 EDT
9/28/1941 02:00 EST
2/09/1942 02:00 EWT
9/30/1945 02:00 EST
4/24/1955 02:00 NY#1
4/30/1967 02:00 US#1
....
NY # 53
Before 11/18/1883 LMT
11/18/1883 12:00 EST
3/31/1918 02:00 EWT
10/27/1918 02:00 EST
3/30/1919 02:00 EWT
10/26/1919 02:00 EST
3/28/1920 02:00 EDT
10/31/1920 02:00 EST
4/29/1934 02:00 EDT
9/30/1934 02:00 EST
4/28/1935 02:00 EDT
9/29/1935 02:00 EST
4/26/1936 02:00 EDT
9/27/1936 02:00 EST
4/25/1937 02:00 EDT
9/26/1937 02:00 EST
4/24/1938 02:00 EDT
9/25/1938 02:00 EST
4/30/1939 02:00 EDT
9/24/1939 02:00 EST
4/28/1940 02:00 EDT
9/29/1940 02:00 EST
4/27/1941 02:00 EDT
9/28/1941 02:00 EST
2/09/1942 02:00 EWT
9/30/1945 02:00 EST
4/24/1955 02:00 NY#1
4/30/1967 02:00 US#1
....
NY # 54
Before 11/18/1883 LMT
11/18/1883 12:00 NY#4
4/26/1936 02:00 NY#1
4/30/1967 02:00 US#1
....
NY # 55
Before 11/18/1883 LMT
11/18/1883 12:00 NY#4
4/29/1923 02:00 EDT
9/30/1923 02:00 EST
4/27/1924 02:00 EDT
9/28/1924 02:00 EST
4/26/1925 02:00 EDT
9/27/1925 02:00 EST
4/25/1926 02:00 EDT
9/26/1926 02:00 EST
4/24/1927 02:00 EDT
9/25/1927 02:00 EST
4/29/1928 02:00 EDT
9/30/1928 02:00 EST
4/28/1929 02:00 EDT
9/29/1929 02:00 EST
4/27/1930 02:00 EDT
9/28/1930 02:00 EST
4/26/1931 02:00 EDT
9/27/1931 02:00 EST
4/24/1932 02:00 EDT
9/25/1932 02:00 EST
4/30/1933 02:00 EDT
9/24/1933 02:00 EST
4/29/1934 02:00 EDT
9/30/1934 02:00 EST
4/28/1935 02:00 EDT
9/29/1935 02:00 EST
4/26/1936 02:00 EDT
9/27/1936 02:00 EST
4/25/1937 02:00 EDT
9/26/1937 02:00 EST
4/24/1938 02:00 EDT
9/25/1938 02:00 EST
4/30/1939 02:00 EDT
9/24/1939 02:00 EST
4/28/1940 02:00 EDT
9/29/1940 02:00 EST
4/27/1941 02:00 EDT
9/28/1941 02:00 EST
2/09/1942 02:00 EWT
9/30/1945 02:00 EST
4/28/1946 02:00 EDT
9/29/1946 02:00 EST
4/27/1947 02:00 EDT
9/28/1947 02:00 EST
4/25/1948 02:00 EDT
9/26/1948 02:00 EST
4/30/1950 02:00 NY#1
4/30/1967 02:00 US#1
....
NY # 56
Before 11/18/1883 LMT
11/18/1883 12:00 EST
3/31/1918 02:00 EWT
10/27/1918 02:00 EST
3/30/1919 02:00 EWT
10/26/1919 02:00 EST
3/28/1920 02:00 EDT
10/31/1920 02:00 EST
4/28/1935 02:00 EDT
9/29/1935 02:00 EST
6/07/1936 02:00 EDT
9/01/1936 02:00 EST
5/30/1937 02:00 EDT
9/07/1937 02:00 EST
6/05/1938 02:00 EDT
9/10/1938 02:00 EST
4/30/1939 02:00 EDT
9/24/1939 02:00 EST
6/02/1940 02:00 NY#1
4/30/1967 02:00 US#1
....
NY # 57
Before 11/18/1883 LMT
11/18/1883 12:00 EST
3/31/1918 02:00 EWT
10/27/1918 02:00 EST
3/30/1919 02:00 EWT
10/26/1919 02:00 EST
3/28/1920 02:00 EDT
10/31/1920 02:00 EST
4/26/1925 02:00 EDT
9/27/1925 02:00 EST
4/25/1926 02:00 EDT
9/26/1926 02:00 EST
4/24/1927 02:00 EDT
9/25/1927 02:00 EST
4/29/1928 02:00 EDT
9/30/1928 02:00 EST
4/28/1929 02:00 EDT
9/29/1929 02:00 EST
4/27/1930 02:00 EDT
9/28/1930 02:00 EST
4/26/1931 02:00 EDT
9/27/1931 02:00 EST
4/24/1932 02:00 EDT
9/25/1932 02:00 EST
4/30/1933 02:00 EDT
9/24/1933 02:00 EST
4/29/1934 02:00 EDT
9/30/1934 02:00 EST
4/28/1935 02:00 EDT
9/29/1935 02:00 EST
4/26/1936 02:00 EDT
9/27/1936 02:00 EST
4/25/1937 02:00 EDT
9/26/1937 02:00 EST
4/24/1938 02:00 EDT
9/25/1938 02:00 EST
4/30/1939 02:00 EDT
9/24/1939 02:00 EST
4/28/1940 02:00 EDT
9/29/1940 02:00 EST
4/27/1941 02:00 EDT
9/28/1941 02:00 EST
2/09/1942 02:00 EWT
9/30/1945 02:00 EST
4/27/1947 02:00 NY#1
4/30/1967 02:00 US#1
....
NY # 58
Before 11/18/1883 LMT
11/18/1883 12:00 NY#4
6/13/1937 02:00 EDT
9/07/1937 02:00 EST
4/24/1938 02:00 NY#1
4/30/1967 02:00 US#1
....
NY # 59
Before 11/18/1883 LMT
11/18/1883 12:00 NY#4
6/25/1940 02:00 EDT
9/10/1940 02:00 EST
2/09/1942 02:00 EWT
9/30/1945 02:00 EST
4/24/1949 02:00 NY#1
4/30/1967 02:00 US#1
....
NY # 60
Before 11/18/1883 LMT
11/18/1883 12:00 NY#4
4/26/1925 02:00 EDT
9/27/1925 02:00 EST
4/30/1939 02:00 NY#1
4/30/1967 02:00 US#1
....
NY # 61
Before 11/18/1883 LMT
11/18/1883 12:00 EST
3/31/1918 02:00 EWT
10/27/1918 02:00 EST
3/30/1919 02:00 EWT
10/26/1919 02:00 EST
3/28/1920 02:00 EDT
10/31/1920 02:00 EST
4/26/1925 02:00 EDT
9/27/1925 02:00 EST
4/25/1926 02:00 EDT
9/26/1926 02:00 EST
4/24/1927 02:00 EDT
9/25/1927 02:00 EST
4/29/1928 02:00 EDT
9/30/1928 02:00 EST
4/28/1929 02:00 EDT
9/29/1929 02:00 EST
4/27/1930 02:00 EDT
9/28/1930 02:00 EST
4/26/1931 02:00 EDT
9/27/1931 02:00 EST
4/24/1932 02:00 EDT
9/25/1932 02:00 EST
4/30/1933 02:00 EDT
9/24/1933 02:00 EST
4/29/1934 02:00 EDT
9/30/1934 02:00 EST
4/28/1935 02:00 EDT
9/29/1935 02:00 EST
4/26/1936 02:00 EDT
9/27/1936 02:00 EST
4/25/1937 02:00 EDT
9/26/1937 02:00 EST
4/24/1938 02:00 EDT
9/25/1938 02:00 EST
4/30/1939 02:00 EDT
9/24/1939 02:00 EST
4/28/1940 02:00 EDT
9/29/1940 02:00 EST
4/27/1941 02:00 EDT
9/28/1941 02:00 EST
2/09/1942 02:00 EWT
9/30/1945 02:00 EST
4/28/1946 02:00 EDT
9/29/1946 02:00 EST
4/24/1949 02:00 NY#1
4/30/1967 02:00 US#1
....
NY # 62
Before 11/18/1883 LMT
11/18/1883 12:00 EST
3/31/1918 02:00 EWT
10/27/1918 02:00 EST
3/30/1919 02:00 EWT
10/26/1919 02:00 EST
3/28/1920 02:00 EDT
10/31/1920 02:00 EST
4/26/1925 02:00 EDT
9/27/1925 02:00 EST
4/25/1926 02:00 EDT
9/26/1926 02:00 EST
4/24/1927 02:00 EDT
9/25/1927 02:00 EST
4/29/1928 02:00 EDT
9/30/1928 02:00 EST
4/28/1929 02:00 EDT
9/29/1929 02:00 EST
4/27/1930 02:00 EDT
9/28/1930 02:00 EST
4/26/1931 02:00 EDT
9/27/1931 02:00 EST
4/24/1932 02:00 EDT
9/25/1932 02:00 EST
4/30/1933 02:00 EDT
10/01/1933 02:00 NY#1
4/30/1967 02:00 US#1
....
NY # 63
Before 11/18/1883 LMT
11/18/1883 12:00 EST
3/31/1918 02:00 EWT
10/27/1918 02:00 EST
3/30/1919 02:00 EWT
10/26/1919 02:00 EST
3/28/1920 02:00 EDT
10/31/1920 02:00 EST
4/26/1931 02:00 EDT
9/27/1931 02:00 EST
4/24/1932 02:00 EDT
9/25/1932 02:00 EST
4/30/1933 02:00 EDT
9/24/1933 02:00 EST
4/29/1934 02:00 EDT
9/30/1934 02:00 EST
4/28/1935 02:00 EDT
9/02/1935 02:00 EST
4/26/1936 02:00 EDT
9/07/1936 02:00 EST
4/25/1937 02:00 NY#1
4/30/1967 02:00 US#1
....
NY # 64
Before 11/18/1883 LMT
11/18/1883 12:00 EST
3/31/1918 02:00 EWT
10/27/1918 02:00 EST
3/30/1919 02:00 EWT
10/26/1919 02:00 EST
3/28/1920 02:00 EDT
10/31/1920 02:00 EST
4/26/1925 02:00 EDT
9/27/1925 02:00 EST
4/25/1926 02:00 EDT
9/26/1926 02:00 EST
4/24/1927 02:00 EDT
9/25/1927 02:00 EST
4/29/1928 02:00 EDT
9/30/1928 02:00 EST
4/28/1929 02:00 EDT
9/29/1929 02:00 EST
4/27/1930 02:00 EDT
9/28/1930 02:00 EST
4/26/1931 02:00 EDT
9/27/1931 02:00 EST
4/24/1932 02:00 EDT
9/25/1932 02:00 EST
4/30/1933 02:00 EDT
9/24/1933 02:00 EST
4/29/1934 02:00 EDT
9/30/1934 02:00 EST
4/28/1935 02:00 EDT
9/29/1935 02:00 EST
4/26/1936 02:00 EDT
9/27/1936 02:00 EST
4/25/1937 02:00 EDT
9/26/1937 02:00 EST
4/24/1938 02:00 EDT
9/25/1938 02:00 EST
4/30/1939 02:00 EDT
9/24/1939 02:00 EST
4/28/1940 02:00 EDT
9/29/1940 02:00 EST
4/27/1941 02:00 EDT
9/28/1941 02:00 EST
2/09/1942 02:00 EWT
9/30/1945 02:00 EST
4/27/1947 02:00 EDT

TIME TABLES

9/28/1947	02:00	EST
4/25/1948	02:00	EDT
9/26/1948	02:00	EST
4/26/1953	02:00	NY#1
4/30/1967	02:00	US#1

NY # 65

Before 11/18/1883		LMT
11/18/1883	12:00	EST
3/31/1918	02:00	EWT
10/27/1918	02:00	EST
3/30/1919	02:00	EWT
10/26/1919	02:00	EST
3/28/1920	02:00	EDT
10/31/1920	02:00	EST
4/26/1931	02:00	EDT
9/27/1931	02:00	EST
2/09/1942	02:00	EWT
9/30/1945	02:00	EST
4/25/1948	02:00	NY#1
4/30/1967	02:00	US#1

NY # 66

Before 11/18/1883		LMT
11/18/1883	12:00	EST
3/31/1918	02:00	EWT
10/27/1918	02:00	EST
3/30/1919	02:00	EWT
10/26/1919	02:00	EST
3/28/1920	02:00	EDT
10/31/1920	02:00	EST
4/26/1931	02:00	EDT
9/27/1931	02:00	EST
4/24/1932	02:00	EDT
9/25/1932	02:00	EST
4/30/1933	02:00	EDT
9/24/1933	02:00	EST
4/29/1934	02:00	EDT
9/30/1934	02:00	EST
4/28/1935	02:00	EDT
9/29/1935	02:00	EST
4/26/1936	02:00	EDT
9/27/1936	02:00	EST
4/25/1937	02:00	EDT
9/26/1937	02:00	EST
4/24/1938	02:00	EDT
10/02/1938	02:00	NY#1
4/30/1967	02:00	US#1

NY # 67

Before 11/18/1883		LMT
11/18/1883	12:00	NY#4
5/12/1940	02:00	EDT
9/02/1940	02:00	EST
4/27/1941	02:00	NY#1
4/30/1967	02:00	US#1

NY # 68

Before 11/18/1883		LMT
11/18/1883	12:00	EST
3/31/1918	02:00	EWT
10/27/1918	02:00	EST
3/30/1919	02:00	EWT
10/26/1919	02:00	EST
3/28/1920	02:00	EDT
10/31/1920	02:00	EST
4/24/1932	02:00	EDT
9/25/1932	02:00	EST
4/30/1933	02:00	EDT
9/24/1933	02:00	EST
4/29/1934	02:00	EDT
9/30/1934	02:00	EST
4/28/1935	02:00	EDT
9/29/1935	02:00	EST
4/26/1936	02:00	EDT
9/27/1936	02:00	EST
4/25/1937	02:00	EDT
9/26/1937	02:00	EST
4/24/1938	02:00	EDT
10/02/1938	02:00	NY#1
4/30/1967	02:00	US#1

NY # 69

Before 11/18/1883		LMT
11/18/1883	12:00	EST
3/31/1918	02:00	EWT
10/27/1918	02:00	EST
3/30/1919	02:00	EWT
10/26/1919	02:00	EST
3/28/1920	02:00	EDT
10/31/1920	02:00	EST
4/26/1931	02:00	EDT
9/27/1931	02:00	EST
4/24/1932	02:00	EDT
9/25/1932	02:00	EST
4/30/1933	02:00	EDT
9/24/1933	02:00	EST
4/29/1934	02:00	EDT
9/30/1934	02:00	EST
4/28/1935	02:00	EDT
9/29/1935	02:00	EST
4/26/1936	02:00	EDT
9/27/1936	02:00	EST
4/25/1937	02:00	EDT
9/26/1937	02:00	EST
4/24/1938	02:00	EDT
9/25/1938	02:00	EST
4/30/1939	02:00	EDT
9/24/1939	02:00	EST
4/28/1940	02:00	EDT
9/29/1940	02:00	EST
4/27/1941	02:00	EDT
9/28/1941	02:00	EST
2/09/1942	02:00	EWT

9/30/1945	02:00	EST
4/27/1947	02:00	NY#1
4/30/1967	02:00	US#1

NY # 70

Before 11/18/1883		LMT
11/18/1883	12:00	NY#4
4/26/1931	02:00	EDT
9/16/1931	02:00	EST
4/24/1932	02:00	NY#1
4/30/1967	02:00	US#1

NY # 71

Before 11/18/1883		LMT
11/18/1883	12:00	EST
3/31/1918	02:00	EWT
10/27/1918	02:00	EST
3/30/1919	02:00	EWT
10/26/1919	02:00	EST
3/28/1920	02:00	EDT
10/31/1920	02:00	EST
4/24/1938	02:00	EDT
9/25/1938	02:00	EST
4/30/1939	02:00	EDT
9/24/1939	02:00	EST
4/28/1940	02:00	EDT
9/29/1940	02:00	EST
4/27/1941	02:00	EDT
9/28/1941	02:00	EST
2/09/1942	02:00	EWT
9/30/1945	02:00	EST
4/29/1951	02:00	NY#1
4/30/1967	02:00	US#1

NY # 72

Before 11/18/1883		LMT
11/18/1883	12:00	EST
3/31/1918	02:00	EWT
10/27/1918	02:00	EST
3/30/1919	02:00	EWT
10/26/1919	02:00	EST
3/28/1920	02:00	EDT
10/31/1920	02:00	EST
4/30/1933	02:00	EDT
9/24/1933	02:00	EST
4/29/1934	02:00	EDT
9/30/1934	02:00	EST
4/28/1935	02:00	EDT
9/29/1935	02:00	EST
4/26/1936	02:00	EDT
9/27/1936	02:00	EST
4/25/1937	02:00	EDT
9/26/1937	02:00	EST
4/24/1938	02:00	EDT
9/25/1938	02:00	EST
4/30/1939	02:00	EDT
9/24/1939	02:00	EST
4/28/1940	02:00	EDT
9/29/1940	02:00	EST
4/27/1941	02:00	EDT
9/28/1941	02:00	EST
2/09/1942	02:00	EWT
9/30/1945	02:00	EST
4/25/1948	02:00	EDT
9/26/1948	02:00	EST
4/24/1955	02:00	NY#1
4/30/1967	02:00	US#1

NY # 73

Before 11/18/1883		LMT
11/18/1883	12:00	NY#5
9/25/1938	02:00	EST
2/09/1942	02:00	EWT
9/30/1945	02:00	EST
4/24/1949	02:00	EDT
9/25/1949	02:00	EST
4/24/1955	02:00	NY#1
4/30/1967	02:00	US#1

NY # 74

Before 11/18/1883		LMT
11/18/1883	12:00	EST
3/31/1918	02:00	EWT
10/27/1918	02:00	EST
3/30/1919	02:00	EWT
10/26/1919	02:00	EST
3/28/1920	02:00	EDT
10/31/1920	02:00	EST
4/26/1931	02:00	EDT
9/27/1931	02:00	EST
4/24/1932	02:00	EDT
9/25/1932	02:00	EST
4/30/1933	02:00	EDT
9/24/1933	02:00	EST
4/29/1934	02:00	EDT
9/30/1934	02:00	EST
4/28/1935	02:00	EDT
9/29/1935	02:00	EST
4/26/1936	02:00	EDT
9/27/1936	02:00	EST
4/25/1937	02:00	EDT
9/26/1937	02:00	EST
4/24/1938	02:00	EDT
9/25/1938	02:00	EST
4/30/1939	02:00	EDT
9/24/1939	02:00	EST
4/28/1940	02:00	EDT
9/29/1940	02:00	EST
4/27/1941	02:00	EDT
9/28/1941	02:00	EST
2/09/1942	02:00	EWT
9/30/1945	02:00	EST
4/25/1948	02:00	EDT
9/26/1948	02:00	EST

4/24/1955	02:00	NY#1
4/30/1967	02:00	US#1

NY # 75

Before 11/18/1883		LMT
11/18/1883	12:00	NY#4
4/24/1938	02:00	EDT
9/25/1938	02:00	EST
4/30/1939	02:00	EDT
9/24/1939	02:00	EST
4/28/1940	02:00	EDT
9/29/1940	02:00	EST
4/27/1941	02:00	EDT
9/28/1941	02:00	EST
2/09/1942	02:00	EWT
9/30/1945	02:00	EST
4/25/1948	02:00	EDT
9/26/1948	02:00	EST
4/24/1955	02:00	NY#1
4/30/1967	02:00	US#1

NY # 76

Before 11/18/1883		LMT
11/18/1883	12:00	EST
3/31/1918	02:00	EWT
10/27/1918	02:00	EST
3/30/1919	02:00	EWT
10/26/1919	02:00	EST
3/28/1920	02:00	EDT
10/31/1920	02:00	EST
4/28/1935	02:00	EDT
9/29/1935	02:00	EST
4/26/1936	02:00	EDT
9/27/1936	02:00	EST
4/25/1937	02:00	EDT
9/26/1937	02:00	EST
4/24/1938	02:00	EDT
9/25/1938	02:00	EST
4/30/1939	02:00	EDT
9/24/1939	02:00	EST
4/28/1940	02:00	EDT
9/29/1940	02:00	EST
4/27/1941	02:00	EDT
9/28/1941	02:00	EST
2/09/1942	02:00	EWT
9/30/1945	02:00	EST
4/25/1948	02:00	EDT
9/26/1948	02:00	EST
4/24/1955	02:00	NY#1
4/30/1967	02:00	US#1

NY # 77

Before 11/18/1883		LMT
11/18/1883	12:00	EST
3/31/1918	02:00	EWT
10/27/1918	02:00	EST
3/30/1919	02:00	EWT
10/26/1919	02:00	EST
3/28/1920	02:00	EDT
10/31/1920	02:00	EST
4/28/1940	02:00	EDT
9/29/1940	02:00	EST
4/27/1941	02:00	EDT
9/28/1941	02:00	EST
2/09/1942	02:00	EWT
9/30/1945	02:00	EST
4/25/1948	02:00	NY#1
4/30/1967	02:00	US#1

NY # 78

Before 11/18/1883		LMT
11/18/1883	12:00	EST
3/31/1918	02:00	EWT
10/27/1918	02:00	EST
3/30/1919	02:00	EWT
10/26/1919	02:00	EST
3/28/1920	02:00	EDT
10/31/1920	02:00	EST
4/30/1939	02:00	EDT
9/24/1939	02:00	EST
2/09/1942	02:00	EWT
9/30/1945	02:00	EST
4/27/1947	02:00	EDT
9/28/1947	02:00	EST
4/25/1948	02:00	EDT
9/26/1948	02:00	EST
4/24/1955	02:00	NY#1
4/30/1967	02:00	US#1

NY # 79

Before 11/18/1883		LMT
11/18/1883	12:00	EST
3/31/1918	02:00	EWT
10/27/1918	02:00	EST
3/30/1919	02:00	EWT
10/26/1919	02:00	EST
3/28/1920	02:00	EDT
10/31/1920	02:00	EST
4/26/1931	02:00	EDT
9/27/1931	02:00	EST
4/24/1932	02:00	EDT
9/25/1932	02:00	EST
4/30/1933	02:00	EDT
9/24/1933	02:00	EST
4/29/1934	02:00	EDT
9/30/1934	02:00	EST
4/28/1935	02:00	EDT
9/29/1935	02:00	EST
4/26/1936	02:00	EDT
9/27/1936	02:00	EST
4/25/1937	02:00	EDT
9/26/1937	02:00	EST
4/24/1938	02:00	EDT
9/25/1938	02:00	EST

4/30/1939	02:00	EDT
9/24/1939	02:00	EST
4/28/1940	02:00	EDT
9/29/1940	02:00	EST
4/27/1941	02:00	EDT
9/28/1941	02:00	EST
2/09/1942	02:00	EWT
9/30/1945	02:00	EST
4/24/1949	02:00	NY#1
4/30/1967	02:00	US#1

NY # 80

Before 11/18/1883		LMT
11/18/1883	12:00	EST
3/31/1918	02:00	EWT
10/27/1918	02:00	EST
3/30/1919	02:00	EWT
10/26/1919	02:00	EST
3/28/1920	02:00	EDT
10/31/1920	02:00	EST
4/30/1933	02:00	EDT
9/24/1933	02:00	EST
4/29/1934	02:00	EDT
9/30/1934	02:00	EST
4/24/1938	02:00	NY#2
4/24/1955	02:00	US#2

NY # 81

Before 11/18/1883		LMT
11/18/1883	12:00	EST
3/31/1918	02:00	EWT
10/27/1918	02:00	EST
3/30/1919	02:00	EWT
10/26/1919	02:00	EST
3/28/1920	02:00	EDT
10/31/1920	02:00	EST
4/26/1925	02:00	EDT
9/27/1925	02:00	EST
4/25/1926	02:00	EDT
9/26/1926	02:00	EST
4/24/1927	02:00	EDT
9/25/1927	02:00	EST
4/29/1928	02:00	EDT
9/30/1928	02:00	EST
4/28/1929	02:00	EDT
9/29/1929	02:00	EST
4/27/1930	02:00	EDT
9/28/1930	02:00	EST
4/26/1931	02:00	EDT
9/27/1931	02:00	EST
4/24/1932	02:00	EDT
9/25/1932	02:00	EST
4/30/1933	02:00	EDT
9/24/1933	02:00	EST
4/29/1934	02:00	EDT
9/30/1934	02:00	EST
4/28/1935	02:00	EDT
9/29/1935	02:00	EST
5/03/1936	02:00	EDT
9/27/1936	02:00	EST
4/25/1937	02:00	EDT
9/26/1937	02:00	EST
4/24/1938	02:00	EDT
9/11/1938	02:00	EST
4/30/1939	02:00	NY#1
4/30/1967	02:00	US#1

NY # 82

Before 11/18/1883		LMT
11/18/1883	12:00	NY#4
5/18/1940	02:00	EDT
9/08/1940	02:00	EST
4/27/1941	02:00	NY#1
4/30/1967	02:00	US#1

NY # 83

Before 11/18/1883		LMT
11/18/1883	12:00	NY#4
5/03/1936	02:00	EDT
9/27/1936	02:00	NY#1
4/30/1967	02:00	US#1

NY # 84

Before 11/18/1883		LMT
11/18/1883	12:00	EST
3/31/1918	02:00	EWT
10/27/1918	02:00	EST
3/30/1919	02:00	EWT
10/26/1919	02:00	EST
3/28/1920	02:00	EDT
10/31/1920	02:00	EST
4/24/1932	02:00	EDT
9/25/1932	02:00	EST
2/09/1942	02:00	EWT
9/30/1945	02:00	EST
4/29/1951	02:00	NY#1
4/30/1967	02:00	US#1

NY # 85

Before 11/18/1883		LMT
11/18/1883	12:00	EST
3/31/1918	02:00	EWT
10/27/1918	02:00	EST
3/30/1919	02:00	EWT
10/26/1919	02:00	EST
3/28/1920	02:00	EDT
10/31/1920	02:00	EST
4/24/1938	02:00	EDT
9/25/1938	02:00	EST
4/30/1939	02:00	EDT
9/24/1939	02:00	EST
2/09/1942	02:00	EWT
9/30/1945	02:00	EST
4/27/1947	02:00	EDT

9/28/1947	02:00	EST
4/25/1948	02:00	EDT
9/26/1948	02:00	EST
4/24/1949	02:00	EDT
9/25/1949	02:00	EST
4/30/1950	02:00	EDT
9/24/1950	02:00	EST
4/29/1951	02:00	EDT
9/30/1951	02:00	EST
4/25/1954	02:00	NY#1
4/30/1967	02:00	US#1

NY # 86

Before 11/18/1883		LMT
11/18/1883	12:00	NY#1
9/25/1921	02:00	EST
7/01/1931	02:00	EDT
9/01/1931	02:00	EST
4/24/1932	02:00	EDT
9/25/1932	02:00	EST
4/30/1933	02:00	EDT
9/24/1933	02:00	EST
4/29/1934	02:00	EDT
9/30/1934	02:00	EST
6/01/1935	02:00	EDT
9/08/1935	02:00	EST
5/31/1936	02:00	EDT
9/06/1936	02:00	EST
5/30/1937	02:00	EDT
9/07/1937	02:00	EST
6/05/1938	02:00	EDT
9/11/1938	02:00	EST
4/30/1939	02:00	NY#1
4/30/1967	02:00	US#1

NY # 87

Before 11/18/1883		LMT
11/18/1883	12:00	NY#4
6/01/1932	02:00	EDT
10/01/1932	02:00	EST
2/09/1942	02:00	EWT
9/30/1945	02:00	EST
4/24/1949	02:00	EDT
9/25/1949	02:00	EST
4/24/1955	02:00	NY#1
4/30/1967	02:00	US#1

NY # 88

Before 11/18/1883		LMT
11/18/1883	12:00	EST
3/31/1918	02:00	EWT
10/27/1918	02:00	EST
3/30/1919	02:00	EWT
10/26/1919	02:00	EST
3/28/1920	02:00	EDT
10/31/1920	02:00	EST
4/30/1933	02:00	EDT
9/24/1933	02:00	EST
4/29/1934	02:00	EDT
9/30/1934	02:00	EST
4/28/1935	02:00	EDT
9/29/1935	02:00	EST
4/26/1936	02:00	EDT
9/27/1936	02:00	EST
4/25/1937	02:00	EDT
9/26/1937	02:00	EST
4/24/1938	02:00	EDT
9/25/1938	02:00	EST
4/30/1939	02:00	EDT
9/24/1939	02:00	EST
4/28/1940	02:00	EDT
9/29/1940	02:00	EST
4/27/1941	02:00	EDT
9/28/1941	02:00	EST
2/09/1942	02:00	EWT
9/30/1945	02:00	EST
4/24/1949	02:00	NY#1
4/30/1967	02:00	US#1

NY # 89

Before 11/18/1883		LMT
11/18/1883	12:00	NY#4
4/30/1939	02:00	EDT
10/01/1939	02:00	EST
4/28/1940	02:00	EDT
9/29/1940	02:00	EST
4/27/1941	02:00	EDT
9/28/1941	02:00	EST
2/09/1942	02:00	EWT
9/30/1945	02:00	EST
4/27/1947	02:00	NY#1
4/30/1967	02:00	US#1

NY # 90

Before 11/18/1883		LMT
11/18/1883	12:00	NY#4
6/01/1931	02:00	EDT
9/01/1931	02:00	EST
4/28/1935	02:00	NY#1
4/30/1967	02:00	US#1

NY # 91

Before 11/18/1883		LMT
11/18/1883	12:00	EST
3/31/1918	02:00	EWT
10/27/1918	02:00	EST
3/30/1919	02:00	EWT
10/26/1919	02:00	EST
3/28/1920	02:00	EDT
10/31/1920	02:00	EST
4/30/1939	02:00	EDT
9/24/1939	02:00	EST
4/28/1940	02:00	EDT
9/29/1940	02:00	EST

TIME TABLES

4/27/1941 02:00 EDT
9/28/1941 02:00 EST
2/09/1942 02:00 EWT
9/30/1945 02:00 EST
4/27/1947 02:00 NY#1
4/30/1967 02:00 US#1
....
NY # 92
Before 11/18/1883 LMT
11/18/1883 12:00 EST
3/31/1918 02:00 EWT
10/27/1918 02:00 EST
3/30/1919 02:00 EWT
10/26/1919 02:00 EST
3/28/1920 02:00 EDT
10/31/1920 02:00 EST
4/30/1939 02:00 EDT
9/24/1939 02:00 EST
4/28/1940 02:00 EDT
9/29/1940 02:00 EST
4/27/1941 02:00 EDT
9/28/1941 02:00 EST
2/09/1942 02:00 EWT
9/30/1945 02:00 EST
4/30/1950 02:00 NY#1
4/30/1967 02:00 US#1
....
NY # 93
Before 11/18/1883 LMT
11/18/1883 12:00 EST
3/31/1918 02:00 EWT
10/27/1918 02:00 EST
3/30/1919 02:00 EWT
10/26/1919 02:00 EST
3/28/1920 02:00 EDT
10/31/1920 02:00 EST
4/30/1939 02:00 EDT
9/24/1939 02:00 EST
4/28/1940 02:00 EDT
9/29/1940 02:00 EST
4/27/1941 02:00 EDT
9/28/1941 02:00 EST
2/09/1942 02:00 EWT
9/30/1945 02:00 EST
4/29/1951 02:00 NY#1
4/30/1967 02:00 US#1
....
NY # 94
Before 11/18/1883 LMT
11/18/1883 12:00 NY#4
6/01/1931 02:00 EDT
10/01/1931 02:00 NY#1
4/30/1967 02:00 US#1
....
NY # 95
Before 11/18/1883 LMT
11/18/1883 12:00 EST
3/31/1918 02:00 EWT
10/27/1918 02:00 EST
3/30/1919 02:00 EWT
10/26/1919 02:00 EST
3/28/1920 02:00 EDT
10/31/1920 02:00 EST
4/28/1940 02:00 EDT
9/29/1940 02:00 EST
2/09/1942 02:00 EWT
9/30/1945 02:00 EST
4/28/1946 02:00 NY#1
4/30/1967 02:00 US#1
....
NY # 96
Before 11/18/1883 LMT
11/18/1883 12:00 EST
3/31/1918 02:00 EWT
10/27/1918 02:00 EST
3/30/1919 02:00 EWT
10/26/1919 02:00 EST
3/28/1920 02:00 EDT
10/31/1920 02:00 EST
4/28/1940 02:00 EDT
9/29/1940 02:00 EST
2/09/1942 02:00 EWT
9/30/1945 02:00 EST
4/25/1948 02:00 EDT
9/26/1948 02:00 EST
4/24/1955 02:00 NY#1
4/30/1967 02:00 US#1
....
NY # 97
Before 11/18/1883 LMT
11/18/1883 12:00 EST
3/31/1918 02:00 EWT
10/27/1918 02:00 EST
3/30/1919 02:00 EWT
10/26/1919 02:00 EST
3/28/1920 02:00 EDT
10/31/1920 02:00 EST
4/28/1940 02:00 EDT
9/29/1940 02:00 EST
5/25/1941 02:00 EDT
9/01/1941 02:00 EST
2/09/1942 02:00 EWT
9/30/1945 02:00 EST
4/25/1948 02:00 NY#1
4/30/1967 02:00 US#1
....
NY # 98
Before 11/18/1883 LMT
11/18/1883 12:00 EST
3/31/1918 02:00 EWT
10/27/1918 02:00 EST
3/30/1919 02:00 EWT
10/26/1919 02:00 EST
3/28/1920 02:00 EDT
10/31/1920 02:00 EST
4/28/1940 02:00 EDT
9/29/1940 02:00 EST
4/27/1941 02:00 EDT
9/28/1941 02:00 EST
2/09/1942 02:00 EWT
9/30/1945 02:00 EST
4/27/1947 02:00 EDT
9/28/1947 02:00 EST
4/25/1948 02:00 EDT
9/26/1948 02:00 EST
4/24/1955 02:00 NY#1
4/30/1967 02:00 US#1
....
NY # 99
Before 11/18/1883 LMT
11/18/1883 12:00 EST
3/31/1918 02:00 EWT
10/27/1918 02:00 EST
3/30/1919 02:00 EWT
10/26/1919 02:00 EST
3/28/1920 02:00 EDT
10/31/1920 02:00 EST
4/28/1940 02:00 EDT
9/29/1940 02:00 EST
4/27/1941 02:00 EDT
9/28/1941 02:00 EST
2/09/1942 02:00 EWT
9/30/1945 02:00 EST
4/27/1947 02:00 NY#1
4/30/1967 02:00 US#1
....
NY # 100
Before 11/18/1883 LMT
11/18/1883 12:00 EST
3/31/1918 02:00 EWT
10/27/1918 02:00 EST
3/30/1919 02:00 EWT
10/26/1919 02:00 EST
3/28/1920 02:00 EDT
10/31/1920 02:00 EST
4/28/1940 02:00 EDT
9/29/1940 02:00 EST
4/27/1941 02:00 EDT
9/28/1941 02:00 EST
2/09/1942 02:00 EWT
9/30/1945 02:00 EST
4/29/1951 02:00 NY#1
4/30/1967 02:00 US#1
....
NY # 101
Before 11/18/1883 LMT
11/18/1883 12:00 EST
3/31/1918 02:00 EWT
10/27/1918 02:00 EST
3/30/1919 02:00 EWT
10/26/1919 02:00 EST
3/28/1920 02:00 EDT
10/31/1920 02:00 EST
4/28/1940 02:00 EDT
9/29/1940 02:00 EST
4/27/1941 02:00 EDT
9/28/1941 02:00 EST
2/09/1942 02:00 EWT
9/30/1945 02:00 EST
4/28/1946 02:00 EDT
9/29/1946 02:00 EST
4/27/1947 02:00 EDT
9/28/1947 02:00 EST
4/25/1948 02:00 EDT
9/26/1948 02:00 EST
4/29/1951 02:00 NY#1
4/30/1967 02:00 US#1
....
NY # 102
Before 11/18/1883 LMT
11/18/1883 12:00 EST
3/31/1918 02:00 EWT
10/27/1918 02:00 EST
3/30/1919 02:00 EWT
10/26/1919 02:00 EST
3/28/1920 02:00 EDT
10/31/1920 02:00 EST
4/30/1939 02:00 EDT
9/24/1939 02:00 EST
4/28/1940 02:00 EDT
9/29/1940 02:00 EST
4/27/1941 02:00 EDT
9/28/1941 02:00 EST
2/09/1942 02:00 EWT
9/30/1945 02:00 EST
4/28/1946 02:00 EDT
9/29/1946 02:00 EST
4/29/1951 02:00 NY#1
4/30/1967 02:00 US#1
....
NY # 103
Before 11/18/1883 LMT
11/18/1883 12:00 EST
3/31/1918 02:00 EWT
10/27/1918 02:00 EST
3/30/1919 02:00 EWT
10/26/1919 02:00 EST
3/28/1920 02:00 EDT
10/31/1920 02:00 EST
4/27/1941 02:00 EDT
9/28/1941 02:00 EST
2/09/1942 02:00 EWT
9/30/1945 02:00 EST
4/27/1947 02:00 EDT
9/28/1947 02:00 EST
4/24/1955 02:00 NY#1
4/30/1967 02:00 US#1
....
NY # 104
Before 11/18/1883 LMT
11/18/1883 12:00 NY#4
4/30/1939 02:00 EDT
9/03/1939 02:00 EST
6/02/1940 02:00 EDT
9/01/1940 02:00 EST
5/25/1941 02:00 EDT
9/07/1941 02:00 EST
2/09/1942 02:00 NY#1
4/30/1967 02:00 US#1
....
NY # 105
Before 11/18/1883 LMT
11/18/1883 12:00 EST
3/31/1918 02:00 EWT
10/27/1918 02:00 EST
3/30/1919 02:00 EWT
10/26/1919 02:00 EST
3/28/1920 02:00 EDT
10/31/1920 02:00 EST
4/27/1941 02:00 EDT
9/28/1941 02:00 EST
2/09/1942 02:00 EWT
9/30/1945 02:00 EST
4/27/1947 02:00 NY#1
4/30/1967 02:00 US#1
....
NY # 106
Before 11/18/1883 LMT
11/18/1883 12:00 EST
3/31/1918 02:00 EWT
10/27/1918 02:00 EST
3/30/1919 02:00 EWT
10/26/1919 02:00 EST
3/28/1920 02:00 EDT
10/31/1920 02:00 EST
4/27/1941 02:00 EDT
9/28/1941 02:00 EST
2/09/1942 02:00 EWT
9/30/1945 02:00 EST
4/25/1948 02:00 NY#1
4/30/1967 02:00 US#1
....
NY # 107
Before 11/18/1883 LMT
11/18/1883 12:00 EST
3/31/1918 02:00 EWT
10/27/1918 02:00 EST
3/30/1919 02:00 EWT
10/26/1919 02:00 EST
3/28/1920 02:00 EDT
10/31/1920 02:00 EST
4/27/1941 02:00 EDT
9/28/1941 02:00 EST
2/09/1942 02:00 EWT
9/30/1945 02:00 EST
4/29/1951 02:00 NY#1
4/30/1967 02:00 US#1
....
NY # 108
Before 11/18/1883 LMT
11/18/1883 12:00 EST
3/31/1918 02:00 EWT
10/27/1918 02:00 EST
3/30/1919 02:00 EWT
10/26/1919 02:00 EST
3/28/1920 02:00 EDT
10/31/1920 02:00 EST
4/27/1941 02:00 EDT
9/28/1941 02:00 EST
2/09/1942 02:00 EWT
9/30/1945 02:00 EST
4/26/1953 02:00 NY#1
4/30/1967 02:00 US#1
....
NY # 109
Before 11/18/1883 LMT
11/18/1883 12:00 EST
3/31/1918 02:00 EWT
10/27/1918 02:00 EST
3/30/1919 02:00 EWT
10/26/1919 02:00 EST
3/28/1920 02:00 EDT
10/31/1920 02:00 EST
4/30/1939 02:00 EDT
9/24/1939 02:00 EST
4/28/1940 02:00 EDT
9/29/1940 02:00 EST
4/27/1941 02:00 EDT
9/28/1941 02:00 EST
2/09/1942 02:00 EWT
9/30/1945 02:00 EST
4/28/1946 02:00 EDT
9/29/1946 02:00 EST
4/29/1951 02:00 NY#1
4/30/1967 02:00 US#1
....
NY # 110
Before 11/18/1883 LMT
11/18/1883 12:00 EST
3/31/1918 02:00 EWT
10/27/1918 02:00 EST
3/30/1919 02:00 EWT
10/26/1919 02:00 EST
3/28/1920 02:00 EDT
10/31/1920 02:00 EST
4/27/1941 02:00 EDT
9/28/1941 02:00 EST
2/09/1942 02:00 EWT
9/30/1945 02:00 EST
4/27/1947 02:00 EDT
9/28/1947 02:00 EST
4/25/1948 02:00 EDT
9/26/1948 02:00 EST
4/30/1950 02:00 EDT
9/24/1950 02:00 EST
4/29/1951 02:00 EDT
9/30/1951 02:00 EST
4/27/1952 02:00 EDT
9/28/1952 02:00 EST
4/24/1955 02:00 NY#1
4/30/1967 02:00 US#1
....
NY # 111
Before 11/18/1883 LMT
11/18/1883 12:00 EST
3/31/1918 02:00 EWT
10/27/1918 02:00 EST
3/30/1919 02:00 EWT
10/26/1919 02:00 EST
3/28/1920 02:00 EDT
10/31/1920 02:00 EST
4/26/1931 02:00 EDT
9/27/1931 02:00 EST
4/24/1932 02:00 EDT
9/25/1932 02:00 EST
4/30/1933 02:00 EDT
10/29/1933 02:00 NY#1
4/30/1967 02:00 US#1
....
NY # 112
Before 11/18/1883 LMT
11/18/1883 12:00 EST
3/31/1918 02:00 EWT
10/27/1918 02:00 EST
3/30/1919 02:00 EWT
10/26/1919 02:00 EST
3/28/1920 02:00 EDT
10/31/1920 02:00 EST
6/01/1931 02:00 EDT
9/01/1931 02:00 EST
4/24/1932 02:00 NY#1
4/30/1967 02:00 US#1
....
NY # 113
Before 11/18/1883 LMT
11/18/1883 12:00 NY#4
5/16/1937 02:00 EDT
9/26/1937 02:00 EST
5/01/1938 02:00 EDT
10/02/1938 02:00 EST
4/30/1939 02:00 EDT
9/24/1939 02:00 EST
5/15/1940 02:00 EDT
9/15/1940 02:00 EST
4/27/1941 02:00 EDT
9/28/1941 02:00 EST
2/09/1942 02:00 EWT
9/30/1945 02:00 EST
4/27/1947 02:00 EDT
9/28/1947 02:00 EST
5/17/1948 02:00 EDT
9/26/1948 02:00 NY#1
4/30/1967 02:00 US#1
....
NY # 114
Before 11/18/1883 LMT
11/18/1883 12:00 EST
3/31/1918 02:00 EWT
10/27/1918 02:00 EST
3/30/1919 02:00 EWT
10/26/1919 02:00 EST
3/28/1920 02:00 EDT
10/31/1920 02:00 EST
4/24/1932 02:00 EDT
9/25/1932 02:00 EST
4/30/1933 02:00 EDT
10/01/1933 02:00 NY#1
4/30/1967 02:00 US#1
....
NY # 115
Before 11/18/1883 LMT
11/18/1883 12:00 NY#4
5/26/1940 02:00 NY#1
4/30/1967 02:00 US#1
....
NY # 116
Before 11/18/1883 LMT
11/18/1883 12:00 EST
3/31/1918 02:00 EWT
10/27/1918 02:00 EST
3/30/1919 02:00 EWT
10/26/1919 02:00 EST
3/28/1920 02:00 EDT
10/31/1920 02:00 EST
6/15/1930 02:00 EDT
8/30/1930 02:00 EST
6/28/1931 02:00 EDT
9/06/1931 02:00 EST
5/07/1939 02:00 EDT
9/24/1939 02:00 EST
4/28/1940 02:00 EDT
10/06/1940 02:00 NY#1
4/30/1967 02:00 US#1
....
NY # 117
Before 11/18/1883 LMT
11/18/1883 12:00 EST
3/31/1918 02:00 EWT
10/27/1918 02:00 EST
3/30/1919 02:00 EWT
10/26/1919 02:00 EST
3/28/1920 02:00 EDT
10/31/1920 02:00 EST
2/09/1942 02:00 EWT
9/30/1945 02:00 EST
4/28/1946 02:00 EDT
9/29/1946 02:00 EST
4/27/1947 02:00 EDT
9/28/1947 02:00 EST
4/25/1948 02:00 EDT
9/26/1948 02:00 EST
4/30/1950 02:00 EDT
9/24/1950 02:00 EST
4/29/1951 02:00 EDT
9/30/1951 02:00 EST
4/24/1955 02:00 NY#1
4/30/1967 02:00 US#1
....
NY # 118
Before 11/18/1883 LMT
11/18/1883 12:00 NY#4
6/21/1941 02:00 EDT
9/01/1941 02:00 EST
2/09/1942 02:00 EWT
9/30/1945 02:00 EST
4/24/1955 02:00 NY#1
4/30/1967 02:00 US#1
....
NY # 119
Before 11/18/1883 LMT
11/18/1883 12:00 EST
3/31/1918 02:00 EWT
10/27/1918 02:00 EST
3/30/1919 02:00 EWT
10/26/1919 02:00 EST
3/28/1920 02:00 EDT
10/31/1920 02:00 EST
4/24/1938 02:00 EDT
9/25/1938 02:00 EST
4/30/1939 02:00 EDT
9/24/1939 02:00 EST
5/12/1940 02:00 EDT
9/03/1940 02:00 EST
4/27/1941 02:00 NY#1
4/30/1967 02:00 US#1
....
NY # 120
Before 11/18/1883 LMT
11/18/1883 12:00 NY#4
6/02/1940 02:00 EDT
9/02/1940 02:00 EST
4/27/1941 02:00 NY#1
4/30/1967 02:00 US#1
....
NY # 121
Before 11/18/1883 LMT
11/18/1883 12:00 NY#4
6/01/1931 02:00 EDT
9/01/1931 02:00 EST
5/29/1932 02:00 EDT
9/05/1932 02:00 EST
5/21/1933 02:00 EDT
9/24/1933 02:00 EST
4/29/1934 02:00 NY#1
4/30/1967 02:00 US#1
....
NY # 122
Before 11/18/1883 LMT
11/18/1883 12:00 EST
3/31/1918 02:00 EWT
10/27/1918 02:00 EST
3/30/1919 02:00 EWT
10/26/1919 02:00 EST
3/28/1920 02:00 EDT
10/31/1920 02:00 EST
4/26/1931 02:00 EDT
9/27/1931 02:00 EST
5/01/1932 02:00 NY#1
4/30/1967 02:00 US#1
....
NY # 123
Before 11/18/1883 LMT
11/18/1883 12:00 NY#4
4/30/1933 02:00 EDT
9/24/1933 02:00 EST
6/01/1936 02:00 EDT
9/27/1936 02:00 EST
4/24/1938 02:00 NY#1
4/30/1967 02:00 US#1
....
NY # 124
Before 11/18/1883 LMT
11/18/1883 12:00 EST
3/31/1918 02:00 EWT
10/27/1918 02:00 EST
3/30/1919 02:00 EWT
10/26/1919 02:00 EST
3/28/1920 02:00 EDT
10/31/1920 02:00 EST
2/09/1942 02:00 EWT
9/30/1945 02:00 EST
4/27/1947 02:00 EDT
9/28/1947 02:00 EST
4/24/1949 02:00 NY#1
4/30/1967 02:00 US#1
....
NY # 125
Before 11/18/1883 LMT
11/18/1883 12:00 EST
3/31/1918 02:00 EWT
10/27/1918 02:00 EST
3/30/1919 02:00 EWT
10/26/1919 02:00 EST
3/28/1920 02:00 EDT
10/31/1920 02:00 EST
2/09/1942 02:00 EWT
9/30/1945 02:00 EST
4/27/1947 02:00 EDT
9/28/1947 02:00 EST
4/30/1950 02:00 NY#1

TIME TABLES

4/30/1967 02:00 US#1

NY # 126
Before 11/18/1883 LMT
11/18/1883 12:00 EST
3/31/1918 02:00 EWT
10/27/1918 02:00 EST
3/30/1919 02:00 EWT
10/26/1919 02:00 EST
3/28/1920 02:00 EDT
10/31/1920 02:00 EST
2/09/1942 02:00 EWT
9/30/1945 02:00 EST
4/27/1947 02:00 EDT
9/28/1947 02:00 EST
4/29/1951 02:00 NY#1
4/30/1967 02:00 US#1

NY # 127
Before 11/18/1883 LMT
11/18/1883 12:00 EST
3/31/1918 02:00 EWT
10/27/1918 02:00 EST
3/30/1919 02:00 EWT
10/26/1919 02:00 EST
3/28/1920 02:00 EDT
10/31/1920 02:00 EST
2/09/1942 02:00 EWT
9/30/1945 02:00 EST
4/27/1947 02:00 EDT
9/28/1947 02:00 EST
4/26/1953 02:00 NY#1
4/30/1967 02:00 US#1

NY # 128
Before 11/18/1883 LMT
11/18/1883 12:00 NY#4
6/02/1935 02:00 EDT
9/02/1935 02:00 EST
6/07/1936 02:00 EDT
9/07/1936 02:00 EST
5/31/1937 02:00 EDT
9/06/1937 02:00 EST
6/05/1938 02:00 EDT
9/04/1938 02:00 EST
6/04/1939 02:00 EDT
9/03/1939 02:00 EST
6/02/1940 02:00 EDT
9/01/1940 02:00 EST
4/27/1941 02:00 EDT
9/28/1941 02:00 EST
2/09/1942 02:00 EWT
9/30/1945 02:00 EST
4/28/1946 02:00 EDT
9/29/1946 02:00 EST
4/27/1947 02:00 EDT
9/28/1947 02:00 EST
4/25/1948 02:00 EDT
9/26/1948 02:00 EST
4/24/1949 02:00 EDT
9/25/1949 02:00 EST
4/29/1951 02:00 NY#1
4/30/1967 02:00 US#1

NY # 129
Before 11/18/1883 LMT
11/18/1883 12:00 NY#4
4/25/1937 02:00 EDT
9/01/1937 02:00 EST
4/24/1938 02:00 EDT
9/25/1938 02:00 EST
5/01/1939 02:00 EDT
9/16/1939 02:00 EST
4/28/1940 02:00 EDT
9/01/1940 02:00 EST
4/27/1941 02:00 NY#1
4/30/1967 02:00 US#1

NY # 130
Before 11/18/1883 LMT
11/18/1883 12:00 EST
3/31/1918 02:00 EWT
10/27/1918 02:00 EST
3/30/1919 02:00 EWT
10/26/1919 02:00 EST
3/28/1920 02:00 EDT
10/31/1920 02:00 EST
2/09/1942 02:00 EWT
9/30/1945 02:00 EST
4/27/1947 02:00 EDT
9/28/1947 02:00 EST
4/25/1948 02:00 EDT
9/26/1948 02:00 EST
4/29/1951 02:00 NY#1
4/30/1967 02:00 US#1

NY # 131
Before 11/18/1883 LMT
11/18/1883 12:00 EST
3/31/1918 02:00 EWT
10/27/1918 02:00 EST
3/30/1919 02:00 EWT
10/26/1919 02:00 EST
3/28/1920 02:00 EDT
10/31/1920 02:00 EST
2/09/1942 02:00 EWT
9/30/1945 02:00 EST
4/27/1947 02:00 EDT
9/28/1947 02:00 EST
4/25/1948 02:00 EDT
9/26/1948 02:00 EST
4/24/1949 02:00 EDT
9/25/1949 02:00 EST
4/30/1950 02:00 EDT
9/24/1950 02:00 EST
4/26/1953 02:00 EDT
9/27/1953 02:00 EST
4/24/1955 02:00 NY#1
4/30/1967 02:00 US#1

NY # 132
Before 11/18/1833 LMT
11/18/1833 12:00 EST
3/31/1918 02:00 EWT
10/27/1918 02:00 EST
3/30/1919 02:00 EWT
10/26/1919 02:00 EST
3/28/1920 02:00 EDT
10/31/1920 02:00 EST
2/09/1942 02:00 EWT
9/30/1945 02:00 EST
4/27/1947 02:00 EDT
9/28/1947 02:00 EST
4/24/1949 02:00 EDT
9/25/1949 02:00 EST
4/29/1951 02:00 NY#1
4/30/1967 02:00 US#1

NY # 133
Before 11/18/1883 LMT
11/18/1883 12:00 EST
3/31/1918 02:00 EWT
10/27/1918 02:00 EST
3/30/1919 02:00 EWT
10/26/1919 02:00 EST
3/28/1920 02:00 EDT
10/31/1920 02:00 EST
2/09/1942 02:00 EWT
9/30/1945 02:00 EST
4/27/1947 02:00 EDT
9/28/1947 02:00 EST
4/25/1948 02:00 EDT
9/26/1948 02:00 EST
4/29/1951 02:00 EDT
9/30/1951 02:00 EST
4/26/1953 02:00 NY#1
4/30/1967 02:00 US#1

NY # 134
Before 11/18/1883 LMT
11/18/1883 12:00 NY#4
6/14/1936 02:00 EDT
9/13/1936 02:00 EST
4/28/1940 02:00 NY#1
4/30/1967 02:00 US#1

NY # 135
Before 11/18/1883 LMT
11/18/1883 12:00 EST
3/31/1918 02:00 EWT
10/27/1918 02:00 EST
3/30/1919 02:00 EWT
10/26/1919 02:00 EST
3/28/1920 02:00 EDT
10/31/1920 02:00 EST
2/09/1942 02:00 EWT
9/30/1945 02:00 EST
4/25/1948 02:00 EDT
9/26/1948 02:00 EST
4/29/1951 02:00 EDT
9/30/1951 02:00 EST
4/24/1955 02:00 NY#1
4/30/1967 02:00 US#1

NY # 136
Before 11/18/1883 LMT
11/18/1883 12:00 NY#4
5/25/1936 02:00 NY#1
4/30/1967 02:00 US#1

NY # 137
Before 11/18/1883 LMT
11/18/1883 12:00 EST
3/31/1918 02:00 EWT
10/27/1918 02:00 EST
3/30/1919 02:00 EWT
10/26/1919 02:00 EST
3/28/1920 02:00 EDT
10/31/1920 02:00 EST
4/28/1940 02:00 EDT
9/29/1940 02:00 EST
2/09/1942 02:00 EWT
9/30/1945 02:00 EST
4/25/1948 02:00 NY#1
4/30/1967 02:00 US#1

NY # 138
Before 11/18/1883 LMT
11/18/1883 12:00 NY#4
5/08/1935 02:00 EDT
9/29/1935 02:00 EST
4/26/1936 02:00 NY#1
4/30/1967 02:00 US#1

NY # 139
Before 11/18/1883 LMT
11/18/1883 12:00 NY#4
6/15/1939 02:00 EDT
9/04/1939 02:00 EST
4/28/1940 02:00 NY#1
4/30/1967 02:00 US#1

NY # 140
Before 11/18/1883 LMT
11/18/1883 12:00 NY#4
4/28/1940 02:00 EDT
9/02/1940 02:00 EST
2/09/1942 02:00 EWT
9/30/1945 02:00 EST
4/27/1947 02:00 NY#1
4/30/1967 02:00 US#1

NY # 141
Before 11/18/1883 LMT
11/18/1883 12:00 EST
3/31/1918 02:00 EWT
10/27/1918 02:00 EST
3/30/1919 02:00 EWT
10/26/1919 02:00 EST
3/28/1920 02:00 EDT
10/31/1920 02:00 EST
2/09/1942 02:00 EWT
9/30/1945 02:00 EST
4/25/1948 02:00 EDT
9/26/1948 02:00 EST
4/24/1949 02:00 EDT
9/25/1949 02:00 EST
4/29/1951 02:00 NY#1
4/30/1967 02:00 US#1

NY # 142
Before 11/18/1883 LMT
11/18/1883 12:00 NY#4
5/31/1931 02:00 EDT
10/01/1931 02:00 EST
4/30/1939 02:00 NY#1
4/30/1967 02:00 US#1

NY # 143
Before 11/18/1883 LMT
11/18/1883 12:00 NY#4
6/02/1940 02:00 EDT
9/02/1940 02:00 EST
4/27/1941 02:00 EDT
9/28/1941 02:00 EST
2/09/1942 02:00 EWT
9/30/1945 02:00 EST
4/25/1948 02:00 EDT
9/26/1948 02:00 EST
4/24/1955 02:00 NY#1
4/30/1967 02:00 US#1

NY # 144
Before 11/18/1883 LMT
11/18/1883 12:00 NY#4
6/20/1941 02:00 EDT
9/01/1941 02:00 EST
2/09/1942 02:00 NY#1
4/30/1967 02:00 US#1

NY # 145
Before 11/18/1883 LMT
11/18/1883 12:00 NY#4
6/27/1937 02:00 EDT
8/29/1937 02:00 EST
6/04/1939 02:00 EDT
9/10/1939 02:00 EST
4/28/1940 02:00 EDT
9/29/1940 02:00 EST
2/09/1942 02:00 EWT
9/30/1945 02:00 EST
4/24/1955 02:00 NY#1
4/30/1967 02:00 US#1

NY # 146
Before 11/18/1883 LMT
11/18/1883 02:00 NY#4
5/06/1939 02:00 EDT
9/30/1939 02:00 EST
4/28/1940 02:00 EDT
9/29/1940 02:00 EST
4/27/1941 02:00 EDT
9/28/1941 02:00 EST
2/09/1942 02:00 EWT
9/30/1945 02:00 EST
4/28/1946 02:00 EDT
9/20/1946 02:00 EST
4/27/1947 02:00 NY#1
4/30/1967 02:00 US#1

NY # 147
Before 11/18/1883 LMT
11/18/1883 12:00 NY#4
6/23/1940 02:00 EDT
9/02/1940 02:00 EST
4/27/1941 02:00 EDT
9/28/1941 02:00 EST
2/09/1942 02:00 EWT
9/30/1945 02:00 EST
4/26/1953 02:00 NY#1
4/30/1967 02:00 US#1

NY # 148
Before 11/18/1883 LMT
11/18/1883 12:00 EST
3/31/1918 02:00 EWT
10/27/1918 02:00 EST
3/30/1919 02:00 EWT
10/26/1919 02:00 EST
3/28/1920 02:00 EDT
10/31/1920 02:00 EST
4/30/1939 02:00 EDT
9/24/1939 02:00 EST
4/28/1940 02:00 EDT
9/02/1940 02:00 EST
4/27/1941 02:00 EDT
9/28/1941 02:00 EST
2/09/1942 02:00 EWT
9/30/1945 02:00 EST
4/29/1951 02:00 NY#1
4/30/1967 02:00 US#1

NY # 149
Before 11/18/1883 LMT
11/18/1883 12:00 NY#4
6/23/1940 02:00 EDT
9/01/1940 02:00 EST
6/20/1941 02:00 EDT
9/01/1941 02:00 EST
2/09/1942 02:00 NY#1
4/30/1967 02:00 US#1

NY # 150
Before 11/18/1883 LMT
11/18/1883 12:00 NY#4
5/14/1940 02:00 EDT
9/02/1940 02:00 EST
4/27/1941 02:00 EDT
9/28/1941 02:00 EST
2/09/1942 02:00 EWT
9/30/1945 02:00 EST
4/28/1946 02:00 EDT
9/29/1946 02:00 EST
4/27/1947 02:00 EDT
9/28/1947 02:00 EST
4/25/1948 02:00 EDT
9/26/1948 02:00 EST
4/24/1955 02:00 NY#1
4/30/1967 02:00 US#1

NY # 151
Before 11/18/1883 LMT
11/18/1883 12:00 NY#4
6/15/1930 02:00 EDT
8/30/1930 02:00 EST
6/28/1931 02:00 EDT
9/06/1931 02:00 EST
5/07/1939 02:00 EDT
9/24/1939 02:00 EST
5/05/1940 02:00 EDT
9/29/1940 02:00 NY#1
4/30/1967 02:00 US#1

NY # 152
Before 11/18/1883 LMT
11/18/1883 12:00 NY#4
6/20/1941 02:00 EDT
9/08/1941 02:00 EST
2/09/1942 02:00 EWT
9/30/1945 02:00 EST
4/27/1947 02:00 EDT
9/28/1947 02:00 EST
4/24/1949 02:00 EDT
9/25/1949 02:00 EST
4/30/1950 02:00 EDT
9/24/1950 02:00 EST
4/26/1953 02:00 NY#1
4/30/1967 02:00 US#1

NY # 153
Before 11/18/1883 LMT
11/18/1883 12:00 NY#1
9/23/1951 02:00 EST
4/27/1952 02:00 NY#1
4/30/1967 02:00 US#1

NY # 154
Before 11/18/1883 LMT
11/18/1883 12:00 NY#4
5/04/1941 02:00 EDT
9/28/1941 02:00 EST
2/09/1942 02:00 EWT
9/30/1945 02:00 EST
4/27/1947 02:00 EDT
9/28/1947 02:00 EST
4/25/1948 02:00 EDT
9/26/1948 02:00 EST
4/24/1949 02:00 EDT
9/25/1949 02:00 EST
4/30/1950 02:00 EDT
9/24/1950 02:00 EST
4/24/1955 02:00 NY#1
4/30/1967 02:00 US#1

NY # 155
Before 11/18/1883 LMT
11/18/1883 12:00 EST
3/31/1918 02:00 EWT
10/27/1918 02:00 EST
3/30/1919 02:00 EWT
10/26/1919 02:00 EST
3/28/1920 02:00 EDT
10/31/1920 02:00 EST
6/23/1940 02:00 EDT
9/01/1940 02:00 EST
6/01/1941 02:00 EDT
8/31/1941 02:00 EST
2/09/1942 02:00 EWT
9/30/1945 02:00 EST
4/27/1947 02:00 NY#1
4/30/1967 02:00 US#1

NY # 156
Before 11/18/1883 LMT
11/18/1883 12:00 NY#4
5/16/1937 02:00 EDT
9/05/1937 02:00 EST
5/12/1940 02:00 EDT
9/03/1940 02:00 EST
4/27/1941 02:00 EDT
9/28/1941 02:00 EST
2/09/1942 02:00 EWT
9/30/1945 02:00 EST
4/25/1948 02:00 NY#1
4/30/1967 02:00 US#1

NY # 157
Before 11/18/1883 LMT
11/18/1883 12:00 NY#4
4/24/1938 02:00 EDT
9/06/1938 02:00 EST
4/30/1939 02:00 EDT
9/24/1939 02:00 EST
4/28/1940 02:00 EDT
9/29/1940 02:00 EST
6/20/1941 02:00 EDT
9/08/1941 02:00 EST
2/09/1942 02:00 EWT
9/30/1945 02:00 EST
4/27/1947 02:00 EDT
9/28/1947 02:00 EST
4/30/1950 02:00 NY#1
4/30/1967 02:00 US#1

NY # 158
Before 11/18/1883 LMT
11/18/1883 12:00 NY#4
6/09/1935 02:00 EDT
9/02/1935 02:00 EST
6/07/1936 02:00 EDT
9/12/1936 02:00 EST
6/06/1937 02:00 EDT
9/06/1937 02:00 EST
6/05/1938 02:00 EDT
9/05/1938 02:00 EST
4/30/1939 02:00 EDT
9/24/1939 02:00 EST
4/28/1940 02:00 EDT
9/29/1940 02:00 EST
2/09/1942 02:00 EWT
9/30/1945 02:00 EST
4/27/1947 02:00 EDT
9/28/1947 02:00 EST
4/26/1953 02:00 NY#1
4/30/1967 02:00 US#1

NY # 159
Before 11/18/1883 LMT
11/18/1883 12:00 NY#4
6/01/1927 02:00 EDT
10/01/1927 02:00 EST
6/01/1928 02:00 EDT
10/01/1928 02:00 EST
6/01/1929 02:00 EDT
10/01/1929 02:00 EST
4/27/1930 02:00 NY#1
4/30/1967 02:00 US#1

NY # 160
Before 11/18/1883 LMT
11/18/1883 12:00 NY#4
4/30/1939 02:00 EDT
10/01/1939 02:00 EST
4/28/1940 02:00 EDT
9/03/1940 02:00 EST
4/27/1941 02:00 NY#1
4/30/1967 02:00 US#1

NY # 161
Before 11/18/1883 LMT
11/18/1883 12:00 NY#4
6/01/1941 02:00 EDT
9/26/1941 02:00 EST
2/09/1942 02:00 EWT
9/30/1945 02:00 EST
4/28/1946 02:00 EDT
9/29/1946 02:00 EST
4/27/1947 02:00 EDT
9/28/1947 02:00 EST
4/25/1948 02:00 EDT
9/26/1948 02:00 EST
4/30/1950 02:00 EDT
9/24/1950 02:00 EST
4/29/1951 02:00 EDT
9/30/1951 02:00 EST
4/24/1955 02:00 NY#1
4/30/1967 02:00 US#1

NY # 162
Before 11/18/1883 LMT
11/18/1883 12:00 NY#1
4/30/1939 02:00 EDT
10/01/1939 02:00 NY#1
4/30/1967 02:00 US#1

NY # 163
Before 11/18/1883 LMT
11/18/1883 12:00 NY#4
6/23/1940 02:00 EDT
9/03/1940 02:00 EST
6/22/1941 02:00 EDT
9/01/1941 02:00 EST
2/09/1942 02:00 EWT
9/30/1945 02:00 EST
4/27/1947 02:00 NY#1
4/30/1967 02:00 US#1

NY # 164
Before 11/18/1883 LMT
11/18/1883 12:00 NY#4
4/28/1940 02:00 EDT
9/02/1940 02:00 EST
4/27/1941 02:00 EDT
9/07/1941 02:00 EST
2/09/1942 02:00 EWT
9/30/1945 02:00 EST
4/24/1955 02:00 NY#1
4/30/1967 02:00 US#1

NY # 165

TIME TABLES

Before 11/18/1883 LMT
11/18/1883 12:00 EST
3/31/1918 02:00 EWT
10/27/1918 02:00 EST
3/30/1919 02:00 EWT
10/26/1919 02:00 EST
3/28/1920 02:00 EDT
10/31/1920 02:00 EST
4/26/1925 02:00 EDT
9/27/1925 02:00 EST
4/25/1926 02:00 EDT
9/26/1926 02:00 EST
4/24/1927 02:00 EDT
9/25/1927 02:00 EST
4/29/1928 02:00 EDT
9/30/1928 02:00 EST
4/28/1929 02:00 EDT
9/29/1929 02:00 EST
4/27/1930 02:00 EDT
9/28/1930 02:00 EST
4/26/1931 02:00 EDT
9/27/1931 02:00 EST
4/30/1932 00:01 EDT
10/01/1932 00:01 EST
4/29/1933 00:01 EDT
9/30/1933 00:01 EST
4/29/1934 00:01 EDT
9/30/1934 00:01 EST
4/28/1935 00:01 EDT
9/29/1935 00:01 EST
4/26/1936 00:01 EDT
9/27/1936 00:01 EST
4/25/1937 00:01 EDT
9/26/1937 00:01 EST
4/24/1938 00:01 EDT
9/25/1938 00:01 EST
4/30/1939 00:01 EDT
9/24/1939 00:01 EST
4/28/1940 00:01 EDT
9/29/1940 00:01 EST
4/27/1941 00:01 EDT
9/28/1941 00:01 EST
2/09/1942 02:00 NY#1
4/30/1967 02:00 US#1

NY # 166
Before 11/18/1883 LMT
11/18/1883 12:00 EST
3/31/1918 02:00 EWT
10/27/1918 02:00 EST
3/30/1919 02:00 EWT
10/26/1919 02:00 EST
3/28/1920 02:00 EDT
10/31/1920 02:00 EST
4/26/1925 02:00 EDT
9/27/1925 02:00 EST
4/25/1926 02:00 EDT
9/26/1926 02:00 EST
4/24/1927 02:00 EDT
9/25/1927 02:00 EST
4/29/1928 02:00 EDT
9/30/1928 02:00 EST
4/28/1929 02:00 EDT
9/29/1929 02:00 EST
4/27/1930 02:00 EDT
9/28/1930 02:00 EST
4/26/1931 02:00 EDT
9/27/1931 02:00 EST
4/03/1932 02:00 EDT
9/25/1932 02:00 EST
4/02/1933 02:00 EDT
9/24/1933 02:00 EST
4/01/1934 02:00 EDT
9/30/1934 02:00 EST
4/07/1935 02:00 EDT
9/29/1935 02:00 EST
4/26/1936 02:00 NY#1
4/30/1967 02:00 US#1

NY # 167
Before 11/18/1883 LMT
11/18/1883 12:00 NY#4
6/01/1941 02:00 EDT
8/31/1941 02:00 EST
2/09/1942 02:00 EWT
9/30/1945 02:00 EST
6/02/1946 02:00 EDT
9/01/1946 02:00 EST
4/29/1951 02:00 NY#1
4/30/1967 02:00 US#1

NY # 168
Before 11/18/1883 LMT
11/18/1883 12:00 NY#4
5/06/1923 02:00 EDT
9/30/1923 02:00 EST
5/04/1924 02:00 EDT
9/28/1924 02:00 EST
5/03/1925 02:00 EDT
9/27/1925 02:00 EST
5/02/1926 02:00 EDT
9/26/1926 02:00 EST
5/08/1927 02:00 EDT
9/25/1927 02:00 EST
5/06/1928 02:00 EDT
9/30/1928 02:00 EST
5/05/1929 02:00 EDT
9/29/1929 02:00 EST
4/30/1933 02:00 EDT
9/30/1933 02:00 EST
2/09/1942 02:00 EWT
9/30/1945 02:00 EST
4/24/1955 02:00 NY#1
4/30/1967 02:00 US#1

NY # 169
Before 11/18/1883 LMT
11/18/1883 12:00 NY#4
5/19/1940 02:00 EDT
9/22/1940 02:00 EST
4/27/1941 02:00 EDT
9/28/1941 02:00 EST
2/09/1942 02:00 EWT
9/30/1945 02:00 EST
4/24/1955 02:00 NY#1
4/30/1967 02:00 US#1

NY # 170
Before 11/18/1883 LMT
11/18/1883 12:00 NY#4
6/15/1930 02:00 EDT
8/30/1930 02:00 EST
4/28/1935 02:00 EDT
9/29/1935 02:00 EST
4/26/1936 02:00 EDT
9/27/1936 02:00 EST
5/07/1939 02:00 EDT
9/24/1939 02:00 EST
5/05/1940 02:00 EDT
9/29/1940 02:00 EST
4/27/1941 02:00 NY#1
4/30/1967 02:00 US#1

NY # 171
Before 11/18/1883 LMT
11/18/1883 12:00 NY#4
6/01/1941 02:00 EDT
9/07/1941 02:00 EST
2/09/1942 02:00 NY#1
4/30/1967 02:00 US#1

NY # 172
Before 11/18/1883 LMT
11/18/1883 12:00 NY#4
6/04/1939 02:00 EDT
9/04/1939 02:00 EST
2/09/1942 02:00 EWT
9/30/1945 02:00 EST
4/24/1955 02:00 NY#1
4/30/1967 02:00 US#1

NY # 173
Before 11/18/1883 LMT
11/18/1883 12:00 EST
3/31/1918 02:00 EWT
10/27/1918 02:00 EST
3/30/1919 02:00 EWT
10/26/1919 02:00 EST
3/28/1920 02:00 EDT
10/31/1920 02:00 EST
6/04/1939 02:00 EDT
9/04/1939 02:00 EST
4/28/1940 02:00 EDT
9/29/1940 02:00 EST
4/27/1941 02:00 EDT
9/28/1941 02:00 EST
2/09/1942 02:00 EWT
9/30/1945 02:00 EST
4/29/1951 02:00 NY#1
4/30/1967 02:00 US#1

NY # 174
Before 11/18/1883 LMT
11/18/1883 12:00 EST
3/31/1918 02:00 EWT
10/27/1918 02:00 EST
3/30/1919 02:00 EWT
10/26/1919 02:00 EST
3/28/1920 02:00 EDT
10/31/1920 02:00 EST
5/06/1923 02:00 EDT
9/30/1923 02:00 EST
5/04/1924 02:00 EDT
9/28/1924 02:00 EST
5/03/1925 02:00 EDT
9/27/1925 02:00 EST
5/02/1926 02:00 EDT
9/26/1926 02:00 EST
5/08/1927 02:00 EDT
9/25/1927 02:00 EST
5/06/1928 02:00 EDT
9/30/1928 02:00 EST
5/05/1929 02:00 EDT
9/29/1929 02:00 EST
4/26/1931 02:00 EDT
9/27/1931 02:00 EST
4/24/1932 02:00 EDT
9/25/1932 02:00 EST
4/30/1933 02:00 EDT
9/24/1933 02:00 EST
4/29/1934 02:00 EDT
9/30/1934 02:00 EST
4/28/1935 02:00 EDT
9/29/1935 02:00 EST
4/26/1936 02:00 EDT
9/27/1936 02:00 EST
4/25/1937 02:00 EDT
9/26/1937 02:00 EST
4/24/1938 02:00 EDT
9/25/1938 02:00 EST
4/30/1939 02:00 EDT
9/24/1939 02:00 EST
4/28/1940 02:00 EDT
9/29/1940 02:00 EST
4/27/1941 02:00 EDT
9/28/1941 02:00 EST
2/09/1942 02:00 EWT
9/30/1945 02:00 EST
4/30/1950 02:00 NY#1
4/30/1967 02:00 US#1

NY # 175
Before 11/18/1883 LMT
11/18/1883 12:00 NY#1
4/24/1932 02:00 EDT
10/30/1932 02:00 EST
4/30/1933 02:00 NY#1
4/30/1967 02:00 US#1

NY # 176
Before 11/18/1883 LMT
11/18/1883 12:00 NY#4
4/30/1939 02:00 EDT
10/01/1939 02:00 EST
4/28/1940 02:00 EDT
9/29/1940 02:00 EST
4/27/1941 02:00 EDT
9/28/1941 02:00 EST
2/09/1942 02:00 EWT
9/30/1945 02:00 EST
4/27/1947 02:00 EDT
9/28/1947 02:00 EST
5/17/1948 02:00 EDT
9/26/1948 02:00 NY#1
4/30/1967 02:00 US#1

NY # 177
Before 11/18/1883 LMT
11/18/1883 12:00 NY#4
4/24/1921 00:01 EDT
9/25/1921 00:01 EST
4/30/1922 00:01 EDT
9/24/1922 00:01 EST
4/29/1923 00:01 EDT
9/30/1923 00:01 EST
4/27/1924 00:01 EDT
9/28/1924 00:01 EST
4/26/1925 00:01 EDT
9/27/1925 00:01 EST
4/25/1926 00:01 EDT
9/26/1926 00:01 EST
4/24/1927 00:01 EDT
9/25/1927 00:01 EST
4/29/1928 00:01 EDT
9/30/1928 00:01 EST
4/28/1929 00:01 EDT
9/29/1929 00:01 EST
4/27/1930 00:01 EDT
9/28/1930 00:01 EST
4/26/1931 00:01 EDT
9/27/1931 00:01 EST
4/24/1932 00:01 EDT
9/25/1932 00:01 EST
4/30/1933 00:01 EDT
9/24/1933 00:01 EST
4/29/1934 00:01 EDT
9/30/1934 00:01 EST
4/28/1935 00:01 EDT
9/29/1935 00:01 EST
4/26/1936 00:01 EDT
9/27/1936 00:01 EST
4/25/1937 00:01 EDT
9/26/1937 00:01 EST
4/24/1938 00:01 EDT
9/25/1938 00:01 EST
4/30/1939 00:01 EDT
9/24/1939 00:01 EST
4/28/1940 00:01 EDT
9/29/1940 00:01 EST
4/27/1941 00:01 EDT
9/28/1941 00:01 EST
2/09/1942 02:00 EWT
9/30/1945 02:00 EST
4/24/1955 02:00 NY#1
4/30/1967 02:00 US#1

NY # 178
Before 11/18/1883 LMT
11/18/1883 12:00 NY#4
5/05/1941 02:00 EDT
9/11/1941 02:00 EST
2/09/1942 02:00 EWT
9/30/1945 02:00 EST
4/25/1948 02:00 NY#1
4/30/1967 02:00 US#1

NY # 179
Before 11/18/1883 LMT
11/18/1883 12:00 EST
3/31/1918 02:00 EWT
10/27/1918 02:00 EST
3/30/1919 02:00 EWT
10/26/1919 02:00 EST
3/28/1920 02:00 EDT
10/31/1920 02:00 EST
4/24/1921 02:00 EDT
9/25/1921 02:00 EST
4/02/1932 02:00 EDT
9/24/1932 02:00 EST
4/02/1933 02:00 EDT
9/24/1933 02:00 EST
4/02/1934 02:00 EDT
9/24/1934 02:00 EST
4/02/1935 02:00 EDT
9/24/1935 02:00 EST
4/02/1936 02:00 EDT
9/24/1936 02:00 EST
4/02/1937 02:00 EDT
9/24/1937 02:00 EST
4/02/1938 02:00 EDT
9/24/1938 02:00 EST
4/02/1939 02:00 EDT
9/24/1939 02:00 EST
4/02/1940 02:00 EDT
9/24/1940 02:00 EST
4/02/1941 02:00 EDT
9/24/1941 02:00 EST
2/09/1942 02:00 NY#1
4/30/1967 02:00 US#1

NY # 180
Before 11/18/1883 LMT
11/18/1883 12:00 NY#4
6/25/1939 02:00 EDT
9/03/1939 02:00 EST
4/28/1940 02:00 NY#1
4/30/1967 02:00 US#1

NY # 181
Before 11/18/1883 LMT
11/18/1883 12:00 NY#4
5/12/1940 02:00 EDT
10/20/1940 02:00 EST
4/26/1941 02:00 EDT
9/01/1941 02:00 EST
2/09/1942 02:00 EWT
9/30/1945 02:00 EST
4/24/1955 02:00 NY#1
4/30/1967 02:00 US#1

NY # 182
Before 11/18/1883 LMT
11/18/1883 12:00 NY#4
4/28/1940 02:00 EDT
9/03/1940 02:00 EST
4/27/1941 02:00 NY#1
4/30/1967 02:00 US#1

NY # 183
Before 11/18/1883 LMT
11/18/1883 12:00 EST
3/31/1918 02:00 EWT
10/27/1918 02:00 EST
3/30/1919 02:00 EWT
10/26/1919 02:00 EST
3/28/1920 02:00 EDT
10/31/1920 02:00 EST
5/06/1923 02:00 EDT
9/30/1923 02:00 EST
5/04/1924 02:00 EDT
9/28/1924 02:00 EST
5/03/1925 02:00 EDT
9/27/1925 02:00 EST
5/02/1926 02:00 EDT
9/26/1926 02:00 EST
5/08/1927 02:00 EDT
9/25/1927 02:00 EST
5/06/1928 02:00 EDT
9/30/1928 02:00 EST
5/05/1929 02:00 EDT
9/29/1929 02:00 EST
4/26/1931 02:00 EDT
9/27/1931 02:00 EST
4/24/1932 02:00 EDT
9/25/1932 02:00 EST
4/30/1933 02:00 EDT
9/30/1933 02:00 EST
4/29/1934 02:00 EDT
9/30/1934 02:00 EST
4/28/1935 02:00 EDT
9/29/1935 02:00 EST
4/26/1936 02:00 EDT
9/27/1936 02:00 EST
4/25/1937 02:00 EDT
9/26/1937 02:00 EST
4/24/1938 02:00 EDT
9/25/1938 02:00 EST
4/30/1939 02:00 EDT
9/24/1939 02:00 EST
4/28/1940 02:00 EDT
9/29/1940 02:00 EST
4/27/1941 02:00 EDT
9/28/1941 02:00 EST
2/09/1942 02:00 EWT
9/30/1945 02:00 EST
4/28/1946 02:00 EDT
9/29/1946 02:00 EST
4/25/1948 02:00 NY#1
4/30/1967 02:00 US#1

NY # 184
Before 11/18/1883 LMT
11/18/1883 12:00 NY#1
4/23/1922 02:00 EDT
9/24/1922 02:00 EST
4/29/1923 02:00 EDT
9/02/1923 02:00 EST
5/30/1924 02:00 EDT
9/01/1924 02:00 EST
5/30/1925 02:00 EDT
9/05/1925 02:00 EST
5/30/1926 02:00 EDT
9/06/1926 02:00 EST
5/08/1927 00:01 EDT
9/25/1927 00:01 EST
4/29/1928 00:01 EDT
9/30/1928 00:01 EST
4/28/1929 00:01 EDT
9/29/1929 00:01 EST
4/27/1930 00:01 EDT
9/28/1930 00:01 EST
4/26/1931 00:01 EDT
9/27/1931 00:01 EST
5/02/1932 00:01 EDT
9/27/1932 00:01 EST
4/30/1933 02:00 EDT
9/24/1933 02:00 EST
4/29/1934 02:00 EDT
9/30/1934 02:00 EST
4/28/1935 02:00 EDT
9/29/1935 02:00 EST
4/26/1936 02:00 EDT
9/27/1936 02:00 EST
4/25/1937 02:00 EDT
9/26/1937 02:00 EST
4/24/1938 02:00 EDT
9/25/1938 02:00 EST
4/30/1939 02:00 EDT
9/24/1939 02:00 EST
4/28/1940 02:00 EDT
9/29/1940 02:00 EST
4/27/1941 02:00 EDT
9/28/1941 02:00 EST
2/09/1942 02:00 EWT
9/30/1945 02:00 EST
4/25/1948 02:00 EDT
9/26/1948 02:00 EST
4/26/1953 02:00 NY#1
4/30/1967 02:00 US#1

NY # 185
Before 11/18/1883 LMT
11/18/1883 12:00 EST
3/31/1918 02:00 EWT
10/27/1918 02:00 EST
3/30/1919 02:00 EWT
10/26/1919 02:00 EST
3/28/1920 02:00 EDT
10/31/1920 02:00 EST
4/28/1940 02:00 EDT
9/29/1940 02:00 EST
4/27/1941 02:00 EDT
10/04/1941 02:00 EST
2/09/1942 02:00 EWT
9/30/1945 02:00 EST
4/28/1946 02:00 EDT
9/29/1946 02:00 EST
4/27/1947 02:00 EDT
9/28/1947 02:00 EST
4/25/1948 02:00 EDT
9/26/1948 02:00 EST
4/24/1949 02:00 EDT
9/25/1949 02:00 EST
4/30/1950 02:00 EDT
9/24/1950 02:00 EST
4/29/1951 02:00 EDT
9/23/1951 02:00 EST
4/27/1952 02:00 NY#1
4/30/1967 02:00 US#1

NY # 186
Before 11/18/1883 LMT
11/18/1883 12:00 NY#4
5/08/1921 02:00 EDT
9/11/1921 02:00 EST
5/14/1922 02:00 EDT
9/10/1922 02:00 EST
5/13/1923 02:00 EDT
9/09/1923 02:00 EST
5/11/1924 02:00 EDT
9/14/1924 02:00 EST
4/30/1939 02:00 NY#1
4/30/1967 02:00 US#1

NY # 187
Before 11/18/1883 LMT
11/18/1883 12:00 NY#4
6/25/1932 02:00 EDT
9/25/1932 02:00 EST
4/30/1933 02:00 EDT
9/24/1933 02:00 EST
6/02/1935 02:00 EDT
9/02/1935 02:00 EST
6/07/1936 02:00 EDT
9/07/1936 02:00 EST
6/06/1937 02:00 EDT
9/06/1937 02:00 EST
6/05/1938 02:00 EDT
9/04/1938 02:00 EST
6/04/1939 02:00 EDT
9/03/1939 02:00 EST
4/28/1940 02:00 EDT
9/29/1940 02:00 EST
4/27/1941 02:00 EDT
9/28/1941 02:00 EST
2/09/1942 02:00 EWT
9/30/1945 02:00 EST
4/28/1946 02:00 EDT
9/29/1946 02:00 EST
4/27/1947 02:00 EDT
9/28/1947 02:00 EST
4/25/1948 02:00 EDT
9/26/1948 02:00 EST
4/24/1949 02:00 EDT
9/25/1949 02:00 EST
4/29/1951 02:00 NY#1
4/30/1967 02:00 US#1

NY # 188
Before 11/18/1883 LMT
11/18/1883 12:00 NY#4
6/16/1940 02:00 EDT
9/01/1940 02:00 EST
6/20/1941 02:00 EDT
9/08/1941 02:00 EST
2/09/1942 02:00 EWT
9/30/1945 02:00 EST
4/27/1947 02:00 NY#1
4/30/1967 02:00 US#1

TIME TABLES

NY # 189

Before 11/18/1883 LMT
11/18/1883 12:00 NY#4
5/22/1921 02:00 EDT
9/25/1921 02:00 EST
5/21/1922 02:00 EDT
9/30/1922 02:00 EST
5/06/1923 02:00 EDT
9/30/1923 02:00 EST
5/17/1925 02:00 EDT
9/13/1925 02:00 EST
5/16/1926 02:00 EDT
9/12/1926 02:00 EST
5/15/1927 02:00 EDT
9/10/1927 02:00 EST
4/29/1928 02:00 EDT
9/30/1928 02:00 EST
4/28/1929 02:00 EDT
9/29/1929 02:00 EST
4/27/1930 02:00 EDT
9/28/1930 02:00 EST
4/26/1931 02:00 EDT
9/27/1931 02:00 EST
4/24/1932 02:00 EDT
9/25/1932 02:00 EST
4/30/1933 02:00 EDT
9/24/1933 02:00 EST
4/29/1934 02:00 EDT
9/30/1934 02:00 EST
4/28/1935 02:00 EDT
9/29/1935 02:00 EST
4/26/1936 02:00 EDT
9/27/1936 02:00 EST
4/25/1937 02:00 EDT
9/26/1937 02:00 EST
4/24/1938 02:00 EDT
9/25/1938 02:00 EST
4/30/1939 02:00 EDT
9/24/1939 02:00 EST
4/28/1940 02:00 EDT
9/29/1940 02:00 EST
4/27/1941 02:00 EDT
9/28/1941 02:00 EST
2/09/1942 02:00 EWT
9/30/1945 02:00 EST
4/25/1948 02:00 EDT
9/26/1948 02:00 EST
4/24/1955 02:00 NY#1
4/30/1967 02:00 US#1

NY # 190

Before 11/18/1883 LMT
11/18/1883 12:00 NY#4
6/01/1927 02:00 EDT
8/31/1927 02:00 EST
5/23/1929 02:00 EDT
9/03/1929 02:00 EST
5/25/1930 02:00 EDT
9/02/1930 02:00 EST
4/26/1931 02:00 EDT
9/27/1931 02:00 EST
5/29/1932 02:00 EDT
9/06/1932 02:00 EST
4/30/1933 02:00 NY#1
4/30/1967 02:00 US#1

NY # 191

Before 11/18/1883 LMT
11/18/1883 12:00 NY#4
5/26/1940 02:00 EDT
9/29/1940 02:00 EST
4/27/1941 02:00 EDT
9/28/1941 02:00 EST
2/09/1942 02:00 EWT
9/30/1945 02:00 EST
4/25/1948 02:00 NY#1
4/30/1967 02:00 US#1

NY # 192

Before 11/18/1883 LMT
11/18/1883 12:00 EST
3/31/1918 02:00 EWT
10/27/1918 02:00 EST
3/30/1919 02:00 EWT
10/26/1919 02:00 EST
3/28/1920 02:00 EDT
10/31/1920 02:00 EST
4/26/1931 02:00 EDT
9/27/1931 02:00 EST
4/24/1932 02:00 EDT
9/25/1932 02:00 EST
4/30/1933 02:00 EDT
9/24/1933 02:00 EST
4/29/1934 02:00 EDT
9/30/1934 02:00 EST
4/28/1935 02:00 EDT
9/29/1935 02:00 EST
4/26/1936 02:00 EDT
9/27/1936 02:00 EST
4/25/1937 02:00 EDT
9/26/1937 02:00 EST
4/24/1938 02:00 EDT
9/25/1938 02:00 EST
4/30/1939 02:00 EDT
9/24/1939 02:00 EST
4/28/1940 02:00 EDT
9/29/1940 02:00 EST
4/27/1941 02:00 EDT
9/28/1941 02:00 EST
2/09/1942 02:00 EWT
9/30/1945 02:00 EST
4/28/1946 02:00 EDT
9/29/1946 02:00 EST
4/27/1947 02:00 EDT
9/28/1947 02:00 EST
4/25/1948 02:00 EDT
9/26/1948 02:00 EST
4/24/1949 02:00 EDT
10/01/1949 00:01 EST
4/30/1950 02:00 NY#1
4/30/1967 02:00 US#1

NY # 193

Before 11/18/1883 LMT
11/18/1883 12:00 EST
3/31/1918 02:00 EWT
10/27/1918 02:00 EST
3/30/1919 02:00 EWT
10/26/1919 02:00 EST
3/28/1920 02:00 EDT
10/31/1920 02:00 EST
4/26/1925 02:00 EDT
9/27/1925 02:00 EST
4/25/1926 02:00 EDT
9/26/1926 02:00 EST
4/24/1927 02:00 EDT
9/25/1927 02:00 EST
4/29/1928 02:00 EDT
9/30/1928 02:00 EST
4/28/1929 02:00 EDT
9/29/1929 02:00 EST
4/27/1930 02:00 EDT
9/28/1930 02:00 EST
4/26/1931 02:00 EDT
9/27/1931 02:00 EST
4/24/1932 02:00 EDT
9/25/1932 02:00 EST
4/30/1933 02:00 EDT
9/24/1933 02:00 EST
4/29/1934 02:00 EDT
9/30/1934 02:00 EST
6/23/1935 02:00 EDT
9/29/1935 02:00 EST
6/04/1936 02:00 EDT
9/05/1936 02:00 EST
6/20/1937 02:00 EDT
9/05/1937 02:00 EST
6/19/1938 02:00 EDT
9/03/1938 02:00 EST
6/18/1939 02:00 EDT
9/03/1939 02:00 EST
6/16/1940 02:00 EDT
9/01/1940 02:00 EST
6/15/1941 02:00 EDT
9/07/1941 02:00 EST
2/09/1942 02:00 EWT
9/30/1945 02:00 EST
4/27/1947 02:00 NY#1
4/30/1967 02:00 US#1

NY # 194

Before 11/18/1883 LMT
11/18/1883 12:00 EST
3/31/1918 02:00 EWT
10/27/1918 02:00 EST
3/30/1919 02:00 EWT
10/26/1919 02:00 EST
3/28/1920 02:00 EDT
10/31/1920 02:00 EST
4/26/1931 02:00 EDT
9/27/1931 02:00 EST
4/24/1932 02:00 EDT
9/25/1932 02:00 EST
4/30/1933 02:00 EDT
10/01/1933 02:00 EST
4/29/1934 02:00 NY#1
4/30/1967 02:00 US#1

NY # 195

Before 11/18/1883 LMT
11/18/1883 12:00 NY#4
6/02/1940 02:00 EDT
9/01/1940 02:00 EST
4/27/1941 02:00 EDT
9/28/1941 02:00 EST
2/09/1942 02:00 EWT
9/30/1945 02:00 EST
4/25/1948 02:00 NY#1
4/30/1967 02:00 US#1

NY # 196

Before 11/18/1883 LMT
11/18/1883 12:00 EST
3/31/1918 02:00 EWT
10/27/1918 02:00 EST
3/30/1919 02:00 EWT
10/26/1919 02:00 EST
3/28/1920 02:00 EDT
10/31/1920 02:00 EST
5/06/1923 02:00 EDT
9/30/1923 02:00 EST
5/04/1924 02:00 EDT
9/28/1924 02:00 EST
5/03/1925 02:00 EDT
9/27/1925 02:00 EST
5/02/1926 02:00 EDT
9/26/1926 02:00 EST
5/08/1927 02:00 EDT
9/25/1927 02:00 EST
5/06/1928 02:00 EDT
9/30/1928 02:00 EST
5/05/1929 02:00 EDT
9/29/1929 02:00 EST
4/27/1930 02:00 EDT
9/28/1930 02:00 EST
4/26/1931 02:00 EDT
9/27/1931 02:00 EST
4/24/1932 02:00 EDT
9/25/1932 02:00 EST
4/30/1933 02:00 EDT
9/24/1933 02:00 EST
4/29/1934 02:00 EDT
9/30/1934 02:00 EST
4/28/1935 02:00 EDT
9/29/1935 02:00 EST
4/26/1936 02:00 EDT
9/27/1936 02:00 EST
4/25/1937 02:00 EDT
9/26/1937 02:00 EST
4/24/1938 02:00 EDT
9/25/1938 02:00 EST
4/30/1939 02:00 EDT
9/24/1939 02:00 EST
4/28/1940 02:00 EDT
9/29/1940 02:00 EST
4/27/1941 02:00 EDT
9/28/1941 02:00 EST
2/09/1942 02:00 EWT
9/30/1945 02:00 EST
4/25/1948 02:00 EDT
9/26/1948 02:00 EST
4/24/1955 02:00 NY#1
4/30/1967 02:00 US#1

NY # 197

Before 11/18/1883 LMT
11/18/1883 12:00 NY#4
5/15/1927 02:00 EDT
9/12/1927 02:00 EST
4/26/1931 02:00 EDT
9/27/1931 02:00 EST
4/24/1932 02:00 EDT
9/25/1932 02:00 EST
5/07/1933 02:00 EDT
9/24/1933 02:00 EST
4/22/1934 02:00 EDT
9/23/1934 02:00 EST
4/28/1935 02:00 NY#1
4/30/1967 02:00 US#1

NY # 198

Before 11/18/1883 LMT
11/18/1883 12:00 NY#4
5/15/1939 02:00 EDT
9/15/1939 02:00 EST
6/15/1940 02:00 EDT
9/01/1940 02:00 EST
5/01/1941 02:00 EDT
9/01/1941 02:00 EST
2/09/1942 02:00 EWT
9/30/1945 02:00 EST
4/25/1948 02:00 NY#1
4/30/1967 02:00 US#1

NY # 199

Before 11/18/1883 LMT
11/18/1883 12:00 NY#1
3/24/1921 02:00 EDT
9/25/1921 02:00 EST
4/29/1923 02:00 EDT
9/30/1923 02:00 EST
5/30/1926 02:00 EDT
9/26/1926 02:00 EST
6/09/1929 02:00 EDT
9/01/1929 02:00 EST
6/08/1930 02:00 EDT
9/07/1930 02:00 EST
6/14/1931 02:00 EDT
9/04/1931 02:00 EST
5/14/1932 02:00 EDT
9/05/1932 02:00 EST
5/21/1933 02:00 EDT
9/24/1933 02:00 EST
4/29/1934 02:00 NY#1
4/30/1967 02:00 US#1

NY # 200

Before 11/18/1883 LMT
11/18/1883 12:00 EST
3/31/1918 02:00 EWT
10/27/1918 02:00 EST
3/30/1919 02:00 EWT
10/26/1919 02:00 EST
3/28/1920 02:00 EDT
10/31/1920 02:00 EST
4/30/1939 02:00 EDT
9/24/1939 02:00 EST
5/11/1940 02:00 EDT
9/14/1940 02:00 EST
4/27/1941 02:00 NY#1
4/30/1967 02:00 US#1

NY # 201

Before 11/18/1883 LMT
11/18/1883 12:00 NY#4
4/26/1925 02:00 EDT
9/27/1925 02:00 EST
5/31/1936 02:00 EDT
9/01/1936 02:00 EST
5/26/1937 02:00 EDT
9/08/1937 02:00 EST
5/29/1938 02:00 EDT
9/04/1938 02:00 EST
5/28/1939 02:00 EDT
9/03/1939 02:00 EST
5/26/1940 02:00 EDT
9/01/1940 02:00 EST
4/27/1941 02:00 NY#1
4/30/1967 02:00 US#1

NY # 202

Before 11/18/1883 LMT
11/18/1883 12:00 NY#1
9/26/1926 02:00 EST
6/05/1927 02:00 EDT
8/28/1927 02:00 EST
4/29/1928 02:00 NY#1
4/30/1967 02:00 US#1

NY # 203

Before 11/18/1883 LMT
11/18/1883 12:00 NY#4
6/02/1940 02:00 EDT
9/01/1940 02:00 EST
5/18/1941 02:00 EDT
9/07/1941 02:00 EST
2/09/1942 02:00 NY#1
4/30/1967 02:00 US#1

NY # 204

Before 11/18/1883 LMT
11/18/1883 12:00 EST
3/31/1918 02:00 EWT
10/27/1918 02:00 EST
3/30/1919 02:00 EWT
10/26/1919 02:00 EST
3/28/1920 02:00 EDT
10/31/1920 02:00 EST
4/24/1921 02:00 EDT
9/25/1921 02:00 EST
6/12/1927 02:00 EDT
9/11/1927 02:00 EST
4/29/1928 02:00 NY#1
4/30/1967 02:00 US#1

NY # 205

Before 11/18/1883 LMT
11/18/1883 12:00 NY#1
9/29/1940 02:00 EST
5/04/1941 02:00 EDT
9/28/1941 02:00 NY#1
4/30/1967 02:00 US#1

NY # 206

Before 11/18/1883 LMT
11/18/1883 12:00 NY#4
5/05/1940 02:00 EDT
9/01/1940 02:00 EST
4/27/1941 02:00 EDT
9/28/1941 02:00 EST
2/09/1942 02:00 EWT
9/30/1945 02:00 EST
4/24/1955 02:00 NY#1
4/30/1967 02:00 US#1

NY # 207

Before 11/18/1883 LMT
11/18/1883 12:00 NY#4
4/25/1937 02:00 EDT
9/26/1937 02:00 EST
6/16/1940 02:00 EDT
9/01/1940 02:00 EST
4/27/1941 02:00 EDT
9/28/1941 02:00 EST
2/09/1942 02:00 EWT
9/30/1945 02:00 EST
4/27/1947 02:00 NY#1
4/30/1967 02:00 US#1

NY # 208

Before 11/18/1883 LMT
11/18/1883 12:00 EST
3/31/1918 02:00 EWT
10/27/1918 02:00 EST
3/30/1919 02:00 EWT
10/26/1919 02:00 EST
3/28/1920 02:00 EDT
10/31/1920 02:00 EST
4/24/1921 02:00 EDT
9/25/1921 02:00 EST
4/06/1930 02:00 EDT
9/28/1930 02:00 EST
4/26/1931 02:00 NY#1
4/30/1967 02:00 US#1

NY # 209

Before 11/18/1883 LMT
11/18/1883 12:00 EST
3/31/1918 02:00 EWT
10/27/1918 02:00 EST
3/30/1919 02:00 EWT
10/26/1919 02:00 EST
3/28/1920 02:00 EDT
10/31/1920 02:00 EST
4/24/1921 02:00 EDT
9/25/1921 02:00 EST
5/30/1926 02:00 EDT
9/12/1926 02:00 EST
5/29/1927 02:00 EDT
9/11/1927 02:00 EST
5/18/1930 02:00 EDT
9/28/1930 02:00 EST
4/30/1939 02:00 EDT
10/01/1939 02:00 EST
4/28/1940 02:00 EDT
9/29/1940 02:00 EST
4/27/1941 02:00 EDT
9/28/1941 02:00 EST
2/09/1942 02:00 EWT
9/30/1945 02:00 EST
4/28/1946 02:00 EDT
9/29/1946 02:00 EST
4/27/1947 02:00 EDT
9/28/1947 02:00 EST
4/25/1948 02:00 EDT
9/26/1948 02:00 EST
4/24/1949 02:00 EDT
9/25/1949 02:00 EST
4/30/1950 02:00 EDT
9/24/1950 02:00 EST
4/29/1951 02:00 EDT
9/23/1951 02:00 EST
4/27/1952 02:00 NY#1
4/30/1967 02:00 US#1

NY # 210

Before 11/18/1883 LMT
11/18/1883 12:00 NY#4
5/01/1921 02:00 EDT
9/02/1921 02:00 EST
4/30/1922 02:00 NY#1
4/30/1967 02:00 US#1

NY # 211

Before 11/18/1883 LMT
11/18/1883 12:00 NY#4
5/15/1927 02:00 EDT
9/01/1927 02:00 EST
4/26/1931 02:00 NY#1
4/30/1967 02:00 US#1

NY # 212

Before 11/18/1883 LMT
11/18/1883 12:00 NY#1
4/24/1921 00:01 EDT
9/25/1921 00:01 EST
4/30/1922 00:01 EDT
9/24/1922 00:01 EST
4/29/1923 00:01 EDT
9/30/1923 00:01 EST
4/27/1924 00:01 EDT
9/28/1924 00:01 EST
4/26/1925 00:01 EDT
9/27/1925 00:01 EST
4/25/1926 00:01 EDT
9/26/1926 00:01 EST
4/24/1927 00:01 EDT
9/25/1927 00:01 EST
4/29/1928 00:01 EDT
9/30/1928 00:01 EST
4/28/1929 00:01 EDT
9/29/1929 00:01 EST
4/27/1930 00:01 EDT
9/28/1930 00:01 EST
4/26/1931 00:01 EDT
9/27/1931 00:01 EST
4/24/1932 00:01 EDT
9/25/1932 00:01 EST
4/30/1933 00:01 EDT
9/24/1933 00:01 EST
4/29/1934 00:01 EDT
9/30/1934 00:01 EST
4/28/1935 00:01 EDT
9/29/1935 00:01 EST
4/26/1936 00:01 EDT
9/27/1936 00:01 EST
4/25/1937 00:01 EDT
9/26/1937 00:01 EST
4/24/1938 00:01 EDT
9/25/1938 00:01 EST
4/30/1939 00:01 EDT
9/24/1939 00:01 EST
4/28/1940 00:01 EDT
9/29/1940 00:01 EST
4/27/1941 00:01 EDT
9/28/1941 00:01 EST
2/09/1942 02:00 EWT
9/30/1945 02:00 EST
4/24/1955 02:00 NY#1
4/30/1967 02:00 US#1

NY # 213

Before 11/18/1883 LMT
11/18/1883 12:00 EST
3/31/1918 02:00 EWT
10/27/1918 02:00 EST
3/30/1919 02:00 EWT
10/26/1919 02:00 EST
3/28/1920 02:00 EDT
10/31/1920 02:00 EST
4/26/1931 02:00 EDT
9/27/1931 02:00 EST
4/24/1932 02:00 EDT
9/25/1932 02:00 EST
4/30/1933 02:00 EDT
9/24/1933 02:00 EST
4/29/1934 02:00 EDT
9/30/1934 02:00 EST
4/28/1935 02:00 EDT
9/29/1935 02:00 EST
4/26/1936 02:00 EDT
9/27/1936 02:00 EST
4/25/1937 02:00 EDT
9/26/1937 02:00 EST
4/24/1938 02:00 EDT
9/25/1938 02:00 EST
4/30/1939 02:00 EDT
9/24/1939 02:00 EST
4/28/1940 02:00 EDT
9/29/1940 02:00 EST
4/27/1941 02:00 EDT
9/28/1941 02:00 EST
2/09/1942 02:00 EWT
9/30/1945 02:00 EST
4/28/1946 02:00 EDT
10/31/1946 02:00 EST
4/27/1947 02:00 NY#1
4/30/1967 02:00 US#1

NY # 214

NEW YORK

TIME TABLES

Date	Time	Zone
Before 11/18/1883		LMT
11/18/1883	12:00	NY#4
4/28/1941	02:00	EDT
9/17/1941	02:00	EST
2/09/1942	02:00	EWT
9/30/1945	02:00	EST
4/24/1955	02:00	NY#1
4/30/1967	02:00	US#1

NY # 215

Date	Time	Zone
Before 11/18/1883		LMT
11/18/1883	12:00	EST
3/31/1918	02:00	EWT
10/27/1918	02:00	EST
3/30/1919	02:00	EWT
10/26/1919	02:00	EST
3/28/1920	02:00	EDT
10/31/1920	02:00	EST
4/26/1925	02:00	EDT
9/27/1925	02:00	EST
4/25/1926	02:00	EDT
9/26/1926	02:00	EST
4/24/1927	02:00	EDT
9/25/1927	02:00	EST
4/29/1928	02:00	EDT
9/30/1928	02:00	EST
4/28/1929	02:00	EDT
9/29/1929	02:00	EST
4/27/1930	02:00	EDT
9/28/1930	02:00	EST
4/26/1931	02:00	EDT
9/27/1931	02:00	EST
4/24/1932	02:00	EDT
9/25/1932	02:00	EST
4/30/1933	02:00	EDT
9/24/1933	02:00	EST
4/29/1934	02:00	EDT
9/30/1934	02:00	EST
4/28/1935	02:00	EDT
9/29/1935	02:00	EST
4/26/1936	02:00	EDT
9/27/1936	02:00	EST
4/25/1937	02:00	EDT
9/26/1937	02:00	EST
4/24/1938	02:00	EDT
9/25/1938	02:00	EST
4/30/1939	02:00	EDT
10/01/1939	02:00	EST
4/28/1940	02:00	EDT
9/29/1940	02:00	EST
4/27/1941	02:00	EDT
9/28/1941	02:00	EST
2/09/1942	02:00	EWT
9/30/1945	02:00	EST
4/28/1946	02:00	EDT
9/30/1946	02:00	EST
4/27/1947	02:00	NY#1
4/30/1967	02:00	US#1

NY # 216

Date	Time	Zone
Before 11/18/1883		LMT
11/18/1883	12:00	NY#4
6/11/1936	02:00	EDT
9/09/1936	02:00	EST
6/11/1937	02:00	EDT
9/10/1937	02:00	EST
6/12/1938	02:00	EDT
9/11/1938	02:00	EST
5/12/1940	02:00	EDT
9/01/1940	02:00	EST
5/12/1941	02:00	EDT
9/08/1941	02:00	NY#4
4/24/1955	02:00	US#2

NY # 217

Date	Time	Zone
Before 11/18/1883		LMT
11/18/1883	12:00	NY#4
4/28/1941	02:00	EDT
9/02/1941	02:00	EST
2/09/1942	02:00	EWT
9/30/1945	02:00	EST
4/29/1951	02:00	NY#1
4/30/1967	02:00	US#1

NY # 218

Date	Time	Zone
Before 11/18/1883		LMT
11/18/1883	12:00	NY#4
4/26/1931	02:00	EDT
9/27/1931	02:00	EST
4/24/1932	02:00	EDT
9/25/1932	02:00	EST
6/01/1939	02:00	EDT
8/31/1939	02:00	EST
6/01/1940	02:00	EDT
8/31/1940	02:00	EST
4/27/1941	02:00	EDT
9/28/1941	02:00	EST
2/09/1942	02:00	EWT
9/30/1945	02:00	EST
4/24/1955	02:00	NY#1
4/30/1967	02:00	US#1

NY # 219

Date	Time	Zone
Before 11/18/1883		LMT
11/18/1883	12:00	EST
3/31/1918	02:00	EWT
10/27/1918	02:00	EST
3/30/1919	02:00	EWT
10/26/1919	02:00	EST
3/28/1920	02:00	EDT
10/31/1920	02:00	EST
4/26/1931	02:00	EDT
9/27/1931	02:00	EST
4/24/1932	02:00	EDT
9/25/1932	02:00	EST
4/30/1933	02:00	EDT
9/24/1933	02:00	EST
4/29/1934	02:00	EDT
9/30/1934	02:00	EST
4/28/1935	02:00	EDT
9/29/1935	02:00	EST
4/26/1936	02:00	EDT
9/27/1936	02:00	EST
4/25/1937	02:00	EDT
9/26/1937	02:00	EST
4/24/1938	02:00	EDT
9/25/1938	02:00	EST
4/30/1939	02:00	EDT
9/24/1939	02:00	EST
4/28/1940	02:00	EDT
9/29/1940	02:00	EST
4/27/1941	02:00	EDT
9/28/1941	02:00	EST
2/09/1942	02:00	EWT
9/30/1945	02:00	EST
4/28/1946	02:00	EDT
10/27/1946	02:00	EST
4/27/1947	02:00	NY#1
4/30/1967	02:00	US#1

NY # 220

Date	Time	Zone
Before 11/18/1883		LMT
11/18/1883	12:00	EST
3/31/1918	02:00	EWT
10/27/1918	02:00	EST
3/30/1919	02:00	EWT
10/26/1919	02:00	EST
3/28/1920	02:00	EDT
10/31/1920	02:00	EST
4/26/1931	02:00	EDT
9/27/1931	02:00	EST
4/02/1932	02:00	EDT
9/24/1932	02:00	EST
4/01/1933	02:00	EDT
9/30/1933	02:00	EST
4/07/1934	02:00	EDT
9/29/1934	02:00	EST
4/06/1935	02:00	EDT
9/28/1935	02:00	EST
4/26/1936	02:00	NY#1
4/30/1967	02:00	US#1

NY # 221

Date	Time	Zone
Before 11/18/1883		LMT
11/18/1883	12:00	NY#4
6/22/1936	02:00	EDT
9/14/1936	02:00	EST
5/30/1937	02:00	EDT
9/12/1937	02:00	EST
4/24/1938	02:00	EDT
9/25/1938	02:00	EST
6/11/1939	02:00	EDT
9/10/1939	02:00	EST
4/28/1940	02:00	NY#1
4/30/1967	02:00	US#1

NY # 222

Date	Time	Zone
Before 11/18/1883		LMT
11/18/1883	12:00	NY#1
9/26/1926	02:00	EST
6/05/1927	02:00	EDT
8/28/1927	02:00	EST
4/29/1928	02:00	NY#1
4/30/1967	02:00	US#1

NY # 223

Date	Time	Zone
Before 11/18/1883		LMT
11/18/1883	12:00	NY#4
4/15/1930	02:00	EDT
10/15/1930	02:00	EST
4/26/1931	02:00	EDT
9/27/1931	02:00	EST
4/24/1932	02:00	EDT
9/25/1932	02:00	EST
4/30/1933	02:00	EDT
9/24/1933	02:00	EST
4/29/1934	02:00	EDT
9/30/1934	02:00	EST
4/28/1935	02:00	EDT
9/29/1935	02:00	EST
4/26/1936	02:00	EDT
9/27/1936	02:00	EST
4/25/1937	02:00	EDT
9/26/1937	02:00	EST
4/24/1938	02:00	EDT
9/25/1938	02:00	EST
4/30/1939	02:00	EDT
9/24/1939	02:00	EST
4/28/1940	02:00	EDT
9/29/1940	02:00	EST
4/27/1941	02:00	EDT
9/28/1941	02:00	EST
2/09/1942	02:00	EWT
9/30/1945	02:00	EST
4/28/1946	02:00	EDT
10/31/1946	02:00	EST
4/27/1947	02:00	NY#1
4/30/1967	02:00	US#1

NY # 224

Date	Time	Zone
Before 11/18/1883		LMT
11/18/1883	12:00	EST
3/31/1918	02:00	EWT
10/27/1918	02:00	EST
3/30/1919	02:00	EWT
10/26/1919	02:00	EST
3/28/1920	02:00	EDT
10/31/1920	02:00	EST
4/30/1939	02:00	EDT
9/24/1939	02:00	EST
4/28/1940	02:00	EDT
9/29/1940	02:00	EST
4/27/1941	02:00	EDT
9/28/1941	02:00	EST
2/09/1942	02:00	EWT
9/30/1945	02:00	EST
4/28/1946	02:00	EDT
9/29/1946	02:00	EST
5/04/1947	02:00	EDT
9/28/1947	02:00	EST
4/25/1948	02:00	NY#1
4/30/1967	02:00	US#1

NY # 225

Date	Time	Zone
Before 11/18/1883		LMT
11/18/1883	12:00	NY#4
4/28/1929	02:00	EDT
9/29/1929	02:00	EST
7/03/1938	02:00	EDT
9/04/1938	02:00	EST
7/02/1939	02:00	EDT
9/03/1939	02:00	EST
6/02/1940	02:00	EDT
9/01/1940	02:00	EST
4/27/1941	02:00	NY#1
4/30/1967	02:00	US#1

NY # 226

Date	Time	Zone
Before 11/18/1883		LMT
11/18/1883	12:00	NY#4
2/09/1942	02:00	EWT
9/30/1945	02:00	EST
4/24/1955	02:00	NY#1
4/30/1967	02:00	US#1

COUNTIES

1 Albany
2 Allegany
3 Bronx
4 Broome
5 Cattaraugus
6 Cayuga
7 Chautauqua
8 Chemung
9 Chenango
10 Clinton
11 Columbia
12 Cortland
13 Delaware
14 Dutchess
15 Erie
16 Essex
17 Franklin
18 Fulton
19 Genesee
20 Greene
21 Hamilton
22 Herkimer
23 Jefferson
24 Kings
25 Lewis
26 Livingston
27 Madison
28 Monroe
29 Montgomery
30 Nassau
31 New York
32 Niagara
33 Oneida
34 Onondaga
35 Ontario
36 Orange
37 Orleans
38 Oswego
39 Otsego
40 Putnam
41 Queens
42 Rensselaer
43 Richmond
44 Rockland
45 St Lawrence
46 Saratoga
47 Schenectady
48 Schoharie
49 Schuyler
50 Seneca
51 Steuben
52 Suffolk
53 Sullivan
54 Tioga
55 Tompkins
56 Ulster
57 Warren
58 Washington
59 Wayne
60 Westchester
61 Wyoming
62 Yates

Place	Table	Lat	Long	Time
Abbotts 5	226	42N13	78w17	5:13:08
Academy 1	1	42N39	73w47	4:55:08
Academy 35	14	42N53	77w17	5:09:08
Accord 56	76	41N48	74w13	4:56:52
Acidalia 53	226	41N51	75w08	5:00:32
Ack 44	4	41N05	73w55	4:55:40
Acra 20	226	42N19	74w03	4:56:12
Adams 23	143	43N49	76w01	5:04:04
Adams Basin 28	226	43N12	77w51	5:11:24
Adams Center 23	143	43N52	76w00	5:04:00
Adams Corners 40	6	41N20	73w52	4:55:28
Adams Cove 23	49	44N00	76w03	5:04:12
Adamsville 58	123	43N25	73w29	4:53:56
Addison 51	13	42N06	77w14	5:08:56
Addison Hill 51	13	41N59	77w19	5:09:16
Adelphi 24	1	40N41	73w58	4:55:52
Adirondack 57	226	43N46	73w45	4:55:00
Adrian 51	20	42N16	77w37	5:10:28
Afton 9	144	42N14	75w32	5:02:08
Afton Lake 9	144	42N14	75w31	5:02:04
Airmont 44	4	41N06	74w07	4:56:28
Airmont Heights 44	4	41N08	74w06	4:56:24
Akins Corners 40	7	41N31	73w36	4:54:24
Akron 15	145	43N01	78w30	5:14:00
Alabama 19	226	43N05	78w22	5:13:28
Albany 1	1	42N39	73w45	4:55:00
Albertson 30	11	40N46	73w39	4:54:36
Albia 42	220	42N43	73w41	4:54:44
Albion 37	146	43N15	78w12	5:12:48
Alcove 1	11	42N28	73w55	4:55:40
Alden 15	38	42N55	78w32	5:14:08
Alden Bend 10	16	44N53	73w39	4:54:36
Alden Center 15	38	42N54	78w30	5:14:00
Alden Manor 30	11	40N42	73w42	4:54:48
Alder Creek 33	14	43N25	75w14	5:00:56
Alexander 19	25	42N55	78w15	5:13:00
Alexandria 23	17	44N18	75w52	5:03:28
Alexandria Bay 23	17	44N20	75w55	5:03:40
Alfred 2	27	42N16	77w48	5:11:12
Allaben 56	88	42N07	74w24	4:57:36
Allard Corners 36	11	41N34	74w11	4:56:44
Allegany 5	20	42N06	78w30	5:14:00
Allegany Indian Reservation 5	226	42N07	78w44	5:14:56
Allen 2	226	42N24	78w01	5:12:04
Allen Center 2	226	42N24	78w01	5:12:04
Allendale 23	143	43N48	76w01	5:04:04
Allens Hill 35	47	42N54	77w25	5:09:40
Allentown 2	226	42N05	78w04	5:12:16
Allenwood 30	1	40N48	73w44	4:54:56
Allerton 3	1	40N53	73w52	4:55:28
Alligerville 56	11	41N50	74w08	4:56:32
Alloway 59	99	43N04	76w59	5:07:56
Alma 2	109	42N03	78w01	5:12:04
Almond 2	71	42N21	77w47	5:11:08
Aloquin 35	14	42N49	77w06	5:08:24
Alpine 49	226	42N19	76w43	5:06:52
Alplaus 47	4	42N51	73w53	4:55:32
Alps 42	226	42N38	73w33	4:54:12
Alsen 20	11	42N09	73w55	4:55:40
Altamont 1	40	42N42	74w02	4:56:08
Altay 49	13	42N31	76w58	5:07:52
Altmar 38	25	43N31	76w00	5:04:00
Alton 59	226	43N13	76w59	5:07:56
Altona 10	124	44N51	73w42	4:54:48
Amagansett 52	11	40N59	72w09	4:48:36
Amawalk 60	16	41N17	73w46	4:55:04
Amber 34	13	42N55	76w20	5:05:20
Ambierville 9	226	42N32	75w23	5:01:32
Amboy 34	25	43N22	75w56	5:03:44
Amboy Center 38	25	43N26	75w54	5:03:36
Amchir 36	1	41N28	74w24	4:57:36
Amenia 14	11	41N47	73w33	4:54:12
Ames 29	7	42N50	74w36	4:58:24
Amherst 15	1	42N59	78w48	5:15:12
Amity 36	11	41N16	74w27	4:57:48
Amity Harbor 52	11	40N41	73w28	4:53:52
Amityville 52	6	40N41	73w25	4:53:40
Amsdell Heights 15	153	42N45	78w51	5:15:24
Amsterdam 29	1	42N56	74w11	4:56:44
Ancram 11	11	42N02	73w35	4:54:20
Ancramdale 11	226	42N00	73w37	4:54:28
Andes 13	226	42N12	74w47	4:59:08
Andover 2	107	42N10	77w48	5:11:12
Andrea Park Estates 60	16	41N17	73w46	4:55:04
Angelica 2	226	42N18	78w02	5:12:08
Angola 15	11	42N38	79w02	5:16:08
Angola on the Lake 15	11	42N39	79w03	5:16:12
Annandale-on-Hudson 14	7	42N01	73w54	4:55:36
Annsville 60	6	41N18	73w56	4:55:44
Ansonia 31	1	40N48	74w06	4:56:24
Antwerp 23	106	44N12	75w37	5:02:28
Apalachin 54	36	42N04	76w09	5:04:36
Apex 13	97	41N58	75w16	5:01:04
Appleton 32	150	43N20	78w39	5:14:36
Apulia 34	91	42N49	76w05	5:04:20
Aquebogue 52	11	40N57	72w37	4:50:28
Aqueduct 47	6	42N47	73w53	4:55:32
Aquetuck 1	1	42N28	73w48	4:55:12
Arcade 61	147	42N32	78w25	5:13:40
Arcadia 59	226	43N06	77w04	5:08:16
Archdale 58	226	43N05	73w30	4:54:00
Archville 60	6	41N07	73w52	4:55:28
Arden 36	4	41N17	74w09	4:56:36

NEW YORK

Ardonia 56 11 41N42 74w03 4:56:12
Ardsley 60 7 41N01 73w50 4:55:20
Ardsley-on-Hudson 60 7 41N02 73w52 4:55:28
Argo Village 30 11 40N42 73w42 4:54:48
Argusville 48 11 42N48 74w37 4:58:28
Argyle 58 226 43N14 73w28 4:53:52
Arietta 21 226 43N32 74w34 4:58:16
Arkport 51 20 42N24 77w42 5:10:48
Arkville 13 42 42N09 74w37 4:58:28
Arkwright 7 15 42N24 79w14 5:16:56
Arlington 14 1 41N42 73w54 4:55:36
Arlyn Oaks 30 11 40N41 73w28 4:53:52
Armonk 60 1 41N08 73w43 4:54:52
Armor 15 153 42N45 78w51 5:15:24
Arrochar 43 1 40N36 74w05 4:56:20
Arthur Manor 60 1 40N59 73w48 4:55:12
Arthursburg 14 226 41N36 73w47 4:55:08
Arverne 41 1 40N36 73w48 4:55:12
Ashantee 26 226 42N55 77w45 5:11:00
Asharoken 52 11 40N56 73w23 4:53:32
Ashford 5 226 42N26 78w39 5:14:36
Ashford Hollow 5 226 42N24 78w37 5:14:28
Ashland 20 226 42N18 74w20 4:57:20
Ashokan 56 11 41N58 74w13 4:56:52
Ashville 7 20 42N06 79w23 5:17:32
Ashville Bay 7 20 42N06 79w23 5:17:32
Ashwood 37 15 43N19 78w23 5:13:32
Assembly Point 41 1 40N47 73w47 4:55:08
Association Island 23 65 43N52 76w12 5:04:48
Astoria 41 1 40N46 73w55 4:55:40
Athens 20 11 42N16 73w49 4:55:16
Athol 57 226 43N29 73w50 4:55:20
Athol Springs 15 11 42N46 78w52 5:15:28
Atlanta 51 14 42N33 77w28 5:09:52
Atlantic 43 11 40N31 74w15 4:57:00
Atlantic Beach 30 11 40N35 73w44 4:54:56
Atlantique 52 11 40N41 73w13 4:52:52
Attica 61 148 42N52 78w17 5:13:08
Attlebury 14 226 41N52 73w43 4:54:52
Atwater 6 13 42N40 76w37 5:06:28
Atwell 22 226 43N27 75w12 5:00:48
Atwood 56 11 41N51 74w09 4:56:36
Auburn 6 13 42N56 76w34 5:06:16
Audubon 31 1 40N50 73w56 4:55:44
Augusta 33 13 42N59 75w30 5:02:00
Aurelius 6 14 42N56 76w40 5:06:40
Auriesville 29 22 42N56 74w19 4:57:16
Aurora 6 13 42N45 76w42 5:06:48
Aurora Tract 34 13 43N07 76w12 5:04:48
Ausable 10 27 44N31 73w36 4:54:24
Ausable Chasm 10 27 44N31 73w28 4:53:52
Au Sable Forks 16 44 44N27 73w41 4:54:44
Austerlitz 11 11 42N19 73w30 4:54:00
Ava 33 226 43N25 75w27 5:01:48
Averill Park 42 226 42N38 73w33 4:54:12
Avoca 51 14 42N25 77w25 5:09:40
Avon 26 20 42N55 77w45 5:11:00
Axeville 5 20 42N14 79w04 5:16:16
Babcock Hill 33 13 42N57 75w15 5:01:00
Babcock Lake 42 11 42N45 73w21 4:53:24
Babylon 52 1 40N42 73w19 4:53:16
Bacon Hill 46 226 43N06 73w35 4:54:20
Baggs Corner 23 45 43N59 75w56 5:03:44
Bainbridge 9 149 42N18 75w29 5:01:56
Baiting Hollow 52 11 40N55 72w45 4:51:00
Bakers Mills 57 49 43N37 74w01 4:56:04
Bakerstand 5 226 42N25 78w30 5:14:00
Balcom 7 217 42N22 79w03 5:16:12
Balcom Beach 2 226 42N24 78w15 5:13:00
Bald Mountain 58 226 43N05 73w30 4:54:00
Baldwin 30 7 40N39 73w36 4:54:24
Baldwin Harbor 30 11 40N39 73w37 4:54:28
Baldwin Heights 5 226 42N05 78w26 5:13:44
Baldwin Place 60 29 41N21 73w46 4:55:04
Baldwinsville 34 91 43N10 76w20 5:05:20
Ballina 27 14 42N56 75w51 5:03:24
Ballston 46 8 42N56 73w53 4:55:32
Ballston Center 46 8 43N01 73w51 4:55:24
Ballston Lake 46 8 42N55 73w49 4:55:16
Ballston Spa 46 8 43N00 73w51 4:55:24
Balltown 7 226 42N28 79w10 5:16:40
Balmat 45 226 44N15 75w24 5:01:36
Balmville 36 1 41N32 74w01 4:56:04
Bangall 14 226 41N53 73w42 4:54:48
Bangor 17 16 44N50 74w26 4:57:44
Bangor Station 17 16 44N50 74w26 4:57:44
Bank Plaza 30 11 40N40 73w34 4:54:16
Barbourville 13 167 42N04 75w25 5:01:40
Barcelona 7 225 42N19 79w34 5:18:16
Barclay Heights 56 215 42N04 73w57 4:55:48
Bardonia 44 4 41N07 74w00 4:56:00
Bar Harbour Shopping Center 30 11 40N51 73w27 4:53:48
Barker 32 150 43N20 78w33 5:14:12
Barkers Grove 58 11 42N54 73w35 4:54:20
Barkersville 46 226 43N05 73w55 4:55:40
Barkertown 26 226 42N32 77w57 5:11:48
Barnerville 48 12 42N41 74w23 4:57:32
Barnes Corners 25 226 43N49 75w49 5:03:16
Barnes Hole 52 11 40N58 72w08 4:48:32
Barneveld 33 82 43N17 75w11 5:00:44
Barnum Island 30 11 40N36 73w39 4:54:36
Barre 37 146 43N10 78w13 5:12:52
Barre Center 37 146 43N15 78w12 5:12:48
Barrington 62 14 42N32 77w02 5:08:08
Barrytown 14 7 42N00 73w56 4:55:44
Barryville 53 20 41N29 74w55 4:59:40
Bartlett 33 211 43N13 75w26 5:01:44
Bartlett Corners 28 13 43N17 77w47 5:11:08
Bartlett Hollow 13 104 42N21 75w10 5:00:40
Barton 54 224 42N04 76w30 5:06:00
Basket 53 226 41N51 75w08 5:00:32
Basom 19 226 43N04 78w24 5:13:36
Batavia 19 142 43N00 78w11 5:12:44
Batchellerville 46 7 43N13 74w10 4:56:40
Bates 48 226 42N27 74w13 4:56:52
Bath 51 14 42N20 77w19 5:09:16
Bath Beach 24 1 40N36 74w00 4:56:00
Battenville 58 226 43N05 73w30 4:54:00
Baxter Estates 30 11 40N50 73w42 4:54:48
Bay 24 1 40N35 73w57 4:55:48
Bayberry 34 13 43N07 76w12 5:04:48
Bayberry Dunes 52 11 40N42 72w59 4:51:56
Baychester 3 1 40N52 73w51 4:55:24
Bay Colony 30 11 40N39 73w37 4:54:28
Bay Park 30 11 40N39 73w40 4:54:40
Bay Point 52 11 40N55 72w27 4:49:48
Bayport 52 11 40N44 73w03 4:52:12
Bay Ridge 24 1 40N37 74w02 4:56:08
Bay Shore 52 1 40N43 73w15 4:53:00
Bay Shores 34 13 42N55 76w20 5:05:20
Bayside 41 1 40N46 73w46 4:55:04
Bay Terrace 41 1 40N46 73w47 4:55:08
Bay Terrace 43 1 40N34 74w07 4:56:28
Bay View 15 11 42N47 78w51 5:15:24
Bay View 24 1 40N38 73w54 4:55:36
Bay View 28 185 43N13 77w36 5:10:24
Bayview 52 11 41N04 72w26 4:49:44
Bayville 30 7 40N55 73w34 4:54:16
Beach Hampton 52 1 40N58 72w08 4:48:32
Beach Ridge 32 1 43N03 78w51 5:15:24
Beachville 51 226 42N24 77w42 5:10:48
Beachwood 7 20 42N06 79w19 5:17:16
Beacon 14 57 41N30 73w58 4:55:52
Beantown 8 226 42N07 76w33 5:06:12
Beards Hollow 48 13 42N38 74w34 4:58:16
Bear Mountain 44 6 41N19 73w59 4:55:56
Bearsville 56 11 42N02 74w09 4:56:36
Beaver Brook 53 226 41N36 75w04 5:00:16
Beaver Dam Lake 36 1 41N31 74w03 4:56:12
Beaver Dams 49 14 42N17 76w58 5:07:52
Beaver Falls 25 226 43N53 75w26 5:01:44
Beaverkill 53 75 41N54 74w50 4:59:20
Beaver Meadow 9 226 42N37 75w36 5:02:24
Beaver River 22 226 43N54 74w55 4:59:40
Beckers Corners 1 11 42N32 73w48 4:55:12
Becks Grove 33 211 43N13 75w26 5:01:44
Bedell 13 42 42N09 74w32 4:58:08
Bedford 60 7 41N12 73w39 4:54:36
Bedford Hills 60 6 41N14 73w42 4:54:48
Bedford-Stuyvesant 24 1 40N41 73w55 4:55:40
Beechertown 45 105 44N48 74w47 4:59:08
Beechurst 41 1 40N47 73w49 4:55:16
Beechwood 28 13 43N10 77w34 5:10:16
Beehive Crossing 42 11 42N54 73w21 4:53:24
Beekman 14 226 41N36 73w42 4:54:48
Beekman Corners 48 11 42N48 74w37 4:58:28
Beekmantown 10 86 44N46 73w29 4:53:56
Beixedon Estates 52 11 41N04 72w26 4:49:44
Belair Road 43 1 40N36 74w05 4:56:20
Belcher 58 213 43N10 73w20 4:53:20
Belcoda 28 226 43N01 77w45 5:11:00
Belden 4 17 42N11 75w38 5:02:32
Belfast 2 20 42N21 78w07 5:12:28
Belfort 25 226 43N48 75w36 5:02:24
Belgium 34 226 43N09 76w20 5:05:20
Belle Isle 34 41 43N05 76w20 5:05:20
Bellerose 41 1 40N43 73w43 4:54:52
Bellerose Terrace 30 1 40N44 73w46 4:55:04
Belle Terre 52 11 40N58 73w04 4:52:16
Belleville 23 226 43N47 76w07 5:04:28
Bellevue 15 7 42N55 78w46 5:15:04
Bellevue 47 1 42N48 73w58 4:55:52
Bellmont 17 226 44N49 74w09 4:56:36
Bellmore 30 7 40N40 73w32 4:54:08
Bellona 62 14 42N46 77w01 5:08:04
Bellport 52 7 40N46 72w56 4:51:44
Bellvale 36 6 41N15 74w19 4:57:16
Bellville 2 226 42N23 78w09 5:12:36
Bellwood 25 226 43N54 75w30 5:02:00
Belmont 2 107 42N14 78w02 5:12:08
Belvidere 2 20 42N13 78w02 5:12:08
Bemis Heights 46 11 42N57 73w39 4:54:36
Bemus Point 7 226 42N10 79w23 5:17:32
Benedict Beach 28 105 43N18 77w55 5:11:40
Bennets 51 226 42N16 77w37 5:10:28
Bennett Bridge 38 25 43N31 76w00 5:04:00
Bennettsburg 49 14 42N25 76w51 5:07:24
Bennetts Corners 27 60 43N05 75w39 5:02:36
Bennettsville 9 149 42N18 75w29 5:01:56
Bennington 61 226 42N50 78w24 5:13:36
Benson 21 226 43N17 74w20 4:57:20
Benson Mines 45 25 44N10 75w02 5:00:08
Benton 62 14 42N43 77w03 5:08:12
Berea 36 11 41N31 74w14 4:56:56
Bergen 19 110 43N05 77w57 5:11:48
Bergen Beach 50 226 42N37 77w33 5:10:12
Bergen Park 52 11 40N51 73w24 4:53:36
Bergholtz 32 1 43N06 78w55 5:15:40
Berkshire 18 226 43N03 74w20 4:57:20
Berkshire 34 13 43N02 76w01 5:04:04
Berkshire 54 226 42N19 76w11 5:04:44
Berkshire Terrace 40 226 41N27 73w40 4:54:40
Berlin 42 11 42N41 73w21 4:53:24
Berne 1 40 42N37 74w05 4:56:20
Bernhards Bay 38 15 43N15 75w56 5:03:44
Berwyn 34 16 42N54 76w06 5:04:24
Best 42 226 42N38 73w33 4:54:12
Bethany 19 13 42N55 78w08 5:12:32
Bethel 14 226 41N59 73w40 4:54:40
Bethel 53 226 41N42 74w50 4:59:20
Bethel Corners 6 226 43N17 76w38 5:06:32
Bethel Grove 55 186 42N28 76w29 5:05:56
Bethford 15 153 42N48 78w49 5:15:16
Bethlehem 1 226 42N36 73w50 4:55:20
Bethlehem Heights 1 11 42N32 73w51 4:55:24
Bethpage 30 11 40N44 73w30 4:54:00
Beukendaal 47 1 42N51 73w57 4:55:48
Beverly Inn Corners 39 226 42N45 75w11 5:00:44
Bible School Park 4 151 42N06 75w58 5:03:52
Bidwell 15 153 42N55 78w53 5:15:32
Big Brook 33 226 43N18 75w23 5:01:32
Big Flats 8 13 42N08 76w54 5:07:36
Big H Shopping Center 52 11 40N51 73w23 4:53:32
Big Indian 56 30 42N06 74w26 4:57:44
Big Island 36 7 41N24 74w20 4:57:20
Big Moose 22 73 43N49 74w55 4:59:40
Big Tree 15 11 42N46 78w50 5:15:20
Big Wolf Lake 17 221 44N14 74w28 4:57:52
Billings 14 226 41N40 73w46 4:55:04
Billington Bay 27 14 43N12 76w02 5:04:08
Billington Heights 15 170 42N47 78w37 5:14:28
Biltmore Shores 30 11 40N41 73w28 4:53:52
Binghamton 4 151 42N06 75w55 5:03:40
Bingley 27 14 42N56 75w51 5:03:24
Binnewater 56 11 41N57 74w00 4:56:00
Bird 5 226 42N25 78w30 5:14:00
Birdsall 2 226 42N24 77w54 5:11:36
Bishopville 2 226 42N24 77w42 5:10:48
Black Brook 10 226 44N31 73w48 4:55:12
Black Creek 2 20 42N17 78w14 5:12:56
Blackmans Corners 10 198 44N58 73w39 4:54:36
Black River 23 12 44N01 75w48 5:03:12
Blackwatch Hills 28 13 43N05 77w28 5:09:52
Blakeley 15 170 42N46 78w37 5:14:28
Blasdell 15 153 42N48 78w50 5:15:20
Blauvelt 44 28 41N04 73w57 4:55:48
Bleecker 18 226 43N10 74w22 4:57:28
Blenheim 48 226 42N29 74w30 4:58:00
Bliss 61 226 42N35 78w15 5:13:00
Blockville 7 226 42N06 79w23 5:17:32
Blodgett Mills 12 41 42N34 76w08 5:04:32
Bloomfield 43 1 40N36 74w08 4:56:32
Bloomingburg 53 11 41N33 74w26 4:57:44
Bloomingdale 16 81 44N24 74w05 4:56:20
Blooming Grove 36 20 41N24 74w11 4:56:44
Bloomington 56 11 41N53 74w03 4:56:12
Bloomville 13 31 42N20 74w48 4:59:12
Blossvale 33 211 43N15 75w27 5:01:48
Blue Mountain 56 215 42N04 73w57 4:55:48
Blue Mountain Lake 21 226 43N51 74w26 4:57:44
Blue Point 52 11 40N45 73w02 4:52:08
Blue Ridge 16 226 43N50 73w46 4:55:04
Blue Stores 11 11 42N08 73w54 4:55:36
Bluff Point 62 14 42N37 77w06 5:08:24
Blythebourne 24 1 40N38 74w00 4:56:00
Boardmanville 5 226 42N05 78w26 5:13:44
Boght Corners 1 1 42N46 73w43 4:54:52
Bohemia 52 11 40N46 73w07 4:52:28
Boiceville 56 37 42N00 74w16 4:57:04
Bolivar 2 24 42N04 78w10 5:12:40
Bolton 57 23 42N03 73w43 4:54:52
Bolton Landing 57 226 43N33 73w43 4:54:52
Bolts Corners 6 13 42N47 76w34 5:06:16
Bombay 17 226 44N56 74w34 4:58:16
Bonney 9 15 42N41 75w34 5:02:16
Bonni Castle 59 226 43N13 76w49 5:07:16
Boonville 33 137 43N29 75w20 5:01:20
Borden 51 13 42N06 77w14 5:08:56
Border City 35 41 42N52 76w59 5:07:56
Borodino 34 13 42N57 76w25 5:05:40
Borough Hall 41 1 40N43 73w50 4:55:20
Boston 15 226 42N39 78w45 5:15:00
Boston Corners 11 79 41N57 73w31 4:54:04
Botanical 3 1 40N52 73w53 4:55:32
Bouckville 27 180 42N53 75w33 5:02:12
Boughton Hill 35 19 42N59 77w25 5:09:40
Boulevard 3 1 40N49 73w54 4:55:36
Boulevard Mall 15 7 42N58 78w48 5:15:12
Boultons Beach 23 12 43N57 76w07 5:04:28
Bouquet 16 129 44N18 73w21 4:53:24
Bournes Beach 7 225 42N19 79w34 5:18:16
Bovina 13 226 42N17 74w45 4:59:00
Bowen 5 20 42N10 78w59 5:15:56

Bowens Corners 38 226 43N19 76w25 5:05:40
Bowerstown 39 13 42N42 74w55 4:59:40
Bowling Green 31 1 40N43 74w01 4:56:04
Bowmansville 15 7 42N56 78w41 5:14:44
Boylston 38 226 43N39 75w57 5:03:48
Boyntonville 42 11 42N54 73w21 4:53:24
Boysen Bay 34 14 43N12 76w02 5:04:08
Braddock Heights 28 226 43N15 77w38 5:10:32
Bradford 51 226 42N20 77w07 5:08:28
Bradley 53 189 41N48 74w45 4:59:00
Braeside 42 11 42N31 73w37 4:54:28
Brainard 42 11 42N30 73w31 4:54:04
Brainards Corners 39 226 42N45 75w11 5:00:44
Brainardsville 17 188 44N52 74w02 4:56:08
Braman Corners 47 226 42N45 74w11 4:56:44
Bramanville 48 12 42N41 74w23 4:57:32
Branchport 62 226 42N36 77w09 5:08:36
Brandon 17 226 44N44 74w25 4:57:40
Brandreth 22 226 43N58 74w25 4:57:40
Brandywine 47 6 42N47 73w54 4:55:36
Brant 15 11 42N35 79w01 5:16:04
Brantingham 25 226 43N41 75w18 5:01:12
Brant Lake 57 11 43N41 73w44 4:54:56
Brasher 45 105 44N53 74w45 4:59:00
Brasher Falls 45 105 44N49 74w47 4:59:08
Brasher Iron Works 45 105 44N48 74w47 4:59:08
Brasie Corners 45 178 44N20 75w28 5:01:52
Breakabeen 48 226 42N36 74w20 4:57:20
Breesport 8 13 42N10 76w44 5:06:56
Breezy Point 41 1 40N43 73w50 4:55:20
Brentwood 52 11 40N47 73w15 4:53:00
Breukelen 24 1 40N38 73w54 4:55:36
Brevoort 24 1 40N41 73w57 4:55:48
Brewerton 34 14 43N14 76w09 5:04:36
Brewster 40 85 41N24 73w37 4:54:28
Brewster Heights 40 85 41N24 73w38 4:54:32
Brewster Hills 40 85 41N25 73w36 4:54:24
Briarcliff Manor 60 1 41N09 73w49 4:55:16
Briar Park 30 11 41N04 73w30 4:54:00
Bridge 32 199 43N07 79w02 5:16:08
Bridgehampton 52 11 40N56 72w18 4:49:12
Bridgeport 27 14 43N12 76w02 5:04:08
Bridgeville 53 197 41N39 74w42 4:58:48
Bridgewater 33 13 42N53 75w15 5:01:00
Brier Hill 45 20 44N32 75w40 5:02:40
Briggs Corner 25 226 43N54 75w30 5:02:00
Brighton 24 1 40N35 73w57 4:55:48
Brighton 28 13 43N08 77w34 5:10:16
Brighton 39 78 42N51 74w59 4:59:56
Brightside 21 226 43N49 74w40 4:58:40
Brightwaters 52 11 40N43 73w16 4:53:04
Brinckerhoff 14 6 41N33 73w52 4:55:28
Brisben 9 130 42N22 75w41 5:02:44
Briscoe 53 189 41N45 74w47 4:59:08
Bristol 35 47 42N49 77w26 5:09:44
Bristol Center 35 14 42N53 77w17 5:09:08
Bristol Springs 35 226 42N37 77w24 5:09:36
Broadacres 4 151 42N07 75w56 5:03:44
Broadalbin 18 226 43N04 74w12 4:56:48
Broad Channel 41 1 40N36 73w49 4:55:16
Broadway 41 1 40N45 73w56 4:55:44
Brockport 28 13 43N13 77w56 5:11:44
Brockville 37 146 43N15 78w12 5:12:48
Brocton 7 160 42N23 79w26 5:17:44
Brodhead 56 37 41N58 74w17 4:57:08
Bronx 3 1 40N51 73w54 4:55:36
Bronxville 60 7 40N56 73w50 4:55:20
Brookdale 45 207 44N45 74w59 4:59:56
Brookfield 27 16 42N50 75w22 5:01:28
Brookhaven 52 11 40N52 73w23 4:53:32
Brooklyn 5 226 42N23 78w45 5:15:00
Brooklyn 24 1 40N38 73w56 4:55:44
Brooklyn Naval Station 24 1 40N42 73w58 4:55:52
Brooksburg 20 226 42N19 74w15 4:57:00
Brooks Grove 26 13 42N43 77w53 5:11:32
Brooktondale 55 226 42N23 76w24 5:05:36
Brookview 42 11 42N32 73w43 4:54:52
Brookville 19 226 42N54 78w16 5:13:04
Brookville 30 11 40N49 73w34 4:54:16
Brookville Park 52 11 40N44 73w13 4:52:52
Broome 48 226 42N30 74w18 4:57:12
Browns Bridge 45 226 44N33 74w56 4:59:44
Browns Crossing 51 13 42N08 77w03 5:08:12
Browns Hollow 29 162 42N52 74w35 4:58:20
Brownsville 24 1 40N40 73w55 4:55:40
Brownsville 35 19 42N59 77w25 5:09:40
Brownville 23 45 44N00 75w59 5:03:56
Bruceville 56 11 41N50 74w08 4:56:32
Brunswick 42 11 42N45 73w37 4:54:28
Brushton 17 152 44N50 74w31 4:58:04
Brutus 6 24 43N03 76w32 5:06:08
Bruynswick 56 11 41N37 74w10 4:56:40
Bryant 31 1 40N46 73w59 4:55:56
Buchanan 60 11 41N16 73w56 4:55:44
Buckhout Corners 60 1 41N09 73w50 4:55:20
Buckingham Estates 44 4 41N08 73w56 4:55:44
Buckleyville 11 10 42N22 73w36 4:54:24
Bucks Bridge 45 226 44N45 75w08 5:00:32
Buckton 45 105 44N48 74w47 4:59:08
Bucyrus Heights 15 11 43N01 78w46 5:15:04
Buel 29 162 42N52 74w35 4:58:20
Buellville 34 13 43N01 76w01 5:04:04
Buena Vista 51 226 42N16 77w37 5:10:28
Buffalo 15 153 42N53 78w53 5:15:32
Bull Hill 22 84 43N14 75w02 5:00:08
Bulls Head 28 209 43N09 77w38 5:10:32
Bulls Head 43 1 40N36 74w08 4:56:32
Bullville 36 11 41N33 74w22 4:57:28
Bundys 38 204 43N27 76w30 5:06:00
Burden Lake 42 226 42N38 73w33 4:54:12
Burdett 49 14 42N25 76w51 5:07:24
Burgoyne 46 226 43N06 73w35 4:54:20
Burke 17 141 44N56 74w11 4:56:44
Burlingham 53 11 41N35 74w23 4:57:32
Burlington 39 226 42N43 75w08 5:00:32
Burlington Flats 39 226 42N45 75w11 5:00:44
Burnhams 7 173 42N21 79w19 5:17:16
Burns 2 20 42N26 77w47 5:11:08
Burns-Whitney Estates 1 1 42N44 73w45 4:55:00
Burnt Hills 46 226 42N55 73w54 4:55:36
Burnwood 13 226 41N59 75w08 5:00:32
Burrs Mills 23 45 43N59 75w56 5:03:44
Burt 32 11 43N19 78w43 5:14:52
Burtonsville 29 12 42N46 74w16 4:57:04
Bushes Landing 25 226 43N54 75w30 5:02:00
Bushnell Basin 28 13 43N05 77w31 5:10:04
Bushnellsville 56 88 42N07 74w24 4:57:36
Bush Terminal 24 1 40N39 74w00 4:56:00
Bushville 19 142 43N00 78w11 5:12:44
Bushville 53 197 41N39 74w42 4:58:48
Bushwick 24 1 40N41 73w56 4:55:44
Buskirk 42 11 42N57 73w26 4:53:44
Busti 7 226 42N03 79w18 5:17:12
Butler 59 226 43N11 76w46 5:07:04
Butlerville 60 16 41N21 73w40 4:54:40
Butterfield 33 222 43N06 75w15 5:01:00
Butternut Grove 13 80 41N56 74w55 4:59:40
Butternuts 39 226 42N28 75w20 5:01:20
Byersville 26 226 42N35 77w56 5:11:44
Byron 19 17 43N05 78w04 5:12:16
Cabinhill 13 226 42N12 74w58 4:59:52
Cadiz 5 226 42N20 78w27 5:13:48
Cadosia 13 97 41N58 75w16 5:01:04
Cadyville 10 14 44N42 73w38 4:54:32
Cahoonzie 36 1 41N23 74w43 4:58:52
Cairo 20 3 42N18 74w00 4:56:00
Calcium 23 45 44N01 75w51 5:03:24
Calcutta 39 14 42N37 74w40 4:58:40
Caledonia 26 4 42N58 77w51 5:11:24
Calico Colony 46 11 42N51 73w48 4:55:12
Callanans Corners 1 1 42N28 73w48 4:55:12
Callicoon 53 20 41N46 75w03 5:00:12
Callicoon Center 53 226 41N50 74w57 4:59:48
Calverton 52 11 40N55 72w45 4:51:00
Cambria 31 226 43N12 78w49 5:15:16
Cambria Heights 41 1 40N42 73w45 4:55:00
Cambridge 58 11 43N02 73w22 4:53:28
Camden 33 14 43N20 75w45 5:03:00
Cameron 51 20 42N13 77w24 5:09:36
Cameron Mills 51 20 42N11 77w22 5:09:28
Camillus 34 13 43N03 76w17 5:05:08
Campbell 51 126 42N14 77w09 5:08:36
Campbell Hall 36 11 41N27 74w16 4:57:04
Camp Hemlock 53 11 41N33 74w26 4:57:44
Camp Hill 44 4 41N11 74w03 4:56:12
Camps Mills 23 45 43N59 75w56 5:03:44
Campville 54 13 42N07 76w03 5:04:12
Camroden 33 211 43N13 75w26 5:01:44
Canaan 11 13 42N23 73w27 4:53:48
Canadice 35 226 42N43 77w33 5:10:12
Canajoharie 29 162 42N54 74w35 4:58:20
Canal Street 31 1 40N43 74w00 4:56:00
Canandaigua 35 14 42N54 77w17 5:09:08
Canarsie 24 1 40N38 73w54 4:55:36
Canaseraga 2 20 42N27 77w45 5:11:00
Canastota 27 92 43N05 75w45 5:03:00
Canawaugus 26 226 42N59 77w51 5:11:24
Candor 54 154 42N13 76w20 5:05:20
Caneadea 2 226 42N24 78w09 5:12:36
Canisteo 51 100 42N16 77w36 5:10:24
Cannon Corners 10 198 44N58 73w39 4:54:36
Canoe Place 52 11 40N52 72w31 4:50:04
Canoga 50 13 42N55 76w24 5:05:36
Canterbury Hill 33 211 43N13 75w26 5:01:44
Canton 45 155 44N36 75w10 5:00:40
Cape Vincent 23 29 44N08 76w15 5:05:00
Capitol 1 1 42N40 73w47 4:55:08
Capitol Hills 36 226 41N21 74w11 4:56:44
Captain Kidd Estates 52 11 40N59 72w32 4:50:08
Cardiff 34 16 42N54 76w06 5:04:24
Carle Place 30 11 40N45 73w37 4:54:28
Carle Terrace 56 114 41N59 74w00 4:56:00
Carlisle 48 226 42N45 74w27 4:57:48
Carlisle Center 48 12 42N43 74w20 4:57:20
Carlisle Gardens 32 190 43N11 78w39 5:14:36
Carlton 37 146 43N20 78w13 5:12:52
Carman 47 6 42N46 73w56 4:55:44
Carmel 40 135 41N26 73w41 4:54:44
Carmel Park Estates 40 226 41N27 73w40 4:54:40
Carmen 1 6 42N46 73w56 4:55:44
Carnegie 15 153 42N45 78w51 5:15:24
Caroga 18 226 43N08 74w29 4:57:56
Caroga Lake 18 226 43N08 74w29 4:57:56
Caroline 55 226 42N23 76w20 5:05:20
Carroll 7 128 42N03 79w06 5:16:24
Carrollton 5 20 42N05 78w36 5:14:24
Carson 51 226 42N16 77w37 5:10:28
Carthage 23 156 43N59 75w37 5:02:28
Cascade 6 13 42N43 76w25 5:05:40
Case 34 16 42N54 76w06 5:04:24
Casowasco 6 13 42N43 76w25 5:05:40
Cass 15 7 42N53 78w49 5:15:16
Cassadaga 7 173 42N20 79w19 5:17:16
Cassville 33 13 42N57 75w15 5:01:00
Castile 61 24 42N38 78w03 5:12:12
Castle 60 1 40N55 73w47 4:55:08
Castle Creek 4 13 42N14 75w55 5:03:40
Castle Hill 3 1 40N51 73w52 4:55:28
Castleton Corners 43 1 40N36 74w08 4:56:32
Castleton on Hudson 42 11 42N32 73w45 4:55:00
Castorland 25 191 43N48 75w29 5:01:56
Catatonk 54 205 42N06 76w16 5:05:04
Catharine 49 226 42N20 76w44 5:06:56
Cathedral 31 1 40N48 73w58 4:55:52
Catlin 8 14 42N15 76w55 5:07:40
Cato 6 24 43N08 76w32 5:06:08
Caton 51 13 42N03 77w01 5:08:04
Catskill 20 1 42N14 73w52 4:55:28
Cattaraugus 5 20 42N20 78w52 5:15:28
Cattaraugus Indian Res 5 42 42N29 78w59 5:15:56
Cattown 39 13 42N43 74w59 4:59:56
Caughdenoy 38 182 43N17 76w09 5:04:36
Cayuga 6 14 42N55 76w44 5:06:56
Cayuga Heights 55 186 42N28 76w30 5:06:00
Cayuta 49 226 42N16 76w41 5:06:44
Cayutaville 49 226 42N19 76w44 5:06:56
Caywood 50 226 42N37 77w21 5:09:24
Cazenovia 27 14 42N56 75w51 5:03:24
Cedarcrest 26 226 42N49 77w40 5:10:40
Cedar Flats 44 6 41N14 73w59 4:55:56
Cedar Hill 1 11 42N32 73w48 4:55:12
Cedarhurst 30 1 40N38 73w44 4:54:56
Cedarvale 34 13 43N01 76w11 5:04:44
Cedarville 22 226 42N56 75w07 5:00:28
Celoron 7 187 42N06 79w17 5:17:08
Cementon 20 11 42N09 73w55 4:55:40
Centenary 44 4 41N09 74w00 4:56:00
Center Berlin 42 11 42N42 73w23 4:53:32
Center Brunswick 42 220 42N43 73w41 4:54:44
Centerbury Hill 33 211 43N13 75w26 5:01:44
Center Cambridge 58 11 43N02 73w23 4:53:32
Centereach 52 11 40N52 73w06 4:52:24
Center Falls 58 226 43N05 73w30 4:54:00
Centerfield 35 14 42N53 77w17 5:09:08
Centerlisle 4 226 42N21 76w00 5:04:00
Center Moriches 52 11 40N48 72w48 4:51:12
Centerport 6 11 42N53 73w23 4:53:32
Centerport 52 11 40N53 73w22 4:53:28
Centerville 2 226 42N29 78w15 5:13:00
Centerville 13 226 41N59 75w08 5:00:32
Center White Creek 58 11 42N57 73w24 4:53:36
Central 41 1 40N42 73w48 4:55:12
Central Bridge 48 12 42N43 74w20 4:57:20
Centralia 7 67 42N16 79w15 5:17:00
Central Islip 52 6 40N47 73w12 4:52:48
Central Nyack 44 1 41N05 73w56 4:55:44
Central Square 38 182 43N17 76w09 5:04:36
Central Valley 36 4 41N20 74w07 4:56:28
Central White Plains 60 1 41N01 73w47 4:55:08
Centre Island 30 11 40N55 73w31 4:54:04
Centre Village 4 17 42N11 75w38 5:02:32
Centuck 60 1 40N58 73w51 4:55:24
Ceres 2 22 42N00 78w16 5:13:04
Chadwicks 33 14 43N01 75w16 5:01:04
Chaffee 15 22 42N34 78w29 5:13:56
Chamberlain Corners 45 226 44N45 75w08 5:00:32
Chambers 8 14 42N17 76w58 5:07:52
Champion 23 119 43N59 75w41 5:02:44
Champion Huddle 23 156 43N59 75w37 5:02:28
Champlain 10 157 44N57 73w26 4:53:44
Champlain Park 10 86 44N43 73w24 4:53:36
Chapel Hill Estates 60 16 41N17 73w46 4:55:04
Chapin 35 14 42N53 77w17 5:09:08
Chappaqua 60 1 41N10 73w46 4:55:04
Charleston 29 12 42N49 74w20 4:57:20
Charleston 43 1 40N38 74w06 4:56:24
Charleston Four Corners 29 7 42N53 74w31 4:58:04
Charlotte 7 67 42N18 79w14 5:16:56
Charlotte 28 226 43N15 77w38 5:10:32
Charlotteville 48 226 42N33 74w40 4:58:40
Charlton 46 226 42N56 73w58 4:55:52
Chase Lake 25 15 43N43 75w24 5:01:36
Chase Mills 45 226 44N51 75w05 5:00:20
Chaseville 39 13 42N32 74w53 4:59:32

NEW YORK

Chasm Falls 17	193	44N51	74w17	4:57:08
Chateaugay 17	188	44N56	74w05	4:56:20
Chatham 11	10	42N21	73w36	4:54:24
Chaumont 23	226	44N04	76w08	5:04:32
Chauncey 60	7	41N01	73w50	4:55:20
Chautauqua 7	158	42N14	79w29	5:17:56
Chazy 10	7	44N53	73w26	4:53:44
Chazy Lake 10	7	44N54	73w48	4:55:12
Chazy Landing 10	7	44N53	73w26	4:53:44
Cheektowaga 15	7	42N54	78w45	5:15:00
Chelsea 14	6	41N33	73w58	4:55:52
Chelsea 43	1	40N36	74w08	4:56:32
Chemung 8	224	42N03	76w37	5:06:28
Chenango 4	13	42N12	75w53	5:03:32
Chenango Bridge 4	13	42N11	75w53	5:03:32
Chenango Forks 4	13	42N14	75w51	5:03:24
Chenango Lake 9	16	42N32	75w31	5:02:04
Cheneys Point 7	226	42N06	79w23	5:17:32
Cheningo 12	16	42N43	76w02	5:04:08
Cherokee 31	1	40N47	73w58	4:55:52
Cherry Creek 7	107	42N18	79w07	5:16:28
Cherry Grove 52	11	40N45	73w05	4:52:20
Cherryplain 42	11	42N38	73w22	4:53:28
Cherrytown 56	72	41N47	74w19	4:57:16
Cherry Valley 39	140	42N48	74w45	4:59:00
Cherry Valley Junction 48	139	42N41	74w29	4:57:56
Cherrywood Shopping Center 30	11	41N04	73w30	4:54:00
Cheshire 35	14	42N53	77w17	5:09:08
Chester 36	4	41N21	74w16	4:57:04
Chesterfield 16	226	44N29	73w28	4:53:52
Chestertown 57	159	43N39	73w48	4:55:12
Chestnut Hill 34	13	43N07	76w12	5:04:48
Chestnut Ridge 32	226	43N09	78w35	5:14:20
Cheviot 11	11	42N08	73w54	4:55:36
Chichester 56	52	42N06	74w19	4:57:16
Childs 37	146	43N15	78w12	5:12:48
Childwold 45	87	44N14	74w36	4:58:24
Chili 28	15	43N06	77w44	5:10:56
Chilson 16	226	43N51	73w25	4:53:40
China 13	167	42N04	75w25	5:01:40
Chinatown 31	1	40N43	74w00	4:56:00
Chipmonk 5	226	42N05	78w30	5:14:00
Chippewa Bay 45	20	44N26	75w46	5:03:04
Chittenango 27	226	43N03	75w52	5:03:28
Chittenango Falls 27	14	42N56	75w51	5:03:24
Choconut Center 4	151	42N07	75w56	5:03:44
Chuckery Corners 33	11	43N04	75w20	5:01:20
Church Street 31	1	40N43	74w00	4:56:00
Churchtown 11	11	42N11	73w35	4:54:20
Churchville 28	161	43N06	77w53	5:11:32
Churchville Greene 28	161	43N06	77w53	5:11:32
Churubusco 10	4	44N57	73w56	4:55:44
Cicero 34	41	43N09	76w05	5:04:20
Cincinnatus 12	226	42N33	75w54	5:03:36
Circleville 36	11	41N31	74w23	4:57:32
City Island 3	1	40N51	73w47	4:55:08
Clairemont Farms 34	13	43N07	76w12	5:04:48
Clare 45	226	44N23	75w00	5:00:00
Claremont Park 3	1	40N51	73w54	4:55:36
Clarence 15	11	43N00	78w40	5:14:40
Clarendon 37	226	43N11	78w03	5:12:12
Clark Heights 14	11	41N45	73w50	4:55:20
Clark Mills 33	11	43N05	75w23	5:01:32
Clarksburg 15	153	42N39	78w54	5:15:36
Clarks Corners 7	226	42N10	79w06	5:16:24
Clarks Mills 58	226	43N05	73w30	4:54:00
Clarkson 28	226	43N15	77w55	5:11:40
Clarkstown 44	4	41N06	73w56	4:55:44
Clarksville 1	11	42N35	73w58	4:55:52
Clarksville 2	226	42N08	78w15	5:13:00
Claryville 53	226	41N55	74w34	4:58:16
Classon 24	1	40N41	73w58	4:55:52
Claverack 11	11	42N14	73w42	4:54:48
Clay 34	13	43N09	76w12	5:04:48
Clayburg 10	136	44N39	73w45	4:55:00
Clayton 23	163	44N14	76w05	5:04:20
Clayville 33	13	42N58	75w15	5:01:00
Clear Creek 5	20	42N14	79w04	5:16:16
Clearfield 15	7	42N59	78w45	5:15:00
Cleaver 13	226	42N10	75w08	5:00:32
Clemons 58	6	43N38	73w27	4:53:48
Clermont 11	226	42N05	73w51	4:55:24
Cleveland 38	15	43N14	75w54	5:03:36
Cleveland Hill 15	7	42N55	78w46	5:15:04
Cleverdale 57	226	43N28	73w39	4:54:36
Cliff Haven 10	86	44N42	73w26	4:53:44
Clifford 38	226	43N19	76w25	5:05:40
Cliffside 39	13	42N32	74w53	4:59:32
Clifton 28	226	43N03	77w49	5:11:16
Clifton 43	1	40N37	74w06	4:56:24
Clifton 45	25	44N11	74w56	4:59:44
Clifton Gardens 46	11	42N51	73w48	4:55:12
Clifton Heights 15	153	42N43	78w56	5:15:44
Clifton Knolls 46	11	42N51	73w48	4:55:12
Clifton Park 46	11	42N52	73w44	4:54:56
Clifton Springs 35	14	42N58	77w08	5:08:32
Climax 20	11	42N22	73w51	4:55:24
Clinton 33	11	43N03	75w23	5:01:32
Clinton Corners 14	226	41N50	73w46	4:55:04
Clintondale 56	11	41N42	74w03	4:56:12
Clinton Heights 42	1	42N39	73w43	4:54:52
Clinton Hollow 14	226	41N44	73w42	4:54:48
Clinton Park 10	86	44N42	73w26	4:53:44
Clinton Park 42	1	42N39	73w43	4:54:52
Clintonville 10	226	44N28	73w35	4:54:20
Clint-Wood Center 28	13	43N09	77w33	5:10:12
Clockville 27	226	43N03	75w45	5:03:00
Clough Corners 4	226	42N20	75w58	5:03:52
Clove 48	139	42N41	74w29	4:57:56
Clover Bank 15	153	42N45	78w53	5:15:32
Clyde 59	99	43N05	76w52	5:07:28
Clymer 7	22	42N02	79w36	5:18:24
Cobb 52	11	40N55	72w21	4:49:24
Cobleskill 48	139	42N41	74w27	4:57:48
Cochecton 53	20	41N41	74w59	4:59:56
Coeymans 1	1	42N29	73w51	4:55:24
Coeymans Hollow 1	1	42N28	73w54	4:55:36
Coffins Mills 45	25	44N11	75w04	5:00:16
Cohocton 51	14	42N31	77w28	5:09:52
Cohoes 1	1	42N46	73w42	4:54:48
Coila 58	11	43N02	73w23	4:53:32
Cokertown 14	7	42N00	73w53	4:55:32
Colchester 13	226	42N04	74w58	4:59:52
Coldbrook 15	1	43N01	78w57	5:15:48
Cold Brook 22	84	43N14	75w02	5:00:08
Coldbrook 47	6	42N46	73w56	4:55:44
Cold Brook Estates 1	6	42N46	73w56	4:55:44
Colden 15	226	42N39	78w41	5:14:44
Coldenham 36	11	41N31	74w14	4:56:56
Colden Hill 36	1	41N31	74w07	4:56:28
Cold Spring 6	13	42N56	76w33	5:06:12
Cold Spring 40	6	41N25	73w57	4:55:48
Cold Spring Harbor 52	1	40N52	73w28	4:53:52
Cold Springs 34	226	43N09	76w20	5:05:20
Cold Springs 51	14	42N20	77w19	5:09:16
Cold Spring Terrace 52	11	40N51	73w23	4:53:32
Coldwater 28	209	43N08	77w43	5:10:52
Colemans Mills 33	222	43N07	75w18	5:01:12
Colesville 4	17	42N10	75w40	5:02:40
Colgate 27	180	42N49	75w33	5:02:12
Collabar 36	11	41N31	74w14	4:56:56
Collamer 28	13	43N17	77w47	5:11:08
Collamer 34	41	43N04	76w04	5:04:16
College 31	1	40N49	73w57	4:55:48
College Park 14	7	42N00	73w53	4:55:32
College Point 41	1	40N47	73w51	4:55:24
Colliersville 39	226	42N29	74w59	4:59:56
Collingwood 34	16	42N54	76w06	5:04:24
Collingwood Estates 32	226	43N20	79w02	5:16:08
Collins 15	42	42N29	78w53	5:15:32
Collins Landing 23	17	44N20	75w55	5:03:40
Collinsville 25	77	44N06	75w40	5:02:40
Colonial Acres 1	11	42N36	73w46	4:55:04
Colonial Acres 60	1	40N59	73w48	4:55:12
Colonial Heights 14	1	41N40	73w54	4:55:36
Colonial Park 31	1	40N50	73w56	4:55:44
Colonial Park 33	211	43N13	75w26	5:01:44
Colonial Springs 52	11	40N45	73w22	4:53:28
Colonial Village 32	199	43N08	78w58	5:15:52
Colonie 1	1	42N44	73w48	4:55:12
Colosse 38	14	43N24	76w08	5:04:32
Colton 45	226	44N33	74w56	4:59:44
Columbia 22	78	42N56	75w02	5:00:08
Columbia University 31	1	40N48	73w58	4:55:52
Columbiaville 11	11	42N19	73w45	4:55:00
Columbus 9	226	42N41	75w22	5:01:28
Columbus Circle 31	1	40N48	74w06	4:56:24
Colvin 34	13	43N01	76w09	5:04:36
Commack 52	11	40N51	73w18	4:53:12
Comstock Tract 34	226	43N09	76w20	5:05:20
Concord 15	218	42N32	78w41	5:14:44
Concord 43	1	40N37	74w06	4:56:24
Conesus 26	20	42N44	77w40	5:10:40
Conesville 48	226	42N24	74w20	4:57:20
Conewango 5	20	42N13	78w59	5:15:56
Conewango Valley 5	20	42N14	79w04	5:16:16
Coney Island 24	1	40N35	73w59	4:55:56
Conger Corners 33	13	42N56	75w23	5:01:32
Congers 44	7	41N09	73w57	4:55:48
Conifer 45	221	44N14	74w28	4:57:52
Conklin 4	226	42N02	75w49	5:03:16
Conklin Forks 4	151	42N05	75w54	5:03:36
Conklingville 46	40	43N19	73w51	4:55:24
Connelly 56	11	41N55	73w59	4:55:56
Connelly Park 7	226	42N06	79w23	5:17:32
Conquest 6	226	43N07	76w39	5:06:36
Constable 17	193	44N57	74w18	4:57:12
Constableville 25	77	44N08	75w34	5:02:16
Constantia 38	226	43N17	75w59	5:03:56
Continental Village 40	11	41N17	73w55	4:55:40
Cook Corners 45	226	44N33	74w56	4:59:44
Cooksburg 1	226	42N27	74w13	4:56:52
Cooks Falls 13	226	41N57	74w59	4:59:56
Cookville 19	164	42N58	78w24	5:13:36
Coolidge Beach 32	226	43N25	78w50	5:15:20
Coonrod 33	211	43N13	75w26	5:01:44
Cooper 31	1	40N44	73w59	4:55:56
Coopers Plains 51	13	42N11	77w08	5:08:32
Cooperstown 39	13	42N42	74w56	4:59:44
Coopersville 10	157	44N59	73w26	4:53:44
Coopersville 26	226	42N35	77w56	5:11:44
Copake 11	11	42N08	73w33	4:54:12
Copake Falls 11	11	42N07	73w31	4:54:04
Copake Lake 11	11	42N11	73w35	4:54:20
Copenhagen 25	156	43N54	75w40	5:02:40
Copiague 52	11	40N41	73w24	4:53:36
Coram 52	11	40N52	73w00	4:52:00
Corbett 13	226	42N05	75w00	5:00:00
Corbettsville 4	226	42N01	75w48	5:03:12
Coreys 17	221	44N14	74w28	4:57:52
Corfu 19	164	42N58	78w24	5:13:36
Corinth 46	7	43N14	73w50	4:55:20
Corners 55	186	42N28	76w29	5:05:56
Corning 51	13	42N09	77w03	5:08:12
Corning Manor 51	13	42N08	77w03	5:08:12
Cornwall 36	165	41N25	74w04	4:56:16
Cornwall Landing 36	165	41N27	74w01	4:56:04
Cornwall on the Hudson 36	165	41N27	74w01	4:56:04
Cornwallville 20	226	42N22	74w10	4:56:40
Corona 41	1	40N45	73w52	4:55:28
Cortland 12	41	42N36	76w11	5:04:44
Cortlandt 60	6	41N17	73w54	4:55:36
Cortlandville 12	41	42N36	76w10	5:04:40
Corwin 32	190	43N15	78w42	5:14:48
Cosmos Heights 12	41	42N35	76w12	5:04:48
Cossayuna 58	213	43N11	73w26	4:53:44
Coss Corners 51	14	42N20	77w19	5:09:16
Cottage 5	217	42N22	79w03	5:16:12
Cottage City 35	14	42N53	77w17	5:09:08
Cottage Park 7	20	42N06	79w19	5:17:16
Cottekill 56	11	41N51	74w06	4:56:24
Cottonwood Point 26	226	42N43	77w41	5:10:44
Country Knolls 46	11	42N55	73w49	4:55:16
Country Life Press 30	11	40N44	73w39	4:54:36
Country Ridge Estates 60	1	41N00	73w40	4:54:40
County Line 32	15	43N19	78w23	5:13:32
Couse 42	1	42N37	73w43	4:54:52
Cove Neck 30	11	40N52	73w30	4:54:00
Coventry 9	33	42N18	75w37	5:02:28
Coventryville 9	149	42N18	75w29	5:01:56
Covert 50	226	42N36	77w36	5:10:24
Coveytown Corners 17	141	44N54	74w10	4:56:40
Covington 61	226	42N50	78w01	5:12:04
Cowlesville 61	38	42N51	78w28	5:13:52
Coxsackie 20	11	42N21	73w48	4:55:12
Crafts 40	226	41N27	73w40	4:54:40
Cragsmoor 56	48	41N40	74w23	4:57:32
Craigs 26	226	42N53	78w01	5:12:04
Craigsville 36	226	41N21	74w16	4:57:04
Crains Mills 12	16	42N43	76w02	5:04:08
Cranberry Creek 18	226	43N06	74w16	4:57:04
Cranberry Lake 45	226	44N13	74w50	4:59:20
Crandall Corners 58	11	42N54	73w35	4:54:20
Cranes Corners 22	184	43N02	75w04	5:00:16
Cranesville 29	1	42N57	74w11	4:56:44
Cranford 3	1	40N54	73w52	4:55:28
Crary Mills 45	155	44N36	75w10	5:00:40
Craryville 11	11	42N11	73w35	4:54:20
Crawford 36	11	41N34	74w20	4:57:20
Creek Locks 56	11	41N53	74w03	4:56:12
Creekside 15	11	42N41	78w47	5:15:08
Crescent 46	11	42N48	73w41	4:54:44
Crescent Beach 28	226	43N15	77w38	5:10:32
Crescent Beach 43	1	40N38	74w06	4:56:24
Crestview Heights 54	13	42N07	76w03	5:04:12
Crestwood 60	1	40N58	73w49	4:55:16
Crittenden 15	38	42N57	78w29	5:13:56
Crocketts 6	226	43N20	76w39	5:06:36
Crofts Corners 40	6	41N20	73w52	4:55:28
Croghan 25	226	43N54	75w24	5:01:36
Crompond 60	6	41N17	73w52	4:55:28
Cropseyville 42	11	42N45	73w33	4:54:12
Cross River 60	16	41N16	73w37	4:54:28
Cross Roads Estates 60	16	41N17	73w46	4:55:04
Croton 49	14	42N16	76w51	5:07:24
Crotona Park 3	1	40N50	73w52	4:55:28
Croton Falls 60	133	41N21	73w40	4:54:40
Croton Heights 60	166	41N15	73w47	4:55:08
Croton-on-Hudson 60	166	41N12	73w53	4:55:32
Crotonville 60	166	41N10	73w51	4:55:24
Crown Point 16	138	43N57	73w29	4:53:56
Crown Village 30	11	40N51	73w27	4:53:48
Crugers 60	6	41N14	73w56	4:55:44
Crum Creek 18	226	43N00	74w41	4:58:44
Crystal Brook 52	11	40N57	73w02	4:52:08
Crystal Dale 25	226	43N54	75w30	5:02:00
Crystal Lake 1	226	42N31	74w08	4:56:32
Crystal Lake 5	226	42N26	78w22	5:13:28
Cuba 2	20	42N13	78w17	5:13:08
Cuddebackville 36	21	41N28	74w36	4:58:24

Cullen 22 78 42N51 74w59 4:59:56
Cummingsville 26 13 42N34 77w42 5:10:48
Curriers 61 147 42N32 78w26 5:13:44
Curry 53 74 41N50 74w39 4:58:36
Currytown 29 7 42N53 74w31 4:58:04
Curtis 51 226 42N14 77w12 5:08:48
Cutchogue 52 11 41N01 72w29 4:49:56
Cutting 7 226 42N03 79w35 5:18:20
Cuyler 12 226 42N44 75w56 5:03:44
Cuylerville 26 13 42N46 77w54 5:11:36
Cypress Hills 24 1 40N41 73w52 4:55:28
Dadville 25 226 43N54 75w30 5:02:00
Dahlia 53 75 41N54 74w50 4:59:20
Dairyland 56 48 41N44 74w29 4:57:56
Dale 61 20 42N49 78w10 5:12:40
Dalton 26 20 42N32 77w57 5:11:48
Damascus 4 226 42N04 75w41 5:02:44
Danby 55 226 42N21 76w28 5:05:52
Danley Corners 61 148 42N52 78w17 5:13:08
Dannemora 10 136 44N43 73w44 4:54:56
Dansville 26 13 42N34 77w42 5:10:48
Danube 22 226 42N59 74w48 4:59:12
Danville 4 167 42N04 75w25 5:01:40
Darien 19 164 42N55 78w23 5:13:32
Darrowsville 57 159 43N39 73w48 4:55:12
Davenport 13 13 42N28 74w51 4:59:24
Davis Park 52 11 40N42 72w59 4:51:56
Daws 19 142 43N00 78w11 5:12:44
Day 46 226 43N19 74w00 4:56:00
Days Rock 22 196 43N00 75w00 5:00:00
Dayton 5 42 42N25 79w00 5:16:00
Daytonville 33 13 42N56 75w23 5:01:32
Deansboro 33 11 43N00 75w26 5:01:44
Debruce 53 75 41N54 74w50 4:59:20
Decatur 39 226 42N39 74w43 4:58:52
Deck 22 196 43N00 75w00 5:00:00
Deckertown 53 75 41N54 74w50 4:59:20
Deerfield 33 11 43N09 75w12 5:00:48
Deerfield 52 11 40N55 72w21 4:49:24
Deerland 21 226 43N58 74w25 4:57:40
Deer Park 52 11 40N46 73w20 4:53:20
Deer River 25 156 43N56 75w36 5:02:24
Deferiet 23 119 44N02 75w41 5:02:44
Defreestville 42 1 42N39 73w43 4:54:52
Degrasse 45 226 44N21 75w05 5:00:20
De Kalb 45 226 44N30 75w21 5:01:24
De Lancey 13 226 42N12 74w58 4:59:52
Delanson 47 98 42N45 74w11 4:56:44
Delaware 1 1 42N39 73w47 4:55:08
Delaware 53 226 41N46 75w00 5:00:00
Delevan 5 108 42N29 78w29 5:13:56
Delhi 13 226 42N17 74w55 4:59:40
Delmar 1 11 42N37 73w49 4:55:16
Delphi Falls 34 226 42N53 75w55 5:03:40
Delray 15 153 42N51 78w46 5:15:04
Dempster Beach 38 204 43N27 76w30 5:06:00
Demster 38 204 43N27 76w30 5:06:00
Denmark 25 15 43N47 75w23 5:01:32
Dennies Hollow 18 226 43N06 74w16 4:57:04
Denning 56 226 41N57 74w29 4:57:56
Dennison Corners 22 196 43N00 75w00 5:00:00
Denton 36 7 41N25 74w24 4:57:36
Denton Hills 52 11 40N53 73w22 4:53:28
Denver 13 42 42N13 74w34 4:58:16
Depauville 23 226 44N08 76w04 5:04:16
Depew 15 7 42N54 78w42 5:14:48
De Peyster 45 226 44N33 75w27 5:01:48
Deposit 4 167 42N04 75w25 5:01:40
Derby 15 11 42N41 78w58 5:15:52
Dering Harbor 52 11 41N06 72w21 4:49:24
De Ruyter 27 226 42N46 75w53 5:03:32
Deuels Corners 15 11 42N47 78w45 5:15:00
Devereux 5 226 42N16 78w40 5:14:40
Devon 52 11 40N58 72w08 4:48:32
Dewey 28 209 43N11 77w39 5:10:36
Dewey Bridge 58 123 43N25 73w29 4:53:56
De Witt 34 13 43N02 76w04 5:04:16
Dewittville 7 158 42N14 79w27 5:17:48
Dexter 23 49 44N00 76w03 5:04:12
Dexterville 38 226 43N19 76w25 5:05:40
Dge 4 13 42N10 75w52 5:03:28
Diamond Hill 22 61 43N03 74w51 4:59:24
Diamond Point 57 226 43N29 73w41 4:54:44
Diana 25 226 43N36 75w41 5:02:44
Dibbletown 33 211 43N15 75w27 5:01:48
Dickersonville 32 226 43N19 78w55 5:15:40
Dickinson Center 17 226 44N43 74w33 4:58:12
Dick-Urban 15 7 42N55 78w42 5:14:48
Dimmick Corners 46 226 43N12 73w39 4:54:36
Dineharts 51 14 42N20 77w19 5:09:16
Divine Corners 53 74 41N46 74w39 4:58:36
Dix 49 14 42N20 76w55 5:07:40
Dix Hills 52 11 40N49 73w21 4:53:24
Dobbs Ferry 60 7 41N01 73w52 4:55:28
Doctors Crossing 19 145 43N01 78w30 5:14:00
Dogtail Corners 14 11 41N39 73w34 4:54:16
Dolgeville 22 168 43N06 74w46 4:59:04
Doonan Corners 13 226 42N20 74w48 4:59:12
Doraville 4 17 42N12 75w36 5:02:24
Doris Park 38 14 43N15 76w00 5:04:00
Dorloo 48 13 42N42 74w35 4:58:20
Dormansville 1 226 42N30 73w59 4:55:56
Douglass 16 226 44N30 73w29 4:53:56
Douglaston 41 1 40N43 73w52 4:55:28

Dover 14 11 41N39 73w34 4:54:16
Dover Plains 14 11 41N45 73w35 4:54:20
Downsville 13 226 42N05 75w00 5:00:00
Doyle 15 7 42N53 78w49 5:15:16
Dresden 62 12 42N41 76w57 5:07:48
Dresden Station 58 6 43N33 73w24 4:53:36
Dresserville 6 13 42N43 76w25 5:05:40
Drews Corner 35 226 44N52 75w12 5:00:48
Dryden 55 13 42N30 76w18 5:05:12
Duane 17 226 44N37 74w15 4:57:00
Duanesburg 47 226 42N47 74w11 4:56:44
Dublin 50 99 43N05 76w52 5:07:28
Duells Corner 15 11 42N45 78w45 5:15:00
Dugway 38 14 43N24 76w08 5:04:32
Dunbar 4 226 42N04 75w41 5:02:44
Dundee 62 169 42N32 76w59 5:07:56
Dunewood 52 11 40N38 73w11 4:52:44
Dunham 33 222 43N06 75w15 5:01:00
Dunham Hollow 42 226 42N38 73w33 4:54:12
Dunham Manor 33 222 43N07 75w18 5:01:12
Dunkirk 7 134 42N29 79w20 5:17:20
Dunnsville 1 40 42N42 74w02 4:56:08
Dunraven 13 226 42N09 74w39 4:58:36
Dunsbach Ferry 1 1 42N46 73w43 4:54:52
Durham 20 226 42N23 74w08 4:56:32
Durhamville 33 13 43N07 75w40 5:02:40
Durkeetown 58 226 43N16 73w35 4:54:20
Durlandville 36 7 41N24 74w20 4:57:20
Dutchess Junction 14 7 41N30 73w58 4:55:52
Dutch Flats 61 226 42N46 78w19 5:13:16
Dutch Hollow 61 226 42N42 78w27 5:13:48
Dwaar Kill 56 226 41N37 74w18 4:57:12
Dykemans 40 226 41N26 73w36 4:54:24
Dyker Heights 24 1 40N37 74w01 4:56:04
Eagle 61 226 42N34 78w15 5:13:00
Eagle Bay 22 226 43N46 74w49 4:59:16
Eagle Bridge 42 11 42N57 73w24 4:53:36
Eagle Center 61 226 42N35 78w15 5:13:00
Eagle Harbor 37 146 43N15 78w15 5:13:00
Eagle Lake 16 226 43N51 73w25 4:53:40
Eagle Mills 42 220 42N43 73w41 4:54:44
Eagle Point 26 13 42N48 77w49 5:11:16
Eagle Valley 36 226 41N10 74w14 4:56:56
Eagle Village 34 13 43N01 76w01 5:04:04
Eagleville 58 213 43N05 73w21 4:53:24
Earlton 20 11 42N21 73w54 4:55:36
Earlville 27 13 42N44 75w33 5:02:12
East 60 1 40N55 73w52 4:55:28
East Amherst 15 11 43N01 78w42 5:14:48
East Arcade 61 147 42N32 78w26 5:13:44
East Atlantic Beach 30 11 40N35 73w43 4:54:52
East Aurora 15 170 42N46 78w37 5:14:28
East Avon 26 20 42N55 77w45 5:11:00
East Bay 59 226 43N13 76w49 5:07:16
East Beekmantown 10 86 44N42 73w26 4:53:44
East Bend Park 14 1 41N40 73w54 4:55:36
East Bennington 61 226 42N54 78w23 5:13:32
East Berkshire 54 226 42N18 76w11 5:04:44
East Berne 1 40 42N37 74w04 4:56:16
East Bethany 19 142 43N00 78w11 5:12:44
East Bloomfield 35 47 42N54 77w25 5:09:40
East Branch 13 226 41N59 75w08 5:00:32
East Brentwood 52 11 40N47 73w15 4:53:00
East Campbell 51 13 42N09 77w06 5:08:24
East Cayuga Heights 55 186 42N28 76w28 5:05:52
East Chatham 11 10 42N25 73w32 4:54:08
East Chester 36 4 41N21 74w16 4:57:04
Eastchester 60 1 40N58 73w49 4:55:16
East Cobleskill 48 12 42N40 74w19 4:57:16
East Coldenham 36 1 41N31 74w03 4:56:12
East Concord 15 218 42N33 78w38 5:14:32
East Corning 51 13 42N08 77w03 5:08:12
East Cutchogue 52 11 41N01 72w29 4:49:56
East De Kalb 45 226 44N30 75w16 5:01:04
East Dickinson 17 226 44N43 74w33 4:58:12
East Durham 20 226 42N22 74w06 4:56:24
East Eden 15 153 42N39 78w54 5:15:36
East Elma 15 170 42N46 78w37 5:14:28
East Elmhurst 41 1 40N46 73w52 4:55:28
East Farmingdale 52 11 40N49 73w27 4:53:48
East Fishkill 14 6 41N34 73w48 4:55:12
East Floyd 33 14 43N14 75w16 5:01:04
East Frankfort 22 184 43N02 75w04 5:00:16
East Freetown 12 13 42N33 76w00 5:04:00
East Gaines 37 146 43N15 78w12 5:12:48
East Galway 46 226 43N05 73w55 4:55:40
East Genoa 6 13 42N40 76w26 5:05:44
East Glenville 47 226 42N52 73w55 4:55:40
East Greenbush 42 1 42N37 73w43 4:54:52
East Greenwich 58 1 43N09 73w24 4:53:36
East Half Hollow Hills 52 11 40N48 73w19 4:53:16
East Hamilton 27 180 42N49 75w28 5:01:52
East Hampton 52 1 40N58 72w11 4:48:44
East Hartford 58 42 43N24 73w16 4:53:04
East Hebron 58 213 43N10 73w20 4:53:20
East Hempstead 30 6 40N42 73w36 4:54:24
East Herkimer 22 183 43N02 74w58 4:59:52
East Hill 55 186 42N28 76w29 5:05:56

East Hills 30 11 40N48 73w38 4:54:32
East Homer 12 41 42N40 76w06 5:04:24
East Hounsfield 23 226 43N49 75w49 5:03:16
East Huntington 52 6 40N52 73w27 4:53:48
East Irvington 60 1 41N03 73w51 4:55:24
East Islip 52 6 40N44 73w12 4:52:48
East Ithaca 55 186 42N28 76w29 5:05:56
East Jefferson 48 226 42N29 74w37 4:58:28
East Jewett 20 23 42N14 74w09 4:56:36
East Kingston 56 11 41N57 74w00 4:56:00
East Koy 61 226 42N34 78w02 5:12:08
East Lake Ronkonkoma 52 11 40N49 73w06 4:52:24
East Lansing 55 13 42N35 76w22 5:05:28
East Leon 5 226 42N20 78w52 5:15:28
East Line 46 11 43N01 73w51 4:55:24
East Maine 4 116 42N07 75w58 5:03:52
East Marion 52 11 41N08 72w20 4:49:20
East Martinsburg 25 226 43N54 75w30 5:02:00
East Masonville 13 13 42N17 75w16 5:01:04
East Massapequa 30 6 40N40 73w26 4:53:44
East McDonough 9 226 42N26 75w36 5:02:24
East Meadow 30 11 40N43 73w34 4:54:16
East Meredith 13 29 42N25 74w53 4:59:32
East Middletown 36 1 41N27 74w24 4:57:36
Eastmor 42 220 42N43 73w41 4:54:44
East Moriches 52 11 40N48 72w45 4:51:00
East Nassau 42 11 42N30 73w30 4:54:00
East Neck 52 11 40N54 73w23 4:53:32
East New York 24 1 40N40 73w54 4:55:36
East Nichols 54 36 42N01 76w22 5:05:28
East Northport 52 7 40N53 73w20 4:53:20
East Norwich 30 11 40N51 73w32 4:54:08
East Oakfield 19 26 43N04 78w16 5:13:04
East Olean 5 101 42N05 78w26 5:13:44
Easton 58 226 43N02 73w32 4:54:08
East Otto 5 226 42N24 78w44 5:14:56
East Palermo 38 182 43N17 76w09 5:04:36
East Palmyra 59 89 43N04 77w09 5:08:36
East Park 14 11 41N47 73w55 4:55:40
East Part 45 105 44N48 74w47 4:59:08
East Patchogue 52 1 40N46 73w00 4:52:00
East Pembroke 19 226 43N00 78w18 5:13:12
East Penfield 28 13 43N05 77w28 5:09:52
East Pharsalia 9 226 42N34 75w43 5:02:52
East Pitcairn 45 226 43N32 75w40 5:02:40
East Pittstown 42 11 42N57 73w26 4:53:44
East Poestenkill 42 226 42N38 73w33 4:54:12
Eastport 52 11 40N50 72w44 4:50:56
East Potter 62 14 42N40 77w03 5:08:12
East Quogue 52 1 40N50 72w35 4:50:20
East Randolph 5 20 42N11 78w57 5:15:48
East Ripley 7 103 42N16 79w43 5:18:52
East Rochester 28 13 43N07 77w29 5:09:56
East Rockaway 30 11 40N39 73w40 4:54:40
East Rodman 23 45 43N59 75w56 5:03:44
East Salamanca 5 14 42N09 78w43 5:14:52
East Schodack 42 68 42N34 73w38 4:54:32
East Schuyler 22 184 43N02 75w04 5:00:16
East Scott 12 41 42N38 76w11 5:04:44
East Seneca 15 153 42N51 78w46 5:15:04
East Setauket 52 11 40N57 73w06 4:52:24
East Shelby 37 112 43N13 78w23 5:13:32
East Side 4 151 42N07 75w53 5:03:32
Eastside 52 11 40N57 72w11 4:48:44
East Sidney 13 104 42N21 75w10 5:00:40
East Springfield 39 140 42N50 74w49 4:59:16
East Steamburg 49 13 42N33 76w40 5:06:40
East Stone Arabia 29 162 42N55 74w35 4:58:20
East Syracuse 34 41 43N04 76w04 5:04:16
East Varick 50 12 42N45 76w50 5:07:20
East Venice 6 13 42N40 76w32 5:06:08
East Vestal 4 151 42N06 75w59 5:03:56
East Victor 35 19 42N59 77w25 5:09:40
East View 60 1 41N04 73w46 4:55:04
East Walden 36 6 41N34 74w11 4:56:44
East Watertown 23 45 43N59 75w56 5:03:44
East Wawarsing 56 48 41N46 74w21 4:57:24
East Whitehall 58 6 43N33 73w24 4:53:36
East White Plains 60 1 41N03 73w45 4:55:00
East Williamson 59 33 43N14 77w09 5:08:36
East Williston 30 11 40N46 73w38 4:54:32
East Wilson 32 226 43N24 78w42 5:14:48
East Windham 20 226 42N20 74w10 4:56:40
East Windsor 4 226 42N04 75w41 5:02:44
East Winfield 22 13 42N53 75w12 5:00:48
Eastwood 34 41 43N04 76w07 5:04:28
East Worcester 39 14 42N37 74w40 4:58:40
Eaton 27 180 42N53 75w38 5:02:32
Eatons Neck 52 11 40N54 73w20 4:53:20
Eavesport 56 11 42N07 73w56 4:55:44
Ebenezer 15 153 42N51 78w46 5:15:04
Eddy 45 155 44N36 75w10 5:00:40

NEW YORK

Eddyville 5 226 42N15 78w48 5:15:12
Eddyville 56 11 41N54 74w02 4:56:08
Eden 15 153 42N39 78w54 5:15:36
Edenville 36 6 41N17 74w25 4:57:40
Edgemere 41 1 40N43 73w50 4:55:20
Edgemont 60 1 40N59 73w48 4:55:12
Edgewater 15 1 43N03 78w55 5:15:40
Edgewater Beach 33 211 43N15 75w27 5:01:48
Edgewater Park 34 13 42N57 76w25 5:05:40
Edgewater Park 45 201 44N42 75w29 5:01:56
Edgewood 20 52 42N08 74w16 4:57:04
Edgewood 52 11 40N47 73w15 4:53:00
Edgewood Garden 34 41 43N05 76w20 5:05:20
Edgewood Park 23 17 44N20 75w55 5:03:40
Edinburg 46 226 43N13 74w06 4:56:24
Edmeston 39 226 42N42 75w15 5:01:00
Edson 4 226 42N04 75w41 5:02:44
Edwards 45 226 44N20 75w15 5:01:00
Edwards Hill 57 49 43N37 74w01 4:56:04
Edwards Park 11 11 42N25 73w27 4:53:48
Edwardsville 45 20 44N27 75w42 5:02:48
Egbertville 43 1 40N34 74w07 4:56:28
Eggertsville 15 7 42N58 78w48 5:15:12
Egypt 28 13 43N05 77w28 5:09:52
Elayne Meadows 46 11 42N48 73w41 4:54:44
Elba 19 171 43N05 78w10 5:12:40
Elbow 58 6 43N33 73w24 4:53:36
Elbridge 34 24 43N03 76w25 5:05:40
Eldred 53 226 41N32 74w53 4:59:32
Elizabethtown 16 50 44N13 73w36 4:54:24
Elizaville 11 226 42N03 73w48 4:55:12
Elka Park 20 23 42N10 74w09 4:56:36
Elk Brook 13 80 41N56 74w55 4:59:40
Elk Creek 39 13 42N33 74w49 4:59:16
Elkdale 5 226 42N09 78w43 5:14:52
Ellenburg 10 18 44N51 73w53 4:55:32
Ellenville 56 48 41N43 74w24 4:57:36
Ellery 7 226 42N10 79w21 5:17:24
Ellicott 7 187 42N08 79w13 5:16:52
Ellicott 15 11 42N47 78w45 5:15:00
Ellicott 15 153 42N54 78w51 5:15:24
Ellicottville 5 172 42N17 78w40 5:14:40
Ellington 7 226 42N13 79w07 5:16:28
Ellisburg 23 226 43N45 76w07 5:04:28
Ellis Hollow 55 186 42N28 76w29 5:05:56
Ellistown 54 224 42N00 76w32 5:06:08
Elma 15 226 42N51 78w38 5:14:32
Elmdale 45 178 44N20 75w28 5:01:52
Elmer Hill 33 211 43N13 75w26 5:01:44
Elm Grove 39 226 42N33 75w15 5:01:00
Elmhurst 7 187 42N06 79w16 5:17:04
Elmhurst 41 1 40N44 73w53 4:55:32
Elmira 8 13 42N06 76w48 5:07:12
Elmira Heights 8 13 42N07 76w49 5:07:16
Elmont 30 1 40N43 73w43 4:54:52
Elm Park 43 1 40N38 74w09 4:56:36
Elmsford 60 6 41N04 73w49 4:55:16
Elm Valley 2 109 42N07 77w57 5:11:48
Elmwood 34 13 43N01 76w10 5:04:40
Elnora 46 11 42N51 73w48 4:55:12
Elsmere 1 11 42N37 73w49 4:55:16
Eltingville 43 11 40N33 74w11 4:56:44
Elton 5 226 42N30 78w29 5:13:56
Elwood 52 11 40N51 73w19 4:53:16
Elwood Farms 52 11 40N51 73w20 4:53:20
Embarkation 24 1 40N43 73w50 4:55:20
Embogcht 20 226 42N13 73w51 4:55:24
Emerson 6 24 43N02 76w37 5:06:28
Emeryville 45 178 44N20 75w28 5:01:52
Eminence 48 13 42N35 74w37 4:58:28
Emmons 39 14 42N27 75w05 5:00:20
Empeyville 33 14 43N20 75w45 5:03:00
Empire State 31 1 40N45 73w59 4:55:56
Endicott 4 13 42N06 76w04 5:04:16
Endwell 4 13 42N06 76w02 5:04:08
Enfield 55 186 42N27 76w37 5:06:28
Englewood 15 1 42N58 78w51 5:15:24
Ensenore 6 13 42N43 76w25 5:05:40
Ephratah 18 226 43N02 74w33 4:58:12
Erieville 27 226 42N51 75w46 5:03:04
Erin 8 226 42N11 76w40 5:06:40
Erwin 51 13 42N09 77w09 5:08:36
Escarpment 32 199 43N09 79w00 5:16:00
Esopus 56 11 41N51 74w00 4:56:00
Esperance 48 12 42N45 74w20 4:57:20
Esplanade 3 1 40N52 73w51 4:55:24
Essex 16 129 44N19 73w21 4:53:24
Etna 55 13 42N29 76w23 5:05:32
Euclid 34 13 43N09 76w13 5:04:52
Evans 15 11 42N39 79w02 5:16:08
Evans Center 15 11 42N39 79w02 5:16:08
Evans Mills 23 26 44N05 75w49 5:03:16
Exeter 39 78 42N48 75w04 5:00:16
Fabius 34 16 42N50 75w59 5:03:56
Factory Village 46 11 43N01 73w51 4:55:24
Factoryville 16 138 43N57 73w25 4:53:40
Fairdale 38 226 43N19 76w35 5:06:20
Fairfield 22 226 43N08 74w55 4:59:40
Fairfield Farms 34 13 43N02 76w01 5:04:04
Fairfield Gardens 1 11 42N42 73w48 4:55:12
Fair Harbor 52 11 40N38 73w11 4:52:44
Fair Haven 6 226 43N19 76w42 5:06:48
Fair Haven 12 41 42N38 76w11 5:04:44
Fairlawn Estates 1 1 42N44 73w45 4:55:00
Fairmount 34 12 43N03 76w15 5:05:00
Fair Oaks 36 1 41N28 74w24 4:57:36
Fairport 28 13 43N06 77w27 5:09:48
Fairview 2 226 42N26 78w22 5:13:28
Fairview 14 11 41N45 73w55 4:55:40
Fairview 60 1 41N03 73w47 4:55:08
Fairview 61 24 42N38 78w03 5:12:12
Fairville 59 22 43N03 77w05 5:08:20
Falconer 7 187 42N07 79w12 5:16:48
Falcon Manor 32 199 43N06 78w58 5:15:52
Falconwood 15 1 43N01 78w57 5:15:48
Falls 32 199 43N05 79w02 5:16:08
Fallsburg 53 74 41N45 74w37 4:58:28
Fancher 37 146 43N15 78w06 5:12:24
Fargo 19 164 42N58 78w24 5:13:36
Farleys Point 6 13 42N50 76w42 5:06:48
Farmers Mills 40 226 41N27 73w40 4:54:40
Farmersville 5 226 42N24 78w23 5:13:32
Farmingdale 30 11 40N44 73w27 4:53:48
Farmington 35 19 42N59 77w20 5:09:20
Farmingville 52 11 40N50 73w02 4:52:08
Farnham 15 22 42N36 79w05 5:16:20
Farragut 24 1 40N39 73w56 4:55:44
Far Rockaway 41 1 40N36 73w45 4:55:00
Fawn Ridge 34 226 43N09 76w20 5:05:20
Fayette 50 13 42N49 76w49 5:07:16
Fayette Manor 34 13 43N02 76w01 5:04:04
Fayetteville 34 13 43N02 76w00 5:04:00
Federal 28 209 43N09 77w37 5:10:28
Federal Reserve 31 1 40N43 73w50 4:55:20
Felts Mills 23 119 44N01 75w46 5:03:04
Fenimore 46 226 41N31 73w42 4:54:48
Fenner 27 226 42N58 75w47 5:03:08
Fenton 4 13 42N11 75w50 5:03:20
Fentonville 7 128 42N03 79w09 5:16:36
Ferenbaugh 51 13 42N08 77w03 5:08:12
Fergusons Corners 62 41 42N52 76w59 5:07:56
Fergusonville 13 13 42N33 74w49 4:59:16
Ferndale 53 72 41N46 74w44 4:58:56
Fernwood 38 226 43N34 76w07 5:04:28
Fernwood 46 226 43N17 73w39 4:54:36
Fernwood 53 226 41N51 75w08 5:00:32
Ferry Village 15 1 43N01 78w57 5:15:48
Feura Bush 1 11 42N35 73w53 4:55:32
Fieldston 3 1 40N53 73w54 4:55:36
Filer Corners 39 226 42N33 75w15 5:01:00
Fillmore 2 226 42N28 78w07 5:12:28
Finchville 36 1 41N28 74w24 4:57:36
Findley Lake 7 226 42N07 79w44 5:18:56
Fine 45 226 44N15 75w08 5:00:32
Fineview 23 163 44N17 76w00 5:04:00
Finger Lakes Manor 35 14 42N53 77w17 5:09:08
Fink Basin 22 61 43N03 74w51 4:59:24
Finnegans Corners 36 7 41N24 74w20 4:57:20
Fire Island Pines 52 11 40N45 73w05 4:52:20
Firthcliffe 36 11 41N26 74w02 4:56:08
Firthcliffe Heights 36 1 41N31 74w03 4:56:12
Fish Creek 25 77 44N08 75w35 5:02:20
Fish Creek 56 215 42N04 73w57 4:55:48
Fish Creek Landing 33 211 43N15 75w27 5:01:48
Fishers 35 13 43N00 77w28 5:09:52
Fishers Island 52 11 41N25 72w00 4:48:00
Fishers Landing 23 163 44N17 76w00 5:04:00
Fisherville 8 13 42N07 76w49 5:07:16
Fish House 18 226 43N03 74w12 4:56:48
Fishkill 14 6 41N32 73w54 4:55:36
Fishkill Plains 14 6 41N36 73w53 4:55:32
Fishs Eddy 13 226 41N58 75w10 5:00:40
Fitch 5 226 42N10 78w23 5:13:32
Five Corners 2 226 42N15 77w47 5:11:08
Five Corners 6 13 42N40 76w32 5:06:08
Five Corners 27 60 43N05 75w39 5:02:36
Five Corners 33 13 42N56 75w23 5:01:32
Fivemile Point 4 20 42N05 75w48 5:03:12
Five Points 35 41 42N52 76w59 5:07:56
Flackville 45 201 44N42 75w29 5:01:56
Flanders 52 11 40N54 72w37 4:50:28
Flatbrook 11 11 42N25 73w27 4:53:48
Flatbush 24 1 40N39 73w56 4:55:44
Flatbush 56 215 42N04 73w57 4:55:48
Flat Creek 29 162 42N52 74w35 4:58:20
Flat Creek 48 226 42N24 74w27 4:57:48
Fleetwood 60 1 40N55 73w50 4:55:20
Fleischmanns 13 42 42N10 74w32 4:58:08
Fleming 6 13 42N53 76w35 5:06:20
Flemingville 54 205 42N06 76w16 5:05:04
Flint 35 14 42N49 77w06 5:08:24
Floral Park 41 1 40N44 73w42 4:54:48
Florence 33 226 43N25 75w45 5:03:00
Florida 36 20 41N20 74w21 4:57:24
Floridaville 6 226 43N10 76w34 5:06:16
Flowerfield Estates 3 1 40N51 73w53 4:55:32
Flower Hill 30 11 40N48 73w41 4:54:44
Flowers 4 226 42N04 75w41 5:02:44
Floyd 33 211 43N13 75w20 5:01:20
Flushing 41 1 40N45 73w49 4:55:16
Fluvanna 7 187 42N06 79w16 5:17:04
Fly Creek 39 13 42N43 74w59 4:59:56
Flying Point 52 11 40N55 72w21 4:49:24
Fly Summit 58 4 43N05 73w30 4:54:00
Folsomdale 61 38 42N51 78w28 5:13:52
Fonda 29 174 42N57 74w22 4:57:28
Foots Corners 26 226 42N43 77w41 5:10:44
Fordham 3 1 40N51 73w54 4:55:36
Forest 10 20 44N54 73w48 4:55:12
Forest Avenue Shoppers Town 43 1 40N38 74w08 4:56:32
Forestburgh 53 226 41N33 74w43 4:58:52
Forest Glen 15 1 40N53 73w50 4:55:20
Forest Hills 41 1 40N42 73w51 4:55:24
Forest Home 55 186 42N28 76w29 5:05:56
Forest Lawn 28 109 42N10 77w59 5:11:56
Forest Park 7 225 42N19 79w34 5:18:16
Forest Park 41 1 40N43 73w50 4:55:20
Forestport 33 226 43N28 75w10 5:00:40
Forestport Station 33 226 43N27 75w12 5:00:48
Forestville 7 226 42N28 79w10 5:16:40
Forge Hollow 33 11 43N00 75w26 5:01:44
Forks 15 7 42N55 78w46 5:15:04
Forsonville 40 6 41N23 73w57 4:55:48
Forsyth 7 226 42N16 79w43 5:18:52
Fort Ann 58 123 43N27 73w30 4:54:00
Fort Covington 17 226 44N59 74w30 4:58:00
Fort Drum 23 12 44N01 75w48 5:03:12
Fort Edward 58 1 43N14 73w33 4:54:12
Fort George 31 1 40N52 73w56 4:55:44
Fort Hamilton 24 1 40N37 74w02 4:56:08
Fort Herkimer 22 183 43N00 75w00 5:00:00
Fort Hunter 29 1 42N57 74w17 4:57:08
Fort Jackson 45 226 44N42 74w43 4:58:52
Fort Jay 31 1 40N43 74w01 4:56:04
Fort Johnson 29 1 42N58 74w14 4:56:56
Fort Miller 58 226 43N16 73w35 4:54:20
Fort Montgomery 36 6 41N20 73w59 4:55:56
Fort Niagara Beach 32 226 43N20 79w02 5:16:08
Fort Plain 29 62 42N56 74w37 4:58:28
Fort Salonga 52 11 40N55 73w18 4:53:12
Fortsville 46 226 43N12 73w39 4:54:36
Fort Tilden 41 1 40N35 73w53 4:55:32
Fort Wadsworth 43 1 40N36 74w05 4:56:20
Fort Washington 31 1 40N50 73w56 4:55:44
Foster 54 205 42N06 76w16 5:05:04
Fosterdale 53 226 41N42 74w58 4:59:52
Fosterville 6 13 42N56 76w33 5:06:12
Foster-Wheeler Junction 26 13 42N34 77w42 5:10:48
Fourth Lake 57 40 43N19 73w50 4:55:20
Fowler 45 226 44N17 75w25 5:01:40
Fowlersville 25 77 44N06 75w40 5:02:40
Fowlerville 15 226 42N38 78w44 5:14:56
Fowlerville 26 226 42N59 77w51 5:11:24
Fox Hill 46 7 43N13 74w10 4:56:40
Frankfort 22 150 43N19 78w34 5:14:16
Frankfort Center 22 184 43N02 75w04 5:00:16
Franklin 13 104 42N21 75w10 5:00:40
Franklin Depot 13 13 42N17 75w16 5:01:04
Franklin D. Roosevelt 31 1 40N46 73w58 4:55:52
Franklin Falls 17 81 44N24 74w05 4:56:20
Franklin Park 34 41 43N04 76w04 5:04:16
Franklin Springs 33 11 43N02 75w24 5:01:36
Franklin Square 30 11 40N43 73w41 4:54:44
Franklinton 48 226 42N36 74w20 4:57:20
Franklinville 5 108 42N20 78w27 5:13:48
Franks Corner 12 41 42N35 76w12 5:04:48
Fraser 13 226 42N17 74w55 4:59:40
Fredonia 7 14 42N26 79w20 5:17:20
Freedom 5 226 42N29 78w23 5:13:32
Freedom Plains 14 11 41N45 73w50 4:55:20
Freehold 20 226 42N22 74w03 4:56:12
Freeman 51 13 42N06 77w14 5:08:56
Freeport 30 175 40N39 73w35 4:54:20
Freetown 52 11 40N57 72w11 4:48:44
Freetown Corners 12 13 42N27 76w02 5:04:08
Freeville 55 13 42N31 76w21 5:05:24
Fremont Center 53 226 41N51 75w02 5:00:08
Fremont Hills 34 41 43N04 76w04 5:04:16
French Creek 7 226 42N03 79w42 5:18:48
Frenchville 33 226 43N18 75w23 5:01:32
French Woods 13 97 41N57 75w17 5:01:08
Fresh Meadows 41 1 40N44 73w47 4:55:08
Fresh Pond 41 1 40N42 73w54 4:55:36
Frewsburg 7 128 42N03 79w10 5:16:40
Friend 62 14 42N40 77w03 5:08:12
Friendship 2 107 42N12 78w08 5:12:32
Friends Point 57 226 43N45 73w30 4:54:00
Frontenac 23 163 44N14 76w05 5:04:20
Frontier Plaza 28 209 43N08 77w43 5:10:52
Front Street 4 151 42N07 75w56 5:03:44
Fruitland 59 226 43N13 77w17 5:09:08
Fruit Valley 38 204 43N27 76w30 5:06:00
Fullerville 45 178 44N20 75w28 5:01:52
Fulmer Valley 2 226 42N09 77w48 5:11:12
Fulton 38 55 43N19 76w25 5:05:40
Fultonham 48 226 42N31 75w03 5:00:12
Fultonville 29 174 42N57 74w22 4:57:28
Furnace Brook 36 226 41N13 74w17 4:57:08
Furnaceville 59 226 43N13 77w17 5:09:08
Furnace Woods 60 11 41N16 73w53 4:55:32
Furniss 38 204 43N27 76w30 5:06:00
Fyler Settlement 27 226 43N00 75w59 5:03:56
Gabriels 17 176 44N26 74w11 4:56:44
Gaines 37 146 43N17 78w12 5:12:48
Gainesville 61 24 42N39 78w08 5:12:32
Galatia 12 13 42N27 76w02 5:04:08
Gale 45 87 44N14 74w34 4:58:16

NEW YORK

Galen 59 99 43N04 76w52 5:07:28
Galeville 34 13 43N07 76w12 5:04:48
Galeville 56 11 41N37 74w10 4:56:40
Gallatin 11 25 42N04 73w43 4:54:52
Gallupville 48 226 42N40 74w14 4:56:56
Galway 46 226 43N02 74w01 4:56:04
Galway Lake 46 226 43N03 74w12 4:56:48
Ganahgote 56 122 41N41 74w09 4:56:36
Gang Mills 51 13 42N09 77w07 5:08:28
Gansevoort 46 226 43N12 73w39 4:54:36
Garbutt 28 226 43N01 77w45 5:11:00
Garden City 30 177 40N44 73w38 4:54:32
Garden Park Estates 1 1 42N40 73w48 4:55:12
Gardenville 15 153 42N51 78w46 5:15:04
Gardiner 56 122 41N42 74w10 4:56:40
Gardiners Bay Estates 52 11 41N08 72w20 4:49:20
Gardners Corners 25 226 43N54 75w30 5:02:00
Gardnersville 48 139 42N41 74w29 4:57:56
Gardnertown 36 1 41N32 74w04 4:56:16
Garfield 42 11 42N33 73w23 4:53:32
Garland 28 226 43N13 77w56 5:11:44
Garnerville 44 6 41N12 73w59 4:55:56
Garnet Lake 57 49 43N37 73w58 4:55:52
Garoga 18 43 43N00 74w22 4:57:28
Garrattsville 39 226 42N39 75w10 5:00:40
Garrison 40 6 41N23 73w57 4:55:48
Garrison Manor 46 226 42N55 73w54 4:55:36
Garwoods 2 226 42N28 77w47 5:11:08
Gaskill 54 205 42N06 76w16 5:05:04
Gasport 32 121 43N11 79w02 5:16:08
Gates 28 209 43N09 77w41 5:10:44
Gayhead 14 226 41N36 73w47 4:55:08
Gay Ridge Estates 60 16 41N17 73w46 4:55:04
Gayville 38 14 43N15 76w00 5:04:00
Geddes 34 13 43N05 76w14 5:04:56
Gedney 60 7 41N01 73w45 4:55:00
Geers Corners 45 226 43N32 75w40 5:02:40
Genegantslet 9 226 42N20 75w46 5:03:04
Genesee 2 226 42N03 78w15 5:13:00
Genesee Falls 61 226 42N34 78w04 5:12:16
Geneseo 26 13 42N48 77w49 5:11:16
Geneva 35 41 42N52 76w59 5:07:56
Genoa 6 13 42N39 76w34 5:06:16
Georgetown 27 226 42N47 75w45 5:03:00
Georgetown Square 15 7 42N59 78w45 5:15:00
Georgtown Station 27 180 42N51 75w37 5:02:28
German 9 226 42N30 75w50 5:03:20
German Flatts 22 183 42N59 74w59 4:59:56
Germantown 11 11 42N08 73w52 4:55:28
Germantown 36 1 41N23 74w41 4:58:44
German Village 28 185 43N13 77w36 5:10:24
Germonds 44 4 41N09 74w00 4:56:00
Gerry 7 120 42N12 79w14 5:16:56
Getzville 15 11 43N02 78w46 5:15:04
Ghent 11 11 42N19 73w39 4:54:36
Gibson 51 13 42N08 77w03 5:08:12
Gibson Landing 51 181 42N24 77w13 5:08:52
Gifford 47 226 42N46 74w08 4:56:32
Gilbert Corners 46 226 43N05 73w47 4:55:08
Gilbert Mills 38 93 43N14 76w18 5:05:12
Gilbertsville 39 226 42N28 75w19 5:01:16
Gilboa 48 226 42N25 74w27 4:57:48
Gilgo Beach 52 11 40N41 73w21 4:53:24
Gilmantown 21 11 42N47 78w50 5:15:20
Glasco 56 215 42N03 73w57 4:55:48
Glass Lake 42 226 42N38 73w33 4:54:12
Glen 29 174 42N55 74w21 4:57:24
Glen Aubrey 4 226 42N15 76w01 5:04:04
Glenburnie 58 226 43N44 73w24 4:53:36
Glencairn 54 224 42N00 76w32 5:06:08
Glen Castle 4 151 42N08 75w53 5:03:32
Glencoe Mills 11 1 42N15 73w47 4:55:08
Glen Cove 30 1 40N52 73w38 4:54:32
Glendale 25 15 43N43 75w24 5:01:36
Glendale 41 1 40N42 73w54 4:55:36
Glenerie 56 215 42N04 73w57 4:55:48
Glenfield 25 15 43N43 75w24 5:01:36
Glenford 56 11 42N00 74w07 4:56:28
Glenham 14 6 41N31 73w56 4:55:44
Glen Haven 6 41 42N38 76w11 5:04:44
Glen Haven 28 185 43N13 77w36 5:10:24
Glenhaven 33 222 43N07 75w18 5:01:12
Glen Head 30 11 40N50 73w38 4:54:32
Glen Island 60 1 40N53 73w47 4:55:08
Glen Lake 46 226 41N31 73w42 4:54:48
Glenmark 59 226 43N11 76w54 5:07:36
Glenmont 1 11 42N36 73w46 4:55:04
Glen Oaks 41 1 40N45 73w43 4:54:52
Glenora 62 13 42N31 76w58 5:07:52
Glen Park 23 45 44N00 75w57 5:03:48
Glens Falls 57 1 43N19 73w39 4:54:36
Glen Spey 53 25 41N29 74w49 4:59:16
Glenville 60 6 41N04 73w50 4:55:20
Glen Wild 53 74 41N39 74w35 4:58:20
Glenwood 15 218 42N37 78w39 5:14:36
Glenwood Landing 30 11 40N48 73w39 4:54:36
Gloversville 18 46 43N03 74w21 4:57:24
Godeffroy 36 21 41N27 74w37 4:58:28
Golden Glow Heights 8 13 42N05 76w50 5:07:20
Goldens Bridge 60 16 41N17 73w40 4:54:40
Goodyears Corners 6 13 42N40 76w37 5:06:28
Goose Bay Estates 52 11 41N04 72w26 4:49:44
Gordon Heights 52 11 40N51 72w58 4:51:52
Gorham 35 14 42N48 77w08 5:08:32
Goshen 36 7 41N24 74w20 4:57:20
Goshen Hills 36 7 41N24 74w20 4:57:20
Gothicville 39 13 42N36 74w45 4:59:00
Goulds Mill 25 77 44N08 75w35 5:02:20
Gouverneur 45 178 44N20 75w28 5:01:52
Governors Island 31 1 40N41 74w01 4:56:04
Gowanda 5 42 42N28 78w56 5:15:44
Gracie 31 1 40N47 73w58 4:55:52
Grafton 42 11 42N46 73w27 4:53:48
Graham Beach 43 1 40N36 74w05 4:56:20
Grahamsville 53 226 41N51 74w33 4:58:12
Granby Center 38 226 43N19 76w25 5:05:40
Grandby 38 226 43N18 76w27 5:05:48
Grand Gorge 13 131 42N22 74w30 4:58:00
Grand Island 15 1 43N01 78w58 5:15:52
Grandview Bay 15 11 42N38 79w03 5:16:12
Grand View Heights 28 226 43N15 77w38 5:10:32
Grand View-on-Hudson 44 4 41N04 73w55 4:55:40
Grandview Park 23 163 44N17 76w02 5:04:08
Grandyle Village 15 1 43N01 78w57 5:15:48
Granger 2 226 42N29 78w01 5:12:04
Grangerville 46 226 43N06 73w35 4:54:20
Granite 56 72 41N47 74w19 4:57:16
Granite Springs 60 16 41N19 73w46 4:55:04
Graniteville 43 1 40N38 74w06 4:56:24
Grant 22 84 43N14 75w02 5:00:08
Grant City 43 1 40N34 74w07 4:56:28
Grant Hollow 42 11 42N50 73w37 4:54:28
Grant Park 30 11 40N39 73w42 4:54:48
Grantville 45 226 44N48 74w59 4:59:56
Granville 58 42 43N24 73w16 4:53:04
Grapeville 20 11 42N22 73w51 4:55:24
Graphite 57 226 43N45 73w30 4:54:00
Grassy Point 44 6 41N14 73w59 4:55:56
Gravesend 24 1 40N36 73w58 4:55:52
Gravesville 22 84 43N13 75w04 5:00:16
Gray 22 84 43N14 75w02 5:00:08
Great Bend 23 119 44N02 75w43 5:02:52
Great Kills 43 1 40N33 74w08 4:56:32
Great Neck 30 1 40N48 73w44 4:54:56
Great Neck Estates 30 1 40N47 73w44 4:54:56
Great River 52 11 40N43 73w09 4:52:36
Great Valley 5 226 42N12 78w38 5:14:32
Greece 28 209 43N14 77w40 5:10:40
Greeley Square 31 1 40N45 73w59 4:55:56
Green Acres 15 1 43N00 78w51 5:15:24
Greenburgh 60 7 41N02 73w49 4:55:16
Green Corners 47 1 42N57 74w11 4:56:44
Green Crest 7 14 42N27 79w20 5:17:20
Greendale 11 1 42N15 73w47 4:55:08
Greene 9 105 42N20 75w46 5:03:04
Greenfield 46 226 43N08 73w51 4:55:24
Greenfield Park 56 48 41N44 74w29 4:57:56
Green Haven 14 226 41N37 73w41 4:54:44
Greenhaven 60 1 40N59 73w42 4:54:48
Greenhurst 7 187 42N07 79w19 5:17:16
Green Island 1 179 42N45 73w42 4:54:48
Greenlawn 52 11 40N52 73w22 4:53:28
Greenpoint 52 11 40N43 73w06 4:52:24
Greenport 52 1 41N06 72w22 4:49:28
Green River 11 11 42N11 73w31 4:54:04
Greenvale 30 11 40N49 73w38 4:54:32
Greenville 20 226 42N25 74w01 4:56:04
Greenville 60 1 41N00 73w49 4:55:16
Greenway 33 211 43N13 75w26 5:01:44
Greenwich 58 1 43N05 73w30 4:54:00
Greenwood 51 226 42N09 77w40 5:10:40
Greenwood Lake 36 226 41N14 74w17 4:57:08
Gregorytown 13 226 42N05 75w00 5:00:00
Greig 25 119 43N59 75w43 5:02:52
Greigsville 26 126 42N50 77w51 5:11:24
Grenell 23 163 44N16 76w03 5:04:12
Greycourt 36 4 41N21 74w16 4:57:04
Gridleyville 54 226 42N17 76w23 5:05:32
Griffins Mills 15 11 42N44 78w40 5:14:40
Griffiss Air Force Base 33 211 43N13 75w26 5:01:44
Grindstone 23 163 44N14 76w05 5:04:20
Grooms Corners 46 4 42N51 73w53 4:55:32
Grooville 53 75 41N54 74w50 4:59:20
Grossinger 53 189 41N46 74w44 4:58:56
Groton 55 13 42N36 76w22 5:05:28
Grove 2 226 42N28 77w55 5:11:40
Groveland 26 13 42N42 77w48 5:11:12
Grover 15 7 42N58 78w48 5:15:12
Grover Hills 16 54 44N05 73w31 4:54:04
Grovernor Corners 48 12 42N43 74w20 4:57:20
Groveville 14 7 41N30 73w58 4:55:52
Grymes Hill 43 1 40N38 74w06 4:56:24
Guilderland 1 6 42N43 73w55 4:55:40
Guilderland Gardens 1 1 42N40 73w48 4:55:12
Guilford 9 149 42N23 75w27 5:01:48
Gulf Summit 4 226 42N04 75w41 5:02:44
Gurn Spring 46 226 43N12 73w39 4:54:36
Guyanoga 62 226 42N36 77w09 5:08:36
Guymard 36 21 41N27 74w37 4:58:28
Gypsum 35 14 42N58 77w08 5:08:32
Hadley 46 40 43N19 73w53 4:55:32
Hadley Bay 7 226 42N09 79w25 5:17:40
Hagaman 29 226 42N58 74w09 4:56:36
Hagedorns Mills 46 226 43N01 74w02 4:56:08
Hagerman 52 11 40N46 73w01 4:52:04
Hague 57 226 43N45 73w30 4:54:00
Hailesboro 45 178 44N18 75w27 5:01:48
Haines Falls 20 2 42N12 74w06 4:56:24
Halcott 20 42 42N13 74w28 4:57:52
Halcottsville 13 42 42N12 74w36 4:58:24
Hales Eddy 13 97 41N57 75w17 5:01:08
Halesite 52 11 40N53 73w25 4:53:40
Half Acre 6 13 42N56 76w33 5:06:12
Half Hollow Hills 52 11 40N47 73w22 4:53:28
Halfmoon 46 11 42N51 73w44 4:54:56
Halfway 34 24 43N02 76w26 5:05:44
Halfway House Corners 45 226 44N45 75w08 5:00:32
Hall 35 14 42N48 77w04 5:08:16
Halls Corners 50 226 42N37 77w33 5:10:12
Halls Corners 61 206 42N44 78w08 5:12:32
Hallsport 2 109 42N07 77w57 5:11:48
Hallsville 29 62 42N56 74w37 4:58:28
Halsey 24 1 40N41 73w55 4:55:40
Halseys Corners 10 86 44N42 73w26 4:53:44
Halsey Valley 54 226 42N13 76w30 5:06:00
Hambletville 13 167 42N04 75w25 5:01:40
Hamburg 15 153 42N45 78w53 5:15:32
Hamburg 20 226 42N13 73w51 4:55:24
Hamburg-on-the-Lake 15 153 42N45 78w51 5:15:24
Hamden 13 226 42N13 74w59 4:59:56
Hamilton 27 180 42N50 75w33 5:02:12
Hamilton Beach 41 1 40N40 73w51 4:55:24
Hamilton Grange 31 1 40N49 73w57 4:55:48
Hamilton Park 43 1 40N38 74w06 4:56:24
Hamlet 7 217 42N22 79w03 5:16:12
Hamlin 28 226 43N19 77w54 5:11:36
Hammertown 14 226 41N59 73w40 4:54:40
Hammond 45 20 44N27 75w42 5:02:48
Hammondsport 51 181 42N25 77w13 5:08:52
Hampshire 51 226 42N07 77w30 5:10:00
Hampton 58 226 43N33 73w17 4:53:08
Hampton Bays 52 11 40N53 72w30 4:50:00
Hamptonburgh 36 11 41N27 74w15 4:57:00
Hampton Manor 42 1 42N39 73w43 4:54:52
Hampton Park 52 11 40N53 72w23 4:49:32
Hancock 13 97 41N57 75w17 5:01:08
Hanfords Bay 7 216 42N33 79w10 5:16:40
Hankins 53 20 41N49 75w05 5:00:20
Hannacroix 20 1 42N26 73w49 4:55:16
Hannawa Falls 45 207 44N37 74w58 4:59:52
Hannibal 38 226 43N19 76w35 5:06:20
Hanover 7 216 42N31 79w08 5:16:32
Harbor Acres 30 11 40N50 73w42 4:54:48
Harbor Heights Park 52 11 40N51 73w23 4:53:32
Harbor Hills 30 1 40N48 73w44 4:54:56
Harbor Isle 30 11 40N36 73w39 4:54:36
Hardenburgh 56 226 42N03 74w37 4:58:28
Hardys 61 24 42N38 78w08 5:12:32
Harford 12 226 42N27 76w13 5:04:52
Harford Mills 12 226 42N25 76w12 5:04:48
Harkness 10 86 44N35 73w32 4:54:08
Harlem 31 1 40N49 73w56 4:55:44
Harlem 15 7 42N58 78w48 5:15:12
Harmon-on-Hudson 60 166 41N12 73w53 4:55:32
Harmon Park 47 1 42N51 73w57 4:55:48
Harmony 7 226 42N03 79w26 5:17:44
Harmony Corners 46 11 43N01 73w51 4:55:24
Harpersfield 13 226 42N27 74w42 4:58:48
Harpursville 4 17 42N11 75w38 5:02:32
Harriet 15 1 42N58 78w51 5:15:24
Harrietstown 17 81 44N20 74w13 4:56:52
Harriman 36 4 41N18 74w09 4:56:36
Harris 53 72 41N43 74w44 4:58:56
Harrisburg 5 226 42N01 78w38 5:14:32
Harrisburg 25 226 43N52 75w21 5:01:24
Harrisburg 57 226 43N25 73w56 4:55:44
Harris Hill 15 7 42N58 78w41 5:14:44
Harrison 60 7 40N59 73w43 4:54:52
Harrisville 25 118 44N09 75w19 5:01:16
Hartfield 7 158 42N14 79w27 5:17:48
Hartford 58 226 43N22 73w25 4:53:40
Hartland 32 226 43N14 78w35 5:14:20
Hart Lot 34 24 43N01 76w28 5:05:52
Hartmans Corners 1 40 42N42 74w02 4:56:08
Hartsdale 60 7 41N01 73w48 4:55:12
Harts Hill 33 222 43N07 75w18 5:01:12
Hartson Point 26 226 42N49 77w40 5:10:40
Hartsville 51 226 42N14 77w41 5:10:44
Hartwick 39 226 42N40 75w03 5:00:12
Hartwick Seminary 39 13 42N39 74w58 4:59:52
Hartwood 53 21 41N28 74w36 4:58:24
Harvard 13 226 41N59 75w08 5:00:32
Hasbrouck 53 74 41N46 74w36 4:58:24
Haselton 33 211 43N13 75w26 5:01:44
Haskell Flats 5 226 42N13 78w17 5:13:08
Haskinville 51 226 42N30 77w30 5:10:00
Hastings 38 182 43N19 76w10 5:04:40

NEW YORK

Hastings-on-Hudson 60
1 40N59 73w53 4:55:32
Hatch's Corner 45
226 44N25 75w09 5:00:36
Hauppauge 52 11 40N50 73w12 4:52:48
Haven 53 11 41N34 74w29 4:57:56
Haverstraw 44 6 41N12 73w58 4:55:52
Haviland 14 11 41N46 73w54 4:55:36
Haviland Hollow 40
7 41N31 73w36 4:54:24
Hawkeye 10 44 44N27 73w41 4:54:44
Hawkinsville 33 226 43N29 75w20 5:01:20
Hawleys 13 226 42N10 75w08 5:00:32
Hawleyton 4 151 42N05 75w54 5:03:36
Hawthorne 60 6 41N07 73w48 4:55:12
Hawthorne Hill 47 6 42N47 73w53 4:55:32
Hawthorne Park 7
225 42N19 79w34 5:18:16
Hawversville 48 226 42N36 74w20 4:57:20
Haydenville 5 226 42N05 78w26 5:13:44
Hayground 52 11 40N55 72w21 4:49:24
Hayt Corners 50 12 42N41 76w47 5:07:08
Hazel 53 75 41N54 74w50 4:59:20
Head of the Harbor 52
11 40N54 73w10 4:52:40
Heathcote 60 1 40N59 73w48 4:55:12
Heatherwood North 52
11 40N56 73w06 4:52:24
Heatherwood South 52
11 40N52 74w49 4:59:16
Heath Grove 34 13 42N55 76w20 5:05:20
Heath Ridge 60 1 40N59 73w48 4:55:12
Hebron 58 226 43N17 73w32 4:54:08
Hecla 33 11 43N07 75w24 5:01:36
Hector 49 226 42N28 76w47 5:07:08
Hedgesville 51 13 42N06 77w14 5:08:56
Helena 45 226 44N55 74w44 4:58:56
Hell Gate 31 1 40N48 73w57 4:55:48
Hemlock 26 226 42N48 77w36 5:10:24
Hempstead 30 6 40N43 73w38 4:54:32
Hempstead Gardens 30
6 40N42 73w39 4:54:36
Hemstreet Park 42 1 42N54 73w41 4:54:44
Henderson 23 65 43N51 76w10 5:04:40
Henderson Harbor 23
65 43N52 76w12 5:04:48
Hendy Creek 8 13 42N02 76w52 5:07:28
Henrietta 28 20 43N04 77w37 5:10:28
Hensonville 20 52 42N17 74w13 4:56:52
Herkimer 22 183 43N02 74w59 4:59:56
Hermitage 51 14 42N20 77w19 5:09:16
Hermitage 61 24 42N38 78w08 5:12:32
Hermon 45 226 44N28 75w14 5:00:56
Herrick Grove 23
226 44N04 76w08 5:04:32
Herricks 30 11 40N45 73w40 4:54:40
Herrings 23 119 44N01 75w40 5:02:40
Hertel 15 226 43N27 78w43 5:14:52
Herthum Heights 33
222 43N07 75w18 5:01:12
Hessville 29 62 42N56 74w37 4:58:28
Heuvelton 45 226 44N37 75w25 5:01:40
Hewittville 45 207 44N45 74w59 4:59:56
Hewlett 30 1 40N39 73w42 4:54:48
Hewlett Bay Park 30
1 40N38 73w42 4:54:48
Hewlett Harbor 30
11 40N39 73w42 4:54:48
Hewlett Neck 30 1 40N38 73w43 4:54:52
Hickeys Corners 46
226 43N05 73w47 4:55:08
Hickory Bush 56 11 41N57 74w00 4:56:00
Hickory Grove 38
204 43N27 76w30 5:06:00
Hicks 8 226 42N07 76w33 5:06:12
Hicksville 30 11 40N46 73w32 4:54:08
Higgins 2 226 42N29 78w20 5:13:20
Higgins Bay 21 226 43N28 74w25 4:57:40
Higginsville 33 13 43N07 75w40 5:02:40
High Bank 10 136 44N39 73w45 4:55:00
High Bridge 3 1 40N50 73w52 4:55:28
High Bridge 34 13 43N02 76w01 5:04:04
High Falls 56 11 41N50 74w08 4:56:32
High Flats 45 226 44N33 74w56 4:59:44
Highland 56 51 41N43 73w58 4:55:52
Highland Falls 36 1 41N22 73w58 4:55:52
Highland Lake 53 25 41N32 74w51 4:59:24
Highland Mills 36
226 41N21 74w08 4:56:32
Highland-on-the-Lake 15
11 42N41 78w58 5:15:52
Highland Park 32
226 43N09 78w35 5:14:20
Highlands 36 1 41N22 73w59 4:55:56
Highlawn 24 1 40N36 73w58 4:55:52
High Market 25 226 44N05 75w27 5:01:48
High Mills 47 226 42N55 73w54 4:55:36
Highmount 56 42 42N09 74w29 4:57:56
High View 53 11 41N33 74w26 4:57:44
High Woods 56 215 42N04 73w57 4:55:48
Hiler 15 1 42N58 78w51 5:15:24
Hillburn 44 4 41N08 74w10 4:56:40
Hillcrest 2 226 42N23 78w09 5:12:36
Hillcrest 4 151 42N08 75w53 5:03:32
Hillcrest 44 4 41N08 74w02 4:56:08
Hillis 14 11 41N38 73w54 4:55:36
Hillsboro 33 14 43N20 75w45 5:03:00
Hillsdale 11 11 42N11 73w32 4:54:08
Hillside 3 1 40N52 73w51 4:55:24
Hillside Heights 30
11 40N45 73w41 4:54:44
Hillside Lake 14 6 41N36 73w53 4:55:32
Hillside Manor 30
11 40N45 73w40 4:54:40
Hillside Park 18 43 43N00 74w22 4:57:28
Hillview 42 1 42N39 73w43 4:54:52
Hilton 28 13 43N17 77w48 5:11:12

Himrod 62 12 42N35 76w57 5:07:48
Hinckley 33 20 43N19 75w07 5:00:28
Hinckleyville 28 14 43N12 77w48 5:11:12
Hindsburg 37 146 43N15 78w12 5:12:48
Hinmans Corners 4
151 42N07 75w56 5:03:44
Hinmansville 38 93 43N14 76w18 5:05:12
Hinsdale 5 20 42N10 78w24 5:13:36
Hinsdale 34 41 43N06 76w08 5:04:32
Hoag Corners 42 11 42N30 73w30 4:54:00
Hobart 13 25 42N22 74w40 4:58:40
Hoboken 39 226 42N38 75w20 5:01:20
Hoffman 32 1 43N04 78w49 5:15:16
Hoffmans 47 94 42N54 74w05 4:56:20
Hoffmeister 21 226 43N23 74w43 4:58:52
Hogansburg 17 226 44N59 74w40 4:58:40
Hogtown 58 123 43N25 73w29 4:53:56
Holbrook 52 11 40N49 73w05 4:52:20
Holbrook-Holtsville 52
11 40N49 73w04 4:52:16
Holcomb 35 47 42N54 77w25 5:09:40
Holcombville 57 49 43N42 73w59 4:55:56
Holiday Manor 35 41 42N52 76w59 5:07:56
Holland 15 22 42N39 78w33 5:14:12
Holland Cove 59 89 43N13 77w12 5:08:48
Holland Patent 33
14 43N15 75w15 5:01:00
Holley 37 117 43N14 78w02 5:12:08
Hollis 41 1 40N43 73w46 4:55:04
Hollis Court 41 1 40N42 73w44 4:54:56
Holliswood 41 1 40N43 73w50 4:55:20
Hollowville 11 11 42N12 73w42 4:54:48
Hollywood 45 87 44N14 74w36 4:58:24
Holmes 14 7 41N31 73w39 4:54:36
Holmesville 9 226 42N31 75w24 5:01:36
Holton Beach 50 226 42N37 77w33 5:10:12
Holtsville 52 11 40N49 73w03 4:52:12
Homecrest 24 1 40N36 73w57 4:55:48
Homer 12 41 42N38 76w11 5:04:44
Homer Hill 5 226 42N05 78w26 5:13:44
Homewood 34 13 43N02 76w01 5:04:04
Homewood Park 15 7 42N55 78w46 5:15:04
Honeoye 35 47 42N48 77w31 5:10:04
Honeoye Falls 28
226 42N57 77w36 5:10:24
Honest Hill 37 226 43N13 78w02 5:12:08
Honeywell Corners 18
226 43N03 74w12 4:56:48
Honk Hill 56 48 41N44 74w22 4:57:28
Honnedaga Lake 33
226 43N27 75w12 5:00:48
Hoopers Valley 54
226 42N01 76w22 5:05:28
Hoosick 42 11 42N53 73w21 4:53:24
Hoosick Falls 42 11 42N54 73w21 4:53:24
Hope 21 226 43N18 74w13 4:56:52
Hope Falls 21 7 43N13 74w10 4:56:40
Hope Farm 14 226 41N44 73w40 4:54:40
Hope Valley 21 7 43N13 74w10 4:56:40
Hopewell 35 14 42N54 77w11 5:08:44
Hopewell Junction 14
226 41N36 73w47 4:55:08
Hopkinton 45 226 44N39 74w44 4:58:56
Horace Harding 41 1 40N45 73w44 4:54:56
Horicon 57 226 43N15 73w44 4:54:56
Hornby 51 226 42N14 77w02 5:08:08
Hornell 51 102 42N20 77w40 5:10:40
Hornellsville 51
102 42N20 77w40 5:10:40
Horseheads 8 13 42N10 76w49 5:07:16
Horton 13 80 41N56 74w55 4:59:40
Horton Estates 60
16 41N20 73w44 4:54:56
Hortonville 53 226 41N46 75w02 5:00:08
Houghton 2 226 42N25 78w10 5:12:40
Hounsfield 23 12 43N57 76w02 5:04:08
Houseville 25 156 44N04 75w35 5:02:20
Housons Corners 48
226 42N36 74w20 4:57:20
Howard 31 1 40N43 74w00 4:56:00
Howard 51 226 42N20 77w31 5:10:04
Howard Beach 41 1 40N40 73w51 4:55:24
Howardville 38 25 43N31 76w00 5:04:00
Howells 36 4 41N29 74w28 4:57:52
Howes Cave 48 12 42N41 74w23 4:57:32
Howlett Hill 34 12 43N03 76w15 5:05:00
Hub 3 1 40N50 73w54 4:55:36
Hubbardsville 27
130 42N49 75w28 5:01:52
Hubbardtown 54 154 42N14 76w20 5:05:20
Hudson 11 1 42N15 73w46 4:55:04
Hudson Falls 58 1 43N18 73w35 4:54:20
Hudson Upper 11 1 42N15 73w47 4:55:08
Hughsonville 14 6 41N35 73w56 4:55:44
Huguenot 36 1 41N25 74w38 4:58:32
Huguenot 43 1 40N38 74w06 4:56:24
Hulberton 37 105 43N15 78w04 5:12:16
Huletts Landing 58
226 43N38 73w31 4:54:04
Hullsville 54 205 42N06 76w16 5:05:04
Humaston 33 211 43N15 75w27 5:01:48
Hume 2 226 42N29 78w08 5:12:32
Humphrey 5 226 42N13 78w31 5:14:04
Humphrey Center 5
226 42N13 78w38 5:14:32
Hunt 26 20 42N33 77w59 5:11:56
Hunter 20 52 42N13 74w13 4:56:52
Hunter Lake 53 53 41N52 74w46 4:59:04
Huntersland 48 226 42N36 74w20 4:57:20
Hunt Hollow 35 226 42N37 77w24 5:09:36
Huntington 52 6 40N52 73w26 4:53:44
Huntington Bay 52
11 40N54 73w24 4:53:36
Huntington Beach 52
11 40N53 73w22 4:53:28
Huntington Station 52
6 40N51 73w25 4:53:40

Huntingtonville 23
45 43N59 75w56 5:03:44
Hunts Corners 12 13 42N27 76w02 5:04:08
Hunts Corners 15 38 42N59 78w35 5:14:20
Hunts Corners 53
226 41N36 75w04 5:00:16
Hurd Corners 14 7 41N34 73w36 4:54:24
Hurley 56 11 41N49 74w06 4:56:24
Hurleyville 53 74 41N44 74w40 4:58:40
Huron 59 226 43N15 76w53 5:07:32
Hyde Park 14 11 41N48 73w54 4:55:36
Hyde Park 39 13 42N42 74w55 4:59:40
Hyndsville 48 139 42N41 74w29 4:57:56
Idle Hour 52 11 40N44 73w08 4:52:32
Idlewood 15 153 42N43 78w56 5:15:44
Ilion 22 184 43N01 75w02 5:00:08
Independence 2 226 42N03 77w47 5:11:08
Index 39 13 42N42 74w55 4:59:40
Indian Castle 22 61 43N03 74w51 4:59:24
Indian Cove 6 13 42N43 76w25 5:05:40
Indian Falls 19 164 42N58 78w24 5:13:36
Indian Kettles 57
226 43N45 73w30 4:54:00
Indian Lake 21 226 43N47 74w16 4:57:04
Indian Park 36 226 41N13 74w17 4:57:08
Indian River 25 226 43N48 75w36 5:02:24
Indian Springs 34
226 43N09 76w20 5:05:20
Indian Village 34
13 42N59 76w09 5:04:36
Ingham Mills 18 61 43N03 74w51 4:59:24
Ingleside 51 226 42N37 77w24 5:09:36
Ingraham 10 226 44N49 73w31 4:54:04
Ings 46 226 43N05 73w47 4:55:08
Inlet 21 226 43N45 74w48 4:59:12
Inman 17 113 44N30 74w07 4:56:28
Interlaken 50 13 42N37 76w44 5:06:56
Interlaken Beach 50
226 42N37 77w33 5:10:12
International Junction 15
1 42N58 78w51 5:15:24
Invale 2 226 42N12 78w08 5:12:32
Inwood 30 11 40N37 73w45 4:55:00
Ionia 35 226 42N56 77w30 5:10:00
Ira 6 226 43N13 76w32 5:06:08
Ireland Corners 56
122 41N41 74w09 4:56:36
Irelandville 49 14 42N23 76w53 5:07:32
Irish Settlement 45
226 44N33 74w56 4:59:44
Irona 10 16 44N53 73w39 4:54:36
Irondequoit 28 185 43N13 77w35 5:10:20
Irondequoit Manor 28
185 43N13 77w36 5:10:24
Irongate 34 13 43N07 76w12 5:04:48
Ironville 16 138 43N57 73w25 4:53:40
Irving 7 216 42N34 79w07 5:16:28
Irvington 60 1 41N02 73w52 4:55:28
Ischua 5 22 42N13 78w24 5:13:36
Island Cottage Beach 28
226 43N15 77w38 5:10:32
Island Park 30 11 40N36 73w39 4:54:36
Islip 52 6 40N44 73w13 4:52:52
Islip Manor 52 6 40N44 73w13 4:52:52
Islip Terrace 52 6 40N45 73w12 4:52:48
Italy 62 226 42N37 77w18 5:09:12
Itaska 4 20 42N20 75w58 5:03:52
Ithaca 55 186 42N27 76w30 5:06:00
Ithaca Junction 6
13 42N56 76w33 5:06:12
Ivanhoe 13 13 42N17 75w16 5:01:04
Ivory 7 128 42N03 79w09 5:16:36
Jackson 58 226 43N04 73w24 4:53:36
Jacksonburg 22 196 43N00 75w00 5:00:00
Jackson Corners 14
7 42N00 73w53 4:55:32
Jackson Heights 41
1 40N45 73w53 4:55:32
Jackson Summit 18
226 43N06 74w16 4:57:04
Jacksonville 34 93 43N14 76w18 5:05:12
Jacksonville 55 13 42N31 76w37 5:06:28
Jacks Reef 34 41 43N05 76w23 5:05:32
Jamaica 41 1 40N43 73w47 4:55:08
Jamesport 52 11 40N57 72w35 4:50:20
Jamestown 7 187 42N06 79w14 5:16:56
Jamestown West 7
187 42N05 79w17 5:17:08
Jamesville 34 13 43N00 76w04 5:04:16
Janesville 48 139 42N41 74w29 4:57:56
Jasper 51 226 42N08 77w30 5:10:00
Java 61 226 42N39 78w23 5:13:32
Java Lake 61 147 42N32 78w26 5:13:44
Java Village 61 226 42N40 78w26 5:13:44
Jay 16 44 44N23 73w43 4:54:52
Jeddo 37 112 43N13 78w23 5:13:32
Jefferson 20 226 42N13 73w51 4:55:24
Jefferson 48 226 42N29 74w37 4:58:28
Jefferson Mall 28
226 43N05 77w38 5:10:32
Jefferson Park 23
13 42N45 77w50 5:11:20
Jefferson Plaza 19
142 43N00 78w11 5:12:44
Jefferson Valley 60
16 41N19 73w45 4:55:00
Jeffersonville 53
226 41N47 74w56 4:59:44
Jenksville 54 226 42N18 76w11 5:04:44
Jericho 10 16 44N53 73w39 4:54:36
Jericho 30 7 40N48 73w32 4:54:08
Jericho 52 11 40N57 72w11 4:48:44
Jersey Colony 52 11 41N04 72w26 4:49:44
Jerusalem 62 226 42N37 77w08 5:08:32
Jerusalem Corners 15
11 42N41 78w58 5:15:52
Jewell 33 15 43N14 75w54 5:03:36

Place		Lat	Long	Time
Jewel Manor 34	13	43N07	76w12	5:04:48
Jewett 20	52	42N15	74w15	4:57:00
Jewettville 15	11	42N44	78w41	5:14:44
Jewettville 23	49	44N00	76w03	5:04:12
John F. Kennedy Internationa 41	1	40N40	73w47	4:55:08
Johnsburg 57	11	42N56	74w01	4:56:04
Johnson 36	11	41N22	74w30	4:58:00
Johnsonburg 61	226	42N46	78w19	5:13:16
Johnson City 4	116	42N07	75w58	5:03:52
Johnson Creek 32	121	43N11	79w02	5:16:08
Johnsonville 42	11	42N55	73w31	4:54:04
Johnstown 18	43	43N00	74w22	4:57:28
Jones Point 44	11	41N17	73w58	4:55:52
Jonesville 46	11	42N51	73w48	4:55:12
Jordan 34	24	43N04	76w29	5:05:56
Jordanville 22	226	42N55	74w57	4:59:48
Junction Boulevard 41	1	40N45	73w53	4:55:32
Junius 50	4	42N59	77w11	5:08:44
Kabob 7	67	42N16	79w15	5:17:00
Kaisertown 36	11	41N31	74w14	4:56:56
Kanona 51	14	42N22	77w22	5:09:28
Kasoag 38	25	43N31	76w00	5:04:00
Katonah 60	1	41N16	73w41	4:54:44
Kattelville 4	151	42N08	75w53	5:03:32
Kattskill Bay 57	226	43N29	73w38	4:54:32
Kauneonga Lake 53	226	41N41	74w50	4:59:20
Kaydeross Park 46	226	43N05	73w47	4:55:08
Kayuta Lake 33	226	43N27	75w12	5:00:48
Kecks Center 18	43	43N00	74w22	4:57:28
Keefers Corners 1	11	42N35	73w53	4:55:32
Keene 16	226	44N14	73w48	4:55:12
Keene Valley 16	226	44N11	73w46	4:55:04
Keeseville 16	20	44N30	73w29	4:53:56
Kelleys 47	226	42N46	74w08	4:56:32
Kelloggsville 6	13	42N43	76w25	5:05:40
Kelly Corners 13	42	42N11	74w36	4:58:24
Kelsey 13	97	41N57	75w17	5:01:08
Kendaia 50	12	42N45	76w50	5:07:20
Kendall 37	105	43N20	78w02	5:12:08
Kendall Mills 28	226	43N13	78w02	5:12:08
Kenilworth 15	1	42N58	78w51	5:15:24
Kenilworth 30	1	40N49	73w45	4:55:00
Kenmore 15	1	42N58	78w52	5:15:28
Kennedy 7	20	42N10	79w06	5:16:24
Kennedy Corner 55	186	42N28	76w29	5:05:56
Kenoza Lake 53	226	41N44	74w57	4:59:48
Kensington 15	7	42N56	78w48	5:15:12
Kensington 24	1	40N39	73w59	4:55:56
Kensington 30	1	40N48	73w43	4:54:52
Kent 37	105	43N20	78w08	5:12:32
Kent 40	226	41N28	73w43	4:54:52
Kent Cliffs 40	226	41N27	73w40	4:54:40
Kents Corners 45	226	44N30	75w16	5:01:04
Kenwood 27	60	43N05	75w39	5:02:36
Kenwood Estates 40	226	41N27	73w40	4:54:40
Kenyonville 37	146	43N19	78w15	5:13:00
Kerhonkson 56	72	41N48	74w19	4:57:16
Kerleys Corners 14	7	42N00	73w53	4:55:32
Kernan 33	222	43N06	75w15	5:01:00
Ketchums Corner 46	11	42N57	73w39	4:54:36
Ketchumville 54	226	42N18	76w11	5:04:44
Keuka 51	226	42N29	77w08	5:08:32
Keuka Park 62	226	42N37	77w19	5:09:16
Kew Gardens 41	1	40N42	73w50	4:55:20
Kiamesha Lake 53	74	41N41	74w40	4:58:40
Kiantone 7	128	42N03	79w12	5:16:48
Kidders 50	226	42N37	77w33	5:10:12
Killawog 4	16	42N24	76w01	5:04:04
Kill Buck 5	20	42N10	78w41	5:14:44
Kimball Stand 7	187	42N06	79w16	5:17:04
Kinderhook 11	11	42N26	73w41	4:54:44
King Ferry 6	13	42N40	76w37	5:06:28
Kingsboro 18	226	43N03	74w20	4:57:20
Kings Bridge 3	1	40N53	73w54	4:55:36
Kingsbury 58	226	43N21	73w33	4:54:12
Kings Park 52	11	40N53	73w16	4:53:04
Kings Point 30	1	40N49	73w46	4:55:04
Kings Settlement 9	200	42N32	75w31	5:02:04
Kings Station 46	226	43N12	73w39	4:54:36
Kingston 56	11	41N56	73w59	4:55:56
Kingsway 24	1	40N36	73w57	4:55:48
Kipps 36	7	41N24	74w20	4:57:20
Kirk 9	226	42N35	75w34	5:02:16
Kirkland 33	11	43N03	75w22	5:01:28
Kirkville 34	226	43N00	75w59	5:03:56
Kirkwood 4	20	42N05	75w48	5:03:12
Kirschnerville 25	226	43N48	75w36	5:02:24
Kisco Park 60	6	41N11	73w44	4:54:56
Kiskatom 20	226	42N13	73w51	4:55:24
Kismet 52	11	40N38	73w13	4:52:52
Kitchawan 60	7	41N13	73w47	4:55:08
Knapp Creek 5	226	42N00	78w30	5:14:00
Knickerbocker 31	1	40N43	73w59	4:55:56
Knights Creek 2	109	42N10	77w59	5:11:56
Knights Eddy 53	1	41N23	74w43	4:58:52
Knowelhurst 57	226	43N25	73w56	4:55:44
Knowlesville 37	115	43N14	78w19	5:13:16
Knowsville 23	45	43N59	75w56	5:03:44
Knox 1	40	42N41	74w07	4:56:28
Knoxboro 33	13	43N00	75w36	5:02:24
Koenig's Point 6	13	42N56	76w33	5:06:12
Kohlertown 53	25	41N32	74w51	4:59:24
Komar Park 46	11	42N55	73w49	4:55:16
Kortright 13	226	42N24	74w47	4:59:08
Kossuth 2	226	42N04	78w10	5:12:40
Kringsbush 18	226	43N00	74w41	4:58:44
Kripplebush 56	11	41N51	74w09	4:56:36
Krumville 56	76	41N53	74w15	4:57:00
Kuckville 37	146	43N19	78w15	5:13:00
Kyserike 56	11	41N50	74w08	4:56:32
Lackawanna 15	153	42N50	78w50	5:15:20
Lacona 38	14	43N39	76w04	5:04:16
Ladentown 44	4	41N11	74w04	4:56:16
Ladleton 56	226	41N55	74w34	4:58:16
LaFargeville 23	226	44N12	75w58	5:03:52
La Fayette 34	20	42N55	76w06	5:04:24
Lafayetteville 14	7	42N00	73w53	4:55:32
La Grange 14	226	41N40	73w49	4:55:16
Lagrange 61	226	42N53	78w01	5:12:04
Lagrangeville 14	226	41N39	73w46	4:55:04
La Guardia Airport 41	1	40N43	73w50	4:55:20
Lairdsville 33	11	43N04	75w20	5:01:20
Lake 36	226	41N18	74w18	4:57:12
Lake Bluff 59	226	43N13	76w49	5:07:16
Lake Bonaparte 25	226	43N32	75w40	5:02:40
Lake Carmel 40	135	41N28	73w40	4:54:40
Lake Charles 40	7	41N31	73w36	4:54:24
Lake Clear 17	176	44N22	74w14	4:56:56
Lake Colby 17	81	44N20	74w08	4:56:32
Lake Como 6	41	42N35	76w12	5:04:48
Lake Delaware 13	226	42N17	74w55	4:59:40
Lake Delta 33	211	43N13	75w26	5:01:44
Lake Erie Beach 15	11	42N38	79w05	5:16:20
Lake Gardens 40	17	41N22	73w44	4:54:56
Lake George 57	1	43N26	73w43	4:54:52
Lake Grove 52	11	40N52	73w08	4:52:32
Lake Hill 56	11	42N04	74w11	4:56:44
Lake Huntington 53	226	41N41	75w00	5:00:00
Lakehurst 60	1	41N04	73w46	4:55:04
Lake Katonah 60	1	41N16	73w41	4:54:44
Lake Katrine 56	114	41N59	74w00	4:56:00
Lake Kitchawan 60	16	41N17	73w33	4:54:12
Lakeland 34	13	43N04	76w14	5:04:56
Lakeland 52	11	40N49	73w06	4:52:24
Lake Lincolndale 60	16	41N22	73w44	4:54:56
Lake Lucille 44	4	41N09	74w00	4:56:00
Lake Luzerne 57	40	43N19	73w50	4:55:20
Lake Mahopac 40	17	41N22	73w44	4:54:56
Lake Minnewaska 56	11	41N45	74w05	4:56:20
Lakemont 62	13	42N31	76w56	5:07:44
Lake Moraine 27	180	42N49	75w33	5:02:12
Lake Osceola 60	16	41N19	73w45	4:55:00
Lake Osiris Colony 36	11	41N34	74w11	4:56:44
Lake Panamoka 52	11	40N54	72w53	4:51:32
Lake Peekskill 40	6	41N21	73w52	4:55:28
Lake Placid 16	1	44N17	73w59	4:55:56
Lake Pleasant 21	226	43N28	74w25	4:57:40
Lakeport 27	226	43N03	75w53	5:03:32
Lake Purdy 60	16	41N20	73w40	4:54:40
Lake Ronkonkoma 52	11	40N50	73w06	4:52:24
Lake Ronkonkoma Heights 52	11	40N49	73w06	4:52:24
Lake Secor 40	17	41N22	73w44	4:54:56
Lakeside 36	226	41N21	74w08	4:56:32
Lakeside 59	226	43N13	77w17	5:09:08
Lakeside Park 1	11	42N42	73w48	4:55:12
Lakeside Park 37	146	43N19	78w15	5:13:00
Lake Station 36	6	41N17	74w20	4:57:20
Lake Success 30	1	40N46	73w43	4:54:52
Lake Sunnyside 41	1	40N47	73w47	4:55:08
Lake Vanare 57	40	43N19	73w50	4:55:20
Lake View 15	153	42N43	78w56	5:15:44
Lakeview 30	11	40N42	73w39	4:54:36
Lakeview 38	204	43N27	76w30	5:06:00
Lakeville 26	20	42N50	77w42	5:10:48
Lakeville 30	11	40N45	73w41	4:54:44
Lakeville Estates 30	11	40N45	73w41	4:54:44
Lakewood 7	20	42N06	79w19	5:17:16
Lamberton 7	14	42N27	79w20	5:17:20
Lambs Corners 1	226	42N25	74w01	4:56:04
Lamont 61	24	42N38	78w03	5:12:12
Lamont Circle 12	41	42N35	76w12	5:04:48
Lamson 34	93	43N14	76w18	5:05:12
Lancaster 15	7	42N54	78w40	5:14:40
Lanesville 20	52	42N08	74w16	4:57:04
Langdon 4	20	42N05	75w48	5:03:12
Langdon Corners 45	155	44N36	75w10	5:00:40
Langford 15	153	42N39	78w54	5:15:36
Lansing 38	204	43N27	76w30	5:06:00
Lansing 55	13	42N33	76w31	5:06:04
Lansingburg 42	11	42N47	73w39	4:54:36
Laona 7	14	42N27	79w20	5:17:20
Lapala 56	11	41N57	74w00	4:56:00
Lapeer 12	13	42N27	76w07	5:04:28
Laphams Mills 10	86	44N35	73w32	4:54:08
Larchmont 60	1	40N56	73w45	4:55:00
Larchmont Manor 60	1	40N57	73w45	4:55:00
La Salle 32	199	43N06	78w58	5:15:52
Lassellsville 18	226	43N00	74w41	4:58:44
Latham 1	1	42N44	73w45	4:55:00
Lathams Corners 9	226	42N32	75w23	5:01:32
Lattingtown 30	11	40N54	73w36	4:54:24
Lattintown 56	6	41N36	73w58	4:55:52
Laughing Waters 52	11	41N04	72w26	4:49:44
Laurel 52	11	40N58	72w34	4:50:16
Laurel Hollow 30	11	40N52	73w29	4:53:56
Laurelton 28	185	43N13	77w36	5:10:24
Laurelton 41	1	40N43	73w50	4:55:20
Laurens 39	226	42N32	75w06	5:00:24
Lava 53	226	41N36	75w04	5:00:16
Lawrence 30	1	40N37	73w44	4:54:56
Lawrence Beach 30	1	40N37	73w44	4:54:56
Lawrence Farms 60	1	41N10	73w46	4:55:04
Lawrenceville 45	16	44N47	74w39	4:58:36
Lawrenceville 56	11	41N50	74w05	4:56:20
Lawtons 15	42	42N32	78w56	5:15:44
Lawyersville 48	13	42N42	74w30	4:58:00
Lebanon 27	13	42N47	75w37	5:02:28
Lebanon Springs 11	11	42N29	73w23	4:53:32
Ledgewood Park 20	226	42N10	74w01	4:56:04
Ledyard 6	13	42N45	76w40	5:06:40
Lee 33	226	43N19	75w30	5:02:00
Leeds 20	11	42N15	73w54	4:55:36
Leedsville 14	11	41N51	73w33	4:54:12
Leeside 40	226	41N27	73w40	4:54:40
Leesville 48	11	42N48	74w37	4:58:28
Lefferts 24	1	40N40	73w57	4:55:48
Leibhardt 56	76	41N48	74w13	4:56:52
Leicester 26	13	42N46	77w53	5:11:32
Lenox 27	226	43N07	75w46	5:03:04
Lenox Furnace 27	226	43N05	75w45	5:03:00
Lenox Hill 31	1	40N46	73w58	4:55:52
Lenox Park 35	41	42N52	76w59	5:07:56
Leon 5	226	42N19	79w00	5:16:00
Leonardsville 27	226	42N49	75w15	5:01:00
Leonta 13	104	42N21	75w10	5:00:40
Le Ray 23	226	44N04	75w47	5:03:08
Le Roy 19	70	42N59	78w00	5:12:00
Le Roy Island 59	226	43N13	76w49	5:07:16
Levanna 6	13	42N45	76w42	5:06:48
Levant 7	187	42N07	79w12	5:16:48
Levittown 30	11	40N44	73w31	4:54:04
Lewbeach 53	226	42N00	74w47	4:59:08
Lewis 16	50	44N16	73w34	4:54:16
Lewisboro 60	16	41N16	73w33	4:54:12
Lewiston 32	121	43N11	79w03	5:16:12
Lewiston Heights 32	199	43N09	79w00	5:16:00
Lewiston Manor 34	13	43N02	76w06	5:04:24
Lexington 20	226	42N13	74w23	4:57:32
Leyden 25	77	44N10	75w38	5:02:32
Liberty 53	189	41N48	74w45	4:59:00
Liberty Gardens 33	211	43N13	75w26	5:01:44
Libertypole 26	13	42N34	77w42	5:10:48
Lido Beach 30	11	40N35	73w38	4:54:32
Lily Dale 7	173	42N21	79w19	5:17:16
Lima 26	226	42N55	77w37	5:10:28
Lime Lake 5	22	42N30	78w29	5:13:56
Limerick 23	49	44N02	76w03	5:04:12
Lime Rock 19	70	42N59	77w59	5:11:56
Limestone 5	20	42N02	78w38	5:14:32
Limestreet 20	226	42N13	73w51	4:55:24
Lincklaen 9	226	42N41	75w50	5:03:20
Lincoln 27	226	43N02	75w44	5:02:56
Lincoln 59	226	43N04	77w18	5:09:12
Lincolndale 60	16	41N19	73w43	4:54:52
Lincoln Park 15	1	42N58	78w51	5:15:24
Lincoln Park 56	11	41N57	74w00	4:56:00
Lincolnton 31	1	40N49	73w56	4:55:44
Lindbergh Court 1	11	42N42	73w48	4:55:12
Linden 19	142	43N00	78w11	5:12:44
Linden Acres 14	7	42N00	73w53	4:55:32
Linden Hill 41	1	40N46	73w49	4:55:16
Lindenhurst 52	9	40N41	73w23	4:53:32
Lindley 51	13	42N01	77w08	5:08:32
Linlithgo 11	11	42N08	73w54	4:55:36
Linwood 26	70	42N54	77w57	5:11:48
Lisbon 45	16	44N44	75w19	5:01:16
Lisle 4	16	42N22	76w03	5:04:12
Litchfield 22	226	42N58	75w09	5:00:36
Lithgow 14	226	41N47	73w41	4:54:44
Little America 38	226	43N34	76w03	5:04:12
Little Bow 45	178	44N20	75w28	5:01:52
Little Britain 36	11	41N28	74w11	4:56:44
Little Canada 19	142	43N00	78w11	5:12:44
Little Falls 14	6	41N36	73w53	4:55:32
Little Falls 22	61	43N03	74w51	4:59:24
Little France 38	182	43N17	76w09	5:04:36
Little Genesee 2	226	42N02	78w13	5:12:52
Little Neck 41	1	40N46	73w45	4:55:00
Little Plains 52	11	40N51	73w20	4:53:20
Little Utica 34	93	43N14	76w18	5:05:12
Little Valley 5	20	42N15	78w48	5:15:12
Littleville 35	14	42N53	77w17	5:09:08
Little York 12	16	42N42	76w10	5:04:40
Little York 36	11	41N18	74w28	4:57:52
Liverpool 34	13	43N06	76w13	5:04:52
Livingston 11	12	42N08	73w47	4:55:08
Livingston Manor	75	41N54	74w50	4:59:20
Livingstonville 48	226	42N36	74w20	4:57:20
Livonia 26	20	42N49	77w40	5:10:40

Livonia Center 26 20 42N49 77w38 5:10:32
Lloyd 56 51 41N43 73w59 4:55:56
Lloyd Harbor 52 11 40N55 73w28 4:53:52
Lochada Lake 53 226 41N29 74w55 4:59:40
Loch Muller 16 49 43N46 73w56 4:55:44
Loch Sheldrake 53 74 41N46 74w39 4:58:36
Lock Berlin 59 99 43N04 76w59 5:07:56
Locke 6 13 42N40 76w26 5:05:44
Lockport 32 190 43N10 78w42 5:14:48
Locksley Park 15 153 42N45 78w51 5:15:24
Lockwood 54 226 42N07 76w33 5:06:12
Locust Grove 25 226 43N29 75w20 5:01:20
Locust Grove 30 7 40N48 73w30 4:54:00
Locust Manor 41 1 40N43 73w50 4:55:20
Locust Point 3 1 40N49 73w49 4:55:16
Locust Valley 30 7 40N53 73w35 4:54:20
Locustwood 30 11 40N42 73w42 4:54:48
Lodi 50 226 42N36 77w22 5:09:28
Lodi Center 50 226 42N37 77w21 5:09:24
Lodi Point 50 226 42N37 77w21 5:09:24
Logan 49 14 42N25 76w51 5:07:24
Logtown 36 1 41N23 74w41 4:58:44
Lombard 7 226 42N16 79w43 5:18:52
Lomond Shore 37 105 43N20 78w02 5:12:08
Lomontville 56 11 41N57 74w00 4:56:00
London Terrace 31 1 40N45 74w00 4:56:00
Lonelyville 52 11 40N38 73w11 4:52:44
Long Beach 30 1 40N35 73w39 4:54:36
Long Branch 34 13 43N07 76w12 5:04:48
Long Branch Manor 34 13 43N07 76w12 5:04:48
Long Bridge 34 24 43N00 76w27 5:05:48
Long Eddy 53 20 41N51 75w08 5:00:32
Long Island 11 40N50 73w00 4:52:00
Long Island City 41 1 40N45 73w56 4:55:44
Long Lake 21 34 43N58 74w25 4:57:40
Long View 7 226 42N06 79w23 5:17:32
Longwood 3 1 40N49 73w54 4:55:36
Loomis 53 189 41N48 74w45 4:59:00
Loomises 7 226 42N06 79w23 5:17:32
Loon Lake 17 113 44N33 74w03 4:56:12
Loon Lake Junction 17 113 44N30 74w07 4:56:28
Lordville 13 97 41N57 75w17 5:01:08
Lorenz Park 11 1 42N15 73w46 4:55:04
Lorings 12 41 42N35 76w12 5:04:48
Lorraine 23 143 43N45 75w58 5:03:52
Lost Valley 29 1 42N57 74w11 4:56:44
Loudonville 1 1 42N43 73w46 4:55:04
Louisville 45 226 44N54 75w01 5:00:04
Lounsberry 54 226 42N01 76w22 5:05:28
Lower Chateaugay Lake 17 188 44N56 74w05 4:56:20
Lower Cincinnatus 12 226 42N33 75w54 5:03:36
Lower Genegantslet Corner 9 226 42N20 75w46 5:03:04
Lower Oswegatchie 45 25 44N11 75w04 5:00:16
Lower Rotterdam 47 1 42N48 73w58 4:55:52
Lower South Bay 34 13 43N09 76w13 5:04:52
Low Hampton 58 226 43N36 73w16 4:53:04
Lowman 8 13 42N02 76w44 5:06:56
Lowville 25 191 43N47 75w29 5:01:56
Ludingtonville 40 7 41N31 73w39 4:54:36
Ludlowville 55 13 42N33 76w32 5:06:08
Lumberland 53 25 41N29 74w49 4:59:16
Luna Park 24 1 40N35 73w59 4:55:56
Luther 42 1 42N37 73w43 4:54:52
Lutheranville 48 226 42N37 74w40 4:58:40
Lycoming 38 15 43N30 76w23 5:05:32
Lyell 28 209 43N10 77w40 5:10:40
Lykers 29 7 42N53 74w31 4:58:04
Lyme 23 226 44N04 76w12 5:04:48
Lynbrook 30 7 40N40 73w40 4:54:40
Lyncourt 34 41 43N04 76w09 5:04:36
Lyndon 5 226 42N18 78w21 5:13:24
Lyndon 34 13 43N02 76w01 5:04:04
Lyndonville 37 15 43N20 78w23 5:13:32
Lynelle Meadows 34 13 43N07 76w12 5:04:48
Lynwood Estates 1 6 42N46 73w56 4:55:44
Lyon Mountain 10 192 44N43 73w55 4:55:40
Lyons 59 99 43N04 77w00 5:08:00
Lyonsdale 25 119 44N05 75w45 5:03:00
Lyons Falls 25 106 43N37 75w22 5:01:28
Lyonsville 56 76 41N48 74w13 4:56:52
Lysander 34 226 43N10 76w21 5:05:24
Mabbettsville 14 226 41N47 73w41 4:54:44
MacDonnell Heights 14 1 41N40 73w54 4:55:36
MacDougall 50 226 42N48 76w53 5:07:32
Macedon 59 226 43N05 77w19 5:09:16
Macedon Center 59 226 43N04 77w18 5:09:12
Machias 5 22 42N25 78w30 5:14:00
Mackey 48 226 42N24 74w27 4:57:48
Macomb 45 20 44N27 75w34 5:02:16
Madison 27 180 42N53 75w31 5:02:04
Madison Center 27 15 43N14 75w54 5:03:36
Madison Park 52 11 40N51 73w20 4:53:20
Madison Square 31 1 40N45 73w59 4:55:56
Madrid 45 132 44N45 75w08 5:00:32
Madrid Springs 45 226 44N45 75w08 5:00:32
Magnolia 7 158 42N15 79w30 5:18:00
Mahopac 40 17 41N22 73w44 4:54:56
Mahopac Falls 40 17 41N22 73w46 4:55:04
Mahopac Hills 40 17 41N22 73w44 4:54:56
Mahopac Point 40 17 41N22 73w44 4:54:56
Mahopac Ridge 40 17 41N22 73w44 4:54:56
Maidstone Park 52 11 40N57 72w11 4:48:44
Maine 4 226 42N11 76w02 5:04:08
Main-Mill 15 7 42N59 78w45 5:15:00
Main Settlement 5 226 42N02 78w20 5:13:20
Malden Bridge 11 10 42N28 73w35 4:54:20
Malden on Hudson 56 215 42N06 73w56 4:55:44
Mallory 38 182 43N19 76w07 5:04:28
Malone 17 193 44N51 74w18 4:57:12
Malta 46 11 42N59 73w48 4:55:12
Malta Ridge 46 11 43N01 73w51 4:55:24
Maltaville 46 11 43N01 73w51 4:55:24
Maltbie Heights 5 42 42N28 78w56 5:15:44
Malverne 30 194 40N41 73w40 4:54:40
Malvic Manor 34 13 43N07 76w12 5:04:48
Mamakating 53 11 41N35 74w29 4:57:56
Mamakating Park 53 11 41N34 74w29 4:57:56
Mamaroneck 60 1 40N57 73w44 4:54:56
Manchester 35 4 42N59 77w11 5:08:44
Manchester Bridge 14 1 41N40 73w54 4:55:36
Mandana 34 13 42N57 76w25 5:05:40
Manhasset 30 6 40N48 73w42 4:54:48
Manhasset Hills 30 11 40N45 73w41 4:54:44
Manhattan 31 1 40N46 73w59 4:55:56
Manhattanville 31 1 40N49 73w57 4:55:48
Manhattanville College 60 7 41N02 73w43 4:54:52
Manheim 22 168 43N04 74w48 4:59:12
Manitou 40 6 41N23 73w57 4:55:48
Manitou Beach 28 13 43N17 77w47 5:11:08
Manlius 34 13 43N03 76w00 5:04:00
Manning 37 226 43N13 78w02 5:12:08
Mannsville 23 14 43N43 76w04 5:04:16
Mannville 1 1 42N43 73w44 4:54:56
Manny Corners 29 1 42N57 74w11 4:56:44
Manorhaven 30 11 40N51 73w43 4:54:52
Manor Kill 48 226 42N24 74w27 4:57:48
Manorton 11 226 42N03 73w48 4:55:12
Manorville 52 11 40N52 72w48 4:51:12
Manorville 56 215 42N04 73w57 4:55:48
Mansfield 5 226 42N18 78w46 5:15:04
Maple Bay 7 226 42N06 79w23 5:17:32
Maplecrest 20 226 42N17 74w11 4:56:44
Mapledale 56 42 42N09 74w37 4:58:28
Maple Grove 21 7 43N13 74w10 4:56:40
Maple Grove 39 226 42N33 75w15 5:01:00
Maple Hill 56 11 41N57 74w00 4:56:00
Maplehurst 5 226 42N10 78w23 5:13:32
Maples 5 226 42N15 78w48 5:15:12
Maple Springs 7 158 42N12 79w25 5:17:40
Mapleton 6 13 42N56 76w33 5:06:12
Mapletown 29 162 42N52 74w35 4:58:20
Maple Valley 39 226 42N39 74w48 4:59:12
Maple View 38 14 43N27 76w09 5:04:36
Maplewood 1 1 42N43 73w44 4:54:56
Maplewood 53 197 41N39 74w42 4:58:48
Marathon 12 13 42N27 76w02 5:04:08
Marble Hill 3 1 40N53 73w54 4:55:36
Marbletown 56 11 41N51 74w09 4:56:36
Marbletown 59 14 43N03 77w05 5:08:20
Marcellus 34 13 42N59 76w20 5:05:20
Marcellus Falls 34 13 42N59 76w20 5:05:20
Marcy 24 1 40N42 73w57 4:55:48
Marcy 33 14 43N10 75w17 5:01:08
Marengo 59 99 43N05 76w52 5:07:28
Margaretville 13 226 42N09 74w39 4:58:36
Mariaville 47 94 42N53 74w05 4:56:20
Marietta 34 13 42N55 76w20 5:05:20
Marilla 15 38 42N50 78w32 5:14:08
Marine Hospital 43 1 40N38 74w06 4:56:24
Mariners Harbor 43 1 40N38 74w09 4:56:36
Marion 59 89 43N09 77w12 5:08:48
Mariposa 9 226 42N39 75w46 5:03:04
Market 15 153 42N53 78w52 5:15:28
Markhams 5 42 42N28 78w56 5:15:44
Marlboro 24 1 40N36 73w58 4:55:52
Marlboro 56 6 41N36 73w58 4:55:52
Marlborough 56 6 41N36 73w58 4:55:52
Marquette 15 1 42N58 78w52 5:15:28
Marshall 2 226 42N21 78w07 5:12:28
Marshall 33 13 42N58 75w24 5:01:36
Marshfield 15 42 42N32 78w56 5:15:44
Marshville 29 162 42N52 74w35 4:58:20
Marshville 45 226 44N28 75w14 5:00:56
Martindale Depot 11 11 42N11 73w35 4:54:20
Martinsburg 25 226 43N57 75w31 5:02:04
Martisco 34 13 42N59 76w20 5:05:20
Martville 6 226 43N17 76w38 5:06:32
Maryknoll 60 166 41N11 73w50 4:55:20
Maryland 39 13 42N33 74w51 4:59:24
Marymount 60 6 41N04 73w51 4:55:24
Masonville 13 226 42N14 75w21 5:01:24
Maspeth 41 1 40N43 73w55 4:55:40
Massapequa 30 6 40N41 73w29 4:53:56
Massapequa Park 30 11 41N02 73w27 4:53:48
Massawepie 45 221 44N14 74w28 4:57:52
Massena 45 195 44N56 74w54 4:59:36
Massena Springs 45 195 44N56 74w54 4:59:36
Masten Lake 53 11 41N34 74w29 4:57:56
Mastic 52 11 40N48 72w52 4:51:28

Mastic Beach 52 11 40N46 72w51 4:51:24
Matinecock 30 11 40N54 73w35 4:54:20
Matteawan 14 7 41N30 73w58 4:55:52
Matteawan State Hospital 14 7 41N30 73w58 4:55:52
Mattituck 52 11 41N00 72w32 4:50:08
Mattydale 34 41 43N06 76w08 5:04:32
Maybrook 36 11 41N29 74w14 4:56:56
Maybury Mills 12 41 42N36 76w06 5:04:24
Mayfield 18 226 43N06 74w15 4:57:00
Mayville 7 158 42N15 79w30 5:18:00
Maywood 1 11 42N42 73w48 4:55:12
Maywood 52 11 40N41 73w28 4:53:52
McClure 4 167 42N04 75w25 5:01:40
McConnellsville 33 226 43N16 75w42 5:02:48
McCormick's Corner 1 6 42N46 73w56 4:55:44
McDonough 9 226 42N30 75w44 5:02:56
McEwens Corners 45 105 44N48 74w41 4:58:44
McGraw 12 41 42N36 76w08 5:04:32
McGrawville 2 226 42N24 78w15 5:13:00
McKeever 22 226 43N27 75w12 5:00:48
McKinley 29 162 42N55 74w35 4:58:20
McKinneys Point 55 186 42N28 76w29 5:05:56
McKinstry Hollow 5 226 42N30 78w29 5:13:56
McKown Park 1 1 42N40 73w48 4:55:12
McKownville 1 1 42N40 73w48 4:55:12
McKownville Estates 1 1 42N40 73w48 4:55:12
McLaughlin Acres 40 17 41N22 73w44 4:54:56
McLean 55 13 42N33 76w17 5:05:08
McNalls 32 121 43N11 79w02 5:16:08
McPherson Point 26 226 42N49 77w40 5:10:40
Meacham 30 11 40N42 73w42 4:54:48
Meadowbrook 36 1 41N31 74w03 4:56:12
Meadowdale 1 40 42N42 74w02 4:56:08
Meadowmere Park 30 11 40N37 73w44 4:54:56
Meadow Run 15 153 42N45 78w51 5:15:24
Meadows 28 226 43N13 77w56 5:11:44
Meads Creek 49 13 42N09 77w06 5:08:24
Mechanicstown 36 1 41N28 74w24 4:57:36
Mechanicville 46 1 42N54 73w41 4:54:44
Mecklenburg 49 226 42N27 76w43 5:06:52
Meco 18 226 43N03 74w20 4:57:20
Mecox 52 11 40N55 72w21 4:49:24
Medford 52 11 40N49 73w00 4:52:00
Medina 37 112 43N13 78w23 5:13:32
Medusa 1 226 42N26 74w08 4:56:32
Medway 20 11 42N22 73w51 4:55:24
Melcourt 3 1 40N50 73w54 4:55:36
Mellenville 11 1 42N15 73w40 4:54:40
Melrose 42 11 42N50 73w37 4:54:28
Melrose Park 6 12 42N55 76w33 5:06:12
Melville 52 11 40N48 73w25 4:53:40
Memphis 34 41 43N05 76w23 5:05:32
Menands 1 11 42N42 73w44 4:54:56
Mendon 28 226 42N59 77w33 5:10:12
Mendon Farms 28 13 43N00 77w34 5:10:16
Menteth Point 35 14 42N53 77w17 5:09:08
Mentz 6 24 43N02 76w38 5:06:32
Meredith 13 29 42N22 74w56 4:59:44
Meridale 13 226 42N22 74w57 4:59:48
Meridian 6 226 43N10 76w32 5:06:08
Merrick 30 1 40N40 73w33 4:54:12
Merrickville 13 13 42N17 75w16 5:01:04
Merriewold 53 197 41N39 74w42 4:58:48
Merriewold Lake 36 226 41N22 74w11 4:56:44
Merrifield 6 13 42N47 76w34 5:06:16
Merrill 10 136 44N43 73w43 4:54:52
Merrillsville 27 60 43N05 75w39 5:02:36
Merrilville 17 221 44N14 74w28 4:57:52
Merriweather Campus 30 11 40N48 73w37 4:54:28
Mertensia 35 19 42N59 77w25 5:09:40
Messengerville 12 13 42N27 76w02 5:04:08
Metropolitan 24 1 40N42 73w57 4:55:48
Mettacahonts 56 76 41N48 74w13 4:56:52
Mexico 38 14 43N28 76w12 5:04:48
Middle Bridge 9 144 42N14 75w31 5:02:04
Middleburg 48 226 42N36 74w20 4:57:20
Middlebury 61 226 42N50 78w08 5:12:32
Middle Falls 58 226 43N07 73w32 4:54:08
Middlefield 39 13 42N41 74w52 4:59:28
Middlefield Center 39 140 42N48 74w45 4:59:00
Middle Granville 58 42 43N26 73w17 4:53:08
Middle Grove 46 226 43N05 73w55 4:55:40
Middle Hope 36 1 41N33 74w00 4:56:00
Middle Island 52 11 40N53 72w57 4:51:48
Middleport 27 180 42N49 75w33 5:02:12
Middleport 32 90 43N13 78w29 5:13:56
Middlesex 62 226 42N42 77w16 5:09:04
Middletown 36 1 41N27 74w25 4:57:40
Middle Village 41 1 40N43 73w52 4:55:28
Middleville 22 226 43N08 74w58 4:59:52
Middleville 52 11 40N54 73w17 4:53:08
Midland Beach 43 1 40N34 74w07 4:56:28
Midtown 31 1 40N45 73w59 4:55:56
Midtown Plaza 28 209 43N09 77w37 5:10:28
Midway 8 14 42N16 76w51 5:07:24
Midwood 24 1 40N37 73w58 4:55:52
Milan 14 226 41N58 73w47 4:55:08
Mileses 53 226 41N50 75w04 5:00:16
Milford 39 15 42N35 74w57 4:59:48
Mill Brook 3 1 40N50 73w54 4:55:36
Millbrook 14 39 41N47 73w42 4:54:48

NEW YORK

Place		Lat.	Long.	Time
Millbrook Heights 14	39	41N47	73w41	4:54:44
Millen Bay 23	226	44N08	76w20	5:05:20
Miller Place 52	11	40N58	73w00	4:52:00
Millers 37	15	43N19	78w23	5:13:32
Millers Mills 22	13	42N53	75w12	5:00:48
Millersport 15	11	43N01	78w42	5:14:48
Millerton 14	79	41N57	73w31	4:54:04
Millertown 42	11	42N55	73w31	4:54:04
Mill Grove 5	226	42N02	78w20	5:13:20
Mill Hook 56	76	41N48	74w13	4:56:52
Mill Neck 30	11	40N54	73w33	4:54:12
Mill Point 29	1	42N57	74w11	4:56:44
Millport 8	14	42N16	76w51	5:07:24
Millsburgh 36	11	41N22	74w30	4:58:00
Mills Mills 2	226	42N28	78w07	5:12:28
Millville 37	112	43N13	78w23	5:13:32
Millwood 60	7	41N12	73w48	4:55:12
Milo 62	14	42N37	77w01	5:08:04
Milo Center 62	14	42N40	77w03	5:08:12
Milo Mills 62	14	42N40	77w03	5:08:12
Milton 46	226	43N02	73w53	4:55:32
Milton 56	1	41N39	73w57	4:55:48
Milton 60	1	40N59	73w42	4:54:48
Mina 7	226	42N07	79w42	5:18:48
Minaville 29	1	42N57	74w11	4:56:44
Minden 29	226	42N56	74w42	4:58:48
Mindenville 29	62	42N56	74w37	4:58:28
Mineola 30	11	40N45	73w38	4:54:32
Mineral Springs 48	139	42N41	74w29	4:57:56
Minerva 16	49	43N47	73w59	4:55:56
Minetto 38	204	43N24	76w29	5:05:56
Mineville 16	54	44N05	73w31	4:54:04
Minisink 36	11	41N20	74w32	4:58:08
Minisink Ford 53	226	41N29	74w55	4:59:40
Minklers Corners 45	195	44N56	74w54	4:59:36
Minnehaha 22	59	43N42	75w00	5:00:00
Minoa 34	226	43N05	76w00	5:04:00
Mitchellsville 51	14	42N20	77w19	5:09:16
Model City 32	199	43N11	78w59	5:15:56
Modena 56	11	41N40	74w07	4:56:28
Modena Gardens 56	11	41N40	74w07	4:56:28
Moffitsville 10	136	44N39	73w45	4:55:00
Mohawk 22	196	43N00	75w00	5:00:00
Mohawk Hill 25	226	43N29	75w20	5:01:20
Mohawk View 1	1	42N44	73w45	4:55:00
Mohegan Lake 60	6	41N19	73w51	4:55:24
Mohonk Lake 56	11	41N45	74w05	4:56:20
Moira 17	125	44N50	74w33	4:58:12
Molyneaux Corners 32	226	43N09	78w35	5:14:20
Mombaccus 56	72	41N47	74w19	4:57:16
Mongaup 53	1	41N23	74w43	4:58:52
Mongaup Valley 53	226	41N40	74w47	4:59:08
Monroe 36	1	41N20	74w11	4:56:44
Monsey 44	4	41N07	74w04	4:56:16
Monsey Heights 44	4	41N07	74w04	4:56:16
Montague 25	226	43N58	75w17	5:01:08
Montario Point 22	14	43N43	76w04	5:04:16
Montauk 52	11	41N03	71w57	4:47:48
Montauk Beach 52	11	41N03	71w57	4:47:48
Montauk Estates 52	11	40N58	72w08	4:48:32
Montclair Colony 52	11	41N06	72w21	4:49:24
Monterey 49	14	42N17	76w58	5:07:52
Monterey Estates 44	4	41N08	73w56	4:55:44
Montezuma 6	25	43N01	76w41	5:06:44
Montgomery 36	11	41N32	74w11	4:56:44
Monticello 53	197	41N39	74w42	4:58:48
Montour 49	14	42N20	76w49	5:07:16
Montour Falls 49	14	42N21	76w51	5:07:24
Montrose 60	7	41N15	73w56	4:55:44
Montville 6	13	42N43	76w25	5:05:40
Moody 17	221	44N14	74w28	4:57:52
Mooers 10	198	44N58	73w39	4:54:36
Mooers Forks 10	198	44N58	73w39	4:54:36
Moores Mill 14	11	41N45	73w50	4:55:20
Moose River 25	77	44N06	75w40	5:02:40
Moravia 6	13	42N43	76w25	5:05:40
Moreau 46	226	43N14	73w39	4:54:36
Morehouse 21	226	43N27	74w43	4:58:52
Moreland 49	14	42N17	76w58	5:07:52
Morey Park 42	11	42N31	73w37	4:54:28
Morgan 31	1	40N45	73w59	4:55:56
Morgan Hill 56	11	41N57	74w00	4:56:00
Morganville 19	70	42N59	78w04	5:12:16
Moriah 16	54	44N03	73w30	4:54:00
Moriches 52	11	40N48	72w51	4:51:24
Morley 45	155	44N36	75w10	5:00:40
Morningside 31	1	40N48	73w57	4:55:48
Morris 39	226	42N33	75w15	5:01:00
Morrisania 3	1	40N50	73w54	4:55:36
Morris Heights 3	1	40N51	73w55	4:55:40
Morrison Heights 36	11	41N31	74w14	4:56:56
Morrisonville 10	86	44N42	73w33	4:54:12
Morris Park 41	1	40N43	73w50	4:55:20
Morristown 45	20	44N35	75w39	5:02:36
Morrisville 27	29	42N53	75w35	5:02:20
Morrisville Station 27	226	42N54	75w39	5:02:36
Morsston 53	75	41N54	74w50	4:59:20
Morton 37	105	43N20	78w00	5:12:00
Moscow Hill 27	180	42N49	75w28	5:01:52
Mosherville 46	226	43N01	74w02	4:56:08
Mosholu 3	1	40N53	73w52	4:55:28
Mosquito Point 20	226	42N19	74w26	4:57:44
Mossyglen 51	13	42N08	77w03	5:08:12
Mott Haven 3	1	40N50	73w54	4:55:36
Mottville 34	24	42N59	76w27	5:05:48
Mountain Dale 53	74	41N41	74w32	4:58:08
Mountain Lodge 36	226	41N21	74w11	4:56:44
Mountain View 17	30	44N44	74w10	4:56:40
Mountainville 36	11	41N31	74w14	4:56:56
Mount Airy 60	166	41N12	73w53	4:55:32
Mount Carmel 3	1	40N52	73w53	4:55:32
Mount Eve 36	7	41N24	74w20	4:57:20
Mount Hope 36	21	41N28	74w31	4:58:04
Mount Hope 60	1	41N00	73w52	4:55:28
Mount Ivy 44	4	41N11	74w03	4:56:12
Mount Kisco 60	6	41N12	73w44	4:54:56
Mount Loretto 43	11	40N31	74w13	4:56:52
Mount Marion 56	215	42N02	73w59	4:55:56
Mount Merion Park 56	215	42N02	73w59	4:55:56
Mount Morris 26	13	42N44	77w52	5:11:28
Mount Pleasant 38	226	43N19	76w25	5:05:40
Mount Pleasant 56	88	42N03	74w17	4:57:08
Mount Prosper 53	11	41N34	74w29	4:57:56
Mount Ross 14	226	41N59	73w40	4:54:40
Mount Sinai 52	11	40N57	73w01	4:52:04
Mount Tremper 56	88	42N03	74w17	4:57:08
Mount Upton 9	226	42N26	75w23	5:01:32
Mount Vernon 15	153	42N45	78w51	5:15:24
Mount Vernon 60	1	40N55	73w50	4:55:20
Mount Vision 39	226	42N35	75w04	5:00:16
Mud Mills 59	14	43N03	77w05	5:08:20
Muitzeskill 42	68	42N29	73w46	4:55:04
Mumford 28	226	42N59	77w52	5:11:28
Mungers Corners 38	226	43N19	76w25	5:05:40
Municipal Building 24	1	40N42	73w59	4:55:56
Munnsville 27	13	42N59	75w35	5:02:20
Munsey Park 30	11	40N48	73w41	4:54:44
Munsons Corners 12	41	42N35	76w12	5:04:48
Murdochs Crossing 37	15	43N19	78w23	5:13:32
Murdock Woods 60	1	40N59	73w48	4:55:12
Murray 37	105	43N15	78w03	5:12:12
Murray Hill 31	1	40N45	73w59	4:55:56
Murray Isle 23	163	44N14	76w05	5:04:20
Muttontown 30	11	40N49	73w32	4:54:08
Myers 55	13	42N32	76w31	5:06:04
Myers Corner 14	6	41N36	73w51	4:55:24
Myers Grove 36	21	41N27	74w37	4:58:28
Nanticoke 4	226	42N17	76w02	5:04:08
Nanuet 44	4	41N05	74w01	4:56:04
Napanoch 56	48	41N44	74w22	4:57:28
Naples 35	226	42N37	77w24	5:09:36
Napoli 5	20	42N13	78w53	5:15:32
Narrowsburg 53	20	41N37	75w04	5:00:16
Nashville 32	1	43N05	78w52	5:15:28
Nashville 7	226	42N28	79w10	5:16:40
Nassau 42	11	42N31	73w37	4:54:28
Nassau Farms 52	11	41N01	72w29	4:49:56
Nassau Point 52	11	41N01	72w29	4:49:56
Nassau Shores 30	11	40N40	73w26	4:53:44
Natural Bridge 23	226	44N04	75w30	5:02:00
Natural Dam 45	178	44N20	75w28	5:01:52
Naumburg 25	191	43N48	75w29	5:01:56
Nauraushaun 44	4	41N04	74w01	4:56:04
Navarino 34	13	42N59	76w20	5:05:20
Nazareth College 28	13	43N09	77w33	5:10:12
Nedrow 34	13	42N59	76w09	5:04:36
Nelliston 29	62	42N56	74w37	4:58:28
Nelson 27	226	42N52	75w45	5:03:00
Nelsonville 40	6	41N26	73w57	4:55:48
Neponsit 41	1	40N35	73w51	4:55:24
Nesconset 52	11	40N50	73w09	4:52:36
Neversink 53	226	41N51	74w35	4:58:20
Nevis 11	5	42N04	73w55	4:55:40
New Albion 5	226	42N18	78w53	5:15:32
Newark 59	14	43N03	77w06	5:08:24
Newark Valley 54	226	42N14	76w11	5:04:44
New Baltimore 20	11	42N25	73w50	4:55:20
New Berlin 9	226	42N37	75w20	5:01:20
New Berlin Junction 9	149	42N18	75w29	5:01:56
New Boston 25	226	43N48	75w19	5:01:16
New Bremen 25	226	43N50	75w36	5:02:24
New Brighton 43	1	40N38	74w07	4:56:28
Newburg 61	24	42N40	78w05	5:12:20
Newburgh 36	1	41N30	74w01	4:56:04
New Cassel 30	11	40N46	73w34	4:54:16
New Castle 60	1	41N11	73w46	4:55:04
New Centerville 38	226	43N34	76w07	5:04:28
New City 44	4	41N09	73w59	4:55:56
New City Park 44	4	41N09	74w00	4:56:00
Newcomb 16	226	43N58	74w10	4:56:40
New Concord 11	10	42N25	73w32	4:54:08
New Dorp 43	1	40N34	74w07	4:56:28
New Dorp Beach 43	1	40N34	74w07	4:56:28
New Ebenezer 15	153	42N51	78w46	5:15:04
New Falconwood 15	1	43N01	78w57	5:15:48
Newfane 32	226	43N17	78w43	5:14:52
Newfield 55	226	42N21	76w35	5:06:20
New Hackensack 14	6	41N37	73w52	4:55:28
New Hamburg 14	6	41N35	73w57	4:55:48
New Hampton 36	7	41N25	74w24	4:57:36
New Hartford 33	11	43N04	75w18	5:01:12
New Haven 38	15	43N29	76w19	5:05:16
New Hempstead 44	4	41N09	74w02	4:56:08
New Hope 6	13	42N43	76w25	5:05:40
New Hudson 2	226	42N18	78w15	5:13:00
New Hurley 56	122	41N41	74w09	4:56:36
New Hyde Park 30	11	40N44	73w41	4:54:44
New Ireland 4	151	42N07	75w56	5:03:44
New Kingston 13	226	42N13	74w41	4:58:44
Newkirk 24	1	40N39	73w57	4:55:48
New Lebanon 11	11	42N28	73w26	4:53:44
New Lisbon 39	226	42N37	75w08	5:00:32
New Lots 24	1	40N41	73w52	4:55:28
New Market 32	199	43N06	79w02	5:16:08
New Milford 36	6	41N14	74w25	4:57:40
New Oregon 15	153	42N39	78w54	5:15:36
New Paltz 56	11	41N45	74w05	4:56:20
Newport 22	20	43N11	75w01	5:00:04
Newport 28	185	43N13	77w36	5:10:24
Newport 34	41	43N05	76w20	5:05:20
New Rochelle 60	1	40N55	73w47	4:55:08
New Russia 16	50	44N10	73w37	4:54:28
New Salem 1	11	42N39	73w56	4:55:44
New Salem 56	11	41N57	74w00	4:56:00
New Scotland 1	11	42N36	73w56	4:55:44
New Springville 43	1	40N38	74w08	4:56:32
New Square 44	4	41N08	74w02	4:56:08
Newstead 15	145	43N01	78w31	5:14:04
New Suffolk 52	11	41N00	72w28	4:49:52
Newton Falls 45	25	44N13	74w59	4:59:56
Newton Hook 11	111	42N24	73w47	4:55:08
Newtonville 1	1	42N43	73w45	4:55:00
Newtown 52	11	40N52	72w31	4:50:04
New Vernon 36	1	41N28	74w24	4:57:36
Newville 22	61	43N03	74w51	4:59:24
New Windsor 36	1	41N28	74w06	4:56:24
New Woodstock 27	226	42N51	75w51	5:03:24
New York 31	1	40N45	73w57	4:55:48
New York Mills 33	222	43N06	75w18	5:01:12
New York Mills Gardens 33	222	43N07	75w18	5:01:12
Niagara 32	199	43N07	78w59	5:15:56
Niagara Falls 32	199	43N06	79w03	5:16:12
Niagara Square 15	153	42N53	78w53	5:15:32
Niagara University 32	199	43N08	79w02	5:16:08
Nichols 51	226	41N59	77w19	5:09:16
Nichols 54	36	42N01	76w22	5:05:28
Nichols Plaza 23	45	43N59	75w56	5:03:44
Nicholville 45	226	44N42	74w40	4:58:40
Niets Crest 7	226	42N06	79w23	5:17:32
Nile 2	226	42N12	78w08	5:12:32
Niles 6	13	42N49	76w24	5:05:36
Nimmonsburg 4	151	42N08	75w53	5:03:32
Nimmonsburg-Chenango Bridge 4	13	42N11	75w53	5:03:32
Nineveh 4	17	42N12	75w36	5:02:24
Nineveh Junction 9	17	42N14	75w31	5:02:04
Niobe 7	20	42N01	79w27	5:17:48
Niskayuna 47	1	42N48	73w53	4:55:32
Nissequogue 52	11	40N54	73w12	4:52:48
Niverville 11	11	42N26	73w40	4:54:40
Noblesboro 22	84	43N14	75w02	5:00:08
Norfolk 45	226	44N48	75w00	5:00:00
Normansville 1	11	42N37	73w49	4:55:16
Norrie Heights 14	219	41N51	73w56	4:55:44
North 60	1	40N57	73w53	4:55:32
North Afton 9	144	42N14	75w31	5:02:04
North Amityville 52	6	40N42	73w25	4:53:40
Northampton 18	7	43N13	74w11	4:56:44
Northampton 52	11	40N55	72w38	4:50:32
North Argyle 58	226	43N14	73w30	4:54:00
North Babylon 52	1	40N44	73w19	4:53:16
North Bailey 15	7	42N58	78w48	5:15:12
North Baldwin 30	11	40N39	73w37	4:54:28
North Ballston Spa 46	8	43N01	73w51	4:55:24
North Bangor 17	16	44N50	74w26	4:57:44
North Bay 33	226	43N14	75w45	5:03:00
North Bay Shore 52	1	40N41	73w13	4:52:52
North Beach 41	1	40N46	73w52	4:55:28
North Bellmore 30	7	40N41	73w32	4:54:08
North Bellport 52	7	40N47	72w57	4:51:48
North Bergen 19	110	43N05	77w57	5:11:48
North Bethlehem 1	1	42N39	73w47	4:55:08
North Blenheim 48	226	42N28	74w27	4:57:48
North Bloomfield 35	226	42N57	77w35	5:10:20
North Boston 15	11	42N41	78w47	5:15:08
North Branch 53	226	41N48	75w00	5:00:00
North Bridgewater 33	13	42N57	75w15	5:01:00
North Broadalbin 18	226	43N03	74w12	4:56:48
North Brookfield 27	13	42N51	75w24	5:01:36
North Burke 17	141	44N54	74w10	4:56:40
Northbush 18	43	43N00	74w22	4:57:28
North Cameron 51	20	42N12	77w24	5:09:36
North Castle 60	1	41N07	73w42	4:54:48
North Cazenovia 27	14	42N56	75w51	5:03:24
North Chatham 11	10	42N29	73w38	4:54:32
North Chemung 8	13	42N02	76w44	5:06:56
North Chili 28	15	43N07	77w48	5:11:12
North Chittenango 27	226	43N03	75w53	5:03:32
North Clymer 7	22	42N04	79w34	5:18:16
North Cohocton 51	14	42N34	77w28	5:09:52
North Collins 15	42	42N36	78w56	5:15:44
North Columbia 22	184	43N01	75w02	5:00:08

NEW YORK

North Corners 45 226 44N44 75w19 5:01:16
North Creek 57 49 43N42 73w59 4:55:56
North Cuba 2 20 42N13 78w17 5:13:08
North Dansville 26 13 42N33 77w42 5:10:48
North Darien 19 164 42N58 78w24 5:13:36
Northeast 14 79 41N57 73w32 4:54:08
Northeast Henrietta 28 13 43N05 77w31 5:10:04
North Easton 58 226 43N05 73w30 4:54:00
North Elba 16 1 44N17 73w58 4:55:52
North End 36 1 41N28 74w24 4:57:36
North Evans 15 11 42N42 78w57 5:15:48
North Fair Haven 6 226 43N19 76w42 5:06:48
North Fenton 4 13 42N14 75w51 5:03:24
Northfield 13 226 42N10 75w08 5:00:32
North Franklin 13 14 42N27 75w05 5:00:20
North Gage 33 222 43N06 75w15 5:01:00
North Gainesville 61 24 42N40 78w05 5:12:20
North Germantown 11 11 42N08 73w54 4:55:36
North Granville 58 42 43N27 73w21 4:53:24
North Great River 52 11 40N47 73w12 4:52:48
North Greece 28 209 43N15 77w44 5:10:56
North Greenbush 42 1 42N41 73w40 4:54:40
North Greenwich 58 1 43N05 73w30 4:54:00
North Hannibal 38 204 43N27 76w30 5:06:00
North Harmony 7 226 42N07 79w25 5:17:40
North Harpersfield 13 226 42N29 74w37 4:58:28
North Hartland 32 150 43N20 78w39 5:14:36
North Haven 52 11 41N01 72w18 4:49:12
North Hebron 58 42 43N24 73w16 4:53:04
North Hempstead 30 1 40N47 73w42 4:54:48
North Highland 40 6 41N26 73w57 4:55:48
North Hills 30 11 40N46 73w41 4:54:44
North Hillsdale 11 11 42N11 73w31 4:54:04
North Hoosick 42 11 42N56 73w21 4:53:24
North Hornell 51 102 42N21 77w40 5:10:40
North Hudson 16 226 44N00 73w46 4:55:04
North Ilion 22 184 43N02 75w04 5:00:16
North Jasper 51 226 42N12 77w24 5:09:36
North Java 61 226 42N41 78w20 5:13:20
North Jay 16 44 44N23 73w44 4:54:56
North Kortright 13 13 42N28 74w51 4:59:24
North Lansing 55 13 42N35 76w22 5:05:28
North Lawrence 45 105 44N48 74w41 4:58:44
North Lindenhurst 52 11 41N01 73w23 4:53:32
North Litchfield 22 184 43N02 75w04 5:00:16
North Lynbrook 30 7 40N40 73w40 4:54:40
North Manlius 34 226 43N00 75w59 5:03:56
North Massapequa 30 6 40N42 73w29 4:53:56
North Merrick 30 1 40N41 73w34 4:54:16
North New Hyde Park 30 11 40N45 73w41 4:54:44
North Norwich 9 200 42N36 75w30 5:02:00
North Olean 5 101 42N05 78w26 5:13:44
North Patchogue 52 1 40N47 73w01 4:52:04
North Pelham 60 1 40N55 73w49 4:55:16
North Pembroke 19 142 43N00 78w11 5:12:44
North Petersburg 42 11 42N45 73w21 4:53:24
North Pharsalia 9 226 42N35 75w34 5:02:16
North Pitcher 9 226 42N37 75w49 5:03:16
North Pole 16 1 44N17 73w59 4:55:56
Northport 52 7 40N54 73w21 4:53:24
North Ridge 32 226 43N09 78w35 5:14:20
North River 57 226 43N44 74w05 4:56:20
North Rockville Centre 30 210 40N40 73w38 4:54:32
North Rose 59 33 43N11 76w53 5:07:32
North Rush 28 27 42N59 77w39 5:10:36
North Russell 45 155 44N36 75w10 5:00:40
North Salem 60 16 41N20 73w36 4:54:24
North Sanford 4 167 42N04 75w25 5:01:40
North Sea 52 11 40N53 72w23 4:49:32
North Seaford 30 11 40N47 73w32 4:54:08
North Settlement 20 226 42N19 74w15 4:57:00
North Shore Beach 52 11 40N57 72w56 4:51:44
Northside 51 13 42N08 77w03 5:08:12
North Smithtown 52 6 40N51 73w14 4:52:56
North Spencer 54 226 42N13 76w30 5:06:00
North Stephentown 42 11 42N33 73w23 4:53:32
North Stockholm 45 20 44N45 74w59 4:59:56
North Syracuse 34 41 43N08 76w07 5:04:28
North Tarrytown 60 6 41N05 73w52 4:55:28
North Tonawanda 32 1 43N02 78w53 5:15:32
Northtown 15 7 42N58 78w48 5:15:12
Northumberland 46 226 43N10 73w38 4:54:32
North Valley Stream 30 7 40N41 73w42 4:54:48
North Victory 6 226 43N17 76w38 5:06:32
Northville 18 7 43N13 74w11 4:56:44
North Wantagh 30 6 41N34 73w30 4:54:00
North Waverly 54 224 42N00 76w32 5:06:08
North Western 33 226 43N20 75w22 5:01:28
North White Plains 60 1 41N03 73w46 4:55:04
North Wilmurt 22 82 43N20 75w11 5:00:44
North Winfield 22 13 42N53 75w12 5:00:48
North Wolcott 59 33 43N13 76w49 5:07:16
North Woodmere 30 1 40N39 73w43 4:54:52
Norton Hill 20 226 42N25 74w04 4:56:16
Norway 22 226 43N13 74w56 4:59:44
Norwich 9 200 42N32 75w32 5:02:08
Norwich Corners 22 14 43N00 75w16 5:01:04
Norwood 45 105 44N45 75w00 5:00:00
Nostrand 24 1 40N35 73w57 4:55:48
Nottingham Estates 32 226 43N09 78w35 5:14:20
Noyac 52 11 40N55 72w27 4:49:48
Number Four 25 226 43N54 75w30 5:02:00
Nunda 26 226 42N35 77w56 5:11:44
Nyack 44 1 41N06 73w56 4:55:44
Oak Beach 52 11 40N38 73w18 4:53:12
Oakbrook 44 4 41N06 74w00 4:56:00
Oakdale 4 116 42N07 75w58 5:03:52
Oakdale 52 11 40N44 73w09 4:52:36
Oakfield 19 26 43N04 78w16 5:13:04
Oak Hill 20 226 42N25 74w09 4:56:36
Oakland 26 226 42N35 77w56 5:11:44
Oakland Gardens 41 1 40N45 73w46 4:55:04
Oak Orchard 37 112 43N13 78w23 5:13:32
Oak Point 3 1 40N50 73w54 4:55:36
Oak Ridge 29 12 42N46 74w16 4:57:04
Oakridge 34 13 43N07 76w12 5:04:48
Oaks Corners 35 13 42N56 77w01 5:08:04
Oak Summit 14 226 41N47 73w41 4:54:44
Oaksville 39 13 42N43 74w59 4:59:56
Oakwood 6 13 42N56 76w33 5:06:12
Oakwood 43 1 40N38 74w06 4:56:24
Oakwood Beach 43 1 40N38 74w06 4:56:24
Oakwood Heights 43 1 40N38 74w06 4:56:24
Oatka 61 206 42N43 78w00 5:12:00
Obernburg 53 226 41N51 75w01 5:00:04
Obi 2 226 42N04 78w10 5:12:40
Occanum 4 226 42N04 75w41 5:02:44
Ocean Bay Park 52 11 40N41 73w13 4:52:52
Ocean Beach 52 11 40N39 73w10 4:52:40
Oceanside 30 11 40N38 73w38 4:54:32
Odessa 49 14 42N20 76w47 5:07:08
Ogden 3 1 40N50 73w52 4:55:28
Ogden 28 14 43N10 77w49 5:11:16
Ogdensburg 45 201 44N42 75w30 5:02:00
Ohio 22 226 43N22 74w57 4:59:48
Ohioville 56 11 41N45 74w05 4:56:20
Oil Springs Indian Res 5 226 42N14 78w19 5:13:16
Oklahoma 28 226 43N12 77w29 5:09:56
Olcott 32 11 43N20 78w43 5:14:52
Old Bethpage 30 11 40N46 73w27 4:53:48
Old Brookville 30 11 40N51 73w36 4:54:24
Old Central Bridge 48 12 42N43 74w20 4:57:20
Old Chatham 11 10 42N26 73w34 4:54:16
Old Chelsa 31 1 40N45 74w00 4:56:00
Old Field 52 11 40N58 73w09 4:52:36
Old Forge 22 203 43N43 74w58 4:59:52
Old Orchard 26 226 42N49 77w40 5:10:40
Old Westbury 30 7 40N47 73w36 4:54:24
Olean 5 101 42N05 78w26 5:13:44
Olive 56 37 41N57 74w15 4:57:00
Olivebridge 56 37 41N55 74w13 4:56:52
Oliverea 56 226 42N04 74w28 4:57:52
Olmstedville 16 49 43N46 73w56 4:55:44
Omar 23 17 44N20 75w55 5:03:40
Onativia 34 16 42N54 76w06 5:04:24
Onchiota 17 113 44N30 74w07 4:56:28
Oneida 27 60 43N06 75w39 5:02:36
Oneida Castle 33 60 43N05 75w38 5:02:32
Oneonta 39 14 42N27 75w04 5:00:16
Onesquethaw 1 11 42N35 73w53 4:55:32
Oniad Lake 14 6 41N35 73w53 4:55:32
Onleys Station 36 1 41N28 74w24 4:57:36
Onondaga 34 13 42N59 76w12 5:04:48
Onondaga Indian Reservation 34 16 42N57 76w09 5:04:36
Ontario 59 33 43N14 77w19 5:09:16
Ontario on the Lake 59 226 43N13 77w17 5:09:08
Onteora Park 20 23 42N12 74w08 4:56:32
Oot Park 34 41 43N04 76w04 5:04:16
Open Meadows 7 226 42N06 79w23 5:17:32
Oppenheim 18 226 43N04 74w42 4:58:48
Oquaga Lake 4 167 42N04 75w25 5:01:40
Oramel 2 226 42N21 78w07 5:12:28
Oran 34 226 42N59 75w56 5:03:44
Orange 49 226 42N20 77w02 5:08:08
Orangeburg 44 4 41N03 73w58 4:55:52
Orange Lake 36 1 41N32 74w06 4:56:24
Orangeport 32 121 43N11 79w02 5:16:08
Orangetown 44 4 41N03 73w57 4:55:48
Orangeville 61 226 42N44 78w15 5:13:00
Orangeville Corners 61 226 42N46 78w19 5:13:16
Orchard Knoll 8 226 42N11 76w49 5:07:16
Orchard Park 15 11 42N46 78w45 5:15:00
Orchard Village 34 12 43N03 76w15 5:05:00
Oregon 52 11 40N59 72w32 4:50:08
Orient 52 11 41N08 72w18 4:49:12
Orienta 60 1 40N57 73w44 4:54:56
Oriental Park 7 226 42N10 79w23 5:17:32
Orient Point 52 11 41N08 72w18 4:49:12
Oriskany 33 202 43N10 75w20 5:01:20
Oriskany Falls 33 202 42N56 75w28 5:01:52
Orlando 5 226 42N15 78w48 5:15:12
Orleans 23 22 44N13 75w58 5:03:52
Orleans 35 14 42N58 77w08 5:08:32
Orleans Four Corners 23 226 44N12 75w58 5:03:52
Orwell 38 226 43N34 75w57 5:03:48
Oscawana 60 166 41N12 73w53 4:55:32
Oscawana Lake 40 6 41N20 73w52 4:55:28
Osceola 25 118 44N08 75w19 5:01:16
Ossian 26 13 42N32 77w47 5:11:08
Ossian Center 26 13 42N34 77w42 5:10:48
Ossining 60 1 41N10 73w55 4:55:40
Oswegatchie 45 201 44N37 75w29 5:01:56
Oswego 38 204 43N27 76w31 5:06:04
Oswego Bitter 34 12 43N03 76w15 5:05:00
Otego 39 104 42N26 75w12 5:00:48
Otisco 34 16 42N52 76w13 5:04:52
Otisco Valley 34 13 42N55 76w20 5:05:20
Otisville 36 21 41N28 74w32 4:58:08
Otsdawa 39 104 42N24 75w11 5:00:44
Otsego 39 203 42N43 74w58 4:59:52
Otselic 9 226 42N40 75w45 5:03:00
Otter Creek 25 15 43N43 75w24 5:01:36
Otter Lake 33 30 43N27 75w12 5:00:48
Ott Meadows 34 13 43N07 76w12 5:04:48
Otto 5 226 42N24 78w44 5:14:56
Ouaquaga 4 17 42N08 75w39 5:02:36
Overlook 46 7 43N15 73w50 4:55:20
Ovid 50 12 42N41 76w49 5:07:16
Ovid Center 50 226 42N37 77w33 5:10:12
Ovington 24 1 40N38 74w01 4:56:04
Owasco 6 13 42N53 76w30 5:06:00
Owego 54 205 42N06 76w16 5:05:04
Owens Mills 8 224 42N01 76w37 5:06:28
Owls Head 17 34 44N44 74w10 4:56:40
Oxbow 23 226 44N17 75w37 5:02:28
Oxford 9 106 42N27 75w36 5:02:24
Oxford 36 226 41N21 74w16 4:57:04
Oyster Bay 30 7 40N52 73w32 4:54:08
Oyster Bay Cove 30 7 40N52 73w30 4:54:00
Ozone Park 41 1 40N41 73w51 4:55:24
Pacama 56 11 41N57 74w00 4:56:00
Paddlefords 35 14 42N53 77w17 5:09:08
Paddy Hill 23 45 44N00 75w59 5:03:56
Paines Hollow 22 196 43N00 75w00 5:00:00
Painted Post 51 13 42N10 77w06 5:08:24
Palatine 29 11 42N57 74w33 4:58:12
Palatine Bridge 29 162 42N55 74w35 4:58:20
Palentown 56 72 41N47 74w19 4:57:16
Palenville 20 226 42N11 74w01 4:56:04
Palermo 38 226 43N22 76w16 5:05:04
Palisades 44 4 41N01 73w55 4:55:40
Palmer 46 7 43N15 73w50 4:55:20
Palmyra 59 89 43N05 77w12 5:08:48
Pamelia 23 45 44N03 75w54 5:03:36
Pamelia Four Corners 23 45 44N05 75w49 5:03:16
Panama 7 226 42N04 79w29 5:17:56
Panther Lake 38 15 43N15 75w56 5:03:44
Pantigo 52 11 40N57 72w11 4:48:44
Paradox 16 226 43N54 73w39 4:54:36
Parcells Corner 7 226 42N28 79w10 5:16:40
Paris 33 13 42N59 75w15 5:01:00
Parish 38 14 43N25 76w08 5:04:32
Parishville 45 226 44N38 74w49 4:59:16
Parkchester 3 1 40N51 73w52 4:55:28
Park Hill 34 41 43N04 76w04 5:04:16
Parkside 41 1 40N43 73w51 4:55:24
Park Slope 24 1 40N40 73w59 4:55:56
Parkston 53 75 41N54 74w50 4:59:20
Parksville 53 53 41N52 74w46 4:59:04
Park Terrace 4 151 42N05 75w54 5:03:36
Park Village 32 1 43N03 78w51 5:15:24
Parkville 24 1 40N37 73w59 4:55:56
Parkway 3 1 40N51 73w52 4:55:28
Parma 28 14 43N16 77w47 5:11:08
Parma Corners 28 14 43N12 77w48 5:11:12
Parson Farms 34 12 43N03 76w15 5:05:00
Pastime Park 50 41 42N52 76w59 5:07:56
Pataukunk 56 72 41N47 74w19 4:57:16
Patchin 15 226 42N38 78w44 5:14:56
Patchin 31 1 40N45 74w00 4:56:00
Patchinville 51 226 42N34 77w36 5:10:24
Patchogue 52 1 40N46 73w01 4:52:04
Patchogue Highlands 52 1 40N46 73w01 4:52:04
Patent 39 226 42N40 75w03 5:00:12
Patria 48 13 42N34 74w30 4:58:00
Patroon 1 1 42N41 73w45 4:55:00
Patterson 40 7 41N31 73w36 4:54:24
Pattersonville 47 94 42N53 74w05 4:56:20
Paul Smiths 17 176 44N26 74w15 4:57:00
Pavilion 19 226 42N53 78w01 5:12:04
Pawling 14 7 41N34 73w36 4:54:24
Payne Beach 28 13 43N17 77w47 5:11:08
Paynesville 2 226 42N02 77w46 5:11:04
Peabrook 13 226 41N51 75w08 5:00:32
Peach Lake 40 226 41N26 73w36 4:54:24

NEW YORK

Peakville 13 226 41N59 75W08 5:00:32
Pearl Creek 61 226 42N50 78W05 5:12:20
Pearl River 44 4 41N04 74W02 4:56:08
Peasleeville 10 86 44N38 73W34 4:54:16
Peat Corners 38 182 43N17 76W09 5:04:36
Pebble Beach 26 226 42N50 77W42 5:10:48
Peck Slip 31 1 40N43 74W00 4:56:00
Pecksville 14 7 41N31 73W39 4:54:36
Peconic 52 11 41N03 72W28 4:49:52
Peekskill 60 1 41N17 73W55 4:55:40
Pekin 32 226 43N10 78W53 5:15:32
Pelham 60 1 40N55 73W49 4:55:16
Pelham Manor 60 1 40N54 73W49 4:55:16
Pelham Parkway 3 1 40N51 73W52 4:55:28
Pellets Island 36 7 41N25 74W24 4:57:36
Pembroke 19 226 43N00 78W23 5:13:32
Penataquit 52 11 40N43 73W15 4:53:00
Pendleton 32 190 43N05 78W44 5:14:56
Penfield 28 13 43N09 77W29 5:09:56
Pennellville 38 182 43N15 76W14 5:04:56
Penn Yan 62 14 42N40 77W03 5:08:12
Peoria 61 226 42N53 78W01 5:12:04
Perch River 23 45 43N59 75W56 5:03:44
Perinton 28 13 43N05 77W27 5:09:48
Perkinsville 51 226 42N32 77W38 5:10:32
Perry 61 206 42N43 78W01 5:12:04
Perry City 49 13 42N33 76W40 5:06:40
Perrysburg 5 42 42N28 79W00 5:16:00
Perrys Mills 10 157 44N59 73W26 4:53:44
Perryville 27 226 43N01 75W48 5:03:12
Persia 5 42 42N24 78W55 5:15:40
Perth 18 226 43N00 74W13 4:56:52
Peru 10 27 44N35 73W32 4:54:08
Peru 34 41 43N05 76W23 5:05:32
Peruville 55 13 42N35 76W22 5:05:28
Peterboro 27 226 42N58 75W41 5:02:44
Petersburg 42 11 42N45 73W21 4:53:24
Peter Stuyvesant 31
1 40N44 73W59 4:55:56
Peth 5 226 42N13 78W38 5:14:32
Petries Corners 25
226 43N54 75W30 5:02:00
Petrolia 2 109 42N07 77W57 5:11:48
Pharsalia 9 226 42N36 75W44 5:02:56
Phelps 35 13 42N58 77W03 5:08:12
Philadelphia 23 77 44N09 75W43 5:02:52
Philipse Manor 60 6 41N04 73W51 4:55:24
Philipstown 40 6 41N24 73W55 4:55:40
Phillipsburg 36 1 41N28 74W24 4:57:36
Phillips Creek 2
226 42N13 78W02 5:12:08
Phillips Mill 7 226 42N10 79W23 5:17:32
Phillipsport 53 48 41N39 74W27 4:57:48
Philmont 11 1 42N15 73W39 4:54:36
Phoenicia 56 88 42N05 74W19 4:57:16
Phoenix 38 93 43N14 76W18 5:05:12
Phoenix Mills 39 13 42N42 74W55 4:59:40
Picketts Corners 10
136 44N39 73W45 4:55:00
Pickettsville 45
226 44N38 74W49 4:59:16
Piercefield 45 87 44N14 74W36 4:58:24
Pierces Corner 45
178 44N20 75W28 5:01:52
Pierceville 27 180 42N51 75W37 5:02:28
Piermont 44 7 41N03 73W55 4:55:40
Pierrepont 45 226 44N33 75W00 5:00:00
Pierrepont Manor 23
143 43N44 76W04 5:04:16
Pierstown 39 13 42N42 74W55 4:59:40
Piffard 26 226 42N50 77W51 5:11:24
Pike 61 226 42N34 78W08 5:12:32
Pike Five Corners 61
226 42N35 78W15 5:13:00
Pilgrim 3 1 40N51 73W51 4:55:24
Pilgrim Corners 36
1 41N28 74W24 4:57:36
Pilgrimport 59 99 43N04 76W59 5:07:56
Pillar Point 23 49 44N00 76W03 5:04:12
Pilot Knob 58 226 43N29 73W38 4:54:32
Pinckney 25 226 43N51 75W13 5:00:52
Pine 1 1 42N40 73W48 4:55:12
Pine Aire 52 11 40N41 73W13 4:52:52
Pine Bush 36 20 41N37 74W18 4:57:12
Pine City 8 13 42N02 76W52 5:07:28
Pine Crest 33 211 43N13 75W26 5:01:44
Pine Grove 25 15 43N43 75W24 5:01:36
Pinegrove Park 1 11 42N42 73W48 4:55:12
Pine Hill 15 7 42N55 78W46 5:15:04
Pine Hill 33 226 43N18 75W37 5:02:28
Pine Hill 56 42 42N08 74W29 4:57:56
Pinehurst 15 153 42N43 78W56 5:15:44
Pine Island 36 11 41N18 74W28 4:57:52
Pine Lake 18 226 43N08 74W29 4:57:56
Pine Meadows 38 25 43N31 76W00 5:04:00
Pine Neck 52 11 40N55 72W27 4:49:48
Pine Neck-West Tiana 52
11 40N51 72W34 4:50:16
Pine Plains 14 226 41N59 73W40 4:54:40
Pine Ridge 1 1 42N40 73W48 4:55:12
Pine Ridge Estates 60
1 41N00 73W40 4:54:40
Pine Valley 8 20 42N14 76W51 5:07:24
Pineville 13 226 42N10 75W08 5:00:32
Pineville 38 25 43N31 76W00 5:04:00
Pine Woods 27 180 42N53 75W33 5:02:12
Pioneer 46 11 43N01 73W51 4:55:24
Piseco 21 226 43N27 74W31 4:58:04
Pitcairn 45 118 44N12 75W16 5:01:04
Pitcher 9 226 42N36 75W50 5:03:20
Pitcher Hill 34 41 43N07 76W08 5:04:32
Pitt 31 1 40N43 73W59 4:55:56
Pittsfield 39 226 42N37 75W16 5:01:04
Pittsford 28 13 43N05 77W31 5:10:04
Pittstown 42 11 42N52 73W31 4:54:04
Plainedge 30 11 40N43 73W29 4:53:56
Plainfield 39 226 42N50 75W12 5:00:48

Plainview 30 11 40N46 73W29 4:53:56
Plainville 34 226 43N10 76W27 5:05:48
Plandome 30 7 40N48 73W42 4:54:48
Plandome Heights 30
7 40N48 73W42 4:54:48
Plandome Manor 30 7 40N49 73W42 4:54:48
Planetarium 31 1 40N47 73W59 4:55:56
Plato 5 226 42N24 78W37 5:14:28
Platt Cove 20 23 42N10 74W09 4:56:36
Plattekill 56 226 41N39 74W04 4:56:16
Platten 37 15 43N19 78W23 5:13:32
Plattsburgh 10 86 44N42 73W28 4:53:52
Plattsburgh Air Force Base 10
86 44N40 73W27 4:53:48
Plaza 41 1 40N45 73W55 4:55:40
Pleasantbrook 39
140 42N48 74W45 4:59:00
Pleasantdale 42 11 42N47 73W39 4:54:36
Pleasant Plains 14
219 41N51 73W56 4:55:44
Pleasant Plains 43
11 40N31 74W13 4:56:52
Pleasant Point 38
204 43N27 76W30 5:06:00
Pleasant Valley 14
226 41N46 73W49 4:55:16
Pleasant Valley 33
13 42N56 75W23 5:01:32
Pleasant Valley 51
14 42N20 77W19 5:09:16
Pleasantville 60 7 41N08 73W47 4:55:08
Plessis 23 17 44N16 75W51 5:03:24
Plumbrook 45 226 44N48 74W59 4:59:56
Plymouth 9 226 42N36 75W37 5:02:28
Pocantico Hills 60
6 41N04 73W51 4:55:24
Poestenkill 42 226 42N41 73W32 4:54:08
Point Au Rouche 10
86 44N42 73W26 4:53:44
Point Breeze 37 105 43N20 78W08 5:12:32
Point Chautauqua 7
158 42N14 79W27 5:17:48
Point Lookout 30 11 40N35 73W35 4:54:20
Point O'Woods 52 6 40N41 73W13 4:52:52
Point Peninsula 23
226 44N05 76W12 5:04:48
Point Pleasant 28
209 43N12 77W34 5:10:16
Point Rochester 35
226 42N37 77W24 5:09:36
Point Rock 33 226 43N18 75W37 5:02:28
Point Vivian 23 17 44N20 75W55 5:03:40
Poland 22 84 43N14 75W04 5:00:16
Poland Center 7 226 42N10 79W06 5:16:24
Polkville 12 41 42N36 76W06 5:04:24
Pomfret 7 15 42N24 79W21 5:17:24
Pomona 44 4 41N12 74W03 4:56:12
Pomona Heights 44 4 41N10 74W04 4:56:16
Pomonok 41 1 40N44 73W47 4:55:08
Pompey 34 14 42N56 75W58 5:03:52
Pompey Center 34 13 43N01 76W01 5:04:04
Ponck Hockie 56 11 41N57 74W00 4:56:00
Pond Eddy 53 25 41N27 74W49 4:59:16
Pond Settlement 45
226 43N32 75W40 5:02:40
Ponquogue 52 11 40N51 72W30 4:50:00
Poolville 27 130 42N47 75W31 5:02:04
Pope Mills 45 226 44N37 75W24 5:01:36
Poplar Beach 50 12 42N45 76W50 5:07:20
Poplar Ridge 6 13 42N44 76W37 5:06:28
Poquott 52 11 40N57 73W05 4:52:20
Portage 26 20 42N34 78W00 5:12:00
Portageville 61 20 42N34 78W02 5:12:08
Port Authority 31 1 40N45 74W00 4:56:00
Port Byron 6 24 43N02 76W37 5:06:28
Port Chester 60 1 41N00 73W40 4:54:40
Port Crane 4 151 42N09 75W53 5:03:32
Port Dickinson 4
151 42N08 75W54 5:03:36
Porter 32 226 43N19 78W59 5:15:56
Porter Corners 46
226 43N09 73W53 4:55:32
Porterville 15 170 42N46 78W37 5:14:28
Port Ewen 56 11 41N54 73W59 4:55:56
Port Gibson 35 89 43N02 77W09 5:08:36
Port Henry 16 54 44N03 73W28 4:53:52
Port Jefferson 52 1 40N57 73W03 4:52:12
Port Jervis 36 1 41N22 74W41 4:58:44
Port Kent 16 4 44N32 73W25 4:53:40
Portland 7 160 42N22 79W28 5:17:52
Portlandville 39 15 42N32 74W58 4:59:52
Port Leyden 25 77 44N06 75W39 5:02:36
Port Ontario 38 226 43N34 76W07 5:04:28
Port Richmond 43 1 40N38 74W08 4:56:32
Portville 5 226 42N03 78W20 5:13:20
Port Washington 30
1 40N50 73W41 4:54:44
Post Creek 8 14 42N17 76W58 5:07:52
Potsdam 45 207 44N40 74W59 4:59:56
Potter 62 226 42N43 77W12 5:08:48
Potter Hollow 1 226 42N27 74W13 4:56:52
Pottersville 57 11 43N44 73W50 4:55:20
Poughkeepsie 14 1 41N42 73W56 4:55:44
Poughquag 14 226 41N37 73W41 4:54:44
Pound Ridge 60 16 41N13 73W35 4:54:20
Pratt 24 1 40N42 73W58 4:55:52
Prattsburg 51 226 42N32 77W17 5:09:08
Pratts Hollow 27
180 42N55 75W36 5:02:24
Prattsville 20 226 42N19 74W26 4:57:44
Preble 12 91 42N44 76W09 5:04:36
Prendergast Point 7
158 42N15 79W30 5:18:00
Presho 51 13 42N02 77W08 5:08:32
Preston 9 226 42N31 75W37 5:02:28
Preston Hollow 1
226 42N27 74W13 4:56:52

Prince 31 1 40N44 74W00 4:56:00
Princes Bay 43 11 40N31 74W13 4:56:52
Princetown 47 11 42N50 74W06 4:56:24
Progress 18 226 43N03 74W20 4:57:20
Prospect 33 82 43N18 75W09 5:00:36
Prospect Heights 42
1 42N39 73W43 4:54:52
Prospect Hill 46 11 42N48 73W41 4:54:44
Prospect Park West 24
1 40N40 73W59 4:55:56
Protection 15 22 42N38 78W33 5:14:12
Providence 46 226 43N06 74W03 4:56:12
Pulaski 38 96 43N34 76W08 5:04:32
Pulteney 51 226 42N31 77W12 5:08:48
Pultneyville 59 226 43N17 77W11 5:08:44
Pulvers Corners 14
5 41N59 73W40 4:54:40
Pumpkin Hill 19 17 43N05 78W04 5:12:16
Purchase 60 7 41N02 73W43 4:54:52
Purdys Mills 10 16 44N53 73W39 4:54:36
Purdy Station 60 16 41N20 73W40 4:54:40
Purling 20 226 42N17 74W00 4:56:00
Putnam 58 29 43N45 73W25 4:53:40
Putnam Lake 40 226 41N29 73W32 4:54:08
Putnam Plaza 40 226 41N27 73W40 4:54:40
Putnam Station 58
226 43N44 73W24 4:53:36
Putnam Valley 40 6 41N22 73W51 4:55:24
Pyrites 45 226 44N31 75W11 5:00:44
Quackenbush Hill 51
13 42N08 77W03 5:08:12
Quackenkill 42 11 42N45 73W33 4:54:12
Quail 1 1 42N40 73W47 4:55:08
Quaker Basin 27 226 42N46 75W53 5:03:32
Quaker Hill 14 7 41N34 73W36 4:54:24
Quaker Springs 46
226 43N06 73W35 4:54:20
Quarry Heights 60 1 41N04 73W45 4:55:00
Quarryville 56 215 42N04 73W57 4:55:48
Queechy 11 11 42N25 73W27 4:53:48
Queens 41 1 40N43 73W52 4:55:28
Queensbridge 41 1 40N45 73W55 4:55:40
Queens Village 41 1 40N42 73W44 4:54:56
Quigley Park 7 226 42N06 79W23 5:17:32
Quinneville 4 13 42N14 75W51 5:03:24
Quioque 52 11 40N49 72W39 4:50:36
Quogue 52 1 40N49 72W36 4:50:24
Raceville 58 226 43N31 73W14 4:52:56
Radio City 31 1 40N46 74W01 4:56:04
Radison 34 226 43N09 76W20 5:05:20
Rainbow Lake 17 176 44N28 74W10 4:56:40
Rainbow Shores 38
226 43N34 76W07 5:04:28
Ralmar Park 47 1 42N51 73W57 4:55:48
Ramapo 44 4 41N09 74W10 4:56:40
Ramona Beach 38 226 43N34 76W07 5:04:28
Rampasture 52 11 40N52 72W31 4:50:04
Randall 29 11 42N55 74W27 4:57:48
Randall Corner 46 7 43N15 73W50 4:55:20
Randallsville 27
180 42N49 75W33 5:02:12
Randolph 5 20 42N10 78W59 5:15:56
Ransomville 32 226 43N14 78W55 5:15:40
Rapids 32 190 43N06 78W38 5:14:32
Raquette Lake 21
226 43N49 74W40 4:58:40
Rathbone 51 20 42N08 77W20 5:09:20
Ravena 1 1 42N28 73W49 4:55:16
Ravenwood 1 11 42N42 73W48 4:55:12
Rawson 2 226 42N13 78W17 5:13:08
Ray Brook 16 83 44N18 74W05 4:56:20
Raymertown 42 220 42N43 73W41 4:54:44
Raymondville 45 226 44N50 74W59 4:59:56
Readburn 13 226 42N10 75W08 5:00:32
Reading 49 14 42N25 76W56 5:07:44
Reber 16 56 44N22 73W23 4:53:32
Rector 25 226 43N54 75W30 5:02:00
Red Creek 52 11 40N52 72W31 4:50:04
Red Creek 59 33 43N15 76W43 5:06:52
Red Falls 20 226 42N19 74W26 4:57:44
Redfield 38 226 43N34 75W49 5:03:16
Redford 10 226 44N37 73W48 4:55:12
Red Hook 14 7 42N00 73W55 4:55:40
Red Hook 24 1 40N41 74W00 4:56:00
Red House 5 20 42N04 78W46 5:15:04
Red Mills 45 201 44N42 75W29 5:01:56
Red Oaks Mill 14 1 41N39 73W52 4:55:28
Red Rock 11 10 42N25 73W32 4:54:08
Red Rock 34 226 43N09 76W20 5:05:20
Redwood 23 17 44N18 75W48 5:03:12
Redwood 52 11 40N55 72W27 4:49:48
Reeds Corner 26 13 42N34 77W42 5:10:48
Reeves Park 52 11 40N55 72W38 4:50:32
Rego Park 41 1 40N44 73W52 4:55:28
Reidsville 1 11 42N39 73W56 4:55:44
Remsen 33 82 43N20 75W11 5:00:44
Remsenburg 52 11 40N48 72W42 4:50:48
Rensselaer 42 208 42N38 73W45 4:55:00
Rensselaer Falls 45
226 44N36 75W19 5:01:16
Rensselaerville 1
226 42N30 74W09 4:56:36
Renwick 55 186 42N28 76W29 5:05:56
Resort 59 226 43N11 76W54 5:07:36
Retsof 26 226 42N50 77W53 5:11:32
Rexford 46 4 42N51 73W53 4:55:32
Rexville 51 226 42N05 77W40 5:10:40
Reydon Shores 52 11 41N04 72W26 4:49:44
Reynoldsville 49 14 42N25 76W51 5:07:24
Rheims 51 181 42N24 77W13 5:08:52
Rhinebeck 14 64 41N56 73W54 4:55:36
Rhinecliff 14 11 41N55 73W57 4:55:48
Ricard 38 25 43N31 76W00 5:04:00
Rice Grove 34 13 42N55 76W20 5:05:20
Riceville 5 226 42N24 78W37 5:14:28
Riceville 18 226 43N03 74W20 4:57:20
Richburg 2 25 42N05 78W09 5:12:36

Richfield 39 78 42N51 75w02 5:00:08
Richfield Springs 39 78 42N51 74w59 4:59:56
Richford 54 226 42N23 76w12 5:04:48
Richland 38 226 43N33 76w07 5:04:28
Richmond 35 47 42N47 77w31 5:10:04
Richmond Hill 41 1 40N42 73w50 4:55:20
Richmond Valley 43 11 40N31 74w15 4:57:00
Richmondville 48 13 42N38 74w34 4:58:16
Richs Corners 37 146 43N15 78w12 5:12:48
Richville 45 226 44N25 75w22 5:01:28
Riders Mills 11 11 42N30 73w31 4:54:04
Ridge 26 13 42N43 77w53 5:11:32
Ridge 52 11 40N54 72w53 4:51:32
Ridgebury 36 7 41N23 74w29 4:57:56
Ridge Mills 33 211 43N13 75w26 5:01:44
Ridgemont 28 209 43N13 77w41 5:10:44
Ridgeway 37 112 43N15 78w23 5:13:32
Ridgewood 32 190 43N15 78w39 5:14:36
Ridgewood 33 222 43N06 75w14 5:00:56
Ridgewood 41 1 40N42 73w54 4:55:36
Rifton 56 11 41N50 74w03 4:56:12
Riga 28 161 43N05 77w53 5:11:32
Rigney Bluff 28 226 43N15 77w38 5:10:32
Riley Cove 46 11 43N01 73w51 4:55:24
Ringdahl Court 33 211 43N13 75w26 5:01:44
Rio 36 1 41N23 74w43 4:58:52
Riparius 57 49 43N40 73w54 4:55:36
Ripley 7 103 42N16 79w43 5:18:52
Rippleton 27 14 42N56 75w51 5:03:24
Risingville 51 226 42N11 77w22 5:09:28
River 28 209 43N08 77w38 5:10:32
Riverdale 3 1 40N54 73w54 4:55:36
Riverdale 33 211 43N13 75w26 5:01:44
Riverhead 52 1 40N55 72w40 4:50:40
Riverside 4 20 42N05 75w48 5:03:12
Riverside 39 12 42N19 75w24 5:01:36
Riverside 46 1 42N54 73w41 4:54:44
Riverside 51 13 42N09 77w05 5:08:20
Riverside Estates 52 11 40N55 72w38 4:50:32
Riverside Manors 32 226 43N25 78w50 5:15:20
Riverside Park 56 11 41N57 74w00 4:56:00
Riverview 10 136 44N39 73w45 4:55:00
Roanoke 19 70 42N59 78w04 5:12:16
Robbins Rest 52 11 40N39 73w09 4:52:36
Roberts Corner 23 65 43N51 76w11 5:04:44
Rochdale 14 1 41N43 73w51 4:55:24
Rochdale Village 41 1 40N41 73w47 4:55:08
Rochester 28 209 43N10 77w37 5:10:28
Rockaway Beach 41 1 40N36 73w49 4:55:16
Rockaway Park 41 1 40N35 73w51 4:55:24
Rockaway Point 41 1 40N43 73w50 4:55:20
Rock City 5 226 42N05 78w26 5:13:44
Rock City 14 7 42N00 73w53 4:55:32
Rock City Falls 46 226 43N04 73w55 4:55:40
Rock Cut 34 13 43N01 76w08 5:04:32
Rockdale 9 226 42N26 75w23 5:01:32
Rockefeller Center 31 1 40N46 73w59 4:55:56
Rock Glen 61 20 42N41 78w07 5:12:28
Rock Hill 53 74 41N38 74w36 4:58:24
Rockhurst 57 226 43N28 73w39 4:54:36
Rockland 44 4 41N03 73w57 4:55:48
Rockland 53 75 41N56 74w51 4:59:24
Rockland Lake 44 4 41N08 73w56 4:55:44
Rock Stream 62 22 42N28 76w56 5:07:44
Rock Tavern 36 11 41N28 74w11 4:56:44
Rock Valley 13 226 41N51 75w08 5:00:32
Rockville 2 20 42N21 78w07 5:12:28
Rockville 36 1 41N28 74w24 4:57:36
Rockville Centre 30 210 40N40 73w39 4:54:36
Rockville Lake 2 226 42N21 78w07 5:12:28
Rockwells Mills 9 226 42N32 75w23 5:01:32
Rockwood 18 43 43N00 74w22 4:57:28
Rocky Point 10 86 44N42 73w26 4:53:44
Rocky Point 52 11 40N57 72w56 4:51:44
Rodman 23 226 43N50 75w55 5:03:40
Roe Park 60 6 41N18 73w53 4:55:32
Roessleville 1 11 42N42 73w49 4:55:16
Rolling Acres 28 14 43N12 77w49 5:11:16
Rolling Hills 28 13 43N05 77w28 5:09:52
Rolling Meadows 56 11 41N57 74w00 4:56:00
Romanoff 40 226 41N27 73w40 4:54:40
Rome 33 211 43N13 75w27 5:01:48
Romulus 50 226 42N42 77w19 5:09:16
Rondaxe 22 203 43N43 74w58 4:59:52
Rondout 56 11 41N57 74w00 4:56:00
Ronkonkoma 52 11 40N48 73w07 4:52:28
Ronkonkoma West 52 11 40N49 73w06 4:52:24
Roosa Gap 53 11 41N33 74w26 4:57:44
Roosevelt 30 1 40N41 73w35 4:54:20
Roosevelt Beach 32 226 43N19 78w52 5:15:28
Roosevelt Field 30 11 40N44 73w39 4:54:36
Rooseveltown 45 226 44N58 74w44 4:58:56
Root 29 11 42N51 74w28 4:57:52
Rosalyn Heights 30 11 40N47 73w38 4:54:32
Roscoe 53 80 41N56 74w55 4:59:40
Rose 59 33 43N10 76w53 5:07:32
Rosebank 43 1 40N36 74w05 4:56:20
Roseboom 39 140 42N43 74w44 4:58:56
Rosecrans Park 42 11 42N31 73w37 4:54:28
Rosedale 41 1 40N39 73w45 4:55:00
Rose Grove 52 11 40N53 72w23 4:49:32
Rose Hill 34 13 42N55 76w20 5:05:20
Roseland 28 226 43N12 77w29 5:09:56
Rosemont Park 42 1 42N39 73w43 4:54:52
Rosendale 56 11 41N51 74w05 4:56:20
Roseton 36 1 41N31 74w03 4:56:12
Rosiere 23 226 44N08 76w20 5:05:20
Roslyn 30 11 40N48 73w39 4:54:36
Roslyn Estates 30 11 40N48 73w40 4:54:40
Roslyn Harbor 30 11 40N48 73w39 4:54:36
Roslyn Heights 30 11 40N47 73w39 4:54:36
Rossburg 2 226 42N30 78w04 5:12:16
Ross Corners 4 13 42N04 76w01 5:04:04
Rossie 45 226 44N21 75w38 5:02:32
Rossman 11 111 42N24 73w47 4:55:08
Ross Mill 7 187 42N07 79w12 5:16:48
Ross's Corners 23 143 43N48 76w01 5:04:04
Rosstown 8 13 42N02 76w52 5:07:28
Rossville 43 11 40N31 74w13 4:56:52
Rotterdam 47 6 42N49 74w01 4:56:04
Rotterdam Junction 47 11 42N52 74w03 4:56:12
Round Lake 46 11 42N56 73w48 4:55:12
Round Top 20 226 42N16 74w02 4:56:08
Rouses Point 10 157 45N00 73w22 4:53:28
Roxbury 13 31 42N17 74w34 4:58:16
Roxbury 41 1 40N43 73w50 4:55:20
Royalton 32 90 43N12 78w33 5:14:12
Ruby 56 13 42N01 74w01 4:56:04
Ruby Corner 45 20 44N27 75w42 5:02:48
Rudeston 21 226 43N28 74w25 4:57:40
Rugby 24 1 40N39 73w56 4:55:44
Rumsey Ridge 32 199 43N09 79w00 5:16:00
Rural Grove 29 7 42N53 74w31 4:58:04
Rural Hill 23 13 42N45 77w50 5:11:20
Rush 28 27 42N59 77w41 5:10:44
Rushford 2 226 42N24 78w15 5:13:00
Rushford Lake 2 226 42N23 78w09 5:12:36
Rushville 62 25 42N46 77w14 5:08:56
Russell 45 226 44N25 75w07 5:00:28
Russell Gardens 30 1 40N47 73w43 4:54:52
Russia 22 84 43N17 75w04 5:00:16
Rutland 23 226 43N58 75w47 5:03:08
Rutland Center 23 45 43N59 75w56 5:03:44
Rutsonville 56 11 41N37 74w10 4:56:40
Ryder 24 1 40N37 73w56 4:55:44
Rye 60 212 40N59 73w41 4:54:44
Rye Hills-Rye Brook 60 212 41N00 73w40 4:54:40
Sabael 21 226 43N45 74w18 4:57:12
Sabattis 21 30 44N05 74w42 4:58:48
Sabbath Day Point 57 226 43N42 73w30 4:54:00
Sacandaga 18 7 43N13 74w10 4:56:40
Sackets Harbor 23 12 43N57 76w07 5:04:28
Sacketts Lake 53 197 41N39 74w42 4:58:48
Saddle Rock 30 1 40N48 73w45 4:55:00
Saddle Rock Estates 30 1 40N48 73w44 4:54:56
Sagaponack 52 11 40N56 72w10 4:48:40
Sages Cottages 52 11 41N06 72w22 4:49:28
Sagetown 8 13 42N02 76w52 5:07:28
Sag Harbor 52 6 41N00 72w18 4:49:12
Sailors Snug Harbor 43 1 40N38 74w06 4:56:24
Saint Albans 41 1 40N42 73w46 4:55:04
Saint Andrew 36 11 41N34 74w11 4:56:44
Saint Armand 16 226 44N24 74w02 4:56:08
Saint Bonaventure 5 226 42N05 78w28 5:13:52
Saint George 43 1 40N38 74w06 4:56:24
Saint Huberts 16 226 44N12 73w47 4:55:08
Saint James 52 11 40N53 73w09 4:52:36
Saint James Heights 52 11 40N52 73w10 4:52:40
Saint John Fisher College 28 13 43N07 77w34 5:10:16
Saint Johnsburg 32 1 43N05 78w53 5:15:32
Saint Johns Place 24 1 40N40 73w57 4:55:48
Saint Johnsville 29 69 43N01 74w41 4:58:44
Saint Lawrence Park 23 17 44N20 75w55 5:03:40
Saint Mary's Park 3 1 40N50 73w54 4:55:36
Saint Regis Falls 17 226 44N41 74w33 4:58:12
Saint Regis Indian Res 17 226 44N59 74w40 4:58:40
Saint Remy 56 11 41N57 74w00 4:56:00
Salamanca 5 14 42N10 78w43 5:14:52
Salem 58 213 43N10 73w20 4:53:20
Salem Center 60 16 41N20 73w40 4:54:40
Salina 34 13 43N06 76w10 5:04:40
Salisbury 22 214 43N09 74w47 4:59:08
Salisbury Center 22 214 43N09 74w47 4:59:08
Salisbury Mills 36 11 41N26 74w08 4:56:32
Salmon River 10 86 44N42 73w26 4:53:44
Saltaire 52 7 40N38 73w12 4:52:48
Salt Point 14 226 41N48 73w48 4:55:12

NEW YORK

Salt Springville 29 140 42N48 74w45 4:59:00
Sammonsville 18 174 42N57 74w22 4:57:28
Samsondale 44 6 41N12 73w59 4:55:56
Samsonville 56 72 41N53 74w18 4:57:12
Sanborn 32 1 43N08 78w53 5:15:32
Sandfordville 45 207 44N40 74w59 4:59:56
Sand Hill 15 145 43N01 78w30 5:14:00
Sand Hill 29 62 42N56 74w37 4:58:28
Sand Lake 42 226 42N37 73w33 4:54:12
Sand Ridge 38 182 43N15 76w14 5:04:56
Sands Point 30 7 40N51 73w42 4:54:48
Sandusky 5 226 42N30 78w23 5:13:32
Sandy Beach 15 1 43N04 78w58 5:15:52
Sandy Creek 38 226 43N38 76w06 5:04:24
Sandy Pond 38 226 43N34 76w07 5:04:28
Sanford 4 226 42N05 75w28 5:01:52
Sangerfield 33 13 42N55 75w23 5:01:32
Sanitaria Springs 4 4 42N09 75w46 5:03:04
San Remo 52 11 40N53 73w13 4:52:52
Santa Clara 17 226 44N38 74w27 4:57:48
Santapoque 52 11 40N43 73w22 4:53:28
Saranac 10 136 44N39 73w45 4:55:00
Saranac Inn 17 16 44N21 74w17 4:57:08
Saranac Lake 17 81 44N20 74w08 4:56:32
Saratoga 46 1 43N04 73w37 4:54:28
Saratoga Springs 46 1 43N05 73w47 4:55:08
Sardinia 15 226 42N34 78w32 5:14:08
Saugerties 56 215 42N05 73w57 4:55:48
Sauquoit 33 14 43N00 75w16 5:01:04
Savannah 59 25 43N05 76w45 5:07:00
Savona 51 20 42N17 77w13 5:08:52
Sawkill 56 11 41N57 74w00 4:56:00
Sawyer 32 1 43N03 78w51 5:15:24
Saxon Park 52 11 40N41 73w13 4:52:52
Sayville 52 7 40N44 73w05 4:52:20
Scarborough 60 7 41N09 73w50 4:55:20
Scarsdale 60 1 40N59 73w49 4:55:16
Scarsdale Park 60 1 40N59 73w48 4:55:12
Schaghticoke 42 11 42N51 73w38 4:54:32
Schaghticoke Hill 42 11 42N54 73w35 4:54:20
Schenectady 47 1 42N49 73w57 4:55:48
Schenevus 39 13 42N33 74w49 4:59:16
Schodack 42 68 42N32 73w41 4:54:44
Schodack Landing 42 68 42N29 73w46 4:55:04
Schoharie 48 12 42N40 74w19 4:57:16
Schroeppel 38 93 43N16 76w17 5:05:08
Schroon 16 5 43N51 73w46 4:55:04
Schroon Lake 16 5 43N50 73w46 4:55:04
Schultzville 14 64 41N56 73w54 4:55:36
Schuluski Estates 46 11 42N48 73w41 4:54:44
Schuyler 22 226 43N06 75w06 5:00:24
Schuyler Falls 10 86 44N39 73w33 4:54:12
Schuyler Lake 39 78 42N47 75w02 5:00:08
Schuylerville 46 1 43N06 73w35 4:54:20
Scio 2 109 42N09 77w59 5:11:56
Sciota 10 226 44N49 73w31 4:54:04
Scipio 6 13 42N48 76w35 5:06:20
Scipioville 6 13 42N47 76w34 5:06:16
Scondondoa 33 60 43N05 75w39 5:02:36
Scotchbush 18 226 43N00 74w41 4:58:44
Scotch Bush 29 1 42N57 74w11 4:56:44
Scotchtown 36 1 41N28 74w22 4:57:28
Scotia 47 7 42N50 73w58 4:55:52
Scott 12 16 42N44 76w14 5:04:56
Scottsburg 26 226 42N40 77w43 5:10:52
Scotts Corners 23 143 43N48 76w01 5:04:04
Scotts Corners 60 16 41N13 73w35 4:54:20
Scottsville 28 226 43N01 77w45 5:11:00
Scranton 15 153 42N44 78w50 5:15:20
Scriba 38 15 43N28 76w25 5:05:40
Scribner Corners 27 60 43N05 75w39 5:02:36
Scuttlehole 52 11 40N56 72w18 4:49:12
Sea Breeze 28 185 43N13 77w36 5:10:24
Sea Cliff 30 6 40N51 73w38 4:54:32
Seaford 30 7 40N40 73w29 4:53:56
Seager 56 42 42N09 74w37 4:58:28
Seamen's Church Institute 31 1 40N43 74w01 4:56:04
Searingtown 30 11 40N46 73w38 4:54:32
Searsburg 49 13 42N33 76w40 5:06:40
Sears Corners 40 226 41N26 73w36 4:54:24
Searsville 36 11 41N31 74w14 4:56:56
Seaview 52 11 40N39 73w09 4:52:36
Second Milo 62 14 42N40 77w03 5:08:12
Secor Gardens 60 1 40N59 73w48 4:55:12
Seeley Creek 8 13 42N02 76w52 5:07:28
Seifert Corners 33 211 43N13 75w26 5:01:44
Selden 52 11 40N52 73w02 4:52:08
Selkirk 1 11 42N32 73w48 4:55:12
Selkirk Beach 38 226 43N34 76w07 5:04:28
Sellecks Corners 45 226 44N33 74w56 4:59:44
Sempronius 6 226 42N44 76w19 5:05:16
Seneca 35 14 42N50 77w05 5:08:20
Seneca Army Depot 50 12 42N45 76w50 5:07:20
Seneca Castle 35 13 42N53 77w06 5:08:24
Seneca Falls 50 14 42N55 76w48 5:07:12
Seneca Hill 38 204 43N27 76w30 5:06:00
Seneca Knolls 34 13 43N04 76w14 5:04:56
Seneca Point 35 226 42N37 77w24 5:09:36
Sennett 6 24 42N58 76w31 5:06:04

Sentinel Heights 34 13 43N01 76W08 5:04:32
Setauket 52 11 40N57 73W07 4:52:28
Settlers Hill 40 226 41N26 73W36 4:54:24
Seven Hills 40 226 41N27 73W40 4:54:40
Seventh Day Hollow 9 226 42N43 75W44 5:02:56
Severance 16 226 43N52 73W44 4:54:56
Seward 48 13 42N42 74W35 4:58:20
Shackport 13 226 42N25 74W53 4:59:32
Shadigee 37 15 43N19 78W23 5:13:32
Shady 56 11 42N04 74W10 4:56:40
Shandaken 56 23 42N05 74W22 4:57:28
Shandelee 53 75 41N54 74W50 4:59:20
Sharon 48 11 42N47 74W36 4:58:24
Sharon Springs 48 11 42N48 74W37 4:58:28
Shawangunk 56 226 41N38 74W16 4:57:04
Shawnee 32 1 43N08 78W53 5:15:32
Sheds 27 226 42N49 75W50 5:03:20
Sheepshead Bay 5 1 40N35 73W56 4:55:44
Shekomeko 14 226 41N59 73W40 4:54:40
Shelby 37 112 43N11 78W23 5:13:32
Shelby Basin 37 112 43N13 78W23 5:13:32
Sheldon 61 226 42N44 78W23 5:13:32
Sheldon Corners 61 226 42N42 78W27 5:13:48
Sheldrake 50 226 42N41 77W21 5:09:24
Sheldrake Springs 50 226 42N37 77W33 5:10:12
Shelter Island 52 11 41N00 72W19 4:49:16
Shelter Island Heights 52 11 41N05 72W21 4:49:24
Shenorock 60 16 41N20 73W44 4:54:56
Sherburne 9 15 42N41 75W30 5:02:00
Sheridan 7 226 42N29 79W14 5:16:56
Sheridan Park 35 41 42N52 76W59 5:07:56
Sherman 7 22 42N10 79W36 5:18:24
Sherman Park 60 7 41N07 73W46 4:55:04
Shermerhorn Landing 45 20 44N27 75W42 5:02:48
Sherrill 33 13 43N05 75W36 5:02:24
Sherwood Knolls 34 12 43N03 76W15 5:05:00
Sherwood Park 42 1 42N39 73W43 4:54:52
Shinhopple 13 226 42N02 75W04 5:00:16
Shinnecock Hills 52 11 40N52 72W31 4:50:04
Shinnecock Indian Res 52 11 40N52 72W25 4:49:40
Shirley 52 11 40N47 72W51 4:51:24
Shokan 56 11 41N58 74W13 4:56:52
Sholam 56 48 41N44 74W22 4:57:28
Shongo 2 226 41N59 77W52 5:11:28
Shooktown 32 226 43N09 78W35 5:14:20
Shore Acres 7 226 42N10 79W23 5:17:32
Shore Acres 28 13 43N17 77W47 5:11:08
Shore Acres 52 11 40N59 72W32 4:50:08
Shoreham 52 11 40N57 72W54 4:51:36
Shore Haven 7 225 42N19 79W34 5:18:16
Shorelands 7 158 42N14 79W27 5:17:48
Shore Oaks 38 204 43N27 76W30 5:06:00
Shorewood 52 11 40N53 73W22 4:53:28
Shortsville 35 4 42N57 77W14 5:08:56
Short Tract 2 226 42N28 78W07 5:12:28
Shrub Oak 60 16 41N20 73W49 4:55:16
Shumla 7 14 42N27 79W20 5:17:20
Shushan 58 213 43N05 73W21 4:53:24
Shutter Corners 48 12 42N40 74W19 4:57:16
Sibleyville 28 226 42N57 77W35 5:10:20
Sidney 13 12 42N19 75W24 5:01:36
Siena 1 1 42N43 73W46 4:55:04
Sillimans Corners 5 226 42N34 78W29 5:13:56
Silver Bay 57 226 43N42 73W30 4:54:00
Silver Creek 7 216 42N33 79W10 5:16:40
Silver Lake 36 1 41N28 74W24 4:57:36
Silver Lake 61 226 42N42 78W01 5:12:04
Silver Lake Village 36 1 41N28 74W24 4:57:36
Silver Springs 61 100 42N40 78W05 5:12:20
Simpsonville 13 13 42N33 74W49 4:59:16
Sinclairville 7 67 42N16 79W16 5:17:04
Sissonville 45 207 44N40 74W59 4:59:56
Skaneateles 34 13 42N57 76W26 5:05:44
Skaneateles Falls 34 24 43N00 76W27 5:05:48
Skerry 17 193 44N51 74W24 4:57:36
Skinnerville 45 105 44N48 74W47 4:59:08
Sky Meadow Farms 60 1 41N00 73W40 4:54:40
Slab City 45 207 44N40 74W59 4:59:56
Slabtown 8 226 42N12 76W48 5:07:12
Slate Hill 36 7 41N23 74W29 4:57:56
Slaterville Springs 55 226 42N24 76W21 5:05:24
Sleepy Hollow Manor 60 6 41N04 73W51 4:55:24
Sleightsburg 56 11 41N54 73W59 4:55:56
Slingerlands 1 11 42N38 73W52 4:55:28
Sliters 42 1 42N37 73W43 4:54:52
Sloan 15 7 42N54 78W47 5:15:08
Sloansville 48 12 42N46 74W20 4:57:20
Sloatsburg 44 4 41N09 74W12 4:56:48
Slyboro 58 42 43N24 73W16 4:53:04
Smallwood 53 226 41N40 74W49 4:59:16
Smartville 38 14 43N39 76W04 5:04:16
Smithboro 54 20 42N02 76W24 5:05:36
Smith Corners 22 196 43N00 75W00 5:00:00
Smithfield 14 11 41N51 73W33 4:54:12
Smithfield 27 226 42N58 75W40 5:02:40
Smiths Basin 58 123 43N25 73W29 4:53:56
Smiths Corner 1 226 42N26 74W08 4:56:32
Smiths Mills 7 226 42N28 79W10 5:16:40
Smithtown 52 6 40N51 73W12 4:52:48
Smithtown Pines 52 6 40N51 73W14 4:52:56
Smith Valley 49 226 42N19 76W44 5:06:56
Smithville 9 226 42N25 75W46 5:03:04
Smithville 23 12 43N52 76W06 5:04:24
Smithville Flats 9 226 42N24 75W49 5:03:16
Smyrna 9 226 42N41 75W37 5:02:28
Snowden 39 226 42N40 75W03 5:00:12
Snufftown 36 7 41N24 74W20 4:57:20
Snyder 15 7 42N58 78W48 5:15:12
Snyders Corners 42 220 42N43 73W41 4:54:44
Snyders Lake 42 220 42N43 73W41 4:54:44
Snyderville 11 226 42N03 73W48 4:55:12
Sodom 40 226 41N26 73W36 4:54:24
Sodom 57 49 43N42 73W59 4:55:56
Sodus 59 108 43N14 77W04 5:08:16
Sodus Center 59 108 43N12 77W01 5:08:04
Sodus Point 59 22 43N16 77W00 5:08:00
Solon 12 41 42N36 76W01 5:04:04
Solsville 27 180 42N55 75W31 5:02:04
Solvay 34 12 43N03 76W13 5:04:52
Somers 60 16 41N19 73W43 4:54:52
Somerset 32 226 43N28 78W33 5:14:12
Somerville 45 178 44N20 75W28 5:01:52
Sonora 51 226 42N17 77W13 5:08:52
Sonyea 26 13 42N41 77W50 5:11:20
Sound Beach 52 11 40N58 72W58 4:51:52
Soundview 3 1 40N50 73W51 4:55:24
South 60 1 40N55 73W53 4:55:32
South Addison 51 13 42N06 77W14 5:08:56
South Alabama 19 226 43N04 78W24 5:13:36
South Albany 1 1 42N28 73W48 4:55:12
South Albion 38 25 43N31 76W00 5:04:00
South Amenia 14 11 41N48 73W34 4:54:16
Southampton 52 6 40N53 72W23 4:49:32
South Amsterdam 29 1 42N55 74W11 4:56:44
South Apalachin 54 36 42N04 76W10 5:04:40
South Argyle 58 226 43N14 73W30 4:54:00
South Attica 61 148 42N52 78W17 5:13:08
South Bay 27 226 43N05 75W45 5:03:00
South Bay Village 58 123 43N25 73W29 4:53:56
South Berne 1 226 42N38 74W08 4:56:32
South Bethlehem 1 11 42N32 73W51 4:55:24
South Bloomfield 35 47 42N54 77W25 5:09:40
South Bolivar 2 24 42N04 78W10 5:12:40
South Bombay 17 125 44N49 74W33 4:58:12
South Bradford 51 226 42N17 77W13 5:08:52
South Bristol 35 226 42N43 77W24 5:09:36
South Brookfield 27 16 42N46 75W17 5:01:08
South Buffalo 15 153 42N52 78W50 5:15:20
South Butler 59 25 43N08 76W46 5:07:04
South Byron 19 70 43N03 78W04 5:12:16
South Cairo 20 3 42N17 73W57 4:55:48
South Cambridge 58 11 42N57 73W26 4:53:44
South Canisteo 51 100 42N16 77W37 5:10:28
South Chili 28 15 43N01 77W45 5:11:00
South Clyde 59 99 43N05 76W52 5:07:28
South Colton 45 226 44N31 74W53 4:59:32
South Columbia 22 78 42N51 74W59 4:59:56
South Corinth 46 7 43N15 73W50 4:55:20
South Corning 51 13 42N07 77W02 5:08:08
South Cortland 12 41 42N35 76W12 5:04:48
South Danby 55 226 42N17 76W23 5:05:32
South Dansville 51 95 42N24 77W42 5:10:48
South Dayton 5 217 42N22 79W03 5:16:12
South Durham 20 226 42N19 74W03 4:56:12
Southeast 40 226 41N24 73W36 4:54:24
Southeast Owasco 6 13 42N43 76W25 5:05:40
South Edmeston 39 226 42N41 75W19 5:01:16
South Edwards 45 226 44N19 75W15 5:01:00
South Fallsburg 53 74 41N43 74W38 4:58:32
South Farmingdale 30 11 40N43 73W26 4:53:44
Southfields 36 4 41N15 74W11 4:56:44
South Floral Park 30 1 40N43 73W42 4:54:48
Southgate Plaza 15 153 42N51 78W46 5:15:04
South Gilboa 48 226 42N25 74W37 4:58:28
South Glens Falls 46 1 43N18 73W38 4:54:32
South Granville 58 42 43N24 73W16 4:53:04
South Greece 28 209 43N13 77W41 5:10:44
South Hamilton 27 13 42N44 75W33 5:02:12
South Hannibal 38 226 43N19 76W35 5:06:20
South Hartford 39 226 42N35 75W04 5:00:16
South Hartford 58 226 43N21 73W22 4:53:28
South Haven 52 11 40N44 73W02 4:52:08
South Hempstead 30 6 40N42 73W37 4:54:28
South Hill 55 186 42N28 76W29 5:05:56
South Holbrook 52 11 40N48 73W04 4:52:16
South Horicon 57 11 43N41 73W45 4:55:00
South Hornell 51 102 42N20 77W40 5:10:40
South Hudson Falls 58 1 43N17 73W35 4:54:20
South Huntington 52 6 40N50 73W25 4:53:40
South Ilion 22 184 43N01 75W02 5:00:08
South Jamesport 52 11 40N56 72W35 4:50:20
South Jefferson 48 226 42N25 74W37 4:58:28
South Jewett 20 52 42N13 74W13 4:56:52
South Kortright 13 226 42N21 74W43 4:58:52
South Lake 40 226 41N27 73W40 4:54:40
South Lebanon 27 13 42N44 75W33 5:02:12
South Lima 26 226 42N51 77W41 5:10:44
South Livonia 26 20 42N49 77W40 5:10:40
South Lockport 32 190 43N09 78W42 5:14:48
South Millbrook 14 39 41N47 73W41 4:54:44
South New Berlin 9 226 42N32 75W23 5:01:32
South Newstead 15 145 43N01 78W30 5:14:00
South Nineveh 4 17 42N11 75W38 5:02:32
South Nyack 44 1 41N05 73W55 4:55:40
Southold 52 6 41N04 72W26 4:49:44
South Olean 5 101 42N05 78W26 5:13:44
South Onondaga 34 13 42N59 76W09 5:04:36
South Otselic 9 226 42N39 75W47 5:03:08
South Owego 54 205 42N06 76W16 5:05:04
South Oxford 9 106 42N26 75W36 5:02:24
South Ozone Park 41 1 40N41 73W49 4:55:16
South Park 15 153 42N51 78W49 5:15:16
South Plainedge 30 11 40N41 73W28 4:53:52
South Plymouth 9 226 42N35 75W34 5:02:16
Southport 8 13 42N02 76W52 5:07:28
South Pulteney 51 181 42N24 77W13 5:08:52
South Richmond Hill 41 1 40N42 73W50 4:55:20
South Ripley 7 103 42N16 79W43 5:18:52
South Russell 45 226 44N25 75W09 5:00:36
South Rutland 23 226 43N54 75W48 5:03:12
South Saint Johnsville 29 62 42N56 74W37 4:58:28
South Salem 60 16 41N17 73W33 4:54:12
South Schodack 42 68 42N31 73W42 4:54:48
South Schroon 16 5 43N48 73W55 4:55:40
South Setauket 52 11 40N56 73W06 4:52:24
South Shore Plaza 15 153 42N45 78W51 5:15:24
South Side 8 13 42N05 76W48 5:07:12
South Sodus 59 22 43N04 76W59 5:07:56
South Stockton 7 67 42N16 79W15 5:17:00
South Stony Brook 52 1 40N54 73W49 4:55:16
South Trenton 33 14 43N17 75W11 5:00:44
South Valley 5 226 42N03 79W00 5:16:00
South Valley 39 140 42N48 74W45 4:59:00
South Valley Stream 30 7 40N39 73W43 4:54:52
South Vandalia 5 22 42N05 78W30 5:14:00
South Vestal 4 13 42N04 76W01 5:04:04
Southview 4 151 42N05 75W54 5:03:36
South Wales 15 22 42N43 78W35 5:14:20
South Warsaw 61 24 42N44 78W08 5:12:32
South Westbury 30 7 40N45 73W34 4:54:16
South Westerlo 1 226 42N27 74W02 4:56:08
Southwest Oswego 38 204 43N27 76W30 5:06:00
South Wilson 32 226 43N24 78W42 5:14:48
Southwood 34 13 43N01 76W08 5:04:32
South Worcester 39 13 42N36 74W45 4:59:00
Spackenkill 14 1 41N40 73W55 4:55:40
Spafford 34 226 42N50 76W17 5:05:08
Sparkill 44 4 41N02 73W56 4:55:44
Sparkle Lake 60 16 41N17 73W46 4:55:04
Sparrow Bush 36 1 41N23 74W43 4:58:52
Sparta 26 13 42N38 77W42 5:10:48
Sparta 60 166 41N10 73W51 4:55:24
Speculator 21 226 43N32 74W21 4:57:24
Speedsville 55 226 42N18 76W11 5:04:44
Speigletown 42 11 42N47 73W39 4:54:36
Spellmans 10 86 44N42 73W26 4:53:44
Spencer 54 226 42N13 76W30 5:06:00
Spencerport 28 14 43N11 77W48 5:11:12
Spencer Settlement 33 211 43N13 75W26 5:01:44
Spencertown 11 10 42N20 73W33 4:54:12
Speonk 52 11 40N49 72W43 4:50:52
Spinnerville 22 184 43N01 75W02 5:00:08
Split Rock 34 12 43N03 76W15 5:05:00
Spragueville 45 226 44N16 75W32 5:02:08
Sprakers 29 7 42N53 74W31 4:58:04
Spring Brook 15 11 42N49 78W41 5:14:44
Springfield 39 226 42N50 74W52 4:59:28
Springfield Gardens 41 1 40N41 73W45 4:55:00

Spring Glen 56 48 41N40 74w26 4:57:44
Spring Lake 6 24 43N02 76w37 5:06:28
Spring Mills 2 226 42N02 77w46 5:11:04
Springport 6 13 42N51 76w40 5:06:40
Springtown 56 11 41N45 74w05 4:56:20
Springvale 9 200 42N32 75w31 5:02:04
Spring Valley 44 4 41N07 74w02 4:56:08
Springville 15 218 42N31 78w40 5:14:40
Springville 52 11 40N52 72w31 4:50:04
Springwater 26 20 42N38 77w36 5:10:24
Springwood Village 14 11 41N47 73w55 4:55:40
Sprout Brook 29 162 42N52 74w35 4:58:20
Sproutville 14 6 41N35 73w51 4:55:24
Spruceton 20 42 42N13 74w31 4:58:04
Staatsburg 14 219 41N51 73w56 4:55:44
Stacy Basin 33 13 43N07 75w40 5:02:40
Stadium 3 1 40N50 73w52 4:55:28
Stafford 19 142 43N00 78w05 5:12:20
Stamford 13 32 42N25 74w37 4:58:28
Standish 10 192 44N43 73w55 4:55:40
Stanford 14 226 41N53 73w42 4:54:48
Stanford Heights 1 1 42N48 73w56 4:55:44
Stanfordville 14 226 41N52 73w43 4:54:52
Stanley 35 14 42N49 77w06 5:08:24
Stanley Manor 34 12 43N03 76w15 5:05:00
Stannards 2 109 42N07 77w57 5:11:48
Stanwix 33 211 43N13 75w26 5:01:44
Stanwix Heights 33 211 43N13 75w26 5:01:44
Stanwood 60 6 41N11 73w44 4:54:56
Stapleton 43 1 40N37 74w06 4:56:24
Starbuckville 57 159 43N39 73w48 4:55:12
Stark 22 226 42N55 74w49 4:59:16
Starkey 62 13 42N31 76w57 5:07:48
Starks Knob 46 226 43N06 73w35 4:54:20
Starkville 22 62 42N56 74w37 4:58:28
Star Lake 45 25 44N10 75w02 5:00:08
State Bridge 33 13 43N07 75w40 5:02:40
State Line 7 226 42N16 79w43 5:18:52
Staten Island 43 1 40N35 74w09 4:56:36
State University 30 11 40N48 73w35 4:54:20
Steamburg 5 20 42N07 78w54 5:15:36
Steam Valley 5 226 42N05 78w26 5:13:44
Stears Corners 23 143 43N46 75w57 5:03:48
Steel City 15 153 42N49 78w49 5:15:16
Steelton 15 153 42N48 78w49 5:15:16
Steinway 41 1 40N46 73w55 4:55:40
Stella 4 151 42N07 75w56 5:03:44
Stella Niagara 32 121 43N12 79w02 5:16:08
Stephens Mills 51 102 42N20 77w40 5:10:40
Stephentown 42 11 42N33 73w24 4:53:36
Sterling 6 226 43N18 76w41 5:06:44
Sterling Forest 36 226 41N11 74w19 4:57:16
Sterling Valley 6 226 43N20 76w39 5:06:36
Stetsonville 39 226 42N35 75w11 5:00:44
Steuben 33 82 43N20 75w15 5:01:00
Steuben Valley 33 14 43N14 75w16 5:01:04
Stever Mill 18 226 43N03 74w12 4:56:48
Stewart Manor 30 11 40N43 73w41 4:54:44
Stilesville 13 167 42N06 75w23 5:01:32
Stillman Village 42 11 42N45 73w21 4:53:24
Stillwater 7 187 42N06 79w16 5:17:04
Stillwater 46 4 42N58 73w41 4:54:44
Stillwater Hill 60 166 41N10 73w51 4:55:24
Stirling 52 11 41N06 72w22 4:49:28
Stissing 14 226 41N52 73w43 4:54:52
Stittville 33 14 43N13 75w17 5:01:08
Stockbridge 27 13 42N59 75w35 5:02:20
Stockholm 45 105 44N45 74w51 4:59:24
Stockport 11 11 42N19 73w45 4:55:00
Stockport 13 97 41N57 75w17 5:01:08
Stockton 7 173 42N18 79w21 5:17:24
Stockwell 33 13 42N56 75w23 5:01:32
Stokes 33 226 43N18 75w31 5:02:04
Stone Arabia 29 62 42N56 74w37 4:58:28
Stone Church 19 110 43N05 77w57 5:11:48
Stonedam 2 226 41N59 77w52 5:11:28
Stone Gate 36 226 41N21 74w11 4:56:44
Stone Mills 23 226 44N12 75w58 5:03:52
Stone Ridge 29 174 42N57 74w22 4:57:28
Stone Ridge 56 11 41N52 74w09 4:56:36
Stony Brook 52 11 40N56 73w09 4:52:36
Stony Creek 23 65 43N49 76w14 5:04:56
Stony Hollow 56 11 41N57 74w00 4:56:00
Stony Point 44 6 41N14 73w59 4:55:56
Stoodley Corners 47 1 42N51 73w57 4:55:48
Stormville 14 17 41N34 73w45 4:55:00
Stottville 11 11 42N17 73w44 4:54:56
Stow 7 226 42N09 79w25 5:17:40
Straits Corners 54 205 42N06 76w16 5:05:04
Stratford 18 226 43N11 74w40 4:58:40
Strathmore 30 11 40N48 73w41 4:54:44
Streetroad 16 226 43N51 73w25 4:53:40
Strykersville 61 226 42N42 78w27 5:13:48
Sturges Corner 13 13 42N28 74w51 4:59:24
Stuyvesant 11 66 42N24 73w45 4:55:00
Stuyvesant 24 1 40N41 73w55 4:55:40
Stuyvesant Falls 11 11 42N21 73w44 4:54:56
Suffern 44 7 41N07 74w09 4:56:36
Suffern Park 44 4 41N08 74w06 4:56:24
Suffolk Plaza 52 11 40N52 74w49 4:59:16
Sugarbush 17 113 44N30 74w07 4:56:28
Sugar Loaf 36 226 41N19 74w17 4:57:08
Sugartown 5 226 42N13 78w38 5:14:32
Sullivan 27 226 43N06 75w53 5:03:32
Sullivanville 8 226 42N11 76w49 5:07:16
Summerhill 6 13 42N39 76w19 5:05:16
Summit 48 13 42N35 74w37 4:58:28
Summit Park 44 4 41N07 74w03 4:56:12
Summit Park Mall 32 199 43N06 78w58 5:15:52
Summitville 53 11 41N37 74w27 4:57:48
Sun 17 141 44N54 74w10 4:56:40
Sundown 56 226 41N53 74w28 4:57:52
Sunmount 17 221 44N14 74w28 4:57:52
Sunny Side 7 187 42N06 79w16 5:17:04
Sunnyside 41 1 40N45 73w55 4:55:40
Sunrise Terrace 4 151 42N06 75w54 5:03:36
Sunset 24 1 40N38 74w01 4:56:04
Sunset Bay 7 216 42N34 79w07 5:16:28
Sunset Bay 7 226 42N10 79w23 5:17:32
Sunset Beach 32 226 43N25 78w50 5:15:20
Sunset Beach 37 146 43N19 78w15 5:13:00
Sunset Manor 33 222 43N07 75w18 5:01:12
Sunside 20 226 42N18 74w00 4:56:00
SUNY 1 1 42N40 73w48 4:55:12
Surprise 20 226 42N24 73w57 4:55:48
Svahn Manor 44 4 41N08 73w56 4:55:44
Swain 2 20 42N29 77w51 5:11:24
Swan Lake 53 189 41N45 74w47 4:59:08
Swartwood 8 226 42N12 76w34 5:06:16
Swastika 10 86 44N38 73w34 4:54:16
Swazey Acres 46 11 42N48 73w41 4:54:44
Sweden 28 226 43N11 77w56 5:11:44
Sweet Meadows 56 1 41N43 73w55 4:55:40
Swenson Drive 14 6 41N36 73w53 4:55:32
Swormville 15 11 43N02 78w42 5:14:48
Sycaway 42 220 42N43 73w41 4:54:44
Sylvan Beach 33 226 43N12 75w44 5:02:56
Sylvan Beach 51 181 42N24 77w13 5:08:52
Sylvan Lake 14 226 41N36 73w47 4:55:08
Syosset 30 7 40N50 73w30 4:54:00
Syracuse 34 41 43N03 76w09 5:04:36
Taberg 33 226 43N18 75w37 5:02:28
Tabor Corners 26 226 42N34 77w36 5:10:24
Taborton 42 226 42N38 73w32 4:54:08
Taconic Lake 42 11 42N45 73w21 4:53:24
Taghkanic 11 226 42N08 73w41 4:54:44
Talcottville 25 226 43N29 75w20 5:01:20
Talcville 45 226 44N19 75w15 5:01:00
Tallman 44 4 41N07 74w06 4:56:24
Tannersville 20 23 42N12 74w08 4:56:32
Tappan 44 16 41N01 73w57 4:55:48
Tarrytown 60 6 41N04 73w52 4:55:28
Tarrytown Heights 60 6 41N04 73w51 4:55:24
Taunton 34 12 43N03 76w13 5:04:52
Taylor 12 226 42N36 75w55 5:03:40
Taylor Settlement 23 143 43N48 76w01 5:04:04
Taylorshire 15 170 42N46 78w37 5:14:28
Teboville 17 193 44N51 74w17 4:57:08
Ten Mile River 53 226 41N36 75w04 5:00:16
Tennanah 53 80 41N56 74w55 4:59:40
Tennanah Lake 53 80 41N56 74w55 4:59:40
Terminal 43 1 40N38 74w06 4:56:24
Terrace Park 45 201 44N42 75w29 5:01:56
Terrys Corners 32 121 43N11 79w02 5:16:08
Terryville 52 11 40N55 73w03 4:52:12
Texas 38 14 43N28 76w14 5:04:56
Texas Valley 12 13 42N27 76w02 5:04:08
Thayer Corners 17 141 44N54 74w10 4:56:40
The Bridges 37 105 43N20 78w08 5:12:32
The Forge 17 188 44N56 74w05 4:56:20
The Forks 5 226 42N34 78w29 5:13:56
The Glen 57 63 43N35 73w52 4:55:28
The Narrows 5 226 42N20 78w27 5:13:48
Thendara 22 59 43N42 75w00 5:00:00
The Plains 58 11 43N02 73w23 4:53:32
Theresa 23 226 44N13 75w48 5:03:12
The Springs 52 11 40N57 72w11 4:48:44
The Terrace 30 11 40N50 73w42 4:54:48
The Vly 56 11 41N51 74w09 4:56:36
Thiells 44 4 41N13 74w01 4:56:04
Thomas Settlement 23 143 43N48 76w01 5:04:04
Thomaston 30 1 40N47 73w43 4:54:52
Thompson 35 4 43N04 76w59 5:07:56
Thompson 53 197 41N39 74w40 4:58:40
Thompson Ridge 36 11 41N34 74w20 4:57:20
Thompsons Lake 1 40 42N42 74w02 4:56:08
Thompsonville 53 74 41N40 74w38 4:58:32
Thomson 58 226 43N07 73w35 4:54:20
Thornton 7 226 42N18 79w06 5:16:24
Thornton Grove 34 13 42N57 76w25 5:05:40
Thornton Heights 34 13 42N57 76w25 5:05:40
Thornwood 60 7 41N07 73w47 4:55:08
Thousand Island Park 23 163 44N17 76w02 5:04:08
Three Mile Bay 23 226 44N05 76w12 5:04:48
Three Rivers 34 13 43N09 76w13 5:04:52
Throgg's Neck 3 1 40N49 73w49 4:55:16
Throop 6 24 42N59 76w36 5:06:24
Thurman 56 11 41N38 73w57 4:55:48
Thurston 51 226 42N14 77w17 5:09:08
Thurston Road 28 209 43N08 77w39 5:10:36

NEW YORK

Tiana 52 11 40N52 72w31 4:50:04
Tiana Shores 52 11 40N50 72w35 4:50:20
Ticonderoga 16 6 43N51 73w26 4:53:44
Tillson 56 11 41N50 74w04 4:56:16
Times Plaza 24 1 40N41 73w59 4:55:56
Times Square 31 1 40N46 73w59 4:55:56
Timothy Heights 14 11 41N45 73w50 4:55:20
Tinkertown 2 226 42N15 77w47 5:11:08
Tioga 54 226 42N06 76w21 5:05:24
Tioga Terrace 54 226 42N04 76w10 5:04:40
Tiona 4 226 42N13 76w11 5:04:44
Tivoli 14 5 42N04 73w55 4:55:40
Toddsville 39 13 42N42 74w55 4:59:40
Toddville 60 6 41N17 73w53 4:55:32
Todt Hill 43 1 40N38 74w06 4:56:24
Toll Gate Corner 5 226 42N02 78w20 5:13:20
Tomhannock 42 11 42N54 73w34 4:54:16
Tomkins Cove 44 1 41N16 73w59 4:55:56
Tomlinson Corners 28 13 43N00 77w34 5:10:16
Tompkins 13 226 42N08 75w16 5:01:04
Tompkins Corners 8 226 42N11 76w49 5:07:16
Tompkins Corners 40 6 41N20 73w52 4:55:28
Tompkins Square 31 1 40N44 73w59 4:55:56
Tompkinsville 43 1 40N38 74w06 4:56:24
Tonawanda 15 1 43N01 78w53 5:15:32
Tonawanda Indian Reservation 15 226 42N35 78w15 5:13:00
Tonawanda Junction 15 1 42N58 78w51 5:15:24
Tonetta Lake Heights 40 226 41N26 73w36 4:54:24
Topps Henrietta Plaza 28 20 43N05 77w38 5:10:32
Torrey 62 12 42N41 76w59 5:07:56
Tottenville 43 11 40N31 74w15 4:57:00
Towerville Corners 7 187 42N06 79w16 5:17:04
Towlesville 51 14 42N20 77w19 5:09:16
Towners 40 7 41N31 73w39 4:54:36
Town Line 15 38 42N53 78w33 5:14:12
Town of Tonawanda 15 1 42N59 78w52 5:15:28
Town Pump 28 14 43N12 77w48 5:11:12
Townsend 49 14 42N23 76w53 5:07:32
Townsendville 50 226 42N37 77w33 5:10:12
Tracy Creek 4 13 42N04 76w01 5:04:04
Trainsmeadow 41 1 40N46 73w53 4:55:32
Transitown 15 7 42N59 78w45 5:15:00
Travis 43 1 40N38 74w06 4:56:24
Treadwell 13 226 42N21 75w03 5:00:12
Tremont 3 1 40N51 73w54 4:55:36
Trenton 33 14 43N15 75w12 5:00:48
Trenton Assembly Park 33 14 43N17 75w11 5:00:44
Trenton Falls 33 14 43N17 75w11 5:00:44
Triangle 4 226 42N22 75w55 5:03:40
Triangle Lake 1 226 42N36 74w20 4:57:20
Tribes Hill 29 1 42N57 74w17 4:57:08
Triborough 31 1 40N48 73w57 4:55:48
Tripoli 12 226 42N44 75w57 5:03:48
Tripoli 58 123 43N25 73w29 4:53:56
Troupsburg 51 226 42N03 77w32 5:10:08
Trout Creek 13 226 42N12 75w17 5:01:08
Trout River 17 193 44N56 74w18 4:57:12
Troy 42 220 42N44 73w41 4:54:44
Truesdale Lake 60 16 41N17 73w33 4:54:12
Trumansburg 55 14 42N33 76w40 5:06:40
Trumbulls Corners 55 226 42N22 76w35 5:06:20
Truthville 58 42 43N27 73w21 4:53:24
Truxton 12 16 42N42 76w02 5:04:08
Tuckahoe 52 11 40N53 72w23 4:49:32
Tuckahoe 60 6 40N57 73w49 4:55:16
Tucker Heights 46 11 42N55 73w49 4:55:16
Tucker Terrace 45 195 44N56 74w54 4:59:36
Tudor 31 1 40N45 73w58 4:55:52
Tully 34 91 42N48 76w07 5:04:28
Tully Valley 34 91 42N48 76w06 5:04:24
Tunnel 4 127 42N13 75w44 5:02:56
Tupper Lake 17 221 44N14 74w28 4:57:52
Turin 25 156 44N01 75w35 5:02:20
Turnwood 56 75 41N54 74w50 4:59:20
Tuscan 39 13 42N36 74w45 4:59:00
Tuscarora 26 13 42N38 77w52 5:11:28
Tuscarora 51 226 42N03 77w15 5:09:00
Tuscarora Indian Reservation 32 121 43N12 78w57 5:15:48
Tusten 53 226 41N35 74w59 4:59:56
Tuthill 56 122 41N41 74w09 4:56:36
Tuxedo 36 6 41N13 74w11 4:56:44
Tuxedo Park 36 6 41N12 74w11 4:56:44
Twelve Corners 28 13 43N07 77w34 5:10:16
Twilight Park 20 23 42N12 74w06 4:56:24
Twin Lakes Village 60 16 41N18 73w35 4:54:20
Twin Orchards 4 13 42N04 76w01 5:04:04
Tyner 9 226 42N26 75w36 5:02:24
Tyre 50 19 42N59 77w24 5:09:36
Tyrone 49 226 42N26 77w04 5:08:16
Ulster 56 7 41N59 73w59 4:55:56
Ulster Heights 56 48 41N43 74w24 4:57:36
Ulster Landing 56 215 42N04 73w57 4:55:48
Ulster Park 56 11 41N51 73w59 4:55:56

NEW YORK

Ulsterville 56 226 41N37 74w18 4:57:12
Ulysses 55 13 42N31 76w37 5:06:28
Unadilla 39 13 42N20 75w19 5:01:16
Unadilla Forks 39
13 42N53 75w12 5:00:48
Underwood Club 16
50 44N10 73w37 4:54:28
Union 4 13 42N07 76w03 5:04:12
Uniondale 30 11 40N43 73w36 4:54:24
Union Falls 10 44 44N27 73w41 4:54:44
Union Hill 59 4 43N13 77w23 5:09:32
Union Mills 18 226 43N03 74w12 4:56:48
Union Springs 6 13 42N51 76w42 5:06:48
Union Vale 14 226 41N41 73w42 4:54:48
Union Valley 9 226 42N46 75w53 5:03:32
Unionville 1 11 42N37 73w49 4:55:16
Unionville 35 13 42N58 77w04 5:08:16
Unionville 36 11 41N18 74w34 4:58:16
Unionville 45 207 44N40 74w59 4:59:56
Unionville 53 226 41N51 74w33 4:58:12
United Nations New York 31
1 40N45 73w58 4:55:52
United States Public Health 43
1 40N37 74w06 4:56:24
University 34 13 43N02 76w07 5:04:28
University Gardens 30
1 40N47 73w43 4:54:52
University Heights 3
1 40N50 73w52 4:55:28
Upper Benson 21 7 43N13 74w10 4:56:40
Upper Brookville 30
11 40N50 73w35 4:54:20
Upper Grand View 44
4 41N05 73w56 4:55:44
Upper Jay 16 226 44N20 73w47 4:55:08
Upper Lisle 4 226 42N20 75w58 5:03:52
Upper Mongaup 53 25 41N29 74w49 4:59:16
Upper Nyack 44 1 41N07 73w56 4:55:44
Upper Red Hook 14 7 42N00 73w53 4:55:32
Upper Union 47 6 42N47 73w53 4:55:32
Upperville 9 15 42N41 75w34 5:02:16
Upton Lake 14 226 41N50 73w46 4:55:04
Uptown 56 11 41N57 74w00 4:56:00
Urbana 51 181 42N25 77w13 5:08:52
Uscc 36 6 41N23 73w57 4:55:48
Ushers 46 11 42N56 73w48 4:55:12
Utica 33 222 43N06 75w14 5:00:56
Utopia 41 1 40N43 73w50 4:55:20
Vail Mills 18 226 43N03 74w12 4:56:48
Vails Gate 36 165 41N27 74w04 4:56:16
Vails Gate Junction 36
165 41N27 74w04 4:56:16
Vail's Grove 40 226 41N26 73w36 4:54:24
Valatie 11 11 42N25 73w41 4:54:44
Valcour 10 86 44N35 73w32 4:54:08
Valhalla 60 7 41N05 73w47 4:55:08
Valley Cottage 44
16 41N07 73w57 4:55:48
Valley Falls 42 11 42N54 73w34 4:54:16
Valley Mills 27 13 42N59 75w35 5:02:20
Valley Pond Estates 60
1 41N16 73w41 4:54:44
Valley Stream 30 7 40N40 73w42 4:54:48
Vallonia Springs 4
17 42N12 75w36 5:02:24
Valois 49 14 42N32 76w53 5:07:32
Van Allen Park 42 1 42N39 73w43 4:54:52
Van Brunt 24 1 40N40 73w59 4:55:56
Van Buren 34 226 43N08 76w20 5:05:20
Van Buren Bay 7 134 42N29 79w20 5:17:20
Van Buren Point 7
160 42N27 79w25 5:17:40
Van Burenville 36 1 41N28 74w24 4:57:36
Van Cortlandtville 60
6 41N19 73w54 4:55:36
Van Cott 3 1 40N53 73w52 4:55:28
Vandalia 5 22 42N05 78w30 5:14:00
Van Del 15 11 42N47 78w45 5:15:00
Vanderveer Station 24
1 40N38 73w57 4:55:48
Van Deusenville 29
162 42N52 74w35 4:58:20
Van Etten 8 226 42N12 76w34 5:06:16
Van Fleet 51 226 41N59 77w19 5:09:16
Van Hornesville 22
226 42N54 74w50 4:59:20
Van Keurens 14 1 41N39 73w56 4:55:44
Van Nest 3 1 40N51 73w52 4:55:28
Varick 50 226 42N47 77w19 5:09:16
Varna 55 186 42N28 76w29 5:05:56
Varysburg 61 226 42N46 78w19 5:13:16
Vaughs Corners 58 1 43N18 73w35 4:54:20
Vega 13 42 42N11 74w36 4:58:24
Venice 6 13 42N43 76w33 5:06:12
Verbank 14 226 41N44 73w43 4:54:52
Verbank Village 14
226 41N44 73w43 4:54:52
Verdoy 1 1 42N44 73w45 4:55:00
Vermillion 38 14 43N28 76w14 5:04:56
Vermontville 17 226 44N27 74w04 4:56:16
Vernal 61 148 42N52 78w17 5:13:08
Vernon 33 13 43N04 75w33 5:02:12
Vernon Valley 52 11 40N53 73w20 4:53:20
Verona 33 13 43N09 75w36 5:02:24
Verona Beach 33 226 43N12 75w44 5:02:56
Verona Mills 33 211 43N13 75w26 5:01:44
Verplanck 60 7 41N15 73w58 4:55:52
Versailles 5 42 42N31 79w00 5:16:00
Vesper 34 91 42N48 76w06 5:04:24
Vestal 4 13 42N03 76w03 5:04:12
Vestal Gardens 4 13 42N04 76w01 5:04:04
Vestal-Twin Orchards 4
13 42N05 76w03 5:04:12
Veteran 8 226 42N14 76w48 5:07:12
Veteran 56 215 42N04 73w57 4:55:48
Veterans Administration Faci 19
142 43N00 78w11 5:12:44

Veterans Administration Hosp 15
7 42N56 78w48 5:15:12
Veterans Hospital 34
13 43N02 76w07 5:04:28
Victor 35 19 43N00 77w26 5:09:44
Victoria 7 226 42N06 79w23 5:17:32
Victory 6 226 43N12 76w39 5:06:36
Victory Heights 8
13 42N07 76w49 5:07:16
Victory Mills 46
226 43N06 73w35 4:54:20
Vienna 33 226 43N14 75w44 5:02:56
Viewmonte 11 11 42N08 73w54 4:55:36
Village 31 1 40N44 74w00 4:56:00
Village of the Branch 52
11 40N51 73w11 4:52:44
Villenova 7 226 42N23 79w07 5:16:28
Vincent 35 14 42N53 77w17 5:09:08
Vine Valley 62 226 42N42 77w16 5:09:04
Vintonton 48 13 42N34 74w30 4:58:00
Viola 44 4 41N08 74w05 4:56:20
Virgil 12 13 42N31 76w11 5:04:44
Vischer Ferry 46 4 42N51 73w53 4:55:32
Vista 60 16 41N12 73w31 4:54:04
Voak 62 14 42N40 77w03 5:08:12
Volney 38 226 43N22 76w23 5:05:32
Volusia 7 225 42N19 79w34 5:18:16
Voorheesville 1 11 42N39 73w56 4:55:44
Vosburg 2 226 42N04 78w10 5:12:40
Vukote 7 226 42N06 79w23 5:17:32
Waccabuc 60 16 41N17 73w36 4:54:24
Waddington 45 226 44N52 75w12 5:00:48
Wadhams 16 58 44N14 73w28 4:53:52
Wadhams Park 45 201 44N42 75w29 5:01:56
Wading River 52 11 40N57 72w50 4:51:20
Wadsworth 26 13 42N49 77w54 5:11:36
Wainscott 52 11 40N56 72w15 4:49:00
Waits 54 205 42N06 76w16 5:05:04
Wakefield 3 1 40N54 73w51 4:55:24
Walden 15 7 42N55 78w46 5:15:04
Walden 36 6 41N34 74w11 4:56:44
Wales 15 22 42N44 78w31 5:14:04
Wales Hollow 15 22 42N43 78w35 5:14:20
Walesville 33 222 43N07 75w18 5:01:12
Walker 28 13 43N17 77w47 5:11:08
Walkers 61 206 42N43 78w00 5:12:00
Walker Valley 56 6 41N38 74w23 4:57:32
Wallace 51 14 42N26 77w28 5:09:52
Wallington 59 108 43N14 77w04 5:08:16
Wallins Corner 29 1 42N57 74w11 4:56:44
Wallkill 56 11 41N37 74w10 4:56:40
Walloomsac 42 11 42N54 73w21 4:53:24
Wall Street 31 1 40N42 74w01 4:56:04
Walton 13 226 42N10 75w08 5:00:32
Walton Lake 36 226 41N21 74w11 4:56:44
Walworth 59 226 43N10 77w18 5:09:12
Wampsville 27 13 43N05 75w42 5:02:48
Wanakah 15 153 42N45 78w54 5:15:36
Wanakena 45 226 44N08 74w55 4:59:40
Wantagh 30 6 40N43 73w31 4:54:04
Wappinger 14 6 41N35 73w54 4:55:36
Wappingers Falls 14
6 41N36 73w55 4:55:40
Wappingers Lake 14
6 41N37 73w54 4:55:36
Ward 2 226 42N13 77w54 5:11:36
Wardwell Settlement 23
143 43N48 76w01 5:04:04
Warners 34 41 43N05 76w20 5:05:20
Warnerville 48 13 42N34 74w30 4:58:00
Warren 22 226 42N54 74w55 4:59:40
Warrensburg 57 223 43N30 73w46 4:55:04
Warrens Corners 32
226 43N09 78w35 5:14:20
Warsaw 61 24 42N45 78w08 5:12:32
Warwick 36 6 41N16 74w22 4:57:28
Washington 14 226 41N47 73w41 4:54:44
Washington Bridge 31
1 40N51 73w56 4:55:44
Washington Heights 36
1 41N28 74w25 4:57:40
Washington Lake 36
1 41N31 74w03 4:56:12
Washington Mills 33
11 43N03 75w16 5:01:04
Washingtonville 36
226 41N26 74w10 4:56:40
Wassaic 14 11 41N48 73w34 4:54:16
Waterboro 7 20 42N10 79w06 5:16:24
Waterburg 55 13 42N33 76w40 5:06:40
Waterford 46 11 42N48 73w41 4:54:44
Water Island 52 11 40N46 73w01 4:52:04
Waterloo 50 14 42N54 76w52 5:07:28
Water Mill 52 11 40N55 72w21 4:49:24
Waterport 37 146 43N19 78w15 5:13:00
Waterside Park 52
11 40N54 73w20 4:53:20
Watertown 23 45 43N59 75w55 5:03:40
Watertown Junction 23
45 43N59 75w56 5:03:44
Watervale 34 13 43N01 76w01 5:04:04
Water Valley 15 153 42N43 78w51 5:15:24
Waterville 33 13 42N56 75w23 5:01:32
Watervliet 1 1 42N44 73w42 4:54:48
Watervliet Arsenal 1
1 42N43 73w44 4:54:56
Watkins Glen 49 14 42N23 76w52 5:07:28
Watson 25 156 43N54 75w38 5:02:32
Watsonville 48 226 42N36 74w20 4:57:20
Wattlesburg 7 226 42N16 79w43 5:18:52
Watts Flats 7 20 42N06 79w23 5:17:32
Wautoma Beach 28 13 43N17 77w47 5:11:08
Wave Crest 41 1 40N43 73w50 4:55:20
Waverly 54 224 42N01 76w32 5:06:08
Wawarsing 56 48 41N45 74w24 4:57:36
Wawayanda 36 7 41N24 74w27 4:57:48
Wayland 51 35 42N34 77w35 5:10:20

Wayne 49 226 42N27 77w08 5:08:32
Wayne Center 59 99 43N04 76w59 5:07:56
Webatuck 14 11 41N39 73w34 4:54:16
Webb 22 226 43N55 74w55 4:59:40
Webbs Mills 8 13 42N02 76w52 5:07:28
Webster 28 33 43N13 77w26 5:09:44
Webster Crossing 26
20 42N40 77w38 5:10:32
Websters Corners 15
11 42N47 78w45 5:15:00
Wedgewood 49 14 42N23 76w53 5:07:32
Weedsport 6 24 43N03 76w34 5:06:16
Wegatchie 45 106 44N12 75w37 5:02:28
Welcome 39 226 42N35 75w04 5:00:16
Wells 21 226 43N24 74w17 4:57:08
Wells Bridge 39 13 42N22 75w15 5:01:00
Wellsburg 8 13 42N01 76w44 5:06:56
Wellsville 2 109 42N07 77w57 5:11:48
Weltonville 54 226 42N13 76w11 5:04:44
Wendelville 32 226 43N04 78w46 5:15:04
Wesley 5 42 42N28 78w56 5:15:44
Wesley Chapel 44 4 41N08 74w06 4:56:24
West Almond 2 71 42N18 77w54 5:11:36
West Amboy 38 182 43N17 76w04 5:04:16
West Amityville 30
6 40N41 73w26 4:53:44
West Babylon 52 1 40N42 73w21 4:53:24
West Bainbridge 9
149 42N18 75w29 5:01:56
West Bangor 17 16 44N50 74w26 4:57:44
West Barre 37 146 43N15 78w12 5:12:48
West Batavia 19 142 43N00 78w11 5:12:44
West Bay Shore 52 1 40N41 73w13 4:52:52
West Berne 1 226 42N38 74w11 4:56:44
West Bethany 19 142 43N00 78w11 5:12:44
West Bloomfield 35
226 42N54 77w31 5:10:04
West Branch 33 226 43N25 75w29 5:01:56
Westbrookville 53
21 41N30 74w34 4:58:16
West Burlington 39
226 42N42 75w11 5:00:44
Westbury 6 226 43N15 76w43 5:06:52
Westbury 30 7 40N45 73w36 4:54:24
West Bush 18 226 43N03 74w20 4:57:20
West Cameron 51 20 42N12 77w24 5:09:36
West Camp 56 11 42N07 73w56 4:55:44
West Candor 54 154 42N14 76w20 5:05:20
West Carthage 23
156 43N59 75w37 5:02:28
West Caton 51 13 42N08 77w03 5:08:12
West Catskill 20 1 42N13 73w51 4:55:24
West Charlton 46 1 42N57 74w11 4:56:44
West Chazy 10 7 44N49 73w31 4:54:04
West Chenango 4 151 42N07 75w56 5:03:44
Westchester 3 1 40N51 73w52 4:55:28
Westchester Heights 3
1 40N51 73w51 4:55:24
West Chili 28 15 43N07 77w48 5:11:12
West Clarksville 2
226 42N08 78w15 5:13:00
West Colesville 4
151 42N07 75w53 5:03:32
West Conesville 48
226 42N24 74w27 4:57:48
West Copake 11 11 42N06 73w28 4:53:52
West Corners 4 13 42N07 76w03 5:04:12
West Coxsackie 20
11 42N21 73w48 4:55:12
Westdale 33 25 43N23 75w49 5:03:16
West Danby 55 226 42N19 76w32 5:06:08
West Davenport 13
135 42N27 74w58 4:59:52
West Delhi 13 226 42N17 74w55 4:59:40
West Dryden 55 13 42N31 76w21 5:05:24
West Durham 20 226 42N24 74w10 4:56:40
West Eaton 27 226 42N51 75w39 5:02:36
West Edmeston 39
226 42N46 75w17 5:01:08
West Ellicott 7 187 42N06 79w16 5:17:04
West Elmira 8 13 42N05 76w51 5:07:24
West End 39 14 42N27 75w06 5:00:24
West Endicott 4 13 42N07 76w03 5:04:12
Westerlea 34 12 43N03 76w15 5:05:00
Westerleigh 43 1 40N38 74w08 4:56:32
Westerlo 1 226 42N31 74w03 4:56:12
Western 33 226 43N20 75w23 5:01:32
Western Pine Knolls 1
1 42N40 73w48 4:55:12
Westernville 33 226 43N18 75w23 5:01:32
West Exeter 39 226 42N48 75w09 5:00:36
West Falls 15 11 42N42 78w41 5:14:44
West Farms 3 1 40N50 73w52 4:55:28
Westfield 7 225 42N20 79w35 5:18:20
Westford 39 13 42N38 74w48 4:59:12
West Fort Ann 58
123 43N25 73w29 4:53:56
West Frankfort 22
184 43N02 75w04 5:00:16
West Fulton 48 226 42N34 74w28 4:57:52
West Gaines 37 146 43N15 78w12 5:12:48
West Galway 18 1 42N57 74w11 4:56:44
Westgate 28 209 43N08 77w43 5:10:52
West Genesee Terrace 34
12 43N03 76w15 5:05:00
West Gilgo Beach 52
11 40N37 73w25 4:53:40
West Glens Falls 57
6 43N19 73w46 4:55:04
West Glenville 47 1 42N57 74w11 4:56:44
West Granville Corners 58
6 43N33 73w24 4:53:36
West Greenville 20
226 42N25 74w01 4:56:04
West Greenwood 51
226 42N08 77w39 5:10:36
West Groton 55 13 42N35 76w22 5:05:28

Westhampton 52 6 40N49 72w40 4:50:40
Westhampton Beach 52 6 40N49 72w39 4:50:36
West Harpersfield 13 226 42N26 74w41 4:58:44
West Haverstraw 44 6 41N13 73w59 4:55:56
West Hebron 58 213 43N14 73w22 4:53:28
West Hempstead 30 6 40N42 73w38 4:54:32
West Henrietta 28 20 43N02 77w40 5:10:40
West Hill 47 1 42N48 73w56 4:55:44
West Hills 52 11 40N50 73w26 4:53:44
West Hoosick 42 11 42N57 73w26 4:53:44
West Huntington 52 6 40N51 73w23 4:53:32
West Hurley 56 11 42N00 74w06 4:56:24
West Islip 52 6 40N42 73w18 4:53:12
West Kendall 37 105 43N20 78w02 5:12:08
West Kill 20 42 42N13 74w31 4:58:04
West Laurens 39 226 42N32 75w05 5:00:20
Westlawn 1 1 42N40 73w48 4:55:12
West Lebanon 11 11 42N29 73w28 4:53:52
West Lee 33 226 43N18 75w31 5:02:04
West Leyden 25 226 43N28 75w28 5:01:52
West Lowville 25 191 43N54 75w30 5:02:00
West Martinsburg 25 226 43N54 75w30 5:02:00
West Mecox 52 11 40N55 72w21 4:49:24
Westmere 1 6 42N41 73w52 4:55:28
West Meredith 13 29 42N25 74w53 4:59:32
West Middleburg 48 226 42N36 74w20 4:57:20
West Middlebury 61 142 43N00 78w11 5:12:44
West Milton 46 11 43N01 73w51 4:55:24
Westminster Park 23 17 44N20 75w55 5:03:40
West Monroe 38 182 43N18 76w05 5:04:20
Westmore Estates 1 1 42N40 73w48 4:55:12
Westmoreland 33 11 43N07 75w27 5:01:48
Westmoreland 52 11 41N05 72w21 4:49:24
West Newark 54 226 42N13 76w11 5:04:44
West New Brighton 43 1 40N38 74w07 4:56:28
West Newburgh 36 1 41N31 74w03 4:56:12
West Nyack 44 1 41N06 73w58 4:55:52
Weston 49 13 42N31 76w58 5:07:52
West Oneonta 39 14 42N28 75w07 5:00:28
Westons Mills 5 22 42N04 78w23 5:13:32
Westover 4 116 42N07 75w58 5:03:52
West Parishville 45 207 44N40 74w59 4:59:56
West Park 56 11 41N48 73w58 4:55:52
West Pawling 14 7 41N34 73w36 4:54:24
West Perry 61 206 42N43 78w00 5:12:00
West Perrysburg 5 42 42N28 79w00 5:16:00
West Perth 18 1 42N57 74w11 4:56:44
West Phoenix 34 93 43N14 76w18 5:05:12
West Pierrepont 45 155 44N36 75w10 5:00:40
West Plattsburg 10 86 44N42 73w33 4:54:12
West Point 36 6 41N24 73w58 4:55:52
Westport 16 58 44N11 73w26 4:53:44
West Portland 7 225 42N19 79w34 5:18:16
West Potsdam 45 207 44N40 74w59 4:59:56
West Richmondville 48 13 42N38 74w34 4:58:16
West Ridge 28 185 43N13 77w39 5:10:36
West Ronkonkoma 52 11 40N49 73w06 4:52:24
West Rush 28 27 42N59 77w42 5:10:48
West Saint James 52 11 40N51 73w14 4:52:56
West Salamanca 5 14 42N09 78w43 5:14:52
West Sand Lake 42 226 42N39 73w36 4:54:24
West Saugerties 56 215 42N04 73w57 4:55:48
West Sayville 52 7 40N44 73w06 4:52:24
West Schuyler 22 222 43N06 75w15 5:01:00
West Seneca 15 153 42N51 78w48 5:15:12
West Shelby 37 112 43N13 78w23 5:13:32
West Shokan 56 37 41N58 74w17 4:57:08
West Slaterville 55 226 42N24 76w21 5:05:24
West Smithtown 52 6 40N51 73w14 4:52:56
West Somerset 32 150 43N20 78w39 5:14:36
West Sparta 26 13 42N37 77w47 5:11:08
West Stephentown 42 11 42N34 73w25 4:53:40
West Stockholm 45 20 44N43 74w54 4:59:36
West Taghkanic 11 226 42N03 73w38 4:54:32
West Tiana 52 11 40N52 72w31 4:50:04
Westtown 36 11 41N20 74w32 4:58:08
West Turin 25 77 44N07 75w34 5:02:16
West Union 51 226 42N03 77w41 5:10:44
Westvale 34 13 43N02 76w13 5:04:52
West Valley 5 226 42N24 78w37 5:14:28
West Valley Falls 42 11 42N54 73w34 4:54:16
Westview 4 151 42N07 75w56 5:03:44
Westview 26 13 42N34 77w42 5:10:48
Westville 39 13 42N33 74w49 4:59:16
Westville Center 17 193 44N56 74w18 4:57:12
West Walworth 59 226 43N04 77w18 5:09:12
West Waterford 46 11 42N48 73w41 4:54:44
West Webster 28 33 43N12 77w29 5:09:56
West Windsor 4 226 42N04 75w41 5:02:44
West Winfield 22 13 42N53 75w12 5:00:48
West Yaphank 52 11 40N49 73w00 4:52:00
Wethersfield 61 226 42N39 78w15 5:13:00
Wethersfield Springs 61 226 42N44 78w08 5:12:32
Wevertown 57 49 43N38 73w57 4:55:48
Whaley Lake 14 7 41N31 73w39 4:54:36
Whallonsburg 16 129 44N16 73w24 4:53:36
Wheatfield 32 1 43N06 78w53 5:15:32
Wheatland 28 226 43N01 77w50 5:11:20
Wheatley 30 11 40N48 73w35 4:54:20
Wheatville 19 226 43N04 78w24 5:13:36
Wheeler 51 14 42N27 77w20 5:09:20
Wheeler Estates 47 11 42N55 73w49 4:55:16
Wheelers 35 47 42N54 77w25 5:09:40
Wheelerville 18 226 43N08 74w29 4:57:56
Whig Corners 39 13 42N42 74w55 4:59:40
Whippleville 17 193 44N49 74w16 4:57:04
Whippoorwill 60 1 41N08 73w43 4:54:52
White Creek 58 11 42N59 73w20 4:53:20
Whiteface 16 1 44N17 73w59 4:55:56
White Fathers 17 113 44N30 74w07 4:56:28
Whitehall 58 6 43N33 73w24 4:53:36
White Lake 33 226 43N31 75w09 5:00:36
White Lake 53 226 41N40 74w50 4:59:20
Whitelaw 27 226 43N05 75w45 5:03:00
White Plains 60 1 41N02 73w46 4:55:04
Whiteport 56 11 41N57 74w00 4:56:00
Whitesboro 33 222 43N07 75w18 5:01:12
Whites Store 9 226 42N32 75w23 5:01:32
Whitestone 41 1 40N47 73w49 4:55:16
Whitestown 33 222 43N07 75w19 5:01:16
White Sulphur Springs 53 189 41N48 74w50 4:59:20
Whitesville 2 226 42N03 77w46 5:11:04
Whitfield 56 76 41N48 74w13 4:56:52
Whitman 13 226 42N15 75w23 5:01:32
Whitney Point 4 36 42N20 75w58 5:03:52
Wiccopee 14 226 41N36 73w47 4:55:08
Wickham Knolls 36 6 41N17 74w20 4:57:20
Wickham Village 36 6 41N17 74w20 4:57:20
Wickman Park 52 11 41N06 72w22 4:49:28
Wilbur 56 11 41N57 74w00 4:56:00
Wildwood 52 11 40N57 72w51 4:51:24
Wileyville 51 226 42N05 77w40 5:10:40
Willard 50 12 42N41 76w52 5:07:28
Willet 12 226 42N27 75w55 5:03:40
Williams Bridge 3 1 40N53 73w52 4:55:28
Williamsburg 24 1 40N42 73w57 4:55:48
Williams Grove 34 13 42N55 76w20 5:05:20
Williams Lake 56 11 41N50 74w05 4:56:20
Williamson 59 33 43N14 77w11 5:08:44
Williamstown 38 25 43N26 75w53 5:03:32
Williamsville 15 55 42N58 78w45 5:15:00
Willing 2 109 42N03 77w54 5:11:36
Williston 15 38 42N54 78w30 5:14:00
Williston Park 30 11 40N46 73w39 4:54:36
Willoughby 5 226 42N13 78w38 5:14:32
Willow 56 11 42N05 74w14 4:56:56
Willow Brook 7 226 42N10 79w23 5:17:32
Willowbrook 43 1 40N38 74w06 4:56:24
Willow Brook Park 47 1 42N51 73w57 4:55:48
Willowemac 53 75 41N54 74w50 4:59:20
Willow Glen 46 1 42N54 73w41 4:54:44
Willow Glen 55 13 42N29 76w18 5:05:12
Willow Grove 6 24 43N02 76w37 5:06:28
Willow Point 4 13 42N04 76w01 5:04:04
Willow Ridge Estates 15 1 43N00 78w51 5:15:24
Willsboro 16 56 44N22 73w24 4:53:36
Willsboro Point 16 56 44N22 73w23 4:53:32
Willseyville 54 226 42N17 76w23 5:05:32
Wilmington 16 129 44N23 73w18 4:53:12
Wilna 23 156 44N02 75w35 5:02:20
Wilson 32 226 43N19 78w50 5:15:20
Wilson Park 60 6 41N04 73w51 4:55:24
Wilton 46 226 43N10 73w43 4:54:52
Winchester 15 153 42N51 78w46 5:15:04
Windecker 25 226 43N54 75w30 5:02:00
Winderest Park 34 12 43N03 76w15 5:05:00
Windham 20 226 42N19 74w13 4:56:52
Winding Ways 34 13 42N57 76w25 5:05:40
Windmill Farms 60 1 41N08 73w43 4:54:52

NEW YORK

Windom 15 153 42N48 78w48 5:15:12
Windsor 4 226 42N04 75w41 5:02:44
Windsor Beach 28 185 43N13 77w36 5:10:24
Winebrook Hills 16 226 43N58 74w10 4:56:40
Winfield 22 226 42N54 75w09 5:00:36
Wingdale 14 11 41N39 73w34 4:54:16
Winona Lake 36 1 41N31 74w03 4:56:12
Winterton 53 11 41N33 74w26 4:57:44
Winthrop 45 105 44N48 74w47 4:59:08
Wirt 2 226 42N08 78w07 5:12:28
Wiscoy 2 226 42N34 78w02 5:12:08
Wisner 36 6 41N17 74w19 4:57:16
Witherbee 16 54 44N05 73w32 4:54:08
Wittenberg 56 11 42N02 74w09 4:56:36
Wolcott 59 33 43N13 76w49 5:07:16
Wolcottsburg 15 226 43N00 78w37 5:14:28
Wolcottsville 32 145 43N01 78w30 5:14:00
Woodbourne 53 74 41N46 74w36 4:58:24
Woodbury 30 6 40N50 73w29 4:53:56
Woodbury Falls 36 226 41N21 74w08 4:56:32
Woodcliff Park 52 11 40N55 72w45 4:51:00
Woodgate 33 226 43N31 75w09 5:00:36
Wood Haven 41 1 40N41 73w51 4:55:24
Woodhull 51 226 42N04 77w23 5:09:32
Woodinville 14 7 41N34 73w36 4:54:24
Woodland 56 88 42N05 74w19 4:57:16
Woodlands 60 1 41N02 73w48 4:55:12
Woodlawn 15 153 42N48 78w51 5:15:24
Woodlawn 3 1 40N54 73w52 4:55:28
Woodlawn 7 226 42N06 79w23 5:17:32
Woodlawn Beach 15 153 42N48 78w49 5:15:16
Woodmere 30 1 40N38 73w42 4:54:48
Woodridge 53 72 41N43 74w34 4:58:16
Woodrow 43 11 40N31 74w13 4:56:52
Woodruff Heights 47 1 42N51 73w57 4:55:48
Woodsburgh 30 11 40N38 73w43 4:54:52
Woods Corners 9 200 42N32 75w31 5:02:04
Woods Falls 10 16 44N53 73w39 4:54:36
Woodside 41 1 40N45 73w55 4:55:40
Woods Mills 10 14 44N42 73w38 4:54:32
Woodstock 56 11 42N02 74w10 4:56:40
Woodsville 26 13 42N34 77w42 5:10:48
Woodville 23 13 42N45 77w50 5:11:20
Woodville 35 226 42N37 77w24 5:09:36
Wooglin 7 158 42N14 79w27 5:17:48
Woolsey 41 1 40N46 73w55 4:55:40
Worcester 39 13 42N36 74w45 4:59:00
Worley Heights 36 226 41N21 74w11 4:56:44
Worth 23 226 43N44 75w51 5:03:24
Worthington 60 1 41N02 73w46 4:55:04
Wright 48 226 42N40 74w13 4:56:52
Wright Park Manor 33 211 43N13 75w26 5:01:44
Wrights Corners 32 190 43N13 78w41 5:14:44
Wrights Corners 34 93 43N14 76w18 5:05:12
Wright Settlement 33 211 43N13 75w26 5:01:44
Wurlitzer Park Village 32 1 43N03 78w51 5:15:24
Wurtemburg 14 64 41N56 73w54 4:55:36
Wurtsboro 53 11 41N34 74w29 4:57:56
Wurtsboro Hills 53 11 41N34 74w29 4:57:56
Wyandanch 52 11 40N45 73w22 4:53:28
Wyatts 47 1 42N51 73w57 4:55:48
Wycoff Heights 24 1 40N42 73w55 4:55:40
Wykagyl 60 1 40N57 73w47 4:55:08
Wynantskill 42 11 42N42 73w39 4:54:36
Wyomanock 42 11 42N33 73w23 4:53:32
Wyoming 61 25 42N50 78w05 5:12:20
Yaddo 46 226 43N05 73w47 4:55:08
Yagerville 56 48 41N44 74w22 4:57:28
Yaleville 45 207 44N45 74w59 4:59:56
Yankee Lake 53 11 41N34 74w29 4:57:56
Yaphank 52 11 40N50 72w59 4:51:56
Yates 37 15 43N21 78w23 5:13:32
Yatesville 62 14 42N40 77w03 5:08:12
Yonkers 60 1 40N56 73w54 4:55:36
York 26 226 42N52 77w53 5:11:32
York Corners 2 109 42N07 77w57 5:11:48
Yorkshire 5 226 42N30 78w30 5:14:00
Yorktown 60 16 41N18 73w47 4:55:08
Yorktown Heights 60 16 41N16 73w47 4:55:08
Yorkville 33 222 43N07 75w16 5:01:04
Young Hickory 51 226 42N03 77w33 5:10:12
Youngs 13 13 42N20 75w19 5:01:16
Youngstown 32 121 43N15 79w03 5:16:12
Youngstown Estates 32 226 43N20 79w02 5:16:08
Youngsville 53 226 41N48 74w54 4:59:36
Yulan 53 226 41N31 74w56 4:59:44
Zena 56 11 42N02 74w07 4:56:28
Zoar 23 143 43N51 75w56 5:03:44

TIME TABLES

NC # 1

Before 11/18/1883 LMT
11/18/1883 12:00 EST
3/31/1918 02:00 EWT
10/27/1918 02:00 EST
3/30/1919 02:00 EWT
10/26/1919 02:00 EST
2/09/1942 02:00 EWT
9/30/1945 02:00 EST
4/24/1966 02:00 US#1

NC # 2

Before 11/18/1883 LMT
11/18/1883 12:00 EST
3/31/1918 02:00 EWT
10/27/1918 02:00 EST
3/30/1919 02:00 EWT
10/26/1919 02:00 EST
2/09/1942 02:00 EWT
9/30/1945 02:00 EST
4/28/1946 02:00 EDT
9/29/1946 02:00 EST
4/24/1966 02:00 US#1

NC # 3

Before 11/18/1883 LMT
11/18/1883 12:00 EST
3/31/1918 02:00 EWT
10/27/1918 02:00 EST
3/30/1919 02:00 EWT
10/26/1919 02:00 EST
2/09/1942 02:00 EWT
9/30/1945 02:00 EST
5/20/1957 00:00 EDT
9/29/1957 02:00 EST
4/24/1966 02:00 US#1

NC # 4

Before 11/18/1883 LMT
11/18/1883 12:00 EST
3/31/1918 02:00 EWT
10/27/1918 02:00 EST
1/01/1919 02:00 CST
3/30/1919 02:00 CWT
10/26/1919 02:00 CST
2/09/1942 02:00 CWT
9/30/1945 02:00 CST
4/28/1946 02:00 CDT
9/29/1946 02:00 CST
9/28/1947 02:00 EST
4/24/1966 02:00 US#1

COUNTIES

1 Alamance
2 Alexander
3 Alleghany
4 Anson
5 Ashe
6 Avery
7 Beaufort
8 Bertie
9 Bladen
10 Brunswick
11 Buncombe
12 Burke
13 Cabarrus
14 Caldwell
15 Camden
16 Carteret
17 Caswell
18 Catawba
19 Chatham
20 Cherokee
21 Chowan
22 Clay
23 Cleveland
24 Columbus
25 Craven
26 Cumberland
27 Currituck
28 Dare
29 Davidson
30 Davie
31 Duplin
32 Durham
33 Edgecombe
34 Forsyth
35 Franklin
36 Gaston
37 Gates
38 Graham
39 Granville
40 Greene
41 Guilford
42 Halifax
43 Harnett
44 Haywood
45 Henderson
46 Hertford
47 Hoke
48 Hyde
49 Iredell
50 Jackson
51 Johnston
52 Jones
53 Lee
54 Lenoir
55 Lincoln
56 McDowell
57 Macon
58 Madison
59 Martin
60 Mecklenburg
61 Mitchell
62 Montgomery
63 Moore
64 Nash
65 New Hanover
66 Northampton
67 Onslow
68 Orange
69 Pamlico
70 Pasquotank
71 Pender
72 Perquimans
73 Person
74 Pitt
75 Polk
76 Randolph
77 Richmond
78 Robeson
79 Rockingham
80 Rowan
81 Rutherford
82 Sampson
83 Scotland
84 Stanly
85 Stokes
86 Surry
87 Swain
88 Transylvania
89 Tyrrell
90 Union
91 Vance
92 Wake
93 Warren
94 Washington
95 Watauga
96 Wayne
97 Wilkes
98 Wilson
99 Yadkin
100 Yancey

Aarons Corner 85 1 36N29 80w27 5:21:48
Abbotts 9 1 34N32 78w43 5:14:52
Abbottsburg 1 34N31 78w44 5:14:56
Abbottsburg 9 1 35N00 79w00 5:16:00
Aberdeen 63 1 35N08 79w26 5:17:44
Abner 62 1 35N24 79w47 5:19:08
Abshers 97 1 36N21 81w01 5:24:04
Acme 24 1 34N19 78w12 5:12:48
Acme 36 1 35N15 81w02 5:24:08
Acorn Hill 37 1 36N27 76w37 5:06:28
Acre 7 1 35N37 76w52 5:07:28
Acton 11 2 35N35 82w36 5:30:24
Adams 95 1 36N13 81w40 5:26:40
Adamsville 96 1 35N22 77w57 5:11:48
Addie 50 2 35N24 83w10 5:32:40
Addor 63 1 35N08 79w26 5:17:44
Adoniram 39 1 36N33 78w47 5:15:08
Advance 30 1 35N57 80w25 5:21:40
Afton 93 1 36N24 78w09 5:12:36
Aho 95 1 36N07 81w40 5:26:40
Ahoskie 46 1 36N17 76w59 5:07:56
Ai 73 1 36N17 78w57 5:15:48
Airboro 96 1 35N22 77w58 5:11:52
Airlie 42 1 36N26 77w55 5:11:40
Alamance 1 1 36N08 79w29 5:17:56
Alarka 87 1 35N21 83w27 5:33:48
Albemarle 84 1 35N21 80w11 5:20:44
Albemarle Beach 94 1 35N53 76w36 5:06:24
Albertson 31 1 35N07 77w48 5:11:12
Albrittons 54 1 35N16 77w35 5:10:20
Alert 35 1 36N24 78w09 5:12:36
Alexander 11 2 35N42 82w37 5:30:28
Alexander Mills 81 1 35N19 81w51 5:27:24
Alexanders Store 60 1 35N16 80w48 5:23:12
Alexis 36 1 35N24 81w07 5:24:28
Alfordsville 78 1 34N38 79w21 5:17:24
Alleghany 29 1 35N32 80w07 5:20:28
Allen 60 1 35N12 80w45 5:23:00
Allendale 47 1 34N52 79w17 5:17:08
Allen Jay 41 1 35N55 79w59 5:19:56
Allensville 73 1 36N24 78w57 5:15:48
All Healing Springs 2 1 35N55 81w10 5:24:40
Alliance 69 1 35N09 76w49 5:07:16
Alligator 89 1 35N56 76w07 5:04:28
Allison 17 1 36N27 79w39 5:18:36
Allreds 62 1 35N24 79w47 5:19:08
Alma 78 1 34N44 79w21 5:17:24
Almond 87 2 35N22 83w34 5:34:16
Altamahaw 1 1 36N11 79w30 5:18:00
Altamont 6 1 36N00 81w57 5:27:48
Altapass 61 1 35N55 82w04 5:28:16
Amantha 95 1 36N15 81w47 5:27:08
Amerotron Mill 78 1 34N49 79w11 5:16:44
Amity 49 1 35N44 80w41 5:22:44
Amity Gardens 60 1 35N14 80w47 5:23:08
Ammon 9 1 34N38 78w33 5:14:12
Anderson 17 1 36N18 79w20 5:17:20
Anderson 28 1 36N04 75w42 5:02:48
Anderson Creek 43 1 35N16 78w56 5:15:44
Anderson Crossroads 42 1 36N26 77w55 5:11:40
Andrews 20 2 35N12 83w49 5:35:16
Angier 43 1 35N31 78w44 5:14:56
Ansonville 4 1 35N06 80w07 5:20:28
Antioch 10 1 34N04 78w09 5:12:36
Antioch 47 1 34N49 79w11 5:16:44
Antioch 58 1 35N48 82w41 5:30:44
Apex 92 1 35N44 78w51 5:15:24
Apple Grove 5 1 36N30 81w30 5:26:00
Aquadale 84 1 35N14 80w07 5:20:28
Aquone 57 1 35N11 83w38 5:34:32
Arabia 47 1 34N59 79w13 5:16:52
Arapahoe 69 1 35N02 76w49 5:07:16
Ararat 86 1 36N24 80w33 5:22:12
Arba 40 1 35N27 77w40 5:10:40
Arcadia 29 1 35N58 80w17 5:21:08
Archdale 76 1 35N56 79w57 5:19:48
Archer 51 1 35N39 78w27 5:13:48
Arcola 93 1 36N24 78w09 5:12:36
Arden 11 1 35N29 82w31 5:30:04
Ardmore 34 1 36N05 80w17 5:21:08
Ardulusa 26 1 35N04 78w53 5:15:32
Argura 50 1 35N16 83w07 5:32:28
Arlington 99 1 36N14 80w50 5:23:20
Armour 24 1 34N20 78w14 5:12:56
Arnold 29 1 35N49 80w15 5:21:00
Artesia 24 1 34N20 78w36 5:14:24
Arthur 74 1 35N35 77w29 5:09:56
Asbury 85 1 36N30 80w35 5:22:20
Ash 10 1 34N04 78w32 5:14:08
Asheboro 76 1 35N43 79w49 5:19:16
Asheville 11 2 35N36 82w33 5:30:12
Ashford 56 1 35N41 82w00 5:28:00
Ash Hill 86 1 36N24 80w33 5:22:12
Ashland 5 1 36N26 81w37 5:26:28
Ashley Heights 47 1 35N08 79w26 5:17:44
Ashton 71 1 34N33 77w55 5:11:40
Ashton Forrest 26 1 35N02 78w57 5:15:48
Ashwood 69 1 35N02 76w41 5:06:44
Askewville 8 1 36N07 76w57 5:07:48
Askin 25 1 35N15 77w04 5:08:16
Aspen 93 1 36N26 77w55 5:11:40
Assembly 44 1 35N32 82w58 5:31:52
Atando 60 1 35N15 80w50 5:23:20
Athens 78 1 34N54 79w01 5:16:04
Atkinson 71 1 34N32 78w10 5:12:40
Atlantic 16 1 34N53 76w20 5:05:20
Atlantic Beach 16 1 34N42 76w44 5:06:56
Atlantic Christian College 98 1 35N44 77w55 5:11:40
Atwell 80 1 35N34 80w41 5:22:44
Auburn 92 1 35N46 78w37 5:14:28
Audubon 65 3 34N13 77w55 5:11:40
Aulander 8 1 36N14 77w07 5:08:28
Aurelian Springs 42 1 36N26 77w55 5:11:40
Aurora 7 1 35N18 76w47 5:07:08
Austin 97 1 36N15 80w52 5:23:28
Austins Mill 84 1 35N27 80w13 5:20:52
Autryville 82 1 35N00 78w39 5:14:36
Aventon 64 1 36N06 77w43 5:10:52
Averasboro 43 1 35N19 78w36 5:14:24
Avery Creek 11 1 35N29 82w36 5:30:24
Avon 28 1 35N21 75w30 5:02:00
Avondale 81 1 35N16 81w48 5:27:12
Axtell 93 1 36N27 78w12 5:12:48
Ayden 74 1 35N28 77w20 5:09:20
Aydlett 27 1 36N20 75w55 5:03:40
Ayersville 79 1 36N25 79w58 5:19:52
Azalea 11 1 35N36 82w31 5:30:04
Azalea 65 3 34N13 77w55 5:11:40
Bachelor 25 1 34N53 76w54 5:07:36
Back Creek 76 1 35N45 79w52 5:19:28
Back Swamp 78 1 34N34 79w07 5:16:28
Badin 84 1 35N24 80w06 5:20:24
Bagley 51 1 35N36 78w07 5:12:28
Bahama 32 1 36N10 78w53 5:15:32
Bailey 64 1 35N47 78w07 5:12:28
Bakers 90 1 34N59 80w33 5:22:12
Bakersville 61 1 36N01 82w10 5:28:40
Bald Creek 100 1 35N55 82w25 5:29:40
Bald Mountain 95 1 36N18 81w36 5:26:24
Bald Mountain 100 1 35N55 82w18 5:29:12
Baldwin 5 1 36N24 81w29 5:25:56
Baldwin 19 1 35N49 79w09 5:16:36
Baldwin 63 1 35N32 79w46 5:19:04
Balfour 45 1 35N21 82w29 5:29:56
Balfours 76 1 35N44 79w48 5:19:12
Ball 5 1 36N30 81w30 5:26:00
Ballards Crossroads 74 1 35N36 77w35 5:10:20
Ballew Store 100 1 35N55 82w18 5:29:12
Balm 6 1 36N10 81w52 5:27:28
Balsam 50 2 35N26 83w05 5:32:20
Balsam Grove 88 1 35N08 82w52 5:31:28
Baltic 31 1 35N00 78w06 5:12:24
Baltimore 9 1 34N26 78w28 5:13:52
Bamboo 95 1 36N07 81w40 5:26:40
Bandana 61 1 36N01 82w09 5:28:36
Bandy 18 1 35N37 81w26 5:25:44
Banks Creek 100 1 35N55 82w18 5:29:12
Banner 51 1 35N23 78w32 5:14:08
Banner Elk 6 1 36N10 81w52 5:27:28
Bannertown 86 1 36N29 80w35 5:22:20
Barbecue 43 1 35N20 79w02 5:16:08
Barber 80 1 35N44 80w38 5:22:32
Barclaysville 43 1 35N30 78w44 5:14:56
Barco 27 1 36N24 75w59 5:03:56
Barham 92 1 35N59 78w30 5:14:00
Barium Springs 49 1 35N43 80w54 5:23:36
Barker Heights 45 1 35N18 82w27 5:29:48
Barkers Creek 50 1 35N24 83w18 5:33:12
Barnardsville 11 1 35N47 82w27 5:29:48
Barnesville 78 1 34N25 79w03 5:16:12
Barrett 3 1 36N33 81w00 5:24:00
Barretts Crossing 46 1 36N30 77w00 5:08:00
Barrier's Mill 13 1 35N24 80w26 5:21:44
Barringer 49 1 35N41 80w50 5:23:20
Barton Creek 92 1 35N57 78w39 5:14:36
Bat Cave 45 1 35N27 82w18 5:29:12
Bath 7 1 35N29 76w49 5:07:16
Baton 14 1 35N48 81w26 5:25:44
Battleboro 64 1 36N02 77w45 5:11:00
Bay 89 1 35N55 76w15 5:05:00
Bayboro 69 1 35N09 76w46 5:07:04
Bayleaf 92 1 35N50 78w40 5:14:40
Baynes 17 1 36N06 79w16 5:17:04
Bayshore Park 16 1 34N42 77w06 5:08:24
Bayview 7 1 35N28 76w49 5:07:16
Beach Spring 72 1 36N11 76w28 5:05:52
Beams Mills 23 1 35N17 81w32 5:26:08
Bear Creek 19 1 35N35 79w28 5:17:52
Bear Creek 67 1 34N43 77w14 5:08:56
Bear Creek Junction 38 1 35N19 83w48 5:35:12
Beard 26 1 35N04 78w53 5:15:32
Beargrass 59 1 35N45 77w07 5:08:28
Bearpond 91 1 36N19 78w24 5:13:36
Bear Poplar 80 1 35N40 80w44 5:22:56
Bearskin 82 1 35N01 78w30 5:14:00
Beaufort 16 1 34N43 76w40 5:06:40
Beaver Creek 5 1 36N24 81w29 5:25:56
Beaverdam 26 1 34N54 78w37 5:14:28
Beaverdam 42 1 36N11 77w40 5:10:40
Beaverdam 44 1 35N35 82w51 5:31:24

Beaver Island 85 1 36N23 80w05 5:20:20
Beckford Junction 37 1 36N27 76w37 5:06:28
Beckwith 7 1 35N37 76w52 5:07:28
Beech 11 1 35N44 82w35 5:30:20
Beech Bottom 6 1 36N05 81w56 5:27:44
Beech Creek 6 1 36N15 81w47 5:27:08
Beechertown 57 1 35N15 83w42 5:34:48
Beech Glenn 58 1 35N51 82w29 5:29:56
Beech Mountain 6 1 36N14 81w56 5:27:44
Bee Log 100 1 35N55 82w18 5:29:12
Belcross 15 1 36N20 76w10 5:04:40
Belews Creek 34 1 36N13 80w05 5:20:20
Belfast 96 1 35N25 77w59 5:11:56
Belgrade 67 1 34N54 77w14 5:08:56
Belhaven 7 1 35N33 76w37 5:06:28
Bellair 25 1 35N06 77w05 5:08:20
Bellarthur 74 1 35N36 77w31 5:10:04
Bellemont 1 1 36N02 79w26 5:17:44
Bell Fork 67 1 34N45 77w26 5:09:44
Bells Cross Roads 49 1 35N42 80w53 5:23:32
Bells Fork 74 1 35N36 77w23 5:09:32
Bell Swamp 10 1 34N09 78w06 5:12:24
Belltown 39 1 36N18 78w35 5:14:20
Bell View 20 1 35N05 84w02 5:36:08
Belmont 36 1 35N14 81w02 5:24:08
Belva 58 1 35N48 82w41 5:30:44
Belvidere 72 1 36N18 76w32 5:06:08
Belwood 23 1 35N25 81w34 5:26:16
Benham 97 1 36N15 80w52 5:23:28
Bennett 19 1 35N34 79w33 5:18:12
Bensalem 63 1 35N20 79w38 5:18:32
Benson 51 1 35N23 78w33 5:14:12
Benton Crossroads 90 1 34N59 80w33 5:22:12
Benton Heights 90 1 34N59 80w33 5:22:12
Bentonsville 51 1 35N20 78w19 5:13:16
Berea 39 1 36N18 78w35 5:14:20
Berryhill 60 1 35N13 80w57 5:23:48
Bertha 27 1 36N17 75w53 5:03:32
Bertie 8 1 36N03 76w57 5:07:48
Bessemer City 36 1 35N17 81w17 5:25:08
Bests 96 1 35N18 77w47 5:11:08
Beta 50 2 35N22 83w14 5:32:56
Bethabara 34 1 36N08 80w18 5:21:12
Bethania 34 1 36N13 80w17 5:21:08
Bethany 49 1 35N51 80w52 5:23:28
Bethel 2 1 35N44 81w21 5:25:24
Bethel 24 1 34N13 78w51 5:15:24
Bethel 44 1 35N33 82w59 5:31:56
Bethel 47 1 34N59 79w13 5:16:52
Bethel 72 1 36N11 76w28 5:05:52
Bethel 74 1 35N48 77w22 5:09:28
Bethel 95 1 36N15 81w46 5:27:04
Bethel Hill 73 1 36N24 78w59 5:15:56
Bethesda 32 1 35N57 78w50 5:15:20
Bethlehem 2 1 35N44 81w21 5:25:24
Bethlehem 46 1 36N21 76w54 5:07:36
Bettie 16 1 34N43 76w39 5:06:36
Beulah 48 1 35N30 76w27 5:05:48
Beulah 51 1 35N36 78w09 5:12:36
Beulah 75 1 35N15 82w38 5:30:32
Beulahtown 51 1 35N36 78w07 5:12:28
Beulaville 31 1 34N55 77w46 5:11:04
Big Creek 85 1 36N31 80w23 5:21:32
Biggs Park 78 1 34N36 79w01 5:16:04
Big Laurel 58 1 35N48 82w41 5:30:44
Big Lick 84 1 35N14 80w19 5:21:16
Big Ridge 50 1 35N10 83w08 5:32:32
Biltmore 11 1 35N34 82w32 5:30:08
Biltmore Forest 11 1 35N34 82w33 5:30:12
Bingham 68 1 35N57 79w12 5:16:48
Bingham Heights 11 1 35N35 82w36 5:30:24
Birdtown 87 1 35N29 83w19 5:33:16
Biscoe 62 1 35N22 79w47 5:19:08
Bishops Cross 7 1 35N35 76w40 5:06:40
Bixby 30 1 35N57 80w25 5:21:40
Blackburn 18 1 35N40 81w13 5:24:52
Black Creek 98 1 35N38 77w56 5:11:44
Black Jack 74 1 35N36 77w23 5:09:32
Black Jack 77 1 35N02 79w50 5:19:20
Blackman 51 1 35N27 78w26 5:13:44
Black Mountain 11 1 35N37 82w19 5:29:16
Black Mountain Sanatorium 11 1 35N37 82w19 5:29:16
Blackwell 17 1 36N31 79w28 5:17:52
Blackwood 68 1 35N55 79w01 5:16:04
Bladenboro 9 1 34N33 78w48 5:15:12
Blades 25 1 34N53 76w54 5:07:36
Blanch 17 1 36N30 79w18 5:17:12
Blantyre 88 1 35N15 82w44 5:30:56
Blevins Store 86 1 36N24 80w43 5:22:52
Blizzards Crossroads 31 1 35N11 78w04 5:12:16
Bloomingdale 78 1 34N28 79w00 5:16:00
Bloomington 84 1 35N21 80w12 5:20:48
Blounts Creek 7 1 35N21 76w58 5:07:52
Blowertown 4 1 34N58 80w05 5:20:20
Blowing Rock 95 1 36N08 81w41 5:26:44
Bluefield 9 1 34N29 78w39 5:14:36
Blue Ridge 11 1 35N37 82w19 5:29:16
Blue Ridge 45 1 35N19 82w28 5:29:52
Blue Ridge 88 1 35N03 82w45 5:31:00
Blue Springs 47 1 34N57 79w18 5:17:12
Blue Wing Church 50 1 35N29 83w19 5:33:16
Bluff 58 1 35N54 82w50 5:31:20
Bly 5 1 36N30 81w30 5:26:00
Boardman 24 1 34N25 78w54 5:15:36
Bobbitt 91 1 36N13 78w26 5:13:44
Boddies Pond 64 1 35N58 77w58 5:11:52
Boger City 55 1 35N29 81w13 5:24:52

Bogue 16 1 34N42 77w02 5:08:08
Boiling Spring Lakes 10 1 34N01 78w03 5:12:12
Boiling Springs 20 1 35N05 84w02 5:36:08
Boiling Springs 23 1 35N15 81w40 5:26:40
Bolivia 10 1 34N04 78w09 5:12:36
Bolling 42 1 36N27 77w40 5:10:40
Bolton 24 1 34N20 78w25 5:13:40
Bonaparte Landing 10 1 33N54 78w27 5:13:48
Bonham Heights 16 1 34N42 76w50 5:07:20
Bonlee 19 1 35N39 79w25 5:17:40
Bonnerton 7 1 35N18 76w47 5:07:08
Bonnetsville 82 1 35N00 78w20 5:13:20
Bonnie Doone 26 1 35N05 78w57 5:15:48
Bonsal 92 1 35N41 78w56 5:15:44
Boogertown 36 1 35N16 81w10 5:24:40
Boomer 97 1 36N04 81w15 5:25:00
Boone 95 1 36N13 81w41 5:26:44
Boones Crossroads 66 1 36N23 77w25 5:09:40
Boonford 61 1 36N01 82w09 5:28:36
Boon Hill 51 1 35N28 78w11 5:12:44
Boon Station 1 1 36N07 79w31 5:18:04
Boonville 99 1 36N14 80w43 5:22:52
Bostic 81 1 35N22 81w50 5:27:20
Bostic Yard 81 1 35N22 81w50 5:27:20
Bottom 86 1 36N30 80w35 5:22:20
Boulevard 79 1 36N30 79w45 5:19:00
Bowdens 31 1 35N03 78w07 5:12:28
Bowditch 100 1 35N55 82w18 5:29:12
Bowmore 47 1 34N59 79w13 5:16:52
Boyd 88 1 35N18 82w39 5:30:36
Boyles Chapel 85 1 36N17 80w21 5:21:24
Bracey 78 1 34N32 79w17 5:17:08
Brackett 56 1 35N33 81w57 5:27:48
Bradfords Cross Roads 49 1 35N51 80w56 5:23:44
Bradshaw 61 1 36N04 82w17 5:29:08
Brake 33 1 35N58 77w48 5:11:12
Brandon 5 1 36N30 81w30 5:26:00
Branon 99 1 36N08 80w40 5:22:40
Brassfield 39 1 36N08 78w36 5:14:24
Brasstown 22 1 35N02 83w57 5:35:48
Braswell 24 1 34N19 78w50 5:15:20
Braswells Crossroads 42 1 36N08 77w25 5:09:40
Brentwood 92 1 35N48 78w38 5:14:32
Brevard 88 1 35N14 82w44 5:30:56
Brewers Crossroads 66 1 36N26 77w34 5:10:16
Brickhaven 19 1 35N38 79w05 5:16:20
Bricks 33 1 36N06 77w43 5:10:52
Brickton 45 1 35N26 82w30 5:30:00
Bridgersville 98 1 35N45 77w40 5:10:40
Bridgeton 25 1 35N07 77w01 5:08:04
Bridgewater 12 1 35N44 81w42 5:26:48
Brief 90 1 35N14 80w30 5:22:00
Briertown 57 1 35N15 83w42 5:34:48
Brightwood 41 1 36N10 79w45 5:19:00
Brindle Town 12 1 35N44 81w42 5:26:48
Brinkleyville 42 1 36N13 77w53 5:11:32
Britts 78 1 34N32 78w58 5:15:52
Broadbay 34 1 36N03 80w13 5:20:52
Broad Creek 16 1 34N43 76w56 5:07:44
Broad River 11 1 35N32 82w16 5:29:04
Broadway 53 1 35N27 79w03 5:16:12
Brocks 67 1 34N54 77w33 5:10:12
Brogden 96 1 35N17 78w04 5:12:16
Brook Cove 85 1 36N18 80w08 5:20:32
Brookford 18 1 35N42 81w21 5:25:24
Brookhaven 92 1 35N50 78w40 5:14:40
Brooks Cross Roads 99 1 36N06 80w46 5:23:04
Brooksdale 73 1 36N24 78w59 5:15:56
Brookside 96 1 35N22 77w58 5:11:52
Brookston 91 1 36N19 78w24 5:13:36
Brower 76 1 35N34 79w38 5:18:32
Brown Marsh 9 1 34N31 78w38 5:14:32
Brown Mountain Beach 14 1 35N54 81w31 5:26:04
Browns Summit 41 1 36N13 79w43 5:18:52
Brownwood 5 1 36N18 81w36 5:26:24
Bruce 41 1 36N12 79w54 5:19:36
Bruce 74 1 35N36 77w23 5:09:32
Brunswick 24 1 34N17 78w42 5:14:48
Brush Creek 100 1 35N59 82w13 5:28:52
Brushy Fork 95 1 36N14 81w43 5:26:52
Brushy Mountain 97 1 36N05 81w06 5:24:24
Bryan 86 1 36N22 80w51 5:23:24
Bryantown 66 1 36N16 77w17 5:09:08
Bryson City 87 2 35N26 83w27 5:33:48
Buckhorn 68 1 36N05 79w10 5:16:40
Buckhorn Cross Roads 98 1 35N36 78w07 5:12:28
Bucklesberry 54 1 35N16 77w35 5:10:20
Buckner 58 1 35N50 82w33 5:30:12
Buck Shoal 99 1 36N07 80w49 5:23:16
Buck Swamp 96 1 35N29 78w03 5:12:12
Buffalo City 28 1 35N53 75w58 5:03:52
Buffalo Cove 14 1 35N54 81w31 5:26:04
Buford 90 1 34N53 80w33 5:22:12
Bug Hill 24 1 34N04 78w41 5:14:44
Buie 78 1 34N44 79w09 5:16:36
Buies Creek 43 1 35N25 78w44 5:14:56
Buladean 61 1 36N07 82w12 5:28:48
Bullhead 40 1 35N31 77w47 5:11:08
Bullock 39 1 36N30 78w33 5:14:12
Bunlevel 43 1 35N19 78w47 5:15:08
Bunn 35 1 35N58 78w15 5:13:00
Bunnlevel 43 1 35N19 78w47 5:15:08
Bunyan 7 1 35N32 77w02 5:08:08

NORTH CAROLINA

Burch 86 1 36N15 80w52 5:23:28
Burden 8 1 36N14 77w07 5:08:28
Burgaw 71 1 34N33 77w56 5:11:44
Burgess 72 1 36N11 76w28 5:05:52
Burke Chapel 12 1 35N44 81w21 5:25:24
Burkemont 12 1 35N44 81w42 5:26:48
Burlington 1 1 36N06 79w26 5:17:44
Burlington Mills 92 1 35N59 78w30 5:14:00
Burningtown 57 1 35N15 83w30 5:34:00
Burnsville 4 1 35N00 80w12 5:20:48
Burnsville 100 1 35N55 82w18 5:29:12
Burnt Mills 15 1 36N27 76w20 5:05:20
Burnt Swamp 78 1 34N42 79w07 5:16:28
Busbee 11 1 35N34 82w32 5:30:08
Bushy Fork 73 1 36N18 79w05 5:16:20
Busick 41 1 36N13 79w43 5:18:52
Busick 100 1 35N55 82w18 5:29:12
Butlers 8 1 36N03 76w57 5:07:48
Butlers Crossroads 82 1 35N00 78w20 5:13:20
Butner 39 1 36N08 78w45 5:15:00
Butters 9 1 34N33 78w50 5:15:20
Butterwood 42 1 36N21 77w51 5:11:24
Buxton 28 1 35N16 75w32 5:02:08
Buzzards Crossroads 8 1 36N12 76w46 5:07:04
Bynum 19 1 35N47 79w09 5:16:36
Cabarrus 13 1 35N14 80w30 5:22:00
Cabin 31 1 35N03 77w45 5:11:00
Cable 1 1 36N00 79w28 5:17:52
Cairo 4 1 34N52 80w00 5:20:00
Calabash 10 1 33N54 78w27 5:13:48
Calahaln 30 1 35N54 80w39 5:22:36
Caldwell 60 1 35N36 81w08 5:24:32
Caldwell 68 1 36N13 78w56 5:15:44
California 28 1 35N54 75w40 5:02:40
California 74 1 35N36 77w35 5:10:20
Call 97 1 36N10 81w08 5:24:32
Callisons 69 1 35N02 76w41 5:06:44
Calvert 88 1 35N14 82w44 5:30:56
Calvin 12 1 35N44 81w42 5:26:48
Calypso 31 1 35N09 78w06 5:12:24
Camden 15 1 36N20 76w10 5:04:40
Cameron 63 1 35N20 79w15 5:17:00
Campbell Creek 7 1 35N18 76w47 5:07:08
Camp Creek 81 1 35N28 81w56 5:27:44
Camp Glenn 16 1 34N42 76w50 5:07:20
Camp Leach 7 1 35N32 77w02 5:08:08
Camp Lejeune 67 1 34N40 77w21 5:09:24
Camp Lejeune Central 67 1 34N44 77w24 5:09:36
Camp Lejeune Junction 67 1 34N43 77w22 5:09:28
Camp Springs 17 1 36N21 79w41 5:18:44
Camp Sutton 90 1 34N59 80w33 5:22:12
Cana 30 1 35N54 80w34 5:22:16
Canada 50 1 35N14 83w01 5:32:04
Canby 62 1 35N13 80w00 5:20:00
Candler 11 2 35N32 82w41 5:30:44
Candler Heights 11 2 35N32 82w41 5:30:44
Candor 62 1 35N18 79w45 5:19:00
Cane Branch 100 1 35N55 82w18 5:29:12
Cane Creek 20 1 35N05 84w02 5:36:08
Cane Creek 61 1 36N01 82w06 5:28:24
Cane River 100 1 35N55 82w25 5:29:40
Canetuck 71 1 34N24 78w10 5:12:40
Caney Fork 50 1 35N19 83w06 5:32:24
Cannon Ferry 21 1 36N13 76w37 5:06:28
Canto 11 1 35N39 82w42 5:30:48
Canton 44 2 35N32 82w50 5:31:20
Cape Carteret 16 1 34N42 77w03 5:08:12
Cape Fear 43 1 35N29 79w03 5:16:12
Cape Fear 65 3 34N13 77w55 5:11:40
Cape Hatteras 48 1 35N30 75w30 5:02:00
Capella 85 1 36N17 80w21 5:21:24
Capelsie 62 1 35N18 79w45 5:19:00
Capernium 34 1 36N01 80w23 5:21:32
Carbonton 19 1 35N28 79w10 5:16:40
Caroleen 81 1 35N17 81w48 5:27:12
Carolina 74 1 35N43 77w17 5:09:08
Carolina Beach 65 3 34N02 77w54 5:11:36
Carolina Hills 45 1 35N26 82w30 5:30:00
Carpenter 92 1 35N49 78w50 5:15:20
Carpenter Bottom 6 1 36N06 81w59 5:27:56
Carr 32 1 35N58 78w45 5:15:00
Carr 68 1 36N06 79w16 5:17:04
Carrboro 68 1 35N55 79w05 5:16:20
Carroll 31 1 35N00 78w06 5:12:24
Carrs 40 1 35N32 77w41 5:10:44
Carter 37 1 36N21 76w36 5:06:24
Carthage 63 1 35N21 79w25 5:17:40
Cartoogechaye 57 1 35N07 83w30 5:34:00
Carvers 9 1 34N26 78w28 5:13:52
Cary 92 1 35N47 78w46 5:15:04
Casar 23 1 35N31 81w37 5:26:28
Cash Corner 69 1 35N09 76w46 5:07:04
Cashiers 50 1 35N06 83w06 5:32:24
Cason Old Field 4 1 34N58 80w05 5:20:20
Castalia 64 1 36N04 78w04 5:12:16
Castle Hayne 65 3 34N21 77w54 5:11:36
Castoria 40 1 35N36 77w42 5:10:48
Casville 17 1 36N27 79w39 5:18:36
Caswell 71 1 34N30 78w09 5:12:36
Caswell Beach 10 1 33N56 78w04 5:12:16
Cataloochee 44 1 35N42 83w04 5:32:16
Catawba 18 1 35N43 81w05 5:24:20
Catawba Heights 36 1 35N15 81w02 5:24:08
Catawba Springs 55 1 35N28 81w01 5:24:04
Catharine Lake 67 1 34N54 77w33 5:10:12
Catheys Creek 88 1 35N12 82w47 5:31:08

 NORTH CAROLINA

Cat Square 55 1 35N33 81W24 5:25:36
Ca-Vel 73 1 36N24 78W59 5:15:56
Cayton 25 1 35N15 77W04 5:08:16
Cecil 44 1 35N29 82W56 5:31:44
Cedar Creek 26 1 35N00 78W46 5:15:04
Cedar Falls 76 1 35N45 79W44 5:18:56
Cedar Fork 31 1 34N55 77W46 5:11:04
Cedar Fork 92 1 35N51 78W50 5:15:20
Cedar Grove 29 1 35N49 80W15 5:21:00
Cedar Grove 68 1 36N10 79W10 5:16:40
Cedar Hill 4 1 34N58 80W05 5:20:20
Cedar Hill 10 1 34N15 78W03 5:12:12
Cedar Island 16 1 34N58 76W19 5:05:16
Cedar Lodge 29 1 35N53 80W05 5:20:20
Cedar Mountain 88 1 35N09 82W39 5:30:36
Cedar Point 16 1 34N42 77W06 5:08:24
Cedarrock 35 1 36N05 78W09 5:12:36
Cedar Valley 14 1 35N54 81W31 5:26:04
Ceffo 73 1 36N24 78W59 5:15:56
Celeste Hinkle 49 1 35N51 80W56 5:23:44
Celo 100 1 35N51 82W12 5:28:48
Center 30 1 35N54 80W34 5:22:16
Center 99 1 36N08 80W40 5:22:40
Center Grove 41 1 36N10 79W50 5:19:20
Centergrove 73 1 36N17 78W57 5:15:48
Centerview 13 1 35N31 80W38 5:22:32
Centerville 35 1 36N11 78W06 5:12:24
Central 9 1 34N41 78W37 5:14:28
Central Falls 76 1 35N46 79W46 5:19:04
Century 92 1 35N47 78W40 5:14:40
Cerro Gordo 24 1 34N17 78W56 5:15:44
Chadbourn 24 1 34N19 78W50 5:15:20
Chadwick Acres 67 1 34N31 77W23 5:09:32
Chalybeate 43 1 35N35 78W48 5:15:12
Chambersburg 49 1 35N46 80W48 5:23:12
Champion 97 1 36N05 81W22 5:25:28
Chapanoke 72 1 36N11 76W28 5:05:52
Chapel Hill 68 1 35N55 79W04 5:16:16
Charity 31 1 34N50 78W02 5:12:08
Charles 49 1 35N51 80W56 5:23:44
Charleston 87 1 35N26 83W25 5:33:40
Charlotte 60 1 35N13 80W51 5:23:24
Charlottetown 60 1 35N13 80W50 5:23:20
Cheek Creek 62 1 35N14 79W52 5:19:28
Cheeks 68 1 36N05 79W12 5:16:48
Cheeks Cross Roads 68 1 36N06 79W16 5:17:04
Cheoah 38 1 35N18 83W49 5:35:16
Cherokee 87 1 35N29 83W19 5:33:16
Cherokee Indian Reservation 87 1 35N29 83W19 5:33:16
Cherry 94 1 35N52 76W24 5:05:36
Cherryfield 88 1 35N14 82W44 5:30:56
Cherrygrove 17 1 36N21 79W41 5:18:44
Cherry Grove 24 1 34N19 78W56 5:15:44
Cherry Lane 3 1 36N26 81W01 5:24:04
Cherry Point 25 1 34N54 76W54 5:07:36
Cherry Springs 56 1 35N38 82W11 5:28:44
Cherryville 36 1 35N23 81W23 5:25:32
Chesterfield 12 1 35N44 81W42 5:26:48
Chestnut Dale 6 1 36N05 81W56 5:27:44
Chestnut Grove 85 1 36N17 80W21 5:21:24
Chestnut Hill 5 1 36N30 81W21 5:25:24
Chestnut Hill 45 1 35N29 82W21 5:29:24
Chicod 74 1 35N29 77W16 5:09:04
Chimney Rock 81 1 35N27 82W10 5:28:40
China Grove 80 1 35N34 80W35 5:22:20
China Grove Cotton Mill Vill 80 1 35N33 80W36 5:22:24
Chinquapin 31 1 34N50 77W49 5:11:16
Chip 62 1 35N13 80W00 5:20:00
Chocowinity 7 1 35N31 77W06 5:08:24
Chublake 73 1 36N24 78W59 5:15:56
Churchill 93 1 36N26 78W05 5:12:20
Churchland 29 1 35N49 80W15 5:21:00
Cid 29 1 35N49 80W15 5:21:00
Cisco 21 1 36N13 76W37 5:06:28
Claremont 18 1 35N43 81W09 5:24:36
Clarendon 24 1 34N13 78W51 5:15:24
Clarksville 30 1 36N00 80W38 5:22:32
Clarkton 9 1 34N29 78W39 5:14:36
Clarrissa 61 1 36N01 82W09 5:28:36
Clay 39 1 36N18 78W35 5:14:20
Clay 41 1 35N58 79W40 5:18:40
Clayroot 74 1 35N28 77W25 5:09:40
Clayton 51 1 35N39 78W28 5:13:52
Clearcreek 60 1 35N12 80W45 5:23:00
Clear Run 82 1 34N47 78W24 5:13:36
Clegg 32 1 35N49 78W50 5:15:20
Clemmons 34 1 36N01 80W23 5:21:32
Clemmonsville 34 1 36N01 80W23 5:21:32
Clemont 82 1 35N00 78W38 5:14:32
Cleveland 80 1 35N44 80W40 5:22:40
Cleveland Springs 23 1 35N17 81W32 5:26:08
Clifdale 26 1 35N02 78W57 5:15:48
Cliffdale 81 1 35N22 81W50 5:27:20
Cliffside 81 1 35N14 81W46 5:27:04
Clifton 5 1 36N28 81W33 5:26:12
Climax 41 1 35N55 79W43 5:18:52
Clinchcross 56 1 35N41 82W00 5:28:00
Clinchfield 56 1 35N41 82W00 5:28:00
Clines 18 1 35N46 81W13 5:24:52
Clingman 97 1 36N13 80W57 5:23:48
Clinton 82 1 35N00 78W20 5:13:20
Cloverdale 93 1 35N46 78W37 5:14:28
Clyde 44 2 35N32 82W55 5:31:40
Coakley 33 1 35N54 77W32 5:10:08
Coalglen 19 1 35N28 79W10 5:16:40
Coalville 20 2 35N12 83W50 5:35:20
Coats 43 1 35N25 78W40 5:14:40
Coats Cross Roads 51 1 35N23 78W33 5:14:12
Cobbs 98 1 35N48 77W52 5:11:28
Cobb Town 33 1 35N40 77W38 5:10:32
Coddle Creek 13 1 35N34 80W48 5:23:12
Cofield 46 1 36N21 76W54 5:07:36
Coinjock 27 1 36N20 75W57 5:03:48
Cokesbury 43 1 35N35 78W48 5:15:12
Cokesbury 91 1 36N19 78W24 5:13:36
Cokey 33 1 35N51 77W42 5:10:48
Colerain 8 1 36N12 76W46 5:07:04
Coleridge 76 1 35N39 79W37 5:18:28
Colewood Acres 93 1 35N48 78W38 5:14:32
Colfax 41 1 36N07 80W01 5:20:04
Colfax 81 1 35N20 81W46 5:27:04
College 32 1 36N00 78W54 5:15:36
College Downs 60 1 35N16 80W48 5:23:12
College Lakes 26 1 35N04 78W53 5:15:32
Collettsville 14 1 35N56 81W41 5:26:44
Collington 28 1 36N04 75W42 5:02:48
Collinsville 75 1 35N11 82W11 5:28:44
Colly 9 1 34N40 78W30 5:14:00
Colon 53 1 35N32 79W02 5:16:08
Colony Park 32 1 36N01 78W56 5:15:44
Columbia 89 1 35N55 76W15 5:05:00
Columbus 75 1 35N15 82W12 5:28:48
Comet 5 1 36N30 81W30 5:26:00
Comfort 52 1 35N00 77W30 5:10:00
Como 46 1 36N30 77W00 5:08:00
Concord 13 1 35N25 80W35 5:22:20
Concord 31 1 34N50 78W02 5:12:08
Concord 73 1 36N24 78W59 5:15:56
Concord 82 1 34N57 78W31 5:14:04
Conetoe 33 1 35N49 77W27 5:09:48
Congleton 74 1 35N49 77W15 5:09:00
Connarista 8 1 36N14 77W07 5:08:28
Connellys Springs 12 1 35N44 81W31 5:26:04
Connestee 88 1 35N14 82W44 5:30:56
Connestee Falls 88 1 35N14 82W44 5:30:56
Conoconnara 42 1 36N14 77W29 5:09:56
Conover 18 1 35N42 81W13 5:24:52
Conrad Hill 29 1 35N48 80W09 5:20:36
Contentnea Neck 54 1 35N22 77W29 5:09:56
Conway 66 1 36N26 77W14 5:08:56
Cooksville 18 1 35N33 81W24 5:25:36
Cooktown 61 1 36N01 82W09 5:28:36
Cooleemee 30 1 35N49 80W33 5:22:12
Cool Spring 49 1 35N44 80W41 5:22:44
Cooper Gap 75 1 35N22 82W12 5:28:48
Coopers 64 1 35N53 77W58 5:11:52
Copeland 86 1 36N24 80W43 5:22:52
Coral Bay 16 1 34N42 76W50 5:07:20
Corapeake 37 1 36N32 76W35 5:06:20
Corbett 17 1 36N06 79W16 5:17:04
Cordova 77 1 34N55 79W49 5:19:16
Core Point 7 1 35N21 76W58 5:07:52
Corinth 19 1 35N38 79W05 5:16:20
Corinth 64 1 35N58 77W58 5:11:52
Cornatzer 30 1 35N54 80W34 5:22:16
Cornelius 60 1 35N29 80W52 5:23:28
Correll Park 80 1 35N39 80W29 5:21:56
Costin 71 1 34N32 78W10 5:12:40
Cottonade 26 1 35N05 78W57 5:15:48
Cotton Grove 29 1 35N43 80W17 5:21:08
Cottonville 84 1 35N14 80W07 5:20:28
Coulwood Hills 60 1 35N14 80W55 5:23:40
Council 9 1 34N25 78W28 5:13:52
Country Park Acres 41 1 36N06 79W49 5:19:16
Countyline 30 1 35N57 80W46 5:23:04
Court House 11 1 35N35 82W30 5:30:00
Court House 15 1 36N21 76W09 5:04:36
Courtney 99 1 36N08 80W40 5:22:40
Cove 25 1 35N11 77W19 5:09:16
Cove City 25 1 35N13 77W19 5:09:16
Cove Creek 44 1 35N33 82W59 5:31:56
Cove Creek 95 1 36N18 81W45 5:27:00
Covington 77 1 35N13 80W00 5:20:00
Cowee 57 1 35N17 83W24 5:33:36
Coxville 74 1 35N28 77W25 5:09:40
Cozart 39 1 36N07 78W41 5:14:44
Crab Creek 45 1 35N17 82W34 5:30:16
Crab Orchard 60 1 35N14 80W44 5:22:56
Crab Point 16 1 34N42 76W50 5:07:20
Crabtree 44 1 35N35 82W55 5:31:40
Craggy 11 2 35N37 82W33 5:30:12
Cramerton 36 1 35N14 81W05 5:24:20
Cranberry 6 1 36N09 81W58 5:27:52
Cranberry Gap 6 1 36N05 81W56 5:27:44
Crawford 27 1 36N26 76W03 5:04:12
Creedmoor 39 1 36N07 78W41 5:14:44
Creeksville 66 1 36N26 77W14 5:08:56
Cremo 8 1 36N12 76W46 5:07:04
Crescent 80 1 35N33 80W24 5:21:36
Creston 5 1 36N25 81W37 5:26:28
Creswell 94 1 35N53 76W24 5:05:36
Cricket 97 1 36N11 81W12 5:24:48
Crisp 33 1 35N45 77W40 5:10:40
Croatan 25 1 35N06 77W05 5:08:20
Croatan 28 1 35N44 75W47 5:03:08
Croft 60 1 35N16 80W48 5:23:12
Crooked Creek 56 1 35N35 82W10 5:28:40
Cross Landing 89 1 35N55 76W15 5:05:00
Cross Mill 56 1 35N41 82W00 5:28:00
Crossnore 6 1 36N01 81W56 5:27:44
Cross Road 86 1 36N30 80W35 5:22:20
Crossway 83 1 34N46 79W28 5:17:52
Crouse 55 1 35N25 81W18 5:25:12
Crowder Mountain 36 1 35N15 81W17 5:25:08
Crowders 36 1 35N16 81W10 5:24:40
Crowells 42 1 36N20 77W35 5:10:20
Crumpler 5 1 36N30 81W24 5:25:36
Crump Town 83 1 34N53 79W22 5:17:28
Cruso 44 1 35N25 82W49 5:31:16
Crusoe Island 24 1 34N20 78W42 5:14:48
Culberson 20 1 35N00 84W09 5:36:36
Culbreth 39 1 36N18 78W35 5:14:20
Cullasaja 57 1 35N11 83W23 5:33:32
Cullowhee 50 1 35N18 83W11 5:32:44
Cumberland 26 1 35N00 78W59 5:15:56
Cumnock 53 1 35N33 79W14 5:16:56
Cunningham 73 1 36N29 79W04 5:16:16
Currie 71 1 34N28 78W06 5:12:24
Currituck 27 1 36N27 76W01 5:04:04
Currituck 48 1 35N31 76W27 5:05:48
Cutshalltown 58 1 35N48 82W41 5:30:44
Cycle 99 1 36N06 80W46 5:23:04
Cypress Creek 24 1 34N20 78W42 5:14:48
Cypress Creek 31 1 34N44 78W00 5:12:00
Cyrus 67 1 34N45 77W26 5:09:44
Dabney 91 1 36N21 78W29 5:13:56
Dale 100 1 36N00 82W14 5:28:56
Dallas 36 1 35N19 81W11 5:24:44
Dalton 85 1 36N20 80W26 5:21:44
Dana 45 1 35N14 82W22 5:29:28
Danbury 85 1 36N25 80W12 5:20:48
Daniels-Rhyne 55 1 35N27 81W16 5:25:04
Dan River 17 1 36N29 79W20 5:17:20
Darby 97 1 36N05 81W22 5:25:28
Darden 59 1 35N49 76W54 5:07:36
Darkridge 6 1 36N09 81W59 5:27:56
Darlington 42 1 36N20 77W35 5:10:20
Davenport Forks 94 1 35N53 76W36 5:06:24
Davidson 60 1 35N30 80W51 5:23:24
Davidson River 88 1 35N15 82W44 5:30:56
Davie Crossroads 30 1 35N54 80W34 5:22:16
Davis 16 1 34N48 76W28 5:05:52
Davistown 33 1 35N47 77W38 5:10:32
Dawson Crossroads 42 1 36N11 77W40 5:10:40
Dawsons Crossroads 54 1 35N16 77W35 5:10:20
Day Book 100 1 35N55 82W18 5:29:12
Days Crossroads 42 1 36N20 77W35 5:10:20
Deans Store 64 1 35N58 77W58 5:11:52
Deep Creek 4 1 34N58 80W05 5:20:20
Deep Gap 95 1 36N14 81W32 5:26:08
Deep River 41 1 35N58 80W00 5:20:00
Deep Run 54 1 35N09 77W42 5:10:48
Deerfield 95 1 36N13 81W40 5:26:40
Dehart 97 1 36N15 81W07 5:24:28
Delco 24 1 34N19 78W13 5:12:52
Delight 23 1 35N25 81W34 5:26:16
Dellview 36 1 35N23 81W25 5:25:40
Dellwood 44 1 35N33 82W59 5:31:56
Delway 82 1 34N50 78W02 5:12:08
Democrat 11 1 35N47 82W27 5:29:48
Dendron 56 1 35N38 82W11 5:28:44
Dennis 34 1 36N18 80W08 5:20:32
Denny 97 1 36N05 81W22 5:25:28
Denton 29 1 35N38 80W06 5:20:24
Denver 55 1 35N32 81W02 5:24:08
Deppe 67 1 34N54 77W14 5:08:56
Derby 77 1 35N04 79W46 5:19:04
Derita 60 1 35N18 80W48 5:23:12
Devotion 86 1 36N24 80W43 5:22:52
Deweese 60 1 35N28 80W50 5:23:20
Dewey Pier 89 1 35N55 76W15 5:05:00
Dexter 39 1 36N18 78W35 5:14:20
Dickerson 39 1 36N18 78W35 5:14:20
Dillingham 11 1 35N45 82W46 5:31:04
Dillsboro 50 2 35N23 83W15 5:33:00
Dillworth 60 1 35N13 80W51 5:23:24
Dimmette 97 1 36N13 80W57 5:23:48
Dismal 82 1 35N06 78W35 5:14:20
Dixie 60 1 35N14 80W53 5:23:32
Dixon 67 1 34N26 77W34 5:10:16
Dobbersville 96 1 35N11 78W04 5:12:16
Dobson 86 1 36N24 80W43 5:22:52
Dockery 97 1 36N21 81W01 5:24:04
Dodgetown 85 1 36N23 79W58 5:19:52
Dodsons Crossroads 68 1 36N05 79W07 5:16:28
Dogwood Acres 76 1 35N42 79W49 5:19:16
Dolinger 5 1 36N30 81W30 5:26:00
Donnaha 34 1 36N15 80W22 5:21:28
Doolie 49 1 35N35 80W49 5:23:16
Dortches 64 1 35N58 77W48 5:11:12
Dosier 34 1 36N09 80W22 5:21:28
Dothan 24 1 34N03 78W53 5:15:32
Double Shoals 23 1 35N25 81W32 5:26:08
Doughton 97 1 36N22 80W56 5:23:44
Douglas Crossroads 7 1 35N32 77W02 5:08:08
Dover 23 1 35N17 81W32 5:26:08
Dover 25 1 35N13 77W26 5:09:44
Dover Mill 23 1 35N17 81W32 5:26:08
Downtown 60 1 35N13 80W51 5:23:24
Downtown 80 1 35N39 80W29 5:21:56
Draco 14 1 35N54 81W31 5:26:04
Drake 64 1 36N03 77W45 5:11:00
Drake Park 26 1 35N02 78W57 5:15:48
Draper 79 1 36N31 79W41 5:18:44
Draughn 33 1 36N06 77W43 5:10:52
Drewry 91 1 36N25 78W17 5:13:08
Drexel 12 1 35N45 81W36 5:26:24
Drivers Store 98 1 35N44 77W55 5:11:40
Druid Hills 45 1 35N19 82W28 5:29:52
Drums Crossroads 18 1 35N40 81W13 5:24:52
Dry Creek 62 1 35N18 79W45 5:19:00
Dry Wells 64 1 35N47 78W13 5:12:52
Duan 18 1 35N40 81W13 5:24:52
Dublin 9 1 34N39 78W43 5:14:52
Duck 28 1 36N04 75W42 5:02:48
Dudley 96 1 35N16 78W02 5:12:08
Dudley Shoals 14 1 35N48 81W26 5:25:44

NORTH CAROLINA

Place		Lat	Long	Time
Duff Creek 31	1	34N46	78w01	5:12:04
Duffies 47	1	34N49	79w11	5:16:44
Duke 32	1	36N00	78w56	5:15:44
Duke 43	1	35N19	78w40	5:14:40
Dukes Crossroads 7	1	35N28	76w49	5:07:16
Dulah 24	1	34N09	78w53	5:15:32
Duncan 43	1	35N35	78w48	5:15:12
Duncans Creek 81	1	35N27	81w43	5:26:52
Dundarrach 47	1	34N56	79w09	5:16:36
Dunn 43	1	35N19	78w37	5:14:28
Dunn Crossroads 98	1	35N48	77w52	5:11:28
Dunns Rock 88	1	35N11	82w42	5:30:48
Dunns Store 42	1	36N08	77w25	5:09:40
Dupree Crossroads 74	1	35N40	77w38	5:10:32
Durants Neck 72	1	36N09	76w19	5:05:16
Durham 32	1	36N00	78w54	5:15:36
Dutchville 39	1	36N08	78w44	5:14:56
Dysartsville 56	1	35N37	81w53	5:27:32
Dysortville 56	1	35N43	81w56	5:27:44
Eagle 49	1	36N06	80w46	5:23:04
Eagle Mills 49	1	36N00	80w45	5:23:00
Eagle Rock 92	1	35N47	78w22	5:13:28
Eagle Springs 63	1	35N17	79w39	5:18:36
Eagletown 66	1	36N16	77w17	5:09:08
Eakers Corner 23	1	35N25	81w34	5:26:16
Earl 23	1	35N12	81w32	5:26:08
Earley 46	1	36N17	76w59	5:07:56
Earpsboro 51	1	35N49	78w19	5:13:16
Easonburg 64	1	35N58	77w48	5:11:12
Easons Crossroads 37	1	36N24	76w45	5:07:00
Easons Store 64	1	35N58	77w48	5:11:12
East Alliance 69	1	35N09	76w49	5:07:16
East Arcadia 9	1	34N20	78w14	5:12:56
Eastatoe 88	1	35N08	82w47	5:31:08
East Bend 99	1	36N13	80w31	5:22:04
East Carolina University 74	1	35N36	77w23	5:09:32
East Durham 32	1	35N59	78w51	5:15:24
East Fayetteville 26	1	35N04	78w53	5:15:32
East Flat Rock 45	1	35N17	82w26	5:29:44
East Fork 44	1	35N30	82w49	5:31:16
East Franklin 57	1	35N11	83w23	5:33:32
East Gastonia 36	1	35N16	81w10	5:24:40
East Goldsboro 16	1	34N45	76w49	5:07:16
East Hickory 18	1	35N44	81w21	5:25:24
East Howellsville 78	1	34N41	78w53	5:15:32
East Lake 28	1	35N53	75w58	5:03:52
East Laport 50	1	35N19	83w11	5:32:44
East Laurinburg 83	1	34N46	79w27	5:17:48
East Lumberton 78	1	34N36	79w01	5:16:04
East Monbo 49	1	35N51	80w56	5:23:44
Eastover 26	1	35N05	78w47	5:15:08
East Rockingham 77	1	34N55	79w46	5:19:04
East Rocky Mount 33	1	35N58	77w48	5:11:12
East Sanford 53	1	35N30	79w08	5:16:32
East Side Park 77	1	34N56	79w46	5:19:04
East Spencer 80	1	35N41	80w26	5:21:44
East Tabor 24	1	34N09	78w53	5:15:32
East Wilmington 65	3	34N13	77w55	5:11:40
Eastwood 63	1	35N18	79w24	5:17:36
Ebbs Chapel 58	1	35N55	82w34	5:30:16
Ebenezer 20	1	35N05	84w02	5:36:08
Echo 78	1	34N32	79w17	5:17:08
Eden 79	1	36N30	79w45	5:19:00
Edenton 21	1	36N04	76w39	5:06:36
Edgar 76	1	35N50	79w52	5:19:28
Edgemont 14	1	36N00	81w47	5:27:08
Edneyville 45	1	35N25	82w19	5:29:16
Edward 7	1	35N19	76w52	5:07:28
Edwards 97	1	36N16	80w56	5:23:44
Edwards Crossroads 3	1	36N30	81w07	5:24:28
Edwards Crossroads 64	1	35N57	78w07	5:12:28
Edwards Crossroads 66	1	36N26	77w14	5:08:56
Edwards Fork 42	1	36N08	77w25	5:09:40
Edwards Junction 25	1	35N06	77w05	5:08:20
Efland 68	1	36N05	79w10	5:16:40
Egypt 100	1	35N59	82w25	5:29:40
Ela 87	1	35N26	83w27	5:33:48
Elams 93	1	36N35	78w00	5:12:00
Elberon 93	1	36N24	78w09	5:12:36
Eldora 86	1	36N23	80w36	5:22:24
Eldorado 62	1	35N28	80w04	5:20:16
Eleanors Crossroads 37	1	36N30	76w46	5:07:04
Elevation 51	1	35N28	78w31	5:14:04
Elf 22	1	35N04	83w49	5:35:16
Elizabeth 60	1	35N13	80w50	5:23:20
Elizabeth City 70	1	36N18	76w14	5:04:56
Elizabethtown 9	1	34N38	78w37	5:14:28
Elkin 86	1	36N15	80w51	5:23:24
Elk Mountain 11	1	35N37	82w33	5:30:12
Elk Park 6	1	36N10	81w59	5:27:56
Elk Shoal 100	1	35N55	82w18	5:29:12
Elkton 9	1	34N29	78w39	5:14:36
Elk Valley 6	1	36N10	81w52	5:27:28
Ellenboro 81	1	35N20	81w45	5:27:00
Ellendale 2	1	35N55	81w16	5:25:04
Eller 29	1	36N04	80w14	5:20:56
Ellerbe 77	1	35N04	79w46	5:19:04
Ellijay 57	1	35N11	83w17	5:33:08
Elliott 82	1	34N59	78w11	5:12:44
Ellisboro 79	1	36N23	79w58	5:19:52
Ellis Crossroads 80	1	35N39	80w29	5:21:56
Ellis Store 8	1	36N03	76w57	5:07:48
Elm City 98	1	35N48	77w52	5:11:28
Elm Grove 52	1	35N16	77w35	5:10:20
Elmore 83	1	34N46	79w28	5:17:52
Elmwood 49	1	35N51	80w56	5:23:44
Elon College 1	1	36N06	79w30	5:18:00
Elrod 78	1	34N32	79w17	5:17:08
Embro 93	1	36N26	78w05	5:12:20
Emerald Isle 16	1	34N41	76w55	5:07:40
Emerson 9	1	34N45	78w51	5:15:24
Emerson 24	1	34N09	78w53	5:15:32
Emerywood 41	1	35N58	80w00	5:20:00
Emit 51	1	35N47	78w12	5:12:48
Emma 11	1	35N35	82w36	5:30:24
Emmons 29	1	35N41	80w06	5:20:24
Encas 98	1	35N44	77w55	5:11:40
Endy 84	1	35N18	80w17	5:21:08
Enfield 42	1	36N11	77w41	5:10:44
Engelhard 48	1	35N31	76w00	5:04:00
Englewood 64	1	35N58	77w48	5:11:12
English 58	1	35N50	82w33	5:30:12
Enka 11	1	35N33	82w39	5:30:36
Enka Village 11	1	35N32	82w38	5:30:32
Ennice 3	1	36N33	81w00	5:24:00
Eno 68	1	36N05	79w02	5:16:08
Enochville 80	1	35N33	80w36	5:22:24
Enola 12	1	35N44	81w42	5:26:48
Enon 99	1	36N08	80w28	5:21:52
Enterprise 29	1	35N49	80w15	5:21:00
Enterprise 93	1	36N26	77w55	5:11:40
Ephesus 30	1	35N54	80w34	5:22:16
Epsom 35	1	36N19	78w24	5:13:36
Erastus 50	1	35N19	83w11	5:32:44
Erect 76	1	35N32	79w46	5:19:04
Ernul 25	1	35N15	77w04	5:08:16
Ervintown 67	1	34N54	77w33	5:10:12
Erwin 43	1	35N20	78w41	5:14:44
Erwin Heights 29	1	35N53	80w05	5:20:20
Essex 42	1	36N15	77w56	5:11:44
Estatoe 61	1	35N55	82w04	5:28:16
Estelle 17	1	36N32	79w12	5:16:48
Ether 62	1	35N26	79w46	5:19:04
Etowah 45	1	35N19	82w36	5:30:24
Eufola 49	1	35N51	80w56	5:23:44
Eure 37	1	36N26	76w51	5:07:24
Eureka 96	1	35N32	77w53	5:11:32
Evansdale 98	1	35N44	77w55	5:11:40
Everetts 59	1	35N50	77w10	5:08:40
Everetts Crossroads 7	1	35N37	76w52	5:07:28
Evergreen 24	1	34N25	78w54	5:15:36
Evergreen Estates 26	1	35N02	78w57	5:15:48
Everhardt 80	1	35N33	80w36	5:22:24
Ewart 61	1	36N01	82w09	5:28:36
Exum 10	1	34N06	78w32	5:14:08
Exway 62	1	35N13	80w00	5:20:00
Fair Bluff 24	1	34N19	79w02	5:16:08
Fairfield 48	1	35N32	76w14	5:04:56
Fairfield 90	1	34N59	80w22	5:21:28
Fair Grove 29	1	35N53	80w05	5:20:20
Fairmont 78	1	34N30	79w07	5:16:28
Fairplains 97	1	36N10	81w08	5:24:32
Fairport 39	1	36N13	78w26	5:13:44
Fairview 11	1	35N31	82w24	5:29:36
Fairview 57	1	35N15	83w42	5:34:48
Fairview 68	1	36N05	79w07	5:16:28
Fairview 90	1	34N59	80w33	5:22:12
Fairview Cross Roads 86	1	36N24	80w43	5:22:52
Faison 31	1	35N07	78w08	5:12:32
Faisons 66	1	36N29	77w27	5:09:48
Faith 80	1	35N35	80w28	5:21:52
Falcon 26	1	35N11	78w39	5:14:36
Falkland 74	1	35N41	77w31	5:10:04
Fall Creek 99	1	36N13	80w36	5:22:24
Falling Creek 54	1	35N17	77w41	5:10:44
Falls 92	1	35N59	78w30	5:14:00
Fallston 23	1	35N26	81w30	5:26:00
Fallstown 49	1	35N42	80w56	5:23:44
Farmer 76	1	35N42	79w49	5:19:16
Farmers Store 5	1	36N30	81w30	5:26:00
Farmington 30	1	36N01	80w32	5:22:08
Farmville 74	1	35N36	77w35	5:10:20
Faro 96	1	35N36	77w49	5:11:16
Faucett 42	1	36N20	77w44	5:10:56
Faucette 1	1	36N11	79w24	5:17:36
Faust 58	1	35N50	82w33	5:30:12
Fayetteville 26	1	35N03	78w53	5:15:32
Federal Building 70	1	36N17	76w14	5:04:56
Federal Point 65	3	34N04	77w54	5:11:36
Feezor 29	1	35N49	80w15	5:21:00
Fentress 41	1	35N59	79w45	5:19:00
Ferguson 97	1	36N05	81w22	5:25:28
Fernside 65	3	34N13	77w55	5:11:40
Ferrells 64	1	35N53	78w10	5:12:40
Fiberville 44	1	35N35	82w51	5:31:24
Fields 54	1	35N18	77w47	5:11:08
Fig 5	1	36N26	81w37	5:26:28
Fines Creek 44	1	35N42	82w58	5:31:52
Finger 84	1	35N24	80w26	5:21:44
Finley 14	1	35N54	81w31	5:26:04
Fires Creek 22	1	35N04	83w49	5:35:16
Fisher Town 13	1	35N31	80w38	5:22:32
Fitch 17	1	36N24	79w20	5:17:20
Five Forks 73	1	36N24	78w59	5:15:56
Five Forks 93	1	36N26	78w05	5:12:20
Five Point 92	1	35N48	78w39	5:14:36
Five Points 7	1	35N32	77w02	5:08:08
Five Points 45	1	36N30	80w35	5:22:20
Five Points 47	1	34N59	79w13	5:16:52
Five Points 77	1	34N56	79w46	5:19:04
Flat Branch 37	1	36N24	76w45	5:07:00
Flat Creek 11	1	35N45	82w33	5:30:12
Flat River 73	1	36N18	78w59	5:15:56
Flat Rock 86	1	36N30	80w35	5:22:20
Flats 57	1	35N01	83w19	5:33:16
Flat Shoals 85	1	36N16	80w14	5:20:56
Flat Springs 6	1	36N09	81w59	5:27:56
Flay 55	1	35N23	81w24	5:25:36
Fleetwood 5	1	36N18	81w31	5:26:04
Fletcher 45	1	35N26	82w30	5:30:00
Flint Hill 62	1	35N22	79w54	5:19:36
Flint Hill 76	1	35N50	79w52	5:19:28
Flint Hill 99	1	36N14	80w30	5:22:00
Floral College 78	1	34N44	79w21	5:17:24
Florence 69	1	35N07	76w39	5:06:36
Flowers 51	1	35N39	78w27	5:13:48
Flowes Store 13	1	35N25	80w36	5:22:24
Floytan Crossroads 91	1	36N19	78w24	5:13:36
Folkstone 67	1	34N26	77w34	5:10:16
Folly 37	1	36N27	76w37	5:06:28
Fontana Dam 38	1	35N26	83w50	5:35:20
Footsville 99	1	36N08	80w40	5:22:40
Forbes 61	1	36N00	82w14	5:28:56
Forbush 99	1	36N07	80w31	5:22:04
Forest 25	1	35N06	77w05	5:08:20
Forest City 81	1	35N20	81w52	5:27:28
Forest Hill 34	1	36N01	80w23	5:21:32
Forest Hills 32	1	35N58	78w55	5:15:40
Forest Hills 65	3	34N13	77w55	5:11:40
Forestville 92	1	35N59	78w30	5:14:00
Fork 30	1	35N54	80w34	5:22:16
Fork Mountain 61	1	36N03	82w10	5:28:40
Fort Barnwell 25	1	35N18	77w20	5:09:20
Fort Bragg 26	1	35N09	79w00	5:16:00
Fort Caswell 10	1	33N56	78w04	5:12:16
Fort Junction 26	1	35N09	78w58	5:15:52
Fort Landing 89	1	35N55	76w15	5:05:00
Fort Macon Village 25	1	34N53	76w54	5:07:36
Fort Raleigh City 28	1	35N54	75w40	5:02:40
Foscoe 95	1	36N10	81w52	5:27:28
Foster Creek 58	1	35N48	82w41	5:30:44
Fountain 31	1	34N50	77w49	5:11:16
Fountain 74	1	34N51	77w38	5:10:32
Fountain Hill 4	1	35N00	80w16	5:21:04
Four Oaks 51	1	35N27	78w26	5:13:44
Fourway 40	1	35N25	77w35	5:10:20
Foys 52	1	35N13	77w26	5:09:44
Francisco 85	1	36N29	80w27	5:21:48
Frank 6	1	36N05	81w56	5:27:44
Franklin 57	1	35N11	83w23	5:33:32
Franklin 80	1	35N39	80w29	5:21:56
Franklin Grove 87	1	35N26	83w27	5:33:48
Franklinton 35	1	36N06	78w27	5:13:48
Franklinville 76	1	35N45	79w44	5:18:56
Franktown 67	1	34N54	77w33	5:10:12
Frazier Crossroads 64	1	35N57	78w07	5:12:28
Fraziers Crossroads 46	1	36N17	76w59	5:07:56
Freedom 60	1	35N14	80w53	5:23:32
Freeland 10	1	34N06	78w32	5:14:08
Freeman 24	1	34N19	78w24	5:13:36
Freemans Mills 41	1	35N58	80w00	5:20:00
Fremont 96	1	35N33	77w58	5:11:52
French Broad 11	1	35N42	82w37	5:30:28
Frenchs Creek 9	1	34N28	78w18	5:13:12
Friendship 31	1	35N00	78w06	5:12:24
Friendship 41	1	36N05	79w54	5:19:36
Friendship 92	1	35N44	78w51	5:15:24
Friendship 99	1	36N14	80w30	5:22:00
Frisco 28	1	35N14	75w37	5:02:28
Frog Level 74	1	35N36	77w23	5:09:32
Frog Level 81	1	35N19	81w52	5:27:28
Frog Pond 84	1	35N13	80w19	5:21:16
Frogsboro 17	1	36N24	79w10	5:16:40
Fruitland 45	1	35N19	82w28	5:29:52
Fruitville 27	1	36N31	75w56	5:03:44
Fulchers Landing 67	1	34N31	77w23	5:09:32
Fulford 10	1	33N54	78w27	5:13:48
Fullers 76	1	35N53	80w05	5:20:20
Fulp 85	1	36N18	80w08	5:20:32
Fulton 30	1	35N52	80w27	5:21:48
Funston 10	1	34N09	78w06	5:12:24
Fuquay-Varina 92	1	35N36	78w49	5:15:16
Furr 84	1	35N15	80w25	5:21:40
Gaddy 78	1	34N27	79w13	5:16:52
Galatia 66	1	36N29	77w27	5:09:48
Gallup Acres 26	1	35N02	78w57	5:15:48
Gamewell 14	1	35N54	81w31	5:26:04
Gap Civil 3	1	36N31	81w08	5:24:32
Gardner 98	1	35N44	77w47	5:11:08
Gardnerville 74	1	35N28	77w25	5:09:40
Gardner Webb College 23	1	35N15	81w40	5:26:40
Garland 82	1	34N47	78w24	5:13:36
Garner 92	1	35N43	78w37	5:14:28
Garners Store 63	1	35N32	79w46	5:19:04
Garren Hill 63	1	35N12	79w28	5:17:52
Garysburg 66	1	36N26	77w34	5:10:16
Gaston 66	1	36N30	77w39	5:10:36
Gastonia 36	1	35N16	81w11	5:24:44
Gastonia East 36	1	35N16	81w10	5:24:40
Gastonia North 36	1	35N16	81w10	5:24:40
Gates 37	1	36N30	76w46	5:07:04
Gatesville 37	1	36N24	76w45	5:07:00
Gause Landing 10	1	33N54	78w27	5:13:48
Gay 50	1	35N22	83w14	5:32:56
Gaylord 7	1	35N28	76w49	5:07:16
Gentry Store 73	1	36N24	78w59	5:15:56
George 66	1	36N19	77w14	5:08:56

Georgetown 54 1 35N16 77w35 5:10:20
Georgeville 13 1 35N18 80w28 5:21:52
Germanton 85 1 36N16 80w14 5:20:56
Gerton 45 1 35N29 82w21 5:29:24
Gethsemane 33 1 36N06 77w43 5:10:52
Gibson 83 1 34N46 79w37 5:18:28
Gibsonville 41 1 36N06 79w32 5:18:08
Giddensville 82 1 34N56 78w10 5:12:40
Gilford City 1 36N04 79w48 5:19:12
Gilkey 81 1 35N26 81w59 5:27:56
Gill 91 1 36N19 78w24 5:13:36
Gillburg 91 1 36N19 78w24 5:13:36
Glade Creek 3 1 36N31 81w00 5:24:00
Glade Valley 3 1 36N29 81w02 5:24:08
Glady Fork 11 1 35N32 82w41 5:30:44
Glass 13 1 35N31 80w38 5:22:32
Glen Alpine 12 1 35N44 81w47 5:27:08
Glen Ayre 61 1 36N01 82w09 5:28:36
Glendale Springs 5
1 36N21 81w23 5:25:32
Glendon 63 1 35N29 79w25 5:17:40
Glenfield 40 1 35N27 77w40 5:10:40
Glen Forest 92 1 35N50 78w40 5:14:40
Glen Lennox 68 1 35N55 79w01 5:16:04
Glenn 68 1 36N01 78w56 5:15:44
Glenola 76 1 35N58 80w00 5:20:00
Glen Raven 1 1 36N07 79w28 5:17:52
Glenrock 11 1 35N36 82w33 5:30:12
Glenview 42 1 36N11 77w40 5:10:40
Glenville 50 1 35N10 83w08 5:32:32
Glenwood 56 1 35N37 81w59 5:27:56
Glenwood 77 1 34N56 79w46 5:19:04
Glenwood Village 92
1 35N50 78w40 5:14:40
Gliden 21 1 36N21 76w36 5:06:24
Glisson 31 1 35N06 77w53 5:11:32
Globe 14 1 36N03 81w42 5:26:48
Gloucester 16 1 34N44 76w32 5:06:08
Gloucester 88 1 35N13 82w53 5:31:32
Gneiss 57 1 35N11 83w23 5:33:32
Goat Neck 89 1 35N55 76w15 5:05:00
Godwin 26 1 35N13 78w41 5:14:44
Golden 81 1 35N22 81w50 5:27:20
Golden Valley 81 1 35N32 81w46 5:27:04
Gold Hill 80 1 35N32 80w24 5:21:36
Gold Mine 35 1 36N11 78w05 5:12:20
Gold Mine 57 1 35N03 83w12 5:32:48
Gold Point 59 1 35N52 77w14 5:08:56
Goldrock 64 1 36N06 77w43 5:10:52
Goldsboro 96 1 35N23 77w59 5:11:56
Goldston 19 1 35N36 79w20 5:17:20
Goodsonville 55 1 35N28 81w15 5:25:00
Goose Creek 15 1 36N17 76w05 5:04:20
Goose Creek 90 1 35N07 80w31 5:22:04
Goose Hollow 24 1 34N19 78w24 5:13:36
Gooseneck 24 1 34N20 78w14 5:12:56
Goose Nest 59 1 35N59 77w19 5:09:16
Goose Pond 8 1 36N12 76w46 5:07:04
Gordonton 73 1 36N16 79w03 5:16:12
Gordontown 29 1 35N49 80w15 5:21:00
Gorman 32 1 36N02 78w53 5:15:32
Goshen 82 1 34N56 78w10 5:12:40
Goshen 97 1 36N09 81w10 5:24:40
Governors Island 87
1 35N26 83w27 5:33:48
Grace 11 1 35N37 82w33 5:30:12
Grace Chapel 14 1 35N48 81w26 5:25:44
Grady 71 1 34N27 78w04 5:12:16
Gradys 96 1 35N14 77w51 5:11:24
Gragg 6 1 35N54 81w31 5:26:04
Graham 1 1 36N05 79w25 5:17:40
Graingers 54 1 35N16 77w35 5:10:20
Grandfather 95 1 36N10 81w52 5:27:28
Grandview 20 1 35N05 84w02 5:36:08
Grandview Heights 95
1 36N13 81w40 5:26:40
Grandy 27 1 36N15 75w53 5:03:32
Granite Falls 14 1 35N48 81w26 5:25:44
Granite Quarry 80 1 35N37 80w26 5:21:44
Grant 76 1 35N40 79w45 5:19:00
Grantham 96 1 35N16 78w12 5:12:48
Granthams 25 1 35N06 77w05 5:08:20
Grantsboro 69 1 35N08 76w51 5:07:24
Grape Creek 20 1 35N05 84w02 5:36:08
Grapevine 58 1 35N48 82w41 5:30:44
Graphite 56 1 35N38 82w11 5:28:44
Grassy Creek 5 1 36N33 81w24 5:25:36
Grassy Creek 61 1 35N55 82w04 5:28:16
Grays Chapel 76 1 35N45 79w41 5:18:44
Grays Creek 26 1 34N54 78w51 5:15:24
Grayson 5 1 36N32 81w40 5:26:40
Great Neck Landing 67
1 34N43 77w14 5:08:56
Great Swamp 96 1 35N33 78w01 5:12:04
Greene 41 1 35N58 79w35 5:18:20
Greene Cove 61 1 36N01 82w09 5:28:36
Greenevers 31 1 34N50 78w02 5:12:08
Greenhill 44 1 35N35 82w51 5:31:24
Green Hill 81 1 35N24 82w03 5:28:12
Greenleaf 96 1 35N22 77w58 5:11:52
Greenlee 56 1 35N38 82w11 5:28:44
Green Level 92 1 35N44 78w51 5:15:24
Greenmountain 100 1 35N59 82w16 5:29:04
Green River 45 1 35N13 82w27 5:29:48
Greenriver 75 1 35N22 81w57 5:27:48
Greensboro 41 1 36N04 79w48 5:19:12
Greens Creek 50 1 35N22 83w14 5:32:56
Green Valley 5 1 36N23 81w43 5:26:52
Greenville 74 1 35N37 77w23 5:09:32
Gregory 27 1 36N23 76w07 5:04:28
Gregory Crossroads 67
1 34N54 77w33 5:10:12
Greystone 91 1 36N19 78w24 5:13:36
Grifton 74 1 35N23 77w26 5:09:44
Grimesdale 45 1 35N19 82w28 5:29:52
Grimesland 74 1 35N34 77w11 5:08:44
Grimshawes 50 1 35N03 83w12 5:32:48
Grissettown 10 1 33N54 78w27 5:13:48
Grissom 39 1 36N07 78w41 5:14:44
Grist 24 1 34N19 78w50 5:15:20
Groomtown 41 1 36N03 79w52 5:19:28
Grove 43 1 35N24 78w40 5:14:40
Grove Hill 93 1 36N26 78w05 5:12:20
Grovemont 11 1 35N37 82w23 5:29:32
Grover 23 1 35N10 81w27 5:25:48
Groves 36 1 35N16 81w10 5:24:40
Growers Crossroads 8
1 36N12 76w46 5:07:04
Guideway 24 1 34N09 78w53 5:15:32
Guilford 41 1 36N04 79w53 5:19:32
Guilford College 41
1 36N06 79w53 5:19:32
Gulf 19 1 35N35 79w20 5:17:20
Gulledge 4 1 34N52 80w06 5:20:24
Gulrock 48 1 35N31 76w00 5:04:00
Gumberry 66 1 36N28 77w30 5:10:00
Gumbranch 67 1 34N45 77w26 5:09:44
Gum Neck 89 1 35N43 76w11 5:04:44
Gumtree 29 1 36N04 80w14 5:20:56
Guntertown 58 1 35N48 82w41 5:30:44
Gupton 35 1 36N08 78w12 5:12:48
Guthrie 34 1 36N07 80w10 5:20:40
Guyton 9 1 34N32 78w48 5:15:12
Gwaltneys 2 1 35N59 81w12 5:24:48
Haddocks Crossroads 74
1 35N32 77w24 5:09:36
Hadley 19 1 35N49 79w17 5:17:08
Half Moon 67 1 34N45 77w26 5:09:44
Halifax 42 1 36N20 77w35 5:10:20
Hall 37 1 36N26 76w51 5:07:24
Halls 46 1 36N17 76w59 5:07:56
Halls 82 1 35N07 78w19 5:13:16
Hallsboro 24 1 34N20 78w36 5:14:24
Halls Ferry Junction 84
1 35N27 80w13 5:20:52
Halls Mills 97 1 36N21 81w14 5:24:56
Halls Store 82 1 35N01 78w30 5:14:00
Hallsville 31 1 34N55 77w46 5:11:04
Hamburg 50 1 35N10 83w08 5:32:32
Hamer 17 1 36N30 79w18 5:17:12
Hamilton 59 1 35N57 77w12 5:08:48
Hamlet 77 1 34N53 79w42 5:18:48
Hampstead 71 1 34N22 77w44 5:10:56
Hampton 29 1 35N58 80w22 5:21:28
Hamptonville 99 1 36N06 80w46 5:23:04
Hamrick 100 1 35N55 82w18 5:29:12
Hamtown 41 1 36N06 79w46 5:19:04
Hancock 21 1 36N04 76w36 5:06:24
Hancock Village 25
1 34N54 76w54 5:07:36
Handy 29 1 35N38 80w07 5:20:28
Hanes 34 1 36N05 80w17 5:21:08
Hannersville 29 1 35N49 80w15 5:21:00
Hanrahans 74 1 35N22 77w26 5:09:44
Happy Valley 14 1 36N00 81w34 5:26:16
Harbinger 27 1 36N06 75w49 5:03:16
Hardees Cross Road 51
1 35N23 78w33 5:14:12
Hardins 36 1 35N19 81w11 5:24:44
Hare 3 1 36N29 81w02 5:24:08
Hargetts Cross Roads 52
1 34N54 77w33 5:10:12
Harkers Island 16 1 34N42 76w34 5:06:16
Harlem Heights 4 1 34N58 80w05 5:20:20
Harlowe 16 1 34N49 76w44 5:06:56
Harmony 49 1 35N58 80w46 5:23:04
Harnett 65 3 34N14 77w51 5:11:24
Harpers Crossroads 19
1 35N37 79w23 5:17:32
Harrell 61 1 36N07 82w12 5:28:48
Harrells 82 1 34N44 78w12 5:12:48
Harrellsville 46 1 36N18 76w48 5:07:12
Harrelsonville 24 1 34N20 78w42 5:14:48
Harris 63 1 35N18 79w24 5:17:36
Harris 81 1 35N15 81w52 5:27:28
Harrisburg 13 1 35N19 80w39 5:22:36
Harris Crossroads 35
1 36N01 78w29 5:13:56
Harris Crossroads 91
1 36N19 78w24 5:13:36
Harris Landing 21 1 36N04 76w36 5:06:24
Harrison Cross Roads 79
1 36N21 79w41 5:18:44
Hartland 14 1 35N54 81w31 5:26:04
Hartman 85 1 36N25 80w13 5:20:52
Harts Store 85 1 36N29 80w14 5:20:56
Harveytown 54 1 35N16 77w35 5:10:20
Haslett 37 1 36N31 76w42 5:06:48
Haslin Corners 7 1 35N32 76w37 5:06:28
Hassell 59 1 35N54 77w17 5:09:08
Hasty 83 1 34N46 79w28 5:17:52
Hatteras 28 1 35N13 75w42 5:02:48
Havelock 25 1 34N53 76w54 5:07:36
Haw 67 1 34N45 77w26 5:09:44
Haw Branch 63 1 35N28 79w10 5:16:40
Haw Branch 67 1 34N54 77w33 5:10:12
Hawk 61 1 36N01 82w09 5:28:36
Haw River 1 1 36N07 79w21 5:17:24
Hawtree 93 1 36N30 78w09 5:12:36
Hayesville 22 1 35N03 83w49 5:35:16
Haymount 26 1 35N03 78w55 5:15:40
Hayne 82 1 35N00 78w38 5:14:32
Hays 97 1 36N15 81w07 5:24:28
Hayti 32 1 36N00 78w54 5:15:36
Haywood 19 1 35N37 79w04 5:16:16
Hazelwood 44 2 35N28 83w00 5:32:00
Healing Spring 29 1 35N38 80w11 5:20:44
Heathsville 42 1 36N11 77w40 5:10:40
Heaton 6 1 36N09 81w59 5:27:56
Hectors Creek 43 1 35N30 78w51 5:15:24
Hedrick Grove 29 1 35N49 80w15 5:21:00
Helens Crossroads 74
1 35N28 77w25 5:09:40
Helton 5 1 36N33 81w28 5:25:52
Hemby 90 1 35N05 80w41 5:22:44
Hemby Bridge 90 1 35N05 80w41 5:22:44
Hemlock 5 1 36N32 81w40 5:26:40
Henderson 91 1 36N20 78w25 5:13:40
Hendersonville 45 1 35N19 82w28 5:29:52
Hendrix 97 1 36N05 81w22 5:25:28
Henrico 66 1 36N32 77w50 5:11:20
Henrietta 81 1 35N16 81w48 5:27:12
Henry River 12 1 35N44 81w21 5:25:24
Hepco 44 1 35N35 82w55 5:31:40
Herrings 82 1 35N08 78w26 5:13:44
Herrings Crossroads 31
1 35N07 77w49 5:11:16
Hertford 72 1 36N11 76w28 5:05:52
Hester 39 1 36N12 78w43 5:14:52
Hesters Store 73 1 36N16 79w03 5:16:12
Hestertown 78 1 34N36 79w01 5:16:04
Hewitt 87 2 35N15 83w42 5:34:48
Hexlena 8 1 36N14 77w07 5:08:28
Hickmans Crossroads 10
1 33N54 78w27 5:13:48
Hickory 18 1 35N44 81w21 5:25:24
Hickory Crossroads 72
1 36N16 76w32 5:06:08
Hickory Grove 60 1 35N13 80w41 5:22:44
Hickory Knoll 57 1 35N11 83w23 5:33:32
Hickory Mountain 19
1 35N42 79w19 5:17:16
Hickory Point 7 1 35N18 76w47 5:07:08
Hickory Rock 35 1 36N08 78w12 5:12:48
Hicks Crossroads 91
1 35N25 80w51 5:23:24
Hiddenite 2 1 35N54 81w05 5:24:20
Higdonville 57 1 35N11 83w23 5:33:32
Higgins 56 1 35N39 81w57 5:27:48
Higgins 100 1 35N55 82w18 5:29:12
Highfalls 63 1 35N29 79w31 5:18:04
Highlands 57 1 35N03 83w12 5:32:48
High Point 41 1 35N57 80w00 5:20:00
High Rock 29 1 35N36 80w13 5:20:52
High Shoals 36 1 35N24 81w12 5:24:48
High Shoals 81 1 35N15 81w48 5:27:12
Highsmiths 82 1 34N57 78w31 5:14:04
Hightowers 17 1 36N18 79w12 5:16:48
Hildebran 12 1 35N43 81w26 5:25:44
Hill Crest 63 1 35N18 79w24 5:17:36
Hillcrest 95 1 36N13 81w40 5:26:40
Hillendale 26 1 35N04 78w53 5:15:32
Hillgirt 45 1 35N19 82w28 5:29:52
Hilliardston 64 1 35N58 77w58 5:11:52
Hillsborough 68 1 36N05 79w07 5:16:28
Hills Crossroads 42
1 36N20 77w35 5:10:20
Hillsdale 30 1 35N57 80w25 5:21:40
Hillsdale 41 1 36N06 79w46 5:19:04
Hill Top 41 1 36N03 79w52 5:19:28
Hilltop 55 1 35N28 81w15 5:25:00
Hines Junction 54 1 35N16 77w35 5:10:20
Hinsons Crossroads 24
1 34N19 79w02 5:16:08
Hiwassee 22 1 35N02 83w45 5:35:00
Hiwassee Dam 20 1 35N05 84w02 5:36:08
Hobbsville 37 1 36N21 76w36 5:06:24
Hobbton 82 1 35N15 78w21 5:13:24
Hobgood 42 1 36N02 77w24 5:09:36
Hobucken 69 1 35N15 76w34 5:06:16
Hodges Gap 95 1 36N13 81w40 5:26:40
Hoffman 77 1 35N02 79w33 5:18:12
Hogback 88 1 35N07 82w55 5:31:40
Hog Island 63 1 35N15 79w17 5:17:08
Holden Beach 10 1 34N01 78w16 5:13:04
Holdens Cross Roads 98
1 35N44 77w55 5:11:40
Holland 92 1 35N35 78w48 5:15:12
Hollemans Crossroads 92
1 35N41 78w56 5:15:44
Hollifield 56 1 35N41 82w00 5:28:00
Hollis 81 1 35N20 81w45 5:27:00
Hollister 42 1 36N15 77w56 5:11:44
Hollow 9 1 34N47 78w50 5:15:20
Holloway 73 1 36N30 78w52 5:15:28
Holly 71 1 34N38 77w43 5:10:52
Holly Grove 8 1 36N17 76w59 5:07:56
Holly Grove 29 1 35N49 80w15 5:21:00
Holly Grove 37 1 36N30 76w34 5:06:16
Holly Ridge 67 1 34N30 77w33 5:10:12
Holly Springs 16 1 34N48 76w52 5:07:28
Holly Springs 57 1 35N11 83w23 5:33:32
Holly Springs 92 1 35N39 78w50 5:15:20
Homestead 60 1 35N14 80w55 5:23:40
Hominy 11 2 35N32 82w41 5:30:44
Honeycutts 82 1 35N03 78w29 5:13:56
Honey Hill 24 1 34N20 78w36 5:14:24
Honey Island 10 1 34N06 78w32 5:14:08
Honey Town 77 1 34N56 79w46 5:19:04
Honolulu 25 1 35N22 77w26 5:09:44
Hoods Crossroads 60
1 35N07 80w43 5:22:52
Hood Swamp 96 1 35N22 77w58 5:11:52
Hookerton 40 1 35N25 77w35 5:10:20
Hooper Hill 10 1 34N15 78w03 5:12:12
Hoopers Creek 45 1 35N25 82w29 5:29:56
Hootentown 7 1 35N32 77w02 5:08:08
Hopedale 1 1 36N06 79w27 5:17:48
Hope Mills 26 1 34N59 78w57 5:15:48
Hopewell 81 1 35N20 81w45 5:27:00
Hopewell 96 1 35N11 78w04 5:12:16
Hopkins 92 1 35N49 78w19 5:13:16
Horse Creek 5 1 36N31 81w35 5:26:20
Horse Shoe 45 1 35N21 82w33 5:30:12
Hosiery Mill 4 1 34N58 80w05 5:20:20

NORTH CAROLINA

Hothouse 20 1 35N01 84w16 5:37:04
Hot Springs 58 2 35N54 82w50 5:31:20
House Creek 92 1 35N51 81w52 5:27:28
Houston 90 1 34N59 80w33 5:22:12
Houstonville 49 1 35N57 80w46 5:23:04
Howards Creek 55 1 35N29 81w21 5:25:24
Hubert 67 1 34N43 77w14 5:08:56
Huckleberry Heights 32 1 36N01 78w56 5:15:44
Hudson 14 1 35N51 81w30 5:26:00
Huffmantown 67 1 34N54 77w33 5:10:12
Hughes 6 1 36N05 81w56 5:27:44
Hugo 54 1 35N22 77w26 5:09:44
Hulls Crossroads 55 1 35N33 81w24 5:25:36
Huntdale 61 1 36N00 82w14 5:28:56
Hunters Bridge 7 1 35N37 76w52 5:07:28
Hunters Mill 37 1 36N24 76w36 5:06:24
Huntersville 60 1 35N25 80w51 5:23:24
Hunting Creek 97 1 36N10 81w08 5:24:32
Huntsboro 39 1 36N18 78w35 5:14:20
Huntsville 79 1 36N19 79w59 5:19:56
Huntsville 99 1 35N54 80w34 5:22:16
Hurdle Mills 73 1 36N16 79w03 5:16:12
Hurricane 5 1 36N34 81w35 5:26:20
Husk 5 1 36N35 81w31 5:26:04
Hyatt Creek 44 1 35N33 82w59 5:31:56
Hydro 84 1 35N13 80w00 5:20:00
Icard 12 1 35N44 81w28 5:25:52
Icaria 21 1 36N13 76w37 5:06:28
Ida 83 1 34N46 79w28 5:17:52
Idlewild 5 1 36N24 81w29 5:25:56
Idlewild 60 1 35N12 80w45 5:23:00
Index 5 1 36N24 81w29 5:25:56
Indian Beach 16 1 34N42 76w50 5:07:20
Indian Hills 50 1 35N26 83w22 5:33:28
Indian Springs 96 1 35N13 77w56 5:11:44
Indian Town 15 1 36N24 76w06 5:04:24
Indian Trail 90 1 35N04 80w40 5:22:40
Indian Woods 8 1 35N58 77w04 5:08:16
Inez 93 1 36N24 78w09 5:12:36
Ingalls 6 1 36N05 81w56 5:27:44
Ingleside 35 1 36N08 78w12 5:12:48
Ingold 82 1 34N50 78w21 5:13:24
Ingram 4 1 34N58 79w59 5:19:56
Ingrams 51 1 35N25 78w25 5:13:40
Institute 54 1 35N20 77w43 5:10:52
Intelligence 79 1 36N23 79w58 5:19:52
Iotla 57 1 35N11 83w23 5:33:32
Iredell 10 1 33N54 78w27 5:13:48
Ironduff 44 1 35N37 82w59 5:31:56
Ironhill 24 1 34N09 78w53 5:15:32
Iron Station 55 1 35N27 81w09 5:24:36
Ironton 55 1 35N29 81w09 5:24:36
Irvins Crossroads 54 1 35N03 77w45 5:11:00
Isenhour 84 1 35N27 80w13 5:20:52
Island Creek 31 1 34N47 77w56 5:11:44
Ita 42 1 36N11 77w40 5:10:40
Ivanhoe 82 1 34N37 78w15 5:13:00
Ivy 58 1 35N46 82w27 5:29:48
Ivy Hill 44 1 35N34 83w05 5:32:20
Ivy Ridge 58 2 35N50 82w33 5:30:12
Jacks Creek 100 1 35N58 82w20 5:29:20
Jackson 66 1 36N23 77w25 5:09:40
Jackson Hill 29 1 35N35 80w07 5:20:28
Jackson Line 87 1 35N26 83w27 5:33:48
Jackson Park 13 1 35N31 80w38 5:22:32
Jacksons Creek 76 1 35N38 80w07 5:20:28
Jacksons Crossroads 54 1 35N16 77w35 5:10:20
Jackson Springs 63 1 35N13 79w38 5:18:32
Jacksons Store 31 1 34N55 77w46 5:11:04
Jacksonville 67 1 34N45 77w26 5:09:44
Jacktown 56 1 35N41 82w00 5:28:00
Jacobs Fork 18 1 35N36 81w19 5:25:16
Jakesville 29 1 35N49 80w15 5:21:00
James City 25 1 35N05 77w02 5:08:08
Jamestown 41 1 36N00 79w56 5:19:44
Jamesville 59 1 35N49 76w54 5:07:36
Janeiro 69 1 35N02 76w50 5:07:20
Jarman Forks 67 1 34N54 77w33 5:10:12
Jarvisburg 27 1 36N09 75w52 5:03:28
Jason 40 1 35N24 77w46 5:11:04
Jasper 25 1 35N06 77w05 5:08:20
Jefferson 5 1 36N25 81w28 5:25:52
Jefferson Park 77 1 34N56 79w46 5:19:04
Jenny Lind 54 1 35N18 77w47 5:11:08
Jericho 17 1 36N24 79w20 5:17:20
Jerome 9 1 34N50 78w44 5:14:56
Jerusalem 30 1 35N50 80w32 5:22:08
Jobs Cabin 97 1 36N15 81w24 5:25:36
Joe 58 1 35N54 82w50 5:31:20
Johns 83 1 34N46 79w28 5:17:52
Johnsons Corner 15 1 36N27 76w20 5:05:20
Johnsontown 29 1 35N53 80w05 5:20:20
Johnsontown 82 1 35N00 78w20 5:13:20
Johnsonville 20 1 35N00 84w10 5:36:40
Johnsonville 43 1 35N17 79w07 5:16:28
Johns River 14 1 35N56 81w41 5:26:44
Johnstown 9 1 34N38 78w33 5:14:12
Jonas Ridge 12 1 35N58 81w53 5:27:32
Jonathan 44 1 35N33 82w59 5:31:56
Jonathans Creek 44 1 35N37 83w02 5:32:08
Jonesboro 53 1 35N27 79w10 5:16:40
Jonesboro Crossing 24 1 34N20 78w36 5:14:24
Jonesboro Heights 53 1 35N28 79w10 5:16:40
Jonestown 54 1 35N03 77w45 5:11:00
Jonesville 99 1 36N14 80w51 5:23:24
Joppa 21 1 36N16 76w32 5:06:08
Joy 12 1 35N44 81w42 5:26:48
Joyceton 14 1 35N54 81w31 5:26:04
Joyners Crossroads 64 1 35N58 77w48 5:11:12
Joynes 97 1 36N21 81w01 5:24:04
Jubilee 29 1 35N45 80w19 5:21:16
Judkins 93 1 36N23 78w00 5:12:00
Jugtown 11 1 35N32 82w41 5:30:44
Jugtown 63 1 35N32 79w46 5:19:04
Julian 41 1 35N54 79w39 5:18:36
Jupiter 11 1 35N46 82w36 5:30:24
Just 58 1 35N50 82w33 5:30:12
Justice 35 1 36N08 78w12 5:12:48
Kalmia 61 1 35N55 82w04 5:28:16
Kannapolis 13 1 35N30 80w37 5:22:28
Kanuga Pines 45 1 35N19 82w28 5:29:52
Kappa 30 1 35N54 80w34 5:22:16
Kapps Mill 86 1 36N19 80w52 5:23:28
Katesville 35 1 36N06 78w27 5:13:48
Keane 32 1 35N58 78w55 5:15:40
Keener 82 1 35N00 78w20 5:13:20
Kelford 8 1 36N11 77w13 5:08:52
Kellersville 95 1 36N10 81w52 5:27:28
Kellum 67 1 34N45 77w26 5:09:44
Kellumtown 67 1 34N43 77w14 5:08:56
Kelly 9 1 34N28 78w19 5:13:16
Kenansville 31 1 34N58 77w58 5:11:52
Kenly 51 1 35N36 78w07 5:12:28
Kennebec 92 1 35N36 78w44 5:14:56
Kennekeet 28 1 35N42 75w39 5:02:36
Kennells Beach 69 1 35N08 76w51 5:07:24
Kernersville 34 1 36N07 80w05 5:20:20
Kerr 82 1 34N44 78w12 5:12:48
Keys Crossroads 37 1 36N21 76w36 5:06:24
Kikers 4 1 35N00 80w16 5:21:04
Kilby 2 1 35N55 81w10 5:24:40
Kilkenny 1 35N38 76w13 5:04:52
Kill Devil Hills 28 1 36N01 75w39 5:02:36
Kimesville 1 1 35N51 79w34 5:18:16
King 85 1 36N17 80w22 5:21:28
King Charles 92 1 35N46 78w37 5:14:28
Kingsboro 33 1 35N58 77w48 5:11:12
Kings Creek 14 1 36N00 81w24 5:25:36
Kings Crossroads 74 1 35N40 77w38 5:10:32
Kings Mountain 23 1 35N15 81w20 5:25:20
King Whites Fork 42 1 36N02 77w24 5:09:36
Kinston 54 1 35N16 77w35 5:10:20
Kinton Fork 39 1 36N18 78w35 5:14:20
Kipling 43 1 35N29 78w49 5:15:16
Kirby 66 1 36N28 77w12 5:08:48
Kittrell 91 1 36N13 78w26 5:13:44
Kitty Fork 82 1 35N00 78w20 5:13:20
Kitty Hawk 28 1 36N04 75w42 5:02:48
Knightdale 92 1 35N47 78w29 5:13:56
Knob Creek 23 1 35N31 81w33 5:26:12
Knob Hill 77 1 34N56 79w46 5:19:04
Knobs 99 1 36N12 80w49 5:23:16
Knotts Island 27 1 36N31 75w56 5:03:44
Kona 61 1 36N01 82w09 5:28:36
Kornbow 26 1 35N05 78w57 5:15:48
Kross Keys 75 1 35N11 82w11 5:28:44
Kure Beach 65 3 34N00 77w54 5:11:36
Kyle 57 1 35N15 83w42 5:34:48
Laboratory 55 1 35N26 81w16 5:25:04
Lackey Hill 87 1 35N26 83w27 5:33:48
Lackey Town 56 1 35N38 82w11 5:28:44
Ladonia 86 1 36N30 80w35 5:22:20
Lafayette 26 1 35N02 78w57 5:15:48
Lagoon 9 1 34N38 78w33 5:14:12
La Grange 54 1 35N19 77w47 5:11:08
Lake Creek 9 1 34N37 78w20 5:13:20
Lakecrest 26 1 35N04 78w53 5:15:32
Lakedale 26 1 35N01 78w55 5:15:40
Lake Junaluska 44 2 35N32 82w58 5:31:52
Lake Landing 48 1 35N29 76w02 5:04:08
Lake Lure 81 1 35N25 82w12 5:28:48
Lake Toxaway 88 1 35N08 82w56 5:31:44
Lakeview 29 1 35N45 80w19 5:21:16
Lakeview 63 1 35N15 79w19 5:17:16
Lakeview Estates 45 1 35N19 82w28 5:29:52
Lake View Park 18 1 35N44 81w21 5:25:24
Lake Waccamaw 24 1 34N20 78w31 5:14:04
Lakewood 32 1 35N58 78w55 5:15:40
Lakewood 45 1 35N19 82w28 5:29:52
Lambert 84 1 35N14 80w26 5:21:44
Lamm 98 1 35N44 77w55 5:11:40
Lamms Crossroads 98 1 35N44 77w55 5:11:40
Lancaster Crossroads 64 1 36N05 78w03 5:12:12
Landis 80 1 35N33 80w37 5:22:28
Lanesboro 4 1 35N00 80w15 5:21:00
Lanes Creek 90 1 34N52 80w23 5:21:32
Lanes Store 81 1 35N29 81w58 5:27:52
Langley Store 64 1 35N58 77w48 5:11:12
Lansdowne 60 1 35N10 80w48 5:23:12
Lansing 5 1 36N29 81w30 5:26:00
Lanvale 10 1 34N15 78w03 5:12:12
Lasker 66 1 36N21 77w18 5:09:12
Lattimore 23 1 35N19 81w40 5:26:40
Lauada 87 1 35N22 83w30 5:34:00
Laurel 58 1 35N48 82w41 5:30:44
Laurel Creek 95 1 36N15 81w50 5:27:20
Laurel Hill 11 1 35N32 82w41 5:30:44
Laurel Hill 83 1 34N49 79w33 5:18:12
Laurel Hills 92 1 35N50 78w40 5:14:40
Laurel Park 45 1 35N19 82w30 5:30:00
Laurel Rock Acres 45 1 35N19 82w28 5:29:52
Laurel Springs 3 1 36N25 81w16 5:25:04
Laurinburg 83 1 34N47 79w28 5:17:52
Laurinburg West 83 1 34N46 79w29 5:17:56
Lawndale 23 1 35N25 81w34 5:26:16
Lawrence 33 1 35N54 77w32 5:10:08
Lawsonville 79 1 36N21 79w41 5:18:44
Lawsonville 85 1 36N29 80w14 5:20:56
Laxon 95 1 36N14 81w33 5:26:12
Laytown 14 1 35N54 81w31 5:26:04
Leaksville 79 1 36N30 79w46 5:19:04
Leaman 63 1 35N26 79w35 5:18:20
Leasburg 17 1 36N24 79w10 5:16:40
Leatherman 57 1 35N11 83w23 5:33:32
Lebanon 32 1 36N06 78w56 5:15:44
Ledbetter 77 1 34N59 79w43 5:18:52
Ledger 61 1 35N58 82w08 5:28:32
Leechville 7 1 35N32 76w37 5:06:28
Lees 24 1 34N13 78w40 5:14:40
Lees Mills 94 1 35N52 76w37 5:06:28
Leesville 92 1 35N54 78w44 5:14:56
Leggett 33 1 35N59 77w35 5:10:20
Leicester 11 1 35N38 82w41 5:30:44
Leland 10 1 34N15 78w03 5:12:12
Lemley 60 1 35N27 80w54 5:23:36
Lemon Springs 53 1 35N23 79w12 5:16:48
Lennon Crossroads 10 1 34N04 78w09 5:12:36
Lennoxville 16 1 34N43 76w39 5:06:36
Lenoir 14 1 35N55 81w32 5:26:08
Lenoir Rhyne 18 1 35N44 81w21 5:25:24
Lester S 54 1 35N16 77w35 5:10:20
Letitia 20 1 35N05 84w02 5:36:08
Level Cross 76 1 35N53 79w49 5:19:16
Level Cross 86 1 36N24 80w43 5:22:52
Levels 89 1 35N55 76w15 5:05:00
Leware 77 1 34N56 79w46 5:19:04
Lewis 39 1 36N18 78w35 5:14:20
Lewisburg 100 1 35N55 82w18 5:29:12
Lewis Fork 97 1 36N09 81w20 5:25:20
Lewiston 8 1 36N07 77w11 5:08:44
Lewisville 34 1 36N05 80w25 5:21:40
Lexington 29 1 35N49 80w15 5:21:00
Liberia 93 1 36N24 78w09 5:12:36
Liberty 76 1 35N51 79w34 5:18:16
Liberty 80 1 35N32 80w20 5:21:20
Liberty Hill 62 1 35N13 80w00 5:20:00
Liddell 54 1 35N14 77w51 5:11:24
Liledown 2 1 35N55 81w10 5:24:40
Lilesville 4 1 34N58 79w59 5:19:56
Lillington 43 1 35N24 78w49 5:15:16
Lilly 15 1 36N27 76w20 5:05:20
Lima 25 1 35N06 77w05 5:08:20
Lincoln Park 63 1 35N08 79w26 5:17:44
Lincolnton 55 1 35N29 81w16 5:25:04
Lindell 40 1 35N36 77w49 5:11:16
Linden 26 1 35N15 78w45 5:15:00
Lineberry 76 1 35N55 79w43 5:18:52
Linville 6 1 36N04 81w52 5:27:28
Linville Falls 12 1 35N57 81w56 5:27:44
Linwood 29 1 35N45 80w19 5:21:16
Lisbon 9 1 34N40 78w15 5:13:00
Litaker 80 1 35N35 80w30 5:22:00
Little Coharie 82 1 34N58 78w31 5:14:04
Little Creek 58 1 35N50 82w33 5:30:12
Littlefield 74 1 35N28 77w25 5:09:40
Little Horse Creek 5 1 36N30 81w30 5:26:00
Little Mountain 56 1 35N43 81w56 5:27:44
Little Pinecreek 58 1 35N48 82w41 5:30:44
Little Richwood 94 1 35N52 76w45 5:07:00
Little River 2 1 35N55 81w10 5:24:40
Little River 63 1 35N13 79w10 5:16:40
Little River 88 1 35N15 82w38 5:30:32
Little Rock Creek 61 1 36N05 82w06 5:28:24
Little Switzerland 56 1 35N51 82w06 5:28:24
Littleton 42 1 36N26 77w54 5:11:36
Livingstons Quarters 83 1 34N49 79w32 5:18:08
Lizzie 40 1 35N27 77w40 5:10:40
Lizzie Cotton Mills 51 1 35N32 78w17 5:13:08
Lloyd Crossroads 46 1 36N18 76w48 5:07:12
Loafers Glory 61 1 36N01 82w09 5:28:36
Lobelia 63 1 35N15 79w17 5:17:08
Locke 80 1 35N39 80w33 5:22:12
Lockwoods Folly 10 1 33N59 78w18 5:13:12
Locust 84 1 35N16 80w26 5:21:44
Locust Grove 100 1 36N00 82w14 5:28:56
Locust Hill 17 1 36N23 79w29 5:17:56
Loftins Crossroad 54 1 35N16 77w35 5:10:20
Logan 81 1 35N22 81w57 5:27:48
Logan Store 81 1 35N26 81w51 5:27:24
Lola 16 1 35N00 76w18 5:05:12
Lomax 97 1 36N13 81w00 5:24:00
Lone Hickory 99 1 36N08 80w40 5:22:40
Long Acre 7 1 35N33 76w56 5:07:44
Long Acres 67 1 34N45 77w26 5:09:44
Long Beach 10 1 33N55 78w07 5:12:28
Longcreek 71 1 34N26 77w53 5:11:32
Long Hill 86 1 36N25 80w33 5:22:12
Longhurst 73 1 36N25 78w58 5:15:52
Longisland 18 1 35N41 80w59 5:23:56
Long Ridge 58 1 35N50 82w33 5:30:12
Long Shoals 55 1 35N28 81w15 5:25:00
Longs Store 73 1 36N24 78w59 5:15:56
Longtown 12 1 35N43 81w56 5:27:44
Longtown 99 1 36N14 80w43 5:22:52

Long View 9 1 34N28 78w19 5:13:16
Longview 18 1 35N44 81w23 5:25:32
Longwood 10 1 34N00 78w33 5:14:12
Longwood Park 77 1 34N55 79w41 5:18:44
Loray 49 1 35N51 80w56 5:23:44
Louisburg 35 1 36N06 78w18 5:13:12
Love Field 50 1 35N22 83w14 5:32:56
Lovejoy 62 1 35N22 79w54 5:19:36
Lovelace 97 1 36N06 81w02 5:24:08
Love Valley 49 1 35N59 80w59 5:23:56
Lowell 36 1 35N16 81w07 5:24:28
Lower Contoe 33 1 35N50 77w28 5:09:52
Lower Fishing Creek 33
1 36N00 77w35 5:10:20
Lower Fork 12 1 35N37 81w34 5:26:16
Lower Hominy 11 1 35N33 82w38 5:30:32
Lower R 33 1 35N47 77w41 5:10:44
Lowes Grove 32 1 35N58 78w55 5:15:40
Lowesville 55 1 35N22 81w06 5:24:24
Lowgap 86 1 36N32 80w52 5:23:28
Lowland 69 1 35N18 76w35 5:06:20
Lucama 98 1 35N39 78w00 5:12:00
Lucia 36 1 35N18 81w01 5:24:04
Luck 58 1 35N44 82w52 5:31:28
Lumber Bridge 78 1 34N53 79w04 5:16:16
Lumberton 78 1 34N37 79w00 5:16:00
Luthers 11 2 35N32 82w41 5:30:44
Lyman 31 1 34N50 77w49 5:11:16
Lynchs Corner 70 1 36N17 76w14 5:04:56
Lynn 75 1 35N14 82w14 5:28:56
Lyon 39 1 36N07 78w41 5:14:44
Mabel 95 1 36N21 81w45 5:27:00
MacClesfield 33 1 35N45 77w40 5:10:40
Macedonia 20 1 35N00 84w10 5:36:40
Macedonia 92 1 35N46 78w43 5:14:52
Macedonia 94 1 35N52 76w45 5:07:00
Machpelah 55 1 35N27 81w09 5:24:36
Mackeys 94 1 35N56 76w37 5:06:28
Macks Village 92 1 35N35 78w48 5:15:12
Maco 10 1 34N15 78w03 5:12:12
Macon 93 1 36N26 78w05 5:12:20
Madison 79 1 36N23 79w58 5:19:52
Maggie Valley 44 1 35N31 83w06 5:32:24
Magnolia 12 1 35N44 81w42 5:26:48
Magnolia 31 1 34N53 78w05 5:12:20
Maiden 18 1 35N35 81w13 5:24:52
Maine 30 1 35N54 80w34 5:22:16
Makatoka 10 1 34N06 78w32 5:14:08
Makleyville 48 1 35N30 76w27 5:05:48
Mallard Creek 60 1 35N18 80w48 5:23:12
Malmo 10 1 34N15 78w03 5:12:12
Malpass Corner 71 1 34N33 77w55 5:11:40
Maltby 20 2 35N10 83w55 5:35:40
Mamers 43 1 35N25 78w56 5:15:44
Mamie 27 1 36N10 75w52 5:03:28
Manchester 26 1 35N11 78w59 5:15:56
Maneys Neck 46 1 36N30 77w01 5:08:04
Mangum 32 1 36N11 78w52 5:15:28
Mangum 77 1 35N13 80w00 5:20:00
Manly 63 1 35N10 79w24 5:17:36
Mannings 64 1 35N57 78w05 5:12:20
Manns Harbor 28 1 35N53 75w46 5:03:04
Mansfield 16 1 34N42 76w50 5:07:20
Mansfield Park 16 1 34N42 76w50 5:07:20
Manson 93 1 36N25 78w17 5:13:08
Manteo 28 1 35N55 75w40 5:02:40
Maple 27 1 36N20 76w07 5:04:28
Maple Cypress 25 1 35N22 77w26 5:09:44
Maple Hill 71 1 34N40 77w42 5:10:48
Maple Springs 97 1 36N11 81w17 5:25:08
Mapleton 46 1 36N26 77w06 5:08:24
Mapleville 35 1 36N08 78w12 5:12:48
Maplewood 77 1 34N56 79w46 5:19:04
Marble 20 2 35N10 83w55 5:35:40
Marcus 62 1 35N13 79w38 5:18:32
Maready 31 1 34N50 77w49 5:11:16
Margaretsville 66 1 36N32 77w21 5:09:24
Margrace 23 1 35N15 81w20 5:25:20
Maribel 69 1 35N09 76w46 5:07:04
Marietta 78 1 34N22 79w07 5:16:28
Marion 56 1 35N41 82w01 5:28:04
Mariposa 55 1 35N22 81w06 5:24:24
Marlboro 74 1 35N36 77w35 5:10:20
Marler 99 1 36N06 80w46 5:23:04
Mar Mac 96 1 35N22 77w58 5:11:52
Marmaduke 93 1 36N26 78w05 5:12:20
Marsh 86 1 36N18 80w45 5:23:00
Marshall 58 2 35N48 82w41 5:30:44
Marshallberg 16 1 34N44 76w31 5:06:04
Mars Hill 58 1 35N50 82w33 5:30:12
Marshville 90 1 35N00 80w26 5:21:44
Marston 77 1 34N59 79w35 5:18:20
Martel Village 11 1 35N37 82w33 5:30:12
Martin Creek 20 1 35N05 84w02 5:36:08
Marvin 90 1 34N56 80w45 5:23:00
Masonboro 65 3 34N10 77w53 5:11:32
Masons Crossroads 83
1 34N46 79w36 5:18:24
Mason Store 43 1 35N24 78w49 5:15:16
Masontown 16 1 34N52 76w25 5:05:40
Massapoag 55 1 35N28 81w15 5:25:00
Mathews Crossroads 64
1 36N05 78w03 5:12:12
Matney 95 1 36N10 81w52 5:27:28
Matrimony 79 1 36N28 79w55 5:19:40
Matthews 60 1 35N07 80w43 5:22:52
Matthewstown 34 1 36N07 80w10 5:20:40
Maury 40 1 35N29 77w35 5:10:20
Maxton 78 1 34N44 79w21 5:17:24
Mayhew 49 1 35N35 80w49 5:23:16
Mayo 79 1 36N27 79w54 5:19:36
Mayodan 79 1 36N25 79w58 5:19:52
Mayos Crossroads 33
1 35N48 77w23 5:09:32
Maysville 52 1 34N54 77w14 5:08:56
Mayview Park 95 1 36N07 81w40 5:26:40
Mazeppa 49 1 35N35 80w49 5:23:16
McAdenville 36 1 35N15 81w05 5:24:20
McArthers Crossroads 83
1 34N46 79w28 5:17:52
McConnell 7 1 35N21 76w58 5:07:52
McConnell 63 1 35N26 79w35 5:18:20
McCullen 82 1 35N00 78w20 5:13:20
McDade 68 1 36N10 79w10 5:16:40
McDaniel 82 1 34N57 78w31 5:14:04
McDaniels 82 1 34N54 78w26 5:13:44
McDonald 78 1 34N33 79w11 5:16:44
McDonalds 78 1 34N31 79w09 5:16:36
McFarlan 4 1 34N49 79w58 5:19:52
McGehees Mill 73 1 36N30 79w09 5:16:36
McGinnis Crossroads 75
1 35N09 81w52 5:27:28
McGrady 97 1 36N21 81w14 5:24:56
McKees 9 1 34N29 78w39 5:14:36
McLamb Crossroads 82
1 35N15 78w21 5:13:24
McLauchlin 47 1 35N00 79w07 5:16:28
McLeansville 41 1 36N07 79w53 5:19:32
McNeills 63 1 35N14 79w20 5:17:20
Meadow 51 1 35N19 78w27 5:13:48
Meadow 85 1 36N18 80w08 5:20:32
Meadow Creek 95 1 36N14 81w32 5:26:08
Meadows 85 1 36N19 80w13 5:20:52
Meadow Summit 79 1 36N30 79w45 5:19:00
Meat Camp 95 1 36N16 81w38 5:26:32
Mebane 1 1 36N06 79w16 5:17:04
Mechanic 76 1 35N42 79w49 5:19:16
Melrose 75 1 35N14 82w21 5:29:24
Melville 1 1 36N05 79w18 5:17:12
Melvin Hill 75 1 35N07 82w09 5:28:36
Menola 46 1 36N17 76w59 5:07:56
Mercer 33 1 35N47 77w38 5:10:32
Meredith 92 1 35N49 78w43 5:14:52
Meredith College 92
1 35N47 78w40 5:14:40
Merrimon 16 1 34N57 76w38 5:06:32
Merritt 69 1 35N06 76w43 5:06:52
Merry Hill 8 1 35N59 76w46 5:07:04
Merry Oaks 19 1 35N38 79w05 5:16:20
Mesic 69 1 35N09 76w46 5:07:04
Metcalf 23 1 35N17 81w32 5:26:08
Method 92 1 35N46 78w43 5:14:52
Methodist College 26
1 35N04 78w53 5:15:32
Mewborns Crossroads 54
1 35N16 77w35 5:10:20
Micaville 100 1 35N55 82w13 5:28:52
Micro 51 1 35N33 78w12 5:12:48
Middle 21 1 36N11 76w40 5:06:40
Middleburg 91 1 36N24 78w19 5:13:16
Middle Creek 92 1 35N36 78w44 5:14:56
Middle Creek Mill 57
1 35N04 83w23 5:33:32
Middle Fork 34 1 36N09 80w12 5:20:48
Middle Fork 88 1 35N14 82w44 5:30:56
Middlesex 64 1 35N47 78w12 5:12:48
Middletown 48 1 35N31 76w00 5:04:00
Midland 13 1 35N14 80w30 5:22:00
Midway 10 1 34N04 78w09 5:12:36
Midway 11 1 35N26 82w30 5:30:00
Midway 13 1 35N31 80w38 5:22:32
Midway 29 1 35N58 80w13 5:20:52
Midway 79 1 36N21 79w41 5:18:44
Midway Park 67 1 34N44 77w21 5:09:24
Mildred 33 1 35N54 77w32 5:10:08
Miles 68 1 36N06 79w16 5:17:04
Millboro 76 1 35N45 79w41 5:18:44
Millbridge 80 1 35N39 80w29 5:21:56
Millbrook 92 1 35N51 78w36 5:14:24
Mill Creek 5 1 36N18 81w36 5:26:24
Mill Creek 10 1 34N09 78w06 5:12:24
Mill Creek 16 1 34N48 76w52 5:07:28
Millennium Church 46
1 36N14 77w07 5:08:28
Millers 2 1 35N50 81w06 5:24:24
Millers Creek 97 1 36N11 81w14 5:24:56
Millersville 2 1 35N55 81w10 5:24:40
Millingport 84 1 35N21 80w12 5:20:48
Millshoal 57 1 35N14 83w19 5:33:16
Millside 23 1 35N17 81w32 5:26:08
Mill Spring 75 1 35N18 82w10 5:28:40
Mills River 45 1 35N22 82w36 5:30:24
Milltown 38 1 35N19 83w48 5:35:12
Milton 17 1 36N32 79w12 5:16:48
Milwaukee 66 1 36N24 77w14 5:08:56
Mineola 7 1 35N32 77w02 5:08:08
Mineral Springs 90
1 34N56 80w40 5:22:40
Mingo 82 1 35N11 78w34 5:14:16
Minneapolis 6 1 36N06 81w59 5:27:56
Minnesott Beach 69
1 35N02 76w50 5:07:20
Minpro 61 1 35N55 82w04 5:28:16
Mint Hill 60 1 35N13 80w41 5:22:44
Mintons Store 46 1 36N20 77w13 5:08:52
Mintonsville 37 1 36N21 76w39 5:06:36
Mintz 82 1 34N57 78w31 5:14:04
Miranda 80 1 35N40 80w44 5:22:56
Misenheimer 84 1 35N29 80w17 5:21:08
Mitchells 8 1 36N12 77w02 5:08:08
Mitchell Village 16
1 34N42 76w50 5:07:20
Mitcheners Crossroads 35
1 36N06 78w27 5:13:48
Mocksville 30 1 35N54 80w34 5:22:16
Moffitt Hill 56 1 35N38 82w11 5:28:44
Mohawk 43 1 35N27 79w03 5:16:12
Mollie 24 1 34N13 78w51 5:15:24
Momeyer 64 1 35N58 77w58 5:11:52
Moncure 19 1 35N38 79w05 5:16:20
Monks Crossroads 82
1 35N15 78w21 5:13:24
Monroe 90 1 34N59 80w33 5:22:12
Monroetown 63 1 35N12 79w28 5:17:52
Monroetown 79 1 36N21 79w41 5:18:44
Montague 71 1 34N32 78w10 5:12:40
Montclair 26 1 35N02 78w57 5:15:48
Montezuma 6 1 36N04 81w54 5:27:36
Montford Cove 56 1 35N36 82w03 5:28:12
Monticello 41 1 36N13 79w43 5:18:52
Montreat 11 1 35N39 82w18 5:29:12
Montrose 47 1 34N59 79w13 5:16:52
Mooresboro 23 1 35N18 81w42 5:26:48
Moores School House 51
1 35N36 78w07 5:12:28
Moores Springs 85 1 36N29 80w27 5:21:48
Mooresville 49 1 35N35 80w48 5:23:12
Mooresville Junction 49
1 35N35 80w49 5:23:16
Moratock 62 1 35N22 79w54 5:19:36
Moravian Falls 97 1 36N06 81w11 5:24:44
Mordecai 92 1 35N48 78w38 5:14:32
Morehead 16 1 34N44 76w48 5:07:12
Morehead City 16 1 34N43 76w43 5:06:52
Morgan's Corner 70
1 36N17 76w14 5:04:56
Morganton 12 1 35N45 81w41 5:26:44
Morgantown 1 1 36N07 79w26 5:17:44
Moriah 73 1 36N13 78w56 5:15:44
Morlan Park 80 1 35N39 80w29 5:21:56
Morning Star 60 1 35N08 80w42 5:22:48
Morris Field 60 1 35N14 80w53 5:23:32
Morris Landing 67 1 34N26 77w34 5:10:16
Morrisville 92 1 35N49 78w50 5:15:20
Mortimer 14 1 35N59 81w45 5:27:00
Morton 1 1 36N12 79w30 5:18:00
Morven 4 1 34N52 80w00 5:20:00
Moseley Hall 54 1 35N18 77w47 5:11:08
Moss 84 1 35N27 80w13 5:20:52
Moss Hill 54 1 35N16 77w35 5:10:20
Mother Vineyard 28
1 35N54 75w40 5:02:40
Motleta 76 1 35N42 79w49 5:19:16
Moultonville 82 1 35N00 78w20 5:13:20
Mountain 50 1 35N12 83w11 5:32:44
Mountain Creek 18 1 35N36 81w01 5:24:04
Mountain Home 45 1 35N23 82w30 5:30:00
Mountain Park 86 1 36N19 80w52 5:23:28
Mountain Valley 45
1 35N09 82w25 5:29:40
Mountain View 85 1 36N17 80w21 5:21:24
Mount Airy 86 1 36N31 80w37 5:22:28
Mount Carmel 62 1 35N13 80w00 5:20:00
Mount Energy 39 1 36N07 78w41 5:14:44
Mount Gilead 13 1 35N25 80w36 5:22:24
Mount Gilead 62 1 35N13 80w00 5:20:00
Mount Herman 14 1 35N54 81w31 5:26:04
Mount Hermon 70 1 36N16 76w18 5:05:12
Mount Holly 36 1 35N18 81w01 5:24:04
Mount Mourne 49 1 35N33 80w51 5:23:24
Mount Olive 9 1 34N38 78w33 5:14:12
Mount Olive 18 1 35N44 81w21 5:25:24
Mount Olive 24 1 34N20 78w42 5:14:48
Mount Olive 48 1 35N32 76w37 5:06:28
Mount Olive 85 1 36N17 80w21 5:21:24
Mount Olive 96 1 35N12 78w04 5:12:16
Mount Pleasant 6 1 36N05 81w56 5:27:44
Mount Pleasant 13 1 35N24 80w26 5:21:44
Mount Pleasant 20 1 35N00 84w10 5:36:40
Mount Pleasant 63 1 35N15 79w17 5:17:08
Mount Pleasant 64 1 35N47 78w07 5:12:28
Mount Pleasant 77 1 35N04 79w46 5:19:04
Mount Pleasant 99 1 36N14 80w43 5:22:52
Mount Sterling 44 1 35N58 83w11 5:32:44
Mount Tabor 34 1 36N08 80w18 5:21:12
Mount Tabor 94 1 35N52 76w24 5:05:36
Mount Tirzah 73 1 36N18 78w51 5:15:24
Mount Ulla 80 1 35N40 80w43 5:22:52
Mount Vernon 80 1 35N44 80w41 5:22:44
Mount Vernon 81 1 35N19 81w52 5:27:28
Mount Vernon Springs 19
1 35N43 79w28 5:17:52
Mount View 36 1 35N15 81w20 5:25:20
Mount Zion 41 1 36N06 79w46 5:19:04
Moxley 97 1 36N21 81w01 5:24:04
Moyock 27 1 36N32 76w10 5:04:40
Mud Castle 66 1 36N23 77w25 5:09:40
Muddy Creek 34 1 36N05 80w17 5:21:08
Muddy Cross 37 1 36N21 76w36 5:06:24
Mulberry 97 1 36N14 81w11 5:24:44
Murchison 100 1 35N55 82w18 5:29:12
Murdocksville 63 1 35N12 79w28 5:17:52
Murfreesboro 46 1 36N27 77w06 5:08:24
Murphy 20 4 35N05 84w02 5:36:08
Murraysville 65 3 34N13 77w55 5:11:40
Murray Town 71 1 34N33 77w55 5:11:40
Musgraves Crossroads 96
1 35N30 77w59 5:11:56
Myers 97 1 36N15 81w07 5:24:28
Myers Park 60 1 35N12 80w50 5:23:20
Myrick 42 1 36N26 77w55 5:11:40
Myrtle Grove 65 3 34N13 77w55 5:11:40
Nags Head 28 1 35N57 75w38 5:02:32
Nahunta 96 1 35N33 77w53 5:11:32
Nakina 24 1 34N08 78w40 5:14:40
Nantahala 87 2 35N15 83w42 5:34:48
Naples 45 1 35N24 82w30 5:30:00
Nashville 64 1 35N58 77w58 5:11:52
Nathans Creek 5 1 36N30 81w24 5:25:36
Nations Village 60
1 35N10 80w51 5:23:24
Navassa 10 1 34N15 78w00 5:12:00
Nebo 56 1 35N43 81w56 5:27:44
Nebo 99 1 36N14 80w43 5:22:52
Nebraska 48 1 35N31 76w00 5:04:00

NORTH CAROLINA

Needmore 80 1 35N46 80w35 5:22:20
Needmore 87 1 35N26 83w27 5:33:48
Neills Creek 43 1 35N26 78w45 5:15:00
Nelson 32 1 35N49 78w50 5:15:20
Neuse 92 1 35N54 78w34 5:14:16
Neuse Crossroads 92 1 35N54 78w34 5:14:16
Neuse Forest 25 1 35N06 77w05 5:08:20
Neuse River 92 1 35N51 78w39 5:14:36
Neverson 98 1 35N46 78w04 5:12:16
New Bern 25 1 35N07 77w03 5:08:12
New Bern Junction 65 3 34N13 77w55 5:11:40
New Bethel 68 1 36N13 78w56 5:15:44
New Bethel 79 1 36N19 79w54 5:19:36
Newbold 26 1 35N04 78w53 5:15:32
New Bridge 11 1 35N37 82w33 5:30:12
New Britton 10 1 34N06 78w32 5:14:08
New Castle 97 1 36N11 80w55 5:23:40
Newdale 100 1 35N55 82w18 5:29:12
Newell 60 1 35N17 80w44 5:22:56
Newfound 11 1 35N39 82w42 5:30:48
New Hill 92 1 35N41 78w56 5:15:44
New Holland 48 1 35N24 76w20 5:05:20
New Home 23 1 35N31 81w37 5:26:28
New Hope 35 1 36N08 78w12 5:12:48
New Hope 92 1 35N48 78w38 5:14:32
New Hope 98 1 35N44 77w55 5:11:40
New Hope Academy 76 1 35N38 80w07 5:20:28
New House 23 1 35N17 81w32 5:26:08
Newland 6 1 36N05 81w56 5:27:44
New Lands 89 1 35N55 76w15 5:05:00
New Leaksville 79 1 36N30 79w45 5:19:00
Newlife 97 1 36N15 81w07 5:24:28
New Light 92 1 36N01 78w38 5:14:32
Newlin 1 1 35N55 79w20 5:17:20
New London 84 1 35N27 80w13 5:20:52
New Market 76 1 35N52 79w53 5:19:32
Newport 16 1 34N48 76w52 5:07:28
New River 95 1 36N14 81w39 5:26:36
New River-Gieger 67 1 34N43 77w27 5:09:48
New Salem 76 1 35N49 79w48 5:19:12
New Salem 90 1 35N07 80w21 5:21:24
Newsom 29 1 35N38 80w07 5:20:28
Newton 18 1 35N40 81w13 5:24:52
Newton Grove 82 1 35N14 78w21 5:13:24
Newtons Crossroads 82 1 34N42 77w59 5:11:56
New Town 77 1 34N54 79w42 5:18:48
Niagara 63 1 35N10 79w24 5:17:36
Nicanor 72 1 36N16 76w32 5:06:08
Nixonton 70 1 36N14 76w12 5:04:48
Nobles Cross Roads 54 1 35N09 77w42 5:10:48
Norfleet 42 1 36N08 77w25 5:09:40
Norlina 93 1 36N27 78w12 5:12:48
Norman 77 1 35N10 79w43 5:18:52
Normanville 61 1 36N01 82w09 5:28:36
Norrington Crossroads 43 1 35N24 78w49 5:15:16
North 34 1 36N08 80w14 5:20:56
North Albemarle 84 1 35N24 80w10 5:20:40
North Asheboro 76 1 35N44 79w49 5:19:16
North Belmont 36 1 35N17 81w02 5:24:08
North Brevard 88 1 35N14 82w44 5:30:56
North Brook 55 1 35N30 81w27 5:25:48
North Burlington 1 1 36N06 79w27 5:17:48
North Catawba 14 1 35N49 81w32 5:26:08
North Charlotte 60 1 35N15 80w50 5:23:20
North Clinton 82 1 35N01 78w18 5:13:12
North Concord 13 1 35N25 80w36 5:22:24
North Cove 56 1 35N51 81w59 5:27:56
North Durham 32 1 36N02 78w53 5:15:32
North Elkin 86 1 36N15 80w52 5:23:28
North Fork 5 1 36N25 81w41 5:26:44
Northgate 32 1 36N00 78w54 5:15:36
North Harlowe 25 1 34N53 76w54 5:07:36
North Henderson 91 1 36N19 78w24 5:13:36
North Lumberton 78 1 34N36 79w01 5:16:04
North Rocky Mount 33 1 35N58 77w48 5:11:12
North Roxboro 73 1 36N24 78w59 5:15:56
Northside 39 1 36N05 78w45 5:15:00
North State Orchards 62 1 35N04 79w46 5:19:04
North West 10 1 34N16 78w03 5:12:12
Northwest 10 1 34N16 78w03 5:12:12
North Whitakers 64 1 36N07 77w48 5:11:12
North Wilkesboro 97 1 36N10 81w09 5:24:36
Norton 50 1 35N19 83w11 5:32:44
Norton 57 1 34N58 83w23 5:33:32
Norwood 84 1 35N14 80w07 5:20:28
Norwood Hollow 6 1 36N10 81w52 5:27:28
Notla 20 1 35N01 84w07 5:36:28
Nutbush 93 1 36N27 78w16 5:13:04
Oakboro 84 1 35N13 80w20 5:21:20
Oak City 59 1 35N58 77w18 5:09:12
Oakdale 41 1 36N00 79w56 5:19:44
Oakdale 47 1 34N59 79w13 5:16:52
Oakdale 49 1 35N51 80w56 5:23:44
Oakdale 60 1 35N14 80w55 5:23:40
Oak Forest 11 1 35N34 82w32 5:30:08
Oak Grove 23 1 35N15 81w20 5:25:20
Oak Grove 32 1 36N00 78w50 5:15:20
Oak Grove 57 1 35N11 83w23 5:33:32
Oak Grove 86 1 36N30 80w35 5:22:20
Oak Hill 12 1 35N44 81w42 5:26:48
Oak Hill 14 1 35N54 81w31 5:26:04
Oak Hill 39 1 36N29 78w43 5:14:52
Oakland 19 1 35N37 79w12 5:16:48
Oakland 88 1 35N06 83w00 5:32:00
Oak Level 64 1 35N57 77w54 5:11:36
Oak Park 11 1 35N29 82w31 5:30:04
Oak Park 20 1 35N05 84w02 5:36:08
Oak Ridge 41 1 36N13 79w59 5:19:56
Oak Ridge 85 1 36N29 80w14 5:20:56
Oak Ridge Park 77 1 34N56 79w46 5:19:04
Oaks 25 1 35N06 77w05 5:08:20
Oakville 93 1 36N26 78w05 5:12:20
Oakwillow 46 1 36N17 76w59 5:07:56
Oakwood Acres 29 1 35N40 80w16 5:21:04
Occoneechee 68 1 36N05 79w07 5:16:28
Ocean Isle Beach 10 1 33N53 78w26 5:13:44
Oconeechee 66 1 36N25 77w31 5:10:04
Ocono Lufty 87 1 35N29 83w19 5:33:16
Ocracoke 48 1 35N07 75w58 5:03:52
Odell 13 1 35N28 80w44 5:22:56
Ogden 22 1 35N02 83w57 5:35:48
Ogreeta 20 1 35N05 84w02 5:36:08
Oine 93 1 36N27 78w12 5:12:48
Okeewemee 62 1 35N22 79w54 5:19:36
Old 34 1 36N09 80w19 5:21:16
Old Bethlehem 93 1 36N24 78w09 5:12:36
Old Dock 24 1 34N20 78w42 5:14:48
Olde Farm 43 1 35N10 78w58 5:15:52
Old Fort 56 1 35N38 82w10 5:28:40
Old Hundred 83 1 34N49 79w32 5:18:08
Old Murphy 20 1 35N05 84w02 5:36:08
Old Richmond 34 1 36N13 80w24 5:21:36
Olds 40 1 35N30 77w37 5:10:28
Old Sparta 33 1 35N45 77w40 5:10:40
Oldtown 34 1 36N08 80w18 5:21:12
Old Trap 15 1 36N17 76w05 5:04:20
Oleander 65 3 34N13 77w55 5:11:40
Olin 49 1 35N55 80w51 5:23:24
Olive Branch 90 1 34N59 80w22 5:21:28
Olive Crossroads 52 1 35N04 77w21 5:09:24
Olive Grove 23 1 35N31 81w37 5:26:28
Olivehill 73 1 36N24 79w04 5:16:16
Olivers Crossroads 18 1 35N40 81w13 5:24:52
Olivette 14 2 35N54 81w31 5:26:04
Olivia 43 1 35N22 79w07 5:16:28
Olympia 69 1 35N06 77w05 5:08:20
Olyphic 24 1 34N09 78w53 5:15:32
O'neals 51 1 35N42 78w14 5:12:56
Onvil 62 1 35N13 80w00 5:20:00
Ophir 62 1 35N28 79w57 5:19:48
Ora Mill 23 1 35N17 81w32 5:26:08
Orange Factory 32 1 36N10 78w53 5:15:32
Orange Grove 68 1 36N05 79w07 5:16:28
Oregon Hill 79 1 36N27 79w39 5:18:36
Oriental 69 1 35N02 76w42 5:06:48
Orion 5 1 36N25 81w28 5:25:52
Orlando 57 1 34N58 83w23 5:33:32
Ormonds 40 1 35N28 77w33 5:10:12
Ormondsville 40 1 35N28 77w25 5:09:40
Orrum 78 1 34N28 79w02 5:16:08
Osborne 77 1 34N54 79w42 5:18:48
Osbornville 97 1 36N02 80w58 5:23:52
Osceola 41 1 36N13 79w43 5:18:52
Osgood 53 1 35N28 79w10 5:16:40
Osmond 17 1 36N24 79w10 5:16:40
Ossipee 1 1 36N06 79w30 5:18:00
Oswalt 49 1 35N42 80w53 5:23:32
Oteen 11 1 35N36 82w31 5:30:04
Otter Creek 33 1 35N43 77w40 5:10:40
Otto 57 1 35N04 83w23 5:33:32
Otway 16 1 34N47 76w33 5:06:12
Outlaws Bridge 31 1 35N14 77w51 5:11:24
Overhills 43 1 35N13 79w01 5:16:04
Overlook 45 1 35N19 82w28 5:29:52
Oxford 39 1 36N19 78w35 5:14:20
Pacolet Valley 75 1 35N12 82w14 5:28:56
Pactolus 74 1 35N38 77w15 5:09:00
Padgett 67 1 34N40 77w42 5:10:48
Paint Fork 11 1 35N47 82w27 5:29:48
Paint Gap 100 1 35N55 82w18 5:29:12
Paint Rock 58 2 35N54 82w50 5:31:20
Palestine 84 1 35N21 80w12 5:20:48
Palmerville 84 1 35N27 80w13 5:20:52
Palmyra 42 1 36N05 77w22 5:09:28
Palo Alto 67 1 34N54 77w14 5:08:56
Pamlico 69 1 35N02 76w41 5:06:44
Pamlico Beach 7 1 35N24 76w36 5:06:24
Pantego 7 1 35N35 76w40 5:06:40
Panther Branch 92 1 35N37 78w39 5:14:36
Panther Creek 44 1 35N35 82w55 5:31:40
Parker 5 1 36N26 81w37 5:26:28
Parkersburg 82 1 34N50 78w27 5:13:48
Parkers Fork 37 1 36N32 76w35 5:06:20
Parks Crossroads 76 1 35N44 79w39 5:18:36
Parkstown 96 1 35N18 77w47 5:11:08
Parkton 78 1 34N54 79w01 5:16:04
Parktown 93 1 36N24 78w09 5:12:36
Parkville 72 1 36N14 76w26 5:05:44
Parkway Forest 11 1 35N36 82w31 5:30:04
Parkwood 13 1 35N25 80w36 5:22:24
Park Wood 32 1 35N54 78w55 5:15:40
Parkwood 32 1 35N54 78w55 5:15:40
Parkwood 63 1 35N18 79w24 5:17:36
Park Yarn 23 1 35N15 81w20 5:25:20
Parmele 59 1 35N49 77w19 5:09:16
Parsonville 97 1 36N11 81w17 5:25:08
Paschall 93 1 36N24 78w09 5:12:36
Pates 78 1 34N41 79w11 5:16:44
Patetown 96 1 35N28 77w56 5:11:44
Patterson 14 1 36N00 81w34 5:26:16
Patterson Springs 23 1 35N17 81w32 5:26:08
Paw Creek 60 1 35N17 80w56 5:23:44
Paynes Store 2 1 35N55 81w10 5:24:40
Paynes Tavern 73 1 36N24 78w59 5:15:56
Peace Haven Estates 34 1 36N07 80w17 5:21:08
Peachland 4 1 35N00 80w16 5:21:04
Peachtree 20 1 35N05 84w02 5:36:08
Peacocks Crossroads 51 1 35N23 78w33 5:14:12
Peak Creek 5 1 36N24 81w18 5:25:12
Pearce Crossroads 35 1 35N49 78w19 5:13:16
Pearces Mill 26 1 35N01 78w55 5:15:40
Pea Ridge 75 1 35N18 82w10 5:28:40
Pecan Grove 42 1 36N08 77w25 5:09:40
Peden 3 1 36N29 81w18 5:25:12
Pee Dee 4 1 34N58 79w59 5:19:56
Pee Dee 62 1 35N16 80w03 5:20:12
Pekin 62 1 35N13 80w00 5:20:00
Peletier 16 1 34N42 77w06 5:08:24
Pelham 17 1 36N31 79w28 5:17:52
Pembroke 78 1 34N41 79w12 5:16:48
Pender Crossroad 98 1 35N48 77w52 5:11:28
Penderlea 71 1 34N42 77w59 5:11:56
Pendleton 66 1 36N28 77w12 5:08:48
Penland 61 1 35N56 82w07 5:28:28
Penny Hill 74 1 35N54 77w32 5:10:08
Penrose 88 1 35N15 82w38 5:30:32
Pensacola 100 1 35N50 82w18 5:29:12
Peoria 95 1 36N15 81w47 5:27:08
Peppers 61 1 36N01 82w09 5:28:36
Perch 86 1 36N20 80w26 5:21:44
Perfection 25 1 35N11 77w19 5:09:16
Perkinsville 95 1 36N13 81w40 5:26:40
Perrytown 8 1 36N12 76w46 5:07:04
Persimmon Creek 20 1 35N05 84w02 5:36:08
Peru 67 1 34N31 77w23 5:09:32
Petersburg 12 1 35N44 81w42 5:26:48
Petersburg 58 1 35N48 82w41 5:30:44
Petersburg 67 1 34N54 77w33 5:10:12
Peters Creek 85 1 36N29 80w14 5:20:56
Petersville 29 1 35N49 80w15 5:21:00
Pfafftown 34 1 36N09 80w22 5:21:28
Philadelphus 78 1 34N45 79w09 5:16:36
Phillips Cross Roads 52 1 35N04 77w21 5:09:24
Phillipsville 44 1 35N35 82w52 5:31:28
Phoenix 10 1 34N15 78w03 5:12:12
Phosphate Junction 7 1 35N31 77w06 5:08:24
Pierceville 15 1 36N27 76w20 5:05:20
Pigeon 44 1 35N33 82w53 5:31:32
Pigeon Roost 61 1 36N00 82w14 5:28:56
Pike Crossroads 96 1 35N30 77w59 5:11:56
Pike Road 7 1 35N41 76w38 5:06:32
Pikeville 96 1 35N30 77w59 5:11:56
Pilot 35 1 35N49 78w19 5:13:16
Pilot 86 1 36N23 80w31 5:22:04
Pilot Mountain 86 1 36N23 80w28 5:21:52
Pinebluff 63 1 35N06 79w28 5:17:52
Pine Hall 85 1 36N19 80w03 5:20:12
Pine Hill 47 1 35N08 79w26 5:17:44
Pinehurst 63 1 35N12 79w28 5:17:52
Pinehurst Park 92 1 35N42 78w37 5:14:28
Pine Knoll 26 1 34N58 78w57 5:15:48
Pine Knoll Shores 16 1 34N42 76w50 5:07:20
Pine Level 51 1 35N31 78w14 5:12:56
Pinelog 22 1 35N02 83w57 5:35:48
Pineola 6 1 36N02 81w54 5:27:36
Pine Ridge 35 1 35N49 78w19 5:13:16
Pine Ridge 86 1 36N30 80w35 5:22:20
Pine Ridge 94 1 35N53 76w36 5:06:24
Pine Swamp 5 1 36N18 81w28 5:25:52
Pinetops 33 1 35N46 77w38 5:10:32
Pinetown 7 1 35N37 76w52 5:07:28
Pine Valley 65 3 34N13 77w55 5:11:40
Pine View 43 1 35N28 79w10 5:16:40
Pineville 60 1 35N05 80w53 5:23:32
Piney Creek 3 1 36N33 81w17 5:25:08
Piney Green 67 1 34N43 77w20 5:09:20
Piney Green 82 1 35N01 78w30 5:14:00
Piney Grove 10 1 34N04 78w09 5:12:36
Piney Grove 25 1 34N53 76w54 5:07:36
Piney Grove 82 1 35N09 78w14 5:12:56
Piney Ridge 82 1 35N00 78w20 5:13:20
Piney Wood 71 1 34N33 77w55 5:11:40
Pin Hook 31 1 34N44 78w00 5:12:00
Pink Hill 54 1 35N03 77w45 5:11:00
Pinkney 36 1 35N16 81w10 5:24:40
Pinkney 96 1 35N32 77w56 5:11:44
Pinkston 4 1 34N58 80w05 5:20:20
Pinnacle 85 1 36N20 80w26 5:21:44
Pireway 24 1 34N09 78w53 5:15:32
Pisgah Forest 88 1 35N15 82w44 5:30:56
Pittmans Store 64 1 36N06 77w43 5:10:52
Pittsboro 19 1 35N43 79w11 5:16:44
Plainview 78 1 34N32 79w17 5:17:08
Plain View 82 1 35N14 78w31 5:14:04
Plateau 18 1 35N33 81w24 5:25:36
Plaza 41 1 36N06 79w49 5:19:16
Plaza 60 1 35N14 80w47 5:23:08
Pleasant Garden 41 1 35N58 79w46 5:19:04
Pleasant Gardens 56 1 35N41 82w00 5:28:00
Pleasant Grove 12 1 35N44 81w42 5:26:48
Pleasant Grove 17 1 36N24 79w20 5:17:20
Pleasant Grove 66 1 36N26 77w34 5:10:16
Pleasant Grove 94 1 35N53 76w36 5:06:24

NORTH CAROLINA

Pleasant Hill 52	1	35N03	77w45	5:11:00
Pleasant Hill 66	1	36N30	77w33	5:10:12
Pleasant Hill 97	1	36N15	80w52	5:23:28
Pleasant Plains 46	1	36N17	76w59	5:07:56
Pleasant View 89	1	35N55	76w15	5:05:00
Pleasantville 79	1	36N23	79w58	5:19:52
Plumtree 6	1	36N02	82w01	5:28:04
Plyler 84	1	35N21	80w12	5:20:48
Plymouth 94	1	35N52	76w43	5:06:52
Pocket 53	1	35N27	79w15	5:17:00
Pocomoke 35	1	36N06	78w27	5:13:48
Point Caswell 71	1	34N32	78w10	5:12:40
Point Harbor 27	1	36N05	75w48	5:03:12
Pole Creek 11	1	35N32	82w41	5:30:44
Polkton 4	1	35N01	80w12	5:20:48
Polkville 23	1	35N25	81w39	5:26:36
Pollocks 52	1	35N04	77w21	5:09:24
Pollocksville 52	1	35N00	77w14	5:08:56
Ponderosa 26	1	35N05	78w57	5:15:48
Pond Mountain 5	1	36N32	81w40	5:26:40
Ponzer 48	1	35N32	76w37	5:06:28
Pookmoke 35	1	36N06	78w27	5:13:48
Pooletown 80	1	35N28	80w16	5:21:04
Poor Town 46	1	36N17	76w59	5:07:56
Pope Air Force Base 26	1	35N08	78w59	5:15:56
Poplar 61	1	36N04	82w21	5:29:24
Poplar Branch 27	1	36N17	75w53	5:03:32
Poplar Grove 82	1	34N56	78w10	5:12:40
Poplar Point 59	1	35N52	77w10	5:08:40
Poplar Springs 85	1	36N17	80w21	5:21:24
Poplar Tent 13	1	35N24	80w39	5:22:36
Porter 84	1	35N14	80w07	5:20:28
Portsmouth 16	1	34N55	76w17	5:05:08
Possumtrot 100	1	35N55	82w18	5:29:12
Potecasi 66	1	36N22	77w14	5:08:56
Potters Hill 31	1	35N03	77w45	5:11:00
Powell Crossroads 37	1	36N21	76w36	5:06:24
Powells Point 27	1	36N10	75w52	5:03:28
Powells Store 79	1	36N27	79w39	5:18:36
Powellsville 8	1	36N14	76w57	5:07:48
Powhatan 51	1	35N39	78w27	5:13:48
Prathers Creek 3	1	36N30	81w14	5:24:56
Prentiss 57	1	35N11	83w23	5:33:32
Prestonville 85	1	36N23	79w58	5:19:52
Price 79	1	36N32	79w55	5:19:40
Price Creek 100	1	35N53	82w23	5:29:32
Princeton 51	1	35N28	78w10	5:12:40
Princeville 33	1	35N53	77w32	5:10:08
Priscilla 36	1	35N16	81w10	5:24:40
Proctorville 78	1	34N29	79w02	5:16:08
Propst Crossroads 18	1	35N40	81w13	5:24:52
Prospect 10	1	34N01	78w16	5:13:04
Prospect Hill 17	1	36N15	79w11	5:16:44
Prosper 24	1	34N19	78w13	5:12:52
Providence 17	1	36N30	79w22	5:17:28
Providence 39	1	36N18	78w35	5:14:20
Providence 56	1	35N41	82w00	5:28:00
Providence 60	1	35N07	80w43	5:22:52
Pumpkin Center 12	1	35N44	81w42	5:26:48
Pumpkin Center 55	1	35N28	81w15	5:25:00
Pumpkin Center 67	1	34N45	77w26	5:09:44
Pumpkintown 50	1	35N22	83w14	5:32:56
Pungo 7	1	35N35	76w40	5:06:40
Purlear 97	1	36N11	81w17	5:25:08
Purley 17	1	36N24	79w20	5:17:20
Purnell 92	1	35N59	78w30	5:14:00
Purvis 78	1	34N32	79w17	5:17:08
Putnam 63	1	35N18	79w24	5:17:36
Pyatte 6	1	36N05	81w56	5:27:44
Quaker Gap 85	1	36N26	80w23	5:21:32
Quaker Meadow 12	1	35N47	81w45	5:27:00
Qualla 50	1	35N28	83w16	5:33:04
Quarry 97	1	36N10	81w08	5:24:32
Quebec 88	1	35N08	82w56	5:31:44
Queen 62	1	35N22	79w54	5:19:36
Quewhiffle 47	1	35N02	79w23	5:17:32
Quick 17	1	36N27	79w39	5:18:36
Quinerly 74	1	35N22	77w26	5:09:44
Quinns Store 31	1	34N55	77w46	5:11:04
Quitsna 8	1	36N03	76w57	5:07:48
Radical 97	1	36N21	81w14	5:24:56
Raeford 47	1	34N59	79w14	5:16:56
Raemon 78	1	34N44	79w21	5:17:24
Raft Swamp 78	1	34N39	79w06	5:16:24
Raleigh 92	1	35N46	78w38	5:14:32
Ramseur 76	1	35N44	79w39	5:18:36
Ramseytown 100	1	36N01	82w22	5:29:28
Randleman 76	1	35N49	79w48	5:19:12
Randolph 60	1	35N10	80w48	5:23:12
Randolph 74	1	35N36	77w23	5:09:32
Ranger 20	1	35N05	84w02	5:36:08
Rankin 41	1	36N06	79w46	5:19:04
Rankin 71	1	34N32	78w10	5:12:40
Ranlo 36	1	35N17	81w08	5:24:32
Ranlo-Smyre 36	1	35N16	81w10	5:24:40
Ransom 24	1	34N19	78w16	5:13:04
Ransomville 7	1	35N32	76w37	5:06:28
Rawls 43	1	35N35	78w48	5:15:12
Raynham 78	1	34N32	79w17	5:17:08
Rebel Acres 92	1	35N48	78w38	5:14:32
Red Banks 78	1	34N44	79w21	5:17:24
Redbug 24	1	34N20	78w36	5:14:24
Red Cross 76	1	35N55	79w43	5:18:52
Red Cross 84	1	35N13	80w19	5:21:16
Reddies River 97	1	36N11	81w14	5:24:56
Red Hill 9	1	34N29	78w39	5:14:36
Red Hill 33	1	36N06	77w43	5:10:52
Red Hill 61	1	36N02	82w15	5:29:00
Red House 17	1	36N30	79w09	5:16:36
Redland 30	1	35N57	80w25	5:21:40
Red Oak 64	1	36N02	77w54	5:11:36
Red Springs 78	1	34N49	79w11	5:16:44
Reeds Cross Roads 29	1	35N49	80w15	5:21:00
Reedy Creek 29	1	35N54	80w20	5:21:20
Reelsboro 69	1	35N06	77w05	5:08:20
Reems Creek 11	1	35N41	82w33	5:30:12
Reepville 55	1	35N33	81w24	5:25:36
Reese 95	1	36N15	81w46	5:27:04
Reeves 24	1	34N08	78w40	5:14:40
Regal 20	1	35N05	84w02	5:36:08
Regan 10	1	34N04	78w32	5:14:08
Register 31	1	34N50	78w02	5:12:08
Rehoboth 66	1	36N23	77w25	5:09:40
Reid 88	1	35N08	82w56	5:31:44
Reidsville 79	1	36N21	79w40	5:18:40
Relief 61	1	36N00	82w14	5:28:56
Rennert 78	1	34N49	79w05	5:16:20
Renston 74	1	35N28	77w25	5:09:40
Republican 8	1	36N03	76w57	5:07:48
Research Triangle Park 32	1	36N00	78w55	5:15:40
Revere 58	1	35N48	82w41	5:30:44
Rex 36	1	35N16	81w10	5:24:40
Rex 78	1	34N51	79w03	5:16:12
Reynolda 34	1	36N08	80w18	5:21:12
Reynoldson 37	1	36N31	76w50	5:07:20
Rheasville 42	1	36N27	77w40	5:10:40
Rhems 52	1	35N06	77w05	5:08:20
Rhine 5	1	36N25	81w28	5:25:52
Rhodes-Rhyne 55	1	35N28	81w15	5:25:00
Rhodhiss 14	1	35N46	81w26	5:25:44
Rhodo 20	1	35N12	83w50	5:35:20
Rhyne Crossroads 71	1	34N33	77w55	5:11:40
Riceville 11	1	35N36	82w31	5:30:04
Richardson 9	1	34N32	78w48	5:15:12
Richfield 84	1	35N28	80w16	5:21:04
Richlands 67	1	34N54	77w34	5:10:16
Richmond Hill 99	1	36N14	80w43	5:22:52
Richmond Mills 83	1	34N49	79w32	5:18:08
Rich Square 66	1	36N16	77w17	5:09:08
Rico 24	1	34N20	78w42	5:14:48
Riddle 15	1	36N24	76w06	5:04:24
Ridenhour 84	1	35N25	80w18	5:21:12
Ridge 36	1	35N16	81w10	5:24:40
Ridgecrest 11	1	35N37	82w17	5:29:08
Ridgefield 41	1	36N06	79w52	5:19:28
Ridgeville 17	1	36N15	79w11	5:16:44
Ridgeway 93	1	36N26	78w14	5:12:56
Riegelwood 24	1	34N20	78w14	5:12:56
Riley 35	1	36N01	78w29	5:13:56
Rimer 13	1	35N25	80w36	5:22:24
Rimertown 13	1	35N28	80w28	5:21:52
Ringwood 42	1	36N11	77w40	5:10:40
Rippys 23	1	35N13	81w32	5:26:08
Ritters 63	1	35N28	79w31	5:18:04
River 23	1	35N11	81w43	5:26:52
River Acres 7	1	35N32	77w02	5:08:08
River Bend 36	1	35N20	81w03	5:24:12
Riverdale 25	1	35N06	77w05	5:08:20
River Haven 84	1	35N21	80w12	5:20:48
Rivermont 54	1	35N16	77w35	5:10:20
River Neck 89	1	35N55	76w15	5:05:00
Riverside 25	1	35N06	77w05	5:08:20
Riverside 25	1	35N22	77w26	5:09:44
Riverside 57	1	35N11	83w23	5:33:32
Riverside 100	1	35N55	82w18	5:29:12
Roanoke Rapids 42	1	36N28	77w40	5:10:40
Roaring Creek 6	1	36N04	82w01	5:28:04
Roaring Gap 3	1	36N24	80w59	5:23:56
Roaring River 97	1	36N13	81w00	5:24:00
Robbins 63	1	35N26	79w35	5:18:20
Robbinsville 38	1	35N19	83w48	5:35:12
Roberdel 77	1	34N56	79w46	5:19:04
Roberdo 62	1	35N13	80w00	5:20:00
Roberson Store 59	1	35N49	77w06	5:08:24
Robersonville 59	1	35N50	77w15	5:09:00
Roberta Mill	1	35N22	80w38	5:22:32
Roberta Mills 13	1	35N25	80w36	5:22:24
Rock Creek 1	1	35N54	79w26	5:17:44
Rockdale 23	1	35N25	81w34	5:26:16
Rockfish 47	1	34N59	79w13	5:16:52
Rockford 86	1	36N13	80w39	5:22:36
Rock Hill 13	1	35N25	80w36	5:22:24
Rockingham 77	1	34N57	79w46	5:19:04
Rock Ridge 98	1	35N44	77w55	5:11:40
Rock Spring 74	1	35N36	77w23	5:09:32
Rockwell 80	1	35N33	80w25	5:21:40
Rockwell Park 60	1	35N16	80w48	5:23:12
Rocky Cross 64	1	35N47	78w12	5:12:48
Rocky Ford 35	1	36N13	78w26	5:13:44
Rockyhock 21	1	36N04	76w36	5:06:24
Rocky Mount 33	1	35N55	77w46	5:11:04
Rocky Pass 56	1	35N43	81w56	5:27:44
Rocky Point 71	1	34N26	77w53	5:11:32
Rocky River 13	1	35N25	80w36	5:22:24
Rocky Springs 62	1	35N13	79w44	5:18:56
Rodanthe 28	1	35N36	75w28	5:01:52
Roduco 37	1	36N28	76w49	5:07:16
Roe	1	35N00	76w19	5:05:16
Rolesville 92	1	35N55	78w27	5:13:48
Rominger 95	1	36N10	81w52	5:27:28
Ronda 97	1	36N13	80w57	5:23:48
Rooks 71	1	34N32	78w10	5:12:40
Roper 94	1	35N53	76w37	5:06:28
Rose 96	1	35N22	77w58	5:11:52
Rose Bay 48	1	35N24	76w20	5:05:20
Roseboro 82	1	34N58	78w31	5:14:04
Roseborough 6	1	36N00	81w47	5:27:08
Rosebud 98	1	35N48	77w52	5:11:28
Rose Hill 31	1	34N50	78w01	5:12:04
Roseland 55	1	35N28	81w15	5:25:00
Roseland 63	1	35N08	79w26	5:17:44
Rosemead 8	1	36N12	76w46	5:07:04
Roseneath 42	1	36N05	77w29	5:09:56
Rosindale 9	1	34N26	78w28	5:13:52
Rosman 88	1	35N09	82w49	5:31:16
Rougemont 32	1	36N13	78w56	5:15:44
Round Peak 86	1	36N30	80w35	5:22:20
Roundtree 74	1	35N28	77w25	5:09:40
Rowan Mill 80	1	35N39	80w30	5:22:00
Rowes Corner 25	1	35N06	77w05	5:08:20
Rowland 78	1	34N32	79w18	5:17:12
Roxboro 73	1	36N24	78w59	5:15:56
Roxobel 8	1	36N11	77w12	5:08:48
Royal 7	1	35N18	76w47	5:07:08
Royal Mills 92	1	35N59	78w30	5:14:00
Royal Oaks 13	1	35N31	80w38	5:22:32
Royal Pines 11	1	35N29	82w31	5:30:04
Rudd 41	1	36N13	79w43	5:18:52
Ruffin 79	1	36N27	79w33	5:18:12
Rural Hall 34	1	36N15	80w18	5:21:12
Rusk 86	1	36N15	80w52	5:23:28
Russtown 10	1	34N04	78w32	5:14:08
Ruth 81	1	35N23	81w57	5:27:48
Rutherford College 12	1	35N45	81w32	5:26:08
Rutherfordton 81	1	35N22	81w58	5:27:52
Rutherwood 45	1	36N13	81w40	5:26:40
Ryes 43	1	35N27	79w03	5:16:12
Ryland 21	1	36N13	76w37	5:06:28
Saddle 3	1	36N33	81w00	5:24:00
Saddletree 78	1	34N43	79w02	5:16:08
Sadler 79	1	36N21	79w41	5:18:44
Saint Helena 71	1	34N33	77w55	5:11:40
Saint John 46	1	36N17	76w59	5:07:56
Saint Johns 21	1	36N04	76w36	5:06:24
Saint Johns 46	1	36N18	77w07	5:08:28
Saint Lewis 33	1	35N45	77w40	5:10:40
Saint Marys 92	1	35N42	78w36	5:14:24
Saint Matthews 92	1	35N48	78w32	5:14:08
Saint Pauls 78	1	34N48	78w58	5:15:52
Salem 12	1	35N44	81w42	5:26:48
Salem 34	1	36N06	80w15	5:21:00
Salem 55	1	35N28	81w15	5:25:00
Salem 64	1	36N06	77w43	5:10:52
Salem 86	1	36N30	80w35	5:22:20
Salemburg 82	1	35N01	78w30	5:14:00
Salem Chapel 34	1	36N12	80w12	5:20:48
Salisbury 80	1	35N40	80w29	5:21:56
Salter Path 16	1	34N41	76w53	5:07:32
Saluda 75	1	35N14	82w21	5:29:24
Salvo 28	1	35N33	75w29	5:01:56
Samaria 64	1	35N47	78w12	5:12:48
Sand Hill 11	1	35N35	82w36	5:30:24
Sandhill 69	1	35N06	77w05	5:08:20
Sands 95	1	36N13	81w40	5:26:40
Sandy Bottom 54	2	35N16	77w35	5:10:20
Sandy Bottoms 83	1	34N46	79w28	5:17:52
Sandy Cross 37	1	36N21	76w36	5:06:24
Sandy Cross 64	1	35N58	77w58	5:11:52
Sandy Grove 29	1	35N49	80w15	5:21:00
Sandymush 11	1	35N40	82w47	5:31:08
Sandy Mush 81	1	35N19	81w52	5:27:28
Sandy Plain 31	1	35N03	77w45	5:11:00
Sandy Plains 75	1	35N11	82w11	5:28:44
Sandy Ridge 41	1	36N07	80w01	5:20:04
Sandy Ridge 85	1	36N30	80w06	5:20:24
Sandy Run 23	1	35N19	81w39	5:26:36
Sanford 53	1	35N29	79w10	5:16:40
Santeetlah 38	1	35N19	83w48	5:35:12
Sapphire 88	1	35N06	83w00	5:32:00
Saratoga 98	1	35N39	77w47	5:11:08
Sarecta Junction 31	1	34N58	77w58	5:11:52
Sassafras Fork 39	1	36N29	78w34	5:14:16
Sassers Mill 52	1	35N13	77w26	5:09:44
Satterwhite 39	1	36N18	78w35	5:14:20
Saulston 96	1	35N25	77w51	5:11:24
Saunook 44	2	35N33	82w59	5:31:56
Sauratown 85	1	36N18	80w08	5:20:32
Savannah 50	1	35N17	83w16	5:33:04
Saw 80	1	35N33	80w36	5:22:24
Saw Mills 14	1	35N48	81w26	5:25:44
Saxapahaw 1	1	35N57	79w19	5:17:16
Saxsony 55	1	35N28	81w15	5:25:00
Sayles Village 11	1	35N34	82w32	5:30:08
Scalesville 41	1	36N12	79w54	5:19:36
Scaly Mountain 57	1	35N01	83w19	5:33:16
Schley 68	1	36N05	79w07	5:16:28
Scholl 83	1	34N54	79w42	5:18:48
Scotch Grove 83	1	34N46	79w28	5:17:52
Scotch Irish 80	1	35N48	80w38	5:22:32
Scotland Neck 42	1	36N08	77w25	5:09:40
Scott Creek 50	1	35N25	83w07	5:32:28
Scotts 49	1	35N45	81w00	5:24:00
Scotts 98	1	35N39	78w01	5:12:04
Scotts Hill 71	1	34N13	77w55	5:11:40
Scotts Store 69	1	35N06	77w05	5:08:20
Scottville 5	1	36N29	81w18	5:25:12
Scranton 48	1	35N30	76w27	5:05:48
Scuffleton 40	1	35N28	77w25	5:09:40
Scuppernong 94	1	35N52	76w24	5:05:36
Seaboard 66	1	36N29	77w26	5:09:44
Seabreeze 65	3	34N13	77w55	5:11:40
Seagate 65	3	34N13	77w55	5:11:40
Seagrove 76	1	35N33	79w46	5:19:04
Sealevel 16	1	34N52	76w23	5:05:32
Seaside 10	1	33N54	78w27	5:13:48
Sedalia 41	1	36N05	79w37	5:18:28
Sedgefield 41	1	36N01	79w54	5:19:36
Sedgefield 60	1	35N11	80w51	5:23:24
Sedgefield Lakes 41	1	36N03	79w52	5:19:28
Sedgefield Park 41	1	36N03	79w52	5:19:28
Sedges Garden 34	1	36N08	80w14	5:20:56
Selica 88	1	35N14	82w44	5:30:56
Selma 51	1	35N32	78w17	5:13:08

Selma Cotton Mills 51 1 35N32 78w17 5:13:08
Selwin 37 1 36N21 76w36 5:06:24
Seminole 43 1 35N27 79w03 5:16:12
Semora 17 1 36N30 79w09 5:16:36
Senia 6 1 36N05 81w56 5:27:44
Setzer Gap 14 1 35N54 81w31 5:26:04
Seven Bridges 78 1 34N44 79w21 5:17:24
Seven Paths 35 1 36N08 78w12 5:12:48
Seven Springs 96 1 35N14 77w51 5:11:24
Severn 66 1 36N31 77w11 5:08:44
Sevier 56 1 35N41 82w00 5:28:00
Seward 34 1 36N09 80w22 5:21:28
Seymour Johnson Air Force Ba 96 1 35N22 77w58 5:11:52
Shacktown 99 1 36N08 80w40 5:22:40
Shady Banks 7 1 35N32 77w02 5:08:08
Shady Brook 13 1 35N31 80w38 5:22:32
Shady Forest 10 1 33N54 78w27 5:13:48
Shady Grove 30 1 35N57 80w26 5:21:44
Shady Grove 52 1 35N16 77w35 5:10:20
Shale Brick 29 1 35N53 80w05 5:20:20
Shaleton 90 1 34N59 80w33 5:22:12
Shallotte 10 1 33N58 78w23 5:13:32
Shallotte Point 10 1 33N54 78w27 5:13:48
Shallowell 53 1 35N28 79w10 5:16:40
Shanghai 82 1 34N50 78w02 5:12:08
Shankle 84 1 35N14 80w07 5:20:28
Shankletown 13 1 35N25 80w36 5:22:24
Shannon 78 1 34N51 79w08 5:16:32
Sharon 15 1 36N27 76w20 5:05:20
Sharon 49 1 35N51 80w56 5:23:44
Sharon 60 1 35N09 80w49 5:23:16
Sharpes 2 1 35N54 81w05 5:24:20
Sharpesburg 49 1 35N55 80w58 5:23:52
Sharp Point 74 1 35N40 77w38 5:10:32
Sharpsburg 33 1 35N53 77w50 5:11:20
Shatley Springs 5 1 36N30 81w24 5:25:36
Shawboro 27 1 36N24 76w06 5:04:24
Shaw Heights 26 1 35N05 78w57 5:15:48
Shawneehaw 95 1 36N11 81w49 5:27:16
Sheffield 30 1 35N54 80w34 5:22:16
Sheffields 63 1 35N28 79w38 5:18:32
Shelby 23 1 35N17 81w32 5:26:08
Shelmerdine 74 1 35N36 77w23 5:09:32
Shelton Town 86 1 36N30 80w35 5:22:20
Shepard 32 1 35N58 78w55 5:15:40
Shephards 49 1 35N35 80w49 5:23:16
Sherrills Ford 18 1 35N37 80w59 5:23:56
Sherwood 95 1 36N15 81w46 5:27:04
Sherwood Forest 11 1 35N37 82w23 5:29:32
Shields Commissary 42 1 36N08 77w25 5:09:40
Shiloh 15 1 36N17 76w05 5:04:20
Shine 40 1 35N28 77w47 5:11:08
Shines Crossroads 40 1 35N27 77w40 5:10:40
Shingle Hollow 81 1 35N22 81w57 5:27:48
Shinnville 49 1 35N35 80w49 5:23:16
Shoal 86 1 36N20 80w26 5:21:44
Shoal Creek 20 1 35N06 84w14 5:36:56
Shoal Creek 50 1 35N26 83w22 5:33:28
Shoals 86 1 36N18 80w30 5:22:00
Shocco 93 1 36N19 78w10 5:12:40
Shoe 97 1 36N16 81w19 5:25:16
Shoofly 39 1 36N12 78w43 5:14:52
Shookville 57 1 35N03 83w12 5:32:48
Shooting Creek 22 1 35N03 83w38 5:34:32
Shopton 60 1 35N13 80w51 5:23:24
Short Off 57 1 35N03 83w12 5:32:48
Shotwell 92 1 35N47 78w29 5:13:56
Shuford 18 1 35N44 81w21 5:25:24
Shulls Mills 95 1 36N13 81w40 5:26:40
Shupings Mill 80 1 35N33 80w24 5:21:36
Sidestown 13 1 35N25 80w36 5:22:24
Sidney 7 1 35N32 76w37 5:06:28
Siler City 19 1 35N44 79w28 5:17:52
Silk Hope 19 1 35N43 79w28 5:17:52
Siloam 86 1 36N19 80w34 5:22:16
Silver City 47 1 34N59 79w13 5:16:52
Silver Creek 12 1 35N41 81w48 5:27:12
Silverdale 67 1 34N43 77w14 5:08:56
Silver Hill 29 1 35N44 80w12 5:20:48
Silver Spring 63 1 35N06 79w28 5:17:52
Silverstone 95 1 36N21 81w45 5:27:00
Silver Valley 29 1 35N49 80w15 5:21:00
Simpson 74 1 35N35 77w17 5:09:08
Simpsonville 79 1 36N19 79w43 5:18:52
Sims 98 1 35N46 78w04 5:12:16
Sioux 100 1 36N00 82w14 5:28:56
Sivey Town 10 1 33N54 78w27 5:13:48
Six Forks 92 1 35N50 78w40 5:14:40
Sixpound 93 1 36N29 78w03 5:12:12
Skibo 26 1 35N02 78w57 5:15:48
Skinnersville 94 1 35N55 76w27 5:05:48
Skyco 28 1 35N54 75w40 5:02:40
Skycrest Village 92 1 35N48 78w38 5:14:32
Skyland 11 1 35N29 82w32 5:30:08
Skyline 63 1 35N15 79w17 5:17:08
Skyway Terrace 83 1 34N44 79w21 5:17:24
Sladesville 48 1 35N30 76w27 5:05:48
Sligo 27 1 36N32 76w10 5:04:40
Sloan 31 1 34N44 78w00 5:12:00
Slocomb 26 1 35N15 78w45 5:15:00
Slocum Village 25 1 34N53 76w54 5:07:36
Slow Creek 20 1 35N10 83w55 5:35:40
Small 7 1 35N18 76w47 5:07:08
Small Cross Roads 21 1 36N04 76w36 5:06:24
Smethport 5 1 36N24 81w29 5:25:56
Smith 31 1 35N00 77w48 5:11:12
Smith Creek 93 1 36N29 78w13 5:12:52

Smith Crossing 24 1 34N20 78w36 5:14:24
Smithfield 51 1 35N31 78w21 5:13:24
Smith Grove 30 1 35N54 80w34 5:22:16
Smiths 78 1 34N46 79w15 5:17:00
Smiths Bridge 57 1 35N04 83w23 5:33:32
Smithtown 99 1 36N14 80w35 5:22:20
Smithville 10 1 33N58 78w10 5:12:40
Smithville 60 1 35N29 80w51 5:23:24
Smoky Creek 12 1 35N48 81w37 5:26:28
Smyre 36 1 35N16 81w10 5:24:40
Smyrna 16 1 34N46 76w31 5:06:04
Snake Bite 8 1 36N05 77w04 5:08:16
Sneads Ferry 67 1 34N31 77w23 5:09:32
Sneads Grove 83 1 34N46 79w28 5:17:52
Snow Camp 1 1 35N54 79w26 5:17:44
Snowden 27 1 36N32 76w10 5:04:40
Snow Hill 40 1 35N27 77w43 5:10:52
Snow Hill 82 1 34N57 78w31 5:14:04
Soapstone Mountain 76 1 35N48 79w33 5:18:12
Sodom 58 1 35N48 82w41 5:30:44
Somers 97 1 36N06 80w55 5:23:40
Somerset 21 1 36N04 76w36 5:06:24
Somerset Hills 92 1 35N48 78w38 5:14:32
Sophia 76 1 35N50 79w52 5:19:28
Soul City 93 1 36N25 78w17 5:13:08
Sound Side 28 1 35N58 75w38 5:02:32
Sound Side 89 1 35N55 76w15 5:05:00
South Albemarle 84 1 35N19 80w11 5:20:44
South Clinton 82 1 34N57 78w19 5:13:16
South Creek 7 1 35N20 76w42 5:06:48
Southern Pines 63 1 35N11 79w24 5:17:36
South Gastonia 36 1 35N16 81w10 5:24:40
South Goldsboro 96 1 35N21 77w59 5:11:56
South Greensboro 41 1 36N03 79w49 5:19:16
South Henderson 91 1 36N19 78w24 5:13:36
South Hominy 11 1 35N32 82w41 5:30:44
South Lexington 29 1 35N49 80w15 5:21:00
South Lowell 32 1 36N10 78w53 5:15:32
South Lumberton 78 1 34N36 79w01 5:16:04
South Mills 15 1 36N27 76w20 5:05:20
Southmont 29 1 35N40 80w16 5:21:04
South Newton 18 1 35N40 81w13 5:24:52
South Point 36 1 35N13 81w06 5:24:24
Southport 10 1 33N55 78w01 5:12:04
South River 16 1 34N43 76w39 5:06:36
South River 82 1 34N46 78w21 5:13:24
South Rocky Mount 33 1 35N58 77w48 5:11:12
South Salisbury 80 1 35N38 80w28 5:21:52
Southside 55 1 35N28 81w15 5:25:00
South Toe 100 1 35N49 82w11 5:28:44
South Wadesboro 4 1 34N57 80w05 5:20:20
South Weldon 42 1 36N25 77w36 5:10:24
Southwest 54 1 35N12 77w32 5:10:08
South Westfield 86 1 36N27 80w30 5:22:00
South Whitakers 64 1 36N02 77w48 5:11:12
South Whiteville 24 1 34N20 78w42 5:14:48
South Williams 24 1 34N08 78w49 5:15:16
South Wilmington 65 3 34N13 77w55 5:11:40
South Wilson 98 1 35N44 77w55 5:11:40
Southwood 54 1 35N16 77w35 5:10:20
Sparta 3 1 36N30 81w07 5:24:28
Spear 6 1 36N02 82w02 5:28:08
Speed 33 1 35N58 77w26 5:09:44
Speedwell 50 1 35N19 83w11 5:32:44
Speights Bridge 40 1 35N35 77w43 5:10:52
Spencer 80 1 35N41 80w26 5:21:44
Spencer Mountain 36 1 35N18 81w07 5:24:28
Spero 76 1 35N42 79w49 5:19:16
Spies 63 1 35N26 79w35 5:18:20
Spindale 81 1 35N22 81w56 5:27:44
Spiveys Corner 82 1 35N19 78w37 5:14:28
Spokane 76 1 35N32 79w46 5:19:04
Spot 27 1 36N07 75w50 5:03:20
Spout Springs 43 1 35N20 79w15 5:17:00
Spray 79 1 36N31 79w46 5:19:04
Spring Creek 58 1 35N47 82w52 5:31:28
Springfield 97 1 36N15 81w07 5:24:28
Springfield Mills 83 1 34N49 79w32 5:18:08
Spring Hill 42 1 36N08 77w25 5:09:40
Spring Hope 25 1 36N06 77w05 5:08:20
Spring Hope 64 1 35N57 78w06 5:12:24
Spring Lake 26 1 35N10 78w58 5:15:52
Spring Valley 41 1 36N03 79w49 5:19:16
Springwood 36 1 35N15 81w02 5:24:08
Spruce Pine 61 1 35N55 82w04 5:28:16
Spurgeon 97 1 36N10 81w08 5:24:32
Stackhouse 58 1 35N48 82w41 5:30:44
Stacy 16 1 34N51 76w25 5:05:40
Stag Park 71 1 34N33 77w55 5:11:40
Staley 76 1 35N48 79w33 5:18:12
Stallings 90 1 35N07 80w43 5:22:52
Stamey Branch 6 1 36N05 81w56 5:27:44
Stanfield 84 1 35N14 80w25 5:21:40
Stanhope 64 1 35N57 78w07 5:12:28
Stanley 36 1 35N21 81w06 5:24:24
Stanleys Store 30 1 35N54 80w34 5:22:16
Stanleyville 34 1 36N12 80w17 5:21:08
Stanton 97 1 36N12 81w20 5:25:20
Stantonsburg 98 1 35N37 77w49 5:11:16

NORTH CAROLINA

Star 62 1 35N24 79w47 5:19:08
Starmount 60 1 35N10 80w51 5:23:24
Starmount 92 1 35N48 78w38 5:14:32
Startown 18 1 35N40 81w13 5:24:52
State Road 86 1 36N19 80w52 5:23:28
Statesville 49 1 35N47 80w53 5:23:32
State University 92 1 35N48 78w41 5:14:44
Stecoah 38 1 35N23 83w41 5:34:44
Stedman 26 1 35N00 78w41 5:14:44
Steeds 62 1 35N32 79w46 5:19:04
Steel Creek 60 1 35N08 80w57 5:23:48
Steele 80 1 35N41 80w38 5:22:32
Steeles 77 1 35N08 79w55 5:19:40
Steen Town 77 1 34N54 79w42 5:18:48
Stella 16 1 34N46 77w09 5:08:36
Stem 39 1 36N12 78w43 5:14:52
Sterlings 78 1 34N24 79w03 5:16:12
Stevens Mill 96 1 35N22 77w58 5:11:52
Stewartsville 83 1 34N45 79w27 5:17:48
Stiles 57 1 35N11 83w23 5:33:32
Stocksville 11 1 35N44 82w35 5:30:20
Stokes 74 1 35N43 77w16 5:09:04
Stokesdale 41 1 36N15 79w59 5:19:56
Stokestown 74 1 35N28 77w25 5:09:40
Stonehaven 60 1 35N10 80w48 5:23:12
Stoneville 79 1 36N28 79w54 5:19:36
Stonewall 69 1 35N08 76w45 5:07:00
Stonewall Jackson Homes 60 1 35N14 80w53 5:23:32
Stonycreek 17 1 36N06 79w30 5:18:00
Stony Fork 11 1 35N32 82w41 5:30:44
Stony Fork 95 1 36N14 81w31 5:26:04
Stony Knoll 86 1 36N24 80w43 5:22:52
Stony Point 2 1 35N52 81w03 5:24:12
Stotts Cross Roads 98 1 35N46 78w04 5:12:16
Stouts 90 1 34N59 80w33 5:22:12
Stovall 39 1 36N27 78w35 5:14:20
Stowe 36 1 35N15 81w02 5:24:08
Straits 16 1 34N46 76w34 5:06:16
Stratford 3 1 36N30 81w07 5:24:28
Strickland Cross Roads 64 1 35N57 78w07 5:12:28
Stubbs 23 1 35N17 81w32 5:26:08
Stump Sound 67 1 34N35 77w29 5:09:56
Stumptown 56 1 35N41 82w00 5:28:00
Stumpy Point 28 1 35N42 75w44 5:02:56
Sturgills 5 1 36N30 81w30 5:26:00
Sugar Fork 57 1 35N08 83w15 5:33:00
Sugar Grove 95 1 36N15 81w47 5:27:08
Sugar Hill 56 1 35N41 82w00 5:28:00
Sugar Loaf 2 1 36N00 81w10 5:24:40
Suit 20 1 35N05 84w02 5:36:08
Sulphur Springs 81 2 35N15 81w55 5:27:40
Summerfield 41 1 36N12 79w54 5:19:36
Summerhaven 11 1 35N37 82w23 5:29:32
Summit 41 1 36N06 79w46 5:19:04
Summit 42 1 36N26 77w55 5:11:40
Summit 97 1 36N11 81w17 5:25:08
Sumner 41 1 35N59 79w50 5:19:20
Sunbury 37 1 36N27 76w37 5:06:28
Sunny Point Military Ocean T 10 1 34N39 77w58 5:11:52
Sunnyside 12 1 35N44 81w42 5:26:48
Sunny Side 28 1 35N54 75w40 5:02:40
Sunnyside 36 1 35N17 81w17 5:25:08
Sunny Side 42 1 36N26 77w55 5:11:40
Sunny View 75 1 35N18 82w10 5:28:40
Sunrise 96 1 35N22 77w58 5:11:52
Sunset Beach 10 1 33N52 78w30 5:14:00
Sunset Harbor 10 1 34N04 78w09 5:12:36
Sunset Hills 18 1 35N44 81w21 5:25:24
Sunset Park 44 1 35N35 82w51 5:31:24
Sunshine 81 1 35N22 81w50 5:27:20
Supply 10 1 34N01 78w16 5:13:04
Surf City 71 1 34N26 77w33 5:10:12
Surl 73 1 36N17 78w57 5:15:48
Sussex 5 1 36N34 81w23 5:25:32
Sutherlands 5 1 36N23 81w43 5:26:52
Sutton Park 90 1 34N59 80w33 5:22:12
Suttons Corner 9 1 34N38 78w33 5:14:12
Suttontown 82 1 34N56 78w10 5:12:40
Swain 94 1 35N53 76w36 5:06:24
Swainsville 23 1 35N17 81w32 5:26:08
Swancreek 99 1 36N14 80w50 5:23:20
Swannanoa 11 1 35N36 82w24 5:29:36
Swannanoa Hills 11 1 35N36 82w31 5:30:04
Swanquarter 48 1 35N25 76w20 5:05:20
Swansboro 67 1 34N39 77w07 5:08:28
Swan Station 53 1 35N23 79w07 5:16:28
Swayney 87 1 35N29 83w19 5:33:16
Sweet Gum 38 1 35N19 83w48 5:35:12
Sweetwater 22 1 35N04 83w53 5:35:32
Sweetwater 95 1 36N15 81w47 5:27:08
Swepsonville 1 1 36N01 79w22 5:17:28
Swift Creek 33 1 36N00 77w43 5:10:52
Swiss 100 1 35N55 82w18 5:29:12
Sylva 50 2 35N23 83w13 5:32:52
Tabernacle 76 1 35N46 79w59 5:19:56
Tabor City 24 1 34N10 78w52 5:15:28
Talleys Crossing 34 1 36N07 80w10 5:20:40
Tallulah Gap 38 1 35N19 83w48 5:35:12
Tally Ho 39 1 36N14 78w43 5:14:52
Tamarack 95 1 36N18 81w36 5:26:24
Tapoco 38 1 35N27 83w56 5:35:44
Tarawa Terrace 67 1 34N43 77w22 5:09:28
Tarboro 33 1 35N54 77w32 5:10:08
Tar Corner 15 1 36N27 76w20 5:05:20
Tar Heel 9 1 34N44 78w47 5:15:08
Tarheel 37 1 36N26 76w51 5:07:24
Tar Landing 67 1 34N45 77w26 5:09:44

NORTH CAROLINA

Tar River 39 1 36N18 78W35 5:14:20
Tate Street 41 1 36N04 79W54 5:19:36
Tatums 24 1 34N24 78W53 5:15:32
Taylor 98 1 35N47 77W57 5:11:48
Taylor Cross Roads 64 1 35N58 77W58 5:11:52
Taylors Bridge 82 1 34N51 78W13 5:12:52
Taylors Corners 52 1 35N04 77W21 5:09:24
Taylors Store 8 1 36N01 76W46 5:07:04
Taylors Store 64 1 35N58 77W58 5:11:52
Taylorsville 2 1 35N55 81W11 5:24:44
Taylortown 63 1 35N12 79W28 5:17:52
Teacheys 31 1 34N46 78W01 5:12:04
Teer 68 1 35N55 79W01 5:16:04
Tennelina 58 1 35N55 83W01 5:32:04
Tennessee Acres 41 1 36N06 79W46 5:19:04
Terrace Gardens 45 1 35N19 82W28 5:29:52
Terra Ceia 7 1 35N35 76W40 5:06:40
Terrell 18 1 35N35 80W59 5:23:56
Terry Fork 58 1 35N50 82W33 5:30:12
Texaco Beach 15 1 36N17 76W05 5:04:20
Texana 20 1 35N05 84W02 5:36:08
The Borough 71 1 34N32 78W10 5:12:40
Thelma 42 1 36N26 77W55 5:11:40
Theta 5 1 36N25 81W28 5:25:52
Thomasboro Crossroads 10 1 33N54 78W27 5:13:48
Thomas Landing 67 1 34N26 77W34 5:10:16
Thomas Valley 50 1 35N26 83W22 5:33:28
Thomasville 29 1 35N53 80W05 5:20:20
Three Mile 6 1 36N05 81W56 5:27:44
Thurman 25 1 35N06 77W05 5:08:20
Thurmond 97 1 36N22 80W56 5:23:44
Tillery 42 1 36N15 77W29 5:09:56
Timberlake 73 1 36N17 78W57 5:15:48
Timothy 82 1 35N19 78W37 5:14:28
Tin City 31 1 34N44 78W00 5:12:00
Tipton Hill 61 1 36N00 82W14 5:28:56
Toast 86 1 36N30 80W38 5:22:32
Tobaccoville 34 1 36N15 80W22 5:21:28
Tobemory 9 1 34N48 78W58 5:15:52
Todd 5 1 36N19 81W36 5:26:24
Todds Crossroads 8 1 36N03 76W57 5:07:48
Toddy 74 1 35N36 77W35 5:10:20
Toecane 61 1 36N01 82W09 5:28:36
Toe River 6 1 35N59 82W00 5:28:00
Toisnot 98 1 35N49 77W50 5:11:20
Tolarsville 78 1 34N48 78W58 5:15:52
Toledo 100 1 36N00 82W14 5:28:56
Toliver 5 1 36N18 81W36 5:26:24
Toluca 23 1 35N25 81W34 5:26:16
Tomahawk 82 1 34N43 78W20 5:13:20
Tom Creek 56 1 35N41 82W00 5:28:00
Tomotla 20 2 35N10 83W55 5:35:40
Topia 3 1 36N29 81W18 5:25:12
Topnot 17 1 36N24 79W20 5:17:20
Topsail 71 1 34N24 77W41 5:10:44
Topsail Beach 71 1 34N22 77W37 5:10:28
Topton 20 2 35N15 83W42 5:34:48
Town Creek 10 1 34N09 78W05 5:12:20
Town Creek 98 1 35N48 77W52 5:11:28
Town Forest 45 1 35N19 82W28 5:29:52
Townsville 91 1 36N30 78W25 5:13:40
Tracy 95 1 36N23 81W43 5:26:52
Tradingford 80 1 35N39 80W29 5:21:56
Tramway 53 1 35N27 79W13 5:16:52
Trap 8 1 36N12 76W46 5:07:04
Traphill 97 1 36N21 80W59 5:23:56
Travis 89 1 35N55 76W15 5:05:00
Treetop 5 1 36N24 81W29 5:25:56
Trent 54 1 35N10 77W44 5:10:56
Trenton 52 1 35N04 77W21 5:09:24
Trent Woods 25 1 35N05 77W06 5:08:24
Triangle 55 1 35N29 81W00 5:24:00
Triangle 92 1 35N49 78W50 5:15:20
Trinity 76 1 35N53 80W00 5:20:00
Trinity 90 1 34N59 80W33 5:22:12
Trotville 37 1 36N21 76W36 5:06:24
Troutman 49 1 35N42 80W53 5:23:32
Troutmans 1 35N42 80W53 5:23:32
Troy 62 1 35N22 79W53 5:19:32
Trust 58 1 35N54 82W50 5:31:20
Tryon 75 1 35N13 82W14 5:28:56
Tuckahoe 52 1 35N01 77W36 5:10:24
Tuckasegee 50 1 35N16 83W07 5:32:28
Tuckerdale 5 1 36N30 81W30 5:26:00
Tulls Creek 27 1 36N27 76W01 5:04:04
Tungsten 91 1 36N19 78W24 5:13:36
Tunis 46 1 36N24 76W56 5:07:44
Turkey 82 1 35N00 78W11 5:12:44
Turlington 43 1 35N19 78W37 5:14:28
Turnbull 9 1 34N47 78W35 5:14:20
Turnersburg 49 1 35N55 80W45 5:23:00
Turners Crossroads 66 1 36N32 77W27 5:09:48
Turnpike 11 2 35N32 82W41 5:30:44
Turtle Mountain Indian Res 95 1 36N12 81W33 5:26:12
Tuscarora 25 1 35N06 77W05 5:08:20
Tuskeegee 38 1 35N19 83W48 5:35:12
Tusquittee 22 1 35N07 83W44 5:34:56
Tuxedo 45 1 35N14 82W26 5:29:44
Twin Lake 10 1 33N54 78W27 5:13:48
Twin Oaks 3 1 36N30 81W07 5:24:28
Tyner 21 1 36N13 76W37 5:06:28
Tyro 29 1 35N49 80W22 5:21:28
Tyson 84 1 35N14 80W13 5:20:52
Ulah 76 1 35N42 79W49 5:19:16
Unahala 87 1 35N26 83W27 5:33:48
Unaka 20 1 35N12 84W08 5:36:32
Uncc 60 1 35N16 80W48 5:23:12
Union 46 1 36N17 76W59 5:07:56
Union 57 1 35N11 83W23 5:33:32
Union Cross 34 1 36N07 80W10 5:20:40
Union Grove 49 1 36N01 80W51 5:23:24
Union Hill 99 1 36N14 80W30 5:22:00
Union Mills 81 1 35N29 81W58 5:27:52
Union Ridge 1 1 36N06 79W27 5:17:48
Unionville 90 1 34N59 80W33 5:22:12
Unity 80 1 35N47 80W35 5:22:20
Upchurch 92 1 35N44 78W51 5:15:24
Upper 21 1 36N16 76W38 5:06:32
Upper Contoe 33 1 35N54 77W24 5:09:36
Upper Creek 12 1 35N52 81W49 5:27:16
Upper Fishing Creek 33 1 36N05 77W38 5:10:32
Upper Fork 12 1 35N39 81W39 5:26:36
Upper Hominy 11 1 35N32 82W43 5:30:52
Upper Little River 43 1 35N24 78W56 5:15:44
Upper Peachtree 20 1 35N05 84W02 5:36:08
Upper Pigeonroost 61 1 36N00 82W14 5:28:56
Upper Poplar 61 1 36N02 82W18 5:29:12
Upton 14 1 35N54 81W31 5:26:04
Upward 45 1 36N30 80W35 5:22:20
Uree 81 1 35N26 82W13 5:28:52
Uwharrie 62 1 35N22 80W00 5:20:00
Valdese 12 1 35N44 81W34 5:26:16
Vale 55 1 35N33 81W24 5:25:36
Valhalla 21 1 36N08 76W40 5:06:40
Valle Crucis 95 1 36N12 81W46 5:27:04
Valley 6 1 36N05 81W56 5:27:44
Valley 20 1 35N11 83W51 5:35:24
Valley Hill 45 1 35N19 82W28 5:29:52
Valmead 14 1 35N54 81W31 5:26:04
Vanceboro 25 1 35N18 77W09 5:08:36
Vandalia 41 1 36N03 79W49 5:19:16
Vandemere 69 1 35N11 76W41 5:06:44
Vander 26 1 35N04 78W53 5:15:32
Vannoy 97 1 36N16 81W19 5:25:16
Varina 92 1 35N35 78W48 5:15:12
Varnum 10 1 34N01 78W16 5:13:04
Vashti 2 1 35N54 81W05 5:24:20
Vass 63 1 35N15 79W17 5:17:08
Vaughan 93 1 36N26 78W00 5:12:00
Vein Mountain 56 1 35N41 82W00 5:28:00
Venters 74 1 35N28 77W25 5:09:40
Verona 67 1 34N40 77W28 5:09:52
Vests 20 1 35N05 84W02 5:36:08
Vicksboro 93 1 36N19 78W24 5:13:36
Victory 36 1 35N16 81W10 5:24:40
Victory Village 68 1 35N55 79W01 5:16:04
Vienna 34 1 36N08 80W23 5:21:32
Viewmont 18 1 35N44 81W21 5:25:24
Vilas 95 1 36N15 81W46 5:27:04
Vina Vista 63 1 35N08 79W26 5:17:44
Vinegar Hill 24 1 34N09 78W53 5:15:32
Violet 20 1 35N12 84W08 5:36:32
Virgilina 39 1 36N33 78W47 5:15:08
Vista 71 1 34N22 77W49 5:11:16
Vixen 100 1 35N55 82W18 5:29:12
Waccamaw 10 1 34N04 78W32 5:14:08
Waco 23 1 35N22 81W26 5:25:44
Wade 26 1 35N10 78W44 5:14:56
Wade Mills 4 1 34N58 80W05 5:20:20
Wadesboro 4 1 34N58 80W05 5:20:20
Wades Point 7 1 35N32 76W37 5:06:28
Wadeville 62 1 35N13 80W00 5:20:00
Wagoner 5 1 36N25 81W28 5:25:52
Wagram 83 1 34N53 79W22 5:17:28
Wake Crossroads 92 1 35N48 78W38 5:14:32
Wakefield 92 1 35N49 78W19 5:13:16
Wake Forest 92 1 35N59 78W30 5:14:00
Wakelon 8 1 36N12 76W46 5:07:04
Wakulla 78 1 34N48 79W15 5:17:00
Walkers Crossroads 92 1 35N59 78W30 5:14:00
Walkersville 90 1 34N56 80W45 5:23:00
Walkertown 34 1 36N10 80W10 5:20:40
Walkertown 43 1 35N15 78W45 5:15:00
Walkertown 80 1 35N33 80W36 5:22:24
Wallace 31 1 34N44 77W59 5:11:56
Wallburg 29 1 36N00 80W08 5:20:32
Walnut 58 1 35N51 82W44 5:30:56
Walnut Cove 85 1 36N18 80W09 5:20:36
Walnut Creek 33 1 35N53 77W38 5:10:32
Walnut Creek 58 1 35N48 82W41 5:30:44
Walnut Creek 96 1 35N22 77W58 5:11:52
Walnut Hill 5 1 36N29 81W26 5:25:44
Walsh 97 1 36N11 81W17 5:25:08
Walstonburg 40 1 35N36 77W42 5:10:48
Waltons Store 67 1 34N45 77W26 5:09:44
Wananish 24 1 34N19 78W32 5:14:08
Wanchese 28 1 35N51 75W38 5:02:32
Warbler 89 1 35N35 76W14 5:04:56
Wards 24 1 34N19 78W50 5:15:20
Wards Corner 71 1 34N33 77W55 5:11:40
Wards Store 64 1 36N06 77W43 5:10:52
Wardsville 37 1 36N27 76W37 5:06:28
Warlick 23 1 35N19 81W25 5:25:40
Warne 22 1 35N00 83W54 5:35:36
Warren Plains 93 1 36N24 78W09 5:12:36
Warrensville 5 1 36N28 81W31 5:26:04
Warrenton 93 1 36N24 78W09 5:12:36
Warren Wilson College 11 1 35N37 82W23 5:29:32
Warrior 14 1 35N54 81W31 5:26:04
Warsaw 31 1 35N00 78W06 5:12:24
Washburn 23 1 35N17 81W32 5:26:08
Washburn Store 81 1 35N22 81W50 5:27:20
Washington 7 1 35N33 77W03 5:08:12
Washington Park 7 1 35N33 77W02 5:08:08
Watauga 57 1 35N11 83W23 5:33:32
Watauga 95 1 36N11 81W45 5:27:00
Waterlily 27 1 36N20 75W57 5:03:48
Waterville 44 1 35N58 83W11 5:32:44
Watha 71 1 34N39 77W58 5:11:52
Watkins 91 1 36N16 78W30 5:14:00
Watson Crossroads 96 1 35N36 78W07 5:12:28
Watts Crossroads 13 1 35N25 80W36 5:22:24
Waughtown 34 1 36N04 80W14 5:20:56
Waverly 58 1 35N50 82W33 5:30:12
Waves 28 1 35N34 75W28 5:01:52
Waxhaw 90 1 34N56 80W45 5:23:00
Waycross 82 1 34N54 78W03 5:12:12
Waynesville 44 2 35N29 83W00 5:32:00
Wayside 47 1 34N59 79W13 5:16:52
Weaversford 5 1 36N30 81W24 5:25:36
Weaverville 11 1 35N42 82W34 5:30:16
Webbs 55 1 35N32 81W02 5:24:08
Webster 50 1 35N20 83W14 5:32:56
Webster Junction 50 1 35N22 83W14 5:32:56
Webtown 96 1 35N22 77W58 5:11:52
Weddington 90 1 34N56 80W45 5:23:00
Weeksville 70 1 36N13 76W10 5:04:40
Welch 21 1 36N13 76W37 5:06:28
Welch Creek 24 1 34N25 78W38 5:14:32
Welcome 29 1 35N55 80W15 5:21:00
Weldon 42 1 36N25 77W36 5:10:24
Wellons Village 32 1 35N59 78W51 5:15:24
Welmar Heights 26 1 35N02 78W57 5:15:48
Wendell 92 1 35N47 78W22 5:13:28
Wenona 94 1 35N35 76W40 5:06:40
Wentworth 79 1 36N24 79W46 5:19:04
Wesleyan College 64 1 35N58 77W48 5:11:12
Wesley Chapel 90 1 34N59 80W33 5:22:12
West 31 1 35N00 78W06 5:12:24
Westarea 26 1 35N05 78W57 5:15:48
West Asheville 11 1 35N35 82W36 5:30:24
West Bend 34 1 36N06 80W25 5:21:40
West Brook 13 1 35N31 80W38 5:22:32
Westbrooks 82 1 35N13 78W25 5:13:40
West Burlington 1 1 36N04 79W29 5:17:56
West Concord 13 1 35N24 80W36 5:22:24
West Cramerton 36 1 35N14 81W05 5:24:20
West Durham 32 1 36N01 78W56 5:15:44
West End 63 1 35N15 79W34 5:18:16
Western Hills 84 1 35N16 80W26 5:21:44
Western Prong 24 1 34N27 78W46 5:15:04
Westfield 86 1 36N29 80W30 5:22:00
West Gastonia 36 1 35N16 81W10 5:24:40
West Hamlet 77 1 34N54 79W42 5:18:48
West Haven 11 1 35N29 82W31 5:30:04
West Hendersonville 45 1 35N19 82W28 5:29:52
West Hillsborough 68 1 36N05 79W07 5:16:28
West Howellsville 78 1 34N43 78W56 5:15:44
West Jefferson 5 1 36N24 81W30 5:26:00
West Jutts Creek 38 1 35N19 83W48 5:35:12
West Lumberton 78 1 34N36 79W01 5:16:04
West Marion 56 1 35N40 82W01 5:28:04
West Market Street 41 1 36N04 79W50 5:19:20
Westminster 81 1 35N22 81W57 5:27:48
Westmont 76 1 35N42 79W49 5:19:16
West New Bern 25 1 35N06 77W05 5:08:20
Westover 92 1 35N46 78W43 5:14:52
Westover 94 1 35N52 76W45 5:07:00
West Rockingham 77 1 34N56 79W46 5:19:04
West Rocky Mount 64 1 35N58 77W48 5:11:12
Westry 64 1 35N58 77W48 5:11:12
West Salisbury 80 1 35N39 80W29 5:21:56
West Sanford 53 1 35N30 79W12 5:16:48
Westside 80 1 35N33 80W36 5:22:24
Wests Mill 57 1 35N11 83W23 5:33:32
West Statesville 49 1 35N46 80W56 5:23:44
West Tarboro 33 1 35N54 77W32 5:10:08
Whaley 6 1 36N09 81W59 5:27:56
Wharton 7 1 35N32 77W02 5:08:08
Whichard 74 1 35N43 77W16 5:09:04
Whispering Pines 63 1 35N15 79W24 5:17:36
Whitakers 64 1 36N06 77W43 5:10:52
White Cross 68 1 35N55 79W01 5:16:04
Whitehead 3 1 36N27 81W08 5:24:32
White Hill 53 1 35N28 79W10 5:16:40
Whitehouse 81 1 35N29 81W58 5:27:52
Whitehurst 74 1 35N49 77W15 5:09:00
White Lake 9 1 34N39 78W30 5:14:00
White Oak 9 1 34N45 78W42 5:14:48
White Oak 37 1 36N28 76W49 5:07:16
White Oak 42 1 36N11 77W40 5:10:40
White Oak 52 1 34N53 77W12 5:08:48
White Oak 64 1 35N58 77W58 5:11:52
White Plains 86 1 36N30 80W35 5:22:20
White Post 7 1 35N28 76W49 5:07:16
Whiterock 58 1 35N48 82W41 5:30:44
White Rock 95 1 36N10 81W52 5:27:28
Whites 8 1 36N06 76W47 5:07:08
Whites Chapel Church 76 1 35N49 80W15 5:21:00
Whites Creek 9 1 34N30 78W32 5:14:08
Whites Crossroads 8 1 36N12 76W46 5:07:04
Whites Garage 17 1 36N24 79W20 5:17:20
White Store 4 1 34N53 80W16 5:21:04

NORTH CAROLINA

White Sulphur Springs 86	1	36N30	80w35	5:22:20
Whiteville 24	1	34N20	78w42	5:14:48
Whitewater 88	1	35N06	83w00	5:32:00
Whitfield Crossroads 54	1	35N14	77w51	5:11:24
Whitnel 14	1	35N53	81w32	5:26:08
Whitsett 41	1	36N04	79w34	5:18:16
Whittier 50	2	35N26	83w22	5:33:28
Whortonville 69	1	35N06	76w43	5:06:52
Whynot 76	1	35N32	79w46	5:19:04
Wiccacanee 66	1	36N27	77w19	5:09:16
Wiggins Crossroads 33	1	35N54	77w32	5:10:08
Wilbanks 98	1	35N48	77w52	5:11:28
Wilbar 97	1	36N16	81w19	5:25:16
Wilbon 92	1	35N35	78w48	5:15:12
Wilbourns Store 39	1	36N33	78w47	5:15:08
Wilders 51	1	35N43	78w21	5:13:24
Wilders Grove 92	1	35N48	78w38	5:14:32
Wildwood 16	1	34N42	76w50	5:07:20
Wilgrove 60	1	35N12	80w45	5:23:00
Wilkerson Cross Roads 98	1	35N36	78w07	5:12:28
Wilkesboro 97	1	36N09	81w10	5:24:40
Wilkinson Boulevard 60	1	35N14	80w53	5:23:32
Willard 71	1	34N42	77w59	5:11:56
Willeyton 37	1	36N30	76w46	5:07:04
William 19	1	35N49	79w01	5:16:04
Williamsboro 91	1	36N21	78w23	5:13:32
Williamsburg 49	1	35N57	80w46	5:23:04
Williamsburg 79	1	36N18	79w36	5:18:24
Williams Cross Roads 96	1	35N11	78w04	5:12:16
Williamson Crossroads 24	1	34N19	78w50	5:15:20
Williamsons 83	1	34N46	79w36	5:18:24
Williamston 59	1	35N51	77w04	5:08:16
Willis Landing 67	1	34N43	77w14	5:08:56
Williston 16	1	34N48	76w31	5:06:04
Willits 50	2	35N22	83w14	5:32:56
Willow 37	1	36N21	76w36	5:06:24
Willow Green 40	1	35N28	77w25	5:09:40
Willow Spring 92	1	35N36	78w44	5:14:56
Wilmar 7	1	35N18	77w09	5:08:36
Wil-mar Park 13	1	35N25	80w36	5:22:24
Wilmington 65	3	34N14	77w55	5:11:40
Wilmington Beach 65	3	34N13	77w55	5:11:40
Wilmot 50	2	35N26	83w22	5:33:28
Wilson 98	1	35N44	77w55	5:11:40
Wilson Creek 14	1	35N58	81w46	5:27:04
Wilson Mills 51	1	35N35	78w22	5:13:28
Wilsons Creek 6	1	36N02	81w50	5:27:20
Wilsons Mill 51	1	35N35	78w21	5:13:24
Wilton 39	1	36N06	78w27	5:13:48
Wind Blow 62	1	35N13	79w38	5:18:32
Winders Cross Roads 99	1	36N06	80w46	5:23:04
Windom 100	1	35N55	82w18	5:29:12
Windsor 8	1	36N00	76w57	5:07:48
Windy Gap 97	1	36N10	81w08	5:24:32
Winfall 72	1	36N13	76w28	5:05:52
Wing 61	1	36N01	82w09	5:28:36
Wingate 90	1	34N59	80w26	5:21:44
Winnabow 10	1	34N09	78w06	5:12:24
Winstead Crossroads 64	1	35N48	77w52	5:11:28
Winsteadville 7	1	35N32	76w37	5:06:28
Winston-Salem 34	1	36N06	80w15	5:21:00
Winter Park 65	3	34N13	77w55	5:11:40
Winterville 74	1	35N32	77w24	5:09:36
Winton 46	1	36N24	76w56	5:07:44
Wise 93	1	36N29	78w10	5:12:40
Wise Forks 52	1	35N13	77w26	5:09:44
Wishart 78	1	34N35	78w55	5:15:40
Wittenberg 2	1	35N50	81w17	5:25:08
Wolf Mountain 50	1	35N16	83w07	5:32:28
Wolf Pit 77	1	34N53	79w47	5:19:08
Wolfscrape 31	1	35N08	77w59	5:11:56
Wood 35	1	36N08	78w12	5:12:48
Woodard 8	1	36N03	76w57	5:07:48
Woodard 98	1	35N44	77w55	5:11:40
Woodburn 10	1	34N15	78w03	5:12:12
Wood Dale 65	3	34N13	77w55	5:11:40
Woodfin 11	1	35N37	82w33	5:30:12
Woodford 5	1	36N18	81w36	5:26:24
Woodington 54	1	35N09	77w36	5:10:24
Woodland 66	1	36N19	77w12	5:08:48
Woodlawn 36	1	35N16	81w07	5:24:28
Woodlawn 56	1	35N47	82w02	5:28:08
Woodleaf 80	1	35N46	80w35	5:22:20
Woodleigh 27	1	36N31	75w56	5:03:44
Woodrow 25	1	35N06	77w05	5:08:20
Woodrow 44	1	35N35	82w51	5:31:24
Woodsdale 73	1	36N29	78w59	5:15:56
Woodside 71	1	34N22	77w49	5:11:16
Woodville 8	1	36N04	77w11	5:08:44
Woodville 72	1	36N11	76w28	5:05:52
Woodville 86	1	36N30	80w35	5:22:20
Woodworth 91	1	36N19	78w24	5:13:36
Wootens Crossroads 24	1	34N29	78w39	5:14:36
Wootens Crossroads 40	1	35N36	77w42	5:10:48
Wootens Crossroads 54	1	35N16	77w35	5:10:20
Wootentown 7	1	35N32	77w02	5:08:08
Worthville 76	1	35N48	79w46	5:19:04
Wrightsboro 65	3	34N13	77w55	5:11:40
Wrightsville 65	3	34N13	77w48	5:11:12
Wrightsville Beach 65	3	34N12	77w48	5:11:12
Yadkin 80	1	35N39	80w29	5:21:56
Yadkin 85	1	36N19	80w22	5:21:28
Yadkin College 29	1	35N53	80w23	5:21:32
Yadkin Junction 65	3	34N13	77w55	5:11:40
Yadkin Junction 80	1	35N39	80w29	5:21:56
Yadkin Valley 14	1	36N01	81w30	5:26:00
Yadkinville 99	1	36N08	80w39	5:22:36
Yamacraw 71	1	34N32	78w10	5:12:40
Yanceyville 17	1	36N24	79w20	5:17:20
Yates Hill 77	1	34N56	79w46	5:19:04
Yatesville 7	1	35N37	76w52	5:07:28
Yaupon Beach 10	1	33N54	78w05	5:12:20
Yeatsville 7	1	35N28	76w49	5:07:16
Yellow Creek 38	1	35N25	83w53	5:35:32
Yeopim 21	1	36N03	76w30	5:06:00
York 93	1	36N25	78w17	5:13:08
Youngsville 35	1	36N01	78w29	5:13:56
Zebulon 92	1	35N49	78w19	5:13:16
Zephyr 86	1	36N15	80w52	5:23:28
Zionville 95	1	36N21	81w45	5:27:00
Zirconia 45	1	35N09	82w25	5:29:40

TIME TABLES

ND # 1

Date	Time	Zone
Before 11/18/1883		LMT
11/18/1883	12:00	CST
3/31/1918	02:00	CWT
10/27/1918	02:00	CST
3/30/1919	02:00	CWT
10/26/1919	02:00	CST
2/09/1942	02:00	CWT
9/30/1945	02:00	CST
4/30/1967	02:00	US#1

ND # 2

Date	Time	Zone
Before 11/18/1883		LMT
11/18/1883	12:00	CST
3/31/1918	02:00	CWT
10/27/1918	02:00	CST
3/30/1919	02:00	CWT
10/26/1919	02:00	CST
2/09/1942	02:00	CWT
9/30/1945	02:00	CST
4/28/1957	02:00	CDT
10/27/1957	02:00	CST
5/31/1958	02:00	CDT
9/02/1958	02:00	CST
5/30/1959	02:00	CDT
9/08/1959	02:00	CST
4/30/1967	02:00	US#1

ND # 3

Date	Time	Zone
Before 11/18/1883		LMT
11/18/1883	12:00	CST
3/31/1918	02:00	CWT
10/27/1918	02:00	CST
3/30/1919	02:00	CWT
10/26/1919	02:00	CST
2/09/1942	02:00	CWT
9/30/1945	02:00	CST
4/28/1957	02:00	CDT
10/27/1957	02:00	CST
4/30/1967	02:00	US#1

ND # 4

Date	Time	Zone
Before 11/18/1883		LMT
11/18/1883	12:00	CST
3/31/1918	02:00	CWT
10/27/1918	02:00	CST
3/30/1919	02:00	CWT
10/26/1919	02:00	CST
2/09/1942	02:00	CWT
9/30/1945	02:00	CST
5/13/1957	00:01	CDT
10/27/1957	02:00	CST
4/30/1967	02:00	US#1

ND # 5

Date	Time	Zone
Before 11/18/1883		LMT
11/18/1883	12:00	CST
3/31/1918	02:00	CWT
10/27/1918	02:00	CST
3/30/1919	02:00	CWT
10/26/1919	02:00	CST
2/09/1942	02:00	CWT
9/30/1945	02:00	CST
4/28/1957	02:00	CDT
5/27/1957	00:01	CST
4/30/1967	02:00	US#1

ND # 6

Date	Time	Zone
Before 11/18/1883		LMT
11/18/1883	12:00	CST
3/31/1918	02:00	CWT
10/27/1918	02:00	CST
3/30/1919	02:00	CWT
10/26/1919	02:00	CST
2/09/1942	02:00	CWT
9/30/1945	02:00	CST
4/28/1957	02:00	CDT
5/25/1957	00:01	CST
4/30/1967	02:00	US#1

ND # 7

Date	Time	Zone
Before 11/18/1883		LMT
11/18/1883	12:00	CST
3/31/1918	02:00	CWT
10/27/1918	02:00	CST
3/30/1919	02:00	CWT
10/26/1919	02:00	CST
2/09/1942	02:00	CWT
9/30/1945	02:00	CST
4/28/1957	02:00	CDT
10/27/1957	02:00	CST
5/31/1958	02:00	CDT
9/02/1958	02:00	CST
5/30/1959	02:00	CDT
9/08/1959	02:00	CST
5/30/1960	02:00	CDT
9/06/1960	02:00	CST
4/30/1967	02:00	US#1

ND # 8

Date	Time	Zone
Before 11/18/1883		LMT
11/18/1883	12:00	CST
3/31/1918	02:00	CWT
10/27/1918	02:00	CST
3/30/1919	02:00	CWT
10/26/1919	02:00	CST
2/09/1942	02:00	CWT
9/30/1945	02:00	CST
4/28/1957	02:00	CDT
10/27/1957	02:00	CST
5/31/1958	02:00	CDT
9/02/1958	02:00	CST
5/30/1959	02:00	CDT
9/08/1959	02:00	CST
5/22/1960	02:00	CDT
9/22/1960	02:00	CST
4/30/1967	02:00	US#1

ND # 9

Date	Time	Zone
Before 11/18/1883		LMT
11/18/1883	12:00	MST
3/31/1918	02:00	MWT
10/27/1918	02:00	MST
3/30/1919	02:00	MWT
10/26/1919	02:00	MST
2/09/1942	02:00	MWT
9/30/1945	02:00	MST
4/30/1967	02:00	US#1

ND # 10

Date	Time	Zone
Before 11/18/1883		LMT
11/18/1883	12:00	MST
3/31/1918	02:00	MWT
10/27/1918	02:00	MST
3/30/1919	02:00	MWT
10/26/1919	02:00	MST
2/09/1942	02:00	MWT
9/30/1945	02:00	MST
5/15/1952	02:00	MDT
9/15/1952	02:00	MST
5/15/1953	02:00	MDT
9/15/1953	02:00	MST
5/15/1954	02:00	MDT
9/15/1954	02:00	MST
5/15/1955	02:00	MDT
9/15/1955	02:00	MST
5/15/1956	02:00	MDT
9/15/1956	02:00	MST
5/15/1957	02:00	MDT
9/15/1957	02:00	MST
5/15/1958	02:00	MDT
9/15/1958	02:00	MST
5/15/1959	02:00	MDT
9/15/1959	02:00	MST
5/15/1960	02:00	CST
4/30/1967	02:00	US#1

COUNTIES

1 Adams
2 Barnes
3 Benson
4 Billings
5 Bottineau
6 Bowman
7 Burke
8 Burleigh
9 Cass
10 Cavalier
11 Dickey
12 Divide
13 Dunn
14 Eddy
15 Emmons
16 Foster
17 Golden Valley
18 Grand Forks
19 Grant
20 Griggs
21 Hettinger
22 Kidder
23 Lamoure
24 Logan
25 McHenry
26 McIntosh
27 McKenzie
28 McLean
29 Mercer
30 Morton
31 Mountrail
32 Nelson
33 Oliver
34 Pembina
35 Pierce
36 Ramsey
37 Ransom
38 Renville
39 Richland
40 Rolette
41 Sargent
42 Sheridan
43 Sioux
44 Slope
45 Stark
46 Steele
47 Stutsman
48 Towner
49 Traill
50 Walsh
51 Ward
52 Wells
53 Williams

Place	Table	Lat	Long	Time
Abercrombie 39	1	46N27	96w44	6:26:56
Absaraka 9	1	46N59	97w24	6:29:36
Adams 50	1	48N25	98w05	6:32:20
Adrian 23	1	46N36	98w33	6:34:12
Agate 40	1	48N37	99w30	6:38:00
Akra 34	1	48N47	97w44	6:30:56
Alamo 53	1	48N35	103w28	6:53:52
Alexander 27	1	47N51	103w39	6:54:36
Alfred 23	1	46N36	99w00	6:36:00
Alice 9	1	46N46	97w33	6:30:12
Alkabo 12	1	48N52	103w53	6:55:32
Almont 30	9	46N44	101w30	6:46:00
Alsen 10	1	48N38	98w42	6:34:48
Ambrose 12	1	48N57	103w29	6:53:56
Amenia 9	1	47N00	97w13	6:28:52
Amidon 44	9	46N29	103w19	6:53:16
Anamoose 25	1	47N53	100w15	6:41:00
Aneta 32	1	47N41	97w59	6:31:56
Anselm 37	1	46N35	97w30	6:30:00
Antler 5	1	48N59	101w17	6:45:08
Appam 53	1	48N35	103w28	6:53:52
Apple Valley 8	1	46N49	100w32	6:42:08
Ardoch 50	1	48N12	97w20	6:29:20
Arena 8	1	47N08	100w10	6:40:40
Argusville 9	1	47N03	96w56	6:27:44
Arnegard 27	1	47N49	103w27	6:53:48
Arthur 9	1	47N06	97w13	6:28:52
Arvilla 18	1	47N55	97w30	6:30:00
Ashley 26	1	46N02	99w22	6:37:28
Auburn 50	1	48N25	97w25	6:29:40
Aurelia 51	1	48N31	101w53	6:47:32
Aylmer 35	1	47N56	100w12	6:40:48
Ayr 9	1	47N03	97w29	6:29:56
Backoo 34	1	48N50	97w43	6:30:52
Baker 3	1	48N10	99w39	6:38:36
Baldwin 8	1	47N02	100w45	6:43:00
Balfour 25	1	47N57	100w32	6:42:08
Balta 35	1	48N10	100w02	6:40:08
Bantry 25	1	48N30	100w37	6:42:28
Barks Spur 48	1	48N38	99w06	6:36:24
Barlow 16	1	47N34	99w09	6:36:36
Barney 39	1	46N16	97w00	6:28:00
Bartlett 36	1	48N03	98w26	6:33:44
Barton 35	1	48N30	100w11	6:40:44
Bathgate 34	1	48N53	97w29	6:29:56
Battleview 7	1	48N35	102w47	6:51:08
Beach 17	9	46N55	104w00	6:56:00
Belcourt 40	1	48N50	99w45	6:39:00
Belden 31	1	48N09	102w22	6:49:28
Belfield 45	9	46N53	103w12	6:52:48
Benedict 28	1	47N50	101w05	6:44:20
Bentley 21	9	46N20	102w04	6:48:16
Berea 2	1	46N56	98w00	6:32:00
Bergen 25	1	48N00	100w43	6:42:52
Berlin 23	1	46N23	98w29	6:33:56
Berthold 51	1	48N19	101w44	6:46:56
Berwick 25	1	48N22	100w15	6:41:00
Beulah 29	9	47N16	101w47	6:47:08
Big Bend 28	1	47N33	101w13	6:44:52
Binford 20	1	47N34	98w21	6:33:24
Bisbee 48	1	48N37	99w23	6:37:32
Bismarck 8	1	46N48	100w47	6:43:08
Blabon 46	1	47N20	97w43	6:30:52
Blaisdell 31	1	48N20	102w05	6:48:20
Blanchard 49	1	47N21	97w13	6:28:52
Bonetraill 53	1	48N26	103w51	6:55:24
Bordulac 16	1	47N23	98w58	6:35:52
Bottineau 5	1	48N50	100w27	6:41:48
Bowbells 7	1	48N48	102w15	6:49:00
Bowdon 52	1	47N28	99w43	6:38:52
Bowesmont 34	1	48N41	97w10	6:28:40
Bowman 6	9	46N11	103w24	6:53:36
Braddock 15	1	46N34	100w06	6:40:24
Brampton 41	1	46N00	97w47	6:31:08
Brantford 14	1	47N36	98w55	6:35:40
Breien 30	9	46N23	100w56	6:43:44
Bremen 52	1	47N45	99w23	6:37:32
Brinsmade 3	1	48N11	99w19	6:37:16
Brocket 36	1	48N13	98w21	6:33:24
Buchanan 47	1	47N04	98w50	6:35:20
Bucyrus 1	9	46N04	102w47	6:51:08
Buffalo 9	1	46N55	97w33	6:30:12
Buffalo Springs 6	9	46N11	103w24	6:53:36
Buford	1	48N00	104w00	6:56:00
Burlington 51	1	48N17	101w26	6:45:44
Burnstad 24	1	46N23	99w38	6:38:32
Burt 21	9	46N22	102w10	6:48:40
Butte 28	1	47N50	100w40	6:42:40
Buttzville 37	1	46N26	97w41	6:30:44
Buxton 49	1	47N36	97w06	6:28:24
Caledonia 49	1	47N28	96w53	6:27:32
Calio 10	1	48N38	98w56	6:35:44
Calvin 10	1	48N51	98w56	6:35:44
Cando 48	1	48N32	99w12	6:36:48
Cannon Ball 43	9	46N25	100w38	6:42:32
Canton 34	1	48N41	97w40	6:30:40
Carbury 5	1	48N53	100w33	6:42:12
Carpio 51	1	48N27	101w43	6:46:52
Carrington 16	1	47N27	99w08	6:36:32
Carson 19	9	46N25	101w34	6:46:16
Cartwright 27	9	47N51	103w56	6:55:44
Cashel 50	1	48N29	97w18	6:29:12
Casselton 9	1	46N54	97w13	6:28:52
Cathay 52	1	47N33	99w25	6:37:40
Cavalier 34	1	48N48	97w37	6:30:28
Cayuga 41	1	46N04	97w23	6:29:32
Center 33	9	47N07	101w18	6:45:12
Central Morton 30	9	46N50	101w30	6:46:00
Central Pierce 35	1	48N09	100w03	6:40:12
Chaffee 9	1	46N46	97w21	6:29:24
Charbonneau 27	1	47N50	103w39	6:54:36
Charlson 27	1	48N04	102w52	6:51:28
Chaseley 52	1	47N27	99w49	6:39:16
Christine 39	1	46N35	96w48	6:27:12
Churchs Ferry 36	1	48N16	99w12	6:36:48
Cleveland 47	1	46N54	99w06	6:36:24
Clifford 49	1	47N21	97w24	6:29:36
Clyde 10	1	48N46	98w54	6:35:36
Cogswell 41	1	46N07	97w47	6:31:08
Coleharbor 28	1	47N33	101w13	6:44:52
Colfax 39	1	46N28	96w53	6:27:32
Colgan 12	1	48N55	103w47	6:55:08
Colgate 46	1	47N15	97w39	6:30:36
Columbus 7	1	48N54	102w47	6:51:08
Concrete 34	1	48N45	97w56	6:31:44
Conway 50	1	48N14	97w41	6:30:44
Cooperstown 20	1	47N27	98w08	6:32:32
Corinth 53	1	48N35	103w28	6:53:52
Coteau 7	1	48N46	102w19	6:49:16
Coulee 31	1	48N33	102w01	6:48:04
Courtenay 47	1	47N13	98w34	6:34:16
Crary 36	1	48N04	98w38	6:34:32
Crete 41	1	46N12	97w58	6:31:52
Crosby 12	1	48N55	103w18	6:53:12
Crystal 34	1	48N36	97w40	6:30:40
Crystal Springs 22	1	46N53	99w28	6:37:52
Cuba 2	1	46N56	98w00	6:32:00
Cummings 49	1	47N31	97w05	6:28:20
Dahlen 32	1	48N09	97w56	6:31:44
Dakota Boys Ranch 51	1	48N20	101w19	6:45:16
Davenport 9	1	46N43	97w04	6:28:16
Dawson 22	1	46N52	99w45	6:39:00
Dazey 2	1	47N11	98w12	6:32:48
Deering 25	1	48N24	101w03	6:44:12
De Lamere 41	1	46N16	97w20	6:29:20
Denbigh 25	1	48N19	100w35	6:42:20
Denhoff 42	1	47N29	100w16	6:41:04
Des Lacs 51	1	48N16	101w34	6:46:16
Des Lacs Valley 51	1	48N39	102w01	6:48:04
Devils Lake 36	3	48N07	98w52	6:35:28
Dickey 23	1	46N32	98w27	6:33:48
Dickinson 45	9	46N53	102w47	6:51:08
Dodge 13	9	47N18	102w12	6:48:48
Dogden Butte 28	1	47N46	100w50	6:43:20
Donnybrook 51	1	48N31	101w53	6:47:32
Dore	9	47N56	104w02	6:56:08
Douglas 51	1	47N51	101w30	6:46:00
Downtown 51	1	48N20	101w19	6:45:16
Doyon 36	1	48N03	98w32	6:34:08
Drake 25	1	47N55	100w23	6:41:32
Drayton 34	3	48N38	97w11	6:28:44
Dresden 10	1	48N46	98w22	6:33:28
Driscoll 8	1	46N51	100w09	6:40:36
Dunn Center 13	9	47N21	102w37	6:50:28
Dunning 5	1	48N41	101w06	6:44:24
Dunseith 40	1	48N50	100w03	6:40:12
Durbin 9	1	46N48	97w09	6:28:36
Dwight 39	1	46N18	96w44	6:26:56
East Adams 1	9	46N04	102w12	6:48:48
East Bowman 6	9	46N08	103w15	6:53:00
East Eddy 14	1	47N45	98w43	6:34:52
East Fairview 27	9	47N51	104w03	6:56:12
East Foster 16	1	47N28	98w41	6:34:44
East Griggs 20	1	47N27	98w07	6:32:28

NORTH DAKOTA

East Hettinger 21 9 46N26 102w22 6:49:28
East Kidder 22 1 46N58 99w38 6:38:32
East La Moure 23 1 46N29 98w18 6:33:12
East Logan 24 1 46N27 99w16 6:37:04
East Mercer 29 9 47N23 101w38 6:46:32
East Ramsey 36 1 48N14 98w27 6:33:48
East Sheridan 42 1 47N31 100w12 6:40:48
East Slope 44 9 46N28 103w07 6:52:28
East Stark 45 9 46N48 102w20 6:49:20
Eckelson 2 1 46N56 98w20 6:33:20
Eckman 5 1 48N40 101w03 6:44:12
Edgeley 23 1 46N22 98w43 6:34:52
Edinburg 50 1 48N30 97w52 6:31:28
Edmore 36 1 48N25 98w27 6:33:48
Edmunds 47 1 47N10 98w54 6:35:36
Egeland 48 1 48N38 99w06 6:36:24
Eldridge 47 1 46N54 98w51 6:35:24
Elgin 19 9 46N24 101w51 6:47:24
Ellendale 11 1 46N00 98w32 6:34:08
Elliott 37 1 46N24 97w49 6:31:16
Embden 9 1 46N54 97w21 6:29:24
Emerado 18 1 47N55 97w22 6:29:28
Emmet 28 1 47N39 101w39 6:46:36
Emrick 52 1 47N33 99w25 6:37:40
Enderlin 37 1 46N38 97w36 6:30:24
Englevale 37 1 46N24 97w55 6:31:40
Epping 53 1 48N17 103w21 6:53:24
Erie 9 1 47N07 97w23 6:29:32
Esmond 3 1 48N02 99w46 6:39:04
Fairdale 50 1 48N30 98w14 6:32:56
Fairfield 4 9 47N11 103w14 6:52:56
Fairmount 39 1 46N03 96w36 6:26:24
Falkirk 28 1 47N22 101w06 6:44:24
Fargo 9 7 46N53 96w48 6:27:12
Fessenden 52 1 47N39 99w38 6:38:32
Fillmore 3 1 48N11 99w48 6:39:12
Fingal 2 1 46N46 97w47 6:31:08
Finley 46 5 47N31 97w50 6:31:20
Flasher 30 9 46N27 101w14 6:44:56
Flaxton 7 1 48N54 102w24 6:49:36
Flora 3 1 47N58 99w32 6:38:08
Fonda 40 1 48N40 99w50 6:39:20
Forbes 11 1 45N57 98w47 6:35:08
Fordville 50 1 48N13 97w48 6:31:12
Forest River 50 1 48N13 97w28 6:29:52
Forest River Colony 18
1 48N15 97w48 6:31:12
Forman 41 1 46N07 97w38 6:30:32
Fort Berthold Indian Res 13
1 47N59 102w29 6:49:56
Fort Clark 33 9 47N14 101w15 6:45:00
Fort Lincoln Estates 8
1 46N49 100w47 6:43:08
Fort Ransom 37 1 46N31 97w56 6:31:44
Fort Rice 30 1 46N32 100w35 6:42:20
Fort Totten 3 1 47N59 99w00 6:36:00
Fort Totten Indian Res 3
1 47N59 99w00 6:36:00
Fortuna 12 1 48N55 103w47 6:55:08
Fort Yates 43 9 46N05 100w38 6:42:32
Four Bears 27 1 47N54 102w49 6:51:16
Four Bears Health Center 27
1 47N59 102w29 6:49:56
Foxholm 51 1 48N22 101w35 6:46:20
Frazier 2 1 47N10 98w27 6:33:48
Freda 9 46N21 101w10 6:44:40
Fredonia 24 1 46N20 99w06 6:36:24
Fryburg 4 9 46N53 103w12 6:52:48
Fullerton 11 1 46N10 98w26 6:33:44
Gackle 24 1 46N38 99w09 6:36:36
Galchutt 39 1 46N23 96w49 6:27:16
Galesburg 49 1 47N16 97w24 6:29:36
Gardar 34 1 48N35 97w53 6:31:32
Gardena 5 1 48N42 100w30 6:42:00
Gardner 9 1 47N09 96w58 6:27:52
Garrison 28 1 47N40 101w25 6:45:40
Garske 36 1 48N17 98w53 6:35:32
Gascoyne 6 9 46N07 103w05 6:52:20
Geneseo 41 1 46N11 97w17 6:29:08
Gilby 18 1 48N05 97w28 6:29:52
Gladstone 45 9 46N52 102w34 6:50:16
Glasston 34 1 48N42 97w27 6:29:48
Glenburn 38 1 48N31 101w13 6:44:52
Glenfield 16 1 47N27 98w34 6:34:16
Glen Ullin 30 9 46N49 101w50 6:47:20
Glenwood Estates 8
1 46N49 100w47 6:43:08
Goldenvalley 29 9 47N17 102w04 6:48:16
Goldwin 47 1 47N09 99w18 6:37:12
Golva 17 9 46N44 103w59 6:55:56
Goodrich 42 1 47N29 100w08 6:40:32
Grace City 16 1 47N33 98w48 6:35:12
Grafton 50 3 48N25 97w25 6:29:40
Grand Forks 18 2 47N55 97w03 6:28:12
Grand Forks Air Force Base 18
1 47N56 97w12 6:28:48
Grandin 9 1 47N14 97w00 6:28:00
Grand Rapids 23 1 46N16 98w18 6:33:12
Grano 38 1 48N37 101w35 6:46:20
Granville 25 1 48N16 100w47 6:43:08
Grassy Butte 27 9 47N24 103w15 6:53:00
Great Bend 39 1 46N09 96w48 6:27:12
Green Acres Estates 8
1 46N49 100w47 6:43:08
Greene 38 1 48N44 101w50 6:47:20
Grenora 53 1 48N37 103w56 6:55:44
Guelph 11 1 46N01 98w14 6:32:56
Guthrie 25 1 48N00 100w23 6:41:32
Gwinner 41 1 46N14 97w40 6:30:40
Hague 15 1 46N02 99w59 6:39:56
Halliday 13 9 47N21 102w20 6:49:20
Hallson 34 1 48N48 97w37 6:30:28
Hamar 14 1 47N51 98w34 6:34:16
Hamberg 52 1 47N46 99w31 6:38:04

Hamilton 34 1 48N48 97w27 6:29:48
Hamlet 53 1 48N38 103w11 6:52:44
Hampden 36 1 48N32 98w40 6:34:40
Hankinson 39 1 46N04 96w54 6:27:36
Hanks 53 1 48N36 103w48 6:55:12
Hanks Corner 10 1 48N45 97w56 6:31:44
Hannaford 20 1 47N19 98w11 6:32:44
Hannah 10 1 48N58 98w42 6:34:48
Hannover 33 9 47N07 101w26 6:45:44
Hansboro 48 1 48N57 99w23 6:37:32
Harlow 3 1 48N10 99w31 6:38:04
Hartland 51 1 48N27 101w43 6:46:52
Harvey 52 1 47N47 99w56 6:39:44
Harwood 9 2 46N59 96w53 6:27:32
Hastings 2 1 46N41 97w58 6:31:52
Hatton 49 1 47N38 97w27 6:29:48
Havana 41 1 45N57 97w37 6:30:28
Havelock 21 9 46N29 102w45 6:51:00
Haynes 1 9 45N59 102w28 6:49:52
Hazelton 15 1 46N29 100w17 6:41:08
Hazen 29 9 47N18 101w38 6:46:32
Heart Butte 19 9 46N29 101w52 6:47:28
Heaton 52 1 47N29 99w33 6:38:12
Hebron 30 9 46N54 102w03 6:48:12
Heil 19 9 46N24 101w42 6:46:48
Heimdal 52 1 47N47 99w39 6:38:36
Hensel 34 1 48N41 97w40 6:30:40
Hensler 33 9 47N16 101w05 6:44:20
Hesper 3 1 47N58 99w32 6:38:08
Hettinger 1 9 46N00 102w39 6:50:36
Hickson 9 1 46N40 96w49 6:27:16
Hillsboro 49 1 47N26 97w03 6:28:12
Holmes 18 1 47N40 97w06 6:28:24
Home On The Range For Boys 17
9 46N55 103w50 6:55:20
Honeyford 18 1 48N05 97w28 6:29:52
Hoople 50 1 48N32 97w38 6:30:32
Hope 46 1 47N19 97w43 6:30:52
Horace 9 1 46N45 96w54 6:27:36
Hovey Mobile Park 10
1 48N29 98w14 6:32:56
Huff 30 10 46N50 100w53 6:43:32
Hull 15 1 46N02 100w00 6:40:00
Hunter 9 1 47N12 97w13 6:28:52
Hurdsfield 52 1 47N27 99w56 6:39:44
Inkster 18 1 48N09 97w39 6:30:36
Jamestown 47 1 46N54 98w42 6:34:48
Jessie 20 1 47N33 98w15 6:33:00
Johnsons Corner 27
1 47N56 102w56 6:51:44
Johnstown 18 1 48N09 97w28 6:29:52
Joliette 34 1 48N49 97w14 6:28:56
Juanita 16 1 47N30 98w41 6:34:44
Jud 23 1 46N32 98w54 6:35:36
Judson 30 9 46N50 101w17 6:45:08
Karlsruhe 25 1 48N06 100w37 6:42:28
Kathryn 2 1 46N41 97w58 6:31:52
Keene 27 1 47N56 102w56 6:51:44
Kelso 49 1 47N24 97w03 6:28:12
Kelvin 40 1 48N49 100w04 6:40:16
Kempton 18 1 47N44 97w34 6:30:16
Kenaston 51 1 48N41 102w05 6:48:20
Kenmare 51 1 48N41 102w05 6:48:20
Kensal 47 1 47N18 98w44 6:34:56
Kief 25 1 47N51 100w31 6:42:04
Killdeer 13 9 47N22 102w45 6:51:00
Kindred 9 1 46N39 97w01 6:28:04
Kintyre 15 1 46N33 99w57 6:39:48
Kloten 32 1 47N43 98w05 6:32:20
Knox 3 1 48N20 99w41 6:38:44
Kongsberg 25 1 48N01 100w50 6:43:20
Kramer 5 1 48N42 100w43 6:42:52
Kulm 23 1 46N18 98w57 6:35:48
Lake Metigoshe 5 1 48N50 100w27 6:41:48
Lake Williams 22 1 47N09 99w47 6:39:08
Lakewood Park 36 1 48N07 98w52 6:35:28
Lakota 32 1 48N02 98w21 6:33:24
La Moure 23 1 46N21 98w18 6:33:12
Landa 5 1 48N54 100w55 6:43:40
Langdon 10 4 48N46 98w22 6:33:28
Lankin 50 1 48N19 97w55 6:31:40
Lansford 5 1 48N38 101w23 6:45:32
Larimore 18 1 47N54 97w38 6:30:32
Lark 19 9 46N27 101w24 6:45:36
Larson 7 1 48N53 102w52 6:51:28
Lawton 36 1 48N18 98w22 6:33:28
Leal 2 1 47N06 98w19 6:33:16
Leeds 3 1 48N17 99w27 6:37:48
Lefor 45 9 46N41 102w34 6:50:16
Lehigh 45 9 46N53 102w47 6:51:08
Lehr 26 1 46N17 99w21 6:37:24
Leith 19 9 46N22 101w38 6:46:32
Leonard 9 1 46N39 97w15 6:29:00
Leroy 34 1 48N55 97w45 6:31:00
Leyden 34 1 48N50 97w43 6:30:52
Lidgerwood 39 1 46N05 97w09 6:28:36
Lignite 7 1 48N53 102w34 6:50:16
Linton 15 1 46N16 100w14 6:40:56
Lisbon 37 1 46N27 97w41 6:30:44
Litchville 2 1 46N39 98w12 6:32:48
Livona 15 1 46N30 100w33 6:42:12
Logan 51 1 48N20 101w19 6:45:16
Loma 10 1 48N38 98w32 6:34:08
Loraine 38 1 48N52 101w34 6:46:16
Lostwood 31 1 48N29 102w25 6:49:40
Lucca 2 1 46N42 97w43 6:30:52
Ludden 11 1 46N01 98w07 6:32:28
Lunds Valley 31 1 48N19 102w23 6:49:32
Luverne 46 1 47N15 97w56 6:31:44
Lynchburg 9 1 46N48 97w09 6:28:36
Maddock 3 1 47N58 99w32 6:38:08
Maida 1 49N00 98w22 6:33:28
Maida 10 1 47N46 98w11 6:32:44
Makoti 51 1 47N58 101w48 6:47:12
Mandan 30 10 46N50 100w54 6:43:36

NORTH DAKOTA

Mandaree 27 1 47N43 102w41 6:50:44
Manfred 52 1 47N42 99w45 6:39:00
Manitou 31 1 48N19 102w32 6:50:08
Manning 13 9 47N14 102w46 6:51:04
Mantador 39 1 46N10 96w59 6:27:56
Manvel 18 1 48N05 97w11 6:28:44
Mapes 32 1 48N02 98w13 6:32:52
Mapleton 9 1 46N53 97w02 6:28:08
Marion 23 1 46N37 98w20 6:33:20
Marmarth 44 9 46N18 103w54 6:55:36
Marshall 13 9 47N08 102w20 6:49:20
Martin 42 1 47N50 100w07 6:40:28
Max 28 1 47N49 101w18 6:45:12
Maxbass 5 1 48N43 101w09 6:44:36
Mayville 49 1 47N30 97w20 6:29:20
Maza 48 1 48N22 99w12 6:36:48
McCanna 18 1 48N00 97w42 6:30:48
McClusky 42 1 47N29 100w27 6:41:48
McGregor 53 1 48N36 102w56 6:51:44
McHenry 16 1 47N35 98w35 6:34:20
McKenzie 8 1 46N50 100w25 6:41:40
McLeod 37 1 46N24 97w18 6:29:12
McVille 32 1 47N46 98w11 6:32:44
Medina 47 1 46N54 99w18 6:37:12
Medora 4 9 46N55 103w31 6:54:04
Mekinock 18 1 48N01 97w22 6:29:28
Melville 16 1 47N27 99w07 6:36:28
Menoken 8 1 46N49 100w32 6:42:08
Mercer 28 1 47N29 100w43 6:42:52
Merricourt 11 1 46N12 98w46 6:35:04
Michigan 32 1 48N01 98w07 6:32:28
Millarton 47 1 46N40 98w45 6:35:00
Milnor 41 1 46N16 97w27 6:29:48
Milton 10 1 48N38 98w03 6:32:12
Minnewaukan 3 1 48N02 99w13 6:36:52
Minot 51 1 48N14 101w18 6:45:12
Minot Base 51 1 48N25 101w20 6:45:20
Minto 50 1 48N17 97w22 6:29:28
Minto West 50 1 48N17 97w31 6:30:04
Moffit 8 1 46N41 100w18 6:41:12
Mohall 38 1 48N46 101w31 6:46:04
Monango 11 1 46N10 98w36 6:34:24
Montpelier 47 1 46N42 98w35 6:34:20
Mooreton 39 1 46N16 96w53 6:27:32
Mott 21 9 46N23 102w20 6:49:20
Mountain 34 1 48N41 97w52 6:31:28
Mount Carmel 10 1 48N46 98w22 6:33:28
Munich 10 1 48N40 98w50 6:35:20
Mylo 40 1 48N38 99w37 6:38:28
Nanson 40 1 48N35 99w47 6:39:08
Napoleon 24 1 46N30 99w46 6:39:04
Nash 50 1 48N28 97w31 6:30:04
Neche 34 1 48N59 97w33 6:30:12
Nekoma 10 1 48N35 98w22 6:33:28
Newburg 5 1 48N43 100w55 6:43:40
New England 21 9 46N32 102w52 6:51:28
New Hradec 13 9 47N00 102w53 6:51:32
New Leipzig 19 9 46N22 101w57 6:47:48
New Rockford 14 1 47N41 99w08 6:36:32
New Salem 30 9 46N51 101w25 6:45:40
New Town 31 1 47N59 102w30 6:50:00
Niagara 18 1 48N00 97w52 6:31:28
Niobe 51 1 48N41 102w13 6:48:52
Nome 2 1 46N41 97w49 6:31:16
Noonan 12 1 48N54 103w01 6:52:04
Norma 38 1 48N44 101w59 6:47:56
North Billings 4 9 47N10 103w15 6:53:00
North Central Mc Lean 28
1 47N44 101w22 6:45:28
Northeast 12 1 48N54 103w19 6:53:16
Northgate 7 1 49N00 102w16 6:49:04
North Kidder 22 1 47N10 99w51 6:39:24
North Lemmon 1 9 45N56 102w10 6:48:40
North Mc Henry 25
1 48N33 100w46 6:43:04
North Nelson 32 1 48N02 98w10 6:32:40
North Pierce 35 1 48N26 99w57 6:39:48
North Ramsey 36 1 48N28 98w37 6:34:28
North Renville 38
1 48N50 101w44 6:46:56
North Sheridan 42
1 47N46 100w20 6:41:20
North Sioux 43 9 46N20 100w41 6:42:44
Northwood 18 1 47N44 97w34 6:30:16
Nortonville 23 1 46N34 98w45 6:35:00
Norwich 25 1 48N15 100w59 6:43:56
Oakes 11 1 46N08 98w06 6:32:24
Oakwood 50 1 48N25 97w25 6:29:40
Oberon 3 1 47N55 99w13 6:36:52
Olga 10 1 48N48 98w03 6:32:12
Omemee 5 1 48N42 100w22 6:41:28
Oriska 2 1 46N56 97w47 6:31:08
Orr 18 1 48N09 97w39 6:30:36
Orrin 35 1 48N06 100w10 6:40:40
Osnabrock 10 1 48N40 98w09 6:32:36
Overly 5 1 48N41 100w09 6:40:36
Page 9 1 47N10 97w34 6:30:16
Palermo 31 1 48N21 102w14 6:48:56
Park River 50 1 48N24 97w45 6:31:00
Parshall 31 1 47N57 102w08 6:48:32
Pekin 32 1 47N48 98w20 6:33:20
Pembina 34 4 48N58 97w15 6:29:00
Penn 36 1 48N13 99w05 6:36:20
Perth 48 1 48N43 99w28 6:37:52
Petersburg 32 1 48N01 98w00 6:32:00
Pettibone 22 1 47N07 99w31 6:38:04
Pick City 29 9 47N31 101w27 6:45:48
Pillsbury 2 1 47N13 97w48 6:31:12
Pingree 47 1 47N10 98w55 6:35:40
Pisek 50 1 48N19 97w43 6:30:52
Plaza 31 1 48N01 101w58 6:47:52
Pleasant Lake 3 1 48N22 99w48 6:39:12
Ponderosa 8 1 46N49 100w47 6:43:08
Porcupine 43 9 46N02 100w55 6:43:40
Portal 7 1 49N00 102w33 6:50:12

Portland 49	1	47N30	97w22	6:29:28
Powers Lake 7	1	48N34	102w39	6:50:36
Prairie View Acres 8	1	46N49	100w47	6:43:08
Price 33	9	47N16	101w05	6:44:20
Prosper 9	2	46N59	96w53	6:27:32
Raleigh 19	9	46N27	101w19	6:45:16
Raub 28	1	47N45	102w03	6:48:12
Rawson 27	1	47N49	103w32	6:54:08
Ray 53	1	48N21	103w10	6:52:40
Reeder 1	9	46N07	102w57	6:51:48
Regan 8	1	47N10	100w32	6:42:08
Regent 21	9	46N25	102w33	6:50:12
Reynolds 18	1	47N40	97w07	6:28:28
Rhame 6	9	46N14	103w39	6:54:36
Richardton 45	9	46N53	102w19	6:49:16
Riverdale 28	1	47N30	101w22	6:45:28
Riverside 9	7	46N55	96w49	6:27:16
Robinson 22	1	47N09	99w47	6:39:08
Rocklake 48	1	48N47	99w15	6:37:00
Rogers 2	1	47N04	98w12	6:32:48
Rolette 40	1	48N40	99w51	6:39:24
Rolla 40	1	48N52	99w37	6:38:28
Rolla Rural 40	1	48N47	99w37	6:38:28
Roseglen 28	1	47N45	101w50	6:47:20
Ross 31	1	48N19	102w33	6:50:12
Roth 5	1	48N55	100w41	6:42:44
Rugby 35	1	48N22	100w00	6:40:00
Ruso 28	1	47N50	100w56	6:43:44
Russell 5	1	48N40	100w54	6:43:36
Ruthville 51	1	48N20	101w19	6:45:16
Rutland 41	1	46N03	97w30	6:30:00
Ryder 51	1	47N55	101w40	6:46:40
Saint Anthony 30	9	46N37	100w55	6:43:40
Saint Benedict 9	1	46N46	96w54	6:27:36
Saint Gertrude 19	9	46N27	101w19	6:45:16
Saint John 40	1	48N57	99w43	6:38:52
Saint Michael 3	1	47N59	98w50	6:35:20
Saint Thomas 34	1	48N37	97w27	6:29:48
Sanborn 2	1	46N57	98w14	6:32:56
Sand Hills 37	1	46N26	97w24	6:29:36
Sanish 31	1	47N58	102w33	6:50:12
Sarles 10	1	48N57	99w00	6:36:00
Sawyer 51	1	48N05	101w03	6:44:12
Schefield 45	9	46N32	102w52	6:51:28
Scranton 6	9	46N09	103w09	6:52:36
Selfridge 43	9	46N02	100w56	6:43:44
Selz 35	1	47N52	99w54	6:39:36
Sentinel Butte 17	9	46N58	103w46	6:55:04
Sharon 46	6	47N36	97w54	6:31:36
Sheldon 37	1	46N35	97w30	6:30:00
Shepard 20	1	47N27	98w07	6:32:28
Sherwood 38	1	48N57	101w38	6:46:32
Sheyenne 14	1	47N50	99w07	6:36:28
Shields 19	9	46N14	101w08	6:44:32
Sibley 2	1	47N13	97w58	6:31:52
Silva 35	1	48N10	99w55	6:39:40
Silver Strip 53	1	48N09	103w37	6:54:28
Simcoe 25	1	48N10	100w52	6:43:28
Sims 30	9	46N43	101w31	6:46:04
Skogmo 42	1	47N52	100w30	6:42:00
Solen 43	9	46N23	100w48	6:43:12
Souris 5	1	48N55	100w41	6:42:44
Southam 36	1	48N04	98w38	6:34:32
South Billings 4	9	46N46	103w26	6:53:44
South Dunn 13	9	47N05	102w36	6:50:24
South Grant 19	9	46N12	101w30	6:46:00
South Heart 45	9	46N52	103w00	6:52:00
South Kidder 22	1	46N47	99w50	6:39:20
South Mc Lean 28	1	47N18	100w55	6:43:40
South Mountrail 31	1	48N01	102w08	6:48:32
South Pierce 35	1	47N57	99w58	6:39:52
South Renville 38	1	48N32	101w32	6:46:08
South Washington 18	1	47N56	97w12	6:28:48
South Wells 52	1	47N26	99w44	6:38:56
Southwest R 12	1	48N48	103w39	6:54:36
Spiritwood 47	1	46N56	98w30	6:34:00
Spiritwood Lake 47	1	46N54	98w43	6:34:52
Spring Brook 53	1	48N18	103w10	6:52:40
Standing Rock Indian Res 43	9	46N06	100w38	6:42:32
Stanley 31	1	48N19	102w23	6:49:32
Stanton 29	9	47N19	101w23	6:45:32
Starkweather 36	1	48N27	98w53	6:35:32
State Hospital 47	1	46N54	98w43	6:34:52
State University 9	7	46N53	96w48	6:27:12
Steele 22	1	46N51	99w55	6:39:40
Sterling 8	1	46N49	100w17	6:41:08
Stirum 41	1	46N13	97w49	6:31:16
Strasburg 15	1	46N08	100w10	6:40:40
Straubville 41	1	46N03	97w54	6:31:36
Streeter 47	1	46N39	99w21	6:37:24
Surrey 51	1	48N14	101w06	6:44:24
Sutton 20	1	47N24	98w27	6:33:48
Sydney	1	46N44	98w46	6:35:04
Sykeston 52	1	47N28	99w24	6:37:36
Taft 49	1	47N24	97w03	6:28:12
Tagus 31	1	48N21	101w56	6:47:44
Tappen 22	1	46N52	99w38	6:38:32
Taylor 45	9	46N54	102w26	6:49:44
Temvik 15	1	46N22	100w15	6:41:00
Thompson 18	1	47N47	97w06	6:28:24
Thorne 40	1	48N40	99w50	6:39:20
Tilden 3	1	48N04	99w15	6:37:00
Tioga 53	1	48N24	102w56	6:51:44
Tokio 3	1	47N55	98w49	6:35:16
Tolley 38	1	48N44	101w50	6:47:20
Tolna 32	1	47N50	98w26	6:33:44
Tower City 9	1	46N56	97w40	6:30:40
Town And Country Shopping Ce 51	1	48N20	101w19	6:45:16
Towner 25	1	48N21	100w25	6:41:40
Trenton 53	1	48N04	103w51	6:55:24
Trotters 17	9	47N19	103w55	6:55:40
Turtle Lake 28	1	47N31	100w54	6:43:36
Turtle Mountain Indian Reser 40	1	48N50	99w45	6:39:00
Turtle Mountains 5	1	48N54	100w20	6:41:20
Tuttle 22	1	47N09	100w00	6:40:00
Twin Buttes 13	9	47N21	102w20	6:49:20
Tyler's Western Village 8	1	46N49	100w47	6:43:08
Underwood 28	1	47N27	101w09	6:44:36
Union 10	1	48N33	97w57	6:31:48
University 18	1	47N56	97w12	6:28:48
Upham 25	1	48N35	100w44	6:42:56
Urbana 2	1	46N56	98w30	6:34:00
Valley City 2	1	46N55	98w00	6:32:00
Velva 25	1	48N04	100w56	6:43:44
Venturia 26	1	46N00	99w33	6:38:12
Verona 23	1	46N22	98w04	6:32:16
Veseleyville 50	1	48N25	97w25	6:29:40
Voltaire 25	1	48N01	100w51	6:43:24
Voss 50	1	48N20	97w27	6:29:48
Wahpeton 39	8	46N16	96w36	6:26:24
Walcott 39	1	46N33	96w56	6:27:44
Wales 10	1	48N54	98w36	6:34:24
Walhalla 34	1	48N55	97w55	6:31:40
Walum 20	1	47N16	98w12	6:32:48
Warren 9	1	46N43	97w04	6:28:16
Warsaw 50	1	48N18	97w23	6:29:32
Warwick 3	1	47N51	98w43	6:34:52
Washburn 28	1	47N17	101w02	6:44:08
Watford City 27	1	47N48	103w17	6:53:08
Webster 36	1	48N17	98w53	6:35:32
Wellsburg 52	1	47N50	99w46	6:39:04
Werner 13	9	47N21	102w27	6:49:48
West Adams 1	9	46N05	102w46	6:51:04
West Bottineau 5	1	48N46	101w24	6:45:36
West Bowman 6	9	46N05	103w41	6:54:44
West Cavalier 10	1	48N46	98w47	6:35:08
West Dickey 11	1	46N07	98w53	6:35:32
West Eddy 14	1	47N43	99w06	6:36:24
West Emmons 15	1	46N17	100w29	6:41:56
West Fargo 9	2	46N52	96w54	6:27:36
Westfield 15	1	46N02	100w12	6:40:48
West Foster 16	1	47N27	99w03	6:36:12
West Griggs 20	1	47N28	98w23	6:33:32
West Hettinger 21	9	46N26	102w45	6:51:00
Westhope 5	1	48N55	101w01	6:44:04
West Logan 24	1	46N28	99w40	6:38:40
West Mc Lean 28	1	47N42	101w55	6:47:40
West Mercer 29	9	47N17	101w57	6:47:48
West Morton 30	9	46N51	101w53	6:47:32
West Oliver 33	9	47N07	101w34	6:46:16
West Sargent 41	1	46N08	97w53	6:31:32
West Slope 44	9	46N27	103w37	6:54:28
West Stark 45	9	46N49	103w06	6:52:24
Wheatland 9	1	46N54	97w21	6:29:24
Wheelock 53	1	48N18	103w15	6:53:00
White Earth 31	1	48N23	102w46	6:51:04
White Shield 28	1	47N39	101w39	6:46:36
Whitman 32	1	48N10	98w07	6:32:28
Wild Rice 9	1	46N46	96w54	6:27:36
Wildrose 53	1	48N38	103w11	6:52:44
Williston 53	1	48N09	103w37	6:54:28
Willow City 5	1	48N36	100w18	6:41:12
Wilton 28	1	47N10	100w47	6:43:08
Wimbledon 2	1	47N10	98w28	6:33:52
Windsor 47	1	46N54	99w03	6:36:12
Wing 8	1	47N09	100w17	6:41:08
Wishek 26	1	46N16	99w33	6:38:12
Wolford 35	1	48N30	99w42	6:38:48
Wolseth 51	1	48N31	101w13	6:44:52
Woods 9	1	46N39	97w15	6:29:00
Woodworth 47	1	47N09	99w23	6:37:32
Wyndmere 39	1	46N16	97w08	6:28:32
Yellowstone 27	9	47N52	104w00	6:56:00
York 3	1	48N19	99w34	6:38:16
Ypsilanti 47	1	46N47	98w34	6:34:16
Zahl 53	1	48N34	103w42	6:54:48
Zap 29	9	47N17	101w55	6:47:40
Zeeland 26	1	45N58	99w50	6:39:20

NORTH DAKOTA

OHIO

TIME TABLES

Zone shifts are uncertain at the zone boundaries for the various changes from Central to Eastern time. During World War II, industrial cities and towns variously ignored the official CWT after February 21, 1943, and used EWT instead, especially during the summer months. We have assumed that the northeast area followed Cleveland, except where newspaper clippings show otherwise. Some of these local differences are not yet documented. During the 1950's, the area observing daylight time gradually spread from the northeast and east westward. But the exact year that particular smaller towns began observing daylight time, and whether the daylight period ended in September or October continues to be uncertain.

OH # 1		
Before	4/01/1893	LMT
4/01/1893	12:00	CST
3/31/1918	02:00	CWT
10/27/1918	02:00	CST
3/30/1919	02:00	CWT
10/26/1919	02:00	CST
9/01/1922	02:00	EST
2/09/1942	02:00	EWT
2/21/1943	02:00	CWT
9/30/1945	02:00	EST
4/30/1967	02:00	US#1

OH # 2		
Before	4/01/1893	LMT
4/01/1893	12:00	CST
3/31/1918	02:00	CWT
10/27/1918	02:00	CST
1/01/1919	02:00	EST
3/30/1919	02:00	EWT
5/17/1919	21:00	CWT
10/26/1919	02:00	CST
3/30/1920	02:00	CDT
10/26/1920	02:00	CST
3/30/1921	02:00	CDT
10/26/1921	02:00	CST
3/30/1922	02:00	CDT
10/26/1922	02:00	CST
3/30/1923	02:00	CDT
10/26/1923	02:00	CST
3/30/1924	02:00	CDT
10/26/1924	02:00	CST
3/30/1925	02:00	CDT
10/26/1925	02:00	CST
3/30/1926	02:00	CDT
9/26/1926	02:00	EST
2/09/1942	02:00	EWT
9/26/1943	02:00	CWT
4/30/1944	02:00	EWT
9/30/1945	02:00	EST
4/25/1948	02:00	EDT
9/26/1948	02:00	EST
4/24/1949	02:00	EDT
9/25/1949	02:00	EST
4/30/1950	02:00	EDT
9/30/1950	02:00	US#5

OH # 3		
Before	4/01/1893	LMT
4/01/1893	12:00	CST
3/31/1918	02:00	CWT
10/27/1918	02:00	CST
3/30/1919	02:00	CWT
10/26/1919	02:00	CST
3/28/1920	02:00	CDT
10/31/1920	02:00	CST
4/02/1921	02:00	CDT
9/25/1921	02:00	CST
4/30/1922	02:00	CDT
9/24/1922	02:00	CST
4/20/1923	02:00	EST
2/09/1942	02:00	EWT
9/26/1943	02:00	CWT
9/30/1945	02:00	EST
4/30/1967	02:00	US#1

OH # 4		
Before	4/01/1893	LMT
4/01/1893	12:00	CST
3/31/1918	02:00	CWT
10/27/1918	02:00	CST
3/30/1919	02:00	CWT
10/26/1919	02:00	CST
8/05/1926	02:00	EST
2/09/1942	02:00	EWT
9/26/1943	02:00	CWT
9/30/1945	02:00	EST
4/30/1967	02:00	US#1

OH # 5		
Before	4/01/1893	LMT
4/01/1893	12:00	CST
3/31/1918	02:00	CWT
10/27/1918	02:00	CST
1/01/1919	02:00	EST
3/30/1919	02:00	EWT
10/26/1919	02:00	EST
2/09/1942	02:00	EWT
2/21/1943	02:00	CWT
9/30/1945	02:00	EST
4/30/1967	02:00	US#1

OH # 6		
Before	4/01/1893	LMT
4/01/1893	12:00	CST
3/31/1918	02:00	CWT
10/27/1918	02:00	CST
1/01/1919	02:00	EST
3/30/1919	02:00	EWT
10/26/1919	02:00	EST
2/09/1942	02:00	EWT
2/21/1943	02:00	CWT
9/30/1945	02:00	EST
4/27/1947	02:00	US#5

OH # 7		
Before	4/01/1893	LMT
4/01/1893	12:00	CST
3/31/1918	02:00	CWT
10/27/1918	02:00	CST
1/01/1919	02:00	EST
3/30/1919	02:00	EWT
10/26/1919	02:00	EST
2/09/1942	02:00	EWT
2/21/1943	02:00	CWT
9/30/1945	02:00	EST
4/25/1948	02:00	EDT
9/26/1948	02:00	EST
4/30/1967	02:00	US#1

OH # 8		
Before	4/01/1893	LMT
4/01/1893	12:00	CST
3/31/1918	02:00	CWT
10/27/1918	02:00	CST
1/01/1919	02:00	EST
3/30/1919	02:00	EWT
10/26/1919	02:00	EST
2/09/1942	02:00	EWT
2/21/1943	02:00	CWT
9/30/1945	02:00	EST
4/25/1948	02:00	EDT
9/26/1948	02:00	EST
4/30/1950	02:00	EDT
9/24/1950	02:00	EST
4/29/1956	02:00	US#5

OH # 9		
Before	4/01/1893	LMT
4/01/1893	12:00	CST
3/31/1918	02:00	CWT
10/27/1918	02:00	CST
1/01/1919	02:00	EST
3/30/1919	02:00	EWT
10/26/1919	02:00	EST
2/09/1942	02:00	EWT
2/21/1943	02:00	CWT
9/30/1945	02:00	EST
4/24/1949	02:00	EDT
9/25/1949	02:00	EST
4/30/1967	02:00	US#1

OH # 10		
Before	4/01/1893	LMT
4/01/1893	12:00	CST
3/31/1918	02:00	CWT
10/27/1918	02:00	CST
1/01/1919	02:00	EST
3/30/1919	02:00	EWT
10/26/1919	02:00	EST
2/09/1942	02:00	EWT
2/21/1943	02:00	CWT
9/30/1945	02:00	EST
4/27/1952	02:00	EDT
9/28/1952	02:00	EST
4/29/1956	02:00	US#5

OH # 11		
Before	4/01/1893	LMT
4/01/1893	12:00	CST
3/31/1918	02:00	CWT
10/27/1918	02:00	CST
1/01/1919	02:00	EST
3/30/1919	02:00	EWT
10/26/1919	02:00	EST
2/09/1942	02:00	EWT
2/21/1943	02:00	CWT
9/30/1945	02:00	EST
4/25/1954	02:00	US#5

OH # 12		
Before	4/01/1893	LMT
4/01/1893	12:00	CST
3/31/1918	02:00	CWT
10/27/1918	02:00	CST
1/01/1919	02:00	EST
3/30/1919	02:00	EWT
10/26/1919	02:00	EST
2/09/1942	02:00	EWT
2/21/1943	02:00	CWT
9/30/1945	02:00	EST
4/24/1955	02:00	EDT
9/25/1955	02:00	EST
4/28/1957	02:00	US#5

OH # 13		
Before	4/01/1893	LMT
4/01/1893	12:00	CST
3/31/1918	02:00	CWT
10/27/1918	02:00	CST
1/01/1919	02:00	EST
3/30/1919	02:00	EWT
10/26/1919	02:00	EST
2/09/1942	02:00	EWT
2/21/1943	02:00	CWT
9/30/1945	02:00	EST
4/24/1955	02:00	US#5

OH # 14		
Before	4/01/1893	LMT
4/01/1893	12:00	CST
3/31/1918	02:00	CWT
10/27/1918	02:00	CST
1/01/1919	02:00	EST
3/30/1919	02:00	EWT
10/26/1919	02:00	EST
2/09/1942	02:00	EWT
2/21/1943	02:00	CWT
9/30/1945	02:00	EST
5/12/1957	02:00	EDT
9/29/1957	02:00	EST
4/28/1963	02:00	EDT
9/29/1963	02:00	EST
4/26/1964	02:00	EDT
9/27/1964	02:00	EST
4/25/1965	02:00	EDT
9/26/1965	02:00	EST
4/24/1966	02:00	US#1

OH # 15		
Before	4/01/1893	LMT
4/01/1893	12:00	CST
3/31/1918	02:00	CWT
10/27/1918	02:00	CST
1/01/1919	02:00	EST
3/30/1919	02:00	EWT
10/26/1919	02:00	EST
2/09/1942	02:00	EWT
2/21/1943	02:00	CWT
9/30/1945	02:00	EST
4/24/1955	02:00	EDT
9/25/1955	02:00	EST
4/29/1956	02:00	EDT
10/28/1956	02:00	EST
4/28/1957	02:00	US#5

OH # 16		
Before	4/01/1893	LMT
4/01/1893	12:00	CST
3/31/1918	02:00	CWT
10/27/1918	02:00	CST
1/01/1919	02:00	EST
3/30/1919	02:00	EWT
10/26/1919	02:00	EST
2/09/1942	02:00	EWT
2/21/1943	02:00	CWT
9/30/1945	02:00	EST
4/28/1957	02:00	US#5

OH # 17		
Before	4/01/1893	LMT
4/01/1893	12:00	CST
3/31/1918	02:00	CWT
10/27/1918	02:00	CST
1/01/1919	02:00	EST
3/30/1919	02:00	EWT
10/26/1919	02:00	EST
2/09/1942	02:00	EWT
2/21/1943	02:00	CWT
9/30/1945	02:00	EST
4/24/1966	02:00	US#2

OH # 18		
Before	4/01/1893	LMT
4/01/1893	12:00	CST
3/31/1918	02:00	CWT
10/27/1918	02:00	CST
1/01/1919	02:00	EST
3/30/1919	02:00	EWT
10/26/1919	02:00	EST
2/09/1942	02:00	EWT
2/21/1943	02:00	CWT
9/30/1945	02:00	EST
6/01/1960	02:00	EDT
9/30/1960	02:00	EST
6/04/1961	02:00	EDT
9/03/1961	02:00	EST
4/29/1962	02:00	EDT
9/30/1962	02:00	EST
6/01/1963	02:00	EDT
8/31/1963	02:00	EST
4/26/1964	02:00	EDT
9/27/1964	02:00	EST
4/25/1965	02:00	US#2

OH # 19		
Before	4/01/1893	LMT
4/01/1893	12:00	CST
3/31/1918	02:00	CWT
10/27/1918	02:00	CST
1/01/1919	02:00	EST
3/30/1919	02:00	EWT
10/26/1919	02:00	EST
2/09/1942	02:00	EWT
2/21/1943	02:00	CWT
9/30/1945	02:00	EST
4/25/1948	02:00	EDT
9/26/1948	02:00	EST
4/28/1957	02:00	US#5

OH # 20		
Before	4/01/1893	LMT
4/01/1893	12:00	CST
3/31/1918	02:00	CWT
10/27/1918	02:00	CST
1/01/1919	02:00	EST
3/30/1919	02:00	EWT
10/26/1919	02:00	EST
2/09/1942	02:00	EWT
2/21/1943	02:00	CWT
9/30/1945	02:00	EST
4/28/1963	02:00	EDT
9/29/1963	02:00	EST
4/26/1964	02:00	EDT
9/27/1964	02:00	EST
4/25/1965	02:00	EDT
9/26/1965	02:00	EST
4/24/1966	02:00	US#1

OH # 21		
Before	4/01/1893	LMT
4/01/1893	12:00	CST
3/31/1918	02:00	CWT
10/27/1918	02:00	CST
1/01/1919	02:00	EST
3/30/1919	02:00	EWT
10/26/1919	02:00	EST
2/09/1942	02:00	EWT
2/21/1943	02:00	CWT
9/30/1945	02:00	EST
4/29/1956	02:00	US#5

OH # 22		
Before	4/01/1893	LMT
4/01/1893	12:00	CST
3/31/1918	02:00	CWT
10/27/1918	02:00	CST
1/01/1919	02:00	EST
3/30/1919	02:00	EWT
10/26/1919	02:00	EST
2/09/1942	02:00	EWT
2/21/1943	02:00	CWT
9/30/1945	02:00	EST
4/24/1955	02:00	US#5

OH # 23		
Before	4/01/1893	LMT
4/01/1893	12:00	CST
3/31/1918	02:00	CWT
10/27/1918	02:00	CST
1/01/1919	02:00	EST
3/30/1919	02:00	EWT
10/26/1919	02:00	EST
2/09/1942	02:00	EWT
2/21/1943	02:00	CWT
9/30/1945	02:00	EST
4/25/1954	02:00	EDT
9/26/1954	02:00	EST
4/24/1955	02:00	EDT
9/25/1955	02:00	EST
4/29/1956	02:00	EDT
9/30/1956	02:00	EST
4/28/1957	02:00	EDT
9/29/1957	02:00	EST
4/27/1958	02:00	EDT
9/28/1958	02:00	EST
4/26/1959	02:00	EDT
9/27/1959	02:00	EST
4/24/1960	02:00	EDT
9/25/1960	02:00	EST
4/30/1961	02:00	EDT
9/24/1961	02:00	EST
4/29/1962	02:00	EDT
9/30/1962	02:00	EST
4/28/1963	02:00	EDT
9/29/1963	02:00	EST
4/26/1964	02:00	EDT
9/27/1964	02:00	EST
4/25/1965	02:00	US#2

OH # 24		
Before	4/01/1893	LMT
4/01/1893	12:00	CST
3/31/1918	02:00	CWT
10/27/1918	02:00	CST
1/01/1919	02:00	EST
3/30/1919	02:00	EWT
10/26/1919	02:00	EST
2/09/1942	02:00	EWT
2/21/1943	02:00	CWT
9/30/1945	02:00	EST
4/24/1955	02:00	EDT
9/25/1955	02:00	EST
4/29/1956	02:00	EDT
9/30/1956	02:00	EST
4/28/1957	02:00	EDT
9/29/1957	02:00	EST
4/27/1958	02:00	EDT
9/28/1958	02:00	EST
4/26/1959	02:00	EDT
9/27/1959	02:00	EST
4/24/1960	02:00	US#2

OH # 25		
Before	4/01/1893	LMT
4/01/1893	12:00	CST
5/01/1914	02:00	EST
3/31/1918	02:00	EWT
10/27/1918	02:00	EST
3/30/1919	02:00	EWT
5/11/1919	02:00	CWT
10/26/1919	02:00	EST
2/09/1942	02:00	EWT
9/26/1943	02:00	CWT
4/30/1944	02:00	EWT
9/24/1944	02:00	CWT
4/29/1945	02:00	EWT
9/30/1945	02:00	EST
4/25/1948	02:00	US#5

OH # 26		
Before	6/15/1890	LMT
6/15/1890	12:00	CST
5/01/1914	02:00	EST
3/31/1918	02:00	EWT
10/27/1918	02:00	EST
3/30/1919	02:00	EWT
5/11/1919	02:00	CWT
10/26/1919	02:00	EST
2/09/1942	02:00	EWT
9/26/1943	02:00	CWT
4/30/1944	02:00	EWT
9/24/1944	02:00	CWT
4/29/1945	02:00	EWT
9/30/1945	02:00	EST
4/25/1948	02:00	US#5

OH # 27		
Before	4/01/1893	LMT
4/01/1893	12:00	CST
3/31/1918	02:00	CWT
10/27/1918	02:00	CST
1/01/1919	02:00	EST
3/30/1919	02:00	CWT
10/26/1919	02:00	CST
3/30/1924	02:00	EST
2/09/1942	02:00	EWT
2/21/1943	02:00	CWT
9/30/1945	02:00	EST
4/30/1967	02:00	US#1

OH # 28		
Before	4/01/1893	LMT
4/01/1893	12:00	CST
3/31/1918	02:00	CWT
10/27/1918	02:00	CST
1/01/1919	02:00	EST
3/30/1919	02:00	CWT
10/26/1919	02:00	CST
3/30/1924	02:00	EST
2/09/1942	02:00	EWT
2/21/1943	02:00	CWT
9/30/1945	02:00	EST
4/27/1947	02:00	EDT
9/28/1947	02:00	EST
4/30/1967	02:00	US#1

OH # 29		
Before	4/01/1893	LMT
4/01/1893	12:00	CST
3/31/1918	02:00	CWT
10/27/1918	02:00	CST
1/01/1919	02:00	EST
3/30/1919	02:00	CWT
10/26/1919	02:00	CST

TIME TABLES

6/01/1920 02:00 EST
2/09/1942 02:00 EWT
9/26/1943 02:00 CWT
4/01/1944 02:00 EWT
9/03/1944 02:00 CWT
4/01/1945 02:00 EWT
9/30/1945 02:00 EST
4/30/1967 02:00 US#1
....
OH # 30
Before 4/01/1893 LMT
4/01/1893 12:00 CST
3/31/1918 02:00 CWT
10/27/1918 02:00 CST
1/01/1919 02:00 EST
3/30/1919 02:00 EWT
6/01/1919 02:00 CWT
10/26/1919 02:00 CST
4/01/1922 02:00 EST
2/09/1942 02:00 EWT
2/21/1943 02:00 CWT
9/30/1945 02:00 EST
4/30/1967 02:00 US#1
....
OH # 31
Before 4/01/1893 LMT
4/01/1893 12:00 CST
3/31/1918 02:00 CWT
10/27/1918 02:00 CST
3/30/1919 02:00 CWT
10/26/1919 02:00 CST
3/28/1920 02:00 CDT
10/31/1920 02:00 CST
3/26/1921 02:00 CDT
10/02/1921 02:00 CST
11/21/1921 02:00 EST
2/09/1942 02:00 EWT
10/01/1943 00:01 CWT
4/01/1944 00:01 EWT
10/01/1944 00:01 CWT
4/01/1945 00:01 EWT
9/30/1945 02:00 EST
4/25/1948 02:00 EDT
9/26/1948 02:00 EST
4/30/1961 02:00 US#2
....
OH # 32
Before 4/01/1893 LMT
4/01/1893 12:00 CST
3/31/1918 02:00 CWT
10/27/1918 02:00 CST
3/30/1919 02:00 CWT
10/26/1919 02:00 CST
3/30/1924 02:00 EST
2/09/1942 02:00 EWT
2/21/1943 02:00 CWT
9/30/1945 02:00 EST
4/30/1967 02:00 US#1
....
OH # 33
Before 4/01/1893 LMT
4/01/1893 12:00 CST
3/31/1918 02:00 CWT
10/27/1918 02:00 CST
3/30/1919 02:00 CWT
10/26/1919 02:00 CST
8/31/1924 00:01 EST
2/09/1942 02:00 EWT
2/21/1943 02:00 CWT
9/30/1945 02:00 EST
4/30/1967 02:00 US#1
....
OH # 34
Before 4/01/1893 LMT
4/01/1893 12:00 CST
3/31/1918 02:00 CWT
10/27/1918 02:00 CST
3/30/1919 02:00 CWT
10/26/1919 02:00 CST
4/03/1927 02:00 EST
2/09/1942 02:00 EWT
2/21/1943 02:00 CWT
9/30/1945 02:00 EST
4/30/1967 02:00 US#1
....
OH # 35
Before 4/01/1893 LMT
4/01/1893 12:00 CST
3/31/1918 02:00 CWT
10/27/1918 02:00 CST
3/30/1919 02:00 CWT
10/26/1919 02:00 CST
4/03/1927 02:00 EST
2/09/1942 02:00 EWT
2/21/1943 02:00 CWT
9/30/1945 02:00 EST
4/24/1955 02:00 US#5
....
OH # 36
Before 4/01/1893 LMT
4/01/1893 12:00 CST
3/31/1918 02:00 CWT
10/27/1918 02:00 CST
3/30/1919 02:00 CWT
10/26/1919 02:00 CST
4/03/1927 02:00 EST
2/09/1942 02:00 EWT
2/21/1943 02:00 CWT
9/30/1945 02:00 EST
4/24/1966 02:00 US#1
....
OH # 37
Before 4/01/1893 LMT
4/01/1893 12:00 CST
3/31/1918 02:00 CWT
10/27/1918 02:00 CST
3/30/1919 02:00 CWT
10/26/1919 02:00 CST
4/03/1927 02:00 EST
2/09/1942 02:00 EWT
2/21/1943 02:00 CWT
9/30/1945 02:00 EST
4/28/1963 02:00 EDT
9/29/1963 02:00 EST
4/26/1964 02:00 EDT
9/27/1964 02:00 EST
4/25/1965 02:00 EDT
9/26/1965 02:00 EST
4/24/1966 02:00 US#1
....
OH # 38
Before 4/01/1893 LMT
4/01/1893 12:00 CST
5/01/1914 02:00 EST
3/31/1918 02:00 EWT
10/27/1918 02:00 EST
3/30/1919 02:00 EWT
10/26/1919 02:00 EST
2/09/1942 02:00 EWT
2/21/1943 02:00 CWT
9/30/1945 02:00 EST
4/30/1967 02:00 US#1
....
OH # 39
Before 1/01/1890 LMT
1/01/1890 12:00 CST
3/31/1918 02:00 CWT
10/27/1918 02:00 CST
3/30/1919 02:00 CWT
10/26/1919 02:00 CST
3/28/1920 02:00 CDT
10/31/1920 02:00 CST
4/03/1921 02:00 CDT
9/25/1921 02:00 CST
4/29/1923 02:00 CDT
9/30/1923 02:00 CST
4/27/1924 02:00 CDT
9/28/1924 02:00 CST
4/26/1925 02:00 CDT
9/27/1925 02:00 CST
4/25/1926 02:00 CDT
9/26/1926 02:00 CST
4/03/1927 02:00 EST
2/09/1942 02:00 EWT
9/26/1943 02:00 CWT
4/02/1944 02:00 EWT
9/03/1944 02:00 CWT
9/30/1945 02:00 EST
4/30/1967 02:00 US#1
....
OH # 40
Before 4/01/1893 LMT
4/01/1893 12:00 CST
3/31/1918 02:00 CWT
10/27/1918 02:00 CST
3/30/1919 02:00 CWT
5/11/1919 02:00 EWT
10/26/1919 02:00 EST
2/09/1942 02:00 EWT
9/26/1943 02:00 CWT
4/30/1944 02:00 EWT
9/24/1944 02:00 CWT
4/29/1945 02:00 EWT
9/30/1945 02:00 EST
4/25/1948 02:00 EDT
9/26/1948 02:00 EST
4/24/1949 02:00 EDT
9/25/1949 02:00 EST
4/29/1956 02:00 EDT
9/30/1956 02:00 EST
4/28/1957 02:00 EDT
9/29/1957 02:00 EST
4/27/1958 02:00 EDT
10/26/1958 02:00 EST
4/26/1959 02:00 EDT
10/25/1959 02:00 EST
4/24/1960 02:00 EDT
10/30/1960 02:00 EST
4/30/1961 02:00 EDT
10/29/1961 02:00 EST
4/29/1962 02:00 EDT
10/28/1962 02:00 EST
4/28/1963 02:00 EDT
10/27/1963 02:00 EST
5/30/1964 02:00 EDT
9/07/1964 02:00 EST
4/25/1965 02:00 US#2
....
OH # 41
Before 4/01/1893 LMT
4/01/1893 12:00 CST
3/31/1918 02:00 CWT
10/27/1918 02:00 CST
3/30/1919 02:00 CWT
10/26/1919 02:00 CST
4/05/1925 02:00 EST
2/09/1942 02:00 EWT
9/26/1943 02:00 CWT
4/02/1944 02:00 EWT
9/03/1944 02:00 CWT
9/30/1945 02:00 EST
4/30/1967 02:00 US#1
....
OH # 42
Before 4/01/1893 LMT
4/01/1893 12:00 CST
3/31/1918 02:00 CWT
10/27/1918 02:00 CST
3/30/1919 02:00 CWT
10/26/1919 02:00 CST
3/28/1920 02:00 CDT
10/31/1920 02:00 CST
4/24/1921 02:00 CDT
9/25/1921 02:00 CST
4/30/1922 02:00 CDT
9/24/1922 02:00 CST
4/29/1923 02:00 CDT
9/30/1923 02:00 CST
4/27/1924 02:00 CDT
9/28/1924 02:00 CST
4/26/1925 02:00 CDT
9/27/1925 02:00 CST
4/25/1926 02:00 CDT
9/26/1926 02:00 EST
2/09/1942 02:00 EWT
9/26/1943 02:00 CWT
4/30/1944 02:00 EWT
9/24/1944 02:00 CWT
4/29/1945 02:00 EWT
9/30/1945 02:00 EST
4/25/1948 02:00 US#5
....
OH # 43
Before 4/01/1893 LMT
4/01/1893 12:00 CST
3/31/1918 02:00 CWT
10/27/1918 02:00 CST
3/30/1919 02:00 CWT
10/26/1919 02:00 CST
3/28/1920 02:00 CDT
10/31/1920 02:00 CST
4/03/1921 02:00 CDT
9/25/1921 02:00 CST
4/02/1922 02:00 CDT
9/24/1922 02:00 CST
4/01/1923 02:00 CDT
9/30/1923 02:00 CST
4/06/1924 02:00 CDT
9/28/1924 02:00 CST
4/05/1925 02:00 CDT
9/27/1925 02:00 CST
4/04/1926 02:00 CDT
9/26/1926 02:00 EST
2/09/1942 02:00 EWT
9/26/1943 02:00 CWT
4/30/1944 02:00 EWT
9/24/1944 02:00 CWT
4/29/1945 02:00 EWT
9/30/1945 02:00 EST
4/25/1948 02:00 EDT
9/26/1948 02:00 EST
4/30/1950 02:00 EDT
9/30/1950 02:00 US#5
....
OH # 44
Before 4/01/1893 LMT
4/01/1893 12:00 CST
3/31/1918 02:00 CWT
10/27/1918 02:00 CST
1/01/1919 02:00 EST
3/30/1919 02:00 EWT
5/17/1919 02:00 CWT
10/26/1919 02:00 EST
2/09/1942 02:00 EWT
9/26/1943 02:00 CWT
4/30/1944 02:00 EWT
9/24/1944 02:00 CWT
4/29/1945 02:00 EWT
9/30/1945 02:00 EST
4/30/1967 02:00 US#1
....
OH # 45
Before 4/01/1893 LMT
4/01/1893 12:00 CST
3/31/1918 02:00 CWT
10/27/1918 02:00 CST
1/01/1919 02:00 EST
3/30/1919 02:00 EWT
5/17/1919 02:00 CWT
10/26/1919 02:00 EST
2/09/1942 02:00 EWT
9/26/1943 02:00 CWT
4/30/1944 02:00 EWT
9/24/1944 02:00 CWT
4/29/1945 02:00 EWT
9/30/1945 02:00 EST
4/28/1946 02:00 US#5
....
OH # 46
Before 4/01/1893 LMT
4/01/1893 12:00 CST
3/31/1918 02:00 CWT
10/27/1918 02:00 CST
1/01/1919 02:00 EST
3/30/1919 02:00 EWT
5/17/1919 02:00 CWT
10/26/1919 02:00 EST
2/09/1942 02:00 EWT
9/26/1943 02:00 CWT
4/30/1944 02:00 EWT
9/24/1944 02:00 CWT
4/29/1945 02:00 EWT
9/30/1945 02:00 EST
4/25/1948 02:00 US#5
....
OH # 47
Before 4/01/1893 LMT
4/01/1893 12:00 CST
3/31/1918 02:00 CWT
10/27/1918 02:00 CST
1/01/1919 02:00 EST
3/30/1919 02:00 EWT
5/17/1919 02:00 CWT
10/26/1919 02:00 EST
2/09/1942 02:00 EWT
9/26/1943 02:00 CWT
4/30/1944 02:00 EWT
9/24/1944 02:00 CWT
4/29/1945 02:00 EWT
9/30/1945 02:00 EST
4/25/1948 02:00 EDT
9/26/1948 02:00 EST
4/24/1949 02:00 EDT
9/25/1949 02:00 EST
4/30/1950 02:00 EDT
9/30/1950 02:00 US#5
....
OH # 48
Before 4/01/1893 LMT
4/01/1893 12:00 CST
3/31/1918 02:00 CWT
10/27/1918 02:00 CST
1/01/1919 02:00 EST
3/30/1919 02:00 EWT
5/17/1919 02:00 CWT
10/26/1919 02:00 EST
2/09/1942 02:00 EWT
9/26/1943 02:00 CWT
4/30/1944 02:00 EWT
9/24/1944 02:00 CWT
4/29/1945 02:00 EWT
9/30/1945 02:00 EST
4/25/1948 02:00 EDT
9/26/1948 02:00 EST
4/24/1949 02:00 EDT
9/25/1949 02:00 EST
4/29/1956 02:00 US#5
....
OH # 49
Before 4/01/1893 LMT
4/01/1893 12:00 CST
3/31/1918 02:00 CWT
10/27/1918 02:00 CST
1/01/1919 02:00 EST
3/30/1919 02:00 EWT
5/17/1919 02:00 CWT
10/26/1919 02:00 EST
2/09/1942 02:00 EWT
9/26/1943 02:00 CWT
4/30/1944 02:00 EWT
9/24/1944 02:00 CWT
4/29/1945 02:00 EWT
9/30/1945 02:00 EST
4/25/1948 02:00 EDT
9/26/1948 02:00 EST
4/24/1949 02:00 EDT
9/25/1949 02:00 EST
4/29/1951 02:00 EDT
9/30/1951 02:00 EST
4/24/1955 02:00 US#5
....
OH # 50
Before 4/01/1893 LMT
4/01/1893 12:00 CST
3/31/1918 02:00 CWT
10/27/1918 02:00 CST
1/01/1919 02:00 EST
3/30/1919 02:00 EWT
5/17/1919 02:00 CWT
10/26/1919 02:00 EST
2/09/1942 02:00 EWT
9/26/1943 02:00 CWT
4/30/1944 02:00 EWT
9/24/1944 02:00 CWT
4/29/1945 02:00 EWT
9/30/1945 02:00 EST
4/25/1948 02:00 EDT
9/26/1948 02:00 EST
4/29/1951 02:00 US#5
....
OH # 51
Before 4/01/1893 LMT
4/01/1893 12:00 CST
3/31/1918 02:00 CWT
10/27/1918 02:00 CST
1/01/1919 02:00 EST
3/30/1919 02:00 EWT
5/17/1919 02:00 CWT
10/26/1919 02:00 EST
2/09/1942 02:00 EWT
9/26/1943 02:00 CWT
4/30/1944 02:00 EWT
9/24/1944 02:00 CWT
4/29/1945 02:00 EWT
9/30/1945 02:00 EST
4/25/1948 02:00 EDT
9/26/1948 02:00 EST
4/24/1949 02:00 EDT
9/25/1949 02:00 EST
4/30/1950 02:00 EDT
9/30/1950 02:00 US#5
....
OH # 52
Before 4/01/1893 LMT
4/01/1893 12:00 CST
3/31/1918 02:00 CWT
10/27/1918 02:00 CST
1/01/1919 02:00 EST
3/30/1919 02:00 EWT
5/17/1919 02:00 CWT
10/26/1919 02:00 EST
2/09/1942 02:00 EWT
9/26/1943 02:00 CWT
4/30/1944 02:00 EWT
9/24/1944 02:00 CWT
4/29/1945 02:00 EWT
9/30/1945 02:00 EST
4/30/1950 02:00 EDT
9/24/1950 02:00 EST
4/29/1951 02:00 EDT
9/30/1951 02:00 EST
4/27/1952 02:00 EDT
9/28/1952 02:00 EST
4/26/1953 02:00 EDT
9/27/1953 02:00 EST
4/25/1954 02:00 EDT
9/26/1954 02:00 EST
4/24/1955 02:00 EDT
9/25/1955 02:00 EST
4/29/1956 02:00 EDT
9/30/1956 02:00 EST
4/28/1957 02:00 EDT
9/29/1957 02:00 EST
4/27/1958 02:00 EDT
9/28/1958 02:00 EST
4/26/1959 02:00 EDT
9/27/1959 02:00 EST
4/24/1960 02:00 US#2
....
OH # 53
Before 4/01/1893 LMT
4/01/1893 12:00 CST
3/31/1918 02:00 CWT
10/27/1918 02:00 CST
1/01/1919 02:00 EST
3/30/1919 02:00 EWT
5/17/1919 02:00 CWT
10/26/1919 02:00 EST
2/09/1942 02:00 EWT
9/26/1943 02:00 CWT
4/30/1944 02:00 EWT
9/24/1944 02:00 CWT
4/29/1945 02:00 EWT
9/30/1945 02:00 EST
4/24/1949 02:00 US#5
....
OH # 54
Before 4/01/1893 LMT
4/01/1893 12:00 CST
3/31/1918 02:00 CWT
10/27/1918 02:00 CST
1/01/1919 02:00 EST
3/30/1919 02:00 EWT
5/17/1919 02:00 CWT
10/26/1919 02:00 EST
2/09/1942 02:00 EWT
9/26/1943 02:00 CWT
4/30/1944 02:00 EWT
9/24/1944 02:00 CWT
4/29/1945 02:00 EWT
9/30/1945 02:00 EST
4/25/1948 02:00 EDT
9/26/1948 02:00 EST
4/24/1949 02:00 EDT
9/25/1949 02:00 EST
4/30/1950 02:00 EDT
9/24/1950 02:00 EST
4/29/1951 02:00 EDT
9/30/1951 02:00 EST
4/27/1952 02:00 EDT
9/28/1952 02:00 EST
4/26/1953 02:00 EDT
9/27/1953 02:00 EST
4/25/1954 02:00 EDT
9/26/1954 02:00 EST
4/24/1955 02:00 EDT
9/25/1955 02:00 EST
4/29/1956 02:00 EDT
10/28/1956 02:00 EST
4/28/1957 02:00 US#5
....
OH # 55
Before 4/01/1893 LMT
4/01/1893 12:00 CST
3/31/1918 02:00 CWT
10/27/1918 02:00 CST
1/01/1919 02:00 EST
3/30/1919 02:00 EWT
5/17/1919 02:00 CWT
10/26/1919 02:00 EST
2/09/1942 02:00 EWT
9/26/1943 02:00 CWT
4/30/1944 02:00 EWT
9/24/1944 02:00 CWT
4/29/1945 02:00 EWT
9/30/1945 02:00 EST
4/29/1951 02:00 EDT
9/30/1951 02:00 EST
4/24/1955 02:00 US#5
....
OH # 56
Before 4/01/1893 LMT
4/01/1893 12:00 CST
3/31/1918 02:00 CWT
10/27/1918 02:00 CST
1/01/1919 02:00 EST
3/30/1919 02:00 EWT
5/17/1919 02:00 CWT
10/26/1919 02:00 EST
2/09/1942 02:00 EWT
9/26/1943 02:00 CWT
4/30/1944 02:00 EWT
9/24/1944 02:00 CWT
4/29/1945 02:00 EWT
9/30/1945 02:00 EST
4/29/1951 02:00 EDT
9/30/1951 02:00 EST
4/29/1956 02:00 US#5
....
OH # 57

TIME TABLES

Before 4/01/1893 LMT
4/01/1893 12:00 CST
3/31/1918 02:00 CWT
10/27/1918 02:00 CST
1/01/1919 02:00 EST
3/30/1919 02:00 EWT
5/17/1919 02:00 CWT
10/26/1919 02:00 EST
2/09/1942 02:00 EWT
9/26/1943 02:00 CWT
4/30/1944 02:00 EWT
9/24/1944 02:00 CWT
4/29/1945 02:00 EWT
9/30/1945 02:00 EST
4/26/1953 02:00 US#5

....

OH # 58
Before 4/01/1893 LMT
4/01/1893 12:00 CST
3/31/1918 02:00 CWT
10/27/1918 02:00 CST
1/01/1919 02:00 EST
3/30/1919 02:00 EWT
5/17/1919 02:00 CWT
10/26/1919 02:00 EST
2/09/1942 02:00 EWT
9/26/1943 02:00 CWT
4/30/1944 02:00 EWT
9/24/1944 02:00 CWT
4/29/1945 02:00 EWT
9/30/1945 02:00 EST
4/25/1954 02:00 US#5

....

OH # 59
Before 4/01/1893 LMT
4/01/1893 12:00 CST
3/31/1918 02:00 CWT
10/27/1918 02:00 CST
1/01/1919 02:00 EST
3/30/1919 02:00 EWT
5/17/1919 02:00 CWT
10/26/1919 02:00 EST
2/09/1942 02:00 EWT
9/26/1943 02:00 CWT
4/30/1944 02:00 EWT
9/24/1944 02:00 CWT
4/29/1945 02:00 EWT
9/30/1945 02:00 EST
4/25/1954 02:00 EDT
9/26/1954 02:00 EST
4/29/1956 02:00 US#5

....

OH # 60
Before 4/01/1893 LMT
4/01/1893 12:00 CST
3/31/1918 02:00 CWT
10/27/1918 02:00 CST
1/01/1919 02:00 EST
3/30/1919 02:00 EWT
5/17/1919 02:00 CWT
10/26/1919 02:00 EST
2/09/1942 02:00 EWT
9/26/1943 02:00 CWT
4/30/1944 02:00 EWT
9/24/1944 02:00 CWT
4/29/1945 02:00 EWT
9/30/1945 02:00 EST
4/24/1955 02:00 US#5

....

OH # 61
Before 4/01/1893 LMT
4/01/1893 12:00 CST
3/31/1918 02:00 CWT
10/27/1918 02:00 CST
1/01/1919 02:00 EST
3/30/1919 02:00 EWT
5/17/1919 02:00 CWT
10/26/1919 02:00 EST
2/09/1942 02:00 EWT
9/26/1943 02:00 CWT
4/30/1944 02:00 EWT
9/24/1944 02:00 CWT
4/29/1945 02:00 EWT
9/30/1945 02:00 EST
4/28/1957 02:00 US#5

....

OH # 62
Before 4/01/1893 LMT
4/01/1893 12:00 CST
3/31/1918 02:00 CWT
10/27/1918 02:00 CST
1/01/1919 02:00 EST
3/30/1919 02:00 EWT
5/17/1919 02:00 CWT
10/26/1919 02:00 EST
2/09/1942 02:00 EWT
9/26/1943 02:00 CWT
4/30/1944 02:00 EWT
9/24/1944 02:00 CWT
4/29/1945 02:00 EWT
9/30/1945 02:00 EST
4/27/1958 02:00 US#5

....

OH # 63
Before 4/01/1893 LMT
4/01/1893 12:00 CST
3/31/1918 02:00 CWT
10/27/1918 02:00 CST
1/01/1919 02:00 EST
3/30/1919 02:00 EWT
5/17/1919 02:00 CWT
10/26/1919 02:00 EST
2/09/1942 02:00 EWT
9/26/1943 02:00 CWT
4/30/1944 02:00 EWT
9/24/1944 02:00 CWT
4/29/1945 02:00 EWT
9/30/1945 02:00 EST
4/24/1955 02:00 EDT
9/25/1955 02:00 EST
4/29/1956 02:00 EDT
10/28/1956 02:00 US#5

....

OH # 64
Before 4/01/1893 LMT
4/01/1893 12:00 CST
3/31/1918 02:00 CWT
10/27/1918 02:00 CST
1/01/1919 02:00 EST
3/30/1919 02:00 EWT
5/17/1919 02:00 CWT
10/26/1919 02:00 EST
2/09/1942 02:00 EWT
9/26/1943 02:00 CWT
4/30/1944 02:00 EWT
9/24/1944 02:00 CWT
4/29/1945 02:00 EWT
9/30/1945 02:00 EST
4/24/1966 02:00 US#2

....

OH # 65
Before 4/01/1893 LMT
4/01/1893 12:00 CST
3/31/1918 02:00 CWT
10/27/1918 02:00 CST
1/01/1919 02:00 EST
3/30/1919 02:00 EWT
5/17/1919 02:00 CWT
10/26/1919 02:00 EST
2/09/1942 02:00 EWT
9/26/1943 02:00 CWT
4/30/1944 02:00 EWT
9/24/1944 02:00 CWT
4/29/1945 02:00 EWT
9/30/1945 02:00 EST
4/25/1948 02:00 EDT
9/26/1948 02:00 EST
4/24/1949 02:00 EDT
9/25/1949 02:00 EST
4/26/1953 02:00 EDT
9/27/1953 02:00 EST
4/29/1956 02:00 US#5

....

OH # 66
Before 4/01/1893 LMT
4/01/1893 12:00 CST
3/31/1918 02:00 CWT
10/27/1918 02:00 CST
1/01/1919 02:00 EST
3/30/1919 02:00 EWT
5/17/1919 02:00 CWT
10/26/1919 02:00 EST
2/09/1942 02:00 EWT
9/26/1943 02:00 CWT
4/30/1944 02:00 EWT
9/24/1944 02:00 CWT
4/29/1945 02:00 EWT
9/30/1945 02:00 EST
4/24/1949 02:00 EDT
9/25/1949 02:00 EST
4/29/1956 02:00 US#5

....

OH # 67
Before 4/01/1893 LMT
4/01/1893 12:00 CST
3/31/1918 02:00 CWT
10/27/1918 02:00 CST
1/01/1919 02:00 EST
3/30/1919 02:00 EWT
5/17/1919 02:00 CWT
10/26/1919 02:00 EST
2/09/1942 02:00 EWT
9/26/1943 02:00 CWT
4/30/1944 02:00 EWT
9/24/1944 02:00 CWT
4/29/1945 02:00 EWT
9/30/1945 02:00 EST
4/29/1956 02:00 US#5

....

OH # 68
Before 4/01/1893 LMT
4/01/1893 12:00 CST
3/31/1918 02:00 CWT
10/27/1918 02:00 CST
1/01/1919 02:00 EST
3/30/1919 02:00 EWT
5/17/1919 02:00 CWT
10/26/1919 02:00 EST
2/09/1942 02:00 EWT
9/26/1943 02:00 CWT
4/30/1944 02:00 EWT
9/24/1944 02:00 CWT
4/29/1945 02:00 EWT
9/30/1945 02:00 EST
4/29/1956 02:00 EDT
9/30/1956 02:00 EST
4/28/1957 02:00 EDT
9/29/1957 02:00 EST
4/27/1958 02:00 EDT
9/28/1958 02:00 EST
4/26/1959 02:00 EDT
9/27/1959 02:00 EST
4/24/1960 02:00 US#2

....

OH # 69
Before 4/01/1893 LMT
4/01/1893 12:00 CST
3/31/1918 02:00 CWT
10/27/1918 02:00 CST
1/01/1919 02:00 EST
3/30/1919 02:00 EWT
5/17/1919 02:00 CWT
10/26/1919 02:00 EST
2/09/1942 02:00 EWT
9/26/1943 02:00 CWT
4/30/1944 02:00 EWT
9/24/1944 02:00 CWT
4/29/1945 02:00 EWT
9/30/1945 02:00 EST
4/28/1957 02:00 EDT
9/29/1957 02:00 EST
4/27/1958 02:00 EDT
9/28/1958 02:00 EST
4/26/1959 02:00 EDT
9/27/1959 02:00 EST
4/24/1960 02:00 EDT
9/25/1960 02:00 EST
4/30/1961 02:00 EDT
9/24/1961 02:00 EST
4/29/1962 02:00 US#2

....

OH # 70
Before 4/01/1893 LMT
4/01/1893 12:00 CST
3/31/1918 02:00 CWT
10/27/1918 02:00 CST
1/01/1919 02:00 EST
3/30/1919 02:00 EWT
5/17/1919 02:00 CWT
10/26/1919 02:00 EST
2/09/1942 02:00 EWT
9/26/1943 02:00 CWT
4/30/1944 02:00 EWT
9/24/1944 02:00 CWT
4/29/1945 02:00 EWT
9/30/1945 02:00 EST
4/24/1955 02:00 US#5

....

OH # 71
Before 4/01/1893 LMT
4/01/1893 12:00 CST
3/31/1918 02:00 CWT
10/27/1918 02:00 CST
1/01/1919 02:00 EST
3/30/1919 02:00 EWT
5/17/1919 02:00 CWT
10/26/1919 02:00 EST
2/09/1942 02:00 EWT
9/26/1943 02:00 CWT
4/30/1944 02:00 EWT
9/24/1944 02:00 CWT
4/29/1945 02:00 EWT
9/30/1945 02:00 EST
4/25/1948 02:00 EDT
9/26/1948 02:00 EST
4/24/1949 02:00 EDT
9/25/1949 02:00 EST
4/30/1950 02:00 EDT
9/24/1950 02:00 EST
4/29/1951 02:00 EDT
9/30/1951 02:00 EST
4/27/1952 02:00 EDT
9/28/1952 02:00 EST
4/26/1953 02:00 EDT
9/27/1953 02:00 EST
4/25/1954 02:00 EDT
9/26/1954 02:00 EST
4/24/1955 02:00 EDT
9/25/1955 02:00 EST
4/29/1956 02:00 EDT
9/30/1956 02:00 EST
4/28/1957 02:00 EDT
9/29/1957 02:00 EST
4/27/1958 02:00 EDT
9/28/1958 02:00 EST
4/26/1959 02:00 EDT
9/27/1959 02:00 EST
4/24/1960 02:00 US#5

....

OH # 72
Before 4/01/1893 LMT
4/01/1893 12:00 CST
3/31/1918 02:00 CWT
10/27/1918 02:00 CST
1/01/1919 02:00 EST
3/30/1919 02:00 EWT
5/17/1919 02:00 CWT
10/26/1919 02:00 EST
2/09/1942 02:00 EWT
9/26/1943 02:00 CWT
4/30/1944 02:00 EWT
9/24/1944 02:00 CWT
4/29/1945 02:00 EWT
9/30/1945 02:00 EST
4/29/1951 02:00 EDT
9/30/1951 02:00 EST
4/27/1952 02:00 EDT
9/28/1952 02:00 EST
4/26/1953 02:00 EDT
9/27/1953 02:00 EST
4/25/1954 02:00 EDT
9/26/1954 02:00 EST
4/24/1955 02:00 EDT
9/25/1955 02:00 EST
4/29/1956 02:00 EDT
9/30/1956 02:00 EST
4/28/1957 02:00 EDT
9/29/1957 02:00 EST
4/27/1958 02:00 EDT
9/28/1958 02:00 EST
4/26/1959 02:00 EDT
9/27/1959 02:00 EST
4/24/1960 02:00 US#2

....

OH # 73
Before 4/01/1893 LMT
4/01/1893 12:00 CST
3/31/1918 02:00 CWT
10/27/1918 02:00 CST
1/01/1919 02:00 EST
3/30/1919 02:00 EWT
5/17/1919 02:00 CWT
10/26/1919 02:00 EST
2/09/1942 02:00 EWT
9/26/1943 02:00 CWT
4/30/1944 02:00 EWT
9/24/1944 02:00 CWT
4/29/1945 02:00 EWT
9/30/1945 02:00 EST
4/24/1955 02:00 US#5

....

OH # 74
Before 4/01/1893 LMT
4/01/1893 12:00 CST
3/31/1918 02:00 CWT
10/27/1918 02:00 CST
1/01/1919 02:00 EST
3/30/1919 02:00 EWT
5/17/1919 02:00 CWT
10/26/1919 02:00 EST
2/09/1942 02:00 EWT
9/26/1943 02:00 CWT
4/30/1944 02:00 EWT
9/24/1944 02:00 CWT
4/29/1945 02:00 EWT
9/30/1945 02:00 EST
4/28/1946 02:00 EDT
9/29/1946 02:00 EST
4/27/1947 02:00 EDT
9/28/1947 02:00 EST
4/25/1948 02:00 EDT
9/26/1948 02:00 EST
4/24/1949 02:00 EDT
9/25/1949 02:00 EST
4/30/1950 02:00 EDT
9/24/1950 02:00 EST
4/29/1951 02:00 EDT
9/30/1951 02:00 EST
4/27/1952 02:00 EDT
9/28/1952 02:00 EST
4/26/1953 02:00 EDT
9/27/1953 02:00 EST
4/25/1954 02:00 EDT
9/26/1954 02:00 EST
4/24/1955 02:00 EDT
9/25/1955 02:00 EST
4/29/1956 02:00 EDT
9/30/1956 02:00 EST
4/28/1957 02:00 EDT
9/29/1957 02:00 EST
4/27/1958 02:00 EDT
10/26/1958 02:00 EST
4/26/1959 02:00 EDT
10/25/1959 02:00 EST
4/24/1960 02:00 EDT
10/30/1960 02:00 EST
4/30/1961 02:00 EDT
10/01/1961 02:00 EST
4/29/1962 02:00 US#2

....

OH # 75
Before 4/01/1893 LMT
4/01/1893 12:00 CST
3/31/1918 02:00 CWT
10/27/1918 02:00 CST
1/01/1919 02:00 EST
3/30/1919 02:00 EWT
5/17/1919 02:00 CWT
10/26/1919 02:00 EST
2/09/1942 02:00 EWT
9/26/1943 02:00 CWT
4/30/1944 02:00 EWT
9/24/1944 02:00 CWT
4/29/1945 02:00 EWT
9/30/1945 02:00 EST
4/28/1946 02:00 EDT
9/29/1946 02:00 EST
4/27/1947 02:00 EDT
9/28/1947 02:00 EST
4/25/1948 02:00 EDT
9/26/1948 02:00 EST
4/24/1949 02:00 EDT
9/25/1949 02:00 EST
4/30/1950 02:00 EDT
9/30/1950 02:00 EST
4/29/1951 02:00 EDT
9/30/1951 02:00 EST
4/27/1952 02:00 EDT
9/28/1952 02:00 EST
4/26/1953 02:00 EDT
9/27/1953 02:00 EST
4/25/1954 02:00 EDT
9/26/1954 02:00 EST
4/24/1955 02:00 EDT
9/25/1955 02:00 EST
4/29/1956 02:00 EDT
9/30/1956 02:00 EST
4/28/1957 02:00 EDT
9/29/1957 02:00 EST
4/27/1958 02:00 EDT
9/07/1958 02:00 EST
4/26/1959 02:00 US#2

....

OH # 76
Before 4/01/1893 LMT
4/01/1893 12:00 CST
3/31/1918 02:00 CWT
10/27/1918 02:00 CST
1/01/1919 02:00 EST
3/30/1919 02:00 EWT
5/17/1919 02:00 CWT
10/26/1919 02:00 EST
2/09/1942 02:00 EWT
9/26/1943 02:00 CWT
4/30/1944 02:00 EWT
9/24/1944 02:00 CWT
4/29/1945 02:00 EWT
9/30/1945 02:00 EST
4/27/1958 02:00 EDT
9/28/1958 02:00 EST
4/26/1959 02:00 EDT
9/27/1959 02:00 EST
4/24/1960 02:00 EDT
9/25/1960 02:00 EST
4/30/1961 02:00 EDT
9/24/1961 02:00 EST
4/29/1962 02:00 US#2

....

OH # 77
Before 4/01/1893 LMT
4/01/1893 12:00 CST
3/31/1918 02:00 CWT
10/27/1918 02:00 CST
1/01/1919 02:00 EST
3/30/1919 02:00 EWT
5/17/1919 02:00 CWT
10/26/1919 02:00 EST
2/09/1942 02:00 EWT
9/26/1943 02:00 CWT
4/30/1944 02:00 EWT
9/24/1944 02:00 CWT
4/29/1945 02:00 EWT
9/30/1945 02:00 EST
4/28/1946 02:00 EDT
9/29/1946 02:00 EST
4/27/1947 02:00 EDT
9/28/1947 02:00 EST
4/25/1948 02:00 EDT
9/26/1948 02:00 EST
4/24/1949 02:00 EDT
9/25/1949 02:00 EST
4/30/1950 02:00 EDT
9/30/1950 02:00 US#5

....

OH # 78
Before 4/01/1893 LMT
4/01/1893 12:00 CST
3/31/1918 02:00 CWT
10/27/1918 02:00 CST
1/01/1919 02:00 EST
3/30/1919 02:00 EWT
5/17/1919 02:00 CWT
10/26/1919 02:00 EST
2/09/1942 02:00 EWT
9/26/1943 02:00 CWT
4/30/1944 02:00 EWT
9/24/1944 02:00 CWT
4/29/1945 02:00 EWT
9/30/1945 02:00 EST
4/25/1954 02:00 EDT
9/26/1954 02:00 EST
4/24/1955 02:00 EDT
9/25/1955 02:00 EST
4/29/1956 02:00 EDT
9/30/1956 02:00 EST
4/28/1957 02:00 EDT
9/29/1957 02:00 EST
4/27/1958 02:00 EDT
9/28/1958 02:00 EST
4/26/1959 02:00 EDT
9/27/1959 02:00 EST
4/24/1960 02:00 EDT
9/25/1960 02:00 EST
4/30/1961 02:00 EDT
9/24/1961 02:00 EST
4/29/1962 02:00 EDT
9/30/1962 02:00 EST
4/28/1963 02:00 EDT
9/29/1963 02:00 EST
4/26/1964 02:00 EDT
9/27/1964 02:00 EST
4/25/1965 02:00 US#2

....

OH # 79
Before 4/01/1893 LMT
4/01/1893 12:00 CST
3/31/1918 02:00 CWT
10/27/1918 02:00 CST
1/01/1919 02:00 EST
3/30/1919 02:00 EWT
5/17/1919 02:00 CWT
10/26/1919 02:00 EST
2/09/1942 02:00 EWT
9/26/1943 02:00 CWT
4/30/1944 02:00 EWT
9/24/1944 02:00 CWT
4/29/1945 02:00 EWT
9/30/1945 02:00 EST
4/26/1959 02:00 EDT
9/27/1959 02:00 EST
4/24/1960 02:00 EDT
9/25/1960 02:00 EST
4/30/1961 02:00 EDT
9/24/1961 02:00 EST
4/29/1962 02:00 US#2

....

OH # 80
Before 4/01/1893 LMT
4/01/1893 12:00 CST
3/31/1918 02:00 CWT

TIME TABLES

10/27/1918 02:00 CST
1/01/1919 02:00 EST
3/30/1919 02:00 EWT
5/17/1919 02:00 CWT
10/26/1919 02:00 EST
2/09/1942 02:00 EWT
9/26/1943 02:00 CWT
4/30/1944 02:00 EWT
9/24/1944 02:00 CWT
4/29/1945 02:00 EWT
9/30/1945 02:00 EST
4/24/1955 02:00 US#3
....

OH # 81
Before 4/01/1893 LMT
4/01/1893 12:00 CST
3/31/1918 02:00 CWT
10/27/1918 02:00 CST
1/01/1919 02:00 EST
3/30/1919 02:00 EWT
5/17/1919 02:00 CWT
10/26/1919 02:00 EST
2/09/1942 02:00 EWT
9/26/1943 02:00 CWT
4/30/1944 02:00 EWT
9/24/1944 02:00 CWT
4/29/1945 02:00 EWT
9/30/1945 02:00 EST
4/25/1948 02:00 EDT
9/26/1948 02:00 EST
4/24/1949 02:00 EDT
9/25/1949 02:00 EST
4/30/1950 02:00 EDT
9/24/1950 02:00 EST
4/29/1951 02:00 EDT
9/30/1951 02:00 EST
4/27/1952 02:00 EDT
9/28/1952 02:00 EST
4/26/1953 02:00 EDT
9/27/1953 02:00 EST
4/25/1954 02:00 EDT
9/26/1954 02:00 EST
4/24/1955 02:00 EDT
9/25/1955 02:00 EST
4/29/1956 02:00 EDT
10/28/1956 02:00 EST
4/28/1957 02:00 EDT
9/29/1957 02:00 EST
4/27/1958 02:00 EDT
9/28/1958 02:00 EST
4/26/1959 02:00 EDT
9/27/1959 02:00 EST
4/24/1960 02:00 EDT
9/25/1960 02:00 EST
4/30/1961 02:00 EDT
9/24/1961 02:00 EST
4/29/1962 02:00 US#2
....

OH # 82
Before 4/01/1893 LMT
4/01/1893 12:00 CST
3/31/1918 02:00 CWT
10/27/1918 02:00 CST
1/01/1919 02:00 EST
3/30/1919 02:00 EWT
5/17/1919 02:00 CWT
10/26/1919 02:00 EST
2/09/1942 02:00 EWT
9/26/1943 02:00 CWT
4/30/1944 02:00 EWT
9/24/1944 02:00 CWT
4/29/1945 02:00 EWT
9/30/1945 02:00 EST
4/27/1958 02:00 EDT
9/28/1958 02:00 EST
4/26/1959 02:00 EDT
9/27/1959 02:00 EST
4/24/1960 02:00 EDT
9/25/1960 02:00 EST
4/30/1961 02:00 EDT
9/24/1961 02:00 EST
4/29/1962 02:00 US#2
....

OH # 83
Before 4/01/1893 LMT
4/01/1893 12:00 CST
3/31/1918 02:00 CWT
10/27/1918 02:00 CST
1/01/1919 02:00 EST
3/30/1919 02:00 EWT
5/17/1919 02:00 CWT
10/26/1919 02:00 EST
2/09/1942 02:00 EWT
9/26/1943 02:00 CWT
4/30/1944 02:00 EWT
9/24/1944 02:00 CWT
4/29/1945 02:00 EWT
9/30/1945 02:00 EST
4/29/1951 02:00 EDT
9/30/1951 02:00 EST
4/29/1956 02:00 EDT
9/30/1956 02:00 EST
4/28/1957 02:00 EDT
9/29/1957 02:00 EST
4/27/1958 02:00 EDT
9/28/1958 02:00 EST
4/26/1959 02:00 EDT
9/27/1959 02:00 EST
4/24/1960 02:00 EDT
9/25/1960 02:00 EST
4/30/1961 02:00 EDT
9/24/1961 02:00 EST
4/29/1962 02:00 US#2
....

OH # 84
Before 4/01/1893 LMT
4/01/1893 12:00 CST
3/31/1918 02:00 CWT
10/27/1918 02:00 CST
1/01/1919 02:00 EST
3/30/1919 02:00 EWT
5/17/1919 02:00 CWT
10/26/1919 02:00 EST
2/09/1942 02:00 EWT
9/26/1943 02:00 CWT
4/30/1944 02:00 EWT
9/24/1944 02:00 CWT
4/29/1945 02:00 EWT
9/30/1945 02:00 EST
4/28/1946 02:00 EDT
9/29/1946 02:00 EST
4/27/1947 02:00 EDT
9/28/1947 02:00 EST
4/25/1948 02:00 EDT
9/26/1948 02:00 EST
4/24/1949 02:00 EDT
9/25/1949 02:00 EST
4/30/1950 02:00 EDT
9/30/1950 02:00 US#5
....

OH # 85
Before 4/01/1893 LMT
4/01/1893 12:00 CST
3/31/1918 02:00 CWT
10/27/1918 02:00 CST
1/01/1919 02:00 EST
3/30/1919 02:00 CWT
10/26/1919 02:00 CST
3/30/1924 02:00 EST
2/09/1942 02:00 EWT
9/26/1943 02:00 CWT
9/30/1945 02:00 EST
4/30/1967 02:00 US#1
....

OH # 86
Before 4/01/1893 LMT
4/01/1893 12:00 CST
3/31/1918 02:00 CWT
10/27/1918 02:00 CST
3/30/1919 02:00 CWT
10/26/1919 02:00 CST
3/30/1924 02:00 EST
2/09/1942 02:00 EWT
9/26/1943 02:00 CWT
9/30/1945 02:00 EST
4/30/1967 02:00 US#1
....

OH # 87
Before 4/01/1893 LMT
4/01/1893 12:00 CST
3/31/1918 02:00 CWT
10/27/1918 02:00 CST
3/30/1919 02:00 CWT
10/26/1919 02:00 CST
4/03/1927 02:00 EST
2/09/1942 02:00 EWT
9/26/1943 02:00 CWT
9/30/1945 02:00 EST
4/30/1967 02:00 US#1
....

OH # 88
Before 2/22/1890 LMT
2/22/1890 12:00 CST
3/31/1918 02:00 CWT
10/27/1918 02:00 CST
3/30/1919 02:00 CWT
10/26/1919 02:00 CST
3/28/1920 02:00 CDT
10/31/1920 02:00 CST
4/02/1921 02:00 CDT
9/25/1921 02:00 CST
4/30/1922 02:00 CDT
9/24/1922 02:00 CST
4/29/1923 02:00 CDT
9/30/1923 02:00 CST
4/27/1924 02:00 CDT
9/28/1924 02:00 CST
4/26/1925 02:00 CDT
9/27/1925 02:00 CST
4/25/1926 02:00 CDT
8/05/1926 02:00 EST
2/09/1942 02:00 EWT
9/26/1943 02:00 CWT
4/30/1944 02:00 EWT
9/24/1944 02:00 CWT
9/30/1945 02:00 EST
4/30/1967 02:00 US#1
....

OH # 89
Before 4/01/1893 LMT
4/01/1893 12:00 CST
3/31/1918 02:00 CWT
10/27/1918 02:00 CST
3/30/1919 02:00 CWT
10/26/1919 02:00 CST
8/31/1924 00:01 EST
2/09/1942 02:00 EWT
2/21/1943 02:00 CWT
4/29/1945 02:00 EWT
9/30/1945 02:00 EST
4/30/1967 02:00 US#1
....

OH # 90
Before 4/01/1893 LMT
4/01/1893 12:00 CST
3/31/1918 02:00 CWT
10/27/1918 02:00 CST
3/30/1919 02:00 CWT
10/26/1919 02:00 CST
4/25/1926 02:00 EST
2/09/1942 02:00 EWT
10/03/1943 03:00 CWT
4/30/1944 03:00 EWT
9/03/1944 03:00 CWT
4/29/1945 03:00 EWT
9/30/1945 02:00 EST
4/30/1967 02:00 US#1
....

OH # 91
Before 4/01/1893 LMT
4/01/1893 12:00 CST
3/31/1918 02:00 CWT
10/27/1918 02:00 CST
3/30/1919 02:00 CWT
10/26/1919 02:00 CST
4/25/1920 02:00 CDT
10/31/1920 02:00 CST
4/24/1921 02:00 CDT
9/25/1921 02:00 CST
4/30/1922 02:00 CDT
9/24/1922 02:00 CST
4/29/1923 02:00 CDT
9/30/1923 02:00 CST
4/27/1924 02:00 CDT
9/28/1924 02:00 CST
4/26/1925 02:00 CDT
9/27/1925 02:00 CST
4/25/1926 02:00 CDT
9/26/1926 02:00 CST
4/03/1927 02:00 EST
2/09/1942 02:00 EWT
2/21/1943 03:00 CWT
4/30/1944 02:00 EWT
9/03/1944 02:00 CWT
4/29/1945 02:00 EWT
5/13/1945 03:00 EST
4/30/1967 02:00 US#1
....

OH # 92
Before 4/01/1893 LMT
4/01/1893 12:00 CST
3/31/1918 02:00 CWT
10/27/1918 02:00 CST
3/30/1919 02:00 CWT
10/26/1919 02:00 CST
3/28/1920 02:00 CDT
10/31/1920 02:00 CST
4/03/1921 02:00 CDT
9/25/1921 02:00 CST
3/26/1922 00:00 EST
2/09/1942 02:00 EWT
2/21/1943 02:00 CWT
4/01/1945 02:00 EWT
9/30/1945 02:00 EST
4/30/1967 02:00 US#1
....

OH # 93
Before 4/01/1893 LMT
4/01/1893 12:00 CST
3/31/1918 02:00 CWT
10/27/1918 02:00 CST
3/30/1919 02:00 CWT
10/26/1919 02:00 CST
4/01/1922 02:00 EST
2/09/1942 02:00 EWT
9/30/1945 02:00 EST
4/30/1967 02:00 US#1
....

OH # 94
Before 4/01/1893 LMT
4/01/1893 12:00 CST
3/31/1918 02:00 CWT
10/27/1918 02:00 CST
3/30/1919 02:00 CWT
10/26/1919 02:00 CST
3/28/1920 02:00 CDT
10/31/1920 02:00 CST
4/03/1921 02:00 CDT
9/25/1921 02:00 CST
4/29/1923 02:00 CDT
9/30/1923 02:00 CST
4/27/1924 02:00 CDT
9/28/1924 02:00 CST
4/26/1925 02:00 CDT
9/27/1925 02:00 CST
4/25/1926 02:00 CDT
9/26/1926 02:00 EST
2/09/1942 02:00 EWT
9/26/1943 02:00 CWT
4/01/1944 02:00 EWT
9/24/1944 02:00 CWT
4/01/1945 02:00 EWT
9/30/1945 02:00 EST
4/30/1967 02:00 US#1
....

OH # 95
Before 4/01/1893 LMT
4/01/1893 12:00 CST
3/31/1918 02:00 CWT
10/27/1918 02:00 CST
1/01/1919 02:00 EST
3/30/1919 02:00 CWT
10/26/1919 02:00 CST
6/06/1920 02:00 EST
2/09/1942 02:00 EWT
9/26/1943 02:00 CWT
2/20/1944 02:00 EWT
9/30/1945 02:00 EST
4/27/1952 02:00 EDT
9/28/1952 02:00 EST
4/26/1953 02:00 EDT
9/27/1953 02:00 EST
4/30/1967 02:00 US#1
....

OH # 96
Before 4/01/1893 LMT
4/01/1893 12:00 CST
3/31/1918 02:00 CWT
10/27/1918 02:00 CST
1/01/1919 02:00 EST
3/30/1919 02:00 CWT
10/26/1919 02:00 CST
3/28/1920 02:00 CDT
10/31/1920 02:00 CST
4/03/1921 02:00 CDT
9/25/1921 02:00 CST
4/30/1922 02:00 CDT
9/24/1922 02:00 CST
4/29/1923 02:00 CDT
9/30/1923 02:00 CST
3/30/1924 02:00 EST
2/09/1942 02:00 EWT
9/26/1943 02:00 CWT
9/30/1945 02:00 EST
4/30/1967 02:00 US#1
....

OH # 97
Before 4/01/1893 LMT
4/01/1893 12:00 CST
3/31/1918 02:00 CWT
10/27/1918 02:00 CST
1/01/1919 02:00 EST
3/30/1919 02:00 CWT
10/26/1919 02:00 CST
3/30/1924 02:00 EST
2/09/1942 02:00 EWT
9/26/1943 02:00 CWT
9/30/1945 02:00 EST
4/30/1967 02:00 US#1
....

OH # 98
Before 4/01/1893 LMT
4/01/1893 12:00 CST
3/31/1918 02:00 CWT
10/27/1918 02:00 CST
1/01/1919 02:00 EST
3/30/1919 02:00 CWT
10/26/1919 02:00 CST
3/30/1924 02:00 EST
2/09/1942 02:00 EWT
9/26/1943 02:00 CWT
9/30/1945 02:00 EST
5/14/1964 02:00 EDT
10/25/1964 02:00 EST
4/30/1967 02:00 US#1
....

OH # 99
Before 4/01/1893 LMT
4/01/1893 12:00 CST
3/31/1918 02:00 CWT
10/27/1918 02:00 CST
3/30/1919 02:00 CWT
10/26/1919 02:00 CST
8/31/1924 00:01 EST
2/09/1942 02:00 EWT
10/31/1943 02:00 CWT
4/02/1944 02:00 EWT
9/24/1944 02:00 CWT
4/01/1945 02:00 EWT
9/30/1945 02:00 EST
4/30/1967 02:00 US#1
....

OH # 100
Before 4/01/1893 LMT
4/01/1893 12:00 CST
3/31/1918 02:00 CWT
10/27/1918 02:00 CST
3/30/1919 02:00 CWT
10/26/1919 02:00 CST
4/03/1927 02:00 EST
2/09/1942 02:00 EWT
9/26/1943 02:00 CWT
4/02/1944 02:00 EWT
9/24/1944 02:00 CWT
9/30/1945 02:00 EST
4/30/1967 02:00 US#1
....

OH # 101
Before 4/01/1893 LMT
4/01/1893 12:00 CST
3/31/1918 02:00 CWT
10/27/1918 02:00 CST
3/30/1919 02:00 CWT
10/26/1919 02:00 CST
4/03/1927 02:00 EST
2/09/1942 02:00 EWT
2/21/1943 02:00 CWT
4/02/1944 02:00 EWT
9/24/1944 02:00 CWT
4/01/1945 02:00 EWT
9/30/1945 02:00 EST
4/30/1967 02:00 US#1
....

OH # 102
Before 4/01/1893 LMT
4/01/1893 12:00 CST
3/31/1918 02:00 CWT
10/27/1918 02:00 CST
3/30/1919 02:00 CWT
10/26/1919 02:00 CST
3/30/1924 02:00 EST
2/09/1942 02:00 EWT
9/26/1943 02:00 CWT
9/30/1945 02:00 EST
4/30/1967 02:00 US#1
....

OH # 103
Before 4/01/1893 LMT
4/01/1893 12:00 CST
3/31/1918 02:00 CWT
10/27/1918 02:00 CST
1/01/1919 02:00 EST
3/30/1919 02:00 EWT
10/26/1919 02:00 EST
2/09/1942 02:00 EWT
9/26/1943 02:00 CWT
9/30/1945 02:00 EST
4/29/1956 02:00 US#5
....

OH # 104
Before 4/01/1893 LMT
4/01/1893 12:00 CST
3/31/1918 02:00 CWT
10/27/1918 02:00 CST
1/01/1919 02:00 EST
3/30/1919 02:00 EWT
10/26/1919 02:00 EST
2/09/1942 02:00 EWT
9/26/1943 02:00 CWT
4/01/1944 02:00 EWT
9/24/1944 02:00 CWT
4/01/1945 02:00 EWT
9/30/1945 02:00 EST
4/30/1967 02:00 US#1
....

OH # 105
Before 4/01/1893 LMT
4/01/1893 12:00 CST
3/31/1918 02:00 CWT
10/27/1918 02:00 CST
1/01/1919 02:00 EST
3/30/1919 02:00 EWT
10/26/1919 02:00 EST
2/09/1942 02:00 EWT
9/30/1945 02:00 EST
4/25/1948 02:00 EDT
9/26/1948 02:00 EST
4/24/1949 02:00 EDT
9/25/1949 02:00 EST
4/30/1950 02:00 EDT
9/30/1950 02:00 EST
4/29/1951 02:00 EDT
9/30/1951 02:00 EST
4/27/1952 02:00 EDT
9/28/1952 02:00 EST
4/26/1953 02:00 EDT
9/27/1953 02:00 EST
4/25/1954 02:00 EDT
9/26/1954 02:00 EST
4/24/1955 02:00 EDT
9/25/1955 02:00 EST
4/29/1956 02:00 US#2
....

OH # 106
Before 4/01/1893 LMT
4/01/1893 12:00 CST
3/31/1918 02:00 CWT
10/27/1918 02:00 CST
1/01/1919 02:00 EST
3/30/1919 02:00 EWT
10/26/1919 02:00 EST
4/27/1941 02:00 EDT
9/28/1941 02:00 EST
2/09/1942 02:00 EWT
9/30/1945 02:00 EST
4/28/1946 02:00 EDT
9/29/1946 02:00 EST
4/27/1947 02:00 EDT
9/28/1947 02:00 EST
4/25/1948 02:00 EDT
9/06/1948 02:00 EST
4/24/1949 02:00 US#3
....

OH # 107
Before 4/01/1893 LMT
4/01/1893 12:00 CST
3/31/1918 02:00 CWT
10/27/1918 02:00 CST
3/30/1919 02:00 CWT
10/26/1919 02:00 CST
3/28/1920 02:00 CDT
10/31/1920 02:00 CST
4/03/1921 02:00 CDT
9/25/1921 02:00 CST
4/30/1922 02:00 CDT
9/24/1922 02:00 CST
4/29/1923 02:00 CDT
9/30/1923 02:00 CST
3/30/1924 02:00 EST
2/09/1942 02:00 EWT
2/21/1943 02:00 CWT
4/02/1944 02:00 EWT
9/03/1944 02:00 CWT
4/01/1945 02:00 EWT
9/30/1945 02:00 EST
4/30/1967 02:00 US#1
....

OH # 108
Before 4/01/1893 LMT
4/01/1893 12:00 CST
3/31/1918 02:00 CWT
10/27/1918 02:00 CST
3/30/1919 02:00 CWT
10/26/1919 02:00 CST
3/30/1924 02:00 EST
2/09/1942 02:00 EWT
2/21/1943 02:00 CWT
4/02/1944 02:00 EWT
9/03/1944 02:00 CWT
4/01/1945 02:00 EWT

TIME TABLES

9/30/1945 02:00 EST
4/30/1967 02:00 US#1
....

OH # 109
Before 4/01/1893 LMT
4/01/1893 12:00 CST
3/31/1918 02:00 CWT
10/27/1918 02:00 CST
1/01/1919 02:00 EST
3/30/1919 02:00 EWT
6/01/1919 02:00 CWT
10/26/1919 02:00 CST
3/30/1924 02:00 EST
2/09/1942 02:00 EWT
2/21/1943 02:00 CWT
4/02/1944 02:00 EWT
9/03/1944 02:00 CWT
9/30/1945 02:00 EST
4/30/1967 02:00 US#1
....

OH # 110
Before 4/01/1893 LMT
4/01/1893 12:00 CST
3/31/1918 02:00 CWT
10/27/1918 02:00 CST
3/30/1919 02:00 CWT
10/26/1919 02:00 CST
4/03/1927 02:00 EST
2/09/1942 02:00 EWT
2/21/1943 02:00 CWT
4/01/1945 02:00 EWT
9/30/1945 02:00 EST
4/30/1967 02:00 US#1
....

OH # 111
Before 4/01/1893 LMT
4/01/1893 12:00 CST
3/31/1918 02:00 CWT
10/27/1918 02:00 CST
3/30/1919 02:00 CWT
10/26/1919 02:00 CST
8/31/1924 00:01 EST
2/09/1942 02:00 EWT
2/21/1943 02:00 CWT
4/01/1945 02:00 EWT
9/30/1945 02:00 EST
4/30/1967 02:00 US#1
....

OH # 112
Before 4/01/1893 LMT
4/01/1893 12:00 CST
3/31/1918 02:00 CWT
10/27/1918 02:00 CST
1/01/1919 02:00 EST
3/30/1919 02:00 EWT
10/26/1919 02:00 EST
2/09/1942 02:00 EWT
2/21/1943 02:00 CWT
4/01/1945 02:00 EWT
9/30/1945 02:00 EST
4/30/1967 02:00 US#1
....

OH # 113
Before 4/01/1893 LMT
4/01/1893 12:00 CST
3/31/1918 02:00 CWT
10/27/1918 02:00 CST
1/01/1919 02:00 EST
3/30/1919 02:00 EWT
10/26/1919 02:00 EST
3/28/1920 02:00 EDT
10/31/1920 02:00 EST
4/24/1921 02:00 EDT
9/25/1921 02:00 EST
4/30/1922 02:00 EDT
9/24/1922 02:00 EST
4/29/1923 02:00 EDT
9/30/1923 02:00 EST
4/27/1924 02:00 EDT
9/28/1924 02:00 EST
4/26/1925 02:00 EDT
9/27/1925 02:00 EST
4/25/1926 02:00 EDT
9/26/1926 02:00 EST
2/09/1942 02:00 EWT
2/21/1943 02:00 CWT
4/01/1945 02:00 EWT
9/30/1945 02:00 EST
4/27/1958 02:00 US#5
....

OH # 114
Before 4/01/1893 LMT
4/01/1893 12:00 CST
3/31/1918 02:00 CWT
10/27/1918 02:00 CST
1/01/1919 02:00 EST
3/30/1919 02:00 EWT
10/26/1919 02:00 EST
2/09/1942 02:00 EWT
2/21/1943 02:00 CWT
4/01/1945 02:00 EWT
9/30/1945 02:00 EST
4/25/1954 02:00 US#5
....

OH # 115
Before 4/01/1893 LMT
4/01/1893 12:00 CST
3/31/1918 02:00 CWT
10/27/1918 02:00 CST
1/01/1919 02:00 EST
3/30/1919 02:00 EWT
10/26/1919 02:00 EST
2/09/1942 02:00 EWT
2/21/1943 02:00 CWT
4/01/1945 02:00 EWT
9/30/1945 02:00 EST
4/28/1957 02:00 US#5
....

OH # 116
Before 4/01/1893 LMT
4/01/1893 12:00 CST
3/31/1918 02:00 CWT
10/27/1918 02:00 CST
1/01/1919 02:00 EST
3/30/1919 02:00 EWT
10/26/1919 02:00 EST
2/09/1942 02:00 EWT
2/21/1943 02:00 CWT
4/01/1945 02:00 EWT
9/30/1945 02:00 EST
4/27/1958 02:00 US#5
....

OH # 117
Before 4/01/1893 LMT
4/01/1893 12:00 CST
3/31/1918 02:00 CWT
10/27/1918 02:00 CST
1/01/1919 02:00 EST
3/30/1919 02:00 EWT
6/01/1919 02:00 CWT
10/26/1919 02:00 CST
3/30/1924 02:00 EST
2/09/1942 02:00 EWT
2/21/1943 02:00 CWT
4/01/1945 02:00 EWT
9/30/1945 02:00 EST
4/30/1967 02:00 US#1
....

OH # 118
Before 4/01/1893 LMT
4/01/1893 12:00 CST
3/31/1918 02:00 CWT
10/27/1918 02:00 CST
3/30/1919 02:00 CWT
10/26/1919 02:00 CST
4/03/1927 02:00 EST
2/09/1942 02:00 EWT
2/21/1943 02:00 CWT
4/29/1945 02:00 EWT
9/30/1945 02:00 EST
4/30/1967 02:00 US#1

COUNTIES

1 Adams
2 Allen
3 Ashland
4 Ashtabula
5 Athens
6 Auglaize
7 Belmont
8 Brown
9 Butler
10 Carroll
11 Champaign
12 Clark
13 Clermont
14 Clinton
15 Columbiana
16 Coshocton
17 Crawford
18 Cuyahoga
19 Darke
20 Defiance
21 Delaware
22 Erie
23 Fairfield
24 Fayette
25 Franklin
26 Fulton
27 Gallia
28 Geauga
29 Greene
30 Guernsey
31 Hamilton
32 Hancock
33 Hardin
34 Harrison
35 Henry
36 Highland
37 Hocking
38 Holmes
39 Huron
40 Jackson
41 Jefferson
42 Knox
43 Lake
44 Lawrence
45 Licking
46 Logan
47 Lorain
48 Lucas
49 Madison
50 Mahoning
51 Marion
52 Medina
53 Meigs
54 Mercer
55 Miami
56 Monroe
57 Montgomery
58 Morgan
59 Morrow
60 Muskingum
61 Noble
62 Ottawa
63 Paulding
64 Perry
65 Pickaway
66 Pike
67 Portage
68 Preble
69 Putnam
70 Richland
71 Ross
72 Sandusky
73 Scioto
74 Seneca
75 Shelby
76 Stark
77 Summit
78 Trumbull
79 Tuscarawas
80 Union
81 Van Wert
82 Vinton
83 Warren
84 Washington
85 Wayne
86 Williams
87 Wood
88 Wyandot

Abanaka 81	34	40N46	84w37	5:38:28
Abbottsville 19	34	39N58	84w33	5:38:12
Aberdeen 8	34	38N39	83w46	5:35:04
Academia 42	108	40N24	82w29	5:29:56
Achor 15	78	40N48	80w32	5:22:08
Acme 52	53	41N01	81w44	5:26:56
Ada 33	34	40N46	83w49	5:35:16
Adams Mills 60	5	40N09	81w57	5:27:48
Adamsville 27	27	38N55	82w18	5:29:12
Adamsville 60	5	40N04	81w53	5:27:32
Adario 70	5	40N56	82w27	5:29:48
Addison 27	27	38N53	82w09	5:28:36
Addyston 31	34	39N08	84w43	5:38:52
Adelphi 71	34	39N28	82w45	5:31:00
Adena 41	23	40N13	80w53	5:23:32
Adrian 74	32	41N03	83w20	5:33:20
Aetnaville 7	23	40N05	80w45	5:23:00
Africa 21	27	40N13	82w53	5:31:32
Afton 13	34	39N05	84w11	5:36:44
Aid 44	34	38N36	82w30	5:30:00
Ainger 86	34	41N35	84w36	5:38:24
Air Material Command 29	34	39N47	84w03	5:36:12
Aitch 56	20	39N47	81w09	5:24:36
Akron 77	2	41N05	81w31	5:26:04
Albany 5	27	39N14	82w12	5:28:48
Al Bar Meadows 31	34	39N11	84w22	5:37:28
Albion 3	44	40N57	82w05	5:28:20
Alcony 55	34	40N03	84w11	5:36:44
Alexander 5	27	39N15	82w07	5:28:28
Alexanders 18	26	41N22	81w40	5:26:40
Alexandersville 57	91	39N40	84w15	5:37:00
Alexandria 45	27	40N05	82w37	5:30:28
Alexis Place 48	31	41N42	83w34	5:34:16
Alfred 53	5	39N14	81w45	5:27:00
Alger 33	34	40N42	83w52	5:35:28
Alikanna 41	106	40N22	80w39	5:22:36
Alledonia 7	21	39N54	80w58	5:23:52
Allen Center 80	33	40N15	83w22	5:33:28
Allensburg 36	34	39N12	83w37	5:34:28
Allensville 82	34	39N16	82w37	5:30:28
Allentown 2	90	40N45	84w10	5:36:40
Allentown 73	34	38N45	82w51	5:31:24
Alliance 76	51	40N55	81w06	5:24:24
Alma 71	34	39N09	83w00	5:32:00
Alpha 29	34	39N43	84w01	5:36:04
Alpine Terrace 13	88	39N06	84w23	5:37:32
Alpine Village 46	34	40N21	83w41	5:34:44
Alta 70	95	40N45	82w31	5:30:04
Altamont Hills 41	106	40N19	80w39	5:22:36
Altamont Park 41	106	40N19	80w39	5:22:36
Alton 25	34	39N55	83w10	5:32:40
Altoona 40	34	39N07	82w33	5:30:12
Alvada 74	32	41N03	83w24	5:33:36
Alvordton 86	34	41N40	84w26	5:37:44
Amanda 23	34	39N39	82w45	5:31:00
Amberley 31	34	39N13	84w26	5:37:44
Amberly 25	107	39N56	82w53	5:31:32
Amboy 4	72	41N56	80w36	5:22:24
Amboy 26	34	41N41	83w57	5:35:48
Amelia 13	34	39N02	84w13	5:36:52
American 2	90	40N46	84w09	5:36:36
Ames 5	5	39N25	82w00	5:28:00
Amesville 5	5	39N24	81w57	5:27:48
Amherst 47	63	41N24	82w14	5:28:56
Amherst Heights 76	54	40N48	81w31	5:26:04
Amity 42	5	40N24	82w29	5:29:56
Amity 49	34	40N07	83w16	5:33:04
Amity 57	34	39N49	84w25	5:37:40
Amlin 25	108	40N03	83w09	5:32:36
Amlin Heights 29	34	39N44	84w02	5:36:08
Amoy 70	95	40N45	82w31	5:30:04
Amsden 74	32	41N13	83w20	5:33:20
Amsterdam 41	67	40N29	80w56	5:23:44
Amsterdam 45	27	39N54	82w27	5:29:48
Anderson 31	34	39N05	84w21	5:37:24
Andersonville 71	34	39N26	83w01	5:32:04
Andis 44	34	38N34	82w35	5:30:20
Andover 4	56	41N36	80w34	5:22:16
Ankenytown 42	5	40N32	82w30	5:30:00
Anna 75	34	40N24	84w11	5:36:44
Annapolis 41	67	40N21	80w48	5:23:12
Ansonia 19	34	40N13	84w38	5:38:32
Antioch 49	34	39N43	83w16	5:33:04
Antioch 56	20	39N40	81w04	5:24:16
Antiquity 56	20	38N58	81w55	5:27:40
Antrim 30	5	40N07	81w22	5:25:28
Antwerp 63	34	41N11	84w44	5:38:56
Apco 67	67	41N10	81w16	5:25:04
Apple Creek 85	62	40N45	81w51	5:27:24
Apple Grove 53	5	38N58	81w55	5:27:40
Appleton 45	27	40N09	82w41	5:30:44
Aquilla 28	62	41N32	81w11	5:24:44
Arabia 44	34	38N40	82w29	5:29:56
Arborcrest Acres 31	34	39N12	84w25	5:37:40
Arcadia 32	33	41N07	83w30	5:34:00
Arcanum 19	34	39N59	84w33	5:38:12
Archbold 26	34	41N31	84w18	5:37:12
Archer 34	21	40N19	81w01	5:24:04
Archers Fork 84	20	39N33	81w04	5:24:16
Arion 73	34	39N03	83w03	5:32:12
Arlington 32	33	40N54	83w39	5:34:36
Arlington 57	34	39N49	84w25	5:37:40
Arlington Heights 31	34	39N13	84w27	5:37:48
Armstrongs Mills 7	21	39N55	80w56	5:23:44
Arnheim 8	34	38N52	83w55	5:35:40
Arnold 80	34	40N07	83w16	5:33:04
Artanna 42	5	40N23	82w23	5:29:32
Arthur 63	34	41N17	84w20	5:37:20
Arwold 55	34	39N58	84w20	5:37:20
Ashland 3	44	40N52	82w19	5:29:16
Ashley 21	27	40N25	82w57	5:31:48
Ashley Corner 73	34	38N45	82w51	5:31:24
Ash Ridge 8	34	38N52	83w55	5:35:40
Ashtabula 4	46	41N52	80w47	5:23:08
Ashville 65	34	39N43	82w57	5:31:48
Assumption 26	34	41N35	83w54	5:35:36
Athens 5	97	39N20	82w06	5:28:24
Atlanta 65	34	39N34	83w11	5:32:44
Atlas 7	21	39N59	81w11	5:24:44
Atlas 67	67	41N10	81w16	5:25:04
Attica 74	32	41N04	82w53	5:31:32
Atwater 67	67	41N01	81w10	5:24:40
Auburn 9	34	39N23	84w42	5:38:48
Auburn Center 17	5	40N54	82w37	5:30:28
Auburn Center 28	67	41N26	81w22	5:25:28
Auburn Corners 28	67	41N17	81w14	5:24:56
Augusta 10	21	40N41	81w02	5:24:08
Ault 7	21	40N00	80w46	5:23:04
Aultman 76	67	40N56	81w28	5:25:52
Aurelius 84	20	39N36	81w26	5:25:44
Aurora 67	46	41N19	81w21	5:25:24
Austin 71	34	39N24	83w10	5:32:40
Austinburg 4	72	41N46	80w51	5:23:24
Austin Square Shopping Ctr 77	67	41N01	81w38	5:26:32
Austintown 50	84	41N06	80w48	5:23:12
Autumn Acres 31	34	39N13	84w35	5:38:20
Ava 61	5	39N50	81w35	5:26:20
Avalon 9	34	39N30	84w23	5:37:32
Avalon 64	27	39N42	82w26	5:29:44

OHIO

Avalon Heights 83
34 39N26 84w12 5:36:48
Avis 69 34 41N01 84w03 5:36:12
Avon 47 65 41N27 82w02 5:28:08
Avondale 7 21 40N01 80w45 5:23:00
Avondale 46 34 40N29 83w56 5:35:44
Avondale 57 91 39N48 84w08 5:36:32
Avondale 60 5 39N47 82w04 5:28:16
Avondale 76 43 40N49 81w26 5:25:44
Avondale Park 45 27 39N54 82w27 5:29:48
Avon Lake 47 65 41N31 82w01 5:28:04
Axtel 22 5 41N25 82w19 5:29:16
Ayersville 20 34 41N17 84w20 5:37:20
Bachman 57 34 39N49 84w25 5:37:40
Bailey Lakes 3 44 40N57 82w23 5:29:32
Baileys Mills 7 21 39N59 81w11 5:24:44
Bainbridge 71 36 39N14 83w16 5:33:04
Bainbridge Center 28
67 41N26 81w22 5:25:28
Bairdstown 87 34 41N11 83w37 5:34:28
Baker 19 34 40N06 84w38 5:38:32
Bakers 47 67 41N09 82w16 5:29:04
Bakersville 16 5 40N21 81w39 5:26:36
Ballville 72 32 41N18 83w08 5:32:32
Baltic 79 16 40N26 81w42 5:26:48
Baltimore 23 27 39N51 82w36 5:30:24
Bangs 42 5 40N24 82w29 5:29:56
Bannock 7 21 40N05 80w55 5:23:40
Bantam 13 34 39N05 84w11 5:36:44
Barberton 77 46 41N00 81w39 5:26:36
Bardwell 8 34 39N02 83w56 5:35:44
Barlow 84 20 39N24 81w39 5:26:36
Barnesburg 31 34 39N13 84w35 5:38:20
Barnesville 7 18 39N59 81w11 5:24:44
Barnhill 79 16 40N27 81w22 5:25:28
Barr 79 16 40N30 81w37 5:26:28
Barretts Mills 36
36 39N14 83w15 5:33:00
Bartles 44 34 38N38 82w40 5:30:40
Bartlett 84 20 39N25 81w49 5:27:16
Bartley Estates 57
91 39N50 84w13 5:36:52
Bartlow 35 34 41N13 83w56 5:35:44
Barton 7 21 40N06 80w51 5:23:24
Bartramville 44 37 38N28 82w25 5:29:40
Bascom 74 32 41N08 83w17 5:33:08
Bashan 53 5 39N05 81w48 5:27:12
Bass Lake 28 67 41N34 81w12 5:24:48
Batavia 13 34 39N05 84w11 5:36:44
Batemantown 42 27 39N56 82w51 5:31:24
Batesville 61 5 39N56 81w17 5:25:08
Bath 77 67 41N11 81w38 5:26:32
Battlesburg 76 67 40N40 81w21 5:25:24
Baughman 85 62 40N51 81w42 5:26:48
Bay 62 93 41N29 83w00 5:32:00
Bayard 15 67 40N44 81w05 5:24:20
Bay Bridge 22 5 41N28 82w49 5:31:16
Bays 87 33 41N18 83w40 5:34:40
Bay Shore 72 30 41N23 82w56 5:31:44
Bayview 4 72 41N32 80w32 5:22:08
Bay View 22 5 41N28 82w49 5:31:16
Bay Village 18 66 41N29 81w56 5:27:44
Bazetta 78 45 41N18 80w46 5:23:04
Beach City 76 21 40N39 81w35 5:26:20
Beachland 18 67 41N35 81w32 5:26:08
Beachwood 18 67 41N29 81w30 5:26:00
Beacon Hill 9 34 39N16 84w24 5:37:36
Beacon Hill 28 67 41N26 81w22 5:25:28
Beallsville 56 20 39N51 81w02 5:24:08
Beals 23 27 39N53 82w45 5:31:00
Beamsville 19 34 40N13 84w29 5:37:56
Bearfield 64 27 39N41 82w03 5:28:12
Beartown 79 16 40N33 81w29 5:25:56
Beatty 12 39 39N55 83w48 5:35:12
Beaumont 5 27 39N20 82w05 5:28:20
Beavan 84 20 39N23 81w14 5:24:56
Beaver 66 34 39N02 82w50 5:31:20
Beaver Creek 29 34 39N43 84w03 5:36:12
Beaverdam 2 34 40N50 83w59 5:35:56
Beaver Park 47 50 41N26 82w10 5:28:40
Beavertown 57 91 39N41 84w09 5:36:36
Beavertown 84 20 39N33 81w04 5:24:16
Becker Highlands 41
106 40N22 80w39 5:22:36
Becks Mills 38 5 40N33 81w55 5:27:40
Bedford 18 70 41N23 81w32 5:26:08
Bedford Heights 18
70 41N23 81w30 5:26:00
Beechcrest 67 67 41N10 81w21 5:25:24
Beechwold 25 107 40N03 83w01 5:32:04
Beechwood 41 106 40N22 80w39 5:22:36
Beechwood 68 34 39N38 84w39 5:38:36
Belden 47 42 41N18 82w06 5:28:24
Belfast 36 34 39N12 83w37 5:34:28
Belfort 76 67 40N50 81w17 5:25:08
Bellaire 7 6 40N01 80w45 5:23:00
Bellaire Gardens 51
27 40N35 83w07 5:32:28
Bellbrook 29 34 39N38 84w04 5:36:16
Belle Center 46 34 40N31 83w44 5:34:56
Bellefontaine 46 99 40N22 83w46 5:35:04
Bellepoint 21 27 40N18 83w04 5:32:16
Belle Valley 61 5 39N47 81w33 5:26:12
Belle Vernon 88 32 40N57 83w11 5:32:44
Belleview Acres 29
34 39N38 84w04 5:36:16
Belleview Heights 68
34 39N51 84w48 5:39:12
Belleview Heights 71
34 39N21 83w00 5:32:00
Bellevue 39 27 41N17 82w51 5:31:24
Bellview Heights 7
21 40N01 80w45 5:23:00
Bellville 70 5 40N37 82w31 5:30:04
Belmont 2 90 40N45 84w06 5:36:24
Belmont 7 13 40N02 81w03 5:24:12
Belmont 9 34 39N22 84w33 5:38:12

Belmont Ridge 7 13 40N12 81w09 5:24:36
Belmore 69 34 41N09 83w56 5:35:44
Beloit 50 67 40N55 81w01 5:24:04
Belpre 84 20 39N17 81w34 5:26:16
Belvedere 41 106 40N22 80w39 5:22:36
Bentley 50 84 41N02 80w33 5:22:12
Bentleyville 18 67 41N25 81w25 5:25:40
Benton 17 33 40N57 83w11 5:32:44
Benton 38 5 40N33 81w55 5:27:40
Benton Ridge 32 34 41N00 83w48 5:35:12
Bentonville 1 34 38N45 83w37 5:34:28
Berea 18 46 41N22 81w52 5:27:28
Bergholz 41 67 40N31 80w53 5:23:32
Berkey 48 34 41N42 83w51 5:35:24
Berkley Heights 57
91 39N41 84w09 5:36:36
Berkshire 21 27 40N15 82w54 5:31:36
Berlin 38 5 40N34 81w48 5:27:12
Berlin Center 50 67 41N01 80w57 5:23:48
Berlin Heights 22 9 41N20 82w30 5:30:00
Berlinville 22 9 41N20 82w30 5:30:00
Bern 5 5 39N25 81w53 5:27:32
Berne 23 27 39N40 82w33 5:30:12
Berne 61 5 39N45 81w31 5:26:04
Bernice 79 16 40N15 81w35 5:26:20
Berrysville 36 34 39N12 83w37 5:34:28
Berwick 74 32 41N04 83w19 5:33:16
Bessemer 5 27 39N26 82w14 5:28:56
Bethany 9 34 39N23 84w23 5:37:32
Bethel 13 34 38N58 84w05 5:36:20
Bethel 49 34 39N43 83w16 5:33:04
Bethesda 7 21 40N01 81w04 5:24:16
Bethlehem 70 5 40N54 82w37 5:30:28
Bettsville 74 32 41N15 83w14 5:32:56
Beulah Beach 22 5 41N25 82w19 5:29:16
Beverly 84 20 39N33 81w38 5:26:32
Beverly Gardens 57
34 39N46 84w06 5:36:24
Bevis 31 34 39N16 84w36 5:38:24
Bexley 25 107 39N58 82w56 5:31:44
Bidwell 27 27 38N55 82w18 5:29:12
Big Island 51 33 40N36 83w14 5:32:56
Biglick 32 33 41N03 83w29 5:33:56
Big Plain 49 34 39N50 83w17 5:33:08
Big Prairie 38 17 40N40 82w06 5:28:24
Big Rock 40 34 39N03 82w50 5:31:20
Big Run 5 5 39N21 81w47 5:27:08
Big Spring 74 32 41N03 83w22 5:33:28
Big Springs 46 33 40N28 83w40 5:34:40
Biltmore Gardens 87
31 41N38 83w29 5:33:56
Bingville 6 34 40N36 83w59 5:35:56
Birds Run 30 5 40N11 81w36 5:26:24
Birmingham 22 5 41N20 82w21 5:29:24
Birmingham 30 5 40N09 81w34 5:26:16
Bishopville 58 5 39N30 82w06 5:28:24
Bismarck 39 32 41N16 82w51 5:31:24
Blackburn 15 67 40N55 80w51 5:23:24
Black Creek 54 34 40N42 84w44 5:38:56
Blackfork 44 34 38N50 82w36 5:30:24
Black Horse 67 67 41N10 81w16 5:25:04
Blacklick 25 27 40N00 82w49 5:31:16
Blacklick Estates 25
27 39N54 82w52 5:31:28
Blackrun 60 5 40N04 82w09 5:28:36
Blacktop 30 5 39N59 81w27 5:25:48
Bladen 27 34 38N35 82w17 5:29:08
Bladensburg 42 5 40N17 82w17 5:29:08
Blaine 7 21 40N04 80w49 5:23:16
Blainesville 7 21 40N07 80w53 5:23:32
Blairmont 34 21 40N13 80w52 5:23:28
Blake 52 60 41N00 81w52 5:27:28
Blakeslee 86 34 41N32 84w44 5:38:56
Blanchard 33 33 40N47 83w39 5:34:36
Blanches Addition 45
27 40N00 82w40 5:30:40
Blanchester 14 34 39N17 83w59 5:35:56
Blendon 25 108 40N06 82w55 5:31:40
Blissfield 16 5 40N24 81w58 5:27:52
Bloom Center 46 34 40N25 83w53 5:35:32
Bloom Center 87 34 41N11 83w33 5:34:12
Bloomdale 87 33 41N11 83w33 5:34:12
Bloomer 55 34 40N07 84w21 5:37:24
Bloomfield 59 27 40N18 82w41 5:30:44
Bloomfield 60 5 39N59 81w46 5:27:04
Bloomfield 84 20 39N35 81w09 5:24:36
Bloomingburg 24 34 39N36 83w24 5:33:36
Bloomingdale 41 67 40N21 80w49 5:23:16
Blooming Grove 59 5 40N57 82w32 5:30:08
Bloomington 14 34 39N29 83w38 5:34:32
Bloomingville 22 5 41N27 82w44 5:30:56
Bloomville 74 32 41N03 83w01 5:32:04
Blue Ash 31 34 39N14 84w23 5:37:32
Blue Ball 9 34 39N30 84w20 5:37:20
Bluebird Beach 47
67 41N25 82w19 5:29:16
Blue Creek 1 34 38N47 83w20 5:33:20
Blue Creek 63 34 41N02 84w38 5:38:32
Blue Rock 60 5 39N48 81w54 5:27:36
Bluffton 2 34 40N54 83w54 5:35:36
Boardman 50 84 41N01 80w39 5:22:36
Bobo 66 34 39N03 82w50 5:31:20
Boden 30 5 39N59 81w46 5:27:04
Bokes Creek 46 33 40N28 83w35 5:34:20
Bolivar 79 16 40N40 81w28 5:25:52
Bolton 76 67 40N55 81w06 5:24:24
Bonn 84 20 39N31 81w25 5:25:40
Bono 48 30 41N33 83w20 5:33:20
Booktown 72 30 41N21 83w08 5:32:32
Bookwalter 24 34 39N39 83w32 5:34:08
Booth 48 30 41N40 83w24 5:33:36
Booth 79 16 40N15 81w35 5:26:20
Boston 36 34 39N12 83w37 5:34:28
Boston 77 67 41N14 81w32 5:26:08
Boston Heights 77
67 41N15 81w30 5:26:00
Boston Mill 77 67 41N14 81w33 5:26:12

Botkins 75 34 40N28 84w11 5:36:44
Boudes Ferry 8 34 38N52 83w55 5:35:40
Boughtonville 39 5 41N03 82w44 5:30:56
Bourneville 71 34 39N17 83w09 5:32:36
Bowerston 34 21 40N25 81w12 5:24:48
Bowersville 29 34 39N35 83w44 5:34:56
Bowling Green 87 33 41N23 83w39 5:34:36
Bowlusville 11 34 40N04 83w42 5:34:48
Boyds Corners 50 67 40N55 81w01 5:24:04
Boydsville 7 21 40N05 80w45 5:23:00
Braceville 78 67 41N14 80w58 5:23:52
Bradbury 53 27 39N00 82w04 5:28:16
Bradford 19 34 40N08 84w26 5:37:44
Bradley 41 67 40N12 80w46 5:23:04
Bradner 87 32 41N20 83w26 5:33:44
Bradrick 44 37 38N27 82w28 5:29:52
Brady 86 34 41N33 84w25 5:37:40
Brady Lake 67 67 41N10 81w19 5:25:16
Bradyville 1 34 38N41 83w36 5:34:24
Braffettsville 19
34 39N51 84w48 5:39:12
Brailey 26 34 41N35 83w54 5:35:36
Branch Hill 13 34 39N15 84w18 5:37:12
Brandon 42 27 40N19 82w31 5:30:04
Brandt 55 34 39N58 84w10 5:36:40
Brandywine 17 33 40N48 82w58 5:31:52
Bratenahl 18 26 41N34 81w36 5:26:24
Bratton 1 34 39N01 83w26 5:33:44
Brecksville 18 67 41N19 81w38 5:26:32
Brecon 31 34 39N17 84w21 5:37:24
Bremen 23 27 39N42 82w26 5:29:44
Brentwood 31 34 39N14 84w32 5:38:08
Brentwood 43 67 41N41 81w21 5:25:24
Brentwood Estates 41
106 40N22 80w39 5:22:36
Brentwood Lake 47
42 41N19 82w05 5:28:20
Brewster 76 67 40N43 81w36 5:26:24
Briarwood Beach 52
73 41N04 81w54 5:27:36
Brice 25 27 39N55 82w50 5:31:20
Briceton 63 34 41N09 84w35 5:38:20
Bridgeport 7 8 40N04 80w45 5:23:00
Bridgeport 33 33 40N48 83w31 5:34:04
Bridges 36 34 39N20 83w34 5:34:16
Bridgetown 31 34 39N10 84w38 5:38:32
Bridgewater 86 34 41N40 84w38 5:38:32
Briggs 18 26 41N24 81w43 5:26:52
Briggsdale 25 107 39N56 83w03 5:32:12
Brighton 12 34 39N55 83w37 5:34:28
Brighton 47 67 41N10 82w19 5:29:16
Brighton 87 31 41N38 83w29 5:33:56
Brightwood 79 16 40N29 81w23 5:25:32
Brilliant 41 67 40N16 80w38 5:22:32
Brimfield 67 67 41N06 81w21 5:25:24
Brinkhaven 42 5 40N28 82w12 5:28:48
Bristol 64 27 39N43 82w13 5:28:52
Bristol Village 66
34 39N09 83w00 5:32:00
Bristolville 78 67 41N23 80w52 5:23:28
Broadacre 41 67 40N21 80w48 5:23:12
Broadmoor Plaza 57
91 39N48 84w17 5:37:08
Broadview Acres 60
5 39N55 82w01 5:28:04
Broadview Heights 18
67 41N19 81w41 5:26:44
Broadway 80 33 40N21 83w25 5:33:40
Broadwell 5 5 39N18 81w54 5:27:36
Brock 19 34 40N13 84w29 5:37:56
Brokaw 58 5 39N33 81w48 5:27:12
Brokensword 17 33 40N48 82w58 5:31:52
Bronson 39 5 41N11 82w36 5:30:24
Brookfield 78 45 41N14 80w34 5:22:16
Brookgate 18 26 41N25 81w48 5:27:12
Brookhill 31 88 39N12 84w32 5:38:08
Brook Hollow 29 34 39N48 84w01 5:36:04
Brooklyn 18 26 41N26 81w47 5:27:08
Brooklyn Heights 18
26 41N25 81w40 5:26:40
Brook Park 18 67 41N24 80w51 5:23:24
Brooks Corner 40 34 39N12 82w41 5:30:44
Brookside 7 21 40N04 80w46 5:23:04
Brookside Estates 25
107 40N05 83w01 5:32:04
Brookville 57 34 39N50 84w25 5:37:40
Brookwood 31 88 39N11 84w27 5:37:48
Broughton 63 34 41N05 84w32 5:38:08
Brown Heights 30 5 40N01 81w35 5:26:20
Brownhelm 47 67 41N23 82w18 5:29:12
Brownsville 45 5 39N57 82w15 5:29:00
Brownsville 56 20 39N36 81w05 5:24:20
Brownsville 71 34 39N21 83w00 5:32:00
Browntown 8 34 38N52 83w55 5:35:40
Brunersburg 20 34 41N18 84w23 5:37:32
Bruno 64 27 39N54 82w27 5:29:48
Brunswick 52 67 41N14 81w51 5:27:24
Brunswick Hills 52
67 41N14 81w51 5:27:24
Brush Ridge 51 27 40N35 83w07 5:32:28
Bryan 86 34 41N28 84w33 5:38:12
Buchanan 66 34 39N09 83w00 5:32:00
Buchtel 5 27 39N28 82w12 5:28:48
Buck 33 34 40N37 83w37 5:34:28
Buckeye 60 5 39N55 82w01 5:28:04
Buckeye Addition 42
5 40N24 82w29 5:29:56
Buckeye Lake 45 27 39N56 82w25 5:29:40
Buckeyeville 30 5 40N01 81w35 5:26:20
Buckhorn 44 34 38N45 82w51 5:31:24
Buckingham 64 27 39N36 82w05 5:28:20
Buckland 6 34 40N37 84w16 5:37:04
Bucks 79 16 40N24 81w39 5:26:36
Buckskin 71 34 39N21 83w18 5:33:12
Bucyrus 17 86 40N48 82w59 5:31:56
Buena Vista 24 34 39N25 83w30 5:34:00
Buena Vista 9 34 39N30 84w23 5:37:32

Buena Vista 37	34	39N35	82w32	5:30:08
Buena Vista 73	34	38N40	83w23	5:33:32
Buffalo 30	5	39N55	81w31	5:26:04
Buford 36	34	39N05	83w51	5:35:24
Bulah 4	72	41N44	80w47	5:23:08
Bulkhead 46	34	40N25	83w53	5:35:32
Bunkerhill 9	34	39N24	84w34	5:38:16
Bunker Hill 38	5	40N33	81w55	5:27:40
Bunker Hill 50	67	40N55	81w01	5:24:04
Burbank 85	62	40N59	82w00	5:28:00
Burghill 78	67	41N20	80w34	5:22:16
Burgoon 72	32	41N16	83w15	5:33:00
Burkettsville 54	34	40N21	84w39	5:38:36
Burkhart 56	20	39N46	81w13	5:24:52
Burlingham 53	27	39N13	82w09	5:28:36
Burlington 26	34	41N31	84w18	5:37:12
Burlington 44	37	38N26	82w33	5:30:12
Burlington 45	27	40N14	82w31	5:30:04
Burnetts Corners 85	76	40N49	81w56	5:27:44
Burnet Woods 31	88	39N09	84w31	5:38:04
Burr Oak 5	27	39N30	82w06	5:28:24
Burr Oaks 49	34	39N43	83w16	5:33:04
Burton 28	73	41N27	81w09	5:24:36
Burtonville 14	34	39N27	83w50	5:35:20
Bushnell 4	72	41N56	80w36	5:22:24
Businessburg 7	21	39N58	80w55	5:23:40
Butler 70	27	40N35	82w26	5:29:44
Butlerville 83	34	39N19	84w06	5:36:24
Byer 40	34	39N11	82w38	5:30:32
Byesville 30	5	39N58	81w32	5:26:08
Byhalia 80	33	40N27	83w28	5:33:52
Byington 66	34	39N06	83w15	5:33:00
Byrd 8	34	38N50	83w43	5:34:52
Byron 29	34	39N44	84w02	5:36:08
Cable 11	34	40N10	83w38	5:34:32
Cadiz 34	21	40N16	81w00	5:24:00
Cadmus 27	34	38N46	82w23	5:29:32
Caesar Creek 29	34	39N36	83w52	5:35:28
Cain Heights 15	105	40N38	80w35	5:22:20
Cairo 2	34	40N50	84w05	5:36:20
Cairo 76	43	40N53	81w24	5:25:36
Calais 56	20	39N58	81w17	5:25:08
Calcutta 15	105	40N38	80w35	5:22:20
Caldwell 61	5	39N45	81w31	5:26:04
Caledonia 51	32	40N38	82w59	5:31:56
Calla 50	67	41N02	80w46	5:23:04
Cambridge 30	116	40N02	81w35	5:26:20
Camden 68	34	39N38	84w39	5:38:36
Cameron 56	20	39N46	80w57	5:23:48
Campbell 50	84	41N05	80w37	5:22:28
Campbellsport 67	67	41N10	81w16	5:25:04
Campbellstown 68	34	39N47	84w46	5:39:04
Camp Creek 58	34	38N59	83w07	5:32:28
Camp Creek 76	67	40N43	81w36	5:26:24
Camp Dennison 31	34	39N12	84w17	5:37:08
Camp Ground 23	27	39N43	82w36	5:30:24
Camp Luther 4	72	41N54	80w46	5:23:04
Campus (Cincinnati) 31	88	39N09	84w30	5:38:00
Canaan 85	58	40N58	81w54	5:27:36
Canaanville 5	27	39N20	82w05	5:28:20
Canal Fulton 76	67	40N53	81w36	5:26:24
Canal Lewisville 16	5	40N16	81w52	5:27:28
Canal Winchester 24	27	39N51	82w48	5:31:12
Candy Town 37	27	39N26	82w14	5:28:56
Canfield 50	67	41N02	80w45	5:23:00
Cannelville 60	5	39N47	82w04	5:28:16
Cannons Creek 44	34	38N38	82w40	5:30:40
Cannons Mills 15	105	40N38	80w35	5:22:20
Canton 76	43	40N48	81w23	5:25:32
Carbondale 5	27	39N23	82w16	5:29:04
Carbon Hill 37	34	39N30	82w29	5:29:56
Cardinal Lake 4	72	41N36	80w52	5:23:28
Cardington 59	27	40N30	82w54	5:31:36
Carey 88	32	40N57	83w23	5:33:32
Carlisle 83	34	39N35	84w19	5:37:16
Carmel 36	34	39N12	83w37	5:34:28
Caroline 74	32	41N04	82w51	5:31:24
Carpenter 53	27	39N14	82w12	5:28:48
Carrington 64	27	39N36	82w05	5:28:20
Carroll 23	27	39N48	82w43	5:30:52
Carrollton 10	103	40N34	81w05	5:24:20
Carrothers 74	32	41N00	82w55	5:31:40
Carryall 63	34	41N13	84w45	5:39:00
Carthage 5	5	39N15	81w52	5:27:28
Carthagena 54	34	40N34	84w33	5:38:12
Carysville 11	34	40N08	84w03	5:36:12
Cassell 30	5	40N01	81w35	5:26:20
Cassella 54	34	40N28	84w34	5:38:16
Casstown 55	34	40N03	84w07	5:36:28
Castalia 22	5	41N24	82w49	5:31:16
Castine 19	34	39N56	84w37	5:38:28
Catawba 12	34	40N01	83w38	5:34:32
Catawba Island 62	93	41N35	82w51	5:31:24
Catbird 1	34	38N41	83w36	5:34:24
Causeway Manor 4	72	41N37	80w36	5:22:24
Cavallo 16	5	40N22	82w09	5:28:36
Cavett 81	34	40N52	84w35	5:38:20
Caywood 84	20	39N27	81w28	5:25:52
Cebee 44	37	38N28	82w25	5:29:40
Cecil 63	34	41N13	84w36	5:38:24
Cedarhill 23	34	39N39	82w45	5:31:00
Cedarhurst 25	107	39N58	82w52	5:31:28
Cedar Mills 1	34	38N47	83w20	5:33:20
Cedar Point 22	5	41N27	82w44	5:30:56
Cedarville 29	34	39N44	83w49	5:35:16
Cedron 13	34	38N52	83w55	5:35:40
Celeryville 39	5	41N03	82w44	5:30:56
Celina 54	34	40N33	84w35	5:38:20
Centenary 27	27	38N46	82w11	5:28:44
Center 30	5	40N01	81w35	5:26:20
Centerburg 42	27	40N18	82w42	5:30:48
Centerfield 36	34	39N21	83w24	5:33:36
Centerpoint 8	34	38N45	83w50	5:35:20
Centerpoint 27	34	38N54	82w35	5:30:20
Center Station 44	34	38N38	82w40	5:30:40
Centerton 39	5	41N03	82w44	5:30:56
Center Village 21	27	40N13	82w53	5:31:32
Centerville 7	21	40N02	81w03	5:24:12
Centerville 8	34	39N02	83w56	5:35:44
Centerville 51	33	40N27	83w11	5:32:44
Centerville 57	34	39N38	84w09	5:36:36
Central 48	31	41N39	83w32	5:34:08
Central College 25	108	40N06	82w56	5:31:44
Centreville 27	34	38N55	82w27	5:29:48
Cessna 33	34	40N42	83w43	5:34:52
Ceylon 22	5	41N24	82w34	5:30:16
Chagrin Falls 18	73	41N26	81w23	5:25:32
Chagrin Harbor 43	67	41N38	81w25	5:25:40
Chalfants 64	27	39N54	82w20	5:29:20
Chambersburg 15	67	40N44	81w05	5:24:20
Chambersburg 27	34	38N41	82w12	5:28:48
Champion 78	45	41N19	80w51	5:23:24
Chandler 41	67	40N21	80w48	5:23:12
Chandlersville 60	5	39N54	81w49	5:27:16
Chapmans 40	34	39N07	82w33	5:30:12
Chardon 28	73	41N35	81w12	5:24:48
Charity Rotch 76	54	40N48	81w31	5:26:04
Charlestown 67	67	41N09	81w09	5:24:36
Charloe 63	34	41N06	84w23	5:37:32
Charm 38	5	40N30	81w47	5:27:08
Chasetown 8	34	39N11	83w57	5:35:48
Chaseville 61	5	39N54	81w32	5:26:08
Chaska Beach 22	5	41N24	82w34	5:30:16
Chatfield 17	32	40N57	82w57	5:31:48
Chatham 45	5	40N07	82w26	5:29:44
Chatham 52	73	41N05	82w01	5:28:04
Chattanooga 54	34	40N38	84w47	5:39:08
Chauncey 5	27	39N24	82w08	5:28:32
Chautauqua 57	34	39N40	84w16	5:37:04
Chenoweth 49	34	39N43	83w16	5:33:04
Cherry Fork 1	34	38N53	83w36	5:34:24
Cherry Grove 13	34	39N04	84w19	5:37:16
Cherry Grove Plaza 31	88	39N06	84w23	5:37:32
Cherry Valley 4	72	41N37	80w42	5:22:48
Chesapeake 44	37	38N26	82w27	5:29:48
Cheshire 21	27	40N13	82w53	5:31:32
Cheshire 27	27	38N57	82w07	5:28:28
Chesswood Acres 31	34	39N13	84w35	5:38:20
Chester 53	5	39N05	81w55	5:27:40
Chester Center 28	67	41N31	81w21	5:25:24
Chesterfield 26	34	41N40	84w10	5:36:40
Chesterhill 58	5	39N29	81w52	5:27:28
Chesterland 28	67	41N31	81w21	5:25:24
Chesterville 59	27	40N28	82w41	5:30:44
Cheviot 31	88	39N10	84w37	5:38:28
Chickasaw 54	34	40N26	84w29	5:37:56
Chili 16	5	40N20	81w44	5:26:56
Chillicothe 71	100	39N20	82w59	5:31:56
Chilo 13	34	38N48	84w08	5:36:32
Chippewa 85	62	40N57	81w42	5:26:48
Chippewa Lake 52	73	41N03	81w54	5:27:36
Chippewa On The Lake 52	73	41N03	81w54	5:27:36
Christiansburg 11	34	40N03	84w02	5:36:08
Chuckery 49	34	40N07	83w29	5:33:56
Churchill 78	84	41N09	80w40	5:22:40
Churchtown 84	20	39N27	81w28	5:25:52
Cincinnati 31	88	39N06	84w31	5:38:04
Circle Green 41	67	40N31	80w52	5:23:28
Circle Hill 5	27	39N26	82w14	5:28:56
Circle Hill 55	34	40N08	84w26	5:37:44
Circleville 65	34	39N36	82w57	5:31:48
City View Heights 9	34	39N26	84w33	5:38:12
Claibourne 80	33	40N25	83w19	5:33:16
Claridon 28	67	41N34	81w12	5:24:48
Claridon 51	27	40N38	82w59	5:31:56
Clarington 56	20	39N46	80w52	5:23:28
Clark 16	5	40N27	81w54	5:27:36
Clark Corners 4	72	41N56	80w36	5:22:24
Clark Corners 52	53	41N01	81w44	5:26:56
Clarksburg 7	21	40N01	80w51	5:23:24
Clarksburg 71	34	39N31	83w09	5:32:36
Clarksfield 39	5	41N12	82w25	5:29:40
Clarkson 15	67	40N48	80w37	5:22:28
Clarksville 14	34	39N24	83w59	5:35:56
Clarksville 64	27	39N42	82w19	5:29:16
Clarktown 73	34	38N53	83w00	5:32:00
Clay 40	34	38N54	82w35	5:30:20
Clay Center 62	93	41N34	83w22	5:33:28
Clay Lick 45	5	40N07	82w26	5:29:44
Claysville 30	5	39N56	81w40	5:26:40
Clayton 1	34	38N41	83w36	5:34:24
Clayton 57	34	39N51	84w21	5:37:24
Clearport 23	27	39N43	82w36	5:30:24
Clearview 47	50	41N26	82w09	5:28:36
Clearview 76	54	40N48	81w31	5:26:04
Clertoma 13	34	39N10	84w18	5:37:12
Cleveland 18	26	41N30	81w42	5:26:48
Cleveland Heights 18	26	41N30	81w34	5:26:16
Cleves 31	34	39N10	84w45	5:39:00
Clifton 29	34	39N48	83w49	5:35:16
Clifton Farms 9	34	39N30	84w23	5:37:32
Climax 59	27	40N33	82w52	5:31:28
Clinton 77	67	40N56	81w38	5:26:32
Clipper Mills 27	27	38N46	82w11	5:28:44
Cloverdale 69	34	41N01	84w18	5:37:12
Cloverhill 64	27	39N43	82w13	5:28:52
Cluff 31	34	39N07	84w21	5:37:24
Clyde 72	38	41N18	82w59	5:31:56
Coach Lite Village 48	34	41N36	83w42	5:34:48
Coalburg 78	84	41N10	80w36	5:22:24
Coal Grove 44	34	38N30	82w39	5:30:36
Coalport 79	16	40N15	81w35	5:26:20
Coalridge 61	5	39N50	81w34	5:26:16
Coal Run 84	20	39N34	81w35	5:26:20
Coalton 40	34	39N07	82w37	5:30:28
Coddingville 52	73	41N08	81w52	5:27:28
Coitsville 50	84	41N05	80w33	5:22:12
Colby 72	30	41N18	82w59	5:31:56
Cold Springs 12	39	39N55	83w48	5:35:12
Coldwater 54	34	40N29	84w38	5:38:32
Colebrook 4	72	41N33	80w47	5:23:08
Colemans 15	67	40N47	80w46	5:23:04
Colerain 7	21	40N07	80w49	5:23:16
Colerain Heights 31	34	39N14	84w36	5:38:24
Colerian 71	34	39N27	82w48	5:31:12
Coles Park 73	34	38N46	82w59	5:31:56
Coletown 19	34	40N06	84w38	5:38:32
College 42	5	40N22	82w23	5:29:32
College Corner 9	34	39N34	84w49	5:39:16
College Hill 30	5	40N01	81w35	5:26:20
College Hill 31	88	39N12	84w32	5:38:08
College Hills 29	34	39N48	84w01	5:36:04
Collins 39	5	41N16	82w30	5:30:00
Collinsville 9	34	39N31	84w37	5:38:28
Collinwood 18	26	41N34	81w34	5:26:16
Colonial Hills 25	107	40N05	83w01	5:32:04
Colton 35	34	41N28	83w57	5:35:48
Columbia 47	67	41N20	81w57	5:27:48
Columbia 76	54	40N48	81w31	5:26:04
Columbia 79	16	40N33	81w29	5:25:56
Columbia 86	34	41N34	84w46	5:39:04
Columbia Center 45	27	40N00	82w40	5:30:40
Columbia Hills Corners 47	21	41N19	81w55	5:27:40
Columbiana 15	47	40N53	80w42	5:22:48
Columbus 25	107	39N58	83w00	5:32:00
Columbus Grove 69	34	40N55	84w04	5:36:16
Columbus Park 22	5	41N27	82w44	5:30:56
Comet 77	67	40N56	81w38	5:26:32
Commercial Point 65	34	39N46	83w04	5:32:16
Compton Park 31	34	39N14	84w32	5:38:08
Compton Woods 31	34	39N14	84w28	5:37:52
Conant 2	34	40N42	84w21	5:37:24
Concord 45	27	40N09	82w41	5:30:44
Condit 21	27	40N15	82w48	5:31:12
Conesville 16	5	40N11	81w54	5:27:36
Congo 64	27	39N36	82w05	5:28:20
Congress 85	62	40N56	82w03	5:28:12
Congress Lake 76	67	40N58	81w20	5:25:20
Conneaut 4	25	41N57	80w34	5:22:16
Conneaut Harbor 4	25	41N56	80w36	5:22:24
Connor 41	67	40N11	80w41	5:22:44
Conotton 34	21	40N25	81w12	5:24:48
Conover 55	34	40N08	84w03	5:36:12
Constitution 84	20	39N21	81w33	5:26:12
Continental 69	34	41N06	84w16	5:37:04
Converse 81	34	40N42	84w21	5:37:24
Convoy 81	34	40N55	84w43	5:38:52
Cooks 24	34	39N43	83w16	5:33:04
Cool Ridge Heights 70	95	40N47	82w30	5:30:00
Coolville 5	5	39N14	81w45	5:27:00
Coonville 37	27	39N23	82w24	5:29:36
Cooper 74	32	41N08	83w00	5:32:00
Cooperdale 16	5	40N13	82w04	5:28:16
Copley 77	67	41N06	81w39	5:26:36
Corinth 78	67	41N26	80w37	5:22:28
Cork 4	72	41N48	80w58	5:23:52
Corner 84	20	39N18	81w34	5:26:16
Cornerville 84	20	39N23	81w24	5:25:36
Corning 64	27	39N36	82w05	5:28:20
Corryville 31	88	39N08	84w31	5:38:04
Corryville 44	37	38N27	82w28	5:29:52
Cortland 78	71	41N20	80w44	5:22:56
Cortsville 12	34	39N50	83w38	5:34:32
Corwin 83	34	39N32	84w05	5:36:20
Coryville 44	34	38N31	82w39	5:30:36
Coshocton 16	5	40N16	81w51	5:27:24
Cottage Grove 77	2	41N00	81w32	5:26:08
Country Acres 29	34	39N48	84w01	5:36:04
Country Club Estates 41	106	40N22	80w39	5:22:36
Country Club Highlands 9	34	39N22	84w33	5:38:12
Country Lane Estates 43	67	41N44	81w14	5:24:56
Cove 40	34	39N04	82w39	5:30:36
Covedale 31	88	39N07	84w37	5:38:28
Coventry 77	2	41N00	81w32	5:26:08
Covington 55	34	40N07	84w21	5:37:24
Cowlesville 55	34	39N58	84w10	5:36:40
Cozaddale 83	34	39N14	84w10	5:36:40
Crabapple 7	21	40N06	80w55	5:23:40
Craig Beach 50	67	41N06	81w00	5:24:00
Craigton 85	79	40N41	82w02	5:28:08
Cranberry 17	32	40N57	82w50	5:31:20
Cranberry Prairie 54	34	40N28	84w34	5:38:16
Crandenbrook 87	31	41N34	83w35	5:34:20
Cranwood 18	26	41N26	81w34	5:26:16
Crawford 88	32	40N57	83w23	5:33:32
Cream City 41	67	40N33	80w44	5:22:56
Creola 82	27	39N19	82w28	5:29:52
Crescent 7	21	40N06	80w55	5:23:40
Crescent Gardens 76	54	40N48	81w31	5:26:04
Crescentville 31	34	39N16	84w24	5:37:36

Crestline 17 28 40N47 82W44 5:30:56
Creston 85 58 40N58 81W54 5:27:36
Crestwood Hills 70 95 40N47 82W30 5:30:00
Cridersville 6 34 40N39 84W09 5:36:36
Crissey 48 34 41N36 83W42 5:34:48
Crooked Tree 61 5 39N40 81W28 5:25:52
Crooksville 64 27 39N46 82W06 5:28:24
Crosby 31 34 39N17 84W44 5:38:56
Cross Creek 41 106 40N21 80W41 5:22:44
Crossenville 64 27 39N42 82W26 5:29:44
Crossroads 76 67 40N43 81W36 5:26:24
Crosstown 8 34 39N04 84W03 5:36:12
Croton 45 27 40N14 82W41 5:30:44
Crown City 27 34 38N36 82W17 5:29:08
Crystal Lakes 12 34 39N53 84W02 5:36:08
Crystal Rock Park 22 5 41N23 82W56 5:31:44
Crystal Springs 76 54 40N50 81W32 5:26:08
Cuba 14 34 39N22 83W52 5:35:28
Culbertson Heights 55 34 40N03 84W11 5:36:44
Cumberland 30 5 39N51 81W40 5:26:40
Cumminsville 31 88 39N10 84W32 5:38:08
Curtice 62 93 41N40 83W16 5:33:04
Custar 87 34 41N17 83W51 5:35:24
Cutler 84 20 39N21 81W47 5:27:08
Cuyahoga Falls 77 2 41N08 81W29 5:25:56
Cuyahoga Heights 18 26 41N26 81W39 5:26:36
Cygnet 87 33 41N14 83W39 5:34:36
Cynthian 75 34 40N18 84W21 5:37:24
Cynthiana 66 34 39N10 83W21 5:33:24
Dabel 57 91 39N43 84W08 5:36:32
Dadsville 68 34 39N44 84W32 5:38:08
Dailyville 66 34 39N09 83W00 5:32:00
Dale 58 5 39N33 81W48 5:27:12
Dalewood 9 34 39N20 84W25 5:37:40
Dallas 17 32 40N43 83W03 5:32:12
Dallasburg 83 34 39N14 84W20 5:37:20
Dalton 85 69 40N48 81W42 5:26:48
Dalzell 84 20 39N34 81W24 5:25:36
Daman Park 9 34 39N30 84W23 5:37:32
Damascus 35 34 41N23 83W57 5:35:48
Damascus 50 67 40N54 80W58 5:23:52
Danbury 62 93 41N32 82W47 5:31:08
Danville 36 34 39N12 83W37 5:34:28
Danville 42 5 40N27 82W16 5:29:04
Danville 53 27 39N03 82W11 5:28:44
Darby Crest 49 34 39N55 83W10 5:32:40
Darbydale 25 34 39N51 83W11 5:32:44
Darbyville 65 34 39N42 83W07 5:32:28
Darlington 60 5 39N55 82W01 5:28:04
Darlington 70 95 40N40 82W30 5:30:00
Darrowville 77 2 41N10 81W28 5:25:52
Darrtown 9 34 39N30 84W40 5:38:40
Dart 84 20 39N29 81W16 5:25:04
Darwin 53 27 39N02 82W02 5:28:08
Davisville 40 34 39N07 82W33 5:30:12
Dawn 19 34 40N13 84W38 5:38:32
Dawson 75 34 40N15 84W20 5:37:20
Day Heights 13 34 39N10 84W18 5:37:12
Dayton 57 91 39N45 84W12 5:36:48
Dayton View 57 91 39N47 84W14 5:36:56
Dean Dale 41 106 40N19 80W39 5:22:36
Deavertown 58 5 39N46 82W06 5:28:24
Decatur 8 34 38N49 83W42 5:34:48
Deep Run 7 21 40N10 80W42 5:22:48
Deerfield 67 67 41N02 81W03 5:24:12
Deering 44 34 38N31 82W39 5:30:36
Deer Park 31 34 39N13 84W23 5:37:32
Deersville 34 21 40N18 81W11 5:24:44
Defiance 20 110 41N17 84W22 5:37:28
De Forest 78 45 41N13 80W47 5:23:08
De Graff 46 34 40N19 83W55 5:35:40
Dekalb 17 33 40N54 82W46 5:31:04
Delano 71 34 39N21 83W00 5:32:00
Delaware 21 117 40N18 83W04 5:32:16
Delhi 31 88 39N06 84W37 5:38:28
Delhi Hills 31 88 39N06 84W36 5:38:24
Delightful 78 67 41N19 80W57 5:23:48
Delisle 19 34 39N58 84W33 5:38:12
Dellroy 10 21 40N33 81W12 5:24:48
Delmont 23 27 39N43 82W36 5:30:24
Delphi 39 5 41N03 82W44 5:30:56
Delphos 2 34 40N51 84W21 5:37:24
Delta 26 34 41N34 84W00 5:36:00
Denmark 4 72 41N45 80W42 5:22:48
Denmark 59 27 40N33 82W52 5:31:28
Dennison 79 114 40N24 81W19 5:25:16
Dent 31 34 39N11 84W39 5:38:36
Denver 71 34 39N09 83W00 5:32:00
Depot 67 67 41N10 81W16 5:25:04
Derby 65 34 39N46 83W13 5:32:52
Derwent 30 5 39N55 81W32 5:26:08
Deshler 35 34 41N13 83W54 5:35:36
Deunquat 88 32 40N57 83W11 5:32:44
Devola 84 20 39N29 81W28 5:25:52
Deweyville 32 34 41N07 83W46 5:35:04
Dexter 53 27 39N05 82W13 5:28:52
Dexter City 61 5 39N39 81W28 5:25:52
Deyarmonville 41 67 40N12 80W46 5:23:04
Dialton 12 39 39N55 83W48 5:35:12
Diamond 67 67 41N06 81W01 5:24:04
Dille 7 21 40N00 80W46 5:23:04
Dillon Falls 60 5 39N55 82W01 5:28:04
Dillonvale 31 34 39N12 84W25 5:37:40
Dillonvale 41 67 40N12 80W46 5:23:04
Dilworth 78 67 41N26 80W37 5:22:28
Dinsmore 75 34 40N26 84W10 5:36:40
Dixie 64 27 39N36 82W12 5:28:48
Dixie Heights 9 34 39N30 84W23 5:37:32
Dixie Heights 57 91 39N50 84W13 5:36:52
Dixon 68 34 39N41 84W45 5:39:00
Dixon 81 34 40N55 84W42 5:38:48
Dixonville 15 105 40N38 80W35 5:22:20

Doanville 5 27 39N26 82W14 5:28:56
Dobbston 44 34 38N33 82W23 5:29:32
Dodds 83 34 39N26 84W12 5:36:48
Dodgeville 4 72 41N36 80W52 5:23:28
Dodson 36 34 39N13 83W48 5:35:12
Dodson 57 34 39N49 84W25 5:37:40
Dodsonville 36 34 39N12 83W49 5:35:16
Dola 33 33 40N47 83W42 5:34:48
Doneys 25 107 39N58 82W52 5:31:28
Donnelsville 12 34 39N55 83W57 5:35:48
Dorcas 53 5 38N58 81W55 5:27:40
Dornbush 31 34 39N13 84W35 5:38:20
Dorset 4 72 41N41 80W40 5:22:40
Dover 79 61 40N32 81W29 5:25:56
Dowling 87 31 41N34 83W35 5:34:20
Downington 53 27 39N14 82W12 5:28:48
Doylestown 85 67 40N58 81W42 5:26:48
Drakes 64 27 39N36 82W05 5:28:20
Drakesburg 67 67 41N14 81W03 5:24:12
Dresden 60 13 40N07 82W01 5:28:04
Drexel 57 91 39N45 84W17 5:37:08
Driftwood 4 72 41N01 80W57 5:23:48
Drinkle 23 34 39N39 82W45 5:31:00
Dry Run 15 105 40N38 80W35 5:22:20
Dry Run 73 34 38N46 82W59 5:31:56
Dublin 25 108 40N06 83W05 5:32:20
Duchouquet 6 34 40N37 84W09 5:36:36
Dudley 33 33 40N36 83W29 5:33:56
Duffy 56 20 39N37 80W55 5:23:40
Duke 66 34 38N55 83W15 5:33:00
Dull 81 34 40N46 84W37 5:38:28
Dumontville 23 27 39N43 82W36 5:30:24
Dunbridge 87 33 41N28 83W37 5:34:28
Duncan Falls 60 5 39N52 81W55 5:27:40
Dundas 82 27 39N12 82W29 5:29:56
Dundee 79 16 40N35 81W37 5:26:28
Dungannon 15 67 40N45 80W56 5:23:44
Dungannon 61 5 39N34 81W31 5:26:20
Dunglen 41 67 40N12 80W49 5:23:16
Dunham 84 20 39N20 81W38 5:26:32
Dunkinsville 1 34 38N51 83W28 5:33:52
Dunkirk 33 33 40N48 83W39 5:34:36
Dunlap 31 34 39N18 84W37 5:38:28
Dupont 69 34 41N03 84W17 5:37:08
Durbin 12 39 39N55 83W48 5:35:12
Durbin 54 34 40N34 84W33 5:38:12
Duvalls 65 34 39N49 82W58 5:31:52
Eagle Beach 62 93 41N31 82W57 5:31:48
Eagle City 12 39 39N55 83W48 5:35:12
Eagle Mills 82 34 39N16 82W47 5:31:08
Eagleport 58 5 39N44 81W55 5:27:40
Eagleville 4 72 41N43 80W50 5:23:20
Eagleville 87 5 40N21 80W48 5:23:12
Earls Island 75 34 40N24 84W22 5:37:28
East 10 21 40N41 80W57 5:23:48
East Akron 77 2 41N04 81W28 5:25:52
East Alliance 50 67 40N54 81W06 5:24:24
East Ashtabula 4 46 41N52 80W49 5:23:16
East Batavia Heights 13 34 39N05 84W11 5:36:44
East Cadiz 34 21 40N16 81W00 5:24:00
East Canton 76 43 40N47 81W17 5:25:08
East Carlisle 47 42 41N22 82W06 5:28:24
East Claridon 28 67 41N32 81W07 5:24:28
East Clayton 5 27 39N26 82W14 5:28:56
East Cleveland 18 26 41N33 81W33 5:26:12
East Conneaut 4 25 41N56 80W36 5:22:24
East Danville 36 34 39N12 83W37 5:34:28
East Defiance 20 34 41N17 84W20 5:37:20
East Delphos 2 34 40N51 84W20 5:37:20
East End 15 105 40N38 80W35 5:22:20
East End 31 88 39N07 84W25 5:37:40
East Fairfield 15 67 40N52 80W37 5:22:28
East Fultonham 60 5 39N51 82W08 5:28:32
East Gardens 87 31 41N38 83W29 5:33:56
East Goshen 50 67 40N55 81W01 5:24:04
East Greenville 76 67 40N51 81W38 5:26:32
Eastlake 43 67 41N40 81W26 5:25:44
East Lawn 87 31 41N35 83W28 5:33:52
East Lewistown 50 67 40N57 80W40 5:22:40
East Liberty 21 27 40N15 82W51 5:31:24
East Liberty 46 33 40N20 83W35 5:34:20
East Liberty 77 2 41N00 81W32 5:26:08
East Liverpool 15 105 40N37 80W35 5:22:20
East Mansfield 70 95 40N47 82W30 5:30:00
East Mecca 78 67 41N19 80W43 5:22:52
East Millersport 23 27 39N54 82W33 5:30:12
East Millfield 5 27 39N26 82W06 5:28:24
East Monroe 36 34 39N21 83W30 5:34:00
East Norwalk 39 5 41N14 82W38 5:30:32
East Norwood 31 88 39N10 84W27 5:37:48
Easton 85 62 40N58 81W47 5:27:08
East Orwell 4 60 41N32 80W53 5:23:32
East Palestine 15 46 40N50 80W33 5:22:12
East Plains 83 34 39N30 84W23 5:37:32
East Richland 7 21 40N06 80W55 5:23:40
East Ringgold 65 27 39N40 82W51 5:31:24
East Rochester 15 67 40N45 81W02 5:24:08
East Side 50 84 41N06 80W37 5:22:28
East Sparta 76 67 40N40 81W21 5:25:24
East Springfield 41 67 40N27 80W52 5:23:28
East Townsend 39 5 41N16 82W30 5:30:00
East Trumbull 4 72 41N39 80W52 5:23:28
East Union 61 5 39N49 81W28 5:25:52
East Union 85 62 40N42 81W52 5:27:28
Eastview 57 34 39N46 84W06 5:36:24
Eastwood 8 34 39N04 84W03 5:36:12

Eaton 68 34 39N45 84W38 5:38:32
Eaton Estates 47 67 41N18 82W01 5:28:04
Eber 24 34 39N34 83W31 5:34:04
Echo 7 21 40N02 80W49 5:23:16
Eckmansville 1 34 38N56 83W38 5:34:32
Eden Park 73 34 38N46 82W59 5:31:56
Edenton 13 34 39N14 84W03 5:36:12
Edenville 88 32 40N49 83W09 5:32:36
Edgefield 24 34 39N39 83W32 5:34:08
Edgefield 76 43 40N50 81W23 5:25:32
Edgemont 31 88 39N12 84W29 5:37:56
Edgerton 86 34 41N27 84W45 5:39:00
Edgewater 18 26 41N29 81W48 5:27:12
Edgewater Beach 45 5 39N54 82W27 5:29:48
Edgewater Park 25 107 39N56 82W53 5:31:32
Edgewood 4 46 41N52 80W48 5:23:12
Edinburg 67 67 41N06 81W09 5:24:36
Edison 59 27 40N33 82W52 5:31:28
Edon 86 34 41N33 84W46 5:39:04
Egypt 6 34 40N24 84W22 5:37:28
Egypt 7 21 39N59 81W11 5:24:44
Eifort 73 34 38N54 82W35 5:30:20
Elba 84 20 39N36 81W25 5:25:40
Elberta Beach 47 67 41N25 82W19 5:29:16
Eldean 55 34 40N03 84W11 5:36:44
Eldon 30 5 39N58 81W17 5:25:08
Eldorado 9 34 39N30 84W23 5:37:32
Eldorado 68 34 39N54 84W41 5:38:44
Elery 35 31 41N38 83W29 5:33:56
Elgin 81 34 40N44 84W28 5:37:52
Elida 2 34 40N47 84W12 5:36:48
Elizabethtown 31 34 39N10 84W48 5:39:12
Elizabethtown 83 34 39N35 84W18 5:37:12
Elkrun 15 67 40N46 80W41 5:22:44
Elkton 15 67 40N46 80W42 5:22:48
Ellerton 57 34 39N40 84W16 5:37:04
Ellet 77 2 41N01 81W28 5:25:52
Elliot 58 5 39N29 81W52 5:27:28
Elliottville 5 27 39N20 82W05 5:28:20
Ellisonville 44 34 38N31 82W39 5:30:36
Elliston 62 93 41N33 83W17 5:33:08
Ellsberry 8 34 38N41 83W46 5:35:04
Ellsworth 50 67 41N02 80W51 5:23:24
Elm Acres 76 54 40N48 81W31 5:26:04
Elm Grove 66 34 39N03 83W10 5:32:40
Elmira 26 34 41N31 84W18 5:37:12
Elmore 62 93 41N29 83W18 5:33:12
Elmville 36 34 39N12 83W37 5:34:28
Elmwood Place 31 88 39N11 84W30 5:38:00
Elroy 19 34 40N13 84W38 5:38:32
Elton 76 54 40N46 81W30 5:26:00
Elyria 47 42 41N22 82W07 5:28:28
Emerald 1 34 38N56 83W38 5:34:32
Emerald 63 34 41N12 84W31 5:38:04
Emerson 41 67 40N12 80W46 5:23:04
Emery Chapel 12 39 39N55 83W48 5:35:12
Empire 41 67 40N30 80W38 5:22:32
England Station 3 44 40N54 82W22 5:29:28
Englewood 57 34 39N53 84W18 5:37:12
Eno 27 27 39N00 82W20 5:29:20
Enoch 61 5 39N39 81W26 5:25:44
Enon 12 34 39N52 83W56 5:35:44
Enterprise 37 27 39N32 82W24 5:29:36
Enterprise 68 34 39N44 84W32 5:38:08
Epworth 70 95 40N45 82W31 5:30:04
Epworth Heights 13 34 39N15 84W17 5:37:08
Era 65 34 39N43 83W16 5:33:04
Erastus 54 34 40N34 84W33 5:38:12
Erhart 52 73 41N08 81W52 5:27:28
Erie 62 93 41N32 83W01 5:32:04
Erieview 18 26 41N29 81W40 5:26:40
Eris 11 34 40N04 83W42 5:34:48
Erlin 72 30 41N21 83W08 5:32:32
Espyville 77 2 41N05 81W33 5:26:12
Essex 80 33 40N26 83W18 5:33:12
Etna 45 27 39N57 82W42 5:30:48
Euclid 18 70 41N34 81W32 5:26:08
Eureka 50 67 40N55 80W41 5:22:44
Evansport 20 34 41N25 84W24 5:37:36
Evansville 78 67 41N08 80W46 5:23:04
Evendale 31 34 39N15 84W26 5:37:44
Everett 77 67 41N14 81W33 5:26:12
Evergreen 84 20 39N27 81W28 5:25:52
Ewing 37 27 39N32 82W24 5:29:36
Ewington 27 27 39N01 82W21 5:29:24
Excello 9 34 39N29 84W25 5:37:40
Fairborn 29 34 39N49 84W02 5:36:08
Fairdale 30 5 40N01 81W35 5:26:20
Fairfax 31 88 39N08 84W24 5:37:36
Fairfax 36 34 39N12 83W37 5:34:28
Fairfield 9 34 39N21 84W34 5:38:16
Fairfield 41 68 40N26 80W46 5:23:04
Fairfield Beach 23 27 39N54 82W27 5:29:48
Fairhaven 68 34 39N38 84W39 5:38:36
Fairhope 76 67 40N50 81W17 5:25:08
Fairlawn 77 67 41N08 81W37 5:26:28
Fair Oaks 13 34 39N05 84W11 5:36:44
Fairplay 9 34 39N22 84W33 5:38:12
Fairplay 41 67 40N21 80W48 5:23:12
Fairpoint 7 21 40N07 80W56 5:23:44
Fairport 43 67 41N45 81W16 5:25:04
Fairport Harbor 43 67 41N45 81W17 5:25:08
Fairview 30 5 40N03 81W14 5:24:56
Fairview 36 34 39N12 83W37 5:34:28
Fairview Heights 41 67 40N28 80W36 5:22:24
Fairview Heights 84 20 39N27 81W28 5:25:52
Fairview Lanes 22 5 41N27 82W44 5:30:56
Fairview Park 18 67 41N26 81W53 5:27:32

Place		Lat	Long	
Fairway View Estates 2	90	40N44	84w09	5:36:36
Fairwind Acres 31	34	39N15	84w22	5:37:28
Fallsburg 45	5	40N06	82w08	5:28:32
Fallsbury 45	5	40N13	82w14	5:28:56
Fargo 59	27	40N25	82w48	5:31:12
Far Hills 57	91	39N43	84w10	5:36:40
Farmdale 78	67	41N26	80w37	5:22:28
Farmer 20	34	41N23	84w38	5:38:32
Farmers 14	34	39N19	83w49	5:35:16
Farmerstown 38	5	40N26	81w41	5:26:44
Farmersville 57	34	39N41	84w26	5:37:44
Farmington 78	67	41N23	80w57	5:23:48
Farnham 4	72	41N56	80w36	5:22:24
Farrington 55	34	40N03	84w11	5:36:44
Fawcett 1	34	38N57	83w24	5:33:36
Fayette 26	34	41N40	84w20	5:37:20
Fayetteville 8	34	39N11	83w57	5:35:48
Fearing 84	20	39N29	81w24	5:25:36
Federal Reserve 18	26	41N29	81w40	5:26:40
Federal Reserve 31	88	39N09	84w30	5:38:00
Feed Springs 34	16	40N24	81w21	5:25:24
Feesburg 8	34	38N52	83w58	5:35:52
Felicity 13	34	38N51	84w06	5:36:24
Fernald 31	34	39N17	84w41	5:38:44
Fernell Heights 13	34	39N07	84w21	5:37:24
Ferry 29	34	40N36	83w59	5:35:56
Fields 47	42	41N22	82w06	5:28:24
Fields Terrace 44	37	38N27	82w28	5:29:52
Filburns Island 75	34	40N24	84w22	5:37:28
Fincastle 8	34	39N01	83w49	5:35:16
Findlay 32	89	41N02	83w39	5:34:36
Findley Gardens 41	67	40N28	80w36	5:22:24
Finneytown 31	88	39N12	84w31	5:38:04
Fire Brick 44	34	38N54	82w35	5:30:20
Firestone Park 77	2	41N03	81w31	5:26:04
Fishback 62	93	41N30	82w52	5:31:28
Fitchville 39	5	41N06	82w29	5:29:56
Five Mile 8	34	39N02	83w56	5:35:44
Five Points 29	34	39N48	84w01	5:36:04
Five Points 50	67	40N57	80w40	5:22:40
Five Points 65	34	39N43	83w16	5:33:04
Five Points 78	67	41N20	80w34	5:22:16
Flatiron 64	27	39N46	82w06	5:28:24
Flat Iron 83	34	39N35	84w18	5:37:12
Flat Rock 74	32	41N14	82w52	5:31:28
Fleatown 45	5	40N07	82w26	5:29:44
Fleetwood Addition 80	33	40N15	83w22	5:33:28
Fleming 84	20	39N23	81w37	5:26:28
Fletcher 55	34	40N09	84w06	5:36:24
Flint 25	107	40N05	83w01	5:32:04
Floodwood 5	27	39N26	82w14	5:28:56
Florence 7	15	40N06	80w44	5:22:56
Florence 22	9	41N20	82w30	5:30:00
Florence 49	34	39N53	83w27	5:33:48
Florence 61	5	39N45	81w31	5:26:04
Florida 35	34	41N20	84w12	5:36:48
Flushing 7	21	40N09	81w04	5:24:16
Fly 56	20	39N34	81w00	5:24:00
Footville 4	72	41N39	80w52	5:23:28
Foraker 33	34	40N42	83w52	5:35:28
Forest 33	33	40N48	83w31	5:34:04
Forestdale 44	34	38N31	82w39	5:30:36
Forest Hills 12	39	39N55	83w48	5:35:12
Forest Park 31	34	39N17	84w34	5:38:16
Forest Park 57	91	39N47	84w13	5:36:52
Forest View 41	106	40N22	80w39	5:22:36
Forestville 31	34	39N04	84w21	5:37:24
Forstoria 87	32	41N11	83w26	5:33:44
Fort Jefferson 19	34	40N06	84w38	5:38:32
Fort Jennings 69	34	40N54	84w18	5:37:12
Fort Loramie 75	34	40N21	84w22	5:37:28
Fort McKinley 57	91	39N48	84w15	5:37:00
Fort Meigs Place 87	31	41N34	83w35	5:34:20
Fort Miami Addition 48	31	41N35	83w40	5:34:40
Fort Recovery 54	34	40N25	84w47	5:39:08
Fort Seneca 74	32	41N13	83w10	5:32:40
Fort Shawnee 2	90	40N41	84w09	5:36:36
Foster 83	34	39N19	84w15	5:37:00
Fosterville 50	84	41N04	80w42	5:22:48
Fostoria 74	32	41N10	83w25	5:33:40
Fountain Park 11	34	40N10	83w32	5:34:08
Fountain Square 31	88	39N07	84w30	5:38:00
Fowler 78	67	41N18	80w40	5:22:40
Fowlers Mill 28	67	41N34	81w12	5:24:48
Fox 10	21	40N36	80w54	5:23:36
Fox 65	34	39N37	82w57	5:31:48
Fox Chase 25	108	40N06	82w56	5:31:44
Frankfort 71	34	39N24	83w11	5:32:44
Franklin 83	34	39N34	84w18	5:37:12
Franklin Furnace 73	34	38N39	82w51	5:31:24
Franklin Square 15	47	40N54	80w45	5:23:00
Frazeysburg 60	5	40N07	82w07	5:28:28
Frederick 55	34	39N58	84w10	5:36:40
Frederick 73	34	38N45	82w51	5:31:24
Fredericksburg 85	44	40N41	81w52	5:27:28
Fredericksdale 61	5	39N49	81w28	5:25:52
Fredericktown 15	105	40N38	80w35	5:22:20
Fredericktown 42	5	40N29	82w33	5:30:12
Fredonia 45	27	40N04	82w31	5:30:04
Freeburg 76	67	40N48	81w10	5:24:40
Freedom 67	67	41N14	81w03	5:24:12
Freedom Station 67	67	41N12	81w09	5:24:36
Freeland 60	5	39N54	81w49	5:27:16
Freeport 34	21	40N12	81w17	5:25:08
Fremont 72	41	41N21	83w07	5:32:28
Frenchtown 19	34	40N13	84w29	5:37:56
Fresno 16	5	40N20	81w44	5:26:56
Friendship 73	34	38N42	83w06	5:32:24
Frontier Park 31	34	39N13	84w35	5:38:20
Frontier Town 50	84	41N02	80w38	5:22:32
Frost 5	5	39N14	81w45	5:27:00
Fruitdale 71	34	39N18	83w21	5:33:24
Fruit Hill 31	34	39N04	84w22	5:37:28
Fryburg 6	34	40N34	84w11	5:36:44
Fryburg 38	5	40N33	81w55	5:27:40
Frytown 57	91	39N43	84w15	5:37:00
Fulda 61	5	39N45	81w31	5:26:04
Fulton 59	27	40N28	82w50	5:31:20
Fultonham 60	5	39N48	82w08	5:28:32
Funk 85	76	40N49	81w56	5:27:44
Gage 27	34	38N46	82w23	5:29:32
Gahanna 25	27	40N01	82w51	5:31:24
Galatea 87	33	41N12	83w39	5:34:36
Galaxy Acres 31	34	39N13	84w35	5:38:20
Galena 21	27	40N13	82w53	5:31:32
Galion 17	112	40N44	82w47	5:31:08
Gallia 27	34	38N46	82w23	5:29:32
Gallipolis 27	97	38N49	82w12	5:28:48
Galloway 25	34	39N55	83w10	5:32:40
Gambier 42	5	40N23	82w23	5:29:32
Ganges 70	5	40N54	82w37	5:30:28
Gann 42	5	40N28	82w12	5:28:48
Gano 9	34	39N18	84w24	5:37:36
Garden 5	5	39N17	81w55	5:27:40
Garden Acres 12	39	39N57	83w47	5:35:08
Garden Acres 70	95	40N47	82w30	5:30:00
Garden City 73	34	38N45	82w51	5:31:24
Garden Isle 52	73	41N01	82w01	5:28:04
Garden Terrace 41	106	40N22	80w39	5:22:36
Garfield 50	67	40N55	80w51	5:23:24
Garfield Heights 18	26	41N26	81w37	5:26:28
Garrettsville 67	46	41N17	81w06	5:24:24
Gasper 68	34	39N41	84w38	5:38:32
Gates Mills 18	67	41N31	81w24	5:25:36
Gath 36	34	39N01	83w49	5:35:16
Gavers 15	67	40N47	80w46	5:23:04
Geauga Lake 67	46	41N19	81w22	5:25:28
Geeburg 50	67	41N02	80w46	5:23:04
Gem Beach 62	93	41N31	82w57	5:31:48
Geneva 4	71	41N48	80w57	5:23:48
Geneva 23	27	39N42	82w26	5:29:44
Geneva-on-the-Lake 4	71	41N52	80w57	5:23:48
Genoa 62	93	41N31	83w22	5:33:28
Georges Run 41	106	40N19	80w39	5:22:36
Georgesville 25	107	39N55	83w03	5:32:12
Georgetown 8	34	38N52	83w54	5:35:36
Gepharts 73	34	38N45	82w51	5:31:24
Gerald 35	34	41N28	84w09	5:36:36
Germano	5	40N25	80w57	5:23:48
Germantown 57	34	39N38	84w22	5:37:28
Germantown 84	20	39N34	81w24	5:25:36
Getaway 44	37	38N27	82w28	5:29:52
Gettysburg 19	34	40N07	84w30	5:38:00
Gettysburg 68	34	39N51	84w48	5:39:12
Geyer 6	34	40N33	84w05	5:36:20
Ghent 77	2	41N08	81w34	5:26:16
Gibisonville 37	34	39N35	82w32	5:30:08
Gibson 30	5	39N58	81w17	5:25:08
Gibson 54	34	40N23	84w45	5:39:00
Gibsonburg 72	32	41N23	83w19	5:33:16
Gilboa 69	34	41N01	83w55	5:35:40
Gilead 59	27	40N33	82w50	5:31:20
Gilmore 79	16	40N19	81w30	5:26:00
Ginger Hill 50	67	40N57	80w34	5:22:16
Ginghamsburg 55	34	39N58	84w10	5:36:40
Girard 78	84	41N09	80w42	5:22:48
Girton 72	32	41N17	83w26	5:33:44
Gist Settlement 36	34	39N20	83w42	5:34:48
Givens 66	34	39N09	83w00	5:32:00
Glade 40	34	39N03	82w50	5:31:20
Gladstone 29	34	39N45	83w49	5:35:16
Glandorf 69	34	41N01	84w05	5:36:20
Glasgow 15	105	40N35	80w39	5:22:36
Glasgow 79	16	40N19	81w30	5:26:00
Glass Rock 64	27	39N54	82w20	5:29:20
Glencoe 7	21	40N01	80w54	5:23:36
Glencoe 31	34	39N14	84w32	5:38:08
Glendale 31	34	39N16	84w28	5:37:52
Glen Este 13	34	39N06	84w16	5:37:04
Glenford 64	5	39N54	82w20	5:29:20
Glengary Heights 25	108	40N06	82w56	5:31:44
Glen Karn 19	34	40N00	84w47	5:39:08
Glenmary 31	34	39N16	84w29	5:37:56
Glenmont 38	5	40N31	82w06	5:28:24
Glenmoor 15	105	40N38	80w35	5:22:20
Glenmore 81	34	40N46	84w37	5:38:28
Glenns Run 7	15	40N06	80w44	5:22:56
Glen Robbins 41	67	40N11	80w41	5:22:44
Glen Roy 40	34	39N07	82w33	5:30:12
Glen Summitt 27	27	39N00	82w20	5:29:20
Glenwillow 18	67	41N22	81w28	5:25:52
Glenwood 68	34	39N44	84w32	5:38:08
Gloria Glens Park 52	73	41N03	81w54	5:27:36
Glouster 5	27	39N30	82w06	5:28:24
Glynwood 6	34	40N34	84w11	5:36:44
Gnadenhutten 79	16	40N22	81w26	5:25:44
Goes 29	34	39N48	83w54	5:35:36
Golda 7	21	40N12	81w09	5:24:36
Golden Corners 85	62	40N59	82w00	5:28:00
Golden Gate 18	67	41N31	81w31	5:26:04
Goldsboro 40	34	40N36	83w59	5:35:56
Golf Manor 31	88	39N11	84w27	5:37:48
Golfway Acres 31	34	39N13	84w35	5:38:20
Good Hope 24	34	39N27	83w22	5:33:28
Goodland Acres 76	67	40N40	81w15	5:25:00
Gordon 19	34	39N56	84w31	5:38:04
Gore 37	27	39N32	82w24	5:29:36
Gorham 26	34	41N40	84w19	5:37:16
Goshen 13	34	39N14	84w10	5:36:40
Goshen 79	16	40N29	81w23	5:25:32
Goulds 41	106	40N19	80w39	5:22:36
Grafton 47	57	41N16	82w04	5:28:16
Grand 51	33	40N40	83w21	5:33:24
Grand Prairie 51	32	40N40	83w07	5:32:28
Grand Rapids 87	34	41N25	83w52	5:35:28
Grand River 43	67	41N45	81w17	5:25:08
Grandview 84	20	39N33	81w06	5:24:24
Grandview Heights 11	34	40N06	83w59	5:35:56
Grandview Heights 25	107	39N59	83w03	5:32:12
Grandview Homes 2	90	40N43	84w06	5:36:24
Grange Hall 65	34	39N43	83w16	5:33:04
Granger 52	67	41N10	81w44	5:26:56
Grant 33	33	40N43	83w34	5:34:16
Granville 45	27	40N03	82w31	5:30:04
Grape Grove 29	34	39N40	83w44	5:34:56
Gratiot 45	5	39N57	82w13	5:28:52
Gratis 68	34	39N37	84w32	5:38:08
Graysville 56	20	39N40	81w11	5:24:44
Graytown 62	93	41N33	83w16	5:33:04
Greasy Ridge 44	34	38N33	82w23	5:29:32
Green Acres 9	34	39N30	84w23	5:37:32
Greenbush 68	34	39N34	84w39	5:38:36
Green Camp 51	33	40N32	83w13	5:32:52
Greencastle 23	27	39N48	82w43	5:30:52
Green Creek 72	30	41N18	83w01	5:32:04
Greenfield 36	34	39N21	83w23	5:33:32
Greenfield Village 31	88	39N12	84w32	5:38:08
Greenford 50	67	40N57	80w48	5:23:12
Green Hills 29	34	39N48	84w01	5:36:04
Greenhills 31	34	39N16	84w32	5:38:08
Greenland 71	34	39N24	83w10	5:32:40
Greenmount 57	91	39N41	84w09	5:36:36
Greensburg 77	67	40N56	81w28	5:25:52
Green Springs 74	30	41N15	83w03	5:32:12
Greens Run 5	27	39N30	82w06	5:28:24
Greens Store 40	34	39N04	82w39	5:30:36
Greentown 76	67	40N56	81w28	5:25:52
Green Valley 42	5	40N24	82w29	5:29:56
Greenview 57	91	39N49	84w15	5:37:00
Greenville 19	110	40N06	84w38	5:38:32
Greenwich 39	5	41N02	82w31	5:30:04
Greenwood 30	5	39N56	81w27	5:25:48
Greenwood Acres 76	54	40N48	81w31	5:26:04
Greer 42	5	40N31	82w07	5:28:28
Grelton 35	34	41N21	84w00	5:36:00
Griffith 31	34	39N09	84w44	5:38:56
Griffith 56	20	39N47	81w09	5:24:36
Griggs 4	72	41N44	80w47	5:23:08
Groesbeck 31	34	39N13	84w35	5:38:20
Groton 22	5	41N21	82w47	5:31:08
Grove City 25	107	39N53	83w06	5:32:24
Groveport 25	34	39N51	82w53	5:31:32
Grover Hill 63	34	41N01	84w29	5:37:56
Guerne 85	76	40N49	81w56	5:27:44
Guernsey 30	5	40N11	81w36	5:26:24
Guilford 15	67	40N47	80w46	5:23:04
Guilford 52	60	41N01	81w49	5:27:16
Gurneyville 14	34	39N27	83w50	5:35:20
Gustavus 78	67	41N28	80w40	5:22:40
Gutman 6	34	40N33	84w05	5:36:20
Guyan 27	34	38N38	82w18	5:29:12
Guysville 5	5	39N17	81w55	5:27:40
Gypsum 62	93	41N30	82w52	5:31:28
Hackney 58	5	39N33	81w38	5:26:32
Hageman 83	34	39N26	84w12	5:36:48
Hale 33	33	40N32	83w33	5:34:12
Haley's Subdivision 79	16	40N33	81w29	5:25:56
Hallock 86	34	41N28	84w33	5:38:12
Halls Corners 78	84	41N08	80w38	5:22:32
Hallsville 71	34	39N27	82w50	5:31:20
Hambden 28	67	41N36	81w09	5:24:36
Hamburg 23	27	39N43	82w36	5:30:24
Hamden 82	34	39N10	82w31	5:30:04
Hamer 36	34	39N10	83w44	5:34:56
Hamersville 8	34	38N55	83w59	5:35:56
Hametown 77	67	41N01	81w38	5:26:32
Hamilton 9	87	39N24	84w34	5:38:16
Hamilton Meadows 25	107	39N54	82w58	5:31:52
Hamler 35	34	41N14	84w02	5:36:08
Hamlet 13	34	39N01	84w13	5:36:52
Hamley Run 5	27	39N20	82w05	5:28:20
Hammondsville 41	67	40N33	80w43	5:22:52
Hanersville 27	27	38N46	82w11	5:28:44
Hanging Rock 44	34	38N34	82w44	5:30:56
Hanley Village 70	95	40N42	82w32	5:30:08
Hannibal 56	20	39N40	80w52	5:23:28
Hanover 34	23	40N23	81w05	5:24:20
Hanover 45	5	40N04	82w16	5:29:04
Hanoverton 15	67	40N45	80w56	5:23:44
Hanville Corners 39	5	41N06	82w37	5:30:28
Happy Hollow 76	67	40N40	81w21	5:25:24
Harbor 4	46	41N52	80w49	5:23:16
Harbor Hills 45	27	39N58	82w28	5:29:52
Harbor View 48	31	41N42	83w27	5:33:48
Hardin 75	34	40N17	84w09	5:36:36
Harding 48	34	41N38	83w51	5:35:24

OHIO

Harding 60 5 39N55 82w01 5:28:04
Hardy 38 5 40N34 81w55 5:27:40
Harlan 83 34 39N19 84w05 5:36:20
Harlan Park 9 34 39N30 84w23 5:37:32
Harlem 21 27 40N10 82w49 5:31:16
Harlem Springs 10 21 40N31 81w00 5:24:00
Harmer 84 20 39N27 81w28 5:25:52
Harmon 76 54 40N46 81w30 5:26:00
Harmony 12 39 39N55 83w48 5:35:12
Harper 46 33 40N22 83w46 5:35:04
Harpersfield 4 72 41N46 80w57 5:23:48
Harpster 88 32 40N44 83w16 5:33:04
Harriett 30 5 40N01 81w35 5:26:20
Harriett 36 34 39N12 83w37 5:34:28
Harriettsville 61 5 39N38 81w20 5:25:20
Harris 62 93 41N29 83w14 5:32:56
Harrisburg 25 34 39N49 83w10 5:32:40
Harrisburg 27 27 38N55 82w18 5:29:12
Harrisburg 76 67 40N50 81w17 5:25:08
Harrison 31 34 39N16 84w49 5:39:16
Harrison Mills 73 34 38N50 82w44 5:30:56
Harrisonville 53 27 39N08 82w08 5:28:32
Harrisville 34 21 40N11 80w53 5:23:32
Harrod 2 34 40N43 83w56 5:35:44
Harshasville 1 34 38N57 83w24 5:33:36
Hartford 78 67 41N19 80w34 5:22:16
Hartland 39 5 41N10 82w30 5:30:00
Hartsgrove 4 72 41N37 80w57 5:23:48
Hartshorn 56 20 39N40 81w11 5:24:44
Hartville 76 67 40N58 81w20 5:25:20
Harveysburg 83 34 39N30 84w01 5:36:04
Haskins 87 34 41N28 83w42 5:34:48
Hasting Hill 73 34 38N46 82w59 5:31:56
Hatch 66 34 39N05 83w01 5:32:04
Hatton 87 33 41N17 83w26 5:33:44
Havana 39 5 41N08 82w45 5:31:00
Havens Corners 25 27 40N00 82w49 5:31:16
Havensport 23 27 39N48 82w43 5:30:52
Haven View 55 34 40N03 84w11 5:36:44
Haverhill 73 34 38N35 82w50 5:31:20
Haviland 63 34 41N02 84w35 5:38:20
Hayden 25 108 40N03 83w09 5:32:36
Haydenville 37 27 39N29 82w20 5:29:20
Hayes Corners 28 67 41N30 81w04 5:24:16
Hayes Place 87 31 41N38 83w29 5:33:56
Hayesville 3 44 40N47 82w16 5:29:04
Haynes 37 34 39N28 82w44 5:30:56
Hays Corner 57 91 39N48 84w17 5:37:08
Hazelwood 31 34 39N15 84w22 5:37:28
Headleys Corners 25 27 40N00 82w49 5:31:16
Heath 45 5 40N02 82w24 5:29:36
Heatherdowns 48 31 41N36 83w38 5:34:32
Hebardville 5 27 39N15 82w10 5:28:40
Hebron 45 27 39N58 82w29 5:29:56
Hecla 44 34 38N31 82w39 5:30:36
Hegemans Landing 75 34 40N24 84w22 5:37:28
Heidelburg Beach 22 5 41N24 82w34 5:30:16
Helena 72 32 41N21 83w18 5:33:12
Helmick 16 5 40N20 82w03 5:28:12
Hemlock 64 27 39N35 82w09 5:28:36
Hemlock Grove 53 5 39N07 81w59 5:27:56
Hempstead 57 91 39N41 84w09 5:36:36
Hendrysburg 7 21 40N04 81w10 5:24:40
Henley 73 34 38N50 83w04 5:32:16
Henrietta 47 67 41N19 82w19 5:29:16
Henry 87 34 41N14 83w43 5:34:52
Hepburn 33 33 40N37 83w28 5:33:52
Hepburn 33 5 39N31 81w18 5:25:12
Hessville 72 30 41N25 83w14 5:32:56
Hestoria 8 34 38N45 83w50 5:35:20
Hickman 45 5 40N07 82w26 5:29:44
Hicksville 20 34 41N18 84w46 5:39:04
Hide-A-Way Hills 23 27 39N42 82w26 5:29:44
Hiett 8 34 38N41 83w46 5:35:04
Higby 71 34 39N21 83w00 5:32:00
Higginsport 8 34 38N47 83w58 5:35:52
High Hill 60 5 39N54 81w49 5:27:16
Highland 36 34 39N20 83w36 5:34:24
Highland Heights 18 67 41N33 81w28 5:25:52
Highland Park 76 54 40N48 81w31 5:26:04
Highland Park 83 34 39N23 84w13 5:36:52
Highland Terrace 7 21 40N06 80w55 5:23:40
Highlandtown 15 21 39N58 81w17 5:25:08
Highpoint 31 34 39N18 84w21 5:37:24
Hill Addition 15 105 40N38 80w35 5:22:20
Hill And Hollow 9 34 39N31 84w44 5:38:56
Hillcrest 15 105 40N35 80w39 5:22:36
Hillcrest 78 75 41N10 80w45 5:23:00
Hillcrest 86 34 41N35 84w36 5:38:24
Hill Grove 19 34 40N12 84w48 5:39:12
Hilliar 42 27 40N19 82w41 5:30:44
Hilliards 25 30 40N02 83w09 5:32:36
Hillman 8 34 38N52 83w55 5:35:40
Hills and Dales 76 43 40N50 81w27 5:25:48
Hills and Dales Shopping Cen 57 91 39N41 84w09 5:36:36
Hillsboro 36 34 39N12 83w37 5:34:28
Hillsboro 41 106 40N19 80w39 5:22:36
Hilltop 25 107 39N57 83w05 5:32:20
Hilltop 55 34 39N58 84w10 5:36:40
Hilltop Acres 31 34 39N14 84w28 5:37:52
Hinckley 52 73 41N14 81w45 5:27:00
Hiram 67 46 41N19 81w09 5:24:36
Hiramsburg 61 5 39N51 81w39 5:26:36
Hitchcock 40 34 38N54 82w35 5:30:20
Hoagland 36 34 39N12 83w37 5:34:28
Hoaglin 81 34 40N57 84w31 5:38:04
Hobson 53 27 39N00 82w04 5:28:16
Hocking 23 34 39N40 82w39 5:30:36
Hockingport 5 5 39N11 81w45 5:27:00
Holden 6 34 40N36 83w59 5:35:56
Holgate 35 34 41N15 84w08 5:36:32
Holiday Valley 12 34 39N48 84w01 5:36:04
Holland 48 34 41N37 83w43 5:34:52
Hollansburg 19 34 40N00 84w48 5:39:12
Hollister 5 27 39N30 82w06 5:28:24
Holloway 7 21 40N10 81w09 5:24:36
Hollowtown 36 34 39N01 83w49 5:35:16
Holman-Stonybrook Shopping C 31 34 39N14 84w20 5:37:20
Holmes 17 32 40N51 83w01 5:32:04
Holmesville 38 5 40N38 81w56 5:27:44
Home Acres 9 34 39N30 84w23 5:37:32
Home Acres 55 34 40N03 84w11 5:36:44
Homedale 25 107 40N03 83w01 5:32:04
Homer 45 27 40N15 82w31 5:30:04
Homerville 52 73 41N02 82w08 5:28:32
Homeside 7 21 40N06 80w55 5:23:40
Homeville 22 5 41N27 82w44 5:30:56
Homewood 9 34 39N22 84w33 5:38:12
Homeworth 15 67 40N50 81w04 5:24:16
Honeytown 85 76 40N49 81w56 5:27:44
Hooker 23 27 39N43 82w36 5:30:24
Hooven 31 34 39N11 84w46 5:39:04
Hopedale 34 21 40N19 80w54 5:23:36
Hopetown 71 34 39N21 83w00 5:32:00
Hopewell 41 67 40N11 80w41 5:22:44
Hopewell 60 5 39N57 82w09 5:28:36
Hopkinsville 83 34 39N20 84w13 5:36:52
Horatio 19 34 40N06 84w38 5:38:32
Horton 46 33 40N25 83w33 5:34:12
Hoskinsville 61 5 39N45 81w31 5:26:04
Houcktown 32 33 40N54 83w38 5:34:32
Houston 75 34 40N15 84w20 5:37:20
Howard 42 5 40N25 82w20 5:29:20
Howenstein 76 67 40N40 81w21 5:25:24
Howland 78 45 41N14 80w46 5:23:04
Hoytville 87 34 41N12 83w47 5:35:08
Hubbard 78 46 41N10 80w34 5:22:16
Huber Heights 57 34 39N50 84w08 5:36:32
Huber Ridge 25 108 40N06 82w56 5:31:44
Hudson 77 47 41N15 81w27 5:25:48
Hue 82 27 39N23 82w24 5:29:36
Hulington 13 34 38N59 84w04 5:36:16
Hull Prairie 87 33 41N23 83w39 5:34:36
Humboldt 71 36 39N14 83w15 5:33:00
Hume 2 90 40N42 84w08 5:36:32
Hunter 7 21 40N01 81w04 5:24:16
Hunterdon 5 27 39N30 82w06 5:28:24
Huntington 47 67 41N09 82w16 5:29:04
Huntington Park 8 34 38N41 83w46 5:35:04
Hunting Valley 18 67 41N28 81w25 5:25:40
Huntsburg 28 67 41N32 81w03 5:24:12
Hunts Corner 39 5 41N16 82w51 5:31:24
Huntsville 9 34 39N30 84w23 5:37:32
Huntsville 46 34 40N26 83w48 5:35:12
Hurford 34 21 40N13 80w52 5:23:28
Huron 22 7 41N24 82w33 5:30:12
Hustead 12 39 39N55 83w48 5:35:12
Hyatts 21 27 40N10 83w06 5:32:24
Hyattville 21 27 40N10 83w06 5:32:24
Hyde Park 31 88 39N08 84w26 5:37:44
Hyde Park 57 91 39N41 84w09 5:36:36
Hyland Park 73 34 38N39 82w52 5:31:28
Iberia 59 27 40N40 82w51 5:31:24
Idaho 66 34 39N05 83w01 5:32:04
Iler 74 32 41N11 83w26 5:33:44
Ilesboro 37 27 39N32 82w24 5:29:36
Immergrun 48 30 41N40 83w24 5:33:36
Independence 18 26 41N23 81w39 5:26:36
Independence 20 34 41N17 84w20 5:37:20
Indian Camp 30 5 40N01 81w35 5:26:20
Indian Hill 31 34 39N11 84w20 5:37:20
Indian Knolls 13 34 39N10 84w18 5:37:12
Indian Ridge 31 34 39N14 84w32 5:38:08
Ingle Mann 68 34 39N51 84w48 5:39:12
Ingomar 68 34 39N44 84w32 5:38:08
Ink 74 32 41N07 83w10 5:32:40
Ira 77 67 41N14 81w33 5:26:12
Iradale 77 2 41N08 81w34 5:26:16
Iron City 46 33 40N22 83w46 5:35:04
Irondale 41 67 40N34 80w44 5:22:56
Irondale 60 21 40N07 82w02 5:28:08
Ironspot 60 5 39N47 82w04 5:28:16
Ironton 44 87 38N32 82w41 5:30:44
Irvington 57 91 39N50 84w13 5:36:52
Irwin 80 34 40N07 83w29 5:33:56
Island Creek 41 106 40N25 80w40 5:22:40
Island View 46 34 40N29 83w56 5:35:44
Isle Saint George 62 93 41N43 82w49 5:31:16
Isleta 16 5 40N16 81w44 5:26:56
Israel 68 34 39N37 84w46 5:39:04
Ithaca 19 34 39N57 84w33 5:38:12
Ivorydale 31 88 39N09 84w30 5:38:00
Jackson 40 34 39N03 82w39 5:30:36
Jackson 85 58 40N58 81w54 5:27:36
Jacksonburgh 9 34 39N32 84w30 5:38:00
Jackson Center 50 67 41N06 80w52 5:23:28
Jackson Center 75 34 40N26 84w03 5:36:12
Jackson Heights 40 34 39N04 82w39 5:30:36
Jackson Heights 41 67 40N11 80w41 5:22:44
Jackson Lake 40 34 38N54 82w35 5:30:20
Jacksontown 45 5 39N58 82w25 5:29:40
Jacksonville 1 34 38N57 83w24 5:33:36
Jacksonville 5 27 39N29 82w05 5:28:20
Jacksonville 12 39 39N55 83w48 5:35:12
Jacktown 9 34 39N30 84w23 5:37:32
Jacobsburg 7 21 39N58 80w55 5:23:40
Jaite 18 26 41N21 81w39 5:26:36
Jamestown 29 34 39N40 83w44 5:34:56
Jasper 66 34 39N03 83w03 5:32:12
Jasper Mills 24 34 39N34 83w31 5:34:04
Jays 19 34 40N06 84w38 5:38:32
Jeddo 41 46 40N28 80w36 5:22:24
Jefferson 4 72 41N44 80w46 5:23:04
Jefferson 23 27 39N48 82w43 5:30:52
Jefferson 85 76 40N49 81w56 5:27:44
Jefferson Estates 65 34 39N37 82w57 5:31:48
Jefferson Heights 41 106 40N19 80w39 5:22:36
Jeffersonville 24 34 39N39 83w34 5:34:16
Jelloway 42 5 40N33 82w18 5:29:12
Jenera 32 34 40N54 83w43 5:34:52
Jenkins Addition 60 5 39N55 82w01 5:28:04
Jep 44 34 38N38 82w40 5:30:40
Jericho 9 34 39N30 84w23 5:37:32
Jerome 80 33 40N10 83w14 5:32:56
Jeromesville 3 44 40N48 82w12 5:28:48
Jerry City 87 33 41N15 83w36 5:34:24
Jersey 45 27 40N05 82w42 5:30:48
Jerusalem 56 20 39N44 81w08 5:24:32
Jethro 15 105 40N38 80w35 5:22:20
Jewell 20 34 41N20 84w17 5:37:08
Jewett 34 11 40N22 81w02 5:24:08
Jobs 37 27 39N30 82w06 5:28:24
Johnson 11 34 40N08 83w59 5:35:56
Johnsons Corners 77 67 41N01 81w38 5:26:32
Johnston 78 67 41N23 80w40 5:22:40
Johnston 79 16 40N33 81w29 5:25:56
Johnstown 45 27 40N09 82w41 5:30:44
Johnsville 57 34 39N42 84w18 5:37:12
Jonesboro 14 34 39N19 83w49 5:35:16
Jonesboro 24 34 39N34 83w31 5:34:04
Jonestown 81 34 40N47 84w27 5:37:48
Joy 58 5 39N29 81w52 5:27:28
Jug Run 41 67 40N12 80w46 5:23:04
Jump 33 5 39N31 81w18 5:25:12
Junction 63 34 41N17 84w20 5:37:20
Junction City 64 27 39N42 82w19 5:29:16
Justus 76 67 40N42 81w35 5:26:20
Kalida 69 34 40N59 84w12 5:36:48
Kamms 18 26 41N28 81w47 5:27:08
Kanauga 27 27 38N46 82w11 5:28:44
Kansas 74 32 41N15 83w17 5:33:08
Kay Subdivision 83 34 39N35 84w18 5:37:12
Keene 16 5 40N21 81w52 5:27:28
Kelleys Island 22 5 41N36 82w42 5:30:48
Kelloggsville 4 72 41N51 80w37 5:22:28
Kemp 2 90 40N42 84w08 5:36:32
Kendall Heights 76 54 40N48 81w31 5:26:04
Kenmore 77 2 41N03 81w34 5:26:16
Kennard 11 34 40N10 83w38 5:34:32
Kennonsburg 61 5 39N58 81w17 5:25:08
Keno 53 5 39N05 81w48 5:27:12
Kenridge 31 34 39N15 84w22 5:37:28
Kensington 15 67 40N44 80w57 5:23:48
Kent 67 46 41N09 81w22 5:25:28
Kenton 33 111 40N39 83w37 5:34:28
Kenwood 31 34 39N12 84w23 5:37:32
Kenwood 34 21 40N13 80w52 5:23:28
Kenwood 48 31 41N40 83w36 5:34:24
Kerr 27 27 38N52 82w16 5:29:04
Kerr 56 20 39N47 81w09 5:24:36
Kessler 55 34 39N58 84w20 5:37:20
Kettering 57 91 39N41 84w10 5:36:40
Kettlersville 75 34 40N26 84w15 5:37:00
Key 7 21 40N01 80w45 5:23:00
Kidron 85 69 40N44 81w45 5:27:00
Kieferville 69 34 41N07 84w10 5:36:40
Kilbourne 21 27 40N20 82w58 5:31:52
Kile 49 34 40N07 83w16 5:33:04
Kilgore 10 21 40N34 81w05 5:24:20
Killbuck 38 5 40N30 81w59 5:27:56
Kilvert 5 5 39N18 81w54 5:27:36
Kimball 22 5 41N19 82w42 5:30:48
Kimberly 5 27 39N26 82w14 5:28:56
Kimbolton 30 5 40N09 81w34 5:26:16
Kingman 14 34 39N27 83w50 5:35:20
King Mines 30 5 39N59 81w27 5:25:48
Kings Corners 70 95 40N42 82w32 5:30:08
Kings Creek 11 34 40N04 83w42 5:34:48
Kingsgate 31 34 39N14 84w32 5:38:08
Kings Mills 83 34 39N21 84w15 5:37:00
Kingston 71 34 39N28 82w55 5:31:40
Kingsville 4 52 41N53 80w41 5:22:44
Kingsville on-the-Lake 4 52 41N54 80w46 5:23:04
Kingsway 72 30 41N21 83w08 5:32:32
Kinnickinnick 71 34 39N21 83w00 5:32:00
Kinsman 78 56 41N27 80w36 5:22:24
Kiousville 49 34 39N43 83w16 5:33:04
Kipling 30 5 40N00 81w30 5:26:00
Kipton 47 67 41N16 82w18 5:29:12
Kirby 88 33 40N49 83w25 5:33:40
Kirkersville 45 27 39N58 82w35 5:30:20
Kirkwood 7 21 40N05 81w11 5:24:44
Kirkwood 75 34 40N17 84w09 5:36:36
Kirkwood Heights 7 21 40N05 80w45 5:23:00
Kirtland 43 67 41N36 81w21 5:25:24
Kirtland Hills 43 67 41N38 81w19 5:25:16
Kitchen 40 34 38N54 82w35 5:30:20
Kitts Hill 44 34 38N34 82w35 5:30:20
Kiwanis Lake 28 67 41N26 81w13 5:24:52

OHIO

Klee 7	21	40N01	80w45	5:23:00
Klondike 78	67	41N19	80w43	5:22:52
Klondyke 15	105	40N38	80w35	5:22:20
Knollwood 29	34	39N45	84w04	5:36:16
Knollwood Village 65	34	39N37	82w57	5:31:48
Knoxville 41	67	40N28	80w36	5:22:24
Kolmont 41	106	40N19	80w39	5:22:36
Kossuth 6	34	40N28	84w34	5:38:16
Krumroy 77	2	41N08	81w34	5:26:16
Kunkle 86	34	41N38	84w30	5:38:00
Kyger 27	27	38N59	82w07	5:28:28
Kylesburg 45	27	39N58	82w28	5:29:52
Lacarne 62	93	41N31	83w03	5:32:12
La Croft 15	105	40N38	80w35	5:22:20
La Fayette 2	34	39N56	83w25	5:33:40
Lafayette 49	34	39N56	83w25	5:33:40
Lafayette 52	73	41N08	81w52	5:27:28
Lafferty 7	21	40N07	81w01	5:24:04
La Grange 44	34	38N31	82w39	5:30:36
Lagrange 47	73	41N14	82w07	5:28:28
Laings 56	20	39N43	81w01	5:24:04
Lake Cable 76	43	40N48	81w19	5:25:16
Lake Fork 3	44	40N48	82w12	5:28:48
Lakeland Beach 38	17	40N40	82w06	5:28:24
Lakeline 43	67	41N40	81w27	5:25:48
Lake Lucerne 28	67	41N26	81w22	5:25:28
Lake Milton 50	73	41N06	81w00	5:24:00
Lakemore 77	2	41N02	81w26	5:25:44
Lake O'Springs 76	43	40N48	81w19	5:25:16
Lakeside 9	34	39N30	84w23	5:37:32
Lakeside 23	27	39N54	82w33	5:30:12
Lakeside 45	5	39N56	82w27	5:29:48
Lakeside 62	93	41N32	82w46	5:31:04
Lake Slagle 76	43	40N53	81w24	5:25:36
Lake Sylvan 12	34	39N55	83w37	5:34:28
Lakeview 46	34	40N29	83w56	5:35:44
Lakeville 38	17	40N40	82w07	5:28:28
Lakewood 18	26	41N29	81w48	5:27:12
Lamira 7	21	40N02	81w03	5:24:12
Lancaster 23	96	39N43	82w36	5:30:24
Landeck 2	34	40N51	84w20	5:37:20
Langsville 53	27	39N03	82w11	5:28:44
Lanier 68	34	39N42	84w33	5:38:12
Lansing 7	21	40N04	80w47	5:23:08
LaPorte 47	42	41N20	82w05	5:28:20
La Rue 51	33	40N35	83w23	5:33:32
Latcha 87	31	41N35	83w28	5:33:52
Latham 66	34	39N06	83w15	5:33:00
Lattasburg 85	62	40N53	82w07	5:28:28
Lattasville 71	34	39N24	83w10	5:32:40
Latty 63	34	41N02	84w31	5:38:04
Laura 55	34	40N00	84w25	5:37:40
Laurel 13	34	38N57	84w17	5:37:08
Laurel 37	34	39N30	82w34	5:30:16
Laurel Ridge 76	43	40N52	81w20	5:25:20
Laurelville 37	34	39N28	82w44	5:30:56
Lawco 44	34	38N38	82w40	5:30:40
Lawndale 76	54	40N48	81w31	5:26:04
Lawrence 44	34	38N38	82w40	5:30:40
Lawrenceville 12	39	39N59	83w52	5:35:28
Lawshe 1	34	38N57	83w24	5:33:36
Lawyerdale Estates 31	34	39N07	84w21	5:37:24
Layhigh 9	34	39N25	84w35	5:38:20
Layland 16	5	40N30	82w00	5:28:00
Layman 84	20	39N21	81w47	5:27:08
Leaper 27	27	38N46	82w11	5:28:44
Leavittsburg 78	45	41N14	80w53	5:23:32
Leavittsville 10	21	40N31	81w14	5:24:56
Lebanon 56	20	39N34	81w24	5:25:36
Lebanon 83	34	39N26	84w13	5:36:52
Lecta 44	34	38N33	82w23	5:29:32
Lee Road 18	26	41N27	81w35	5:26:20
Leesburg 36	34	39N21	83w33	5:34:12
Lees Creek 14	34	39N25	83w39	5:34:36
Leesville 10	21	40N27	81w13	5:24:52
Leesville Cross Roads 17	33	40N47	82w44	5:30:56
Leetonia 15	47	40N53	80w44	5:22:56
Lehmkuhl Landing 75	34	40N24	84w22	5:37:28
Leipsic 69	34	41N06	83w59	5:35:56
Leistville 65	34	39N37	82w57	5:31:48
Lelan 83	34	39N26	84w12	5:36:48
Lemert 17	33	40N57	83w11	5:32:44
Lemon 9	34	39N29	84w24	5:37:36
Lemoyne 87	32	41N30	83w28	5:33:52
Lena 55	34	40N08	84w03	5:36:12
Lenox 4	72	41N41	80w47	5:23:08
Leo 40	34	39N07	82w33	5:30:12
Leon 4	72	41N41	80w40	5:22:40
Leonardsburg 21	27	40N18	83w04	5:32:16
Lerado 13	34	39N04	84w03	5:36:12
Le Sourdsville 9	34	39N27	84w25	5:37:40
Lester 52	73	41N08	81w52	5:27:28
Letart 53	5	38N55	81w53	5:27:32
Letart Falls 53	5	38N54	81w56	5:27:44
Levanna 8	34	38N45	83w50	5:35:20
Lewis 8	34	38N50	84w00	5:36:00
Lewis Addition 41	106	40N22	80w39	5:22:36
Lewisburg 68	34	39N51	84w33	5:38:12
Lewis Center 21	27	40N12	83w01	5:32:04
Lewistown 46	33	40N25	83w53	5:35:32
Lewisville 56	20	39N46	81w13	5:24:52
Lexington 70	95	40N41	82w35	5:30:20
Lexington 76	67	40N55	81w06	5:24:24
Liberty 57	91	39N43	84w15	5:37:00
Liberty Center 35	34	41N27	84w01	5:36:04
Liberty Plaza 78	84	41N08	80w38	5:22:32
Lick 40	34	39N03	82w37	5:30:28
Licking View 60	5	39N55	82w01	5:28:04
Lickskillet 71	34	39N16	82w47	5:31:08
Liebs Island 23	27	39N54	82w33	5:30:12
Lightsville 19	34	40N17	84w38	5:38:32
Lilly Chapel 49	34	39N56	83w17	5:33:08
Lima 2	90	40N44	84w06	5:36:24
Limaville 76	67	40N59	81w08	5:24:32
Lime City 87	31	41N32	83w34	5:34:16
Limecrest 12	39	39N55	83w48	5:35:12
Limerick 40	34	39N04	82w39	5:30:36
Limestone 62	93	41N33	83w16	5:33:04
Limestone City 12	39	39N55	83w48	5:35:12
Lincoln 59	27	40N28	82w51	5:31:24
Lincoln 70	95	40N47	82w30	5:30:00
Lincoln Heights 31	34	39N14	84w28	5:37:52
Lincoln Heights 70	95	40N45	82w31	5:30:04
Lincoln Village 25	107	39N57	83w07	5:32:28
Lincolnville 36	34	39N12	83w37	5:34:28
Lindair Estates 12	39	39N55	83w48	5:35:12
Lindale 13	34	38N59	84w13	5:36:52
Lindentree 10	21	40N37	81w23	5:25:32
Lindenwald 9	34	39N22	84w33	5:38:12
Lindsey 72	30	41N25	83w13	5:32:52
Linndale 18	26	41N27	81w46	5:27:04
Linnville 44	34	38N34	82w28	5:29:52
Linnville 45	5	39N54	82w27	5:29:48
Linton 16	5	40N11	81w42	5:26:48
Linworth 25	107	40N05	83w01	5:32:04
Lisbon 12	34	39N50	83w38	5:34:32
Lisbon 15	67	40N46	80w46	5:23:04
Lisman 44	34	38N38	82w40	5:30:40
Litchfield 52	73	41N10	82w02	5:28:08
Lithopolis 23	34	39N48	82w49	5:31:16
Little Chicago 65	34	39N43	82w58	5:31:52
Little Farms 25	107	39N57	83w07	5:32:28
Little Hocking 84	20	39N16	81w42	5:26:48
Little Richmond 57	34	39N49	84w25	5:37:40
Little Sandusky 88	32	40N44	83w16	5:33:04
Little Walnut 65	34	39N43	82w58	5:31:52
Little Washington 70	95	40N45	82w31	5:30:04
Little York 57	91	39N50	84w13	5:36:52
Little York 77	67	41N21	81w32	5:26:08
Livingston 25	107	39N56	82w53	5:31:32
Lloydsville 7	21	40N06	80w55	5:23:40
Lock 42	27	40N18	82w41	5:30:44
Lockbourne 25	34	39N49	82w58	5:31:52
Lockbourne Base 25	34	39N49	82w57	5:31:48
Lockington 75	34	40N12	84w14	5:36:56
Lockland 31	34	39N14	84w28	5:37:52
Locks 71	34	39N21	83w00	5:32:00
Lock Two 6	34	40N26	84w22	5:37:28
Lockville 23	27	39N48	82w43	5:30:52
Lockwood 78	67	41N28	80w52	5:23:28
Lockwood Corners 77	2	41N00	81w32	5:26:08
Locust Corner 13	34	39N02	84w17	5:37:08
Locust Grove 1	34	38N57	83w24	5:33:36
Locust Grove 50	67	40N55	80w51	5:23:24
Locust Lake 13	34	39N02	84w14	5:36:56
Locust Point 62	93	41N31	83w08	5:32:32
Locust Ridge 8	34	39N04	84w03	5:36:12
Lodi 52	73	41N02	82w01	5:28:04
Logan 37	27	39N32	82w25	5:29:40
Logansville 46	34	40N19	83w55	5:35:40
Lombardsville 73	34	38N50	83w04	5:32:16
London 49	101	39N53	83w27	5:33:48
London 70	5	40N54	82w37	5:30:28
Londonderry 30	5	40N12	81w16	5:25:04
Londonderry 71	34	39N16	82w48	5:31:12
Long 19	34	40N06	84w38	5:38:32
Long Beach 62	93	41N31	83w08	5:32:32
Long Bottom 53	5	39N05	81w48	5:27:12
Long Run 41	67	40N12	80w46	5:23:04
Longstreth 37	27	39N26	82w14	5:28:56
Longview Heights 5	27	39N20	82w05	5:28:20
Longvue 84	20	39N27	81w28	5:25:52
Lorain 47	50	41N28	82w11	5:28:44
Loramie 75	34	40N14	84w22	5:37:28
Lordstown 78	45	41N10	80w52	5:23:28
Lore City 30	5	39N59	81w28	5:25:52
Lostcreek 55	34	40N05	84w04	5:36:16
Lost Creek Addition 2	90	40N43	84w06	5:36:24
Lottridge 5	5	39N14	81w45	5:27:00
Louden 1	34	38N57	83w24	5:33:36
Louden 79	16	40N33	81w29	5:25:56
Loudonville 3	5	40N38	82w14	5:28:56
Louisville 1	35	38N57	83w24	5:33:36
Louisville 76	67	40N50	81w16	5:25:04
Loveland 31	34	39N16	84w16	5:37:04
Lovell 88	33	40N46	83w21	5:33:24
Lowell 74	32	41N07	83w10	5:32:40
Lowell 84	20	39N32	81w31	5:26:04
Lowellville 50	84	41N02	80w32	5:22:08
Lower Newport 84	20	39N23	81w14	5:24:56
Lower Salem 84	20	39N34	81w24	5:25:36
Loyal Oak 77	67	41N01	81w38	5:26:32
Lucas 70	5	40N42	82w25	5:29:40
Lucasburg 30	5	39N58	81w32	5:26:08
Lucasville 73	34	38N53	83w00	5:32:00
Lucerne 42	27	40N29	82w32	5:30:08
Luckey 87	32	41N27	83w29	5:33:56
Ludington 64	27	39N36	82w05	5:28:20
Ludlow 84	20	39N34	81w12	5:24:48
Ludlow Falls 55	34	40N00	84w21	5:37:24
Lugbill Addition 26	34	41N31	84w18	5:37:12
Lumberton 14	34	39N27	83w50	5:35:20
Luray 45	27	39N58	82w28	5:29:52
Lykens 17	32	40N57	83w02	5:32:08
Lyme 39	5	41N15	82w48	5:31:12
Lynchburg 15	67	40N44	80w57	5:23:48
Lynchburg 36	34	39N15	83w48	5:35:12
Lyndhurst 18	67	41N31	81w30	5:26:00
Lyndon 71	34	39N21	83w19	5:33:16
Lynn 33	34	40N38	83w43	5:34:52
Lynx 1	34	38N46	83w25	5:33:40
Lyons 26	34	41N42	84w04	5:36:16
Lyra 73	34	38N45	82w51	5:31:24
Lytle 83	34	39N32	84w05	5:36:20
Lytton 26	34	41N34	84w00	5:36:00
Macedon 54	34	40N29	84w37	5:38:28
Macedonia 77	58	41N19	81w31	5:26:04
Mack 31	34	39N10	84w39	5:38:36
Macksburg 84	20	39N38	81w28	5:25:52
Macon 8	34	38N58	83w44	5:34:56
Maddox 1	34	38N41	83w36	5:34:24
Madeira 31	34	39N11	84w22	5:37:28
Madison 43	46	41N46	81w03	5:24:12
Madisonburg 85	76	40N49	81w56	5:27:44
Madison Lake Area 49	34	39N53	83w27	5:33:48
Madison Mills 24	34	39N39	83w20	5:33:20
Madison-on-the-Lake 43	46	41N48	81w04	5:24:16
Madisonville 31	34	39N10	84w23	5:37:32
Magnetic Springs 80	33	40N22	83w16	5:33:04
Magnolia 76	21	40N39	81w18	5:25:12
Maineville 83	34	39N19	84w14	5:36:56
Mainsville 64	27	39N43	82w13	5:28:52
Malaga 56	20	39N51	81w09	5:24:36
Malinta 35	34	41N19	84w02	5:36:08
Mallet Creek 52	73	41N08	81w52	5:27:28
Malta 58	5	39N38	81w54	5:27:36
Malvern 10	21	40N42	81w11	5:24:44
Manchester 1	34	38N41	83w36	5:34:24
Manchester 77	2	41N00	81w32	5:26:08
Mandale 63	34	41N01	84w17	5:37:08
Manhattan 41	106	40N22	80w39	5:22:36
Mannhassett Village 83	34	39N22	84w17	5:37:08
Mansfield 70	95	40N45	82w31	5:30:04
Mantua 67	46	41N17	81w14	5:24:56
Maple Corner 29	34	39N44	84w02	5:36:08
Maple Grove 71	34	39N21	83w00	5:32:00
Maple Heights 18	26	41N25	81w34	5:26:16
Maple Heights 61	5	39N46	81w31	5:26:04
Maple Lake 41	68	40N26	80w46	5:23:04
Maple Ridge 50	67	40N55	81w06	5:24:24
Mapleshade 27	27	38N46	82w11	5:28:44
Mapleton 76	43	40N48	81w19	5:25:16
Maple Valley 77	2	41N05	81w35	5:26:20
Maplewood 75	34	40N23	84w02	5:36:08
Marathon 13	34	39N09	84w01	5:36:04
Marble Cliff 25	107	39N59	83w04	5:32:16
Marble Furnace 1	34	38N57	83w24	5:33:36
Marblehead 62	93	41N32	82w44	5:30:56
Marchand 76	43	40N53	81w24	5:25:36
Marcy 18	26	41N26	81w37	5:26:28
Marcy 23	27	39N51	82w48	5:31:12
Marengo 59	27	40N24	82w49	5:31:16
Margaretta 22	5	41N25	82w48	5:31:12
Maria Stein 54	34	40N24	84w28	5:37:52
Mariemont 31	34	39N09	84w23	5:37:32
Marietta 84	113	39N25	81w27	5:25:48
Marion 51	98	40N35	83w08	5:32:32
Mark 20	34	41N18	84w38	5:38:32
Marlan Acres 31	34	39N14	84w32	5:38:08
Marlboro 76	67	40N55	81w06	5:24:24
Marne 45	5	40N07	82w26	5:29:44
Marquis 50	67	41N02	80w46	5:23:04
Marr 56	20	39N40	81w15	5:25:00
Marseilles 88	33	40N42	83w24	5:33:36
Marshall 36	34	39N09	83w29	5:33:56
Marshallville 85	62	40N54	81w44	5:26:56
Martel 51	27	40N40	82w55	5:31:40
Martin 62	32	41N33	83w20	5:33:20
Martinsburg 42	5	40N16	82w21	5:29:24
Martins Ferry 7	15	40N06	80w44	5:22:56
Martinsville 14	34	39N19	83w49	5:35:16
Mary Ann 45	5	40N09	82w19	5:29:16
Marygrove 48	34	41N35	83w54	5:35:36
Marysville 80	33	40N14	83w22	5:33:28
Mason 83	34	39N22	84w19	5:37:16
Mason Heights 83	34	39N22	84w17	5:37:08
Massie 83	34	39N29	84w02	5:36:08
Massieville 71	34	39N16	82w58	5:31:52
Massillon 76	54	40N48	81w32	5:26:08
Masury 78	46	41N13	80w32	5:22:08
Matville 65	34	39N48	83w09	5:32:36
Maud 9	34	39N21	84w23	5:37:32
Maumee 48	31	41N34	83w39	5:34:36
Maustown 9	34	39N24	84w27	5:37:48
Maximo 76	67	40N53	81w11	5:24:44
Maxtown 21	27	40N06	82w56	5:31:44
Maxville 64	27	39N42	82w19	5:29:16
Mayfield 9	34	39N30	84w23	5:37:32
Mayfield 18	67	41N33	81w29	5:25:56
Mayfield Heights 18	67	41N31	81w28	5:25:52
Mayflower Village 76	54	40N48	81w31	5:26:04
May-Green Shopping Center 18	67	41N31	81w32	5:26:08
May Hill 1	34	38N56	83w34	5:34:16
Maynard 7	21	40N07	80w53	5:23:32
Maysville 2	34	40N46	83w51	5:35:24
Maysville 85	62	40N45	81w50	5:27:20
McArthur 82	34	39N15	82w29	5:29:56
McCance 85	62	40N41	81w52	5:27:28
McCartyville 75	34	40N23	84w10	5:36:40
McClaimsville 49	34	39N43	83w16	5:33:04
McClainville 7	21	40N01	80w45	5:23:00

McClintocksburg 67 58 41N11 80w59 5:23:56
McClure 35 34 41N22 83w57 5:35:48
McComb 32 34 41N07 83w48 5:35:12
McConnelsville 58 5 39N39 81w51 5:27:24
McCormick 27 27 38N46 82w11 5:28:44
McCracken Corners 15 67 40N55 80w51 5:23:24
McCuneville 64 27 39N38 82w14 5:28:56
McCutchenville 88 32 40N59 83w16 5:33:04
McDermott 73 34 38N50 83w04 5:32:16
McDonald 78 75 41N10 80w45 5:23:00
McDonaldsville 76 43 40N53 81w24 5:25:36
McFarlands Corners 28 67 41N26 81w22 5:25:28
McGill 63 34 41N05 84w44 5:38:56
McGonigle 9 34 39N27 84w41 5:38:44
McGuffey 33 34 40N42 83w47 5:35:08
McIntyre 41 67 40N21 80w48 5:23:12
McKay 3 5 40N38 82w14 5:28:56
McKean 45 27 40N10 82w31 5:30:04
McKinley Heights 78 75 41N12 80w45 5:23:00
McLean 75 34 40N22 84w21 5:37:24
McLeish 5 27 39N30 82w06 5:28:24
McLuney 64 27 39N46 82w06 5:28:24
McMorran 46 33 40N22 83w46 5:35:04
McWhorters Acres 9 34 39N25 84w35 5:38:20
McZena 3 64 40N40 82w07 5:28:28
Mead 7 21 39N58 80w50 5:23:20
Meade 65 34 39N29 82w55 5:31:40
Meadowbrook 60 5 39N55 82w01 5:28:04
Meadowbrook Lake 77 2 41N10 81w28 5:25:52
Meadow Lawn 9 34 39N30 84w23 5:37:32
Mecca 78 67 41N23 80w44 5:22:56
Mechanic 38 5 40N29 81w52 5:27:28
Mechanicsburg 11 34 40N03 83w33 5:34:12
Mechanicsburg 17 33 40N54 82w46 5:31:04
Mechanicsburg 85 76 40N49 81w56 5:27:44
Mechanicstown 10 21 40N37 80w57 5:23:48
Mechanicsville 4 72 41N48 80w58 5:23:52
Medina 52 73 41N08 81w52 5:27:28
Medway 12 34 39N53 84w02 5:36:08
Meeker 51 33 40N39 83w18 5:33:12
Meigs 58 5 39N39 81w51 5:27:24
Meigsville 58 5 39N38 81w45 5:27:00
Melbern 86 34 41N28 84w33 5:38:12
Melmore 74 32 41N01 83w07 5:32:28
Melody Lake 60 5 39N55 82w01 5:28:04
Melrose 63 34 41N06 84w25 5:37:40
Melvin 14 34 39N27 83w50 5:35:20
Memphis 14 34 39N20 83w34 5:34:16
Mendon 54 34 40N40 84w31 5:38:04
Mentor 43 48 41N40 81w21 5:25:24
Mentor Headlands 43 48 41N41 81w21 5:25:24
Mentor-on-the-Lake 43 48 41N43 81w22 5:25:28
Mercer 54 34 40N40 84w31 5:38:04
Mercerville 27 27 38N46 82w11 5:28:44
Mermill 87 33 41N20 83w39 5:34:36
Mesopotamia 78 67 41N27 80w57 5:23:48
Metamora 26 34 41N42 83w55 5:35:40
Metzger 71 34 39N21 83w00 5:32:00
Mexico 88 32 40N57 83w11 5:32:44
Meyers Lake 76 43 40N49 81w24 5:25:36
Miami 31 34 39N13 84w42 5:38:48
Miami Heights 31 88 39N10 84w36 5:38:24
Miamisburg 57 34 39N38 84w17 5:37:08
Miamitown 31 34 39N13 84w42 5:38:48
Miami University 9 34 39N31 84w44 5:38:56
Miami Villa 57 91 39N49 84w15 5:37:00
Miamiville 13 34 39N13 84w18 5:37:12
Mid City 57 91 39N45 84w11 5:36:44
Middle Bass 62 93 41N41 82w50 5:31:20
Middleboro 83 34 39N22 84w08 5:36:32
Middlebourne 30 5 39N58 81w17 5:25:08
Middlebranch 76 67 40N54 81w20 5:25:20
Middleburg 46 34 40N18 83w35 5:34:20
Middleburg 61 5 39N45 81w31 5:26:04
Middleburgh Heights 18 67 41N22 81w49 5:27:16
Middlebury 42 5 40N31 82w35 5:30:20
Middlebury 81 34 40N55 84w42 5:38:48
Middlefield 28 74 41N28 81w05 5:24:20
Middle Point 81 34 40N51 84w27 5:37:48
Middleport 53 97 39N00 82w03 5:28:12
Middleton 15 67 40N55 80w41 5:22:44
Middleton 40 34 39N07 82w33 5:30:12
Middleton Corner 29 34 39N44 84w02 5:36:08
Middletown 9 3 39N31 84w24 5:37:36
Middletown 11 34 40N10 83w38 5:34:32
Middletown 17 33 40N44 82w47 5:31:08
Midland 14 34 39N18 83w54 5:35:36
Midpark 18 26 41N24 81w46 5:27:04
Midtown 60 5 39N55 82w01 5:28:04
Midvale 79 16 40N26 81w23 5:25:32
Midway 7 21 40N06 80w55 5:23:40
Midway 49 34 39N45 83w29 5:33:56
Midway Mall 47 42 41N22 82w06 5:28:24
Mifflin 3 44 40N54 82w22 5:29:28
Milan 22 38 41N18 82w37 5:30:28
Milford 13 34 39N11 84w18 5:37:12
Milford Center 80 34 40N11 83w26 5:33:44
Mill 79 16 40N23 81w20 5:25:20
Millbrook 85 76 40N49 81w56 5:27:44
Millbury 87 30 41N34 83w25 5:33:40
Millcreek 80 33 40N13 83w14 5:32:56
Milledgeville 24 34 39N36 83w35 5:34:20
Miller 42 27 40N19 82w30 5:30:00
Miller 44 34 38N35 82w17 5:29:08
Miller City 69 34 41N06 84w08 5:36:32
Millersburg 38 5 40N33 81w55 5:27:40
Millersport 23 27 39N54 82w32 5:30:08
Millerstown 11 34 40N06 83w59 5:35:56
Millersville 72 32 41N19 83w17 5:33:08
Millertown 64 27 39N36 82w05 5:28:20
Millfield 5 27 39N26 82w06 5:28:24
Millport 15 67 40N44 80w57 5:23:48
Millport 65 34 39N43 82w58 5:31:52
Millsboro 70 95 40N45 82w31 5:30:04
Millsbury 87 30 41N34 83w26 5:33:44
Millville 9 34 39N23 84w39 5:38:36
Millville 50 67 40N55 80w51 5:23:24
Millwood 30 5 39N58 81w17 5:25:08
Millwood 42 5 40N27 82w16 5:29:04
Milton Center 87 34 41N19 83w50 5:35:20
Miltonsburg 56 20 39N49 81w10 5:24:40
Miltonville 9 34 39N30 84w28 5:37:52
Mineral 5 27 39N19 82w13 5:28:52
Mineral City 79 21 40N36 81w22 5:25:28
Mineral Ridge 78 68 41N08 80w46 5:23:04
Minersville 53 5 39N07 82w00 5:28:00
Minerva 76 21 40N44 81w06 5:24:24
Minerva Park 25 107 40N04 82w57 5:31:48
Minford 73 34 38N52 82w52 5:31:28
Mingo 11 34 40N13 83w38 5:34:32
Mingo Junction 41 106 40N19 80w37 5:22:28
Minster 6 34 40N24 84w23 5:37:32
Mishler 67 67 41N03 81w24 5:25:36
Mississinawa 19 34 40N19 84w45 5:39:00
Mitiwanga 22 5 41N24 82w34 5:30:16
Modest 13 34 39N14 84w10 5:36:40
Modoc 5 27 39N30 82w06 5:28:24
Moffit Heights 76 54 40N48 81w31 5:26:04
Mogadore 77 67 41N03 81w23 5:25:32
Mohawk 16 5 40N20 82w03 5:28:12
Mohican 3 44 40N46 82w11 5:28:44
Mohicanville 3 44 40N48 82w12 5:28:48
Moline 87 31 41N36 83w30 5:34:00
Momeneetown 48 31 41N38 83w29 5:33:56
Monclova 48 34 41N34 83w46 5:35:04
Monclova Gardens 48 34 41N35 83w40 5:34:40
Monday Creek 64 27 39N38 82w20 5:29:20
Monfort Heights 31 34 39N13 84w35 5:38:20
Monnett 17 32 40N43 83w02 5:32:08
Mononcue 88 32 40N46 83w21 5:33:24
Monroe 9 34 39N27 84w22 5:37:28
Monroe Center 4 72 41N56 80w36 5:22:24
Monroe Mills 42 5 40N25 82w20 5:29:20
Monroeville 39 27 41N15 82w42 5:30:48
Monroeville 41 67 40N36 80w50 5:23:20
Monterey 69 34 40N57 84w21 5:37:24
Montezuma 54 34 40N29 84w37 5:38:28
Montgomery 31 34 39N14 84w21 5:37:24
Monticello 81 34 40N42 84w21 5:37:24
Montpelier 86 34 41N35 84w37 5:38:28
Montra 75 34 40N23 84w10 5:36:40
Montrose 77 2 41N08 81w34 5:26:16
Montville 28 67 41N36 81w03 5:24:12
Moons 24 34 39N34 83w31 5:34:04
Moorefield 12 39 39N55 83w48 5:35:12
Moorefield 34 21 40N12 81w09 5:24:36
Moores Fork 13 34 39N18 83w59 5:35:56
Moores Junction 64 27 39N46 82w06 5:28:24
Mooresville 71 34 39N21 83w00 5:32:00
Moraine 57 91 39N42 84w14 5:36:56
Moreland 85 76 40N49 81w56 5:27:44
Moreland Hills 18 67 41N26 81w27 5:25:48
Morgan Center 27 27 39N00 82w20 5:29:20
Morgandale 78 45 41N14 80w49 5:23:16
Morgan Place 57 34 39N51 84w18 5:37:12
Morgansville 58 5 39N39 81w52 5:27:28
Morgantown 50 84 41N02 80w38 5:22:32
Morgantown 66 34 39N08 83w12 5:32:48
Morges 10 21 40N39 81w18 5:25:12
Morning Sun 68 34 39N38 84w39 5:38:36
Morral 51 32 40N41 83w13 5:32:52
Morris 42 29 40N26 82w30 5:30:00
Morris Apartments 57 91 39N50 84w13 5:36:52
Morrisons 60 5 39N55 82w01 5:28:04
Morristown 5 27 39N24 82w08 5:28:32
Morristown 7 21 40N04 81w05 5:24:20
Morrisville 14 34 39N27 83w50 5:35:20
Morrow 83 34 39N21 84w08 5:36:32
Moscow 13 34 38N52 84w14 5:36:56
Moss Run 84 20 39N27 81w28 5:25:52
Moulton 6 34 40N36 84w16 5:37:04
Moultrie 15 67 40N44 81w05 5:24:20
Moundbuilders 45 5 40N07 82w26 5:29:44
Moundsville 61 5 39N45 81w31 5:26:04
Mound View 48 31 41N40 83w24 5:33:36
Mount Air 25 107 40N05 83w01 5:32:04
Mount Blanchard 32 33 40N54 83w34 5:34:16
Mount Carmel 13 34 39N07 84w21 5:37:24
Mount Carmel 72 30 41N18 82w59 5:31:56
Mount Carmel Heights 13 34 39N07 84w21 5:37:24
Mount Cory 32 34 40N56 83w48 5:35:12
Mount Eaton 85 62 40N42 81w42 5:26:48
Mount Ephraim 61 5 39N49 81w28 5:25:52
Mount Everett 84 20 39N27 81w28 5:25:52
Mount Forest Trails 13 34 39N07 84w21 5:37:24
Mount Gilead 59 27 40N33 82w50 5:31:20
Mount Healthy 31 34 39N14 84w33 5:38:12
Mount Healthy Heights 31 34 39N14 84w32 5:38:08
Mount Holly 13 34 39N02 84w13 5:36:52

Mount Holly 83 34 39N32 84w05 5:36:20
Mount Hope 38 5 40N38 81w47 5:27:08
Mount Jefferson 75 34 40N15 84w20 5:37:20
Mount Joy 73 34 38N52 83w11 5:32:44
Mount Liberty 42 27 40N21 82w38 5:30:32
Mount Olive 13 34 38N59 84w04 5:36:16
Mount Orab 8 34 39N02 83w55 5:35:40
Mount Perry 64 27 39N53 82w13 5:28:52
Mount Pisgah 13 34 38N57 84w17 5:37:08
Mount Pleasant 37 27 39N32 82w24 5:29:36
Mount Pleasant 41 67 40N11 80w48 5:23:12
Mount Pleasant 72 30 41N16 82w51 5:31:24
Mount Pleasant 76 43 40N53 81w24 5:25:36
Mount Repose 13 34 39N12 84w13 5:36:52
Mount Saint Joseph 31 88 39N06 84w39 5:38:36
Mount Sterling 49 34 39N43 83w16 5:33:04
Mount Union 76 67 40N55 81w06 5:24:24
Mount Vernon 42 29 40N23 82w29 5:29:56
Mount Victory 33 33 40N32 83w32 5:34:08
Mountville 58 5 39N30 82w06 5:28:24
Mount Washington 31 88 39N06 84w23 5:37:32
Mowrystown 36 34 39N02 83w45 5:35:00
Moxahala 64 27 39N40 82w08 5:28:32
Moxahala Park 60 5 39N55 82w01 5:28:04
Mudsock 25 108 40N01 83w08 5:32:32
Mudsock 27 34 38N46 82w23 5:29:32
Muhlenberg 65 34 39N42 83w07 5:32:28
Mulberry 13 34 39N11 84w15 5:37:00
Mule Town 73 34 38N51 82w52 5:31:28
Muncie Hollow 72 30 41N21 83w08 5:32:32
Munroe Falls 77 67 41N09 81w26 5:25:44
Munson 28 67 41N32 81w15 5:25:00
Murdock 83 34 39N14 84w20 5:37:20
Murlin Heights 57 91 39N50 84w13 5:36:52
Murray City 37 27 39N31 82w10 5:28:40
Museville 60 5 39N53 81w49 5:27:16
Mutual 11 34 40N05 83w38 5:34:32
Myersville 77 67 40N59 81w25 5:25:40
Naceville 66 34 39N05 83w23 5:33:32
Nankin 3 44 40N55 82w17 5:29:08
Napoleon 35 34 41N23 84w08 5:36:32
Nash Corners 65 34 39N37 82w57 5:31:48
Nashport 60 5 40N04 82w09 5:28:36
Nashville 19 34 40N06 84w38 5:38:32
Nashville 38 5 40N36 82w07 5:28:28
Nashville 55 34 40N03 84w11 5:36:44
National Road 45 27 39N58 82w28 5:29:52
Navarre 76 54 40N45 81w29 5:25:56
Neals Corner 8 34 38N59 84w04 5:36:16
Neapolis 48 34 41N30 83w52 5:35:28
Neave 19 34 40N02 84w39 5:38:36
Needmore 2 34 40N51 84w20 5:37:20
Neel 8 34 38N45 83w50 5:35:20
Neelysville 58 5 39N39 81w51 5:27:24
Neffs 7 10 40N02 80w49 5:23:16
Negley 15 67 40N48 80w32 5:22:08
Nellie 16 5 40N20 82w05 5:28:20
Nelson 67 67 41N19 81w03 5:24:12
Nelsonville 5 27 39N26 82w14 5:28:56
Neptune 54 34 40N36 84w30 5:38:00
Nettle Lake 86 34 41N35 84w36 5:38:24
Nevada 88 32 40N49 83w09 5:32:36
Neville 13 34 38N49 84w12 5:36:48
New Albany 25 27 40N05 82w50 5:31:20
New Albany 50 67 40N55 80w51 5:23:24
New Alexander 15 67 40N45 81w02 5:24:08
New Alexandria 41 67 40N17 80w41 5:22:44
New Antioch 14 34 39N27 83w50 5:35:20
Newark 45 92 40N03 82w24 5:29:36
New Athens 34 21 40N11 81w00 5:24:00
New Baltimore 31 34 39N16 84w40 5:38:40
New Baltimore 76 67 40N55 81w06 5:24:24
New Bavaria 35 34 41N12 84w10 5:36:40
New Bedford 16 5 40N26 81w41 5:26:44
Newberry 55 34 40N08 84w23 5:37:32
New Bloomington 51 33 40N35 83w19 5:33:16
New Boston 73 34 38N45 82w56 5:31:44
New Bremen 6 34 40N26 84w23 5:37:32
New Buffalo 50 67 41N02 80w46 5:23:04
Newburg 18 26 41N26 81w37 5:26:28
Newburgh Heights 18 26 41N27 81w40 5:26:40
New Burlington 14 34 39N34 83w58 5:35:52
New Burlington 31 34 39N14 84w32 5:38:08
Newbury 28 67 41N28 81w15 5:25:00
New California 80 34 40N07 83w16 5:33:04
New Carlisle 12 34 39N56 84w02 5:36:08
New Castle 7 21 39N51 81w03 5:24:12
Newcastle 16 5 40N21 82w10 5:28:40
New Castle 44 34 38N31 82w39 5:30:36
New Chicago 57 91 39N43 84w15 5:37:00
New Cleveland 69 34 41N01 84w03 5:36:12
Newcomerstown 79 12 40N15 81w35 5:26:20
New Concord 60 5 40N00 81w04 5:24:16
New Cumberland 79 16 40N37 81w23 5:25:32
New Cumberland 44 40N30 80w36 5:22:24
New Dover 80 33 40N15 83w22 5:33:28
Newell 41 67 40N15 80w50 5:23:20
Newell Run 84 20 39N23 81w14 5:24:56
New England 5 5 39N18 81w54 5:27:36
New Floodwood 5 27 39N26 82w14 5:28:56
New Franklin 76 67 40N44 81w05 5:24:20

New Garden 15 67 40N45 80w56 5:23:44
New Germany 29 34 39N46 84w06 5:36:24
New Guilford 16 5 40N22 82w09 5:28:36
New Hagerstown 10 21 40N25 81w12 5:24:48
New Hampshire 6 34 40N33 83w57 5:35:48
New Harmony 8 34 39N04 84w03 5:36:12
New Harrisburg 10 21 40N34 81w05 5:24:20
New Harrison 19 34 40N08 84w26 5:37:44
New Haven 31 34 39N17 84w44 5:38:56
New Haven 39 5 41N02 82w41 5:30:44
New Holland 65 34 39N33 83w17 5:33:08
Newhope 8 34 38N58 83w55 5:35:40
New Hope 68 34 39N45 84w38 5:38:32
New Jasper 29 34 39N39 83w49 5:35:16
New Knoxville 6 34 40N30 84w18 5:37:12
New Lebanon 57 34 39N45 84w23 5:37:32
New Lexington 64 109 39N43 82w13 5:28:52
New Lexington 68 34 39N44 84w32 5:38:08
New Liberty 15 67 40N51 80w32 5:22:08
New London 39 5 41N05 82w24 5:29:36
New Lyme 4 72 41N37 80w47 5:23:08
New Madison 19 34 39N58 84w43 5:38:52
Newman 51 27 40N27 83w11 5:32:44
Newman 76 54 40N48 81w31 5:26:04
New Market 36 34 39N09 83w40 5:34:40
New Marshfield 5 27 39N19 82w13 5:28:52
New Martinsburg 24 34 39N21 83w24 5:33:36
New Matamoras 84 20 39N31 81w04 5:24:16
New Miami 9 34 39N26 84w32 5:38:08
New Middletown 50 67 40N57 80w34 5:22:16
New Milford 67 67 41N06 81w13 5:24:52
New Moorefield 12 34 40N00 83w43 5:34:52
New Moscow 16 5 40N16 81w52 5:27:28
New Paris 68 34 39N51 84w48 5:39:12
New Petersburg 36 34 39N16 83w27 5:33:48
New Philadelphia 79 115 40N30 81w27 5:25:48
New Pittsburg 85 76 40N49 81w56 5:27:44
New Pittsburgh 17 5 41N00 82w40 5:30:40
New Plymouth 82 27 39N23 82w24 5:29:36
New Plymouth Heights 73 34 38N39 82w52 5:31:28
Newport 49 34 39N53 83w27 5:33:48
Newport 75 34 40N21 84w22 5:37:28
Newport 79 16 40N24 81w21 5:25:24
Newport 84 20 39N23 81w14 5:24:56
New Reading 64 16 40N24 81w21 5:25:24
New Richmond 13 34 38N57 84w17 5:37:08
New Riegel 74 32 41N03 83w19 5:33:16
New Rochester 87 33 41N25 83w28 5:33:52
New Rome 25 34 39N57 83w09 5:32:36
New Rumley 34 11 40N22 81w01 5:24:04
New Salem 23 27 39N49 82w32 5:30:08
New Salisbury 15 67 40N33 80w43 5:22:52
New Somerset 41 67 40N28 80w36 5:22:24
New Springfield 50 67 40N55 80w36 5:22:24
New Stark 32 33 40N50 83w39 5:34:36
New Straitsville 64 27 39N35 82w14 5:28:56
New Strasburg 23 34 39N39 82w45 5:31:00
Newton Falls 78 58 41N11 80w59 5:23:56
Newtonsville 13 34 39N11 84w05 5:36:20
Newtown 31 34 39N08 84w22 5:37:28
New Town 37 34 39N30 82w11 5:28:44
Newtown 41 67 40N12 80w46 5:23:04
New Vienna 14 34 39N19 83w42 5:34:48
Newville 70 5 40N40 82w19 5:29:16
New Washington 17 32 40N58 82w51 5:31:24
New Waterford 15 61 40N52 80w37 5:22:28
Newway 45 27 40N09 82w41 5:30:44
New Weston 19 34 40N20 84w39 5:38:36
New Winchester 17 33 40N48 82w58 5:31:52
Ney 20 34 41N23 84w32 5:38:08
Nicholsville 13 34 38N59 84w04 5:36:16
Nile 73 34 38N42 83w09 5:32:36
Niles 78 75 41N11 80w46 5:23:04
Nimishillen 76 67 40N51 81w16 5:25:04
Nimisila 77 67 40N56 81w38 5:26:32
Nipgen 71 36 39N14 83w15 5:33:00
Noble 18 67 41N36 81w31 5:26:04
Normandy Heights 9 34 39N22 84w33 5:38:12
Norris 55 34 39N58 84w20 5:37:20
North 34 23 40N23 81w06 5:24:24
Northampton 77 2 41N10 81w32 5:26:08
North Auburn 17 33 40N54 82w46 5:31:04
North Baltimore 87 33 41N11 83w41 5:34:44
North Bend 31 34 39N09 84w45 5:39:00
North Benton 50 67 40N59 81w01 5:24:04
North Bloomfield 78 67 41N28 80w52 5:23:28
North Brewster 76 67 40N43 81w36 5:26:24
North Bristol 78 67 41N23 80w52 5:23:28
Northbrook 31 34 39N15 84w35 5:38:20
North Canton 76 43 40N53 81w24 5:25:36
North Clippinger 31 34 39N11 84w22 5:37:28
North College Hill 31 88 39N13 84w33 5:38:12
North Condit 21 27 40N15 82w51 5:31:24
North Creek 69 34 41N09 84w13 5:36:52
North Dayton 57 91 39N47 84w10 5:36:40
North Eaton 47 42 41N18 82w06 5:28:24
North Fairfield 39 5 41N06 82w37 5:30:28
North Feesburg 8 34 38N55 83w59 5:35:56
Northfield 77 67 41N20 81w32 5:26:08
North Findlay 32 89 41N03 83w39 5:34:36
North Folk Village 71 34 39N21 83w00 5:32:00
North Georgetown 15 67 40N51 80w59 5:23:56
North Greenfield 46 33 40N25 83w33 5:34:12
North Hampton 12 34 39N59 83w56 5:35:44
North Hill 77 2 41N06 81w31 5:26:04
North Hills 37 34 39N32 82w24 5:29:36
North Hills Estates 31 88 39N12 84w32 5:38:08
North Houston 75 34 40N15 84w20 5:37:20
North Industry 76 43 40N45 81w24 5:25:36
North Jackson 50 67 41N06 80w52 5:23:28
North Kenova 44 37 38N26 82w33 5:30:12
North Kingsville 4 52 41N54 80w42 5:22:48
Northland 25 107 40N04 82w58 5:31:52
North Lawrence 76 67 40N51 81w38 5:26:32
North Lewisburg 11 34 40N13 83w33 5:34:12
North Liberty 42 5 40N39 82w30 5:30:00
North Lima 50 61 40N57 80w40 5:22:40
North Madison 43 67 41N48 81w04 5:24:16
North Monroeville 39 5 41N15 82w42 5:30:48
Northmoor 57 34 39N51 84w18 5:37:12
North Mount Vernon 42 5 40N24 82w29 5:29:56
North Olmsted 18 50 41N25 81w56 5:27:44
North Perry 43 67 41N47 81w09 5:24:36
North Randall 18 67 41N26 81w32 5:26:08
Northridge 12 39 39N55 83w48 5:35:12
Northridge 57 91 39N50 84w13 5:36:52
North Ridgeville 47 67 41N23 82w01 5:28:04
North Robinson 17 27 40N47 82w51 5:31:24
North Royalton 18 67 41N19 81w44 5:26:56
North Salem 30 5 40N09 81w34 5:26:16
North Side 50 84 41N07 80w39 5:22:36
North Star 19 34 40N20 84w34 5:38:16
North Summit Shopping Center 77 67 41N19 81w30 5:26:00
North Uniontown 36 34 39N12 83w37 5:34:28
Northup 27 27 38N47 82w17 5:29:08
Northville 11 34 40N04 83w42 5:34:48
Northwest 25 107 40N03 83w05 5:32:20
Northwest 86 34 41N40 84w45 5:39:00
Northwood 46 33 40N31 83w44 5:34:56
Northwood 87 31 41N37 83w30 5:34:00
North Woodbury 59 95 40N40 82w30 5:30:00
North Zanesville 60 104 39N58 82w01 5:28:04
Norton 21 27 40N27 83w05 5:32:20
Norton 77 67 41N02 81w39 5:26:36
Norwalk 39 44 41N15 82w37 5:30:28
Norwich 60 5 39N58 81w49 5:27:16
Norwood 31 88 39N10 84w27 5:37:48
Norwood 84 20 39N27 81w28 5:25:52
Nottingham 34 21 40N15 81w10 5:24:40
Nova 3 44 41N02 82w18 5:29:12
Novelty 28 67 41N28 81w23 5:25:32
Oakdale 5 27 39N30 82w06 5:28:24
Oakdale 57 91 39N41 84w09 5:36:36
Oakdale 76 54 40N48 81w31 5:26:04
Oakfield 64 27 39N46 82w06 5:28:24
Oakfield 78 67 41N28 80w52 5:23:28
Oak Grove 84 20 39N27 81w28 5:25:52
Oak Harbor 62 93 41N30 83w09 5:32:36
Oak Hill 40 34 38N54 82w35 5:30:20
Oakland 9 34 39N28 84w23 5:37:32
Oakland 14 34 39N27 83w50 5:35:20
Oakland 23 34 39N39 82w45 5:31:00
Oakland Park 25 107 40N03 82w58 5:31:52
Oakley 31 88 39N09 84w27 5:37:48
Oak Park 34 21 40N16 81w00 5:24:00
Oak Run 49 34 39N49 83w21 5:33:24
Oakshade 26 34 41N40 84w09 5:36:36
Oak Shade 26 34 41N33 84w08 5:36:32
Oakthorpe 23 27 39N54 82w27 5:29:48
Oakwood 57 91 39N43 84w11 5:36:44
Oakwood 63 34 41N06 84w23 5:37:32
Oberlin 47 46 41N18 82w13 5:28:52
Oberlin Beach 22 5 41N24 82w34 5:30:16
Obetz 25 107 39N53 82w57 5:31:48
Oceola 17 33 40N51 83w06 5:32:24
Oco 7 21 40N06 80w55 5:23:40
O'Connor Landing 46 33 40N31 83w44 5:34:56
Octa 24 34 39N37 83w36 5:34:24
Ogden 14 34 39N27 83w50 5:35:20
Ogontz 22 9 41N20 82w30 5:30:00
Ohio City 81 34 40N46 84w37 5:38:28
Ohio Furnace 73 34 38N31 82w39 5:30:36
Ohio Junction 7 15 40N06 80w44 5:22:56
Ohltown 50 67 41N06 80w45 5:23:00
Okeana 9 34 39N21 84w46 5:39:04
Okolona 35 34 41N21 84w13 5:36:52
Old Fort 74 32 41N14 83w09 5:32:36
Old Plymouth Heights 73 34 38N39 82w52 5:31:28
Old Straitsville 64 27 39N35 82w14 5:28:56
Oldtown 29 34 39N44 84w02 5:36:08
Old Washington 30 5 40N02 81w27 5:25:48
Old West End 48 31 41N40 83w33 5:34:12
Olena 39 5 41N09 82w33 5:30:12
Olive 61 5 39N45 81w31 5:26:04

OHIO

Olive Branch 13 34 39N05 84w14 5:36:56
Olive Green 21 27 40N15 82w51 5:31:24
Olivegreen 61 5 39N45 81w31 5:26:04
Oliver 1 34 38N54 83w30 5:34:00
Olivesburg 70 5 40N54 82w22 5:29:28
Olivett 7 21 39N59 81w11 5:24:44
Olmsted 18 50 41N23 81w55 5:27:40
Olmsted Falls 18 50 41N22 81w54 5:27:36
Olszeski 41 67 40N12 80w46 5:23:04
Omega 66 34 39N09 82w55 5:31:40
Oneida 9 34 39N29 84w24 5:37:36
Oneida 10 21 40N41 81w11 5:24:44
Ontario 70 95 40N46 82w36 5:30:24
Opperman 30 5 39N51 81w39 5:26:36
Oran 75 34 40N15 84w20 5:37:20
Orange 16 5 40N15 81w35 5:26:20
Orange 18 67 41N27 81w28 5:25:52
Orangeville 78 67 41N20 80w31 5:22:04
Orbiston 37 34 39N30 82w06 5:28:24
Orchard Island 46 34 40N29 83w56 5:35:44
Orchard Park Heights 70 95 40N42 82w32 5:30:08
Oregon 48 30 41N38 83w25 5:33:40
Oregonia 83 34 39N27 84w06 5:36:24
Oreville 37 27 39N35 82w14 5:28:56
Orient 65 34 39N48 83w09 5:32:36
Orland 82 27 39N23 82w24 5:29:36
Orrville 85 69 40N50 81w46 5:27:04
Orwell 4 60 41N32 80w52 5:23:28
Osgood 19 34 40N20 84w30 5:38:00
Osnaburg 76 67 40N47 81w16 5:25:04
Ostrander 21 33 40N16 83w13 5:32:52
Otsego 60 5 40N07 81w46 5:27:04
Ottawa 69 34 41N01 84w03 5:36:12
Ottawa Hills 48 31 41N40 83w38 5:34:32
Ottokee 26 34 41N33 84w08 5:36:32
Ottoville 69 34 40N58 84w16 5:37:04
Otway 73 34 38N52 83w11 5:32:44
Outville 45 27 40N00 82w40 5:30:40
Overlook 57 34 39N46 84w06 5:36:24
Overlook Hills 41 106 40N22 80w39 5:22:36
Overpeck 9 34 39N27 84w31 5:38:04
Overton 85 76 40N49 81w56 5:27:44
Owens Hill 60 5 39N55 82w01 5:28:04
Owensville 13 34 39N07 84w08 5:36:32
Oxford 9 34 39N31 84w45 5:39:00
Ozark 56 20 39N51 81w03 5:24:12
Padanaram 4 72 41N37 80w36 5:22:24
Padua 54 34 40N25 84w46 5:39:04
Page Manor 57 34 39N46 84w06 5:36:24
Pagetown 59 27 40N25 82w48 5:31:12
Painesville 43 46 41N43 81w15 5:25:00
Painesville on the Lake 43 46 41N44 81w14 5:24:56
Painters Creek 19 34 39N58 84w33 5:38:12
Paintersville 29 34 39N40 83w44 5:34:56
Palestine 19 34 40N03 84w45 5:39:00
Palmyra 42 27 40N29 82w32 5:30:08
Palmyra 67 67 41N06 81w03 5:24:12
Palos 5 27 39N30 82w06 5:28:24
Pancoastburg 24 34 39N34 83w31 5:34:04
Pandora 69 34 40N57 83w58 5:35:52
Pansy 14 34 39N18 83w59 5:35:56
Paradise 50 67 41N02 80w46 5:23:04
Paradise Hill 3 44 40N54 82w22 5:29:28
Paris 76 67 40N48 81w10 5:24:40
Parkdale 31 34 39N17 84w31 5:38:04
Parkertown 22 5 41N20 82w47 5:31:08
Park Layne 12 34 39N56 84w02 5:36:08
Parkman 28 67 41N22 81w04 5:24:16
Park Place 31 34 39N14 84w28 5:37:52
Park Ridge Acres 12 39 39N55 83w50 5:35:20
Parkview Heights 31 88 39N12 84w32 5:38:08
Parlett 41 21 40N16 81w00 5:24:00
Parma 18 26 41N23 81w43 5:26:52
Parma Heights 18 26 41N23 81w46 5:27:04
Parral 79 16 40N34 81w30 5:26:00
Parrott 24 34 39N34 83w31 5:34:04
Pasadena 57 91 39N41 84w09 5:36:36
Pasco 75 34 40N17 84w09 5:36:36
Pataskala 45 27 40N00 82w41 5:30:44
Patmos 50 67 40N55 80w51 5:23:24
Patriot 27 34 38N46 82w23 5:29:32
Patterson 33 33 40N47 83w32 5:34:08
Pattersonville 10 21 40N44 81w05 5:24:20
Pattin Addition 84 20 39N27 81w28 5:25:52
Pattonville 40 34 39N04 82w39 5:30:36
Paulding 63 34 41N08 84w35 5:38:20
Pavonia 70 95 40N45 82w31 5:30:04
Pawnee 52 73 41N01 82w01 5:28:04
Paxton 71 36 39N14 83w14 5:32:56
Payne 63 34 41N05 84w44 5:38:56
Pearlbrook 18 26 41N27 81w42 5:26:48
Pease 7 21 40N05 80w46 5:23:04
Pebble 66 34 39N08 83w08 5:32:32
Pedro 44 34 38N38 82w40 5:30:40
Peebles 1 34 38N57 83w24 5:33:36
Pee Pee 66 34 39N08 83w01 5:32:04
Pekin 10 21 40N44 81w05 5:24:20
Pekin 41 106 40N22 80w39 5:22:36
Pekin 83 34 39N26 84w12 5:36:48
Pemberton 75 34 40N18 84w02 5:36:08
Pemberville 87 32 41N25 83w28 5:33:52
Penfield 47 67 41N10 82w07 5:28:28
Peniel 27 34 38N46 82w23 5:29:32
Peninsula 77 67 41N14 81w33 5:26:12
Pennsville 58 5 39N35 81w51 5:27:24
Penn View 4 72 41N37 80w36 5:22:24
Peoli 79 16 40N15 81w35 5:26:20
Peoria 9 34 39N31 84w44 5:38:56

Peoria 80 33 40N19 83w27 5:33:48
Pepper Pike 18 67 41N29 81w29 5:25:56
Perintown 13 34 39N08 84w14 5:36:56
Perkins 22 5 41N24 82w42 5:30:48
Perry 43 46 41N47 81w08 5:24:32
Perry Addition 73 34 38N53 83w00 5:32:00
Perry Heights 76 54 40N48 81w31 5:26:04
Perrysburg 87 31 41N34 83w38 5:34:32
Perrysburg Heights 87 31 41N34 83w35 5:34:20
Perrysville 3 44 40N40 82w19 5:29:16
Perrysville 10 23 40N23 81w05 5:24:20
Perryton 45 5 40N06 82w08 5:28:32
Peru 39 5 41N15 82w42 5:30:48
Petersburg 10 21 40N34 81w05 5:24:20
Petersburg 40 34 39N04 82w39 5:30:36
Petersburg 50 67 40N55 80w32 5:22:08
Petrea 40 34 39N04 82w39 5:30:36
Petroleum 78 45 41N14 80w32 5:22:08
Pettisville 26 34 41N32 84w14 5:36:56
Pfeiffer Station 33 5 39N31 81w18 5:25:12
Phalanx 78 46 41N19 80w57 5:23:48
Pharisburg 80 33 40N15 83w22 5:33:28
Phillipsburg 57 34 39N54 84w24 5:37:36
Philo 60 5 39N49 81w55 5:27:40
Philothea 54 34 40N29 84w37 5:38:28
Phoneton 55 34 39N54 84w08 5:36:32
Pickaway 65 34 39N32 82w55 5:31:40
Pickerington 23 27 39N53 82w45 5:31:00
Pickrelltown 46 34 40N16 83w46 5:35:04
Piedmont 34 21 40N11 81w12 5:24:48
Pierce 13 34 39N02 84w16 5:37:04
Pierpont 4 72 41N45 80w34 5:22:16
Pigeon Run 76 54 40N48 81w31 5:26:04
Piketon 66 34 39N04 83w01 5:32:04
Pikeville 19 34 39N21 83w24 5:33:36
Pine Grove 44 34 38N38 82w40 5:30:40
Pinegrove 53 5 39N07 82w00 5:28:00
Pinehurst 84 20 39N27 81w28 5:25:52
Pine Valley 41 67 40N12 80w46 5:23:04
Piney Fork 41 67 40N15 80w50 5:23:20
Pinkerman 73 34 38N50 82w44 5:30:56
Pioneer 86 34 41N41 84w33 5:38:12
Piqua 55 34 40N09 84w15 5:37:00
Pisgah 9 34 39N19 84w22 5:37:28
Pitchin 12 39 39N55 83w48 5:35:12
Pitsburg 19 34 39N59 84w29 5:37:56
Pitt 88 32 40N46 83w15 5:33:00
Pittsburgh Junction 34 21 40N21 81w00 5:24:00
Pittsfield 47 67 41N14 82w13 5:28:52
Plain City 49 34 40N06 83w15 5:33:00
Plainfield 16 5 40N12 81w41 5:26:44
Plain View 56 20 39N47 81w09 5:24:36
Plainville 31 34 39N10 84w23 5:37:32
Plankton 17 33 40N57 83w11 5:32:44
Planktown 70 5 40N58 82w36 5:30:24
Plantation Acres 31 88 39N12 84w32 5:38:08
Plants 53 5 38N58 81w55 5:27:40
Plantsville 58 5 39N29 81w52 5:27:28
Plattsburg 12 34 39N50 83w38 5:34:32
Plattsville 75 34 40N17 84w09 5:36:36
Playhouse Square 18 26 41N30 81w41 5:26:44
Pleasant 25 34 39N52 83w11 5:32:44
Pleasant Bend 35 34 41N13 84w10 5:36:40
Pleasant City 30 5 39N54 81w32 5:26:08
Pleasant Corners 25 107 39N55 83w03 5:32:12
Pleasant Grove 60 5 39N55 82w01 5:28:04
Pleasant Hill 5 27 39N20 82w05 5:28:20
Pleasant Hill 41 106 40N22 80w39 5:22:36
Pleasant Hill 55 34 40N03 84w21 5:37:24
Pleasant Hills 31 34 39N14 84w32 5:38:08
Pleasant Home 85 62 40N57 82w05 5:28:20
Pleasant Plain 83 34 39N17 84w07 5:36:28
Pleasant Run 31 34 39N14 84w32 5:38:08
Pleasant Run Farms 31 34 39N17 84w31 5:38:04
Pleasant Valley 16 5 40N16 81w52 5:27:28
Pleasant Valley 18 26 41N24 81w43 5:26:52
Pleasant Valley 71 34 39N21 83w00 5:32:00
Pleasant View 24 34 39N39 83w32 5:34:08
Pleasant View 29 34 39N48 84w01 5:36:04
Pleasantville 23 27 39N49 82w32 5:30:08
Plumwood 49 34 39N53 83w27 5:33:48
Plymouth 70 27 41N00 82w40 5:30:40
Plymouth Center 4 46 41N52 80w49 5:23:16
Poast Town 9 34 39N30 84w23 5:37:32
Poetown 8 34 38N55 83w59 5:35:56
Point 25 107 39N56 83w03 5:32:12
Point Isabel 13 34 38N52 84w13 5:36:52
Point Place 48 31 41N42 83w30 5:34:00
Point Pleasant 13 34 38N54 84w14 5:36:56
Poland 50 84 41N01 80w37 5:22:28
Polk 3 44 40N57 82w13 5:28:52
Pomeroy 53 97 39N02 82w02 5:28:08
Pond Run 73 34 38N40 83w23 5:33:32
Poplargrove 66 34 38N57 83w24 5:33:36
Portage 87 33 41N20 83w39 5:34:36
Portage Lakes 77 2 41N00 81w32 5:26:08
Port Clinton 62 93 41N31 82w57 5:31:48
Porter 27 27 38N55 82w18 5:29:12
Porterfield 84 20 39N18 81w34 5:26:16
Portersville 64 27 39N36 82w05 5:28:20
Port Homer 41 67 40N28 80w36 5:22:24
Port Jefferson 75 34 40N20 84w06 5:36:24
Portland 53 5 39N06 81w46 5:27:04
Portsmouth 73 94 38N44 83w00 5:32:00
Port Union 9 34 39N20 84w28 5:37:52
Port Washington 79 16 40N20 81w31 5:26:04
Port William 14 34 39N33 83w47 5:35:08
Possum Woods 12 39 39N55 83w48 5:35:12
Post Town 9 34 39N30 84w23 5:37:32
Post Town 57 91 39N48 84w17 5:37:08
Potsdam 55 34 39N58 84w26 5:37:44
Pottersburg 80 33 40N15 83w22 5:33:28
Pottery Additon 41 106 40N22 80w39 5:22:36
Powell 21 32 40N10 83w05 5:32:20
Powellsville 73 34 38N39 82w52 5:31:28
Powers 26 34 41N41 84w20 5:37:20
Powhatan Point 7 21 39N52 80w49 5:23:16
Powhatton 11 34 40N04 83w42 5:34:48
Pratts Fork 5 27 39N13 82w09 5:28:36
Prattsville 82 27 39N15 82w29 5:29:56
Pravo 41 67 40N33 80w43 5:22:52
Prentiss 69 34 41N06 84w00 5:36:00
Preston Addition 73 34 38N53 83w00 5:32:00
Price Hill 31 88 39N07 84w35 5:38:20
Pricetown 36 34 39N12 83w37 5:34:28
Pricetown 78 67 41N06 81w00 5:24:00
Princeton 9 34 39N23 84w27 5:37:48
Proctor 67 67 41N10 81w16 5:25:04
Proctorville 44 37 38N26 82w23 5:29:32
Prospect 51 27 40N27 83w11 5:32:44
Providence 48 34 41N28 83w52 5:35:28
Provident 7 21 40N06 80w55 5:23:40
Provincial Point 31 34 39N07 84w21 5:37:24
Public Square 18 26 41N27 81w44 5:26:56
Pulaski 86 34 41N28 84w31 5:38:04
Pulaskiville 59 27 40N33 82w50 5:31:20
Pulse 36 34 39N02 83w56 5:35:44
Pultney 7 21 40N01 80w48 5:23:12
Puntenneyville 1 34 38N40 83w23 5:33:32
Puritas Park 18 26 41N26 81w48 5:27:12
Purity 45 5 40N11 82w25 5:29:40
Pusheta 6 34 40N31 84w10 5:36:40
Put-in-Bay 62 93 41N41 82w49 5:31:16
Putnam Place 84 20 39N27 81w28 5:25:52
Pymatuning Park 4 72 41N37 80w36 5:22:24
Pyrmont 57 34 39N49 84w25 5:37:40
Pyro 40 34 38N54 82w35 5:30:20
Quaker City 30 5 39N58 81w17 5:25:08
Quaker Hill 50 67 40N55 81w03 5:24:12
Qualey 84 20 39N21 81w47 5:27:08
Queen Acres 9 34 39N24 84w39 5:38:36
Quincy 46 34 40N18 83w58 5:35:52
Raccoon 27 34 38N55 82w24 5:29:36
Raccoon Island 27 27 38N46 82w11 5:28:44
Racine 53 5 38N58 81w55 5:27:40
Radcliff 82 27 39N08 82w23 5:29:32
Radio Heights 15 105 40N38 80w35 5:22:20
Radnor 21 33 40N23 83w09 5:32:36
Ragersville 79 16 40N30 81w37 5:26:28
Raiders Run 31 34 39N12 84w25 5:37:40
Rainsboro 36 34 39N13 83w25 5:33:40
Ramsey 41 67 40N12 80w46 5:23:04
Randolph 67 67 41N02 81w15 5:25:00
Range 49 34 39N45 83w25 5:33:40
Ransom 68 34 39N44 84w32 5:38:08
Rarden 73 34 38N55 83w15 5:33:00
Ratcliffburg 82 34 39N16 82w47 5:31:08
Rathbone 21 27 40N18 83w04 5:32:16
Rathbone 84 20 39N27 81w28 5:25:52
Rathbone Heights 84 20 39N27 81w28 5:25:52
Ravenna 67 46 41N09 81w15 5:25:00
Rawson 32 34 40N58 83w46 5:35:04
Ray 82 34 39N12 82w41 5:30:44
Rayland 41 67 40N11 80w41 5:22:44
Raymond 80 33 40N20 83w28 5:33:52
Rays Corners 4 72 41N44 80w47 5:23:08
Reading 15 67 40N51 80w59 5:23:56
Reading 31 34 39N14 84w28 5:37:52
Recker Heights 55 34 40N10 84w16 5:37:04
Recovery 54 34 40N26 84w46 5:39:04
Red Bank 31 34 39N10 84w23 5:37:32
Redbird 43 67 41N48 81w04 5:24:16
Red Coach Farm 57 91 39N41 84w09 5:36:36
Redfield 64 27 39N43 82w13 5:28:52
Red Fox 67 67 41N10 81w21 5:25:24
Redhaw 3 44 40N57 82w13 5:28:52
Red Lion 83 34 39N29 84w15 5:37:00
Redoak 8 34 38N45 83w50 5:35:20
Red River 19 34 40N08 84w26 5:37:44
Redtown 5 27 39N30 82w06 5:28:24
Reed 74 32 41N07 82w52 5:31:28
Reedsburg 85 76 40N49 81w56 5:27:44
Reedsmills 41 67 40N21 80w48 5:23:12
Reedsville 53 5 39N07 81w45 5:27:00
Reedtown 74 32 41N04 82w51 5:31:24
Reedurban 76 43 40N47 81w25 5:25:40
Reese Station 25 107 39N54 82w58 5:31:52
Reesville 14 34 39N29 83w41 5:34:44
Rehoboth 64 27 39N43 82w13 5:28:52
Reily 9 34 39N26 84w46 5:39:04
Reinersville 58 5 39N41 81w40 5:26:40
Reminderville 77 67 41N20 81w24 5:25:36
Remington 31 34 39N14 84w20 5:37:20
Remson Corners 52 73 41N08 81w52 5:27:28
Rendville 64 27 39N37 82w05 5:28:20

Reno 84 20 39N23 81w24 5:25:36
Reno Beach 48 30 41N40 83w16 5:33:04
Renrock 61 5 39N51 81w39 5:26:36
Rensselaer Park 31 88 39N12 84w29 5:37:56
Republic 74 32 41N08 83w01 5:32:04
Resaca 49 34 40N07 83w16 5:33:04
Revenge 23 27 39N43 82w36 5:30:24
Reynoldsburg 25 27 39N57 82w48 5:31:12
Reynolds Corners 48 31 41N39 83w41 5:34:44
Rhodesdale 41 67 40N11 80w41 5:22:44
Rialto 9 34 39N20 84w25 5:37:40
Rice 69 34 41N07 84w10 5:36:40
Rice 72 30 41N26 83w06 5:32:24
Riceland 85 62 40N51 81w46 5:27:04
Richfield 77 67 41N14 81w38 5:26:32
Richfield Center 48 34 41N42 83w51 5:35:24
Richfield Heights 77 67 41N14 81w38 5:26:32
Rich Hill 42 27 40N18 82w41 5:30:44
Rich Hill 60 5 39N52 81w47 5:27:08
Richland 46 33 40N31 83w44 5:34:56
Richmond 41 68 40N26 80w46 5:23:04
Richmond Center 4 72 41N37 80w36 5:22:24
Richmond Dale 71 34 39N12 82w49 5:31:16
Richmond Heights 18 67 41N34 81w30 5:26:00
Richville 76 43 40N47 81w25 5:25:40
Richwood 80 33 40N26 83w18 5:33:12
Rickenbacker Air Force Base 25 108 39N49 82w57 5:31:48
Ridgefield 39 5 41N15 82w41 5:30:44
Ridgeland 40 34 39N04 82w39 5:30:36
Ridgeton 17 33 40N48 82w58 5:31:52
Ridgeview 47 42 41N22 82w06 5:28:24
Ridgeville 35 34 41N27 84w17 5:37:08
Ridgeville 83 34 39N26 84w12 5:36:48
Ridgeville Corners 35 34 41N26 84w16 5:37:04
Ridgeway 33 33 40N31 83w35 5:34:20
Ridgewood 60 5 39N55 82w01 5:28:04
Ridgewood Heights 57 91 39N45 84w17 5:37:08
Rigrish 73 34 38N46 82w59 5:31:56
Rimer 69 34 40N55 84w04 5:36:16
Rinard Mills 56 20 39N35 81w09 5:24:36
Ringgold 58 5 39N39 81w52 5:27:28
Rio Grande 27 34 38N53 82w23 5:29:32
Ripley 8 34 38N45 83w51 5:35:24
Risingsun 87 32 41N17 83w26 5:33:44
Rittman 85 46 40N58 81w47 5:27:08
River Corners 52 73 41N06 82w07 5:28:28
Riverdale 66 34 39N05 83w01 5:32:04
River Edge 18 67 41N25 81w51 5:27:24
Riverlea 25 107 40N05 83w02 5:32:08
Riverside 57 91 39N47 84w07 5:36:28
Riverside Park 79 16 40N24 81w21 5:25:24
River Styx 52 73 41N08 81w52 5:27:28
Riverview 7 21 40N01 80w45 5:23:00
Riverview 84 20 39N27 81w28 5:25:52
Rix Mills 60 5 39N59 81w46 5:27:04
Roachester 83 34 39N22 84w08 5:36:32
Roads 40 34 39N05 82w33 5:30:12
Roanoke 79 16 40N24 81w21 5:25:24
Roberts 60 5 39N47 82w04 5:28:16
Robertsville 76 67 40N46 81w11 5:24:44
Robins 30 5 39N58 81w32 5:26:08
Robtown 65 34 39N43 82w58 5:31:52
Robyville 34 21 40N13 80w52 5:23:28
Rochester 47 67 41N08 82w18 5:29:12
Rochester Place 87 31 41N38 83w29 5:33:56
Rockbridge 37 34 39N35 82w32 5:30:08
Rock Camp 15 67 40N47 80w46 5:23:04
Rock Camp 44 34 38N32 82w33 5:30:12
Rock Creek 4 72 41N40 80w52 5:23:28
Rockdale 9 34 39N22 84w33 5:38:12
Rockford 54 34 40N41 84w39 5:38:36
Rockhill 7 21 40N10 81w05 5:24:20
Rockland 84 20 39N18 81w34 5:26:16
Rock Mills 24 34 39N34 83w31 5:34:04
Rockport 2 34 40N55 84w04 5:36:16
Rockville 1 34 38N40 83w23 5:33:32
Rock Way 12 39 39N56 83w49 5:35:16
Rockwood 44 37 38N27 82w28 5:29:52
Rockyhill 40 34 39N04 82w39 5:30:36
Rocky Ridge 62 93 41N32 83w12 5:32:48
Rocky River 18 26 41N28 81w51 5:27:24
Rodney 27 27 38N51 82w18 5:29:12
Rogers 15 67 40N48 80w37 5:22:28
Rokeby Lock 58 5 39N39 81w51 5:27:24
Rolandus 53 5 38N58 81w55 5:27:40
Rollersville 72 32 41N23 83w20 5:33:20
Rolling Mill Park 9 34 39N30 84w23 5:37:32
Rome 4 72 41N36 80w52 5:23:28
Rome 44 37 38N28 82w25 5:29:40
Rome 70 5 40N58 82w36 5:30:24
Rome Station 4 72 41N36 80w52 5:23:28
Romohr Acres 13 34 39N07 84w21 5:37:24
Roosevelt 57 91 39N45 84w15 5:37:00
Rootstown 67 67 41N06 81w14 5:24:56
Roscoe 16 5 40N16 81w52 5:27:28
Rose 10 21 40N36 81w16 5:25:04
Rosedale 49 34 40N07 83w29 5:33:56
Rose Farm 58 5 39N46 82w06 5:28:24
Rose Hill 19 34 40N20 84w39 5:38:36
Roseland 70 95 40N46 82w34 5:30:16
Roselawn 31 88 39N11 84w27 5:37:48
Roselms 63 34 41N01 84w29 5:37:56
Rosemont 50 67 41N06 80w52 5:23:28
Rosemount 73 34 38N48 82w58 5:31:52
Roseville 60 5 39N49 82w05 5:28:20

Rosewood 11	34	40N13	83w58	5:35:52
Roslyn 57	91	39N41	84w09	5:36:36
Ross 9	34	39N19	84w39	5:38:36
Rossburg 19	34	40N17	84w38	5:38:32
Rossford 87	31	41N36	83w34	5:34:16
Rossmoyne 31	34	39N12	84w25	5:37:40
Rossville 9	34	39N25	84w35	5:38:20
Roswell 79	16	40N29	81w21	5:25:24
Round Bottom 56	20	39N46	80w52	5:23:28
Roundhead 33	33	40N34	83w50	5:35:20
Rousculp 2	90	40N42	84w08	5:36:32
Rowsburg 3	44	40N52	82w09	5:28:36
Roxabell 71	34	39N24	83w10	5:32:40
Roxanna 29	34	39N32	84w05	5:36:20
Roxbury 58	5	39N33	81w48	5:27:12
Royalton 23	27	39N44	82w46	5:31:04
Royersville 44	34	38N31	82w39	5:30:36
Rubyville 73	34	38N46	82w59	5:31:56
Rudolph 87	33	41N18	83w40	5:34:40
Ruggles 3	44	41N02	82w25	5:29:40
Ruggles Beach 22	5	41N24	82w34	5:30:16
Rumley 34	11	40N23	81w01	5:24:04
Rumley 75	34	40N23	84w10	5:36:40
Runnymede 9	34	39N30	84w23	5:37:32
Rural 13	34	38N51	84w05	5:36:20
Ruraldale 60	5	39N53	81w49	5:27:16
Rushmore 69	34	40N54	84w17	5:37:08
Rush Run 41	67	40N11	80w41	5:22:44
Rushsylvania 46	33	40N28	83w41	5:34:44
Rushtown 73	34	38N50	83w04	5:32:16
Rushville 23	27	39N46	82w26	5:29:44
Russell 28	67	41N28	81w21	5:25:24
Russell 36	34	39N12	83w37	5:34:28
Russell Heights 15	105	40N35	80w39	5:22:36
Russells 60	5	39N55	82w01	5:28:04
Russells Point 46	34	40N28	83w54	5:35:36
Russellville 8	34	38N52	83w47	5:35:08
Russia 75	34	40N14	84w24	5:37:36
Rutland 53	27	39N03	82w08	5:28:32
Rye Beach 22	5	41N24	82w34	5:30:16
Sabina 14	34	39N29	83w38	5:34:32
Sagamore Hills 77	67	41N19	81w34	5:26:16
Sahara Sands 76	54	40N48	81w31	5:26:04
Saint Albans 45	27	40N05	82w36	5:30:24
Saint Bernard 31	88	39N10	84w30	5:38:00
Saint Clairsville 7	22	40N05	80w54	5:23:36
Saint Henry 54	34	40N25	84w38	5:38:32
Saint Joe 7	21	40N01	80w45	5:23:00
Saint Johns 6	34	40N33	84w05	5:36:20
Saint Joseph 54	34	40N25	84w46	5:39:04
Saint Joseph 67	67	41N01	81w10	5:24:40
Saint Joseph 86	34	41N28	84w45	5:39:00
Saint Louisville 45	5	40N10	82w25	5:29:40
Saint Martin 8	34	39N13	83w55	5:35:40
Saint Marys 6	34	40N33	84w24	5:37:36
Saint Paris 11	34	40N08	83w58	5:35:52
Saint Pauls 65	34	39N43	82w58	5:31:52
Saint Peters 54	34	40N25	84w46	5:39:04
Saint Rosa 54	34	41N00	84w35	5:38:20
Saint Sebastian 54	34	40N26	84w29	5:37:56
Saint Stephens 74	32	41N04	82w51	5:31:24
Saint Wendelin 54	34	40N28	84w34	5:38:16
Salem 15	77	40N54	80w52	5:23:28
Salem Center 53	27	39N03	82w11	5:28:44
Salem Heights 15	77	40N55	80w51	5:23:24
Salesville 30	5	39N58	81w17	5:25:08
Saline 41	67	40N32	80w42	5:22:48
Salineville 15	67	40N37	80w50	5:23:20
Salisbury 53	27	39N03	82w03	5:28:12
Saltair 13	34	38N59	84w04	5:36:16
Saltillo 64	27	39N43	82w13	5:28:52
Salt Lick 64	27	39N37	82w12	5:28:48
Salt Rock 51	33	40N40	83w15	5:33:00
Salt Run 41	67	40N11	80w41	5:22:44
Samantha 36	34	39N20	83w34	5:34:16
Sand Beach 62	93	41N31	83w08	5:32:32
Sand Hill 22	5	41N27	82w44	5:30:56
Sand Hill 73	34	38N45	82w51	5:31:24
Sand Hill 84	20	39N23	81w24	5:25:36
Sand Ridge 5	27	39N26	82w06	5:28:24
Sandrun 37	27	39N26	82w14	5:28:56
Sandusky 22	40	41N27	82w42	5:30:48
Sandy Springs 1	34	38N40	83w23	5:33:32
Sandyville 79	16	40N38	81w23	5:25:32
San Margherita 25	107	39N57	83w05	5:32:20
Santa Fe 6	34	40N34	84w11	5:36:44
Santoy 64	27	39N36	82w05	5:28:20
Sarahsville 61	5	39N49	81w28	5:25:52
Sardinia 8	34	39N00	83w49	5:35:16
Sardis 56	20	39N37	80w55	5:23:40
Savannah 3	44	40N58	82w22	5:29:28
Saville Estates 57	34	39N46	84w06	5:36:24
Savona 19	34	40N06	84w38	5:38:32
Sawyerwood 77	2	41N08	81w34	5:26:16
Saybrook 4	46	41N50	80w53	5:23:32
Sayler Park 31	88	39N08	84w38	5:38:32
Sayre 64	27	39N46	82w06	5:28:24
Schauers Acres 12	34	39N53	84w02	5:36:08
Schley 84	20	39N23	81w14	5:24:56
Schoenbrunn 79	16	40N29	81w23	5:25:32
Schooleys 71	34	39N21	83w00	5:32:00
Schrader 71	34	39N21	83w00	5:32:00
Schumm 81	34	40N45	84w47	5:39:08
Scio 34	23	40N24	81w05	5:24:20
Sciotodale 73	34	38N46	82w59	5:31:56
Scioto Furnace 73	34	38N48	82w46	5:31:04
Sciotoville 73	34	38N46	82w59	5:31:56
Scipio 9	34	39N21	84w46	5:39:04
Scotch Ridge 87	33	41N25	83w28	5:33:52
Scott 81	34	40N59	84w35	5:38:20
Scottown 44	34	38N33	82w23	5:29:32
Scotts Crossing 2	34	40N51	84w20	5:37:20
Scroggsfield 10	21	40N34	81w05	5:24:20
Scrub Ridge 1	34	38N47	83w20	5:33:20
Seal 66	34	39N05	82w58	5:31:52
Seal 88	32	40N49	83w09	5:32:36
Seaman 1	34	38N57	83w34	5:34:16
Sebring 50	59	40N55	81w03	5:24:12
Secedar Corners 78	84	41N10	80w36	5:22:24
Sedalia 49	34	39N45	83w29	5:33:56
Seilcrest Acres 83	34	39N14	84w20	5:37:20
Sellers Point 23	27	39N54	82w33	5:30:12
Selma 12	34	39N47	83w43	5:34:52
Senecaville 30	5	39N56	81w27	5:25:48
Senior 83	34	39N22	84w08	5:36:32
Sentinel 4	72	41N41	80w40	5:22:40
Seven Hills 18	26	41N23	81w41	5:26:44
Seven Hills 31	34	39N14	84w32	5:38:08
Seven Mile 9	34	39N29	84w33	5:38:12
Seventeen 79	16	40N21	81w26	5:25:44
Seville 52	60	41N01	81w52	5:27:28
Seward 26	34	41N42	84w04	5:36:16
Sewellsville 7	21	39N59	81w11	5:24:44
Shade 5	27	39N13	82w02	5:28:08
Shadeville 25	108	39N49	82w58	5:31:52
Shady Glen 41	67	40N28	80w36	5:22:24
Shady Glen 71	34	39N21	83w00	5:32:00
Shady Grove 29	34	39N48	84w01	5:36:04
Shadyside 7	21	39N59	80w45	5:23:00
Shadyside 15	105	40N38	80w35	5:22:20
Shaker Crossing 57	91	39N41	84w09	5:36:36
Shaker Heights 18	73	41N29	81w32	5:26:08
Shalersville 67	67	41N15	81w16	5:25:04
Shandon 9	34	39N20	84w43	5:38:52
Shanesville 79	16	40N30	81w37	5:26:28
Shannon 60	5	40N07	82w02	5:28:08
Sharon 61	5	39N44	81w34	5:26:16
Sharon Center 52	53	41N06	81w44	5:26:56
Sharon Hills 25	107	40N05	83w01	5:32:04
Sharon Park 2	90	40N44	84w09	5:36:36
Sharon Park 9	34	39N24	84w33	5:38:12
Sharonville 31	34	39N16	84w25	5:37:40
Sharon West 78	45	41N14	80w31	5:22:04
Sharpsburg 5	5	39N26	81w55	5:27:40
Shartz Road 83	34	39N35	84w18	5:37:12
Shauck 59	27	40N37	82w40	5:30:40
Shawnee 64	27	39N36	82w13	5:28:52
Shawnee Hills 21	108	40N10	83w08	5:32:32
Shawnee Meadows 2	90	40N42	84w08	5:36:32
Shawtown 32	34	41N07	83w46	5:35:04
Shawville 47	42	41N22	82w06	5:28:24
Shay 84	20	39N33	81w04	5:24:16
Sheffield 47	67	41N28	82w05	5:28:20
Sheffield Lake 47	67	41N29	82w06	5:28:24
Shelby 70	85	40N53	82w40	5:30:40
Shelby Junction 70	85	40N54	82w37	5:30:28
Shell Beach 23	27	39N54	82w27	5:29:48
Shenandoah 70	5	41N02	82w32	5:30:08
Shepard 25	107	40N00	82w56	5:31:44
Sheridan 44	37	38N26	82w33	5:30:12
Sherman 39	5	41N10	82w48	5:31:12
Sherman 70	95	40N46	82w34	5:30:16
Sherman 77	67	41N01	81w38	5:26:32
Sherritts 44	34	38N42	82w28	5:29:52
Sherrodsville 10	21	40N32	81w14	5:24:56
Sherwood 20	34	41N17	84w33	5:38:12
Shiloh 8	34	38N59	84w04	5:36:16
Shiloh 57	91	39N49	84w15	5:37:00
Shiloh 70	5	40N58	82w36	5:30:24
Shinrock 22	9	41N21	82w32	5:30:08
Shore 18	67	41N37	81w31	5:26:04
Short Creek 34	21	40N11	80w55	5:23:40
Short Hills 57	91	39N41	84w09	5:36:36
Shreve 85	79	40N41	82w01	5:28:04
Sidney 75	34	40N17	84w09	5:36:36
Signal 15	67	40N47	80w46	5:23:04
Silica 48	34	41N41	83w45	5:35:00
Silo 67	67	41N17	81w14	5:24:56
Silver Creek 29	34	39N39	83w44	5:34:56
Silver Creek 52	53	41N01	81w44	5:26:56
Silver Lake 77	2	41N09	81w28	5:25:52
Silverton 31	34	39N12	84w24	5:37:36
Simons 4	72	41N32	80w32	5:22:08
Singing Hills 57	91	39N40	84w15	5:37:00
Sinking Spring 36	34	39N04	83w23	5:33:32
Sixteen Mile Stand 31	34	39N14	84w20	5:37:20
Skyline Acres 31	34	39N14	84w32	5:38:08
Slabtown 2	90	40N45	84w06	5:36:24
Slickaway 8	34	38N41	83w46	5:35:04
Sligo 14	34	39N27	83w50	5:35:20
Slocums 73	34	38N46	82w59	5:31:56
Smith Corners 50	67	41N06	80w45	5:23:00
Smithfield 41	67	40N15	80w48	5:23:12
Smithville 85	62	40N53	81w55	5:27:40
Smithville 88	32	40N46	83w21	5:33:24
Smyrna 34	21	40N12	81w09	5:24:36
Snodes 50	67	40N55	81w01	5:24:04
Snyderville 12	39	39N55	83w48	5:35:12
Soaptown 78	67	41N08	80w46	5:23:04
Socialville 83	34	39N19	84w20	5:37:20
Solon 18	46	41N23	81w27	5:25:48
Somerdale 79	16	40N34	81w22	5:25:28
Somerford 49	34	39N58	83w30	5:34:00
Somers 68	34	39N37	84w39	5:38:36
Somerset 64	27	39N48	82w18	5:29:12
Somerton 7	21	39N54	81w08	5:24:32
Somerville 9	34	39N34	84w38	5:38:32
Sonora 60	5	39N59	81w54	5:27:36
South Amherst 47	67	41N21	82w15	5:29:00
South Arlington 77	2	41N03	81w30	5:26:00
South Bloomfield 65	34	39N43	82w59	5:31:56
South Bloomingville 37	34	39N25	82w36	5:30:24
Southbrook 57	91	39N41	84w09	5:36:36
South Charleston 12	34	39N50	83w38	5:34:32
South Clippinger 31	34	39N11	84w22	5:37:28
South Condit 21	27	40N15	82w51	5:31:24
Southdale 57	91	39N41	84w09	5:36:36
South Enon Estates 12	34	39N52	83w56	5:35:44
Southern Hills 57	91	39N41	84w09	5:36:36
Southern Knoll 9	34	39N31	84w44	5:38:56
South Euclid 18	70	41N31	81w32	5:26:08
South Excello 9	34	39N29	84w25	5:37:40
South Highlands 9	34	39N30	84w23	5:37:32
South Hill Park 48	34	41N36	83w42	5:34:48
Southington 78	67	41N18	80w57	5:23:48
South Kingman 14	34	39N27	83w50	5:35:20
Southland 18	26	41N24	81w46	5:27:04
Southland Shopping Center 51	27	40N35	83w07	5:32:28
South Lebanon 83	34	39N22	84w13	5:36:52
South Logan 37	33	39N32	82w24	5:29:36
South Lorain 47	50	41N26	82w09	5:28:36
South Madison 43	67	41N48	81w04	5:24:16
South Milford 13	34	39N10	84w18	5:37:12
South Mount Vernon 42	29	40N23	82w30	5:30:00
South Newbury 28	67	41N28	81w09	5:24:36
South Olive 61	5	39N45	81w31	5:26:04
South Park 18	26	41N22	81w40	5:26:40
South Park 88	32	40N46	83w21	5:33:24
South Perry 37	34	39N30	82w40	5:30:40
South Plymouth 24	34	39N34	83w31	5:34:04
South Point 44	37	38N25	82w35	5:30:20
South Russell 28	67	41N26	81w19	5:25:16
South Salem 71	34	39N20	83w18	5:33:12
South Shore Park 48	31	41N38	83w29	5:33:56
South Side 50	84	41N04	80w40	5:22:40
South Side 79	16	40N29	81w23	5:25:32
South Solon 49	34	39N44	83w37	5:34:28
South Vernon 42	5	40N24	82w29	5:29:56
South Vienna 12	34	39N55	83w37	5:34:28
South Webster 73	34	38N49	82w44	5:30:56
Southwest 70	95	40N44	82w31	5:30:04
South West Hubbard 78	84	41N10	80w36	5:22:24
South Woodbury 59	27	40N25	82w48	5:31:12
Southworth 2	34	40N51	84w20	5:37:20
South Zanesville 60	104	39N54	82w02	5:28:08
Spargursville 71	34	39N14	83w10	5:32:40
Sparta 59	27	40N24	82w42	5:30:48
Speaker's Addition 41	106	40N22	80w39	5:22:36
Speidel 7	21	40N01	81w04	5:24:16
Spencer 52	73	41N06	82w08	5:28:32
Spencer 60	21	40N04	81w54	5:27:36
Spencerville 2	34	40N43	84w21	5:37:24
Sprigg 1	34	38N42	83w38	5:34:32
Springboro 83	34	39N33	84w14	5:36:56
Springbrook 22	5	41N23	82w56	5:31:44
Springcreek 55	34	40N10	84w11	5:36:44
Springdale 31	34	39N17	84w29	5:37:56
Springfield 12	39	39N55	83w49	5:35:16
Spring Hills 11	34	40N16	83w46	5:35:04
Spring Meadows 31	34	39N14	84w32	5:38:08
Spring Mill 70	95	40N45	82w31	5:30:04
Spring Mountain 16	5	40N20	82w03	5:28:12
Springside 73	34	38N45	82w51	5:31:24
Springvale 13	34	39N13	84w11	5:36:44
Spring Valley 29	34	39N37	83w59	5:35:56
Spring Valley 47	42	41N22	82w06	5:28:24
Spring Valley 48	34	41N36	83w42	5:34:48
Springville 74	32	40N57	83w23	5:33:32
Springville 85	79	40N41	82w02	5:28:08
Springwood 9	34	39N31	84w44	5:38:56
Stafford 56	20	39N43	81w17	5:25:08
Standardsburg 39	5	41N15	82w42	5:30:48
Standley 20	34	41N15	84w08	5:36:32
Stanleyville 84	20	39N31	81w25	5:25:40
Stanwood 76	54	40N46	81w30	5:26:00
Starr 37	27	39N26	82w22	5:29:28
Staunton 24	34	39N34	83w31	5:34:04
Staunton 55	34	40N03	84w10	5:36:40
Steam Corners 59	95	40N42	82w32	5:30:08
Steinersville 7	21	39N52	80w49	5:23:16
Stella 82	27	39N19	82w28	5:29:52
Stelvideo 19	34	40N06	84w38	5:38:32
Sterling 85	58	40N58	81w51	5:27:24
Sterling Heights 83	34	39N35	84w18	5:37:12
Steuben 39	5	41N15	82w42	5:30:48
Steubenville 41	106	40N22	80w37	5:22:28
Stewart 5	5	39N18	81w54	5:27:36

Stewartsville 7 21 40N01 80w51 5:23:24
Stillwater 79 16 40N19 81w19 5:25:16
Stillwater Junction 57 91 39N45 84w17 5:37:08
Stillwell 38 5 40N30 82w00 5:28:00
Stiversville 53 5 39N06 81w46 5:27:04
Stockdale 66 34 38N57 82w51 5:31:24
Stockport 58 5 39N33 81w48 5:27:12
Stockton 9 34 39N22 84w33 5:38:12
Stock Yards 31 88 39N09 84w33 5:38:12
Stone 60 5 39N53 81w49 5:27:16
Stone Creek 79 16 40N24 81w33 5:26:12
Stonelick 13 34 39N08 84w09 5:36:36
Stony Prairie 72 32 41N22 83w09 5:32:36
Stony Ridge 87 32 41N31 83w30 5:34:00
Stonyrill 83 34 39N30 84w23 5:37:32
Stoudertown 23 27 39N51 82w37 5:30:28
Stout 1 34 38N40 83w23 5:33:32
Stoutsville 23 34 39N36 82w50 5:31:20
Stovertown 60 5 39N55 82w01 5:28:04
Stow 77 67 41N10 81w26 5:25:44
Strasburg 79 24 40N36 81w32 5:26:08
Stratford 21 27 40N18 83w04 5:32:16
Stratton 41 67 40N31 80w38 5:22:32
Streetsboro 67 67 41N15 81w21 5:25:24
Stringtown 5 27 39N20 82w05 5:28:20
Stringtown 8 34 38N45 83w50 5:35:20
Stringtown 13 34 38N51 84w05 5:36:20
Stringtown 65 34 39N29 82w55 5:31:40
Strongsville 18 67 41N19 81w50 5:27:20
Stroup Corners 78 67 41N23 80w59 5:23:56
Struthers 50 84 41N04 80w39 5:22:36
Stryker 86 34 41N30 84w25 5:37:40
Stuart Manor 41 106 40N22 80w39 5:22:36
Suffield 67 67 41N02 81w22 5:25:28
Sugar Bush Knolls 67 67 41N12 81w21 5:25:24
Sugarcreek 79 16 40N30 81w37 5:26:28
Sugar Grove 23 27 39N38 82w33 5:30:12
Sugar Grove 41 67 40N28 80w36 5:22:24
Sugar Grove 73 34 38N46 82w59 5:31:56
Sugar Grove Hill 12 39 39N55 83w50 5:35:20
Sugar Ridge 87 33 41N23 83w39 5:34:36
Sugar Tree Ridge 36 34 39N04 83w40 5:34:40
Sugar Valley 68 34 39N45 84w38 5:38:32
Sullivan 3 44 41N02 82w14 5:28:56
Sulphurgrove 57 34 39N50 84w08 5:36:32
Sulphur Lick 71 34 39N21 83w00 5:32:00
Sulphur Springs 17 27 40N52 82w53 5:31:32
Summerfield 61 5 39N48 81w20 5:25:20
Summerford 49 34 39N53 83w27 5:33:48
Summerside 13 34 39N07 84w21 5:37:24
Summerside Estates 13 34 39N07 84w21 5:37:24
Summersville 80 33 40N26 83w18 5:33:12
Summit 56 20 39N46 81w13 5:24:52
Summit 71 34 39N21 83w00 5:32:00
Summit 78 84 41N10 80w42 5:22:48
Summit Station 45 27 40N00 82w45 5:31:00
Summitville 15 67 40N41 80w53 5:23:32
Sumner 53 5 39N05 81w55 5:27:40
Sunbury 21 27 40N15 82w51 5:31:24
Sunbury 57 34 39N37 84w22 5:37:28
Sundale 60 5 39N58 81w49 5:27:16
Sunfish 66 34 39N02 83w12 5:32:48
Sunny Acres 41 106 40N22 80w39 5:22:36
Sunnyland 12 39 39N55 83w48 5:35:12
Sunny Meade 30 5 40N01 81w35 5:26:20
Sunsbury 56 20 39N50 81w02 5:24:08
Sunset Heights 7 21 40N05 80w45 5:23:00
Sunset Point 43 67 41N44 81w14 5:24:56
Sunshine 1 34 38N40 83w23 5:33:32
Sunshine Park 41 106 40N22 80w39 5:22:36
Sun Valley 25 107 39N56 82w53 5:31:32
Superior 86 34 41N34 84w38 5:38:32
Surfside 43 67 41N38 81w25 5:25:40
Surrey Hill 78 45 41N13 80w47 5:23:08
Sutton 53 5 39N01 81w55 5:27:40
Swan 82 34 39N21 82w28 5:29:52
Swan Creek 26 34 41N32 83w56 5:35:44
Swanders 75 34 39N55 83w37 5:34:28
Swanktown 57 34 39N49 84w25 5:37:40
Swanton 26 34 41N35 83w54 5:35:36
Swickards Additions 41 106 40N22 80w39 5:22:36
Switzerland 56 20 39N49 80w54 5:23:36
Sybene 44 37 38N26 82w33 5:30:12
Sycamore 31 34 39N15 84w22 5:37:28
Sycamore 88 32 40N57 83w10 5:32:40
Sycamore Valley 56 20 39N40 81w15 5:25:00
Sychar Road 42 5 40N24 82w29 5:29:56
Sylvania 48 34 41N43 83w42 5:34:48
Symmes Corner 9 34 39N22 84w33 5:38:12
Syracuse 53 5 39N00 82w00 5:28:00
Taborville 28 67 41N26 81w22 5:25:28
Tacoma 7 21 39N59 81w11 5:24:44
Taft 31 34 39N12 84w25 5:37:40
Tallmadge 77 2 41N06 81w27 5:25:48
Tama 54 34 40N34 84w33 5:38:12
Tarlton 65 34 39N33 82w47 5:31:08
Tate 13 34 38N58 84w05 5:36:20
Tatmans 64 27 39N36 82w05 5:28:20
Tawawa 75 34 40N17 84w09 5:36:36
Taylor 80 33 40N21 83w23 5:33:32
Taylor Creek 33 33 40N33 83w41 5:34:44
Taylor Farm Acres 76 54 40N50 81w32 5:26:08
Taylorsburg 57 34 39N51 84w21 5:37:24
Taylors Creek 31 34 39N13 84w41 5:38:44
Taylor Station 25 107 39N58 82w52 5:31:28
Taylorsville 36 34 39N12 83w37 5:34:28
Taylortown 41 67 40N28 80w36 5:22:24
Taylortown 70 5 40N54 82w37 5:30:28
Tedrow 26 34 41N33 84w08 5:36:32
Teegarden 15 67 40N47 80w46 5:23:04
Temperanceville 7 21 39N59 81w11 5:24:44
Terminal Junction 7 15 40N06 80w44 5:22:56
Terrace Park 31 34 39N10 84w18 5:37:12
Terre Haute 11 34 40N04 83w42 5:34:48
Terry Acres 29 34 39N48 84w01 5:36:04
Texas 17 32 40N57 83w06 5:32:24
Texas 35 34 41N27 84w00 5:36:00
Thackery 11 34 40N04 83w42 5:34:48
Thatcher 65 34 39N37 82w57 5:31:48
The Avenue 78 45 41N14 80w32 5:22:08
The Bend 20 34 41N17 84w20 5:37:20
Thelma City 50 67 40N55 81w06 5:24:24
The Plains 5 27 39N22 82w08 5:28:32
The Village Of Indian Hill 31 34 39N11 84w22 5:37:28
Thivener 27 27 38N46 82w11 5:28:44
Thompson 28 67 41N41 81w03 5:24:12
Thompson Place 15 105 40N38 80w35 5:22:20
Thorn 64 27 39N54 82w26 5:29:44
Thornville 64 27 39N54 82w25 5:29:40
Thorny Acres 83 34 39N30 84w23 5:37:32
Thrifton 71 34 39N21 83w24 5:33:36
Thurman 27 27 38N55 82w27 5:29:48
Thurston 23 27 39N50 82w33 5:30:12
Tiffin 74 1 41N07 83w11 5:32:44
Tiltonsville 41 67 40N10 80w42 5:22:48
Timberlake 43 67 41N40 81w27 5:25:48
Tinny 72 32 41N20 83w18 5:33:12
Tipp City 55 34 39N58 84w11 5:36:44
Tippecanoe 34 21 40N16 81w17 5:25:08
Tipton 63 34 41N02 84w35 5:38:20
Tiro 17 32 40N54 82w46 5:31:04
Tiverton 16 5 40N25 82w10 5:28:40
Toboso 45 5 40N03 82w13 5:28:52
Tod 17 32 40N51 83w06 5:32:24
Todds 58 5 39N33 81w48 5:27:12
Toledo 48 31 41N39 83w33 5:34:12
Tomlison Addition 73 34 38N53 83w00 5:32:00
Tontogany 87 34 41N25 83w45 5:35:00
Torch 5 5 39N14 81w45 5:27:00
Toronto 41 80 40N28 80w36 5:22:24
Town and Country Estates 57 91 39N41 84w09 5:36:36
Townwood 69 34 41N06 84w00 5:36:00
Tradersville 49 34 39N53 83w27 5:33:48
Trail 38 5 40N35 81w37 5:26:28
Trail Run 56 20 39N33 81w04 5:24:16
Tranquility 1 34 38N56 83w34 5:34:16
Trebeins 29 34 39N44 84w02 5:36:08
Tremont City 12 34 40N01 83w50 5:35:20
Trenton 9 34 39N29 84w28 5:37:52
Triadelphia 58 5 39N39 81w52 5:27:28
Trimble 5 34 39N30 82w10 5:28:40
Trinway 60 5 40N09 82w01 5:28:04
Tri-Village 25 107 40N00 83w03 5:32:12
Trotwood 57 34 39N48 84w18 5:37:12
Trowbridge 62 93 41N33 83w16 5:33:04
Troy 55 34 40N02 84w12 5:36:48
Truetown 5 27 39N26 82w06 5:28:24
Trumbull 4 72 41N40 80w57 5:23:48
Truro 25 27 39N57 82w49 5:31:16
Tucson 71 34 39N21 83w00 5:32:00
Tunnel 84 20 39N27 81w28 5:25:52
Tunnel Hill 16 5 40N20 82w03 5:28:12
Tuppers Plains 53 5 39N10 81w51 5:27:24
Turpin Hills 31 34 39N07 84w21 5:37:24
Tuscarawas 79 16 40N24 81w24 5:25:36
Twenty Mile Stand 83 34 39N14 84w20 5:37:20
Twightwee 31 34 39N14 84w20 5:37:20
Twin Lakes 2 90 40N43 84w06 5:36:24
Twin Lakes 67 67 41N10 81w21 5:25:24
Twinsburg 77 67 41N19 81w27 5:25:48
Twinsburg Heights 77 67 41N20 81w27 5:25:48
Twin Valley 73 34 38N46 82w59 5:31:56
Tymochtee 88 32 40N57 83w15 5:33:00
Tyndall 16 5 40N16 81w52 5:27:28
Tyrrell 78 67 41N16 80w34 5:22:16
Uhrichsville 79 19 40N24 81w21 5:25:24
Union 57 34 39N51 84w18 5:37:12
Union City 19 34 40N12 84w48 5:39:12
Union Furnace 37 27 39N28 82w22 5:29:28
Union Landing Siding 44 34 38N31 82w39 5:30:36
Union Plains 8 34 39N02 83w56 5:35:44
Unionport 41 67 40N21 80w51 5:23:24
Uniontown 7 21 40N06 80w55 5:23:40
Uniontown 76 67 40N59 81w25 5:25:40
Unionvale 34 21 40N16 81w56 5:27:44
Unionville 4 72 41N47 81w00 5:24:00
Unionville 58 5 39N39 81w51 5:27:24
Unionville Center 80 34 40N09 83w20 5:33:20
Uniopolis 6 34 40N36 84w05 5:36:20
Unity 1 34 38N48 83w32 5:34:08
Unity 15 67 40N53 80w34 5:22:16
University Heights 18 73 41N29 81w32 5:26:08
University View 25 107 40N00 83w03 5:32:12
Upland Heights 41 67 40N10 80w42 5:22:48
Upper 44 34 38N33 82w39 5:30:36
Upper Arlington 9 34 39N30 84w23 5:37:32

OHIO

Upper Arlington 25 107 40N00 83w04 5:32:16
Upper Dayton View 57 91 39N47 84w14 5:36:56
Upper Sandusky 88 102 40N50 83w17 5:33:08
Urbana 11 110 40N07 83w45 5:35:00
Urbancrest 25 107 39N54 83w06 5:32:24
Utica 45 5 40N14 82w27 5:29:48
Utopia 13 34 38N52 83w55 5:35:40
Valley 15 67 40N55 80w51 5:23:24
Valley City 52 67 41N14 81w56 5:27:44
Valley Crossing 25 107 39N54 82w58 5:31:52
Valleydale 31 88 39N12 84w29 5:37:56
Valley Hi 46 33 40N21 83w41 5:34:44
Valley View 18 26 41N22 81w40 5:26:40
Valley View 25 107 39N57 83w05 5:32:20
Valley View 41 67 40N21 80w48 5:23:12
Valley View 73 34 38N46 82w59 5:31:56
Valley View Heights 13 34 39N07 84w21 5:37:24
Valley View Village 60 5 39N55 82w01 5:28:04
Valleywood 29 34 39N43 84w06 5:36:24
Vanatta 45 5 40N07 82w26 5:29:44
Van Buren 32 33 41N08 83w39 5:34:36
Vanburen 45 5 40N07 82w26 5:29:44
Vandalia 57 34 39N54 84w12 5:36:48
Vanlue 32 33 40N58 83w29 5:33:56
Van Wert 81 118 40N52 84w35 5:38:20
Vaughnsville 69 34 40N53 84w09 5:36:36
Vega 40 34 38N55 82w27 5:29:48
Venedocia 81 34 40N47 84w28 5:37:52
Venice 22 5 41N27 82w44 5:30:56
Venice 74 32 41N03 82w52 5:31:28
Venice Heights 78 45 41N13 80w47 5:23:08
Vera Cruz 8 34 39N11 83w57 5:35:48
Vermilion 22 81 41N25 82w22 5:29:28
Vermilion-on-the-Lake 47 81 41N25 82w19 5:29:16
Vernon 44 34 38N38 82w40 5:30:40
Vernon 70 5 40N54 82w37 5:30:28
Vernon 78 67 41N27 80w36 5:22:24
Vernon Heights 51 5 40N35 83w07 5:32:28
Verona 68 34 39N53 84w29 5:37:56
Versailles 19 34 40N13 84w29 5:37:56
Vesuvius 44 34 38N38 82w40 5:30:40
Veterans Administration 57 91 39N46 84w12 5:36:48
Veto 84 20 39N18 81w34 5:26:16
Vickery 72 30 41N23 82w56 5:31:44
Vicksville 58 5 39N30 82w06 5:28:24
Vienna 78 82 41N14 80w40 5:22:40
Vigo 71 34 39N21 83w00 5:32:00
Viking Village 13 34 39N07 84w21 5:37:24
Villa 12 39 39N57 83w47 5:35:08
Villa Nova 6 34 40N33 84w22 5:37:28
Vincent 47 42 41N25 82w07 5:28:28
Vincent 84 20 39N23 81w40 5:26:40
Vine Street 43 67 41N38 81w25 5:25:40
Vinton 27 27 38N59 82w21 5:29:24
Violet 23 27 39N53 82w46 5:31:04
Virginia 16 5 40N11 81w57 5:27:48
Wabash 54 34 40N33 84w45 5:39:00
Waco 76 43 40N47 81w22 5:25:28
Wade 84 20 39N33 81w04 5:24:16
Wadsworth 52 46 41N02 81w44 5:26:56
Waggoner Place 87 31 41N34 83w35 5:34:20
Wagram 45 27 40N00 82w40 5:30:40
Wahlsburg 8 34 38N52 83w55 5:35:40
Wainwright 79 16 40N25 81w26 5:25:44
Waite Hill 43 67 41N37 81w23 5:25:32
Wakefield 66 34 38N58 83w01 5:32:04
Wakeman 39 5 41N15 82w24 5:29:36
Walbridge 87 31 41N35 83w29 5:33:56
Waldo 51 27 40N28 83w05 5:32:20
Walhonding 16 5 40N22 82w09 5:28:36
Walhonding 30 5 39N54 81w32 5:26:08
Wallace Heights 41 67 40N28 80w36 5:22:24
Walnut Creek 38 5 40N33 81w43 5:26:52
Walnut Grove 46 33 40N22 83w46 5:35:04
Walnut Hills 31 88 39N08 84w29 5:37:56
Walnut Hills 40 34 39N04 82w39 5:30:36
Walnut Hills 76 54 40N48 81w31 5:26:04
Walnutrun 49 34 39N53 83w27 5:33:48
Walton Hills 18 67 41N21 81w34 5:26:16
Wamsley 1 34 38N52 83w11 5:32:44
Wapakoneta 6 118 40N34 84w12 5:36:48
Ward 37 27 39N31 82w14 5:28:56
Ward Town 8 34 38N45 83w50 5:35:20
Wardwood Acres 31 34 39N13 84w35 5:38:20
Warner 84 20 39N34 81w25 5:25:40
Warnock 7 21 40N01 80w56 5:23:44
Warren 78 45 41N14 80w49 5:23:16
Warrensburg 21 33 40N16 83w13 5:32:52
Warrensville 18 67 41N26 81w30 5:26:00
Warrensville Heights 18 67 41N27 81w32 5:26:08
Warrenton 41 67 40N11 80w41 5:22:44
Warsaw 16 5 40N20 82w01 5:28:04
Warwick 77 67 40N56 81w38 5:26:32
Warwick 79 16 40N24 81w25 5:25:40
Washington Court House 24 4 39N32 83w26 5:33:44
Washingtonville 15 67 40N55 80w46 5:23:04
Waterford 42 27 40N29 82w32 5:30:08
Waterford 84 20 39N33 81w39 5:26:36
Waterloo 5 27 39N20 82w14 5:28:56
Waterloo 23 27 39N51 82w48 5:31:12
Waterloo 44 34 38N42 82w28 5:29:52

Watertown 84 20 39N28 81w38 5:26:32
Waterville 48 34 41N30 83w43 5:34:52
Watkins 80 33 40N15 83w22 5:33:28
Wattsville 10 21 40N37 80w57 5:23:48
Wauseon 26 34 41N33 84w08 5:36:32
Waverly 66 34 39N08 82w59 5:31:56
Waverly Gables 66 34 39N09 83w00 5:32:00
Way 56 20 39N40 81w11 5:24:44
Wayland 67 67 41N10 81w04 5:24:16
Wayne 4 72 41N32 80w32 5:22:08
Wayne 87 33 41N18 83w29 5:33:56
Wayne Lakes Parke 19 34 40N06 84w38 5:38:32
Waynesburg 17 33 40N54 82w46 5:31:04
Waynesburg 76 67 40N40 81w15 5:25:00
Waynesfield 6 34 40N36 83w59 5:35:56
Waynesville 83 34 39N32 84w05 5:36:20
Weathersfield 78 75 41N10 80w45 5:23:00
Weaver Station 19 34 40N06 84w38 5:38:32
Webb 7 21 40N00 80w46 5:23:04
Webb Summit 37 27 39N32 82w24 5:29:36
Webertown 36 34 39N14 83w47 5:35:08
Webster 19 34 40N08 84w26 5:37:44
Webster 87 33 41N27 83w32 5:34:08
Wegee 7 21 40N00 80w46 5:23:04
Weller 70 5 40N56 82w27 5:29:48
Wellington 47 55 41N10 82w13 5:28:52
Wellington Park 31 34 39N14 84w32 5:38:08
Wellman 83 34 39N32 84w05 5:36:20
Wells 41 67 40N16 80w41 5:22:44
Wellston 40 87 39N07 82w32 5:30:08
Wellsville 15 105 40N35 80w39 5:22:36
Welshfield 28 67 41N23 81w09 5:24:36
Welshtown 53 5 39N07 82w00 5:28:00
Wengerlawn 57 34 39N49 84w25 5:37:40
Wernert 48 31 41N42 83w36 5:34:24
Wesley 84 20 39N25 81w48 5:27:12
West 15 67 40N46 81w02 5:24:08
West Akron 77 2 41N04 81w32 5:26:08
West Alexandria 68 34 39N45 84w32 5:38:08
West Andover 4 56 41N37 80w36 5:22:24
Westarado 76 54 40N48 81w31 5:26:04
West Austintown 50 67 41N06 80w45 5:23:00
West Bedford 16 5 40N20 82w03 5:28:12
West Bellaire 7 6 40N01 80w45 5:23:00
West Belpre 84 20 39N18 81w34 5:26:16
West Berlin 21 27 40N18 83w04 5:32:16
Westboro 14 34 39N17 83w55 5:35:40
West Brookfield 76 54 40N48 81w31 5:26:04
West Carlisle 16 5 40N06 82w08 5:28:32
West Carlisle 47 42 41N22 82w06 5:28:24
West Carrollton 57 91 39N40 84w15 5:37:00
West Charleston 55 34 39N58 84w10 5:36:40
West Chesapeake 44 37 38N27 82w28 5:29:52
West Chester 9 34 39N20 84w25 5:37:40
West Chester 79 16 40N16 81w17 5:25:08
West Clarksfield 39 5 41N15 82w24 5:29:36
West Elkton 68 34 39N35 84w33 5:38:12
West End 4 46 41N52 80w49 5:23:16
West Enon Estates 12 34 39N52 83w56 5:35:44
Western Hills 31 88 39N07 84w37 5:38:28
Western Reserve Estates 77 67 41N15 81w28 5:25:52
Westerville 25 27 40N08 82w56 5:31:44
West Fairport 43 67 41N45 81w17 5:25:08
West Farmington 78 67 41N23 80w58 5:23:52
Westfield 15 105 40N38 80w35 5:22:20
Westfield 59 27 40N25 82w57 5:31:48
Westfield Center 52 73 41N06 81w56 5:27:44
West Florence 68 34 39N45 84w38 5:38:32
Westhope 35 34 41N13 83w54 5:35:36
West Independence 32 33 41N11 83w26 5:33:44
West Jefferson 49 34 39N57 83w17 5:33:08
West Jefferson 86 34 41N35 84w36 5:38:24
West Lafayette 16 5 40N16 81w44 5:26:56
Westlake 18 67 41N27 81w56 5:27:44
West Lakeville 4 72 41N56 80w36 5:22:24
West Lancaster 24 34 39N39 83w32 5:34:08
Westland 30 5 39N58 81w40 5:26:40
West Lebanon 85 62 40N48 81w41 5:26:44
West Leipsic 69 34 41N06 84w00 5:36:00
West Liberty 17 33 40N47 82w44 5:30:56
West Liberty 46 34 40N15 83w45 5:35:00
West Liberty 59 27 40N25 82w48 5:31:12
West Lodi 74 32 41N16 82w51 5:31:24
West Logan 37 27 39N32 82w24 5:29:36
West London 49 34 39N53 83w27 5:33:48
West Manchester 68 34 39N54 84w38 5:38:32
West Mansfield 46 33 40N24 83w33 5:34:12
West Marietta 84 20 39N27 81w28 5:25:52
West Marysville 80 33 40N24 82w29 5:29:56
West Mecca 78 67 41N19 80w43 5:22:52
West Middletown 9 3 39N32 84w25 5:37:40
West Millgrove 87 33 41N15 83w30 5:34:00
West Milton 55 34 39N58 84w20 5:37:20
Westminster 2 34 40N42 83w55 5:35:40
West Newton 2 34 40N42 83w55 5:35:40
West Oberlin 47 46 41N18 82w13 5:28:52
Weston 87 34 41N21 83w48 5:35:12
West Park 18 26 41N28 81w47 5:27:08
West Park 32 89 41N03 83w39 5:34:36
West Park 41 106 40N22 80w39 5:22:36
West Park 76 54 40N48 81w31 5:26:04
West Point 15 67 40N43 80w42 5:22:48
West Point 59 27 40N44 82w47 5:31:08
West Portsmouth 73 34 38N46 83w02 5:32:08
West Powhatan 7 21 39N52 80w49 5:23:16
West Richfield 77 67 41N14 81w39 5:26:36
West Rushville 23 27 39N46 82w26 5:29:44
West Salem 85 62 40N58 82w07 5:28:28
West Side 50 84 41N06 80w42 5:22:48
West Sonora 68 34 39N51 84w32 5:38:08
West Toledo 48 31 41N42 83w34 5:34:16
West Town 51 5 40N35 83w07 5:32:28
West Union 1 34 38N48 83w33 5:34:12
West Unity 86 34 41N35 84w26 5:37:44
West View 18 67 41N21 81w54 5:27:36
Westview 47 67 41N20 81w57 5:27:48
Westville 11 34 40N07 83w51 5:35:24
Westville 15 67 40N55 81w01 5:24:04
Westville Lake 15 67 40N55 81w01 5:24:04
West Warren 78 45 41N14 80w51 5:23:24
West Wheeling 7 21 40N01 80w45 5:23:00
West Williamsfield 4 72 41N32 80w32 5:22:08
Westwood 31 88 39N10 84w36 5:38:24
Westwood 41 106 40N22 80w39 5:22:36
Westwood 85 76 40N49 81w56 5:27:44
Westwood Estates 41 106 40N22 80w39 5:22:36
West Woodville 13 34 39N18 83w59 5:35:56
Wetsel 81 34 40N51 84w27 5:37:48
Weymouth 52 73 41N08 81w52 5:27:28
Wharton 88 33 40N52 83w28 5:33:52
Wheelersburg 73 34 38N44 82w51 5:31:24
Wheeling Creek 7 21 40N05 80w45 5:23:00
Whetstone 17 32 40N46 82w54 5:31:36
Whigville 61 5 39N48 81w20 5:25:20
Whipple 84 20 39N31 81w25 5:25:40
Whistler 65 34 39N29 82w55 5:31:40
White Cottage 60 5 39N52 82w06 5:28:24
White Eyes 16 5 40N20 81w44 5:26:56
Whitehall 25 107 39N58 82w53 5:31:32
Whitehouse 48 34 41N31 83w48 5:35:12
White Oak 8 34 39N04 83w44 5:34:56
Whiteoak 24 34 39N43 83w16 5:33:04
White Oak 31 34 39N13 84w35 5:38:20
White Oak Meadows 31 34 39N13 84w35 5:38:20
White Oaks 41 106 40N22 80w39 5:22:36
White Pond 77 67 41N06 81w38 5:26:32
White's Landing 22 5 41N23 82w56 5:31:44
White Sulphur 21 33 40N16 83w13 5:32:52
Whiteville 26 34 41N42 83w55 5:35:40
Whitewater 31 34 39N12 84w46 5:39:04
Whitfield 57 34 39N40 84w16 5:37:04
Wick 4 49 41N32 80w32 5:22:08
Wickliffe 43 49 41N36 81w28 5:25:52
Widowville 3 44 40N54 82w22 5:29:28
Wiggonsville 13 34 38N59 84w04 5:36:16
Wilberforce 29 34 39N43 83w53 5:35:32
Wilbren 64 27 39N43 82w13 5:28:52
Wildare 78 67 41N19 80w43 5:22:52
Wildbrook Acres 31 34 39N14 84w32 5:38:08
Wildwood 9 34 39N30 84w23 5:37:32
Wilgus 44 34 38N34 82w28 5:29:52
Wilkesville 82 27 39N05 82w20 5:29:20
Wilkins Corners 45 5 40N07 82w26 5:29:44
Willard 39 5 41N03 82w44 5:30:56
Willetsville 36 34 39N12 83w37 5:34:28
Williamsburg 13 34 39N03 84w04 5:36:16
Williams Center 86 34 41N28 84w33 5:38:12
Williams Corner 13 34 39N05 84w11 5:36:44
Williamsdale 9 34 39N26 84w32 5:38:08
Williamsfield 4 83 41N33 80w36 5:22:24
Williamsport 59 27 40N33 82w50 5:31:20
Williamsport 65 34 39N35 83w07 5:32:28
Williamstown 32 33 40N50 83w39 5:34:36
Williston 62 93 41N36 83w20 5:33:20
Willobee 43 67 41N38 81w25 5:25:40
Willoughby 43 46 41N39 81w24 5:25:36
Willoughby Hills 43 46 41N35 81w26 5:25:44
Willow 18 26 41N28 81w39 5:26:36
Willow Brook Heights 76

OHIO

43 40N52 81w20 5:25:20
Willowcrest 50 67 40N57 80w40 5:22:40
Willowdell 19 34 40N13 84w29 5:37:56
Willow Grove 7 6 40N01 80w45 5:23:00
Willow Lakes 60 5 39N55 82w01 5:28:04
Willowville 13 34 39N06 84w15 5:37:00
Willowick 43 49 41N38 81w28 5:25:52
Willow Wood 44 34 38N34 82w28 5:29:52
Wills 30 5 40N01 81w23 5:25:32
Wills Creek 16 5 40N11 81w53 5:27:32
Willshire 81 34 40N45 84w48 5:39:12
Willshire Heights 83 34 39N35 84w18 5:37:12
Wilmington 14 34 39N27 83w50 5:35:20
Wilmot 76 21 40N39 81w39 5:26:36
Wilson 56 20 39N51 81w03 5:24:12
Wiltondale 31 34 39N10 83w21 5:33:24
Winameg 26 34 41N34 84w00 5:36:00
Winchester 1 34 38N58 83w37 5:34:28
Winchester 40 34 39N04 82w39 5:30:36
Windchester Hills 20 34 41N17 84w20 5:37:20
Windham 67 53 41N14 81w04 5:24:16
Windsor 4 72 41N32 80w56 5:23:44
Windsor 70 95 40N45 82w31 5:30:04
Windsor 83 34 39N18 84w06 5:36:24
Windsor Mills 4 72 41N32 80w56 5:23:44
Winesburg 38 5 40N37 81w42 5:26:48
Winfield 79 16 40N33 81w29 5:25:56
Wingett Run 84 20 39N32 81w14 5:24:56
Wingston 87 33 41N18 83w40 5:34:40
Winkle 36 34 39N07 83w43 5:34:52
Winona 15 67 40N50 80w54 5:23:36
Winterdale 41 106 40N22 80w39 5:22:36
Winterset 30 5 39N59 81w27 5:25:48
Wintersville 41 106 40N22 80w41 5:22:44
Wisterman 69 34 41N07 84w10 5:36:40
Withamsville 13 34 39N04 84w17 5:37:08
Wolf 79 16 40N15 81w35 5:26:20
Wolfhurst 7 21 40N05 80w45 5:23:00
Wolf Run 41 67 40N30 80w54 5:23:36
Wonderland 25 107 40N01 82w53 5:31:32
Woodbourne 57 91 39N39 84w12 5:36:48
Woodington 19 34 40N06 84w38 5:38:32
Woodlawn 31 34 39N15 84w28 5:37:52
Woodmere 18 67 41N28 81w29 5:25:56
Woods 9 34 39N31 84w44 5:38:56
Woodsdale 9 34 39N26 84w29 5:37:56
Woodsfield 56 14 39N46 81w07 5:24:28
Woodside 87 33 41N20 83w26 5:33:44
Woodstock 11 34 40N10 83w32 5:34:08
Woodville 72 32 41N27 83w22 5:33:28
Woodville Gardens 87 31 41N38 83w29 5:33:56
Woodworth 50 67 40N59 80w40 5:22:40
Wooster 85 76 40N48 81w56 5:27:44
Wooster Heights 70 95 40N45 82w31 5:30:04
Worstville 63 34 41N05 84w44 5:38:56
Worthington 25 107 40N05 83w01 5:32:04
Wren 81 34 40N48 84w47 5:39:08
Wright-Patterson Air Force B 29 34 39N47 84w03 5:36:12
Wrightsville 1 34 38N41 83w36 5:34:24
Wrightview 29 34 39N48 84w01 5:36:04
Wrightview Heights 29 34 39N48 84w01 5:36:04
Wyandot 88 32 40N49 83w09 5:32:36
Wyoming 31 34 39N14 84w29 5:37:56
Wyoming Meadows 31 34 39N14 84w32 5:38:08
Xavier 31 88 39N09 84w29 5:37:56
Xenia 29 87 39N41 83w56 5:35:44
Yale 62 93 41N36 83w20 5:33:20
Yale 67 67 41N02 81w03 5:24:12
Yankeeburg 84 20 39N23 81w14 5:24:56
Yankee Hills 78 67 41N16 80w34 5:22:16
Yankee Lake 78 67 41N16 80w34 5:22:16
Yankeetown 8 34 38N55 83w59 5:35:56
Yatesville 24 34 39N36 83w24 5:33:36
Yellow Bud 71 34 39N21 83w00 5:32:00
Yellow Creek 15 67 40N36 80w41 5:22:44
Yellow Springs 29 34 39N48 83w53 5:35:32
Yoder 2 90 40N42 84w08 5:36:32
York 41 67 40N13 80w52 5:23:28
Yorkshire 19 34 40N20 84w30 5:38:00
Yorkville 41 21 40N09 80w43 5:22:52
Youba 5 5 39N14 81w45 5:27:00
Young Hickory 60 5 39N51 81w39 5:26:36
Youngs 73 34 38N52 83w11 5:32:44
Youngs Corners 52 73 41N08 81w52 5:27:28
Youngstown 50 84 41N06 80w39 5:22:36
Youngsville 1 34 38N56 83w34 5:34:16
Zaleski 82 27 39N17 82w24 5:29:36
Zane 46 33 40N17 83w36 5:34:24
Zanesfield 46 33 40N21 83w41 5:34:44
Zanesville 60 104 39N56 82w01 5:28:04
Zann's Corners 66 34 39N09 83w00 5:32:00
Zeno 60 5 39N51 81w39 5:26:36
Zenz City 54 34 40N25 84w46 5:39:04
Zimmerman 29 34 39N46 84w06 5:36:24
Zoar 79 16 39N21 84w11 5:36:44
Zoarville 79 16 40N35 81w24 5:25:36
Zone 26 34 41N41 84w20 5:37:20

OKLAHOMA

TIME TABLES

OK # 1

Before 11/18/1883		LMT
11/18/1883	12:00	CST
3/31/1918	02:00	CWT
10/27/1918	02:00	CST
3/30/1919	02:00	CWT
10/26/1919	02:00	CST
2/09/1942	02:00	CWT
9/30/1945	02:00	CST
4/30/1967	02:00	US#1

OK # 2

Before 11/18/1883		LMT
11/18/1883	12:00	CST
3/31/1918	02:00	CWT
10/27/1918	02:00	CST
3/30/1919	02:00	CWT
10/26/1919	02:00	CST
2/09/1942	02:00	CWT
9/30/1945	02:00	CST
5/28/1962	02:00	CDT
11/13/1962	02:00	CST
4/30/1967	02:00	US#1

OK # 3

Before 11/18/1883		LMT
11/18/1883	12:00	CST
3/31/1918	02:00	CWT
10/27/1918	02:00	CST
3/30/1919	02:00	CWT
10/26/1919	02:00	CST
2/09/1942	02:00	CWT
9/30/1945	02:00	CST
6/13/1966	02:00	CDT
10/30/1966	02:00	US#1

OK # 4

Before 11/18/1883		LMT
11/18/1883	12:00	MST
3/31/1918	02:00	MWT
10/27/1918	02:00	MST
3/30/1919	02:00	MWT
10/26/1919	02:00	MST
3/08/1921	02:00	CST
2/09/1942	02:00	CWT
9/30/1945	02:00	CST
4/30/1967	02:00	US#1

COUNTIES

1 Adair
2 Alfalfa
3 Atoka
4 Beaver
5 Beckham
6 Blaine
7 Bryan
8 Caddo
9 Canadian
10 Carter
11 Cherokee
12 Choctaw
13 Cimarron
14 Cleveland
15 Coal
16 Comanche
17 Cotton
18 Craig
19 Creek
20 Custer
21 Delaware
22 Dewey
23 Ellis
24 Garfield
25 Garvin
26 Grady
27 Grant
28 Greer
29 Harmon
30 Harper
31 Haskell
32 Hughes
33 Jackson
34 Jefferson
35 Johnston
36 Kay
37 Kingfisher
38 Kiowa
39 Latimer
40 Le Flore
41 Lincoln
42 Logan
43 Love
44 McClain
45 McCurtain
46 McIntosh
47 Major
48 Marshall
49 Mayes
50 Murray
51 Muskogee
52 Noble
53 Nowata
54 Okfuskee
55 Oklahoma
56 Okmulgee
57 Osage
58 Ottawa
59 Pawnee
60 Payne
61 Pittsburg
62 Pontotoc
63 Pottawatomie
64 Pushmataha
65 Roger Mills
66 Rogers
67 Seminole
68 Sequoyah
69 Stephens
70 Texas
71 Tillman
72 Tulsa
73 Wagoner
74 Washington
75 Washita
76 Woods
77 Woodward

Place	Table	Lat.	Long.	Time
Achille 7	1	33N50	96w23	6:25:32
Acme 26	1	34N47	97w58	6:31:52
Ada 62	1	34N46	96w41	6:26:44
Adair 49	1	36N26	95w16	6:21:04
Adams 70	4	36N45	101w05	6:44:20
Adamson 61	1	34N55	95w33	6:22:12
Addington 34	1	34N15	97w58	6:31:52
Adel 64	1	34N32	95w45	6:23:00
Admiral 72	1	36N10	95w55	6:23:40
Afton 58	1	36N41	94w58	6:19:52
Agawam 26	1	34N53	97w57	6:31:48
Agra 41	1	35N54	96w53	6:27:32
Ahloso 62	1	34N44	96w38	6:26:32
Ahpeatone 17	1	34N21	98w18	6:33:12
Akins 68	1	35N28	94w47	6:19:08
Albany 7	1	33N53	96w10	6:24:40
Albert 8	1	35N14	98w25	6:33:40
Albion 64	1	34N40	95w06	6:20:24
Alderson 61	1	34N54	95w41	6:22:44
Aledo 22	1	35N52	99w21	6:37:24
Alex 26	1	34N55	97w47	6:31:08
Alfalfa 8	1	35N13	98w36	6:34:24
Aline 2	1	36N31	98w27	6:33:48
Allen 62	1	34N53	96w25	6:25:40
Allison 7	1	33N56	96w26	6:25:44
Alluwe 53	1	36N37	95w32	6:22:08
Alma 69	1	34N25	97w37	6:30:28
Alpers 10	1	34N31	97w21	6:29:24
Alsuma	1	36N06	95w52	6:23:28
Altus 33	1	34N38	99w20	6:37:20
Altus Air Force Base 33	1	34N39	99w19	6:37:16
Alva 76	1	36N48	98w40	6:34:40
Amber 26	1	35N10	97w53	6:31:32
Amber Pocasset 26	1	35N08	97w53	6:31:32
Ames 47	1	36N15	98w11	6:32:44
Amorita 2	1	36N56	98w18	6:33:12
Anadarko 8	1	35N04	98w15	6:33:00
Antioch 25	1	34N37	97w24	6:29:36
Antioch 48	1	34N05	96w46	6:27:04
Antlers 64	1	34N14	95w37	6:22:28
Apache 8	1	34N54	98w22	6:33:28
Apperson 57	1	36N42	96w44	6:26:56
Apple 12	1	34N08	95w21	6:21:24
Aqua Park 68	1	35N28	94w47	6:19:08
Arapaho 20	1	35N34	98w58	6:35:52
Arcadia 55	1	35N40	97w20	6:29:20
Ardmore 10	1	34N10	97w08	6:28:32
Arkoma 40	1	35N21	94w26	6:17:44
Arlington 41	1	35N29	96w41	6:26:44
Armstrong 7	1	34N03	96w21	6:25:24
Arnett 23	1	36N08	99w46	6:39:04
Arnett 29	1	34N41	99w55	6:39:40
Arpelar 61	1	34N53	95w57	6:23:48
Arthur 69	1	34N28	98w00	6:32:00
Asher 63	1	34N59	96w56	6:27:44
Ashland 61	1	34N46	96w04	6:24:16
Asphaltum 34	1	34N10	97w36	6:30:24
Atoka 3	1	34N23	96w08	6:24:32
Atwood 32	1	34N57	96w20	6:25:20
Avant 57	1	36N29	96w04	6:24:16
Avard 76	1	36N42	98w47	6:35:08
Avery 41	1	35N53	96w45	6:27:00
Aydelotte 63	1	35N20	96w59	6:27:56
Babbs 38	1	35N02	99w06	6:36:24
Bache 61	1	34N54	95w39	6:22:36
Bacone 51	1	35N45	95w22	6:21:28
Bailey 26	1	34N39	97w57	6:31:48
Baker 70	4	36N52	101w01	6:44:04
Baldhill 56	1	35N37	95w58	6:23:52
Balko 4	4	36N38	100w41	6:42:44
Ballard 1	1	36N07	94w34	6:18:16
Banner 9	1	35N32	97w57	6:31:48
Banty 7	1	34N00	96w02	6:24:08
Barber 11	1	35N53	94w54	6:19:36
Barnsdall 57	1	36N34	96w10	6:24:40
Baron 1	1	35N59	94w34	6:18:16
Bartlesville 74	2	36N45	95w59	6:23:56
Battiest 45	1	34N24	94w56	6:19:44
Baum 10	1	34N11	97w03	6:28:12
Bearden 54	1	35N21	96w23	6:25:32
Beaver 4	1	36N49	100w31	6:42:04
Bee 35	1	34N09	96w22	6:25:28
Beggs 56	1	35N45	96w04	6:24:16
Beland 51	1	35N45	95w22	6:21:28
Belmont 63	1	35N29	96w41	6:26:44
Belva	1	36N30	98w59	6:35:56
Belzoni 64	1	34N14	95w37	6:22:28
Bengal 39	1	34N58	94w43	6:18:52
Benmartin 73	1	35N52	95w31	6:22:04
Bennington 7	1	34N00	96w02	6:24:08
Bentley 3	1	34N13	96w04	6:24:16
Berlin 65	1	35N27	99w36	6:38:24
Bernice 21	1	36N37	94w55	6:19:40
Bessie 75	1	35N23	98w59	6:35:56
Bethany 55	1	35N31	97w38	6:30:32
Bethel 45	1	34N22	94w51	6:19:24
Bethel Acres 63	1	35N19	97w02	6:28:08
Big Cabin 18	1	36N32	95w14	6:20:56
Big Rocks 64	1	34N14	95w37	6:22:28
Big Spring 32	1	35N14	96w14	6:24:56
Billings 52	1	36N32	97w27	6:29:48
Binger 8	1	35N18	98w21	6:33:24
Bishop 23	1	36N07	100w02	6:40:08
Bison 24	1	36N12	97w53	6:31:32
Bixby 72	1	35N57	95w53	6:23:32
Blackburn 59	1	36N22	96w36	6:26:24
Blackgum 68	1	35N30	94w58	6:19:52
Blackwell 36	1	36N48	97w17	6:29:08
Blair 33	1	34N47	99w20	6:37:20
Blanchard 44	1	35N08	97w39	6:30:36
Blanco 61	1	34N45	95w46	6:23:04
Blocker 61	1	35N04	95w34	6:22:16
Blue 7	1	34N00	96w23	6:25:32
Bluejacket 18	1	36N48	95w04	6:20:16
Bluff 12	1	34N02	95w42	6:22:48
Boatman 49	1	36N16	95w11	6:20:44
Boehler 3	1	34N02	95w52	6:23:28
Boggy Depot 3	1	34N23	96w08	6:24:32
Bois D'Arc 36	1	36N45	97w00	6:28:00
Boise City 13	4	36N44	102w31	6:50:04
Bokchito 7	1	34N01	96w09	6:24:36
Bokhoma 45	1	33N49	94w35	6:18:20
Bokoshe 40	1	35N11	94w47	6:19:08
Boley 54	1	35N29	96w29	6:25:56
Bond 46	1	35N28	95w31	6:22:04
Boone 8	1	34N54	98w22	6:33:28
Boss 45	1	33N54	94w49	6:19:16
Boswell 12	1	34N02	95w52	6:23:28
Boulevard 14	1	35N14	97w25	6:29:40
Bowden 19	1	36N06	96w01	6:24:04
Bowlegs 67	1	35N09	96w40	6:26:40
Bowring 57	1	35N57	95w53	6:23:32
Box 68	1	35N30	94w58	6:19:52
Boynton 51	1	35N39	95w39	6:22:36
Braden 40	1	35N15	94w37	6:18:28
Bradley 26	1	34N53	97w42	6:30:48
Brady 25	1	34N39	97w10	6:28:40
Braggs 51	1	35N40	95w12	6:20:48
Braman 36	1	36N56	97w20	6:29:20
Bray 69	1	34N38	97w49	6:31:16
Breckinridge 24	1	36N26	97w44	6:30:56
Brent 68	1	35N28	94w47	6:19:08
Briartown 51	1	35N18	95w14	6:20:56
Bridgeport 8	1	35N33	98w23	6:33:32
Brinkman 28	1	35N01	99w33	6:38:12
Bristow 19	1	35N50	96w23	6:25:32
Britton 55	1	35N34	97w32	6:30:08
Brock 10	1	34N11	97w03	6:28:12
Broken Arrow 72	1	36N03	95w48	6:23:12
Broken Bow 45	1	34N02	94w44	6:18:56
Bromide 15	1	34N26	96w30	6:26:00
Brooken 31	1	35N20	95w03	6:20:12
Brooksville 63	1	35N12	96w58	6:27:52
Brown 7	1	34N00	96w23	6:25:32
Broxton 8	1	34N54	98w22	6:33:28
Bruno 3	1	34N20	96w02	6:24:08
Brushy 68	1	35N28	94w47	6:19:08
Bryant 56	1	35N23	96w04	6:24:16
Buffalo 30	1	36N50	99w38	6:38:32
Bunch 1	1	35N41	94w46	6:19:04
Burbank 57	1	36N42	96w44	6:26:56
Burg 3	1	34N43	95w51	6:23:24
Burlington 2	1	36N54	98w25	6:33:40
Burmah 22	1	35N51	98w58	6:35:52
Burneyville 43	1	33N54	97w17	6:29:08
Burns Flat 75	1	35N21	99w10	6:36:40
Burt 71	1	34N24	99w01	6:36:04
Bushyhead 66	1	36N32	95w26	6:21:44
Butler 20	1	35N38	99w11	6:36:44
Butner 67	1	35N09	96w30	6:26:00
Byars 44	1	34N53	97w03	6:28:12
Byng 62	1	34N47	96w40	6:26:40
Byron 2	1	36N54	98w18	6:33:12
Cache 16	1	34N38	98w38	6:34:32
Caddo 7	1	34N07	96w16	6:25:04
Cade 7	1	34N00	96w02	6:24:08
Cairo 15	1	34N31	96w13	6:24:52
Calera 7	1	33N56	96w26	6:25:44
Calhoun 40	1	35N08	94w40	6:18:40
Calumet 9	1	35N36	98w07	6:32:28
Calvin 32	1	34N58	96w15	6:25:00
Camargo 22	1	36N01	99w17	6:37:08
Cambria 39	1	34N51	95w34	6:22:16
Cambridge 38	1	34N59	99w15	6:37:00
Cameron 40	1	35N08	94w32	6:18:08
Cameron College 16	1	34N37	98w25	6:33:40
Camp Houston 76	1	36N46	99w07	6:36:28
Canadian 61	1	35N11	95w39	6:22:36
Canadian City 9	1	35N32	97w57	6:31:48
Caney 3	1	34N14	96w13	6:24:52
Canton 6	1	36N03	98w35	6:34:20
Canute 75	1	35N25	99w17	6:37:08
Capitol Hill 55	1	35N26	97w32	6:30:08
Capron 76	1	36N54	98w35	6:34:20
Cardin 58	1	36N58	94w50	6:19:20
Carleton 6	1	35N51	98w25	6:33:40
Carmen 2	1	36N35	98w28	6:33:52
Carnegie 8	1	35N06	98w36	6:34:24
Carney 41	1	35N48	97w01	6:28:04
Carpenter 65	1	35N25	99w25	6:37:40
Carrier 24	1	36N29	98w02	6:32:08
Carson 32	1	35N06	96w08	6:24:32
Carter 5	1	35N13	99w30	6:38:00
Carter 11	1	35N52	94w58	6:19:52
Carter Nine 57	1	36N42	96w44	6:26:56
Carter Park 55	1	35N26	97w26	6:29:44
Cartersville 31	1	35N18	94w46	6:19:04
Cartwright 7	1	33N51	96w34	6:26:16
Cashion 37	1	35N48	97w41	6:30:44
Castle 54	1	35N28	96w23	6:25:32
Catale 66	1	36N25	95w13	6:20:52
Catesby 23	1	36N30	99w58	6:39:52
Catoosa 66	1	36N11	95w45	6:23:00
Cement 8	1	34N56	98w08	6:32:32
Center 62	1	34N48	96w49	6:27:16
Centrahoma 15	1	34N37	96w21	6:25:24

Central Atoka 3 1 34N18 96w00 6:24:00
Centralia 18 1 36N48 95w21 6:21:24
Central Washita 75 1 35N17 98w57 6:35:48
Ceres 52 1 36N28 97w11 6:28:44
Cerrogordo 45 1 33N51 94w39 6:18:36
Cestos 22 1 36N09 99w06 6:36:24
Chandler 41 1 35N42 96w53 6:27:32
Chase 51 1 35N45 95w22 6:21:28
Chattanooga 16 1 34N25 98w39 6:34:36
Checotah 46 1 35N28 95w31 6:22:04
Chelsea 66 1 36N32 95w26 6:21:44
Cherokee 2 1 36N45 98w21 6:33:24
Chester 47 1 36N13 98w55 6:35:40
Chewey 1 1 36N07 94w34 6:18:16
Cheyenne 65 1 35N37 99w40 6:38:40
Chickasha 26 1 35N03 97w58 6:31:52
Childers 53 1 36N47 95w38 6:22:32
Chilocco 36 1 36N59 97w04 6:28:16
Chitwood 26 1 34N57 97w56 6:31:44
Choctaw 55 1 35N29 97w16 6:29:04
Choska 73 1 36N03 95w42 6:22:48
Chouteau 49 1 36N11 95w21 6:21:24
Christie 1 1 35N57 94w41 6:18:44
Cimarron 55 1 35N31 97w29 6:29:56
Cimmaron City 42 1 36N00 97w37 6:30:28
Cisco 45 1 33N54 94w49 6:19:16
Citra 32 1 34N53 96w24 6:25:36
Civit 25 1 34N44 97w13 6:28:52
Claremore 66 1 36N19 95w36 6:22:24
Clarita 15 1 34N29 96w26 6:25:44
Clarksville 73 1 35N52 95w31 6:22:04
Claud 69 1 34N28 98w00 6:32:00
Clayton 64 1 34N35 95w21 6:21:24
Clayton Lake 64 1 34N35 95w21 6:21:24
Clear Lake 4 1 36N34 100w13 6:40:52
Clearview 54 1 35N24 96w11 6:24:44
Clebit 45 1 34N21 94w52 6:19:28
Clemscot 10 1 34N20 97w28 6:29:52
Cleo 1 36N24 98w26 6:33:44
Cleora 21 1 36N39 94w56 6:19:44
Cleo Springs 47 1 36N25 98w26 6:33:44
Cleveland 59 1 36N19 96w28 6:25:52
Clinton 20 1 35N31 98w58 6:35:52
Clinton Junction 20 1 35N31 98w58 6:35:52
Cloud Chief 75 1 35N20 99w05 6:36:20
Cloudy 64 1 34N18 95w17 6:21:08
Clyde 27 1 36N51 97w49 6:31:16
Coalgate 15 1 34N32 96w13 6:24:52
Coalton 56 1 35N28 95w56 6:23:44
Cobb 7 1 34N00 96w23 6:25:32
Cogar 8 1 35N19 97w56 6:31:44
Colbert 7 1 33N51 96w30 6:26:00
Colcord 21 1 36N16 94w42 6:18:48
Cold Springs 38 1 34N48 99w00 6:36:00
Cole 44 1 35N06 97w34 6:30:16
Coleman 35 1 34N16 96w25 6:25:40
College 60 1 36N07 97w04 6:28:16
Collinsville 72 1 36N22 95w51 6:23:24
Colony 75 1 35N21 98w41 6:34:44
Comanche 69 1 34N22 97w58 6:31:52
Commerce 58 1 36N56 94w53 6:19:32
Concho 9 1 35N32 97w57 6:31:48
Connerville 35 1 34N27 96w38 6:26:32
Conser 40 1 34N53 94w36 6:18:24
Coodys Bluff 53 1 36N42 95w38 6:22:32
Cookietown 17 1 34N11 98w28 6:33:52
Cookson 11 1 35N42 94w58 6:19:52
Cooperton 38 1 34N52 98w52 6:35:28
Copan 74 1 36N54 95w56 6:23:44
Corbett 14 1 34N58 97w14 6:28:56
Cordell 75 1 35N17 98w59 6:35:56
Corinne 64 1 34N12 95w21 6:21:24
Corn 75 1 35N23 98w47 6:35:08
Cornish 34 1 34N10 97w36 6:30:24
Corum 69 1 34N22 97w58 6:31:52
Cottonwood 15 1 34N31 96w13 6:24:52
Council Hill 51 1 35N33 95w39 6:22:36
Countyline 69 1 34N27 97w35 6:30:20
Courtney 43 1 33N56 97w30 6:30:00
Covington 24 1 36N18 97w35 6:30:20
Cowden 75 1 35N20 99w05 6:36:20
Coweta 73 1 35N57 95w39 6:22:36
Cowlington 40 1 35N18 94w47 6:19:08
Cox City 26 1 34N43 97w44 6:30:56
Coyle 42 1 35N57 97w14 6:28:56
Craig 61 1 34N56 95w46 6:23:04
Cravens 39 1 34N57 95w05 6:20:20
Crawford 65 1 35N50 99w48 6:39:12
Creosote 12 1 34N01 95w31 6:22:04
Crescent 42 1 35N57 97w36 6:30:24
Criner 44 1 35N01 97w22 6:29:28
Cromwell 67 1 35N21 96w27 6:25:48
Crowder 61 1 35N08 95w40 6:22:40
Crystal 3 1 34N12 95w57 6:23:48
Cumberland 48 1 34N04 96w36 6:26:24
Curtis 77 1 36N27 99w08 6:36:32
Cushing 60 1 35N59 96w45 6:27:00
Custer City 20 1 35N40 98w53 6:35:32
Cyril 8 1 34N54 98w12 6:32:48
Dacoma 76 1 36N40 98w34 6:34:16
Daisy 3 1 34N32 95w45 6:23:00
Dale 63 1 35N24 97w03 6:28:12
Damon 39 1 34N55 95w19 6:21:16
Darwin 64 1 34N14 95w37 6:22:28
Davenport 41 1 35N42 96w46 6:27:04
Davidson 71 1 34N14 99w05 6:36:20
Davis 50 1 34N30 97w07 6:28:28
Dawson 72 1 36N09 95w59 6:23:56
Deer Creek 27 1 36N48 97w31 6:30:04
Degnan 39 1 34N55 95w19 6:21:16
Dela 64 1 34N14 95w37 6:22:28
Delaware 53 1 36N47 95w39 6:22:36
Del City 55 1 35N26 97w26 6:29:44

Delhi 5 1 35N18 99w38 6:38:32
Denman 39 1 34N57 95w05 6:20:20
Dennis 21 1 36N48 95w21 6:21:24
Denoya 57 1 36N42 96w44 6:26:56
Denver 14 1 35N14 97w25 6:29:40
Depew 19 1 35N48 96w31 6:26:04
Depot 61 1 34N56 95w46 6:23:04
Devol 17 1 34N11 98w35 6:34:20
Dewar 56 1 35N28 95w56 6:23:44
Dewey 74 1 36N48 95w56 6:23:44
Dibble 44 1 35N02 97w38 6:30:32
Dickson 10 1 34N11 96w59 6:27:56
Dighton 56 1 35N28 95w56 6:23:44
Dillard 10 1 34N10 97w25 6:29:40
Dill City 75 1 35N17 99w08 6:36:32
Disney 49 1 36N29 95w01 6:20:04
Dixon 67 1 35N09 96w30 6:26:00
Donaldson 72 1 36N09 95w57 6:23:48
Dotyville 58 1 36N53 94w53 6:19:32
Dougherty 50 1 34N24 97w03 6:28:12
Douglas 24 1 36N16 97w40 6:30:40
Douthat 58 1 36N53 94w53 6:19:32
Dover 37 1 35N59 97w55 6:31:40
Dow 61 1 34N52 95w36 6:22:24
Downtown 55 1 35N29 97w32 6:30:08
Doyle 69 1 34N37 97w30 6:30:00
Drake 50 1 34N32 96w55 6:27:40
Driftwood 2 1 36N53 98w22 6:33:28
Drummond 24 1 36N18 98w02 6:32:08
Drumright 19 1 35N59 96w36 6:26:24
Duke 33 1 34N40 99w34 6:38:16
Dunbar 64 1 34N35 95w21 6:21:24
Duncan 69 1 34N30 97w57 6:31:48
Dunjee Park 55 1 35N29 97w22 6:29:28
Durant 7 1 34N00 96w23 6:25:32
Durham 65 1 35N51 99w56 6:39:44
Durwood 10 1 34N11 97w03 6:28:12
Dustin 32 1 35N16 96w02 6:24:08
Dutton 26 1 35N12 97w58 6:31:52
Eagle City 6 1 35N56 98w35 6:34:20
Eagletown 45 1 34N02 94w34 6:18:16
Eakly 8 1 35N18 98w34 6:34:16
Earl 35 1 34N11 96w51 6:27:24
Earlsboro 63 1 35N16 96w48 6:27:12
East Bryan 7 1 34N02 96w01 6:24:04
East Canadian 9 1 35N35 97w48 6:31:12
East Cherokee 11 1 35N51 94w51 6:19:24
East Coal 15 1 34N33 96w14 6:24:56
Eastern 55 1 35N29 97w29 6:29:56
Eastern Oklahoma A&M College 39 1 34N55 95w19 6:21:16
East Jackson 33 1 34N43 99w13 6:36:52
East Jessie 15 1 34N39 96w31 6:26:04
East Johnston 35 1 34N17 96w30 6:26:00
East Logan 42 1 35N52 97w15 6:29:00
East Love 43 1 33N55 97w08 6:28:32
East Major 47 1 36N21 98w14 6:32:56
East Mayes 49 1 36N23 95w05 6:20:20
East Mc Clain 44 1 34N54 97w08 6:28:32
East Murray 50 1 34N30 96w57 6:27:48
East Ninnekah 26 1 34N57 97w56 6:31:44
East Noble 52 1 36N26 97w06 6:28:24
East Roger Mills 65 1 35N43 99w27 6:37:48
East Side 74 2 36N45 95w59 6:23:56
East Tillman 71 1 34N17 98w44 6:34:56
Echota 1 1 35N49 94w37 6:18:28
Eddy 36 1 36N41 97w34 6:30:16
Edgewater Park 16 1 34N54 98w22 6:33:28
Edmond 55 1 35N39 97w29 6:29:56
Edna 19 1 35N50 96w23 6:25:32
Eldon 11 1 35N54 94w59 6:19:56
Eldorado 33 1 34N28 99w39 6:38:36
Elgin 16 1 34N47 98w18 6:33:12
Elk City 5 1 35N25 99w25 6:37:40
Elmer 33 1 34N29 99w21 6:37:24
Elmore City 25 1 34N37 97w25 6:29:40
Elmwood 4 4 36N37 100w31 6:42:04
El Reno 9 1 35N32 97w57 6:31:48
El Reno Junction 9 1 35N32 97w57 6:31:48
Emerson Center 17 1 34N21 98w18 6:33:12
Emet 35 1 34N15 96w33 6:26:12
Empire 69 1 34N26 98w02 6:32:08
Enid 24 1 36N24 97w53 6:31:32
Enos 48 1 34N00 96w43 6:26:52
Enterprise 31 1 35N07 95w22 6:21:28
Enville 43 1 33N56 97w07 6:28:28
Eram 56 1 35N39 95w39 6:22:36
Erick 5 1 35N13 99w52 6:39:28
Erin Springs 25 1 34N49 97w36 6:30:24
Ethel 64 1 34N14 95w37 6:22:28
Etta 11 1 35N53 94w54 6:19:36
Eucha 21 1 36N22 94w53 6:19:32
Euchee Creek 72 1 36N08 96w03 6:24:12
Eufaula 46 1 35N17 95w35 6:22:20
Eva 70 4 36N48 101w54 6:47:36
Ewing 20 1 35N31 98w58 6:35:52
Fairfax 57 1 36N34 96w42 6:26:48
Fairland 58 3 36N45 94w51 6:19:24
Fairmont 24 1 36N21 97w43 6:30:52
Fair Oaks 73 1 36N09 95w40 6:22:40
Fair Valley 76 1 36N48 98w40 6:34:40
Fairview 47 1 36N16 98w29 6:33:56
Falconhead 43 1 33N54 97w17 6:29:08
Falfa 39 1 34N45 95w03 6:20:12
Fallis 41 1 35N45 97w07 6:28:28
Fallon 12 1 34N01 95w31 6:22:04
Fame 46 1 35N17 95w35 6:22:20
Fanshaw 40 1 34N57 94w55 6:19:40
Fanshawe 40 1 34N57 94w55 6:19:40
Fargo 23 1 36N22 99w37 6:38:28
Farley 55 1 35N29 97w34 6:30:16

OKLAHOMA

Farris 3 1 34N16 95w52 6:23:28
Faxon 16 1 34N28 98w35 6:34:20
Fay 22 1 35N49 98w39 6:34:36
Featherston 61 1 35N07 95w22 6:21:28
Felker 45 1 34N00 95w06 6:20:24
Felt 13 4 36N34 102w48 6:51:12
Fern 30 1 36N26 99w24 6:37:36
Fillmore 35 1 34N16 96w25 6:25:40
Finley 64 1 34N20 95w30 6:22:00
Fisher 72 1 36N08 96w03 6:24:12
Fittstown 62 1 34N37 96w38 6:26:32
Fitzhugh 62 1 34N40 96w46 6:27:04
Fleetwood 34 1 33N54 97w56 6:31:44
Fletcher 16 1 34N50 98w15 6:33:00
Flint 21 1 36N11 94w34 6:18:16
Floris 4 1 36N54 100w32 6:42:08
Fob 48 1 34N00 96w43 6:26:52
Folsom 35 1 34N16 96w25 6:25:40
Foraker 57 1 36N52 96w34 6:26:16
Forest Hill 40 1 34N53 94w36 6:18:24
Forest Park 55 1 35N32 97w26 6:29:44
Forgan 4 1 36N54 100w32 6:42:08
Forman 68 1 35N24 94w36 6:18:24
Forney 12 1 34N01 95w31 6:22:04
Forrester 40 1 34N53 94w36 6:18:24
Fort Cobb 8 1 35N06 98w26 6:33:44
Fort Coffee 40 1 35N15 94w37 6:18:28
Fort Gibson 51 1 35N48 95w15 6:21:00
Fort Reno 9 1 35N32 97w57 6:31:48
Fort Sill 16 1 34N41 98w26 6:33:44
Fort Supply 77 1 36N35 99w35 6:38:20
Fort Towson 12 1 34N01 95w16 6:21:04
Foss 75 1 35N27 99w10 6:36:40
Foster 25 1 34N37 97w30 6:30:00
Fox 10 1 34N22 97w30 6:30:00
Foyil 66 1 36N26 95w31 6:22:04
Francis 62 1 34N52 96w36 6:26:24
Franklin 14 1 35N14 97w25 6:29:40
Frederick 71 1 34N23 99w01 6:36:04
Freedom 76 1 36N46 99w07 6:36:28
Friendship 33 1 34N39 99w19 6:37:16
Frisco 62 1 36N25 95w08 6:20:32
Frogville 12 1 34N01 95w31 6:22:04
Fugate 3 1 34N28 96w03 6:24:12
Gaddy 63 1 35N20 96w59 6:27:56
Gage 23 1 36N19 99w45 6:39:00
Gans 68 1 35N23 94w41 6:18:44
Gap 3 1 34N43 95w54 6:23:36
Garber 24 1 36N26 97w35 6:30:20
Garland 31 1 35N20 95w03 6:20:12
Garvin 45 1 33N57 94w56 6:19:44
Gas City 69 1 34N22 97w58 6:31:52
Gate 4 1 36N51 100w04 6:40:16
Gay 12 1 34N01 95w31 6:22:04
Geary 6 1 35N38 98w19 6:33:16
Gene Autry 10 1 34N19 97w02 6:28:08
Georgetown 51 1 35N48 95w15 6:21:00
Geronimo 16 1 34N29 98w23 6:33:32
Gerty 32 1 34N50 96w17 6:25:08
Gibson 73 1 35N57 95w22 6:21:28
Gideon 11 1 35N54 94w59 6:19:56
Gilmore 40 1 35N03 94w37 6:18:28
Glencoe 60 1 36N14 96w56 6:27:44
Glendale 40 1 34N57 94w38 6:18:32
Glenn 10 1 34N19 97w08 6:28:32
Glenoak 53 2 36N45 95w59 6:23:56
Glenpool 72 1 35N57 96w01 6:24:04
Glover 45 1 34N01 94w44 6:18:56
Golden 45 1 34N02 94w54 6:19:36
Goldsby 44 1 35N09 97w29 6:29:56
Goltry 2 1 36N32 98w09 6:32:36
Good 12 1 34N01 95w31 6:22:04
Goodlake 45 1 33N51 94w39 6:18:36
Goodland 12 1 34N01 95w31 6:22:04
Goodwater 45 1 33N55 94w34 6:18:16
Goodwell 70 4 36N36 101w38 6:46:32
Gore 68 1 35N32 95w07 6:20:28
Gotebo 38 1 35N04 98w53 6:35:32
Gould 29 1 34N40 99w47 6:39:08
Gowen 39 1 34N53 95w29 6:21:56
Grace 3 1 34N43 95w54 6:23:36
Gracemont 8 1 35N11 98w16 6:33:04
Grady 34 1 34N01 97w40 6:30:40
Graham 10 1 34N20 97w28 6:29:52
Grainola 57 1 36N56 96w39 6:26:36
Grandfield 71 1 34N14 98w41 6:34:44
Grand Lake Towne 49 1 36N30 95w02 6:20:08
Granite 28 1 34N58 99w23 6:37:32
Grant 12 1 33N57 95w31 6:22:04
Gray 4 4 36N34 100w49 6:43:16
Gray Horse 57 1 36N33 96w39 6:26:36
Grayson 56 1 35N30 95w52 6:23:28
Greenfield 6 1 35N44 98w23 6:33:32
Green Pastures 55 1 35N29 97w22 6:29:28
Greig 55 1 36N47 95w38 6:22:32
Griggs 13 4 36N30 101w47 6:47:08
Grimes 65 1 35N28 99w46 6:39:04
Grove 21 1 36N36 94w46 6:19:04
Gulf Junction 9 1 35N32 97w57 6:31:48
Guthrie 42 1 35N53 97w25 6:29:40
Guymon 70 4 36N41 101w29 6:45:56
Haileyville 61 1 34N51 95w35 6:22:20
Hall Addition 72 1 36N08 96w03 6:24:12
Hallett 59 1 36N14 96w34 6:26:16
Hall Park 14 1 35N14 97w24 6:29:36
Hamden 12 1 34N14 95w37 6:22:28
Hamilton 67 1 35N09 96w30 6:26:00
Hammon 65 1 35N38 99w23 6:37:32
Hanna 46 1 35N16 95w54 6:23:36
Hanson 68 1 35N28 94w47 6:19:08
Happyland 62 1 34N47 96w40 6:26:40
Harden City 62 1 34N36 96w36 6:26:24
Hardesty 70 4 36N37 101w12 6:44:48

OKLAHOMA

Hardy 36	1	36N58	96w48	6:27:12
Harjo 63	1	35N08	96w47	6:27:08
Harmon 23	1	36N09	99w32	6:38:08
Harrah 55	1	35N29	97w10	6:28:40
Harris 45	1	33N45	94w44	6:18:56
Hartshorne 61	1	34N51	95w34	6:22:16
Haskell 51	1	35N50	95w40	6:22:40
Haskew 76	1	36N46	99w07	6:36:28
Hastings 34	1	34N14	98w07	6:32:28
Haw Creek 40	1	34N51	94w38	6:18:32
Hawley 27	1	36N40	98w03	6:32:12
Haworth 45	1	33N51	94w39	6:18:36
Hayward 24	1	36N18	97w35	6:30:20
Haywood 61	1	34N53	95w57	6:23:48
Headrick 33	1	34N38	99w09	6:36:36
Healdton 10	1	34N14	97w29	6:29:56
Healdton Central 10	1	34N14	97w29	6:29:56
Heavener 40	1	34N53	94w36	6:18:24
Helena 2	1	36N33	98w16	6:33:04
Hendrix 7	1	33N46	96w24	6:25:36
Hennepin 25	1	34N31	97w21	6:29:24
Hennessey 37	1	36N06	97w54	6:31:36
Henryetta 56	1	35N27	95w59	6:23:56
Herd 57	1	36N52	96w13	6:24:52
Herring 65	1	35N38	99w23	6:37:32
Hess 33	1	34N29	99w21	6:37:24
Hester 28	1	34N48	99w26	6:37:44
Hewitt 10	1	34N10	97w25	6:29:40
Hext 5	1	35N13	99w52	6:39:28
Hickory 50	1	34N33	97w21	6:29:24
Hicks Addition 55	1	35N29	97w22	6:29:28
Higgins 39	1	34N55	95w19	6:21:16
Hill 40	1	35N08	94w32	6:18:08
Hillsdale 24	1	36N34	97w59	6:31:56
Hill Top 32	1	34N54	96w06	6:24:24
Hinton 8	1	35N28	98w21	6:33:24
Hird 62	1	34N47	96w40	6:26:40
Hitchcock 6	1	35N58	98w21	6:33:24
Hitchita 46	1	35N31	95w45	6:23:00
Hobart 38	1	35N01	99w06	6:36:24
Hockerville 58	1	36N57	94w44	6:18:56
Hodgen 40	1	34N51	94w38	6:18:32
Hoffman 56	1	35N29	95w51	6:23:24
Hog Shooter 74	2	36N45	95w59	6:23:56
Holdenville 32	1	35N05	96w24	6:25:36
Holley Creek 45	1	34N01	94w44	6:18:56
Hollis 29	1	34N41	99w55	6:39:40
Hollister 71	1	34N21	98w52	6:35:28
Hollywood 14	1	35N14	97w25	6:29:40
Homer 62	1	34N47	96w40	6:26:40
Homestead 6	1	36N09	98w24	6:33:36
Hominy 57	1	36N25	96w24	6:25:36
Honobia 40	1	34N33	94w57	6:19:48
Hontubby 40	1	34N53	94w36	6:18:24
Hooker 70	4	36N52	101w13	6:44:52
Hopeton 76	1	36N41	98w40	6:34:40
Hotulke 63	1	35N16	96w56	6:27:44
Howe 40	1	34N57	94w38	6:18:32
Hoyt 31	1	35N16	95w18	6:21:12
Hughes 39	1	34N57	95w05	6:20:20
Hugo 12	1	34N01	95w31	6:22:04
Hulah	1	36N56	96w02	6:24:08
Hulbert 11	1	35N56	95w05	6:20:20
Hulen 17	1	34N21	98w18	6:33:12
Humphreys 33	1	34N33	99w14	6:36:56
Hunter 24	1	36N34	97w40	6:30:40
Hyde Park 51	1	35N45	95w22	6:21:28
Hydro 8	1	35N33	98w35	6:34:20
Idabel 45	1	33N54	94w50	6:19:20
Indiahoma 16	1	34N37	98w45	6:35:00
Indianola 61	1	35N10	95w46	6:23:04
Ingalls 60	1	36N07	97w04	6:28:16
Ingersoll 2	1	36N48	98w24	6:33:36
Inola 66	1	36N09	95w31	6:22:04
Iona 50	1	34N32	96w55	6:27:40
Iron Post 19	1	35N50	96w23	6:25:32
Irving 34	1	34N03	97w58	6:31:52
Isabella 47	1	36N14	98w21	6:33:24
Jackson 7	1	34N00	96w02	6:24:08
Jacktown 41	1	35N30	96w54	6:27:36
Jamestown 66	1	36N32	95w42	6:22:48
Jay 21	1	36N25	94w48	6:19:12
Jefferson 27	1	36N43	97w48	6:31:12
Jenks 72	1	36N01	95w58	6:23:52
Jennings 59	1	36N11	96w34	6:26:16
Jesse 62	1	34N39	96w31	6:26:04
Jester 28	1	35N02	99w31	6:38:04
Jet 2	1	36N40	98w11	6:32:44
Jimtown 43	1	33N54	97w17	6:29:08
Joburn 3	1	34N28	96w13	6:24:52
Johnsonville 44	1	34N54	97w07	6:28:28
Jones 55	1	35N34	97w17	6:29:08
Joy 50	1	34N39	97w10	6:28:40
Jumbo 64	1	34N26	95w44	6:22:56
Kadashan 73	1	36N03	95w42	6:22:48
Kansas 21	1	36N12	94w48	6:19:12
Karen Park 55	1	35N28	97w24	6:29:36
Katie 25	1	34N37	97w24	6:29:36
Kaw City 36	1	36N46	96w50	6:27:20
Keefeton 51	1	35N36	95w21	6:21:24
Keetonville 66	1	36N19	95w37	6:22:28
Kellond 64	1	34N14	95w37	6:22:28
Kellyville 19	1	35N57	96w13	6:24:52
Kemp 7	1	33N46	96w21	6:25:24
Kendrick 41	1	35N47	96w46	6:27:04
Kenefic 7	1	34N09	96w22	6:25:28
Kenefick 7	1	34N09	96w22	6:25:28
Kent 12	1	34N02	95w42	6:22:48
Kenton 13	4	36N54	102w58	6:51:52
Kenwood 21	1	36N19	94w59	6:19:56
Keota 31	1	35N15	94w55	6:19:40
Ketchum 18	1	36N32	95w01	6:20:04
Keyes 13	4	36N49	102w15	6:49:00
Keystone Lake 19	1	36N05	96w25	6:25:40
Kiamichi 64	1	34N37	95w17	6:21:08
Kiefer 19	1	35N57	96w04	6:24:16
Kildare 36	1	36N48	97w03	6:28:12
Kingfisher 37	1	35N52	97w56	6:31:44
Kingston 48	1	34N00	96w43	6:26:52
Kinta 31	1	35N07	95w14	6:20:56
Kiowa 61	1	34N43	95w54	6:23:36
Knowles 4	1	36N53	100w12	6:40:48
Komalty 38	1	35N02	99w06	6:36:24
Konawa 67	1	34N58	96w45	6:27:00
Kosoma 64	1	34N19	95w39	6:22:36
Krebs 61	1	34N56	95w43	6:22:52
Krebs Junction 61	1	34N56	95w46	6:23:04
Kremlin 24	1	36N33	97w50	6:31:20
Kulli 45	1	33N54	94w49	6:19:16
Lacey 37	1	36N07	98w05	6:32:20
Lahoma 24	1	36N23	98w05	6:32:20
Lake Aluma 55	1	35N32	97w27	6:29:48
Lake Creek 28	1	34N58	99w23	6:37:32
Lake Hiwasse 55	1	35N40	97w20	6:29:20
Lake Humphreys 69	1	34N39	97w57	6:31:48
Lakeside Village 16	1	34N46	98w17	6:33:08
Lake Station 72	1	36N09	96w02	6:24:08
Lake Valley 75	1	35N04	98w52	6:35:28
Lakewest 7	1	34N02	95w52	6:23:28
Lamar 32	1	35N06	96w08	6:24:32
Lambert 2	1	36N41	98w25	6:33:40
Lamont 27	1	36N41	97w50	6:31:20
Lane 3	1	34N18	95w59	6:23:56
Langley 49	1	36N28	95w03	6:20:12
Langston 42	1	35N56	97w15	6:29:00
Lark 48	1	34N00	96w43	6:26:52
Last Chance 54	1	35N26	96w18	6:25:12
Laverne 30	1	36N43	99w54	6:39:36
Lawrence 62	1	34N40	96w46	6:27:04
Lawton 16	1	34N37	98w25	6:33:40
Leach 21	1	36N12	94w57	6:19:48
Lebanon 48	1	33N59	96w55	6:27:40
Leedey 22	1	35N52	99w21	6:37:24
Leflore 40	1	34N54	94w59	6:19:56
Lehigh 15	1	34N28	96w13	6:24:52
Lenapah 53	1	36N51	95w38	6:22:32
Lenna 46	1	35N23	95w46	6:23:04
Lenora 22	1	36N03	99w04	6:36:16
Leon 43	1	33N53	97w26	6:29:44
Leonard 72	1	35N55	95w48	6:23:12
Lep 57	1	36N48	96w43	6:26:52
Lequire 31	1	35N06	95w13	6:20:52
Lewisville 31	1	35N07	95w14	6:20:56
Lexington 14	1	35N01	97w20	6:29:20
Liberty 7	1	33N47	96w24	6:25:36
Liberty 68	1	35N24	94w36	6:18:24
Lima 67	1	35N10	96w36	6:26:24
Limestone 39	1	34N55	95w19	6:21:16
Lincolnville 58	1	36N57	94w44	6:18:56
Lindsay 25	1	34N50	97w38	6:30:32
Linn 48	1	34N05	96w46	6:27:04
Little 67	1	35N14	96w41	6:26:44
Little Axe 14	1	35N14	97w25	6:29:40
Little Chief 57	1	36N34	96w42	6:26:48
Little City 48	1	34N05	96w37	6:26:28
Loco 69	1	34N50	97w38	6:30:32
Locust Grove 49	1	36N12	95w10	6:20:40
Lodi 39	1	34N57	95w05	6:20:20
Logan 4	4	36N34	100w13	6:40:52
Lona 31	1	35N07	95w14	6:20:56
Lone Grove 10	1	34N11	97w16	6:29:04
Lone Wolf 38	1	34N59	99w15	6:37:00
Long 68	1	35N24	94w36	6:18:24
Longdale 6	1	36N08	98w33	6:34:12
Lookeba 8	1	35N22	98w22	6:33:28
Lookout 76	1	36N57	99w16	6:37:04
Lotsee 72	1	36N08	96w13	6:24:52
Loveland 71	1	34N18	98w46	6:35:04
Lovell 42	1	36N04	97w38	6:30:32
Loving 40	1	34N53	94w36	6:18:24
Loyal 37	1	35N58	98w07	6:32:28
Lucien 52	1	36N17	97w27	6:29:48
Lugert 38	1	34N54	99w16	6:37:04
Lula 62	1	34N42	96w26	6:25:44
Luther 55	1	35N40	97w12	6:28:48
Lutie 39	1	34N55	95w16	6:21:04
Lynn Addition 57	1	36N24	96w13	6:24:52
Lyons 1	1	35N49	94w37	6:18:28
Macomb 63	1	35N09	97w01	6:28:04
Madden 53	1	36N42	95w38	6:22:32
Madill 48	1	34N06	96w46	6:27:04
Maguire 14	1	35N09	97w23	6:29:32
Manard 11	1	35N48	95w15	6:21:00
Manchester 27	1	37N00	98w02	6:32:08
Mangum 28	1	34N53	99w30	6:38:00
Manitou 71	1	34N30	98w59	6:35:56
Mannford 19	1	36N07	96w21	6:25:24
Manning 61	1	34N55	95w33	6:22:12
Mannsville 35	1	34N11	96w53	6:27:32
Maple 68	1	35N24	94w36	6:18:24
Maramec 59	1	36N15	96w41	6:26:44
Marble City 68	1	35N35	94w49	6:19:16
Marietta 43	1	33N56	97w07	6:28:28
Marland 52	1	36N34	97w09	6:28:36
Marlow 69	1	34N39	97w58	6:31:52
Marshall 42	1	36N09	97w38	6:30:32
Martha 33	1	34N44	99w23	6:37:32
Martin 51	1	35N45	95w22	6:21:28
Mason 54	1	35N34	96w21	6:25:24
Matoy 7	1	34N07	96w16	6:25:04
Maud 63	1	35N08	96w46	6:27:04
Maxwell 62	1	34N47	96w40	6:26:40
May 30	1	36N37	99w45	6:39:00
Mayfield 5	1	35N20	99w53	6:39:32
Maysville 25	1	34N49	97w24	6:29:36
Mazie 49	1	36N06	95w22	6:21:28
McAlester 61	1	34N56	95w46	6:23:04
McBride 48	1	33N56	96w38	6:26:32
McCurtain 31	1	35N09	94w58	6:19:52
McKey 68	1	35N30	94w58	6:19:52
McKiddyville 14	1	35N01	97w20	6:29:20
McKnight 29	1	34N41	99w55	6:39:40
McLain 51	1	35N45	95w22	6:21:28
McLoud 63	1	35N26	97w06	6:28:24
McMan 10	1	34N14	97w29	6:29:56
McMillan 48	1	34N05	96w56	6:27:44
McTees Store 38	1	34N59	99w15	6:37:00
McWillie 2	1	36N31	98w27	6:33:48
Mead 7	1	34N00	96w31	6:26:04
Medford 27	1	36N48	97w44	6:30:56
Medicine Park 16	1	34N44	98w30	6:34:00
Meeker 41	1	35N30	96w54	6:27:36
Meers 16	1	34N47	98w35	6:34:20
Mehan 60	1	36N07	97w04	6:28:16
Mellette 46	1	35N17	95w35	6:22:20
Melvin 11	1	34N56	95w54	6:23:36
Memorial 51	1	35N45	95w22	6:21:28
Meno 47	1	36N23	98w11	6:32:44
Meridian 42	1	35N51	97w15	6:29:00
Messer 12	1	34N01	95w31	6:22:04
Miami 58	1	36N53	94w53	6:19:32
Micawber 54	1	35N38	96w25	6:25:40
Middleberg 26	1	35N06	97w44	6:30:56
Middleton 36	1	36N53	97w03	6:28:12
Midlothian 41	1	35N42	96w53	6:27:32
Midway 3	1	34N31	96w13	6:24:52
Midwest City 55	1	35N27	97w24	6:29:36
Milburn 35	1	34N15	96w33	6:26:12
Milfay 19	1	35N45	96w34	6:26:16
Mill Creek 35	1	34N24	96w49	6:27:16
Miller 64	1	34N19	95w39	6:22:36
Millerton 45	1	33N59	95w01	6:20:04
Milo 10	1	34N20	97w21	6:29:24
Milton 40	1	35N09	94w58	6:19:52
Minco 26	1	35N19	97w57	6:31:48
Mineral Heights 58	1	36N59	94w50	6:19:20
Mocane 4	1	36N54	100w32	6:42:08
Moffett 68	1	35N25	95w27	6:21:48
Monroe 40	1	35N00	94w31	6:18:04
Moodys 11	1	36N02	94w58	6:19:52
Moon 45	1	33N51	94w39	6:18:36
Moore 14	1	35N20	97w29	6:29:56
Mooreland 77	1	36N26	99w12	6:36:48
Moorewood 20	1	35N44	99w21	6:37:24
Moravia 5	1	35N02	99w31	6:38:04
Morris 56	1	35N36	95w51	6:23:24
Morrison 52	1	36N18	97w01	6:28:04
Morse 54	1	35N26	96w18	6:25:12
Mounds 19	1	35N53	96w04	6:24:16
Mountain Park 38	1	34N42	98w57	6:35:48
Mountain View 38	1	35N00	98w45	6:35:00
Mount Herman 45	1	34N01	94w44	6:18:56
Moyers 64	1	34N19	95w39	6:22:36
Mudsand 12	1	34N02	95w42	6:22:48
Muldrow 68	1	35N24	94w36	6:18:24
Mulhall 42	1	36N04	97w24	6:29:36
Murphy 49	1	36N12	95w10	6:20:40
Muse 40	1	34N40	94w46	6:19:04
Muskogee 51	1	35N45	95w22	6:21:28
Mustang 9	1	35N23	97w43	6:30:52
Mutual 77	1	36N14	99w10	6:36:40
Narcissa 58	1	36N53	94w53	6:19:32
Nardin 36	1	36N48	97w27	6:29:48
Nash 27	1	36N40	98w03	6:32:12
Nashoba 64	1	34N29	95w13	6:20:52
Nashville	1	36N40	98w03	6:32:12
Natura 56	1	35N44	96w04	6:24:16
Navina 42	1	35N53	97w26	6:29:44
Nebo 50	1	34N32	96w55	6:27:40
Needmore 14	1	35N09	97w23	6:29:32
Neff 40	1	35N03	94w37	6:18:28
Neill 25	1	34N50	97w37	6:30:28
Nelagoney	1	36N36	96w15	6:25:00
Nelagony 57	1	36N24	96w13	6:24:52
Nelson 12	1	34N14	95w37	6:22:28
Newalla 55	1	35N29	97w32	6:30:08
New Alluwe 53	1	36N37	95w29	6:21:56
Newby 19	1	35N50	96w23	6:25:32
Newcastle 44	1	35N15	97w36	6:30:24
New Cordell 75	1	35N18	98w59	6:35:56
Newkirk 36	1	36N53	97w03	6:28:12
New Liberty 5	1	35N18	99w38	6:38:32
New Lima 67	1	35N10	96w36	6:26:24
New Oberlin 12	1	34N02	95w52	6:23:28
Newport 10	1	34N11	97w03	6:28:12
New Prue 57	1	36N15	96w16	6:25:04
New Tulsa 73	1	36N04	95w40	6:22:40
New Woodville 48	1	33N58	96w39	6:26:36
Nichols Hills 55	1	35N33	97w33	6:30:12
Nicoma Park 55	1	35N30	97w19	6:29:16
Nicut 68	1	35N24	94w36	6:18:24
Nida 35	1	34N09	96w22	6:25:28
Niles 9	1	35N28	98w21	6:33:24
Ninnekah 26	1	34N57	97w56	6:31:44
Noble 14	1	35N08	97w24	6:29:36
Noel 76	1	36N48	98w40	6:34:40
Nolia 64	1	34N29	95w13	6:20:52
Non 32	1	34N58	96w15	6:25:00
Norfolk 60	1	35N59	96w46	6:27:04
Norge 26	1	34N59	98w00	6:32:00
Norman 14	1	35N13	97w26	6:29:44
Norris 39	1	34N57	95w05	6:20:20
North Alfalfa 2	1	36N51	98w19	6:33:16
North Atoka 3	1	34N32	95w54	6:23:36
North Beaver 4	1	36N53	100w40	6:42:40
North Canadian 9	1	35N40	97w57	6:31:48
North Central Bryan 7	1	34N04	96w12	6:24:48

 OKLAHOMA

North Central Pittsburg 61	1	35N07	95w46	6:23:04
North Central Pontotoc 62	1	34N51	96w37	6:26:28
North Cherokee 11	1	36N04	94w59	6:19:56
North Cleveland 14	1	35N18	97w23	6:29:32
North Craig 18	1	36N55	95w09	6:20:36
North Enid 24	1	36N26	97w52	6:31:28
North Logan 42	1	36N06	97w30	6:30:00
North Marshall 48	1	34N05	96w48	6:27:12
North McAlester 61	1	34N56	95w46	6:23:04
North Mc Curtain 45	1	34N24	94w45	6:19:00
North Miami 58	1	36N55	94w53	6:19:32
North Pushmataha 64	1	34N36	95w16	6:21:04
Northside 72	1	36N11	95w59	6:23:56
Northwest 55	1	35N29	97w32	6:30:08
Nowata 53	1	36N42	95w38	6:22:32
Noxie 53	1	36N55	95w48	6:23:12
Nursery 7	1	34N00	96w23	6:25:32
Nuyaka 56	1	35N39	96w08	6:24:32
Oak Grove 60	1	35N59	96w37	6:26:28
Oak Grove 73	1	36N02	95w48	6:23:12
Oak Hill 45	1	34N01	94w44	6:18:56
Oakhurst 72	1	36N05	96w04	6:24:16
Oakland 48	1	34N06	96w48	6:27:12
Oakman 62	1	34N47	96w40	6:26:40
Oakridge 19	1	36N05	96w04	6:24:16
Oaks 21	1	36N10	94w51	6:19:24
Oakwood 22	1	35N56	98w42	6:34:48
Oberlin 7	1	34N02	95w52	6:23:28
Ochelata 74	1	36N36	95w59	6:23:56
Octavia 40	1	34N32	94w42	6:18:48
Oglesby 74	1	36N38	95w51	6:23:24
Oil Center 62	1	34N47	96w40	6:26:40
Oil City 10	1	34N10	97w25	6:29:40
Oilton 19	1	36N05	96w35	6:26:20
Okarche 37	1	35N44	97w58	6:31:52
Okay 73	1	35N51	95w19	6:21:16
Okeene 6	1	36N07	98w19	6:33:16
Okemah 54	1	35N26	96w19	6:25:16
Okesa 57	2	36N45	95w59	6:23:56
Okfuskee 54	1	35N26	96w18	6:25:12
Oklahoma City 55	1	35N30	97w30	6:30:00
Oklahoma College Of Liberal 26	1	35N02	97w57	6:31:48
Okmulgee 56	1	35N37	95w58	6:23:52
Oktaha 51	1	35N35	95w29	6:21:56
Old Allison 7	1	33N56	96w26	6:25:44
Oleta 64	1	34N12	95w21	6:21:24
Olive 19	1	35N59	96w37	6:26:28
Olney 15	1	34N31	96w13	6:24:52
Olustee 33	1	34N33	99w25	6:37:40
Omega 37	1	35N52	98w12	6:32:48
Oneta 73	1	36N02	95w48	6:23:12
Oolagah 66	1	36N27	95w43	6:22:52
Oologah 66	1	36N27	95w42	6:22:48
Optima 70	4	36N46	101w21	6:45:24
Orienta 47	1	36N21	98w29	6:33:56
Orion 47	1	36N17	98w29	6:33:56
Orlando 42	1	36N09	97w23	6:29:32
Orr 43	1	34N02	97w32	6:30:08
Osage 57	1	36N17	96w25	6:25:40
Osage Hills Estates 72	1	36N08	96w03	6:24:12
Osage Indian Reservation 57	1	36N24	96w13	6:24:52
Oscar 34	1	33N59	97w45	6:31:00
Ottawa 58	1	36N53	94w53	6:19:32
Overbrook 43	1	34N04	97w09	6:28:36
Owasso 72	1	36N16	95w51	6:23:24
Pacific Junction 9	1	35N32	97w57	6:31:48
Paden 54	1	35N30	96w34	6:26:16
Page 40	1	34N43	94w33	6:18:12
Panama 40	1	35N10	94w40	6:18:40
Panola 39	1	34N56	95w13	6:20:52
Paoli 25	1	34N50	97w16	6:29:04
Paradise Hill 68	1	35N28	94w47	6:19:08
Parker 15	1	34N31	96w13	6:24:52
Park Hill 11	1	35N52	94w58	6:19:52
Parkland 41	1	35N54	96w52	6:27:28
Patterson 39	1	34N55	95w19	6:21:16
Pauls Valley 25	1	34N44	97w13	6:28:52
Pawhuska 57	1	36N40	96w20	6:25:20
Pawnee 59	1	36N20	96w48	6:27:12
Paw Paw 68	1	35N24	94w36	6:18:24
Payson 41	1	35N30	96w54	6:27:36
Pearson 63	1	35N04	96w56	6:27:44
Pearsonia 57	1	36N24	96w13	6:24:52
Peckham 36	1	36N53	97w10	6:28:40
Peggs 11	1	36N05	95w06	6:20:24
Pensacola 49	1	36N27	95w08	6:20:32
Peoria 58	1	36N55	94w40	6:18:40
Perkins 60	1	35N58	97w02	6:28:08
Pernell 25	1	34N34	97w31	6:30:04
Perry 52	1	36N17	97w17	6:29:08
Pershing 57	1	36N34	96w10	6:24:40
Petersburg 34	1	34N10	97w36	6:30:24
Pettit 11	1	35N52	94w58	6:19:52
Pharoah 54	1	35N25	96w07	6:24:28
Phillips 15	1	34N30	96w13	6:24:52
Picher 58	1	36N59	94w50	6:19:20
Pickens 45	1	34N23	95w02	6:20:08
Pickett 62	1	34N47	96w40	6:26:40
Piedmont 9	1	35N38	97w45	6:31:00
Pierce 46	1	35N28	95w31	6:22:04
Pike 43	1	33N56	97w07	6:28:28
Pine Ridge 8	1	35N06	98w26	6:33:44
Pine Springs 3	1	34N16	95w52	6:23:28
Piney 1	1	35N49	94w37	6:18:28
Pink 63	1	35N16	96w56	6:27:44
Pioneer Park 16	1	34N37	98w25	6:33:40
Pittsburg 61	1	34N43	95w51	6:23:24
Plainview 28	1	35N02	99w31	6:38:04
Plainview 76	1	36N46	99w07	6:36:28
Platter 7	1	33N54	96w32	6:26:08
Pleasant Hill 45	1	33N51	94w39	6:18:36
Plunkettville 45	1	34N25	94w29	6:17:56
Pocasset 26	1	35N12	97w58	6:31:52
Pocola 40	1	35N14	94w29	6:17:56
Pollard 45	1	33N51	94w39	6:18:36
Ponca City 36	1	36N42	97w05	6:28:20
Pondcreek 27	1	36N40	97w48	6:31:12
Pontotoc 35	1	35N25	96w07	6:24:28
Pooleville 10	1	34N25	97w24	6:29:36
Port 75	1	35N10	99w10	6:36:40
Porter 73	1	35N52	95w31	6:22:04
Porter Hill 16	1	34N46	98w17	6:33:08
Porum 51	1	35N22	95w16	6:21:04
Potapo 3	1	34N28	96w03	6:24:12
Poteau 40	1	35N03	94w37	6:18:28
Powell 48	1	33N56	96w53	6:27:32
Prague 41	1	35N29	96w41	6:26:44
Prairie Hill 33	1	34N40	99w34	6:38:16
Prattville 72	1	36N08	96w03	6:24:12
Preston 56	1	35N43	95w59	6:23:56
Proctor 1	1	35N58	94w47	6:19:08
Prue 57	1	36N15	96w16	6:25:04
Pruitt 10	1	34N25	97w31	6:30:04
Pryor 49	1	36N19	95w19	6:21:16
Pumpkin Center 16	1	34N37	98w25	6:33:40
Pumpkin Center 56	1	35N36	95w51	6:23:24
Purcell 44	1	35N01	97w22	6:29:28
Purdy 25	1	34N50	97w37	6:30:28
Putnam 22	1	35N51	98w58	6:35:52
Pyramid Corners 18	1	36N50	95w04	6:20:16
Qualls 11	1	35N52	94w58	6:19:52
Quapaw 58	1	36N58	94w47	6:19:08
Quay 59	1	36N10	96w42	6:26:48
Quinlan 77	1	36N27	99w03	6:36:12
Quinton 61	1	35N07	95w22	6:21:28
Raiford 46	1	35N17	95w35	6:22:20
Ralston 59	1	36N30	96w44	6:26:56
Ramona 74	1	36N32	95w55	6:23:40
Ranch Acres 72	1	36N08	95w57	6:23:48
Ranchwood Manor 14	1	35N27	97w31	6:30:04
Randlett 17	1	34N11	98w28	6:33:52
Ratliff City 10	1	34N27	97w31	6:30:04
Rattan 64	1	34N12	95w25	6:21:40
Ravia 35	1	34N14	96w45	6:27:00
Reagan 35	1	34N14	96w41	6:26:44
Reck 10	1	34N10	97w25	6:29:40
Redbird 73	1	35N54	95w36	6:22:24
Redden 3	1	34N30	95w51	6:23:24
Red Hill 31	1	35N16	94w55	6:19:40
Red Horse 55	1	35N28	97w24	6:29:36
Redland 68	1	35N24	94w36	6:18:24
Red Oak 39	1	34N57	95w05	6:20:20
Redrock 52	1	36N28	97w11	6:28:44
Reed 28	1	34N54	99w42	6:38:48
Reeves 51	1	35N45	95w22	6:21:28
Reichert 40	1	34N53	94w36	6:18:24
Remus 63	1	35N20	96w59	6:27:56
Renfrow 27	1	36N55	97w39	6:30:36
Rentiesville 46	1	35N31	95w30	6:22:00
Retrop 5	1	35N10	99w22	6:37:28
Rexroat 10	1	34N10	97w25	6:29:40
Reydon 65	1	35N39	99w55	6:39:40
Rhea 22	1	35N52	99w21	6:37:24
Richards	1	34N46	98w23	6:33:32
Richards Spur 16	1	34N46	98w17	6:33:08
Richland 9	1	35N30	97w45	6:31:00
Richville 61	1	34N56	95w46	6:23:04
Ringling 34	1	34N11	97w36	6:30:24
Ringold 45	1	34N13	95w08	6:20:32
Ringwood 47	1	36N23	98w15	6:33:00
Ripley 60	1	36N01	96w54	6:27:36
Roberta 7	1	34N00	96w23	6:25:32
Rock Island 40	1	35N08	94w32	6:18:08
Rock Island Junction 9	1	35N32	97w57	6:31:48
Rocky 75	1	35N09	99w04	6:36:16
Roff 62	1	34N38	96w50	6:27:20
Roland 68	1	35N25	94w31	6:18:04
Roll 65	1	35N47	99w43	6:38:52
Roosevelt 38	1	34N51	99w01	6:36:04
Rose 49	1	36N13	95w02	6:20:08
Rosedale 44	1	34N55	97w11	6:28:44
Rosston 30	1	36N49	99w56	6:39:44
Rossville 41	1	35N42	97w04	6:28:16
Row 21	1	36N16	94w41	6:18:44
Rubottom 43	1	33N58	97w29	6:29:56
Rufe 45	1	34N07	95w09	6:20:36
Rush Springs 26	1	34N47	97w58	6:31:52
Russell 28	1	34N53	99w30	6:38:00
Russellville 61	1	35N07	95w22	6:21:28
Russett 35	1	34N11	96w51	6:27:24
Ryan 34	1	34N01	97w57	6:31:48
Sacred Heart 63	1	34N58	96w46	6:27:04
Sageeyah 66	1	36N19	95w37	6:22:28
Saint Louis 63	1	35N04	96w52	6:27:28
Salem 46	1	35N28	95w56	6:23:44
Salina 49	1	36N18	95w09	6:20:36
Sallisaw 68	1	35N28	94w47	6:19:08
Salt Fork 27	1	36N38	97w35	6:30:20
Sandbluff 12	1	34N02	95w52	6:23:28
Sand Creek	1	36N51	98w01	6:32:04
Sand Point 7	1	34N00	96w31	6:26:04
Sand Springs 72	1	36N09	96w07	6:24:28
Sansbois 31	1	35N07	95w14	6:20:56
Sapulpa 19	1	36N00	96w07	6:24:28
Sardis 64	1	34N39	95w25	6:21:40
Sasakwa 67	1	34N57	96w31	6:26:04
Savanna 61	1	34N50	95w51	6:23:24
Sawyer 12	1	34N01	95w23	6:21:32
Sayre 5	1	35N18	99w38	6:38:32
Schlegal 60	1	35N59	96w46	6:27:04
Schoeb Switch 2	1	36N46	98w23	6:33:32
Schoolton 67	1	35N26	96w18	6:25:12
Schulter 56	1	35N31	95w57	6:23:48
Scipio 61	1	35N03	95w58	6:23:52
Scott 8	1	35N28	98w21	6:33:24
Scraper 11	1	35N54	94w59	6:19:56
Scullin 50	1	34N31	96w52	6:27:28
Scullyville 40	1	35N15	94w37	6:18:28
Seiling 22	1	36N02	98w47	6:35:08
Selman 30	1	36N48	99w30	6:38:00
Seminole 67	1	35N14	96w41	6:26:44
Sentinel 75	1	35N09	99w11	6:36:44
Sequoyah 66	1	36N19	95w37	6:22:28
Seward 42	1	35N48	97w29	6:29:56
Shady Point 40	1	35N08	94w40	6:18:40
Shamrock 19	1	35N56	96w35	6:26:20
Sharon 77	1	36N17	99w20	6:37:20
Shartel 55	1	35N31	97w32	6:30:08
Shattuck 23	1	36N16	99w53	6:39:32
Shawnee 63	1	35N20	96w55	6:27:40
Shay 48	1	34N00	96w43	6:26:52
Sheridan 16	1	34N37	98w25	6:33:40
Sherwood 45	1	34N01	94w44	6:18:56
Shidler 57	1	36N47	96w40	6:26:40
Shinewell 45	1	33N51	94w39	6:18:36
Shults 45	1	33N54	94w49	6:19:16
Sickles 8	1	35N22	98w22	6:33:28
Sill 16	1	34N41	98w30	6:34:00
Silo 7	1	34N03	96w29	6:25:56
Silver City 19	1	36N11	96w34	6:26:16
Simon 43	1	34N04	97w09	6:28:36
Simpson 48	1	34N05	96w46	6:27:04
Skedee 59	1	36N23	96w42	6:26:48
Skiatook 72	1	36N22	96w00	6:24:00
Slapout 4	1	36N37	100w07	6:40:28
Slaughterville 14	1	35N01	97w20	6:29:20
Slick 19	1	35N47	96w16	6:25:04
Smelter Prairie 74	2	36N45	95w59	6:23:56
Smith Lee 7	1	34N00	96w02	6:24:08
Smith Village 55	1	35N27	97w27	6:29:48
Smithville 45	1	34N28	94w39	6:18:36
Snow 64	1	34N24	95w25	6:21:40
Snyder 38	1	34N40	98w57	6:35:48
Sobol 64	1	34N01	95w16	6:21:04
Soper 12	1	34N02	95w42	6:22:48
Southard 6	1	36N04	98w29	6:33:56
South Beaver 4	1	36N39	100w29	6:41:56
South Bryan 7	1	33N47	96w21	6:25:24
South Canadian 9	1	35N26	97w58	6:31:52
South Central Pontotoc 62	1	34N38	96w39	6:26:36
South Cherokee 11	1	35N48	94w58	6:19:52
South Cleveland 14	1	35N04	97w13	6:28:52
South Coffeyville 53	1	36N59	95w37	6:22:28
Southeast 72	1	36N06	95w53	6:23:32
South Ellis 23	1	36N05	99w44	6:38:56
South Hughes 32	1	34N53	96w16	6:25:04
South Jefferson 34	1	34N02	97w51	6:31:24
South Kay 36	1	36N41	97w07	6:28:28
South Latimer 39	1	34N45	95w14	6:20:56
South Le Flore 40	1	34N32	94w41	6:18:44
South Marshall 48	1	33N56	96w46	6:27:04
South Roger Mills 65	1	35N28	99w46	6:39:04
Southside 72	1	36N06	95w58	6:23:52
South Wagoner 73	1	35N51	95w30	6:22:00
Southwest 55	1	35N26	97w33	6:30:12
South Woods 76	1	36N34	98w42	6:34:48
Sparks 41	1	35N37	96w49	6:27:16
Spaulding 32	1	35N05	96w24	6:25:36
Spavinaw 49	1	36N23	95w03	6:20:12
Speer 12	1	34N07	95w33	6:22:12
Spelter City 56	1	35N28	95w56	6:23:44
Spencer 55	1	35N31	97w23	6:29:32
Spencerville 12	1	34N08	95w21	6:21:24
Sperry 72	1	36N18	95w59	6:23:56
Spiro 40	1	35N15	94w37	6:18:28
Sportsmen Acres 49	1	36N18	95w19	6:21:16
Springer 10	1	34N19	97w08	6:28:32
Spring Lake Park 55	1	35N31	97w29	6:29:56
Stafford 20	1	35N33	99w07	6:36:28
Stanley 64	1	34N35	95w21	6:21:24
Stapp 40	1	34N51	94w38	6:18:32
Star 31	1	35N16	94w55	6:19:40
State Capitol 55	1	35N31	97w30	6:30:00
Stecker 8	1	34N57	98w19	6:33:16
Steedman 62	1	34N53	96w24	6:25:36
Steen 24	1	36N25	97w52	6:31:28
Sterling 16	1	34N45	98w10	6:32:40
Stidham 46	1	35N22	95w42	6:22:48
Stigler 31	1	35N15	95w08	6:20:32
Stillwater 60	1	36N07	97w04	6:28:16
Stilwell 1	1	35N49	94w38	6:18:32
Stock Yards 55	1	35N27	97w33	6:30:12
Stonebluff 73	1	35N49	95w41	6:22:44
Stonewall 62	1	34N39	96w32	6:26:08
Stony Point 40	1	35N15	94w37	6:18:28
Story 25	1	34N49	97w25	6:29:40

OKLAHOMA

Straight 70	4	36N41	101w29	6:45:56
Strang 49	1	36N25	95w08	6:20:32
Stratford 25	1	34N48	96w58	6:27:52
Stringtown 3	1	34N28	99w36	6:38:24
Stringtown 17	1	34N21	98w18	6:33:12
Strong City 65	1	35N40	99w36	6:38:24
Stroud 41	1	35N45	96w40	6:26:40
Stuart 32	1	34N54	96w06	6:24:24
Sugden 34	1	34N05	97w59	6:31:56
Sullivan Village 16	1	34N37	98w25	6:33:40
Sulphur 50	1	34N31	96w58	6:27:52
Summerfield 40	1	34N58	94w43	6:18:52
Summit 51	1	35N40	95w26	6:21:44
Sumner 52	1	36N19	97w07	6:28:28
Sunkist 12	1	34N02	95w52	6:23:28
Sunray 69	1	34N25	97w58	6:31:52
Sweetwater 65	1	35N25	99w55	6:39:40
Swink 12	1	34N01	95w12	6:20:48
Tabler 26	1	35N03	97w49	6:31:16
Taft 51	1	35N46	95w32	6:22:08
Tahlequah 11	1	35N55	94w58	6:19:52
Tahona 40	1	35N08	94w32	6:18:08
Talala 66	1	36N32	95w42	6:22:48
Talihina 40	1	34N45	95w03	6:20:12
Tallant 57	1	36N34	96w10	6:24:40
Taloga 22	1	36N02	98w58	6:35:52
Tamaha 31	1	35N24	94w59	6:19:56
Tangier 77	1	36N26	99w24	6:37:36
Tatums 10	1	34N29	97w28	6:29:52
Taylor 17	1	34N11	98w28	6:33:52
Tecumseh 63	1	35N15	96w56	6:27:44
Tegarden 76	1	36N48	98w40	6:34:40
Temple 17	1	34N16	98w14	6:32:56
Teresita 11	1	36N13	95w02	6:20:08
Terlton 59	1	36N11	96w29	6:25:56
Terral 34	1	33N54	97w57	6:31:48
Texanna 46	1	35N28	95w31	6:22:04
Texas Junction 9	1	35N32	97w57	6:31:48
Texhoma 70	4	36N30	101w47	6:47:08
Texola 5	1	35N13	100w00	6:40:00
Thackerville 43	1	33N48	97w09	6:28:36
The Village 55	1	35N34	97w33	6:30:12
Thomas 20	1	35N45	98w45	6:35:00
Ti 61	1	34N45	95w46	6:23:04
Tiawah 66	1	36N19	95w37	6:22:28
Tidal 19	1	35N59	96w37	6:26:28
Tidmore 67	1	35N14	96w41	6:26:44
Tinker Air Force Base 55	1	35N29	97w32	6:30:08
Tipton 71	1	34N30	99w08	6:36:32
Tishomingo 35	1	34N14	96w41	6:26:44
Titanic 1	1	35N49	94w37	6:18:28
Tom 45	1	33N44	94w35	6:18:20
Tonkawa 36	1	36N41	97w18	6:29:12
Topsy 21	1	36N24	95w03	6:20:12
Treece 58	1	36N59	94w50	6:19:20
Tribbey 63	1	35N07	97w04	6:28:16
Trousdale 63	1	34N58	97w02	6:28:08
Troy 35	1	34N23	96w50	6:27:20
Tryon 41	1	35N52	96w58	6:27:52
Tucker 40	1	35N18	94w44	6:18:56
Tullahassee 73	1	35N50	95w26	6:21:44
Tulsa 72	1	36N10	95w55	6:23:40
Tupelo 15	1	34N36	96w26	6:25:44
Turkey Ford 21	1	36N35	94w48	6:19:12
Turley 72	1	36N14	95w58	6:23:52
Turpin 4	4	36N52	100w52	6:43:28
Tushka 3	1	34N19	96w10	6:24:40
Tuskahoma 64	1	34N37	95w17	6:21:08
Tuskegee 19	1	35N50	96w23	6:25:32
Tussy 10	1	34N30	97w33	6:30:12
Tuttle 26	1	35N17	97w49	6:31:16
Tuxedo Park 74	2	36N45	95w59	6:23:56
Twin Cities 61	1	34N51	95w36	6:22:24
Twin Hills 56	1	35N37	95w58	6:23:52
Twin Oaks 21	1	36N10	94w51	6:19:24
Tyler 48	1	34N05	96w46	6:27:04
Tyrone 70	4	36N57	101w04	6:44:16
Uncas 36	1	36N48	96w56	6:27:44
Unger 12	1	34N02	95w52	6:23:28
Union 72	1	36N02	95w48	6:23:12
Union City 9	1	35N23	97w57	6:31:48
Union Valley 62	1	34N39	96w31	6:26:04
University 24	1	36N25	97w52	6:31:28
University 63	1	35N20	96w59	6:27:56
Upson 68	1	35N30	94w58	6:19:52
Utica 7	1	33N54	96w14	6:24:56
Valley Brook 55	1	35N25	97w29	6:29:56
Valley Drive 72	1	36N08	96w03	6:24:12
Valley Park 66	1	36N19	95w37	6:22:28
Valliant 45	1	34N00	95w06	6:20:24
Vamoosa 67	1	34N58	96w46	6:27:04
Vance Air Force Base 24	1	36N25	97w52	6:31:28
Vanoss 62	1	34N46	96w52	6:27:28
Velma 69	1	34N28	97w40	6:30:40
Vera 74	1	36N27	95w53	6:23:32
Verden 26	1	35N05	98w05	6:32:20
Verdigris 66	1	36N19	95w37	6:22:28
Vernon 46	1	35N13	95w56	6:23:44
Vian 68	1	35N30	94w58	6:19:52
Vici 22	1	36N09	99w18	6:37:12
Victory 33	1	34N33	99w25	6:37:40
Vinco 60	1	35N58	97w02	6:28:08
Vining 2	1	36N40	98w11	6:32:44
Vinita 18	1	36N39	95w09	6:20:36
Vinson 29	1	34N54	99w52	6:39:28
Virgil 12	1	34N01	95w22	6:21:28
Vista 63	1	34N58	96w46	6:27:04
Vivian 46	1	35N17	95w35	6:22:20
Wade 7	1	34N00	96w02	6:24:08
Wagoner 73	1	35N58	95w22	6:21:28
Wainwright 51	1	35N37	95w34	6:22:16
Wakita 27	1	36N53	97w55	6:31:40
Walls 40	1	34N57	95w05	6:20:20
Wallville 25	1	34N50	97w37	6:30:28
Walnut 9	1	35N27	98w14	6:32:56
Walters 17	1	34N22	98w19	6:33:16
Wanette 63	1	34N58	97w02	6:28:08
Wann 53	1	36N55	95w48	6:23:12
Wapanucka 35	1	34N23	96w26	6:25:44
Wardville 3	1	34N39	96w02	6:24:08
Warner 51	1	35N30	95w18	6:21:12
Warr Acres 55	1	35N32	99w01	6:36:04
Warren 33	1	34N47	99w20	6:37:20
Warwick 41	1	35N41	97w00	6:28:00
Washington 44	1	35N04	97w29	6:29:56
Washita 8	1	35N06	98w21	6:33:24
Washunga 36	1	36N47	96w50	6:27:20
Watchorn 59	1	36N18	97w01	6:28:04
Waterloo 42	1	35N39	97w29	6:29:56
Watonga 6	1	35N51	98w25	6:33:40
Watova 53	1	36N37	95w39	6:22:36
Watson 45	1	34N27	94w33	6:18:12
Watts 1	1	36N07	94w34	6:18:16
Wauhillau 1	1	35N49	94w37	6:18:28
Waukomis 24	1	36N17	97w54	6:31:36
Waurika 34	1	34N10	98w00	6:32:00
Wayne 44	1	34N55	97w19	6:29:16
Waynoka 76	1	36N35	98w53	6:35:32
Wealand 58	1	36N53	94w53	6:19:32
Weatherford 20	1	35N32	98w43	6:34:52
Weathers 61	1	34N39	95w35	6:22:20
Webb 22	1	36N01	99w17	6:37:08
Webb City 57	1	36N48	96w42	6:26:48
Webbers Falls 51	1	35N31	95w08	6:20:32
Wekiwa 72	1	36N08	96w03	6:24:12
Welch 18	1	36N52	95w06	6:20:24
Weleetka 54	1	35N20	96w08	6:24:32
Welling 11	1	35N53	94w54	6:19:36
Wellston 41	1	35N42	97w04	6:28:16
Welty 54	1	35N38	96w25	6:25:40
West Atoka 3	1	34N17	96w17	6:25:08
West Canadian 9	1	35N38	98w12	6:32:48
West Central Pontotoc 62	1	34N46	96w50	6:27:20
West Central Stephens 69	1	34N31	97w58	6:31:52
West Choctaw 12	1	34N01	95w47	6:23:08
West Coal 15	1	34N34	96w25	6:25:40
West Haskell 31	1	35N12	95w19	6:21:16
West Jackson 33	1	34N34	99w33	6:38:12
West Johnston 35	1	34N20	96w34	6:26:16
West Love 43	1	33N57	97w25	6:29:40
West Murray 50	1	34N32	97w07	6:28:28
Westport 59	1	36N18	96w28	6:25:52
West Siloam Springs 21	1	36N11	94w35	6:18:20
West Texas 70	4	36N47	101w51	6:47:24
West Tulsa 72	1	36N06	96w01	6:24:04
Westville 1	1	36N00	94w34	6:18:16
West Woods 76	1	36N50	99w09	6:36:36
Wetumka 32	1	35N14	96w15	6:25:00
Wewoka 67	1	35N09	96w30	6:26:00
Wheatland 55	1	35N29	97w32	6:30:08
Wheeless 13	4	36N43	102w54	6:51:36
White Bead 25	1	34N46	97w18	6:29:12
White Eagle 36	1	36N45	97w00	6:28:00
Whitefield 31	1	35N15	95w14	6:20:56
White Oak 18	1	36N31	95w09	6:20:36
Whitesboro 40	1	34N41	94w53	6:19:32
Whittier 72	1	36N09	95w59	6:23:56
Wilburton 39	1	34N55	95w19	6:21:16
Wild Horse 57	1	36N25	96w24	6:25:36
Williams 40	1	35N08	94w32	6:18:08
Willis 48	1	34N00	96w43	6:26:52
Willow 28	1	35N03	99w31	6:38:04
Will Rogers 55	1	35N27	97w31	6:30:04
Wilson 10	1	34N10	97w26	6:29:44
Wimer 18	1	37N00	95w37	6:22:28
Winganon 66	1	36N32	95w26	6:21:44
Wirt 10	1	34N14	97w29	6:29:56
Wister 40	1	34N58	94w43	6:18:52
Wolco 57	1	36N34	96w10	6:24:40
Wolf 67	1	35N08	96w47	6:27:08
Woodford 10	1	34N19	97w08	6:28:32
Woodlawn Park 55	1	35N31	97w39	6:30:36
Woods 55	1	35N29	97w16	6:29:04
Woodville 48	1	33N58	96w39	6:26:36
Woodward 77	1	36N26	99w24	6:37:36
Wright City 45	1	34N08	95w00	6:20:00
Wyandotte 58	1	36N48	94w44	6:18:56
Wybark 51	1	35N45	95w22	6:21:28
Wye 63	1	35N09	97w01	6:28:04
Wynnewood 25	1	34N39	97w10	6:28:40
Wynona 57	1	36N33	96w20	6:25:20
Yale 60	1	36N07	96w42	6:26:48
Yanush 39	1	34N43	95w19	6:21:16
Yarnaby 7	1	33N47	96w24	6:25:36
Yeager 32	1	35N09	96w21	6:25:24
Yewed 2	1	36N41	98w25	6:33:40
Yonkers 73	1	36N12	95w10	6:20:40
Yost 60	1	36N13	96w56	6:27:44
Yuba 7	1	33N53	96w10	6:24:40
Yukon 9	1	35N31	97w45	6:31:00
Zafra 40	1	34N31	94w30	6:18:00
Zena 21	1	36N29	94w53	6:19:32
Zoe 40	1	34N51	94w38	6:18:32

TIME TABLES

OR # 1
Before 11/18/1883 LMT
11/18/1883 12:00 MST
3/31/1918 02:00 MWT
10/27/1918 02:00 MST
3/30/1919 02:00 MWT
10/26/1919 02:00 MST
2/09/1942 02:00 MWT
9/30/1945 02:00 MST
4/28/1963 02:00 MDT
10/27/1963 02:00 MST
4/26/1964 02:00 MDT
10/25/1964 02:00 MST
4/25/1965 02:00 MDT
10/31/1965 02:00 MST
4/30/1967 02:00 MDT
10/29/1967 02:00 MST
4/28/1968 02:00 MDT
10/27/1968 02:00 MST
4/27/1969 02:00 MDT
10/26/1969 02:00 MST
4/26/1970 02:00 MDT
10/25/1970 02:00 MST
4/25/1971 02:00 MDT
10/31/1971 02:00 MST
4/30/1972 02:00 MDT
10/29/1972 02:00 MST
4/29/1973 02:00 MDT
10/28/1973 02:00 MST
2/03/1974 02:00 MDT
10/27/1974 02:00 MST
2/23/1975 02:00 US#1

OR # 2
Before 11/18/1883 LMT
11/18/1883 12:00 PST
3/31/1918 02:00 PWT
10/27/1918 02:00 PST
3/30/1919 02:00 PWT
10/26/1919 02:00 PST
2/09/1942 02:00 PWT
9/30/1945 02:00 PST
4/30/1950 02:00 PDT
9/24/1950 02:00 PST
4/29/1951 02:00 PDT
9/30/1951 02:00 PST
4/28/1963 02:00 PDT
10/27/1963 02:00 PST
4/26/1964 02:00 PDT
10/25/1964 02:00 PST
4/25/1965 02:00 PDT
10/31/1965 02:00 PST
4/24/1966 02:00 PDT
10/30/1966 02:00 PST
4/30/1967 02:00 US#1

OR # 3
Before 11/18/1883 LMT
11/18/1883 12:00 PST
3/31/1918 02:00 PWT
10/27/1918 02:00 PST
3/30/1919 02:00 PWT
10/26/1919 02:00 PST
2/09/1942 02:00 PWT
9/30/1945 02:00 PST
4/30/1950 02:00 PDT
9/24/1950 02:00 PST
4/29/1951 02:00 PDT
9/30/1951 02:00 PST
4/27/1952 02:00 PDT
9/28/1952 02:00 PST
4/28/1963 02:00 PDT
10/27/1963 02:00 PST
4/26/1964 02:00 PDT
10/25/1964 02:00 PST
4/25/1965 02:00 PDT
10/31/1965 02:00 PST
4/24/1966 02:00 PDT
10/30/1966 02:00 PST
4/30/1967 02:00 US#1

OR # 4
Before 11/18/1883 LMT
11/18/1883 12:00 PST
3/31/1918 02:00 PWT
10/27/1918 02:00 PST
3/30/1919 02:00 PWT
10/26/1919 02:00 PST
2/09/1942 02:00 PWT
9/30/1945 02:00 PST
4/30/1950 02:00 PDT
9/24/1950 02:00 PST
4/29/1951 02:00 PDT
9/30/1951 02:00 PST
5/07/1961 01:00 PDT
9/24/1961 02:00 PST
4/29/1962 02:00 PDT
9/29/1962 02:00 PST
4/28/1963 02:00 PDT
10/27/1963 02:00 PST
4/26/1964 02:00 PDT
10/25/1964 02:00 PST
4/25/1965 02:00 PDT
10/31/1965 02:00 PST
4/24/1966 02:00 PDT
10/30/1966 02:00 PST
4/30/1967 02:00 US#1

OR # 5
Before 11/18/1883 LMT
11/18/1883 12:00 PST
3/31/1918 02:00 PWT
10/27/1918 02:00 PST
3/30/1919 02:00 PWT
10/26/1919 02:00 PST
2/09/1942 02:00 PWT
9/30/1945 02:00 PST
4/30/1950 02:00 PDT
9/24/1950 02:00 PST
4/29/1951 02:00 PDT
9/30/1951 02:00 PST
4/27/1952 02:00 PDT
9/28/1952 02:00 PST
5/07/1961 01:00 PDT
9/24/1961 02:00 PST
4/29/1962 02:00 PDT
9/29/1962 02:00 PST
4/28/1963 02:00 PDT
10/27/1963 02:00 PST
4/26/1964 02:00 PDT
10/25/1964 02:00 PST
4/25/1965 02:00 PDT
10/31/1965 02:00 PST
4/24/1966 02:00 PDT
10/30/1966 02:00 PST
4/30/1967 02:00 US#1

OR # 6
Before 11/18/1883 LMT
11/18/1883 12:00 PST
3/31/1918 02:00 PWT
10/27/1918 02:00 PST
3/30/1919 02:00 PWT
10/26/1919 02:00 PST
2/09/1942 02:00 PWT
9/30/1945 02:00 PST
4/24/1949 02:00 PDT
9/25/1949 02:00 PST
4/30/1950 02:00 PDT
9/24/1950 02:00 PST
4/29/1951 02:00 PDT
9/30/1951 02:00 PST
4/27/1952 02:00 PDT
9/28/1952 02:00 PST
5/07/1961 01:00 PDT
9/24/1961 02:00 PST
4/29/1962 02:00 PDT
9/29/1962 02:00 PST
4/28/1963 02:00 PDT
10/27/1963 02:00 PST
4/26/1964 02:00 PDT
10/25/1964 02:00 PST
4/25/1965 02:00 PDT
10/31/1965 02:00 PST
4/24/1966 02:00 PDT
10/30/1966 02:00 PST
4/30/1967 02:00 US#1

OR # 7
Before 11/18/1883 LMT
11/18/1883 12:00 PST
3/31/1918 02:00 PWT
10/27/1918 02:00 PST
3/30/1919 02:00 PWT
10/26/1919 02:00 PST
2/09/1942 02:00 PWT
9/30/1945 02:00 PST
4/30/1950 02:00 PDT
9/24/1950 02:00 PST
4/29/1951 02:00 PDT
9/30/1951 02:00 PST
4/29/1962 02:00 PDT
9/29/1962 02:00 PST
4/28/1963 02:00 PDT
10/27/1963 02:00 PST
4/26/1964 02:00 PDT
10/25/1964 02:00 PST
4/25/1965 02:00 PDT
10/31/1965 02:00 PST
4/24/1966 02:00 PDT
10/30/1966 02:00 PST
4/30/1967 02:00 US#1

OR # 8
Before 11/18/1883 LMT
11/18/1883 12:00 PST
3/31/1918 02:00 PWT
10/27/1918 02:00 PST
3/30/1919 02:00 PWT
10/26/1919 02:00 PST
2/09/1942 02:00 PWT
9/30/1945 02:00 PST
4/30/1950 02:00 PDT
9/24/1950 02:00 PST
4/29/1951 02:00 PDT
9/30/1951 02:00 PST
4/27/1952 02:00 PDT
9/28/1952 02:00 PST
4/29/1962 02:00 PDT
9/29/1962 02:00 PST
4/28/1963 02:00 PDT
10/27/1963 02:00 PST
4/26/1964 02:00 PDT
10/25/1964 02:00 PST
4/25/1965 02:00 PDT
10/31/1965 02:00 PST
4/24/1966 02:00 PDT
10/30/1966 02:00 PST
4/30/1967 02:00 US#1

OR # 9
Before 11/18/1883 LMT
11/18/1883 12:00 PST
3/31/1918 02:00 PWT
10/27/1918 02:00 PST
3/30/1919 02:00 PWT
10/26/1919 02:00 PST
2/09/1942 02:00 PWT
9/30/1945 02:00 PST
4/30/1950 02:00 PDT
9/24/1950 02:00 PST
4/29/1951 02:00 PDT
9/30/1951 02:00 PST
5/27/1962 02:00 PDT
9/29/1962 02:00 PST
4/28/1963 02:00 PDT
10/27/1963 02:00 PST
4/26/1964 02:00 PDT
10/25/1964 02:00 PST
4/25/1965 02:00 PDT
10/31/1965 02:00 PST
4/24/1966 02:00 PDT
10/30/1966 02:00 PST
4/30/1967 02:00 US#1

OR # 10
Before 11/18/1883 LMT
11/18/1883 12:00 PST
3/31/1918 02:00 PWT
10/27/1918 02:00 PST
3/30/1919 02:00 PWT
10/26/1919 02:00 PST
2/09/1942 02:00 PWT
9/30/1945 02:00 PST
4/24/1949 02:00 PDT
9/25/1949 02:00 PST
4/30/1950 02:00 PDT
9/04/1950 02:00 PST
4/29/1951 02:00 PDT
9/30/1951 02:00 PST
4/27/1952 02:00 PDT
9/28/1952 02:00 PST
5/07/1961 01:00 PDT
9/24/1961 02:00 PST
4/29/1962 02:00 PDT
9/29/1962 02:00 PST
4/28/1963 02:00 PDT
10/27/1963 02:00 PST
4/26/1964 02:00 PDT
10/25/1964 02:00 PST
4/25/1965 02:00 PDT
10/31/1965 02:00 PST
4/24/1966 02:00 PDT
10/30/1966 02:00 PST
4/30/1967 02:00 US#1

OR # 11
Before 11/18/1883 LMT
11/18/1883 12:00 PST
3/31/1918 02:00 PWT
10/27/1918 02:00 PST
3/30/1919 02:00 PWT
10/26/1919 02:00 PST
2/09/1942 02:00 PWT
9/30/1945 02:00 PST
4/30/1950 02:00 PDT
9/24/1950 02:00 PST
4/29/1951 02:00 PDT
9/30/1951 02:00 PST
4/29/1962 02:00 PDT
9/29/1962 02:00 PST
4/28/1963 02:00 PDT
10/27/1963 02:00 PST
4/26/1964 02:00 PDT
10/25/1964 02:00 PST
4/25/1965 02:00 PDT
10/31/1965 02:00 PST
4/24/1966 02:00 PDT
10/30/1966 02:00 PST
4/30/1967 02:00 US#1

OR # 12
Before 11/18/1883 LMT
11/18/1883 12:00 PST
3/31/1918 02:00 PWT
10/27/1918 02:00 PST
3/30/1919 02:00 PWT
10/26/1919 02:00 PST
2/09/1942 02:00 PWT
9/30/1945 02:00 PST
4/25/1948 02:00 PDT
9/26/1948 02:00 PST
4/24/1949 02:00 PDT
9/11/1949 02:00 PST
4/30/1950 02:00 PDT
9/24/1950 02:00 PST
4/29/1951 02:00 PDT
9/30/1951 02:00 PST
4/30/1952 02:00 PDT
9/28/1952 02:00 PST
5/07/1961 01:00 PDT
9/24/1961 02:00 PST
4/29/1962 02:00 PDT
9/29/1962 02:00 PST
4/28/1963 02:00 PDT
10/27/1963 02:00 PST
4/26/1964 02:00 PDT
10/25/1964 02:00 PST
4/25/1965 02:00 PDT
10/31/1965 02:00 PST
4/24/1966 02:00 PDT
10/30/1966 02:00 PST
4/30/1967 02:00 US#1

OR # 13
Before 11/18/1883 LMT
11/18/1883 12:00 PST
3/31/1918 02:00 PWT
10/27/1918 02:00 PST
3/30/1919 02:00 PWT
10/26/1919 02:00 PST
2/09/1942 02:00 PWT
9/30/1945 02:00 PST
4/24/1949 02:00 PDT
9/25/1949 02:00 PST
4/30/1950 02:00 PDT
9/24/1950 02:00 PST
4/29/1951 02:00 PDT
9/30/1951 02:00 PST
4/29/1962 02:00 PDT
9/29/1962 02:00 PST
4/28/1963 02:00 PDT
10/27/1963 02:00 PST
4/26/1964 02:00 PDT
10/25/1964 02:00 PST
4/25/1965 02:00 PDT
10/31/1965 02:00 PST
4/24/1966 02:00 PDT
10/30/1966 02:00 PST
4/30/1967 02:00 US#1

OR # 14
Before 11/18/1883 LMT
11/18/1883 12:00 PST
3/31/1918 02:00 PWT
10/27/1918 02:00 PST
3/30/1919 02:00 PWT
10/26/1919 02:00 PST
2/09/1942 02:00 PWT
9/30/1945 02:00 PST
4/24/1949 02:00 PDT
9/25/1949 02:00 PST
4/30/1950 02:00 PDT
9/24/1950 02:00 PST
4/29/1951 02:00 PDT
9/30/1951 02:00 PST
4/27/1952 02:00 PDT
9/28/1952 02:00 PST
4/29/1962 02:00 PDT
9/29/1962 02:00 PST
4/28/1963 02:00 PDT
10/27/1963 02:00 PST
4/26/1964 02:00 PDT
10/25/1964 02:00 PST
4/25/1965 02:00 PDT
10/31/1965 02:00 PST
4/24/1966 02:00 PDT
10/30/1966 02:00 PST
4/30/1967 02:00 US#1

OR # 15
Before 11/18/1883 LMT
11/18/1883 12:00 PST
3/31/1918 02:00 PWT
10/27/1918 02:00 PST
3/30/1919 02:00 PWT
10/26/1919 02:00 PST
2/09/1942 02:00 PWT
9/30/1945 02:00 PST
4/24/1949 02:00 PDT
9/25/1949 02:00 PST
4/30/1950 02:00 PDT
9/24/1950 02:00 PST
4/29/1951 02:00 PDT
9/30/1951 02:00 PST
4/28/1963 02:00 PDT
10/27/1963 02:00 PST
4/26/1964 02:00 PDT
10/25/1964 02:00 PST
4/25/1965 02:00 PDT
10/31/1965 02:00 PST
4/24/1966 02:00 PDT
10/30/1966 02:00 PST
4/30/1967 02:00 US#1

OR # 16
Before 11/18/1883 LMT
11/18/1883 12:00 PST
3/31/1918 02:00 PWT
10/27/1918 02:00 PST
3/30/1919 02:00 PWT
10/26/1919 02:00 PST
2/09/1942 02:00 PWT
9/30/1945 02:00 PST
4/25/1948 02:00 PDT
9/26/1948 02:00 PST
4/30/1950 02:00 PDT
9/24/1950 02:00 PST
4/29/1951 02:00 PDT
9/30/1951 02:00 PST
4/28/1963 02:00 PDT
10/27/1963 02:00 PST
4/26/1964 02:00 PDT
10/25/1964 02:00 PST
4/25/1965 02:00 PDT
10/31/1965 02:00 PST
4/24/1966 02:00 PDT
10/30/1966 02:00 PST
4/30/1967 02:00 US#1

OR # 17
Before 11/18/1883 LMT
11/18/1883 12:00 PST
3/31/1918 02:00 PWT
10/27/1918 02:00 PST
3/30/1919 02:00 PWT
10/26/1919 02:00 PST
2/09/1942 02:00 PWT
9/30/1945 02:00 PST
4/24/1949 02:00 PDT
9/25/1949 02:00 PST
4/30/1950 02:00 PDT
9/24/1950 02:00 PST
4/29/1951 02:00 PDT
9/30/1951 02:00 PST
5/07/1961 01:00 PDT
9/24/1961 02:00 PST
4/29/1962 02:00 PDT
9/29/1962 02:00 PST
4/28/1963 02:00 PDT
10/27/1963 02:00 PST
4/26/1964 02:00 PDT
10/25/1964 02:00 PST
4/25/1965 02:00 PDT
10/31/1965 02:00 PST
4/24/1966 02:00 PDT
10/30/1966 02:00 PST
4/30/1967 02:00 US#1

COUNTIES

1 Baker
2 Benton
3 Clackamas
4 Clatsop
5 Columbia
6 Coos
7 Crook
8 Curry
9 Deschutes
10 Douglas
11 Gilliam
12 Grant
13 Harney
14 Hood River
15 Jackson
16 Jefferson
17 Josephine
18 Klamath
19 Lake
20 Lane
21 Lincoln
22 Linn
23 Malheur
24 Marion
25 Morrow
26 Multnomah
27 Polk
28 Sherman
29 Tillamook
30 Umatilla
31 Union
32 Wallowa
33 Wasco
34 Washington
35 Wheeler
36 Yamhill

Place	Table	Lat	Long	Time
Acorn Park 20	8	44N05	123w08	8:12:32
Ada 10	2	43N44	124w07	8:16:28
Adams 30	2	45N46	118w34	7:54:16
Adel 19	2	42N11	119w54	7:59:36
Adrian 23	1	43N45	117w04	7:48:16
Agate Beach 21	11	44N41	124w04	8:16:16
Agness 8	2	42N34	124w05	8:16:20
Aims 3	12	45N32	122w26	8:09:44
Airlie 27	2	44N51	123w14	8:12:56

OREGON

Airport 26	12	45N34	122w34	8:10:16
Albany 22	13	44N38	123w06	8:12:24
Albany Yard 22	13	44N38	123w06	8:12:24
Albee 30	2	45N08	118w56	7:55:44
Alder Creek 3	4	45N24	122w16	8:09:04
Aldrich Point 4	14	46N11	123w50	8:15:20
Alfalfa 9	8	44N04	121w18	8:05:12
Alicel 31	2	45N18	117w48	7:51:12
Alkali Lake 19	2	42N11	120w22	8:01:28
Allegany 6	2	43N26	124w02	8:16:08
Allston 5	12	45N24	122w39	8:10:36
Aloha 34	5	45N30	122w52	8:11:28
Alpine 2	2	44N20	123w22	8:13:28
Alsea 2	2	44N23	123w36	8:14:24
Altamont 18	3	42N12	121w44	8:06:56
Alvadore 20	2	44N08	123w16	8:13:04
Amity 36	13	45N07	123w12	8:12:48
Andrews 13	2	43N35	119w03	7:56:12
Anlauf 10	2	43N40	123w19	8:13:16
Annex 23	1	44N15	116w58	7:47:52
Antelope 33	2	44N55	120w43	8:02:52
Apiary 5	12	45N24	122w39	8:10:36
Applegate 15	2	42N16	123w10	8:12:40
Apple Valley 5	4	45N45	122w52	8:11:28
Arago 6	2	43N04	124w08	8:16:32
Arcadia 23	1	43N53	117w00	7:48:00
Arch Cape 4	11	45N49	123w58	8:15:52
Ardenwald 3	12	45N26	122w37	8:10:28
Arlington 11	2	45N43	120w12	8:00:48
Arock 23	1	42N55	117w32	7:50:08
Ashland 15	2	42N12	122w43	8:10:52
Ashwood 16	2	44N44	120w45	8:03:00
Astoria 4	14	46N11	123w50	8:15:20
Athena 30	2	45N49	118w30	7:54:00
Aumsville 24	2	44N51	122w52	8:11:28
Aurora 24	2	45N13	122w46	8:11:04
Austin 12	2	44N36	118w30	7:54:00
Austin Junction 12	2	44N36	118w30	7:54:00
Avon 5	12	45N24	122w39	8:10:36
Azalea 10	2	42N48	123w16	8:13:04
Badger Mountain 20	2	44N04	123w23	8:13:32
Baker 1	9	44N47	117w50	7:51:20
Baker Valley 1	2	44N50	117w46	7:51:04
Ballston 27	15	45N06	123w24	8:13:36
Bancroft 6	2	43N04	124w08	8:16:32
Bandon 6	2	43N07	124w25	8:17:40
Banks 34	4	45N37	123w07	8:12:28
Barlow 3	4	45N15	122w43	8:10:52
Barton 3	4	45N26	122w23	8:09:32
Barview 6	2	43N20	124w19	8:17:16
Barview 29	11	45N34	123w55	8:15:40
Bates 12	2	44N36	118w30	7:54:00
Battin 3	12	45N29	122w33	8:10:12
Bay City 29	7	45N31	123w53	8:15:32
Bayshore 21	2	44N26	124w04	8:16:16
Bayside Garden 29	11	45N43	123w54	8:15:36
Bayview 21	2	44N26	124w04	8:16:16
Beatty 18	2	42N27	121w16	8:05:04
Beaver 29	2	45N17	123w49	8:15:16
Beavercreek 3	4	45N18	122w34	8:10:16
Beaver Marsh 18	2	43N13	121w47	8:07:08
Beaverton 34	12	45N29	122w48	8:11:12
Beburg 34	12	45N29	122w48	8:11:12
Beck 20	2	44N02	123w52	8:15:28
Belleview 15	2	42N12	122w42	8:10:48
Bellevue 36	14	45N13	123w12	8:12:48
Bellfountain 2	2	44N19	123w18	8:13:12
Bend 9	8	44N04	121w19	8:05:16
Berlin 22	2	44N31	122w53	8:11:32
Bethany 34	6	45N31	122w58	8:11:52
Bethel 27	2	44N56	123w14	8:12:56
Bethel Heights 27	15	44N56	123w00	8:12:00
Beulah 23	1	43N45	118w05	7:52:20
Beverly Beach 21	2	44N38	124w03	8:16:12
Biggs 28	2	45N40	120w50	8:03:20
Bingham 15	2	42N19	122w58	8:11:52
Bingham Springs 30	2	45N46	118w34	7:54:16
Birkenfeld 5	4	46N06	123w12	8:12:48
Black Butte Ranch 9	2	44N17	121w33	8:06:12
Black Rock 27	2	44N49	123w30	8:14:00
Blaine 29	2	45N17	123w49	8:15:16
Blalock 11	2	45N42	120w22	8:01:28
Blodgett 2	2	44N38	123w27	8:13:48
Blooming 34	6	45N31	123w03	8:12:12
Blue River 20	2	44N09	122w20	8:09:20
Bly 18	2	42N24	121w03	8:04:12
Boardman 25	2	45N51	119w43	7:58:52
Bolton 3	12	45N24	122w39	8:10:36
Bonanza 18	2	42N12	121w24	8:05:36
Bonita 34	12	45N27	122w46	8:11:04
Bonneville 26	4	45N38	121w57	8:07:48
Bonnie Lure Park 3	4	45N21	122w21	8:09:24
Bonny Slope 26	12	45N33	122w49	8:11:16
Boring 3	4	45N26	122w23	8:09:32
Boyd 33	2	45N27	121w08	8:04:32
Boyer 29	2	45N04	123w37	8:14:28
Bradwood 4	2	46N06	123w12	8:12:48
Breitenbush 24	2	44N44	122w09	8:08:36
Briarwood 3	12	45N25	122w42	8:10:48
Brickerville 20	2	44N02	123w52	8:15:28
Bridal Veil 26	4	45N33	122w11	8:08:44
Bridge 6	2	43N01	124w00	8:16:00
Bridgeport 1	2	44N29	117w45	7:51:00
Bridgeport 27	2	44N55	123w19	8:13:16
Bridgeton 26	12	45N29	122w41	8:10:44
Brighton 29	2	45N34	123w55	8:15:40
Brightwood 3	4	45N23	122w03	8:08:12
Broadacres 24	10	45N42	121w31	8:06:04
Broadbent 6	2	43N01	124w09	8:16:36
Brockway 10	2	43N07	123w25	8:13:40
Brogan 23	1	44N15	117w31	7:50:04
Brookings 8	2	42N03	124w17	8:17:08
Brooklyn 26	12	45N29	122w33	8:10:12
Brooks 24	15	44N56	123w03	8:12:12
Brothers 9	2	43N49	120w36	8:02:24
Brownlee 1	2	44N49	116w56	7:47:44
Brownsmead 4	2	46N13	123w32	8:14:08
Brownsville 22	2	44N24	122w59	8:11:56
Brush College 27	15	44N57	123w05	8:12:20
Bryant 3	12	45N25	122w42	8:10:48
Buchanan 2	7	44N34	123w16	8:13:04
Buchanan 13	2	43N35	119w03	7:56:12
Buck Fork 10	2	43N01	123w18	8:13:12
Buckley 28	2	45N22	120w47	8:03:08
Buell 27	15	45N06	123w24	8:13:36
Buena Vista 27	2	44N51	123w11	8:12:44
Bull Mountain 34	12	45N25	122w48	8:11:12
Bullrun 3	4	45N24	122w16	8:09:04
Bunker Hill 6	2	43N22	124w12	8:16:48
Buoy Depot 4	14	46N11	123w50	8:15:20
Burlington 26	12	45N39	122w50	8:11:20
Burns 13	2	43N35	119w03	7:56:12
Burns Junction 23	1	42N59	117w03	7:48:12
Burnt Woods 21	2	44N36	123w37	8:14:28
Butte Falls 15	2	42N33	122w34	8:10:16
Butteville 24	2	45N13	122w46	8:11:04
Buxton 34	4	45N43	123w09	8:12:36
Cairo 23	1	44N01	116w58	7:47:52
Calapooia 10	2	43N26	123w17	8:13:08
Calapooya 22	2	44N24	122w36	8:10:24
Camas Valley 10	2	43N02	123w40	8:14:40
Camp Sherman 16	2	44N28	121w38	8:06:32
Camp Twelve 21	11	44N43	123w55	8:15:40
Campus 2	7	44N34	123w16	8:13:04
Canary 20	2	43N53	124w06	8:16:24
Canby 3	4	45N16	122w42	8:10:48
Canemah 3	12	45N23	122w36	8:10:24
Cannon Beach 4	11	45N54	123w58	8:15:52
Cannon Beach Junction 4	11	46N00	123w55	8:15:40
Canyon City 12	2	44N23	118w57	7:55:48
Canyonville 10	2	42N56	123w17	8:13:08
Cape Meares 29	2	45N27	123w50	8:15:20
Carlton 36	2	45N18	123w11	8:12:44
Carnation 34	6	45N31	123w03	8:12:12
Carpenterville 8	2	42N13	124w17	8:17:08
Carson 1	2	44N53	117w06	7:48:24
Carus 3	12	45N23	122w36	8:10:24
Carver 3	12	45N25	122w34	8:10:16
Cascade Gorge 15	2	42N39	122w49	8:11:16
Cascade Locks 14	4	45N40	121w54	8:07:36
Cascade Summit 18	2	43N35	122w02	8:08:08
Cascadia 22	2	44N24	122w29	8:09:56
Cave Junction 17	2	42N10	123w39	8:14:36
Cayuse 30	2	45N41	118w33	7:54:12
Cecil 25	2	45N37	119w58	7:59:52
Cedar Dale 3	12	45N29	122w44	8:10:56
Cedar Hills 34	12	45N30	122w47	8:11:08
Cedarhurst Park 3	4	45N21	122w43	8:10:52
Cedar Mill 34	12	45N30	122w47	8:11:08
Celilo 33	2	45N36	121w11	8:04:44
Central 26	12	45N31	122w41	8:10:44
Central Point 15	2	42N23	122w55	8:11:40
Charleston 6	2	43N21	124w20	8:17:20
Charlestown 30	2	45N50	119w18	7:57:12
Chehalem 36	14	45N20	123w01	8:12:04
Chehalem Mountain 34	4	45N25	123w00	8:12:00
Chelsea 18	3	42N13	121w45	8:07:00
Chemawa 24	2	45N02	122w57	8:11:48
Chemult 18	2	43N13	121w47	8:07:08
Chenoweth 33	2	45N37	121w13	8:04:52
Cherry Grove 34	4	45N31	123w15	8:13:00
Cherryville 3	4	45N24	122w16	8:09:04
Cheshire 20	2	44N11	123w17	8:13:08
Chiloquin 18	2	42N35	121w52	8:07:28
Chitwood 21	2	44N37	123w56	8:15:44
Christmas Valley 19	2	43N08	120w56	8:03:44
City Of The Dalles 33	2	45N36	121w11	8:04:44
Clackamas 3	12	45N25	122w34	8:10:16
Clackamas Heights 3	12	45N23	122w36	8:10:24
Clarkes 3	4	45N17	122w32	8:10:08
Clarno 35	2	44N55	120w43	8:02:52
Clatskanie 5	4	46N06	123w12	8:12:48
Clatsop Plains 4	14	46N03	123w55	8:15:40
Clear Lake 24	2	45N02	123w00	8:12:00
Cleveland 10	3	43N11	123w22	8:13:28
Clifton 4	2	46N06	123w12	8:12:48
Cloverdale 9	2	44N17	121w11	8:04:44
Cloverdale 20	2	43N55	123w01	8:12:04
Cloverdale 29	11	45N12	123w53	8:15:32
Coaledo 6	2	43N20	124w14	8:16:56
Coburg 20	2	44N10	123w04	8:12:16
College Crest 20	8	44N04	123w05	8:12:20
Colton 3	4	45N10	122w25	8:09:40
Columbia 5	4	45N53	122w53	8:11:32
Columbia City 5	17	45N53	122w49	8:11:16
Columbia Hall 33	2	45N36	121w11	8:04:44
Concomly 24	2	45N07	122w54	8:11:36
Concord 3	12	45N26	122w37	8:10:28
Condon 11	2	45N14	120w11	8:00:44
Cook 3	12	45N25	122w42	8:10:48
Cooper Mountain 34	4	45N28	122w53	8:11:32
Coos Bay 6	2	43N22	124w13	8:16:52
Cooston 6	2	43N24	124w14	8:16:56
Coquille 6	2	43N11	124w11	8:16:44
Corbett 26	4	45N31	122w20	8:09:20
Cornelius 34	6	45N31	123w03	8:12:12
Cornelius Pass 26	12	45N35	122w48	8:11:12
Cornucopia 1	2	45N00	117w12	7:48:48
Coronado Shores 21	11	44N56	124w01	8:16:04
Corvallis 2	7	44N34	123w16	8:13:04
Cottage Grove 20	3	43N48	123w03	8:12:12
Cottrell 3	4	45N26	122w23	8:09:32
Country Estate 2	7	44N34	123w16	8:13:04
Courtrock 12	2	44N49	119w25	7:57:40
Cove 31	2	45N18	117w49	7:51:16
Cove Orchard 36	2	45N26	123w08	8:12:32
Crabtree 22	2	44N38	122w54	8:11:36
Crane 13	2	43N25	118w35	7:54:20
Crater Lake 18	2	42N54	122w08	8:08:32
Crawfordsville 22	2	44N21	122w51	8:11:24
Crescent 18	2	43N28	121w42	8:06:48
Crescent Lake 18	2	43N31	121w58	8:07:52
Crescent Lake Junction 18	2	43N31	121w58	8:07:52
Creston 26	12	45N29	122w36	8:10:24
Creswell 20	2	43N55	123w01	8:12:04
Crockett 30	2	45N59	118w23	7:53:32
Crooked River 7	2	44N10	120w30	8:02:00
Crow 20	8	44N04	123w05	8:12:20
Crowfoot 22	2	44N31	122w53	8:11:32
Crowley 27	2	44N56	123w14	8:12:56
Cully 26	12	45N34	122w36	8:10:24
Culp Creek 20	2	43N42	122w50	8:11:20
Culver 16	2	44N32	121w13	8:04:52
Currinsville 3	4	45N21	122w43	8:10:52
Curtin 10	2	43N43	123w12	8:12:48
Cushman 20	2	43N59	124w03	8:16:12
Cutler City 21	11	44N57	124w01	8:16:04
Dairy 18	2	42N14	121w31	8:06:04
Dale 12	2	44N59	118w57	7:55:48
Dallas 27	2	44N55	123w19	8:13:16
Dalles 33	7	45N36	121w10	8:04:40
Damascus 3	12	45N25	122w34	8:10:16
Damascus Heights 3	4	45N26	122w23	8:09:32
Danner 23	1	42N59	117w03	7:48:12
Dawson 2	2	44N22	123w25	8:13:40
Days Creek 10	2	42N58	123w10	8:12:40
Dayton 36	2	45N12	123w04	8:12:16
Dayville 12	2	44N28	119w32	7:58:08
Dead Ox Flat 23	1	44N09	116w57	7:47:48
Deadwood 20	2	44N06	123w45	8:15:00
Dee 14	4	45N36	121w37	8:06:28
Deer Island 5	4	45N56	122w51	8:11:24
De Lake 21	2	45N00	123w52	8:15:28
Delena 5	4	46N06	123w12	8:12:48
Dellwood 6	2	43N20	124w14	8:16:56
Delmoor 4	11	46N10	123w55	8:15:40
Denmark 8	2	42N56	124w27	8:17:48
Depoe Bay 21	11	44N49	124w04	8:16:16
Deschutes 9	8	44N04	121w18	8:05:12
Deschutes Junction 9	8	44N04	121w18	8:05:12
Detroit 24	2	44N44	122w09	8:08:36
Dever 22	13	44N40	123w03	8:12:12
Dew Valley 6	2	43N07	124w24	8:17:36
Dexter 20	2	43N55	122w49	8:11:16
Diamond 13	2	42N47	118w55	7:55:40
Diamond Lake 18	2	43N09	121w48	8:07:12
Diamond Lake Junction 18	2	43N13	121w47	8:07:08
Dickey Prairie 3	12	45N29	122w44	8:10:56
Dillard 10	2	43N06	123w26	8:13:44
Dilley 34	6	45N31	123w03	8:12:12
Disston 20	2	43N42	122w46	8:11:04
Dixonville 10	3	43N11	123w22	8:13:28
Dodge 3	4	45N21	122w43	8:10:52
Dodson 26	4	45N38	121w57	8:07:48
Dolph Corner 27	2	44N55	123w19	8:13:16
Donald 24	2	45N13	122w50	8:11:20
Donnybrook 16	2	44N44	120w45	8:03:00
Dora 6	2	43N10	123w59	8:15:56
Dorena 20	2	43N43	122w52	8:11:28
Douglas Gardens 20	3	44N03	123w00	8:12:00
Dover 3	4	45N24	122w16	8:09:04
Drain 10	2	43N40	123w19	8:13:16
Draperville 22	13	44N38	123w06	8:12:24
Drew 10	2	42N56	122w57	8:11:48
Drewsey 13	2	43N31	118w35	7:54:20
Drift Creek 21	2	44N26	124w04	8:16:16
Dryland 3	4	45N16	122w41	8:10:44
Dufur 33	2	45N27	121w08	8:04:32
Dukes Valley 14	10	45N42	121w31	8:06:04
Dundee 36	14	45N17	123w01	8:12:04
Dunes 20	2	43N55	124w06	8:16:24
Durham 34	12	45N24	122w45	8:11:00
Durkee 1	2	44N35	117w28	7:49:52
Eagle Creek 3	4	45N21	122w21	8:09:24
Eagle Crest Corners 27	15	44N57	123w05	8:12:20
Eagle Point 15	2	42N28	122w48	8:11:12
Eagle Valley 1	2	44N51	117w18	7:49:12
East Bend 9	8	44N04	121w16	8:05:04
East Gardiner 10	2	43N42	124w06	8:16:24
East Gresham 26	12	45N31	122w28	8:09:52
East Lake 9	2	43N40	121w30	8:06:00
East Milwaukie 3	12	45N26	122w37	8:10:28
East Parkrose 26	12	45N32	122w31	8:10:04

OREGON

East Portland 26	12	45N31	122w38	8:10:32
Eastside 6	2	43N19	124w05	8:16:20
Eastwood 10	3	43N11	123w22	8:13:28
Echo 30	2	45N45	119w12	7:56:48
Eckman Lake 21	2	44N26	124w04	8:16:16
Eddyville 21	2	44N38	123w47	8:15:08
Edenbower 10	3	43N11	123w22	8:13:28
Elgarose 10	3	43N11	123w22	8:13:28
Elgin 31	2	45N34	117w55	7:51:40
Elk City 21	2	44N37	123w56	8:15:44
Elkhorn 24	2	44N48	122w48	8:11:12
Elk Lake 9	8	44N04	121w18	8:05:12
Elkton 10	2	43N38	123w34	8:14:16
Ellendale 27	2	44N55	123w19	8:13:16
Ellingson Mill 12	2	44N26	118w12	7:52:48
Elliott Prairie 3	4	45N09	122w51	8:11:24
Elmira 20	2	44N04	123w21	8:13:24
Elmonica 34	12	45N29	122w48	8:11:12
Elsie 4	2	45N52	123w36	8:14:24
Elwood 3	4	45N10	122w26	8:09:44
Emerald Heights 4	14	46N11	123w50	8:15:20
Empire 6	2	43N20	124w14	8:16:56
Englewood 6	2	43N20	124w14	8:16:56
Englewood 26	12	45N25	122w42	8:10:48
Enterprise 32	2	45N25	117w17	7:49:08
Eola 27	15	44N57	123w05	8:12:20
Eola 36	14	45N13	123w12	8:12:48
Eola Crest 36	13	45N07	123w12	8:12:48
Errol Heights 26	12	45N28	122w36	8:10:24
Estacada 3	4	45N17	122w20	8:09:20
Eugene 20	8	44N05	123w04	8:12:16
Evans Valley 15	2	42N32	123w07	8:12:28
Fairfield 24	2	45N07	122w54	8:11:36
Fair Oaks 3	12	45N26	122w37	8:10:28
Fairoaks 10	2	43N23	123w19	8:13:16
Fairview 22	2	44N31	122w53	8:11:32
Fairview 26	12	43N13	124w05	8:16:20
Fairview 29	2	45N27	123w50	8:15:20
Falcon Heights 18	2	42N09	121w47	8:07:08
Fall Creek 20	2	43N58	122w49	8:11:16
Falls City 27	2	44N52	123w26	8:13:44
Faraday 3	4	45N21	122w43	8:10:52
Fargo 24	2	45N13	122w46	8:11:04
Faubion 3	4	45N21	121w57	8:07:48
Fayetteville 22	2	44N28	123w07	8:12:28
Federal 26	12	45N29	122w41	8:10:44
Fern Corner 27	2	44N55	123w19	8:13:16
Fern Hill 4	14	46N11	123w50	8:15:20
Fern Hill 5	12	45N24	122w39	8:10:36
Ferns 27	2	44N55	123w19	8:13:16
Fernwood 3	6	45N19	122w55	8:11:40
Fields 13	2	42N28	118w37	7:54:28
Fields 20	2	43N43	122w28	8:09:52
Finn Rock 20	8	44N04	123w05	8:12:20
Fir Grove 20	8	44N04	123w05	8:12:20
Firlock 34	12	45N27	122w46	8:11:04
Fir Villa 27	2	44N55	123w19	8:13:16
Firwood 3	4	45N24	122w16	8:09:04
Fishers Mill 3	12	45N23	122w36	8:10:24
Fish Lake Resort 15	2	42N28	122w48	8:11:12
Five Corners 19	2	42N11	120w22	8:01:28
Flavel 4	11	46N10	123w55	8:15:40
Flora 32	2	45N54	117w19	7:49:16
Florence 20	2	43N58	124w07	8:16:28
Foots Creek 15	2	42N23	123w04	8:12:16
Forest Grove 34	6	45N31	123w07	8:12:28
Forest Park 26	12	45N32	122w43	8:10:52
Forfar 21	2	44N38	124w03	8:16:12
Fort Hill 27	15	45N04	123w29	8:13:56
Fort Klamath 18	2	42N42	122w00	8:08:00
Fort Rock 19	2	43N21	121w03	8:04:12
Fort Stevens 4	11	46N12	123w57	8:15:48
Fortune Branch 10	2	42N44	123w26	8:13:44
Fort Vannoy 17	2	42N27	123w24	8:13:36
Fossil 35	2	45N00	120w13	8:00:52
Foster 22	2	44N25	122w40	8:10:40
Four Corners 24	15	44N56	122w58	8:11:52
Fox 12	2	44N39	119w09	7:56:36
Franklin 20	3	44N13	123w12	8:12:48
Freewater 30	2	45N56	118w23	7:53:32
Frenchglen 13	2	42N50	118w55	7:55:40
Friend 33	2	45N21	121w16	8:05:04
Fruitdale 17	2	42N22	123w19	8:13:16
Fruitland 24	15	44N56	123w00	8:12:00
Fruitvale 21	2	44N38	124w03	8:16:12
Gales Creek 34	6	45N31	123w03	8:12:12
Galice 17	2	42N31	123w25	8:13:40
Garden Home 34	12	45N27	122w46	8:11:04
Gardiner 10	2	43N44	124w07	8:16:28
Garfield 3	4	45N21	122w43	8:10:52
Garibaldi 29	11	45N34	123w55	8:15:40
Gaston 34	4	45N26	123w08	8:12:32
Gates 24	2	44N45	122w25	8:09:40
Gateway 16	2	44N38	121w08	8:04:32
Gaylord 6	2	43N04	124w08	8:16:32
Gazley 10	2	43N01	123w18	8:13:12
Gearhart 4	14	46N01	123w55	8:15:40
George 3	4	45N21	122w43	8:10:52
Gervais 24	2	45N07	122w54	8:11:36
Gibbon 30	2	45N42	118w21	7:53:24
Gilbert 26	12	45N29	122w33	8:10:12
Gilchrist 18	2	43N29	121w41	8:06:44
Gillespie Corners 20	8	44N02	123w06	8:12:24
Gilliams 27	2	44N55	123w19	8:13:16
Gladstone 3	12	45N23	122w36	8:10:24
Gladtidings 3	12	45N29	122w44	8:10:56
Glasgow 6	2	43N24	124w14	8:16:56
Glenada 20	2	43N57	124w06	8:16:24
Glenbrook 2	2	44N19	123w18	8:13:12
Glendale 10	2	42N44	123w26	8:13:44
Glendale Junction 10	2	42N44	123w26	8:13:44
Glendoveer 26	12	45N32	122w31	8:10:04
Gleneden Beach 21	11	44N56	124w01	8:16:04
Glengary 10	3	43N11	123w22	8:13:28
Glenmorrie 3	12	45N25	122w42	8:10:48
Glenwood 20	8	44N04	123w05	8:12:20
Glenwood 34	4	45N39	123w16	8:13:04
Glide 10	2	43N18	123w06	8:12:24
Globe 20	2	44N02	123w35	8:14:20
Goble 5	4	45N59	122w55	8:11:40
Gold Beach 8	2	42N25	124w25	8:17:40
Gold Hill 15	2	42N26	123w03	8:12:12
Gooseberry 25	2	45N30	119w49	7:59:16
Gopher 36	15	45N06	123w24	8:13:36
Goshen 20	3	44N00	123w01	8:12:04
Government Camp 3	4	45N18	121w45	8:07:00
Grande Ronde 31	2	45N22	118w03	7:52:12
Grand Ronde 27	2	45N04	123w37	8:14:28
Grandview 16	2	44N28	121w41	8:06:44
Granite 12	2	44N49	118w25	7:53:40
Granite Hill 17	2	42N31	123w19	8:13:16
Grants Pass 17	2	42N26	123w19	8:13:16
Grass Valley 28	2	45N22	120w47	8:03:08
Gravelford 6	2	43N04	124w08	8:16:32
Green 10	2	43N09	123w23	8:13:32
Green Acres 6	2	43N20	124w14	8:16:56
Greenacres 10	2	43N41	123w48	8:15:12
Greenberry 2	7	44N34	123w16	8:13:04
Greenburg 34	12	45N27	122w46	8:11:04
Greenhorn 1	2	44N47	118w18	7:53:12
Greenleaf 20	2	44N07	123w40	8:14:40
Green Springs Mountain 15	2	42N07	122w23	8:09:32
Greenville 22	2	44N24	122w36	8:10:24
Greenville 34	6	45N31	123w03	8:12:12
Gresham 26	12	45N30	122w26	8:09:44
Grizzly 16	2	44N38	121w08	8:04:32
Hager 18	3	42N13	121w45	8:07:00
Haines 1	2	44N55	117w56	7:51:44
Halfway 1	2	44N58	117w05	7:48:20
Halls Ferry 24	15	44N54	123w02	8:12:08
Halsey 22	2	44N23	123w07	8:12:28
Hamilton 12	2	44N44	119w18	7:57:12
Hammond 4	11	46N12	123w57	8:15:48
Hampton 9	2	43N40	120w14	8:00:56
Hamricks Corner 3	4	45N16	122w41	8:10:44
Happy Valley 3	12	45N25	122w35	8:10:20
Harbor 8	2	42N03	124w10	8:16:40
Hardman 25	2	45N10	119w41	7:58:44
Harlan 21	2	44N33	123w42	8:14:48
Harmony 3	12	45N26	122w37	8:10:28
Harney 13	2	43N35	119w03	7:56:12
Harper 23	1	43N52	117w37	7:50:28
Harriman 18	3	42N13	121w45	8:07:00
Harrisburg 22	3	44N16	123w10	8:12:40
Hathaway Mead 29	2	45N27	123w50	8:15:20
Hauser 6	2	43N30	124w13	8:16:52
Hayesville 24	15	44N58	122w59	8:11:56
Hazeldale 34	12	45N29	122w48	8:11:12
Hazel Green 24	15	44N58	123w00	8:12:00
Hazelwood 26	12	45N32	122w31	8:10:04
Hebo 29	11	45N14	123w52	8:15:28
Heceta Beach 20	2	43N57	124w06	8:16:24
Heceta Junction 20	2	43N57	124w06	8:16:24
Helix 30	2	45N51	118w39	7:54:36
Helvetia 34	6	45N31	122w58	8:11:52
Hemlock 20	2	43N46	122w31	8:10:04
Henley 18	2	42N10	121w43	8:06:52
Heppner 25	2	45N21	119w33	7:58:12
Hereford 1	2	44N32	118w11	7:52:44
Hermiston 30	2	45N51	119w17	7:57:08
Highland 3	4	45N15	122w22	8:09:28
Highway 24	2	45N09	122w51	8:11:24
Hildebrand 18	2	42N12	121w24	8:05:36
Hilgard 31	2	45N21	118w14	7:52:56
Hillsboro 34	6	45N31	122w59	8:11:56
Hillsview 3	12	45N31	122w28	8:09:52
Hines 13	2	43N34	119w05	7:56:20
Holbrook 26	12	45N35	122w48	8:11:12
Holdman 30	2	45N47	118w48	7:55:12
Holladay Park 26	12	45N33	122w38	8:10:32
Holland 17	2	42N08	123w32	8:14:08
Holley 22	2	44N21	122w47	8:11:08
Hollywood 24	15	44N58	123w00	8:12:00
Homestead 1	2	45N02	116w51	7:47:24
Hood River 14	10	45N43	121w31	8:06:04
Hopewell 36	15	44N57	123w05	8:12:20
Horton 20	3	44N13	123w12	8:12:48
Hoskins 2	2	44N41	123w28	8:13:52
Howell 24	4	45N00	122w53	8:11:32
Hubbard 24	2	45N11	122w48	8:11:12
Huber 34	12	45N29	122w48	8:11:12
Hugo 17	2	42N25	123w20	8:13:20
Hunter Creek 8	2	42N25	124w25	8:17:40
Huntington 1	2	44N21	117w16	7:49:04
Idanha 24	2	44N42	122w05	8:08:20
Idaville 29	11	45N31	123w53	8:15:32
Idleyld Park 10	2	43N19	123w02	8:12:08
Illahe 8	2	42N34	124w05	8:16:20
Illinois Valley 17	2	42N10	123w39	8:14:36
Imbler 31	2	45N28	117w58	7:51:52
Imnaha 32	2	45N32	116w52	7:47:28
Independence 27	2	44N51	123w11	8:12:44
Indian Ford 9	2	44N17	121w33	8:06:12
Indian Village 13	2	43N35	119w03	7:56:12
Inglis 5	4	46N06	123w12	8:12:48
Interlachen 26	12	45N32	122w26	8:09:44
Ione 25	2	45N30	119w50	7:59:20
Ironside 23	1	44N19	117w57	7:51:48
Irrigon 25	2	45N54	119w30	7:58:00
Irving 20	8	44N04	123w05	8:12:20
Island 3	12	45N26	122w37	8:10:28
Island City 31	2	45N21	118w03	7:52:12
Ivy 4	14	46N11	123w50	8:15:20
Jacksonville 15	2	42N19	122w57	8:11:48
Jacktown 34	12	45N29	122w48	8:11:12
Jamieson 23	1	44N11	117w26	7:49:44
Jasper 20	8	44N04	123w05	8:12:20
Jeffers Garden 4	14	46N11	123w50	8:15:20
Jefferson 24	2	44N43	123w01	8:12:04
Jerome Prairie 17	2	42N24	123w25	8:13:40
Jewell 4	2	45N55	123w30	8:14:00
John Day 12	2	44N25	118w57	7:55:48
Johnson City 3	12	45N26	122w37	8:10:28
Jonesboro 23	1	43N45	118w05	7:52:20
Jordan 22	2	44N42	122w51	8:11:24
Jordan 23	1	42N53	117w29	7:49:56
Jordan Valley 23	1	42N59	117w03	7:48:12
Joseph 32	2	45N21	117w14	7:48:56
Junction City 20	3	44N13	123w12	8:12:48
Juntura 23	1	43N45	118w05	7:52:20
Kahneeta Hot Springs 33	2	44N46	121w16	8:05:04
Kamela 31	2	45N26	118w24	7:53:36
Kansas City 34	6	45N31	123w03	8:12:12
Keating 1	9	44N47	117w50	7:51:20
Keizer 24	15	44N59	123w01	8:12:04
Kellogg 10	2	43N25	123w18	8:13:12
Kelly Butte 26	12	45N30	122w33	8:10:12
Kelso 3	4	45N26	122w23	8:09:32
Kendall 26	12	45N29	122w36	8:10:24
Keno 18	2	42N08	121w56	8:07:44
Kent 28	2	45N12	120w42	8:02:48
Kenton 26	12	45N34	122w41	8:10:44
Kerby 17	2	42N12	123w39	8:14:36
Kernville 21	11	44N57	124w01	8:16:04
Kilts 16	2	44N44	120w45	8:03:00
Kimberly 12	2	44N46	119w39	7:58:36
King 34	12	45N26	122w47	8:11:08
King City 34	12	45N27	122w46	8:11:04
Kingston 22	2	44N48	122w48	8:11:12
Kings Valley 2	2	44N42	123w26	8:13:44
Kingwood 27	15	44N57	123w05	8:12:20
Kinton 34	12	45N29	122w48	8:11:12
Kinzua 35	2	44N59	120w03	8:00:12
Kirk 18	2	42N45	121w50	8:07:20
Kiwanda Beach 29	2	45N21	123w11	8:12:44
Klamath Agency 18	2	42N37	121w56	8:07:44
Klamath Falls 18	3	42N13	121w46	8:07:04
Knappa 4	2	46N11	123w35	8:14:20
Labish Village 24	15	44N58	123w00	8:12:00
Lacomb 22	2	44N36	122w46	8:11:04
Ladd 3	12	45N25	122w42	8:10:48
Ladd Hill 3	4	45N18	122w46	8:11:04
Lafayette 36	2	45N15	123w07	8:12:28
La Grande 31	2	45N20	118w05	7:52:20
Lakecreek 15	2	42N26	122w37	8:10:28
Lake Grove 3	12	45N25	122w42	8:10:48
Lake Of The Woods 18	3	42N13	121w45	8:07:00
Lake Oswego 3	12	45N25	122w40	8:10:40
Lake Shore 18	2	42N13	121w53	8:07:32
Lakeside 6	2	43N35	124w11	8:16:44
Lakeview 19	3	42N11	120w21	8:01:24
Lakewood 3	12	45N25	122w42	8:10:48
Lancaster 20	3	44N13	123w12	8:12:48
Langell 18	2	42N14	121w07	8:04:28
Langlois 8	2	42N56	124w27	8:17:48
Langrell 1	2	44N53	117w06	7:48:24
La Pine 9	2	43N40	121w30	8:06:00
Larwood 22	2	44N42	122w51	8:11:24
Latham 20	2	43N48	123w04	8:12:16
Latourell Falls 26	4	45N38	121w57	8:07:48
Laurel 34	6	45N31	122w58	8:11:52
Laurel Grove 6	2	43N07	124w24	8:17:36
Laurelwood 34	4	45N26	123w08	8:12:32
Laurelwood Academy 34	4	45N26	123w08	8:12:32
Lawen 13	2	43N27	118w48	7:55:12
Leaburg 20	8	44N04	123w05	8:12:20
Lebanon 22	2	44N32	122w55	8:11:40
Lee 6	2	43N08	124w11	8:16:44
Lee's Camp 29	12	45N27	122w30	8:10:00
Lehman Hot Springs 30	2	45N08	118w56	7:55:44
Leland 17	2	42N38	123w27	8:13:48
Lents 26	12	45N29	122w33	8:10:12
Lewis And Clark 4	2	46N07	123w51	8:15:24
Lewisburg 2	2	44N39	123w15	8:13:00
Lewisville 27	2	44N51	123w14	8:12:56
Lexington 25	2	45N27	119w42	7:58:48
Libby 6	2	43N20	124w14	8:16:56
Liberal 3	12	45N29	122w44	8:10:56
Liberty 22	2	44N24	122w36	8:10:24
Lime 1	2	44N21	117w16	7:49:04
Lincoln 15	2	42N12	122w42	8:10:48
Lincoln Beach 21	11	44N49	124w04	8:16:16
Lincoln City 21	11	44N57	124w01	8:16:04
Linnton 26	12	45N35	122w48	8:11:12
Little Albany 21	2	44N25	123w54	8:15:36
Locoda 5	4	46N06	123w12	8:12:48

Logan 3 12 45N23 122w36 8:10:24
Logsden 21 2 44N45 123w47 8:15:08
London 20 2 43N48 123w04 8:12:16
Lone Elder 3 4 45N16 122w41 8:10:44
Lonerock 11 2 45N05 119w53 7:59:32
Long Creek 12 2 44N43 119w06 7:56:24
Lookingglass 10 2 43N11 123w29 8:13:56
Looking Glass 31 2 45N34 117w55 7:51:40
Lorane 20 2 43N50 123w14 8:12:56
Lorella 18 2 42N12 121w24 8:05:36
Lostine 32 2 45N29 117w26 7:49:44
Lowell 20 2 43N55 122w47 8:11:08
Lower Bridge 9 2 44N21 121w11 8:04:44
Lunnville 36 2 45N21 123w11 8:12:44
Lyons 22 2 44N47 122w37 8:10:28
Macksburg 3 4 45N16 122w41 8:10:44
Macleay 24 15 44N56 123w00 8:12:00
Madras 16 11 44N38 121w08 8:04:32
Malheur Junction 23 1 43N58 117w01 7:48:04
Malin 18 2 42N01 121w24 8:05:36
Manhattan Beach 29 11 45N34 123w55 8:15:40
Manning 34 6 45N31 122w58 8:11:52
Manzanita 29 2 45N43 123w56 8:15:44
Mapleton 20 2 44N02 123w52 8:15:28
Maplewood 26 12 45N27 122w44 8:10:56
Marcola 20 2 44N10 122w52 8:11:28
Marion 24 2 44N45 122w56 8:11:44
Marion Forks 22 2 44N37 122w13 8:08:52
Market 6 2 43N20 124w14 8:16:56
Marlene Village 34 12 45N29 122w48 8:11:12
Marmot 3 4 45N24 122w16 8:09:04
Marquam 3 4 45N04 122w47 8:11:08
Marshland 5 4 46N08 123w14 8:12:56
Martin Manor 34 12 45N30 122w47 8:11:08
Marylhurst 3 12 45N24 122w39 8:10:36
Mason Additions 7 2 44N18 120w51 8:03:24
Maupin 33 2 45N11 121w05 8:04:20
Mayger 5 4 46N06 123w12 8:12:48
May Park 31 2 45N20 118w04 7:52:16
Mayville 11 2 45N05 120w12 8:00:48
Maywood Park 26 12 45N33 122w34 8:10:16
McCoy 27 2 44N56 123w14 8:12:56
McCredie Springs 20 2 43N43 122w17 8:09:08
McEwen 1 2 44N47 118w18 7:53:12
McKee 24 2 45N09 122w51 8:11:24
McKee Bridge 15 2 42N19 122w58 8:11:52
McKenzie 20 2 44N08 122w27 8:09:48
McKenzie Bridge 20 2 44N11 122w10 8:08:40
McKinley 6 2 43N02 124w08 8:16:32
McMinnville 36 14 45N13 123w12 8:12:48
McNary 30 2 45N55 119w17 7:57:08
McNulty 5 17 45N50 122w50 8:11:20
Meacham 30 2 45N31 118w25 7:53:40
Meadowbrook 3 12 45N29 122w44 8:10:56
Meadow View 20 3 44N13 123w12 8:12:48
Meda 29 11 45N12 123w53 8:15:32
Medford 15 3 42N19 122w52 8:11:28
Medical Springs 31 2 45N12 117w38 7:50:32
Mehama 24 2 44N48 122w48 8:11:12
Melrose 10 2 43N16 123w34 8:14:16
Melrose Acres 7 2 44N18 120w51 8:03:24
Melville 4 14 46N11 123w50 8:15:20
Merlin 17 2 42N31 123w25 8:13:40
Merrill 18 2 42N01 121w36 8:06:24
Metolius 16 2 44N35 121w11 8:04:44
Metzger 34 12 45N26 122w44 8:10:56
Middle Siuslaw 20 2 44N09 123w46 8:15:04
Midland 18 2 42N08 121w49 8:07:16
Midway 26 12 45N31 122w30 8:10:00
Midway 34 6 45N31 122w58 8:11:52
Midway 36 2 45N04 123w37 8:14:28
Mikkalo 11 2 45N28 120w14 8:00:56
Miles Crossing 4 14 46N11 123w50 8:15:20
Mill City 24 2 44N45 122w29 8:09:56
Miller 22 2 44N23 123w05 8:12:20
Millersburg 22 13 44N38 123w06 8:12:24
Millican 9 8 44N04 121w18 8:05:12
Millington 6 2 43N20 124w14 8:16:56
Millwood 10 2 43N22 123w28 8:13:52
Milo 10 2 42N56 123w03 8:12:12
Milton 30 2 45N56 118w23 7:53:32
Milton-Freewater 30 2 45N56 118w23 7:53:32
Milwaukie 3 12 45N27 122w38 8:10:32
Milwaukie Heights 3 12 45N26 122w37 8:10:28
Minam 32 2 45N38 117w43 7:50:52
Minerva 20 2 43N57 124w06 8:16:24
Minnow 20 2 43N55 122w49 8:11:16
Mission 30 16 45N40 118w48 7:55:12
Mist 5 4 46N00 123w15 8:13:00
Mitchell 35 2 44N34 120w09 8:00:36
Modeville 27 2 44N51 123w11 8:12:44
Modoc Point 18 2 42N27 121w52 8:07:28
Mohawk 20 3 44N03 123w00 8:12:00
Mohawk Junction 20 3 44N03 123w00 8:12:00
Mohler 29 11 45N43 123w54 8:15:36
Molalla 3 5 45N09 122w35 8:10:20
Monitor 24 2 45N09 122w51 8:11:24
Monmouth 27 2 44N51 123w14 8:12:56
Monroe 2 2 44N19 123w18 8:13:12
Montgomery Ranch 9 8 44N04 121w18 8:05:12
Monument 12 2 44N49 119w25 7:57:40
Moody 21 2 44N38 124w03 8:16:12
Morgan 25 2 45N30 119w49 7:59:16
Moro 28 2 45N29 120w44 8:02:56
Mosier 33 2 45N41 121w24 8:05:36
Mountaindale 34 6 45N31 123w03 8:12:12
Mount Angel 24 4 45N04 122w48 8:11:12
Mount Hood 3 4 45N22 122w05 8:08:20
Mount Hood 14 4 45N33 121w34 8:06:16
Mount Vernon 12 2 44N25 119w07 7:56:28
Mount View 15 2 42N12 122w42 8:10:48
Mulino 3 4 45N13 122w33 8:10:12
Mulloy 34 4 45N21 122w50 8:11:20
Multnomah 26 12 45N27 122w43 8:10:52
Mundorf 3 4 45N16 122w41 8:10:44
Munkers 22 2 44N42 122w51 8:11:24
Murphy 17 2 42N21 123w20 8:13:20
Murphys Camp 10 2 43N41 123w48 8:15:12
Myrick 30 2 45N46 118w34 7:54:16
Myrtle Creek 10 2 43N01 123w17 8:13:08
Myrtle Point 6 2 43N04 124w08 8:16:32
Narrows 13 2 43N35 119w03 7:56:12
Nashville 21 2 44N32 123w21 8:13:24
Neahkahnie 29 11 45N43 123w54 8:15:36
Nedonna 29 11 45N34 123w55 8:15:40
Needy 3 4 45N16 122w41 8:10:44
Nehalem 29 2 45N44 123w43 8:14:52
Nelscott 21 11 44N57 124w01 8:16:04
Neotsu 21 11 45N00 123w59 8:15:56
Nesika Beach 8 2 42N29 124w24 8:17:36
Neskowin 29 11 45N10 123w53 8:15:32
Netarts 29 11 45N26 123w57 8:15:48
Newberg 36 14 45N18 122w58 8:11:52
New Bridge 1 2 44N46 117w10 7:48:40
New Era 3 4 45N16 122w41 8:10:44
New Idaho 19 2 42N11 120w22 8:01:28
New Idanha 22 2 44N37 122w13 8:08:52
New Pine Creek 19 2 42N00 120w18 8:01:12
Newport 21 7 44N39 124w03 8:16:12
Newton Creek 10 3 43N11 123w22 8:13:28
Ninety One 3 4 45N16 122w41 8:10:44
Nixon 22 2 44N23 123w05 8:12:20
Nonpareil 10 2 43N23 123w19 8:13:16
North Albany 2 13 44N40 123w07 8:12:28
North Bayside 6 2 43N30 124w10 8:16:40
North Beach 20 2 43N57 124w06 8:16:24
North Bend 6 2 43N24 124w14 8:16:56
North Howell 24 2 45N00 122w47 8:11:08
North Plains 34 4 45N36 123w00 8:12:00
North Powder 31 2 45N02 117w55 7:51:40
North Santiam 24 2 44N51 122w52 8:11:28
North Side 24 2 45N00 122w47 8:11:08
North Siuslaw 20 2 44N06 123w59 8:15:56
North Sweet Home 22 2 44N28 122w42 8:10:48
North Umpqua 10 2 43N17 123w01 8:12:04
Norway 6 2 43N06 124w09 8:16:36
Norwood 34 12 45N23 122w46 8:11:04
Noti 20 2 44N03 123w27 8:13:48
Nyssa 23 1 43N54 117w02 7:48:08
Oakdale 27 2 44N55 123w19 8:13:16
Oak Grove 3 12 45N25 122w38 8:10:32
Oak Grove 14 10 45N42 121w31 8:06:04
Oakland 10 2 43N25 123w18 8:13:12
Oaklawn 3 4 45N09 122w51 8:11:24
Oakridge 20 3 43N45 122w28 8:09:52
Oakville 22 2 44N28 123w07 8:12:28
O'Brien 17 2 42N04 123w42 8:14:48
Oceanside 29 11 45N28 123w58 8:15:52
Ochoco 7 2 44N22 120w46 8:03:04
Odell 14 4 45N38 121w32 8:06:08
Old Colton 3 4 45N10 122w26 8:09:44
Old Town 10 2 43N25 123w18 8:13:12
Olene 18 2 42N10 121w38 8:06:32
Olex 11 2 45N43 120w12 8:00:48
Olney 4 2 46N07 123w45 8:15:00
O'Neil Corners 3 4 45N16 122w41 8:10:44
Ontario 23 1 44N02 116w58 7:47:52
Ophir 8 2 42N34 124w23 8:17:32
Orchard View 36 14 45N13 123w12 8:12:48
Oregon Caves 17 2 42N10 123w39 8:14:36
Oregon City 3 12 45N21 122w36 8:10:24
Orenco 34 6 45N31 122w58 8:11:52
Oretech 18 3 42N13 121w45 8:07:00
Oretown 29 11 45N12 123w53 8:15:32
Orient 26 4 45N29 122w20 8:09:20
Orleans 22 13 44N38 123w06 8:12:24
Oswego 3 12 45N25 122w40 8:10:40
Otis 21 2 45N01 123w57 8:15:48
Otter Rock 21 11 44N45 124w03 8:16:12
Owyhee 23 1 43N49 117w07 7:48:28
Owyhee Corners 23 1 43N53 117w00 7:48:00
Oxbow 1 2 45N02 116w51 7:47:24
Pacific City 29 11 45N12 123w57 8:15:48
Page 22 13 44N38 123w06 8:12:24
Paisley 19 2 42N42 120w32 8:02:08
Palestine 2 13 44N38 123w06 8:12:24
Paradise Park 3 4 45N21 122w43 8:10:52
Parkdale 14 4 45N31 121w36 8:06:24
Parker 27 2 44N51 123w11 8:12:44
Parkersburg 6 2 43N07 124w24 8:17:36
Park Place 3 12 45N22 122w33 8:10:12
Parkrose 26 12 45N34 122w33 8:10:12
Parkrose Heights 26 12 45N33 122w34 8:10:16
Paulina 7 2 44N08 119w58 7:59:52
Pedee 27 2 44N51 123w14 8:12:56
Peel 10 2 43N18 123w06 8:12:24
Pelican City 18 3 42N13 121w45 8:07:00
Pendair Heights 30 16 45N40 118w48 7:55:12
Pendleton 30 16 45N40 118w47 7:55:08
Pendleton Junction 30 16 45N40 118w48 7:55:12
Peoria 22 2 44N28 123w07 8:12:28
Perry 31 2 45N20 118w05 7:52:20
Perrydale 27 4 45N03 123w16 8:13:04
Philomath 2 2 44N32 123w22 8:13:28
Phoenix 15 2 42N16 122w49 8:11:16
Piedmont 26 12 45N34 122w38 8:10:32
Pike 36 2 45N21 123w11 8:12:44
Pilot Rock 30 2 45N29 118w50 7:55:20
Pine 1 2 44N52 117w05 7:48:20
Pine Grove 14 10 45N42 121w31 8:06:04
Pine Grove 33 2 45N11 121w05 8:04:20
Pine Ridge 18 2 42N35 121w52 8:07:28
Pioneer 26 12 45N31 122w41 8:10:44
Pistol River 8 2 42N17 124w24 8:17:36
Pittsburg 5 4 45N52 123w11 8:12:44
Placer 17 2 42N38 123w19 8:13:16
Plainview 9 8 44N04 121w18 8:05:12
Plainview 22 2 44N28 123w07 8:12:28
Pleasant Hill 20 2 43N57 122w56 8:11:44
Pleasant Home 26 12 45N31 122w28 8:09:52
Pleasant Valley 1 9 44N47 117w50 7:51:20
Pleasant Valley 17 2 42N31 123w25 8:13:40
Pleasant Valley 26 12 45N28 122w27 8:09:48
Pleasant Valley 29 2 45N27 123w50 8:15:20
Plush 19 2 42N25 119w54 7:59:36
Poe Valley 18 2 42N14 121w31 8:06:04
Polk Station 27 2 44N55 123w19 8:13:16
Pondosa 31 2 45N01 117w38 7:50:32
Pony Village 6 2 43N24 124w14 8:16:56
Portland 26 12 45N32 122w37 8:10:28
Portland Zoo Railway 26 12 45N30 122w42 8:10:48
Port Orford 8 2 42N45 124w30 8:18:00
Post 7 2 44N10 120w29 8:01:56
Powell Butte 7 2 44N15 121w01 8:04:04
Powell Butte 26 12 45N29 122w31 8:10:04
Powellhurst 26 12 45N30 122w31 8:10:04
Powell Valley 26 12 45N31 122w28 8:09:52
Powers 6 2 42N53 124w04 8:16:16
Prairie City 12 2 44N28 118w43 7:54:52
Pratum 24 15 44N56 123w00 8:12:00
Prescott 5 4 46N03 122w53 8:11:32
Princeton 13 2 43N15 118w35 7:54:20
Prineville 7 8 44N18 120w51 8:03:24
Progress 34 12 45N29 122w48 8:11:12
Prospect 15 2 42N45 122w29 8:09:56
Prosper 6 2 43N07 124w24 8:17:36
Quatama 34 12 45N29 122w48 8:11:12
Quinaby 24 15 44N58 123w00 8:12:00
Quincy 5 4 46N09 123w10 8:12:40
Quines Creek 10 2 42N44 123w26 8:13:44
Rainier 5 4 46N05 122w56 8:11:44
Rajneesh 33 2 44N55 120w43 8:02:52
Rajneeshpuram 33 2 44N50 120w29 8:01:56
Raleigh Hills 34 12 45N30 122w47 8:11:08
Ramsey Hall 33 2 45N27 121w08 8:04:32
Randolph 6 2 43N07 124w24 8:17:36
Redland 3 4 45N20 122w27 8:09:48
Redmond 9 8 44N17 121w11 8:04:44
Reedsport 10 2 43N42 124w06 8:16:24
Reedville 34 12 45N29 122w48 8:11:12
Remote 6 2 43N00 123w54 8:15:36
Reservation 30 2 45N40 118w34 7:54:16
Rhododendron 3 4 45N20 121w55 8:07:40
Rice Hill 10 2 43N25 123w18 8:13:12
Richardson 20 2 44N02 123w35 8:14:20
Richland 1 2 44N46 117w10 7:48:40
Rickreall 27 2 44N56 123w14 8:12:56
Riddle 10 2 42N57 123w22 8:13:28
Rieth 30 2 45N40 118w54 7:55:36
Riley 13 2 43N32 119w28 7:57:52
Ritter 12 2 44N54 119w08 7:56:32
River Crest 3 12 45N23 122w36 8:10:24
River Grove 3 12 45N25 122w42 8:10:48
River Road 20 8 44N05 123w08 8:12:32
Riverside 22 13 44N38 123w06 8:12:24
Riverside 23 2 43N32 118w10 7:52:40
Riverton 6 2 43N10 124w16 8:17:04
Riverview 5 4 45N52 123w11 8:12:44
Riverview 20 3 44N13 123w12 8:12:48
Roads End 21 11 45N01 123w57 8:15:48
Roberts 24 15 44N54 123w02 8:12:08
Robertson 3 12 45N26 122w37 8:10:28
Robinwood 3 12 45N24 122w39 8:10:36
Rockaway 29 7 45N37 123w57 8:15:48
Rock Creek 1 2 44N55 117w56 7:51:44
Rock Creek 11 2 45N43 120w12 8:00:48
Rockford 14 10 45N42 121w31 8:06:04
Rockwood 26 12 45N33 122w31 8:10:04
Rocky Point 18 3 42N13 121w45 8:07:00
Rogue Elk 15 2 43N50 123w14 8:12:56
Rogue River 15 2 42N26 123w10 8:12:40
Rome 23 1 42N59 117w03 7:48:12
Roseburg 10 3 43N13 123w20 8:13:20
Rose City Park 26 12 45N32 122w36 8:10:24
Rosedale 24 15 44N54 123w02 8:12:08
Rose Lodge 21 11 45N01 123w52 8:15:28
Rosemont 3 12 45N24 122w39 8:10:36
Rowena 33 2 44N55 123w19 8:13:16
Roy 34 4 45N37 123w07 8:12:28
Ruch 15 2 42N14 123w03 8:12:12
Rufus 28 2 45N42 120w44 8:02:56
Ruggs 25 2 45N24 119w37 7:58:28
Russellville 26 12 45N31 122w33 8:10:12
Rye Valley 1 2 44N21 117w16 7:49:04
Saginaw 20 3 43N11 123w22 8:13:28
Saint Benedict 24 4 45N03 122w46 8:11:04

Saint Helens 5 17 45N52 122w48 8:11:12
Saint Johns 26 12 45N35 122w43 8:10:52
Saint Joseph 36 14 45N13 123w12 8:12:48
Saint Louis 24 2 45N07 122w54 8:11:36
Saint Paul 24 2 45N12 122w58 8:11:52
Salem 24 15 44N56 123w02 8:12:08
Salmon Harbor 10 2 43N42 124w06 8:16:24
Salt Creek 27 2 44N55 123w19 8:13:16
Sams Valley 15 2 42N28 122w51 8:11:24
Sand Lake 29 11 45N12 123w53 8:15:32
Sandy 3 5 45N24 122w16 8:09:04
San Marine 21 2 44N19 124w06 8:16:24
Santa Clara 20 2 44N06 123w08 8:12:32
Saunders Lake 6 2 43N24 124w14 8:16:56
Scappoose 5 5 45N45 122w53 8:11:32
Schefflin 34 6 45N31 123w03 8:12:12
Scholls 34 6 45N31 122w58 8:11:52
Scio 22 2 44N42 122w51 8:11:24
Scofield 34 4 45N41 123w12 8:12:48
Scottsburg 10 2 43N39 123w49 8:15:16
Scotts Mills 24 2 45N02 122w40 8:10:40
Seal Rock 21 2 44N30 124w05 8:16:20
Searose Beach 20 2 44N19 124w06 8:16:24
Seaside 4 14 46N00 123w56 8:15:44
Seghers 34 4 45N26 123w08 8:12:32
Sellwood Moreland 26 12 45N29 122w38 8:10:32
Selma 17 2 42N17 123w37 8:14:28
Seneca 12 2 44N08 118w58 7:55:52
Sewell 34 6 45N31 122w58 8:11:52
Shadowood 3 12 45N24 122w39 8:10:36
Shady Cove 15 2 42N37 122w49 8:11:16
Shady Dell 3 12 45N29 122w44 8:10:56
Shady Pine 18 3 42N13 121w45 8:07:00
Shaniko 33 2 45N00 120w45 8:03:00
Shaw 24 2 44N51 122w52 8:11:28
Shedd 22 2 44N28 123w07 8:12:28
Shelburn 22 2 44N42 122w51 8:11:24
Sheridan 36 15 45N06 123w24 8:13:36
Sherwood 34 4 45N21 122w50 8:11:20
Shiloh Basin 5 17 45N52 122w48 8:11:12
Shorewood 6 2 43N24 124w14 8:16:56
Sidney 24 2 44N43 123w00 8:12:00
Siletz 21 2 44N43 123w55 8:15:40
Siltcoos 20 2 43N53 124w04 8:16:16
Silver Lake 19 2 43N08 121w03 8:04:12
Silverton 24 4 45N01 122w47 8:11:08
Silverton Hills 24 2 44N59 122w43 8:10:52
Silvies 12 2 43N35 119w03 7:56:12
Silvies Landing 12 2 43N35 119w03 7:56:12
Simnasho 33 2 44N58 121w21 8:05:24
Siskiyou 15 2 42N04 122w37 8:10:28
Sisters 9 2 44N18 121w33 8:06:12
Sitkum 6 2 43N04 124w08 8:16:32
Six Corners 34 4 45N21 122w50 8:11:20
Sixes 8 2 42N49 124w29 8:17:56
Skelley 10 2 43N36 123w17 8:13:08
Skipanon 4 11 46N10 123w55 8:15:40
Skyland 3 12 45N25 122w42 8:10:48
Skyline 26 12 45N39 122w51 8:11:24
Smithfield 27 2 44N55 123w19 8:13:16
Smith Lake 26 12 45N36 122w41 8:10:44
Smock 33 2 45N15 121w10 8:04:40
Sodaville 22 2 44N29 122w52 8:11:28
Southbeach 21 2 44N37 124w03 8:16:12
South Corvallis 2 7 44N32 123w18 8:13:12
South Grants Pass 17 2 42N25 123w20 8:13:20
South Junction 33 2 44N51 121w05 8:04:20
South Lebanon 22 2 44N32 122w54 8:11:36
South Medford 15 2 42N20 122w57 8:11:48
South Oswego 3 12 45N25 122w42 8:10:48
South Scappoose 5 4 45N45 122w52 8:11:28
South Side 20 8 44N02 123w06 8:12:24
South Siuslaw 20 2 43N56 124w03 8:16:12
South Sweet Home 22 2 44N22 122w32 8:10:08
South Umpqua 10 2 42N51 123w08 8:12:32
Spicer 22 2 44N31 122w53 8:11:32
Sprague River 18 2 42N27 121w30 8:06:00
Spray 35 2 44N50 119w48 7:59:12
Springbrook 36 14 45N18 122w58 8:11:52
Springdale 26 12 45N32 122w26 8:09:44
Springfield 20 3 44N03 123w01 8:12:04
Springwater 3 4 45N21 122w43 8:10:52
Stafford 3 4 45N20 122w46 8:11:04
Staleys Junction 34 4 45N41 123w12 8:12:48
Stanfield 30 2 45N47 119w13 7:56:52
Starkey 31 2 45N16 118w18 7:53:12
Stayton 24 2 44N48 122w48 8:11:12
Steamboat 10 2 43N19 123w02 8:12:08
Stephens 10 2 43N25 123w18 8:13:12
Stewart Lennox Addition 18 3 42N13 121w45 8:07:00
Stimson Mill 34 4 45N26 123w08 8:12:32
Sublimity 24 2 44N50 122w47 8:11:08
Summer Lake 19 2 42N58 120w47 8:03:08
Summerville 31 2 45N29 118w00 7:52:00
Summit 2 2 44N38 123w35 8:14:20
Sumner 6 2 43N20 124w14 8:16:56
Sumpter 1 2 44N45 118w12 7:52:48
Sunnycrest 36 2 45N11 122w48 8:11:12
Sunnyside 3 12 45N25 122w34 8:10:16
Sunnyside 30 2 45N56 118w23 7:53:32
Sunny Valley 17 2 42N38 123w22 8:13:28
Sunriver 9 8 44N04 121w18 8:05:12
Sunset 3 12 45N24 122w39 8:10:36
Sunset Beach 4 11 46N10 123w55 8:15:40
Suplee 7 2 44N08 119w58 7:59:52
Surf Pines 4 11 46N10 123w55 8:15:40
Surprise Valley 10 2 43N01 123w18 8:13:12
Sutherlin 10 2 43N23 123w19 8:13:16
Suver 27 2 44N51 123w11 8:12:44
Suver Junction 27 2 44N51 123w14 8:12:56
Svensen 4 2 46N10 123w40 8:14:40
Sweet Home 22 2 44N24 122w44 8:10:56
Swisshome 20 2 44N04 123w48 8:15:12
Sylvan 26 12 45N30 122w43 8:10:52
Table Rock 15 2 42N22 122w56 8:11:44
Taft 21 11 44N57 124w01 8:16:04
Takilma 17 2 42N03 123w37 8:14:28
Talbot 24 2 44N43 123w00 8:12:00
Talent 15 2 42N15 122w47 8:11:08
Tallman 22 2 44N34 122w58 8:11:52
Tangent 22 2 44N33 123w07 8:12:28
Taylorville 4 2 46N06 123w12 8:12:48
Telocaset 31 2 45N06 117w49 7:51:16
Tenmile 10 2 43N05 123w34 8:14:16
Tennessee 22 2 44N35 122w55 8:11:40
Terrebonne 9 2 44N21 121w11 8:04:44
Thatcher 34 6 45N31 123w03 8:12:12
The Dalles 33 7 45N36 121w10 8:04:40
Thornhollow 30 2 45N46 118w34 7:54:16
Three Lynx 3 4 45N21 122w43 8:10:52
Three Pines 17 2 42N25 123w20 8:13:20
Three Rocks 29 11 45N01 123w57 8:15:48
Tide 20 2 44N03 123w48 8:15:12
Tide Creek 5 4 45N56 122w51 8:11:24
Tidewater 21 2 44N25 123w54 8:15:36
Tierra Del Mar 29 11 45N12 123w53 8:15:32
Tigard 34 12 45N26 122w46 8:11:04
Tillamook 29 2 45N27 123w51 8:15:24
Tiller 10 2 42N56 122w57 8:11:48
Timber 34 4 45N43 123w18 8:13:12
Timber Grove 3 4 45N17 122w32 8:10:08
Toketee Falls 10 2 43N19 123w02 8:12:08
Toledo 21 2 44N37 123w56 8:15:44
Tollgate 30 2 45N49 118w25 7:53:40
Tolovana Park 4 11 45N52 123w57 8:15:48
Top 12 2 44N49 119w25 7:57:40
Tophill 34 4 45N41 123w12 8:12:48
Trail 15 2 42N39 122w49 8:11:16
Trent 20 2 43N55 122w49 8:11:16
Triangle Lake 20 2 44N08 123w35 8:14:20
Tri City 10 2 43N01 123w18 8:13:12
Trout Creek 13 2 43N35 119w03 7:56:12
Troutdale 26 12 45N32 122w23 8:09:32
Troy 32 2 45N34 117w32 7:50:08
Tryon 26 12 45N27 122w42 8:10:48
Tualatin 34 12 45N23 122w46 8:11:04
Tumalo 9 2 44N14 121w22 8:05:28
Turner 24 2 44N51 122w57 8:11:48
Twelve Mile 26 12 45N31 122w28 8:09:52
Twickenham 35 2 44N34 120w09 8:00:36
Twin Rocks 29 11 45N34 123w55 8:15:40
Twomile 6 2 43N07 124w24 8:17:36
Tyee 10 2 43N22 123w28 8:13:52
Tygh Valley 33 2 45N15 121w10 8:04:40
Ukiah 30 2 45N08 118w56 7:55:44
Umapine 30 2 45N59 118w30 7:54:00
Umatilla 30 2 45N55 119w21 7:57:24
Umatilla Indian Reservation 30 2 44N46 121w16 8:05:04
Umpqua 10 2 43N22 123w28 8:13:52
Union 31 2 45N13 117w52 7:51:28
Union Creek 15 2 42N55 122w27 8:09:48
Union Gap 10 2 43N25 123w18 8:13:12
Union Mills 3 4 45N13 122w35 8:10:20
Union Point 22 2 44N24 122w56 8:11:44
Unionvale 36 2 45N13 123w04 8:12:16
Unity 1 2 44N26 118w12 7:52:48
Unity 20 2 43N58 122w49 8:11:16
University of Oregon 20 8 44N04 123w05 8:12:20
University Park 26 12 45N35 122w43 8:10:52
Upper Farm 21 2 44N45 123w47 8:15:08
Upper Highland 3 4 45N17 122w32 8:10:08
Upper Siuslaw 20 2 43N55 123w22 8:13:28
Upper Soda 22 2 44N24 122w29 8:09:56
Upper Walla Walla 30 2 45N56 118w17 7:53:08
Vale 23 1 43N59 117w15 7:49:00
Valley Falls 19 2 42N11 120w22 8:01:28
Valley Junction 27 15 45N04 123w29 8:13:56
Valsetz 27 2 44N50 123w39 8:14:36
Vandervert Ranch 9 8 44N04 121w18 8:05:12
Vanport 26 12 45N35 122w41 8:10:44
Vaughn 20 2 44N03 123w21 8:13:24
Venator 13 2 43N25 118w35 7:54:20
Veneta 20 2 44N03 123w21 8:13:24
Verboort 34 6 45N31 123w03 8:12:12
Vernonia 5 4 45N52 123w11 8:12:44
Vida 20 2 44N09 122w34 8:10:16
Vinemaple 4 11 46N00 123w55 8:15:40
Viola 3 4 45N21 122w43 8:10:52
Vista 24 15 44N54 123w02 8:12:08
Waconda 24 2 45N07 122w54 8:11:36
Wagontire 13 2 43N35 119w03 7:56:12
Wakonda Beach 21 2 44N26 124w04 8:16:16
Walden 20 2 43N48 123w04 8:12:16
Waldport 21 2 44N26 124w04 8:16:16
Walker 20 2 43N55 123w01 8:12:04
Wallace Bridge 27 15 45N04 123w29 8:13:56

OREGON

Wallowa 32 2 45N34 117w32 7:50:08
Walterville 20 2 44N04 122w48 8:11:12
Walton 20 2 44N02 123w35 8:14:20
Wamic 33 2 45N14 121w16 8:05:04
Wankers Corners 3 12 45N24 122w39 8:10:36
Wapato 36 2 45N26 123w08 8:12:32
Wapinitia 33 2 45N07 121w16 8:05:04
Warm Springs 16 2 44N46 121w16 8:05:04
Warm Springs Indian Res 16 2 44N46 121w16 8:05:04
Warner Valley 19 2 42N29 119w47 7:59:08
Warren 5 4 45N50 122w55 8:11:40
Warrendale 26 4 45N38 121w57 8:07:48
Warrenton 4 8 46N10 123w56 8:15:44
Wasco 28 2 45N36 120w42 8:02:48
Waterloo 22 2 44N30 122w49 8:11:16
Watseco 29 11 45N34 123w55 8:15:40
Waverly Heights 3 12 45N26 122w37 8:10:28
Weatherby 1 2 44N35 117w28 7:49:52
Wecoma Beach 21 11 44N57 124w01 8:16:04
Wedderburn 8 2 42N26 124w25 8:17:40
Welches 3 4 45N21 121w58 8:07:52
Wemme 3 4 45N21 121w58 8:07:52
West 4 11 46N10 123w55 8:15:40
Westfall 23 1 44N00 117w43 7:50:52
Westfir 20 2 43N45 122w31 8:10:04
West Haven 34 12 45N30 122w47 8:11:08
Westlake 20 2 43N53 124w06 8:16:24
West Linn 3 12 45N22 122w38 8:10:32
West Main 15 2 42N22 122w56 8:11:44
West Oak 20 2 43N43 122w28 8:09:52
Weston 30 2 45N49 118w26 7:53:44
Westport 4 2 46N08 123w23 8:13:32
West Powellhurst 26 12 45N29 122w33 8:10:12
West Rainier 5 12 45N24 122w39 8:10:36
West Saint Helens 5 17 45N52 122w48 8:11:12
West Salem 27 15 44N57 123w05 8:12:20
West Scio 22 2 44N42 122w51 8:11:24
West Side 19 2 42N11 120w22 8:01:28
West Side 20 8 44N05 123w08 8:12:32
West Slope 34 12 45N30 122w46 8:11:04
West Stayton 24 2 44N51 122w52 8:11:28
West Sweet Home 22 2 44N26 122w44 8:10:56
West Union 34 6 45N31 122w58 8:11:52
West Vale 23 1 43N58 117w22 7:49:28
Westwood 3 12 45N26 122w37 8:10:28
West Woodburn 24 2 45N09 122w51 8:11:24
Wetmore 35 2 44N59 120w03 8:00:12
Weyerhaeuser Townsite 18 3 42N13 121w45 8:07:00
Wheatland 36 15 44N57 123w05 8:12:20
Wheeler 29 7 45N41 123w53 8:15:32
Wheeler Heights 29 11 45N41 123w53 8:15:32
Whiskey Hill 3 4 45N11 122w48 8:11:12
White City 15 2 42N26 122w51 8:11:24
Whiteson 36 14 45N09 123w12 8:12:48
Whitney 1 2 44N47 118w18 7:53:12
Wichita 3 12 45N26 122w37 8:10:28
Wilark 5 4 45N45 122w52 8:11:28
Wilbur 10 2 43N19 123w21 8:13:24
Wilderville 17 2 42N21 123w32 8:14:08
Wildwood 3 4 44N55 120w43 8:02:52
Willamette 3 12 45N24 122w39 8:10:36
Willamette City 20 2 43N43 122w28 8:09:52
Willamina 36 15 45N05 123w29 8:13:56
Williams 17 2 42N15 123w16 8:13:04
Willowcreek 23 1 43N59 117w15 7:49:00
Willowdale 16 2 44N38 121w08 8:04:32
Willsburg Junction 3 12 45N26 122w37 8:10:28
Wilson Beach 29 2 45N27 123w50 8:15:20
Wilsonia 3 12 45N25 122w42 8:10:48
Wilsonville 3 4 45N18 122w46 8:11:04
Wimer 15 2 42N26 123w10 8:12:40
Winberry 20 2 43N58 122w49 8:11:16
Winchester 10 2 43N17 123w21 8:13:24
Winchester Bay 10 2 43N41 124w10 8:16:40
Windmaster Corner 14 10 45N42 121w31 8:06:04
Winema Beach 29 11 45N12 123w53 8:15:32
Wingville 1 2 44N54 118w01 7:52:04
Winston 10 2 43N07 123w25 8:13:40
Winterville 6 2 43N07 124w24 8:17:36
Wistful Vista 16 2 44N38 121w08 8:04:32
Witch Hazel 34 6 45N31 122w58 8:11:52
Wocus 18 2 42N17 121w48 8:07:12
Wolf Creek 17 2 42N42 123w24 8:13:36
Wonder 17 2 42N23 123w28 8:13:52
Woodburn 24 2 45N09 122w51 8:11:24
Woods 29 11 45N12 123w53 8:15:32
Woodson 5 4 46N06 123w12 8:12:48
Wood Village 26 12 45N32 122w24 8:09:36
Worden 18 2 42N02 121w52 8:07:28
Wren 2 2 44N32 123w21 8:13:24
Wyeth 14 4 45N40 121w53 8:07:32
Yachats 21 2 44N19 124w06 8:16:24
Yamhill 36 2 45N22 123w16 8:13:04
Yampo 36 13 45N07 123w12 8:12:48
Yankton 5 17 45N52 122w48 8:11:12
Yaquina 21 2 44N38 124w03 8:16:12
Yoder 3 4 45N10 122w41 8:10:44
Yoncalla 10 2 43N36 123w17 8:13:08
Yonna 18 2 42N12 121w24 8:05:36
Zigzag 3 4 45N20 121w55 8:07:40

TIME TABLES

The law requiring that birth times be recorded in EST was in effect until April 12, 1971. But this law was infrequently observed. Daylight time was widely observed during the 1950's. However this is not fully documented for smaller towns.

PA # 1		
Before	4/13/1887	LMT
4/13/1887	12:00	EST
3/31/1918	02:00	EWT
10/27/1918	02:00	EST
3/30/1919	02:00	EWT
10/26/1919	02:00	EST
2/09/1942	02:00	EWT
9/30/1945	02:00	US#2

PA # 2		
Before	4/13/1887	LMT
4/13/1887	12:00	EST
3/31/1918	02:00	EWT
10/27/1918	02:00	EST
3/30/1919	02:00	EWT
10/26/1919	02:00	EST
4/24/1938	02:00	US#2

PA # 3		
Before	4/13/1887	LMT
4/13/1887	12:00	EST
3/31/1918	02:00	EWT
10/27/1918	02:00	EST
3/30/1919	02:00	EWT
10/26/1919	02:00	EST
4/27/1941	02:00	US#2

PA # 4		
Before	4/13/1887	LMT
4/13/1887	12:00	EST
3/31/1918	02:00	EWT
10/27/1918	02:00	EST
3/30/1919	02:00	EWT
10/26/1919	02:00	EST
2/09/1942	02:00	EWT
9/30/1945	02:00	EST
4/27/1947	02:00	US#2

PA # 5		
Before	4/13/1887	LMT
4/13/1887	12:00	EST
3/31/1918	02:00	EWT
10/27/1918	02:00	EST
3/30/1919	02:00	EWT
10/26/1919	02:00	EST
2/09/1942	02:00	EWT
9/30/1945	02:00	EST
4/24/1949	02:00	US#2

PA # 6		
Before	4/13/1887	LMT
4/13/1887	12:00	EST
3/31/1918	02:00	EWT
10/27/1918	02:00	EST
3/30/1919	02:00	EWT
10/26/1919	02:00	EST
2/09/1942	02:00	EWT
9/30/1945	02:00	EST
4/29/1956	02:00	US#2

PA # 7		
Before	4/13/1887	LMT
4/13/1887	12:00	EST
3/31/1918	02:00	EWT
10/27/1918	02:00	EST
3/30/1919	02:00	EWT
10/26/1919	02:00	EST
2/09/1942	02:00	EWT
9/30/1945	02:00	EST
4/26/1953	02:00	US#2

PA # 8		
Before	4/13/1887	LMT
4/13/1887	12:00	EST
3/31/1918	02:00	EWT
10/27/1918	02:00	EST
3/30/1919	02:00	EWT
10/26/1919	02:00	EST
4/26/1931	02:00	US#2

PA # 9		
Before	4/13/1887	LMT
4/13/1887	12:00	EST
3/31/1918	02:00	EWT
10/27/1918	02:00	EST
3/30/1919	02:00	EWT
10/26/1919	02:00	EST
4/24/1921	02:00	US#2

PA # 10		
Before	4/13/1887	LMT
4/13/1887	12:00	EST
3/31/1918	02:00	EWT
10/27/1918	02:00	EST
3/30/1919	02:00	EWT
10/26/1919	02:00	EST
4/26/1925	02:00	US#2

PA # 11		
Before	4/13/1887	LMT
4/13/1887	12:00	EST
3/31/1918	02:00	EWT
10/27/1918	02:00	EST
3/30/1919	02:00	EWT
10/26/1919	02:00	EST
4/24/1921	02:00	EDT
9/25/1921	02:00	EST
4/30/1922	02:00	EDT
9/24/1922	02:00	EST
4/29/1923	02:00	EDT
9/30/1923	02:00	EST
4/27/1924	02:00	EDT
9/28/1924	02:00	EST
4/26/1925	02:00	EDT
9/27/1925	02:00	EST
4/25/1926	02:00	EDT
9/26/1926	02:00	EST
4/24/1927	02:00	EDT
9/25/1927	02:00	EST
4/29/1928	02:00	EDT
9/30/1928	02:00	EST
4/28/1929	02:00	EDT
9/29/1929	02:00	EST
4/27/1930	02:00	EDT
9/28/1930	02:00	EST
4/26/1931	02:00	EDT
9/27/1931	02:00	EST
4/24/1932	02:00	EDT
9/25/1932	02:00	EST
4/30/1933	02:00	EDT
9/24/1933	02:00	EST
4/29/1934	02:00	EDT
9/30/1934	02:00	EST
4/28/1935	02:00	EDT
9/29/1935	02:00	EST
4/26/1936	02:00	EDT
9/27/1936	02:00	EST
4/25/1937	02:00	EDT
9/26/1937	02:00	EST
4/24/1938	02:00	EDT
9/25/1938	02:00	EST
4/30/1939	02:00	EDT
9/24/1939	02:00	EST
4/28/1940	02:00	EDT
9/29/1940	02:00	EST
4/27/1941	02:00	EDT
9/28/1941	02:00	EST
2/09/1942	02:00	EWT
9/30/1945	02:00	EST
4/28/1946	02:00	EDT
9/29/1946	02:00	EST
4/27/1947	02:00	EDT
9/28/1947	02:00	EST
4/25/1948	02:00	EDT
9/26/1948	02:00	EST
4/24/1949	02:00	EDT
9/25/1949	02:00	EST
4/30/1950	02:00	EDT
9/24/1950	02:00	EST
4/29/1951	02:00	EDT
9/30/1951	02:00	EST
4/27/1952	02:00	EDT
9/28/1952	02:00	EST
4/26/1953	02:00	EDT
9/27/1953	02:00	EST
4/25/1954	02:00	EDT
9/26/1954	02:00	EST
4/24/1955	02:00	EDT
9/25/1955	02:00	EST
4/29/1956	02:00	EDT
9/30/1956	02:00	EST
4/28/1957	02:00	EDT
9/29/1957	02:00	EST
4/27/1958	02:00	EDT
9/28/1958	02:00	EST
4/26/1959	02:00	EDT
9/27/1959	02:00	EST
4/24/1960	02:00	EDT
9/25/1960	02:00	EST
4/30/1961	02:00	EDT
9/24/1961	02:00	EST
4/29/1962	02:00	US#2

PA # 12		
Before	4/13/1887	LMT
4/13/1887	12:00	EST
3/31/1918	02:00	EWT
10/27/1918	02:00	EST
3/30/1919	02:00	EWT
10/26/1919	02:00	EST
4/28/1929	02:00	US#2

PA # 13		
Before	4/13/1887	LMT
4/13/1887	12:00	EST
3/31/1918	02:00	EWT
10/27/1918	02:00	EST
3/30/1919	02:00	EWT
10/26/1919	02:00	EST
4/27/1930	02:00	US#2

PA # 14		
Before	4/13/1887	LMT
4/13/1887	12:00	EST
3/31/1918	02:00	EWT
10/27/1918	02:00	EST
3/30/1919	02:00	EWT
10/26/1919	02:00	EST
4/30/1933	02:00	US#2

PA # 15		
Before	4/13/1887	LMT
4/13/1887	12:00	EST
3/31/1918	02:00	EWT
10/27/1918	02:00	EST
3/30/1919	02:00	EWT
10/26/1919	02:00	EST
4/28/1935	02:00	US#2

PA # 16		
Before	4/13/1887	LMT
4/13/1887	12:00	EST
3/31/1918	02:00	EWT
10/27/1918	02:00	EST
3/30/1919	02:00	EWT
10/26/1919	02:00	EST
4/24/1932	02:00	EDT
9/25/1932	02:00	EST
4/24/1938	02:00	US#2

PA # 17		
Before	4/13/1887	LMT
4/13/1887	12:00	PA#8
9/30/1945	02:00	EST
4/24/1949	02:00	US#2

PA # 18		
Before	4/13/1887	LMT
4/13/1887	12:00	EST
3/31/1918	02:00	EWT
10/27/1918	02:00	EST
3/30/1919	02:00	EWT
10/26/1919	02:00	EST
4/29/1934	02:00	EDT
9/30/1934	02:00	EST
4/28/1935	02:00	EDT
9/29/1935	02:00	EST
4/26/1936	02:00	EDT
9/27/1936	02:00	EST
2/09/1942	02:00	EWT
9/30/1945	02:00	EST
4/28/1946	02:00	US#2

PA # 19		
Before	4/13/1887	LMT
4/13/1887	12:00	PA#8
4/29/1956	02:00	EDT
9/30/1956	02:00	EST
4/28/1957	02:00	US#2

PA # 20		
Before	4/13/1887	LMT
4/13/1887	12:00	EST
3/31/1918	02:00	EWT
10/27/1918	02:00	EST
3/30/1919	02:00	EWT
10/26/1919	02:00	EST
4/28/1935	02:00	EDT
9/29/1935	02:00	EST
2/09/1942	02:00	EWT
9/30/1945	02:00	EST
4/28/1946	02:00	US#2

PA # 21		
Before	4/13/1887	LMT
4/13/1887	12:00	EST
3/31/1918	02:00	EWT
10/27/1918	02:00	EST
3/30/1919	02:00	EWT
10/26/1919	02:00	EST
5/05/1935	02:00	EDT
9/29/1935	02:00	PA#1
4/30/1967	02:00	US#1

PA # 22		
Before	4/13/1887	LMT
4/13/1887	12:00	EST
3/31/1918	02:00	EWT
10/27/1918	02:00	EST
3/30/1919	02:00	EWT
10/26/1919	02:00	EST
4/30/1939	02:00	EDT
9/24/1939	02:00	EST
2/09/1942	02:00	EWT
9/30/1945	02:00	EST
4/29/1951	02:00	US#2

PA # 23		
Before	4/13/1887	LMT
4/13/1887	12:00	EST
3/31/1918	02:00	EWT
10/27/1918	02:00	EST
3/30/1919	02:00	EWT
10/26/1919	02:00	EST
4/29/1934	02:00	US#2

PA # 24		
Before	4/13/1887	LMT
4/13/1887	12:00	PA#2
9/25/1938	02:00	EST
4/27/1941	02:00	US#2

PA # 25		
Before	4/13/1887	LMT
4/13/1887	12:00	EST
3/31/1918	02:00	EWT
10/27/1918	02:00	EST
3/30/1919	02:00	EWT
10/26/1919	02:00	EST
4/30/1939	02:00	US#2

PA # 26		
Before	4/13/1887	LMT
4/13/1887	12:00	EST
3/31/1918	02:00	EWT
10/27/1918	02:00	EST
3/30/1919	02:00	EWT
10/26/1919	02:00	EST
4/30/1933	02:00	EDT
9/24/1933	02:00	PA#2
4/30/1967	02:00	US#1

PA # 27		
Before	4/13/1887	LMT
4/13/1887	12:00	EST
3/31/1918	02:00	EWT
10/27/1918	02:00	EST
3/30/1919	02:00	EWT
10/26/1919	02:00	EST
4/28/1940	02:00	US#2

PA # 28		
Before	4/13/1887	LMT
4/13/1887	12:00	EST
3/31/1918	02:00	EWT
10/27/1918	02:00	EST
3/30/1919	02:00	EWT
10/26/1919	02:00	EST
4/26/1936	02:00	US#2

PA # 29		
Before	4/13/1887	LMT
4/13/1887	12:00	EST
3/31/1918	02:00	EWT
10/27/1918	02:00	EST
3/30/1919	02:00	EWT
10/26/1919	02:00	EST
4/28/1940	02:00	EDT
9/29/1940	02:00	EST
4/27/1941	02:00	EDT
9/28/1941	02:00	EST
2/09/1942	02:00	EWT
9/30/1945	02:00	EST
4/26/1953	02:00	US#2

PA # 30		
Before	4/13/1887	LMT
4/13/1887	12:00	EST
3/31/1918	02:00	EWT
10/27/1918	02:00	EST
3/30/1919	02:00	EWT
10/26/1919	02:00	EST
4/24/1932	02:00	EDT
9/25/1932	02:00	EST
4/26/1936	02:00	US#2

PA # 31		
Before	4/13/1887	LMT
4/13/1887	12:00	EST
3/31/1918	02:00	EWT
10/27/1918	02:00	EST
3/30/1919	02:00	EWT
10/26/1919	02:00	EST
4/24/1932	02:00	EDT
9/25/1932	02:00	EST
4/30/1933	02:00	EDT
9/24/1933	02:00	EST
4/29/1934	02:00	EDT
9/30/1934	02:00	EST
4/24/1938	02:00	US#2

PA # 32		
Before	4/13/1887	LMT
4/13/1887	12:00	PA#8
9/27/1931	02:00	EST
4/30/1932	02:00	US#2

PA # 33		
Before	4/13/1887	LMT
4/13/1887	12:00	EST
3/31/1918	02:00	EWT
10/27/1918	02:00	EST
3/30/1919	02:00	EWT
10/26/1919	02:00	EST
4/27/1941	02:00	EDT
9/28/1941	02:00	EST
2/09/1942	02:00	EWT
9/30/1945	02:00	EST
4/28/1946	02:00	EDT
9/29/1946	02:00	EST
4/27/1947	02:00	EDT
9/28/1947	02:00	EST
4/25/1948	02:00	EDT
9/26/1948	02:00	EST
4/24/1949	02:00	EDT
9/25/1949	02:00	EST
4/30/1950	02:00	EDT
9/24/1950	02:00	EST
4/29/1951	02:00	EDT
9/30/1951	02:00	EST
4/27/1952	02:00	EDT
9/28/1952	02:00	EST
4/26/1953	02:00	EDT
9/27/1953	02:00	EST
4/25/1954	02:00	EDT
9/26/1954	02:00	EST
4/24/1955	02:00	EDT
10/30/1955	02:00	EST
4/29/1956	02:00	EDT
9/30/1956	02:00	EST
4/28/1957	02:00	EDT
9/29/1957	02:00	EST
4/27/1958	02:00	EDT
9/28/1958	02:00	EST
4/26/1959	02:00	EDT
9/27/1959	02:00	EST
4/24/1960	02:00	EDT
9/25/1960	02:00	EST
4/30/1961	02:00	US#2

PA # 34		
Before	4/13/1887	LMT
4/13/1887	12:00	PA#3
2/09/1942	02:00	EWT
9/30/1945	02:00	EST
4/27/1947	02:00	EDT
9/28/1947	02:00	EST
4/25/1948	02:00	EDT
9/26/1948	02:00	EST
4/24/1949	02:00	EDT
9/25/1949	02:00	EST
4/30/1950	02:00	EDT
9/24/1950	02:00	EST
4/29/1951	02:00	EDT
9/30/1951	02:00	EST
4/27/1952	02:00	EDT
9/28/1952	02:00	EST
4/29/1956	02:00	US#2

PA # 35		
Before	4/13/1887	LMT
4/13/1887	12:00	EST
3/31/1918	02:00	EWT
10/27/1918	02:00	EST
3/30/1919	02:00	EWT
10/26/1919	02:00	EST
4/27/1941	02:00	EDT
9/28/1941	02:00	EST
2/09/1942	02:00	EWT
9/30/1945	02:00	EST
4/26/1953	02:00	US#2

PA # 36		
Before	4/13/1887	LMT
4/13/1887	12:00	EST
3/31/1918	02:00	EWT
10/27/1918	02:00	EST
3/30/1919	02:00	EWT
10/26/1919	02:00	EST
4/27/1941	02:00	EDT
9/28/1941	02:00	EST
2/09/1942	02:00	EWT
9/30/1945	02:00	EST
4/27/1947	02:00	EDT
9/28/1947	02:00	EST
4/25/1948	02:00	EDT
9/26/1948	02:00	EST
4/24/1949	02:00	EDT
9/25/1949	02:00	EST
4/30/1950	02:00	EDT
9/24/1950	02:00	EST
4/29/1951	02:00	EDT
9/30/1951	02:00	EST
4/27/1952	02:00	EDT
9/28/1952	02:00	EST
4/26/1953	02:00	EDT
9/27/1953	02:00	EST
4/25/1954	02:00	EDT
9/26/1954	02:00	EST
4/24/1955	02:00	EDT
9/25/1955	02:00	EST
4/29/1956	02:00	EDT
9/30/1956	02:00	EST
4/28/1957	02:00	US#2

PA # 37		
Before	4/13/1887	LMT
4/13/1887	12:00	EST
3/31/1918	02:00	EWT
10/27/1918	02:00	EST
3/30/1919	02:00	EWT
10/26/1919	02:00	EST
4/27/1941	02:00	EDT
9/28/1941	02:00	EST
2/09/1942	02:00	EWT
9/30/1945	02:00	EST
4/29/1956	02:00	US#2

PA # 38		
Before	4/13/1887	LMT
4/13/1887	12:00	EST
3/31/1918	02:00	EWT
10/27/1918	02:00	EST
3/30/1919	02:00	EWT
10/26/1919	02:00	EST
4/27/1941	02:00	EDT
9/28/1941	02:00	EST
2/09/1942	02:00	EWT
9/30/1945	02:00	EST

PENNSYLVANIA

4/30/1950 02:00 US#2
....
PA # 39
Before 4/13/1887 LMT
4/13/1887 12:00 PA#8
9/27/1931 02:00 EST
4/28/1940 02:00 EDT
9/29/1940 02:00 EST
4/27/1941 02:00 EDT
9/28/1941 02:00 EST
2/09/1942 02:00 EWT
9/30/1945 02:00 EST
4/28/1946 02:00 EDT
9/29/1946 02:00 EST
4/27/1947 02:00 EDT
9/28/1947 02:00 EST
4/25/1948 02:00 EDT
9/26/1948 02:00 EST
4/24/1949 02:00 EDT
9/25/1949 02:00 EST
4/30/1950 02:00 EDT
9/24/1950 02:00 EST
4/29/1951 02:00 EDT
9/30/1951 02:00 EST
4/27/1952 02:00 EDT
9/28/1952 02:00 EST
4/26/1953 02:00 EDT
9/27/1953 02:00 EST
4/25/1954 02:00 EDT
9/26/1954 02:00 EST
4/24/1955 02:00 EDT
9/25/1955 02:00 EST
4/29/1956 02:00 EDT
10/28/1956 02:00 EST
4/28/1957 02:00 EDT
10/27/1957 02:00 EST
4/27/1958 02:00 EDT
9/28/1958 02:00 EST
4/26/1959 02:00 US#2
....
PA # 40
Before 4/13/1887 LMT
4/13/1887 12:00 PA#1
9/28/1947 02:00 EST
4/26/1953 02:00 US#2
....
PA # 41
Before 4/13/1887 LMT
4/13/1887 12:00 PA#1
9/29/1946 02:00 EST
4/24/1949 02:00 US#2
....
PA # 42
Before 4/13/1887 LMT
4/13/1887 12:00 PA#1
4/24/1955 02:00 EDT
9/25/1955 02:00 EST
4/29/1956 02:00 EDT
9/30/1956 02:00 EST
4/28/1957 02:00 EDT
9/29/1957 02:00 EST
4/27/1958 02:00 US#2
....
PA # 43
Before 4/13/1887 LMT
4/13/1887 12:00 PA#1
9/29/1946 02:00 EST
4/26/1953 02:00 US#2
....
PA # 44
Before 4/13/1887 LMT
4/13/1887 12:00 PA#1
4/24/1955 02:00 EDT
9/25/1955 02:00 EST
4/29/1956 02:00 US#2
....
PA # 45
Before 4/13/1887 LMT
4/13/1887 12:00 EST
3/31/1918 02:00 EWT
10/27/1918 02:00 EST
3/30/1919 02:00 EWT
10/26/1919 02:00 EST
4/28/1935 02:00 EDT
9/29/1935 02:00 EST
4/26/1936 02:00 EDT
9/27/1936 02:00 EST
2/09/1942 02:00 EWT
9/30/1945 02:00 EST
4/28/1946 02:00 EDT
9/29/1946 02:00 EST
4/27/1947 02:00 EDT
9/28/1947 02:00 EST
4/25/1948 02:00 EDT
9/26/1948 02:00 EST
4/24/1949 02:00 EDT
9/25/1949 02:00 EST
4/30/1950 02:00 EDT
9/24/1950 02:00 EST
4/29/1951 02:00 EDT
9/30/1951 02:00 EST
4/27/1952 02:00 EDT
9/28/1952 02:00 EST
4/26/1953 02:00 EDT
9/27/1953 02:00 EST
4/25/1954 02:00 EDT
9/26/1954 02:00 EST
4/24/1955 02:00 EDT
9/25/1955 02:00 EST
4/29/1956 02:00 US#2
....
PA # 46
Before 4/13/1887 LMT
4/13/1887 12:00 PA#8
4/29/1934 02:00 EDT
10/27/1934 02:00 US#2
....
PA # 47
Before 4/13/1887 LMT
4/13/1887 12:00 PA#8
4/26/1936 02:00 EDT
10/25/1936 02:00 US#2
....
PA # 48
Before 4/13/1887 LMT
4/13/1887 12:00 PA#4
9/28/1952 02:00 EST
4/29/1956 02:00 US#2
....
PA # 49
Before 4/13/1887 LMT
4/13/1887 12:00 EST
3/31/1918 02:00 EWT
10/27/1918 02:00 EST
3/30/1919 02:00 EWT
10/26/1919 02:00 EST
4/26/1936 02:00 EDT
9/27/1936 02:00 EST
4/28/1940 02:00 US#2
....
PA # 50
Before 4/13/1887 LMT
4/13/1887 12:00 EST
3/31/1918 02:00 EWT
10/27/1918 02:00 EST
3/30/1919 02:00 EWT
10/26/1919 02:00 EST
2/09/1942 02:00 EWT
9/30/1945 02:00 EST
4/27/1947 02:00 EDT
9/28/1947 02:00 EST
4/25/1948 02:00 EDT
9/26/1948 02:00 EST
4/24/1949 02:00 EDT
9/25/1949 02:00 EST
4/30/1950 02:00 EDT
9/24/1950 02:00 EST
4/29/1951 02:00 EDT
9/30/1951 02:00 EST
4/27/1952 02:00 EDT
9/28/1952 02:00 EST
4/26/1953 02:00 EDT
9/27/1953 02:00 EST
4/25/1954 02:00 EDT
9/26/1954 02:00 EST
4/24/1955 02:00 EDT
9/25/1955 02:00 EST
4/29/1956 02:00 EDT
9/30/1956 02:00 EST
4/28/1957 02:00 EDT
9/29/1957 02:00 EST
4/27/1958 02:00 EDT
9/28/1958 02:00 EST
4/26/1959 02:00 EDT
9/27/1959 02:00 EST
4/24/1960 02:00 EDT
9/25/1960 02:00 EST
4/30/1961 02:00 US#2
....
PA # 51
Before 4/13/1887 LMT
4/13/1887 12:00 EST
3/31/1918 02:00 EWT
10/27/1918 02:00 EST
3/30/1919 02:00 EWT
10/26/1919 02:00 EST
2/09/1942 02:00 EWT
9/30/1945 02:00 EST
4/25/1948 02:00 US#2
....
PA # 52
Before 4/13/1887 LMT
4/13/1887 12:00 EST
3/31/1918 02:00 EWT
10/27/1918 02:00 EST
3/30/1919 02:00 EWT
10/26/1919 02:00 EST
2/09/1942 02:00 EWT
9/30/1945 02:00 EST
4/25/1948 02:00 EDT
9/26/1948 02:00 EST
4/26/1953 02:00 US#2
....
PA # 53
Before 4/13/1887 LMT
4/13/1887 12:00 EST
3/31/1918 02:00 EWT
10/27/1918 02:00 EST
3/30/1919 02:00 EWT
10/26/1919 02:00 EST
2/09/1942 02:00 EWT
9/30/1945 02:00 EST
4/25/1948 02:00 EDT
9/26/1948 02:00 EST
4/24/1949 02:00 EDT
9/25/1949 02:00 EST
4/30/1950 02:00 EDT
9/24/1950 02:00 EST
4/29/1951 02:00 EDT
9/30/1951 02:00 EST
4/27/1952 02:00 EDT
9/28/1952 02:00 EST
4/26/1953 02:00 EDT
9/27/1953 02:00 EST
4/25/1954 02:00 EDT
9/26/1954 02:00 EST
4/24/1955 02:00 EDT
10/30/1955 02:00 EST
4/29/1956 02:00 EDT
10/28/1956 02:00 EST
4/28/1957 02:00 EDT
10/27/1957 02:00 EST
4/27/1958 02:00 EDT
9/28/1958 02:00 EST
4/26/1959 02:00 EDT
9/27/1959 02:00 EST
4/24/1960 02:00 EDT
9/25/1960 02:00 EST
4/30/1961 02:00 US#2
....
PA # 54
Before 4/13/1887 LMT
4/13/1887 12:00 EST
3/31/1918 02:00 EWT
10/27/1918 02:00 EST
3/30/1919 02:00 EWT
10/26/1919 02:00 EST
2/09/1942 02:00 EWT
9/30/1945 02:00 EST
4/27/1947 02:00 EDT
9/28/1947 02:00 EST
4/25/1948 02:00 EDT
9/26/1948 02:00 EST
4/24/1949 02:00 EDT
9/25/1949 02:00 EST
4/30/1950 02:00 EDT
9/24/1950 02:00 EST
4/29/1951 02:00 EDT
9/30/1951 02:00 EST
4/27/1952 02:00 EDT
9/28/1952 02:00 EST
4/26/1953 02:00 EDT
9/27/1953 02:00 EST
4/25/1954 02:00 EDT
9/26/1954 02:00 EST
4/24/1955 02:00 EDT
10/02/1955 02:00 EST
4/29/1956 02:00 EDT
9/30/1956 02:00 EST
4/28/1957 02:00 EDT
9/29/1957 02:00 EST
4/27/1958 02:00 EDT
9/28/1958 02:00 EST
4/26/1959 02:00 EDT
9/27/1959 02:00 EST
4/24/1960 02:00 EDT
9/25/1960 02:00 EST
4/30/1961 02:00 EDT
9/24/1961 02:00 EST
4/29/1962 02:00 US#2
....
PA # 55
Before 4/13/1887 LMT
4/13/1887 12:00 EST
3/31/1918 02:00 EWT
10/27/1918 02:00 EST
3/30/1919 02:00 EWT
10/26/1919 02:00 EST
2/09/1942 02:00 EWT
9/30/1945 02:00 EST
4/25/1948 02:00 EDT
9/26/1948 02:00 EST
4/24/1949 02:00 EDT
9/25/1949 02:00 EST
4/30/1950 02:00 EDT
9/24/1950 02:00 EST
4/29/1951 02:00 EDT
9/30/1951 02:00 EST
4/27/1952 02:00 EDT
9/28/1952 02:00 EST
4/26/1953 02:00 EDT
9/27/1953 02:00 EST
4/25/1954 02:00 EDT
9/26/1954 02:00 EST
4/24/1955 02:00 EDT
9/25/1955 02:00 EST
4/29/1956 02:00 EDT
9/30/1956 02:00 EST
4/28/1957 02:00 EDT
9/29/1957 02:00 EST
4/27/1958 02:00 EDT
9/28/1958 02:00 EST
4/26/1959 02:00 EDT
9/27/1959 02:00 EST
4/24/1960 02:00 EDT
9/25/1960 02:00 EST
4/30/1961 02:00 US#2
....
PA # 56
Before 4/13/1887 LMT
4/13/1887 12:00 EST
3/31/1918 02:00 EWT
10/27/1918 02:00 EST
3/30/1919 02:00 EWT
10/26/1919 02:00 EST
2/09/1942 02:00 EWT
9/30/1945 02:00 EST
4/30/1950 02:00 US#2
....
PA # 57
Before 4/13/1887 LMT
4/13/1887 12:00 EST
3/31/1918 02:00 EWT
10/27/1918 02:00 EST
3/30/1919 02:00 EWT
10/26/1919 02:00 EST
2/09/1942 02:00 EWT
9/30/1945 02:00 EST
4/25/1948 02:00 EDT
9/26/1948 02:00 EST
4/26/1953 02:00 EDT
9/27/1953 02:00 EST
4/25/1954 02:00 EDT
9/26/1954 02:00 EST
4/24/1955 02:00 EDT
10/09/1955 02:00 EST
4/29/1956 02:00 EDT
9/30/1956 02:00 EST
4/28/1957 02:00 EDT
9/29/1957 02:00 EST
4/27/1958 02:00 EDT
9/28/1958 02:00 EST
4/26/1959 02:00 EDT
9/27/1959 02:00 EST
4/24/1960 02:00 US#2
....
PA # 58
Before 4/13/1887 LMT
4/13/1887 12:00 PA#3
9/01/1941 02:00 PA#1
4/30/1967 02:00 US#1
....
PA # 59
Before 4/13/1887 LMT
4/13/1887 12:00 EST
3/31/1918 02:00 EWT
10/27/1918 02:00 EST
3/30/1919 02:00 EWT
10/26/1919 02:00 EST
2/09/1942 02:00 EWT
9/30/1945 02:00 EST
4/29/1951 02:00 US#2
....
PA # 60
Before 4/13/1887 LMT
4/13/1887 12:00 EST
3/31/1918 02:00 EWT
10/27/1918 02:00 EST
3/30/1919 02:00 EWT
10/26/1919 02:00 EST
2/09/1942 02:00 EWT
9/30/1945 02:00 EST
4/29/1951 02:00 EDT
9/30/1951 02:00 EST
4/29/1956 02:00 US#2
....
PA # 61
Before 4/13/1887 LMT
4/13/1887 12:00 EST
3/31/1918 02:00 EWT
10/27/1918 02:00 EST
3/30/1919 02:00 EWT
10/26/1919 02:00 EST
4/27/1941 02:00 EDT
9/26/1941 02:00 PA#1
4/30/1967 02:00 US#1
....
PA # 62
Before 4/13/1887 LMT
4/13/1887 12:00 EST
3/31/1918 02:00 EWT
10/27/1918 02:00 EST
3/30/1919 02:00 EWT
10/26/1919 02:00 EST
2/09/1942 02:00 EWT
9/30/1945 02:00 EST
4/26/1953 02:00 EDT
9/27/1953 02:00 EST
4/25/1954 02:00 EDT
9/26/1954 02:00 EST
4/24/1955 02:00 EDT
10/02/1955 00:00 EST
4/29/1956 02:00 EDT
9/30/1956 02:00 EST
4/28/1957 02:00 EDT
9/29/1957 02:00 EST
4/27/1958 02:00 EDT
9/28/1958 02:00 EST
4/26/1959 02:00 EDT
9/27/1959 02:00 EST
4/24/1960 02:00 US#2
....
PA # 63
Before 4/13/1887 LMT
4/13/1887 12:00 PA#7
4/24/1955 02:00 EDT
9/25/1955 02:00 EST
4/29/1956 02:00 EDT
9/30/1956 02:00 EST
4/28/1957 02:00 EDT
9/29/1957 02:00 EST
4/27/1958 02:00 EDT
9/28/1958 02:00 EST
4/26/1959 02:00 EDT
9/27/1959 02:00 EST
4/24/1960 02:00 US#2
....
PA # 64
Before 4/13/1887 LMT
4/13/1887 12:00 EST
3/31/1918 02:00 EWT
10/27/1918 02:00 EST
3/30/1919 02:00 EWT
10/26/1919 02:00 EST
2/09/1942 02:00 EWT
9/30/1945 02:00 EST
4/25/1954 02:00 US#2
....
PA # 65
Before 4/13/1887 LMT
4/13/1887 12:00 EST
3/31/1918 02:00 EWT
10/27/1918 02:00 EST
3/30/1919 02:00 EWT
10/26/1919 02:00 EST
2/09/1942 02:00 EWT
9/30/1945 02:00 EST
4/24/1955 02:00 US#2
....
PA # 66
Before 4/13/1887 LMT
4/13/1887 12:00 EST
3/31/1918 02:00 EWT
10/27/1918 02:00 EST
3/30/1919 02:00 EWT
10/26/1919 02:00 EST
2/09/1942 02:00 EWT
9/30/1945 02:00 EST
4/29/1956 02:00 EDT
9/30/1956 02:00 EST
4/28/1957 02:00 US#2
....
PA # 67
Before 4/13/1887 LMT
4/13/1887 12:00 EST
3/31/1918 02:00 EWT
10/27/1918 02:00 EST
3/30/1919 02:00 EWT
10/26/1919 02:00 EST
4/26/1931 02:00 EDT
9/27/1931 02:00 EST
4/24/1932 02:00 EDT
9/25/1932 02:00 EST
4/30/1933 02:00 EDT
9/24/1933 02:00 EST
4/29/1934 02:00 EDT
9/30/1934 02:00 EST
4/28/1935 02:00 EDT
9/29/1935 02:00 EST
4/26/1936 02:00 EDT
9/27/1936 02:00 EST
4/25/1937 02:00 EDT
9/26/1937 02:00 EST
4/24/1938 02:00 EDT
9/25/1938 02:00 EST
4/30/1939 02:00 EDT
9/24/1939 02:00 EST
4/28/1940 02:00 EDT
9/29/1940 02:00 EST
4/27/1941 02:00 EDT
9/28/1941 02:00 EST
2/09/1942 02:00 EWT
9/30/1945 02:00 EST
4/28/1946 02:00 EDT
9/29/1946 02:00 EST
4/27/1947 02:00 EDT
9/28/1947 02:00 EST
4/25/1948 02:00 EDT
9/26/1948 02:00 EST
4/24/1949 02:00 EDT
9/25/1949 02:00 EST
4/30/1950 02:00 EDT
9/24/1950 02:00 EST
4/29/1951 02:00 EDT
9/30/1951 02:00 EST
4/27/1952 02:00 EDT
9/28/1952 02:00 EST
4/26/1953 02:00 EDT
9/27/1953 02:00 EST
4/25/1954 02:00 EDT
9/26/1954 02:00 EST
4/24/1955 02:00 EDT
10/30/1955 02:00 EST
4/29/1956 02:00 EDT
10/28/1956 02:00 EST
4/28/1957 02:00 EDT
9/29/1957 02:00 EST
4/27/1958 02:00 EDT
9/28/1958 02:00 EST
4/26/1959 02:00 US#2
....
PA # 68
Before 4/13/1887 LMT
4/13/1887 12:00 PA#3
4/27/1958 02:00 EDT
9/28/1958 02:00 EST
4/26/1959 02:00 EDT
9/27/1959 02:00 EST
4/24/1960 02:00 EDT
9/25/1960 02:00 EST
4/30/1961 02:00 US#2
....
PA # 69
Before 4/13/1887 LMT
4/13/1887 12:00 EST
3/31/1918 02:00 EWT
10/27/1918 02:00 EST
3/30/1919 02:00 EWT
10/26/1919 02:00 EST
2/09/1942 02:00 EWT
9/30/1945 02:00 EST
4/28/1946 02:00 EDT
9/29/1946 02:00 EST
4/27/1947 02:00 EDT
9/28/1947 02:00 EST
4/29/1951 02:00 US#2
....
PA # 70
Before 4/13/1887 LMT
4/13/1887 12:00 EST
3/31/1918 02:00 EWT
10/27/1918 02:00 EST
3/30/1919 02:00 EWT
10/26/1919 02:00 EST
2/09/1942 02:00 EWT

PENNSYLVANIA

9/30/1945 02:00 EST
4/28/1946 02:00 EDT
9/29/1946 02:00 EST
4/27/1947 02:00 EDT
9/28/1947 02:00 EST
4/25/1948 02:00 EDT
9/26/1948 02:00 EST
4/24/1949 02:00 EDT
9/25/1949 02:00 EST
4/30/1950 02:00 EDT
9/24/1950 02:00 EST
4/29/1951 02:00 EDT
9/30/1951 02:00 EST
4/27/1952 02:00 EDT
9/28/1952 02:00 EST
4/26/1953 02:00 EDT
9/27/1953 02:00 EST
4/25/1954 02:00 EDT
9/26/1954 02:00 EST
4/29/1956 02:00 EDT
9/30/1956 02:00 EST
4/28/1957 02:00 EDT
9/29/1957 02:00 EST
4/27/1958 02:00 US#2

PA # 71
Before 4/13/1887 LMT
4/13/1887 12:00 PA#3
9/28/1952 02:00 EST
4/29/1956 02:00 US#2

PA # 72
Before 4/13/1887 LMT
4/13/1887 12:00 EST
3/31/1918 02:00 EWT
10/27/1918 02:00 EST
3/30/1919 02:00 EWT
10/26/1919 02:00 EST
4/30/1933 02:00 EDT
9/24/1933 02:00 EST
4/27/1941 02:00 EDT
9/28/1941 02:00 EST
2/09/1942 02:00 EWT
9/30/1945 02:00 EST
4/28/1946 02:00 EDT
9/29/1946 02:00 EST
4/27/1947 02:00 EDT
9/28/1947 02:00 EST
4/25/1948 02:00 EDT
9/26/1948 02:00 EST
4/24/1949 02:00 EDT
9/25/1949 02:00 EST
4/30/1950 02:00 EDT
9/24/1950 02:00 EST
4/29/1956 02:00 US#2

PA # 73
Before 4/13/1887 LMT
4/13/1887 12:00 PA#1
4/24/1955 02:00 EDT
9/25/1955 02:00 EST
4/29/1956 02:00 EDT
9/30/1956 02:00 EST
4/28/1957 02:00 EDT
9/29/1957 02:00 EST
4/27/1958 02:00 EDT
9/28/1958 02:00 EST
4/26/1959 02:00 EDT
9/27/1959 02:00 EST
4/24/1960 02:00 US#2

PA # 74
Before 4/13/1887 LMT
4/13/1887 12:00 EST
3/31/1918 02:00 EWT
10/27/1918 02:00 EST
3/30/1919 02:00 EWT
10/26/1919 02:00 EST
4/24/1921 02:00 EDT
9/25/1921 02:00 EST
4/30/1922 02:00 EDT
9/24/1922 02:00 EST
4/29/1923 02:00 EDT
9/30/1923 02:00 EST
4/27/1924 02:00 EDT
9/28/1924 02:00 EST
4/26/1925 02:00 EDT
9/27/1925 02:00 EST
4/25/1926 02:00 EDT
9/26/1926 02:00 EST
4/24/1927 02:00 EDT
9/25/1927 02:00 EST
4/29/1928 02:00 EDT
9/30/1928 02:00 EST
4/28/1929 02:00 EDT
9/29/1929 02:00 EST
4/27/1930 02:00 EDT
9/28/1930 02:00 EST
4/26/1931 02:00 EDT
9/27/1931 02:00 EST
4/24/1932 02:00 EDT
9/25/1932 02:00 EST
4/30/1933 02:00 EDT
9/24/1933 02:00 EST
4/29/1934 02:00 EDT
9/30/1934 02:00 EST
4/28/1935 02:00 EDT
9/29/1935 02:00 EST
4/26/1936 02:00 EDT
9/27/1936 02:00 EST
4/25/1937 02:00 EDT
9/26/1937 02:00 EST
4/24/1938 02:00 EDT
9/25/1938 02:00 EST
4/30/1939 02:00 EDT
9/24/1939 02:00 EST
4/28/1940 02:00 EDT
9/29/1940 02:00 EST
4/27/1941 02:00 EDT
9/28/1941 02:00 EST
2/09/1942 02:00 EWT
9/30/1945 02:00 EST
4/28/1946 02:00 EDT
9/29/1946 02:00 EST
4/27/1947 02:00 EDT
9/28/1947 02:00 EST
4/25/1948 02:00 EDT
9/26/1948 02:00 EST
4/24/1949 02:00 EDT
9/25/1949 02:00 EST
4/30/1950 02:00 EDT
9/24/1950 02:00 EST
4/29/1951 02:00 EDT
9/30/1951 02:00 EST
4/27/1952 02:00 EDT
9/28/1952 02:00 EST
4/26/1953 02:00 EDT
9/27/1953 02:00 EST
4/25/1954 02:00 EDT
9/26/1954 02:00 EST
4/24/1955 02:00 EDT
10/30/1955 02:00 EST
4/29/1956 02:00 EDT
9/30/1956 02:00 EST
4/28/1957 02:00 EDT
9/29/1957 02:00 EST
4/27/1958 02:00 EDT
9/28/1958 02:00 EST
4/26/1959 02:00 EDT
9/27/1959 02:00 EST
4/24/1960 02:00 US#2

PA # 75
Before 4/13/1887 LMT
4/13/1887 12:00 PA#3
4/28/1946 02:00 EDT
9/29/1946 02:00 EST
4/27/1947 02:00 EDT
9/28/1947 02:00 EST
4/25/1948 02:00 EDT
9/26/1948 02:00 EST
4/24/1949 02:00 EDT
9/25/1949 02:00 EST
4/30/1950 02:00 EDT
9/24/1950 02:00 EST
4/29/1951 02:00 EDT
9/30/1951 02:00 EST
4/27/1952 02:00 EDT
9/28/1952 02:00 EST
4/26/1953 02:00 EDT
9/27/1953 02:00 EST
4/25/1954 02:00 EDT
9/26/1954 02:00 EST
4/24/1955 02:00 EDT
9/25/1955 02:00 EST
4/29/1956 02:00 EDT
9/30/1956 02:00 EST
4/28/1957 02:00 US#2

PA # 76
Before 4/13/1887 LMT
4/13/1887 12:00 EST
3/31/1918 02:00 EWT
10/27/1918 02:00 EST
3/30/1919 02:00 EWT
10/26/1919 02:00 EST
2/09/1942 02:00 EWT
9/30/1945 02:00 EST
4/28/1946 02:00 EDT
9/29/1946 02:00 EST
4/27/1947 02:00 EDT
9/28/1947 02:00 EST
4/25/1948 02:00 EDT
9/26/1948 02:00 EST
4/24/1949 02:00 EDT
9/25/1949 02:00 EST
4/30/1950 02:00 EDT
9/24/1950 02:00 EST
4/29/1951 02:00 EDT
9/30/1951 02:00 EST
4/27/1952 02:00 EDT
9/28/1952 02:00 EST
4/26/1953 02:00 EDT
9/27/1953 02:00 EST
4/25/1954 02:00 EDT
9/26/1954 02:00 EST
4/24/1955 02:00 EDT
9/25/1955 02:00 EST
4/29/1956 02:00 EDT
10/28/1956 02:00 EST
4/28/1957 02:00 EDT
9/29/1957 02:00 EST
4/27/1958 02:00 EDT
9/28/1958 02:00 EST
4/26/1959 02:00 US#2

PA # 77
Before 4/13/1887 LMT
4/13/1887 12:00 EST
3/31/1918 02:00 EWT
10/27/1918 02:00 EST
3/30/1919 02:00 EWT
10/26/1919 02:00 EST
4/27/1930 02:00 EDT
9/28/1930 02:00 EST
4/26/1931 02:00 EDT
9/27/1931 02:00 EST
4/24/1932 02:00 EDT
9/25/1932 02:00 EST
4/30/1933 02:00 EDT
9/24/1933 02:00 EST
4/29/1934 02:00 EDT
9/30/1934 02:00 EST
4/28/1935 02:00 EDT
9/29/1935 02:00 EST
4/26/1936 02:00 EDT
9/27/1936 02:00 EST
4/25/1937 02:00 EDT
9/26/1937 02:00 EST
4/24/1938 02:00 EDT
9/25/1938 02:00 EST
4/30/1939 02:00 EDT
9/24/1939 02:00 EST
4/28/1940 02:00 EDT
9/29/1940 02:00 EST
4/27/1941 02:00 EDT
9/28/1941 02:00 EST
2/09/1942 02:00 EWT
9/30/1945 02:00 EST
4/28/1946 02:00 EDT
9/29/1946 02:00 EST
4/29/1956 02:00 EDT
9/30/1956 02:00 EST
4/28/1957 02:00 US#2

PA # 78
Before 4/13/1887 LMT
4/13/1887 12:00 EST
3/31/1918 02:00 EWT
10/27/1918 02:00 EST
3/30/1919 02:00 EWT
10/26/1919 02:00 EST
4/27/1924 02:00 US#2

PA # 79
Before 4/13/1887 LMT
4/13/1887 12:00 EST
3/31/1918 02:00 EWT
10/27/1918 02:00 EST
3/30/1919 02:00 EWT
10/26/1919 02:00 EST
2/09/1942 02:00 EWT
9/30/1945 02:00 EST
4/27/1947 02:00 EDT
9/28/1947 02:00 EST
4/25/1948 02:00 EDT
9/26/1948 02:00 EST
4/24/1949 02:00 EDT
9/25/1949 02:00 EST
4/30/1950 02:00 EDT
9/24/1950 02:00 EST
4/29/1951 02:00 EDT
9/30/1951 02:00 EST
4/27/1952 02:00 EDT
9/28/1952 02:00 EST
4/26/1953 02:00 EDT
9/27/1953 02:00 EST
4/25/1954 02:00 EDT
9/26/1954 02:00 EST
4/24/1955 02:00 EDT
9/25/1955 02:00 EST
4/29/1956 02:00 EDT
9/30/1956 02:00 EST
4/28/1957 02:00 EDT
9/29/1957 02:00 EST
4/27/1958 02:00 EDT
9/28/1958 02:00 EST
4/26/1959 02:00 US#2

PA # 80
Before 4/13/1887 LMT
4/13/1887 12:00 EST
3/31/1918 02:00 EWT
10/27/1918 02:00 EST
3/30/1919 02:00 EWT
10/26/1919 02:00 EST
4/24/1932 02:00 US#2

PA # 81
Before 4/13/1887 LMT
4/13/1887 12:00 PA#1
4/24/1955 02:00 EDT
9/25/1955 02:00 EST
4/29/1956 02:00 EDT
9/30/1956 02:00 EST
4/28/1957 02:00 EDT
9/29/1957 02:00 EST
4/27/1958 02:00 EDT
9/28/1958 02:00 EST
4/26/1959 02:00 EDT
9/27/1959 02:00 EST
4/24/1960 02:00 EDT
9/25/1960 02:00 EST
4/30/1961 02:00 US#2

PA # 82
Before 4/13/1887 LMT
4/13/1887 12:00 EST
3/31/1918 02:00 EWT
10/27/1918 02:00 EST
3/30/1919 02:00 EWT
10/26/1919 02:00 EST
2/09/1942 02:00 EWT
9/30/1945 02:00 EST
4/28/1946 02:00 EDT
9/29/1946 02:00 EST
4/27/1947 02:00 EDT
9/28/1947 02:00 EST
4/25/1948 02:00 EDT
9/26/1948 02:00 EST
4/24/1949 02:00 EDT
9/25/1949 02:00 EST
4/30/1950 02:00 EDT
9/24/1950 02:00 EST
4/29/1951 02:00 EDT
9/30/1951 02:00 EST
4/27/1952 02:00 EDT
9/28/1952 02:00 EST
4/26/1953 02:00 EDT
9/27/1953 02:00 EST
4/25/1954 02:00 EDT
9/26/1954 02:00 EST
4/24/1955 02:00 EDT
9/25/1955 02:00 EST
4/29/1956 02:00 EDT
9/30/1956 02:00 EST
4/28/1957 02:00 EDT
9/29/1957 02:00 EST
4/27/1958 02:00 EDT
9/28/1958 02:00 EST
4/26/1959 02:00 US#2

PA # 83
Before 4/13/1887 LMT
4/13/1887 12:00 EST
3/31/1918 02:00 EWT
10/27/1918 02:00 EST
3/30/1919 02:00 EWT
10/26/1919 02:00 EST
4/30/1939 02:00 EDT
9/24/1939 02:00 EST
2/09/1942 02:00 EWT
9/30/1945 02:00 EST
4/28/1946 02:00 EDT
9/29/1946 02:00 EST
4/27/1947 02:00 EDT
9/28/1947 02:00 EST
4/25/1948 02:00 EDT
9/26/1948 02:00 EST
4/24/1949 02:00 EDT
9/25/1949 02:00 EST
4/30/1950 02:00 EDT
9/24/1950 02:00 EST
4/29/1951 02:00 EDT
9/30/1951 02:00 EST
4/27/1952 02:00 EDT
9/28/1952 02:00 EST
4/26/1953 02:00 EDT
9/27/1953 02:00 EST
4/25/1954 02:00 EDT
9/26/1954 02:00 EST
4/24/1955 02:00 EDT
9/25/1955 02:00 EST
4/29/1956 02:00 EDT
9/30/1956 02:00 EST
4/28/1957 02:00 EDT
9/29/1957 02:00 EST
4/27/1958 02:00 EDT
9/28/1958 02:00 EST
4/26/1959 02:00 EDT
9/27/1959 02:00 EST
4/24/1960 02:00 EDT
9/25/1960 02:00 EST
4/30/1961 02:00 US#2

PA # 84
Before 4/13/1887 LMT
4/13/1887 12:00 EST
3/31/1918 02:00 EWT
10/27/1918 02:00 EST
3/30/1919 02:00 EWT
10/26/1919 02:00 EST
4/29/1934 02:00 EDT
9/30/1934 02:00 EST
4/28/1935 02:00 EDT
9/29/1935 02:00 EST
4/26/1936 02:00 EDT
9/27/1936 02:00 EST
4/25/1937 02:00 EDT
9/26/1937 02:00 EST
4/24/1938 02:00 EDT
9/25/1938 02:00 EST
4/30/1939 02:00 EDT
9/24/1939 02:00 EST
4/28/1940 02:00 EDT
9/29/1940 02:00 EST
4/27/1941 02:00 EDT
9/28/1941 02:00 EST
2/09/1942 02:00 EWT
9/30/1945 02:00 EST
4/28/1946 02:00 EDT
9/29/1946 02:00 EST
4/27/1947 02:00 EDT
9/28/1947 02:00 EST
4/25/1948 02:00 EDT
9/26/1948 02:00 EST
4/24/1949 02:00 EDT
9/25/1949 02:00 EST
4/30/1950 02:00 EDT
9/24/1950 02:00 EST
4/29/1951 02:00 EDT
9/30/1951 02:00 EST
4/27/1952 02:00 EDT
9/28/1952 02:00 EST
4/26/1953 02:00 EDT
9/27/1953 02:00 EST
4/25/1954 02:00 EDT
9/26/1954 02:00 EST
4/24/1955 02:00 EDT
9/25/1955 02:00 EST
4/29/1956 02:00 US#2

PA # 85
Before 4/13/1887 LMT
4/13/1887 12:00 EST
3/31/1918 02:00 EWT
10/27/1918 02:00 EST
3/30/1919 02:00 EWT
10/26/1919 02:00 EST
4/24/1938 02:00 EDT
9/25/1938 02:00 EST
4/30/1939 02:00 EDT
9/24/1939 02:00 EST
4/28/1940 02:00 EDT
9/29/1940 02:00 EST
4/27/1941 02:00 EDT
9/28/1941 02:00 EST
2/09/1942 02:00 EWT
9/30/1945 02:00 EST
4/28/1946 02:00 EDT
9/29/1946 02:00 EST
4/27/1947 02:00 EDT
9/28/1947 02:00 EST
4/25/1948 02:00 EDT
9/26/1948 02:00 EST
4/24/1949 02:00 EDT
9/25/1949 02:00 EST
4/30/1950 02:00 EDT
9/24/1950 02:00 EST
4/29/1951 02:00 EDT
9/30/1951 02:00 EST
4/27/1952 02:00 EDT
9/28/1952 02:00 EST
4/26/1953 02:00 EDT
9/27/1953 02:00 EST
4/25/1954 02:00 EDT
9/26/1954 02:00 EST
4/24/1955 02:00 EDT
9/25/1955 02:00 EST
4/29/1956 02:00 EDT
9/30/1956 02:00 EST
4/28/1957 02:00 EDT
9/29/1957 02:00 EST
4/27/1958 02:00 EDT
9/28/1958 02:00 EST
4/26/1959 02:00 EDT
9/27/1959 02:00 EST
4/24/1960 02:00 US#2

PA # 86
Before 4/13/1887 LMT
4/13/1887 12:00 EST
3/31/1918 02:00 EWT
10/27/1918 02:00 EST
3/30/1919 02:00 EWT
10/26/1919 02:00 EST
4/24/1938 02:00 EDT
9/25/1938 02:00 EST
4/30/1939 02:00 EDT
9/24/1939 02:00 EST
4/28/1940 02:00 EDT
9/29/1940 02:00 EST
4/27/1941 02:00 EDT
9/28/1941 02:00 EST
2/09/1942 02:00 EWT
9/30/1945 02:00 EST
4/29/1956 02:00 US#2

PA # 87
Before 4/13/1887 LMT
4/13/1887 12:00 PA#3
9/29/1946 02:00 EST
4/29/1956 02:00 US#2

PA # 88
Before 4/13/1887 LMT
4/13/1887 12:00 EST
3/31/1918 02:00 EWT
10/27/1918 02:00 EST
3/30/1919 02:00 EWT
10/26/1919 02:00 EST
2/09/1942 02:00 EWT
9/30/1945 02:00 EST
4/27/1947 02:00 EDT
9/28/1947 02:00 EST
4/25/1948 02:00 EDT
9/26/1948 02:00 EST
4/24/1949 02:00 EDT
9/25/1949 02:00 EST
4/30/1950 02:00 EDT
9/24/1950 02:00 EST
4/29/1951 02:00 EDT
9/30/1951 02:00 EST
4/27/1952 02:00 EDT
9/28/1952 02:00 EST
4/26/1953 02:00 EDT
9/27/1953 02:00 EST
4/25/1954 02:00 EDT
9/26/1954 02:00 EST
4/24/1955 02:00 EDT
9/25/1955 02:00 EST
4/29/1956 02:00 US#2

PA # 89
Before 4/13/1887 LMT
4/13/1887 12:00 PA#5
4/24/1955 02:00 EDT
9/25/1955 02:00 EST
4/29/1956 02:00 EDT
9/30/1956 02:00 EST
4/28/1957 02:00 EDT
9/29/1957 02:00 EST
4/27/1958 02:00 US#2

PA # 90

TIME TABLES

Before 4/13/1887 LMT
4/13/1887 12:00 EST
3/31/1918 02:00 EWT
10/27/1918 02:00 EST
3/30/1919 02:00 EWT
10/26/1919 02:00 EST
4/29/1928 02:00 US#2

PA # 91
Before 4/13/1887 LMT
4/13/1887 12:00 EST
3/31/1918 02:00 EWT
10/27/1918 02:00 EST
3/30/1919 02:00 EWT
10/26/1919 02:00 EST
4/28/1940 02:00 EDT
9/02/1940 02:00 EST
4/27/1941 02:00 EDT
9/28/1941 02:00 EST
2/09/1942 02:00 EWT
9/30/1945 02:00 EST
4/28/1946 02:00 EDT
9/29/1946 02:00 EST
4/27/1947 02:00 EDT
9/28/1947 02:00 EST
4/25/1948 02:00 EDT
9/26/1948 02:00 EST
4/24/1949 02:00 EDT
9/25/1949 02:00 EST
4/30/1950 02:00 EDT
9/24/1950 02:00 EST
4/29/1951 02:00 EDT
9/30/1951 02:00 EST
4/27/1952 02:00 EDT
9/28/1952 02:00 EST
4/26/1953 02:00 EDT
9/27/1953 02:00 EST
4/25/1954 02:00 EDT
9/26/1954 02:00 EST
4/24/1955 02:00 EDT
9/25/1955 02:00 EST
4/29/1956 02:00 EDT
10/28/1956 02:00 EST
4/28/1957 02:00 EDT
9/29/1957 02:00 EST
4/27/1958 02:00 EDT
9/28/1958 02:00 EST
4/26/1959 02:00 EDT
9/27/1959 02:00 EST
4/24/1960 02:00 US#2

PA # 92
Before 4/13/1887 LMT
4/13/1887 12:00 EST
3/31/1918 02:00 EWT
10/27/1918 02:00 EST
3/30/1919 02:00 EWT
10/26/1919 02:00 EST
2/09/1942 02:00 EWT
9/30/1945 02:00 EST
4/25/1948 02:00 EDT
9/26/1948 02:00 EST
4/26/1953 02:00 EDT
9/27/1953 02:00 EST
4/25/1954 02:00 EDT
9/26/1954 02:00 EST
4/24/1955 02:00 EDT
9/25/1955 02:00 EST
4/29/1956 02:00 EDT
9/30/1956 02:00 EST
4/28/1957 02:00 EDT
9/29/1957 02:00 EST
4/27/1958 02:00 EDT
9/28/1958 02:00 EST
4/26/1959 02:00 EDT
9/27/1959 02:00 EST
4/24/1960 02:00 US#2

PA # 93
Before 4/13/1887 LMT
4/13/1887 12:00 EST
3/31/1918 02:00 EWT
10/27/1918 02:00 EST
3/30/1919 02:00 EWT
10/26/1919 02:00 EST
2/09/1942 02:00 EWT
9/30/1945 02:00 EST
4/27/1947 02:00 EDT
9/28/1947 02:00 EST
4/29/1956 02:00 US#2

PA # 94
Before 4/13/1887 LMT
4/13/1887 12:00 EST
3/31/1918 02:00 EWT
10/27/1918 02:00 EST
3/30/1919 02:00 EWT
10/26/1919 02:00 EST
2/09/1942 02:00 EWT
9/30/1945 02:00 EST
4/24/1955 02:00 EDT
9/25/1955 02:00 EST
4/29/1956 02:00 EDT
9/30/1956 02:00 EST
4/28/1957 02:00 EDT
9/29/1957 02:00 EST
4/27/1958 02:00 EDT
9/28/1958 02:00 EST
4/26/1959 02:00 EDT
9/27/1959 02:00 EST
4/24/1960 02:00 US#2

PA # 95
Before 4/13/1887 LMT
4/13/1887 12:00 EST
3/31/1918 02:00 EWT
10/27/1918 02:00 EST
3/30/1919 02:00 EWT
10/26/1919 02:00 EST
4/24/1921 02:00 EDT
9/25/1921 02:00 EST
4/30/1922 02:00 EDT
9/24/1922 02:00 EST
4/29/1923 02:00 EDT
9/30/1923 02:00 EST
4/27/1924 02:00 EDT
9/28/1924 02:00 EST
4/26/1925 02:00 EDT
9/27/1925 02:00 EST
4/25/1926 02:00 EDT
9/26/1926 02:00 EST
4/24/1927 02:00 EDT
9/25/1927 02:00 EST
4/29/1928 02:00 EDT
9/30/1928 02:00 EST
4/28/1929 02:00 EDT
9/29/1929 02:00 EST
4/27/1930 02:00 EDT
9/28/1930 02:00 EST
4/26/1931 02:00 EDT
9/27/1931 02:00 EST
4/24/1932 02:00 EDT
9/25/1932 02:00 EST
4/30/1933 02:00 EDT
9/24/1933 02:00 EST
4/29/1934 02:00 EDT
9/30/1934 02:00 EST
4/28/1935 02:00 EDT
9/29/1935 02:00 EST
4/26/1936 02:00 EDT
9/27/1936 02:00 EST
4/25/1937 02:00 EDT
9/26/1937 02:00 EST
4/24/1938 02:00 EDT
9/25/1938 02:00 EST
4/30/1939 02:00 EDT
9/24/1939 02:00 EST
4/28/1940 02:00 EDT
9/29/1940 02:00 EST
4/27/1941 02:00 EDT
9/28/1941 02:00 EST
2/09/1942 02:00 EWT
9/30/1945 02:00 EST
4/28/1946 02:00 EDT
9/29/1946 02:00 EST
4/27/1947 02:00 EDT
9/28/1947 02:00 EST
4/25/1948 02:00 EDT
9/26/1948 02:00 EST
4/24/1949 02:00 EDT
9/25/1949 02:00 EST
4/30/1950 02:00 EDT
9/24/1950 02:00 EST
4/29/1951 02:00 EDT
9/30/1951 02:00 EST
4/27/1952 02:00 EDT
9/28/1952 02:00 EST
4/26/1953 02:00 EDT
9/27/1953 02:00 EST
4/25/1954 02:00 EDT
9/26/1954 02:00 EST
4/24/1955 02:00 EDT
10/30/1955 02:00 EST
4/29/1956 02:00 EDT
10/28/1956 02:00 EST
4/28/1957 02:00 EDT
9/29/1957 02:00 EST
4/27/1958 02:00 EDT
9/28/1958 02:00 EST
4/26/1959 02:00 US#2

PA # 96
Before 4/13/1887 LMT
4/13/1887 12:00 EST
3/31/1918 02:00 EWT
10/27/1918 02:00 EST
3/30/1919 02:00 EWT
10/26/1919 02:00 EST
4/24/1921 02:00 EDT
9/25/1921 02:00 EST
4/30/1922 02:00 EDT
9/24/1922 02:00 EST
4/29/1923 02:00 EDT
9/30/1923 02:00 EST
4/27/1924 02:00 EDT
9/28/1924 02:00 EST
4/26/1925 02:00 EDT
9/27/1925 02:00 EST
4/25/1926 02:00 EDT
9/26/1926 02:00 EST
4/24/1927 02:00 EDT
9/25/1927 02:00 EST
4/29/1928 02:00 EDT
9/30/1928 02:00 EST
4/28/1929 02:00 EDT
9/29/1929 02:00 EST
4/27/1930 02:00 EDT
9/28/1930 02:00 EST
4/26/1931 02:00 EDT
9/27/1931 02:00 EST
4/24/1932 02:00 EDT
9/25/1932 02:00 EST
4/30/1933 02:00 EDT
9/24/1933 02:00 EST
4/29/1934 02:00 EDT
9/30/1934 02:00 EST
4/28/1935 02:00 EDT
9/29/1935 02:00 EST
4/26/1936 02:00 EDT
9/27/1936 02:00 EST
4/25/1937 02:00 EDT
9/26/1937 02:00 EST
4/24/1938 02:00 EDT
9/25/1938 02:00 EST
4/30/1939 02:00 EDT
9/24/1939 02:00 EST
4/28/1940 02:00 EDT
9/29/1940 02:00 EST
4/27/1941 02:00 EDT
9/28/1941 02:00 EST
2/09/1942 02:00 EWT
9/30/1945 02:00 EST
4/26/1953 02:00 US#2

PA # 97
Before 4/13/1887 LMT
4/13/1887 12:00 EST
3/31/1918 02:00 EWT
10/27/1918 02:00 EST
3/30/1919 02:00 EWT
10/26/1919 02:00 EST
4/30/1932 02:00 US#2

PA # 98
Before 4/13/1887 LMT
4/13/1887 12:00 EST
3/31/1918 02:00 EWT
10/27/1918 02:00 EST
3/30/1919 02:00 EWT
10/26/1919 02:00 EST
2/09/1942 02:00 EWT
9/30/1945 02:00 EST
4/25/1954 02:00 US#3

PA # 99
Before 4/13/1887 LMT
4/13/1887 12:00 PA#3
9/21/1948 02:00 EST
4/24/1949 02:00 US#2

PA # 100
Before 4/13/1887 LMT
4/13/1887 12:00 EST
3/31/1918 02:00 EWT
10/27/1918 02:00 EST
3/30/1919 02:00 EWT
10/26/1919 02:00 EST
2/09/1942 02:00 EWT
9/30/1945 02:00 EST
4/28/1946 02:00 EDT
9/29/1946 02:00 EST
4/27/1947 02:00 EDT
9/28/1947 02:00 EST
4/25/1948 02:00 EDT
9/26/1948 02:00 EST
4/24/1949 02:00 EDT
9/25/1949 02:00 EST
4/30/1950 02:00 EDT
9/24/1950 02:00 EST
4/29/1951 02:00 EDT
9/30/1951 02:00 EST
4/27/1952 02:00 EDT
9/28/1952 02:00 EST
4/26/1953 02:00 EDT
9/27/1953 02:00 EST
4/25/1954 02:00 EDT
9/26/1954 02:00 EST
4/24/1955 02:00 EDT
9/25/1955 02:00 EST
4/29/1956 02:00 EDT
10/28/1956 02:00 EST
4/28/1957 02:00 EDT
9/29/1957 02:00 EST
4/27/1958 02:00 US#2

PA # 101
Before 4/13/1887 LMT
4/13/1887 12:00 PA#8
4/24/1955 02:00 EDT
9/25/1955 02:00 EST
4/29/1956 02:00 EDT
10/28/1956 02:00 EST
4/28/1957 02:00 EDT
10/27/1957 02:00 EST
4/27/1958 02:00 EDT
9/28/1958 02:00 EST
4/26/1959 02:00 US#2

PA # 102
Before 4/13/1887 LMT
4/13/1887 12:00 EST
3/31/1918 02:00 EWT
10/27/1918 02:00 EST
3/30/1919 02:00 EWT
10/26/1919 02:00 EST
4/28/1940 02:00 EDT
9/29/1940 02:00 EST
4/27/1941 02:00 EDT
9/01/1941 02:00 EST
2/09/1942 02:00 EWT
9/30/1945 02:00 EST
4/28/1946 02:00 US#2

PA # 103
Before 4/13/1887 LMT
4/13/1887 12:00 EST
3/31/1918 02:00 EWT
10/27/1918 02:00 EST
3/30/1919 02:00 EWT
10/26/1919 02:00 EST
2/09/1942 02:00 EWT
9/30/1945 02:00 EST
6/01/1946 02:00 EDT
8/31/1946 02:00 EST
4/25/1948 02:00 EDT
9/26/1948 02:00 EST
4/26/1953 02:00 US#2

PA # 104
Before 4/13/1887 LMT
4/13/1887 12:00 PA#3
9/15/1947 02:00 EST
4/25/1948 02:00 US#2

PA # 105
Before 4/13/1887 LMT
4/13/1887 12:00 EST
3/31/1918 02:00 EWT
10/27/1918 02:00 EST
3/30/1919 02:00 EWT
10/26/1919 02:00 EST
2/09/1942 02:00 EWT
9/30/1945 02:00 EST
4/25/1948 02:00 EDT
9/26/1948 02:00 EST
4/24/1949 02:00 EDT
9/04/1949 02:00 EST
4/30/1950 02:00 US#2

PA # 106
Before 4/13/1887 LMT
4/13/1887 12:00 EST
3/31/1918 02:00 EWT
10/27/1918 02:00 EST
3/30/1919 02:00 EWT
10/26/1919 02:00 EST
2/09/1942 02:00 EWT
9/30/1945 02:00 EST
4/27/1947 02:00 EDT
9/28/1947 02:00 EST
4/29/1948 02:00 EDT
9/01/1948 02:00 EST
4/24/1949 02:00 US#2

PA # 107
Before 7/01/1887 LMT
7/01/1887 12:00 EST
3/31/1918 02:00 EWT
10/27/1918 02:00 EST
3/30/1919 02:00 EWT
10/26/1919 02:00 EST
4/17/1921 02:00 EDT
10/23/1921 02:00 EST
4/16/1922 02:00 EDT
10/22/1922 02:00 EST
4/15/1923 02:00 EDT
10/28/1923 02:00 EST
4/20/1924 02:00 EDT
10/26/1924 02:00 EST
4/19/1925 02:00 EDT
10/25/1925 02:00 EST
4/18/1926 02:00 EDT
10/24/1926 02:00 EST
4/17/1927 02:00 EDT
10/23/1927 02:00 EST
4/15/1928 02:00 EDT
10/28/1928 02:00 EST
4/21/1929 02:00 EDT
10/27/1929 02:00 EST
4/20/1930 02:00 EDT
10/26/1930 02:00 EST
4/19/1931 02:00 EDT
10/25/1931 02:00 EST
4/17/1932 02:00 EDT
10/23/1932 02:00 EST
4/16/1933 02:00 EDT
10/22/1933 02:00 EST
4/15/1934 02:00 EDT
10/28/1934 02:00 EST
4/21/1935 02:00 EDT
10/27/1935 02:00 EST
4/19/1936 02:00 EDT
10/25/1936 02:00 EST
4/18/1937 02:00 EDT
10/24/1937 02:00 EST
4/17/1938 02:00 EDT
10/23/1938 02:00 EST
4/16/1939 02:00 EDT
10/22/1939 02:00 EST
5/13/1940 02:00 EDT
9/02/1940 02:00 EST
4/27/1941 02:00 EDT
9/28/1941 02:00 EST
2/09/1942 02:00 EWT
9/30/1945 02:00 EST
4/28/1946 02:00 EDT
9/29/1946 02:00 EST
4/27/1947 02:00 EDT
9/28/1947 02:00 EST
4/25/1948 02:00 EDT
9/26/1948 02:00 EST
4/24/1949 02:00 EDT
9/25/1949 02:00 EST
4/30/1950 02:00 EDT
9/24/1950 02:00 EST
4/29/1951 02:00 EDT
9/30/1951 02:00 EST
4/27/1952 02:00 EDT
9/28/1952 02:00 EST
4/26/1953 02:00 EDT
9/27/1953 02:00 EST
4/25/1954 02:00 EDT
9/26/1954 02:00 EST
4/24/1955 02:00 EDT
9/25/1955 02:00 EST
4/29/1956 02:00 EDT
9/30/1956 02:00 EST
4/28/1957 02:00 EDT
9/29/1957 02:00 EST
4/27/1958 02:00 EDT
9/28/1958 02:00 EST
4/26/1959 02:00 EDT
9/27/1959 02:00 EST
4/24/1960 02:00 US#2

PA # 108
Before 4/13/1887 LMT
4/13/1887 12:00 PA#2
9/24/1939 02:00 EST
5/01/1941 02:00 EDT
10/01/1941 02:00 EST
2/09/1942 02:00 EWT
9/30/1945 02:00 EST
4/29/1951 02:00 US#2

PA # 109
Before 4/13/1887 LMT
4/13/1887 12:00 PA#3
9/26/1948 02:00 EST
4/30/1949 02:00 US#2

PA # 110
Before 4/13/1887 LMT
4/13/1887 12:00 PA#4
4/30/1950 02:00 EDT
9/30/1950 02:00 EST
4/29/1951 02:00 EDT
9/30/1951 02:00 EST
4/27/1952 02:00 EDT
9/28/1952 02:00 EST
4/29/1956 02:00 US#2

PA # 111
Before 4/13/1887 LMT
4/13/1887 12:00 PA#1
9/26/1948 02:00 EST
4/27/1949 02:00 US#2

PA # 112
Before 4/13/1887 LMT
4/13/1887 12:00 EST
3/31/1918 02:00 EWT
10/27/1918 02:00 EST
3/30/1919 02:00 EWT
10/26/1919 02:00 EST
4/30/1933 02:00 EDT
9/24/1933 02:00 EST
4/25/1937 02:00 EDT
9/26/1937 02:00 EST
2/09/1942 02:00 EWT
9/30/1945 02:00 EST
4/28/1946 02:00 EDT
9/29/1946 02:00 EST
4/27/1947 02:00 EDT
9/28/1947 02:00 EST
4/25/1948 02:00 EDT
9/26/1948 02:00 EST
4/24/1949 02:00 EDT
9/25/1949 02:00 EST
4/30/1950 02:00 EDT
9/30/1950 02:00 EST
4/29/1951 02:00 EDT
9/30/1951 02:00 EST
4/27/1952 02:00 EDT
9/28/1952 02:00 EST
4/26/1953 02:00 EDT
9/27/1953 02:00 EST
4/25/1954 02:00 EDT
9/26/1954 02:00 EST
4/24/1955 02:00 EDT
10/30/1955 02:00 EST
4/29/1956 02:00 EDT
9/30/1956 02:00 EST
4/28/1957 02:00 EDT
9/29/1957 02:00 EST
4/27/1958 02:00 EDT
9/28/1958 02:00 EST
4/26/1959 02:00 US#2

PA # 113
Before 4/13/1887 LMT
4/13/1887 12:00 EST
3/31/1918 02:00 EWT
10/27/1918 02:00 EST
3/30/1919 02:00 EWT
10/26/1919 02:00 EST
2/09/1942 02:00 EWT
9/30/1945 02:00 EST
4/28/1946 02:00 EDT
10/31/1946 02:00 US#2

PA # 114
Before 1/01/1887 LMT
1/01/1887 12:00 EST
3/31/1918 02:00 EWT
10/27/1918 02:00 EST
3/30/1919 02:00 EWT
10/26/1919 02:00 EST
3/28/1920 02:00 EDT
10/31/1920 02:00 EST
4/24/1921 02:00 US#2

PA # 115
Before 4/13/1887 LMT
4/13/1887 12:00 EST

PENNSYLVANIA

TIME TABLES

3/31/1918 02:00 EWT
10/27/1918 02:00 EST
3/30/1919 02:00 EWT
10/26/1919 02:00 EST
2/09/1942 02:00 EWT
9/30/1945 02:00 EST
4/25/1948 02:00 EDT
9/26/1948 02:00 EST
4/24/1949 02:00 EDT
9/25/1949 02:00 EST
4/30/1950 02:00 EDT
9/30/1950 02:00 US#2

PA # 116

Before 4/13/1887 LMT
4/13/1887 12:00 EST
3/31/1918 02:00 EWT
10/27/1918 02:00 EST
3/30/1919 02:00 EWT
10/26/1919 02:00 EST
2/09/1942 02:00 EWT
9/30/1945 02:00 EST
4/25/1948 02:00 EDT
9/26/1948 02:00 EST
4/30/1949 02:00 EDT
9/25/1949 02:00 US#2

PA # 117

Before 4/13/1887 LMT
4/13/1887 12:00 PA#3
4/30/1950 02:00 EDT
9/30/1950 02:00 EST
4/29/1951 02:00 EDT
9/30/1951 02:00 EST
4/27/1952 02:00 EDT
9/28/1952 02:00 EST
4/26/1953 02:00 EDT
9/27/1953 02:00 EST
4/25/1954 02:00 EDT
9/26/1954 02:00 EST
4/24/1955 02:00 EDT
10/30/1955 02:00 EST
4/29/1956 02:00 EDT
9/30/1956 02:00 EST
4/28/1957 02:00 US#2

PA # 118

Before 4/13/1887 LMT
4/13/1887 12:00 PA#8
9/29/1940 02:00 EST
5/01/1941 02:00 EDT
10/01/1941 02:00 US#2

PA # 119

Before 4/13/1887 LMT
4/13/1887 12:00 EST
3/31/1918 02:00 EWT
10/27/1918 02:00 EST
3/30/1919 02:00 EWT
10/26/1919 02:00 EST
4/30/1933 02:00 EDT
9/24/1933 02:00 EST
4/29/1934 02:00 EDT
9/30/1934 02:00 EST
4/28/1935 02:00 EDT
9/29/1935 02:00 EST
4/26/1936 02:00 EDT
9/27/1936 02:00 EST
4/25/1937 02:00 EDT
9/26/1937 02:00 EST
4/24/1938 02:00 EDT
9/25/1938 02:00 EST
4/30/1939 02:00 EDT
9/24/1939 02:00 EST
4/28/1940 02:00 EDT
9/29/1940 02:00 EST
4/27/1941 02:00 EDT
9/28/1941 02:00 EST
2/09/1942 02:00 EWT
9/30/1945 02:00 EST
4/28/1946 02:00 EDT
9/29/1946 02:00 EST
4/27/1947 02:00 EDT
9/28/1947 02:00 EST
4/25/1948 02:00 EDT
9/26/1948 02:00 EST
4/24/1949 02:00 EDT
9/25/1949 02:00 EST
4/30/1950 02:00 EDT
9/30/1950 02:00 EST
4/29/1951 02:00 US#2

PA # 120

Before 4/13/1887 LMT
4/13/1887 12:00 EST
3/31/1918 02:00 EWT
10/27/1918 02:00 EST
3/30/1919 02:00 EWT
10/26/1919 02:00 EST
6/14/1937 02:00 EDT
9/02/1937 02:00 EST
6/03/1939 02:00 EDT
9/04/1939 02:00 EST
4/28/1940 02:00 EDT
9/29/1940 02:00 EST
4/27/1941 02:00 EDT
9/28/1941 02:00 EST
2/09/1942 02:00 EWT
9/30/1945 02:00 EST
4/28/1946 02:00 EDT
9/29/1946 02:00 EST
4/27/1947 02:00 EDT
9/28/1947 02:00 EST
4/25/1948 02:00 EDT
9/26/1948 02:00 EST
4/24/1949 02:00 EDT
9/25/1949 02:00 EST
4/30/1950 02:00 EDT
9/24/1950 02:00 EST
4/29/1951 02:00 EDT
9/23/1951 02:00 EST
4/27/1952 02:00 EDT
9/28/1952 02:00 EST
4/26/1953 02:00 EDT
9/27/1953 02:00 EST
4/25/1954 02:00 EDT
9/26/1954 02:00 EST
4/24/1955 02:00 EDT
9/25/1955 02:00 EST
4/29/1956 02:00 EDT
9/30/1956 02:00 EST
4/28/1957 02:00 US#2

PA # 121

Before 4/13/1887 LMT
4/13/1887 12:00 EST
3/31/1918 02:00 EWT
10/27/1918 02:00 EST
3/30/1919 02:00 EWT
10/26/1919 02:00 EST
3/28/1920 02:00 EDT
10/30/1920 02:00 EST
4/24/1921 02:00 EDT
9/25/1921 02:00 EST
4/30/1922 02:00 EDT
9/24/1922 02:00 EST
4/29/1923 02:00 EDT
9/30/1923 02:00 EST
4/27/1924 02:00 EDT
9/28/1924 02:00 EST
4/26/1925 02:00 EDT
9/27/1925 02:00 EST
4/25/1926 02:00 EDT
9/26/1926 02:00 EST
4/24/1927 02:00 EDT
9/25/1927 02:00 EST
4/29/1928 02:00 EDT
9/30/1928 02:00 EST
4/28/1929 02:00 EDT
9/29/1929 02:00 EST
4/27/1930 02:00 EDT
9/28/1930 02:00 EST
4/26/1931 02:00 EDT
9/27/1931 02:00 EST
4/24/1932 02:00 EDT
9/25/1932 02:00 EST
4/29/1933 00:01 EDT
9/31/1933 00:01 EST
4/28/1934 00:01 EDT
9/29/1934 00:01 EST
5/04/1935 00:01 EDT
9/28/1935 00:01 EST
5/02/1936 00:01 EDT
10/03/1936 00:01 EST
5/01/1937 00:01 EDT
10/02/1937 00:01 EST
4/30/1938 00:01 EDT
10/01/1938 00:01 EST
4/29/1939 00:01 EDT
9/30/1939 00:01 EST
5/04/1940 00:01 EDT
9/28/1940 00:01 EST
5/03/1941 00:01 EDT
10/04/1941 00:01 EST
2/09/1942 02:00 EWT
9/30/1945 02:00 EST
4/28/1946 02:00 EDT
9/29/1946 02:00 EST
4/27/1947 02:00 EDT
9/28/1947 02:00 EST
4/25/1948 02:00 EDT
9/26/1948 02:00 EST
4/24/1949 02:00 EDT
9/25/1949 02:00 EST
4/30/1950 02:00 EDT
9/24/1950 02:00 EST
4/29/1951 02:00 EDT
9/30/1951 02:00 EST
4/27/1952 02:00 EDT
9/28/1952 02:00 EST
4/26/1953 02:00 EDT
9/27/1953 02:00 EST
4/25/1954 02:00 EDT
9/26/1954 02:00 EST
4/24/1955 02:00 EDT
10/30/1955 02:00 EST
4/29/1956 02:00 EDT
9/30/1956 02:00 EST
4/28/1957 02:00 EDT
9/29/1957 02:00 EST
4/27/1958 02:00 EDT
9/28/1958 02:00 EST
4/26/1959 02:00 US#2

PA # 122

Before 4/13/1887 LMT
4/13/1887 12:00 PA#6
9/27/1964 02:00 EST
4/25/1965 02:00 US#2

PA # 123

Before 4/13/1887 LMT
4/13/1887 12:00 EST
3/31/1918 02:00 EWT
10/27/1918 02:00 EST
3/30/1919 02:00 EWT
10/26/1919 02:00 EST
2/09/1942 02:00 EWT
9/30/1945 02:00 EST
4/30/1950 02:00 EDT
9/30/1950 02:00 EST
4/29/1951 02:00 US#2

COUNTIES

1 Adams
2 Allegheny
3 Armstrong
4 Beaver
5 Bedford
6 Berks
7 Blair
8 Bradford
9 Bucks
10 Butler
11 Cambria
12 Cameron
13 Carbon
14 Centre
15 Chester
16 Clarion
17 Clearfield
18 Clinton
19 Columbia
20 Crawford
21 Cumberland
22 Dauphin
23 Delaware
24 Elk
25 Erie
26 Fayette
27 Forest
28 Franklin
29 Fulton
30 Greene
31 Huntingdon
32 Indiana
33 Jefferson
34 Juniata
35 Lackawanna
36 Lancaster
37 Lawrence
38 Lebanon
39 Lehigh
40 Luzerne
41 Lycoming
42 McKean
43 Mercer
44 Mifflin
45 Monroe
46 Montgomery
47 Montour
48 Northampton
49 Northumberland
50 Perry
51 Philadelphia
52 Pike
53 Potter
54 Schuylkill
55 Snyder
56 Somerset
57 Sullivan
58 Susquehanna
59 Tioga
60 Union
61 Venango
62 Warren
63 Washington
64 Wayne
65 Westmoreland
66 Wyoming
67 York

Place		Lat	Long	Time
Aaronsburg 14	52	40N54	77w27	5:09:48
Abbott 53	6	41N38	77w42	5:10:48
Abbottstown 1	1	39N53	76w59	5:07:56
Aberdeen 35	4	41N20	75w32	5:02:08
Aberdeen 36	2	40N10	76w36	5:06:24
Abington 46	2	40N07	75w07	5:00:28
Abrahamsville 64	6	41N46	75w03	5:00:12
Academia 34	7	40N32	77w24	5:09:36
Academy Corners 59	6	41N57	77w26	5:09:44
Acahela 45	94	41N06	75w36	5:02:24
Accomac 67	1	40N01	76w36	5:06:24
Acheson 63	6	40N07	80w25	5:21:40
Ackermanville 46	17	40N49	75w17	5:01:08
Acme 65	6	40N08	79w26	5:17:44
Acmetonia 2	14	40N33	79w49	5:19:16
Acosta 56	6	40N07	79w04	5:16:16
Adah 26	51	39N54	79w55	5:19:40
Adams 3	6	40N53	79w36	5:18:24
Adamsburg 65	3	40N19	79w39	5:18:36
Adams Corner 10	6	41N02	80w03	5:20:12
Adamsdale 54	27	40N38	76w10	5:04:40
Adams Hill 65	25	40N20	79w43	5:18:52
Adamstown 36	27	40N15	76w03	5:04:12
Adamsville 20	63	41N31	80w22	5:21:28
Addingham 23	9	39N57	75w18	5:01:12
Addison 56	53	39N45	79w21	5:17:24
Adelaide 26	104	40N01	79w35	5:18:20
Admire 67	39	39N56	76w51	5:07:24
Adrian 3	15	40N53	79w32	5:18:08
Advance 32	72	40N41	79w12	5:16:48
Africa 28	51	39N50	77w55	5:11:40
Aiden Lair 46	1	40N09	75w12	5:00:48
Aiken 42	6	41N54	78w32	5:14:08
Airville 67	1	39N50	76w24	5:05:36
Airydale 31	85	40N26	77w56	5:11:44
Akeley 62	6	41N56	79w08	5:16:32
Akersville 29	6	39N57	78w14	5:12:56
Akron 36	28	40N09	76w12	5:04:48
Aladdin 3	2	40N41	79w40	5:18:40
Alaska 33	34	41N10	79w05	5:16:20
Alba 8	7	41N42	76w50	5:07:20
Albany 6	56	40N37	75w53	5:03:32
Albany 26	56	40N02	79w55	5:19:40
Alberts Corners 40	20	41N14	75w52	5:03:28
Albidale 46	1	40N09	75w03	5:00:12
Albion 25	7	41N54	80w22	5:21:28
Albion 33	51	40N56	78w58	5:15:52
Albrightsville 13	94	41N02	75w37	5:02:28
Alburtis 39	13	40N31	75w36	5:02:24
Alcoa Center 65	14	40N34	79w45	5:19:00
Aldan 23	9	39N55	75w17	5:01:08
Alden 40	21	41N12	76w00	5:04:00
Aldenville 64	6	41N39	75w22	5:01:28
Alderson 40	6	41N22	76w02	5:04:08
Aldham 15	8	40N08	75w31	5:02:04
Aldovin 66	59	41N32	75w57	5:03:48
Aleppo 30	7	39N46	79w59	5:19:56
Alexander Springs 44	6	40N36	77w44	5:10:56
Alexandria 31	7	40N34	78w06	5:12:24
Alfarata 44	1	40N42	77w19	5:09:16
Alford 58	59	41N46	75w43	5:02:52
Alice 65	6	40N08	79w26	5:17:44
Alicia 26	51	40N02	79w55	5:19:40
Alicia 30	51	39N48	79w55	5:19:40
Alinda 50	6	40N21	77w18	5:09:12
Aline 55	6	40N43	77w01	5:08:04
Aliquippa 4	13	40N37	80w15	5:21:00
Allandale 21	12	40N14	76w57	5:07:48
Allegany 53	6	41N52	77w54	5:11:36
Allegheny 2	114	40N28	80w01	5:20:04
Allegheny Acres 2	114	40N20	80w05	5:20:20
Alleghenyville 6	101	40N18	75w59	5:03:56
Allemans 17	54	40N41	78w30	5:14:00
Allen 21	1	40N10	77w05	5:08:20
Allen 48	13	40N43	75w29	5:01:56
Allen Crest 39	13	40N39	75w30	5:02:00
Allendale Farms 23	9	39N58	75w22	5:01:28
Allenport 31	85	40N23	77w53	5:11:32
Allenport 63	115	40N05	79w51	5:19:24
Allens Mills 33	6	41N06	78w53	5:15:32
Allensville 44	7	40N32	77w49	5:11:16
Allentown 39	13	40N37	75w29	5:01:56
Allenvale 56	6	40N01	79w05	5:16:20
Allenwood 60	73	41N07	76w54	5:07:36
Allis Hollow 8	60	41N51	76w21	5:05:24
Allison 26	51	39N59	79w52	5:19:28
Allison Heights 26	51	39N59	79w52	5:19:28
Allison Park 2	114	40N33	79w58	5:19:52
Allport 11	92	40N40	78w47	5:15:08
Allport 17	4	40N58	78w12	5:12:48
Almaden 17	63	40N46	78w25	5:13:40
Almedia 19	4	41N01	76w23	5:05:32
Almont 9	8	40N24	75w24	5:01:36
Alpha 46	17	40N51	75w17	5:01:08
Alpine 67	12	40N08	76w52	5:07:28
Alsace 6	101	40N23	75w52	5:03:28
Alsace Manor 6	101	40N24	75w55	5:03:40
Alta Manor 7	33	40N31	78w25	5:13:40
Altamont 54	27	40N47	76w14	5:04:56
Altenwald 28	100	39N45	77w34	5:10:16
Alton 15	13	39N57	75w36	5:02:24
Altoona 7	33	40N31	78w24	5:13:36
Alum Bank 5	6	40N11	78w37	5:14:28
Alum Rock 16	1	41N11	79w43	5:18:52
Aluta 46	8	40N45	75w18	5:01:12
Alverda 32	6	40N38	78w52	5:15:28
Alverton 65	111	40N08	79w35	5:18:20
Amaranth 29	6	39N45	78w11	5:12:44
Amasa 35	1	41N32	75w32	5:02:08
Amberson 28	1	40N10	77w41	5:10:44
Ambler 46	8	40N09	75w13	5:00:52
Ambler Farms 23	9	39N53	75w18	5:01:12
Ambler Highlands 46	9	40N07	75w14	5:00:56
Ambridge 4	13	40N36	80w14	5:20:56

Ambridge Heights 4	13	40N35	80w13	5:20:52
Ambrose 32	6	40N46	79w03	5:16:12
Amend 26	80	39N54	79w44	5:18:56
Amesville 17	4	40N50	78w21	5:13:24
Amity 63	6	40N02	80w12	5:20:48
Amity Hall 50	51	40N24	77w02	5:08:08
Amsbry 11	55	40N29	78w33	5:14:12
Amsterdam 43	6	41N10	80w05	5:20:20
Amwell 63	3	40N05	80w12	5:20:48
Analomink 45	23	41N03	75w13	5:00:52
Ancient Oaks 39	13	40N33	75w34	5:02:16
Andalusia 9	9	40N06	74w56	4:59:44
Anderson 44	73	40N33	77w38	5:10:32
Andersonburg 50	6	40N22	77w21	5:09:24
Andersontown 67	1	40N00	76w58	5:07:52
Andover 29	66	39N59	78w04	5:12:16
Andreas 54	1	40N45	75w48	5:03:12
Andrews Bridge 36	23	39N58	76w00	5:04:00
Andrews Plan 4	13	40N37	80w16	5:21:04
Andrews Settlement 53	6	41N59	77w52	5:11:28
Angelica 6	101	40N18	75w59	5:03:56
Angels 64	6	41N19	75w19	5:01:16
Anita 33	51	41N00	78w58	5:15:52
Annaline Village 23	90	39N50	75w25	5:01:40
Annin 42	7	41N53	78w19	5:13:16
Annin Creek 42	7	41N52	78w20	5:13:20
Annisville 10	6	41N05	79w41	5:18:44
Annville 38	8	40N20	76w31	5:06:04
Anselma 15	8	40N06	75w37	5:02:28
Ansonia 59	6	41N45	77w18	5:09:12
Ansonville 17	54	40N46	78w33	5:14:12
Antes Fort 41	7	41N12	77w14	5:08:56
Anthracite 38	8	40N17	76w25	5:05:40
Antis 7	50	40N36	78w20	5:13:20
Antrim 59	6	41N38	77w17	5:09:08
Apolacon 58	6	41N57	76w06	5:04:24
Apollo 3	4	40N35	79w34	5:18:16
Appenzell 45	23	41N00	75w13	5:00:52
Applebachsville 9	13	40N29	75w25	5:01:40
Applewold 3	15	40N48	79w31	5:18:04
Aquashicola 13	8	40N49	75w35	5:02:20
Aqueduct 50	51	40N24	77w02	5:08:08
Aquetong 9	8	40N22	74w56	4:59:44
Ararat 58	59	41N49	75w31	5:02:04
Arbor 67	1	39N52	76w37	5:06:28
Arbuckle 25	58	41N54	79w51	5:19:24
Arcadia 32	6	40N47	78w51	5:15:24
Arcadia 36	1	39N47	76w11	5:04:44
Archbald 35	1	41N30	75w34	5:02:16
Arch Rock 34	7	40N35	77w24	5:09:36
Arch Spring 7	11	40N40	78w13	5:12:52
Arcola 46	8	40N09	75w27	5:01:48
Ardara 65	25	40N22	79w44	5:18:56
Ardenheim 31	81	40N30	78w01	5:12:04
Arden Mines 63	3	40N11	80w16	5:21:04
Ardmore 23	9	40N00	75w17	5:01:08
Ardmore Manor 23	9	40N01	75w17	5:01:08
Ardmore Park 23	9	40N01	75w17	5:01:08
Ardsley 46	9	40N07	75w10	5:00:40
Arendtsville 1	1	39N55	77w18	5:09:12
Arensberg 26	6	39N59	80w00	5:20:00
Argentine 10	6	41N05	79w50	5:19:20
Argus 9	8	40N24	75w24	5:01:36
Aristes 19	27	40N49	76w20	5:05:20
Arlingham 46	9	40N06	75w15	5:01:00
Arlingham Hills 46	9	40N06	75w15	5:01:00
Arlington 23	9	39N58	75w18	5:01:12
Arlington 64	6	41N27	75w23	5:01:32
Arlington Heights 45	23	41N00	75w13	5:00:52
Arlington Knolls 39	13	40N39	75w30	5:02:00
Arlington Park 2	114	40N23	79w49	5:19:16
Armagh 32	7	40N28	79w02	5:16:08
Armbrust 65	111	40N13	79w33	5:18:12
Armenia 8	7	41N45	76w52	5:07:28
Arndts 46	80	40N48	75w32	5:02:08
Arnold 65	14	40N35	79w46	5:19:04
Arnold City 26	1	40N08	79w52	5:19:28
Arnot 59	6	41N40	77w08	5:08:32
Arnots Addition 54	27	40N43	76w11	5:04:44
Arona 65	3	40N16	79w40	5:18:40
Aronimink 23	9	39N57	75w18	5:01:12
Aronimink Estates 23	9	39N57	75w18	5:01:12
Aronimink Heights 23	9	39N57	75w18	5:01:12
Aronimink Park 23	9	39N57	75w18	5:01:12
Aronwald 23	90	40N00	75w23	5:01:32
Arrowhead Lake 45	1	41N06	75w31	5:02:04
Arsenal 2	114	40N28	79w57	5:19:48
Artemas 5	6	39N45	78w27	5:13:48
Arthurs 16	37	41N15	79w28	5:17:52
Arundel Village 46	1	40N11	75w10	5:00:40
Asaph 59	6	41N45	77w18	5:09:12
Asbury 25	107	42N05	80w04	5:20:16
Ashbury 19	4	41N05	76w25	5:05:40
Ashfield 13	80	40N47	75w43	5:02:52
Ashland 17	4	40N51	78w16	5:13:04
Ashland 54	27	40N47	76w21	5:05:24
Ashley 40	20	41N13	75w54	5:03:36
Ashtola 56	123	40N15	78w50	5:15:20
Ashville 11	63	40N34	78w33	5:14:12
Askam 40	20	41N13	75w54	5:03:36
Aspers 1	1	39N59	77w14	5:08:56
Aspinwall 2	114	40N29	79w55	5:19:40
Aston 23	90	39N52	75w26	5:01:44
Aston Manor 23	90	39N51	75w22	5:01:28
Asylum 8	60	41N43	76w22	5:05:28
Atco 64	6	41N36	75w04	5:00:16
Atglen 15	8	39N57	75w58	5:03:52
Athens 8	1	41N58	76w31	5:06:04
Athol 6	8	40N18	75w44	5:02:56
Atkinsons Mills 44	7	40N30	77w45	5:11:00
Atlantic 17	59	40N50	78w21	5:13:24
Atlantic 20	59	41N30	80w21	5:21:24
Atlantic 65	3	40N24	79w25	5:17:40
Atlas 49	27	40N48	76w26	5:05:44
Atlasburg 63	6	40N20	80w23	5:21:32
Atwood 3	6	40N45	79w16	5:17:04
Auburn 54	3	40N36	76w05	5:04:20
Auburn Center 58	6	41N39	76w10	5:04:40
Auburn Four Corners 58	60	41N42	75w55	5:03:40
Audenried 13	42	40N58	76w00	5:04:00
Audubon 46	90	40N08	75w25	5:01:40
Aughwick 31	85	40N23	77w53	5:11:32
Augustaville 49	82	40N52	76w47	5:07:08
Aultman 32	6	40N34	79w16	5:17:04
Austin 53	6	41N38	78w06	5:12:24
Austinburg 59	6	41N57	77w26	5:09:44
Austin Heights 35	18	41N22	75w44	5:02:56
Austinville 8	7	41N50	76w48	5:07:12
Avalon 2	114	40N30	80w04	5:20:16
Avella 63	6	40N32	80w28	5:21:52
Avis 18	7	41N11	77w19	5:09:16
Avoca 40	1	41N20	75w45	5:03:00
Avon 38	8	40N21	76w23	5:05:32
Avondale 15	8	39N50	75w47	5:03:08
Avondale Knolls 23	90	39N54	75w22	5:01:28
Avon Heights 38	8	40N20	76w26	5:05:44
Avonmore 65	116	40N32	79w28	5:17:52
Axemann 14	70	40N53	77w45	5:11:00
Ayr 29	66	39N54	78w01	5:12:04
Bachmanville 22	31	40N17	76w39	5:06:36
Bacton 15	47	40N03	75w35	5:02:20
Baden 4	13	40N38	80w14	5:20:56
Baederwood 46	9	40N06	75w09	5:00:36
Bagdad 65	4	40N38	79w37	5:18:28
Baggaley 65	3	40N19	79w23	5:17:32
Baidland 63	1	40N11	79w54	5:19:36
Bailey 50	1	40N29	77w08	5:08:32
Baileys Corner 8	7	41N43	76w47	5:07:08
Baileyville 14	6	40N42	78w00	5:12:00
Bainbridge 36	2	40N05	76w40	5:06:40
Bair 67	67	39N58	76w44	5:06:56
Bairdford 2	6	40N38	79w53	5:19:32
Bakers Crossroads 11	57	40N38	78w39	5:14:36
Bakers Summit 5	3	40N16	78w25	5:13:40
Baker Station 15	1	39N49	75w50	5:03:20
Bakerstown 2	6	40N39	79w56	5:19:44
Bakersville 56	6	40N01	79w05	5:16:20
Bala-Cynwyd 46	9	40N00	75w14	5:00:56
Bald Eagle 7	11	40N40	78w13	5:12:52
Bald Eagle 18	7	41N07	77w31	5:10:04
Bald Hill 17	6	41N05	78w17	5:13:08
Baldwin 2	114	40N23	79w59	5:19:56
Baldwin 23	90	39N51	75w22	5:01:28
Balliettsville 39	13	40N40	75w30	5:02:00
Balls Mills 41	7	41N19	77w05	5:08:20
Bally 6	3	40N24	75w35	5:02:20
Balsinger 26	80	39N54	79w46	5:19:04
Bamford 36	97	40N06	76w25	5:05:40
Banard Town 4	8	40N46	80w20	5:21:20
Banetown 63	3	40N11	80w16	5:21:04
Bangor 48	17	40N52	75w13	5:00:52
Banian Junction 17	6	40N50	78w26	5:13:44
Banner Ridge 17	122	40N51	78w43	5:14:52
Bannerville 55	1	40N42	77w19	5:09:16
Banning 26	104	40N03	79w39	5:18:36
Barbours 41	82	41N14	77w01	5:08:04
Bard 5	6	39N57	78w39	5:14:36
Baresville 67	1	39N48	76w59	5:07:56
Bareville 36	28	40N05	76w11	5:04:44
Barkeyville 61	6	41N11	79w59	5:19:56
Barking 2	14	40N29	79w44	5:18:56
Barlow 1	1	39N49	77w11	5:08:44
Barmouth 46	9	40N01	75w15	5:01:00
Barnards 3	59	40N53	79w15	5:17:00
Barnes 11	63	40N36	78w45	5:15:00
Barnes 62	3	41N42	79w02	5:16:08
Barnesboro 11	92	40N40	78w47	5:15:08
Barneston 15	27	40N06	75w55	5:03:40
Barnesville 54	27	40N48	76w20	5:05:20
Barnett 27	6	41N22	79w10	5:16:40
Barneytown 31	85	40N24	77w56	5:11:44
Barnitz 21	16	40N12	77w11	5:08:44
Barnsley 15	3	39N47	75w59	5:03:56
Barr 11	92	40N37	78w49	5:15:16
Barree 31	6	40N40	77w49	5:11:16
Barren Hill 46	90	40N05	75w16	5:01:04
Barret Plan 4	13	40N37	80w16	5:21:04
Barrett 17	1	41N02	78w27	5:13:48
Barrett 45	84	41N12	75w16	5:01:04
Barronvale 56	4	39N55	79w11	5:16:44
Barr Slope 32	6	40N43	79w01	5:16:04
Barrville 44	73	40N40	77w36	5:10:24
Barry 54	27	40N43	76w25	5:05:40
Barry Heights 46	90	40N08	75w21	5:01:24
Bart 36	23	39N56	76w04	5:04:16
Barto 6	2	40N23	75w37	5:02:28
Bartonsville 45	1	41N00	75w17	5:01:08
Bartville 36	23	39N58	76w00	5:04:00
Basket 6	101	40N23	75w54	5:03:36
Bassards Corners 46	80	40N48	75w32	5:02:08
Bastress 41	64	41N11	77w07	5:08:28
Bath 48	13	40N44	75w24	5:01:36
Bath Addition 9	9	40N08	74w51	4:59:24
Bath Manor 9	9	40N08	74w51	4:59:24
Battle Hollow 33	6	41N06	78w53	5:15:32
Bauerstown 2	114	40N29	79w59	5:19:56
Baumgardner 36	8	39N59	76w17	5:05:08
Baumstown 6	8	40N16	75w48	5:03:12
Bausman 36	8	40N02	76w18	5:05:12
Bavington 63	6	40N23	80w20	5:21:20
Baxter 33	6	41N10	79w13	5:16:52
Beachdale 56	79	39N52	79w04	5:16:16
Beach Haven 40	1	41N04	76w11	5:04:44
Beach Lake 64	6	41N36	75w09	5:00:36
Beadling 2	114	40N20	80w05	5:20:20
Beale 34	6	40N30	77w31	5:10:04
Beallsville 63	51	40N04	80w02	5:20:08
Bear Creek 40	1	41N13	75w46	5:03:04
Bear Gap 49	1	40N52	76w33	5:06:12
Bear Lake 62	6	42N00	79w30	5:18:00
Bear Rocks 26	6	40N08	79w26	5:17:44
Beartown 28	100	39N45	77w34	5:10:16
Beartown 36	27	40N06	75w59	5:03:56
Bear Valley 49	27	40N48	76w33	5:06:12
Beatty 65	3	40N19	79w23	5:17:32
Beatty Hills 23	9	39N58	75w22	5:01:28
Beaufort Farms 22	12	40N17	76w53	5:07:32
Beaumont 66	6	41N22	76w02	5:04:08
Beaver 4	19	40N42	80w19	5:21:16
Beaver Acres 2	114	40N28	80w05	5:20:20
Beaver Brook 40	42	40N58	76w00	5:04:00
Beaver Center 20	6	41N46	80w22	5:21:28
Beaverdale 11	63	40N19	78w42	5:14:48
Beaverdale 49	27	40N48	76w25	5:05:40
Beaver Dam 25	3	41N55	79w39	5:18:36
Beaver Falls 4	8	40N46	80w20	5:21:20
Beaver Lake 41	6	41N21	76w35	5:06:20
Beaver Meadows 13	42	40N56	75w55	5:03:40
Beaver Springs 55	6	40N45	77w13	5:08:52
Beavertown 7	51	40N19	78w20	5:13:20
Beavertown 31	6	40N16	78w04	5:12:16
Beavertown 55	6	40N45	77w11	5:08:44
Beavertown 67	1	40N07	77w02	5:08:08
Beaver Valley 11	54	40N43	78w31	5:14:04
Beccaria 17	54	40N46	78w31	5:14:04
Bechtelsville 6	2	40N22	75w38	5:02:32
Beckersville 6	101	40N18	75w59	5:03:56
Becks 54	49	40N41	76w12	5:04:48
Bedford 5	70	40N01	78w30	5:14:00
Bedminster 9	1	40N27	75w14	5:00:56
Beech Creek 18	7	41N05	77w36	5:10:24
Beechersville 1	1	39N56	77w15	5:09:00
Beech Flats 8	103	41N39	76w51	5:07:24
Beech Glen 57	6	41N21	76w35	5:06:20
Beechmont 2	114	40N27	80w08	5:20:32
Beechtree 33	5	41N15	78w48	5:15:12
Beechwood 12	106	41N31	78w14	5:12:56
Beechwood Park 23	90	39N52	75w23	5:01:32
Beersville 48	13	40N41	75w22	5:01:28
Beesons 26	80	39N52	79w42	5:18:48
Beham 63	6	40N06	80w31	5:22:04
Bela 16	1	41N03	79w39	5:18:36
Belair Park 36	8	40N04	76w19	5:05:16
Belardy 9	9	40N08	74w51	4:59:24
Belden 5	70	39N58	78w31	5:14:04
Belfast 29	60	39N53	78w09	5:12:36
Belfast 46	8	40N45	75w18	5:01:12
Belfast Junction 46	12	40N41	75w14	5:00:56
Belian Village 35	18	41N22	75w43	5:02:52
Belknap 3	59	40N53	79w15	5:17:00
Bell Acres 2	13	40N35	80w10	5:20:40
Bellaire 36	2	40N10	76w36	5:06:24
Bella Vista 41	82	41N15	76w55	5:07:40
Belle Bridge 2	8	40N17	79w50	5:19:20
Bellefonte 14	70	40N55	77w47	5:11:08
Bellegrove 38	8	40N20	76w31	5:06:04
Bellemont 36	9	40N01	76w08	5:04:32
Belle Valley 25	107	42N05	80w04	5:20:16
Belle Vernon 63	1	40N08	79w52	5:19:28
Belleville 44	6	40N36	77w44	5:10:56
Bellevue 2	114	40N30	80w04	5:20:16
Bell Mountain 35	18	41N26	75w40	5:02:40
Bell Point 65	4	40N33	79w33	5:18:12
Bellrun 42	7	42N00	78w16	5:13:04
Bells Landing 17	122	40N51	78w43	5:14:52
Bells Mills 33	51	40N56	78w58	5:15:52
Belltown 44	1	40N42	77w19	5:09:16
Bellwood 7	50	40N36	78w20	5:13:20
Belmont 11	74	40N17	78w53	5:15:32
Belmont Corner 64	59	41N44	75w26	5:01:44
Belmont Hills 9	9	40N06	74w56	4:59:44
Belmont Homes 11	74	40N17	78w53	5:15:32
Belmont Terrace 46	90	40N05	75w22	5:01:28
Belsano 11	63	40N31	78w52	5:15:28
Belsena Mills 17	6	40N50	78w26	5:13:44
Belton 4	121	40N52	80w16	5:21:04
Ben Avon 2	114	40N30	80w05	5:20:20
Ben Avon 32	72	40N38	79w09	5:16:36
Ben Avon Heights 2	114	40N31	80w04	5:20:16
Bencetown 32	6	40N43	79w01	5:16:04
Bendersville 1	1	39N59	77w15	5:09:00
Bendertown 19	4	41N05	76w25	5:05:40
Benedicks 67	1	40N00	76w58	5:07:52
Benezette 24	6	41N19	78w23	5:13:32
Benfer 55	6	40N45	77w13	5:08:52
Benjamin 9	8	40N25	75w23	5:01:32
Benner 14	9	40N52	77w48	5:11:12
Bensalem 9	9	40N06	74w57	4:59:48

PENNSYLVANIA

Bens Creek 11 55 40N25 78w37 5:14:28
Benson 56 74 40N12 78w56 5:15:44
Bentley Creek 8 7 42N01 76w44 5:06:56
Bentleyville 63 51 40N07 80w01 5:20:04
Benton 19 56 41N12 76w23 5:05:32
Benvenue 22 1 40N24 77w02 5:08:08
Benzinger 24 36 41N26 78w33 5:14:12
Bergey 46 8 40N17 75w23 5:01:32
Berkeley Hills 2 114 40N33 80w01 5:20:04
Berkley 6 101 40N23 75w56 5:03:44
Berkleys Mill 56 79 39N49 79w02 5:16:08
Berkshire Heights 6 101 40N19 75w59 5:03:56
Berlin 56 6 39N55 78w57 5:15:48
Berlin Junction 1 1 39N52 77w03 5:08:12
Berlinsville 46 8 40N45 75w36 5:02:24
Bermudian 1 1 40N07 77w02 5:08:08
Bern 6 101 40N24 75w59 5:03:56
Berne 6 80 40N33 75w59 5:03:56
Bernharts 6 101 40N23 75w56 5:03:44
Bernice 57 60 41N29 76w23 5:05:32
Bernville 6 3 40N26 76w07 5:04:28
Berrysburg 22 4 40N36 76w49 5:07:16
Berrytown 8 7 41N57 76w48 5:07:12
Bertha 63 7 40N23 80w24 5:21:36
Berwick 19 1 41N03 76w14 5:04:56
Berwinsdale 17 54 40N46 78w33 5:14:12
Berwyn 15 90 40N03 75w26 5:01:44
Besco 63 6 39N59 80w03 5:20:12
Bessemer 2 114 40N24 79w52 5:19:28
Bessemer 37 1 40N59 80w30 5:22:00
Bessemer 65 111 40N09 79w33 5:18:12
Bessemer Terrace 2 114 40N24 79w50 5:19:20
Best 2 114 40N22 79w54 5:19:36
Best Station 39 8 40N45 75w37 5:02:28
Bethany 64 59 41N37 75w17 5:01:08
Bethayres 46 9 40N07 75w04 5:00:16
Bethel 6 1 40N28 76w18 5:05:12
Bethel 11 54 40N29 78w43 5:14:52
Bethel 43 117 41N10 80w27 5:21:48
Bethel Hill 46 8 40N15 75w17 5:01:08
Bethel Park 2 114 40N20 80w01 5:20:04
Bethesda 36 1 39N50 76w19 5:05:16
Bethlehem 17 122 40N51 78w43 5:14:52
Bethlehem 48 13 40N37 75w23 5:01:32
Bethton 9 8 40N19 75w19 5:01:16
Betula 42 93 41N49 78w27 5:13:48
Betzwood 46 90 40N08 75w21 5:01:24
Beulah 2 114 40N27 79w50 5:19:20
Beulah 17 6 40N48 78w24 5:13:36
Beverly Estates 36 8 40N04 76w19 5:05:16
Beverly Heights 38 8 40N20 76w26 5:05:44
Beverly Hills 7 33 40N31 78w25 5:13:40
Beyer 32 6 40N47 79w12 5:16:48
Biddle 65 25 40N20 79w41 5:18:44
Biesecker Gap 28 100 39N45 77w34 5:10:16
Big Beaver 4 121 40N49 80w22 5:21:28
Big Cove Tannery 29 66 39N51 78w03 5:12:12
Big Creek 13 8 40N50 75w42 5:02:48
Biggertown 41 6 41N14 76w31 5:06:04
Bigler 17 6 40N50 78w26 5:13:44
Biglerville 1 56 39N56 77w15 5:09:00
Big Mine Run Junction 54 27 40N47 76w21 5:05:24
Bigmount 67 1 40N00 76w58 5:07:52
Big Pond 8 7 41N50 76w48 5:07:12
Big Run 33 51 40N59 78w53 5:15:32
Big Shanty 42 6 41N52 78w40 5:14:40
Bingen 48 13 40N36 75w23 5:01:32
Bingham 42 6 41N52 78w40 5:14:40
Bingham 53 6 41N57 77w47 5:11:08
Binnstown 63 114 40N29 79w50 5:19:20
Bino 28 1 39N48 77w44 5:10:56
Birchardville 58 60 41N50 75w53 5:03:32
Birchrunville 15 8 40N08 75w39 5:02:36
Bird in Hand 36 96 40N02 76w11 5:04:44
Birdsboro 6 8 40N16 75w49 5:03:16
Birdville 2 14 40N37 79w44 5:18:56
Birdville 31 85 40N24 77w56 5:11:44
Birmingham 15 13 39N57 75w36 5:02:24
Birmingham 31 11 40N40 78w13 5:12:52
Bishop 63 114 40N20 80w11 5:20:44
Bishtown 17 6 41N00 78w21 5:13:24
Bitner 26 105 39N59 79w37 5:18:28
Bittersville 67 1 39N55 76w35 5:06:20
Bitumen 18 7 41N18 77w51 5:11:24
Bixler 50 6 40N22 77w21 5:09:24
Black 8 41 41N46 76w27 5:05:48
Black 56 4 39N55 79w08 5:16:32
Blackash 20 6 41N38 79w59 5:19:56
Black Bear 6 101 40N20 75w53 5:03:32
Blackburn 65 25 40N22 79w44 5:18:56
Black Creek 40 1 40N59 76w11 5:04:44
Black Creek Junction 13 60 40N57 75w49 5:03:16
Black Diamond 63 1 40N11 79w54 5:19:36
Blackgap 28 1 39N55 77w34 5:10:16
Blackhawk 4 8 40N46 80w20 5:21:20
Blackhorse 15 32 39N58 75w55 5:03:40
Black Horse 23 90 39N55 75w22 5:01:28
Black Horse 46 90 40N08 75w21 5:01:24
Black Lick 32 98 40N28 79w12 5:16:48
Blacklog 31 6 40N15 77w53 5:11:32
Blackman 40 20 41N15 75w53 5:03:32
Black Ridge 2 114 40N28 79w50 5:19:20
Blacks Corner 20 77 41N40 80w07 5:20:28
Blacktown 43 66 41N14 80w14 5:20:56
Black Walnut 66 6 41N39 76w10 5:04:40
Blackwell 59 6 41N33 77w23 5:09:32
Blain 50 6 40N20 77w31 5:10:04
Blain City 17 54 40N45 78w32 5:14:08
Blaine 63 6 40N11 80w24 5:21:36
Blaine Hill 2 8 40N16 79w53 5:19:32
Blainsport 36 1 40N16 76w07 5:04:28
Blair 7 33 40N24 78w25 5:13:40
Blairs 16 6 41N14 79w32 5:18:08
Blairs Mills 31 6 40N17 77w43 5:10:52
Blairsville 32 35 40N26 79w16 5:17:04
Blairtown 30 1 39N54 80w11 5:20:44
Blakely 35 18 41N28 75w37 5:02:28
Blakes 59 6 41N41 77w04 5:08:16
Blakeslee 45 94 41N06 75w36 5:02:24
Blanchard 2 7 40N40 79w50 5:19:20
Blanchard 14 7 41N04 77w36 5:10:24
Blanco 3 6 40N47 79w17 5:17:08
Blandburg 11 63 40N41 78w25 5:13:40
Blandon 6 101 40N26 75w53 5:03:32
Blanket Hill 3 15 40N49 79w32 5:18:08
Blawnox 2 114 40N30 79w52 5:19:28
Bloom 17 7 41N01 78w38 5:14:32
Bloomfield 2 114 40N28 79w57 5:19:48
Bloomingdale 13 80 40N50 75w51 5:03:24
Bloomingdale 36 8 40N04 76w19 5:05:16
Bloomingdale 40 1 41N09 76w10 5:04:40
Blooming Glen 9 1 40N22 75w15 5:01:00
Blooming Grove 52 6 41N23 75w06 5:00:24
Blooming Grove 67 1 39N48 76w59 5:07:56
Bloomington 17 7 40N57 78w33 5:14:12
Bloomington 35 4 41N20 75w32 5:02:08
Blooming Valley 20 6 41N41 80w02 5:20:08
Bloomsburg 19 4 41N00 76w27 5:05:48
Bloomsdale Gardens 9 9 40N09 74w51 4:59:24
Bloserville 21 1 40N10 77w24 5:09:36
Bloss 59 6 41N40 77w07 5:08:28
Blossburg 59 59 41N41 77w04 5:08:16
Blosser Hill 26 7 39N44 79w52 5:19:28
Blossom Hill 36 8 40N04 76w19 5:05:16
Blossom Valley 36 8 40N04 76w19 5:05:16
Blough 56 6 40N09 78w55 5:15:40
Blue Ball 36 27 40N07 76w03 5:04:12
Blue Bell 46 8 40N09 75w16 5:01:04
Blue Bell Farms 46 8 40N10 75w17 5:01:08
Blue Bell Gardens 46 8 40N10 75w17 5:01:08
Blue Goose Mine 16 1 41N03 79w39 5:18:36
Blue Hill 55 82 40N48 76w52 5:07:28
Blue Jay 27 3 41N42 79w02 5:16:08
Blueknob 7 33 40N28 78w25 5:13:40
Blue Marsh 6 101 40N18 76w00 5:04:00
Blue Mountain Camps 45 23 41N00 75w11 5:00:44
Blue Ridge Summit 28 1 39N43 77w28 5:09:52
Bluff 30 6 39N45 80w18 5:21:12
Blystone Mill 20 3 41N48 80w03 5:20:12
Blythe 54 27 40N44 76w07 5:04:28
Blytheburn 40 20 41N14 75w52 5:03:28
Blythedale 2 8 40N17 79w49 5:19:16
Blythewood 9 8 40N21 75w13 5:00:52
Boalsburg 14 9 40N47 77w47 5:11:08
Boardman 17 122 40N50 78w41 5:14:44
Bobtown 30 7 39N46 79w59 5:19:56
Bodines 41 7 41N27 76w59 5:07:56
Boggstown 28 1 40N04 77w50 5:11:20
Boggsville 3 2 40N44 79w45 5:19:00
Bohemia 52 6 41N29 75w11 5:00:44
Bohrmans Mill 54 27 40N38 76w10 5:04:40
Boiling Springs 21 2 40N09 77w09 5:08:36
Bolivar 65 7 40N24 79w09 5:16:36
Bolivar Run 42 102 41N57 78w39 5:14:36
Boltz 32 7 40N25 79w01 5:16:04
Bonair 9 1 40N12 75w05 5:00:20
Bon Air 11 74 40N21 78w54 5:15:36
Bon Air 23 9 40N00 75w18 5:01:12
Bon Aire 10 3 40N53 79w53 5:19:32
Bondsville 15 46 40N00 75w42 5:02:48
Bon Meade 2 13 40N33 80w15 5:21:00
Bonnair 67 3 39N48 76w44 5:06:56
Bonneauville 1 1 39N49 77w08 5:08:32
Bonny Brook 21 16 40N12 77w11 5:08:44
Bonus 10 6 41N05 79w41 5:18:44
Booneville 18 7 41N02 77w18 5:09:12
Boon Terrace 63 2 40N15 80w13 5:20:52
Booth Corner 23 90 39N50 75w25 5:01:40
Boothwyn 23 90 39N50 75w26 5:01:44
Boothwyn Highlands 23 90 39N50 75w25 5:01:40
Boquet 65 3 40N23 79w36 5:18:24
Bordnersville 38 1 40N22 77w43 5:10:52
Borland Manor 63 2 40N16 80w11 5:20:44
Borough 4 19 40N41 80w20 5:21:20
Bortondale 23 90 39N55 75w22 5:01:28
Bossardsville 45 23 41N00 75w13 5:00:52
Boston 2 9 40N19 79w49 5:19:16
Boston Run 54 3 40N49 76w08 5:04:32
Boswell 56 6 40N10 79w02 5:16:08
Botts 67 67 39N57 76w42 5:06:48
Boulevard 51 9 40N02 75w04 5:00:16
Bourne 8 60 41N51 76w30 5:06:00
Bovard 10 6 41N06 79w54 5:19:36
Bovard 65 99 40N19 79w30 5:18:00
Bowdertown 32 63 40N44 78w49 5:15:16
Bower Hill 2 114 40N22 80w05 5:20:20
Bowers 6 8 40N29 75w45 5:03:00
Bowersville 33 51 40N56 78w58 5:15:52
Bowie 43 6 41N16 80w08 5:20:32
Bowling Green 23 90 39N55 75w22 5:01:28
Bowman Addition 67 1 39N48 76w59 5:07:56
Bowmans 54 3 40N49 76w08 5:04:32
Bowmansdale 21 12 40N10 76w59 5:07:56
Bowmans Store 67 1 39N46 76w50 5:07:20
Bowmanstown 13 8 40N48 75w40 5:02:40
Bowmansville 36 27 40N10 76w04 5:04:16
Bowood Mines No. 1 26 51 39N48 79w49 5:19:16
Boyce 2 114 40N20 80w05 5:20:20
Boyds Mills 64 6 41N40 75w04 5:00:16
Boydstown 10 6 40N57 79w45 5:19:00
Boydtown 49 27 40N48 76w33 5:06:12
Boyers 10 6 41N07 79w54 5:19:36
Boyers Junction 6 8 40N27 75w50 5:03:20
Boyertown 6 2 40N20 75w38 5:02:32
Boynton 56 79 39N46 79w04 5:16:16
Brackenridge 2 14 40N36 79w44 5:18:56
Brackney 58 6 41N59 75w56 5:03:44
Braddock 2 114 40N24 79w52 5:19:28
Braddock Hills 2 114 40N25 79w52 5:19:28
Braden Plan 30 6 39N59 80w03 5:20:12
Bradenville 65 3 40N24 79w25 5:17:40
Bradford 42 102 41N58 78w38 5:14:32
Bradford Hills 15 13 40N00 75w39 5:02:36
Bradfordwoods 2 6 40N38 80w05 5:20:20
Bradley Junction 11 54 40N29 78w43 5:14:52
Bradleytown 61 6 41N30 79w52 5:19:28
Bradys Bend 3 1 40N59 79w39 5:18:36
Braeburn 65 14 40N33 79w42 5:18:48
Braintrim 66 59 41N38 76w08 5:04:32
Braman 64 6 41N49 75w05 5:00:20
Branch 54 27 40N41 76w17 5:05:08
Branch Dale 54 27 40N41 76w20 5:05:20
Branchton 10 6 41N04 79w59 5:19:56
Branchville 25 107 42N00 80w09 5:20:36
Brandamore 15 9 40N03 75w50 5:03:20
Brandonville 54 56 40N52 76w14 5:04:56
Brandt 58 59 41N57 75w37 5:02:28
Brandtsville 21 12 40N12 77w00 5:08:00
Brandy Camp 24 6 41N19 78w41 5:14:44
Brandywine Homes 15 9 39N59 75w50 5:03:20
Brandywine Manor 15 9 40N04 75w49 5:03:16
Brandywine Summit 23 4 39N55 75w30 5:02:00
Brandywine Village 46 90 40N06 75w23 5:01:32
Bratton 44 7 40N29 77w42 5:10:48
Brave 30 6 39N44 80w16 5:21:04
Braznell 26 51 40N01 79w50 5:19:20
Breadysville 9 1 40N12 75w05 5:00:20
Breakneck 26 104 40N01 79w35 5:18:20
Bredinville 10 3 40N51 79w56 5:19:44
Breezewood 2 114 40N33 80w01 5:20:04
Breezewood 5 6 40N00 78w15 5:13:00
Breezy Corner 6 8 40N27 75w50 5:03:20
Breinigsville 39 9 40N33 75w38 5:02:32
Breinizer 65 98 40N26 79w16 5:17:04
Brent 37 6 41N07 80w15 5:21:00
Brentwood 2 114 40N22 79w59 5:19:56
Breslau 40 20 41N14 75w52 5:03:28
Breton Hills 9 1 40N12 75w05 5:00:20
Bretonville 17 6 40N51 78w34 5:14:16
Briarbrook 40 20 41N14 75w52 5:03:28
Briarcliff 23 9 39N54 75w18 5:01:12
Briar Creek 19 1 41N03 76w17 5:05:08
Briarwood 9 1 42N08 75w53 5:03:32
Brickchurch 3 15 40N46 79w32 5:18:08
Brickerville 36 8 40N09 76w18 5:05:12
Brick Tavern 9 13 40N29 75w25 5:01:40
Bridesburg 51 9 40N00 75w05 5:00:20
Bridgeburg 3 15 40N53 79w32 5:18:08
Bridgeport 1 1 39N56 77w15 5:09:00
Bridgeport 13 60 41N04 75w46 5:03:04
Bridgeport 17 7 40N57 78w33 5:14:12
Bridgeport 36 8 40N02 76w17 5:05:08
Bridgeport 46 90 40N06 75w21 5:01:24
Bridgeport 50 6 40N21 77w18 5:09:12
Bridgeport 65 111 40N09 79w33 5:18:12
Bridgeton 9 7 40N33 75w06 5:00:24
Bridgeton 67 1 39N44 76w31 5:06:04
Bridgetown 9 97 40N10 74w55 4:59:40
Bridge Valley 9 8 40N18 75w05 5:00:20
Bridgeville 2 114 40N22 80w07 5:20:28
Bridgewater 9 9 40N06 74w56 4:59:44
Bridgewater Farms 23 90 39N52 75w23 5:01:32
Brier Hill 26 51 39N59 79w50 5:19:20
Briggsville 40 1 41N03 76w13 5:04:52
Brighton 4 8 40N42 80w22 5:21:28
Brighton 23 9 39N58 75w18 5:01:12
Brightside 9 9 40N08 74w51 4:59:24
Brightwood 2 114 40N20 80w02 5:20:08
Brilhart 67 67 39N59 76w46 5:07:04
Brinkerton 65 99 40N18 79w34 5:18:16
Brintons 15 13 39N57 75w36 5:02:24
Briquette 2 10 40N22 79w51 5:19:24
Brisbin 17 4 40N50 78w21 5:13:24
Briscoe Springs 43 6 41N10 80w05 5:20:20
Bristol 9 9 40N06 74w51 4:59:24
Bristoria 30 6 39N56 80w23 5:21:32
Brittany Farms 9 2 40N20 75w18 5:01:12
Britton Run 20 56 41N50 79w41 5:18:44
Broad Acres 43 6 41N10 80w05 5:20:20
Broad Axe 46 1 40N09 75w12 5:00:48
Broad Ford 26 104 40N01 79w35 5:18:20
Broadlawn Highlands 2 114 40N20 80w05 5:20:20
Broad Street 40 42 40N58 76w00 5:04:00
Broad Top 31 6 40N09 78w13 5:12:52
Broadview 2 14 40N37 79w44 5:18:56
Broadway 40 1 41N09 76w10 5:04:40
Broadway Manor 9 9 40N08 74w51 4:59:24
Brock 30 6 39N47 80w13 5:20:52

Brockie 67 67 39N57 76w42 5:06:48
Brockport 24 5 41N16 78w44 5:14:56
Brockton 54 1 40N45 76w04 5:04:16
Brockway 33 5 41N15 78w47 5:15:08
Brodbecks 67 1 39N46 76w50 5:07:20
Brodhead 48 13 40N39 75w21 5:01:24
Brodheadsville 45 1 40N55 75w24 5:01:36
Brogue 67 1 39N52 76w29 5:05:56
Broguevlle 67 1 39N50 76w34 5:06:16
Brokenstraw 62 3 41N51 79w19 5:17:16
Brommerstown 54 1 40N36 76w05 5:04:20
Brookdale 11 74 40N23 78w50 5:15:20
Brookdale 58 50 41N58 75w45 5:03:00
Brookes Mills 7 33 40N28 78w25 5:13:40
Brookfield 59 6 41N58 77w32 5:10:08
Brookhaven 23 90 39N52 75w23 5:01:32
Brookhaven Gardens 23 90 39N52 75w23 5:01:32
Brookland 53 6 41N54 77w46 5:11:04
Brookline 2 114 40N24 80w01 5:20:04
Brookline 23 9 40N00 75w18 5:01:12
Brooklyn 58 59 41N45 75w49 5:03:16
Brook Park 60 70 40N58 76w54 5:07:36
Brookside 21 82 40N03 77w32 5:10:08
Brookside 25 107 42N08 80w01 5:20:04
Brookside 41 7 41N23 77w03 5:08:12
Brookside 54 9 40N36 76w23 5:05:32
Brookside 67 1 40N00 76w58 5:07:52
Brookside Farms 2 114 40N20 80w05 5:20:20
Brookston 27 3 41N42 79w02 5:16:08
Brookthorpe Hills 23 9 39N58 75w22 5:01:28
Brookvale 26 104 40N01 79w35 5:18:20
Brookville 33 34 41N10 79w05 5:16:20
Brookwater Park 46 8 40N12 75w28 5:01:52
Broomall 23 1 39N59 75w22 5:01:28
Brothersvalley 56 6 39N55 78w59 5:15:56
Brotherton 56 6 39N56 78w57 5:15:48
Broughton 2 114 40N19 79w59 5:19:56
Brownbacks 15 118 40N11 75w33 5:02:12
Browndale 64 59 41N39 75w28 5:01:52
Brownfield 26 80 39N51 79w43 5:18:52
Brownhill 20 3 41N48 80w03 5:20:12
Browns 40 1 41N19 75w46 5:03:04
Brownsburg 9 8 40N22 74w56 4:59:44
Brownsdale 10 6 40N46 79w58 5:19:52
Brownstone 22 12 40N16 76w43 5:06:52
Brownstown 3 4 40N32 79w30 5:18:00
Brownstown 11 74 40N20 78w56 5:15:44
Brownstown 26 1 40N07 79w50 5:19:20
Brownstown 36 28 40N07 76w13 5:04:52
Brownsville 6 80 40N20 76w05 5:04:20
Brownsville 26 1 40N01 79w53 5:19:32
Brownsville 28 1 39N55 77w34 5:10:16
Brownsville 54 27 40N49 76w12 5:04:48
Brownsville Junction 26 51 40N02 79w55 5:19:40
Brownsville Township 26 51 40N02 79w55 5:19:40
Browntown 8 6 41N40 76w16 5:05:04
Browntown 40 1 41N19 75w47 5:03:08
Browntown 63 6 40N17 80w28 5:21:52
Bruceton 2 114 40N22 79w58 5:19:52
Bruin 10 6 41N04 79w44 5:18:56
Brumbaugh Crossing 31 3 40N26 78w07 5:12:28
Brunnerville 36 8 40N09 76w18 5:05:12
Brush Creek 29 6 39N56 78w14 5:12:56
Brushmeadway 7 33 40N25 78w24 5:13:36
Brushtown 1 1 39N48 76w59 5:07:56
Brushtown 21 1 40N10 77w24 5:09:36
Brush Valley 32 6 40N32 79w04 5:16:16
Brushville 8 6 41N46 76w11 5:04:44
Brushville 58 59 41N57 75w37 5:02:28
Bryan 3 59 40N53 79w15 5:17:00
Bryan 26 104 40N03 79w39 5:18:36
Bryan Hill 32 72 40N38 79w09 5:16:36
Bryan Mills 41 81 41N14 76w44 5:06:56
Bryansville 67 7 39N44 76w19 5:05:16
Bryant 2 114 40N34 80w00 5:20:00
Bryn Athyn 46 1 40N09 75w04 5:00:16
Bryn Gweled 9 1 40N11 75w03 5:00:12
Bryn Mawr 2 114 40N26 79w53 5:19:32
Bryn Mawr 46 9 40N01 75w19 5:01:16
Brysonia 1 1 39N56 77w15 5:09:00
Bucher 17 6 40N50 78w26 5:13:44
Buck 36 27 39N54 76w10 5:04:40
Buck 40 6 41N10 75w41 5:02:44
Buckeye 65 111 40N09 79w33 5:18:12
Buck Hill Falls 45 84 41N11 75w16 5:01:04
Buckhorn 11 63 40N34 78w33 5:14:12
Buckhorn 19 4 41N00 76w25 5:05:40
Buckingham 9 8 40N19 75w04 5:00:16
Buckman Village 23 90 39N51 75w22 5:01:28
Buckmanville 9 8 40N22 74w56 4:59:44
Buck Mountain 13 60 40N57 75w49 5:03:16
Buck Mountain 54 27 40N48 76w20 5:05:20
Buck Run 15 9 39N59 75w50 5:03:20
Buck Run 32 6 40N40 79w00 5:16:00
Buck Run 54 27 40N42 76w20 5:05:20
Buckstown 56 6 40N07 78w57 5:15:48
Bucksville 9 1 40N31 75w10 5:00:40
Bucktown 15 8 40N11 75w40 5:02:40
Buck Valley 29 6 39N45 78w11 5:12:44
Buells Corners 20 56 41N50 79w41 5:18:44
Buena Vista 2 8 40N16 79w48 5:19:12
Buena Vista 7 11 40N40 78w13 5:12:52
Buena Vista 10 6 40N57 79w45 5:19:00
Buena Vista 26 104 40N02 79w40 5:18:40
Buena Vista 28 100 39N45 77w34 5:10:16
Buena Vista 36 23 39N59 76w02 5:04:08
Buena Vista Springs 28 100 39N45 77w34 5:10:16
Buffalo 63 6 40N14 80w22 5:21:28
Buffalo Cross Roads 60 70 40N58 76w54 5:07:36
Buffalo Mills 3 7 40N50 79w38 5:18:32
Buffalo Mills 5 7 39N57 78w39 5:14:36
Buffalo Run 14 63 40N48 78w03 5:12:12
Buffalo Springs 38 8 40N20 76w26 5:05:44
Buffalo Valley 3 6 40N50 79w38 5:18:32
Buffington 26 51 39N56 79w50 5:19:20
Buffington 32 6 40N31 78w57 5:15:48
Buhl 43 117 41N15 80w30 5:22:00
Buhls 10 6 40N46 80w04 5:20:16
Bulger 63 64 40N23 80w20 5:21:20
Bullion 61 6 41N17 79w44 5:18:56
Bullis Mill 42 40 41N57 78w23 5:13:32
Bullskin 26 111 40N05 79w32 5:18:08
Bully Hill 61 109 41N25 79w50 5:19:20
Bunches 67 12 40N14 76w51 5:07:24
Bungalow Park 39 13 40N37 75w31 5:02:04
Bunker Hill 38 8 40N20 76w26 5:05:44
Bunker Hill 54 49 40N41 76w12 5:04:48
Bunkertown 34 1 40N38 77w17 5:09:08
Bunola 2 8 40N14 79w56 5:19:44
Burd Coleman Village 38 8 40N17 76w25 5:05:40
Burgettstown 63 4 40N23 80w23 5:21:32
Burlington 8 60 41N47 76w36 5:06:24
Burnham 44 73 40N38 77w34 5:10:16
Burning Well 42 75 41N40 78w49 5:15:16
Burnside 17 6 40N49 78w47 5:15:08
Burnside 23 9 39N55 75w19 5:01:16
Burnside 49 27 40N48 76w33 5:06:12
Burnstown 37 121 40N52 80w16 5:21:04
Burnt Cabins 29 6 40N05 77w54 5:11:36
Burnwood 58 6 41N52 75w31 5:02:04
Burrows 53 6 41N44 77w39 5:10:36
Burson Plan 30 6 39N59 80w03 5:20:12
Bursonville 9 12 40N36 75w12 5:00:48
Burtville 53 6 41N49 78w17 5:13:08
Bush Addition 14 70 40N53 77w45 5:11:00
Bushkill 52 3 41N06 75w00 5:00:00
Bushkill Center 46 8 40N45 75w18 5:01:12
Bush Patch 35 18 41N22 75w44 5:02:56
Bustleton 51 9 40N05 75w02 5:00:08
Bute 26 80 39N57 79w42 5:18:48
Butler 10 3 40N52 79w54 5:19:36
Butler Junction 10 2 40N40 79w42 5:18:48
Buttermilk Falls 65 110 40N15 79w14 5:16:56
Buttonwood 40 20 41N15 75w53 5:03:32
Buttonwood 41 7 41N23 77w03 5:08:12
Buttonwood Glen 9 8 40N21 75w13 5:00:52
Buttonwood Manor 9 8 40N21 75w13 5:00:52
Butztown 48 13 40N39 75w21 5:01:24
Buyerstown 36 23 40N00 76w06 5:04:24
Byers 15 80 40N03 75w40 5:02:40
Byersdale 4 13 40N38 80w12 5:20:48
Byrnedale 24 7 41N17 78w30 5:14:00
Byrnesville 19 27 40N48 76w21 5:05:24
Byromtown 27 6 41N28 79w07 5:16:28
Bywood 23 9 39N58 75w18 5:01:12
Bywood Heights 23 9 39N58 75w18 5:01:12
Cable Hollow 62 6 41N56 79w08 5:16:32
Cabot 10 6 40N46 79w46 5:19:04
Cacoossing 6 101 40N18 76w00 5:04:00
Cadis 8 6 42N06 76w16 5:05:04
Cadogan 3 15 40N45 79w35 5:18:20
Caernarvon 6 27 40N10 75w53 5:03:32
Cains 36 23 39N59 76w02 5:04:08
Cairnbrook 56 63 40N07 78w49 5:15:16
Caldwell 18 76 41N08 77w28 5:09:52
Caledonia 24 7 41N17 78w30 5:14:00
Caledonia Park 28 1 39N55 77w34 5:10:16
California 9 13 40N29 75w25 5:01:40
California 47 73 41N06 76w52 5:07:28
California 63 1 40N04 79w54 5:19:36
Calkins 64 6 41N40 75w04 5:00:16
Callapoose 64 4 41N20 75w32 5:02:08
Callensburg 16 6 41N08 79w33 5:18:12
Callery 10 6 40N44 80w02 5:20:08
Callimont 56 79 39N49 79w02 5:16:08
Caln 15 46 40N00 75w47 5:03:08
Calumet 65 6 40N13 79w28 5:17:52
Calvert 41 7 41N23 77w03 5:08:12
Calvert Hills 7 33 40N31 78w25 5:13:40
Calvin 31 6 40N20 78w02 5:12:08
Camargo 36 27 39N54 76w10 5:04:40
Cambra 40 6 41N12 76w18 5:05:12
Cambria 11 54 40N29 78w45 5:15:00
Cambridge 15 27 40N05 75w57 5:03:48
Cambridge Springs 20 3 41N48 80w04 5:20:16
Camden Hill 2 114 40N22 79w54 5:19:36
Cameron 12 106 41N31 78w14 5:12:56
Cammal 41 6 41N24 77w28 5:09:52
Camp Akiba 45 17 40N56 75w19 5:01:16
Campbelltown 38 31 40N17 76w35 5:06:20
Campbelltown 42 75 41N40 78w49 5:15:16
Camp Curtin 22 12 40N17 76w53 5:07:32
Camp Grove 49 51 40N43 76w51 5:07:24
Camp Hill 2 114 40N25 80w05 5:20:20
Camp Hill 21 12 40N14 76w56 5:07:44
Camp Jo-Ann 65 14 40N31 79w41 5:18:44
Camp Mystic 25 3 41N48 80w03 5:20:12
Camp Perry 43 6 41N24 80w11 5:20:44
Campton 2 14 40N37 79w44 5:18:56
Camptown 8 6 41N44 76w14 5:04:56
Canaan 64 6 41N34 75w24 5:01:36
Canadensis 45 84 41N12 75w15 5:01:00

PENNSYLVANIA

Canadohta Lake 20 58 41N54 79w51 5:19:24
Canal 61 6 41N29 79w57 5:19:48
Canan Station 7 33 40N31 78w25 5:13:40
Candlebrook 46 90 40N05 75w22 5:01:28
Candor 63 51 40N24 80w19 5:21:16
Cannelton 4 8 40N49 80w25 5:21:40
Canoe 32 51 40N53 78w57 5:15:48
Canoe Camp 59 59 41N50 77w01 5:08:04
Canoe Creek 7 33 40N25 78w24 5:13:36
Canoe Ridge 32 51 40N53 78w56 5:15:44
Canonsburg 63 2 40N16 80w11 5:20:44
Canton 8 103 41N39 76w51 5:07:24
Caprivi 21 16 40N12 77w11 5:08:44
Carbon 13 8 40N48 75w36 5:02:24
Carbon 31 6 40N13 78w10 5:12:40
Carbon 65 99 40N18 79w34 5:18:16
Carbon Center 10 3 40N53 79w53 5:19:32
Carbondale 35 1 41N35 75w30 5:02:00
Cardale 26 51 39N57 79w52 5:19:28
Cardington 23 9 39N58 75w18 5:01:12
Carlisle 21 16 40N12 77w12 5:08:48
Carlisle Barracks 21 2 40N13 77w10 5:08:40
Carlisle Springs 21 16 40N12 77w11 5:08:44
Carlton 43 59 41N29 80w01 5:20:04
Carmichaels 30 51 39N54 79w59 5:19:56
Carnegie 2 114 40N24 80w05 5:20:20
Carnot 2 13 40N31 80w13 5:20:52
Carnwath 17 6 40N53 78w32 5:14:08
Carpenter Corner 43 6 41N20 80w06 5:20:24
Carpenter Town 35 44 41N32 75w44 5:02:56
Carpentertown 65 111 40N09 79w33 5:18:12
Carrier 33 59 41N08 79w11 5:16:44
Carroll 18 7 41N02 77w18 5:09:12
Carroll Park 19 4 41N00 76w25 5:05:40
Carroll Park 23 9 39N59 75w16 5:01:04
Carrolltown 11 63 40N36 78w43 5:14:52
Carroll Valley 1 1 39N47 77w22 5:09:28
Carson 2 114 40N25 79w59 5:19:56
Carsontown 41 6 41N19 77w22 5:09:28
Carsonville 22 24 40N28 76w56 5:07:44
Carter Camp 53 6 41N44 77w39 5:10:36
Cartwright 24 5 41N16 78w44 5:14:56
Carver Court 15 9 39N59 75w50 5:03:20
Carversville 9 8 40N23 75w04 5:00:16
Carverton 40 20 41N19 75w51 5:03:24
Casanova 14 4 40N57 78w10 5:12:40
Cascade 41 7 41N27 76w54 5:07:36
Casey Tract 9 1 40N13 75w01 5:00:04
Cashtown 1 1 39N53 77w22 5:09:28
Cashtown 28 42 39N56 77w40 5:10:40
Cassandra 11 55 40N24 78w38 5:14:32
Casselman 56 4 39N53 79w13 5:16:52
Cassville 31 6 40N18 78w02 5:12:08
Castanea 18 76 41N07 77w25 5:09:40
Caste Village 2 114 40N22 79w58 5:19:52
Castle Garden 12 7 41N21 78w08 5:12:32
Castle Rock 23 90 40N00 75w23 5:01:32
Castle Shannon 2 114 40N21 80w02 5:20:08
Castle Valley 9 2 40N20 75w18 5:01:12
Castlewood 37 112 41N00 80w21 5:21:24
Castor 51 9 40N02 75w04 5:00:16
Cataract 17 6 41N10 78w04 5:12:16
Catasauqua 39 13 40N39 75w28 5:01:52
Catawissa 19 4 40N57 76w28 5:05:52
Catharine 7 3 40N31 78w12 5:12:48
Cavettsville 65 25 40N22 79w44 5:18:56
Ceasetown 40 1 41N12 76w04 5:04:16
Cecil 63 114 40N20 80w11 5:20:44
Cedarbrook 46 9 40N05 75w09 5:00:36
Cedarbrook Hills 46 9 40N05 75w09 5:00:36
Cedar Brook-Melrose Park 46 9 40N05 75w07 5:00:28
Cedar Cliff Manor 21 12 40N14 76w57 5:07:48
Cedar Heights 46 8 40N08 75w17 5:01:08
Cedar Hollow 15 8 40N02 75w31 5:02:04
Cedarhurst 2 114 40N23 80w04 5:20:16
Cedar Knoll 15 9 39N59 75w50 5:03:20
Cedar Lane 36 27 40N07 76w02 5:04:08
Cedar Ledge 8 103 41N39 76w51 5:07:24
Cedar Ridge 1 1 39N52 77w03 5:08:12
Cedar Run 41 6 41N31 77w27 5:09:48
Cedars 46 8 40N13 75w22 5:01:28
Cedar Springs 18 76 41N06 77w29 5:09:56
Cedarville 15 8 40N15 75w39 5:02:36
Celia 4 121 40N49 80w12 5:20:48
Cementon 39 13 40N39 75w30 5:02:00
Centennial 1 1 39N48 76w59 5:07:56
Centennial Hills 9 1 40N12 75w05 5:00:20
Center 2 14 40N29 79w44 5:18:56
Center 34 7 40N35 77w24 5:09:36
Center 50 6 40N22 77w21 5:09:24
Center Bridge 9 8 40N22 74w56 4:59:44
Center Hill 3 15 40N49 79w32 5:18:08
Center Mills 1 1 39N59 77w15 5:09:00
Center Moreland 66 59 41N32 75w57 5:03:48
Centerport 6 80 40N29 76w00 5:04:00
Center Road 20 7 41N40 80w27 5:21:48
Center Square 46 8 40N10 75w17 5:01:08
Center Square Greens 46 90 40N08 75w21 5:01:24
Centertown 43 6 41N10 80w05 5:20:20
Center Union 31 81 40N30 78w01 5:12:04
Center Valley 3 15 40N46 79w32 5:18:08
Center Valley 39 13 40N32 75w24 5:01:36
Centerville 5 70 39N58 78w31 5:14:04

Centerville 36 8 40N02 76w17 5:05:08
Centerville 50 1 40N33 77w09 5:08:36
Centerville 63 51 40N03 79w59 5:19:56
Centerville 65 111 40N13 79w36 5:18:24
Centerville 65 6 40N09 79w44 5:18:56
Centerville 67 3 39N48 76w44 5:06:56
Central 2 10 40N21 79w51 5:19:24
Central 19 6 41N12 76w23 5:05:32
Central 63 3 40N11 80w16 5:21:04
Central 65 111 40N10 79w35 5:18:20
Central City 14 70 40N57 77w47 5:11:08
Central City 56 63 40N07 78w49 5:15:16
Central Highlands 2 8 40N17 79w50 5:19:20
Centralia 19 27 40N48 76w21 5:05:24
Central Manor 36 26 40N00 76w28 5:05:52
Central Park 2 8 40N17 79w50 5:19:20
Central Wharf 2 114 40N24 79w54 5:19:36
Centre Hall 14 64 40N51 77w41 5:10:44
Centre Hill 14 64 40N51 77w34 5:10:16
Century 26 51 40N02 79w55 5:19:40
Ceres 42 7 41N58 78w16 5:13:04
Cessna 5 70 39N58 78w31 5:14:04
Cetronia 39 13 40N37 75w31 5:02:04
Ceylon 30 51 39N54 79w58 5:19:52
Chadds Ford 23 13 39N52 75w36 5:02:24
Chadville 26 80 39N54 79w44 5:18:56
Chain 54 1 40N41 76w00 5:04:00
Chain Bridge 9 1 40N12 75w05 5:00:20
Chaintown 65 111 40N06 79w35 5:18:20
Chalfant 2 114 40N25 79w50 5:19:20
Chalfont 9 2 40N20 75w18 5:01:12
Chalkhill 26 6 39N51 79w37 5:18:28
Challenge 24 5 41N16 78w44 5:14:56
Chalybeate 5 70 39N58 78w31 5:14:04
Chambersburg 28 42 39N56 77w40 5:10:40
Chambers Hill 22 12 40N16 76w49 5:07:16
Chambers Mill 63 3 40N11 80w16 5:21:04
Chambersville 32 72 40N42 79w10 5:16:40
Champion 26 6 40N02 79w18 5:17:12
Chanceford 67 1 39N53 76w29 5:05:56
Chandler Plan 3 15 40N46 79w32 5:18:08
Chandlers Valley 62 3 41N56 79w18 5:17:12
Chaneysville 5 6 39N42 78w34 5:14:16
Chapel 6 2 40N26 75w32 5:02:08
Chapel Downs 2 14 40N33 79w49 5:19:16
Chapel Hill 46 1 40N09 75w03 5:00:12
Chapman 48 13 40N45 75w24 5:01:36
Chapman 55 51 40N42 76w52 5:07:28
Chapman Lake 35 1 41N32 75w32 5:02:08
Chapmanville 6 41N36 79w50 5:19:20
Charleroi 63 1 40N08 79w54 5:19:36
Charleston 43 117 41N15 80w30 5:22:00
Charleston 59 6 41N45 77w14 5:08:56
Charlestown 15 8 40N06 75w33 5:02:12
Charlestown 28 51 39N50 77w55 5:11:40
Charlesville 5 70 39N58 78w31 5:14:04
Charlottsville 7 11 40N40 78w13 5:12:52
Charlton 18 76 41N08 77w28 5:09:52
Charlton 22 12 40N19 76w48 5:07:12
Charmian 28 1 39N43 77w28 5:09:52
Charnita 1 1 39N47 77w22 5:09:28
Charteroak 31 81 40N35 78w03 5:12:12
Charter Oaks 25 107 42N05 80w04 5:20:16
Charterwood 2 114 40N33 80w01 5:20:04
Chartiers 63 2 40N15 80w14 5:20:56
Chartiers Terrace 2 114 40N25 80w05 5:20:20
Chase 40 20 41N20 75w56 5:03:44
Chatham 15 8 39N51 75w49 5:03:16
Chatham Park 23 9 40N00 75w18 5:01:12
Chatham Run 18 76 41N08 77w28 5:09:52
Chatham Village 23 9 40N00 75w18 5:01:12
Chatwood 15 13 39N58 75w35 5:02:20
Chauncey 40 20 41N15 75w57 5:03:48
Chelsea 23 90 39N50 75w25 5:01:40
Cheltenham 46 9 40N04 75w06 5:00:24
Cherokee Ranch 6 101 40N24 75w55 5:03:40
Cherry City 2 114 40N31 79w57 5:19:48
Cherry Corner 17 122 40N51 78w43 5:14:52
Cherrydale 46 90 40N05 75w16 5:01:04
Cherry Flats 59 59 41N45 77w05 5:08:20
Cherry Grove 31 6 40N12 77w59 5:11:56
Cherry Grove 62 6 41N41 79w09 5:16:36
Cherry Hill 25 7 41N54 80w22 5:21:28
Cherryhill 32 6 40N39 79w00 5:16:00
Cherry Hill 46 8 40N45 75w18 5:01:12
Cherry Lane 3 4 40N35 79w34 5:18:16
Cherry Ridge 64 59 41N32 75w17 5:01:08
Cherry Run 60 6 40N52 77w18 5:09:12
Cherrytown 31 3 40N23 78w10 5:12:40
Cherry Tree 32 63 40N44 78w48 5:15:12
Cherry Tree 61 74 41N38 79w40 5:18:40
Cherry Valley 10 6 40N21 80w21 5:21:24
Cherryville 48 8 40N45 75w33 5:02:12
Cherryville 54 27 40N34 76w24 5:05:36
Chesney Downs 23 9 39N56 75w20 5:01:20
Chester 23 90 39N51 75w22 5:01:28
Chesterfield 17 54 40N45 78w32 5:14:08
Chester Heights 23 4 39N54 75w28 5:01:52
Chester Hill 17 113 40N53 78w14 5:12:56
Chester Plaza 23 90 39N52 75w23 5:01:32
Chester Springs 15 8 40N06 75w37 5:02:28
Chester Township 23 90 39N51 75w22 5:01:28
Chester Valley Knoll 15 8 40N02 75w31 5:02:04
Chesterville 15 8 39N47 75w46 5:03:04
Chestnut Crossroads 21 82 40N03 77w32 5:10:08
Chestnut Grove 17 7 40N58 78w36 5:14:24
Chestnut Hill 25 107 42N05 80w04 5:20:16
Chestnut Hill 36 26 40N02 76w31 5:06:04
Chestnuthill 45 1 40N57 75w24 5:01:36
Chestnut Hill 46 12 40N41 75w14 5:00:56
Chestnut Hill 51 9 40N04 75w12 5:00:48
Chestnut Level 36 27 39N54 76w10 5:04:40
Chestnut Ridge 26 51 39N59 79w49 5:19:16
Chestnut Ridge 36 8 40N02 76w20 5:05:20
Chestnut View 36 8 40N04 76w19 5:05:16
Chest Springs 11 63 40N35 78w37 5:14:28
Cheswick 2 119 40N32 79w48 5:19:12
Chevy Chase Heights 32 72 40N38 79w09 5:16:36
Chewton 37 121 40N53 80w20 5:21:20
Cheyney 23 4 39N56 75w32 5:02:08
Chickasaw 3 64 40N55 79w28 5:17:52
Chickory 11 74 40N21 78w54 5:15:36
Chicora 10 6 40N57 79w45 5:19:00
Childs 35 1 41N34 75w32 5:02:08
Chillisquaque 49 70 40N58 76w51 5:07:24
China Hall 9 9 40N06 74w56 4:59:44
Chinchilla 35 45 41N30 75w43 5:02:52
Chippewa 4 8 40N46 80w23 5:21:32
Choconut 58 6 41N58 76w01 5:04:04
Christiana 36 23 39N58 76w00 5:04:00
Christian Springs 46 8 40N45 75w18 5:01:12
Christmans 13 80 40N52 75w44 5:02:56
Christy Manor 3 15 40N44 79w32 5:18:08
Chrome 15 3 39N45 76w01 5:04:04
Chrystal 53 6 41N55 78w01 5:12:04
Chulasky 49 6 40N58 76w36 5:06:24
Church Hill 26 51 39N53 79w52 5:19:28
Church Hill 27 6 41N35 79w24 5:17:36
Church Hill 28 51 39N50 77w55 5:11:40
Church Hill Manor 44 73 40N40 77w36 5:10:24
Churchill 2 114 40N26 79w48 5:19:12
Churchill Valley 2 114 40N28 79w50 5:19:20
Churchtown 36 27 40N08 75w58 5:03:52
Churchville 5 7 40N16 78w31 5:14:04
Churchville 9 56 40N11 75w01 5:00:04
Churchville 46 8 40N45 75w16 5:01:04
Cinnamon Hills 46 90 40N05 75w22 5:01:28
Circle Ville 14 9 40N48 77w52 5:11:28
Circleville 65 25 40N20 79w43 5:18:52
Cisna Run 50 6 40N22 77w21 5:09:24
Cito 29 66 39N56 78w00 5:12:00
Clairton 2 8 40N18 79w53 5:19:32
Clairton Junction 2 114 40N22 79w54 5:19:36
Clamtown 54 27 40N48 75w58 5:03:52
Clappertown 7 3 40N28 78w12 5:12:48
Clapp Farm 61 9 41N25 79w42 5:18:48
Clappville 20 7 41N44 79w46 5:19:04
Clara 53 6 41N53 78w07 5:12:28
Clarence 14 7 41N03 77w57 5:11:48
Clarendon 62 3 41N47 79w06 5:16:24
Claridge 65 3 40N22 79w37 5:18:28
Clarington 27 6 41N20 79w07 5:16:28
Clarion 16 37 41N13 79w23 5:17:32
Clark 43 6 41N17 80w25 5:21:40
Clark Manor 4 13 40N37 80w16 5:21:04
Clarksburg 32 6 40N32 79w23 5:17:32
Clarks Green 35 45 41N30 75w43 5:02:52
Clarks Mills 43 6 41N24 80w11 5:20:44
Clarks Summit 35 45 41N30 75w42 5:02:48
Clarkstown 41 83 41N12 76w47 5:07:08
Clarksville 30 6 39N59 80w03 5:20:12
Claussville 39 13 40N38 75w35 5:02:20
Clay 36 30 40N11 76w11 5:04:44
Clay Hill 28 42 39N56 77w40 5:10:40
Claylick 28 51 39N50 77w55 5:11:40
Claypoole Heights 32 72 40N38 79w09 5:16:36
Claysburg 7 3 40N18 78w27 5:13:48
Claysville 63 6 40N07 80w25 5:21:40
Clayton 6 2 40N24 75w35 5:02:20
Claytonia 10 6 41N02 80w03 5:20:12
Clearbrook 23 9 39N56 75w16 5:01:04
Clearbrook Village 46 1 40N11 75w06 5:00:24
Clearfield 17 1 41N02 78w27 5:13:48
Clearfield 46 8 40N45 75w18 5:01:12
Clear Ridge 29 6 40N03 78w02 5:12:08
Clear Run 17 56 41N07 78w46 5:15:04
Clear Spring 67 1 40N07 77w02 5:08:08
Clearview 36 8 40N04 76w19 5:05:16
Clearview Estates 4 13 40N37 80w16 5:21:04
Clearville 5 6 39N55 78w23 5:13:32
Cleona 38 8 40N21 76w29 5:05:56
Clermont 42 59 41N44 78w39 5:14:36
Cleveland 19 27 40N52 76w27 5:05:48
Cleversburg 21 82 40N03 77w32 5:10:08
Cliff Mine 114 40N27 80w12 5:20:48
Clifford 58 59 41N41 75w34 5:02:16
Clifton 22 80 40N12 76w43 5:06:52
Clifton 35 4 41N15 75w33 5:02:12
Clifton Heights 23 9 39N56 75w18 5:01:12
Climax 3 6 40N59 79w23 5:17:32
Climax 16 6 40N59 79w23 5:17:32
Climax 32 29 40N23 79w04 5:16:16
Clinton 2 6 40N29 80w18 5:21:12
Clinton 2 6 40N29 80w18 5:21:12
Clinton 3 2 40N41 79w41 5:18:44
Clintondale 18 76 41N06 77w29 5:09:56
Clintonville 61 6 41N12 79w53 5:19:32
Cloe 33 51 40N56 78w58 5:15:52

PENNSYLVANIA

Clonmell 15 1 39N49 75w50 5:03:20
Clover 33 34 41N09 79w10 5:16:40
Cloverdale Park 46 8 40N16 75w15 5:01:00
Clover Hill 63 51 40N02 79w58 5:19:52
Clover Park 6 101 40N19 75w57 5:03:48
Clover Run 17 122 40N51 78w43 5:14:52
Clune 32 6 40N34 79w18 5:17:12
Cly 67 80 40N07 76w43 5:06:52
Clyde 32 29 40N23 79w04 5:16:16
Clyde 48 13 40N45 75w24 5:01:36
Clymer 32 52 40N40 79w01 5:16:04
Coal 49 27 40N48 76w33 5:06:12
Coal Brook 26 104 40N01 79w35 5:18:20
Coal Cabin Beach 67 1 39N44 76w19 5:05:16
Coal Castle 54 49 40N41 76w12 5:04:48
Coal Center 63 1 40N04 79w54 5:19:36
Coal City 61 6 41N17 79w44 5:18:56
Coaldale 22 1 40N34 76w42 5:06:48
Coaldale 54 80 40N49 75w55 5:03:40
Coal Glen 33 5 41N13 78w50 5:15:20
Coal Hill 61 9 41N25 79w42 5:18:48
Coal Hollow 24 36 41N21 78w37 5:14:28
Coalmont 31 51 40N13 78w12 5:12:48
Coalport 13 80 40N52 75w44 5:02:56
Coalport 17 54 40N45 78w32 5:14:08
Coal Run 17 4 40N51 78w16 5:13:04
Coal Run 49 27 40N47 76w33 5:06:12
Coaltown 10 6 41N02 80w03 5:20:12
Coaltown 37 112 41N00 80w21 5:21:24
Coal Valley 2 6 39N56 80w03 5:20:12
Coatesville 15 9 39N59 75w50 5:03:20
Cobblerville 21 1 40N10 77w24 5:09:36
Cobbs Corners 62 56 41N50 79w41 5:18:44
Cobham 62 6 41N41 79w24 5:17:36
Coburn 7 33 40N31 78w25 5:13:40
Coburn 14 52 40N52 77w28 5:09:52
Cocalico 36 28 40N14 76w08 5:04:32
Cochran Acres 4 13 40N37 80w16 5:21:04
Cochrans Mill 2 8 40N18 79w54 5:19:36
Cochrans Mills 3 15 40N46 79w32 5:18:08
Cochranton 20 59 41N31 80w03 5:20:12
Cochranville 15 8 39N54 75w55 5:03:40
Cocolamus 34 6 40N39 77w13 5:08:52
Codorus 67 3 39N47 76w47 5:07:08
Coffeetown 38 31 40N19 76w36 5:06:24
Coffeetown 39 13 40N36 75w28 5:01:52
Coffeetown 46 12 40N41 75w14 5:00:56
Cogan House 41 6 41N25 77w10 5:08:40
Cogan Station 41 7 41N19 77w05 5:08:20
Cokeburg 63 51 40N06 80w04 5:20:16
Cokeburg Junction 63 51 40N07 80w01 5:20:04
Cold Point 46 90 40N07 75w16 5:01:04
Cold Spring 15 8 40N15 75w39 5:02:36
Cold Spring 28 1 39N55 77w34 5:10:16
Cold Spring 38 27 40N31 76w34 5:06:16
Cold Spring 67 3 39N51 76w46 5:07:04
Colebrook 18 7 41N13 77w32 5:10:08
Colebrook 38 7 40N14 76w31 5:06:04
Colebrookdale 6 2 40N21 75w39 5:02:36
Colegrove 42 93 41N49 78w27 5:13:48
Coleman 56 6 40N03 79w00 5:16:00
Colemanville 36 1 39N53 76w22 5:05:28
Colerain 31 6 40N37 78w08 5:12:32
Colerain Forge 31 6 40N37 78w08 5:12:32
Coles 54 3 40N49 76w08 5:04:32
Colesburg 53 66 41N46 78w01 5:12:04
Coles Creek 19 6 41N12 76w23 5:05:32
Colesville 39 13 40N36 75w23 5:01:32
Coleville 14 70 40N53 77w45 5:11:00
Coleville 42 93 41N49 78w27 5:13:48
Colfax 31 81 40N30 78w01 5:12:04
College 14 9 40N48 77w49 5:11:16
College 46 12 40N41 75w14 5:00:56
College Heights 6 101 40N23 75w56 5:03:44
College Hill 4 8 40N46 80w20 5:21:20
College Misericordia 40 20 41N20 75w56 5:03:44
College Park 46 9 40N06 75w15 5:01:00
College Park 60 70 40N58 76w54 5:07:36
Collegeville 46 8 40N11 75w28 5:01:52
Colley 57 6 41N25 76w18 5:05:12
Collier 2 114 40N23 80w07 5:20:28
Collier 26 80 39N54 79w44 5:18:56
Collingdale 23 9 39N55 75w17 5:01:08
Collins 36 27 39N54 76w10 5:04:40
Collinsburg 65 61 40N14 79w46 5:19:04
Collinsville 67 1 39N50 76w24 5:05:36
Collomsville 41 82 41N14 77w01 5:08:04
Colmar 46 8 40N16 75w15 5:01:00
Colona 4 13 40N40 80w17 5:21:08
Colonial Crest 22 12 40N16 76w49 5:07:16
Colonial Hills 6 101 40N18 76w00 5:04:00
Colonial Hills 44 73 40N36 77w34 5:10:16
Colonial Manor 36 8 40N02 76w20 5:05:20
Colonial Park 22 12 40N18 76w50 5:07:20
Colonial Park 23 9 39N56 75w20 5:01:20
Colonial Park 36 28 40N05 76w11 5:04:44
Colonial Village 15 90 40N02 75w22 5:01:28
Columbia 36 26 40N02 76w30 5:06:00
Columbia Cross Roads 8 7 41N50 76w48 5:07:12
Columbus 62 3 41N57 79w35 5:18:20
Colver 11 54 40N33 78w47 5:15:08
Colwyn 23 9 39N55 75w15 5:01:00
Colza 62 3 41N55 79w39 5:18:36
Comly 47 6 41N06 76w46 5:07:04
Commerce 51 9 39N58 75w09 5:00:36
Commodore 32 6 40N43 78w57 5:15:48

PENNSYLVANIA

Compass 15 23 39N59 76W02 5:04:08
Concord 28 1 40N15 77W42 5:10:48
Concordville 23 4 39N53 75W31 5:02:04
Conemaugh 11 74 40N21 78W54 5:15:36
Conestoga 36 8 39N57 76W21 5:05:24
Conestoga Farms 23 1 39N52 75W35 5:02:20
Conestoga Woods 36 8 40N02 76W18 5:05:12
Coneville 53 29 41N58 78W11 5:12:44
Conewago Heights 67 1 40N04 76W43 5:06:52
Conewango 62 120 41N53 79W11 5:16:44
Confluence 56 53 39N49 79W21 5:17:24
Conger 63 3 40N10 80W16 5:21:04
Congo 46 2 40N23 75W37 5:02:28
Congruity 65 6 40N24 79W30 5:18:00
Conifer 33 6 41N08 79W11 5:16:44
Connaughton 46 90 40N05 75W17 5:01:08
Conneaut Lake 20 6 41N36 80W18 5:21:12
Conneaut Lake Park 20 6 41N36 80W19 5:21:16
Conneautville 20 6 41N46 80W22 5:21:28
Connellsville 26 104 40N01 79W35 5:18:20
Connersville 49 27 40N48 76W25 5:05:40
Connerton 54 27 40N47 76W17 5:05:08
Connoquenessing 10 6 40N49 80W01 5:20:04
Conoy 36 2 40N07 76W40 5:06:40
Conrad 53 6 41N38 78W06 5:12:24
Conshohocken 46 90 40N04 75W19 5:01:16
Continental 51 9 39N57 75W09 5:00:36
Conway 4 13 40N40 80W14 5:20:56
Conyngham 40 42 40N59 76W04 5:04:16
Cook 65 6 40N11 79W19 5:17:16
Cooke 21 1 40N02 77W19 5:09:16
Cookport 32 6 40N43 78W57 5:15:48
Cooksburg 27 6 41N20 79W12 5:16:48
Cooks Mills 5 51 39N50 78W43 5:14:52
Cooks Run 18 7 41N18 77W51 5:11:24
Coolbaugh 45 84 41N12 75W25 5:01:40
Coolbaughs 45 1 41N06 75W00 5:00:00
Coolspring 26 80 39N52 79W42 5:18:48
Coolspring 33 6 41N03 79W05 5:16:20
Coolspring 43 66 41N16 80W13 5:20:52
Cool Valley 63 2 40N16 80W11 5:20:44
Coon Corners 20 77 41N40 80W07 5:20:28
Coon Hunter 55 6 40N47 77W03 5:08:12
Coontown 42 75 41N40 78W49 5:15:16
Coopersburg 39 13 40N31 75W23 5:01:32
Cooper Settlement 17 6 41N01 78W07 5:12:28
Cooperstown 10 6 40N43 79W56 5:19:44
Cooperstown 61 6 41N30 79W52 5:19:28
Cooperstown 65 3 40N19 79W23 5:17:32
Coopersville 36 23 39N58 76W00 5:04:00
Copella 48 13 40N45 75W24 5:01:36
Copes Bridge 15 13 39N57 75W36 5:02:24
Copesville 15 13 39N57 75W36 5:02:24
Coplay 39 13 40N40 75W30 5:02:00
Coral 32 71 40N30 79W11 5:16:44
Coraopolis 2 114 40N31 80W10 5:20:40
Coraopolis Heights 2 114 40N30 80W10 5:20:40
Corinne 15 13 39N57 75W36 5:02:24
Cork Lane 40 1 41N19 75W47 5:03:08
Corliss 2 114 40N27 80W04 5:20:16
Corner Ketch 15 46 40N00 75W42 5:02:48
Corner Store 15 8 40N08 75W31 5:02:04
Corning 39 13 40N29 75W30 5:02:00
Cornish 26 7 39N44 79W52 5:19:28
Cornog 15 80 40N02 75W41 5:02:44
Cornplanter 61 9 41N28 79W40 5:18:40
Cornpropst 31 81 40N30 78W01 5:12:04
Cornwall 38 8 40N17 76W25 5:05:40
Cornwells Heights 8 9 40N05 74W57 4:59:48
Corpers Homes 46 90 40N05 75W16 5:01:04
Corrine 15 13 39N57 75W36 5:02:24
Corry 25 3 41N55 79W39 5:18:36
Corsica 33 6 41N10 79W13 5:16:52
Cortez 33 51 40N56 78W58 5:15:52
Cortez 35 6 41N27 75W23 5:01:32
Corwins Corners 42 102 41N57 78W39 5:14:36
Corydon 42 6 41N56 78W51 5:15:24
Coryville 42 93 41N53 78W24 5:13:36
Costello 53 6 41N38 78W06 5:12:24
Cosytown 28 1 39N48 77W44 5:10:56
Cottage 31 81 40N35 78W03 5:12:12
Cottage Grove 37 112 41N00 80W20 5:21:20
Cottage Hill 16 6 41N00 79W20 5:17:20
Cottageville 9 8 40N21 75W13 5:00:52
Cotton Town 7 3 40N18 78W27 5:13:48
Couchtown 50 6 40N22 77W21 5:09:24
Coudersport 53 66 41N46 78W01 5:12:04
Coulters 2 8 40N18 79W48 5:19:12
Council Crest 40 42 40N58 76W00 5:04:00
Country Acres 46 90 40N05 75W16 5:01:04
Country Club Estates 23 9 39N55 75W19 5:01:16
Country Club Estates 36 8 40N04 76W19 5:05:16
Country Club Estates 46 90 40N05 75W16 5:01:04
Country Club Heights 36 8 40N04 76W19 5:05:16
Country Gardens 36 28 40N05 76W11 5:04:44
Country Hills 65 25 40N20 79W43 5:18:52
Coupon 11 33 40N32 78W31 5:14:04
Courtdale 40 20 41N17 75W55 5:03:40
Courtney 63 1 40N13 79W58 5:19:52
Cove 50 51 40N24 77W02 5:08:08
Cove Gap 28 51 39N50 77W55 5:11:40
Coventryville 15 8 40N15 75W39 5:02:36
Coverdale 2 114 40N20 80W02 5:20:08
Coverdale 7 3 40N28 78W12 5:12:48
Coverdale 37 8 40N51 80W23 5:21:32
Coveville 45 84 41N12 75W15 5:01:00
Coveytown 57 60 41N31 76W24 5:05:36
Covington 59 59 41N45 77W05 5:08:20
Covode 32 51 40N56 78W58 5:15:52
Cowan 60 6 40N55 77W03 5:08:12
Cowanesque 59 6 41N56 77W30 5:10:00
Cowansburg 65 4 40N15 79W45 5:19:00
Cowanshannock 3 6 40N48 79W18 5:17:12
Cowans Village 28 51 39N55 77W54 5:11:36
Cowansville 3 6 40N53 79W36 5:18:24
Cowden 63 2 40N19 80W13 5:20:52
Coxeville 13 42 40N56 75W55 5:03:40
Coxton 40 1 41N21 75W46 5:03:04
Coy 32 71 40N33 79W10 5:16:40
Coy Junction 32 71 40N33 79W10 5:16:40
Coyleville 10 6 40N52 79W44 5:18:56
Crabapple 30 6 39N55 80W26 5:21:44
Crabtree 65 3 40N22 79W28 5:17:52
Cracker Jack 63 1 40N11 79W54 5:19:36
Crackersport 39 13 40N37 75W31 5:02:04
Crafton 2 114 40N26 80W04 5:20:16
Craig 35 44 41N32 75W44 5:02:56
Craigheads 21 16 40N12 77W11 5:08:44
Craigs 54 3 40N49 76W08 5:04:32
Craigs Meadow 45 23 41N00 75W11 5:00:44
Craigsville 3 6 40N51 79W39 5:18:36
Craley 67 2 39N57 76W31 5:06:04
Cramer 32 7 40N25 79W01 5:16:04
Cranberry 40 42 40N58 76W00 5:04:00
Cranberry 61 1 41N21 79W43 5:18:52
Cranberry Ridge 40 42 40N58 76W00 5:04:00
Cranesville 25 7 41N54 80W21 5:21:24
Crates 16 6 41N02 79W15 5:17:00
Crawford 18 7 41N06 77W16 5:09:04
Crawfordtown 33 51 40N59 78W58 5:15:52
Creamery 46 8 40N13 75W25 5:01:40
Creekside 32 72 40N41 79W12 5:16:48
Creighton 2 14 40N35 79W47 5:19:08
Crenshaw 33 5 41N15 78W48 5:15:12
Crescent 2 13 40N33 80W14 5:20:56
Crescentdale 37 121 40N53 80W20 5:21:20
Crescent Heights 63 51 40N03 79W57 5:19:48
Crescent Hills 2 114 40N28 79W50 5:19:20
Crescent Lake 45 84 41N06 75W15 5:01:00
Cresco 45 84 41N09 75W17 5:01:08
Cresmont 54 27 40N47 76W14 5:04:56
Cress 28 100 39N45 77W34 5:10:16
Cresson 11 55 40N28 78W36 5:14:24
Cressona 54 27 40N38 76W12 5:04:48
Crestmont 18 76 41N08 77W28 5:09:52
Crestmont 46 2 40N09 75W07 5:00:28
Crestmont Village 4 13 40N37 80W16 5:21:04
Crestview 46 1 40N11 75W06 5:00:24
Crestview 46 12 40N41 75W14 5:00:56
Creswell 36 8 39N57 76W21 5:05:24
Criders Corners 10 6 40N41 80W06 5:20:24
Croft 17 6 41N05 78W20 5:13:20
Cromby 15 8 40N08 75W31 5:02:04
Cromwell 31 6 40N14 77W55 5:11:40
Crooked Creek 31 81 40N30 78W01 5:12:04
Crooked Creek 59 6 41N51 77W17 5:09:08
Crookham 63 114 40N15 80W00 5:20:00
Crosby 42 93 41N45 78W24 5:13:36
Cross Creek 63 6 40N18 80W25 5:21:40
Cross Fork 53 6 41N29 77W49 5:11:16
Crossgrove 55 1 40N42 77W19 5:09:16
Crossingville 20 6 41N53 80W08 5:20:32
Cross Keys 1 1 39N52 77W03 5:08:12
Cross Keys 7 33 40N28 78W25 5:13:40
Cross Keys 9 8 40N21 75W13 5:00:52
Cross Keys 34 6 40N22 77W36 5:10:24
Crossroads 48 13 40N45 75W24 5:01:36
Cross Roads 67 1 39N49 76W34 5:06:16
Crosswicks 46 9 40N06 75W09 5:00:36
Crown 16 6 41N23 79W16 5:17:04
Croydon 9 9 40N06 74W54 4:59:36
Croyle 11 63 40N22 78W45 5:15:00
Crozar Terrace 23 90 39N51 75W22 5:01:28
Crozer Park Gardens 23 90 39N51 75W22 5:01:28
Crucible 30 6 39N57 79W58 5:19:52
Crum Creek Manor 23 90 39N51 75W22 5:01:28
Crum Lynne 23 9 39N53 75W20 5:01:20
Crystal 53 6 41N55 78W01 5:12:04
Crystal Lake 58 59 41N39 75W28 5:01:52
Crystal Spring 29 6 39N57 78W14 5:12:56
Cuba Mills 34 7 40N35 77W24 5:09:36
Cuddy 2 114 40N21 80W09 5:20:36
Cuddy Hill 2 114 40N21 80W09 5:20:36
Culmerville 2 6 40N39 79W51 5:19:24
Culp 7 33 40N31 78W25 5:13:40
Culpepper Woods 46 90 40N05 75W16 5:01:04
Cumberland Park 21 12 40N14 76W57 5:07:48
Cumberland Valley 5 51 39N49 78W39 5:14:36
Cumberland Village 30 51 39N54 79W58 5:19:52
Cumbola 54 27 40N43 76W08 5:04:32
Cummings 41 6 41N20 77W20 5:09:20
Cummingstown 21 16 40N12 77W11 5:08:44
Cummingswood Park 65 6 40N08 79W26 5:17:44
Cumru 6 101 40N18 75W57 5:03:48
Cuneo 24 36 41N21 78W37 5:14:28
Cupola 15 27 40N06 75W55 5:03:40
Curley Hill 9 8 40N21 75W13 5:00:52
Curllsville 16 6 41N06 79W27 5:17:48
Curren Terrace 46 90 40N08 75W21 5:01:24
Curry Run 17 122 40N51 78W43 5:14:52
Curryville 7 51 40N17 78W20 5:13:20
Curtin 14 6 41N06 77W46 5:11:04
Curtis Hills 46 9 40N05 75W09 5:00:36
Curtis Park 14 113 40N54 78W13 5:12:52
Curtis Park 23 9 39N54 75W17 5:01:08
Curtisville 2 6 40N39 79W51 5:19:24
Curwensville 17 1 40N58 78W31 5:14:04
Cussewago 20 6 41N48 80W13 5:20:52
Custards 20 59 41N31 80W03 5:20:12
Custer City 42 102 41N54 78W39 5:14:36
Custis Woods 46 9 40N07 75W10 5:00:40
Cyclone 42 6 41N50 78W35 5:14:20
Cymbria Mine 11 92 40N40 78W47 5:15:08
Cynwyd Estates 46 9 40N01 75W15 5:01:00
Cynwyd Hills 46 9 40N01 75W15 5:01:00
Cypher 5 6 40N09 78W16 5:13:04
Daggett 59 6 41N59 76W56 5:07:44
Dagus 24 36 41N21 78W37 5:14:28
Daguscahonda 24 36 41N25 78W44 5:14:56
Dagus Mines 24 36 41N21 78W37 5:14:28
Dahoga 24 7 41N35 78W41 5:14:44
Daisytown 11 74 40N19 78W54 5:15:36
Daisytown 63 51 40N03 79W57 5:19:48
Dale 6 2 40N23 75W37 5:02:28
Dale 11 74 40N19 78W54 5:15:36
Dale Summit 14 9 40N48 77W52 5:11:28
Daleville 15 23 39N53 75W55 5:03:40
Daleville 35 4 41N20 75W32 5:02:08
Dalevue 14 9 40N48 77W52 5:11:28
Daley 56 63 40N07 78W49 5:15:16
Dallas 40 1 41N20 75W58 5:03:52
Dallas City 42 102 41N57 78W39 5:14:36
Dallastown 67 7 39N54 76W39 5:06:36
Dalmatia 49 51 40N39 76W54 5:07:36
Dalton 35 44 41N32 75W44 5:02:56
Damascus 64 6 41N42 75W07 5:00:28
Danboro 9 8 40N21 75W08 5:00:32
Danielsville 48 80 40N48 75W32 5:02:08
Dannersville 48 13 40N41 75W22 5:01:28
Danville 47 70 40N58 76W37 5:06:28
Darby 23 9 39N55 75W16 5:01:04
Dark Water 54 27 40N43 76W11 5:04:44
Darlington 4 64 40N49 80W26 5:21:44
Darlington 23 90 39N55 75W22 5:01:28
Darlington 65 110 40N15 79W14 5:16:56
Darlington Corners 15 13 39N57 75W36 5:02:24
Darragh 65 3 40N16 79W41 5:18:44
Dartmouth Hills 46 90 40N05 75W22 5:01:28
Dauberville 6 80 40N27 75W59 5:03:56
Daugherty 4 8 40N45 80W17 5:21:08
Dauphin 22 12 40N22 76W56 5:07:44
Davidsburg 67 1 40N00 76W58 5:07:52
Davidson 26 104 40N01 79W35 5:18:20
Davidson 57 6 41N20 76W28 5:05:52
Davidson Heights 4 13 40N35 80W16 5:21:04
Davidsville 56 74 40N14 78W56 5:15:44
Davis Grove 46 1 40N11 75W10 5:00:40
Davistown 30 6 39N46 80W02 5:20:08
Davisville 9 1 40N11 75W03 5:00:12
Dawson 26 104 40N03 79W39 5:18:36
Dawson Manor 46 1 40N11 75W06 5:00:24
Dawson Ridge 4 19 40N42 80W19 5:21:16
Day 16 37 41N12 79W20 5:17:20
Daylesford 15 90 40N03 75W26 5:01:44
Dayton 3 59 40N53 79W15 5:17:00
Dayton 22 1 40N35 76W37 5:06:28
Deal 56 79 39N49 79W02 5:16:08
Dean 11 33 40N36 78W29 5:13:56
Deanville 3 6 41N00 79W20 5:17:20
Dearth 26 80 39N54 79W44 5:18:56
Deckard 20 59 41N31 80W03 5:20:12
Deckers Point 32 6 40N46 79W03 5:16:12
Deemers Cross Roads 33 6 41N06 78W53 5:15:32
Deemston 63 51 40N02 80W02 5:20:08
Deep Run 9 8 40N25 75W23 5:01:32
Deep Valley 30 6 39N46 80W25 5:21:40
Deer Creek 43 6 41N27 80W08 5:20:32
Deercroft 46 90 40N05 75W16 5:01:04
Deer Lake 26 6 39N51 79W37 5:18:28
Deer Lake 54 80 40N37 76W03 5:04:12
Deer Park 9 8 40N22 74W56 4:59:44
Defiance 5 51 40N10 78W14 5:12:56
Degolia 42 102 41N57 78W39 5:14:36
Deiblers 49 6 40N58 76W36 5:06:24
Delabole 48 17 40N52 75W15 5:01:00
De Lancey 33 51 40N59 78W58 5:15:52
Delano 54 60 40N51 76W04 5:04:16
Delaware Grove 43 66 41N19 80W16 5:21:04
Delaware Run 49 73 41N06 76W52 5:07:28
Delaware Water Gap 45 23 41N00 75W09 5:00:36
Dellville 50 51 40N24 77W02 5:08:08
Delmar 59 6 41N43 77W20 5:09:20
Delmont 65 6 40N25 79W34 5:18:16
Delphi 46 8 40N16 75W28 5:01:52
Delps 46 80 40N48 75W32 5:02:08
Delta 67 1 39N44 76W20 5:05:20
Delta Manor 48 13 40N39 75W21 5:01:24
Demmler 2 114 40N23 79W49 5:19:16
Demmler Transfer 2 114 40N23 79W49 5:19:16

PENNSYLVANIA

Dempseytown 61 109 41N25 79w50 5:19:20
Denbeau Heights 63 51 40N02 79w55 5:19:40
Denbo 63 51 40N02 79w58 5:19:52
Denholm 34 7 40N35 77w24 5:09:36
Dennison 40 60 41N06 75w50 5:03:20
Dennys Mill 10 6 40N46 79w46 5:19:04
Dents Run 24 7 41N21 78w08 5:12:32
Denver 36 28 40N14 76w08 5:04:32
Deodate 22 2 40N10 76w36 5:06:24
Deringer 40 60 40N56 76w10 5:04:40
Derrick City 42 102 41N58 78w35 5:14:20
Derrs 19 6 41N12 76w23 5:05:32
Derry 65 3 40N20 79w18 5:17:12
Derry Church 22 31 40N17 76w39 5:06:36
Derwood Park 23 9 39N53 75w21 5:01:24
Derwyn 46 9 40N01 75w15 5:01:00
Deshon Manor 10 3 40N53 79w53 5:19:32
Desire 33 6 41N06 78w53 5:15:32
De Turksville 54 9 40N36 76w23 5:05:32
Devault 15 8 40N05 75w32 5:02:08
Devon 15 90 40N03 75w25 5:01:40
Dewart 49 73 41N07 76w53 5:07:32
Dewey Heights 39 13 40N39 75w30 5:02:00
De Young 24 6 41N34 78w54 5:15:36
Diamond 61 74 41N38 79w40 5:18:40
Diamondtown 49 27 40N48 76w25 5:05:40
Diamondville 32 6 40N40 79w00 5:16:00
Dice 60 6 40N55 77w03 5:08:12
Dickerson Run 26 104 40N02 79w40 5:18:40
Dickey 28 51 39N50 77w55 5:11:40
Dickinson 21 1 40N06 77w15 5:09:00
Dicksonburg 20 6 41N46 80w22 5:21:28
Dickson City 35 18 41N28 75w37 5:02:28
Dieners Hall 54 49 40N41 76w12 5:04:48
Dilliner 30 7 39N45 79w56 5:19:44
Dillinger 39 13 40N33 75w31 5:02:04
Dillingersville 39 13 40N29 75w30 5:02:00
Dillontown 64 6 41N51 75w14 5:00:56
Dillsburg 67 1 40N07 77w02 5:08:08
Dillsburg Junction 21 12 40N12 77w00 5:08:00
Dilltown 32 6 40N29 79w00 5:16:00
Dilworthtown 15 13 39N57 75w36 5:02:24
Dime 3 4 40N39 79w32 5:18:08
Dimeling 17 1 41N02 78w27 5:13:48
Dimock 58 60 41N45 75w55 5:03:40
Dingman 51 1 41N21 74w55 4:59:40
Dingmans Ferry 52 3 41N13 74w52 4:59:28
Dipple Manor 40 42 40N58 76w00 5:04:00
Distant 3 6 40N59 79w22 5:17:28
District 6 9 40N26 75w40 5:02:40
Dividing Ridge 56 6 39N56 78w57 5:15:48
Dixonville 32 6 40N43 79w01 5:16:04
Doe Run 15 9 39N59 75w50 5:03:20
Dog Town 3 15 40N46 79w32 5:18:08
Dogtown 19 4 41N00 76w25 5:05:40
Dogtown 40 1 41N09 76w10 5:04:40
Dogtown 55 82 40N48 76w52 5:07:28
Dogwood Acres 9 1 40N11 75w03 5:00:12
Dolington 9 8 40N14 74w56 4:59:44
Dombach Manor 36 8 40N04 76w19 5:05:16
Donaghmore 38 8 40N20 76w26 5:05:44
Donaldson 54 9 40N38 76w24 5:05:36
Donaldson Crossroads 63 2 40N16 80w11 5:20:44
Donation 31 81 40N30 78w01 5:12:04
Donegal 65 6 40N07 79w23 5:17:32
Donegal Heights 36 2 40N07 76w31 5:06:04
Donegal Springs 36 2 40N07 76w31 5:06:04
Donerville 36 8 40N02 76w20 5:05:20
Donnally Mills 50 1 40N33 77w09 5:08:36
Donnellytown 21 16 40N12 77w11 5:08:44
Donohoe 65 3 40N19 79w23 5:17:32
Donora 63 1 40N11 79w52 5:19:28
Dooleyville 49 27 40N48 76w25 5:05:40
Dora 30 51 39N48 79w55 5:19:40
Dora 33 51 40N56 78w58 5:15:52
Doris 11 74 40N20 78w56 5:15:44
Dormont 2 114 40N24 80w02 5:20:08
Dorneyville 39 13 40N37 75w31 5:02:04
Dornsife 49 51 40N45 76w48 5:07:12
Dorothy 65 3 40N19 79w23 5:17:32
Dorrance 40 6 41N06 76w01 5:04:04
Dorset 54 1 40N41 76w00 5:04:00
Dorseyville 2 114 40N35 79w53 5:19:32
Dott 29 6 39N45 78w11 5:12:44
Dotters Corners 45 9 40N52 75w27 5:01:48
Doubling Gap 21 1 40N10 77w24 5:09:36
Douglass 6 28 40N18 75w40 5:02:40
Douglassville 6 8 40N15 75w44 5:02:56
Doutyville 49 27 40N48 76w33 5:06:12
Dover 67 1 40N00 77w08 5:08:32
Down East 15 8 40N02 75w31 5:02:04
Downey 56 6 39N56 78w57 5:15:48
Downieville 10 6 40N41 80w00 5:20:00
Downing Hills 15 46 40N00 75w42 5:02:48
Downingtown 15 80 40N01 75w42 5:02:48
Downtown 26 80 39N54 79w44 5:18:56
Doylesburg 28 1 40N13 77w42 5:10:48
Doyles Mills 34 7 40N34 77w25 5:09:40
Doylestown 9 8 40N19 75w08 5:00:32
Drake 37 6 41N07 80w15 5:21:00
Drakes Mills 20 3 41N48 80w03 5:20:12
Draketown 56 53 39N49 79w21 5:17:24
Drane 17 4 40N51 78w16 5:13:04
Draper 59 6 41N45 77w18 5:09:12
Drauckers 17 56 41N03 78w43 5:14:52
Dravosburg 2 114 40N21 79w54 5:19:36
Dreher 64 6 41N18 75w21 5:01:24
Drehersville 54 1 40N38 76w05 5:04:20
Drennen 65 14 40N34 79w45 5:19:00
Dresher 46 9 40N09 75w10 5:00:40
Drexelbrook 23 9 39N57 75w18 5:01:12
Drexel Gardens 23 9 39N57 75w18 5:01:12
Drexel Heights 48 13 40N41 75w22 5:01:28
Drexel Hill 23 9 39N57 75w18 5:01:12
Drexel Hills 21 12 40N14 76w51 5:07:24
Drexel Manor 23 9 39N57 75w18 5:01:12
Drexel Park 23 9 39N57 75w18 5:01:12
Drexel Plaza 23 9 39N56 75w16 5:01:04
Drifting 17 6 41N01 78w07 5:12:28
Drifton 40 42 41N01 75w54 5:03:36
Driftwood 12 64 41N20 78w08 5:12:32
Drinker 35 4 41N20 75w32 5:02:08
Drocton 18 73 41N20 77w45 5:11:00
Druid Hills 40 20 41N20 75w56 5:03:44
Drummond 24 5 41N16 78w44 5:14:56
Drumore 36 1 39N50 76w15 5:05:00
Drums 40 42 41N01 76w00 5:04:00
Drury Run 18 73 41N20 77w45 5:11:00
Dry Hill 26 104 40N01 79w35 5:18:20
Dry Run 28 1 40N10 77w45 5:11:00
Dry Tavern 30 6 39N57 80w00 5:20:00
Dry Valley Crossroads 60 70 40N55 76w51 5:07:24
Dryville 6 9 40N30 75w40 5:02:40
Dublin 9 8 40N24 75w16 5:01:04
Dublin Mills 29 6 40N03 78w02 5:12:08
Du Bois 17 56 41N07 78w46 5:15:04
Duboistown 41 82 41N13 77w02 5:08:08
Dudley 31 6 40N12 78w11 5:12:44
Duff City 2 13 40N33 80w10 5:20:40
Duffield 28 42 39N56 77w40 5:10:40
Duhring 27 6 41N28 79w07 5:16:28
Duke Center 42 6 41N57 78w29 5:13:56
Dunbar 26 105 39N59 79w37 5:18:28
Duncan 59 6 41N39 77w15 5:09:00
Duncannon 50 51 40N23 77w02 5:08:08
Duncansville 7 33 40N25 78w26 5:13:44
Duncott 54 49 40N41 76w12 5:04:48
Dundaff 58 1 41N34 75w32 5:02:08
Dundore 55 51 40N42 76w52 5:07:28
Dungarvin 31 6 40N42 78w08 5:12:32
Dunkard 30 7 39N45 79w59 5:19:56
Dunkelbergers 49 27 40N48 76w33 5:06:12
Dunlap Creek Junction 26 51 40N02 79w55 5:19:40
Dunlap Creek Village 26 1 39N59 79w53 5:19:32
Dunlevy 63 115 40N07 79w52 5:19:28
Dunlo 11 63 40N18 78w43 5:14:52
Dunminning 23 90 40N00 75w23 5:01:32
Dunmore 35 18 41N25 75w38 5:02:32
Dunn 63 3 40N10 80w16 5:21:04
Dunningsville 63 2 40N11 80w08 5:20:32
Dunningtown 65 6 40N25 79w38 5:18:32
Dunns Eddy 62 3 41N51 79w14 5:16:56
Dunnstable 18 76 41N11 77w24 5:09:36
Dunnstown 18 76 41N08 77w28 5:09:52
Dupont 40 1 41N19 75w45 5:03:00
Duquesne 2 10 40N22 79w51 5:19:24
Duquesne Wharf 2 10 40N22 79w51 5:19:24
Durbin 30 6 39N55 80w26 5:21:44
Durham 9 1 40N34 75w13 5:00:52
Durham Furnace 9 12 40N35 75w13 5:00:52
Durlach 36 30 40N11 76w11 5:04:44
Durrell 8 41 41N46 76w27 5:05:48
Duryea 40 1 41N21 75w46 5:03:04
Duryea Junction 40 1 41N21 75w46 5:03:04
Dushore 57 60 41N31 76w24 5:05:36
Dutch Hill 16 1 41N03 79w39 5:18:36
Dutch Hill 26 51 39N59 79w55 5:19:40
Dutch Settlement 11 63 40N23 78w40 5:14:40
Dutton Mill 15 13 39N57 75w36 5:02:24
Dyberry 64 59 41N38 75w18 5:01:12
Dyerstown 9 8 40N21 75w13 5:00:52
Dysart 11 63 40N36 78w31 5:14:04
Eagle Farms 23 9 40N00 75w18 5:01:12
Eagle Foundry 31 6 40N12 78w08 5:12:32
Eagle Heights 23 9 40N00 75w18 5:01:12
Eaglehurst 25 107 42N05 80w04 5:20:16
Eagle Rock 61 9 41N25 79w42 5:18:48
Eagles Mere 57 6 41N25 76w35 5:06:20
Eagles Mere Park 57 6 41N25 76w35 5:06:20
Eagleville 14 7 41N04 77w36 5:10:24
Eagleville 46 90 40N09 75w24 5:01:36
Earlington 46 1 40N19 75w22 5:01:28
Earlston 5 6 40N01 78w22 5:13:28
Earlville 6 8 40N19 75w44 5:02:56
Earnestville 14 4 40N51 78w16 5:13:04
East Allen 48 13 40N42 75w25 5:01:40
East Altoona 7 33 40N31 78w25 5:13:40
East Ararat 58 6 41N52 75w31 5:02:04
East Athens 8 1 41N58 76w31 5:06:04
East Bangor 46 17 40N53 75w11 5:00:44
East Benton 35 44 41N32 75w44 5:02:56
East Berlin 1 1 39N56 76w59 5:07:56
East Berwick 40 1 41N04 76w14 5:04:56
East Bethlehem 63 6 40N00 80w00 5:20:00
East Bradford 15 13 39N58 75w39 5:02:36
East Bradford 42 102 41N57 78w39 5:14:36
East Brady 16 1 40N59 79w37 5:18:28
East Branch 62 56 41N50 79w41 5:18:44
East Brandywine 15 46 40N02 75w45 5:03:00
Eastbrook 37 112 41N00 80w21 5:21:24
East Brunswick 54 1 40N41 76w00 5:04:00
East Buffalo 60 70 40N56 76w55 5:07:40
East Buffalo 63 3 40N11 80w16 5:21:04
East Butler 10 3 40N53 79w51 5:19:24
East Caln 15 13 40N01 75w41 5:02:44
East Cameron 49 27 40N47 76w26 5:05:44
East Canton 8 103 41N39 76w51 5:07:24
East Carroll 11 63 40N35 78w41 5:14:44
East Charleston 59 59 41N50 77w01 5:08:04
East Chillisquaque 49 6 41N00 76w48 5:07:12
East Cocalico 36 28 40N14 76w06 5:04:24
East Conemaugh 11 74 40N21 78w53 5:15:32
East Connellsville 26 104 40N01 79w35 5:18:20
East Coventry 15 8 40N12 75w37 5:02:28
East Deer 2 14 40N35 79w47 5:19:08
East Donegal 36 2 40N06 76w34 5:06:16
East Drumore 36 27 39N52 76w10 5:04:40
East Du Bois 17 56 41N07 78w46 5:15:04
East Du Bois Junction 17 56 41N07 78w46 5:15:04
East Earl 36 27 40N08 76w02 5:04:08
East End 17 1 41N02 78w27 5:13:48
East Fairfield 20 59 41N33 80w05 5:20:20
East Falls 51 9 40N01 75w11 5:00:44
East Faxon 41 82 41N15 76w58 5:07:52
East Finley 63 6 40N04 80w23 5:21:32
East Franklin 3 15 40N51 79w34 5:18:16
East Fredericktown 26 51 39N59 79w55 5:19:40
East Freedom 7 3 40N21 78w26 5:13:44
East Germantown 51 9 40N03 75w10 5:00:40
East Goshen 15 13 40N00 75w33 5:02:12
East Greenville 46 2 40N25 75w31 5:02:04
East Hanover 38 8 40N20 76w31 5:06:04
East Hempfield 36 8 40N04 76w23 5:05:32
East Herrick 8 6 41N46 76w11 5:04:44
East Hickory 27 6 41N35 79w24 5:17:36
East Honesdale 64 22 41N36 75w16 5:01:04
East Hopewell 67 1 39N48 76w32 5:06:08
East Huntingdon 65 111 40N08 79w36 5:18:24
East Jermyn 35 1 41N32 75w32 5:02:08
East Kane 42 75 41N40 78w49 5:15:16
East Keating 18 7 41N19 77w58 5:11:52
East Lackawannock 43 66 41N12 80w17 5:21:08
East Lampeter 36 8 40N02 76w14 5:04:56
Eastland 36 3 39N45 76w01 5:04:04
Eastland Hills 28 100 39N45 77w34 5:10:16
Eastland Hills 36 8 40N02 76w17 5:05:08
East Lansdowne 23 9 39N57 75w16 5:01:04
East Lawn 46 8 40N45 75w18 5:01:12
Eastlawn Gardens 46 8 40N45 75w18 5:01:12
East Lawrenceville 59 59 42N00 77w08 5:08:32
East Lemon 66 59 41N32 75w57 5:03:48
East Lenox 58 59 41N43 75w29 5:01:56
East Lewisburg 49 70 41N01 76w51 5:07:24
East Liberty 2 114 40N28 79w55 5:19:40
East Mahanoy Junction 54 27 40N48 76w20 5:05:20
East Mahoning 32 6 40N49 79w03 5:16:12
East Manchester 67 67 40N03 76w42 5:06:48
East Marianna 63 6 40N02 80w06 5:20:24
East Marlborough 15 8 39N53 75w43 5:02:52
East McKeesport 2 114 40N23 79w49 5:19:16
East Mead 20 77 41N38 80w04 5:20:16
East Millsboro 26 6 39N59 80w00 5:20:00
East Mines 54 27 40N43 76w11 5:04:44
East Monongahela 2 1 40N11 79w54 5:19:36
Eastmont 2 114 40N28 79w50 5:19:20
Eastmont 11 74 40N18 78w55 5:15:40
Eastmont 67 1 40N00 76w58 5:07:52
East Muncy 41 83 41N12 76w47 5:07:08
East Nantmeal 15 1 40N08 75w43 5:02:52
East New Castle 37 112 41N00 80w21 5:21:24
East Newport 50 1 40N29 77w08 5:08:32
East Norriton 46 8 40N10 75w21 5:01:24
East Norwegian 54 27 40N43 76w10 5:04:40
East Nottingham 15 3 39N45 75w58 5:03:52
East Oakmont 2 10 40N21 79w49 5:19:16
Easton 16 7 41N06 79w30 5:18:00
Easton 48 12 40N41 75w13 5:00:52
East Oreland 46 9 40N07 75w11 5:00:44
East Penn 13 80 40N46 75w44 5:02:56
East Pennsboro 21 12 40N17 76w56 5:07:44
East Petersburg 36 8 40N06 76w21 5:05:24
East Pikeland 15 8 40N08 75w34 5:02:16
East Pittsburgh 2 114 40N24 79w50 5:19:20
Eastpoint 59 7 41N34 76w57 5:07:48
East Prospect 67 2 39N58 76w32 5:06:08
East Providence 5 6 40N01 78w16 5:13:04
East Riverside 26 51 39N54 79w55 5:19:40
East Rochester 4 13 40N42 80w16 5:21:04
East Rockhill 9 8 40N27 75w21 5:01:24
Eastrun 32 6 40N46 79w03 5:16:12
East Rush 58 60 41N42 75w55 5:03:40
East Saint Clair 5 6 40N08 78w34 5:14:16

East Salem 34 7 40N35 77w24 5:09:36
East Sharpsburg 7 3 40N20 78w24 5:13:36
East Side 13 60 41N04 75w46 5:03:04
East Smethport 42 93 41N49 78w26 5:13:44
East Smithfield 8 6 41N52 76w38 5:06:32
East Springfield 25 68 41N58 80w24 5:21:36
East Stroudsburg 45 23 41N00 75w11 5:00:44
East Swiftwater 45 84 41N06 75w20 5:01:20
East Taylor 11 74 40N22 78w53 5:15:32
East Texas 39 13 40N33 75w33 5:02:12
East Titusville 20 74 41N38 79w40 5:18:40
East Towanda 8 41 41N46 76w27 5:05:48
Easttown 15 90 40N02 75w26 5:01:44
Easttown Woods 15 90 40N03 75w26 5:01:44
East Troy 8 7 41N46 76w44 5:06:56
East Union 54 60 40N53 76w08 5:04:32
East Uniontown 26 80 39N54 79w42 5:18:48
Eastvale 4 8 40N46 80w19 5:21:16
East Vandergrift 65 4 40N36 79w34 5:18:16
East View 30 1 39N54 80w11 5:20:44
Eastville 18 7 41N02 77w18 5:09:12
East Vincent 15 118 40N11 75w35 5:02:20
Eastvue 2 114 40N28 79w50 5:19:20
East Washington 63 3 40N10 80w14 5:20:56
East Waterford 34 6 40N22 77w36 5:10:24
East Weissport 13 8 40N50 75w42 5:02:48
East Wheatfield 32 7 40N27 79w01 5:16:04
East Whiteland 15 47 40N03 75w33 5:02:12
East William Penn 54 27 40N49 76w12 5:04:48
Eastwood 2 114 40N28 79w50 5:19:20
Eastwood 65 99 40N18 79w31 5:18:04
East Yoe 67 1 39N52 76w37 5:06:28
East York 67 67 39N59 76w46 5:07:04
Eaton 66 59 41N30 75w58 5:03:52
Eatonville 66 59 41N32 75w57 5:03:48
Eau Claire 10 1 41N08 79w48 5:19:12
Ebenezer 38 8 40N20 76w26 5:05:44
Ebensburg 11 54 40N29 78w44 5:14:56
Eberhardt 2 114 40N34 80w00 5:20:00
Eberhardt 10 3 40N53 79w53 5:19:32
Eberleys Mill 21 12 40N14 76w57 5:07:48
Ebervale 40 42 40N59 75w56 5:03:44
Echo 3 59 40N53 79w15 5:17:00
Echo 11 74 40N23 78w50 5:15:20
Echo Lake 45 23 41N00 75w11 5:00:44
Echo Valley 23 90 40N00 75w23 5:01:32
Echo Valley 54 9 40N38 76w24 5:05:36
Eckenrode Mill 11 57 40N38 78w39 5:14:36
Eckert 39 13 40N37 75w31 5:02:04
Eckley 40 60 40N57 75w49 5:03:16
Eckville 6 56 40N37 75w53 5:03:32
Economy 4 13 40N37 80w11 5:20:44
Eddington 9 9 40N06 74w56 4:59:44
Eddington Gardens 9 9 40N06 74w56 4:59:44
Eddystone 23 90 39N52 75w21 5:01:24
Eddyville 3 6 41N00 79w20 5:17:20
Edelman 46 8 40N45 75w18 5:01:12
Eden 36 27 39N55 76w08 5:04:32
Edenborn 26 51 39N53 79w52 5:19:28
Edenburg 6 80 40N33 75w59 5:03:56
Eden Croft 46 1 40N09 75w03 5:00:12
Edendale 14 4 40N51 78w16 5:13:04
Eden Heights 36 8 40N04 76w19 5:05:16
Edenville 28 42 39N56 77w40 5:10:40
Edgecliff 65 14 40N34 79w45 5:19:00
Edgegrove 1 1 39N48 76w59 5:07:56
Edge Hill 46 9 40N07 75w10 5:00:40
Edgely 9 9 40N08 74w50 4:59:20
Edgemont 22 12 40N18 76w50 5:07:20
Edgemont 23 4 39N57 75w28 5:01:52
Edgemont 46 8 40N45 75w36 5:02:24
Edgemont Farms 15 90 40N00 75w23 5:01:32
Edges Mill 15 46 40N00 75w42 5:02:48
Edgewater 2 14 40N31 79w50 5:19:20
Edgewater Park 9 9 40N12 74w49 4:59:16
Edgewater Terrace 65 3 40N19 79w23 5:17:32
Edgewood 2 114 40N26 79w53 5:19:32
Edgewood 49 27 40N48 76w33 5:06:12
Edgewood 56 64 40N01 79w05 5:16:20
Edgewood Acres 2 114 40N26 79w53 5:19:32
Edgewood Grove 56 6 40N01 79w05 5:16:20
Edgewood Park 9 9 40N12 74w49 4:59:16
Edgewood Park 23 9 39N58 75w22 5:01:28
Edgeworth 2 13 40N34 80w13 5:20:52
Edie 56 6 40N01 79w05 5:16:20
Edinboro 25 3 41N52 80w08 5:20:32
Edinburg 37 112 41N01 80w26 5:21:44
Edison 9 8 40N21 75w13 5:00:52
Edisonville 36 96 39N59 76w11 5:04:44
Edmon 3 4 40N32 79w30 5:18:00
Edna 65 3 40N19 79w39 5:18:36
Edwardsville 40 20 41N16 75w54 5:03:36
Effort 45 1 40N56 75w26 5:01:44
Egypt 33 5 41N15 78w48 5:15:12
Egypt 39 13 40N39 75w30 5:02:00
Egypt Mills 52 6 41N06 75w00 5:00:00
Ehrenfeld 11 63 40N22 78w47 5:15:08
Eichelbergertown 5 6 40N09 78w16 5:13:04
Eidenau 10 6 40N48 80w08 5:20:32
Eighty Four 63 2 40N11 80w08 5:20:32
Ekastown 10 2 40N44 79w45 5:19:00
Elam 23 4 39N55 75w30 5:02:00
Elberta 7 33 40N31 78w25 5:13:40
Elbon 24 5 41N16 78w44 5:14:56
Elbrook 28 100 39N45 77w34 5:10:16
Elco 63 115 40N05 79w52 5:19:28
Elder 11 63 40N41 78w41 5:14:44
Elders Ridge 32 116 40N29 79w27 5:17:48
Eldersville 63 6 40N21 80w29 5:21:56
Elderton 3 6 40N42 79w20 5:17:20
Eldora 36 1 39N47 76w11 5:04:44
Eldora 63 1 40N11 79w54 5:19:36
Eldorado 10 6 41N05 79w41 5:18:44
Eldred 42 40 41N58 78w23 5:13:32
Eldredsville 57 6 41N29 76w36 5:06:24
Elephant 9 8 40N25 75w23 5:01:32
Eleven Mile 53 6 41N59 77w52 5:11:28
Elfinwild 2 114 40N34 80w00 5:20:00
Elgin 25 7 41N55 79w45 5:19:00
Elgin Park 23 90 40N00 75w23 5:01:32
Elim 11 74 40N19 78w56 5:15:44
Elimsport 41 6 41N08 77w01 5:08:04
Elizabeth 2 8 40N16 79w53 5:19:32
Elizabethtown 36 2 40N09 76w36 5:06:24
Elizabethville 22 4 40N33 76w49 5:07:16
Elk City 16 6 41N14 79w32 5:18:08
Elk Creek 25 7 41N54 80w18 5:21:12
Elkdale 15 1 41N01 75w20 5:01:20
Elkdale 58 59 41N43 75w29 5:01:56
Elk Grove 19 6 41N12 76w23 5:05:32
Elkhorn 2 8 40N14 79w56 5:19:44
Elkins Park 46 9 40N05 75w08 5:00:32
Elk Lake 58 60 41N42 75w55 5:03:40
Elkland 59 6 41N59 77w19 5:09:16
Elk Lick 56 79 39N46 79w07 5:16:28
Elk Run Junction 33 51 40N56 78w58 5:15:52
Elkview 15 7 39N49 75w50 5:03:20
Ellen Gowan 54 27 40N49 76w12 5:04:48
Ellenton 41 103 41N39 76w51 5:07:24
Ellerslie 9 9 40N06 74w56 4:59:44
Elliger Park 46 9 40N07 75w14 5:00:56
Elliottsburg 50 6 40N21 77w16 5:09:04
Elliotts Mills 37 6 41N02 80w03 5:20:12
Elliottson 21 16 40N12 77w11 5:08:44
Elliottsville 26 6 39N48 79w34 5:18:16
Ellisburg 53 6 41N59 77w52 5:11:28
Ellport 37 121 40N52 80w16 5:21:04
Ellrod 2 10 40N21 79w51 5:19:24
Ellsworth 63 51 40N07 80w01 5:20:04
Ellwood City 37 121 40N52 80w17 5:21:08
Elm 36 1 40N12 76w21 5:05:24
Elmer 53 6 41N55 77w32 5:10:08
Elmhurst 35 4 41N23 75w33 5:02:12
Elmo 16 6 41N14 79w32 5:18:08
Elmora 11 63 40N36 78w45 5:15:00
Elmwood 67 67 39N57 76w42 5:06:48
Elora 10 6 41N02 80w03 5:20:12
Elrama 63 8 40N15 79w56 5:19:44
Elrico 65 6 40N28 79w31 5:18:04
Elroy 46 8 40N19 75w19 5:01:16
Elstie 11 63 40N34 78w33 5:14:12
Elstonville 36 8 40N06 76w22 5:05:28
Elton 11 123 40N17 78w48 5:15:12
Elverson 15 56 40N09 75w50 5:03:20
Elwood Park 63 3 40N11 80w16 5:21:04
Elwyn 23 90 39N54 75w25 5:01:40
Elwyn Terrace 36 8 40N06 76w22 5:05:28
Elysburg 49 1 40N52 76w33 5:06:12
Emanuelsville 48 13 40N45 75w24 5:01:36
Emblem 2 10 40N21 79w49 5:19:16
Embreeville 15 8 39N56 75w44 5:02:56
Emeigh 11 92 40N42 78w47 5:15:08
Emerald 30 6 39N59 80w03 5:20:12
Emerald 39 8 40N45 75w38 5:02:32
Emerickville 33 34 41N10 79w05 5:16:20
Emigh Run 32 63 40N44 78w49 5:15:16
Emigsville 67 67 40N01 76w44 5:06:56
Emlenton 61 1 41N11 79w43 5:18:52
Emmaus 39 13 40N32 75w30 5:02:00
Emmaville 29 6 39N57 78w14 5:12:56
Emporium 12 106 41N31 78w14 5:12:56
Emporium Junction 12 106 41N31 78w14 5:12:56
Emsworth 2 114 40N30 80w05 5:20:20
Endeavor 27 6 41N35 79w23 5:17:32
Enders 22 24 40N28 76w56 5:07:44
Energy 37 112 41N00 80w21 5:21:24
Enfield 46 9 40N07 75w11 5:00:44
Engles Lake 45 84 41N06 75w20 5:01:20
Englesville 6 2 40N20 75w38 5:02:32
Englewood 54 27 40N47 76w14 5:04:56
English Center 41 6 41N19 77w22 5:09:28
Enhaut 22 12 40N14 76w50 5:07:20
Enid 29 6 40N05 78w10 5:12:40
Enlow 2 51 40N27 80w15 5:21:00
Ennisville 31 81 40N30 78w01 5:12:04
Enola 21 12 40N16 76w55 5:07:40
Enon 63 64 40N00 80w28 5:21:52
Enon Valley 37 6 40N51 80w27 5:21:48
Enterline 22 24 40N28 76w56 5:07:44
Enterprise 43 6 41N10 80w05 5:20:20
Enterprise 49 27 40N46 76w30 5:06:00
Enterprise 62 74 41N38 79w40 5:18:40
Entlerville 21 1 40N10 77w24 5:09:36
Entriken 31 6 40N20 78w12 5:12:48
Ephrata 36 30 40N11 76w11 5:04:44
Equinunk 64 6 41N51 75w14 5:00:56
Ercildoun 15 9 39N57 75w51 5:03:24
Erdenheim 46 9 40N04 75w12 5:00:48
Erdman 22 1 40N34 76w42 5:06:48
Erhard 17 6 40N53 78w32 5:14:08
Erie 25 107 42N08 80w05 5:20:20
Erlen 46 9 40N03 75w08 5:00:32

PENNSYLVANIA

Erly 50 6 40N21 77w16 5:09:04
Ernest 32 72 40N41 79w10 5:16:40
Erney 67 1 40N00 76w58 5:07:52
Erwinna 9 1 40N30 75w04 5:00:16
Eshbach 6 2 40N22 75w38 5:02:32
Eshcol 50 1 40N33 77w09 5:08:36
Espy 19 4 41N00 76w25 5:05:40
Espyville Station 20 7 41N36 80w29 5:21:56
Essington 23 9 39N52 75w18 5:01:12
Estella 57 6 41N29 76w36 5:06:24
Esterly 6 101 40N20 75w53 5:03:32
Esther 4 19 40N40 80w24 5:21:36
Estherton 22 12 40N17 76w53 5:07:32
Etna 2 114 40N30 79w57 5:19:48
Etters 67 1 40N09 76w45 5:07:00
Euclid 10 3 40N53 79w53 5:19:32
Eulalia 53 66 41N45 78w00 5:12:00
Eureka 9 8 40N13 75w17 5:01:08
Eureka 11 123 40N15 78w50 5:15:20
Eureka 65 6 40N09 79w44 5:18:56
Eustontown 38 8 40N20 76w26 5:05:44
Evans 26 80 39N54 79w44 5:18:56
Evansburg 46 8 40N12 75w28 5:01:52
Evans City 10 108 40N46 80w04 5:20:16
Evans Falls 66 59 41N32 75w57 5:03:48
Evanston 65 3 40N16 79w41 5:18:44
Evansville 6 80 40N29 75w53 5:03:32
Evansville 19 1 41N04 76w15 5:05:00
Evendale 34 6 40N41 77w07 5:08:28
Everett 5 70 40N01 78w23 5:13:32
Evergreen 8 60 41N36 76w27 5:05:48
Evergreen Park 39 13 40N39 75w30 5:02:00
Everhartville 50 1 40N29 77w08 5:08:32
Everson 26 111 40N05 79w35 5:18:20
Ewalt 2 114 40N28 80w01 5:20:04
Ewings Mill 32 6 40N37 79w01 5:16:04
Ewingsville 2 114 40N25 80w05 5:20:20
Excelsior 49 27 40N46 76w30 5:06:00
Exchange 47 6 40N58 76w36 5:06:24
Exeter 40 1 41N20 75w49 5:03:16
Export 65 6 40N25 79w38 5:18:32
Exton 15 13 40N02 75w37 5:02:28
Eyers Grove 19 6 41N05 76w31 5:06:04
Eynon 35 18 41N28 75w37 5:02:28
Factoryville 46 17 40N53 75w12 5:00:48
Factoryville 66 44 41N34 75w47 5:03:08
Fagleysville 46 2 40N19 75w37 5:02:28
Fair Acres 67 12 40N14 76w51 5:07:24
Fairbank 26 51 39N57 79w53 5:19:32
Fairbrook 14 6 40N42 78w00 5:12:00
Fairchance 26 51 39N49 79w45 5:19:00
Fairdale 30 51 39N53 79w58 5:19:52
Fairdale 58 60 41N50 75w53 5:03:32
Fairfield 1 1 39N47 77w22 5:09:28
Fairfield 25 107 42N08 80w01 5:20:04
Fairfield 63 6 40N02 80w06 5:20:24
Fair Grounds 30 6 39N56 80w03 5:20:12
Fairhaven Heights 2 114 40N23 79w49 5:19:16
Fairhill 9 8 40N17 75w18 5:01:12
Fairhill 51 9 40N00 75w09 5:00:36
Fairhope 26 1 40N08 79w52 5:19:28
Fairhope 56 51 39N51 78w48 5:15:12
Fairland 36 8 40N09 76w18 5:05:12
Fairlawn 41 7 41N19 77w05 5:08:20
Fairless Hills 9 97 40N10 74w53 4:59:32
Fairmont 65 25 40N20 79w43 5:18:52
Fairmount 36 27 39N54 76w10 5:04:40
Fairmount 40 6 41N17 76w16 5:05:04
Fairmount 51 9 39N59 75w10 5:00:40
Fairmount City 16 6 41N01 79w19 5:17:16
Fairmount Springs 40 6 41N12 76w23 5:05:32
Fairoaks 2 13 40N35 80w13 5:20:52
Fairoaks 46 1 40N11 75w10 5:00:40
Fair Plain 25 68 42N01 80w21 5:21:24
Fairplay 1 1 39N49 77w11 5:08:44
Fairview 7 33 40N31 78w25 5:13:40
Fairview 17 4 40N57 78w14 5:12:56
Fairview 25 68 42N02 80w15 5:21:00
Fairview 28 100 39N45 77w34 5:10:16
Fairview 33 51 40N56 78w58 5:15:52
Fairview 43 66 41N19 80w16 5:21:04
Fairview 44 73 40N36 77w34 5:10:16
Fairview 49 27 40N48 76w33 5:06:12
Fairview Drive 67 1 39N48 76w59 5:07:56
Fairview Heights 2 114 40N31 79w53 5:19:32
Fairview Heights 6 80 40N25 75w58 5:03:52
Fairview Heights 40 20 41N14 75w52 5:03:28
Fairview Hills 40 20 41N14 75w52 5:03:28
Fairview Knolls 46 12 40N41 75w14 5:00:56
Fairview Park 15 13 39N57 75w36 5:02:24
Fairview Park 36 8 40N02 76w20 5:05:20
Fairview Park 40 20 41N14 75w52 5:03:28
Fairview Village 46 90 40N10 75w23 5:01:32
Fairville 15 8 39N51 75w38 5:02:32
Fairville 60 70 40N58 76w54 5:07:36
Falconcrest 15 13 39N57 75w36 5:02:24
Fallentimber 11 54 40N41 78w30 5:14:00
Fallen Timbers 26 7 39N44 79w52 5:19:28
Falling Spring 28 42 39N56 77w40 5:10:40
Falling Spring 50 6 40N21 77w18 5:09:12
Fallowfield 63 51 40N09 79w57 5:19:48
Falls 66 6 41N28 75w51 5:03:24
Falls Creek 17 59 41N09 78w48 5:15:12
Fallsington 9 9 40N11 74w49 4:59:16
Fallston 4 19 40N43 80w19 5:21:16

 PENNSYLVANIA

Place		Lat	Long	Time
Falmouth 36	2	40N05	76w40	5:06:40
Fannett 28	1	40N12	77w43	5:10:52
Fannettsburg 28	1	40N04	77w50	5:11:20
Faraday Park 23	9	39N54	75w20	5:01:20
Farmdale 36	2	40N07	76w31	5:06:04
Farmers 67	39	39N56	76w51	5:07:24
Farmers Mills 14	64	40N51	77w34	5:10:16
Farmers Valley 8	52	41N47	76w47	5:07:08
Farmers Valley 42	93	41N49	78w27	5:13:48
Farmersville 36	30	40N11	76w11	5:04:44
Farmersville 46	12	40N41	75w14	5:00:56
Farmington 26	6	39N48	79w34	5:18:16
Farmington 39	13	40N35	75w28	5:01:52
Farm School 9	8	40N21	75w13	5:00:52
Farquhar Estates 67	67	39N57	76w42	5:06:48
Farragut 41	82	41N15	76w55	5:07:40
Farrandsville 18	7	41N11	77w31	5:10:04
Farrell 43	117	41N13	80w30	5:22:00
Farview 6	101	40N19	75w57	5:03:48
Farwell 18	73	41N20	77w45	5:11:00
Fassett 8	7	41N57	76w48	5:07:12
Faunce 17	122	40N50	78w41	5:14:44
Fawn Grove 67	1	39N44	76w28	5:05:52
Faxon 41	82	41N15	76w59	5:07:56
Fayette 34	1	40N39	77w16	5:09:04
Fayette 37	6	41N07	80w15	5:21:00
Fayette City 26	1	40N06	79w50	5:19:20
Fayetteville 28	1	39N55	77w33	5:10:12
Fayfield 67	67	39N59	76w46	5:07:04
Fay Terrace 43	59	41N24	80w23	5:21:32
Fearnot 54	27	40N38	76w36	5:06:24
Feasterville 9	1	40N09	75w00	5:00:00
Feasterville-Trevose 9	97	40N10	74w55	4:59:40
Federal 2	114	40N23	80w09	5:20:36
Federal Reserve 2	114	40N27	79w58	5:19:52
Federal Reserve 51	9	39N57	75w09	5:00:36
Federal Square 22	12	40N16	76w53	5:07:32
Fell 35	1	41N36	75w29	5:01:56
Fellsburg 65	1	40N11	79w49	5:19:16
Fellwick 46	9	40N07	75w14	5:00:56
Felton 67	7	39N51	76w34	5:06:16
Feltonville 23	90	39N51	75w22	5:01:28
Fenelton 10	6	40N52	79w44	5:18:56
Ferguson 2	114	40N34	80w00	5:20:00
Fergusonville 9	9	40N08	74w51	4:59:24
Fermanagh 34	7	40N36	77w23	5:09:32
Fern Brook 40	20	41N20	75w56	5:03:44
Ferndale 9	1	40N32	75w11	5:00:44
Ferndale 11	74	40N17	78w55	5:15:40
Ferndale 49	27	40N48	76w33	5:06:12
Ferndale 54	1	40N54	76w13	5:04:52
Fern Glen 40	60	40N56	76w10	5:04:40
Fern Hill 15	13	39N57	75w36	5:02:24
Fernridge 45	84	41N03	75w28	5:01:52
Fern Village 46	1	40N11	75w06	5:00:24
Fernville 19	4	41N00	76w25	5:05:40
Fernway 10	6	40N48	80w08	5:20:32
Fernwood 17	63	40N46	78w25	5:13:40
Fernwood 23	9	39N56	75w16	5:01:04
Fernwood-Yeadon 23	9	39N56	75w16	5:01:04
Ferrelton 56	6	40N07	78w57	5:15:48
Fertigs 61	6	41N22	79w29	5:17:56
Fertility 36	8	40N02	76w17	5:05:08
Fetterville 36	27	40N06	75w59	5:03:56
Fiddlers Green 11	63	40N23	78w40	5:14:40
Fidelity 51	9	39N57	75w09	5:00:36
Fieldmore Springs 20	74	41N38	79w40	5:18:40
Fieldson Crossroad 30	51	39N48	79w55	5:19:40
Fifficktown 11	74	40N22	78w51	5:15:24
Fiketown 26	6	39N44	79w27	5:17:48
Filbert 26	51	39N57	79w53	5:19:32
Fillmore 14	70	40N53	77w45	5:11:00
Finch Hill 35	1	41N34	75w32	5:02:08
Findlay 2	6	40N29	80w18	5:21:12
Findley 43	66	41N13	80w11	5:20:44
Finland 9	2	40N24	75w30	5:02:00
Finley Mills 33	51	40N56	78w58	5:15:52
Finleyville 5	51	40N10	78w13	5:12:52
Finleyville 63	114	40N15	80w01	5:20:04
Fisher 16	6	41N16	79w15	5:17:00
Fisherdale 19	1	40N52	76w33	5:06:12
Fisher Heights 63	1	40N11	79w54	5:19:36
Fishers Corner 23	90	39N51	75w22	5:01:28
Fishers Ferry 49	82	40N52	76w47	5:07:08
Fishertown 5	6	40N08	78w35	5:14:20
Fishertown 11	74	40N22	78w51	5:15:24
Fisherville 15	46	40N00	75w42	5:02:48
Fisherville 22	24	40N28	76w56	5:07:44
Fishingcreek 19	6	41N08	76w21	5:05:24
Fiske 11	54	40N41	78w30	5:14:00
Fitz Henry 65	6	40N09	79w44	5:18:56
Five Corners 20	7	41N44	79w46	5:19:04
Fiveforks 28	100	39N45	77w34	5:10:16
Five Points 4	13	40N34	80w16	5:21:04
Five Points 4	6	40N41	80w28	5:21:52
Five Points 6	101	40N20	75w53	5:03:32
Five Points 15	8	39N51	75w43	5:02:52
Five Points 17	122	40N50	78w41	5:14:44
Five Points 25	107	42N05	80w04	5:20:16
Five Points 32	72	40N41	79w12	5:16:48
Five Points 40	6	40N58	76w05	5:04:20
Five Points 43	6	41N16	80w08	5:20:32
Five Points 46	8	40N10	75w17	5:01:08
Five Points 49	6	41N06	76w46	5:07:04
Five Points 65	99	40N18	79w34	5:18:16
Fivepointville 36	28	40N14	76w08	5:04:32
Flat Rock 26	6	39N44	79w27	5:17:48
Flatwoods 26	104	40N02	79w40	5:18:40
Fleetville 35	44	41N36	75w43	5:02:52
Fleetwing Estates 9	9	40N09	74w51	4:59:24
Fleetwood 6	8	40N27	75w49	5:03:16
Fleming 14	7	40N54	77w53	5:11:32
Flemington 18	76	41N08	77w28	5:09:52
Flicksville 46	15	40N49	75w12	5:00:48
Flinton 11	54	40N43	78w31	5:14:04
Flintville 38	8	40N20	76w26	5:05:44
Floradale 1	1	39N56	77w15	5:09:00
Floreffe 2	8	40N17	79w56	5:19:44
Florence 63	6	40N26	80w26	5:21:44
Florida Park 23	90	40N00	75w23	5:01:32
Florin 36	2	40N07	76w31	5:06:04
Flourtown 46	9	40N06	75w13	5:00:52
Flourtown Gardens 46	9	40N06	75w15	5:01:00
Fogelsville 39	13	40N35	75w38	5:02:32
Folcroft 23	9	39N53	75w17	5:01:08
Foleys Siding 2	114	40N22	80w00	5:20:00
Folsom 23	9	39N53	75w20	5:01:20
Folstown 40	20	41N14	75w52	5:03:28
Fombell 4	121	40N49	80w12	5:20:48
Font 15	46	40N00	75w42	5:02:48
Fontana 38	8	40N20	76w26	5:05:44
Footedale 26	51	39N56	79w50	5:19:20
Foot Of Ten 7	33	40N28	78w25	5:13:40
Forbes Road 65	99	40N21	79w31	5:18:04
Force 24	7	41N15	78w30	5:14:00
Ford City 3	15	40N46	79w32	5:18:08
Ford Cliff 3	15	40N45	79w32	5:18:08
Ford View 3	15	40N46	79w32	5:18:08
Fordville 67	39	39N56	76w51	5:07:24
Fordyce 30	1	39N54	80w11	5:20:44
Forest Castle 40	1	41N20	75w49	5:03:16
Forest City 58	59	41N39	75w28	5:01:52
Forest Grove 2	114	40N29	80w08	5:20:32
Forest Grove 9	8	40N18	75w04	5:00:16
Foresthill 60	6	40N55	77w03	5:08:12
Forest Hills 2	114	40N26	79w50	5:19:20
Forest Hills 36	28	40N05	76w11	5:04:44
Forest Hills Manor 46	1	40N09	75w03	5:00:12
Forest Inn 13	8	40N50	75w42	5:02:48
Forest Knolls 46	8	40N04	76w26	5:05:44
Forest Lake 58	6	41N53	75w59	5:03:56
Forest Lake Park 52	6	41N28	75w03	5:00:12
Forest Park 9	2	40N20	75w18	5:01:12
Forest Park 40	20	41N15	75w53	5:03:32
Forestville 10	6	41N06	80w00	5:20:00
Forestville 15	1	39N49	75w50	5:03:20
Forestville 54	49	40N41	76w12	5:04:48
Forge 7	11	40N40	78w13	5:12:52
Forks 19	4	41N05	76w25	5:05:40
Forkston 66	6	41N30	76w08	5:04:32
Forksville 57	6	41N29	76w36	5:06:24
Fort Fetter 7	33	40N25	78w24	5:13:36
Fort Hill 56	53	39N50	79w16	5:17:04
Fort Hunter 22	12	40N17	76w53	5:07:32
Fort Littleton 29	6	40N04	77w58	5:11:52
Fort Loudon 28	51	39N55	77w54	5:11:36
Fortney 67	12	40N08	76w52	5:07:28
Fort Roberston 50	6	40N22	77w21	5:09:24
Fort Washington 46	9	40N08	75w13	5:00:52
Forty Fort 40	20	41N17	75w52	5:03:28
Fossilville 5	6	39N57	78w39	5:14:36
Foster 32	116	40N29	79w27	5:17:48
Foster Brook 42	102	41N57	78w39	5:14:36
Fostoria 7	11	40N40	78w13	5:12:52
Foundryville 19	1	41N04	76w15	5:05:00
Fountain 54	27	40N39	76w30	5:06:00
Fountain Dale 1	1	39N47	77w22	5:09:28
Fountain House 20	59	41N44	80w07	5:20:28
Fountain Springs 54	27	40N47	76w21	5:05:24
Fountainville 9	8	40N20	75w09	5:00:36
Foustown 67	67	39N58	76w47	5:07:08
Foustwell 56	6	40N11	78w59	5:15:56
Fowler Heights 32	72	40N38	79w09	5:16:36
Fowlersville 19	1	41N04	76w15	5:05:00
Foxburg 11	92	40N18	78w44	5:14:56
Foxburg 16	1	41N09	79w41	5:18:44
Fox Chapel 2	114	40N31	79w53	5:19:32
Fox Chase 36	8	40N04	76w19	5:05:16
Fox Chase 51	9	40N04	75w05	5:00:20
Fox Chase Manor 46	9	40N05	75w07	5:00:28
Foxcroft 23	9	39N58	75w22	5:01:28
Foxdale 65	111	40N13	79w36	5:18:24
Fox Hill 28	100	39N45	77w34	5:10:16
Fox Hill 40	20	41N15	75w53	5:03:32
Foxtown 65	111	40N14	79w35	5:18:20
Foxtown Hill 45	23	41N00	75w13	5:00:52
Foxwood Park 23	9	39N58	75w22	5:01:28
Frackville 54	27	40N47	76w14	5:04:56
Frailey 54	9	40N38	76w25	5:05:40
Francis 25	68	41N59	80w19	5:21:16
Francis Mine 63	6	40N23	80w24	5:21:36
Franconia 46	8	40N18	75w21	5:01:24
Frank 2	8	40N16	79w48	5:19:12
Frankford 51	9	40N01	75w06	5:00:24
Frankfort Springs 4	6	40N29	80w26	5:21:44
Franklin 61	109	41N24	79w50	5:19:20
Franklin Center 23	90	39N55	75w22	5:01:28
Franklin Corners 25	7	41N53	80w08	5:20:32
Franklindale 8	60	41N43	76w28	5:05:52
Franklin Farms 63	3	40N11	80w16	5:21:04
Franklin Forks 58	60	41N50	75w53	5:03:32
Franklin Furnace 28	42	39N56	77w40	5:10:40
Franklin Hill 58	50	41N58	75w45	5:03:00
Franklin Park 2	114	40N35	80w06	5:20:24
Franklintown 67	1	40N05	77w02	5:08:08
Franklinville 31	6	40N37	78w08	5:12:32
Frankstown 7	33	40N27	78w21	5:13:24
Frazer 15	47	40N02	75w34	5:02:16
Frederick 46	8	40N18	75w32	5:02:08
Fredericksburg 3	6	41N00	79w43	5:18:52
Fredericksburg 7	51	40N19	78w20	5:13:20
Fredericksburg 20	77	41N39	80w11	5:20:44
Fredericksburg 38	1	40N27	76w26	5:05:44
Fredericksville 6	9	40N30	75w40	5:02:40
Fredericktown 63	6	40N00	80w00	5:20:00
Fredericktown Hill 63	6	40N01	80w00	5:20:00
Fredonia 43	66	41N19	80w16	5:21:04
Freeburg 55	4	40N46	76w56	5:07:44
Freedom 4	13	40N41	80w15	5:21:00
Freehold 62	6	41N57	79w26	5:17:44
Freeland 40	42	41N01	75w54	5:03:36
Freemansburg 48	12	40N41	75w10	5:00:40
Freemansburg Heights 48	13	40N39	75w21	5:01:24
Freemansville 6	101	40N19	75w57	5:03:48
Freeport 3	2	40N41	79w41	5:18:44
Freeport 25	91	42N13	79w50	5:19:20
Freeport 30	6	39N46	80w25	5:21:40
Freeport Junction 3	2	40N41	79w41	5:18:44
Frenchs Corners 3	15	40N53	79w32	5:18:08
Frenchtown 20	6	41N38	79w59	5:19:56
Frenchville 17	6	41N06	78w13	5:12:52
Freys Grove 22	80	40N12	76w43	5:06:52
Freysville 67	1	39N52	76w37	5:06:28
Fricks 9	8	40N17	75w16	5:01:04
Fricks Lock 15	8	40N15	75w39	5:02:36
Friedens 39	8	40N45	75w37	5:02:28
Friedens 56	6	40N03	79w00	5:16:00
Friedensburg 54	27	40N36	76w15	5:05:00
Friedensville 39	13	40N39	75w21	5:01:24
Friendship Heights 26	51	39N47	79w52	5:19:28
Friendship Village 15	9	39N59	75w50	5:03:20
Friendsville 58	6	41N55	76w03	5:04:12
Friesville 7	3	40N18	78w27	5:13:48
Frisbie 54	1	40N38	76w05	5:04:20
Frisco 4	121	40N52	80w16	5:21:04
Fritztown 6	101	40N18	76w00	5:04:00
Frogtown 3	1	40N59	79w37	5:18:28
Frogtown 16	6	41N00	79w20	5:17:20
Frogtown 31	6	40N42	78w08	5:12:32
Frogtown 67	12	40N14	76w51	5:07:24
Frostburg 33	51	40N58	79w02	5:16:08
Frugality 11	54	40N41	78w30	5:14:00
Fruitville 36	8	40N04	76w19	5:05:16
Fruitville 46	8	40N16	75w28	5:01:52
Frush Valley 6	101	40N23	75w56	5:03:44
Frutcheys 45	23	41N00	75w11	5:00:44
Fryburg 16	6	41N21	79w26	5:17:44
Frye 63	1	40N11	79w54	5:19:36
Frystown 6	25	40N23	76w18	5:05:12
Fullerton 39	13	40N38	75w29	5:01:56
Fulmor Heights 46	1	40N11	75w06	5:00:24
Fulton 36	1	39N47	76w11	5:04:44
Fulton Run 32	72	40N38	79w09	5:16:36
Furlong 9	8	40N18	75w05	5:00:20
Furnace Run 3	15	40N53	79w32	5:18:08
Furniss 36	1	39N47	76w11	5:04:44
Gabby Heights 63	3	40N11	80w16	5:21:04
Gabelsville 6	2	40N20	75w38	5:02:32
Gahagen 56	63	40N05	78w50	5:15:20
Gaibleton 32	6	40N44	79w06	5:16:24
Gaines 59	6	41N45	77w34	5:10:16
Galeton 53	6	41N44	77w39	5:10:36
Galilee 64	6	41N44	75w09	5:00:36
Gallagher 18	7	41N16	77w27	5:09:48
Gallagherville 15	46	40N00	75w42	5:02:48
Gallatin 2	1	40N11	79w54	5:19:36
Gallitzin 11	55	40N29	78w33	5:14:12
Galloway 61	109	41N25	79w50	5:19:20
Gamble 41	7	41N23	76w56	5:07:44
Ganister 7	3	40N28	78w14	5:12:56
Gans 26	51	39N45	79w49	5:19:16
Gap 36	23	39N59	76w02	5:04:08
Gapsville 5	6	40N00	78w15	5:13:00
Garards Fort 30	6	39N49	80w02	5:20:08
Gardeau 42	75	41N40	78w49	5:15:16
Garden City 2	114	40N26	79w47	5:19:08
Garden City 23	90	39N55	75w22	5:01:28
Gardendale 23	90	39N50	75w25	5:01:40
Garden Hills 36	8	40N02	76w20	5:05:20
Garden View 41	82	41N15	77w03	5:08:12
Gardenview 44	73	40N40	77w36	5:10:24
Gardenville 9	8	40N22	75w07	5:00:28
Gardner 37	112	41N00	80w21	5:21:24
Gardners 1	1	40N00	77w12	5:08:48
Garfield 6	1	40N26	76w07	5:04:28
Garland 62	7	41N49	79w27	5:17:48
Garman 11	92	40N40	78w47	5:15:08
Garrett 56	79	39N52	79w04	5:16:16
Garrettford 23	9	39N57	75w18	5:01:12
Garrett Hill 23	90	40N02	75w19	5:01:16
Garretts Run 3	15	40N49	79w32	5:18:08
Garrison 30	6	39N46	80w25	5:21:40
Garvers Ferry 65	2	40N41	79w41	5:18:44
Gascola 2	114	40N28	79w50	5:19:20

Gaskill 33 6 40N57 78W51 5:15:24
Gastonville 63 114 40N15 79W59 5:19:56
Gastown 3 6 40N40 79W18 5:17:12
Gatchellville 67 1 39N44 76W31 5:06:04
Gates 26 51 39N54 79W55 5:19:40
Gatesburg 14 6 40N42 78W08 5:12:32
Gateway Center 2
114 40N27 79W59 5:19:56
Gauff Hill 39 13 40N39 75W21 5:01:24
Gayly 2 114 40N27 80W09 5:20:36
Gaysport 7 33 40N25 78W24 5:13:36
Gearhartville 17
113 40N54 78W13 5:12:52
Geeseytown 7 33 40N25 78W24 5:13:36
Geiger 56 6 40N03 79W00 5:16:00
Geigertown 6 8 40N12 75W50 5:03:20
Geistown 11 74 40N18 78W52 5:15:28
Gelatt 58 6 41N50 75W36 5:02:24
General Warren Village 15
8 40N02 75W31 5:02:04
General Wayne 46 9 40N01 75W15 5:01:00
Genesee 53 6 42N00 77W53 5:11:32
Geneva 20 59 41N36 80W19 5:21:16
Geneva Hill 4 8 40N46 80W20 5:21:20
Georges 26 51 39N50 79W46 5:19:04
Georgetown 1 56 39N45 77W05 5:08:20
Georgetown 3 4 40N38 79W36 5:18:24
Georgetown 4 6 40N39 80W30 5:22:00
Georgetown 40 20 41N15 75W53 5:03:32
Georgetown 46 8 40N45 75W18 5:01:12
Georgeville 32 6 40N46 79W03 5:16:12
German 26 51 39N53 79W52 5:19:28
German Corners 39 8 40N42 75W42 5:02:48
Germania 53 6 41N44 77W39 5:10:36
Germans 13 8 40N50 75W42 5:02:48
Germansville 39 8 40N42 75W42 5:02:48
Germantown 1 56 39N45 77W05 5:08:20
Germantown 28 1 39N55 77W34 5:10:16
Germantown 51 9 39N57 75W10 5:00:40
Germany 1 56 39N44 77W06 5:08:24
Geryville 9 2 40N24 75W30 5:02:00
Getty Heights 32 72 40N38 79W09 5:16:36
Gettysburg 1 1 39N50 77W14 5:08:56
Gettysburg Junction 21
16 40N12 77W11 5:08:44
Ghennes Heights 63
1 40N11 79W54 5:19:36
Ghent 8 60 41N51 76W30 5:06:00
Gibbon Glade 26 6 39N44 79W36 5:18:24
Gibraltar 6 8 40N17 75W52 5:03:28
Gibson 58 6 41N48 75W39 5:02:36
Gibson 63 51 40N07 80W00 5:20:00
Gibsonia 2 114 40N38 79W58 5:19:52
Gibsonton 65 1 40N08 79W52 5:19:28
Gifford 42 6 41N51 78W36 5:14:24
Gilbert 45 1 40N55 75W26 5:01:44
Gilberton 54 27 40N48 76W14 5:04:56
Gilbertsville 46 2 40N19 75W37 5:02:28
Gilfoyl 27 6 41N28 79W07 5:16:28
Gillespie 26 1 40N07 79W50 5:19:20
Gillett 8 7 41N57 76W48 5:07:12
Gill Hall 2 8 40N18 79W54 5:19:36
Gilmore 26 80 39N54 79W44 5:18:56
Gilmore 30 6 39N45 80W20 5:21:20
Gilmore 42 102 41N58 78W34 5:14:16
Gilmore 63 51 40N22 80W14 5:20:56
Gilmore Acres 2 114 40N28 79W50 5:19:20
Gilpin 3 4 40N40 79W36 5:18:24
Ginger Hill 63 1 40N11 79W54 5:19:36
Ginter 17 63 40N46 78W23 5:13:32
Ginther 54 27 40N48 75W58 5:03:52
Gipsy 32 6 40N48 78W53 5:15:32
Girard 25 68 42N00 80W19 5:21:16
Girardville 54 27 40N47 76W17 5:05:08
Girty 3 6 40N39 79W25 5:17:40
Gitts Run 67 1 39N48 76W59 5:07:56
Gladden 2 114 40N21 80W11 5:20:44
Gladden Heights 63
51 40N22 80W14 5:20:56
Glade 56 6 39N56 78W57 5:15:48
Glade 62 3 41N52 79W06 5:16:24
Glade City 56 79 39N49 79W02 5:16:08
Glade Mills 6 40N44 79W56 5:19:44
Glades 67 67 39N59 76W46 5:07:04
Gladstone 23 9 39N56 75W16 5:01:04
Gladwyne 46 9 40N02 75W17 5:01:08
Glasgow 4 6 40N38 80W30 5:22:00
Glasgow 11 54 40N42 78W27 5:13:48
Glasgow 46 8 40N15 75W39 5:02:36
Glass City 14 113 40N54 78W13 5:12:52
Glassmere 2 14 40N35 79W47 5:19:08
Glassport 2 8 40N19 79W54 5:19:36
Glassworks 30 51 39N48 79W55 5:19:40
Glatfelter 67 3 39N51 76W46 5:07:04
Gleason 59 103 41N39 76W51 5:07:24
Gleasonton 18 7 41N21 77W42 5:10:48
Glen Acres 15 13 39N57 75W36 5:02:24
Glen Ashton Farms 9
9 40N06 74W56 4:59:44
Glenburn 35 44 41N31 75W44 5:02:56
Glen Campbell 32 6 40N49 78W50 5:15:20
Glen Carbon 54 49 40N41 76W12 5:04:48
Glencoe 56 6 39N49 78W51 5:15:24
Glendale 2 114 40N24 80W06 5:20:24
Glendale 9 8 40N22 74W56 4:59:44
Glendale 40 1 41N19 75W46 5:03:04
Glendale Gardens 23
9 39N54 75W18 5:01:12
Glendon 46 12 40N40 75W14 5:00:56
Glendon 54 3 40N49 76W08 5:04:32
Glen Dower 54 49 40N41 76W12 5:04:48
Glenfield 2 114 40N31 80W08 5:20:32
Glen Forney 28 100 39N45 77W34 5:10:16
Glenhall 15 13 39N57 75W36 5:02:24
Glen Hazel 24 7 41N35 78W41 5:14:44
Glenhope 17 54 40N48 78W30 5:14:00

PENNSYLVANIA

Glenhurst 46 1 40N09 75W04 5:00:16
Gleniron 60 7 40N53 77W08 5:08:32
Glenloch 15 97 40N02 75W35 5:02:20
Glen Lyon 40 1 41N10 76W05 5:04:20
Glen Mawr 41 81 41N14 76W44 5:06:56
Glen Mills 23 4 39N55 75W30 5:02:00
Glenmoore 15 1 40N06 75W47 5:03:08
Glen Moore 36 8 40N04 76W19 5:05:16
Glenolden 23 9 39N54 75W18 5:01:12
Glen Richey 17 1 40N57 78W29 5:13:56
Glen Riddle 23 90 39N54 75W26 5:01:44
Glen Rock 67 3 39N48 76W44 5:06:56
Glen Rose 15 9 39N59 75W50 5:03:20
Glen Roy 15 3 39N45 76W01 5:04:04
Glenruadh 25 107 42N05 80W04 5:20:16
Glen Savage 56 1 40N07 79W50 5:19:20
Glenshaw 2 114 40N32 79W58 5:19:52
Glenside 46 9 40N06 75W09 5:00:36
Glenside Gardens 46
9 40N07 75W10 5:00:40
Glenside Heights 46
9 40N07 75W10 5:00:40
Glen Summit 40 20 41N14 75W52 5:03:28
Glenview 2 114 40N31 79W58 5:19:52
Glenville 67 3 39N47 76W47 5:07:08
Glenwall Village 4
13 40N37 80W16 5:21:04
Glenwillard 2 13 40N34 80W13 5:20:52
Glenwood 22 12 40N18 76W50 5:07:20
Glenwood 58 89 41N38 75W47 5:03:08
Glenworth 54 49 40N41 76W12 5:04:48
Glosser View 41 82 41N14 77W01 5:08:04
Glyndon 20 56 41N50 79W41 5:18:44
Gnatstown 67 1 39N48 76W59 5:07:56
Godfrey 3 4 40N38 79W37 5:18:28
Goff 10 6 41N06 79W54 5:19:36
Goheenville 3 64 40N55 79W28 5:17:52
Gold 53 6 41N52 77W51 5:11:24
Golden Hill 66 6 41N39 76W10 5:04:40
Goldsboro 67 1 40N09 76W45 5:07:00
Golf Villa 23 9 40N00 75W18 5:01:12
Good 28 100 39N45 77W34 5:10:16
Goodhope 21 12 40N12 77W00 5:08:00
Good Intent 63 6 40N07 80W25 5:21:40
Goodmans Corners 61
6 41N22 79W29 5:17:56
Goods Corner 11 74 40N20 78W56 5:15:44
Good Spring 54 9 40N38 76W24 5:05:36
Goodtown 56 6 39N56 78W57 5:15:48
Goodville 34 6 40N34 77W14 5:08:56
Goodville 36 27 40N08 76W00 5:04:00
Goodyear 21 1 40N00 77W12 5:08:48
Goosetown 15 9 39N59 75W50 5:03:20
Gordon 54 27 40N45 76W20 5:05:20
Gordonville 36 9 40N01 76W08 5:04:32
Goshen 17 6 41N07 78W23 5:13:32
Goshenville 15 13 39N57 75W36 5:02:24
Gosser Hill 65 4 40N38 79W37 5:18:28
Gouglersville 6 101 40N18 76W00 5:04:00
Gouldsboro 64 4 41N15 75W27 5:01:48
Gowen City 49 1 40N45 76W32 5:06:08
Grace Park 23 9 39N54 75W20 5:01:20
Graceton 32 71 40N30 79W10 5:16:40
Graceville 5 6 40N01 78W22 5:13:28
Gracey 29 66 39N59 78W04 5:12:16
Gradwohl Terrace 48
13 40N39 75W21 5:01:24
Gradyville 23 4 39N57 75W28 5:01:52
Graham 17 6 41N02 78W13 5:12:52
Grampian 17 7 40N58 78W37 5:14:28
Grampian Hills 41
82 41N14 77W01 5:08:04
Grand Valley 62 6 41N43 79W32 5:18:08
Grand View 3 15 40N49 79W32 5:18:08
Grandview 32 72 40N38 79W09 5:16:36
Grandview 63 1 40N11 79W54 5:19:36
Grandview Heights 36
8 40N04 76W19 5:05:16
Grand View Heights 46
90 40N08 75W21 5:01:24
Grandview Park 24
36 41N26 78W34 5:14:16
Grand View Park 46
8 40N12 75W28 5:01:52
Grandview Terrace 67
67 39N57 76W42 5:06:48
Grange 33 51 40N56 78W58 5:15:52
Grange Corners 20 6 40N47 79W14 5:16:56
Grange Hall Center 20
6 40N47 79W14 5:16:56
Grangeville 67 1 39N48 76W59 5:07:56
Granite 1 1 39N49 77W11 5:08:44
Grant 32 6 40N47 78W57 5:15:48
Grant City 37 6 40N56 80W08 5:20:32
Grantham 21 12 40N09 77W00 5:08:00
Grant Station 24 6 41N19 78W23 5:13:32
Grantville 22 1 40N23 76W39 5:06:36
Granville 44 73 40N33 77W38 5:10:32
Granville 63 51 40N02 79W58 5:19:52
Granville Center 8
7 41N43 76W47 5:07:08
Granville Summit 8
7 41N43 76W47 5:07:08
Grapeville 65 99 40N19 79W36 5:18:24
Grassflat 17 6 41N00 78W07 5:12:28
Grassmere Park 19 6 41N12 76W23 5:05:32
Grassy Island 35 18 41N28 75W36 5:02:24
Graterford 46 8 40N13 75W27 5:01:48
Gratton 32 98 40N28 79W12 5:16:48
Gratz 22 1 40N37 76W43 5:06:52
Gratztown 65 61 40N13 79W46 5:19:04
Gravity 64 59 41N27 75W23 5:01:32
Gray 30 6 39N56 80W23 5:21:32
Gray 56 6 40N08 79W05 5:16:20
Graydon 67 1 39N50 76W34 5:06:16
Grays Landing 26 51 39N51 79W54 5:19:36

Graysville 30 6 39N56 80W23 5:21:32
Graysville 31 6 40N37 78W08 5:12:32
Grazier 56 6 40N11 78W59 5:15:56
Grazierville 7 11 40N40 78W13 5:12:52
Greason 21 16 40N12 77W11 5:08:44
Great Bend 58 50 41N58 75W45 5:03:00
Greble 38 25 40N23 76W18 5:05:12
Greece City 10 6 40N57 79W45 5:19:00
Greeley 52 6 41N25 75W00 5:00:00
Green Acres 67 67 39N59 76W46 5:07:04
Greenawalds 39 13 40N37 75W31 5:02:04
Greenbank 36 27 40N07 76W05 5:04:20
Greenbrier 14 64 40N51 77W34 5:10:16
Greenbrier 23 90 40N00 75W23 5:01:32
Greenbrier 49 6 40N43 76W44 5:06:56
Greenburr 18 7 41N02 77W18 5:09:12
Greenbury 54 49 40N41 76W12 5:04:48
Greencastle 28 70 39N47 77W44 5:10:56
Greencrest Park 43
59 41N24 80W23 5:21:32
Greendale 42 75 41N40 78W49 5:15:16
Greene 36 1 39N47 76W14 5:04:56
Greene Junction 26
104 40N01 79W35 5:18:20
Greenfield 43 66 41N14 80W14 5:20:56
Greenfield Manor 6
101 40N21 75W56 5:03:44
Green Fields 22 1 40N35 76W37 5:06:28
Green Grove 35 18 41N28 75W36 5:02:24
Green Hill 15 13 39N57 75W36 5:02:24
Green Hill 67 67 39N57 76W42 5:06:48
Green Hills 23 9 39N54 75W17 5:01:08
Green Lane 46 8 40N20 75W28 5:01:52
Greenlawn Park 9 9 40N08 74W51 4:59:24
Greenmount 1 1 39N49 77W11 5:08:44
Greenock 2 3 40N19 79W49 5:19:16
Green Park 50 6 40N23 77W19 5:09:16
Green Point 38 1 40N22 77W43 5:10:52
Green Ridge 23 90 39N52 75W23 5:01:32
Green Ridge 40 42 40N58 76W00 5:04:00
Green Ridge 67 67 39N59 76W46 5:07:04
Greenridge Farms 46
1 40N09 75W03 5:00:12
Greensboro 30 51 39N48 79W55 5:19:40
Greensburg 65 99 40N18 79W33 5:18:12
Greens Landing 8 1 41N58 76W31 5:06:04
Greenspring 21 1 40N10 77W24 5:09:36
Green Springs 1 1 39N48 76W59 5:07:56
Greenstone 1 1 39N54 77W01 5:08:04
Greentown 52 6 41N19 75W18 5:01:12
Green Tree 15 8 40N02 75W30 5:02:00
Green Tree 2 114 40N25 80W05 5:20:20
Green Valley 2 114 40N23 79W49 5:19:16
Green Valley 33 34 41N10 79W05 5:16:20
Green Valley Acres 23
9 39N58 75W18 5:01:12
Greenview Park 23 9 40N00 75W18 5:01:12
Greenvillage 28 42 39N56 77W40 5:10:40
Greenville 17 6 41N00 78W07 5:12:28
Greenville 43 69 41N24 80W23 5:21:32
Greenwald 65 3 40N24 79W25 5:17:40
Greenwich 6 8 40N34 75W49 5:03:16
Greenwich 11 92 40N40 78W47 5:15:08
Greenwood 7 33 40N31 78W25 5:13:40
Greenwood 19 6 41N07 76W32 5:06:08
Greenwood 26 104 40N01 79W35 5:18:20
Greenwood 28 1 39N55 77W34 5:10:16
Greenwood 35 18 41N22 75W43 5:02:52
Greenwood Hills 22
12 40N18 76W50 5:07:20
Greenwood Village 10
3 40N53 79W53 5:19:32
Gregg 2 114 40N27 80W08 5:20:32
Gregory 40 20 41N16 75W54 5:03:36
Grenoble 9 1 40N12 75W05 5:00:20
Gresham 20 74 41N38 79W40 5:18:40
Greshville 6 2 40N20 75W38 5:02:32
Gretna 63 3 40N11 80W16 5:21:04
Grier City 54 27 40N48 76W20 5:05:20
Griers Corner 9 8 40N20 75W09 5:00:36
Griesemersville 6 2 40N20 75W38 5:02:32
Griffiths 42 75 41N40 78W49 5:15:16
Grill 6 101 40N19 75W57 5:03:48
Grimesville 41 82 41N14 77W01 5:08:04
Grimville 6 8 40N31 75W47 5:03:08
Grindstone 26 51 40N01 79W50 5:19:20
Gringo 4 13 40N34 80W17 5:21:08
Grisemore 32 6 40N40 79W00 5:16:00
Groffdale 36 27 40N07 76W05 5:04:20
Grovania 47 6 40N58 76W36 5:06:24
Grove 12 6 41N22 78W03 5:12:12
Grove 15 13 39N57 75W36 5:02:24
Grove Chapel 32 72 40N38 79W09 5:16:36
Grove City 43 70 41N10 80W05 5:20:20
Grover 8 7 41N37 76W52 5:07:28
Groveton 2 114 40N30 80W08 5:20:32
Grugan 18 7 41N15 77W36 5:10:24
Gruvertown 46 17 40N53 75W12 5:00:48
Guernsey 1 1 39N56 77W15 5:09:00
Guffey 42 59 41N44 78W39 5:14:36
Guffey 65 25 40N20 79W43 5:18:52
Guilford 28 42 39N54 77W37 5:10:28
Guilford Springs 28
42 39N56 77W40 5:10:40
Guitonville 27 6 41N28 79W07 5:16:28
Guldens 1 1 39N49 77W11 5:08:44
Gulich 17 63 40N46 78W24 5:13:36
Gulph Mills 46 90 40N05 75W17 5:01:08
Gump 30 1 39N54 80W11 5:20:44
Gum Tree 15 9 39N59 75W50 5:03:20
Guth 39 13 40N37 75W31 5:02:04
Guthriesville 15 46 40N02 75W46 5:03:04
Guthsville 39 13 40N38 75W35 5:02:20
Guyasuta 2 114 40N30 79W56 5:19:44
Guys Mills 20 6 41N38 79W59 5:19:56
Gwynedd 46 8 40N12 75W15 5:01:00

Gwynedd Square 46 8 40N15 75w17 5:01:08
Gwynedd Valley 46 8 40N11 75w16 5:01:04
Haafsville 39 9 40N33 75w38 5:02:32
Hackelbernie 13 80 40N52 75w44 5:02:56
Hackett 63 114 40N15 80w03 5:20:12
Haddenville 26 80 39N54 79w44 5:18:56
Haddock 54 42 40N58 76w00 5:04:00
Hadley 43 6 41N25 80w14 5:20:56
Haffey 2 114 40N29 79w50 5:19:20
Hagersville 9 8 40N25 75w23 5:01:32
Hahnstown 36 30 40N11 76w11 5:04:44
Hahntown 65 25 40N19 79w43 5:18:52
Haines 14 6 40N54 77w22 5:09:28
Haines Acres 67 67 39N59 76w46 5:07:04
Haleeka 41 7 41N19 77w05 5:08:20
Halfmoon 14 63 40N46 78w02 5:12:08
Halford Hills 46 90 40N08 75w21 5:01:24
Halfville 36 8 40N09 76w18 5:05:12
Halfway 38 8 40N20 76w26 5:05:44
Halifax 22 24 40N28 76w56 5:07:44
Hall 2 114 40N26 79w47 5:19:08
Hallam 67 1 40N00 76w36 5:06:24
Hallowell 46 1 40N11 75w10 5:00:40
Halls 41 83 41N12 76w47 5:07:08
Hallstead 58 50 41N58 75w45 5:03:00
Hallston 10 6 41N02 80w03 5:20:12
Hallton 24 6 41N17 79w07 5:16:28
Hallwood 40 1 41N12 76w04 5:04:16
Halsey 42 75 41N40 78w49 5:15:16
Hamburg 6 80 40N33 75w59 5:03:56
Hametown 67 3 39N48 76w44 5:06:56
Hamill 32 6 40N49 78w59 5:15:56
Hamilton 33 7 40N55 79w05 5:16:20
Hamilton 49 82 40N52 76w47 5:07:08
Hamiltonban 1 1 39N48 77w24 5:09:36
Hamilton Park 36 8 40N02 76w20 5:05:20
Hamilton Square 45 23 41N00 75w13 5:00:52
Hamlin 38 1 40N27 76w26 5:05:44
Hamlin 64 6 41N24 75w24 5:01:36
Hammersley Fork 18 7 41N26 77w55 5:11:40
Hammett 25 107 42N08 80w01 5:20:04
Hammond 59 59 41N54 77w08 5:08:32
Hammondville 26 111 40N09 79w33 5:18:12
Hamorton 15 8 39N52 75w39 5:02:36
Hampden 6 101 40N21 75w55 5:03:40
Hampden 21 12 40N15 76w58 5:07:52
Hampshire Heights 65 99 40N18 79w34 5:18:16
Hampton 1 1 39N52 77w03 5:08:12
Hampton 2 114 40N35 79w57 5:19:48
Hancock 6 9 40N30 75w40 5:02:40
Haneyville 18 76 41N08 77w28 5:09:52
Hanlin 63 6 40N23 80w24 5:21:36
Hannahstown 10 6 40N46 79w46 5:19:04
Hannastown 65 3 40N21 79w30 5:18:00
Hannasville 61 59 41N31 80w03 5:20:12
Hanover 40 21 41N12 76w00 5:04:00
Hanover 48 13 40N39 75w21 5:01:24
Hanover 67 1 39N48 76w59 5:07:56
Hanoverdale 22 1 41N09 79w41 5:18:44
Hanover Green 40 20 41N15 75w53 5:03:32
Hanover Heights 15 8 40N15 75w39 5:02:36
Hanover Junction 67 3 39N51 76w46 5:07:04
Hansotte Plan 3 15 40N46 79w32 5:18:08
Happy Valley 40 1 41N20 75w49 5:03:16
Harbor 37 112 41N00 80w21 5:21:24
Harborcreek 25 107 42N09 79w58 5:19:52
Harbor Woods 15 47 40N03 75w33 5:02:12
Harding 40 6 41N28 75w51 5:03:24
Harford 58 59 41N46 75w43 5:02:52
Harford Heights 65 25 40N20 79w43 5:18:52
Harlansburg 37 112 41N00 80w21 5:21:24
Harleigh 40 42 40N59 75w58 5:03:52
Harlem 6 2 40N23 75w37 5:02:28
Harleysville 46 8 40N17 75w23 5:01:32
Harmar 2 14 40N33 79w50 5:19:20
Harmar Heights 2 14 40N33 79w49 5:19:16
Harmarville 2 114 40N31 79w53 5:19:32
Harmonsburg 20 6 41N40 80w19 5:21:16
Harmonville 46 90 40N05 75w17 5:01:08
Harmony 10 6 40N48 80w08 5:20:32
Harmony 17 7 40N45 78w41 5:14:44
Harmony 33 51 40N56 78w58 5:15:52
Harmony Grove 67 1 40N00 76w58 5:07:52
Harmony Hill 15 46 40N00 75w42 5:02:48
Harmonyville 15 8 40N15 75w39 5:02:36
Harnedsville 56 53 39N49 79w21 5:17:24
Harpers 46 8 40N45 75w36 5:02:24
Harper Tavern 38 8 40N20 76w31 5:06:04
Harper Village 2 13 40N37 80w16 5:21:04
Harriman 9 9 40N08 74w51 4:59:24
Harris 14 6 40N48 77w45 5:11:00
Harris Acres 14 9 40N48 77w52 5:11:28
Harrisburg 22 12 40N16 76w53 5:07:32
Harrison 2 14 40N37 79w44 5:18:56
Harrison City 65 3 40N21 79w39 5:18:36
Harrison Valley 53 6 41N57 77w39 5:10:36
Harrisonville 29 66 39N59 78w04 5:12:16
Harristown 36 9 40N01 76w08 5:04:32
Harrisville 10 6 41N08 80w01 5:20:04
Harrity 13 8 40N50 75w42 5:02:48
Harrow 9 1 40N31 75w10 5:00:40
Harshaville 4 6 40N29 80w18 5:21:12
Hartleton 60 6 40N54 77w09 5:08:36
Hartley 5 70 39N58 78w31 5:14:04
Hartley 60 6 40N53 77w13 5:08:52
Hartranft 46 90 40N08 75w21 5:01:24
Hartsfield 59 6 41N33 77w06 5:08:24
Hartstown 20 63 41N33 80w23 5:21:32
Hartsville 9 1 40N12 75w05 5:00:20
Harvey Junction 40 20 41N16 75w54 5:03:36
Harveys Lake 40 6 41N22 76w02 5:04:08
Harveyville 40 1 41N09 76w10 5:04:40
Harwick 2 119 40N33 79w48 5:19:12
Harwood Mines 40 42 40N58 76w00 5:04:00
Harwood Park 23 9 39N58 75w18 5:01:12
Hasson Heights 61 9 41N25 79w42 5:18:48
Hastings 11 92 40N40 78w43 5:14:52
Hatboro 46 17 40N11 75w06 5:00:24
Hatfield 26 80 39N54 79w44 5:18:56
Hatfield 46 8 40N17 75w18 5:01:12
Hauto 13 1 40N52 75w49 5:03:16
Haverford 46 9 40N01 75w18 5:01:12
Haverford Park Apartments 23 9 40N01 75w17 5:01:08
Havertown 23 9 39N58 75w18 5:01:12
Hawkeye 65 111 40N08 79w35 5:18:20
Hawk Run 17 113 40N55 78w13 5:12:52
Hawksville 36 27 39N54 76w10 5:04:40
Hawley 64 6 41N28 75w11 5:00:44
Hawstone 44 73 40N36 77w34 5:10:16
Hawthorn 16 6 41N01 79w17 5:17:08
Hawthorne 16 6 41N01 79w17 5:17:08
Haycock 9 8 40N30 75w18 5:01:12
Haycock Run 9 8 40N25 75w23 5:01:32
Haydentown 26 51 39N48 79w49 5:19:16
Hayesville 15 3 39N47 75w59 5:03:56
Hayfield 20 77 41N43 80w13 5:20:52
Haynie 16 37 41N15 79w28 5:17:52
Hays 26 80 39N54 79w44 5:18:56
Hays Grove 21 1 40N10 77w24 5:09:36
Hays Mills 56 79 39N49 79w02 5:16:08
Haysville 2 114 40N32 80w09 5:20:36
Haysville 10 6 41N00 79w43 5:18:52
Hayti 15 9 39N59 75w51 5:03:24
Hazel Hurst 42 6 41N42 78w35 5:14:20
Hazel Kirk 63 1 40N11 79w54 5:19:36
Hazelwood 2 13 40N40 80w14 5:20:56
Hazen 33 6 41N12 78w58 5:15:52
Hazle 40 42 40N58 76w00 5:04:00
Hazleton 40 42 40N57 75w59 5:03:56
Hazle Village 40 42 40N58 76w00 5:04:00
Hazzard 63 1 40N11 79w54 5:19:36
Headlee Heights 30 6 39N49 80w02 5:20:08
Heart Lake 58 60 41N50 75w53 5:03:32
Heath 33 6 41N20 79w01 5:16:04
Heatherwold 23 90 39N54 75w22 5:01:28
Heath Station 33 6 41N24 78w56 5:15:44
Heathville 33 6 41N08 79w11 5:16:44
Hebe 49 51 40N43 76w51 5:07:24
Heberlig 21 1 40N10 77w24 5:09:36
Hebron 38 8 40N20 76w26 5:05:44
Hebron 53 6 41N52 78w03 5:12:12
Hebron Center 53 8 40N16 75w15 5:01:00
Heckescherville 54 27 40N43 76w17 5:05:08
Heckton 22 12 40N17 76w53 5:07:32
Hecktown 48 13 40N39 75w21 5:01:24
Hecla 54 1 40N41 76w00 5:04:00
Hector 53 6 41N51 77w39 5:10:36
Hegins 54 27 40N39 76w30 5:06:00
Heidelberg 2 114 40N24 80w05 5:20:20
Heidlersburg 1 1 39N49 77w11 5:08:44
Heilmandale 38 8 40N20 76w26 5:05:44
Heilwood 32 6 40N37 78w55 5:15:40
Heistersburg 26 6 39N59 80w00 5:20:00
Helen Furnace 16 37 41N12 79w22 5:17:28
Helfenstein 54 27 40N45 76w27 5:05:48
Helfrick Spring Apartments 39 13 40N39 75w30 5:02:00
Helixville 5 6 40N03 78w39 5:14:36
Hellam 67 64 40N01 76w36 5:06:24
Hellen Mills 24 6 40N45 76w04 5:04:16
Hellertown 48 13 40N35 75w21 5:01:24
Helvetia 17 56 41N03 78w43 5:14:52
Hemlock 19 4 41N01 76w31 5:06:04
Hemlock 62 120 41N52 79w09 5:16:36
Hemlock Grove 57 6 41N21 76w35 5:06:20
Henderson 43 6 41N20 80w06 5:20:24
Henderson Park 46 90 40N05 75w22 5:01:28
Hendersonville 63 114 40N18 80w09 5:20:36
Hendleton 6 101 40N19 75w57 5:03:48
Hendricks 46 8 40N19 75w27 5:01:48
Henningsville 6 13 40N31 75w36 5:02:24
Henrietta 7 51 40N19 78w20 5:13:20
Henry Clay 26 6 39N46 79w27 5:17:48
Henrys Bend 61 9 41N25 79w42 5:18:48
Henryville 45 84 41N06 75w15 5:01:00
Hensel 36 27 39N54 76w10 5:04:40
Hensingerville 39 13 40N31 75w36 5:02:24
Hepburn 41 7 41N20 77w03 5:08:12
Hepburn Heights 41 7 41N19 77w05 5:08:20
Hepburnia 17 7 40N58 78w36 5:14:24
Hepburnville 41 7 41N19 77w05 5:08:20
Hephzibah 15 9 39N59 75w50 5:03:20
Hepler 54 1 40N40 76w37 5:06:28
Herbert 26 51 39N57 79w53 5:19:32
Hercules 46 8 40N45 75w16 5:01:04
Hereford 6 1 40N27 75w34 5:02:16
Heritage Hills 2 8 40N17 79w50 5:19:20
Herman 10 3 40N50 79w49 5:19:16
Hermine No. 2 65 25 40N20 79w43 5:18:52
Herminie 65 25 40N16 79w43 5:18:52
Hermitage 43 117 41N15 80w30 5:22:00
Herndon 49 51 40N43 76w51 5:07:24
Herrick Center 58 59 41N44 75w29 5:01:56
Herrickville 8 6 41N40 76w16 5:05:04
Herrville 36 8 39N59 76w17 5:05:08
Hershey 22 31 40N17 76w39 5:06:36

PENNSYLVANIA

Hershey Heights 1 1 39N48 76w59 5:07:56
Heshbon 32 98 40N26 79w16 5:17:04
Heshbon Park 41 82 41N14 77w01 5:08:04
Hessdale 36 96 39N59 76w11 5:04:44
Hesston 31 3 40N26 78w07 5:12:28
Hetlerville 19 1 41N03 76w13 5:04:52
Hettesheimer Corners 66 6 41N25 76w03 5:04:12
Hiawatha 64 6 41N55 75w28 5:01:52
Hibbs 26 51 39N56 79w53 5:19:32
Hickernell 20 6 41N48 80w22 5:21:28
Hickman 2 114 40N27 80w08 5:20:32
Hickory 63 51 40N18 80w18 5:21:12
Hickory Corners 43 117 41N15 80w30 5:22:00
Hickory Corners 49 6 40N39 76w54 5:07:36
Hickory Grove 58 59 41N57 75w37 5:02:28
Hickory Heights 37 112 41N00 80w21 5:21:24
Hickoryhill 15 3 39N45 75w55 5:03:40
Hickory Hills 9 9 40N12 74w49 4:59:16
Hickorytown 21 16 40N12 77w11 5:08:44
Hickorytown 46 90 40N08 75w21 5:01:24
Hickox 53 6 41N59 77w52 5:11:28
Hicks Ferry 40 1 41N04 76w15 5:05:00
Hicks Hill 3 116 40N32 79w28 5:17:52
Hidden Valley 46 90 40N05 75w22 5:01:28
Higgins Corners 10 6 41N05 79w50 5:19:20
Highcliff 2 114 40N31 80w03 5:20:12
Highfield 10 3 40N51 79w54 5:19:36
High House 26 51 39N48 79w49 5:19:16
Highland 2 114 40N33 80w01 5:20:04
Highland 4 8 40N49 80w25 5:21:40
Highland 40 20 41N20 75w54 5:03:36
Highland 65 99 40N21 79w32 5:18:08
Highland Acres 36 8 40N02 76w17 5:05:08
Highland Corners 24 75 41N40 78w49 5:15:16
Highland Farms 9 1 40N13 75w01 5:00:04
Highland Meadows 2 8 40N17 79w50 5:19:20
Highland Park 11 74 40N17 78w53 5:15:32
Highland Park 21 12 40N14 76w57 5:07:48
Highland Park 23 9 39N58 75w18 5:01:12
Highland Park 25 107 42N05 80w04 5:20:16
Highland Park 44 73 40N36 77w34 5:10:16
Highland Park 46 12 40N41 75w14 5:00:56
Highland View 9 1 40N13 75w01 5:00:04
High Meadows 23 90 39N55 75w22 5:01:28
Highmount 67 1 40N01 76w36 5:06:24
High Park 46 1 40N11 75w06 5:00:24
Highrock 67 1 39N50 76w24 5:05:36
High Spire 22 12 40N13 76w47 5:07:08
Highville 36 8 39N57 76w21 5:05:24
Hill Church 6 2 40N20 75w38 5:02:32
Hill Church 63 2 40N16 80w11 5:20:44
Hill City 61 1 41N21 79w43 5:18:52
Hillcrest 2 114 40N20 80w02 5:20:08
Hillcrest 4 13 40N37 80w16 5:21:04
Hill Crest 26 104 40N01 79w35 5:18:20
Hillcrest 43 117 41N14 80w29 5:21:56
Hill Crest 46 9 40N03 75w08 5:00:32
Hillcrest 67 67 39N57 76w42 5:06:48
Hillcroft 67 67 39N57 76w42 5:06:48
Hilldale 40 20 41N15 75w53 5:03:32
Hiller 26 1 40N01 79w54 5:19:36
Hilliards 10 6 41N05 79w50 5:19:20
Hillman 32 51 40N56 78w58 5:15:52
Hillsboro 56 123 40N15 78w50 5:15:20
Hillsdale 32 6 40N45 78w53 5:15:32
Hillsgrove 57 6 41N26 76w43 5:06:52
Hillside 39 13 40N38 75w35 5:02:20
Hillside 40 20 41N20 75w56 5:03:44
Hillside 54 49 40N41 76w12 5:04:48
Hillside 65 3 40N20 79w18 5:17:12
Hillside Junction 35 18 41N22 75w43 5:02:52
Hillside Village 9 8 40N21 75w13 5:00:52
Hills Terrace 54 3 40N49 76w08 5:04:32
Hillsview 65 110 40N15 79w14 5:16:56
Hillsville 37 1 41N01 80w30 5:22:00
Hill Top Acres 3 15 40N46 79w32 5:18:08
Hilltop Acres 36 8 40N02 76w20 5:05:20
Hilltown 1 1 39N56 77w15 5:09:00
Hilltown 9 8 40N22 75w18 5:01:12
Hillville 3 6 41N00 79w43 5:18:52
Hilton 67 1 40N00 76w58 5:07:52
Hinkletown 9 1 40N26 75w09 5:00:36
Hinkletown 36 30 40N11 76w11 5:04:44
Hinkson Corner 23 90 39N54 75w22 5:01:28
Hiyasota 56 6 40N11 78w59 5:15:56
Hobart 67 1 39N48 76w59 5:07:56
Hobbie 40 1 41N04 76w08 5:04:32
Hoblitzell 5 51 39N50 78w43 5:14:52
Hockersville 21 1 40N10 77w24 5:09:36
Hockersville 22 31 40N17 76w39 5:06:36
Hoernerstown 22 12 40N16 76w43 5:06:52
Hoffer 55 51 40N42 76w52 5:07:28
Hoffman 39 8 40N45 75w37 5:02:28
Hoffmansville 46 8 40N18 75w32 5:02:08
Hogestown 21 12 40N12 77w00 5:08:00
Hoguetown 11 55 40N28 78w35 5:14:20
Hokendauqua 39 13 40N39 75w30 5:02:00
Holbrook 30 6 39N51 80w19 5:21:16
Holicong 9 8 40N20 75w02 5:00:08
Holiday Park 2 14 40N29 79w44 5:18:56
Holland 9 8 40N11 74w59 4:59:56
Hollenback 40 6 41N04 76w05 5:04:20
Hollentown 11 54 40N41 78w30 5:14:00
Hollers Hill 40 42 40N58 76w00 5:04:00

Holley Heights 67 67 39N58 76w47 5:07:08
Hollidaysburg 7 33 40N26 78w24 5:13:36
Hollinger 36 8 40N02 76w20 5:05:20
Hollisterville 64 4 41N20 75w32 5:02:08
Hollsopple 56 66 40N11 78w59 5:15:56
Hollywood 17 7 41N17 78w30 5:14:00
Hollywood 40 42 40N58 76w00 5:04:00
Hollywood 46 9 40N05 75w07 5:00:28
Hollywood 67 67 39N57 76w42 5:06:48
Hollywood Heights 67 67 39N57 76w42 5:06:48
Holmes 23 9 39N55 75w19 5:01:16
Holmesburg 51 9 40N03 75w02 5:00:08
Holters Crossing 14 63 41N01 77w39 5:10:36
Holtwood 36 7 39N50 76w20 5:05:20
Home 32 6 40N44 79w06 5:16:24
Home Acres 67 67 39N57 76w42 5:06:48
Homecamp 17 6 41N05 78w39 5:14:36
Homeland 36 8 40N04 76w19 5:05:16
Home Park 39 13 40N39 75w30 5:02:00
Homer 53 66 41N43 78w01 5:12:04
Homer City 32 71 40N32 79w10 5:16:40
Homer Gap 7 33 40N31 78w25 5:13:40
Homestead 2 114 40N24 79w55 5:19:40
Homestead Park 2 114 40N24 79w54 5:19:36
Homesville 54 27 40N47 76w21 5:05:24
Hometown 54 27 40N49 75w59 5:03:56
Homets Ferry 8 60 41N40 76w16 5:05:04
Homeville 15 3 39N52 75w59 5:03:56
Homeville 2 114 40N22 79w54 5:19:36
Homeville 15 59 41N31 80w03 5:20:12
Homewood 2 114 40N27 79w54 5:19:36
Homewood 4 121 40N49 80w20 5:21:20
Homewood 67 1 40N07 77w02 5:08:08
Honeoye 53 29 41N58 78w11 5:12:44
Honesdale 64 22 41N34 75w16 5:01:04
Honey Brook 15 27 40N05 75w55 5:03:40
Honey Grove 34 6 40N24 77w33 5:10:12
Honey Pot 40 21 41N12 76w00 5:04:00
Hoodville 61 1 41N11 79w43 5:18:52
Hooker 10 6 41N00 79w43 5:18:52
Hookstown 4 6 40N37 80w28 5:21:52
Hoover 26 51 39N53 79w52 5:19:28
Hooverhurst 32 6 40N50 78w50 5:15:20
Hoovers 62 3 41N42 79w02 5:16:08
Hooversville 56 6 40N09 78w55 5:15:40
Hooverville 65 7 40N25 79w01 5:16:04
Hop Bottom 58 89 41N42 75w46 5:03:04
Hopeland 36 28 40N14 76w16 5:05:04
Hopewell 5 6 40N09 78w16 5:13:04
Hopewell 15 3 39N47 75w59 5:03:56
Hoppenville 46 2 40N24 75w30 5:02:00
Hopwood 26 80 39N53 79w42 5:18:48
Hormtown 33 6 41N06 78w53 5:15:32
Horn Brook 8 41 41N46 76w27 5:05:48
Hornby 25 91 42N13 79w50 5:19:20
Horning 2 114 40N23 79w59 5:19:56
Horningford 44 73 40N36 77w34 5:10:16
Horrell 7 33 40N25 78w24 5:13:36
Horseshoe Heights 36 8 40N02 76w17 5:05:08
Horsham 46 1 40N11 75w08 5:00:32
Horton 24 5 41N17 78w43 5:14:52
Hortons Corners 8 6 41N40 76w16 5:05:04
Hosensack 39 13 40N29 75w30 5:02:00
Hosensock 54 27 40N48 76w20 5:05:20
Hospital 46 90 40N08 75w21 5:01:24
Host 6 1 40N22 76w11 5:04:44
Hostetter 65 3 40N16 79w24 5:17:36
Hottelville 27 6 41N28 79w07 5:16:28
Houserville 14 9 40N48 77w52 5:11:28
Houston 63 2 40N15 80w13 5:20:52
Houston City 40 1 41N19 75w46 5:03:04
Housum 28 42 39N56 77w40 5:10:40
Houtzdale 17 4 40N50 78w21 5:13:24
Hovey 3 1 41N08 79w41 5:18:44
Howard 2 114 40N24 79w54 5:19:36
Howard 12 106 41N31 78w14 5:12:56
Howard 14 63 41N01 77w40 5:10:40
Howell Park 2 8 40N17 79w50 5:19:20
Howellville 15 90 40N03 75w26 5:01:44
Howersville 46 8 40N45 75w36 5:02:24
Howerton 48 13 40N41 75w22 5:01:28
Hoytdale 4 121 40N53 80w20 5:21:20
Hoytville 59 6 41N36 77w18 5:09:12
Hublersburg 14 63 40N58 77w37 5:10:28
Hubley 54 27 40N38 76w37 5:06:28
Huckenberry 17 6 40N59 78w08 5:12:32
Hudson 17 113 40N54 78w13 5:12:52
Hudson 40 20 41N15 75w53 5:03:32
Hudsondale 13 60 40N57 75w49 5:03:16
Huefner 16 6 41N19 79w22 5:17:28
Huey 16 7 41N05 79w31 5:18:04
Huff 32 29 40N23 79w04 5:16:16
Huffs Church 6 13 40N31 75w36 5:02:24
Hughes Park 46 90 40N05 75w22 5:01:28
Hughestown 40 1 41N20 75w46 5:03:04
Hughesville 41 81 41N14 76w44 5:06:56
Hughs 40 1 41N12 76w04 5:04:16
Hulltown 26 104 40N03 79w39 5:18:36
Hulmeville 9 97 40N09 74w55 4:59:40
Hulmeville Park 9 97 40N10 74w55 4:59:40
Hulton 2 14 40N31 79w50 5:19:20
Humbolt 40 42 40N58 76w00 5:04:00
Hummels Store 6 101 40N18 75w59 5:03:56
Hummelstown 22 12 40N16 76w43 5:06:52
Hummels Wharf 55 82 40N50 76w50 5:07:20
Humphreys 65 99 40N18 79w34 5:18:16
Humphreyville 15 9 39N59 75w50 5:03:20
Hundred Spring 31 11 40N40 78w13 5:12:52
Hungry Hollow 3 4 40N38 79w37 5:18:28
Hunker 65 111 40N12 79w37 5:18:28
Hunlock 40 1 41N14 76w06 5:04:24
Hunlock Creek 40 1 41N12 76w04 5:04:16
Hunlock Gardens 40 1 41N12 76w04 5:04:16
Hunter 49 27 40N48 76w33 5:06:12
Hunter Hill 46 90 40N07 75w16 5:01:04
Hunters Run 21 56 40N00 77w12 5:08:48
Hunterstown 1 1 39N49 77w11 5:08:44
Huntersville 41 83 41N12 76w47 5:07:08
Huntingdon 31 81 40N30 78w01 5:12:04
Huntingdon Furnace 31 11 40N40 78w13 5:12:52
Huntingdon Heights 65 25 40N20 79w43 5:18:52
Huntingdon Manor 36 28 40N05 76w11 5:04:44
Huntingdon Meadows 46 1 40N09 75w03 5:00:12
Huntingdon Valley 46 1 40N09 75w03 5:00:12
Hunting Park 51 9 40N01 75w09 5:00:36
Huntington Mills 40 1 41N11 76w14 5:04:56
Huntley 12 7 41N21 78w08 5:12:32
Huntsdale 21 16 40N12 77w11 5:08:44
Huntsville 40 20 41N20 75w56 5:03:44
Husband 56 6 40N01 79w05 5:16:20
Huskin 56 63 40N07 78w49 5:15:16
Hustons Mill 21 12 40N12 77w00 5:08:00
Hustontown 29 6 40N03 78w02 5:12:08
Hutchins 42 59 41N44 78w39 5:14:36
Hutchinson 26 80 39N54 79w44 5:18:56
Hutchinson 65 61 40N13 79w44 5:18:56
Hyde 17 1 41N01 78w28 5:13:52
Hyde Park 6 101 40N23 75w56 5:03:44
Hyde Park 65 4 40N38 79w35 5:18:20
Hydes 24 5 41N16 78w44 5:14:56
Hydetown 20 7 41N39 79w43 5:18:52
Hyde Villa 6 101 40N23 75w56 5:03:44
Hyndman 5 51 39N49 78w43 5:14:52
Hynemansville 39 1 40N41 75w45 5:03:00
Hyner 18 7 41N20 77w39 5:10:36
Icedale 15 27 40N06 75w55 5:03:40
Icedale Mobile Homes 15 27 40N06 75w55 5:03:40
Ickesburg 50 7 40N27 77w21 5:09:24
Idaho 3 6 40N40 79w18 5:17:12
Idamar 32 7 40N43 79w01 5:16:04
Idaville 1 1 40N01 77w12 5:08:48
Idetown 40 6 41N22 76w02 5:04:08
Idlewood 2 114 40N26 80w04 5:20:16
Imler 5 7 40N12 78w31 5:14:04
Imlertown 5 70 39N58 78w31 5:14:04
Immaculata 15 8 40N01 75w35 5:02:20
Imperial 2 51 40N27 80w15 5:21:00
Independence 55 51 40N42 76w52 5:07:28
Independence 63 6 40N15 80w31 5:22:04
Indiana 32 72 40N37 79w09 5:16:36
Indian Crossing 42 40 41N57 78w23 5:13:32
Indian Head 26 6 40N01 79w24 5:17:36
Indian Head 26 6 40N01 79w24 5:17:36
Indian King 15 13 39N57 75w36 5:02:24
Indian Lake 56 63 40N03 78w52 5:15:28
Indianland 46 8 40N45 75w36 5:02:24
Indian Mountain Lake 13 1 40N57 75w29 5:01:56
Indianola 2 14 40N34 79w52 5:19:28
Indian Pines 2 114 40N26 80w04 5:20:16
Indian Town Gap 12 40N20 76w50 5:07:20
Indian Village 1 1 39N48 76w59 5:07:56
Industry 4 19 40N40 80w24 5:21:36
Inez 53 66 41N46 78w01 5:12:04
Ingleby 14 6 40N54 77w21 5:09:24
Inglenook 22 24 40N28 76w56 5:07:44
Ingleside 11 74 40N17 78w53 5:15:32
Inglesmith 5 6 39N45 78w27 5:13:48
Ingomar 2 114 40N35 80w04 5:20:16
Ingram 2 114 40N27 80w04 5:20:16
Inkerman 40 1 41N19 75w47 5:03:08
Intercourse 36 23 40N02 76w06 5:04:24
Iola 19 6 41N07 76w32 5:06:08
Iona 38 8 40N20 76w26 5:05:44
Irishtown 1 1 39N52 77w03 5:08:12
Irishtown 17 7 40N58 78w36 5:14:24
Irishtown 42 6 41N52 78w40 5:14:40
Irishtown 43 66 41N14 80w14 5:20:56
Iron Bridge 26 111 40N09 79w33 5:18:12
Iron Springs 1 1 39N47 77w22 5:09:28
Ironton 39 13 40N40 75w30 5:02:00
Ironville 7 11 40N40 78w13 5:12:52
Ironville 36 26 40N02 76w31 5:06:04
Irvin 2 114 40N22 79w54 5:19:36
Irvine 62 3 41N50 79w17 5:17:08
Irving 54 9 40N36 76w23 5:05:32
Irvona 17 54 40N46 78w33 5:14:12
Irwin 65 25 40N20 79w43 5:18:52
Isabella 26 51 39N57 79w56 5:19:44
Iselin 32 6 40N34 79w23 5:17:32
Iselin Heights 17 56 41N07 78w46 5:15:04
Island Park 49 82 40N52 76w47 5:07:08
Ithan 23 90 40N02 75w20 5:01:20
Itley 25 7 41N53 80w08 5:20:32
Iva 36 9 40N01 76w08 5:04:32
Ivarea 25 7 41N54 80w20 5:21:20
Ivyland 9 1 40N12 75w04 5:00:16
Ivy Mills 23 4 39N54 75w28 5:01:52
J & B Junction 42 59 41N44 78w39 5:14:36
Jacks Mountain 1 1 39N47 77w22 5:09:28
Jackson 58 6 41N50 75w36 5:02:24
Jackson Center 43 6 41N16 80w08 5:20:32
Jackson Corner 31 81 40N30 78w01 5:12:04

PENNSYLVANIA

Jackson Hall 28 42 39N56 77w40 5:10:40
Jackson Knolls 37 112 41N00 80w21 5:21:24
Jackson Summit 59 6 41N59 76w56 5:07:44
Jacksonville 14 63 41N01 77w39 5:10:36
Jacksonville 32 6 40N33 79w17 5:17:08
Jacksonville 39 56 40N37 75w53 5:03:32
Jacksonville 48 13 40N45 75w24 5:01:36
Jacksonwald 6 101 40N20 75w53 5:03:32
Jacksville 10 6 41N02 80w03 5:20:12
Jacktown 65 25 40N20 79w43 5:18:52
Jacktown Acres 65 25 40N20 79w43 5:18:52
Jacobs Creek 65 6 40N08 79w45 5:19:00
Jacobs Mills 67 1 39N48 76w59 5:07:56
Jacobus 67 3 39N53 76w42 5:06:48
Jalappa 6 80 40N33 75w59 5:03:56
James City 24 75 41N37 78w51 5:15:24
James Creek 31 3 40N23 78w10 5:12:40
James Manor 9 8 40N21 75w13 5:00:52
Jamestown 11 63 40N23 78w40 5:14:40
Jamestown 13 8 40N50 75w42 5:02:48
Jamestown 43 63 41N29 80w27 5:21:48
Jamesville 48 13 40N45 75w24 5:01:36
Jamison 9 8 40N16 75w05 5:00:20
Jamison 26 80 39N54 79w44 5:18:56
Jamison City 19 6 41N12 76w23 5:05:32
Japan 40 20 41N20 75w54 5:03:36
Jarrettown 46 1 40N09 75w12 5:00:48
Jay 24 7 41N18 78w30 5:14:00
Jeanesville 40 42 40N58 76w00 5:04:00
Jeannette 65 3 40N19 79w37 5:18:28
Jeddo 40 6 41N59 75w54 5:03:36
Jednota 22 80 40N12 76w43 5:06:52
Jefferis Crossing 26 80 39N54 79w44 5:18:56
Jefferson 2 8 40N18 79w55 5:19:40
Jefferson 30 6 39N56 80w03 5:20:12
Jefferson 54 1 40N36 76w05 5:04:20
Jefferson 63 6 40N17 80w28 5:21:52
Jefferson Center 10 3 40N53 79w53 5:19:32
Jeffersonville 46 90 40N08 75w21 5:01:24
Jenkins 40 20 41N18 75w48 5:03:12
Jenkintown 46 9 40N06 75w08 5:00:32
Jenkintown Manor 46 9 40N05 75w07 5:00:28
Jenks 27 6 41N28 79w07 5:16:28
Jenner 56 6 40N11 79w03 5:16:12
Jenners 56 6 40N09 79w02 5:16:08
Jennerstown 56 6 40N10 79w04 5:16:16
Jennersville 15 1 39N49 75w50 5:03:20
Jenningsville 66 59 41N34 76w04 5:04:16
Jericho 12 116 40N29 79w27 5:17:48
Jericho Mills 34 7 40N35 77w24 5:09:36
Jericho Valley 9 8 40N22 74w56 4:59:44
Jermyn 35 1 41N32 75w33 5:02:12
Jerome 56 74 40N13 78w59 5:15:56
Jerome Junction 56 6 40N11 78w59 5:15:56
Jersey Mills 41 6 41N21 77w25 5:09:40
Jersey Shore 41 73 41N12 77w15 5:09:00
Jerseytown 19 4 41N00 76w25 5:05:40
Jessup 35 1 41N28 75w34 5:02:16
Jessup-Peckville 35 1 41N28 75w34 5:02:16
Jewell 2 114 40N20 80w02 5:20:08
Jewtown 32 6 40N37 78w55 5:15:40
Jim Thorpe 13 80 40N52 75w44 5:02:56
Joanna 6 56 40N11 75w52 5:03:28
Jobs Corners 59 6 41N59 76w56 5:07:44
Joffre 63 6 40N23 80w22 5:21:28
Johnsonburg 24 36 41N29 78w41 5:14:44
Johnson Greene 40 20 41N15 75w57 5:03:48
Johnsons Corner 23 1 39N52 75w35 5:02:20
Johnstown 11 74 40N19 78w55 5:15:40
Johnstown 60 6 40N55 77w03 5:08:12
Johnsville 9 1 40N12 75w05 5:00:20
John Wanamaker 51 9 39N57 75w09 5:00:36
Jo Jo 42 75 41N40 78w49 5:15:16
Jollett 54 9 40N38 76w24 5:05:36
Joller 31 6 40N11 78w07 5:12:28
Jollytown 30 2 40N41 79w41 5:18:44
Jonas 45 9 40N52 75w27 5:01:48
Jones 24 7 41N34 78w40 5:14:40
Jones Mills 65 6 40N05 79w21 5:17:24
Jones Terrace 46 12 40N41 75w14 5:00:56
Jonestown 19 4 41N05 76w25 5:05:40
Jonestown 38 1 40N22 77w43 5:10:52
Jonestown 54 49 40N41 76w12 5:04:48
Jonestown 63 1 40N08 79w54 5:19:36
Jordan 39 8 40N42 75w42 5:02:48
Jordan Park Apartments 39 13 40N39 75w30 5:02:00
Jordan Valley 39 8 40N42 75w42 5:02:48
Josephine 32 98 40N27 79w13 5:16:52
Jugtown 28 100 39N45 77w34 5:10:16
Julian 14 7 40N52 77w58 5:11:52
Jumonville 26 80 39N52 79w42 5:18:48
Juneau 32 51 40N53 78w56 5:15:44
Junedale 13 42 40N55 75w57 5:03:48
June Meadows 46 1 40N09 75w03 5:00:12
Juniata 7 33 40N31 78w25 5:13:40
Juniata 26 105 39N59 79w37 5:18:28
Juniata 50 1 40N29 77w12 5:08:48
Juniata Gap 7 33 40N31 78w25 5:13:40
Juniata Terrace 44 73 40N35 77w35 5:10:20
Just A Farm 46 1 40N09 75w03 5:00:12
Justus 35 45 41N30 75w43 5:02:52
Kaiserville 66 59 41N37 76w03 5:04:12
Kammerer 63 2 40N11 80w08 5:20:32
Kane 42 75 41N40 78w49 5:15:16

Kanesholm 42 75 41N40 78w49 5:15:16
Kaneville 61 9 41N25 79w42 5:18:48
Kantner 56 6 40N08 78w58 5:15:52
Kantz 55 82 40N48 76w52 5:07:28
Kaolin 15 8 39N48 75w44 5:02:56
Kapp Heights 49 82 40N54 76w48 5:07:12
Karen 63 51 40N02 79w55 5:19:40
Karns 2 14 40N37 79w44 5:18:56
Karns City 10 1 40N59 79w43 5:18:52
Karthaus 17 6 41N07 78w07 5:12:28
Kaseville 47 6 40N58 76w36 5:06:24
Kasiesville 28 51 39N50 77w55 5:11:40
Kaska 54 27 40N44 76w07 5:04:28
Kasson 42 93 41N49 78w27 5:13:48
Kauffman 28 42 39N56 77w40 5:10:40
Kaufmann's 2 114 40N22 80w03 5:20:12
Kaufmann's-McKnight Road 2 114 40N33 80w01 5:20:04
Kaylor 3 7 40N57 79w45 5:19:00
Kaywin 39 13 40N38 75w23 5:01:32
Kearney 5 51 40N10 78w13 5:12:52
Kearsarge 25 107 42N05 80w04 5:20:16
Keating 18 7 41N18 77w51 5:11:24
Keating Junction 18 7 41N18 77w51 5:11:24
Keating Summit 53 75 41N40 78w49 5:15:16
Kecksburg 65 111 40N09 79w33 5:18:12
Kedron Park 23 9 39N54 75w20 5:01:20
Keech 53 6 41N59 77w52 5:11:28
Keelersville 9 8 40N25 75w23 5:01:32
Keeneyville 59 6 41N52 77w19 5:09:16
Keepville 25 7 41N54 80w22 5:21:28
Keewaydin 17 6 41N06 78w13 5:12:52
Keffer 65 110 40N15 79w14 5:16:56
Kehley Run Junction 54 27 40N49 76w12 5:04:48
Keifertown 26 111 40N06 79w35 5:18:20
Keisters 10 6 41N02 80w03 5:20:12
Keisterville 26 80 39N57 79w48 5:19:12
Kelayres 54 60 40N54 76w00 5:04:00
Kellers Church 9 8 40N25 75w23 5:01:32
Kellersville 45 23 41N00 75w13 5:00:52
Kellettville 27 6 41N30 79w27 5:17:48
Kelly 3 15 40N46 79w32 5:18:08
Kelly 60 70 41N00 76w55 5:07:40
Kelly Crossroads 60 70 40N58 76w54 5:07:36
Kelly Point 60 70 40N58 76w54 5:07:36
Kellytown 17 122 40N50 78w41 5:14:44
Kellytown 59 59 41N50 77w01 5:08:04
Kellyville 23 9 39N57 75w18 5:01:12
Kelton 15 1 39N49 75w53 5:03:32
Kemblesville 15 1 39N45 75w50 5:03:20
Kemmererville 45 23 41N00 75w13 5:00:52
Kempton 6 56 40N37 75w53 5:03:32
Kendall 4 6 40N39 80w30 5:22:00
Kendall Creek 42 102 41N57 78w39 5:14:36
Kendrick 17 4 40N50 78w21 5:13:24
Kenhorst 6 101 40N19 75w57 5:03:48
Kenilworth 15 8 40N14 75w38 5:02:32
Kenmawr 2 114 40N29 80w07 5:20:28
Kennard 43 59 41N24 80w23 5:21:32
Kennedy 2 114 40N29 80w06 5:20:24
Kennedy 59 6 41N45 77w18 5:09:12
Kennedy Mill 37 6 40N56 80w08 5:20:32
Kennerdell 61 6 41N17 79w44 5:18:56
Kennett 15 8 39N51 75w41 5:02:44
Kennett Square 15 8 39N51 75w43 5:02:52
Kenny 2 114 40N22 79w54 5:19:36
Kenny Row 26 51 39N56 79w50 5:19:20
Kennywood 2 114 40N22 79w54 5:19:36
Kensington 51 9 39N59 75w08 5:00:32
Kent 32 6 40N33 79w17 5:17:08
Kenwick Village 36 8 40N04 76w19 5:05:16
Kenwood 32 6 40N40 79w00 5:16:00
Kepner 54 1 40N41 76w00 5:04:00
Kepple Hill 3 4 40N37 79w34 5:18:16
Kepples Corner 10 6 40N57 79w45 5:19:00
Kernsville 39 13 40N38 75w35 5:02:20
Kerr 17 114 40N18 80w09 5:20:36
Kerrmoor 17 7 40N57 78w33 5:14:12
Kerrsville 21 16 40N12 77w11 5:08:44
Kerrtown 20 77 41N40 80w07 5:20:28
Kersey 24 36 41N22 78w36 5:14:24
Kesslerville 46 8 40N45 75w18 5:01:12
Ketcham 40 20 41N20 75w56 5:03:44
Keys 67 1 39N50 76w34 5:06:16
Keystone 24 5 41N16 78w44 5:14:56
Keystone 40 20 41N15 75w53 5:03:32
Keystone 56 79 39N49 79w02 5:16:08
Keystone 65 25 40N16 79w43 5:18:52
Khedive 30 51 39N54 79w58 5:19:52
Kidder 13 94 41N04 75w40 5:02:40
Kilbuck 2 114 40N31 80w06 5:20:24
Kilgore 43 6 41N20 80w06 5:20:24
Killinger 22 1 40N33 76w57 5:07:48
Kimberton 15 8 40N08 75w34 5:02:16
Kimbles 52 6 41N29 75w11 5:00:44
Kimmell 5 7 40N15 78w30 5:14:00
Kimmelton 56 6 40N07 78w57 5:15:48
Kim Plan 65 25 40N20 79w43 5:18:52
Kinderhook 36 26 40N02 76w31 5:06:04
Kindts Corner 6 80 40N30 75w58 5:03:52
King 5 7 40N12 78w32 5:14:08
King of Prussia 46 90 40N05 75w23 5:01:32
Kingsdale 1 56 39N45 77w05 5:08:20
Kingsley 27 59 41N32 79w16 5:17:04
Kingsley 58 59 41N46 75w43 5:02:52
Kings Manor 46 90 40N05 75w22 5:01:28
Kingston 40 20 41N16 75w54 5:03:36
Kingston 65 3 40N19 79w23 5:17:32
Kingston-Forty Fort 40 20 41N16 75w54 5:03:36
Kingsville 16 6 41N08 79w11 5:16:44
Kingswood Park 9 9 40N08 74w51 4:59:24
Kingview 26 111 40N06 79w35 5:18:20
Kingwood 56 4 39N52 79w14 5:16:56
Kinkora Heights 50 51 40N24 77w02 5:08:08
Kinlock 65 14 40N34 79w45 5:19:00
Kinney 53 6 41N59 77w52 5:11:28
Kinport 11 63 40N44 78w49 5:15:16
Kintnersville 9 1 40N31 75w11 5:00:44
Kinzers 36 23 40N00 76w06 5:04:24
Kirby 30 1 39N54 80w11 5:20:44
Kirklyn 23 9 39N58 75w18 5:01:12
Kirks Mills 36 3 39N45 76w01 5:04:04
Kirkwood 36 3 39N51 76w03 5:04:12
Kirwan Heights 2 114 40N22 80w06 5:20:24
Kiskimere 3 4 40N37 79w34 5:18:16
Kiskiminetas 3 4 40N35 79w29 5:17:56
Kissel Hill 36 8 40N09 76w18 5:05:12
Kissimmee 55 6 40N47 77w03 5:08:12
Kissingers Mill 16 7 41N02 79w30 5:18:00
Kistler 44 85 40N23 77w52 5:11:28
Kistler 50 6 40N22 77w21 5:09:24
Kitches Corners 43 59 41N24 80w23 5:21:32
Kittanning 3 15 40N49 79w31 5:18:04
Kittanning Heights 3 15 40N50 79w33 5:18:12
Klahr 7 3 40N18 78w27 5:13:48
Klecknersville 48 13 40N45 75w24 5:01:36
Kleinfeltersville 38 25 40N18 76w17 5:05:08
Kline 54 60 40N54 76w00 5:04:00
Klines Corner 6 9 40N30 75w40 5:02:40
Klines Grove 49 82 40N52 76w47 5:07:08
Klinesville 6 1 40N34 75w53 5:03:32
Klinesville 36 26 40N02 76w31 5:06:04
Klingerstown 54 1 40N40 76w37 5:06:28
Klondike 42 6 41N52 78w40 5:14:40
Klondyke 44 73 40N36 77w34 5:10:16
Knapp 59 6 41N45 77w18 5:09:12
Knauers 6 101 40N18 75w59 5:03:56
Knauertown 15 1 40N10 75w44 5:02:56
Knepper 28 100 39N45 77w34 5:10:16
Knightsbridge 2 114 40N26 80w04 5:20:16
Knightsville 31 85 40N24 77w56 5:11:44
Knobsville 29 66 39N56 78w00 5:12:00
Knoebel's Grove 49 1 40N52 76w33 5:06:12
Knousetown 34 1 40N33 77w09 5:08:36
Knowltonwood 23 90 39N54 75w23 5:01:32
Knox 4 121 40N52 80w16 5:21:04
Knox 16 35 41N14 79w32 5:18:08
Knox Dale 33 34 41N13 79w03 5:16:12
Knoxlyn 1 1 39N49 77w11 5:08:44
Knoxville 26 51 40N02 79w55 5:19:40
Knoxville 59 6 41N57 77w27 5:09:48
Kohinoor Junction 54 27 40N49 76w12 5:04:48
Koonsville 40 1 41N09 76w10 5:04:40
Koppel 4 121 40N50 80w20 5:21:20
Korn Krest 40 20 41N15 75w53 5:03:32
Kossuth 16 6 41N17 79w34 5:18:16
Kralltown 67 1 39N56 76w59 5:07:56
Kratzerville 55 82 40N48 76w52 5:07:28
Kraussdale 39 2 40N25 75w31 5:02:04
Krayn 11 123 40N15 78w50 5:15:20
Kreamer 55 6 40N49 76w58 5:07:52
Kreidersville 48 13 40N41 75w22 5:01:28
Kremis 43 59 41N24 80w23 5:21:32
Kresgeville 45 1 40N57 75w29 5:01:56
Kreutz Creek 67 1 40N01 76w36 5:06:24
Kricktown 6 101 40N18 76w00 5:04:00
Krings 11 74 40N17 78w53 5:15:32
Krocksville 39 13 40N37 75w31 5:02:04
Krumrine 14 9 40N48 77w52 5:11:28
Krumsville 6 1 40N34 75w53 5:03:32
Kuhnsville 39 13 40N35 75w28 5:01:52
Kuhntown 30 6 39N45 80w18 5:21:12
Kulp 19 4 40N57 76w28 5:05:52
Kulpmont 49 27 40N48 76w29 5:05:56
Kulps Corner 9 8 40N25 75w23 5:01:32
Kulpsville 8 40N14 75w20 5:01:20
Kulptown 6 8 40N15 75w44 5:02:56
Kunkle 40 20 41N20 75w56 5:03:44
Kunkletown 45 9 40N51 75w27 5:01:48
Kushequa 42 75 41N40 78w49 5:15:16
Kutztown 6 8 40N31 75w47 5:03:08
Kutztown 38 25 40N23 76w18 5:05:12
Kylers Corner 24 36 41N21 78w37 5:14:28
Kylertown 17 6 41N00 78w07 5:12:28
Kyleville 67 1 39N50 76w24 5:05:36
La Anna 52 84 41N09 75w17 5:01:08
La Belle 26 51 39N59 79w55 5:19:40
Laboratory 63 3 40N11 80w16 5:21:04
Labott 67 39 39N56 76w51 5:07:24
Lacey Park 9 1 40N12 75w05 5:00:20
Laceyville 66 59 41N39 76w10 5:04:40
Lack 34 6 40N22 77w41 5:10:44
Lackawannock 43 6 41N12 80w21 5:21:24
Lackawaxen 52 59 41N29 75w03 5:00:12
Laddsburg 8 60 41N36 76w27 5:05:48
Ladona 53 66 41N46 78w01 5:12:04
Lafayette 42 6 41N48 78w41 5:14:44
Lafayette Hill 46 90 40N06 75w16 5:01:04
Lafayette Park 46 90 40N05 75w16 5:01:04
Lafferty Hill 2 114 40N23 79w59 5:19:56
Laflin 40 1 41N18 75w47 5:03:08
La Gonda 63 3 40N11 80w16 5:21:04

PENNSYLVANIA

Lahaska 9 8 40N20 75w06 5:00:24
Laings Garden 9 9 40N08 74w51 4:59:24
Laird 3 6 40N50 79w38 5:18:32
Lairdsville 41 6 41N14 76w36 5:06:24
La Jose 17 122 40N50 78w41 5:14:44
Lake Ariel 64 59 41N27 75w23 5:01:32
Lake Carey 66 59 41N32 75w57 5:03:48
Lake City 25 68 42N01 80w21 5:21:24
Lake Como 64 6 41N51 75w20 5:01:20
Lake Harmony 13 94 41N04 75w36 5:02:24
Lake Lynn 26 7 39N44 79w52 5:19:28
Lakemont 7 33 40N30 78w24 5:13:36
Lakemont Terrace 7 33 40N31 78w25 5:13:40
Lake Pleasant 25 58 41N54 79w51 5:19:24
Lake Sheridan 35 89 41N38 75w47 5:03:08
Lakeside 58 50 41N53 75w44 5:02:56
Laketon 40 6 41N22 76w02 5:04:08
Laketon Heights 2 114 40N28 79w50 5:19:20
Lakeview 58 59 41N57 75w37 5:02:28
Lakeview Heights 22 12 40N16 76w49 5:07:16
Lakeville 64 7 41N26 75w17 5:01:08
Lake Winola 66 6 41N30 75w50 5:03:20
Lakewood 25 107 42N08 80w09 5:20:36
Lakewood 64 6 41N51 75w22 5:01:28
Lamar 18 76 41N04 77w26 5:09:44
Lamartine 16 37 41N12 79w22 5:17:28
Lamberton 26 51 39N50 79w53 5:19:32
Lambertsville 56 6 40N07 78w57 5:15:48
Lambs Creek 59 59 41N50 77w01 5:08:04
Lamokin Village 23 90 39N51 75w22 5:01:28
La Mott 46 9 40N05 75w07 5:00:28
Lampeter 36 8 40N00 76w14 5:04:56
Lanark 39 13 40N32 75w24 5:01:36
Lancaster 36 8 40N02 76w19 5:05:16
Lancaster Junction 36 8 40N06 76w22 5:05:28
Landenberg 15 8 39N47 75w46 5:03:04
Lander 62 6 41N56 79w08 5:16:32
Landingville 54 27 40N38 76w07 5:04:28
Landisburg 50 6 40N21 77w19 5:09:16
Landis Farms 36 8 40N04 76w19 5:05:16
Landis Store 6 2 40N20 75w38 5:02:32
Landis Valley 36 8 40N02 76w18 5:05:12
Landisville 36 97 40N06 76w25 5:05:40
Landreth Manor 9 9 40N08 74w51 4:59:24
Landstreet 56 6 40N11 78w59 5:15:56
Lane 3 2 40N41 79w41 5:18:44
Lanesboro 58 59 41N57 75w35 5:02:20
Lanes Mills 33 5 41N15 78w48 5:15:12
Langdon 41 7 41N31 76w57 5:07:48
Langdondale 5 6 40N09 78w16 5:13:04
Langeloth 63 6 40N23 80w24 5:21:36
Langford Hills 23 9 39N58 75w22 5:01:28
Langhorne 9 97 40N10 74w55 4:59:40
Langhorne Gables 9 97 40N10 74w55 4:59:40
Langhorne Gardens 9 97 40N10 74w55 4:59:40
Langhorne Manor 9 97 40N10 74w55 4:59:40
Langhorne Terrace 9 97 40N10 74w55 4:59:40
Lansdale 46 8 40N14 75w17 5:01:08
Lansdowne 23 9 39N56 75w16 5:01:04
Lansdowne Park Gardens 23 9 39N55 75w16 5:01:04
Lanse 17 6 40N59 78w08 5:12:32
Lansford 13 80 40N50 75w53 5:03:32
Lantz Corners 42 59 41N44 78w39 5:14:36
Lapark 36 9 40N01 76w08 5:04:32
Lapidea Hills 23 90 39N54 75w22 5:01:28
La Plume 35 44 41N33 75w45 5:03:00
Laporte 57 6 41N25 76w30 5:06:00
Larabee 42 40 41N57 78w23 5:13:32
Larchmont 23 90 40N00 75w23 5:01:32
Larchmont Square 23 90 40N00 75w23 5:01:32
Lardintown 10 2 40N44 79w45 5:19:00
Large 2 8 40N18 79w54 5:19:36
Larimer 65 25 40N21 79w44 5:18:56
Larkin Knoll 23 90 39N50 75w25 5:01:40
Larkins Corner 23 90 39N50 75w25 5:01:40
Larksville 40 20 41N15 75w56 5:03:44
Larrys Creek 41 6 41N14 77w15 5:09:00
Larryville 41 6 41N14 77w15 5:09:00
Larue 67 3 39N48 76w44 5:06:56
Lathrop 58 89 41N41 75w49 5:03:16
Latimore 1 1 40N01 77w05 5:08:20
Latrobe 65 3 40N19 79w23 5:17:32
Lattimer Mines 40 42 41N00 75w57 5:03:48
Laubachs 19 6 41N12 76w23 5:05:32
Laughlin Corner 4 6 40N39 80w30 5:22:00
Laughlintown 65 110 40N13 79w12 5:16:48
Laurel 21 1 40N00 77w12 5:08:48
Laurel 67 1 39N50 76w34 5:06:16
Laurel Bend 9 9 40N08 74w51 4:59:24
Laureldale 6 101 40N23 75w56 5:03:44
Laurel Gardens 2 114 40N32 80w01 5:20:04
Laurel Gardens 40 42 40N58 76w00 5:04:00
Laurel Hill 26 105 39N59 79w37 5:18:28
Laurel Hill 63 51 40N22 80w14 5:20:56
Laurel Lake 58 6 41N59 75w56 5:03:44
Laurel Park 60 6 40N53 77w08 5:08:32
Laurel Run 40 20 41N13 75w52 5:03:28
Laurelton 60 6 40N53 77w12 5:08:48
Laurelville 26 111 40N09 79w33 5:18:12
Laurelville 36 27 40N07 76w05 5:04:20
Laurys Station 39 8 40N43 75w32 5:02:08

PENNSYLVANIA

Lausanne 13	60	40N58	75w49	5:03:16
Lavansville 56	6	40N01	79w05	5:16:20
Lavelle 54	27	40N46	76w22	5:05:28
Laverock 46	9	40N04	75w12	5:00:48
Lawn 38	2	40N13	76w32	5:06:08
Lawnherst 46	12	40N41	75w14	5:00:56
Lawnton 22	12	40N16	76w49	5:07:16
Lawrence 63	114	40N18	80w07	5:20:28
Lawrence Park 23	9	39N58	75w22	5:01:28
Lawrence Park 25	107	42N09	80w01	5:20:04
Lawrenceville 35	1	41N21	75w46	5:03:04
Lawrenceville 59	59	42N00	77w08	5:08:32
Lawsonham 16	7	41N02	79w30	5:18:00
Lawson Heights 65	3	40N18	79w23	5:17:32
Lawsville Center 58	60	41N50	75w53	5:03:32
Lawton 58	6	41N47	76w04	5:04:16
Layfield 46	2	40N19	75w37	5:02:28
Layton 26	6	40N05	79w44	5:18:56
Leacock 36	27	40N03	76w07	5:04:28
Leaders Heights 67	67	39N57	76w42	5:06:48
Leaf Park 36	8	40N02	76w20	5:05:20
Leak Run 2	114	40N26	79w47	5:19:08
Leaman Place 36	9	40N01	76w08	5:04:32
Leamersville 7	33	40N28	78w25	5:13:40
Leasuresville 10	2	40N44	79w45	5:19:00
Leather Corner Post 39	13	40N38	75w35	5:02:20
Leatherwood 16	6	41N00	79w20	5:17:20
Lebanon 38	8	40N20	76w26	5:05:44
Lebanon Church 2	114	40N22	79w54	5:19:36
Lebo 50	6	40N21	77w18	5:09:12
Le Boeuf 25	35	41N53	79w57	5:19:48
Le Boeuf Gardens 25	35	41N56	79w59	5:19:56
Leck Kill 49	1	40N43	76w38	5:06:32
Leckrone 26	51	39N52	79w53	5:19:32
Lecontes Mills 17	6	41N05	78w17	5:13:08
Lederach 46	8	40N16	75w24	5:01:36
Ledgedale 64	6	41N20	75w24	5:01:36
Lee 40	1	41N11	76w04	5:04:16
Leechburg 3	4	40N38	79w36	5:18:24
Leedon Estates 23	9	39N53	75w20	5:01:20
Leedon Gardens 23	9	39N53	75w20	5:01:20
Lee Mine 40	21	41N12	76w00	5:04:00
Lee Park 40	20	41N15	75w53	5:03:32
Leeper 16	6	41N22	79w18	5:17:12
Leesburg 43	6	41N07	80w15	5:21:00
Lees Cross Roads 21	82	40N03	77w32	5:10:08
Leesport 6	80	40N27	75w58	5:03:52
Leet 2	13	40N35	80w12	5:20:48
Leetonia 59	6	41N31	77w27	5:09:48
Leetsdale 2	13	40N34	80w13	5:20:52
Lehigh 35	6	41N15	75w27	5:01:48
Lehigh Furnace 39	8	40N45	75w37	5:02:28
Lehigh Gap 39	8	40N45	75w37	5:02:28
Lehighton 13	80	40N50	75w43	5:02:52
Lehigh University 48	13	40N36	75w23	5:01:32
Lehigh Valley 39	13	40N38	75w23	5:01:32
Lehman 40	6	41N19	76w01	5:04:04
Lehman 67	95	39N53	76w52	5:07:28
Leibeyville 54	1	40N41	76w00	5:04:00
Leidy 18	7	41N25	77w52	5:11:28
Leinbachs 6	101	40N23	75w56	5:03:44
Leisenring 26	104	40N00	79w39	5:18:36
Leith 26	80	39N54	79w44	5:18:56
Leithsville 48	13	40N35	75w20	5:01:20
Lemasters 28	51	39N52	77w52	5:11:28
Lemon 66	59	41N37	75w55	5:03:40
Lemont 14	9	40N48	77w49	5:11:16
Lemont Furnace 26	80	39N55	79w40	5:18:40
Lemoyne 21	12	40N15	76w54	5:07:36
Lenape 15	13	39N55	75w38	5:02:32
Lenape Heights 3	15	40N46	79w31	5:18:04
Lenape Park 3	15	40N46	79w32	5:18:08
Lenhartsville 6	1	40N34	75w53	5:03:32
Lenker Manor 22	12	40N16	76w49	5:07:16
Lenkerville 22	1	40N33	76w57	5:07:48
Lenni 23	4	39N54	75w27	5:01:48
Lenni Heights 23	90	39N54	75w26	5:01:44
Lennox Park 23	90	39N52	75w23	5:01:32
Lenover 15	32	39N58	75w55	5:03:40
Lenox 58	89	41N41	75w42	5:02:48
Lenoxville 58	6	41N40	75w38	5:02:32
Leola 36	28	40N05	76w11	5:04:44
Leolyn 59	7	41N34	76w57	5:07:48
Leona 8	52	41N47	76w47	5:07:08
Leonard 17	1	41N02	78w27	5:13:48
Leopard 15	90	40N03	75w26	5:01:44
Leopard Lakes 15	90	40N03	75w26	5:01:44
Le Raysville 8	6	41N51	76w11	5:04:44
Lernerville	2	40N44	79w46	5:19:04
Le Roy 8	7	41N41	76w43	5:06:52
Lester 23	9	40N00	75w09	5:00:36
Letort 36	26	40N00	76w28	5:05:52
Letterkenny 28	1	40N04	77w41	5:10:44
Letterkenny Army Depot 28	42	39N56	77w40	5:10:40
Level Corner 41	64	41N14	77w08	5:08:32
Level Green 65	25	40N24	79w43	5:18:52
Levittown	9	40N09	74w51	4:59:24
Lewisberry 67	12	40N08	76w52	5:07:28
Lewisburg 60	70	40N58	76w54	5:07:36
Lewis Run 42	6	41N52	78w40	5:14:40
Lewistown 44	73	40N36	77w34	5:10:16
Lewistown 54	27	40N48	75w58	5:03:52
Lewistown Junction 44	73	40N36	77w34	5:10:16
Lewisville	6	41N54	77w46	5:11:04
Lewisville 15	1	39N43	75w53	5:03:32
Lewisville 32	6	40N32	79w23	5:17:32
Lexington 36	8	40N09	76w18	5:05:12
Liberty 59	6	41N34	77w06	5:08:24
Liberty Corners 8	41	41N46	76w27	5:05:48
Liberty Square 36	1	39N48	76w15	5:05:00
Library 2	114	40N18	80w02	5:20:08
Licking 16	6	41N08	79w33	5:18:12
Licking Creek 29	66	39N59	78w05	5:12:20
Lickingville 16	6	41N23	79w22	5:17:28
Lightner 67	67	39N58	76w47	5:07:08
Lightstreet 19	4	41N02	76w25	5:05:40
Ligonier 65	110	40N15	79w14	5:16:56
Lilly 11	55	40N26	78w37	5:14:28
Lillyville 4	121	40N49	80w12	5:20:48
Lima 23	4	39N55	75w26	5:01:44
Limehill 8	6	41N40	76w16	5:05:04
Limekiln 6	8	40N21	75w48	5:03:12
Limeport 39	13	40N31	75w27	5:01:48
Limerick 46	8	40N14	75w32	5:02:08
Lime Ridge 19	4	41N00	76w25	5:05:40
Lime Rock 36	8	40N09	76w18	5:05:12
Limestone 16	37	41N08	79w20	5:17:20
Limestoneville 47	70	41N01	76w51	5:07:24
Lime Valley 36	8	39N59	76w17	5:05:08
Limeville 36	23	39N59	76w02	5:04:08
Lincoln 2	8	40N17	79w50	5:19:20
Lincoln 36	30	40N11	76w11	5:04:44
Lincoln Acres 65	25	40N20	79w43	5:18:52
Lincoln Colliery 54	9	40N36	76w23	5:05:32
Lincoln Heights 6	8	40N16	75w48	5:03:12
Lincoln Heights 65	3	40N20	79w37	5:18:28
Lincoln Hill 63	3	40N11	80w16	5:21:04
Lincoln Park 2	114	40N28	79w50	5:19:20
Lincoln Park 6	101	40N19	76w00	5:04:00
Lincoln Park 23	9	39N54	75w17	5:01:08
Lincoln Terrace 46	12	40N41	75w14	5:00:56
Lincoln University 15	3	39N48	75w56	5:03:44
Lincolnville 20	7	41N44	79w46	5:19:04
Lincolnway 67	67	39N58	76w47	5:07:08
Linconia 9	97	40N10	74w55	4:59:40
Lindaville 58	89	41N42	75w46	5:03:04
Lindberg Terrace 46	118	40N11	75w33	5:02:12
Linden 41	64	41N14	77w08	5:08:32
Linden 63	2	40N14	80w08	5:20:32
Linden Hall 14	64	40N51	77w41	5:10:44
Lindsey 33	51	40N56	78w58	5:15:52
Line Lexington 9	8	40N17	75w16	5:01:04
Line Mountain 49	6	40N40	76w37	5:06:28
Linesville 20	7	41N39	80w26	5:21:44
Linfield 46	8	40N13	75w32	5:02:08
Linglestown 22	12	40N19	76w48	5:07:12
Linhart 2	114	40N27	79w50	5:19:20
Linn 26	51	40N01	79w50	5:19:20
Linntown 60	70	40N58	76w54	5:07:36
Linwood 23	90	39N49	75w26	5:01:44
Linwood Terrace 23	90	39N50	75w25	5:01:40
Lionville 15	13	40N03	75w39	5:02:36
Lippincott 30	1	39N54	80w11	5:20:44
Lisburn 21	12	40N12	77w00	5:08:00
Listie 56	6	40N02	79w01	5:16:04
Listonburg 56	53	39N45	79w19	5:17:16
Litchfield 8	6	41N57	76w26	5:05:44
Lithia Springs 49	82	40N54	76w48	5:07:12
Lithia Valley 66	44	41N34	75w47	5:03:08
Lititz 36	8	40N09	76w18	5:05:12
Little Beaver 37	6	40N53	80w28	5:21:52
Little Britain 36	1	39N47	76w06	5:04:24
Little Chapel 64	6	41N27	75w23	5:01:32
Little Chicago 30	51	39N54	79w58	5:19:52
Little Cooley 20	7	41N44	79w46	5:19:04
Little Corners 20	77	41N40	80w07	5:20:28
Little Gap 13	9	40N52	75w27	5:01:48
Little Germany 50	6	40N21	77w16	5:09:04
Little Hope 25	91	42N13	79w50	5:19:20
Little Italy 9	1	40N15	75w02	5:00:08
Little Kansas 44	7	40N30	77w45	5:11:00
Little Mahanoy 49	6	40N46	76w46	5:07:04
Little Marsh 59	6	41N53	77w24	5:09:36
Little Meadows 58	6	41N59	76w08	5:04:32
Littles Corners 20	77	41N40	80w07	5:20:28
Littlestown 1	56	39N45	77w05	5:08:20
Little Washington 21	1	40N10	77w24	5:09:36
Live Easy 30	51	39N54	79w58	5:19:52
Liverpool 50	1	40N34	77w00	5:08:00
Livonia 14	6	40N57	77w27	5:09:48
Llandrilla 46	9	40N01	75w15	5:01:00
Llanerch Manor 23	9	40N00	75w18	5:01:12
Llanfair 11	63	40N18	78w43	5:14:52
Llangelan Hills 23	90	40N00	75w23	5:01:32
Llewellyn 54	27	40N40	76w17	5:05:08
Lloydell 11	63	40N16	78w42	5:14:48
Lloydesville 65	3	40N19	79w23	5:17:32
Loag 15	27	40N08	75w50	5:03:20
Lobachsville 6	101	40N23	75w54	5:03:36
Lochiel 60	70	40N58	76w54	5:07:36
Locke Mills 44	7	40N43	77w35	5:10:20
Lock Haven 18	76	41N08	77w28	5:09:52
Lock No. 4 63	1	40N08	79w54	5:19:36
Lockport 18	76	41N08	77w28	5:09:52
Lockport 44	73	40N36	77w34	5:10:16
Lockport 65	7	40N24	79w09	5:16:36
Locksley 23	4	39N55	75w30	5:02:00
Lockview 63	1	40N08	79w54	5:19:36
Locust 19	27	40N53	76w23	5:05:32
Locust 32	6	40N49	78w59	5:15:56
Locustdale 19	27	40N47	76w23	5:05:32
Locust Gap 49	27	40N46	76w26	5:05:44
Locust Grove 15	13	39N57	75w36	5:02:24
Locust Grove 67	67	39N59	76w46	5:07:04
Locust Point 21	12	40N12	77w00	5:08:00
Locust Ridge 2	114	40N30	79w59	5:19:56
Locust Run 34	6	40N34	77w14	5:08:56
Locust Summit 49	27	40N46	76w26	5:05:44
Locust Valley 39	13	40N31	75w23	5:01:32
Locust Valley 54	27	40N48	76w20	5:05:20
Lofty 54	42	40N58	76w00	5:04:00
Logan 7	33	40N30	78w24	5:13:36
Logan 51	9	40N02	75w09	5:00:36
Logan Mills 18	7	41N02	77w18	5:09:12
Logans Ferry 2	14	40N34	79w45	5:19:00
Logans Ferry Heights 2	14	40N34	79w45	5:19:00
Logansport 3	15	40N46	79w32	5:18:08
Loganton 18	7	41N02	77w19	5:09:16
Loganville 67	3	39N51	76w42	5:06:48
Log Pile 63	3	40N11	80w16	5:21:04
London 43	6	41N10	80w05	5:20:20
London Britain 15	1	39N45	75w47	5:03:08
London Grove 15	8	39N50	75w49	5:03:16
Lonely Acres 11	63	40N36	78w42	5:14:48
Lone Pine 63	3	40N11	80w16	5:21:04
Long Acre Park 23	9	39N56	75w16	5:01:04
Long Branch 63	115	40N06	79w53	5:19:32
Longfellow 44	73	40N36	77w34	5:10:16
Longlevel 67	26	40N01	76w32	5:06:08
Long Pond 45	84	41N03	75w28	5:01:52
Long Run 13	8	40N50	75w42	5:02:48
Longstown 67	67	39N59	76w46	5:07:04
Longswamp 6	9	40N30	75w39	5:02:36
Longview 2	114	40N20	80w02	5:20:08
Longwood 15	8	39N52	75w40	5:02:40
Lookabough Corners 3	4	40N38	79w37	5:18:28
Lookout 64	6	41N47	75w11	5:00:44
Loomis Park 40	20	41N15	75w53	5:03:32
Loop Station 7	33	40N25	78w24	5:13:36
Lopez 57	6	41N27	76w20	5:05:20
Lorain 11	74	40N18	78w53	5:15:32
Lorane 6	101	40N20	75w53	5:03:32
Lorberry 54	9	40N36	76w23	5:05:32
Lords Valley 52	6	41N29	75w11	5:00:44
Lorenton 41	6	41N36	77w18	5:09:12
Loretto 11	55	40N31	78w38	5:14:32
Loschs 34	1	40N38	77w17	5:09:08
Loshs Run 50	51	40N24	77w02	5:08:08
Lost Creek 54	27	40N49	76w14	5:04:56
Lottsville 62	6	42N00	79w30	5:18:00
Lovedale 2	8	40N17	79w50	5:19:20
Lovejoy 32	6	40N43	78w57	5:15:48
Lovell 25	3	41N55	79w39	5:18:36
Lovelton 66	59	41N34	76w04	5:04:16
Lovely 5	6	40N11	78w37	5:14:28
Lover 63	1	40N08	79w54	5:19:36
Lowber 26	1	40N07	79w50	5:19:20
Lowber 65	61	40N15	79w46	5:19:04
Lower 13	8	40N49	75w34	5:02:16
Lower Allen 21	12	40N13	76w56	5:07:44
Lower Alsace 6	101	40N20	75w53	5:03:32
Lower Askam 40	20	41N13	75w54	5:03:36
Lower Augusta 49	82	40N48	76w48	5:07:12
Lower Burrell 65	14	40N36	79w44	5:18:56
Lower Chanceford 67	1	39N49	76w23	5:05:32
Lower Chichester 23	90	39N50	75w25	5:01:40
Lower Frankford 21	1	40N14	77w18	5:09:12
Lower Frederick 46	8	40N17	75w29	5:01:56
Lower Gwynedd 46	8	40N11	75w14	5:00:56
Lower Heidelberg 6	101	40N21	76w03	5:04:12
Lower Longswamp 6	9	40N30	75w40	5:02:40
Lower Macungie 39	13	40N33	75w34	5:02:16
Lower Mahanoy 49	51	40N40	76w53	5:07:32
Lower Makefield 9	9	40N14	74w50	4:59:20
Lower Merion 46	90	40N02	75w18	5:01:12
Lower Mifflin 21	1	40N14	77w26	5:09:44
Lower Milford 39	13	40N28	75w28	5:01:52
Lower Moreland 46	1	40N08	75w03	5 00:12
Lower Mount Bethel 46	15	40N48	75w10	5:00:40
Lower Nazareth 48	8	40N43	75w20	5:01:20
Lower Orchard 9	9	40N09	74w51	4:59:24
Lower Oxford 15	3	39N48	75w59	5:03:56
Lower Paxton 22	12	40N19	76w48	5:07:12
Lower Peanut 26	6	40N00	79w47	5:19:08
Lower Pottsgrove 46	8	40N16	75w36	5:02:24
Lower Providence 46	90	40N08	75w26	5:01:44
Lower Sagon 49	6	40N53	76w41	5:06:44
Lower Salford 46	8	40N16	75w24	5:01:36
Lower Saucon 48	13	40N35	75w21	5:01:24
Lower Southampton 9	1	40N09	74w59	4:59:56
Lower Swatara 22	80	40N13	76w46	5:07:04
Lower Turkeyfoot 56	53	39N52	79w21	5:17:24
Lower Tyrone 26	104	40N04	79w39	5:18:36
Lower Windsor 67	2	39N58	76w32	5:06:08
Lower Yoder 11	74	40N20	78w57	5:15:48
Lowhill 39	1	40N39	75w39	5:02:36
Low Hill 63	51	40N02	79w58	5:19:52
Lowville 25	7	42N00	79w48	5:19:12
Loyalhanna 65	116	40N27	79w27	5:17:48
Loyalsock 41	82	41N17	76w59	5:07:56

PENNSYLVANIA

Loyalsockville 41 82 41N15 76W55 5:07:40
Loyalton 22 1 40N34 76W42 5:06:48
Loyalville 40 20 41N20 75W56 5:03:44
Loysburg 5 6 40N10 78W23 5:13:32
Loysville 50 6 40N22 77W21 5:09:24
Lucernemines 32 71 40N33 79W08 5:16:32
Lucesco 65 4 40N38 79W37 5:18:28
Lucinda 16 6 41N19 79W22 5:17:28
Luciusboro 32 71 40N33 79W10 5:16:40
Lucknow 22 12 40N17 76W53 5:07:32
Lucky 67 1 39N50 76W34 5:06:16
Lucon 46 2 40N20 75W20 5:01:20
Lucy Crossing 46 12 40N41 75W14 5:00:56
Lucy Furnace 44 85 40N23 77W53 5:11:32
Ludlow 42 3 41N44 78W57 5:15:48
Ludwigs Corner 15 80 40N02 75W41 5:02:44
Luke Fidler 49 27 40N48 76W33 5:06:12
Lumber 12 7 41N27 78W11 5:12:44
Lumber City 17 7 40N56 78W34 5:14:16
Lumberville 9 1 40N24 75W03 5:00:12
Lundys Lane 25 7 41N54 80W22 5:21:28
Lungerville 41 6 41N14 76W31 5:06:04
Lurgan 28 56 40N09 77W38 5:10:32
Luthersburg 17 56 41N03 78W43 5:14:52
Luthers Mills 8 41 41N46 76W27 5:05:48
Lutztown 21 16 40N12 77W11 5:08:44
Lutzville 5 6 40N01 78W22 5:13:28
Luxor 65 3 40N20 79W29 5:17:56
Luzerne 26 51 39N59 79W55 5:19:40
Luzerne 40 20 41N17 75W54 5:03:36
Lycippus 65 3 40N19 79W23 5:17:32
Lycoming 41 7 41N18 77W06 5:08:24
Lykens 22 1 40N34 76W42 5:06:48
Lyleville 17 54 40N45 78W32 5:14:08
Lynch 27 6 41N36 79W03 5:16:12
Lynchville 24 36 41N26 78W34 5:14:16
Lyndell 15 80 40N04 75W45 5:03:00
Lyndon 36 8 40N02 76W17 5:05:08
Lyndora 10 3 40N51 79W56 5:19:44
Lynn 39 1 40N40 75W47 5:03:08
Lynn 58 60 41N42 75W55 5:03:40
Lynnewood Gardens 46 9 40N05 75W07 5:00:28
Lynnport 39 1 40N41 75W48 5:03:12
Lynnville 39 1 40N41 75W45 5:03:00
Lynnwood 26 1 40N08 79W52 5:19:28
Lynnwood 40 20 41N15 75W53 5:03:32
Lynnwood Park 23 9 40N00 75W18 5:01:12
Lynoak 6 101 40N19 75W57 5:03:48
Lynwood 6 101 40N19 75W57 5:03:48
Lyons 6 8 40N29 75W45 5:03:00
Lyons Run Mine 65 25 40N22 79W44 5:18:56
Lyon Station 6 8 40N29 75W45 5:03:00
Lyon Valley 39 1 40N41 75W45 5:03:00
Mable 54 27 40N47 76W21 5:05:24
Mable Hill 30 7 39N45 79W56 5:19:44
MacArthur 4 13 40N37 80W16 5:21:04
Macdonaldton 56 6 39N56 78W57 5:15:48
Macedonia 8 41 41N46 76W27 5:05:48
Macedonia 34 7 40N35 77W24 5:09:36
Mackeyville 18 76 41N03 77W28 5:09:52
Macungie 39 13 40N31 75W33 5:02:12
Maddensville 31 6 40N03 78W02 5:12:08
Madera 17 6 40N50 78W26 5:13:44
Madge 24 75 41N40 78W49 5:15:16
Madison 65 3 40N15 79W41 5:18:44
Madisonburg 14 64 40N55 77W31 5:10:04
Madisonville 35 4 41N20 75W32 5:02:08
Madley 5 6 39N57 78W39 5:14:36
Magee 62 6 41N41 79W24 5:17:36
Magill Heights 2 114 40N20 80W05 5:20:20
Magnolia Gardens 9 9 40N08 74W51 4:59:24
Mahaffey 17 6 40N53 78W44 5:14:56
Mahanoy 54 3 40N49 76W08 5:04:32
Mahanoy City 54 3 40N49 76W09 5:04:36
Mahanoy Plane 54 3 40N49 76W08 5:04:32
Mahoning 3 64 40N55 79W28 5:17:52
Mahoningtown 37 112 41N00 80W20 5:21:20
Maiden Creek 6 80 40N28 75W54 5:03:36
Main 19 4 40N59 76W23 5:05:32
Mainesburg 59 59 41N47 77W07 5:08:28
Mainland 46 8 40N15 75W22 5:01:28
Mainsville 28 82 40N03 77W32 5:10:08
Mainville 19 4 41N00 76W25 5:05:40
Maitland 44 73 40N36 77W34 5:10:16
Maizeville 54 27 40N48 76W14 5:04:56
Majeriks Corners 25 35 41N56 79W59 5:19:56
Makefield Village 9 9 40N12 74W49 4:59:16
Malden Place 63 51 40N02 79W55 5:19:40
Malta 49 6 40N39 76W54 5:07:36
Maltby 40 20 41N16 75W54 5:03:36
Malvern 15 8 40N02 75W31 5:02:04
Mammoth 65 111 40N12 79W28 5:17:52
Mamont 65 6 40N29 79W35 5:18:20
Manada Gap 22 12 40N19 76W48 5:07:12
Manatawny 6 101 40N23 75W54 5:03:36
Manayunk 51 9 40N01 75W14 5:00:56
Mance 56 79 39N49 79W02 5:16:08
Manchester 67 35 40N04 76W43 5:06:52
Mandata 49 51 40N43 76W51 5:07:24
Manheim 36 2 40N10 76W24 5:05:36
Manifold 2 40N12 80W13 5:20:52
Manito 65 3 40N19 79W23 5:17:32
Mann 5 6 39N46 78W24 5:13:36
Mannitto Haven 65 3 40N24 79W25 5:17:40
Manns Choice 5 6 40N00 78W36 5:14:24
Mannsville 50 1 40N29 77W08 5:08:32
Manoa 23 9 40N00 75W18 5:01:12
Manoa Heights 23 9 40N00 75W18 5:01:12
Manor 32 6 40N37 79W01 5:16:04
Manor 65 25 40N20 79W40 5:18:40
Manor Hill 31 81 40N30 78W01 5:12:04
Manor Park Terrace 3 15 40N46 79W32 5:18:08
Manor Ridge 36 8 40N02 76W20 5:05:20
Manorville 3 15 40N47 79W31 5:18:04
Manown 2 1 40N11 79W54 5:19:36
Mansfield 59 59 41N48 77W05 5:08:20
Mantzville 54 1 40N45 75W48 5:03:12
Maple Beach 9 9 40N08 74W51 4:59:24
Maple Crest 15 47 40N03 75W33 5:02:12
Mapledale 61 109 41N25 79W50 5:19:20
Maple Glen 46 1 40N11 75W11 5:00:44
Maple Glen 63 51 40N02 79W55 5:19:40
Maple Grove 6 13 40N31 75W36 5:02:24
Maple Grove 15 3 39N47 75W59 5:03:56
Maple Grove 16 7 41N02 79W30 5:18:00
Maple Grove Park 6 101 40N18 75W59 5:03:56
Maple Hill 41 82 41N10 76W53 5:07:32
Maple Hill 54 27 40N49 76W12 5:04:48
Maplelake 35 4 41N20 75W32 5:02:08
Maple Manor 40 42 40N58 76W00 5:04:00
Maple Ridge 56 6 40N11 78W59 5:15:56
Mapleton 31 85 40N24 77W56 5:11:44
Mapleton Depot 31 85 40N24 77W56 5:11:44
Mapletown 30 51 39N48 79W55 5:19:40
Maplewood 9 8 40N21 75W13 5:00:52
Maplewood 64 6 41N27 75W23 5:01:32
Maplewood Heights 40 20 41N20 75W56 5:03:44
Maplewood Park 23 9 39N56 75W18 5:01:12
Maplewood Terrace 65 99 40N18 79W34 5:18:16
Marble 16 6 41N20 79W26 5:17:44
Marble Hall 46 90 40N05 75W16 5:01:04
Marchand 32 6 40N51 79W02 5:16:08
Marcus Hook 23 90 39N49 75W25 5:01:40
Marengo 14 6 40N42 78W08 5:12:32
Margaret 3 15 40N49 79W32 5:18:08
Margaretta Furnace 67 1 40N01 76W36 5:06:24
Margo Gardens 9 9 40N08 74W51 4:59:24
Marguerite 65 3 40N16 79W28 5:17:52
Marianna 63 7 40N02 80W06 5:20:24
Mariasville 61 1 41N11 79W43 5:18:52
Marienville 27 6 41N28 79W08 5:16:32
Marietta 36 26 40N04 76W33 5:06:12
Marion 28 42 39N52 77W42 5:10:48
Marion Center 32 6 40N46 79W03 5:16:12
Marion Heights 49 27 40N49 76W28 5:05:52
Marion Hill 4 8 40N44 80W18 5:21:12
Mark Acres 65 25 40N20 79W43 5:18:52
Markelsville 50 1 40N29 77W08 5:08:32
Markes 28 51 39N50 77W55 5:11:40
Market Square 51 9 40N04 75W12 5:00:48
Markle 65 4 40N35 79W39 5:18:36
Marklesburg 31 3 40N23 78W10 5:12:40
Markleton 56 4 39N52 79W14 5:16:56
Markleysburg 26 6 39N44 79W27 5:17:48
Markton 33 51 41N00 79W02 5:16:08
Markvue Manor 65 25 40N20 79W43 5:18:52
Marlboro 15 8 39N51 75W43 5:02:52
Marlborough 46 2 40N22 75W27 5:01:48
Mar Lin 54 27 40N41 76W15 5:05:00
Marple 23 9 39N58 75W22 5:01:28
Marple Gardens 23 9 39N58 75W22 5:01:28
Marple Heights 23 9 39N58 75W22 5:01:28
Marple Summit Estates 23 9 39N58 75W22 5:01:28
Marple Woods 23 9 39N58 75W22 5:01:28
Marron 17 7 40N57 78W33 5:14:12
Mars 10 3 40N42 80W01 5:20:04
Marsh 15 1 40N09 75W50 5:03:20
Marsh 28 100 39N45 77W34 5:10:16
Marshall 2 6 40N39 80W06 5:20:24
Marshall Heights 32 98 40N28 79W12 5:16:48
Marshalls Creek 45 85 41N03 75W08 5:00:32
Marshall Terrace 23 90 39N50 75W25 5:01:40
Marshallton 15 13 39N57 75W41 5:02:44
Marshallton 49 27 40N48 76W33 5:06:12
Marshbrook 35 44 41N32 75W44 5:02:56
Marshburg 42 6 41N52 78W40 5:14:40
Marsh Hill 41 7 41N23 77W03 5:08:12
Marshlands 59 6 41N45 77W34 5:10:16
Marsh Run 67 12 40N14 76W51 5:07:24
Marshview 8 41 41N46 76W27 5:05:48
Marshwood 35 1 41N28 75W34 5:02:16
Marsteller 11 92 40N39 78W47 5:15:08
Marstown 54 9 40N36 76W23 5:05:32
Martha Furnace 14 7 40N52 77W58 5:11:52
Martic 36 1 39N53 76W18 5:05:12
Martic Forge 36 1 39N53 76W22 5:05:28
Marticville 36 1 39N53 76W22 5:05:28
Martin 26 51 39N48 79W55 5:19:40
Martindale 11 63 40N23 78W40 5:14:40
Martindale 36 27 40N09 76W05 5:04:20
Martinsburg 7 51 40N19 78W20 5:13:20
Martins Corner 15 9 39N59 75W50 5:03:20
Martins Creek 48 15 40N47 75W11 5:00:44
Martins Ferry 30 51 39N48 79W55 5:19:40
Martinsville 67 1 39N55 76W35 5:06:20
Martzville 19 1 41N04 76W15 5:05:00
Marvel Gardens 23 9 39N53 75W21 5:01:24
Marvindale 42 93 41N49 78W27 5:13:48
Marwood 10 6 40N48 79W47 5:19:08
Mary D 54 27 40N46 76W03 5:04:12
Marysville 50 12 40N21 76W56 5:07:44
Marywood College 35 18 41N25 75W39 5:02:36
Mascot 36 1 40N02 76W10 5:04:40
Mason-Dixon 28 1 39N48 77W44 5:10:56
Masontown 26 51 39N51 79W54 5:19:36
Masseyburg 31 81 40N35 78W03 5:12:12
Masten 41 7 41N32 76W48 5:07:12
Mastersonville 36 8 40N06 76W22 5:05:28
Mast Hope 52 6 41N29 75W03 5:00:12
Matamoras 22 24 40N28 76W56 5:07:44
Matamoras 52 3 41N22 74W42 4:58:48
Mateer 3 15 40N46 79W32 5:18:08
Mather 30 6 39N56 80W04 5:20:16
Mattawana 44 7 40N30 77W44 5:10:56
Matthews Run 62 3 41N51 79W14 5:16:56
Mausdale 47 6 40N59 76W38 5:06:32
Maxatawny 6 9 40N32 75W44 5:02:56
Maxwell 26 51 39N59 79W55 5:19:40
Mayberry 47 6 40N55 76W33 5:06:12
Mayburg 27 3 41N42 79W02 5:16:08
Mayfair 51 9 40N03 75W02 5:00:08
Mayfield 35 1 41N32 75W32 5:02:08
Mayfield East 67 67 39N58 76W44 5:06:56
Mayport 16 6 41N02 79W15 5:17:00
Maysville 3 6 40N34 79W27 5:17:48
Maysville 43 59 41N24 80W23 5:21:32
Maysville 49 27 40N47 76W33 5:06:12
Maytown 36 2 40N04 76W35 5:06:20
Maytown 67 12 40N08 76W52 5:07:28
Mayville 37 112 41N00 80W20 5:21:20
Maze 34 6 40N34 77W14 5:08:56
Mazeppa 60 70 40N58 76W54 5:07:36
McAdoo 54 60 40N54 76W00 5:04:00
McAdoo Heights 54 60 40N54 76W00 5:04:00
McAlevys Fort 31 81 40N30 78W01 5:12:04
McAlisterville 34 1 40N38 77W17 5:09:08
McCalmont 33 51 41N02 78W58 5:15:52
McCance 65 110 40N15 79W14 5:16:56
McCandless 2 114 40N34 80W02 5:20:08
McCartney 17 7 40N50 78W26 5:13:44
McCauley 17 4 40N50 78W21 5:13:24
McChesneytown 65 3 40N19 79W23 5:17:32
McClarran 65 3 40N19 79W23 5:17:32
McClellan 22 24 40N28 76W56 5:07:44
McClellandtown 26 51 39N53 79W52 5:19:28
McClellan Heights 67 67 39N57 76W42 5:06:48
McClintock 61 9 41N25 79W42 5:18:48
McClure 26 111 40N09 79W33 5:18:12
McClure 55 1 40N42 77W19 5:09:16
McConnellsburg 29 66 39N56 78W00 5:12:00
McConnells Mill 63 2 40N16 80W11 5:20:44
McConnellstown 31 81 40N27 78W05 5:12:20
McCoysville 34 7 40N34 77W25 5:09:40
McCrea 21 1 40N10 77W24 5:09:36
McCullocks Mills 34 6 40N24 77W33 5:10:12
McCullough 65 25 40N22 79W41 5:18:44
McDonald 63 51 40N22 80W14 5:20:56
McDowell Corners 43 6 41N10 80W05 5:20:20
McElhattan 18 64 41N10 77W22 5:09:28
McEwensville 49 73 41N05 76W49 5:07:16
McGees Mills 17 6 40N53 78W46 5:15:04
McGillstown 38 1 40N22 77W43 5:10:52
McGovern 63 2 40N14 80W13 5:20:52
McGrann 3 15 40N47 79W31 5:18:04
McGregor 3 59 40N53 79W15 5:17:00
McHenry 41 6 41N24 77W28 5:09:52
McIlhaney 45 1 40N55 75W24 5:01:36
McIntyre 32 6 40N34 79W18 5:17:12
McIntyre 41 7 41N31 76W57 5:07:48
McKean 25 107 42N00 80W09 5:20:36
McKeansburg 54 1 40N41 76W00 5:04:00
McKee 7 3 40N21 78W26 5:13:44
McKee Half Falls 55 51 40N42 76W52 5:07:28
McKeesport 2 10 40N21 79W51 5:19:24
McKees Rocks 2 114 40N28 80W05 5:20:20
McKinley 46 9 40N05 75W07 5:00:28
McKinley Hill 26 7 39N44 79W54 5:19:36
McKinney 28 1 40N06 77W38 5:10:32
McKnight 114 40N33 80W02 5:20:08
McKnightstown 1 1 39N52 77W20 5:09:20
McKnight Village 2 114 40N33 80W01 5:20:04
McLane 25 107 42N00 80W09 5:20:36
McMichaels 45 23 41N00 75W13 5:00:52
McMurray 63 114 40N17 80W05 5:20:20
McNett 41 7 41N34 76W51 5:07:24
McPherron 17 122 40N50 78W41 5:14:44
McQueston Corners 43 6 41N25 80W14 5:20:56
McSherrystown 1 6 39N48 77W01 5:08:04
McSparren 36 1 39N47 76W11 5:04:44
McVeytown 44 7 40N30 77W45 5:11:00
McVille 3 2 40N41 79W41 5:18:44
McWilliams 3 6 41N00 79W20 5:17:20
Mead 62 3 41N47 79W05 5:16:20
Meadia Heights 36 8 40N02 76W17 5:05:08
Meadowbrook 26 80 39N54 79W44 5:18:56
Meadowbrook 46 9 40N06 75W09 5:00:36
Meadowbrook Manor 15 47 40N03 75W33 5:02:12
Meadow Gap 31 6 40N15 77W53 5:11:32
Meadow Lands 63 2 40N13 80W14 5:20:56
Meadowood 10 3 40N51 79W56 5:19:44
Meadowview Estates 36 28 40N05 76W11 5:04:44
Meadow Wood 4 13 40N37 80W16 5:21:04
Meadville 20 77 41N39 80W09 5:20:36
Mechanicsburg 21 12 40N13 77W00 5:08:00

PENNSYLVANIA

Mechanics Grove 36 27 39N54 76w10 5:04:40
Mechanicsville 9 8 40N21 75w05 5:00:20
Mechanicsville 16 37 41N12 79w22 5:17:28
Mechanicsville 36 8 40N06 76w22 5:05:28
Mechanicsville 39 13 40N37 75w31 5:02:04
Mechanicsville 54 49 40N41 76w12 5:04:48
Meckesville 13 94 41N02 75w37 5:02:28
Mecks Corner 50 1 40N25 77w12 5:08:48
Media 23 90 39N55 75w23 5:01:32
Medix Run 24 7 41N17 78w30 5:14:00
Meeker 40 20 41N20 75w56 5:03:44
Megargee 15 9 39N59 75w50 5:03:20
Mehoopany 66 59 41N34 76w04 5:04:16
Meiser 55 6 40N47 77w03 5:08:12
Meiserville 55 6 40N43 77w01 5:08:04
Melcroft 26 6 40N03 79w24 5:17:36
Mellingertown 65 111 40N09 79w33 5:18:12
Melrose 6 101 40N20 75w53 5:03:32
Melrose 26 51 39N59 79w55 5:19:40
Melrose 58 59 41N57 75w37 5:02:28
Melrose Park 46 9 40N04 75w08 5:00:32
Mench 5 6 40N01 78w22 5:13:28
Mendenhall 15 8 39N51 75w39 5:02:36
Mendon 65 111 40N10 79w37 5:18:28
Menges Mills 67 95 39N52 76w54 5:07:36
Menno 44 7 40N34 77w47 5:11:08
Mentcle 32 6 40N38 78w52 5:15:28
Mercer 43 66 41N14 80w15 5:21:00
Mercersburg 28 51 39N50 77w54 5:11:36
Mercur 8 41 41N46 76w24 5:05:36
Meredith 3 6 40N47 79w17 5:17:08
Meridian 10 3 40N51 79w58 5:19:52
Merion 46 9 40N00 75w15 5:01:00
Merion Golf Manor 23 9 40N01 75w17 5:01:08
Merion Park 46 90 40N02 75w18 5:01:12
Merion Square 46 90 40N02 75w18 5:01:12
Merion Station 46 90 40N02 75w18 5:01:12
Merion View 46 90 40N05 75w22 5:01:28
Meriwether Farms 15 13 39N57 75w36 5:02:24
Merrian 49 27 40N48 76w25 5:05:40
Merrill 4 19 40N40 80w24 5:21:36
Merrittstown 26 51 39N58 79w53 5:19:32
Merryall 8 6 41N40 76w16 5:05:04
Mertztown 6 9 40N30 75w40 5:02:40
Merwin 4 40N32 79w39 5:18:36
Merwinsburg 45 1 40N56 75w26 5:01:44
Merwood 23 9 40N00 75w18 5:01:12
Meshoppen 66 59 41N37 76w03 5:04:12
Messmore 26 51 39N53 79w52 5:19:28
Metal 28 1 40N04 77w50 5:11:20
Metcalf 65 14 40N34 79w45 5:19:00
Mexico 34 7 40N32 77w21 5:09:24
Meyersdale 56 79 39N49 79w02 5:16:08
Meyersville 39 13 40N37 75w31 5:02:04
Mickley Gardens 39 13 40N39 75w30 5:02:00
Middleboro 25 107 42N00 80w09 5:20:36
Middleburg 40 60 41N04 75w46 5:03:04
Middleburg 55 6 40N47 77w03 5:08:12
Middlebury 59 6 41N52 77w16 5:09:04
Middle Churches 65 111 40N09 79w33 5:18:12
Middle City 51 9 39N57 75w10 5:00:40
Middle Creek 55 1 40N46 77w16 5:09:04
Middle Lancaster 10 6 40N48 80w08 5:20:32
Middle Paxton 22 12 40N23 76w55 5:07:40
Middleport 54 1 40N44 76w05 5:04:20
Middlesex 21 16 40N12 77w11 5:08:44
Middle Smithfield 45 1 41N06 75w06 5:00:24
Middle Spring 21 82 40N03 77w32 5:10:08
Middleswarth 55 6 40N47 77w03 5:08:12
Middle Taylor 11 74 40N22 78w55 5:15:40
Middleton 17 122 40N51 78w43 5:14:52
Middletown 22 80 40N12 76w44 5:06:56
Middletown 48 13 40N39 75w21 5:01:24
Middletown 65 111 40N13 79w36 5:18:24
Middletown Center 58 6 41N55 76w03 5:04:12
Middletown Heights 23 90 39N55 75w22 5:01:28
Midland 4 2 40N15 80w13 5:20:52
Midvale 40 20 41N16 75w51 5:03:24
Midvalley 19 27 40N49 76w23 5:05:32
Midway 1 1 39N48 76w59 5:07:56
Midway 38 8 40N20 76w26 5:05:44
Midway 63 51 40N22 80w18 5:21:12
Midway 65 99 40N18 79w34 5:18:16
Mifflin 34 7 40N34 77w25 5:09:40
Mifflinburg 60 4 40N55 77w03 5:08:12
Mifflin Junction 2 114 40N22 79w58 5:19:52
Mifflintown 34 7 40N35 77w24 5:09:36
Mifflinville 19 1 41N02 76w18 5:05:12
Milan 8 60 41N54 76w32 5:06:08
Milanville 64 6 41N40 75w04 5:00:16
Mildred 57 6 41N29 76w23 5:05:32
Mile Run 49 82 40N52 76w47 5:07:08
Miles 14 6 40N57 77w24 5:09:36
Milesburg 14 70 40N57 77w47 5:11:08
Milesville 2 1 40N11 79w54 5:19:36
Milford 52 2 41N19 74w48 4:59:12
Milford Manor 9 9 40N12 74w49 4:59:16
Milford Square 9 2 40N21 75w24 5:01:36
Milfred Terrace 63 6 39N59 80w00 5:20:00
Militia Hill 46 9 40N07 75w14 5:00:56
Millardsville 38 25 40N23 76w18 5:05:12
Millbach 38 1 40N21 76w13 5:04:52
Millbach Springs 38 1 40N21 76w13 5:04:52
Millbank 23 9 39N58 75w18 5:01:12
Millbank 65 110 40N15 79w14 5:16:56
Millbourne 23 9 39N58 75w15 5:01:00
Millbrook 14 9 40N48 77w52 5:11:28
Millbrook 43 6 41N16 80w08 5:20:32
Mill City 66 44 41N32 75w44 5:02:56
Mill Creek 31 85 40N26 77w56 5:11:44
Mill Creek 54 49 40N41 76w12 5:04:48
Millcreek Township 25 107 42N08 80w09 5:20:36
Milledgeville 43 59 41N29 80w01 5:20:04
Miller Heights 48 13 40N39 75w21 5:01:24
Miller Manor 48 13 40N41 75w22 5:01:28
Miller Run 56 6 40N09 78w55 5:15:40
Millers 20 3 41N48 80w03 5:20:12
Millersburg 22 1 40N32 76w58 5:07:52
Miller Shaft 11 63 40N23 78w40 5:14:40
Millerstown 2 14 40N39 79w48 5:19:12
Millerstown 7 51 40N19 78w20 5:13:20
Millerstown 16 6 41N20 79w26 5:17:44
Millerstown 50 1 40N33 77w09 5:08:36
Millersville 36 8 40N00 76w22 5:05:28
Millerton 59 6 41N59 76w56 5:07:44
Millertown 26 6 40N01 79w24 5:17:36
Mill Grove 19 4 40N57 76w28 5:05:52
Mill Hall 18 76 41N06 77w29 5:09:56
Millheim 14 52 40N54 77w29 5:09:56
Milligantown 6 44N34 79w41 5:18:44
Millmont 60 7 40N53 77w08 5:08:32
Mill Park 46 8 40N15 75w39 5:02:36
Millport 36 28 40N05 76w11 5:04:44
Millport 53 6 41N55 78w01 5:12:04
Millrift 52 6 41N25 74w45 4:59:00
Mill Run 7 3 40N53 79w53 5:19:32
Mill Run 17 7 41N13 78w34 5:14:16
Mill Run 26 6 39N57 79w27 5:17:48
Mills 53 6 41N57 77w41 5:10:44
Millsboro 63 7 39N59 80w00 5:20:00
Millstone 24 6 41N24 79w01 5:16:04
Milltown 8 1 41N58 76w31 5:06:04
Milltown 15 13 39N58 75w33 5:02:12
Millvale 2 114 40N29 79w58 5:19:52
Millview 57 6 41N29 76w36 5:06:24
Mill Village 25 59 41N53 80w10 5:20:40
Millville 19 7 41N07 76w32 5:06:08
Millway 36 8 40N09 76w18 5:05:12
Millwood 65 3 40N20 79w18 5:17:12
Milmont Park 23 9 39N53 75w20 5:01:20
Milnesville 40 42 40N59 75w59 5:03:56
Milnor 28 1 39N48 77w44 5:10:56
Milroy 44 7 40N43 77w35 5:10:20
Milton 3 59 40N53 79w15 5:17:00
Milton 49 70 41N01 76w51 5:07:24
Milton Grove 36 2 40N07 76w31 5:06:04
Milwaukee 35 45 41N30 75w43 5:02:52
Mina 53 66 41N46 78w01 5:12:04
Mineral 61 6 41N19 79w58 5:19:52
Mineral Point 11 74 40N23 78w50 5:15:20
Mineral Springs 17 1 41N00 78w22 5:13:28
Miners Village 38 8 40N17 76w25 5:05:40
Minersville 54 27 40N41 76w16 5:05:04
Minesite 39 13 40N35 75w28 5:01:52
Mingoville 14 63 40N56 77w39 5:10:36
Minisink Hills 45 23 41N00 75w08 5:00:32
Miola 16 37 41N12 79w22 5:17:28
Miquon 46 90 40N04 75w16 5:01:04
Miquon Hills 46 90 40N05 75w17 5:01:08
Misertown 45 84 41N06 75w15 5:01:00
Mission Hill 36 8 40N04 76w19 5:05:16
Mitchell Park 46 1 40N11 75w06 5:00:24
Mix Run 12 7 41N21 78w08 5:12:32
Mocanaqua 40 1 41N09 76w08 5:04:32
Mocking Bird Hill 65 25 40N20 79w43 5:18:52
Model Village 23 90 39N50 75w25 5:01:40
Modena 15 9 39N58 75w48 5:03:12
Moffitty 30 7 39N45 79w56 5:19:44
Mogees 46 90 40N08 75w21 5:01:24
Mohns Hill 6 101 40N18 76w00 5:04:00
Mohnton 6 101 40N17 75w59 5:03:56
Mohrsville 6 80 40N28 75w59 5:03:56
Molino 54 1 40N38 76w05 5:04:20
Mollenauer 2 114 40N20 80w02 5:20:08
Molltown 6 8 40N27 75w50 5:03:20
Monaca 4 13 40N41 80w17 5:21:08
Monaghan 67 12 40N08 76w58 5:07:52
Monarch 26 105 39N59 79w37 5:18:28
Monessen 65 1 40N09 79w54 5:19:36
Mongul 28 82 40N03 77w32 5:10:08
Moninger 63 2 40N15 80w13 5:20:52
Moniteau 10 6 41N00 79w54 5:19:36
Monocacy Station 6 8 40N16 75w46 5:03:04
Monongahela 63 1 40N12 79w56 5:19:44
Monongahela Junction 2 10 40N22 79w51 5:19:24
Monroe 9 1 40N31 75w11 5:00:44
Monroe 16 6 41N14 79w32 5:18:08
Monroe Heights 2 114 40N26 79w47 5:19:08
Monroeton 8 60 41N43 76w29 5:05:56
Monroeville 2 114 40N26 79w45 5:19:00
Monroeville Mall 2 114 40N26 79w47 5:19:08
Mont Alto 28 7 39N51 77w34 5:10:16
Montandon 49 70 40N58 76w51 5:07:24
Mont Clare 46 8 40N08 75w30 5:02:00
Montdale 35 18 41N28 75w36 5:02:24
Montebello 50 51 40N24 77w02 5:08:08
Montello 6 101 40N18 76w00 5:04:00
Monterey 6 8 40N31 75w47 5:03:08
Monterey 28 1 39N43 77w28 5:09:52
Monterey 36 28 40N05 76w11 5:04:44
Montgomery 41 82 41N10 76w53 5:07:32
Montgomery Ferry 50 1 40N29 77w08 5:08:32
Montgomery Square 46 8 40N15 75w15 5:01:00
Montgomeryville 46 8 40N15 75w15 5:01:00
Montmorenci 24 36 41N25 78w44 5:14:56
Montour 2 114 40N27 79w58 5:19:52
Montour 19 4 40N59 76w30 5:06:00
Montour Junction 2 114 40N30 80w10 5:20:40
Montoursville 41 82 41N15 76w55 5:07:40
Montrose 6 101 40N19 75w57 5:03:48
Montrose 58 60 41N50 75w53 5:03:32
Montrose Hill 2 114 40N30 79w51 5:19:24
Montsera 21 16 40N12 77w11 5:08:44
Monument 14 7 41N04 77w35 5:10:20
Monvue 26 51 39N51 79w54 5:19:36
Moon 2 13 40N31 80w14 5:20:56
Moon Crest 2 114 40N30 80w10 5:20:40
Moon Run 2 114 40N28 80w05 5:20:20
Moonstown 38 1 40N21 76w13 5:04:52
Moore 48 9 40N47 75w25 5:01:40
Mooredale 21 16 40N12 77w11 5:08:44
Mooresburg 47 56 40N58 76w36 5:06:24
Moores Corners 10 6 41N02 80w03 5:20:12
Moorestown 48 13 40N45 75w24 5:01:36
Moorheadville 25 91 42N13 79w50 5:19:20
Moosic 35 18 41N22 75w43 5:02:52
Morado 4 8 40N46 80w20 5:21:20
Morann 17 4 40N48 78w21 5:13:24
Moravia 37 121 40N53 80w20 5:21:20
Moravian 48 13 40N38 75w23 5:01:32
Mordansville 19 4 41N00 76w25 5:05:40
Morea Colliery 54 3 40N48 76w10 5:04:40
Moreland 41 6 41N12 76w39 5:06:36
Moreland Farms 46 1 40N11 75w06 5:00:24
Moreland Manor 46 1 40N11 75w06 5:00:24
Morewood 46 1 40N11 75w06 5:00:24
Morgan 2 114 40N21 80w09 5:20:36
Morgan 26 104 40N01 79w35 5:18:20
Morgan Hill 2 114 40N21 80w09 5:20:36
Morgans Hill 46 12 40N41 75w14 5:00:56
Morgantown 6 3 40N09 75w54 5:03:36
Morrell 26 105 39N59 79w37 5:18:28
Morris 59 6 41N36 77w18 5:09:12
Morris Crossroads 26 7 39N44 79w52 5:19:28
Morrisdale 17 7 40N57 78w14 5:12:56
Morris Run 59 6 41N41 77w01 5:08:04
Morrisville 9 9 40N13 74w47 4:59:08
Morrisville 30 1 39N54 80w11 5:20:44
Morrows Corner 3 15 40N53 79w32 5:18:08
Morstein 15 8 40N01 75w35 5:02:20
Morton 23 9 39N55 75w20 5:01:20
Mortonville 15 9 39N59 75w50 5:03:20
Morwood 46 8 40N19 75w24 5:01:36
Morysville 6 2 40N20 75w38 5:02:32
Moscow 35 4 41N20 75w31 5:02:04
Moselem 6 80 40N33 75w59 5:03:56
Moselem Springs 6 8 40N27 75w50 5:03:20
Mosgrove 3 7 40N55 79w28 5:17:52
Moshannon 14 7 41N02 78w00 5:12:00
Mosherville 8 7 41N57 76w48 5:07:12
Mosiertown 20 59 41N44 80w07 5:20:28
Mosserville 39 1 40N41 75w45 5:03:00
Moss Plan 4 19 40N42 80w17 5:21:08
Mostoller 56 6 40N07 78w57 5:15:48
Moudy Hill 11 63 40N23 78w40 5:14:40
Moulstown 67 1 39N48 76w59 5:07:56
Mount Aetna 6 25 40N25 76w18 5:05:12
Mountaindale 11 54 40N41 78w30 5:14:00
Mountain Grove 40 4 41N00 76w25 5:05:40
Mountainhome 45 84 41N11 75w17 5:01:08
Mountain Lake 8 41 41N46 76w27 5:05:48
Mountain Top 40 20 41N14 75w52 5:03:28
Mount Airy 16 7 41N06 79w30 5:18:00
Mount Airy 36 28 40N13 76w09 5:04:36
Mount Airy 51 9 40N03 75w11 5:00:44
Mount Airy Terrace 40 20 41N20 75w56 5:03:44
Mount Allen 21 12 40N12 77w00 5:08:00
Mount Alton 42 6 41N52 78w40 5:14:40
Mount Bethel 48 8 40N54 75w07 5:00:28
Mount Braddock 26 104 39N57 79w39 5:18:36
Mount Carbon 54 49 40N40 76w11 5:04:44
Mount Carmel 49 27 40N48 76w25 5:05:40
Mount Chestnut Springs 10 3 40N53 79w53 5:19:32
Mount Cobb 35 6 41N27 75w23 5:01:32
Mount Eagle 14 63 41N01 77w39 5:10:36
Mount Etna 7 3 40N28 78w12 5:12:48
Mount Gretna 38 8 40N15 76w28 5:05:52
Mount Gretna Heights 38 8 40N15 76w28 5:05:52
Mount Holly Springs 21 2 40N07 77w12 5:08:48
Mount Hope 1 56 39N47 77w22 5:09:28
Mount Hope 36 8 40N06 76w22 5:05:28
Mount Independence 26 80 39N55 79w40 5:18:40
Mount Jackson 37 112 41N00 80w21 5:21:24
Mount Jewett 42 38 41N44 78w39 5:14:36
Mount Joy 17 1 41N02 78w27 5:13:48
Mount Joy 36 2 40N07 76w30 5:06:00
Mount Joy 65 111 40N09 79w33 5:18:12
Mount Laffee 54 49 40N41 76w12 5:04:48
Mount Laurel 40 42 40N58 76w00 5:04:00
Mount Lebanon 2 114 40N23 80w03 5:20:12

PENNSYLVANIA

Mount Misery 1 1 39N52 77w03 5:08:12
Mount Morris 30 6 39N44 80w04 5:20:16
Mount Nebo 2 114 40N33 80w06 5:20:24
Mount Nebo 36 1 39N53 76w22 5:05:28
Mount Oliver 2 114 40N25 79w59 5:19:56
Mount Patrick 50 1 40N34 77w00 5:08:00
Mount Penn 6 101 40N20 75w54 5:03:36
Mount Pleasant 1 1 39N48 76w59 5:07:56
Mount Pleasant 6 1 40N26 76w07 5:04:28
Mount Pleasant 23
90 40N02 75w22 5:01:28
Mount Pleasant 34 7 40N35 77w24 5:09:36
Mount Pleasant 38 8 40N20 76w26 5:05:44
Mount Pleasant 44 7 40N43 77w35 5:10:20
Mount Pleasant 46
17 40N53 75w12 5:00:48
Mount Pleasant 50 6 40N20 77w31 5:10:04
Mount Pleasant 54
49 40N41 76w12 5:04:48
Mount Pleasant 59 6 41N36 77w18 5:09:12
Mount Pleasant 65
111 40N09 79w33 5:18:12
Mount Pleasant 67 1 40N07 77w02 5:08:08
Mount Pleasant Mills 55
6 40N43 77w01 5:08:04
Mount Pocono 45 84 41N07 75w22 5:01:28
Mountrock 21 16 40N12 77w11 5:08:44
Mount Rock 28 82 40N03 77w32 5:10:08
Mount Rock 44 73 40N36 77w34 5:10:16
Mount Royal 67 1 40N00 76w58 5:07:52
Mount Sterling 26
51 39N51 79w54 5:19:36
Mount Tabor 1 1 40N00 77w12 5:08:48
Mount Troy 2 114 40N28 80w01 5:20:04
Mount Union 28 1 39N55 77w34 5:10:16
Mount Union 31 85 40N23 77w53 5:11:32
Mount Vernon 2 8 40N18 79w48 5:19:12
Mount Vernon 15 3 39N47 75w59 5:03:56
Mount Vernon 36 23 39N59 76w02 5:04:08
Mountville 36 8 40N03 76w26 5:05:44
Mount Washington 2
114 40N26 80w01 5:20:04
Mount Washington 4
8 40N46 80w20 5:21:20
Mount Wilson 38 8 40N20 76w26 5:05:44
Mount Wolf 67 7 40N04 76w43 5:06:52
Mount Zion 21 16 40N12 77w11 5:08:44
Mount Zion 38 8 40N20 76w26 5:05:44
Mount Zion 40 1 41N20 75w49 5:03:16
Mount Zion 45 23 41N00 75w11 5:00:44
Mount Zion 67 67 39N59 76w46 5:07:04
Moween 65 116 40N29 79w27 5:17:48
Mowersville 28 82 40N03 77w32 5:10:08
Mowry 54 27 40N47 76w21 5:05:24
Moyer 26 104 40N01 79w35 5:18:20
Moylan 23 90 39N55 75w23 5:01:32
Mozart 9 8 40N18 75w05 5:00:20
Muddycreek 10 6 40N56 80w07 5:20:28
Muddy Creek Forks 67
1 39N50 76w24 5:05:36
Muhlenberg 6 101 40N24 75w56 5:03:44
Muhlenberg 40 1 41N12 76w04 5:04:16
Muhlenberg Park 6
101 40N23 75w56 5:03:44
Muir 54 27 40N36 76w31 5:06:04
Mullertown 67 1 39N48 76w59 5:07:56
Mumbauersville 9 2 40N24 75w30 5:02:00
Mummasburg 1 1 39N49 77w11 5:08:44
Muncy 41 83 41N12 76w47 5:07:08
Muncy Creek 41 83 41N12 76w45 5:07:00
Muncy Valley 57 6 41N21 76w35 5:06:20
Munderf 33 34 41N10 79w05 5:16:20
Mundys Corner 11 74 40N21 78w54 5:15:36
Munhall 2 114 40N25 79w54 5:19:36
Munhall Terrace 2
114 40N22 79w54 5:19:36
Munntown 63 2 40N11 80w08 5:20:32
Munson 17 7 40N57 78w10 5:12:40
Munster 11 55 40N28 78w39 5:14:36
Murdock 56 6 40N01 79w05 5:16:20
Murdocksville 2 6 40N29 80w18 5:21:12
Murphy Siding 26
104 40N01 79w35 5:18:20
Murrell 36 30 40N11 76w11 5:04:44
Murrinsville 10 6 41N06 79w54 5:19:36
Murry Hill 63 2 40N16 80w10 5:20:40
Murrysville 65 114 40N26 79w39 5:18:36
Muse 63 2 40N18 80w12 5:20:48
Mustard 2 8 40N17 79w50 5:19:20
Mutual 65 99 40N18 79w34 5:18:16
Myersburg 8 41 41N46 76w24 5:05:36
Myerstown 21 1 40N00 77w12 5:08:48
Myerstown 38 25 40N22 76w19 5:05:16
Mylo Park 11 54 40N29 78w43 5:14:52
Myobeach 66 59 41N37 76w03 5:04:12
Myoma 10 6 40N44 80w02 5:20:08
Myrtle 42 7 42N00 78w16 5:13:04
Mystic 25 3 41N48 80w03 5:20:12
Naceville 9 8 40N24 75w24 5:01:36
Nadine 2 114 40N29 79w50 5:19:20
Naginey 44 7 40N43 77w35 5:10:20
Nan Lynn Gardens 9
1 40N12 75w05 5:00:20
Nansen 24 75 41N40 78w49 5:15:16
Nanticoke 40 21 41N12 76w00 5:04:00
Nantmeal Village 15
80 40N02 75w41 5:02:44
Nanty Glo 11 63 40N28 78w50 5:15:20
Naomi 26 1 40N07 79w50 5:19:20
Napier 5 6 40N05 78w39 5:14:36
Napierville 36 30 40N11 76w11 5:04:44
Narberth 46 9 40N01 75w16 5:01:04
Narbrook Park 23 9 40N00 75w16 5:01:04
Narrows Creek 17 56 41N07 78w46 5:15:04
Narvon 36 27 40N06 75w59 5:03:56
Nashville 32 6 40N49 78w59 5:15:56
Nashville 67 95 39N53 76w52 5:07:28
Nassau Village 23 9 39N53 75w20 5:01:20
Natalie 49 27 40N48 76w25 5:05:40
National Hill 2 114 40N21 80w09 5:20:36
Natrona 2 14 40N37 79w44 5:18:56
Natrona Heights 2
14 40N37 79w44 5:18:56
Nauvoo 59 6 41N36 77w18 5:09:12
Naval Hospital 51 9 39N55 75w11 5:00:44
Navarro 48 13 40N41 75w22 5:01:28
Nay Aug 35 18 41N25 75w38 5:02:32
Nazareth 48 8 40N44 75w19 5:01:16
Nealmont 7 11 40N40 78w13 5:12:52
Neasons Hill 20 77 41N40 80w07 5:20:28
Neath 8 6 41N50 76w11 5:04:44
Nectarine 61 6 41N10 80w00 5:20:00
Ned 30 6 39N46 80w25 5:21:40
Needful 17 6 41N00 78w21 5:13:24
Needmore 29 6 39N51 78w09 5:12:36
Neelyton 31 6 40N10 77w50 5:11:20
Neffs 39 8 40N42 75w37 5:02:28
Neffs Mills 31 81 40N35 78w03 5:12:12
Neffsville 36 8 40N04 76w19 5:05:16
Neiffer 46 8 40N16 75w28 5:01:52
Neiltown 27 6 41N36 79w35 5:18:20
Neiman 67 3 39N48 76w44 5:06:56
Nellie 26 104 40N02 79w40 5:18:40
Nelson 59 59 41N59 77w14 5:08:56
Nemacolin 30 51 39N53 79w56 5:19:44
Neola 45 23 41N00 75w13 5:00:52
Nescopeck 40 1 41N03 76w13 5:04:52
Neshaminy 9 8 40N14 75w08 5:00:32
Neshaminy Falls 9
97 40N10 74w55 4:59:40
Neshaminy Hills 9
97 40N10 74w55 4:59:40
Neshaminy Valley 9
9 40N06 74w56 4:59:44
Neshaminy Woods 9
97 40N10 74w55 4:59:40
Neshannock 37 112 41N03 80w21 5:21:24
Neshannock Falls 37
6 41N07 80w15 5:21:00
Nesquehoning 13 1 40N52 75w49 5:03:16
Nether Providence 23
90 39N54 75w22 5:01:28
Neville 2 114 40N31 80w08 5:20:32
Neville Island 2
114 40N31 80w08 5:20:32
New Albany 8 60 41N36 76w27 5:05:48
New Alexandria 65 3 40N24 79w25 5:17:40
New Baltimore 56 6 39N59 78w46 5:15:04
New Baltimore 67 1 39N48 76w59 5:07:56
New Beaver 37 121 40N53 80w22 5:21:28
New Bedford 37 6 41N06 80w30 5:22:00
New Berlin 60 6 40N53 76w59 5:07:56
New Berlinville 6 2 40N21 75w38 5:02:32
Newberry 41 82 41N14 77w01 5:08:04
Newberry 67 12 40N08 76w48 5:07:12
Newberrytown 67 1 40N09 76w45 5:07:00
New Bethlehem 16 87 41N00 79w20 5:17:20
New Bloomfield 50 1 40N25 77w11 5:08:44
Newboro 26 51 39N56 79w50 5:19:20
New Bridgeville 67
1 39N52 76w37 5:06:28
New Brighton 4 19 40N44 80w19 5:21:16
New Britain 9 56 40N20 75w15 5:01:00
New Buena Vista 5 6 40N00 78w36 5:14:24
New Buffalo 50 3 40N27 76w58 5:07:52
Newburg 7 33 40N31 78w25 5:13:40
Newburg 21 82 40N08 77w33 5:10:12
Newburg 46 8 40N45 75w18 5:01:12
Newburg Homes 46 12 40N41 75w14 5:00:56
New Castle 37 112 41N00 80w21 5:21:24
New Centerville 56
4 39N57 79w12 5:16:48
New Chester 1 1 39N52 77w03 5:08:12
New Columbia 60 70 41N02 76w52 5:07:28
New Columbus 13 1 40N52 75w49 5:03:16
New Columbus 40 6 41N11 76w18 5:05:12
Newcomer 26 80 39N54 79w44 5:18:56
New Cumberland 21
12 40N14 76w53 5:07:32
New Cumberland Army Depot 67
12 40N16 76w53 5:07:32
New Danville 36 8 40N02 76w20 5:05:20
New Derry 65 3 40N24 79w25 5:17:40
New Eagle 63 1 40N13 79w57 5:19:48
Newell 26 115 40N05 79w54 5:19:36
New Enterprise 5 6 40N10 78w25 5:13:40
New Era 8 60 41N36 76w27 5:05:48
Newfield 2 114 40N29 79w50 5:19:20
Newfield 53 6 41N54 77w46 5:11:04
New Florence 65 7 40N23 79w05 5:16:20
Newfoundland 64 6 41N18 75w19 5:01:16
New Franklin 28 42 39N56 77w40 5:10:40
New Freedom 67 27 39N44 76w42 5:06:48
New Freeport 30 6 39N46 80w26 5:21:44
New Galena 9 2 40N20 75w18 5:01:12
New Galilee 4 8 40N50 80w24 5:21:36
New Garden 15 8 39N49 75w45 5:03:00
New Geneva 26 51 39N47 79w52 5:19:28
New Germantown 50 6 40N19 77w34 5:10:16
New Germany 11 63 40N23 78w40 5:14:40
New Grenada 29 6 40N11 78w07 5:12:28
New Hamburg 43 66 41N19 80w16 5:21:04
New Hanover 46 2 40N19 75w34 5:02:16
New Hanover Square 46
8 40N18 75w32 5:02:08
Newhard 39 8 40N45 75w37 5:02:28
New Holland 36 27 40N06 76w05 5:04:20
New Hope 9 8 40N22 74w57 4:59:48
New Ireland 25 58 41N54 79w51 5:19:24
New Jerusalem 6 8 40N27 75w50 5:03:20
New Kensington 65
14 40N34 79w46 5:19:04
New Kingstown 21 56 40N14 77w05 5:08:20
Newkirk 54 27 40N48 75w58 5:03:52
New Lebanon 43 6 41N25 80w05 5:20:20
New Lexington 56 4 39N55 79w11 5:16:44
Newlin 15 8 39N55 75w44 5:02:56
Newlin 19 4 40N57 76w28 5:05:52
New London 15 3 39N47 75w53 5:03:32
New London 17 54 40N45 78w32 5:14:08
New London 62 6 41N41 79w24 5:17:36
Newlonsburg 65 114 40N26 79w40 5:18:40
New Mahoning 13 8 40N50 75w42 5:02:48
Newmanstown 38 1 40N21 76w13 5:04:52
Newmansville 16 6 41N30 79w27 5:17:48
New Market 67 12 40N14 76w51 5:07:24
New Milford 58 50 41N52 75w44 5:02:56
New Millport 17 6 40N53 78w32 5:14:08
New Milltown 36 23 40N00 76w06 5:04:24
New Mines 54 27 40N41 76w20 5:05:20
New Oxford 1 88 39N52 77w04 5:08:16
New Paris 5 6 40N07 78w39 5:14:36
New Park 67 1 39N44 76w31 5:06:04
New Philadelphia 54
27 40N43 76w07 5:04:28
Newport 37 121 40N53 80w20 5:21:20
Newport 50 1 40N29 77w08 5:08:32
Newportville 9 9 40N10 74w51 4:59:24
Newportville Terrace 9
9 40N08 74w54 4:59:36
New Providence 36
27 39N56 76w12 5:04:48
New Richmond 20 6 41N38 79w59 5:19:56
New Ringgold 54 1 40N41 76w00 5:04:00
Newry 7 33 40N24 78w26 5:13:44
New Salem 26 51 39N56 79w50 5:19:20
New Salem 67 67 39N54 76w47 5:07:08
New Schaefferstown 6
1 40N26 76w07 5:04:28
New Sewickley 4 6 40N43 80w13 5:20:52
New Sheffield 4 13 40N36 80w16 5:21:04
Newside 39 8 40N45 75w37 5:02:28
New Smithville 39 8 40N31 75w47 5:03:08
New Stanton 65 111 40N13 79w37 5:18:28
New Texas 2 14 40N29 79w44 5:18:56
New Texas 36 1 39N47 76w11 5:04:44
Newton 35 44 41N27 75w46 5:03:04
Newtonburg 17 122 40N51 78w43 5:14:52
Newton Hamilton 44
85 40N24 77w50 5:11:20
Newton Lake 35 1 41N34 75w32 5:02:08
Newtown 9 8 40N14 74w57 4:59:48
New Town 14 4 40N51 78w16 5:13:04
Newtown 23 90 40N00 75w23 5:01:32
Newtown 36 26 40N02 76w31 5:06:04
Newtown 39 9 40N33 75w38 5:02:32
Newtown 40 20 41N13 75w54 5:03:36
Newtown Heights 23
90 40N00 75w23 5:01:32
Newtown Square 23 8 39N59 75w24 5:01:36
New Tripoli 39 1 40N41 75w45 5:03:00
New Vernon 43 6 41N24 80w08 5:20:32
Newville 9 2 40N20 75w18 5:01:12
Newville 21 1 40N10 77w24 5:09:36
Newville 36 4 40N33 76w49 5:07:16
New Virginia 43 117 41N15 80w30 5:22:00
New Washington 17
122 40N49 78w42 5:14:48
New Wilmington 37 6 41N07 80w20 5:21:20
Niagara 64 59 41N44 75w26 5:01:44
Niantic 46 2 40N23 75w37 5:02:28
Nicetown 51 9 40N01 75w09 5:00:36
Nicholson 66 89 41N38 75w47 5:03:08
Nickel Mines 36 9 40N01 76w08 5:04:32
Nickleville 61 1 41N11 79w43 5:18:52
Nicklin 61 109 41N25 79w50 5:19:20
Nicktown 11 92 40N37 78w48 5:15:12
Nilan 26 51 39N45 79w49 5:19:16
Niles 61 109 41N25 79w50 5:19:20
Niles Valley 59 6 41N51 77w17 5:09:08
Ninepoints 36 23 39N55 76w03 5:04:12
Nine Row 11 54 40N33 78w47 5:15:08
Nineveh 16 27 40N47 76w21 5:05:24
Nineveh 30 6 39N57 80w19 5:21:16
Nippenose 41 6 41N11 77w13 5:08:52
Nisbet 41 64 41N13 77w07 5:08:28
Nittany 14 63 41N01 77w39 5:10:36
Niverton 56 6 39N44 79w08 5:16:32
Nixon 10 3 40N53 79w53 5:19:32
Noble 46 9 40N06 75w09 5:00:36
Noblestown 2 51 40N23 80w13 5:20:52
Nockamixon 9 1 40N31 75w11 5:00:44
Nolo 32 6 40N37 79w01 5:16:04
Nook 34 7 40N34 77w25 5:09:40
Nordmont 57 6 41N21 76w35 5:06:20
Normal 13 8 40N50 75w42 5:02:48
Normalville 26 6 40N00 79w27 5:17:48
Norristown 46 90 40N07 75w21 5:01:24
Norrisville 20 6 41N46 80w22 5:21:28
North 8 41 41N48 76w28 5:05:52
North Abington 35
44 41N33 75w42 5:02:48
Northampton 48 13 40N41 75w30 5:02:00
Northampton Hills 9
1 40N11 75w03 5:00:12
North Annville 38 1 40N21 76w32 5:06:08
North Apollo 3 4 40N36 79w34 5:18:16
North Ardmore 46 9 40N00 75w17 5:01:08
North Aronimink 23
9 39N58 75w18 5:01:12
North Bangor 46 17 40N53 75w12 5:00:48
North Barnesboro 11
92 40N40 78w47 5:15:08
North Beaver 37 112 40N57 80w26 5:21:44
North Belle Vernon 65
1 40N08 79w52 5:19:28
North Bend 18 7 41N21 77w42 5:10:48

North Bessemer 2 114 40N28 79W50 5:19:20
North Bethlehem 63 51 40N06 80W06 5:20:24
North Bingham 53 6 41N59 77W46 5:11:04
North Braddock 2 114 40N25 79W52 5:19:28
North Branch 66 6 41N33 76W11 5:04:44
Northbrook 15 8 39N55 75W41 5:02:44
Northbrook Hills 36 8 40N04 76W19 5:05:16
North Buffalo 3 15 40N46 79W35 5:18:20
North Butler 10 3 40N53 79W53 5:19:32
North Catasauqua 48 13 40N40 75W29 5:01:56
North Centre 19 6 41N04 76W21 5:05:24
North Charleroi 63 1 40N09 79W55 5:19:40
North Codorus 67 95 39N52 76W49 5:07:16
North Connellsville 26 104 40N02 79W35 5:18:20
North Cornwall 38 8 40N19 76W27 5:05:48
North Coventry 15 8 40N13 75W41 5:02:44
North East 25 91 42N13 79W50 5:19:20
North Edinburg 37 112 41N01 80W26 5:21:44
North End 40 20 41N16 75W51 5:03:24
North Essington 23 9 39N52 75W17 5:01:08
North Fayette 2 51 40N25 80W14 5:20:56
North Fogelsville 39 9 40N33 75W38 5:02:32
North Fork 53 6 41N55 77W32 5:10:08
North Franklin 63 3 40N09 80W16 5:21:04
North Fredericktown 63 6 40N01 80W00 5:20:00
North Freedom 3 6 41N02 79W15 5:17:00
North Hamilton 9 8 40N21 75W13 5:00:52
North Heidelberg 6 1 40N24 76W07 5:04:28
North Hills 46 9 40N07 75W10 5:00:40
North Hopewell 67 1 39N49 76W36 5:06:24
North Huntingdon 65 25 40N20 79W44 5:18:56
North Irwin 65 25 40N20 79W43 5:18:52
North Jackson 58 59 41N57 75W37 5:02:28
North Larchmont 23 90 40N00 75W23 5:01:32
North Lebanon 38 8 40N22 76W25 5:05:40
North Liberty 43 6 41N10 80W05 5:20:20
North Londonderry 38 1 40N20 76W35 5:06:20
North Mahoning 32 6 40N53 79W03 5:16:12
North Manheim 54 27 40N39 76W09 5:04:36
North McKees Rocks 2 114 40N28 80W05 5:20:20
North Mehoopany 66 59 41N34 76W04 5:04:16
North Middleton 21 16 40N14 77W12 5:08:48
Northmoreland 66 6 41N26 75W56 5:03:44
North Mountain 41 6 41N21 76W35 5:06:20
North Newton 21 1 40N09 77W27 5:09:48
North Oakland 10 6 40N57 79W45 5:19:00
North Orwell 8 60 41N51 76W21 5:05:24
North Philadelphia 51 9 40N00 75W10 5:00:40
North Philipsburg 14 113 40N54 78W13 5:12:52
North Pine Grove 16 6 41N25 79W14 5:16:56
North Point 5 51 40N10 78W13 5:12:52
Northpoint 32 6 40N54 79W08 5:16:32
North Radcliffe 9 9 40N08 74W51 4:59:24
North Rochester 4 19 40N42 80W17 5:21:08
North Rome 8 41 41N46 76W24 5:05:36
North Scottdale 65 111 40N06 79W35 5:18:20
North Scranton 35 18 41N26 75W40 5:02:40
North Sewickley 4 121 40N48 80W17 5:21:08
North Shenango 20 7 41N36 80W28 5:21:52
North Springfield 25 51 42N00 80W26 5:21:44
North Strabane 63 2 40N14 80W09 5:20:36
North Towanda 8 41 41N46 76W27 5:05:48
Northumberland 49 82 40N54 76W48 5:07:12
North Vandergrift 3 4 40N36 79W34 5:18:16
North Versailles 2 9 40N23 79W49 5:19:16
Northvue 10 3 40N53 79W53 5:19:32
North Wales 46 8 40N13 75W17 5:01:08
North Warren 62 120 41N52 79W09 5:16:36
North Washington 10 6 41N03 79W49 5:19:16
North Washington 65 4 40N32 79W36 5:18:24
North Waynesburg 30 100 39N45 77W34 5:10:16
North Weissport 13 8 40N50 75W42 5:02:48
North Whitehall 39 8 40N40 75W35 5:02:20
Northwood 7 11 40N40 78W13 5:12:52
North Woodbury 7 51 40N17 78W19 5:13:16
North York 67 67 39N59 76W44 5:06:56
Norvelt 65 111 40N12 79W30 5:18:00
Norwegian 54 49 40N41 76W14 5:04:56
Norwich 42 6 41N42 78W23 5:13:32
Norwin Heights 65 25 40N20 79W43 5:18:52
Norwood 2 114 40N28 80W05 5:20:20
Norwood 23 9 39N53 75W18 5:01:12
Norwood Acres 23 9 39N53 75W18 5:01:12
Norwood Park 23 9 39N53 75W18 5:01:12
Nossville 31 6 40N17 77W43 5:10:52
Nottingham 9 1 40N08 74W58 4:59:52
Nottingham 15 3 39N45 76W01 5:04:04
Nowrytown 32 116 40N29 79W27 5:17:48
Noxen 66 6 41N26 76W04 5:04:16
Noyes 18 7 41N17 77W50 5:11:20
Nuangola 40 1 41N09 75W59 5:03:56
Nuangola Station 40 20 41N14 75W52 5:03:28
Number Fifty Six 51 9 39N57 75W09 5:00:36
Numidia 19 27 40N53 76W24 5:05:36
Nu Mine 3 6 40N48 79W18 5:17:12
Nuremberg 54 60 40N56 76W10 5:04:40
Nuremburg 21 1 40N56 76W11 5:04:44
Nyesville 28 42 39N56 77W40 5:10:40
Oakbottom 36 27 39N54 76W10 5:04:40
Oakdale 2 114 40N24 80W11 5:20:44
Oakdale 40 20 41N20 75W54 5:03:36
Oakdale Manor 9 9 40N12 74W49 4:59:16
Oakeola 23 9 39N54 75W18 5:01:12
Oakford 9 1 40N09 74W58 4:59:52
Oakford Park 65 3 40N20 79W37 5:18:28
Oak Forest 30 1 39N54 80W11 5:20:44
Oak Grove 17 4 40N57 78W14 5:12:56
Oak Grove 54 9 40N36 76W23 5:05:32
Oakgrove 65 110 40N15 79W14 5:16:56
Oak Hall 14 9 40N46 77W48 5:11:12
Oak Hill 2 114 40N27 79W50 5:19:20
Oak Hill 2 114 40N23 79W49 5:19:16
Oak Hill 17 6 41N07 78W07 5:12:28
Oak Hill 35 18 41N22 75W43 5:02:52
Oakland 2 114 40N27 79W57 5:19:48
Oakland 37 112 41N00 80W21 5:21:24
Oakland 58 59 41N57 75W37 5:02:28
Oakland Beach 20 6 41N36 80W19 5:21:16
Oakland Mills 34 1 40N37 77W19 5:09:16
Oak Lane 46 9 40N04 75W07 5:00:28
Oaklane Manor 46 9 40N05 75W08 5:00:32
Oakleigh 22 12 40N16 76W49 5:07:16
Oaklyn 49 82 40N52 76W47 5:07:08
Oakmont 2 14 40N32 79W50 5:19:20
Oakmont 11 74 40N17 78W53 5:15:32
Oakmont 23 9 40N00 75W18 5:01:12
Oakmont Park 23 9 40N00 75W18 5:01:12
Oak Park 46 8 40N15 75W17 5:01:08
Oak Park 49 82 40N54 76W48 5:07:12
Oak Park Trailer Camp 46 8 40N17 75W18 5:01:12
Oak Ridge 3 6 41N00 79W18 5:17:12
Oakryn 36 1 39N47 76W11 5:04:44
Oaks 46 8 40N08 75W27 5:01:48
Oak Shade 36 27 39N54 76W10 5:04:40
Oakview 23 9 39N57 75W18 5:01:12
Oakview Park 23 9 39N57 75W18 5:01:12
Oakville 21 23 39N59 76W02 5:04:08
Oakville 65 3 40N19 79W23 5:17:32
Oakwood 37 112 41N00 80W22 5:21:28
Oakwood Park 40 20 41N15 75W53 5:03:32
Oalmer Park 46 12 40N41 75W14 5:00:56
Obelisk 46 8 40N17 75W29 5:01:56
Oberlin 22 12 40N14 76W50 5:07:20
Oberlin Gardens 22 12 40N14 76W50 5:07:20
Observatory 2 114 40N29 80W01 5:20:04
Odenthal 11 63 40N23 78W40 5:14:40
Odenwelder 46 12 40N41 75W14 5:00:56
Odin 53 66 41N46 78W01 5:12:04
Ogden 23 90 39N50 75W27 5:01:48
Ogdensburg 59 7 41N34 76W57 5:07:48
Ogle 10 6 40N42 80W01 5:20:04
Ogle 56 6 40N13 78W43 5:14:52
Ogletown 56 123 40N15 78W50 5:15:20
Ogontz 46 9 40N04 75W07 5:00:28
Ogontz Campus 46 2 40N07 75W07 5:00:28
O'hara 2 114 40N30 79W54 5:19:36
Ohio 2 114 40N33 80W06 5:20:24
Ohiopyle 26 4 39N52 79W30 5:18:00
Ohioview 4 19 40N40 80W24 5:21:36
Ohioville 4 6 40N41 80W30 5:22:00
Ohl 33 6 41N08 79W11 5:16:44
Oil City 11 55 40N24 78W38 5:14:32
Oil City 61 9 41N26 79W42 5:18:48
Oil Creek 61 9 41N25 79W42 5:18:48
Oklahoma 17 56 41N07 78W46 5:15:04
Oklahoma 65 4 40N35 79W34 5:18:16
Okome 41 6 41N21 77W25 5:09:40
Olanta 17 122 40N50 78W41 5:14:44
Old Boston 40 1 41N19 75W46 5:03:04
Old Clarendon 62 3 41N47 79W06 5:16:24
Old Concord 63 3 40N10 80W16 5:21:04
Old Crabtree 65 3 40N19 79W23 5:17:32
Old Enon 37 6 40N51 80W27 5:21:48
Old Forge 35 18 41N22 75W45 5:03:00
Oldframe 26 51 39N48 79W49 5:19:16
Old Junction 56 6 40N01 79W05 5:16:20
Old Line 36 8 40N06 76W22 5:05:28
Old Lycoming 41 82 41N16 77W05 5:08:20
Old Meadow 65 111 40N06 79W35 5:18:20
Old Orchard 46 12 40N41 75W14 5:00:56
Old Port 34 7 40N32 77W24 5:09:36
Old Stanton 65 111 40N13 79W36 5:18:24
Old Zionsville 39 13 40N29 75W31 5:02:04
Oleopolis 61 9 41N25 79W42 5:18:48
Oley 6 1 40N22 75W46 5:03:04
Oley Furnace 6 101 40N23 75W54 5:03:36
Oliphant Furnace 26 80 39N51 79W44 5:18:56
Oliveburg 33 51 41N00 79W02 5:16:08
Oliver 26 80 39N55 79W43 5:18:52
Olivers Mills 40 20 41N15 75W53 5:03:32
Olivet 3 116 40N32 79W28 5:17:52
Olney 51 9 40N02 75W07 5:00:28
Olyphant 35 18 41N28 75W36 5:02:24
Oneida 10 3 40N53 79W53 5:19:32
Oneida 31 81 40N33 77W58 5:11:52
Oneida 54 60 40N54 76W08 5:04:32
Oneida Junction 40 42 40N58 76W00 5:04:00
Onnalinda 11 63 40N19 78W42 5:14:48
Ono 38 1 40N24 76W32 5:06:08
Ontario 63 51 40N06 80W04 5:20:16
Ontelaunee 6 80 40N27 75W57 5:03:48
Opp 41 83 41N12 76W47 5:07:08
Oppermans Corner 15 8 40N06 75W37 5:02:28
Option 2 114 40N22 79W58 5:19:52
Orange 19 6 41N06 76W25 5:05:40
Orange 40 20 41N20 75W56 5:03:44
Orangeville 19 4 41N05 76W25 5:05:40
Orbisonia 31 6 40N15 77W54 5:11:36
Orchard Beach 25 91 42N13 79W50 5:19:20
Orchard Crossing 7 11 40N40 78W13 5:12:52
Orchard Hill 65 111 40N09 79W33 5:18:12
Orchard Hills 3 4 40N35 79W32 5:18:08
Orchard Hills 23 90 39N55 75W22 5:01:28
Orchard Park 36 8 40N04 76W19 5:05:16
Orefield 39 13 40N38 75W35 5:02:20
Oregon 36 28 40N05 76W11 5:04:44
Oregon 64 59 41N39 75W13 5:00:52
Oregon Hill 41 6 41N36 77W18 5:09:12
Ore Hill 7 3 40N20 78W24 5:13:36
Oreland 46 9 40N07 75W11 5:00:44
Oreland Gardens 46 9 40N07 75W11 5:00:44
Oreminea 7 3 40N28 78W12 5:12:48
Ore Valley 67 67 39N57 76W42 5:06:48
Oreville 6 9 40N30 75W40 5:02:40
Orient 26 51 39N57 79W52 5:19:28
Oriental 34 1 40N34 77W00 5:08:00
Oriole 41 6 41N14 77W15 5:09:00
Ormrod 39 13 40N40 75W30 5:02:00
Ormsby 42 6 41N48 78W33 5:14:12
Orners Corner 7 33 40N31 78W25 5:13:40
Orrstown 28 1 40N04 77W37 5:10:28
Orrtanna 1 4 39N51 77W22 5:09:28
Orrville 2 119 40N33 79W47 5:19:08
Orson 64 6 41N49 75W27 5:01:48
Orvilla 46 8 40N17 75W18 5:01:12
Orviston 14 7 41N06 77W45 5:11:00
Orwell 8 6 41N53 76W16 5:05:04
Orwigsburg 54 1 40N39 76W06 5:04:24
Orwin 54 27 40N36 76W33 5:06:12
Osborne 2 13 40N32 80W10 5:20:40
Osceola 59 6 41N59 77W21 5:09:24
Osceola Mills 17 4 40N51 78W16 5:13:04
Osgood 43 59 41N24 80W23 5:21:32
Oshanter 17 1 41N02 78W27 5:13:48
Ostend 17 122 40N51 78W43 5:14:52
Osterburg 5 7 40N16 78W31 5:14:04
Osterhout 66 59 41N32 75W57 5:03:48
Oswayo 53 6 41N55 78W01 5:12:04
Ottawa 47 6 40N58 76W36 5:06:24
Otter Creek 43 59 41N24 80W18 5:21:12
Otto 42 6 41N57 78W29 5:13:56
Ottown 5 6 40N01 78W22 5:13:28
Ottsville 9 1 40N26 75W08 5:00:32
Ott Town 5 6 40N01 78W22 5:13:28
Outcrop 26 51 39N48 79W49 5:19:16
Outlet 40 20 41N20 75W56 5:03:44
Outwood 54 9 40N36 76W23 5:05:32
Oval 41 64 41N13 77W07 5:08:28
Overbrook 51 9 39N59 75W16 5:01:04
Overbrook Hills 46 9 39N59 75W16 5:01:04
Overfield 66 6 41N31 75W50 5:03:20
Overholt Acres 65 25 40N20 79W43 5:18:52
Overleigh 46 9 40N01 75W15 5:01:00
Overlook 36 8 40N04 76W19 5:05:16
Overton 8 60 41N35 76W32 5:06:08
Overview 21 12 40N20 76W59 5:07:56
Owensdale 26 104 40N01 79W35 5:18:20
Oxford 15 3 39N47 75W59 5:03:56
Oyster Point 36 8 40N02 76W17 5:05:08
P&OV Junction 2 114 40N28 80W05 5:20:20
P & W Patch 63 6 40N17 80W28 5:21:52
Packer 13 80 40N54 75W53 5:03:32
Packerton 13 8 40N50 75W42 5:02:48
Pageville 25 7 41N54 80W22 5:21:28
Paint 56 123 40N15 78W50 5:15:20
Painter Run 59 59 41N54 77W08 5:08:32
Paintersville 44 6 40N39 77W27 5:09:48
Paintersville 65 111 40N13 79W36 5:18:24
Paintertown 65 25 40N20 79W43 5:18:52
Paisley 30 51 39N54 79W58 5:19:52
Palestine 17 4 40N57 78W14 5:12:56
Paletown 9 8 40N25 75W23 5:01:32
Palm 46 2 40N26 75W32 5:02:08
Palmdale 22 31 40N18 76W37 5:06:28
Palmer 20 6 41N46 80W22 5:21:28
Palmer 46 8 40N42 75W16 5:01:04
Palmer Heights 46 12 40N41 75W14 5:00:56
Palmerton 13 8 40N48 75W37 5:02:28
Palmyra 38 31 40N18 76W36 5:06:24
Palo Alto 5 51 39N50 78W43 5:14:52
Palo Alto 54 49 40N41 76W10 5:04:40
Palomino Farms 9 8 40N15 75W08 5:00:32
Pancoast 33 6 41N06 78W53 5:15:32
Panic 33 6 41N06 78W53 5:15:32
Panorama Village 14 9 40N48 77W52 5:11:28
Pansy 33 6 41N08 79W11 5:16:44
Pansy Hill 38 8 40N20 76W26 5:05:44
Panther 52 6 41N19 75W19 5:01:16

PENNSYLVANIA

PENNSYLVANIA

Paoli 15	8	40N02	75w29	5:01:56
Paper Mills 46	1	40N09	75w04	5:00:16
Paradise 36	9	40N02	76w08	5:04:32
Paradise 54	9	40N36	76w23	5:05:32
Paradise Falls 45	84	41N09	75w17	5:01:08
Paradise Valley 45	84	41N09	75w17	5:01:08
Pardee 17	113	40N54	78w13	5:12:52
Pardeesville 40	42	41N00	75w57	5:03:48
Pardoe 43	66	41N14	80w14	5:20:56
Pardus 33	6	41N06	78w53	5:15:32
Paris 63	6	40N23	80w24	5:21:36
Park 65	4	40N37	79w34	5:18:16
Parkchester 15	13	39N57	75w36	5:02:24
Park Crest 54	27	40N48	76w20	5:05:20
Parker 10	6	41N04	79w44	5:18:56
Parker City 3	6	41N05	79w41	5:18:44
Parker Ford 15	8	40N13	75w36	5:02:24
Parkersville 15	13	39N57	75w36	5:02:24
Parkesburg 15	32	39N58	75w55	5:03:40
Park Gate 37	121	40N52	80w16	5:21:04
Park Heights 67	1	39N48	76w59	5:07:56
Parkhill 11	74	40N22	78w52	5:15:28
Park Hills 14	9	40N48	77w52	5:11:28
Park Hills 67	1	39N48	76w59	5:07:56
Parkland 9	97	40N10	74w55	4:59:40
Park Manor 6	101	40N19	75w57	5:03:48
Park Meadows 65	25	40N20	79w43	5:18:52
Park Place 54	3	40N49	76w08	5:04:32
Parks 3	4	40N39	79w32	5:18:08
Parkside 23	90	39N52	75w23	5:01:32
Parkside Courts 39	13	40N37	75w31	5:02:04
Parkside Manor 23	90	39N52	75w23	5:01:32
Parktown Estates 9	9	40N12	74w49	4:59:16
Parkview 2	114	40N31	79w53	5:19:32
Parkview Gardens 39	13	40N39	75w30	5:02:00
Park View Heights 14	70	40N53	77w45	5:11:00
Parkville 67	1	39N47	76w58	5:07:52
Parkway Center 2	114	40N26	80w03	5:20:12
Parkway Manor 39	13	40N37	75w31	5:02:04
Parkwood 32	6	40N40	79w18	5:17:12
Park Wynne Estates 23	9	39N58	75w22	5:01:28
Parnassus 65	14	40N34	79w45	5:19:00
Parrs Mill 19	4	40N57	76w28	5:05:52
Parryville 13	8	40N49	75w40	5:02:40
Parsonville 10	6	41N01	79w44	5:18:56
Parsonville 17	4	40N50	78w21	5:13:24
Parvin 18	76	41N06	77w29	5:09:56
Paschall 51	9	39N56	75w14	5:00:56
Passmore 6	2	40N22	75w38	5:02:32
Patchel Run 61	109	41N25	79w50	5:19:20
Patchinville 17	63	40N44	78w49	5:15:16
Patterson 4	8	40N45	80w20	5:21:20
Patterson Grove 40	1	41N09	76w10	5:04:40
Patterson Heights 4	8	40N45	80w20	5:21:20
Patterson Hill 2	8	40N17	79w50	5:19:20
Pattersons Mill 63	6	40N17	80w28	5:21:52
Patterson Township 4	8	40N46	80w20	5:21:20
Pattersonville 54	1	40N52	76w14	5:04:56
Patton 11	57	40N38	78w39	5:14:36
Pattonville 3	15	40N46	79w32	5:18:08
Paulton 65	4	40N34	79w35	5:18:20
Paupack 52	6	41N27	75w16	5:01:04
Pavia 5	7	40N12	78w31	5:14:04
Paxinos 49	1	40N51	76w36	5:06:24
Paxtang 22	12	40N16	76w50	5:07:20
Paxtang Manor 22	12	40N16	76w49	5:07:16
Paxton 22	1	40N39	76w54	5:07:36
Paxtonia 22	12	40N16	76w49	5:07:16
Paxtonville 55	6	40N46	77w05	5:08:20
Peacedale 15	3	39N47	75w59	5:03:56
Peach Bottom 67	7	39N45	76w21	5:05:24
Peach Bottom Village 36	1	39N47	76w11	5:04:44
Peach Glen 1	1	39N59	77w15	5:09:00
Pealertown 19	4	41N05	76w25	5:05:40
Peanut 37	112	41N01	80w26	5:21:44
Peanut 65	3	40N20	79w18	5:17:12
Pearl 61	6	41N22	79w56	5:19:44
Pebble Acres 9	8	40N21	75w13	5:00:52
Pebble Hill 9	8	40N21	75w13	5:00:52
Pecan 61	6	41N22	79w56	5:19:44
Pechin 26	105	39N59	79w37	5:18:28
Pecks Pond 52	6	41N14	74w53	4:59:32
Peckville 35	1	41N29	75w35	5:02:20
Pemberton 31	11	40N40	78w13	5:12:52
Pen Argyl 48	17	40N52	75w16	5:01:04
Penarth 46	9	40N01	75w15	5:01:00
Penbrook 22	12	40N17	76w51	5:07:24
Pencoyd 46	9	40N02	75w15	5:01:00
Pendle Hill 23	90	39N54	75w22	5:01:28
Penfield 17	7	41N13	78w35	5:14:20
Penfield 23	9	40N00	75w18	5:01:12
Penfield Downs 46	9	39N59	75w16	5:01:04
Penllyn 46	8	40N10	75w17	5:01:08
Pen Mar 28	100	39N45	77w34	5:10:16
Penn 65	3	40N20	79w38	5:18:32
Penn Allen 46	8	40N45	75w18	5:01:12
Pennbrook 46	8	40N15	75w17	5:01:08
Penn Center 51	9	39N57	75w10	5:00:40
Penncraft 26	6	39N59	80w00	5:20:00
Penndel 9	97	40N09	74w55	4:59:40
Pennersville 28	100	39N45	77w34	5:10:16
Pennfield 9	9	40N08	74w51	4:59:24
Penn Five 14	4	40N51	78w16	5:13:04
Penn Forest 13	1	40N58	75w39	5:02:36
Penn Glyn 65	25	40N20	79w43	5:18:52
Pennhall 14	64	40N51	77w34	5:10:16
Penn Heights 67	1	39N48	76w59	5:07:56
Penn Hill 36	1	39N47	76w11	5:04:44
Penn Hill Apartments 23	9	39N52	75w20	5:01:20
Penn Hill Homes 23	9	39N52	75w20	5:01:20
Penn Hills 2	114	40N28	79w52	5:19:28
Pennline 20	7	41N40	80w27	5:21:48
Penn Pines 23	9	39N56	75w18	5:01:12
Penn Pitt 30	51	39N48	79w55	5:19:40
Penn Ridge 2	114	40N28	79w50	5:19:20
Penn Rose 2	114	40N29	79w50	5:19:20
Penn Rose Park 36	8	40N04	76w19	5:05:16
Penn Run 32	6	40N37	79w01	5:16:04
Pennsburg 46	2	40N23	75w29	5:01:56
Pennsbury 15	1	39N52	75w37	5:02:28
Pennsbury Heights 9	9	40N12	74w49	4:59:16
Pennsbury Village 2	114	40N26	80w04	5:20:16
Penns Creek 55	6	40N52	77w04	5:08:16
Pennsdale 41	81	41N15	76w48	5:07:12
Pennside 6	101	40N20	75w53	5:03:32
Pennside 25	7	41N54	80w22	5:21:28
Penns Park 9	8	40N16	75w00	5:00:00
Penn Square 46	90	40N08	75w21	5:01:24
Pennsville 26	104	40N01	79w35	5:18:20
Pennsville 48	13	40N41	75w22	5:01:28
Penns Woods 65	25	40N20	79w43	5:18:52
Pennsylvania Furnace 31	6	40N42	78w00	5:12:00
Penn Valley 46	9	40N00	75w16	5:01:04
Penn Valley Terrace 9	97	40N10	74w55	4:59:40
Penn Village 46	8	40N15	75w39	5:02:36
Pennville 67	1	39N48	77w00	5:08:00
Pennwyn 6	101	40N19	75w57	5:03:48
Penn Wynne 46	9	39N59	75w16	5:01:04
Penobscot 40	20	41N14	75w52	5:03:28
Penowa 63	6	40N17	80w28	5:21:52
Penryn 36	1	40N12	76w22	5:05:28
Pequea 36	8	39N58	76w18	5:05:12
Percy 26	80	39N55	79w40	5:18:40
Perdix 50	51	40N24	77w02	5:08:08
Perkasie 9	8	40N22	75w18	5:01:12
Perkiomen 46	8	40N14	75w28	5:01:52
Perkiomen Heights 46	2	40N24	75w30	5:02:00
Perkiomen Junction 15	8	40N08	75w31	5:02:04
Perkiomen Village 46	8	40N12	75w28	5:01:52
Perkiomenville 46	8	40N19	75w29	5:01:56
Perrine Corners 43	6	41N20	80w06	5:20:24
Perrymont 2	114	40N33	80w01	5:20:04
Perryopolis 26	6	40N05	79w45	5:19:00
Perry Square 25	107	42N08	80w05	5:20:20
Perrysville 2	114	40N32	80w02	5:20:08
Perrysville 65	116	40N32	79w28	5:17:52
Perryville	4	40N31	79w32	5:18:08
Perryville 16	6	41N05	79w41	5:18:44
Perryville 41	7	41N19	77w05	5:08:20
Perulack 34	6	40N22	77w36	5:10:24
Petersburg 31	81	40N34	78w03	5:12:12
Petersburg 43	6	41N25	80w14	5:20:56
Peters Corner 9	8	40N21	75w05	5:00:20
Peters Creek 2	8	40N18	79w54	5:19:36
Peters Store 39	8	40N45	75w37	5:02:28
Petersville 48	13	40N41	75w22	5:01:28
Petrolia 10	6	41N01	79w43	5:18:52
Pettis 20	77	41N40	80w07	5:20:28
Pew 16	6	41N02	79w15	5:17:00
Pheasant Hill 36	8	40N04	76w19	5:05:16
Philadelphia 51	9	39N57	75w10	5:00:40
Philipsburg 14	113	40N54	78w13	5:12:52
Philipsburg 63	1	40N04	79w54	5:19:36
Phillips 26	80	39N54	79w44	5:18:56
Phillips 59	6	41N55	77w32	5:10:08
Phillipston 16	7	41N02	79w30	5:18:00
Phillipsville 15	9	39N59	75w50	5:03:20
Phillipsville 25	7	42N00	79w48	5:19:12
Philmont 46	1	40N09	75w03	5:00:12
Philmont Manor 46	1	40N09	75w03	5:00:12
Philmont Park 46	1	40N09	75w03	5:00:12
Phoenix Park 54	49	40N41	76w12	5:04:48
Phoenixville 15	8	40N08	75w31	5:02:04
Piatt 41	64	41N13	77w13	5:08:52
Picture Rocks 41	6	41N17	76w43	5:06:52
Pierce 2	8	40N18	79w54	5:19:36
Pierce 3	6	41N02	79w15	5:17:00
Pierceville 67	3	39N48	76w44	5:06:56
Pigeon 27	6	41N28	79w07	5:16:28
Pikeland 15	8	40N06	75w37	5:02:28
Piketown 22	12	40N19	76w48	5:07:12
Pikeville 6	101	40N23	75w54	5:03:36
Pilgrim Gardens 23	9	39N57	75w18	5:01:12
Pilgrimham 16	6	41N14	79w32	5:18:08
Pillow 22	4	40N38	76w48	5:07:12
Pine 18	7	41N10	77w22	5:09:28
Pine Avenue 25	107	42N06	80w03	5:20:12
Pine Bank 30	6	39N45	80w18	5:21:12
Pinecrest 9	97	40N10	74w55	4:59:40
Pinecroft 7	33	40N31	78w25	5:13:40
Pinedale 54	1	40N38	76w05	5:04:20
Pine Flats 32	6	40N40	79w00	5:16:00
Pine Forge 6	8	40N17	75w42	5:02:48
Pine Glen 14	6	41N07	78w07	5:12:28
Pine Glen 44	7	40N30	77w44	5:10:56
Pine Grove 50	6	40N22	77w21	5:09:24
Pine Grove 54	27	40N33	76w23	5:05:32
Pine Grove Furnace 21	1	40N00	77w12	5:08:48
Pine Grove Mills 14	9	40N44	77w53	5:11:32
Pine Hall 14	9	40N48	77w52	5:11:28
Pine Hill 3	15	40N49	79w32	5:18:08
Pine Hill 54	49	40N41	76w12	5:04:48
Pine Hill 56	6	39N56	78w57	5:15:48
Pine Ridge 23	90	39N55	75w22	5:01:28
Pine Run 9	8	40N21	75w13	5:00:52
Pine Run 41	64	41N14	77w08	5:08:32
Pine Summit 19	6	41N07	76w32	5:06:08
Pine Swamp 15	1	40N09	75w50	5:03:20
Pinetown 67	12	40N08	76w52	5:07:28
Pinetree 65	111	40N06	79w35	5:18:20
Pine Valley 62	3	41N56	79w35	5:18:20
Pine View 40	20	41N14	75w52	5:03:28
Pineville 9	8	40N18	75w00	5:00:00
Pineville 62	6	41N43	79w32	5:18:08
Piney 16	6	41N08	79w28	5:17:52
Piney Fork 2	114	40N17	80w00	5:20:00
Pink 64	6	41N27	75w23	5:01:32
Pinola 28	82	40N03	77w32	5:10:08
Pipersville 9	1	40N26	75w09	5:00:36
Pitcairn 2	114	40N24	79w47	5:19:08
Pitman 54	1	40N43	76w31	5:06:04
Pitt Gas 30	6	39N59	80w03	5:20:12
Pittock 2	114	40N28	80w05	5:20:20
Pittsburgh 2	114	40N26	80w01	5:20:04
Pittsburgh Plate Plan 3	15	40N46	79w32	5:18:08
Pittsburgh Valley 36	8	39N57	76w21	5:05:24
Pittsfield 62	7	41N50	79w26	5:17:44
Pittston 40	1	41N19	75w47	5:03:08
Pittsville 61	6	41N17	79w44	5:18:56
Plainfield 21	2	40N12	77w17	5:09:08
Plainfield 46	15	40N49	75w15	5:01:00
Plainfield 67	1	40N09	76w45	5:07:00
Plain Grove 37	6	41N04	80w09	5:20:36
Plains 40	20	41N16	75w50	5:03:20
Plainsville 40	20	41N16	75w51	5:03:24
Plainview 1	1	39N49	77w11	5:08:44
Planebrook 15	8	40N02	75w31	5:02:04
Plank 59	6	41N36	77w18	5:09:12
Platea 25	7	41N57	80w20	5:21:20
Plateau Heights 20	77	41N40	80w07	5:20:28
Plattsville 11	92	40N40	78w43	5:14:52
Plaza 10	3	40N53	79w53	5:19:32
Plaza Heights 67	1	39N48	76w59	5:07:56
Pleasant 62	3	41N48	79w11	5:16:44
Pleasant Corners 13	8	40N50	75w42	5:02:48
Pleasant Gap 14	70	40N52	77w45	5:11:00
Pleasant Grove 36	1	39N47	76w11	5:04:44
Pleasant Grove 63	6	40N07	80w25	5:21:40
Pleasant Grove 67	80	40N07	76w43	5:06:52
Pleasant Hall 28	1	40N03	77w39	5:10:36
Pleasant Hill 17	6	41N00	78w07	5:12:28
Pleasant Hill 17	113	40N54	78w13	5:12:52
Pleasant Hill 23	90	39N55	75w22	5:01:28
Pleasant Hill 32	72	40N38	79w09	5:16:36
Pleasant Hill 37	121	40N49	80w12	5:20:48
Pleasant Hill 38	8	40N20	76w27	5:05:48
Pleasant Hill 67	1	39N48	76w59	5:07:56
Pleasant Hills 2	114	40N20	79w58	5:19:52
Pleasant Hills 22	12	40N19	76w48	5:07:12
Pleasant Mount 64	59	41N44	75w26	5:01:44
Pleasant Union 56	79	39N49	79w02	5:16:08
Pleasant Unity 65	3	40N15	79w28	5:17:52
Pleasant Valley 6	80	40N25	75w58	5:03:52
Pleasant Valley 7	33	40N31	78w25	5:13:40
Pleasant Valley 9	13	40N29	75w25	5:01:40
Pleasant Valley 36	8	40N02	76w18	5:05:12
Pleasant Valley 54	9	40N36	76w23	5:05:32
Pleasant Valley 65	3	40N23	79w40	5:18:40
Pleasantview 4	8	40N46	80w20	5:21:20
Pleasant View 14	70	40N53	77w45	5:11:00
Pleasant View 22	12	40N16	76w43	5:06:52
Pleasantview 34	7	40N32	77w24	5:09:36
Pleasant View 67	1	39N52	76w37	5:06:28
Pleasant Village 7	33	40N31	78w25	5:13:40
Pleasantville 2	14	40N37	79w44	5:18:56
Pleasantville 5	6	40N11	78w37	5:14:28
Pleasantville 61	6	41N36	79w35	5:18:20
Pleasureville 67	67	40N01	76w43	5:06:52
Pleasureville Heights 67	67	39N59	76w46	5:07:04
Plum 2	14	40N29	79w47	5:19:08
Plum 61	74	41N38	79w40	5:18:40
Plumbridge 9	9	40N09	74w51	4:59:24
Plum Creek 2	14	40N29	79w44	5:18:56
Plumcreek 3	6	40N43	79w21	5:17:24
Plumer 61	9	41N25	79w42	5:18:48
Plummer 26	51	39N53	79w52	5:19:28
Plumsock 15	90	40N00	75w23	5:01:32
Plumstead 9	8	40N24	75w09	5:00:36
Plumsteadville 9	8	40N23	75w09	5:00:36
Plumville 32	6	40N48	79w11	5:16:44
Plunketts Creek 41	6	41N24	76w47	5:07:0[illegible]

PENNSYLVANIA

Plymouth 40	20	41N14	75w57	5:03:48
Plymouth Center 46	90	40N07	75w16	5:01:04
Plymouth Junction 40	20	41N15	75w57	5:03:48
Plymouth Meeting 46	90	40N06	75w17	5:01:08
Plymouth Valley 46	90	40N08	75w21	5:01:24
Plymptonville 17	1	41N02	78w27	5:13:48
Pocahontas 56	79	39N49	79w02	5:16:08
Pocono 45	84	41N04	75w18	5:01:12
Pocono Lake 45	3	41N06	75w31	5:02:04
Pocono Lake Preserve 45	84	41N06	75w28	5:01:52
Pocono Manor 45	84	41N06	75w22	5:01:28
Pocono Park 45	23	41N00	75w13	5:00:52
Pocono Pines 45	84	41N05	75w29	5:01:56
Pocono Summit 45	84	41N07	75w24	5:01:36
Pocono Summit Estates 45	84	41N07	75w24	5:01:36
Pocopson 15	13	39N54	75w37	5:02:28
Pogue 31	6	40N12	77w59	5:11:56
Point 5	6	40N03	78w39	5:14:36
Point 49	82	40N56	76w47	5:07:08
Point Breeze 2	114	40N29	79w50	5:19:20
Point Breeze 51	9	39N55	75w11	5:00:44
Point Marion 26	7	39N44	79w54	5:19:36
Point Phillip 48	13	40N45	75w24	5:01:36
Point Pleasant 9	1	40N25	75w04	5:00:16
Point View 7	3	40N28	78w12	5:12:48
Pokeytown 56	6	40N07	78w57	5:15:48
Poland 30	7	39N45	79w56	5:19:44
Polk 61	6	41N22	79w56	5:19:44
Polk Junction 61	6	41N22	79w56	5:19:44
Polktown 28	100	39N45	77w34	5:10:16
Polk Valley 48	13	40N35	75w20	5:01:20
Pomeroy 15	32	39N58	75w53	5:03:32
Pomeroy Heights 15	32	39N59	75w50	5:03:20
Pond Bank 28	42	39N56	77w40	5:10:40
Pond Creek 40	60	41N04	75w46	5:03:04
Pond Eddy 52	6	41N27	74w49	4:59:16
Pond Hill 40	1	41N04	76w08	5:04:32
Pont 25	7	41N54	80w22	5:21:28
Pools Corner 9	8	40N21	75w13	5:00:52
Poplar Grove 26	104	40N01	79w35	5:18:20
Poplar Grove 36	8	40N09	76w18	5:05:12
Portage 11	63	40N23	78w41	5:14:44
Portage Creek 42	6	41N49	78w17	5:13:08
Port Allegany 42	3	41N49	78w17	5:13:08
Port Barnett 33	34	41N10	79w05	5:16:20
Port Blanchard 40	1	41N19	75w47	5:03:08
Port Carbon 54	27	40N42	76w10	5:04:40
Port Clinton 54	80	40N35	76w02	5:04:08
Porter 33	51	40N56	78w58	5:15:52
Porters Sideling 67	1	39N44	76w54	5:07:36
Portersville 10	6	40N56	80w08	5:20:32
Port Griffith 40	1	41N19	75w47	5:03:08
Port Indian 46	90	40N08	75w21	5:01:24
Port Jenkins 40	60	41N04	75w46	5:03:04
Port Kennedy 46	90	40N05	75w22	5:01:28
Portland 48	8	40N55	75w06	5:00:24
Portland Mills 24	59	41N23	78w50	5:15:20
Port Matilda 14	63	40N48	78w03	5:12:12
Port Providence 46	8	40N08	75w31	5:02:04
Port Royal 34	7	40N32	77w23	5:09:32
Port Trevorton 55	51	40N42	76w52	5:07:28
Port Vue 2	10	40N20	79w52	5:19:28
Possum Hollow 37	121	40N53	80w20	5:21:20
Potetown 7	3	40N20	78w24	5:13:36
Potosi 67	3	39N48	76w44	5:06:56
Potter Brook 59	6	41N55	77w32	5:10:08
Pottersdale 17	6	41N10	78w04	5:12:16
Potters Mills 14	64	40N51	77w34	5:10:16
Potterville 8	60	41N51	76w21	5:05:24
Potts Grove 49	6	41N00	76w48	5:07:12
Pottstown 46	8	40N15	75w39	5:02:36
Pottstown Landing 15	8	40N15	75w39	5:02:36
Pottsville 54	49	40N41	76w12	5:04:48
Powder Valley 39	13	40N29	75w30	5:02:00
Powell 8	60	41N42	76w31	5:06:04
Powells Valley 22	24	40N28	76w56	5:07:44
Powelton 14	4	40N49	78w14	5:12:56
Powys 41	7	41N19	77w05	5:08:20
Poyntelle 64	6	41N49	75w25	5:01:40
Prentisvale 42	40	41N57	78w23	5:13:32
Prescott 38	8	40N20	76w26	5:05:44
Prescottville 33	6	41N06	78w53	5:15:32
President 61	6	41N27	79w33	5:18:12
Presidential Heights 2	114	40N33	80w01	5:20:04
Presque Isle 25	107	42N08	80w09	5:20:36
Pressston 2	114	40N28	80w05	5:20:20
Presto 2	114	40N23	80w07	5:20:28
Preston 40	20	41N13	75w54	5:03:36
Preston 64	6	41N51	75w25	5:01:40
Preston Hill 54	27	40N47	76w17	5:05:08
Preston Park 64	6	41N53	75w22	5:01:28
Pretoria 56	6	40N11	78w59	5:15:56
Price 45	84	41N08	75w13	5:00:52
Priceburg 35	18	41N27	75w37	5:02:28
Pricedale 65	1	40N08	79w51	5:19:24
Pricetown 6	8	40N27	75w50	5:03:20
Priceville 64	6	41N51	75w14	5:00:56
Primos 23	9	39N56	75w18	5:01:12
Primos-Secane 23	9	39N56	75w18	5:01:12
Primrose 63	51	40N22	80w16	5:21:04
Princeton 37	112	41N00	80w21	5:21:24
Pringle 40	20	41N17	75w54	5:03:36
Prittstown 26	111	40N09	79w33	5:18:12
Proctor 41	82	41N14	77w01	5:08:04
Progress 22	12	40N18	76w50	5:07:20
Prompton 64	7	41N35	75w20	5:01:20
Prospect 10	6	40N54	80w03	5:20:12
Prospect Gardens 36	8	40N02	76w17	5:05:08
Prospect Heights 48	13	40N39	75w21	5:01:24
Prospect Hill 35	18	41N28	75w36	5:02:24
Prospect Park 12	106	41N31	78w14	5:12:56
Prospect Park 23	9	39N53	75w18	5:01:12
Prospectville 46	1	40N13	75w11	5:00:44
Prosperity 63	3	40N10	80w16	5:21:04
Providence 36	78	39N55	76w14	5:04:56
Providence Downe 23	90	39N55	75w22	5:01:28
Providence Square 46	8	40N12	75w28	5:01:52
Providence Village 23	90	39N54	75w22	5:01:28
Provins Works 26	51	39N51	79w54	5:19:36
Pughtown 15	8	40N10	75w40	5:02:40
Pulaski 37	51	41N07	80w26	5:21:44
Pulasri 4	8	40N44	80w18	5:21:12
Punxsutawney 33	51	40N57	78w58	5:15:52
Purcell 5	6	39N55	78w23	5:13:32
Purchase Line 32	6	40N43	78w57	5:15:48
Puritan 11	63	40N23	78w40	5:14:40
Puritan 26	51	39N53	79w52	5:19:28
Putnam 59	59	41N45	77w05	5:08:20
Putnamville 62	6	41N56	79w08	5:16:32
Putneyville 3	6	41N00	79w20	5:17:20
Puzzletown 7	33	40N28	78w25	5:13:40
Pymatuning 43	59	41N20	80w25	5:21:40
Pyrra 3	15	40N46	79w32	5:18:08
Quakake 54	60	40N51	76w02	5:04:08
Quaker Hills 36	8	40N01	76w21	5:05:24
Quaker Lake 58	6	41N59	75w56	5:03:44
Quakertown 9	8	40N27	75w21	5:01:24
Quaker Valley 1	1	39N56	77w15	5:09:00
Quarryville 36	27	39N54	76w10	5:04:40
Quecreek 56	6	40N06	79w05	5:16:20
Queen 5	7	40N16	78w31	5:14:04
Queen 27	6	41N35	79w24	5:17:36
Queen City 19	4	40N57	76w28	5:05:52
Queens Grant 9	9	40N12	74w49	4:59:16
Queens Run 18	76	41N08	77w28	5:09:52
Queenstown 3	6	41N00	79w43	5:18:52
Quemahoning 56	6	40N08	78w58	5:15:52
Quentin 38	8	40N17	76w26	5:05:44
Quicks Bend 8	6	41N38	76w15	5:05:00
Quicktown 35	4	41N20	75w32	5:02:08
Quiggleville 41	7	41N19	77w05	5:08:20
Quincy 28	100	39N49	77w33	5:10:12
Raccoon 4	64	40N36	80w22	5:21:28
Racine 4	8	40N46	80w20	5:21:20
Radebaugh 65	99	40N18	79w34	5:18:16
Radnor 23	90	40N02	75w22	5:01:28
Rahn 54	80	40N48	75w56	5:03:44
Rahns 46	8	40N12	75w28	5:01:52
Railroad 67	27	39N46	76w42	5:06:48
Raineytown 26	104	40N03	79w39	5:18:36
Rainsburg 5	6	39N54	78w31	5:14:04
Ralpho 49	1	40N51	76w33	5:06:12
Ralphton 56	6	40N07	78w57	5:15:48
Ralston 41	7	41N30	76w57	5:07:48
Ramey 17	6	40N48	78w24	5:13:36
Ramsay Terrace 65	111	40N09	79w33	5:18:12
Ramsey 41	6	41N14	77w15	5:09:00
Ranavilla 21	12	40N14	76w57	5:07:48
Rand 2	114	40N23	79w59	5:19:56
Randolph 20	6	41N38	79w57	5:19:48
Rankin 2	114	40N25	79w53	5:19:32
Ranshaw 49	27	40N47	76w33	5:06:12
Rapho 36	1	40N10	76w27	5:05:48
Rasleytown 46	17	40N52	75w15	5:01:00
Rasselas 24	59	41N35	78w41	5:14:44
Rathbun 24	106	41N31	78w14	5:12:56
Rathmel 33	6	41N06	78w53	5:15:32
Rattigan 10	6	40N57	79w45	5:19:00
Raubsville 46	12	40N41	75w14	5:00:56
Rauchtown 18	7	41N14	77w15	5:09:00
Rauschs 54	1	40N41	76w00	5:04:00
Raven Creek 19	6	41N12	76w23	5:05:32
Raven Run 54	27	40N49	76w14	5:04:56
Ravine 54	27	40N34	76w24	5:05:36
Rawlinsville 36	1	39N50	76w19	5:05:16
Rayburn 3	15	40N50	79w29	5:17:56
Raymilton 61	6	41N22	79w56	5:19:44
Raymond 53	6	41N59	77w52	5:11:28
Rayne 32	6	40N43	79w07	5:16:28
Raytown 32	6	40N50	78w50	5:15:20
Rea 63	6	40N17	80w24	5:21:36
Reade 11	63	40N41	78w26	5:13:44
Reading 6	101	40N20	75w56	5:03:44
Reading Gardens 6	101	40N20	75w53	5:03:32
Reading Mines 56	6	40N07	78w57	5:15:48
Reagantown 65	111	40N10	79w37	5:18:28
Reamstown 36	28	40N13	76w07	5:04:28
Reamstown Heights 36	28	40N13	76w07	5:04:28
Rebel Hill 46	90	40N05	75w17	5:01:08
Rebersburg 14	6	40N57	77w27	5:09:48
Rebuck 49	6	40N43	76w44	5:06:56
Rector 65	110	40N12	79w15	5:17:00
Red Bank 60	64	40N55	77w03	5:08:12
Redbird 11	63	40N23	78w40	5:14:40
Red Bridge 28	42	39N56	77w40	5:10:40
Red Bridge 42	75	41N40	78w49	5:15:16
Redclyffe 27	6	41N28	79w07	5:16:28
Red Cross 49	4	40N45	76w47	5:07:08
Redds Mill 63	1	40N08	79w54	5:19:36
Red Hill 7	33	40N31	78w25	5:13:40
Red Hill 46	2	40N23	75w29	5:01:56
Redington 48	13	40N35	75w20	5:01:20
Red Lion 6	13	40N33	75w34	5:02:16
Red Lion 15	8	39N51	75w43	5:02:52
Red Lion 67	7	39N54	76w36	5:06:24
Red Mill 33	56	41N09	78w45	5:15:00
Red Oak 35	6	41N27	75w23	5:01:32
Red Rock 40	6	41N12	76w23	5:05:32
Red Rock 42	102	41N58	78w34	5:14:16
Red Rose Gate 9	9	40N09	74w51	4:59:24
Redrun 36	28	40N13	76w09	5:04:36
Redstone 26	51	39N59	79w50	5:19:20
Redstone Junction 26	80	39N55	79w43	5:18:52
Reduction 65	6	40N09	79w44	5:18:56
Reed 22	3	40N25	76w58	5:07:52
Reed 49	1	40N51	76w36	5:06:24
Reeder 9	8	40N22	74w56	4:59:44
Reeders 45	1	41N01	75w20	5:01:20
Reeds Gap 34	6	40N24	77w33	5:10:12
Reeds Road 15	46	40N00	75w42	5:02:48
Reedsville 44	73	40N40	77w36	5:10:24
Reels Corners 56	63	40N05	78w50	5:15:20
Reese 7	33	40N25	78w24	5:13:36
Reesedale 3	15	40N53	79w32	5:18:08
Reevesdale 54	27	40N48	75w58	5:03:52
Refton 36	8	39N57	76w14	5:04:56
Regency Park 2	14	40N29	79w44	5:18:56
Register 40	6	41N10	76w20	5:05:20
Rehrersburg 6	1	40N27	76w15	5:05:00
Reidsburg 16	37	41N12	79w22	5:17:28
Reiffton 6	101	40N20	75w53	5:03:32
Reightown 7	50	40N36	78w20	5:13:20
Reilly 54	9	40N40	76w20	5:05:20
Reillys 11	57	40N38	78w39	5:14:36
Reinerton 54	27	40N36	76w33	5:06:12
Reinholds 36	56	40N16	76w07	5:04:28
Reinoeldville 38	8	40N20	76w26	5:05:44
Reissing 63	114	40N20	80w11	5:20:44
Reistville 38	25	40N23	76w18	5:05:12
Reitz No. 2 56	63	40N07	78w49	5:15:16
Relay 67	1	39N54	76w38	5:06:32
Reliance 46	8	40N19	75w19	5:01:16
Renfrew 10	6	40N46	79w58	5:19:52
Rennerdale 2	114	40N25	80w05	5:20:20
Reno 61	109	41N25	79w50	5:19:20
Renova 18	73	41N20	77w45	5:11:00
Renovo 18	73	41N20	77w45	5:11:00
Renton 2	14	40N29	79w44	5:18:56
Renton Junction 2	14	40N29	79w44	5:18:56
Republic 26	51	39N58	79w53	5:19:32
Republican 63	1	40N04	79w54	5:19:36
Reserve 2	114	40N29	79w59	5:19:56
Reserve Township 2	114	40N28	80w01	5:20:04
Reservoir 7	33	40N25	78w24	5:13:36
Retort 14	4	40N49	78w14	5:12:56
Revere 9	1	40N31	75w10	5:00:40
Revloc 11	54	40N29	78w46	5:15:04
Rew 42	6	41N54	78w32	5:14:08
Reward 50	1	40N33	77w09	5:08:36
Rexford 59	6	41N45	77w34	5:10:16
Rexis 32	6	40N29	78w55	5:15:40
Rexmont 38	8	40N17	76w25	5:05:40
Rextown 39	8	40N45	75w37	5:02:28
Reyburn 40	1	41N09	76w10	5:04:40
Reynolds 54	27	40N48	75w58	5:03:52
Reynoldsdale 5	6	40N07	78w39	5:14:36
Reynolds Heights 43	59	41N24	80w23	5:21:32
Reynoldsville 33	48	41N06	78w53	5:15:32
Rheems 36	2	40N08	76w34	5:06:16
Rhone 40	21	41N12	76w00	5:04:00
Ribot 31	81	40N35	78w03	5:12:12
Rice 40	1	41N09	75w57	5:03:48
Rices Landing 30	6	39N57	80w00	5:20:00
Riceville 20	7	41N47	79w48	5:19:12
Richards Grove 41	6	41N14	76w31	5:06:04
Richboro 9	1	40N13	75w01	5:00:04
Richboro Manor 9	1	40N13	75w01	5:00:04
Richeyville 63	51	40N02	79w58	5:19:52
Richfield 34	6	40N41	77w07	5:08:28
Richfol 63	2	40N16	80w11	5:20:44
Rich Hill 9	13	40N29	75w25	5:01:40
Richhill 30	6	39N54	80w27	5:21:48
Rich Hill 63	2	40N14	80w13	5:20:52
Richland 2	56	40N38	79w57	5:19:48
Richland 38	25	40N22	76w16	5:05:04
Richlandtown 9	13	40N30	75w23	5:01:32
Richmond 46	17	40N53	75w12	5:00:48
Richmond 51	9	40N00	75w07	5:00:28
Richmondale 35	59	41N39	75w28	5:01:52
Richmond Furnace 28	51	39N55	77w54	5:11:36
Riddlesburg 5	51	40N10	78w15	5:13:00
Riddlewood 23	90	39N55	75w22	5:01:28
Riderville 42	6	41N52	78w40	5:14:40
Ridgebury 8	7	41N57	76w43	5:06:52
Ridge Park 6	101	40N19	75w57	5:03:48
Ridge Valley 9	8	40N24	75w24	5:01:36
Ridgeview 22	12	40N19	76w48	5:07:12
Ridge View 65	111	40N09	79w33	5:18:12
Ridgeview Park 65	3	40N20	79w18	5:17:12
Ridgeville 47	6	40N58	76w36	5:06:24
Ridgewood 6	8	40N16	75w48	5:03:12
Ridgewood 40	20	41N16	75w51	5:03:24
Ridgewood Farm 15	13	39N57	75w36	5:02:24
Ridgewood Park 23	9	40N00	75w18	5:01:12
Ridgway 24	36	41N25	78w44	5:14:56
Ridley 23	9	39N53	75w20	5:01:20
Ridley Farms 23	9	39N54	75w20	5:01:20
Ridley Gardens 23	9	39N55	75w19	5:01:16

Ridley Park 23 9 39n53 75w20 5:01:20
Ridley Parkview 23 9 39n53 75w20 5:01:20
Riegelsville 9 12 40n36 75w12 5:00:48
Riggs 8 60 41n51 76w30 5:06:00
Rillton 65 25 40n17 79w44 5:18:56
Rimer 3 7 40n55 79w28 5:17:52
Rimersburg 16 43 41n03 79w30 5:18:00
Rimerton 3 64 40n55 79w28 5:17:52
Rinely 67 1 39n45 76w35 5:06:20
Ringdale 57 60 41n31 76w24 5:05:36
Ringertown 65 6 40n25 79w35 5:18:20
Ringgold 33 6 41n00 79w10 5:16:40
Ringing Hill 46 8 40n15 75w39 5:02:36
Ringing Rock Park 46 8 40n15 75w39 5:02:36
Ringtown 6 9 40n30 75w40 5:02:40
Ringtown 54 56 40n51 76w14 5:04:56
Risher Mine Siding 2 114 40n22 79w54 5:19:36
Rising Sun 39 8 40n45 75w37 5:02:28
Rittenhouse Gap 6 13 40n33 75w34 5:02:16
Ritzie Village 22 12 40n19 76w48 5:07:12
River Hill 2 1 40n11 79w54 5:19:36
Riverside 11 74 40n17 78w53 5:15:32
Riverside 35 18 41n28 75w37 5:02:28
Riverside 49 6 40n57 76w39 5:06:36
Riverside Junction 35 18 41n28 75w37 5:02:28
Riverton 46 17 40n53 75w12 5:00:48
River Valley 2 14 40n33 79w49 5:19:16
River View 3 6 40n30 78w52 5:15:28
Riverview 4 8 40n46 80w20 5:21:20
Riverview 17 1 41n02 78w27 5:13:48
River View 63 1 40n12 79w57 5:19:48
Riverview Acres 39 8 40n45 75w37 5:02:28
River View Park 6 101 40n23 75w56 5:03:44
Rixford 42 6 41n56 78w30 5:14:00
Roadside 28 100 39n45 77w34 5:10:16
Roaring Branch 59 7 41n34 76w57 5:07:48
Roaring Brook 35 4 41n23 75w33 5:02:12
Roaring Creek 19 1 40n54 76w21 5:05:24
Roaring Spring 7 3 40n20 78w24 5:13:36
Robb 65 29 40n23 79w04 5:16:16
Robert Bruce West 46 1 40n11 75w06 5:00:24
Robertsdale 31 6 40n11 78w07 5:12:28
Robertsville 33 51 40n56 78w58 5:15:52
Robeson 6 8 40n15 75w52 5:03:28
Robeson Extension 7 3 40n28 78w12 5:12:48
Robesonia 6 56 40n21 76w08 5:04:32
Robin Hood Lakes 45 8 40n20 75w28 5:01:52
Robinson 32 7 40n24 79w09 5:16:36
Rocherty 38 8 40n20 76w26 5:05:44
Rochester 4 19 40n42 80w17 5:21:08
Rochester Mills 32 6 40n49 78w59 5:15:56
Rochester Township 4 19 40n42 80w17 5:21:08
Rock 54 9 40n36 76w23 5:05:32
Rockdale 9 9 40n08 74w51 4:59:24
Rockdale 20 3 41n48 79w58 5:19:52
Rockdale 23 90 39n52 75w23 5:01:32
Rockdale 33 56 41n09 78w45 5:15:00
Rockdale 39 8 40n45 75w37 5:02:28
Rockefeller 49 82 40n50 76w44 5:06:56
Rock Glen 40 1 40n58 76w11 5:04:44
Rockhill 9 8 40n24 75w24 5:01:36
Rockhill 31 56 40n15 77w54 5:11:36
Rockhill 36 8 39n57 76w21 5:05:24
Rockhill Furnace 31 6 40n15 77w54 5:11:36
Rockingham 56 63 40n07 78w49 5:15:16
Rock Lake 64 59 41n44 75w26 5:01:44
Rockland 61 7 41n17 79w44 5:18:56
Rockledge 46 9 40n05 75w06 5:00:24
Rockport 13 60 40n57 75w49 5:03:16
Rockrimmin Ridge 36 28 40n05 76w11 5:04:44
Rock Run 15 9 39n59 75w50 5:03:20
Rocksprings 14 6 40n42 78w00 5:12:00
Rocks Works 26 80 39n54 79w44 5:18:56
Rockton 17 6 41n05 78w39 5:14:36
Rocktown 65 111 40n10 79w35 5:18:20
Rockville 3 15 40n46 79w32 5:18:08
Rockville 11 74 40n22 78w51 5:15:24
Rockville 15 27 40n06 75w55 5:03:40
Rockville 22 12 40n17 76w53 5:07:32
Rockville 34 7 40n35 77w24 5:09:36
Rockville 44 6 40n36 77w44 5:10:56
Rockville 46 80 40n48 75w32 5:02:08
Rockville 67 3 39n48 76w44 5:06:56
Rockwood 38 8 40n20 76w26 5:05:44
Rockwood 56 4 39n55 79w09 5:16:36
Rock Works 26 51 39n51 79w54 5:19:36
Rocky Glen 35 18 41n22 75w43 5:02:52
Rocky Grove 61 109 41n24 79w50 5:19:20
Rocky Hill 15 13 39n57 75w36 5:02:24
Rodman 7 3 40n20 78w24 5:13:36
Rodney 65 6 40n08 79w26 5:17:44
Roedersville 54 9 40n36 76w23 5:05:32
Rogers Mills 26 6 40n00 79w27 5:17:48
Rogers Stop 63 1 40n08 79w54 5:19:36
Rogerstown 26 104 40n01 79w35 5:18:20
Rogersville 30 1 39n53 80w16 5:21:04
Rogertown 62 3 41n47 79w06 5:16:24
Rohrerstown 36 8 40n03 76w22 5:05:28
Rohrsburg 19 4 41n05 76w25 5:05:40
Roler 67 1 40n00 76w58 5:07:52
Rolfe 24 36 41n30 78w41 5:14:44
Rolling Glen 15 47 40n03 75w33 5:02:12
Rolling Hills 6 101 40n19 75w57 5:03:48
Rolling Hills 39 13 40n39 75w30 5:02:00
Rolling Park 23 90 39n51 75w22 5:01:28
Romansville 15 9 39n59 75w50 5:03:20
Rome 8 60 41n51 76w21 5:05:24
Ronco 26 51 39n52 79w55 5:19:40
Ronks 36 1 40n02 76w10 5:04:40
Rook 2 114 40n26 80w03 5:20:12
Roots Crossing 7 11 40n40 78w13 5:12:52
Roscoe 63 115 40n05 79w52 5:19:28
Rose 33 34 41n08 79w06 5:16:24
Roseann 44 7 40n43 77w35 5:10:20
Rose Bud 17 54 40n45 78w32 5:14:08
Roseburg 50 1 40n29 77w08 5:08:32
Rosecrans 18 7 41n02 77w18 5:09:12
Rose Crest 2 114 40n26 79w47 5:19:08
Rosedale 2 114 40n29 79w50 5:19:20
Rosedale 9 13 40n29 75w24 5:01:36
Rosedale 15 1 39n52 75w35 5:02:20
Rosedale 26 80 39n54 79w44 5:18:56
Rosedale Heights 2 114 40n29 79w50 5:19:20
Roseglen 50 51 40n24 77w02 5:08:08
Rosehill 51 9 40n01 75w09 5:00:36
Roselawn 7 33 40n31 78w25 5:13:40
Rosemont 46 90 40n02 75w19 5:01:16
Rose Point 37 112 41n00 80w21 5:21:24
Roses 27 6 41n28 79w07 5:16:28
Roseto 46 17 40n53 75w13 5:00:52
Rose Tree 23 90 39n56 75w24 5:01:36
Rosetree Woods 23 9 39n58 75w22 5:01:28
Rose Valley 23 90 39n54 75w23 5:01:32
Rose Valley 46 1 40n09 75w12 5:00:48
Rose Valley Acres 23 90 39n55 75w22 5:01:28
Roseville 33 34 41n10 79w05 5:16:20
Roseville 36 8 40n04 76w19 5:05:16
Roseville 59 59 41n52 76w58 5:07:52
Rosewood Gardens 9 1 40n12 75w05 5:00:20
Roslyn 15 13 39n57 75w36 5:02:24
Roslyn 46 2 40n08 75w07 5:00:28
Ross Common 45 17 40n54 75w19 5:01:16
Rossford 3 15 40n46 79w32 5:18:08
Rossiter 32 51 40n54 78w56 5:15:44
Rosslyn Farms 2 114 40n26 80w06 5:20:24
Rossmere 36 8 40n04 76w19 5:05:16
Rossmoyne 21 12 40n14 76w57 5:07:48
Ross Siding 41 6 41n24 77w28 5:09:52
Rosston 3 15 40n45 79w33 5:18:12
Rossville 67 1 40n03 76w56 5:07:44
Rostraver 65 1 40n10 79w49 5:19:16
Rote 18 76 41n06 77w29 5:09:56
Rothsville 36 28 40n09 76w15 5:05:00
Rough And Ready 54 1 40n40 76w37 5:06:28
Roulette 53 6 41n47 78w09 5:12:36
Round Top 1 1 39n49 77w11 5:08:44
Roundtown 67 67 39n58 76w47 5:07:08
Rouseville 61 9 41n28 79w42 5:18:48
Rouzerville 28 100 39n44 77w32 5:10:08
Rowes Run 26 51 40n01 79w50 5:19:20
Rowland 52 59 41n28 75w03 5:00:12
Rowland Park 46 9 40n05 75w08 5:00:32
Roxborough 51 9 40n03 75w14 5:00:56
Roxbury 21 12 40n12 77w00 5:08:00
Roxbury 28 1 40n07 77w40 5:10:40
Roxbury 56 6 39n56 78w57 5:15:48
Royal 26 51 39n59 79w49 5:19:16
Royal 58 89 41n38 75w47 5:03:08
Royalton 22 80 40n11 76w43 5:06:52
Royer 7 3 40n28 78w12 5:12:48
Royersford 46 118 40n11 75w33 5:02:12
Roystone 62 3 41n42 79w02 5:16:08
Rozel Park 9 1 40n11 75w03 5:00:12
Ruble 26 51 39n48 79w49 5:19:16
Ruchsville 39 13 40n40 75w30 5:02:00
Rudytown 67 12 40n14 76w51 5:07:24
Ruffcreek 30 3 40n10 80w16 5:21:04
Ruffs Dale 65 111 40n10 79w37 5:18:28
Ruggles 66 6 41n22 76w02 5:04:08
Rumilla 46 8 40n19 75w19 5:01:16
Rummel 56 123 40n15 78w50 5:15:20
Rummerfield 8 6 41n40 76w16 5:05:04
Rundell 20 6 41n46 80w22 5:21:28
Runville 14 70 40n53 77w45 5:11:00
Rupert 19 4 41n00 76w25 5:05:40
Rural Ridge 2 14 40n35 79w50 5:19:20
Rural Valley 3 6 40n48 79w19 5:17:16
Ruscombmanor 6 8 40n26 75w49 5:03:16
Rush 58 60 41n50 75w53 5:03:32
Rushland 9 56 40n15 75w02 5:00:08
Rushtown 49 6 40n58 76w36 5:06:24
Rushville 58 59 41n55 75w38 5:02:32
Russell 62 6 41n56 79w08 5:16:32
Russell Hill 66 59 41n32 75w57 5:03:48
Russellton 2 14 40n37 79w50 5:19:20
Russellville 15 3 39n50 75w57 5:03:48
Russellville 31 3 40n23 78w10 5:12:40
Rutan 30 6 39n51 80w19 5:21:16
Rutherford 22 12 40n16 76w49 5:07:16
Ruthford 11 63 40n20 78w45 5:15:00
Ruthfred Acres 2 114 40n20 80w02 5:20:08
Rutland 59 59 41n52 76w59 5:07:56
Rutledge 23 9 39n54 75w20 5:01:20
Rutledgedale 64 6 41n42 75w04 5:00:16
Ryan 54 60 40n48 76w04 5:04:16
Ryans Corner 9 8 40n14 74w56 4:59:44
Rydal 46 9 40n06 75w06 5:00:24
Ryde 44 7 40n30 77w45 5:11:00
Rye 50 12 40n20 77w02 5:08:08
Rye 67 1 39n54 76w38 5:06:32
Ryeland 6 1 40n22 76w11 5:04:44

PENNSYLVANIA

Ryerson Station 30 6 39n55 80w26 5:21:44
Rynd Farm 61 9 41n25 79w42 5:18:48
Ryot 5 6 40n11 78w37 5:14:28
Sabinsville 59 6 41n52 77w31 5:10:04
Sabula 17 56 41n07 78w46 5:15:04
Sackett 24 75 41n40 78w49 5:15:16
Saco 8 60 41n51 76w30 5:06:00
Sacramento 54 27 40n38 76w36 5:06:24
Sadsburyville 15 32 39n59 75w54 5:03:36
Saegersville 39 8 40n42 75w42 5:02:48
Saegertown 20 59 41n43 80w09 5:20:36
Safe Harbor 36 8 39n57 76w21 5:05:24
Sagamore 3 6 40n47 79w14 5:16:56
Sagamore 26 6 40n01 79w24 5:17:36
Saginaw 67 1 40n04 76w42 5:06:48
Sagon 49 27 40n48 76w33 5:06:12
Saint Albans 23 90 40n00 75w23 5:01:32
Saint Augustine 11 63 40n36 78w31 5:14:04
Saint Benedict 11 92 40n38 78w44 5:14:56
Saint Boniface 11 57 40n40 78w41 5:14:44
Saint Charles 16 6 41n00 79w20 5:17:20
Saint Clair 54 27 40n43 76w12 5:04:48
Saint Clair 65 99 40n18 79w34 5:18:16
Saint Clair Acres 2 114 40n20 80w05 5:20:20
Saint Clairsville 5 7 40n10 78w31 5:14:04
Saint Davids 23 90 40n02 75w22 5:01:28
Saint George 61 6 41n17 79w44 5:18:56
Saint Johns 40 42 41n02 76w00 5:04:00
Saint Joseph 58 6 41n55 76w03 5:04:12
Saint Lawrence 6 101 40n19 75w53 5:03:32
Saint Lawrence 11 57 40n38 78w39 5:14:36
Saint Leonard 9 8 40n14 74w56 4:59:44
Saint Marys 24 36 41n26 78w34 5:14:16
Saint Michael 11 63 40n20 78w46 5:15:04
Saint Nicholas 54 3 40n49 76w08 5:04:32
Saint Paul 56 79 39n49 79w02 5:16:08
Saint Peters 15 56 40n11 75w44 5:02:56
Saint Petersburg 16 1 41n10 79w39 5:18:36
Saint Thomas 28 1 39n55 77w47 5:11:08
Saint Vincent 65 3 40n19 79w23 5:17:32
Saint Vincent College 65 3 40n19 79w23 5:17:32
Salco 56 6 39n56 78w57 5:15:48
Salem 17 56 41n07 78w46 5:15:04
Salem 28 42 39n56 77w40 5:10:40
Salem 43 59 41n24 80w23 5:21:32
Salem 55 82 40n48 76w52 5:07:28
Salem Harbor 9 9 40n06 74w56 4:59:44
Salemville 5 6 40n10 78w25 5:13:40
Salford 46 8 40n20 75w25 5:01:40
Salford Heights 46 8 40n17 75w23 5:01:32
Salfordville 46 8 40n18 75w26 5:01:44
Salida 2 114 40n23 79w59 5:19:56
Salina 65 116 40n31 79w30 5:18:00
Salisbury 56 79 39n45 79w05 5:16:20
Salisbury Heights 36 23 39n59 76w02 5:04:08
Salisbury Junction 56 79 39n49 79w02 5:16:08
Salix 11 63 40n18 78w46 5:15:04
Salladasburg 41 6 41n17 77w14 5:08:56
Salona 18 76 41n05 77w28 5:09:52
Saltillo 31 6 40n13 78w00 5:12:00
Saltlick 26 6 40n03 79w24 5:17:36
Saltsburg 32 116 40n29 79w27 5:17:48
Salunga 36 97 40n06 76w25 5:05:40
Saluvia 29 66 39n59 78w04 5:12:16
Sample Heights 2 114 40n30 79w59 5:19:56
Sample Run 32 6 40n40 79w00 5:16:00
Sampson 63 1 40n11 79w54 5:19:36
Sanatoga 46 8 40n15 75w36 5:02:24
Sanatoga Park 46 8 40n15 75w39 5:02:36
Sanbourn 17 4 40n50 78w21 5:13:24
Sandbeach 22 31 40n17 76w39 5:06:36
Sand Hill 38 8 40n20 76w26 5:05:44
Sandhill 45 17 40n56 75w19 5:01:16
Sand Patch 56 79 39n49 79w02 5:16:08
Sand Springs 40 42 41n01 76w00 5:04:00
Sandts Eddy 46 12 40n41 75w14 5:00:56
Sandy 17 56 41n06 78w46 5:15:04
Sandy Bank 23 90 39n55 75w22 5:01:28
Sandy Creek 2 114 40n29 79w50 5:19:20
Sandy Hill 46 90 40n08 75w21 5:01:24
Sandy Hollow 16 7 41n02 79w30 5:18:00
Sandy Lake 43 6 41n21 80w05 5:20:20
Sandy Plains 63 6 39n59 80w03 5:20:12
Sandy Ridge 14 4 40n49 78w14 5:12:56
Sandy Run 30 51 39n48 79w55 5:19:40
Sandy Run 40 20 41n20 75w54 5:03:36
Sandy Valley 33 6 41n06 78w53 5:15:32
Sandyville 52 6 41n06 75w00 5:00:00
Sanford 62 3 41n50 79w23 5:17:32
Sankertown 11 55 40n28 78w35 5:14:20
Sarah Furnace 16 7 41n02 79w30 5:18:00
Sardis 65 14 40n30 79w42 5:18:48
Sartwell 42 40 41n57 78w23 5:13:32
Sarver 10 2 40n44 79w45 5:19:00
Sarversville 10 2 40n44 79w45 5:19:00
Sassamansville 46 2 40n20 75w34 5:02:16
Satterfield 57 60 41n31 76w24 5:05:36
Satterfield Junction 57 60 41n31 76w24 5:05:36
Saulsburg 31 81 40n30 78w01 5:12:04
Saville 50 6 40n26 77w20 5:09:20
Sawtown 61 9 41n25 79w42 5:18:48

Sawyer City 42 102 41N57 78w39 5:14:36
Saxonburg 10 6 40N45 79w49 5:19:16
Saxton 5 51 40N13 78w15 5:13:00
Saybrook 62 3 41N42 79w02 5:16:08
Saylorsburg 45 17 40N54 75w19 5:01:16
Sayre 8 1 41N59 76w32 5:06:08
Scalp Level 11 123 40N15 78w51 5:15:24
Scandia 62 6 41N56 79w08 5:16:32
Scarlets Mill 6 8 40N14 75w51 5:03:24
Scenery Hill 63 51 40N05 80w04 5:20:16
Scenic Hills 23 9 39N56 75w20 5:01:20
Schaefferstown 38 25 40N18 76w18 5:05:12
Schellsburg 5 6 40N03 78w39 5:14:36
Schenley 3 2 40N41 79w40 5:18:40
Schnecksville 39 8 40N41 75w36 5:02:24
Schoeneck 36 28 40N13 76w09 5:04:36
Schoeneck 46 8 40N45 75w18 5:01:12
Schoentown 54 27 40N42 76w10 5:04:40
Schofer 6 8 40N31 75w47 5:03:08
School Lane 36 8 40N02 76w20 5:05:20
School Lane Hills 36 8 40N02 76w18 5:05:12
Schubert 6 1 40N28 76w18 5:05:12
Schultzville 6 2 40N23 75w37 5:02:28
Schultzville 35 45 41N30 75w43 5:02:52
Schuster Heights 10 2 40N41 79w41 5:18:44
Schuyler 47 6 41N06 76w46 5:07:04
Schuylkill 51 9 39N56 75w11 5:00:44
Schuylkill Haven 54 27 40N38 76w10 5:04:40
Schuylkill Hills 46 90 40N08 75w21 5:01:24
Schwenksville 46 8 40N16 75w28 5:01:52
Sciota 45 17 40N56 75w19 5:01:16
Sconnelltown 15 13 39N57 75w36 5:02:24
Scotch Hill 16 6 41N22 79w18 5:17:12
Scotch Hollow 17 4 40N51 78w16 5:13:04
Scotia 2 8 40N18 79w54 5:19:36
Scotland 28 42 39N58 77w35 5:10:20
Scotrun 45 84 41N04 75w19 5:01:16
Scott Center 64 6 41N55 75w28 5:01:52
Scottdale 65 111 40N06 79w35 5:18:20
Scott Haven 65 1 40N14 79w48 5:19:12
Scottsville 4 13 40N37 80w16 5:21:04
Scott Township 2 114 40N25 80w05 5:20:20
Scranton 35 18 41N25 75w40 5:02:40
Scrubgrass 61 1 41N12 79w47 5:19:08
Scullton 56 4 39N55 79w11 5:16:44
Scyoc 50 6 40N22 77w36 5:10:24
Seagers 41 83 41N12 76w47 5:07:08
Seamentown 32 6 40N43 78w57 5:15:48
Seanor 56 74 40N13 78w54 5:15:36
Searights 26 80 39N54 79w44 5:18:56
Sebring 59 6 41N33 77w06 5:08:24
Secane 23 9 39N56 75w18 5:01:12
Secane Highlands 23 9 39N56 75w18 5:01:12
Seek 54 80 40N49 75w55 5:03:40
Seelyville 64 22 41N36 75w16 5:01:04
Seemsville 48 13 40N41 75w22 5:01:28
Seger 65 3 40N20 79w18 5:17:12
Seidersville 48 13 40N36 75w23 5:01:32
Seipstown 39 9 40N33 75w38 5:02:32
Seisholtzville 6 13 40N33 75w34 5:02:16
Seitzland 67 3 39N48 76w44 5:06:56
Seitzville 67 3 39N51 76w46 5:07:04
Selea 31 6 40N12 77w59 5:11:56
Selinsgrove 55 82 40N48 76w52 5:07:28
Sellersville 9 8 40N24 75w24 5:01:36
Seltzer 54 27 40N42 76w14 5:04:56
Seminole 3 6 40N58 79w20 5:17:20
Seneca 61 9 41N23 79w42 5:18:48
Seneca Valley 65 25 40N20 79w43 5:18:52
Sereno 19 6 41N07 76w32 5:06:08
Sergeant 42 7 41N40 78w32 5:14:08
Seven Pines 34 7 40N32 77w24 5:09:36
Sevenpoints 49 82 40N52 76w47 5:07:08
Seven Springs 56 6 40N02 79w18 5:17:12
Seven Stars 1 1 39N56 77w15 5:09:00
Seven Stars 34 1 40N33 77w09 5:08:36
Seven Valleys 67 3 39N51 76w46 5:07:04
Seward 65 7 40N25 79w01 5:16:04
Sewickley 2 13 40N32 80w12 5:20:48
Sewickley Heights 2 13 40N34 80w09 5:20:36
Sewickley Hills 2 114 40N34 80w07 5:20:28
Seybertown 3 1 40N59 79w37 5:18:28
Seyfert 6 8 40N16 75w48 5:03:12
Shade 56 63 40N07 78w50 5:15:20
Shade Gap 31 6 40N11 77w52 5:11:28
Shadeland 20 6 41N48 80w22 5:21:28
Shades Glen 40 60 41N04 75w46 5:03:04
Shade Valley 31 6 40N17 77w43 5:10:52
Shadle 55 111 40N09 79w33 5:18:12
Shado-wood Village 32 72 40N38 79w09 5:16:36
Shadow Shuttle 2 114 40N28 79w50 5:19:20
Shady Grove 28 100 39N47 77w40 5:10:40
Shady Plain 3 4 40N36 79w30 5:18:00
Shadyside 2 114 40N27 79w56 5:19:44
Shaffer 17 56 41N07 78w46 5:15:04
Shaffers Corner 26 80 39N51 79w43 5:18:52
Shaffersville 31 81 40N30 78w01 5:12:04
Shaft 54 27 40N49 76w12 5:04:48
Shafton 65 25 40N20 79w43 5:18:52
Shaler 2 114 40N32 79w58 5:19:52
Shalercrest 2 114 40N31 79w57 5:19:48
Shamokin 49 27 40N47 76w34 5:06:16
Shamokin Dam 55 82 40N51 76w49 5:07:16
Shamrock 26 80 39N54 79w44 5:18:56
Shamrock Station 6 9 40N30 75w40 5:02:40
Shaner 65 25 40N20 79w43 5:18:52
Shaners Crossroads 65 4 40N38 79w37 5:18:28
Shanesville 6 2 40N20 75w38 5:02:32
Shanksville 56 6 40N01 78w54 5:15:36
Shanktown 32 6 40N42 78w58 5:15:52
Shannondale 16 6 41N02 79w15 5:17:00
Shannon Heights 2 114 40N28 79w50 5:19:20
Shanor Heights 10 3 40N53 79w53 5:19:32
Sharon 43 117 41N14 80w31 5:22:04
Sharon Center 53 29 41N58 78w11 5:12:44
Sharon Hill 23 9 39N54 75w16 5:01:04
Sharon Park 23 9 39N54 75w17 5:01:08
Sharpsburg 2 114 40N30 79w56 5:19:44
Sharpsburg 31 85 40N26 77w56 5:11:44
Sharps Hill 2 114 40N30 79w56 5:19:44
Sharpsville 43 117 41N15 80w29 5:21:56
Sharrertown 63 51 40N03 79w57 5:19:48
Shartlesville 6 1 40N31 76w06 5:04:24
Shavertown 40 20 41N20 75w56 5:03:44
Shawanese 40 6 41N21 76w02 5:04:08
Shaw Mine 63 51 40N22 80w14 5:20:56
Shaw Mines 56 79 39N49 79w02 5:16:08
Shawmut 24 5 41N16 78w44 5:14:56
Shawnee On Delaware 45 85 41N01 75w07 5:00:28
Shaws 20 77 41N40 80w07 5:20:28
Shawtown 65 25 40N20 79w43 5:18:52
Shawville 17 1 41N04 78w22 5:13:28
Shay 3 6 40N44 79w27 5:17:48
Sheakleyville 43 6 41N27 80w12 5:20:48
Shearerburg 65 4 40N38 79w37 5:18:28
Sheatown 40 21 41N12 76w00 5:04:00
Sheeder 15 118 40N11 75w33 5:02:12
Sheerlund Forest 6 101 40N19 75w57 5:03:48
Sheffield 62 3 41N42 79w02 5:16:08
Shehawken 64 6 41N55 75w28 5:01:52
Shellsville 22 3 40N23 76w39 5:06:36
Shelly 9 13 40N29 75w25 5:01:40
Shellytown 7 3 40N28 78w12 5:12:48
Shelocta 32 6 40N40 79w18 5:17:12
Shelvey 24 36 41N21 78w37 5:14:28
Shenandoah 54 27 40N49 76w12 5:04:48
Shenandoah Heights 54 1 40N50 76w12 5:04:48
Shenandoah Junction 54 27 40N49 76w12 5:04:48
Shenango 43 59 41N23 80w24 5:21:36
Shenkel 15 8 40N15 75w39 5:02:36
Shenks Ferry 67 1 39N52 76w29 5:05:56
Shepherdstown 21 12 40N12 77w00 5:08:00
Sheppton 54 60 40N54 76w07 5:04:28
Sherersville 39 13 40N37 75w31 5:02:04
Sheridan 38 1 40N21 76w13 5:04:52
Sheridan 54 27 40N36 76w33 5:06:12
Sherman 64 6 42N04 75w25 5:01:40
Shermans Dale 50 6 40N20 77w11 5:08:44
Shermansville 20 6 41N36 80w19 5:21:16
Sherrett 3 6 40N53 79w36 5:18:24
Sheshequin 8 60 41N52 76w27 5:05:48
Shetters Grove 67 67 39N58 76w44 5:06:56
Shickshinny 40 1 41N09 76w09 5:04:36
Shields 2 13 40N33 80w10 5:20:40
Shieldsburg 65 3 40N24 79w25 5:17:40
Shillington 6 101 40N18 75w58 5:03:52
Shiloh 67 67 39N58 76w47 5:07:08
Shimerville 39 13 40N33 75w31 5:02:04
Shimpstown 28 51 39N50 77w55 5:11:40
Shindle 44 1 40N42 77w19 5:09:16
Shinglehouse 53 29 41N58 78w12 5:12:48
Shingletown 14 9 40N48 77w52 5:11:28
Shintown 18 73 41N20 77w45 5:11:00
Shipmans Eddy 62 120 41N52 79w09 5:16:36
Shippensburg 21 82 40N03 77w31 5:10:04
Shippenville 16 37 41N15 79w28 5:17:52
Shippingport 4 6 40N37 80w26 5:21:44
Shirks Corner 46 8 40N16 75w28 5:01:52
Shirley 31 85 40N21 77w52 5:11:28
Shirleysburg 31 85 40N18 77w53 5:11:32
Shoaf 26 51 39N48 79w49 5:19:16
Shocks Mills 36 26 40N04 76w33 5:06:12
Shoemaker 11 63 40N23 78w40 5:14:40
Shoemakers 45 23 41N00 75w11 5:00:44
Shoemakers 54 3 40N49 76w08 5:04:32
Shoemakersville 6 80 40N30 75w58 5:03:52
Shoenberger 31 11 40N40 78w13 5:12:52
Shoenersville 39 13 40N35 75w28 5:01:52
Shohola 52 6 41N26 74w56 4:59:44
Shope Gardens 22 80 40N12 76w43 5:06:52
Shorbes Hill 67 1 39N48 76w59 5:07:56
Shortsville 59 6 41N51 77w17 5:09:08
Shraders 44 73 40N40 77w36 5:10:24
Shrewsbury 67 27 39N46 76w41 5:06:44
Shumans 19 4 41N00 76w25 5:05:40
Shunk 57 6 41N33 76w44 5:06:56
Sickles Corner 7 33 40N31 78w25 5:13:40
Siddonsburg 67 1 40N07 77w02 5:08:08
Sidman 11 63 40N20 78w45 5:15:00
Siegfried 48 13 40N41 75w22 5:01:28
Sigel 33 6 41N17 79w07 5:16:28
Siglerville 44 7 40N43 77w35 5:10:20
Sigmund 39 13 40N29 75w30 5:02:00
Sigsbee 30 51 39N48 79w55 5:19:40
Silkworth 40 1 41N12 76w04 5:04:16
Silvara 8 6 41N39 76w10 5:04:40
Silver Creek 54 27 40N43 76w07 5:04:28
Silverdale 9 8 40N24 75w21 5:01:24
Silver Ford Heights 44 85 40N23 77w53 5:11:32

PENNSYLVANIA

Silver Lake 9 8 40N14 74w56 4:59:44
Silver Lake 58 6 41N58 75w56 5:03:44
Silver Lake 67 12 40N08 76w52 5:07:28
Silver Spring 36 8 40N04 76w26 5:05:44
Silverville 10 2 40N42 79w44 5:18:56
Simmonstown 36 23 39N59 76w02 5:04:08
Simpson 35 1 41N36 75w30 5:02:00
Simpson Store 30 6 40N00 80w28 5:21:52
Singersville 22 12 40N22 76w56 5:07:44
Sinking Spring 6 101 40N19 76w01 5:04:04
Sinking Valley 7 33 40N31 78w25 5:13:40
Sinnamahoning 12 7 41N19 78w06 5:12:24
Sinsheim 67 95 39N53 76w52 5:07:28
Sipes Mill 29 6 39N51 78w09 5:12:36
Sipesville 56 6 40N06 79w06 5:16:24
Six Mile Run 5 51 40N10 78w13 5:12:52
Six Points 10 6 41N05 79w41 5:18:44
Sizerville 12 106 41N31 78w14 5:12:56
Skelp 7 33 40N31 78w25 5:13:40
Skidmore 37 112 41N00 80w21 5:21:24
Skinners Eddy 66 6 41N39 76w10 5:04:40
Skippack 46 8 40N14 75w24 5:01:36
Skyline Heights 67 67 39N59 76w46 5:07:04
Skyline View 22 1 40N21 76w43 5:06:52
Skytop 45 84 41N14 75w15 5:01:00
Slabtown 17 63 40N44 78w49 5:15:16
Slabtown 28 26 40N01 76w32 5:06:08
Slackwater 36 8 40N01 76w21 5:05:24
Slatedale 39 8 40N45 75w40 5:02:40
Slatefield 46 80 40N48 75w32 5:02:08
Slateford 46 8 40N54 75w07 5:00:28
Slate Hill 67 1 39N44 76w19 5:05:16
Slate Lick 3 2 40N46 79w39 5:18:36
Slate Run 41 6 41N28 77w30 5:10:00
Slate Valley 46 80 40N48 75w32 5:02:08
Slateville 39 56 40N37 75w53 5:03:32
Slatington 39 8 40N45 75w37 5:02:28
Slickport 11 92 40N40 78w43 5:14:52
Slickville 65 6 40N28 79w31 5:18:04
Sligo 16 6 41N06 79w29 5:17:56
Slippery Rock 10 6 41N02 80w03 5:20:12
Slippery Rock Park 10 6 41N02 80w03 5:20:12
Slocum 40 1 41N09 76w02 5:04:08
Slocum Corners 40 1 41N04 76w08 5:04:32
Slovan 63 6 40N22 80w23 5:21:32
Smallwood 63 51 40N02 79w58 5:19:52
Smethport 42 93 41N49 78w27 5:13:48
Smicksburg 32 6 40N27 78w59 5:15:56
Smiley 26 80 39N54 79w44 5:18:56
Smith 63 6 40N22 80w23 5:21:32
Smith Bridge 30 6 39N55 80w26 5:21:44
Smithdale 2 1 40N14 79w48 5:19:12
Smithfield 26 51 39N48 79w49 5:19:16
Smithfield 31 81 40N30 78w01 5:12:04
Smithfield 45 85 41N02 75w08 5:00:32
Smithfield Center 31 81 40N29 78w02 5:12:08
Smith Gardens 67 1 40N04 76w43 5:06:52
Smithland 16 6 41N00 79w20 5:17:20
Smithmill 17 63 40N46 78w25 5:13:40
Smithport 32 6 40N50 78w50 5:15:20
Smiths 67 95 39N53 76w52 5:07:28
Smiths Corner 9 1 40N25 75w04 5:00:16
Smiths Ferry 4 6 40N41 80w28 5:21:52
Smithton 65 6 40N09 79w44 5:18:56
Smithtown 9 1 40N26 75w09 5:00:36
Smithtown 33 56 41N09 78w45 5:15:00
Smithville 36 27 39N56 76w12 5:04:48
Smock 26 6 40N00 79w47 5:19:08
Smokeless 32 29 40N23 79w04 5:16:16
Smokerun 17 6 40N48 78w26 5:13:44
Smoketown 9 13 40N29 75w25 5:01:40
Smoketown 28 42 39N56 77w40 5:10:40
Smoketown 36 8 40N02 76w12 5:04:48
Smullton 14 52 40N53 77w29 5:09:56
Smyerstown 32 51 40N53 78w56 5:15:44
Smyrna 36 23 39N58 76w00 5:04:00
Snake Spring Valley 5 70 40N02 78w25 5:13:40
Snedekerville 8 7 41N50 76w48 5:07:12
Snively Corners 16 6 41N14 79w32 5:18:08
Snowball Gate 9 9 40N09 74w51 4:59:24
Snowden 2 114 40N18 80w00 5:20:00
Snowdenville 15 118 40N11 75w33 5:02:12
Snow Shoe 14 7 41N02 77w57 5:11:48
Snyder Corner 67 1 39N52 76w37 5:06:28
Snyders 54 1 40N41 76w00 5:04:00
Snydersburg 16 6 41N21 79w21 5:17:24
Snydersville 45 23 41N00 75w13 5:00:52
Snydertown 14 63 41N01 77w39 5:10:36
Snydertown 26 104 40N01 79w35 5:18:20
Snydertown 49 6 40N53 76w41 5:06:44
Snydertown 65 3 40N24 79w25 5:17:40
Snyderville 3 59 40N53 79w15 5:17:00
Sober 14 64 40N51 77w34 5:10:16
Soldier 33 6 41N06 78w53 5:15:32
Solebury 9 8 40N23 75w00 5:00:00
Solomons Gap 40 20 41N14 75w52 5:03:28
Somerset 56 6 40N01 79w05 5:16:20
Somers Lane 59 59 42N00 77w08 5:08:32
Somerton 51 56 40N06 75w02 5:00:08
Somerville 3 1 40N59 79w37 5:18:28
Sonestown 57 6 41N21 76w33 5:06:12
Sonman 11 63 40N23 78w40 5:14:40
Soradoville 44 1 40N42 77w19 5:09:16
Soudersburg 36 96 40N01 76w09 5:04:36
Souderton 46 8 40N19 75w19 5:01:16
Soukesburg 11 74 40N22 78w51 5:15:24
South Abington 35 45 41N29 75w42 5:02:48
Southampton 9 1 40N11 75w03 5:00:12
South Annville 38 8 40N18 76w31 5:06:04

South Ardmore 23 9 40N00 75w18 5:01:12
South Auburn 58 59 41N37 76w03 5:04:12
South Beaver 4 6 40N46 80w27 5:21:48
South Bend 3 6 40N38 79w23 5:17:32
South Bethlehem 3 6 41N00 79w20 5:17:20
South Bradford 42 102 41N57 78w39 5:14:36
South Buffalo 3 2 40N44 79w38 5:18:32
South Burgettstown 63 6 40N23 80w24 5:21:36
South Canaan 64 6 41N31 75w24 5:01:36
South Carnegie 2 114 40N25 80w05 5:20:20
South Centre 19 6 41N02 76w21 5:05:24
South Clarksville 30 6 39N59 80w03 5:20:12
South Clearfield 17 1 41N02 78w27 5:13:48
South Coatesville 15 9 39N58 75w49 5:03:16
South Connellsville 26 104 40N01 79w35 5:18:20
South Coventry 15 8 40N11 75w40 5:02:40
South Creek 8 7 41N57 76w47 5:07:08
Southdale 40 1 41N09 76w10 5:04:40
South Duquesne 2 10 40N22 79w51 5:19:24
South Easton 46 12 40N41 75w14 5:00:56
South Eaton 66 59 41N32 75w57 5:03:48
Southerwood 65 6 40N08 79w26 5:17:44
South Fayette 2 114 40N21 80w09 5:20:36
South Fork 11 62 40N22 78w48 5:15:12
South Franklin 63 3 40N07 80w18 5:21:12
South Gibson 58 6 41N44 75w38 5:02:32
South Greensburg 65 99 40N17 79w33 5:18:12
South Hanover 22 31 40N17 76w43 5:06:52
South Heidelberg 6 80 40N19 76w06 5:04:24
South Heights 4 13 40N34 80w14 5:20:56
South Hermitage 36 27 40N06 75w59 5:03:56
South Hills 2 114 40N24 80w02 5:20:08
South Huntingdon 65 4 40N11 79w43 5:18:52
South Lakemont 7 33 40N30 78w24 5:13:36
South Lebanon 38 8 40N20 76w23 5:05:32
South Londonderry 38 2 40N14 76w33 5:06:12
South Mahoning 32 6 40N53 79w09 5:16:36
South Manheim 54 27 40N36 76w09 5:04:36
South Meadville 20 77 41N40 80w07 5:20:28
South Media 23 90 39N55 75w22 5:01:28
South Middleton 21 2 40N09 77w10 5:08:40
Southmont 11 74 40N19 78w56 5:15:44
South Montrose 58 60 41N48 75w54 5:03:36
South Mountain 28 1 39N51 77w30 5:10:00
South New Castle 37 112 40N59 80w21 5:21:24
South Newton 21 1 40N05 77w24 5:09:36
South Oil City 61 9 41N25 79w42 5:18:48
South Park 2 114 40N18 80w00 5:20:00
South Perkasie 9 8 40N25 75w23 5:01:32
South Philipsburg 14 113 40N53 78w13 5:12:52
South Pottstown 15 8 40N14 75w39 5:02:36
South Pymatuning 43 117 41N18 80w29 5:21:56
South Renovo 18 73 41N20 77w44 5:10:56
South Shenango 20 63 41N32 80w27 5:21:48
South Side 35 18 41N24 75w40 5:02:40
South Sterling 64 65 41N16 75w20 5:01:20
South Strabane 63 3 40N10 80w12 5:20:48
South Tamaqua 54 27 40N48 75w58 5:03:52
South Temple 6 101 40N24 75w55 5:03:40
South Towanda 8 41 41N46 76w27 5:05:48
South Union 26 80 39N53 79w44 5:18:56
South Uniontown 26 80 39N54 79w45 5:19:00
South Versailles 2 9 40N18 79w48 5:19:12
Southview 63 51 40N20 80w16 5:21:04
Southwark 51 9 39N56 75w09 5:00:36
South Waverly 8 1 42N00 76w32 5:06:08
Southwest 65 111 40N12 79w31 5:18:04
Southwest Greensburg 65 99 40N18 79w33 5:18:12
South Whitehall 39 13 40N36 75w32 5:02:08
South Williamsport 41 82 41N14 77w00 5:08:00
South Woodbury 5 6 40N10 78w25 5:13:40
Southwood Hills 67 67 39N57 76w42 5:06:48
Spangler 11 92 40N39 78w47 5:15:08
Spangsville 6 2 40N20 75w38 5:02:32
Sparta 20 56 41N48 79w42 5:18:48
Sparta 63 3 40N10 80w16 5:21:04
Spartansburg 20 56 41N49 79w41 5:18:44
Spears Grove 34 6 40N22 77w36 5:10:24
Speedwell 36 8 40N09 76w18 5:05:12
Speers 63 1 40N07 79w53 5:19:32
Spike Island 14 4 40N51 78w16 5:13:04
Spike Island 35 18 41N22 75w43 5:02:52
Spindley City 11 55 40N29 78w33 5:14:12
Spinnerstown 9 8 40N26 75w26 5:01:44
Split Rock 13 94 41N04 75w36 5:02:24
Sporting Hill 21 12 40N12 77w00 5:08:00
Sporting Hill 36 8 40N06 76w22 5:05:28
Sportsburg 33 51 40N56 78w58 5:15:52
Spraggs 30 6 39N47 80w13 5:20:52
Sprankle Mills 33 6 41N00 79w07 5:16:28
Spring Bank 14 52 40N53 77w29 5:09:56
Springboro 20 6 41N48 80w22 5:21:28
Spring Brook 35 1 41N18 75w37 5:02:28
Spring Church 3 4 40N36 79w29 5:17:56
Spring City 15 118 40N11 75w33 5:02:12
Spring Creek 39 13 40N31 75w36 5:02:24
Spring Creek 62 7 41N53 79w32 5:18:08
Springdale 2 119 40N32 79w47 5:19:08
Springdell 15 9 39N59 75w50 5:03:20
Springettsbury 67 67 39N59 76w41 5:06:44
Springfield 8 7 41N50 76w48 5:07:12
Springfield 21 1 40N10 77w24 5:09:36
Springfield 23 9 39N57 75w20 5:01:20
Springfield Park 23 9 39N56 75w20 5:01:20
Spring Garden 9 8 40N14 74w56 4:59:44
Spring Garden 36 23 40N00 76w06 5:04:24
Spring Garden 51 9 39N59 75w09 5:00:36
Spring Garden 54 27 40N38 76w10 5:04:40
Spring Garden 60 73 41N07 76w54 5:07:36
Spring Garden 65 111 40N09 79w33 5:18:12
Spring Garden 67 67 39N57 76w43 5:06:52
Spring Garden Township 67 67 39N57 76w42 5:06:48
Spring Glen 54 27 40N38 76w37 5:06:28
Spring Grove 67 95 39N53 76w52 5:07:28
Springhaven Estates 23 90 39N54 75w22 5:01:28
Springhill 8 6 41N40 76w16 5:05:04
Spring Hill 11 63 40N22 78w40 5:14:40
Spring Hill 23 9 39N56 75w18 5:01:12
Springhope 5 6 40N03 78w39 5:14:36
Spring House 46 8 40N11 75w14 5:00:56
Spring Mill 46 90 40N05 75w17 5:01:08
Spring Mills 14 64 40N51 77w35 5:10:20
Springmont 6 101 40N19 76w00 5:04:00
Spring Mount 31 6 40N42 78w08 5:12:32
Spring Mount 46 8 40N17 75w28 5:01:52
Spring Run 28 1 40N09 77w47 5:11:08
Springs 56 6 39N44 79w09 5:16:36
Springtown 9 13 40N33 75w18 5:01:12
Springtown 28 1 40N04 77w50 5:11:20
Springtown 40 20 41N14 75w52 5:03:28
Springtown 49 73 41N06 76w52 5:07:28
Springvale 67 1 39N52 76w37 5:06:28
Spring Valley 6 101 40N24 75w55 5:03:40
Spring Valley 9 8 40N21 75w13 5:00:52
Spring Valley 17 4 40N56 78w17 5:13:08
Spring Valley 48 13 40N36 75w23 5:01:32
Spring Valley Estates 28 42 39N56 77w40 5:10:40
Springville 21 2 40N09 77w09 5:08:36
Springville 36 23 40N00 76w06 5:04:24
Springville 58 60 41N42 75w55 5:03:40
Springville 61 6 41N22 79w56 5:19:44
Sproul 7 3 40N16 78w28 5:13:52
Spruce Creek 31 7 40N37 78w08 5:12:32
Spruce Hill 34 6 40N28 77w28 5:09:52
Sprucetown 26 7 39N44 79w54 5:19:36
Spry 67 67 39N57 76w42 5:06:48
Square Corner 1 1 39N49 77w11 5:08:44
Squirrel Hill 2 114 40N26 79w55 5:19:40
Stack Town 36 2 40N05 76w40 5:06:40
Stafore Estates 48 13 40N39 75w21 5:01:24
Stahlstown 65 6 40N09 79w19 5:17:16
Stairville 40 1 41N04 76w08 5:04:32
Stalker 64 6 41N49 75w05 5:00:20
Stambaugh 26 80 39N55 79w40 5:18:40
Standard 65 111 40N09 79w33 5:18:12
Standard Shaft 65 111 40N09 79w33 5:18:12
Standing Stone 8 60 41N46 76w20 5:05:20
Stanhope 54 9 40N36 76w23 5:05:32
Stanley 17 56 41N07 78w46 5:15:04
Stanton 33 34 41N10 79w05 5:16:20
Stanton Heights 65 111 40N13 79w36 5:18:24
Stanwood 9 9 40N06 74w57 4:59:48
Stanwood Gardens 9 9 40N06 74w56 4:59:44
Starbrick 62 120 41N52 79w09 5:16:36
Starford 32 6 40N42 78w58 5:15:52
Star Junction 26 6 40N04 79w46 5:19:04
Starks 35 18 41N22 75w43 5:02:52
Starkville 66 89 41N38 75w47 5:03:08
Starlight 64 6 41N54 75w20 5:01:20
Starners Station 21 1 40N00 77w12 5:08:48
Starr 27 6 41N32 79w22 5:17:28
Starr 62 6 41N43 79w32 5:18:08
Starrucca 64 59 41N54 75w28 5:01:52
Starview 67 1 40N04 76w42 5:06:48
State College 14 9 40N48 77w52 5:11:28
State Hill 6 101 40N18 76w00 5:04:00
State Hill 15 23 39N59 76w02 5:04:08
State Line 5 51 39N50 78w43 5:14:52
Stateline 25 7 42N16 79w43 5:18:52
State Line 28 1 39N43 77w43 5:10:52
Steamburg 20 7 41N40 80w27 5:21:48
Steel City 48 13 40N36 75w23 5:01:32
Steelstown 38 8 40N20 76w31 5:06:04
Steelton 22 12 40N14 76w50 5:07:20
Steelville 15 23 39N54 75w57 5:03:48
Steene 64 1 41N35 75w24 5:01:36
Steffins Hill 4 8 40N46 80w20 5:21:20
Steinsburg 9 13 40N29 75w25 5:01:40
Steinsville 39 56 40N37 75w53 5:03:32
Stemlersville 13 8 40N50 75w42 5:02:48
Sterling 17 4 40N50 78w21 5:13:24
Sterling 64 6 41N20 75w24 5:01:36
Sterling Run 12 7 41N25 78w12 5:12:48
Sterlingworth 39 13 40N37 75w31 5:02:04

PENNSYLVANIA

Sterrettania 25 107 42N04 80w10 5:20:40
Steuben 20 7 41N41 79w49 5:19:16
Stevens 8 56 41N46 76w10 5:04:40
Stevens 36 28 40N13 76w09 5:04:36
Stevens Point 58 59 41N57 75w37 5:02:28
Stevenstown 67 1 40N07 77w02 5:08:08
Stevensville 8 6 41N46 76w11 5:04:44
Stewardson 53 6 41N33 77w44 5:10:56
Stewart 26 6 39N53 79w29 5:17:56
Stewart Run 27 6 41N36 79w35 5:18:20
Stewartstown 67 1 39N45 76w36 5:06:24
Stewartsville 65 25 40N20 79w43 5:18:52
Stickney 42 102 41N57 78w39 5:14:36
Sticks 67 3 39N47 76w47 5:07:08
Stier 46 17 40N53 75w12 5:00:48
Stifflertown 17 63 40N44 78w49 5:15:16
Stiles 39 13 40N39 75w30 5:02:00
Still Creek 54 27 40N48 75w58 5:03:52
Stilleys Siding 2 8 40N18 79w54 5:19:36
Stillwater 19 6 41N09 76w22 5:05:28
Stillwater Lake Estates 45 84 41N07 75w24 5:01:36
Stiltz 67 3 39N48 76w44 5:06:56
Stines Corner 39 1 40N41 75w45 5:03:00
Stobo 4 13 40N40 80w16 5:21:04
Stockdale 63 115 40N05 79w51 5:19:24
Stockertown 48 8 40N45 75w16 5:01:04
Stockton 40 42 40N58 76w00 5:04:00
Stoddartsville 40 94 41N06 75w36 5:02:24
Stokesdale 59 6 41N45 77w18 5:09:12
Stoneboro 43 66 41N20 80w07 5:20:28
Stone Church 46 8 40N54 75w07 5:00:28
Stone Glen 22 12 40N22 76w56 5:07:44
Stoneham 62 3 41N47 79w06 5:16:24
Stone Hill 36 8 39N57 76w21 5:05:24
Stonehurst 9 1 40N11 75w03 5:00:12
Stonehurst 23 9 39N58 75w18 5:01:12
Stonehurst Hills 23 9 39N58 75w18 5:01:12
Stone Row 5 6 40N09 78w16 5:13:04
Stonerstown 5 51 40N13 78w14 5:12:56
Stonersville 6 8 40N16 75w48 5:03:12
Stonetown 6 8 40N16 75w48 5:03:12
Stonevilla 65 99 40N18 79w34 5:18:16
Stoneybreak 29 6 39N45 78w11 5:12:44
Stonington 49 82 40N52 76w47 5:07:08
Stonybrook 67 67 39N59 76w46 5:07:04
Stonybrook Heights 67 67 39N59 76w46 5:07:04
Stony Creek Mills 6 101 40N20 75w53 5:03:32
Stonyfork 59 6 41N45 77w18 5:09:12
Stony Point 9 1 40N31 75w11 5:00:44
Stony Point 20 6 41N36 80w19 5:21:16
Stony Point 28 1 40N09 77w47 5:11:08
Stony Point 30 6 39N56 80w03 5:20:12
Stony Run 6 1 40N37 75w49 5:03:16
Stoopville 9 8 40N14 74w56 4:59:44
Stormstown 14 63 40N48 78w03 5:12:12
Stormville 45 23 41N00 75w13 5:00:52
Stottsville 15 32 39N58 75w53 5:03:32
Stouchsburg 6 1 40N22 76w11 5:04:44
Stoufferstown 28 42 39N56 77w40 5:10:40
Stoughstown 21 82 40N03 77w32 5:10:08
Stover 31 11 40N40 78w13 5:12:52
Stoverdale 22 12 40N16 76w43 5:06:52
Stoverstown 67 95 39N53 76w52 5:07:28
Stowe 46 8 40N15 75w39 5:02:36
Stowell 66 6 41N39 76w10 5:04:40
Stowe Township 2 114 40N28 80w05 5:20:20
Stoystown 56 6 40N06 78w57 5:15:48
Straban 1 1 39N52 77w10 5:08:40
Strabane 63 2 40N15 80w12 5:20:48
Strafford 15 90 40N03 75w24 5:01:36
Strangford 32 98 40N26 79w16 5:17:04
Strasburg 36 96 39N59 76w11 5:04:44
Strattanville 16 37 41N12 79w20 5:17:20
Strausstown 6 1 40N29 76w11 5:04:44
Strawberry Ridge 47 6 40N58 76w36 5:06:24
Strawbridge 41 6 41N21 76w35 5:06:20
Straw Pump 65 25 40N20 79w43 5:18:52
Stremmels 1 1 39N49 77w11 5:08:44
Strickhousers 67 3 39N51 76w46 5:07:04
Stricklerstown 38 1 40N21 76w13 5:04:52
Strinestown 67 1 40N04 76w43 5:06:52
Stringtown 3 15 40N46 79w32 5:18:08
Stringtown 30 51 39N54 79w58 5:19:52
Strobleton 16 6 41N30 79w27 5:17:48
Strodes Mills 44 73 40N36 77w34 5:10:16
Stronach 17 7 40N57 78w33 5:14:12
Strong 49 27 40N48 76w25 5:05:40
Strongstown 32 6 40N33 78w55 5:15:40
Stroud 45 23 41N01 75w13 5:00:52
Stroudsburg 45 23 40N59 75w12 5:00:48
Strum 26 51 39N48 79w49 5:19:16
Studa 63 6 40N17 80w28 5:21:52
Stull 66 6 41N25 76w03 5:04:12
Stump Creek 33 6 41N01 78w50 5:15:20
Stumptown 17 4 40N51 78w16 5:13:04
Sturgeon 2 51 40N23 80w13 5:20:52
Sturgis 35 18 41N28 75w36 5:02:24
Suburban Village 15 13 39N57 75w36 5:02:24
Suedburg 54 9 40N36 76w23 5:05:32
Sugarcreek 61 109 41N25 79w50 5:19:20
Sugargrove 62 6 41N59 79w21 5:17:24
Sugar Hill 33 5 41N15 78w48 5:15:12
Sugar Loaf 6 40N59 76w05 5:04:20
Sugar Notch 40 20 41N12 75w56 5:03:44
Sugar Run 8 6 41N38 76w15 5:05:00
Sugartown 15 8 40N02 75w31 5:02:04
Sullivan 26 80 39N52 79w42 5:18:48
Sullivan 59 59 41N48 76w57 5:07:48

PENNSYLVANIA

Sulphur Springs 50 51 40N24 77w02 5:08:08
Summerdale 21 12 40N18 76w56 5:07:44
Summerhill 11 63 40N23 78w46 5:15:04
Summer Hill 19 1 41N04 76w15 5:05:00
Summerville 33 6 41N08 79w11 5:16:44
Summerville 58 50 41N58 75w45 5:03:00
Summit 11 55 40N28 78w35 5:14:20
Summit 42 102 41N57 78w39 5:14:36
Summit Grove Camp 67 27 39N44 76w42 5:06:48
Summit Hill 13 80 40N49 75w51 5:03:24
Summit Lawn 39 13 40N35 75w28 5:01:52
Summit Mills 56 79 39N49 79w02 5:16:08
Summit Station 54 1 40N34 76w12 5:04:48
Sumneytown 46 8 40N20 75w27 5:01:48
Sunbeam 28 42 39N56 77w40 5:10:40
Sunbrook 7 33 40N28 78w25 5:13:40
Sunbury 49 82 40N52 76w48 5:07:12
Sundale 9 1 40N30 75w04 5:00:16
Sunderlinville 53 6 41N52 77w31 5:10:04
Sunnybrook 46 9 40N07 75w11 5:00:44
Sunnybrook Estates 23 9 39N53 75w18 5:01:12
Sunnyburn 67 1 39N50 76w24 5:05:36
Sunny Side 2 1 40N11 79w54 5:19:36
Sunnyside 37 112 41N00 80w21 5:21:24
Sunnyside 38 8 40N20 76w26 5:05:44
Sunnyside 49 27 40N48 76w33 5:06:12
Sunset Hills 4 13 40N37 80w16 5:21:04
Sunset Manor 67 67 39N58 76w44 5:06:56
Sunset Pines 18 76 41N08 77w28 5:09:52
Sunset Valley 65 25 40N19 79w44 5:18:56
Sunshine 26 51 39N48 79w55 5:19:40
Sunshine 40 1 41N09 76w10 5:04:40
Sun Valley 45 1 40N56 75w26 5:01:44
Sun Village 23 90 39N51 75w22 5:01:28
Sunville 61 6 41N30 79w52 5:19:28
Superior 26 51 40N02 79w55 5:19:40
Superior 65 3 40N20 79w18 5:17:12
Suplee 15 27 40N06 75w55 5:03:40
Surrey Hills 23 90 40N00 75w23 5:01:32
Surveyor 17 1 41N02 78w27 5:13:48
Suscon 40 1 41N19 75w46 5:03:04
Susquehanna 58 59 41N57 75w37 5:02:28
Susquehanna Bridge 17 1 41N02 78w27 5:13:48
Susquehanna Depot 58 59 41N57 75w36 5:02:24
Sutersville 65 1 40N14 79w48 5:19:12
Sutervile 65 1 40N14 79w48 5:19:12
Swales 34 1 40N38 77w17 5:09:08
Swan Acres 2 114 40N33 80w01 5:20:04
Swart 30 1 39N56 80w15 5:21:00
Swarthmore 23 9 39N55 75w21 5:01:24
Swarthmorwood 23 9 39N54 75w20 5:01:20
Swartzville 36 1 40N16 76w07 5:04:28
Swatara 54 9 40N38 76w24 5:05:36
Swatara Station 22 31 40N17 76w39 5:06:36
Swede Hill 65 99 40N18 79w34 5:18:16
Swedeland 46 90 40N08 75w21 5:01:24
Sweden 53 66 41N46 77w55 5:11:40
Sweden Valley 53 66 41N46 78w01 5:12:04
Swedesburg 46 90 40N06 75w21 5:01:24
Swedetown 11 92 40N40 78w43 5:14:52
Swedetown 65 111 40N06 79w35 5:18:20
Sweeney Plan 65 1 40N08 79w52 5:19:28
Sweet Valley 40 6 41N17 76w09 5:04:36
Swengel 60 6 40N54 77w08 5:08:32
Swiftwater 45 84 41N06 75w20 5:01:20
Swineford 55 6 40N47 77w03 5:08:12
Swissdale 18 76 41N08 77w28 5:09:52
Swissvale 2 114 40N25 79w53 5:19:32
Switzer 39 1 40N41 75w45 5:03:00
Swoyerville 40 20 41N18 75w53 5:03:32
Sybertsville 40 6 41N00 76w05 5:04:20
Sycamore 30 1 39N56 80w15 5:21:00
Sycamore Mills 23 90 39N55 75w22 5:01:28
Sygan 2 114 40N22 80w06 5:20:24
Sygan Hill 2 114 40N22 80w06 5:20:24
Sykesville 33 56 41N03 78w50 5:15:20
Sylmar 15 3 39N45 76w01 5:04:04
Sylvan 28 51 39N50 77w55 5:11:40
Sylvan Dell 6 101 40N20 75w53 5:03:32
Sylvan Dell 41 82 41N14 77w01 5:08:04
Sylvan Grove 17 4 40N57 78w14 5:12:56
Sylvan Hills 7 33 40N25 78w24 5:13:36
Sylvania 8 7 41N48 76w52 5:07:28
Syner 38 8 40N20 76w31 5:06:04
Table Rock 1 1 39N56 77w15 5:09:00
Tacony 51 9 40N01 75w03 5:00:12
Tafton 52 6 41N24 75w11 5:00:44
Talley Cavey 2 114 40N36 79w57 5:19:48
Talmage 36 28 40N07 76w13 5:04:52
Talmar 19 6 41N12 76w23 5:05:32
Tamanend 54 27 40N48 75w58 5:03:52
Tamaqua 54 27 40N48 75w58 5:03:52
Tamarack 18 7 41N29 77w49 5:11:16
Tamiment 52 6 41N09 75w02 5:00:08
Tank 40 6 40N58 76w05 5:04:20
Tannersville 45 84 41N03 75w19 5:01:16
Tannery 40 60 41N04 75w46 5:03:04
Tanoma 32 6 40N40 79w00 5:16:00
Tarentum 2 14 40N36 79w46 5:19:04
Tarrs 65 111 40N10 79w35 5:18:20
Tarrtown 3 15 40N53 79w32 5:18:08
Tatamy 46 15 40N44 75w15 5:01:00
Tatesville 5 6 40N01 78w22 5:13:28
Taylor 35 18 41N23 75w43 5:02:52
Taylor Highlands 31 81 40N30 78w01 5:12:04
Tayloria 36 3 39N47 75w59 5:03:56
Taylorstown 63 6 40N10 80w23 5:21:32
Taylorsville 9 8 40N14 74w56 4:59:44
Taylorville 32 6 40N43 78w57 5:15:48
Taylorville 54 27 40N47 76w21 5:05:24
Teagarden Homes 30 6 39N59 80w03 5:20:12
Tearing Run 32 71 40N33 79w10 5:16:40
Teedyskung Lake 52 6 41N28 75w03 5:00:12
Teepleville 20 3 41N48 80w03 5:20:12
Telford 46 2 40N20 75w20 5:01:20
Tell 31 6 40N15 77w46 5:11:04
Temple 6 101 40N24 75w55 5:03:40
Templeton 3 64 40N55 79w28 5:17:52
Ten Mile 63 6 40N02 80w12 5:20:48
Tenmile Bottom 61 9 41N23 79w42 5:18:48
Tenth Avenue 39 13 40N38 75w23 5:01:32
Terminal 23 9 39N58 75w18 5:01:12
Terrace 2 114 40N22 79w54 5:19:36
Terre Hill 36 27 40N10 76w03 5:04:12
Terry 8 60 41N39 76w20 5:05:20
Terrytown 8 6 41N40 76w16 5:05:04
Texas 64 22 41N33 75w15 5:01:00
Tharptown 49 27 40N48 76w33 5:06:12
The Pines 1 1 39N52 77w03 5:08:12
Thomas 63 2 40N14 80w06 5:20:24
Thomas Mills 56 6 40N11 78w59 5:15:56
Thomasville 67 39 39N56 76w51 5:07:24
Thompson 58 6 41N52 75w31 5:02:04
Thompson No. 1 26 1 39N59 79w53 5:19:32
Thompson No. 2 26 51 39N56 79w50 5:19:20
Thompsontown 17 122 40N50 78w41 5:14:44
Thompsontown 34 7 40N34 77w14 5:08:56
Thompsonville 63 2 40N16 80w11 5:20:44
Thornburg 2 114 40N26 80w05 5:20:20
Thornbury 15 4 39N55 75w34 5:02:16
Thorndale 15 46 40N00 75w45 5:03:00
Thorndale Heights 15 46 40N00 75w42 5:02:48
Thornhurst 35 6 41N15 75w27 5:01:48
Thornton 23 4 39N54 75w32 5:02:08
Three Springs 31 6 40N12 77w59 5:11:56
Three Tuns 46 1 40N09 75w12 5:00:48
Throop 35 18 41N27 75w37 5:02:28
Thumptown 59 74 40N19 78w54 5:15:36
Tidal 3 64 40N55 79w28 5:17:52
Tidedale 32 71 40N33 79w10 5:16:40
Tidioute 62 6 41N41 79w24 5:17:36
Tiffany 58 60 41N50 75w53 5:03:32
Tilden 6 80 40N33 76w01 5:04:04
Tillotson 20 58 41N54 79w51 5:19:24
Timberly Heights 10 3 40N53 79w53 5:19:32
Timberwyck 23 90 39N55 75w22 5:01:28
Timblin 33 6 40N58 79w13 5:16:52
Timbuck 42 6 41N52 78w40 5:14:40
Time 30 6 39N57 80w19 5:21:16
Tinicum 9 1 40N26 75w09 5:00:36
Tioga 59 59 41N55 77w08 5:08:32
Tiona 62 3 41N45 79w03 5:16:12
Tionesta 27 35 41N30 79w28 5:17:52
Tippecanoe 26 6 40N00 79w47 5:19:08
Tipton 7 50 40N38 78w18 5:13:12
Tire Hill 56 74 40N16 78w55 5:15:40
Titusville 20 74 41N38 79w41 5:18:44
Tivoli 41 81 41N14 76w44 5:06:56
Toboyne 50 6 40N17 77w36 5:10:24
Toby 16 7 41N04 79w30 5:18:00
Toby 24 36 41N21 78w37 5:14:28
Tobyhanna 45 84 41N11 75w25 5:01:40
Tobyhanna Army Depot 45 84 41N11 75w25 5:01:40
Todd 31 6 40N16 78w04 5:12:16
Todmorron 23 90 39N54 75w22 5:01:28
Toftrees 14 9 40N48 77w52 5:11:28
Toland 21 1 40N00 77w12 5:08:48
Tolna 67 27 39N44 76w42 5:06:48
Tomb 41 6 41N14 77w15 5:09:00
Tompkins 59 59 41N59 77w14 5:08:56
Tompkinsville 35 1 41N32 75w32 5:02:08
Tomstown 28 100 39N45 77w34 5:10:16
Tooley Corners 35 4 41N20 75w32 5:02:08
Topton 6 9 40N30 75w42 5:02:48
Torpedo 62 3 41N50 79w23 5:17:32
Torrance 65 98 40N25 79w14 5:16:56
Torresdale 51 9 40N04 75w00 5:00:00
Toughkenamon 15 8 39N50 75w46 5:03:04
Towamencin 46 8 40N15 75w19 5:01:16
Towamensing 13 80 40N52 75w35 5:02:20
Towanda 8 41 41N46 76w27 5:05:48
Tower City 54 27 40N35 76w33 5:06:12
Tower Hill No. 1 26 1 39N59 79w53 5:19:32
Tower Hill No. 2 26 51 39N58 79w53 5:19:32
Towerville 15 9 39N59 75w50 5:03:20
Town Hill 40 1 41N09 76w10 5:04:40
Town Line 40 1 41N09 76w10 5:04:40
Townville 20 6 41N41 79w53 5:19:32
Trade City 32 6 40N27 78w59 5:15:56
Tradesville 9 2 40N20 75w18 5:01:12
Trafford 65 114 40N23 79w46 5:19:04
Trailwood 40 20 41N15 75w53 5:03:32
Trainer 23 90 39N50 75w25 5:01:40
Transfer 43 6 41N25 80w05 5:20:20
Trappe 46 8 40N12 75w28 5:01:52
Trauger 65 3 40N19 79w23 5:17:32
Traymore 9 1 40N12 75w05 5:00:20
Tredyffrin 15 90 40N04 75w26 5:01:44
Treehaven 2 114 40N20 80w02 5:20:08
Trees Mills 65 6 40N26 79w33 5:18:12
Treichlers 48 8 40N44 75w33 5:02:12
Tremont 54 9 40N38 76w23 5:05:32
Trent 56 6 40N02 79w18 5:17:12
Trenton 54 3 40N49 76w08 5:04:32
Tresckow 13 42 40N55 75w58 5:03:52
Tresslarville 64 6 41N27 75w23 5:01:32
Treveskyn 2 114 40N21 80w09 5:20:36
Trevorton 49 56 40N47 76w41 5:06:44
Trevose 9 1 40N09 74w59 4:59:56
Trewigtown 46 8 40N16 75w15 5:01:00
Trexler 6 56 40N37 75w53 5:03:32
Trexlertown 39 13 40N33 75w36 5:02:24
Trimmer Manor 67 67 39N58 76w44 5:06:56
Trindle Spring 21 12 40N12 77w00 5:08:00
Triumph 62 7 41N45 79w24 5:17:36
Trooper 46 90 40N09 75w24 5:01:36
Trotter 26 104 40N01 79w35 5:18:20
Trotwood 2 114 40N20 80w05 5:20:20
Trout Run 41 7 41N23 77w03 5:08:12
Trouts Crossing 65 111 40N09 79w33 5:18:12
Troutville 17 56 41N02 78w47 5:15:08
Troxelville 55 6 40N48 77w12 5:08:48
Troy 8 52 41N47 76w47 5:07:08
Troy 17 113 40N54 78w13 5:12:52
Troy Hill 3 15 40N49 79w32 5:18:08
Truce 36 27 39N54 76w10 5:04:40
Trucksville 40 20 41N20 75w56 5:03:44
Trucksville Gardens 40 20 41N20 75w56 5:03:44
Truemans 27 3 41N42 79w02 5:16:08
Truesdale Terrace 40 20 41N13 75w54 5:03:36
Truittsburg 16 6 41N01 79w19 5:17:16
Truman 12 106 41N31 78w14 5:12:56
Trumbauersville 9 13 40N28 75w29 5:01:56
Trunkeyville 27 6 41N41 79w24 5:17:36
Truxall 65 4 40N33 79w32 5:18:08
Tryonville 20 7 41N44 79w46 5:19:04
Tuckerton 6 101 40N23 75w56 5:03:44
Tullytown 9 9 40N08 74w49 4:59:16
Tulpehocken 6 25 40N26 76w16 5:05:04
Tunkhannock 66 59 41N32 75w57 5:03:48
Tunnelhill 11 55 40N29 78w33 5:14:12
Tunnelton 32 116 40N29 79w27 5:17:48
Turbett 34 7 40N31 77w22 5:09:28
Turbotville 49 6 41N06 76w46 5:07:04
Turbut 49 73 41N02 76w49 5:07:16
Turkey City 16 1 41N11 79w37 5:18:28
Turkeyfoot 28 42 39N56 77w40 5:10:40
Turkey Run 54 27 40N49 76w12 5:04:48
Turkeytown 65 61 40N13 79w46 5:19:04
Turnersville 20 63 41N29 80w26 5:21:44
Turnip Hole 16 1 41N11 79w43 5:18:52
Turnpike 67 27 39N46 76w41 5:06:44
Turtle Creek 2 114 40N24 79w50 5:19:20
Turtlepoint 42 7 41N52 78w20 5:13:20
Tuscarora 34 7 40N32 77w24 5:09:36
Tuscarora 54 27 40N46 76w02 5:04:08
Tusculam 21 82 40N03 77w32 5:10:08
Tusseyville 14 64 40N51 77w41 5:10:44
Twickinham Village 46 9 40N07 75w10 5:00:40
Twilight 63 1 40N07 79w54 5:19:36
Twin Bridge Farm 15 13 39N57 75w36 5:02:24
Twin Bridges 63 1 40N08 79w54 5:19:36
Twin Brooks 67 67 39N58 76w44 5:06:56
Twin Lakes 52 6 41N28 74w55 4:59:40
Twin Oaks 9 9 40N09 74w51 4:59:24
Twin Oaks 23 90 39N52 75w23 5:01:32
Twin Oaks Farms 23 90 39N52 75w23 5:01:32
Twin Rocks 11 63 40N30 78w52 5:15:28
Two Taverns 1 1 39N49 77w11 5:08:44
Tyler 17 7 41N13 78w34 5:14:16
Tylerdale 63 3 40N11 80w16 5:21:04
Tyler Hill 64 6 41N42 75w04 5:00:16
Tylersburg 16 6 41N23 79w19 5:17:16
Tylersport 46 1 40N21 75w23 5:01:32
Tylersville 18 7 40N59 77w26 5:09:44
Tyre 2 51 40N26 80w17 5:21:08
Tyrone 7 11 40N40 78w14 5:12:56
Uhlerstown 9 1 40N32 75w03 5:00:12
Uledi 26 80 39N54 79w46 5:19:04
Ulster 8 60 41N51 76w30 5:06:00
Ulysses 53 6 41N54 77w46 5:11:04
Unicorn 36 27 39N54 76w10 5:04:40
Union 36 3 39N51 76w03 5:04:12
Union Center 59 103 41N39 76w51 5:07:24
Union City 25 58 41N54 79w51 5:19:24
Union Dale 58 59 41N43 75w30 5:02:00
Union Deposit 22 31 40N17 76w39 5:06:36
Union Furnace 31 11 40N40 78w13 5:12:52
Union Hill 13 8 40N50 75w42 5:02:48
Union Mills 44 6 40N36 77w44 5:10:56
Union Square 36 8 40N06 76w22 5:05:28
Uniontown 26 80 39N54 79w44 5:18:56
Uniontown 32 63 40N44 78w49 5:15:16
Uniontown 67 1 40N07 77w02 5:08:08
Uniontown North 26 80 39N54 79w44 5:18:56
Union Trust 2 114 40N27 79w59 5:19:56
Unionville 4 19 40N42 80w17 5:21:08
Unionville 6 8 40N15 75w44 5:02:56
Unionville 9 8 40N17 75w18 5:01:12
Unionville 10 3 40N53 79w53 5:19:32
Unionville 14 70 40N55 77w53 5:11:32
Unionville 15 8 39N54 75w44 5:02:56
Union Water Works 38 8 40N20 76w31 5:06:04
United 65 111 40N13 79w30 5:18:00
Unity 2 3 40N17 79w26 5:17:44
Unity House 52 6 41N08 75w02 5:00:08
Unity Junction 2 14 40N29 79w44 5:18:56
Unityville 41 6 41N14 76w31 5:06:04
Universal 2 114 40N28 79w50 5:19:20
University Heights 48 13 40N36 75w23 5:01:32

PENNSYLVANIA

University Park 14 9 40N48 77w52 5:11:28
Upland 23 90 39N51 75w23 5:01:32
Upland Park 23 9 40N00 75w18 5:01:12
Upland Terrace 46 9 40N01 75w15 5:01:00
Upper Allen 21 12 40N11 76w59 5:07:56
Upper Augusta 49 82 40N53 76w45 5:07:00
Upper Bern 6 1 40N31 76w06 5:04:24
Upper Black Eddy 9 9 40N34 75w06 5:00:24
Upper Burrell 65 6 40N33 79w40 5:18:40
Upper Chichester 23 90 39N50 75w26 5:01:44
Upper Darby 23 9 39N58 75w16 5:01:04
Upper Dublin 46 1 40N09 75w11 5:00:44
Upper Exeter 40 1 41N20 75w49 5:03:16
Upper Fairfield 41 6 41N18 76w52 5:07:28
Upper Frankford 21 1 40N14 77w22 5:09:28
Upper Frederick 46 8 40N19 75w31 5:02:04
Upper Glasgow 46 8 40N15 75w39 5:02:36
Upper Gwynedd 46 8 40N13 75w17 5:01:08
Upper Hanover 46 2 40N25 75w31 5:02:04
Upper Lawn 38 31 40N19 76w36 5:06:24
Upper Leacock 36 8 40N05 76w12 5:04:48
Upper Lehigh 40 20 41N20 75w54 5:03:36
Upper Lehigh Junction 40 60 41N04 75w46 5:03:04
Upper Macungie 39 13 40N34 75w37 5:02:28
Upper Mahanoy 49 1 40N43 76w38 5:06:32
Upper Mahantango 54 1 40N40 76w37 5:06:28
Upper Makefield 9 8 40N18 74w54 4:59:36
Upper Merion 46 90 40N05 75w22 5:01:28
Upper Middletown 26 6 40N00 79w47 5:19:08
Upper Mifflin 21 1 40N12 77w30 5:10:00
Upper Milford 39 13 40N30 75w31 5:02:04
Upper Mill 21 2 40N07 77w11 5:08:44
Upper Moreland 46 2 40N10 75w06 5:00:24
Upper Mount Bethel 46 8 40N54 75w08 5:00:32
Upper Nazareth 48 8 40N44 75w21 5:01:24
Upper Orchard 9 9 40N09 74w51 4:59:24
Upper Oxford 15 3 39N51 75w57 5:03:48
Upper Paxton 22 1 40N34 76w55 5:07:40
Upper Peanut 26 6 40N00 79w47 5:19:08
Upper Pottsgrove 46 8 40N17 75w38 5:02:32
Upper Reese 7 33 40N25 78w24 5:13:36
Upper Sagon 49 6 40N53 76w41 5:06:44
Upper Salford 46 8 40N18 75w27 5:01:48
Upper Saucon 39 13 40N32 75w25 5:01:40
Upper Southampton 9 1 40N11 75w02 5:00:08
Upper St. Clair 2 114 40N20 80w05 5:20:20
Upper Strasburg 28 1 40N04 77w43 5:10:52
Upper Tulpehocken 6 1 40N30 76w10 5:04:40
Upper Turkeyfoot 56 6 39N54 79w17 5:17:08
Upper Tyrone 26 111 40N05 79w35 5:18:20
Upper Uwchlan 15 80 40N05 75w43 5:02:52
Upper Yoder 11 74 40N18 78w57 5:15:48
Upton 28 1 39N48 77w44 5:10:56
Uptown 2 114 40N27 79w59 5:19:56
Urban 49 51 40N43 76w51 5:07:24
Urey 32 6 40N50 78w50 5:15:20
Uriah 21 1 40N00 77w12 5:08:48
Ursina 56 53 39N49 79w20 5:17:20
Ursina Junction 56 53 39N49 79w21 5:17:24
U. S. Naval Base 51 9 39N53 75w10 5:00:40
Uswick 64 6 41N29 75w11 5:00:44
Utahville 17 54 40N45 78w32 5:14:08
Utica 61 59 41N26 79w58 5:19:52
Uwchlan 15 80 40N03 75w40 5:02:40
Uwchland 15 80 40N05 75w41 5:02:44
Vail 7 11 40N40 78w13 5:12:52
Valencia 10 6 40N41 79w59 5:19:56
Valier 33 51 40N55 79w03 5:16:12
Vallamont Hills 41 82 41N14 77w01 5:08:04
Valley Falls 46 1 40N09 75w03 5:00:12
Valley Forge 15 8 40N06 75w28 5:01:52
Valley Forge 67 67 39N59 76w46 5:07:04
Valley Forge Estates 15 90 40N02 75w22 5:01:28
Valley Forge Homes 46 90 40N05 75w22 5:01:28
Valley Forge Manor 46 8 40N08 75w31 5:02:04
Valley Furnace 54 27 40N43 76w07 5:04:28
Valley Green 23 9 39N57 75w18 5:01:12
Valley View 11 74 40N20 78w56 5:15:44
Valley View 14 70 40N53 77w45 5:11:00
Valley View 36 8 40N06 76w22 5:05:28
Valley View 54 27 40N39 76w33 5:06:12
Valley View Acres 23 90 40N00 75w23 5:01:32
Valley View Farms 23 9 39N56 75w20 5:01:20
Valley View Farms 46 1 40N09 75w03 5:00:12
Valley View Heights 3 15 40N46 79w32 5:18:08
Van 61 1 41N21 79w43 5:18:52
Van Buren 63 3 40N10 80w16 5:21:04
Vance 63 3 40N11 80w16 5:21:04
Vances Mills 26 80 39N54 79w44 5:18:56
Vanceville 63 2 40N11 80w08 5:20:32
Vanderbilt 26 104 40N02 79w40 5:18:40
Vandergrift 65 4 40N36 79w34 5:18:16
Vandergrift Heights 65 4 40N37 79w34 5:18:16
Vandling 35 59 41N38 75w28 5:01:52
Vandyke 34 7 40N35 77w24 5:09:36
Vankirk 63 3 40N11 80w16 5:21:04
Van Meter 65 6 40N08 79w45 5:19:00
Van Ormer 11 54 40N41 78w30 5:14:00
Vanport 4 19 40N41 80w20 5:21:20
Van Voorhis 63 51 40N10 79w58 5:19:52
Van Wert 34 7 40N35 77w24 5:09:36
Varden 64 6 41N27 75w23 5:01:32
Vaux Town 9 8 40N21 75w13 5:00:52
Venango 20 3 41N47 80w07 5:20:28
Venetia 63 114 40N15 80w03 5:20:12
Venice 63 2 40N19 80w14 5:20:56
Venus 61 6 41N22 79w29 5:17:56
Vera Cruz 39 13 40N33 75w31 5:02:04
Verdilla 55 82 40N48 76w52 5:07:28
Vere Cruz 36 1 40N16 76w07 5:04:28
Vernfield 46 8 40N17 75w23 5:01:32
Vernon 20 77 41N38 80w13 5:20:52
Vernon 66 59 41N32 75w57 5:03:48
Vernondale 25 107 42N05 80w04 5:20:16
Vernon Park 51 9 40N02 75w10 5:00:40
Verona 2 14 40N31 79w51 5:19:24
Versailles 2 9 40N19 79w50 5:19:20
Vestaburg 63 51 40N01 79w59 5:19:56
Vesta Heights 63 6 40N01 80w00 5:20:00
Vesta No 6 63 51 40N02 79w58 5:19:52
Veterans Hospital 2 114 40N27 79w58 5:19:52
Veterans Hospital 40 20 41N15 75w53 5:03:32
Vicksburg 7 33 40N25 78w24 5:13:36
Vicksburg 60 70 40N56 76w59 5:07:56
Victory 61 7 41N19 79w54 5:19:36
Victory Heights 61 109 41N25 79w50 5:19:20
Victory Hills 63 1 40N11 79w54 5:19:36
Vienna 63 6 40N06 80w31 5:22:04
Viennese Woods 2 114 40N30 79w59 5:19:56
Village 2 114 40N20 80w05 5:20:20
Village Green 23 90 39N52 75w26 5:01:44
Village of Olde Hickory 36 8 40N04 76w19 5:05:16
Villa Green 67 67 39N57 76w42 5:06:48
Villa Maria 37 6 41N05 80w30 5:22:00
Villanova 23 90 40N02 75w20 5:01:20
Vincent 15 118 40N11 75w33 5:02:12
Vinco 11 74 40N21 78w54 5:15:36
Vinemont 6 1 40N16 76w07 5:04:28
Vintage 36 9 40N01 76w08 5:04:32
Vintondale 11 63 40N29 78w55 5:15:40
Violet Hill 67 1 40N21 77w18 5:09:12
Vira 44 73 40N36 77w34 5:10:16
Virginia Mills 1 1 39N47 77w22 5:09:28
Virginville 6 8 40N31 75w52 5:03:28
Voganville 36 30 40N11 76w11 5:04:44
Vogleyville 10 3 40N53 79w53 5:19:32
Volant 37 6 41N07 80w15 5:21:00
Vosburg 66 59 41N32 75w57 5:03:48
Vowinckel 16 6 41N25 79w14 5:16:56
Vulcan 54 27 40N48 76w20 5:05:20
Wabash 2 114 40N26 80w03 5:20:12
Wadesville 54 49 40N41 76w12 5:04:48
Wadsworth 51 9 40N04 75w10 5:00:40
Wagner 44 1 40N42 77w19 5:09:16
Wagnersville 46 12 40N41 75w14 5:00:56
Wago Junction 67 7 40N04 76w42 5:06:48
Wagontown 15 9 40N01 75w51 5:03:24
Wahlville 10 6 40N46 80w04 5:20:16
Wahnetah 13 80 40N52 75w44 5:02:56
Wakena 65 116 40N29 79w27 5:17:48
Walbert 39 13 40N37 75w31 5:02:04
Walcksville 13 8 40N50 75w42 5:02:48
Walkchalk 3 15 40N49 79w32 5:18:08
Walkers Mill 2 114 40N24 80w08 5:20:32
Walkertown 63 51 40N03 79w57 5:19:48
Wall 2 114 40N24 79w47 5:19:08
Wallace 15 80 40N05 75w46 5:03:04
Wallace Junction 25 68 41N59 80w19 5:21:16
Wallaceton 17 7 40N58 78w17 5:13:08
Wallaceville 61 74 41N38 79w40 5:18:40
Waller 19 6 41N12 76w23 5:05:32
Wallingford 23 90 39N54 75w22 5:01:28
Wallingford Hills 23 90 39N54 75w22 5:01:28
Wallis Run 41 7 41N23 77w03 5:08:12
Wall Rose 4 13 40N38 80w12 5:20:48
Walls Corners 35 44 41N32 75w44 5:02:56
Wallsville 35 44 41N32 75w44 5:02:56
Walltown 17 7 40N58 78w36 5:14:24
Walmo 37 112 41N00 80w21 5:21:24
Walnut 4 8 40N49 80w25 5:21:40
Walnut 34 7 40N32 77w24 5:09:36
Walnut Bend 61 9 41N25 79w42 5:18:48
Walnut Bottom 21 1 40N05 77w24 5:09:36
Walnut Gardens 39 13 40N39 75w30 5:02:00
Walnut Grove 50 1 40N29 77w08 5:08:32
Walnut Hill 26 80 39N54 79w44 5:18:56
Walnut Hill 30 7 39N45 79w56 5:19:44
Walnutport 46 8 40N45 75w36 5:02:24
Walnuttown 6 8 40N27 75w50 5:03:20
Walsall 11 74 40N17 78w53 5:15:32
Walston 33 51 40N58 79w01 5:16:04
Walston Junction 33 51 40N56 78w58 5:15:52
Walters 46 12 40N41 75w14 5:00:56
Waltersburg 26 80 39N59 79w46 5:19:04
Waltonville 22 12 40N16 76w43 5:06:52
Waltz 65 111 40N10 79w37 5:18:28
Waltzvale 17 6 40N48 78w24 5:13:36
Wampum 37 121 40N54 80w21 5:21:24
Wanamakers 39 56 40N37 75w53 5:03:32
Wanamie 40 21 41N12 76w00 5:04:00
Wandin 32 6 40N43 78w57 5:15:48
Wanneta 25 7 41N54 80w22 5:21:28
Wapwallopen 40 1 41N04 76w08 5:04:32
Ward 23 4 39N53 75w31 5:02:04
Ward 59 7 41N41 76w56 5:07:44
Warfordsburg 29 6 39N45 78w11 5:12:44
Warminster 9 1 40N12 75w06 5:00:24
Warner 63 1 40N08 79w54 5:19:36
Warren 62 120 41N51 79w09 5:16:36
Warren Center 8 6 41N56 76w11 5:04:44
Warrendale 2 6 40N39 80w05 5:20:20
Warrens Mill 56 79 39N49 79w02 5:16:08
Warrensville 41 82 41N20 76w57 5:07:48
Warrington 9 8 40N14 75w08 5:00:32
Warrior Ridge 31 81 40N35 78w03 5:12:12
Warrior Run 40 20 41N11 75w57 5:03:48
Warriors Mark 31 6 40N42 78w08 5:12:32
Warsaw 33 6 41N14 78w59 5:15:56
Warsaw 35 18 41N25 75w38 5:02:32
Warsaw 40 20 41N15 75w53 5:03:32
Warwick 15 1 40N10 75w47 5:03:08
Washington 63 3 40N10 80w15 5:21:00
Washington Boro 36 26 40N00 76w28 5:05:52
Washington Crossing 9 1 40N18 74w52 4:59:28
Washington Heights 21 12 40N15 76w54 5:07:36
Washington Hill 46 8 40N15 75w39 5:02:36
Washington Square 46 90 40N08 75w21 5:01:24
Washingtonville 47 6 41N03 76w41 5:06:44
Waterfall 29 6 40N08 78w04 5:12:16
Waterford 25 35 41N57 79w59 5:19:56
Waterford 65 110 40N15 79w14 5:16:56
Waterloo 34 6 40N22 77w36 5:10:24
Waterloo Mills 15 90 40N03 75w26 5:01:44
Waterman 32 71 40N33 79w10 5:16:40
Waterside 5 51 40N14 78w22 5:13:28
Waterson 16 37 41N12 79w20 5:17:20
Waterton 40 1 41N09 76w10 5:04:40
Waterville 41 6 41N19 77w22 5:09:28
Watkins 11 63 40N36 78w42 5:14:48
Watrous 59 6 41N45 77w34 5:10:16
Watson Crossing 62 3 41N47 79w06 5:16:24
Watson Farm 27 6 41N28 79w07 5:16:28
Watson Run 20 6 41N36 80w19 5:21:16
Watsontown 49 73 41N05 76w52 5:07:28
Watters 10 6 40N46 80w02 5:20:08
Wattersonville 3 6 40N53 79w36 5:18:24
Watts 50 3 40N28 76w59 5:07:56
Wattsburg 25 7 42N00 79w49 5:19:16
Waverly 35 45 41N32 75w42 5:02:48
Waverly Heights 23 9 39N57 75w18 5:01:12
Waverly Manor 23 9 39N57 75w18 5:01:12
Wawa 23 4 39N54 75w28 5:01:52
Wawaset 15 13 39N57 75w36 5:02:24
Waymart 64 1 41N35 75w24 5:01:36
Wayne 23 90 40N03 75w23 5:01:32
Waynecastle 28 1 39N48 77w44 5:10:56
Wayne Heights 28 100 39N45 77w33 5:10:12
Waynesboro 28 100 39N45 77w35 5:10:20
Waynesburg 30 1 39N54 80w11 5:20:44
Waynesville 22 24 40N28 76w56 5:07:44
Weatherly 13 60 40N57 75w50 5:03:20
Weaverland 36 27 40N07 76w02 5:04:08
Weaver Mill 65 110 40N12 79w15 5:17:00
Weaversville 48 13 40N41 75w22 5:01:28
Weavertown 6 8 40N15 75w44 5:02:56
Weavertown 36 96 40N02 76w11 5:04:44
Weavertown 38 8 40N13 76w26 5:05:44
Weavertown 63 2 40N16 80w11 5:20:44
Weber City 12 106 41N31 78w14 5:12:56
Webster 65 114 40N23 80w04 5:20:16
Webster Mills 29 66 39N56 78w00 5:12:00
Weedville 24 7 41N17 78w30 5:14:00
Wegley 65 25 40N20 79w43 5:18:52
Wehnwood 7 33 40N31 78w25 5:13:40
Weidasville 39 8 40N41 75w36 5:02:24
Weidmanville 36 30 40N11 76w11 5:04:44
Weigelstown 67 1 40N00 76w58 5:07:52
Weigh Scale 49 27 40N48 76w33 5:06:12
Weikert 60 7 40N52 77w18 5:09:12
Weilersville 39 13 40N31 75w36 5:02:24
Weinel Cross Roads 65 4 40N38 79w37 5:18:28
Weir Lake 45 9 40N52 75w27 5:01:48
Weisel 9 8 40N25 75w23 5:01:32
Weisenberg 39 9 40N36 75w42 5:02:48
Weishample 54 27 40N39 76w30 5:06:00
Weissport 13 8 40N50 75w42 5:02:48
Weldon 46 9 40N07 75w10 5:00:40
Wellersburg 56 6 39N44 78w51 5:15:24
Welliversville 19 4 41N00 76w25 5:05:40
Wellsboro 59 6 41N45 77w18 5:09:12
Wellscreek 56 6 40N03 79w00 5:16:00
Wells Tannery 29 6 40N05 78w10 5:12:40
Wellsville 67 1 40N03 76w56 5:07:44
Welsh Hill 58 59 41N43 75w29 5:01:56
Welsh Run 28 1 39N48 77w44 5:10:56
Welty 65 111 40N09 79w33 5:18:12
Weltys 28 100 39N45 77w34 5:10:16
Wendel 65 25 40N17 79w41 5:18:44
Wenks 1 1 39N59 77w15 5:09:00

Wennersville 39 13 40N37 75w31 5:02:04
Wentling Corners 16 6 41N14 79w32 5:18:08
Werleys Corner 39 1 40N41 75w45 5:03:00
Wernersville 6 80 40N20 76w05 5:04:20
Wertzville 21 12 40N12 77w00 5:08:00
Wescosville 39 13 40N36 75w29 5:01:56
Wesley 61 6 41N10 80w00 5:20:00
Wesley Chapel 11 74 40N21 78w54 5:15:36
Wesleyville 25 107 42N09 80w00 5:20:00
West 31 6 40N38 77w59 5:11:56
West Abington 35 44 41N32 75w46 5:03:04
West Acres 60 70 40N58 76w54 5:07:36
West Alexander 63 6 40N06 80w31 5:22:04
West Aliquippa 4 13 40N37 80w16 5:21:04
West Ambler 46 1 40N09 75w12 5:00:48
West Annville 38 8 40N20 76w31 5:06:04
West Apollo 65 4 40N35 79w34 5:18:16
West Auburn 58 6 41N39 76w10 5:04:40
Westaway 46 90 40N05 75w16 5:01:04
West Bangor 46 17 40N53 75w12 5:00:48
West Bangor 67 1 39N44 76w19 5:05:16
West Beaver 55 1 40N45 77w19 5:09:16
West Bellevue 2 114 40N30 80w04 5:20:16
West Bend 26 6 39N59 80w00 5:20:00
West Berwick 19 1 41N04 76w15 5:05:00
West Bethlehem 63 6 40N02 80w05 5:20:20
West Bingham 53 6 41N59 77w52 5:11:28
West Bolivar 65 7 40N24 79w09 5:16:36
West Bradford 15 46 39N58 75w43 5:02:52
West Branch 11 92 40N40 78w47 5:15:08
West Branch 53 6 41N41 77w42 5:10:48
West Brandywine 15 9 40N03 75w49 5:03:16
West Bridgewater 4 19 40N42 80w19 5:21:16
West Bristol 9 9 40N06 74w54 4:59:36
Westbrook Park 23 9 39N56 75w18 5:01:12
West Brownsville 63 1 40N02 79w53 5:19:32
West Brunswick 54 1 40N38 76w04 5:04:16
West Buffalo 60 6 40N57 77w03 5:08:12
West Burlington 8 7 41N46 76w40 5:06:40
West Caln 15 9 40N01 75w53 5:03:32
West Cameron 49 1 40N45 76w39 5:06:36
West Carroll 11 63 40N36 78w44 5:14:56
West Catasauqua 39 13 40N39 75w30 5:02:00
West Chester 15 13 39N58 75w36 5:02:24
West Chillisquaque 49 70 40N58 76w51 5:07:24
West Clifford 58 59 41N43 75w29 5:01:56
West Cocalico 36 28 40N16 76w09 5:04:36
West Conshohocken 46 90 40N04 75w19 5:01:16
West Cornwall 38 8 40N16 76w27 5:05:48
West Creek 12 106 41N31 78w14 5:12:56
West Cressona 54 27 40N38 76w12 5:04:48
West Damascus 64 6 41N42 75w04 5:00:16
West Decatur 17 4 40N56 78w17 5:13:08
West Deer 2 6 40N38 79w52 5:19:28
West Derry 65 3 40N20 79w19 5:17:16
West Donegal 36 2 40N08 76w37 5:06:28
West Earl 36 28 40N08 76w11 5:04:44
West Easton 46 12 40N41 75w14 5:00:56
West Eldred 42 40 41N57 78w23 5:13:32
West Elizabeth 2 8 40N16 79w54 5:19:36
West Ellwood Junction 4 121 40N50 80w20 5:21:20
West End 22 12 40N16 76w53 5:07:32
West Enola 21 12 40N16 76w55 5:07:40
West Etna 2 114 40N31 79w57 5:19:48
West Export 65 6 40N25 79w38 5:18:32
West Fairfield 65 29 40N23 79w04 5:16:16
West Fairview 21 12 40N17 76w55 5:07:40
Westfall 51 2 41N23 74w45 4:59:00
West Falls 66 6 41N28 75w51 5:03:24
West Fayetteville 28 1 39N55 77w34 5:10:16
Westfield 59 6 41N55 77w32 5:10:08
Westfield Terrace 67 12 40N14 76w51 5:07:24
West Finley 63 6 40N01 80w28 5:21:52
Westford 20 63 41N29 80w26 5:21:44
West Franklin 3 6 40N51 79w39 5:18:36
West Franklin 8 60 41N43 76w28 5:05:52
West Freedom 16 6 41N05 79w41 5:18:44
Westgate Hills 23 9 40N00 75w18 5:01:12
Westgate Hills 48 13 40N39 75w21 5:01:24
West Goshen 15 13 39N59 75w36 5:02:24
West Goshen Hills 15 13 39N57 75w36 5:02:24
West Goshen Park 15 13 39N57 75w36 5:02:24
West Grove 15 1 39N49 75w50 5:03:20
West Hamburg 6 80 40N33 75w59 5:03:56
West Hanover 22 12 40N22 76w45 5:07:00
West Hazleton 40 42 40N58 76w01 5:04:04
West Hemlock 47 6 41N02 76w35 5:06:20
West Hempfield 36 26 40N04 76w27 5:05:48
West Hickory 27 6 41N34 79w25 5:17:40
West Hill 21 16 40N12 77w11 5:08:44
West Hills Estates 41 82 41N14 77w01 5:08:04
West Hills Shopping Center 2 114 40N30 80w10 5:20:40
West Hoffman 2 114 40N34 80w00 5:20:00
West Homestead 2 114 40N24 79w55 5:19:40
Westinghouse Village 23 9 39N52 75w17 5:01:08
West Jeannette 65 3 40N20 79w37 5:18:28
West Keating 18 7 41N13 78w02 5:12:08
West Kittanning 3 15 40N48 79w32 5:18:08
West Lampeter 36 8 40N00 76w16 5:05:04
West Lancaster 36 8 40N02 76w20 5:05:20
Westland 63 2 40N17 80w16 5:21:04
West Lawn 6 101 40N20 76w00 5:04:00
West Lawn 60 70 40N58 76w54 5:07:36
West Lebanon 32 6 40N35 79w22 5:17:28
West Lebanon 38 8 40N21 76w27 5:05:48
West Leechburg 65 4 40N38 79w37 5:18:28
West Leisenring 26 80 39N57 79w42 5:18:48
West Lenox 58 59 41N46 75w43 5:02:52
West Leroy 8 103 41N39 76w51 5:07:24
West Liberty 10 6 41N00 80w04 5:20:16
West Liberty 17 56 41N07 78w46 5:15:04
West Library 2 114 40N20 80w02 5:20:08
Westline 42 6 41N47 78w47 5:15:08
West Mahanoy 54 27 40N48 76w15 5:05:00
West Mahoning 32 6 40N53 79w09 5:16:36
West Manayunk 46 9 39N59 75w16 5:01:04
West Manchester 67 39 39N57 76w52 5:07:28
West Manheim 67 1 39N45 76w57 5:07:48
West Marietta 36 26 40N04 76w33 5:06:12
West Marlborough 15 8 39N54 75w48 5:03:12
West Mayfield 4 121 40N47 80w20 5:21:20
West Mead 20 77 41N38 80w08 5:20:32
West Meyersdale 56 79 39N49 79w02 5:16:08
West Middlesex 43 117 41N10 80w27 5:21:48
West Middletown 63 6 40N15 80w26 5:21:44
West Mifflin 2 114 40N22 79w54 5:19:36
West Milton 60 70 41N01 76w52 5:07:28
Westminster 25 107 42N04 80w09 5:20:36
Westminster 40 20 41N15 75w53 5:03:32
Westminster Manor 2 114 40N20 80w05 5:20:20
West Monocacy 6 8 40N15 75w44 5:02:56
Westmont 11 74 40N19 78w58 5:15:52
Westmont 38 8 40N20 76w26 5:05:44
West Monterey 16 1 41N03 79w39 5:18:36
Westmoreland 65 25 40N20 79w41 5:18:44
West Moshannon 17 4 40N50 78w21 5:13:24
West Myerstown 38 25 40N23 76w18 5:05:12
West Nanticoke 40 21 41N12 76w00 5:04:00
West Nantmeal 15 1 40N07 75w49 5:03:16
West New Kensington 2 14 40N35 79w47 5:19:08
West Newton 65 61 40N13 79w46 5:19:04
West Nicholson 66 89 41N38 75w47 5:03:08
West Norriton 46 90 40N08 75w22 5:01:28
West Nottingham 15 3 39N45 76w03 5:04:12
Weston 40 1 40N57 76w09 5:04:36
Weston Place 54 27 40N49 76w12 5:04:48
Westover 17 7 40N45 78w40 5:14:40
West Overton 65 111 40N06 79w35 5:18:20
Westover Woods 46 90 40N08 75w21 5:01:24
West Park 2 114 40N28 80w05 5:20:20
West Park 51 9 39N59 75w14 5:00:56
West Pen Argyl 46 17 40N52 75w15 5:01:00
West Penn 54 1 40N44 75w53 5:03:32
West Pennsboro 21 1 40N11 77w20 5:09:20
West Perry 55 6 40N42 77w06 5:08:24
West Pike 53 6 41N47 77w43 5:10:52
West Pikeland 15 8 40N05 75w37 5:02:28
West Pike Run 63 51 40N04 79w57 5:19:48
West Pittsburg 37 112 40N56 80w22 5:21:28
West Pittston 40 1 41N20 75w48 5:03:12
West Pittston Junction 40 112 40N56 80w22 5:21:28
West Plaza 25 107 42N08 80w09 5:20:36
West Point 11 74 40N23 78w50 5:15:20
West Point 46 8 40N13 75w18 5:01:12
Westport 18 7 41N18 77w51 5:11:24
West Pottsgrove 46 28 40N17 75w40 5:02:40
West Providence 5 6 40N01 78w21 5:13:24
West Reading 6 101 40N20 75w57 5:03:48
West Renovo 18 73 41N20 77w45 5:11:00
West Ridge 25 107 42N04 80w09 5:20:36
West Ridge 36 8 40N02 76w20 5:05:20
West Rockhill 9 2 40N25 75w27 5:01:48
West Sadsbury 15 8 39N58 75w57 5:03:48
West Saint Clair 5 6 40N11 78w38 5:14:32
West Salem 43 63 41N24 80w26 5:21:44
West Salisbury 56 79 39N45 79w06 5:16:24
West Scranton 35 18 41N25 75w41 5:02:44
West Sheffield 62 3 41N42 79w02 5:16:08
West Shenango 20 63 41N31 80w30 5:22:00
West Side 40 21 41N12 76w00 5:04:00
West Side 65 61 40N13 79w46 5:19:04
West Spring Creek 62 3 41N55 79w39 5:18:36
West Springfield 25 7 41N57 80w29 5:21:56
West Sunbury 10 6 41N00 79w54 5:19:36
West Tarentum 2 14 40N37 79w44 5:18:56
West Taylor 11 74 40N22 78w57 5:15:48
West Telford 46 2 40N20 75w20 5:01:20
Westtown 15 4 39N56 75w33 5:02:12
Westtown Acres 15 13 39N57 75w36 5:02:24
West Union 30 1 39N56 80w15 5:21:00

West Valley 3 15 40N49 79w32 5:18:08
West Vandergrift 65 4 40N36 79w35 5:18:20
West View 2 114 40N31 80w02 5:20:08
Westville 33 5 41N13 78w50 5:15:20
West Vincent 15 8 40N08 75w39 5:02:36
West Warren 8 6 42N01 76w22 5:05:28
West Waynesburg 30 1 39N54 80w11 5:20:44
West Wheatfield 32 7 40N26 79w07 5:16:28
West Whiteland 15 13 40N01 75w37 5:02:28
West William Penn 54 27 40N49 76w12 5:04:48
West Willow 36 8 39N58 76w17 5:05:08
West Wilmerding 2 114 40N23 79w49 5:19:16
West Winfield 10 6 40N46 79w46 5:19:04
Westwood 11 74 40N19 78w56 5:15:44
Westwood Hills 2 10 40N20 79w52 5:19:28
Westwood Park 23 9 40N00 75w18 5:01:12
West Wyoming 40 20 41N19 75w51 5:03:24
West Wyomissing 6 101 40N19 76w00 5:04:00
West York 67 67 39N57 76w46 5:07:04
West Zollarsville 63 6 40N02 80w06 5:20:24
Wetmore 42 75 41N39 78w49 5:15:16
Wetona 8 7 41N50 76w48 5:07:12
Wexford 2 114 40N38 80w03 5:20:12
Weyant 5 7 40N12 78w31 5:14:04
Wharton 53 6 41N38 78w06 5:12:24
Wheatfield 50 1 40N24 77w05 5:08:20
Wheatland 43 117 41N12 80w30 5:22:00
Wheatland Hills 36 8 40N02 76w18 5:05:12
Wheeler 26 104 40N01 79w35 5:18:20
Wheelerville 57 6 41N33 76w44 5:06:56
Whipkeys-Dam 56 4 39N52 79w14 5:16:56
Whiskerville 10 6 41N05 79w50 5:19:20
Whitaker 2 114 40N24 79w53 5:19:32
White 26 6 40N04 79w26 5:17:44
White 32 116 40N29 79w27 5:17:48
White Bear 6 8 40N16 75w48 5:03:12
White Deer 60 70 41N03 76w55 5:07:40
White Hall 1 56 39N45 77w05 5:08:20
Whitehall 2 114 40N22 79w59 5:19:56
Whitehall 39 13 40N39 75w30 5:02:00
White Hall 47 6 40N58 76w36 5:06:24
Whitehall Park 46 90 40N08 75w21 5:01:24
White Haven 40 60 41N04 75w47 5:03:08
White Hill 21 12 40N14 76w57 5:07:48
White Horse 15 90 40N00 75w23 5:01:32
White Horse 36 23 39N59 76w02 5:04:08
White House 26 51 39N48 79w49 5:19:16
Whiteland Crest 15 47 40N03 75w33 5:02:12
Whiteland Farms 15 8 40N02 75w31 5:02:04
Whiteley 30 1 39N49 80w08 5:20:32
Whitemarsh 46 9 40N06 75w15 5:01:00
Whitemarsh Downs 46 9 40N07 75w11 5:00:44
Whitemarsh Estates 46 90 40N05 75w16 5:01:04
Whitemarsh Greens 46 90 40N05 75w16 5:01:04
Whitemarsh Hills 46 90 40N05 75w16 5:01:04
Whitemarsh Valley Farms 46 90 40N05 75w16 5:01:04
White Marsh Village 23 9 39N56 75w20 5:01:20
White Mills 64 59 41N32 75w12 5:00:48
White Oak 2 8 40N20 79w49 5:19:16
White Oak 36 8 40N06 76w22 5:05:28
White Pine 41 7 41N23 77w03 5:08:12
Whitesburg 3 15 40N49 79w32 5:18:08
Whites Crossing 35 1 41N34 75w32 5:02:08
Whites Ferry 66 59 41N32 75w57 5:03:48
Whites Hill 65 111 40N14 79w35 5:18:20
Whiteside 17 4 40N50 78w21 5:13:24
Whitesprings 60 6 40N55 77w03 5:08:12
Whitestown 10 6 40N54 80w03 5:20:12
Whites Valley 64 59 41N44 75w26 5:01:44
White Township 4 8 40N46 80w20 5:21:20
White Valley 65 6 40N25 79w38 5:18:32
Whitfield 6 101 40N19 76w00 5:04:00
Whitford 15 47 40N03 75w33 5:02:12
Whitney 65 3 40N15 79w25 5:17:40
Whitpain 46 8 40N10 75w17 5:01:08
Whitsett 26 6 40N07 79w46 5:19:04
Wick 10 6 41N02 80w03 5:20:12
Wick City 3 15 40N49 79w32 5:18:08
Wickerham Manor 63 1 40N11 79w54 5:19:36
Wickerton 15 1 39N49 75w50 5:03:20
Wickham Village 4 13 40N37 80w16 5:21:04
Wickhaven 26 6 40N07 79w46 5:19:04
Wiconisco 22 1 40N35 76w42 5:06:48
Wiconisco Center 22 1 40N34 76w41 5:06:44
Widener College 23 90 39N51 75w22 5:01:28
Widnoon 3 64 40N58 79w28 5:17:52
Wiegletown 37 112 41N00 80w21 5:21:24
Wiester 65 6 40N29 79w37 5:18:28
Wiggans 54 3 40N49 76w08 5:04:32
Wila 50 1 40N29 77w08 5:08:32
Wilawana 8 1 41N58 76w31 5:06:04
Wilbur 56 6 40N07 78w57 5:15:48
Wilburton 19 27 40N49 76w23 5:05:32

Wilco Hill 65 114 40N23 80W04 5:20:16
Wilcox 24 64 41N35 78W41 5:14:44
Wildcat 16 7 41N02 79W30 5:18:00
Wilden Acres 46 12 40N41 75W14 5:00:56
Wildwood 2 114 40N36 79W58 5:19:52
Wiley 67 1 39N45 76W35 5:06:20
Wiley Heights 30 51 39N54 79W58 5:19:52
Wilgus 32 6 40N50 78W50 5:15:20
Wilkes-Barre 40 20 41N15 75W53 5:03:32
Wilkins 2 114 40N25 79W50 5:19:20
Wilkinsburg 2 114 40N26 79W53 5:19:32
Willet 32 72 40N41 79W12 5:16:48
William Penn Annex 51 9 40N00 75W09 5:00:36
William Penn Manor 48 13 40N39 75W21 5:01:24
Williams 33 51 40N56 78W58 5:15:52
Williamsburg 7 3 40N28 78W12 5:12:48
Williamsburg 16 37 41N12 79W22 5:17:28
Williams Grove 21 12 40N12 77W00 5:08:00
Williamson 28 1 39N51 77W48 5:11:12
Williamsport 41 82 41N15 77W00 5:08:00
Williamstown 22 1 40N35 76W37 5:06:28
Williamstown 63 6 39N59 80W03 5:20:12
Willistown 15 8 40N01 75W30 5:02:00
Willock 2 114 40N22 79W58 5:19:52
Willopenn 9 1 40N11 75W03 5:00:12
Willowburn 23 90 40N02 75W20 5:01:20
Willowdale 15 8 39N53 75W43 5:02:52
Willow Grove 37 112 41N00 80W21 5:21:24
Willow Grove 46 2 40N09 75W07 5:00:28
Willow Grove Naval Air Stati 46 2 40N09 75W07 5:00:28
Willow Hill 28 1 40N06 77W48 5:11:12
Willow Springs 19 4 41N00 76W25 5:05:40
Willow Springs 65 25 40N20 79W43 5:18:52
Willow Street 36 8 39N59 76W17 5:05:08
Willow View Heights 36 8 40N02 76W17 5:05:08
Wills Creek 5 51 39N50 78W43 5:14:52
Wilmer 15 8 40N08 75W31 5:02:04
Wilmerding 2 114 40N24 79W49 5:19:16
Wilmington 37 6 41N06 80W20 5:21:20
Wilmore 11 63 40N23 78W43 5:14:52
Wilmore Heights 11 63 40N23 78W40 5:14:40
Wilmot 8 6 41N37 76W15 5:05:00
Wilpen 65 110 40N17 79W12 5:16:48
Wilshire Hills 36 8 40N02 76W20 5:05:20
Wilshire Hills 67 67 39N59 76W46 5:07:04
Wilson 2 8 40N18 79W54 5:19:36
Wilson 48 12 40N41 75W14 5:00:56
Wilson Creek 56 4 39N55 79W11 5:16:44
Wilsons Corners 15 8 40N08 75W31 5:02:04
Wimmers 35 59 41N27 75W23 5:01:32
Winburne 17 7 40N58 78W08 5:12:32
Windber 56 123 40N14 78W50 5:15:20
Winder Village 9 9 40N08 74W51 4:59:24
Windfall 8 7 41N43 76W47 5:07:08
Windgap 48 17 40N51 75W17 5:01:08
Windham Center 8 6 42N01 76W22 5:05:28
Winding Hill 21 12 40N12 77W00 5:08:00
Winding Hill Heights 21 12 40N12 77W00 5:08:00
Wind Ridge 30 6 39N55 80W26 5:21:44
Windsor 67 1 39N55 76W35 5:06:20
Windsor Castle 6 80 40N33 75W59 5:03:56
Windsor Farms 22 12 40N17 76W53 5:07:32
Windsor Park 21 12 40N12 77W00 5:08:00
Windsor Park 67 67 39N57 76W42 5:06:48
Windward Heights 10 3 40N53 79W53 5:19:32
Winfield 10 2 40N46 79W44 5:18:56
Winfield 60 70 40N55 76W51 5:07:24
Wingate 14 70 40N56 77W49 5:11:16
Winona Homes 23 9 39N53 75W18 5:01:12
Winslow 33 6 41N06 78W53 5:15:32
Winstead 26 7 39N44 79W54 5:19:36
Winterburne 17 7 41N13 78W34 5:14:16
Winterdale 64 6 41N57 75W17 5:01:08
Winterstown 67 1 39N50 76W37 5:06:28
Wintersville 6 25 40N22 76W16 5:05:04
Wireton 2 13 40N33 80W14 5:20:56
Wiscasset 45 84 41N08 75W22 5:01:28
Wishaw 33 6 41N06 78W53 5:15:32
Wismer 9 1 40N26 75W09 5:00:36
Wissahickon Village 46 90 40N05 75W16 5:01:04
Wissinoming 51 9 40N01 75W03 5:00:12
Witinski Villa 40 20 41N13 75W54 5:03:36
Witmer 36 8 40N03 76W13 5:04:52
Wittmer 2 114 40N31 79W58 5:19:52
Wolf 41 81 41N16 76W44 5:06:56
Wolf Creek 43 6 41N13 80W04 5:20:16
Wolfdale 63 3 40N12 80W17 5:21:08
Wolfsburg 5 70 39N58 78W31 5:14:04
Wolfs Corner 16 6 41N30 79W27 5:17:48
Wolfs Crossroads 49 2 40N12 77W17 5:09:08
Wolftown 2 114 40N24 79W52 5:19:28
Wolverton 49 6 40N57 76W39 5:06:36
Womelsdorf 6 56 40N22 76W11 5:04:44
Wood 31 6 40N11 78W06 5:12:24
Woodale 45 23 41N00 75W11 5:00:44
Woodbine 67 1 39N50 76W24 5:05:36
Woodbourne 9 97 40N10 74W55 4:59:40
Woodbridgetown 26 51 39N48 79W49 5:19:16
Woodbury 5 51 40N14 78W22 5:13:28
Woodchoppertown 6 2 40N20 75W38 5:02:32
Woodcock 20 3 41N46 80W05 5:20:20
Woodcrest 15 13 39N57 75W36 5:02:24
Wooddale 26 111 40N09 79W33 5:18:12
Woodhill 9 8 40N14 74W56 4:59:44
Woodland 17 7 41N00 78W21 5:13:24
Woodland 44 73 40N40 77W36 5:10:24
Woodland Heights 61 9 41N24 79W42 5:18:48
Woodland Park 41 82 41N14 77W01 5:08:04
Woodland View 67 67 39N59 76W46 5:07:04
Woodlawn 4 13 40N37 80W16 5:21:04
Woodlawn 36 8 40N02 76W20 5:05:20
Woodlawn 39 13 40N37 75W31 5:02:04
Woodlawn 65 3 40N20 79W37 5:18:28
Woodlyn 23 9 39N52 75W20 5:01:20
Woodlyn Manor 23 9 39N53 75W21 5:01:24
Woodlyn Park 23 9 39N53 75W21 5:01:24
Woodmere Park 23 9 40N00 75W18 5:01:12
Woodrow 63 6 40N17 80W22 5:21:28
Woodside 9 8 40N14 74W53 4:59:32
Woodside 26 51 39N48 79W49 5:19:16
Woodside 40 20 41N20 75W54 5:03:36
Woodstown 56 6 40N11 78W59 5:15:56
Woodvale Heights 11 74 40N19 78W54 5:15:36
Woodview 23 90 40N00 75W23 5:01:32
Woodville 2 114 40N25 80W05 5:20:20
Woodward 14 6 40N54 77W21 5:09:24
Woodycrest 14 9 40N48 77W52 5:11:28
Woolrich 18 7 41N12 77W23 5:09:32
Wopsononock 7 6 40N36 78W31 5:14:04
Worcester 46 8 40N12 75W21 5:01:24
Worden Place 40 6 41N22 76W02 5:04:08
Worleytown 28 1 39N48 77W44 5:10:56
Worman 6 8 40N15 75W44 5:02:56
Wormleysburg 21 12 40N16 76W54 5:07:36
Worthington 3 6 40N50 79W38 5:18:32
Worthville 33 6 41N02 79W08 5:16:32
Woxall 46 8 40N19 75W27 5:01:48
Wright 40 6 41N07 75W55 5:03:40
Wrights 42 6 41N49 78W17 5:13:08
Wrights Corners 42 93 41N49 78W27 5:13:48
Wrightsdale 36 1 39N47 76W11 5:04:44
Wrightstown 9 1 40N17 75W01 5:00:04
Wrightsville 62 3 41N50 79W23 5:17:32
Wrightsville 67 26 40N01 76W32 5:06:08

Wurtemburg 4 121 40N52 80W16 5:21:04
Wyalusing 8 60 41N40 76W16 5:05:04
Wyano 65 4 40N12 79W42 5:18:48
Wyattville 61 109 41N25 79W50 5:19:20
Wycombe 9 1 40N17 75W01 5:00:04
Wydnor 48 13 40N36 75W23 5:01:32
Wyebrooke 15 27 40N06 75W55 5:03:40
Wylandville 63 2 40N11 80W08 5:20:32
Wyncote 46 9 40N05 75W09 5:00:36
Wyncote Hills 46 9 40N05 75W09 5:00:36
Wyncroft 23 90 39N55 75W22 5:01:28
Wyndham Hills 67 67 39N57 76W42 5:06:48
Wyndmoor 46 9 40N05 75W11 5:00:44
Wyndmoor Valley 46 9 40N07 75W11 5:00:44
Wynglade Park 23 9 40N00 75W18 5:01:12
Wynn 26 80 39N54 79W44 5:18:56
Wynnewood 9 9 40N12 74W49 4:59:16
Wynnewood 46 9 40N00 75W17 5:01:08
Wyola 23 90 40N00 75W23 5:01:32
Wyoming 40 20 41N19 75W50 5:03:20
Wyoming Camp Ground 40 20 41N20 75W56 5:03:44
Wyomissing 6 101 40N20 75W59 5:03:56
Wyomissing Hills 6 101 40N20 75W59 5:03:56
Wyomissing Junction 6 101 40N19 75W59 5:03:56
Wysox 8 41 41N47 76W24 5:05:36
Yardley 9 9 40N15 74W50 4:59:20
Yardley Farms 9 9 40N12 74W49 4:59:16
Yarnell 14 70 40N53 77W45 5:11:00
Yatesboro 3 6 40N48 79W20 5:17:20
Yatesville 40 1 41N18 75W47 5:03:08
Yatesville 54 27 40N49 76W12 5:04:48
Yeadon 23 9 39N56 75W15 5:01:00
Yeagertown 44 73 40N38 77W35 5:10:20
Yellow Creek 5 6 40N09 78W16 5:13:04
Yellow Hammer 27 3 41N45 79W03 5:16:12
Yellow House 6 8 40N15 75W44 5:02:56
Yerkes 46 8 40N10 75W27 5:01:48
Yocumtown 67 9 40N09 76W45 5:07:00
Yoe 67 7 39N55 76W38 5:06:32
York 67 67 39N58 76W44 5:06:56
Yorkana 67 2 39N59 76W35 5:06:20
York Gardens 46 1 40N11 75W06 5:00:24
York Haven 67 80 40N07 76W43 5:06:52
Yorklyn 67 67 39N59 76W46 5:07:04
York New Salem 67 67 39N54 76W47 5:07:08
York Run 26 80 39N54 79W44 5:18:56
Yorkshire 67 67 39N59 76W46 5:07:04
York Springs 1 1 40N00 77W07 5:08:28
Yostville 35 4 41N20 75W32 5:02:08
Youngdale 18 7 41N10 77W22 5:09:28
Youngsburg 15 9 39N59 75W50 5:03:20
Youngstown 40 42 41N01 75W54 5:03:36
Youngstown 65 3 40N17 79W22 5:17:28
Youngsville 46 80 40N48 75W32 5:02:08
Youngsville 62 3 41N51 79W19 5:17:16
Youngwood 65 111 40N14 79W35 5:18:20
Yukon 65 4 40N13 79W41 5:18:44
Zebleys Corner 23 90 39N50 75W25 5:01:40
Zelienople 10 86 40N48 80W08 5:20:32
Zerbe 54 9 40N38 76W24 5:05:36
Zieglerville 46 8 40N17 75W29 5:01:56
Zion 14 70 40N53 77W45 5:11:00
Zion 40 1 41N20 75W49 5:03:16
Zion Grove 54 1 40N54 76W13 5:04:52
Zionhill 9 13 40N29 75W24 5:01:36
Zion Hill 16 6 41N08 79W33 5:18:12
Zions View 67 67 39N58 76W47 5:07:08
Zionsville 39 13 40N29 75W30 5:02:00
Zollarsville 63 6 40N02 80W06 5:20:24
Zooks Corner 36 8 40N02 76W17 5:05:08
Zooks Dam 34 7 40N35 77W24 5:09:36
Zora 1 1 39N47 77W22 5:09:28
Zucksville 46 12 40N41 75W14 5:00:56
Zullinger 28 100 39N46 77W38 5:10:32

TIME TABLES

Before 3/28/1899		LMT
3/28/1899	12:00	AST
5/03/1942	00:00	AWT
9/30/1945	02:00	AST

COUNTIES

1 Aguadilla
2 Arecibo
3 Bayamon
4 Guayama
5 Humacao
6 Mayaguez
7 Ponce
8 San Juan

Place	Lat	Long	Time
Adjuntas 6	18N10	66w43	4:26:52
Aguada 1	18N23	67w11	4:28:44
Aguadilla 1	18N26	67w09	4:28:36
Aguas Buenas 4	18N15	66w06	4:24:24
Aibonito 7	18N08	66w16	4:25:04
Anasco 6	18N17	67w08	4:28:32
Arecibo 2	18N28	66w43	4:26:52
Arenal 4	17N59	66w19	4:25:16
Arroyo 4	17N58	66w04	4:24:16
Asomante 2	18N23	66w36	4:26:24
Bahomamey 1	18N20	66w59	4:27:56
Barceloneta 2	18N27	66w32	4:26:08
Barinas 6	18N01	66w51	4:27:24
Barranquitas 4	18N11	66w18	4:25:12
Bayamon 3	18N24	66w09	4:24:36
Boca Chica 7	17N59	66w32	4:26:08
Boqueroen 6	18N02	67w10	4:28:40
Botijas 7	18N15	66w22	4:25:28
Cabo Rojo 6	18N05	67w09	4:28:36
Caguas 4	18N14	66w02	4:24:08
Camuy 1	18N29	66w51	4:27:24
Canovanas 3	18N23	65w54	4:23:36
Carolina 3	18N23	65w57	4:23:48
Catano 8	18N27	66w07	4:24:28
Cayey 4	18N07	66w10	4:24:40
Ceiba 5	18N16	65w39	4:22:36
Central Aguirre 4	17N57	66w13	4:24:52
Centro Puntas 1	18N22	67w16	4:29:04
Charco Hondo 2	18N25	66w43	4:26:52
Ciales 2	18N20	66w28	4:25:52
Cidra 4	18N11	66w10	4:24:40
Coamo 7	18N05	66w22	4:25:28
Collores 7	18N12	66w37	4:26:28
Colonia Providencia 4	17N59	66w00	4:24:00
Comereo 4	18N13	66w14	4:24:56
Comerio 4	18N13	66w14	4:24:56
Coqui 4	17N59	66w14	4:24:56
Corcega 1	18N19	67w15	4:29:00
Corozal 3	18N21	66w17	4:25:08
Coto Laurel 7	18N03	66w33	4:26:12
Culebra 5	18N18	65w18	4:21:12
Daguao 5	18N14	65w41	4:22:44
Dewey 5	18N18	65w18	4:21:12
Domingo Ruiz 2	18N27	66w41	4:26:44
Dorado 2	18N28	66w16	4:25:04
Dos Bocas 2	18N20	66w40	4:26:40
El Campamento 2	18N22	66w28	4:25:52
El Coto 2	18N28	66w44	4:26:56
El Faro 6	18N00	66w47	4:27:08
El Minao 3	18N22	66w05	4:24:20
El Polvorin 2	18N26	66w17	4:25:08
Ensenada 6	17N58	66w56	4:27:44
Esperanza	18N06	65w28	4:21:52
Fajardo 5	18N20	65w39	4:22:36
Feliciano 1	18N28	67w08	4:28:32
Florida 2	18N22	66w34	4:26:16
Florida 5	18N14	65w47	4:23:08
Guaenica 6	17N59	66w55	4:27:40
Guanabana 6	18N01	67w07	4:28:28
Guanica 6	17N58	66w55	4:27:40
Guayama 4	17N59	66w07	4:24:28
Guayanilla 6	18N01	66w47	4:27:08
Guaynabo 3	18N22	66w07	4:24:28
Gurabo 5	18N16	65w58	4:23:52
Hatillo 1	18N29	66w49	4:27:16
Hato Rey 3	18N25	66w03	4:24:12
Hormigueros 6	18N09	67w08	4:28:32
Humacao 5	18N09	65w50	4:23:20
Indiera Alta 6	18N09	66w53	4:27:32
Isabel Segunda	18N09	65w27	4:21:48
Isabela 1	18N30	67w01	4:28:04
Jayuga 7	18N14	66w36	4:26:24
Jayuya 7	18N13	66w36	4:26:24
Jobos 4	17N58	66w10	4:24:40
Joyuda 6	18N07	67w11	4:28:44
Juana Diaz 7	18N03	66w31	4:26:04
Juncos 5	18N14	65w55	4:23:40
La Cuesta 2	18N25	66w49	4:27:16
La Esperanza 3	18N22	66w07	4:24:28
Lajas 6	18N03	67w04	4:28:16
Lares 6	18N18	66w53	4:27:32
Las Arenas 6	18N02	67w09	4:28:36
Las Flores 7	18N03	66w22	4:25:28
Las Mareas 4	17N56	66w09	4:24:36
Las Marias 6	18N15	67w00	4:28:00
Las Palmas 4	17N59	66w02	4:24:08
Las Piedras 5	18N11	65w52	4:23:28
Las Pinas 5	18N15	65w55	4:23:40
Las Vegas 6	18N11	67w02	4:28:08
Loiza Aldea	18N26	65w53	4:23:32
Los Llanos 7	18N03	66w24	4:25:36
Los Rabanos 6	18N11	66w50	4:27:20
Luquillo 5	18N22	65w43	4:22:52
Machuchal 6	18N03	66w56	4:27:44
Mamayes 5	18N22	65w46	4:23:04
Manati 2	18N26	66w29	4:25:56
Mani 6	18N15	67w10	4:28:40
Maricao 6	18N11	66w59	4:27:56
Maunabo 4	18N01	65w54	4:23:36
Mayaguez 6	18N12	67w09	4:28:36
Moca 1	18N24	67w07	4:28:28
Montebello 2	18N22	66w31	4:26:04
Mora 1	18N28	67w02	4:28:08
Morovis 2	18N20	66w24	4:25:36
Naguabo 5	18N13	65w44	4:22:56
Naranjito 3	18N18	66w15	4:25:00
Orocovis 7	18N14	66w23	4:25:32
Palmarejo 6	18N03	67w05	4:28:20
Palmer 5	18N22	65w46	4:23:04
Palo Blanco 2	18N26	66w39	4:26:36
Palo Seco 8	18N28	66w09	4:24:36
Parguera 6	17N59	67w03	4:28:12
Paso Seco 7	17N59	66w23	4:25:32
Pastillo 7	17N59	66w29	4:25:56
Patillas 4	18N00	66w01	4:24:04
Penuelas 6	18N03	66w43	4:26:52
Perchas 6	18N19	66w59	4:27:56
Playa de Fajardo 5	18N20	65w38	4:22:32
Playa de Guayanes 5	18N04	65w49	4:23:16
Playa de Guayanilla 6	18N01	66w46	4:27:04
Playa De Humacao 5	18N10	65w45	4:23:00
Playa de Naguabo 5	18N12	65w43	4:22:52
Playa de Ponce 7	17N59	66w37	4:26:28
Poblado Cerro Gordo 2	18N29	66w20	4:25:20
Poblado Jacuaguas 7	18N03	66w32	4:26:08
Poblado Mediania Alta	18N26	65w50	4:23:20
Poblados Abalos 6	18N11	67w09	4:28:36
Poblado Santana 2	18N27	66w40	4:26:40
Ponce 7	18N01	66w37	4:26:28
Pueblito de Ponce 1	18N26	66w58	4:27:52
Pueblo Nuevo 1	18N28	66w51	4:27:24
Puerto Real 6	18N05	67w11	4:28:44
Punta Santiago 5	18N10	65w45	4:23:00
Quebrada Seca 5	18N14	65w40	4:22:40
Quebradillas 1	18N29	66w56	4:27:44
Rincon 1	18N20	67w15	4:29:00
Rio Canias 7	18N03	66w26	4:25:44
Rio Grande	18N23	65w50	4:23:20
Rio Jueyes 7	18N01	66w20	4:25:20
Rio Piedras 3	18N24	66w03	4:24:12
Rosario 6	18N10	67w05	4:28:20
Sabana 5	18N20	65w44	4:22:56
Sabana Grande 6	18N05	66w58	4:27:52
Sabana Llana 6	18N02	66w15	4:25:00
Saint Just 3	18N23	66w00	4:24:00
Salinas 4	17N59	66w18	4:25:12
San Antonio 1	18N30	67w07	4:28:28
San Felipe 4	17N58	66w13	4:24:52
San German 6	18N05	67w03	4:28:12
San Juan 8	18N28	66w07	4:24:28
San Lorenzo 5	18N11	65w58	4:23:52
San Sebastian 1	18N20	66w59	4:27:56
Santa Isabel 7	17N58	66w24	4:25:36
Santa Maria	18N09	65w26	4:21:44
San Turce 8	18N27	66w05	4:24:20
Soroco 5	18N22	65w38	4:22:32
Tablones 5	18N15	65w45	4:23:00
Toa Alta 3	18N23	66w15	4:25:00
Toa Baja 3	18N27	66w15	4:25:00
Trujillo Alto 3	18N22	66w01	4:24:04
Utuado 2	18N16	66w42	4:26:48
Vega Alta 2	18N25	66w20	4:25:20
Vega Baja 2	18N27	66w23	4:25:32
Vertedero 6	18N05	66w15	4:25:00
Victoria 1	18N25	67w10	4:28:40
Vieques	18N09	65w27	4:21:48
Villalba 7	18N08	66w30	4:26:00
Villa Perez 6	18N12	66w47	4:27:08
Yabucoa 5	18N03	65w53	4:23:32
Yauco 6	18N02	66w51	4:27:24

RHODE ISLAND

TIME TABLES

RI # 1

Date	Time	Zone
Before 11/18/1883		LMT
11/18/1883	12:00	EST
3/31/1918	02:00	EWT
10/27/1918	02:00	EST
3/30/1919	02:00	EWT
10/26/1919	02:00	EST
4/29/1923	02:00	EDT
9/30/1923	02:00	EST
4/27/1924	02:00	EDT
9/28/1924	02:00	EST
4/26/1925	02:00	EDT
9/27/1925	02:00	EST
4/25/1926	02:00	EDT
9/26/1926	02:00	EST
4/24/1927	02:00	EDT
9/25/1927	02:00	EST
4/29/1928	02:00	EDT
9/30/1928	02:00	EST
4/28/1929	02:00	EDT
9/29/1929	02:00	EST
4/27/1930	02:00	EDT
9/28/1930	02:00	EST
4/26/1931	02:00	EDT
9/27/1931	02:00	EST
4/24/1932	02:00	EDT
9/25/1932	02:00	EST
4/30/1933	02:00	EDT
9/24/1933	02:00	EST
4/29/1934	02:00	EDT
9/30/1934	02:00	EST
4/28/1935	02:00	EDT
9/29/1935	02:00	EST
4/26/1936	02:00	EDT
9/27/1936	02:00	EST
4/25/1937	02:00	EDT
9/26/1937	02:00	EST
4/24/1938	02:00	EDT
10/01/1938	02:00	EST
4/30/1939	02:00	EDT
9/24/1939	02:00	EST
4/28/1940	02:00	EDT
9/29/1940	02:00	EST
4/27/1941	02:00	EDT
9/28/1941	02:00	EST
2/09/1942	02:00	US#2

RI # 2

Date	Time	Zone
Before 11/18/1883		LMT
11/18/1883	12:00	EST
3/31/1918	02:00	EWT
10/27/1918	02:00	EST
3/30/1919	02:00	EWT
10/26/1919	02:00	EST
4/27/1924	02:00	EDT
9/28/1924	02:00	EST
4/26/1925	02:00	EDT
9/27/1925	02:00	EST
4/25/1926	02:00	EDT
9/26/1926	02:00	EST
4/24/1927	02:00	EDT
9/25/1927	02:00	EST
4/29/1928	02:00	EDT
9/30/1928	02:00	EST
4/28/1929	02:00	EDT
9/29/1929	02:00	EST
4/27/1930	02:00	EDT
9/28/1930	02:00	EST
4/26/1931	02:00	EDT
9/27/1931	02:00	EST
4/24/1932	02:00	EDT
9/25/1932	02:00	EST
4/30/1933	02:00	EDT
9/24/1933	02:00	EST
4/29/1934	02:00	EDT
9/30/1934	02:00	EST
4/28/1935	02:00	EDT
9/29/1935	02:00	EST
4/26/1936	02:00	EDT
9/27/1936	02:00	EST
4/25/1937	02:00	EDT
9/26/1937	02:00	EST
4/24/1938	02:00	EDT
10/01/1938	02:00	EST
4/30/1939	02:00	EDT
9/24/1939	02:00	EST
4/28/1940	02:00	EDT
9/29/1940	02:00	EST
4/27/1941	02:00	EDT
9/28/1941	02:00	EST
2/09/1942	02:00	US#2

COUNTIES

1 Bristol
2 Kent
3 Newport
4 Providence
5 Washington

Place		Lat	Long	Time
Abbott Run Valley 4	1	41N55	71w24	4:45:36
Adamsville 3	1	41N33	71w08	4:44:32
Albion 4	1	41N57	71w27	4:45:48
Allendale 4	1	41N50	71w28	4:45:52
Allenton 5	1	41N38	71w27	4:45:48
Alton 5	1	41N26	71w42	4:46:48
Annawomscutt 1	1	41N44	71w19	4:45:16
Annex 4	1	41N49	71w25	4:45:40
Anthony 2	1	41N41	71w34	4:46:16
Apple Blossom 4	1	41N47	71w26	4:45:44
Arcadia 5	1	41N30	71w43	4:46:52
Arctic 2	1	41N42	71w30	4:46:00
Arkwright 2	1	41N41	71w34	4:46:16
Arlington 4	1	41N47	71w26	4:45:44
Armington Corner 4	1	41N49	71w22	4:45:28
Arnold Mills 4	1	41N55	71w24	4:45:36
Arnold's Neck 2	1	41N42	71w26	4:45:44
Ashaway 5	1	41N25	71w47	4:47:08
Ashton 4	1	41N56	71w26	4:45:44
Atlantic Beach 5	1	41N22	71w50	4:47:20
Attleboro	1	41N56	71w17	4:45:08
Auburn 4	1	41N47	71w26	4:45:44
Austin 5	1	41N35	71w32	4:46:08
Avondale 5	1	41N22	71w50	4:47:20
Barberville 5	1	41N30	71w43	4:46:52
Barrington 1	1	41N44	71w19	4:45:16
Bayridge 2	1	41N40	71w28	4:45:52
Bay Spring 1	1	41N44	71w19	4:45:16
Bay View 4	1	41N49	71w22	4:45:28
Beach Terrace 1	1	41N41	71w16	4:45:04
Bellefonte 4	1	41N47	71w26	4:45:44
Belleville 5	1	41N38	71w27	4:45:48
Berkeley 4	1	41N55	71w25	4:45:40
Beverage Hill 4	1	41N53	71w23	4:45:32
Black Plain 5	1	41N35	71w32	4:46:08
Block Island 5	1	41N10	71w34	4:46:16
Bonnet Shores 5	1	41N23	71w28	4:45:52
Boon Lake 5	1	41N35	71w32	4:46:08
Bowdish Lake 4	1	41N55	71w40	4:46:40
Boyden Heights 4	1	41N49	71w22	4:45:28
Bradford 5	1	41N23	71w45	4:47:00
Branch Village 4	1	42N00	71w30	4:46:00
Brenton Village 3	1	41N30	71w19	4:45:16
Bridgeport 3	1	41N38	71w12	4:44:48
Bridgeton 4	1	41N57	71w42	4:46:48
Bridgetown 5	1	41N30	71w25	4:45:40
Briggs Beach 3	1	41N30	71w10	4:44:40
Bristol 1	1	41N40	71w16	4:45:04
Bristol Colony 3	1	41N36	71w20	4:45:20
Bristol Ferry 3	1	41N38	71w15	4:45:00
Bristol Highlands 1	1	41N41	71w16	4:45:04
Bristol Narrows 1	1	41N41	71w16	4:45:04
Broadway 3	1	41N30	71w19	4:45:16
Brookfield 4	1	41N47	71w26	4:45:44
Brown 4	1	41N49	71w26	4:45:44
Brush Neck Cove 2	1	41N42	71w26	4:45:44
Bullocks Point 4	1	41N49	71w22	4:45:28
Burdickville 5	1	41N24	71w45	4:47:00
Burrillville 4	1	41N57	71w40	4:46:40
Canonchet 5	1	41N30	71w43	4:46:52
Carolina 5	1	41N28	71w40	4:46:40
Carpenters Beach 5	1	41N26	71w30	4:46:00
Carpenters Corner 4	1	41N49	71w22	4:45:28
Cedar Grove 5	1	41N35	71w32	4:46:08
Cedar Point 3	1	41N29	71w22	4:45:28
Cedar Tree Point 2	1	41N42	71w26	4:45:44
Centerdale 4	1	41N50	71w28	4:45:52
Centerville 2	1	41N42	71w30	4:46:00
Centerville 5	1	41N30	71w43	4:46:52
Central Falls 4	1	41N53	71w24	4:45:36
Charlestown 5	1	41N23	71w39	4:46:36
Charlestown Beach 5	1	41N23	71w45	4:47:00
Chepachet 4	1	41N55	71w40	4:46:40
Cherry Valley 4	1	41N55	71w40	4:46:40
Cherry Valley Beach 4	1	41N55	71w40	4:46:40
Chopmist 4	1	41N50	71w35	4:46:20
Clarke's Village 3	1	41N29	71w22	4:45:28
Clayville 4	1	41N47	71w41	4:46:44
Clyde 2	1	41N42	71w30	4:46:00
Coasters Harbor 3	1	41N30	71w19	4:45:16
Coddington Point 3	1	41N30	71w19	4:45:16
Coggeshall 1	1	41N44	71w16	4:45:04
Cold Springs Beach 5	1	41N38	71w27	4:45:48
Columbia Heights 5	1	41N27	71w38	4:46:32
Common Fence Point 3	1	41N36	71w15	4:45:00
Commons 3	1	41N30	71w10	4:44:40
Comstock Gardens 4	1	41N47	71w26	4:45:44
Conanicut Park 3	1	41N29	71w22	4:45:28
Conimicut 2	1	41N43	71w23	4:45:32
Corey's Lane 3	1	41N36	71w15	4:45:00
Coventry 2	1	41N42	71w34	4:46:16
Cranston 4	1	41N47	71w26	4:45:44
Crescent Park 4	1	41N49	71w22	4:45:28
Crompton 2	1	41N42	71w30	4:46:00
Cross Mills 5	1	41N23	71w45	4:47:00
Cumberland 4	1	41N57	71w25	4:45:40
Cumberland Hill 4	1	41N55	71w24	4:45:36
Curtis Corners 5	1	41N27	71w30	4:46:00
Darlington 4	1	41N53	71w23	4:45:32
Davisville 5	1	41N38	73w12	4:52:48
Diamond Hill 4	1	41N55	71w24	4:45:36
Dryden Heights 2	1	41N44	71w24	4:45:36
Dunns Corners 5	1	41N22	71w50	4:47:20
Durfee Hill 4	1	41N55	71w40	4:46:40
Eagleville 3	1	41N38	71w12	4:44:48
East Greenwich 2	1	41N40	71w27	4:45:48
East Matunuck 5	1	41N26	71w30	4:46:00
East Providence 4	1	41N48	71w22	4:45:28
East Providence Wharf 4	1	41N49	71w22	4:45:28
East Side 4	1	41N50	71w24	4:45:36
East Warren 1	1	41N44	71w16	4:45:04
Echo Lake 4	1	41N55	71w40	4:46:40
Eden Park 4	1	41N47	71w26	4:45:44
Edgewood 4	1	41N48	71w25	4:45:40
Elmwood 4	1	41N48	71w26	4:45:44
Enos 4	1	41N47	71w26	4:45:44
Escoheag 5	1	41N35	71w32	4:46:08
Esmond 4	1	41N53	71w30	4:46:00
Exeter 5	1	41N34	71w36	4:46:24
Fairbanks Corner 2	1	41N41	71w44	4:46:56
Fairmount 4	1	42N00	71w30	4:46:00
Finast 4	1	41N49	71w22	4:45:28
Fisherville 5	1	41N35	71w32	4:46:08
Fiskeville 4	1	41N46	71w27	4:45:48
Fogland Point 3	1	41N38	71w12	4:44:48
Forestdale 4	1	42N01	71w34	4:46:16
Fort Adams 3	1	41N30	71w19	4:45:16
Foster 4	2	41N47	71w44	4:46:56
Frenchtown 2	1	41N40	71w28	4:45:52
Friar 4	1	41N49	71w26	4:45:44
Fruit Hill 4	1	41N50	71w28	4:45:52
Galilee 5	1	41N23	71w28	4:45:52
Garden City 4	1	41N47	71w28	4:45:52
Gaspee Point 2	1	41N44	71w24	4:45:36
Gazzaville 4	1	41N57	71w39	4:46:36
Geneva 4	1	41N50	71w28	4:45:52
Georgiaville 4	1	41N53	71w30	4:46:00
Glendale 4	1	41N58	71w38	4:46:32
Globe 4	1	42N00	71w30	4:46:00
Glocester 4	1	41N53	71w40	4:46:40
Goat Island 3	1	41N30	71w19	4:45:16
Goulds 5	1	41N27	71w30	4:46:00
Graniteville 4	1	41N49	71w30	4:46:00
Grants Mills 4	1	41N58	71w28	4:45:52
Greene 2	1	41N41	71w44	4:46:56
Green Hill 5	1	41N26	71w30	4:46:00
Greenville 4	1	41N52	71w33	4:46:12
Greystone 4	1	41N50	71w28	4:45:52
Hamilton 5	1	41N38	71w27	4:45:48
Hamlet 4	1	42N00	71w30	4:46:00
Hampden Meadows 1	1	41N44	71w19	4:45:16
Harmony 4	1	41N53	71w36	4:46:24
Harris 2	1	41N41	71w34	4:46:16
Harrisville 4	1	41N58	71w41	4:46:44
Haversham 5	1	41N22	71w50	4:47:20
Hog Island 3	1	41N41	71w16	4:45:04
Homestead 3	1	41N36	71w20	4:45:20
Hope 4	1	41N44	71w34	4:46:16
Hope Valley 5	1	41N30	71w43	4:46:52
Hopkins Hollow 2	1	41N41	71w44	4:46:56
Hopkinton 5	1	41N27	71w45	4:47:00
Howard 4	1	41N47	71w28	4:45:52
Hoxsie 2	1	41N43	71w23	4:45:32
Hughesdale 4	1	41N49	71w30	4:46:00
Indian Lake Shores 5	1	41N26	71w30	4:46:00
Island Park 3	1	41N36	71w15	4:45:00
Jackson 4	1	41N46	71w27	4:45:48
Jamestown 3	1	41N31	71w22	4:45:28
Jamestown Center 3	1	41N29	71w22	4:45:28
Jamestown Shores 3	1	41N29	71w22	4:45:28
Jerusalem 5	1	41N26	71w30	4:46:00
Johnston 4	1	41N50	71w30	4:46:00
Kent Corner 4	1	41N49	71w22	4:45:28
Kent Heights 4	1	41N49	71w22	4:45:28
Kenyon 5	1	41N27	71w38	4:46:32
Kingston 5	1	41N29	71w32	4:46:08
Knightsville 4	1	41N47	71w26	4:45:44
La Fayette 5	1	41N38	71w27	4:45:48
Lake Bel Air 4	1	42N00	71w30	4:46:00
Lake Mishnock 2	1	41N41	71w34	4:46:16
Langworthy Corner 5	1	41N22	71w50	4:47:20
Laurel Hill 4	1	41N57	71w42	4:46:48
Laurel Park 1	1	41N44	71w16	4:45:04
Leonard Corner 4	1	41N49	71w22	4:45:28
Liberty 5	1	41N32	71w31	4:46:04
Limerock 4	1	41N54	71w25	4:45:40
Lincoln 4	1	41N55	71w26	4:45:44
Lippit 2	1	41N42	71w30	4:46:00
Lippitt Estate 4	1	41N55	71w24	4:45:36
Little Compton 3	1	41N32	71w10	4:44:40
Lonsdale 4	1	41N54	71w25	4:45:40
Lymansville 4	1	41N50	71w28	4:45:52
Manton 4	1	41N49	71w30	4:46:00
Manville 4	1	41N58	71w28	4:45:52
Maple Root Village 2	1	41N41	71w34	4:46:16
Mapleville 4	1	41N57	71w39	4:46:36
Marieville 4	1	41N51	71w26	4:45:44
Matunuck 5	1	41N26	71w30	4:46:00
Meshanticut 4	1	41N47	71w26	4:45:44
Middletown 3	1	41N32	71w18	4:45:12
Misquamicut 5	1	41N22	71w50	4:47:20
Mohegan 4	1	42N00	71w30	4:46:00
Mohegan Bluffs 5	1	41N10	71w34	4:46:16
Mooresfield 5	1	41N30	71w25	4:45:40
Moosup Valley 4	1	41N41	71w44	4:46:56
Moscow 5	1	41N30	71w43	4:46:52
Mount Saint Joseph College 5	1	41N26	71w30	4:46:00
Mount Vernon 4	1	41N51	71w46	4:47:04
Mount View 5	1	41N38	71w27	4:45:48
Nannaquaket 3	1	41N38	71w12	4:44:48
Narragansett 5	1	41N26	71w27	4:45:48
Narragansett Heights 3	1	41N38	71w12	4:44:48
Narragansett Pier 5	1	41N25	71w28	4:45:52
Nasonville 4	1	42N00	71w30	4:46:00
Natick 2	1	41N42	71w26	4:45:44
Naval Training Station 3	1	41N30	71w19	4:45:16
Nayatt 1	1	41N44	71w19	4:45:16
New Harbor 5	1	41N10	71w34	4:46:16
Newport 3	1	41N29	71w19	4:45:16
New Shoreham 5	1	41N10	71w35	4:46:20
Nichols Corner 2	1	41N40	71w28	4:45:52
Nooseneck 2	1	41N41	71w34	4:46:16
North 4	1	41N50	71w26	4:45:44
North Foster 4	1	41N51	71w46	4:47:04
North Kingstown 5	1	41N36	71w27	4:45:48
North Providence 4	1	41N51	71w28	4:45:52
North Quidnessett 5	1	41N38	71w27	4:45:48

North Scituate 4 1 41N50 71w35 4:46:20
North Smithfield 4 1 41N59 71w33 4:46:12
Oakland 4 1 41N58 71w39 4:46:36
Oak Lawn 4 1 41N47 71w26 4:45:44
Old Harbor 5 1 41N10 71w34 4:46:16
Olney Arnold Estates 4 1 41N47 71w26 4:45:44
Olneyville 4 1 41N49 71w27 4:45:48
Pascoag 4 1 41N57 71w42 4:46:48
Pawtucket 4 1 41N53 71w23 4:45:32
Peace Dale 5 1 41N27 71w30 4:46:00
Perryville 5 1 41N26 71w30 4:46:00
Pettaquamscutt Lake Shores 5 1 41N30 71w25 4:45:40
Phenix 2 1 41N42 71w30 4:46:00
Phillipsdale 4 1 41N49 71w22 4:45:28
Pleasant View 4 1 41N53 71w23 4:45:32
Plum Beach 5 1 41N30 71w25 4:45:40
Plum Point 5 1 41N30 71w25 4:45:40
Poccasett Heights 3 1 41N38 71w15 4:45:00
Point Judith 5 1 41N23 71w28 4:45:52
Popasquash Point 1 1 41N41 71w16 4:45:04
Poplar Point 5 1 41N38 71w27 4:45:48
Portsmouth 3 1 41N36 71w15 4:45:00
Potowomut 2 1 41N49 71w30 4:46:00
Potter Hill 5 1 41N22 71w50 4:47:20
Primrose 4 1 42N00 71w30 4:46:00
Print Works 4 1 41N47 71w26 4:45:44
Providence 4 1 41N49 71w24 4:45:36
Prudence Island 3 1 41N36 71w20 4:45:20
Prudence Park 3 1 41N36 71w20 4:45:20
Quaker Hill 3 1 41N36 71w15 4:45:00
Quidnessett 5 1 41N38 71w27 4:45:48
Quidnick 2 1 41N41 71w34 4:46:16
Quinnville 4 1 41N54 71w25 4:45:40
Quonochontaug 5 1 41N24 71w45 4:47:00
Rice City 2 1 41N41 71w44 4:46:56
Rice Plat 4 1 41N50 71w35 4:46:20
Richmond 5 1 41N29 71w39 4:46:36
River Point 2 1 41N42 71w30 4:46:00
Riverside 4 1 41N47 71w22 4:45:28
Rockville 5 1 41N31 71w46 4:47:04

Rocky Brook 5 1 41N27 71w30 4:46:00
Rumford 4 1 41N50 71w22 4:45:28
Rumstick Point 1 1 41N44 71w19 4:45:16
Sakonnet 3 1 41N30 71w10 4:44:40
Sandy Point 2 1 41N40 71w28 4:45:52
Sandy Point 5 1 41N10 71w34 4:46:16
Saunderstown 5 1 41N30 71w25 4:45:40
Saundersville 4 1 41N50 71w35 4:46:20
Saylesville 4 1 41N54 71w25 4:45:40
Saylesville Highlands 4 1 41N54 71w25 4:45:40
Scituate 4 2 41N49 71w37 4:46:28
Shady Harbor 5 1 41N22 71w50 4:47:20
Shannock 5 1 41N27 71w38 4:46:32
Shelter Harbor 5 1 41N22 71w50 4:47:20
Shores Acres 5 1 41N38 71w27 4:45:48
Simmonsville 4 1 41N49 71w30 4:46:00
Slatersville 4 1 42N00 71w35 4:46:20
Slocum 5 1 41N32 71w31 4:46:04
Smithfield 4 1 41N53 71w32 4:46:08
Social 4 1 42N00 71w30 4:46:00
Sockanosset 4 1 41N47 71w26 4:45:44
South Foster 4 1 41N51 71w46 4:47:04
South Hopkinton 5 1 41N24 71w45 4:47:00
South Kingstown 5 1 41N27 71w32 4:46:08
South Warren 1 1 41N44 71w16 4:45:04
Sprague Park 5 1 41N23 71w28 4:45:52
Spragueville 4 1 41N53 71w30 4:46:00
Spring Grove 4 1 41N55 71w40 4:46:40
Spring Lake Beach 4 1 41N58 71w38 4:46:32
Squantum 4 1 41N49 71w22 4:45:28
Stillwater 4 1 41N53 71w30 4:46:00
Summit 2 1 41N41 71w44 4:46:56
Tarkiln 4 1 42N00 71w30 4:46:00
The Anchorage 3 1 41N31 71w18 4:45:12
The Hummocks 3 1 41N36 71w15 4:45:00
Thornton 4 1 41N49 71w30 4:46:00
Tiverton 3 1 41N38 71w12 4:44:48
Tiverton Four Corners 3 1 41N38 71w12 4:44:48
Tonomy Hill 3 1 41N30 71w19 4:45:16
Touisset Highlands 1 1 41N44 71w16 4:45:04
Tuckertown 5 1 41N26 71w30 4:46:00

RHODE ISLAND

Tunipus 3 1 41N30 71w10 4:44:40
Union Village 4 1 42N00 71w30 4:46:00
Usquepaug 5 1 41N29 71w34 4:46:16
Valley Falls 4 1 41N55 71w24 4:45:36
Vaughn Hollow 2 1 41N41 71w44 4:46:56
Wakefield 5 1 41N26 71w30 4:46:00
Walnut Hill 4 1 42N00 71w30 4:46:00
Warren 1 1 41N43 71w16 4:45:04
Warren Point 3 1 41N30 71w10 4:44:40
Warwick 2 1 41N42 71w28 4:45:52
Warwick Neck 2 1 41N43 71w23 4:45:32
Washington Park 4 1 41N47 71w26 4:45:44
Watch Hill 5 1 41N22 71w50 4:47:20
Watchmocket Square 4 1 41N49 71w22 4:45:28
Waterford 4 1 42N01 71w30 4:46:00
Waterman Four Corners 4 1 41N50 71w35 4:46:20
Weekapaug 5 1 41N22 71w50 4:47:20
West Barrington 1 1 41N44 71w19 4:45:16
Westcott 2 1 41N42 71w30 4:46:00
Westcott Beach 4 1 41N55 71w40 4:46:40
Westerly 5 1 41N22 71w50 4:47:20
West Greenville 4 1 41N52 71w33 4:46:12
West Greenwich 2 1 41N37 71w37 4:46:28
West Greenwich Center 2 1 41N41 71w44 4:46:56
West Kingston 5 1 41N29 71w34 4:46:16
West Warwick 2 1 41N43 71w32 4:46:08
Weybosset Hill 4 1 41N49 71w25 4:45:40
Whipple 4 1 41N58 71w39 4:46:36
White Rock 5 1 41N22 71w50 4:47:20
Wilde's Corner 2 1 41N42 71w26 4:45:44
Wild Goose Point 5 1 41N38 71w27 4:45:48
Wood Estates 2 1 41N41 71w34 4:46:16
Wood River Junction 5 1 41N26 71w42 4:46:48
Woodville 4 1 41N50 71w28 4:45:52
Woodville 5 1 41N30 71w43 4:46:52
Woonsocket 4 1 42N00 71w31 4:46:04
Wyoming 5 1 41N31 71w42 4:46:48
Yorktown Manor 5 1 41N38 71w27 4:45:48

SOUTH CAROLINA

TIME TABLES

Date	Time	Zone
Before 11/18/1883		LMT
11/18/1883	12:00	EST
3/31/1918	02:00	EWT
10/27/1918	02:00	EST
3/30/1919	02:00	EWT
10/26/1919	02:00	EST
2/09/1942	02:00	EWT
9/30/1945	02:00	EST
4/30/1967	02:00	US#1

COUNTIES

1 Abbeville
2 Aiken
3 Allendale
4 Anderson
5 Bamberg
6 Barnwell
7 Beaufort
8 Berkeley
9 Calhoun
10 Charleston
11 Cherokee
12 Chester
13 Chesterfield
14 Clarendon
15 Colleton
16 Darlington
17 Dillon
18 Dorchester
19 Edgefield
20 Fairfield
21 Florence
22 Georgetown
23 Greenville
24 Greenwood
25 Hampton
26 Horry
27 Jasper
28 Kershaw
29 Lancaster
30 Laurens
31 Lee
32 Lexington
33 McCormick
34 Marion
35 Marlboro
36 Newberry
37 Oconee
38 Orangeburg
39 Pickens
40 Richland
41 Saluda
42 Spartanburg
43 Sumter
44 Union
45 Williamsburg
46 York

Place	Lat.	Long.	Offset
Abbeville 1	34N11	82w23	5:29:32
Abney 28	34N33	80w35	5:22:20
Adamsburg 44	34N43	81w37	5:26:28
Adams Run 10	32N44	80w21	5:21:24
Adamsville 35	34N40	79w33	5:18:12
Adger 20	34N22	81w05	5:24:20
Adrian 26	33N51	79w03	5:16:12
Aiken 2	33N34	81w43	5:26:52
Airport 42	34N54	81w56	5:27:44
Albemarle 10	32N48	80w00	5:20:00
Alcolu 14	33N45	80w13	5:20:52
Alcot 31	34N13	80w15	5:21:00
Algary 24	34N23	82w21	5:29:24
Alice Mill 39	34N50	82w37	5:30:28
Allendale 3	33N01	81w18	5:25:12
Alliance 20	34N21	81w08	5:24:32
Allsbrook 26	34N03	78w53	5:15:32
Alta Vista 40	34N02	80w59	5:23:56
Alvin 8	33N22	79w48	5:19:12
American Spinning 23	34N52	82w23	5:29:32
Ampere 24	34N12	82w09	5:28:36
Anderson 4	34N31	82w39	5:30:36
Andrews 22	33N27	79w34	5:18:16
Angelus 13	34N39	80w23	5:21:32
Angle Siding 7	32N27	80w44	5:22:56
Ansel 23	34N56	82w13	5:28:52
Antioch 28	34N15	80w36	5:22:24
Antioch 29	34N42	80w47	5:23:08
Antreville 1	34N18	82w40	5:30:40
Appleton 3	33N04	81w29	5:25:56
Appleton Mills 4	34N31	82w39	5:30:36
Aragon Mills 12	34N43	81w13	5:24:52
Arcadia 42	34N58	81w59	5:27:56
Arcadia Lakes 40	34N03	80w58	5:23:52
Ardincaple 40	34N02	81w04	5:24:16
Ariail 39	34N51	82w38	5:30:32
Arial 39	34N50	82w37	5:30:28
Ariel Cross Roads 34	34N12	79w15	5:17:00
Arkwright 42	34N55	81w56	5:27:44
Arlington 42	34N56	82w13	5:28:52
Armenia 12	34N43	81w13	5:24:52
Arthurtown 40	34N00	81w03	5:24:12
Asbury 11	35N04	81w38	5:26:32
Ashepoo 15	32N44	80w37	5:22:28
Ashland 31	34N13	80w15	5:21:00
Ashley Heights 10	32N52	79w59	5:19:56
Ashley Junction 10	32N54	80w00	5:20:00
Ashton 15	33N01	80w58	5:23:52
Ashwood 31	34N01	80w17	5:21:08
Atkins 31	34N04	80w05	5:20:20
Atlantic Beach 26	33N48	78w43	5:14:52
Attaway 41	34N00	81w46	5:27:04
Auburn 16	34N23	80w05	5:20:20
Avondale 10	32N48	80w00	5:20:00
Awendaw 10	33N03	79w37	5:18:28
Aynor 26	34N00	79w12	5:16:48
Babbtown 23	34N41	82w11	5:28:44
Badham 18	33N12	80w39	5:22:36
Baileys Landing 7	32N29	80w59	5:23:56
Bald Rock 44	34N43	81w37	5:26:28
Baldwin Mills 12	34N43	81w13	5:24:52
Ballentine 40	34N08	81w14	5:24:56
Bamberg 5	33N16	81w05	5:24:20
Barkersville 25	32N45	80w56	5:23:44
Barksdale 30	34N37	82w07	5:28:28
Barnes 4	34N18	82w40	5:30:40
Barnwell 6	33N15	81w23	5:25:32
Barr 32	33N59	81w14	5:24:56
Barrineau 14	33N52	79w45	5:19:00
Barton 3	32N57	81w14	5:24:56
Bascomville 12	34N43	81w01	5:24:04
Batesburg 32	33N54	81w33	5:26:12
Batesville 23	34N51	82w21	5:29:24
Bath 2	33N31	81w51	5:27:24
Baton Rouge 12	34N43	81w13	5:24:52
Battlecreek 37	34N47	83w16	5:33:04
Bayboro 26	34N03	78w53	5:15:32
Bay View 40	34N02	80w59	5:23:56
Bear Swamp 10	32N50	80w05	5:20:20
Beaufort 7	32N26	80w40	5:22:40
Beaufort 29	34N42	80w47	5:23:08
Beaufort Station 7	32N28	80w42	5:22:48
Beckhamville 12	34N34	80w54	5:23:36
Beech Island 2	33N26	81w52	5:27:28
Bel-Clear Heights 2	33N31	81w56	5:27:44
Beldoc 3	33N04	81w29	5:25:56
Belle Isle Gardens 22	32N32	80w46	5:23:04
Belle Mead 23	34N51	82w23	5:29:32
Bellinger 27	32N17	81w04	5:24:16
Bells 15	33N00	80w49	5:23:16
Belmont 23	34N51	82w24	5:29:36
Belmont 40	34N03	81w02	5:24:08
Belton 4	34N31	82w30	5:30:00
Belvedere 2	33N32	81w57	5:27:48
Belvedere 40	34N02	80w59	5:23:56
Belvedere Estates 8	32N55	80w00	5:20:00
Ben Avon 42	34N56	81w56	5:27:44
Bendale 40	34N03	81w02	5:24:08
Bennett 10	32N52	79w59	5:19:56
Bennettsville 35	34N37	79w41	5:18:44
Berea 23	34N54	82w27	5:29:48
Berkeley Hills 8	32N55	80w00	5:20:00
Berlin 2	33N34	81w18	5:25:12
Bethany 46	35N07	81w14	5:24:56
Bethear 2	33N39	81w22	5:25:28
Bethera 8	33N12	79w47	5:19:08
Bethune 28	34N25	80w21	5:21:24
Biddle 20	34N22	81w05	5:24:20
Bigcreek 41	34N11	81w52	5:27:28
Bingham 17	34N20	79w26	5:17:44
Bird Town 16	34N23	80w05	5:20:20
Bishopville 31	34N13	80w15	5:21:00
Blacks 41	33N52	81w44	5:26:56
Blacksburg 11	35N07	81w31	5:26:04
Blackstock 12	34N34	81w08	5:24:32
Blackville 6	33N22	81w16	5:25:04
Blair 20	34N25	81w23	5:25:32
Blair Mills 4	34N31	82w30	5:30:00
Blairville 46	34N57	81w20	5:25:20
Blake 15	32N41	80w51	5:23:24
Blakedale 24	34N12	82w09	5:28:36
Blakely 45	33N36	79w51	5:19:24
Blenheim 35	34N31	79w39	5:18:36
Bloomingvale 45	33N27	79w35	5:18:20
Bloomville 14	33N43	80w17	5:21:08
Blossom 21	34N00	79w34	5:18:16
Blue Brick 34	34N12	79w32	5:18:08
Blue Town 35	34N37	79w41	5:18:44
Bluff Estates 40	33N59	80w57	5:23:48
Bluffton 7	32N14	80w52	5:23:28
Blythewood 40	34N13	80w58	5:23:52
Boiling Springs 42	35N03	81w57	5:27:48
Bolen 38	33N30	80w52	5:23:28
Bon Air Terrace 43	33N55	80w21	5:21:24
Bonham 44	34N43	81w37	5:26:28
Bonneau 8	33N16	79w58	5:19:52
Bookgreen 22	33N33	79w02	5:16:08
Bordeaux 33	33N55	82w18	5:29:12
Borden 43	34N04	80w29	5:21:56
Bowling Green 46	35N09	81w12	5:24:48
Bowman 38	33N21	80w41	5:22:44
Bowyer 38	33N20	80w25	5:21:40
Boyden Arbor 40	34N02	80w57	5:23:48
Boykin 28	34N12	80w31	5:22:04
Bradley 24	34N03	82w15	5:29:00
Bradleyville 2	33N31	81w56	5:27:44
Branchville 38	33N15	80w49	5:23:16
Brand 30	34N31	82w00	5:28:00
Brandon 23	34N51	82w26	5:29:44
Brannon 42	35N03	82w05	5:28:20
Branwood 23	34N52	82w25	5:29:40
Brazen Crossroads 21	34N00	79w34	5:18:16
Breeze Hill 2	33N31	81w51	5:27:24
Brentwood 10	32N52	79w59	5:19:56
Brewerton 30	34N24	82w15	5:29:00
Briarcliffe Acres 26	33N39	78w56	5:15:44
Brighton 25	32N36	81w15	5:25:00
Brighton Beach 7	32N14	80w52	5:23:28
Brightsville 35	34N46	79w36	5:18:24
Bristow 35	34N31	79w39	5:18:36
Britton 43	33N55	80w21	5:21:24
Britton Neck 34	33N56	79w25	5:17:40
Brittons Neck 34	33N53	79w19	5:17:16
Britts 33	33N55	82w18	5:29:12
Broadway 14	33N44	80w28	5:21:52
Broadway Lake 4	34N31	82w39	5:30:36
Brockington 45	33N40	79w50	5:19:20
Brogdon 43	33N55	80w21	5:21:24
Brook Forest 23	34N49	82w24	5:29:36
Brook Green Park 21	34N12	79w45	5:19:00
Brooklyn 29	34N42	80w47	5:23:08
Brooksville 26	33N49	78w40	5:14:40
Brownsville 18	33N01	80w11	5:20:44
Brownsville 35	34N31	79w39	5:18:36
Broxton 15	33N01	80w57	5:23:48
Bruner 40	33N54	80w53	5:23:32
Brunson 25	32N56	81w11	5:24:44
Brunsons Crossroads 45	33N44	79w29	5:17:56
Brushy Creek 4	34N45	82w31	5:30:04
Buckingham Landing 7	32N13	80w45	5:23:00
Bucksport 26	33N40	79w06	5:16:24
Bucksville 26	33N51	79w03	5:16:12
Buffalo 44	34N44	81w41	5:26:44
Bullock Creek 46	34N57	81w20	5:25:20
Burgess 26	33N33	79w02	5:16:08
Burnettown 2	33N31	81w51	5:27:24
Burton 7	32N27	80w44	5:22:56
Bynum 45	33N40	79w50	5:19:20
Byrd 18	33N11	80w35	5:22:20
Cades 45	33N47	79w47	5:19:08
Caesars Head 23	35N03	82w45	5:31:00
Calhoun 39	34N41	82w48	5:31:12
Calhoun Falls 1	34N06	82w36	5:30:24
Callison 24	34N03	82w15	5:29:00
Camden 28	34N16	80w36	5:22:24
Cameron 9	33N34	80w43	5:22:52
Camp Creek 29	34N42	80w47	5:23:08
Camp Croft 42	34N56	81w56	5:27:44
Campfield 22	33N22	79w17	5:17:08
Camp Ground 40	34N11	81w04	5:24:16
Campobello 42	35N07	82w09	5:28:36
Campton 42	35N03	82w05	5:28:20
Canaan 42	34N56	81w56	5:27:44
Canadys 15	33N03	80w37	5:22:28
Cane Savannah 43	33N55	80w21	5:21:24
Cannadys	33N03	80w37	5:22:28
Capehart 7	32N28	80w48	5:23:12
Capitol 40	34N01	81w00	5:24:00
Capitol View 40	33N59	80w57	5:23:48
Carlisle 44	34N36	81w28	5:25:52
Carmel 29	34N36	80w40	5:22:40
Carolina Mills 17	34N25	79w22	5:17:28
Caromi Village 8	33N00	80w06	5:20:24
Cartersville 21	34N08	79w57	5:19:48
Carver Heights 40	34N02	80w59	5:23:56
Carvers Bay 22	33N44	79w29	5:17:56
Cash 13	34N42	79w53	5:19:32
Cashville 42	34N44	82w02	5:28:08
Caskey 29	34N42	80w47	5:23:08
Cassatt 28	34N22	80w26	5:21:44
Catarrh 13	34N39	80w23	5:21:32
Catawba 46	34N51	80w55	5:23:40
Cateechee 39	34N46	82w46	5:31:04
Cauthens Crossroads 29	34N42	80w47	5:23:08
Cayce 32	33N58	81w04	5:24:16
Cedar Springs 10	32N39	80w08	5:20:32
Cedar Terrace 40	33N59	80w57	5:23:48
Celriver 46	34N56	81w01	5:24:04
Cementon 38	33N20	80w25	5:21:40
Centenary 34	34N02	79w21	5:17:24
Central 39	34N44	82w47	5:31:08
Central Pacolet 42	34N55	81w45	5:27:00
Chapin 32	34N11	81w21	5:25:24
Chappell	34N11	81w52	5:27:28
Chappells 36	34N11	81w52	5:27:28
Charleston 10	32N46	79w56	5:19:44
Charleston Base 10	32N54	80w04	5:20:16
Charleston Heights 10	32N51	80w00	5:20:00
Charleston Yard 10	32N51	79w55	5:19:40
Cheddar 4	34N31	82w30	5:30:00
Cheraw 13	34N42	79w53	5:19:32
Cherokee 42	34N56	81w56	5:27:44
Cherokee Falls 11	35N04	81w32	5:26:08

Cherokee Forest 23	34N53	82w21	5:29:24
Cherry Grove Beach 26	33N50	78w39	5:14:36
Cherry Hill 8	33N12	80w01	5:20:04
Cherry Road 46	34N56	81w01	5:24:04
Chesnee 42	35N09	81w52	5:27:28
Chester 12	34N43	81w12	5:24:48
Chesterfield 13	34N44	80w05	5:20:20
Chestnut Hills 23	34N49	82w24	5:29:36
Chickasaw Point 37	34N31	82w59	5:31:56
Chick Springs 23	34N53	82w21	5:29:24
Chicora 10	32N51	79w57	5:19:48
Chicora Place 10	32N52	79w59	5:19:56
Choppee 22	33N22	79w17	5:17:08
Citadel 10	32N48	79w57	5:19:48
City View 23	34N52	82w25	5:29:40
Claremont 43	33N55	80w21	5:21:24
Clarks Hill 33	33N40	82w11	5:28:44
Claussen 21	34N12	79w45	5:19:00
Clayton 20	34N30	81w25	5:25:40
Clearmont 37	34N40	83w06	5:32:24
Clearspring 23	34N43	82w18	5:29:12
Clearwater 2	33N30	81w54	5:27:36
Clemson 39	34N41	82w50	5:31:20
Clemson University 39	34N41	82w48	5:31:12
Cleora 19	33N47	81w56	5:27:44
Cleveland 23	35N04	82w31	5:30:04
Clifton 42	34N59	81w49	5:27:16
Clinton 30	34N29	81w53	5:27:32
Clio 35	34N35	79w33	5:18:12
Clover 46	35N07	81w14	5:24:56
Clubhouse Crossroads 18	33N06	80w19	5:21:16
Club House Crossroads 32	33N55	81w23	5:25:32
Clyde 16	34N28	80w15	5:21:00
Cochrantown 26	33N51	79w03	5:16:12
Cokesbury 24	34N17	82w15	5:29:00
Cold Point 30	34N31	82w00	5:28:00
Colliers 19	33N44	82w12	5:28:48
Collins 12	34N48	81w01	5:24:04
Columbia 40	34N00	81w03	5:24:12
Coneross 37	34N40	83w06	5:32:24
Conestee 23	34N47	82w20	5:29:20
Congaree 40	33N53	80w41	5:22:44
Converse 42	34N59	81w50	5:27:20
Conway 26	33N51	79w03	5:16:12
Cooks Crossroads 30	34N41	82w11	5:28:44
Cooley Springs 42	35N09	81w52	5:27:28
Cool Spring 26	34N00	79w12	5:16:48
Cooper 45	33N52	79w45	5:19:00
Coosaw 7	32N32	80w46	5:23:04
Coosawhatchie 27	32N35	80w56	5:23:44
Cope 38	33N23	81w00	5:24:00
Cordesville 8	33N11	79w47	5:19:08
Cordova 38	33N26	80w55	5:23:40
Cornwell 12	34N37	81w10	5:24:40
Coronaca	34N16	82w06	5:28:24
Coronaco 24	34N12	82w09	5:28:36
Cottageville 15	32N56	80w29	5:21:56
Couchtown 2	33N34	81w44	5:26:56
Country Club Estates 46	34N56	81w01	5:24:04
Courtenay 37	34N41	82w56	5:31:44
Coward 21	33N58	79w45	5:19:00
Cowards 21	33N59	79w45	5:19:00
Cowpens 42	35N01	81w48	5:27:12
Cox 36	34N17	81w37	5:26:28
Crane Forest 40	34N03	81w02	5:24:08
Crayton Manor Apartments 4	34N31	82w39	5:30:36
Crescent 42	34N44	82w02	5:28:08
Crescent Beach 26	33N49	78w40	5:14:40
Creston 9	33N34	80w43	5:22:52
Crestview 16	34N12	79w45	5:19:00
Crocketville 25	32N55	81w05	5:24:20
Crosland Park 2	33N34	81w44	5:26:56
Cross 8	33N21	80w08	5:20:32
Cross Anchor 42	34N39	81w51	5:27:24
Cross Hill 30	34N18	81w59	5:27:56
Cross Keys 44	34N35	81w39	5:26:36
Crosswell 39	34N50	82w37	5:30:28
Crouch 41	34N00	81w46	5:27:04
Cummings 25	32N47	80w59	5:23:56
Cusaac Crossroads 21	34N05	79w46	5:19:04
Cypress Crossroads 31	34N10	80w04	5:20:16
Cypress Fork 14	33N45	80w13	5:20:52
Dacusville 39	34N50	82w37	5:30:28
Daisy 26	34N03	78w53	5:15:32
Dale 7	32N33	80w41	5:22:44
Dalewood 24	34N18	82w40	5:30:40
Dalzell 43	34N01	80w26	5:21:44
Danwood 21	34N05	79w46	5:19:04
Darlington 16	34N18	79w52	5:19:28
Daufuskie Island 7	32N06	80w52	5:23:28
Davis Crossroads 14	33N37	80w21	5:21:24
Davis Station 14	33N36	80w16	5:21:04
Dawkins 20	34N25	81w23	5:25:32
Deans 4	34N23	82w42	5:30:48
Deer Park 10	32N52	79w59	5:19:56
De Kalb 28	34N19	80w36	5:22:24
Delmar 41	33N55	81w28	5:25:52
Delphia 46	35N00	81w14	5:24:56
Delta 44	34N30	81w37	5:26:28
Denmark 5	33N19	81w09	5:24:36
Denny 41	34N00	81w46	5:27:04
Denny Terrace 40	34N03	81w02	5:24:08
Dentsville 40	34N04	80w58	5:23:52
Deweys Hill 10	32N54	80w00	5:20:00
Dillon 17	34N25	79w22	5:17:28
Dixiana 32	33N59	81w05	5:24:20
Dixie 29	34N42	80w47	5:23:08
Doddville 42	35N03	82w05	5:28:20
Dog Bluff 26	34N00	79w12	5:16:48
Donalds 1	34N23	82w21	5:29:24
Doneraile 16	34N19	79w53	5:19:32
Dongola 26	33N51	79w03	5:16:12
Dorange 18	33N12	80w39	5:22:36
Dorchester 18	33N08	80w24	5:21:36
Dorchester Estates 18	33N01	80w11	5:20:44
Dorchester-Waylyn 10	32N52	79w59	5:19:56
Douglass 20	34N21	81w08	5:24:32
Dovesville 16	34N24	79w54	5:19:36
Drake 35	34N31	79w39	5:18:36
Drawdy 15	32N57	80w40	5:22:40
Drayton 42	34N58	81w54	5:27:36
Draytonville 11	35N04	81w38	5:26:32
Drexel Lake Hills 40	34N02	80w58	5:23:52
Dry Branch 2	33N25	81w41	5:26:44
Dubose 43	34N01	80w17	5:21:08
Du Bose Crossroads 31	34N01	80w17	5:21:08
Du Bose Park 28	34N15	80w36	5:22:24
Dudley 13	34N46	80w23	5:21:32
Duew 1	34N20	82w23	5:29:32
Due West 1	34N20	82w23	5:29:32
Duford 26	34N14	79w09	5:16:36
Dunbar 22	33N22	79w17	5:17:08
Dunbar 35	34N35	79w32	5:18:08
Duncan 42	34N56	82w08	5:28:32
Dunean 23	34N51	82w24	5:29:36
Dunes 26	33N39	78w56	5:15:44
Dunkins Mill 43	34N06	80w32	5:22:08
Dupont 10	32N48	80w00	5:20:00
Dusty Bend 28	34N15	80w36	5:22:24
Dutch Fork 40	34N04	81w08	5:24:32
Dutchman 42	34N50	81w52	5:27:28
Dyson 24	34N10	82w01	5:28:04
Eadytown 8	33N26	80w01	5:20:04
Earle Homes 4	34N31	82w39	5:30:36
Earles 45	33N27	79w35	5:18:20
Earlwood Park 16	34N18	79w53	5:19:32
Early Branch 25	32N45	80w56	5:23:44
Easley 39	34N50	82w36	5:30:24
Eastatoe 39	34N59	82w48	5:31:12
East Gaffney 11	35N05	81w38	5:26:32
East Gantt 23	34N49	82w24	5:29:36
East Greer 42	34N56	82w13	5:28:52
East Hartsville 16	34N23	80w05	5:20:20
East Hopewell 11	35N04	81w26	5:25:44
Eastmont 40	33N59	80w57	5:23:48
Eastover 40	33N52	80w41	5:22:44
East View 23	34N39	82w28	5:29:52
Eau Claire 40	34N03	81w02	5:24:08
Ebenezer 21	34N12	79w45	5:19:00
Ebenezer 46	34N56	81w01	5:24:04
Eden 30	34N37	82w07	5:28:28
Edgefield 19	33N47	81w56	5:27:44
Edgemoor 12	34N48	81w01	5:24:04
Edgewater Park 10	32N48	80w00	5:20:00
Edgewood 40	34N02	80w59	5:23:56
Edisto Beach 10	32N34	80w17	5:21:08
Edisto Island 10	32N34	80w17	5:21:08
Edmund 32	33N59	81w14	5:24:56
Effingham 21	34N05	79w46	5:19:04
Ehrhardt 5	33N06	81w01	5:24:04
Elgin 28	34N10	80w48	5:23:12
Elgin 29	34N42	80w47	5:23:08
Elko 6	33N23	81w23	5:25:32
Elliott 31	34N06	80w10	5:20:40
Elloree 38	33N32	80w34	5:22:16
Emory 41	34N00	81w46	5:27:04
Enoree 42	34N39	81w58	5:27:52
Epworth 24	34N05	82w03	5:28:12
Equinox Mill 4	34N31	82w39	5:30:36
Estill 25	32N45	81w15	5:25:00
Eulala 41	34N00	81w46	5:27:04
Eulonia 34	33N56	79w25	5:17:40
Eureka 2	33N42	81w46	5:27:04
Eutaw Springs 38	33N24	80w20	5:21:20
Eutawville 38	33N24	80w21	5:21:24
Evans Crossroad 29	34N42	80w47	5:23:08
Evergreen 21	34N05	79w46	5:19:04
Evergreen Hills 4	34N31	82w39	5:30:36
Fairfax 3	32N59	81w15	5:25:00
Fairfield 7	32N13	80w45	5:23:00
Fairfiled Terrace 40	34N03	81w02	5:24:08
Fairforest 42	34N58	82w01	5:28:04
Fairforest Finishing Plant 42	34N58	82w01	5:28:04
Fairmont 42	34N57	81w58	5:27:52
Fairmont Mills 42	34N53	82w03	5:28:12
Fair Play 37	34N31	82w59	5:31:56
Fairview 23	34N41	82w11	5:28:44
Fairview Crossroads 32	33N55	81w28	5:25:52
Farrels Crossroads 5	33N15	80w49	5:23:16
Farrow Terrace 40	34N03	81w02	5:24:08
Fechtig 25	32N45	80w56	5:23:44
Federal 23	34N51	82w23	5:29:32
Felderville 38	33N32	80w34	5:22:16
Fenwick Hills 10	32N39	80w08	5:20:32
Ferndale 10	32N54	80w00	5:20:00
Filbert 46	35N00	81w14	5:24:56
Fingerville 42	35N09	82w02	5:28:08
Finklea 26	34N03	78w53	5:15:32
Finland 5	33N19	81w09	5:24:36
Five Forks 4	34N39	82w47	5:31:08
Five Forks 23	34N43	82w18	5:29:12
Five Forks 39	34N47	82w42	5:30:48
Five Points 40	34N00	81w00	5:24:00
Flat Rock 4	34N31	82w39	5:30:36
Fletcher 35	34N40	79w33	5:18:12
Florence 21	34N12	79w46	5:19:04
Florence West 21	34N11	79w48	5:19:12
Floyd Dale 17	34N19	79w20	5:17:20
Floyds 26	34N10	79w03	5:16:12
Folly Beach 10	32N39	79w56	5:19:44
Folly Field 7	32N13	80w45	5:23:00
Forest 18	33N08	80w24	5:21:36
Forest 39	35N01	82w44	5:30:56
Forest Acres 40	34N01	80w59	5:23:56
Forest Beach 7	32N13	80w45	5:23:00
Forest Lake 40	34N01	80w57	5:23:48
Foreston 14	33N38	80w04	5:20:16
Fork 4	34N31	82w53	5:31:32
Fork 17	34N17	79w16	5:17:04
Fork Shoals 23	34N41	82w11	5:28:44
Fort Jackson 40	34N01	81w00	5:24:00
Fort Lawn 12	34N42	80w54	5:23:36
Fort Mill 46	35N00	80w57	5:23:48
Fort Motte 9	33N44	80w42	5:22:48
Fortner 39	35N04	82w31	5:30:04
Fountain Inn 23	34N42	82w12	5:28:48
Four Holes 38	33N20	80w25	5:21:40
Four Mile 10	32N48	79w52	5:19:28
Fowler 45	33N40	79w50	5:19:20
Fox Town 2	33N34	81w44	5:26:56
Fraserville 22	33N26	79w07	5:16:28
Freedman 10	32N34	80w17	5:21:08
Friendfield 21	33N55	79w45	5:19:00
Friendship 24	34N12	82w09	5:28:36
Fripp Island 7	32N24	80w35	5:22:20
Fripp Landing 7	32N29	80w59	5:23:56
Frogmore 7	32N24	80w35	5:22:20
Fruit Hill 41	34N00	81w46	5:27:04
Furman 25	32N41	81w11	5:24:44
Gable 14	33N49	80w06	5:20:24
Gadsden 40	33N51	80w46	5:23:04
Gaffney 11	35N05	81w39	5:26:36
Gaillard Crossroads 43	34N01	80w26	5:21:44
Galaxy 40	33N59	80w57	5:23:48
Galivants Ferry 26	34N03	79w15	5:17:00
Gantt 23	34N47	82w24	5:29:36
Gapway 34	34N12	79w15	5:17:00
Garden City Beach 26	33N33	79w02	5:16:08
Gardens Corner 7	32N41	80w51	5:23:24
Garnett 25	32N36	81w15	5:25:00
Gaston 32	33N49	81w05	5:24:20
Gayle Mill 12	34N43	81w13	5:24:52
Georgetown 22	33N23	79w17	5:17:08
Gifford 25	32N52	81w14	5:24:56
Gilbert 32	33N56	81w24	5:25:36
Gillespie 13	34N38	80w03	5:20:12
Gillisonville 27	32N29	80w59	5:23:56
Givhans 18	33N06	80w19	5:21:16
Glass Hill 26	33N51	79w03	5:16:12
Glendale 42	34N57	81w50	5:27:20
Glenn Springs 42	34N50	81w52	5:27:28
Glenwood 39	34N50	82w37	5:30:28
Gloverville 2	33N31	81w50	5:27:20
Gluck 4	34N27	82w40	5:30:40
Glympville 36	34N16	81w25	5:25:40
Godsey 24	34N10	82w01	5:28:04
Golden Grove 23	34N42	82w27	5:29:48
Golightly 42	34N56	81w56	5:27:44
Gooches 29	34N42	80w47	5:23:08
Goodwins Crossroads 30	34N28	81w53	5:27:32
Goose Creek 8	32N59	80w02	5:20:08
Goretown 26	34N03	78w53	5:15:32
Gourdin 45	33N31	79w53	5:19:32
Govan 5	33N13	81w11	5:24:44
Gowensville 23	35N11	82w11	5:28:44
Grace 29	34N42	80w47	5:23:08
Grahamville 26	33N51	79w03	5:16:12
Grahamville 27	32N29	80w59	5:23:56
Gramling 42	35N04	82w10	5:28:40
Graniteville 2	33N34	81w49	5:27:16
Graves 22	33N29	79w22	5:17:28
Gray Court 30	34N36	82w07	5:28:28
Grays 27	32N45	80w56	5:23:44
Grays Hill 7	32N30	80w45	5:23:00
Great Falls 12	34N34	80w54	5:23:36
Greeleyville 45	33N35	80w00	5:20:00
Greenbrier 20	34N22	81w05	5:24:20
Green Pond 15	32N44	80w37	5:22:28
Green Pond 42	34N44	82w02	5:28:08
Green Sea 26	34N08	78w59	5:15:56
Greenview 40	34N03	81w02	5:24:08
Greenville 23	34N51	82w24	5:29:36
Greenwood 24	34N12	82w10	5:28:40
Greenwood Shores 24	34N10	82w01	5:28:04
Greer 23	34N56	82w14	5:28:56
Greer Mill 23	34N56	82w13	5:28:52
Grendel Mills 24	34N12	82w09	5:28:36
Gresham 34	33N56	79w25	5:17:40
Grover 18	33N06	80w36	5:22:24
Guess 13	34N46	80w14	5:20:56
Gurley 26	34N03	78w53	5:15:32
Guthries 46	34N52	81w14	5:24:56
Hadden Heights 42	34N57	81w58	5:27:52
Hagood 43	34N06	80w32	5:22:08
Halsellville 12	34N43	81w13	5:24:52
Hamburg 2	33N31	81w56	5:27:44
Hamer 17	34N29	79w20	5:17:20
Hammond 4	34N31	82w39	5:30:36
Hammond 26	33N51	79w03	5:16:12
Hammond Crossroads 9	33N40	80w47	5:23:08
Hampton 25	32N52	81w07	5:24:28
Hampton Heights 23	34N53	82w21	5:29:24
Hampton Park Terrace 10	32N48	79w57	5:19:48
Hanahan 8	32N55	80w00	5:20:00

SOUTH CAROLINA

Hand 26 33N51 79w03 5:16:12
Hannah 21 34N00 79w34 5:18:16
Hardeeville 27 32N17 81w05 5:24:20
Hardy 19 33N31 81w56 5:27:44
Harleyville 18 33N13 80w27 5:21:48
Harmony 19 33N50 81w48 5:27:12
Harmony 46 34N51 80w55 5:23:40
Harris 24 34N12 82w09 5:28:36
Hartsville 16 34N23 80w04 5:20:16
Harveytown 42 34N57 82w07 5:28:28
Haskell Heights 40 34N03 81w02 5:24:08
Hayne 42 34N57 81w58 5:27:52
Hazelwood Acres 40 33N59 80w57 5:23:48
Heath Springs 29 34N36 80w40 5:22:40
Hebron 45 33N47 79w47 5:19:08
Helena 36 34N17 81w37 5:26:28
Hemingway 45 33N45 79w27 5:17:48
Hemlock 12 34N43 81w13 5:24:52
Hendersonville 32N48 81w43 5:26:52
Hendersonville 15 32N57 80w40 5:22:40
Heriots Crossroads 43 34N13 80w15 5:21:00
Hibernia 41 33N51 81w37 5:26:28
Hickory Grove 26 33N51 79w03 5:16:12
Hickory Grove 46 34N59 81w25 5:25:40
Hickory Tavern 30 34N37 82w07 5:28:28
Highland 23 35N04 82w16 5:29:04
Highland Park 8 32N55 80w00 5:20:00
Highway Four Forty One 43 33N55 80w21 5:21:24
Hilda 6 33N16 81w15 5:25:00
Hillcrest Acres 4 34N31 82w30 5:30:00
Hillcrest Heights 4 34N37 82w29 5:29:56
Hilton 40 34N10 81w21 5:25:24
Hilton Head 32N13 80w45 5:23:00
Hilton Head Island 7 32N13 80w45 5:23:00
Hobbs Cross Road 43 33N55 80w21 5:21:24
Hobcaw Point 10 32N48 79w52 5:19:28
Hodges 24 34N17 82w15 5:29:00
Hollands Store 4 34N23 82w42 5:30:48
Holly Hill 38 33N19 80w25 5:21:40
Holly Springs 37 34N40 83w06 5:32:24
Holly Springs 42 35N03 82w05 5:28:20
Hollywood 10 32N44 80w14 5:20:56
Hollywood 41 34N00 81w46 5:27:04
Hollywood Hills 40 34N03 81w02 5:24:08
Holmesville 17 34N21 79w10 5:16:40
Holtson Crossroads 41 33N54 81w33 5:26:12
Homeland Park 4 34N31 82w39 5:30:36
Homewood 26 33N53 79w03 5:16:12
Honea Path 4 34N27 82w24 5:29:36
Honey Hill 8 33N11 79w38 5:18:32
Hoodtown 46 34N57 81w20 5:25:20
Hopewell 46 34N59 81w25 5:25:40
Hopkins 40 33N54 80w53 5:23:32
Horatio 43 34N01 80w33 5:22:12
Horeb 20 34N22 81w05 5:24:20
Horrel Hill 40 33N57 80w51 5:23:24
Horsegall 25 32N51 81w05 5:24:20
Howard 26 34N03 78w53 5:15:32
Hoyt Heights 43 33N55 80w21 5:21:24
Huger 8 33N06 79w48 5:19:12
Hunley Park 10 32N52 80w03 5:20:12
Hyman 21 34N00 79w34 5:18:16
Independents 40 33N59 80w57 5:23:48
Indian 45 33N45 79w35 5:18:20
Industrial 46 34N56 81w01 5:24:04
Ingleside 42 35N11 82w11 5:28:44
Inman 42 35N03 82w05 5:28:20
Inman Mills 42 35N02 82w06 5:28:24
Irmo 32 34N05 81w11 5:24:44
Irvines Landing 24 34N12 82w09 5:28:36
Irwin 29 34N42 80w49 5:23:16
Islandton 15 32N55 80w56 5:23:44
Isle of Palms 10 32N47 79w48 5:19:12
Iva 4 34N19 82w40 5:30:40
Jackson 2 33N20 81w47 5:27:08
Jacksonboro 15 32N46 80w27 5:21:48
Jacksonham 29 34N56 80w45 5:23:00
Jackson Mill 42 34N57 82w06 5:28:24
Jalapa 36 34N17 81w37 5:26:28
James Island 10 32N44 79w57 5:19:48
Jamestown 8 33N17 79w42 5:18:48
Jamison 38 33N30 80w52 5:23:28
Jedburg 18 33N01 80w11 5:20:44
Jefferson 13 34N39 80w23 5:21:32
Jenkinsville 20 34N16 81w17 5:25:08
Jennys 3 32N57 81w14 5:24:56
Jericho 10 32N45 80w18 5:21:12
Joanna 30 34N25 81w49 5:27:16
Jocasse 37 34N54 82w59 5:31:56
Johns 44 34N50 81w41 5:26:44
Johns Island 10 32N47 80w07 5:20:28
Johnson City 42 34N57 81w58 5:27:52
Johnson Crossroads 2 33N25 81w41 5:26:44
Johnsonville 21 33N49 79w27 5:17:48
Johnston 19 33N50 81w48 5:27:12
Johnstown 2 33N30 81w52 5:27:28
Jones Crossroads 2 33N51 81w37 5:26:28
Jones Crossroads 29 34N42 80w47 5:23:08
Jonesville 44 34N50 81w41 5:26:44
Jordan 14 33N36 80w12 5:20:48
Jordania 37 34N41 82w56 5:31:44
Judson 23 34N51 82w26 5:29:44
Kathwood 32 33N59 81w05 5:24:20
Kelly 44 34N43 81w37 5:26:28
Kellytown 16 34N23 80w05 5:20:20
Kelton 44 34N50 81w41 5:26:44
Kemper 17 34N21 79w10 5:16:40
Kensington 22 33N22 79w17 5:17:08
Keowee 37 34N41 82w56 5:31:44
Kershaw 28 34N33 80w35 5:22:20

Key 35 34N31 79w39 5:18:36
Kilgore 42 34N39 81w58 5:27:52
Killgo 28 34N15 80w36 5:22:24
Killian 40 34N03 81w02 5:24:08
Kinards 36 34N23 81w46 5:27:04
King Circle 29 34N42 80w47 5:23:08
Kingsburg 21 33N49 79w27 5:17:48
Kings Creek 11 35N04 81w26 5:25:44
Kingstree 45 33N40 79w50 5:19:20
Kingville 40 33N45 80w45 5:23:00
Kirkland 28 34N15 80w36 5:22:24
Kirksey 24 34N02 82w02 5:28:08
Kirkwood 28 34N15 80w36 5:22:24
Kitchings Mill 2 33N34 81w18 5:25:12
Kline 6 33N08 81w21 5:25:24
Klondike Crossroads 26 33N51 79w03 5:16:12
Kneece 32 33N54 81w33 5:26:12
Knightsville 18 33N01 80w11 5:20:44
Knox 12 34N43 81w13 5:24:52
Ladson 10 32N59 80w06 5:20:24
La France 4 34N37 82w45 5:31:00
Lake City 21 33N52 79w45 5:19:00
Lake Forest 23 34N51 82w21 5:29:24
Lake Lanier 23 35N11 82w11 5:28:44
Lakemont 23 35N04 82w31 5:30:04
Lake Murray Shores 41 33N55 81w28 5:25:52
Lake Shores 24 34N12 82w09 5:28:36
Lake Swamp 16 34N13 80w00 5:20:00
Lake View 17 34N21 79w10 5:16:40
Lamar 16 34N10 80w04 5:20:16
Lambs 10 32N52 79w59 5:19:56
Lancaster 29 34N43 80w46 5:23:04
Lando 12 34N46 81w01 5:24:04
Landrum 42 35N11 82w11 5:28:44
Lands End 7 32N24 80w35 5:22:20
Landsford 12 34N46 80w57 5:23:48
Lane 45 33N32 79w53 5:19:32
Lanford 30 34N39 81w58 5:27:52
Langley 2 33N31 81w50 5:27:20
Lathem 39 34N50 82w37 5:30:28
Latta 17 34N21 79w26 5:17:44
Laurel Bay 7 32N27 80w47 5:23:08
Laurens 30 34N30 82w01 5:28:04
Leawood 23 34N51 82w24 5:29:36
Lebanon 4 34N31 82w39 5:30:36
Lebanon 20 34N22 81w05 5:24:20
Leeds 12 34N36 81w28 5:25:52
Leesburg 40 33N59 80w57 5:23:48
Leesville 32 33N55 81w31 5:26:04
Legareville 10 32N39 80w08 5:20:32
Lena 25 32N45 81w12 5:24:48
Leo 21 33N52 79w45 5:19:00
Leslie 46 34N56 81w01 5:24:04
Lesslie 46 34N53 80w58 5:23:52
Lester 35 34N37 79w41 5:18:44
Level Land 1 34N18 82w40 5:30:40
Lewis 12 34N43 81w13 5:24:52
Lewis Cross Roads 16 34N18 79w53 5:19:32
Lexington 32 34N00 81w14 5:24:56
Liberty 39 34N48 82w42 5:30:48
Liberty Hill 10 32N54 80w00 5:20:00
Liberty Hill 28 34N29 80w48 5:23:12
Liberty Hill 33 33N55 82w18 5:29:12
Limehouse 27 32N17 81w04 5:24:16
Limp 41 34N00 81w46 5:27:04
Lincoln Shire 40 34N03 81w02 5:24:08
Lincolnville 10 33N01 80w09 5:20:36
Lions Beach 8 33N12 80w01 5:20:04
Litchfield Beach 22 33N26 79w07 5:16:28
Little Africa 42 35N09 81w52 5:27:28
Little Camden 40 34N00 81w03 5:24:12
Little Mountain 36 34N12 81w25 5:25:40
Little River 26 33N53 78w37 5:14:28
Little Rock 17 34N29 79w24 5:17:36
Livingston 38 33N33 81w07 5:24:28
Lobeco 7 32N33 80w45 5:23:00
Lockhart 44 34N47 81w28 5:25:52
Lockhart Junction 44 34N50 81w41 5:26:44
Lodge 15 33N04 80w56 5:23:44
Lone Star 9 33N38 80w35 5:22:20
Long Bay Estates 26 33N39 78w56 5:15:44
Longcreek 37 34N46 83w12 5:32:48
Long Point 26 34N03 78w53 5:15:32
Long Ridge 8 33N12 80w01 5:20:04
Longs 26 33N56 78w44 5:14:56
Longtown 20 34N18 80w58 5:23:52
Loris 26 34N04 78w53 5:15:32
Lowndesville 1 34N13 82w39 5:30:36
Lowrys 12 34N48 81w14 5:24:56
Lucknow 31 34N13 80w15 5:21:00
Lugoff 28 34N13 80w40 5:22:40
Luray 25 32N49 81w14 5:24:56
Lydia 16 34N17 80w07 5:20:28
Lydia Mills 30 34N28 81w53 5:27:32
Lykesland 40 33N54 80w53 5:23:32
Lyman 42 34N57 82w07 5:28:28
Lynchburg 31 34N04 80w04 5:20:16
Lyndhurst 6 33N15 81w22 5:25:28
Macedon 32 33N59 81w14 5:24:56
Maddens 30 34N31 82w00 5:28:00
Madison 2 33N34 81w48 5:27:12
Madison 37 34N38 83w12 5:32:48
Mangums 13 34N46 80w23 5:21:32
Manning 14 33N42 80w13 5:20:52
Manville 31 34N13 80w15 5:21:00
Maple Crossroads 26 33N51 79w03 5:16:12
Marietta 23 35N01 82w30 5:30:00
Marine Corps Air Station 7 32N27 80w44 5:22:56
Marion 34 34N11 79w24 5:17:36
Marlboro 35 34N37 79w41 5:18:44

Mars Bluff 21 34N12 79w45 5:19:00
Martin 3 33N04 81w29 5:25:56
Marysville 22 33N26 79w07 5:16:28
Maryville 10 32N48 80w00 5:20:00
Maryville 22 33N22 79w17 5:17:08
Mathews Heights 24 34N12 82w09 5:28:36
Mauldin 23 34N47 82w19 5:29:16
Mauldins Mill 25 32N52 81w07 5:24:28
May 17 34N21 79w10 5:16:40
Mayesville 43 34N00 80w13 5:20:52
Mayfair 23 34N53 82w21 5:29:24
Mayo 42 35N05 81w52 5:27:28
Mayo Mills 42 35N05 81w52 5:27:28
Mayson 41 33N59 81w05 5:24:20
McBee 13 34N28 80w15 5:21:00
McBeth 8 33N18 79w58 5:19:52
McClellanville 10 33N05 79w28 5:17:52
McColl 35 34N40 79w33 5:18:12
McConnells 46 34N52 81w14 5:24:56
McCormick 33 33N55 82w18 5:29:12
McCutchen Crossroads 31 34N13 80w15 5:21:00
McKenzie Crossroads 21 33N56 79w56 5:19:44
McKeown 12 34N43 81w13 5:24:52
McPhersonville 25 32N45 80w56 5:23:44
Meadows 44 34N43 81w37 5:26:28
Mechanicsville 16 34N18 79w53 5:19:32
Mechanicsville 31 34N13 80w15 5:21:00
Meggett 10 32N43 80w14 5:20:56
Melrose 2 33N25 81w41 5:26:44
Melrose 10 32N48 80w00 5:20:00
Merchant 41 34N00 81w46 5:27:04
Meriwether 33N39 82w10 5:28:40
Middendorf 13 34N23 80w05 5:20:20
Midland Park 8 32N52 79w59 5:19:56
Midway 5 33N16 81w05 5:24:20
Midway 28 34N22 80w26 5:21:44
Midway 29 34N42 80w47 5:23:08
Midway Village 26 33N39 78w56 5:15:44
Miley 25 32N57 81w02 5:24:08
Milford Springs 24 34N12 82w09 5:28:36
Millers Crossroads 19 33N44 82w12 5:28:48
Millett 3 33N04 81w29 5:25:56
Millettville 33N05 81w31 5:26:04
Millford 43 33N44 80w28 5:21:52
Mill Village 35 34N37 79w41 5:18:44
Millwood 45 33N40 79w50 5:19:20
Millwood Gardens 43 33N55 80w21 5:21:24
Minturn 17 34N32 79w29 5:17:56
Mitchellville 27 32N29 80w59 5:23:56
Mitford 20 34N34 80w54 5:23:36
Mixville 2 33N33 81w48 5:27:12
Modoc 33 33N44 82w13 5:28:52
Monaghan 23 34N51 82w26 5:29:44
Monarch 44 34N42 81w34 5:26:16
Monarch Mills 44 34N43 81w36 5:26:24
Moncks Corner 8 33N12 80w01 5:20:04
Monetta 41 33N46 81w34 5:26:16
Montague 23 34N51 82w24 5:29:36
Monticello 20 34N21 81w18 5:25:12
Montmorenci 2 33N32 81w38 5:26:32
Montrose 13 34N42 79w53 5:19:32
Moore 42 34N50 82w00 5:28:00
Moores Crossroads 45 33N47 79w47 5:19:08
Morgan 11 35N07 81w47 5:27:08
Morgana 33N36 82w04 5:28:16
Morningside 23 34N51 82w21 5:29:24
Morrell 21 34N08 79w57 5:19:48
Morris Acres 10 32N39 80w08 5:20:32
Moselle 15 32N55 80w56 5:23:44
Moss 19 33N47 81w56 5:27:44
Motbridge 43 34N04 80w05 5:20:20
Mountain Brook 40 33N59 80w57 5:23:48
Mountain Rest 37 34N51 83w07 5:32:28
Mountain View 42 35N09 81w52 5:27:28
Mount Carmel 33 34N00 82w31 5:30:04
Mount Croghan 13 34N46 80w14 5:20:56
Mount Gallagher 30 34N24 82w15 5:29:00
Mount Holly 8 33N02 80w02 5:20:08
Mount Olive 26 34N14 79w09 5:16:36
Mount Pisgah 28 34N31 80w29 5:21:56
Mount Pleasant 10 32N47 79w52 5:19:28
Mount View 23 34N53 82w21 5:29:24
Mountville 30 34N22 81w57 5:27:48
Mount Willing 41 34N00 81w46 5:27:04
Mount Zion 28 34N16 80w32 5:22:08
Mullins 34 34N12 79w15 5:17:00
Murraysville 8 33N12 80w01 5:20:04
Murrells Inlet 22 33N33 79w02 5:16:08
Myers 10 32N52 79w59 5:19:56
Myrtle Beach 26 33N42 78w53 5:15:32
Myrtle Island 7 32N14 80w52 5:23:28
Naval Base 10 32N51 79w55 5:19:40
Naval Hospital 7 32N27 80w44 5:22:56
Neeses 38 33N33 81w07 5:24:28
Nesmith 45 33N39 79w31 5:18:04
Nevadun 27 32N29 80w59 5:23:56
Nevitt Forest 4 34N31 82w39 5:30:36
Newberry 36 34N17 81w37 5:26:28
New Cut 29 34N42 80w47 5:23:08
New Easley Highway 23 34N51 82w26 5:29:44
New Ellenton 2 33N28 81w41 5:26:44
New Holland Crossroads 2 33N54 81w33 5:26:12
New Hope 21 33N58 79w45 5:19:00
New Prospect 42 35N03 82w05 5:28:20
Newry 37 34N43 82w55 5:31:40
New Town 17 34N25 79w22 5:17:28
New Zion 14 33N51 80w02 5:20:08
Nichols 34 34N14 79w09 5:16:36
Nimmons 39 34N59 82w48 5:31:12

SOUTH CAROLINA

Nine Times 39 34N59 82w48 5:31:12
Ninety Six 24 34N10 82w01 5:28:04
Nixons Crossroads 26 33N52 78w40 5:14:40
Nixonville 26 33N51 79w03 5:16:12
Nixville 25 32N45 81w15 5:25:00
Noisette Creek 10 32N52 79w56 5:19:44
Norris 39 34N46 82w46 5:31:04
North 38 33N37 81w06 5:24:24
North Anderson 4 34N31 82w39 5:30:36
North Augusta 2 33N30 81w59 5:27:56
Northbridge 10 32N48 80w00 5:20:00
North Charleston 10 32N53 80w00 5:20:00
North Forest Beach 7 32N13 80w45 5:23:00
Northgate 21 34N12 79w45 5:19:00
North Hartsville 16 34N24 80w04 5:20:16
North Litchfield Beach 22 33N26 79w07 5:16:28
North Mullins 34 34N12 79w15 5:17:00
North Myrtle Beach 26 33N49 78w40 5:14:40
North Pacolet 42 35N07 82w09 5:28:36
North Santee 22 33N22 79w17 5:17:08
North Summerville 18 33N01 80w11 5:20:44
North Winyah Heights 22 33N22 79w17 5:17:08
Norway 38 33N27 81w07 5:24:28
Oak Dale 14 33N51 80w02 5:20:08
Oak Grove 17 34N20 79w26 5:17:44
Oak Hill 2 33N25 81w41 5:26:44
Oakhurst 29 34N33 80w35 5:22:20
Oakland 7 32N27 80w44 5:22:56
Oakland 10 32N48 80w00 5:20:00
Oakland Cross Roads 17 34N29 79w20 5:17:20
Oakland Mill 36 34N17 81w37 5:26:28
Oakley 8 33N07 80w01 5:20:04
Oak Ridge 29 34N36 80w40 5:22:40
Oakvale 23 34N42 82w27 5:29:48
Oakway 37 34N35 83w00 5:32:00
Oakwood 2 33N34 81w44 5:26:56
Oatland 22 33N22 79w17 5:17:08
Oats 16 34N10 80w04 5:20:16
Ocean Drive Beach 26 33N49 78w40 5:14:40
Ocean Forest 26 33N39 78w56 5:15:44
Ogden 46 34N56 81w01 5:24:04
Olanta 21 33N56 79w56 5:19:44
Olar 5 33N11 81w11 5:24:44
Old House 27 32N29 80w59 5:23:56
Old Madison 37 34N38 83w12 5:32:48
Olga 39 35N02 82w30 5:30:00
Olympia 40 34N00 81w03 5:24:12
Ora 30 34N35 82w00 5:28:00
Orangeburg 38 33N30 80w52 5:23:28
Orrs 12 34N43 81w13 5:24:52
Orrville 4 34N31 82w39 5:30:36
Orum 21 34N00 79w34 5:18:16
Osborn 10 32N44 80w21 5:21:24
Osceola 29 34N51 80w51 5:23:24
Oswego 43 34N01 80w17 5:21:08
Otranto 8 32N52 79w59 5:19:56
Outland 22 33N44 79w29 5:17:56
Overbrook 23 34N51 82w21 5:29:24
Owdoms 41 34N00 81w46 5:27:04
Owings 30 34N37 82w07 5:28:28
Pacolet 42 34N54 81w46 5:27:04
Pacolet Mills 42 34N55 81w45 5:27:00
Pacolet Park 42 34N55 81w45 5:27:00
Padgetts 15 33N05 80w49 5:23:16
Pageland 13 34N46 80w24 5:21:36
Paint Hill 28 34N15 80w36 5:22:24
Palmer Subdivision 4 34N31 82w39 5:30:36
Palmetto 16 34N18 79w53 5:19:32
Palmetto Fort 10 32N48 79w52 5:19:28
Palmetto Plaza 43 33N55 80w21 5:21:24
Pamplico 21 34N00 79w34 5:18:16
Panola 14 33N44 80w28 5:21:52
Panola 24 34N12 82w09 5:28:36
Paramount Park 23 34N49 82w24 5:29:36
Paris 23 34N55 82w22 5:29:28
Parkers Ferry 10 32N44 80w21 5:21:24
Parkersville 22 33N26 79w07 5:16:28
Park Place 23 34N52 82w23 5:29:32
Parksville 33 33N47 82w13 5:28:52
Parlers 38 33N29 80w29 5:21:56
Parris Island 7 32N20 80w41 5:22:44
Patrick 13 34N34 80w03 5:20:12
Pauline 42 34N50 81w52 5:27:28
Pawleys Island 22 33N26 79w07 5:16:28
Paxville 14 33N44 80w22 5:21:28
Peach Valley 42 34N58 81w57 5:27:48
Peak 36 34N14 81w19 5:25:16
Pecan Terrace 23 34N49 82w24 5:29:36
Pecan Way Terrace 38 33N30 80w52 5:23:28
Peedee 34 34N12 79w32 5:18:08
Pelham 23 34N56 82w13 5:28:52
Pelion 32 33N46 81w15 5:25:00
Pelzer 4 34N39 82w28 5:29:52
Pendleton 4 34N39 82w47 5:31:08
Peniel Crossroads 21 34N08 79w57 5:19:48
Percival Crossroads 37 34N40 83w06 5:32:24
Perry 2 33N38 81w19 5:25:16
Philip 10 32N48 79w52 5:19:28
Phoenix 24 34N12 82w09 5:28:36
Pickens 39 34N53 82w42 5:30:48
Pickens Mill 39 34N53 82w42 5:30:48
Pickensville 39 34N50 82w37 5:30:28
Pickett Post 37 34N46 83w04 5:32:16

Piedmont 23 34N42 82w28 5:29:52
Piercetown 4 34N37 82w29 5:29:56
Pierpont 10 32N48 80w00 5:20:00
Pimlico 8 33N12 80w01 5:20:04
Pinecrest 10 32N48 80w00 5:20:00
Pinehurst 18 33N01 80w11 5:20:44
Pinehurst 24 34N12 82w09 5:28:36
Pinehurst-Sheppard Park 18 33N01 80w11 5:20:44
Pine Island 26 33N39 78w56 5:15:44
Pineland 27 32N36 81w10 5:24:40
Pineridge 16 34N28 80w15 5:21:00
Pineridge 32 33N55 81w07 5:24:28
Pineville 8 33N26 80w01 5:20:04
Pinewood 43 33N44 80w27 5:21:48
Piney Grove 42 35N01 81w48 5:27:12
Pinopolis 8 33N14 80w02 5:20:08
Pisgah 43 34N06 80w32 5:22:08
Plains 13 34N39 80w23 5:21:32
Plantersville 22 33N33 79w13 5:16:52
Pleasant Hill 29 34N36 80w40 5:22:40
Pleasant Lane 19 33N55 82w01 5:28:04
Pleasant Valley 23 34N49 82w24 5:29:36
Pocataligo 27 32N41 80w51 5:23:24
Poe 23 34N52 82w23 5:29:32
Polk Village 7 32N27 80w44 5:22:56
Pomaria 36 34N16 81w25 5:25:40
Pontiac 40 34N07 80w54 5:23:36
Poovey Estate 29 34N42 80w47 5:23:08
Poplar Springs 42 34N50 82w00 5:28:00
Port Royal 7 32N23 80w42 5:22:48
Port Royal Plantation 7 32N13 80w45 5:23:00
Poston 21 33N53 79w26 5:17:44
Powdersville 4 34N50 82w37 5:30:28
Pregnall 18 33N08 80w24 5:21:36
Primus 29 34N42 80w47 5:23:08
Princeton 30 34N30 82w17 5:29:08
Pritchardville 7 32N14 80w52 5:23:28
Privateer 43 33N49 80w23 5:21:32
Promised Land 24 34N03 82w15 5:29:00
Prospect Crossroads 21 33N52 79w45 5:19:00
Prosperity 36 34N12 81w32 5:26:08
Purysburgh 27 32N17 81w04 5:24:16
Quinby 21 34N14 79w44 5:18:56
Quinby Estates 21 34N12 79w45 5:19:00
Quinby Forest 21 34N12 79w45 5:19:00
Rains 34 34N06 79w19 5:17:16
Rantowles 10 32N43 80w14 5:20:56
Ravenel 10 32N46 80w15 5:21:00
Ravenwood 40 34N02 80w58 5:23:52
Red Bank 32 33N59 81w14 5:24:56
Red Bluff Crossroads 26 34N03 78w53 5:15:32
Red Hill 31 34N15 80w36 5:22:24
Red River 46 34N57 80w58 5:23:52
Red Top 10 32N39 80w08 5:20:32
Reevesville 18 33N12 80w39 5:22:36
Reidville 42 34N52 82w07 5:28:28
Rembert 43 34N06 80w32 5:22:08
Renfrew 23 34N58 82w26 5:29:44
Renno 30 34N28 81w53 5:27:32
Rhems 22 33N22 79w17 5:17:08
Ribault Park 7 32N27 80w44 5:22:56
Richburg 12 34N43 81w01 5:24:04
Richland 37 34N41 83w01 5:32:04
Richland Springs 41 34N00 81w46 5:27:04
Richmond Hills 23 34N52 82w23 5:29:32
Richtex 20 34N11 81w11 5:24:44
Ridgecrest 2 33N34 81w44 5:26:56
Ridge Cut 25 32N45 80w56 5:23:44
Ridgeland 27 32N29 80w59 5:23:56
Ridge Spring 41 33N51 81w40 5:26:40
Ridgeville 18 33N06 80w19 5:21:16
Ridgeway 20 34N18 80w58 5:23:52
Ridgewood 10 33N00 80w06 5:20:24
Ridgewood 40 34N03 81w02 5:24:08
Rimini 14 33N40 80w30 5:22:00
Rion 20 34N18 81w08 5:24:32
Ritter 15 32N47 80w38 5:22:32
River 41 34N07 81w44 5:26:56
Riverdale 17 34N25 79w22 5:17:28
River Falls 23 35N02 82w30 5:30:00
Riverland Terrace 10 32N48 80w00 5:20:00
Rivers Annex 10 32N48 79w57 5:19:48
Riverside 1 34N24 82w15 5:29:00
Riverside 4 34N31 82w39 5:30:36
Riverside 23 34N52 82w27 5:29:48
Riverside 29 34N42 80w47 5:23:08
Riverside Park 40 33N51 80w56 5:23:44
Robat 44 34N43 81w37 5:26:28
Robertville 27 32N36 81w15 5:25:00
Robinson 16 34N28 80w15 5:21:00
Rock Bluff 45 33N40 79w50 5:19:20
Rock Hill 46 34N56 81w01 5:24:04
Rockton 20 34N22 81w05 5:24:20
Rockville 32N36 81w12 5:24:48
Rockville 10 32N39 80w11 5:20:44
Rocky Bottom 39 34N59 82w48 5:31:12
Rocky River 1 34N18 82w40 5:30:40
Roddy 46 34N51 80w55 5:23:40
Rodman 12 34N46 81w05 5:24:20
Roebuck 42 34N53 81w58 5:27:52
Roseida 7 32N27 80w44 5:22:56
Rosemont 10 32N50 79w58 5:19:52
Rosinville 18 33N11 80w35 5:22:20
Round O 15 32N56 80w32 5:22:08
Rowell 12 34N51 80w55 5:23:40
Rowesville 38 33N22 80w50 5:23:20
Ruby 13 34N44 80w11 5:20:44
Ruffin 15 33N00 80w49 5:23:16
Russell 37 34N54 83w09 5:32:36
Russellville 8 33N24 79w58 5:19:52

Saint Andrews 10 32N48 80w01 5:20:04
Saint Andrews 32 33N51 80w56 5:23:44
Saint Charles 31 34N05 80w13 5:20:52
Saint George 18 33N11 80w35 5:22:20
Saint Helena 7 32N24 80w36 5:22:24
Saint Matthews 9 33N40 80w46 5:23:04
Saint Paul 14 33N37 80w21 5:21:24
Saint Paul Forks 26 33N51 79w03 5:16:12
Saint Pauls 10 32N45 80w17 5:21:08
Saint Stephen 8 33N24 79w55 5:19:40
Salak 24 34N12 82w09 5:28:36
Salem 21 34N00 79w34 5:18:16
Salem 37 34N54 82w58 5:31:52
Salem Crossroads 20 34N25 81w23 5:25:32
Salkehatchie 15 32N41 80w51 5:23:24
Salley 2 33N34 81w18 5:25:12
Salters 45 33N36 79w51 5:19:24
Saluca 24 34N12 82w09 5:28:36
Saluda 41 34N00 81w46 5:27:04
Saluda Gardens 32 33N59 81w05 5:24:20
Saluda Terrace 32 33N59 81w05 5:24:20
Samaria 32 33N54 81w33 5:26:12
Sampit 22 33N22 79w17 5:17:08
Sanders Corner 43 34N01 80w33 5:22:12
Sandwood 40 34N02 80w58 5:23:52
Sandy Flat 23 34N53 82w21 5:29:24
Sandy Springs 4 34N36 82w45 5:31:00
Sans Souci 23 34N52 82w23 5:29:32
Sans Souci Heights 23 34N52 82w23 5:29:32
Santee 38 33N29 80w29 5:21:56
Santee Circle 8 33N12 80w01 5:20:04
Santuc 44 34N36 81w28 5:25:52
Sardinia 14 33N49 80w03 5:20:12
Sardis 21 34N04 79w56 5:19:44
Sato 5 33N19 81w09 5:24:36
Savannah Bluff 26 33N51 79w03 5:16:12
Saxon 42 34N58 81w58 5:27:52
Saylors Crossroads 4 34N31 82w30 5:30:00
Scanlonville 10 32N48 79w52 5:19:28
Schofield 5 33N12 81w11 5:24:44
Schultz Hill 2 33N31 81w56 5:27:44
Scotia 25 32N41 81w15 5:25:00
Scottsville 43 33N59 80w13 5:20:52
Scranton 21 33N55 79w45 5:19:00
Seaboard Junction 13 34N42 79w53 5:19:32
Seabrook 7 32N32 80w46 5:23:04
Sea Pines 7 32N13 80w45 5:23:00
Sedalia 44 34N43 81w37 5:26:28
Segars 16 34N23 80w05 5:20:20
Seigling 3 33N00 81w18 5:25:12
Seivern 2 33N39 81w22 5:25:28
Sellers 34 34N17 79w28 5:17:52
Selma 17 34N25 79w22 5:17:28
Seneca 37 34N41 82w57 5:31:48
Seven Mile 10 32N48 79w52 5:19:28
Shady Rest 35 34N37 79w41 5:18:44
Shamokin 28 34N15 80w36 5:22:24
Shannontown 43 33N54 80w20 5:21:20
Sharon 46 34N57 81w20 5:25:20
Sharon Park 23 34N51 82w24 5:29:36
Shaw 43 33N58 80w29 5:21:56
Shaw Air Force Base 43 33N58 80w29 5:21:56
Shaw Heights 43 33N58 80w29 5:21:56
Sheldon 7 32N36 80w48 5:23:12
Shell 26 33N51 79w03 5:16:12
Shell Point 7 32N27 80w44 5:22:56
Shelton 20 34N30 81w25 5:25:40
Shepard 28 34N22 80w26 5:21:44
Sheppard Park 18 33N01 80w11 5:20:44
Sherwood Archer 42 33N34 81w44 5:26:56
Shiloh 43 33N58 80w02 5:20:08
Shipyard Plantations 7 32N13 80w45 5:23:00
Shirley 25 32N36 81w15 5:25:00
Shoals Junction 24 34N21 82w17 5:29:08
Shoreswood 42 34N57 81w58 5:27:52
Shulerville 8 33N11 79w38 5:18:32
Silver 14 33N43 80w17 5:21:08
Silverstreet 36 34N13 81w43 5:26:52
Simmonsville 22 33N22 79w17 5:17:08
Simpson 20 34N18 80w58 5:23:52
Simpsonville 23 34N44 82w15 5:29:00
Singleton 9 33N40 80w47 5:23:08
Six Mile 10 32N52 79w59 5:19:56
Six Mile 39 34N48 82w49 5:31:16
Skyview Terrace 40 33N51 80w56 5:23:44
Slansville 18 33N01 80w11 5:20:44
Slater 23 35N03 82w33 5:30:12
Slighs 36 34N13 81w32 5:26:08
Smallwood 20 34N18 80w58 5:23:52
Smith 46 34N56 81w01 5:24:04
Smithboro 17 34N12 79w15 5:17:00
Smith Mills 22 33N44 79w29 5:17:56
Smoaks 15 33N05 80w49 5:23:16
Smyrna 46 35N02 81w24 5:25:36
Snelling 6 33N15 81w27 5:25:48
Sniders Crossroads 15 33N00 80w49 5:23:16
Snowden 10 32N48 79w52 5:19:28
Socastee 26 33N39 78w56 5:15:44
Society Hill 16 34N31 79w51 5:19:24
Sol Legare Island 10 32N47 79w56 5:19:44
South Bennettsville 35 34N37 79w41 5:18:44
South Congaree 32 33N54 81w08 5:24:32
Southern 42 35N00 81w58 5:27:52
Southern Shops 42 35N00 81w59 5:27:56
South Forest Estates 23 34N49 82w24 5:29:36
South Greenwood 24 34N12 82w09 5:28:36

SOUTH CAROLINA

South Hartsville 16 34N23 80w05 5:20:20
South Hills 44 34N43 81w37 5:26:28
South Lynchburg 31 34N04 80w05 5:20:20
South Mullins 34 34N12 79w15 5:17:00
Southside 11 34N57 81w41 5:26:44
Southside 21 34N12 79w45 5:19:00
South Windermere 10 32N48 80w00 5:20:00
Spartanburg 42 34N56 81w57 5:27:48
Springdale 29 34N42 80w47 5:23:08
Springdale 32 33N59 81w05 5:24:20
Springfield 38 33N30 81w17 5:25:08
Spring Hill 31 34N06 80w32 5:22:08
Springmaid Beach 26 33N39 78w56 5:15:44
Spring Mills 29 34N33 80w35 5:22:20
Springwood 40 34N02 80w59 5:23:56
Stallsville 18 33N01 80w11 5:20:44
Stark Terrace 40 34N03 81w02 5:24:08
Starr 4 34N23 82w41 5:30:44
Startex 42 34N56 82w05 5:28:20
Stateburg 43 33N55 80w21 5:21:24
State College 38 33N30 80w52 5:23:28
Steedman 32 33N55 81w28 5:25:52
Stiefeltown 2 33N33 81w48 5:27:12
Stockman 36 34N13 81w32 5:26:08
Stokes 15 32N57 80w40 5:22:40
Stokes Bridge 31 34N13 80w15 5:21:00
Stoneboro 28 34N36 80w40 5:22:40
Stone Station 42 34N57 81w58 5:27:52
Stoney Hill 36 34N13 81w32 5:26:08
Stover 20 34N21 81w08 5:24:32
Strangeville 38 33N30 80w52 5:23:28
Stratford Forest 23 34N51 82w24 5:29:36
Strawberry 8 33N12 80w01 5:20:04
Strother 20 34N25 81w23 5:25:32
Stuart Point 7 32N32 80w46 5:23:04
Stuckey 45 33N44 79w31 5:18:04
Sullivans Island 10 32N46 79w51 5:19:24
Summer Hill 2 33N31 81w56 5:27:44
Summerland 32 33N54 81w33 5:26:12
Summerton 14 33N36 80w20 5:21:20
Summerville 18 33N01 80w11 5:20:44
Summit 32 33N55 81w25 5:25:40
Summit View 23 34N51 82w24 5:29:36
Sumter 43 33N55 80w21 5:21:24
Sunnyside 42 34N56 82w13 5:28:52
Sunset 39 34N59 82w48 5:31:12
Surfside Beach 26 33N37 78w59 5:15:56
Suttons 45 33N27 79w35 5:18:20
Swansea 32 33N44 81w06 5:24:24
Sweden 5 33N19 81w09 5:24:36
Sweetwater 2 33N31 81w56 5:27:44
Switzer 42 34N50 82w00 5:28:00
Switzerland 27 32N26 81w00 5:24:00
Sycamore 3 33N02 81w13 5:24:52
Syracuse 16 34N18 79w53 5:19:32
Talatha 2 33N25 81w41 5:26:44
Tamassee 37 34N53 83w02 5:32:08
Tanglewood 23 34N51 82w26 5:29:44
Tarboro 27 32N28 81w06 5:24:24
Tatum 35 34N39 79w35 5:18:20
Taxahaw 29 34N33 80w35 5:22:20
Taylors 23 34N56 82w29 5:29:56
Temperance 34 34N11 79w24 5:17:36
Ten Mile 10 32N48 79w52 5:19:28
Terrells Crossroads 45 33N47 79w47 5:19:08
The Dunes 26 33N39 78w56 5:15:44
The Farms 8 32N55 80w00 5:20:00
The Groves 10 32N48 79w52 5:19:28
Thor 32 33N46 81w14 5:24:56
Thorn Hill 28 34N28 80w41 5:22:44
Tigerville 23 35N05 82w25 5:29:40
Tillman 27 32N28 81w06 5:24:24
Timmonsville 21 34N08 79w57 5:19:48
Tirzah 46 35N00 81w14 5:24:56
Toddville 26 33N46 79w05 5:16:20
Tokeena Crossroads 37 34N41 82w56 5:31:44
Toney Creek 4 34N31 82w30 5:30:00
Townville 4 34N34 82w54 5:31:36
Toxaway 4 34N31 82w39 5:30:36
Tradesville 29 34N46 80w33 5:22:12
Tranquil Acres 18 33N01 80w11 5:20:44
Travelers Rest 23 34N58 82w27 5:29:48
Trenton 19 33N45 81w51 5:27:24
Triangle 4 34N31 82w30 5:30:00
Trio 45 33N29 79w43 5:18:52
Troy 24 33N59 82w17 5:29:08
Tuckertown 44 34N36 81w28 5:25:52
Turbeville 14 33N54 80w01 5:20:04
Turkey 45 33N35 79w36 5:18:24
Twin Lake Hill 40 33N59 80w57 5:23:48
Ulmer 3 33N06 81w13 5:24:52
Ulmers 3 33N03 81w16 5:25:04
Una 16 34N10 80w04 5:20:16
Union 20 34N22 81w05 5:24:20
Union 44 34N43 81w37 5:26:28
Union Bleachery 23 34N52 82w23 5:29:32
Union Crossroads 14 33N51 80w02 5:20:08
Unity 29 34N56 80w45 5:23:00
University 40 34N01 81w00 5:24:00
Utica 37 34N41 82w56 5:31:44
Valencia Heights 40 34N00 81w00 5:24:00
Valley Falls 42 34N58 81w57 5:27:48
Vance 38 33N26 80w25 5:21:40
Van Wyck 29 34N56 80w51 5:23:24
Varnville 25 32N51 81w05 5:24:20
Vaucluse 2 33N37 81w49 5:27:16
Verdery 24 34N07 82w15 5:29:00
Victor Mills Village 42 34N56 82w13 5:28:52
Waccamaw 22 33N29 79w07 5:16:28
Waddell Gardens 7 32N27 80w44 5:22:56
Wade-hampton 23 34N53 82w20 5:29:20
Wadmalaw Island 10 32N39 80w11 5:20:44
Wadsworth 42 34N57 81w58 5:27:52
Wagener 2 33N39 81w22 5:25:28
Walhalla 37 34N46 83w04 5:32:16
Wallace 35 34N44 79w49 5:19:16
Walnut Grove 42 34N50 81w52 5:27:28
Walterboro 15 32N55 80w40 5:22:40
Wampee 26 33N56 78w44 5:14:56
Wando 8 32N56 79w50 5:19:20
Wando Woods 10 32N52 79w59 5:19:56
Ward 41 33N52 81w44 5:26:56
Wards 41 33N52 81w44 5:26:56
Ware Place 23 34N39 82w28 5:29:52
Ware Shoals 24 34N24 82w15 5:29:00
Warrenville 2 33N33 81w48 5:27:12
Warsaw 45 33N27 79w35 5:18:20
Wateree 40 33N49 80w38 5:22:32
Waterloo 30 34N22 82w03 5:28:12
Watkins Store 2 33N25 81w41 5:26:44
Watsonia 41 33N51 81w37 5:26:28
Watts Mills 30 34N31 82w00 5:28:00
Wattsville 30 34N31 82w00 5:28:00
Waverly Mills 22 33N26 79w07 5:16:28
Waylyn 10 32N51 80w00 5:20:00
Wedgefield 43 33N53 80w31 5:22:04
Welcome 4 34N31 82w39 5:30:36
Welcome 23 34N51 82w26 5:29:44
Wellford 42 34N57 82w06 5:28:24
Wesleyan 39 34N43 82w47 5:31:08
West Andrews 22 33N27 79w35 5:18:20
Westcliff 23 35N02 82w30 5:30:00
West Columbia 32 33N59 81w04 5:24:16
West Florence 21 34N12 79w45 5:19:00
West Gantt 23 34N49 82w24 5:29:36
Westminster 37 34N40 83w06 5:32:24
Westover Acres 32 33N59 81w05 5:24:20
West Pelzer 4 34N39 82w28 5:29:52
West Springs 44 34N43 81w45 5:27:00
West Union 37 34N45 83w03 5:32:12
West View 42 34N56 82w00 5:28:00
Westville 23 34N51 82w26 5:29:44
Westville 28 34N27 80w36 5:22:24
Whetstone 37 34N54 83w09 5:32:36
Whipper Barony 10 32N52 79w59 5:19:56
White Bluff 29 34N33 80w35 5:22:20
White Hall 15 32N41 80w51 5:23:24
Whitehall 24 34N12 82w09 5:28:36
Whitehall Terrace 10 32N48 79w52 5:19:28
White Horse Heights 23 34N51 82w26 5:29:44
White Oak 20 34N28 81w07 5:24:28
White Plains 4 34N37 82w29 5:29:56
White Pond 2 33N24 81w25 5:25:40
White Rock 40 34N09 81w16 5:25:04
White Stone 42 34N54 81w48 5:27:12
Whitesville 8 33N12 80w01 5:20:04
Whitmire 36 34N30 81w37 5:26:28
Whitney 42 34N59 81w56 5:27:44
Whitney Heights 42 34N58 81w57 5:27:48
Wilder 8 33N18 79w58 5:19:52
Wiles Crossroads 9 33N44 80w42 5:22:48
Wilkins 7 32N27 80w44 5:22:56
Wilkinsville 11 35N04 81w38 5:26:32
Williams 15 33N03 80w50 5:23:20
Williamsburg 45 33N28 79w39 5:18:36
Williams Estate 29 34N42 80w47 5:23:08
Williamston 4 34N37 82w29 5:29:56
Willington 33 33N58 82w28 5:29:52
Williston 6 33N24 81w25 5:25:40
Wilson 14 33N40 80w07 5:20:28
Wilsons Cross Roads 16 34N18 79w53 5:19:32
Windsor 2 33N29 81w31 5:26:04
Windsor Estates 40 34N02 80w59 5:23:56
Windsor Lake Park 40 34N02 80w58 5:23:52
Windsor Park 13 34N42 79w53 5:19:32
Windy Hill 21 34N12 79w45 5:19:00
Windy Hill Beach 26 33N49 78w40 5:14:40
Winnsboro 20 34N23 81w05 5:24:20
Winnsboro Mills 20 34N22 81w05 5:24:20
Winona 21 34N12 79w45 5:19:00
Winthrop College 46 34N56 81w01 5:24:04
Wisacky 31 34N09 80w12 5:20:48
Wolfton 38 33N37 81w06 5:24:24
Woodburn Hills 42 34N57 81w51 5:27:24
Woodfield 40 34N02 80w58 5:23:52
Woodfields 23 34N49 82w24 5:29:36
Woodford 38 33N40 81w06 5:24:24
Woodrow 31 34N01 80w26 5:21:44
Woodruff 42 34N45 82w02 5:28:08
Woods Chapel 42 34N56 82w11 5:28:44
Woodside 23 34N51 82w26 5:29:44
Woodville 23 34N39 82w23 5:29:32
Woodward 20 34N21 81w08 5:24:32
Workman 45 33N51 80w02 5:20:08
Yauhannah 22 33N22 79w17 5:17:08
Yeamans Hall 8 32N55 80w00 5:20:00
Yemassee 25 32N41 80w51 5:23:24
Yenome 6 33N08 81w21 5:25:24
Yonges Island 10 32N41 80w14 5:20:56
Yorba Village 7 32N36 80w48 5:23:12
York 46 35N00 81w15 5:25:00
Youngs 30 34N44 82w02 5:28:08
Zion 34 34N12 79w15 5:17:00

TIME TABLES

SD # 1

Before 11/18/1883		LMT
11/18/1883	12:00	CST
3/31/1918	02:00	CWT
10/27/1918	02:00	CST
3/30/1919	02:00	CWT
10/26/1919	02:00	CST
2/09/1942	02:00	CWT
9/30/1945	02:00	CST
4/30/1967	02:00	US#1

SD # 2

Before 11/18/1883		LMT
11/18/1883	12:00	CST
3/31/1918	02:00	CWT
10/27/1918	02:00	CST
3/30/1919	02:00	CWT
10/26/1919	02:00	CST
2/09/1942	02:00	CWT
9/30/1945	02:00	CST
5/13/1957	02:00	CDT
9/29/1957	02:00	CST
4/30/1967	02:00	US#1

SD # 3

Before 11/18/1883		LMT
11/18/1883	12:00	MST
3/31/1918	02:00	MWT
10/27/1918	02:00	MST
3/30/1919	02:00	MWT
10/26/1919	02:00	MST
2/09/1942	02:00	MWT
9/30/1945	02:00	MST
4/30/1967	02:00	US#1

SD # 4

Before 11/18/1883		LMT
11/18/1883	12:00	MST
3/31/1918	02:00	MWT
10/27/1918	02:00	MST
3/30/1919	02:00	MWT
10/26/1919	02:00	MST
2/09/1942	02:00	MWT
9/30/1945	02:00	MST
4/24/1966	02:00	US#1

COUNTIES

1 Aurora
2 Beadle
3 Bennett
4 Bon Homme
5 Brookings
6 Brown
7 Brule
8 Buffalo
9 Butte
10 Campbell
11 Charles Mix
12 Clark
13 Clay
14 Codington
15 Corson
16 Custer
17 Davison
18 Day
19 Deuel
20 Dewey
21 Douglas
22 Edmunds
23 Fall River
24 Faulk
25 Grant
26 Gregory
27 Haakon
28 Hamlin
29 Hand
30 Hanson
31 Harding
32 Hughes
33 Hutchinson
34 Hyde
35 Jackson
36 Jerauld
37 Jones
38 Kingsbury
39 Lake
40 Lawrence
41 Lincoln
42 Lyman
43 McCook
44 McPherson
45 Marshall
46 Meade
47 Mellette
48 Miner
49 Minnehaha
50 Moody
51 Pennington
52 Perkins
53 Potter
54 Roberts
55 Sanborn
56 Shannon
57 Spink
58 Stanley
59 Sully
60 Todd
61 Tripp
62 Turner
63 Union
64 Walworth
65 Washabaugh
66 Yankton
67 Ziebach

Place		Lat	Long	Time
Aberdeen 6	1	45N28	98w29	6:33:56
Academy 11	1	43N27	99w05	6:36:20
Ada 52	3	45N21	102w24	6:49:36
Adrian 22	1	45N33	99w11	6:36:44
Agar 59	1	44N50	100w05	6:40:20
Agency 54	1	45N31	97w02	6:28:08
Akaska 64	1	45N20	100w07	6:40:28
Alban 25	1	45N12	96w32	6:26:08
Albee 25	1	45N03	96w33	6:26:12
Albion 4	1	42N57	97w56	6:31:44
Alcester 63	1	43N01	96w38	6:26:32
Alden 29	1	44N41	99w06	6:36:24
Alexandria 30	1	43N39	97w47	6:31:08
Allen 3	3	43N17	101w56	6:47:44
Alliance 50	1	43N54	96w29	6:25:56
Allison 6	1	45N49	98w40	6:34:40
Alpena 36	1	44N11	98w22	6:33:28
Alpha 29	1	44N35	98w59	6:35:56
Altamont 19	1	44N50	96w42	6:26:48
Alto 54	1	45N26	97w10	6:28:40
Alton 5	1	44N19	96w35	6:26:20
Altoona 2	1	44N35	98w24	6:33:36
America 7	1	43N33	99w11	6:36:44
Ames 29	1	44N31	98w59	6:35:56
Amherst 45	1	45N44	97w55	6:31:40
Anderson 52	3	45N41	102w16	6:49:04
Andover 18	1	45N25	97w54	6:31:36
Anina 36	1	43N59	98w38	6:34:32
Annin 42	1	43N59	100w04	6:40:16
Antelope 60	4	43N18	100w39	6:42:36
Antelope Valley 19	1	44N56	96w29	6:25:56
Applegate 42	1	44N08	100w05	6:40:20
Appomattox 53	1	45N08	100w07	6:40:28
Arcade 24	1	44N56	99w01	6:36:04
Ardmore 23	3	43N01	103w40	6:54:40
Arena 53	1	45N12	99w52	6:39:28
Argentine 23	3	43N26	103w59	6:55:56
Argo 5	1	44N30	96w42	6:26:48
Arlington 38	1	44N22	97w08	6:28:32
Arlington Beach 5	1	44N22	97w08	6:28:32
Armour 21	1	43N19	98w21	6:33:24
Arpan 9	3	44N40	103w33	6:54:12
Artas 10	1	45N53	99w49	6:39:16
Artesian 55	1	44N01	97w55	6:31:40
Artichoke 53	1	44N56	100w06	6:40:24
Ashton 57	1	45N00	98w30	6:34:00
Astoria 19	1	44N34	96w33	6:26:12
Athol 57	1	45N01	98w36	6:34:24
Aurora 5	1	44N17	96w41	6:26:44
Aurora Center 1	1	43N35	98w27	6:33:48
Avon 4	1	43N00	98w04	6:32:16
Avon Springs 53	1	44N56	99w45	6:39:00
Badger 38	1	44N29	97w12	6:28:48
Bad Nation 47	4	43N36	100w22	6:41:28
Badus 39	1	44N09	97w11	6:28:44
Bailey 42	1	43N48	99w41	6:38:44
Baltic 49	1	43N46	96w44	6:26:56
Bancroft 38	1	44N30	97w45	6:31:00
Bangor 5	1	44N20	97w03	6:28:12
Barnard 6	1	45N44	98w30	6:34:00
Batesland 56	3	43N08	102w06	6:48:24
Bath 6	1	45N28	98w19	6:33:16
Bear Butte 46	3	44N25	103w31	6:54:04
Bear Creek 20	3	45N01	101w26	6:45:44
Beaver 48	1	43N53	97w47	6:31:08
Beaver Creek 61	1	43N03	100w10	6:40:40
Beck 52	3	45N10	102w39	6:50:36
Becker 54	1	45N33	96w50	6:27:20
Belford 1	1	43N53	98w22	6:33:28
Belle 22	1	45N33	98w54	6:35:36
Belle Fourche 9	3	44N40	103w51	6:55:24
Belle Plaine 57	1	44N51	98w09	6:32:36
Belle Prairie 2	1	44N14	97w55	6:31:40
Belleview 48	1	44N09	97w26	6:29:44
Belvidere 35	3	43N50	101w16	6:45:04
Bemis 19	1	44N50	96w51	6:27:24
Benedict 55	1	44N04	97w54	6:31:36
Beotia 57	1	45N11	98w12	6:32:48
Beresford 63	1	43N05	96w47	6:27:08
Bethel 13	1	42N57	97w06	6:28:24
Bethlehem 46	3	44N17	103w31	6:54:04
Big Bend 51	3	44N06	103w09	6:52:36
Big Buffalo 35	3	43N52	102w01	6:48:04
Big Sioux 63	1	42N32	96w30	6:26:00
Big Springs 63	1	42N57	96w38	6:26:32
Big Stone 25	1	45N17	96w31	6:26:04
Big Stone City 25	1	45N18	96w28	6:25:52
Bijou Hills 7	1	43N31	99w09	6:36:36
Bison 52	3	45N31	102w28	6:49:52
Black 61	1	43N23	99w57	6:39:48
Black Dog 42	1	43N42	99w34	6:38:16
Black Hawk 46	3	44N09	103w19	6:53:16
Blackpipe 47	3	43N26	101w06	6:44:24
Blacktail 40	3	44N21	103w46	6:55:04
Blendon 17	1	43N48	98w16	6:33:04
Blinsmon 50	1	43N54	96w35	6:26:20
Blom 19	1	44N35	96w42	6:26:48
Blooming Valley 25	1	45N15	97w10	6:28:40
Blumengard Colony 24	1	45N10	99w07	6:36:28
Blunt 32	1	44N31	99w59	6:39:56
Bonesteel 26	1	43N04	98w57	6:35:48
Bon Homme 4	1	42N53	97w46	6:31:04
Bon Homme Colony 4	1	42N52	97w32	6:30:08
Bonilla 2	1	44N35	98w30	6:34:00
Bossko 54	1	45N46	97w10	6:28:40
Bovine 37	1	44N08	100w52	6:43:28
Bowdle 22	1	45N27	99w39	6:38:36
Box Elder 51	3	44N07	103w04	6:52:16
Bradley 12	1	45N05	97w39	6:30:36
Brainard 6	1	45N44	98w24	6:33:36
Bramhall 34	1	44N30	99w22	6:37:28
Brandon 49	1	43N35	96w35	6:26:20
Brandon Terrace 49	1	43N35	96w34	6:26:16
Brandt 19	1	44N40	96w38	6:26:32
Brantford 28	1	44N46	97w23	6:29:32
Brentford 57	1	45N10	98w19	6:33:16
Bretton 32	1	44N31	99w51	6:39:24
Bridger 67	3	44N33	101w55	6:47:40
Bridgewater 43	1	43N33	97w30	6:30:00
Bristol 18	1	45N21	97w45	6:31:00
Britton 45	1	45N48	97w45	6:31:00
Broadland 2	1	44N30	98w21	6:33:24
Brookfield 43	1	43N49	97w20	6:29:20
Brookings 5	1	44N19	96w48	6:27:12
Brooklyn 41	1	43N07	96w52	6:27:28
Brothersfield 62	1	43N28	97w06	6:28:24
Bruce 5	1	44N26	96w54	6:27:36
Brunson 61	1	43N28	99w48	6:39:12
Bryan 11	1	43N08	98w17	6:33:08
Bryant 28	1	44N35	97w28	6:29:52
Buffalo 31	3	45N35	103w33	6:54:12
Buffalo Gap 16	3	43N30	103w19	6:53:16
Buffalo Trading Post 49	1	43N47	96w56	6:27:44
Bull Creek 61	1	43N28	99w35	6:38:20
Bullhead 15	3	45N46	101w05	6:44:20
Burbank 13	1	42N45	96w50	6:27:20
Burdette 29	1	44N41	98w46	6:35:04
Burdick 52	3	45N47	102w23	6:49:32
Burk 49	1	43N48	96w50	6:27:20
Burke 26	1	43N11	99w18	6:37:12
Burr Oak 2	1	44N14	98w38	6:34:32
Bushnell 5	1	44N20	96w38	6:26:32
Butler 18	1	45N15	97w43	6:30:52
Cactus Flat 35	3	43N58	102w05	6:48:20
Cadillac 15	3	45N52	101w01	6:44:04
Cambria 6	1	45N33	98w17	6:33:08
Campbell 29	1	44N41	99w16	6:37:04
Camp Crook 31	3	45N33	103w59	6:55:56
Canistota 43	1	43N36	97w18	6:29:12
Canning 32	1	44N22	100w20	6:41:20
Canova 48	1	43N53	97w30	6:30:00
Canton 41	1	43N18	96w35	6:26:20
Capa 37	3	44N07	100w59	6:43:56
Capital 33	1	43N13	97w42	6:30:48
Capitola 57	1	44N45	98w02	6:32:08
Caputa 51	3	44N00	102w59	6:51:56
Carl 44	1	45N48	98w48	6:35:12
Carlisle 6	1	45N39	98w40	6:34:40
Carlock 26	1	43N02	99w28	6:37:52
Carlton 29	1	44N46	98w53	6:35:32
Carlyle 2	1	44N15	98w24	6:33:36
Carpenter 12	1	44N38	97w55	6:31:40
Carr 53	1	45N07	99w46	6:39:04
Carroll 11	1	43N28	98w46	6:35:04
Carter 61	3	43N23	100w12	6:40:48
Carthage 48	1	44N10	97w43	6:30:52
Cash 52	3	45N36	102w39	6:50:36
Castalia 11	1	43N23	99w00	6:36:00
Castle Rock 9	3	44N58	103w26	6:53:44
Castlewood 28	1	44N44	97w02	6:28:08
Cattron 53	1	44N57	100w15	6:41:00
Cavour 2	1	44N22	98w02	6:32:08
Cedar 29	1	44N21	99w14	6:36:56
Cedarbutte 47	3	43N35	101w01	6:44:04
Cedar Lake 3	3	43N04	101w18	6:45:12
Center 1	1	43N33	98w37	6:34:28
Center 43	1	43N44	97w23	6:29:32
Center Point 62	1	43N10	97w14	6:28:56
Centerville 62	1	43N07	96w58	6:27:52
Central City 40	3	44N22	103w46	6:55:04
Central Point 18	1	45N17	97w18	6:29:12
Chamberlain 7	1	43N49	99w20	6:37:20
Chance 52	3	45N23	102w16	6:49:04
Chancellor 62	1	43N22	96w59	6:27:56
Chaudoin 52	3	45N15	102w24	6:49:36
Chautauqua 39	1	44N00	97w07	6:28:28
Chelsea 24	1	45N10	98w45	6:35:00
Cherry Creek 67	3	44N36	101w30	6:46:00
Chery 36	1	44N09	98w38	6:34:32
Chester 39	1	43N54	96w56	6:27:44
Cheyenne 51	3	44N23	102w11	6:48:44
Cheyenne Crossing 40	3	44N21	103w46	6:55:04
Cheyenne River Indian Res 20	3	45N00	101w13	6:44:52
Childstown 62	1	43N18	97w20	6:29:20
Choteau Creek 11	1	43N09	98w10	6:32:40
Civil Bend 63	1	42N37	96w39	6:26:36
Claire City 54	1	45N52	97w06	6:28:24
Clare 50	1	44N04	96w42	6:26:48
Claremont 6	1	45N40	98w01	6:32:04
Clark 12	1	44N53	97w44	6:30:56
Clark Colony 57	1	44N55	97w56	6:31:44
Clarno 39	1	43N54	97w18	6:29:12
Clayton 33	1	43N26	97w41	6:30:44
Clearfield 61	1	43N10	100w02	6:40:08
Clear Lake 19	1	44N45	96w41	6:26:44
Clearwater 48	1	43N59	97w26	6:29:44
Clinton 48	1	43N59	97w47	6:31:08
Cloyd Valley 22	1	45N22	99w31	6:38:04
Clyde 2	1	44N20	98w17	6:33:08
Cody 47	4	43N38	100w32	6:42:08
Collins 12	1	44N35	97w40	6:30:40
Colman 50	1	43N59	96w49	6:27:16
Colome 61	1	43N16	99w43	6:38:52
Colton 49	1	43N47	96w56	6:27:44
Columbia 6	1	45N37	98w19	6:33:16
Commerce 49	1	43N31	96w42	6:26:48
Como 29	1	44N15	99w13	6:36:52
Conata 51	3	43N48	102w12	6:48:48

SOUTH DAKOTA

Concord 39 1 44N04 97w18 6:29:12
Conde 57 1 45N09 98w06 6:32:24
Condon 61 1 43N33 99w42 6:38:48
Cooper 1 1 43N48 98w37 6:34:28
Corn Creek 47 3 43N31 101w10 6:44:40
Cornwall 57 1 44N40 98w17 6:33:08
Corona 54 1 45N20 96w46 6:27:04
Corsica 21 1 43N25 98w24 6:33:36
Corson 49 1 43N37 96w34 6:26:16
Cortlandt 22 1 45N27 98w46 6:35:04
Cottonwood 35 3 43N58 101w54 6:47:36
Cottonwood Lake 22 1 45N28 99w31 6:38:04
Cottonwood Valley 47 4 43N36 100w54 6:43:36
Crandall 18 1 45N10 98w06 6:32:24
Crandon 57 1 44N45 98w24 6:33:36
Crazy Horse 16 3 43N46 103w36 6:54:24
Creighton 51 3 44N15 102w13 6:48:52
Cresbard 24 1 45N10 98w57 6:35:48
Crocker 12 1 45N06 97w47 6:31:08
Crooked Creek 51 3 43N57 102w23 6:49:32
Crooks 49 1 43N40 96w49 6:27:16
Cross Plains 33 1 43N27 97w57 6:31:48
Crow 36 1 44N04 98w52 6:35:28
Crow Creek Indian Res 8 1 44N03 99w26 6:37:44
Crow Lake 36 1 43N59 98w45 6:35:00
Crystal Lake 1 1 43N38 98w38 6:34:32
Cunningham 53 1 45N02 99w52 6:39:28
Curlew 61 1 43N33 100w11 6:40:44
Custer 16 3 43N46 103w36 6:54:24
Dale 36 1 44N09 98w31 6:34:04
Dallas 26 1 43N14 99w31 6:38:04
Dalzell 46 3 44N19 102w32 6:50:08
Daneville 62 1 43N08 97w06 6:28:24
Dante 11 1 43N02 98w11 6:32:44
Davis 62 1 43N16 96w59 6:27:56
Day 12 1 44N51 97w40 6:30:40
Deadwood 40 3 44N23 103w44 6:54:56
Dearborn 2 1 44N20 98w24 6:33:36
De Grey 32 1 44N19 99w56 6:39:44
Delaney 15 3 45N36 101w55 6:47:40
Delapre 41 1 43N28 96w49 6:27:16
Delaware 41 1 43N13 96w52 6:27:28
Dell Rapids 49 1 43N50 96w43 6:26:52
Delmont 21 1 43N16 98w10 6:32:40
Dempster 28 1 44N41 96w56 6:27:44
Denby 56 3 43N04 102w20 6:49:20
Denver 38 1 44N23 97w12 6:28:48
De Smet 38 1 44N23 97w33 6:30:12
Devoe 24 1 45N07 98w54 6:35:36
Dewey 3 43N32 104w02 6:56:08
De Witt 52 3 45N47 102w07 6:48:28
Dexter 14 1 45N06 97w17 6:29:08
Diana 55 1 43N59 97w54 6:31:36
Dickens 26 1 43N07 99w29 6:37:56
Dimock 33 1 43N29 97w59 6:31:56
Dixon 26 1 43N23 99w29 6:37:56
Dog Ear 61 1 43N13 99w57 6:39:48
Doland 57 1 44N54 98w06 6:32:24
Dolton 62 1 43N30 97w23 6:29:32
Dorman 42 1 43N59 99w50 6:39:20
Douglas 34 1 44N41 99w29 6:37:56
Draper 37 1 43N56 100w32 6:42:08
Dryden 23 3 43N10 103w18 6:53:12
Dry Wood Lake 54 1 45N36 97w07 6:28:28
Duell 52 3 45N21 102w39 6:50:36
Dumarce 45 1 45N47 97w24 6:29:36
Dunkel 37 1 43N52 100w31 6:42:04
Dupree 67 3 45N03 101w36 6:46:24
Eagle Butte 20 3 45N00 101w14 6:44:56
Earling 42 1 43N53 99w57 6:39:48
East Choteau 21 1 43N14 98w10 6:32:40
Easter 54 1 45N37 96w55 6:27:40
East Hanson 6 1 45N22 98w02 6:32:08
East Rondell 6 1 45N17 98w17 6:33:08
East Sioux Falls 49 1 43N31 96w42 6:26:48
Eden 45 1 45N37 97w25 6:29:40
Edens 26 1 43N18 99w28 6:37:52
Edgemont 23 3 43N18 103w50 6:55:20
Edgerton 30 1 43N43 97w40 6:30:40
Edison 49 1 43N43 96w35 6:26:20
Edna 42 1 43N44 99w55 6:39:40
Egan 50 1 44N00 96w39 6:26:36
Egeland 18 1 45N11 97w18 6:29:12
Elida 53 1 44N57 99w53 6:39:32
Elk Point 63 1 42N41 96w41 6:26:44
Elkton 5 1 44N14 96w29 6:25:56
Elliott 55 1 43N54 98w16 6:33:04
Ellis 49 1 43N31 96w42 6:26:48
Elliston 61 1 43N13 99w35 6:38:20
Ellisville 24 1 44N57 99w30 6:38:00
Ellston 26 1 43N02 99w08 6:36:32
Ellsworth 46 3 44N10 103w06 6:52:24
Ellsworth Air Force Base 46 3 44N10 103w06 6:52:24
Elmira 14 1 44N56 97w04 6:28:16
Elmore 40 3 44N21 103w46 6:55:04
Elm Springs 46 3 44N19 102w32 6:50:08
Elm Springs Colony 33 1 43N33 97w59 6:31:56
Elrod 12 1 44N51 97w33 6:30:12
Elroy 24 1 45N07 99w30 6:38:00
Elvira 8 1 44N03 98w59 6:35:56
Emanuel 4 1 43N07 97w56 6:31:44
Emerson 24 1 45N12 99w01 6:36:04
Emery 30 1 43N36 97w37 6:30:28
Emmet 63 1 42N57 96w45 6:27:00
Empire 9 3 44N37 103w24 6:53:36
Englewood 52 3 45N16 102w07 6:48:28
Enning 46 3 44N35 102w34 6:50:16
Epiphany 30 1 43N53 97w30 6:30:00
Erwin 38 1 44N29 97w27 6:29:48
Esmond 38 1 44N16 97w46 6:31:04
Estelline 28 1 44N35 96w54 6:27:36
Ethan 17 1 43N33 97w59 6:31:56
Eureka 44 1 45N46 99w38 6:38:32
Exline 57 1 44N51 98w39 6:34:36
Fair 33 1 43N13 97w56 6:31:44
Fairburn 16 3 43N41 103w13 6:52:52
Fairfax 26 1 43N02 98w54 6:35:36
Fairfield 2 1 44N30 98w16 6:33:04
Fairland 42 1 43N53 99w28 6:37:52
Fairpoint 3 44N45 102w48 6:51:12
Fairpoint 46 3 43N41 103w12 6:52:48
Fairview 41 1 43N13 96w29 6:25:56
Faith 46 3 45N02 102w02 6:48:08
Farmer 30 1 43N43 97w41 6:30:44
Farmingdale 51 3 43N57 102w53 6:51:32
Faulkton 24 1 45N02 99w08 6:36:32
Fayette 53 1 45N12 100w07 6:40:28
Fedora 48 1 44N01 97w48 6:31:12
Ferney 6 1 45N20 98w06 6:32:24
Firesteel 20 3 45N26 101w17 6:45:08
Flandreau 50 1 44N03 96w36 6:26:24
Flandreau Indian Reservation 50 1 44N03 96w35 6:26:20
Flat Butte 51 3 43N52 102w05 6:48:20
Flat Creek 52 3 45N52 102w16 6:49:04
Fleetwood 49 1 43N35 96w34 6:26:16
Flint Rock 52 3 45N05 102w03 6:48:12
Florence 14 1 45N03 97w20 6:29:20
Floyd 55 1 44N09 98w02 6:32:08
Forbes 11 1 43N27 98w53 6:35:32
Fordham 12 1 44N46 97w55 6:31:40
Forestburg 55 1 44N02 98w04 6:32:16
Forest City 53 1 45N02 100w15 6:41:00
Fort 45 1 45N38 97w32 6:30:08
Fort Pierre 58 4 44N21 100w22 6:41:28
Fort Thompson 8 1 44N03 99w26 6:37:44
Fountain 22 1 45N27 98w54 6:35:36
Foxton 12 1 44N45 97w33 6:30:12
Frankfort 57 1 44N53 98w18 6:33:12
Franklin 39 1 44N00 97w07 6:28:28
Franklyn 6 1 45N43 98w40 6:34:40
Frederick 6 1 45N50 98w31 6:34:04
Fredlund 52 3 45N41 102w39 6:50:36
Freedom 24 1 45N12 99w09 6:36:36
Freeman 33 1 43N21 97w26 6:29:44
Fremont 50 1 44N09 96w50 6:27:20
Froehlich Addition 49 1 43N31 96w42 6:26:48
Fruitdale 9 3 44N40 103w42 6:54:48
Fuller 14 1 45N01 97w16 6:29:04
Fulton 30 1 43N44 97w49 6:31:16
Galena 40 3 44N23 103w44 6:54:56
Gales 1 1 43N38 98w44 6:34:56
Gannvalley 8 1 44N02 98w59 6:35:56
Garden City 12 1 44N57 97w35 6:30:20
Garden Prairie 6 1 45N17 98w10 6:32:40
Garland 6 1 45N39 98w24 6:33:36
Garretson 49 1 43N43 96w30 6:26:00
Gary 19 1 44N48 96w27 6:25:48
Gayville 66 1 42N53 97w10 6:28:40
Geddes 11 1 43N15 98w42 6:34:48
Gem 6 1 45N22 98w20 6:33:20
Geneseo 54 1 45N22 96w41 6:26:44
Georgia 25 1 45N01 96w42 6:26:48
German 33 1 43N18 97w56 6:31:44
Gettysburg 53 1 45N01 99w57 6:39:48
Gilbert 29 1 44N35 98w46 6:35:04
Glad Valley 67 3 45N24 101w47 6:47:08
Glen 22 1 45N28 99w24 6:37:36
Glencross 20 3 45N27 100w55 6:43:40
Glendale 29 1 44N18 99w05 6:36:20
Glendale Colony 57 1 44N52 98w18 6:33:12
Glendo 52 3 45N42 102w53 6:51:32
Glenham 64 1 45N32 100w16 6:41:04
Glover 22 1 45N23 99w24 6:37:36
Goodwill 54 1 45N36 97w02 6:28:08
Goodwin 19 1 44N53 96w51 6:27:24
Goose Lake 11 1 43N13 98w34 6:34:16
Graceland 14 1 44N56 97w26 6:29:44
Graceville Colony 39 1 44N00 97w22 6:29:28
Grafton 48 1 44N09 97w33 6:30:12
Grand 29 1 44N29 98w45 6:35:00
Grandfield 27 3 44N26 101w13 6:44:52
Grand Meadow 49 1 43N43 96w58 6:27:52
Grand River 52 3 45N53 102w38 6:50:32
Grand Valley 15 3 45N41 101w55 6:47:40
Grange 19 1 44N35 96w49 6:27:16
Grant Center 25 1 45N12 96w42 6:26:48
Great Bend 58 1 44N56 98w25 6:33:40
Greenfield 6 1 45N49 98w17 6:33:08
Greenfield 13 1 42N45 96w50 6:27:20
Green Grass 20 3 45N10 101w15 6:45:00
Greenland 43 1 43N37 97w11 6:28:44
Greenleaf 29 1 44N35 99w07 6:36:28
Green Valley 48 1 44N04 97w40 6:30:40
Greenway 1 45N55 99w43 6:38:52
Greenwood 11 1 43N04 98w18 6:33:12
Greenwood 61 1 43N38 100w02 6:40:08
Gregory 26 1 43N14 99w26 6:37:44
Grenville 18 1 45N28 97w23 6:29:32
Groton 6 1 45N27 98w06 6:32:24
Grouse Creek 42 1 43N59 99w57 6:39:48
Groveland 57 1 44N56 98w40 6:34:40
Grovena 50 1 43N59 96w35 6:26:20
Grover 14 1 44N54 97w07 6:28:28
Hague 12 1 44N40 97w47 6:31:08
Hall 52 3 45N20 102w32 6:50:08
Hamill 61 1 43N36 99w41 6:38:44
Hamlin 28 1 44N46 96w57 6:27:48
Hammer 54 1 45N51 96w55 6:27:40
Hancock 4 1 42N52 98w03 6:32:12
Hanna 40 3 44N21 103w46 6:55:04
Hanson 30 1 43N43 97w54 6:31:36
Harmon 54 1 45N47 96w43 6:26:52
Harrington 3 3 43N10 101w15 6:45:00
Harrisburg 41 1 43N26 96w42 6:26:48
Harrison 21 1 43N26 98w32 6:34:08
Harrold 32 1 44N31 99w44 6:38:56
Hart 54 1 45N47 96w55 6:27:40
Hartford 49 1 43N38 96w57 6:27:48
Hartford Beach 54 1 45N20 96w46 6:27:04
Havana 19 1 44N46 96w49 6:27:16
Hayes 58 3 44N22 101w01 6:44:04
Hayti 28 1 44N40 97w13 6:28:52
Hayward Addition 49 1 43N31 96w42 6:26:48
Hazel 28 1 44N46 97w23 6:29:32
Hecla 6 1 45N53 98w09 6:32:36
Henden 48 1 44N04 97w26 6:29:44
Henry 14 1 44N53 97w28 6:29:52
Hereford 46 3 44N23 102w54 6:51:36
Herman 39 1 43N59 97w11 6:28:44
Hermosa 16 3 43N50 103w12 6:52:48
Herreid 10 1 45N50 100w04 6:40:16
Herrick 26 1 43N07 99w11 6:36:44
Herried 1 45N50 100w04 6:40:16
Hetland 38 1 44N23 97w14 6:28:56
Hiawatha Beach 54 1 45N25 96w52 6:27:28
Hickman 45 1 45N38 97w48 6:31:12
Hidden Timber 4 43N14 100w25 6:41:40
Hidewood 19 1 44N40 96w50 6:27:20
Highmore 34 1 44N31 99w27 6:37:48
Hiland 29 1 44N19 98w53 6:35:32
Hill City 51 3 43N56 103w35 6:54:20
Hillhead 45 1 45N52 97w17 6:29:08
Hillsdale 24 1 44N56 98w54 6:35:36
Hillside 21 1 43N25 98w25 6:33:40
Hillside 22 1 45N17 99w24 6:37:36
Hillside Colony 57 1 44N54 98w06 6:32:24
Hillsview 44 1 45N40 99w34 6:38:16
Hilmoe 42 1 43N48 100w10 6:40:40
Hisega 51 3 44N06 103w09 6:52:36
Hisle 65 3 43N24 101w45 6:47:00
Hitchcock 2 1 44N38 98w25 6:33:40
Hoffman 44 1 45N50 99w03 6:36:12
Holabird 34 1 44N32 99w36 6:38:24
Holden 29 1 44N40 98w53 6:35:32
Holland 21 1 43N28 98w32 6:34:08
Holmquist 18 1 45N20 97w31 6:30:04
Holsclaw 61 1 43N08 100w10 6:40:40
Home 62 1 43N28 96w59 6:27:56
Homer 18 1 45N32 97w48 6:31:12
Hooker 62 1 43N10 97w05 6:28:20
Hoover 9 3 45N07 103w16 6:53:04
Hope 42 1 43N59 100w18 6:41:12
Hopper 1 1 43N43 98w22 6:33:28
Horse Creek 52 3 45N53 102w53 6:51:32
Hosmer 22 1 45N34 99w28 6:37:52
Hot Springs 23 3 43N26 103w29 6:53:56
Houghton 6 1 45N46 98w13 6:32:52
Hoven 53 1 45N15 99w47 6:39:08
Howard 48 1 44N01 97w32 6:30:08
Howell 29 1 44N46 99w00 6:36:00
Howes 46 3 44N37 102w03 6:48:12
Hub City 13 1 42N46 96w55 6:27:40
Hudgins 52 3 45N41 102w07 6:48:28
Hudson 41 1 43N08 96w27 6:25:48
Huffton 6 1 45N40 98w01 6:32:04
Huggins 61 1 43N02 100w05 6:40:20
Hulbert 29 1 44N25 98w45 6:35:00
Humboldt 49 1 43N39 97w05 6:28:20
Huntley 22 1 45N28 99w09 6:36:36
Hurley 62 1 43N17 97w05 6:28:20
Huron 2 1 44N22 98w13 6:32:52
Huron Colony 2 1 44N21 98w13 6:32:52
Ideal 61 1 43N33 99w54 6:39:36
Igloo 3 43N12 103w52 6:55:28
Illinois 34 1 44N46 99w29 6:37:56
Imlay 51 3 43N45 102w22 6:49:28
Indian Creek 35 3 43N57 101w23 6:45:32
Interior 35 3 43N44 101w59 6:47:56
Iona 42 1 43N33 99w26 6:37:44
Ipswich 22 1 45N27 99w02 6:36:08
Irene 13 1 43N05 97w10 6:28:40
Iron Lightning 67 3 45N03 101w36 6:46:24
Iroquois 38 1 44N22 97w51 6:31:24
Irwin 61 1 43N18 99w36 6:38:24
Isabel 20 3 45N24 101w26 6:45:44
James 6 1 45N27 98w06 6:32:24
Jamesville 66 1 43N08 97w27 6:29:48
Jasper 30 1 43N43 97w47 6:31:08
Java 64 1 45N30 99w53 6:39:32
Jefferson 63 1 42N36 96w34 6:26:16
Jewett 35 3 43N57 101w34 6:46:16
Johnson Siding 51 3 44N06 103w09 6:52:36
Jones 26 1 43N07 99w21 6:37:24
Jordan 61 1 43N23 100w04 6:40:16
Joubert 21 1 43N28 98w39 6:34:36
Junction City 63 1 42N45 96w50 6:27:20
Junius 39 1 44N00 97w15 6:29:00
Kadoka 35 3 43N50 101w31 6:46:04
Kampeska 14 1 44N51 97w18 6:29:12
Kassel 33 1 43N18 97w34 6:30:16
Kaylor 33 1 43N11 97w50 6:31:20
Keldron 15 3 45N56 101w48 6:47:12
Kellogg 2 1 44N14 98w31 6:34:04
Kenel 15 3 45N55 100w29 6:41:56
Kennebec 42 1 43N54 99w52 6:39:28
Kennedy 11 1 43N13 98w18 6:33:12
Kent 22 1 45N17 98w54 6:35:36
Keyapaha 61 1 43N07 100w08 6:40:32
Keystone 51 3 43N54 103w25 6:53:40

Kidder 45 1 45N53 97w43 6:30:52
Kilborn 25 1 45N17 96w48 6:27:12
Kimball 7 1 43N45 98w57 6:35:48
King 61 1 43N33 99w48 6:39:12
Kingsburg 4 1 42N51 97w54 6:31:36
Kirley 3 44N32 101w19 6:45:16
Kolls 37 1 44N02 100w38 6:42:32
Kones Corner 28 1 44N44 97w02 6:28:08
Kosciusko 18 1 45N30 97w17 6:29:08
Kranzburg 14 1 44N54 96w55 6:27:40
Kulm 33 1 43N18 98w03 6:32:12
Kyle 56 3 43N26 102w10 6:48:40
La Belle 45 1 45N53 97w25 6:29:40
La Bolt 25 1 45N03 96w41 6:26:44
Ladner 3 45N50 103w44 6:54:56
Ladner 31 3 43N26 102w10 6:48:40
Lafayette 42 1 43N59 99w35 6:38:20
Lafoon 24 1 45N02 99w01 6:36:04
Lake Andes 11 1 43N09 98w32 6:34:08
Lake Byron 2 1 44N35 98w10 6:32:40
Lake Campbell 50 1 44N19 96w47 6:27:08
Lake City 45 1 45N44 97w25 6:29:40
Lake Creek 51 3 44N02 102w04 6:48:16
Lake Flat 51 3 44N02 102w18 6:49:12
Lake George 11 1 43N28 99w00 6:36:00
Lake Hendricks 5 1 44N29 96w29 6:25:56
Lake Hill 51 3 44N02 102w11 6:48:44
Lake Norden 28 1 44N35 97w13 6:28:52
Lake Preston 38 1 44N22 97w23 6:29:32
Lakeside 46 3 44N11 102w35 6:50:20
Lake Sinai 5 1 44N15 97w04 6:28:16
Laketon 5 1 44N30 97w04 6:28:16
Lake View 39 1 43N59 97w04 6:28:16
Lamro 61 1 43N23 99w50 6:39:20
Landing Creek 26 1 43N17 98w37 6:34:28
Lane 36 1 44N04 98w26 6:33:44
Langford 45 1 45N36 97w50 6:31:20
Lansing 6 1 45N48 98w09 6:32:36
Lantry 20 3 45N01 101w26 6:45:44
La Plant 20 3 45N09 100w39 6:42:36
La Prairie 57 1 45N13 98w22 6:33:28
La Roche 11 1 43N28 99w07 6:36:28
La Valley 41 1 43N23 96w45 6:27:00
Lead 40 3 44N21 103w46 6:55:04
Lebanon 53 1 45N04 99w46 6:39:04
Lee 54 1 45N27 96w54 6:27:36
Lemmon 52 3 45N57 102w10 6:48:40
Lennox 41 1 43N21 96w53 6:27:32
Leola 44 1 45N43 98w56 6:35:44
Le Roy 39 1 44N04 97w04 6:28:16
Lesterville 66 1 43N02 97w35 6:30:20
Le Sueur 38 1 44N30 97w46 6:31:04
Letcher 55 1 43N54 98w08 6:32:32
Lien 54 1 45N53 96w55 6:27:40
Lily 18 1 45N11 97w41 6:30:44
Limestone 23 3 43N10 103w11 6:52:44
Linden Beach 54 1 45N20 96w46 6:27:04
Linn 29 1 44N51 98w53 6:35:32
Lisbon 17 1 43N38 98w09 6:32:36
Little Buffalo 35
3 43N52 101w51 6:47:24
Little Oak 15 3 45N31 101w10 6:44:40
Lockwood 54 1 45N22 96w34 6:26:16
Lodgepole 52 3 45N48 102w40 6:50:40
Lodi 57 1 44N51 98w24 6:33:36
Lone Rock 50 1 43N53 96w29 6:25:56
Lone Tree 50 1 44N00 96w39 6:26:36
Long Hollow 54 1 45N41 97w10 6:28:40
Longlake 44 1 45N51 99w12 6:36:48
Long Lake Colony 44
1 45N38 98w46 6:35:04
Longvalley 65 3 43N28 101w30 6:46:00
Loomer 23 3 43N02 103w08 6:52:32
Loomis 17 1 43N48 98w06 6:32:24
Lowe 19 1 44N56 96w35 6:26:20
Lower Brule 1 44N05 99w34 6:38:16
Lower Brule Indian Res 42
1 44N22 100w20 6:41:20
Lowry 64 1 45N19 99w59 6:39:56
Loyalton 22 1 45N17 99w17 6:37:08
Lucas 26 1 43N17 99w13 6:36:52
Ludlow 31 3 45N50 103w23 6:53:32
Lund 42 1 43N59 100w11 6:40:44
Lura 25 1 45N11 97w07 6:28:28
Lyman 1 43N53 99w44 6:38:56
Lyon 7 1 43N53 98w59 6:35:56
Lyons 49 1 43N43 96w50 6:27:20
Madison 39 1 44N00 97w07 6:28:28
Madsen Beach 54 1 45N25 96w52 6:27:28
Mahto 15 3 45N46 100w39 6:42:36
Maltby 52 3 45N26 102w45 6:51:00
Manchester 38 1 44N23 97w41 6:30:44
Manderson 56 3 43N14 102w28 6:49:52
Mansfield 57 1 45N15 98w34 6:34:16
Mapleton 49 1 43N38 96w42 6:26:48
Marcus 46 3 44N40 102w17 6:49:08
Marcy Colony 33 1 43N24 97w59 6:31:56
Marindahl 66 1 43N02 97w13 6:28:52
Marion 62 1 43N25 97w16 6:29:04
Marlar 36 1 44N09 98w52 6:35:28
Marlow 45 1 45N52 97w17 6:29:08
Marshfield 52 3 45N36 102w27 6:49:48
Martin 3 3 43N11 101w44 6:46:56
Marty 11 1 43N00 98w26 6:33:44
Marvin 25 1 45N16 96w55 6:27:40
Mathews 38 1 44N15 97w34 6:30:16
Mattison 27 3 44N18 101w20 6:45:20
Maurine 46 3 45N01 102w36 6:50:24
Maxwell Colony 33
1 43N09 97w43 6:30:52
Maydell 12 1 45N01 97w33 6:30:12
Mayfield 66 1 43N07 97w20 6:29:20
Mazeppa 25 1 45N12 96w58 6:27:52
McClure 42 1 44N09 100w11 6:40:44
McCook Lake 63 1 42N36 96w34 6:26:16
McIntosh 15 3 45N55 101w21 6:45:24
McKinley 45 1 45N47 97w17 6:29:08
McLaughlin 15 3 45N49 100w49 6:43:16
McNeely 61 1 43N12 99w50 6:39:20
Meadow 52 3 45N32 102w13 6:48:52
Meckling 13 1 42N51 97w04 6:28:16
Medary 5 1 44N15 96w49 6:27:16
Media 36 1 44N04 98w38 6:34:32
Mellette 57 1 45N09 98w30 6:34:00
Melrose 25 1 45N17 96w40 6:26:40
Menno 33 1 43N14 97w34 6:30:16
Mercier 6 1 45N28 98w40 6:34:40
Merton 12 1 44N46 97w39 6:30:36
Middleton 62 1 43N18 96w59 6:27:56
Midland 27 3 44N04 101w10 6:44:40
Midway 66 1 43N05 97w10 6:28:40
Milbank 25 1 45N13 96w38 6:26:32
Milesville 27 3 44N28 101w41 6:46:44
Milford 2 1 44N35 98w02 6:32:08
Millboro 61 1 43N04 99w58 6:39:52
Miller 29 1 44N31 98w59 6:35:56
Miller Dale Colony 29
1 44N31 98w59 6:35:56
Milltown 33 1 43N25 97w48 6:31:12
Mina 22 1 45N26 98w45 6:35:00
Miner 48 1 44N04 97w47 6:31:08
Minnesota 54 1 45N53 97w02 6:28:08
Miranda 24 1 44N58 98w58 6:35:52
Mission 60 4 43N18 100w39 6:42:36
Mission Hill 66 1 42N55 97w17 6:29:08
Mission Ridge 58 4 44N41 100w46 6:43:04
Mitchell 17 1 43N43 98w02 6:32:08
Mobridge 64 1 45N32 100w26 6:41:44
Modena 22 1 45N33 99w39 6:38:36
Molan 33 1 43N13 97w27 6:29:48
Mondamin 29 1 44N16 99w05 6:36:20
Monroe 62 1 43N29 97w13 6:28:52
Montpelier 22 1 45N23 99w16 6:37:04
Montrose 43 1 43N42 97w11 6:28:44
Moreau 52 3 45N13 102w17 6:49:08
Morgan 37 3 43N57 101w00 6:44:00
Morningside 2 1 44N21 98w13 6:32:52
Morningside 42 1 43N34 99w35 6:38:20
Morristown 15 3 45N56 101w43 6:46:52
Morton 18 1 45N17 97w26 6:29:44
Mosher 47 4 43N28 100w18 6:41:12
Mound City 10 1 45N44 100w04 6:40:16
Mount Pleasant 12
1 44N56 97w40 6:30:40
Mount Vernon 17 1 43N43 98w16 6:33:04
Mud Butte 46 3 45N00 102w54 6:51:36
Mullen 37 3 43N46 100w45 6:43:00
Murdo 37 1 43N53 100w43 6:42:52
Mussman 37 1 43N57 100w25 6:41:40
Myron 24 1 45N07 99w01 6:36:04
Mystic 51 3 43N56 103w34 6:54:16
Nance 2 1 44N35 98w41 6:34:44
Naples 12 1 44N46 97w31 6:30:04
Navan 15 3 45N52 101w23 6:45:32
Nemo 40 3 44N12 103w30 6:54:00
Newark 45 1 45N54 97w48 6:31:12
New Effington 54 1 45N51 96w55 6:27:40
Newell 9 3 44N43 103w25 6:53:40
New Elm Springs Colony 33
1 43N33 97w59 6:31:56
New Holland 21 1 43N26 98w36 6:34:24
New Hope 6 1 45N17 98w40 6:34:40
Newport 45 1 45N38 97w55 6:31:40
New Underwood 51 3 44N06 102w50 6:51:20
New Witten 61 1 43N26 100w05 6:40:20
Nisland 9 3 44N40 103w33 6:54:12
Nora 63 1 43N01 96w38 6:26:32
Norbeck 24 1 45N10 99w07 6:36:28
Nordland 45 1 45N50 97w31 6:30:04
Norris 47 3 43N28 101w12 6:44:48
North Bryant 22 1 45N33 99w16 6:37:04
North Detroit 6 1 45N48 98w02 6:32:08
North Eagle Butte 20
3 45N00 101w13 6:44:52
North Riverside 53
1 45N12 100w13 6:40:52
North Sioux City 63
1 42N32 96w29 6:25:56
Northville 57 1 45N09 98w35 6:34:20
Norton Acres 49 1 43N31 96w42 6:26:48
Nowlin 3 44N03 101w18 6:45:12
Nunda 39 1 44N10 97w01 6:28:04
Nutley 18 1 45N33 97w26 6:29:44
Oacoma 42 1 43N48 99w24 6:37:36
Oak Gulch 18 1 45N11 97w56 6:31:44
Oak Hollow 33 1 43N13 98w02 6:32:08
Oak Lake 5 1 44N30 96w35 6:26:20
Oakwood 5 1 44N25 96w56 6:27:44
Odessa 22 1 45N23 99w39 6:38:36
Oelrichs 23 3 43N11 103w14 6:52:56
Oglala 56 3 43N17 102w44 6:50:56
Ohio 29 1 44N19 98w59 6:35:56
Okaton 37 3 43N53 100w53 6:43:32
Okreek 60 4 43N22 100w23 6:41:32
Ola 7 1 43N37 99w12 6:36:48
Oldham 38 1 44N14 97w19 6:29:16
Olean 57 1 45N08 98w02 6:32:08
Olivet 33 1 43N14 97w40 6:30:40
Olsonville 60 4 42N52 100w33 6:42:12
Onaka 24 1 45N12 99w28 6:37:52
Oneida 55 1 44N04 98w02 6:32:08
O'neil 24 1 45N07 99w23 6:37:32
Oneota 6 1 45N43 98w32 6:34:08
One Road 54 1 45N33 97w08 6:28:32
Onida 59 1 44N42 100w04 6:40:16
Ontario 29 1 44N46 99w14 6:36:56
Opal 46 3 44N54 102w30 6:50:00
Opdahl 28 1 44N40 97w19 6:29:16
Oral 23 3 43N24 103w16 6:53:04
Ordway 6 1 45N33 98w25 6:33:40
Orient 24 1 44N54 99w05 6:36:20
Orland 39 1 43N54 97w11 6:28:44
Ortley 54 1 45N20 97w12 6:28:48
Osceola 38 1 44N28 97w50 6:31:20
Oslo 5 1 44N15 96w56 6:27:44
Ottumwa 27 3 44N14 101w21 6:45:24
Owanka 51 3 44N01 102w35 6:50:20
Owattonna 53 1 44N57 100w00 6:40:00
Oxford 28 1 44N45 97w13 6:28:52
Pahapesto 61 1 43N38 100w10 6:40:40
Palatine 1 1 43N48 98w23 6:33:32
Palisade 49 1 43N43 96w28 6:25:52
Palmyra 6 1 45N54 98w40 6:34:40
Parade 20 3 45N02 101w06 6:44:24
Park 29 1 44N51 98w59 6:35:56
Parker 62 1 43N24 97w08 6:28:32
Parkston 33 1 43N24 97w59 6:31:56
Parmelee 60 3 43N19 101w02 6:44:08
Parnell 5 1 44N14 96w35 6:26:20
Patricia 3 3 43N11 101w44 6:46:56
Patten 1 1 43N54 98w44 6:34:56
Pearl Creek 2 1 44N14 98w02 6:32:08
Pearl Creek Colony 2
1 44N22 97w51 6:31:24
Pearsons Corner 66
1 43N10 97w05 6:28:20
Pedro 51 3 44N15 102w12 6:48:48
Peever 54 1 45N33 96w57 6:27:48
Pelican 14 1 44N51 97w11 6:28:44
Pembrook 22 1 45N33 98w49 6:35:16
Peninsula Park 39
1 44N00 96w58 6:27:52
Perkins 4 1 42N51 97w54 6:31:36
Philip 27 3 44N02 101w40 6:46:40
Phipps 14 1 45N01 97w26 6:29:44
Pickerel 18 1 45N28 97w23 6:29:32
Pickstown 11 1 43N04 98w32 6:34:08
Piedmont 46 3 44N14 103w24 6:53:36
Pierpont 18 1 45N30 97w50 6:31:20
Pierre 32 1 44N22 100w21 6:41:24
Pine Creek 47 4 43N31 100w52 6:43:28
Pine Ridge 56 3 43N02 102w33 6:50:12
Pine Ridge Indian Res 3
3 43N01 102w33 6:50:12
Plain Center 11 1 43N08 98w24 6:33:36
Plainfield 7 1 43N43 98w51 6:35:24
Plainview 3 44N36 102w10 6:48:40
Plainview 46 3 43N01 102w33 6:50:12
Plainview Colony 22
1 45N27 99w02 6:36:08
Plankinton 1 1 43N43 98w29 6:33:56
Plano 30 1 43N48 97w54 6:31:36
Plateau 52 3 45N31 102w53 6:51:32
Plato 29 1 44N51 98w46 6:35:04
Platte 11 1 43N23 98w51 6:35:24
Pleasant Grove 7 1 43N32 98w58 6:35:52
Pleasant Lake 1 1 43N38 98w30 6:34:00
Pleasant Ridge 15
3 45N31 101w24 6:45:36
Pluma 40 3 44N23 103w44 6:54:56
Plummer 7 1 43N53 98w51 6:35:24
Pollock 10 1 45N55 100w17 6:41:08
Polo 29 1 44N54 99w05 6:36:20
Porcupine 56 3 43N14 102w20 6:49:20
Portage 6 1 45N54 98w04 6:32:16
Portland 19 1 44N56 96w42 6:26:48
Potato Creek 65 3 43N32 102w00 6:48:00
Powell 22 1 45N17 99w02 6:36:08
Prairie 63 1 43N02 96w45 6:27:00
Prairie City 52 3 45N32 102w48 6:51:12
Prairie View 15 3 45N52 101w31 6:46:04
Presho 42 1 43N54 100w04 6:40:16
Preston 5 1 44N30 96w57 6:27:48
Pringle 16 3 43N37 103w36 6:54:24
Progressive 61 1 43N27 100w10 6:40:40
Prospect 47 3 43N41 101w05 6:44:20
Prosper 17 1 43N38 98w01 6:32:04
Provo 23 3 43N12 103w50 6:55:20
Pukwana 7 1 43N47 99w11 6:36:44
Pulaski 24 1 45N07 99w08 6:36:32
Pumpkin Center 49
1 43N39 97w05 6:28:20
Pure Water 47 4 43N27 100w37 6:42:28
Putney 6 1 45N34 98w11 6:32:44
Quinn 51 3 43N59 102w08 6:48:32
Quinn Table 51 3 44N00 102w14 6:48:56
Raber 32 1 44N18 99w51 6:39:24
Racine 18 1 45N22 97w25 6:29:40
Rainbow 52 3 45N31 102w24 6:49:36
Rainy Creek 51 3 44N18 102w11 6:48:44
Ralph 31 3 45N46 103w04 6:52:16
Rames 61 1 43N02 99w49 6:39:16
Ramona 39 1 44N07 97w13 6:28:52
Ramsey 43 1 43N48 97w11 6:28:44
Randolph 6 1 45N19 98w18 6:33:12
Rapid City 51 3 44N05 103w14 6:52:56
Raritan 18 1 45N27 97w33 6:30:12
Rauville 14 1 45N01 97w05 6:28:20
Ravenna 55 1 43N54 97w54 6:31:36
Ravinia 11 1 43N08 98w26 6:33:44
Raymond 12 1 44N55 97w56 6:31:44
Red Elm 67 3 45N05 101w48 6:47:12
Redfield 57 1 44N53 98w31 6:34:04
Red Fish 47 4 43N48 101w00 6:44:00
Redig 31 3 45N16 103w33 6:54:12
Red Iron Lake 45 1 45N41 97w17 6:29:08
Red Lake 7 1 43N43 99w11 6:36:44
Redowl 46 3 44N42 102w33 6:50:12
Red Rock 49 1 43N38 96w28 6:25:52
Red Scaffold 67 3 44N37 102w03 6:48:12
Red Shirt 56 3 43N40 102w54 6:51:36
Redstone 48 1 44N09 97w47 6:31:08
Ree 11 1 42N56 98w17 6:33:08
Ree Heights 29 1 44N31 99w12 6:36:48
Reliance 42 1 43N53 99w36 6:38:24

SOUTH DAKOTA

Place	Zone	Lat	Long	Time
Renel Heights 51	3	44N10	103w06	6:52:24
Renner 49	1	43N39	96w43	6:26:52
Reva 31	3	45N33	103w05	6:52:20
Revillo 25	1	45N01	96w34	6:26:16
Rex 42	1	43N53	99w42	6:38:48
Rhoades 26	1	43N13	99w20	6:37:20
Rhoda 11	1	43N18	98w45	6:35:00
Richfield 57	1	44N50	98w02	6:32:08
Richland 63	1	42N46	96w39	6:26:36
Rich Valley 37	1	44N02	100w25	6:41:40
Ridgeland 15	3	45N31	100w36	6:42:24
Ridgeview 20	3	45N05	100w48	6:43:12
Ring Thunder 47	4	43N26	100w52	6:43:28
Riverside 30	1	43N43	98w02	6:32:08
Riverside Colony 2	1	44N21	98w13	6:32:52
Riverview 50	1	44N09	96w43	6:26:52
Robins 23	3	43N16	103w11	6:52:44
Rochford 51	3	44N07	103w43	6:54:52
Rock Creek 48	1	43N53	97w40	6:30:40
Rockdale 29	1	44N25	99w06	6:36:24
Rockerville 51	3	43N58	103w21	6:53:24
Rockford 52	3	45N42	102w23	6:49:32
Rockham 24	1	44N55	98w49	6:35:16
Rockport 30	1	43N39	97w47	6:31:08
Rocky Ford 47	3	43N36	101w08	6:44:32
Rolling Green 15	3	45N47	101w54	6:47:36
Roscoe 22	1	45N27	99w20	6:37:20
Rose 42	1	43N48	99w55	6:39:40
Rosebud 60	4	43N14	100w51	6:43:24
Rosebud Indian Reservation 26	3	43N14	100w51	6:43:24
Rosedale Colony 30	1	43N43	98w02	6:32:08
Rosefield 62	1	43N23	97w20	6:29:20
Rose Hill 29	1	44N19	98w45	6:35:00
Roseland 61	1	43N38	99w40	6:38:40
Rosette 22	1	45N33	99w03	6:36:12
Rosholt 54	2	45N52	96w44	6:26:56
Roslyn 18	1	45N30	97w29	6:29:56
Roswell 48	1	44N00	97w42	6:30:48
Rouse 11	1	42N56	98w10	6:32:40
Rowe 42	1	44N09	100w19	6:41:16
Rowena 49	1	43N31	96w33	6:26:12
Roy 53	1	45N01	99w46	6:39:04
Rumford 23	3	43N08	103w42	6:54:48
Rumpus Ridge 43	1	43N36	97w18	6:29:12
Running Bird 47	4	43N36	101w00	6:44:00
Running Water 4	1	42N48	98w01	6:32:04
Rusk 18	1	45N17	97w33	6:30:12
Rutland 39	1	44N05	96w58	6:27:52
Saint Charles 26	1	43N05	99w06	6:36:24
Saint Francis 60	4	43N09	100w54	6:43:36
Saint Lawrence 29	1	44N31	98w56	6:35:44
Saint Onge 40	3	44N33	103w43	6:54:52
Salem 43	1	43N44	97w23	6:29:32
Sand Creek 2	1	44N20	98w38	6:34:32
Sangamon 22	1	45N33	99w24	6:37:36
Sanner 53	1	45N01	100w07	6:40:28
Saratoga 24	1	45N07	99w16	6:37:04
Savo 6	1	45N54	98w25	6:33:40
Savoy 40	3	44N21	103w46	6:55:04
Scandinavia 19	1	44N35	96w32	6:26:08
Scenic 51	3	43N47	102w33	6:50:12
Schriever 26	1	43N07	98w58	6:35:52
Scotch Cap 52	3	45N31	102w39	6:50:36
Scotland 4	1	43N09	97w43	6:30:52
Scovil 37	1	43N57	100w53	6:43:32
Seim 52	3	45N46	102w15	6:49:00
Selby 64	1	45N31	100w02	6:40:08
Seneca 24	1	45N04	99w31	6:38:04
Seven Mile Corner	3	43N50	101w40	6:46:40
Shadehill 52	3	45N46	102w11	6:48:44
Shady Beach 54	1	45N20	96w46	6:27:04
Sharon 33	1	43N18	97w49	6:31:16
Shelby 6	1	45N42	98w11	6:32:44
Sheridan 14	1	44N51	97w04	6:28:16
Sherman 49	1	43N45	96w28	6:25:52
Shyne 51	3	44N06	102w26	6:49:44
Sidney 52	3	45N42	102w46	6:51:04
Signal 11	1	43N17	98w52	6:35:28
Silver City 51	3	44N05	103w34	6:54:16
Silver Creek 55	1	44N04	98w09	6:32:36
Silverlake 33	1	43N28	97w28	6:29:52
Sinai 5	1	44N15	97w03	6:28:12
Sioux 42	1	43N46	100w17	6:41:08
Sioux Falls 49	1	43N33	96w44	6:26:56
Sioux Valley 63	1	42N52	96w37	6:26:28
Sisseton 54	1	45N40	97w03	6:28:12
Sisseton Indian Reservation 14	1	45N40	97w03	6:28:12
Skyway 51	3	44N10	103w06	6:52:24
Slim Butte 23	3	43N05	103w11	6:52:44
Smith 7	1	43N43	99w05	6:36:20
Smiths Park 39	1	44N00	96w58	6:27:52
Smithwick 23	3	43N18	103w13	6:52:52
So Dak Park 54	1	45N25	96w52	6:27:28
Soldier Creek 60	4	43N18	100w39	6:42:36
Sorum 52	3	45N27	102w56	6:51:44
South Creek 37	3	44N03	100w59	6:43:56
South Detroit 6	1	45N43	98w02	6:32:08
South Forest City 53	1	44N57	100w21	6:41:24
South Riverside 53	1	45N07	100w15	6:41:00
South Shore 14	1	45N07	96w56	6:27:44
Spearfish 40	3	44N30	103w52	6:55:28
Spencer 43	1	43N44	97w36	6:30:24
Spink 63	1	42N51	96w45	6:27:00
Spink Colony 57	1	44N52	98w18	6:33:12
Spirit Lake 38	1	44N30	97w35	6:30:20
Spirit Mound 13	1	42N52	96w57	6:27:48
Split Rock 49	1	43N32	96w35	6:26:20
Spring Creek 50	1	44N09	96w35	6:26:20
Spring Creek 60	4	43N09	100w54	6:43:36
Springfield 4	1	42N49	97w54	6:31:36
Spring Grove 54	1	45N28	97w03	6:28:12
Spring Hill 29	1	44N25	99w14	6:36:56
Spring Valley 62	1	43N17	97w05	6:28:20
Spring Valley Colony 36	1	44N05	98w34	6:34:16
Standing Rock Indian Res 15	3	45N00	101w13	6:44:52
Stanley Corner 43	1	43N30	97w23	6:29:32
Star 13	1	43N03	97w05	6:28:20
Star Prairie 61	1	43N13	100w05	6:40:20
Starr 33	1	43N28	98w03	6:32:12
Stena 45	1	45N48	97w54	6:31:36
Stephan 34	1	44N15	99w27	6:37:48
Sterling 5	1	44N25	96w49	6:27:16
Stewart 61	1	43N07	99w43	6:38:52
Stickney 1	1	43N35	98w26	6:33:44
Stockholm 25	1	45N06	96w48	6:27:12
Stone Bridge 28	1	44N44	97w02	6:28:08
Stoneville 46	3	44N44	102w39	6:50:36
Stony Butte 42	1	44N04	100w18	6:41:12
Storla 1	1	43N52	98w21	6:33:24
Strandburg 25	1	45N03	96w46	6:27:04
Stratford 6	1	45N19	98w18	6:33:12
Strool 52	3	45N31	102w46	6:51:04
Sturgis 46	3	44N25	103w31	6:54:04
Sully 61	1	43N23	99w36	6:38:24
Summit 54	1	45N18	97w02	6:28:08
Sumner 57	1	45N01	98w10	6:32:40
Sunnyside 51	3	44N13	102w18	6:49:12
Sunnyview 5	1	44N19	96w47	6:27:08
Sun Prairie 43	1	43N48	97w27	6:29:48
Surprise Valley 47	3	43N29	101w01	6:44:04
Susquehanna 33	1	43N23	98w04	6:32:16
Sverdrup 49	1	43N43	96w42	6:26:48
Swan Lake 62	1	43N13	97w06	6:28:24
Sweet 33	1	43N13	97w35	6:30:20
Swett 3	3	43N11	101w44	6:46:56
Sylvia 42	1	43N44	100w02	6:40:08
Table Mountain 31	3	45N53	103w37	6:54:28
Tabor 4	1	42N57	97w40	6:30:40
Tacoma Park 6	1	45N37	98w19	6:33:16
Tamworth 24	1	45N01	99w09	6:36:36
Taopi 49	1	43N48	96w58	6:27:52
Tea 41	1	43N27	96w50	6:27:20
Terraville 40	3	44N22	103w46	6:55:04
Tetonka 57	1	45N07	98w18	6:33:12
Theresa 2	1	44N25	98w17	6:33:08
Thomas 28	1	44N40	97w12	6:28:48
Thorp 12	1	45N01	97w41	6:30:44
Three Rivers 57	1	44N57	98w31	6:34:04
Thunder Butte 67	3	45N13	101w40	6:46:40
Thunder Hawk 15	3	45N53	101w54	6:47:36
Tilford 46	3	44N18	103w26	6:53:44
Timber Lake 20	3	45N26	101w05	6:44:20
Tobin 17	1	43N33	98w09	6:32:36
Tolstoy 53	1	45N13	99w36	6:38:24
Toronto 19	1	44N34	96w39	6:26:36
Torrey Lake 7	1	43N33	98w50	6:35:20
Tracy 42	1	44N04	100w11	6:40:44
Trail 52	3	45N55	102w16	6:49:04
Trail City 20	3	45N28	100w44	6:42:56
Trent 50	1	43N54	96w39	6:26:36
Trenton 5	1	44N15	96w42	6:26:48
Tripp 33	1	43N13	97w58	6:31:52
Troy 25	1	45N02	96w52	6:27:28
Truro 1	1	43N32	98w30	6:34:00
Tschetter Colony 33	1	43N22	97w41	6:30:44
Tulare 57	1	44N44	98w31	6:34:04
Turkey Ridge 62	1	43N17	97w05	6:28:20
Turkey Valley 66	1	43N07	97w13	6:28:52
Turner 62	1	43N13	96w59	6:27:56
Turton 57	1	45N03	98w06	6:32:24
Tuthill 3	3	43N09	101w30	6:46:00
Twin 31	3	45N53	103w00	6:52:00
Twin Brooks 25	1	45N12	96w47	6:27:08
Twin Butte 15	3	45N31	101w56	6:47:44
Twin Lake 55	1	43N59	98w16	6:33:04
Tyndall 4	1	43N00	97w52	6:31:28
Union Center 46	3	44N34	102w40	6:50:40
Unityville 43	1	43N48	97w27	6:29:48
University 5	1	44N19	96w47	6:27:08
Upper Red Owl 46	3	44N44	102w39	6:50:36
Usta 52	3	45N01	102w02	6:48:08
Utica 66	1	42N59	97w30	6:30:00
Vail 52	3	45N36	102w46	6:51:04
Vale 9	3	44N37	103w24	6:53:36
Valley Springs 49	1	43N35	96w28	6:25:52
Valley View 66	1	42N57	97w11	6:28:44
Van Metre 37	3	44N07	100w44	6:42:56
Van Order 34	1	44N25	99w21	6:37:24
Vayland 29	1	44N27	98w42	6:34:48
Veblen 45	1	45N52	97w17	6:29:08
Vedin Corner 66	1	43N05	97w10	6:28:40
Verdon 6	1	45N15	98w06	6:32:24
Vermillion 13	1	42N47	96w56	6:27:44
Vermont 22	1	45N17	99w16	6:37:04
Vessey 31	3	45N53	103w08	6:52:32
Vetal 3	3	43N13	101w23	6:45:32
Viborg 62	1	43N10	97w05	6:28:20
Vickers 52	3	45N26	102w31	6:50:04
Victor 54	1	45N52	96w44	6:26:56
Vienna 12	1	44N42	97w30	6:30:00
Viewfield 46	3	44N06	102w50	6:51:20
Viking 52	3	45N53	102w45	6:51:00
Vilas 48	1	44N01	97w36	6:30:24
Villa Ranchaero 51	3	44N08	103w04	6:52:16
Villa Trailer Court 51	3	44N10	103w06	6:52:24
Viola 36	1	43N59	98w30	6:34:00
Virgil 2	1	44N17	98w25	6:33:40
Virginia 63	1	43N00	96w32	6:26:08
Vivian 42	1	43N56	100w18	6:41:12
Volga 5	1	44N19	96w56	6:27:44
Volin 66	1	42N58	97w11	6:28:44
Volunteer 46	3	44N25	103w31	6:54:04
Vrooman 52	3	45N05	102w46	6:51:04
Wachter 44	1	45N54	98w47	6:35:08
Wacker 44	1	45N54	99w02	6:36:08
Wagner 11	1	43N05	98w18	6:33:12
Wahehe 11	1	42N58	98w24	6:33:36
Wakonda 13	1	43N00	97w06	6:28:24
Wakpala 15	3	45N40	100w32	6:42:08
Waldro 7	1	43N48	98w58	6:35:52
Walker 15	3	45N55	101w05	6:44:20
Wall 51	3	44N00	102w14	6:48:56
Wallace 14	1	45N05	97w29	6:29:56
Wall Lake 49	1	43N33	96w57	6:27:48
Walnut Grove 21	1	43N28	98w25	6:33:40
Walshtown 66	1	43N02	97w20	6:29:20
Wanblee 65	3	43N34	101w40	6:46:40
War Creek 37	1	44N08	100w30	6:42:00
Ward 50	1	44N09	96w28	6:25:52
Warner 6	1	45N20	98w30	6:34:00
Wasta 51	3	44N04	102w27	6:49:48
Watauga 15	3	45N55	101w32	6:46:08
Watertown 14	1	44N54	97w07	6:28:28
Waubay 18	1	45N20	97w18	6:29:12
Waverly 14	1	44N54	97w07	6:28:28
Weaver 61	1	43N18	99w57	6:39:48
Weber 44	1	45N53	98w54	6:35:36
Webster 18	1	45N20	97w31	6:30:04
Webster Grove 49	1	43N31	96w42	6:26:48
Wecota 24	1	45N10	99w07	6:36:28
Wellington 49	1	43N33	97w05	6:28:20
Wentworth 39	1	44N00	96w58	6:27:52
Wesley 24	1	45N07	98w46	6:35:04
Wessington 2	1	44N27	98w42	6:34:48
Wessington Springs 36	1	44N05	98w34	6:34:16
Westerville 13	1	42N46	96w55	6:27:40
West Hanson 6	1	45N22	98w10	6:32:40
Weston 45	1	45N43	97w55	6:31:40
Westover 37	1	43N47	100w39	6:42:36
West Point 7	1	43N54	99w14	6:36:56
Westport 6	1	45N39	98w31	6:34:04
West Rondell 6	1	45N17	98w24	6:33:36
Weta 35	3	43N46	101w51	6:47:24
Wetonka 44	1	45N37	98w46	6:35:04
Wewela 61	1	43N01	99w47	6:39:08
Wheatland 18	1	45N11	97w26	6:29:44
Wheaton 29	1	44N47	98w45	6:35:00
Whetstone 26	1	43N13	98w59	6:35:56
White 5	1	44N26	96w39	6:26:36
White Butte 52	3	45N56	102w22	6:49:28
White Hill 52	3	45N36	102w53	6:51:32
Whitehorse 20	3	45N16	100w53	6:43:32
White Lake 1	1	43N44	98w43	6:34:52
White Owl 46	3	44N36	102w26	6:49:44
White Rivers 47	4	43N34	100w45	6:43:00
White Rock 54	1	45N55	96w35	6:26:20
Whiteside 2	1	44N30	98w40	6:34:40
White Swan 11	1	43N05	98w31	6:34:04
Whitewood 40	3	44N28	103w39	6:54:36
Whitney 52	3	45N34	102w03	6:48:12
Wicksville 51	3	44N06	102w35	6:50:20
Wilbur 7	1	43N37	98w50	6:35:20
William Hamilton 34	1	44N35	99w22	6:37:28
Williams Creek 37	1	43N49	100w24	6:41:36
Willow 44	1	45N44	98w48	6:35:12
Willow Creek 61	1	43N07	99w57	6:39:48
Willow Lake 12	1	44N38	97w38	6:30:32
Wilmot 54	1	45N25	96w52	6:27:28
Winfred 39	1	44N00	97w22	6:29:28
Winner 61	1	43N22	99w52	6:39:28
Winsor 5	1	44N25	97w04	6:28:16
Wismer 45	1	45N47	97w27	6:29:48
Witten 61	1	43N26	100w05	6:40:20
Wittenberg 33	1	43N19	97w42	6:30:48
Wolf Creek 33	1	43N23	97w35	6:30:20
Wolf Creek Colony 33	1	43N15	97w41	6:30:44
Wolsey 2	1	44N25	98w28	6:33:52
Wood 47	4	43N30	100w29	6:41:56
Woodland 12	1	45N02	97w48	6:31:12
Woonsocket 55	1	44N03	98w17	6:33:08
Worthen 30	1	43N33	97w55	6:31:40
Worthing 41	1	43N20	96w46	6:27:04
Wortman 61	1	43N08	100w04	6:40:16
Wounded Knee 56	3	43N08	102w22	6:49:28
Wright 61	1	43N13	100w10	6:40:40
Wyandotte 52	3	45N16	102w50	6:51:20
Yale 2	1	44N26	97w59	6:31:56
Yankton 66	1	42N53	97w23	6:29:32
Yankton Indian Reservation 11	1	43N14	98w26	6:33:44
Zell 24	1	44N54	98w44	6:34:56
Zeona 52	3	45N12	102w55	6:51:40
Zickrick 37	1	43N47	100w31	6:42:04

TIME TABLES

TN # 1
Before 11/18/1883 LMT
11/18/1883 12:00 EST
3/31/1918 02:00 EWT
10/27/1918 02:00 EST
3/30/1919 02:00 EWT
10/26/1919 02:00 EST
2/09/1942 02:00 EWT
9/30/1945 02:00 EST
4/30/1967 02:00 US#1

TN # 2
Before 11/18/1883 LMT
11/18/1883 12:00 EST
3/31/1918 02:00 EWT
10/27/1918 02:00 EST
3/30/1919 02:00 EWT
10/26/1919 02:00 EST
2/09/1942 02:00 EWT
9/30/1945 02:00 EST
4/28/1946 02:00 EDT
7/01/1946 00:01 EST
4/30/1967 02:00 US#1

TN # 3
Before 11/18/1883 LMT
11/18/1883 12:00 CST
3/31/1918 02:00 CWT
10/27/1918 02:00 CST
3/30/1919 02:00 CWT
10/26/1919 02:00 CST
2/09/1942 02:00 CWT
9/30/1945 02:00 CST
4/30/1967 02:00 US#1

TN # 4
Before 11/18/1883 LMT
11/18/1883 12:00 CST
3/31/1918 02:00 CWT
10/27/1918 02:00 CST
3/30/1919 02:00 CWT
10/26/1919 02:00 CST
7/06/1941 00:01 CDT
9/28/1941 02:00 CST
2/09/1942 02:00 CWT
9/30/1945 02:00 CST
5/09/1946 00:01 CDT
9/29/1946 02:00 CST
5/11/1947 00:01 CDT
9/28/1947 00:01 CST
4/25/1948 00:01 CDT
9/26/1948 00:01 CST
4/29/1956 00:01 CDT
10/28/1956 00:01 CST
4/30/1967 02:00 US#1

TN # 5
Before 11/18/1883 LMT
11/18/1883 12:00 CST
3/31/1918 02:00 CWT
10/27/1918 02:00 CST
3/30/1919 02:00 CWT
10/26/1919 02:00 CST
2/09/1942 02:00 CWT
9/30/1945 02:00 CST
5/02/1948 00:01 CDT
8/22/1948 00:01 CST
4/30/1967 02:00 US#1

TN # 6
Before 11/18/1883 LMT
11/18/1883 12:00 CST
3/31/1918 02:00 CWT
10/27/1918 02:00 CST
3/30/1919 02:00 CWT
10/26/1919 02:00 CST
7/14/1941 00:01 CDT
9/28/1941 02:00 CST
2/09/1942 02:00 CWT
9/30/1945 02:00 CST
4/25/1948 00:01 CDT
8/22/1948 02:00 CST
4/30/1967 02:00 US#1

TN # 7
Before 11/18/1883 LMT
11/18/1883 12:00 CST
3/31/1918 02:00 CWT
10/27/1918 02:00 CST
3/30/1919 02:00 CWT
10/26/1919 02:00 CST
7/28/1941 00:01 CDT
9/08/1941 00:01 CST
2/09/1942 02:00 CWT
9/30/1945 02:00 CST
4/30/1967 02:00 US#1

TN # 8
Before 11/18/1883 LMT
11/18/1883 12:00 CST
3/31/1918 02:00 CWT
10/27/1918 02:00 CST
3/30/1919 02:00 CWT
10/26/1919 02:00 CST
7/21/1941 00:01 CDT
9/28/1941 00:01 CST
2/09/1942 02:00 CWT
9/30/1945 02:00 CST
4/30/1967 02:00 US#1

TN # 9
Before 11/18/1883 LMT
11/18/1883 12:00 CST
3/31/1918 02:00 CWT
10/27/1918 02:00 CST
3/30/1919 02:00 CWT
10/26/1919 02:00 CST
7/21/1941 00:01 CDT
9/28/1941 02:00 CST
2/09/1942 02:00 CWT
9/30/1945 02:00 CST
4/30/1967 02:00 US#1

TN # 10
Before 11/18/1883 LMT
11/18/1883 12:00 CST
3/31/1918 02:00 CWT
10/27/1918 02:00 CST
3/30/1919 02:00 CWT
10/26/1919 02:00 CST
7/21/1941 00:01 CDT
9/28/1941 02:00 CST
2/09/1942 02:00 CWT
9/30/1945 02:00 CST
5/02/1948 00:01 CDT
9/26/1948 00:01 CST
4/30/1967 02:00 US#1

TN # 11
Before 11/18/1883 LMT
11/18/1883 12:00 CST
3/31/1918 02:00 CWT
10/27/1918 02:00 CST
3/30/1919 02:00 CWT
10/26/1919 02:00 CST
2/09/1942 02:00 CWT
9/30/1945 02:00 CST
4/25/1948 00:01 CDT
9/26/1948 00:01 CST
4/30/1967 02:00 US#1

TN # 12
Before 11/18/1883 LMT
11/18/1883 12:00 CST
3/31/1918 02:00 CWT
10/27/1918 02:00 CST
3/30/1919 02:00 CWT
10/26/1919 02:00 CST
7/24/1941 00:01 CDT
9/28/1941 02:00 CST
2/09/1942 02:00 CWT
9/30/1945 02:00 CST
4/30/1967 02:00 US#1

TN # 13
Before 11/18/1883 LMT
11/18/1883 12:00 CST
3/31/1918 02:00 CWT
10/27/1918 02:00 CST
3/30/1919 02:00 CWT
10/26/1919 02:00 CST
7/24/1941 00:01 CDT
9/28/1941 02:00 CST
2/09/1942 02:00 CWT
9/30/1945 02:00 CST
5/18/1947 00:01 CDT
9/28/1947 00:01 CST
5/02/1948 00:01 CDT
9/26/1948 00:01 CST
4/30/1967 02:00 US#1

TN # 14
Before 11/18/1883 LMT
11/18/1883 12:00 CST
3/31/1918 02:00 CWT
10/27/1918 02:00 CST
3/30/1919 02:00 CWT
10/26/1919 02:00 CST
8/06/1941 00:01 CDT
9/15/1941 00:01 CST
2/09/1942 02:00 CWT
9/30/1945 02:00 CST
4/30/1967 02:00 US#1

TN # 15
Before 11/18/1883 LMT
11/18/1883 12:00 CST
3/31/1918 02:00 CWT
10/27/1918 02:00 CST
3/30/1919 02:00 CWT
10/26/1919 02:00 CST
7/21/1941 00:01 CDT
9/28/1941 02:00 CST
2/09/1942 02:00 CWT
9/30/1945 02:00 CST
5/01/1948 00:01 CDT
9/20/1948 00:01 CST
4/30/1967 02:00 US#1

TN # 16
Before 11/18/1883 LMT
11/18/1883 12:00 CST
3/31/1918 02:00 CWT
10/27/1918 02:00 CST
3/30/1919 02:00 CWT
10/26/1919 02:00 CST
8/10/1941 00:01 CDT
9/07/1941 00:01 CST
2/09/1942 02:00 CWT
9/30/1945 02:00 CST
4/30/1967 02:00 US#1

TN # 17
Before 11/18/1883 LMT
11/18/1883 12:00 CST
3/31/1918 02:00 CWT
10/27/1918 02:00 CST
3/30/1919 02:00 CWT
10/26/1919 02:00 CST
8/06/1941 00:01 CDT
9/07/1941 00:01 CST
2/09/1942 02:00 CWT
9/30/1945 02:00 CST
4/30/1967 02:00 US#1

TN # 18
Before 11/18/1883 LMT
11/18/1883 12:00 CST
3/31/1918 02:00 CWT
10/27/1918 02:00 CST
3/30/1919 02:00 CWT
10/26/1919 02:00 CST
7/28/1941 00:01 CDT
9/28/1941 02:00 CST
2/09/1942 02:00 CWT
9/30/1945 02:00 CST
4/30/1967 02:00 US#1

TN # 19
Before 11/18/1883 LMT
11/18/1883 12:00 CST
3/31/1918 02:00 CWT
10/27/1918 02:00 CST
3/30/1919 02:00 CWT
10/26/1919 02:00 CST
7/28/1941 00:01 CDT
9/28/1941 02:00 CST
2/09/1942 02:00 CWT
9/30/1945 02:00 CST
5/25/1947 00:01 CDT
9/28/1947 00:01 CST
4/30/1967 02:00 US#1

TN # 20
Before 11/18/1883 LMT
11/18/1883 12:00 CST
3/31/1918 02:00 CWT
10/27/1918 02:00 CST
3/30/1919 02:00 CWT
10/26/1919 02:00 CST
7/28/1941 00:01 CDT
9/28/1941 00:01 CST
2/09/1942 02:00 CWT
9/30/1945 02:00 CST
4/30/1967 02:00 US#1

TN # 21
Before 11/18/1883 LMT
11/18/1883 12:00 CST
3/31/1918 02:00 CWT
10/27/1918 02:00 CST
3/30/1919 02:00 CWT
10/26/1919 02:00 CST
8/07/1941 00:01 CDT
9/28/1941 02:00 CST
2/09/1942 02:00 CWT
9/30/1945 02:00 CST
4/30/1967 02:00 US#1

TN # 22
Before 11/18/1883 LMT
11/18/1883 12:00 CST
3/31/1918 02:00 CWT
10/27/1918 02:00 CST
3/30/1919 02:00 CWT
10/26/1919 02:00 CST
7/14/1941 00:01 CDT
9/28/1941 00:01 CST
2/09/1942 02:00 CWT
9/30/1945 02:00 CST
4/30/1967 02:00 US#1

TN # 23
Before 11/18/1883 LMT
11/18/1883 12:00 CST
3/31/1918 02:00 CWT
10/27/1918 02:00 CST
3/30/1919 02:00 CWT
10/26/1919 02:00 CST
8/10/1941 12:00 CDT
9/13/1941 12:00 CST
2/09/1942 02:00 CWT
9/30/1945 02:00 CST
4/30/1967 02:00 US#1

TN # 24
Before 11/18/1883 LMT
11/18/1883 12:00 CST
3/31/1918 02:00 CWT
10/27/1918 02:00 CST
3/30/1919 02:00 CWT
10/26/1919 02:00 CST
8/06/1941 18:00 CDT
9/06/1941 00:01 CST
2/09/1942 02:00 CWT
9/30/1945 02:00 CST
4/30/1967 02:00 US#1

TN # 25
Before 11/18/1883 LMT
11/18/1883 12:00 CST
3/31/1918 02:00 CWT
10/27/1918 02:00 CST
3/30/1919 02:00 CWT
10/26/1919 02:00 CST
8/09/1941 00:01 CDT
9/15/1941 00:01 CST
2/09/1942 02:00 CWT
9/30/1945 02:00 CST
4/30/1967 02:00 US#1

TN # 26
Before 11/18/1883 LMT
11/18/1883 12:00 CST
3/31/1918 02:00 CWT
10/27/1918 02:00 CST
3/30/1919 02:00 CWT
10/26/1919 02:00 CST
7/29/1941 00:01 CDT
9/08/1941 00:01 CST
2/09/1942 02:00 CWT
9/30/1945 02:00 CST
4/30/1967 02:00 US#1

TN # 27
Before 11/18/1883 LMT
11/18/1883 12:00 CST
3/31/1918 02:00 CWT
10/27/1918 02:00 CST
3/30/1919 02:00 CWT
10/26/1919 02:00 CST
2/09/1942 02:00 CWT
9/30/1945 02:00 CST
4/25/1948 00:01 CDT
9/26/1948 00:01 CST
4/30/1967 02:00 US#1

TN # 28
Before 11/18/1883 LMT
11/18/1883 12:00 CST
3/31/1918 02:00 CWT
10/27/1918 02:00 CST
3/30/1919 02:00 CWT
10/26/1919 02:00 CST
7/14/1941 00:01 CDT
9/08/1941 00:01 CST
2/09/1942 02:00 CWT
9/30/1945 02:00 CST
4/30/1967 02:00 US#1

TN # 29
Before 11/18/1883 LMT
11/18/1883 12:00 CST
3/31/1918 02:00 CWT
10/27/1918 02:00 CST
3/30/1919 02:00 CWT
10/26/1919 02:00 CST
7/27/1941 00:01 CDT
9/28/1941 02:00 CST
2/09/1942 02:00 CWT
9/30/1945 02:00 CST
4/30/1967 02:00 US#1

TN # 30
Before 11/18/1883 LMT
11/18/1883 12:00 CST
3/31/1918 02:00 CWT
10/27/1918 02:00 CST
3/30/1919 02:00 CWT
10/26/1919 02:00 CST
7/14/1941 00:01 CDT
9/28/1941 02:00 CST
2/09/1942 02:00 CWT
9/30/1945 02:00 CST
4/26/1948 00:01 CDT
9/26/1948 00:01 CST
4/30/1967 02:00 US#1

TN # 31
Before 11/18/1883 LMT
11/18/1883 12:00 CST
3/31/1918 02:00 CWT
10/27/1918 02:00 CST
3/30/1919 02:00 CWT
10/26/1919 02:00 CST
7/13/1941 00:01 CDT
9/28/1941 02:00 CST
2/09/1942 02:00 CWT
9/30/1945 02:00 CST
4/30/1967 02:00 US#1

TN # 32
Before 11/18/1883 LMT
11/18/1883 12:00 CST
3/31/1918 02:00 CWT
10/27/1918 02:00 CST
3/30/1919 02:00 CWT
10/26/1919 02:00 CST
7/07/1941 00:01 CDT
9/28/1941 02:00 CST
2/09/1942 02:00 CWT
9/30/1945 02:00 CST
4/30/1967 02:00 US#1

TN # 33
Before 11/18/1883 LMT
11/18/1883 12:00 CST
3/31/1918 02:00 CWT
10/27/1918 02:00 CST
3/30/1919 02:00 CWT
10/26/1919 02:00 CST
7/21/1941 00:01 CDT
9/28/1941 02:00 CST
2/09/1942 02:00 CWT
9/30/1945 02:00 CST
5/25/1947 00:01 CDT
9/28/1947 00:01 CST
4/30/1967 02:00 US#1

TN # 34
Before 11/18/1883 LMT
11/18/1883 12:00 CST
3/31/1918 02:00 CWT
10/27/1918 02:00 CST
3/30/1919 02:00 CWT
10/26/1919 02:00 CST
7/06/1941 00:01 CDT
9/28/1941 02:00 CST
2/09/1942 02:00 CWT
9/30/1945 02:00 CST
4/25/1948 00:01 CDT
9/26/1948 00:01 CST
4/30/1967 02:00 US#1

TN # 35
Before 11/18/1883 LMT
11/18/1883 12:00 CST
3/31/1918 02:00 CWT
10/27/1918 02:00 CST
3/30/1919 02:00 CWT
10/26/1919 02:00 CST
7/08/1941 00:01 CDT
9/28/1941 02:00 CST
2/09/1942 02:00 CWT
9/30/1945 02:00 CST
5/02/1948 00:01 CDT
9/26/1948 00:01 CST
4/30/1967 02:00 US#1

TN # 36
Before 11/18/1883 LMT
11/18/1883 12:00 CST
3/31/1918 02:00 CWT
10/27/1918 02:00 CST
3/30/1919 02:00 CWT
10/26/1919 02:00 CST
7/16/1941 00:01 CDT
9/28/1941 02:00 CST
2/09/1942 02:00 CWT
9/30/1945 02:00 CST
4/30/1967 02:00 US#1

TN # 37
Before 11/18/1883 LMT
11/18/1883 12:00 CST
3/31/1918 02:00 CWT
10/27/1918 02:00 CST
3/30/1919 02:00 CWT
10/26/1919 02:00 CST
7/06/1941 00:01 CDT
9/28/1941 02:00 CST
2/09/1942 02:00 CWT
9/30/1945 02:00 CST
5/03/1948 00:01 CDT
9/26/1948 00:01 CST
4/30/1967 02:00 US#1

TN # 38
Before 11/18/1883 LMT
11/18/1883 12:00 CST
3/31/1918 02:00 CWT
10/27/1918 02:00 CST
3/30/1919 02:00 CWT
10/26/1919 02:00 CST
7/08/1941 00:01 CDT
9/28/1941 02:00 CST
2/09/1942 02:00 CWT
9/30/1945 02:00 CST
4/25/1948 00:01 CDT
9/26/1948 00:01 CST
4/30/1967 02:00 US#1

TN # 39
Before 11/18/1883 LMT
11/18/1883 12:00 CST
3/31/1918 02:00 CWT
10/27/1918 02:00 CST
3/30/1919 02:00 CWT
10/26/1919 02:00 CST
5/12/1940 02:00 CDT
9/08/1940 02:00 CST
8/06/1941 00:01 CDT
9/28/1941 02:00 CST
2/09/1942 02:00 CWT
9/30/1945 02:00 CST
4/30/1967 02:00 US#1

TN # 40
Before 11/18/1883 LMT
11/18/1883 12:00 CST
3/31/1918 02:00 CWT
10/27/1918 02:00 CST
3/30/1919 02:00 CWT
10/26/1919 02:00 CST
8/06/1941 00:01 CDT
9/28/1941 02:00 CST
2/09/1942 02:00 CWT
9/30/1945 02:00 CST
4/30/1967 02:00 US#1

TN # 41
Before 11/18/1883 LMT
11/18/1883 12:00 CST
3/31/1918 02:00 CWT
10/27/1918 02:00 CST
3/30/1919 02:00 CWT
10/26/1919 02:00 CST
2/09/1942 02:00 CWT
9/30/1945 02:00 CST
5/02/1948 00:01 CDT
9/26/1948 00:01 CST
4/30/1967 02:00 US#1

TN # 42
Before 11/18/1883 LMT
11/18/1883 12:00 CST
3/31/1918 02:00 CWT
10/27/1918 02:00 CST
3/30/1919 02:00 CWT
10/26/1919 02:00 CST

TIME TABLES

7/06/1941 00:01 CDT
9/28/1941 02:00 CST
2/09/1942 02:00 CWT
9/30/1945 02:00 CST
5/26/1947 00:01 CDT
9/27/1947 23:59 CST
5/23/1948 23:59 CDT
9/26/1948 00:01 CST
4/30/1967 02:00 US#1

TN # 43
Before 11/18/1883 LMT
11/18/1883 12:00 CST
3/31/1918 02:00 CWT
10/27/1918 02:00 CST
3/30/1919 02:00 CWT
10/26/1919 02:00 CST
7/06/1941 00:01 CDT
9/28/1941 02:00 CST
2/09/1942 02:00 CWT
9/30/1945 02:00 CST
4/25/1948 00:01 CDT
9/26/1948 00:01 CST
4/30/1967 02:00 US#1

TN # 44
Before 11/18/1883 LMT
11/18/1883 12:00 CST
3/31/1918 02:00 CWT
10/27/1918 02:00 CST
3/30/1919 02:00 CWT
10/26/1919 02:00 CST
8/10/1941 12:00 CDT
9/08/1941 00:01 CST
2/09/1942 02:00 CWT
9/30/1945 02:00 CST
4/30/1967 02:00 US#1

TN # 45
Before 11/18/1883 LMT
11/18/1883 12:00 CST
3/31/1918 02:00 CWT
10/27/1918 02:00 CST
3/30/1919 02:00 CWT
10/26/1919 02:00 CST
8/09/1941 00:01 CDT
9/26/1941 02:00 CST
2/09/1942 02:00 CWT
9/30/1945 02:00 CST
4/30/1967 02:00 US#1

TN # 46
Before 11/18/1883 LMT
11/18/1883 12:00 CST
3/31/1918 02:00 CWT
10/27/1918 02:00 CST
3/30/1919 02:00 CWT
10/26/1919 02:00 CST
7/13/1941 00:01 CDT
9/29/1941 00:01 CST
2/09/1942 02:00 CWT
9/30/1945 02:00 CST
4/30/1967 02:00 US#1

TN # 47
Before 11/18/1883 LMT
11/18/1883 12:00 CST
3/31/1918 02:00 CWT
10/27/1918 02:00 CST
3/30/1919 02:00 CWT
10/26/1919 02:00 CST
8/07/1941 00:01 CDT
8/28/1941 00:01 CST
2/09/1942 02:00 CWT
9/30/1945 02:00 CST
4/30/1967 02:00 US#1

TN # 48
Before 11/18/1883 LMT
11/18/1883 12:00 CST
3/31/1918 02:00 CWT
10/27/1918 02:00 CST
3/30/1919 02:00 CWT
10/26/1919 02:00 CST
7/10/1941 00:01 CDT
9/28/1941 02:00 CST
2/09/1942 02:00 CWT
9/30/1945 02:00 CST
5/13/1946 00:01 CDT
9/29/1946 00:01 CST
6/13/1947 00:01 CDT
9/26/1947 00:01 CST
4/25/1948 00:01 CDT
9/26/1948 00:01 CST
4/30/1967 02:00 US#1

TN # 49
Before 11/18/1883 LMT
11/18/1883 12:00 CST
3/31/1918 02:00 CWT
10/27/1918 02:00 CST
3/30/1919 02:00 CWT
10/26/1919 02:00 CST
7/06/1941 00:01 CDT
9/28/1941 02:00 CST
2/09/1942 02:00 CWT
9/30/1945 02:00 CST
4/30/1967 02:00 US#1

TN # 50
Before 11/18/1883 LMT
11/18/1883 12:00 CST
3/31/1918 02:00 CWT
10/27/1918 02:00 CST
3/30/1919 02:00 CWT
10/26/1919 02:00 CST
7/06/1941 00:01 CDT
9/28/1941 02:00 CST
2/09/1942 02:00 CWT
9/30/1945 02:00 CST
4/30/1967 02:00 US#1

TN # 51
Before 11/18/1883 LMT
11/18/1883 12:00 CST
3/31/1918 02:00 CWT
10/27/1918 02:00 CST
3/30/1919 02:00 CWT
10/26/1919 02:00 CST
2/09/1942 02:00 CWT
9/30/1945 02:00 CST
9/28/1947 02:00 EST
4/30/1967 02:00 US#1

TN # 52
Before 11/18/1883 LMT
11/18/1883 12:00 CST
3/31/1918 02:00 CWT
10/27/1918 02:00 CST
3/30/1919 02:00 CWT
10/26/1919 02:00 CST
7/23/1941 00:01 CDT
9/28/1941 02:00 CST
2/09/1942 02:00 CWT
9/30/1945 02:00 CST
9/28/1947 02:00 EST
4/30/1967 02:00 US#1

TN # 53
Before 11/18/1883 LMT
11/18/1883 12:00 CST
3/31/1918 02:00 CWT
10/27/1918 02:00 CST
3/30/1919 02:00 CWT
10/26/1919 02:00 CST
7/21/1941 00:01 CDT
9/28/1941 00:01 CST
2/09/1942 02:00 CWT
9/30/1945 02:00 CST
9/28/1947 02:00 EST
4/30/1967 02:00 US#1

TN # 54
Before 11/18/1883 LMT
11/18/1883 12:00 CST
3/31/1918 02:00 CWT
10/27/1918 02:00 CST
3/30/1919 02:00 CWT
10/26/1919 02:00 CST
7/21/1941 00:01 CDT
9/28/1941 02:00 CST
2/09/1942 02:00 CWT
9/30/1945 02:00 CST
9/28/1947 02:00 EST
4/30/1967 02:00 US#1

TN # 55
Before 11/18/1883 LMT
11/18/1883 12:00 CST
3/31/1918 02:00 CWT
10/27/1918 02:00 CST
3/30/1919 02:00 CWT
10/26/1919 02:00 CST
7/22/1941 00:01 CDT
9/28/1941 02:00 CST
2/09/1942 02:00 CWT
9/30/1945 02:00 CST
9/28/1947 02:00 EST
4/30/1967 02:00 US#1

TN # 56
Before 11/18/1883 LMT
11/18/1883 12:00 CST
3/31/1918 02:00 CWT
10/27/1918 02:00 CST
3/30/1919 02:00 CWT
10/26/1919 02:00 CST
2/09/1942 02:00 CWT
9/30/1945 02:00 CST
4/03/1960 02:00 EST
4/30/1967 02:00 US#1

TN # 57
Before 11/18/1883 LMT
11/18/1883 12:00 CST
3/31/1918 02:00 CWT
10/27/1918 02:00 CST
3/30/1919 02:00 CWT
10/26/1919 02:00 CST
7/21/1941 00:01 CDT
9/28/1941 02:00 CST
2/09/1942 02:00 CWT
9/30/1945 02:00 CST
4/03/1960 02:00 EST
4/30/1967 02:00 US#1

TN # 58
Before 11/18/1883 LMT
11/18/1883 12:00 CST
3/31/1918 02:00 CWT
10/27/1918 02:00 CST
3/30/1919 02:00 CWT
10/26/1919 02:00 CST
7/28/1941 00:01 CDT
9/28/1941 02:00 CST
2/09/1942 02:00 CWT
9/30/1945 02:00 CST
4/03/1960 02:00 EST
4/30/1967 02:00 US#1

TN # 59
Before 11/18/1883 LMT
11/18/1883 12:00 CST
3/31/1918 02:00 CWT
10/27/1918 02:00 CST
3/30/1919 02:00 CWT
10/26/1919 02:00 CST
7/21/1941 00:01 CDT
9/28/1941 02:00 CST
2/09/1942 02:00 CWT
9/30/1945 02:00 CST
4/27/1946 02:00 EST
4/30/1967 02:00 US#1

TN # 60
Before 11/18/1883 LMT
11/18/1883 12:00 CST
3/31/1918 02:00 CWT
10/27/1918 02:00 CST
3/30/1919 02:00 CWT
10/26/1919 02:00 CST
7/26/1941 00:01 CDT
9/28/1941 02:00 CST
2/09/1942 02:00 CWT
9/30/1945 02:00 CST
4/27/1946 02:00 EST
4/30/1967 02:00 US#1

TN # 61
Before 11/18/1883 LMT
11/18/1883 12:00 CST
3/31/1918 02:00 CWT
10/27/1918 02:00 CST
3/30/1919 02:00 CWT
10/26/1919 02:00 CST
7/21/1941 00:01 CDT
9/28/1941 00:01 CST
2/09/1942 02:00 CWT
9/30/1945 02:00 CST
4/27/1947 02:00 CDT
9/28/1947 02:00 CST
4/25/1948 00:01 CDT
9/26/1948 00:01 CST
8/14/1949 02:00 EST
4/30/1967 02:00 US#1

TN # 62
Before 11/18/1883 LMT
11/18/1883 12:00 CST
3/31/1918 02:00 CWT
10/27/1918 02:00 CST
3/30/1919 02:00 CWT
10/26/1919 02:00 CST
7/23/1941 00:01 CDT
9/28/1941 02:00 CST
2/09/1942 02:00 CWT
9/30/1945 02:00 CST
9/29/1947 02:00 EST
4/30/1967 02:00 US#1

TN # 63
Before 11/18/1883 LMT
11/18/1883 12:00 CST
3/31/1918 02:00 CWT
10/27/1918 02:00 CST
3/30/1919 02:00 CWT
10/26/1919 02:00 CST
2/09/1942 02:00 CWT
9/30/1945 02:00 CST
4/28/1946 00:01 EST
4/30/1967 02:00 US#1

TN # 64
Before 11/18/1883 LMT
11/18/1883 12:00 CST
3/31/1918 02:00 CWT
10/27/1918 02:00 CST
3/30/1919 02:00 CWT
10/26/1919 02:00 CST
7/20/1941 23:00 CDT
9/28/1941 02:00 CST
2/09/1942 02:00 CWT
9/30/1945 02:00 CST
4/28/1946 00:01 EST
4/30/1967 02:00 US#1

TN # 65
Before 11/18/1883 LMT
11/18/1883 12:00 CST
3/31/1918 02:00 CWT
10/27/1918 02:00 CST
3/30/1919 02:00 CWT
10/26/1919 02:00 CST
7/21/1941 00:01 CDT
9/28/1941 00:01 CST
2/09/1942 02:00 CWT
9/30/1945 02:00 CST
4/28/1946 00:01 EST
4/30/1967 02:00 US#1

TN # 66
Before 11/18/1883 LMT
11/18/1883 12:00 CST
3/31/1918 02:00 CWT
10/27/1918 02:00 CST
3/30/1919 02:00 CWT
10/26/1919 02:00 CST
7/23/1941 00:01 CDT
9/28/1941 00:01 CST
2/09/1942 02:00 CWT
9/30/1945 02:00 CST
4/28/1946 00:01 EST
4/30/1967 02:00 US#1

TN # 67
Before 11/18/1883 LMT
11/18/1883 12:00 CST
3/31/1918 02:00 CWT
10/27/1918 02:00 CST
3/30/1919 02:00 CWT
10/26/1919 02:00 CST
7/21/1941 00:01 CDT
9/28/1941 02:00 CST
2/09/1942 02:00 CWT
9/30/1945 02:00 CST
4/28/1946 00:01 EST
4/30/1967 02:00 US#1

TN # 68
Before 11/18/1883 LMT
11/18/1883 12:00 CST
3/31/1918 02:00 CWT
10/27/1918 02:00 CST
3/30/1919 02:00 CWT
10/26/1919 02:00 CST
7/22/1941 00:01 CDT
9/28/1941 02:00 CST
2/09/1942 02:00 CWT
9/30/1945 02:00 CST
4/28/1946 00:01 EST
4/30/1967 02:00 US#1

TN # 69
Before 11/18/1883 LMT
11/18/1883 12:00 CST
3/31/1918 02:00 CWT
10/27/1918 02:00 CST
3/30/1919 02:00 CWT
10/26/1919 02:00 CST
7/20/1941 23:00 CDT
9/28/1941 02:00 CST
2/09/1942 02:00 CWT
9/30/1945 02:00 CST
4/28/1946 00:01 EST
4/30/1967 02:00 US#1

TN # 70
Before 11/18/1883 LMT
11/18/1883 12:00 CST
3/31/1918 02:00 CWT
10/27/1918 02:00 CST
3/30/1919 02:00 CWT
10/26/1919 02:00 CST
7/21/1941 00:01 CDT
9/28/1941 02:00 CST
2/09/1942 02:00 CWT
9/30/1945 02:00 CST
5/05/1946 00:01 EST
4/30/1967 02:00 US#1

TN # 71
Before 11/18/1883 LMT
11/18/1883 12:00 CST
3/31/1918 02:00 CWT
10/27/1918 02:00 CST
3/30/1919 02:00 CWT
10/26/1919 02:00 CST
7/21/1941 00:01 CDT
9/28/1941 02:00 CST
2/09/1942 02:00 CWT
9/30/1945 02:00 CST
4/27/1947 02:00 EST
4/30/1967 02:00 US#1

TN # 72
Before 11/18/1883 LMT
11/18/1883 12:00 CST
3/31/1918 02:00 CWT
10/27/1918 02:00 CST
3/30/1919 02:00 CWT
10/26/1919 02:00 CST
7/21/1941 00:01 CDT
9/28/1941 02:00 CST
2/09/1942 02:00 CWT
9/30/1945 02:00 CST
4/28/1947 00:01 EST
4/30/1967 02:00 US#1

TN # 73
Before 11/18/1883 LMT
11/18/1883 12:00 CST
3/31/1918 02:00 CWT
10/27/1918 02:00 CST
3/30/1919 02:00 CWT
10/26/1919 02:00 CST
7/28/1941 00:01 CDT
9/28/1941 02:00 CST
2/09/1942 02:00 CWT
9/30/1945 02:00 CST
4/28/1947 00:01 EST
4/30/1967 02:00 US#1

TN # 74
Before 11/18/1883 LMT
11/18/1883 12:00 CST
3/31/1918 02:00 CWT
10/27/1918 02:00 CST
3/30/1919 02:00 CWT
10/26/1919 02:00 CST
7/21/1941 00:01 CDT
9/28/1941 02:00 CST
2/09/1942 02:00 CWT
9/30/1945 02:00 CST
8/21/1949 02:00 EST
4/30/1967 02:00 US#1

TN # 75
Before 11/18/1883 LMT
11/18/1883 12:00 CST
3/31/1918 02:00 CWT
10/27/1918 02:00 CST
1/01/1919 02:00 EST
3/30/1919 02:00 EWT
10/26/1919 02:00 EST
2/09/1942 02:00 EWT
9/30/1945 02:00 EST
4/30/1967 02:00 US#1

COUNTIES

1 Anderson
2 Bedford
3 Benton
4 Bledsoe
5 Blount
6 Bradley
7 Campbell
8 Cannon
9 Carroll
10 Carter
11 Cheatham
12 Chester
13 Claiborne
14 Clay
15 Cocke
16 Coffee
17 Crockett
18 Cumberland
19 Davidson
20 Decatur
21 Dekalb
22 Dickson
23 Dyer
24 Fayette
25 Fentress
26 Franklin
27 Gibson
28 Giles
29 Grainger
30 Greene
31 Grundy
32 Hamblen
33 Hamilton
34 Hancock
35 Hardeman
36 Hardin
37 Hawkins
38 Haywood
39 Henderson
40 Henry
41 Hickman
42 Houston
43 Humphreys
44 Jackson
45 Jefferson
46 Johnson
47 Knox
48 Lake
49 Lauderdale
50 Lawrence
51 Lewis
52 Lincoln
53 Loudon
54 McMinn
55 McNairy
56 Macon
57 Madison
58 Marion
59 Marshall
60 Maury
61 Meigs
62 Monroe
63 Montgomery
64 Moore
65 Morgan
66 Obion
67 Overton
68 Perry
69 Pickett
70 Polk
71 Putnam
72 Rhea
73 Roane
74 Robertson
75 Rutherford
76 Scott
77 Sequatchie
78 Sevier
79 Shelby
80 Smith
81 Stewart
82 Sullivan
83 Sumner
84 Tipton
85 Trousdale
86 Unicoi
87 Union
88 Van Buren
89 Warren
90 Washington
91 Wayne
92 Weakley
93 White
94 Williamson
95 Wilson

Acklen 19 4 36N08 86W48 5:47:12
Acton 55 3 35N04 88W25 5:53:40
Adair 57 3 35N43 88W57 5:55:48
Adams 74 3 36N35 87W04 5:48:16
Adams Crossroads 22 3 36N05 87W23 5:49:32
Adamsville 55 3 35N14 88W23 5:53:32
Aetna 41 3 35N48 87W27 5:49:48
Afton 30 65 36N12 82W44 5:30:56
Airport 19 4 36N08 86W42 5:46:48
Airport Estates 19 4 36N06 86W45 5:47:00
Air View 31 3 35N26 85W43 5:42:52
Akard Addition 82 2 36N35 82W11 5:28:44
Alamo 17 14 35N47 89W07 5:56:28
Albany 30 65 36N13 82W48 5:31:12
Albright 83 42 36N23 86W26 5:45:44
Alcoa 5 64 35N50 83W59 5:35:56
Alder Branch 78 60 35N49 83W33 5:34:12
Alder Springs 7 66 36N23 84W07 5:36:28
Alder Springs 87 52 36N15 83W48 5:35:12
Alexandria 21 3 36N05 86W02 5:44:08
Algood 71 34 36N12 85W27 5:41:48
Allardt 25 3 36N23 84W53 5:39:32
Allen Grove 15 65 35N49 83W15 5:33:00
Allens 38 24 35N36 89W16 5:57:04
Allens Chapel 21 11 35N57 85W49 5:43:16
Allensville 78 60 35N49 83W33 5:34:12
Allisona 75 3 35N48 86W40 5:46:40
Allons 67 3 36N27 85W21 5:41:24
Allred 67 3 36N20 85W11 5:40:44
Almaville 75 3 35N53 86W33 5:46:12
Almira 84 3 35N29 89W43 5:58:52
Alpha 32 67 36N12 83W23 5:33:32
Alpha Heights 32 67 36N13 83W17 5:33:08
Alpine 67 3 36N24 85W13 5:40:52
Altamont 31 3 35N26 85W44 5:42:56
Alto 26 18 35N13 86W05 5:44:20
Alton Hill 56 3 36N32 86W02 5:44:08
Alton Park 33 61 35N01 85W19 5:41:16
Alumwell 37 70 36N24 83W00 5:32:00
Amanda 93 3 35N56 85W28 5:41:52
Amis 37 70 36N24 83W00 5:32:00
Amis Chapel 37 70 36N28 82W51 5:31:24
Amity Heights 82 2 36N35 82W11 5:28:44
Amqui 19 4 36N16 86W43 5:46:52
Anderson 26 18 35N05 85W56 5:43:44
Anderson Heights 82 1 36N32 82W19 5:29:16
Andersonville 1 62 36N12 84W02 5:36:08
Anglea 83 50 36N29 86W19 5:45:16
Annadel 65 56 36N13 84W39 5:38:36
Anthony Hill 28 3 35N09 87W06 5:48:24
Antioch 19 4 36N04 86W40 5:46:40
Antioch 44 27 36N21 85W39 5:42:36
Antioch 53 68 35N48 84W16 5:37:04
Antioch 84 3 35N27 89W49 5:59:16
Antioch Harbor Resort 40 3 36N15 88W09 5:52:36
Apison 33 61 35N01 85W01 5:40:04
Appleton 50 29 35N03 87W19 5:49:16
Applewood 33 61 35N08 85W19 5:41:16
Arcadia 82 2 36N34 82W33 5:30:12
Archer 59 30 35N27 86W48 5:47:12
Archville 70 72 35N11 84W30 5:38:00
Ardmore 28 3 35N00 86W51 5:47:24
Arkland 60 3 35N37 87W13 5:48:52
Arlington 42 3 36N19 87W42 5:50:48
Arlington 79 40 35N18 89W40 5:58:40
Armathwaite 25 3 36N23 84W53 5:39:32
Armona 5 64 35N46 83W58 5:35:52
Armour 60 31 35N37 87W02 5:48:08
Arms Mill 87 52 36N15 83W48 5:35:12
Arno 94 3 35N48 86W40 5:46:40
Arnold Engineering Developme 16 13 35N21 86W12 5:44:48
Arnolds Chapel 71 3 36N09 85W38 5:42:32
Arp 49 28 35N45 89W32 5:58:08
Arrington 94 3 35N52 86W43 5:46:52
Arrow 60 9 35N32 87W12 5:48:48
Arrowhead 47 67 35N56 83W54 5:35:36
Arthur 13 51 36N33 83W40 5:34:40
Asbury 16 12 35N28 86W05 5:44:20
Asbury 38 3 35N28 89W24 5:57:36
Asbury 47 67 36N00 83W53 5:35:32
Asbury 69 3 36N33 84W58 5:39:52
Ashburn 74 35 36N30 86W53 5:47:32
Ashbury 81 3 36N19 87W50 5:51:20
Ashland 91 3 35N19 87W46 5:51:04
Ashland City 11 10 36N17 87W04 5:48:16
Ashland Hills 63 32 36N32 87W22 5:49:28
Ashport 49 3 35N46 89W47 5:59:08
Ashwood 60 31 35N37 87W02 5:48:08
Asia 26 19 35N11 86W07 5:44:28
Aspen Hill 28 22 35N12 87W02 5:48:08
Athens 54 71 35N27 84W36 5:38:24
Athens Rural 54 71 35N27 84W38 5:38:32
Atoka 84 3 35N26 89W47 5:59:08
Atwood 9 3 35N59 88W41 5:54:44
Auburntown 8 3 35N57 86W05 5:44:20
Austin Springs 92 3 36N30 88W43 5:54:52
Avoca 82 1 36N32 82W13 5:28:52
Avondale 27 8 35N50 88W55 5:55:40
Avondale 29 55 36N17 83W31 5:34:04
Avondale 83 43 36N18 86W37 5:46:28
Avondale Springs 29 55 36N17 83W31 5:34:04
Aymett Town 28 22 35N12 87W02 5:48:08
Bacchus 13 51 36N27 83W34 5:34:16
Bacon Gap 73 67 35N52 84W31 5:38:04
Bagdad 44 3 36N23 85W57 5:43:48
Bailey 79 40 35N03 89W40 5:58:40
Baileyton 30 65 36N20 82W50 5:31:20
Bailey Town 15 65 35N58 83W11 5:32:44
Bairds Mills 95 34 36N12 86W18 5:45:12
Baker Crossroads 18 15 35N57 85W02 5:40:08
Bakers 19 4 36N18 86W43 5:46:52
Bakers Crossroads 93 3 35N56 85W28 5:41:52
Bakerton 14 3 36N32 85W51 5:43:24
Bakertown 19 4 36N06 86W45 5:47:00
Bakerville 43 3 35N55 87W51 5:51:24
Bakewell 33 61 35N21 85W08 5:40:32
Bald Point 29 55 36N21 83W25 5:33:40
Ball Camp 47 67 35N58 83W58 5:35:52
Ball Play 70 72 35N04 84W44 5:38:56
Balltown 54 54 35N20 84W32 5:38:08
Bangham 71 34 36N11 85W28 5:41:52
Banner 78 59 35N43 83W31 5:34:04
Banner Hill 86 1 36N08 82W25 5:29:40
Banner Springs 25 3 36N26 84W56 5:39:44
Baptist 19 4 36N09 86W47 5:47:08
Baptist Ridge 14 3 36N25 85W27 5:41:48
Barfield 75 37 35N51 86W23 5:45:32
Bargerton 39 25 35N39 88W23 5:53:32
Barkertown 31 3 35N21 85W34 5:42:16
Barnard 73 67 35N46 84W34 5:38:16
Barnardsville 73 67 35N52 84W31 5:38:04
Barnesville 50 29 35N26 87W18 5:49:12
Barr 49 3 35N53 89W24 5:57:36
Barren Plains 74 3 36N36 86W53 5:47:32
Barretville 79 40 35N20 89W53 5:59:32
Barrons Corner 27 21 36N04 89W00 5:56:00
Barthelia 85 45 36N24 86W19 5:45:16
Bartlebaugh 33 61 35N05 85W12 5:40:48
Bartlett 79 40 35N13 89W51 5:59:24
Barton Springs 32 67 36N13 83W17 5:33:08
Bates Hill 89 46 35N42 85W46 5:43:04
Bath Springs 20 3 35N26 88W05 5:52:20
Batley 1 62 36N05 84W08 5:36:32
Baucom 16 12 35N28 86W05 5:44:20
Baugh Spring 6 53 35N07 84W59 5:39:56
Baxter 71 3 36N09 85W38 5:42:32
Bazel Town 73 67 35N56 84W33 5:38:12
Beacon 20 3 35N39 88W07 5:52:28
Beans Creek 26 18 35N03 86W16 5:45:04
Bean Station 29 55 36N20 83W20 5:33:20
Bear Creek 76 58 36N33 84W27 5:37:48
Beardstown 68 3 35N46 87W47 5:51:08
Bear Spring 81 3 36N29 87W50 5:51:20
Beartown 82 2 36N34 82W33 5:30:12
Beaver 84 3 35N29 89W43 5:58:52
Beaverdam Springs 41 3 35N40 87W42 5:50:48
Beaver Ridge 47 67 35N58 83W58 5:35:52
Beckwith 95 49 36N12 86W31 5:46:04
Bedford 2 3 35N28 86W34 5:46:16
Beech Bluff 57 3 35N36 88W38 5:54:32
Beech Bottom 56 3 36N32 86W02 5:44:08
Beech Creek 37 70 36N27 82W47 5:31:08
Beech Fork 7 66 36N18 84W13 5:36:52
Beech Grove 1 62 36N13 84W09 5:36:36
Beechgrove 16 12 35N38 86W14 5:44:56
Beech Grove 29 55 36N21 83W25 5:33:40
Beech Grove 85 45 36N23 86W10 5:44:40
Beech Grove 92 3 36N09 88W48 5:55:12
Beech Hill 28 22 35N12 87W02 5:48:08
Beech Hill 56 3 36N23 86W10 5:44:40
Beechnut 82 1 36N32 82W19 5:29:16
Beech Springs 78 60 35N59 83W37 5:34:28
Beersheba Springs 31 3 35N28 85W39 5:42:36
Bel Air 60 31 35N37 87W02 5:48:08
Bel Aire 16 13 35N21 86W12 5:44:48
Bel Aire 75 37 35N51 86W23 5:45:32
Bel-aire Heights 26 19 35N11 86W07 5:44:28
Bel-air Estates 63 32 36N32 87W22 5:49:28
Belfast 59 3 35N25 86W42 5:46:48
Belk 21 11 35N57 85W49 5:43:16
Bell Buckle 2 5 35N35 86W21 5:45:24
Bell Campground 47 67 36N02 84W02 5:36:08
Belle Aire 93 3 35N56 85W28 5:41:52
Belle Brook Estate 82 2 36N35 82W11 5:28:44
Belle Eagle 38 24 35N36 89W16 5:57:04
Belle Founte 6 53 35N09 84W52 5:39:28
Belle Meade 5 64 35N46 83W58 5:35:52
Belle Meade 19 4 36N07 86W52 5:47:28
Belleview 52 9 35N03 86W34 5:46:16
Belleville 52 9 35N09 86W35 5:46:20
Bellevue 19 4 36N04 86W57 5:47:48
Bellevue Estates 54 54 35N20 84W32 5:38:08
Bells 17 3 35N43 89W05 5:56:20
Bellsburg 22 3 36N11 87W20 5:49:20
Bell Town 11 9 36N06 87W07 5:48:28
Bellview 4 3 35N36 85W11 5:40:44
Bellview 52 9 35N09 86W35 5:46:20
Bellwood 95 34 36N12 86W18 5:45:12
Belmont 1 62 36N12 84W02 5:36:08
Belmont 16 12 35N28 86W05 5:44:20
Belvidere 26 18 35N08 86W12 5:44:48
Bemis 57 14 35N35 88W49 5:55:16
Bending Chestnut 94 48 35N57 86W53 5:47:32
Ben Stockton 25 3 36N26 84W56 5:39:44
Benton 70 72 35N10 84W39 5:38:36
Berclair 79 40 35N06 89W54 5:59:36
Berlin 59 30 35N27 86W48 5:47:12
Berry Hill 19 4 36N07 86W47 5:47:08
Berry's Chapel 94 48 35N59 86W52 5:47:28
Bertha 34 51 36N34 83W03 5:32:12
Bethany 89 46 35N42 85W46 5:43:04
Bethel 1 62 36N05 84W08 5:36:32
Bethel 3 3 36N04 88W06 5:52:24
Bethel 9 3 36N00 88W25 5:53:40
Bethel 11 10 36N16 87W04 5:48:16
Bethel 21 11 35N57 85W49 5:43:16
Bethel 28 3 35N02 87W00 5:48:00
Bethel 60 3 35N44 87W08 5:48:32
Bethel Springs 55 3 35N14 88W36 5:54:24
Bethesda 30 65 36N14 82W41 5:30:44
Bethesda 94 3 35N48 86W40 5:46:40
Bethlehem 40 3 36N26 88W18 5:52:48
Bethlehem 62 67 35N31 84W22 5:37:28
Bethlehem 94 48 35N57 86W53 5:47:32
Bethpage 83 50 36N29 86W19 5:45:16
Betsy Willis 16 12 35N25 85W58 5:43:52
Beulah 30 65 36N12 83W03 5:32:12
Beverly 47 67 36N02 83W56 5:35:44
Beverly Hills 47 67 36N03 83W53 5:35:32
Bible Hill 20 3 35N39 88W07 5:52:28
Big Barren Creek 13 51 36N25 83W41 5:34:44
Big Boy Junction 23 16 36N02 89W23 5:57:32
Bigbyville 60 31 35N37 87W02 5:48:08
Big Creek 34 51 36N32 83W13 5:32:52
Big Creek 37 70 36N24 83W00 5:32:00
Big Creek 62 67 35N31 84W22 5:37:28
Big Ivy 36 23 35N14 88W14 5:52:56
Big Lick 18 15 35N57 85W02 5:40:08
Big Mountain 65 51 36N02 84W20 5:37:20
Big Piney 53 68 35N44 84W21 5:37:24

TENNESSEE

Big Ridge Park 87
52 36N15 83w48 5:35:12
Big Rock 81 3 36N35 87w46 5:51:04
Big Sandy 3 3 36N14 88w05 5:52:20
Big Spring 5 64 35N46 84w08 5:36:32
Big Spring 10 1 36N20 82w13 5:28:52
Big Spring 61 54 35N31 84w47 5:39:08
Big Springs 57 3 35N29 88w43 5:54:52
Big Springs 67 22 36N23 85w19 5:41:16
Big Springs 75 36 35N43 86w24 5:45:36
Big War Creek 34 51 36N27 83w14 5:32:56
Biltmore 10 1 36N22 82w15 5:29:00
Binfield 5 64 35N42 84w04 5:36:16
Bingham 94 48 35N57 86w53 5:47:32
Binghamton 79 39 35N09 89w59 5:59:56
Birchwood 33 61 35N22 85w00 5:40:00
Bird Crossroads 78
60 35N49 83w33 5:34:12
Birnam Wood 33 61 35N08 85w19 5:41:16
Bishop 23 16 36N02 89w23 5:57:32
Black Center 3 3 36N04 88w06 5:52:24
Black Creek 76 58 36N21 84w35 5:38:20
Black Fox 6 53 35N09 84w52 5:39:28
Black Fox 29 55 36N17 83w36 5:34:24
Black Jack 16 12 35N28 86w05 5:44:20
Blackman 75 37 35N51 86w23 5:45:32
Blackwell 29 55 36N17 83w31 5:34:04
Blaine 29 55 36N10 83w39 5:34:36
Blair 73 67 35N56 84w33 5:38:12
Blair Gap 82 2 36N34 82w33 5:30:12
Blakeville 52 9 35N19 86w38 5:46:32
Blanche 52 9 35N00 86w40 5:46:40
Blaney Forest 33 61 35N01 85w14 5:40:56
Blanton Chapel 16
12 35N28 86w05 5:44:20
Bledsoe 52 9 35N19 86w38 5:46:32
Bledsoe 83 50 36N29 86w19 5:45:16
Block City 37 70 36N32 82w41 5:30:44
Block House 5 64 35N46 83w58 5:35:52
Blondy 51 3 35N33 87w34 5:50:16
Bloomingdale 82 1 36N35 82w28 5:29:52
Bloomington 69 3 36N34 85w08 5:40:32
Bloomington Heights 82
2 36N34 82w33 5:30:12
Bloomington Springs 71
3 36N12 85w37 5:42:28
Blount Hills 5 64 35N46 83w58 5:35:52
Blountville 82 1 36N32 82w19 5:29:16
Blowing Springs 1
62 36N05 84w08 5:36:32
Bluefields 19 4 36N09 86w41 5:46:44
Blue Goose 39 25 35N39 88w23 5:53:32
Bluegrass 47 67 35N52 84w08 5:36:32
Blue Hill 89 46 35N42 85w46 5:43:04
Blue Ridge 82 2 36N35 82w11 5:28:44
Blue Spring 10 1 36N20 82w13 5:28:52
Blue Springs 21 11 35N57 85w49 5:43:16
Bluff City 82 1 36N28 82w16 5:29:04
Bluff Creek 80 3 36N07 86w02 5:44:08
Bluhmtown 21 11 35N57 85w49 5:43:16
Board Valley 93 3 35N56 85w28 5:41:52
Boatland 25 3 36N26 84w56 5:39:44
Bobtown 26 18 35N12 85w55 5:43:40
Bodenham 28 22 35N12 87w02 5:48:08
Bogota 23 16 36N10 89w26 5:57:44
Bohannon Addition 54
71 35N27 84w36 5:38:24
Bold Spring 43 3 35N58 87w41 5:50:44
Bolivar 35 3 35N16 89w00 5:56:00
Bolton 79 40 35N17 89w40 5:58:40
Boma 71 3 36N08 85w41 5:42:44
Bon Air 93 3 35N57 85w22 5:41:28
Bon Aqua 41 3 35N56 87w19 5:49:16
Bon Aqua Junction 41
3 35N55 87w21 5:49:24
Bon De Croft 93 3 35N54 85w22 5:41:28
Bone Cave 88 3 35N47 85w35 5:42:20
Bonicord 23 16 36N02 89w23 5:57:32
Bonnertown 50 29 35N03 87w19 5:49:16
Bonny Kate 47 67 35N56 83w54 5:35:36
Bonsack 67 3 36N14 85w10 5:40:40
Bonwood 57 3 35N39 88w53 5:55:32
Boom 69 3 36N26 85w15 5:41:00
Boone 90 75 36N24 82w26 5:29:44
Boones Creek 90 75 36N18 82w28 5:29:52
Booneville 52 9 35N09 86w35 5:46:20
Boonshill 52 9 35N11 86w45 5:47:00
Boothspoint 23 16 36N02 89w23 5:57:32
Bordeaux 19 4 36N12 86w50 5:47:20
Boston 94 3 35N51 87w03 5:48:12
Bowen 29 55 36N17 83w31 5:34:04
Bowman 18 15 35N57 85w02 5:40:08
Bowmantown 90 63 36N15 82w33 5:30:12
Boyd 47 67 35N52 84w08 5:36:32
Boyds Creek 78 60 35N49 83w33 5:34:12
Brace 50 29 35N26 87w18 5:49:12
Brackentown 83 50 36N35 86w31 5:46:04
Bradburn Hill 30 65 36N13 82w48 5:31:12
Bradbury 73 67 35N52 84w31 5:38:04
Braden 24 3 35N23 89w34 5:58:16
Bradford 27 21 36N05 88w49 5:55:16
Bradleytown 23 16 36N03 89w29 5:57:56
Bradyville 8 3 35N44 86w10 5:44:40
Braemar 10 1 36N17 82w10 5:28:40
Brainerd 33 61 35N02 85w14 5:40:56
Brakebill 62 67 35N31 84w22 5:37:28
Branchville 2 3 35N19 86w38 5:46:32
Branchville 26 18 35N03 86w16 5:45:04
Bransford 83 50 36N29 86w19 5:45:16
Bratcher 89 46 35N42 85w46 5:43:04
Brattontown 56 3 36N32 86w02 5:44:08
Braxton 8 3 35N49 86w04 5:44:16
Bray 34 51 36N21 83w25 5:33:40
Brayton 4 3 35N27 85w05 5:40:20
Braytown 1 62 36N09 84w23 5:37:32
Brazil 27 8 35N58 88w57 5:55:48
Brentlawn 74 35 36N30 86w53 5:47:32
Brentwood 94 3 36N02 86w47 5:47:08
Brentwood Mall 94 3 36N02 86w47 5:47:08
Brewer Addition 54
71 35N27 84w36 5:38:24
Brewstertown 65 51 36N21 84w35 5:38:20
Briar Thicket 15 65 36N03 83w11 5:32:44
Briarwood 63 32 36N32 87w22 5:49:28
Briceville 1 62 36N11 84w11 5:36:44
Brick Church 28 22 35N12 87w02 5:48:08
Bride 84 44 35N34 89w42 5:58:48
Bridgeport 15 65 35N56 83w09 5:32:36
Bridwell Heights 82
1 36N32 82w19 5:29:16
Brighton 84 3 35N29 89w43 5:58:52
Bristol 82 2 36N36 82w11 5:28:44
Britton Ford 40 3 36N15 88w09 5:52:36
Brittontown 30 65 36N12 82w44 5:30:56
Brittsville 61 54 35N17 84w57 5:39:48
Broad Acres 47 67 36N02 84w02 5:36:08
Broadmoor 23 16 36N02 89w23 5:57:32
Broadview 60 31 35N37 87w02 5:48:08
Broadway 39 25 35N39 88w23 5:53:32
Brockdell 4 3 35N36 85w11 5:40:44
Brooks Ferry 44 27 36N21 85w39 5:42:36
Brookside 7 66 36N20 84w23 5:37:32
Brotherton 71 34 36N11 85w28 5:41:52
Browder 53 68 35N48 84w16 5:37:04
Browder 58 8 35N04 85w39 5:42:36
Brown Cross Roads 50
29 35N04 87w26 5:49:44
Browningtown 26 18 35N21 86w12 5:44:48
Brown Mill 26 18 35N03 86w16 5:45:04
Browns 56 3 36N32 86w02 5:44:08
Brownsville 38 24 35N36 89w16 5:57:04
Broylesville 90 63 36N13 82w38 5:30:32
Bruceton 9 3 36N03 88w15 5:53:00
Bruceville 23 16 36N02 89w23 5:57:32
Bruner Grove 15 65 36N03 83w11 5:32:44
Brunswick 79 40 35N16 89w46 5:59:04
Brush Creek 77 3 35N22 85w23 5:41:32
Brush Creek 80 3 36N07 86w02 5:44:08
Brushy Creek 94 3 35N59 87w07 5:48:28
Bryant Station 60 3 35N27 86w48 5:47:12
Bryson 28 3 35N07 86w48 5:47:12
Buchanan 40 3 36N26 88w12 5:52:48
Buckeye 7 66 36N25 84w18 5:37:12
Buck Lodge 83 50 36N35 86w31 5:46:04
Buckner 21 11 35N57 85w49 5:43:16
Bucktown 36 23 35N14 88w14 5:52:56
Bucktown 53 68 35N48 84w16 5:37:04
Buena Vista 9 3 35N59 88w17 5:53:08
Buffalo 43 3 35N58 87w47 5:51:08
Buffalo Springs 29
55 36N17 83w31 5:34:04
Buffalo Valley 71 3 36N08 85w47 5:43:08
Bufords 28 3 35N23 87w00 5:48:00
Bugscuffle 2 5 35N32 86w20 5:45:20
Buladeen 10 1 36N20 82w13 5:28:52
Bullards Gap 44 27 36N21 85w39 5:42:36
Bull Creek 76 58 36N25 84w29 5:37:56
Bullet Creek 62 70 35N11 84w30 5:38:00
Bull Run 19 4 36N16 87w04 5:48:16
Bulls Gap 37 70 36N15 83w05 5:32:20
Bumpass Cove 86 1 36N08 82w25 5:29:40
Bumpus Mills 81 3 36N36 87w50 5:51:20
Buncombe 82 1 36N32 82w19 5:29:16
Bungalow Town 5 64 35N46 83w58 5:35:52
Bunker Hill 28 22 35N12 87w02 5:48:08
Buntontown 46 1 36N20 82w00 5:28:00
Buntyn 79 39 35N07 89w57 5:59:48
Burbank 10 1 36N12 82w05 5:28:20
Burchfield Heights 47
67 35N59 84w18 5:37:12
Burem 37 70 36N24 83w00 5:32:00
Burke 18 9 35N36 85w11 5:40:44
Burlington 47 67 36N00 83w53 5:35:32
Burlington Heights 6
53 35N09 84w52 5:39:28
Burlison 84 3 35N34 89w46 5:59:04
Burns 22 3 36N03 87w19 5:49:16
Burnt Church 36 23 35N14 88w14 5:52:56
Burristown 44 3 36N24 85w34 5:42:16
Burrville 65 56 36N18 84w45 5:39:00
Burt 8 3 35N49 86w04 5:44:16
Burton 37 70 36N24 83w00 5:32:00
Burwood 94 3 35N48 86w55 5:47:40
Busby 50 29 35N04 87w26 5:49:44
Busselltown 53 68 35N48 84w16 5:37:04
Butler 46 1 36N25 81w57 5:27:48
Butlers Landing 14
11 36N33 85w30 5:42:00
Bybee 15 65 36N03 83w11 5:32:44
Bybee 89 46 35N42 85w46 5:43:04
Byrdstown 69 3 36N34 85w08 5:40:32
Cabin Row 63 3 36N22 87w18 5:49:12
Cades 27 8 35N59 88w47 5:55:08
Cades Cove 5 64 35N40 83w45 5:35:00
Caffey 55 3 35N02 88w34 5:54:16
Cagle 77 3 35N22 85w23 5:41:32
Cainsville 95 49 35N56 86w17 5:45:08
Cairo 17 14 35N47 89w07 5:56:28
Cairo 83 42 36N23 86w26 5:45:44
Cairo Bend 95 34 36N12 86w18 5:45:12
Calderwood 5 64 35N46 83w58 5:35:52
Calfkiller 71 3 36N09 85w16 5:41:04
Calhoun 16 12 35N28 86w05 5:44:20
Calhoun 54 54 35N18 84w45 5:39:00
Calico 61 54 35N31 84w47 5:39:08
Calistia 74 3 36N33 86w42 5:46:48
Calls 16 12 35N16 86w08 5:44:32
Camargo 52 9 35N09 86w35 5:46:20
Cambria 54 54 35N16 84w33 5:38:12
Camden 3 7 36N04 88w06 5:52:24
Campaign 89 3 35N46 85w38 5:42:32
Camp Austin 65 51 35N59 84w33 5:38:12
Campbell Army Airfield 63
3 36N38 87w28 5:49:52
Campbell Junction 18
15 35N57 85w02 5:40:08
Campbells 60 3 35N29 86w59 5:47:56
Campbells Station 60
3 35N29 86w59 5:47:56
Campbellsville 28 3 35N20 87w08 5:48:32
Campcreek 30 65 36N13 82w48 5:31:12
Camp Marymount 94 3 35N59 87w07 5:48:28
Camp Monterey Lake 71
3 36N09 85w16 5:41:04
Candlewyck 82 2 36N35 82w11 5:28:44
Cane Ridge 19 4 36N05 86w39 5:46:36
Caney Branch 30 65 36N13 82w48 5:31:12
Caney Spring 59 30 35N27 86w48 5:47:12
Capital Hill 76 58 36N25 84w29 5:37:56
Capitol Hill 26 18 35N16 86w08 5:44:32
Capleville 79 40 35N01 89w54 5:59:36
Car Branch 13 51 36N26 83w36 5:34:24
Cardiff 73 70 35N52 84w41 5:38:44
Carlisle 81 3 36N29 87w50 5:51:20
Carlock 54 54 35N20 84w32 5:38:08
Carnegie 90 75 36N19 82w21 5:29:24
Carpenter Campground 5
64 35N46 83w58 5:35:52
Carriage Hill 33 61 35N08 85w19 5:41:16
Carroll Reece 90 75 36N19 82w21 5:29:24
Carson Spring 15 65 35N58 83w11 5:32:44
Carter 10 1 36N25 82w05 5:28:20
Carters Creek 60 31 35N37 87w02 5:48:08
Carthage 80 41 36N15 85w57 5:43:48
Carthage Junction 80
3 36N09 85w57 5:43:48
Cartwright 77 3 35N12 85w31 5:42:04
Cartwright 80 3 36N23 85w57 5:43:48
Caryville 7 66 36N18 84w13 5:36:52
Cassville 93 3 35N56 85w28 5:41:52
Castalian Springs 83
50 36N24 86w19 5:45:16
Castle Heights 15
65 35N58 83w11 5:32:44
Cat Corner 66 3 36N16 89w11 5:56:44
Cates 48 3 36N23 89w29 5:57:56
Catlettsburg 78 60 35N49 83w33 5:34:12
Cato 85 3 36N22 86w03 5:44:12
Catons Grove 15 65 35N49 83w15 5:33:00
Cave 93 3 35N51 85w31 5:42:04
Cave Spring 13 51 36N27 83w34 5:34:16
Cavvia 9 3 35N53 88w09 5:52:36
Cawood 13 51 36N27 83w55 5:35:40
Cedar Bluff 47 67 35N57 84w05 5:36:20
Cedar Bluff 78 60 35N49 83w33 5:34:12
Cedarbluff 85 3 36N12 86w18 5:45:12
Cedar Chapel 35 3 35N20 89w09 5:56:36
Cedarcreek 30 65 36N13 82w48 5:31:12
Cedarfork 13 51 36N27 83w34 5:34:16
Cedar Fork 53 68 35N40 84w24 5:37:36
Cedar Grove 9 3 35N49 88w36 5:54:24
Cedar Grove 10 1 36N19 82w21 5:29:24
Cedar Grove 43 3 35N58 87w47 5:51:08
Cedar Grove 82 2 36N34 82w33 5:30:12
Cedar Hill 74 3 36N33 87w00 5:48:00
Cedars 95 49 36N06 86w25 5:45:40
Cedar Springs 54 71 35N27 84w36 5:38:24
Cedar Valley 82 2 36N35 82w11 5:28:44
Celina 14 11 36N33 85w30 5:42:00
Center 17 3 35N47 89w00 5:56:00
Center 40 3 36N23 88w29 5:53:56
Center 50 29 35N15 87w20 5:49:20
Center 62 70 35N22 84w18 5:37:12
Center Grove 26 18 35N21 86w12 5:44:48
Center Grove 44 27 36N21 85w39 5:42:36
Center Hill 8 3 35N49 86w04 5:44:16
Center Point 12 3 35N23 88w26 5:53:44
Center Point 50 29 35N10 87w21 5:49:24
Center Point 77 3 35N18 85w22 5:41:28
Center Point 81 3 36N29 87w50 5:51:20
Center Star 41 3 35N44 87w17 5:49:08
Centersville 53 68 35N40 84w10 5:36:40
Centertown 89 3 35N44 85w55 5:43:40
Centerview 15 65 36N04 83w09 5:32:36
Centerville 30 65 36N13 82w38 5:30:32
Centerville 41 3 35N47 87w28 5:49:52
Centerville 95 34 36N12 86w18 5:45:12
Central 10 1 36N19 82w21 5:29:24
Central 27 8 35N58 88w57 5:55:48
Central 49 28 35N45 89w32 5:58:08
Central 66 3 36N21 89w03 5:56:12
Central 90 75 36N19 82w21 5:29:24
Central Heights 82
1 36N32 82w19 5:29:16
Central Point 29 55 36N17 83w31 5:34:04
Central State Hospital 19
4 36N08 86w42 5:46:48
Centreville 95 34 36N12 86w18 5:45:12
Cerro Gordo 36 23 35N14 88w14 5:52:56
Chalklevel 3 3 36N04 88w06 5:52:24
Chalk Level 37 70 36N21 82w59 5:31:56
Chambers 55 3 35N04 88w25 5:53:40
Champ 52 9 35N13 86w28 5:45:52
Chandler 5 64 35N49 84w03 5:36:12
Chantay Acres 60 31 35N37 87w02 5:48:08
Chapel Hill 59 3 35N38 86w43 5:46:52
Chapel Hill 60 9 35N32 87w12 5:48:48
Chapman Grove 73 67 35N52 84w31 5:38:04
Chapmansboro 11 9 36N21 87w10 5:48:40
Charity 64 3 35N09 86w35 5:46:20
Charleston 6 53 35N17 84w45 5:39:00
Charleston 84 3 35N28 89w24 5:57:36
Charleys Branch 1
62 36N09 84w23 5:37:32
Charlotte 22 3 36N11 87w21 5:49:24

TENNESSEE

Chaska 7 66 36N27 84W04 5:36:16
Chattanooga 33 61 35N03 85W19 5:41:16
Cheap Hill 11 9 36N21 87W10 5:48:40
Cherokee Heights 5 64 35N46 83W58 5:35:52
Cherokee Hills 73 67 35N52 84W31 5:38:04
Cherokee Hills 78 60 35N49 83W33 5:34:12
Cherokee Park 5 64 35N46 83W58 5:35:52
Cherry 49 3 35N40 89W34 5:58:16
Cherrybrook 47 67 36N00 83W58 5:35:52
Cherry Hill 21 3 36N05 85W44 5:42:56
Cherry Valley 95 9 36N06 86W08 5:44:32
Chesney 87 52 36N15 83W40 5:34:40
Chesterfield 39 25 35N39 88W23 5:53:32
Chestnutbloom 32 67 36N13 83W17 5:33:08
Chestnut Bluff 17 3 35N53 89W24 5:57:36
Chestnut Grove 68 3 35N37 87W50 5:51:20
Chestnut Grove 81 3 36N29 87W50 5:51:20
Chestnut Grove 87 52 36N15 83W48 5:35:12
Chestnut Hill 45 67 35N58 83W20 5:33:20
Chestnut Mound 80 3 36N12 85W50 5:43:20
Chestnutridge 52 9 35N19 86W38 5:46:32
Chestoa 86 1 36N08 82W25 5:29:40
Chestua 62 67 35N31 84W22 5:37:28
Chestuee 6 53 35N09 84W52 5:39:28
Chewalla 55 3 35N01 88W39 5:54:36
Chic 23 16 36N03 89W29 5:57:56
Chickamauga 33 61 35N02 85W11 5:40:44
Chickasaw Heights 40 26 36N18 88W19 5:53:16
Childers Hill 36 3 35N09 88W19 5:53:16
Chilhowee 78 60 35N53 83W44 5:34:56
Chilhowee View 5 64 35N46 83W58 5:35:52
China Grove 27 21 36N08 88W55 5:55:40
Chinubee 50 29 35N08 87W32 5:50:08
Chipman 83 50 36N29 86W19 5:45:16
Chittum 13 51 36N27 83W34 5:34:16
Choptack 37 70 36N24 83W00 5:32:00
Chota 5 64 35N46 83W58 5:35:52
Christiana 75 36 35N43 86W24 5:45:36
Christian Bend 37 70 36N32 82W41 5:30:44
Christie Hill 5 64 35N46 83W58 5:35:52
Christmasville 9 3 36N08 88W31 5:54:04
Chuckey 30 65 36N14 82W41 5:30:44
Church Hill 37 70 36N31 82W43 5:30:52
Churchton 23 16 36N07 89W16 5:57:04
Citico Beach 62 67 35N35 84W15 5:37:00
Clacks Gap 73 67 35N56 84W33 5:38:12
Clairfield 13 51 36N33 83W57 5:35:48
Clareville 27 21 36N12 89W01 5:56:04
Clark Addition 5 64 35N46 83W58 5:35:52
Clarkrange 25 3 36N11 85W01 5:40:04
Clarksburg 9 3 35N52 88W24 5:53:36
Clarksville 63 32 36N32 87W21 5:49:24
Clarksville Base 63 3 36N38 87W28 5:49:52
Clarktown 93 3 35N56 85W28 5:41:52
Claxton 1 62 36N02 84W02 5:36:08
Claxton 54 71 35N27 84W36 5:38:24
Claybrook 57 3 35N39 88W53 5:55:32
Clayton 66 3 36N20 89W10 5:56:40
Clear Springs 30 65 36N13 82W38 5:30:32
Clear Springs 47 67 36N04 83W44 5:34:56
Clear Springs 54 54 35N18 84W45 5:39:00
Clearwater 54 71 35N27 84W36 5:38:24
Clementsville 14 3 36N32 85W51 5:43:24
Cleveland 6 53 35N10 84W53 5:39:32
Clevenger 15 65 35N58 83W11 5:32:44
Cliff Springs 67 3 36N09 85W16 5:41:04
Clifton City 91 3 35N23 88W00 5:52:00
Clifty 18 9 35N56 85W28 5:41:52
Clinchmore 7 66 36N15 84W18 5:37:12
Clinton 1 62 36N06 84W08 5:36:32
Clopton 84 3 35N29 89W43 5:58:52
Cloud Creek 37 70 36N24 83W00 5:32:00
Clouds 13 51 36N27 83W34 5:34:16
Clouse Hill 31 3 35N16 85W44 5:42:56
Clovercroft 94 48 35N57 86W53 5:47:32
Cloverdale 66 3 36N16 89W19 5:57:16
Cloverdale 79 40 35N20 89W53 5:59:32
Cloverhill 5 64 35N46 83W58 5:35:52
Cloverhill 19 4 36N09 86W41 5:46:44
Cloverport 35 3 35N21 88W57 5:55:48
Club Springs 80 3 36N09 85W57 5:43:48
Coal Chute 10 1 36N20 82W13 5:28:52
Coalfield 65 51 36N03 84W26 5:37:44
Coal Hill 65 51 35N56 84W33 5:38:12
Coalmont 31 3 35N20 85W42 5:42:48
Cobbs 17 3 35N43 89W05 5:56:20
Coble 41 3 35N43 87W36 5:50:24
Coffee Landing 36 3 35N14 88W23 5:53:32
Coffee Ridge 86 1 36N08 82W25 5:29:40
Cokercreek 62 70 35N16 84W17 5:37:08
Cold Spring 4 3 35N36 85W11 5:40:44
Cold Spring 46 1 36N29 81W48 5:27:12
Cold Springs 5 64 35N44 83W49 5:35:16
Cold Springs 37 70 36N28 82W51 5:31:24
Coldwater 52 9 35N09 86W35 5:46:20
Coleman Heights 59 30 35N27 86W48 5:47:12
Colesburg 22 3 36N05 87W23 5:49:32
Coles Store 71 3 36N09 85W38 5:42:32
Coletown 70 73 34N59 84W22 5:37:28
College 4 3 35N22 85W23 5:41:32
College 5 64 35N46 83W58 5:35:52
Collegedale 33 61 35N04 85W03 5:40:12
College Grove 94 3 35N47 86W41 5:46:44
College Park 10 1 36N19 82W21 5:29:24
College Park Estates 5 64 35N46 83W58 5:35:52

Colliers Corner 45 67 36N07 83W30 5:34:00
Collierville 79 40 35N03 89W40 5:58:40
Collins 31 3 35N21 85W34 5:42:16
Collins 37 70 36N24 83W00 5:32:00
Collinwood 91 3 35N10 87W44 5:50:56
Colonial Heights 82 2 36N29 82W30 5:30:00
Columbia 60 31 35N37 87W02 5:48:08
Columbus Hill 44 27 36N21 85W39 5:42:36
Comfort 58 8 35N01 85W43 5:42:52
Commerce 95 9 36N06 86W08 5:44:32
Como 40 3 36N18 88W31 5:54:04
Compton 75 37 35N51 86W23 5:45:32
Conasauga 1 62 35N59 84W18 5:37:12
Conasauga 70 72 35N00 84W44 5:38:56
Concord 9 3 36N00 88W25 5:53:40
Concord 27 8 35N58 88W57 5:55:48
Concord 47 67 35N52 84W08 5:36:32
Concord 75 3 35N45 86W32 5:46:08
Conklin 90 75 36N18 82W28 5:29:52
Conyersville 40 3 36N27 88W20 5:53:20
Cookeville 71 34 36N10 85W30 5:42:00
Cool Springs 27 21 36N12 89W11 5:56:44
Coopers 9 3 36N02 88W15 5:53:00
Coopertown 74 3 36N27 87W01 5:48:04
Copperhill 70 73 35N00 84W23 5:37:32
Corbin Hill 65 51 36N02 84W20 5:37:20
Cordell 76 58 36N25 84W29 5:37:56
Corder Cross Roads 52 9 35N08 86W28 5:45:52
Cordova 79 40 35N09 89W47 5:59:08
Corinth 47 67 36N02 83W56 5:35:44
Corinth 83 50 36N35 86W31 5:46:04
Cornersville 59 3 35N22 86W50 5:47:20
Coro Lake 79 39 35N04 90W04 6:00:16
Corona 84 3 35N28 90W11 6:00:44
Corryton 47 67 36N09 83W47 5:35:08
Cortner 2 3 35N27 86W15 5:45:00
Cosby 15 65 35N54 83W13 5:32:52
Cottage Grove 40 3 36N22 88W27 5:53:48
Cottage Home 95 49 36N00 85W58 5:43:52
Cotton Lake 84 44 35N34 89W42 5:58:48
Cottonport 61 54 35N31 84W47 5:39:08
Cottontown 83 50 36N27 86W32 5:46:08
Cotula 7 66 36N27 84W04 5:36:16
Couchville 19 4 36N12 86W37 5:46:28
Coulterville 33 61 35N23 85W07 5:40:28
Counce 36 3 35N03 88W16 5:53:04
Country Club Estates 82 2 36N35 82W11 5:28:44
County Line 29 55 36N20 83W22 5:33:28
Countyline 64 33 35N17 86W22 5:45:28
Cove Creek 7 66 36N18 84W13 5:36:52
Cove Creek 10 1 36N12 82W05 5:28:20
Cove Creek Cascades 78 60 35N49 83W33 5:34:12
Covington 84 44 35N34 89W39 5:58:36
Cowan 26 18 35N10 86W01 5:44:04
Cowanstown 46 1 36N20 82W00 5:28:00
Cowards 47 67 35N58 83W58 5:35:52
Cowenville 80 3 36N09 85W57 5:43:48
Coxville 17 3 35N50 88W55 5:55:40
Cozyette 20 3 35N50 88W02 5:52:08
Crab Orchard 18 9 35N55 84W53 5:39:32
Crabtree 10 1 36N12 82W05 5:28:20
Craggie Hope 11 9 36N06 87W07 5:48:28
Craigfield 94 3 35N56 87W19 5:49:16
Crandull 46 1 36N31 81W56 5:27:44
Cranmore Cove 72 74 35N01 85W11 5:40:44
Craveltown 80 3 36N23 85W57 5:43:48
Cravenstown 67 3 36N16 85W05 5:40:20
Crawford 67 3 36N14 85W11 5:40:44
Crenshaw 47 67 35N56 83W54 5:35:36
Crescent 75 37 35N51 86W23 5:45:32
Creson 52 9 35N09 86W35 5:46:20
Creston 18 15 35N57 85W02 5:40:08
Crestwood 73 67 35N52 84W31 5:38:04
Crestwood Hills 47 67 36N02 83W56 5:35:44
Crewstown 50 29 35N15 87W20 5:49:20
Crieve Hall 19 4 36N06 86W45 5:47:00
Crippen Gap 47 67 36N02 83W56 5:35:44
Crisp Spring 89 3 35N36 85W49 5:43:16
Crockett 66 3 36N21 89W03 5:56:12
Crockett Mills 17 3 35N52 89W10 5:56:40
Cronanville 48 3 36N23 89W29 5:57:56
Cross 82 1 36N32 82W19 5:29:16
Cross Anchor 30 65 36N13 82W48 5:31:12
Cross Bridges 60 9 35N32 87W12 5:48:48
Cross Keys 94 3 35N48 86W40 5:46:40
Crossland 40 3 36N30 88W19 5:53:16
Cross Plains 74 3 36N33 86W42 5:46:48
Crossroads 17 3 35N43 89W05 5:56:20
Crossroads 36 23 35N14 88W14 5:52:56
Crossroads 50 29 35N10 87W21 5:49:24
Crosstown 79 39 35N08 90W00 6:00:00
Crosstown 84 3 35N26 89W47 5:59:08
Crossville 18 15 35N57 85W02 5:40:08
Crow 22 3 36N03 87W19 5:49:16
Crowley Store 92 3 36N09 88W48 5:55:12
Crucifer 39 3 35N35 88W32 5:54:08
Crump 36 3 35N13 88W20 5:53:20
Crystal 66 3 36N25 89W03 5:56:12
Crystal Springs 52 9 35N08 86W28 5:45:52
Cuba 37 70 36N21 83W14 5:32:56
Cuba 79 40 35N20 89W53 5:59:32
Cub Creek 44 27 36N21 85W39 5:42:36
Culleoka 60 3 35N29 86W59 5:47:56
Culpepper 8 3 35N50 86W10 5:44:40
Cumberland City 81 3 36N23 87W38 5:50:32
Cumberland Furnace 22 3 36N16 87W22 5:49:28

Cumberland Gap 13 51 36N36 83W40 5:34:40
Cumberland Heights 31 3 35N20 85W43 5:42:52
Cumberland Heights 63 3 36N29 87W23 5:49:32
Cumberland Plateau 4 3 35N39 85W15 5:41:00
Cumberland Springs 72 74 35N01 85W11 5:40:44
Cumberland View 7 66 36N20 84W11 5:36:44
Cummingsville 88 3 35N56 85W28 5:41:52
Cunningham 63 3 36N24 87W23 5:49:32
Curlee 8 3 35N49 86W04 5:44:16
Currie 27 21 36N04 89W00 5:56:00
Curve 49 28 35N45 89W32 5:58:08
Cusick 78 60 35N53 83W43 5:34:52
Cuzick 53 68 35N48 84W16 5:37:04
Cypress 17 14 35N47 89W07 5:56:28
Cypress Creek 40 3 36N26 88W12 5:52:48
Cypress Inn 91 3 35N01 87W49 5:51:16
Cyruston 52 9 35N09 86W35 5:46:20
Daisy 33 61 35N15 85W11 5:40:44
Dale Hollow 14 11 36N33 85W30 5:42:00
Dalewood 19 4 36N13 86W44 5:46:56
Dallas Gardens 33 61 35N16 85W11 5:40:44
Dallas Hills 33 61 35N16 85W11 5:40:44
Dancyville 38 3 35N28 89W24 5:57:36
Dandridge 45 67 36N01 83W25 5:33:40
Dante 47 67 35N58 83W58 5:35:52
Darden 39 3 35N38 88W13 5:52:52
Daus 77 3 35N19 85W26 5:41:44
Davidson 25 3 36N16 85W05 5:40:20
Davis Chapel 9 3 36N00 88W25 5:53:40
Davy Crockett 30 65 36N13 82W48 5:31:12
Daylight 89 46 35N42 85W46 5:43:04
Daysville 18 9 35N52 84W41 5:38:44
Dayton 72 74 35N30 85W01 5:40:04
Daytona Hills 33 61 35N06 85W17 5:41:08
Dayton Spur 18 15 35N57 85W02 5:40:08
Deanburg 12 3 35N29 88W43 5:54:52
Deans 41 3 35N48 87W27 5:49:48
DeArmond 73 67 35N56 84W33 5:38:12
Deason 2 5 35N35 86W21 5:45:24
Decatur 61 54 35N31 84W47 5:39:08
Decaturville 20 3 35N35 88W07 5:52:28
Decherd 26 18 35N13 86W05 5:44:20
Deep Springs 1 62 36N05 84W03 5:36:12
Deerfield 50 29 35N18 87W30 5:50:00
Deerfield Acres 82 2 36N35 82W11 5:28:44
Deer Lodge 65 56 36N12 84W46 5:39:04
Defeated 80 41 36N15 85W57 5:43:48
Delano 70 72 35N16 84W33 5:38:12
Delina 59 3 35N22 86W50 5:47:20
Dellrose 52 9 35N07 86W48 5:47:12
Dellwood 5 64 35N46 83W58 5:35:52
Del Rio 15 65 35N53 83W00 5:32:00
Demory 7 66 36N23 84W07 5:36:28
Denmark 57 3 35N31 89W00 5:56:00
Dennis Cove 10 1 36N17 82W10 5:28:40
Denny Seminary 71 3 36N05 85W44 5:42:56
Denton 15 65 35N49 83W15 5:33:00
Dentville 54 54 35N16 84W33 5:38:12
Denver 8 3 35N50 86W10 5:44:40
Denver 43 3 36N03 87W56 5:51:44
De Priest Bend 68 3 35N46 87W47 5:51:08
De Rossett 93 3 35N57 85W19 5:41:16
Detroit 84 3 35N33 89W48 5:59:12
Devonia 1 62 36N09 84W23 5:37:32
Diana 28 3 35N22 86W50 5:47:20
Dibrell 89 3 35N47 85W46 5:43:04
Dickel 16 13 35N21 86W12 5:44:48
Dickson 22 3 36N05 87W23 5:49:32
Difficult 80 3 36N23 85W57 5:43:48
Dill 4 3 35N36 85W11 5:40:44
Dilley 13 51 36N33 83W59 5:35:56
Dillton 75 37 35N51 86W23 5:45:32
Disco 5 64 35N46 84W08 5:36:32
Dismal 21 3 36N00 85W58 5:43:52
Disney 7 66 36N13 84W09 5:36:36
Dixie 66 3 36N28 89W13 5:56:52
Dixie Lee Junction 47 67 35N48 84W16 5:37:04
Dixon Springs 80 3 36N22 86W03 5:44:12
Dixonville 84 3 35N20 89W53 5:59:32
Doaks Cross Roads 95 34 36N12 86W18 5:45:12
Dockery 6 53 35N17 84W46 5:39:04
Dodson 93 3 35N56 85W28 5:41:52
Dodson Estates 19 4 36N16 86W37 5:46:28
Doeville 46 1 36N20 82W00 5:28:00
Dog Hill 17 3 35N49 89W14 5:56:56
Dogtown 10 1 36N20 82W13 5:28:52
Dog Town 31 3 35N20 85W43 5:42:52
Dogwood 73 67 35N52 84W31 5:38:04
Dollar 9 3 35N36 88W38 5:54:32
Donelson 19 4 36N10 86W40 5:46:40
Donnels Chapel 75 3 35N50 86W10 5:44:40
Dorton 18 15 35N57 85W02 5:40:08
Dossett 1 62 36N05 84W08 5:36:32
Dotson 29 55 36N17 83W36 5:34:24
Dotson Branch 44 3 36N11 85W28 5:41:52
Dotson's Camp Ground 29 55 36N17 83W36 5:34:24
Dotsontown 30 65 36N13 82W38 5:30:32
Dotsonville 63 3 36N33 87W31 5:50:04
Double Bridges 49 3 35N53 89W24 5:57:36
Double Springs 71 3 36N09 85W38 5:42:32
Douglas 94 48 35N57 86W53 5:47:32
Douglas Estates 45 67 36N01 83W25 5:33:40
Dover 81 3 36N29 87W50 5:51:20

Dowelltown 21 3 36N01 85w57 5:43:48
Dowler Heights 33 61 35N08 85w19 5:41:16
Downtown 5 64 35N46 83w58 5:35:52
Doyle 93 3 35N51 85w31 5:42:04
Draper Cross Roads 56 3 36N32 86w02 5:44:08
Dresden 92 47 36N18 88w42 5:54:48
Driftwood 82 2 36N35 82w11 5:28:44
Drop 93 3 35N56 85w28 5:41:52
Drummonds 84 3 35N27 89w56 5:59:44
Drycreek 90 75 36N18 82w28 5:29:52
Dry Hills 49 3 35N53 89w24 5:57:36
Duck Creek 34 51 36N32 83w13 5:32:52
Duck River 41 3 35N44 87w17 5:49:08
Ducktown 70 73 35N02 84w23 5:37:32
Ducktown 90 63 36N13 82w38 5:30:32
Dudney Hill 44 27 36N21 85w39 5:42:36
Due West 19 4 36N16 86w43 5:46:52
Duff 7 66 36N27 84w04 5:36:16
Dukedom 92 3 36N30 88w43 5:54:52
Dulaney 30 65 36N13 82w48 5:31:12
Dull 22 3 36N11 87w20 5:49:20
Dumplin 45 67 36N06 83w33 5:34:12
Dunbar 20 3 35N26 88w05 5:52:20
Duncan Hills 33 61 35N06 85w17 5:41:08
Dunlap 77 3 35N23 85w23 5:41:32
Dunn Creek 78 60 35N48 83w23 5:33:32
Duplex 94 48 35N57 86w53 5:47:32
Du Pont 78 60 35N53 83w43 5:34:52
Durhamville 49 28 35N45 89w32 5:58:08
Dutch 29 55 36N17 83w36 5:34:24
Dutch Valley 1 62 36N05 84w08 5:36:32
Dycus 44 3 36N24 85w48 5:43:12
Dyer 27 21 36N04 89w00 5:56:00
Dyersburg 23 16 36N02 89w23 5:57:32
Dyllis 73 67 35N56 84w33 5:38:12
Dyson Grove 46 1 36N20 82w00 5:28:00
Eads 79 40 35N12 89w39 5:58:36
Eagan 13 51 36N33 83w59 5:35:56
Eagle Creek 3 3 35N53 88w09 5:52:36
Eagle Furnace 73 70 35N52 84w41 5:38:44
Eagleton Village 5 64 35N48 83w57 5:35:48
Eagleville 75 36 35N45 86w39 5:46:36
East 19 4 36N11 86w45 5:47:00
East Acres 79 40 35N20 89w53 5:59:32
Eastbrook 26 18 35N16 86w08 5:44:32
East Chattanooga 33 61 35N04 85w14 5:40:56
East Chester 12 3 35N28 88w32 5:54:08
East Cleveland 6 53 35N09 84w51 5:39:24
East Due West 19 4 36N16 86w43 5:46:52
East Erin 42 3 36N17 87w36 5:50:24
East Etowah 54 54 35N20 84w32 5:38:08
East Fork 78 60 35N49 83w33 5:34:12
Eastgate Center 33 61 35N02 85w14 5:40:56
East Jamestown 25 3 36N26 84w56 5:39:44
East Kingsport 82 2 36N33 82w31 5:30:04
East Lake 33 61 35N01 85w17 5:41:08
Eastland 93 3 35N56 85w28 5:41:52
East Memphis 79 39 35N07 89w57 5:59:48
East Miller's Cove 5 64 35N44 83w49 5:35:16
East Ridge 33 61 34N59 85w13 5:40:52
Eastside 8 3 35N49 86w04 5:44:16
East Side 10 1 36N20 82w13 5:28:52
East Side 22 3 36N03 87w19 5:49:16
Eastside 82 2 36N33 82w31 5:30:04
East Siding 1 62 36N05 84w08 5:36:32
East Springbrook 5 64 35N47 83w59 5:35:56
East Sweetwater 62 67 35N36 84w28 5:37:52
East Union 57 3 35N39 88w53 5:55:32
Eastview 30 65 36N13 82w48 5:31:12
Eastview 55 3 35N02 88w33 5:54:12
East View 61 54 35N17 84w57 5:39:48
Eastwood 75 3 36N01 86w34 5:46:16
Eaton 27 8 35N58 89w08 5:56:32
Eaton Crossroad 53 68 35N48 84w16 5:37:04
Eaton Forest 53 68 35N48 84w16 5:37:04
Ebenezer 58 8 35N04 85w39 5:42:36
Edenwold 19 4 36N16 86w43 5:46:52
Edgefield 82 2 36N35 82w11 5:28:44
Edgemont 15 65 35N59 83w15 5:33:00
Edgemont 82 2 36N35 82w11 5:28:44
Edgemoor 1 62 36N05 84w08 5:36:32
Edgewood 23 16 36N07 89w16 5:57:04
Edgewood Acres 5 64 35N46 83w58 5:35:52
Edgewood Heights 1 62 36N02 84w02 5:36:08
Edith 49 28 35N45 89w32 5:58:08
Edna 45 67 36N09 83w25 5:33:40
Edwina 15 65 35N58 83w11 5:32:44
Eidson 37 70 36N30 83w05 5:32:20
Elba 24 3 35N03 89w33 5:58:12
Elbethel 2 6 35N29 86w27 5:45:48
Elbridge 66 3 36N16 89w19 5:57:16
Elgin 76 58 36N20 84w36 5:38:24
Elizabeth 17 3 35N54 89w15 5:57:00
Elizabethton 10 1 36N21 82w13 5:28:52
Elkhead 31 3 35N19 85w53 5:43:32
Elkhorn 40 26 36N18 88w19 5:53:16
Elk Mills 10 1 36N20 82w00 5:28:00
Elk Mill Village 52 9 35N09 86w35 5:46:20
Elkmont 78 59 35N43 83w31 5:34:04
Elkton 28 3 35N04 86w53 5:47:32
Elk Valley 7 66 36N29 84w15 5:37:00
Ellendale 79 40 35N14 89w49 5:59:16
Ellis Mills 42 3 36N23 87w38 5:50:32
Elm Springs 29 55 36N17 83w36 5:34:24
Elmwood 80 3 36N13 85w53 5:43:32
Elora 52 9 35N01 86w21 5:45:24
Elverton 73 67 35N56 84w33 5:38:12
Elza 1 62 35N59 84w18 5:37:12
Embreeville 90 75 36N08 82w25 5:29:40
Embreeville Junction 90 75 36N18 82w23 5:29:32
Emerts Cove 78 60 35N49 83w33 5:34:12
Emery Mill 4 3 35N36 85w11 5:40:44
Emmett 82 2 36N35 82w11 5:28:44
Emory Gap 73 67 35N56 84w33 5:38:12
Emory Heights 1 62 35N59 84w18 5:37:12
Emory Heights 73 67 35N56 84w33 5:38:12
Englewood 54 71 35N26 84w29 5:37:56
Englewood 66 3 36N25 89w03 5:56:12
English Mountain Resort 78 60 35N49 83w33 5:34:12
Enigma 80 3 36N08 85w47 5:43:08
Eno 22 3 36N05 87w23 5:49:32
Enon 56 3 36N32 85w51 5:43:24
Ensor 71 3 36N09 85w38 5:42:32
Enterprise 37 70 36N21 82w59 5:31:56
Enterprise 60 9 35N32 87w12 5:48:48
Enville 12 3 35N23 88w26 5:53:44
Epperson 62 70 35N22 84w18 5:37:12
Erasmus 18 15 35N57 85w02 5:40:08
Erie 53 68 35N39 84w34 5:38:16
Erin 42 3 36N19 87w42 5:50:48
Ernestville 86 1 36N08 82w25 5:29:40
Erwin 86 1 36N09 82w25 5:29:40
Essary Springs 35 3 35N03 88w48 5:55:12
Estes Kefauver 90 75 36N19 82w21 5:29:24
Estill Springs 26 18 35N16 86w08 5:44:32
Ethridge 50 29 35N19 87w18 5:49:12
Etowah 54 54 35N20 84w32 5:38:08
Etter 69 3 36N34 85w08 5:40:32
Euchee 61 54 35N40 84w40 5:38:40
Eulia 56 3 36N34 86w15 5:45:00
Eureka 6 53 35N09 84w52 5:39:28
Eureka 73 70 35N52 84w41 5:38:44
Eurekaton 38 3 35N20 89w09 5:56:36
Eva 3 3 36N04 88w00 5:52:00
Evanston 34 51 36N32 83w13 5:32:52
Evansville 23 16 36N02 89w23 5:57:32
Evensville 72 74 35N34 84w57 5:39:48
Evergreen 10 1 36N12 82w05 5:28:20
Evins Mill 21 11 35N57 85w49 5:43:16
Ewingville 94 48 35N57 86w53 5:47:32
Excell 63 32 36N32 87w22 5:49:28
Factory 91 3 35N19 87w46 5:51:04
Fair Acres 82 2 36N35 82w11 5:28:44
Fairfield 2 5 35N32 86w20 5:45:20
Fairfield 32 67 36N13 83w17 5:33:08
Fairfield 41 3 35N48 87w27 5:49:48
Fairfield 83 50 36N34 86w15 5:45:00
Fairfield Glade 18 15 35N57 85w02 5:40:08
Fair Garden 78 60 35N49 83w33 5:34:12
Fairgrounds 2 6 35N29 86w27 5:45:48
Fairlane Estates 2 6 35N29 86w27 5:45:48
Fairmont 33 61 35N08 85w19 5:41:16
Fairmont 82 2 36N35 82w11 5:28:44
Fairview 5 64 35N46 83w58 5:35:52
Fairview 6 53 35N09 84w52 5:39:28
Fairview 10 1 36N17 82w10 5:28:40
Fairview 14 3 36N27 85w21 5:41:24
Fairview 16 12 35N27 86w15 5:45:00
Fairview 25 3 36N26 84w56 5:39:44
Fairview 27 21 36N12 89w01 5:56:04
Fairview 29 55 36N21 83w25 5:33:40
Fairview 57 3 35N50 88w55 5:55:40
Fairview 61 54 35N31 84w47 5:39:08
Fairview 69 3 36N34 85w08 5:40:32
Fairview 71 34 36N11 85w28 5:41:52
Fairview 76 58 36N25 84w29 5:37:56
Fairview 81 3 36N29 87w50 5:51:20
Fairview 89 46 35N42 85w46 5:43:04
Fairview 90 75 36N18 82w28 5:29:52
Fairview 94 3 35N59 87w07 5:48:28
Fairview Heights 45 67 36N01 83w25 5:33:40
Fairview Heights 60 31 35N37 87w02 5:48:08
Faix 69 3 36N34 85w08 5:40:32
Falcon 55 3 35N10 88w35 5:54:20
Fall Branch 90 63 36N25 82w37 5:30:28
Falling Water 33 61 35N06 85w15 5:41:00
Fallriver 50 29 35N10 87w21 5:49:24
Falls Mill 26 18 35N08 86w11 5:44:44
Fanchers Mills 93 3 35N56 85w28 5:41:52
Farmers Exchange 41 3 35N33 87w34 5:50:16
Farmers Valley 68 3 35N29 87w50 5:51:20
Farmington 59 30 35N27 86w48 5:47:12
Farner 70 73 35N09 84w19 5:37:16
Farragut 47 67 35N52 84w08 5:36:32
Farris Chapel 26 19 35N11 86w07 5:44:28
Farrport 5 64 35N47 83w59 5:35:56
Faulkner Springs 89 46 35N42 85w46 5:43:04
Faxon 3 3 36N14 88w05 5:52:20
Fayette Corners 24 3 35N21 89w14 5:56:56
Fayetteville 52 9 35N09 86w34 5:46:16
Federal Reserve 19 4 36N09 86w47 5:47:08
Felker 6 53 35N09 84w52 5:39:28
Fennel Store 29 55 36N09 83w42 5:34:48
Fernvale 94 48 35N57 86w53 5:47:32
Fernwood 32 67 36N13 83w17 5:33:08
Field Crest 60 31 35N37 87w02 5:48:08
Fielden Store 45 67 36N06 83w33 5:34:12
Fikes Mill 60 3 35N37 87w13 5:48:52
Fincastle 7 66 36N24 84w01 5:36:04
Findlay 93 3 35N56 85w28 5:41:52
Finger 55 3 35N22 88w36 5:54:24
Finley 23 16 36N02 89w29 5:57:56
Fisherville 79 40 35N09 89w42 5:58:48
Fishery 86 1 36N08 82w25 5:29:40
Fish Springs 10 1 36N20 82w00 5:28:00
Fisk University 19 4 36N09 86w47 5:47:08
Five Points 50 29 35N03 87w19 5:49:16
Five Points 57 3 35N29 88w43 5:54:52
Five Points 72 74 35N01 85w11 5:40:44
Flag Branch 30 65 36N13 82w48 5:31:12
Flag Pond 86 1 36N03 82w31 5:30:04
Flat Branch Junction 31 3 35N16 85w44 5:42:56
Flat Creek 2 6 35N29 86w27 5:45:48
Flat Gap 34 51 36N26 83w14 5:32:56
Flatgap 45 67 36N07 83w30 5:34:00
Flat Hollow 7 66 36N27 83w55 5:35:40
Flattop 33 61 35N16 85w11 5:40:44
Flatwood 84 3 35N33 89w48 5:59:12
Flat Woods 50 29 35N19 87w18 5:49:12
Flat Woods 68 3 35N29 87w50 5:51:20
Flewellyn 74 35 36N30 86w53 5:47:32
Flintville 52 9 35N04 86w25 5:45:40
Flippin 49 28 35N45 89w32 5:58:08
Florence 75 37 35N51 86w23 5:45:32
Flourville 90 75 36N18 82w28 5:29:52
Flowers 3 3 36N04 88w06 5:52:24
Flowertown 16 12 35N27 86w15 5:45:00
Fly 60 3 35N44 87w08 5:48:32
Fochee 53 68 35N44 84w21 5:37:24
Forbus 25 3 36N34 85w01 5:40:04
Ford 53 68 35N48 84w16 5:37:04
Fordtown 82 2 36N27 82w31 5:30:04
Forest Chapel 83 50 36N34 86w15 5:45:00
Forest Grove 19 4 36N10 86w46 5:47:04
Forest Grove 61 54 35N31 84w47 5:39:08
Forest Hill 5 64 35N46 83w58 5:35:52
Forest Hill 43 3 36N05 87w47 5:51:08
Forest Hills 2 6 35N29 86w27 5:45:48
Forest Hills 19 4 36N06 86w50 5:47:20
Forest Hills 59 30 35N27 86w48 5:47:12
Forest Hills 82 2 36N35 82w11 5:28:44
Forest Mills 16 12 35N28 86w05 5:44:20
Forked Deer 38 3 35N50 89w25 5:57:40
Fork Mountain 1 62 36N08 84w25 5:37:40
Fork Of Pike 21 3 36N00 85w58 5:43:52
Fork Ridge 13 51 36N37 83w44 5:34:56
Forks Of The River 80 3 36N13 85w51 5:43:24
Forrest Hills 60 31 35N37 87w02 5:48:08
Forrest Park 16 13 35N21 86w12 5:44:48
Fort Campbell 63 3 36N36 87w33 5:50:12
Fort Loudon Estates 53 68 35N48 84w16 5:37:04
Fosterville 75 3 35N39 86w24 5:45:36
Foundry Hill 40 3 36N27 88w20 5:53:20
Fountain City 47 67 36N02 83w56 5:35:44
Fountain Head 83 50 36N35 86w31 5:46:04
Fountain Heights 60 3 35N33 86w58 5:47:52
Four Point 27 21 36N04 88w49 5:55:16
Four Way 2 6 35N29 86w27 5:45:48
Fowler Grove 15 65 36N03 83w11 5:32:44
Fowlers 3 3 36N04 88w06 5:52:24
Fowlkes 23 16 35N57 89w20 5:57:20
Fox Bluff 11 10 36N16 87w04 5:48:16
Foxbranch 34 51 36N34 83w03 5:32:12
Frankewing 28 3 35N12 86w51 5:47:24
Frankfort 65 56 36N13 84w39 5:38:36
Franklin 94 48 35N55 86w52 5:47:28
Fraterville 1 62 36N13 84w09 5:36:36
Frayser 79 39 35N13 90w00 6:00:00
Fredonia 16 12 35N28 86w05 5:44:20
Fredonia 63 32 36N32 87w22 5:49:28
Free Hills 14 11 36N33 85w30 5:42:00
Freeland 40 3 36N26 88w12 5:52:48
Freewill 44 27 36N21 85w39 5:42:36
Fremont 66 3 36N25 89w03 5:56:12
French Broad 15 65 35N55 83w01 5:32:04
Frettin 35 3 35N04 88w53 5:55:32
Friendship 17 3 35N55 89w14 5:56:56
Friendship 33 61 35N07 85w08 5:40:32
Friendship 37 70 36N26 83w14 5:32:56
Friends Station 45 67 36N06 83w33 5:34:12
Friendsville 5 64 35N46 84w08 5:36:32
Frisco 37 70 36N32 82w41 5:30:44
Frog Jump 17 3 35N53 89w24 5:57:36
Frog Jump 27 8 35N58 88w57 5:55:48
Front Street 79 39 35N08 90w03 6:00:12
Frost Bottom 1 62 36N02 84w20 5:37:20
Fruitland 27 21 35N54 88w56 5:55:44
Fruitvale 17 3 35N45 89w02 5:56:08
Fruit Valley 2 3 35N45 86w32 5:46:08
Fry 32 67 36N13 83w17 5:33:08
Fulton 49 3 35N40 89w34 5:58:16
Furnace 46 1 36N29 81w48 5:27:12
Gabtown 90 63 36N25 82w37 5:30:28
Gadsden 17 3 35N47 88w59 5:55:56
Gail 12 3 35N26 88w39 5:54:36
Gainesboro 44 27 36N21 85w39 5:42:36
Gainsville 84 44 35N25 89w32 5:58:08
Gaitherville 50 29 35N15 87w20 5:49:20
Galaxy Heights 33 61 35N06 85w15 5:41:00
Galbraith Springs 37 70 36N21 83w14 5:32:56
Galen 56 3 36N32 86w02 5:44:08
Gallatin 83 42 36N24 86w27 5:45:48
Gallaway 24 3 35N20 89w37 5:58:28
Gandy 50 29 35N15 87w20 5:49:20

Gann 27 20 35N55 88w46 5:55:04
Gapcreek 10 1 36N20 82w13 5:28:52
Gardner 92 3 36N21 88w51 5:55:24
Garland 84 3 35N35 89w46 5:59:04
Garretts 20 3 35N35 88w07 5:52:28
Gassaway 8 3 36N00 85w58 5:43:52
Gates 49 3 35N50 89w24 5:57:36
Gath 89 46 35N42 85w46 5:43:04
Gatlinburg 78 59 35N43 83w31 5:34:04
Gattistown 52 9 35N13 86w28 5:45:52
Gause 74 3 36N21 87w10 5:48:40
Gentry 71 3 36N09 85w38 5:42:32
Georgetown 33 61 35N17 84w57 5:39:48
George W. Lee 79 39 35N08 90w03 6:00:12
Germantown 19 4 36N10 86w46 5:47:04
Germantown 79 40 35N05 89w49 5:59:16
Gibbs 47 67 36N07 83w51 5:35:24
Gibbs 66 3 36N25 89w03 5:56:12
Gibbs Cross Roads 56 3 36N23 85w57 5:43:48
Gibson 27 21 35N53 88w51 5:55:24
Gift 84 44 35N34 89w42 5:58:48
Gilchrist 55 3 35N14 88w23 5:53:32
Gillises Mills 36 23 35N14 88w14 5:52:56
Gilmore 57 3 35N39 88w53 5:55:32
Gilt Edge 84 3 35N33 89w50 5:59:20
Gin House Lake 84 3 35N27 89w49 5:59:16
Gladdice 44 27 36N21 85w39 5:42:36
Glades 65 56 36N12 84w46 5:39:04
Glades 78 59 35N43 83w31 5:34:04
Gladeville 95 49 36N07 86w25 5:45:40
Glass 66 3 36N16 89w11 5:56:44
Gleason 92 3 36N13 88w37 5:54:28
Glen 16 12 35N25 85w58 5:43:52
Glen Alice 73 70 35N52 84w41 5:38:44
Glencliff 19 4 36N06 86w45 5:47:00
Glendale 19 4 36N07 86w52 5:47:28
Glendale 33 61 35N05 85w19 5:41:16
Glendale 53 68 35N40 84w10 5:36:40
Glendale 60 31 35N37 87w02 5:48:08
Glendale Estates 28 22 35N12 87w02 5:48:08
Glen Mary 76 58 36N21 84w35 5:38:20
Glenmore Estates 5 64 35N46 83w58 5:35:52
Glenobey 25 3 36N26 84w56 5:39:44
Glenview 16 12 35N28 86w05 5:44:20
Glenview 19 4 36N08 86w42 5:46:48
Glenwilde 22 3 36N16 87w22 5:49:28
Glimp 49 3 35N40 89w34 5:58:16
Glover Hill 58 8 35N04 85w39 5:42:36
Gnat Hill 16 12 35N28 86w05 5:44:20
Goat City 27 21 35N48 88w46 5:55:04
Godwin 60 31 35N37 87w02 5:48:08
Goffton 71 34 36N11 85w28 5:41:52
Goin 13 51 36N26 83w36 5:34:24
Golddust 49 28 35N45 89w32 5:58:08
Goldpoint 33 61 35N06 85w15 5:41:00
Goodbars 89 3 35N48 85w37 5:42:28
Goodfield 61 54 35N31 84w47 5:39:08
Good Hope 7 66 36N35 84w08 5:36:32
Good Hope 23 16 36N07 89w16 5:57:04
Goodlettsville 19 4 36N19 86w43 5:46:52
Good Luck 27 21 36N08 88w59 5:55:56
Goodspring 28 3 35N09 87w06 5:48:24
Good Springs 54 54 35N20 84w32 5:38:08
Goose Horn 56 3 36N27 85w40 5:42:40
Gooseneck 5 64 35N46 84w08 5:36:32
Gordon 28 22 35N12 87w02 5:48:08
Gordonsburg 51 3 35N33 87w34 5:50:16
Gordonsville 80 3 36N10 85w56 5:43:44
Gorman 43 3 36N06 87w38 5:50:32
Goshen 37 70 36N32 82w41 5:30:44
Gossburg 16 12 35N38 86w14 5:44:56
Graball 27 20 35N55 88w46 5:55:04
Graball 83 50 36N35 86w31 5:46:04
Graham 41 3 35N52 87w28 5:49:52
Grand Junction 35 3 35N04 89w06 5:56:24
Grandview 47 67 35N56 83w54 5:35:36
Grandview 72 74 35N45 84w50 5:39:20
Grandview Terrace 82 2 36N35 82w11 5:28:44
Granite 1 62 36N05 84w08 5:36:32
Grant 80 3 36N11 85w56 5:43:44
Grantsboro 7 66 36N23 84w07 5:36:28
Granville 44 3 36N16 85w48 5:43:12
Grasshopper 33 61 35N22 85w00 5:40:00
Grassland 94 48 35N57 86w53 5:47:32
Grassy Cove 18 15 35N57 85w02 5:40:08
Grassy Creek 70 73 34N59 84w22 5:37:28
Grassy Fork 15 65 35N49 83w09 5:32:36
Gratio 66 3 36N16 89w11 5:56:44
Gravel Hill 55 3 35N02 88w34 5:54:16
Gravel Hill 90 63 36N13 82w38 5:30:32
Gravelly Hill 45 67 36N07 83w30 5:34:00
Gravelly Hills 5 64 35N49 84w03 5:36:12
Gravelotte 11 10 36N16 87w04 5:48:16
Graveltown 80 3 36N19 86w01 5:44:04
Graveston 47 67 36N10 83w49 5:35:16
Gray 90 75 36N25 82w29 5:29:56
Gray Acres 82 2 36N35 82w11 5:28:44
Graymere Manor 60 31 35N37 87w02 5:48:08
Graysville 72 74 35N27 85w08 5:40:32
Graytown 41 3 35N48 87w27 5:49:48
Greater Hendersonville 83 43 36N17 86w37 5:46:28
Green Acres 28 22 35N12 87w02 5:48:08
Green Acres 47 67 35N58 83w58 5:35:52
Greenback 53 68 35N40 84w10 5:36:40
Greenbrier 11 10 36N16 87w04 5:48:16
Green Brier 69 3 36N34 85w08 5:40:32
Green Brier 74 3 36N26 86w48 5:47:12
Greeneville 30 65 36N10 82w50 5:31:20
Greenfield 92 3 36N09 88w48 5:55:12
Green Grove 56 3 36N23 86w10 5:44:40
Greenhaw 26 18 35N13 86w05 5:44:20
Green Hill 89 46 35N42 85w46 5:43:04
Green Hill 95 49 36N09 86w39 5:46:36
Green Hills 19 4 36N06 86w50 5:47:20
Green Hills 60 31 35N37 87w02 5:48:08
Green Hills Village 19 4 36N06 86w50 5:47:20
Green Meadow 6 53 35N17 84w46 5:39:04
Greenvale 95 9 36N06 86w08 5:44:32
Green Valley 47 67 35N56 84w00 5:36:00
Green Valley 56 3 36N32 86w02 5:44:08
Green Village 37 70 36N32 82w41 5:30:44
Greenwood 56 3 36N32 85w51 5:43:24
Greenwood 95 34 36N12 86w18 5:45:12
Greystone 30 65 36N13 82w48 5:31:12
Greystone Estates 82 2 36N35 82w11 5:28:44
Griffith 4 3 36N03 88w35 5:54:20
Griffith Creek 58 8 35N12 85w31 5:42:04
Grimsley 25 3 36N16 84w59 5:39:56
Grinders 41 3 35N48 87w27 5:49:48
Gronanville 48 3 36N23 89w29 5:57:56
Gruetli 31 3 35N22 85w40 5:42:40
Gudger 62 67 35N31 84w22 5:37:28
Guild 58 8 35N03 85w32 5:42:08
Gulf Park 47 67 35N56 84w00 5:36:00
Gum 75 37 35N51 86w23 5:45:32
Gum Creek 26 18 35N13 86w05 5:44:20
Gum Flat 17 3 35N43 89w05 5:56:20
Gum Spring 15 65 35N58 83w11 5:32:44
Gum Springs 56 3 36N23 85w57 5:43:48
Guntown 37 70 36N24 83w00 5:32:00
Guys 55 3 35N02 88w34 5:54:16
Habersham 7 66 36N29 84w07 5:36:28
Hackberry 63 3 36N26 87w29 5:49:56
Hales Point 49 3 35N53 89w24 5:57:36
Halesville 21 3 36N00 85w58 5:43:52
Haletown 58 8 35N02 85w32 5:42:08
Haley 2 5 35N32 86w20 5:45:20
Halls 49 3 35N53 89w24 5:57:36
Halls Crossroads 47 67 36N05 83w56 5:35:44
Halls Hill 75 37 35N51 86w23 5:45:32
Halls Mills 2 6 35N29 86w27 5:45:48
Hambright 70 72 35N11 84w30 5:38:00
Hamburg 36 3 35N09 88w19 5:53:16
Hamillville 33 61 35N06 85w15 5:41:00
Hamlin Town 13 51 36N33 83w57 5:35:48
Hampshire 60 3 35N36 87w18 5:49:12
Hampton 10 1 36N17 82w10 5:28:40
Hampton Station 63 32 36N32 87w22 5:49:28
Handleyton 74 3 36N35 86w31 5:46:04
Hanging Limb 67 3 36N14 85w10 5:40:40
Happy Top 18 9 35N45 84w50 5:39:20
Happy Valley 5 64 35N33 84w06 5:36:24
Happy Valley 10 1 36N18 82w18 5:29:12
Harbin 73 70 35N52 84w41 5:38:44
Harbison 47 67 36N10 83w49 5:35:16
Hardin Estates 53 68 35N48 84w16 5:37:04
Hardin Valley 47 67 35N56 84w11 5:36:44
Hardison Mill 60 31 35N37 87w02 5:48:08
Hardy 67 3 36N11 85w28 5:41:52
Hardy Acres 60 31 35N37 87w02 5:48:08
Harmon 46 1 36N31 81w56 5:27:44
Harmony 26 18 35N10 86w12 5:44:48
Harmony 88 3 35N47 85w35 5:42:20
Harmony Grove 15 65 35N55 83w01 5:32:04
Harmony Hills 82 2 36N34 82w33 5:30:12
Harms 52 9 35N09 86w35 5:46:20
Harpeth 94 48 35N57 86w53 5:47:32
Harpeth Valley Park 19 4 36N10 86w46 5:47:04
Harriman 73 67 35N56 84w33 5:38:12
Harriman Junction 73 67 35N56 84w33 5:38:12
Harris 66 3 36N25 89w03 5:56:12
Harrisburg 78 60 35N49 83w33 5:34:12
Harrison 33 61 35N07 85w08 5:40:32
Harrison Hills 53 68 35N48 84w16 5:37:04
Harrogate 13 51 36N35 83w40 5:34:40
Harrtown 82 1 36N32 82w19 5:29:16
Hartford 15 65 35N49 83w09 5:32:36
Hartmantown 90 75 36N18 82w28 5:29:52
Hartsville 85 45 36N24 86w09 5:44:36
Hatchie 57 3 35N28 89w05 5:56:20
Havley Springs 32 67 36N13 83w17 5:33:08
Havron Chapel 58 8 35N04 85w39 5:42:36
Haydenburg 44 3 36N27 85w40 5:42:40
Hayes Fork 81 3 36N29 87w50 5:51:20
Haynesfield 82 2 36N35 82w11 5:28:44
Hays 24 3 35N04 89w24 5:57:36
Haysboro 19 4 36N13 86w44 5:46:56
Haysville 56 3 36N32 86w02 5:44:08
Head Of Barren 13 51 36N26 83w36 5:34:24
Heard 69 3 36N23 85w19 5:41:16
Heatoncreek 10 1 36N12 82w05 5:28:20
Hebron 35 3 35N16 89w00 5:56:00
Heiskell 47 67 36N05 84w03 5:36:12
Helena 25 3 36N26 84w56 5:39:44
Helenwood 76 58 36N26 84w33 5:38:12
Heloise 23 16 36N03 89w29 5:57:56
Helton 21 3 36N05 86w02 5:44:08
Heltonville 29 55 36N20 83w22 5:33:28
Henardtown 37 70 36N24 83w00 5:32:00
Henderson 12 3 35N26 88w38 5:54:32
Hendersonville 83 43 36N18 86w37 5:46:28
Hendon 4 3 35N27 85w05 5:40:20

Hendron 47 67 35N56 83w54 5:35:36
Henley 26 18 35N13 86w05 5:44:20
Henning 49 3 35N40 89w33 5:58:12
Henrietta 11 10 36N16 87w04 5:48:16
Henry 40 3 36N12 88w25 5:53:40
Henrys Crossroads 78 60 36N00 83w38 5:34:32
Henry Street 32 67 36N13 83w17 5:33:08
Henryville 50 29 35N26 87w18 5:49:12
Hensley Chapel 93 3 35N56 85w28 5:41:52
Heritage Hills 5 64 35N46 83w58 5:35:52
Hermitage 19 4 36N12 86w37 5:46:28
Hermitage Hills 19 4 36N12 86w37 5:46:28
Hermitage Springs 14 3 36N35 85w47 5:43:08
Hermon 30 65 36N12 82w44 5:30:56
Hiawassee 89 3 35N36 85w49 5:43:16
Hickerson 16 13 35N21 86w12 5:44:48
Hickey 71 3 36N05 85w44 5:42:56
Hickman 80 3 36N09 85w57 5:43:48
Hickory Bend 19 4 36N09 86w41 5:46:44
Hickory Flat 9 3 35N49 88w36 5:54:24
Hickory Flats 55 3 35N14 88w23 5:53:32
Hickory Grove 27 8 35N58 88w57 5:55:48
Hickory Grove 83 50 36N24 86w19 5:45:16
Hickory Grove 89 46 35N42 85w46 5:43:04
Hickory Heights 59 30 35N27 86w48 5:47:12
Hickory Point 63 32 36N32 87w22 5:49:28
Hickory Star Landing 87 52 36N15 83w48 5:35:12
Hickory Tree 82 1 36N28 82w15 5:29:00
Hickory Valley 35 3 35N09 89w08 5:56:32
Hickory Valley 87 52 36N15 83w48 5:35:12
Hickory Withe 24 3 35N15 89w35 5:58:20
Hicks Chapel 58 8 35N12 85w31 5:42:04
Hicksville 57 3 35N39 88w53 5:55:32
Hico 9 3 36N00 88w25 5:53:40
Highcliff 7 66 36N35 84w08 5:36:32
Highland 44 27 36N21 85w39 5:42:36
Highland 66 3 36N25 89w03 5:56:12
Highland 67 22 36N23 85w19 5:41:16
Highland 91 3 35N10 87w44 5:50:56
Highland Academy 83 50 36N35 86w31 5:46:04
Highland Acres 5 64 35N46 83w58 5:35:52
Highland Forest 73 70 35N52 84w41 5:38:44
Highland Heights 19 4 36N13 86w46 5:47:04
Highland Heights 28 22 35N12 87w02 5:48:08
Highland Heights 60 31 35N37 87w02 5:48:08
Highland Heights 79 40 35N10 89w54 5:59:36
Highland Junction 25 3 36N16 85w05 5:40:20
Highland Park 33 61 35N01 85w16 5:41:04
Highland Park 53 68 35N48 84w16 5:37:04
Highland Park 60 31 35N37 87w02 5:48:08
Highland Springs 29 55 36N09 83w42 5:34:48
Highlandview 47 67 35N56 83w54 5:35:36
High Point 15 65 35N58 83w11 5:32:44
High Point 65 56 36N12 84w46 5:39:04
Highway One Hundred 19 4 36N07 86w52 5:47:28
Hilham 67 3 36N23 85w26 5:41:44
Hillcrest 32 67 36N13 83w17 5:33:08
Hillcrest 59 30 35N27 86w48 5:47:12
Hilldale 63 32 36N32 87w22 5:49:28
Hilliard 9 3 36N00 88w25 5:53:40
Hillsboro 16 12 35N25 85w58 5:43:52
Hillsdale 56 3 36N22 86w03 5:44:12
Hills View 54 54 35N23 84w42 5:38:48
Hilltop 2 6 35N29 86w27 5:45:48
Hilltop 63 1 36N20 82w00 5:28:00
Hilltop 75 38 35N59 86w31 5:46:04
Hill Top 90 75 36N19 82w21 5:29:24
Hillvale 1 62 36N05 84w08 5:36:32
Hillville 38 3 35N26 89w14 5:56:56
Hillwood 19 4 36N07 86w52 5:47:28
Hindscreek 1 62 36N05 84w08 5:36:32
Hinds Creek Valley 87 52 36N15 83w48 5:35:12
Hinkle 36 3 35N27 88w18 5:53:12
Hinkledale 9 3 36N08 88w31 5:54:04
Hitchcox 4 3 35N36 85w11 5:40:44
Hiwassee College 62 67 35N31 84w22 5:37:28
Hixson 33 61 35N09 85w14 5:40:56
Hodges 45 67 36N06 83w33 5:34:12
Hoggtown 80 41 36N15 85w57 5:43:48
Hohenwald 51 3 35N33 87w33 5:50:12
Holiday City 79 40 35N03 89w54 5:59:36
Holiday Hills 73 67 35N52 84w31 5:38:04
Holladay 3 3 35N52 88w09 5:52:36
Holladay 71 34 36N11 85w28 5:41:52
Holland Mill 30 65 36N12 82w44 5:30:56
Hollow Rock 9 3 36N02 88w16 5:53:04
Hollow Springs 8 3 35N44 86w10 5:44:40
Holly Grove 38 3 35N43 89w05 5:56:20
Holly Grove 59 30 35N27 86w48 5:47:12
Holly Grove 84 3 35N29 89w43 5:58:52
Holly Leaf 9 3 36N01 88w37 5:54:28
Holly Springs 67 22 36N23 85w19 5:41:16
Hollywood 33 61 35N08 85w19 5:41:16
Hollywood 60 3 35N29 86w59 5:47:56
Hollywood 79 39 35N11 89w57 5:59:48
Holston Hills 82 2 36N35 82w11 5:28:44
Holston Institute 82 1 36N32 82w19 5:29:16

TENNESSEE

Place	No.	Lat.	Long.	Time
Holston Valley 82	1	36N34	82w03	5:28:12
Holtland 59	3	35N42	86w42	5:46:48
Holts Corner 59	3	35N38	86w42	5:46:48
Holttown 15	65	35N58	83w11	5:32:44
Holy Hill 46	1	36N29	81w48	5:27:12
Homestead 18	15	35N57	85w02	5:40:08
Homeway Village 16	13	35N21	86w12	5:44:48
Honeycutt 37	70	36N24	83w00	5:32:00
Hood Lake 50	29	35N15	87w20	5:49:20
Hoodoo 16	12	35N38	86w14	5:44:56
Hookers Bend 36	3	35N19	88w21	5:53:24
Hoop 13	51	36N27	83w34	5:34:16
Hoovers Gap 75	36	35N43	86w24	5:45:36
Hopewell 6	53	35N09	84w52	5:39:28
Hopewell 9	3	35N51	88w40	5:54:40
Hopewell 19	4	36N09	86w39	5:46:36
Hopewell 84	3	35N29	89w43	5:58:52
Hopewell Springs 62	67	35N31	84w22	5:37:28
Hopson 10	1	36N12	82w05	5:28:20
Hornbeak 66	3	36N20	89w18	5:57:12
Hornertown 41	3	35N40	87w42	5:50:48
Hornsby 35	3	35N14	88w50	5:55:20
Horse Creek 82	2	36N34	82w33	5:30:12
Horse Shoe 10	1	36N20	82w13	5:28:52
Housley Addition 54	71	35N27	84w36	5:38:24
Houston 91	3	35N10	87w56	5:51:44
Howard 62	67	35N35	84w15	5:37:00
Howard Springs 18	15	35N57	85w02	5:40:08
Howell 52	9	35N14	86w37	5:46:28
Howell Hill 52	9	35N09	86w35	5:46:20
Howley 9	3	35N49	88w36	5:54:24
Hubbard 5	64	35N46	83w58	5:35:52
Huffman 65	56	36N15	84w40	5:38:40
Hugarth 25	3	36N26	84w56	5:39:44
Hughey 52	9	35N09	86w35	5:46:20
Hulan Hollow 86	1	36N08	82w25	5:29:40
Humboldt 27	8	35N50	88w55	5:55:40
Hunter 10	1	36N20	82w13	5:28:52
Hunters Point 95	34	36N12	86w18	5:45:12
Huntersville 57	3	35N34	88w55	5:55:40
Huntingdon 9	3	36N00	88w26	5:53:44
Huntland 26	18	35N03	86w16	5:45:04
Huntsville 53	68	35N48	84w16	5:37:04
Huntsville 76	58	36N25	84w29	5:37:56
Hurdlow 64	3	35N08	86w11	5:44:44
Hurley 36	3	35N04	88w25	5:53:40
Huron 39	3	35N35	88w32	5:54:08
Hurricane Hill 49	28	35N45	89w32	5:58:08
Hurricane Mills 43	3	35N58	87w47	5:51:08
Hustburg 43	3	36N03	87w56	5:51:44
Hutchings 93	3	35N56	85w28	5:41:52
Hutsell 54	71	35N27	84w36	5:38:24
Hyndsver 92	3	36N21	88w51	5:55:24
Iconium 8	3	35N49	86w04	5:44:16
Idaho 50	29	35N10	87w21	5:49:24
Idaville 84	3	35N26	89w47	5:59:08
Ideal Valley 72	74	35N41	84w52	5:39:28
Idlewild 27	8	35N59	88w48	5:55:12
Idlewild 54	71	35N27	84w36	5:38:24
Idlewild 60	31	35N37	87w02	5:48:08
Imperial Estates 47	67	35N58	83w58	5:35:52
Independence 34	51	36N31	83w02	5:32:08
Independence 67	3	36N26	85w15	5:41:00
India 40	26	36N18	88w19	5:53:16
Indian Bluff 1	62	36N11	84w11	5:36:44
Indian Cave 29	55	36N09	83w42	5:34:48
Indian Mound 21	3	35N56	85w28	5:41:52
Indian Mound 81	3	36N30	87w42	5:50:48
Indian Ridge 29	55	36N09	83w42	5:34:48
Indian Springs 82	1	36N32	82w26	5:29:44
Ingleside Hill 54	71	35N27	84w36	5:38:24
Inglewood 19	4	36N13	86w44	5:46:56
Irish Cut 15	65	35N58	83w11	5:32:44
Iron 50	29	35N02	87w30	5:50:00
Iron City 50	29	35N01	87w35	5:50:20
Irving College 89	3	35N36	85w36	5:42:24
Isabella 70	73	35N02	84w21	5:37:24
Isham 76	58	36N33	84w27	5:37:48
Isoline 18	15	35N57	85w02	5:40:08
Isom 60	3	35N36	87w18	5:49:12
Ivy 62	70	35N11	84w30	5:38:00
Ivydell 7	66	36N23	84w07	5:36:28
Ivy Point 19	4	36N18	86w43	5:46:52
Ivyton 67	3	36N24	85w14	5:40:56
Jacksboro 7	66	36N20	84w11	5:36:44
Jacks Creek 12	3	35N28	88w31	5:54:04
Jackson 57	14	35N37	88w49	5:55:16
Jackson Heights 60	31	35N37	87w02	5:48:08
Jackson Heights 75	37	35N51	86w23	5:45:32
Jackson Square 1	62	35N59	84w18	5:37:12
Jackson Suburban 57	14	35N36	88w49	5:55:16
Jakestown 75	37	35N51	86w23	5:45:32
Jalapa 62	70	35N22	84w18	5:37:12
Jamestown 25	3	36N26	84w56	5:39:44
Jarrell 9	3	36N08	88w31	5:54:04
Jasper 58	8	35N05	85w38	5:42:32
Jaybird 15	65	35N58	83w11	5:32:44
Jaybird 32	67	36N13	83w17	5:33:08
Jeannette 20	3	35N39	88w07	5:52:28
Jearoldstown 30	65	36N21	82w43	5:30:52
Jefferson 21	11	35N57	85w49	5:43:16
Jefferson City 45	67	36N07	83w30	5:34:00
Jefferson Estates 45	67	36N09	83w25	5:33:40
Jellico 7	66	36N35	84w08	5:36:32
Jena 53	68	35N40	84w10	5:36:40
Jenkins Hill 78	60	35N49	83w33	5:34:12
Jenkinsville 23	16	36N02	89w23	5:57:32
Jere Baxter 19	4	36N13	86w44	5:46:56
Jessie 89	46	35N42	85w46	5:43:04
Jewell 92	47	36N17	88w42	5:54:48
Jimtown 15	65	35N58	83w11	5:32:44
Joelton 19	4	36N10	86w46	5:47:04
John Sevier 47	67	36N03	83w50	5:35:20
Johnson City 90	75	36N19	82w21	5:29:24
Johnsons Chapel 21	3	35N56	85w28	5:41:52
Johnsons Grove 17	3	35N43	89w05	5:56:20
Johnsons Store 37	70	36N32	82w41	5:30:44
Johnstown 16	13	35N21	86w12	5:44:48
Johntown 85	45	36N23	86w10	5:44:40
Jones 38	3	35N43	89w05	5:56:20
Jonesboro 90	75	36N18	82w29	5:29:56
Jones Chapel 69	3	36N34	85w08	5:40:32
Jones Cove 78	60	35N49	83w33	5:34:12
Jones Mill 40	3	36N23	88w29	5:53:56
Jones Valley 41	3	35N44	87w08	5:48:32
Jonesville 73	63	36N02	84w20	5:37:20
Joppa 29	55	36N17	83w31	5:34:04
Jordonia 19	4	36N13	86w50	5:47:20
Jug Town 75	37	35N51	86w23	5:45:32
Juno 39	25	35N39	88w23	5:53:32
Kansas 83	42	36N23	86w26	5:45:44
Karns 47	67	35N59	84w08	5:36:32
Kedron 28	3	35N02	87w00	5:48:00
Kedron 60	3	35N45	86w55	5:47:40
Keefe 48	3	36N16	89w29	5:57:56
Keeling 38	3	35N28	89w24	5:57:36
Keenburg 10	1	36N20	82w13	5:28:52
Keese 26	18	35N13	86w05	5:44:20
Kelley Town 73	63	36N02	84w20	5:37:20
Kelso 52	9	35N08	86w28	5:45:52
Keltonburg 21	11	35N57	85w49	5:43:16
Kemmer Hill 72	74	35N41	84w52	5:39:28
Kempville 80	41	36N15	85w57	5:43:48
Kendricks Creek 82	2	36N31	82w32	5:30:08
Kenneytown 30	65	36N13	82w48	5:31:12
Kenton 66	3	36N12	89w01	5:56:04
Kenwood 63	32	36N32	87w22	5:49:28
Kepler 37	70	36N24	83w00	5:32:00
Kerrville 79	40	35N20	89w53	5:59:32
Kettle Mills 60	3	35N36	87w18	5:49:12
Key 93	3	35N56	85w28	5:41:52
Keys Chapel 2	6	35N29	86w27	5:45:48
Key Station 46	1	36N23	81w43	5:26:52
Keystone 90	75	36N19	82w21	5:29:24
Killians Chapel 31	3	35N26	85w43	5:42:52
Kilsyth 7	66	36N27	84w04	5:36:16
Kimball 58	8	35N02	85w41	5:42:44
Kimberlin Heights 47	67	35N56	83w48	5:35:12
Kimery 92	3	36N09	88w48	5:55:12
Kimmins 51	3	35N37	87w32	5:50:08
King 7	66	36N33	83w57	5:35:48
Kingfield 94	48	35N57	86w53	5:47:32
Kingsport 82	2	36N33	82w33	5:30:12
Kingsport North 82	2	36N34	82w33	5:30:12
King Springs 90	75	36N19	82w21	5:29:24
Kingston 73	67	35N52	84w31	5:38:04
Kingston Hills 47	67	35N56	84w00	5:36:00
Kingston Springs 11	9	36N06	87w07	5:48:28
Kingston Woods 47	67	35N56	84w00	5:36:00
Kinzel Springs 5	64	35N40	83w45	5:35:00
Kirk 24	3	35N03	89w40	5:58:40
Kirkland 52	9	35N00	86w40	5:46:40
Kirkland 94	3	35N48	86w40	5:46:40
Kite 37	70	36N24	83w00	5:32:00
Kittrell 75	3	35N48	86w15	5:45:00
Kline 26	19	35N11	86w07	5:44:28
Knapp 1	62	36N13	84w09	5:36:36
Knob Creek 49	28	35N45	89w32	5:58:08
Knob Creek 78	60	35N52	83w39	5:34:36
Knoxville 47	67	35N58	83w55	5:35:40
Kodak 78	60	36N00	83w38	5:34:32
Koko 38	3	35N28	89w24	5:57:36
Kyles Ford 34	51	36N34	83w03	5:32:12
Laager 31	3	35N22	85w36	5:42:24
Laconia 24	3	35N17	89w15	5:57:00
Lacy 35	3	35N04	88w53	5:55:32
Ladds 58	8	34N59	85w30	5:42:00
Lafayette 56	3	36N31	86w02	5:44:08
La Follette 7	66	36N23	84w07	5:36:28
La Grange 24	3	35N03	89w15	5:57:00
La Guardo 95	34	36N12	86w18	5:45:12
Lake City 1	62	36N13	84w09	5:36:36
Lake Crest 82	2	36N31	82w32	5:30:08
Lake Drive 48	3	36N23	89w29	5:57:56
Lake Harbor Estates 33	61	35N05	85w12	5:40:48
Lakemont 5	64	35N49	84w03	5:36:12
Lakemont Cabin Area 37	70	36N21	83w14	5:32:56
Lakemont Heights 73	70	35N52	84w41	5:38:44
Lakemoor 47	67	35N56	83w54	5:35:36
Lakemoore 32	67	36N13	83w17	5:33:08
Lake Placid 12	3	35N26	88w39	5:54:36
Lakeshore Estates 33	61	35N05	85w12	5:40:48
Lake Side 33	61	35N06	85w15	5:41:00
Lakeside 62	67	35N35	84w15	5:37:00
Lakesite 33	61	35N16	85w11	5:40:44
Lake Tansi 18	15	35N57	85w02	5:40:08
Lake Tullahoma Estates 16	13	35N21	86w12	5:44:48
Lakeview 32	67	36N13	83w17	5:33:08
Lakeview 54	71	35N27	84w36	5:38:24
Lake View Heights 73	67	35N56	84w33	5:38:12
Lakeview Manor 40	3	36N15	88w09	5:52:36
Lakeview Park 45	67	36N01	83w25	5:33:40
Lakewood 19	4	36N09	86w39	5:46:36
Lamar 79	39	35N06	89w59	5:59:56
Lambert 24	3	35N14	89w21	5:57:24
Lamont 74	35	36N30	86w53	5:47:32
Lamontville 54	54	35N18	84w45	5:39:00
Lancaster 80	3	36N08	85w51	5:43:24
Lancaster Hill 80	3	36N09	85w57	5:43:48
Lancing 65	56	36N09	84w42	5:38:48
Lane 23	16	36N16	89w11	5:56:44
Laneview 27	8	35N58	88w57	5:55:48
Lanier 5	64	35N38	84w03	5:36:12
Lantana 18	9	35N49	85w06	5:40:24
Lanton 60	31	35N37	87w02	5:48:08
Lascassas 75	3	35N58	86w19	5:45:16
Lassiter Corner 66	3	36N20	89w18	5:57:12
Latham 92	47	36N17	88w42	5:54:48
Laurel 1	62	36N05	84w08	5:36:32
Laurel 78	60	35N49	83w33	5:34:12
Laurel Bloomery 46	1	36N34	81w46	5:27:04
Laurelburg 88	3	35N47	85w35	5:42:20
Laurel Cove 88	3	35N45	85w27	5:41:48
Laurel Grove 1	62	36N11	84w11	5:36:44
La Vergne 75	3	36N01	86w35	5:46:20
Lavinia 9	3	35N51	88w40	5:54:40
Law 39	25	35N39	88w23	5:53:32
Law Chapel 5	64	35N46	83w58	5:35:52
Lawnville 73	67	35N52	84w31	5:38:04
Lawrenceburg 50	29	35N14	87w20	5:49:20
Lawton 55	3	35N10	88w35	5:54:20
Leach 9	3	35N56	88w29	5:53:56
Leadvale 45	67	36N06	83w17	5:33:08
Leama 75	37	35N51	86w23	5:45:32
Leaman 34	51	36N32	83w13	5:32:52
Leapwood 55	3	35N14	88w23	5:53:32
Lea Springs 29	55	36N09	83w42	5:34:48
Leatherwood 91	3	35N19	87w46	5:51:04
Lebanon 95	34	36N12	86w18	5:45:12
Lee 4	3	35N36	85w11	5:40:44
Leesburg 90	75	36N18	82w28	5:29:52
Lee Valley 37	70	36N32	83w13	5:32:52
Leeville 95	34	36N12	86w18	5:45:12
Leftwich 60	31	35N37	87w02	5:48:08
Legate 81	3	36N30	87w42	5:50:48
Leighs Chapel 84	44	35N34	89w42	5:58:48
Leighton 57	3	35N32	89w00	5:56:00
Leinart 1	62	36N05	84w08	5:36:32
Leipers Fork 94	3	35N54	87w00	5:48:00
Lenoir City 53	69	35N48	84w16	5:37:04
Lenox 23	16	36N05	89w30	5:58:00
Leoma 50	29	35N10	87w21	5:49:24
Leonard 82	2	36N35	82w11	5:28:44
Leoni 8	3	35N49	86w04	5:44:16
Lewisburg 59	30	35N27	86w48	5:47:12
Lewis Chapel 77	3	35N22	85w23	5:41:32
Lewis Park 51	3	35N33	87w34	5:50:16
Lewis Store 16	12	35N38	86w14	5:44:56
Lexie 26	18	35N08	86w11	5:44:44
Lexie Crossroads 26	18	35N08	86w11	5:44:44
Lexington 39	25	35N39	88w24	5:53:36
Liberty 3	3	36N04	88w06	5:52:24
Liberty 20	3	35N31	88w14	5:52:56
Liberty 21	3	36N00	85w58	5:43:52
Liberty 26	19	35N11	86w07	5:44:28
Liberty 28	3	35N02	87w00	5:48:00
Liberty 44	3	36N16	85w48	5:43:12
Liberty 46	1	36N29	81w48	5:27:12
Liberty 52	9	35N09	86w35	5:46:20
Liberty 65	51	36N06	84w36	5:38:24
Liberty 83	50	36N29	86w19	5:45:16
Liberty 92	3	36N13	88w37	5:54:28
Liberty Grove 50	29	35N04	87w26	5:49:44
Liberty Hill 15	65	35N58	83w11	5:32:44
Liberty Hill 29	55	36N17	83w36	5:34:24
Liberty Hill 54	71	35N25	84w29	5:37:56
Liberty Hill 94	3	35N56	87w19	5:49:16
Lick Creek 3	3	36N14	88w05	5:52:20
Lick Creek 20	3	35N39	88w07	5:52:28
Lickskillet 87	52	36N15	83w48	5:35:12
Lickton 19	4	36N18	86w43	5:46:52
Lightfoot 49	28	35N45	89w32	5:58:08
Lillamay 11	10	36N16	87w04	5:48:16
Lillydale 86	1	36N08	82w25	5:29:40
Lily Grove 13	51	36N26	83w36	5:34:24
Limbs 92	3	36N14	88w50	5:55:20
Limestone 90	63	36N14	82w38	5:30:32
Limestone Cove 86	1	36N12	82w21	5:29:24
Linary 18	15	35N57	85w02	5:40:08
Lincoln 52	9	35N09	86w35	5:46:20
Lincoln Park 59	30	35N27	86w48	5:47:12
Lincoya Hills 19	4	36N09	86w41	5:46:44
Linden 68	3	35N37	87w50	5:51:20
Lindenwood 66	3	36N28	89w03	5:56:12
Link 75	36	35N43	86w24	5:45:36
Linton 19	4	36N08	86w48	5:47:12
Linwood 95	34	36N12	86w18	5:45:12
Lisbon 35	3	35N04	88w53	5:55:32
Little Bigby 60	3	35N35	87w05	5:48:20
Littlecrab 25	3	36N26	84w56	5:39:44
Little Doe 46	1	36N20	82w00	5:28:00
Little Earren 13	51	36N26	83w36	5:34:24
Little Emory 73	67	35N56	84w33	5:38:12

Little Hope 75 37 35N51 86w23 5:45:32
Little Hope 91 3 35N19 87w46 5:51:04
Littlelot 41 3 35N51 87w16 5:49:04
Little Milligan 10 1 36N20 82w00 5:28:00
Little River 5 64 35N46 83w58 5:35:52
Little White Oak 7 66 36N27 84w04 5:36:16
Litton 4 3 35N36 85w11 5:40:44
Liverwort 63 32 36N32 87w22 5:49:28
Livingston 67 22 36N23 85w19 5:41:16
Lobelville 68 3 35N46 87w47 5:51:08
Locke 79 40 35N20 89w53 5:59:32
Lockertsville 11 10 36N16 87w04 5:48:16
Lockmiller Addition 54 71 35N27 84w36 5:38:24
Locust Springs 30 65 36N12 82w44 5:30:56
Lodge 58 8 35N01 85w43 5:42:52
Logans Lake 55 3 35N22 88w36 5:54:24
Lois 64 3 35N13 86w28 5:45:52
Lomax Crossroads 51 3 35N33 87w34 5:50:16
Lone Mountain 13 51 36N24 83w35 5:34:20
Lone Oak 63 3 36N23 87w20 5:49:20
Lone Oak 77 3 35N08 85w19 5:41:16
Lone Star 82 2 36N34 82w33 5:30:12
Long Branch 50 29 35N15 87w20 5:49:20
Long Creek 15 65 36N00 83w06 5:32:24
Long Island 82 2 36N31 82w32 5:30:08
Long Rock 9 3 36N00 88w25 5:53:40
Longs Mills 54 71 35N27 84w36 5:38:24
Longtown 24 3 35N25 89w32 5:58:08
Lonoke 27 21 36N12 89w01 5:56:04
Lonsdale 47 67 35N58 83w58 5:35:52
Lookout Mountain 33 61 34N59 85w21 5:41:24
Lookout Valley 33 61 35N01 85w20 5:41:20
Loonewood 88 3 35N45 85w27 5:41:48
Loretto 50 29 35N05 87w26 5:49:44
Lorraine 74 74 35N41 84w52 5:39:28
Lost Creek 93 3 35N56 85w28 5:41:52
Lost Mountain 30 65 36N13 82w48 5:31:12
Loudon 53 68 35N45 84w20 5:37:20
Louise 63 3 36N16 87w22 5:49:28
Louisville 5 64 35N49 84w03 5:36:12
Love Joy 67 3 36N09 85w16 5:41:04
Lovelace 30 65 36N14 82w41 5:30:44
Love Lady 69 3 36N34 85w08 5:40:32
Love Station 86 1 36N08 82w25 5:29:40
Lovetown 60 9 35N32 87w12 5:48:48
Lower Mockeson 50 29 35N10 87w21 5:49:24
Lower Rutherford Creek 60 3 35N39 86w57 5:47:48
Lowland 32 67 36N09 83w12 5:32:48
Lowryville 36 23 35N14 88w14 5:52:56
Luckett 49 28 35N45 89w32 5:58:08
Lucky 89 46 35N42 85w46 5:43:04
Lucy 79 40 35N20 89w53 5:59:32
Lulaville 29 55 36N17 83w31 5:34:04
Lunns Store 59 3 35N38 86w42 5:46:48
Lupton City 33 61 35N07 85w16 5:41:04
Luray 39 3 35N38 88w30 5:54:00
Lusk 4 3 35N22 85w23 5:41:32
Luskville 54 54 35N18 84w45 5:39:00
Luther 34 51 36N32 83w13 5:32:52
Luttrell 53 68 35N40 84w24 5:37:36
Luttrell 87 52 36N12 83w45 5:35:00
Lutts 91 3 35N09 87w56 5:51:44
Lyles 41 3 35N55 87w21 5:49:24
Lynchburg 64 33 35N17 86w22 5:45:28
Lynn Garden 82 2 36N35 82w34 5:30:16
Lynnville 28 3 35N23 87w00 5:48:00
Macedonia 9 3 36N08 88w31 5:54:04
Macedonia 66 3 36N12 89w01 5:56:04
Macedonia 93 3 36N02 85w31 5:42:04
Mace's Hill 80 3 36N19 86w01 5:44:04
Macon 24 3 35N09 89w30 5:58:00
Maddox 36 23 35N14 88w14 5:52:56
Madie 48 3 36N16 89w29 5:57:56
Madison 19 4 36N16 86w42 5:46:48
Madison College 19 4 36N16 86w43 5:46:52
Madison Hall 57 3 35N39 88w53 5:55:32
Madisonville 62 67 35N31 84w22 5:37:28
Maggart 80 3 36N13 85w53 5:43:32
Magnolia 42 3 36N19 87w50 5:51:20
Major 95 34 36N12 86w18 5:45:12
Malesus 57 3 35N33 88w50 5:55:20
Mallory 79 39 35N04 90w04 6:00:16
Mallorys 94 48 35N57 86w53 5:47:32
Maloney Heights 47 67 35N56 83w54 5:35:36
Maloneyville 47 67 36N02 83w56 5:35:44
Manchester 16 12 35N29 86w05 5:44:20
Mankinville 75 37 35N51 86w23 5:45:32
Manlyville 40 3 36N15 88w09 5:52:36
Mansfield 40 3 36N11 88w17 5:53:08
Mansford 26 19 35N11 86w07 5:44:28
Manskers Island 19 4 36N16 86w43 5:46:52
Manson 25 3 36N26 84w56 5:39:44
Maple Grove 14 3 36N27 85w21 5:41:24
Maple Grove 56 3 36N32 86w02 5:44:08
Maple Grove 61 54 35N40 84w40 5:38:40
Maple Hill 82 2 36N35 82w11 5:28:44
Maplehurst 82 1 36N28 82w15 5:29:00
Maples 1 62 36N05 84w08 5:36:32
Maplewood 19 4 36N13 86w44 5:46:56
Marbledale 47 67 35N58 83w49 5:35:16
Marble Hall 37 70 36N24 83w00 5:32:00
Marble Hill 5 64 35N46 84w08 5:36:32
Marble Hill 64 3 35N11 86w07 5:44:28
Marble Plains 26 19 35N11 86w07 5:44:28
Marbleton 86 1 36N12 82w21 5:29:24
Marguerite 32 67 36N13 83w17 5:33:08
Marion 13 51 36N33 83w57 5:35:48
Marion 63 3 36N16 87w22 5:49:28
Markham 48 3 36N23 89w29 5:57:56
Marlow 1 62 36N05 84w08 5:36:32
Marlyn Hills 82 2 36N35 82w11 5:28:44
Marrowbone 11 10 36N16 87w04 5:48:16
Marshall Heights 59 30 35N27 86w48 5:47:12
Martel Estates 53 68 35N48 84w16 5:37:04
Martha 95 34 36N12 86w18 5:45:12
Martha Washington 25 3 36N11 85w01 5:40:04
Martin 92 3 36N21 88w51 5:55:24
Martin Creek 71 3 36N09 85w38 5:42:32
Martin Springs 58 8 35N01 85w43 5:42:52
Marvin 30 65 36N11 82w57 5:31:48
Mary Chapel 29 55 36N20 83w22 5:33:28
Marys Grove 52 9 35N00 86w40 5:46:40
Maryville 5 64 35N46 83w58 5:35:52
Mascot 47 67 36N04 83w45 5:35:00
Mason 84 44 35N25 89w32 5:58:08
Mason Grove 17 3 35N50 88w55 5:55:40
Masonhall 66 3 36N12 89w01 5:56:04
Masseyville 12 3 35N14 88w36 5:54:24
Match 60 31 35N37 87w02 5:48:08
Maupin Row 90 75 36N19 82w21 5:29:24
Maury City 17 3 35N49 89w14 5:56:56
Maxey 23 16 36N07 89w16 5:57:04
Maxwell 26 18 35N08 86w11 5:44:44
May Acres 45 67 36N09 83w25 5:33:40
Mayland 18 9 36N03 85w12 5:40:48
Maynardville 87 52 36N15 83w48 5:35:12
Mayview Heights 47 67 36N02 84w02 5:36:08
McAnna 66 3 36N20 89w10 5:56:40
McBurg 52 9 35N11 86w51 5:47:24
McCains 60 31 35N37 87w02 5:48:08
McClamerys Stand 91 3 35N10 87w44 5:50:56
McCloud 37 70 36N24 83w00 5:32:00
McClures Bend 80 41 36N15 85w57 5:43:48
McCoinsville 44 27 36N21 85w39 5:42:36
McConnell 66 3 36N21 88w51 5:55:24
McCookville 78 60 35N49 83w33 5:34:12
McCullough 23 16 36N02 89w23 5:57:32
McDonald 6 53 35N07 84w59 5:39:56
McElroy 88 3 35N51 85w31 5:42:04
McEwan 43 3 36N06 87w38 5:50:32
McEwen 43 3 36N07 87w38 5:50:32
McIllwain 3 3 35N53 88w09 5:52:36
McKenzie 9 3 36N08 88w31 5:54:04
McKinley 90 75 36N19 82w21 5:29:24
McKinnon 42 3 36N19 87w54 5:51:36
McLemoresville 9 3 35N59 88w35 5:54:20
McLin's Corner 17 3 35N54 89w15 5:57:00
McMahan 78 60 35N49 83w33 5:34:12
McMinnville 89 46 35N41 85w46 5:43:04
McMinnville Plaza 89 46 35N42 85w46 5:43:04
McNairy 55 3 35N19 88w37 5:54:28
McPheeter Bend 37 70 36N32 82w41 5:30:44
Meacham 23 16 36N02 89w23 5:57:32
Meadorville 56 3 36N32 86w02 5:44:08
Meadow 53 68 35N40 84w10 5:36:40
Meadow Branch 29 55 36N20 83w22 5:33:28
Meadowbrook 5 64 35N46 83w58 5:35:52
Meadow Mead 40 26 36N18 88w19 5:53:16
Meadow View 33 61 35N17 84w57 5:39:48
Meadowview 50 29 35N15 87w20 5:49:20
Meadowview Gardens 73 67 35N56 84w33 5:38:12
Meagsville 44 27 36N21 85w39 5:42:36
Mechanicsville 8 3 35N57 85w49 5:43:16
Medford 1 62 36N13 84w09 5:36:36
Medina 27 21 35N48 88w46 5:55:04
Medon 57 3 35N28 88w56 5:55:44
Melbourne 1 62 36N05 84w03 5:36:12
Melrose 19 4 36N07 86w47 5:47:08
Melville Hill 33 61 35N16 85w11 5:40:44
Melvine 4 3 35N36 85w11 5:40:44
Melwood 12 3 35N14 88w36 5:54:24
Memorial 14 3 36N32 85w51 5:43:24
Memphis 79 39 35N08 90w03 6:00:12
Memphis State University 79 39 35N07 89w57 5:59:48
Mengelwood 23 16 36N05 89w30 5:58:00
Mentor 5 64 35N49 84w01 5:36:04
Mercer 57 3 35N29 89w02 5:56:08
Meredith Cave 7 66 36N23 84w07 5:36:28
Merry Oaks 19 4 36N09 86w41 5:46:44
Michie 55 3 35N03 88w26 5:53:44
Middleburg 35 3 35N16 89w00 5:56:00
Middleburg 39 3 35N31 88w14 5:52:56
Middle City 23 16 36N02 89w23 5:57:32
Middle Creek 78 60 35N49 83w33 5:34:12
Middle Fork 39 3 35N36 88w35 5:54:20
Middle Settlement 5 64 35N49 84w03 5:36:12
Middleton 35 3 35N04 88w53 5:55:32
Middle Valley 33 61 35N10 85w13 5:40:52
Middle Valley Estates 33 61 35N06 85w15 5:41:00
Midfields 82 2 36N34 82w34 5:30:16
Midland 75 3 35N35 86w21 5:45:24
Midtown 73 67 35N56 84w33 5:38:12
Midway 15 65 35N55 83w01 5:32:04
Midway 21 11 35N57 85w49 5:43:16
Midway 23 16 36N03 89w29 5:57:56
Midway 26 18 35N12 85w55 5:43:40
Midway 30 65 36N11 82w59 5:31:56

Midway 47 67 36N04 83w41 5:34:44
Midway 66 3 36N25 89w03 5:56:12
Midway 69 3 36N30 85w10 5:40:40
Mifflin 12 3 35N36 88w35 5:54:20
Milan 27 20 35N55 88w46 5:55:04
Milburnton 30 65 36N13 82w38 5:30:32
Miles Crossroads 14 3 36N32 85w51 5:43:24
Mile Straight 33 61 35N16 85w11 5:40:44
Milky Way 28 22 35N12 87w02 5:48:08
Mill Brook 90 63 36N13 82w38 5:30:32
Mill Creek 1 62 36N12 84w02 5:36:08
Mill Creek 41 3 35N55 87w21 5:49:24
Mill Creek 65 56 36N15 84w40 5:38:40
Mill Creek 71 34 36N11 85w28 5:41:52
Milldale 74 35 36N30 86w53 5:47:32
Milledgeville 55 3 35N22 88w22 5:53:28
Miller's Cove 5 64 35N44 83w49 5:35:16
Millersville 83 50 36N18 86w43 5:46:52
Millertown 47 67 36N00 83w53 5:35:32
Millican 78 60 35N49 83w33 5:34:12
Milligan College 10 1 36N18 82w18 5:29:12
Millington 79 40 35N21 89w54 5:59:36
Millsfield 23 16 36N07 89w22 5:57:28
Mill Spring 45 67 36N06 83w33 5:34:12
Milltown 44 3 36N27 85w40 5:42:40
Milo 4 3 35N41 84w52 5:39:28
Milton 75 3 35N56 86w11 5:44:44
Mimms 19 4 36N06 86w45 5:47:00
Mimosa 52 9 35N09 86w35 5:46:20
Mimosa Estates 5 64 35N49 84w03 5:36:12
Mineral Park 6 53 35N07 84w59 5:39:56
Minnick 66 3 36N16 89w11 5:56:44
Minor Hill 28 3 35N04 87w09 5:48:36
Mint 5 64 35N46 83w58 5:35:52
Miser Station 5 64 35N49 84w03 5:36:12
Miston 23 16 36N10 89w29 5:57:56
Mitchell 74 3 36N35 86w31 5:46:04
Mitchellville 83 50 36N38 86w32 5:46:08
Mixie 9 3 36N02 88w16 5:53:04
Moccasin 91 3 35N19 87w46 5:51:04
Model 81 3 36N39 87w59 5:51:56
Mohawk 30 65 36N11 83w04 5:32:16
Mohawk Crossroad 30 65 36N15 83w05 5:32:20
Molino 52 9 35N09 86w35 5:46:20
Mona 75 37 35N51 86w23 5:45:32
Monoville 80 3 36N18 85w59 5:43:56
Monroe 67 3 36N26 85w15 5:41:00
Montague 19 4 36N16 86w43 5:46:52
Monteagle 31 3 35N15 85w50 5:43:20
Monterey 71 3 36N09 85w16 5:41:04
Montezuma 12 3 35N26 88w39 5:54:36
Montgomery Junction 76 58 36N20 84w23 5:37:32
Montvale 5 64 35N46 83w58 5:35:52
Moodyville 69 3 36N34 85w08 5:40:32
Mooneyham 88 3 35N45 85w27 5:41:48
Moons 40 3 36N15 88w09 5:52:36
Moore 64 33 35N17 86w21 5:45:24
Mooresburg 37 70 36N22 83w12 5:32:48
Moores Chapel 27 20 35N55 88w46 5:55:04
Mooresville 59 30 35N27 86w48 5:47:12
Mooring 48 3 36N16 89w29 5:57:56
Morgan Springs 72 74 35N01 85w11 5:40:44
Morganton 53 68 35N40 84w10 5:36:40
Morgantown 72 74 35N01 85w11 5:40:44
Morganville 58 8 35N12 85w31 5:42:04
Morley 7 66 36N33 84w03 5:36:12
Morny 19 4 36N10 86w46 5:47:04
Morris Chapel 3 3 36N04 88w06 5:52:24
Morris Chapel 36 3 35N16 88w19 5:53:16
Morrison 89 3 35N36 85w55 5:43:40
Morrison City 82 2 36N35 82w34 5:30:16
Morrison Creek 44 27 36N21 85w39 5:42:36
Morristown 32 67 36N13 83w18 5:33:12
Moscow 24 3 35N04 89w24 5:57:36
Mosheim 30 65 36N11 82w57 5:31:48
Moss 14 3 36N36 85w37 5:42:28
Mossy Grove 65 51 35N56 84w33 5:38:12
Mountain City 46 1 36N29 81w48 5:27:12
Mountain Dale 86 1 36N08 82w25 5:29:40
Mountain Home 90 75 36N20 82w21 5:29:24
Mountain View 16 12 35N28 86w05 5:44:20
Mountain View Acres 26 19 35N11 86w07 5:44:28
Mount Airy 77 3 35N22 85w23 5:41:32
Mount Carmel 20 3 35N35 88w07 5:52:28
Mount Carmel 30 65 36N15 83w05 5:32:20
Mount Carmel 37 70 36N33 82w40 5:30:40
Mount Carmel 84 44 35N34 89w42 5:58:48
Mount Crest 4 3 35N36 85w11 5:40:44
Mount Denson 74 35 36N30 86w53 5:47:32
Mount Gilead 39 3 35N49 88w36 5:54:24
Mount Harmony 54 71 35N31 84w32 5:38:08
Mount Herman 92 3 36N09 88w48 5:55:12
Mount Horeb 45 67 36N07 83w30 5:34:00
Mount Joy 60 9 35N32 87w12 5:48:48
Mount Juliet 95 49 36N12 86w31 5:46:04
Mount Lebanon 50 29 35N15 87w20 5:49:20
Mount Leo 89 46 35N42 85w46 5:43:04
Mount Moriah 3 3 36N04 88w06 5:52:24
Mount Nebo 50 29 35N02 87w30 5:50:00
Mount Olive 31 3 35N42 85w46 5:43:04
Mount Olive 47 67 35N53 83w56 5:35:44
Mount Olive 58 8 35N12 85w31 5:42:04
Mount Olive 75 37 35N51 86w23 5:45:32
Mount Pelia 92 3 36N21 88w51 5:55:24
Mount Pisgah 93 3 35N49 85w36 5:42:24
Mount Pleasant 30 65 36N13 82w48 5:31:12
Mount Pleasant 40 3 36N26 88w12 5:52:48

Mount Pleasant 60 9 35N32 87w12 5:48:48
Mount Pleasant 71 34 36N11 85w28 5:41:52
Mount Pleasant 76 58 36N21 84w35 5:38:20
Mount Tucker Addition 82 1 36N32 82w19 5:29:16
Mount Union 69 3 36N34 85w08 5:40:32
Mount Vernon 18 9 35N52 84w41 5:38:44
Mount Vernon 62 67 35N25 84w22 5:37:28
Mount Vernon 75 3 35N45 86w32 5:46:08
Mount View 19 4 36N06 86w45 5:47:00
Mount View 31 3 35N14 85w50 5:43:20
Mount View 76 58 36N21 84w35 5:38:20
Mount Vinson 55 3 35N10 88w26 5:53:44
Mount Zion 62 67 35N35 84w15 5:37:00
Mount Zion 63 3 36N16 87w22 5:49:28
Mount Zion 89 46 35N42 85w46 5:43:04
Mourberry 93 3 35N56 85w28 5:41:52
Mowbray 33 61 35N16 85w11 5:40:44
Muddy Pond 67 3 36N09 85w16 5:41:04
Mud Tavern 19 4 36N09 86w41 5:46:44
Mulberry 52 9 35N13 86w28 5:45:52
Mulberry Gap 34 51 36N32 83w13 5:32:52
Mulberry Hill 81 3 36N29 87w50 5:51:20
Mullican 78 60 35N54 83w29 5:33:56
Mulloy 83 50 36N27 86w32 5:46:08
Munford 84 3 35N27 89w49 5:59:16
Murfreesboro 75 37 35N51 86w24 5:45:36
Murray Store 54 71 35N31 84w32 5:38:08
Nameless 44 3 36N12 85w37 5:42:28
Nankipoo 49 3 35N53 89w24 5:57:36
Napier 51 3 35N33 87w34 5:50:16
Narrow Valley 29 55 36N17 83w31 5:34:04
Nash 71 3 36N09 85w38 5:42:32
Nashville 19 4 36N10 86w47 5:47:08
Natco 60 31 35N37 87w02 5:48:08
Natural Bridge 15 65 36N00 83w06 5:32:24
Nauvoo 23 16 36N02 89w23 5:57:32
Naval Air Station Memphis 79 40 35N20 89w53 5:59:32
Naval Hospital 79 40 35N20 89w53 5:59:32
Neapolis 60 31 35N37 87w02 5:48:08
Neboville 27 21 36N07 89w16 5:57:04
Needmore 32 67 36N16 83w08 5:32:32
Needmore 59 30 35N27 86w48 5:47:12
Needmore 63 3 36N30 87w42 5:50:48
Neptune 11 10 36N16 87w04 5:48:16
Neubert 47 67 35N54 83w51 5:35:24
Neva 46 1 36N21 81w54 5:27:36
Newark 93 3 36N11 85w28 5:41:52
Newbern 23 16 36N07 89w16 5:57:04
New Bethel 54 54 35N20 84w32 5:38:08
New Canton 37 70 36N32 82w41 5:30:44
New Castle 35 3 35N20 89w09 5:56:36
Newcomb 7 66 36N33 84w10 5:36:40
New Corinth 29 55 36N17 83w31 5:34:04
New Deal 83 50 36N27 86w32 5:46:08
New Dellrose 52 9 35N07 86w48 5:47:12
New Due West 19 4 36N16 86w43 5:46:52
Newell Station 78 60 35N53 83w43 5:34:52
New Harmony 4 3 35N36 85w11 5:40:44
New Harmony 56 3 36N23 86w10 5:44:40
New Herman 2 6 35N29 86w27 5:45:48
New Hope 34 51 36N32 83w13 5:32:52
New Hope 37 70 36N24 83w00 5:32:00
New Hope 42 3 36N19 87w50 5:51:20
New Hope 44 3 36N25 85w27 5:41:48
New Hope 52 9 35N09 86w35 5:46:20
New Hope 58 8 35N01 85w43 5:42:52
New Hope 94 3 35N59 87w07 5:48:28
New Johnsonville 43 3 36N01 87w58 5:51:52
New Loyston 87 52 36N12 84w02 5:36:08
New Markam 48 3 36N23 89w29 5:57:56
New Market 45 67 36N06 83w33 5:34:12
New Middleton 80 3 36N11 85w56 5:43:44
New Midway 73 67 35N52 84w31 5:38:04
Newport 15 65 35N58 83w11 5:32:44
New Prospect 50 29 35N15 87w20 5:49:20
New Providence 63 3 36N33 87w23 5:49:32
New River 76 58 36N23 84w33 5:38:12
New Salem 33 61 35N16 85w11 5:40:44
New Salem 44 27 36N21 85w39 5:42:36
New Tazewell 13 51 36N27 83w36 5:34:24
Newton 18 15 35N57 85w02 5:40:08
New Town 59 3 35N22 86w50 5:47:20
Newtown 70 73 34N59 84w22 5:37:28
New Union 16 12 35N28 86w05 5:44:20
New Victory 90 75 36N18 82w28 5:29:52
New Zion 9 3 36N00 88w25 5:53:40
New Zion 56 3 36N34 86w15 5:45:00
Nicks Creek 7 66 36N25 84w29 5:37:56
Nine Mile 4 3 35N36 85w11 5:40:44
Niota 54 71 35N31 84w33 5:38:12
Nixon 36 3 35N07 88w16 5:53:04
Noah 16 12 35N28 86w05 5:44:20
Nolensville 94 3 35N57 86w40 5:46:40
Nonaburg 54 71 35N25 84w29 5:37:56
Norene 95 49 36N04 86w15 5:45:00
Norma 76 58 36N20 84w23 5:37:32
Normandy 2 3 35N27 86w16 5:45:04
Norris 1 62 36N12 84w04 5:36:16
North 19 4 36N10 86w48 5:47:12
North 79 39 35N10 90w01 6:00:04
North Cannon 8 3 35N52 86w03 5:44:12
North Chattanooga 33 61 35N05 85w19 5:41:16
Northcott 82 2 36N34 82w33 5:30:12
Northcutts Cove 31 3 35N42 85w46 5:43:04
Northeast 19 4 36N13 86w46 5:47:04
Northern Hills 33 61 35N06 85w15 5:41:00
North Etowah 54 54 35N20 84w32 5:38:08
North Fork Holston 82 2 36N34 82w36 5:30:24
North Glen Estates 33 61 35N06 85w15 5:41:00
North Huntingdon 9 3 36N03 88w23 5:53:32
North Johnson City 90 75 36N19 82w21 5:29:24
North Knoxville 47 67 36N00 83w55 5:35:40
North Liberty 54 71 35N27 84w36 5:38:24
North Of The River 44 3 36N24 85w44 5:42:56
Northpoint 62 67 35N36 84w28 5:37:52
Northport 15 65 35N58 83w11 5:32:44
North Riverside 51 3 35N33 87w34 5:50:16
North Side 57 3 35N39 88w53 5:55:32
North Side 80 3 36N21 85w57 5:43:48
North Springs 44 3 36N27 85w40 5:42:40
Norwood 1 62 36N02 84w20 5:37:20
Norwood 47 67 36N00 83w58 5:35:52
Notchy 62 67 35N31 84w22 5:37:28
Nough 15 65 35N53 83w01 5:32:04
Nubia 83 50 36N34 86w15 5:45:00
Nucarbon 50 29 35N10 87w21 5:49:24
Number One 83 42 36N23 86w26 5:45:44
Nunnelly 41 3 35N52 87w28 5:49:52
Nutbush 38 3 35N43 89w23 5:57:32
Oak City 78 60 35N53 83w43 5:34:52
Oakdale 37 70 36N28 82w51 5:31:24
Oakdale 65 56 36N00 84w36 5:38:24
Oak Dale 67 3 36N26 85w15 5:41:00
Oakdale 93 3 35N56 85w28 5:41:52
Oakfield 57 3 35N43 88w48 5:55:12
Oak Grove 7 66 36N13 84w09 5:36:36
Oak Grove 10 1 36N20 82w13 5:28:52
Oak Grove 22 3 36N05 87w23 5:49:32
Oak Grove 26 18 35N13 86w05 5:44:20
Oak Grove 28 3 35N09 87w06 5:48:24
Oak Grove 36 23 35N14 88w14 5:52:56
Oak Grove 45 67 36N01 83w25 5:33:40
Oak Grove 51 3 35N33 87w34 5:50:16
Oak Grove 53 68 35N48 84w16 5:37:04
Oak Grove 58 8 35N12 85w31 5:42:04
Oakgrove 69 3 36N26 85w15 5:41:00
Oak Grove 70 72 35N11 84w39 5:38:36
Oak Grove 83 50 36N29 86w19 5:45:16
Oak Grove 84 44 35N34 89w42 5:58:48
Oak Grove 89 3 35N36 85w49 5:43:16
Oak Grove 90 75 36N18 82w28 5:29:52
Oak Grove Heights 47 67 35N58 83w58 5:35:52
Oak Hill 18 15 35N57 85w02 5:40:08
Oak Hill 19 4 36N05 86w47 5:47:08
Oak Hill 40 3 36N02 88w16 5:53:04
Oak Hill 67 3 36N16 85w22 5:41:28
Oak Hill 69 3 36N34 85w08 5:40:32
Oak Hill 82 2 36N35 82w11 5:28:44
Oakhurst 5 64 35N46 83w58 5:35:52
Oakknob 56 3 36N32 86w02 5:44:08
Oakland 24 3 35N14 89w31 5:58:04
Oakland 89 46 35N42 85w46 5:43:04
Oakland 90 63 36N15 82w33 5:30:12
Oakleigh Estates 82 2 36N35 82w11 5:28:44
Oakley 67 3 36N27 85w21 5:41:24
Oak Park 16 13 35N21 86w12 5:44:48
Oakplain 11 10 36N16 87w04 5:48:16
Oak Plains 63 32 36N32 87w22 5:49:28
Oak Ridge 1 62 36N01 84w16 5:37:04
Oak View 5 64 35N44 83w49 5:35:16
Oakwood 63 3 36N32 87w35 5:50:20
Obion 66 3 36N16 89w12 5:56:48
Ocana 83 43 36N18 86w37 5:46:28
Ocoee 70 72 35N07 84w43 5:38:52
O'connors 93 3 35N56 85w28 5:41:52
Odd Fellows Hall 28 22 35N12 87w02 5:48:08
Odens Bend 83 42 36N23 86w26 5:45:44
Offutt 1 62 36N05 84w08 5:36:32
Ogden 72 74 35N01 85w11 5:40:44
Oglesby 19 4 36N06 86w45 5:47:00
Okalona 67 22 36N23 85w19 5:41:16
Okolona 10 1 36N19 82w21 5:29:24
Okolona 37 70 36N32 82w41 5:30:44
Old Antioch 44 27 36N21 85w39 5:42:36
Olde Mill 33 61 35N06 85w15 5:41:00
Oldfort 70 72 35N04 84w44 5:38:56
Old Fremont 66 3 36N25 89w03 5:56:12
Old Glory 5 64 35N46 83w58 5:35:52
Old Hickory 19 4 36N15 86w39 5:46:36
Old Hometown 79 39 35N02 90w03 6:00:12
Old Lawton 55 3 35N10 88w35 5:54:20
Old Salem 26 18 35N03 86w16 5:45:04
Old Springville 40 3 36N15 88w09 5:52:36
Olive Branch 49 28 35N45 89w32 5:58:08
Olivehill 36 3 35N16 88w05 5:52:20
Oliver Springs 73 63 36N03 84w20 5:37:20
Olivet 36 23 35N14 88w14 5:52:56
Oneida 76 58 36N30 84w31 5:38:04
Only 41 3 35N53 87w35 5:50:20
Ooltewah 33 61 35N04 85w04 5:40:16
Opossum 49 28 35N45 89w32 5:58:08
Oral 73 67 35N48 84w16 5:37:04
Orebank 82 2 36N33 82w28 5:29:52
Ore Spring 92 47 36N17 88w42 5:54:48
Orlinda 74 3 36N36 86w43 5:46:52
Orme 58 8 35N01 85w49 5:43:16
Orysa 49 28 35N45 89w32 5:58:08

TENNESSEE

Osage 40 26 36N18 88w19 5:53:16
Ostella 59 30 35N27 86w48 5:47:12
Oswego 7 66 36N35 84w08 5:36:32
Otes 37 70 36N21 82w59 5:31:56
Ottway 30 65 36N13 82w48 5:31:12
Overall 75 3 35N49 86w29 5:45:56
Overlook 5 64 35N46 83w58 5:35:52
Overstreets 14 11 36N33 85w30 5:42:00
Ovilla 50 29 35N15 87w20 5:49:20
Ovoca 16 13 35N21 86w12 5:44:48
Owl City 48 3 36N23 89w29 5:57:56
Owlhollow 26 19 35N11 86w07 5:44:28
Owl Hoot 48 3 36N16 89w29 5:57:56
Ozone 18 9 35N53 84w49 5:39:16
Pactolus 82 2 36N31 82w32 5:30:08
Pailo 4 3 35N22 85w23 5:41:32
Paint Rock 53 68 35N44 84w21 5:37:24
Paint Rock 73 67 35N39 84w34 5:38:16
Palestine 39 25 35N39 88w23 5:53:32
Palestine 74 35 36N30 86w53 5:47:32
Pall Mall 25 3 36N33 84w58 5:39:52
Palmer 31 3 35N21 85w34 5:42:16
Palmersville 92 3 36N24 88w35 5:54:20
Palmetto 2 3 35N27 86w48 5:47:12
Palmyra 63 3 36N26 87w29 5:49:56
Pandora 46 1 36N20 82w00 5:28:00
Paperville 82 2 36N35 82w11 5:28:44
Paragon Mills 19 4 36N06 86w45 5:47:00
Parham 83 50 36N27 86w32 5:46:08
Paris 40 26 36N18 88w19 5:53:16
Parkburg 57 3 35N29 88w43 5:54:52
Parker 69 3 36N33 84w58 5:39:52
Parker Crossroads 39 3 35N48 88w22 5:53:28
Parkey 34 51 36N32 83w13 5:32:52
Park Lane 63 32 36N32 87w22 5:49:28
Park Settlement 78 60 35N49 83w33 5:34:12
Park Shore 33 61 35N06 85w15 5:41:00
Parksville 70 72 35N04 84w42 5:38:48
Parkview 73 70 35N52 84w41 5:38:44
Parrottsville 15 65 36N00 83w04 5:32:16
Parsons 20 3 35N39 88w08 5:52:32
Paschall 94 48 35N57 86w53 5:47:32
Pasquo 19 4 36N06 86w50 5:47:20
Pate Hill 30 65 36N11 82w57 5:31:48
Patterson 75 3 36N36 87w07 5:48:28
Patty 70 72 35N16 84w33 5:38:12
Paulette 87 52 36N15 83w48 5:35:12
Payne Cove 31 3 35N19 85w53 5:43:32
Paynes Store 85 3 36N29 86w19 5:45:16
Peabody 7 66 36N23 84w07 5:36:28
Peak 1 62 36N05 84w08 5:36:32
Peakland 61 54 35N31 84w47 5:39:08
Peanut 15 65 36N00 83w06 5:32:24
Pea Ridge 21 3 36N00 85w58 5:43:52
Pea Ridge 50 29 35N15 87w20 5:49:20
Pearl City 52 9 35N09 86w35 5:46:20
Peavine 18 15 35N57 85w02 5:40:08
Peeled Chestnut 93 3 35N56 85w28 5:41:52
Pegram 11 9 36N06 87w03 5:48:12
Pelham 31 3 35N18 85w51 5:43:24
Pence 23 16 36N10 89w29 5:57:56
Pennine 72 74 35N41 84w52 5:39:28
Pennington Bend 19 4 36N09 86w41 5:46:44
Pennington Chapel 87 52 36N17 83w36 5:34:24
Perkins Hill 60 31 35N37 87w02 5:48:08
Perrin Hollow 29 55 36N09 83w42 5:34:48
Perry 57 3 35N39 88w53 5:55:32
Perryville 20 3 35N37 88w02 5:52:08
Persia 37 70 36N24 83w00 5:32:00
Petersburg 37 70 36N24 83w00 5:32:00
Petersburg 52 9 35N19 86w38 5:46:32
Petros 65 51 36N06 84w27 5:37:48
Petway 11 10 36N16 87w04 5:48:16
Peytonsville 94 48 35N57 86w53 5:47:32
Philadelphia 44 3 36N12 85w37 5:42:28
Philadelphia 53 68 35N41 84w24 5:37:36
Philippi 21 11 35N57 85w49 5:43:16
Phillippy 48 3 36N23 89w29 5:57:56
Pickwatina Place 54 71 35N27 84w36 5:38:24
Pickwick 36 3 35N03 88w18 5:53:12
Pickwick Dam 36 3 35N03 88w14 5:52:56
Piedmont 45 67 36N01 83w25 5:33:40
Pierce 66 3 36N30 88w53 5:55:32
Pigeon Forge 78 60 35N48 83w33 5:34:12
Pigeon River Estates 78 60 35N49 83w33 5:34:12
Pikeville 4 3 35N36 85w11 5:40:44
Pillowville 92 3 36N08 88w31 5:54:04
Pilot Knob 30 65 36N15 83w05 5:32:20
Pilot Knob 83 42 36N23 86w26 5:45:44
Pilot Mountain 65 56 36N13 84w39 5:38:36
Pinecrest 7 66 36N20 84w11 5:36:44
Pine Crest 10 1 36N19 82w21 5:29:24
Pine Grove 30 65 36N13 82w48 5:31:12
Pine Grove 53 68 35N44 84w21 5:37:24
Pine Grove 78 60 35N49 83w33 5:34:12
Pine Grove 88 3 35N45 85w27 5:41:48
Pine Haven 25 3 36N26 84w56 5:39:44
Pinehaven 79 40 35N20 89w53 5:59:32
Pine Hill 6 53 35N07 84w59 5:39:56
Pine Hill 58 8 35N12 85w31 5:42:04
Pineland 61 54 35N31 84w47 5:39:08
Pine Orchard 65 51 35N59 84w33 5:38:12
Pine Point 40 3 36N15 88w09 5:52:36
Pine Ridge 45 67 36N06 83w17 5:33:08
Pine Ridge 70 73 35N09 84w19 5:37:16
Pine Top 53 68 35N48 84w16 5:37:04

Pine Tree Estates 33 61 35N06 85W15 5:41:00
Pineview Heights 16 13 35N21 86W12 5:44:48
Pineville 32 67 36N13 83W17 5:33:08
Pinewood 41 3 35N52 87W28 5:49:52
Piney 53 68 35N44 84W21 5:37:24
Piney 88 3 35N45 85W27 5:41:48
Piney Flats 82 1 36N25 82W20 5:29:20
Pin Hook 87 52 36N15 83W48 5:35:12
Pinnacle 11 9 36N10 86W46 5:47:04
Pinnacle 78 60 35N49 83W33 5:34:12
Pinson 57 3 35N29 88W43 5:54:52
Pioneer 7 66 36N25 84W19 5:37:16
Piperton 24 3 35N03 89W40 5:58:40
Pisgah 21 11 35N57 85W49 5:43:16
Pisgah 28 22 35N12 87W02 5:48:08
Pisgah 79 40 35N03 89W54 5:59:36
Pittman Center 78 59 35N43 83W31 5:34:04
Plainfield 5 64 35N46 83W58 5:35:52
Plainview 87 52 36N12 83W45 5:35:00
Plant 43 3 36N03 87W56 5:51:44
Plateau 18 15 35N57 85W02 5:40:08
Plateau Of The Barrens 8 3 35N43 86W02 5:44:08
Pleasant Grove 2 6 35N29 86W27 5:45:48
Pleasant Grove 52 9 35N09 86W35 5:46:20
Pleasant Grove 58 8 35N04 85W39 5:42:36
Pleasant Grove 76 58 36N33 84W27 5:37:48
Pleasant Grove 83 50 36N34 86W15 5:45:00
Pleasant Hill 14 3 36N27 85W21 5:41:24
Pleasant Hill 18 9 35N59 85W12 5:40:48
Pleasant Hill 49 3 35N40 89W34 5:58:16
Pleasant Hill 61 73 35N40 84W40 5:38:40
Pleasant Hill 64 33 35N17 86W22 5:45:28
Pleasant Hill 70 72 34N59 84W22 5:37:28
Pleasant Hill 78 60 35N49 83W33 5:34:12
Pleasant Point 13 51 36N26 83W36 5:34:24
Pleasant Point 50 29 35N04 87W26 5:49:44
Pleasant Ridge 8 3 35N49 86W04 5:44:16
Pleasant Ridge 26 18 35N03 86W16 5:45:04
Pleasant Shade 80 3 36N23 85W57 5:43:48
Pleasant Valley 83 50 36N27 86W32 5:46:08
Pleasant Valley 90 75 36N18 82W28 5:29:52
Pleasant View 8 3 35N49 86W04 5:44:16
Pleasant View 11 9 36N22 87W08 5:48:32
Pleasantville 41 3 35N40 87W42 5:50:48
Plunkets Creek 80 3 36N11 85W56 5:43:44
Pocahontas 16 12 35N36 85W49 5:43:16
Pocahontas 35 3 35N03 88W48 5:55:12
Poga 10 1 36N20 82W00 5:28:00
Point Pleasant 15 65 35N58 83W11 5:32:44
Polk 66 3 36N21 89W03 5:56:12
Pollard 42 3 36N19 87W42 5:50:48
Pomona 18 15 35N57 85W02 5:40:08
Pomona 22 3 36N05 87W23 5:49:32
Pond 22 3 36N05 87W23 5:49:32
Ponderosa Hills 47 67 36N02 84W02 5:36:08
Ponders Gap 73 67 35N40 84W40 5:38:40
Pond Grove 73 70 35N52 84W41 5:38:44
Pond Hill 54 71 35N27 84W36 5:38:24
Pope 57 3 35N45 88W52 5:55:28
Pope 68 3 35N37 87W50 5:51:20
Poplar 1 62 36N05 84W08 5:36:32
Poplar Grove 1 62 36N05 84W08 5:36:32
Poplar Grove 43 3 36N06 87W38 5:50:32
Poplar Grove 71 34 36N11 85W28 5:41:52
Poplar Hill 28 3 35N02 87W00 5:48:00
Poplar Hill 54 71 35N27 84W36 5:38:24
Poplar Springs 39 25 35N39 88W23 5:53:32
Poplar Springs 53 68 35N44 84W21 5:37:24
Poplar Springs 67 3 36N11 85W28 5:41:52
Poplar Springs 73 67 35N52 84W31 5:38:04
Poplar Top 60 3 35N38 87W15 5:49:00
Poplins Crossroads 2 3 35N37 86W35 5:46:20
Porter Court 40 26 36N18 88W19 5:53:16
Porterfield 8 3 35N56 86W11 5:44:44
Porter Gap 49 3 35N53 89W24 5:57:36
Portland 83 50 36N35 86W31 5:46:04
Port Royal 63 3 36N35 87W04 5:48:16
Port Serena 33 61 35N06 85W15 5:41:00
Postelle 70 73 35N03 84W24 5:37:36
Post Oak 71 34 36N11 85W28 5:41:52
Post Oak 73 70 35N52 84W41 5:38:44
Poteet 67 3 36N24 85W14 5:40:56
Pottsville 60 31 35N37 87W02 5:48:08
Powder Springs 29 55 36N15 83W40 5:34:40
Powell 47 67 36N02 84W02 5:36:08
Powells Crossroads 58 8 35N12 85W31 5:42:04
Powell Station 47 67 36N03 84W02 5:36:08
Prairie Creek 33 61 35N16 85W11 5:40:44
Prairie Peninsula 33 61 35N06 85W15 5:41:00
Prairie Plains 16 12 35N25 85W58 5:43:52
Pressmens Home 37 70 36N27 83W04 5:32:16
Prestige 49 28 35N45 89W32 5:58:08

Price 49 3 35N40 89W45 5:59:00
Price 93 3 35N56 85W28 5:41:52
Primm Springs 41 3 35N49 87W15 5:49:00
Proctor City 48 3 36N23 89W29 5:57:56
Prospect 5 64 35N44 83W49 5:35:16
Prospect 6 53 35N09 84W52 5:39:28
Prospect 28 3 35N02 87W00 5:48:00
Prospect 52 9 35N09 86W35 5:46:20
Prosperity 56 3 36N32 85W51 5:43:24
Prosperity 95 49 35N57 86W06 5:44:24
Protemus 66 3 36N20 89W10 5:56:40
Providence 19 4 36N06 86W45 5:47:00
Providence 31 3 35N13 86W05 5:44:20
Providence 57 3 35N39 88W53 5:55:32
Providence 83 50 36N34 86W15 5:45:00
Pruden 13 51 36N35 83W54 5:35:36
Pryor Ridge 58 8 35N16 85W44 5:42:56
Puckett 75 3 35N45 86W32 5:46:08
Pulaski 28 22 35N12 87W02 5:48:08
Pumpkintown 56 3 36N32 86W02 5:44:08
Puncheon Camp 29 55 36N17 83W36 5:34:24
Punkton 15 65 35N55 83W01 5:32:04
Purdy 55 3 35N10 88W35 5:54:20
Puryear 40 3 36N27 88W20 5:53:20
Pyburns 36 23 35N14 88W14 5:52:56
Quebeck 93 3 35N49 85W34 5:42:16
Quincy 17 14 35N47 89W07 5:56:28
Quito 84 3 35N20 89W53 5:59:32
Raccoon Valley 87 52 36N15 83W48 5:35:12
Rader 30 65 36N13 82W48 5:31:12
Rafter 62 70 35N22 84W18 5:37:12
Ragsdale 16 12 35N28 86W05 5:44:20
Raines 79 39 35N02 90W03 6:00:12
Raleigh 79 40 35N12 89W55 5:59:40
Ralston 92 3 36N21 88W51 5:55:24
Ramah 50 29 35N10 87W21 5:49:24
Ramer 55 3 35N04 88W37 5:54:28
Ramsey 47 67 36N00 83W53 5:35:32
Randolph 84 3 35N26 89W47 5:59:08
Range 10 1 36N22 82W17 5:29:08
Ranger 57 3 35N39 88W53 5:55:32
Rankin 15 65 35N58 83W11 5:32:44
Rascal Town 50 29 35N04 87W26 5:49:44
Raus 2 3 35N21 86W12 5:44:48
Raven Branch 15 65 35N49 83W09 5:32:36
Ravenscroft 93 3 35N56 85W28 5:41:52
Rayon Terrace 10 1 36N20 82W13 5:28:52
Rays Chapel 2 3 35N38 86W42 5:46:48
Raysville 64 3 35N21 86W12 5:44:48
Readyville 8 3 35N50 86W10 5:44:40
Reagan 39 3 35N31 88W20 5:53:20
Red Ash 7 66 36N18 84W13 5:36:52
Red Bank 33 61 35N07 85W16 5:41:04
Red Bankwhite Oak 33 61 35N07 85W17 5:41:08
Red Boiling Springs 56 3 36N32 85W51 5:43:24
Red Hill 6 53 35N09 84W52 5:39:28
Red Hill 13 51 35N59 84W18 5:37:12
Red Hill 16 12 35N28 86W05 5:44:20
Red Hill 25 3 36N26 84W56 5:39:44
Red Hill 58 8 35N12 85W31 5:42:04
Red Hill 69 3 36N34 85W08 5:40:32
Red House 29 55 36N09 83W42 5:34:48
Red Row 60 9 35N32 87W12 5:48:48
Redstone 82 2 36N35 82W11 5:28:44
Reed Spring 53 68 35N40 84W24 5:37:36
Reeds Store 75 3 35N48 86W40 5:46:40
Reedtown 15 65 35N58 83W11 5:32:44
Reel Cove 58 8 35N12 85W31 5:42:04
Rehoboth 23 16 36N02 89W23 5:57:32
Reliance 70 72 35N11 84W30 5:38:00
Reubensville 83 50 36N35 86W31 5:46:04
Reverie 84 3 35N32 90W00 6:00:00
Revilo 50 29 35N10 87W21 5:49:24
Rheatown 30 65 36N14 82W41 5:30:44
Rialto 84 44 35N34 89W42 5:58:48
Rice Bend 86 1 36N01 82W33 5:30:12
Riceville 54 54 35N23 84W42 5:38:48
Rich 28 3 35N23 87W00 5:48:00
Rich Acres 90 75 36N19 82W21 5:29:24
Richard City 58 8 35N00 85W44 5:42:56
Richardson 84 3 35N26 89W47 5:59:08
Rich Crossing 26 18 35N03 86W16 5:45:04
Richland 19 4 36N07 86W52 5:47:28
Richland 29 55 36N09 83W42 5:34:48
Richmond 2 3 35N19 86W38 5:46:32
Richs Crossing 26 18 35N03 86W16 5:45:04
Richwood 23 16 36N02 89W23 5:57:32
Rickman 67 3 36N16 85W23 5:41:32
Riddle Store 54 71 35N36 84W28 5:37:52
Riddleton 80 3 36N19 86W01 5:44:04
Ridenour 87 52 36N12 84W02 5:36:08
Ridge 13 51 36N27 83W34 5:34:16
Ridgedale 18 9 35N56 85W28 5:41:52
Ridgedale 82 2 36N35 82W11 5:28:44
Ridgely 48 3 36N16 89W29 5:57:56
Ridgeside 33 61 35N02 85W15 5:41:00
Ridgetop 51 3 35N36 87W18 5:49:12
Ridgetop 74 3 36N24 86W46 5:47:04
Ridgeville 64 33 35N17 86W22 5:45:28
Ridley 60 31 35N37 87W02 5:48:08
Riggs 94 3 35N48 86W40 5:46:40
Right 36 3 35N19 88W21 5:53:24
Rinda 92 3 36N09 88W48 5:55:12
Ringgold 63 32 36N32 87W22 5:49:28
Rinnie 18 15 35N57 85W02 5:40:08
Riovista 10 1 36N20 82W13 5:28:52
Ripley 49 28 35N45 89W32 5:58:08
Ritchie 13 51 36N27 83W34 5:34:16
Ritta 47 67 36N02 83W56 5:35:44
Riva Lake Camp 26 19 35N11 86W07 5:44:28

TENNESSEE

Riverdale 47 67 36N00 83W53 5:35:32
River Heights 60 31 35N37 87W02 5:48:08
River Hill 86 1 36N08 82W25 5:29:40
River Hill 93 3 35N56 85W28 5:41:52
River Oaks 33 61 35N07 85W08 5:40:32
Riversburg 28 22 35N12 87W02 5:48:08
Riverside 16 12 35N28 86W05 5:44:20
Riverside 19 4 36N13 86W50 5:47:20
Riverside 60 31 35N37 87W02 5:48:08
Riverside 79 39 35N07 89W59 5:59:56
Riverton 25 3 36N26 84W56 5:39:44
Riverview 13 51 36N35 83W39 5:34:36
Riverview 86 1 36N08 82W25 5:29:40
Riverview 88 3 35N47 85W35 5:42:20
Rives 66 3 36N21 89W03 5:56:12
Roan Mountain 10 1 36N12 82W04 5:28:16
Roaring Springs 30 65 36N12 82W44 5:30:56
Roarks Cove 26 18 35N13 86W05 5:44:20
Robbins 69 3 36N34 85W08 5:40:32
Robbins 76 58 36N21 84W35 5:38:20
Roberts 71 3 36N05 85W44 5:42:56
Robertson Fork 59 3 35N23 87W00 5:48:00
Robinson Crossroads 47 67 35N52 84W08 5:36:32
Rockbridge 83 50 36N29 86W19 5:45:16
Rock City 80 41 36N15 85W57 5:43:48
Rock City 82 2 36N33 82W31 5:30:04
Rock Creek 59 3 35N31 86W44 5:46:56
Rock Creek 69 3 36N26 84W56 5:39:44
Rock Creek 86 1 36N08 82W25 5:29:40
Rockdale 60 9 35N32 87W12 5:48:48
Rockford 5 64 35N50 83W56 5:35:44
Rock Hill 34 51 36N34 83W03 5:32:12
Rock Hill 39 25 35N39 88W23 5:53:32
Rock Hill 82 1 36N22 82W17 5:29:08
Rock House 85 3 36N18 86W37 5:46:28
Rock Island 89 3 35N48 85W37 5:42:28
Rockland 83 43 36N18 86W37 5:46:28
Rock Springs 23 16 36N02 89W23 5:57:32
Rock Springs 39 3 35N48 88W22 5:53:28
Rock Springs 75 38 35N59 86W31 5:46:04
Rock Springs 82 2 36N31 82W32 5:30:08
Rockvale 75 3 35N45 86W32 5:46:08
Rockville 62 67 35N36 84W28 5:37:52
Rockwood 73 70 35N52 84W41 5:38:44
Rockwood Hill 30 65 36N13 82W48 5:31:12
Rocky Branch 5 64 35N44 83W49 5:35:16
Rocky Fork 75 38 35N59 86W31 5:46:04
Rocky Fork 86 1 36N02 82W33 5:30:12
Rocky Grove 78 60 35N49 83W15 5:33:00
Rocky Mound 56 3 36N34 86W15 5:45:00
Rocky Point 71 34 36N11 85W28 5:41:52
Rocky Ridge 67 3 36N26 85W15 5:41:00
Rocky Spring 62 67 35N31 84W22 5:37:28
Roddy 72 74 35N41 84W52 5:39:28
Roe 32 67 36N13 83W17 5:33:08
Roe Junction 32 67 36N13 83W17 5:33:08
Roellen 23 16 36N02 89W17 5:57:08
Rogana 83 50 36N29 86W19 5:45:16
Rogers Spring 35 3 35N04 88W53 5:55:32
Rogersville 37 70 36N24 83W01 5:32:04
Rolling Acres 45 67 36N09 83W25 5:33:40
Rolling Fields 60 31 35N37 87W02 5:48:08
Rolling Hills 32 67 36N13 83W17 5:33:08
Rolling Hills 59 30 35N27 86W48 5:47:12
Rome 80 3 36N16 86W04 5:44:16
Romeo 30 65 36N15 83W05 5:32:20
Roneys Store 66 3 36N20 89W18 5:57:12
Rose Creek 55 3 35N10 88W35 5:54:20
Rosedale 1 62 36N10 84W21 5:37:24
Rose Hill 57 3 35N39 88W53 5:55:32
Rose Hill 87 52 36N15 83W48 5:35:12
Rosemark 79 40 35N22 89W46 5:59:04
Rose Valley 81 3 36N30 87W42 5:50:48
Roseville 2 5 35N32 86W20 5:45:20
Roslin 25 3 36N26 84W56 5:39:44
Ross Camp Ground 37 70 36N32 82W41 5:30:44
Rosser 9 3 36N00 88W25 5:53:40
Rossview 63 32 36N32 87W22 5:49:28
Rossville 24 3 35N05 89W33 5:58:12
Rotherwood 37 70 36N32 82W41 5:30:44
Roughpoint 44 27 36N21 85W39 5:42:36
Round Pond 63 32 36N32 87W22 5:49:28
Roundtop 95 49 36N05 86W02 5:44:08
Routon 40 3 36N12 88W25 5:53:40
Rover 2 3 35N40 86W36 5:46:24
Rowland 89 3 35N48 85W37 5:42:28
Rowland Station 89 3 35N48 85W37 5:42:28
Royal 2 6 35N29 86W27 5:45:48
Royal Blue 7 66 36N25 84W18 5:37:12
Royal Oak 16 12 35N28 86W05 5:44:20
Royal Oaks 60 31 35N37 87W02 5:48:08
Royer Estates 75 37 35N51 86W23 5:45:32
Rucker 75 37 35N51 86W23 5:45:32
Rudderville 94 48 35N57 86W53 5:47:32
Rudolph 38 24 35N36 89W16 5:57:04
Rugby 65 56 36N22 84W42 5:38:48
Rural Hill 19 4 36N08 86W42 5:46:48
Rural Vale 62 70 35N22 84W18 5:37:12
Russel Fork 7 66 36N27 84W04 5:36:16
Russell Hill 56 3 36N23 85W57 5:43:48
Russellville 32 67 36N15 83W12 5:32:48
Rutherford 27 21 36N08 88W59 5:55:56
Ruthton 82 2 36N35 82W11 5:28:44
Ruthville 92 3 36N21 88W51 5:55:24
Rutledge 29 55 36N17 83W31 5:34:04
Rutledge Falls 16 12 35N28 86W05 5:44:20
Rutledge Hills 16 12 35N25 85W58 5:43:52
Ryall Springs 33 61 35N02 85W08 5:40:32

Place		Lat.	Long.	Time
Sadie 10	1	36N20	82w13	5:28:52
Sadlers 71	3	36N09	85w38	5:42:32
Sadlersville 74	3	36N36	87w07	5:48:28
Safely 89	46	35N42	85w46	5:43:04
Safford 39	3	35N38	88w13	5:52:52
Sagetown 70	72	35N11	84w39	5:38:36
Sailors Rest 63	3	36N23	87w38	5:50:32
Saint Andrews 26	18	35N14	85w54	5:43:36
Saint Bethlehem 63	3	36N34	87w18	5:49:12
Saint Clair 37	70	36N15	83w05	5:32:20
Saint Elmo 33	61	35N00	85w20	5:41:20
Saint James 30	65	36N13	82w48	5:31:12
Saint John 14	3	36N27	85w21	5:41:24
Saint Joseph 50	29	35N02	87w30	5:50:00
Saint Paul 84	3	35N26	89w47	5:59:08
Sainville 16	12	35N28	86w05	5:44:20
Sale Creek 33	61	35N23	85w07	5:40:28
Salem 15	65	36N00	83w06	5:32:24
Salem 51	3	35N48	87w27	5:49:48
Salem 63	32	36N32	87w22	5:49:28
Salem 84	3	35N26	89w47	5:59:08
Salem 92	3	36N14	88w50	5:55:20
Saltillo 36	3	35N23	88w13	5:52:52
Samburg 66	3	36N23	89w21	5:57:24
Sampson 4	3	35N36	85w11	5:40:44
Sanders 31	3	35N16	85w44	5:42:56
Sandlick 13	51	36N26	83w36	5:34:24
Sand Springs 71	3	36N09	85w16	5:41:04
Sandy Hook 60	9	35N32	87w12	5:48:48
Sandy Lane 62	70	35N22	84w18	5:37:12
Sandy Ridge 45	67	36N01	83w25	5:33:40
Sandy Spring 74	3	36N33	87w00	5:48:00
Sanford 54	54	35N23	84w42	5:38:48
Sanford Hill 12	3	35N26	88w39	5:54:36
Sango 63	32	36N32	87w22	5:49:28
Sante Fe 60	3	35N45	87w08	5:48:32
Sardis 15	65	35N58	83w11	5:32:44
Sardis 39	3	35N32	88w18	5:53:12
Saulsbury 35	3	35N03	89w05	5:56:20
Saundersville 83	43	36N18	86w37	5:46:28
Savannah 36	23	35N14	88w15	5:53:00
Sawyers Mill 3	3	36N04	88w06	5:52:24
Scandlyn 73	63	36N02	84w20	5:37:20
Scattersville 83	50	36N35	86w31	5:46:04
Scenic Heights 26	19	35N11	86w07	5:44:28
Scoot Mill 30	65	36N12	83w03	5:32:12
Scottsboro 19	4	36N13	86w50	5:47:20
Scotts Hill 39	3	35N31	88w15	5:53:00
Screamer 60	9	35N32	87w12	5:48:48
Seeber Flats 1	62	36N11	84w11	5:36:44
Selmer 55	3	35N10	88w36	5:54:24
Sequatchie 58	8	35N07	85w36	5:42:24
Sequatchie Valley 4	3	35N36	85w12	5:40:48
Sequoia Grove 6	53	35N09	84w52	5:39:28
Serles 35	3	35N16	89w00	5:56:00
Servilla 70	72	35N11	84w30	5:38:00
Seven Islands 47	67	35N56	83w54	5:35:36
Seven Oaks 47	67	35N52	84w08	5:36:32
Sevier Home 47	67	35N53	83w51	5:35:24
Sevierville 78	60	35N52	83w34	5:34:16
Sewanee 26	18	35N12	85w55	5:43:40
Sewee 61	54	35N31	84w32	5:38:08
Seymour 78	60	35N53	83w43	5:34:52
Shacklett 11	9	36N06	87w07	5:48:28
Shadowlawn 79	40	35N17	89w40	5:58:40
Shady Grove 16	12	35N55	85w35	5:42:20
Shady Grove 33	61	35N16	85w11	5:40:44
Shady Grove 47	67	35N52	84w08	5:36:32
Shady Grove 52	9	34N59	86w25	5:45:40
Shady Grove 63	32	36N32	87w22	5:49:28
Shady Hill 39	25	35N39	88w23	5:53:32
Shady Rest 89	46	35N42	85w46	5:43:04
Shady Valley 46	1	36N32	81w54	5:27:36
Shallowford 86	1	36N08	82w25	5:29:40
Shandy 35	3	35N16	89w00	5:56:00
Sharon 92	3	36N14	88w50	5:55:20
Sharon Park 60	31	35N37	87w02	5:48:08
Sharp Place 25	3	36N26	84w56	5:39:44
Sharps Chapel 87	52	36N21	83w50	5:35:20
Sharpsville 75	37	35N51	86w23	5:45:32
Shawanee 13	51	36N35	83w38	5:34:32
Shawnette 91	3	35N10	87w44	5:50:56
Shelby Center 79	40	35N12	89w54	5:59:36
Shelby Forest 79	40	35N19	89w54	5:59:36
Shelbyville 2	6	35N29	86w28	5:45:52
Shell Creek 10	1	36N12	82w05	5:28:20
Shellsford 89	46	35N42	85w46	5:43:04
Shenandoah Heights 10	1	36N19	82w21	5:29:24
Shepherd 33	61	35N02	85w12	5:40:48
Shepherd Forest 33	61	35N08	85w19	5:41:16
Shepp 38	3	35N28	89w24	5:57:36
Sherwood 26	18	35N05	85w56	5:43:44
Sherwood Estates 1	62	36N05	84w08	5:36:32
Sheybogan 8	3	35N49	86w04	5:44:16
Shiloh 29	55	36N17	83w31	5:34:04
Shiloh 36	3	35N09	88w19	5:53:16
Shiloh 37	70	36N32	83w13	5:32:52
Shiloh 43	3	36N06	87w38	5:50:32
Shiloh 44	3	36N11	85w28	5:41:52
Shiloh 63	3	36N16	87w22	5:49:28
Shiloh 75	37	35N51	86w23	5:45:32
Shingleton 46	1	36N29	81w48	5:27:12
Shining Rock 21	11	35N57	85w49	5:43:16
Shipetown 47	67	36N04	83w44	5:34:56
Shipley 71	34	36N11	85w28	5:41:52
Shipps Bend 41	3	35N48	87w27	5:49:48
Shirley 25	3	36N23	84w53	5:39:32
Shirleyton 58	8	35N12	85w31	5:42:04
Shooks 47	67	35N56	83w54	5:35:36
Shop Spring 95	49	36N08	86w13	5:44:52
Short Tail Springs 33	61	35N07	85w08	5:40:32
Shouns 46	1	36N27	81w48	5:27:12
Shubert 51	3	35N33	87w34	5:50:16
Siam 10	1	36N20	82w13	5:28:52
Sideview 83	42	36N23	86w26	5:45:44
Sidonia 92	3	36N14	88w50	5:55:20
Signal Hills 33	61	35N05	85w19	5:41:16
Signal Mountain 33	61	35N07	85w21	5:41:24
Silerton 35	3	35N21	88w47	5:55:08
Silica 7	66	36N18	84w13	5:36:52
Siloam 56	3	36N33	86w10	5:44:40
Silvacola 82	1	36N32	82w19	5:29:16
Silver City 32	67	36N15	83w12	5:32:48
Silverhill 75	37	35N51	86w23	5:45:32
Silver Lake 46	1	36N29	81w48	5:27:12
Silver Point 71	3	36N05	85w44	5:42:56
Silver Ridge 53	68	35N48	84w16	5:37:04
Silvertop 42	3	36N06	87w38	5:50:32
Simonton 84	3	35N29	89w43	5:58:52
Sims Spring 2	6	35N29	86w27	5:45:48
Singleton 2	6	35N29	86w27	5:45:48
Singleton 5	64	35N49	84w03	5:36:12
Singtown 83	50	36N35	86w31	5:46:04
Sitka 27	20	35N55	88w46	5:55:04
Sixmile 5	64	35N46	83w58	5:35:52
Skaggston 47	67	36N05	83w45	5:35:00
Skinem 52	9	35N09	86w35	5:46:20
Skinner Crossroads 30	65	36N12	83w03	5:32:12
Skullbone 27	21	36N04	88w49	5:55:16
Skyline Park 33	61	35N08	85w19	5:41:16
Slatestone 1	62	36N11	84w11	5:36:44
Slatesville 95	9	36N06	86w08	5:44:32
Slayden 22	3	36N18	87w28	5:49:52
Slick Rock 76	58	36N21	84w35	5:38:20
Slide 37	70	36N21	82w59	5:31:56
Smartt 89	3	35N38	85w50	5:43:20
Smith Chapel 44	3	36N11	85w28	5:41:52
Smithfield 62	70	35N22	84w18	5:37:12
Smithland 52	9	35N08	86w28	5:45:52
Smiths Chapel 56	3	36N32	85w51	5:43:24
Smiths Fork 36	3	35N17	88w02	5:52:08
Smith Springs 19	4	36N09	86w41	5:46:44
Smithville 21	11	35N58	85w49	5:43:16
Smoky Junction 76	58	36N20	84w23	5:37:32
Smyrna 9	3	35N59	88w17	5:53:08
Smyrna 69	3	36N34	85w08	5:40:32
Smyrna 75	38	35N59	86w31	5:46:04
Smyrna 89	46	35N42	85w46	5:43:04
Sneedville 34	51	36N32	83w13	5:32:52
Snell 75	37	35N51	86w23	5:45:32
Snow Hill 33	61	35N14	85w03	5:40:12
Snows Hill 21	3	36N01	85w57	5:43:48
Soddy 33	61	35N17	85w10	5:40:40
Soddy-Daisy 33	61	35N15	85w08	5:40:32
Solo 84	44	35N34	89w42	5:58:48
Solway 47	67	35N59	84w11	5:36:44
Somerville 24	17	35N15	89w21	5:57:24
South 19	4	36N09	86w45	5:47:00
Southall 94	48	35N57	86w53	5:47:32
South Bradley 6	53	35N03	84w56	5:39:44
South Cannon 8	3	35N46	86w04	5:44:16
South Carthage 80	41	36N14	85w57	5:43:48
South Cleveland 6	53	35N07	84w52	5:39:28
South Clinton 1	62	36N04	84w08	5:36:32
South Columbia 60	31	35N37	87w02	5:48:08
South Covington 84	44	35N34	89w42	5:58:48
South Daisy 33	61	35N16	85w11	5:40:44
South Dyersburg 23	16	36N02	89w23	5:57:32
Southern Hills 60	31	35N37	87w02	5:48:08
South Etowah 54	54	35N20	84w32	5:38:08
South Fulton 66	3	36N30	88w52	5:55:28
Southgate 79	39	35N04	90w04	6:00:16
South Hall 5	64	35N47	83w59	5:35:56
South Harriman 73	67	35N56	84w33	5:38:12
South Huntingdon 9	3	35N55	88w29	5:53:56
South Knoxville 47	67	35N56	83w54	5:35:36
Southland Mall 79	39	35N02	90w03	6:00:12
South Liberty 54	54	35N23	84w42	5:38:48
South Pittsburg 58	8	35N01	85w42	5:42:48
Southport 60	3	35N29	86w59	5:47:56
Southside 60	31	35N37	87w02	5:48:08
Southside 63	3	36N22	87w18	5:49:12
South Side 80	3	36N11	86w00	5:44:00
South Tunnel 83	50	36N29	86w28	5:45:52
Sparkman 88	3	35N51	85w31	5:42:04
Sparta 93	3	35N56	85w28	5:41:52
Spear Springs 37	70	36N24	83w00	5:32:00
Speedwell 13	51	36N27	83w55	5:35:40
Spencer 88	3	35N45	85w28	5:41:52
Spencers Mill 22	3	36N03	87w19	5:49:16
Spot 41	3	35N52	87w28	5:49:52
Spout Springs 66	3	36N20	89w18	5:57:12
Springbrook 5	64	35N47	83w59	5:35:56
Spring City 72	74	35N42	84w50	5:39:20
Spring Creek 57	3	35N46	88w41	5:54:44
Springdale 13	51	36N27	83w34	5:34:16
Springdale 82	2	36N31	82w32	5:30:08
Springfield 74	35	36N31	86w53	5:47:32
Spring Hill 38	3	35N28	89w24	5:57:36
Spring Hill 39	3	35N35	88w32	5:54:08
Spring Hill 42	3	36N19	87w42	5:50:48
Spring Hill 60	3	35N45	86w56	5:47:44
Spring Hill 93	3	35N56	85w28	5:41:52
Spring Place 47	67	36N00	83w53	5:35:32
Springville 40	3	36N14	88w11	5:52:44
Spruce Pine 37	70	36N21	83w14	5:32:56
Spurgeon 90	75	36N18	82w28	5:29:52
Staffords Store 92	3	36N09	88w48	5:55:12
Staffordtown 70	73	34N59	84w22	5:37:28
Stahlman 19	4	36N10	86w47	5:47:08
Stainville 1	62	36N11	84w11	5:36:44
Stanfield 7	66	36N28	84w17	5:37:08
Stanley Junction 76	58	36N30	84w31	5:38:04
Stanton 38	3	35N28	89w24	5:57:36
Stantonville 55	3	35N12	88w27	5:53:48
Star Point 69	3	36N34	85w08	5:40:32
Statesville 95	9	36N01	86w08	5:44:32
State University 90	75	36N19	82w21	5:29:24
Static 69	3	36N36	85w04	5:40:16
Station Camp 83	50	36N27	86w32	5:46:08
Stayton 22	3	36N16	87w22	5:49:28
Stella 28	3	35N02	87w05	5:48:20
Stephen Holston 82	2	36N35	82w11	5:28:44
Stephens 65	51	36N02	84w20	5:37:20
Sterling Park 33	61	35N06	85w15	5:41:00
Stewart 42	3	36N19	87w50	5:51:20
Stinking Creek 7	66	36N23	84w07	5:36:28
Stiversville 60	3	35N29	86w59	5:47:56
Stock Creek 47	67	35N56	83w54	5:35:36
Stockton 25	3	36N26	84w56	5:39:44
Stockton Valley 53	68	35N44	84w21	5:37:24
Stokes 23	16	35N54	89w15	5:57:00
Stokes Crossing 2	5	35N32	86w20	5:45:20
Stone 44	27	36N21	85w39	5:42:36
Stone River 19	4	36N12	86w37	5:46:28
Stone River Estates 19	4	36N12	86w37	5:46:28
Stones River Homes 75	38	35N59	86w31	5:46:04
Stonewall 80	3	36N09	85w57	5:43:48
Stoney Fork 76	58	36N18	84w13	5:36:52
Stony Creek 10	1	36N24	82w05	5:28:20
Stony Gap 34	51	36N32	83w13	5:32:52
Stony Point 37	70	36N28	82w51	5:31:24
Strahl 37	70	36N21	82w59	5:31:56
Strawberry Plains 45	67	36N04	83w41	5:34:44
Striggersville 37	70	36N24	83w00	5:32:00
Stringtown 63	3	36N33	87w31	5:50:04
Stroudsville 74	3	36N33	87w00	5:48:00
Sugar Creek 44	27	36N21	85w39	5:42:36
Sugar Forks 45	67	36N01	83w25	5:33:40
Sugar Grove 6	53	35N09	84w52	5:39:28
Sugar Grove 73	67	35N56	84w33	5:38:12
Sugar Grove 83	50	36N34	86w15	5:45:00
Sugarlimb 53	68	35N44	84w21	5:37:24
Sugar Tree 20	3	35N50	88w02	5:52:08
Suggs Creek 95	49	36N12	86w31	5:46:04
Sullivan Gardens 82	2	36N29	82w35	5:30:20
Sulphur 67	22	36N23	85w19	5:41:16
Sulphura 83	50	36N35	86w31	5:46:04
Sulphur Creek 41	3	35N40	87w42	5:50:48
Sulphur Springs 1	62	36N05	84w08	5:36:32
Sulphur Springs 58	8	35N12	85w31	5:42:04
Sulphur Springs 90	63	36N23	82w34	5:30:16
Sumac 28	22	35N12	87w02	5:48:08
Summer City 4	3	35N36	85w11	5:40:44
Summerfield 31	3	35N16	85w44	5:42:56
Summer Shade 67	3	36N27	85w21	5:41:24
Summertown 33	61	35N08	85w19	5:41:16
Summertown 50	29	35N26	87w18	5:49:12
Summit 33	61	35N04	85w04	5:40:16
Summit 37	70	36N15	83w05	5:32:20
Summit 63	32	36N32	87w22	5:49:28
Summit Knobs 33	61	35N04	85w10	5:40:40
Summitville 16	12	35N34	85w59	5:43:56
Sunbright 65	56	36N15	84w40	5:38:40
Sunny Brook 82	2	36N35	82w11	5:28:44
Sunny Hill 38	24	35N36	89w16	5:57:04
Sunny Hills 82	2	36N35	82w11	5:28:44
Sunnyside 34	51	36N32	83w13	5:32:52
Sunnyside 60	31	35N37	87w02	5:48:08
Sunnyside 66	3	36N25	89w03	5:56:12
Sunnyside 82	1	36N32	82w19	5:29:16
Sunrise 29	55	36N17	83w31	5:34:04
Sunrise 41	3	35N48	87w27	5:49:48
Sunset Hills 32	67	36N13	83w17	5:33:08
Surgoinsville 37	70	36N30	82w52	5:31:28
Sutherland 46	1	36N38	81w47	5:27:08
Swan Bluff 41	3	35N48	87w27	5:49:48
Swann Chapel 45	67	36N01	83w25	5:33:40
Swannsylvania 45	67	36N01	83w25	5:33:40
Sweet Lips 12	3	35N26	88w39	5:54:36
Sweeton Hill 31	3	35N20	85w43	5:42:52
Sweetwater 62	67	35N36	84w28	5:37:52
Swift 36	23	35N14	88w14	5:52:56
Sycamore 13	51	36N27	83w29	5:33:56
Sycamore 71	34	36N11	85w28	5:41:52
Sycamore Hall 13	51	36N27	83w34	5:34:16
Sycamore Landing 43	3	36N05	87w47	5:51:08
Sykes 80	3	36N07	86w02	5:44:08
Sylvia 22	3	36N05	87w23	5:49:32
Tabernacle 38	24	35N36	89w16	5:57:04

Tabernacle 84	3	35N31	89w32	5:58:08
Tabor 18	15	35N57	85w02	5:40:08
Tackett Creek 7	66	36N27	84w04	5:36:16
Taft 52	9	35N01	86w43	5:46:52
Talbott 45	67	36N09	83w25	5:33:40
Tallassee 5	64	35N33	84w04	5:36:16
Talley 59	3	35N19	86w38	5:46:32
Tampico 29	55	36N17	83w31	5:34:04
Tanglewood 80	41	36N15	85w57	5:43:48
Tarlton 31	3	35N42	85w46	5:43:04
Tarpley 28	22	35N12	87w02	5:48:08
Tasso 6	53	35N13	84w48	5:39:12
Tate Springs 29	55	36N20	83w22	5:33:28
Tatesville 31	3	35N21	85w34	5:42:16
Taylor Cross Roads 2	3	35N37	86w35	5:46:20
Taylors 24	3	35N14	89w21	5:57:24
Taylors Cross Roads 67	3	36N26	85w15	5:41:00
Taylorsville 60	3	35N36	87w18	5:49:12
Taylorsville 95	34	36N12	86w18	5:45:12
Tazewell 13	51	36N27	83w34	5:34:16
Teachers College 19	4	36N09	86w47	5:47:08
Teague 35	3	35N27	88w52	5:55:28
Tekoa 47	67	35N58	83w58	5:35:52
Telford 90	63	36N13	82w35	5:30:20
Tellico Hills 54	71	35N27	84w36	5:38:24
Tellico Plains 62	70	35N22	84w18	5:37:12
Temperance Hall 21	3	36N00	85w58	5:43:52
Templeton 23	16	36N07	89w16	5:57:04
Templow 85	3	36N29	86w19	5:45:16
Ten Mile 61	54	35N40	84w40	5:38:40
Tennemo 23	16	36N10	89w29	5:57:56
Tennessee City 22	3	36N06	87w31	5:50:04
Tennessee Hills 82	2	36N35	82w11	5:28:44
Tennessee Ridge 42	3	36N19	87w47	5:51:08
Terrell 92	3	36N21	88w51	5:55:24
Terry 9	3	35N49	88w36	5:54:24
Terry Creek 7	66	36N28	84w17	5:37:08
Theodore 51	3	35N33	87w34	5:50:16
Theta 60	3	35N47	87w03	5:48:12
The Wye 1	62	36N13	84w09	5:36:36
Thick 59	3	35N38	86w42	5:46:48
Thomas 71	3	36N09	85w38	5:42:32
Thomas Addition 82	2	36N34	82w34	5:30:16
Thomas Bridge 82	1	36N28	82w15	5:29:00
Thomasville 11	10	36N16	87w04	5:48:16
Thompsons Station 94	3	35N48	86w55	5:47:40
Thompsons Store 14	11	36N33	85w30	5:42:00
Thorngrove 47	67	36N04	83w41	5:34:44
Thorn Hill 29	55	36N22	83w26	5:33:44
Thornton Heights 47	67	35N52	84w08	5:36:32
Three Churches 91	3	35N10	87w44	5:50:56
Three Oaks 50	29	35N19	87w18	5:49:12
Three Point 49	3	35N41	89w44	5:58:56
Three Points 47	67	36N02	83w56	5:35:44
Three Springs 32	67	36N15	83w12	5:32:48
Three Way 27	8	35N50	88w55	5:55:40
Throckmorton 81	3	36N30	87w42	5:50:48
Thula 30	65	36N12	83w03	5:32:12
Thurman Addition 78	60	35N49	83w33	5:34:12
Tibbs 38	24	35N36	89w16	5:57:04
Tidwell 22	3	36N05	87w23	5:49:32
Tidwell 41	3	35N56	87w19	5:49:16
Tigertown 32	67	36N13	83w17	5:33:08
Tiger Valley 10	1	36N13	82w12	5:28:48
Tigrett 23	16	35N59	89w14	5:56:56
Timberlake 39	25	35N39	88w23	5:53:32
Timberlinks 33	61	35N08	85w19	5:41:16
Timesville 33	61	35N08	85w19	5:41:16
Timothy 67	3	36N25	85w27	5:41:48
Tinch 25	3	36N26	84w56	5:39:44
Tin Cup 3	3	36N04	88w06	5:52:24
Tinsleys Bottom 44	3	36N33	85w30	5:42:00
Tiprell 13	51	36N36	83w40	5:34:40
Tipton 47	67	35N56	83w54	5:35:36
Tipton 84	3	35N25	89w49	5:59:16
Tiptonville 48	3	36N23	89w29	5:57:56
Tip Top 93	3	35N56	85w28	5:41:52
Tom Murray 57	3	35N39	88w53	5:55:32
Toone 35	3	35N21	88w57	5:55:48
Top of the World Estates 5	64	35N33	84w06	5:36:24
Topside 47	67	35N56	83w54	5:35:36
Topsy 91	3	35N19	87w46	5:51:04
Toqua 62	67	35N35	84w15	5:37:00
Tottys 41	3	35N44	87w17	5:49:08
Toulon 38	3	35N45	89w32	5:58:08
Towee 70	72	35N11	84w30	5:38:00
Town Acres 30	65	36N13	82w48	5:31:12
Town Creek 13	51	36N27	83w55	5:35:40
Towne Hills 33	61	35N06	85w15	5:41:00
Townsend 5	64	35N41	83w45	5:35:00
Tracy City 31	3	35N16	85w44	5:42:56
Trade 46	1	36N23	81w43	5:26:52
Tranquility 54	71	35N27	84w36	5:38:24
Travisville 69	3	36N33	84w58	5:39:52
Treadway 34	51	36N26	83w14	5:32:56
Treeville 47	67	36N02	84w02	5:36:08
Trenton 27	8	35N59	88w56	5:55:44
Trent Valley 34	51	36N32	83w13	5:32:52
Trentville 47	67	36N04	83w41	5:34:44
Trevecca-College 19	4	36N09	86w45	5:47:00

Trevilion 7	66	36N33	84w03	5:36:12
Trezevant 9	3	36N01	88w37	5:54:28
Trigonia 53	68	35N46	83w58	5:35:52
Trimble 23	16	36N12	89w11	5:56:44
Triune 94	3	35N52	86w43	5:46:52
Trousdale 89	3	35N36	85w49	5:43:16
Troy 66	3	36N20	89w10	5:56:40
Trundel Crossroad 78	60	35N53	83w43	5:34:52
Tuckahoe 47	67	36N04	83w41	5:34:44
Tuckers Crossroads 95	34	36N12	86w18	5:45:12
Tullahoma 16	13	35N22	86w13	5:44:52
Tulu 55	3	35N04	88w25	5:53:40
Tumbling 92	3	36N08	88w31	5:54:04
Tuppertown 1	62	36N02	84w20	5:37:20
Turley 7	66	36N18	84w13	5:36:52
Turnbull 22	3	36N03	87w19	5:49:16
Turners Station 83	50	36N34	86w15	5:45:00
Turnersville 74	3	36N33	87w00	5:48:00
Turnpike 38	24	35N36	89w16	5:57:04
Turtletown 70	73	35N07	84w21	5:37:24
Tusculum 30	65	36N10	82w45	5:31:00
Tusculum College 30	65	36N10	82w46	5:31:04
Twin Oak 71	3	36N09	85w38	5:42:32
Twin Oaks 82	2	36N34	82w34	5:30:16
Twinton 67	3	36N14	85w10	5:40:40
Twomey 41	3	35N48	87w27	5:49:48
Tyner Hills 33	61	35N02	85w11	5:40:44
Tyson 27	21	36N12	89w01	5:56:04
Uceba 5	64	35N53	83w43	5:34:52
Una 19	4	36N08	86w42	5:46:48
Unaka Springs 86	1	36N08	82w25	5:29:40
Underhill 21	3	36N02	85w54	5:43:36
Unicoi 86	1	36N12	82w21	5:29:24
Union 38	24	35N36	89w16	5:57:04
Union 65	51	36N02	84w20	5:37:20
Union 73	67	35N52	84w31	5:38:04
Union Camp 56	3	36N32	86w02	5:44:08
Union City 66	3	36N26	89w03	5:56:12
Union Grove 5	64	35N46	84w08	5:36:32
Union Grove 54	71	35N31	84w32	5:38:08
Union Grove 61	54	35N31	84w47	5:39:08
Union Heights 32	67	36N13	83w17	5:33:08
Union Hill 14	3	36N35	85w37	5:42:28
Union Hill 19	4	36N18	86w43	5:46:52
Union Hill 39	3	35N31	88w20	5:53:20
Union Hill 84	3	35N26	89w47	5:59:08
Union Mcminn 54	71	35N31	84w32	5:38:08
Union Ridge 2	5	35N32	86w20	5:45:20
Union Temple 30	65	36N12	82w44	5:30:56
Unionville 2	3	35N37	86w34	5:46:16
Unionville 23	16	35N53	89w24	5:57:36
Unitia 53	68	35N40	84w10	5:36:40
Unity 67	3	36N27	85w21	5:41:24
University 47	67	35N57	83w56	5:35:44
University Of Tennessee 92	3	36N21	88w51	5:55:24
University Of The South 26	18	35N12	85w55	5:43:40
Upchurch 30	65	36N12	82w44	5:30:56
Upper Big Bigby 60	9	35N30	87w12	5:48:48
Upper Mockeson 50	29	35N10	87w21	5:49:24
Upper Shell Creek 10	1	36N12	82w05	5:28:20
Upper Sinking 41	3	35N40	87w42	5:50:48
Uptonville 57	3	35N28	89w05	5:56:20
Uptown 47	67	35N59	83w56	5:35:44
Uptown Nashville 19	4	36N10	86w47	5:47:08
Vaden 43	3	36N06	87w38	5:50:32
Valdeau 33	61	35N06	85w17	5:41:08
Vale 9	3	36N06	88w15	5:53:00
Valleybrook 33	61	35N06	85w15	5:41:00
Valley Creek 13	51	36N33	83w57	5:35:48
Valley Forge 10	1	36N19	82w11	5:28:44
Valley Hills 82	2	36N35	82w11	5:28:44
Valleyhome 32	67	36N13	83w17	5:33:08
Valley View 1	62	36N05	84w08	5:36:32
Valley View 46	1	36N29	81w48	5:27:12
Van Benber Springs 13	51	36N27	83w55	5:35:40
Van Blarcom 19	4	36N09	86w51	5:47:24
Van Dyke 40	26	36N18	88w19	5:53:16
Vanleer 22	3	36N14	87w27	5:49:48
Vannatta 2	6	35N29	86w27	5:45:48
Vanntown 52	9	34N59	86w25	5:45:40
Vardy 34	51	36N32	83w13	5:32:52
Vasper 7	66	36N18	84w13	5:36:52
Vaughn's Gap 19	4	36N07	86w52	5:47:28
Vaughns Grove 27	8	35N58	88w57	5:55:48
Vernon 41	3	35N52	87w28	5:49:52
Vernon Heights 82	2	36N33	82w31	5:30:04
Verona 59	30	35N27	86w48	5:47:12
Versailles 75	3	35N45	86w32	5:46:08
Vesta 95	34	36N12	86w18	5:45:12
Vestal 47	67	35N55	83w57	5:35:48
Viar 23	16	36N02	89w23	5:57:32
Victoria 58	8	35N09	85w33	5:42:12
Victory 7	66	36N23	84w07	5:36:28
Vildo 35	3	35N20	89w09	5:56:36
Vine 95	34	36N12	86w18	5:45:12
Vinegar Hill 82	2	36N35	82w11	5:28:44
Vine Ridge 67	3	36N14	85w10	5:40:40
Viola 89	3	35N32	85w52	5:43:28
Virtue 47	67	35N52	84w08	5:36:32
Vise 20	3	35N35	88w07	5:52:28
Volunteer Heights 18	15	35N57	85w02	5:40:08
Vonore 62	67	35N36	84w14	5:36:56
Vose 5	64	35N47	83w59	5:35:56

Waco 28	3	35N23	87w00	5:48:00
Walden 33	61	35N08	85w19	5:41:16
Walden Creek 78	60	35N49	83w33	5:34:12
Waldens Ridge 72	74	35N01	85w11	5:40:44
Wales 28	22	35N12	87w02	5:48:08
Walker 79	39	35N04	90w04	6:00:16
Walkertown 30	65	36N12	82w44	5:30:56
Walkertown 36	23	35N14	88w14	5:52:56
Wallace Acres 59	30	35N27	86w48	5:47:12
Walland 5	64	35N44	83w49	5:35:16
Walling 93	3	35N49	85w36	5:42:24
Walnut Grove 27	21	36N12	89w01	5:56:04
Walnut Grove 36	23	35N14	88w14	5:52:56
Walnut Grove 49	28	35N45	89w32	5:58:08
Walnut Grove 61	54	35N31	84w47	5:39:08
Walnut Grove 83	50	36N27	86w32	5:46:08
Walnut Grove 84	3	35N33	89w48	5:59:12
Walnut Hill 17	3	35N43	89w05	5:56:20
Walnut Hill 73	67	35N56	84w33	5:38:12
Walnut Hill 82	2	36N35	82w11	5:28:44
Walnut Log 66	3	36N34	89w11	5:56:44
Walnut Shade 56	3	36N32	85w51	5:43:24
Walter Crossroad 30	65	36N13	82w48	5:31:12
Walterhill 75	3	35N57	86w23	5:45:32
Wa-Ni Village 29	55	36N17	83w31	5:34:04
Warren 24	3	35N14	89w21	5:57:24
Warrens Bluff 39	25	35N39	88w23	5:53:32
Warrensburg 30	65	36N11	82w59	5:31:56
Wartburg 65	51	36N06	84w36	5:38:24
Wartrace 2	5	35N32	86w20	5:45:20
Warwicktown 87	52	36N15	83w48	5:35:12
Washburn 29	55	36N18	83w36	5:34:24
Washington 72	74	35N01	85w11	5:40:44
Washington College 90	63	36N13	82w38	5:30:32
Washington Heights 33	61	35N04	85w14	5:40:56
Watauga 10	1	36N22	82w18	5:29:12
Watauga Point 10	1	36N20	82w13	5:28:52
Waterstown 5	64	35N44	83w49	5:35:16
Watertown 95	9	36N06	86w08	5:44:32
Water Valley 60	3	35N44	87w08	5:48:32
Waterville 6	53	35N09	84w52	5:39:28
Watkins 21	11	35N57	85w49	5:43:16
Watt Heights 54	54	35N18	84w45	5:39:00
Watts Bar Dam 72	74	35N37	84w47	5:39:08
Watts Bar Estates 72	74	35N41	84w52	5:39:28
Waverly 43	3	36N05	87w48	5:51:12
Wayland Springs 50	29	35N02	87w30	5:50:00
Waynesboro 91	3	35N19	87w46	5:51:04
Wayside 89	46	35N42	85w46	5:43:04
Weakly 28	3	35N15	87w20	5:49:20
Wear Valley 78	60	35N46	83w37	5:34:28
Weaver 82	1	36N31	82w09	5:28:36
Webber City 50	29	35N19	87w18	5:49:12
Webbs Chapel 21	11	35N57	85w49	5:43:16
Webbtown 56	3	36N32	86w02	5:44:08
Wedgewood Hills 47	67	35N52	84w08	5:36:32
Welchland 88	3	35N45	85w27	5:41:48
Welch's Camp 7	66	36N18	84w13	5:36:52
Well Spring 7	66	36N27	83w55	5:35:40
Wellsville 5	64	35N46	83w58	5:35:52
Wellwood 38	3	35N43	89w05	5:56:20
Wesleyanna 54	71	35N27	84w36	5:38:24
West 19	4	36N09	86w51	5:47:24
West 27	20	35N55	88w46	5:55:04
West Bradley 6	53	35N13	84w56	5:39:44
West Chester 12	3	35N24	88w41	5:54:44
Westel 18	57	35N52	84w45	5:39:00
West Emory 47	67	35N52	84w08	5:36:32
West End 15	65	35N58	83w11	5:32:44
West Erin 42	3	36N18	87w45	5:51:00
West Fork 67	3	36N24	85w14	5:40:56
West Greene 30	65	36N13	82w48	5:31:12
West Haven 60	31	35N37	87w02	5:48:08
West Knoxville 47	67	35N56	84w00	5:36:00
West Maryville 5	64	35N46	83w58	5:35:52
West Meade 16	12	35N28	86w05	5:44:20
West Meade 19	4	36N07	86w52	5:47:28
West Meade 60	31	35N37	87w02	5:48:08
West Miller Cove 5	64	35N44	83w49	5:35:16
Westmoreland 83	50	36N34	86w15	5:45:00
West Nashville 19	4	36N09	86w51	5:47:24
Westover 57	3	35N37	88w53	5:55:32
Westpoint 50	29	35N08	87w32	5:50:08
Westport 9	3	35N54	88w19	5:53:16
West Ridge 37	70	36N35	82w38	5:30:32
West Riverside 89	46	35N42	85w46	5:43:04
West Robbin 76	58	36N21	84w35	5:38:20
West Shiloh 55	3	35N09	88w23	5:53:32
Westside Heights 16	13	35N21	86w12	5:44:48
West Springbrook 5	64	35N47	83w59	5:35:56
Westwood 16	13	35N21	86w12	5:44:48
Westwood 60	31	35N37	87w02	5:48:08
Westwood 79	39	35N04	90w04	6:00:16
Westwood Gardens 57	3	35N39	88w53	5:55:32
Westwood Hills 5	64	35N46	83w58	5:35:52
Westwood Homes 16	12	35N28	86w05	5:44:20
Wetmore 70	72	35N16	84w33	5:38:12
Wheel 2	6	35N29	86w27	5:45:48
Wheelerton 28	3	35N07	86w48	5:47:12
Whitaker 2	6	35N29	86w27	5:45:48
White 79	40	35N06	89w54	5:59:36
White Acres 59	30	35N27	86w48	5:47:12

Place		Lat.	Long.	Time
White Bluff 22	3	36N06	87w13	5:48:52
White Bridge 19	4	36N07	86w52	5:47:28
White City 31	3	35N16	85w44	5:42:56
White Fern 39	3	35N36	88w38	5:54:32
Whitehaven 79	39	35N01	90w02	6:00:08
Whitehead 59	30	35N27	86w48	5:47:12
Whitehead Hills 10	1	36N12	82w05	5:28:20
White Hill 74	3	36N18	86w43	5:46:52
White Hill 88	3	35N47	85w35	5:42:20
White Horn 37	70	36N15	83w05	5:32:20
White House 74	3	36N29	86w36	5:46:24
White Oak 7	66	36N27	84w04	5:36:16
White Oak 33	61	35N06	85w17	5:41:08
Whiteoak 56	3	36N32	86w02	5:44:08
White Oak 65	51	35N59	84w33	5:38:12
White Oak Flat 22	3	36N11	87w20	5:49:20
White Oaks 16	12	35N28	86w05	5:44:20
White Pine 45	67	36N07	83w17	5:33:08
Whitesand 30	65	36N13	82w48	5:31:12
Whitesburg 32	67	36N16	83w08	5:32:32
White Schoolhouse Corners 65	51	36N02	84w20	5:37:20
Whites Creek 19	4	36N10	86w46	5:47:04
White's Creek 72	74	35N41	84w52	5:39:28
Whiteside 58	8	35N01	85w33	5:42:12
Whiteville 35	3	35N20	89w09	5:56:36
Whitleyville 44	3	36N27	85w40	5:42:40
Whitlock 40	26	36N18	88w19	5:53:16
Whitwell 58	8	35N12	85w31	5:42:04
Widow Town 78	60	35N49	83w33	5:34:12
Wilder 25	3	36N16	85w05	5:40:20
Wilder Chapel 26	18	35N13	86w05	5:44:20
Wildersville 39	3	35N47	88w22	5:53:28
Wildwood 5	64	35N49	83w49	5:35:16
Wildwood Lake 6	53	35N09	84w52	5:39:28
Wilkerson 13	51	36N33	83w57	5:35:48
Wilkinsville 84	3	35N20	89w53	5:59:32
Willard 85	45	36N23	86w10	5:44:40
Willette 56	3	36N27	85w52	5:43:28
Williams 49	28	35N45	89w32	5:58:08
Williams 56	3	36N32	86w02	5:44:08
Williamsburg 54	54	35N20	84w32	5:38:08
Williamsport 60	3	35N37	87w13	5:48:52
Williams Springs 29	55	36N17	83w36	5:34:24
Willis 34	51	36N34	83w03	5:32:12
Willis Spring 70	72	35N04	84w44	5:38:56
Williston 24	3	35N10	89w22	5:57:28
Wilson Station 62	67	35N25	84w29	5:37:56
Wilsonville 15	65	35N58	83w11	5:32:44
Winchester 26	19	35N11	86w07	5:44:28
Winchester Springs 26	19	35N11	86w07	5:44:28
Windle 67	22	36N23	85w19	5:41:16
Windletown 67	3	36N14	85w10	5:40:40
Windrock 1	62	36N02	84w20	5:37:20
Windrow 75	3	35N45	86w32	5:46:08
Windy City 57	3	35N50	88w55	5:55:40
Windy Hill 82	2	36N35	82w11	5:28:44
Winesap 18	15	35N57	85w02	5:40:08
Winfield 76	58	36N32	84w25	5:37:40
Wingo 9	3	36N01	88w37	5:54:28
Winklers 56	3	36N32	85w51	5:43:24
Winner 10	1	36N20	82w13	5:28:52
Winona 76	58	36N23	84w27	5:37:48
Winton Town 16	12	35N28	86w05	5:44:20
Wirmingham 67	3	36N26	85w15	5:41:00
Witt 32	67	36N09	83w17	5:33:08
Wolf Creek 15	65	35N55	83w01	5:32:04
Wolf Creek 21	3	36N05	85w44	5:42:56
Wolf Creek 72	74	35N41	84w52	5:39:28
Wolf River 25	3	36N33	84w58	5:39:52
Woodbine 19	4	36N06	86w45	5:47:00
Woodbury 8	3	35N50	86w04	5:44:16
Woodcliff 71	3	36N09	85w16	5:41:04
Wooddale 47	67	36N00	83w53	5:35:32
Woodland 38	3	35N34	89w08	5:56:32
Woodland Acres 47	67	35N56	84w00	5:36:00
Woodland Mills 66	3	36N30	89w04	5:56:16
Woodlawn 18	15	35N57	85w02	5:40:08
Woodlawn 53	68	35N48	84w16	5:37:04
Woodlawn 63	3	36N33	87w31	5:50:04
Woodlawn 90	75	36N18	82w28	5:29:52
Woodlawn 91	3	35N10	87w44	5:50:56
Woodrow 82	1	36N32	82w19	5:29:16
Woods Ferry 83	42	36N23	86w26	5:45:44
Woodstock 79	40	35N20	89w53	5:59:32
Woods Valley 22	3	36N16	87w22	5:49:28
Woodville 38	3	35N45	89w32	5:58:08
Woody 18	15	35N57	85w02	5:40:08
Wooldridge 7	66	36N35	84w08	5:36:32
Woolworth 43	3	36N19	87w42	5:50:48
Wrencoe 19	4	36N06	86w45	5:47:00
Wright 84	3	35N29	89w43	5:58:52
Wrigley 41	3	35N54	87w21	5:49:24
Wyatts Chapel 81	3	36N29	87w50	5:51:20
Wyatt Village 29	55	36N20	83w22	5:33:28
Wyly 3	3	36N04	88w06	5:52:24
Wynnburg 48	3	36N20	89w29	5:57:56
Yager 89	46	35N42	85w46	5:43:04
Yankeetown 93	3	35N56	85w28	5:41:52
Yateston 93	3	35N49	85w36	5:42:24
Yell 59	30	35N27	86w48	5:47:12
Yellow Creek 42	3	36N19	87w42	5:50:48
Yett Addition 78	60	35N49	83w33	5:34:12
Yorkely 28	3	35N23	87w00	5:48:00
Yorkville 27	21	36N05	89w07	5:56:28
Youngville 74	35	36N30	86w53	5:47:32
Y Section 90	75	36N19	82w21	5:29:24
Yukon 52	9	35N00	86w40	5:46:40
Yuma 9	3	35N51	88w20	5:53:20
Yum Yum 24	3	35N14	89w21	5:57:24
Zacharytown 47	67	36N10	83w49	5:35:16
Zack 3	3	36N04	88w06	5:52:24
Zion Grove 78	60	35N49	83w33	5:34:12
Zion Hill 37	70	36N24	83w00	5:32:00

TENNESSEE

TIME TABLES

TX # 1

Date	Time	Zone
Before 11/18/1883		LMT
11/18/1883	12:00	CST
3/31/1918	02:00	CWT
10/27/1918	02:00	CST
3/30/1919	02:00	CWT
10/26/1919	02:00	CST
2/09/1942	02:00	CWT
9/30/1945	02:00	CST
4/30/1967	02:00	US#1

TX # 2

Date	Time	Zone
Before 11/18/1883		LMT
11/18/1883	12:00	MST
3/31/1918	02:00	MWT
10/27/1918	02:00	MST
3/30/1919	02:00	MWT
10/26/1919	02:00	MST
2/09/1942	02:00	MWT
9/30/1945	02:00	MST
4/30/1967	02:00	US#1

TX # 3

Date	Time	Zone
Before 11/18/1883		LMT
11/18/1883	12:00	CST
3/31/1918	02:00	CWT
10/27/1918	02:00	CST
11/27/1918	02:00	MST
3/30/1919	02:00	MWT
10/26/1919	02:00	MST
3/07/1921	02:00	CST
2/09/1942	02:00	CWT
9/30/1945	02:00	CST
4/30/1967	02:00	US#1

COUNTIES

1 Anderson
2 Andrews
3 Angelina
4 Aransas
5 Archer
6 Armstrong
7 Atascosa
8 Austin
9 Bailey
10 Bandera
11 Bastrop
12 Baylor
13 Bee
14 Bell
15 Bexar
16 Blanco
17 Borden
18 Bosque
19 Bowie
20 Brazoria
21 Brazos
22 Brewster
23 Briscoe
24 Brooks
25 Brown
26 Burleson
27 Burnet
28 Caldwell
29 Calhoun
30 Callahan
31 Cameron
32 Camp
33 Carson
34 Cass
35 Castro
36 Chambers
37 Cherokee
38 Childress
39 Clay
40 Cochran
41 Coke
42 Coleman
43 Collin
44 Collingsworth
45 Colorado
46 Comal
47 Comanche
48 Concho
49 Cooke
50 Coryell
51 Cottle
52 Crane
53 Crockett
54 Crosby
55 Culberson
56 Dallam
57 Dallas
58 Dawson
59 Deaf Smith
60 Delta
61 Denton
62 De Witt
63 Dickens
64 Dimmit
65 Donley
66 Duval
67 Eastland
68 Ector
69 Edwards
70 Ellis
71 El Paso
72 Erath
73 Falls
74 Fannin
75 Fayette
76 Fisher
77 Floyd
78 Foard
79 Fort Bend
80 Franklin
81 Freestone
82 Frio
83 Gaines
84 Galveston
85 Garza
86 Gillespie
87 Glasscock
88 Goliad
89 Gonzales
90 Gray
91 Grayson
92 Gregg
93 Grimes
94 Guadalupe
95 Hale
96 Hall
97 Hamilton
98 Hansford
99 Hardeman
100 Hardin
101 Harris
102 Harrison
103 Hartley
104 Haskell
105 Hays
106 Hemphill
107 Henderson
108 Hidalgo
109 Hill
110 Hockley
111 Hood
112 Hopkins
113 Houston
114 Howard
115 Hudspeth
116 Hunt
117 Hutchinson
118 Irion
119 Jack
120 Jackson
121 Jasper
122 Jeff Davis
123 Jefferson
124 Jim Hogg
125 Jim Wells
126 Johnson
127 Jones
128 Karnes
129 Kaufman
130 Kendall
131 Kenedy
132 Kent
133 Kerr
134 Kimble
135 King
136 Kinney
137 Kleberg
138 Knox
139 Lamar
140 Lamb
141 Lampasas
142 La Salle
143 Lavaca
144 Lee
145 Leon
146 Liberty
147 Limestone
148 Lipscomb
149 Live Oak
150 Llano
151 Loving
152 Lubbock
153 Lynn
154 McCulloh
155 McLean
156 McMullen
157 Madison
158 Marion
159 Martin
160 Mason
161 Matagorda
162 Maverick
163 Medina
164 Menard
165 Midland
166 Milam
167 Mills
168 Mitchell
169 Montague
170 Montgomery
171 Moore
172 Morris
173 Motley
174 Nacogdoches
175 Navarro
176 Newton
177 Nolan
178 Nueces
179 Ochiltree
180 Oldham
181 Orange
182 Palo Pinto
183 Panola
184 Parker
185 Parmer
186 Pecos
187 Polk
188 Potter
189 Presidio
190 Rains
191 Randall
192 Reagan
193 Real
194 Red River
195 Reeves
196 Refugio
197 Roberts
198 Robertson
199 Rockwall
200 Runnels
201 Rusk
202 Sabine
203 San Augustine
204 San Jacinto
205 San Patricio
206 San Saba
207 Schleicher
208 Scurry
209 Shackelford
210 Shelby
211 Sherman
212 Smith
213 Somervell
214 Starr
215 Stephens
216 Sterling
217 Stonewall
218 Sutton
219 Swisher
220 Tarrant
221 Taylor
222 Terrell
223 Terry
224 Throckmorton
225 Titus
226 Tom Green
227 Travis
228 Trinity
229 Tyler
230 Upshur
231 Upton
232 Uvalde
233 Val Verde
234 Van Zandt
235 Victoria
236 Walker
237 Waller
238 Ward
239 Washington
240 Webb
241 Wharton
242 Wheeler
243 Wichita
244 Wilbarger
245 Willacy
246 Williamson
247 Wilson
248 Winkler
249 Wise
250 Wood
251 Yoakum
252 Young
253 Zapata
254 Zavala

Place		Lat	Long	Time
Abbott 109	1	31N53	97w04	6:28:16
Aberdeen 44	3	34N51	100w10	6:40:40
Aberfoyle 116	1	33N22	96w04	6:24:16
Abernathy 95	1	33N50	101w51	6:47:24
Abilene 221	1	32N28	99w43	6:38:52
Abilene Christian College 221	1	32N28	99w44	6:38:56
Ables Springs 129	1	32N45	96w29	6:25:56
Abner 129	1	32N45	96w29	6:25:56
Abram 108	1	26N13	98w20	6:33:20
Acacia Lake 31	1	25N55	97w29	6:29:56
Acala 115	2	31N18	105w51	7:03:24
Ace 187	1	30N31	94w50	6:19:20
Ackerly 58	1	32N32	101w43	6:46:52
Acton 111	1	32N27	97w47	6:31:08
Acuff 152	1	33N35	101w51	6:47:24
Acworth 194	1	33N36	95w03	6:20:12
Adams Gardens 31	1	26N11	97w39	6:30:36
Adamsville 141	1	31N18	98w10	6:32:40
Addicks	1	29N47	95w39	6:22:36
Addielou 194	1	33N34	95w10	6:20:40
Addison 57	1	32N58	96w50	6:27:20
Addran 112	1	33N08	95w36	6:22:24
Adell 184	1	32N48	98w01	6:32:04
Ad Hall 166	1	30N51	96w59	6:27:56
Adkins 15	1	29N23	98w24	6:33:36
Admiral 30	1	32N24	99w24	6:37:36
Adrian 180	3	35N16	102w40	6:50:40
Adsul 176	1	30N39	93w54	6:15:36
Ady 188	3	35N29	102w08	6:48:32
Aero Vista 71	2	31N50	106w23	7:05:32
Afton 63	1	33N46	100w49	6:43:16
Agnes 184	1	32N59	97w47	6:31:08
Agua Dulce 178	1	27N47	97w55	6:31:40
Agua Nueva 124	1	26N54	98w36	6:34:24
Aguilares 240	1	27N27	99w05	6:36:20
Aiken 77	1	34N09	101w32	6:46:08
Aiken 210	1	31N48	94w11	6:16:44
Air 160	1	30N45	99w14	6:36:56
Airlawn 57	1	32N50	96w50	6:27:20
Airport City 15	1	29N34	98w14	6:32:56
Air Terminal 165	1	32N00	102w05	6:48:20
Airville 14	1	31N06	97w21	6:29:24
Alabama Creek 228	1	31N03	95w08	6:20:32
Alamo 108	1	26N11	98w07	6:32:28
Alamo Alto 71	2	31N27	106w05	7:04:20
Alamo Heights 15	1	29N28	98w28	6:33:52
Alanreed 90	3	35N13	100w44	6:42:56
Alazan 174	1	31N40	94w38	6:18:32
Alba 250	1	32N48	95w38	6:22:32
Albany 209	1	32N44	99w18	6:37:12
Albert 86	1	30N12	98w36	6:34:24
Albert Thomas 101	1	29N47	95w23	6:21:32
Albion 194	1	33N52	95w02	6:20:08
Aldine 101	1	29N56	95w23	6:21:32
Aldine Estates 101	1	29N55	95w20	6:21:20
Aldine Gardens 101	1	29N55	95w20	6:21:20
Aldine Meadows 101	1	29N55	95w20	6:21:20
Aledo 184	1	32N42	97w36	6:30:24
Aleman 97	1	31N42	98w07	6:32:28
Alexander 72	1	32N04	98w12	6:32:48
Alexanders Store 210	1	31N46	93w52	6:15:28
Aley 107	1	32N26	96w05	6:24:20
Alfred 125	1	27N53	97w59	6:31:56
Algerita 206	1	31N12	98w44	6:34:56
Algoa 84	1	29N24	95w14	6:20:56
Alice 125	1	27N45	98w05	6:32:20
Alice Rural 125	1	27N41	98w05	6:32:20
Alief 101	1	29N43	95w36	6:22:24
Allamoore 115	2	31N05	105w00	7:00:00
Allen 43	1	33N06	96w40	6:26:40
Allenfarm 21	1	30N24	96w14	6:24:56
Allenhurst 161	1	28N59	95w58	6:23:52
Allens Chapel 74	1	33N34	96w00	6:24:00
Allens Point 74	1	33N35	95w54	6:23:36
Alleyton 45	1	29N42	96w29	6:25:56
Allison 242	3	35N36	100w06	6:40:24
Alma 70	1	32N17	96w33	6:26:12
Almeda 101	1	29N38	95w26	6:21:44
Almont 19	1	33N30	94w37	6:18:28

TEXAS

Aloe 235 1 28N46 97w05 6:28:20
Alpine 22 1 30N22 103w40 6:54:40
Alsa 234 1 32N43 96w00 6:24:00
Alsdorf 70 1 32N20 96w38 6:26:32
Altair 45 1 29N34 96w27 6:25:48
Alta Loma 84 1 29N22 95w05 6:20:20
Alto 37 1 31N39 95w04 6:20:16
Altoga 43 1 33N08 96w37 6:26:28
Alton 108 1 26N13 98w20 6:33:20
Alto Springs 73 1 31N18 96w38 6:26:32
Alum 247 1 29N14 97w58 6:31:52
Alum Creek 11 1 30N07 97w19 6:29:16
Alvarado 126 1 32N24 97w13 6:28:52
Alvin 20 1 29N26 95w15 6:21:00
Alvord 249 1 33N22 97w42 6:30:48
Amarillo 188 3 35N13 101w50 6:47:20
Ambia 139 1 33N38 95w42 6:22:48
Ambrose 91 1 33N37 96w24 6:25:36
Ames 50 1 31N25 97w43 6:30:52
Ames 146 1 30N03 94w45 6:19:00
Amherst 140 1 34N01 102w25 6:49:40
Amistad 233 1 29N21 100w50 6:43:20
Ammansville 75 1 29N54 96w52 6:27:28
Amy 60 1 33N22 95w41 6:22:44
Anadarko 201 1 31N58 94w49 6:19:16
Anahuac 36 1 29N46 94w41 6:18:44
Anchor 20 1 29N09 95w27 6:21:48
Ander 88 1 28N40 97w23 6:29:32
Anderson 93 1 30N29 95w59 6:23:56
Andice 246 1 30N38 97w40 6:30:40
Andrews 2 1 32N19 102w33 6:50:12
Angelo State University 226
1 31N28 100w27 6:41:48
Angleton 20 1 29N10 95w26 6:21:44
Angleton South 20
1 29N09 95w27 6:21:48
Angus 175 1 32N06 96w31 6:26:04
Anna 43 1 33N21 96w33 6:26:12
Annarose 149 1 28N20 98w07 6:32:28
Anneta 184 1 32N44 97w31 6:30:04
Anneville 249 1 33N05 97w34 6:30:16
Annona 194 1 33N35 94w55 6:19:40
Anson 127 1 32N45 99w54 6:39:36
Anson Jones 101 1 29N47 95w22 6:21:28
Antelope 119 1 33N26 98w22 6:33:28
Anthony 71 2 31N59 106w36 7:06:24
Antioch 34 1 33N07 94w10 6:16:40
Antioch 60 1 33N22 95w41 6:22:44
Antioch 107 1 32N18 95w29 6:21:56
Antioch 113 1 31N08 95w27 6:21:48
Antioch 157 1 31N02 95w45 6:23:00
Antioch 201 1 32N09 94w48 6:19:12
Antioch 210 1 31N48 94w11 6:16:44
Anton 110 1 33N49 102w10 6:48:40
Apolonia 93 1 30N29 95w59 6:23:56
Appleby 174 1 31N43 94w36 6:18:24
Apple Springs 228
1 31N14 94w58 6:19:52
Aquilla 109 1 31N51 97w13 6:28:52
Aransas Pass 205 1 27N59 97w09 6:28:36
Arbala 112 1 33N08 95w36 6:22:24
Arbor 113 1 31N22 95w11 6:20:44
Arcadia 84 1 29N23 95w07 6:20:28
Arcadia 210 1 31N48 94w11 6:16:44
Archer 5 1 33N34 98w30 6:34:00
Archer City 5 1 33N36 98w38 6:34:32
Arcola 79 1 29N31 95w28 6:21:52
Arden 118 1 31N28 100w27 6:41:48
Ardis Heights 116
1 33N08 96w07 6:24:28
Argenta 149 1 28N06 97w50 6:31:20
Argo 225 1 33N16 94w54 6:19:36
Argyle 61 1 33N07 97w11 6:28:44
Ariola 100 1 30N22 94w19 6:17:16
Arlam 201 1 31N50 94w30 6:18:00
Arlie 38 1 34N26 100w13 6:40:52
Arlington 220 1 32N44 97w07 6:28:28
Arlington Downs 220
1 32N43 97w06 6:28:24
Arlington Heights 220
1 32N44 97w23 6:29:32
Armstrong 131 1 26N56 97w47 6:31:08
Arneckeville 62 1 29N06 97w17 6:29:08
Arnett 50 1 31N27 97w54 6:31:36
Arnett 110 1 33N35 102w22 6:49:28
Arney 35 3 34N45 101w52 6:47:28
Arp 212 1 32N14 95w04 6:20:16
Arroyo 31 1 26N11 97w39 6:30:36
Art 160 1 30N44 99w07 6:36:28
Artesia Wells 142
1 28N17 99w17 6:37:08
Arthur City 139 1 33N52 95w31 6:22:04
Arvana 58 1 32N44 101w58 6:47:52
Asa 155 1 31N33 97w10 6:28:40
Ash 107 1 32N12 95w51 6:23:24
Ash 113 1 31N19 95w27 6:21:48
Ashby 161 1 28N42 96w13 6:24:52
Asherton 64 1 28N27 99w46 6:39:04
Ashland 230 1 32N43 94w45 6:19:00
Ashmore 83 1 32N55 102w20 6:49:20
Ashtola 65 3 34N56 100w53 6:43:32
Ashwood 161 1 29N03 95w42 6:22:48
Ashworth 129 1 32N35 96w17 6:25:08
Asia 187 1 31N00 94w50 6:19:20
Askew 112 1 33N04 95w28 6:21:52
Aspermont 217 1 33N08 100w14 6:40:56
Astin 198 1 30N53 96w36 6:26:24
Astrodome 101 1 29N42 95w25 6:21:40
Atascosa 15 1 29N16 98w44 6:34:56
Ater 50 1 31N25 97w43 6:30:52
Athens 107 1 32N12 95w51 6:23:24
Atlanta 34 1 33N07 94w10 6:16:40
Atlas 139 1 33N40 95w31 6:22:04
Atlee 142 1 28N02 99w21 6:37:24
Atoy 37 1 31N48 95w09 6:20:36

Atreco 123 1 29N55 93w56 6:15:44
Attoyac 174 1 31N40 94w38 6:18:32
Atwell 30 1 32N23 98w59 6:35:56
Aubrey 61 1 33N18 96w59 6:27:56
Auburn 70 1 32N16 97w11 6:28:44
Augusta 113 1 31N29 95w29 6:21:56
Aurora 249 1 33N03 97w28 6:29:52
Austin 227 1 30N17 97w45 6:31:00
Austonio 113 1 31N11 95w38 6:22:32
Austwell 196 1 28N23 96w51 6:27:24
Authon 184 1 32N48 98w01 6:32:04
Avalon 70 1 32N12 96w48 6:27:12
Avery 194 1 33N33 94w47 6:19:08
Avinger 34 1 32N54 94w33 6:18:12
Avoca 127 1 32N52 99w43 6:38:52
Avondale 31 1 26N11 97w39 6:30:36
Avondale 220 1 32N47 97w21 6:29:24
Axtell 155 1 31N40 96w58 6:27:52
Azle 220 1 32N54 97w33 6:30:12
Bacliff 84 1 29N31 94w59 6:19:56
Bagby 74 1 33N35 95w54 6:23:36
Bagwell 194 1 33N40 95w10 6:20:40
Bahia Mar 31 1 26N05 97w08 6:28:32
Bailey 74 1 33N26 96w10 6:24:40
Baileyboro 9 1 34N04 102w32 6:50:08
Baileys Prairie 20
1 29N08 95w30 6:22:00
Baileyville 166 1 31N04 96w58 6:27:52
Bainer 140 1 33N55 102w20 6:49:20
Bainville 128 1 28N49 97w51 6:31:24
Baird 30 1 32N24 99w24 6:37:36
Baker 184 1 32N45 97w43 6:30:52
Bakersfield 186 1 30N54 102w18 6:49:12
Balch Springs 57 1 32N43 96w38 6:26:32
Balcones Heights 15
1 29N29 98w33 6:34:12
Bald Hill 3 1 30N15 95w32 6:22:08
Baldwin 102 1 32N42 94w07 6:16:28
Ballinger 200 1 31N45 99w57 6:39:48
Balmorhea 195 1 30N59 103w45 6:55:00
Balsora 249 1 33N13 97w46 6:31:04
Bammel 101 1 30N01 95w28 6:21:52
Banana Junction 155
1 31N34 97w10 6:28:40
Bancroft 181 1 30N06 93w46 6:15:04
Bandera 10 1 29N44 99w05 6:36:20
Bandera Falls 10 1 29N43 98w56 6:35:44
Bangs 25 1 31N43 99w08 6:36:32
Bankersmith 130 1 30N17 98w52 6:35:28
Banquete 178 1 27N48 97w48 6:31:12
Barbarosa 94 1 29N42 98w08 6:32:32
Barclay 73 1 31N12 97w02 6:28:08
Bardwell 70 1 32N16 96w42 6:26:48
Barker 101 1 29N47 95w41 6:22:44
Barkman 19 1 33N28 94w17 6:17:08
Barksdale 69 1 29N44 100w02 6:40:08
Barnes 187 1 30N55 94w50 6:19:20
Barnhart 118 1 31N08 101w10 6:44:40
Barnum 187 1 30N57 94w40 6:18:40
Barrett 101 1 29N53 95w04 6:20:16
Barry 175 1 32N06 96w38 6:26:32
Barstow 238 1 31N28 103w24 6:53:36
Bartlett 14 1 30N48 97w26 6:29:44
Bartley Woods 74 1 33N34 96w00 6:24:00
Bartons Chapel 119
1 33N13 98w10 6:32:40
Bartonville 61 1 33N07 97w11 6:28:44
Barwise 77 1 33N59 101w20 6:45:20
Basin Springs 91 1 33N41 96w51 6:27:24
Bassett 19 1 33N19 94w34 6:18:16
Bastrop 11 1 30N07 97w19 6:29:16
Bastrop Bayou 20 1 29N09 95w27 6:21:48
Bastrop Beach 20 1 29N09 95w27 6:21:48
Bateman 11 1 29N58 97w27 6:29:48
Batesville 254 1 28N58 99w37 6:38:28
Batson 100 1 30N15 94w37 6:18:28
Battle 155 1 31N33 96w50 6:27:20
Baxter 107 1 32N12 95w51 6:23:24
Bay City 161 1 28N59 95w58 6:23:52
Bay Oaks 101 1 29N39 95w01 6:20:04
Bayou 202 1 31N21 93w51 6:15:24
Bayou Chantilly 84
1 29N27 95w03 6:20:12
Bay Plaza 101 1 29N46 95w00 6:20:00
Bayside 196 1 28N06 97w13 6:28:52
Bayside Terrace 101
1 29N38 95w01 6:20:04
Baytown 101 1 29N43 94w59 6:19:56
Bayview 31 1 26N08 97w24 6:29:36
Bay View 84 1 29N31 94w59 6:19:56
Baywood 101 1 29N34 95w01 6:20:04
Bazette 175 1 32N08 96w14 6:24:56
Beach 170 1 30N19 95w28 6:21:52
Beach City 36 1 29N46 95w00 6:20:00
Beacon Hill 15 1 29N28 98w32 6:34:08
Beadle 161 1 28N54 96w03 6:24:12
Bear Grass 145 1 31N22 96w09 6:24:36
Beasley 79 1 29N30 95w55 6:23:40
Beattie 47 1 31N54 98w36 6:34:24
Beaukiss 246 1 30N21 97w22 6:29:28
Beaumont 123 1 30N05 94w06 6:16:24
Beaumont Place 101
1 29N50 95w13 6:20:52
Beauxart Gardens 123
1 30N03 94w06 6:16:24
Beaver Dam 19 1 33N30 94w37 6:18:28
Bebe 89 1 29N25 97w38 6:30:32
Beck 140 1 34N04 102w32 6:50:08
Becker 129 1 32N35 96w17 6:25:08
Becton 152 1 33N40 101w32 6:46:08
Bedford 220 1 32N51 97w08 6:28:32
Bedias 93 1 30N47 95w57 6:23:48
Beecaves 227 1 30N16 97w48 6:31:12
Beech Grove 121 1 30N55 94w00 6:16:00
Bee House 50 1 31N24 98w05 6:32:20

Beeville 13 1 28N24 97w45 6:31:00
Beeville Rural 13
1 28N23 97w43 6:30:52
Behring Store 94 1 29N35 97w58 6:31:52
Bel Air 102 1 32N34 94w25 6:17:40
Belcherville 169 1 33N48 97w50 6:31:20
Belfalls 14 1 31N10 97w12 6:28:48
Belgrade 176 1 30N44 93w39 6:14:36
Belk 139 1 33N52 95w31 6:22:04
Bellaire 101 1 29N42 95w28 6:21:52
Bell Branch 70 1 32N11 96w53 6:27:32
Belle Plain 171 3 35N52 101w58 6:47:52
Bellevue 39 1 33N38 98w01 6:32:04
Bellmead 155 1 31N35 97w06 6:28:24
Bells 91 1 33N37 96w25 6:25:40
Bellville 8 1 29N57 96w15 6:25:00
Belmont 89 1 29N32 97w41 6:30:44
Belott 113 1 31N19 95w27 6:21:48
Belton 14 1 31N03 97w28 6:29:52
Ben Arnold 166 1 30N58 96w59 6:27:56
Benavides 66 1 27N36 98w25 6:33:40
Ben Bolt 125 1 27N39 98w05 6:32:20
Benbrook 220 1 32N41 97w28 6:29:52
Benchley 198 1 30N45 96w27 6:25:48
Bend 206 1 31N06 98w31 6:34:04
Ben Franklin 60 1 33N28 95w46 6:23:04
Ben Hur 147 1 31N31 96w44 6:26:56
Benjamin 138 1 33N35 99w48 6:39:12
Bennett 184 1 32N43 98w03 6:32:12
Benoit 200 1 31N47 99w50 6:39:20
Benonine 242 3 35N13 100w09 6:40:36
Ben Wheeler 234 1 32N27 95w42 6:22:48
Berclair 88 1 28N32 97w36 6:30:24
Berea 158 1 32N49 94w25 6:17:40
Bergheim 130 1 29N50 98w35 6:34:20
Bergstrom Air Force Base 227
1 30N13 97w40 6:30:40
Berlin 239 1 30N10 96w24 6:25:36
Bernardo 45 1 29N51 96w20 6:25:20
Berryville 107 1 32N03 95w30 6:22:00
Bertram 27 1 30N45 98w03 6:32:12
Bess 66 1 28N20 98w07 6:32:28
Bessmay 121 1 30N28 93w57 6:15:48
Best 192 1 31N13 101w37 6:46:28
Bethany 183 1 32N22 94w03 6:16:12
Bethel 1 1 31N50 95w50 6:23:20
Bethel 70 1 32N24 96w50 6:27:20
Bethel 107 1 32N12 95w51 6:23:24
Bethel 200 1 31N45 99w57 6:39:48
Bethlehem 19 1 33N30 94w37 6:18:28
Bethlehem 109 1 31N57 97w19 6:29:16
Bethlehem 230 1 32N44 94w57 6:19:48
Betner 139 1 33N40 95w31 6:22:04
Bettie 230 1 32N49 94w58 6:19:52
Beverly 155 1 31N32 97w09 6:28:36
Beverly Hills 43 1 33N08 96w37 6:26:28
Beverly Hills 57 1 32N44 96w53 6:27:32
Beverly Hills 155
1 31N31 97w09 6:28:36
Beversville 246 1 30N28 97w24 6:29:36
Bevil Oaks 123 1 30N09 94w16 6:17:04
Biardstown 139 1 33N34 95w30 6:22:00
Big Bend National Park 22
1 29N16 103w17 6:53:08
Bigfoot 82 1 29N03 98w52 6:35:28
Biggs 71 2 31N50 106w23 7:05:32
Biggs Field 71 2 31N50 106w23 7:05:32
Bighill 147 1 31N25 96w34 6:26:16
Big Lake 192 1 31N12 101w28 6:45:52
Big Sandy 230 1 32N35 95w07 6:20:28
Big Spring 114 1 32N15 101w28 6:45:52
Big Wells 64 1 28N34 99w34 6:38:16
Billington 147 1 31N40 96w58 6:27:52
Biloxi 176 1 30N44 93w39 6:14:36
Birch 26 1 30N21 96w32 6:26:08
Birdville 220 1 32N48 97w15 6:29:00
Birome 109 1 31N49 96w58 6:27:52
Birthright 112 1 33N08 95w36 6:22:24
Biry 163 1 29N09 98w54 6:35:36
Bisbee 220 1 32N37 97w11 6:28:44
Bishop 178 1 27N35 97w48 6:31:12
Bivins 34 1 33N01 94w12 6:16:48
Black 185 3 34N41 102w47 6:51:08
Blackfoot 1 1 31N53 95w38 6:22:32
Black Jack 37 1 32N08 95w07 6:20:28
Blackland 199 1 32N59 96w20 6:25:20
Blackoak 112 1 33N04 95w28 6:21:52
Blackwell 177 1 32N05 100w19 6:41:16
Blair 221 1 32N28 99w49 6:39:16
Blakeney 194 1 33N34 95w10 6:20:40
Blanchard 187 1 30N43 94w56 6:19:44
Blanco 16 1 30N06 98w25 6:33:40
Blanconia 13 1 28N23 97w42 6:30:48
Bland 181 1 30N06 93w46 6:15:04
Blandlake 203 1 31N32 94w07 6:16:28
Blanket 25 1 31N49 98w47 6:35:08
Blanks 28 1 29N53 97w40 6:30:40
Blanton 200 1 31N45 99w57 6:39:48
Bleakwood 176 1 30N32 93w49 6:15:16
Bledsoe 40 1 33N38 103w01 6:52:04
Bleiblerville 8 1 30N00 96w27 6:25:48
Blessing 161 1 28N52 96w13 6:24:52
Blevins 73 1 31N15 97w30 6:30:00
Blewett 232 1 29N11 100w02 6:40:08
Blocker 102 1 32N34 94w25 6:17:40
Blodgett 225 1 33N00 94w58 6:19:52
Bloomburg 34 1 33N08 94w04 6:16:16
Bloomdale 43 1 33N08 96w37 6:26:28
Bloomfield 49 1 33N24 96w57 6:27:48
Blooming Grove 175
1 32N06 96w43 6:26:52
Bloomington 235 1 28N39 96w54 6:27:36
Blossom 139 1 33N40 95w23 6:21:32
Blue 144 1 30N25 97w01 6:28:04
Bluegrove 39 1 33N40 98w14 6:32:56

Blue Haven Estates 116 1 32N43 96W00 6:24:00
Blue Mound 220 1 32N52 97W21 6:29:24
Blue Ridge 43 1 33N18 96W24 6:25:36
Blue Ridge 73 1 31N13 96W47 6:27:08
Bluetown 31 1 26N04 97W50 6:31:20
Blue Water Key 107 1 32N18 95W29 6:21:56
Bluff Dale 72 1 32N21 98W01 6:32:04
Bluff Springs 184 1 32N46 97W28 6:29:52
Bluff Springs 227 1 30N13 97W44 6:30:56
Bluffton 150 1 30N49 98W30 6:34:00
Bluff View 25 1 31N44 98W58 6:35:52
Blum 109 1 32N06 97W21 6:29:24
Blumenthal 86 1 30N17 98W52 6:35:28
Bluntzer 178 1 27N48 97W41 6:30:44
Bob Harris 101 1 29N42 95W12 6:20:48
Bobville 170 1 30N22 95W46 6:23:04
Boca Chica 31 1 25N55 97W29 6:29:56
Boerne 130 1 29N47 98W44 6:34:56
Bogata 194 1 33N28 95W13 6:20:52
Bogus Springs 34 1 33N01 94W12 6:16:48
Bois D Arc 1 1 31N46 95W38 6:22:32
Boling 241 1 29N16 95W57 6:23:48
Bolivar 61 1 33N21 97W11 6:28:44
Bolivar Peninsula 84 1 29N25 94W38 6:18:32
Bomarton 12 1 33N31 99W26 6:37:44
Bon Ami 121 1 30N39 93W54 6:15:36
Bonanza 112 1 33N07 95W44 6:22:56
Bonanza 170 1 30N23 95W42 6:22:48
Bonham 74 1 33N35 96W11 6:24:44
Bonita 169 1 33N46 97W36 6:30:24
Bonner 108 1 26N12 98W15 6:33:00
Bonney 20 1 29N09 95W27 6:21:48
Bonnie View 196 1 28N14 97W19 6:29:16
Bono 126 1 32N20 97W31 6:30:04
Bon Wier 176 1 30N44 93W39 6:14:36
Booker 148 3 36N27 100W32 6:42:08
Boonsville 249 1 33N13 97W46 6:31:04
Booth 79 1 29N32 95W39 6:22:36
Boquillas 22 1 29N16 103W17 6:53:08
Borden 45 1 29N42 96W47 6:27:08
Borderland 71 2 31N52 106W35 7:06:20
Bordersville 101 1 29N56 95W17 6:21:08
Borger 117 3 35N39 101W24 6:45:36
Bosqueville 155 1 31N34 97W10 6:28:40
Boston 19 1 33N28 94W25 6:17:40
Bovina 185 3 34N31 102W53 6:51:32
Bowie 169 1 33N34 97W51 6:31:24
Box Church 147 1 31N32 96W32 6:26:08
Boxelder 194 1 33N35 94W55 6:19:40
Box Quarter 198 1 30N59 96W41 6:26:44
Boxwood 230 1 32N48 94W43 6:18:52
Boyce 70 1 32N24 96W50 6:27:20
Boyd 74 1 33N35 96W11 6:24:44
Boyd 249 1 33N05 97W34 6:30:16
Boyd Lodge 208 1 32N35 101W00 6:44:00
Boydston 90 3 35N12 101W06 6:44:24
Boys Ranch 180 3 35N32 102W15 6:49:00
Boz 70 1 32N24 96W50 6:27:20
Bozar 167 1 31N28 98W34 6:34:16
Brachfield 201 1 32N03 94W39 6:18:36
Bracken 46 1 29N30 98W25 6:33:40
Brackettville 136 1 29N19 100W25 6:41:40
Brad 182 1 32N45 98W30 6:34:00
Bradford 1 1 31N53 95W38 6:22:32
Bradshaw 221 1 32N06 99W54 6:39:36
Brady 154 1 31N09 99W20 6:37:20
Brady 210 1 31N48 94W11 6:16:44
Branch 43 1 33N08 96W37 6:26:28
Branchville 166 1 30N59 96W41 6:26:44
Brandon 109 1 32N03 96W58 6:27:52
Bransford 220 1 32N54 97W09 6:28:36
Branton 67 1 32N06 98W58 6:35:52
Brashear 112 1 33N07 95W44 6:22:56
Brazoria 20 1 29N03 95W34 6:22:16
Brazos 182 1 32N40 98W08 6:32:32
Brazos Point 18 1 32N04 97W30 6:30:00
Brazosport 20 1 29N00 95W21 6:21:24
Breckenridge 215 1 32N45 98W54 6:35:36
Bremond 198 1 31N10 96W41 6:26:44
Brenham 239 1 30N10 96W24 6:25:36
Brentwood Manor 235 1 28N48 96W59 6:27:56
Breslau 143 1 29N31 97W00 6:28:00
Briar 184 1 33N00 97W33 6:30:12
Briaroaks 126 1 32N33 97W20 6:29:20
Briary 166 1 31N04 96W58 6:27:52
Brice 96 1 34N43 100W54 6:43:36
Bridge City 181 1 30N01 93W51 6:15:24
Bridgeport 249 1 33N13 97W45 6:31:00
Briggs 27 1 30N53 97W56 6:31:44
Bright Star 190 1 32N47 95W38 6:22:32
Bright Star 234 1 32N43 96W00 6:24:00
Briscoe 242 3 35N35 100W17 6:41:08
Bristol 70 1 32N20 96W38 6:26:32
Britton 70 1 32N33 97W04 6:28:16
Broaddus 203 1 31N18 94W16 6:17:04
Broadway 54 1 33N40 101W14 6:44:56
Broadway 139 1 33N40 95W31 6:22:04
Broadway Junction 139 1 33N40 95W31 6:22:04
Brock 184 1 32N45 97W43 6:30:52
Brock Junction 184 1 32N45 97W43 6:30:52
Brogado 195 1 30N59 103W44 6:54:56
Bronco 251 1 33N15 103W04 6:52:16
Bronson 202 1 31N21 94W01 6:16:04
Bronte 41 1 31N53 100W18 6:41:12
Brooke Army Medical Center 15 1 29N27 98W27 6:33:48
Brookeland 202 1 31N09 94W00 6:16:00
Brookesmith 25 1 31N35 99W04 6:36:16
Brook Hollow 57 1 32N49 96W51 6:27:24
Brooks Air Force Base 15 1 29N21 98W26 6:33:44
Brookshire 237 1 29N47 95W57 6:23:48
Brookside 20 1 29N36 95W19 6:21:16
Brookside Village 1 29N35 95W20 6:21:20
Brookston 139 1 33N38 95W42 6:22:48
Broome 216 1 31N51 100W59 6:43:56
Browndell 121 1 31N09 94W00 6:16:00
Brownfield 223 1 33N11 102W17 6:49:08
Browning 212 1 32N30 95W10 6:20:40
Brownsboro 28 1 29N53 97W40 6:30:40
Brownsboro 107 1 32N17 95W35 6:22:20
Brownsville 31 1 25N54 97W30 6:30:00
Brownwood 25 1 31N43 98W59 6:35:56
Brownwood 181 1 30N06 93W46 6:15:04
Broyles 1 1 31N46 95W38 6:22:32
Bruceville 155 1 31N19 97W14 6:28:56
Bruceville-Eddy 155 1 31N19 97W14 6:28:56
Brumley 230 1 33N00 94W58 6:19:52
Brundage 64 1 28N34 99W40 6:38:40
Bruner 181 1 30N06 93W46 6:15:04
Bruni 240 1 27N26 98W50 6:35:20
Brunswick 37 1 31N39 95W04 6:20:16
Brushy Creek 1 1 31N46 95W38 6:22:32
Bryan 21 1 30N40 96W22 6:25:28
Bryans Mill 34 1 33N12 94W21 6:17:24
Bryson 119 1 33N10 98W23 6:33:32
B.U. 155 1 31N31 97W08 6:28:32
Buchanan Dam 150 1 30N45 98W25 6:33:40
Buck 187 1 30N43 94W56 6:19:44
Buckeye 161 1 28N54 96W03 6:24:12
Buckholts 166 1 30N52 97W07 6:28:28
Buckhorn 8 1 29N57 96W15 6:25:00
Buckhorn 176 1 30N44 93W39 6:14:36
Buckingham 57 1 32N56 96W43 6:26:52
Buckner 184 1 32N31 98W03 6:32:12
Buda 105 1 30N05 97W51 6:31:24
Buena Vista 15 1 29N21 98W30 6:34:00
Buffalo 145 1 31N28 96W04 6:24:16
Buffalo Gap 221 1 32N17 99W50 6:39:20
Buffalo Gap 227 1 30N16 97W48 6:31:12
Buffalo Springs 39 1 33N38 98W01 6:32:04
Buford 168 1 32N24 100W52 6:43:28
Bug Tussle 74 1 33N25 95W56 6:23:44
Bula 9 1 33N55 102W39 6:50:36
Bulcher 49 1 33N39 97W23 6:29:32
Bullard 212 1 32N08 95W19 6:21:16
Bulverde 46 1 29N33 98W26 6:33:44
Buna 121 1 30N26 93W58 6:15:52
Bunavista 117 3 35N39 101W28 6:45:52
Buncomb 183 1 32N09 94W20 6:17:20
Bunger 252 1 33N06 98W35 6:34:20
Bunker Hill 101 1 29N47 95W32 6:22:08
Bunker Hill 139 1 33N46 95W39 6:22:36
Bunker Hill Village 101 1 29N46 95W32 6:22:08
Bunyan 72 1 32N05 98W20 6:33:20
Burbank Gardens 57 1 32N44 96W59 6:27:56
Burgess 14 1 30N56 97W14 6:28:56
Burkburnett 243 1 34N06 98W34 6:34:16
Burke 3 1 31N14 94W46 6:19:04
Burkett 42 1 32N00 99W13 6:36:52
Burkeville 176 1 31N00 93W40 6:14:40
Burleigh 8 1 29N57 96W15 6:25:00
Burleson 126 1 32N33 97W19 6:29:16
Burlington 166 1 31N01 97W00 6:28:00
Burnell 128 1 28N49 97W51 6:31:24
Burnet 27 1 30N45 98W14 6:32:56
Burns 19 1 33N28 94W17 6:17:08
Burns 49 1 33N24 96W57 6:27:48
Burr 241 1 29N19 96W06 6:24:24
Burrow 116 1 32N59 96W20 6:25:20
Burton 239 1 30N11 96W42 6:26:48
Busby 76 1 31N40 94W53 6:19:32
Bushland 188 3 35N11 102W04 6:48:16
Bustamante 253 1 27N00 99W07 6:36:28
Busterville 110 1 33N25 102W09 6:48:36
Butler 11 1 30N19 97W18 6:29:12
Butler 81 1 31N35 95W51 6:23:24
Byers 39 1 34N04 98W11 6:32:44
Bynum 109 1 31N58 97W00 6:28:00
Byrd 70 1 32N20 96W38 6:26:32
Cactus 171 3 36N02 102W00 6:48:00
Caddo 215 1 32N43 98W40 6:34:40
Caddo Mills 116 1 33N04 96W14 6:24:56
Cadiz 13 1 28N23 97W42 6:30:48
Caesar 13 1 28N49 97W51 6:31:24
Cain City 86 1 30N11 98W45 6:35:00
Calaveras 247 1 29N08 98W09 6:32:36
Caldwell 26 1 30N32 96W42 6:26:48
Caledonia 201 1 31N54 94W24 6:17:36
Calf Creek 154 1 31N08 99W20 6:37:20
Call 176 1 30N35 93W48 6:15:12
Callihan 156 1 28N29 98W21 6:33:24
Callisburg 49 1 33N38 97W08 6:28:32
Calvary 250 1 32N40 95W29 6:21:56
Calvert 198 1 30N59 96W40 6:26:40
Calvin 11 1 30N07 97W19 6:29:16
Camden 187 1 30N55 94W44 6:18:56
Cameron 166 1 30N51 96W59 6:27:56
Camey 61 1 33N09 96W50 6:27:20
Camilla 204 1 30N36 95W08 6:20:32
Camp Alzafar 130 1 29N48 98W45 6:35:00
Campbell 116 1 33N09 95W57 6:23:48
Campbellton 7 1 28N45 98W18 6:33:12
Camp Bullis 15 1 29N23 98W36 6:34:24
Camp Dallas 61 1 33N09 96W50 6:27:20
Campo Alto 108 1 26N12 98W09 6:32:36
Camp Providence 187 1 30N43 94W56 6:19:44
Camp Ruby 187 1 30N43 94W56 6:19:44
Camps 92 1 32N27 94W44 6:18:56
Camp San Saba 154 1 31N00 99W16 6:37:04
Camp Scenic 133 1 30N04 99W14 6:36:56
Camp Springs 208 1 32N38 100W46 6:43:04
Camp Stanley 15 1 29N26 98W30 6:34:00
Camp Stewart 133 1 30N04 99W20 6:37:20
Campti 210 1 31N48 94W11 6:16:44
Camp Verde 133 1 29N54 99W06 6:36:24
Camp Willow 94 1 29N42 98W08 6:32:32
Camp Wood 193 1 29N40 100W01 6:40:04
Canada Verde 247 1 29N08 98W09 6:32:36
Canadian 106 3 35N55 100W23 6:41:32
Canadian River Breaks 188 3 35N17 101W52 6:47:28
Candelaria 1 30N08 104W41 6:58:44
Caney 112 1 33N08 95W36 6:22:24
Caney 161 1 28N59 95W58 6:23:52
Caney City 107 1 32N10 96W01 6:24:04
Cannon 91 1 33N25 96W34 6:26:16
Canton 234 1 32N33 95W52 6:23:28
Canutillo 71 2 31N55 106W36 7:06:24
Canyon 152 1 33N35 101W51 6:47:24
Canyon 191 3 34N59 101W55 6:47:40
Canyon Creek 43 1 32N57 96W44 6:26:56
Canyon Creek Square 43 1 32N57 96W44 6:26:56
Canyon Lake 46 1 29N42 98W08 6:32:32
Canyon Valley 54 1 33N24 101W20 6:45:20
Capitol 227 1 30N17 97W44 6:30:56
Caplen 84 1 29N31 94W29 6:17:56
Capps Corner 169 1 33N42 97W31 6:30:04
Cap Rock 54 1 33N29 101W24 6:45:36
Caps 221 1 32N23 99W51 6:39:24
Caradan 167 1 31N28 98W34 6:34:16
Carancahua 120 1 28N42 96W13 6:24:52
Carbon 67 1 32N16 98W50 6:35:20
Carbondale 19 1 33N20 94W21 6:17:24
Cardinal 107 1 32N12 95W51 6:23:24
Carey 38 1 34N28 100W20 6:41:20
Carey Estates 101 1 29N34 95W01 6:20:04
Carlisle 228 1 30N57 95W23 6:21:32
Carlos 93 1 30N29 95W59 6:23:56
Carlsbad 226 1 31N36 100W38 6:42:32
Carlton 97 1 31N55 98W10 6:32:40
Carmine 75 1 30N09 96W41 6:26:44
Carmona 187 1 31N00 94W50 6:19:20
Caro 174 1 31N40 94W38 6:18:32
Carricitos 31 1 26N08 97W38 6:30:32
Carrizo Springs 64 1 28N31 99W52 6:39:28
Carroll 212 1 32N20 95W18 6:21:12
Carrollton 57 1 32N57 96W55 6:27:40
Carson 74 1 33N47 96W01 6:24:04
Carswell Air Force Base 220 1 32N45 97W26 6:29:44
Carta Valley 69 1 29N48 100W41 6:42:44
Carterville 34 1 33N00 94W22 6:17:28
Carthage 183 1 32N09 94W20 6:17:20
Cartwright 250 1 32N58 95W17 6:21:08
Casa Piedra 1 29N44 104W03 6:56:12
Casey 71 2 31N35 106W14 7:04:56
Cash 116 1 33N00 96W07 6:24:28
Cason 172 1 33N02 94W49 6:19:16
Cass 34 1 33N08 94W03 6:16:12
Castell 150 1 30N42 98W58 6:35:52
Castle Hill Estates 220 1 32N46 97W28 6:29:52
Castle Hills 15 1 29N31 98W31 6:34:04
Castolon 22 1 29N08 103W31 6:54:04
Castroville 163 1 29N21 98W53 6:35:32
Catarina 64 1 28N21 99W37 6:38:28
Cat Spring 8 1 29N51 96W20 6:25:20
Cave Springs 102 1 32N34 94W25 6:17:40
Cavines 139 1 33N40 95W31 6:22:04
Cavitt 50 1 31N25 97W31 6:30:04
Cawthon 21 1 30N23 96W05 6:24:20
Cayote 18 1 31N39 97W28 6:29:52
Cayuga 1 1 31N58 95W59 6:23:56
Cedar Creek 11 1 30N05 97W30 6:30:00
Cedar Creek 237 1 30N06 96W02 6:24:08
Cedar Grove 3 1 30N15 95W32 6:22:08
Cedar Hill 57 1 32N35 96W58 6:27:52
Cedar Hill 77 1 34N07 101W27 6:45:48
Cedar Lake 161 1 28N54 95W38 6:22:32
Cedar Lane 161 1 28N58 95W45 6:23:00
Cedar Mills 91 1 33N41 96W51 6:27:24
Cedar Park 246 1 30N30 97W49 6:31:16
Cedar Point 36 1 29N46 95W00 6:20:00
Cedar Springs 73 1 31N04 96W58 6:27:52
Cedar Springs 230 1 32N48 94W43 6:18:52
Cedar Valley 227 1 30N16 97W48 6:31:12
Cee Vee 51 1 34N13 100W27 6:41:48
Cego 73 1 31N15 97W30 6:30:00
Cele 227 1 30N21 97W33 6:30:12
Celeste 116 1 33N18 96W12 6:24:48
Celina 43 1 33N19 96W47 6:27:08
Center 147 1 31N32 96W32 6:26:08
Center 210 1 31N48 94W11 6:16:44
Center City 167 1 31N28 98W25 6:33:40
Center Line 26 1 30N21 96W32 6:26:08
Center Mill 111 1 32N27 97W47 6:31:08
Center Point 32 1 33N00 94W58 6:19:52
Center Point 70 1 32N11 96W53 6:27:32
Center Point 114 1 32N14 101W28 6:45:52
Center Point 116 1 33N08 96W07 6:24:28
Center Point 133 1 29N56 99W01 6:36:04
Center Point 183 1 32N19 94W31 6:18:04
Center Point 184 1 32N46 97W28 6:29:52
Center Point 230 1 32N34 95W00 6:20:00

Centerview 145	1	31N16	95w59	6:23:56
Centerville 57	1	32N54	96w37	6:26:28
Centerville 145	1	31N16	95w59	6:23:56
Centerville 228	1	31N03	95w08	6:20:32
Centex 105	1	29N53	97w56	6:31:44
Central 3	1	31N27	94w52	6:19:28
Central 37	1	31N39	95w04	6:20:16
Central 220	1	32N45	97w20	6:29:20
Central Gardens 123	1	29N57	93w59	6:15:56
Central Heights 123	1	29N57	93w59	6:15:56
Central Heights 174	1	31N40	94w38	6:18:32
Centralia 228	1	31N16	95w02	6:20:08
Central Park 101	1	29N45	95w19	6:21:16
Cestohowa 128	1	28N59	98w01	6:32:04
Chaffee Village 14	1	31N08	97w46	6:31:04
Chalk 51	1	33N53	100w13	6:40:52
Chalk Bluff 155	1	31N34	97w10	6:28:40
Chalk Mountain 72	1	32N13	98w13	6:32:52
Chalybeate 250	1	32N58	95w17	6:21:08
Chambersville 43	1	33N08	96w37	6:26:28
Chambliss 43	1	33N21	96w33	6:26:12
Chance 26	1	30N21	96w32	6:26:08
Chances Store 26	1	30N21	96w32	6:26:08
Chandler 107	1	32N18	95w29	6:21:56
Channelview 101	1	29N47	95w08	6:20:32
Channelwood 101	1	29N46	95w09	6:20:36
Channing 103	3	35N41	102w20	6:49:20
Chapel Hill 212	1	32N20	95w18	6:21:12
Chapman 201	1	32N09	94w48	6:19:12
Chapman Ranch 178	1	27N35	97w27	6:29:48
Chappel 206	1	31N12	98w44	6:34:56
Chappell Hill 239	1	30N09	96w15	6:25:00
Charco 88	1	28N40	97w23	6:29:32
Charleston 57	1	32N46	96w37	6:26:28
Charleston 60	1	33N23	95w32	6:22:08
Charlie 39	1	33N52	98w33	6:34:12
Charlotte 7	1	28N52	98w43	6:34:52
Chase 13	1	28N22	97w40	6:30:40
Chase Field 13	1	28N23	97w42	6:30:48
Chat 109	1	32N01	97w07	6:28:28
Chatfield 175	1	32N14	96w25	6:25:40
Cheapside 89	1	29N17	97w24	6:29:36
Cheek 123	1	30N03	94w06	6:16:24
Cheneyboro 175	1	32N06	96w31	6:26:04
Cherokee 206	1	30N59	98w43	6:34:52
Cherry Spring 86	1	30N17	98w52	6:35:28
Chester 229	1	30N56	94w36	6:18:24
Chesterville 45	1	29N32	96w04	6:24:16
Cheyenne	1	31N59	103w08	6:52:32
Chico 249	1	33N18	97w48	6:31:12
Chicota 139	1	33N52	95w34	6:22:16
Chief 129	1	32N35	96w17	6:25:08
Chihuahua 108	1	26N13	98w20	6:33:20
Childress 38	1	34N25	100w13	6:40:52
Chillicothe 99	1	34N15	99w31	6:38:04
Chilton 73	1	31N17	97w04	6:28:16
China 123	1	30N03	94w20	6:17:20
China Grove 15	1	29N23	98w21	6:33:24
China Grove 208	1	32N38	100w46	6:43:04
China Spring 155	1	31N39	97w18	6:29:12
Chinati 189	1	29N33	104w23	6:57:32
Chireno 174	1	31N30	94w21	6:17:24
Chisholm	1	32N50	96w22	6:25:28
Chita 228	1	30N57	95w23	6:21:32
Choate 128	1	28N46	97w45	6:31:00
Chocolate Bayou 20	1	29N24	95w14	6:20:56
Choice 210	1	31N48	94w11	6:16:44
Chriesman 26	1	30N36	96w46	6:27:04
Christine 7	1	28N47	98w30	6:34:00
Christoval 226	1	31N12	100w30	6:42:00
Chuckville 67	1	32N06	98w58	6:35:52
Church Hill 201	1	32N09	94w48	6:19:12
Churchill Bridge 20	1	29N02	95w34	6:22:16
Cibolo 94	1	29N34	98w14	6:32:56
Circle 37	1	31N48	95w09	6:20:36
Circle 140	1	34N11	102w14	6:48:56
Circle Back 9	1	34N04	102w32	6:50:08
Circleville 246	1	30N34	97w25	6:29:40
Cisco 67	1	32N23	98w59	6:35:56
Cistern 75	1	29N49	97w13	6:28:52
Citrus City 108	1	26N13	98w20	6:33:20
Clairemont	1	33N10	100w45	6:43:00
Clairette 72	1	31N59	98w02	6:32:08
Clara 243	1	33N57	98w40	6:34:40
Clardy 139	1	33N35	95w24	6:21:36
Clarendon 65	3	34N56	100w53	6:43:32
Clareville 13	1	28N23	97w42	6:30:48
Clark 146	1	30N18	95w07	6:20:28
Clarks 29	1	28N37	96w38	6:26:32
Clarksville 194	1	33N37	95w03	6:20:12
Clarksville City 92	1	32N31	94w52	6:19:28
Clarkwood 178	1	27N48	97w30	6:30:00
Claude 6	3	35N07	101w22	6:45:28
Clauene 110	1	33N28	102w23	6:49:32
Clawson 3	1	30N15	95w32	6:22:08
Clay 26	1	30N23	96w21	6:25:24
Clayton 123	1	29N57	93w59	6:15:56
Clayton 183	1	32N06	94w29	6:17:56
Claytonville 76	1	32N28	100w24	6:41:36
Claytonville 219	1	34N22	101w45	6:47:00
Clear Lake 43	1	33N08	96w37	6:26:28
Clear Lake City 101	1	29N33	95w07	6:20:28
Clear Lake Shores 84	1	29N32	95w01	6:20:04
Clear Springs	1	29N41	98w04	6:32:16
Clearview 11	1	30N07	97w19	6:29:16
Cleburne 126	1	32N21	97w23	6:29:32
Clegg 149	1	28N20	98w07	6:32:28
Clemons 237	1	29N47	95w57	6:23:48
Clemville 161	1	29N00	96w08	6:24:32
Cleo	1	30N36	99w53	6:39:32
Cleveland 146	1	30N21	95w05	6:20:20
Clever Creek 210	1	31N12	100w30	6:42:00
Cliffside 188	3	35N12	101w53	6:47:32
Clifton 18	1	31N47	97w35	6:30:20
Clifton 234	1	32N43	96w00	6:24:00
Climax 43	1	33N11	96w30	6:26:00
Cline 232	1	29N15	100w05	6:40:20
Clint 71	2	31N35	106w14	7:04:56
Clinton 62	1	29N06	97w17	6:29:08
Clinton 116	1	33N04	96w14	6:24:56
Clodine 79	1	29N35	95w46	6:23:04
Close City 85	1	33N12	101w23	6:45:32
Cloudy 57	1	32N44	96w59	6:27:56
Cloverleaf 101	1	29N46	95w10	6:20:40
Club Lake Estates 212	1	32N20	95w18	6:21:12
Clute City 20	1	29N01	95w24	6:21:36
Clyde 30	1	32N24	99w30	6:38:00
Coady 101	1	29N46	95w00	6:20:00
Coahoma 114	1	32N18	101w18	6:45:12
Coal Mine 163	1	29N14	98w48	6:35:12
Cobbs 129	1	32N45	96w29	6:25:56
Coble	1	33N36	102w31	6:50:04
Cochran 8	1	30N02	96w08	6:24:32
Cockrell Hill 57	1	32N44	96w53	6:27:32
Coffee City 107	1	32N03	95w30	6:22:00
Coffeyville 230	1	32N48	94w43	6:18:52
Coit 147	1	31N18	96w38	6:26:32
Coke 250	1	33N04	95w28	6:21:52
Colaboz 31	1	26N08	97w38	6:30:32
Coldhill 212	1	32N20	95w18	6:21:12
Coldspring 204	1	30N35	95w07	6:20:28
Coleman 42	1	31N50	99w26	6:37:44
Colfax 234	1	32N33	95w52	6:23:28
College Hill 19	1	33N30	94w37	6:18:28
Collegeport 161	1	28N43	96w11	6:24:44
College Station 21	1	30N37	96w21	6:25:24
Colleyville 220	1	32N53	97w09	6:28:36
Collinsville 91	1	33N34	96w55	6:27:40
Colmesneil 229	1	30N54	94w25	6:17:40
Cologne 88	1	28N48	96w59	6:27:56
Colonial 155	1	31N33	97w10	6:28:40
Colony 75	1	29N41	97w06	6:28:24
Colorado City 168	1	32N24	100w52	6:43:28
Coltexo 90	3	35N26	100w48	6:43:12
Colton 227	1	30N13	97w44	6:30:56
Columbus 45	1	29N42	96w33	6:26:12
Comal 46	1	29N39	98w13	6:32:52
Comanche 47	1	31N54	98w36	6:34:24
Combes 31	1	26N15	97w44	6:30:56
Combine 57	1	32N40	96w36	6:26:24
Comfort 130	1	29N58	98w55	6:35:40
Commerce 116	1	33N15	95w54	6:23:36
Como 112	1	33N03	95w28	6:21:52
Comstock 233	1	29N41	101w10	6:44:40
Comyn 47	1	32N07	98w32	6:34:08
Concan 232	1	29N30	99w43	6:38:52
Concepcion 66	1	27N24	98w21	6:33:24
Concho 48	1	31N30	99w55	6:39:40
Concord 37	1	32N04	95w03	6:20:12
Concord 116	1	33N08	96w07	6:24:28
Concord 145	1	31N16	96w09	6:24:36
Concord 201	1	31N55	94w41	6:18:44
Concrete 62	1	29N14	97w18	6:29:12
Cone 54	1	33N48	101w23	6:45:32
Conlen 56	3	36N14	102w15	6:49:00
Connor 157	1	31N01	95w55	6:23:40
Conroe 170	1	30N19	95w27	6:21:48
Content 200	1	31N59	99w38	6:38:32
Converse 15	1	29N31	98w19	6:33:16
Conway 33	3	35N13	101w23	6:45:32
Cooks Point 26	1	30N37	96w37	6:26:28
Cooks Store 1	1	31N50	95w50	6:23:20
Cookville 225	1	33N11	94w51	6:19:24
Cool 184	1	32N48	98w01	6:32:04
Coolidge 147	1	31N45	96w39	6:26:36
Cooper 60	1	33N23	95w42	6:22:48
Cooper Creek 61	1	33N11	97w04	6:28:16
Copano Village 4	1	28N02	97w03	6:28:12
Copeville 43	1	33N05	96w25	6:25:40
Coppell 57	1	32N57	97w01	6:28:04
Copperas Cove 50	1	31N08	97w54	6:31:36
Copper Canyon 61	1	33N07	97w11	6:28:44
Corbet 175	1	32N00	96w32	6:26:08
Cordele 120	1	28N59	96w39	6:26:36
Corinth 61	1	33N09	97w04	6:28:16
Corinth 127	1	33N00	99w42	6:38:48
Corinth 145	1	31N28	96w04	6:24:16
Corinth 234	1	32N41	95w43	6:22:52
Corley 19	1	33N20	94w21	6:17:24
Cornersville 112	1	32N58	95w17	6:21:08
Cornett 34	1	33N12	94w41	6:18:44
Cornudas	2	31N47	105w28	7:01:52
Coronado 71	2	31N44	106w21	7:05:24
Corpus Christi 178	1	27N47	97w24	6:29:36
Corpus Christi West 178	1	27N51	97w45	6:31:00
Corral City 61	1	33N07	97w11	6:28:44
Corrigan 187	1	31N00	94w50	6:19:20
Corry 140	1	34N04	101w51	6:47:24
Corsicana 175	1	32N06	96w28	6:25:52
Corsicana Junction 175	1	32N06	96w31	6:26:04
Coryell 50	1	31N39	97w28	6:29:52
Cost 89	1	29N26	97w32	6:30:08
Cotton 74	1	33N35	96w11	6:24:44
Cotton Center 74	1	33N35	96w11	6:24:44
Cotton Center 95	1	34N01	102w02	6:48:08
Cottondale 249	1	33N09	97w41	6:30:44
Cotton Gin 81	1	31N38	96w17	6:25:08
Cotton Mill 91	1	33N45	96w34	6:26:16
Cottonwood 30	1	32N24	99w24	6:37:36
Cottonwood 73	1	31N23	97w13	6:28:52
Cottonwood 157	1	30N55	96w07	6:24:28
Cotulla 142	1	28N26	99w14	6:36:56
Coughran 7	1	28N57	98w25	6:33:40
Country Campus 236	1	30N43	95w33	6:22:12
Country Club Estates 68	1	31N52	102w22	6:49:28
Country Club Terrace 235	1	28N48	96w59	6:27:56
County Line 32	1	33N00	94w58	6:19:52
County Line 95	1	33N41	102w00	6:48:00
Coupland 246	1	30N28	97w23	6:29:32
Courtney 93	1	30N16	96w04	6:24:16
Cove 36	1	29N46	95w00	6:20:00
Cove City 181	1	30N04	93w45	6:15:00
Cove Spring 37	1	31N58	95w16	6:21:04
Covington 109	1	32N11	97w16	6:29:04
Cox 230	1	32N44	94w57	6:19:48
Coyanosa 186	1	31N11	102w58	6:51:52
Coy City 128	1	28N50	98w02	6:32:08
Crabb 79	1	29N35	95w46	6:23:04
Crabbs Prairie 236	1	30N43	95w33	6:22:12
Craft 37	1	31N58	95w16	6:21:04
Crafton 249	1	33N18	97w48	6:31:12
Craig 201	1	32N09	94w48	6:19:12
Crandall 129	1	32N38	96w27	6:25:48
Crane 52	1	31N24	102w21	6:49:24
Cranfills Gap 18	1	31N48	97w47	6:31:08
Crawford 155	1	31N32	97w27	6:29:48
Creagleville 234	1	32N41	95w43	6:22:52
Crecy 228	1	31N03	95w08	6:20:32
Creechville 70	1	32N20	96w38	6:26:32
Creedmoor 227	1	30N13	97w44	6:30:56
Crescent 241	1	29N19	96w06	6:24:24
Crescent Heights 107	1	32N12	95w51	6:23:24
Cresson 111	1	32N32	97w37	6:30:28
Cresthaven 15	1	29N31	98w31	6:34:04
Crestwood 68	1	31N52	102w22	6:49:28
Crews 200	1	31N58	99w58	6:39:52
Crimcrest 201	1	32N09	94w48	6:19:12
Crisp 70	1	32N20	96w38	6:26:32
Crockett 113	1	31N19	95w27	6:21:48
Crosby 101	1	29N55	95w04	6:20:16
Crosbyton 54	1	33N40	101w14	6:44:56
Cross 93	1	30N46	96w05	6:24:20
Cross 156	1	28N55	98w33	6:34:12
Cross Cut 25	1	32N02	99w08	6:36:32
Cross Plains 30	1	32N08	99w11	6:36:44
Cross Roads 47	1	31N57	98w44	6:34:56
Cross Roads 60	1	33N22	95w41	6:22:44
Cross Roads 61	1	33N18	96w59	6:27:56
Crossroads 102	1	32N34	94w25	6:17:40
Cross Roads 107	1	32N03	95w58	6:23:52
Crossroads 112	1	33N08	95w36	6:22:24
Cross Roads 166	1	30N51	96w59	6:27:56
Cross Roads 201	1	32N22	94w52	6:19:28
Croton 63	1	33N50	100w30	6:42:00
Crow 250	1	32N35	95w12	6:20:48
Crowell 78	1	33N59	99w43	6:38:52
Crowley 220	1	32N35	97w22	6:29:28
Cruz Calle 66	1	27N24	98w21	6:33:24
Cryer Creek 175	1	32N06	96w38	6:26:32
Crystal Beach 84	1	29N23	94w46	6:19:04
Crystal City 254	1	28N41	99w50	6:39:20
Crystal Falls 215	1	32N45	98w55	6:35:40
Crystal Lake 1	1	31N46	95w38	6:22:32
Cuadrilla 71	2	31N35	106w14	7:04:56
Cuba 126	1	32N21	97w23	6:29:32
Cuero 62	1	29N06	97w17	6:29:08
Culleoka 43	1	33N08	96w37	6:26:28
Cumby 112	1	33N08	95w50	6:23:20
Cundiff 119	1	33N19	98w00	6:32:00
Cuney 37	1	32N02	95w25	6:21:40
Cunningham 139	1	33N26	95w21	6:21:24
Currie 175	1	31N48	96w28	6:25:52
Curtis 121	1	30N55	94w04	6:16:16
Curvitas 108	1	26N14	98w34	6:34:16
Cushing 174	1	31N49	94w50	6:19:20
Cusseta 34	1	33N10	94w33	6:18:12
Cut 113	1	31N13	95w29	6:21:56
Cut and Shoot 170	1	30N19	95w28	6:21:52
Cuthand 194	1	33N28	95w13	6:20:52
Cuthbert 168	1	32N24	100w52	6:43:28
Cyclone 14	1	31N01	97w00	6:28:00
Cypress 80	1	32N58	95w17	6:21:08
Cypress 101	1	29N58	95w42	6:22:48
Cypress Bend 101	1	29N51	95w30	6:22:00
Cypress Creek Estates 101	1	29N58	95w42	6:22:48
Cypress Mill 16	1	30N35	98w20	6:33:20
Dabney 232	1	29N13	99w47	6:39:08
Da Costa 235	1	28N48	96w59	6:27:56
Dacus 170	1	30N23	95w42	6:22:48
Daffan 227	1	30N21	97w33	6:30:12
Daingerfield 172	1	33N02	94w44	6:18:56
Daisetta 146	1	30N07	94w39	6:18:36
Dalby Springs 19	1	33N30	94w37	6:18:28
Dale 28	1	29N56	97w34	6:30:16
Dale Crest 234	1	32N41	95w43	6:22:52
Dalhart 56	3	36N04	102w31	6:50:04
Dallardsville 187	1	30N38	94w38	6:18:32
Dallas 57	1	32N47	96w49	6:27:16

TEXAS

Place		Lat.	Long.	Time
Dal-nor 57	1	32N57	96w53	6:27:32
Dalrock 57	1	32N54	96w37	6:26:28
Dalton 34	1	33N12	94w41	6:18:44
Dalworth 57	1	32N44	96w59	6:27:56
Dalworthington Gardens 220	1	32N42	97w09	6:28:36
Dalys 113	1	31N29	95w29	6:21:56
Damon 20	1	29N17	95w44	6:22:56
Danbury 20	1	29N14	95w21	6:21:24
Danciger 20	1	29N10	95w49	6:23:16
Danevang 241	1	29N03	96w13	6:24:52
Daniel 113	1	31N19	95w27	6:21:48
Daniels 183	1	32N09	94w20	6:17:20
Daniels 239	1	30N20	96w10	6:24:40
Danville 92	1	32N22	94w52	6:19:28
Daphane 80	1	33N09	94w58	6:19:52
Darco 102	1	32N25	94w26	6:17:44
Darrouzett 148	3	36N27	100w20	6:41:20
Daugherty 190	1	32N52	95w46	6:23:04
Davenport 194	1	33N34	95w10	6:20:40
Davilla 166	1	30N47	97w16	6:29:04
Davis Prairie 147	1	31N25	96w34	6:26:16
Davisville 3	1	30N15	95w32	6:22:08
Davisville 145	1	31N16	95w59	6:23:56
Dawn 59	3	34N55	102w12	6:48:48
Dawson 175	1	31N54	96w43	6:26:52
Dayton 146	1	30N03	94w54	6:19:36
Deadwood 183	1	32N09	94w20	6:17:20
Dean 39	1	33N54	98w30	6:34:00
Dean 110	1	33N41	102w00	6:48:00
Deanville 26	1	30N26	96w45	6:27:00
De Berry 183	1	32N18	94w10	6:16:40
Decatur 249	1	33N14	97w35	6:30:20
Decker 177	1	32N05	100w19	6:41:16
Decker Prairie 170	1	30N13	95w45	6:23:00
Deep Water Point Estates 43	1	33N05	96w25	6:25:40
Deer Creek 39	1	33N49	98w12	6:32:48
Deer Park 101	1	29N43	95w08	6:20:32
De Kalb 19	1	33N31	94w37	6:18:28
Delbert L. Atkinson 101	1	29N39	95w11	6:20:44
De Leon 47	1	32N07	98w32	6:34:08
Delhi 28	1	29N56	97w18	6:29:12
Delia 147	1	31N45	96w53	6:27:32
Dell City 115	2	31N56	105w12	7:00:48
Del Mar Hills 240	1	27N31	99w30	6:38:00
Delmita 214	1	26N41	98w25	6:33:40
Del Monte 123	1	29N57	93w59	6:15:56
Delray 183	1	32N09	94w20	6:17:20
Del Rio 233	1	29N22	100w54	6:43:36
Delrose 230	1	32N44	94w57	6:19:48
Del Valle 227	1	30N12	97w40	6:30:40
Delwin 51	1	34N01	100w18	6:41:12
Democrat 47	1	31N54	98w36	6:34:24
Denhawken 247	1	29N14	97w58	6:31:52
Denison 91	1	33N45	96w33	6:26:12
Denning 203	1	31N32	94w07	6:16:28
Dennis 184	1	32N37	97w56	6:31:44
Denny 73	1	31N18	96w38	6:26:32
Denson Spring 1	1	31N29	95w29	6:21:56
Denton 30	1	32N24	99w30	6:38:00
Denton 61	1	33N13	97w08	6:28:32
Denver City 251	1	32N58	102w50	6:51:20
Denver Harbor 101	1	29N47	95w19	6:21:16
Deport 139	1	33N32	95w19	6:21:16
Derby 82	1	28N46	99w08	6:36:32
Dermott 208	1	32N51	101w01	6:44:04
Dernal 235	1	28N48	96w59	6:27:56
Desdemona 67	1	32N16	98w33	6:34:12
Desert 43	1	33N23	96w24	6:25:36
De Soto 57	1	32N35	96w51	6:27:24
Dessau 227	1	30N18	97w43	6:30:52
Detmold 166	1	30N37	97w12	6:28:48
Detroit 194	1	33N40	95w16	6:21:04
Devers 146	1	30N02	94w36	6:18:24
Devine 163	1	29N08	98w54	6:35:36
Dew 81	1	31N36	96w09	6:24:36
Dewalt 79	1	29N33	95w34	6:22:16
Dewees 247	1	29N08	98w09	6:32:36
Dewey 169	1	33N32	97w33	6:30:12
Deweyville 176	1	30N18	93w45	6:15:00
Dewville 89	1	29N16	97w46	6:31:04
Dexter 49	1	33N38	97w08	6:28:32
D'Hanis 163	1	29N20	99w17	6:37:08
Dial 74	3	35N39	101w26	6:45:44
Dialville 37	1	31N52	95w14	6:20:56
Diana 230	1	32N43	94w45	6:19:00
Diboll 3	1	31N11	94w47	6:19:08
Dicey 184	1	32N45	97w43	6:30:52
Dickens 63	1	33N37	100w50	6:43:20
Dickinson 84	1	29N28	95w03	6:20:12
Dickson Cove 116	1	32N54	96w05	6:24:20
Dido 220	1	32N47	97w21	6:29:24
Dies 229	1	30N47	94w25	6:17:40
Dike 112	1	33N14	95w29	6:21:56
Dilley 82	1	28N40	99w10	6:36:40
Dilworth 89	1	29N30	97w27	6:29:48
Dime Box 144	1	30N21	96w49	6:27:16
Dimmitt 35	3	34N33	102w19	6:49:16
Dimple 194	1	33N36	95w03	6:20:12
Dinero 149	1	28N14	97w58	6:31:52
Ding Dong 14	1	31N07	97w46	6:31:04
Dinsmore 241	1	29N19	96w06	6:24:24
Direct 139	1	33N46	95w39	6:22:36
Dirgin 201	1	32N16	94w35	6:18:20
Dittlinger 46	1	29N40	98w11	6:32:44
Divide 41	1	31N54	100w29	6:41:56
Divot 82	1	28N40	99w10	6:36:40
Dixie 91	1	33N40	96w54	6:27:36
Dixon 116	1	33N08	96w07	6:24:28
Doans 244	1	34N09	99w18	6:37:12
Dobbin 170	1	30N22	95w46	6:23:04
Dobrowolski 7	1	28N55	98w33	6:34:12
Doc Brown 181	1	30N06	93w46	6:15:04
Dodd City 74	1	33N33	96w02	6:24:08
Dodge 236	1	30N45	95w24	6:21:36
Dodson 44	3	34N46	99w56	6:39:44
Dogridge 14	1	31N03	97w28	6:29:52
Dogwood 229	1	30N47	94w25	6:17:40
Dogwood Acres 170	1	29N47	95w23	6:21:32
Dolen 146	1	30N18	95w07	6:20:28
Domino 34	1	33N09	94w09	6:16:36
Donelton 116	1	32N57	95w56	6:23:44
Donie 81	1	31N29	96w13	6:24:52
Donna 108	1	26N10	98w03	6:32:12
Doole 154	1	31N24	99w36	6:38:24
Dorchester 91	1	33N32	96w41	6:26:44
Doss 34	1	33N00	94w22	6:17:28
Doss 86	1	30N27	99w08	6:36:32
Dot 73	1	31N15	97w30	6:30:00
Dothan 67	1	32N23	98w59	6:35:56
Dotson 183	1	32N04	94w34	6:18:16
Double Bayou 36	1	29N41	94w38	6:18:32
Double Oak 61	1	33N07	97w11	6:28:44
Doucette 229	1	30N49	94w26	6:17:44
Dougherty 77	1	33N57	101w05	6:44:20
Douglass 174	1	31N40	94w53	6:19:32
Douglassville 34	1	33N12	94w21	6:17:24
Doule 147	1	31N32	96w32	6:26:08
Downing 47	1	31N54	98w36	6:34:24
Downsville 155	1	31N31	97w08	6:28:32
Downtown 20	1	28N58	95w25	6:21:40
Downtown 21	1	30N40	96w22	6:25:28
Downtown 31	1	25N55	97w29	6:29:56
Downtown 57	1	32N51	96w58	6:27:52
Downtown 92	1	32N27	94w44	6:18:56
Downtown 108	1	26N12	98w15	6:33:00
Downtown 178	1	27N45	97w24	6:29:36
Downtown 188	3	35N11	101w51	6:47:24
Dozier 44	3	35N13	100w15	6:41:00
Drane 175	1	32N06	96w31	6:26:04
Drasco 200	1	31N58	99w58	6:39:52
Draw 153	1	33N10	101w48	6:47:12
Dreka 210	1	31N46	93w52	6:15:28
Dresden 175	1	32N06	96w38	6:26:32
Dreyer 89	1	29N26	97w10	6:28:40
Dreyfoos 106	3	36N07	100w02	6:40:08
Driftwood 105	1	30N07	98w02	6:32:08
Dripping Springs 105	1	30N12	98w05	6:32:20
Driscoll 178	1	27N41	97w45	6:31:00
Drop 61	1	33N07	97w17	6:29:08
Dryden 222	1	30N03	102w07	6:48:28
Dubina 75	1	29N41	96w54	6:27:36
Dublin 72	1	32N05	98w21	6:33:24
Dudley 30	1	32N28	99w44	6:38:56
Duffau 72	1	32N05	98w00	6:32:00
Duke 79	1	29N21	95w28	6:21:52
Dulin 25	1	31N33	99w07	6:36:28
Dumas 171	3	35N52	101w58	6:47:52
Dumont 135	1	33N50	100w30	6:42:00
Dunbar 190	1	32N52	95w46	6:23:04
Duncans Woods 181	1	30N06	93w46	6:15:04
Duncanville 57	1	32N39	96w55	6:27:40
Dundee	1	33N44	98w54	6:35:36
Dunlap 51	1	34N01	100w18	6:41:12
Dunlay 163	1	29N21	99w00	6:36:00
Dunn 208	1	32N34	100w53	6:43:32
Dunnan 170	1	29N47	95w23	6:21:32
Duplex 74	1	33N43	96w09	6:24:36
Durango 73	1	31N12	97w02	6:28:08
Duster 47	1	32N07	98w42	6:34:48
Dye Mound 169	1	33N42	97w31	6:30:04
Dyersdale 101	1	29N52	95w20	6:21:20
Dyess Air Force Base 221	1	32N25	99w48	6:39:12
Eagle Lake 45	1	29N35	96w20	6:25:20
Eagle Mountain 220	1	32N49	97w24	6:29:36
Eagle Mountain Acres 220	1	32N39	97w14	6:28:56
Eagle Pass 162	1	28N43	100w30	6:42:00
Early 25	1	31N45	98w57	6:35:48
Earlywine 239	1	30N10	96w24	6:25:36
Earth 140	1	34N14	102w24	6:49:36
East Afton 63	1	33N46	100w49	6:43:16
East Austin 227	1	30N16	97w42	6:30:48
East Bernard 241	1	29N32	96w04	6:24:16
East Bexar 15	1	29N27	98w19	6:33:16
East Central 71	2	31N39	106w15	7:05:00
East Columbia 20	1	29N08	95w39	6:22:36
East Crockett 53	1	30N46	101w12	6:44:48
East Direct 139	1	33N46	95w39	6:22:36
East Ector 68	1	31N54	102w24	6:49:36
Easterly 198	1	31N06	96w23	6:25:32
Eastex Oaks Village 101	1	29N56	95w17	6:21:08
Eastgate 146	1	30N03	94w53	6:19:32
East Grand 57	1	32N47	96w45	6:27:00
East Grayson 91	1	33N40	96w26	6:25:44
East Hamilton 210	1	31N46	93w52	6:15:28
East Houston 101	1	29N50	95w18	6:21:12
Eastland 67	1	32N24	98w49	6:35:16
East Liberty 210	1	31N48	94w11	6:16:44
East Mayfield 202	1	31N21	93w51	6:15:24
East Mountain 230	1	32N44	94w57	6:19:48
East Oak Cliff 57	1	32N44	96w49	6:27:16
Easton 92	1	32N23	94w35	6:18:20
East Point 250	1	32N58	95w17	6:21:08
East River 101	1	30N18	95w07	6:20:28
East Side 58	1	32N44	101w58	6:47:52
East Side 183	1	32N18	94w10	6:16:40
East Stamford 127	1	33N00	99w42	6:38:48
East Tawakoni 190	1	32N53	95w56	6:23:44
East Tempe 187	1	30N43	94w56	6:19:44
East Terrell 222	1	30N14	102w00	6:48:00
East Tom Green 226	1	31N27	100w15	6:41:00
Eastvale 61	1	33N03	97w03	6:28:12
East View 92	1	32N22	94w52	6:19:28
Eastwood 101	1	29N43	95w19	6:21:16
Eaton 198	1	31N01	96w29	6:25:56
Ebenezer 32	1	33N00	94w58	6:19:52
Ebony 167	1	31N34	98w40	6:34:40
Echo 42	1	31N49	99w26	6:37:44
Echo 181	1	30N06	93w46	6:15:04
Echols 147	1	31N45	96w39	6:26:36
Eckert 86	1	30N24	98w42	6:34:48
Ecleto 128	1	29N05	97w50	6:31:20
Ector 74	1	33N37	96w19	6:25:16
Edcouch 108	1	26N18	97w58	6:31:52
Eddy 155	1	31N18	97w15	6:29:00
Eden 48	1	31N13	99w51	6:39:24
Edgar 62	1	29N12	97w14	6:28:56
Edge 21	1	30N53	96w18	6:25:12
Edgecliff 220	1	32N40	97w21	6:29:24
Edgewood 234	1	32N42	95w53	6:23:32
Edgeworth 14	1	30N56	97w14	6:28:56
Edhube 74	1	33N35	96w11	6:24:44
Edinburg 108	1	26N18	98w10	6:32:40
Edith 41	1	31N54	100w29	6:41:56
Edmonson 95	1	34N17	101w54	6:47:36
Edna 120	1	28N59	96w39	6:26:36
Edna Hill 72	1	32N05	98w20	6:33:20
Edom 234	1	32N23	95w36	6:22:24
Edroy 205	1	27N59	97w41	6:30:44
Egan 126	1	32N21	97w23	6:29:32
Egypt 170	1	30N13	95w45	6:23:00
Egypt 241	1	29N30	96w20	6:25:20
Eight Mile 102	1	32N34	94w25	6:17:40
Elbert 224	1	33N16	99w00	6:36:00
El Campo 241	1	29N12	96w16	6:25:04
El Centro 214	1	26N41	98w25	6:33:40
Eldorado 207	1	30N52	100w36	6:42:24
Eldorado Center 175	1	31N54	96w43	6:26:52
Electra 243	1	34N02	98w55	6:35:40
Elevation 166	1	30N43	96w52	6:27:28
El Gato 108	1	26N12	98w09	6:32:36
Elgin 11	1	30N21	97w22	6:29:28
Eli 96	1	34N44	100w32	6:42:08
Eliasville 252	1	32N57	98w46	6:35:04
El Indio 162	1	28N31	100w19	6:41:16
El Jardin 31	1	25N55	97w29	6:29:56
El Jardin Del Mar 101	1	29N34	95w01	6:20:04
Elk 155	1	31N40	96w58	6:27:52
Elkhart 1	1	31N38	95w35	6:22:20
El Lago 101	1	29N34	95w01	6:20:04
Ellinger 75	1	29N50	96w42	6:26:48
Elliott 198	1	31N01	96w29	6:25:56
Elliott 244	1	34N05	99w02	6:36:08
Ellwood 152	1	33N34	101w54	6:47:36
Elmaton 161	1	28N57	96w05	6:24:20
Elmdale 221	1	32N25	99w46	6:39:04
Elmendorf 15	1	29N15	98w20	6:33:20
Elm Flat 175	1	32N08	96w14	6:24:56
Elm Grove 37	1	31N48	95w09	6:20:36
Elm Grove 75	1	29N42	97w18	6:29:12
Elm Grove 241	1	29N35	96w20	6:25:20
Elm Mott 155	1	31N40	97w06	6:28:24
Elmo 129	1	32N43	96w10	6:24:40
Elmont 91	1	33N25	96w34	6:26:16
Elmwood 1	1	31N46	95w38	6:22:32
Eloise 73	1	31N13	96w47	6:27:08
El Oso 128	1	28N49	97w51	6:31:24
El Paso 71	2	31N45	106w29	7:05:56
Elroy 227	1	30N12	97w40	6:30:40
Elsa 108	1	26N18	98w00	6:32:00
El Sauz 214	1	26N35	98w52	6:35:28
Elstone 163	1	29N21	99w08	6:36:32
El Toro 120	1	28N59	96w39	6:26:36
Elwood 74	1	33N47	96w01	6:24:04
Elwood 157	1	31N02	95w45	6:23:00
Ely 74	1	33N35	96w16	6:25:04
Elysian Fields 102	1	32N22	94w11	6:16:44
Emberson 139	1	33N46	95w39	6:22:36
Emblem 112	1	33N08	95w36	6:22:24
Emhouse 175	1	32N10	96w35	6:26:20
Emilee 229	1	30N47	94w25	6:17:40
Emmett 175	1	32N05	96w48	6:27:12
Emory 190	1	32N52	95w46	6:23:04
Enchanted Oaks 107	1	32N22	95w59	6:23:56
Encinal 142	1	28N02	99w21	6:37:24
Encino 24	1	26N56	98w08	6:32:32
Energy 47	1	31N46	98w22	6:33:28
Engelman 108	1	26N18	98w00	6:32:00
Engle 75	1	29N41	96w54	6:27:36
English 194	1	33N38	94w52	6:19:28
Enloe 60	1	33N26	95w39	6:22:36
Ennis 70	1	32N20	96w38	6:26:32
Enoch 230	1	32N44	94w57	6:19:48
Enochs 9	1	33N52	102w46	6:51:04
Enos 237	1	29N47	95w57	6:23:48
Ensign 70	1	32N20	96w38	6:26:32
Enterprise 37	1	31N58	95w16	6:21:04
Enterprise 234	1	32N43	96w00	6:24:00
Eola 48	1	31N32	99w49	6:39:16
Eolian 215	1	32N45	98w55	6:35:40
Era 49	1	33N30	97w17	6:29:08

TEXAS

Erath 155 1 31N34 97w10 6:28:40
Erin 121 1 30N55 94w00 6:16:00
Erwin 93 1 30N29 95w59 6:23:56
Esbon 150 1 30N52 98w49 6:35:16
Escobares 214 1 26N23 98w49 6:35:16
Escobas 253 1 27N04 99w01 6:36:04
Eskota 76 1 32N29 100w07 6:40:28
Esperanza 115 2 31N15 105w48 7:03:12
Esseville 149 1 28N38 98w16 6:33:04
Estacado 54 1 33N40 101w32 6:46:08
Estacado 152 1 33N52 101w36 6:46:24
Estelline 96 1 34N33 100w26 6:41:44
Estes 4 1 27N57 97w07 6:28:28
Estes 102 1 32N27 94w44 6:18:56
Estes Addition 249
1 33N00 97w29 6:29:56
Ethel 91 1 33N34 96w54 6:27:36
Etoile 174 1 31N23 94w26 6:17:44
Etter 171 3 36N02 102w00 6:48:00
Eubank Acres 227 1 30N22 97w41 6:30:44
Eula 30 1 32N24 99w30 6:38:00
Eulalie 201 1 31N54 94w24 6:17:36
Euless 220 1 32N50 97w05 6:28:20
Eulogy 18 1 32N04 97w30 6:30:00
Eureka 175 1 32N01 96w18 6:25:12
Eustace 107 1 32N18 96w01 6:24:04
Evadale 121 1 30N21 94w05 6:16:20
Evant 50 1 31N29 98w09 6:32:36
Evergreen 204 1 30N31 95w15 6:21:00
Everitt 204 1 30N18 95w07 6:20:28
Everman 220 1 32N38 97w17 6:29:08
Ewell 230 1 32N44 94w57 6:19:48
Exchange Park 57 1 32N50 96w50 6:27:20
Exell 171 3 35N38 101w59 6:47:56
Eylau 19 1 33N26 94w04 6:16:16
Ezzell 143 1 29N17 96w54 6:27:36
Fabens 71 2 31N30 106w10 7:04:40
Fairbanks 101 1 29N51 95w30 6:22:00
Fairchilds 79 1 29N24 95w50 6:23:20
Fairdale 202 1 31N21 93w51 6:15:24
Fairfield 81 1 31N44 96w10 6:24:40
Fairland 27 1 30N35 98w20 6:33:20
Fairlie 116 1 33N15 95w54 6:23:36
Fairmount 202 1 31N21 93w51 6:15:24
Fairoaks 147 1 31N29 96w13 6:24:52
Fair Park 57 1 32N47 96w46 6:27:04
Fair Play 183 1 32N15 94w27 6:17:48
Fairview 9 1 34N04 102w32 6:50:08
Fairview 18 1 31N39 97w28 6:29:52
Fairview 43 1 33N09 96w38 6:26:32
Fairview 101 1 29N45 95w24 6:21:36
Fairview 111 1 32N27 97w47 6:31:08
Fairview 114 1 32N14 101w28 6:45:52
Fairview 201 1 31N52 94w59 6:19:56
Fairview 247 1 29N08 98w09 6:32:36
Fairview 249 1 33N03 97w28 6:29:52
Fairy 97 1 31N59 98w02 6:32:08
Faker 32 1 33N00 94w58 6:19:52
Falcon 253 1 26N38 99w06 6:36:24
Falcon Heights 214
1 26N35 99w08 6:36:32
Falcon Village 214
1 26N35 99w08 6:36:32
Falfurrias 24 1 27N14 98w09 6:32:36
Fallon 147 1 31N41 96w29 6:25:56
Falls City 128 1 28N59 98w01 6:32:04
Fannett 123 1 29N55 94w15 6:17:00
Fannin 88 1 28N42 97w14 6:28:56
Fargo 244 1 34N09 99w18 6:37:12
Farmer 54 1 33N41 101w23 6:45:32
Farmers Branch 57
1 32N56 96w54 6:27:36
Farmers Valley 244
1 34N09 99w18 6:37:12
Farmersville 43 1 33N10 96w22 6:25:28
Farmington 91 1 33N27 96w45 6:27:00
Farnsworth 179 3 36N19 100w58 6:43:52
Farrar 147 1 31N27 96w17 6:25:08
Farrsville 176 1 30N59 93w49 6:15:16
Farwell 185 3 34N23 103w02 6:52:08
Fashing 7 1 28N47 98w08 6:32:32
Fate 199 1 32N56 96w23 6:25:32
Faught 139 1 33N40 95w31 6:22:04
Faulkner 139 1 32N37 96w47 6:27:08
Fawil 176 1 30N44 93w39 6:14:36
Fayburg 43 1 33N18 96w24 6:25:36
Fayetteville 75 1 29N54 96w41 6:26:44
Faysville 108 1 26N25 98w08 6:32:32
Fedor 144 1 30N25 97w01 6:28:04
Fentress 28 1 29N45 97w47 6:31:08
Fergus 116 1 33N08 96w07 6:24:28
Ferris 70 1 32N32 96w40 6:26:40
Field Creek 150 1 30N54 98w59 6:35:56
Fieldton 140 1 34N03 102w18 6:49:12
Fife 154 1 31N24 99w22 6:37:28
Figridge 36 1 29N47 94w23 6:17:32
Files Valley 109 1 32N10 97w09 6:28:36
Fincastle 107 1 32N03 95w30 6:22:00
Fink 91 1 33N46 96w40 6:26:40
Finney 95 1 34N17 101w43 6:46:52
Finney 135 1 34N01 100w18 6:41:12
Fischer 46 1 29N58 98w16 6:33:04
Fish Branch 204 1 30N30 95w00 6:20:00
Fisk 42 1 31N49 99w26 6:37:44
Fitze 174 1 31N50 94w30 6:18:00
Fitzhugh 105 1 30N17 97w46 6:31:04
Five Points 70 1 32N24 96w50 6:27:20
Flagg 35 3 34N33 102w19 6:49:16
Flamingo Bay 101 1 29N34 95w01 6:20:04
Flanagan 201 1 32N19 94w31 6:18:04
Flat 50 1 31N19 97w38 6:30:32
Flat Fork 210 1 31N57 94w15 6:17:00
Flatonia 75 1 29N41 97w07 6:28:28
Flats 190 1 32N50 95w53 6:23:32
Flatwood 234 1 32N27 95w42 6:22:48
Fletcher 100 1 30N16 94w11 6:16:44
Flint 212 1 32N12 95w21 6:21:24
Flint Creek 252 1 33N06 98w35 6:34:20
Flo 145 1 31N26 95w55 6:23:40
Flomot 173 1 34N14 100w59 6:43:56
Flora 112 1 33N14 95w29 6:21:56
Florence 246 1 30N51 97w48 6:31:12
Florence Hill 57 1 32N40 97w01 6:28:04
Floresville 247 1 29N08 98w10 6:32:40
Florey 2 1 32N27 102w36 6:50:24
Flour Bluff 178 1 27N39 97w18 6:29:12
Flowella 24 1 27N13 98w09 6:32:36
Flower Mound 61 1 33N01 97w05 6:28:20
Floy 75 1 29N41 97w06 6:28:24
Floyd 116 1 33N08 96w07 6:24:28
Floydada 77 1 33N59 101w20 6:45:20
Fluvanna 208 1 32N53 101w09 6:44:36
Flynn 145 1 31N09 96w08 6:24:32
Foard City 78 1 33N59 99w43 6:38:52
Fodice 113 1 31N08 95w27 6:21:48
Follett 148 3 36N26 100w08 6:40:32
Foncine 43 1 33N08 96w37 6:26:28
Fondren 101 1 29N32 95w07 6:20:28
Foot 43 1 33N08 96w37 6:26:28
Ford Oaks 227 1 30N14 97w47 6:31:08
Fords Corner 203 1 31N32 94w07 6:16:28
Fordtran 235 1 29N17 97w09 6:28:36
Forest 37 1 31N31 95w01 6:20:04
Forestburg 169 1 33N32 97w33 6:30:12
Forest Chapel 139
1 33N52 95w31 6:22:04
Forest Cove 101 1 29N56 95w17 6:21:08
Forest Glade 147 1 31N39 96w31 6:26:04
Forest Grove 43 1 33N08 96w37 6:26:28
Forest Grove 107 1 32N18 95w29 6:21:56
Forest Hill 139 1 33N35 95w54 6:23:36
Forest Hill 220 1 32N41 97w16 6:29:04
Forest Hill 250 1 32N48 95w27 6:21:48
Forest Hills 212 1 32N20 95w18 6:21:12
Forney 129 1 32N45 96w28 6:25:52
Forreston 70 1 32N15 96w52 6:27:28
Forsan 114 1 32N07 101w22 6:45:28
Fort Belknap Park 252
1 33N12 98w44 6:34:56
Fort Bliss 71 2 31N48 106w25 7:05:40
Fort Davis 122 1 30N35 103w54 6:55:36
Fort Gates 50 1 31N24 97w42 6:30:48
Fort Griffin 209 1 32N44 99w18 6:37:12
Fort Hancock 115 2 31N18 105w51 7:03:24
Fort Hood 14 1 31N08 97w45 6:31:00
Fort McKavett 164
1 30N50 100w06 6:40:24
Fort Ringgold 214
1 26N23 98w49 6:35:16
Fort Sam Houston 15
1 29N27 98w27 6:33:48
Fort Spunky 111 1 32N21 97w23 6:29:32
Fort Stockton 186
1 30N53 102w53 6:51:32
Fort Wolters 182 1 32N50 98w04 6:32:16
Fort Worth 220 1 32N45 97w18 6:29:12
Foster 79 1 29N35 95w46 6:23:04
Foster 223 1 33N11 102w16 6:49:04
Foster Place 101 1 29N41 95w22 6:21:28
Foster Store 26 1 30N32 96w42 6:26:48
Fouke 250 1 32N35 95w12 6:20:48
Four Corners 20 1 29N02 95w34 6:22:16
Four Corners 170 1 30N19 95w28 6:21:52
Four Way 171 3 35N41 102w20 6:49:20
Fowlerton 142 1 28N28 98w48 6:35:12
Fox 184 1 32N45 97w43 6:30:52
Frame Switch 246 1 30N34 97w25 6:29:40
Francis 181 1 30N06 93w46 6:15:04
Francitas 120 1 28N52 96w20 6:25:20
Frankel City 2 1 32N23 102w47 6:51:08
Frankell 215 1 32N28 98w41 6:34:44
Franklin 198 1 31N02 96w29 6:25:56
Frankston 1 1 32N03 95w30 6:22:00
Frankston Lake 1 1 32N03 95w30 6:22:00
Fred 229 1 30N34 94w10 6:16:40
Fredericksburg 86
1 30N16 98w52 6:35:28
Fredonia 92 1 32N22 94w52 6:19:28
Fredonia 160 1 30N56 99w07 6:36:28
Fredonia Hill 174
1 31N40 94w38 6:18:32
Freedom 155 1 31N33 97w08 6:28:32
Freemound 49 1 33N39 97w23 6:29:32
Freeport 20 1 28N57 95w21 6:21:24
Freer 66 1 27N53 98w37 6:34:28
Freestone 81 1 31N33 96w15 6:25:00
Freeway Oaks 170 1 29N47 95w23 6:21:32
Frelsburg 45 1 29N53 96w29 6:25:56
Frenstat 26 1 30N32 96w42 6:26:48
Fresenius 100 1 30N16 94w11 6:16:44
Fresno 79 1 29N32 95w27 6:21:48
Freyburg 75 1 29N41 96w54 6:27:36
Friar 201 1 32N16 94w59 6:19:56
Friday 228 1 31N07 95w16 6:21:04
Friendship 121 1 30N51 93w45 6:15:00
Friendship 140 1 34N04 102w32 6:50:08
Friendship 212 1 32N34 94w55 6:19:40
Friendship 234 1 32N41 95w43 6:22:52
Friendship 246 1 30N43 97w26 6:29:44
Friendswood 84 1 29N32 95w12 6:20:48
Friona 185 3 34N38 102w43 6:50:52
Frio Town 82 1 28N54 99w06 6:36:24
Frisco 43 1 33N09 96w49 6:27:16
Fritch 117 3 35N38 101w36 6:46:24
Frognot 43 1 33N18 96w24 6:25:36
Front 183 1 32N18 94w10 6:16:40
Fronton 214 1 26N24 99w05 6:36:20
Frosa 147 1 31N39 96w47 6:27:08
Frost 175 1 32N05 96w49 6:27:16
Fruitland 169 1 33N30 97w48 6:31:12
Fruitvale 234 1 32N41 95w48 6:23:12
Frydek 8 1 29N47 96w09 6:24:36
Fulbright 194 1 33N40 95w16 6:21:04
Fuller Springs 3 1 30N15 95w32 6:22:08
Fulshear 79 1 29N41 95w54 6:23:36
Fulton 4 1 28N04 97w02 6:28:08
Fulton Beach 4 1 28N04 97w02 6:28:08
Funston 127 1 32N45 99w48 6:39:12
Furney Richardson 81
1 31N38 96w17 6:25:08
Fussel 201 1 31N58 94w49 6:19:16
Gail 17 1 32N46 101w27 6:45:48
Gainesville 49 1 33N38 97w08 6:28:32
Galena Park 101 1 29N44 95w14 6:20:56
Gallatin 37 1 31N54 95w09 6:20:36
Gallaway 183 1 31N58 93w57 6:15:48
Galle 94 1 29N39 97w50 6:31:20
Galloway 34 1 33N07 94w10 6:16:40
Galveston 84 1 29N18 94w48 6:19:12
Galveston Island 84
1 29N14 94w56 6:19:44
Ganado 120 1 29N02 96w31 6:26:04
Gano 246 1 30N37 97w12 6:28:48
Garceno 214 1 26N23 98w49 6:35:16
Garciasville 214 1 26N19 98w43 6:34:52
Garden Acres 220 1 32N36 97w19 6:29:16
Garden City 87 1 31N52 101w29 6:45:56
Garden City 101 1 29N51 95w27 6:21:48
Gardendale 142 1 28N31 99w13 6:36:52
Garden Ridge 46 1 29N30 98w25 6:33:40
Garden Valley 38 1 34N23 100w04 6:40:16
Garden Valley 212
1 32N31 95w25 6:21:40
Garden Villas 235
1 28N48 96w59 6:27:56
Garfield 62 1 28N59 97w30 6:30:00
Garfield 227 1 30N11 97w34 6:30:16
Garland 19 1 33N30 94w37 6:18:28
Garland 57 1 32N55 96w38 6:26:32
Garner 184 1 32N45 97w43 6:30:52
Garrett 70 1 32N22 96w39 6:26:36
Garretts Bluff 139
1 33N52 95w31 6:22:04
Garrison 174 1 31N49 94w30 6:18:00
Garth 101 1 29N46 95w00 6:20:00
Garvin 249 1 33N05 97w34 6:30:16
Garwood 45 1 29N27 96w24 6:25:36
Gary 183 1 32N02 94w22 6:17:28
Gasco 57 1 32N39 96w56 6:27:44
Gasoline 23 1 34N22 101w03 6:44:12
Gastonia 129 1 32N44 96w25 6:25:40
Gatesville 50 1 31N26 97w45 6:31:00
Gatewood 101 1 29N55 95w20 6:21:20
Gause 166 1 30N47 96w43 6:26:52
Gay Hill 239 1 30N10 96w24 6:25:36
Geneva 202 1 31N29 93w55 6:15:40
Genoa 101 1 29N38 95w16 6:21:04
George 157 1 31N03 96w07 6:24:28
Georgetown 246 1 30N38 97w41 6:30:44
George West 149 1 28N14 98w04 6:32:16
Georgia 139 1 33N46 95w39 6:22:36
Gerald 155 1 31N33 97w09 6:28:36
Geronimo 94 1 29N40 97w58 6:31:52
Gethsemane 158 1 32N46 94w21 6:17:24
Gholson 155 1 31N36 97w06 6:28:24
Gibtown 119 1 33N43 96w40 6:26:40
Giddings 144 1 30N11 96w56 6:27:44
Gilbert 3 1 30N15 95w32 6:22:08
Gilchrist 84 1 29N31 94w29 6:17:56
Giles 65 3 34N49 100w35 6:42:20
Gill 102 1 32N34 94w25 6:17:40
Gillett 128 1 29N03 97w50 6:31:20
Gilliland 138 1 33N45 99w49 6:39:16
Gilmer 181 1 30N06 93w46 6:15:04
Gilmer 230 1 32N44 94w57 6:19:48
Gilpin 63 1 33N29 100w51 6:43:24
Ginger 190 1 32N47 95w38 6:22:32
Girard 132 1 33N22 100w40 6:42:40
Girvin 186 1 31N05 102w24 6:49:36
Givens 139 1 33N40 95w31 6:22:04
Gladewater 92 1 32N33 94w56 6:19:44
Glad Tidings 100 1 30N22 94w19 6:17:16
Gladwater 225 1 33N09 94w58 6:19:52
Glass 213 1 32N03 97w45 6:31:00
Glaze City 89 1 29N26 97w10 6:28:40
Glazier 106 3 36N01 100w16 6:41:04
Glecker 143 1 29N41 96w54 6:27:36
Glen Cove 42 1 31N52 99w26 6:37:44
Glen Cove 84 1 29N33 95w03 6:20:12
Glencrest 220 1 32N42 97w16 6:29:04
Glendale 228 1 31N01 95w18 6:21:12
Glenfawn 201 1 31N49 94w50 6:19:20
Glen Flora 241 1 29N21 96w12 6:24:48
Glenn 63 1 33N46 100w49 6:43:16
Glenn Heights 57 1 32N37 96w51 6:27:24
Glenrio 59 3 35N11 103w03 6:52:12
Glen Rose 213 1 32N14 97w45 6:31:00
Glenwood 230 1 32N38 94w51 6:19:24
Glidden 45 1 29N42 96w35 6:26:20
Globe 139 1 33N46 95w39 6:22:36
Glory 139 1 33N40 95w31 6:22:04
Gober 74 1 33N28 96w05 6:24:20
Godley 126 1 32N27 97w45 6:31:00
Gold 86 1 30N17 98w52 6:35:28
Golden 250 1 32N44 95w34 6:22:16
Golden Acres 101 1 29N42 95w10 6:20:40
Gold Finch 82 1 29N03 98w52 6:35:28
Goldsboro 42 1 32N04 99w41 6:38:44
Goldsmith 68 1 31N59 102w37 6:50:28
Goldthwaite 167 1 31N27 98w34 6:34:16
Goliad 88 1 28N40 97w23 6:29:32
Golinda 73 1 31N23 97w13 6:28:52
Gomez 223 1 33N11 102w23 6:49:32
Gonzales 89 1 29N30 97w27 6:29:48
Goober Hill 210 1 31N39 93w56 6:15:44

TEXAS

Goodfellow Air Force Base 226	1	31N28	100w27	6:41:48
Good Hope 210	1	31N48	94w11	6:16:44
Goodland 9	1	33N52	102w59	6:51:56
Goodlett 99	3	34N20	99w53	6:39:32
Goodlow Park 175	1	32N08	96w14	6:24:56
Goodnight 6	3	35N02	101w11	6:44:44
Goodnight 175	1	32N08	96w14	6:24:56
Goodrich 187	1	30N36	94w57	6:19:48
Goodville 73	1	31N12	97w02	6:28:08
Gordon 153	1	33N12	101w23	6:45:32
Gordon 182	1	32N33	98w22	6:33:28
Gordonville 91	1	33N48	96w51	6:27:24
Goree 138	1	33N28	99w31	6:38:04
Gorman 67	1	32N12	98w41	6:34:44
Goshen 236	1	30N43	95w33	6:22:12
Gossett 129	1	32N26	96w05	6:24:20
Gouldbusk 42	1	31N33	99w29	6:37:56
Graceton 230	1	32N44	94w57	6:19:48
Graford 182	1	32N56	98w14	6:32:56
Graham 252	1	33N06	98w35	6:34:20
Graham Chapel 85	1	33N12	101w23	6:45:32
Granbury 111	1	32N27	97w47	6:31:08
Grand Bluff 183	1	32N15	94w27	6:17:48
Grandfalls 238	1	31N20	102w51	6:51:24
Grand Lake 170	1	30N19	95w28	6:21:52
Grand Prairie 57	1	32N45	97w00	6:28:00
Grand Saline 234	1	32N41	95w43	6:22:52
Grandview 19	1	33N26	94w04	6:16:16
Grandview 58	1	32N44	101w58	6:47:52
Grandview 126	1	32N16	97w11	6:28:44
Grange Hall 102	1	32N34	94w25	6:17:40
Granger 246	1	30N43	97w26	6:29:44
Granite Shoals 27	1	30N35	98w24	6:33:36
Granite Shoals Lake Shores 150	1	30N40	98w26	6:33:44
Granjeno 108	1	26N13	98w20	6:33:20
Grapeland 113	1	31N30	95w29	6:21:56
Grapevine 220	1	32N56	97w05	6:28:20
Grassland 153	1	33N12	101w23	6:45:32
Gravel Slough 57	1	32N32	96w40	6:26:40
Gray 158	1	32N47	94w05	6:16:20
Grayback 244	1	34N02	98w55	6:35:40
Grayburg 100	1	30N07	94w25	6:17:40
Grays Chapel 1	1	31N46	95w38	6:22:32
Grays Prairie 129	1	32N31	96w23	6:25:32
Graytown 247	1	29N08	98w09	6:32:36
Great Southwest 220	1	32N45	97w06	6:28:24
Green 128	1	28N44	97w52	6:31:28
Green Acres 212	1	32N20	95w18	6:21:12
Greenfield Acres 68	1	31N52	102w22	6:49:28
Green Hill 225	1	33N09	94w58	6:19:52
Green Lake 29	1	28N37	96w38	6:26:32
Greens Bayou 101	1	29N47	95w12	6:20:48
Green Valley 61	1	33N18	96w59	6:27:56
Greenview 112	1	33N07	95w44	6:22:56
Greenview Hills 57	1	32N51	96w58	6:27:52
Greenville 116	1	33N08	96w07	6:24:28
Greenvine 239	1	30N11	96w36	6:26:24
Greenwood 112	1	33N11	95w20	6:21:20
Greenwood 165	1	32N00	102w05	6:48:20
Greenwood 184	1	32N45	97w43	6:30:52
Greenwood 194	1	33N36	95w03	6:20:12
Greenwood 249	1	33N23	97w29	6:29:56
Gregg 227	1	30N21	97w33	6:30:12
Greggton 92	1	32N27	94w44	6:18:56
Gregory 205	1	27N56	97w18	6:29:12
Gresham 212	1	32N20	95w18	6:21:12
Grey Forest 15	1	29N37	98w41	6:34:44
Gribble 57	1	32N56	96w52	6:27:28
Grice 230	1	32N44	94w57	6:19:48
Griffin 37	1	32N08	95w07	6:20:28
Griffing 123	1	29N55	93w56	6:15:44
Griffing Park 123	1	29N55	93w55	6:15:40
Griffith 40	1	33N43	102w45	6:51:00
Griffith 70	1	32N26	97w06	6:28:24
Grigsby 210	1	31N48	94w11	6:16:44
Grindstone 81	1	31N44	96w10	6:24:40
Grit 160	1	30N47	99w19	6:37:16
Grit 190	1	32N47	95w38	6:22:32
Groceville 170	1	30N19	95w28	6:21:52
Groesbeck 147	1	31N31	96w32	6:26:08
Groom 33	3	35N12	101w06	6:44:24
Grosvenor 25	1	31N44	98w58	6:35:52
Groves 123	1	29N56	93w55	6:15:40
Groveton 228	1	31N04	95w08	6:20:32
Grow 135	1	34N01	100w18	6:41:12
Gruenau 62	1	28N59	97w30	6:30:00
Gruene 46	1	29N44	98w06	6:32:24
Grulla 214	1	26N16	98w39	6:34:36
Gruver 98	3	36N16	101w24	6:45:36
Guadalupe 235	1	28N45	96w55	6:27:40
Guajillo 66	1	27N45	98w05	6:32:20
Guerra 124	1	26N53	98w54	6:35:36
Guilbeau 15	1	29N24	98w30	6:34:00
Gulf Camp 238	1	31N35	102w53	6:51:32
Gum Springs 102	1	32N27	94w44	6:18:56
Gun Barrel City 107	1	32N22	95w59	6:23:56
Gunsight 215	1	32N23	98w59	6:35:56
Gunter 91	1	33N27	96w45	6:27:00
Gustine 47	1	31N51	98w24	6:33:36
Guthrie 135	1	33N37	100w19	6:41:16
Guy 79	1	29N21	95w47	6:23:08
Guys Store 145	1	31N16	95w59	6:23:56
Hackberry 15	1	29N24	98w28	6:33:52
Hackberry 51	1	34N01	100w18	6:41:12
Hagansport 80	1	33N22	95w06	6:20:24
Haid 241	1	29N13	96w02	6:24:08
Hail 74	1	33N34	96w00	6:24:00
Hainesville 250	1	32N43	95w22	6:21:28
Halbert 210	1	31N46	93w52	6:15:28
Hale Center 95	1	34N04	101w51	6:47:24
Halesboro 194	1	33N28	95w13	6:20:52
Halfway 95	1	34N11	101w57	6:47:48
Hall 206	1	31N17	99w03	6:36:12
Hallettsville 143	1	29N27	96w57	6:27:48
Hallsburg 155	1	31N36	97w06	6:28:24
Halls Store 183	1	32N22	94w03	6:16:12
Hallsville 102	1	32N30	94w35	6:18:20
Halsted 75	1	29N54	96w52	6:27:28
Haltom City 220	1	32N48	97w16	6:29:04
Hamby 221	1	32N28	99w44	6:38:56
Hamilton 97	1	31N42	98w07	6:32:28
Hamlin 127	1	32N53	100w08	6:40:32
Hammond 198	1	31N06	96w43	6:26:52
Hamon 89	1	29N30	97w27	6:29:48
Hampton 229	1	30N56	94w36	6:18:24
Hamshire 123	1	29N52	94w19	6:17:16
Hancock 58	1	32N44	101w58	6:47:52
Handley 220	1	32N45	97w13	6:28:52
Handy 166	1	30N39	97w00	6:28:00
Hankamer 36	1	29N51	94w38	6:18:32
Hannibal 72	1	32N13	98w13	6:32:52
Hanover 166	1	30N51	96w59	6:27:56
Hanson 210	1	31N58	94w03	6:16:12
Happy 219	3	34N45	101w52	6:47:28
Happy Hill 126	1	32N24	97w13	6:28:52
Happy Union 95	1	34N11	101w43	6:46:52
Happy Valley 221	1	32N03	100w07	6:40:28
Harbin 72	1	32N05	98w20	6:33:20
Hardin 100	1	30N22	94w19	6:17:16
Hardin 146	1	30N09	94w44	6:18:56
Hardin-Simmons 221	1	32N28	99w44	6:38:56
Hardy 169	1	33N42	97w31	6:30:04
Hare 246	1	30N34	97w25	6:29:40
Hargill 108	1	26N27	98w01	6:32:04
Harker Heights 14	1	31N05	97w39	6:30:36
Harkeyville 206	1	31N13	98w47	6:35:08
Harlandale 15	1	29N21	98w29	6:33:56
Harleton 102	1	32N41	94w35	6:18:20
Harlingen 31	1	26N12	97w42	6:30:48
Harmon 139	1	33N35	95w54	6:23:36
Harmony 1	1	31N46	95w48	6:23:12
Harmony 184	1	32N45	97w43	6:30:52
Harmony 201	1	32N16	94w59	6:19:56
Harmony Hill 201	1	32N19	94w31	6:18:04
Harper 86	1	30N18	99w15	6:37:00
Harpersville 215	1	32N45	98w55	6:35:40
Harriet 226	1	31N28	100w27	6:41:48
Harrisburg 101	1	29N43	95w17	6:21:08
Harrisburg 121	1	30N55	94w00	6:16:00
Harrisdale 68	1	31N52	102w22	6:49:28
Harrison 155	1	31N28	96w56	6:27:44
Harrold 244	1	34N05	99w02	6:36:08
Hart 35	1	34N23	102w07	6:48:28
Hartburg 176	1	30N06	93w46	6:15:04
Hart Camp 140	1	33N55	102w20	6:49:20
Hartley 103	3	35N53	102w24	6:49:36
Hart Spur 220	1	32N50	97w10	6:28:40
Hartzo 158	1	32N46	94w21	6:17:24
Harvard 32	1	33N00	94w58	6:19:52
Harvest Heights 101	1	29N51	95w27	6:21:48
Harvey 21	1	30N40	96w22	6:25:28
Harwood 89	1	29N40	97w30	6:30:00
Haskell 104	1	33N10	99w44	6:38:56
Haslam 210	1	31N58	94w03	6:16:12
Haslet 220	1	32N59	97w21	6:29:24
Hasse 47	1	31N56	98w29	6:33:56
Hatchel 200	1	31N51	99w57	6:39:48
Hatchetville 112	1	33N14	95w29	6:21:56
Havana 108	1	26N13	98w20	6:33:20
Hawkins 250	1	32N35	95w12	6:20:48
Hawley 127	1	32N37	99w49	6:39:16
Hawthorne 236	1	30N32	95w29	6:21:56
Hayden 234	1	32N43	96w00	6:24:00
Haynesville 243	1	34N05	98w55	6:35:40
Headsville 198	1	31N18	96w38	6:26:32
Heald 242	3	35N14	100w36	6:42:24
Hearne 198	1	30N53	96w36	6:26:24
Heath 199	1	32N50	96w29	6:25:56
Hebbronville 124	1	27N18	98w41	6:34:44
Hebron 61	1	33N02	96w52	6:27:28
Heckville 152	1	33N46	101w40	6:46:40
Hedley 65	3	34N52	100w39	6:42:36
Hedwigs Hill 160	1	30N45	99w14	6:36:56
Hedwig Village 101	1	29N47	95w32	6:22:08
Hefner 138	1	33N28	99w31	6:38:04
Heidelberg 108	1	26N09	97w55	6:31:40
Heidenheimer 14	1	31N01	97w18	6:29:12
Heights 84	1	29N23	94w57	6:19:48
Helena 128	1	28N57	97w50	6:31:20
Helmic 228	1	31N03	95w08	6:20:32
Helotes 15	1	29N35	98w41	6:34:44
Helotes Park Estates 15	1	29N37	98w41	6:34:44
Helotes Ranch Acres 15	1	29N37	98w41	6:34:44
Hemphill 202	1	31N20	93w51	6:15:24
Hempstead 237	1	30N06	96w05	6:24:20
Henderson 201	1	32N09	94w48	6:19:12
Henkhaus 143	1	29N26	97w10	6:28:40
Henly 105	1	30N10	98w05	6:32:20
Henning 174	1	31N50	94w30	6:18:00
Henrietta 39	1	33N49	98w12	6:32:48
Henrys Chapel 37	1	32N08	95w07	6:20:28
Hereford 59	3	34N49	102w24	6:49:36
Heritage Hills 227	1	30N22	97w41	6:30:44
Hermleigh 208	1	32N38	100w46	6:43:04
Hermosa 195	1	31N25	103w30	6:54:00
Herring 226	1	31N28	100w27	6:41:48
Herty 3	1	31N21	94w41	6:18:44
Hester 175	1	32N06	96w31	6:26:04
Hewitt 155	1	31N23	97w12	6:28:48
Hext 164	1	30N52	99w32	6:38:08
Hickmuntown 227	1	30N23	97w45	6:31:00
Hickory Creek 61	1	33N07	97w03	6:28:12
Hickory Creek 116	1	33N18	96w12	6:24:48
Hickory Grove 61	1	33N07	97w02	6:28:08
Hickory Ridge 202	1	31N21	93w51	6:15:24
Hickston 89	1	29N42	97w18	6:29:12
Hico 97	1	31N59	98w02	6:32:08
Hidalgo 108	1	26N06	98w16	6:33:04
Hidden Valley 101	1	29N51	95w27	6:21:48
Higginbotham 83	1	32N58	102w50	6:51:20
Higgins 148	3	36N07	100w02	6:40:08
High 139	1	33N38	95w42	6:22:48
Highbank	1	31N10	96w50	6:27:20
High Hill 75	1	29N41	96w54	6:27:36
High Island 84	1	29N34	94w24	6:17:36
Highland 72	1	32N05	98w20	6:33:20
Highland Acres 91	1	33N46	96w40	6:26:40
Highland Acres 101	1	29N51	95w27	6:21:48
Highland Acres 116	1	32N57	95w56	6:23:44
Highland Addition 101	1	29N51	95w27	6:21:48
Highland Addition 184	1	32N58	97w41	6:30:44
Highland Bayou 84	1	29N21	95w01	6:20:04
Highland Estates 235	1	28N48	96w59	6:27:56
Highland Heights	1	29N53	95w27	6:21:48
Highland Hills 15	1	29N22	98w27	6:33:48
Highland Park 57	1	32N50	96w48	6:27:12
Highlands 101	1	29N49	95w03	6:20:12
Highland Village 61	1	33N03	97w03	6:28:12
Highland Village 101	1	29N45	95w29	6:21:56
Hiland Shores 91	1	33N46	96w40	6:26:40
Hilda 160	1	30N45	99w14	6:36:56
Hill 11	1	30N07	97w19	6:29:16
Hill City 111	1	32N23	97w55	6:31:40
Hill Country Village 15	1	29N35	98w29	6:33:56
Hillcrest 20	1	29N23	95w13	6:20:52
Hill Crest 21	1	30N40	96w22	6:25:28
Hillcrest 45	1	29N42	96w33	6:26:12
Hillebrandt 123	1	30N03	94w06	6:16:24
Hillister 229	1	30N40	94w23	6:17:32
Hillje 241	1	29N11	96w17	6:25:08
Hills 144	1	30N13	97w07	6:28:28
Hillsboro 109	1	32N01	97w08	6:28:32
Hillside Gardens 101	1	29N55	95w20	6:21:20
Hilltop Lakes 145	1	31N03	96w07	6:24:28
Hilshire Village 101	1	29N47	95w29	6:21:56
Hinckley 139	1	33N40	95w31	6:22:04
Hindes 7	1	28N55	98w33	6:34:12
Hines 244	1	34N09	99w18	6:37:12
Hinkles Ferry 20	1	29N02	95w34	6:22:16
Hiram 129	1	32N43	96w00	6:24:00
Hitchcock 84	1	29N21	95w01	6:20:04
Hitchland 98	3	36N30	101w19	6:45:16
Hix 26	1	30N47	96w43	6:26:52
Hoard 250	1	32N40	95w29	6:21:56
Hobbs 76	1	32N38	100w46	6:43:04
Hobson 128	1	28N57	97w59	6:31:56
Hochheim 62	1	29N19	97w17	6:29:08
Hockley 101	1	30N02	95w51	6:23:24
Hockley Mine 101	1	30N02	95w51	6:23:24
Hodges 127	1	32N37	99w49	6:39:16
Hodgson 19	1	33N30	94w37	6:18:28
Hoen 155	1	31N45	96w53	6:27:32
Hogg 26	1	30N32	96w42	6:26:48
Holcombs Store 37	1	31N48	95w09	6:20:36
Holiday 61	1	33N03	97w03	6:28:12
Holiday Estates 116	1	32N43	96w00	6:24:00
Holiday Hills 190	1	32N57	95w56	6:23:44
Holland 14	1	30N53	97w24	6:29:36
Holland Quarters 183	1	32N09	94w20	6:17:20
Holliday 5	1	33N49	98w42	6:34:48
Hollis 157	1	31N01	95w55	6:23:40
Holly 113	1	31N08	95w27	6:21:48
Holly Grove 187	1	30N43	94w56	6:19:44
Holly Springs 121	1	30N55	94w00	6:16:00
Hollywood 123	1	29N57	93w59	6:15:56
Hollywood Heights 123	1	29N57	93w59	6:15:56
Hollywood Park 15	1	29N36	98w29	6:33:56
Holman 75	1	29N42	96w47	6:27:08
Homer 3	1	30N15	95w32	6:22:08
Hondo 163	1	29N21	99w09	6:36:36
Honea 170	1	30N23	95w42	6:22:48
Honey Grove 74	1	33N35	95w55	6:23:40
Honey Island 100	1	30N24	94w27	6:17:48
Hood 49	1	33N38	97w08	6:28:32

 TEXAS

Hooks 19	1	33N28	94w16	6:17:04
Hoover 90	3	35N36	100w51	6:43:24
Hoovers Valley 27	1	30N46	98w14	6:32:56
Hope 143	1	29N17	97w09	6:28:36
Hopewell 80	1	33N11	95w13	6:20:52
Hopewell 113	1	31N19	95w27	6:21:48
Horn Hill 147	1	31N32	96w32	6:26:08
Hornsby Bend 227	1	30N16	97w42	6:30:48
Horton 60	1	33N15	95w54	6:23:36
Horton 183	1	32N18	94w10	6:16:40
Hostyn 75	1	29N54	96w52	6:27:28
Houmont Park 101	1	29N50	95w14	6:20:56
Houston 101	1	29N46	95w22	6:21:28
Houston Heights 101	1	29N48	95w25	6:21:40
Howard 70	1	32N24	96w50	6:27:20
Howardwick 65	3	34N56	100w53	6:43:32
Howe 91	1	33N30	96w37	6:26:28
Howellville 101	1	29N43	95w35	6:22:20
Howland 139	1	33N32	95w38	6:22:32
Howth 237	1	30N06	96w02	6:24:08
Hoxie 246	1	30N34	97w25	6:29:40
Hoyt 250	1	32N47	95w38	6:22:32
Hoyte 166	1	30N51	96w59	6:27:56
Hub 185	3	34N38	102w43	6:50:52
Hubbard 109	1	31N51	96w48	6:27:12
Hubert 205	1	28N06	97w50	6:31:20
Huckabay 72	1	32N20	98w18	6:33:12
Hudson 3	1	31N19	94w50	6:19:20
Huffines 34	1	33N01	94w12	6:16:48
Huffman 101	1	30N01	95w06	6:20:24
Hufsmith 101	1	30N07	95w36	6:22:24
Hughes Springs 34	1	33N00	94w38	6:18:32
Hulen Park 84	1	29N23	94w57	6:19:48
Hull 146	1	30N09	94w39	6:18:36
Humble 101	1	30N00	95w16	6:21:04
Humble Government Wells Camp 66	1	27N53	98w37	6:34:28
Humble Hieghts 101	1	29N56	95w17	6:21:08
Hungerford 241	1	29N24	96w05	6:24:20
Hunt 116	1	33N08	96w07	6:24:28
Hunt 133	1	30N04	99w20	6:37:20
Hunter 46	1	29N48	98w01	6:32:04
Hunters Creek Village 101	1	29N47	95w31	6:22:04
Huntington 3	1	31N17	94w34	6:18:16
Huntsville 236	1	30N43	95w33	6:22:12
Hurlwood 152	1	33N35	102w02	6:48:08
Hurnville 39	1	33N49	98w12	6:32:48
Huron 109	1	31N57	97w19	6:29:16
Hurst 220	1	32N49	97w09	6:28:36
Hurstown 210	1	31N46	93w52	6:15:28
Hurst Springs 50	1	31N47	97w35	6:30:20
Hutchins 57	1	32N39	96w43	6:26:52
Hutto 246	1	30N33	97w33	6:30:12
Huxley 210	1	31N46	93w52	6:15:28
Hye 16	1	30N15	98w34	6:34:16
Hylton 177	1	32N05	100w19	6:41:16
Hyman 168	1	32N14	101w28	6:45:52
Iago 241	1	29N16	95w57	6:23:48
Iatan 168	1	32N22	101w01	6:44:04
Ida 91	1	33N31	96w23	6:25:32
Idalou 152	1	33N40	101w41	6:46:44
Idlewild 57	1	32N44	96w59	6:27:56
Ike 70	1	32N24	96w50	6:27:20
Illinois Bend 169	1	33N42	97w31	6:30:04
Impact 221	1	32N30	99w45	6:39:00
Imperial 186	1	31N11	102w49	6:51:16
Inadale 208	1	32N33	100w41	6:42:44
Independence 239	1	30N19	96w21	6:25:24
India 70	1	32N32	96w37	6:26:28
Indian Creek 25	1	31N44	98w58	6:35:52
Indian Gap 97	1	31N42	98w07	6:32:28
Indian Hill 176	1	31N00	93w42	6:14:48
Indianola 29	1	28N37	96w38	6:26:32
Indian Rock 230	1	32N44	94w57	6:19:48
Indio 189	1	29N33	104w23	6:57:32
Industrial 57	1	32N47	96w49	6:27:16
Industry 8	1	29N58	96w30	6:26:00
Inez 235	1	28N54	96w47	6:27:08
Ingleside 205	1	27N53	97w13	6:28:52
Ingleside on the Bay 205	1	27N53	97w12	6:28:48
Ingram 133	1	30N05	99w14	6:36:56
Inks Lake Village 150	1	30N45	98w25	6:33:40
Inwood 57	1	32N51	96w49	6:27:16
Iola 93	1	30N46	96w05	6:24:20
Iowa Colony 20	1	29N21	95w28	6:21:52
Iowa Park 243	1	33N57	98w40	6:34:40
Ira 208	1	32N35	101w00	6:44:00
Iraan 186	1	30N55	101w54	6:47:36
Iredell 18	1	31N59	97w52	6:31:28
Ireland 50	1	31N25	97w43	6:30:52
Irene 109	1	31N59	96w52	6:27:28
Ironton 37	1	31N55	95w23	6:21:32
Irving 57	1	32N49	96w56	6:27:44
Irvington 101	1	29N50	95w23	6:21:32
Isla 202	1	31N26	93w51	6:15:24
Island 84	1	29N18	94w50	6:19:20
Island 157	1	31N02	95w45	6:23:00
Italy 70	1	32N11	96w53	6:27:32
Itasca 109	1	32N10	97w09	6:28:36
Ivan 215	1	32N53	98w44	6:34:56
Ivanhoe 74	1	33N43	96w09	6:24:36
Iverson 109	1	32N07	96w57	6:27:48
Izoro 141	1	31N07	97w54	6:31:36
Jacinto City 101	1	29N46	95w13	6:20:52
Jacksboro 119	1	33N13	98w10	6:32:40
Jackson 158	1	32N46	94w21	6:17:24
Jackson 210	1	31N58	94w03	6:16:12
Jackson 234	1	32N26	95w58	6:23:52
Jacksonville 37	1	31N58	95w17	6:21:08
Jacobia 116	1	33N08	96w07	6:24:28
Jacobs 201	1	32N16	94w59	6:19:56
Jamaica Beach 84	1	29N18	94w50	6:19:20
James 113	1	31N22	95w11	6:20:44
James 210	1	31N48	94w11	6:16:44
James Moody 235	1	28N48	96w59	6:27:56
Jamestown 176	1	30N51	93w45	6:15:00
J. And L. Ranchland 101	1	29N56	95w17	6:21:08
Jappa 27	1	30N45	98w03	6:32:12
Jardin 116	1	33N15	95w54	6:23:36
Jarrell 246	1	30N45	97w35	6:30:20
Jarvis College 250	1	32N35	95w12	6:20:48
Jasper 121	1	30N55	94w00	6:16:00
Jasper Heights 102	1	32N34	94w25	6:17:40
Jayton 132	1	33N15	100w34	6:42:16
Jean 252	1	33N18	98w37	6:34:28
Jeans 229	1	31N01	94w23	6:17:32
Jeddo 11	1	29N56	97w18	6:29:12
Jefferson 158	1	32N46	94w21	6:17:24
Jenkins 172	1	33N02	94w44	6:18:56
Jennings 139	1	33N40	95w31	6:22:04
Jensen Drive 101	1	29N48	95w20	6:21:20
Jericho 65	3	34N56	100w53	6:43:32
Jericho 210	1	31N48	94w11	6:16:44
Jermyn 119	1	33N16	98w23	6:33:32
Jersey Village 101	1	29N53	95w34	6:22:16
Jester 175	1	31N57	96w37	6:26:28
Jewett 145	1	31N22	96w09	6:24:36
J. Frank Dobie 15	1	29N24	98w25	6:33:40
Jiba 129	1	32N35	96w17	6:25:08
Jim Ned 221	1	32N10	99w50	6:39:20
Joaquin 210	1	31N58	94w03	6:16:12
Joe Pool 57	1	32N43	96w51	6:27:24
John Allen 101	1	29N47	95w24	6:21:36
John Foster 101	1	29N42	95w12	6:20:48
Johnson 223	1	33N11	102w16	6:49:04
Johnson City 16	1	30N17	98w25	6:33:40
Johnsons Station 220	1	32N41	97w08	6:28:32
Johnstown 170	1	30N19	95w28	6:21:52
Johnstown 234	1	32N43	96w00	6:24:00
Johnsville 72	1	31N59	98w02	6:32:08
Johntown 194	1	33N25	95w10	6:20:40
Joinerville 201	1	32N11	94w55	6:19:40
Joliet 28	1	29N41	97w39	6:30:36
Jolly 39	1	33N52	98w21	6:33:24
Jollyville 246	1	30N31	97w41	6:30:44
Jonah 246	1	30N38	97w40	6:30:40
Jones 234	1	32N41	95w43	6:22:52
Jonesboro 50	1	31N37	97w53	6:31:32
Jones Creek 20	1	28N58	95w28	6:21:52
Jones Creek 241	1	29N11	96w17	6:25:08
Jones Prairie 166	1	30N51	96w59	6:27:56
Jonestown 227	1	30N35	97w51	6:31:24
Jonesville 102	1	32N30	94w07	6:16:28
Joplin 119	1	33N06	98w00	6:32:00
Jordans Store 210	1	31N46	93w52	6:15:28
Josephine 43	1	33N04	96w19	6:25:16
Joshua 126	1	32N28	97w23	6:29:32
Josserand 228	1	31N03	95w08	6:20:32
Jot 'Em Down 60	1	33N25	95w56	6:23:44
Jourdanton 7	1	28N55	98w33	6:34:12
Joy 39	1	33N49	98w12	6:32:48
Joy 212	1	32N34	94w55	6:19:40
Jozye 157	1	31N01	95w55	6:23:40
Jud 104	1	33N19	99w51	6:39:24
Judson 92	1	32N35	94w45	6:19:00
Juliff 79	1	29N27	95w28	6:21:52
Junction 134	1	30N29	99w46	6:39:04
Juno	1	30N09	101w07	6:44:28
Juno 233	1	31N32	99w49	6:39:16
Jupiter Pharmacy 57	1	32N57	96w44	6:26:56
Justiceburg 85	1	33N03	101w12	6:44:48
Justin 61	1	33N05	97w18	6:29:12
Kadane Corner 243	1	33N52	98w50	6:35:20
Kalgary 54	1	33N12	101w23	6:45:32
Kamay 243	1	33N53	98w49	6:35:16
Kamey 29	1	28N38	96w45	6:27:00
Kanawha 194	1	33N40	95w16	6:21:04
Kane 108	1	26N12	98w15	6:33:00
Karen 170	1	30N13	95w45	6:23:00
Karnack 102	1	32N40	94w10	6:16:40
Karnes City 128	1	28N53	97w54	6:31:36
Katemcy 160	1	30N55	99w15	6:37:00
Katy 101	1	29N47	95w49	6:23:16
Kaufman 129	1	32N35	96w19	6:25:16
Kayare 31	1	26N11	97w39	6:30:36
Kay Bee Heights 50	1	31N08	97w46	6:31:04
Keechi 145	1	31N28	96w04	6:24:16
Keenan 170	1	30N19	95w39	6:22:36
Keene 126	1	32N24	97w20	6:29:20
Keeter 249	1	33N05	97w34	6:30:16
Keith 93	1	30N46	96w05	6:24:20
Keller 220	1	32N56	97w15	6:29:00
Keller Corner 31	1	25N55	97w29	6:29:56
Kellerville 242	3	35N22	100w30	6:42:00
Kelly 43	1	33N21	96w33	6:26:12
Kelly Air Force Base 15	1	29N23	98w35	6:34:20
Kellyville 158	1	32N46	94w21	6:17:24
Kelsay 124	1	26N57	98w08	6:32:32
Kelsey 230	1	32N44	94w57	6:19:48
Kelton 242	3	35N26	100w17	6:41:08
Keltys 3	1	31N22	94w45	6:19:00
Kemah 84	1	29N33	95w01	6:20:04
Kemp 129	1	32N26	96w14	6:24:56
Kempner 141	1	31N05	98w00	6:32:00
Kendalia 130	1	29N58	98w31	6:34:04
Kendleton 79	1	29N27	96w00	6:24:00
Kenedy 128	1	28N49	97w51	6:31:24
Kenefick 146	1	30N07	94w52	6:19:28
Kennard 113	1	31N22	95w11	6:20:44
Kennedale 220	1	32N39	97w13	6:28:52
Kennedy Shores 31	1	25N55	97w29	6:29:56
Kenney 8	1	30N03	96w20	6:25:20
Kensing 60	1	33N26	95w39	6:22:36
Kent	1	31N04	104w13	6:56:52
Kentuckytown 91	1	33N31	96w23	6:25:32
Kenwood Place 101	1	29N55	95w20	6:21:20
Kerens 175	1	32N08	96w14	6:24:56
Kermit 248	1	31N52	103w06	6:52:24
Kerrick 56	3	36N30	102w15	6:49:00
Kerrville 133	1	30N03	99w08	6:36:32
Kerrville Rural 133	1	30N02	99w07	6:36:28
Kevin 146	1	30N18	95w07	6:20:28
Key 58	1	32N44	101w48	6:47:12
Kickapoo 1	1	32N03	95w30	6:22:00
Kildare 34	1	32N57	94w15	6:17:00
Kildare Junction 34	1	33N01	94w12	6:16:48
Kilgore 92	1	32N23	94w53	6:19:32
Killeen 14	1	31N07	97w44	6:30:56
Kilowatt 181	1	30N06	93w46	6:15:04
Kimball 18	1	32N04	97w30	6:30:00
Kimbro 227	1	30N21	97w33	6:30:12
Kinard Estates 181	1	30N06	93w46	6:15:04
King 50	1	31N24	98w03	6:32:12
King 194	1	33N35	94w55	6:19:40
King City 146	1	30N18	95w07	6:20:28
Kingola 244	1	34N08	99w09	6:36:36
Kingsbury 94	1	29N39	97w50	6:31:20
Kingsland 150	1	30N40	98w26	6:33:44
Kingsley 57	1	32N54	96w37	6:26:28
Kingsmill	3	35N29	101w04	6:44:16
Kings Mill 90	3	35N33	100w58	6:43:52
Kingston 116	1	33N08	96w07	6:24:28
Kingsville 137	1	27N31	97w52	6:31:28
Kingsville Rural 137	1	27N28	97w45	6:31:00
Kingsville Station 137	1	27N30	97w49	6:31:16
Kinkler 143	1	29N27	96w56	6:27:44
Kinwood	1	29N55	95w19	6:21:16
Kiomatia 194	1	33N40	95w16	6:21:04
Kirby 15	1	29N28	98w23	6:33:32
Kirbyville 121	1	30N40	93w54	6:15:36
Kirk 147	1	31N33	96w50	6:27:20
Kirkland 38	1	34N23	100w04	6:40:16
Kirkpatrick Addition 212	1	32N20	95w18	6:21:12
Kirtley 75	1	30N00	97w09	6:28:36
Kirvin 81	1	31N46	96w20	6:25:20
Kitchenville 227	1	30N14	97w47	6:31:08
Kittrell 236	1	30N57	95w23	6:21:32
Kleberg 57	1	32N41	96w36	6:26:24
Klein 101	1	30N09	95w25	6:21:40
Klondike 58	1	32N44	101w58	6:47:52
Klondike 60	1	33N20	95w46	6:23:04
Klump 239	1	30N10	96w24	6:25:36
Knapp 208	1	32N35	101w00	6:44:00
Knickerbocker 226	1	31N16	100w38	6:42:32
Knippa 232	1	29N18	99w38	6:38:32
Knott 114	1	32N24	101w39	6:46:36
Knox City 138	1	33N25	99w49	6:39:16
Knoxville 134	1	30N18	99w15	6:37:00
Koerth 143	1	29N27	96w56	6:27:44
Kohrville 101	1	30N01	95w35	6:22:20
Kokomo 67	1	32N13	98w40	6:34:40
Koockville 160	1	30N45	99w14	6:36:56
Kopperl 18	1	32N04	97w30	6:30:00
Kosciusko 247	1	29N14	97w58	6:31:52
Kosse 147	1	31N18	96w38	6:26:32
Kountze 100	1	30N22	94w19	6:17:16
Kovar 11	1	29N41	97w06	6:28:24
Krem 57	1	32N54	96w37	6:26:28
Kress 219	1	34N22	101w45	6:47:00
Krugerville 61	1	33N18	96w59	6:27:56
Krum 61	1	33N16	97w14	6:28:56
Kurten 21	1	30N47	96w16	6:25:04
Kyle 105	1	29N59	97w53	6:31:32
Kyote 7	1	29N03	98w52	6:35:28
Labatt 247	1	29N08	98w09	6:32:36
Labelle 123	1	29N53	94w13	6:16:52
La Blanca 108	1	26N17	98w02	6:32:08
La Casita 214	1	26N23	98w49	6:35:16
Laceola 157	1	31N03	96w07	6:24:28
Lackland 15	1	29N23	98w37	6:34:28
Lackland Air Force Base 15	1	29N23	98w36	6:34:24
La Coste 163	1	29N19	98w49	6:35:16
La Cour 146	1	30N04	94w48	6:19:12
Lacy 228	1	31N03	95w08	6:20:32
Lacy-Lakeview 155	1	31N41	97w06	6:28:24
Ladonia 74	1	33N25	95w57	6:23:48
LaFayette 230	1	33N00	94w58	6:19:52
La Feria 31	1	26N09	97w49	6:31:16
La Gloria 214	1	26N46	98w29	6:33:56
Lago Vista 246	1	30N35	97w51	6:31:24
La Grange 75	1	29N54	96w52	6:27:28
Laguna Heights 31	1	26N05	97w08	6:28:32
Laguna Park 18	1	31N51	97w23	6:29:32

Laguna Vista 31	1	26N06	97w11	6:28:44
Laird Hill 201	1	32N21	94w54	6:19:36
La Isla 71	2	31N30	106w12	7:04:48
Lajitas 22	1	29N16	103w46	6:55:04
La Joya 108	1	26N14	98w27	6:33:48
La Junta 184	1	32N55	97w36	6:30:24
Lake 249	1	33N13	97w46	6:31:04
Lake Alaska 20	1	29N09	95w27	6:21:48
Lake Barbara 20	1	29N01	95w23	6:21:32
Lake Brownwood 25	1	31N44	98w58	6:35:52
Lake Cherokee 92	1	32N09	94w48	6:19:12
Lake Corsicana 175	1	32N06	96w31	6:26:04
Lake Creek 60	1	33N27	95w35	6:22:20
Lake Cypress 101	1	29N58	95w42	6:22:48
Lake Dallas 61	1	33N07	97w01	6:28:04
Lake Estates 170	1	30N23	95w42	6:22:48
Lake Halbert 175	1	32N06	96w31	6:26:04
Lakehills 10	1	29N43	98w56	6:35:44
Lake Jackson 20	1	29N03	95w27	6:21:48
Lake Jackson Farms 20	1	29N02	95w26	6:21:44
Lake Kiowa 49	1	33N38	97w08	6:28:32
Lakeland 170	1	30N19	95w28	6:21:52
Lakeland Heights 57	1	32N43	96w59	6:27:56
Lakeland Hills 227	1	30N16	97w48	6:31:12
Lakeland Park 227	1	30N23	97w45	6:31:00
Lake Placid 94	1	29N35	97w58	6:31:52
Lakeport 92	1	32N24	94w42	6:18:48
Lake Shore 25	1	31N44	98w58	6:35:52
Lakeside 84	1	29N32	95w01	6:20:04
Lakeside 220	1	32N49	97w28	6:29:52
Lakeside City 5	1	33N52	98w33	6:34:12
Lakeside Hieghts 150	1	30N40	98w26	6:33:44
Lakeside Village 18	1	32N01	97w36	6:30:24
Lake Tanglewood 191	3	35N11	101w51	6:47:24
Lake Thomas 208	1	32N35	101w00	6:44:00
Laketon 90	3	35N33	100w58	6:43:52
Lake Victor 27	1	31N04	98w11	6:32:44
Lakeview 14	1	31N03	97w28	6:29:52
Lakeview 57	1	32N44	96w59	6:27:56
Lakeview 77	1	33N59	101w20	6:45:20
Lakeview 96	1	34N40	100w42	6:42:48
Lakeview 123	1	29N55	93w56	6:15:44
Lakeview 153	1	33N20	102w12	6:48:48
Lakeview 155	1	31N36	97w06	6:28:24
Lakeview 181	1	30N09	94w01	6:16:04
Lakeview 219	3	34N32	101w46	6:47:04
Lakeview 220	1	32N49	97w24	6:29:36
Lakeview Estates 234	1	32N43	96w00	6:24:00
Lakeway 227	1	30N17	97w46	6:31:04
Lakewood 57	1	32N49	96w45	6:27:00
Lakewood 101	1	29N46	95w00	6:20:00
Lakewood 181	1	30N09	94w01	6:16:04
Lakewood Harbor 18	1	31N47	97w35	6:30:20
Lake Worth 220	1	32N49	97w24	6:29:36
Lake Worth Village 220	1	32N48	97w27	6:29:48
Lamar 4	1	28N08	97w00	6:28:00
Lamar Park 178	1	27N44	97w24	6:29:36
La Marque 84	1	29N23	94w58	6:19:52
Lamar Tech 123	1	30N03	94w06	6:16:24
Lamasco 74	1	33N47	96w01	6:24:04
Lamesa 58	1	32N44	101w58	6:47:52
Lamkin 47	1	31N49	98w16	6:33:04
Lampasas 141	1	31N04	98w11	6:32:44
Lanark 34	1	33N09	94w09	6:16:36
Lancaster 57	1	32N35	96w45	6:27:00
Landrum 31	1	26N08	97w38	6:30:32
Lane 116	1	33N18	96w12	6:24:48
Lane City 241	1	29N13	96w02	6:24:08
Lanely 81	1	31N28	96w04	6:24:16
Laneport 246	1	30N34	97w25	6:29:40
Lane Prairie 126	1	32N21	97w23	6:29:32
Laneville 201	1	31N58	94w49	6:19:16
Langtry 233	1	29N49	101w34	6:46:16
Lanham 97	1	31N37	97w53	6:31:32
Lanier 34	1	33N00	94w22	6:17:28
Lannius 74	1	33N35	96w04	6:24:16
La Paloma 31	1	26N03	97w40	6:30:40
Lapham 15	1	29N33	98w31	6:34:04
La Porte 101	1	29N40	95w01	6:20:04
La Pryor 254	1	28N57	99w51	6:39:24
Laredo 240	1	27N30	99w30	6:38:00
La Reforma 214	1	26N41	98w22	6:33:28
Lariat 185	3	34N20	102w55	6:51:40
Lark 33	3	35N12	101w14	6:44:56
Larue 107	1	32N07	95w41	6:22:44
La Salle 120	1	28N47	96w40	6:26:40
Lasara 245	1	26N28	97w55	6:31:40
Las Milpas 108	1	26N12	98w10	6:32:40
Las Rusias 31	1	26N08	97w38	6:30:32
Lassater 158	1	32N54	94w33	6:18:12
Latch 230	1	32N44	94w57	6:19:48
Latex 183	1	32N21	94w06	6:16:24
Latexo 113	1	31N24	95w29	6:21:56
La Tijera 108	1	26N10	98w03	6:32:12
Latium 239	1	30N11	96w36	6:26:24
Laughlin 233	1	29N21	100w46	6:43:04
Laughlin Air Force Base 233	1	29N21	100w50	6:43:20
Laureles 31	1	26N07	97w26	6:29:44
Laurel Heights 15	1	29N27	98w30	6:34:00
La Vernia 247	1	29N21	98w07	6:32:28
La Villa 108	1	26N18	97w55	6:31:40
Lavon 43	1	33N02	96w26	6:25:44
Lavon Beach Estates 43	1	33N10	96w22	6:25:28
Lavon Shores Estates 43	1	33N08	96w37	6:26:28
Law 21	1	30N40	96w22	6:25:28
La Ward 120	1	28N51	96w28	6:25:52
Lawn 221	1	32N08	99w45	6:39:00
Lawrence 129	1	32N45	96w29	6:25:56
Lawrence Springs 234	1	32N41	95w43	6:22:52
Lawson 57	1	32N42	96w34	6:26:16
Lawsonville 201	1	31N55	94w41	6:18:44
Lazare 51	1	34N17	100w00	6:40:00
Lazbuddie 185	3	34N23	102w37	6:50:28
Leaday 42	1	31N34	99w40	6:38:40
League City 84	1	29N31	95w06	6:20:24
Leagueville 107	1	32N17	95w45	6:23:00
Leakey 193	1	29N44	99w46	6:39:04
Leander 246	1	30N35	97w51	6:31:24
Leary 19	1	33N28	94w13	6:16:52
Lebanon 43	1	33N09	96w50	6:27:20
Ledbetter 75	1	30N09	96w48	6:27:12
Ledbetter Hills 57	1	32N44	96w53	6:27:32
Leedale 14	1	30N56	97w14	6:28:56
Lees 87	1	32N14	101w28	6:45:52
Leesburg 32	1	32N59	95w05	6:20:20
Leesville 89	1	29N25	97w45	6:31:00
Lefors 90	3	35N26	100w48	6:43:12
Leggett 187	1	30N49	94w52	6:19:28
Legion 133	1	30N03	99w09	6:36:36
Lehman 40	1	33N37	102w48	6:51:12
Leigh 102	1	32N36	94w08	6:16:32
Lela 242	3	35N14	100w21	6:41:24
Lelia Lake 65	3	34N54	100w46	6:43:04
Leming 7	1	29N04	98w29	6:33:56
Lena 75	1	29N57	97w02	6:28:08
Lenorah 159	1	32N18	101w53	6:47:32
Lenz 128	1	28N47	97w59	6:31:56
Leo 49	1	33N14	97w35	6:30:20
Leo 144	1	30N25	97w01	6:28:04
Leona 145	1	31N09	95w58	6:23:52
Leonard 74	1	33N23	96w15	6:25:00
Leon Junction 50	1	31N21	97w36	6:30:24
Leon Springs 15	1	29N48	98w45	6:35:00
Leon Valley 15	1	29N28	98w38	6:34:32
Leroy 155	1	31N44	97w01	6:28:04
Lesley 96	1	34N40	100w42	6:42:48
Le Tourneau 92	1	32N27	94w44	6:18:56
Levelland 110	1	33N35	102w23	6:49:32
Leveretts Chapel 201	1	32N16	94w59	6:19:56
Levi 155	1	31N23	97w13	6:28:52
Levita 50	1	31N25	97w43	6:30:52
Lewisville 61	1	33N03	97w00	6:28:00
Lewisville Valley 61	1	33N03	97w03	6:28:12
Lexington 144	1	30N25	97w01	6:28:04
Libby 174	1	31N40	94w38	6:18:32
Liberty 146	1	30N03	94w48	6:19:12
Liberty 152	1	33N35	101w51	6:47:24
Liberty 176	1	30N51	93w45	6:15:00
Liberty 201	1	32N09	94w48	6:19:12
Liberty City 92	1	32N34	94w55	6:19:40
Liberty Grove 57	1	32N53	96w30	6:26:00
Liberty Hill 109	1	31N57	97w19	6:29:16
Liberty Hill 166	1	30N39	97w00	6:28:00
Liberty Hill 246	1	30N40	97w55	6:31:40
Liggett 57	1	32N51	96w58	6:27:52
Lilac 166	1	30N37	97w12	6:28:48
Lilbert 174	1	31N44	94w54	6:19:36
Lillard 100	1	30N16	94w11	6:16:44
Lillian 126	1	32N30	97w11	6:28:44
Lilly 44	3	34N51	100w10	6:40:40
Lily Island 187	1	30N55	94w44	6:18:56
Lincoln 144	1	30N17	96w58	6:27:52
Lincoln Park 61	1	33N18	96w59	6:27:56
Lindale 212	1	32N31	95w25	6:21:40
Lindberg 220	1	32N41	97w13	6:28:52
Linden 34	1	33N01	94w22	6:17:28
Lindenau 62	1	29N07	97w22	6:29:28
Lindsay 49	1	33N38	97w13	6:28:52
Lingleville 72	1	32N15	98w23	6:33:32
Link Five 101	1	29N40	95w02	6:20:08
Linkwood Estates 220	1	32N44	97w31	6:30:04
Linn 108	1	26N34	98w07	6:32:28
Linwood 37	1	31N39	95w04	6:20:16
Lipan 111	1	32N31	98w03	6:32:12
Lipscomb 148	3	36N14	100w16	6:41:04
Lissie 241	1	29N33	96w13	6:24:52
Littig 227	1	30N19	97w27	6:29:48
Little Cypress 181	1	30N10	93w46	6:15:04
Little Elm 61	1	33N10	96w56	6:27:44
Littlefield 140	1	33N55	102w20	6:49:20
Little Hope 250	1	32N58	95w17	6:21:08
Little Mexico 186	1	30N54	102w53	6:51:32
Little River 14	1	30N59	97w22	6:29:28
Lively 129	1	32N26	96w05	6:24:20
Live Oak 15	1	29N33	98w20	6:33:20
Liveoak 182	1	32N31	98w03	6:32:12
Liverpool 20	1	29N18	95w17	6:21:08
Livingston 187	1	30N43	94w56	6:19:44
Llano 150	1	30N45	98w41	6:34:44
Lobo 55	1	30N54	104w47	6:59:08
Lochridge 20	1	29N21	95w28	6:21:52
Locker 206	1	31N16	98w57	6:35:48
Lockett 244	1	34N05	99w22	6:37:28
Lockettville 110	1	33N25	102w09	6:48:36
Lockhart 28	1	29N53	97w40	6:30:40
Lockney 77	1	34N07	101w27	6:45:48
Loco 38	1	34N26	100w13	6:40:52
Locust 91	1	33N46	96w40	6:26:40
Lodi 158	1	32N53	94w17	6:17:08
Lodwick 158	1	32N46	94w21	6:17:24
Loeb 100	1	30N11	94w11	6:16:44
Loebau 144	1	30N17	96w52	6:27:28
Logan 183	1	31N58	93w57	6:15:48
Lohn 154	1	31N19	99w25	6:37:40
Loire 247	1	28N58	98w29	6:33:56
Lois 49	1	33N29	97w10	6:28:40
Lolaville 43	1	33N09	96w50	6:27:20
Lolita 120	1	28N50	96w33	6:26:12
Loma 236	1	30N37	95w53	6:23:32
Loma Alta	1	29N55	100w46	6:43:04
Loma Vista 254	1	28N57	99w37	6:38:28
Lomax 101	1	29N41	95w03	6:20:12
Lomax 114	1	32N14	101w28	6:45:52
Lometa 141	1	31N13	98w24	6:33:36
Lomo Alta 156	1	28N28	98w33	6:34:12
London 134	1	30N41	99w35	6:38:20
Lone Camp 182	1	32N46	98w18	6:33:12
Lone Cedar 70	1	32N05	96w48	6:27:12
Lone Elm 70	1	32N24	96w50	6:27:20
Lone Elm 129	1	32N45	96w30	6:26:00
Lone Grove 150	1	30N49	98w35	6:34:20
Lone Mountain 230	1	32N44	94w57	6:19:48
Lone Oak 15	1	29N23	98w24	6:33:36
Lone Oak 116	1	33N00	95w57	6:23:48
Lone Pine 1	1	31N46	95w38	6:22:32
Lone Star 14	1	31N07	97w46	6:31:04
Lone Star 77	1	34N07	101w27	6:45:48
Lone Star 172	1	32N55	94w43	6:18:52
Lone Star 225	1	33N11	94w51	6:19:24
Long Branch 67	1	32N16	98w50	6:35:20
Long Branch 183	1	32N04	94w34	6:18:16
Longfellow 186	1	30N10	102w38	6:50:32
Long Lake 1	1	31N46	95w38	6:22:32
Long Mott 29	1	28N29	96w46	6:27:04
Long Point 79	1	29N24	95w50	6:23:20
Long Point 101	1	29N48	95w30	6:22:00
Long Point 102	1	32N42	94w07	6:16:28
Longpoint 239	1	30N11	96w36	6:26:24
Longview 92	1	32N30	94w44	6:18:56
Longview Heights 102	1	32N27	94w44	6:18:56
Longworth 76	1	32N39	100w21	6:41:24
Looneyville 174	1	31N49	94w50	6:19:20
Loop 83	1	32N55	102w25	6:49:40
Lopeno 253	1	26N43	99w07	6:36:28
Lopezville 108	1	26N12	98w09	6:32:36
Loraine 168	1	32N25	100w43	6:42:52
Lorena 155	1	31N23	97w13	6:28:52
Lorenzo 54	1	33N40	101w32	6:46:08
Los Angeles 142	1	28N28	99w00	6:36:00
Los Coyotes 245	1	26N25	97w48	6:31:12
Los Cuates 31	1	26N08	97w38	6:30:32
Los Ebanos 108	1	26N14	98w34	6:34:16
Los Fresnos 31	1	26N04	97w29	6:29:56
Los Indios 31	1	26N03	97w45	6:31:00
Los Jardines 15	1	29N25	98w34	6:34:16
Losoya 15	1	29N21	98w30	6:34:00
Los Saenz 214	1	26N24	99w00	6:36:00
Lott 73	1	31N12	97w02	6:28:08
Louise 241	1	29N06	96w24	6:25:36
Love Chapel 34	1	33N00	94w38	6:18:32
Lovelace 109	1	32N01	97w07	6:28:28
Lovelady 113	1	31N08	95w27	6:21:48
Lovell Lake 123	1	30N06	94w09	6:16:36
Loving 252	1	33N16	98w31	6:34:04
Lowake 48	1	31N34	100w05	6:40:20
Lowry Crossing 43	1	33N08	96w37	6:26:28
Loyal Valley 160	1	30N35	99w00	6:36:00
Loyola Beach 137	1	27N18	97w49	6:31:16
Lozano 31	1	26N11	97w32	6:30:08
Lubbock 152	1	33N35	101w51	6:47:24
Lucas 43	1	33N05	96w35	6:26:20
Luckenback 86	1	30N17	98w52	6:35:28
Lucky Ridge 249	1	33N05	97w34	6:30:16
Lueders 127	1	32N48	99w37	6:38:28
Luella 91	1	33N38	96w36	6:26:24
Lufkin 3	1	31N21	94w44	6:18:56
Lufkin Junction 212	1	32N20	95w18	6:21:12
Luling 28	1	29N41	97w39	6:30:36
Lull 108	1	26N17	98w10	6:32:40
Lumberton 100	1	30N16	94w11	6:16:44
Lums Chapel 140	1	33N50	102w20	6:49:20
Lund 227	1	30N21	97w22	6:29:28
Lusk 224	1	33N01	99w03	6:36:12
Luther 114	1	32N14	101w28	6:45:52
Lutie 44	3	35N01	100w13	6:40:52
Luxello 15	1	29N29	98w27	6:33:48
Lydia 194	1	33N27	94w46	6:19:04
Lyford 245	1	26N25	97w48	6:31:12
Lynchburg 101	1	29N46	95w05	6:20:20
Lyncrest 101	1	29N52	95w20	6:21:20
Lyons 26	1	30N23	96w34	6:26:16
Lytle 7	1	29N14	98w48	6:35:12
Lytton Springs 28	1	29N56	97w34	6:30:16
Mabank 129	1	32N22	96w06	6:24:24
Mabelle 12	1	33N35	99w16	6:37:04
Mabry 194	1	33N36	95w03	6:20:12
Macdona 15	1	29N20	98w42	6:34:48
Macedonia 19	1	33N26	94w04	6:16:16
Macedonia 146	1	30N18	95w07	6:20:28
Mackay 241	1	29N19	96w06	6:24:24
Macon 80	1	33N09	94w58	6:19:52
Macune 203	1	31N32	94w07	6:16:28
Macy 21	1	30N54	96w24	6:25:36
Madero 108	1	26N13	98w20	6:33:20
Madisonville 157	1	30N57	95w55	6:23:40
Magasco 202	1	31N17	93w59	6:15:56
Magnet 241	1	29N09	95w59	6:23:56

TEXAS

Magnolia 170 1 30N13 95w45 6:23:00
Magnolia Beach 29 1 28N34 96w33 6:26:12
Magnolia Gardens 101 1 29N53 95w06 6:20:24
Magnolia Springs 121 1 30N44 94w02 6:16:08
Magpetco 123 1 29N58 93w59 6:15:56
Mahl 174 1 31N40 94w38 6:18:32
Mahomet 27 1 30N45 98w03 6:32:12
Mahoney 112 1 33N08 95w36 6:22:24
Main Place 57 1 32N47 96w47 6:27:08
Majors 80 1 33N11 95w13 6:20:52
Malakoff 107 1 32N10 96w01 6:24:04
Mallard 169 1 33N40 97w43 6:30:52
Malone 109 1 31N55 96w54 6:27:36
Malta 19 1 33N28 94w25 6:17:40
Mambrino 111 1 32N27 97w47 6:31:08
Manchaca 227 1 30N08 97w50 6:31:20
Manchester 194 1 33N51 95w10 6:20:40
Manda 227 1 30N21 97w33 6:30:12
Mangum 67 1 32N24 98w49 6:35:16
Manheim 144 1 30N13 97w07 6:28:28
Mankin 107 1 32N09 96w05 6:24:20
Mankins 5 1 33N47 98w48 6:35:12
Manor 227 1 30N21 97w33 6:30:12
Mansfield 220 1 32N34 97w09 6:28:36
Manvel 20 1 29N28 95w21 6:21:24
Maple 9 1 33N51 102w54 6:51:36
Maple Crest Acres 181 1 30N09 94w01 6:16:04
Maple Springs 225 1 33N09 94w58 6:19:52
Mapleton 113 1 31N19 95w27 6:21:48
Marathon 22 1 30N12 103w15 6:53:00
Marble Falls 27 1 30N35 98w16 6:33:04
March Trailer Court 116 1 32N43 96w00 6:24:00
Marfa 189 1 30N19 104w01 6:56:04
Margaret 78 1 34N03 99w39 6:38:36
Marie 200 1 31N53 100w18 6:41:12
Marietta 34 1 33N10 94w33 6:18:12
Marilee 43 1 33N27 96w45 6:27:00
Marion 94 1 29N37 98w07 6:32:28
Marion West 158 1 32N48 94w30 6:18:00
Markham 161 1 28N58 96w04 6:24:16
Markley 252 1 33N16 98w31 6:34:04
Marlin 73 1 31N18 96w54 6:27:36
Marquez 145 1 31N14 96w15 6:25:00
Marshall 102 1 32N33 94w23 6:17:32
Marshall Ford 227 1 30N23 97w45 6:31:00
Marston 187 1 30N43 94w56 6:19:44
Mart 155 1 31N33 96w50 6:27:20
Martindale 28 1 29N52 97w49 6:31:16
Martins Mills 234 1 32N25 95w48 6:23:12
Martin Springs 112 1 33N08 95w36 6:22:24
Martinsville 174 1 31N39 94w25 6:17:40
Marvin 139 1 33N40 95w31 6:22:04
Marvin 198 1 30N59 96w41 6:26:44
Mary Hardin-Baylor 14 1 31N03 97w28 6:29:52
Maryneal 177 1 32N14 100w27 6:41:48
Marysville 49 1 33N46 97w20 6:29:20
Mason 160 1 30N45 99w14 6:36:56
Massey Lake 1 1 31N50 95w50 6:23:20
Masterson 171 3 35N38 101w58 6:47:52
Matador 173 1 34N01 100w49 6:43:16
Matagorda 161 1 28N42 95w58 6:23:52
Mathis 205 1 28N06 97w50 6:31:20
Matinburg 32 1 33N00 94w58 6:19:52
Mattox 176 1 31N00 93w42 6:14:48
Maud 19 1 33N20 94w21 6:17:24
Mauriceville 181 1 30N12 93w52 6:15:28
Maurin 89 1 29N30 97w27 6:29:48
Maverick 200 1 31N50 100w12 6:40:48
Maxdale 14 1 31N07 97w46 6:31:04
Maxey 139 1 33N38 95w42 6:22:48
Maxwell 28 1 29N53 97w48 6:31:12
May 25 1 31N59 98w55 6:35:40
Maydelle 37 1 31N48 95w18 6:21:12
Mayfield 109 1 32N10 97w09 6:28:36
Mayflower 176 1 31N00 93w42 6:14:48
Mayflower 201 1 32N19 94w31 6:18:04
Mayhill 61 1 33N11 97w04 6:28:16
Maynard 204 1 30N32 95w29 6:21:56
Maypearl 70 1 32N19 97w01 6:28:04
Maysfield 166 1 30N54 96w51 6:27:24
McAdoo 63 1 33N44 101w00 6:44:00
McAllen 108 1 26N12 98w14 6:32:56
McBeth 20 1 29N09 95w27 6:21:48
McCamey 231 1 31N08 102w14 6:48:56
McCaulley 76 1 32N47 100w13 6:40:52
McClanahan 73 1 31N18 96w53 6:27:32
McColl 108 1 26N12 98w15 6:33:00
McCoy 7 1 28N52 98w21 6:33:24
McCoy 77 1 33N59 101w20 6:45:20
McCoy 129 1 32N50 96w06 6:24:24
McCoy 183 1 32N02 94w22 6:17:28
McDade 11 1 30N17 97w14 6:28:56
McElroy 202 1 31N15 93w58 6:15:52
McFaddin 235 1 28N33 97w01 6:28:04
McGalin 121 1 30N27 93w57 6:15:48
McGregor 155 1 31N27 97w24 6:29:36
McKee 171 3 36N01 101w49 6:47:16
McKibben 98 3 36N12 101w12 6:44:48
McKinney 43 1 33N12 96w37 6:26:28
McKnight 201 1 32N09 94w48 6:19:12
McLean 90 3 35N14 100w36 6:42:24
McLendon 199 1 32N53 96w30 6:26:00
McLendon-Chisholm 199 1 32N53 96w30 6:26:00
McLeod 34 1 32N57 94w05 6:16:20

McMahan 28 1 29N56 97w34 6:30:16
McMillin 206 1 31N12 98w44 6:34:56
McMurray 221 1 32N25 99w46 6:39:04
McNair 101 1 29N49 95w02 6:20:08
McNair Village 14 1 31N08 97w46 6:31:04
McNary 115 2 31N15 105w48 7:03:12
McNeil 28 1 29N41 97w39 6:30:36
McNeil 227 1 30N27 97w43 6:30:52
McQueeney 94 1 29N35 98w02 6:32:08
Meador Grove 14 1 31N18 97w22 6:29:28
Meadow 223 1 33N20 102w12 6:48:48
Mecca 157 1 31N03 96w07 6:24:28
Medical Center 57 1 32N49 96w49 6:27:16
Medicine Mound 99 1 34N11 99w36 6:38:24
Medill 139 1 33N40 95w31 6:22:04
Medina 10 1 29N48 99w15 6:37:00
Medina Base 15 1 29N23 98w36 6:34:24
Meeker 123 1 30N06 94w09 6:16:36
Meeks 14 1 31N01 97w00 6:28:00
Megargel 5 1 33N27 98w56 6:35:44
Meldrum 210 1 31N57 94w15 6:17:00
Melissa 43 1 33N17 96w34 6:26:16
Melody Hills 220 1 32N50 97w17 6:29:08
Melrose 92 1 32N22 94w52 6:19:28
Melrose 174 1 31N34 94w29 6:17:56
Melton 116 1 33N08 96w07 6:24:28
Melvin 154 1 31N12 99w35 6:38:20
Memorial Park 101 1 29N47 95w32 6:22:08
Memphis 96 1 34N44 100w33 6:42:12
Menard 164 1 30N55 99w47 6:39:08
Mendoza 28 1 30N01 97w41 6:30:44
Menlow 109 1 31N53 97w05 6:28:20
Mentone 151 1 31N42 103w36 6:54:24
Mentz 45 1 29N42 96w33 6:26:12
Mercedes 108 1 26N09 97w55 6:31:40
Mercer's Gap 47 1 31N54 98w36 6:34:24
Merchandise Mart 57 1 32N47 96w48 6:27:12
Mercury 154 1 31N28 99w10 6:36:40
Mereta 226 1 31N27 100w08 6:40:32
Meridian 18 1 31N56 97w39 6:30:36
Merit 116 1 33N13 96w17 6:25:08
Merkel 221 1 32N28 100w01 6:40:04
Merle 26 1 30N21 96w32 6:26:08
Mertens 109 1 32N04 96w54 6:27:36
Mertzon 118 1 31N16 100w49 6:43:16
Mesa 71 2 31N32 106w10 7:04:40
Mesquite 17 1 32N58 101w50 6:47:20
Mesquite 57 1 32N46 96w36 6:26:24
Metcalf Gap 182 1 32N33 98w30 6:34:00
Mexia 147 1 31N41 96w29 6:25:56
Mexico 116 1 32N54 96w05 6:24:20
Meyers Village 68 1 31N52 102w22 6:49:28
Meyersville 62 1 28N55 97w21 6:29:24
Miami 197 3 35N42 100w38 6:42:32
Mickey 77 1 34N07 101w27 6:45:48
Mico 163 1 29N32 98w56 6:35:44
Middleton 145 1 31N16 95w59 6:23:56
Middle Water 103 3 35N51 102w47 6:51:08
Midfield 161 1 28N56 96w13 6:24:52
Midkiff 231 1 31N38 101w50 6:47:20
Midland 165 1 32N00 102w05 6:48:20
Midline 170 1 30N18 95w07 6:20:28
Midlothian 70 1 32N29 97w00 6:28:00
Midway 14 1 31N03 97w28 6:29:52
Midway 32 1 33N00 94w58 6:19:52
Midway 58 1 32N44 101w58 6:47:52
Midway 74 1 33N35 96w11 6:24:44
Midway 109 1 32N01 97w07 6:28:28
Midway 143 1 29N26 97w10 6:28:40
Midway 152 1 33N32 101w35 6:46:20
Midway 157 1 31N02 95w45 6:23:00
Midway 170 1 30N18 95w07 6:20:28
Midway 205 1 27N59 97w24 6:29:36
Midway 208 1 32N38 100w46 6:43:04
Midway 212 1 32N30 95w10 6:20:40
Midyett 183 1 32N18 94w10 6:16:40
Miguel 82 1 29N03 98w52 6:35:28
Milam 202 1 31N26 93w51 6:15:24
Milano 166 1 30N43 96w52 6:27:28
Milburn 154 1 31N13 99w13 6:36:52
Mildred 175 1 32N06 96w31 6:26:04
Mile High 115 2 31N11 105w21 7:01:24
Miles 200 1 31N36 100w11 6:40:44
Milford 70 1 32N07 96w57 6:27:48
Mill Creek 239 1 30N10 96w24 6:25:36
Miller Grove 32 1 33N00 94w58 6:19:52
Miller Grove 112 1 33N08 95w50 6:23:20
Millersview 48 1 31N25 99w45 6:39:00
Millett 142 1 28N35 99w12 6:36:48
Millheim 8 1 29N47 96w09 6:24:36
Millican 21 1 30N28 96w12 6:24:48
Milligan 43 1 33N08 96w37 6:26:28
Mill Pond 174 1 31N40 94w38 6:18:32
Millsap 184 1 32N45 98w01 6:32:04
Millwood 43 1 32N59 96w20 6:25:20
Milton 139 1 33N32 95w19 6:21:16
Minden 201 1 32N01 94w42 6:18:48
Mineola 250 1 32N40 95w29 6:21:56
Mineral 13 1 29N34 98w08 6:32:32
Mineral Heights 116 1 33N08 96w07 6:24:28
Mineral Wells 182 1 32N48 98w07 6:32:28
Minerva 166 1 30N46 96w59 6:27:56
Mings Chapel 230 1 32N44 94w57 6:19:48
Mingus 182 1 32N32 98w25 6:33:40
Minter 139 1 33N35 95w24 6:21:36
Minters Chapel 220 1 32N57 97w07 6:28:28

Mirando City 240 1 27N26 99w00 6:36:00
Mission 108 1 26N13 98w19 6:33:16
Mission Valley 46 1 29N42 98w08 6:32:32
Mission Valley 235 1 28N48 96w59 6:27:56
Missouri City 79 1 29N37 95w32 6:22:08
Mixon 37 1 32N08 95w07 6:20:28
Mobeetie 242 3 35N31 100w26 6:41:44
Moffatt 14 1 31N12 97w28 6:29:52
Moffett 3 1 30N15 95w32 6:22:08
Monadale 246 1 30N33 97w33 6:30:12
Monahans 238 1 31N36 102w54 6:51:36
Monaville 237 1 30N06 96w02 6:24:08
Monkstown 74 1 33N48 95w56 6:23:44
Monroe 201 1 32N22 94w52 6:19:28
Monroe City 36 1 29N47 94w35 6:18:20
Mont 143 1 29N27 96w56 6:27:44
Montague 169 1 33N40 97w43 6:30:52
Montague Village 50 1 31N07 97w50 6:31:20
Montalba 1 1 31N53 95w38 6:22:32
Mont Belvieu 36 1 29N51 94w53 6:19:32
Monte Alto 108 1 26N22 97w58 6:31:52
Montell 232 1 29N13 99w47 6:39:08
Monteola 13 1 28N49 97w51 6:31:24
Montgomery 170 1 30N23 95w42 6:22:48
Montgomery Gardens 212 1 32N20 95w18 6:21:12
Monthalia 89 1 29N26 97w32 6:30:08
Monticello 225 1 33N09 94w58 6:19:52
Moody 155 1 31N18 97w21 6:29:24
Moonshine Hill 101 1 30N00 95w14 6:20:56
Moore 82 1 29N03 99w01 6:36:04
Moore's Chapel 74 1 33N35 96w11 6:24:44
Moores Crossing 227 1 30N12 97w40 6:30:40
Moores Station 1 32N11 95w34 6:22:16
Moore Station 107 1 32N07 95w41 6:22:44
Mooresville 73 1 31N17 97w04 6:28:16
Mooring 21 1 30N40 96w22 6:25:28
Morales 120 1 29N08 96w46 6:27:04
Moran 209 1 32N33 99w10 6:36:40
Moravia 143 1 29N41 96w54 6:27:36
Morgan 18 1 32N01 97w37 6:30:28
Morgan Mill 72 1 32N23 98w10 6:32:40
Morgan's Point 101 1 29N41 94w59 6:19:56
Morgan's Point Resort 14 1 31N03 97w28 6:29:52
Morrill 37 1 31N39 95w04 6:20:16
Morris Ranch 86 1 30N17 98w52 6:35:28
Morse 98 3 36N04 101w29 6:45:56
Morton 40 1 33N44 102w46 6:51:04
Morton 102 1 32N43 94w45 6:19:00
Morton Valley 67 1 32N28 98w49 6:35:16
Moscow 187 1 30N55 94w50 6:19:20
Mosheim 18 1 31N39 97w28 6:29:52
Moss Bluff 146 1 30N04 94w48 6:19:12
Moss Hill 146 1 30N15 94w45 6:19:00
Mostyn 170 1 30N13 95w45 6:23:00
Moulton 143 1 29N35 97w09 6:28:36
Mound 50 1 31N21 97w38 6:30:32
Mound City 1 1 31N29 95w29 6:21:56
Mountain 50 1 31N25 97w43 6:30:52
Mountain Creek 57 1 32N44 96w59 6:27:56
Mountain Home 133 1 30N10 99w22 6:37:28
Mountain Peak 70 1 32N31 97w11 6:28:44
Mountain Springs 49 1 33N24 96w57 6:27:48
Mount Blanco 54 1 33N40 101w14 6:44:56
Mount Calm 109 1 31N46 96w53 6:27:32
Mount Calvary 183 1 32N09 94w20 6:17:20
Mount Carmel 243 1 34N02 98w55 6:35:40
Mount Enterprise 201 1 31N55 94w41 6:18:44
Mount Enterprise 250 1 32N40 95w29 6:21:56
Mount Houston 101 1 29N54 95w18 6:21:12
Mount Joy 60 1 33N22 95w41 6:22:44
Mount Lucas 149 1 28N13 97w58 6:31:52
Mount Olive 143 1 29N26 97w10 6:28:40
Mount Pleasant 225 1 33N09 94w58 6:19:52
Mount Selman 37 1 32N04 95w17 6:21:08
Mount Sharp 105 1 30N10 98w05 6:32:20
Mount Sylvan 212 1 32N27 95w28 6:21:52
Mount Union 121 1 30N39 93w54 6:15:36
Mount Vernon 80 1 33N11 95w13 6:20:52
Mount Zion 237 1 29N47 95w57 6:23:48
Mozelle 42 1 31N49 99w26 6:37:44
Muddig 116 1 33N25 95w56 6:23:44
Mudville 21 1 30N40 96w22 6:25:28
Muellersville 239 1 30N10 96w24 6:25:36
Muenster 49 1 33N39 97w23 6:29:32
Mulberry 74 1 33N40 96w14 6:24:56
Muldoon 75 1 29N49 97w04 6:28:16
Muleshoe 9 1 34N13 102w43 6:50:52
Mullin 167 1 31N33 98w40 6:34:40
Mullins Prairie 75 1 29N54 96w52 6:27:28
Mumford 198 1 30N44 96w34 6:26:16
Muncy 77 1 34N07 101w27 6:45:48
Munday 138 1 33N27 99w38 6:38:32
Mungerville 58 1 32N44 101w58 6:47:52
Munson 199 1 32N59 96w20 6:25:20
Murchison 107 1 32N17 95w45 6:23:00

TEXAS

Murphy 43 1 33N01 96w37 6:26:28
Murray 252 1 33N06 98w35 6:34:20
Murryhill 152 1 33N33 101w53 6:47:32
Musgrove 80 1 32N58 95w17 6:21:08
Mustang 61 1 33N24 96w57 6:27:48
Mustang 147 1 31N45 96w39 6:26:36
Mustang 175 1 32N06 96w31 6:26:04
Myra 49 1 33N39 97w23 6:29:32
Myrtle Springs 234 1 32N37 95w56 6:23:44
Naaman 57 1 32N54 96w37 6:26:28
Nacogdoches 174 1 31N36 94w39 6:18:36
Nada 45 1 29N24 96w23 6:25:32
Nadeau 84 1 29N23 94w57 6:19:48
Nancy 3 1 31N09 94w26 6:17:44
Naples 172 1 33N12 94w41 6:18:44
Naruna 27 1 31N04 98w11 6:32:44
Nash 19 1 33N26 94w08 6:16:32
Nash 70 1 32N15 96w52 6:27:28
Nassau Bay 101 1 29N47 95w23 6:21:32
Nat 174 1 31N49 94w50 6:19:20
Natalia 163 1 29N11 98w52 6:35:28
Natural Bridge Caverns 15 1 29N30 98w25 6:33:40
Naval Air 178 1 27N39 97w18 6:29:12
Navarro 175 1 31N57 96w41 6:26:44
Navarro Mills 175 1 31N57 96w37 6:26:28
Navasota 93 1 30N23 96w05 6:24:20
Navo 61 1 33N09 96w50 6:27:20
Nazareth 35 3 34N33 102w06 6:48:24
Neals Valley 70 1 32N20 96w38 6:26:32
Necessity 215 1 32N45 98w55 6:35:40
Nechanitz 75 1 30N09 96w48 6:27:12
Neches 1 1 31N52 95w30 6:22:00
Neches Indian Village 37 1 31N39 95w04 6:20:16
Neches Junction 123 1 29N55 93w56 6:15:44
Nederland 123 1 29N59 94w00 6:16:00
Needmore 9 1 34N04 102w32 6:50:08
Needmore 223 1 33N20 102w20 6:49:20
Needville 79 1 29N24 95w50 6:23:20
Negley 194 1 33N36 95w03 6:20:12
Neinda 127 1 32N53 100w08 6:40:32
Nell 149 1 28N49 97w51 6:31:24
Nelsonville 8 1 29N57 96w15 6:25:00
Nelta 112 1 33N14 95w29 6:21:56
Nemo 213 1 32N16 97w39 6:30:36
Nesbitt 102 1 32N36 94w28 6:17:52
Nesbitt 198 1 31N10 96w41 6:26:44
Neuville 210 1 31N41 94w09 6:16:36
Nevada 43 1 33N02 96w23 6:25:32
Newark 249 1 33N00 97w29 6:29:56
New Baden 198 1 31N03 96w26 6:25:44
New Berlin 94 1 29N35 97w58 6:31:52
New Boston 19 1 33N28 94w25 6:17:40
New Braunfels 46 1 29N42 98w08 6:32:32
Newburg 47 1 31N54 98w36 6:34:24
Newby 145 1 31N22 96w09 6:24:36
New Caney 170 1 30N09 95w13 6:20:52
Newcastle 252 1 33N12 98w44 6:34:56
New Clarkson 166 1 31N04 96w58 6:27:52
New Colony 34 1 33N00 94w22 6:17:28
New Corn Hill 246 1 30N49 97w36 6:30:24
New Deal 152 1 33N44 101w50 6:47:20
New Fountain 163 1 29N21 99w08 6:36:32
Newgulf 241 1 29N15 95w57 6:23:48
New Harmony 210 1 31N46 93w52 6:15:28
New Harmony 212 1 32N20 95w18 6:21:12
Newharp 169 1 33N32 97w33 6:30:12
New Hebron 102 1 32N21 94w06 6:16:24
New Home 153 1 33N20 101w55 6:47:40
New Hope 37 1 31N58 95w16 6:21:04
New Hope 43 1 33N08 96w37 6:26:28
New Hope 57 1 32N46 96w37 6:26:28
New Hope 107 1 32N20 95w37 6:22:28
New Hope 127 1 33N00 99w42 6:38:48
New Hope 201 1 32N22 94w52 6:19:28
New Hope 204 1 30N18 95w07 6:20:28
New Hope 212 1 32N20 95w18 6:21:12
New Hope 250 1 32N40 95w29 6:21:56
Newlin 96 1 34N35 100w27 6:41:48
New London 201 1 32N15 94w56 6:19:44
New Lynn 153 1 33N10 101w48 6:47:12
Newman 71 2 31N52 106w26 7:05:44
New Mine 32 1 33N00 94w58 6:19:52
New Mobeetie 3 35N32 100w26 6:41:44
New Moore 153 1 32N58 101w50 6:47:20
New Mountain 230 1 32N44 94w57 6:19:48
Newport 39 1 33N28 98w01 6:32:04
Newport 101 1 29N54 95w04 6:20:16
New Prospect 201 1 32N09 94w48 6:19:12
New Prospect 210 1 31N54 94w24 6:17:36
New Salem 182 1 32N36 98w13 6:32:52
New Salem 201 1 32N09 94w48 6:19:12
Newsome 32 1 32N59 95w08 6:20:32
New Summerfield 37 1 31N59 95w06 6:20:24
New Sweden 227 1 30N21 97w33 6:30:12
New Taiton 241 1 29N19 96w20 6:25:20
Newton 176 1 30N51 93w46 6:15:04
New Ulm 8 1 29N53 96w29 6:25:56
New Waverly 236 1 30N32 95w29 6:21:56
New Wehdem 8 1 30N10 96w24 6:25:36
New Willard 187 1 30N48 94w55 6:19:40
New York 107 1 32N07 95w41 6:22:44
Neylandville 116 1 33N12 96w00 6:24:00
Nickel 89 1 29N30 97w27 6:29:48
Nickelberry 34 1 33N10 94w33 6:18:12
Nickel Creek 55 1 32N25 104w14 6:56:56
Niederwald 105 1 29N59 97w53 6:31:32
Nigton 228 1 31N13 94w58 6:19:52
Nile 166 1 30N37 97w12 6:28:48
Nimitz 15 1 29N33 98w31 6:34:04
Nimrod 67 1 32N23 98w59 6:35:56
Nineveh 145 1 31N28 96w04 6:24:16
Nix 141 1 31N04 98w11 6:32:44
Nixon 89 1 29N16 97w46 6:31:04
Noack 246 1 30N34 97w25 6:29:40
Nobility 74 1 33N25 96w03 6:24:12
Noble 139 1 33N36 95w49 6:23:16
Nockenut 247 1 29N14 97w58 6:31:52
Nocona 169 1 33N47 97w44 6:30:56
Nogalus 228 1 31N03 95w08 6:20:32
Nolan 177 1 32N16 100w15 6:41:00
Nolanville 14 1 31N05 97w36 6:30:24
Nome 123 1 30N02 94w25 6:17:40
Nona 100 1 30N22 94w19 6:17:16
Noodle 127 1 32N28 99w49 6:39:16
Noonday 212 1 32N15 95w24 6:21:36
Nopal 62 1 28N59 97w30 6:30:00
Nordheim 62 1 28N55 97w37 6:30:28
Norias 131 1 26N47 97w47 6:31:08
Normandy 1 28N55 100w36 6:42:24
Normandy 162 1 29N43 99w46 6:39:04
Normangee 145 1 31N02 96w07 6:24:28
Normanna 13 1 28N32 97w47 6:31:08
Norman's Crossing 246 1 30N34 97w25 6:29:40
Norse 18 1 31N47 97w35 6:30:20
North Amarillo 188 3 35N14 101w48 6:47:12
North Austin 227 1 30N18 97w43 6:30:52
Northaven 57 1 32N53 96w51 6:27:24
North Broadway 15 1 29N33 98w29 6:33:56
North Cedar 228 1 31N13 94w58 6:19:52
North Cleveland 146 1 30N21 95w06 6:20:24
North College 152 1 33N34 101w52 6:47:28
North Cowden 1 32N01 102w31 6:50:04
Northcrest 155 1 31N38 97w06 6:28:24
Northcrest Estates 235 1 28N48 96w59 6:27:56
Northfield 173 1 34N17 100w36 6:42:24
Northgate 235 1 28N48 96w59 6:27:56
North Groesbeck 99 1 34N18 99w44 6:38:56
North Houston 101 1 29N56 95w30 6:22:00
North Houston Heights 101 1 29N52 95w20 6:21:20
North Jefferson 158 1 32N46 94w21 6:17:24
North Jim Hogg 124 1 27N14 98w45 6:35:00
Northlake 61 1 33N08 97w16 6:29:04
Northline Terrace 101 1 29N50 95w23 6:21:32
North Oaks 227 1 30N22 97w41 6:30:44
North Port Arthur 123 1 29N55 93w56 6:15:44
North Prairie 73 1 31N17 97w04 6:28:16
North Randall 191 3 35N06 101w52 6:47:28
North Richland Hills 220 1 32N50 97w14 6:28:56
North River 38 1 34N40 100w12 6:40:48
Northrup 144 1 30N11 96w56 6:27:44
North Rusk 37 1 31N48 95w09 6:20:36
North San Pedro 178 1 27N48 97w41 6:30:44
North Shepherd 101 1 29N47 95w23 6:21:32
North Sherman 91 1 33N38 96w36 6:26:24
North Shore 101 1 29N56 95w17 6:21:08
North Texarkana 19 1 33N26 94w04 6:16:16
North Uvalde 232 1 29N13 99w47 6:39:08
North Vidor 181 1 30N09 94w01 6:16:04
Northwest 220 1 32N53 97w29 6:29:56
Northwest 227 1 30N20 97w44 6:30:56
North Zulch 157 1 30N55 96w07 6:24:28
Norton 200 1 31N52 100w08 6:40:32
Norwood 203 1 31N32 94w07 6:16:28
Notla 179 3 36N24 100w48 6:43:12
Notrees 68 1 31N55 102w45 6:51:00
Novice 42 1 31N59 99w37 6:38:28
Novice 139 1 33N40 95w31 6:22:04
Novohrad 143 1 29N35 97w09 6:28:36
Noxville 134 1 30N18 99w15 6:37:00
Nugent 127 1 32N28 99w44 6:38:56
Nursery 235 1 28N56 97w06 6:28:24
Nuway 71 2 32N00 106w36 7:06:24
Oakalla 27 1 31N06 97w41 6:30:44
Oak Dale 72 1 32N13 98w13 6:32:52
Oak Flat 174 1 31N49 94w50 6:19:20
Oak Flat 201 1 31N55 94w41 6:18:44
Oak Forest 89 1 29N30 97w35 6:30:20
Oak Grove 19 1 33N33 94w47 6:19:08
Oak Grove 70 1 32N20 96w38 6:26:32
Oak Grove 220 1 32N33 97w20 6:29:20
Oak Grove 250 1 32N48 95w27 6:21:48
Oak Hill 126 1 32N21 97w23 6:29:32
Oak Hill 201 1 32N09 94w48 6:19:12
Oak Hill 227 1 30N14 97w52 6:31:28
Oakhurst 204 1 30N44 95w19 6:21:16
Oak Island 36 1 29N46 94w42 6:18:48
Oak Knoll 220 1 32N48 97w15 6:29:00
Oak Lake 155 1 31N36 97w06 6:28:24
Oakland 37 1 31N48 95w09 6:20:36
Oakland 45 1 29N36 96w50 6:27:20
Oakland 181 1 30N06 93w46 6:15:04
Oakland 201 1 32N09 94w48 6:19:12
Oakland 234 1 32N33 95w52 6:23:28
Oak Park 133 1 30N03 99w09 6:36:36
Oak Ridge 19 1 33N30 94w37 6:18:28
Oak Ridge 129 1 32N45 96w29 6:25:56
Oak Ridge 174 1 31N40 94w38 6:18:32
Oak Ridge 184 1 32N45 97w43 6:30:52
Oaks 13 1 28N49 97w51 6:31:24
Oaks 220 1 32N47 97w24 6:29:36
Oakville 149 1 29N11 98w52 6:35:28
Oakwood 145 1 31N35 95w51 6:23:24
Oatmeal 27 1 30N45 98w03 6:32:12
O'Brien 104 1 33N23 99w50 6:39:20
Ocee 155 1 31N32 97w27 6:29:48
Ochoa 189 1 29N33 104w23 6:57:32
Odds 147 1 31N25 96w34 6:26:16
Odell 244 3 34N21 99w25 6:37:40
Odem 205 1 27N57 97w35 6:30:20
Odessa 68 1 31N52 102w23 6:49:32
Odom 234 1 32N22 95w59 6:23:56
O'Donnell 153 1 32N58 101w50 6:47:20
Oenaville 14 1 31N06 97w21 6:29:24
O'Farrell 34 1 33N07 94w10 6:16:40
Ogg 191 3 34N45 101w52 6:47:28
Oglesby 50 1 31N25 97w30 6:30:00
Oilla 181 1 30N06 93w46 6:15:04
Oilton 240 1 27N27 98w59 6:35:56
Ojuelas 240 1 27N26 99w00 6:36:00
Oklahoma 170 1 30N13 95w45 6:23:00
Oklahoma Flat 110 1 33N55 102w20 6:49:20
Oklahoma Lane 185 3 34N23 103w02 6:52:08
Oklaunion 244 1 34N08 99w09 6:36:36
Okra 67 1 32N16 98w50 6:35:20
Ola 129 1 32N35 96w17 6:25:08
Old Boston 19 1 33N28 94w25 6:17:40
Old Brazoria 20 1 29N02 95w34 6:22:16
Old Dime Box 144 1 30N21 96w50 6:27:20
Olden 67 1 32N25 98w45 6:35:00
Oldenburg 75 1 29N54 96w52 6:27:28
Old Glory 217 1 33N08 100w03 6:40:12
Old Larissa 37 1 32N08 95w19 6:21:16
Old Laurel 176 1 30N27 93w57 6:15:48
Old London 201 1 32N15 94w55 6:19:40
Old Mobeetie 242 3 35N31 100w26 6:41:44
Old Moulton 143 1 29N35 97w09 6:28:36
Old Ocean 20 1 29N05 95w45 6:23:00
Old River 26 1 30N30 96w27 6:25:48
Old River Terrace 101 1 29N46 95w09 6:20:36
Old Round Rock 246 1 30N31 97w41 6:30:44
Old Salem 176 1 30N37 93w53 6:15:32
Old Union 19 1 33N21 94w31 6:18:04
Old Union 147 1 31N25 96w34 6:26:16
Old Union 220 1 32N57 97w07 6:28:28
Oletha 147 1 31N25 96w34 6:26:16
Olfen 200 1 31N39 100w03 6:40:12
Olin 97 1 31N59 98w02 6:32:08
Olivia 29 1 28N37 96w38 6:26:32
Ollie 187 1 30N49 94w52 6:19:28
Olmito 31 1 26N01 97w32 6:30:08
Olmos 13 1 28N15 97w41 6:30:44
Olmos Park 15 1 29N28 98w29 6:33:56
Olney 252 1 33N22 98w45 6:35:00
Olton 140 1 34N11 102w08 6:48:32
Omaha 172 1 33N11 94w45 6:19:00
Onalaska 187 1 30N48 95w07 6:20:28
Opdyke 110 1 33N36 102w17 6:49:08
Opelika 107 1 32N17 95w45 6:23:00
Oplin 30 1 32N24 99w30 6:38:00
O'Quinn 75 1 29N54 96w52 6:27:28
Oran 182 1 32N56 98w15 6:33:00
Orange 181 1 30N06 93w44 6:14:56
Orangedale 13 1 28N23 97w42 6:30:48
Orangefield 181 1 30N04 93w51 6:15:24
Orange Grove 125 1 27N58 97w56 6:31:44
Orangeville 74 1 33N31 96w23 6:25:32
Orchard 79 1 29N36 95w58 6:23:52
Ore 230 1 32N48 94w43 6:18:52
Orient 226 1 31N39 100w20 6:41:20
Orla 195 1 31N50 103w55 6:55:40
Orme 220 1 32N43 97w06 6:28:24
Orrs 158 1 32N54 94w33 6:18:12
Orton Hill 174 1 31N40 94w38 6:18:32
Osage 50 1 31N25 97w43 6:30:52
Oscar 14 1 31N06 97w21 6:29:24
Osceola 109 1 32N10 97w09 6:28:36
Otis Chalk 114 1 32N07 101w22 6:45:28
Ottine 89 1 29N36 97w35 6:30:20
Otto 73 1 31N27 96w48 6:27:12
Ovalo 221 1 32N10 99w49 6:39:16
Overton 201 1 32N16 94w59 6:19:56
Ovilla 57 1 32N32 96w53 6:27:32
Owens 25 1 31N59 98w55 6:35:40
Owens 54 1 33N34 101w21 6:45:24
Owensville 198 1 31N01 96w29 6:25:56
Owentown 1 32N26 95w12 6:20:48
Oxford 150 1 30N45 98w41 6:34:44
Oyster Creek 20 1 28N58 95w25 6:21:40
Ozona 53 1 30N43 101w12 6:44:48
Pacio 60 1 33N26 95w39 6:22:36
Packery 239 1 30N10 96w24 6:25:36
Padgett 252 1 33N22 98w45 6:35:00
Paducah 51 1 34N01 100w18 6:41:12
Pagoda 228 1 30N57 95w23 6:21:32
Paige 11 1 30N13 97w07 6:28:28
Paint Rock 48 1 31N31 99w55 6:39:40
Paisano Annex 71 2 31N46 106w26 7:05:44
Pakan 242 3 35N13 100w15 6:41:00
Palacios 161 1 28N42 96w13 6:24:52
Palava 76 1 32N28 100w24 6:41:36
Palestine 1 1 31N46 95w38 6:22:32
Palestine 187 1 30N56 94w36 6:18:24
Palito Blanco 125 1 27N35 98w11 6:32:44
Palmer 70 1 32N26 96w40 6:26:40
Palmetto 204 1 30N44 95w19 6:21:16

Place		Lat.	Long.	Time
Palmhurst 108	1	26N15	98w18	6:33:12
Palmview 108	1	26N17	98w10	6:32:40
Palm Village 31	1	25N55	97w29	6:29:56
Palo Alto 178	1	27N35	97w48	6:31:12
Paloduro 6	3	34N56	100w53	6:43:32
Palo Pinto 182	1	32N46	98w18	6:33:12
Paluxy 111	1	32N16	97w54	6:31:36
Pampa 90	3	35N32	100w58	6:43:52
Pancake 50	1	31N37	97w53	6:31:32
Pandale 233	1	30N43	101w12	6:44:48
Pandora 247	1	29N15	97w50	6:31:20
Panhandle 33	3	35N21	101w23	6:45:32
Panna Maria 128	1	28N57	97w48	6:31:12
Panola 183	1	32N21	94w06	6:16:24
Panorama Estates 116	1	32N43	96w00	6:24:00
Panorama Village 170	1	30N19	95w28	6:21:52
Pantego 220	1	32N43	97w09	6:28:36
Pantex 33	3	35N20	101w35	6:46:20
Papalote 13	1	28N10	97w36	6:30:24
Paradise 249	1	33N09	97w41	6:30:44
Paris 139	1	33N40	95w33	6:22:12
Park 75	1	29N54	96w52	6:27:28
Park Cities 57	1	32N50	96w47	6:27:08
Parker 43	1	33N06	96w40	6:26:40
Parker 126	1	32N16	97w11	6:28:44
Park Glen 101	1	29N44	95w35	6:22:20
Park Hill Estate 15	1	29N27	98w30	6:34:00
Park Place 101	1	29N41	95w17	6:21:08
Park Springs 249	1	33N27	97w46	6:31:04
Parkview Estates 94	1	29N35	97w58	6:31:52
Parkwood 121	1	30N27	93w57	6:15:48
Parnell 96	1	34N31	100w36	6:42:24
Parvin 61	1	33N19	96w47	6:27:08
Pasadena 101	1	29N43	95w13	6:20:52
Patilo 72	1	32N31	98w03	6:32:12
Patman 34	1	32N54	94w33	6:18:12
Patrich 201	1	31N55	94w41	6:18:44
Patricia 58	1	32N33	102w01	6:48:04
Patrick 57	1	32N32	96w40	6:26:40
Patroon 210	1	31N38	93w59	6:15:56
Pattison 237	1	29N49	96w00	6:24:00
Patton 155	1	31N39	97w28	6:29:52
Patton 170	1	30N12	95w10	6:20:40
Pattonville 139	1	33N35	95w24	6:21:36
Pauline 99	1	34N18	99w44	6:38:56
Pauline 107	1	32N18	96w00	6:24:00
Pauls Store 210	1	31N46	93w52	6:15:28
Pawelekville 128	1	28N59	98w01	6:32:04
Pawnee 13	1	28N39	98w00	6:32:00
Paxton 210	1	31N58	94w03	6:16:12
Payne Springs 107	1	32N18	96w00	6:24:00
Peaceful Valley 212	1	32N20	95w18	6:21:12
Peach Creek 241	1	29N19	96w06	6:24:24
Peacock 217	1	33N11	100w24	6:41:36
Peadenville 182	1	32N49	98w04	6:32:16
Pearl 50	1	31N24	98w03	6:32:12
Pearland 20	1	29N34	95w17	6:21:08
Pearl City 62	1	29N17	97w09	6:28:36
Pear Ridge 123	1	29N55	93w56	6:15:44
Pearsall 82	1	28N54	99w06	6:36:24
Pearson 163	1	29N09	98w54	6:35:36
Pearsons Chapel 113	1	31N08	95w27	6:21:48
Pear Valley 154	1	31N19	99w30	6:38:00
Peaster 184	1	32N52	97w52	6:31:28
Pebble Beach 43	1	33N05	96w25	6:25:40
Pecan Gap 60	1	33N26	95w51	6:23:24
Pecangrove 50	1	31N25	97w31	6:30:04
Pecos 195	1	31N26	103w30	6:54:00
Peden 220	1	32N57	97w32	6:30:08
Pedigo 229	1	30N47	94w25	6:17:40
Peeltown 129	1	32N31	96w23	6:25:32
Peerless 112	1	33N08	95w36	6:22:24
Peggy 7	1	28N44	98w11	6:32:44
Pelham 175	1	31N51	96w48	6:27:12
Pendelton 202	1	31N21	93w51	6:15:24
Pendleton 14	1	31N12	97w21	6:29:24
Penelope 109	1	31N52	96w56	6:27:44
Peniel 116	1	33N08	96w07	6:24:28
Penitas 108	1	26N17	98w27	6:33:48
Penland 91	1	33N37	96w24	6:25:36
Pennington 228	1	31N11	95w14	6:20:56
Penwell 68	1	31N45	102w36	6:50:24
Peoria 109	1	32N01	97w07	6:28:28
Pep 110	1	33N49	102w33	6:50:12
Percilla 113	1	31N33	95w24	6:21:36
Perezville 108	1	26N13	98w20	6:33:20
Perico 56	3	36N23	103w01	6:52:04
Pernitas Point 149	1	28N01	97w53	6:31:32
Perrin 91	1	33N02	98w04	6:32:16
Perrin 119	1	33N43	96w40	6:26:40
Perrin Air Force Base 119	1	33N43	96w40	6:26:40
Perry 73	1	31N25	96w55	6:27:40
Perry Landing 20	1	28N58	95w25	6:21:40
Perryton 179	3	36N24	100w48	6:43:12
Perryville 250	1	32N44	94w57	6:19:48
Personville 147	1	31N32	96w23	6:25:32
Pert 1	1	31N46	95w38	6:22:32
Peters 8	1	29N51	96w11	6:24:44
Petersburg 95	1	33N52	101w36	6:46:24
Peterson 123	1	29N57	93w59	6:15:56
Peters Prairie 194	1	33N36	95w03	6:20:12
Petersville 62	1	29N17	97w09	6:28:36
Petrolia 39	1	34N01	98w14	6:32:56
Petronila 178	1	27N48	97w41	6:30:44
Petteway 198	1	31N10	96w41	6:26:44
Pettibone 166	1	30N51	96w59	6:27:56
Pettit 47	1	31N51	98w24	6:33:36
Pettit 110	1	33N42	102w32	6:50:08
Pettus 13	1	28N37	97w48	6:31:12
Petty 139	1	33N36	95w49	6:23:16
Petty 153	1	33N10	101w48	6:47:12
Pettys Chapel 175	1	32N06	96w31	6:26:04
Pflugerville 227	1	30N26	97w37	6:30:28
Phalba 234	1	32N22	95w59	6:23:56
Pharr 108	1	26N12	98w11	6:32:44
Phelan 11	1	30N07	97w19	6:29:16
Phelps 236	1	30N42	95w27	6:21:48
Phillips 117	3	35N42	101w22	6:45:28
Phillipsburg 239	1	30N10	96w24	6:25:36
Phillips Camp 98	3	36N16	101w24	6:45:36
Philrich 117	3	35N39	101w26	6:45:44
Philview Camp 117	3	35N39	101w26	6:45:44
Pickens 107	1	32N12	95w51	6:23:24
Pickett 175	1	32N06	96w31	6:26:04
Pickton 112	1	33N02	95w24	6:21:36
Pickwick 182	1	32N56	98w15	6:33:00
Pidcoke 50	1	31N17	97w53	6:31:32
Piedmont 93	1	30N29	95w59	6:23:56
Pierce 241	1	29N14	96w12	6:24:48
Pierces Chapel 37	1	31N58	95w16	6:21:04
Pike 43	1	33N18	96w24	6:25:36
Pilgrims Rest 190	1	32N52	95w46	6:23:04
Pilot Grove 91	1	33N31	96w23	6:25:32
Pilot Knob 227	1	30N13	97w44	6:30:56
Pilot Point 61	1	33N24	96w58	6:27:52
Pine 32	1	33N00	94w58	6:19:52
Pine Forest 112	1	33N04	95w28	6:21:52
Pine Forest 181	1	30N11	94w02	6:16:08
Pine Grove 101	1	29N56	95w17	6:21:08
Pine Grove 176	1	30N51	93w45	6:15:00
Pine Grove 181	1	30N06	93w46	6:15:04
Pine Hill 37	1	31N58	95w16	6:21:04
Pinehill 201	1	32N06	94w39	6:18:36
Pinehurst 170	1	30N10	95w41	6:22:44
Pinehurst 181	1	30N07	93w48	6:15:12
Pine Island 123	1	30N06	94w09	6:16:36
Pine Lake 170	1	30N23	95w42	6:22:48
Pineland 202	1	31N15	93w58	6:15:52
Pine Prairie 236	1	30N43	95w33	6:22:12
Pine Ridge 100	1	30N22	94w19	6:17:16
Pine Springs 55	1	32N25	104w14	6:56:56
Pine Valley 3	1	31N12	94w47	6:19:08
Pine Valley 204	1	30N32	95w29	6:21:56
Pineview 250	1	32N58	95w17	6:21:08
Pinewood 92	1	32N27	94w44	6:18:56
Pinewood Estates 100	1	30N06	94w09	6:16:36
Piney Grove 170	1	30N13	95w45	6:23:00
Piney Grove 230	1	33N00	94w58	6:19:52
Piney Point 101	1	29N47	95w32	6:22:08
Piney Point Village 101	1	29N46	95w31	6:22:04
Pinnacle 230	1	32N34	95w00	6:20:00
Pioneer 67	1	32N07	99w05	6:36:20
Pioneer Town 105	1	30N00	98w06	6:32:24
Pipe Creek 10	1	29N43	98w56	6:35:44
Pirtle 201	1	32N16	94w59	6:19:56
Pitner Junction 201	1	32N16	94w59	6:19:56
Pitts 170	1	29N56	95w17	6:21:08
Pittsburg 32	1	33N00	94w58	6:19:52
Pittsville	1	30N04	95w14	6:20:56
Placedo 235	1	28N41	96w50	6:27:20
Placid 154	1	31N19	99w11	6:36:44
Plains 251	1	33N11	102w50	6:51:20
Plainview 95	1	34N11	101w43	6:46:52
Plainview 202	1	31N15	93w58	6:15:52
Plano 43	1	33N01	96w42	6:26:48
Plantation 20	1	29N02	95w26	6:21:44
Plantersville 93	1	30N21	95w53	6:23:32
Plaska 96	1	34N36	100w39	6:42:36
Plateau 55	1	31N04	104w34	6:58:16
Pleak 79	1	29N35	95w46	6:23:04
Pleasant Glade	1	32N53	97w06	6:28:24
Pleasant Grove 73	1	31N04	96w58	6:27:52
Pleasant Grove 201	1	32N09	94w48	6:19:12
Pleasant Grove 230	1	32N34	95w00	6:20:00
Pleasant Grove 250	1	32N58	95w17	6:21:08
Pleasant Hill 16	1	30N17	98w25	6:33:40
Pleasant Hill 67	1	32N23	98w59	6:35:56
Pleasant Hill 187	1	31N00	94w50	6:19:20
Pleasant Hill 239	1	30N10	96w24	6:25:36
Pleasanton 7	1	28N58	98w29	6:33:56
Pleasant Point 126	1	32N24	97w13	6:28:52
Pleasant Ridge 107	1	32N03	95w30	6:22:00
Pleasant Ridge 145	1	31N16	95w59	6:23:56
Pleasant Ridge 183	1	32N09	94w20	6:17:20
Pleasant Run 57	1	32N37	96w51	6:27:24
Pleasant Valley 57	1	32N54	96w37	6:26:28
Pleasant Valley 85	1	33N12	101w23	6:45:32
Pleasant Valley 182	1	32N49	98w04	6:32:16
Pleasant Valley 243	1	33N56	98w35	6:34:20
Pledger 161	1	29N11	95w55	6:23:40
Pluck 187	1	31N00	94w50	6:19:20
Plum 75	1	29N56	96w58	6:27:52
Plum Grove 146	1	30N18	95w07	6:20:28
Poe Prairie 184	1	32N45	98w01	6:32:04
Poesville 18	1	32N01	97w36	6:30:24
Poetry 129	1	32N45	96w29	6:25:56
Point 190	1	32N56	95w52	6:23:28
Pointblank 204	1	30N45	95w13	6:20:52
Point Comfort 29	1	28N41	96w33	6:26:12
Point Enterprise 147	1	31N41	96w29	6:25:56
Polar 132	1	32N51	101w01	6:44:04
Pollok 3	1	31N27	94w52	6:19:28
Polytechnic 220	1	32N43	97w16	6:29:04
Ponder 61	1	33N11	97w17	6:29:08
Pone 201	1	31N58	94w49	6:19:16
Ponta 37	1	31N58	95w16	6:21:04
Pontotoc 160	1	30N55	98w59	6:35:56
Pony 200	1	31N45	99w57	6:39:48
Poolville 184	1	32N58	97w52	6:31:28
Porfirio 245	1	26N29	97w47	6:31:08
Port Acres 123	1	29N55	93w56	6:15:44
Portairs 178	1	27N45	97w25	6:29:40
Port Alto 29	1	28N40	96w25	6:25:40
Port Aransas 178	1	27N47	97w11	6:28:44
Port Arthur 123	1	29N54	93w56	6:15:44
Port Bolivar 84	1	29N23	94w46	6:19:04
Port Brownsville 31	1	25N55	97w25	6:29:40
Porter 170	1	30N06	95w14	6:20:56
Porter Springs 113	1	31N15	95w37	6:22:28
Port Isabel 31	1	26N05	97w12	6:28:48
Portland 205	1	27N53	97w20	6:29:20
Port Lavaca 29	1	28N37	96w38	6:26:32
Port Mansfield	1	26N34	97w26	6:29:44
Port Neches 123	1	30N00	93w58	6:15:52
Port O'Connor 29	1	28N27	96w24	6:25:36
Portway Acres 31	1	25N55	97w29	6:29:56
Porvenir 189	1	30N34	104w29	6:57:56
Posey 112	1	33N08	95w36	6:22:24
Posey 152	1	33N44	101w43	6:46:52
Post 85	1	33N12	101w23	6:45:32
Postoak 81	1	31N38	96w17	6:25:08
Post Oak 113	1	31N08	95w27	6:21:48
Postoak 119	1	33N34	97w51	6:31:24
Postoak 139	1	33N40	95w16	6:21:04
Postoak Point 8	1	29N53	96w29	6:25:56
Poteet 7	1	29N02	98w35	6:34:20
Poth 247	1	29N04	98w05	6:32:20
Potosi 221	1	32N28	99w44	6:38:56
Potters Point 158	1	32N46	94w21	6:17:24
Pottsboro 91	1	33N46	96w40	6:26:40
Pottsville 97	1	31N40	98w19	6:33:16
Powderly 139	1	33N49	95w31	6:22:04
Powell 175	1	32N07	96w20	6:25:20
Powell Point 79	1	29N27	96w00	6:24:00
Poynor 107	1	32N04	95w36	6:22:24
Prade Ranch 193	1	30N10	99w22	6:37:28
Praesel 166	1	30N39	97w00	6:28:00
Praha 75	1	29N41	97w06	6:28:24
Prairie Dell 14	1	30N57	97w32	6:30:08
Prairie Grove 147	1	31N41	96w29	6:25:56
Prairie Hill 147	1	31N39	96w47	6:27:08
Prairie Hill 239	1	30N10	96w24	6:25:36
Prairie Lea 28	1	29N44	97w45	6:31:00
Prairie Point 49	1	33N32	97w33	6:30:12
Prairie Springs 126	1	32N33	97w20	6:29:20
Prairie Valley 169	1	33N47	97w44	6:30:56
Prairie View 237	1	30N06	95w59	6:23:56
Prairieville 129	1	32N22	95w59	6:23:56
Prattville 60	1	33N22	95w41	6:22:44
Premont 125	1	27N22	98w07	6:32:28
Presidio 189	1	29N34	104w22	6:57:28
Preston 57	1	32N52	96w48	6:27:12
Preston Road Highlands 43	1	33N00	96w49	6:27:16
Preston Shores 91	1	33N46	96w40	6:26:40
Price 60	1	33N22	95w41	6:22:44
Price 123	1	29N57	93w59	6:15:56
Price 201	1	32N08	94w57	6:19:48
Priddy 167	1	31N41	98w31	6:34:04
Primera 31	1	26N14	97w46	6:31:04
Primrose 234	1	32N27	95w42	6:22:48
Princeton 43	1	33N10	96w30	6:26:00
Pringle 117	3	35N57	101w27	6:45:48
Pritchett 230	1	32N40	95w01	6:20:04
Proctor 47	1	31N59	98w26	6:33:44
Proffit 252	1	33N12	98w44	6:34:56
Progreso 108	1	26N06	97w58	6:31:52
Progress 9	1	34N14	102w44	6:50:56
Progress 182	1	32N49	98w04	6:32:16
Promenade 57	1	32N57	96w44	6:26:56
Prospect 158	1	32N46	94w21	6:17:24
Prosper 43	1	33N14	96w48	6:27:12
Providence 3	1	30N15	95w32	6:22:08
Providence 187	1	30N43	94w56	6:19:44
Providence 234	1	32N41	95w43	6:22:52
Provident City 45	1	29N06	96w25	6:25:40
Pruett 34	1	32N46	94w21	6:17:24
Pruitt 234	1	32N41	95w43	6:22:52
Puerto Rico 108	1	26N34	98w09	6:32:36
Pullman 188	3	35N10	101w53	6:47:32
Pumphrey 200	1	31N58	99w58	6:39:52
Pumpkin 204	1	30N32	95w29	6:21:56
Pumpkin Center 58	1	32N44	101w58	6:47:52

TEXAS

Pumpkin Center 67 1 32N24 98W49 6:35:16
Pumpville 233 1 29N57 101W44 6:46:56
Punkin Center 184 1 32N45 97W43 6:30:52
Purdon 175 1 31N57 96W37 6:26:28
Purley 80 1 33N05 95W16 6:21:04
Purmela 50 1 31N29 97W58 6:31:52
Pursley 175 1 31N57 96W37 6:26:28
Purves 72 1 32N05 98W20 6:33:20
Putnam 30 1 32N22 99W12 6:36:48
Pyote 238 1 31N32 103W08 6:52:32
Pyron 208 1 32N27 100W33 6:42:12
Quail 44 3 34N54 100W24 6:41:36
Quanah 99 1 34N18 99W45 6:39:00
Quarry 239 1 30N18 96W30 6:26:00
Queen City 34 1 33N09 94W09 6:16:36
Quemado 162 1 28N57 100W37 6:42:28
Quicksand 176 1 30N51 93W45 6:15:00
Quinlan 116 1 32N55 96W08 6:24:32
Quintana 20 1 28N58 95W25 6:21:40
Quitaque 23 1 34N22 101W04 6:44:16
Quitman 250 1 32N48 95W27 6:21:48
Rabb 178 1 27N48 97W41 6:30:44
Rabbs 143 1 29N27 96W56 6:27:44
Rabbs Prairie 75 1 29N54 96W52 6:27:28
Raccoon Bend 8 1 29N57 96W15 6:25:00
Racetrack 60 1 33N22 95W41 6:22:44
Rachal 24 1 26N53 98W08 6:32:32
Radium 127 1 32N45 99W54 6:39:36
Ragtown 139 1 33N52 95W31 6:22:04
Rainbow 213 1 32N16 97W43 6:30:52
Raisin 235 1 28N45 97W07 6:28:28
Raleigh 175 1 32N05 96W48 6:27:12
Ralls 54 1 33N41 101W23 6:45:32
Ramah 210 1 31N57 94W15 6:17:00
Ramireno 253 1 27N03 99W27 6:37:48
Ramirez 66 1 27N21 98W25 6:33:40
Ramona 108 1 26N10 97W59 6:31:56
Ramsey 45 1 29N42 96W33 6:26:12
Ranchito 31 1 26N08 97W38 6:30:32
Rancho Allegre Addition 125 1 27N45 98W05 6:32:20
Rancho Viejo 124 1 27N19 98W41 6:34:44
Randolph 15 1 33N29 96W15 6:25:00
Randolph 74 1 29N32 98W17 6:33:08
Randolph Air Force Base 15 1 29N32 98W19 6:33:16
Ranger 67 1 32N28 98W41 6:34:44
Rangerville 31 1 26N08 97W42 6:30:48
Rankin 70 1 32N20 96W38 6:26:32
Rankin 231 1 31N13 101W56 6:47:44
Ratama 82 1 28N40 99W10 6:36:40
Ratcliff 113 1 31N24 95W08 6:20:32
Ratcliff 203 1 31N32 94W07 6:16:28
Ratibor 14 1 31N06 97W21 6:29:24
Rattan 60 1 33N22 95W41 6:22:44
Ravenna 74 1 33N40 96W15 6:25:00
Rayburn 146 1 30N25 94W56 6:19:44
Rayford 170 1 30N09 95W25 6:21:40
Rayland 78 1 34N09 99W18 6:37:12
Raymondville 245 1 26N29 97W47 6:31:08
Ray Point 149 1 28N28 98W11 6:32:44
Raywood 146 1 30N02 94W40 6:18:40
Razor 139 1 33N52 95W31 6:22:04
Reagan 73 1 31N13 96W47 6:27:08
Reagan Wells 232 1 29N13 99W47 6:39:08
Reagor Springs 70 1 32N24 96W50 6:27:20
Realitos 66 1 27N27 98W32 6:34:08
Reavilon 116 1 33N08 96W07 6:24:28
Redbank 19 1 33N32 94W16 6:17:04
Red Bird 57 1 32N39 96W56 6:27:44
Red Bluff 101 1 29N34 95W01 6:20:04
Red Bluff 195 1 31N49 103W55 6:55:40
Red Cut Heights 19 1 33N26 94W04 6:16:16
Redfield 174 1 31N40 94W38 6:18:32
Redford 189 1 29N27 104W11 6:56:44
Red Gate 108 1 26N30 98W08 6:32:32
Red Hill 34 1 33N00 94W22 6:17:28
Red Lake 81 1 31N35 95W51 6:23:24
Redland 3 1 30N15 95W32 6:22:08
Redland 145 1 31N16 95W59 6:23:56
Redland 234 1 32N23 95W30 6:22:00
Redlawn 37 1 31N39 95W04 6:20:16
Redlick 19 1 33N26 94W04 6:16:16
Redmond Terrace 21 1 30N37 96W20 6:25:20
Red Oak 70 1 32N31 96W48 6:27:12
Red Oak 129 1 32N35 96W17 6:25:08
Red Ranger 14 1 30N56 97W14 6:28:56
Red Rock 11 1 29N58 97W27 6:29:48
Red Springs 12 1 33N37 99W25 6:37:40
Red Springs 19 1 33N26 94W04 6:16:16
Red Springs 212 1 32N31 95W25 6:21:40
Red Town 3 1 30N15 95W32 6:22:08
Redwater 19 1 33N22 94W15 6:17:00
Redwood 94 1 29N53 97W56 6:31:44
Reedville 28 1 29N53 97W48 6:31:12
Reese 37 1 31N58 95W16 6:21:04
Reese 152 1 33N36 102W02 6:48:08
Reese Air Force Base 152 1 33N35 101W51 6:47:24
Reese Village 152 1 33N35 101W51 6:47:24
Refuge 113 1 31N29 95W29 6:21:56
Refugio 196 1 28N18 97W17 6:29:08
Regency 167 1 31N34 98W40 6:34:40
Rehobeth 183 1 32N09 94W20 6:17:20
Reilly Springs 112 1 33N08 95W36 6:22:24
Rek Hill 75 1 29N54 96W41 6:26:44
Reklaw 37 1 31N52 94W59 6:19:56
Relampago 108 1 26N09 97W55 6:31:40
Reliance 21 1 30N40 96W22 6:25:28
Rendon 220 1 32N35 97W14 6:28:56
Renner 43 1 32N59 96W47 6:27:08
Reno 139 1 33N40 95W31 6:22:04
Reno 184 1 32N46 97W28 6:29:52
Retreat 175 1 32N03 96W29 6:25:56
Retta 126 1 32N33 97W20 6:29:20
Reynard 113 1 31N29 95W29 6:21:56
Rhea 185 3 34N38 102W43 6:50:52
Rhea Mills 43 1 33N08 96W37 6:26:28
Rhineland 138 1 33N27 99W37 6:38:28
Rhome 249 1 33N03 97W28 6:29:52
Rhonesboro 230 1 32N34 95W00 6:20:00
Ricardo 137 1 27N25 97W51 6:31:24
Rice 175 1 32N15 96W30 6:26:00
Rice 212 1 32N20 95W18 6:21:12
Rices Crossing 246 1 30N34 97W25 6:29:40
Richards 93 1 30N32 95W51 6:23:24
Richardson 57 1 32N57 96W44 6:26:56
Richardson Heights Village 57 1 32N57 96W44 6:26:56
Richland 175 1 31N56 96W26 6:25:44
Richland 190 1 32N56 95W52 6:23:28
Richland Hills 220 1 32N49 97W14 6:28:56
Richland Park 220 1 32N49 97W12 6:28:48
Richland Springs 206 1 31N16 98W57 6:35:48
Richmond 79 1 29N35 95W46 6:23:04
Richwood 20 1 29N03 95W24 6:21:36
Richwood Village 20 1 29N02 95W24 6:21:36
Riderville 183 1 32N09 94W20 6:17:20
Ridge 167 1 31N34 98W40 6:34:40
Ridge 198 1 31N09 96W19 6:25:16
Ridgecrest 21 1 30N40 96W22 6:25:28
Ridgecrest 123 1 29N57 93W59 6:15:56
Ridgecrest 181 1 30N06 93W46 6:15:04
Ridgeway 112 1 33N11 95W46 6:23:04
Ridings 74 1 33N40 96W14 6:24:56
Riesel 155 1 31N29 96W55 6:27:40
Rincon 214 1 26N23 98W49 6:35:16
Ringgold 169 1 33N49 97W57 6:31:48
Rio Farms 108 1 26N18 97W58 6:31:52
Rio Frio 193 1 29N38 99W44 6:38:56
Rio Grande 1 26N23 98W49 6:35:16
Rio Grande City 214 1 26N23 98W49 6:35:16
Rio Hondo 31 1 26N14 97W35 6:30:20
Riomedina 163 1 29N26 98W53 6:35:32
Rio Pecos 52 1 31N05 102W21 6:49:24
Rio Rico 108 1 26N09 97W55 6:31:40
Rios 66 1 27N27 98W16 6:33:04
Rio Vista 126 1 32N14 97W23 6:29:32
Rising Star 67 1 32N06 98W58 6:35:52
Rita 26 1 30N47 96W43 6:26:52
Riverbottom 204 1 30N45 95W13 6:20:52
Riverby 74 1 33N47 96W01 6:24:04
River Hill 183 1 32N09 94W20 6:17:20
River Hills 227 1 30N23 97W45 6:31:00
River Oaks 101 1 30N11 95W42 6:22:48
River Oaks 220 1 32N46 97W24 6:29:36
Riverside 220 1 32N47 97W18 6:29:12
Riverside 236 1 30N51 95W24 6:21:36
Riverside Crest 101 1 29N56 95W17 6:21:08
River Terrace 101 1 30N18 95W07 6:20:28
Riviera 137 1 27N18 97W49 6:31:16
Riviera Beach 137 1 27N18 97W49 6:31:16
Roane 175 1 32N10 96W23 6:25:32
Roanoke 61 1 33N00 97W14 6:28:56
Roans Prairie 93 1 30N35 95W57 6:23:48
Roaring Springs 173 1 33N54 100W52 6:43:28
Robbins 145 1 31N22 96W09 6:24:36
Robert Lee 41 1 31N54 100W29 6:41:56
Robertson 54 1 33N40 101W32 6:46:08
Robinson 155 1 31N28 97W07 6:28:28
Robstown 178 1 27N47 97W40 6:30:40
Roby 76 1 32N45 100W23 6:41:32
Rochelle 154 1 31N14 99W13 6:36:52
Rochester 104 1 33N19 99W51 6:39:24
Rock Creek 23 1 34N28 101W18 6:45:12
Rock Creek 155 1 31N34 97W10 6:28:40
Rockdale 166 1 30N39 97W00 6:28:00
Rockett 70 1 32N24 96W50 6:27:20
Rockhill 43 1 33N08 96W37 6:26:28
Rock Hill 250 1 32N48 95W27 6:21:48
Rockhouse 8 1 29N53 96W29 6:25:56
Rock Island 45 1 29N32 96W34 6:26:16
Rock Island 187 1 31N00 94W50 6:19:20
Rockland 229 1 31N01 94W23 6:17:32
Rockne 11 1 30N07 97W19 6:29:16
Rockport 4 1 28N02 97W03 6:28:12
Rocksprings 69 1 30N01 100W13 6:40:52
Rockwall 199 1 32N56 96W28 6:25:52
Rockwood 42 1 31N30 99W22 6:37:28
Rocky Branch 172 1 33N12 94W41 6:18:44
Rocky Hill 73 1 31N18 96W53 6:27:32
Roddy 234 1 32N22 95W59 6:23:56
Rodney 175 1 31N54 96W43 6:26:52
Roganville 121 1 30N48 93W54 6:15:36
Rogers 14 1 30N56 97W14 6:28:56
Rogers Hill 155 1 31N48 97W06 6:28:24
Rogerslacy 108 1 26N15 97W50 6:31:20
Rolla 44 3 34N51 100W10 6:40:40
Rolling Hills 116 1 32N57 95W56 6:23:44
Rolling Oaks 234 1 32N43 96W00 6:24:00
Rollingwood 227 1 30N16 97W47 6:31:08
Roma 214 1 26N24 99W05 6:36:20
Romayor 146 1 30N27 94W50 6:19:20
Romero 103 3 35N44 102W56 6:51:44
Romney 67 1 32N06 98W58 6:35:52
Roosevelt 134 1 30N29 100W03 6:40:12
Roosevelt 152 1 33N35 101W51 6:47:24
Ropesville 110 1 33N26 102W09 6:48:36
Rosalie 194 1 33N28 95W13 6:20:52
Rosanky 11 1 29N56 97W18 6:29:12
Roscoe 177 1 32N27 100W32 6:42:08
Rosebud 73 1 31N04 96W59 6:27:56
Rose City 181 1 30N09 94W01 6:16:04
Rosedale 73 1 31N13 96W47 6:27:08
Rose Hill 57 1 32N54 96W37 6:26:28
Rose Hill 101 1 30N05 95W36 6:22:24
Rose Hill Acres 100 1 30N12 94W12 6:16:48
Rosenberg 79 1 29N34 95W49 6:23:16
Rosenthal 155 1 31N23 97W13 6:28:52
Rosevine 202 1 31N21 94W01 6:16:04
Rosewood 230 1 32N44 94W57 6:19:48
Rosharon 20 1 29N21 95W28 6:21:52
Rosita 66 1 27N47 98W26 6:33:44
Rosita 214 1 26N23 98W49 6:35:16
Ross 155 1 31N43 97W07 6:28:28
Ross City 114 1 32N14 101W28 6:45:52
Rosser 129 1 32N28 96W27 6:25:48
Rosston 49 1 33N29 97W27 6:29:48
Rossville 7 1 29N02 98W35 6:34:20
Roswell 18 1 31N47 97W35 6:30:20
Rotan 76 1 32N51 100W28 6:41:52
Round Mountain 16 1 30N26 98W21 6:33:24
Round Prairie 175 1 32N08 96W14 6:24:56
Round Rock 246 1 30N31 97W41 6:30:44
Round Timber 12 1 33N35 99W16 6:37:04
Round Top 75 1 30N04 96W42 6:26:48
Roundup 110 1 33N46 102W06 6:48:24
Rowden 30 1 32N24 99W24 6:37:36
Rowena 200 1 31N39 100W03 6:40:12
Rowlett 57 1 32N54 96W34 6:26:16
Roxton 139 1 33N33 95W44 6:22:56
Royal Lane 57 1 32N54 96W48 6:27:12
Royalty 238 1 31N22 102W52 6:51:28
Roy Miller 178 1 27N47 97W26 6:29:44
Roy Royall 101 1 29N52 95W20 6:21:20
Royse City 199 1 32N59 96W20 6:25:20
Royston 76 1 32N45 100W23 6:41:32
Rucker 47 1 32N10 98W36 6:34:24
Rudolph 131 1 26N41 97W46 6:31:04
Rugby 194 1 33N32 95W19 6:21:16
Ruidosa 1 29N59 104W41 6:58:44
Rule 104 1 33N11 99W54 6:39:36
Rumley 141 1 31N05 98W00 6:32:00
Runge 128 1 28N53 97W43 6:30:52
Rural Shade 175 1 32N08 96W14 6:24:56
Rushing 175 1 31N48 96W28 6:25:52
Rush Prairie 175 1 32N05 96W48 6:27:12
Rusk 37 1 31N48 95W09 6:20:36
Rutersville 75 1 29N57 96W48 6:27:12
Rye 146 1 30N27 94W46 6:19:04
Rylie 57 1 32N46 96W37 6:26:28
Sabanna 67 1 32N23 98W59 6:35:56
Sabathany 184 1 32N45 97W43 6:30:52
Sabinal 232 1 29N19 99W28 6:37:52
Sabine 123 1 29N43 93W52 6:15:28
Sabine Pass 123 1 29N49 94W14 6:16:56
Sabinetown 202 1 31N21 93W51 6:15:24
Sachse 57 1 32N59 96W36 6:26:24
Sacul 174 1 31N50 94W56 6:19:44
Sadler 91 1 33N41 96W51 6:27:24
Sagerton 104 1 33N05 99W58 6:39:52
Saginaw 220 1 32N52 97W22 6:29:28
Saint Clair City 212 1 32N08 95W07 6:20:28
Saint Francis 188 3 35N14 101W48 6:47:12
Saint Francis Village 220 1 32N35 97W22 6:29:28
Saint Hedwig 15 1 29N25 98W12 6:32:48
Saint Jo 169 1 33N42 97W31 6:30:04
Saint Lawrence 87 1 31N52 101W29 6:45:56
Saint Louis 212 1 32N20 95W18 6:21:12
Saint Paul 43 1 33N01 96W32 6:26:08
Saint Paul 73 1 31N18 96W53 6:27:32
Saint Paul 205 1 28N06 97W33 6:30:12
Saint Paul 237 1 30N06 96W02 6:24:08
Salado 14 1 30N57 97W32 6:30:08
Salem 212 1 32N08 95W07 6:20:28
Salesville 182 1 32N55 98W05 6:32:20
Salineno 214 1 26N31 99W07 6:36:28
Salmon 1 1 31N37 95W35 6:22:20
Salona 169 1 33N34 97W51 6:31:24
Salt Flat 115 2 31N45 105W05 7:00:20
Salt Gap 154 1 31N18 99W36 6:38:24
Saltillo 112 1 33N11 95W20 6:21:20
Salty 166 1 30N39 97W00 6:28:00
Sam Houston 101 1 29N47 95W23 6:21:32
Sam Houston College 236 1 30N43 95W33 6:22:12
Samnorwood 44 3 35N03 100W17 6:41:08
Sam Rayburn 121 1 30N55 94W00 6:16:00
San Angelo 226 1 31N28 100W26 6:41:44
San Antonio 15 1 29N25 98W30 6:34:00
San Augustine 203 1 31N32 94W07 6:16:28
San Benito 31 1 26N08 97W38 6:30:32
San Carlos 108 1 26N17 98W10 6:32:40
Sanco 41 1 31N54 100W29 6:41:56
Sand 58 1 32N44 101W58 6:47:52
Sanderson 222 1 30N09 102W24 6:49:36
Sand Flat 190 1 32N52 95W46 6:23:04
Sandflat 212 1 32N20 95W18 6:21:12
Sand Flat 234 1 32N41 95W43 6:22:52

Place	Zone	Lat	Long	Time
Sand Hill 77	1	33N59	101w20	6:45:20
Sand Hill 230	1	32N44	94w57	6:19:48
Sandia 125	1	28N01	97w53	6:31:32
San Diego 66	1	27N46	98w14	6:32:56
Sand Lake 70	1	32N20	96w38	6:26:32
Sandoval 246	1	30N34	97w25	6:29:40
Sand Ridge 113	1	31N19	95w27	6:21:48
Sand Springs 114	1	32N17	101w20	6:45:20
Sandusky 91	1	33N40	96w54	6:27:36
Sandy 16	1	30N22	98w28	6:33:52
Sandy Corner 241	1	29N11	96w17	6:25:08
Sandy Creek 166	1	30N43	96w52	6:27:28
Sandy Fork 89	1	29N40	97w30	6:30:00
Sandy Harbor 150	1	30N35	98w20	6:33:20
Sandy Hill 239	1	30N10	96w24	6:25:36
Sandy Point 20	1	29N23	95w29	6:21:56
San Elizario 71	2	31N35	106w16	7:05:04
San Felipe 8	1	29N48	96w06	6:24:24
Sanford 117	3	35N42	101w32	6:46:08
San Gabriel 166	1	30N37	97w12	6:28:48
Sanger 61	1	33N22	97w10	6:28:40
San Geromino 15	1	29N37	98w41	6:34:44
San Isidro 214	1	26N43	98w27	6:33:48
San Jacinto 188	3	35N12	101w53	6:47:32
San Jacinto 236	1	30N43	95w33	6:22:12
San Jose 66	1	27N45	98w05	6:32:20
San Juan 108	1	26N11	98w09	6:32:36
San Juan 178	1	27N48	97w24	6:29:36
San Juan Community 108	1	26N17	98w10	6:32:40
San Leanna 8	1	30N17	97w44	6:30:56
San Leon 84	1	29N29	94w55	6:19:40
San Marcos 105	1	29N53	97w56	6:31:44
San Patricio 178	1	28N06	97w50	6:31:20
San Pedro 178	1	27N48	97w41	6:30:44
San Perlita 245	1	26N30	97w39	6:30:36
San Saba 206	1	31N12	98w43	6:34:52
Sansom Park Village 220	1	32N48	97w24	6:29:36
Santa Anna 42	1	31N45	99w20	6:37:20
Santa Catarina 214	1	26N23	98w49	6:35:16
Santa Cruz 214	1	26N23	98w49	6:35:16
Santa Elena 214	1	26N46	98w29	6:33:56
Santa Maria 31	1	26N05	97w51	6:31:24
Santa Monica 245	1	26N29	97w47	6:31:08
Santa Rosa 31	1	26N16	97w50	6:31:20
Santo 182	1	32N36	98w13	6:32:52
San Ygnacio 253	1	27N03	99w26	6:37:44
Saragosa 195	1	31N02	103w39	6:54:36
Saratoga 100	1	30N17	94w31	6:18:04
Sarco 88	1	28N40	97w23	6:29:32
Sardis 70	1	32N31	97w11	6:28:44
Sargent 161	1	28N59	95w58	6:23:52
Sarita 131	1	27N13	97w47	6:31:08
Sash 74	1	33N35	95w54	6:23:36
Saspamco 247	1	29N14	98w18	6:33:12
Satin 73	1	31N21	97w02	6:28:08
Satsuma 101	1	29N51	95w30	6:22:00
Sattler 46	1	29N59	98w16	6:33:04
Saturn 89	1	29N42	97w18	6:29:12
Sauer 166	1	30N51	96w59	6:27:56
Sauney Stand 239	1	30N09	96w16	6:25:04
Savage 54	1	33N41	101w23	6:45:32
Savoy 74	1	33N36	96w22	6:25:28
Sayard 226	1	31N28	100w27	6:41:48
Sayers 11	1	30N07	97w19	6:29:16
Sayersville	1	30N14	97w20	6:29:20
Scallorn 167	1	31N13	98w23	6:33:32
Schattel 82	1	29N03	98w52	6:35:28
Schertz 94	1	29N33	98w16	6:33:04
Schoenau 8	1	29N53	96w29	6:25:56
School Land 89	1	29N16	97w46	6:31:04
Schroeder 88	1	28N40	97w23	6:29:32
Schulenburg 75	1	29N41	96w54	6:27:36
Schumansville 94	1	29N42	98w08	6:32:32
Schwab City 187	1	30N43	94w56	6:19:44
Schwertner 246	1	30N49	97w31	6:30:04
Scotland 5	1	33N40	98w28	6:33:52
Scott 234	1	32N43	96w00	6:24:00
Scottsville 102	1	32N32	94w14	6:16:56
Scroggins 80	1	32N58	95w11	6:20:44
Scurry 129	1	32N31	96w23	6:25:32
Seabrook 101	1	29N34	95w02	6:20:08
Sea Crest Park 36	1	29N46	95w00	6:20:00
Seadrift 29	1	28N25	96w43	6:26:52
Seagoville 57	1	32N38	96w32	6:26:08
Seagraves 83	1	32N57	102w34	6:50:16
Seale 198	1	31N25	96w34	6:26:16
Sealy 8	1	29N47	96w09	6:24:36
Seaton 14	1	31N03	97w13	6:28:52
Sea Willow 28	1	29N53	97w40	6:30:40
Sebastian 245	1	26N21	97w48	6:31:12
Sebastopol 228	1	30N57	95w23	6:21:32
Seco Mines 162	1	28N43	100w29	6:41:56
Security 170	1	30N18	95w07	6:20:28
Sedalia 43	1	33N25	96w34	6:26:16
Sefcikville 14	1	31N06	97w21	6:29:24
Seglar 15	1	29N16	98w44	6:34:56
Segno 187	1	30N35	94w41	6:18:44
Segovia 134	1	30N29	99w46	6:39:04
Seguin 94	1	29N34	97w58	6:31:52
Sejita 66	1	27N27	98w32	6:34:08
Selden 72	1	32N13	98w13	6:32:52
Selfs 74	1	33N35	95w54	6:23:36
Selma 15	1	29N35	98w19	6:33:16
Selman City 201	1	32N11	94w58	6:19:52
Seminary Hill 220	1	32N41	97w20	6:29:20
Seminole 83	1	32N43	102w39	6:50:36
Senior 15	1	29N17	98w39	6:34:36
Serbin 144	1	30N11	96w56	6:27:44
Serna 15	1	29N30	98w25	6:33:40
Seth Ward 95	1	34N13	101w42	6:46:48
Settles Addition 114	1	32N14	101w28	6:45:52
Seven Oaks 187	1	30N49	94w52	6:19:28
Seven Pines 230	1	32N44	94w57	6:19:48
Seven Points 107	1	32N26	96w05	6:24:20
Seven Sisters 66	1	28N01	98w31	6:34:04
Sexton 202	1	31N32	94w07	6:16:28
Sexton City 201	1	32N16	94w59	6:19:56
Seymore 112	1	33N08	95w36	6:22:24
Seymour 12	1	33N35	99w16	6:37:04
Seymour West 12	1	33N36	99w22	6:37:28
Shadow Glen 101	1	29N46	95w09	6:20:36
Shadowland 194	1	33N32	95w19	6:21:16
Shady Grove 3	1	31N12	94w47	6:19:08
Shady Grove 37	1	31N48	95w09	6:20:36
Shady Grove 57	1	32N48	97w01	6:28:04
Shady Grove 175	1	31N57	96w37	6:26:28
Shady Grove 230	1	32N34	95w00	6:20:00
Shady Oaks 220	1	32N50	97w10	6:28:40
Shady Shores 61	1	33N10	97w02	6:28:08
Shady Trees 101	1	29N56	95w17	6:21:08
Shafter 189	1	29N49	104w18	6:57:12
Shallowater 152	1	33N41	102w00	6:48:00
Shamrock 57	1	32N37	96w51	6:27:24
Shamrock 242	3	35N13	100w15	6:41:00
Shamrock Shores 25	1	31N44	98w58	6:35:52
Shanklerville 176	1	31N00	93w40	6:14:40
Shannon 39	1	33N49	98w12	6:32:48
Sharon 212	1	32N20	95w18	6:21:12
Sharp 166	1	30N45	97w10	6:28:40
Sharpstown 101	1	29N42	95w31	6:22:04
Sharyland 108	1	26N13	98w20	6:33:20
Shavano Park 15	1	29N34	98w33	6:34:12
Shaw Bend 206	1	31N12	98w44	6:34:56
Shawnee Shores Estates 116	1	32N54	96w05	6:24:20
Sheffield 186	1	30N41	101w49	6:47:16
Shelby 8	1	30N01	96w36	6:26:24
Shelbyville 210	1	31N46	94w05	6:16:20
Sheldon 101	1	29N52	95w08	6:20:32
Shenandoah 170	1	30N19	95w28	6:21:52
Shep 221	1	32N03	100w07	6:40:28
Shepherd 204	1	30N30	95w00	6:20:00
Sheppard Air Force Base 243	1	33N59	98w31	6:34:04
Shepphard 176	1	30N27	93w57	6:15:48
Shepton 43	1	32N58	96w46	6:27:04
Sheridan 45	1	29N30	96w40	6:26:40
Sherman 91	1	33N38	96w36	6:26:24
Sherman Junction 91	1	33N45	96w34	6:26:16
Sherry 194	1	33N36	95w03	6:20:12
Sherwood 118	1	31N16	100w49	6:43:16
Sherwood Shores 27	1	30N35	98w20	6:33:20
Shields 42	1	31N44	99w19	6:37:16
Shiloh 11	1	30N07	97w19	6:29:16
Shiloh 57	1	32N54	96w37	6:26:28
Shiloh 146	1	30N04	94w48	6:19:12
Shiloh 147	1	31N41	96w29	6:25:56
Shiloh 246	1	30N35	97w18	6:29:12
Shiner 143	1	29N26	97w10	6:28:40
Shirley 112	1	33N08	95w36	6:22:24
Shiro 93	1	30N37	95w53	6:23:32
Shive 97	1	31N42	98w07	6:32:28
Shoreacres 101	1	29N36	95w01	6:20:04
Short 210	1	31N48	94w11	6:16:44
Sidney 47	1	31N57	98w44	6:34:56
Sierra Blanca 115	2	31N11	105w22	7:01:28
Silas 210	1	31N54	94w24	6:17:36
Siloam 19	1	33N30	94w37	6:18:28
Siloam 47	1	31N51	98w24	6:33:36
Siloam 246	1	30N21	97w22	6:29:28
Silsbee 100	1	30N21	94w11	6:16:44
Silver 41	1	32N04	100w40	6:42:40
Silver City 166	1	30N51	96w59	6:27:56
Silver City 175	1	31N57	96w37	6:26:28
Silver City 194	1	33N36	95w03	6:20:12
Silver Lake 234	1	32N41	95w43	6:22:52
Silverton 23	1	34N28	101w19	6:45:16
Silver Valley 42	1	31N58	99w33	6:38:12
Simmons 149	1	28N28	98w11	6:32:44
Simmonsville 14	1	32N44	94w57	6:19:48
Simms 19	1	33N21	94w31	6:18:04
Simonton 79	1	29N41	95w58	6:23:52
Simpsonville 161	1	28N42	96w13	6:24:52
Simsboro 81	1	31N38	96w17	6:25:08
Sinclair City 212	1	32N08	95w07	6:20:28
Singleton 93	1	30N39	95w58	6:23:52
Sinton 205	1	28N02	97w31	6:30:04
Sipe Springs 47	1	31N54	98w36	6:34:24
Sisterdale 130	1	29N48	98w45	6:35:00
Sivells Bend 49	1	33N38	97w08	6:28:32
Six Points 178	1	27N46	97w24	6:29:36
Skellytown 33	3	35N34	101w11	6:44:44
Skidmore 13	1	28N15	97w41	6:30:44
Slate Shoals 139	1	33N40	95w31	6:22:04
Slaton 152	1	33N26	101w39	6:46:36
Slay 175	1	32N05	96w48	6:27:12
Slide 152	1	33N35	101w51	6:47:24
Slidell 249	1	33N22	97w23	6:29:32
Slocum 1	1	31N38	95w28	6:21:52
Slutter 45	1	29N42	96w33	6:26:12
Small 234	1	32N42	95w53	6:23:32
Smetana 21	1	30N40	96w22	6:25:28
Smiley 89	1	29N16	97w38	6:30:32
Smith Grove 113	1	31N08	95w27	6:21:48
Smith Hill 19	1	33N28	94w17	6:17:08
Smithland 158	1	32N49	94w10	6:16:40
Smith Oaks 91	1	33N38	96w36	6:26:24
Smith Point 36	1	29N32	94w46	6:19:04
Smiths Bend 18	1	31N47	97w35	6:30:20
Smith Springs 72	1	32N13	98w13	6:32:52
Smithville 11	1	30N01	97w10	6:28:40
Smithwick 27	1	30N35	98w20	6:33:20
Smitty 107	1	32N12	95w51	6:23:24
Smyer 110	1	33N35	102w10	6:48:40
Smyrna 34	1	33N07	94w10	6:16:40
Snap 183	1	32N09	94w20	6:17:20
Sneedville 51	1	34N01	100w18	6:41:12
Snook 26	1	30N29	96w28	6:25:52
Snow 145	1	31N03	96w07	6:24:28
Snow Hill 43	1	33N10	96w22	6:25:28
Snow Hill 187	1	31N00	94w50	6:19:20
Snyder 208	1	32N44	100w55	6:43:40
Socorro 71	2	31N39	106w18	7:05:12
Soda 187	1	30N43	94w56	6:19:44
Soda Springs 184	1	32N45	98w01	6:32:04
Sodville 205	1	28N02	97w31	6:30:04
Solms 46	1	29N42	98w08	6:32:32
Somerset 15	1	29N14	98w40	6:34:40
Somerville 26	1	30N21	96w32	6:26:08
Soncy 188	3	35N12	101w53	6:47:32
Sonoma 70	1	32N20	96w33	6:26:12
Sonora 218	1	30N34	100w39	6:42:36
Sorrels 241	1	29N19	96w06	6:24:24
Sorters 170	1	29N47	95w23	6:21:32
Soules Chapel 230	1	32N44	94w57	6:19:48
Sourlake 100	1	30N09	94w25	6:17:40
South 21	1	30N37	96w20	6:25:20
South Amarillo 188	3	35N10	101w53	6:47:32
South Austin 227	1	30N14	97w47	6:31:08
South Bend 252	1	33N00	98w40	6:34:40
South Bexar 15	1	29N16	98w29	6:33:56
South Bosque 155	1	31N32	97w11	6:28:44
South Brazos 20	1	30N31	96w16	6:25:04
South Brice 96	1	34N56	100w53	6:43:32
South Dallas 57	1	32N45	96w46	6:27:04
Southeast 220	1	32N37	97w12	6:28:48
South Elm 166	1	30N52	97w08	6:28:32
South End 123	1	30N03	94w06	6:16:24
South Fort Worth 220	1	32N44	97w20	6:29:20
South Gale 91	1	33N45	96w34	6:26:16
South Groveton 228	1	31N03	95w08	6:20:32
South Hanlon 215	1	32N45	98w55	6:35:40
South Houston 101	1	29N40	95w14	6:20:56
South Jim Hogg 124	1	26N56	98w49	6:35:16
Southlake 220	1	32N57	97w07	6:28:28
Southland 85	1	33N22	101w33	6:46:12
Southland 241	1	29N11	96w17	6:25:08
Southland Acres 220	1	32N43	97w06	6:28:24
South Laredo 240	1	27N31	99w30	6:38:00
South Liberty 146	1	30N04	94w48	6:19:12
Southmayd 91	1	33N38	96w46	6:27:04
Southmore 101	1	29N44	95w22	6:21:28
South Oak Cliff 57	1	32N43	96w48	6:27:12
South Padre Island 31	1	26N05	97w08	6:28:32
South Park 101	1	29N40	95w20	6:21:20
South Plains 77	1	34N13	101w19	6:45:16
South Post Oak 101	1	29N39	95w29	6:21:56
South Purmela 50	1	31N29	97w58	6:31:52
South Rockwall 199	1	32N52	96w23	6:25:32
South San Antonio 15	1	29N22	98w33	6:34:12
South Sand Hills 9	1	33N57	102w49	6:51:16
South San Pedro 178	1	27N47	97w41	6:30:44
South Side Place 101	1	29N42	95w26	6:21:44
South Sulphur 116	1	33N22	96w04	6:24:16
South Temple 14	1	31N06	97w21	6:29:24
South Texarkana 19	1	33N26	94w04	6:16:16
South Texas Medical Center 15	1	29N30	98w35	6:34:20
Southton 15	1	29N21	98w30	6:34:00
Southwest 220	1	32N38	97w27	6:29:48
Sowells Bluff 74	1	33N40	96w14	6:24:56
Sowers 57	1	32N51	96w58	6:27:52
Spade 140	1	33N56	102w09	6:48:36
Spanish Camp 241	1	29N19	96w06	6:24:24
Spanish Fort 169	1	33N47	97w44	6:30:56
Sparenberg 58	1	32N44	101w58	6:47:52
Sparks 14	1	30N53	97w24	6:29:36
Speaks 143	1	29N15	96w42	6:26:48
Spearman 98	3	36N12	101w12	6:44:48
Speegleville 155	1	31N32	97w11	6:28:44
Spicewood 27	1	30N29	98w10	6:32:40
Spillers Store 145	1	31N09	95w58	6:23:52
Splendora 170	1	30N14	95w10	6:20:40
Spofford 136	1	29N10	100w25	6:41:40
Spooner 181	1	30N06	93w46	6:15:04
Spring	1	30N05	95w25	6:21:40
Spring Branch 46	1	29N53	98w25	6:33:40
Spring Creek 86	1	30N17	98w52	6:35:28
Spring Creek 206	1	31N16	98w57	6:35:48
Spring Creek 224	1	33N27	98w56	6:35:44
Spring Creek Acres 235	1	28N48	96w59	6:27:56
Springdale 34	1	33N09	94w09	6:16:36
Springfield 1	1	31N53	95w38	6:22:32

Springfield 125 1 27N45 98w05 6:32:20
Springfield 147 1 31N41 96w29 6:25:56
Spring Hill 19 1 33N30 94w37 6:18:28
Spring Hill 92 1 32N34 94w48 6:19:12
Spring Hill 94 1 29N35 97w58 6:31:52
Springhill 175 1 31N54 96w43 6:26:52
Spring Lake 140 1 34N14 102w18 6:49:12
Spring Seat 145 1 31N22 96w09 6:24:36
Springtown 184 1 32N58 97w41 6:30:44
Spring Valley 101 1 29N47 95w30 6:22:00
Spring Valley 155 1 31N18 97w22 6:29:28
Sprinkle 227 1 30N18 97w43 6:30:52
Spur 63 1 33N28 100w52 6:43:28
Spurger 229 1 30N42 94w11 6:16:44
Stacy 154 1 31N29 99w36 6:38:24
Staff 67 1 32N24 98w49 6:35:16
Stafford 79 1 29N37 95w34 6:22:16
Stagecoach 170 1 30N13 95w45 6:23:00
Stairtown 28 1 29N43 97w44 6:30:56
Stamford 127 1 32N57 99w48 6:39:12
Stampede 14 1 31N18 97w22 6:29:28
Stamps 230 1 32N44 94w57 6:19:48
Stanfield 39 1 33N49 98w12 6:32:48
Stanton 159 1 32N08 101w48 6:47:12
Staples 94 1 29N47 97w50 6:31:20
Star 167 1 31N28 98w19 6:33:16
Star Harbor 107 1 32N10 96w01 6:24:04
Starrville 212 1 32N30 95w10 6:20:40
Startzville 46 1 29N42 98w08 6:32:32
Steeltown 123 1 29N57 93w55 6:15:40
Steep Hollow 21 1 30N40 96w22 6:25:28
Stegal 9 1 33N52 102w59 6:51:56
Stellar 75 1 29N49 97w04 6:28:16
Stephen Creek 204 1 30N42 95w11 6:20:44
Stephenville 72 1 32N13 98w12 6:32:48
Sterley 77 1 34N13 101w24 6:45:36
Sterling City 216 1 31N50 101w00 6:44:00
Sterrett 70 1 32N24 96w50 6:27:20
Stewards Mill 81 1 31N53 96w19 6:25:16
Stewart 201 1 32N09 94w48 6:19:12
Stewart Heights 101 1 29N46 95w00 6:20:00
Stieren 89 1 29N40 97w30 6:30:00
Stiles 192 1 31N25 101w34 6:46:16
Stilson 146 1 30N03 94w53 6:19:32
Stinnett 117 3 35N50 101w27 6:45:48
Stith 127 1 32N28 99w49 6:39:16
Stockard 107 1 32N12 95w51 6:23:24
Stockdale 247 1 29N14 97w58 6:31:52
Stockholm 108 1 26N25 97w48 6:31:12
Stockman 210 1 31N49 94w24 6:17:36
Stock Yards 220 1 32N47 97w21 6:29:24
Stoneburg 169 1 33N40 97w54 6:31:36
Stoneham 93 1 30N21 95w55 6:23:40
Stonewall 86 1 30N14 98w40 6:34:40
Stony 61 1 33N11 97w17 6:29:08
Stormville 250 1 32N48 95w27 6:21:48
Stout 250 1 32N58 95w17 6:21:08
Stowell 36 1 29N47 94w23 6:17:32
Stranger 73 1 31N18 96w38 6:26:32
Stratford 211 3 36N20 102w04 6:48:16
Stratton 62 1 29N06 97w17 6:29:08
Stratton Ridge 20 1 28N58 95w25 6:21:40
Strawn 182 1 32N33 98w30 6:34:00
Streeter 160 1 30N46 99w23 6:37:32
Streetman 81 1 31N53 96w19 6:25:16
Strickland 202 1 31N15 93w58 6:15:52
String Prairie 11 1 29N53 97w21 6:29:24
Structure 246 1 30N21 97w22 6:29:28
Stuart Place 31 1 26N11 97w39 6:30:36
Study Butte 22 1 29N19 103w37 6:54:28
Sturdivant 182 1 32N49 98w04 6:32:16
Sturgeon 49 1 33N40 96w54 6:27:36
Sturgis Mill 202 1 31N21 93w51 6:15:24
Styx 129 1 32N26 96w05 6:24:20
Sublett 220 1 32N31 97w09 6:28:36
Sublime 143 1 29N29 96w48 6:27:12
Sudan 140 1 34N04 102w32 6:50:08
Suffolk 230 1 32N44 94w57 6:19:48
Sugar Land 79 1 29N37 95w38 6:22:32
Sugar Valley 161 1 29N03 95w42 6:22:48
Sullivan 94 1 29N39 97w50 6:31:20
Sullivan 108 1 26N16 98w28 6:33:52
Sullivan City 108 1 26N16 98w34 6:34:16
Sulphur Bluff 112 1 33N22 95w24 6:21:36
Sulphur Springs 3 1 31N09 94w26 6:17:44
Sulphur Springs 112 1 33N08 95w36 6:22:24
Sulphur Springs 201 1 31N49 94w50 6:19:20
Sul Ross 22 1 30N20 103w39 6:54:36
Summerfield 35 3 34N44 102w31 6:50:04
Summerfield 230 1 32N44 94w57 6:19:48
Summerville 89 1 29N30 97w27 6:29:48
Sumner 139 1 33N45 95w41 6:22:44
Sun 91 1 33N45 96w34 6:26:16
Sundown 110 1 33N28 102w27 6:49:48
Sunniland 149 1 28N28 98w11 6:32:44
Sunnyside 35 1 34N24 102w19 6:49:16
Sunny Side 237 1 29N55 96w04 6:24:16
Sunnyslope 19 1 33N26 94w04 6:16:16
Sunnyvale 57 1 32N48 96w34 6:26:16
Sun Oil Camp 214 1 26N41 98w25 6:33:40
Sunray 171 3 36N01 101w49 6:47:16
Sunrise 73 1 31N17 96w53 6:27:32

Sunrise Beach Village 150 1 30N45 98w41 6:34:44
Sunset 152 1 33N34 101w57 6:47:48
Sunset 169 1 33N27 97w46 6:31:04
Sunset Heights 68 1 31N52 102w22 6:49:28
Sunset Valley 227 1 30N14 97w49 6:31:16
Suntide 178 1 27N49 97w31 6:30:04
Sunview 158 1 32N48 94w43 6:18:52
Surf Oaks 101 1 29N34 95w01 6:20:04
Surfside 20 1 28N58 95w25 6:21:40
Sutherland Springs 247 1 29N17 98w03 6:32:12
Swamp City 92 1 32N34 94w55 6:19:40
Swan 212 1 32N20 95w18 6:21:12
Swan Lagoon 101 1 29N47 95w23 6:21:32
Swanson Hill 1 1 31N46 95w38 6:22:32
Swearingen 51 1 34N01 100w18 6:41:12
Sweeny 20 1 29N03 95w42 6:22:48
Sweeny Switch 149 1 28N06 97w50 6:31:20
Sweet Home 143 1 29N21 97w04 6:28:16
Sweetwater 47 1 31N54 98w36 6:34:24
Sweetwater 177 1 32N28 100w25 6:41:40
Swenson 217 1 33N13 100w19 6:41:16
Swift 174 1 31N40 94w38 6:18:32
Swiss Alp 75 1 29N41 96w54 6:27:36
Sycamore 176 1 31N00 93w40 6:14:40
Sylvan 139 1 33N40 95w31 6:22:04
Sylvan Beach 101 1 29N40 95w02 6:20:08
Sylvester 76 1 32N43 100w15 6:41:00
Tabor 21 1 30N40 96w22 6:25:28
Tacoma 183 1 32N09 94w20 6:17:20
Tadmor 113 1 31N22 95w11 6:20:44
Taft 205 1 27N59 97w24 6:29:36
Taft Southwest 205 1 27N59 97w24 6:29:36
Tahoka 153 1 33N10 101w48 6:47:12
Taiton 241 1 29N11 96w17 6:25:08
Talco 225 1 33N22 95w06 6:20:24
Talpa 42 1 31N47 99w43 6:38:52
Talty 129 1 32N45 96w29 6:25:56
Tamega 27 1 30N45 98w03 6:32:12
Tamina 170 1 30N11 95w27 6:21:48
Tanglewood 144 1 30N30 96w59 6:27:56
Tarkington Prairie 146 1 30N18 95w07 6:20:28
Tarleton 72 1 32N13 98w13 6:32:52
Tarpley 10 1 29N39 99w17 6:37:08
Tarrant 220 1 32N50 97w06 6:28:24
Tarver 109 1 31N57 97w19 6:29:16
Tarzan 159 1 32N18 101w58 6:47:52
Tate Springs 220 1 32N43 97w06 6:28:24
Tatum 201 1 32N19 94w31 6:18:04
Tavener 79 1 29N32 96w04 6:24:16
Taylor 246 1 30N34 97w24 6:29:36
Taylor Lake Village 101 1 29N35 95w03 6:20:12
Taylorsville 28 1 29N58 97w27 6:29:48
Taylor Town 139 1 33N40 95w31 6:22:04
Taylorville 74 1 33N25 96w03 6:24:12
T.C.U. 220 1 32N44 97w20 6:29:20
Teague 81 1 31N38 96w17 6:25:08
Teaselville 212 1 32N08 95w19 6:21:16
Tech 152 1 33N34 101w52 6:47:28
Tecula 37 1 31N58 95w16 6:21:04
Tehuacana 147 1 31N45 96w33 6:26:12
Telegraph 134 1 30N20 99w54 6:39:36
Telephone 74 1 33N47 96w01 6:24:04
Telferner 235 1 28N51 96w53 6:27:32
Telico 70 1 32N20 96w38 6:26:32
Tell 38 1 34N23 100w24 6:41:36
Temple 14 1 31N06 97w21 6:29:24
Tenaha 210 1 31N57 94w15 6:17:00
Tenneryville 92 1 32N27 94w44 6:18:56
Tennessee Colony 1 1 31N50 95w50 6:23:20
Tennyson 41 1 31N45 100w17 6:41:08
Terlingua 22 1 29N19 103w36 6:54:24
Terrell 129 1 32N44 96w17 6:25:08
Terrell Hills 15 1 29N29 98w27 6:33:48
Terrell Wells 15 1 29N21 98w30 6:34:00
Terrys Chapel 73 1 31N04 96w58 6:27:52
Terryville 62 1 29N17 97w09 6:28:36
Texarkana 19 1 33N26 94w06 6:16:24
Texas City 84 1 29N24 94w54 6:19:36
Texhoma 211 3 36N30 101w47 6:47:08
Texline 56 3 36N23 103w02 6:52:08
Texon 192 1 31N13 101w42 6:46:48
Texroy 117 3 35N34 101w10 6:44:40
Thalia 78 1 33N59 99w32 6:38:08
Thayer 108 1 26N09 97w55 6:31:40
Thedford 212 1 32N31 95w25 6:21:40
The Grove 50 1 31N16 97w32 6:30:08
The Heights 20 1 29N24 95w14 6:20:56
The Knobbs 144 1 30N17 97w15 6:29:00
Thelma 15 1 29N21 98w30 6:34:00
Thelma 147 1 31N32 96w32 6:26:08
The Meadows 79 1 29N38 95w33 6:22:12
Theon 246 1 30N49 97w36 6:30:24
Thermo 112 1 33N08 95w36 6:22:24
Thicket 100 1 30N24 94w38 6:18:32
Thomas 230 1 33N00 94w58 6:19:52
Thomaston 62 1 29N00 97w09 6:28:36
Thompson 101 1 29N51 95w30 6:22:00
Thompsons 79 1 29N30 95w35 6:22:20
Thompsonville 89 1 29N42 97w18 6:29:12
Thornberry 39 1 33N52 98w33 6:34:12
Thorndale 166 1 30N37 97w12 6:28:48
Thornton 147 1 31N25 96w34 6:26:16
Thorntonville 238 1 31N35 102w53 6:51:32
Thorp Spring 111 1 32N27 97w47 6:31:08
Thrall 246 1 30N35 97w18 6:29:12

TEXAS

Three Leagues 159 1 32N31 101w43 6:46:52
Three Point 227 1 30N31 97w41 6:30:44
Three Rivers 149 1 28N28 98w11 6:32:44
Thrifty 25 1 31N44 98w58 6:35:52
Throckmorton 224 1 33N11 99w11 6:36:44
Thurber 72 1 32N32 98w25 6:33:40
Tidehaven 161 1 28N54 96w09 6:24:36
Tidwell 116 1 33N08 96w07 6:24:28
Tidwell Prairie 198 1 31N10 96w41 6:26:44
Tigertown 139 1 33N35 95w54 6:23:36
Tigua 71 2 31N44 106w21 7:05:24
Tilden 156 1 28N28 98w33 6:34:12
Tilmon 28 1 29N56 97w34 6:30:16
Timber Cove 101 1 29N34 95w01 6:20:04
Timberlake 101 1 29N58 95w42 6:22:48
Timberlane Acres 170 1 29N47 95w23 6:21:32
Timothy 175 1 32N14 96w25 6:25:40
Timpson 210 1 31N54 94w24 6:17:36
Tin Top 184 1 32N45 97w43 6:30:52
Tioga 91 1 33N28 96w55 6:27:40
Tira 112 1 33N08 95w36 6:22:24
Tivoli 196 1 28N27 96w53 6:27:32
Tivydale 86 1 30N17 98w52 6:35:28
Tobe Hahn 123 1 30N06 94w09 6:16:36
Toco 139 1 33N38 95w42 6:22:48
Tod 101 1 29N34 95w01 6:20:04
Todd City 1 1 31N46 95w38 6:22:32
Togo 11 1 30N00 97w09 6:28:36
Tokio 223 1 33N11 102w35 6:50:20
Tolar 111 1 32N23 97w55 6:31:40
Tolbert 244 1 34N09 99w18 6:37:12
Toledo 176 1 31N00 93w40 6:14:40
Tolosa 129 1 32N26 96w05 6:24:20
Tomball 101 1 30N06 95w37 6:22:28
Tom Bean 91 1 33N31 96w29 6:25:56
Tool 107 1 32N26 96w05 6:24:20
Topsey 50 1 31N07 97w54 6:31:36
Tornillo 71 2 31N27 106w05 7:04:20
Toto 184 1 32N58 97w52 6:31:28
Tours 155 1 31N48 97w06 6:28:24
Tow 150 1 30N53 98w28 6:33:52
Town Bluff 229 1 30N47 94w25 6:17:40
Town Hall 57 1 32N46 96w37 6:26:28
Toyah 195 1 31N19 103w48 6:55:12
Toyahvale 195 1 30N57 103w47 6:55:08
Tracy 166 1 30N52 97w08 6:28:32
Trammells 79 1 29N38 95w26 6:21:44
Travis 73 1 31N12 97w02 6:28:08
Travis Peak 227 1 30N35 98w20 6:33:20
Trawick 174 1 31N46 94w45 6:19:00
Trent 221 1 32N29 100w07 6:40:28
Trenton 74 1 33N26 96w20 6:25:20
Trevat 228 1 31N03 95w08 6:20:32
Tri Cities 107 1 32N12 95w51 6:23:24
Trickham 42 1 31N44 99w19 6:37:16
Trinidad 107 1 32N09 96w06 6:24:24
Trinity 228 1 30N57 95w22 6:21:28
Trinity Mills 57 1 32N57 96w53 6:27:32
Trinity Park 43 1 33N01 96w32 6:26:08
Tripp 57 1 32N46 96w37 6:26:28
Tropical Acres 235 1 28N48 96w59 6:27:56
Troup 212 1 32N09 95w07 6:20:28
Trout Creek 176 1 30N37 93w53 6:15:32
Troy 14 1 31N12 97w18 6:29:12
Truby 127 1 32N37 99w49 6:39:16
Truce 119 1 33N28 98w01 6:32:04
Trumbull 70 1 32N29 96w40 6:26:40
Truscott 138 1 33N45 99w49 6:39:16
Tucker 1 1 31N41 95w44 6:22:56
Tuleta 13 1 28N34 97w48 6:31:12
Tulia 219 3 34N32 101w46 6:47:04
Tulip 74 1 33N49 96w08 6:24:32
Tulsita 13 1 28N49 97w51 6:31:24
Tundra 234 1 32N28 95w53 6:23:32
Tunis 26 1 30N33 96w31 6:26:04
Tupelo 175 1 32N15 96w30 6:26:00
Turkey 96 1 34N24 100w54 6:43:36
Turlington 81 1 31N44 96w10 6:24:40
Turnersville 50 1 31N36 97w46 6:31:04
Turnersville 227 1 30N05 97w51 6:31:24
Turnertown 201 1 32N11 94w58 6:19:52
Turney 37 1 31N58 95w16 6:21:04
Turtle Bayou 36 1 29N46 94w42 6:18:48
Tuscola 221 1 32N12 99w48 6:39:12
Tuxedo 127 1 32N56 99w57 6:39:48
Twitchell 179 3 36N24 100w48 6:43:12
Twitty 242 3 35N19 100w14 6:40:56
T.W.U. 61 1 33N13 97w08 6:28:32
Tye 221 1 32N27 99w52 6:39:28
Tyler 212 1 32N21 95w18 6:21:12
Tylers Bluff 49 1 33N42 97w31 6:30:04
Tynan 13 1 28N10 97w45 6:31:00
Type 11 1 30N21 97w22 6:29:28
Type 246 1 30N21 97w22 6:29:28
Uhland 105 1 29N59 97w53 6:31:32
Umbarger 191 3 34N57 102w07 6:48:28
Uncertain 102 1 32N42 94w07 6:16:28
Union 152 1 33N26 101w39 6:46:36
Union 208 1 32N44 101w00 6:44:00
Union 223 1 33N11 102w16 6:49:04
Union Bower 57 1 32N51 96w58 6:27:52
Union Grove 230 1 32N34 94w55 6:19:40
Union High 175 1 31N54 96w43 6:26:52
Union Hill 18 1 32N04 97w30 6:30:00
Union Hill 230 1 32N44 94w57 6:19:48
Union Springs 174 1 31N40 94w38 6:18:32
Union Valley 116 1 32N59 96w20 6:25:20
Union Valley 247 1 29N16 97w46 6:31:04
Unity 139 1 33N46 95w39 6:22:36

TEXAS

Universal City 15 1 29N33 98w17 6:33:08
University 227 1 30N17 97w44 6:30:56
University Hill 61 1 33N11 97w04 6:28:16
University Of Dallas 57 1 32N51 96w58 6:27:52
University of Texas at El Pa 71 2 31N47 106w30 7:06:00
University Park 15 1 29N28 98w35 6:34:20
University Park 57 1 32N51 96w48 6:27:12
University Park 243 1 33N52 98w33 6:34:12
Upper Meyersville 62 1 28N59 97w30 6:30:00
Upshaw 174 1 31N40 94w53 6:19:32
Upton 11 1 30N01 97w16 6:29:04
Urbana 204 1 30N30 95w00 6:20:00
Utley 11 1 30N07 97w19 6:29:16
Utopia 232 1 29N37 99w32 6:38:08
Uvalde 232 1 29N13 99w47 6:39:08
Valdasta 43 1 33N18 96w24 6:25:36
Valentine 122 1 30N35 104w30 6:58:00
Valera 42 1 31N45 99w33 6:38:12
Valleycreek 74 1 33N25 96w03 6:24:12
Valley-hi 15 1 29N25 98w37 6:34:28
Valley Lodge 79 1 29N41 95w58 6:23:52
Valley Mills 18 1 31N40 97w28 6:29:52
Valley Spring 150 1 30N52 98w49 6:35:16
Valley View 49 1 33N29 97w10 6:28:40
Valley View 62 1 29N06 97w17 6:29:08
Valley View 155 1 31N33 97w08 6:28:32
Valley View 168 1 32N24 100w52 6:43:28
Valley View 200 1 31N45 99w57 6:39:48
Valley View 230 1 32N44 94w57 6:19:48
Valley View 243 1 33N57 98w40 6:34:40
Valley Wells 64 1 28N34 99w34 6:38:16
Val Verde 166 1 30N52 97w08 6:28:32
Van 234 1 32N31 95w38 6:22:32
Van Alstyne 91 1 33N25 96w35 6:26:20
Vance 193 1 29N44 100w02 6:40:08
Vancourt 226 1 31N21 100w11 6:40:44
Vandalia 194 1 33N36 95w03 6:20:12
Vandenburg 163 1 29N21 99w08 6:36:32
Vanderbilt 120 1 28N49 96w37 6:26:28
Vanderpool 10 1 29N45 99w33 6:38:12
Vandyke 47 1 31N54 98w36 6:34:24
Vanetia 145 1 31N14 96w16 6:25:04
Van Horn 55 1 31N03 104w50 6:59:20
Van Raub 15 1 29N48 98w45 6:35:00
Van Vleck 161 1 29N01 95w53 6:23:32
Varisco 21 1 30N40 96w22 6:25:28
Vasco 60 1 33N26 95w39 6:22:36
Vashti 39 1 33N38 98w01 6:32:04
Vattmanville 137 1 27N18 97w49 6:31:16
Vaughan 109 1 32N01 97w07 6:28:28
Vealmoor 114 1 32N14 101w28 6:45:52
Veal Station 184 1 32N58 97w41 6:30:44
Vega 180 3 35N15 102w26 6:49:44
Ventura 170 1 30N13 95w45 6:23:00
Venus 126 1 32N26 97w06 6:28:24
Vera 138 1 33N38 99w34 6:38:16
Verdi 7 1 28N58 98w29 6:33:56
Verhalen 195 1 31N08 103w36 6:54:24
Verhelle 62 1 29N06 97w17 6:29:08
Veribest 226 1 31N29 100w16 6:41:04
Vernon 244 1 34N09 99w17 6:37:08
Verona 43 1 33N18 96w24 6:25:36
Veterans Administration 14 1 31N06 97w21 6:29:24
Veterans Administration 155 1 31N31 97w09 6:28:36
Viboras 214 1 26N45 98w50 6:35:20
Vick 48 1 31N21 100w11 6:40:44
Vickery 57 1 32N54 96w44 6:26:56
Victoria 147 1 31N33 96w50 6:27:20
Victoria 235 1 28N48 97w00 6:28:00
Victory City 19 1 33N28 94w17 6:17:08
Victory Gardens 181 1 30N06 93w46 6:15:04
Vidauri 196 1 28N26 97w08 6:28:32
Vidor 181 1 30N07 94w01 6:16:04
Vienna 143 1 29N27 96w56 6:27:44
View 221 1 32N21 99w53 6:39:32
Vigo Park 219 3 34N39 101w30 6:46:00
Vilas 14 1 30N53 97w24 6:29:36
Villa Cavazos 31 1 25N55 97w29 6:29:56
Village 57 1 32N50 96w47 6:27:08
Village 165 1 32N00 102w05 6:48:20
Village Mills 100 1 30N30 94w24 6:17:36
Villa Nueva 31 1 25N55 97w29 6:29:56
Villareales 214 1 26N23 98w49 6:35:16
Vincent 114 1 32N29 101w14 6:44:56
Vineyard 119 1 33N10 97w59 6:31:56
Vinton 71 2 32N00 106w36 7:06:24
Viola 178 1 27N50 97w31 6:30:04
Violet 178 1 27N47 97w36 6:30:24
Virginia Point 84 1 29N18 94w50 6:19:20
Vistula 113 1 31N08 95w27 6:21:48
Voca 154 1 31N01 99w11 6:36:44
Volente 227 1 30N35 97w51 6:31:24
Von Ormy 15 1 29N17 98w39 6:34:36
Voss 42 1 31N37 99w34 6:38:16
Votaw 100 1 30N26 94w41 6:18:44
Voth 123 1 30N09 94w10 6:16:40
Waco 155 1 31N33 97w09 6:28:36
Wadsworth 161 1 28N50 95w56 6:23:44
Waelder 89 1 29N42 97w18 6:29:12
Wainwright 15 1 29N27 98w27 6:33:48
Waka 179 3 36N17 101w03 6:44:12
Wake 54 1 33N44 101w00 6:44:00
Wakefield 187 1 31N00 94w50 6:19:20
Waketon 61 1 33N03 97w03 6:28:12
Wake Village 19 1 33N25 94w06 6:16:24
Walburg 246 1 30N44 97w35 6:30:20
Waldeck 75 1 30N09 96w48 6:27:12
Walden Woods 170 1 29N47 95w23 6:21:32
Waldrip 154 1 31N19 99w25 6:37:40
Walhalla 75 1 30N04 96w42 6:26:48
Walkers Mill 102 1 32N30 94w34 6:18:16
Wall 226 1 31N22 100w18 6:41:12
Wallace 234 1 32N33 95w52 6:23:28
Wallace Chapel 230 1 33N00 94w58 6:19:52
Waller 237 1 30N04 95w56 6:23:44
Wallis 8 1 29N38 96w04 6:24:16
Wallisville 36 1 29N50 94w44 6:18:56
Walnut Forest 227 1 30N22 97w41 6:30:44
Walnut Grove 43 1 33N08 96w37 6:26:28
Walnut Grove 183 1 32N09 94w20 6:17:20
Walnut Grove 212 1 32N08 95w07 6:20:28
Walnut Springs 18 1 32N03 97w45 6:31:00
Walnut Springs 70 1 32N32 96w40 6:26:40
Walston Springs 1 1 31N46 95w38 6:22:32
Walton 34 1 32N52 93w59 6:15:56
Walton 234 1 32N12 95w51 6:23:24
Wamba 19 1 33N26 94w04 6:16:16
Waples 111 1 32N29 97w43 6:30:52
Warda 75 1 30N03 96w55 6:27:40
Ward Prairie 81 1 31N44 96w10 6:24:40
Wards Creek 19 1 33N21 94w31 6:18:04
Waring 130 1 29N57 98w48 6:35:12
Warlock 158 1 32N54 94w33 6:18:12
Warren 229 1 30N37 94w24 6:17:36
Warren City 92 1 32N33 94w54 6:19:36
Warrenton 75 1 30N01 96w44 6:26:56
Warsaw 129 1 32N35 96w17 6:25:08
Washburn 6 3 35N11 101w34 6:46:16
Washington 239 1 30N20 96w09 6:24:36
Waskom 102 1 32N29 94w04 6:16:16
Wastella 177 1 32N27 100w33 6:42:12
Watauga 1 32N52 97w16 6:29:04
Waterloo 91 1 33N45 96w34 6:26:16
Waterloo 246 1 30N34 97w25 6:29:40
Waterman 210 1 31N48 94w11 6:16:44
Waters Bluff 212 1 32N30 95w10 6:20:40
Water Valley 226 1 31N40 100w43 6:42:52
Waterwood 204 1 30N44 95w19 6:21:16
Watson 27 1 31N04 98w11 6:32:44
Watsonville 220 1 32N31 97w09 6:28:36
Watt 147 1 31N33 96w50 6:27:20
Waverly 204 1 30N32 95w29 6:21:56
Waxahachie 70 1 32N24 96w51 6:27:24
Wayside 6 3 34N48 101w33 6:46:12
Wayside 153 1 33N19 101w44 6:46:56
Wealthy 145 1 31N03 96w07 6:24:28
Weatherford 184 1 32N46 97w48 6:31:12
Weatherford Junction 126 1 32N21 97w23 6:29:32
Weaver 112 1 33N11 95w20 6:21:20
Webb 220 1 32N38 97w05 6:28:20
Webb Air Force Base 114 1 32N14 101w28 6:45:52
Webberville 227 1 30N21 97w33 6:30:12
Webbville 42 1 32N00 99w13 6:36:52
Webster 101 1 29N32 95w07 6:20:28
Weches 113 1 31N33 95w14 6:20:56
Wedgewood 220 1 32N40 97w22 6:29:28
Weedhaven 120 1 28N37 96w38 6:26:32
Weeping Mary 37 1 31N39 95w04 6:20:16
Weesatche 88 1 28N51 97w27 6:29:48
Weimar 45 1 29N42 96w47 6:27:08
Weinert 94 1 29N39 97w50 6:31:20
Weinert 104 1 33N19 99w40 6:38:40
Weir 246 1 30N41 97w35 6:30:20
Weirville 112 1 33N08 95w36 6:22:24
Welch 58 1 32N56 102w08 6:48:32
Welcome 8 1 29N58 96w30 6:26:00
Welcome Valley 72 1 32N13 98w13 6:32:52
Weldon 113 1 31N01 95w34 6:22:16
Welfare 130 1 29N48 98w45 6:35:00
Wellborn 21 1 30N32 96w18 6:25:12
Wellington 44 3 34N51 100w13 6:40:52
Wellman 223 1 33N03 102w26 6:49:44
Wells 37 1 31N29 94w56 6:19:44
Wells 153 1 32N58 101w50 6:47:20
Wentworth 234 1 32N33 95w52 6:23:28
Weser 88 1 28N40 97w23 6:29:32
Weslaco 108 1 26N10 98w00 6:32:00
Weslaco Farm Labor Center 108 1 26N10 97w59 6:31:56
Wesley 239 1 30N10 96w24 6:25:36
Wesley Grove 236 1 30N37 95w53 6:23:32
West 155 1 31N48 97w06 6:28:24
West Austin 227 1 30N17 97w46 6:31:04
West Baytown 101 1 29N46 95w00 6:20:00
West Bluff 181 1 30N06 93w46 6:15:04
West Brazos 20 1 30N39 96w29 6:25:56
Westbrook 168 1 32N21 101w01 6:44:04
West Carlisle 152 1 33N35 101w58 6:47:52
West Cliff 14 1 31N03 97w28 6:29:52
West Columbia 20 1 29N09 95w39 6:22:36
West Crockett 53 1 30N47 101w39 6:46:36
West End 8 1 29N58 96w28 6:25:52
West End 241 1 29N11 96w17 6:25:08
Westfield 101 1 30N01 95w24 6:21:36
Westfield 241 1 29N11 96w17 6:25:08
Westgate 101 1 29N58 95w42 6:22:48
West Glaveston 84 1 29N18 94w50 6:19:20
Westheimer 101 1 29N44 95w32 6:22:08
Westhoff 62 1 29N12 97w28 6:29:52
Westlake 61 1 32N59 97w10 6:28:40
West Lake Hills 227 1 30N20 97w48 6:31:12
Westlawn 181 1 30N06 93w46 6:15:04
West Mineola 250 1 32N40 95w29 6:21:56
Westminster 43 1 33N22 96w28 6:25:52
West Mountain 230 1 32N37 94w55 6:19:40
West Odessa 68 1 31N52 102w22 6:49:28
Weston 43 1 33N21 96w40 6:26:40
West Orange 181 1 30N04 93w48 6:15:12
Westover 12 1 33N30 99w01 6:36:04
Westover 68 1 31N52 102w22 6:49:28
Westover Hills 220 1 32N45 97w24 6:29:36
West Payne 241 1 29N11 96w17 6:25:08
Westphalia 73 1 31N12 97w02 6:28:08
West Point 75 1 29N57 97w02 6:28:08
West Point 153 1 33N10 101w48 6:47:12
West Port Arthur 123 1 29N55 93w56 6:15:44
West Side 123 1 30N06 94w09 6:16:36
West Sinton 205 1 27N57 97w35 6:30:20
West Tawakoni 116 1 32N54 96w01 6:24:04
West Temple 187 1 30N43 94w56 6:19:44
West Terrell 222 1 30N07 102w23 6:49:32
West Texarkana 19 1 33N26 94w04 6:16:16
West Texas 191 3 34N59 101w55 6:47:40
West University Place 101 1 29N42 95w26 6:21:44
West Vernon 244 1 34N09 99w18 6:37:12
Westview 155 1 31N32 97w11 6:28:44
Westville 228 1 30N57 95w23 6:21:32
Westway 59 3 34N49 102w24 6:49:36
Westway 71 2 31N55 106w36 7:06:24
Westworth 220 1 32N46 97w24 6:29:36
Westworth Village 220 1 32N47 97w24 6:29:36
Wetmore 15 1 29N34 98w25 6:33:40
Wetsel 43 1 33N08 96w37 6:26:28
Whaley 19 1 33N28 94w25 6:17:40
Wharton 241 1 29N19 96w06 6:24:24
Wheatland 220 1 32N44 97w27 6:29:48
Wheeler 242 3 35N27 100w16 6:41:04
Wheelock 198 1 30N54 96w24 6:25:36
Whispering Oaks 190 1 32N57 95w56 6:23:44
White City 244 1 34N09 99w18 6:37:12
White Deer 33 3 35N26 101w10 6:44:40
Whiteface 40 1 33N36 102w37 6:50:28
Whiteflat 173 1 34N06 100w53 6:43:32
White Hall 14 1 31N18 97w22 6:29:28
White Hall 50 1 31N25 97w43 6:30:52
White Hall 93 1 30N23 96w05 6:24:20
Whitehouse 212 1 32N14 95w15 6:21:00
Whiteland 154 1 31N12 99w35 6:38:20
White Mound 91 1 33N38 96w36 6:26:24
White Oak 92 1 32N32 94w51 6:19:24
White Oaks 170 1 29N47 95w23 6:21:32
White Rock 57 1 32N50 96w42 6:26:48
White Rock 91 1 33N45 96w34 6:26:16
White Rock 116 1 33N18 96w12 6:24:48
White Rock 194 1 33N36 95w03 6:20:12
White Rock 203 1 31N32 94w07 6:16:28
Whitesboro 91 1 33N39 96w54 6:27:36
White Settlement 220 1 32N46 97w27 6:29:48
Whites Ranch 36 1 29N47 94w23 6:17:32
Whitestar 173 1 34N14 100w59 6:43:56
Whitestone 246 1 30N35 97w51 6:31:24
Whiteway 97 1 31N34 97w58 6:31:52
Whitewright 91 1 33N31 96w24 6:25:36
Whitharral 110 1 33N44 102w20 6:49:20
Whitman 239 1 30N10 96w24 6:25:36
Whitney 109 1 31N57 97w19 6:29:16
Whitsett 149 1 28N38 98w16 6:33:04
Whitson 50 1 31N18 97w22 6:29:28
Whitt 184 1 32N57 98w01 6:32:04
Whitton 234 1 32N33 95w52 6:23:28
Whon 42 1 31N30 99w18 6:37:12
Wichita Falls 243 1 33N54 98w30 6:34:00
Wichita Valley Farms 243 1 31N33 97w08 6:28:32
Wickett 238 1 31N34 103w00 6:52:00
Wied 143 1 29N27 96w56 6:27:44
Wieland 116 1 33N08 96w07 6:24:28
Wiergate 176 1 31N00 93w42 6:14:48
Wiggins 34 1 33N01 94w12 6:16:48
Wiggins 155 1 31N48 97w06 6:28:24
Wigginsville 170 1 30N19 95w28 6:21:52
Wilcox 26 1 30N27 96w23 6:25:32
Wilderville 73 1 31N04 96w58 6:27:52
Wild Horse 55 1 31N03 104w50 6:59:20
Wildorado 180 3 35N13 102w12 6:48:48
Wild Peach 20 1 29N02 95w34 6:22:16
Wildwood 100 1 30N30 94w24 6:17:36
Wilford Hall U.S.A.F. Hospit 15 1 29N23 98w36 6:34:24
Wilkins 230 1 32N34 95w00 6:20:00
Wilkinson 225 1 33N09 94w58 6:19:52
Willacy County Housing Autho 245 1 26N29 97w47 6:31:08
Willamar 245 1 26N29 97w47 6:31:08
William Beaumont General Hos 71 2 31N47 106w25 7:05:40
William Penn 239 1 30N10 96w24 6:25:36
William Rice 101 1 29N43 95w25 6:21:40
Williams 25 1 31N59 98w55 6:35:40

Place	Zone	Lat	Long	Time
Williamsburg 139	1	33N40	95w31	6:22:04
Williamsburg 143	1	29N27	96w56	6:27:44
William Spear Addition 229	1	32N20	95w18	6:21:12
Willis 170	1	30N25	95w29	6:21:56
Willow City 86	1	30N24	98w42	6:34:48
Willow Grove 14	1	31N18	97w22	6:29:28
Willow Grove 155	1	31N32	97w11	6:28:44
Willow Grove 210	1	31N58	94w03	6:16:12
Willow Oak 230	1	32N44	94w57	6:19:48
Willow Park 184	1	32N44	97w38	6:30:32
Willow Point 249	1	33N13	97w46	6:31:04
Willow Springs 75	1	29N54	96w41	6:26:44
Willow Springs 190	1	32N52	95w46	6:23:04
Willow Springs 204	1	30N36	95w08	6:20:32
Wills Point 234	1	32N43	96w01	6:24:04
Wilmer 57	1	32N35	96w41	6:26:44
Wilmeth 200	1	31N58	99w58	6:39:52
Wilson 153	1	33N19	101w44	6:46:56
Wimberley 105	1	30N00	98w06	6:32:24
Winchell 25	1	31N25	99w09	6:36:36
Winchester 75	1	30N01	97w01	6:28:04
Windcrest 15	1	29N31	98w23	6:33:32
Windom 74	1	33N34	96w00	6:24:00
Windthorst 5	1	33N34	98w26	6:33:44
Winedale 75	1	30N11	96w36	6:26:24
Winfield 225	1	33N10	95w07	6:20:28
Winfree 36	1	29N52	94w50	6:19:20
Winfree 181	1	30N06	93w46	6:15:04
Wingate 200	1	32N03	100w07	6:40:28
Wink 248	1	31N45	103w09	6:52:36
Winkler 81	1	31N53	96w19	6:25:16
Winnie 36	1	29N49	94w23	6:17:32
Winningkoff 43	1	33N08	96w37	6:26:28
Winnsboro 250	1	32N58	95w17	6:21:08
Winona 212	1	32N29	95w10	6:20:40
Winslow 109	1	32N01	97w07	6:28:28
Winter Haven 64	1	28N37	99w51	6:39:24
Winters 200	1	31N58	99w58	6:39:52
Witting 143	1	29N35	97w09	6:28:36
Wizard Wells 119	1	33N13	98w10	6:32:40
Wolfe City 116	1	33N22	96w04	6:24:16
Wolf Flat 96	1	34N24	100w54	6:43:36
Wolfforth 152	1	33N30	102w01	6:48:04
Womack 18	1	31N47	97w35	6:30:20
Woodbine 49	1	33N37	97w01	6:28:04
Woodbranch 170	1	30N11	95w11	6:20:44
Woodbury 109	1	32N01	97w07	6:28:28
Woodlake 228	1	31N02	95w02	6:20:08
Woodland 194	1	33N48	95w17	6:21:08
Woodland Hills 57	1	32N40	96w54	6:27:36
Woodlawn 3	1	30N15	95w32	6:22:08
Woodlawn 102	1	32N40	94w21	6:17:24
Woodley 102	1	32N34	94w25	6:17:40
Woodrow 152	1	33N27	101w50	6:47:20
Woods 183	1	31N57	94w15	6:17:00
Woodsboro 196	1	28N14	97w20	6:29:20
Woodson 224	1	33N01	99w03	6:36:12
Wood Springs 212	1	32N31	95w25	6:21:40
Woodville 229	1	30N47	94w25	6:17:40
Woodway 155	1	31N30	97w13	6:28:52
Woody Acres 170	1	29N47	95w23	6:21:32
Woosley 190	1	32N56	95w52	6:23:28
Wortham 81	1	31N47	96w28	6:25:52
Worthing 143	1	29N27	96w56	6:27:44
Wright City 201	1	32N16	94w59	6:19:56
Wrightsboro 89	1	29N22	97w34	6:30:16
Wylie 43	1	33N01	96w33	6:26:12
Wylie 221	1	32N25	99w46	6:39:04
Yale 80	1	33N11	95w13	6:20:52
Yancey 116	1	33N08	96w07	6:24:28
Yancey 163	1	29N08	99w09	6:36:36
Yantis 250	1	32N56	95w35	6:22:20
Yarboro 93	1	30N23	96w05	6:24:20
Yard 1	1	31N50	95w50	6:23:20
Yarrelton 166	1	30N52	97w08	6:28:32
Yates 134	1	30N41	99w35	6:38:20
Yellow Mound 67	1	32N24	98w49	6:35:16
Yellowpine 202	1	31N21	93w51	6:15:24
Yescas 31	1	26N08	97w38	6:30:32
Yetes 109	1	31N57	97w19	6:29:16
Yoakum 143	1	29N17	97w09	6:28:36
Yorktown 62	1	28N59	97w30	6:30:00
Young 81	1	31N44	96w10	6:24:40
Youngsport 14	1	31N07	97w46	6:31:04
Yowell 60	1	33N15	95w54	6:23:36
Ysleta 71	2	31N44	106w21	7:05:24
Yucote Acres 43	1	33N08	96w37	6:26:28
Zabcikville 14	1	31N06	97w21	6:29:24
Zapata 253	1	26N55	99w16	6:37:04
Zavalla 3	1	31N10	94w26	6:17:44
Zephyr 25	1	31N41	98w48	6:35:12
Zionsville 239	1	30N10	96w24	6:25:36
Zipp City 57	1	32N46	96w37	6:26:28
Zipperlenville 73	1	31N04	96w58	6:27:52
Zippville 94	1	29N35	97w58	6:31:52
Zorn 94	1	29N53	97w56	6:31:44
Zuehl 94	1	29N34	98w08	6:32:32
Zunkerville 128	1	28N49	97w51	6:31:24
Zybach 106	3	35N35	100w17	6:41:08

TEXAS

TIME TABLES

UT # 1			UT # 2		
Before 11/18/1883		LMT	Before 11/18/1883		LMT
11/18/1883	12:00	MST	11/18/1883	12:00	PST
3/31/1918	02:00	MWT	3/31/1918	02:00	PWT
10/27/1918	02:00	MST	10/27/1918	02:00	PST
3/30/1919	02:00	MWT	3/30/1919	02:00	PWT
10/26/1919	02:00	MST	10/26/1919	02:00	PST
2/09/1942	02:00	MWT	2/09/1942	02:00	PWT
9/30/1945	02:00	MST	9/30/1945	02:00	PST
4/30/1967	02:00	US#1	4/24/1966	02:00	PDT
....			10/30/1966	02:00	PST
			4/30/1967	02:00	PDT
			10/29/1967	02:00	PST
			4/28/1968	02:00	PDT
			10/27/1968	02:00	PST
			4/27/1969	02:00	MDT
			4/27/1969	02:00	US#1

COUNTIES

1 Beaver
2 Box Elder
3 Cache
4 Carbon
5 Daggett
6 Davis
7 Duchesne
8 Emery
9 Garfield
10 Grand
11 Iron
12 Juab
13 Kane
14 Millard
15 Morgan
16 Piute
17 Rich
18 Salt Lake
19 San Juan
20 Sanpete
21 Sevier
22 Summit
23 Tooele
24 Uintah
25 Utah
26 Wasatch
27 Washington
28 Wayne
29 Weber

Abraham 14	1	39N20	112w40	7:30:40
Adamsville 1	1	38N16	112w48	7:31:12
Alpine 25	1	40N27	111w47	7:27:08
Alta 18	1	40N35	111w52	7:27:28
Altamont 7	1	40N22	110w19	7:21:16
Alton 13	1	37N26	112w29	7:29:56
Altonah 7	1	40N24	110w18	7:21:12
Amalga 3	1	41N52	111w54	7:27:36
American Fork 25	1	40N23	111w48	7:27:12
Anchorage 6	1	41N07	112w01	7:28:04
Aneth 19	1	37N13	109w11	7:16:44
Angle 16	1	38N06	111w59	7:27:56
Annabella 21	1	38N42	112w04	7:28:16
Antimony 9	1	38N07	112w00	7:28:00
Arcadia 7	1	40N10	110w14	7:20:56
Arsenal 6	1	41N07	112w01	7:28:04
Atwood 18	1	40N40	111w54	7:27:36
Aurora 21	1	38N55	111w56	7:27:44
Austin 21	1	38N38	112w07	7:28:28
Avon 3	1	41N38	111w51	7:27:24
Axtell 20	1	39N03	111w50	7:27:20
Bauer 23	1	40N27	112w22	7:29:28
Bear River 2	2	41N41	112w11	7:28:44
Bear River City 2	2	41N37	112w08	7:28:32
Beaver 1	1	38N17	112w38	7:30:32
Beaverdam 2	1	41N46	112w06	7:28:24
Beeton 2	1	41N42	112w05	7:28:20
Belmont Heights 18	1	40N35	111w52	7:27:28
Benchland 2	1	41N46	112w05	7:28:20
Benjamin 25	1	40N07	111w39	7:26:36
Ben Lomond 29	1	41N16	111w58	7:27:52
Bennion 18	1	40N39	111w58	7:27:52
Benson 3	1	41N51	111w52	7:27:28
Beryl 11	1	37N54	113w40	7:34:40
Bicknell 28	1	38N20	111w33	7:26:12
Bingham 18	1	40N33	112w05	7:28:20
Bingham Canyon 18	1	40N32	112w09	7:28:36
Birdseye 25	1	39N56	111w33	7:26:12
Blanding 19	1	37N37	109w29	7:17:56
Bluebell 7	1	40N22	110w13	7:20:52
Bluff 19	1	37N17	109w33	7:18:12
Bluffdale 18	1	40N34	111w57	7:27:48
Bonanza 24	1	40N01	109w11	7:16:44
Boneta 7	1	40N22	110w17	7:21:08
Bonnie 25	1	40N17	111w41	7:26:44
Bothwell 2	2	41N43	112w16	7:29:04
Boulder 9	1	37N55	111w25	7:25:40
Bountiful 6	1	40N53	111w53	7:27:32
Bowery Haven 21	1	38N46	112w05	7:28:20
Brendel 10	1	38N58	109w43	7:18:52
Bridgeland 7	1	40N10	110w14	7:20:56
Brigham City 2	1	41N31	112w01	7:28:04
Brighton 18	1	40N38	111w50	7:27:20
Brooklyn 21	1	38N41	112w09	7:28:36
Bryce Canyon 9	1	37N38	112w10	7:28:40
Bunker Spur 25	1	40N17	111w41	7:26:44
Burbank 14	1	38N24	113w00	7:32:00
Burmester 23	2	40N42	112w27	7:29:48
Burrville 21	1	38N46	112w05	7:28:20
Burton 18	1	40N43	111w54	7:27:36
Bushnell 2	1	41N30	112w00	7:28:00
Butlerville 18	1	40N38	111w49	7:27:16
Cache Junction 3	1	41N50	112w00	7:28:00
Caineville 28	1	38N18	111w25	7:25:40
Camp Williams 18	1	40N34	111w57	7:27:48
Cannonville 9	1	37N34	112w03	7:28:12
Carbonville 4	1	39N36	110w48	7:23:12
Castle Dale 8	1	39N13	111w01	7:24:04
Castle Gate 4	1	39N44	110w52	7:23:28
Castleton 10	1	38N34	109w33	7:18:12
Cedar	1	39N24	110w27	7:21:48
Cedar Breaks Lodge 11	1	37N43	113w03	7:32:12
Cedar City 11	1	37N41	113w04	7:32:16
Cedar Fort 25	1	40N20	112w06	7:28:24
Cedar Valley 25	1	40N20	112w06	7:28:24
Cedarview 7	1	40N27	110w04	7:20:16
Center Creek 26	1	40N29	111w26	7:25:44
Centerfield 20	1	39N08	111w49	7:27:16
Centerville 6	1	40N55	111w52	7:27:28
Central 21	1	38N38	112w07	7:28:28
Central 27	1	37N25	113w38	7:34:32
Charleston 26	1	40N28	111w28	7:25:52
Chester 20	1	39N29	111w28	7:25:52
Christianburg 20	1	39N09	111w49	7:27:16
Circleville 16	1	38N10	112w16	7:29:04
Cisco 10	1	38N58	109w19	7:17:16
Clarkston 3	2	41N55	112w03	7:28:12
Clawson 8	1	39N08	111w06	7:24:24
Clear Creek 2	2	42N00	113w17	7:33:08
Clear Creek 4	1	39N39	111w09	7:24:36
Clearfield 6	1	41N07	112w02	7:28:08
Cleveland 8	1	39N21	110w51	7:23:24
Clifton 6	1	41N07	112w01	7:28:04
Clinton 6	1	41N08	112w02	7:28:08
Clover 23	1	40N14	112w26	7:29:44
Clyde 25	1	40N17	111w41	7:26:44
Coalville 22	1	40N55	111w24	7:25:36
College 3	1	41N43	111w49	7:27:16
Collinston 2	1	41N46	112w06	7:28:24
Colton 25	1	39N51	111w01	7:24:04
Columbia	1	39N31	110w23	7:21:32
Como Springs 15	1	41N02	111w40	7:26:40
Copperton 18	1	40N32	112w09	7:28:36
Corinne 2	2	41N33	112w07	7:28:28
Cornish 3	2	41N58	111w57	7:27:48
Cottonwood 18	1	40N35	111w47	7:27:08
Cottonwood Heights 18	1	40N40	111w50	7:27:20
Cottonwood Meadows 18	1	40N40	111w50	7:27:20
Cove 3	1	41N55	111w48	7:27:12
Cove Fort 14	1	38N17	112w38	7:30:32
Crescent 18	1	40N35	111w52	7:27:28
Croydon 15	1	41N04	111w31	7:26:04
Crystal Springs 2	1	41N38	112w05	7:28:20
Cushing 18	1	40N37	111w53	7:27:32
Daniel 26	1	40N29	111w26	7:25:44
Defas Park 7	1	40N26	110w48	7:23:12
Defense Depot Ogden 29	1	41N13	111w58	7:27:52
Delta 14	1	39N21	112w35	7:30:20
Deseret 14	2	39N17	112w39	7:30:36
Devils Slide 15	1	41N04	111w33	7:26:12
Deweyville 2	1	41N42	112w05	7:28:20
Dragerton 4	1	39N33	110w25	7:21:40
Draper 18	1	40N32	111w52	7:27:28
Dry Fork 24	1	40N27	109w32	7:18:08
Duchesne 7	1	40N10	110w24	7:21:36
Dugway 23	2	40N14	112w45	7:31:00
Dutch John 5	1	40N55	109w24	7:17:36
East Carbon 4	1	39N33	110w25	7:21:40
East Daggett 5	1	40N56	109w12	7:16:48
Eastland Township 19	1	37N52	109w20	7:17:20
East Layton 6	1	41N05	111w56	7:27:44
East Millcreek 18	1	40N42	111w49	7:27:16
East Wellington 4	1	39N33	110w44	7:22:56
Eastwood Hills 18	1	40N43	111w51	7:27:24
Echo 22	1	40N59	111w27	7:25:48
Eden 29	1	41N18	111w49	7:27:16
Edgemont 25	1	40N15	111w40	7:26:40
Elberta 25	1	39N57	111w57	7:27:48
Elgin 10	1	39N00	110w09	7:20:36
Elmo 8	1	39N23	110w49	7:23:16
Elsinore 21	1	38N41	112w09	7:28:36
Elwood 2	2	41N41	112w08	7:28:32
Emery 8	1	38N55	111w15	7:25:00
Emigration 18	1	40N43	111w47	7:27:08
Emory 22	1	41N03	111w19	7:25:16
Enoch 11	1	37N47	113w02	7:32:08
Enterprise 15	1	41N02	111w40	7:26:40
Enterprise 27	1	37N34	113w43	7:34:52
Ephraim 20	1	39N22	111w35	7:26:20
Erda 23	1	40N32	112w18	7:29:12
Escalante 9	1	37N47	111w36	7:26:24
Esk Dale 14	2	38N56	114w02	7:36:08
Etna 2	2	41N42	113w53	7:35:32
Eureka 12	1	39N58	112w07	7:28:28
Fairfield 25	1	40N16	112w06	7:28:24
Fairgrounds 18	1	40N49	111w56	7:27:44
Fairview 20	1	39N38	111w26	7:25:44
Farmington 6	1	40N59	111w53	7:27:32
Farr West 29	1	41N16	111w58	7:27:52
Faust 23	1	40N11	112w24	7:29:36
Fayette 20	1	39N14	111w51	7:27:24
Ferron 8	1	39N05	111w08	7:24:32
Fielding 2	2	41N49	112w07	7:28:28
Fillmore 14	1	38N58	112w20	7:29:20
Fish Lake 21	1	38N46	112w05	7:28:20
Flowell 14	1	38N58	112w20	7:29:20
Foothill 18	1	40N44	111w50	7:27:20
Fort Duchesne 24	1	40N17	109w52	7:19:28
Fountain Green 20	1	39N38	111w38	7:26:32
Francis 22	1	40N37	111w17	7:25:08
Freedom 20	1	39N32	111w35	7:26:20
Freeport Center 6	1	41N07	112w01	7:28:04
Fremont 28	1	38N27	111w37	7:26:28
Fruita 28	1	38N17	111w15	7:25:00
Fruit Heights 6	1	41N03	111w55	7:27:40
Fruitland 7	1	40N13	110w51	7:23:24
Garden City 17	1	41N57	111w24	7:25:36
Garland 2	2	41N45	112w10	7:28:40
Garrison 14	2	38N56	114w02	7:36:08
Genola 25	1	40N01	111w50	7:27:20
Gilluly 25	1	40N15	111w40	7:26:40
Glen Canyon	1	37N01	111w34	7:26:16
Glendale 13	1	37N19	112w36	7:30:24
Glenwood 21	1	38N46	111w59	7:27:56
Gooseberry 21	1	38N57	111w51	7:27:24
Gorder 29	1	41N12	111w58	7:27:52
Goshen 25	1	39N57	111w54	7:27:36
Goshute	2	39N53	114w00	7:36:00
Granger 18	1	40N42	111w58	7:27:52
Granger-Hunter 18	1	40N42	111w58	7:27:52
Granite 18	1	40N35	111w52	7:27:28
Granite Park 18	1	40N42	111w53	7:27:32
Grantsville 23	2	40N36	112w28	7:29:52
Greendale 5	1	40N55	109w24	7:17:36
Greenfield Village 18	1	40N40	111w50	7:27:20
Green Lake 5	1	41N00	109w43	7:18:52
Green River 8	1	39N00	110w10	7:20:40
Greenville 1	1	38N15	112w43	7:30:52
Greenwich 16	1	38N26	111w55	7:27:40
Grouse Creek 2	2	41N42	113w53	7:35:32
Grover 28	1	38N17	111w29	7:25:56
Gunlock 27	1	37N17	113w46	7:35:04
Gunnison 20	1	39N09	111w49	7:27:16
Gusher 24	1	40N18	109w49	7:19:16
Hailstone 26	1	40N29	111w26	7:25:44
Hanksville 28	1	38N22	110w43	7:22:52
Hanna 7	1	40N26	110w48	7:23:12
Hardy Beet Spur 25	1	40N21	111w45	7:27:00
Harrisburg Junction 27	1	37N07	113w35	7:34:20
Harrisville 29	1	41N17	111w59	7:27:56
Harrisville Heights 29	1	41N13	111w58	7:27:52
Hatch 9	1	37N39	112w26	7:29:44
Hatton 14	1	38N48	112w26	7:29:44
Heber 26	1	40N31	111w25	7:25:40
Helper 4	1	39N41	110w51	7:23:24
Henefer 22	1	41N01	111w30	7:26:00
Henrieville 9	1	37N34	112w00	7:28:00
Hermitage 29	1	41N16	111w58	7:27:52
Herriman 18	1	40N34	111w57	7:27:48
Hiawatha 4	1	39N29	111w01	7:24:04
Hildale 27	1	37N01	112w58	7:31:52
Hill Air Force Base 6	1	41N14	111w57	7:27:48
Hill Creek 24	1	39N43	109w35	7:18:20

UTAH

Hilldale 27	1	37N01	112w58	7:31:52
Hinckley 14	2	39N20	112w40	7:30:40
Hite 9	1	37N53	110w33	7:22:12
Holden 14	1	39N06	112w16	7:29:04
Holladay 18	1	40N40	111w50	7:27:20
Honeyville 2	1	41N38	112w04	7:28:16
Hooper 29	2	41N15	112w07	7:28:28
Howell 2	2	41N48	112w27	7:29:48
Hoytsville 22	1	40N55	111w24	7:25:36
Hunter 18	1	40N43	112w00	7:28:00
Huntington 8	1	39N20	110w58	7:23:52
Huntsville 29	1	41N16	111w46	7:27:04
Hurricane 27	1	37N11	113w17	7:33:08
Hyde Park 3	1	41N48	111w49	7:27:16
Hyrum 3	1	41N31	111w45	7:27:00
Ibapah 23	2	40N02	113w59	7:35:56
Indianola 20	1	39N38	111w26	7:25:44
Ioka 7	1	40N27	110w04	7:20:16
Ivins 27	1	37N08	113w41	7:34:44
Jensen 24	1	40N22	109w20	7:17:20
Jericho	1	39N45	112w57	7:31:48
Jordan 18	1	40N36	111w57	7:27:48
Joseph 21	1	38N38	112w13	7:28:52
Junction 16	1	38N14	112w13	7:28:52
Kamas 22	1	40N38	111w17	7:25:08
Kanab 13	1	37N03	112w32	7:30:08
Kanarraville 11	1	37N32	113w11	7:32:44
Kanesville 29	2	41N15	112w07	7:28:28
Kanosh 14	1	38N48	112w26	7:29:44
Kaysville 6	1	41N02	111w56	7:27:44
Kearns 18	1	40N39	112w00	7:28:00
Keetley 26	1	40N29	111w26	7:25:44
Kenilworth 4	1	39N41	110w48	7:23:12
Kimball Junction 22	1	40N39	111w29	7:25:56
Kingston 16	1	38N13	112w11	7:28:44
Knudsen Corner 18	1	40N38	111w50	7:27:20
Koosharem 21	1	38N31	111w53	7:27:32
Lake Point 23	1	40N32	112w18	7:29:12
Lake Shore 25	1	40N07	111w39	7:26:36
Lakeside Resort 21	1	38N31	111w53	7:27:32
Laketown 17	1	41N49	111w19	7:25:16
Lakeview 25	1	40N15	111w40	7:26:40
Lapoint 24	1	40N24	109w48	7:19:12
Lark 18	1	40N31	112w06	7:28:24
La Sal 19	1	38N20	109w15	7:17:00
La Verkin 27	1	37N12	113w16	7:33:04
Lawrence 8	1	39N20	110w58	7:23:52
Layton 6	1	41N04	111w58	7:27:52
Leamington 14	1	39N32	112w17	7:29:08
Leeds 27	1	37N14	113w22	7:33:28
Leeton 24	1	40N27	110w04	7:20:16
Lehi 25	1	40N24	111w51	7:27:24
Leland 25	1	40N07	111w39	7:26:36
Levan 12	1	39N33	111w52	7:27:28
Lewiston 3	1	41N59	111w51	7:27:24
Liberty 29	1	41N18	111w49	7:27:16
Lincoln 23	1	40N32	112w18	7:29:12
Lindon 25	1	40N20	111w43	7:26:52
Littleton 15	1	41N02	111w40	7:26:40
Loa 28	1	38N24	111w39	7:26:36
Logan 3	1	41N44	111w50	7:27:20
Long Valley Junction 13	1	37N26	112w29	7:29:56
Lucin	2	41N21	113w54	7:35:36
Lund 11	1	38N00	113w26	7:33:44
Lyman 28	1	38N24	111w35	7:26:20
Lynn 2	2	41N52	113w42	7:34:48
Lynndyl 14	1	39N31	112w22	7:29:28
Madsen 2	1	41N38	112w05	7:28:20
Maeser 24	1	40N28	109w35	7:18:20
Magna 18	1	40N42	112w06	7:28:24
Mammoth 12	1	39N57	112w07	7:28:28
Manderfield 1	1	38N22	112w39	7:30:36
Manila 5	1	40N59	109w43	7:18:52
Manti 20	1	39N16	111w38	7:26:32
Mantua 2	1	41N30	111w57	7:27:48
Mapleton 25	1	40N08	111w35	7:26:20
Marion 22	1	40N37	111w16	7:25:04
Marriott 29	1	41N16	111w58	7:27:52
Martin 4	1	39N41	110w51	7:23:24
Marysvale 16	1	38N27	112w14	7:28:56
Mayfield 20	1	39N07	111w43	7:26:52
Meadow 14	1	38N53	112w24	7:29:36
Meadowville 17	1	41N49	111w19	7:25:16
Mendon 3	1	41N42	111w59	7:27:56
Mexican Hat 19	1	37N09	109w52	7:19:28
Middleton 27	1	37N07	113w35	7:34:20
Midvale 18	1	40N37	111w54	7:27:36
Midway 26	1	40N31	111w28	7:25:52
Milburn 20	1	39N38	111w26	7:25:44
Milford 1	1	38N24	113w01	7:32:04
Millcreek 18	1	40N43	111w51	7:27:24
Mills 12	1	39N29	112w02	7:28:08
Millville 3	1	41N41	111w50	7:27:20
Milton 15	1	41N02	111w40	7:26:40
Minersville 1	1	38N13	112w56	7:31:44
Moab 10	1	38N35	109w33	7:18:12
Modena	1	37N48	113w56	7:35:44
Molen 8	1	39N05	111w08	7:24:32
Mona 12	1	39N49	111w51	7:27:24
Monarch 7	1	40N27	110w04	7:20:16
Monroe 21	1	38N38	112w07	7:28:28
Montezuma Creek 19	1	37N17	109w20	7:17:20
Monticello 19	1	37N52	109w21	7:17:24
Monument Valley 19	1	37N09	109w52	7:19:28
Moore 8	1	39N05	111w08	7:24:32
Morgan 15	1	41N02	111w41	7:26:44
Moroni 20	1	39N32	111w35	7:26:20
Mountain Green 15	1	41N02	111w40	7:26:40
Mountain Home 7	1	40N24	110w23	7:21:32
Mount Carmel 13	1	37N15	112w40	7:30:40
Mount Olympus 18	1	40N41	111w48	7:27:12
Mount Pleasant 20	1	39N33	111w27	7:25:48
Murray 18	1	40N40	111w53	7:27:32
Myton 7	1	40N12	110w04	7:20:16
Naples 24	1	40N27	109w32	7:18:08
Navajo 19	1	37N11	109w31	7:18:04
Neola 7	1	40N26	110w02	7:20:08
Nephi 12	1	39N43	111w50	7:27:20
Newcastle 11	1	37N40	113w33	7:34:12
New Harmony 27	1	37N29	113w19	7:33:16
Newton 3	2	41N52	112w00	7:28:00
Nibley 3	1	41N40	111w50	7:27:20
North Creek 1	1	38N17	112w38	7:30:32
North Davis 6	1	41N06	112w00	7:28:00
North Logan 3	1	41N46	111w48	7:27:12
North Ogden 29	1	41N19	111w58	7:27:52
North Salt Lake 6	1	40N50	111w55	7:27:40
Oak City 14	1	39N22	112w20	7:29:20
Oak Creek 20	1	39N38	111w26	7:25:44
Oakley 22	1	40N43	111w18	7:25:12
Oasis 14	1	39N18	112w38	7:30:32
Ogden 29	1	41N13	111w58	7:27:52
Ogden Valley 29	1	41N18	111w44	7:26:56
Olmstead 25	1	40N15	111w40	7:26:40
Onaqui 23	1	40N13	112w23	7:29:32
Ophir 23	1	40N22	112w15	7:29:00
Orangeville 8	1	39N14	111w03	7:24:12
Orderville 13	1	37N17	112w38	7:30:32
Orem 25	1	40N19	111w42	7:26:48
Ouray 24	1	40N06	109w41	7:18:44
Pallas 18	1	40N40	111w54	7:27:36
Palmyra 25	1	40N07	111w39	7:26:36
Panguitch 9	1	37N50	112w26	7:29:44
Paradise 3	1	41N34	111w50	7:27:20
Paragonah 11	1	37N53	112w46	7:31:04
Park City 22	1	40N43	111w32	7:26:08
Park Terrace 18	1	40N43	111w51	7:27:24
Park Valley 2	2	41N49	113w20	7:33:20
Parowan 11	1	37N51	112w50	7:31:20
Partoun 12	2	39N42	113w49	7:35:16
Payson 25	1	40N03	111w44	7:26:56
Penrose 2	1	41N42	112w09	7:28:36
Peoa 22	1	40N44	111w21	7:25:24
Perry 2	1	41N28	112w02	7:28:08
Petersboro 3	1	41N42	111w59	7:27:56
Peterson 15	1	41N02	111w40	7:26:40
Pickleville 17	1	41N55	111w23	7:25:32
Pine Cliff 22	1	40N55	111w24	7:25:36
Pine Valley 27	1	37N23	113w31	7:34:04
Pinto 11	1	37N40	113w33	7:34:12
Pintura 27	1	37N21	113w16	7:33:04
Pioneer 18	1	40N46	111w53	7:27:32
Plain City 29	2	41N18	112w06	7:28:24
Pleasant Green Acres 18	1	40N44	112w01	7:28:04
Pleasant Grove 25	1	40N22	111w44	7:26:56
Pleasant View 25	1	40N15	111w40	7:26:40
Pleasant View 29	1	41N19	112w00	7:28:00
Plymouth 2	2	41N53	112w09	7:28:36
Portage 2	2	41N59	112w14	7:28:56
Porterville 15	1	40N59	111w41	7:26:44
Price 4	1	39N36	110w49	7:23:16
Promontory Point 2	2	41N13	112w25	7:29:40
Providence 3	1	41N43	111w49	7:27:16
Provo 25	1	40N14	111w39	7:26:36
Randlett 24	1	40N14	109w48	7:19:12
Randolph 17	1	41N40	111w11	7:24:44
Redmond 21	1	39N00	111w52	7:27:28
Redwood 18	1	40N42	111w56	7:27:44
Richfield 21	1	38N46	112w05	7:28:20
Richmond 3	1	41N56	111w48	7:27:12
Richville 15	1	41N02	111w40	7:26:40
Riverdale 29	1	41N11	112w00	7:28:00
River Heights 3	1	41N43	111w50	7:27:20
Riverside 2	2	41N48	112w10	7:28:40
Riverton 18	1	40N31	111w56	7:27:44
Rockville 27	1	37N10	113w02	7:32:08
Roosevelt 7	1	40N18	109w59	7:19:56
Roper 18	1	40N43	111w54	7:27:36
Rosette 2	2	41N49	113w20	7:33:20
Round Valley 17	1	41N49	111w19	7:25:16
Roy 29	1	41N10	112w02	7:28:08
Rubys Inn 9	1	37N40	112w10	7:28:40
Saint George 27	1	37N11	113w42	7:34:48
Saint John 23	2	40N21	112w26	7:29:44
Salem 25	1	40N03	111w40	7:26:40
Salina 21	1	38N58	111w51	7:27:24
Saltair	2	40N46	112w06	7:28:24
Salt Lake City 18	1	40N45	111w53	7:27:32
Sandy 18	1	40N35	111w52	7:27:28
Sandy City 18	1	40N36	111w53	7:27:32
Santa Clara 27	1	37N08	113w39	7:34:36
Santaquin 25	1	39N59	111w47	7:27:08
Scipio 14	2	39N15	112w06	7:28:24
Scofield 4	1	39N44	111w10	7:24:40
Sevier 21	1	38N35	112w15	7:29:00
Sherwood Park 18	1	40N35	111w52	7:27:28
Shivwits 27	1	37N11	113w45	7:35:00
Sigurd 21	1	38N50	111w58	7:27:52
Silver Fork 18	1	40N45	111w52	7:27:28
Skull Valley Indian Reservat 23	1	40N17	109w52	7:19:28
Slaterville 29	1	41N16	111w58	7:27:52
Smithfield 3	1	41N50	111w50	7:27:20
Smoot 25	1	40N15	111w40	7:26:40
Snowville 2	2	41N58	112w43	7:30:52
Snyderville 22	1	40N39	111w29	7:25:56
Soldier Summit 26	1	39N56	111w05	7:24:20
South Cottonwood 18	1	40N38	111w50	7:27:20
South Davis 6	1	40N52	111w53	7:27:32
South Jordan 18	1	40N34	111w57	7:27:48
South Ogden 29	1	41N11	111w58	7:27:52
South Salt Lake 18	1	40N43	111w53	7:27:32
South Weber 6	1	41N08	111w57	7:27:48
Spanish Fork 25	1	40N07	111w39	7:26:36
Spring City 20	1	39N29	111w30	7:26:00
Springdale 27	1	37N11	113w00	7:32:00
Springdell 25	1	40N15	111w40	7:26:40
Spring Glen 4	1	39N40	110w51	7:23:24
Spring Lake 25	1	40N02	111w44	7:26:56
Springville 25	1	40N10	111w37	7:26:28
Spry 9	1	37N49	112w26	7:29:44
Standardville 4	1	39N41	110w51	7:23:24
Standrod 2	2	42N01	113w17	7:33:08
Stansbury Park 23	1	40N32	112w18	7:29:12
Starr 12	1	39N49	111w51	7:27:24
Sterling 20	1	39N12	111w42	7:26:48
Stockton 23	1	40N27	112w22	7:29:28
Stoddard 15	1	41N02	111w40	7:26:40
Strawberry Valley 26	1	40N04	111w04	7:24:16
Sugar House 18	1	40N43	111w51	7:27:24
Sugarville 14	1	39N21	112w35	7:30:20
Sulphurdale	1	38N34	112w35	7:30:20
Summit 11	1	37N48	112w56	7:31:44
Sundance 25	1	40N15	111w40	7:26:40
Sunnyside 4	1	39N34	110w23	7:21:32
Sunset 6	1	41N08	112w01	7:28:04
Sutherland 14	1	39N21	112w35	7:30:20
Swan Creek 17	1	41N56	111w23	7:25:32
Syracuse 6	1	41N06	112w03	7:28:12
Tabiona 7	1	40N21	110w43	7:22:52
Talmage 7	1	40N21	110w26	7:21:44
Taylor 29	1	41N13	111w58	7:27:52
Taylorsville 18	1	40N40	111w54	7:27:36
Teasdale 28	1	38N17	111w29	7:25:56
Terra 23	2	40N14	112w45	7:31:00
Thatcher 2	1	41N42	112w09	7:28:36
Thistle	1	40N00	111w30	7:26:00
Thompson 10	1	38N58	109w43	7:18:52
Thompsonville 16	1	38N27	112w14	7:28:56
Tod Park	1	40N30	112w20	7:29:20
Tooele 23	1	40N32	112w18	7:29:12
Tooele Army Depot 23	1	40N32	112w18	7:29:12
Toquerville 27	1	37N15	113w17	7:33:08
Torrey 28	1	38N18	111w25	7:25:40
Tremonton 2	2	41N43	112w10	7:28:40
Trenton 3	2	41N55	111w56	7:27:44
Tridell 24	1	40N27	109w51	7:19:24
Tropic 9	1	37N37	112w05	7:28:20
Trout Creek 12	2	39N42	113w50	7:35:20
Uintah 29	1	41N09	111w56	7:27:44
Union 18	1	40N37	111w53	7:27:32
Unitah And Ouray Indian Rese 7	1	40N59	111w53	7:27:32
University 25	1	40N15	111w40	7:26:40
Upalco 7	1	40N17	110w13	7:20:52
Upton 22	1	40N55	111w24	7:25:36
Utah State University 3	1	41N43	111w49	7:27:16
Utida 3	1	41N58	111w57	7:27:48
Uvada	1	37N43	114w03	7:36:12
Val Verda 6	1	40N53	111w53	7:27:32
Venice 21	1	38N46	112w05	7:28:20
Vermillion 21	1	38N51	111w58	7:27:52
Vernal 24	1	40N27	109w32	7:18:08
Vernon 23	2	40N06	112w26	7:29:44
Veyo 27	1	37N20	113w41	7:34:44
Vineyard 25	1	40N17	111w41	7:26:44
Virgin 27	1	37N12	113w11	7:32:44
Vivian Park 25	1	40N15	111w40	7:26:40
Wahsatch	1	41N12	111w06	7:24:24
Wales 20	1	39N29	111w38	7:26:32
Wallsburg 26	1	40N23	111w25	7:25:40
Wanship 22	1	40N49	111w24	7:25:36
Warren 29	1	41N16	111w58	7:27:52
Washington 27	1	37N08	113w31	7:34:04
Washington Terrace 29	1	41N11	111w59	7:27:56
Wellington 4	1	39N32	110w44	7:22:56
Wellsville 3	1	41N38	111w56	7:27:44
Wendover 23	2	40N44	114w02	7:36:08
West Bountiful 6	1	40N54	111w54	7:27:36
West Box Elder 2	2	41N41	113w32	7:34:08
West Daggett 5	1	40N58	109w43	7:18:52
West Jordan 18	1	40N37	111w57	7:27:48
West Juab 12	2	39N43	113w06	7:32:24
West Kaysville 6	1	41N03	111w57	7:27:48
West Layton 6	1	41N04	111w57	7:27:48
West Point 6	1	41N07	112w03	7:28:12
West Side 24	1	40N19	109w52	7:19:28
West Warren 29	1	41N16	111w58	7:27:52
West Weber 29	1	41N13	111w58	7:27:52
Wheelon 2	1	41N46	112w06	7:28:24
White Canyon	1	37N49	110w26	7:21:44
White City 18	1	40N34	111w52	7:27:28
Whiterocks 24	1	40N28	109w56	7:19:44
Wicks 25	1	40N15	111w40	7:26:40
Wildwood 25	1	40N15	111w40	7:26:40
Willard 2	1	41N25	112w02	7:28:08
Wilson 29	1	41N13	111w58	7:27:52
Woodland 22	1	40N37	111w16	7:25:04
Woodrow 14	1	39N21	112w35	7:30:20
Woodruff 17	1	41N31	111w10	7:24:40
Woods Cross 6	1	40N53	111w54	7:27:36
Woodside	1	39N16	110w21	7:21:24
Yost 2	2	41N58	113w33	7:34:12
Zane	1	37N56	113w35	7:34:20
Zion National Park 27	1	37N11	113w00	7:32:00

TIME TABLES

VT # 1		
Before 11/18/1883		LMT
11/18/1883	12:00	EST
3/31/1918	02:00	EWT
10/27/1918	02:00	EST
3/30/1919	02:00	EWT
10/26/1919	02:00	EST
2/09/1942	02:00	EWT
9/30/1945	02:00	EST
4/24/1955	02:00	US#2

VT # 2		
Before 11/18/1883		LMT
11/18/1883	12:00	EST
3/31/1918	02:00	EWT
10/27/1918	02:00	EST
3/30/1919	02:00	EWT
10/26/1919	02:00	EST
4/24/1938	02:00	US#2

VT # 3		
Before 11/18/1883		LMT
11/18/1883	12:00	EST
3/31/1918	02:00	EWT
10/27/1918	02:00	EST
3/30/1919	02:00	EWT
10/26/1919	02:00	EST
4/30/1939	02:00	US#2

VT # 4		
Before 11/18/1883		LMT
11/18/1883	12:00	EST
3/31/1918	02:00	EWT
10/27/1918	02:00	EST
3/30/1919	02:00	EWT
10/26/1919	02:00	EST
4/28/1940	02:00	US#2

VT # 5		
Before 11/18/1883		LMT
11/18/1883	12:00	EST
3/31/1918	02:00	EWT
10/27/1918	02:00	EST
3/30/1919	02:00	EWT
10/26/1919	02:00	EST
4/27/1941	02:00	US#2

VT # 6		
Before 11/18/1883		LMT
11/18/1883	12:00	EST
3/31/1918	02:00	EWT
10/27/1918	02:00	EST
3/30/1919	02:00	EWT
10/26/1919	02:00	EST
2/09/1942	02:00	EWT
9/30/1945	02:00	EST
4/28/1946	02:00	US#2

VT # 7		
Before 11/18/1883		LMT
11/18/1883	12:00	EST
3/31/1918	02:00	EWT
10/27/1918	02:00	EST
3/30/1919	02:00	EWT
10/26/1919	02:00	EST
2/09/1942	02:00	EWT
9/30/1945	02:00	EST
4/27/1947	02:00	US#2

VT # 8		
Before 11/18/1883		LMT
11/18/1883	12:00	EST
3/31/1918	02:00	EWT
10/27/1918	02:00	EST
3/30/1919	02:00	EWT
10/26/1919	02:00	EST
2/09/1942	02:00	EWT
9/30/1945	02:00	EST
4/25/1948	02:00	US#2

VT # 9		
Before 11/18/1883		LMT
11/18/1883	12:00	EST
3/31/1918	02:00	EWT
10/27/1918	02:00	EST
3/30/1919	02:00	EWT
10/26/1919	02:00	EST
2/09/1942	02:00	EWT
9/30/1945	02:00	EST
4/24/1949	02:00	US#2

VT # 10		
Before 11/18/1883		LMT
11/18/1883	12:00	EST
3/31/1918	02:00	EWT
10/27/1918	02:00	EST
3/30/1919	02:00	EWT
10/26/1919	02:00	EST
2/09/1942	02:00	EWT
9/30/1945	02:00	EST
4/29/1951	02:00	US#2

VT # 11		
Before 11/18/1883		LMT
11/18/1883	12:00	EST
3/31/1918	02:00	EWT
10/27/1918	02:00	EST
3/30/1919	02:00	EWT
10/26/1919	02:00	EST
2/09/1942	02:00	EWT
9/30/1945	02:00	EST
4/27/1952	02:00	US#2

VT # 12		
Before 11/18/1883		LMT
11/18/1883	12:00	EST
3/31/1918	02:00	EWT
10/27/1918	02:00	EST
3/30/1919	02:00	EWT
10/26/1919	02:00	EST
4/27/1941	02:00	EDT
9/28/1941	02:00	EST
2/09/1942	02:00	EWT
9/30/1945	02:00	EST
4/24/1955	02:00	US#2

VT # 13		
Before 11/18/1883		LMT
11/18/1883	12:00	EST
3/31/1918	02:00	EWT
10/27/1918	02:00	EST
3/30/1919	02:00	EWT
10/26/1919	02:00	EST
4/28/1935	02:00	US#2

VT # 14		
Before 11/18/1883		LMT
11/18/1883	12:00	EST
3/31/1918	02:00	EWT
10/27/1918	02:00	EST
3/30/1919	02:00	EWT
10/26/1919	02:00	EST
2/09/1942	02:00	EWT
9/30/1945	02:00	EST
4/25/1948	02:00	EDT
9/26/1948	02:00	EST
4/24/1955	02:00	US#2

VT # 15		
Before 11/18/1883		LMT
11/18/1883	12:00	EST
3/31/1918	02:00	EWT
10/27/1918	02:00	EST
3/30/1919	02:00	EWT
10/26/1919	02:00	EST
4/26/1936	02:00	US#2

VT # 16		
Before 11/18/1883		LMT
11/18/1883	12:00	EST
3/31/1918	02:00	EWT
10/27/1918	02:00	EST
3/30/1919	02:00	EWT
10/26/1919	02:00	EST
4/26/1931	02:00	US#2

VT # 17		
Before 11/18/1883		LMT
11/18/1883	12:00	EST
3/31/1918	02:00	EWT
10/27/1918	02:00	EST
3/30/1919	02:00	EWT
10/26/1919	02:00	EST
4/28/1940	02:00	EDT
9/29/1940	02:00	EST
4/27/1941	02:00	EDT
9/28/1941	02:00	EST
2/09/1942	02:00	EWT
9/30/1945	02:00	EST
4/24/1955	02:00	US#2

VT # 18		
Before 11/18/1883		LMT
11/18/1883	12:00	EST
3/31/1918	02:00	EWT
10/27/1918	02:00	EST
3/30/1919	02:00	EWT
10/26/1919	02:00	EST
2/09/1942	02:00	EWT
9/30/1945	02:00	EST
4/24/1949	02:00	EDT
9/25/1949	02:00	EST
4/30/1950	02:00	EDT
9/24/1950	02:00	EST
4/24/1955	02:00	US#2

VT # 19		
Before 11/18/1883		LMT
11/18/1883	12:00	EST
3/31/1918	02:00	EWT
10/27/1918	02:00	EST
3/30/1919	02:00	EWT
10/26/1919	02:00	EST
4/30/1939	02:00	EDT
9/24/1939	02:00	EST
4/28/1940	02:00	EDT
9/29/1940	02:00	EST
4/27/1941	02:00	EDT
9/28/1941	02:00	EST
2/09/1942	02:00	EWT
9/30/1945	02:00	EST
4/24/1955	02:00	US#2

VT # 20		
Before 11/18/1883		LMT
11/18/1883	12:00	EST
3/31/1918	02:00	EWT
10/27/1918	02:00	EST
3/30/1919	02:00	EWT
10/26/1919	02:00	EST
2/09/1942	02:00	EWT
9/30/1945	02:00	EST
4/27/1947	02:00	EDT
9/28/1947	02:00	EST
4/25/1948	02:00	EDT
9/26/1948	02:00	EST
4/24/1949	02:00	EDT
9/25/1949	02:00	EST
4/24/1955	02:00	US#2

VT # 21		
Before 11/18/1883		LMT
11/18/1883	12:00	EST
3/31/1918	02:00	EWT
10/27/1918	02:00	EST
3/30/1919	02:00	EWT
10/26/1919	02:00	EST
4/24/1938	02:00	EDT
9/25/1938	02:00	EST
4/30/1939	02:00	EDT
9/24/1939	02:00	EST
4/28/1940	02:00	EDT
9/29/1940	02:00	EST
4/27/1941	02:00	EDT
9/28/1941	02:00	EST
2/09/1942	02:00	EWT
9/30/1945	02:00	EST
4/24/1955	02:00	US#2

VT # 22		
Before 11/18/1883		LMT
11/18/1883	12:00	EST
3/31/1918	02:00	EWT
10/27/1918	02:00	EST
3/30/1919	02:00	EWT
10/26/1919	02:00	EST
2/09/1942	02:00	EWT
9/30/1945	02:00	EST
4/27/1947	02:00	EDT
9/28/1947	02:00	EST
4/25/1948	02:00	EDT
9/26/1948	02:00	EST
4/24/1949	02:00	EDT
9/25/1949	02:00	EST
4/30/1950	02:00	EDT
9/24/1950	02:00	EST
4/24/1955	02:00	US#2

VT # 23		
Before 11/18/1883		LMT
11/18/1883	12:00	EST
3/31/1918	02:00	EWT
10/27/1918	02:00	EST
3/30/1919	02:00	EWT
10/26/1919	02:00	EST
4/30/1922	02:00	EDT
9/24/1922	02:00	EST
4/29/1923	02:00	EDT
9/30/1923	02:00	EST
4/27/1924	02:00	EDT
9/28/1924	02:00	EST
4/26/1925	02:00	EDT
9/27/1925	02:00	EST
4/25/1926	02:00	EDT
9/26/1926	02:00	EST
4/24/1927	02:00	EDT
9/25/1927	02:00	EST
4/29/1928	02:00	EDT
9/30/1928	02:00	EST
4/28/1929	02:00	EDT
9/29/1929	02:00	EST
4/27/1930	02:00	EDT
9/28/1930	02:00	EST
4/26/1931	02:00	EDT
9/27/1931	02:00	EST
4/24/1932	02:00	EDT
9/25/1932	02:00	EST
4/30/1933	02:00	EDT
10/01/1933	02:00	EST
4/28/1935	02:00	US#2

VT # 24		
Before 11/18/1883		LMT
11/18/1883	12:00	EST
3/31/1918	02:00	EWT
10/27/1918	02:00	EST
3/30/1919	02:00	EWT
10/26/1919	02:00	EST
4/28/1929	02:00	EDT
9/29/1929	02:00	EST
4/27/1930	02:00	EDT
9/28/1930	02:00	EST
4/26/1931	02:00	EDT
9/27/1931	02:00	EST
5/24/1936	02:00	EDT
9/27/1936	02:00	EST
4/25/1937	02:00	US#2

VT # 25		
Before 11/18/1883		LMT
11/18/1883	12:00	EST
3/31/1918	02:00	EWT
10/27/1918	02:00	EST
3/30/1919	02:00	EWT
10/26/1919	02:00	EST
4/24/1938	02:00	EDT
9/25/1938	02:00	EST
4/30/1939	02:00	EDT
9/24/1939	02:00	EST
4/28/1940	02:00	EDT
9/29/1940	02:00	EST
4/27/1941	02:00	EDT
9/28/1941	02:00	EST
2/09/1942	02:00	EWT
9/30/1945	02:00	EST
4/27/1947	02:00	US#2

VT # 26		
Before 11/18/1883		LMT
11/18/1883	12:00	EST
3/31/1918	02:00	EWT
10/27/1918	02:00	EST
3/30/1919	02:00	EWT
10/26/1919	02:00	EST
4/24/1938	02:00	EDT
9/25/1938	02:00	EST
4/30/1939	02:00	EDT
9/24/1939	02:00	EST
4/28/1940	02:00	EDT
9/29/1940	02:00	EST
4/27/1941	02:00	EDT
9/28/1941	02:00	EST
2/09/1942	02:00	EWT
9/30/1945	02:00	EST
4/25/1948	02:00	US#2

VT # 27		
Before 11/18/1883		LMT
11/18/1883	12:00	EST
3/31/1918	02:00	EWT
10/27/1918	02:00	EST
3/30/1919	02:00	EWT
10/26/1919	02:00	EST
4/25/1937	02:00	US#2

VT # 28		
Before 11/18/1883		LMT
11/18/1883	12:00	EST
3/31/1918	02:00	EWT
10/27/1918	02:00	EST
3/30/1919	02:00	EWT
10/26/1919	02:00	EST
4/24/1938	02:00	EDT
9/25/1938	02:00	EST
4/30/1939	02:00	EDT
9/24/1939	02:00	EST
4/28/1940	02:00	EDT
9/29/1940	02:00	EST
4/27/1941	02:00	EDT
9/28/1941	02:00	EST
2/09/1942	02:00	EWT
9/30/1945	02:00	EST
4/25/1948	02:00	EDT
9/26/1948	02:00	EST
4/24/1949	02:00	EDT
9/25/1949	02:00	EST
4/30/1950	02:00	EDT
9/24/1950	02:00	EST
4/24/1955	02:00	US#2

VT # 29		
Before 11/18/1883		LMT
11/18/1883	12:00	EST
3/31/1918	02:00	EWT
10/27/1918	02:00	EST
3/30/1919	02:00	EWT
10/26/1919	02:00	EST
4/29/1934	02:00	EDT
9/30/1934	02:00	EST
4/28/1935	02:00	EDT
9/29/1935	02:00	EST
4/26/1936	02:00	EDT
9/27/1936	02:00	EST
4/25/1937	02:00	EDT
9/26/1937	02:00	EST
4/24/1938	02:00	EDT
9/25/1938	02:00	EST
4/30/1939	02:00	EDT
9/24/1939	02:00	EST
4/28/1940	02:00	EDT
9/29/1940	02:00	EST
4/27/1941	02:00	EDT
9/28/1941	02:00	EST
2/09/1942	02:00	EWT
9/30/1945	02:00	EST
4/27/1947	02:00	EDT
9/28/1947	02:00	EST
4/29/1951	02:00	US#2

VT # 30		
Before 11/18/1883		LMT
11/18/1883	12:00	EST
3/31/1918	02:00	EWT
10/27/1918	02:00	EST
3/30/1919	02:00	EWT
10/26/1919	02:00	EST
4/30/1939	02:00	EDT
9/24/1939	02:00	EST
4/28/1940	02:00	EDT
9/29/1940	02:00	EST
4/27/1941	02:00	EDT
9/28/1941	02:00	EST
2/09/1942	02:00	EWT
9/30/1945	02:00	EST
4/27/1947	02:00	US#2

VT # 31		
Before 11/18/1883		LMT
11/18/1883	12:00	EST
3/31/1918	02:00	EWT
10/27/1918	02:00	EST
3/30/1919	02:00	EWT
10/26/1919	02:00	EST
4/24/1938	02:00	EDT
9/25/1938	02:00	EST
2/09/1942	02:00	EWT
9/30/1945	02:00	EST
4/24/1949	02:00	US#2

VT # 32		
Before 11/18/1883		LMT
11/18/1883	12:00	EST
3/31/1918	02:00	EWT
10/27/1918	02:00	EST
3/30/1919	02:00	EWT
10/26/1919	02:00	EST
4/30/1939	02:00	EDT
9/24/1939	02:00	EST
4/28/1940	02:00	EDT
9/29/1940	02:00	EST
4/27/1941	02:00	EDT
9/28/1941	02:00	EST
2/09/1942	02:00	EWT
9/30/1945	02:00	EST
4/29/1951	02:00	US#2

VT # 33		
Before 11/18/1883		LMT
11/18/1883	12:00	EST
3/31/1918	02:00	EWT
10/27/1918	02:00	EST
3/30/1919	02:00	EWT
10/26/1919	02:00	EST
4/28/1935	02:00	EDT
9/29/1935	02:00	EST
4/26/1936	02:00	EDT
9/27/1936	02:00	EST
4/24/1938	02:00	US#2

VT # 34		
Before 11/18/1883		LMT
11/18/1883	12:00	EST
3/31/1918	02:00	EWT
10/27/1918	02:00	EST
3/30/1919	02:00	EWT
10/26/1919	02:00	EST
4/30/1939	02:00	EDT
9/24/1939	02:00	EST
4/28/1940	02:00	EDT
9/29/1940	02:00	EST
4/27/1941	02:00	EDT
9/28/1941	02:00	EST
2/09/1942	02:00	EWT
9/30/1945	02:00	EST
4/27/1947	02:00	EDT
9/28/1947	02:00	EST
4/25/1948	02:00	EDT
9/26/1948	02:00	EST
4/24/1949	02:00	EDT
9/25/1949	02:00	EST
4/24/1955	02:00	US#2

VT # 35		
Before 11/18/1883		LMT
11/18/1883	12:00	EST
3/31/1918	02:00	EWT
10/27/1918	02:00	EST
3/30/1919	02:00	EWT
10/26/1919	02:00	EST
4/30/1939	02:00	EDT
9/24/1939	02:00	EST
4/28/1940	02:00	EDT
9/29/1940	02:00	EST
4/27/1941	02:00	EDT
9/28/1941	02:00	EST
2/09/1942	02:00	EWT
9/30/1945	02:00	EST
4/28/1946	02:00	EDT
9/29/1946	02:00	EST
4/25/1948	02:00	US#2

VT # 36		
Before 11/18/1883		LMT
11/18/1883	12:00	EST
3/31/1918	02:00	EWT
10/27/1918	02:00	EST
3/30/1919	02:00	EWT
10/26/1919	02:00	EST
4/25/1937	02:00	EDT
9/26/1937	02:00	EST
4/28/1940	02:00	US#2

VT # 37		
Before 11/18/1883		LMT
11/18/1883	12:00	EST
3/31/1918	02:00	EWT
10/27/1918	02:00	EST
3/30/1919	02:00	EWT
10/26/1919	02:00	EST
4/25/1937	02:00	EDT
9/26/1937	02:00	EST
4/24/1938	02:00	EDT
9/25/1938	02:00	EST
4/30/1939	02:00	EDT
9/24/1939	02:00	EST
4/28/1940	02:00	EDT
9/29/1940	02:00	EST
4/27/1941	02:00	EDT
9/28/1941	02:00	EST
2/09/1942	02:00	EWT
9/30/1945	02:00	EST
4/24/1955	02:00	US#2

VT # 38		
Before 11/18/1883		LMT
11/18/1883	12:00	EST
3/31/1918	02:00	EWT
10/27/1918	02:00	EST
3/30/1919	02:00	EWT
10/26/1919	02:00	EST
4/27/1941	02:00	EDT
9/28/1941	02:00	EST
2/09/1942	02:00	EWT
9/30/1945	02:00	EST
4/27/1947	02:00	US#2

VT # 39		
Before 11/18/1883		LMT
11/18/1883	12:00	EST
3/31/1918	02:00	EWT

TIME TABLES

10/27/1918 02:00 EST
3/30/1919 02:00 EWT
10/26/1919 02:00 EST
4/27/1941 02:00 EDT
9/28/1941 02:00 EST
2/09/1942 02:00 EWT
9/30/1945 02:00 EST
4/29/1951 02:00 US#2

VT # 40
Before 11/18/1883 LMT
11/18/1883 12:00 EST
3/31/1918 02:00 EWT
10/27/1918 02:00 EST
3/30/1919 02:00 EWT
10/26/1919 02:00 EST
2/09/1942 02:00 EWT
9/30/1945 02:00 EST
4/24/1949 02:00 EDT
9/25/1949 02:00 EST
4/29/1951 02:00 US#2

VT # 41
Before 11/18/1883 LMT
11/18/1883 12:00 EST
3/31/1918 02:00 EWT
10/27/1918 02:00 EST
3/30/1919 02:00 EWT
10/26/1919 02:00 EST
2/09/1942 02:00 EWT
9/30/1945 02:00 EST
4/24/1949 02:00 EDT
9/25/1949 02:00 EST
4/29/1951 02:00 EDT
9/30/1951 02:00 EST
4/26/1953 02:00 US#2

VT # 42
Before 11/18/1883 LMT
11/18/1883 12:00 EST
3/31/1918 02:00 EWT
10/27/1918 02:00 EST
3/30/1919 02:00 EWT
10/26/1919 02:00 EST
4/28/1940 02:00 EDT
9/29/1940 02:00 EST
5/18/1941 02:00 EDT
9/21/1941 02:00 EST
2/09/1942 02:00 EWT
9/30/1945 02:00 EST
4/24/1955 02:00 US#2

VT # 43
Before 11/18/1883 LMT
11/18/1883 12:00 EST
3/31/1918 02:00 EWT
10/27/1918 02:00 EST
3/30/1919 02:00 EWT
10/26/1919 02:00 EST
4/28/1940 02:00 EDT
9/29/1940 02:00 EST
5/01/1941 02:00 EDT
10/01/1941 02:00 EST
2/09/1942 02:00 EWT
9/30/1945 02:00 EST
4/25/1948 02:00 US#2

VT # 44
Before 11/18/1883 LMT
11/18/1883 12:00 EST
3/31/1918 02:00 EWT
10/27/1918 02:00 EST
3/30/1919 02:00 EWT
10/26/1919 02:00 EST
5/28/1939 02:00 EDT
9/10/1939 02:00 EST
5/26/1940 02:00 EDT
9/08/1940 02:00 EST
5/25/1941 02:00 EDT
9/14/1941 02:00 EST
2/09/1942 02:00 EWT
9/30/1945 02:00 EST
4/27/1952 02:00 EDT
9/28/1952 02:00 EST
4/24/1955 02:00 US#2

VT # 45
Before 11/18/1883 LMT
11/18/1883 12:00 EST
3/31/1918 02:00 EWT
10/27/1918 02:00 EST
3/30/1919 02:00 EWT
10/26/1919 02:00 EST
4/24/1938 02:00 EDT
9/25/1938 02:00 EST
4/30/1939 02:00 EDT
9/24/1939 02:00 EST
4/28/1940 02:00 EDT
9/29/1940 02:00 EST
4/27/1941 02:00 EDT
9/28/1941 02:00 EST
2/09/1942 02:00 EWT
9/30/1945 02:00 EST
4/28/1946 02:00 EDT
9/29/1946 02:00 EST
4/27/1947 02:00 EDT
9/28/1947 02:00 EST
4/25/1948 02:00 EDT
9/26/1948 02:00 EST
5/01/1949 02:00 EDT
9/25/1949 02:00 EST
4/25/1954 02:00 US#2

VT # 46
Before 11/18/1883 LMT
11/18/1883 12:00 EST
3/31/1918 02:00 EWT
10/27/1918 02:00 EST
3/30/1919 02:00 EWT
10/26/1919 02:00 EST
5/07/1939 02:00 EDT
9/24/1939 02:00 EST
5/05/1940 02:00 EDT
9/29/1940 02:00 EST
5/04/1941 02:00 EDT
9/28/1941 02:00 EST
2/09/1942 02:00 EWT
9/30/1945 02:00 EST
4/24/1955 02:00 US#2

VT # 47
Before 11/18/1883 LMT
11/18/1883 12:00 EST
3/31/1918 02:00 EWT
10/27/1918 02:00 EST
3/30/1919 02:00 EWT
10/26/1919 02:00 EST
5/01/1938 02:00 EDT
10/01/1938 02:00 EST
5/01/1939 02:00 EDT
10/01/1939 02:00 EST
5/01/1940 02:00 EDT
10/01/1940 02:00 EST
5/01/1941 02:00 EDT
10/01/1941 02:00 EST
2/09/1942 02:00 US#2

VT # 48
Before 11/18/1883 LMT
11/18/1883 12:00 EST
3/31/1918 02:00 EWT
10/27/1918 02:00 EST
3/30/1919 02:00 EWT
10/26/1919 02:00 EST
5/26/1939 02:00 EDT
9/03/1939 02:00 EST
5/26/1940 02:00 EDT
9/01/1940 02:00 EST
5/25/1941 02:00 EDT
9/07/1941 02:00 EST
2/09/1942 02:00 EWT
9/30/1945 02:00 EST
4/25/1948 02:00 EDT
9/26/1948 02:00 EST
4/24/1955 02:00 US#2

VT # 49
Before 11/18/1883 LMT
11/18/1883 12:00 EST
3/31/1918 02:00 EWT
10/27/1918 02:00 EST
3/30/1919 02:00 EWT
10/26/1919 02:00 EST
4/30/1939 02:00 EDT
9/24/1939 02:00 EST
5/01/1940 02:00 EDT
10/01/1940 02:00 EST
5/01/1941 02:00 EDT
10/01/1941 02:00 EST
2/09/1942 02:00 US#2

VT # 50
Before 11/18/1883 LMT
11/18/1883 12:00 EST
3/31/1918 02:00 EWT
10/27/1918 02:00 EST
3/30/1919 02:00 EWT
10/26/1919 02:00 EST
4/24/1938 02:00 EDT
10/29/1938 02:00 EST
4/30/1939 02:00 EDT
9/24/1939 02:00 EST
5/01/1940 02:00 EDT
10/01/1940 02:00 EST
5/01/1941 02:00 EDT
10/01/1941 02:00 EST
2/09/1942 02:00 EWT
9/30/1945 02:00 EST
4/29/1951 02:00 US#2

VT # 51
Before 11/18/1883 LMT
11/18/1883 12:00 EST
3/31/1918 02:00 EWT
10/27/1918 02:00 EST
3/30/1919 02:00 EWT
10/26/1919 02:00 EST
4/25/1937 02:00 EDT
9/26/1937 02:00 EST
5/29/1938 02:00 EDT
9/11/1938 02:00 EST
5/28/1939 02:00 EDT
9/10/1939 02:00 EST
5/26/1940 02:00 EDT
9/08/1940 02:00 EST
5/25/1941 02:00 EDT
9/14/1941 02:00 EST
2/09/1942 02:00 EWT
9/30/1945 02:00 EST
4/28/1946 02:00 US#2

VT # 52
Before 11/18/1883 LMT
11/18/1883 12:00 EST
3/31/1918 02:00 EWT
10/27/1918 02:00 EST
3/30/1919 02:00 EWT
10/26/1919 02:00 EST
4/28/1940 02:00 EDT
10/27/1940 02:00 EST
4/27/1941 02:00 EDT
10/26/1941 02:00 EST
2/09/1942 02:00 EWT
9/30/1945 02:00 EST
4/24/1955 02:00 US#2

VT # 53
Before 11/18/1883 LMT
11/18/1883 12:00 EST
3/31/1918 02:00 EWT
10/27/1918 02:00 EST
3/30/1919 02:00 EWT
10/26/1919 02:00 EST
4/28/1940 02:00 EDT
9/29/1940 02:00 EST
4/27/1941 02:00 EDT
9/28/1941 02:00 EST
2/09/1942 02:00 EWT
9/30/1945 02:00 EST
4/27/1947 02:00 US#2

VT # 54
Before 11/18/1883 LMT
11/18/1883 12:00 EST
3/31/1918 02:00 EWT
10/27/1918 02:00 EST
3/30/1919 02:00 EWT
10/26/1919 02:00 EST
2/09/1942 02:00 EWT
9/30/1945 02:00 EST
4/29/1951 02:00 EDT
9/30/1951 02:00 EST
4/24/1955 02:00 US#2

VT # 55
Before 11/18/1883 LMT
11/18/1883 12:00 EST
3/31/1918 02:00 EWT
10/27/1918 02:00 EST
3/30/1919 02:00 EWT
10/26/1919 02:00 EST
2/09/1942 02:00 EWT
9/30/1945 02:00 EST
4/29/1951 02:00 EDT
9/30/1951 02:00 EST
4/27/1952 02:00 EDT
9/28/1952 02:00 EST
4/26/1953 02:00 EDT
9/27/1953 02:00 EST
4/25/1954 02:00 EDT
9/26/1954 02:00 EST
4/24/1955 02:00 US#2

VT # 56
Before 11/18/1883 LMT
11/18/1883 12:00 EST
3/31/1918 02:00 EWT
10/27/1918 02:00 EST
3/30/1919 02:00 EWT
10/26/1919 02:00 EST
5/29/1938 02:00 EDT
9/25/1938 02:00 EST
4/30/1939 02:00 EDT
9/24/1939 02:00 EST
4/28/1940 02:00 EDT
9/29/1940 02:00 EST
4/27/1941 02:00 EDT
9/28/1941 02:00 EST
2/09/1942 02:00 EWT
9/30/1945 02:00 EST
4/27/1947 02:00 US#2

VT # 57
Before 11/18/1883 LMT
11/18/1883 12:00 EST
3/31/1918 02:00 EWT
10/27/1918 02:00 EST
3/30/1919 02:00 EWT
10/26/1919 02:00 EST
4/25/1937 02:00 EDT
9/26/1937 02:00 EST
4/30/1939 02:00 US#2

VT # 58
Before 11/18/1883 LMT
11/18/1883 12:00 EST
3/31/1918 02:00 EWT
10/27/1918 02:00 EST
3/30/1919 02:00 EWT
10/26/1919 02:00 EST
4/28/1935 02:00 EDT
9/29/1935 02:00 EST
4/26/1936 02:00 EDT
9/27/1936 02:00 EST
4/25/1937 02:00 EDT
9/26/1937 02:00 EST
4/24/1938 02:00 EDT
9/25/1938 02:00 EST
4/30/1939 02:00 EDT
9/24/1939 02:00 EST
4/28/1940 02:00 EDT
9/29/1940 02:00 EST
4/27/1941 02:00 EDT
9/28/1941 02:00 EST
2/09/1942 02:00 EWT
9/30/1945 02:00 EST
4/24/1955 02:00 US#2

VT # 59
Before 11/18/1883 LMT
11/18/1883 12:00 EST
3/31/1918 02:00 EWT
10/27/1918 02:00 EST
3/30/1919 02:00 EWT
10/26/1919 02:00 EST
4/24/1938 02:00 EDT
9/25/1938 02:00 EST
4/30/1939 02:00 EDT
9/24/1939 02:00 EST
2/09/1942 02:00 EWT
9/30/1945 02:00 EST
4/28/1946 02:00 US#2

VT # 60
Before 11/18/1883 LMT
11/18/1883 12:00 EST
3/31/1918 02:00 EWT
10/27/1918 02:00 EST
3/30/1919 02:00 EWT
10/26/1919 02:00 EST
4/30/1939 02:00 EDT
9/24/1939 02:00 EST
4/27/1941 02:00 EDT
9/28/1941 02:00 EST
2/09/1942 02:00 EWT
9/30/1945 02:00 EST
4/24/1955 02:00 US#2

VT # 61
Before 11/18/1883 LMT
11/18/1883 12:00 EST
3/31/1918 02:00 EWT
10/27/1918 02:00 EST
3/30/1919 02:00 EWT
10/26/1919 02:00 EST
5/08/1937 02:00 EDT
9/26/1937 02:00 EST
4/24/1938 02:00 US#2

VT # 62
Before 11/18/1883 LMT
11/18/1883 12:00 EST
3/31/1918 02:00 EWT
10/27/1918 02:00 EST
3/30/1919 02:00 EWT
10/26/1919 02:00 EST
4/25/1937 02:00 EDT
9/26/1937 02:00 EST
4/24/1938 02:00 EDT
9/25/1938 02:00 EST
4/30/1939 02:00 EDT
9/24/1939 02:00 EST
4/28/1940 02:00 EDT
9/29/1940 02:00 EST
4/27/1941 02:00 EDT
9/28/1941 02:00 EST
2/09/1942 02:00 EWT
9/30/1945 02:00 EST
4/27/1947 02:00 US#2

VT # 63
Before 11/18/1883 LMT
11/18/1883 12:00 EST
3/31/1918 02:00 EWT
10/27/1918 02:00 EST
3/30/1919 02:00 EWT
10/26/1919 02:00 EST
4/30/1939 02:00 EDT
9/24/1939 02:00 EST
4/27/1941 02:00 EDT
9/28/1941 02:00 EST
2/09/1942 02:00 EWT
9/30/1945 02:00 EST
4/27/1947 02:00 US#2

VT # 64
Before 11/18/1883 LMT
11/18/1883 12:00 EST
3/31/1918 02:00 EWT
10/27/1918 02:00 EST
3/30/1919 02:00 EWT
10/26/1919 02:00 EST
4/24/1938 02:00 EDT
9/25/1938 02:00 EST
4/30/1939 02:00 EDT
9/24/1939 02:00 EST
4/27/1941 02:00 EDT
9/28/1941 02:00 EST
2/09/1942 02:00 EWT
9/30/1945 02:00 EST
4/27/1947 02:00 US#2

VT # 65
Before 11/18/1883 LMT
11/18/1883 12:00 EST
3/31/1918 02:00 EWT
10/27/1918 02:00 EST
3/30/1919 02:00 EWT
10/26/1919 02:00 EST
4/25/1937 02:00 EDT
9/26/1937 02:00 EST
4/24/1938 02:00 EDT
9/25/1938 02:00 EST
4/30/1939 02:00 EDT
9/24/1939 02:00 EST
4/28/1940 02:00 EDT
9/29/1940 02:00 EST
4/27/1941 02:00 EDT
9/28/1941 02:00 EST
2/09/1942 02:00 EWT
9/30/1945 02:00 EST
4/28/1946 02:00 EDT
9/29/1946 02:00 EST
4/25/1948 02:00 US#2

VT # 66
Before 11/18/1883 LMT
11/18/1883 12:00 EST
3/31/1918 02:00 EWT
10/27/1918 02:00 EST
3/30/1919 02:00 EWT
10/26/1919 02:00 EST
4/24/1938 02:00 EDT
9/25/1938 02:00 EST
4/30/1939 02:00 EDT
9/24/1939 02:00 EST
4/28/1940 02:00 EDT
9/29/1940 02:00 EST
4/27/1941 02:00 EDT
9/28/1941 02:00 EST
2/09/1942 02:00 EWT
9/30/1945 02:00 EST
4/25/1948 02:00 EDT
9/26/1948 02:00 EST
4/24/1949 02:00 EDT
9/25/1949 02:00 EST
4/30/1950 02:00 EDT
9/24/1950 02:00 EST
4/29/1951 02:00 EDT
9/30/1951 02:00 EST
4/26/1953 02:00 US#2

VT # 67
Before 11/18/1883 LMT
11/18/1883 12:00 EST
3/31/1918 02:00 EWT
10/27/1918 02:00 EST
3/30/1919 02:00 EWT
10/26/1919 02:00 EST
2/09/1942 02:00 EWT
9/30/1945 02:00 EST
4/28/1946 02:00 EDT
9/29/1946 02:00 EST
4/25/1948 02:00 EDT
9/26/1948 02:00 EST
4/27/1952 02:00 US#2

COUNTIES

1 Addison
2 Bennington
3 Caledonia
4 Chittenden
5 Essex
6 Franklin
7 Grand Isle
8 Lamoille
9 Orange
10 Orleans
11 Rutland
12 Washington
13 Windham
14 Windsor

VERMONT

Abnaki 7	11	44N49	73w18	4:53:12
Adamant 12	1	44N20	72w31	4:50:04
Addison 1	1	44N05	73w21	4:53:24
Albany 10	5	44N44	72w21	4:49:24
Alburg 7	31	44N59	73w18	4:53:12
Alburgh 7	31	44N59	73w18	4:53:12
Alburgh Springs 7	31	44N59	73w18	4:53:12
Alburg Springs 7	31	44N59	73w18	4:53:12
Alfrecha 11	24	43N34	72w58	4:51:52
Alpine Village 12	1	44N07	72w51	4:51:24
Ames Hill 13	1	42N52	72w43	4:50:52
Amsden 14	1	43N22	72w31	4:50:04
Andover 14	5	43N17	72w43	4:50:52
Arlington 2	27	43N04	73w11	4:52:44
Arlington Center 2	27	43N04	73w09	4:52:36
Arnold Bay 1	66	44N10	73w15	4:53:00
Ascutney 14	6	43N24	72w25	4:49:40
Athens 13	1	43N07	72w35	4:50:20
Avalon Beach 11	1	43N36	73w14	4:52:56
Averill 5	1	44N56	71w41	4:46:44
Bailey's Mills 14	1	43N27	72w32	4:50:08
Bakersfield 6	12	44N47	72w48	4:51:12
Baltimore 14	1	43N21	72w34	4:50:16
Barnard 14	1	43N46	72w37	4:50:28
Barnet 3	17	44N18	72w03	4:48:12
Barnumtown 1	63	44N07	73w09	4:52:36
Barre 12	27	44N12	72w30	4:50:00
Barton 10	17	44N45	72w11	4:48:44
Bartonsville 13	39	43N14	72w32	4:50:08
Basin Harbor 1	66	44N10	73w15	4:53:00
Bayside 4	15	44N30	73w11	4:52:44
Beanville 9	2	43N55	72w40	4:50:40
Beaulieu's Corner 6	1	44N56	73w03	4:52:12
Beebe Plain 10	37	45N00	72w09	4:48:36
Beecher Falls 5	26	45N01	71w31	4:46:04
Bellows Falls 13	2	43N08	72w27	4:49:48
Belmont 11	1	43N25	72w49	4:51:16
Belvidere 8	12	44N46	72w41	4:50:44
Belvidere Corners 8	1	44N45	72w41	4:50:44
Belvidere Junction 8	1	44N41	72w46	4:51:04
Bennington 2	23	42N53	73w12	4:52:48
Bennington College 2	23	42N53	73w12	4:52:48
Benson 11	1	43N42	73w19	4:53:16
Benson Landing 11	1	43N42	73w19	4:53:16
Berkshire 6	1	44N58	72w46	4:51:04
Berlin 12	12	44N12	72w36	4:50:24
Bethel 14	25	43N50	72w38	4:50:32
Bethel Gilead 14	2	43N55	72w40	4:50:40
Binghamville 6	1	44N39	72w53	4:51:32
Birdland 7	1	44N49	73w18	4:53:12
Bliss Pond 12	1	44N20	72w31	4:50:04
Blissville 11	1	43N31	73w14	4:52:56
Bloomfield 5	12	44N48	71w38	4:46:32
Blossoms Corners 11	1	43N21	73w15	4:53:00
Bolton 4	1	44N23	72w54	4:51:36
Bolton Valley 4	49	44N24	73w00	4:52:00
Boltonville 9	1	44N09	72w04	4:48:16
Bomoseen 11	1	43N39	73w12	4:52:48
Bondville 2	1	43N09	72w53	4:51:32
Bordoville 6	1	44N54	72w48	4:51:12
Bowlsville 11	1	43N27	72w52	4:51:28
Bradford 9	33	44N01	72w09	4:48:36
Bragg 14	35	43N43	72w19	4:49:16
Braintree 9	12	43N58	72w43	4:50:52
Brandon 11	2	43N48	73w06	4:52:24
Brattleboro 13	13	42N51	72w34	4:50:16
Bread Loaf 1	56	44N01	73w10	4:52:40
Bridgewater 14	17	43N36	72w39	4:50:36
Bridgewater Corners 14	1	43N35	72w40	4:50:40
Bridport 1	1	43N59	73w21	4:53:24
Brighton 5	1	44N48	71w52	4:47:28
Brimstone Corner 9	1	43N52	72w16	4:49:04
Brimstone Corners 11	1	43N21	73w11	4:52:44
Bristol 1	19	44N08	73w05	4:52:20
Brockways Mills 13	1	43N16	72w36	4:50:24
Brookfield 9	17	44N02	72w35	4:50:20
Brookline 13	12	43N01	72w37	4:50:28
Brookside 4	1	44N37	73w01	4:52:04
Brookside 13	1	42N57	72w46	4:51:04
Brooksville 1	56	44N01	73w10	4:52:40
Brownington 10	1	44N49	72w08	4:48:32
Brownsville 14	1	43N28	72w28	4:49:52
Brunswick 5	1	44N44	71w40	4:46:40
Buck Hollow 6	1	44N40	73w01	4:52:04
Buels Gore 4	1	44N13	72w57	4:51:48
Burke 3	17	44N37	71w56	4:47:44
Burke Mountain 3	1	44N35	71w56	4:47:44
Burlington 4	15	44N29	73w12	4:52:48
Burnham Hill 12	1	44N30	72w22	4:49:28
Burnham Hollow 11	1	43N29	73w07	4:52:28
Button Bay 1	66	44N10	73w15	4:53:00
Cabot 12	42	44N25	72w18	4:49:12
Cadys Falls 8	1	44N34	72w36	4:50:24
Calais 12	1	44N22	72w27	4:49:48
Cambridge 8	1	44N39	72w53	4:51:32
Cambridge Junction 8	1	44N39	72w50	4:51:20
Cambridgeport 13	1	43N09	72w33	4:50:12
Canaan 5	2	44N59	71w35	4:46:20
Castleton 11	26	43N37	73w11	4:52:44
Cavendish 14	3	43N24	72w36	4:50:24
Cedar Beach 4	1	44N19	73w15	4:53:00
Center Rutland 11	24	43N36	73w01	4:52:04
Centerville 8	1	44N36	72w37	4:50:28
Charleston 10	1	44N51	72w01	4:48:04
Charlotte 4	43	44N19	73w14	4:52:56
Checkerberry 4	2	44N38	73w07	4:52:28
Chelsea 9	12	43N59	72w27	4:49:48
Chester 14	34	43N17	72w36	4:50:24
Chester Depot 14	10	43N16	72w35	4:50:20
Chimney Corner 4	2	44N38	73w07	4:52:28
Chimney Point 1	66	44N10	73w15	4:53:00
Chipman Lake 11	36	43N21	73w00	4:52:00
Chipmans Point 1	1	43N48	73w18	4:53:12
Chippenhook 11	27	43N36	73w03	4:52:12
Chiselville 2	27	43N04	73w09	4:52:36
Chittenden 11	1	43N43	72w57	4:51:48
Clarendon 11	24	43N33	72w59	4:51:56
Clarendon Springs 11	27	43N36	73w03	4:52:12
Cleveland Corner 8	1	44N34	72w36	4:50:24
Colbyville 12	1	44N18	72w45	4:51:00
Colchester 4	15	44N33	73w12	4:52:48
Cold River 11	30	43N29	72w53	4:51:32
Coles Corner 3	2	44N25	72w01	4:48:04
Concord 5	2	44N26	71w53	4:47:32
Concord Corner 5	1	44N26	71w53	4:47:32
Cookville 9	1	44N01	72w17	4:49:08
Copperfield 9	1	43N58	72w19	4:49:16
Corinth 9	1	44N02	72w17	4:49:08
Corinth Corners 9	1	44N01	72w17	4:49:08
Cornwall 1	1	43N57	73w14	4:52:56
Coventry 10	1	44N53	72w14	4:48:56
Craftsbury 10	17	44N39	72w23	4:49:32
Craftsbury Common 10	1	44N39	72w23	4:49:32
Cream Hill 1	1	43N59	73w19	4:53:16
Crown Point 1	66	44N10	73w15	4:53:00
Crystal Beach 11	1	43N39	73w12	4:52:48
Cuttingsville 11	30	43N29	72w53	4:51:32
Danby 11	36	43N21	73w03	4:52:12
Danby Corners 11	36	43N21	73w00	4:52:00
Danville 3	19	44N25	72w09	4:48:36
Derby 10	37	44N58	72w08	4:48:32
Derby Line 10	37	45N00	72w06	4:48:24
Dewey's Mills 14	1	43N39	72w25	4:49:40
Dorset 2	57	43N15	73w06	4:52:24
Dover 13	17	42N58	72w50	4:51:20
Downers 14	1	43N22	72w31	4:50:04
Downingville 1	1	44N08	73w05	4:52:20
Dows 3	1	44N30	72w22	4:49:28
Dowsville 12	1	44N15	72w46	4:51:04
Dummerston 13	5	42N56	72w35	4:50:20
Duxbury 12	1	44N16	72w48	4:51:12
Eagle Point 10	1	44N56	72w13	4:48:52
East Albany 10	1	44N48	72w17	4:49:08
East Alburgh 7	31	44N59	73w18	4:53:12
East Arlington 2	27	43N04	73w09	4:52:36
East Barnard 14	1	43N49	72w31	4:50:04
East Barre 12	27	44N12	72w30	4:50:00
East Berkshire 6	1	44N56	72w42	4:50:48
East Bethel 14	1	43N50	72w38	4:50:32
East Braintree 9	2	43N55	72w40	4:50:40
East Brookfield 9	2	43N55	72w40	4:50:40
East Burke 3	1	44N35	71w56	4:47:44
East Cabot 12	1	44N24	72w18	4:49:12
East Calais 12	1	44N22	72w26	4:49:44
East Cambridge 8	1	44N39	72w50	4:51:20
East Charleston 10	1	44N38	72w21	4:49:24
East Charlotte 4	1	44N19	73w15	4:53:00
East Clarendon 11	24	43N34	72w58	4:51:52
East Concord 5	6	44N26	71w53	4:47:32
East Corinth 9	1	44N04	72w13	4:48:52
East Craftsbury 10	1	44N38	71w38	4:46:32
East Dorset 2	57	43N15	73w04	4:52:16
East Dover 13	1	42N57	72w46	4:51:04
East Dummerston 13	2	42N59	72w31	4:50:04
East Elmore 8	1	44N33	72w27	4:49:48
East Enosburg 6	44	44N54	72w48	4:51:12
East Fairfield 6	1	44N47	72w52	4:51:28
East Fletcher 6	1	44N39	72w50	4:51:20
East Franklin 6	1	44N59	72w55	4:51:40
East Granville 1	64	44N06	72w44	4:50:56
East Hardwick 3	1	44N30	72w22	4:49:28
East Haven 5	1	44N39	71w50	4:47:20
East Highgate 6	1	44N56	73w03	4:52:12
East Hubbardton 11	1	43N37	73w11	4:52:44
East Jamaica 13	1	43N06	72w47	4:51:08
East Johnson 8	1	44N38	72w41	4:50:44
East Lyndon 3	1	44N32	72w00	4:48:00
East Middlebury 1	1	43N58	73w06	4:52:24
East Monkton 1	1	44N08	73w05	4:52:20
East Montpelier 12	27	44N17	72w31	4:50:04
East Montpelier Center 12	27	44N16	72w34	4:50:16
East Orange 9	1	44N07	72w19	4:49:16
East Peacham 3	1	44N20	72w10	4:48:40
East Pittsford 11	24	43N36	72w59	4:51:56
East Poultney 11	1	43N32	73w13	4:52:52
East Putney 13	2	42N59	72w31	4:50:04
East Randolph 9	1	43N57	72w33	4:50:12
East Roxbury 12	27	44N09	72w39	4:50:36
East Rupert 2	1	43N21	73w11	4:52:44
East Ryegate 3	1	44N12	72w04	4:48:16
East Sheldon 6	1	44N54	72w48	4:51:12
East Shoreham 1	1	43N54	73w19	4:53:16
East St. Johnsbury 3	1	44N26	71w57	4:47:48
East Sutton Ridge 3	1	44N38	72w02	4:48:08
East Thetford 9	1	43N49	72w11	4:48:44
East Wallingford 11	2	43N27	72w52	4:51:28
East Warren 12	1	44N07	72w51	4:51:24
Eden 8	1	44N43	72w32	4:50:08
Eden Mills 8	1	44N43	72w32	4:50:08
Egypt 6	1	44N47	72w52	4:51:28
Elmore 8	1	44N30	72w30	4:50:00
Ely 9	53	43N53	72w11	4:48:44
Enosburg 6	44	44N52	72w46	4:51:04
Enosburg Center 6	44	44N54	72w48	4:51:12
Enosburg Falls 6	44	44N55	72w48	4:51:12
Essex 4	27	44N31	73w04	4:52:16
Essex Junction 4	27	44N29	73w07	4:52:28
Ethan Allen Shopping Center 4	15	44N30	73w11	4:52:44
Evansville 10	1	44N49	72w12	4:48:48
Fairfax 6	17	44N40	73w01	4:52:04
Fairfax Falls 6	1	44N40	73w01	4:52:04
Fairfield 6	1	44N49	72w56	4:51:44
Fairground 6	1	44N53	72w57	4:51:48
Fair Haven 11	45	43N36	73w16	4:53:04
Fairlee 9	3	43N54	72w09	4:48:36
Fays Corner 4	49	44N24	73w00	4:52:00
Fayston 12	1	44N13	72w51	4:51:24
Ferdinand 5	1	44N44	71w46	4:47:04
Fernville 1	1	43N48,	73w05	4:52:20
Ferrisburg 1	7	44N13	73w15	4:53:00
Fieldsville 14	27	43N29	72w23	4:49:32
Fletcher 6	1	44N43	72w54	4:51:36
Florence 11	53	43N43	73w04	4:52:16
Fonda 6	51	44N55	73w07	4:52:28
Forest Dale 11	1	43N50	73w03	4:52:12
Foxville 9	27	44N12	72w30	4:50:00
Franklin 6	1	44N59	72w55	4:51:40
Freedleyville 2	1	43N14	73w01	4:52:04
Gageville 13	1	43N08	72w27	4:49:48
Gallup Mills 5	1	44N26	71w53	4:47:32
Garfield 8	1	44N34	72w36	4:50:24
Gassetts 14	4	43N16	72w35	4:50:20
Gaysville 14	1	43N47	72w42	4:50:48
Georgia 6	12	44N44	73w07	4:52:28
Georgia Plain 6	2	44N38	73w07	4:52:28
Gilman 5	58	44N25	71w43	4:46:52
Glover 10	1	44N41	72w14	4:48:56
Goodrich Four Corners 14	35	43N43	72w19	4:49:16
Goose City 14	1	42N57	72w46	4:51:04
Goose Green 9	1	44N01	72w17	4:49:08
Gordon Landing 7	1	44N43	73w18	4:53:12
Goshen 1	1	43N52	73w00	4:52:00
Goulds Mills 14	1	43N18	72w29	4:49:56
Grafton 13	17	43N10	72w37	4:50:28
Grahamville 14	61	43N24	72w42	4:50:48
Granby 5	1	44N36	71w43	4:46:52
Grand Isle 7	38	44N43	73w18	4:53:12
Graniteville 12	27	44N12	72w30	4:50:00
Granville 1	12	44N00	72w50	4:51:20
Green Bay 3	1	44N13	72w12	4:48:48
Greenbush 14	1	43N22	72w31	4:50:04
Green Mountain 4	49	44N24	73w00	4:52:00
Green River 13	13	42N51	72w34	4:50:16
Greensboro 12	12	44N36	72w17	4:49:08
Greensboro Bend 10	1	44N33	72w16	4:49:04
Greens Corners 6	65	44N49	73w05	4:52:20
Groton 3	17	44N13	72w15	4:49:00
Grout 13	6	43N05	72w27	4:49:48
Guildhall 5	6	44N34	71w34	4:46:16
Guilford 13	17	42N47	72w37	4:50:28
Halifax 13	12	42N47	72w46	4:51:04
Halls Lake 9	1	44N09	72w04	4:48:16
Hammondsville 14	1	43N27	72w32	4:50:08
Hancock 1	12	43N56	72w51	4:51:24
Hanksville 4	1	44N14	73w04	4:52:16
Hardscrabble 14	1	43N18	72w29	4:49:56
Hardwick 3	46	44N30	72w22	4:49:28
Hardwick Steet 3	1	44N30	72w22	4:49:28
Harmonyville 13	1	43N03	72w40	4:50:40
Harrisville 13	13	42N51	72w34	4:50:16
Hartford 14	17	43N40	72w23	4:49:32
Hartland 14	59	43N32	72w24	4:49:36
Hartland Four Corners 14	59	43N33	72w26	4:49:44
Harvey 3	1	44N25	72w09	4:48:36
Healdville 11	10	43N26	72w46	4:51:04
Heartwellville 2	1	42N46	72w57	4:51:48
Hectorville 6	1	44N53	72w37	4:50:28
Hewitts Corners 14	1	43N43	72w29	4:49:56
Highgate 6	60	44N58	73w02	4:52:08
Highgate Falls 6	1	44N56	73w03	4:52:12
Highgate Springs 6	60	44N58	72w59	4:51:56
Hinesburg 4	17	44N19	73w06	4:52:24
Hinesburg 13	13	42N51	72w34	4:50:16
Holden 11	1	43N42	73w01	4:52:04
Holland 10	1	44N58	72w01	4:48:04
Hortonia 11	1	43N48	73w18	4:53:12
Hortonville 11	1	43N27	72w49	4:51:16
Houghtonville 13	1	43N10	72w37	4:50:28
Hubbard Corner 6	65	44N49	73w05	4:52:20
Hubbardton 11	1	43N43	73w11	4:52:44
Huntington 4	1	44N19	72w58	4:51:52
Huntville 6	1	44N40	73w01	4:52:04
Hutchins 6	1	44N53	72w37	4:50:28
Hyde Park 8	17	44N36	72w37	4:50:28
Hydeville 11	14	43N36	73w14	4:52:56
Indian Point 10	1	44N56	72w13	4:48:52
Inwood 3	1	44N18	72w03	4:48:12
Ira 11	1	43N32	73w04	4:52:16
Irasburg 10	12	44N45	72w17	4:49:08
Irasville 12	1	44N11	72w50	4:51:20
Island Pond 5	1	44N49	71w53	4:47:32

VERMONT

Isle La Motte 7 9 44N51 73w20 4:53:20
Jacksonville 13 1 42N48 72w49 4:51:16
Jamaica 13 17 43N13 72w46 4:51:04
Jay 10 12 44N58 72w28 4:49:52
Jay Peak 10 1 45N00 72w24 4:49:36
Jeffersonville 8 19 44N39 72w50 4:51:20
Jenneville 14 27 43N29 72w23 4:49:32
Jericho 4 1 44N29 72w58 4:51:52
Jerusalem 1 1 44N08 73w05 4:52:20
Joes Pond 3 1 44N25 72w12 4:48:48
Johnson 8 19 44N38 72w41 4:50:44
Jonesville 4 1 44N23 72w56 4:51:44
Kansas 2 27 43N04 73w09 4:52:36
Keeler Bay 7 1 44N39 73w19 4:53:16
Kendall 14 1 43N49 72w11 4:48:44
Kendricks Corner 14 1 43N20 72w31 4:50:04
Killington 11 1 43N40 72w46 4:51:04
Kimball 10 1 44N45 72w11 4:48:44
Kirby 3 12 44N31 71w56 4:47:44
Lake Dunmore 1 1 43N54 73w06 4:52:24
Lake Elmore 8 1 44N33 72w31 4:50:04
Lake Fairlee 9 1 43N53 72w11 4:48:44
Lake Hortonia 11 1 43N36 73w16 4:53:04
Lake Morey 9 1 43N55 72w09 4:48:36
Lake Park 10 1 44N56 72w13 4:48:52
Lake Raponda 13 1 42N52 72w52 4:51:28
Lake Rescue 14 61 43N24 72w42 4:50:48
Lake Saint Catherine 11 1 43N31 73w14 4:52:56
Lakewood 6 51 44N55 73w07 4:52:28
Landgrove 2 1 43N16 72w51 4:51:24
Lapham Bay 1 1 43N59 73w19 4:53:16
Larrabees Point 1 10 43N54 73w19 4:53:16
Leicester 1 41 43N52 73w05 4:52:20
Leicester Junction 1 41 43N51 73w09 4:52:36
Lemington 5 1 44N53 71w34 4:46:16
Lewiston 14 6 43N43 72w19 4:49:16
Lillieville 14 1 43N50 72w38 4:50:32
Lincoln 1 12 44N06 72w58 4:51:52
Londonderry 13 21 43N12 72w49 4:51:16
Long Point 1 7 44N15 73w13 4:52:52
Lowell 10 12 44N48 72w27 4:49:48
Lower Cabot 12 1 44N21 72w21 4:49:24
Lower Granville 1 1 43N59 72w51 4:51:24
Lower Narrows 3 1 44N25 72w12 4:48:48
Lower Plain 9 33 44N00 72w07 4:48:28
Lower Village 8 1 44N28 72w41 4:50:44
Lower Waterford 3 1 44N21 71w54 4:47:36
Lower Websterville 12 27 44N12 72w30 4:50:00
Ludlow 14 61 43N24 72w42 4:50:48
Lunenburg 5 19 44N28 71w42 4:46:48
Lyman 14 25 43N39 72w19 4:49:16
Lyndon 3 1 44N31 72w01 4:48:04
Lyndon Corners 3 1 44N31 72w01 4:48:04
Lyndonville 3 19 44N32 72w00 4:48:00
Mackville 3 1 44N30 72w22 4:49:28
Madonna 8 1 44N39 72w50 4:51:20
Mad River Glen 12 1 44N11 72w50 4:51:20
Maidstone 5 6 44N39 71w37 4:46:28
Maidstone Lake 5 1 44N45 71w37 4:46:28
Mallets Bay 4 15 44N30 73w11 4:52:44
Manchester 2 62 43N10 73w04 4:52:16
Manchester Depot 2 62 43N11 73w03 4:52:12
Maple Dell 14 1 43N18 72w29 4:49:56
Maquam 6 51 44N55 73w07 4:52:28
Marlboro 13 12 42N52 72w44 4:50:56
Marlboro College 13 1 42N52 72w43 4:50:52
Marshfield 12 1 44N19 72w23 4:49:32
Mary Meyer 13 1 43N03 72w40 4:50:40
McIndoe Falls 3 1 44N16 72w04 4:48:16
Mechanicsville 4 49 44N24 73w00 4:52:00
Medburyville 13 1 42N52 72w52 4:51:28
Melville 6 65 44N49 73w05 4:52:20
Mendon 11 17 43N39 72w54 4:51:36
Merrill Corner 9 1 44N48 72w17 4:49:08
Middlebury 1 56 44N01 73w10 4:52:40
Middlesex 12 4 44N17 72w38 4:50:32
Middlesex Center 12 27 44N16 72w34 4:50:16
Middletown 14 17 43N16 72w36 4:50:24
Middletown Springs 11 19 43N29 73w07 4:52:28
Mile Point 1 66 44N10 73w15 4:53:00
Miles Pond 5 6 44N26 71w53 4:47:32
Mill Village 9 1 43N58 72w19 4:49:16
Mill Village 10 1 44N39 72w23 4:49:32
Milton 4 2 44N38 73w07 4:52:28
Miltonboro 4 2 44N38 73w07 4:52:28
Missisquoi 6 1 45N00 72w40 4:50:40
Monkton 1 1 44N13 73w08 4:52:32
Monkton Ridge 1 7 44N15 73w13 4:52:52
Montgomery 6 17 44N53 72w36 4:50:24
Montpelier 12 27 44N16 72w35 4:50:20
Moretown 12 17 44N16 72w44 4:50:56
Moretown Common 12 1 44N15 72w46 4:51:04
Morgan 10 12 44N54 71w59 4:47:56
Morristown 8 17 44N33 72w37 4:50:28
Morrisville 8 1 44N34 72w36 4:50:24
Morses Mills 3 2 44N23 72w02 4:48:08
Moscow 8 1 44N26 72w43 4:50:52
Mosquitoville 3 1 44N12 72w04 4:48:16
Mount Holly 11 40 43N26 72w48 4:51:12
Mount Snow 13 1 42N56 72w50 4:51:20
Mount Tabor 11 1 43N22 72w56 4:51:44
Nashville 4 1 44N30 73w00 4:52:00
Neshobe Beach 11 1 43N39 73w12 4:52:48
Newark 3 1 44N42 71w55 4:47:40
Newark Hollow 3 1 44N38 71w59 4:47:56
New Boston 14 1 43N47 72w45 4:51:00
Newbury 9 4 44N06 72w06 4:48:24
Newfane 13 17 42N59 72w39 4:50:36
New Haven 1 63 44N06 73w09 4:52:36
New Haven Mills 1 1 44N08 73w05 4:52:20
Newport 10 19 44N56 72w13 4:48:52
North Bennington 2 16 42N56 73w15 4:53:00
North Burlington 4 15 44N29 73w13 4:52:52
North Calais 12 1 44N22 72w26 4:49:44
North Cambridge 8 1 44N39 72w50 4:51:20
North Clarendon 11 24 43N34 72w58 4:51:52
North Concord 5 6 44N26 71w53 4:47:32
North Danville 3 2 44N25 72w01 4:48:04
North Derby 10 1 44N56 72w13 4:48:52
North Dorset 2 10 43N14 73w01 4:52:04
North Duxbury 12 1 44N18 72w45 4:51:00
North Fairfax 6 1 44N40 73w01 4:52:04
North Fayston 12 1 44N15 72w46 4:51:04
North Ferrisburg 1 7 44N15 73w13 4:52:52
Northfield 12 27 44N09 72w40 4:50:40
Northfield Falls 12 27 44N10 72w39 4:50:36
North Hartland 14 18 43N35 72w21 4:49:24
North Hero 7 38 44N49 73w18 4:53:12
North Hyde Park 8 1 44N36 72w37 4:50:28
North Landgrove 2 1 43N14 72w49 4:51:16
North Montpelier 12 27 44N18 72w27 4:49:48
North Orwell 1 1 43N48 73w18 4:53:12
North Peacham 3 1 44N25 72w12 4:48:48
North Pomfret 14 1 43N43 72w29 4:49:56
North Pownal 2 33 42N48 73w16 4:53:04
North Randolph 9 2 43N55 72w40 4:50:40
North Royalton 14 30 43N49 72w34 4:50:16
North Rupert 2 1 43N21 73w11 4:52:44
North Shaftsbury 2 62 43N08 73w04 4:52:16
North Sheldon 6 1 44N54 72w59 4:51:56
North Sherburne 11 1 43N40 72w46 4:51:04
North Shrewsbury 11 30 43N29 72w53 4:51:32
North Springfield 14 21 43N20 72w31 4:50:04
North Thetford 9 6 43N51 72w11 4:48:44
North Troy 10 17 45N00 72w24 4:49:36
North Tunbridge 9 1 43N53 72w30 4:50:00
North Westminster 13 1 43N07 72w27 4:49:48
North Windham 13 1 43N14 72w49 4:51:16
North Wolcott 8 1 44N37 72w28 4:49:52
Norton 5 54 45N00 71w48 4:47:12
Norwich 14 35 43N42 72w19 4:49:16
Oakland 6 65 44N49 73w05 4:52:20
Oil City 9 1 43N52 72w23 4:49:32
Old Bennington 2 23 42N52 73w13 4:52:52
Old Church 14 2 43N55 72w40 4:50:40
Olympus 14 1 43N50 72w38 4:50:32
Orange 9 12 44N10 72w23 4:49:32
Orchard Lane 14 1 43N18 72w29 4:49:56
Orleans 10 19 44N49 72w12 4:48:48
Orwell 1 22 43N49 73w18 4:53:12
Panton 1 1 44N09 73w18 4:53:12
Paper Mill Village 2 16 42N56 73w15 4:53:00
Passumpsic 3 2 44N23 72w02 4:48:08
Pawlet 11 12 43N22 73w11 4:52:44
Peacham 3 17 44N20 72w12 4:48:48
Peach Four Corners 9 4 44N04 72w08 4:48:32
Pearl 7 1 44N43 73w18 4:53:12
Peaseville 14 1 43N16 72w36 4:50:24
Pedden Acres 14 1 43N18 72w29 4:49:56
Pekin 12 1 44N17 72w25 4:49:40
Perkinsville 14 1 43N22 72w31 4:50:04
Peru 2 17 43N15 72w54 4:51:36
Peth 9 2 43N55 72w40 4:50:40
Pierces Corner 11 24 43N34 72w58 4:51:52
Pikes Falls 13 1 43N06 72w47 4:51:08
Pittsfield 11 12 43N46 72w49 4:51:16
Pittsford 11 28 43N43 73w01 4:52:04
Plainfield 12 19 44N17 72w26 4:49:44
Pleasant Valley 8 1 44N39 72w53 4:51:32
Plymouth 14 12 43N32 72w43 4:50:52
Plymouth Kingdom 14 1 43N32 72w43 4:50:52
Plymouth Union 14 1 43N32 72w43 4:50:52
Pomfret 14 12 43N44 72w30 4:50:00
Post Mills 9 1 43N53 72w16 4:49:04
Potash Bay 1 66 44N10 73w15 4:53:00
Potash Point 1 66 44N10 73w15 4:53:00
Pottersville 8 1 44N33 72w27 4:49:48
Poultney 11 47 43N31 73w14 4:52:56
Pownal 2 4 42N46 73w14 4:52:56
Prindle Corner 4 1 44N19 73w15 4:53:00
Proctor 11 3 43N40 73w02 4:52:08
Proctorsville 14 2 43N23 72w38 4:50:32
Prosper 14 1 43N38 72w31 4:50:04
Putnamville 12 27 44N16 72w34 4:50:16
Putney 13 2 42N58 72w31 4:50:04
Quechee 14 1 43N39 72w25 4:49:40
Ralston Corner 5 1 44N26 71w53 4:47:32
Randolph 9 2 43N55 72w40 4:50:40
Rawsonville 13 1 43N12 72w49 4:51:16
Reading 14 1 43N30 72w34 4:50:16
Readsboro 2 17 42N46 72w57 4:51:48
Readsboro Falls 2 1 42N46 72w57 4:51:48
Red Village 3 1 44N32 72w00 4:48:00
Reedville 14 1 43N16 72w36 4:50:24
Rhode Island Corner 4 49 44N24 73w00 4:52:00
Rices Mills 9 1 43N50 72w15 4:49:00
Richford 6 48 45N00 72w41 4:50:44
Richmond 4 49 44N24 73w00 4:52:00
Ricker Mills 3 1 44N13 72w12 4:48:48
Ripton 1 1 44N00 73w00 4:52:00
Riverton 12 12 44N12 72w38 4:50:32
Robinson 14 1 43N52 72w49 4:51:16
Rochester 14 19 43N53 72w48 4:51:12
Rockingham 13 32 43N11 72w30 4:50:00
Rockville 1 1 44N08 73w05 4:52:20
Rocky Dale 1 1 44N08 73w05 4:52:20
Round Pond 9 1 44N11 72w09 4:48:36
Roxbury 12 64 44N05 72w44 4:50:56
Roxbury Flat 12 64 44N06 72w44 4:50:56
Royalton 14 30 43N52 72w33 4:50:12
Rupert 2 17 43N16 73w11 4:52:44
Russellville 11 30 43N29 72w53 4:51:32
Russtown 14 25 43N39 72w19 4:49:16
Rutland 11 24 43N37 72w58 4:51:52
Ryegate 3 12 44N13 72w07 4:48:28
Saint Albans 6 65 44N49 73w05 4:52:20
Saint Albans Bay 6 65 44N49 73w08 4:52:32
Saint Albans Hill 6 65 44N49 73w05 4:52:20
Saint George 4 1 44N23 73w08 4:52:32
Saint Johnsbury 3 2 44N25 72w01 4:48:04
Saint Rocks 6 65 44N49 73w05 4:52:20
Salisbury 1 11 43N56 73w06 4:52:24
Samsonville 6 1 44N54 72w48 4:51:12
Sanderson Corner 6 1 44N40 73w01 4:52:04
Sandgate 2 1 43N10 73w12 4:52:48
Saxtons River 13 19 43N08 72w31 4:50:04
Scottsville 11 36 43N21 73w00 4:52:00
Searsburg 2 12 42N54 72w58 4:51:52
Shadow Lake 10 1 44N42 72w11 4:48:44
Shady Rill 12 27 44N16 72w34 4:50:16
Shaftsbury 2 29 43N01 73w11 4:52:44
Sharon 14 17 43N47 72w26 4:49:44
Shawville 6 1 44N59 72w55 4:51:40
Sheddsville 14 27 43N29 72w23 4:49:32
Sheffield 3 17 44N37 72w07 4:48:28
Sheffield Square 3 1 44N36 72w07 4:48:28
Shelburne 4 50 44N23 73w14 4:52:56
Shelburne Falls 4 50 44N23 73w14 4:52:56
Shelburne Road Section 4 15 44N27 73w12 4:52:48
Sheldon 6 17 44N53 72w57 4:51:48
Sheldon Junction 6 1 44N53 72w57 4:51:48
Sheldon Springs 6 1 44N54 72w59 4:51:56
Sherburne 11 1 43N40 72w47 4:51:08
Shoreham 1 10 43N54 73w19 4:53:16
Shrewsbury 11 17 43N32 72w51 4:51:24
Simonsville 14 1 43N16 72w36 4:50:24
Simpsonville 13 1 43N03 72w40 4:50:40
Smith Four Corners 3 1 44N30 72w22 4:49:28
Smithville 14 61 43N24 72w42 4:50:48
Sodom 2 16 42N56 73w15 4:53:00
South Albany 10 1 44N44 72w14 4:48:56
South Alburg 7 31 44N59 73w18 4:53:12
South Barre 12 27 44N12 72w30 4:50:00
South Burlington 4 15 44N27 73w10 4:52:40
South Cabot 12 1 44N21 72w21 4:49:24
South Cambridge 8 1 44N39 72w50 4:51:20
South Corinth 9 33 44N00 72w07 4:48:28
South Danville 3 1 44N25 72w09 4:48:36
South Dorset 2 57 43N13 73w04 4:52:16
South Duxbury 12 1 44N15 72w46 4:51:04
South End 11 36 43N21 73w00 4:52:00
South Hero 7 38 44N39 73w19 4:53:16
South Lincoln 1 1 44N08 73w05 4:52:20
South Londonderry 13 1 43N12 72w49 4:51:16
South Lunenburg 5 19 44N26 71w41 4:46:44
South Newbury 9 4 44N03 72w05 4:48:20
South Newfane 13 1 42N56 72w43 4:50:52
South Northfield 12 27 44N09 72w39 4:50:36
South Peacham 3 1 44N18 72w03 4:48:12
South Pomfret 14 1 43N40 72w32 4:50:08
South Poultney 11 1 43N31 73w14 4:52:56
South Randolph 9 1 43N49 72w31 4:50:04
South Reading 14 1 43N23 72w38 4:50:32
South Richford 6 1 45N00 72w40 4:50:40
South Royalton 14 30 43N49 72w31 4:50:04
South Ryegate 3 1 44N11 72w09 4:48:36
South Starksboro 1 1 44N14 73w04 4:52:16
South Strafford 9 1 43N50 72w22 4:49:28
South Tunbridge 9 1 43N49 72w31 4:50:04
South Vershire 9 1 43N58 72w19 4:49:16
South Walden 3 1 44N30 72w22 4:49:28
South Wallingford 11 25 43N25 73w00 4:52:00
South Wardsboro 13 1 43N02 72w47 4:51:08
South Washington 9 1 44N06 72w26 4:49:44
South Wheelock 3 1 44N32 72w00 4:48:00
South Windham 13 1 43N05 72w43 4:50:52
South Woodbury 12 1 44N22 72w26 4:49:44
South Woodstock 14 1 43N34 72w32 4:50:08
Spoonerville 14 1 43N16 72w35 4:50:20

VERMONT

Springfield 14	21	43N18	72w29	4:49:56
Stamford 2	17	42N45	73w04	4:52:16
Stannard 3	1	44N33	72w14	4:48:56
Starksboro 1	1	44N14	73w02	4:52:08
Stevens Mills 6	1	45N00	72w40	4:50:40
Stevensville 4	1	44N32	72w57	4:51:48
Stockbridge 14	12	43N46	72w44	4:50:56
Stowe 8	19	44N28	72w41	4:50:44
Strafford 9	1	43N52	72w22	4:49:28
Stratton 13	1	43N03	72w55	4:51:40
Stratton Mountain 13	1	43N12	72w49	4:51:16
Stump Station 1	1	43N54	73w19	4:53:16
Sudbury 11	1	43N47	73w12	4:52:48
Summer Point 1	66	44N10	73w15	4:53:00
Summit 11	20	43N27	72w49	4:51:16
Sunderland 2	10	43N04	73w05	4:52:20
Sutton 3	17	44N38	72w01	4:48:04
Swanton 6	51	44N55	73w08	4:52:32
Tafts Corner 4	1	43N38	72w28	4:49:52
Taftsville 14	1	43N38	72w28	4:49:52
Talcville 14	1	43N52	72w49	4:51:16
Tarbellville 11	1	43N27	72w52	4:51:28
Taylorville 3	1	44N30	72w22	4:49:28
The Bluffs 10	1	44N56	72w13	4:48:52
The Island 14	1	43N17	72w48	4:51:12
Thetford 9	17	43N50	72w14	4:48:56
Thompsonburg 13	1	43N14	72w49	4:51:16
Thompson's Point 4	1	44N19	73w15	4:53:00
Tinmouth 11	1	43N27	73w03	4:52:12
Topsham 9	12	44N08	72w15	4:49:00
Topsham Four Corners 9	1	44N04	72w13	4:48:52
Townshend 13	17	43N04	72w39	4:50:36
Trow Hill 12	27	44N12	72w30	4:50:00
Troy 10	1	44N56	72w23	4:49:32
Tunbridge 9	12	43N54	72w29	4:49:56
Tyson 14	61	43N24	72w42	4:50:48
Una Bella 2	23	42N53	73w12	4:52:48
Underhill 4	1	44N32	72w54	4:51:36
Union Village 9	1	43N49	72w11	4:48:44
Upper Graniteville 12	27	44N12	72w30	4:50:00
Upper Narrows 3	1	44N25	72w12	4:48:48
Vergennes 1	66	44N10	73w15	4:53:00
Vernon 13	4	42N46	72w31	4:50:04
Vershire 9	12	43N58	72w19	4:49:16
Vershire Heights 9	1	43N58	72w19	4:49:16
Victory 5	1	44N33	71w49	4:47:16
Waitsfield 12	17	44N07	72w49	4:51:16
Waitsfield Common 12	1	44N11	72w50	4:51:20
Waits River 9	1	44N07	72w19	4:49:16
Walden 3	1	44N29	72w15	4:49:00
Walden Heights 3	1	44N25	72w12	4:48:48
Wallingford 11	25	43N28	72w59	4:51:56
Wallispond 5	1	45N00	71w32	4:46:08
Waltham 1	1	44N08	73w14	4:52:56
Wardsboro 13	17	43N02	72w49	4:51:16
Warren 12	17	44N07	72w51	4:51:24
Warrens Gore 5	1	44N55	71w52	4:47:28
Washington 9	17	44N05	72w26	4:49:44
Washington Heights 9	1	44N33	72w31	4:50:04
Waterbury 12	27	44N20	72w46	4:51:04
Waterford 3	1	44N23	71w57	4:47:48
Waterville 8	1	44N42	72w46	4:51:04
Weathersfield 14	17	43N23	72w28	4:49:52
Weathersfield Bow 14	1	43N18	72w29	4:49:56
Websterville 12	27	44N10	72w28	4:49:52
Wells 11	12	43N25	73w11	4:52:44
Wells River 9	6	44N09	72w04	4:48:16
West Addison 1	66	44N10	73w15	4:53:00
West Arlington 2	27	43N04	73w09	4:52:36
West Barnet 3	1	44N19	72w08	4:48:32
West Berkshire 6	1	44N54	72w48	4:51:12
West Bolton 4	1	44N30	73w00	4:52:00
West Branch 8	1	44N28	72w41	4:50:44
West Brattleboro 13	13	42N51	72w34	4:50:16
West Bridgewater 11	1	43N35	72w40	4:50:40
West Bridport 1	1	43N59	73w19	4:53:16
West Brookfield 9	2	43N55	72w40	4:50:40
West Burke 3	1	44N39	71w59	4:47:56
West Castleton 11	1	43N36	73w16	4:53:04
West Charleston 10	1	44N54	72w03	4:48:12
West Corinth 9	1	44N01	72w17	4:49:08
West Cornwall 1	56	44N01	73w10	4:52:40
West Danville 3	1	44N25	72w12	4:48:48
West Derby 10	1	44N56	72w13	4:48:52
West Dover 13	1	42N56	72w51	4:51:24
West Dummerston 13	1	42N56	72w37	4:50:28
West Enosburg 6	44	44N54	72w48	4:51:12
West Fairlee 9	12	43N56	72w14	4:48:56
Westfield 10	1	44N53	72w26	4:49:44
Westford 4	1	44N36	73w01	4:52:04
West Georgia 6	65	44N49	73w05	4:52:20
West Glover 10	1	44N44	72w14	4:48:56
West Groton 3	1	44N13	72w12	4:48:48
West Halifax 13	1	42N46	72w46	4:51:04
West Hartford 14	53	43N43	72w25	4:49:40
West Haven 11	1	43N39	73w21	4:53:24
West Hill 6	1	44N54	72w48	4:51:12
West Lincoln 1	1	44N08	73w05	4:52:20
West Milton 4	2	44N38	73w07	4:52:28
Westminster 13	4	43N04	72w32	4:50:08
Westminster Station 13	6	43N05	72w27	4:49:48
Westmore 10	12	44N45	72w03	4:48:12
West Newbury 9	4	44N04	72w08	4:48:32
West Norwich 14	35	43N43	72w19	4:49:16
Weston 14	12	43N19	72w47	4:51:08
Weston Priory 14	1	43N17	72w48	4:51:12
West Pawlet 11	3	43N21	73w15	4:53:00
West Rupert 2	1	43N14	73w15	4:53:00
West Rutland 11	8	43N38	73w04	4:52:16
West Salisbury 1	1	43N54	73w06	4:52:24
West Springfield 14	21	43N18	72w29	4:49:56
West Swanton 6	51	44N55	73w07	4:52:28
West Topsham 9	1	44N07	72w19	4:49:16
West Townshend 13	1	43N05	72w43	4:50:52
West Wardsboro 13	1	43N02	72w51	4:51:24
West Waterford 3	2	44N25	72w01	4:48:04
West Windsor 14	12	43N29	72w29	4:49:56
West Woodstock 14	1	43N38	72w31	4:50:04
Weybridge 1	55	44N03	73w13	4:52:52
Weybridge Hill 1	56	44N01	73w10	4:52:40
Wheelock 3	1	44N33	72w07	4:48:28
White River Junction 14	25	43N39	72w19	4:49:16
Whitesville 14	1	43N23	72w37	4:50:28
Whiting 1	67	43N52	73w12	4:52:48
Whitingham 13	17	42N47	72w52	4:51:28
Wilder 14	35	43N40	72w19	4:49:16
Williamstown 9	52	44N07	72w32	4:50:08
Williamsville 13	1	42N46	72w41	4:50:44
Williston 4	12	44N26	73w06	4:52:24
Williston Road Section 4	15	44N28	73w10	4:52:40
Wilmington 13	19	42N52	72w52	4:51:28
Windham 13	12	43N11	72w43	4:50:52
Windsor 14	27	43N29	72w24	4:49:36
Winhall 2	17	43N10	72w56	4:51:44
Winooski 4	15	44N29	73w11	4:52:44
Winooski Park 4	15	44N30	73w11	4:52:44
Wolcott 8	1	44N34	72w27	4:49:48
Woodbury 12	12	44N26	72w25	4:49:40
Woodford 2	12	42N53	73w05	4:52:20
Woodford Hollow 2	23	42N53	73w12	4:52:48
Woodstock 14	21	43N36	72w33	4:50:12
Worcester 12	12	44N23	72w34	4:50:16

TIME TABLES

VA # 1
Before 11/18/1883 LMT
11/18/1883 12:00 EST
3/31/1918 02:00 EWT
10/27/1918 02:00 EST
3/30/1919 02:00 EWT
10/26/1919 02:00 EST
2/09/1942 02:00 EWT
9/30/1945 02:00 EST
5/11/1947 02:00 EDT
9/28/1947 02:00 EST
5/02/1948 02:00 EDT
9/26/1948 02:00 EST
4/24/1949 02:00 EDT
9/25/1949 02:00 EST
5/04/1950 02:00 EDT
9/24/1950 02:00 EST
4/29/1951 02:00 EDT
9/30/1951 02:00 EST
4/27/1952 02:00 EDT
9/28/1952 02:00 EST
4/30/1953 02:00 EDT
9/27/1953 02:00 EST
4/25/1954 02:00 US#3

VA # 2
Before 11/18/1883 LMT
11/18/1883 12:00 EST
3/31/1918 02:00 EWT
10/27/1918 02:00 EST
3/30/1919 02:00 EWT
10/26/1919 02:00 EST
2/09/1942 02:00 EWT
9/30/1945 02:00 EST
5/05/1950 02:00 EDT
9/24/1950 02:00 EST
4/29/1951 02:00 EDT
9/30/1951 02:00 EST
4/27/1952 02:00 EDT
9/28/1952 02:00 EST
4/30/1953 02:00 EDT
9/27/1953 02:00 EST
4/25/1954 02:00 US#3

VA # 3
Before 11/18/1883 LMT
11/18/1883 12:00 EST
3/31/1918 02:00 EWT
10/27/1918 02:00 EST
3/30/1919 02:00 EWT
10/26/1919 02:00 EST
2/09/1942 02:00 EWT
9/30/1945 02:00 EST
5/02/1948 02:00 EDT
9/26/1948 02:00 EST
4/24/1949 02:00 EDT
9/25/1949 02:00 EST
6/28/1950 02:00 EDT
9/24/1950 02:00 EST
4/29/1951 02:00 EDT
9/30/1951 02:00 EST
4/27/1952 02:00 EDT
9/28/1952 02:00 EST
4/30/1953 02:00 EDT
9/27/1953 02:00 EST
4/25/1954 02:00 US#3

VA # 4
Before 11/18/1883 LMT
11/18/1883 12:00 EST
3/31/1918 02:00 EWT
10/27/1918 02:00 EST
3/30/1919 02:00 EWT
10/26/1919 02:00 EST
2/09/1942 02:00 EWT
9/30/1945 02:00 EST
5/31/1962 00:00 EDT
9/04/1962 00:00 EST
5/31/1963 00:00 EDT
9/03/1963 00:00 EST
6/01/1964 00:00 EDT
9/07/1964 00:00 EST
6/07/1965 00:00 EDT
9/06/1965 00:00 EST
4/24/1966 02:00 US#1

VA # 5
Before 11/18/1883 LMT
11/18/1883 12:00 EST
3/31/1918 02:00 EWT
10/27/1918 02:00 EST
3/30/1919 02:00 EWT
10/26/1919 02:00 EST
2/09/1942 02:00 EWT
9/30/1945 02:00 EST
4/28/1946 02:00 EDT
9/29/1946 02:00 EST
5/31/1962 00:00 EDT
9/04/1962 00:00 EST
5/31/1963 00:00 EDT
9/03/1963 00:00 EST
6/01/1964 00:00 EDT
9/07/1964 00:00 EST
6/07/1965 00:00 EDT
9/06/1965 00:00 EST
4/24/1966 02:00 US#1

VA # 6
Before 11/18/1883 LMT
11/18/1883 12:00 EST
3/31/1918 02:00 EWT
10/27/1918 02:00 EST
3/30/1919 02:00 EWT
10/26/1919 02:00 EST
2/09/1942 02:00 EWT
9/30/1945 02:00 EST
4/28/1946 02:00 EDT
9/30/1946 00:00 EST
4/25/1948 02:00 EDT
9/26/1948 02:00 EST
4/27/1952 02:00 EDT
9/28/1952 02:00 EST
5/31/1962 00:00 EDT
9/04/1962 00:00 EST
5/31/1963 00:00 EDT
9/03/1963 00:00 EST
6/01/1964 00:00 EDT
9/07/1964 00:00 EST
6/07/1965 00:00 EDT
9/06/1965 00:00 EST
4/24/1966 02:00 US#1

VA # 7
Before 11/18/1883 LMT
11/18/1883 12:00 EST
3/31/1918 02:00 EWT
10/27/1918 02:00 EST
3/30/1919 02:00 EWT
10/26/1919 02:00 EST
2/09/1942 02:00 EWT
9/30/1945 02:00 EST
4/28/1946 02:00 EDT
9/30/1946 02:00 EST
4/25/1948 02:00 US#5

VA # 8
Before 11/18/1883 LMT
11/18/1883 12:00 EST
3/31/1918 02:00 EWT
10/27/1918 02:00 EST
3/30/1919 02:00 EWT
10/26/1919 02:00 EST
2/09/1942 02:00 EWT
9/30/1945 02:00 EST
4/25/1948 02:00 US#5

VA # 9
Before 11/18/1883 LMT
11/18/1883 12:00 EST
3/31/1918 02:00 EWT
10/27/1918 02:00 EST
3/30/1919 02:00 EWT
10/26/1919 02:00 EST
2/09/1942 02:00 EWT
9/30/1945 02:00 EST
4/25/1948 02:00 EDT
9/26/1948 02:00 EST
4/24/1949 02:00 EDT
9/25/1949 02:00 EST
4/30/1950 02:00 EDT
9/24/1950 02:00 EST
4/29/1951 02:00 EDT
9/30/1951 02:00 EST
4/27/1952 02:00 EDT
9/28/1952 02:00 EST
4/30/1961 02:00 EDT
10/01/1961 02:00 EST
5/31/1962 00:00 EDT
9/04/1962 00:00 EST
5/31/1963 00:00 EDT
9/03/1963 00:00 EST
6/01/1964 00:00 EDT
9/07/1964 00:00 EST
6/07/1965 00:00 EDT
9/06/1965 00:00 EST
4/24/1966 02:00 US#1

VA # 10
Before 11/18/1883 LMT
11/18/1883 12:00 EST
3/31/1918 02:00 EWT
10/27/1918 02:00 EST
3/30/1919 02:00 EWT
10/26/1919 02:00 EST
2/09/1942 02:00 EWT
9/30/1945 02:00 EST
4/27/1952 02:00 US#5

VA # 11
Before 11/18/1883 LMT
11/18/1883 12:00 EST
3/31/1918 02:00 EWT
10/27/1918 02:00 EST
3/30/1919 02:00 EWT
10/26/1919 02:00 EST
2/09/1942 02:00 EWT
9/30/1945 02:00 EST
4/29/1956 02:00 US#5

VA # 12
Before 11/18/1883 LMT
11/18/1883 12:00 EST
3/31/1918 02:00 EWT
10/27/1918 02:00 EST
3/30/1919 02:00 EWT
10/26/1919 02:00 EST
2/09/1942 02:00 EWT
9/30/1945 02:00 EST
4/29/1956 02:00 EDT
9/30/1956 02:00 EST
4/30/1961 02:00 EDT
10/01/1961 02:00 EST
5/31/1962 00:00 EDT
9/04/1962 00:00 EST
5/31/1963 00:00 EDT
9/03/1963 00:00 EST
6/01/1964 00:00 EDT
9/07/1964 00:00 EST
6/07/1965 00:00 EDT
9/06/1965 00:00 EST
4/24/1966 02:00 US#1

VA # 13
Before 11/18/1883 LMT
11/18/1883 12:00 EST
3/31/1918 02:00 EWT
10/27/1918 02:00 EST
3/30/1919 02:00 EWT
10/26/1919 02:00 EST
2/09/1942 02:00 EWT
9/30/1945 02:00 EST
4/26/1959 02:00 EDT
10/25/1959 02:00 EST
4/30/1961 02:00 EDT
10/29/1961 02:00 EST
5/31/1962 00:00 EDT
9/04/1962 00:00 EST
5/31/1963 00:00 EDT
9/03/1963 00:00 EST
6/01/1964 00:00 EDT
9/07/1964 00:00 EST
6/07/1965 00:00 EDT
9/06/1965 00:00 EST
4/24/1966 02:00 US#1

VA # 14
Before 11/18/1883 LMT
11/18/1883 12:00 EST
3/31/1918 02:00 EWT
10/27/1918 02:00 EST
3/30/1919 02:00 EWT
10/26/1919 02:00 EST
2/09/1942 02:00 EWT
9/30/1945 02:00 EST
4/30/1961 02:00 EDT
10/29/1961 02:00 EST
5/31/1962 00:00 EDT
9/04/1962 00:00 EST
5/31/1963 00:00 EDT
9/03/1963 00:00 EST
6/01/1964 00:00 EDT
9/07/1964 00:00 EST
6/07/1965 00:00 EDT
9/06/1965 00:00 EST
4/24/1966 02:00 US#1

VA # 15
Before 11/18/1883 LMT
11/18/1883 12:00 EST
3/31/1918 02:00 EWT
10/27/1918 02:00 EST
3/30/1919 02:00 EWT
10/26/1919 02:00 EST
2/09/1942 02:00 EWT
9/30/1945 02:00 EST
5/31/1962 00:00 EDT
9/04/1962 00:00 EST
5/31/1963 00:00 EDT
9/03/1963 00:00 EST
4/30/1967 02:00 US#1

VA # 16
Before 11/18/1883 LMT
11/18/1883 12:00 EST
3/31/1918 02:00 EWT
10/27/1918 02:00 EST
3/30/1919 02:00 EWT
10/26/1919 02:00 EST
2/09/1942 02:00 EWT
9/30/1945 02:00 EST
5/03/1961 02:00 EDT
10/29/1961 02:00 EST
5/31/1962 00:00 EDT
9/04/1962 00:00 EST
5/31/1963 00:00 EDT
9/03/1963 00:00 EST
6/01/1964 00:00 EDT
9/07/1964 00:00 EST
6/07/1965 00:00 EDT
9/06/1965 00:00 EST
4/24/1966 02:00 US#1

VA # 17
Before 11/18/1883 LMT
11/18/1883 12:00 EST
3/31/1918 02:00 EWT
10/27/1918 02:00 EST
3/30/1919 02:00 EWT
10/26/1919 02:00 EST
2/09/1942 02:00 EWT
9/30/1945 02:00 EST
4/30/1961 00:00 EDT
10/01/1961 02:00 EST
5/31/1962 00:00 EDT
9/04/1962 00:00 EST
5/31/1963 00:00 EDT
9/03/1963 00:00 EST
6/01/1964 00:00 EDT
9/07/1964 00:00 EST
6/07/1965 00:00 EDT
9/06/1965 00:00 EST
4/24/1966 02:00 US#1

VA # 18
Before 11/18/1883 LMT
11/18/1883 12:00 EST
3/31/1918 02:00 EWT
10/27/1918 02:00 EST
3/30/1919 02:00 EWT
10/26/1919 02:00 EST
2/09/1942 02:00 EWT
9/30/1945 02:00 EST
5/23/1961 02:00 EDT
10/29/1961 02:00 EST
5/31/1962 00:00 EDT
9/04/1962 00:00 EST
5/31/1963 00:00 EDT
9/03/1963 00:00 EST
6/01/1964 00:00 EDT
9/07/1964 00:00 EST
6/07/1965 00:00 EDT
9/06/1965 00:00 EST
4/24/1966 02:00 US#1

VA # 19
Before 11/18/1883 LMT
11/18/1883 12:00 EST
3/31/1918 02:00 EWT
10/27/1918 02:00 EST
3/30/1919 02:00 EWT
10/26/1919 02:00 EST
2/09/1942 02:00 EWT
9/30/1945 02:00 EST
5/15/1961 00:00 EDT
10/29/1961 02:00 EST
5/31/1962 00:00 EDT
9/04/1962 00:00 EST
5/31/1963 00:00 EDT
9/03/1963 00:00 EST
6/01/1964 00:00 EDT
9/07/1964 00:00 EST
6/07/1965 00:00 EDT
9/06/1965 00:00 EST
4/24/1966 02:00 US#1

VA # 20
Before 11/18/1883 LMT
11/18/1883 12:00 EST
3/31/1918 02:00 EWT
10/27/1918 02:00 EST
3/30/1919 02:00 EWT
10/26/1919 02:00 EST
2/09/1942 02:00 EWT
9/30/1945 02:00 EST
4/30/1961 02:00 EDT
5/06/1961 02:00 EST
5/31/1962 00:00 EDT
9/04/1962 00:00 EST
5/31/1963 00:00 EDT
9/03/1963 00:00 EST
6/01/1964 00:00 EDT
9/07/1964 00:00 EST
6/07/1965 00:00 EDT
9/06/1965 00:00 EST
4/24/1966 02:00 US#1

VA # 21
Before 11/18/1883 LMT
11/18/1883 12:00 EST
3/31/1918 02:00 EWT
10/27/1918 02:00 EST
3/30/1919 02:00 EWT
10/26/1919 02:00 EST
2/09/1942 02:00 EWT
9/30/1945 02:00 EST
4/30/1961 02:00 EDT
9/04/1961 00:00 EST
5/31/1962 00:00 EDT
9/04/1962 00:00 EST
5/31/1963 00:00 EDT
9/03/1963 00:00 EST
6/01/1964 00:00 EDT
9/07/1964 00:00 EST
6/07/1965 00:00 EDT
9/06/1965 00:00 EST
4/24/1966 02:00 US#1

VA # 22
Before 11/18/1883 LMT
11/18/1883 12:00 EST
3/31/1918 02:00 EWT
10/27/1918 02:00 EST
3/30/1919 02:00 EWT
10/26/1919 02:00 EST
2/09/1942 02:00 EWT
9/30/1945 02:00 EST
4/30/1961 02:00 EDT
10/01/1961 02:00 EST
5/31/1962 00:00 EDT
9/04/1962 00:00 EST
5/31/1963 00:00 EDT
9/03/1963 00:00 EST
6/01/1964 00:00 EDT
9/07/1964 00:00 EST
6/07/1965 00:00 EDT
9/06/1965 00:00 EST
4/24/1966 02:00 US#1

VA # 23
Before 11/18/1883 LMT
11/18/1883 12:00 EST
3/31/1918 02:00 EWT
10/27/1918 02:00 EST
3/30/1919 02:00 EWT
10/26/1919 02:00 EST
2/09/1942 02:00 EWT
9/30/1945 02:00 EST
4/30/1961 02:00 EDT
10/15/1961 02:00 EST
5/31/1962 00:00 EDT
9/04/1962 00:00 EST
5/31/1963 00:00 EDT
9/03/1963 00:00 EST
6/01/1964 00:00 EDT
9/07/1964 00:00 EST
6/07/1965 00:00 EDT
9/06/1965 00:00 EST
4/24/1966 02:00 US#1

VA # 24
Before 11/18/1883 LMT
11/18/1883 12:00 EST
3/31/1918 02:00 EWT
10/27/1918 02:00 EST
3/30/1919 02:00 EWT
10/26/1919 02:00 EST
2/09/1942 02:00 EWT
9/30/1945 02:00 EST
4/29/1956 02:00 EDT
9/30/1956 02:00 EST
4/28/1957 02:00 EDT
9/29/1957 02:00 EST
4/27/1958 02:00 EDT
10/26/1958 02:00 EST
4/26/1959 02:00 EDT
10/25/1959 02:00 EST
4/24/1960 02:00 EDT
10/30/1960 02:00 EST
4/30/1961 02:00 EDT
10/01/1961 02:00 EST
4/29/1962 02:00 US#2

VA # 25
Before 11/18/1883 LMT
11/18/1883 12:00 EST
3/31/1918 02:00 EWT
10/27/1918 02:00 EST
3/30/1919 02:00 EWT
10/26/1919 02:00 EST
2/09/1942 02:00 EWT
9/30/1945 02:00 EST
4/28/1946 02:00 EDT
9/29/1946 02:00 EST
4/30/1967 02:00 US#1

VA # 26
Before 11/18/1883 LMT
11/18/1883 12:00 CST
3/31/1918 02:00 CWT
10/27/1918 02:00 CST
3/30/1919 02:00 CWT
10/26/1919 02:00 CST
2/09/1942 02:00 CWT
9/30/1945 02:00 CST
3/02/1946 02:00 EST
5/31/1962 00:00 EDT
9/04/1962 00:00 EST
5/31/1963 00:00 EDT
9/03/1963 00:00 EST
4/30/1967 02:00 US#1

COUNTIES

1 Accomack
2 Albemarle
3 Alleghany
4 Amelia
5 Amherst
6 Appomattox
7 Arlington
8 Augusta
9 Bath
10 Bedford
11 Bland
12 Botetourt
13 Brunswick
14 Buchanan
15 Buckingham
16 Campbell
17 Caroline
18 Carroll
19 Charles City
20 Charlotte
21 Chesterfield
22 Clarke
23 Craig
24 Culpeper
25 Cumberland
26 Dickenson
27 Dinwiddie
28 Essex
29 Fairfax
30 Fauquier
31 Floyd
32 Fluvanna
33 Franklin
34 Frederick
35 Giles
36 Gloucester
37 Goochland
38 Grayson
39 Greene
40 Greensville
41 Halifax
42 Hanover
43 Henrico
44 Henry
45 Highland
46 Isle of Wight
47 James City
48 King and Queen
49 King George
50 King William
51 Lancaster
52 Lee
53 Loudoun
54 Louisa
55 Lunenburg
56 Madison
57 Mathews
58 Mecklenburg
59 Middlesex
60 Montgomery
61 Nansemond
62 Nelson
63 New Kent
64 Northampton
65 Northumberland
66 Nottoway
67 Orange
68 Page
69 Patrick
70 Pittsylvania
71 Powhatan
72 Prince Edward
73 Prince George
74 Prince William
75 Pulaski
76 Rappahannock
77 Richmond
78 Roanoke
79 Rockbridge
80 Rockingham
81 Russell
82 Scott
83 Shenandoah
84 Smyth
85 Southampton
86 Spotsylvania
87 Stafford
88 Surry
89 Sussex
90 Tazewell
91 Warren
92 Washington
93 Westmoreland
94 Wise
95 Wythe
96 York
97 Alexandria
98 Bedford
99 Bristol
100 Buena Vista
101 Charlottesville
102 Chesapeake
103 Clifton Forge
104 Colonial Heights
105 Covington
106 Danville
107 Emporia
108 Fairfax
109 Falls Church
110 Franklin
111 Fredericksburg
112 Galax
113 Hampton
114 Harrisonburg
115 Hopewell
116 Lexington
117 Lynchburg
118 Manassas
119 Manassas Park
120 Martinsville
121 Newport News
122 Norfolk
123 Norton
124 Petersburg
125 Portsmouth
126 Radford
127 Richmond
128 Roanoke
129 Salem
130 South Boston
131 Staunton
132 Suffolk
133 Virginia Beach
134 Waynesboro
135 Williamsburg
136 Winchester

Abbot 23	4	37N30	80W07	5:20:28
Abilene 20	4	37N03	78W39	5:14:36
Abingdon 92	15	36N43	81W59	5:27:56
Accomac 1	4	37N43	75W40	5:02:40
Accotink 29	3	38N42	77W09	5:08:36
Accotink Heights 29	1	38N50	77W12	5:08:48
Accotink Springs 29	3	38N45	77W12	5:08:48
Achilles 36	4	37N17	76W27	5:05:48
Achsah 56	4	38N20	78W10	5:12:40
Acorn 93	19	38N01	76W39	5:06:36
Acquinton 50	14	37N43	77W06	5:08:24
Acredale 133	6	36N49	76W09	5:04:36
Ada 30	19	38N52	77W52	5:11:28
Aden 74	14	38N42	77W35	5:10:20
Adial 62	14	37N50	78W44	5:14:56
Adkins Store 19	14	37N27	77W02	5:08:08
Adner 36	4	37N36	76W36	5:06:24
Adria 90	4	37N08	81W31	5:26:04
Adsit 13	4	36N45	77W42	5:10:48
Advance Mills 2	14	38N14	78W22	5:13:28
Adwolf 84	15	36N50	81W31	5:26:04
Afton 62	14	38N02	78W50	5:15:20
Agnewville 74	13	38N39	77W16	5:09:04
Agricola 5	16	37N30	79W08	5:16:32
Ahoy Acres 102	6	36N50	76W25	5:05:40
Aiken Summit 44	4	36N40	79W43	5:18:52
Aily 26	15	36N59	82W17	5:29:08
Airlie 30	19	38N44	77W44	5:10:56
Airmont 53	14	39N08	77W46	5:11:04
Ajax 70	4	36N34	79W44	5:18:56
Alanthus 24	4	38N30	77W54	5:11:36
Alban Woods 74	13	38N39	77W16	5:09:04
Alberene 2	14	37N53	78W37	5:14:28
Alberta 13	4	36N52	77W53	5:11:32
Albin 34	9	39N11	78W10	5:12:40
Alcoma 15	4	37N32	78W37	5:14:28
Aldie 53	4	38N59	77W39	5:10:36
Alexandria 97	1	38N48	77W03	5:08:12
Alfonso 51	4	37N48	76W31	5:06:04
Algren 102	6	36N50	76W25	5:05:40
Alhambra 5	16	37N43	79W04	5:16:16
Alice Heights 21	22	37N27	77W28	5:09:52
Allegany Spring 60	4	37N10	80W15	5:21:00
Alleghany 3	4	37N45	80W14	5:20:56
Allen 26	15	37N10	82W22	5:29:28
Allens Creek 62	14	37N33	78W52	5:15:28
Allen Shop Corner 48	4	37N40	76W53	5:07:32
Allenslevel 15	4	37N33	78W28	5:13:52
Allison Gap 84	15	36N54	81W47	5:27:08
Allisonia 75	4	36N56	80W44	5:22:56
Allmondsville 36	4	37N25	76W32	5:06:08
Allwington 30	19	38N44	77W44	5:10:56
Allwood 5	16	37N35	79W03	5:16:12
Alma 68	14	38N35	78W30	5:14:00
Almagro 106	4	36N35	79W23	5:17:32
Almira 94	15	37N08	82W36	5:30:24
Alonzaville 83	14	38N55	78W28	5:13:52
Alpha 15	4	37N33	78W28	5:13:52
Alpine 29	1	38N50	77W12	5:08:48
Alpine 83	14	38N39	78W40	5:14:40
Alps 17	22	38N01	77W22	5:09:28
Alsop 86	22	38N12	77W35	5:10:20
Altavista 16	16	37N06	79W17	5:17:08
Alto 5	16	37N54	79W12	5:16:48
Alton 41	4	36N34	79W00	5:16:00
Alum Ridge 31	4	36N58	80W24	5:21:36
Alvarado 92	15	36N43	81W58	5:27:52
Amburg 59	4	37N33	76W20	5:05:20
Amelia Court House 4	4	37N21	77W59	5:11:56
Americana Apartments 29	1	38N50	77W12	5:08:48
Amherst 5	16	37N35	79W03	5:16:12
Amherst 29	3	38N48	77W16	5:09:04
Amissville 76	14	38N40	78W00	5:12:00
Ammon 4	4	37N13	77W46	5:11:04
Amonate 90	4	37N12	81W38	5:26:32
Ampthill 21	22	37N27	77W28	5:09:52
Amsterdam 12	4	37N28	79W55	5:19:40
Andersonville 15	4	37N28	78W34	5:14:16
Andover 94	26	36N55	82W48	5:31:12
Andrew Lewis Place 78	4	37N17	80W03	5:20:12
Angola 25	4	37N18	78W24	5:13:36
Ankum 13	4	36N46	77W51	5:11:24
Annalee Heights 29	3	38N52	77W13	5:08:52
Annandale 29	1	38N50	77W12	5:08:48
Annandale Acres 29	1	38N50	77W12	5:08:48
Annandale Gardens 29	1	38N50	77W12	5:08:48
Annandale Terrace 29	1	38N50	77W12	5:08:48
Annex 8	21	38N09	79W05	5:16:20
Ante 13	14	36N41	77W32	5:10:08
Antioch 32	4	37N48	78W29	5:13:56
Antlers 58	4	36N40	78W23	5:13:32
Appalachia 94	26	36N54	82W47	5:31:08
Apple Grove 54	14	37N53	77W54	5:11:36
Appomattox 6	4	37N21	78W50	5:15:20
Aqua 79	14	37N53	79W17	5:17:08
Aquia 87	4	38N27	77W22	5:09:28
Aragona Acres 133	6	36N52	76W00	5:04:00
Aragona Village 133	6	36N53	76W08	5:04:32
Ararat 69	4	36N36	80W31	5:22:04
Arbor Estates 132	5	36N44	76W35	5:06:20
Arborhill 8	21	38N03	79W13	5:16:52
Arcadia 12	4	37N32	79W41	5:18:44
Arch Mills 12	4	37N32	79W41	5:18:44
Arco 91	14	38N55	78W12	5:12:48
Arcola 53	4	38N57	77W32	5:10:08
Arcturus 29	1	38N45	77W04	5:08:16
Ardmore 108	3	38N51	77W15	5:09:00
Argyle Heights 87	4	38N23	77W27	5:09:48
Ark 36	4	37N26	76W35	5:06:20
Arlington 7	1	38N53	77W07	5:08:28
Arlington 115	14	37N17	77W18	5:09:12
Arlington Hall 7	1	38N52	77W06	5:08:24
Armel 34	9	39N11	78W10	5:12:40
Arnolds Corner 49	22	38N16	77W11	5:08:44
Aroda 56	4	38N20	78W14	5:12:56
Arrington 62	14	37N41	78W54	5:15:36
Arritt 3	4	37N47	79W59	5:19:56
Arrowhead 133	6	36N51	76W09	5:04:36
Arthur 60	4	37N10	80W15	5:21:00
Artrip 81	15	36N57	82W09	5:28:36
Arvonia 15	4	37N41	78W20	5:13:20
Asberrys 90	4	36N58	81W38	5:26:32
Ashburn 53	4	39N03	77W29	5:09:56
Ashby 25	4	37N30	78W15	5:13:00
Ashby 91	14	38N55	78W12	5:12:48
Ashland 42	22	37N46	77W29	5:09:56
Ashton Glen 74	2	38N47	77W28	5:09:52
Ashville 30	19	38N52	77W52	5:11:28
Ashwood 9	4	38N00	79W50	5:19:20
Aspen 20	4	37N05	78W45	5:15:00
Aspenwall 20	4	37N03	78W56	5:15:44
Assawoman 1	4	37N52	75W32	5:02:08
Athlone 80	22	38N37	78W48	5:15:12
Atkins 84	15	36N53	81W23	5:25:32
Atlantic 1	4	37N56	75W32	5:02:08
Atlantic Park 133	6	36N48	76W01	5:04:04
Atlee 42	22	37N37	77W22	5:09:28
Attoway 84	15	36N50	81W31	5:26:04
Auburn 30	19	38N39	77W39	5:10:36
Augusta Springs 8	21	38N06	79W19	5:17:16
Aura Heights 29	1	38N51	77W09	5:08:36
Austinville 95	4	36N51	80W55	5:23:40
Avalon 65	18	37N55	76W28	5:05:52
Avalon 102	6	36N50	76W16	5:05:04
Avalon Terrace 133	6	36N51	76W09	5:04:36
Averett 58	4	36N34	78W42	5:14:48
Avon 62	14	38N02	78W50	5:15:20
Avon Forest 29	3	38N48	77W20	5:09:20
Axtel 15	4	37N44	78W40	5:14:40
Axton 44	4	36N40	79W43	5:18:52
Aylett 50	14	37N47	77W06	5:08:24
Aylor 56	4	38N23	78W16	5:13:04
Azalea Court 43	17	37N36	77W27	5:09:48
Bachelors Hall 70	4	36N35	79W23	5:17:32
Backbay 133	6	36N51	76W06	5:04:24
Back Creek 34	4	39N10	78W17	5:13:08
Bacon 20	4	36N51	78W37	5:14:28
Bacova 9	4	38N03	79W51	5:19:24
Bacova Junction 9	4	38N00	79W50	5:19:20
Baden 26	15	37N09	82W27	5:29:48
Bagby 17	22	38N01	77W22	5:09:28
Bagleys Mills 55	4	36N44	78W07	5:12:28
Bailey 90	4	37N15	81W17	5:25:08
Baileys Crossroads 29	1	38N51	77W08	5:08:32
Balcony Falls 79	14	37N38	79W27	5:17:48
Ballards Crossroads 46	4	36N43	76W50	5:07:20
Balls Hills 29	1	38N55	77W11	5:08:44
Ballsville 71	14	37N30	78W04	5:12:16
Baltimore Corner 27	22	37N09	77W44	5:10:56
Balty 17	22	37N55	77W29	5:09:56
Banco 56	4	38N27	78W15	5:13:00
Bandy 90	4	37N09	81W42	5:26:48
Bane 35	4	37N20	80W44	5:22:56
Banners Corner 81	15	36N54	82W17	5:29:08
Bannockburn Estates 29	3	38N51	77W15	5:09:00
Barbour 67	14	38N12	78W16	5:13:04
Barbours Creek 23	4	37N30	80W07	5:20:28
Barboursville 67	14	38N10	78W17	5:13:08
Barcroft Hills 29	1	38N51	77W09	5:08:36
Barcroft Woods 29	1	38N51	77W09	5:08:36
Barfoot 33	4	37N00	79W53	5:19:32
Barham 88	4	37N10	76W58	5:07:52
Barhamsville 63	14	37N27	76W50	5:07:20
Barkers Crossroads 29	3	38N45	77W12	5:08:48
Barley 40	20	36N41	77W32	5:10:08
Barlow Corners 96	23	37N17	76W43	5:06:52
Barnesville 20	4	36N47	78W37	5:14:28
Barnett 81	15	37N00	81W59	5:27:56
Barnetts 19	14	37N20	77W04	5:08:16
Barren Ridge 8	21	38N09	79W05	5:16:20
Barren Springs 95	4	36N47	80W48	5:23:12
Barrett Acres 132	5	36N44	76W35	5:06:20
Barrett Corner 85	4	36N58	76W59	5:07:56
Bartlett 46	4	36N57	76W34	5:06:16
Bartlick 26	15	37N12	82W18	5:29:12
Bartonville 34	9	39N11	78W10	5:12:40
Barytes 92	25	36N36	82W11	5:28:44
Bascomb Church 81	15	37N00	81W59	5:27:56
Basic 134	22	38N04	78W54	5:15:36
Baskerville 58	4	36N41	78W16	5:13:04
Bassett 44	4	36N46	79W59	5:19:56
Bassett Forks 44	4	36N46	79W59	5:19:56
Bastian 11	4	37N09	81W09	5:24:36
Basye 83	14	38N48	78W47	5:15:08
Batesville 2	14	38N00	78W43	5:14:52
Battery 28	14	37N55	76W52	5:07:28
Battery Park 43	17	37N36	77W29	5:09:56
Battery Park 46	4	37N00	76W35	5:06:20

Battle Creek 68 14 38N35 78W30 5:14:00
Battlefield Acres 43 22 37N40 77W30 5:10:00
Battlefield Farms 42 22 37N37 77W22 5:09:28
Battlefield Park 73 22 37N13 77W26 5:09:44
Battletown 22 4 39N08 77W55 5:11:40
Bavon 57 4 37N20 76W17 5:05:08
Bay 113 4 37N01 76W19 5:05:16
Bayberry Estates 49 12 38N20 77W03 5:08:12
Bay Colony 133 6 36N52 76W00 5:04:00
Bayford 64 4 37N29 75W56 5:03:44
Bay Lake Beach 133 6 36N53 76W08 5:04:32
Baylake Pines 133 6 36N53 76W08 5:04:32
Baynesville 93 19 38N06 76W50 5:07:20
Bayside 133 6 36N53 76W08 5:04:32
Bay View 64 4 37N16 76W00 5:04:00
Bayville Park 133 6 36N53 76W08 5:04:32
Baywood 38 4 36N40 80W55 5:23:40
Beach 21 22 37N23 77W31 5:10:04
Beacon Manor 29 1 38N46 77W04 5:08:16
Bealeton 30 19 38N34 77W46 5:11:04
Beamantown 94 26 36N56 82W47 5:31:08
Beamon 132 5 36N44 76W35 5:06:20
Bear Wallow 14 15 37N11 81W48 5:27:12
Beaverdam 42 22 37N53 77W34 5:10:16
Beaverlett 57 4 37N24 76W19 5:05:16
Beazley 17 14 37N55 76W52 5:07:28
Beckham 6 4 37N21 78W59 5:15:56
Bedford 83 14 38N49 78W34 5:14:16
Bedford 98 4 37N20 79W31 5:18:04
Bee 26 15 37N07 82W10 5:28:40
Beech Grove 133 6 36N49 76W09 5:04:36
Beech Springs 52 26 36N40 83W07 5:32:28
Beechwood 58 4 36N36 78W09 5:12:36
Beechwood Hills 16 14 37N24 79W10 5:16:40
Beechwood Manor 73 22 37N17 77W18 5:09:12
Beechwood Park 43 22 37N32 77W19 5:09:16
Bel Air 29 3 38N52 77W13 5:08:52
Beldor 80 14 38N24 78W37 5:14:28
Belfast Mills 81 15 37N05 81W46 5:27:04
Belfield 40 20 36N43 77W33 5:10:12
Bellair 2 14 38N02 78W29 5:13:56
Bell Air 87 4 38N23 77W27 5:09:48
Bellamy 36 4 37N23 76W35 5:06:20
Bellamy 82 26 36N41 82W45 5:31:00
Bellany Manor 133 6 36N51 76W09 5:04:36
Bellbluff 21 22 37N27 77W28 5:09:52
Belleair 29 3 38N48 77W16 5:09:04
Bellefonte 66 4 37N07 77W57 5:11:48
Belle Forest 29 3 38N51 77W15 5:09:00
Belle Haven 1 4 37N32 75W52 5:03:28
Belle Haven 29 1 38N46 77W04 5:08:16
Belle Haven 133 6 36N51 76W07 5:04:28
Belle Meade 30 19 38N54 78W05 5:12:20
Belle Meadows 92 25 36N36 82W11 5:28:44
Belle View 29 1 38N46 77W04 5:08:16
Bellevue 127 17 37N36 77W27 5:09:48
Bells Cross Road 86 22 38N12 77W35 5:10:20
Bells Cross Roads 54 14 38N02 78W00 5:12:00
Bells Mill 102 6 36N47 76W15 5:05:00
Bell Spur 69 4 36N44 80W25 5:21:40
Bells Valley 79 14 37N59 79W30 5:18:00
Bellwood 21 22 37N27 77W28 5:09:52
Bellwood Manor 21 22 37N27 77W28 5:09:52
Belmont 29 3 38N42 77W14 5:08:56
Belmont 74 13 38N39 77W16 5:09:04
Belmont 86 22 38N12 77W35 5:10:20
Belmont 101 14 38N02 78W29 5:13:56
Belmont Acres 21 22 37N27 77W28 5:09:52
Belmont Farms 60 4 37N08 80W24 5:21:36
Belmont Park 53 4 39N03 77W29 5:09:56
Belona 71 14 37N29 77W55 5:11:40
Belspring 75 4 37N11 80W36 5:22:24
Belvedere 29 1 38N51 77W09 5:08:36
Belvidere Beach 49 22 38N23 77W27 5:09:48
Belvoir 30 19 38N52 77W52 5:11:28
Bena 36 4 37N16 76W27 5:05:48
Benefit 102 4 36N41 76W16 5:05:04
Benham 92 25 36N36 82W11 5:28:44
Ben Hur 52 26 36N44 83W05 5:32:20
Bennetts Harbor 132 5 36N44 76W35 5:06:20
Bennett Springs 78 4 37N17 80W03 5:20:12
Benns Church 46 4 36N59 76W38 5:06:32
Bensley 21 22 37N27 77W28 5:09:52
Bent Creek 6 4 37N33 78W52 5:15:28
Bent Mountain 78 4 37N09 80W07 5:20:28
Bentonville 91 14 38N50 78W19 5:13:16
Bergton 80 22 38N46 78W57 5:15:48
Berkeley 2 14 38N02 78W29 5:13:56
Berkley 122 6 36N50 76W17 5:05:08
Berlin 85 4 36N54 76W54 5:07:36
Berlin And Ivor 85 4 36N52 76W57 5:07:48
Bermuda 21 22 37N23 77W25 5:09:40
Bermuda Hundred 21 22 37N23 77W26 5:09:44
Berrys 22 4 39N06 78W04 5:12:16
Berryville 22 14 39N09 77W59 5:11:56
Berthaville 49 22 38N16 77W11 5:08:44
Berton 35 4 37N20 80W44 5:22:56
Bess 3 4 37N47 79W59 5:19:56
Bestland 28 4 37N50 76W53 5:07:32
Bethel 30 19 38N44 77W44 5:10:56
Bethel 74 13 38N39 77W16 5:09:04
Bethel 91 14 38N55 78W12 5:12:48
Bethel 96 4 37N07 76W26 5:05:44
Bethel Manor 96 4 37N07 76W31 5:06:04
Beulah Church 28 14 37N55 76W52 5:07:28
Beulah Village 21 22 37N27 77W28 5:09:52
Beulahville 50 14 37N51 77W11 5:08:44
Beverly Forest 29 3 38N45 77W12 5:08:48
Beverly Heights 129 4 37N17 80W03 5:20:12
Beverly Hills 43 22 37N36 77W32 5:10:08
Beverly Manor 8 21 38N08 79W03 5:16:12
Beverly Manor 29 1 38N55 77W11 5:08:44
Beverlyville 65 18 37N51 76W17 5:05:08
Big Fork 58 4 36N44 78W07 5:12:28
Big Island 10 4 37N32 79W22 5:17:28
Big Laurel 94 15 37N01 82W35 5:30:20
Big Lick 78 4 37N19 79W51 5:19:24
Big River 8 21 37N59 79W30 5:18:00
Big Rock 14 15 37N21 82W11 5:28:44
Big Spring 68 14 38N46 78W23 5:13:32
Big Stone Gap 94 26 36N52 82W47 5:31:08
Big Vein 90 4 37N18 81W21 5:25:24
Biltmore 43 22 37N40 77W30 5:10:00
Binns Hall 19 14 37N20 77W04 5:08:16
Birch Creek 41 4 36N42 79W06 5:16:24
Birchleaf 26 15 37N11 82W16 5:29:04
Birch Town 1 4 37N56 75W22 5:01:28
Birdneck Acres 133 6 36N52 76W00 5:04:00
Birdsnest 64 4 37N26 75W53 5:03:32
Birmingham 90 4 37N05 81W46 5:27:04
Biscoe 48 4 37N48 77W03 5:08:12
Bishop 90 4 37N13 81W40 5:26:40
Bishops Corner 55 4 36N58 78W07 5:12:28
Blackberry 44 4 36N44 80W02 5:20:08
Black Creek 63 14 37N32 77W10 5:08:40
Blackey 14 15 37N23 82W00 5:28:00
Blackford 81 15 37N01 81W59 5:27:56
Blacklick 95 4 36N55 81W13 5:24:52
Blackridge 58 4 36N39 78W04 5:12:16
Blacksburg 60 4 37N14 80W25 5:21:40
Blacksburg 79 14 37N44 79W21 5:17:24
Blacksburg 92 15 36N48 81W46 5:27:04
Blackstone 66 4 37N04 78W00 5:12:00
Black Walnut 41 4 36N38 78W55 5:15:40
Blackwater 52 26 36N38 83W03 5:32:12
Blackwater 133 6 36N51 76W06 5:04:24
Blackwater Bridge 133 6 36N51 76W06 5:04:24
Blackwells Chapel 92 15 36N46 81W52 5:27:28
Blackwood 94 15 36N59 82W38 5:30:32
Blainville 68 14 38N40 78W27 5:13:48
Blairs 70 4 36N41 79W23 5:17:32
Blakes 57 4 37N30 76W22 5:05:28
Bland 11 4 37N06 81W07 5:24:28
Blantons 17 22 37N55 77W29 5:09:56
Bleak 30 19 38N36 77W44 5:10:56
Blendon 66 4 37N09 78W03 5:12:12
Blessing 95 4 36N57 81W05 5:24:20
Blevinstown 29 3 38N51 77W15 5:09:00
Bloomfield 53 4 39N07 77W50 5:11:20
Bloomingdale 43 17 37N36 77W29 5:09:56
Blowing Rock 26 15 37N09 82W27 5:29:48
Bloxom 1 4 37N50 75W38 5:02:32
Bluefield 90 4 37N15 81W17 5:25:08
Blue Grass 45 4 38N26 79W38 5:18:32
Bluemont 53 4 39N07 77W50 5:11:20
Blue Ridge 12 4 37N23 79W49 5:19:16
Blue Ridge Shores 54 14 38N02 78W00 5:12:00
Bluestone 58 4 36N43 78W32 5:14:08
Boaz 46 4 36N43 76W50 5:07:20
Bocock 16 14 37N24 79W10 5:16:40
Body Camp 10 4 37N20 79W31 5:18:04
Bohannon 57 4 37N24 76W22 5:05:28
Boiling Spring 3 4 37N42 80W07 5:20:28
Boissevain 90 4 37N17 81W23 5:25:32
Bolar 9 4 38N13 79W41 5:18:44
Bolling Store 18 4 36N46 80W44 5:22:56
Bolton 81 15 37N00 81W59 5:27:56
Bon Air 21 22 37N31 77W34 5:10:16
Bondtown 94 15 37N00 82W28 5:29:52
Bonniemill Gardens 29 3 38N45 77W12 5:08:48
Bonny Blue 52 26 36N49 83W03 5:32:12
Bonsack 78 4 37N19 79W55 5:19:40
Boone 102 6 36N50 76W25 5:05:40
Boones Mill 33 4 37N07 79W57 5:19:48
Boonesville 2 14 38N15 78W32 5:14:08
Boonsboro 10 14 37N26 79W11 5:16:44
Bordeaux 29 3 38N58 77W22 5:09:28
Borkey Store 42 22 37N37 77W22 5:09:28
Boston 24 4 38N33 78W08 5:12:32
Boston 132 5 36N44 76W35 5:06:20
Boswells Store 87 4 38N25 77W24 5:09:36
Boswells Tavern 54 14 38N09 78W11 5:12:44
Botha 30 19 38N44 77W44 5:10:56
Boudar Gardens 43 17 37N36 77W29 5:09:56
Boulevard Estates 29 3 38N51 77W15 5:09:00
Bowers Corner 13 4 36N39 77W57 5:11:48
Bowers Hill 102 6 36N50 76W25 5:05:40
Bowlers Wharf 28 14 37N55 76W52 5:07:28
Bowling 52 26 36N40 83W07 5:32:28
Bowling Green 17 22 38N03 77W21 5:09:24
Bowmans 83 14 38N49 78W34 5:14:16
Boxley Hills 78 4 37N19 79W55 5:19:40
Boxwood 44 4 36N40 79W43 5:18:52
Boyce 22 4 39N06 78W04 5:12:16

Boyd Tavern 2 14 38N02 78W40 5:14:40
Boydton 58 4 36N40 78W24 5:13:36
Boykins 85 4 36N35 77W12 5:08:48
Boys Home 3 4 37N47 79W59 5:19:56
Bracey 58 4 36N36 78W09 5:12:36
Braddock Hills 29 1 38N50 77W12 5:08:48
Bradford Acres 133 6 36N53 76W08 5:04:32
Bradley Forest 74 2 38N47 77W28 5:09:52
Bradshaw 78 4 37N13 80W14 5:20:56
Branchville 85 4 36N35 77W15 5:09:00
Brand 8 21 38N09 79W05 5:16:20
Brandon 73 22 37N13 77W04 5:08:16
Brandons Store 13 4 37N05 78W00 5:12:00
Brandy Creek Estates 42 22 37N37 77W22 5:09:28
Brandy Station 24 4 38N30 77W54 5:11:36
Brays 28 14 37N55 76W52 5:07:28
Breaks 26 15 37N18 82W17 5:29:08
Brecon Ridge 29 3 38N51 77W15 5:09:00
Bremo Bluff 32 4 37N42 78W18 5:13:12
Bren Mar Park 29 1 38N49 77W09 5:08:36
Brentsville 74 14 38N41 77W30 5:10:00
Brentwood 102 6 36N46 76W21 5:05:24
Briarcliff 78 4 37N23 79W49 5:19:16
Briarwood 92 25 36N36 82W11 5:28:44
Bridgetown 64 4 37N24 75W54 5:03:36
Bridgewater 80 22 38N23 78W59 5:15:56
Bridle Creek 38 4 36N37 81W09 5:24:36
Briery 72 4 37N02 78W29 5:13:56
Briery Branch 80 22 38N25 78W57 5:15:48
Briggs 22 14 39N09 77W59 5:11:56
Brighton Square 29 1 38N49 77W09 5:08:36
Brightwood 56 4 38N25 78W12 5:12:48
Brilyn Park 29 1 38N53 77W13 5:08:52
Brink 40 20 36N41 77W32 5:10:08
Brinton 31 4 37N02 80W10 5:20:40
Bristol 99 25 36N36 82W11 5:28:44
Bristow 29 1 38N50 77W12 5:08:48
Bristow 74 14 38N44 77W32 5:10:08
Bristow Village 29 1 38N50 77W12 5:08:48
Britain 53 4 39N16 77W38 5:10:32
Britton Hills Farms 43 17 37N34 77W29 5:09:56
Broaddus 62 14 37N43 78W51 5:15:24
Broadford 84 15 36N56 81W41 5:26:44
Broad Rock 127 17 37N29 77W29 5:09:56
Broad Run 74 14 38N59 77W29 5:09:56
Broad Run Farms 53 4 39N00 77W24 5:09:36
Broadway 80 22 38N37 78W48 5:15:12
Brockroad 86 22 38N12 77W35 5:10:20
Brodnax 13 4 36N43 78W02 5:12:08
Brokenburg 86 22 38N09 77W43 5:10:52
Brooke 87 4 38N23 77W23 5:09:32
Brookfield 29 3 38N54 77W26 5:09:44
Brookfield 87 4 38N23 77W27 5:09:48
Brookhaven 29 1 38N55 77W11 5:08:44
Brookland 43 22 37N38 77W29 5:09:56
Brookland Estates 29 3 38N43 77W09 5:08:36
Brookland Gardens 43 17 37N36 77W29 5:09:56
Brookley Acres 43 22 37N40 77W30 5:10:00
Brooklyn 41 4 36N37 79W12 5:16:48
Brookneal 16 16 37N03 78W57 5:15:48
Brook Vale 51 4 37N46 76W28 5:05:52
Brookwood 133 6 36N51 76W07 5:04:28
Brosville 70 4 36N37 79W37 5:18:28
Brown Field 74 14 38N31 77W18 5:09:12
Brownsburg 79 14 37N56 79W19 5:17:16
Browns Corner 51 4 37N50 76W26 5:05:44
Browns Corner 63 14 37N32 77W10 5:08:40
Browns Cove 2 14 38N04 78W42 5:14:48
Browns Store 55 4 36N58 78W06 5:12:24
Browns Store 65 18 37N55 76W28 5:05:52
Brown Town 5 16 37N35 79W03 5:16:12
Browntown 91 14 38N50 78W19 5:13:16
Broyhill Crest 29 1 38N50 77W12 5:08:48
Broyhill Park 29 3 38N52 77W13 5:08:52
Bruce 102 6 36N50 76W25 5:05:40
Brucetown 34 4 39N15 78W04 5:12:16
Bruington 48 4 37N47 77W00 5:08:00
Bruno 82 26 36N39 82W28 5:29:52
Brunswick 13 4 36N46 77W51 5:11:24
Brush Tavern 16 14 37N24 79W10 5:16:40
Bruton 96 23 37N17 76W40 5:06:40
Bryan Park 43 17 37N36 77W29 5:09:56
Bryan Parkway 43 17 37N36 77W29 5:09:56
Bryant 62 14 37N46 78W59 5:15:56
Bryants Corner 40 20 36N41 77W32 5:10:08
Bryn Mawr 29 1 38N55 77W11 5:08:44
Buchanan 12 4 37N32 79W41 5:18:44
Buckhall 74 2 38N47 77W28 5:09:52
Buckhorn 58 4 36N44 78W15 5:13:00
Buckingham 2 14 38N02 78W29 5:13:56
Buckingham 15 4 37N33 78W33 5:14:12
Buckland 74 14 38N48 77W37 5:10:28
Bucknell Heights 29 1 38N46 77W04 5:08:16
Bucknell Manor 29 1 38N46 77W04 5:08:16
Buckner 54 14 37N58 77W46 5:11:04
Buckroe Beach 113 4 37N04 76W19 5:05:16
Buckton 91 14 39N00 78W22 5:13:28
Bucu 26 15 36N57 82W09 5:28:36
Buell 102 6 36N46 76W21 5:05:24
Buena 24 4 38N19 78W04 5:12:16
Buena Vista 100 14 37N44 79W21 5:17:24
Buffalo Forge 79 14 37N38 79W27 5:17:48
Buffalo Gap 8 21 38N10 79W12 5:16:48
Buffalo Hill 5 16 37N35 79W03 5:16:12

Buffalo Hills 29 1 38N52 77w12 5:08:48
Buffalo Junction 58 4 36N36 78w38 5:14:32
Buffalo Ridge 69 4 36N38 80w16 5:21:04
Buffalo Springs 58 4 36N36 78w38 5:14:32
Bufford Cross Roads 40 20 36N41 77w32 5:10:08
Buford 21 22 37N29 77w33 5:10:12
Bull Run 29 3 38N50 77w26 5:09:44
Bull Run Estates 29 3 38N50 77w26 5:09:44
Bumpass 54 14 37N58 77w46 5:11:04
Bundy 52 26 36N52 82w54 5:31:36
Bungalow City 43 22 37N32 77w19 5:09:16
Burdette 85 4 36N41 76w56 5:07:44
Burgess 65 18 37N53 76w21 5:05:24
Burgundy Farms 29 3 38N43 77w09 5:08:36
Burgundy Manor 29 1 38N47 77w05 5:08:20
Burgundy Village 29 3 38N43 77w09 5:08:36
Burke 29 3 38N48 77w16 5:09:04
Burke Heights 29 3 38N48 77w16 5:09:04
Burke Hills 29 3 38N48 77w16 5:09:04
Burkes Garden 90 4 37N06 81w21 5:25:24
Burkes Shop 17 22 38N07 77w25 5:09:40
Burketown 8 21 38N17 78w55 5:15:40
Burkeville 66 4 37N11 78w12 5:12:48
Burks Fork 31 4 36N49 80w29 5:21:56
Burlington Mills 75 4 37N06 80w41 5:22:44
Burnleys 2 14 38N10 78w17 5:13:08
Burnley Town 9 4 37N17 81w23 5:25:32
Burnside Farms 42 22 37N37 77w22 5:09:28
Burnsville 9 4 38N11 79w39 5:18:36
Burnt Chimneys 33 4 37N04 79w53 5:19:32
Burnt Store 58 4 36N42 78w06 5:12:24
Burr Hill 67 14 38N21 77w51 5:11:24
Burrowsville 73 22 37N08 77w14 5:08:56
Burson Place 92 25 36N36 82w11 5:28:44
Burton 133 6 36N53 76w08 5:04:32
Burtons Ford 94 15 36N58 82w18 5:29:12
Burtons Shop 90 4 37N08 81w31 5:26:04
Bush Hill 29 3 38N43 77w09 5:08:36
Bush Hill Woods 29 3 38N43 77w09 5:08:36
Bushy 59 4 37N34 76w26 5:05:44
Bustleburg 79 14 37N47 79w26 5:17:44
Butterworth 27 22 37N03 77w37 5:10:28
Butts 102 6 36N47 76w15 5:05:00
Butts Corner 29 3 38N48 77w20 5:09:20
Butylo 59 4 37N46 76w41 5:06:44
Bybee 32 4 37N56 78w13 5:12:52
Byllesby 18 4 36N50 80w58 5:23:52
Byno 82 25 36N36 82w11 5:28:44
Bynum Store 58 4 36N48 78w28 5:13:52
Byrd 37 4 37N47 78w03 5:12:12
Byrdton 65 18 37N43 76w23 5:05:32
Cabin Point 88 4 37N10 76w58 5:07:52
Cadet 94 26 36N56 82w47 5:31:08
Caira 25 4 37N30 78w15 5:13:00
Caledonia 37 4 37N45 78w10 5:12:40
Callaghan 3 4 37N49 80w04 5:20:16
Callands 70 4 36N49 79w35 5:18:20
Callao 65 18 37N58 76w34 5:06:16
Callaville 13 4 36N45 77w42 5:10:48
Callaway 33 4 37N01 80w03 5:20:12
Callison 9 4 38N00 79w50 5:19:20
Calno 50 14 37N46 77w22 5:09:28
Calvary 83 14 38N53 78w31 5:14:04
Calverton 30 19 38N38 77w40 5:10:40
Calvin 52 26 36N52 82w54 5:31:36
Cambria 60 4 37N08 80w24 5:21:36
Cambridge 21 22 37N29 77w33 5:10:12
Camelot 29 1 38N50 77w12 5:08:48
Camm 15 4 37N38 78w50 5:15:20
Camp 84 15 36N47 81w25 5:25:40
Camp Appalachia 3 4 37N47 79w59 5:19:56
Camp Barrett 87 4 38N30 77w26 5:09:44
Campbell 2 14 38N02 78w40 5:14:40
Camp Pickett 13 4 37N05 78w00 5:12:00
Camps Mill 132 5 36N44 76w35 5:06:20
Cana 18 4 36N35 80w40 5:22:40
Candlewax 81 15 37N01 81w59 5:27:56
Cannady 14 15 37N14 82w06 5:28:24
Canova 74 2 38N47 77w28 5:09:52
Canterburg 34 4 39N06 78w13 5:12:52
Canterbury 43 22 37N36 77w32 5:10:08
Canterbury Hills 2 14 38N02 78w29 5:13:56
Canterbury Woods 29 1 38N50 77w12 5:08:48
Canton 82 26 36N38 83w03 5:32:12
Cap 18 4 36N43 80w49 5:23:16
Capahosic 36 4 37N25 76w32 5:06:08
Cape Charles 64 4 37N16 76w01 5:04:04
Cape Henry Shores 133 6 36N52 76w00 5:04:00
Capeville 64 4 37N14 75w57 5:03:48
Capon Road 83 14 39N00 78w22 5:13:28
Capron 85 4 36N42 77w10 5:08:40
Carbo 81 15 36N57 82w09 5:28:36
Cardinal 57 4 37N25 76w23 5:05:32
Cardinal Forest 29 3 38N49 77w14 5:08:56
Cardwell 37 4 37N38 77w48 5:11:12
Cardwell Town 84 15 36N53 81w46 5:27:04
Caret 28 4 37N59 76w58 5:07:52
Carfax 94 15 37N00 82w28 5:29:52
Carloover 9 4 38N00 79w50 5:19:20
Carlson Store 51 4 37N55 76w28 5:05:52
Carlton Corner 48 4 37N40 76w53 5:07:32
Carolanne Farms 133 6 36N51 76w09 5:04:36
Carriage Hill 29 3 38N55 77w14 5:08:56
Carriage Hill 133 6 36N51 76w07 5:04:28
Carrie 26 15 36N57 82w09 5:28:36
Carrollton 46 4 36N57 76w34 5:06:16
Carrsbrook 2 14 38N02 78w29 5:13:56
Carrsville 46 4 36N43 76w50 5:07:20
Carsley 88 4 37N02 77w07 5:08:28
Carson 27 22 37N02 77w24 5:09:36
Carsonville 38 4 36N37 81w09 5:24:36
Carters Bridge 2 14 38N02 78w29 5:13:56
Carters Mills 69 4 36N36 80w31 5:22:04
Carters Store 86 22 38N12 77w35 5:10:20
Cartersville 25 4 37N40 78w06 5:12:24
Carterton 81 15 37N00 81w59 5:27:56
Carver Gardens 96 23 37N17 76w43 5:06:52
Carysbrook 32 4 37N49 78w15 5:13:00
Casanova 30 19 38N40 77w43 5:10:52
Cascade 70 4 36N34 79w40 5:18:40
Cash 36 4 37N25 76w32 5:06:08
Cash Corner 2 14 38N09 78w11 5:12:44
Cashville 1 4 37N43 75w44 5:02:56
Caskie 62 14 37N33 78w52 5:15:28
Castle Craig 16 16 37N14 79w17 5:17:08
Castleton 76 14 38N36 78w06 5:12:24
Castlewood 81 15 36N55 82w16 5:29:04
Catalpa 24 14 38N30 78w00 5:12:00
Catawba 41 4 36N56 78w57 5:15:48
Catawba 78 4 37N20 79w59 5:19:56
Catharpin 74 14 38N51 77w34 5:10:16
Catherton 118 2 38N47 77w28 5:09:52
Catlett 30 19 38N39 77w39 5:10:36
Cauthronville 48 4 37N53 77w04 5:08:16
Cavalcade 29 1 38N50 77w12 5:08:48
Cavalier Park 133 6 36N52 76w00 5:04:00
Cave Mountain 79 14 37N37 79w30 5:18:00
Cave Spring 78 4 37N14 80w01 5:20:04
Cavetown 68 14 38N40 78w27 5:13:48
Caylor 52 26 36N38 83w30 5:34:00
Cedar Bluff 90 4 37N05 81w46 5:27:04
Cedar Bluff 92 15 36N38 81w47 5:27:08
Cedar Branch 84 15 36N53 81w46 5:27:04
Cedar Creek 9 4 38N02 79w51 5:19:24
Cedar Creek 34 4 39N02 78w17 5:13:08
Cedar Forest 70 4 37N04 79w06 5:16:24
Cedar Fork 17 22 37N55 77w29 5:09:56
Cedar Grove 58 4 36N44 78w07 5:12:28
Cedar Grove 64 4 37N16 76w00 5:04:00
Cedarhill 70 4 36N50 79w24 5:17:36
Cedar Lawn 43 17 37N32 77w24 5:09:36
Cedar Level 73 22 37N17 77w18 5:09:12
Cedar Mountain 24 4 38N24 78w02 5:12:08
Cedar Run 30 19 38N40 77w40 5:10:40
Cedar Springs 29 3 38N50 77w26 5:09:44
Cedar Springs 84 15 36N54 81w16 5:25:04
Cedar View 1 4 37N35 75w47 5:03:08
Cedarville 91 14 38N55 78w12 5:12:48
Cedarville 92 15 36N46 81w52 5:27:28
Cedon 17 22 38N07 77w25 5:09:40
Celt 39 14 38N18 78w26 5:13:44
Centenary 15 4 37N43 78w31 5:14:04
Center Cross 28 4 37N48 76w47 5:07:08
Center Star 27 22 37N11 77w38 5:10:32
Centerville 8 21 38N23 78w59 5:15:56
Centerville 37 4 37N36 77w42 5:10:48
Centerville 41 4 36N43 78w54 5:15:36
Centerville 47 23 37N17 76w43 5:06:52
Centerville 54 14 38N01 77w54 5:11:36
Central 7 1 38N53 77w07 5:08:28
Central 127 17 37N33 77w26 5:09:44
Central Garage 50 14 37N41 77w01 5:08:04
Central Point 17 22 37N59 77w08 5:08:32
Centreville 29 1 38N50 77w26 5:09:44
Chamberlayne Heights 21 22 37N38 77w26 5:09:44
Champlain 28 4 38N01 77w00 5:08:00
Chancellor 86 22 38N17 77w37 5:10:28
Chantilly 29 3 38N54 77w26 5:09:44
Chapel 22 14 39N06 78w01 5:12:04
Charlemont 10 4 37N32 79w22 5:17:28
Charles City 19 14 37N21 77w04 5:08:16
Charlie Hope 13 4 36N42 78w02 5:12:08
Charlotte Court House 20 4 37N03 78w39 5:14:36
Charlottesville 101 14 38N02 78w30 5:14:00
Chase City 58 4 36N48 78w28 5:13:52
Chatham 70 4 36N50 79w24 5:17:36
Chatham Heights 87 4 38N23 77w27 5:09:48
Chatham Hill 84 15 36N53 81w46 5:27:04
Chatmoss 44 4 36N40 79w52 5:19:28
Cheapside 64 4 37N16 76w00 5:04:00
Check 31 4 37N02 80w10 5:20:40
Cheriton 64 4 37N17 75w58 5:03:52
Cherry Hill 74 14 38N36 77w19 5:09:16
Cherrystone 64 4 37N17 75w58 5:03:52
Chesapeake 102 6 36N50 76w17 5:05:08
Chesapeake Beach 133 6 36N53 76w08 5:04:32
Chesconessex 1 4 37N43 75w44 5:02:56
Chesopeian 133 6 36N51 76w07 5:04:28
Chester 21 22 37N21 77w27 5:09:48
Chesterbrook 29 1 38N55 77w11 5:08:44
Chesterbrooke Mews 29 1 38N55 77w11 5:08:44
Chesterbrook Gardens 29 1 38N55 77w11 5:08:44
Chesterbrook Woods 29 1 38N55 77w11 5:08:44
Chester Estates 92 25 36N36 82w11 5:28:44
Chesterfield 21 22 37N23 77w31 5:10:04
Chester Gap 76 14 38N51 78w08 5:12:32
Chester Park 29 3 38N42 77w14 5:08:56
Chestnut Hill 29 1 38N50 77w12 5:08:48
Chestnut Hill 49 22 38N16 77w11 5:08:44
Chestnut Knob 44 4 36N40 79w52 5:19:28
Chestnut Level 70 4 36N41 79w22 5:17:28
Chestnut Yard 18 4 36N43 80w49 5:23:16
Chevalle 74 2 38N47 77w28 5:09:52
Chewings Corner 86 22 38N02 77w38 5:10:32
Chickahominy Haven 47 14 37N24 76w55 5:07:40
Childress 60 4 37N08 80w24 5:21:36
Childry 41 4 36N56 78w57 5:15:48
Chilesburg 17 22 37N55 77w29 5:09:56
Chilhowie 84 15 36N48 81w41 5:26:44
Chiltons 93 19 38N06 76w50 5:07:20
Chincoteague 1 4 37N56 75w23 5:01:32
Chisford 93 19 38N06 76w50 5:07:20
Christchurch 59 4 37N37 76w33 5:06:12
Christensons Corner 47 23 37N17 76w43 5:06:52
Christian 8 21 38N10 79w12 5:16:48
Christiansburg 60 4 37N08 80w25 5:21:40
Christie 41 4 36N33 78w47 5:15:08
Chuckatuck 61 4 36N48 76w36 5:06:24
Chula 4 4 37N23 77w54 5:11:36
Churchill 29 3 38N54 77w13 5:08:52
Churchland 125 6 36N52 76w18 5:05:12
Church Road 27 22 37N11 77w38 5:10:32
Church View 59 4 37N41 76w41 5:06:44
Churchville 8 21 38N14 79w10 5:16:40
Cifax 10 4 37N22 79w23 5:17:32
Cismont 2 14 38N02 78w40 5:14:40
Civic Center 127 17 37N33 77w26 5:09:44
Clam 1 4 37N50 75w37 5:02:28
Clancie 48 4 37N33 76w44 5:06:56
Claraville 65 18 37N55 76w28 5:05:52
Claremont 88 4 37N14 76w58 5:07:52
Claresville 40 20 36N41 77w32 5:10:08
Clarkes Gap 53 14 39N07 77w34 5:10:16
Clarksville 58 4 36N37 78w34 5:14:16
Clarksville 92 15 36N48 81w46 5:27:04
Clarkton 41 4 36N56 78w57 5:15:48
Clary 83 14 39N00 78w22 5:13:28
Claudville 69 4 36N35 80w25 5:21:40
Clay Bank 36 4 37N25 76w32 5:06:08
Claypool Hill 90 4 37N05 81w43 5:26:52
Clays Mills 41 4 36N45 78w47 5:15:08
Clayville 71 14 37N29 77w55 5:11:40
Clear Brook 34 4 39N15 78w06 5:12:24
Clearbrook 78 4 37N14 79w57 5:19:48
Clearfield 29 3 38N49 77w13 5:08:52
Clearfork 11 4 37N09 81w09 5:24:36
Clear Fork 90 4 37N14 81w22 5:25:28
Clearview Manor 29 1 38N55 77w11 5:08:44
Clearwater Park 3 4 37N47 79w59 5:19:56
Clell 14 15 37N13 82w00 5:28:00
Clermont Woods 29 3 38N43 77w09 5:08:36
Cleveland 81 15 36N57 82w09 5:28:36
Clifdale 3 4 37N47 79w59 5:19:56
Cliffield 90 4 37N05 81w43 5:26:52
Clifford 5 16 37N39 79w02 5:16:08
Cliffview 18 4 36N40 80w55 5:23:40
Clifton 29 1 38N47 77w23 5:09:32
Clifton 67 14 38N19 78w04 5:12:16
Cliftondale 3 4 37N49 79w50 5:19:20
Clifton Forge 103 4 37N49 79w50 5:19:20
Climax 70 4 36N50 79w24 5:17:36
Clinchburg 92 15 36N50 81w49 5:27:16
Clinchco 26 15 37N10 82w22 5:29:28
Clinchport 82 26 36N41 82w45 5:31:00
Clintwood 26 15 37N09 82w28 5:29:52
Clito 38 4 36N43 80w59 5:23:56
Clocks Corner 17 22 38N07 77w25 5:09:40
Clopton 36 4 37N21 76w31 5:06:04
Clover 41 4 36N50 78w44 5:14:56
Cloverdale 12 4 37N22 79w54 5:19:36
Cloverdale 32 4 37N42 78w18 5:13:12
Clover Hill 80 22 38N25 78w57 5:15:48
Cloverland 43 17 37N34 77w26 5:09:44
Cloyd 75 4 37N09 80w40 5:22:40
Club Court 43 17 37N36 77w27 5:09:48
Cluster Springs 41 4 36N37 78w56 5:15:44
Coalcreek 18 4 36N40 80w55 5:23:40
Coal Mine 83 14 39N00 78w22 5:13:28
Cobbdale 108 3 38N51 77w15 5:09:00
Cobbs 64 4 37N16 76w00 5:04:00
Cobbs Creek 57 4 37N30 76w24 5:05:36
Cobham 2 14 38N04 78w16 5:13:04
Cobham 88 4 37N07 76w47 5:07:08
Cochran 13 4 36N52 77w53 5:11:32
Cody 41 4 36N56 78w57 5:15:48
Coeburn 94 15 36N57 82w28 5:29:52
Cohoke 50 14 37N33 76w48 5:07:12
Coke 36 4 37N17 76w30 5:06:00
Colchester 29 3 38N42 77w14 5:08:56
Cold Harbor 42 22 37N37 77w15 5:09:00
Cold Harbor Farms 42 22 37N37 77w22 5:09:28
Coldwater 48 4 37N38 76w42 5:06:48
Coleman Falls 10 4 37N30 79w18 5:17:12
Coles 74 2 38N43 77w27 5:09:48
Coles Point 93 19 38N09 76w38 5:06:32
Colier 95 4 36N49 81w11 5:24:44
Colleen 62 14 37N41 78w54 5:15:36
College 111 24 38N23 77w27 5:09:48
College Park 131 21 38N09 79w05 5:16:20
College Park 125 6 36N52 76w18 5:05:12
Colley 26 15 37N11 82w16 5:29:04
Collierstown 79 14 37N47 79w26 5:17:44
Collingwood 29 1 38N45 77w04 5:08:16
Collins 17 22 38N07 77w25 5:09:40
Collinsville 34 4 39N19 78w18 5:13:12

VIRGINIA

Place		Lat	Long	Time
Collinsville 44	4	36N43	79w55	5:19:40
Collinwood 81	15	37N00	81w59	5:27:56
Cologne 48	4	37N32	76w41	5:06:44
Colonial Beach 93	19	38N15	76w58	5:07:52
Colonial Farms 29	3	38N45	77w08	5:08:32
Colonial Heights 92	25	36N36	82w11	5:28:44
Colonial Heights 104	22	37N15	77w25	5:09:40
Colonial Port Trailer Park 74	13	38N39	77w16	5:09:04
Colosse 46	4	36N43	76w50	5:07:20
Colthurst 2	14	38N02	78w29	5:13:56
Coltons Mill 10	4	37N20	79w31	5:18:04
Columbia 32	4	37N52	78w10	5:12:40
Columbia Furnace 83	14	38N49	78w34	5:14:16
Columbian Grove 55	4	36N52	78w12	5:12:48
Columbia Park 73	22	37N17	77w18	5:09:12
Columbia Pines 29	1	38N50	77w12	5:08:48
Colvin Run 29	3	39N00	77w15	5:09:00
Comans Well 89	4	36N46	77w17	5:09:08
Comers Rock 38	4	36N43	81w11	5:24:44
Comet 46	4	36N59	76w38	5:06:32
Community 29	3	38N45	77w06	5:08:24
Comorn 49	22	38N23	77w27	5:09:48
Compton 68	14	38N46	78w23	5:13:32
Conaway 14	15	37N21	82w12	5:28:48
Concord 13	4	36N57	77w47	5:11:08
Concord 16	16	37N21	78w59	5:15:56
Concord Wharf 64	4	37N27	75w55	5:03:40
Conde 30	19	38N52	77w52	5:11:28
Confederate Heights 43	17	37N34	77w26	5:09:44
Conicville 83	14	38N50	78w42	5:14:48
Conner Grove 31	4	36N51	80w29	5:21:56
Conners Valley 95	4	37N00	80w45	5:23:00
Cook Terrace Annex 96	4	37N12	76w27	5:05:48
Cooktown 29	3	38N58	77w22	5:09:28
Coolspring 29	1	38N45	77w04	5:08:16
Coolwell 5	16	37N35	79w03	5:16:12
Cootes Store 80	22	38N37	78w48	5:15:12
Copeland 9	4	37N49	79w50	5:19:20
Cople 93	19	38N04	76w38	5:06:32
Copper Hill 31	4	37N05	80w08	5:20:32
Copper Valley 31	4	37N08	80w34	5:22:16
Corbin 17	22	38N12	77w23	5:09:32
Cordova 24	14	38N28	78w00	5:12:00
Corinth 85	4	36N54	76w54	5:07:36
Corneals Store 42	22	37N37	77w22	5:09:28
Cornetts Store 38	4	36N42	81w26	5:25:44
Cornland 102	6	36N47	76w15	5:05:00
Corn Valley 81	15	37N01	81w59	5:27:56
Cornwall 79	14	37N44	79w21	5:17:24
Coulson 18	4	36N43	80w49	5:23:16
Coulwood 81	15	37N01	81w59	5:27:56
Council 14	15	37N01	81w59	5:27:56
Countis Corner 92	25	36N36	82w11	5:28:44
Country Club Hills 108	3	38N51	77w15	5:09:00
Country Club Lake 74	14	38N36	77w19	5:09:16
Country Club View 29	3	38N51	77w15	5:09:00
Counts 26	15	36N59	82w17	5:29:08
Court House 7	1	38N53	77w06	5:08:24
Courthouse 89	4	36N55	77w18	5:09:12
Courtland 85	4	36N43	77w04	5:08:16
Courtland Park 29	1	38N51	77w09	5:08:36
Courtney 43	22	37N40	77w30	5:10:00
Cove Creek 11	4	37N09	81w09	5:24:36
Cove Creek 90	4	37N08	81w31	5:26:04
Covesville 2	14	37N53	78w43	5:14:52
Covingston Corner 17	22	37N52	77w27	5:09:48
Covington 105	4	37N47	79w59	5:19:56
Coxs Chapel 38	4	36N35	81w20	5:25:20
Crab Orchard 94	15	37N00	82w28	5:29:52
Crackers Neck 94	26	36N56	82w47	5:31:08
Craddockville 1	4	37N35	75w52	5:03:28
Cradock 125	6	36N49	76w20	5:05:20
Craigs Mills 92	25	36N36	82w11	5:28:44
Craig Springs 23	4	37N30	80w07	5:20:28
Craigsville 8	21	38N05	79w23	5:17:32
Crandon 11	4	37N06	81w07	5:24:28
Cranes Nest 94	15	37N00	82w28	5:29:52
Craney Island Estates 42	22	37N37	77w22	5:09:28
Creeds 133	6	36N51	76w06	5:04:24
Crescent Hill 115	14	37N17	77w18	5:09:12
Cresthill 30	19	38N50	78w00	5:12:00
Crestview 43	22	37N35	77w31	5:10:04
Crestwood 102	6	36N47	76w15	5:05:00
Crestwood Manor 29	1	38N50	77w12	5:08:48
Crewe 66	4	37N10	78w08	5:12:32
Criders 80	22	38N45	79w00	5:16:00
Criglersville 56	4	38N23	78w16	5:13:04
Crimora 8	21	38N09	78w51	5:15:24
Cripple Creek 95	4	36N49	81w06	5:24:24
Critz 69	4	36N38	80w09	5:20:36
Croaker 47	23	37N17	76w43	5:06:52
Crockett 95	4	36N53	81w12	5:24:48
Crockett Springs 60	4	37N10	80w15	5:21:00
Crossbrook 94	26	36N55	82w48	5:31:12
Crosses Corner 42	22	37N46	77w22	5:09:28
Cross Junction 34	4	39N19	78w18	5:13:12
Crosskeys 80	22	38N21	78w56	5:15:44
Crossroads 41	4	36N56	78w57	5:15:48
Crossroads 78	4	37N19	79w55	5:19:40
Cross Roads 83	14	38N45	78w39	5:14:36
Crosswinds 29	3	38N47	77w12	5:08:48
Crouch 48	4	37N48	76w47	5:07:08
Crows 3	4	37N47	79w59	5:19:56
Crozet 2	14	38N04	78w42	5:14:48
Crozier 37	4	37N38	77w48	5:11:12
Cruise 69	4	36N38	80w16	5:21:04
Crymes Store 55	4	36N59	78w14	5:12:56
Crystal Acres 133	6	36N52	76w00	5:04:00
Crystal Beach 1	4	37N43	75w44	5:02:56
Crystal Hill 41	4	36N52	78w55	5:15:40
Cuckoo 54	14	37N57	77w52	5:11:28
Cullen 20	4	37N07	78w39	5:14:36
Culls 64	4	37N16	76w00	5:04:00
Culmore 29	1	38N51	77w09	5:08:36
Culpeper 24	14	38N29	78w00	5:12:00
Cumberland 25	4	37N30	78w15	5:13:00
Cummings Heights 92	15	36N43	81w58	5:27:52
Cumnor 48	4	37N40	76w53	5:07:32
Cunningham 32	4	37N50	78w22	5:13:28
Curdsville 15	4	37N30	78w26	5:13:44
Currioman Landing 93	19	38N06	76w50	5:07:20
Cuscowilla 58	4	36N40	78w23	5:13:32
Customhouse 122	6	36N54	76w16	5:05:04
Cypress 61	4	36N41	76w32	5:06:08
Cypress Chapel 132	5	36N44	76w35	5:06:20
Cyrandall Valley 29	3	38N55	77w14	5:08:56
Dabneys 54	14	37N45	77w48	5:11:12
Dahlgren 49	12	38N20	77w03	5:08:12
Dahlia 40	20	36N32	77w32	5:10:08
Dalbys 64	4	37N16	76w00	5:04:00
Dale 21	22	37N25	77w30	5:10:00
Dale City 74	14	38N37	77w18	5:09:12
Dale Enterprise 80	22	38N27	78w52	5:15:28
Dale Ridge 94	15	37N00	82w28	5:29:52
Daleville 12	4	37N25	79w55	5:19:40
Dalhart 38	4	36N40	80w55	5:23:40
Damascus 92	15	36N38	81w47	5:27:08
Dam Neck 133	6	36N47	75w58	5:03:52
Danbury Forest 29	3	38N49	77w13	5:08:52
Daniel 67	14	38N13	78w06	5:12:24
Daniel Boone 82	26	36N38	82w34	5:30:16
Danieltown 13	4	36N52	77w53	5:11:32
Danripple 41	4	36N43	78w54	5:15:36
Dante 81	15	36N59	82w18	5:29:12
Danville 106	4	36N36	79w23	5:17:32
Darlington Heights 72	4	37N12	78w37	5:14:28
Darnell Town 52	26	36N52	82w54	5:31:36
Darvills 27	22	37N06	77w48	5:11:12
Darwin 26	15	37N09	82w27	5:29:48
Daugherty 1	4	37N43	75w40	5:02:40
Davenport 14	15	37N06	82w08	5:28:32
Davis 79	14	37N56	79w14	5:16:56
Davis 83	14	39N01	78w23	5:13:32
Davis Corner 133	6	36N51	76w09	5:04:36
Davis Wharf 1	4	37N33	75w53	5:03:32
Daw 81	15	37N02	81w55	5:27:40
Dawlegs Corners 133	6	36N51	76w06	5:04:24
Dawn 17	22	37N52	77w27	5:09:48
Dayton 80	22	38N25	78w56	5:15:44
Deatonville 4	4	37N18	78w06	5:12:24
DeBree 122	6	36N52	76w17	5:05:08
De Busk Mill 92	15	36N48	81w46	5:27:04
Deel 14	15	37N14	82w06	5:28:24
Deep Creek 1	4	37N43	75w44	5:02:56
Deep Creek 102	6	36N46	76w21	5:05:24
Deep Hole 1	4	37N56	75w22	5:01:28
Deerfield 8	21	38N12	79w25	5:17:40
Deerfield Estates 21	22	37N23	77w31	5:10:04
Deerock 62	14	37N50	78w44	5:14:56
Deer Park 74	2	38N47	77w28	5:09:52
DeJarnett 17	22	38N01	77w22	5:09:28
De Kalb 82	26	36N45	82w35	5:30:20
Delaplane 30	19	38N55	77w55	5:11:40
Delaware 85	4	36N41	76w56	5:07:44
Delmar 92	15	36N38	81w47	5:27:08
Deltaville 59	4	37N33	76w20	5:05:20
Delton 75	4	37N00	80w45	5:23:00
Denaro 4	4	37N21	77w59	5:11:56
Denbigh 121	4	37N07	76w31	5:06:04
Dendron 88	4	37N03	76w56	5:07:44
Denmark 79	14	37N47	79w26	5:17:44
Denniston 41	4	36N34	79w00	5:16:00
Derby 94	26	36N58	82w47	5:31:08
Desha 28	14	37N55	76w52	5:07:28
Deshazo Corner 48	4	37N44	76w55	5:07:40
Deskins 14	15	37N14	82w06	5:28:24
Detrick 83	14	38N52	78w24	5:13:36
Devonshire Gardens 29	3	38N52	77w13	5:08:52
Dewey 10	4	37N22	79w49	5:19:16
Dewey 94	15	37N08	82w36	5:30:24
DeWitt 27	22	37N02	77w39	5:10:36
Diamond Springs 133	6	36N53	76w08	5:04:32
Diascund 47	14	37N24	76w55	5:07:40
Dickensdale 43	17	37N34	77w29	5:09:56
Dickensonville 81	15	36N54	82w17	5:29:08
Dickinson Store 86	22	37N58	77w46	5:11:04
Diggs 57	4	37N26	76w16	5:05:04
Dillwyn 15	4	37N32	78w27	5:13:48
Dinwiddie 27	22	37N05	77w35	5:10:20
Dinwiddie Gardens 27	22	37N13	77w26	5:09:44
Disputanta 73	22	37N08	77w14	5:08:56
Ditchley 65	18	37N43	76w23	5:05:32
Dixie 32	4	37N46	78w16	5:13:04
Dixie 57	4	37N30	76w28	5:05:52
Dixie Hill 29	3	38N51	77w15	5:09:00
Dockery 58	4	36N44	78w07	5:12:28
Dodds Store 5	16	37N35	79w03	5:16:12
Doe Hill 45	4	38N26	79w27	5:17:48
Dogue 49	22	38N14	77w13	5:08:52
Dogwood Hill 131	21	38N09	79w05	5:16:20
Dogwood Knoll 42	22	37N37	77w22	5:09:28
Dolphin 13	4	36N50	77w47	5:11:08
Donkey 94	15	37N08	82w36	5:30:24
Donna Lee Gardens 29	1	38N53	77w13	5:08:52
Dooms 8	21	38N04	78w54	5:15:36
Doran 90	4	37N06	81w50	5:27:20
Dorcas 8	21	38N21	79w05	5:16:20
Dorchester 94	15	36N59	82w38	5:30:32
Dorchester Junction 94	15	36N59	82w38	5:30:32
Doswell 42	22	37N52	77w27	5:09:48
Dot 52	26	36N46	83w02	5:32:08
Double Tollgate 22	4	39N03	78w06	5:12:24
Dover 37	4	37N39	77w43	5:10:52
Dover 53	14	38N58	77w44	5:10:56
Doveville 29	3	38N51	77w15	5:09:00
Dowden Terrace 29	1	38N49	77w09	5:08:36
Downings 77	4	37N53	76w38	5:06:32
Doylesville 2	14	38N04	78w42	5:14:48
Dozier Corner 102	6	36N47	76w15	5:05:00
Dragonville 48	4	37N40	76w53	5:07:32
Drakes Branch 20	4	37N00	78w36	5:14:24
Dranesville 29	1	38N56	77w12	5:08:48
Draper 75	4	37N00	80w46	5:23:04
Drewryville 85	4	36N43	77w19	5:09:16
Drill 81	15	37N01	81w59	5:27:56
Dry Branch 75	4	37N12	80w37	5:22:28
Dryburg 41	4	36N45	78w47	5:15:08
Dryden 52	26	36N47	82w57	5:31:48
Dry Fork 70	4	36N45	79w24	5:17:36
Dry Fork 94	15	37N00	82w28	5:29:52
Duane 50	14	37N47	77w06	5:08:24
Dublin 75	4	37N06	80w41	5:22:44
Dudley 41	4	36N46	78w56	5:15:44
Duffield 82	26	36N43	82w48	5:31:12
Dugspur 18	4	36N49	80w37	5:22:28
Dumbarton 43	17	37N36	77w29	5:09:56
Dumfries 74	14	38N34	77w18	5:09:12
Dunbar 94	26	36N58	82w47	5:31:08
Dunbrooke 28	14	37N55	76w52	5:07:28
Duncan Gap 94	15	37N01	82w35	5:30:20
Duncans Mills 82	26	36N41	82w45	5:31:00
Dundalow 132	5	36N44	76w35	5:06:20
Dundas 55	4	36N55	78w01	5:12:04
Dunford Town 90	4	37N09	81w42	5:26:48
Dungannon 82	15	36N50	82w28	5:29:52
Dunlop 104	22	37N23	77w28	5:09:52
Dunn Loring 29	3	38N53	77w14	5:08:56
Dunn Loring Woods 29	3	38N55	77w14	5:08:56
Dunnsville 28	4	37N51	76w49	5:07:16
Dutton 36	4	37N30	76w28	5:05:52
Duty 14	15	37N07	82w10	5:28:40
Dwale 26	15	37N09	82w27	5:29:48
Dwina 94	15	37N00	82w28	5:29:52
Dye 81	15	37N02	81w55	5:27:40
Dyke 39	14	38N15	78w32	5:14:08
Eads 7	1	38N51	77w05	5:08:20
Eagle Rock 12	4	37N38	79w48	5:19:12
Earlhurst 3	4	37N47	79w59	5:19:56
Earls 4	4	37N15	77w49	5:11:16
Earlysville 2	14	38N10	78w29	5:13:56
Earmans 80	22	38N27	78w52	5:15:28
East Brook 16	14	37N24	79w10	5:16:40
East Chesapeake 102	6	36N49	76w14	5:04:56
East End 127	17	37N33	77w24	5:09:36
Eastern 35	4	37N19	80w36	5:22:24
Eastern Park 133	6	36N51	76w07	5:04:28
Eastham 2	14	38N02	78w29	5:13:56
East Highland Park 43	17	37N34	77w26	5:09:44
East Honaker 81	15	37N01	81w59	5:27:56
East Lexington 79	14	37N47	79w26	5:17:44
Eastmoreland 43	17	37N32	77w24	5:09:36
East Norton 123	15	36N59	82w38	5:30:32
Eastover 132	5	36N44	76w35	5:06:20
Eastover Gardens 43	17	37N32	77w24	5:09:36
East Point 1	4	37N43	75w44	5:02:56
East Radford 126	4	37N08	80w34	5:22:16
East Stone Gap 94	26	36N52	82w45	5:31:00
East Suffolk Gardens 132	5	36N44	76w35	5:06:20
Eastville 64	4	37N21	75w57	5:03:48
East Woodford 29	3	38N55	77w14	5:08:56
East Wytheville 95	4	37N00	81w05	5:24:20
Ebenezer 70	4	36N50	79w14	5:16:56
Ebony 13	4	36N35	78w00	5:12:00
Edge 16	16	37N10	79w05	5:16:20
Edgehill 49	22	38N16	77w11	5:08:44
Edgehill Park 27	22	37N13	77w26	5:09:44
Edgemont 105	4	37N47	79w59	5:19:56
Edgemont Park 92	15	36N43	81w58	5:27:52
Edgerton 13	4	36N46	77w51	5:11:24
Edgewood 73	22	37N13	77w17	5:09:08
Edinburg 83	14	38N49	78w34	5:14:16

Edmonds Corner 102
6 36N50 76W16 5:05:04
Edom 80 22 38N31 78W50 5:15:20
Edsall Park 29 3 38N49 77W13 5:08:52
Edwards Shop 24 4 38N31 77W51 5:11:24
Edwardsville 65 18 37N54 76W28 5:05:52
Eggbornsville 24 4 38N35 77W59 5:11:56
Eggleston 35 4 37N17 80W37 5:22:28
Eheart 67 14 38N10 78W17 5:13:08
Elam 72 4 37N18 78W34 5:14:16
Elberon 88 4 37N05 76W53 5:07:32
Elephant Fork 132 5 36N44 76W35 5:06:20
Elevon 17 22 38N01 77W00 5:08:00
Elizabeth River Shores 133
6 36N51 76W09 5:04:36
Elizabeth River Terrace 133
6 36N51 76W09 5:04:36
Elk Creek 38 4 36N40 81W10 5:24:40
Elk Garden 81 15 37N00 81W59 5:27:56
Elk Hill 37 4 37N43 78W05 5:12:20
Elkins 29 1 38N55 77W11 5:08:44
Elko 43 22 37N33 77W22 5:09:28
Elkrun 30 19 38N36 77W44 5:10:56
Elkton 80 14 38N25 78W37 5:14:28
Elkwood 24 4 38N31 77W51 5:11:24
Ellerson 42 22 37N37 77W22 5:09:28
Ellett 60 4 37N08 80W24 5:21:36
Elliston 60 4 37N13 80W14 5:20:56
Ellisville 54 14 38N02 78W00 5:12:00
Elma 62 14 37N43 78W51 5:15:24
Elmo 41 4 36N41 79W08 5:16:32
Elmont 42 22 37N45 77W29 5:09:56
Elmwood Estates 29
1 38N55 77W11 5:08:44
El-Nido 29 1 38N55 77W11 5:08:44
Elon 5 16 37N29 79W07 5:16:28
Elsom 48 4 37N32 76W46 5:07:04
Elvan 53 4 39N16 77W38 5:10:32
Elysian Woods 74 13 38N39 77W16 5:09:04
Emmerton 77 4 37N58 76W46 5:07:04
Emory 92 15 36N47 81W50 5:27:20
Emporia 107 20 36N41 77W32 5:10:08
Endicott 33 4 36N55 80W01 5:20:04
Enfield 50 14 37N42 77W09 5:08:36
Engleside 29 3 38N45 77W08 5:08:32
Engleside Village 29
3 38N45 77W08 5:08:32
Enon 87 4 38N23 77W27 5:09:48
Eona 18 4 36N46 80W44 5:22:56
Eppes Fork 58 4 36N30 78W25 5:13:40
Erica 93 19 38N06 76W50 5:07:20
Ervinton 26 15 37N03 82W20 5:29:20
Esmont 2 14 37N50 78W37 5:14:28
Esserville 94 15 36N59 82W38 5:30:32
Essex Mill 28 4 37N51 76W49 5:07:16
Estes 76 14 38N36 78W06 5:12:24
Estillville 82 26 36N38 82W37 5:30:28
Ethel 77 4 37N58 76W46 5:07:04
Etlan 56 4 38N32 78W16 5:13:04
Etna Mills 50 14 37N46 77W22 5:09:28
Etter 95 4 36N54 81W16 5:25:04
Ettrick 21 22 37N13 77W26 5:09:44
Euclid 133 6 36N51 76W09 5:04:36
Euclid Place 133 6 36N51 76W09 5:04:36
Eureka 20 4 37N02 78W29 5:13:56
Eureka Mills 20 4 37N02 78W29 5:13:56
Eureka Park 133 6 36N51 76W07 5:04:28
Eustaces Corner 30
19 38N36 77W44 5:10:56
Everets 132 5 36N44 76W35 5:06:20
Evergreen 6 4 37N18 78W47 5:15:08
Evergreen Hills 92
25 36N36 82W11 5:28:44
Evington 16 16 37N14 79W17 5:17:08
Evol 16 16 37N10 79W05 5:16:20
Ewell 47 23 37N17 76W43 5:06:52
Ewing 52 26 36N38 83W26 5:33:44
Exeter 94 26 36N53 82W51 5:31:24
Exmore 64 4 37N32 75W50 5:03:20
Faber 62 14 37N50 78W44 5:14:56
Fagg 60 4 37N08 80W24 5:21:36
Fairfax 108 3 38N51 77W18 5:09:12
Fairfax Acres 29 3 38N51 77W15 5:09:00
Fairfax Circle 108
3 38N51 77W15 5:09:00
Fairfax Forest 29 3 38N51 77W15 5:09:00
Fairfax Heights 108
3 38N51 77W15 5:09:00
Fairfax Station 29
3 38N48 77W20 5:09:20
Fairfax Villa 29 3 38N51 77W15 5:09:00
Fairfax Woods 108 3 38N51 77W15 5:09:00
Fairfield 28 4 37N51 76W49 5:07:16
Fairfield 79 14 37N53 79W17 5:17:08
Fairhaven 29 1 38N47 77W05 5:08:20
Fair Hill 29 3 38N51 77W15 5:09:00
Fairland 29 1 38N49 77W09 5:08:36
Fairlawn 75 4 37N09 80W34 5:22:16
Fairlawn 105 4 37N47 79W59 5:19:56
Fairlee 29 3 38N51 77W15 5:09:00
Fair Meadows 133 6 36N51 76W09 5:04:36
Fair Meadows Estates 133
6 36N51 76W09 5:04:36
Fair Oaks 43 22 37N32 77W19 5:09:16
Fair Oaks 108 3 38N51 77W15 5:09:00
Fair Port 65 18 37N51 76W17 5:05:08
Fairview 29 3 38N45 77W06 5:08:24
Fairview 58 4 36N48 78W28 5:13:52
Fairview 60 4 37N04 80W27 5:21:48
Fairview 64 4 37N16 76W00 5:04:00
Fairview 68 14 38N40 78W27 5:13:48
Fairview 82 26 36N41 82W45 5:31:00
Fairview 108 3 38N51 77W15 5:09:00
Fairview Beach 49
22 38N23 77W27 5:09:48
Fairview Heights 103
4 37N49 79W50 5:19:20
Fairview Heights 116
14 37N47 79W26 5:17:44
Fairview Manor 102
6 36N49 76W14 5:04:56
Fairwood 38 4 36N42 81W26 5:25:44
Fairwood Acres 29 3 38N48 77W20 5:09:20
Falconerville 5 16 37N35 79W03 5:16:12
Falling Creek 21 22 37N27 77W28 5:09:52
Falling Spring 3 4 37N54 79W59 5:19:56
Falls Church 109 1 38N53 77W10 5:08:40
Falls Hill 29 3 38N54 77W13 5:08:52
Falls Mills 90 4 37N16 81W19 5:25:16
Falmouth 87 24 38N20 77W28 5:09:52
Fancy Gap 18 4 36N36 80W41 5:22:44
Fancy Hill 5 16 37N35 79W03 5:16:12
Farmers 17 22 38N07 77W25 5:09:40
Farmers Fork 77 4 37N58 76W46 5:07:04
Farmers Store 95 4 36N58 80W57 5:23:48
Farmingdale 73 22 37N17 77W18 5:09:12
Farmington 2 14 38N02 78W29 5:13:56
Farmington 43 22 37N36 77W32 5:10:08
Farmville 72 4 37N18 78W24 5:13:36
Farnham 77 4 37N53 76W38 5:06:32
Fauquier Springs 30
19 38N44 77W44 5:10:56
Favonia 95 4 36N57 81W05 5:24:20
Fawcett Gap 34 9 39N11 78W10 5:12:40
Fayette Park 43 17 37N34 77W26 5:09:44
Featherstone 74 13 38N39 77W16 5:09:04
Featherstone Shores 74
13 38N39 77W16 5:09:04
Featherstone Terrace 74
13 38N39 77W16 5:09:04
Federal Reserve 127
17 37N32 77W28 5:09:52
Fentress 133 6 36N52 76W00 5:04:00
Fenwick Park 29 3 38N52 77W13 5:08:52
Ferncliff 54 14 37N53 78W08 5:12:32
Ferndale Gardens 27
22 37N13 77W26 5:09:44
Ferrell 49 22 38N16 77W11 5:08:44
Ferrum 33 4 36N55 80W01 5:20:04
Ferry Farms 87 4 38N23 77W27 5:09:48
Fieldale 44 4 36N43 79W57 5:19:48
Fife 37 4 37N44 78W04 5:12:16
Fifty Seven Mile Siding 89
4 37N02 77W07 5:08:28
File 17 22 38N03 77W21 5:09:24
Fincastle 12 4 37N30 79W53 5:19:32
Finchley 58 4 36N37 78W34 5:14:16
Fine Creek Mills 71
14 37N29 77W55 5:11:40
Finneywood 58 4 36N48 78W28 5:13:52
Fishers Hill 83 14 38N59 78W24 5:13:36
Fishersville 8 21 38N06 78W58 5:15:52
Fitzhugh 13 4 36N46 77W51 5:11:24
Five Forks 5 16 37N35 79W03 5:16:12
Five Forks 10 4 37N20 79W31 5:18:04
Five Forks 27 22 37N11 77W38 5:10:32
Five Forks 41 4 36N43 78W54 5:15:36
Five Forks 47 23 37N17 76W43 5:06:52
Five Forks 56 4 38N13 78W06 5:12:24
Five Forks 62 14 37N33 78W52 5:15:28
Five Forks 72 4 37N14 78W41 5:14:44
Five Forks 115 14 37N17 77W18 5:09:12
Five Mile Fork 86
22 38N17 77W33 5:10:12
Five Oaks 90 4 37N08 81W31 5:26:04
Flagpond 82 26 36N38 83W03 5:32:12
Flat Gap 94 15 37N08 82W36 5:30:24
Flatridge 38 4 36N47 81W25 5:25:40
Flat Run 67 14 38N18 77W49 5:11:16
Flat Spur 26 15 36N59 82W17 5:29:08
Flatwoods 12 4 37N30 79W53 5:19:32
Fleeburg 68 14 38N29 78W37 5:14:28
Fleenors 92 25 36N36 82W11 5:28:44
Fleet 122 6 36N56 76W19 5:05:16
Fleeton 65 18 37N49 76W17 5:05:08
Flemington 26 15 37N09 82W27 5:29:48
Fletcher 39 14 38N18 78W26 5:13:44
Flint Hill 10 4 37N11 79W37 5:18:28
Flint Hill 29 3 38N55 77W14 5:08:56
Flint Hill 76 14 38N46 78W06 5:12:24
Flood 45 4 38N20 79W29 5:17:56
Floris 29 3 38N58 77W22 5:09:28
Floyd 31 4 36N55 80W19 5:21:16
Folly 65 18 37N51 76W17 5:05:08
Foneswood 77 4 38N06 76W54 5:07:36
Ford 27 22 37N09 77W44 5:10:56
Ford Park 102 6 36N49 76W14 5:04:56
Forest 10 4 37N22 79W17 5:17:08
Forest Hill 127 17 37N28 77W28 5:09:52
Forest Hills 133 6 36N52 76W02 5:04:08
Forest Lake Hills 42
22 37N37 77W22 5:09:28
Forest Lodge Acres 43
22 37N40 77W30 5:10:00
Forestville 29 3 39N00 77W15 5:09:00
Forestville 83 14 38N41 78W41 5:14:44
Fork 91 14 38N55 78W16 5:13:04
Fork Ridge 90 4 37N07 81W52 5:27:28
Fork Shop 48 4 37N37 76W47 5:07:08
Forks of Buffalo 5
16 37N35 79W03 5:16:12
Forksville 58 4 36N45 78W03 5:12:12
Fork Union 32 4 37N46 78W16 5:13:04
Formosa 20 4 36N54 78W42 5:14:48
Fort Belvoir 29 8 38N43 77W09 5:08:36
Fort Blackmore 82
26 36N46 82W35 5:30:20
Fort Chiswell 95 4 36N58 80W56 5:23:44
Fort Defiance 8 21 38N15 78W57 5:15:48
Fortener Addition 84
15 36N50 81W31 5:26:04
Fort Eustis 121 10 37N09 76W35 5:06:20
Fort Hill 43 22 37N35 77W31 5:10:04
Fort Hill 117 14 37N24 79W10 5:16:40
Fort Hunt 29 3 38N43 77W04 5:08:16
Fort Lee 73 11 37N15 77W20 5:09:20
Fort Lewis Terrace 129
4 37N17 80W03 5:20:12
Fort Lyons Heights 29
1 38N47 77W05 5:08:20
Fort Mitchell 55 4 36N55 78W29 5:13:56
Fort Monroe 113 7 37N00 76W18 5:05:12
Fort Myer 7 8 38N53 77W04 5:08:16
Fort Story 133 6 36N55 76W01 5:04:04
Foster 57 4 37N27 76W23 5:05:32
Fosters Falls 95 4 36N53 80W51 5:23:24
Foundation Park 102
6 36N49 76W14 5:04:56
Four Corners 29 3 38N55 77W14 5:08:56
Four Mile Fork 86
22 38N23 77W27 5:09:48
Fourway 90 4 37N08 81W31 5:26:04
Fox 38 4 36N37 81W09 5:24:36
Foxlee 53 4 39N00 77W24 5:09:36
Fox Mill Estates 29
3 38N58 77W22 5:09:28
Foxwells 51 14 37N39 76W23 5:05:32
Fractionville 92 15 36N43 81W58 5:27:52
Fraleytown 82 26 36N43 82W48 5:31:12
Francisco 15 4 37N26 78W34 5:14:16
Franconia 29 3 38N47 77W10 5:08:40
Franklin 110 4 36N41 76W56 5:07:44
Franklin Forest 29
1 38N55 77W11 5:08:44
Franklin Heights 33
4 37N00 79W53 5:19:32
Franklin Park 29 1 38N55 77W11 5:08:44
Franks Mill 8 21 38N09 79W05 5:16:20
Franktown 64 4 37N28 75W53 5:03:32
Frederick Hall 54
14 37N59 77W49 5:11:16
Fredericksburg 111
24 38N18 77W28 5:09:52
Freeling 26 15 37N09 82W27 5:29:48
Freeman 13 4 36N45 77W42 5:10:48
Freemont 18 4 36N46 80W44 5:22:56
Freeport 36 4 37N25 76W32 5:06:08
Freeshade Corner 59
4 37N33 76W27 5:05:48
Free Union 2 14 38N09 78W34 5:14:16
Fremac 133 6 36N52 76W00 5:04:00
Fremont 26 15 37N10 82W22 5:29:28
Friendship 92 15 36N48 81W46 5:27:04
Fries 38 4 36N43 80W59 5:23:56
Fringer 12 4 37N32 79W41 5:18:44
Front Royal 91 14 38N55 78W12 5:12:48
Front Royal Junction 91
14 38N55 78W12 5:12:48
Fugate Hill 81 15 37N00 81W59 5:27:56
Fugua Farms 21 22 37N27 77W28 5:09:52
Fulkerson 82 26 36N38 82W24 5:29:36
Fulks Run 80 22 38N40 78W55 5:15:40
Furnace 68 14 38N24 78W37 5:14:28
Furnace Hill 84 15 36N50 81W31 5:26:04
Furnace Mountain 53
14 39N07 77W34 5:10:16
Gainesboro 34 4 39N16 78W14 5:12:56
Gaines Mill Estates 42
22 37N37 77W22 5:09:28
Gainesville 74 14 38N48 77W37 5:10:28
Gala 12 4 37N38 79W48 5:19:12
Galax 112 4 36N40 80W56 5:23:44
Galts Mill 5 14 37N25 79W08 5:16:32
Gapstore 90 4 37N05 81W46 5:27:04
Garden 14 15 37N13 81W53 5:27:32
Gardenwood Park 133
6 36N53 76W08 5:04:32
Gardner 81 15 37N01 81W59 5:27:56
Gardners Cross Roads 54
14 38N01 77W54 5:11:36
Garfield Estates 74
13 38N39 77W16 5:09:04
Gargatha 1 4 37N47 75W39 5:02:36
Garland Heights 21
22 37N27 77W28 5:09:52
Garnett 42 22 37N52 77W27 5:09:48
Garrisonville 87 4 38N29 77W26 5:09:44
Garysville 73 22 37N17 77W18 5:09:12
Gasburg 13 4 36N34 77W54 5:11:36
Gate City 82 26 36N38 82W35 5:30:20
Gatewood 86 22 38N12 77W35 5:10:20
Gaynor Heights 44 4 36N40 79W52 5:19:28
Geer 39 14 38N18 78W26 5:13:44
Geneva Park 102 6 36N46 76W21 5:05:24
Genito 71 14 37N29 77W55 5:11:40
Genoa 80 22 38N40 78W55 5:15:40
Georges Fork 26 15 37N09 82W27 5:29:48
Georges Mill 53 4 39N16 77W38 5:10:32
Georges Tavern 37 4 37N41 77W53 5:11:32
Georgetown 83 14 38N45 78W39 5:14:36
George Washington 87
4 38N17 77W23 5:09:32
George Washington 97
1 38N50 77W04 5:08:16
George Washington Park 133
6 36N51 76W07 5:04:28
Gertie 102 4 36N41 76W16 5:05:04
Gether 17 22 37N55 77W12 5:08:48
Getz 83 14 38N45 78W39 5:14:36
Gholsonville 13 4 36N39 77W57 5:11:48
Gibson Station 52
26 36N38 83W26 5:33:44
Gidsville 5 16 37N35 79W03 5:16:12

VIRGINIA

Gilbert Gardens 43	17	37N32	77w24	5:09:36
Giles 4	4	37N21	77w58	5:11:52
Gills 4	4	37N18	78w06	5:12:24
Gilmore Mills 79	14	37N37	79w30	5:18:00
Gladehill 33	4	36N59	79w46	5:19:04
Gladesboro 18	4	36N46	80w44	5:22:56
Glade Spring 92	15	36N47	81w47	5:27:08
Gladeville 94	15	37N01	82w36	5:30:24
Gladstone 62	14	37N33	78w52	5:15:28
Gladys 16	16	37N10	79w05	5:16:20
Glamorgan 94	15	37N01	82w35	5:30:20
Glasgow 79	14	37N38	79w27	5:17:48
Glass 36	4	37N17	76w30	5:06:00
Glasses Store 52	26	36N40	83w07	5:32:28
Glen Alden 29	3	38N51	77w15	5:09:00
Glen Allen 21	22	37N40	77w30	5:10:00
Glen Allen Heights 43	22	37N40	77w30	5:10:00
Glen Echo 77	17	37N33	77w24	5:09:36
Glen Forest 29	1	38N51	77w09	5:08:36
Glen Gary 29	1	38N55	77w11	5:08:44
Glenita 82	26	36N41	82w45	5:31:00
Glen Lyn 35	4	37N22	80w52	5:23:28
Glenmore 15	4	37N44	78w40	5:14:40
Glenns 36	4	37N36	76w36	5:06:24
Glen Oaks 29	3	38N48	77w16	5:09:04
Glenrochie 92	15	36N43	81w58	5:27:52
Glenvar 78	4	37N17	80w03	5:20:12
Glen Wilton 12	4	37N45	79w49	5:19:16
Glenwood 70	4	36N35	79w22	5:17:28
Glenwood Farms 43	17	37N33	77w24	5:09:36
Gloucester 36	4	37N25	76w32	5:06:08
Gloucester Point 36	4	37N15	76w30	5:06:00
Goad Heights 78	4	37N23	79w49	5:19:16
Goblintown 69	4	36N38	80w16	5:21:04
Golansville 17	22	37N55	77w29	5:09:56
Goldbond 35	4	37N23	80w40	5:22:40
Golddale 67	14	38N16	77w58	5:11:52
Gold Hill 15	4	37N42	78w18	5:13:12
Goldmans Corner 17	22	38N10	77w12	5:08:48
Goldvein 30	19	38N27	77w39	5:10:36
Gonyon 65	18	37N55	76w28	5:05:52
Goochland 37	4	37N41	77w53	5:11:32
Goode 10	4	37N22	79w23	5:17:32
Goods Mills 80	22	38N23	78w48	5:15:12
Goodview 10	4	37N09	79w40	5:18:40
Goodwins Ferry 35	4	37N18	80w30	5:22:00
Goose Pimple Junction 92	25	36N36	82w11	5:28:44
Gordon 67	14	38N16	77w48	5:11:12
Gordonsville 67	14	38N09	78w11	5:12:44
Gore 34	4	39N16	78w20	5:13:20
Goshen 79	14	37N59	79w30	5:18:00
Gossan Junction 18	4	36N40	80w55	5:23:40
Government 95	4	36N57	81w05	5:24:20
Grady 70	4	36N49	79w35	5:18:20
Grafton 96	4	37N10	76w27	5:05:48
Grafton Village 87	4	38N23	77w27	5:09:48
Grahams Forge 95	4	36N58	80w57	5:23:48
Grandin Road 128	4	37N15	79w59	5:19:56
Grangeville 1	4	37N39	75w44	5:02:56
Granite Springs 86	22	38N12	77w35	5:10:20
Grant's Field 27	22	37N13	77w26	5:09:44
Grapefield 11	4	37N09	81w09	5:24:36
Grassfield 102	6	36N46	76w21	5:05:24
Grassland 67	14	38N16	77w58	5:11:52
Grass Ridge 29	1	38N55	77w11	5:08:44
Gratton 90	4	37N08	81w31	5:26:04
Gravel Ridge 16	16	37N10	79w05	5:16:20
Graves Mill 56	4	38N25	78w22	5:13:28
Graves Store 10	4	37N10	79w28	5:17:52
Gray 89	4	36N46	77w17	5:09:08
Grays Hill Village 29	3	38N42	77w09	5:08:36
Graysontown 60	4	37N08	80w34	5:22:16
Great Bridge 102	6	36N47	76w15	5:05:00
Great Falls 29	3	39N00	77w15	5:09:00
Great Neck Manor 133	6	36N52	76w02	5:04:08
Green Acres 108	3	38N51	77w15	5:09:00
Greenbackville 1	4	38N01	75w23	5:01:32
Green Bay 72	4	37N08	78w19	5:13:16
Greenbriar 29	3	38N51	77w15	5:09:00
Greenbush 1	4	37N45	75w41	5:02:44
Green Cove 92	15	36N38	81w47	5:27:08
Greendale 43	17	37N36	77w29	5:09:56
Greendale 92	15	36N43	81w58	5:27:52
Greendale Manor 43	17	37N34	77w29	5:09:56
Greenfield 62	14	38N02	78w50	5:15:20
Greenfield 70	4	36N57	79w22	5:17:28
Green Hill 16	16	37N10	79w05	5:16:20
Greenlee 79	14	37N37	79w30	5:18:00
Green Meadows Point 102	6	36N50	76w25	5:05:40
Greenmount 80	22	38N27	78w52	5:15:28
Green Pond 70	4	36N50	79w24	5:17:36
Green Spring 34	9	39N11	78w10	5:12:40
Green Spring 54	14	38N05	78w09	5:12:36
Green Springs 54	14	38N09	78w11	5:12:44
Green Springs 92	15	36N43	81w58	5:27:52
Green Valley 92	25	36N36	82w11	5:28:44
Greenville 8	21	38N00	79w10	5:16:40
Greenville 30	19	38N42	77w35	5:10:20
Greenway 22	4	39N03	78w05	5:12:20
Greenway 29	3	38N58	77w14	5:08:56
Greenway Downs 29	3	38N52	77w13	5:08:52
Greenway Hills 108	3	38N51	77w15	5:09:00
Greenway Wharf 36	4	37N18	76w25	5:05:40
Greenwich 74	14	38N42	77w35	5:10:20
Greenwich 133	6	36N51	76w09	5:04:36
Greenwood 2	14	38N04	78w45	5:15:00
Greenwood 43	22	37N40	77w30	5:10:00
Gregory Corner 58	4	36N42	78w30	5:14:00
Gressitt 48	4	37N29	76w43	5:06:52
Gretna 70	4	36N57	79w22	5:17:28
Greys Corner 93	19	38N02	76w35	5:06:20
Griffinsburg 24	14	38N28	78w00	5:12:00
Griffith 3	4	37N49	79w50	5:19:20
Griffiths Corner 93	19	38N02	76w35	5:06:20
Grimes 34	9	39N11	78w10	5:12:40
Grimsleyville 14	15	37N05	81w52	5:27:28
Grimstead 57	4	37N30	76w18	5:05:12
Grindall Creek 21	22	37N27	77w28	5:09:52
Grit 70	16	37N06	79w18	5:17:12
Grizzard 89	4	36N37	77w33	5:10:12
Grosclose 95	4	36N54	81w16	5:25:04
Grotons 1	4	37N55	75w37	5:02:28
Grottoes 80	22	38N16	78w50	5:15:20
Grove 47	23	37N17	76w43	5:06:52
Grove Hill 68	14	38N29	78w37	5:14:28
Groveland 133	6	36N51	76w07	5:04:28
Groveton 29	1	38N46	77w05	5:08:20
Groveton Gardens 29	1	38N47	77w05	5:08:20
Groveton Heights 29	1	38N47	77w05	5:08:20
Grubbs Store 54	14	38N02	78w00	5:12:00
Grundy 14	15	37N17	82w06	5:28:24
Guilford 1	4	37N50	75w37	5:02:28
Guilford 29	3	38N43	77w09	5:08:36
Guilford 88	4	37N09	76w59	5:07:56
Guinea 17	22	38N09	77w26	5:09:44
Guinea Mills 25	4	37N30	78w15	5:13:00
Gum Fork 36	4	37N25	76w32	5:06:08
Gum Spring 54	14	37N46	77w54	5:11:36
Gum Tree 42	22	37N45	77w29	5:09:56
Gunton Park 95	4	36N58	80w57	5:23:48
Gwathmey 42	22	37N45	77w29	5:09:56
Gwynn 57	4	37N30	76w17	5:05:08
Hacksneck 1	4	37N39	75w52	5:03:28
Haddonfield 94	15	37N08	82w36	5:30:24
Hadens Store 37	4	37N44	78w04	5:12:16
Hadensville 37	4	37N49	78w00	5:12:00
Hadlock 64	4	37N27	75w55	5:03:40
Hagans 52	26	36N40	83w07	5:32:28
Hague 93	19	38N04	76w39	5:06:36
Hale Creek 14	15	37N15	81w55	5:27:40
Halenhurst 108	3	38N51	77w15	5:09:00
Hales Bottom 90	4	37N15	81w17	5:25:08
Halfway 30	19	38N52	77w46	5:11:04
Halifax 41	4	36N46	78w56	5:15:44
Hall Addition 84	15	36N50	81w31	5:26:04
Halliahurst Park 78	4	37N23	79w49	5:19:16
Hallieford 57	4	37N30	76w20	5:05:20
Hallowing Point River Estate 29	3	38N42	77w14	5:08:56
Hallsboro 21	22	37N29	77w34	5:10:16
Hallwood 1	4	37N53	75w36	5:02:24
Hamburg 68	14	38N40	78w27	5:13:48
Hamburg 83	14	38N49	78w34	5:14:16
Hamilton 53	14	39N08	77w40	5:10:40
Hamiltontown 94	15	36N59	82w38	5:30:32
Hamlin 81	15	36N54	82w17	5:29:08
Hampden 72	4	37N11	78w28	5:13:52
Hampden Sydney 72	4	37N14	78w28	5:13:52
Hampton 113	6	37N02	76w21	5:05:24
Hampton Institute 113	6	37N01	76w21	5:05:24
Hampton Roads 122	6	36N56	76w19	5:05:16
Hanckel 92	15	36N46	81w52	5:27:28
Handsom 85	4	36N39	77w02	5:08:08
Hanging Rock 78	4	37N17	80w03	5:20:12
Hanover 42	22	37N46	77w22	5:09:28
Hansonville 81	15	37N00	81w59	5:27:56
Happy Creek 91	14	38N54	78w09	5:12:36
Harborton 1	4	37N40	75w50	5:03:20
Harbor View 29	3	38N42	77w14	5:08:56
Harcum 36	4	37N25	76w32	5:06:08
Hardesty 91	14	38N55	78w12	5:12:48
Hardings 65	18	37N43	76w23	5:05:32
Hardware 32	4	37N48	78w29	5:13:56
Hardwood 82	15	36N50	82w28	5:29:52
Hardy 10	4	37N14	79w49	5:19:16
Hardy 46	4	36N58	76w43	5:06:52
Hardyville 59	4	37N33	76w23	5:05:32
Hare Valley 64	4	37N27	75w55	5:03:40
Hargraves 29	1	38N47	77w07	5:08:28
Harless 60	4	37N08	80w24	5:21:36
Harman 14	15	37N18	82w12	5:28:48
Harman Junction 14	15	37N17	82w06	5:28:24
Harmony 41	4	36N34	79w00	5:16:00
Harmony 83	14	38N49	78w34	5:14:16
Harmony Village 59	4	37N35	76w28	5:05:52
Harrell Siding 132	5	36N44	76w35	5:06:20
Harrisonburg 114	22	38N27	78w52	5:15:28
Harriston 8	21	38N16	78w49	5:15:16
Harrisville 83	14	38N57	78w26	5:13:44
Harrowgate 21	22	37N23	77w26	5:09:44
Harryhogan 65	18	37N58	76w34	5:06:16
Hartfield 59	4	37N33	76w27	5:05:48
Harts Shop 54	14	38N01	77w54	5:11:36
Hartwood 87	4	38N25	77w35	5:10:20
Hassen Heights 92	25	36N36	82w11	5:28:44
Hatchers 71	14	37N29	77w55	5:11:40
Hat Creek 16	16	37N03	78w56	5:15:44
Hatton 2	14	37N48	78w29	5:13:56
Hattontown 29	3	38N58	77w22	5:09:28
Hawkinstown 83	14	38N45	78w39	5:14:36
Hawthorne 76	14	38N35	78w14	5:12:56
Hawthorne 123	15	36N59	82w38	5:30:32
Hayes 36	4	37N17	76w30	5:06:00
Hayfield 29	3	38N43	77w09	5:08:36
Hayfield 34	4	39N14	78w17	5:13:08
Hayfield Farms 29	3	38N43	77w09	5:08:36
Haymarket 74	14	38N49	77w38	5:10:32
Haynesville 77	4	37N57	76w40	5:06:40
Haysi 26	15	37N12	82w18	5:29:12
Haytokah 66	4	37N11	78w11	5:12:44
Haywood 56	4	38N27	78w15	5:13:00
Hazel 26	15	36N59	82w17	5:29:08
Hazel Heights 92	25	36N36	82w11	5:28:44
Hazel River 24	4	38N35	77w59	5:11:56
Head Waters 45	4	38N19	79w25	5:17:40
Healing Springs 9	4	37N58	79w52	5:19:28
Health Science 127	17	37N33	77w26	5:09:44
Healys 59	4	37N33	76w27	5:05:48
Heards 2	14	38N02	78w50	5:15:20
Heathsville 65	18	37N55	76w29	5:05:56
Hebron 8	21	38N09	79w05	5:16:20
Hebron 18	4	36N40	80w55	5:23:40
Hebron 27	22	37N08	77w52	5:11:28
Hechler Village 43	17	37N33	77w24	5:09:36
Helmet 48	4	37N48	77w03	5:08:12
Hematite 3	4	37N47	79w59	5:19:56
Hemlock 31	4	37N10	80w15	5:21:00
Hendricks Store 10	4	37N11	79w37	5:18:28
Henleys Fork 48	4	37N43	77w01	5:08:04
Henleys Store 5	16	37N35	79w03	5:16:12
Henry 33	4	36N50	79w59	5:19:56
Henry Clay Heights 42	22	37N37	77w22	5:09:28
Henry Crossroads 89	4	36N50	77w28	5:09:52
Henrytown 84	15	36N53	81w46	5:27:04
Hepners 83	14	38N45	78w39	5:14:36
Herald 26	15	37N00	82w28	5:29:52
Heritage Square 29	1	38N50	77w12	5:08:48
Heritage Village 29	1	38N50	77w12	5:08:48
Herman 20	4	36N56	78w40	5:14:40
Hermitage 8	21	38N04	78w54	5:15:36
Hermitage Court 43	17	37N36	77w29	5:09:56
Hermitage Farms 43	17	37N36	77w29	5:09:56
Hermitage Park 43	17	37N36	77w29	5:09:56
Hermosa 41	4	36N56	78w57	5:15:48
Herndon 29	1	38N58	77w23	5:09:32
Herndon Heights 29	3	38N58	77w22	5:09:28
Herndon Junction 29	3	38N58	77w22	5:09:28
Hewlett 42	22	37N55	77w35	5:10:20
Hickory 102	6	36N46	76w21	5:05:24
Hickory Flat 18	4	36N40	80w55	5:23:40
Hickory Grove 74	14	38N40	77w29	5:09:56
Hickory Hill 2	14	38N02	78w29	5:13:56
Hickory Sign Post 47	23	37N17	76w43	5:06:52
Hicksford 40	20	36N35	77w38	5:10:32
Hicksville 11	4	37N09	81w09	5:24:36
Hiddenbrook 29	3	38N58	77w22	5:09:28
Hidenwood 121	4	37N04	76w29	5:05:56
Highland 75	4	37N06	80w41	5:22:44
Highland Gardens 43	17	37N34	77w26	5:09:44
Highland Home 87	4	38N23	77w27	5:09:48
Highland Park 74	2	38N47	77w28	5:09:52
Highland Park 115	14	37N17	77w18	5:09:12
Highland Springs 43	22	37N33	77w20	5:09:20
High Meadows 92	25	36N36	82w11	5:28:44
High Point 115	14	37N17	77w18	5:09:12
High Rock 95	4	36N46	80w44	5:22:56
Hightown 45	4	38N26	79w38	5:18:32
Hilander Park 92	25	36N36	82w11	5:28:44
Hill 82	26	36N38	82w34	5:30:16
Hillbrook 29	1	38N50	77w12	5:08:48
Hillbrook Forest 29	1	38N50	77w12	5:08:48
Hillcrest 25	4	37N30	78w15	5:13:00
Hillcrest Estates 74	2	38N47	77w28	5:09:52
Hillsboro 53	14	39N12	77w43	5:10:52
Hillsdale 132	5	36N44	76w35	5:06:20
Hillsman Corner 16	14	37N24	79w10	5:16:40
Hillsville 18	4	36N46	80w44	5:22:56
Hill Top 120	4	36N40	79w52	5:19:28
Hilltop 133	6	36N52	76w00	5:04:00
Hillwood 29	3	38N52	77w13	5:08:52
Hiltons 82	26	36N39	82w28	5:29:52
Hinesville 70	4	36N45	79w24	5:17:36
Hinnom 93	19	38N06	76w50	5:07:20
Hinton 80	22	38N28	78w58	5:15:52
Hitesburg 41	4	36N33	78w47	5:15:08
Hiwassee 75	4	36N58	80w43	5:22:52
Hixburg 6	4	37N14	78w41	5:14:44
Hoadly 74	14	38N41	77w22	5:09:28
Hockley 48	4	37N33	76w48	5:07:12
Hockman 90	4	37N15	81w17	5:25:08
Hodges 16	16	37N10	79w05	5:16:20

 VIRGINIA

Hodges Ferry 102 6 36N50 76w25 5:05:40
Hodgesville 33 4 37N00 79w53 5:19:32
Hoges Chapel 35 4 37N20 80w38 5:22:32
Holcomb Rock 10 14 37N26 79w11 5:16:44
Holdcroft 19 14 37N20 77w04 5:08:16
Holiday Point 132 5 36N44 76w35 5:06:20
Holland 61 4 36N41 76w47 5:07:08
Hollinbrook Park 29 3 38N45 77w06 5:08:24
Hollindale 29 3 38N45 77w06 5:08:24
Hollin Hall Village 29 1 38N45 77w04 5:08:16
Hollin Hills 29 3 38N45 77w06 5:08:24
Hollins 78 4 37N24 79w51 5:19:24
Hollins College 78 4 37N21 79w57 5:19:48
Hollinswood 29 3 38N55 77w14 5:08:56
Holloday 86 14 38N01 77w54 5:11:36
Holly Brook 11 4 37N06 81w07 5:24:28
Holly Forest 29 3 38N48 77w20 5:09:20
Holly Glen Estates 43 22 37N40 77w30 5:10:00
Holly Park 29 3 38N51 77w15 5:09:00
Hollyridge 87 4 38N23 77w27 5:09:48
Hollywood 132 5 36N44 76w35 5:06:20
Holman 80 22 38N38 78w46 5:15:04
Holmes Run Acres 29 3 38N52 77w13 5:08:52
Holmes Run Heights 29 1 38N50 77w12 5:08:48
Holmes Run Park 29 3 38N52 77w13 5:08:52
Holston 92 15 36N43 81w58 5:27:52
Holston Mill 84 15 36N50 81w31 5:26:04
Holts Crossing 16 16 37N10 79w05 5:16:20
Holy Neck 61 4 36N41 76w43 5:06:52
Home Creek 14 15 37N17 82w06 5:28:24
Home Crest 29 3 38N52 77w13 5:08:52
Homeville 89 4 37N02 77w07 5:08:28
Homewood 29 3 38N48 77w16 5:09:04
Honaker 81 15 37N01 81w59 5:27:56
Honaker Junction 81 15 37N01 81w59 5:27:56
Honey Branch 94 15 36N58 82w18 5:29:12
Honeycamp 26 15 37N09 82w27 5:29:48
Honeyville 68 14 38N35 78w30 5:14:00
Hood 56 4 38N21 78w23 5:13:32
Hopeful 54 14 37N58 77w46 5:11:04
Hopeton 1 4 37N47 75w39 5:02:36
Hopewell 115 14 37N18 77w17 5:09:08
Hopkins 1 4 37N47 75w39 5:02:36
Horizon Hills 92 25 36N36 82w11 5:28:44
Horners 93 19 38N06 76w50 5:07:20
Horntown 1 4 37N58 75w28 5:01:52
Horse Gap 94 15 37N08 82w36 5:30:24
Horse Head 65 18 37N55 76w28 5:05:52
Horse Pasture 44 4 36N37 79w59 5:19:56
Horsepen 90 4 37N14 81w31 5:26:04
Horsey 1 4 37N56 75w34 5:02:16
Hotchkiss 9 4 37N59 79w36 5:18:24
Hot Springs 9 4 38N00 79w50 5:19:20
Howardsville 2 14 37N44 78w40 5:14:40
Howertons 28 4 37N50 76w53 5:07:32
Howland 65 18 37N55 76w28 5:05:52
Hubbard Junction 81 15 37N01 81w59 5:27:56
Hubbard Springs 52 26 36N40 83w07 5:32:28
Huddle 95 4 36N57 81w05 5:24:20
Huddleston 10 4 37N10 79w28 5:17:52
Hudgins 57 4 37N28 76w20 5:05:20
Huffman 23 4 37N18 80w30 5:22:00
Huff Store 18 4 36N49 80w37 5:22:28
Huffville 31 4 37N03 80w22 5:21:28
Huguenot 71 14 37N31 77w47 5:11:08
Hulls Chapel 87 4 38N23 77w27 5:09:48
Hume 30 19 38N50 78w00 5:12:00
Hunter 29 3 38N55 77w14 5:08:56
Hunterdale 85 4 36N41 76w56 5:07:44
Hunter Estates 29 3 38N40 77w11 5:08:44
Hunters Valley 29 3 38N55 77w14 5:08:56
Hunting Creek 29 1 38N47 77w05 5:08:20
Hunting Ridge 29 1 38N55 77w11 5:08:44
Huntington 29 1 38N48 77w04 5:08:16
Huntington 43 22 37N36 77w32 5:10:08
Huntington 133 6 36N51 76w09 5:04:36
Huntly 76 14 38N50 78w07 5:12:28
Hunton 43 22 37N40 77w30 5:10:00
Hunts Village 29 3 38N51 77w15 5:09:00
Hupp 80 22 38N38 78w46 5:15:04
Hurley 14 15 37N25 82w01 5:28:04
Hurricane 14 15 37N08 82w03 5:28:12
Hurricane 94 15 37N01 82w35 5:30:20
Hurt 70 16 37N06 79w18 5:17:12
Huske 89 4 36N57 77w24 5:09:36
Hustle 28 4 38N02 77w04 5:08:16
Hutton Heights 43 22 37N40 77w30 5:10:00
Hyacinth 65 18 37N59 76w35 5:06:20
Hybla Valley 29 1 38N46 77w06 5:08:24
Hybla Valley Farms 29 3 38N45 77w06 5:08:24
Hyco 41 4 36N43 78w54 5:15:36
Hylas 42 22 37N43 77w41 5:10:44
Iberis 51 4 37N46 76w28 5:05:52
Ida 68 14 38N40 78w27 5:13:48
Idlewilde 105 4 37N47 79w59 5:19:56
Idylwood 29 3 38N54 77w13 5:08:52
Igo 49 22 38N23 77w27 5:09:48
Imboden 94 26 36N58 82w47 5:31:08
Independence 38 4 36N37 81w09 5:24:36
Independent Hill 74 2 38N47 77w28 5:09:52
Index 49 22 38N12 77w05 5:08:20
Indian 90 4 37N05 81w46 5:27:04
Indian Gap 14 15 37N14 82w06 5:28:24
Indian Neck 48 4 37N54 77w02 5:08:08
Indian River 102 6 36N49 76w14 5:04:56
Indian River Estates 133 6 36N51 76w09 5:04:36
Indian River Park 102 6 36N49 76w14 5:04:56
Indian Rock 12 4 37N32 79w41 5:18:44
Indian Run Park 29 1 38N49 77w09 5:08:36
Indian Springs 29 1 38N49 77w09 5:08:36
Indiantown 67 14 38N18 77w49 5:11:16
Indian Valley 31 4 36N55 80w31 5:22:04
Indika 46 4 36N49 76w45 5:07:00
Inez 54 14 37N58 77w46 5:11:04
Ingham 68 14 38N29 78w37 5:14:28
Ingles 75 4 37N02 80w39 5:22:36
Ingleside 29 1 38N55 77w11 5:08:44
Ingram 41 4 36N45 79w10 5:16:40
Inlet 24 14 38N28 78w00 5:12:00
Inlet 133 6 36N52 76w00 5:04:00
Inman 94 26 36N54 82w48 5:31:12
Ino 48 4 37N48 76w47 5:07:08
Interior 35 4 37N23 80w40 5:22:40
Intervale 3 4 37N47 79w59 5:19:56
Ira 14 15 37N25 82w07 5:28:28
Irisburg 44 4 36N40 79w43 5:18:52
Iriswood 44 4 36N40 79w47 5:19:08
Irondale 94 26 36N56 82w47 5:31:08
Iron Gate 3 4 37N48 79w48 5:19:12
Irongate 74 2 38N47 77w28 5:09:52
Ironto 60 4 37N13 80w14 5:20:56
Irving 10 4 37N21 79w37 5:18:28
Irvington 51 14 37N40 76w25 5:05:40
Irwin 37 4 37N42 77w55 5:11:40
Island Creek 18 4 36N46 80w44 5:22:56
Island Ford 80 14 38N24 78w37 5:14:28
Isle Of Wight 46 4 36N54 76w43 5:06:52
Isom 26 15 37N09 82w27 5:29:48
Ivakota 29 3 38N47 77w23 5:09:32
Ivandale 77 4 37N58 76w46 5:07:04
Ivanhoe 95 4 36N50 80w58 5:23:52
Ivor 85 4 36N54 76w54 5:07:36
Ivy 2 14 38N05 78w35 5:14:20
Ivyview 41 4 36N45 79w06 5:16:24
Jackson Creek 59 4 37N33 76w20 5:05:20
Jackson Hills 29 3 39N00 77w15 5:09:00
Jackson River 3 4 37N47 79w52 5:19:28
Jacksons Ferry 95 4 36N51 80w55 5:23:40
Jaffa 106 4 36N35 79w23 5:17:32
Jamaica 59 4 37N42 76w40 5:06:40
James River 15 4 37N36 78w41 5:14:44
James River Estates 37 17 37N32 77w24 5:09:36
James Store 36 4 37N28 76w28 5:05:52
Jamestown 47 14 37N13 76w47 5:07:08
Jamesville 64 4 37N31 75w56 5:03:44
Janey 14 15 37N13 82w00 5:28:00
Jarman Gap 2 14 38N04 78w42 5:14:48
Jarratt 89 4 36N48 77w28 5:09:52
Jasper 52 26 36N43 82w48 5:31:12
Java 70 4 36N50 79w14 5:16:56
Jefferson 29 3 38N52 77w13 5:08:52
Jefferson 71 14 37N29 77w55 5:11:40
Jefferson 92 15 36N50 81w53 5:27:32
Jefferson Apartments 29 3 38N52 77w13 5:08:52
Jefferson Manor 29 1 38N47 77w05 5:08:20
Jefferson Mews 29 3 38N58 77w22 5:09:28
Jefferson Park 73 22 37N17 77w18 5:09:12
Jeffersonton 24 4 38N38 77w55 5:11:40
Jefferson Village 29 3 38N52 77w13 5:08:52
Jeffersonville 90 4 37N09 81w34 5:26:16
Jeffress 58 4 36N37 78w34 5:14:16
Jenkins Bridge 1 4 37N55 75w37 5:02:28
Jennings 66 4 37N11 78w07 5:12:28
Jennings Gap 8 21 38N14 79w10 5:16:40
Jennings Mission 82 26 36N38 82w34 5:30:16
Jennings Store 82 26 36N41 82w45 5:31:00
Jericho 18 4 36N43 80w49 5:23:16
Jericho 132 5 36N44 76w34 5:06:16
Jermantown 108 3 38N51 77w15 5:09:00
Jerome 83 14 38N49 78w34 5:14:16
Jersey 49 22 38N13 77w08 5:08:32
Jerusalem 85 4 36N46 77w00 5:08:00
Jessup Farms 21 22 37N27 77w28 5:09:52
Jetersville 4 4 37N18 78w06 5:12:24
Jett 95 4 36N46 80w44 5:22:56
Jewell Hollow 68 14 38N40 78w27 5:13:48
Jewell Ridge 90 4 37N11 81w48 5:27:12
Jewell Valley 14 15 37N15 81w48 5:27:12
Johnson 82 26 36N44 82w26 5:29:44
Johnson Creek 69 4 36N36 80w31 5:22:04
Johnsons Corner 29 3 38N50 77w26 5:09:44
Johnsontown 64 4 37N24 75w54 5:03:36
Johnston 83 14 38N52 78w26 5:13:44
Joliffs 102 6 36N50 76w25 5:05:40
Jolivue 8 21 38N09 79w05 5:16:20
Jollett 68 14 38N24 78w37 5:14:28
Jones 86 22 38N12 77w35 5:10:20
Jonesboro 13 4 37N05 78w00 5:12:00
Jones Corner 17 22 38N03 77w21 5:09:24
Jones Corner 29 1 38N55 77w11 5:08:44
Jones Creek 120 4 36N40 79w52 5:19:28
Jones Store 20 4 36N47 78w37 5:14:28
Jonesville 52 26 36N41 83w07 5:32:28
Jordan Mines 3 4 37N41 80w07 5:20:28
Josephine 94 15 36N59 82w38 5:30:32
Joshua Falls 5 14 37N25 79w08 5:16:32
Joyce Heights 108 3 38N51 77w15 5:09:00
Justisville 1 4 37N47 75w39 5:02:36
Ka 82 15 36N50 82w28 5:29:52
Kamp Washington 108 3 38N51 77w15 5:09:00
Karo 91 14 38N55 78w12 5:12:48
Kathmoor 29 3 38N43 77w09 5:08:36
Kayoulah 75 4 36N56 80w44 5:22:56
Kecoughtan 113 6 37N01 76w20 5:05:20
Keeling 70 4 36N43 79w17 5:17:08
Keene 2 14 37N52 78w33 5:14:12
Keene Homes 29 1 38N45 77w04 5:08:16
Keene Mill Manor 29 3 38N49 77w14 5:08:56
Keen Mountain 14 15 37N12 81w59 5:27:56
Keever 16 16 37N10 79w05 5:16:20
Keezletown 80 22 38N25 78w48 5:15:12
Keith 50 14 37N47 77w06 5:08:24
Keller 1 4 37N37 75w46 5:03:04
Kelley View 94 26 36N58 82w47 5:31:08
Kellys Ford 24 4 38N32 77w49 5:11:16
Kelsa 14 15 37N25 82w07 5:28:28
Kemmerer Gem No. Ø2 52 26 36N49 83w03 5:32:12
Kemps Place 43 17 37N32 77w24 5:09:36
Kempsville 133 6 36N51 76w09 5:04:36
Kempsville Colony 133 6 36N51 76w09 5:04:36
Kempsville Garden 133 6 36N51 76w09 5:04:36
Kempsville Heights 133 6 36N51 76w09 5:04:36
Kenady 26 15 37N05 82w27 5:29:48
Kenbridge 55 4 36N58 78w08 5:12:32
Kendall Grove 64 4 37N21 75w56 5:03:44
Kennard 77 4 37N58 76w46 5:07:04
Kent 95 4 36N57 81w01 5:24:04
Kent Gardens 29 1 38N55 77w11 5:08:44
Kentland Farms 29 3 38N58 77w22 5:09:28
Kents Store 32 4 37N53 78w08 5:12:32
Kentuck 70 4 36N36 79w18 5:17:12
Kenwood 42 22 37N45 77w29 5:09:56
Kenwood 115 14 37N17 77w18 5:09:12
Keokee 52 26 36N52 82w54 5:31:36
Kerfoot 30 19 38N55 77w55 5:11:40
Kermit 82 26 36N38 82w34 5:30:16
Kerns 82 26 36N46 82w35 5:30:20
Kernstown 136 9 39N11 78w10 5:12:40
Kerrs Creek 80 22 37N50 79w31 5:18:04
Kesslers Mill 129 4 37N17 80w03 5:20:12
Keswick 2 14 38N02 78w40 5:14:40
Ketron 92 25 36N36 82w11 5:28:44
Ketrontown 82 26 36N34 82w33 5:30:12
Keysville 20 4 37N02 78w29 5:13:56
Key West 2 14 38N02 78w29 5:13:56
Keywood 92 15 36N48 81w46 5:27:04
Kibler 69 4 36N36 80w31 5:22:04
Kidds Fork 17 22 38N03 77w21 5:09:24
Kidville 8 21 38N06 78w58 5:15:52
Kiels Gardens 29 3 38N51 77w15 5:09:00
Kilby 132 5 36N44 76w35 5:06:20
Kilby Shores 132 5 36N44 76w35 5:06:20
Kildare Annex 43 17 37N34 77w29 5:09:56
Kilmarnock 51 14 37N43 76w23 5:05:32
Kilmarnock Wharf 51 14 37N43 76w23 5:05:32
Kimages 19 14 37N20 77w04 5:08:16
Kimballton 35 4 37N20 80w41 5:22:44
Kimberling 11 4 37N06 81w07 5:24:28
Kinderhook 39 14 38N18 78w26 5:13:44
Kindrick 95 4 36N57 81w05 5:24:20
King And Queen 48 4 37N40 76w53 5:07:32
King George 49 22 38N16 77w11 5:08:44
Kings Fork 132 5 36N44 76w35 5:06:20
Kings Hill 43 17 37N32 77w24 5:09:36
Kingsland 21 22 37N27 77w28 5:09:52
Kings Manor 29 1 38N55 77w11 5:08:44
Kings Park 29 3 38N49 77w13 5:08:52
Kings Point 47 23 37N17 76w43 5:06:52
Kings Store 31 4 37N05 80w08 5:20:32
Kingston 16 16 37N14 79w17 5:17:08
Kingstown 78 4 37N24 79w51 5:19:24
Kingsville 72 4 37N18 78w24 5:13:36
Kingtown 99 25 36N36 82w11 5:28:44
King William 50 14 37N41 77w01 5:08:04
Kino 28 14 37N55 76w52 5:07:28
Kinsale 93 19 38N02 76w35 5:06:20
Kiptopeke 64 4 37N16 76w00 5:04:00
Kiptopeke Beach 64 4 37N16 76w00 5:04:00
Kire 35 4 37N26 80w31 5:22:04
Kirkside 29 3 38N45 77w06 5:08:24
Klocks Corner 17 22 38N07 77w25 5:09:40
Klotz 35 4 37N20 80w41 5:22:44
Knightly 8 21 38N15 78w57 5:15:48
Knox 14 15 37N24 82w03 5:28:12
Koehler 44 4 36N40 79w52 5:19:28
Konnarock 92 15 36N39 81w38 5:26:32
Laban 57 4 37N24 76w19 5:05:16
Laburnum Manor 43 17 37N34 77w26 5:09:44
Lacey Spring 80 22 38N32 78w46 5:15:04
Lackey 96 4 37N12 76w27 5:05:48
La Crosse 58 4 36N42 78w06 5:12:24
Ladd 8 21 38N04 78w54 5:15:36
Ladysmith 17 22 38N01 77w31 5:10:04
Lafayette 60 4 37N14 80w19 5:21:16
Lafayette Boulevard 122 6 36N53 76w16 5:05:04
Lahore 67 14 38N12 77w58 5:11:52
Lake 65 18 37N57 76w31 5:06:04
Lake 87 4 38N23 77w27 5:09:48
Lake Barcroft 29 1 38N51 77w09 5:08:36
Lake Hills 29 3 38N42 77w14 5:08:56

VIRGINIA

Place	Zone	Lat.	Long.	Time
Lake Jackson 74	2	38n47	77w28	5:09:52
Lake Ridge 74	13	38n39	77w16	5:09:04
Lakes 10	4	37n11	79w30	5:18:00
Lake Shores 133	6	36n53	76w08	5:04:32
Lakeside 43	22	37n37	77w29	5:09:56
Lakeside 129	4	37n17	80w03	5:20:12
Lakeside Hills 43	17	37n36	77w29	5:09:56
Lakeside Village 25	4	37n40	78w06	5:12:24
Lake Smith 133	6	36n53	76w08	5:04:32
Lakesmith Terrace 133	6	36n53	76w08	5:04:32
Lakevile Estates 133	6	36n51	76w09	5:04:36
Lakewood 29	1	38n51	77w09	5:08:36
Lambsburg 18	4	36n35	80w46	5:23:04
Lanahan 33	4	36n55	80w01	5:20:04
Lancaster 51	4	37n46	76w28	5:05:52
Landmark Square 74	2	38n47	77w28	5:09:52
Land of Promise 133	6	36n51	76w06	5:04:24
Land O'Pines 21	22	37n23	77w31	5:10:04
Landtown 133	6	36n49	76w09	5:04:36
Lanes Corner 86	22	38n12	77w35	5:10:20
Lanesville 50	14	37n41	77w01	5:08:04
Laneview 28	4	37n45	76w44	5:06:56
Lanexa 63	14	37n24	76w55	5:07:40
Langhorne Acres 29	3	38n51	77w15	5:09:00
Langley 29	3	38n54	77w13	5:08:52
Langley Air Force Base 113	11	37n05	76w21	5:05:24
Langley Forest 29	1	38n55	77w11	5:08:44
Langley Ridge 29	1	38n55	77w11	5:08:44
Lankford Corner 51	4	37n55	76w28	5:05:52
Lantz Mills 83	14	38n49	78w34	5:14:16
Lara 65	18	37n46	76w28	5:05:52
Lark 90	4	37n06	81w48	5:27:12
Lark Downs 133	6	36n51	76w09	5:04:36
Larkspur 133	6	36n51	76w09	5:04:36
Larwood Acres 92	25	36n36	82w11	5:28:44
Laswell 95	4	36n58	80w57	5:23:48
Laurel 43	22	37n39	77w31	5:10:04
Laurel 81	15	37n01	81w59	5:27:56
Laureldale 92	15	36n38	81w47	5:27:08
Laurel Dell 43	17	37n36	77w29	5:09:56
Laurel Fork 18	4	36n43	80w36	5:22:24
Laurel Grove 29	3	37n16	76w00	5:04:00
Laurel Grove 70	4	36n37	79w12	5:16:48
Laurel Grove Estates 42	22	37n37	77w22	5:09:28
Laurel Heights 43	17	37n36	77w29	5:09:56
Laurel Hill 8	21	38n09	79w05	5:16:20
Laurel Hill 83	14	39n03	78w22	5:13:28
Laurel Mills 76	14	38n36	78w06	5:12:24
Laurel Park 43	17	37n36	77w29	5:09:56
Lavender 60	4	37n10	80w15	5:21:00
Lawndale Farms 43	17	37n32	77w24	5:09:36
Lawrenceville 13	4	36n46	77w51	5:11:24
Lawrenceville Hills 13	4	36n46	77w51	5:11:24
Lawson 46	4	36n59	76w38	5:06:32
Lawson Forest 133	6	36n53	76w08	5:04:32
Lawsons Store 58	4	36n48	78w28	5:13:52
Lawyers 16	14	37n24	79w10	5:16:40
Layman 80	22	38n27	78w52	5:15:28
LC Page 122	6	36n55	76w13	5:04:52
Lead Mines 95	4	36n52	80w54	5:23:36
Leakesville Junction 70	4	36n34	79w40	5:18:40
Leaksville 68	14	38n40	78w27	5:13:48
Lebanon 81	15	36n54	82w05	5:28:20
Lebanon Church 83	14	39n03	78w22	5:13:28
Leck 26	15	37n00	82w28	5:29:52
Leda 41	4	36n56	78w57	5:15:48
Lee 37	4	37n38	77w48	5:11:12
Lee Boulevard Heights 29	1	38n52	77w12	5:08:48
Leedstown 93	19	38n15	76w58	5:07:52
Lee Forest 29	3	38n51	77w15	5:09:00
Lee Hall 121	4	37n10	76w33	5:06:12
Lee Hill 86	24	38n15	77w28	5:09:52
Lee-Hi Village 29	3	38n51	77w15	5:09:00
Leeland 87	24	38n20	77w25	5:09:40
Lee Manor 29	3	38n51	77w15	5:09:00
Leemaster 14	15	37n14	82w06	5:28:24
Lee Meadows 29	3	38n51	77w15	5:09:00
Lee Mont 1	4	37n47	75w41	5:02:44
Lee Park 43	22	37n33	77w22	5:09:28
Leesburg 53	14	39n07	77w34	5:10:16
Leesville 16	16	37n09	79w18	5:17:12
Lee Town 14	15	37n17	82w06	5:28:24
Leetown 34	4	39n14	78w07	5:12:28
Leewood 29	3	38n49	77w13	5:08:52
Legato 29	3	38n51	77w15	5:09:00
Leigh Mill 29	3	39n00	77w15	5:09:00
Leithton 53	14	38n58	77w44	5:10:56
Lenah 53	4	38n59	77w39	5:10:36
Lennig 41	4	36n54	78w55	5:15:40
Lenox 133	6	36n48	76w01	5:04:04
Leon 56	4	38n26	78w09	5:12:36
Leona Mines 52	26	36n49	83w03	5:32:12
Leonard 92	25	36n36	82w11	5:28:44
Leonardo Store 52	26	36n38	83w26	5:33:44
Lerty 93	19	38n06	76w50	5:07:20
Lester Manor 50	14	37n41	77w01	5:08:04
Level Run 70	16	37n06	79w18	5:17:12
Levi 53	4	38n59	77w39	5:10:36
Levisa 14	15	37n21	82w12	5:28:48
Lewinsville 29	1	38n55	77w11	5:08:44
Lewinsville Heights 29	1	38n55	77w11	5:08:44
Lewisetta 65	18	38n00	76w28	5:05:52
Lewis Gardens 43	22	37n33	77w22	5:09:28
Lewis Park 29	3	38n51	77w15	5:09:00
Lewis Store 32	4	37n48	78w29	5:13:56
Lewiston 55	4	36n59	78w16	5:13:04
Lexington 116	14	37n47	79w27	5:17:48
Liberia Woods 118	2	38n47	77w28	5:09:52
Liberty 41	4	36n56	78w57	5:15:48
Liberty 90	4	37n08	81w31	5:26:04
Lick Fork 26	15	37n00	82w28	5:29:52
Lickinghole 37	4	37n43	77w55	5:11:40
Lick Run 12	4	37n38	79w48	5:19:12
Lifestyle 29	3	38n58	77w22	5:09:28
Lightfoot 47	14	37n20	76w45	5:07:00
Lignum 24	4	38n25	77w50	5:11:20
Lilian 65	18	37n52	76w18	5:05:12
Lima 106	4	36n35	79w23	5:17:32
Lime Hill 92	25	36n36	82w11	5:28:44
Limeton 91	14	38n50	78w19	5:13:16
Lincoln 53	14	39n07	77w42	5:10:48
Lincolnia 29	1	38n50	77w09	5:08:36
Lincolnia Heights 29	1	38n49	77w09	5:08:36
Lincolnia Park 29	1	38n49	77w09	5:08:36
Lincoln Park 29	3	38n51	77w15	5:09:00
Lindell 92	15	36n43	81w58	5:27:52
Linden 91	14	38n54	78w05	5:12:20
Lindenwood 78	4	37n23	79w49	5:19:16
Lindsay 2	14	38n09	78w11	5:12:44
Linkhorn Park 133	6	36n52	76w00	5:04:00
Linville 80	22	38n31	78w50	5:15:20
Lipps 94	15	37n00	82w25	5:29:40
Lipscomb 8	21	38n01	79w02	5:16:08
Lithia 12	4	37n29	79w45	5:19:00
Little Creek 133	6	36n53	76w08	5:04:32
Little Montgomery 60	4	37n04	80w47	5:23:08
Little Neck Village 133	6	36n51	76w07	5:04:28
Little Plymouth 48	4	37n38	76w48	5:07:12
Little River 31	4	36n58	80w15	5:21:00
Little River Hills 108	3	38n51	77w15	5:09:00
Little River Pines 29	3	38n51	77w15	5:09:00
Littleton 89	4	37n02	77w07	5:08:28
Little Vienna Estates 29	3	38n55	77w14	5:08:56
Littlevine 18	4	36n46	80w44	5:22:56
Litwalton 51	4	37n46	76w28	5:05:52
Litz 92	15	36n48	81w46	5:27:04
Lively 51	4	37n47	76w31	5:06:04
Livingston 86	22	38n10	77w47	5:11:08
Lloyd Place 132	5	36n43	76w34	5:06:16
Locher 79	14	37n38	79w27	5:17:48
Loch Laird 100	14	37n44	79w21	5:17:24
Loch Laird Junction 100	14	37n44	79w21	5:17:24
Loch Leven 55	4	36n51	78w04	5:12:16
Loch Lomond 74	2	38n47	77w28	5:09:52
Lockett 72	4	37n16	78w17	5:13:08
Lockhart Flats 26	15	37n09	82w27	5:29:48
Locust Creek 54	14	37n58	77w46	5:11:04
Locust Dale 56	4	38n19	78w12	5:12:48
Locust Grove 31	4	37n03	80w10	5:20:40
Locust Grove 67	14	38n18	77w49	5:11:16
Locust Hill 59	4	37n36	76w31	5:06:04
Locust Hill 95	4	36n58	80w57	5:23:48
Locust Mound 1	4	37n39	75w44	5:02:56
Locustville 1	4	37n39	75w41	5:02:44
Lodge 65	18	37n58	76w34	5:06:16
Lodi 92	15	36n48	81w46	5:27:04
Lodore 4	4	37n21	77w59	5:11:56
Lofton 8	21	37n56	79w14	5:16:56
Logan 86	22	38n12	77w35	5:10:20
Loisdale 29	3	38n45	77w12	5:08:48
Lomax 82	26	36n46	82w35	5:30:20
Lombardy Grove 58	4	36n44	78w07	5:12:28
London Bridge 133	6	36n52	76w02	5:04:08
London Towne 29	3	38n50	77w26	5:09:44
Lone Fountain 8	21	38n14	79w10	5:16:40
Lone Gum 10	4	37n10	79w28	5:17:52
Longbottom 14	15	37n17	82w06	5:28:24
Long Branch 26	15	36n59	82w17	5:29:08
Long Branch 29	3	38n49	77w15	5:09:00
Long Dale 3	4	37n49	79w50	5:19:20
Longdale 43	22	37n40	77w30	5:10:00
Longdale Furnace 3	4	37n49	79w50	5:19:20
Longfork 8	21	38n23	78w59	5:15:56
Long Island 16	16	37n04	79w06	5:16:24
Long Marsh 22	14	39n11	78w01	5:12:04
Long Mountain 16	16	37n19	79w03	5:16:12
Long Ridge 102	6	36n46	76w21	5:05:24
Longshoal 18	4	36n56	80w44	5:22:56
Longshop 60	4	37n08	80w24	5:21:36
Long Spur 11	4	37n06	80w41	5:22:44
Longview 46	4	36n59	76w38	5:06:32
Looney's Creek 14	15	37n17	82w06	5:28:24
Loretto 28	4	38n05	77w03	5:08:12
Lorfax Heights 29	3	38n42	77w14	5:08:56
Lorne 17	22	37n55	77w29	5:09:56
Lorton 29	3	38n42	77w14	5:08:56
Lorton Valley 29	3	38n42	77w14	5:08:56
Lost Corner 22	9	39n11	78w10	5:12:40
Lottsburg 65	18	37n59	76w35	5:06:20
Loudoun Heights 53	4	39n19	77w44	5:10:56
Louisa 54	14	38n01	78w00	5:12:00
Love 62	14	38n06	78w52	5:15:28
Love Mills 92	15	36n48	81w41	5:26:44
Loves Shop 41	4	36n46	78w56	5:15:44
Lovettsville 53	4	39n16	77w39	5:10:36
Lovingston 62	14	37n46	78w52	5:15:28
Lower Brandon 73	22	37n10	76w58	5:07:52
Lower Elk Creek 38	4	36n43	81w11	5:24:44
Lower Exeter 94	26	36n53	82w51	5:31:24
Lowery Hills 92	25	36n36	82w11	5:28:44
Lowesville 5	16	37n43	79w04	5:16:16
Lowmoor 3	4	37n47	79w53	5:19:32
Lowry 10	4	37n21	79w26	5:17:44
Luck 70	4	36n50	79w14	5:16:56
Lucketts 53	14	39n07	77w34	5:10:16
Lucky Hill 30	19	38n32	77w49	5:11:16
Lumberton 89	4	37n02	77w07	5:08:28
Lummis 132	5	36n44	76w35	5:06:20
Lunenburg 55	4	36n58	78w16	5:13:04
Luray 68	14	38n40	78w28	5:13:52
Lurich 35	4	37n20	80w48	5:23:12
Lusters Gate 60	4	37n14	80w25	5:21:40
Luttrellville 65	18	37n58	76w34	5:06:16
Lydia 39	14	38n18	78w26	5:13:44
Lyells 77	4	37n58	76w46	5:07:04
Lyman Park 74	14	38n31	77w18	5:09:12
Lynchburg 117	14	37n25	79w09	5:16:36
Lynch Station 16	16	37n09	79w18	5:17:12
Lyndhurst 8	21	38n06	78w52	5:15:28
Lynndale Estates 133	6	36n51	76w07	5:04:28
Lynn Grove 43	17	37n34	77w26	5:09:44
Lynnhaven 133	6	36n51	76w07	5:04:28
Lynnhaven Acres 133	6	36n51	76w07	5:04:28
Lynnhaven Colony 133	6	36n52	76w00	5:04:00
Lynn Haven Hills 78	4	37n23	79w49	5:19:16
Lynnhaven Shores 133	6	36n52	76w00	5:04:00
Lynn Spring 81	15	37n02	81w55	5:27:40
Lynnwood 80	22	38n18	78w49	5:15:16
Lynnwood 133	6	36n51	76w07	5:04:28
Lynwood 74	13	38n39	77w16	5:09:04
Mabe 82	26	36n41	82w45	5:31:00
Macanie 83	14	38n45	78w39	5:14:36
Mace Springs 82	26	36n39	82w28	5:29:52
Machipongo 64	4	37n24	75w54	5:03:36
Machodoc 93	19	38n06	76w43	5:06:52
Mackall Hill 29	1	38n55	77w11	5:08:44
Mack Creek Village 75	4	36n58	80w43	5:22:52
Macon 71	14	37n34	78w01	5:12:04
Madison 56	4	38n23	78w15	5:13:00
Madison College 114	22	38n27	78w52	5:15:28
Madison Heights 5	14	37n25	79w08	5:16:32
Madison Mills 56	4	38n17	78w09	5:12:36
Madison Run 67	14	38n09	78w11	5:12:44
Madisonville 20	4	37n11	78w42	5:14:48
Madrid 8	21	38n04	78w54	5:15:36
Madrillon Farms 29	3	38n55	77w14	5:08:56
Maggie 23	4	37n30	80w07	5:20:28
Magnolia 132	5	36n44	76w35	5:06:20
Magnolia Gardens 132	5	36n44	76w35	5:06:20
Magruder 96	23	37n17	76w43	5:06:52
Maidens 37	4	37n40	77w53	5:11:32
Maiden Spring 90	4	37n06	81w45	5:27:00
Major 10	4	37n32	79w22	5:17:28
Major 38	4	36n35	81w20	5:25:20
Makemie Park 1	4	37n54	75w33	5:02:12
Makleys Corner 29	3	38n48	77w20	5:09:20
Malbrook 29	1	38n52	77w12	5:08:48
Malcolm 92	25	36n36	82w11	5:28:44
Malibu 133	6	36n51	76w07	5:04:28
Mallow 3	4	37n47	79w59	5:19:56
Malmaison 70	4	36n41	79w22	5:17:28
Manakin 37	4	37n36	77w42	5:10:48
Manakin Farms 37	4	37n36	77w42	5:10:48
Manakin-Sabot 37	4	37n36	77w42	5:10:48
Manassas 118	2	38n45	77w28	5:09:52
Manassas Park 119	2	38n47	77w28	5:09:52
Manchester 21	22	37n28	77w30	5:10:00
Maness 52	26	36n49	83w03	5:32:12
Mangohick 50	14	37n48	77w14	5:08:56
Mannboro 4	4	37n15	77w49	5:11:16
Mann Ford 82	26	36n38	82w34	5:30:16
Mannoni 60	4	37n08	80w24	5:21:36
Manquin 50	14	37n42	77w09	5:08:36
Manry 85	4	36n58	76w59	5:07:56
Mantua 29	3	38n51	77w15	5:09:00
Mantua Hills 29	3	38n51	77w15	5:09:00
Manville 82	26	36n38	82w34	5:30:16
Maple Grove 29	3	38n43	77w09	5:08:36
Maple Grove 93	19	38n15	76w58	5:07:52
Maple Terrace 29	3	38n51	77w15	5:09:00
Maple Terrace 133	6	36n52	76w00	5:04:00
Mapleton 133	6	36n49	76w09	5:04:36
Maplewood 4	4	37n21	77w59	5:11:56
Mappsburg 1	4	37n35	75w47	5:03:08
Mappsville 1	4	37n51	75w34	5:02:16
Marcem 82	26	36n38	82w34	5:30:16
Marengo 58	4	36n42	78w06	5:12:24
Marford 132	5	36n44	76w35	5:06:20
Margo 86	22	38n12	77w35	5:10:20
Marion 84	15	36n50	81w31	5:26:04
Marion Hill 43	17	37n32	77w24	5:09:36
Marionville 64	4	37n27	75w51	5:03:24
Markham 30	19	38n54	77w59	5:11:56
Markham 70	4	36n57	79w22	5:17:28

 VIRGINIA

Place		Lat.	Long.	Time
Marksville 68	14	38N35	78w29	5:13:56
Marlan Forest 29	1	38N46	77w04	5:08:16
Marlboro 21	22	37N29	77w29	5:09:56
Marlboro 34	4	39N02	78w17	5:13:08
Marlbrook 79	14	37N54	79w12	5:16:48
Marmora 27	22	37N11	77w38	5:10:32
Marrowbone Heights 44	4	36N33	79w51	5:19:24
Marshall 30	19	38N52	77w52	5:11:28
Marshall Farms 29	3	38N50	77w26	5:09:44
Martha Gap 26	15	37N12	82w18	5:29:12
Martin Siding 64	4	37N24	75w54	5:03:36
Martins Store 5	14	37N25	79w08	5:16:32
Martins Store 41	4	36N56	78w57	5:15:48
Martins Store 62	14	38N02	78w50	5:15:20
Martinsville 120	4	36N41	79w52	5:19:28
Marumsco Acres 74	13	38N39	77w16	5:09:04
Marumsco Hills 74	13	38N39	77w16	5:09:04
Marumsco Village 74	13	38N39	77w16	5:09:04
Marumsco Woods 74	13	38N39	77w16	5:09:04
Marvin 14	15	37N05	81w52	5:27:28
Marye 86	22	38N12	77w35	5:10:20
Mary Lee Park 29	3	38N45	77w08	5:08:32
Marysville 16	16	37N10	79w05	5:16:20
Maryus 36	4	37N17	76w24	5:05:36
Mascot 48	4	37N38	76w42	5:06:48
Mason 29	1	38N52	77w10	5:08:40
Mason Cove 78	4	37N17	80w03	5:20:12
Mason Creek 129	4	37N17	80w03	5:20:12
Masonville 29	1	38N50	77w12	5:08:48
Massaponax 86	22	38N23	77w27	5:09:48
Massie 75	4	37N07	80w47	5:23:08
Massies Mill 62	14	37N47	79w00	5:16:00
Mathews 57	4	37N26	76w19	5:05:16
Matoaca 21	22	37N15	77w28	5:09:52
Mattaponi 48	4	37N32	76w46	5:07:04
Mauck 68	14	38N35	78w30	5:14:00
Maurertown 83	14	38N55	78w28	5:13:52
Mavisdale 14	15	37N12	82w01	5:28:04
Max 18	4	36N40	80w55	5:23:40
Max Creek 75	4	36N58	80w43	5:22:52
Maxie 14	15	37N18	82w11	5:28:44
Max Meadows 95	4	36N58	80w57	5:23:48
Maxwell 90	4	37N08	81w31	5:26:04
Mayberry 69	4	36N44	80w25	5:21:40
Maybrook 35	4	37N20	80w38	5:22:32
Mayfair Place 43	17	37N33	77w24	5:09:36
Mayfield 43	17	37N34	77w29	5:09:56
Mayfield Farms 42	22	37N37	77w22	5:09:28
Mayflower 5	16	37N35	79w03	5:16:12
Mayland 80	22	38N37	78w48	5:15:12
Mayo 41	4	36N34	78w53	5:15:32
Mayo 44	4	36N37	80w00	5:20:00
Mayo River 69	4	36N38	80w09	5:20:36
Maysville 15	4	37N33	78w33	5:14:12
Maytown 94	15	37N00	82w28	5:29:52
McAdam 75	4	37N04	80w47	5:23:08
McCall Gap 92	15	36N48	81w46	5:27:04
McClung 9	4	37N59	79w36	5:18:24
McClure 26	15	37N06	82w22	5:29:28
McConnell 82	26	36N38	82w34	5:30:16
McCorkle 82	26	36N39	82w28	5:29:52
McCoy 60	4	37N13	80w37	5:22:28
McCrady 84	15	36N53	81w46	5:27:04
McDonalds Mill 60	4	37N14	80w25	5:21:40
McDonald's Small Farms 43	22	37N40	77w30	5:10:00
McDowell 45	4	38N20	79w29	5:17:56
McGaheysville 80	22	38N22	78w44	5:14:56
McHenry 86	22	38N12	77w35	5:10:20
McKendree 41	4	36N46	78w56	5:15:44
McKenney 27	22	36N59	77w43	5:10:52
McKinley 8	21	38N03	79w13	5:16:52
McLean 29	1	38N56	77w11	5:08:44
McLean Estates 29	1	38N55	77w11	5:08:44
McLean Hamlet 29	1	38N55	77w11	5:08:44
McLean Manor 29	1	38N55	77w11	5:08:44
McMullen 39	14	38N18	78w26	5:13:44
McNeals Corner 51	4	37N46	76w28	5:05:52
Meade 28	14	37N55	76w52	5:07:28
Meadowbrook 21	22	37N27	77w28	5:09:52
Meadowcreek 38	4	36N40	80w55	5:23:40
Meadowcrest 92	25	36N36	82w11	5:28:44
Meadowood 43	17	37N36	77w27	5:09:48
Meadows of Dan 69	4	36N44	80w25	5:21:40
Meadows Of Newgate 29	3	38N50	77w26	5:09:44
Meadow View 21	22	37N27	77w28	5:09:52
Meadowview 43	22	37N32	77w19	5:09:16
Meadowview 92	15	36N46	81w52	5:27:28
Meadsville 41	4	36N50	79w03	5:16:12
Meadville 41	4	36N56	78w57	5:15:48
Mears 1	4	37N51	75w36	5:02:24
Mearsville 1	4	37N51	75w36	5:02:24
Mechanicsburg 11	4	37N09	80w58	5:23:52
Mechanicsville 42	22	37N36	77w22	5:09:28
Mechanicsville 80	22	38N38	78w46	5:15:04
Mechums River 2	14	38N02	78w29	5:13:56
Media Park 43	17	37N32	77w24	5:09:36
Meetze 30	19	38N44	77w44	5:10:56
Meherrin 72	4	37N06	78w22	5:13:28
Melfa 1	4	37N39	75w45	5:03:00
Melrose 16	16	37N10	79w05	5:16:20
Melrose 128	4	37N18	79w59	5:19:56
Melrose Gardens 74	14	38N33	77w19	5:09:16
Melton 54	14	38N09	78w11	5:12:44
Memorial Heights 29	1	38N47	77w05	5:08:20
Mendota 92	26	36N42	82w19	5:29:16
Mentow 10	4	37N10	79w28	5:17:52
Mercer 53	14	39N01	77w45	5:11:00
Meredithville 13	4	36N48	77w57	5:11:48
Meridan Park 29	1	38N53	77w13	5:08:52
Merrifield 29	1	38N52	77w14	5:08:56
Merrimac 60	4	37N08	80w24	5:21:36
Merrimac Mines 60	4	37N08	80w24	5:21:36
Merritt Hills 130	4	36N43	78w54	5:15:36
Merry Oaks 29	3	38N55	77w14	5:08:56
Merry Point 51	4	37N43	76w29	5:05:56
Messongo 1	4	37N55	75w37	5:02:28
Metomkin 1	4	37N47	75w39	5:02:36
Metompkin 1	4	37N48	75w36	5:02:24
Mew 81	15	36N54	82w17	5:29:08
Michaux 71	14	37N29	77w55	5:11:40
Middlebrook 8	21	38N03	79w13	5:16:52
Middleburg 53	14	38N58	77w44	5:10:56
Middleridge 29	3	38N51	77w15	5:09:00
Middle River 8	21	38N12	78w53	5:15:32
Middleton 43	17	37N36	77w29	5:09:56
Middleton Gardens 129	4	37N17	80w03	5:20:12
Middletown 34	4	39N02	78w17	5:13:08
Middletown Farm 96	23	37N17	76w43	5:06:52
Midland 30	19	38N36	77w44	5:10:56
Midlothian 21	22	37N30	77w39	5:10:36
Mid-Town 125	6	36N50	76w20	5:05:20
Midway 20	4	37N07	78w49	5:15:16
Midway 41	4	36N33	78w47	5:15:08
Midway 58	4	36N41	78w16	5:13:04
Mike 16	16	37N21	78w59	5:15:56
Mila 65	18	37N55	76w28	5:05:52
Milan 122	6	36N53	76w18	5:05:12
Miles 57	4	37N25	76w22	5:05:28
Miles Store 57	4	37N25	76w23	5:05:32
Milestone 51	4	37N46	76w28	5:05:52
Milford 17	22	38N01	77w22	5:09:28
Millboro 9	4	37N59	79w36	5:18:24
Millboro Springs 9	4	37N59	79w36	5:18:24
Mill Creek Park 29	1	38N50	77w12	5:08:48
Milldale 91	14	38N55	78w12	5:12:48
Millenbeck 51	4	37N46	76w28	5:05:52
Miller Park 117	14	37N24	79w10	5:16:40
Miller School 2	14	38N02	78w29	5:13:56
Millers Tavern 28	4	37N50	76w57	5:07:48
Mill Gap 45	4	38N25	79w35	5:18:20
Mill Run Acres 29	3	39N00	77w15	5:09:00
Milltown 53	4	39N16	77w38	5:10:32
Millwood 22	4	39N04	78w02	5:12:08
Milteer Acres 132	5	36N44	76w35	5:06:20
Mineral 54	14	38N01	77w55	5:11:40
Miners Store 52	26	36N40	83w07	5:32:28
Mine Run 67	14	38N16	77w58	5:11:52
Minnieville 74	13	38N39	77w16	5:09:04
Minor 28	14	37N55	76w52	5:07:28
Mint Spring 8	21	38N04	79w06	5:16:24
Miona 1	4	37N59	75w32	5:02:08
Miskimon 51	4	37N55	76w28	5:05:52
Mission Home 39	14	38N17	78w37	5:14:28
Mitchells 24	4	38N23	78w02	5:12:08
Mitchells Store 17	22	37N52	77w27	5:09:48
Mitchelltown 9	4	38N01	79w49	5:19:16
Mobjack 57	4	37N23	76w21	5:05:24
Moccasin Gap 82	26	36N38	82w33	5:30:12
Modern 113	6	37N01	76w25	5:05:40
Modest Town 1	4	37N49	75w34	5:02:16
Moffats Creek 8	21	38N03	79w13	5:16:52
Mollusk 51	4	37N44	76w33	5:06:12
Monaskon 51	4	37N46	76w28	5:05:52
Monday 31	4	36N44	80w25	5:21:40
Moneta 10	4	37N11	79w37	5:18:28
Money Point 102	6	36N50	76w16	5:05:04
Moneys Corner 29	3	38N58	77w22	5:09:28
Monroe 5	16	37N30	79w08	5:16:32
Monroe Hall 93	19	38N15	76w58	5:07:52
Montague 28	4	37N45	76w44	5:06:56
Montebello 62	14	37N52	79w08	5:16:32
Monterey 45	4	38N25	79w35	5:18:20
Montevideo 80	22	38N23	78w48	5:15:12
Montevue 2	14	38N02	78w29	5:13:56
Montezuma 80	22	38N25	78w57	5:15:48
Montezuma Gardens 43	17	37N33	77w24	5:09:36
Montford 67	14	38N13	78w06	5:12:24
Monticello 2	14	38N02	78w29	5:13:56
Monticello Woods 29	3	38N45	77w12	5:08:48
Montpelier 42	22	37N46	77w22	5:09:28
Montpelier Station 67	14	38N14	78w11	5:12:44
Montrose 43	17	37N32	77w24	5:09:36
Montrose Heights 127	17	37N32	77w24	5:09:36
Montrose Terrace 43	17	37N32	77w24	5:09:36
Montross 93	19	38N06	76w50	5:07:20
Montvale 10	4	37N23	79w44	5:18:56
Monument Heights 43	22	37N35	77w31	5:10:04
Moon 57	4	37N29	77w35	5:10:20
Mooreland Farms 43	22	37N36	77w32	5:10:08
Moores Corner 87	4	38N25	77w24	5:09:36
Moores Store 83	14	38N41	78w41	5:14:44
Moorings 88	4	37N02	76w56	5:07:44
Moran 72	4	37N16	78w17	5:13:08
Morattico 51	4	37N47	76w38	5:06:32
Morefield 81	15	36N58	82w18	5:29:12
Morgarts Beach 46	4	36N59	76w38	5:06:32
Morningside Hills 92	15	36N43	81w58	5:27:52
Morning Star 68	14	38N40	78w27	5:13:48
Morrisdale 21	22	37N23	77w26	5:09:44
Morrison Farms 43	22	37N32	77w19	5:09:16
Morrisonville 53	4	39N16	77w38	5:10:32
Morrisville 30	19	38N30	77w42	5:10:48
Morven 4	4	37N21	77w59	5:11:56
Mosby 29	3	38N52	77w13	5:08:52
Mosby Woods 29	3	38N51	77w15	5:09:00
Moscow 8	21	38N21	79w05	5:16:20
Moseley 71	14	37N29	77w47	5:11:08
Moss Crest 29	3	38N55	77w14	5:08:56
Moss Run 3	4	37N47	79w59	5:19:56
Mossy Creek 8	21	38N23	78w59	5:15:56
Motley 70	16	37N06	79w18	5:17:12
Motorun 57	4	37N21	76w18	5:05:12
Mountain Falls 34	9	39N11	78w10	5:12:40
Mountain Gap 53	14	39N07	77w34	5:10:16
Mountain Grove 9	4	38N03	79w47	5:19:08
Mountain Lake 35	4	37N20	80w38	5:22:32
Mountain View 35	4	37N17	80w37	5:22:28
Mountain View 49	22	38N23	77w27	5:09:48
Mountain View 75	4	37N06	80w41	5:22:44
Mountain View 79	14	37N44	79w21	5:17:24
Mountain View 92	15	36N43	81w58	5:27:52
Mount Airy 70	4	36N56	79w12	5:16:48
Mount Alto 2	14	37N50	78w36	5:14:24
Mount Blanco 21	22	37N23	77w26	5:09:44
Mount Carmel 41	4	36N35	79w04	5:16:16
Mount Carmel 84	15	36N50	81w31	5:26:04
Mountcastle 63	14	37N27	77w02	5:08:08
Mount Clifton 83	14	38N45	78w39	5:14:36
Mount Clinton 80	22	38N27	78w52	5:15:28
Mount Crawford 80	22	38N21	78w56	5:15:44
Mountfair 2	14	38N04	78w42	5:14:48
Mount Garland 54	14	38N01	77w54	5:11:36
Mount Gilead 53	14	39N06	77w43	5:10:52
Mount Hermon 70	4	36N35	79w23	5:17:32
Mount Heron 14	15	37N13	82w00	5:28:00
Mount Holly 93	19	38N06	76w43	5:06:52
Mount Jackson 83	14	38N45	78w39	5:14:36
Mount Landing 28	14	37N55	76w52	5:07:28
Mount Laurel 41	4	36N50	78w44	5:14:56
Mount Meridian 8	21	38N16	78w49	5:15:16
Mount Olive 83	14	38N57	78w26	5:13:44
Mount Pisgah 8	21	38N15	78w58	5:15:52
Mount Pleasant 5	16	37N35	79w03	5:16:12
Mount Sidney 8	21	38N15	78w58	5:15:52
Mount Solon 8	21	38N21	79w05	5:16:20
Mount Tabor 60	4	37N17	80w21	5:21:24
Mount Vernon 29	3	38N39	77w06	5:08:24
Mount Vernon Cedars 29	3	38N45	77w08	5:08:32
Mount Vernon Forest 29	3	38N45	77w08	5:08:32
Mount Vernon Grove 29	3	38N45	77w08	5:08:32
Mount Vernon Hills 29	3	38N45	77w08	5:08:32
Mount Vernon Park 29	3	38N45	77w08	5:08:32
Mount Vernon Square Apartmen 29	3	38N45	77w06	5:08:24
Mount Vernon Terrace 29	3	38N45	77w08	5:08:32
Mount Vernon Valley 29	3	38N45	77w08	5:08:32
Mount Vernon Woods 29	3	38N45	77w08	5:08:32
Mountville 53	14	38N58	77w44	5:10:56
Mount Vinco 15	4	37N32	78w37	5:14:28
Mount Williams 34	9	39N11	78w10	5:12:40
Mount Zephyr 29	3	38N45	77w08	5:08:32
Mount Zion 16	16	37N10	79w05	5:16:20
Mouth of Laurel 90	4	37N05	81w46	5:27:04
Mouth of Wilson 38	4	36N35	81w20	5:25:20
Mulch 77	4	37N53	76w38	5:06:32
Mumpower 92	25	36N36	82w11	5:28:44
Munden 133	6	36N51	76w06	5:04:24
Mundy Point 65	18	37N58	76w34	5:06:16
Munson Hill 29	1	38N51	77w09	5:08:36
Murden's Corner 133	6	36N49	76w09	5:04:36
Murphy 14	15	37N14	82w06	5:28:24
Murrayfield 92	15	36N48	81w46	5:27:04
Museville 70	4	36N50	79w24	5:17:36
Musket Hills 74	2	38N47	77w28	5:09:52
Mustoe 45	4	38N20	79w39	5:18:36
Myrtle 132	5	36N44	76w35	5:06:20
Nace 12	4	37N25	79w53	5:19:32
Naffs 33	4	37N07	79w57	5:19:48
Nahor 32	4	37N51	78w16	5:13:04
Nain 34	9	39N11	78w10	5:12:40
Namozine 4	4	37N11	77w38	5:10:32
Nancy Wrights Corner 17	22	38N07	77w25	5:09:40
Nandua 1	4	37N35	75w47	5:03:08
Nansemond 132	5	36N44	76w35	5:06:20
Nansemond Shores 132	5	36N44	76w35	5:06:20
Naola 5	16	37N30	79w08	5:16:32
Narrows 35	4	37N20	80w49	5:23:16
Naruna 16	16	37N06	79w00	5:16:00
Nash Ford 81	15	36N57	82w09	5:28:36
Nashs Store 52	26	36N38	83w26	5:33:44
Nasons 67	14	38N13	78w06	5:12:24
Nassawadox 64	4	37N28	75w52	5:03:28
Nathalie 41	4	36N56	78w57	5:15:48

VIRGINIA

National Airport 7 1 38N55 77w01 5:08:04
National Heights 43 17 37N32 77w24 5:09:36
Natural Bridge 79 14 37N38 79w33 5:18:12
Natural Bridge Station 79 14 37N37 79w30 5:18:00
Natural Well 3 4 38N00 79w50 5:19:20
Naval Air Station 122 7 36N56 76w19 5:05:16
Naval Amphibious Base 133 7 36N52 76w11 5:04:44
Naval Hospital 125 7 36N51 76w18 5:05:12
Naval Weapons Station 96 11 37N12 76w27 5:05:48
Navy 29 8 38N51 77w15 5:09:00
Navy Annex 7 8 38N52 77w06 5:08:24
Navy Yard 125 7 36N49 76w18 5:05:12
Naxera 36 4 37N20 76w27 5:05:48
Neabsco 74 14 38N39 77w20 5:09:20
Nealy Ridge 26 15 37N10 82w22 5:29:28
Nebo 84 15 37N01 81w21 5:25:24
Needmore 94 15 36N59 82w38 5:30:32
Needwood 17 22 37N52 77w27 5:09:48
Neenah 93 19 38N06 76w50 5:07:20
Neersville 53 4 39N19 77w44 5:10:56
Negro Foot 42 22 37N46 77w22 5:09:28
Nellysford 62 14 37N54 78w52 5:15:28
Nelson 58 4 36N34 78w42 5:14:48
Nelson Estates 43 17 37N32 77w24 5:09:36
Nelsonia 1 4 37N49 75w35 5:02:20
Nelson Park 96 23 37N17 76w43 5:06:52
Nethers 56 4 38N34 78w17 5:13:08
Nettleridge 69 4 36N38 80w16 5:21:04
New Alexandria 29 1 38N48 77w03 5:08:12
New Baltimore 30 19 38N44 77w44 5:10:56
Newbern 75 4 37N04 80w42 5:22:48
New Bohemia 73 22 37N08 77w14 5:08:56
New Canton 15 4 37N42 78w18 5:13:12
New Castle 23 4 37N30 80w07 5:20:28
New Church 1 4 37N59 75w32 5:02:08
Newcomb Hall 101 14 38N02 78w29 5:13:56
New Copley Hill 2 14 38N02 78w29 5:13:56
New Design 106 4 36N35 79w23 5:17:32
New Garden 81 15 37N03 81w58 5:27:52
New Glasgow 5 16 37N35 79w03 5:16:12
New Hampden 45 4 38N30 79w33 5:18:12
New Hope 8 21 38N12 78w54 5:15:36
New Hope 19 14 37N20 77w04 5:08:16
Newington 29 3 38N40 77w11 5:08:44
Newington Station 29 3 38N47 77w12 5:08:48
Newington Woods 29 3 38N47 77w12 5:08:48
New Kent 63 14 37N31 76w59 5:07:56
Newland 77 4 37N58 76w46 5:07:04
New London 16 16 37N22 79w17 5:17:08
New Market 83 14 38N39 78w40 5:14:40
New Point 57 4 37N21 76w17 5:05:08
Newport 35 4 37N18 80w30 5:22:00
Newport 46 4 36N56 76w36 5:06:24
Newport 68 14 38N29 78w37 5:14:28
Newport News 121 6 36N59 76w25 5:05:40
New Post 86 22 38N23 77w27 5:09:48
New Quarry 84 15 36N53 81w46 5:27:04
New River 75 4 37N08 80w35 5:22:20
News Ferry 41 4 36N43 78w54 5:15:36
Newsoms 85 4 36N38 77w08 5:08:32
New Store 15 4 37N18 78w24 5:13:36
Newtown 48 4 37N55 77w08 5:08:32
Newtown 51 4 37N46 76w28 5:05:52
Newtown 80 14 38N25 78w36 5:14:24
New Upton 36 4 37N25 76w32 5:06:08
Newville 73 22 37N08 77w14 5:08:56
Newville 89 4 36N52 77w11 5:08:44
Niceleytown 3 4 37N49 79w50 5:19:20
Nickelsville 82 26 36N45 82w25 5:29:40
Niday 11 4 37N20 80w48 5:23:12
Nightingale Trailer Park 29 3 38N45 77w06 5:08:24
Nimmo 133 6 36N49 76w09 5:04:36
Nimrod Hall 9 4 37N59 79w36 5:18:24
Ninde 49 12 38N16 77w03 5:08:12
Nineveh 91 14 38N55 78w12 5:12:48
Nokesville 74 14 38N42 77w35 5:10:20
Nomini Grove 93 19 38N02 76w45 5:07:00
Nora 26 15 37N04 82w21 5:29:24
Nordick 92 15 36N42 82w18 5:29:12
Norfolk 122 6 36N51 76w17 5:05:08
Norfolk Highlands 102 6 36N49 76w14 5:04:56
Norge 47 14 37N22 76w46 5:07:04
Norland 26 15 37N09 82w27 5:29:48
Norman 24 14 38N28 78w00 5:12:00
North 7 1 38N54 77w08 5:08:32
North 57 4 37N27 76w25 5:05:40
North Anna 42 22 37N52 77w27 5:09:48
North Bristol 99 25 36N36 82w11 5:28:44
Northeast 33 4 37N05 79w48 5:19:12
North Emporia 107 20 36N41 77w32 5:10:08
North Fork 53 14 39N10 77w43 5:10:52
North Fork 84 15 36N55 81w38 5:26:32
North Gap 11 4 37N14 81w06 5:24:24
North Grundy 14 15 37N19 82w03 5:28:12
North Holston 84 15 36N53 81w46 5:27:04
North Jerico 132 5 36N44 76w35 5:06:20
North Linkhorn Park 133 6 36N52 76w00 5:04:00
North Pine Ridge 29 3 38N51 77w15 5:09:00
North Pulaski 75 4 37N05 80w46 5:23:04
North Run Hills 43 17 37N36 77w29 5:09:56
Northside 127 17 37N34 77w26 5:09:44
North Springfield 29 3 38N48 77w12 5:08:48
North Stanton 41 4 36N56 78w57 5:15:48
North Tazewell 90 4 37N08 81w31 5:26:04
North View 58 4 36N43 78w14 5:12:56
North Virginia Beach 133 6 36N52 76w00 5:04:00
North Wellville 66 4 37N05 78w00 5:12:00
Northwest 33 4 37N04 79w59 5:19:56
Northwest 102 4 36N41 76w16 5:05:04
North Woodley 29 1 38N53 77w13 5:08:52
Norton 123 15 36N56 82w38 5:30:32
Nortonsville 2 14 38N15 78w32 5:14:08
Norvello 58 4 36N40 78w23 5:13:32
Norview 122 6 36N53 76w14 5:04:56
Norwood 10 4 37N22 79w17 5:17:08
Norwood 62 14 37N39 78w49 5:15:16
Nottingham 82 26 36N38 82w34 5:30:16
Nottoway 66 4 37N08 78w05 5:12:20
Novelty 33 4 36N59 79w38 5:18:32
Novum 56 4 38N29 78w08 5:12:32
Nurney 132 5 36N44 76w35 5:06:20
Nurneysville 132 5 36N44 76w35 5:06:20
Nutbush 55 4 36N59 78w14 5:12:56
Nuttall 36 4 37N25 76w32 5:06:08
Nuttsville 51 4 37N48 76w33 5:06:12
Oak 63 14 37N24 76w55 5:07:40
Oak Forest 25 4 37N30 78w15 5:13:00
Oak Grove 18 4 36N43 80w49 5:23:16
Oak Grove 53 4 38N58 77w22 5:09:28
Oak Grove 65 18 37N50 76w26 5:05:44
Oak Grove 93 19 38N15 76w58 5:07:52
Oak Grove 102 6 36N46 76w21 5:05:24
Oak Hall 1 4 37N56 75w33 5:02:12
Oak Hill 43 17 37N33 77w24 5:09:36
Oak Hill 68 14 38N46 78w23 5:13:32
Oakhurst 73 22 37N13 77w26 5:09:44
Oaklette 102 6 36N49 76w14 5:04:56
Oak Level 41 4 36N46 78w56 5:15:44
Oaklevel 44 4 36N46 79w59 5:19:56
Oakley 28 4 37N48 76w47 5:07:08
Oakley 78 4 37N17 80w03 5:20:12
Oakpark 56 4 38N22 78w10 5:12:40
Oak Ridge 29 3 38N55 77w14 5:08:56
Oakridge 132 5 36N44 76w35 5:06:20
Oakridge Estates 74 2 38N47 77w28 5:09:52
Oakridge Estates 132 5 36N44 76w35 5:06:20
Oakshade 24 4 38N35 77w59 5:11:56
Oakton 29 3 38N53 77w18 5:09:12
Oaktree 53 4 39N00 77w24 5:09:36
Oaktree 96 23 37N17 76w43 5:06:52
Oak Valley 29 3 38N55 77w14 5:08:56
Oak Valley Estates 29 3 38N55 77w14 5:08:56
Oak View 43 17 37N36 77w29 5:09:56
Oakville 6 4 37N21 78w50 5:15:20
Oakwood 14 15 37N13 82w00 5:28:00
Oakwood 29 3 38N43 77w09 5:08:36
Oatlands 53 14 39N07 77w34 5:10:16
Occoquan 74 13 38N41 77w16 5:09:04
Occupacia 28 4 38N03 77w01 5:08:04
Oceana 133 6 36N48 76w01 5:04:04
Oceana Gardens 133 6 36N48 76w01 5:04:04
Oceana Naval Air Station 133 7 36N49 76w02 5:04:08
Ocean Park 133 6 36N53 76w08 5:04:32
Ocean View 122 6 36N56 76w15 5:05:00
Ocoonita 52 26 36N40 83w07 5:32:28
Odricks Corner 29 1 38N55 77w11 5:08:44
Office Hall 49 22 38N16 77w11 5:08:44
Oilville 37 4 37N42 77w47 5:11:08
Olaf 78 4 37N17 80w03 5:20:12
Old 38 4 36N37 80w57 5:23:48
Old Church 42 22 37N37 77w22 5:09:28
Old Creek Estates 29 3 38N51 77w15 5:09:00
Old Dominion 2 14 37N47 78w42 5:14:48
Old Dominion Gardens 29 1 38N55 77w11 5:08:44
Olde Forge 29 3 38N51 77w15 5:09:00
Olde Towne 97 1 38N49 77w05 5:08:20
Oldewood 29 3 38N54 77w13 5:08:52
Oldfield 133 6 36N52 76w00 5:04:00
Old Glade Spring 92 15 36N48 81w46 5:27:04
Oldhams 93 19 38N00 76w40 5:06:40
Old Somerset 67 14 38N13 78w13 5:12:52
Old Tavern 30 19 38N52 77w46 5:11:04
Oldtown 38 4 36N40 80w55 5:23:40
Old Well 20 4 37N05 78w45 5:15:00
Olinger 52 26 36N56 82w47 5:31:08
Olive 125 6 36N49 76w21 5:05:24
Oliver Estates 29 3 39N00 77w15 5:09:00
Omaha 26 15 37N09 82w27 5:29:48
Omega 41 4 36N43 78w54 5:15:36
Onancock 1 4 37N43 75w45 5:03:00
Onemo 57 4 37N24 76w16 5:05:04
Onley 1 4 37N41 75w43 5:02:52
Ontario 20 4 37N00 78w36 5:14:24
Opal 30 19 38N44 77w44 5:10:56
Opequon 34 4 39N04 78w13 5:12:52
Ophelia 65 18 37N55 76w17 5:05:08
Oranda 83 14 39N00 78w22 5:13:28
Orange 67 14 38N15 78w07 5:12:28
Orange Hunt 29 3 38N45 77w12 5:08:48
Orbit 46 4 36N49 76w45 5:07:00
Orchid 54 14 38N01 77w54 5:11:36
Ordinary 36 4 37N19 76w31 5:06:04
Ore Bank 15 4 37N41 78w20 5:13:20
Oreton 94 26 36N56 82w47 5:31:08
Oriskany 12 4 37N37 79w59 5:19:56
Orkney Springs 83 14 38N48 78w49 5:15:16
Orlando 132 5 36N44 76w35 5:06:20
Orlean 30 19 38N45 77w58 5:11:52
Orleans Village 29 1 38N49 77w09 5:08:36
Oronoco 5 16 37N54 79w12 5:16:48
Osaka 94 26 36N54 82w47 5:31:08
Osbornes Chapel 52 26 36N38 83w03 5:32:12
Osborns Gap 26 15 37N09 82w27 5:29:48
Osborns Store 90 4 36N58 81w38 5:26:32
Osbos 10 4 37N27 79w31 5:18:04
Osceola 92 15 36N43 81w58 5:27:52
Osso 49 22 38N23 77w27 5:09:48
Otey 60 4 37N10 80w15 5:21:00
Othma 37 4 37N45 77w55 5:11:40
Otter Hill 10 4 37N20 79w31 5:18:04
Otter River 16 16 37N09 79w18 5:17:12
Otterville 10 4 37N20 79w31 5:18:04
Ottobine 80 22 38N25 78w57 5:15:48
Ottoman 51 4 37N46 76w28 5:05:52
Overall 68 14 38N50 78w19 5:13:16
Owens 49 22 38N20 77w12 5:08:48
Owenton 48 4 37N53 77w06 5:08:24
Ox Hill 29 3 38N54 77w26 5:09:44
Oyster 64 4 37N17 75w55 5:03:40
Ozeana 28 4 37N51 76w49 5:07:16
Paces 41 4 36N43 78w54 5:15:36
Paeonian Springs 53 14 39N09 77w37 5:10:28
Page 14 15 37N13 82w00 5:28:00
Page 17 22 38N07 77w25 5:09:40
Page Hollow 84 15 36N53 81w46 5:27:04
Paineville 4 4 37N18 78w06 5:12:24
Paint Bank 23 4 37N34 80w16 5:21:04
Painter 1 4 37N35 75w47 5:03:08
Paint Lick 90 4 37N05 81w43 5:26:52
Palls 50 14 37N41 77w01 5:08:04
Palmer 51 14 37N39 76w23 5:05:32
Palmer Crossroads 58 4 36N27 78w12 5:12:48
Palmer Springs 58 4 36N34 78w17 5:13:08
Palmyra 32 4 37N52 78w16 5:13:04
Palmyra 132 5 36N44 76w35 5:06:20
Palos 80 22 38N40 78w55 5:15:40
Pampa 36 4 37N25 76w32 5:06:08
Pamplin City 6 4 37N16 78w41 5:14:44
Panoramic Hills 29 1 38N50 77w12 5:08:48
Pardee 94 26 37N00 82w45 5:31:00
Paris 30 19 39N00 77w57 5:11:48
Park 84 15 36N51 81w34 5:26:16
Park 134 22 38N04 78w54 5:15:36
Parker 86 22 38N18 77w49 5:11:16
Parkfairfax 97 1 38N50 77w05 5:08:20
Parklawn 29 1 38N49 77w09 5:08:36
Park Lee Place 21 22 37N27 77w28 5:09:52
Parksley 1 4 37N47 75w39 5:02:36
Park View 80 22 38N27 78w52 5:15:28
Parkview 102 6 36N46 76w21 5:05:24
Parkview 121 6 37N01 76w26 5:05:44
Parkwood 29 1 38N51 77w09 5:08:36
Parkwood Estates 92 25 36N36 82w11 5:28:44
Parnassus 8 21 37N48 76w31 5:06:04
Parrish Court 105 4 37N47 79w59 5:19:56
Parrott 75 4 37N12 80w37 5:22:28
Partlow 86 22 38N02 77w38 5:10:32
Passapatanzy 49 22 38N23 77w27 5:09:48
Passing 17 22 38N03 77w21 5:09:24
Pastoria 1 4 37N47 75w39 5:02:36
Pastures 8 21 38N11 79w15 5:17:00
Patna 45 4 38N12 79w34 5:18:16
Patrick Henry 16 16 37N07 79w00 5:16:00
Patrick Henry Heights 42 22 37N37 77w22 5:09:28
Patrick Springs 69 4 36N39 80w12 5:20:48
Patterson 14 15 37N16 81w58 5:27:52
Pattersons Store 63 14 37N32 77w10 5:08:40
Pattonsville 82 26 36N43 82w48 5:31:12
Pauls Cross Roads 28 4 37N52 76w55 5:07:40
Paytes 86 22 38N13 77w49 5:11:16
Peach Bottom 38 4 36N40 80w55 5:23:40
Peaks 10 4 37N27 79w31 5:18:04
Peaks 42 22 37N46 77w22 5:09:28
Peapatch 14 15 37N11 81w48 5:27:12
Pearch 10 14 37N26 79w11 5:16:44
Pearisburg 35 4 37N20 80w44 5:22:56
Pearly 14 15 37N17 82w06 5:28:24
Peary 57 4 37N22 76w17 5:05:08
Pedlar 5 16 37N37 79w15 5:17:00
Pedlar Mills 5 16 37N30 79w08 5:16:32
Pedro 28 4 38N06 77w08 5:08:32
Pemberton 37 4 37N41 77w53 5:11:32
Pembroke 35 4 37N19 80w38 5:22:32
Pembroke Manor 133 6 36N51 76w09 5:04:36
Pender 29 3 38N52 77w22 5:09:28
Penderbrook 29 3 38N51 77w15 5:09:00
Penderwood 29 3 38N53 77w18 5:09:12
Pendletons 54 14 38N01 77w54 5:11:36
Penhook 33 4 36N59 79w38 5:18:32
Penn Daw 29 1 38N47 77w05 5:08:20
Penn Daw Terrace 29 1 38N46 77w04 5:08:16

Pennington Gap 52
26 36N46 83W02 5:32:08
Penn Laird 80 22 38N23 78W48 5:15:12
Pennsand 82 26 36N38 82W34 5:30:16
Penns Store 69 4 36N37 80W00 5:20:00
Penola 17 22 37N55 77W29 5:09:56
Pentagon 7 1 38N52 77W06 5:08:24
Penvir 35 4 37N20 80W48 5:23:12
Peola Mills 56 4 38N39 78W14 5:12:56
Pepper 60 4 37N08 80W34 5:22:16
Perrin 36 4 37N17 76W30 5:06:00
Perrowville 10 4 37N22 79W17 5:17:08
Perryville 84 15 36N53 81W46 5:27:04
Perth 41 4 36N56 78W57 5:15:48
Petersburg 124 22 37N14 77W24 5:09:36
Peters Creek 69 4 36N36 80W17 5:21:08
Peterson Chapel 82
26 36N43 82W48 5:31:12
Petsworth 36 4 37N29 76W37 5:06:28
Phenix 20 4 37N05 78W45 5:15:00
Philadelphia 132 5 36N44 76W35 5:06:20
Philbeck Crossroads 58
4 36N42 78W30 5:14:00
Phillip 92 25 36N36 82W11 5:28:44
Phillis 58 4 36N40 78W23 5:13:32
Philomont 53 4 39N03 77W44 5:10:56
Philpott 44 4 36N46 79W59 5:19:56
Phlegar 35 4 37N20 80W48 5:23:12
Phoebus 113 4 37N01 76W19 5:05:16
Piankitank 57 4 37N29 76W20 5:05:20
Pickadat Corner 21
22 37N23 77W28 5:09:52
Pickaway 70 4 36N45 79W06 5:16:24
Pickwick 29 3 38N48 77W20 5:09:20
Pico 12 4 37N32 79W41 5:18:44
Piedmont 8 21 38N16 78W49 5:15:16
Piedmont 76 14 38N40 78W14 5:12:56
Pierces Corner 51 4 37N46 76W28 5:05:52
Pierces Shop 67 14 38N13 78W06 5:12:24
Pigg River 70 4 36N59 79W28 5:17:52
Pilgrams Knob 14 15 37N15 81W55 5:27:40
Pilot 60 4 37N03 80W22 5:21:28
Pimmit Hills 29 3 38N55 77W13 5:08:52
Pine 75 4 37N00 80W45 5:23:00
Pineaire 132 5 36N44 76W35 5:06:20
Pine Creek 18 4 36N50 80W42 5:22:48
Pinecrest 29 1 38N49 77W09 5:08:36
Pinecrest Heights 29
1 38N50 77W12 5:08:48
Pinedale 43 22 37N36 77W32 5:10:08
Pine Grove 68 14 38N35 78W30 5:14:00
Pine Grove 92 15 36N42 82W18 5:29:12
Pine Hill 42 22 37N37 77W22 5:09:28
Pine Ridge 29 3 38N51 77W15 5:09:00
Pinero 36 4 37N30 76W32 5:06:08
Pine Springs 29 3 38N52 77W13 5:08:52
Pinetia 102 6 36N49 76W14 5:04:56
Pine Top 59 4 37N34 76W25 5:05:40
Pine Tree 71 14 37N39 78W05 5:12:20
Pinetta 36 4 37N25 76W32 5:06:08
Pineville 80 22 38N22 78W44 5:14:56
Pinewood Gardens 133
6 36N51 76W07 5:04:28
Pinewood Lawns 29 3 38N45 77W08 5:08:32
Pinewood Park 74 2 38N47 77W28 5:09:52
Pinewood South 29 3 38N45 77W08 5:08:32
Piney Grove 41 4 36N45 78W47 5:15:08
Piney River 62 14 37N43 79W02 5:16:08
Piney Run 29 3 38N43 77W09 5:08:36
Piper Gap 18 4 36N40 80W49 5:23:16
Pipers Gap 18 4 36N40 80W55 5:23:40
Pisgah 90 4 37N08 81W31 5:26:04
Pitmans Corner 51 4 37N39 76W27 5:05:48
Pittston 70 4 36N37 79W12 5:16:48
Pittsville 70 4 36N59 79W28 5:17:52
Plains 80 22 38N38 78W49 5:15:16
Plain View 48 4 37N30 76W30 5:06:00
Plasterco 92 15 36N53 81W46 5:27:04
Pleasant Gap 70 4 36N45 79W24 5:17:36
Pleasant Grove 55 4 37N02 78W23 5:13:32
Pleasant Grove 58 4 36N44 78W07 5:12:28
Pleasant Hill 80 22 38N27 78W52 5:15:28
Pleasant Hill 132 5 36N43 76W35 5:06:20
Pleasant Ridge 29 1 38N50 77W12 5:08:48
Pleasant Ridge 133
6 36N52 76W00 5:04:00
Pleasant Shade 40
20 36N41 77W32 5:10:08
Pleasant Valley 53
4 38N54 77W26 5:09:44
Pleasant Valley 80
22 38N23 78W54 5:15:36
Pleasantview 5 16 37N30 79W08 5:16:32
Plum Creek 92 15 36N48 81W46 5:27:04
Plum Point 63 14 37N33 76W48 5:07:12
Plum Tree 54 14 37N58 77W46 5:11:04
Plunkettsville 131
21 38N09 79W05 5:16:20
Plymouth 55 4 37N00 78W11 5:12:44
Plymouth Park 102 6 36N49 76W14 5:04:56
Poages Mill 78 4 37N15 80W01 5:20:04
Pocahontas 90 4 37N18 81W21 5:25:24
Pocahontas Village 133
6 36N51 76W09 5:04:36
Pocoshock 127 17 37N29 77W33 5:10:12
Poetown 14 15 37N17 82W06 5:28:24
Poff 31 4 36N54 80W16 5:21:04
Pohick 29 3 38N43 77W12 5:08:48
Pohick Estates 29 3 38N42 77W14 5:08:56
Pohick River Pines 29
3 38N42 77W14 5:08:56
Poindexters 42 22 37N45 77W29 5:09:56
Point Eastern 17 22 37N55 77W29 5:09:56
Point of View 133 6 36N51 76W09 5:04:36
Point of Woods 74 2 38N47 77W28 5:09:52
Point Pleasant 11 4 37N06 81W07 5:24:28
Pole Green 42 22 37N37 77W22 5:09:28
Pollard 4 4 37N18 78W06 5:12:24
Pons 46 4 36N54 76W54 5:07:36
Poole 27 22 37N11 77W38 5:10:32
Poplar Camp 95 4 36N53 80W51 5:23:24
Poplar Cove 1 4 37N43 75W44 5:02:56
Poplar Heights 29 1 38N53 77W13 5:08:52
Poplar Hill 29 1 38N50 77W12 5:08:48
Poplar Hill 35 4 37N20 80W44 5:22:56
Poplar Inn 17 22 38N01 77W22 5:09:28
Poquoson 96 4 37N08 76W24 5:05:36
Port Dumfries 74 14 38N33 77W19 5:09:16
Porter 2 14 37N50 78W36 5:14:24
Porters Cross Roads 95
4 36N57 81W05 5:24:20
Port Haywood 57 4 37N23 76W19 5:05:16
Portlock 102 6 36N50 76W16 5:05:04
Port Republic 80 22 38N18 78W49 5:15:16
Port Richmond 50 14 37N33 76W48 5:07:12
Port Royal 17 22 38N10 77W12 5:08:48
Portsmouth 125 6 36N50 76W18 5:05:12
Post Oak 86 22 38N12 77W35 5:10:20
Potato Creek 38 4 36N35 81W20 5:25:20
Potomac 49 22 38N19 77W08 5:08:32
Potomac 97 1 38N49 77W04 5:08:16
Potomac Beach 93 19 38N15 76W58 5:07:52
Potomac Hills 29 1 38N55 77W11 5:08:44
Potomac Mills 93 19 38N06 76W50 5:07:20
Potomac Run 87 4 38N23 77W27 5:09:48
Potters Flats 26 15 37N19 82W21 5:29:24
Poulson 1 4 37N51 75W36 5:02:24
Pound 94 15 37N08 82W36 5:30:24
Pounding Mill 90 4 37N05 81W43 5:26:52
Powcan 48 4 37N47 77W00 5:08:00
Powell 82 26 36N39 82W51 5:31:24
Powells Corner 133
6 36N51 76W09 5:04:36
Powells Store 10 4 37N32 79W22 5:17:28
Powell Store 2 14 37N50 78W36 5:14:24
Powellton 13 4 36N39 77W47 5:11:08
Powhatan 71 14 37N32 77W55 5:11:40
Prater 14 15 37N12 82W07 5:28:28
Pratts 56 4 38N21 78W16 5:13:04
Premier 90 4 37N07 81W52 5:27:28
Preston 44 4 36N40 79W52 5:19:28
Preston Hills 92 25 36N36 82W11 5:28:44
Preston King 7 1 38N53 77W08 5:08:32
Prices Fork 60 4 37N13 80W27 5:21:48
Prices Store 5 14 37N25 79W08 5:16:32
Prilliman 33 4 36N55 80W01 5:20:04
Prince George 73 22 37N13 77W17 5:09:08
Princess Anne 133 6 36N49 76W09 5:04:36
Princess Anne Hills 133
6 36N52 76W00 5:04:00
Princess Anne Plaza 133
6 36N51 76W07 5:04:28
Proffit 2 14 38N02 78W29 5:13:56
Proffits Store 32 4 37N48 78W29 5:13:56
Progress 33 4 36N59 79W38 5:18:32
Prospect 72 4 37N18 78W34 5:14:16
Prospectdale 35 4 37N20 80W44 5:22:56
Prospect Hill 29 1 38N55 77W11 5:08:44
Providence 41 4 36N56 78W57 5:15:48
Providence Church 132
5 36N44 76W35 5:06:20
Providence Forge 63
14 37N27 77W02 5:08:08
Providence Park 43
17 37N34 77W26 5:09:44
Providence Terrace 102
6 36N50 76W16 5:05:04
Provost 71 14 37N29 77W55 5:11:40
Public Fork 41 4 36N56 78W40 5:14:40
Pulaski 75 4 37N03 80W47 5:23:08
Pullens 70 4 36N34 79W44 5:18:56
Pumpkin Center 11 4 37N06 81W07 5:24:28
Pungo 133 6 36N49 76W09 5:04:36
Pungoteague 1 4 37N36 75W47 5:03:08
Purcellville 53 14 39N08 77W43 5:10:52
Purchase 82 26 36N41 82W45 5:31:00
Purdy 40 20 36N49 77W36 5:10:24
Puryear Corner 58 4 36N37 78W34 5:14:16
Putnam 81 15 37N01 81W59 5:27:56
Quail Oaks 21 22 37N27 77W28 5:09:52
Quantico 74 11 38N31 77W17 5:09:08
Quantico Station 74
11 38N31 77W18 5:09:12
Quarry 84 15 36N53 81W46 5:27:04
Queens Lake 96 23 37N17 76W43 5:06:52
Quicksburg 83 14 38N41 78W41 5:14:44
Quicks Mill 8 21 38N09 79W05 5:16:20
Quinby 1 4 37N33 75W44 5:02:56
Quinque 39 14 38N15 78W24 5:13:36
Quinton 63 14 37N32 77W10 5:08:40
Quoit 31 4 36N44 80W25 5:21:40
Rabat 41 4 36N56 78W57 5:15:48
Raccoon Ford 24 14 38N28 78W00 5:12:00
Radford 126 4 37N08 80W35 5:22:20
Radford College 126
4 37N08 80W34 5:22:16
Radiant 56 4 38N19 78W13 5:12:52
Ragged Point Beach 93
19 38N09 76W38 5:06:32
Rainswood 65 18 37N55 76W28 5:05:52
Ralco 55 4 36N58 78W07 5:12:28
Raleigh Heights 102
6 36N50 76W16 5:05:04
Ramoth 87 4 38N25 77W24 5:09:36
Ramsey 123 15 36N59 82W38 5:30:32
Randolph 20 4 36N54 78W42 5:14:48
Randolph 25 4 37N22 78W22 5:13:28
Randolph Corner 53
4 39N07 77W50 5:11:20
Random Hill 29 3 38N51 77W15 5:09:00

Rangeley 44 4 36N42 79W57 5:19:48
Ransons 15 4 37N33 78W28 5:13:52
Raphine 79 14 37N56 79W14 5:16:56
Rapidan 24 4 38N19 78W04 5:12:16
Rappahannock Academy 17
22 38N11 77W17 5:09:08
Rapps Mill 79 14 37N47 79W26 5:17:44
Raven 90 4 37N05 81W52 5:27:28
Ravensworth 29 3 38N49 77W13 5:08:52
Ravensworth Farms 29
3 38N49 77W13 5:08:52
Ravensworth Grove 29
1 38N50 77W12 5:08:48
Ravensworth Park 29
1 38N50 77W12 5:08:48
Ravenwood 29 1 38N52 77W12 5:08:48
Rawhide 52 26 36N52 82W54 5:31:36
Rawley Springs 80
22 38N28 78W58 5:15:52
Rawlings 13 4 36N57 77W47 5:11:08
Raymondale 29 3 38N52 77W13 5:08:52
Raynor 46 4 36N54 76W54 5:07:36
Rayo 86 22 38N12 77W35 5:10:20
Rayon Terrace 105 4 37N47 79W59 5:19:56
Readus 83 14 38N49 78W34 5:14:16
Reba 10 4 37N20 79W31 5:18:04
Rectortown 30 19 38N55 77W52 5:11:28
Red Apple Orchard 62
14 37N43 78W51 5:15:24
Redart 57 4 37N28 76W18 5:05:12
Red Ash 90 4 37N07 81W52 5:27:28
Red Bank 41 4 36N37 78W46 5:15:04
Red Bank 64 4 37N27 75W51 5:03:24
Red Eye 70 4 36N50 79W24 5:17:36
Red Fox Forest 29 1 38N50 77W12 5:08:48
Red Hill 2 14 37N57 78W38 5:14:32
Red House 20 4 37N11 78W49 5:15:16
Redlawn 58 4 36N36 78W09 5:12:36
Red Mills 8 21 38N09 78W51 5:15:24
Red Oak 13 4 36N54 77W52 5:11:28
Red Oak 20 4 36N47 78W37 5:14:28
Red Valley 33 4 37N04 79W53 5:19:32
Redwood 33 4 37N01 79W49 5:19:16
Reed Creek 44 4 36N46 79W56 5:19:44
Reed Creek 52 26 36N52 82W54 5:31:36
Reedtown 133 6 36N53 76W08 5:04:32
Reedville 65 18 37N51 76W17 5:05:08
Reedy Church 17 22 37N53 77W22 5:09:28
Reese Shop 20 4 36N54 78W42 5:14:48
Reflection Place 29
3 38N58 77W22 5:09:28
Refuge 34 4 39N06 78W13 5:12:52
Regina 51 4 37N48 76W25 5:05:40
Rehoboth 55 4 36N55 78W24 5:13:36
Rehoboth Church 51
14 37N43 76W23 5:05:32
Reids Ferry 132 5 36N44 76W35 5:06:20
Reids Grove 29 1 38N55 77W11 5:08:44
Reliance 91 14 39N00 78W15 5:13:00
Relief 34 9 39N11 78W10 5:12:40
Remington 30 19 38N32 77W49 5:11:16
Remlik 59 4 37N38 76W34 5:06:16
Remo 65 18 37N49 76W23 5:05:32
Renan 70 4 36N57 79W22 5:17:28
Republican Grove 41
4 36N57 79W03 5:16:12
Rescue 46 4 37N00 76W34 5:06:16
Reservoir Hill 105
4 37N47 79W59 5:19:56
Rest 34 4 39N15 78W06 5:12:24
Reston 29 3 38N58 77W21 5:09:24
Retreat 33 4 37N00 79W53 5:19:32
Return 17 22 38N10 77W12 5:08:48
Reva 24 4 38N29 78W08 5:12:32
Rexburg 28 14 37N55 76W52 5:07:28
Reynolds Store 34 4 39N19 78W18 5:13:12
Rhoadesville 67 14 38N12 77W55 5:11:40
Rhodes 46 4 36N49 76W45 5:07:00
Rice 72 4 37N16 78W17 5:13:08
Riceville 70 4 36N50 79W14 5:16:56
Richardson 18 4 36N46 80W44 5:22:56
Richardsville 24 4 38N24 77W44 5:10:56
Rich Creek 35 4 37N23 80W49 5:23:16
Richfield 78 4 37N16 80W02 5:20:08
Richlands 90 4 37N06 81W48 5:27:12
Richmond 127 17 37N33 77W27 5:09:48
Richmond Beach 28
14 37N55 76W52 5:07:28
Richmond Heights 43
17 37N32 77W24 5:09:36
Richpatch 3 4 37N47 79W59 5:19:56
Rich Valley 84 15 36N53 81W46 5:27:04
Ridge 43 22 37N36 77W32 5:10:08
Ridgecrest 29 3 38N53 77W18 5:09:12
Ridgelea Estates 29
3 38N51 77W15 5:09:00
Ridge Manor 29 3 38N51 77W15 5:09:00
Ridge View 29 3 38N43 77W09 5:08:36
Ridgeway 41 4 36N45 79W06 5:16:24
Ridgeway 44 4 36N35 79W52 5:19:28
Riggs 82 26 36N41 82W45 5:31:00
Rileyville 68 14 38N46 78W23 5:13:32
Riner 60 4 37N04 80W27 5:21:48
Ringgold 70 4 36N36 79W18 5:17:12
Ripplemead 35 4 37N20 80W41 5:22:44
Rip Rap 41 4 36N33 78W47 5:15:08
Rivanna 2 14 38N06 78W23 5:13:32
Riverdale 41 4 36N43 78W54 5:15:36
Riverdale 85 4 36N39 77W02 5:08:08
Riverdale 113 6 37N01 76W25 5:05:40
Riverhead 8 21 38N01 79W09 5:16:36
Rivermont 8 21 38N01 79W02 5:16:08
Rivermont 21 22 37N23 77W26 5:09:44
Rivermont 105 4 37N47 79W59 5:19:56
Rivermont 117 14 37N26 79W11 5:16:44

River Oaks 29	1	38N55	77w11	5:08:44
Riverside 79	14	37N44	79w21	5:17:24
Riverside Estates 29	3	38N45	77w08	5:08:32
Riverside Gardens 29	1	38N45	77w04	5:08:16
Riverside Park Homes 102	6	36N49	76w14	5:04:56
Riverton 91	14	38N57	78w12	5:12:48
Riverview 94	15	37N00	82w28	5:29:52
Riverview Marina Apartments 74	13	38N39	77w16	5:09:04
Riverville 5	16	37N33	78w52	5:15:28
Rives 73	22	37N11	77w21	5:09:24
Rixeyville 24	4	38N35	77w59	5:11:56
Roanes 36	4	37N25	76w32	5:06:08
Roanoke 128	4	37N16	79w56	5:19:44
Roaringfork 94	26	36N58	82w47	5:31:08
Roaring Park 94	26	36N58	82w47	5:31:08
Roaring Run 12	4	37N32	79w41	5:18:44
Robbin Dale Farms 43	22	37N33	77w22	5:09:28
Robbins Chapel 52	26	36N52	82w54	5:31:36
Robbins Corner 133	6	36N53	76w08	5:04:32
Roberson 94	15	37N06	82w36	5:30:24
Roberts 47	14	37N13	76w38	5:06:32
Robertson 56	4	38N27	78w14	5:12:56
Robertsons 10	4	37N20	79w31	5:18:04
Robin Park 43	22	37N32	77w19	5:09:16
Robinson 75	4	37N03	80w50	5:23:20
Robinwood 43	17	37N32	77w24	5:09:36
Robley 77	4	37N53	76w38	5:06:32
Robnel 118	2	38N47	77w28	5:09:52
Rochelle 56	4	38N17	78w16	5:13:04
Rockbridge Baths 79	14	37N54	79w24	5:17:36
Rock Castle 37	4	37N41	77w53	5:11:32
Rockdell 81	15	36N53	81w57	5:27:48
Rockfish 62	14	37N57	78w51	5:15:24
Rock Hill 87	4	38N27	77w28	5:09:52
Rockland 91	14	38N55	78w12	5:12:48
Rockland Village 29	3	38N54	77w26	5:09:44
Rock Lick 14	15	37N20	82w10	5:28:40
Rock Mills 76	14	38N36	78w06	5:12:24
Rock Springs 21	22	37N27	77w28	5:09:52
Rock Springs 29	1	38N51	77w09	5:08:36
Rocktown 92	25	36N36	82w11	5:28:44
Rockville 42	22	37N43	77w41	5:10:44
Rocky Gap 11	4	37N15	81w06	5:24:24
Rocky Mount 33	4	37N00	79w53	5:19:32
Rocky Station 52	26	36N46	83w01	5:32:04
Roda 94	26	36N58	82w47	5:31:08
Rodden 41	4	36N56	78w57	5:15:48
Rodophil 4	4	37N18	78w06	5:12:24
Roetown 92	15	36N38	81w47	5:27:08
Rogers 60	4	37N04	80w27	5:21:48
Rohoic 27	22	37N12	77w27	5:09:48
Rolling Brook 74	13	38N39	77w16	5:09:04
Rolling Hill 20	4	37N11	78w49	5:15:16
Rolling Hills 29	3	38N45	77w08	5:08:32
Rolling Valley 29	3	38N45	77w12	5:08:48
Rollins Fork 49	22	38N11	77w04	5:08:16
Roman 8	21	38N15	78w58	5:15:52
Rondo 70	4	36N50	79w24	5:17:36
Roosevelt Park 43	17	37N33	77w24	5:09:36
Roseann 14	15	37N21	82w03	5:28:12
Rose Bower 6	4	37N21	78w50	5:15:20
Rosedale 81	15	36N58	81w56	5:27:44
Rosehill 82	26	36N40	83w22	5:33:28
Rose Hill 29	3	38N43	77w09	5:08:36
Rose Hill Farms 29	1	38N47	77w07	5:08:28
Roseland 62	14	37N46	78w59	5:15:56
Rosemont 29	1	38N55	77w11	5:08:44
Rosemont 132	5	36N44	76w35	5:06:20
Rosemont 133	6	36N51	76w07	5:04:28
Roseville 87	4	38N25	77w24	5:09:36
Roslyn Hills 43	22	37N36	77w32	5:10:08
Rosslyn 7	1	38N53	77w05	5:08:20
Roth 14	15	37N16	81w58	5:27:52
Rough Creek 20	4	37N05	78w45	5:15:00
Round Bottom 11	4	37N20	80w48	5:23:12
Round Hill 53	14	39N08	77w46	5:11:04
Round Top 94	15	37N01	82w35	5:30:20
Roundtree 29	3	38N52	77w13	5:08:52
Rowanta 27	22	37N02	77w24	5:09:36
Rowanty 27	22	37N05	77w33	5:10:12
Rowe 14	15	37N07	82w02	5:28:08
Roxbury 19	14	37N27	77w02	5:08:08
Roxbury 43	22	37N36	77w32	5:10:08
Royal City 14	15	37N17	82w06	5:28:24
Royal Court 29	1	38N50	77w12	5:08:48
Royal Oak 84	15	36N49	81w31	5:26:04
Ruark 59	4	37N33	76w20	5:05:20
Ruby 87	4	38N30	77w31	5:10:04
Ruckersville 39	14	38N14	78w22	5:13:28
Rue 1	4	37N47	75w39	5:02:36
Ruff 57	4	37N24	76w19	5:05:16
Ruffin 2	14	37N47	78w42	5:14:48
Rugby 38	4	36N35	81w20	5:25:20
Rural Retreat 95	4	36N54	81w17	5:25:08
Rushmere 46	4	37N04	76w41	5:06:44
Russell 81	15	37N01	81w59	5:27:56
Russell Creek 94	15	36N58	82w18	5:29:12
Rustburg 16	16	37N17	79w06	5:16:24
Rustic 19	14	37N20	77w04	5:08:16
Rutherford 29	3	38N51	77w15	5:09:00
Rutherglen 17	22	37N56	77w28	5:09:52
Ruthland 43	17	37N36	77w29	5:09:56
Ruthville 19	14	37N17	77w02	5:08:08
Ryan 53	4	39N03	77w29	5:09:56
Rye Cove 82	26	36N41	82w45	5:31:00
Rye Valley 84	15	36N45	81w32	5:26:08
Sabot 37	4	37N36	77w42	5:10:48
Sadler Heights 132	5	36N44	76w35	5:06:20
Sago 33	4	36N59	79w38	5:18:32
Saint Brides 102	4	36N41	76w16	5:05:04
Saint Charles 52	26	36N48	83w04	5:32:16
Saint Clair 90	4	37N15	81w17	5:25:08
Saint Clair Bottom 84	15	36N48	81w41	5:26:44
Saint Davids Church 83	14	38N48	78w27	5:13:48
Saint Just 67	14	38N16	77w58	5:11:52
Saint Luke 83	14	38N53	78w31	5:14:04
Saint Paul 94	15	36N54	82w19	5:29:16
Saint Peters 63	14	37N31	77w04	5:08:16
Saint Stephens 30	19	38N39	77w39	5:10:36
Saint Stephens Church 48	4	37N48	77w03	5:08:12
Salem 24	14	38N28	78w00	5:12:00
Salem 129	4	37N18	80w03	5:20:12
Salem 133	6	36N49	76w09	5:04:36
Salisbury 21	22	37N29	77w34	5:10:16
Salona Village 29	1	38N55	77w11	5:08:44
Saltpetre 12	4	37N38	79w48	5:19:12
Saltville 84	15	36N53	81w46	5:27:04
Saluda 59	4	37N36	76w36	5:06:24
Salvia 48	4	37N48	77w03	5:08:12
Samos 59	4	37N38	76w34	5:06:16
Samuel Miller 2	14	37N59	78w43	5:14:52
Sanburne Park 43	22	37N33	77w22	5:09:28
Sand Bridge Beach 133	6	36N49	76w09	5:04:36
Sandidges 5	16	37N35	79w03	5:16:12
Sand Lick 26	15	37N09	82w17	5:29:08
Sandston 43	22	37N31	77w19	5:09:16
Sandy Hook 37	4	37N45	77w55	5:11:40
Sandy Level 70	4	36N34	79w44	5:18:56
Sandy River 70	4	36N40	79w43	5:18:52
Sanford 1	4	37N55	75w40	5:02:40
Sangerville 8	21	38N23	78w59	5:15:56
Sanville 44	4	36N46	79w59	5:19:56
Sapony 27	22	36N58	77w37	5:10:28
Sarah 57	4	37N24	76w16	5:05:04
Saratoga 29	3	38N47	77w12	5:08:48
Saratoga Place 132	5	36N43	76w36	5:06:24
Sassafras 36	4	37N25	76w32	5:06:08
Saumsville 83	14	38N55	78w28	5:13:52
Saunders 127	17	37N33	77w27	5:09:48
Savage Crossing 132	5	36N44	76w35	5:06:20
Savageville 1	4	37N43	75w44	5:02:56
Savedge 88	4	37N10	76w58	5:07:52
Saxe 20	4	36N56	78w40	5:14:40
Saxis 1	4	37N56	75w43	5:02:52
Sayersville 90	4	37N09	81w42	5:26:48
Scarboroughs Neck 1	4	37N32	75w52	5:03:28
Scenic Park 92	25	36N36	82w11	5:28:44
Schley 36	4	37N23	76w27	5:05:48
Schneiders Crossroads 29	3	38N50	77w26	5:09:44
Schuyler 62	14	37N47	78w42	5:14:48
Scott 30	19	38N55	77w48	5:11:12
Scott Addition 92	15	36N43	81w58	5:27:52
Scottie Farms 43	22	37N32	77w19	5:09:16
Scottsburg 41	4	36N45	78w48	5:15:12
Scotts Crossroads 58	4	36N48	78w28	5:13:52
Scotts Fork 4	4	37N21	77w59	5:11:56
Scottsville 2	14	37N48	78w30	5:14:00
Scrabble 76	14	38N33	78w08	5:12:32
Scruggs 33	4	37N11	79w37	5:18:28
Seaboard 90	4	37N06	81w48	5:27:12
Seaford 96	4	37N12	76w26	5:05:44
Sealston 49	22	38N16	77w20	5:09:20
Sea Pines 133	6	36N52	76w00	5:04:00
Seatack 133	6	36N52	76w00	5:04:00
Seaview 64	4	37N16	75w57	5:03:48
Seawright Spring 8	21	38N15	78w58	5:15:52
Sebrell 85	4	36N47	77w08	5:08:32
Sedalia 10	4	37N32	79w22	5:17:28
Seddon 11	4	37N07	81w07	5:24:28
Sedgefield Manor 43	17	37N36	77w29	5:09:56
Sedley 85	4	36N46	76w59	5:07:56
Selden 36	4	37N25	76w32	5:06:08
Selma 3	4	37N48	79w51	5:19:24
Selton 26	15	36N59	82w17	5:29:08
Seminary 52	26	36N56	82w47	5:31:08
Seneca 16	16	37N10	79w05	5:16:20
Seng Camp 14	15	37N11	81w48	5:27:12
Senora 51	4	37N46	76w28	5:05:52
Seven Corners 29	1	38N52	77w09	5:08:36
Seven Fountains 83	14	38N52	78w24	5:13:36
Seven Mile Ford 84	15	36N49	81w38	5:26:32
Seven Pines 43	22	37N33	77w22	5:09:28
Seven Pines Villa 43	22	37N33	77w22	5:09:28
Severn 36	4	37N18	76w25	5:05:40
Shacklefords 48	4	37N33	76w44	5:06:56
Shadow 57	4	37N21	76w18	5:05:12
Shadowlawn Heights 133	6	36N52	76w00	5:04:00
Shadow Valley 92	25	36N36	82w11	5:28:44
Shadwell 2	14	38N01	78w24	5:13:36
Shady Grove 39	14	38N17	78w37	5:14:28
Shady Grove 41	4	36N33	78w47	5:15:08

Shady Grove 92	15	36N43	81w58	5:27:52
Shady Lane 62	14	37N43	79w02	5:16:08
Shady Oak 29	3	39N00	77w15	5:09:00
Shadyside 64	4	37N24	75w54	5:03:36
Shakerag 9	4	38N03	79w47	5:19:08
Shaklefords Fork 48	4	37N33	76w44	5:06:56
Shanghai 48	4	37N37	76w47	5:07:08
Shannon Hills 44	4	36N33	79w51	5:19:24
Sharon 11	4	37N02	81w19	5:25:16
Sharps 77	4	37N49	76w42	5:06:48
Shawnee 34	9	39N09	78w09	5:12:36
Shawsville 60	4	37N10	80w15	5:21:00
Shawver Mill 90	4	37N08	81w31	5:26:04
Sheep Town 18	4	36N51	80w55	5:23:40
Sheffield Court 21	22	37N29	77w33	5:10:12
Shelby 56	4	38N23	78w16	5:13:04
Shelfar 54	14	38N01	77w54	5:11:36
Shelton 133	6	36N53	76w08	5:04:32
Shenandoah 68	14	38N29	78w37	5:14:28
Shenandoah 115	14	37N17	77w18	5:09:12
Shenandoah Caverns 83	14	38N41	78w41	5:14:44
Shenandoah Iron Works 68	14	38N32	78w35	5:14:20
Shenandoah Place 43	22	37N35	77w31	5:10:04
Shepherds Hill 52	26	36N52	82w54	5:31:36
Shepherds Store 32	4	37N47	78w10	5:12:40
Sherando 8	21	37N59	78w58	5:15:52
Sherwill 16	16	37N21	78w59	5:15:56
Sherwood 29	1	38N53	77w13	5:08:52
Sherwood Forest 8	21	38N09	79w05	5:16:20
Sherwood Forest 130	4	36N43	78w54	5:15:36
Sherwood Hall 29	3	38N45	77w06	5:08:24
Sheva 70	4	36N50	79w24	5:17:36
Shields 1	4	37N32	75w52	5:03:28
Shiloh 49	22	38N14	77w05	5:08:20
Shiny Rock 58	4	36N37	78w34	5:14:16
Shipman 62	14	37N43	78w51	5:15:24
Ships Corner 133	6	36N49	76w09	5:04:36
Shirley Acres 29	3	38N42	77w14	5:08:56
Shirley Duke 97	1	38N49	77w07	5:08:28
Shirley Gate Park 29	3	38N51	77w15	5:09:00
Shirley Springs 29	3	38N45	77w12	5:08:48
Shirlington 7	1	38N51	77w05	5:08:20
Shockeysville 34	9	39N11	78w10	5:12:40
Shockoe 70	4	36N50	79w24	5:17:36
Shores 32	4	37N51	78w16	5:13:04
Shorewood 102	6	36N50	76w25	5:05:40
Short Lane 36	4	37N25	76w32	5:06:08
Short Pump 43	22	37N40	77w30	5:10:00
Shorts Creek 18	4	36N51	80w55	5:23:40
Shorts Store 93	19	38N04	76w39	5:06:36
Shortt Gap 14	15	37N09	81w53	5:27:32
Shreveport Park 43	22	37N32	77w19	5:09:16
Shrevewood 29	3	38N54	77w13	5:08:52
Shumansville 17	22	37N56	77w17	5:09:08
Shumate 35	4	37N20	80w48	5:23:12
Siddon 58	4	36N34	78w42	5:14:48
Sideburn 29	3	38N51	77w15	5:09:00
Sigma 133	6	36N49	76w09	5:04:36
Signpine 36	4	37N25	76w32	5:06:08
Siler 34	9	39N11	78w10	5:12:40
Silva 1	4	37N59	75w32	5:02:08
Silver Beach 64	4	37N31	75w56	5:03:44
Silver Springs 29	3	38N43	77w09	5:08:36
Simeon 2	14	38N02	78w29	5:13:56
Simmonsville 23	4	37N27	80w19	5:21:16
Simonsdale 125	6	36N49	76w21	5:05:24
Simonson 77	4	37N53	76w38	5:06:32
Simpkins 64	4	37N16	76w00	5:04:00
Simpsons 31	4	37N02	80w13	5:20:52
Sinai 41	4	36N43	78w54	5:15:36
Singer 78	4	37N17	80w03	5:20:12
Singers Glen 80	22	38N33	78w55	5:15:40
Sinking Creek 23	4	37N30	80w07	5:20:28
Sinnickson 1	4	37N58	75w28	5:01:52
Sissons Corner 65	18	37N55	76w28	5:05:52
Skeetrock 26	15	37N09	82w27	5:29:48
Skeggs 14	15	37N07	82w02	5:28:08
Skiminoe 96	23	37N17	76w43	5:06:52
Skippers 40	20	36N37	77w33	5:10:12
Skipwith 58	4	36N42	78w30	5:14:00
Skipwith Farms 43	22	37N36	77w32	5:10:08
Skipworth Farms 135	23	37N17	76w43	5:06:52
Skyland 68	14	38N40	78w27	5:13:48
Skymont 131	21	38N09	79w05	5:16:20
Sky View Park 29	3	38N45	77w08	5:08:32
Slabtown 51	4	37N46	76w28	5:05:52
Slabtown 82	26	36N38	82w34	5:30:16
Slate 14	15	37N17	82w06	5:28:24
Slate Mills 76	14	38N33	78w08	5:12:32
Slate River 15	4	37N41	78w30	5:14:00
Slates Corner 40	20	36N41	77w32	5:10:08
Sleepy Hole 61	4	36N48	76w31	5:06:04
Sleepy Hollow 29	3	38N52	77w13	5:08:52
Sleepy Hollow Estates 29	1	38N52	77w12	5:08:48
Sleepy Hollow Estates 43	22	37N36	77w32	5:10:08
Sleepy Hollow Manor 29	1	38N52	77w12	5:08:48

Sleepy Hollow Run 29 1 38N50 77w12 5:08:48
Sleepy Hollow Woods 29 1 38N50 77w12 5:08:48
Sliders 15 4 37N28 78w34 5:14:16
Smithfield 46 4 36N59 76w38 5:06:32
Smith River 69 4 36N46 80w13 5:20:52
Smiths Cross Roads 58 4 36N44 78w07 5:12:28
Smoky 13 4 36N46 77w51 5:11:24
Snake Creek 18 4 36N46 80w44 5:22:56
Snapp 92 15 36N48 81w46 5:27:04
Snell 86 22 38N12 77w35 5:10:20
Snowden 5 16 37N36 79w24 5:17:36
Snowden 29 1 38N45 77w04 5:08:16
Snowflake 82 26 36N38 82w34 5:30:16
Snow Hill 48 4 37N33 76w44 5:06:56
Snowville 75 4 37N04 80w47 5:23:08
Soapstone 70 4 36N40 79w43 5:18:52
Soles 57 4 37N30 76w28 5:05:52
Solomons Store 43 22 37N40 77w30 5:10:00
Somers 51 4 37N46 76w28 5:05:52
Somerset 67 14 38N13 78w13 5:12:52
Somerville 30 19 38N31 77w37 5:10:28
Sonans 70 4 36N50 79w24 5:17:36
Sorocco 132 5 36N44 76w35 5:06:20
South 7 1 38N52 77w06 5:08:24
Southampton 113 6 37N02 76w21 5:05:24
South Anna 42 22 37N48 77w41 5:10:44
Southanna 54 14 38N01 77w54 5:11:36
South Boston 130 4 36N42 78w54 5:15:36
South Clinchfield 81 15 36N57 82w09 5:28:36
Southeast 33 4 36N55 79w45 5:19:00
Southern Pine 27 22 37N13 77w26 5:09:44
South Fairview 102 6 36N49 76w14 5:04:56
South Garden 2 14 37N57 78w38 5:14:32
South Grundy 14 15 37N16 82w05 5:28:20
South Hill 58 4 36N44 78w08 5:12:32
South Hill 102 6 36N50 76w16 5:05:04
South Jackson 83 14 38N45 78w39 5:14:36
South Martinsville 120 4 36N40 79w52 5:19:28
South Norfolk 102 6 36N50 76w16 5:05:04
Southport 74 13 38N39 77w16 5:09:04
Southridge 29 1 38N55 77w11 5:08:44
South Roanoke 128 4 37N14 79w57 5:19:48
South Salem 129 4 37N17 80w03 5:20:12
Southside 6 4 37N18 78w51 5:15:24
Southside 127 17 37N29 77w29 5:09:56
South Suffolk 132 5 36N44 76w35 5:06:20
Southwest 33 4 36N56 80w01 5:20:04
South Woodley 29 3 38N52 77w13 5:08:52
Spainville 66 4 37N05 78w00 5:12:00
Sparkling Springs 80 22 38N31 78w50 5:15:20
Sparta 17 22 37N59 77w14 5:08:56
Speedwell 95 4 36N50 81w05 5:24:20
Spencer 44 4 36N37 80w01 5:20:04
Sperryville 76 14 38N39 78w14 5:12:56
Spitler 68 14 38N40 78w27 5:13:48
Spivey Mill 82 26 36N38 82w34 5:30:16
Spivey Store 82 26 36N38 82w34 5:30:16
Splashdam 26 15 37N12 82w18 5:29:12
Spotswood 67 14 38N14 78w07 5:12:28
Spotsylvania 86 22 38N12 77w36 5:10:24
Spottswood 8 21 37N57 79w13 5:16:52
Spout Spring 6 4 37N21 78w55 5:15:40
Springbrook Forest 29 3 38N51 77w15 5:09:00
Spring Creek 80 22 38N24 79w02 5:16:08
Springcreek 80 22 38N24 79w02 5:16:08
Springdale 43 17 37N34 77w26 5:09:44
Springdale 92 25 36N36 82w11 5:28:44
Springfield 29 3 38N47 77w11 5:08:44
Springfield 68 14 38N40 78w27 5:13:48
Springfield 79 14 37N32 79w41 5:18:44
Springfield Estates 29 3 38N45 77w12 5:08:48
Springfield Forest 29 3 38N45 77w12 5:08:48
Springfield Woods 29 3 38N45 77w12 5:08:48
Spring Garden 70 4 36N41 79w22 5:17:28
Spring Garden 99 25 36N36 82w11 5:28:44
Spring Grove 88 4 37N10 76w58 5:07:52
Springhaven Estates 29 1 38N55 77w11 5:08:44
Spring Hill 8 21 38N09 79w05 5:16:20
Spring Hill 29 1 38N55 77w11 5:08:44
Spring Meadows 42 22 37N37 77w22 5:09:28
Spring Mills 6 4 37N21 78w59 5:15:56
Springvale 29 3 39N00 77w15 5:09:00
Spring Valley 38 4 36N43 80w59 5:23:56
Springville 90 4 37N08 81w31 5:26:04
Springwood 12 4 37N32 79w41 5:18:44
Sprouse's Corner 15 4 37N33 78w28 5:13:52
Stacy 14 15 37N17 82w06 5:28:24
Stafford 87 4 38N25 77w25 5:09:40
Staffordshire 21 22 37N29 77w33 5:10:12
Staffordsville 35 4 37N15 80w41 5:22:44
Stage Bridge 62 14 37N43 78w51 5:15:24
Stage Junction 32 4 37N45 78w10 5:12:40
Staleys Cross Roads 95 4 36N54 81w16 5:25:04
Stanardsville 39 14 38N18 78w26 5:13:44
Stanley 68 14 38N35 78w30 5:14:00
Stanleytown 44 4 36N44 79w57 5:19:48
Stanleytown 82 26 36N41 82w45 5:31:00
Staples Mill 43 17 37N36 77w29 5:09:56
Stapleton 5 14 37N25 79w08 5:16:32
Starkey 78 4 37N12 80w00 5:20:00
Starnes 82 26 36N46 82w35 5:30:20
Star Tannery 34 4 39N05 78w26 5:13:44
Station Hills 29 3 38N48 77w20 5:09:20
Staunton 131 21 38N09 79w04 5:16:16
Staunton Park 131 21 38N09 79w05 5:16:20
Staunton River 70 4 37N02 79w16 5:17:04
Steeleburg 90 4 37N05 81w46 5:27:04
Steeles Tavern 8 21 37N56 79w12 5:16:48
Steinman 26 15 37N10 82w22 5:29:28
Stella 69 4 36N38 80w12 5:20:48
Stemphleytown 80 22 38N25 78w57 5:15:48
Stephens 94 15 37N01 82w35 5:30:20
Stephens City 34 4 39N05 78w13 5:12:52
Stephenson 34 4 39N14 78w07 5:12:28
Sterling 53 4 39N01 77w26 5:09:44
Sterling Park 53 4 39N00 77w24 5:09:36
Stevensburg 24 4 38N26 77w50 5:11:20
Stevens Creek 38 4 36N44 81w00 5:24:00
Stevensville 48 4 37N44 76w53 5:07:32
Stewart 127 17 37N34 77w29 5:09:56
Stewartsburg 79 14 37N44 79w21 5:17:24
Stewartsville 10 4 37N23 79w49 5:19:16
Stickleys 29 1 38N47 77w07 5:08:28
Stingray Point 59 4 37N33 76w20 5:05:20
Stith 41 4 36N50 78w44 5:14:56
Stockton 44 4 36N40 79w43 5:18:52
Stoddert 25 4 37N18 78w24 5:13:36
Stokesland 106 4 36N35 79w23 5:17:32
Stokesville 8 21 38N21 79w05 5:16:20
Stone Bridge 22 4 39N03 78w06 5:12:24
Stone Creek 52 26 36N46 83w02 5:32:08
Stonega 94 26 36N57 82w48 5:31:12
Stonehouse 47 14 37N24 76w48 5:07:12
Stone Mountain 10 4 37N20 79w31 5:18:04
Stones Mill 95 4 36N57 81w05 5:24:20
Stone Springs 114 22 38N27 78w52 5:15:28
Stonewall 6 4 37N21 78w59 5:15:56
Stonewall Acres 74 2 38N47 77w28 5:09:52
Stonewall Manor 29 3 38N55 77w14 5:08:56
Stony 82 15 36N50 82w28 5:29:52
Stony Battery 84 15 36N50 81w31 5:26:04
Stony Creek 89 4 36N57 77w24 5:09:36
Stony Man 68 14 38N40 78w27 5:13:48
Stony Point 2 14 38N02 78w29 5:13:56
Stony Point Mills 25 4 37N30 78w15 5:13:00
Stormont 59 4 37N36 76w36 5:06:24
Story 85 4 36N43 77w04 5:08:16
Stott 46 4 36N49 76w45 5:07:00
Stovall 41 4 36N56 78w57 5:15:48
Stover 8 21 38N14 79w10 5:16:40
Straightstone 70 4 37N04 79w06 5:16:24
Strasburg 83 14 38N59 78w22 5:13:28
Strasburg Junction 83 14 39N00 78w22 5:13:28
Stratford 29 1 38N45 77w04 5:08:16
Stratford 93 19 38N09 76w51 5:07:24
Stratford Hills 127 17 37N28 77w28 5:09:52
Stratford Landing 29 1 38N45 77w04 5:08:16
Stratford-on-the-Potomac 29 1 38N45 77w04 5:08:16
Stratford Village 43 17 37N34 77w26 5:09:44
Strathmeade Springs 29 1 38N50 77w12 5:08:48
Strathmore 32 4 37N42 78w18 5:13:12
Stringtown 22 14 39N09 77w59 5:11:56
Stroupes Store 95 4 36N57 81w05 5:24:20
Stuart 69 4 36N38 80w16 5:21:04
Stuarts Draft 8 21 38N02 79w02 5:16:08
Stubbs 86 22 38N12 77w35 5:10:20
Studley 42 22 37N40 77w17 5:09:08
Stukeley Hall Farms 43 17 37N36 77w27 5:09:48
Stumptown 53 14 39N07 77w34 5:10:16
Sturgeon 13 4 36N50 77w45 5:11:00
Suburban Apartments 43 17 37N34 77w29 5:09:56
Sudley 74 2 38N47 77w28 5:09:52
Suffolk 132 5 36N44 76w35 5:06:20
Sugar Grove 84 15 36N47 81w25 5:25:40
Sugarland Run 53 4 39N00 77w24 5:09:36
Sugar Loaf 78 4 37N15 80w01 5:20:04
Suiter 11 4 37N06 81w07 5:24:28
Sulgrave Manor 29 3 38N45 77w08 5:08:32
Sulphur Springs 18 4 36N46 80w53 5:23:32
Sulphur Springs 82 15 36N50 82w28 5:29:52
Sumerduck 30 19 38N28 77w44 5:10:56
Summerdeon 8 21 38N03 79w13 5:16:52
Summit 84 15 36N47 81w25 5:25:40
Summit 86 22 38N23 77w27 5:09:48
Sun 81 15 36N54 82w17 5:29:08
Sunbeam 85 4 36N39 77w02 5:08:08
Sunlight 86 22 38N12 77w35 5:10:20
Sunnybank 65 18 37N51 76w17 5:05:08
Sunnybrook Estates 74 2 38N47 77w28 5:09:52
Sunny Ridge 29 3 38N43 77w09 5:08:36
Sunnyside 25 4 37N30 78w15 5:13:00
Sunnyside 34 9 39N11 78w10 5:12:40
Sunny View 29 3 38N45 77w08 5:08:32
Sunray 102 6 36N50 76w25 5:05:40
Sunset Heights 43 17 37N32 77w24 5:09:36
Sunset Hills 29 3 38N58 77w22 5:09:28
Sunset Manor 29 1 38N49 77w09 5:08:36

Sunset Village 129 4 37N17 80w03 5:20:12
Supply 28 4 38N06 77w08 5:08:32
Surrey Square 29 3 38N51 77w15 5:09:00
Surry 88 4 37N08 76w50 5:07:20
Susan 57 4 37N22 76w19 5:05:16
Sussex 89 4 36N55 77w17 5:09:08
Sutherland 27 22 37N12 77w34 5:10:16
Sutherland 94 15 36N59 82w38 5:30:32
Sutherlin 70 4 36N37 79w12 5:16:48
Sutton Place 29 3 38N51 77w15 5:09:00
Swansonville 70 4 36N45 79w24 5:17:36
Sweet Briar 5 16 37N33 79w04 5:16:16
Sweet Chalybeate 3 4 37N47 79w59 5:19:56
Sweet Hall 50 14 37N33 76w48 5:07:12
Swift Creek 104 22 37N23 77w28 5:09:52
Swift Run 80 14 38N24 78w37 5:14:28
Swimley 22 14 39N09 77w59 5:11:56
Swinks Mill 29 1 38N55 77w11 5:08:44
Swoope 8 21 38N10 79w12 5:16:48
Swords Creek 81 15 37N02 81w55 5:27:40
Sycamore 70 4 36N57 79w22 5:17:28
Syclon 53 14 39N07 77w34 5:10:16
Sydnorsville 33 4 37N00 79w53 5:19:32
Sylvania Heights 86 22 38N23 77w27 5:09:48
Sylvatus 18 4 36N46 80w44 5:22:56
Syria 56 4 38N29 78w20 5:13:20
Syringa 59 4 37N35 76w27 5:05:48
Tabb 96 4 37N07 76w31 5:06:04
Tabscott 37 4 37N45 78w10 5:12:40
Tacoma 94 15 37N00 82w28 5:29:52
Taft 51 14 37N39 76w23 5:05:32
Tall Oaks 29 1 38N50 77w12 5:08:48
Tallysville 63 14 37N31 76w59 5:07:56
Tamworth 25 4 37N39 78w05 5:12:20
Tangier 1 4 37N49 76w00 5:04:00
Tanglewood 102 6 36N49 76w14 5:04:56
Tannersville 90 4 36N58 81w38 5:26:32
Tappahannock 28 14 37N56 76w52 5:07:28
Tarpon 26 15 37N09 82w27 5:29:48
Tarters Store 95 4 36N57 81w05 5:24:20
Tasley 1 4 37N43 75w42 5:02:48
Tasso 94 15 37N01 82w35 5:30:20
Tatum 67 14 38N16 77w58 5:11:52
Tauxemont 29 1 38N45 77w04 5:08:16
Taylors Store 33 4 37N04 79w53 5:19:32
Taylorstown 53 14 39N07 77w34 5:10:16
Taylors Valley 92 15 36N38 81w47 5:27:08
Taylorsville 42 22 37N52 77w27 5:09:48
Taylorwood Estates 102 6 36N50 76w25 5:05:40
Tazewell 90 4 37N07 81w31 5:26:04
Teas 84 15 36N47 81w25 5:25:40
Temperance 5 16 37N40 79w03 5:16:12
Temperanceville 1 4 37N54 75w33 5:02:12
Temple Hill 81 15 36N54 82w17 5:29:08
Templeman 93 19 38N05 76w47 5:07:08
Templeton 73 22 37N05 77w18 5:09:12
Tenso 26 15 37N10 82w22 5:29:28
Tenth Legion 80 22 38N37 78w48 5:15:12
Terrys Fork 31 4 37N02 80w10 5:20:40
Tetotum 49 22 38N16 77w11 5:08:44
Thalia Manor 133 6 36N51 76w07 5:04:28
Thalia Shores 133 6 36N51 76w07 5:04:28
Thaxton 10 4 37N21 79w37 5:18:28
The Cedars 84 15 36N50 81w31 5:26:04
The English Hills 29 3 38N48 77w20 5:09:20
The Hollow 69 4 36N36 80w31 5:22:04
The Islands 1 4 37N56 75w22 5:01:28
The Knolls 74 13 38N39 77w16 5:09:04
Thelma 54 14 38N09 78w11 5:12:44
The Manors 74 13 38N39 77w16 5:09:04
The Meadows 2 14 38N02 78w29 5:13:56
Theological Seminary 97 1 38N49 77w07 5:08:28
The Plains 30 19 38N52 77w47 5:11:08
The Ridge 58 4 36N40 78w23 5:13:32
Thessalia 35 4 37N20 80w44 5:22:56
Theta 16 16 37N10 79w05 5:16:20
The Timbers 29 3 38N45 77w12 5:08:48
The Villas 74 13 38N39 77w16 5:09:04
Thomas Bridge 84 15 36N50 81w31 5:26:04
Thomas Corner 122 6 36N51 76w14 5:04:56
Thomasson Park 74 14 38N31 77w18 5:09:12
Thomas Terrace 16 14 37N24 79w10 5:16:40
Thomastown 9 4 38N00 79w50 5:19:20
Thompson Valley 90 4 37N08 81w31 5:26:04
Thornburg 86 22 38N08 77w31 5:10:04
Thornhill 67 14 38N13 78w06 5:12:24
Thoroughfare 74 14 38N50 77w43 5:10:52
Thoroughgood 133 6 36N53 76w08 5:04:32
Three Chopt 43 22 37N37 77w32 5:10:08
Three Forks 16 16 37N17 79w06 5:16:24
Three Spring 92 25 36N36 82w11 5:28:44
Threeway 93 19 38N04 76w39 5:06:36
Tibitha 65 18 37N51 76w17 5:05:08
Ticktown 1 4 37N43 75w40 5:02:40
Tidemill 36 4 37N17 76w30 5:06:00
Tidewater 77 4 37N58 76w46 5:07:04
Tidwells 93 19 38N06 76w50 5:07:20
Tignor 17 22 38N01 77w22 5:09:28
Timberlake 16 16 37N21 79w14 5:16:56
Timberly Heights 73 22 37N13 77w17 5:09:08
Timber Ridge 79 14 37N47 79w26 5:17:44
Timberville 80 22 38N39 78w47 5:15:08
Timothy Park 29 3 38N45 77w08 5:08:32
Tindall 31 4 37N02 80w19 5:21:16

VIRGINIA

Tiny 26	15	37N11	82w16	5:29:04
Tiptop 90	4	37N13	81w26	5:25:44
Tito 82	26	36N43	82w48	5:31:12
Tivis 26	15	37N12	82w18	5:29:12
Toano 47	14	37N23	76w48	5:07:12
Tobaccoville 71	14	37N21	77w59	5:11:56
Todds Tavern 86	22	38N12	77w35	5:10:20
Toga 15	4	37N30	78w38	5:14:32
Tola 20	4	37N05	78w45	5:15:00
Tomahawk 70	4	36N50	79w24	5:17:36
Toms Bottom 26	15	37N12	82w18	5:29:12
Toms Brook 83	14	38N57	78w26	5:13:44
Toms Creek 94	15	37N00	82w28	5:29:52
Tookland 14	15	37N17	82w06	5:28:24
Topnot 83	14	39N00	78w22	5:13:28
Topping 59	4	37N35	76w28	5:05:52
Totaro 13	4	36N46	77w51	5:11:24
Totten 91	14	38N55	78w12	5:12:48
Town and Country Estates 29	3	38N55	77w14	5:08:56
Townsend 64	4	37N11	75w57	5:03:48
Trammel 26	15	37N01	82w18	5:29:12
Trantwood Shores 133	6	36N52	76w02	5:04:08
Trapp 53	4	39N00	77w53	5:11:32
Tree Brooke 29	3	38N53	77w18	5:09:12
Tremont Gardens 29	3	38N52	77w13	5:08:52
Trenholm 71	14	37N29	77w55	5:11:40
Trent Mill 25	4	37N30	78w15	5:13:00
Trevilians 54	14	37N35	76w28	5:05:52
Triangle 74	14	38N33	77w20	5:09:20
Trigg 35	4	37N20	80w44	5:22:56
Triplet 13	4	36N37	77w46	5:11:04
Trone 34	4	39N16	78w20	5:13:20
Trout Dale 38	4	36N42	81w26	5:25:44
Troutville 12	4	37N25	79w53	5:19:32
Trower 1	4	37N36	75w41	5:02:44
Troy 32	4	37N52	78w20	5:13:20
Trueblue 67	14	38N28	78w00	5:12:00
Truhart 48	4	37N38	76w48	5:07:12
Truxillo 4	4	37N21	77w59	5:11:56
Tuckahoe 43	22	37N36	77w34	5:10:16
Tuckahoe Park 43	22	37N36	77w32	5:10:08
Tuckahoe Village 43	22	37N36	77w32	5:10:08
Tucker Hill 93	19	38N02	76w35	5:06:20
Tuggle 72	4	37N18	78w24	5:13:36
Tulip 34	4	39N06	78w13	5:12:52
Tunstall 63	14	37N31	76w59	5:07:56
Tunstall 70	4	36N37	79w29	5:17:56
Turbeville 41	4	36N37	79w02	5:16:08
Turkey Fork 38	4	36N43	81w11	5:24:44
Turnbull 30	19	38N44	77w44	5:10:56
Turner Store 13	4	36N48	77w57	5:11:48
Tuxamount 29	1	38N45	77w04	5:08:16
Twymans Mill 56	4	38N23	78w16	5:13:04
Tye River 62	14	37N39	78w57	5:15:48
Tyler Park 29	3	38N52	77w13	5:08:52
Tylerton 87	4	38N23	77w27	5:09:48
Tyro 62	14	37N49	79w00	5:16:00
Tysons Corner 29	3	38N55	77w14	5:08:56
Tysons Green 29	3	38N55	77w14	5:08:56
Union 10	4	37N21	79w37	5:18:28
Union Hall 33	4	37N00	79w41	5:18:44
Union Level 58	4	36N43	78w14	5:12:56
Uniontown 29	3	38N50	77w26	5:09:44
Unionville 67	14	38N16	77w58	5:11:52
Unison 53	14	39N08	77w46	5:11:04
Unity 85	4	36N52	76w50	5:07:20
University of Virginia 101	14	38N02	78w29	5:13:56
University Gardens Apartment 101	14	38N02	78w29	5:13:56
University Heights 43	22	37N36	77w32	5:10:08
University Of Richmond 127	17	37N32	77w28	5:09:52
Uno 56	4	38N17	78w16	5:13:04
Unthanks 52	26	36N40	83w07	5:32:28
Upper Brandon 73	22	37N10	76w58	5:07:52
Upperville 30	19	39N00	77w53	5:11:32
Upright 28	4	37N50	76w53	5:07:32
Upshaw 50	14	37N47	77w06	5:08:24
Urbanna 59	4	37N38	76w35	5:06:20
Vails Mill 92	15	36N38	81w47	5:27:08
Valaho 82	15	36N50	82w28	5:29:52
Vale 29	3	38N53	77w18	5:09:12
Valentine Hills 43	17	37N36	77w29	5:09:56
Valentines 13	4	36N35	77w50	5:11:20
Valley 12	4	37N23	79w53	5:19:32
Valley Brook 29	3	38N52	77w13	5:08:52
Valley Creek 82	15	36N45	82w25	5:29:40
Valley Mills 8	21	38N10	79w12	5:16:48
Valley Ridge 3	4	37N47	79w59	5:19:56
Valley Springs 9	4	37N57	79w51	5:19:24
Valley Stream 102	6	36N49	76w14	5:04:56
Valley View 29	1	38N47	77w05	5:08:20
Valleywood 74	13	38N39	77w16	5:09:04
Van Buren Furnace 83	14	38N55	78w28	5:13:52
Vanderpool 45	4	38N25	79w35	5:18:20
Vandyke 14	15	37N05	81w52	5:27:28
Vanlear 8	21	38N01	79w02	5:16:08
Vannoy Acres 29	3	38N51	77w15	5:09:00
Vannoy Park 29	3	38N47	77w23	5:09:32
Vansant 14	15	37N14	82w06	5:28:24
Varina 43	22	37N30	77w20	5:09:20
Vaucluse 34	4	39N06	78w13	5:12:52
Vaughn 68	14	38N40	78w27	5:13:48
Vawters Shore 54	14	38N02	78w00	5:12:00
Venia 14	15	37N01	81w59	5:27:56
Vera 6	4	37N21	78w50	5:15:20
Verbena 68	14	38N24	78w37	5:14:28
Verdi 82	26	36N41	82w45	5:31:00
Verdon 42	22	37N52	77w27	5:09:48
Vernon Hill 41	4	36N45	79w06	5:16:24
Verona 8	21	38N12	79w01	5:16:04
Vertain Park 29	3	38N51	77w15	5:09:00
Vesta 69	4	36N43	80w22	5:21:28
Vests Store 71	14	37N29	77w55	5:11:40
Vesuvius 79	14	37N54	79w12	5:16:48
Veterans Administration Hosp 127	17	37N33	77w26	5:09:44
Vicey 14	15	37N12	82w18	5:29:12
Vicker 60	4	37N08	80w24	5:21:36
Vicksville 85	4	36N46	76w59	5:07:56
Victoria 55	4	37N00	78w14	5:12:56
Victoria Hills 21	22	37N23	77w26	5:09:44
Vienna 29	3	38N54	77w16	5:09:04
Viers 26	15	37N12	82w18	5:29:12
Viewtown 76	14	38N38	78w02	5:12:08
Village 65	18	37N57	76w36	5:06:24
Villa Heights 44	4	36N40	79w52	5:19:28
Villa Loring 29	3	38N55	77w14	5:08:56
Villamay 29	1	38N46	77w04	5:08:16
Villamont 10	4	37N24	79w47	5:19:08
Villboro 17	22	38N07	77w25	5:09:40
Vint Hill Farms 30	19	38N44	77w44	5:10:56
Vinthill Farms Station 30	19	38N45	77w41	5:10:44
Vinton 78	4	37N17	79w53	5:19:32
Virgilina 41	4	36N33	78w47	5:15:08
Virginia Beach 133	6	36N51	75w59	5:03:56
Virginia City 94	15	36N58	82w18	5:29:12
Virginia Estates 29	3	38N42	77w14	5:08:56
Virginia Heights 43	17	37N32	77w24	5:09:36
Virginia Hills 29	3	38N43	77w09	5:08:36
Virginia Hills 92	25	36N36	82w11	5:28:44
Virginia Union University 127	17	37N33	77w27	5:09:48
Virginia Village Apartments 29	1	38N49	77w09	5:08:36
Vir-mar Beach 65	18	37N55	76w28	5:05:52
Vista 16	16	37N09	79w17	5:17:08
Volens 41	4	36N56	79w01	5:16:04
Volney 38	4	36N37	81w23	5:25:32
Vulcan 67	14	38N16	77w58	5:11:52
Wabun 78	4	37N17	80w03	5:20:12
Wachapreague 1	4	37N36	75w42	5:02:48
Wadesville 22	14	39N09	77w59	5:11:56
Wake 59	4	37N34	76w26	5:05:44
Wakefield 89	4	36N58	76w59	5:07:56
Wakefield Chapel 29	1	38N50	77w12	5:08:48
Wakefield Chapel Woods 29	1	38N50	77w12	5:08:48
Wakefield Forest 29	1	38N50	77w12	5:08:48
Wake Forest 60	4	37N08	80w24	5:21:36
Wakenva 26	15	36N59	82w17	5:29:08
Waldrop 54	14	38N09	78w11	5:12:44
Walhaven 29	3	38N43	77w09	5:08:36
Walkerford 5	16	37N33	78w52	5:15:28
Walkers Creek 79	14	37N55	79w22	5:17:28
Walkers Store 65	18	37N51	76w17	5:05:08
Walker Store 58	4	36N48	78w28	5:13:52
Walkerton 48	4	37N44	77w01	5:08:04
Wallace 92	15	36N39	82w08	5:28:32
Wallaces Store 20	4	37N00	78w36	5:14:24
Wallaceton 102	6	36N47	76w15	5:05:00
Walmsley 65	18	37N57	76w32	5:06:08
Walnut Grove 92	15	36N42	82w18	5:29:12
Walnut Hill 124	22	37N13	77w26	5:09:44
Walnut Point 65	18	37N55	76w28	5:05:52
Walter Heights 29	1	38N55	77w11	5:08:44
Walters 46	4	36N46	76w51	5:07:24
Walters Woods 29	1	38N52	77w12	5:08:48
Walton 20	4	37N04	78w32	5:14:08
Walton 60	4	37N08	80w24	5:21:36
Walton Furnace 95	4	36N58	80w57	5:23:48
Waltons Store 10	4	37N10	79w28	5:17:52
Ward 14	15	37N29	82w04	5:28:16
Wardell 90	4	37N05	81w46	5:27:04
Wards Mill 18	4	36N40	80w55	5:23:40
Wardtown 64	4	37N32	75w53	5:03:32
Ware 36	4	37N26	76w30	5:06:00
Ware Neck 36	4	37N24	76w27	5:05:48
Wares Crossroads 54	14	38N01	77w54	5:11:36
Wares Wharf 28	4	37N51	76w49	5:07:16
Warfield 13	4	36N54	77w50	5:11:20
Warminster 62	14	37N38	78w50	5:15:20
Warm Springs 9	4	38N03	79w47	5:19:08
Warner 59	4	37N38	76w39	5:06:36
Warren 2	14	37N48	78w29	5:13:56
Warrenton 30	19	38N43	77w48	5:11:12
Warren Woods 108	3	38N51	77w15	5:09:00
Warsaw 77	4	37N58	76w46	5:07:04
Warwick 121	6	37N02	76w27	5:05:48
Washington 76	14	38N43	78w10	5:12:40
Washington City 130	4	36N43	78w54	5:15:36
Washington Corner 17	22	38N07	77w25	5:09:40
Washington Park 40	20	36N41	77w32	5:10:08
Watauga 92	15	36N43	81w58	5:27:52
Waterford 53	4	39N11	77w37	5:10:28
Waterlick 91	14	39N00	78w22	5:13:28
Waterloo 22	4	39N03	78w06	5:12:24
Water View 59	4	37N43	76w37	5:06:28
Watson 53	14	39N07	77w34	5:10:16
Wattsville 1	4	37N56	75w30	5:02:00
Waugh 10	4	37N32	79w22	5:17:28
Waverly 89	4	37N02	77w06	5:08:24
Waxpool 53	4	38N57	77w32	5:10:08
Wayland 21	22	37N29	77w33	5:10:12
Wayland 82	26	36N38	82w34	5:30:16
Wayne 8	21	38N06	78w54	5:15:36
Waynesboro 134	22	38N04	78w53	5:15:32
Waynewood 29	1	38N45	77w04	5:08:16
Wayside 19	14	37N20	77w04	5:08:16
Weal 70	4	36N50	79w24	5:17:36
Webbtown 22	14	39N09	77w55	5:11:56
Weber City 82	26	36N37	82w33	5:30:12
Wedgewood 43	22	37N36	77w32	5:10:08
Weedonville 49	22	38N18	77w11	5:08:44
Weems 51	4	37N39	76w27	5:05:48
Weir Creek 63	14	37N29	76w50	5:07:20
Weirwood 64	4	37N27	75w52	5:03:28
Welchs 17	22	38N07	77w25	5:09:40
Welcome 49	22	38N13	77w08	5:08:32
Welfleet 74	3	38N43	77w09	5:08:36
Weller 14	15	37N17	82w06	5:28:24
Wellesley 53	14	39N07	77w34	5:10:16
Wellford 77	4	37N58	76w46	5:07:04
Wellington 29	1	38N45	77w04	5:08:16
Wellington 74	2	38N47	77w28	5:09:52
Wellington Heights 29	1	38N45	77w04	5:08:16
West Augusta 8	21	38N17	79w20	5:17:20
West Bottom 32	4	37N42	78w18	5:13:12
Westbourne 43	17	37N34	77w29	5:09:56
West Chesapeake 102	6	36N50	76w16	5:05:04
Westchester 21	22	37N29	77w33	5:10:12
Westchester 29	3	38N51	77w15	5:09:00
Westdale 43	22	37N36	77w32	5:10:08
West Dante 26	15	37N04	82w21	5:29:24
West End 131	21	38N09	79w05	5:16:20
West End Manor 43	22	37N36	77w32	5:10:08
Western 35	4	37N20	80w50	5:23:20
Western 124	22	37N13	77w26	5:09:44
West Falls Church 109	1	38N53	77w13	5:08:52
Westfield 99	25	36N36	82w11	5:28:44
West Fredericksburg 111	24	38N23	77w27	5:09:48
West Galax 112	4	36N40	80w55	5:23:40
West Gate of Lomond 74	2	38N47	77w28	5:09:52
Westgrove 29	1	38N46	77w04	5:08:16
Westham 43	22	37N36	77w32	5:10:08
Westhampton 29	3	38N54	77w13	5:08:52
Westhampton 127	17	37N35	77w31	5:10:04
West Hopewell 115	14	37N17	77w18	5:09:12
West Landing 102	6	36N47	76w15	5:05:00
West Lawn 29	3	38N52	77w13	5:08:52
West Lewinsville Heights 29	1	38N55	77w11	5:08:44
West Lexington 79	14	37N47	79w26	5:17:44
West McLean 29	1	38N55	77w11	5:08:44
Westmont 29	1	38N55	77w11	5:08:44
Westmoreland 93	19	38N04	76w34	5:06:16
Westmoreland Heights 29	3	38N54	77w13	5:08:52
Westmoreland Park 29	1	38N53	77w13	5:08:52
West Munden 102	6	36N50	76w16	5:05:04
Westover 19	14	37N20	77w04	5:08:16
Westover Hills 40	20	36N41	77w32	5:10:08
Westover Hills 70	4	36N35	79w23	5:17:32
West Petersburg 27	22	37N13	77w26	5:09:44
West Point 50	14	37N32	76w48	5:07:12
West Springfield 29	3	38N47	77w14	5:08:56
Wests Store 41	4	36N56	78w57	5:15:48
Westview 8	21	38N10	79w12	5:16:48
West View 37	4	37N41	77w53	5:11:32
Westview Hills 29	3	38N45	77w12	5:08:48
Westville 57	4	37N23	76w20	5:05:20
Westwood 3	4	37N47	79w59	5:19:56
Westwood 43	22	37N35	77w31	5:10:04
Westwood Estates 92	15	36N43	81w58	5:27:52
Westwood Park 29	1	38N53	77w13	5:08:52
West Wytheville 95	4	36N59	81w08	5:24:32
Weyanoke 29	1	38N49	77w09	5:08:36
Weyers Cave 8	21	38N17	78w55	5:15:40
Whaleyville 61	4	36N35	76w41	5:06:44
Wheatfield 83	14	39N03	78w22	5:13:28
Wheatland 53	14	39N10	77w43	5:10:52
Whitacre 34	4	39N20	78w20	5:13:20
White Chapel 51	4	37N44	76w32	5:06:08
White City 40	20	36N41	77w32	5:10:08
White Gate 35	4	37N20	80w44	5:22:56
White Hall 2	14	38N09	78w39	5:14:36
White Hall 34	9	39N11	78w10	5:12:40
White Hill 8	21	38N01	79w02	5:16:08
White House 58	4	36N34	78w42	5:14:48
White Marsh 36	4	37N21	76w31	5:06:04
White Mill 92	15	36N43	81w58	5:27:52
White Oak 41	4	36N46	78w56	5:15:44
White Oak 87	4	38N23	77w27	5:09:48
White Oaks 29	1	38N46	77w04	5:08:16
Whiteoak Swamp 43	22	37N33	77w22	5:09:28
White Plains 13	4	36N39	77w57	5:11:48
White Post 22	4	39N00	77w00	5:08:00
White Shoals 52	26	36N39	83w14	5:32:56
White Shop 50	14	37N41	77w01	5:08:04

VIRGINIA

White Stone 51	14	37N39	76w23	5:05:32
Whitethorne 60	4	37N12	80w34	5:22:16
Whitetop 38	4	36N36	81w38	5:26:32
Whiteville 25	4	37N30	78w15	5:13:00
Whitewood 14	15	37N15	81w52	5:27:28
Whitfield 106	4	36N35	79w23	5:17:32
Whitley 46	4	36N49	76w45	5:07:00
Whitlock 54	14	38N09	78w11	5:12:44
Whitmell 70	4	36N45	79w24	5:17:36
Whittle 70	4	36N50	79w24	5:17:36
Wickford 29	3	38N43	77w09	5:08:36
Wicomico 36	4	37N17	76w31	5:06:04
Wicomico 65	18	37N47	76w22	5:05:28
Wicomico Church 65	18	37N49	76w23	5:05:32
Widewater 87	4	38N25	77w24	5:09:36
Wightman 58	4	36N48	78w28	5:13:52
Wilburdale 29	1	38N50	77w12	5:08:48
Wilda 8	21	38N01	79w02	5:16:08
Wilde Acres 34	9	39N11	78w10	5:12:40
Wilder 81	15	36N57	82w09	5:28:36
Wilderness 67	14	38N20	77w44	5:10:56
Wilderness Corner 86	22	38N12	77w35	5:10:20
Wildwood 29	3	38N42	77w14	5:08:56
Wildwood 32	4	37N51	78w16	5:13:04
Wildwood 43	17	37N36	77w27	5:09:48
Wilkinsons Store 27	22	37N11	77w38	5:10:32
Wilkinson Terrace 21	22	37N27	77w28	5:09:52
Will 49	22	38N16	77w11	5:08:44
Williamsburg 135	23	37N16	76w43	5:06:52
Williamsburg Manor 29	1	38N45	77w04	5:08:16
Williams Mill 82	26	36N38	82w34	5:30:16
Williams Mills 55	4	37N02	78w29	5:13:56
Williamson Road 128	4	37N19	79w55	5:19:40
Williamsville 9	4	38N12	79w35	5:18:20
Williamsville 83	14	38N41	78w41	5:14:44
Willis 26	15	37N14	82w20	5:29:20
Willis 31	4	36N51	80w29	5:21:56
Willis Store 52	26	36N40	83w07	5:32:28
Willisville 53	4	39N00	77w53	5:11:32
Willis Wharf 64	4	37N31	75w48	5:03:12
Willow 5	16	37N35	79w03	5:16:12
Willowbrook 54	14	37N58	77w46	5:11:04
Willow Grove 64	4	37N16	76w00	5:04:00
Willow Lawn 43	17	37N34	77w29	5:09:56
Willow Run 29	1	38N50	77w12	5:08:48
Willow Spring 81	15	37N00	81w59	5:27:56
Willow Springs 29	3	38N51	77w15	5:09:00
Willow Tree 52	26	36N38	83w26	5:33:44
Willow Woods 29	1	38N50	77w12	5:08:48
Wills Corner 46	4	36N59	76w38	5:06:32
Willston 29	1	38N52	77w12	5:08:48
Wilmington 32	4	37N51	78w16	5:13:04
Wilroy 132	5	36N44	76w35	5:06:20
Wilson 92	15	36N38	82w07	5:28:28
Wilson Creek 38	4	36N39	81w23	5:25:32
Wilson Grove 75	4	37N04	80w47	5:23:08
Wilsons 27	22	37N08	77w52	5:11:28
Wilton Woods 29	3	38N43	77w09	5:08:36
Winchester 136	9	39N11	78w10	5:12:40
Windcliff 43	17	37N36	77w29	5:09:56
Windmill Point 51	14	37N39	76w23	5:05:32
Windsor 46	4	36N49	76w45	5:07:00
Windsordale 43	22	37N36	77w32	5:10:08
Windsor Estates 29	3	38N43	77w09	5:08:36
Windsor Shades 63	14	37N27	77w02	5:08:08
Windsor Woods 133	6	36N51	76w07	5:04:28
Windy Hill Estates 42	22	37N37	77w22	5:09:28
Winfall 16	16	37N10	79w05	5:16:20
Wingina 62	14	37N38	78w50	5:15:20
Winningham 66	4	37N11	78w08	5:12:32
Winslow Hills 29	3	38N43	77w09	5:08:36
Winston 24	14	38N28	78w00	5:12:00
Wintergreen 62	14	37N50	78w44	5:14:56
Winterham 4	4	37N21	77w59	5:11:56
Winterpock 21	22	37N21	77w43	5:10:52
Wirtz 33	4	37N04	79w53	5:19:32
Wise 94	15	36N59	82w35	5:30:20
Wisharts Point 1	4	37N54	75w30	5:02:00
Wistar Farms 43	17	37N36	77w29	5:09:56
Witch Duck 133	6	36N51	76w09	5:04:36
Witch Duck Point 133	6	36N53	76w08	5:04:32
Withams 1	4	37N57	75w35	5:02:20
Wittens Mills 90	4	37N08	81w31	5:26:04
Wolfglade 18	4	36N40	80w55	5:23:40
Wolford 14	15	37N22	81w59	5:27:56
Wolftown 56	4	38N21	78w21	5:13:24
Wolf Trap 41	4	36N43	78w54	5:15:36
Womacks 20	4	37N03	78w39	5:14:36
Wood 82	26	36N46	82w35	5:30:20
Woodberry Forest 56	4	38N18	78w08	5:12:32
Woodbridge 74	13	38N40	77w15	5:09:00
Woodbrook 2	14	38N02	78w29	5:13:56
Woodburn Heights 29	1	38N50	77w12	5:08:48
Woodford 17	22	38N07	77w25	5:09:40
Woodhouse Corner 133	6	36N49	76w09	5:04:36
Woodland Hills 92	15	36N43	81w58	5:27:52
Woodlawn 18	4	36N43	80w49	5:23:16
Woodlawn Manor 29	3	38N45	77w08	5:08:32
Woodlawn Mansion 29	3	38N42	77w09	5:08:36
Woodlawn Park 29	3	38N45	77w08	5:08:32
Woodlawn Terrace 29	3	38N45	77w08	5:08:32
Woodlawn Terrace 43	22	37N33	77w22	5:09:28
Woodlee 131	21	38N09	79w05	5:16:20
Woodley Hills 29	3	38N45	77w08	5:08:32
Woodman Terrace 43	17	37N36	77w29	5:09:56
Woodmont 21	22	37N29	77w33	5:10:12
Woodridge 2	14	37N48	78w29	5:13:56
Woodrow Wilson 8	21	38N06	78w58	5:15:52
Woodrum 8	21	38N09	79w05	5:16:20
Woods Cross Roads 36	4	37N29	76w37	5:06:28
Woodside Estates 29	1	38N55	77w11	5:08:44
Woodson 5	16	37N43	79w04	5:16:16
Woodstock 83	14	38N53	78w30	5:14:00
Woodville 76	14	38N36	78w11	5:12:44
Woodway 52	26	36N46	83w02	5:32:08
Woolsey 74	14	38N40	77w29	5:09:56
Woolwine 69	4	36N47	80w17	5:21:08
Worlds 70	4	36N49	79w35	5:18:20
Worsham 72	4	37N18	78w24	5:13:36
Worshams 71	14	37N29	77w55	5:11:40
Wren 20	4	37N05	78w45	5:15:00
Wright 122	6	36N55	76w17	5:05:08
Wrights Shop 5	14	37N25	79w08	5:16:32
Wright Woods 29	3	38N42	77w09	5:08:36
Wurno 75	4	37N04	80w47	5:23:08
Wylliesburg 20	4	36N52	78w36	5:14:24
Wyndale 92	15	36N43	81w58	5:27:52
Wythe 113	6	37N00	76w23	5:05:32
Wytheville 95	4	36N57	81w05	5:24:20
Yacht Haven Estates 29	3	38N45	77w08	5:08:32
Yadkin 102	6	36N46	76w21	5:05:24
Yale 89	4	36N51	77w17	5:09:08
Yancey Mills 2	14	38N04	78w42	5:14:48
Yanceyville 54	14	38N02	78w00	5:12:00
Yards 90	4	37N17	81w19	5:25:16
Yellow Springs 92	15	36N46	81w52	5:27:28
Yellow Tavern 43	22	37N40	77w30	5:10:00
Yokum Station 52	26	36N50	82w53	5:31:32
York Manor 43	22	37N32	77w19	5:09:16
Yorkshire 74	2	38N47	77w27	5:09:48
Yorkshire Acres 74	2	38N47	77w28	5:09:52
Yorkshire Park 74	2	38N47	77w28	5:09:52
York Terrace 96	23	37N17	76w43	5:06:52
Yorktown 96	4	37N14	76w30	5:06:00
Yost 9	4	37N59	79w36	5:18:24
Youngers Store 41	4	36N46	78w56	5:15:44
Yuma 82	26	36N38	82w34	5:30:16
Zacata 93	19	38N07	76w47	5:07:08
Zanoni 36	4	37N22	76w29	5:05:56
Zenda 80	22	38N27	78w52	5:15:28
Zepp 83	14	38N55	78w28	5:13:52
Zion 40	20	36N32	77w28	5:09:52
Zion 54	14	38N09	78w11	5:12:44
Zion Crossroads 54	14	38N09	78w11	5:12:44
Zuni 46	4	36N52	76w50	5:07:20

WASHINGTON

TIME TABLES

WA # 1

Before 11/18/1883		LMT
11/18/1883	12:00	PST
3/31/1918	02:00	PWT
10/27/1918	02:00	PST
3/30/1919	02:00	PWT
10/26/1919	02:00	PST
2/09/1942	02:00	PWT
9/30/1945	02:00	PST
4/30/1961	02:00	PDT
9/24/1961	02:00	PST
4/29/1962	02:00	PDT
9/30/1962	02:00	PST
4/28/1963	02:00	US#2

WA # 2

Before 11/18/1883		LMT
11/18/1883	12:00	PST
3/31/1918	02:00	PWT
10/27/1918	02:00	PST
3/30/1919	02:00	PWT
10/26/1919	02:00	PST
2/09/1942	02:00	PWT
9/30/1945	02:00	PST
5/02/1950	02:00	PDT
9/24/1950	02:00	PST
4/30/1961	02:00	PDT
9/24/1961	02:00	PST
4/29/1962	02:00	PDT
9/30/1962	02:00	PST
4/28/1963	02:00	US#2

WA # 3

Before 11/18/1883		LMT
11/18/1883	12:00	PST
3/31/1918	02:00	PWT
10/27/1918	02:00	PST
3/30/1919	02:00	PWT
10/26/1919	02:00	PST
2/09/1942	02:00	PWT
9/30/1945	02:00	PST
4/30/1950	02:00	PDT
9/24/1950	02:00	PST
4/30/1961	02:00	PDT
9/24/1961	02:00	PST
4/29/1962	02:00	PDT
9/30/1962	02:00	PST
4/28/1963	02:00	US#2

WA # 4

Before 11/18/1883		LMT
11/18/1883	12:00	PST
3/31/1918	02:00	PWT
10/27/1918	02:00	PST
3/30/1919	02:00	PWT
10/26/1919	02:00	PST
2/09/1942	02:00	PWT
9/30/1945	02:00	PST
6/01/1949	00:01	PDT
9/01/1949	00:01	PST
4/29/1951	02:00	PDT
9/30/1951	02:00	PST
6/01/1952	02:00	PDT
9/28/1952	02:00	PST
4/30/1961	02:00	PDT
9/24/1961	02:00	PST
4/29/1962	02:00	PDT
9/30/1962	02:00	PST
4/28/1963	02:00	US#2

WA # 5

Before 11/18/1883		LMT
11/18/1883	12:00	PST
3/31/1918	02:00	PWT
10/27/1918	02:00	PST
3/30/1919	02:00	PWT
10/26/1919	02:00	PST
2/09/1942	02:00	PWT
9/30/1945	02:00	PST
6/01/1949	00:01	PDT
9/01/1949	00:01	PST
6/02/1950	02:00	PDT
9/07/1950	02:00	PST
4/30/1961	02:00	PDT
9/24/1961	02:00	PST
4/29/1962	02:00	PDT
9/30/1962	02:00	PST
4/28/1963	02:00	US#2

WA # 6

Before 11/18/1883		LMT
11/18/1883	12:00	PST
3/31/1918	02:00	PWT
10/27/1918	02:00	PST
3/30/1919	02:00	PWT
10/26/1919	02:00	PST
2/09/1942	02:00	PWT
9/30/1945	02:00	PST
6/01/1949	00:01	PDT
8/31/1949	00:01	PST
4/30/1950	02:00	PDT
9/24/1950	02:00	PST
4/30/1961	02:00	PDT
9/24/1961	02:00	PST
4/29/1962	02:00	PDT
9/30/1962	02:00	PST
4/28/1963	02:00	US#2

WA # 7

Before 11/18/1883		LMT
11/18/1883	12:00	PST
3/31/1918	02:00	PWT
10/27/1918	02:00	PST
3/30/1919	02:00	PWT
10/26/1919	02:00	PST
2/09/1942	02:00	PWT
9/30/1945	02:00	PST
6/01/1949	00:01	PDT
9/01/1949	00:01	PST
4/30/1961	02:00	PDT
9/24/1961	02:00	PST
4/29/1962	02:00	PDT
9/30/1962	02:00	PST
4/28/1963	02:00	US#2

WA # 8

Before 11/18/1883		LMT
11/18/1883	12:00	PST
3/31/1918	02:00	PWT
10/27/1918	02:00	PST
3/30/1919	02:00	PWT
10/26/1919	02:00	PST
5/07/1933	02:00	PDT
8/27/1933	02:00	PST
2/09/1942	02:00	PWT
9/30/1945	02:00	PST
6/03/1948	00:01	PDT
9/25/1948	00:01	PST
6/01/1949	02:00	PDT
9/25/1949	02:00	PST
4/30/1950	02:00	PDT
9/24/1950	02:00	PST
4/29/1951	02:00	PDT
9/30/1951	02:00	PST
4/30/1961	02:00	PDT
9/24/1961	02:00	PST
4/29/1962	02:00	PDT
9/30/1962	02:00	PST
4/28/1963	02:00	US#2

WA # 9

Before 11/18/1883		LMT
11/18/1883	12:00	PST
3/31/1918	02:00	PWT
10/27/1918	02:00	PST
3/30/1919	02:00	PWT
10/26/1919	02:00	PST
2/09/1942	02:00	PWT
9/30/1945	02:00	PST
6/01/1949	00:01	PDT
9/25/1949	00:01	PST
5/02/1950	02:00	PDT
9/24/1950	02:00	PST
4/29/1951	02:00	PDT
9/30/1951	02:00	PST
6/01/1952	02:00	PDT
9/28/1952	02:00	PST
4/30/1961	02:00	PDT
9/24/1961	02:00	PST
4/29/1962	02:00	PDT
9/30/1962	02:00	PST
4/28/1963	02:00	US#2

WA # 10

Before 11/18/1883		LMT
11/18/1883	12:00	PST
3/31/1918	02:00	PWT
10/27/1918	02:00	PST
3/30/1919	02:00	PWT
10/26/1919	02:00	PST
2/09/1942	02:00	PWT
9/30/1945	02:00	PST
4/27/1952	02:00	PDT
9/28/1952	02:00	PST
4/30/1961	02:00	PDT
9/24/1961	02:00	PST
4/29/1962	02:00	PDT
9/30/1962	02:00	PST
4/28/1963	02:00	US#2

WA # 11

Before 11/18/1883		LMT
11/18/1883	12:00	PST
3/31/1918	02:00	PWT
10/27/1918	02:00	PST
3/30/1919	02:00	PWT
10/26/1919	02:00	PST
5/07/1933	02:00	PDT
8/27/1933	02:00	PST
2/09/1942	02:00	PWT
9/30/1945	02:00	PST
6/01/1948	00:01	PDT
8/31/1948	00:01	PST
6/01/1949	00:01	PDT
9/01/1949	00:01	PST
4/30/1950	02:00	PDT
9/24/1950	02:00	PST
4/30/1961	02:00	PDT
9/24/1961	02:00	PST
4/29/1962	02:00	PDT
9/30/1962	02:00	PST
4/28/1963	02:00	US#2

WA # 12

Before 11/18/1883		LMT
11/18/1883	12:00	PST
3/31/1918	02:00	PWT
10/27/1918	02:00	PST
3/30/1919	02:00	PWT
10/26/1919	02:00	PST
2/09/1942	02:00	PWT
9/30/1945	02:00	PST
6/01/1949	00:01	PDT
9/30/1949	00:01	PST
4/30/1950	02:00	PDT
9/24/1950	02:00	PST
4/29/1951	02:00	PDT
9/30/1951	02:00	PST
6/01/1952	02:00	PDT
9/28/1952	02:00	PST
4/30/1961	02:00	PDT
9/24/1961	02:00	PST
4/29/1962	02:00	PDT
9/30/1962	02:00	PST
4/28/1963	02:00	US#2

WA # 13

Before 11/18/1883		LMT
11/18/1883	12:00	PST
3/31/1918	02:00	PWT
10/27/1918	02:00	PST
3/30/1919	02:00	PWT
10/26/1919	02:00	PST
2/09/1942	02:00	PWT
9/30/1945	02:00	PST
6/01/1948	00:01	PDT
9/25/1948	00:01	PST
6/01/1949	00:01	PDT
9/30/1949	00:01	PST
4/30/1950	02:00	PDT
9/24/1950	02:00	PST
4/29/1951	02:00	PDT
9/30/1951	02:00	PST
4/27/1952	02:00	PDT
9/28/1952	02:00	PST
4/30/1961	02:00	PDT
9/24/1961	02:00	PST
4/29/1962	02:00	PDT
9/30/1962	02:00	PST
4/28/1963	02:00	US#2

WA # 14

Before 11/18/1883		LMT
11/18/1883	12:00	PST
3/31/1918	02:00	PWT
10/27/1918	02:00	PST
3/30/1919	02:00	PWT
10/26/1919	02:00	PST
2/09/1942	02:00	PWT
9/30/1945	02:00	PST
6/14/1948	00:01	PDT
9/25/1948	00:01	PST
4/30/1961	02:00	PDT
9/24/1961	02:00	PST
4/29/1962	02:00	PDT
9/30/1962	02:00	PST
4/28/1963	02:00	US#2

WA # 15

Before 11/18/1883		LMT
11/18/1883	12:00	PST
3/31/1918	02:00	PWT
10/27/1918	02:00	PST
3/30/1919	02:00	PWT
10/26/1919	02:00	PST
2/09/1942	02:00	PWT
9/30/1945	02:00	PST
4/24/1949	00:01	PDT
9/01/1949	00:01	PST
4/30/1950	02:00	PDT
9/24/1950	02:00	PST
4/27/1952	02:00	PDT
9/28/1952	02:00	PST
4/30/1961	02:00	PDT
9/24/1961	02:00	PST
4/29/1962	02:00	PDT
9/30/1962	02:00	PST
4/28/1963	02:00	US#2

WA # 16

Before 11/18/1883		LMT
11/18/1883	12:00	PST
3/31/1918	02:00	PWT
10/27/1918	02:00	PST
3/30/1919	02:00	PWT
10/26/1919	02:00	PST
2/09/1942	02:00	PWT
9/30/1945	02:00	PST
6/01/1949	02:00	PDT
9/30/1949	02:00	PST
4/30/1950	02:00	PDT
9/03/1950	02:00	PST
4/30/1961	02:00	PDT
9/24/1961	02:00	PST
4/29/1962	02:00	PDT
9/30/1962	02:00	PST
4/28/1963	02:00	US#2

WA # 17

Before 11/18/1883		LMT
11/18/1883	12:00	PST
3/31/1918	02:00	PWT
10/27/1918	02:00	PST
3/30/1919	02:00	PWT
10/26/1919	02:00	PST
5/10/1933	02:00	PDT
8/31/1933	02:00	PST
2/09/1942	02:00	PWT
9/30/1945	02:00	PST
6/01/1948	00:01	PDT
9/25/1948	00:01	PST
6/01/1949	00:01	PDT
9/01/1949	00:01	PST
6/02/1950	02:00	PDT
9/07/1950	02:00	PST
4/29/1951	02:00	PDT
9/30/1951	02:00	PST
4/30/1961	02:00	PDT
9/24/1961	02:00	PST
4/29/1962	02:00	PDT
9/30/1962	02:00	PST
4/28/1963	02:00	US#2

WA # 18

Before 11/18/1883		LMT
11/18/1883	12:00	PST
3/31/1918	02:00	PWT
10/27/1918	02:00	PST
3/30/1919	02:00	PWT
10/26/1919	02:00	PST
2/09/1942	02:00	PWT
9/30/1945	02:00	PST
6/01/1948	00:01	PDT
9/25/1948	00:01	PST
6/01/1949	00:01	PDT
9/01/1949	00:01	PST
6/02/1950	02:00	PDT
9/07/1950	02:00	PST
4/30/1961	02:00	PDT
9/24/1961	02:00	PST
4/29/1962	02:00	PDT
9/30/1962	02:00	PST
4/28/1963	02:00	US#2

WA # 19

Before 11/18/1883		LMT
11/18/1883	12:00	PST
3/31/1918	02:00	PWT
10/27/1918	02:00	PST
3/30/1919	02:00	PWT
10/26/1919	02:00	PST
2/09/1942	02:00	PWT
9/30/1945	02:00	PST
6/01/1948	00:01	PDT
9/25/1948	00:01	PST
4/30/1961	02:00	PDT
9/24/1961	02:00	PST
4/29/1962	02:00	PDT
9/30/1962	02:00	PST
4/28/1963	02:00	US#2

WA # 20

Before 11/18/1883		LMT
11/18/1883	12:00	PST
3/31/1918	02:00	PWT
10/27/1918	02:00	PST
3/30/1919	02:00	PWT
10/26/1919	02:00	PST
2/09/1942	02:00	PWT
9/30/1945	02:00	PST
6/01/1952	02:00	PDT
9/28/1952	02:00	PST
4/30/1961	02:00	PDT
9/24/1961	02:00	PST
4/29/1962	02:00	PDT
9/30/1962	02:00	PST
4/28/1963	02:00	US#2

WA # 21

Before 11/18/1883		LMT
11/18/1883	12:00	PST
3/31/1918	02:00	PWT
10/27/1918	02:00	PST
3/30/1919	02:00	PWT
10/26/1919	02:00	PST
2/09/1942	02:00	PWT
9/30/1945	02:00	PST
6/06/1948	00:01	PDT
9/25/1948	00:01	PST
4/30/1961	02:00	PDT
9/24/1961	02:00	PST
4/29/1962	02:00	PDT
9/30/1962	02:00	PST
4/28/1963	02:00	US#2

WA # 22

Before 11/18/1883		LMT
11/18/1883	12:00	PST
3/31/1918	02:00	PWT
10/27/1918	02:00	PST
3/30/1919	02:00	PWT
10/26/1919	02:00	PST
2/09/1942	02:00	PWT
9/30/1945	02:00	PST
6/03/1948	00:01	PDT
9/25/1948	00:01	PST
5/01/1952	02:00	PDT
9/28/1952	02:00	PST
4/30/1961	02:00	PDT
9/24/1961	02:00	PST
4/29/1962	02:00	PDT
9/30/1962	02:00	PST
4/28/1963	02:00	US#2

WA # 23

Before 11/18/1883		LMT
11/18/1883	12:00	PST
3/31/1918	02:00	PWT
10/27/1918	02:00	PST
3/30/1919	02:00	PWT
10/26/1919	02:00	PST
2/09/1942	02:00	PWT
9/30/1945	02:00	PST
6/01/1949	00:01	PDT
9/01/1949	00:01	PST
4/30/1950	02:00	PDT
9/24/1950	02:00	PST
4/29/1951	02:00	PDT
9/30/1951	02:00	PST
6/01/1952	02:00	PDT
9/01/1952	02:00	PST
4/30/1961	02:00	PDT
9/24/1961	02:00	PST
4/29/1962	02:00	PDT
9/30/1962	02:00	PST
4/28/1963	02:00	US#2

WA # 24

Before 11/18/1883		LMT
11/18/1883	12:00	PST
3/31/1918	02:00	PWT
10/27/1918	02:00	PST
3/30/1919	02:00	PWT
10/26/1919	02:00	PST
5/07/1933	02:00	PDT
8/27/1933	02:00	PST
2/09/1942	02:00	PWT
9/30/1945	02:00	PST
6/01/1948	00:01	PDT
9/25/1948	00:01	PST
6/01/1949	00:01	PDT
9/30/1949	00:01	PST
4/30/1950	02:00	PDT
9/24/1950	02:00	PST
6/01/1952	02:00	PDT
9/28/1952	02:00	PST
4/30/1961	02:00	PDT
9/24/1961	02:00	PST
4/29/1962	02:00	PDT
9/30/1962	02:00	PST
4/28/1963	02:00	US#2

WA # 25

Before 11/18/1883		LMT
11/18/1883	12:00	PST
3/31/1918	02:00	PWT
10/27/1918	02:00	PST
3/30/1919	02:00	PWT
10/26/1919	02:00	PST
2/09/1942	02:00	PWT
9/30/1945	02:00	PST
6/01/1949	00:01	PDT
9/30/1949	00:01	PST
5/02/1950	02:00	PDT
9/24/1950	02:00	PST
4/30/1961	02:00	PDT
9/24/1961	02:00	PST
4/29/1962	02:00	PDT
9/30/1962	02:00	PST
4/28/1963	02:00	US#2

WA # 26

Before 11/18/1883		LMT
11/18/1883	12:00	PST
3/31/1918	02:00	PWT
10/27/1918	02:00	PST
3/30/1919	02:00	PWT
10/26/1919	02:00	PST
2/09/1942	02:00	PWT
9/30/1945	02:00	PST
6/03/1948	00:01	PDT
9/25/1948	00:01	PST
6/01/1949	00:01	PDT
9/30/1949	00:01	PST
4/30/1950	02:00	PDT
9/24/1950	02:00	PST
4/29/1951	02:00	PDT
9/30/1951	02:00	PST
4/30/1961	02:00	PDT
9/24/1961	02:00	PST
4/29/1962	02:00	PDT
9/30/1962	02:00	PST
4/28/1963	02:00	US#2

WA # 27

Before 11/18/1883		LMT
11/18/1883	12:00	PST
3/31/1918	02:00	PWT
10/27/1918	02:00	PST
3/30/1919	02:00	PWT
10/26/1919	02:00	PST
2/09/1942	02:00	PWT
9/30/1945	02:00	PST
6/01/1949	00:01	PDT
9/01/1949	00:01	PST
4/30/1950	02:00	PDT
9/24/1950	02:00	PST
4/29/1951	02:00	PDT
9/30/1951	02:00	PST
6/01/1952	02:00	PDT
9/28/1952	02:00	PST
4/30/1961	02:00	PDT
9/24/1961	02:00	PST
4/29/1962	02:00	PDT
9/30/1962	02:00	PST
4/28/1963	02:00	US#2

WA # 28

Before 11/18/1883		LMT
11/18/1883	12:00	PST
3/31/1918	02:00	PWT
10/27/1918	02:00	PST
3/30/1919	02:00	PWT
10/26/1919	02:00	PST
2/09/1942	02:00	PWT
9/30/1945	02:00	PST
4/24/1949	00:01	PDT
9/01/1949	00:01	PST
4/30/1950	02:00	PDT
9/24/1950	02:00	PST
4/29/1951	02:00	PDT
9/30/1951	02:00	PST
4/27/1952	02:00	PDT
9/28/1952	02:00	PST
4/30/1961	02:00	PDT
9/24/1961	02:00	PST
4/29/1962	02:00	PDT
9/30/1962	02:00	PST
4/28/1963	02:00	US#2

TIME TABLES

WA # 29

Date	Time	Zone
Before 11/18/1883		LMT
11/18/1883	12:00	PST
3/31/1918	02:00	PWT
10/27/1918	02:00	PST
3/30/1919	02:00	PWT
10/26/1919	02:00	PST
2/09/1942	02:00	PWT
9/30/1945	02:00	PST
6/20/1948	00:01	PDT
9/25/1948	00:01	PST
4/30/1961	02:00	PDT
9/24/1961	02:00	PST
4/29/1962	02:00	PDT
9/30/1962	02:00	PST
4/28/1963	02:00	US#2

WA # 30

Date	Time	Zone
Before 11/18/1883		LMT
11/18/1883	12:00	PST
3/31/1918	02:00	PWT
10/27/1918	02:00	PST
3/30/1919	02:00	PWT
10/26/1919	02:00	PST
2/09/1942	02:00	PWT
9/30/1945	02:00	PST
6/01/1948	00:01	PDT
9/25/1948	00:01	PST
4/30/1950	02:00	PDT
9/24/1950	02:00	PST
4/29/1951	02:00	PDT
9/30/1951	02:00	PST
6/01/1952	02:00	PDT
9/28/1952	02:00	PST
4/30/1961	02:00	PDT
9/24/1961	02:00	PST
4/29/1962	02:00	PDT
9/30/1962	02:00	PST
4/28/1963	02:00	US#2

WA # 31

Date	Time	Zone
Before 11/18/1883		LMT
11/18/1883	12:00	PST
3/31/1918	02:00	PWT
10/27/1918	02:00	PST
3/30/1919	02:00	PWT
10/26/1919	02:00	PST
2/09/1942	02:00	PWT
9/30/1945	02:00	PST
6/01/1949	00:01	PDT
9/30/1949	00:01	PST
4/30/1961	02:00	PDT
9/24/1961	02:00	PST
4/29/1962	02:00	PDT
9/30/1962	02:00	PST
4/28/1963	02:00	US#2

WA # 32

Date	Time	Zone
Before 11/18/1883		LMT
11/18/1883	12:00	PST
3/31/1918	02:00	PWT
10/27/1918	02:00	PST
3/30/1919	02:00	PWT
10/26/1919	02:00	PST
2/09/1942	02:00	PWT
9/30/1945	02:00	PST
6/01/1948	00:01	PDT
9/25/1948	00:01	PST
4/24/1949	00:01	PDT
9/11/1949	00:01	PST
4/30/1950	02:00	PDT
9/24/1950	02:00	PST
4/29/1951	02:00	PDT
9/30/1951	02:00	PST
4/27/1952	02:00	PDT
9/28/1952	02:00	PST
4/30/1961	02:00	PDT
9/24/1961	02:00	PST
4/29/1962	02:00	PDT
9/30/1962	02:00	PST
4/28/1963	02:00	US#2

WA # 33

Date	Time	Zone
Before 11/18/1883		LMT
11/18/1883	12:00	PST
3/31/1918	02:00	PWT
10/27/1918	02:00	PST
3/30/1919	02:00	PWT
10/26/1919	02:00	PST
2/09/1942	02:00	PWT
9/30/1945	02:00	PST
6/03/1948	00:01	PDT
9/25/1948	00:01	PST
6/01/1949	00:01	PDT
8/31/1949	00:01	PST
4/30/1950	02:00	PDT
9/24/1950	02:00	PST
4/30/1961	02:00	PDT
9/24/1961	02:00	PST
4/29/1962	02:00	PDT
9/30/1962	02:00	PST
4/28/1963	02:00	US#2

WA # 34

Date	Time	Zone
Before 11/18/1883		LMT
11/18/1883	12:00	PST
3/31/1918	02:00	PWT
10/27/1918	02:00	PST
3/30/1919	02:00	PWT
10/26/1919	02:00	PST
2/09/1942	02:00	PWT
9/30/1945	02:00	PST
6/01/1949	00:01	PDT
8/31/1949	00:01	PST
4/30/1950	02:00	PDT
9/24/1950	02:00	PST
6/01/1952	02:00	PDT
9/28/1952	02:00	PST
4/30/1961	02:00	PDT
9/24/1961	02:00	PST
4/29/1962	02:00	PDT
9/30/1962	02:00	PST
4/28/1963	02:00	US#2

WA # 35

Date	Time	Zone
Before 11/18/1883		LMT
11/18/1883	12:00	PST
3/31/1918	02:00	PWT
10/27/1918	02:00	PST
3/30/1919	02:00	PWT
10/26/1919	02:00	PST
2/09/1942	02:00	PWT
9/30/1945	02:00	PST
6/13/1950	02:00	PDT
9/07/1950	02:00	PST
4/30/1961	02:00	PDT
9/24/1961	02:00	PST
4/29/1962	02:00	PDT
9/30/1962	02:00	PST
4/28/1963	02:00	US#2

WA # 36

Date	Time	Zone
Before 11/18/1883		LMT
11/18/1883	12:00	PST
3/31/1918	02:00	PWT
10/27/1918	02:00	PST
3/30/1919	02:00	PWT
10/26/1919	02:00	PST
5/14/1933	02:00	PDT
8/27/1933	02:00	PST
2/09/1942	02:00	PWT
9/30/1945	02:00	PST
6/01/1948	00:01	PDT
9/25/1948	00:01	PST
6/01/1949	00:01	PDT
9/01/1949	00:01	PST
5/01/1950	02:00	PDT
9/24/1950	02:00	PST
4/29/1951	02:00	PDT
9/30/1951	02:00	PST
6/01/1952	02:00	PDT
9/28/1952	02:00	PST
4/30/1961	02:00	PDT
9/24/1961	02:00	PST
4/29/1962	02:00	PDT
9/30/1962	02:00	PST
4/28/1963	02:00	US#2

WA # 37

Date	Time	Zone
Before 11/18/1883		LMT
11/18/1883	12:00	PST
3/31/1918	02:00	PWT
10/27/1918	02:00	PST
3/30/1919	02:00	PWT
10/26/1919	02:00	PST
2/09/1942	02:00	PWT
9/30/1945	02:00	PST
6/01/1948	00:01	PDT
9/25/1948	00:01	PST
6/01/1949	00:01	PDT
9/30/1949	00:01	PST
5/02/1950	02:00	PDT
9/24/1950	02:00	PST
4/30/1961	02:00	PDT
9/24/1961	02:00	PST
4/29/1962	02:00	PDT
9/30/1962	02:00	PST
4/28/1963	02:00	US#2

WA # 38

Date	Time	Zone
Before 11/18/1883		LMT
11/18/1883	12:00	PST
3/31/1918	02:00	PWT
10/27/1918	02:00	PST
3/30/1919	02:00	PWT
10/26/1919	02:00	PST
2/09/1942	02:00	PWT
9/30/1945	02:00	PST
6/01/1949	00:01	PDT
9/30/1949	00:01	PST
4/30/1950	02:00	PDT
9/24/1950	02:00	PST
4/29/1951	02:00	PDT
9/30/1951	02:00	PST
4/30/1961	02:00	PDT
9/24/1961	02:00	PST
4/29/1962	02:00	PDT
9/30/1962	02:00	PST
4/28/1963	02:00	US#2

WA # 39

Date	Time	Zone
Before 11/18/1883		LMT
11/18/1883	12:00	PST
3/31/1918	02:00	PWT
10/27/1918	02:00	PST
3/30/1919	02:00	PWT
10/26/1919	02:00	PST
2/09/1942	02:00	PWT
9/30/1945	02:00	PST
6/03/1948	00:01	PDT
9/25/1948	00:01	PST
5/30/1949	00:01	PDT
9/01/1949	00:01	PST
4/29/1951	02:00	PDT
9/30/1951	02:00	PST
6/01/1952	02:00	PDT
9/28/1952	02:00	PST
4/30/1961	02:00	PDT
9/24/1961	02:00	PST
4/29/1962	02:00	PDT
9/30/1962	02:00	PST
4/28/1963	02:00	US#2

WA # 40

Date	Time	Zone
Before 11/18/1883		LMT
11/18/1883	12:00	PST
3/31/1918	02:00	PWT
10/27/1918	02:00	PST
3/30/1919	02:00	PWT
10/26/1919	02:00	PST
2/09/1942	02:00	PWT
9/30/1945	02:00	PST
6/01/1949	00:01	PDT
9/30/1949	00:01	PST
4/30/1950	02:00	PDT
9/24/1950	02:00	PST
4/29/1951	02:00	PDT
9/30/1951	02:00	PST
5/05/1952	02:00	PDT
10/05/1952	02:00	PST
4/30/1961	02:00	PDT
9/24/1961	02:00	PST
4/29/1962	02:00	PDT
9/30/1962	02:00	PST
4/28/1963	02:00	US#2

WA # 41

Date	Time	Zone
Before 11/18/1883		LMT
11/18/1883	12:00	PST
3/31/1918	02:00	PWT
10/27/1918	02:00	PST
3/30/1919	02:00	PWT
10/26/1919	02:00	PST
2/09/1942	02:00	PWT
9/30/1945	02:00	PST
4/24/1949	02:00	PDT
9/25/1949	02:00	PST
5/02/1950	02:00	PDT
9/24/1950	02:00	PST
6/10/1951	02:00	PDT
9/02/1951	02:00	PST
4/29/1956	02:00	PDT
9/29/1956	02:00	PST
4/30/1961	02:00	PDT
9/24/1961	02:00	PST
4/29/1962	02:00	PDT
9/30/1962	02:00	PST
4/28/1963	02:00	US#2

WA # 42

Date	Time	Zone
Before 11/18/1883		LMT
11/18/1883	12:00	PST
3/31/1918	02:00	PWT
10/27/1918	02:00	PST
3/30/1919	02:00	PWT
10/26/1919	02:00	PST
2/09/1942	02:00	PWT
9/30/1945	02:00	PST
4/24/1949	00:01	PDT
9/01/1949	00:01	PST
4/27/1952	02:00	PDT
9/28/1952	02:00	PST
4/30/1961	02:00	PDT
9/24/1961	02:00	PST
4/29/1962	02:00	PDT
9/30/1962	02:00	PST
4/28/1963	02:00	US#2

WA # 43

Date	Time	Zone
Before 11/18/1883		LMT
11/18/1883	12:00	PST
3/31/1918	02:00	PWT
10/27/1918	02:00	PST
3/30/1919	02:00	PWT
10/26/1919	02:00	PST
2/09/1942	02:00	PWT
9/30/1945	02:00	PST
4/24/1949	00:01	PDT
9/01/1949	00:01	PST
4/30/1961	02:00	PDT
9/24/1961	02:00	PST
4/29/1962	02:00	PDT
9/30/1962	02:00	PST
4/28/1963	02:00	US#2

WA # 44

Date	Time	Zone
Before 11/18/1883		LMT
11/18/1883	12:00	PST
3/31/1918	02:00	PWT
10/27/1918	02:00	PST
3/30/1919	02:00	PWT
10/26/1919	02:00	PST
5/07/1933	02:00	PDT
8/27/1933	02:00	PST
2/09/1942	02:00	PWT
9/30/1945	02:00	PST
6/01/1948	00:01	PDT
9/25/1948	00:01	PST
6/01/1949	00:01	PDT
9/30/1949	00:01	PST
4/30/1950	02:00	PDT
9/24/1950	02:00	PST
4/29/1951	02:00	PDT
9/30/1951	02:00	PST
6/01/1952	02:00	PDT
9/28/1952	02:00	PST
4/30/1961	02:00	PDT
9/24/1961	02:00	PST
4/29/1962	02:00	PDT
9/30/1962	02:00	PST
4/28/1963	02:00	US#2

WA # 45

Date	Time	Zone
Before 11/18/1883		LMT
11/18/1883	12:00	PST
3/31/1918	02:00	PWT
10/27/1918	02:00	PST
3/30/1919	02:00	PWT
10/26/1919	02:00	PST
2/09/1942	02:00	PWT
9/30/1945	02:00	PST
6/01/1948	00:01	PDT
9/25/1948	00:01	PST
4/30/1950	02:00	PDT
9/24/1950	02:00	PST
4/29/1951	02:00	PDT
9/30/1951	02:00	PST
4/30/1961	02:00	PDT
9/24/1961	02:00	PST
4/29/1962	02:00	PDT
9/30/1962	02:00	PST
4/28/1963	02:00	US#2

WA # 46

Date	Time	Zone
Before 11/18/1883		LMT
11/18/1883	12:00	PST
3/31/1918	02:00	PWT
10/27/1918	02:00	PST
3/30/1919	02:00	PWT
10/26/1919	02:00	PST
2/09/1942	02:00	PWT
9/30/1945	02:00	PST
6/01/1948	00:01	PDT
9/25/1948	00:01	PST
5/01/1950	02:00	PDT
9/25/1950	02:00	PST
4/30/1961	02:00	PDT
9/24/1961	02:00	PST
4/29/1962	02:00	PDT
9/30/1962	02:00	PST
4/28/1963	02:00	US#2

WA # 47

Date	Time	Zone
Before 11/18/1883		LMT
11/18/1883	12:00	PST
3/31/1918	02:00	PWT
10/27/1918	02:00	PST
3/30/1919	02:00	PWT
10/26/1919	02:00	PST
2/09/1942	02:00	PWT
9/30/1945	02:00	PST
6/06/1948	00:01	PDT
9/25/1948	00:01	PST
4/29/1951	02:00	PDT
9/30/1951	02:00	PST
6/01/1952	02:00	PDT
9/28/1952	02:00	PST
4/30/1961	02:00	PDT
9/24/1961	02:00	PST
4/29/1962	02:00	PDT
9/30/1962	02:00	PST
4/28/1963	02:00	US#2

WA # 48

Date	Time	Zone
Before 11/18/1883		LMT
11/18/1883	12:00	PST
3/31/1918	02:00	PWT
10/27/1918	02:00	PST
3/30/1919	02:00	PWT
10/26/1919	02:00	PST
5/07/1933	02:00	PDT
8/27/1933	02:00	PST
2/09/1942	02:00	PWT
9/30/1945	02:00	PST
4/30/1961	02:00	PDT
9/24/1961	02:00	PST
4/29/1962	02:00	PDT
9/30/1962	02:00	PST
4/28/1963	02:00	US#2

WA # 49

Date	Time	Zone
Before 11/18/1883		LMT
11/18/1883	12:00	PST
3/31/1918	02:00	PWT
10/27/1918	02:00	PST
3/30/1919	02:00	PWT
10/26/1919	02:00	PST
5/07/1933	02:00	PDT
8/27/1933	02:00	PST
2/09/1942	02:00	PWT
9/30/1945	02:00	PST
6/01/1948	00:01	PDT
9/25/1948	00:01	PST
6/01/1949	00:01	PDT
9/01/1949	00:01	PST
4/30/1950	02:00	PDT
9/24/1950	02:00	PST
4/29/1951	02:00	PDT
9/30/1951	02:00	PST
5/17/1952	02:00	PDT
9/28/1952	02:00	PST
4/30/1961	02:00	PDT
9/24/1961	02:00	PST
4/29/1962	02:00	PDT
9/30/1962	02:00	PST
4/28/1963	02:00	US#2

WA # 50

Date	Time	Zone
Before 11/18/1883		LMT
11/18/1883	12:00	PST
3/31/1918	02:00	PWT
10/27/1918	02:00	PST
3/30/1919	02:00	PWT
10/26/1919	02:00	PST
2/09/1942	02:00	PWT
9/30/1945	02:00	PST
6/01/1949	00:01	PDT
9/30/1949	00:01	PST
4/30/1950	02:00	PDT
9/24/1950	02:00	PST
4/27/1952	02:00	PDT
9/28/1952	02:00	PST
4/30/1961	02:00	PDT
9/24/1961	02:00	PST
4/29/1962	02:00	PDT
9/30/1962	02:00	PST
4/28/1963	02:00	US#2

WA # 51

Date	Time	Zone
Before 11/18/1883		LMT
11/18/1883	12:00	PST
3/31/1918	02:00	PWT
10/27/1918	02:00	PST
3/30/1919	02:00	PWT
10/26/1919	02:00	PST
5/07/1933	02:00	PDT
8/27/1933	02:00	PST
2/09/1942	02:00	PWT
9/30/1945	02:00	PST
6/01/1948	00:01	PDT
9/25/1948	00:01	PST
4/24/1949	00:01	PDT
9/11/1949	00:01	PST
5/01/1950	02:00	PDT
9/24/1950	02:00	PST
4/29/1951	02:00	PDT
9/30/1951	02:00	PST
4/27/1952	02:00	PDT
9/28/1952	02:00	PST
4/30/1961	02:00	PDT
9/24/1961	02:00	PST
4/29/1962	02:00	PDT
9/30/1962	02:00	PST
4/28/1963	02:00	US#2

WA # 52

Date	Time	Zone
Before 11/18/1883		LMT
11/18/1883	12:00	PST
3/31/1918	02:00	PWT
10/27/1918	02:00	PST
3/30/1919	02:00	PWT
10/26/1919	02:00	PST
5/07/1933	02:00	PDT
8/27/1933	02:00	PST
2/09/1942	02:00	PWT
9/30/1945	02:00	PST
6/03/1948	00:01	PDT
9/25/1948	00:01	PST
4/30/1961	02:00	PDT
9/24/1961	02:00	PST
4/29/1962	02:00	PDT
9/30/1962	02:00	PST
4/28/1963	02:00	US#2

WA # 53

Date	Time	Zone
Before 11/18/1883		LMT
11/18/1883	12:00	PST
3/31/1918	02:00	PWT
10/27/1918	02:00	PST
3/30/1919	02:00	PWT
10/26/1919	02:00	PST
2/09/1942	02:00	PWT
9/30/1945	02:00	PST
4/24/1949	00:01	PDT
9/01/1949	00:01	PST
4/30/1950	02:00	PDT
9/24/1950	02:00	PST
4/29/1951	02:00	PDT
9/30/1951	02:00	PST
4/30/1961	02:00	PDT
9/24/1961	02:00	PST
4/29/1962	02:00	PDT
9/30/1962	02:00	PST
4/28/1963	02:00	US#2

COUNTIES

1 Adams
2 Asotin
3 Benton
4 Chelan
5 Clallam
6 Clark
7 Columbia
8 Cowlitz
9 Douglas
10 Ferry
11 Franklin
12 Garfield
13 Grant
14 Grays Harbor
15 Island
16 Jefferson
17 King
18 Kitsap
19 Kittitas
20 Klickitat
21 Lewis
22 Lincoln
23 Mason
24 Okanogan
25 Pacific
26 Pend Oreille
27 Pierce
28 San Juan
29 Skagit
30 Skamania
31 Snohomish
32 Spokane
33 Stevens
34 Thurston
35 Wahkiakum
36 Walla Walla
37 Whatcom
38 Whitman
39 Yakima

Aberdeen 14 8 46N59 123W50 8:15:20
Aberdeen Gardens 14
1 46N58 123W45 8:15:00
Academy 32 1 47N26 117W23 7:49:32
Acme 37 1 48N43 122W12 8:08:48
Adco 13 1 47N23 119W29 7:57:56
Addy 33 1 48N21 117W50 7:51:20
Adelaide 17 9 47N19 122W14 8:08:56
Adelma Beach 16 31 48N07 122W47 8:11:08
Adna 21 5 46N38 123W04 8:12:16
Adrian 13 1 47N23 119W29 7:57:56
Aeneas 24 1 48N33 118W59 7:55:56
Agate Beach 5 2 48N08 123W44 8:14:56
Agnew 5 2 48N06 123W24 8:13:36
Ahtanum 39 1 46N34 120W37 8:02:28
Airway Heights 32
1 47N43 117W40 7:50:40
Ajlune 21 1 46N31 122W26 8:09:44
Aladdin 33 1 48N33 117W54 7:51:36
Albion 38 1 46N48 117W15 7:49:00
Alder 27 6 46N48 122W17 8:09:08
Alder Grove 14 1 46N59 123W36 8:14:24
Alderton 27 6 47N10 122W14 8:08:56
Alderwood Manor 31
1 47N50 122W17 8:09:08
Alger 29 1 48N28 122W19 8:09:16
Algona 17 9 47N17 122W15 8:09:00
Allen 29 1 48N31 122W21 8:09:24
Allentown 17 4 47N30 122W15 8:09:00
Allyn 23 1 47N23 122W50 8:11:20
Almira 22 1 47N43 118W56 7:55:44
Almota 1 46N42 117W28 7:49:52
Aloha 14 1 47N12 124W10 8:16:40
Alpental 17 4 47N32 121W49 8:07:16
Alpha 21 5 46N35 122W42 8:10:48
Alstown 1 47N34 120W00 8:00:00
Altoona 35 1 46N16 123W39 8:14:36
Amanda Park 14 1 47N28 123W54 8:15:36
Amber 32 1 47N21 117W43 7:50:52
Amboy 6 1 45N55 122W27 8:09:48
American Lake 27 6 47N09 122W33 8:10:12
Ames Lake 17 4 47N39 122W09 8:08:36
Anacortes 29 1 48N30 122W37 8:10:28
Anatone 2 1 46N08 117W08 7:48:32
Anderson Island 27
6 47N11 122W42 8:10:48
Annapolis 18 1 47N33 122W37 8:10:28
Appleton 20 1 45N49 121W16 8:05:04
Appleyard 4 1 47N26 120W19 8:01:16
Arden 33 1 48N33 117W54 7:51:36
Ardenvoir 4 1 47N44 120W22 8:01:28
Argyle 28 1 48N32 123W01 8:12:04
Ariel 8 3 45N57 122W34 8:10:16
Arletta 27 6 47N20 122W35 8:10:20
Arlington 31 1 48N12 122W08 8:08:32
Arlington Heights 31
1 48N12 122W07 8:08:28
Armar 31 24 48N04 122W10 8:08:40
Arnada Park Annex 6
51 45N39 122W40 8:10:40
Arrowhead 17 4 47N43 122W13 8:08:52
Arrowhead 27 6 47N09 122W33 8:10:12
Artic 14 1 46N57 123W46 8:15:04
Ashford 27 6 46N46 122W02 8:08:08
Asotin 2 1 46N20 117W03 7:48:12
Auburn 17 9 47N18 122W14 8:08:56
Ault Field 15 2 48N20 122W39 8:10:36
Austin 15 2 48N01 122W32 8:10:08
Avon 29 1 48N25 122W19 8:09:16
Avondale 17 4 47N39 122W09 8:08:36
Ayer 36 1 46N35 118W23 7:53:32
Azwell 4 1 47N57 119W52 7:59:28
B & G 31 24 47N58 122W14 8:08:56
Baby Island Heights 15
2 48N02 122W24 8:09:36
Baird 9 1 47N37 119W17 7:57:08
Bakerview 37 11 48N45 122W29 8:09:56
Ballard 17 44 47N41 122W22 8:09:28
Bangor 18 1 47N39 122W42 8:10:48
Barberton 6 51 45N40 122W37 8:10:28
Baring 17 4 47N46 121W29 8:05:56
Barstow 10 1 48N36 118W03 7:52:12
Basin City 11 1 46N35 119W00 7:56:00
Battle Ground 6 10 45N47 122W32 8:10:08
Battle Point 18 1 47N38 122W31 8:10:04
Bay Center 25 1 46N38 123W57 8:15:48
Bay City 14 1 46N58 123W45 8:15:00
Bayne 17 4 47N18 121W55 8:07:40
Bayview 29 1 48N25 122W19 8:09:16
Beacon Hill 8 32 46N10 122W55 8:11:40
Beaux Arts 17 4 47N36 122W12 8:08:48
Beaux Arts Village 17
4 47N35 122W12 8:08:48
Beaver 5 2 48N03 124W19 8:17:16
Beaver Valley 16 1 47N56 122W44 8:10:56
Beckett Point 16
31 48N07 122W47 8:11:08
Belfair 23 1 47N27 122W50 8:11:20
Bellevue 17 4 47N37 122W12 8:08:48
Bellingham 37 11 48N46 122W29 8:09:56

Belmont 38 1 47N06 117W10 7:48:40
Belvedere 24 1 48N03 118W59 7:55:56
Bench Drive 14 1 46N58 123W45 8:15:00
Benge 1 1 46N55 118W06 7:52:24
Bennett Hill 37 11 48N45 122W29 8:09:56
Benton City 3 1 46N16 119W29 7:57:56
Berrydale 17 4 47N20 122W08 8:08:32
Bethel 18 1 47N30 122W37 8:10:28
Beverly 13 1 46N50 119W56 7:59:44
Beverly Beach 15 2 48N01 122W32 8:10:08
Beverly Park 31 24 47N58 122W14 8:08:56
Bickleton 20 1 45N58 120W21 8:01:24
Big Lake 29 1 48N24 122W14 8:08:56
Bingen 20 1 45N43 121W28 8:05:52
Birch 17 4 47N12 121W59 8:07:56
Birch Bay 37 1 48N59 122W45 8:11:00
Birdsview 29 1 48N32 121W46 8:07:04
Bitter Lake 17 4 47N44 122W21 8:09:24
Black Diamond 17 4 47N19 122W00 8:08:00
Black Lake 33 1 48N33 117W54 7:51:36
Black River 17 4 47N30 122W15 8:09:00
Black River Junction 17
40 47N29 122W12 8:08:48
Blaine 37 1 48N59 122W45 8:11:00
Blakely Island 28
1 48N30 122W37 8:10:28
Blanchard 29 1 48N36 122W25 8:09:40
Blewett 4 1 47N36 120W40 8:02:40
Blue Creek 33 1 48N17 117W43 7:50:52
Blueslide 26 1 48N19 117W17 7:49:08
Blyn 5 2 48N05 123W06 8:12:24
Bodie 24 1 48N44 118W59 7:55:56
Bogachiel 5 2 47N57 124W23 8:17:32
Boise 17 1 47N11 122W01 8:08:04
Boistfort 21 5 46N40 122W58 8:11:52
Bonneville Spur 37
11 48N45 122W29 8:09:56
Bonney Lake 27 6 47N11 122W11 8:08:44
Boston Harbor 34
36 47N08 122W54 8:11:36
Bothell 17 12 47N46 122W12 8:08:48
Bow 29 1 48N34 122W24 8:09:36
Boyds 10 1 48N43 118W08 7:52:32
Brady 14 1 46N59 123W36 8:14:24
Breidablick 18 1 47N44 122W38 8:10:32
Bremer 21 7 46N33 122W22 8:09:28
Bremerton 18 13 47N34 122W38 8:10:32
Brewster 24 14 48N06 119W47 7:59:08
Bridgeport 9 1 48N00 119W40 7:58:40
Bridle Trail 17 4 47N41 122W12 8:08:48
Brier 31 1 47N50 122W15 8:09:00
Brinnon 16 1 47N41 122W54 8:11:36
Broadway 17 44 47N38 122W18 8:09:12
Brookdale 27 6 47N09 122W27 8:09:48
Brooklyn 25 1 46N47 123W31 8:14:04
Browns Point 27 49 47N18 122W26 8:09:44
Brownstown 39 1 46N24 120W32 8:02:08
Brownsville 18 1 47N39 122W37 8:10:28
Brush Prairie 6 1 45N44 122W33 8:10:12
Bryant 31 1 48N15 122W09 8:08:36
Bryn Mawr 17 40 47N30 122W14 8:08:56
Buckley 27 6 47N10 122W02 8:08:08
Bucoda 34 7 46N48 122W52 8:11:28
Buena 39 1 46N26 120W19 8:01:16
Buena Vista 15 2 48N14 122W21 8:09:24
Bunker 21 5 46N40 122W58 8:11:52
Burbank 36 1 46N12 119W01 7:56:04
Burbank Heights 36
1 46N14 119W07 7:56:28
Burien 17 4 47N28 122W21 8:09:24
Burley 18 1 47N25 122W38 8:10:32
Burlington 29 1 48N28 122W20 8:09:20
Burnett 27 6 47N10 122W02 8:08:08
Burton 17 4 47N23 122W28 8:09:52
Bush Point 15 2 48N02 122W36 8:10:24
Calville 1 48N33 117W54 7:51:36
Cama Beach 15 2 48N14 122W21 8:09:24
Camano City 15 2 48N14 122W21 8:09:24
Camas 6 15 45N35 122W24 8:09:36
Camden 1 48N03 117W14 7:48:56
Camelot 17 9 47N19 122W14 8:08:56
Camp Union 18 1 47N35 122W40 8:10:40
Campus 37 11 48N45 122W29 8:09:56
Capitol Hill 17 44 47N38 122W18 8:09:12
Capsante 29 1 48N30 122W37 8:10:28
Carbonado 27 6 47N05 122W03 8:08:12
Carlisle 14 1 47N07 124W05 8:16:20
Carlsborg 5 2 47N14 122W17 8:09:08
Carlson 21 7 46N43 122W11 8:08:44
Carlton 24 1 48N15 120W07 8:00:28
Carlyle 17 4 47N43 122W13 8:08:52
Carnation 17 4 47N39 121W55 8:07:40
Carriage Hill 18 1 46N31 122W09 8:08:36
Carrolls 8 3 46N04 122W52 8:11:28
Carson 30 1 45N44 121W49 8:07:16
Cascade Vista 17
40 47N29 122W12 8:08:48
Cashmere 4 1 47N31 120W28 8:01:52
Castle Rock 8 16 46N17 122W54 8:11:36
Cathcart 31 1 47N51 122W06 8:08:24

Cathlamet 35 1 46N12 123W23 8:13:32
Cavelero Beach 15
2 48N14 122W21 8:09:24
Cedardale 29 1 48N25 122W19 8:09:16
Cedar Falls 17 4 47N22 121W47 8:07:08
Cedar Grove 17 4 47N26 122W03 8:08:12
Cedarhome 31 1 48N14 122W21 8:09:24
Cedarhurst 17 1 47N29 122W29 8:09:56
Cedar Mountain 17
40 47N29 122W12 8:08:48
Cedarview 27 6 47N13 122W15 8:09:00
Cedarville 14 1 46N50 123W14 8:12:56
Cedonia 33 1 48N09 118W10 7:52:40
Center 16 1 47N49 122W53 8:11:32
Centerville 20 1 45N45 120W54 8:03:36
Centralia 21 17 46N43 122W58 8:11:52
Central Park 14 1 46N58 123W41 8:14:44
Central Valley 18
1 47N44 122W38 8:10:32
Ceres 21 5 46N40 122W58 8:11:52
Charter Oak 6 1 45N47 122W32 8:10:08
Chattaroy 32 1 47N53 117W21 7:49:24
Chehalis 21 18 46N40 122W58 8:11:52
Chehalis Indian Reservation 14
1 46N49 123W12 8:12:48
Chelan 4 1 47N51 120W01 8:00:04
Chelan Falls 4 1 47N48 119W59 7:59:56
Chelatchie 6 1 45N55 122W27 8:09:48
Chelsea Park 17 4 47N26 122W21 8:09:24
Cheney 32 1 47N30 117W35 7:50:20
Chenois Creek 14 1 46N59 123W53 8:15:32
Chenowith 30 1 45N44 121W32 8:06:08
Cherokee Bay Park 17
4 47N25 122W03 8:08:12
Cherry Crest 17 4 47N35 122W10 8:08:40
Cherry Gardens 17
4 47N45 121W59 8:07:56
Chesaw 24 1 48N57 119W03 7:56:12
Chewelah 33 1 48N17 117W43 7:50:52
Chico 18 1 47N37 122W43 8:10:52
Chimacum 16 1 48N01 122W46 8:11:04
Chinook 25 1 46N16 123W57 8:15:48
Christopher 17 9 47N19 122W14 8:08:56
Chuckanut Village 37
11 48N45 122W29 8:09:56
Chumstick 4 1 47N36 120W40 8:02:40
Cinebar 21 7 46N36 122W32 8:10:08
Clallam Bay 5 2 48N15 124W16 8:17:04
Claquato 21 5 46N40 122W58 8:11:52
Claremont 31 24 47N58 122W14 8:08:56
Clarkston 2 1 46N25 117W03 7:48:12
Clarkston Heights 2
1 46N24 117W03 7:48:12
Clayton 33 1 48N00 117W33 7:50:12
Clearbrook 37 1 49N00 122W16 8:09:04
Clearlake 29 1 48N28 122W14 8:08:56
Clearview 31 1 47N50 122W07 8:08:28
Clearwater 16 1 47N57 124W23 8:17:32
Cle Elum 19 1 47N12 120W56 8:03:44
Cleveland 20 1 45N44 120W12 8:00:48
Cliffdell 19 1 46N56 121W04 8:04:16
Cline 33 1 48N03 117W44 7:50:56
Clinton 15 2 47N59 122W21 8:09:24
Clipper 37 1 48N49 122W13 8:08:52
Cloverdale 8 3 46N01 122W51 8:11:24
Cloverland 2 1 46N20 117W02 7:48:08
Clover Park 27 6 47N10 122W32 8:10:08
Clyde Hill 17 4 47N38 122W13 8:08:52
Coal Creek 8 32 46N09 122W56 8:11:44
Coal Creek 17 4 47N33 122W04 8:08:16
Coalfield 17 4 47N30 122W07 8:08:28
Cohasset Beach 14
1 46N53 124W07 8:16:28
Colbert 32 1 47N50 117W20 7:49:20
Colby 18 1 47N32 122W38 8:10:32
Colchester 18 1 47N32 122W38 8:10:32
Cole's Corner 4 1 47N36 120W40 8:02:40
Colfax 38 1 46N53 117W22 7:49:28
College Place 36 1 46N03 118W23 7:53:32
Colton 38 1 46N34 117W08 7:48:32
Columbia 17 44 47N34 122W17 8:09:08
Columbia Beach 15
2 47N59 122W22 8:09:28
Columbia Heights 8
32 46N10 122W56 8:11:44
Colville 33 1 48N33 117W54 7:51:36
Colville Indian Agency 24
1 48N10 118W58 7:55:52
Colville Indian Reservation 10
1 48N10 118W58 7:55:52
Colvos 17 1 47N29 122W29 8:09:56
Conconully 24 1 48N34 119W45 7:59:00
Concora 17 4 47N24 122W17 8:09:08
Concrete 29 1 48N32 121W45 8:07:00
Conifer View 17 4 47N43 122W13 8:08:52
Connell 11 1 46N40 118W52 7:55:28
Conway 29 1 48N21 122W21 8:09:24
Cook 30 1 45N43 121W28 8:05:52
Copalis Beach 14 1 47N07 124W10 8:16:40

WASHINGTON

Copalis Crossing 14	1	47N07	124w05	8:16:20
Cornwall 37	11	48N45	122w29	8:09:56
Cosmopolis 14	1	46N57	123w46	8:15:04
Cottage Lake 17	4	47N45	122w09	8:08:36
Cottonwood Beach 37	1	48N59	122w45	8:11:00
Cougar 8	3	46N03	122w18	8:09:12
Coulee City 13	1	47N37	119w17	7:57:08
Coulee Dam 24	19	47N58	118w58	7:55:52
Country Homes 32	48	47N45	117w24	7:49:36
Coupeville 15	2	48N13	122w41	8:10:44
Cove 17	1	47N27	122w31	8:10:04
Covington 17	4	47N21	122w07	8:08:28
Cowiche 39	1	46N40	120w43	8:02:52
Craige 2	1	46N08	117w08	7:48:32
Crescent Beach 5	2	48N08	123w44	8:14:56
Crescent Valley 27	6	47N20	122w35	8:10:20
Creston 22	1	47N46	118w31	7:54:04
Crewport 39	1	46N20	120w11	8:00:44
Crocker 27	6	47N06	122w12	8:08:48
Cromwell 27	6	47N20	122w35	8:10:20
Crystal Mountain 27	6	47N12	121w59	8:07:56
Crystal Springs 27	6	47N14	122w32	8:10:08
Cumberland 17	4	47N17	121w56	8:07:44
Cunningham 1	1	46N49	118w48	7:55:12
Curlew 10	1	48N53	118w36	7:54:24
Curtis 21	5	46N35	123w07	8:12:28
Cushman Dam 23	1	47N24	123w09	8:12:36
Cusick 26	1	48N20	117w18	7:49:12
Custer 37	1	48N55	122w38	8:10:32
Dabob 16	1	47N49	122w53	8:11:32
Dahlia 35	1	46N20	123w38	8:14:32
Daisy 33	1	48N22	118w10	7:52:40
Dalkena 26	1	48N15	117w14	7:48:56
Dallesport 20	1	45N37	121w10	8:04:40
Danville 10	1	49N00	118w30	7:54:00
Darlington 31	24	47N58	122w14	8:08:56
Darrington 31	1	48N15	121w36	8:06:24
Dash Point 27	49	47N19	122w26	8:09:44
Davenport 22	1	47N39	118w09	7:52:36
Davis Terrace 8	3	46N09	122w54	8:11:36
Day Creek 29	1	48N30	122w14	8:08:56
Day Island 27	6	47N14	122w32	8:10:08
Dayton 7	1	46N19	117w59	7:51:56
Dayton 23	1	47N13	123w06	8:12:24
Decatur 28	1	48N30	122w37	8:10:28
Deckerville 23	1	47N00	123w24	8:13:36
Deep Creek 32	1	47N39	117w43	7:50:52
Deep River 35	1	46N21	123w41	8:14:44
Deer Harbor 28	1	48N37	123w00	8:12:00
Deer Lake 33	1	48N04	117w38	7:50:32
Deer Park 32	1	47N57	117w28	7:49:52
Dellesta Park 37	11	48N45	122w29	8:09:56
Delta Junction 31	24	47N58	122w14	8:08:56
Deming 37	1	48N50	122w13	8:08:52
Denison 32	1	47N57	117w28	7:49:52
Denny Creek 17	4	47N30	121w47	8:07:08
Denny Park 17	4	47N41	122w12	8:08:48
Des Moines 17	4	47N24	122w20	8:09:20
Dewey 29	1	48N30	122w37	8:10:28
Diablo 37	1	48N58	121w08	8:04:32
Diamond 38	1	46N53	117w22	7:49:28
Diamond Lake 26	1	48N11	117w01	7:48:04
Dieringer 27	6	47N14	122w14	8:08:56
Dines Point 15	2	48N06	122w34	8:10:16
Disautel 24	1	48N22	119w14	7:56:56
Discovery Bay 16	31	48N07	122w47	8:11:08
Dishman 32	1	47N40	117w16	7:49:04
Dixie 36	1	46N08	118w09	7:52:36
Dockton 17	4	47N22	122w28	8:09:52
Dodge 12	1	46N28	117w36	7:50:24
Doebay 28	1	48N37	122w50	8:11:20
Dollar Corner 6	1	45N47	122w32	8:10:08
Donald 39	1	46N29	120w24	8:01:36
Doris 19	1	46N52	120w01	8:00:04
Doty 21	7	46N38	123w17	8:13:08
Douglas 9	1	47N37	120w00	8:00:00
Downing 9	44	47N38	122w20	8:09:20
Draper Spring 20	1	46N01	121w17	8:05:08
Driftwood Shores 15	2	48N14	122w21	8:09:24
Dryad 21	5	46N40	122w58	8:11:52
Dryden 4	1	47N33	120w34	8:02:16
Dungeness 5	2	48N09	123w07	8:12:28
Du Pont 27	6	47N06	122w38	8:10:32
Dusty 38	1	46N49	117w39	7:50:36
Duvall 17	4	47N45	121w59	8:07:56
Duwamish 17	4	47N24	122w17	8:09:08
Eagledale 18	1	47N37	122w31	8:10:04
Earlington 17	40	47N29	122w12	8:08:48
Earlmount 17	4	47N39	122w09	8:08:36
East Auburn 17	9	47N19	122w14	8:08:56
East Coulee Dam 24	1	47N58	118w59	7:55:56
East Farms 32	1	47N44	117w04	7:48:16
Eastgate 17	4	47N34	122w08	8:08:32
Eastgate 36	1	46N04	118w20	7:53:20
East Hill 17	30	47N24	122w15	8:09:00
East Olympia 34	36	46N58	122w50	8:11:20
Easton 19	1	47N14	121w11	8:04:44
East Port Orchard 18	1	47N32	122w38	8:10:32
East Quilcene 16	1	47N49	122w53	8:11:32
East Redmond 17	4	47N39	122w09	8:08:36
East Selah 39	19	46N36	120w29	8:01:56
Eastsound 28	1	48N42	122w55	8:11:40
East Spokane 32	48	47N41	117w25	7:49:40
East Stanwood 31	1	48N14	122w21	8:09:24
East Union 17	44	47N37	122w18	8:09:12
East Wenatchee 9	1	47N25	120w18	8:01:12
East Wenatchee Bench 9	1	47N26	120w18	8:01:12
Eatonville 27	6	46N52	122w16	8:09:04
Echo 33	1	48N33	117w54	7:51:36
Echo Lake 17	4	47N44	122w21	8:09:24
Eden 35	1	46N20	123w38	8:14:32
Edgecomb 31	1	48N12	122w07	8:08:28
Edgemont 27	6	47N14	122w17	8:09:08
Edgemoor 37	11	48N45	122w29	8:09:56
Edgewater 31	24	47N58	122w14	8:08:56
Edgewood 27	6	47N15	122w18	8:09:12
Edison 29	1	48N33	122w27	8:09:48
Edmonds 31	20	47N49	122w23	8:09:32
Edwall 22	1	47N30	117w57	7:51:48
Eglon 18	2	47N52	122w31	8:10:04
Elbe 27	6	46N46	122w12	8:08:48
Elberton 38	1	46N59	117w13	7:48:52
Eldon 23	1	47N33	123w03	8:12:12
Electric City 13	1	47N56	119w02	7:56:08
Electron 27	6	47N06	122w12	8:08:48
Elgin 27	6	47N20	122w35	8:10:20
Elk 32	1	48N01	117w17	7:49:08
Elkcoal 17	4	47N22	121w52	8:07:28
Elk Plain 27	6	47N06	122w25	8:09:40
Ellensburg 19	21	47N00	120w32	8:02:08
Ellisford 24	1	48N47	119w24	7:57:36
Ellisport 17	4	47N25	122w26	8:09:44
Ellisville 17	4	47N30	121w47	8:07:08
Ellsworth 6	1	45N39	122w35	8:10:20
Elma 14	22	47N00	123w25	8:13:40
Elmer City 24	1	48N00	118w57	7:55:48
Eltopia 11	1	46N27	119w01	7:56:04
Emden	1	47N06	118w07	7:52:28
Emerald Hills 17	4	47N35	122w10	8:08:40
Endicott 38	1	46N56	117w41	7:50:44
Enetai 18	1	47N35	122w36	8:10:24
Enterprise 33	1	48N04	118w12	7:52:48
Entiat 4	1	47N40	120w13	8:00:52
Entiat Lake 9	1	47N45	120w05	8:00:20
Enumclaw 17	23	47N12	121w59	8:07:56
Enumclaw Plateau 17	4	47N16	122w00	8:08:00
Ephrata 13	1	47N19	119w33	7:58:12
Erlands Point 18	1	47N36	122w42	8:10:48
Espanola 32	1	47N36	117w45	7:51:00
Estes 38	1	46N44	117w00	7:48:00
Ethel 21	5	46N32	122w44	8:10:56
Etna 6	1	45N54	122w45	8:11:00
Eufaula Heights 8	32	46N09	122w56	8:11:44
Eureka 36	1	46N18	118w37	7:54:28
Evaline 21	5	46N30	122w56	8:11:44
Evans	1	48N43	118w01	7:52:04
Everett 31	24	47N59	122w12	8:08:48
Evergreen 6	1	45N39	122w35	8:10:20
Everson 37	1	48N55	122w21	8:09:24
Ewan 38	1	47N07	117w44	7:50:56
Fairchild 32	1	47N37	117w38	7:50:32
Fairchild Air Force Base 32	1	47N38	117w38	7:50:32
Fairfield 32	1	47N23	117w11	7:48:44
Fairholm 5	2	48N06	123w24	8:13:36
Fairmont 31	24	47N54	122w14	8:08:56
Fairview 39	19	46N35	120w28	8:01:52
Fall City 17	4	47N34	121w53	8:07:32
Fargher Lake 6	1	45N52	122w40	8:10:40
Farmer 9	1	47N37	119w49	7:59:16
Farmington 38	1	47N05	117w03	7:48:12
Federal 17	44	47N36	122w20	8:09:20
Federal Reservation 3	1	46N30	119w33	7:58:12
Federal Way 17	4	47N18	122w19	8:09:16
Felida 6	51	45N40	122w37	8:10:28
Ferncliff 18	1	47N38	122w31	8:10:04
Ferndale 37	1	48N51	122w36	8:10:24
Fern Hill 27	49	47N14	122w28	8:09:52
Fern Prairie 6	1	45N35	122w24	8:09:36
Fernwood 18	1	47N32	122w38	8:10:32
Fife 27	6	47N15	122w21	8:09:24
Fife Heights 27	6	47N14	122w20	8:09:20
Finley 3	1	46N09	119w02	7:56:08
Finn Hall 8	3	45N54	122w45	8:11:00
Fircrest 27	49	47N14	122w31	8:10:04
Firdale 25	39	46N41	123w44	8:14:56
Firwood 27	6	47N12	122w20	8:09:20
Fisher 6	1	45N35	122w24	8:09:36
Five Corners 34	7	46N57	122w36	8:10:24
Fletcher Bay 18	1	47N38	122w31	8:10:04
Florence 31	1	48N14	122w21	8:09:24
Fobes Hill 31	1	47N13	122w15	8:09:00
Foothill 32	48	47N42	117w22	7:49:28
Ford 33	1	47N55	117w49	7:51:16
Fordair 13	1	47N37	119w17	7:57:08
Fords Prairie 21	5	46N44	122w59	8:11:56
Forest 21	5	46N40	122w58	8:11:52
Forest Beach 23	1	47N27	122w50	8:11:20
Forest Beach 27	6	47N20	122w35	8:10:20
Forest City 18	1	47N32	122w38	8:10:32
Forest Hills Addition 32	48	47N43	117w25	7:49:40
Forest Park 17	4	47N45	122w17	8:09:08
Forks 5	25	47N57	124w23	8:17:32
Fort Lawton 17	4	47N40	122w25	8:09:40
Fort Lewis 27	6	47N06	122w35	8:10:20
Fort Rains 30	1	45N39	121w56	8:07:44
Four Corners 16	31	48N07	122w47	8:11:08
Four Corners 18	1	47N44	122w38	8:10:32
Four Corners 34	7	46N57	122w36	8:10:24
Four Lakes 32	1	47N34	117w36	7:50:24
Fourth Plain 6	51	45N38	122w37	8:10:28
Fox Island 27	6	47N16	122w38	8:10:32
Fragaria 18	1	47N26	122w33	8:10:12
Frances 25	1	46N33	123w30	8:14:00
Freeland 15	2	48N01	122w32	8:10:08
Freeman 32	1	47N31	117w12	7:48:48
Friday Harbor 28	1	48N32	123w01	8:12:04
Fruitland 33	1	48N04	118w12	7:52:48
Fruitvale 39	19	46N37	120w33	8:02:12
Gales Addition 5	2	48N06	123w24	8:13:36
Galvin 21	5	46N45	123w02	8:12:08
Gardena 36	1	46N02	118w40	7:54:40
Garden City 14	1	47N03	123w16	8:13:04
Gardenville 27	49	47N16	122w24	8:09:36
Gardiner 16	1	48N03	122w55	8:11:40
Garfield 38	1	47N01	117w09	7:48:36
Garland 32	48	47N41	117w25	7:49:40
Garrett 36	1	46N03	118w25	7:53:40
Gate 34	7	46N51	123w08	8:12:32
Geiger Field 32	1	47N38	117w30	7:50:00
Geiger Heights 32	1	47N36	117w29	7:49:56
Geneva 37	11	48N45	122w24	8:09:36
George 13	1	47N05	119w53	7:59:32
Georgetown 17	4	47N22	121w59	8:07:56
Getchell 31	1	48N12	122w07	8:08:28
Gibraltar 29	1	48N30	122w37	8:10:28
Gibson Creek 14	1	46N50	123w14	8:12:56
Gifford 33	1	48N18	118w09	7:52:36
Gig Harbor 27	34	47N20	122w35	8:10:20
Gig Harbor Peninsula 27	6	47N19	122w37	8:10:28
Gilberton 18	1	47N38	122w36	8:10:24
Gilmore Corners 8	3	46N19	122w44	8:10:56
Glacier 37	1	48N53	121w57	8:07:48
Gleed 39	1	46N40	120w37	8:02:28
Glen Acres 17	4	47N27	122w28	8:09:52
Glen Cove 16	31	48N07	122w47	8:11:08
Glencove 27	6	47N20	122w35	8:10:20
Glendale 15	1	47N56	122w22	8:09:28
Glenoma 21	7	46N31	122w10	8:08:40
Glenrose 32	1	47N40	117w17	7:49:08
Glenwood 18	1	47N32	122w38	8:10:32
Glenwood 20	1	46N01	121w17	8:05:08
Gold Bar 31	1	47N51	121w42	8:06:48
Goldendale 20	1	45N49	120w50	8:03:20
Goldendale Observatory 20	1	45N50	120w49	8:03:16
Goodnoe Hills 20	1	45N45	120w29	8:01:56
Gooseprairie 39	1	46N54	121w16	8:05:04
Gorst 18	1	47N32	122w42	8:10:48
Govan 22	1	47N45	118w42	7:54:48
Graham 27	6	47N03	122w18	8:09:12
Grand Coulee 13	1	47N57	119w00	7:56:00
Grand Mound 34	7	46N44	122w59	8:11:56
Grandview 39	1	46N15	119w54	7:59:36
Granger 39	1	46N21	120w11	8:00:44
Granite Falls 31	1	48N05	121w58	8:07:52
Grant Road Addition 9	1	47N26	120w19	8:01:16
Granville Grange 31	1	48N05	121w58	8:07:52
Grapeview 23	1	47N20	122w50	8:11:20
Grassmere 29	1	48N32	121w46	8:07:04
Gravelly Lake 27	6	47N10	122w32	8:10:08
Gray Gables 14	1	46N59	123w53	8:15:32
Grayland 14	1	46N49	124w06	8:16:24
Grays Harbor City 14	1	46N59	123w53	8:15:32
Grays River 35	1	46N21	123w37	8:14:28
Greenacres 32	1	47N40	117w10	7:48:40
Greenbank 15	2	48N06	122w35	8:10:20
Green Bluff 32	48	47N45	117w23	7:49:32
Green Mountain 6	1	45N54	122w45	8:11:00
Greenwater 17	4	47N12	121w59	8:07:56
Greenwood 14	1	46N58	123w45	8:15:00
Greenwood 17	44	47N41	122w21	8:09:24
Grisdale 14	1	47N22	123w37	8:14:28
Grotto 17	4	47N44	121w26	8:05:44
Guemes 29	1	48N30	122w37	8:10:28
Guerrier 21	5	46N40	122w58	8:11:52
Hadlock 16	1	48N02	122w45	8:11:00
Halterman 31	1	48N12	122w07	8:08:28
Hamilton 29	1	48N31	122w00	8:08:00
Hansville 18	1	47N55	122w33	8:10:12
Happy Valley 37	11	48N45	122w29	8:09:56
Harbor Center 15	2	48N01	122w32	8:10:08
Harbor Heights 17	4	47N23	122w28	8:09:52
Harbor Heights 27	6	47N03	122w15	8:09:00
Harmony 21	5	46N32	122w35	8:10:20
Harper 18	1	47N31	122w34	8:10:16
Harrah 39	1	46N24	120w33	8:02:12
Harrington 22	1	47N29	118w15	7:53:00
Harstine 23	1	47N13	123w06	8:12:24
Hartford 31	1	48N01	122w04	8:08:16
Hartland 20	1	45N42	121w17	8:05:08
Hartline 13	1	47N41	119w06	7:56:24
Harwood 39	19	46N36	120w32	8:02:08
Hatton 1	1	46N47	118w50	7:55:20
Havillah 24	1	48N42	119w26	7:57:44
Hay 38	1	46N41	117w55	7:51:40
Hayes 8	3	45N54	122w45	8:11:00
Hayes Park 32	48	47N42	117w22	7:49:28
Hayford 32	1	47N36	117w34	7:50:16
Hazel 31	1	48N12	122w07	8:08:28
Hazel Dell 6	51	45N39	122w40	8:10:40
Hazelwood 17	40	47N29	122w12	8:08:48
Hazelwood 32	48	47N39	117w27	7:49:48
Heather 25	1	46N48	124w06	8:16:24
Heisson 6	1	45N50	122w30	8:10:00
Herron Island 27	6	47N15	122w46	8:11:04
Highland 2	1	46N24	117w03	7:48:12
Highland 6	1	45N52	122w40	8:10:40
Highland 31	1	48N01	122w04	8:08:16
Highland Park 8	3	46N09	122w54	8:11:36
Highlands 17	40	47N29	122w12	8:08:48
High Point 17	4	47N32	121w59	8:07:56
Hillgrove 14	1	47N03	123w16	8:13:04
Hilltop 17	4	47N35	122w10	8:08:40
Hillyard 32	48	47N42	117w22	7:49:28
Hobart 17	4	47N22	121w58	8:07:52

Hockinson 6 1 45N44 122w33 8:10:12
Hoh Indian Reservation 16
1 47N44 124w25 8:17:40
Hoko 5 2 48N16 124w18 8:17:12
Holcomb 25 39 46N41 123w44 8:14:56
Holden Village 4 1 47N50 120w01 8:00:04
Holly 18 1 47N33 122w59 8:11:56
Hollywood 17 4 47N45 122w09 8:08:36
Holman 25 1 46N20 124w03 8:16:12
Home 27 6 47N17 122w46 8:11:04
Home Acres 31 24 47N58 122w14 8:08:56
Home Valley 30 1 45N41 121w53 8:07:32
Hood 30 1 45N44 121w34 8:06:16
Hoodsport 23 1 47N24 123w09 8:12:36
Hoogdal 29 1 48N30 122w14 8:08:56
Hooper 38 1 46N45 118w09 7:52:36
Hoquiam 14 26 46N59 123w53 8:15:32
Horizon View 17 4 47N35 122w10 8:08:40
Horseshoe Lake 18
1 47N32 122w38 8:10:32
Houghton 17 4 47N40 122w12 8:08:48
Humptulips 14 1 47N14 123w57 8:15:48
Hunters 33 1 48N07 118w12 7:52:48
Hunts Point 17 4 47N38 122w13 8:08:52
Huntsville 7 1 46N17 118w06 7:52:24
Husum 20 1 45N48 121w29 8:05:56
Hyak 19 4 47N24 121w24 8:05:36
Illahee 14 1 46N59 123w53 8:15:32
Illahee 18 1 47N35 122w40 8:10:40
Ilwaco 25 1 46N19 124w03 8:16:12
Image 6 1 45N39 122w35 8:10:20
Impach 10 1 48N18 118w12 7:52:48
Inchelium 10 1 48N18 118w12 7:52:48
Index 31 1 47N50 121w33 8:06:12
Indian Beach 15 2 48N14 122w21 8:09:24
Indianola 18 1 47N45 122w31 8:10:04
Inglewood 17 4 47N43 122w13 8:08:52
Intercity 31 24 47N58 122w14 8:08:56
International 17
44 47N38 122w20 8:09:20
Ione 26 1 48N45 117w25 7:49:40
Irby 22 1 47N22 118w51 7:55:24
Irondale 16 31 48N07 122w47 8:11:08
Island Center 18 1 47N38 122w31 8:10:04
Island Lake 18 1 47N44 122w38 8:10:32
Island View 3 1 46N14 119w14 7:56:56
Issaquah 17 27 47N32 122w02 8:08:08
Issaquah Plateau 17
4 47N33 122w01 8:08:04
Iverson 5 2 48N01 124w23 8:17:32
Jamieson Park 32
48 47N39 117w27 7:49:48
Jared 26 1 48N20 117w18 7:49:12
Johnson 38 1 46N38 117w08 7:48:32
Jorden 31 1 48N12 122w07 8:08:28
Jovita 27 6 47N12 122w20 8:09:20
Joyce 5 2 48N08 123w44 8:14:56
Juanita 17 4 47N42 122w12 8:08:48
Junction City 14 1 46N58 123w45 8:15:00
Juniper Beach 15 2 48N14 122w21 8:09:24
Kahlotus 11 1 46N39 118w33 7:54:12
Kalaloch 16 1 47N36 124w22 8:17:28
Kalama 8 28 46N01 122w51 8:11:24
Kalber 21 5 46N35 123w07 8:12:28
Kamilche 23 1 47N13 123w06 8:12:24
Kanaskat 17 4 47N19 121w54 8:07:36
Kangley 17 4 47N22 121w53 8:07:32
Kapowsin 27 6 46N59 122w13 8:08:52
Keller 10 1 48N05 118w41 7:54:44
Kellogg Marsh 31 1 48N12 122w07 8:08:28
Kellys Korner 34
36 46N58 122w50 8:11:20
Kelso 8 28 46N09 122w54 8:11:36
Kendall 37 1 48N49 122w13 8:08:52
Kenmore 17 4 47N46 122w14 8:08:56
Kennard Corner 31
1 47N43 122w13 8:08:52
Kennewick 3 29 46N12 119w07 7:56:28
Kennydale 17 40 47N31 122w12 8:08:48
Kenroy 9 1 47N26 120w19 8:01:16
Kent 17 30 47N23 122w14 8:08:56
Kettle Falls 33 1 48N37 118w03 7:52:12
Kewa 10 1 48N12 118w17 7:53:08
Key Center 27 6 47N20 122w35 8:10:20
Keyport 18 1 47N42 122w38 8:10:32
Kid Valley 8 3 46N20 122w41 8:10:44
Kiesling 32 48 47N38 117w24 7:49:36
Kingsgate 17 4 47N41 122w12 8:08:48
Kingston 18 1 47N48 122w30 8:10:00
Kiona 3 1 46N16 119w29 7:57:56
Kirkland 17 27 47N41 122w13 8:08:52
Kitsap Lake 18 1 47N35 122w40 8:10:40
Kittitas 19 1 46N59 120w25 8:01:40
Klaber 21 5 46N35 123w07 8:12:28
Klickitat 20 1 45N49 121w09 8:04:36
Klipsan Beach 25 1 46N30 124w03 8:16:12
Knab 21 5 46N26 122w51 8:11:24
Koontzville 1 48N01 118w57 7:55:48
Kosmos 21 7 46N30 122w11 8:08:44
Krain 17 4 47N12 121w59 8:07:56
Krupp 13 1 47N25 118w59 7:55:56
Kruse 31 24 48N04 122w10 8:08:40
K Street 27 49 47N15 122w29 8:09:56
Kummer 17 4 47N19 122w00 8:08:00
Lacamas 21 5 46N35 122w42 8:10:48
La Center 6 10 45N52 122w40 8:10:40
Lacey 34 36 47N02 122w49 8:11:16
La Conner 29 21 48N23 122w30 8:10:00
Lacrosse 38 1 46N49 117w53 7:51:32
Lagoon Point 15 2 48N06 122w34 8:10:16
La Grande 27 6 46N50 122w19 8:09:16
Lake Alice 17 4 47N34 121w53 8:07:32
Lakebay 27 6 47N15 122w46 8:11:04
Lake City 17 44 47N43 122w18 8:09:12
Lake City 27 6 47N09 122w34 8:10:16
Lake Crescent 5 2 48N06 123w24 8:13:36
Lake Dolloff 17 9 47N19 122w14 8:08:56

Lake Forest Park 17
4 47N46 122w16 8:09:04
Lake Heights 17 4 47N37 122w09 8:08:36
Lake Hills 17 4 47N36 122w08 8:08:32
Lake Joy 17 4 47N39 121w55 8:07:40
Lakeland Village 32
1 47N34 117w41 7:50:44
Lake Leota 17 4 47N45 122w09 8:08:36
Lake Louise 27 6 47N09 122w33 8:10:12
Lake Retreat 17 4 47N21 121w59 8:07:56
Lakeridge 17 4 47N30 122w15 8:09:00
Lakes 27 6 47N10 122w32 8:10:08
Lake Sawyer 17 30 47N24 122w15 8:09:00
Lake Shore 6 51 45N40 122w37 8:10:28
Lakeside 4 1 47N50 120w01 8:00:04
Lake Stevens 31 1 48N01 122w04 8:08:16
Lakeview 27 6 47N09 122w29 8:09:56
Lakeview Park 13 1 47N23 119w29 7:57:56
Lake Washington 17
4 47N44 122w13 8:08:52
Lake Wilderness 17
4 47N25 122w03 8:08:12
Lakewood 31 1 48N09 122w13 8:08:52
Lakewood Center 27
6 47N11 122w32 8:10:08
Lakota 17 4 47N20 122w22 8:09:28
Lamona 22 1 47N22 118w29 7:53:56
Lamont 38 1 47N12 117w54 7:51:36
Lancaster 1 47N02 117w40 7:50:40
Langley 15 2 48N02 122w25 8:09:40
La Push 5 2 47N55 124w38 8:18:32
Larimers Corner 31
1 47N55 122w05 8:08:20
Latah 32 1 47N17 117w09 7:48:36
Laurel 20 1 45N57 121w23 8:05:32
Laurel 37 11 48N45 122w29 8:09:56
Laurel Heights 31
24 47N58 122w14 8:08:56
Laurier 10 1 49N00 118w13 7:52:52
Lawrence 37 1 48N55 122w21 8:09:24
Leadpoint 33 1 48N55 117w35 7:50:20
Leavenworth 4 1 47N36 120w40 8:02:40
Lebam 25 1 46N34 123w33 8:14:12
Leland 16 1 47N53 122w53 8:11:32
Lemolo 18 1 47N44 122w38 8:10:32
Lester 17 4 47N12 121w29 8:05:56
Lexington 8 3 46N11 122w54 8:11:36
Liberty 19 1 47N14 120w42 8:02:48
Liberty Lake 32 1 47N41 117w05 7:48:20
Lilliwaup 23 1 47N28 123w07 8:12:28
Lincoln 22 1 47N50 118w25 7:53:40
Lind 1 1 46N58 118w37 7:54:28
Lindberg 21 7 46N33 122w22 8:09:28
Lisabuela 17 4 47N25 122w31 8:10:04
Littell 21 5 46N40 122w58 8:11:52
Little Falls 22 1 47N55 117w49 7:51:16
Littlerock 34 7 46N54 123w01 8:12:04
Lochsloy 31 1 48N01 122w04 8:08:16
Locke 26 1 48N20 117w18 7:49:12
Lofall 18 1 47N44 122w38 8:10:32
Lone Pine 24 1 47N58 118w59 7:55:56
Long Beach 25 1 46N21 124w03 8:16:12
Longbranch 27 6 47N13 122w46 8:11:04
Long Lake 18 1 47N32 122w38 8:10:32
Long Lake 22 1 47N50 117w51 7:51:24
Longmire 27 6 46N45 121w49 8:07:16
Longview 8 32 46N08 122w57 8:11:48
Loomis 24 1 48N49 119w38 7:58:32
Loon Lake 33 1 48N04 117w38 7:50:32
Lopez 28 1 48N31 122w54 8:11:36
Lost Creek 26 1 48N37 117w22 7:49:28
Loveland 27 6 47N06 122w25 8:09:40
Lowden 36 1 46N03 118w35 7:54:20
Lowell 31 24 47N58 122w14 8:08:56
Lower Peninsula 27
6 47N14 122w43 8:10:52
Lower Snoqualmie Valley 17
4 47N43 122w04 8:08:16
Lucerne 4 1 48N12 120w36 8:02:24
Lummi Indian Reservation 37
1 48N47 122w38 8:10:32
Lummi Island 37 1 48N43 122w41 8:10:44
Lyle 20 1 45N42 121w17 8:05:08
Lyman 29 1 48N32 122w04 8:08:16
Lynden 37 1 48N57 122w27 8:09:48
Lynwood 32 1 47N49 122w19 8:09:16
Lynwood Center 18
1 47N38 122w31 8:10:04
Mabana 15 2 48N06 122w25 8:09:40
Mabton 39 1 46N13 120w00 8:00:00
Machias 31 1 47N55 122w05 8:08:20
Madigan General Hospital 27
49 47N14 122w28 8:09:52
Madrona Beach 15 2 48N14 122w21 8:09:24
Mae 13 1 47N09 119w18 7:57:12
Magnolia 17 44 47N39 122w24 8:09:36
Magnolia Beach 17
4 47N23 122w29 8:09:56
Makah Indian Reservation 5
2 48N22 124w37 8:18:28
Malaga 4 1 47N20 120w16 8:01:04
Malden 38 1 47N14 117w29 7:49:56
Malo 10 1 48N48 118w36 7:54:24
Malone 14 1 46N58 123w20 8:13:20
Malott 24 1 48N17 119w42 7:58:48
Maltby 31 4 47N48 122w07 8:08:28
Manchester 18 1 47N33 122w33 8:10:12
Manette 18 1 47N35 122w40 8:10:40
Manito 32 48 47N38 117w24 7:49:36
Manito Club Estates 32
48 47N38 117w24 7:49:36
Manitou Beach 18 1 47N40 122w30 8:10:00
Manor 6 1 45N47 122w32 8:10:08
Mansfield 9 1 47N49 119w38 7:58:32
Manson 4 1 47N53 120w09 8:00:36
Manzanita 17 4 47N22 122w28 8:09:52
Manzanita 18 1 47N41 122w33 8:10:12

Maple Beach 18 1 47N38 122w51 8:11:24
Maple Falls 37 1 48N56 122w05 8:08:20
Maple Grove 5 2 48N06 123w24 8:13:36
Maple Valley 17 4 47N25 122w03 8:08:12
Maplewood 17 40 47N28 122w10 8:08:40
Maplewood 27 6 47N12 122w20 8:09:20
Marble 1 48N51 117w54 7:51:36
Marblemount 29 1 48N32 121w26 8:05:44
Marcellus 1 47N14 118w24 7:53:36
Marcus 33 1 48N40 118w04 7:52:16
Marengo 1 1 47N01 118w12 7:52:48
Marietta 37 1 48N47 122w36 8:10:24
Marine Drive 18 1 47N35 122w40 8:10:40
Markham 14 1 46N58 123w45 8:15:00
Marlin 13 1 47N25 118w59 7:55:56
Marshal 32 48 47N35 117w23 7:49:32
Marshall 32 1 47N34 117w30 7:50:00
Maryhill 20 1 45N41 120w49 8:03:16
Marys Corner 21 5 46N33 122w49 8:11:16
Marysville 31 24 48N03 122w11 8:08:44
Mason City 24 1 47N58 119w02 7:56:08
Matlock 23 1 47N14 123w25 8:13:40
Matneys Spur 10 1 48N36 118w03 7:52:12
Mattawa 13 1 46N44 119w54 7:59:36
Maxwelton 15 2 47N56 122w26 8:09:44
Maytown 34 36 47N02 122w51 8:11:24
Mazama 24 1 48N36 120w24 8:01:36
McChord 27 10 47N08 122w29 8:09:56
McChord Air Force Base 27
10 47N07 122w35 8:10:20
McCleary 14 1 47N03 123w16 8:13:04
McDonald 13 1 47N04 119w13 7:56:52
McDonald 21 5 46N40 122w58 8:11:52
McGowan 25 1 46N16 123w57 8:15:48
McKees Beach 31 1 48N14 122w21 8:09:24
McKenna 27 6 46N56 122w33 8:10:12
McMicken Heights 17
4 47N24 122w17 8:09:08
McMillin 27 6 47N08 122w14 8:08:56
McMurray 29 1 48N19 122w14 8:08:56
Mead 32 1 47N46 117w21 7:49:24
Meadow Brook 17 4 47N32 121w49 8:07:16
Meadowdale 31 1 47N51 122w20 8:09:20
Meadow Glade 6 1 45N47 122w32 8:10:08
Medical Lake 32 1 47N34 117w41 7:50:44
Medical Lake Rural 32
1 47N32 117w39 7:50:36
Medina 17 4 47N37 122w14 8:08:56
Medina Heights 17
4 47N35 122w10 8:08:40
Meeker 27 6 47N12 122w20 8:09:20
Megler 25 1 46N15 123w51 8:15:24
Melbourne 14 1 46N57 123w37 8:14:28
Menlo 25 1 46N38 123w39 8:14:36
Menlo Park 27 6 47N14 122w32 8:10:08
Mercer Island 17 4 47N35 122w15 8:09:00
Meredith 17 9 47N19 122w14 8:08:56
Meridan Heights 17
30 47N24 122w15 8:09:00
Meridian Heights 17
4 47N22 122w07 8:08:28
Merritt 4 1 47N47 120w50 8:03:20
Mesa 11 1 46N35 119w00 7:56:00
Metaline 26 1 48N51 117w24 7:49:36
Metaline Falls 26
1 48N52 117w22 7:49:28
Methow 24 1 48N08 120w00 8:00:00
Metreco 27 6 47N07 122w35 8:10:20
Miami Beach 18 1 47N38 122w51 8:11:24
Mica 32 1 47N33 117w13 7:48:52
Midland 27 49 47N10 122w24 8:09:36
Midland Acres 6 1 45N35 122w24 8:09:36
Midvale Corner 15
2 47N59 122w22 8:09:28
Midway 17 30 47N24 122w15 8:09:00
Midway 27 6 47N20 122w35 8:10:20
Milan 32 1 47N58 117w20 7:49:20
Milco 8 3 46N09 122w54 8:11:36
Miles 22 1 47N55 118w18 7:53:12
Miller River 17 4 47N43 121w22 8:05:28
Milltown 29 1 48N14 122w21 8:09:24
Millwood 32 1 47N41 117w17 7:49:08
Milton 27 4 47N15 122w19 8:09:16
Mineral 21 7 46N43 122w11 8:08:44
Minnehaha 6 51 45N40 122w39 8:10:36
Mirror Lake 17 9 47N19 122w14 8:08:56
Mission Beach 31
24 48N03 122w16 8:09:04
Mobase 27 6 47N06 122w35 8:10:20
Moclips 14 1 47N14 124w13 8:16:52
Mohler 22 1 47N24 118w20 7:53:20
Mold 9 1 47N37 119w17 7:57:08
Molson 24 1 48N59 119w12 7:56:48
Mondovi 22 1 47N41 118w01 7:52:04
Monitor 4 1 47N29 120w25 8:01:40
Monohan 17 4 47N35 122w04 8:08:16
Monroe 31 1 47N51 121w58 8:07:52
Monroe Junction 31
1 47N51 121w59 8:07:56
Monse 24 1 48N09 119w41 7:58:44
Monta Vista 27 6 47N10 122w32 8:10:08
Montborne 29 1 48N25 122w19 8:09:16
Montesano 14 33 46N59 123w36 8:14:24
Moorlands 17 4 47N43 122w13 8:08:52
Moran Prairie 32
48 47N38 117w24 7:49:36
Morgan Acres 32 48 47N42 117w22 7:49:28
Morganville 17 4 47N19 122w00 8:08:00
Morton 21 7 46N34 122w17 8:09:08
Moses Lake 13 1 47N08 119w17 7:57:08
Moses Lake North 13
1 47N09 119w18 7:57:12
Mossyrock 21 7 46N32 122w29 8:09:56
Mountain View 37 1 48N51 122w05 8:10:24
Mountain View Beach 15
2 48N14 122w21 8:09:24
Mount Brook 20 1 45N44 121w29 8:05:56

Mount Hope 32 1 47N23 117w10 7:48:40
Mountlake Terrace 31
1 47N47 122w19 8:09:16
Mount Pleasant 5 2 48N06 123w24 8:13:36
Mount Rainier 27 6 47N01 121w57 8:07:48
Mount Spokane 32 1 47N47 117w08 7:48:32
Mount Vernon 29 3 48N25 122w20 8:09:20
Moxee City 39 1 46N33 120w23 8:01:32
Muckleshoot Indian Res 17
1 47N15 122w07 8:08:28
Mukilteo 31 1 47N57 122w18 8:09:12
Murphy's Corner 31
24 47N58 122w14 8:08:56
Naches 39 1 46N44 120w42 8:02:48
Nahcotta 25 1 46N30 124w02 8:16:08
Napavine 21 5 46N35 122w54 8:11:36
Naselle 25 1 46N22 123w49 8:15:16
National 27 6 46N46 122w02 8:08:08
Navy Yard City 18
1 47N33 122w40 8:10:40
Neah Bay 5 2 48N22 124w37 8:18:28
Neilton 14 1 47N25 123w53 8:15:32
Nemah 25 1 46N31 123w53 8:15:32
Nespelem 24 1 48N10 118w59 7:55:56
Newaukum 17 9 47N15 122w14 8:08:56
Newaukum 21 5 46N40 122w58 8:11:52
Newcastle 17 40 47N29 122w12 8:08:48
Newhalem 37 1 48N40 121w15 8:05:00
New London 14 1 47N03 123w56 8:15:44
Newman Lake 32 1 47N44 117w04 7:48:16
Newport 17 4 47N35 122w10 8:08:40
Newport 26 1 48N11 117w03 7:48:12
Newport Hills 17 4 47N37 122w09 8:08:36
Newport Shores 17
4 47N37 122w09 8:08:36
Newton 14 1 46N59 123w53 8:15:32
Nighthawk 24 1 48N58 119w38 7:58:32
Nile 39 1 46N44 120w42 8:02:48
Nine Mile Falls 32
1 47N47 117w33 7:50:12
Nisqually 34 6 47N04 122w42 8:10:48
Nisqually Indian Reservation 27
1 47N00 122w41 8:10:44
Nisson 14 1 46N59 123w53 8:15:32
Nooksack 37 1 48N56 122w19 8:09:16
Nordland 16 1 48N03 122w41 8:10:44
Norman 31 1 48N14 122w21 8:09:24
Normandy Park 17 4 47N26 122w21 8:09:24
North Avon 29 1 48N25 122w19 8:09:16
North Bend 17 4 47N30 121w47 8:07:08
North Bonneville 30
1 45N39 121w57 8:07:48
North Central 32
48 47N42 117w26 7:49:44
North City 17 4 47N45 122w19 8:09:16
North Cove 25 1 46N42 123w59 8:15:56
North Fort Lewis 27
6 47N06 122w35 8:10:20
Northgate 17 44 47N43 122w18 8:09:12
North Highline 17
44 47N30 122w20 8:09:20
North Lake 17 9 47N19 122w14 8:08:56
North Lynnwood 31
1 47N50 122w17 8:09:08
Northport 33 1 48N55 117w48 7:51:12
North Prosser 3 1 46N12 119w46 7:59:04
North Puyallup 27
6 47N12 122w17 8:09:08
Norwood Village 17
4 47N35 122w10 8:08:40
Novelty 17 4 47N51 121w59 8:07:56
Oakbrook 27 6 47N09 122w33 8:10:12
Oakesdale 38 1 47N08 117w15 7:49:00
Oak Harbor 15 2 48N18 122w39 8:10:36
Oak Park 6 1 45N35 122w24 8:09:36
Oakville 14 35 46N51 123w14 8:12:56
Obrien 17 30 47N24 122w15 8:09:00
Ocean City 14 1 47N04 124w10 8:16:40
Ocean Park 25 1 46N30 124w03 8:16:12
Ocean Shores 14 1 46N59 123w53 8:15:32
Ocean Shores Estates 14
1 46N59 123w53 8:15:32
Oceanside 25 1 46N21 124w03 8:16:12
Ocosta 14 1 46N58 123w45 8:15:00
Odessa 22 1 47N20 118w41 7:54:44
Offutt Lake 34 36 47N02 122w51 8:11:24
Ohop 27 6 46N57 122w12 8:08:48
Okanogan 24 14 48N22 119w35 7:58:20
Olalla 18 1 47N26 122w33 8:10:12
Old Willapa 25 39 46N41 123w44 8:14:56
Olga 28 1 48N37 122w50 8:11:20
Olalla Valley 18
1 47N26 122w33 8:10:12
Olympia 17 4 47N35 122w10 8:08:40
Olympia 34 36 47N03 122w53 8:11:32
Olympic View 18 1 47N42 122w44 8:10:56
Omak 24 14 48N25 119w31 7:58:04
Onalaska 21 5 46N35 122w42 8:10:48
Onion Creek 33 1 48N33 117w54 7:51:36
Opportunity 32 1 47N39 117w15 7:49:00
Orcas 28 1 48N36 122w57 8:11:48
Orchard Avenue 32
48 47N41 117w25 7:49:40
Orchard Heights 18
1 47N31 122w36 8:10:24
Orchard Prairie 32
48 47N42 117w22 7:49:28
Orchards 6 1 45N39 122w35 8:10:20
Orient 10 1 48N52 118w12 7:52:48
Orillia 17 30 47N24 122w15 8:09:00
Orin 33 1 48N33 117w54 7:51:36
Orondo 9 1 47N38 120w13 8:00:52
Oroville 24 1 48N56 119w26 7:57:44
Orting 27 6 47N06 122w12 8:08:48
Osceola 17 4 47N12 121w59 8:07:56
Oso 31 1 48N16 121w56 8:07:44
Ostrander 8 7 46N12 122w53 8:11:32
Othello 1 1 46N50 119w10 7:56:40
Otis Orchards 32 1 47N42 117w13 7:48:52
Outlook 39 1 46N20 120w05 8:00:20
Overlake 17 4 47N35 122w09 8:08:36
Overlook 18 1 47N32 122w38 8:10:32
Oyhat 14 1 46N59 123w53 8:15:32
Oysterville 25 1 46N33 124w02 8:16:08
Ozette 5 2 48N15 124w16 8:17:04
Pacific 17 9 47N16 122w15 8:09:00
Pacific Beach 14 1 47N13 124w12 8:16:48
Packwood 21 7 46N36 121w40 8:06:40
Palisades 9 1 47N25 119w54 7:59:36
Palmer 17 4 47N19 121w54 8:07:36
Palouse 38 1 46N55 117w04 7:48:16
Palouse Falls 38 1 46N43 118w12 7:52:48
Paradise 6 1 45N54 122w45 8:11:00
Paradise Inn 27 6 46N47 121w44 8:06:56
Park 37 1 48N30 122w14 8:08:56
Parker 39 1 46N30 120w28 8:01:52
Parkland 27 49 47N09 122w26 8:09:44
Park Rapids 33 1 48N33 117w54 7:51:36
Parkwater 32 48 47N41 117w25 7:49:40
Parkwood 18 1 47N32 122w38 8:10:32
Pasadena Park 32 1 47N40 117w17 7:49:08
Pasco 11 29 46N14 119w06 7:56:24
Pasco West 11 1 46N14 119w09 7:56:36
Pataha City 12 1 46N28 117w32 7:50:08
Pateros 24 1 48N03 119w54 7:59:36
Paterson 3 1 45N56 119w36 7:58:24
Pearcot 9 1 47N26 120w19 8:01:16
Pearson 18 1 47N44 122w38 8:10:32
Pe Ell 21 7 46N34 123w18 8:13:12
Penn Cove Park 15
2 48N19 122w39 8:10:36
Peone 32 48 47N45 117w23 7:49:32
Perrinville 31 1 47N47 122w20 8:09:20
Peshastin 4 1 47N34 120w36 8:02:24
Picnic Point 27 6 47N20 122w35 8:10:20
Pillar Rock 35 1 46N20 123w38 8:14:32
Pine City 38 1 47N12 117w31 7:50:04
Pinecroft 32 48 47N40 117w20 7:49:20
Pinehurst 31 24 47N58 122w14 8:08:56
Pine Lake 17 4 47N33 122w04 8:08:16
Pinkney City 33 1 48N33 117w54 7:51:36
Plain 4 1 47N46 120w39 8:02:36
Plaza 32 1 47N19 117w23 7:49:32
Pleasant Beach 18
1 47N38 122w31 8:10:04
Pleasant Prairie 32
48 47N42 117w22 7:49:28
Pleasant Valley 6
51 45N40 122w37 8:10:28
Pleasant Valley 37
1 48N51 122w36 8:10:24
Plumb 34 7 46N56 122w51 8:11:24
Plymouth 3 1 45N56 119w21 7:57:24
Point Ellice 25 1 46N16 123w57 8:15:48
Point Roberts 37 1 48N59 123w05 8:12:20
Point White 18 1 47N38 122w31 8:10:04
Pomeroy 12 1 46N28 117w36 7:50:24
Pomona 39 19 46N36 120w32 8:02:08
Ponder 27 6 47N10 122w32 8:10:08
Ponderosa Estates 27
6 47N13 122w15 8:09:00
Pontius Park 31 1 47N43 122w13 8:08:52
Portage 17 4 47N24 122w26 8:09:44
Port Angeles 5 37 48N07 123w27 8:13:48
Port Blakely 18 1 47N38 122w31 8:10:04
Porter 14 1 46N56 123w18 8:13:12
Port Gamble 18 1 47N51 122w35 8:10:20
Port Gamble Indian Res 18
1 47N54 122w34 8:10:16
Port Ludlow 16 1 47N56 122w41 8:10:44
Port Madison 18 1 47N38 122w31 8:10:04
Port Madison Indian Res 18
1 47N43 122w38 8:10:32
Port Orchard 18 1 47N32 122w38 8:10:32
Port Stanley 28 1 48N31 122w54 8:11:36
Port Townsend 16
31 48N07 122w45 8:11:00
Possession 15 1 47N55 122w23 8:09:32
Potlatch 23 1 47N22 123w09 8:12:36
Poulsbo 18 1 47N44 122w39 8:10:36
Prairie 29 1 48N30 122w14 8:08:56
Prairie Center 15
2 48N13 122w40 8:10:40
Prairie Ridge 27 6 47N13 122w15 8:09:00
Preachers Slough 14
1 46N59 123w36 8:14:24
Prescott 36 1 46N18 118w19 7:53:16
Preston 17 4 47N31 121w56 8:07:44
Proctor 27 49 47N17 122w30 8:10:00
Proebstel 32 1 45N39 122w35 8:10:20
Prosser 3 1 46N12 119w46 7:59:04
Puget Island 35 1 46N13 123w23 8:13:32
Pullman 38 1 46N44 117w10 7:48:40
Purdy 27 6 47N23 122w38 8:10:32
Puyallup 27 38 47N12 122w18 8:09:12
Queen Anne 17 44 47N36 122w21 8:09:24
Queensborough 31 1 47N43 122w13 8:08:52
Queensgate 17 4 47N43 122w13 8:08:52
Queets 16 1 47N32 124w20 8:17:20
Quendall 17 40 47N29 122w12 8:08:48
Quilcene 16 1 47N49 122w53 8:11:32
Quillayute Indian Res 5
1 47N54 124w38 8:18:32
Quinault 14 1 47N28 123w51 8:15:24
Quinault Indian Reservation 14
1 47N21 124w17 8:17:08
Quincy 13 1 47N14 119w51 7:59:24
Rainier 34 7 46N53 122w41 8:10:44
Ralston 1 1 46N59 118w21 7:53:24
Randle 21 7 46N32 121w57 8:07:48
Raugust 13 1 47N09 119w18 7:57:12
Ravensdale 17 4 47N21 121w59 8:07:56
Raymond 25 39 46N41 123w44 8:14:56
Reardan 22 1 47N40 117w53 7:51:32

Redmond 17 27 47N41 122w07 8:08:28
Redondo 17 4 47N21 122w20 8:09:20
Rees Corner 31 1 47N55 122w05 8:08:20
Renton 17 40 47N29 122w12 8:08:48
Republic 10 1 48N39 118w44 7:54:56
Retsil 18 1 47N33 122w36 8:10:24
Revere 1 47N05 117w56 7:51:44
Rexville 29 1 48N25 122w19 8:09:16
Rhododendron Park 27
6 47N13 122w15 8:09:00
Rice 33 1 48N26 118w10 7:52:40
Richardson 28 1 48N27 122w54 8:11:36
Richland 3 41 46N17 119w18 7:57:12
Richmond Beach 17
20 47N46 122w23 8:09:32
Richmond Highlands 17
4 47N46 122w21 8:09:24
Ridgecrest 17 4 47N45 122w17 8:09:08
Ridgefield 6 42 45N49 122w45 8:11:00
Rimrock 39 1 46N44 120w42 8:02:48
Ringold 11 1 46N35 119w00 7:56:00
Ritzville 1 1 47N08 118w23 7:53:32
Riverside 24 1 48N30 119w30 7:58:00
Riverside 31 1 48N12 122w07 8:08:28
Riverton 17 4 47N24 122w17 8:09:08
Riverton Heights 17
4 47N28 122w17 8:09:08
Robe 31 1 48N06 121w49 8:07:16
Robinswood 17 4 47N35 122w10 8:08:40
Roche Harbor 28 1 48N32 123w01 8:12:04
Rochester 34 7 46N49 123w06 8:12:24
Rockford 32 1 47N27 117w08 7:48:32
Rock Island 9 1 47N22 120w08 8:00:32
Rockport 29 1 48N29 121w36 8:06:24
Rocky Butte 9 1 48N06 119w47 7:59:08
Rocky Point 8 3 46N09 122w54 8:11:36
Rocky Point 15 2 48N14 122w21 8:09:24
Rocky Point 18 1 47N36 122w40 8:10:40
Rollingbay 18 1 47N40 122w30 8:10:00
Ronald 19 1 47N14 121w01 8:04:04
Roosevelt 31 1 47N54 122w01 8:08:04
Rosalia 38 1 47N14 117w22 7:49:28
Rosario 28 1 48N39 122w52 8:11:28
Rosburg 35 1 46N20 123w38 8:14:32
Rosedale 27 6 47N20 122w39 8:10:36
Rose Hill 17 4 47N41 122w12 8:08:48
Rosehilla 17 4 47N22 122w28 8:09:52
Rosewood 32 48 47N43 117w25 7:49:40
Roslyn 19 1 47N13 120w59 8:03:56
Roy 27 6 47N00 122w33 8:10:12
Royal 13 1 46N47 119w32 7:58:08
Royal City 13 1 46N54 119w38 7:58:32
Ruby 26 1 48N31 117w18 7:49:12
Ruff 13 1 47N10 119w00 7:56:00
Ruston 27 6 47N18 122w31 8:10:04
Ryderwood 8 43 46N23 123w03 8:12:12
Sagehill 11 1 46N35 119w00 7:56:00
Saginaw 14 1 47N00 123w24 8:13:36
Saint Andrews 9 1 47N38 119w30 7:58:00
Saint John 38 1 47N06 117w35 7:50:20
Saint Urbans 21 5 46N30 122w56 8:11:44
Salkum 21 7 46N32 122w38 8:10:32
Salmon Creek 6 51 45N40 122w37 8:10:28
Samish Island 29 1 48N31 122w21 8:09:24
San de Fuca 15 2 48N14 122w43 8:10:52
Sandy Hook Park 18
1 47N44 122w38 8:10:32
Sandy Shores 17 4 47N22 122w28 8:09:52
Sappho 5 2 48N04 124w16 8:17:04
Sara 6 1 45N49 122w45 8:11:00
Satsop 14 1 47N00 123w29 8:13:56
Satus 39 1 46N17 120w09 8:00:36
Sawyer 39 1 46N28 120w22 8:01:28
Saxon 37 1 48N43 122w12 8:08:48
Scandia 18 1 47N43 122w39 8:10:36
Scenic 17 4 47N43 121w09 8:04:36
Schawana 13 1 46N50 119w56 7:59:44
Schneiders Prairie 34
36 47N02 122w51 8:11:24
Schwarder 39 1 46N33 120w32 8:02:08
Scopa 17 40 47N29 122w12 8:08:48
Seabeck 18 1 47N38 122w50 8:11:20
Seabold 18 1 47N38 122w31 8:10:04
Sea First 17 44 47N36 122w20 8:09:20
Seahurst 17 4 47N28 122w22 8:09:28
Seatons Grove 24 1 47N58 118w59 7:55:56
Seattle 17 44 47N36 122w20 8:09:20
Seattle Heights 31
20 47N49 122w20 8:09:20
Seaview 25 1 46N20 124w03 8:16:12
Sedro Woolley 29 1 48N30 122w14 8:08:56
Sekiu 5 2 48N16 124w18 8:17:12
Selah 39 19 46N39 120w32 8:02:08
Selleck 17 4 47N23 121w52 8:07:28
Sequim 5 25 48N05 123w06 8:12:24
Seven Mile 32 1 47N44 117w29 7:49:56
Sharon 32 48 47N38 117w24 7:49:36
Shaw Island 28 1 48N35 122w56 8:11:44
Shelton 23 45 47N13 123w06 8:12:24
Sheridan Beach 17
4 47N45 122w17 8:09:08
Sheridan Park 18 1 47N35 122w40 8:10:40
Sherwood Forest 17
4 47N35 122w10 8:08:40
Shine 16 1 47N52 122w39 8:10:36
Shoalwater Indian Res 25
1 46N42 124w01 8:16:04
Shore Acres 27 6 47N19 122w35 8:10:20
Shoreline 17 4 47N45 122w20 8:09:20
Shorewood Beach 27
6 47N16 122w38 8:10:32
Shoultes 31 1 48N05 122w10 8:08:40
Sifton 6 1 45N39 122w35 8:10:20
Sightly 8 3 46N20 122w41 8:10:44
Silvana 31 1 48N12 122w15 8:09:00
Silvana Terraces 31
1 48N14 122w21 8:09:24

WASHINGTON

Place		Lat	Long	Time
Silver Beach 37	11	48N45	122w29	8:09:56
Silver Creek 21	5	46N32	122w35	8:10:20
Silverdale 18	1	47N39	122w42	8:10:48
Silverlake 8	3	46N18	122w49	8:11:16
Silver Lake 31	24	47N58	122w14	8:08:56
Silverton 31	1	48N05	121w35	8:06:20
Similk Beach 29	1	48N27	122w34	8:10:16
Sisco Heights 31	1	48N12	122w07	8:08:28
Sixth Avenue 27	49	47N16	122w29	8:09:56
Skamania 30	1	45N37	122w03	8:08:12
Skamokawa 35	1	46N16	123w27	8:13:48
Skokomish Indian Reservation 23	1	47N22	123w09	8:12:36
Skykomish 17	4	47N42	121w22	8:05:28
Skyway 17	4	47N30	122w15	8:09:00
Sleepy Hollow 35	1	46N16	123w27	8:13:48
Smokey Point 31	1	48N12	122w07	8:08:28
Smyrna 13	1	46N54	119w38	7:58:32
Snake River 11	1	46N23	118w41	7:54:44
Snee-oosh-Beach 29	1	48N23	122w29	8:09:56
Snohomish 31	46	47N55	122w06	8:08:24
Snoqualmie 17	4	47N31	121w49	8:07:16
Snoqualmie Falls 17	4	47N32	121w49	8:07:16
Snoqualmie National Forest 17	4	47N29	121w31	8:06:04
Snoqualmie Pass 17	4	47N32	121w49	8:07:16
Snug Harbor 5	2	48N42	122w40	8:10:40
Soap Lake 13	1	47N23	119w29	7:57:56
Sol Duc Hot Springs 5	2	48N06	123w24	8:13:36
South Aberdeen 14	1	46N58	123w45	8:15:00
South Aberdeen Junction 14	1	46N58	123w45	8:15:00
South Bay 34	36	47N02	122w51	8:11:24
South Bellingham 37	11	48N45	122w29	8:09:56
South Bend 25	47	46N40	123w48	8:15:12
South Benton 3	1	46N01	119w28	7:57:52
South Broadway 39	1	46N34	120w31	8:02:04
South Cle Elum 19	1	47N11	120w57	8:03:48
South Colby 18	1	47N06	122w25	8:09:40
South Elma 14	1	47N00	123w24	8:13:36
Southgate 27	6	47N10	122w32	8:10:08
South Highline 17	4	47N26	122w19	8:09:16
South Montesano 14	1	46N59	123w36	8:14:24
South Prairie 27	6	47N08	122w06	8:08:24
South Snohomish 31	1	47N54	122w07	8:08:28
South Tacoma 27	49	47N12	122w28	8:09:52
Southworth 18	1	47N31	122w30	8:10:00
Spanaway 27	6	47N06	122w26	8:09:44
Spangle 32	1	47N26	117w23	7:49:32
Spear 32	48	47N40	117w21	7:49:24
Spee-bi-dah 31	24	48N04	122w10	8:08:40
Spirit 33	1	48N33	117w54	7:51:36
Spirit Lake 30	1	46N16	122w09	8:08:36
Spokane 32	48	47N40	117w24	7:49:36
Spokane Indian Reservation 33	1	47N53	117w59	7:51:56
Sprague 22	1	47N18	117w59	7:51:56
Springdale 33	1	48N04	117w45	7:51:00
Spring Glen 17	4	47N34	121w52	8:07:28
Squaxon Island Indian Res 23	1	47N12	122w54	8:11:36
Stampede 17	4	47N12	121w29	8:05:56
Stanwood 31	1	48N15	122w23	8:09:32
Starbuck 7	1	46N31	118w07	7:52:28
Star Lake 17	4	47N22	122w17	8:09:08
Startup 31	1	47N52	121w44	8:06:56
State Camp 35	1	46N15	123w19	8:13:16
Stehekin 4	1	48N19	120w39	8:02:36
Steilacoom 27	6	47N11	122w36	8:10:24
Steptoe 38	1	47N00	117w21	7:49:24
Sterling 29	1	48N30	122w14	8:08:56
Stevenson 30	20	45N42	121w53	8:07:32
Stiebels Corner 18	1	47N44	122w33	8:10:12
Stillwater 17	4	47N39	121w55	8:07:40
Stonehenge Replica 20	1	45N42	120w49	8:03:16
Strandell 37	1	48N55	122w21	8:09:24
Stratford 13	1	47N26	119w17	7:57:08
Stringtown 25	1	46N18	124w02	8:16:08
Sultan 31	1	47N52	121w49	8:07:16
Sumach 39	19	46N36	120w29	8:01:56
Sumas 37	1	49N00	122w16	8:09:04
Summit 27	4	47N22	122w01	8:08:04
Summit Park 29	1	48N30	122w37	8:10:28
Sumner 27	6	47N12	122w14	8:08:56
Sundale 20	1	45N44	120w12	8:00:48
Sundins Beach 15	2	48N14	122w21	8:09:24
Sunlight Beach 15	2	47N59	122w22	8:09:28
Sunny Bay 27	6	47N20	122w35	8:10:20
Sunnydale 17	4	47N28	122w20	8:09:20
Sunnyside 31	24	47N58	122w14	8:08:56
Sunnyside 39	1	46N20	120w00	8:00:00
Sunnyslope 18	1	47N30	122w44	8:10:56
Sunrise Beach 27	6	47N21	122w34	8:10:16
Sunrise Point 15	2	48N14	122w21	8:09:24
Sunset 36	1	47N05	117w35	7:50:20
Sunset Beach 14	1	47N14	124w13	8:16:52
Sunset Beach 15	2	48N14	122w21	8:09:24
Sunset Beach 23	6	47N14	122w34	8:10:16
Sun Village 17	4	47N43	122w13	8:08:52
Suquamish 18	1	47N44	122w33	8:10:12
Swan Trail 31	24	47N58	122w14	8:08:56
Swinomish Indian Reservation 29	1	48N25	122w32	8:10:08
Sylvan 27	6	47N16	122w38	8:10:32
Synarep 24	1	48N31	119w20	7:57:20
Tacoma 27	49	47N14	122w26	8:09:44
Tacoma Junction 27	6	47N14	122w20	8:09:20
Tahlequah 17	4	47N20	122w30	8:10:00
Taholah 14	1	47N21	124w17	8:17:08
Tahuya 23	1	47N22	123w03	8:12:12
Tampico 39	19	46N36	120w32	8:02:08
Tanglewild 34	36	47N02	122w51	8:11:24
Tanner 17	4	47N30	121w47	8:07:08
Teanaway 19	1	47N12	120w56	8:03:44
Tekoa 38	1	47N14	117w04	7:48:16
Telma 4	1	47N36	120w40	8:02:40
Tenino 34	50	46N51	122w51	8:11:24
Terminal Annex 32	48	47N42	117w25	7:49:40
Terrace Heights 39	1	46N36	120w26	8:01:44
Terrys Corner 15	2	48N14	122w21	8:09:24
Thomas 17	30	47N21	122w14	8:08:56
Thompson Place 34	36	47N02	122w51	8:11:24
Thornton 38	1	47N07	117w23	7:49:32
Thorp 19	1	47N04	120w40	8:02:40
Thrall 19	1	47N00	120w32	8:02:08
Thrashers Corner 31	1	47N43	122w13	8:08:52
Three Lakes 31	1	47N57	122w01	8:08:04
Thrift 27	6	47N03	122w15	8:09:00
Tieton 39	1	46N42	120w46	8:03:04
Tiger 26	1	48N42	117w24	7:49:36
Tillicum 27	6	47N07	122w32	8:10:08
Tillicum Beach 15	2	48N14	122w21	8:09:24
Times Square 17	44	47N37	122w20	8:09:20
Tokeland 25	1	46N42	123w59	8:15:56
Toledo 21	5	46N26	122w51	8:11:24
Tonasket 24	1	48N42	119w26	7:57:44
Toppenish 39	1	46N23	120w19	8:01:16
Touchet 36	1	46N02	118w40	7:54:40
Toutle 8	3	46N20	122w41	8:10:44
Town and Country 32	48	47N43	117w25	7:49:40
Tracyton 18	1	47N36	122w39	8:10:36
Trafton 31	1	48N12	122w07	8:08:28
Trend 17	4	47N41	122w12	8:08:48
Trentwood 32	1	47N42	117w13	7:48:52
Tri-Cities 11	1	46N14	119w06	7:56:24
Trinidad 13	1	47N14	119w51	7:59:24
Trout Lake 20	1	46N00	121w32	8:06:08
Trunbull 32	1	47N26	117w33	7:50:12
Tukwila 17	4	47N29	122w16	8:09:04
Tulalip 31	1	48N04	122w17	8:09:08
Tulalip Indian Reservation 31	1	48N05	122w15	8:09:00
Tulalip Shores 31	24	48N04	122w10	8:08:40
Tumtum 33	1	47N53	117w41	7:50:44
Tumwater 34	36	47N01	122w54	8:11:36
Turner Corner 31	1	47N55	122w05	8:08:20
Twisp 24	1	48N22	120w07	8:00:28
Tyee 5	2	48N04	124w21	8:17:24
Tyler 32	1	47N26	117w47	7:51:08
Underwood 30	1	45N44	121w32	8:06:08
Union 23	1	47N22	123w06	8:12:24
Union Gap 39	1	46N33	120w28	8:01:52
Union Mill 34	36	47N02	122w51	8:11:24
Uniontown 38	1	46N32	117w05	7:48:20
University of Washington 17	44	47N40	122w19	8:09:16
University Place 27	6	47N14	122w32	8:10:08
Upper Mill 17	4	47N12	121w56	8:07:44
Upper Preston 17	4	47N30	121w54	8:07:36
Upper Snoqualmie Valley 17	4	47N32	121w49	8:07:16
Urban 29	1	48N37	122w42	8:10:48
Usk 26	1	48N19	117w17	7:49:08
Utsaladdy 15	2	48N14	122w21	8:09:24
Vader 21	7	46N24	122w58	8:11:52
Vail 34	7	46N51	122w40	8:10:40
Valhalla 17	4	47N43	122w13	8:08:52
Valley 33	1	48N11	117w44	7:50:56
Valleyford 32	1	47N33	117w13	7:48:52
Van Buren 37	1	48N55	122w21	8:09:24
Vancouver 6	51	45N38	122w40	8:10:40
Van Horn 29	1	48N32	121w46	8:07:04
Vantage 19	1	46N58	119w59	7:59:56
Van Zandt 37	1	48N47	122w11	8:08:44
Vashon 17	4	47N27	122w28	8:09:52
Vashon Center 17	4	47N27	122w28	8:09:52
Vashon Heights 17	4	47N27	122w28	8:09:52
Vashon Island 17	4	47N26	122w28	8:09:52
Vaughn 27	6	47N21	122w46	8:11:04
Veazey 17	9	47N19	122w14	8:08:56
Venersborg 6	1	45N47	122w32	8:10:08
Venice 18	1	47N40	122w34	8:10:16
Veradale 32	1	47N39	117w13	7:48:52
Verlot 31	1	48N05	121w58	8:07:52
Vesta 14	1	46N57	123w46	8:15:04
Veterans Administration Hosp 6	51	45N38	122w37	8:10:28
Veterans Administration Hosp 36	48	46N04	118w22	7:53:28
View 6	1	45N52	122w40	8:10:40
View Park 18	1	47N32	122w38	8:10:32
Villa Beach 27	6	47N11	122w42	8:10:48
Virginia 18	1	47N43	122w38	8:10:32
Vision Acres 8	3	46N09	122w54	8:11:36
Wabash 17	4	47N12	121w59	8:07:56
Wahkiacus 20	1	45N49	121w06	8:04:24
Waitsburg 36	1	46N16	118w09	7:52:36
Waldron 28	1	48N41	123w02	8:12:08
Walla Walla 36	48	46N04	118w20	7:53:20
Wallicut 25	1	46N18	124w02	8:16:08
Wallingford 17	44	47N41	122w21	8:09:24
Wallula 36	1	46N05	118w54	7:55:36
Walnut Grove 6	1	45N39	122w35	8:10:20
Wapato 39	1	46N27	120w25	8:01:40
Warden 13	1	46N58	119w02	7:56:08
Warm Beach 31	1	48N10	122w22	8:09:28
Warren 27	6	47N20	122w35	8:10:20
Washougal 6	10	45N35	122w21	8:09:24
Washtucna 1	1	46N45	118w19	7:53:16
Waterville 9	1	47N39	120w04	8:00:16
Wauconda 24	1	48N44	118w59	7:55:56
Waukon 22	1	47N32	117w51	7:51:24
Wauna 27	6	47N23	122w39	8:10:36
Waunch Prairie 21	5	46N44	122w59	8:11:56
Wautauga Beach 18	1	47N32	122w38	8:10:32
Waverly 32	1	47N21	117w14	7:48:56
Wawawai 38	1	46N38	117w23	7:49:32
Wedgwood 17	44	47N41	122w18	8:09:12
Wegoe 27	6	47N06	122w35	8:10:20
Weikel 39	19	46N36	120w32	8:02:08
Weir Park 6	1	45N35	122w24	8:09:36
Welcome 37	1	48N49	122w13	8:08:52
Wellpinit 33	1	47N53	117w59	7:51:56
Wenatchee 4	52	47N25	120w19	8:01:16
Wenatchee Heights 4	1	47N26	120w19	8:01:16
Wenatchee Suburban 4	1	47N26	120w20	8:01:20
West Blakely 18	1	47N38	122w31	8:10:04
West Clarkston 2	1	46N24	117w03	7:48:12
West Coulee 9	1	47N58	118w59	7:55:56
Westfair 17	9	47N19	122w14	8:08:56
Westlake 13	1	47N06	119w20	7:57:20
West Park 18	1	47N35	122w40	8:10:40
Westport 14	1	46N53	124w06	8:16:24
West Richland 3	41	46N18	119w20	7:57:20
West Seattle 17	44	47N33	122w23	8:09:32
West Side 39	19	46N36	120w32	8:02:08
West Sound 28	1	48N42	122w55	8:11:40
West Wenatchee 4	1	47N27	120w20	8:01:20
Westwood 18	1	47N38	122w31	8:10:04
Weyerhauser 27	6	46N52	122w16	8:09:04
Wheeler 13	1	47N08	119w10	7:56:40
Whidbey Island Naval Air Sta 15	2	48N19	122w39	8:10:36
White Center 17	4	47N26	122w21	8:09:24
White Pass 39	1	46N44	120w42	8:02:48
Whites 14	1	47N00	123w24	8:13:36
White Salmon 20	1	45N44	121w29	8:05:56
White Swan 39	1	46N23	120w44	8:02:56
Whitman Nat Hist Site 36	48	46N02	118w28	7:53:52
Whitstran 3	1	46N12	119w46	7:59:04
Wickersham 37	1	48N40	122w13	8:08:52
Wilbur 22	1	47N46	118w42	7:54:48
Wilburton 17	4	47N35	122w10	8:08:40
Wildcat Lake 18	1	47N35	122w40	8:10:40
Wilderness Village 17	4	47N25	122w03	8:08:12
Wildwood 21	5	46N35	123w07	8:12:28
Wiley 39	19	46N36	120w29	8:01:56
Wilkeson 27	6	47N07	122w03	8:08:12
Willada 38	1	47N05	117w35	7:50:20
Willapa 25	39	46N41	123w44	8:14:56
Willard 30	1	45N43	121w28	8:05:52
Willow Grove 8	32	46N09	122w56	8:11:44
Wilma	1	46N41	117w09	7:48:36
Wilson Creek 13	1	47N25	119w07	7:56:28
Winchester 13	1	47N15	119w43	7:58:52
Winlock 21	5	46N30	122w56	8:11:44
Winona 38	1	46N57	117w48	7:51:12
Winslow 18	19	47N38	122w31	8:10:04
Winthrop 24	1	48N29	120w11	8:00:44
Winton 4	1	47N44	120w44	8:02:56
Wishkah 14	1	46N58	123w45	8:15:00
Wishram 20	1	45N40	120w58	8:03:52
Withrow	1	47N42	119w48	7:59:12
Wollochet 27	6	47N16	122w35	8:10:20
Woodinville 17	4	47N45	122w09	8:08:36
Woodland 8	53	45N54	122w45	8:11:00
Woodland 31	1	48N14	122w21	8:09:24
Woodland Beach 15	2	48N14	122w21	8:09:24
Woodlawn 14	1	46N59	123w53	8:15:32
Woodmont Beach 17	4	47N21	122w19	8:09:16
Woodway 31	20	47N47	122w23	8:09:32
Wycoff 18	1	47N35	122w40	8:10:40
Wye Lake 18	1	47N32	122w38	8:10:32
Wymer	1	46N50	120w28	8:01:52
Yacolt 6	1	45N52	122w25	8:09:40
Yakima 39	19	46N37	120w30	8:02:00
Yakima Indian Reservation 39	1	46N23	120w30	8:02:00
Yale 8	3	45N57	122w34	8:10:16
Yardley 32	48	47N41	117w25	7:49:40
Yarrow Point 17	4	47N39	122w13	8:08:52
Yelm 34	7	46N57	122w36	8:10:24
Yoman Ferry 27	6	47N11	122w42	8:10:48
Zenith 17	4	47N23	122w20	8:09:20
Zillah 39	1	46N24	120w15	8:01:00

WEST VIRGINIA

TIME TABLES

WV # 1
Before 7/01/1887 LMT
7/01/1887 12:00 EST
3/31/1918 02:00 EWT
10/27/1918 02:00 EST
3/30/1919 02:00 EWT
10/26/1919 02:00 EST
2/09/1942 02:00 EWT
9/30/1945 02:00 EST
4/28/1963 02:00 EDT
9/29/1963 02:00 EST
4/26/1964 02:00 EDT
9/27/1964 02:00 EST
4/25/1965 02:00 EDT
9/26/1965 02:00 EST
4/24/1966 02:00 US#1

WV # 2
Before 7/01/1887 LMT
7/01/1887 12:00 EST
3/31/1918 02:00 EWT
10/27/1918 02:00 EST
3/30/1919 02:00 EWT
10/26/1919 02:00 EST
2/09/1942 02:00 EWT
9/30/1945 02:00 EST
4/28/1963 02:00 US#2

WV # 3
Before 7/01/1887 LMT
7/01/1887 12:00 EST
3/31/1918 02:00 EWT
10/27/1918 02:00 EST
3/30/1919 02:00 EWT
10/26/1919 02:00 EST
2/09/1942 02:00 EWT
9/30/1945 02:00 EST
4/30/1950 02:00 EDT
9/24/1950 02:00 EST
4/29/1951 02:00 EDT
9/30/1951 02:00 EST
4/27/1952 02:00 EDT
9/28/1952 02:00 EST
4/26/1953 02:00 EDT
9/27/1953 02:00 EST
4/25/1954 02:00 EDT
9/26/1954 02:00 EST
4/24/1955 02:00 EDT
9/25/1955 02:00 EST
4/29/1956 02:00 EDT
9/30/1956 02:00 EST
4/28/1957 02:00 EDT
10/27/1957 02:00 EST
4/27/1958 02:00 EDT
10/26/1958 02:00 EST
4/26/1959 02:00 EDT
10/25/1959 02:00 EST
4/24/1960 02:00 EDT
10/30/1960 02:00 EST
4/30/1961 02:00 EDT
10/29/1961 02:00 EST
4/29/1962 02:00 EDT
9/30/1962 02:00 EST
4/28/1963 02:00 US#2

WV # 4
Before 7/01/1887 LMT
7/01/1887 12:00 EST
3/31/1918 02:00 EWT
10/27/1918 02:00 EST
3/30/1919 02:00 EWT
10/26/1919 02:00 EST
2/09/1942 02:00 EWT
9/30/1945 02:00 EST
4/29/1951 02:00 EDT
9/30/1951 02:00 EST
4/27/1952 02:00 EDT
9/28/1952 02:00 EST
4/26/1953 02:00 EDT
9/27/1953 02:00 EST
4/25/1954 02:00 EDT
9/26/1954 02:00 EST
4/24/1955 02:00 EDT
9/25/1955 02:00 EST
4/29/1956 02:00 EDT
9/30/1956 02:00 EST
4/28/1957 02:00 EDT
10/27/1957 02:00 EST
4/27/1958 02:00 EDT
10/26/1958 02:00 EST
4/26/1959 02:00 EDT
10/25/1959 02:00 EST
4/24/1960 02:00 EDT
10/30/1960 02:00 EST
4/30/1961 02:00 EDT
10/29/1961 02:00 EST
4/29/1962 02:00 EDT
9/30/1962 02:00 EST
4/28/1963 02:00 US#2

WV # 5
Before 7/01/1887 LMT
7/01/1887 12:00 EST
3/31/1918 02:00 EWT
10/27/1918 02:00 EST
3/30/1919 02:00 EWT
10/26/1919 02:00 EST
2/09/1942 02:00 EWT
9/30/1945 02:00 EST
4/27/1952 02:00 EDT
9/28/1952 02:00 EST
4/26/1953 02:00 EDT
9/27/1953 02:00 EST
4/25/1954 02:00 EDT
9/26/1954 02:00 EST
4/24/1955 02:00 EDT
9/25/1955 02:00 EST
4/29/1956 02:00 EDT
9/30/1956 02:00 EST
4/28/1957 02:00 EDT
9/29/1957 02:00 EST
4/27/1958 02:00 EDT
9/28/1958 02:00 EST
4/26/1959 02:00 EDT
9/27/1959 02:00 EST
4/24/1960 02:00 EDT
9/25/1960 02:00 EST
4/30/1961 02:00 EDT
9/24/1961 02:00 EST
4/29/1962 02:00 EDT
9/30/1962 02:00 EST
4/28/1963 02:00 EDT
9/29/1963 02:00 EST
4/26/1964 02:00 EDT
9/27/1964 02:00 EST
4/25/1965 02:00 EDT
9/26/1965 02:00 EST
4/24/1966 02:00 US#1

WV # 6
Before 7/01/1887 LMT
7/01/1887 12:00 EST
3/31/1918 02:00 EWT
10/27/1918 02:00 EST
3/30/1919 02:00 EWT
10/26/1919 02:00 EST
2/09/1942 02:00 EWT
9/30/1945 02:00 EST
4/27/1952 02:00 EDT
9/28/1952 02:00 EST
4/26/1953 02:00 EDT
9/27/1953 02:00 EST
4/25/1954 02:00 EDT
9/26/1954 02:00 EST
4/24/1955 02:00 EDT
9/25/1955 02:00 EST
4/29/1956 02:00 EDT
9/30/1956 02:00 EST
4/28/1957 02:00 EDT
9/29/1957 02:00 EST
4/27/1958 02:00 US#2

WV # 7
Before 7/01/1887 LMT
7/01/1887 12:00 EST
3/31/1918 02:00 EWT
10/27/1918 02:00 EST
3/30/1919 02:00 EWT
10/26/1919 02:00 EST
2/09/1942 02:00 EWT
9/30/1945 02:00 EST
4/27/1952 02:00 EDT
9/28/1952 02:00 EST
4/28/1963 02:00 US#2

WV # 8
Before 7/01/1887 LMT
7/01/1887 12:00 EST
3/31/1918 02:00 EWT
10/27/1918 02:00 EST
3/30/1919 02:00 EWT
10/26/1919 02:00 EST
2/09/1942 02:00 EWT
9/30/1945 02:00 EST
4/26/1953 02:00 EDT
9/27/1953 02:00 EST
4/25/1954 02:00 EDT
9/26/1954 02:00 EST
4/24/1955 02:00 EDT
9/25/1955 02:00 EST
4/29/1956 02:00 EDT
9/30/1956 02:00 EST
4/28/1957 02:00 EDT
10/27/1957 02:00 EST
4/27/1958 02:00 US#2

WV # 9
Before 7/01/1887 LMT
7/01/1887 12:00 EST
3/31/1918 02:00 EWT
10/27/1918 02:00 EST
3/30/1919 02:00 EWT
10/26/1919 02:00 EST
2/09/1942 02:00 EWT
9/30/1945 02:00 EST
4/26/1953 02:00 EDT
9/27/1953 02:00 EST
4/25/1954 02:00 EDT
9/26/1954 02:00 EST
4/24/1955 02:00 EDT
9/25/1955 02:00 EST
4/29/1956 02:00 EDT
9/30/1956 02:00 EST
4/28/1957 02:00 EDT
9/29/1957 02:00 EST
4/27/1958 02:00 EDT
9/28/1958 02:00 EST
4/26/1959 02:00 EDT
9/27/1959 02:00 EST
4/24/1960 02:00 US#2

WV # 10
Before 7/01/1887 LMT
7/01/1887 12:00 EST
3/31/1918 02:00 EWT
10/27/1918 02:00 EST
3/30/1919 02:00 EWT
10/26/1919 02:00 EST
2/09/1942 02:00 EWT
9/30/1945 02:00 EST
4/25/1954 02:00 EDT
9/26/1954 02:00 EST
4/24/1955 02:00 EDT
9/25/1955 02:00 EST
4/29/1956 02:00 EDT
9/30/1956 02:00 EST
4/28/1957 02:00 EDT
9/29/1957 02:00 EST
4/27/1958 02:00 EDT
9/28/1958 02:00 EST
4/26/1959 02:00 EDT
9/27/1959 02:00 EST
4/24/1960 02:00 EDT
9/25/1960 02:00 EST
4/30/1961 02:00 EDT
9/24/1961 02:00 EST
4/29/1962 02:00 EDT
9/30/1962 02:00 EST
4/28/1963 02:00 EDT
9/29/1963 02:00 EST
4/26/1964 02:00 EDT
9/27/1964 02:00 EST
4/25/1965 02:00 EDT
9/26/1965 02:00 EST
4/24/1966 02:00 US#1

WV # 11
Before 7/01/1887 LMT
7/01/1887 12:00 EST
3/31/1918 02:00 EWT
10/27/1918 02:00 EST
3/30/1919 02:00 EWT
10/26/1919 02:00 EST
2/09/1942 02:00 EWT
9/30/1945 02:00 EST
4/25/1954 02:00 EDT
9/26/1954 02:00 EST
4/24/1955 02:00 EDT
9/25/1955 02:00 EST
4/29/1956 02:00 EDT
9/30/1956 02:00 EST
4/28/1957 02:00 EDT
9/29/1957 02:00 EST
4/27/1958 02:00 EDT
9/28/1958 02:00 EST
4/26/1959 02:00 EDT
9/27/1959 02:00 EST
4/24/1960 02:00 EDT
9/25/1960 02:00 EST
4/30/1961 02:00 EDT
9/24/1961 02:00 EST
4/29/1962 02:00 US#2

WV # 12
Before 7/01/1887 LMT
7/01/1887 12:00 EST
3/31/1918 02:00 EWT
10/27/1918 02:00 EST
3/30/1919 02:00 EWT
10/26/1919 02:00 EST
2/09/1942 02:00 EWT
9/30/1945 02:00 EST
4/28/1957 02:00 EDT
9/29/1957 02:00 EST
4/27/1958 02:00 EDT
9/28/1958 02:00 EST
4/26/1959 02:00 EDT
9/27/1959 02:00 EST
4/24/1960 02:00 EDT
9/25/1960 02:00 EST
4/30/1961 02:00 EDT
9/24/1961 02:00 EST
4/29/1962 02:00 US#2

WV # 13
Before 7/01/1887 LMT
7/01/1887 12:00 EST
3/31/1918 02:00 EWT
10/27/1918 02:00 EST
3/30/1919 02:00 EWT
10/26/1919 02:00 EST
2/09/1942 02:00 EWT
9/30/1945 02:00 EST
4/24/1955 02:00 EDT
9/25/1955 02:00 EST
4/29/1956 02:00 EDT
9/30/1956 02:00 EST
4/28/1957 02:00 EDT
10/27/1957 02:00 EST
4/27/1958 02:00 US#2

WV # 14
Before 7/01/1887 LMT
7/01/1887 12:00 EST
3/31/1918 02:00 EWT
10/27/1918 02:00 EST
3/30/1919 02:00 EWT
10/26/1919 02:00 EST
2/09/1942 02:00 EWT
9/30/1945 02:00 EST
4/29/1956 02:00 EDT
9/30/1956 02:00 EST
4/28/1957 02:00 EDT
9/29/1957 02:00 EST
4/27/1958 02:00 EDT
9/28/1958 02:00 EST
4/26/1959 02:00 EDT
9/27/1959 02:00 EST
4/24/1960 02:00 EDT
9/25/1960 02:00 EST
4/30/1961 02:00 EDT
9/24/1961 02:00 EST
4/29/1962 02:00 EDT
9/30/1962 02:00 EST
4/28/1963 02:00 EDT
9/29/1963 02:00 EST
4/26/1964 02:00 EDT
9/27/1964 02:00 EST
4/25/1965 02:00 EDT
9/26/1965 02:00 EST
4/24/1966 02:00 US#1

WV # 15
Before 7/01/1887 LMT
7/01/1887 12:00 EST
3/31/1918 02:00 EWT
10/27/1918 02:00 EST
3/30/1919 02:00 EWT
10/26/1919 02:00 EST
2/09/1942 02:00 EWT
9/30/1945 02:00 EST
4/29/1956 02:00 EDT
9/30/1956 02:00 EST
4/28/1957 02:00 EDT
10/27/1957 02:00 EST
4/27/1958 02:00 US#2

WV # 16
Before 7/01/1887 LMT
7/01/1887 12:00 EST
3/31/1918 02:00 EWT
10/27/1918 02:00 EST
3/30/1919 02:00 EWT
10/26/1919 02:00 EST
2/09/1942 02:00 EWT
9/30/1945 02:00 EST
4/29/1956 02:00 EDT
9/30/1956 02:00 EST
4/28/1957 02:00 EDT
9/29/1957 02:00 EST
4/27/1958 02:00 EDT
9/28/1958 02:00 EST
4/26/1959 02:00 EDT
9/27/1959 02:00 EST
4/24/1960 02:00 US#2

WV # 17
Before 7/01/1887 LMT
7/01/1887 12:00 EST
3/31/1918 02:00 EWT
10/27/1918 02:00 EST
3/30/1919 02:00 EWT
10/26/1919 02:00 EST
2/09/1942 02:00 EWT
9/30/1945 02:00 EST
4/28/1957 02:00 EDT
9/29/1957 02:00 EST
4/27/1958 02:00 EDT
9/28/1958 02:00 EST
4/26/1959 02:00 EDT
9/27/1959 02:00 EST
4/24/1960 02:00 EDT
9/25/1960 02:00 EST
4/30/1961 02:00 EDT
9/24/1961 02:00 EST
4/29/1962 02:00 EDT
9/30/1962 02:00 EST
4/28/1963 02:00 EDT
9/29/1963 02:00 EST
4/26/1964 02:00 EDT
9/27/1964 02:00 EST
4/25/1965 02:00 EDT
9/26/1965 02:00 EST
4/24/1966 02:00 US#1

WV # 18
Before 7/01/1887 LMT
7/01/1887 12:00 EST
3/31/1918 02:00 EWT
10/27/1918 02:00 EST
3/30/1919 02:00 EWT
10/26/1919 02:00 EST
2/09/1942 02:00 EWT
9/30/1945 02:00 EST
4/28/1957 02:00 EDT
9/29/1957 02:00 EST
4/28/1963 02:00 EDT
9/29/1963 02:00 EST
4/26/1964 02:00 EDT
9/27/1964 02:00 EST
4/25/1965 02:00 EDT
9/26/1965 02:00 EST
4/24/1966 02:00 US#1

WV # 19
Before 7/01/1887 LMT
7/01/1887 12:00 EST
3/31/1918 02:00 EWT
10/27/1918 02:00 EST
3/30/1919 02:00 EWT
10/26/1919 02:00 EST
2/09/1942 02:00 EWT
9/30/1945 02:00 EST
4/29/1962 02:00 US#2

WV # 20
Before 7/01/1887 LMT
7/01/1887 12:00 EST
3/31/1918 02:00 EWT
10/27/1918 02:00 EST
3/30/1919 02:00 EWT
10/26/1919 02:00 EST
2/09/1942 02:00 EWT
9/30/1945 02:00 EST
5/06/1962 02:00 EDT
9/03/1962 02:00 EST
4/28/1963 02:00 EDT
9/29/1963 02:00 EST
4/26/1964 02:00 EDT
9/27/1964 02:00 EST
4/25/1965 02:00 EDT
9/26/1965 02:00 EST
4/24/1966 02:00 US#1

WV # 21
Before 7/01/1887 LMT
7/01/1887 12:00 EST
3/31/1918 02:00 EWT
10/27/1918 02:00 EST
3/30/1919 02:00 EWT
10/26/1919 02:00 EST
2/09/1942 02:00 EWT
9/30/1945 02:00 EST
4/30/1950 02:00 EDT
10/29/1950 02:00 EST
4/29/1951 02:00 EDT
9/30/1951 02:00 EST
4/27/1952 02:00 EDT
9/28/1952 02:00 EST
4/26/1953 02:00 EDT
9/27/1953 02:00 EST
4/25/1954 02:00 EDT
9/26/1954 02:00 EST
4/24/1955 02:00 EDT
9/25/1955 02:00 EST
4/29/1956 02:00 EDT
9/30/1956 02:00 EST
4/28/1957 02:00 EDT
10/27/1957 02:00 EST
4/27/1958 02:00 US#2

WV # 22
Before 7/01/1887 LMT
7/01/1887 12:00 EST
3/31/1918 02:00 EWT
10/27/1918 02:00 EST
3/30/1919 02:00 EWT
10/26/1919 02:00 EST
4/25/1937 00:01 EDT
9/05/1937 00:01 EST
2/09/1942 02:00 EWT
9/30/1945 02:00 EST
4/29/1956 02:00 EDT
9/30/1956 02:00 EST
4/28/1957 02:00 EDT
9/29/1957 02:00 EST
4/27/1958 02:00 EDT
9/28/1958 02:00 EST
4/26/1959 02:00 EDT
9/27/1959 02:00 EST
4/24/1960 02:00 EDT
9/25/1960 02:00 EST
4/30/1961 02:00 EDT
9/24/1961 02:00 EST
4/29/1962 02:00 EDT
9/30/1962 02:00 EST
4/28/1963 02:00 EDT
9/29/1963 02:00 EST
4/26/1964 02:00 EDT
9/27/1964 02:00 EST
4/25/1965 02:00 EDT
9/26/1965 02:00 EST
4/24/1966 02:00 US#1

WV # 23
Before 7/01/1887 LMT
7/01/1887 12:00 EST
3/31/1918 02:00 EWT
10/27/1918 02:00 EST
3/30/1919 02:00 EWT
10/26/1919 02:00 EST
2/09/1942 02:00 EWT
9/30/1945 02:00 EST
4/25/1948 02:00 EDT
9/26/1948 02:00 EST
4/24/1949 02:00 EDT
9/25/1949 02:00 EST
5/27/1950 02:00 EDT
9/01/1950 02:00 EST
4/29/1951 02:00 EDT
9/30/1951 02:00 EST
4/27/1952 02:00 EDT
9/28/1952 02:00 EST
4/26/1953 02:00 EDT
9/27/1953 02:00 EST
4/25/1954 02:00 EDT
9/26/1954 02:00 EST
4/24/1955 02:00 EDT
9/25/1955 02:00 EST
4/29/1956 02:00 EDT
9/30/1956 02:00 EST
4/28/1957 02:00 EDT
9/29/1957 02:00 EST
4/27/1958 02:00 EDT
9/28/1958 02:00 EST
4/26/1959 02:00 EDT
9/27/1959 02:00 EST
4/24/1960 02:00 EDT
9/25/1960 02:00 EST
4/30/1961 02:00 EDT
9/24/1961 02:00 EST
4/29/1962 02:00 US#2

WV # 24
Before 7/01/1887 LMT
7/01/1887 12:00 EST
3/31/1918 02:00 EWT
10/27/1918 02:00 EST
3/30/1919 02:00 EWT
10/26/1919 02:00 EST

TIME TABLES

2/09/1942 02:00 EWT
9/30/1945 02:00 EST
4/27/1947 02:00 EDT
9/28/1947 02:00 EST
4/25/1948 02:00 EDT
9/26/1948 02:00 EST
4/24/1949 02:00 EDT
9/25/1949 02:00 EST
4/29/1956 02:00 EDT
9/30/1956 02:00 EST
4/28/1957 02:00 EDT
9/29/1957 02:00 EST
4/27/1958 02:00 EDT
9/28/1958 02:00 EST
4/26/1959 02:00 EDT
9/27/1959 02:00 EST
4/24/1960 02:00 EDT
9/25/1960 02:00 EST
4/30/1961 02:00 EDT
9/24/1961 02:00 EST
4/29/1962 02:00 EDT
9/30/1962 02:00 EST
4/28/1963 02:00 EDT
9/29/1963 02:00 EST
4/26/1964 02:00 EDT
9/27/1964 02:00 EST
4/25/1965 02:00 EDT
9/26/1965 02:00 EST
4/24/1966 02:00 US#1

WV # 25
Before 7/01/1887 LMT
7/01/1887 12:00 EST
3/31/1918 02:00 EWT
10/27/1918 02:00 EST
3/30/1919 02:00 EWT
10/26/1919 02:00 EST
2/09/1942 02:00 EWT
9/30/1945 02:00 EST
4/28/1946 02:00 EDT
9/29/1946 02:00 EST
4/24/1949 02:00 EDT
9/25/1949 02:00 EST
4/30/1950 02:00 EDT
9/24/1950 02:00 EST
4/29/1956 02:00 EDT
9/30/1956 02:00 EST
4/28/1957 02:00 EDT
9/29/1957 02:00 EST
4/27/1958 02:00 EDT
9/28/1958 02:00 EST
4/26/1959 02:00 EDT
9/27/1959 02:00 EST
4/24/1960 02:00 EDT
9/25/1960 02:00 EST
4/30/1961 02:00 EDT
9/24/1961 02:00 EST
4/29/1962 02:00 EDT
9/30/1962 02:00 EST
4/28/1963 02:00 EDT
9/29/1963 02:00 EST
4/26/1964 02:00 EDT
9/27/1964 02:00 EST
4/25/1965 02:00 EDT
9/26/1965 02:00 EST
4/24/1966 02:00 US#1

WV # 26
Before 7/01/1887 LMT
7/01/1887 12:00 EST
3/31/1918 02:00 EWT
10/27/1918 02:00 EST
3/30/1919 02:00 EWT
10/26/1919 02:00 EST
2/09/1942 02:00 EWT
9/30/1945 02:00 EST
4/28/1946 02:00 EDT
9/29/1946 02:00 EST
4/28/1957 02:00 EDT
9/29/1957 02:00 EST
4/27/1958 02:00 EDT
9/28/1958 02:00 EST
4/26/1959 02:00 EDT
9/27/1959 02:00 EST
4/24/1960 02:00 EDT
9/25/1960 02:00 EST
4/30/1961 02:00 EDT
9/24/1961 02:00 EST
4/29/1962 02:00 EDT
9/30/1962 02:00 EST
4/28/1963 02:00 EDT
9/29/1963 02:00 EST
4/26/1964 02:00 EDT
9/27/1964 02:00 EST
4/25/1965 02:00 EDT
9/26/1965 02:00 EST
4/24/1966 02:00 US#1

WV # 27
Before 7/01/1887 LMT
7/01/1887 12:00 EST
3/31/1918 02:00 EWT
10/27/1918 02:00 EST
3/30/1919 02:00 EWT
10/26/1919 02:00 EST
2/09/1942 02:00 EWT
9/30/1945 02:00 EST
4/25/1948 02:00 EDT
9/26/1948 02:00 EST
4/24/1949 02:00 EDT
9/25/1949 02:00 EST
4/30/1950 02:00 EDT
9/24/1950 02:00 EST
4/29/1951 02:00 EDT
9/30/1951 02:00 EST
4/27/1952 02:00 EDT
9/28/1952 02:00 EST
4/26/1953 02:00 EDT
9/27/1953 02:00 EST
4/25/1954 02:00 EDT
9/26/1954 02:00 EST
4/24/1955 02:00 EDT
9/25/1955 02:00 EST
4/29/1956 02:00 EDT
9/30/1956 02:00 EST
4/27/1958 02:00 EDT
10/26/1958 02:00 EST
4/26/1959 02:00 EDT
9/27/1959 02:00 EST
4/24/1960 02:00 EDT
9/25/1960 02:00 EST
4/23/1961 02:00 EDT
9/24/1961 02:00 EST
4/29/1962 02:00 US#2

WV # 28
Before 7/01/1887 LMT
7/01/1887 12:00 EST
3/31/1918 02:00 EWT
10/27/1918 02:00 EST
3/30/1919 02:00 EWT
10/26/1919 02:00 EST
4/27/1941 02:00 EDT
10/28/1941 02:00 EST
2/09/1942 02:00 EWT
9/30/1945 02:00 EST
4/28/1946 02:00 EDT
9/29/1946 02:00 EST
4/27/1947 02:00 EDT
9/28/1947 02:00 EST
4/25/1948 02:00 EDT
9/26/1948 02:00 EST
4/24/1949 02:00 EDT
9/25/1949 02:00 EST
4/30/1950 02:00 EDT
9/24/1950 02:00 EST
4/28/1957 02:00 EDT
9/29/1957 02:00 EST
4/27/1958 02:00 EDT
9/28/1958 02:00 EST
4/26/1959 02:00 EDT
9/27/1959 02:00 EST
4/24/1960 02:00 EDT
9/25/1960 02:00 EST
4/30/1961 02:00 EDT
9/24/1961 02:00 EST
4/29/1962 02:00 EDT
9/30/1962 02:00 EST
4/28/1963 02:00 EDT
9/29/1963 02:00 EST
4/26/1964 02:00 EDT
9/27/1964 02:00 EST
4/25/1965 02:00 EDT
9/26/1965 02:00 EST
4/24/1966 02:00 US#1

WV # 29
Before 7/01/1887 LMT
7/01/1887 12:00 EST
3/31/1918 02:00 EWT
10/27/1918 02:00 EST
3/30/1919 02:00 EWT
10/26/1919 02:00 EST
4/27/1941 02:00 EDT
10/28/1941 02:00 EST
2/09/1942 02:00 EWT
9/30/1945 02:00 EST
4/28/1957 02:00 EDT
9/29/1957 02:00 EST
4/27/1958 02:00 EDT
9/28/1958 02:00 EST
4/26/1959 02:00 EDT
9/27/1959 02:00 EST
4/24/1960 02:00 EDT
9/25/1960 02:00 EST
4/30/1961 02:00 EDT
9/24/1961 02:00 EST
4/29/1962 02:00 US#2

WV # 30
Before 7/01/1887 LMT
7/01/1887 12:00 EST
3/31/1918 02:00 EWT
10/27/1918 02:00 EST
3/30/1919 02:00 EWT
10/26/1919 02:00 EST
2/09/1942 02:00 EWT
9/30/1945 02:00 EST
4/24/1949 02:00 EDT
9/25/1949 02:00 EST
4/28/1963 02:00 US#2

WV # 31
Before 7/01/1887 LMT
7/01/1887 12:00 EST
3/31/1918 02:00 EWT
10/27/1918 02:00 EST
3/30/1919 02:00 EWT
10/26/1919 02:00 EST
2/09/1942 02:00 EWT
9/30/1945 02:00 EST
4/28/1946 02:00 EDT
9/29/1946 02:00 EST
4/26/1953 02:00 EDT
9/27/1953 02:00 EST
4/25/1954 02:00 EDT
9/26/1954 02:00 EST
4/24/1955 02:00 EDT
9/25/1955 02:00 EST
4/29/1956 02:00 EDT
9/30/1956 02:00 EST
4/28/1957 02:00 EDT
9/29/1957 02:00 EST
4/27/1958 02:00 EDT
9/28/1958 02:00 EST
4/26/1959 02:00 EDT
9/27/1959 02:00 EST
4/24/1960 02:00 EDT
9/25/1960 02:00 EST
4/30/1961 02:00 EDT
9/24/1961 02:00 EST
4/29/1962 02:00 US#2

WV # 32
Before 7/01/1887 LMT
7/01/1887 12:00 EST
3/31/1918 02:00 EWT
10/27/1918 02:00 EST
3/30/1919 02:00 EWT
10/26/1919 02:00 EST
4/28/1941 02:00 EDT
10/28/1941 02:00 EST
2/09/1942 02:00 EWT
9/30/1945 02:00 EST
4/25/1948 02:00 EDT
9/26/1948 02:00 EST
4/24/1949 02:00 EDT
9/25/1949 02:00 EST
4/30/1950 02:00 EDT
9/24/1950 02:00 EST
4/29/1951 02:00 EDT
9/30/1951 02:00 EST
4/27/1952 02:00 EDT
9/28/1952 02:00 EST
4/26/1953 02:00 EDT
9/27/1953 02:00 EST
4/25/1954 02:00 EDT
9/26/1954 02:00 EST
4/24/1955 02:00 EDT
9/25/1955 02:00 EST
4/29/1956 02:00 EDT
9/30/1956 02:00 EST
4/28/1957 02:00 EDT
9/29/1957 02:00 EST
4/27/1958 02:00 EDT
9/28/1958 02:00 EST
4/26/1959 02:00 EDT
9/27/1959 02:00 EST
4/24/1960 02:00 EDT
10/30/1960 02:00 EST
4/30/1961 02:00 EDT
10/29/1961 02:00 EST
4/29/1962 02:00 EDT
10/28/1962 02:00 EST
4/28/1963 02:00 EDT
10/27/1963 02:00 EST
4/26/1964 02:00 EDT
10/25/1964 02:00 EST
4/25/1965 02:00 EDT
10/24/1965 02:00 EST
4/24/1966 02:00 US#1

WV # 33
Before 7/01/1887 LMT
7/01/1887 12:00 EST
3/31/1918 02:00 EWT
10/27/1918 02:00 EST
3/30/1919 02:00 EWT
10/26/1919 02:00 EST
4/27/1941 02:00 EDT
10/28/1941 02:00 EST
2/09/1942 02:00 EWT
9/30/1945 02:00 EST
4/25/1948 02:00 EDT
9/26/1948 02:00 EST
4/24/1949 02:00 EDT
9/25/1949 02:00 EST
4/30/1950 02:00 EDT
9/24/1950 02:00 EST
4/29/1951 02:00 EDT
9/30/1951 02:00 EST
4/27/1952 02:00 EDT
9/28/1952 02:00 EST
4/26/1953 02:00 EDT
9/27/1953 02:00 EST
4/25/1954 02:00 EDT
9/26/1954 02:00 EST
4/24/1955 02:00 EDT
9/25/1955 02:00 EST
4/29/1956 02:00 EDT
9/30/1956 02:00 EST
4/28/1957 02:00 EDT
9/29/1957 02:00 EST
4/27/1958 02:00 EDT
9/28/1958 02:00 EST
4/26/1959 02:00 EDT
9/27/1959 02:00 EST
4/24/1960 02:00 US#2

WV # 34
Before 3/31/1887 LMT
3/31/1887 12:00 EST
3/31/1918 02:00 EWT
10/27/1918 02:00 EST
3/30/1919 02:00 EWT
10/26/1919 02:00 EST
4/26/1937 02:00 EDT
10/27/1937 02:00 EST
4/27/1941 02:00 EDT
10/28/1941 02:00 EST
2/09/1942 02:00 EWT
9/30/1945 02:00 EST
4/28/1946 02:00 EDT
9/29/1946 02:00 EST
4/27/1947 02:00 EDT
9/28/1947 02:00 EST
4/25/1948 02:00 EDT
9/26/1948 02:00 EST
4/24/1949 02:00 EDT
9/25/1949 02:00 EST
4/30/1950 02:00 EDT
9/24/1950 02:00 EST
4/29/1951 02:00 EDT
9/30/1951 02:00 EST
4/27/1952 02:00 EDT
9/28/1952 02:00 EST
4/26/1953 02:00 EDT
9/27/1953 02:00 EST
4/25/1954 02:00 EDT
9/26/1954 02:00 EST
4/24/1955 02:00 EDT
9/25/1955 02:00 EST
4/29/1956 02:00 EDT
9/30/1956 02:00 EST
4/28/1957 02:00 EDT
9/29/1957 02:00 EST
4/27/1958 02:00 US#2

WV # 35
Before 7/01/1887 LMT
7/01/1887 12:00 EST
3/31/1918 02:00 EWT
10/27/1918 02:00 EST
3/30/1919 02:00 EWT
10/26/1919 02:00 EST
4/27/1941 02:00 EDT
9/28/1941 02:00 EST
2/09/1942 02:00 EWT
9/30/1945 02:00 EST
4/29/1956 02:00 EDT
9/30/1956 02:00 EST
4/28/1957 02:00 EDT
9/29/1957 02:00 EST
4/27/1958 02:00 EDT
9/28/1958 02:00 EST
4/26/1959 02:00 EDT
9/27/1959 02:00 EST
4/24/1960 02:00 EDT
9/25/1960 02:00 EST
4/30/1961 02:00 EDT
9/24/1961 02:00 EST
4/29/1962 02:00 EDT
9/30/1962 02:00 EST
4/28/1963 02:00 EDT
9/29/1963 02:00 EST
4/26/1964 02:00 EDT
9/27/1964 02:00 EST
4/25/1965 02:00 EDT
9/26/1965 02:00 EST
4/24/1966 02:00 US#1

COUNTIES

1 Barbour
2 Berkeley
3 Boone
4 Braxton
5 Brooke
6 Cabell
7 Calhoun
8 Clay
9 Doddridge
10 Fayette
11 Gilmer
12 Grant
13 Greenbrier
14 Hampshire
15 Hancock
16 Hardy
17 Harrison
18 Jackson
19 Jefferson
20 Kanawha
21 Lewis
22 Lincoln
23 Logan
24 McDowell
25 Marion
26 Marshall
27 Mason
28 Mercer
29 Mineral
30 Mingo
31 Monongalia
32 Monroe
33 Morgan
34 Nicholas
35 Ohio
36 Pendelton
37 Pleasants
38 Pocahontas
39 Preston
40 Putnam
41 Raleigh
42 Randolph
43 Ritchie
44 Roane
45 Summers
46 Taylor
47 Tucker
48 Tyler
49 Upshur
50 Wayne
51 Webster
52 Wetzel
53 Wirt
54 Wood
55 Wyoming

Aarrons Fork 20	1	38N26	81W29	5:25:56
Abbott 49	1	38N59	80W13	5:20:52
Abney 41	1	37N42	81W12	5:24:48
Abraham 41	1	37N47	80W57	5:23:48
Accoville 23	1	37N46	81W50	5:27:20
Acme 20	1	38N04	81W27	5:25:48
Ada 28	20	37N16	81W14	5:24:56
Adaline 26	21	39N50	80W34	5:22:16
Adamston 17	24	39N16	80W19	5:21:16
Adamsville 17	1	39N24	80W18	5:21:12
Addison 51	1	38N29	80W25	5:21:40
Adkin 24	1	37N21	81W30	5:26:00
Adlai 37	1	39N24	81W12	5:24:48
Adolph 42	1	38N44	79W58	5:19:52
Adrian 49	1	38N54	80W17	5:21:08
Advent 18	1	38N37	81W34	5:26:16
Afton 39	12	39N27	79W33	5:18:12
Aggregate 42	35	38N56	79W51	5:19:24
Ajax 30	1	37N48	82W17	5:29:08
Albright 39	12	39N30	79W39	5:18:36
Alderson 32	1	37N44	80W38	5:22:32
Alexander 49	1	38N47	80W13	5:20:52
Algoma 24	1	37N25	81W26	5:25:44
Alice 11	1	39N03	80W50	5:23:20
Alkol 22	1	38N10	81W56	5:27:44
Allen 33	11	39N38	78W10	5:12:40
Allendale 26	34	40N04	80W42	5:22:48
Allen Junction 55	1	37N35	81W21	5:25:24
Allensville 2	2	39N33	78W00	5:12:00
Allister 52	2	39N34	80W44	5:22:56
Alloy 10	14	38N08	81W17	5:25:08
Alma 48	2	39N26	80W49	5:23:16
Almoris 34	1	38N17	80W51	5:23:24

 WEST VIRGINIA

Alpena 42	1	38N55	79W42	5:18:48
Alpha 17	14	39N13	80W21	5:21:24
Alpoca 55	1	37N33	81W23	5:25:32
Alta 10	1	38N12	81W11	5:24:44
Altizer 7	1	38N47	81W08	5:24:32
Alton 49	1	38N54	80W17	5:21:08
Alum Bridge 21	1	39N02	80W40	5:22:40
Alum Creek 20	1	38N17	81W48	5:27:12
Alvon 13	14	37N48	80W18	5:21:12
Alvord 44	1	38N48	81W21	5:25:24
Alvy 48	2	39N27	80W42	5:22:48
Amandaville 20	18	38N23	81W49	5:27:16
Amboy 39	12	39N21	79W34	5:18:16
Ambrosia 27	1	38N52	82W08	5:28:32
Ameagle 41	1	37N57	81W25	5:25:40
Amelia 20	1	38N17	81W17	5:25:08
Ames 10	18	38N04	81W04	5:24:16
Amherstdale 23	1	37N47	81W49	5:27:16
Amma 44	1	38N34	81W16	5:25:04
Anawalt 24	1	37N20	81W26	5:25:44
Andersonville 26	21	39N50	80W34	5:22:16
Andrew 3	1	38N08	81W41	5:26:44
Anjean 13	1	37N58	80W41	5:22:44
Anmoore 17	24	39N16	80W18	5:21:12
Annamoriah 7	1	38N57	81W14	5:24:56
Annamoriah Flats 7	1	38N56	81W14	5:24:56
Ansted 10	1	38N08	81W06	5:24:24
Anthony 13	1	37N54	80W20	5:21:20
Anthony Creek 13	1	37N56	80W12	5:20:48
Antioch 9	1	39N18	80W47	5:23:08
Aplin 18	1	38N46	81W33	5:26:12
Apple Farm 7	1	38N48	81W04	5:24:16
Apple Grove 24	1	37N28	81W49	5:27:16
Apple Grove 27	1	38N39	82W10	5:28:40
Aracoma 23	1	37N52	81W59	5:27:56
Arborland Acres 20	18	38N23	81W49	5:27:16
Arbovale 38	1	38N26	79W49	5:19:16
Arbuckle 27	1	38N44	82W02	5:28:08
Arbutus Park 17	24	39N16	80W19	5:21:16
Archer 52	2	39N32	80W39	5:22:36
Archer Heights 5	32	40N24	80W33	5:22:12
Arcola 51	1	38N25	80W33	5:22:12
Ardel 50	1	38N13	82W27	5:29:48
Arden 1	1	39N13	80W00	5:20:00
Arden 2	27	39N25	77W58	5:11:52
Argonne 23	1	37N51	82W03	5:28:12
Argyle 23	1	37N50	81W52	5:27:28
Arista	1	37N28	81W16	5:25:04
Arkansas 16	1	39N02	78W45	5:15:00
Arlee 27	1	38N50	82W08	5:28:32
Arlington 17	24	39N16	80W19	5:21:16
Arlington 49	1	38N50	80W21	5:21:24
Arnett 41	1	37N50	81W26	5:25:44
Arnette 4	1	38N46	80W44	5:22:56
Arnettsville 31	28	39N39	79W58	5:19:52
Arnold Hill 42	35	38N56	79W51	5:19:24
Arnoldsburg 7	1	38N48	81W07	5:24:28
Arroyo 15	9	40N30	80W37	5:22:28
Arthur 12	1	39N04	79W07	5:16:28
Arthurdale 39	12	39N30	79W49	5:19:16
Artie 41	1	37N56	81W22	5:25:28
Arvilla 37	1	39N28	81W06	5:24:24
Asbury 13	1	37N49	80W34	5:22:16
Asbury Church 16	1	39N02	78W45	5:15:00
Asco 24	1	37N30	81W38	5:26:32
Ashford 3	1	38N11	81W42	5:26:48
Ashland 24	1	37N25	81W21	5:25:24
Ashley 9	1	39N18	80W47	5:23:08
Ashton 27	1	38N38	82W10	5:28:40
Aspinall 21	14	38N52	80W36	5:22:24
Astor 46	1	39N16	80W08	5:20:32
Astor Junction 46	1	39N16	80W08	5:20:32
Atenville 22	1	38N02	82W07	5:28:28
Athens 28	1	37N25	81W01	5:24:04
Atwood 48	2	39N34	80W44	5:22:56
Auburn 43	1	39N06	80W51	5:23:24
Audra 1	1	38N59	80W13	5:20:52
Augusta 14	1	39N18	78W38	5:14:32
Augusta 28	1	37N22	81W05	5:24:20
Aurora 39	12	39N19	79W33	5:18:12
Austen 39	12	39N23	79W51	5:19:24
Auto 13	1	37N58	80W19	5:21:16
Auvil 47	1	39N10	79W42	5:18:48
Auville 24	1	37N28	81W49	5:27:16
Avis 45	14	37N40	80W53	5:23:32
Avon 9	1	39N14	80W41	5:22:44
Avondale 9	1	39N18	80W47	5:23:08
Avondale 24	1	37N25	81W47	5:27:08
Bablin 21	1	38N49	80W28	5:21:52
Backus 10	1	37N52	80W51	5:23:24
Baden 27	1	38N45	81W57	5:27:48
Baileysville 55	1	37N35	81W40	5:26:40
Baisden 30	1	37N33	81W55	5:27:40
Baker 16	1	39N02	78W45	5:15:00
Baker Heights 2	27	39N28	77W58	5:11:52
Baker Park 20	18	38N23	81W49	5:27:16
Baker Ridge 31	28	39N39	79W58	5:19:52
Bakerton 19	3	39N22	77W46	5:11:04
Bald Knob 3	1	37N52	81W38	5:26:32
Baldwin 11	1	38N58	80W45	5:23:00
Ballard 32	1	37N29	80W47	5:23:08
Ballengee 45	1	37N37	80W44	5:22:56
Balls Gap 6	1	38N26	82W08	5:28:32
Bamboo 34	1	38N09	80W44	5:22:56
Bancroft 40	1	38N31	81W50	5:27:20
Bandytown 3	1	37N56	81W38	5:26:32
Banks 49	1	38N48	80W19	5:21:16
Barboursville 6	1	38N24	82W18	5:29:12
Bardane 19	2	39N23	77W53	5:11:32
Bargers Springs 45	1	37N34	80W47	5:23:08
Barker 1	1	39N03	79W56	5:19:44
Barker 52	2	39N34	80W41	5:22:44

Barkers Ridge 55	1	37N31	81W21	5:25:24
Barksdale 45	14	37N40	80W53	5:23:32
Barn 28	1	37N35	81W06	5:24:24
Barnabus 23	1	37N45	82W00	5:28:00
Barnet Run 51	1	38N30	80W46	5:23:04
Barrackville 25	17	39N30	80W10	5:20:40
Barrett 3	1	37N53	81W40	5:26:40
Barrs 44	1	38N48	81W21	5:25:24
Barry Mine 46	1	39N16	80W08	5:20:32
Bartley 24	1	37N20	81W45	5:27:00
Bartow 38	14	38N31	79W47	5:19:08
Basin 55	1	37N30	81W20	5:25:20
Basnettsville 25	17	39N36	80W15	5:21:00
Basore 16	1	38N52	78W52	5:15:28
Bath 33	11	39N37	78W14	5:12:56
Battelle 31	17	39N41	80W20	5:21:20
Baxter 25	17	39N33	80W09	5:20:36
Bayard 12	1	39N16	79W22	5:17:28
Bear Creek 4	1	38N40	80W46	5:23:04
Beard Heights 38	1	38N13	80W05	5:20:20
Beards Fork 10	14	38N04	81W14	5:24:56
Bear Mountain Mine 1	1	39N13	80W09	5:20:36
Bearsville 48	2	39N30	80W54	5:23:36
Beartown 24	1	37N23	81W49	5:27:16
Beason 43	1	39N17	80W58	5:23:52
Beatrice 43	1	39N04	81W05	5:24:20
Beatysville 18	1	39N08	81W44	5:26:56
Beaver 34	1	38N19	80W38	5:22:32
Beaver 41	18	37N45	81W08	5:24:32
Beaver Pond 28	20	37N18	81W12	5:24:48
Bebee 52	12	39N39	80W51	5:23:24
Becco 23	1	37N47	81W49	5:27:16
Beckley 41	18	37N47	81W11	5:24:44
Beckley Junction 41	18	37N46	81W13	5:24:52
Beckwith 10	1	38N06	81W09	5:24:36
Bedington 2	27	39N28	77W58	5:11:52
Beech Bottom 5	33	40N14	80W39	5:22:36
Beech Creek 30	1	37N37	82W04	5:28:16
Beech Glen 34	1	38N14	81W12	5:24:48
Beechgrove 43	1	39N17	80W58	5:23:52
Beech Hill 27	1	38N43	81W58	5:27:52
Beechwood 31	28	39N39	79W58	5:19:52
Beechwood 54	14	39N17	81W32	5:26:08
Beechwood 55	1	37N35	81W21	5:25:24
Beelick Knob 10	1	37N52	80W51	5:23:24
Beeson 28	1	37N28	81W12	5:24:48
Belfont 4	1	38N38	80W52	5:23:28
Belgrove 18	1	38N41	81W40	5:26:40
Belington 1	1	39N02	79W56	5:19:44
Bellburn 13	1	38N03	80W43	5:22:52
Belle 20	1	38N14	81W33	5:26:12
Bellepoint 45	14	37N40	80W53	5:23:32
Belleville 54	1	39N08	81W44	5:26:56
Bellmeade 27	1	38N52	82W08	5:28:32
Bellview 25	17	39N28	80W10	5:20:40
Bellwood 10	1	37N58	80W46	5:23:04
Belmont 37	1	39N23	81W16	5:25:04
Belva 34	1	38N14	81W12	5:24:48
Bemis 42	1	38N49	79W45	5:19:00
Benbush 47	1	39N09	79W30	5:18:00
Bendale 21	1	39N03	80W28	5:21:52
Bennett 21	1	38N56	80W30	5:22:00
Benson 17	1	39N07	80W25	5:21:40
Bens Run 48	2	39N28	81W06	5:24:24
Benton Ferry 25	17	39N28	80W10	5:20:40
Bentree 34	1	38N17	81W12	5:24:48
Benwood 26	13	40N01	80W44	5:22:56
Benwood Junction 26	13	40N02	80W45	5:23:00
Berea 43	1	39N08	80W56	5:23:44
Bergoo 51	1	38N29	80W18	5:21:12
Berkeley 2	27	39N28	77W58	5:11:52
Berkeley Springs 33	11	39N38	78W14	5:12:56
Berlin 21	1	39N03	80W28	5:21:52
Bernie 22	1	38N14	81W59	5:27:56
Berryburg 1	1	39N16	80W08	5:20:32
Berryburg Mine No. 1 1	1	39N16	80W08	5:20:32
Berry Siding 4	1	38N43	80W39	5:22:36
Berryville 33	11	39N38	78W14	5:12:56
Bertha Hill 31	28	39N41	79W59	5:19:56
Berwind 24	1	37N16	81W40	5:26:40
Beryl 29	6	39N26	78W59	5:15:56
Besoco 41	1	37N38	81W14	5:24:56
Bessemer 2	27	39N28	77W58	5:11:52
Bethany 5	9	40N12	80W33	5:22:12
Bethel 36	1	38N41	79W11	5:16:44
Bethel Place 54	1	39N16	81W40	5:26:40
Bethesada 50	1	38N13	82W27	5:29:48
Bethlehem 17	1	39N24	80W18	5:21:12
Bethlehem 35	34	40N03	80W42	5:22:48
Betty Zane 35	34	40N04	80W42	5:22:48
Beverly 42	1	38N51	79W53	5:19:32
Beverly Hills 6	5	38N25	82W25	5:29:40
Beverly Hills 25	17	39N28	80W10	5:20:40
Bias 30	1	37N42	82W11	5:28:44
Bickmore 8	1	38N23	81W07	5:24:28
Big Battle 9	1	39N17	80W34	5:22:16
Bigbend 7	1	38N58	81W10	5:24:40
Big Chimney 20	14	38N24	81W32	5:26:08
Big Creek 23	1	38N00	82W03	5:28:12
Big Four 24	1	37N26	81W30	5:26:00
Big Isaac 9	1	39N17	80W34	5:22:16
Big Moses 48	2	39N26	80W49	5:23:16
Big Mountain 20	1	38N13	81W26	5:25:44
Big Otter 8	1	38N36	81W03	5:24:12
Big Run 25	17	39N32	80W20	5:21:20
Big Run 26	21	39N50	80W34	5:22:16
Big Run 51	1	38N34	80W27	5:21:48
Big Run 52	2	39N35	80W35	5:22:20
Big Sandy 20	1	38N30	81W22	5:25:28
Big Sandy 24	1	37N28	81W42	5:26:48

Bigson 3	1	37N58	81W43	5:26:52
Big Springs 7	1	38N59	81W04	5:24:16
Big Sycamore 8	1	38N22	81W10	5:24:40
Billings 44	1	38N54	81W25	5:25:40
Bim 3	1	37N55	81W41	5:26:44
Bingamon 25	17	39N27	80W15	5:21:00
Bingamon Junction 25	17	39N27	80W15	5:21:00
Bingham 13	1	38N00	80W44	5:22:56
Birch 4	1	38N38	80W54	5:23:36
Birch River 34	1	38N30	80W46	5:23:04
Birchton 41	18	37N59	81W32	5:26:08
Birds Creek 39	12	39N23	79W51	5:19:24
Bishop 24	1	37N13	81W40	5:26:40
Bismarck 12	1	39N17	79W14	5:16:56
Blackberry City 30	1	37N37	82W10	5:28:40
Black Betsy 40	1	38N28	81W49	5:27:16
Black Bottom 23	1	37N52	81W59	5:27:56
Black Eagle 55	1	37N35	81W23	5:25:32
Black Fork 47	1	39N05	79W40	5:18:40
Blackhawk 20	22	38N21	81W38	5:26:32
Blacksville 31	17	39N43	80W13	5:20:52
Blaine 29	2	39N23	79W12	5:16:48
Blair 19	2	39N17	77W47	5:11:08
Blair 23	1	37N53	81W52	5:27:28
Blairton 2	27	39N28	77W58	5:11:52
Blakeley 20	1	38N18	81W18	5:25:12
Blandville 9	1	39N15	80W43	5:22:52
Blaser 39	19	39N24	79W45	5:19:00
Blocton 30	1	37N47	82W21	5:29:24
Bloomery 14	1	39N23	78W26	5:13:44
Bloomery 19	23	39N17	77W52	5:11:28
Bloomingrose 3	1	38N08	81W38	5:26:32
Blount 20	1	38N19	81W26	5:25:44
Blue 48	2	39N30	80W54	5:23:36
Blue Creek 20	1	38N27	81W27	5:25:48
Bluefield 28	20	37N16	81W13	5:24:52
Blue Jay 41	1	37N44	81W08	5:24:32
Blue Ridge Acres 19	3	39N19	77W44	5:10:56
Blue Rock 42	1	38N44	79W58	5:19:52
Bluestone 28	20	37N16	81W14	5:24:56
Blue Sulphur 13	1	37N49	80W39	5:22:36
Blue Sulphur Springs 13	1	37N44	80W39	5:22:36
Blueville 46	14	39N20	80W01	5:20:04
Bluewell 28	20	37N16	81W14	5:24:56
Blundon 20	1	38N26	81W29	5:25:56
Board 27	1	38N54	81W56	5:27:44
Boaz 54	1	39N22	81W30	5:26:00
Bob White 3	1	37N57	81W43	5:26:52
Boggs 51	1	38N28	80W38	5:22:32
Bolair 51	1	38N26	80W27	5:21:48
Bolivar 19	3	39N19	77W45	5:11:00
Bolt 41	1	37N46	81W25	5:25:40
Bomont 8	1	38N27	81W14	5:24:56
Bonnie 4	1	38N46	80W44	5:22:56
Bonnivale 54	1	39N11	81W32	5:26:08
Booher 48	2	39N26	80W49	5:23:16
Boomer 10	14	38N09	81W17	5:25:08
Boonesborough 10	14	38N07	81W16	5:25:04
Booth 31	17	39N36	80W01	5:20:04
Booths Creek 46	1	39N22	80W08	5:20:32
Boothsville 25	17	39N28	80W10	5:20:40
Borderland 30	1	37N43	82W19	5:29:16
Borgman 39	19	39N24	79W45	5:19:00
Bottom Creek 24	1	37N26	81W30	5:26:00
Bowan Ridge 6	5	38N24	82W26	5:29:44
Bowden 42	1	38N55	79W43	5:18:52
Bowlby 31	28	39N41	79W59	5:19:56
Bowles 22	1	38N17	82W06	5:28:24
Boyd 49	1	38N50	80W21	5:21:24
Boyer 38	1	38N26	79W49	5:19:16
Bozoo 32	1	37N28	80W50	5:23:20
Bradley 3	1	38N09	81W44	5:26:56
Bradley 41	1	37N52	81W12	5:24:48
Bradshaw 24	1	37N21	81W48	5:27:12
Braeholm 23	1	37N47	81W49	5:27:16
Bragg 41	1	37N47	80W57	5:23:48
Bramwell 28	1	37N20	81W19	5:25:16
Branchland 22	1	38N13	82W12	5:28:48
Brandonville 39	12	39N40	79W37	5:18:28
Brandywine 36	1	38N38	79W15	5:17:00
Braxton 4	1	38N46	80W44	5:22:56
Bream 20	1	38N26	81W29	5:25:56
Breeden 30	1	37N56	82W16	5:29:04
Brenton 55	1	37N36	81W38	5:26:32
Bretz 39	12	39N32	79W48	5:19:12
Bretz 47	1	39N06	79W41	5:18:44
Brewsterdale 24	1	37N14	81W31	5:26:04
Briarwood Estates 54	14	39N17	81W32	5:26:08
Brick Church 50	1	38N07	82W36	5:30:24
Bridgeport 17	1	39N17	80W15	5:21:00
Bridgeport Hill 17	1	39N17	80W15	5:21:00
Bridgeway 48	2	39N30	80W54	5:23:36
Brighton	1	38N48	82W03	5:28:12
Brink 25	17	39N32	80W20	5:21:20
Bristol 17	1	39N17	80W31	5:22:04
Broaddus 1	1	39N09	80W03	5:20:12
Broadmoor 54	1	39N16	81W40	5:26:40
Broad Oaks 17	24	39N16	80W19	5:21:16
Brohard 53	1	39N02	81W11	5:24:44
Brookhaven 31	28	39N39	79W58	5:19:52
Brooklyn 10	18	38N03	81W06	5:24:24
Brooklyn Junction 52	12	39N39	80W51	5:23:24
Brooks 45	14	37N44	80W54	5:23:36
Brookside 39	12	39N19	79W33	5:18:12
Brounland 20	22	38N20	81W38	5:26:32
Brown 17	1	39N24	80W29	5:21:56
Brownlow 46	14	39N20	80W01	5:20:04
Brownsburg 38	1	38N13	80W05	5:20:20

WEST VIRGINIA

Browns Creek 24 1 37N27 81w34 5:26:16
Browns Mills 39 28 39N39 79w58 5:19:52
Brownsville 10 1 38N10 81w11 5:24:44
Brownsville 21 1 39N03 80w28 5:21:52
Brownton 1 1 39N13 80w09 5:20:36
Bruceton Mills 39 12 39N40 79w38 5:18:32
Bruno 23 1 37N42 81w52 5:27:28
Brush Fork 28 20 37N16 81w14 5:24:56
Brushy run 36 1 38N48 79w17 5:17:08
Brydon 46 1 39N16 80w05 5:20:20
Bryson 41 1 37N44 81w18 5:25:12
Bubbling Spring 14 1 39N18 78w26 5:13:44
Buck 45 14 37N40 80w53 5:23:32
Buckeye 38 1 38N11 80w08 5:20:32
Buckhannon 49 1 39N00 80w14 5:20:56
Bud 55 1 37N32 81w23 5:25:32
Buffalo 40 1 38N37 81w59 5:27:56
Buffalo Creek 50 14 38N24 82w35 5:30:20
Buff Lick 20 1 38N13 81w26 5:25:44
Bula 31 17 39N42 80w18 5:21:12
Bulger 22 1 38N10 81w56 5:27:44
Bull 50 1 37N54 82w27 5:29:48
Bull Run 39 12 39N33 79w48 5:19:12
Bulltown 4 1 38N47 80w35 5:22:20
Bunker Hill 2 2 39N20 78w03 5:12:12
Bunker Hill 20 14 38N21 81w44 5:26:56
Bunners Ridge 25 17 39N28 80w10 5:20:40
Burchfield 52 2 39N36 80w30 5:22:00
Burlington 29 2 39N20 78w55 5:15:40
Burning Springs 20 14 38N15 81w33 5:26:12
Burning Springs 53 1 39N01 81w14 5:24:56
Burnsville 4 14 38N52 80w40 5:22:40
Burnsville Junction 4 14 38N51 80w40 5:22:40
Burnt Factory 33 11 39N38 78w14 5:12:56
Burnt House 43 1 39N03 80w59 5:23:56
Burnwell 20 1 38N03 81w23 5:25:32
Burton 52 2 39N40 80w26 5:21:44
Butchersville 21 1 39N03 80w28 5:21:52
Cabin Creek 20 1 38N10 81w27 5:25:48
Cabin Run 29 2 39N26 78w54 5:15:36
Cabins 12 1 39N00 79w08 5:16:32
Cabot 3 1 38N01 81w38 5:26:32
Cabot Station 7 1 38N55 81w06 5:24:24
Cacapon 33 2 39N33 78w22 5:13:28
Cairo 43 1 39N13 81w09 5:24:36
Caldwell 13 1 37N47 80w24 5:21:36
Calis 26 21 39N50 80w34 5:22:16
Callaway 41 1 37N54 81w10 5:24:40
Calvert 20 18 38N23 81w49 5:27:16
Calvin 34 1 38N20 80w43 5:22:52
Cambria 17 1 39N23 80w21 5:21:24
Camden 21 1 39N03 80w34 5:22:16
Camden On Gauley 51 1 38N22 80w36 5:22:24
Cameo 3 1 38N08 82w01 5:28:04
Cameron 26 21 39N50 80w34 5:22:16
Camp 9 1 39N23 80w49 5:23:16
Campbelltown 38 1 38N13 80w05 5:20:20
Camp Creek 28 1 37N30 81w06 5:24:24
Campus 55 1 37N44 81w41 5:26:44
Canaan 49 1 38N50 80w21 5:21:24
Canaan Heights 47 1 39N08 79w28 5:17:52
Canaan Valley 47 1 39N08 79w28 5:17:52
Canebrake 24 1 37N15 81w39 5:26:36
Cane Fork 20 1 38N05 81w27 5:25:48
Canfield 4 1 38N40 80w43 5:22:52
Canfield 42 35 38N56 79w51 5:19:24
Cannelton 10 1 38N12 81w18 5:25:12
Canton 9 1 39N18 80w47 5:23:08
Cantwell 43 1 39N13 81w03 5:24:12
Canvas 34 1 38N16 80w46 5:23:04
Capehart 27 1 38N45 81w57 5:27:48
Capels 24 1 37N27 81w36 5:26:24
Capitol 20 22 38N21 81w37 5:26:28
Capon Bridge 14 1 39N18 78w26 5:13:44
Capon Springs 14 1 39N08 78w29 5:13:56
Carbon 20 1 38N02 81w25 5:25:40
Carbondale 10 1 38N12 81w18 5:25:12
Caretta 24 1 37N20 81w41 5:26:44
Carl 34 1 38N09 80w41 5:22:44
Carlisle 10 1 37N57 81w10 5:24:40
Carl Lee Ray 54 1 39N16 81w40 5:26:40
Carlos 24 1 37N23 81w49 5:27:16
Carolina 25 17 39N29 80w16 5:21:04
Carroll 22 1 38N17 82w06 5:28:24
Carrollton 1 1 39N05 80w08 5:20:32
Carswell 24 1 37N26 81w30 5:26:00
Carter 49 1 38N53 80w18 5:21:12
Cascade 39 12 39N29 79w49 5:19:16
Cashmere 32 1 37N29 80w47 5:23:08
Cass 38 1 38N24 79w55 5:19:40
Cassity 42 1 38N53 79w59 5:19:56
Cassville 31 17 39N40 80w04 5:20:16
Catawba 25 17 39N32 80w05 5:20:20
Cave 36 1 38N39 79w20 5:17:20
Cazy 3 1 37N57 81w43 5:26:52
Cedar Grove 20 1 38N13 81w26 5:25:44
Cedar Grove 54 14 39N17 81w32 5:26:08
Cedarville 11 1 38N50 80w49 5:23:16
Centennial 32 1 37N34 80w24 5:21:36
Center Hill 53 1 39N04 81w24 5:25:36
Center Point 9 1 39N24 80w38 5:22:32
Centerville 48 2 39N26 80w51 5:23:24
Centerville 50 1 38N15 82w36 5:30:24
Central 9 1 39N17 80w51 5:23:24
Central 54 14 39N17 81w32 5:26:08
Centralia 4 1 38N37 80w34 5:22:16
Central Station 9 1 39N18 80w50 5:23:20
Centreville 48 2 39N24 80w52 5:23:28
Century 1 1 39N06 80w11 5:20:44
Century No. 2 1 1 39N05 80w08 5:20:32
Ceredo 50 16 38N21 82w33 5:30:12
Ceres 28 20 37N16 81w14 5:24:56
Cham 23 1 37N50 81w52 5:27:28
Chapel 4 1 38N40 80w46 5:23:04
Chapman 4 14 38N52 80w36 5:22:24
Chapman 51 1 38N29 80w25 5:21:40
Chapman Addition 5 33 40N17 80w37 5:22:28
Chapmanville 23 1 37N59 82w01 5:28:04
Charles 19 23 39N18 77w51 5:11:24
Charleston 20 22 38N21 81w38 5:26:32
Charles Town 19 23 39N17 77w52 5:11:28
Charlton Heights 10 1 38N15 81w15 5:25:00
Charmco 13 1 38N00 80w44 5:22:56
Chatham Hill 25 17 39N31 80w15 5:21:00
Chattaroy 30 1 37N42 82w17 5:29:08
Chauncey 23 1 37N46 81w59 5:27:56
Cheat Neck 31 28 39N39 79w58 5:19:52
Chelyan 20 1 38N12 81w30 5:26:00
Cherokee 20 1 38N04 81w27 5:25:48
Cherry Falls 51 1 38N29 80w25 5:21:40
Cherry Grove 36 1 38N38 79w31 5:18:04
Cherry Run 33 10 39N38 78w02 5:12:08
Chesapeake 20 1 38N13 81w32 5:26:08
Chesapeake 25 17 39N28 80w10 5:20:40
Chester 15 9 40N37 80w34 5:22:16
Chesterville 54 1 39N11 81w32 5:26:08
Chestnut Heights 5 33 40N17 80w37 5:22:28
Chestnut Hill 15 32 40N24 80w35 5:22:20
Chestnut Ridge 31 28 39N39 79w58 5:19:52
Chiefton 17 24 39N16 80w19 5:21:16
Chimney Corner 10 1 38N10 81w11 5:24:44
Chloe 7 1 38N42 81w05 5:24:20
Christian 23 1 37N42 81w52 5:27:28
Church 52 2 39N40 80w27 5:21:48
Churchville 21 1 39N03 80w34 5:22:16
Cicerone 44 1 38N42 81w25 5:25:40
Cinco 20 22 38N21 81w38 5:26:32
Cinderella 30 1 37N41 82w16 5:29:04
Circleville 36 1 38N40 79w30 5:18:00
Cirtsville 41 18 37N47 81w11 5:24:44
Cisco 43 1 39N11 81w16 5:25:04
Claremont 10 1 37N58 81w05 5:24:20
Clarence 44 1 38N46 81w33 5:26:12
Clark 17 14 39N16 80w22 5:21:28
Clark 24 1 37N25 81w26 5:25:44
Clarksburg 17 14 39N17 80w21 5:21:24
Clay 8 1 38N28 81w05 5:24:20
Clay Junction 8 1 38N29 81w05 5:24:20
Claypool 23 1 37N44 81w49 5:27:16
Claypool 45 1 37N52 80w51 5:23:24
Claysville 29 2 39N22 79w02 5:16:08
Clayton 45 1 37N44 80w39 5:22:36
Clearco 1 38N06 80w34 5:22:16
Clear Creek 41 1 37N55 81w21 5:25:24
Clear Fork 55 1 37N38 81w41 5:26:44
Clearview 35 6 40N08 80w41 5:22:44
Clem 4 1 38N38 80w56 5:23:44
Clemtown 1 1 39N13 79w56 5:19:44
Clendenin 20 1 38N29 81w21 5:25:24
Cleveland 51 1 38N44 80w24 5:21:36
Clifftop 10 1 38N00 80w56 5:23:44
Clifton 27 1 39N01 82w02 5:28:08
Clifton Mills 39 12 39N40 79w38 5:18:32
Clinton 3 1 37N53 81w40 5:26:40
Clinton 31 17 39N33 79w58 5:19:52
Clinton 35 6 40N06 80w36 5:22:24
Clintonville 13 1 37N54 80w36 5:22:24
Clio 44 1 38N33 81w19 5:25:16
Clothier 23 1 37N57 81w49 5:27:16
Clouston 26 21 39N50 80w34 5:22:16
Clover 44 1 38N48 81w21 5:25:24
Clover 47 1 39N09 79w46 5:19:04
Cloverdale 32 1 37N24 80w48 5:23:12
Clover Lick 38 1 38N22 79w58 5:19:52
Clyde 20 22 38N22 81w38 5:26:32
Clyde 52 2 39N38 80w41 5:22:44
Coal 17 14 39N18 80w22 5:21:28
Coalburg 20 1 38N11 81w28 5:25:52
Coal City 41 1 37N41 81w12 5:24:48
Coaldale 28 1 37N21 81w21 5:25:24
Coal Fork 20 1 38N06 81w27 5:25:48
Coal Mountain 55 1 37N41 81w44 5:26:56
Coalridge 20 1 38N29 81w21 5:25:24
Coalton 42 1 38N54 79w58 5:19:52
Coal Valley 23 1 37N57 81w49 5:27:16
Coalwood 24 1 37N23 81w39 5:26:36
Coburn 52 2 39N36 80w30 5:22:00
Coco 20 1 38N26 81w29 5:25:56
Coe 34 1 38N22 80w36 5:22:24
Cofoco 20 1 38N06 81w27 5:25:48
Coketon 47 1 39N08 79w31 5:18:04
Colcord 41 1 37N57 81w27 5:25:48
Cold Stream 14 1 39N18 78w26 5:13:44
Coldwater 9 1 39N14 80w41 5:22:44
Colebank 1 1 39N13 79w56 5:19:44
Coleman 50 1 38N07 82w28 5:29:52
Colfax 25 17 39N26 80w08 5:20:32
Colliers 5 32 40N22 80w33 5:22:12
Collinsdale 10 1 38N03 81w23 5:25:32
Collins Settlement 21 1 38N52 80w28 5:21:52
Cologne 27 1 38N47 81w56 5:27:44
Colored Hill 28 1 37N22 81w07 5:24:28
Columbia 10 14 38N08 81w18 5:25:12
Combs Addition 23 1 37N44 81w49 5:27:16
Comfort 3 1 38N07 81w37 5:26:28
Conaway 48 2 39N30 80w54 5:23:36
Concord 39 12 39N23 79w51 5:19:24
Confidence 40 1 38N32 81w54 5:27:36
Congo 15 9 40N37 80w36 5:22:24
Conings 11 1 39N01 80w46 5:23:04
Cool Ridge 41 1 37N39 81w06 5:24:24
Cooper 28 1 37N19 81w19 5:25:16
Coopertown 3 1 38N04 81w34 5:26:16
Copen 4 1 38N50 80w44 5:22:56
Copley 21 1 39N03 80w28 5:21:52
Copper 27 1 38N51 81w59 5:27:56
Cora 23 1 37N50 82w02 5:28:08
Cordova 13 1 38N00 80w22 5:21:28
Core 31 17 39N41 80w07 5:20:28
Corinne 55 1 37N35 81w21 5:25:24
Corinth 39 12 39N25 79w30 5:18:00
Corley 1 1 39N01 79w56 5:19:44
Corley 4 1 38N44 80w36 5:22:24
Corliss 10 1 37N58 80w46 5:23:04
Cornstalk 13 1 37N57 80w32 5:22:08
Cornwallis 43 1 39N13 81w09 5:24:36
Corrinne 55 1 37N35 81w21 5:25:24
Corton 20 1 38N29 81w16 5:25:04
Costa 3 1 38N10 81w43 5:26:52
Cottageville 18 1 38N52 81w49 5:27:16
Cottle 34 1 38N21 80w40 5:22:40
Cotton 44 1 38N33 81w19 5:25:16
Cottontown 52 2 39N40 80w26 5:21:44
Countsville 44 1 38N42 81w25 5:25:40
Courtright 17 1 39N17 80w15 5:21:00
Cove 15 32 40N24 80w35 5:22:20
Cove Gap 50 1 38N06 82w15 5:29:00
Covel 55 1 37N29 81w20 5:25:20
Cowen 51 1 38N25 80w34 5:22:16
Cox Landing 6 1 38N31 82w18 5:29:12
Coxs Mills 11 1 39N03 80w50 5:23:20
Coxtown 21 1 39N03 80w28 5:21:52
Crab Orchard 41 18 37N45 81w14 5:24:56
Crag 13 1 37N58 80w46 5:23:04
Craigmoor 17 14 39N13 80w21 5:21:24
Craigsville 34 1 38N20 80w39 5:22:36
Cranberry 41 18 37N49 81w12 5:24:48
Craneco 23 1 37N48 81w45 5:27:00
Cranesville 39 12 39N27 79w33 5:18:12
Crany 55 1 37N41 81w38 5:26:32
Crave Creek 26 21 39N51 80w36 5:22:24
Crawford 21 1 38N52 80w26 5:21:44
Crawley 13 1 37N56 80w39 5:22:36
Creamery 32 1 37N44 80w39 5:22:36
Crede 20 22 38N22 81w38 5:26:32
Cremo 7 1 38N57 81w16 5:25:04
Crescent 10 1 38N11 81w21 5:25:24
Cressmont 8 1 38N29 81w05 5:24:20
Creston 53 1 38N57 81w16 5:25:04
Crichton 13 1 38N03 80w43 5:22:52
Crickmer 10 1 37N56 80w54 5:23:36
Crook 3 1 37N56 81w41 5:26:44
Crooked Creek 23 1 37N53 81w59 5:27:56
Crosby 8 1 38N20 81w11 5:24:44
Cross Creek 5 8 40N19 80w34 5:22:16
Cross Lanes 20 18 38N25 81w50 5:27:20
Crossroads 31 17 39N41 80w20 5:21:20
Crow 41 18 37N45 81w08 5:24:32
Crown 23 1 37N46 81w51 5:27:24
Crown 31 28 39N39 79w58 5:19:52
Crown Hill 20 1 38N12 81w25 5:25:40
Crow Summit 18 1 38N57 81w46 5:27:04
Crum 50 1 37N54 82w27 5:29:48
Crumpler 24 1 37N26 81w21 5:25:24
Crystal 28 1 37N22 81w13 5:24:52
Crystal Lake 9 1 39N18 80w47 5:23:08
Crystal Springs 42 35 38N56 79w51 5:19:24
Crystal Springs 54 1 39N16 81w40 5:26:40
Cubana 42 1 38N52 80w08 5:20:32
Cucumber 24 1 37N17 81w38 5:26:32
Culloden 6 1 38N25 82w03 5:28:12
Cumberland Heights 28 20 37N16 81w14 5:24:56
Cunard 10 1 38N00 81w02 5:24:08
Curry 40 1 38N23 82w00 5:28:00
Curtin 51 1 38N28 80w22 5:21:28
Curtis 44 1 38N48 81w28 5:25:52
Curtisville 25 17 39N32 80w20 5:21:20
Cusicks Crossing 52 2 39N40 80w26 5:21:44
Custer Addition 17 24 39N16 80w19 5:21:16
Cutlips 4 1 38N46 80w44 5:22:56
Cuzzart 39 12 39N36 79w34 5:18:16
Cyclone 55 1 37N44 81w41 5:26:44
Cyrus 50 14 38N24 82w35 5:30:20
Czar 42 1 38N42 80w12 5:20:48
Dabney 23 1 37N49 81w55 5:27:40
Dahmer 36 1 38N39 79w20 5:17:20
Dailey 42 1 38N48 79w54 5:19:36
Daisy 23 1 38N00 82w02 5:28:08
Dakota 25 17 39N28 80w10 5:20:40
Dale 48 2 39N32 80w39 5:22:36
Dallas 26 4 40N01 80w32 5:22:08
Dallison 54 1 39N11 81w23 5:25:32
Dameron 41 1 37N47 81w20 5:25:20
Dan 24 1 37N21 81w48 5:27:12
Danese 10 1 37N56 80w54 5:23:36
Daniels 41 1 37N45 81w07 5:24:28
Dans Run 29 2 39N27 78w42 5:14:48
Danville 3 18 38N05 81w50 5:27:20
Darkesville 2 2 39N22 78w03 5:12:12
Dartmont 3 1 38N11 81w42 5:26:48
Dartmoor 1 1 39N01 79w56 5:19:44
Davenport 48 31 39N34 81w00 5:24:00
Davin 23 1 37N44 81w49 5:27:16
Davis 23 1 37N50 82w04 5:28:16
Davis 47 1 39N08 79w28 5:17:52
Davis Creek 20 1 38N17 81w48 5:27:12
Davisville 54 1 39N12 81w30 5:26:00
Davy 24 1 37N29 81w39 5:26:36
Dawes 20 1 38N09 81w27 5:25:48

WEST VIRGINIA

Dawmont 17 14 39N21 80w21 5:21:24
Dawson 13 1 37N51 80w43 5:22:52
Daybrook 31 17 39N36 80w15 5:21:00
Daysville 49 1 38N59 80w13 5:20:52
Deansville 49 1 38N59 80w13 5:20:52
Deanville 21 1 39N03 80w28 5:21:52
Decota 20 1 38N04 81w27 5:25:48
Deep Valley 25 17 39N32 80w20 5:21:20
Deep Valley 48 2 39N16 80w54 5:23:36
Deep Water 10 14 38N07 81w16 5:25:04
Deer Creek 38 1 38N24 79w55 5:19:40
Deer Run 36 1 38N39 79w20 5:17:20
Deer Walk 54 1 39N11 81w23 5:25:32
Dehue 23 1 37N49 81w55 5:27:40
De Kalb 11 1 38N58 80w56 5:23:44
Delbarton 30 1 37N43 82w11 5:28:44
Dellslow 31 17 39N37 79w53 5:19:32
Delong 37 1 39N24 81w12 5:24:48
Delray 14 1 39N13 78w36 5:14:24
Dempsey 10 18 38N03 81w06 5:24:24
Denver 26 21 39N50 80w34 5:22:16
Denver 39 19 39N24 79w45 5:19:00
Denver Heights 26 21 39N50 80w34 5:22:16
Derryhale 10 1 37N54 81w10 5:24:40
Despard 17 24 39N17 80w19 5:21:16
Dessie 4 1 38N38 80w52 5:23:28
Devon 30 1 37N37 82w04 5:28:16
Dewitt 10 1 37N59 81w09 5:24:36
Diamond 20 14 38N15 81w33 5:26:12
Diamond 23 1 37N50 82w04 5:28:16
Diana 51 1 38N34 80w27 5:21:48
Dickson 50 14 38N20 82w27 5:29:48
Dille 8 1 38N29 80w50 5:23:20
Dingess 30 1 37N52 82w10 5:28:40
Dingy 4 1 38N36 80w51 5:23:24
Dink 8 1 38N32 81w02 5:24:08
Dixie 34 1 38N15 81w12 5:24:48
Doane 50 1 38N01 82w26 5:29:44
Dobra 23 1 37N55 81w50 5:27:20
Dock 20 18 38N23 81w49 5:27:16
Dog Patch 23 1 37N49 82w00 5:28:00
Dola 17 1 39N23 80w21 5:21:24
Donaldson 51 1 38N25 80w33 5:22:12
Doortown 51 1 38N29 80w25 5:21:40
Dorcas 12 1 38N56 79w06 5:16:24
Dorothy 41 18 37N57 81w29 5:25:56
Dothan 10 1 37N58 81w13 5:24:52
Dott 28 1 37N29 81w15 5:25:00
Douglas 7 1 38N42 81w05 5:24:20
Douglas 47 1 39N09 79w30 5:18:00
Drennen 34 1 38N16 81w00 5:24:00
Drews Creek 41 1 37N52 81w29 5:25:56
Droop 38 1 38N06 80w17 5:21:08
Drybranch 20 1 38N11 81w28 5:25:52
Dry Creek 41 1 37N52 81w28 5:25:52
Dryfork 42 1 38N58 79w30 5:18:00
Dry Hill 41 18 37N47 81w11 5:24:44
Dubree 10 1 38N03 81w00 5:24:00
Duck 8 1 38N35 80w56 5:23:44
Dudeon 18 1 38N41 81w40 5:26:40
Dudley Gap 6 1 38N26 82w08 5:28:32
Duffields 19 2 39N22 77w51 5:11:24
Duffy 21 1 38N49 80w28 5:21:52
Duhring 28 1 37N21 81w16 5:25:04
Dukes 44 1 38N54 81w32 5:26:08
Dunbar 20 14 38N22 81w44 5:26:56
Dunbar Village 20 14 38N23 81w45 5:27:00
Duncan 18 1 38N54 81w35 5:26:20
Dundon 8 1 38N29 81w05 5:24:20
Dunloup 10 1 37N54 81w10 5:24:40
Dunlow 50 1 38N01 82w26 5:29:44
Dunmore 38 1 38N22 79w53 5:19:32
Dunns 28 1 37N35 81w06 5:24:24
Duo 13 1 37N58 80w41 5:22:44
Dupont Circle 54 1 39N16 81w40 5:26:40
Dupont City 20 14 38N15 81w33 5:26:12
Durbin 38 14 38N33 79w50 5:19:20
Durgon 16 1 39N03 78w58 5:15:52
Dutchman 43 1 39N05 81w12 5:24:48
Dutch Ridge 20 1 38N29 81w21 5:25:24
Duval 22 1 38N13 81w56 5:27:44
Dyer 51 1 38N25 80w33 5:22:12
Eagle 10 1 38N11 81w21 5:25:24
Eagle 17 1 39N23 80w22 5:21:28
Earling 23 1 37N46 81w55 5:27:40
Earnshaw 52 2 39N35 80w22 5:21:28
East Bank 20 1 38N13 81w27 5:25:48
East Beckley 41 18 37N47 81w11 5:24:44
East Dailey 42 1 38N51 79w52 5:19:28
Eastgulf 41 1 37N38 81w17 5:25:08
East Kermit 30 1 37N50 82w24 5:29:36
East Lynn 50 1 38N10 82w23 5:29:32
East Nitro 20 18 38N25 81w50 5:27:20
East Oak Hill 10 1 37N59 81w09 5:24:36
Easton 31 28 39N39 79w58 5:19:52
East Pea Ridge 6 5 38N25 82w25 5:29:40
East Rainelle 1 37N58 80w47 5:23:08
East River 28 1 37N22 81w03 5:24:12
East Salem 17 1 39N17 80w34 5:22:16
Eastside 25 17 39N28 80w10 5:20:40
East View 17 24 39N16 80w18 5:21:12
East Williamson 30 1 37N41 82w16 5:29:04
Eaton 54 1 39N11 81w23 5:25:32
Eccles 41 1 37N47 81w16 5:25:04
Echo 50 1 38N13 82w27 5:29:48
Eckman 1 37N24 81w28 5:25:52
Eden 35 34 40N04 80w42 5:22:48
Eden 49 1 38N50 80w21 5:21:24
Edgarton 30 1 37N34 82w09 5:28:36
Edgemont 25 17 39N28 80w10 5:20:40
Edgewood 17 24 39N16 80w19 5:21:16
Edgewood 35 34 40N04 80w42 5:22:48
Edison 28 20 37N16 81w14 5:24:56
Edmond 10 1 38N04 81w02 5:24:08
Edna 31 28 39N39 79w58 5:19:52
Edray 38 1 38N16 80w04 5:20:16
Edwight 41 1 37N53 81w31 5:26:04
Effler 24 1 37N20 81w26 5:25:44
Egeria 41 1 37N36 81w12 5:24:48
Eggleton 40 1 38N17 82w06 5:28:24
Eglon 39 12 39N18 79w31 5:18:04
Elana 44 1 38N36 81w11 5:24:44
Eldora 25 17 39N28 80w10 5:20:40
Eleanor 40 1 38N32 81w56 5:27:44
Elgood 28 1 37N24 80w56 5:23:44
Elizabeth 53 1 39N04 81w24 5:25:36
Elk 47 1 39N05 79w38 5:18:32
Elk City 1 1 39N09 80w03 5:20:12
Elk Forest 20 22 38N21 81w37 5:26:28
Elk Garden 29 2 39N23 79w09 5:16:36
Elkhorn 24 1 37N23 81w23 5:25:32
Elkhurst 8 1 38N29 81w12 5:24:48
Elkins 42 35 38N55 79w51 5:19:24
Elkridge 10 14 38N05 81w19 5:25:16
Elkridge 24 1 37N25 81w26 5:25:44
Elk Run Junction 3 18 37N59 81w32 5:26:08
Elkview 20 1 38N27 81w29 5:25:56
Elkwater 42 1 38N43 79w59 5:19:56
Ella 26 4 39N43 80w49 5:23:16
Ellamore 42 1 38N56 80w06 5:20:24
Ellenboro 43 1 39N16 81w03 5:24:12
Elliber Spring 29 2 39N14 78w56 5:15:44
Ellison 45 1 37N39 80w59 5:23:56
Ellsworth 48 2 39N31 80w52 5:23:28
Elm Grove 35 34 40N04 80w42 5:22:48
Elmira 4 1 38N39 80w59 5:23:56
Elm Terrace 35 34 40N04 80w42 5:22:48
Elmwood 27 1 38N45 81w57 5:27:48
Elmwood 50 1 38N13 82w27 5:29:48
Elmwood Heights 54 1 39N24 81w27 5:25:48
Eloise 50 1 38N01 82w26 5:29:44
Elton 45 1 37N50 80w48 5:23:12
Emma 40 1 38N36 81w44 5:26:56
Emmart 21 1 38N52 80w28 5:21:52
Emmett 23 1 37N41 81w50 5:27:20
Emmons 3 1 38N11 81w42 5:26:48
Emoryville 29 2 39N23 79w09 5:16:36
Endicott 52 2 39N42 80w31 5:22:04
Engle 19 3 39N19 77w44 5:10:56
Enoch 8 1 38N29 81w05 5:24:20
Enon 34 1 38N17 80w51 5:23:24
Enterprise 17 1 39N25 80w17 5:21:08
Enterprise 53 1 39N02 81w24 5:25:36
Entry 36 1 38N39 79w20 5:17:20
Epperly 41 1 37N40 81w14 5:24:56
Erbacon 51 1 38N31 80w35 5:22:20
Erie 17 14 39N20 80w20 5:21:20
Erin 24 1 37N27 81w42 5:26:48
Erwin 39 12 39N21 79w41 5:18:44
Eskdale 20 1 38N05 81w27 5:25:48
Estar 18 1 38N53 81w51 5:27:24
Esty 13 1 38N00 80w22 5:21:28
Etam 39 12 39N21 79w41 5:18:44
Ethel 23 1 37N52 81w54 5:27:36
Euclid 7 1 38N42 81w02 5:24:08
Eunice 41 18 37N58 81w32 5:26:08
Eureka 37 1 39N22 81w17 5:25:08
Evans 18 1 38N49 81w47 5:27:08
Evansdale 31 28 39N39 79w58 5:19:52
Evansville 39 12 39N21 79w57 5:19:48
Evenwood 42 1 38N55 79w42 5:18:48
Everett 48 2 39N31 81w04 5:24:16
Everettville 31 17 39N34 80w04 5:20:16
Evergreen 49 1 38N53 80w18 5:21:12
Evergreen Hills 18 1 38N52 81w49 5:27:16
Everson 25 17 39N28 80w10 5:20:40
Excelsior 24 1 37N18 81w41 5:26:44
Excelsior 49 1 38N59 80w13 5:20:52
Exchange 4 1 38N46 80w44 5:22:56
Extra 40 1 38N37 81w59 5:27:56
Factory 33 11 39N38 78w14 5:12:56
Fairdale 41 1 37N47 81w21 5:25:24
Fairfax 47 1 39N09 79w30 5:18:00
Fairlea 13 14 37N48 80w27 5:21:48
Fairmont 25 25 39N29 80w09 5:20:36
Fairmor 31 28 39N39 79w58 5:19:52
Fairplain 18 1 38N49 81w42 5:26:48
Fairview 25 17 39N36 80w15 5:21:00
Fairview 26 4 39N43 80w49 5:23:16
Fairview 27 1 38N54 81w56 5:27:44
Fairview 30 1 37N41 82w16 5:29:04
Fairview 54 1 39N16 81w40 5:26:40
Fallen Timber 52 2 39N30 80w34 5:22:16
Falling Rock 20 1 38N28 81w24 5:25:36
Falling Springs 13 1 38N01 80w20 5:21:20
Falling Waters 2 2 39N34 77w55 5:11:40
Falls 10 1 38N11 81w13 5:24:52
Falls 12 1 39N07 79w10 5:16:40
Falls Mill 4 1 38N47 80w33 5:22:12
Falls Mills 48 2 39N31 81w04 5:24:16
Fallsview 10 14 38N08 81w17 5:25:08
Far 52 2 39N34 80w44 5:22:56
Farley 45 1 37N32 80w58 5:23:52
Farmington 25 17 39N31 80w15 5:21:00
Farnum 17 14 39N20 80w20 5:21:20
Faulkner 42 1 38N55 79w42 5:18:48
Fayetteville 10 18 38N03 81w06 5:24:24
Federal 28 20 37N16 81w14 5:24:56
Federal 37 1 39N24 81w12 5:24:48
Federal Mine 25 17 39N33 80w11 5:20:44
Fellowsville 39 12 39N20 79w50 5:19:20
Fenwick 34 14 38N14 80w35 5:22:20
Ferguson 50 1 38N01 82w26 5:29:44
Ferrell 20 18 38N23 81w49 5:27:16
Ferrellsburg 22 1 38N02 82w06 5:28:24
Fetterman 46 12 39N23 79w58 5:19:52
Finch 43 1 39N16 81w03 5:24:12
Finley 20 1 38N17 81w48 5:27:12
Fireco 41 1 37N39 81w12 5:24:48
Fisher 16 1 39N03 79w00 5:16:00
Fitzpatrick 41 18 37N47 81w11 5:24:44
Five Forks 7 1 38N58 81w04 5:24:16
Five Forks 39 12 39N40 79w38 5:18:32
Five Forks 43 1 39N13 81w03 5:24:12
Fivemile 20 1 38N20 81w30 5:26:00
Fivemile 27 1 38N50 82w08 5:28:32
Flat Rock 27 1 38N52 82w08 5:28:32
Flats 16 1 39N14 78w56 5:15:44
Flats 41 1 37N52 81w29 5:25:56
Flat Top 28 1 37N35 81w06 5:24:24
Flat Top Lake 41 1 37N37 81w07 5:24:28
Flatwoods 4 1 38N43 80w39 5:22:36
Flatwoods 18 1 38N57 81w46 5:27:04
Flemington 46 1 39N16 80w08 5:20:32
Fletcher 18 1 38N39 81w36 5:26:24
Flinderation 17 1 39N17 80w31 5:22:04
Flint 9 1 39N18 80w47 5:23:08
Flipping 28 1 37N21 81w16 5:25:04
Floe 8 1 38N39 81w02 5:24:08
Flower 4 1 38N50 80w46 5:23:04
Foch 3 18 38N02 81w47 5:27:08
Fola 8 1 38N22 81w07 5:24:28
Follansbee 5 8 40N20 80w36 5:22:24
Folsom 52 2 39N28 80w31 5:22:04
Forest Hill 45 1 37N34 80w48 5:23:12
Forest Hills 35 34 40N04 80w42 5:22:48
Fork Lick 51 1 38N28 80w22 5:21:28
Forksburg 25 17 39N28 80w10 5:20:40
Forks Of Cacapon 14 19 39N32 78w28 5:13:52
Forks of Coal 20 1 38N17 81w48 5:27:12
Forks Of Hurricane 50 1 38N07 82w36 5:30:24
Fort Ashby 29 2 39N30 78w46 5:15:04
Fort Branch 23 1 37N52 81w54 5:27:36
Fort Gay 50 1 38N07 82w36 5:30:24
Fort Grande 31 17 39N34 80w04 5:20:16
Fort Henry Mall 35 34 40N04 80w42 5:22:48
Fort Martin 31 28 39N41 79w59 5:19:56
Fort Neal 54 14 39N17 81w32 5:26:08
Fort Run 16 1 39N03 78w58 5:15:52
Fort Seybert 36 1 38N41 79w12 5:16:48
Fort Spring 13 14 37N46 80w28 5:21:52
Foster 3 18 38N06 81w47 5:27:08
Fosterville 3 1 38N06 81w37 5:26:28
Four Mile 52 2 39N34 80w41 5:22:44
Four States 25 17 39N29 80w19 5:21:16
Frame 20 1 38N26 81w29 5:25:56
Frametown 4 1 38N38 80w52 5:23:28
Francis 17 17 39N28 80w10 5:20:40
Francis 41 1 37N36 81w18 5:25:12
Frank 38 14 38N33 79w48 5:19:12
Frankford 13 1 37N56 80w23 5:21:32
Frankfort 29 2 39N34 78w47 5:15:08
Franklin 5 33 40N17 80w37 5:22:28
Franklin 26 4 39N43 80w49 5:23:16
Franklin 36 1 38N39 79w20 5:17:20
Fraziers Bottom 40 1 38N34 81w59 5:27:56
Freed 7 1 39N02 81w11 5:24:44
Freeman 28 1 37N19 81w19 5:25:16
Freemansburg 21 1 39N03 80w28 5:21:52
Freemans Creek 21 1 39N05 80w34 5:22:16
Freeport 39 12 39N27 79w33 5:18:12
Freeport 53 1 39N11 81w23 5:25:32
Freeze Fork 23 1 37N52 81w54 5:27:36
French Creek 49 1 38N53 80w18 5:21:12
Frenchton 49 1 38N52 80w22 5:21:28
Frew 48 2 39N30 80w54 5:23:36
Friars Hill 13 1 38N01 80w28 5:21:52
Friendly 48 2 39N31 81w04 5:24:16
Friendly View 41 1 37N52 81w28 5:25:52
Frogtown 23 1 37N50 82w04 5:28:16
Frost 38 1 38N16 79w53 5:19:32
Frozen Camp 18 1 38N54 81w32 5:26:08
Fry 22 1 38N02 82w06 5:28:24
Fulton 35 34 40N04 80w42 5:22:48
Gaines 49 1 38N50 80w21 5:21:24
Gallagher 20 1 38N10 81w24 5:25:36
Gallipolis Ferry 27 1 38N47 82w12 5:28:48
Galloway 1 1 39N13 80w09 5:20:36
Galloway Junction 1 1 39N13 80w09 5:20:36
Galmish 52 2 39N34 80w41 5:22:44
Gandeeville 44 1 38N42 81w25 5:25:40
Gap Mills 32 1 37N34 80w25 5:21:40
Gap of the Ridge 28 20 37N16 81w14 5:24:56
Garden Village 25 17 39N28 80w10 5:20:40
Gardner 28 1 37N22 81w05 5:24:20
Garfield 18 1 38N54 81w33 5:26:12
Garland 24 1 37N25 81w47 5:27:08
Garretts Bend 22 1 38N15 81w53 5:27:32
Garrison 3 18 38N00 81w31 5:26:04
Garten 10 18 38N03 81w06 5:24:24
Garwood 55 1 37N30 81w20 5:25:20
Gary 1 37N22 81w33 5:26:12
Gassaway 4 1 38N41 80w47 5:23:08
Gaston 21 1 39N03 80w28 5:21:52
Gaston Junction 25 17 39N28 80w10 5:20:40
Gates 32 1 37N35 80w33 5:22:12
Gatewood 10 18 38N03 81w06 5:24:24
Gauley Bridge 10 1 38N10 81w12 5:24:48
Gauley Mills 51 1 38N22 80w35 5:22:20

WEST VIRGINIA

Gawthrop 49 1 38N59 80W13 5:20:52
Gay 18 1 38N46 81W33 5:26:12
Gaymont 10 1 38N08 81W06 5:24:24
Geary 44 1 38N35 81W14 5:24:56
Gem 4 14 38N50 80W40 5:22:40
Genoa 50 1 38N07 82W28 5:29:52
Georges Run 48 2 39N18 80W47 5:23:08
Georgetown 2 2 39N33 78W00 5:12:00
Georgetown 21 1 39N00 80W23 5:21:32
Georgetown 26 21 39N50 80W34 5:22:16
Georgetown 31 28 39N39 79W58 5:19:52
Gerrardstown 2 2 39N25 78W06 5:12:24
Ghent 41 1 37N37 81W07 5:24:28
Gilbert 30 1 37N37 81W52 5:27:28
Gilboa 34 1 38N18 80W57 5:23:48
Giles 20 1 38N09 81W27 5:25:48
Gilkerson 50 1 38N10 82W23 5:29:32
Gill 22 1 38N07 82W11 5:28:44
Gillman Bottom 23 1 37N44 81W49 5:27:16
Gilman 42 35 38N56 79W51 5:19:24
Gilmer 11 14 38N53 80W43 5:22:52
Gip 4 1 38N39 80W59 5:23:56
Given 18 1 38N44 81W44 5:26:56
Glace 32 1 37N41 80W20 5:21:20
Glade Farms 39 12 39N40 79W38 5:18:32
Glade Springs 41 1 37N45 81W07 5:24:28
Gladesville 39 12 39N24 79W52 5:19:28
Glade View 51 1 38N25 80W33 5:22:12
Gladwin 47 1 38N55 79W42 5:18:48
Glady 42 1 38N48 79W43 5:18:52
Glady Creek 25 17 39N28 80W10 5:20:40
Glasgow 20 1 38N13 81W25 5:25:40
Glen 8 1 38N24 81W15 5:25:00
Glenalum 30 1 37N33 81W58 5:27:52
Glencoe 10 1 38N02 81W16 5:25:04
Glen Dale 26 34 40N02 80W43 5:22:52
Glendale Heights 26
34 40N02 80W43 5:22:52
Glen Daniel 41 1 37N47 81W20 5:25:20
Glendon 4 1 38N36 80W51 5:23:24
Glen Easton 26 4 39N50 80W39 5:22:36
Glen Elk 17 24 39N16 80W19 5:21:16
Glen Falls 17 24 39N16 80W19 5:21:16
Glen Ferris 10 14 38N09 81W13 5:24:52
Glen Fork 55 1 37N42 81W32 5:26:08
Glengary 2 2 39N23 78W10 5:12:40
Glenhayes 50 1 38N01 82W31 5:30:04
Glen Hedrick 41 18 37N45 81W08 5:24:32
Glen Jean 10 1 37N56 81W09 5:24:36
Glenmore 42 35 38N56 79W51 5:19:24
Glen Morgan 41 18 37N45 81W10 5:24:40
Glenray 45 1 37N44 80W39 5:22:36
Glen Rogers 55 1 37N43 81W25 5:25:40
Glen View 41 18 37N45 81W14 5:24:56
Glenville 11 1 38N56 80W50 5:23:20
Glen White 41 1 37N44 81W17 5:25:08
Glenwood 27 1 38N36 82W11 5:28:44
Glenwood 35 34 40N04 80W42 5:22:48
Glenwood Park 28 20 37N16 81W14 5:24:56
Glover Gap 25 17 39N35 80W22 5:21:28
Godby 23 1 37N58 82W01 5:28:04
Godfrey 28 1 37N23 81W17 5:25:08
Goffs 43 1 39N05 81W02 5:24:08
Goldtown 18 1 38N41 81W40 5:26:40
Goodhope 17 1 39N10 80W21 5:21:24
Goodman 30 1 37N42 82W17 5:29:08
Gordon 3 1 37N59 81W42 5:26:48
Gore 14 1 39N23 78W35 5:14:20
Gore 17 24 39N16 80W19 5:21:16
Gormania 12 1 39N18 79W21 5:17:24
Gormley 49 1 38N56 80W06 5:20:24
Goshen 49 1 38N50 80W21 5:21:24
Gould 49 1 38N53 80W18 5:21:12
Grace 44 1 38N54 81W25 5:25:40
Grafton 46 14 39N21 80W02 5:20:08
Graham 27 1 38N58 81W58 5:27:52
Graham Heights 25
17 39N28 80W07 5:20:28
Grand Central Mall 54
14 39N17 81W32 5:26:08
Grandview 41 18 37N45 81W08 5:24:32
Grangeville 25 17 39N32 80W20 5:21:20
Grantsville 7 1 38N55 81W06 5:24:24
Grant Town 25 17 39N33 80W11 5:20:44
Granville 31 28 39N39 80W00 5:20:00
Grapevine 24 1 37N23 81W49 5:27:16
Grassy Meadows 13 1 37N50 80W43 5:22:52
Grave Creek 26 21 39N51 80W36 5:22:24
Graydon 10 1 38N08 81W05 5:24:20
Graysville 26 4 39N43 80W49 5:23:16
Great Cacapon 33 11 39N37 78W17 5:13:08
Green 52 2 39N34 80W45 5:23:00
Green Bank 38 1 38N25 79W50 5:19:20
Green Bottom 6 1 38N31 82W18 5:29:12
Green Castle 53 1 39N11 81W23 5:25:32
Greendale 34 1 38N14 81W12 5:24:48
Green Hill 52 12 39N39 80W51 5:23:24
Greenland 12 1 39N07 79W10 5:16:40
Greenland 54 1 39N16 81W40 5:26:40
Greensburg 2 27 39N28 77W58 5:11:52
Green Spring 14 1 39N32 78W37 5:14:28
Greenstown 10 1 37N59 81W09 5:24:36
Green Sulphur 45 1 37N47 80W50 5:23:20
Green Sulphur Springs 45
1 37N49 80W50 5:23:20
Green Valley 28 20 37N16 81W14 5:24:56
Greenview 3 18 38N05 81W50 5:27:20
Greenville 32 1 37N33 80W41 5:22:44
Greenwood 3 1 37N52 81W38 5:26:32
Greenwood 9 1 39N16 80W54 5:23:36
Greer 27 1 38N52 82W08 5:28:32
Greer 31 28 39N39 79W58 5:19:52
Greggsville 35 34 40N04 80W42 5:22:48
Grey Eagle 30 1 37N50 82W24 5:29:36
Griffithsville 22 1 38N14 81W59 5:27:56
Grimms Landing 27 1 38N40 81W57 5:27:48
Grippe 20 22 38N20 81W38 5:26:32
Grove 9 1 39N14 80W41 5:22:44
Grubbs Corner 2 27 39N28 77W58 5:11:52
Guardian 51 1 38N38 80W28 5:21:52
Gum Spring 31 28 39N39 79W58 5:19:52
Gunville 27 1 38N45 81W57 5:27:48
Guthrie 20 22 38N22 81W40 5:26:40
Guyan 23 1 37N56 82W01 5:28:04
Guyandotte 6 14 38N24 82W22 5:29:28
Guyan Estates 6 1 38N25 82W17 5:29:08
Guyan Terrace 23 1 37N52 81W59 5:27:56
Gypsy 17 1 39N22 80W19 5:21:16
Hackers Creek 21 1 39N04 80W24 5:21:36
Hacker Valley 51 1 38N39 80W23 5:21:32
Hagans 31 17 39N41 80W07 5:20:28
Hager 22 1 38N11 82W05 5:28:20
Hales Gap 28 20 37N16 81W14 5:24:56
Hall 1 1 38N59 80W13 5:20:52
Hallburg 8 1 38N35 80W56 5:23:44
Halleck 31 28 39N39 79W58 5:19:52
Halltown 19 2 39N19 77W48 5:11:12
Hambleton 47 1 39N05 79W39 5:18:36
Hamilton 34 1 38N25 80W46 5:23:04
Hamlin 22 1 38N17 82W06 5:28:24
Hampden 30 1 37N39 81W57 5:27:48
Hancock 33 19 39N42 78W10 5:12:40
Handley 20 1 38N11 81W22 5:25:28
Hanna 54 1 39N11 81W23 5:25:32
Hannahsville 47 1 39N10 79W42 5:18:48
Hannan 27 1 38N35 82W07 5:28:28
Hansford 20 1 38N12 81W24 5:25:36
Hany 50 1 38N01 82W26 5:29:44
Hardee 30 1 37N47 82W15 5:29:00
Harding 42 1 39N01 79W56 5:19:44
Hardy 28 1 37N22 81W05 5:24:20
Harewood 10 14 38N09 81W17 5:25:08
Harley 44 1 38N38 81W24 5:25:36
Harlin 9 1 39N18 80W47 5:23:08
Harman 42 1 38N55 79W32 5:18:08
Harmco 55 1 37N35 81W23 5:25:32
Harmony 44 1 38N41 81W29 5:25:56
Harmony Grove 31 28 39N39 79W58 5:19:52
Harper 36 1 38N39 79W20 5:17:20
Harper 41 1 37N48 81W16 5:25:04
Harper 44 1 38N41 81W29 5:25:56
Harper Heights 41
18 37N47 81W11 5:24:44
Harpers Ferry 19 3 39N20 77W44 5:10:56
Harpertown 42 35 38N56 79W51 5:19:24
Harris 54 1 39N09 81W43 5:26:52
Harris Ferry 54 1 39N12 81W42 5:26:48
Harrison 8 1 38N31 80W57 5:23:48
Harrisville 43 1 39N13 81W03 5:24:12
Harters Hill 25 17 39N27 80W15 5:21:00
Hartford 27 1 39N00 81W59 5:27:56
Hartford City 27 1 39N00 81W59 5:27:56
Hartland 8 1 38N29 81W05 5:24:20
Hartmansville 29 2 39N23 79W09 5:16:36
Harts 22 1 38N02 82W07 5:28:28
Harts Creek 22 1 38N02 82W07 5:28:28
Harvey 10 1 37N56 81W08 5:24:32
Harvey 30 1 37N54 82W13 5:28:52
Hastings 52 2 39N33 80W40 5:22:40
Hatcher 28 1 37N22 81W05 5:24:20
Hatcher 55 1 37N41 81W38 5:26:32
Hatfield Bottom 30
1 37N37 82W10 5:28:40
Haywood 17 1 39N23 80W20 5:21:20
Haywood Junction 17
1 39N23 80W20 5:21:20
Hazelgreen 43 1 39N05 81W00 5:24:00
Hazelton 39 12 39N39 79W32 5:18:08
Hazelwood 42 1 38N51 79W52 5:19:28
Heaters 4 1 38N46 80W38 5:22:32
Heavener Grove 49 1 38N59 80W13 5:20:52
Hebron 37 1 39N22 81W01 5:24:04
Hedgesville 2 2 39N33 78W00 5:12:00
Hedgeview 23 1 37N51 82W01 5:28:04
Heizer 40 1 38N28 81W49 5:27:16
Helen 41 1 37N38 81W19 5:25:16
Helens Run 25 17 39N27 80W15 5:21:00
Helvetia 42 1 38N42 80W12 5:20:48
Hemlock 49 1 38N42 80W12 5:20:48
Hemlock Hollow 10 1 37N52 80W59 5:23:56
Hemphill 24 1 37N26 81W35 5:26:20
Henderson 27 1 38N50 82W08 5:28:32
Hendricks 47 1 39N05 79W38 5:18:32
Henlawson 23 1 37N54 81W59 5:27:56
Henning 13 1 37N56 80W23 5:21:32
Henrietta 7 1 38N55 81W06 5:24:24
Henry 8 1 38N29 81W06 5:24:24
Hensley Heights 23
1 37N45 81W53 5:27:32
Hepzibah 17 14 39N20 80W20 5:21:20
Hepzibah 46 1 39N17 80W15 5:21:00
Hereford 18 1 38N54 81W32 5:26:08
Herndon 55 1 37N30 81W20 5:25:20
Herndon Heights 55
1 37N30 81W20 5:25:20
Hernshaw 20 1 38N13 81W36 5:26:24
Herold 4 1 38N34 80W49 5:23:16
Herring 39 12 39N33 79W48 5:19:12
Hettie 4 1 38N49 80W28 5:21:52
Hetzel 23 1 37N52 81W54 5:27:36
Hewett 3 1 37N58 81W51 5:27:24
Hiawatha 28 1 37N26 81W15 5:25:00
Hickman Run 25 17 39N28 80W10 5:20:40
Hickory 27 1 38N52 82W08 5:28:32
Hico 10 1 38N07 81W00 5:24:00
Hicumbottom 20 22 38N21 81W38 5:26:32
Highland 43 1 39N18 81W03 5:24:12
Highland Lake Terrace 54
1 39N16 81W40 5:26:40
Highland Park 42 35 38N56 79W51 5:19:24
Highlawns 25 17 39N32 80W07 5:20:28
High View 14 1 39N14 78W25 5:13:40
Hildebrand 31 28 39N39 79W58 5:19:52
Hillcrest 25 17 39N28 80W10 5:20:40
Hilldale 45 14 37N40 80W53 5:23:32
Hillsboro 38 1 38N08 80W13 5:20:52
Hillsdale 32 1 37N40 80W33 5:22:12
Hilltop 10 1 37N56 81W09 5:24:36
Hillview 6 5 38N25 82W23 5:29:32
Hillview 25 17 39N28 80W10 5:20:40
Hillview Terrace 26
21 39N51 80W36 5:22:24
Hilton Village 10 1 37N58 80W46 5:23:04
Hinch 30 1 37N37 82W04 5:28:16
Hines 13 1 37N59 80W43 5:22:52
Hinkleville 49 1 38N59 80W13 5:20:52
Hinton 45 14 37N40 80W54 5:23:36
Hiorra 39 12 39N23 79W51 5:19:24
Hite 25 17 39N32 80W07 5:20:28
Hitop 20 1 38N17 81W17 5:25:08
Hix 45 1 37N44 80W49 5:23:16
Hodgesville 49 1 39N04 80W12 5:20:48
Hogsett 27 1 38N47 82W12 5:28:48
Hokes Mill 13 14 37N45 80W28 5:21:52
Holbrook 43 1 39N12 80W52 5:23:28
Holden 23 1 37N50 82W04 5:28:16
Holly 20 1 38N04 81W27 5:25:48
Holly Grove 20 1 38N12 81W24 5:25:36
Holly Hill Church 16
1 39N02 78W45 5:15:00
Hollywood 32 1 37N35 80W33 5:22:12
Homeland 21 1 39N07 80W25 5:21:40
Hometown 40 1 38N32 81W51 5:27:24
Homewood 21 1 39N03 80W28 5:21:52
Hominy Falls 34 1 38N09 80W44 5:22:56
Hoodsville 25 17 39N32 80W07 5:20:28
Hoo Hoo 41 1 37N44 81W18 5:25:12
Hookersville 34 1 38N17 80W51 5:23:24
Hooverson Heights 5
32 40N21 80W34 5:22:16
Hoover Town 49 1 38N53 80W18 5:21:12
Hopewell 1 1 39N09 80W03 5:20:12
Hopewell 10 1 38N08 81W05 5:24:20
Hopewell 25 17 39N28 80W10 5:20:40
Hopewell 39 12 39N40 79W38 5:18:32
Hopkins Fork 3 1 38N01 81W38 5:26:32
Horner 21 1 39N00 80W23 5:21:32
Horsepen 24 1 37N14 81W31 5:26:04
Horse Shoe Run 39
12 39N17 79W31 5:18:04
Horton 42 1 38N49 79W33 5:18:12
Hosterman 38 14 38N33 79W50 5:19:20
Hotchkiss 41 1 37N41 81W20 5:25:20
Hoult 25 17 39N28 80W10 5:20:40
Howells Mill 6 1 38N26 82W13 5:28:52
Howesville 39 19 39N24 79W45 5:19:00
Hoy 14 1 39N22 78W31 5:14:04
Hubball 22 1 38N13 82W12 5:28:48
Hubbardstown 50 1 38N15 82W36 5:30:24
Hudson 39 12 39N30 79W39 5:18:36
Huff Creek 55 1 37N33 81W48 5:27:12
Huff Junction 23 1 37N44 81W51 5:27:24
Hughart 13 1 37N54 80W36 5:22:24
Hughes 17 1 39N21 80W19 5:21:16
Hugheston 20 1 38N12 81W22 5:25:28
Hugo 40 1 38N32 81W54 5:27:36
Hull 24 1 37N28 81W49 5:27:16
Humphrey 54 1 39N08 81W44 5:26:56
Hundred 52 7 39N41 80W28 5:21:52
Hunt 23 1 37N45 81W53 5:27:32
Huntersville 38 1 38N12 79W59 5:19:56
Hunting Ground 36 1 38N38 79W31 5:18:04
Huntington 6 5 38N25 82W27 5:29:48
Hur 7 1 38N52 81W07 5:24:28
Hurricane 40 1 38N26 82W02 5:28:08
Hurst 21 1 39N03 80W42 5:22:48
Hutchinson 23 1 37N49 81W55 5:27:40
Hutchinson 25 17 39N27 80W15 5:21:00
Huttonsville 42 1 38N43 79W59 5:19:56
Iaeger 24 1 37N28 81W49 5:27:16
Idamay 25 17 39N30 80W16 5:21:04
Imperial Junction 20
1 38N03 81W23 5:25:32
Independence 8 1 38N20 81W11 5:24:44
Independence 18 1 38N54 81W40 5:26:40
Independence 39 12 39N24 79W52 5:19:28
Indian 20 18 38N23 81W49 5:27:16
Indian Meadows 6 1 38N26 82W13 5:28:52
Indian Mills 45 1 37N32 80W49 5:23:16
Indore 8 1 38N22 81W10 5:24:40
Industrial 17 24 39N16 80W19 5:21:16
Industry 7 1 39N00 81W12 5:24:48
Ingleside 28 1 37N19 81W03 5:24:12
Ingram Branch 10 1 38N02 81W16 5:25:04
Inkerman 16 1 39N02 78W45 5:15:00
Institute 20 14 38N23 81W46 5:27:04
Intermont 14 1 39N05 78W36 5:14:24
Inwood 2 2 39N22 78W03 5:12:12
Ireland 21 1 38N49 80W28 5:21:52
Irish Corner 13 14 37N43 80W28 5:21:52
Irona 39 12 39N28 79W41 5:18:44
Iroquis 55 1 37N35 81W19 5:25:16
Island Creek 23 1 37N47 82W01 5:28:04
Isom 23 1 37N56 81W54 5:27:36
Israel 39 19 39N24 79W45 5:19:00
Iuka 48 2 39N30 80W54 5:23:36
Ivanhoe 49 1 38N56 80W14 5:20:56
Ivy 49 1 38N59 80W13 5:20:52
Ivydale 8 1 38N32 81W02 5:24:08
Jacksonburg 52 2 39N32 80W39 5:22:36
Jacksons Mills 21 1 39N03 80W28 5:21:52
Jacox 38 1 38N08 80W13 5:20:52
Jamestown 19 2 39N15 77W58 5:11:52
Jamison Mine No. 9 25
17 39N31 80W15 5:21:00

Place		Lat	Long	Time
Jane Lew 21	1	39N07	80w25	5:21:40
Janie 3	18	37N59	81w32	5:26:08
Jarrods Valley 3	18	37N59	81w32	5:26:08
Jarvisville 17	1	39N17	80w28	5:21:52
Jawood 41	1	37N36	81w19	5:25:16
Jayenn 25	17	39N28	80w10	5:20:40
Jeffrey 3	1	37N58	81w49	5:27:16
Jenkinjones	1	37N18	81w25	5:25:40
Jenks 22	1	38N11	82w05	5:28:20
Jenky 10	1	38N07	81w00	5:24:00
Jenningston 47	1	38N55	79w42	5:18:48
Jenny Gap 41	1	37N44	81w18	5:25:12
Jere 31	17	39N40	80w03	5:20:12
Jerrys Run 54	1	39N08	81w44	5:26:56
Jerryville	1	38N25	80w18	5:21:12
Jimtown 17	1	39N23	80w21	5:21:24
Jimtown 33	11	39N38	78w14	5:12:56
Job 42	1	38N52	79w33	5:18:12
Jockeycamp Run 9	1	39N18	80w47	5:23:08
Jodie 10	1	38N14	81w09	5:24:36
Joetown 25	17	39N32	80w20	5:21:20
Johnnycake 24	1	37N28	81w49	5:27:16
Johnsontown 2	2	39N33	78w00	5:12:00
Johnsontown 19	2	39N23	77w53	5:11:32
Johnstown 17	1	39N10	80w21	5:21:24
Joker 7	1	38N56	81w14	5:24:56
Jonben 41	1	37N39	81w12	5:24:48
Jones Springs 2	2	39N30	78w06	5:12:24
Jordan 25	17	39N33	80w05	5:20:20
Jordan Run 12	1	39N07	79w10	5:16:40
Josephine 41	1	37N37	81w13	5:24:52
Josephs Mills 48	2	39N26	80w49	5:23:16
Joy 9	1	39N12	80w52	5:23:28
Judson 45	1	37N44	80w39	5:22:36
Judy Gap 36	1	38N45	79w26	5:17:44
Julia 13	1	38N00	80w22	5:21:28
Julian 3	1	38N09	81w51	5:27:24
Jumping Branch 45	1	37N39	80w59	5:23:56
Junction 14	1	39N19	78w52	5:15:28
Junior 1	1	38N59	79w57	5:19:48
Justice	1	37N35	81w50	5:27:20
Justice Addition 23	1	37N52	81w59	5:27:56
Kabletown 19	23	39N14	77w54	5:11:36
Kalamazoo 1	1	39N09	80w03	5:20:12
Kanawha 54	1	39N12	81w27	5:25:48
Kanawha City 20	22	38N19	81w35	5:26:20
Kanawha Drive 11	1	38N56	80w50	5:23:20
Kanawha Falls 10	1	38N08	81w12	5:24:48
Kanawha Head 49	1	38N46	80w21	5:21:24
Kanawha Station 54	1	39N12	81w30	5:26:00
Kanetown 39	19	39N24	79w45	5:19:00
Kasson 1	1	39N13	79w53	5:19:32
Katy 25	17	39N28	80w10	5:20:40
Katy Lick 17	24	39N16	80w19	5:21:16
Kayford 20	1	38N01	81w27	5:25:48
Kearneysville 19	2	39N23	77w53	5:11:32
Kedron 49	1	38N59	80w13	5:20:52
Keenan 32	1	37N35	80w33	5:22:12
Kegley 28	1	37N24	81w08	5:24:32
Keister 13	14	37N48	80w27	5:21:48
Keith 3	1	38N04	81w34	5:26:16
Kelly Hill 20	1	38N29	81w21	5:25:24
Kellysville 28	1	37N21	80w56	5:23:44
Kenna 18	1	38N41	81w40	5:26:40
Kenova 50	14	38N24	82w35	5:30:20
Kent 26	4	39N43	80w49	5:23:16
Kentuck 18	1	38N39	81w36	5:26:24
Kentucky 34	1	38N13	80w41	5:22:44
Kera Landing 18	1	38N53	81w51	5:27:24
Kerens 42	1	39N01	79w49	5:19:16
Kermit 30	1	37N50	82w24	5:29:36
Keslers Cross Lanes 34	1	38N14	80w56	5:23:44
Kessel 16	1	39N03	79w00	5:16:00
Kessler 13	1	37N59	80w40	5:22:40
Kettle 44	1	38N42	81w25	5:25:40
Key 36	1	38N45	79w26	5:17:44
Keyrock 55	1	37N35	81w32	5:26:08
Keyser 29	6	39N26	78w59	5:15:56
Keystone 24	1	37N25	81w27	5:25:48
Kiahsville 50	1	38N06	82w20	5:29:20
Kidwell 48	2	39N30	80w54	5:23:36
Kieffer 13	1	37N56	80w36	5:22:24
Kilarm Junction 25	17	39N28	80w10	5:20:40
Killarney 41	1	37N38	81w17	5:25:08
Kilsyth 10	1	37N53	81w11	5:24:44
Kimball 24	1	37N26	81w30	5:26:00
Kimberly 10	14	38N08	81w18	5:25:12
Kincaid 10	1	38N02	81w16	5:25:04
Kincheloe 17	1	39N07	80w25	5:21:40
Kinder 22	1	38N10	82w11	5:28:44
Kingmont 25	17	39N27	80w11	5:20:44
Kingston 10	1	37N58	81w18	5:25:12
Kingstown 52	2	39N35	80w35	5:22:20
Kingsville 42	1	38N54	79w58	5:19:52
Kingwood 39	12	39N28	79w41	5:18:44
Kirby 14	1	39N11	78w44	5:14:56
Kirbyton 3	1	38N06	81w37	5:26:28
Kirk 30	1	37N52	82w10	5:28:40
Kirt 1	1	39N04	79w49	5:19:16
Kistler 23	1	37N46	81w52	5:27:28
Kitchen 23	1	37N58	82w01	5:28:04
Kitsonville 21	1	39N03	80w28	5:21:52
Kline 36	1	38N48	79w17	5:17:08
Klines Gap 12	1	39N07	79w10	5:16:40
Knawl 4	1	38N52	80w28	5:21:52
Knob Fork 52	2	39N39	80w33	5:22:12
Knobs 32	1	37N35	80w33	5:22:12
Knollwood 20	22	38N22	81w38	5:26:32
Knottsville 46	12	39N18	79w58	5:19:52
Kodol 52	2	39N38	80w41	5:22:44
Kopperston	1	37N45	81w35	5:26:20
Krollitz 24	1	37N28	81w49	5:27:16
Kyle 6	5	38N24	82w29	5:29:56
Lacoma 55	1	37N44	81w41	5:26:44
Lafayette 37	1	39N22	81w03	5:24:12
La Frank 34	14	38N14	80w32	5:22:08
Lahmansville 12	1	39N08	79w05	5:16:20
Lake 23	1	37N56	81w54	5:27:36
Lake Floyd 17	1	39N17	80w31	5:22:04
Lake Ridge 17	1	39N17	80w15	5:21:00
Lake Ron 54	1	39N16	81w40	5:26:40
Lake Washington 40	1	38N26	82w01	5:28:04
Lamberton 43	1	39N16	81w03	5:24:12
Lanark 41	18	37N50	81w09	5:24:36
Landes 12	1	39N19	78w52	5:15:28
Landisburg 10	1	37N56	80w54	5:23:36
Lando Mines 30	1	37N42	82w11	5:28:44
Landville 23	1	37N43	81w52	5:27:28
Laneville 47	1	38N58	79w25	5:17:40
Lanham 40	1	38N28	81w49	5:27:16
Lansing 10	18	38N04	81w04	5:24:16
Lantz 1	1	38N56	80w06	5:20:24
Largent 33	11	39N37	78w17	5:13:08
Larkmead 54	14	39N17	81w32	5:26:08
Lashmeet 28	1	37N25	81w12	5:24:48
Lauckport 54	14	39N17	81w32	5:26:08
Laura Lee Mine 17	1	39N23	80w21	5:21:24
Laurel Branch 32	1	37N34	80w16	5:21:04
Laurel Court 4	1	38N40	80w43	5:22:52
Laurel Dale 29	2	39N22	79w02	5:16:08
Laurel Hill 22	1	38N08	82w12	5:28:48
Laurel Iron Works 31	28	39N39	79w58	5:19:52
Laurel Point 31	28	39N39	79w58	5:19:52
Lavalette 50	14	38N20	82w27	5:29:48
Lawn 13	1	37N52	80w51	5:23:24
Lawrenceville 15	9	40N37	80w34	5:22:16
Lawton 10	1	37N52	80w59	5:23:56
Layland 10	1	37N54	80w58	5:23:52
Layopolis 11	1	38N55	80w45	5:23:00
Layville 3	1	38N08	81w54	5:27:36
Leachtown 54	1	39N04	81w24	5:25:36
Lead Mine 47	1	39N10	79w42	5:18:48
Leadsville 42	35	38N57	79w51	5:19:24
Leander 10	1	38N10	81w02	5:24:08
Leatherwood 30	1	37N40	81w51	5:27:24
Lee 10	1	37N54	81w10	5:24:40
Lee Creek 54	1	39N12	81w42	5:26:48
Leet 22	1	38N04	82w05	5:28:20
Leetown 19	2	39N23	77w53	5:11:32
Leevale 41	18	37N59	81w32	5:26:08
Leewood 20	1	38N04	81w27	5:25:48
Left Hand 44	1	38N37	81w15	5:25:00
Lego 41	1	37N38	81w14	5:24:56
Lehew 14	1	39N12	78w26	5:13:44
Leivasy 34	1	38N09	80w41	5:22:44
Lenore 30	1	37N48	82w17	5:29:08
Lenox 39	12	39N30	79w39	5:18:36
Leon 27	1	38N45	81w58	5:27:52
Leonard 13	1	38N00	80w22	5:21:28
Leopold 9	1	39N08	80w45	5:23:00
Lerona 28	1	37N30	80w59	5:23:56
Le Roy 18	1	38N54	81w33	5:26:12
Lesage 6	1	38N31	82w18	5:29:12
Leslie 13	1	38N03	80w43	5:22:52
Lester 41	1	37N44	81w18	5:25:12
Letart 27	1	38N54	81w56	5:27:44
Letherbark 7	1	38N47	81w08	5:24:32
Letter Gap 11	1	38N53	80w55	5:23:40
Levels 14	1	39N29	78w33	5:14:12
Lewis 27	1	38N51	82w05	5:28:20
Lewisburg 13	14	37N48	80w27	5:21:48
Lex 24	1	37N21	81w48	5:27:12
Liberty 17	24	39N16	80w19	5:21:16
Liberty 40	1	38N36	81w44	5:26:56
Lick Creek 45	1	37N32	80w58	5:23:52
Lick Fork 10	18	38N03	81w06	5:24:24
Licking 47	1	39N13	79w44	5:18:56
Lico 20	22	38N20	81w38	5:26:32
Lightburn 21	1	39N07	80w25	5:21:40
Lila 24	1	37N20	81w26	5:25:44
Lillydale 32	1	37N33	80w41	5:22:44
Lilly Grove 28	1	37N22	81w04	5:24:16
Lilly Park 13	1	37N58	80w46	5:23:04
Lima 48	2	39N26	80w45	5:23:00
Limestone 26	21	39N51	80w36	5:22:24
Limestone 29	6	39N26	78w59	5:15:56
Limestone Hill 53	1	39N04	81w24	5:25:36
Linden 44	1	38N43	81w13	5:24:52
Lindside 32	1	37N27	80w40	5:22:40
Lindytown 3	1	37N55	81w37	5:26:28
Link 48	2	39N34	80w44	5:22:56
Linn 11	1	39N01	80w43	5:22:52
Linwood 38	1	38N25	80w08	5:20:32
Little 48	2	39N31	81w04	5:24:16
Little Birch 4	1	38N35	80w43	5:22:52
Little Falls 31	17	39N33	80w00	5:20:00
Little Georgetown 2	2	39N33	78w00	5:12:00
Little Italy 8	1	38N32	81w02	5:24:08
Little Italy 42	1	38N49	79w33	5:18:12
Little Laurel Creek 34	14	38N14	80w32	5:22:08
Little Levels 38	1	38N08	80w14	5:20:56
Littlesburg 28	20	37N16	81w14	5:24:56
Littleton 52	2	39N42	80w32	5:22:08
Lively 10	1	37N57	81w10	5:24:40
Liverpool 18	1	38N54	81w32	5:26:08
Livingston 20	1	38N10	81w24	5:25:36
Lizemores 8	1	38N20	81w11	5:24:44
Lloydsville 4	1	38N46	80w44	5:22:56
Lobata 30	1	37N39	82w11	5:28:44
Lobelia 38	1	38N08	80w13	5:20:52
Lochgelly 10	18	38N01	81w09	5:24:36
Lockbridge 45	1	37N50	80w51	5:23:24
Lockhart 18	1	38N54	81w40	5:26:40
Lockney 11	1	38N51	80w58	5:23:52
Lockwood 34	1	38N16	81w03	5:24:12
Lodgeville 17	1	39N17	80w15	5:21:00
Logan 23	1	37N51	81w59	5:27:56
Logansport 25	17	39N32	80w20	5:21:20
Lomax 24	1	37N19	81w42	5:26:48
London 20	1	38N12	81w22	5:25:28
Lonetree 48	2	39N30	80w54	5:23:36
Longacre 10	14	38N10	81w18	5:25:12
Long Branch 10	1	37N55	81w16	5:25:04
Longdale 27	1	38N54	81w56	5:27:44
Longpole 24	1	37N28	81w49	5:27:16
Long Run 9	1	39N17	80w34	5:22:16
Longview 1	1	39N05	80w08	5:20:32
Lookout 10	1	38N04	80w59	5:23:56
Loom 14	1	39N18	78w38	5:14:32
Looneyville 44	1	38N41	81w18	5:25:12
Loop 18	1	38N41	81w40	5:26:40
Lorado 23	1	37N48	81w43	5:26:52
Lorentz 49	1	39N01	80w18	5:21:12
Lorton Lick 28	20	37N16	81w14	5:24:56
Lory 3	18	38N05	81w50	5:27:20
Lost City 16	1	38N56	78w50	5:15:20
Lost Creek 17	1	39N10	80w21	5:21:24
Lost River 16	1	38N55	78w51	5:15:24
Loudendale 20	22	38N20	81w38	5:26:32
Loudenville 26	21	39N50	80w34	5:22:16
Loudon 20	22	38N18	81w40	5:26:40
Louise 5	33	40N17	80w37	5:22:28
Loveridge 13	1	38N00	80w22	5:21:28
Lovern 28	1	37N22	81w05	5:24:20
Lowdell 54	1	39N04	81w33	5:26:12
Lowell 45	1	37N41	80w44	5:22:56
Lower Belle 20	14	38N15	81w33	5:26:12
Lower Falls 20	18	38N23	81w49	5:27:16
Low Gap 3	18	38N04	81w49	5:27:16
Lowney 30	1	37N56	82w16	5:29:04
Lowsville 31	17	39N34	80w04	5:20:16
Lubeck 54	1	39N14	81w38	5:26:32
Lucas 10	1	38N08	81w05	5:24:20
Lucerne 11	1	39N03	80w50	5:23:20
Lucretia 46	14	39N20	80w01	5:20:04
Lumberport 17	1	39N23	80w21	5:21:24
Lundale 23	1	37N48	81w45	5:27:00
Lyburn 23	1	37N48	81w56	5:27:44
Lynn 30	1	37N37	82w10	5:28:40
Lynn Camp 26	4	39N50	80w39	5:22:36
Lynwinn 41	1	37N41	81w15	5:25:00
Lyon 39	12	39N25	79w51	5:19:24
Lyonsville 34	1	38N17	80w51	5:23:24
Maben 55	1	37N38	81w23	5:25:32
Mabie 42	1	38N53	79w59	5:19:56
Mabscott 41	18	37N46	81w12	5:24:48
MacArthur 41	18	37N45	81w13	5:24:52
MacCorkle 22	1	38N15	81w53	5:27:32
MacDale 31	17	39N43	80w13	5:20:52
MacDonald 10	1	37N54	81w10	5:24:40
MacDunn 10	14	38N05	81w19	5:25:16
Mace 38	1	38N30	80w03	5:20:12
MacFarlan 43	1	39N05	81w12	5:24:48
Macksville 36	1	38N50	79w23	5:17:32
Macomber 39	12	39N21	79w41	5:18:44
Madam Creek 45	14	37N40	80w53	5:23:32
Madeline 41	1	37N36	81w19	5:25:16
Madison 3	18	38N04	81w49	5:27:16
Madison Run 39	12	39N19	79w33	5:18:12
Magnolia 33	19	39N34	78w26	5:13:44
Magnolia 49	1	38N53	80w18	5:21:12
Mahan 10	1	38N02	81w21	5:25:24
Maher 30	1	37N41	82w16	5:29:04
Mahone 43	1	39N06	81w05	5:24:20
Maidsville 31	28	39N41	79w59	5:19:56
Majorsville 26	4	40N01	80w32	5:22:08
Malcom Spring Heights 6	1	38N26	82w08	5:28:32
Malden 20	14	38N18	81w33	5:26:12
Mallory 23	1	37N44	81w51	5:27:24
Mammoth 20	1	38N16	81w22	5:25:28
Man 23	1	37N45	81w53	5:27:32
Mandeville 45	1	37N28	80w50	5:23:20
M And K Junction 39	12	39N21	79w41	5:18:44
Manheim 39	12	39N22	79w41	5:18:44
Manila 3	1	37N58	82w01	5:28:04
Manleys Church 25	17	39N28	80w10	5:20:40
Mannings 19	3	39N19	77w44	5:10:56
Mannington 25	26	39N32	80w21	5:21:24
Manown 39	12	39N28	79w41	5:18:44
Mansfield 1	1	39N09	80w03	5:20:12
Manus 23	1	37N51	82w03	5:28:12
Maple Acres 28	20	37N16	81w14	5:24:56
Maple Fork 41	1	37N54	81w10	5:24:40
Maple Lake 17	1	39N17	80w15	5:21:00
Maple Meadow 41	1	37N44	81w18	5:25:12
Maple Point 25	17	39N30	80w10	5:20:40
Maple View 28	20	37N16	81w14	5:24:56
Maplewood 10	1	37N56	80w56	5:23:44
Marcus 51	1	38N25	80w33	5:22:12
Marfrance 13	1	38N04	80w41	5:22:44
Margaret 17	1	39N24	80w29	5:21:56
Marie 45	1	37N29	80w47	5:23:08
Marie Heights 54	14	39N17	81w32	5:26:08
Marine 24	1	37N29	81w39	5:26:36
Market 9	1	39N14	80w41	5:22:44
Markwood 29	2	39N20	78w55	5:15:40
Marlaing Addition 20	18	38N23	81w49	5:27:16
Marland Heights 5	32	40N24	80w35	5:22:20
Marlinton 38	1	38N13	80w06	5:20:24
Marlowe 2	2	39N34	77w54	5:11:36
Marmet 20	14	38N15	81w34	5:26:16
Marquess 39	19	39N24	79w45	5:19:00

Marrtown 54 14 39N17 81w32 5:26:08
Marshall 18 1 38N54 81w32 5:26:08
Marshall Terrace 5
33 40N17 80w37 5:22:28
Marshall University 6
5 38N25 82w25 5:29:40
Marsh Fork 41 1 37N52 81w28 5:25:52
Marshville 17 1 39N17 80w31 5:22:04
Martha 6 1 38N25 82w17 5:29:08
Martinsburg 2 27 39N27 77w58 5:11:52
Marvel 10 1 38N08 81w06 5:24:24
Mason 27 1 39N01 82w02 5:28:08
Masontown 39 12 39N33 79w48 5:19:12
Masonville 12 1 38N57 79w06 5:16:24
Masseyville 41 1 37N51 81w27 5:25:48
Matewan 30 1 37N37 82w10 5:28:40
Matheny 54 1 39N16 81w40 5:26:40
Mathias 16 1 38N53 78w52 5:15:28
Matoaka 28 1 37N25 81w15 5:25:00
Maud 52 12 39N39 80w51 5:23:24
Mavis 4 1 38N38 80w52 5:23:28
Maxine 3 1 38N07 81w37 5:26:28
Maxwell Acres 26 21 39N51 80w36 5:22:24
Maxwelton 13 1 37N52 80w25 5:21:40
Maybeury 1 37N22 81w22 5:25:28
Maynor 41 18 37N47 81w11 5:24:44
Maysel 8 1 38N29 81w07 5:24:28
Maysville 12 1 39N07 79w10 5:16:40
McAlpin 41 1 37N42 81w15 5:25:00
McCauley 16 1 39N02 78w45 5:15:00
McClellan 25 17 39N23 80w38 5:22:32
McCloud 30 1 37N52 82w10 5:28:40
McComas 6 1 38N20 82w15 5:29:00
McComas 28 1 37N23 81w17 5:25:08
McConnell 23 1 37N50 81w58 5:27:52
McCreery 41 1 37N52 81w06 5:24:24
McElroy 48 2 39N26 80w45 5:23:00
McGee 46 14 39N20 80w01 5:20:04
McGraws 55 1 37N40 81w28 5:25:52
McGuire Park 21 1 39N03 80w28 5:21:52
McIntire 17 14 39N20 80w20 5:21:20
McKeefrey 26 21 39N51 80w36 5:22:24
McKim 37 1 39N22 81w08 5:24:32
McKinleyville 5 33 40N17 80w37 5:22:28
McMechen 26 15 39N59 80w44 5:22:56
McRoss 13 1 37N58 80w46 5:23:04
McWhorter 17 1 39N08 80w23 5:21:32
Mead 41 1 37N37 81w16 5:25:04
Meadland 46 1 39N17 80w15 5:21:00
Meador 30 1 37N37 82w04 5:28:16
Meadow Bluff 13 1 37N59 80w42 5:22:48
Meadow Bridge 10 1 37N52 80w51 5:23:24
Meadowbrook 17 1 39N21 80w19 5:21:16
Meadowbrook 20 22 38N21 81w37 5:26:28
Meadowbrook 27 1 38N52 82w08 5:28:32
Meadow Creek 45 1 37N49 80w55 5:23:40
Meadowdale 25 17 39N28 80w10 5:20:40
Meadowville 1 1 39N01 79w56 5:19:44
Meadville 48 2 39N28 81w06 5:24:24
Mechanicsburg 14 1 39N21 78w45 5:15:00
Mechanicstown 19 23 39N17 77w52 5:11:28
Medina 18 1 38N57 81w46 5:27:04
Medley 12 1 39N11 79w04 5:16:16
Meighen 26 4 39N50 80w39 5:22:36
Melissa 6 1 38N25 82w17 5:29:08
Mellin 43 1 39N13 81w03 5:24:12
Melrose 28 1 37N25 81w01 5:24:04
Melrose 54 1 39N16 81w40 5:26:40
Melville 23 1 37N51 81w58 5:27:52
Meredith Springs 25
17 39N28 80w10 5:20:40
Meriden 1 1 39N09 80w03 5:20:12
Merrimac 30 1 37N41 82w16 5:29:04
Metalton 41 1 37N47 81w16 5:25:04
Metz 25 17 39N35 80w22 5:21:28
Miami 20 1 38N10 81w27 5:25:48
Micco 23 1 37N48 81w59 5:27:56
Middlebourne 48 2 39N30 80w54 5:23:36
Middle Fork 42 1 38N43 80w08 5:20:32
Middle Grave Creek 26
21 39N51 80w36 5:22:24
Middle Run 4 1 38N38 80w52 5:23:28
Middletown 34 14 38N14 80w32 5:22:08
Middleway 19 2 39N20 77w56 5:11:44
Midkiff 22 1 38N10 82w11 5:28:44
Midland 42 35 38N56 79w51 5:19:24
Midway 1 1 39N01 79w56 5:19:44
Midway 28 20 37N16 81w14 5:24:56
Midway 40 1 38N32 81w54 5:27:36
Midway 41 1 37N43 81w15 5:25:00
Mifflin 23 1 37N57 81w49 5:27:16
Milam 16 1 38N49 79w06 5:16:24
Milam 55 1 37N40 81w28 5:25:52
Mile Branch 24 1 37N25 81w47 5:27:08
Millard 44 1 38N48 81w21 5:25:24
Millbrook 14 1 39N18 78w26 5:13:44
Mill Creek 42 1 38N44 79w58 5:19:52
Mill Creek Road 13
1 37N59 80w43 5:22:52
Millersville 25 17 39N28 80w10 5:20:40
Millertown 46 14 39N20 80w01 5:20:04
Mill Point 38 1 38N09 80w11 5:20:44
Mill Run 36 1 38N48 79w16 5:17:04
Mill Run 47 1 39N05 79w38 5:18:32
Millstone 7 1 38N48 81w06 5:24:24
Millstone 30 1 37N42 82w11 5:28:44
Milltown 3 1 38N01 81w38 5:26:32
Millville 19 2 39N17 77w47 5:11:08
Millwood 18 1 38N53 81w51 5:27:24
Milo 7 1 38N43 81w13 5:24:52
Milroy 12 1 38N58 79w10 5:16:40
Milton 6 1 38N26 82w08 5:28:32
Minden 10 1 37N59 81w07 5:24:28
Mineral City 23 1 37N44 81w49 5:27:16
Mineralwells 54 1 39N11 81w32 5:26:08

Minerva 22 1 38N13 82w12 5:28:48
Mingo 42 1 38N31 80w04 5:20:16
Mink Shoals 20 22 38N22 81w38 5:26:32
Minnehaha Springs 38
1 38N10 79w59 5:19:56
Minnie 52 12 39N39 80w51 5:23:24
Minnora 7 1 38N43 81w06 5:24:24
Miracle Run 31 17 39N36 80w15 5:21:00
Missouri Branch 50
1 38N01 82w26 5:29:44
Mitchell 36 1 38N39 79w20 5:17:20
Mitchell Branch 30
1 37N39 82w08 5:28:32
Mitchell Heights 23
1 37N54 81w59 5:27:56
Moatstown 36 1 38N31 79w22 5:17:28
Moatsville 1 1 39N13 79w56 5:19:44
Mobley 52 2 39N30 80w34 5:22:16
Mohegan 24 1 37N27 81w36 5:26:24
Molers 19 30 39N26 77w48 5:11:12
Monarch 20 1 38N13 81w26 5:25:44
Monaville 23 1 37N49 82w00 5:28:00
Monclo 23 1 37N55 81w50 5:27:20
Monitor 32 1 37N38 80w31 5:22:04
Monkeytown 36 1 38N45 79w26 5:17:44
Monongah 25 17 39N28 80w13 5:20:52
Montana Mines 25 17 39N32 80w07 5:20:28
Montcalm 28 1 37N21 81w15 5:25:00
Montcoal 41 18 37N55 81w32 5:26:08
Monterville 42 1 38N34 80w06 5:20:24
Montgomery 10 17 38N11 81w19 5:25:16
Montgomery Heights 10
1 38N11 81w21 5:25:24
Montpelier 17 24 39N16 80w19 5:21:16
Montrose 42 1 39N04 79w49 5:19:16
Moore 47 1 39N04 79w49 5:19:16
Moorefield 16 1 39N04 78w58 5:15:52
Mooresville 31 17 39N41 80w07 5:20:28
Morgan 18 1 39N05 81w48 5:27:12
Morgan 31 28 39N37 79w55 5:19:40
Morgan Heights 31
28 39N39 79w58 5:19:52
Morgansville 9 1 39N18 80w47 5:23:08
Morgantown 31 28 39N38 79w57 5:19:48
Morning Star 44 1 38N48 81w21 5:25:24
Morrall Mine 1 1 39N09 80w03 5:20:12
Morris 34 1 38N30 80w46 5:23:04
Morristown 53 1 39N04 81w24 5:25:36
Morrisvale 3 1 38N08 81w54 5:27:36
Mossy 10 1 37N57 81w10 5:24:40
Mound 20 14 38N23 81w45 5:27:00
Moundsville 26 4 39N55 80w44 5:22:56
Mountain 43 1 39N21 80w55 5:23:40
Mountain Cove 10 1 38N08 81w03 5:24:12
Mountaindale 39 12 39N40 79w38 5:18:32
Mountain Mission 19
3 39N19 77w44 5:10:56
Mountain View 39 19 39N24 79w45 5:19:00
Mount Alto 18 1 38N52 81w53 5:27:32
Mount Carbon 10 14 38N08 81w18 5:25:12
Mount Clare 17 14 39N13 80w21 5:21:24
Mount De Chantel 35
34 40N04 80w42 5:22:48
Mount Echo 35 6 40N05 80w34 5:22:16
Mount Gay 23 1 37N51 82w00 5:28:00
Mount Harmony 25 17 39N28 80w10 5:20:40
Mount Home 8 1 38N32 81w02 5:24:08
Mount Hope 10 18 37N54 81w10 5:24:40
Mount Hope 44 1 38N38 81w24 5:25:36
Mount Hope 54 1 39N02 81w24 5:25:36
Mount Liberty 1 1 39N09 80w03 5:20:12
Mount Lookout 34 1 38N10 80w55 5:23:40
Mount Nebo 34 1 38N12 80w51 5:23:24
Mount Olive 27 1 38N38 82w10 5:28:40
Mount Olive 44 1 38N48 81w21 5:25:24
Mount Olivet 26 34 40N04 80w42 5:22:48
Mount Olivet 28 1 37N22 81w13 5:24:52
Mount Pleasant 19 2 39N15 77w58 5:11:52
Mount Storm 12 1 39N17 79w15 5:17:00
Mount Tabor 41 18 37N47 81w11 5:24:44
Mount Vernon 39 12 39N31 79w48 5:19:12
Mount Vernon 40 1 38N26 82w01 5:28:04
Mountview 45 1 37N39 81w06 5:24:24
Mount Welcome 44 1 38N38 81w24 5:25:36
Mount Zion 7 1 38N52 81w07 5:24:28
Mount Zion 47 1 39N10 79w42 5:18:48
Mouth of Seneca 36
1 38N50 79w23 5:17:32
Moyers 36 1 38N31 79w22 5:17:28
Mozart 35 34 40N04 80w42 5:22:48
Mozer 36 1 38N48 79w17 5:17:08
Mud 22 1 38N08 82w01 5:28:04
Muddlety 34 1 38N17 80w51 5:23:24
Mudfork 7 1 38N42 81w05 5:24:20
Mudfork 23 1 37N51 82w03 5:28:12
Mullens 55 1 37N35 81w23 5:25:32
Mullensville 55 1 37N35 81w32 5:26:08
Munday 53 1 39N00 81w12 5:24:48
Murphy 1 1 38N59 80w13 5:20:52
Murphy 43 1 39N05 81w06 5:24:24
Murphytown 54 1 39N14 81w27 5:25:48
Murraysville 18 1 39N05 81w48 5:27:12
Muses Bottom 18 1 39N05 81w48 5:27:12
Mustang Acres 54 14 39N17 81w32 5:26:08
Myerstown 19 23 39N17 77w52 5:11:28
Myra 22 1 38N13 82w07 5:28:28
Myrtle 3 1 38N09 81w40 5:26:40
Myrtle 30 1 37N46 82w12 5:28:48
Nabob 20 1 38N01 81w25 5:25:40
Nallen 10 1 38N07 80w53 5:23:32
Nancys Run 44 1 38N48 81w21 5:25:24
Naoma 41 1 37N52 81w29 5:25:56
Napier 4 1 38N47 80w35 5:22:20
Narrows Run 51 1 38N38 80w28 5:21:52
National 31 28 39N39 79w58 5:19:52

Naugatuck 30 1 37N47 82w21 5:29:24
Naval Ordnance Plant 20
14 38N21 81w42 5:26:48
Neal 50 14 38N24 82w35 5:30:20
Neals Run 14 1 39N22 78w31 5:14:04
Nebo 8 1 38N38 81w02 5:24:08
Nebo 49 1 38N59 80w13 5:20:52
Needmore 16 1 39N02 78w45 5:15:00
Neibert 23 1 37N48 81w56 5:27:44
Nelco 30 1 37N41 82w16 5:29:04
Nellis 3 1 38N09 81w44 5:26:56
Nelson 3 1 38N01 81w38 5:26:32
Nemours 28 1 37N18 81w18 5:25:12
Neola 13 1 37N58 80w08 5:20:32
Neptune 18 1 39N05 81w48 5:27:12
Nestlow 50 1 38N10 82w23 5:29:32
Nestorville 1 1 39N11 79w55 5:19:40
Nettie 34 1 38N13 80w41 5:22:44
Neville 41 18 37N47 81w11 5:24:44
New 41 1 37N47 80w57 5:23:48
Newark 53 1 39N07 81w24 5:25:36
Newberne 11 1 39N03 80w54 5:23:36
Newburg 39 12 39N23 79w51 5:19:24
New Creek 29 2 39N22 79w02 5:16:08
New Cumberland 15 9 40N30 80w37 5:22:28
Newdale 52 12 39N39 80w51 5:23:24
Newell 15 9 40N37 80w36 5:22:24
New England 54 1 39N12 81w42 5:26:48
New England Heights 54
1 39N16 81w40 5:26:40
New Era 18 1 38N54 81w40 5:26:40
New Hamlin 22 1 38N17 82w06 5:28:24
New Haven 27 1 38N59 81w58 5:27:52
New Hill 31 17 39N40 80w04 5:20:16
New Hope 28 1 37N22 81w05 5:24:20
New Interest 42 1 39N03 79w49 5:19:16
Newlon 49 1 38N45 80w14 5:20:56
New Manchester 15 9 40N32 80w34 5:22:16
New Martinsville 52
29 39N39 80w52 5:23:28
New Milton 9 1 39N14 80w41 5:22:44
New Thacker 30 1 37N36 82w08 5:28:32
Newton 44 1 38N36 81w11 5:24:44
Newtown 30 1 37N38 82w05 5:28:20
Newtown Mall 35 34 40N04 80w42 5:22:48
Newville 4 1 38N41 80w35 5:22:20
Next 48 31 39N34 81w00 5:24:00
Nicolette 54 14 39N17 81w32 5:26:08
Nicut 7 1 38N42 81w02 5:24:08
Nile 34 1 38N17 80w51 5:23:24
Nimitz 45 1 37N39 80w58 5:23:52
Nitro 20 18 38N25 81w51 5:27:24
Nitro Park Addition 20
18 38N25 81w50 5:27:20
Nobe 7 1 38N59 81w02 5:24:08
Nolan 30 1 37N45 82w19 5:29:16
Nollville 2 27 39N28 77w58 5:11:52
Normantown 11 1 38N51 80w56 5:23:44
North Berkeley 33
11 39N38 78w14 5:12:56
North Fairmont 25
17 39N28 80w10 5:20:40
Northfork 24 1 37N25 81w26 5:25:44
North Hill 18 1 38N49 81w42 5:26:48
North Matewan 30 1 37N38 82w09 5:28:36
North Mitchell Heights 23
1 37N52 81w59 5:27:56
North Mountain 2 2 39N33 78w00 5:12:00
North Parkersburg 54
14 39N17 81w32 5:26:08
North Ravenswood 18
1 38N57 81w46 5:27:04
North River Mills 14
1 39N18 78w26 5:13:44
North View 17 24 39N16 80w19 5:21:16
Norton 42 1 38N56 79w57 5:19:48
Norway 25 17 39N28 80w10 5:20:40
Numan 9 1 39N17 80w34 5:22:16
Nuriva 55 1 37N35 81w23 5:25:32
Nuttall 10 1 38N05 80w59 5:23:56
Nutter Farm 43 1 39N11 81w16 5:25:04
Nutter Fort 17 24 39N16 80w19 5:21:16
Nutterville 13 1 38N03 80w42 5:22:48
Oak Acres 54 1 39N16 81w40 5:26:40
Oakdale 17 1 39N32 80w20 5:21:20
Oak Flat 36 1 38N37 79w15 5:17:00
Oak Hill 10 17 37N59 81w09 5:24:36
Oak Hill 18 1 38N49 81w42 5:26:48
Oakmont 29 2 39N23 79w09 5:16:36
Oakmont 35 34 40N04 80w42 5:22:48
Oakvale 28 1 37N20 80w58 5:23:52
Oakview Heights 50
14 38N24 82w35 5:30:20
Oakwood Estates 54
14 39N17 81w32 5:26:08
O'Brion 8 1 38N35 80w56 5:23:44
Oceana 55 1 37N42 81w38 5:26:32
Odaville 18 1 38N54 81w40 5:26:40
Odd 41 1 37N36 81w12 5:24:48
Ohley 20 1 38N06 81w27 5:25:48
Olcott 20 22 38N20 81w38 5:26:32
Old Arthur 12 1 39N04 79w07 5:16:28
Old Fields 16 1 39N08 78w57 5:15:48
Omar 23 1 37N45 82w00 5:28:00
Omps 33 11 39N38 78w14 5:12:56
Ona 6 1 38N26 82w13 5:28:52
Onego 36 1 38N51 79w26 5:17:44
O'Neil 17 14 39N18 80w24 5:21:36
Oney Gap 28 1 37N22 81w05 5:24:20
Onoto 38 1 38N13 80w05 5:20:20
Opekiska 31 17 39N28 80w10 5:20:40
Opequon 2 27 39N29 77w55 5:11:40
Oral Lake 17 1 39N17 80w15 5:21:00
Orchard 32 1 37N29 80w47 5:23:08
Organ Cave 13 14 37N45 80w28 5:21:52

WEST VIRGINIA

Orgas 3	1	38N04	81w34	5:26:16
Orient Hill 13	1	38N00	80w44	5:22:56
Orlando 21	14	38N52	80w36	5:22:24
Orleans Road 33	11	39N37	78w17	5:13:08
Orma 7	1	38N45	81w06	5:24:24
Orr 39	12	39N27	79w33	5:18:12
Ortin Heights 40	18	38N25	81w50	5:27:20
Orville 23	1	37N50	81w52	5:27:28
Osage 31	17	39N39	80w01	5:20:04
Osborne 20	1	38N29	81w21	5:25:24
Osbornes Mills 44	1	38N29	81w21	5:25:24
Oscar 13	1	38N00	80w22	5:21:28
O'Toole 24	1	37N20	81w26	5:25:44
Otsego 55	1	37N35	81w23	5:25:32
Ottawa 3	1	37N58	81w49	5:27:16
Otto 44	1	38N48	81w21	5:25:24
Ovapa 8	1	38N32	81w11	5:24:44
Overfield 1	1	39N09	80w03	5:20:12
Owings 17	1	39N23	80w16	5:21:04
Oxford 9	1	39N12	80w52	5:23:28
Packs Branch 10	1	37N54	81w10	5:24:40
Packsville 41	18	37N57	81w31	5:26:04
Pad 44	1	38N38	81w24	5:25:36
Paden City 52	31	39N36	80w57	5:23:48
Page 10	14	38N03	81w16	5:25:04
Paint Creek Junction 20	1	38N13	81w25	5:25:40
Palace Valley 49	1	38N42	80w12	5:20:48
Palestine 13	1	37N44	80w39	5:22:36
Palestine 53	1	39N02	81w24	5:25:36
Pansy 12	1	39N00	79w07	5:16:28
Paradise 40	1	38N36	81w44	5:26:56
Parchment Valley 18	1	38N49	81w42	5:26:48
Parcoal 51	1	38N27	80w23	5:21:32
Pardee 23	1	37N48	81w43	5:26:52
Park Addition 5	33	40N17	80w37	5:22:28
Parkersburg 54	14	39N16	81w34	5:26:16
Parkview 35	34	40N04	80w42	5:22:48
Parkview 46	14	39N20	80w01	5:20:04
Par Metta Crest 54	1	39N20	81w22	5:25:28
Parsley Bottom 30	1	37N48	82w17	5:29:08
Parsons 47	1	39N06	79w41	5:18:44
Patterson Creek 29	2	39N34	78w44	5:14:56
Paw Paw 33	19	39N32	78w28	5:13:52
Pax 10	1	37N55	81w16	5:25:04
Peach Creek 23	1	37N53	81w59	5:27:56
Peanut 25	17	39N32	80w20	5:21:20
Pear 41	1	37N47	80w57	5:23:48
Pecks Mill 23	1	37N56	81w59	5:27:56
Pecks Run 49	1	38N59	80w13	5:20:52
Peeltree 1	1	39N05	80w08	5:20:32
Peewee 53	1	38N54	81w33	5:26:12
Pemberton 41	1	37N43	81w13	5:24:52
Pence Springs 45	1	37N41	80w44	5:22:56
Peniel 44	1	38N54	81w25	5:25:40
Pennsboro 43	1	39N17	80w58	5:23:52
Pentress 31	17	39N42	80w10	5:20:40
Peora 17	1	39N24	80w18	5:21:12
Pepper 1	1	39N17	80w15	5:21:00
Perkins 11	1	38N47	80w56	5:23:44
Perry 16	1	39N05	78w36	5:14:24
Persinger 34	1	38N17	80w51	5:23:24
Petersburg 12	1	39N00	79w07	5:16:28
Peterson 21	1	38N56	80w30	5:22:00
Peterstown 32	1	37N24	80w48	5:23:12
Petroleum 43	1	39N11	81w16	5:25:04
Pettit Heights 5	33	40N14	80w39	5:22:36
Pettry 28	1	37N25	81w01	5:24:04
Pettry Bottom 41	1	37N53	81w31	5:26:04
Pettus 41	18	37N58	81w32	5:26:08
Peytona 3	1	38N09	81w43	5:26:52
Pharoah 50	1	38N15	82w36	5:30:24
Phico 23	1	37N58	82w01	5:28:04
Philippi 1	1	39N09	80w03	5:20:12
Philoah 40	1	38N36	81w44	5:26:56
Piatt 20	14	38N15	81w33	5:26:12
Pickaway 32	1	37N38	80w31	5:22:04
Pickens 42	1	38N39	80w13	5:20:52
Pickle Street 21	1	39N02	80w40	5:22:40
Pickshin 41	1	37N38	81w14	5:24:56
Pie 30	1	37N39	82w00	5:28:00
Piedmont 29	11	39N27	79w03	5:16:12
Pierce 47	1	39N09	79w30	5:18:00
Pierpont 31	28	39N39	79w58	5:19:52
Pierpont 55	1	37N38	81w23	5:25:32
Pigeon 44	1	38N32	81w12	5:24:48
Pike 43	1	39N17	81w05	5:24:20
Pikeside 2	27	39N28	77w58	5:11:52
Pinch 20	1	38N25	81w29	5:25:56
Pine Bluff 17	1	39N24	80w18	5:21:12
Pine Creek 23	1	37N50	82w04	5:28:16
Pine Grove 20	18	38N25	81w50	5:27:20
Pine Grove 25	17	39N28	80w10	5:20:40
Pine Grove 52	2	39N34	80w41	5:22:44
Pineknob 41	1	37N52	81w29	5:25:56
Pineville 55	1	37N35	81w32	5:26:08
Piney 52	2	39N34	80w44	5:22:56
Piney View 41	1	37N50	81w08	5:24:32
Pinoak 28	1	37N25	81w12	5:24:48
Pipestem 45	1	37N32	80w56	5:23:44
Pisgah 39	12	39N40	79w38	5:18:32
Pleasant Creek 1	1	39N09	80w03	5:20:12
Pleasant Dale 14	1	39N18	78w38	5:14:32
Pleasant Hill 7	1	38N55	81w06	5:24:24
Pleasant Home 54	1	39N08	81w44	5:26:56
Pleasant Run 47	1	39N01	79w49	5:19:16
Pleasant Valley 15	32	40N24	80w35	5:22:20
Pleasant Valley 25	17	39N28	80w10	5:20:40
Pleasant Valley 26	21	39N50	80w34	5:22:16
Pleasant Valley 35	34	40N04	80w42	5:22:48
Pleasant View 18	1	38N57	81w46	5:27:04
Pleasant View 22	1	38N13	82w12	5:28:48
Pleasant View 25	17	39N32	80w07	5:20:28
Pleasure Valley 1	1	39N04	79w49	5:19:16
Pliny 40	1	38N37	81w59	5:27:56
Plum Orchard 18	1	38N49	81w42	5:26:48
Pluto 41	14	37N40	80w53	5:23:32
Plymouth 40	1	38N31	81w51	5:27:24
Poca 40	1	38N28	81w49	5:27:16
Pocatalico 20	1	38N29	81w40	5:26:40
Poe 34	1	38N15	80w58	5:23:52
Point Lick Junction 20	22	38N21	81w38	5:26:32
Point Mills 35	6	40N06	80w36	5:22:24
Point Pleasant 27	1	38N51	82w08	5:28:32
Points 14	1	39N26	78w37	5:14:28
Polard 48	2	39N30	80w54	5:23:36
Polemic 4	1	38N40	80w43	5:22:52
Polk Gap 55	1	37N38	81w23	5:25:32
Pondco 3	1	37N55	81w40	5:26:40
Pond Creek 54	1	39N08	81w44	5:26:56
Pond Gap 20	1	38N17	81w17	5:25:08
Pond Junction 3	18	38N04	81w49	5:27:16
Pool 34	1	38N10	80w52	5:23:28
Port Amherst 20	22	38N21	81w38	5:26:32
Porters Falls 52	2	39N35	80w47	5:23:08
Porterwood 47	1	39N04	79w49	5:19:16
Portland 39	12	39N27	79w35	5:18:20
Porto Rico 9	1	39N14	80w41	5:22:44
Posey 41	1	37N48	81w25	5:25:40
Potomac 35	6	40N06	80w31	5:22:04
Potomac Manor 29	2	39N23	79w12	5:16:48
Potomac Park 2	2	39N34	77w54	5:11:36
Powell 25	17	39N28	80w10	5:20:40
Powell Creek 3	18	38N04	81w49	5:27:16
Powellton 10	14	38N05	81w19	5:25:16
Pratt 20	1	38N13	81w25	5:25:40
Prenter 3	1	38N01	81w38	5:26:32
Price 22	1	38N10	82w11	5:28:44
Price Hill 3	18	38N04	81w49	5:27:16
Price Hill 41	1	37N54	81w10	5:24:40
Price Hill Junction 10	1	37N54	81w10	5:24:40
Pricetown 21	1	39N03	80w28	5:21:52
Pricetown 52	2	39N30	80w34	5:22:16
Prichard 50	1	38N15	82w36	5:30:24
Priestly 22	1	38N17	81w48	5:27:12
Prince 10	1	37N52	81w04	5:24:16
Princeton 28	1	37N22	81w06	5:24:24
Princewick 41	1	37N40	81w14	5:24:56
Procious 8	1	38N29	81w12	5:24:48
Proctor 52	2	39N43	80w49	5:23:16
Propstburg 36	1	38N37	79w15	5:17:00
Prospect Valley 17	1	39N24	80w18	5:21:12
Prosperity 41	18	37N50	81w12	5:24:48
Prudence 10	1	37N56	81w08	5:24:32
Prunty 43	1	39N13	81w03	5:24:12
Pruntytown 46	14	39N20	80w05	5:20:20
Pullman 43	1	39N11	80w57	5:23:48
Pumpkintown 42	1	38N54	79w58	5:19:52
Purgitsville 14	1	39N14	78w56	5:15:44
Puritan 30	1	37N41	82w10	5:28:40
Pursglove 31	17	39N40	80w01	5:20:04
Pursley 48	31	39N34	81w00	5:24:00
Quaker 50	1	38N01	82w26	5:29:44
Quarrier 20	1	38N01	81w25	5:25:40
Queens 49	1	38N52	80w08	5:20:32
Queen Shoals 8	1	38N29	81w21	5:25:24
Quick 20	1	38N29	81w21	5:25:24
Quiet Dell 17	14	39N13	80w21	5:21:24
Quincy 20	14	38N15	81w33	5:26:12
Quinland 3	18	38N02	81w47	5:27:08
Quinnimont 10	1	37N51	81w03	5:24:12
Quinwood 13	1	38N04	80w42	5:22:48
Rachel 25	17	39N31	80w18	5:21:12
Racine 3	1	38N09	81w40	5:26:40
Racy 43	1	39N11	81w16	5:25:04
Rada 14	1	39N14	78w56	5:15:44
Radnor 50	1	38N05	82w27	5:29:48
Ragland 30	1	37N43	82w08	5:28:32
Rainelle 13	1	37N58	80w47	5:23:08
Raines Corner 32	1	37N27	80w40	5:22:40
Raintown 38	1	38N09	80w11	5:20:44
Raleigh 41	18	37N46	81w11	5:24:44
Ramage 3	1	37N59	81w49	5:27:16
Ramp 45	1	37N47	80w53	5:23:32
Ramsey 10	1	38N10	81w02	5:24:08
Rand 20	14	38N17	81w34	5:26:16
Randall 31	28	39N39	80w00	5:20:00
Ranger 22	1	38N07	82w11	5:28:44
Rangoon 1	1	39N04	80w06	5:20:24
Ranson 19	23	39N18	77w52	5:11:28
Raven 34	1	38N17	80w51	5:23:24
Ravencliff 55	1	37N42	81w29	5:25:56
Raven Rock 37	1	39N24	81w12	5:24:48
Raven Rocks 14	1	39N27	78w42	5:14:48
Ravenswood 18	1	38N57	81w46	5:27:04
Rawl 30	1	37N39	82w13	5:28:52
Rayburn 27	1	38N52	82w08	5:28:32
Raymond City 40	1	38N28	81w49	5:27:16
Reader 52	2	39N34	80w44	5:22:56
Reamer 20	1	38N29	81w21	5:25:24
Red Creek 47	1	39N00	79w30	5:18:00
Redhill 54	14	39N17	81w32	5:26:08
Red House 40	1	38N32	81w54	5:27:36
Red Jacket 30	1	37N39	82w08	5:28:32
Red Run 47	1	39N05	79w38	5:18:32
Red Spring 10	1	37N52	80w51	5:23:24
Redstar 10	1	37N56	81w09	5:24:36
Red Sulphur 32	1	37N27	80w45	5:23:00
Red Sulphur Springs 32	1	37N29	80w47	5:23:08
Red Warrior Junction 20	1	38N04	81w27	5:25:48
Reedson 19	2	39N22	77w51	5:11:24
Reedsville 39	12	39N31	79w48	5:19:12
Reedy 44	1	38N54	81w26	5:25:44
Reedyville 44	1	38N48	81w21	5:25:24
Reger 49	1	38N59	80w13	5:20:52
Renick 13	1	38N00	80w22	5:21:28
Renicks Valley 13	1	38N00	80w22	5:21:28
Reno 39	12	39N20	79w46	5:19:04
Rensford 20	22	38N21	81w38	5:26:32
Replete 51	1	38N42	80w28	5:21:52
Republic 20	1	38N02	81w25	5:25:40
Reston 3	18	38N04	81w49	5:27:16
Revere 11	1	38N59	81w02	5:24:08
Reynolds 20	22	38N20	81w38	5:26:32
Reynoldsville 17	1	39N17	80w26	5:21:44
Rhodell 41	1	37N36	81w18	5:25:12
Richard 31	28	39N39	79w58	5:19:52
Richardson 7	1	38N47	81w08	5:24:32
Richland 13	14	37N48	80w27	5:21:48
Richland 35	6	40N08	80w40	5:22:40
Richmond 41	1	37N45	80w59	5:23:56
Richwood 34	14	38N14	80w32	5:22:08
Rider 17	1	39N10	80w21	5:21:24
Ridersville 33	11	39N38	78w14	5:12:56
Ridgedale 31	28	39N39	79w58	5:19:52
Ridge Farms 25	17	39N32	80w07	5:20:28
Ridgeley 29	2	39N38	78w46	5:15:04
Ridgeview 3	1	38N08	81w46	5:27:04
Ridgeway 2	2	39N18	78w05	5:12:20
Riffle 4	1	38N45	80w44	5:22:56
Rift 24	1	37N18	81w41	5:26:44
Rig 16	1	39N02	79w04	5:16:16
Riley 41	18	37N49	81w10	5:24:40
Rinehart 17	1	39N24	80w29	5:21:56
Ringold 31	28	39N39	79w58	5:19:52
Rio 14	1	39N08	78w40	5:14:40
Ripley 18	1	38N49	81w43	5:26:52
Ripley Landing 18	1	38N53	81w51	5:27:24
Ripling Waters 18	1	38N35	81w36	5:26:24
Rippon 19	2	39N13	77w54	5:11:36
Rita 23	1	37N46	81w55	5:27:40
Ritchie 35	34	40N03	80w43	5:22:52
Riverbend 20	18	38N23	81w49	5:27:16
Riverlake Estates 20	18	38N23	81w49	5:27:16
Riverlawn 20	18	38N23	81w49	5:27:16
Riverside 20	1	38N13	81w25	5:25:40
Riverside 31	28	39N39	79w58	5:19:52
Riverside 54	14	39N17	81w32	5:26:08
Riverton 36	1	38N45	79w26	5:17:44
Rivesville 25	17	39N32	80w07	5:20:28
Rivesville Junction 25	17	39N32	80w07	5:20:28
Roach 6	1	38N25	82w17	5:29:08
Roanoke 21	1	38N56	80w30	5:22:00
Roaring Creek 42	1	38N54	79w59	5:19:56
Roberts 9	1	39N18	80w47	5:23:08
Robertsburg 40	1	38N39	81w57	5:27:48
Robey 17	1	39N23	80w21	5:21:24
Robinette 23	1	37N47	81w49	5:27:16
Robinson 27	1	38N54	82w04	5:28:16
Robson 10	14	38N06	81w15	5:25:00
Rock 28	1	37N24	81w13	5:24:52
Rock Camp 32	1	37N27	80w40	5:22:40
Rock Castle 18	1	38N43	81w47	5:27:08
Rock Cave 49	1	38N50	80w21	5:21:24
Rock Creek 3	18	38N05	81w50	5:27:20
Rock Creek 41	1	37N51	81w27	5:25:48
Rockford 17	1	39N10	80w21	5:21:24
Rock Forge 31	28	39N39	79w58	5:19:52
Rock Gap 33	2	39N32	78w15	5:13:00
Rock Lake 25	17	39N28	80w10	5:20:40
Rock Lake Village 20	14	38N21	81w44	5:26:56
Rock Lick 10	1	37N59	81w07	5:24:28
Rocklick 26	21	39N50	80w34	5:22:16
Rock Oak 16	1	39N02	78w45	5:15:00
Rockport 54	1	39N04	81w33	5:26:12
Rock Run 9	1	39N18	80w47	5:23:08
Rocksdale 7	1	38N47	81w08	5:24:32
Rockton 4	1	38N38	80w52	5:23:28
Rockville 22	1	38N10	82w11	5:28:44
Rocky Fork 20	22	38N22	81w40	5:26:40
Rodemer 39	12	39N27	79w33	5:18:12
Roderfield 24	1	37N27	81w42	5:26:48
Rohr 39	12	39N33	79w48	5:19:12
Rolfe 24	1	37N25	81w23	5:25:32
Rollins Branch 55	1	37N41	81w38	5:26:32
Romance 18	1	38N35	81w36	5:26:24
Romines Mills 17	1	39N10	80w21	5:21:24
Romney 14	1	39N21	78w45	5:15:00
Romont 10	1	38N08	81w06	5:24:24
Ronceverte 13	14	37N45	80w28	5:21:52
Ronda 20	1	38N10	81w27	5:25:48
Roneys Point 35	6	40N06	80w36	5:22:24
Roseby Rock 26	21	39N51	80w36	5:22:24
Rosedale 10	1	37N59	81w09	5:24:36
Rosedale 11	1	38N44	80w57	5:23:48
Rosedale 31	28	39N41	79w59	5:19:56
Rosemont 46	1	39N16	80w10	5:20:40
Roseville Addition 20	5	38N25	82w27	5:29:48
Rossmore 23	1	37N49	81w58	5:27:52
Rough Run 12	1	38N48	79w17	5:17:08
Round Bottom 52	2	39N41	80w27	5:21:48
Round Knob 40	1	38N37	81w59	5:27:56
Rowlesburg 39	12	39N21	79w40	5:18:40
Roxalana 20	14	38N23	81w45	5:27:00
Roxalana 44	1	38N41	81w18	5:25:12
Ruddle 36	1	38N39	79w20	5:17:20
Rumble 3	1	38N11	81w42	5:26:48
Runa 34	1	38N09	80w51	5:23:24
Rupert 13	1	37N58	80w41	5:22:44

WEST VIRGINIA

Place		Lat	Long	Time
Rush Creek 44	1	38N48	81w21	5:25:24
Rusk 43	1	39N11	81w16	5:25:04
Russelldale 29	2	39N20	78w55	5:15:40
Russellville 13	1	38N05	80w54	5:23:36
Russett 7	1	38N55	81w06	5:24:24
Ruth 20	22	38N20	81w38	5:26:32
Ruthbelle 39	12	39N30	79w39	5:18:36
Rutherford 43	1	39N13	81w03	5:24:12
Ryanville 17	1	39N17	80w15	5:21:00
Rymer 25	17	39N32	80w20	5:21:20
Sabine 55	1	37N41	81w30	5:26:00
Sabraton 31	28	39N39	79w58	5:19:52
Sago 49	1	38N59	80w13	5:20:52
Saint Albans 20	18	38N23	81w50	5:27:20
Saint Clara 9	1	39N04	80w42	5:22:48
Saint Cloud 31	17	39N41	80w27	5:21:48
Saint George 47	1	39N11	79w38	5:18:32
Saint Joe 39	12	39N30	79w39	5:18:36
Saint Joseph 26	4	39N43	80w49	5:23:16
Saint Marys 37	1	39N23	81w12	5:24:48
Salem 17	1	39N17	80w34	5:22:16
Salt Hill 18	1	38N49	81w42	5:26:48
Salt Lick 4	1	38N48	80w35	5:22:20
Saltlick Bridge 4	1	38N46	80w38	5:22:32
Saltpetre 50	1	38N05	82w34	5:30:16
Salt Rock 6	1	38N19	82w13	5:28:52
Salt Sulphur Springs 32	1	37N35	80w33	5:22:12
Saltwell 17	1	39N17	80w15	5:21:00
Sam Black Church 13	1	37N54	80w36	5:22:24
Sand Creek 22	1	38N07	82w11	5:28:44
Sanderson 20	1	38N29	81w21	5:25:24
Sand Fork 11	1	38N55	80w45	5:23:00
Sand Hill 26	4	40N00	80w35	5:22:20
Sandlick 28	20	37N16	81w14	5:24:56
Sand Lick Junction 46	1	39N16	80w05	5:20:20
Sand Ridge 7	1	38N48	81w04	5:24:16
Sand Run 49	1	38N59	80w13	5:20:52
Sandstone 45	1	37N47	80w53	5:23:32
Sandy Huff 24	1	37N28	81w49	5:27:16
Sandy River 24	1	37N26	81w50	5:27:20
Sandy Summit 44	1	38N54	81w32	5:26:08
Sandyville 18	1	38N54	81w40	5:26:40
Sanford 25	17	39N28	80w10	5:20:40
Sanger 10	1	37N59	81w09	5:24:36
Sanoma 53	1	39N02	81w24	5:25:36
Sarah Ann 23	1	37N43	81w59	5:27:56
Sardis 17	1	39N20	80w25	5:21:40
Sarton 32	1	37N35	80w38	5:22:32
Sassafras 27	1	38N59	82w04	5:28:16
Sattes 20	18	38N25	81w50	5:27:20
Saulsbury 54	1	39N11	81w32	5:26:08
Saulsville 55	1	37N40	81w28	5:25:52
Saunders 23	1	37N48	81w43	5:26:52
Saxman 34	14	38N14	80w35	5:22:20
Saxon 41	1	37N48	81w25	5:25:40
Scarbro 10	1	37N57	81w10	5:24:40
Scarlet 30	1	37N42	82w11	5:28:44
Scary 40	18	38N23	81w49	5:27:16
Scherr 12	1	39N12	79w10	5:16:40
Schrader 20	1	38N26	81w29	5:25:56
Schultz 37	1	39N19	81w15	5:25:00
Scott 4	1	38N38	80w52	5:23:28
Scott Depot 40	1	38N27	81w55	5:27:40
Scotts 42	1	38N58	79w30	5:18:00
Scrabble 2	30	39N26	77w48	5:11:12
Seaman 44	1	38N54	81w32	5:26:08
Secondcreek 32	1	37N39	80w29	5:21:56
Sedalia 9	1	39N17	80w34	5:22:16
Seebert 38	1	38N08	80w11	5:20:44
Selbyville 49	1	38N45	80w14	5:20:56
Selwyn 30	1	37N50	82w24	5:29:36
Seminole 17	1	39N22	80w19	5:21:16
Seng Creek 3	18	37N59	81w32	5:26:08
Servia 4	1	38N37	80w57	5:23:48
Seth 3	1	38N06	81w37	5:26:28
Seven Pines 25	17	39N32	80w20	5:21:20
Sewell Mountain 10	1	37N58	80w55	5:23:40
Shady Brook 21	1	39N03	80w28	5:21:52
Shady Spring 41	1	37N42	81w06	5:24:24
Shafer 47	1	39N10	79w42	5:18:48
Shamrock 23	1	37N50	82w02	5:28:08
Shanghai 2	2	39N27	78w08	5:12:32
Shanks 14	1	39N19	78w41	5:14:44
Shannondale 19	3	39N19	77w44	5:10:56
Sharon 20	1	38N10	81w27	5:25:48
Sharon Heights 30	1	37N37	81w52	5:27:28
Sharples 23	1	37N55	81w50	5:27:20
Shawvers Crossing 13	1	37N58	80w41	5:22:44
Shegon 23	1	37N51	82w03	5:28:12
Shenandoah Junction 19	2	39N22	77w51	5:11:24
Shepherdstown 19	30	39N25	77w49	5:11:16
Sheridan 22	1	38N13	82w12	5:28:48
Sherman 18	1	38N59	81w46	5:27:04
Sherrard 26	34	40N04	80w42	5:22:48
Sherwood 9	1	39N18	80w47	5:23:08
Shiloh 41	1	37N47	81w20	5:25:20
Shiloh 48	2	39N31	81w04	5:24:16
Shinnston 17	1	39N24	80w18	5:21:12
Shirley 48	2	39N24	80w46	5:23:04
Shively 23	1	37N55	82w05	5:28:20
Shoals 50	14	38N20	82w28	5:29:52
Shock 11	1	38N47	80w58	5:23:52
Short Creek 5	9	40N11	80w41	5:22:44
Short Creek Valley 5	34	40N04	80w42	5:22:48
Short Gap 29	6	39N26	78w59	5:15:56
Short Line Junction 17	24	39N16	80w19	5:21:16
Shrewsbury 20	1	38N12	81w28	5:25:52
Shriver 31	17	39N40	80w03	5:20:12
Sias 22	1	38N11	82w05	5:28:20
Sidneyville 18	1	38N49	81w42	5:26:48
Sigman 40	1	38N32	81w54	5:27:36
Silver Grove 19	3	39N19	77w44	5:10:56
Silver Hill 52	12	39N39	80w51	5:23:24
Silver Lake 39	12	39N17	79w31	5:18:04
Silverton 18	1	38N57	81w46	5:27:04
Simoda 36	1	38N45	79w26	5:17:44
Simpson 46	1	39N18	80w15	5:21:00
Sinclair 39	12	39N13	79w56	5:19:44
Sinks Grove 32	1	37N40	80w33	5:22:12
Sir Johns Run 33	11	39N38	78w14	5:12:56
Sissonville 20	1	38N32	81w38	5:26:32
Sistersville 48	31	39N34	81w00	5:24:00
Six 24	1	37N23	81w39	5:26:36
Six Mile 3	18	38N05	81w50	5:27:20
Skeetersville 19	2	39N22	77w51	5:11:24
Skelton 41	18	37N49	81w11	5:24:44
Skidmore 18	1	38N49	81w42	5:26:48
Skin Creek 21	1	38N58	80w23	5:21:32
Slab Fork 41	1	37N41	81w20	5:25:20
Slabtown 30	1	37N37	81w52	5:27:28
Slagle 23	1	37N50	81w52	5:27:28
Slanesville 14	1	39N23	78w32	5:14:08
Slate 54	1	39N11	81w30	5:26:00
Slatyfork 38	1	38N25	80w08	5:20:32
Sleepy Creek 33	10	39N38	78w05	5:12:20
Smithburg 9	1	39N17	80w44	5:22:56
Smithers 10	1	38N11	81w18	5:25:12
Smithfield 19	2	39N23	77w53	5:11:32
Smithfield 52	2	39N30	80w34	5:22:16
Smithtown 31	28	39N39	79w58	5:19:52
Smithville 25	17	39N32	80w07	5:20:28
Smithville 43	1	39N04	81w06	5:24:24
Smoke Hole 36	1	38N48	79w17	5:17:08
Smoot 13	1	37N53	80w40	5:22:40
Snider 39	12	39N28	79w41	5:18:44
Snowden 22	1	38N14	81w58	5:27:52
Snow Flake 13	14	37N45	80w32	5:22:08
Snow Hill 20	22	38N21	81w37	5:26:28
Sod 22	1	38N15	81w53	5:27:32
Sodom 23	1	37N55	81w50	5:27:20
Somerville 54	1	39N16	81w40	5:26:40
Sophia 41	1	37N43	81w15	5:25:00
South Bluefield 28	20	37N16	81w14	5:24:56
South Charleston 20	14	38N21	81w44	5:26:56
South Fork 16	1	38N59	79w01	5:16:04
South Grafton 46	14	39N20	80w01	5:20:04
South Hills 31	28	39N39	79w58	5:19:52
South Madison 3	18	38N04	81w49	5:27:16
South Malden 20	22	38N21	81w38	5:26:32
South Park 21	1	39N07	80w25	5:21:40
South Parkersburg 54	14	39N17	81w32	5:26:08
Southside 27	1	38N43	81w58	5:27:52
South Side Junction 10	1	37N58	81w05	5:24:20
Southwest 9	1	39N10	80w50	5:23:20
South Worthington 25	17	39N27	80w15	5:21:00
Spangler 20	1	38N17	81w17	5:25:08
Spanishburg 28	1	37N27	81w07	5:24:28
Spears 22	1	38N10	82w11	5:28:44
Speed 44	1	38N48	81w21	5:25:24
Speedway 28	1	37N25	81w01	5:24:04
Spelter 17	1	39N21	80w19	5:21:16
Spencer 44	1	38N48	81w21	5:25:24
Spice 38	1	38N08	80w13	5:20:52
Sprague 41	18	37N48	81w13	5:24:52
Sprattsville 30	1	37N37	81w52	5:27:28
Spread 8	1	38N29	81w05	5:24:20
Sprigg 30	1	37N38	82w12	5:28:48
Spring Creek 13	1	38N00	80w22	5:21:28
Spring Creek 53	1	38N57	81w20	5:25:20
Spring Dale 10	1	37N53	80w48	5:23:12
Springdale 35	34	40N04	80w42	5:22:48
Springfield 14	1	39N27	78w42	5:14:48
Spring Fork 20	22	38N21	81w38	5:26:32
Spring Gap 14	1	39N22	78w31	5:14:04
Spring Hill 17	24	39N16	80w19	5:21:16
Spring Hill 20	14	38N21	81w44	5:26:56
Spring Mills 2	2	39N33	78w00	5:12:00
Spring Valley 50	5	38N24	82w26	5:29:44
Spruce Valley 23	1	37N53	81w50	5:27:20
Spurlockville 22	1	38N08	82w01	5:28:04
Squire	1	37N14	81w37	5:26:28
Stafford 30	1	37N36	81w54	5:27:36
Stanaford 41	18	37N49	81w10	5:24:40
Standard 20	1	38N10	81w24	5:25:36
Star City 31	28	39N40	79w59	5:19:56
Staten 7	1	38N48	81w04	5:24:16
Statler Run 31	17	39N36	80w15	5:21:00
Statts Mills 18	1	38N45	81w38	5:26:32
Stealey 17	24	39N16	80w19	5:21:16
Steele 54	1	39N05	81w35	5:26:20
Steeles 55	1	37N28	81w49	5:27:16
Steelton 52	12	39N39	80w51	5:23:24
Steep Gut Hollow 30	1	37N45	82w19	5:29:16
Stephenson 55	1	37N35	81w19	5:25:16
Steptown 50	1	37N50	82w24	5:29:36
Stevenburg 39	19	39N24	79w45	5:19:00
Stewart 54	14	39N17	81w32	5:26:08
Stewartstown 31	28	39N39	79w58	5:19:52
Stickney 41	1	37N54	81w32	5:26:08
Stillman 49	1	38N50	80w21	5:21:24
Stinson 7	1	38N42	81w05	5:24:20
Stirrat 23	1	37N44	82w00	5:28:00
Stohrs Cross Roads 33	11	39N38	78w14	5:12:56
Stollings 23	1	37N51	81w58	5:27:52
Stone Branch 23	1	37N58	82w01	5:28:04
Stonecoal 50	1	37N50	82w24	5:29:36
Stonewall 20	22	38N22	81w38	5:26:32
Stonewall 50	1	38N08	82w21	5:29:24
Stonewood 17	24	39N15	80w19	5:21:16
Stony Bottom 38	1	38N22	79w58	5:19:52
Stony River 12	1	39N17	79w14	5:16:56
Stotesbury 41	1	37N42	81w15	5:25:00
Stouts Mills 11	1	38N54	80w44	5:22:56
Stover 41	1	37N47	81w20	5:25:20
Stowe 23	1	37N48	81w45	5:27:00
Straight Fork 49	1	38N52	80w26	5:21:44
Strange Creek 4	1	38N34	80w54	5:23:36
Streby 12	1	39N07	79w10	5:16:40
Streeter 45	1	37N38	81w01	5:24:04
Stringtown 1	1	39N01	79w56	5:19:44
Stringtown 25	17	39N32	80w20	5:21:20
Stringtown 42	1	38N58	79w30	5:18:00
Stringtown 44	1	38N48	81w21	5:25:24
Strouds 51	1	38N22	80w36	5:22:24
Stumptown 11	1	38N51	81w00	5:24:00
Sturgisson 31	28	39N39	79w58	5:19:52
Sugar Camp 9	1	39N14	80w41	5:22:44
Sugar Grove 36	1	38N30	79w21	5:17:24
Sugar Tree 22	1	38N14	81w59	5:27:56
Sugar Valley 39	12	39N40	79w38	5:18:32
Sullivan 41	1	37N42	81w12	5:24:48
Sullivan 42	35	38N56	79w51	5:19:24
Sully 42	1	38N55	79w42	5:18:48
Sulphur 29	2	39N23	79w09	5:16:36
Sumerco 22	1	38N14	81w54	5:27:36
Summerlee 10	1	38N00	81w10	5:24:40
Summers 9	1	39N12	80w52	5:23:28
Summersville 34	1	38N17	80w51	5:23:24
Summit 22	1	38N14	81w54	5:27:36
Summit 54	14	39N17	81w32	5:26:08
Summit Park 17	24	39N16	80w19	5:21:16
Summit Point 19	2	39N15	77w58	5:11:52
Sun 10	1	37N56	81w09	5:24:36
Sunbeam 23	1	37N52	81w54	5:27:36
Suncrest 31	28	39N39	79w58	5:19:52
Sundial 41	1	37N53	81w31	5:26:04
Sun Flower 44	1	38N54	81w32	5:26:08
Sun Hill 55	1	37N38	81w41	5:26:44
Sunlight 13	1	38N01	80w28	5:21:52
Sunset Acres 21	1	39N03	80w28	5:21:52
Sunset Beach 31	28	39N39	79w58	5:19:52
Sunset Court 23	1	37N58	82w01	5:28:04
Sunshine 25	17	39N32	80w20	5:21:20
Sun Valley 15	32	40N24	80w35	5:22:20
Sun Valley 17	24	39N16	80w19	5:21:16
Sun Valley 20	18	38N23	81w49	5:27:16
Superior Bottom 23	1	37N45	82w00	5:28:00
Surosa 30	1	37N37	82w10	5:28:40
Surveyor 41	1	37N46	81w19	5:25:16
Sutton 4	1	38N40	80w43	5:22:52
Swamp Run 49	1	38N59	80w13	5:20:52
Swandale 8	1	38N30	81w03	5:24:12
Sweeneysburg 41	18	37N47	81w11	5:24:44
Sweetland 22	1	38N16	82w03	5:28:12
Sweet Run 50	14	38N24	82w35	5:30:20
Sweet Springs 32	1	37N38	80w15	5:21:00
Swiss 34	1	38N14	81w08	5:24:32
Switzer 23	1	37N48	81w59	5:27:56
Sycamore 7	1	38N48	81w05	5:24:20
Sycamore 17	1	39N17	80w28	5:21:52
Sycamore 23	1	37N50	82w04	5:28:16
Sycamore Junction 30	1	37N41	82w16	5:29:04
Sydnor Addition 30	1	37N36	82w08	5:28:32
Sylvester 3	18	38N01	81w33	5:26:12
Tablerock 41	18	37N45	81w08	5:24:32
Tablers 2	2	39N22	78w03	5:12:12
Tacy 1	1	39N09	80w03	5:20:12
Tad 20	1	38N20	81w30	5:26:00
Tague 4	1	38N38	80w52	5:23:28
Talbott 1	1	39N01	79w56	5:19:44
Talcott 45	1	37N41	80w44	5:22:56
Tallmansville 49	1	38N55	80w11	5:20:44
Tamcliff 30	1	37N37	81w52	5:27:28
Tams 41	1	37N40	81w18	5:25:12
Tango 22	1	38N17	82w06	5:28:24
Tanner 11	1	38N59	80w57	5:23:48
Tannery 16	1	39N03	78w58	5:15:52
Taplin 23	1	37N46	81w54	5:27:36
Tappan 46	14	39N20	80w01	5:20:04
Tarico Heights 2	2	39N20	78w03	5:12:12
Tariff 44	1	38N41	81w12	5:24:48
Tate 4	1	38N36	80w51	5:23:24
Tavennersville 54	14	39N17	81w32	5:26:08
Taylorville 30	1	37N42	82w11	5:28:44
Teaberry 13	14	37N48	80w27	5:21:48
Teays 40	1	38N26	81w57	5:27:48
Teays Valley 40	1	38N29	82w00	5:28:00
Tekram 30	1	37N42	82w11	5:28:44
Tempa 45	1	37N44	80w39	5:22:36
Tenmile 17	1	39N18	80w31	5:22:04
Ten Mile 49	1	38N55	80w11	5:20:44
Tennerton 49	1	38N59	80w13	5:20:52
Tera Rosa 54	1	39N16	81w40	5:26:40
Terra Alta 39	12	39N27	79w33	5:18:12
Terry 41	1	37N52	81w06	5:24:24
Tesla 4	1	38N36	80w43	5:22:52
Teter 49	1	39N05	80w08	5:20:32
Teterton 36	1	38N51	79w26	5:17:44
Thacker 30	1	37N36	82w08	5:28:32
Thacker Mines 30	1	37N36	82w08	5:28:32
Thayer 10	1	37N55	81w02	5:24:08
The Flats 31	28	39N39	79w58	5:19:52
The Mileground 31	28	39N39	79w58	5:19:52
The Y 18	1	38N54	81w40	5:26:40
Thoburn 25	17	39N28	80w10	5:20:40

WEST VIRGINIA

Thomas 47	1	39N09	79w30	5:18:00
Thompson Town 23	1	37N50	82w04	5:28:16
Thornhill 28	1	37N23	81w17	5:25:08
Thornton 46	12	39N21	79w57	5:19:48
Thornwood 38	14	38N31	79w47	5:19:08
Three Churches 14	1	39N24	78w39	5:14:36
Threefork Bridge 39	12	39N24	79w52	5:19:28
Three Mile 20	1	38N26	81w29	5:25:56
Thurmond 10	1	37N58	81w05	5:24:20
Thursday 43	1	39N04	81w05	5:24:20
Tidewater 24	1	37N26	81w30	5:26:00
Tilden 41	1	37N42	81w12	5:24:48
Timber Ridge 33	2	39N28	78w16	5:13:04
Tioga 34	1	38N25	80w40	5:22:40
Tolleys 41	1	37N46	81w19	5:25:16
Toll Gate 43	1	39N16	80w55	5:23:40
Tomahawk 2	2	39N33	78w00	5:12:00
Toney 22	1	38N02	82w06	5:28:24
Toneyfork 55	1	37N41	81w38	5:26:32
Tophet 45	1	37N32	80w58	5:23:52
Topins Grove 18	1	39N05	81w48	5:27:12
Tornado 20	18	38N20	81w51	5:27:24
Tourison 10	18	38N03	81w06	5:24:24
Town 41	18	37N48	81w13	5:24:52
Town Hill 12	1	39N00	79w07	5:16:28
Trace 30	1	37N52	82w10	5:28:40
Trace Fork 20	22	38N21	81w38	5:26:32
Traphill 41	1	37N46	81w20	5:25:20
Triadelphia 35	6	40N06	80w36	5:22:24
Triplett 8	1	38N29	81w05	5:24:20
Triune 31	28	39N39	79w58	5:19:52
Trout 13	1	38N01	80w28	5:21:52
Troy 11	1	39N03	80w48	5:23:12
Troy Town 23	1	37N51	82w03	5:28:12
Trubada 11	1	38N56	80w50	5:23:20
True 45	1	37N35	80w56	5:23:44
Tuckahoe 13	14	37N48	80w18	5:21:12
Tucker 53	1	39N03	81w31	5:26:04
Tug River 30	1	37N42	82w15	5:29:00
Tunnelton 39	19	39N24	79w45	5:19:00
Turkey Gap 28	1	37N29	81w15	5:25:00
Turkey Knob 10	1	37N54	81w10	5:24:40
Turner Douglass 39	12	39N23	79w28	5:17:52
Turnertown 21	1	39N03	80w28	5:21:52
Turtle Creek 3	18	38N02	81w52	5:27:28
Twilight 3	1	37N55	81w37	5:26:28
Twistville 4	1	38N38	80w52	5:23:28
Two Lick 17	1	39N07	80w25	5:21:40
Two Run 53	1	39N02	81w24	5:25:36
Tygart 54	14	39N13	81w33	5:26:12
Tyler 48	2	39N26	80w49	5:23:16
Tyler Heights 20	22	38N22	81w40	5:26:40
Tyrone 31	28	39N39	79w58	5:19:52
Tyson Store 44	1	38N48	81w21	5:25:24
Uffington 31	28	39N39	79w58	5:19:52
Uler 44	1	38N37	81w09	5:24:36
Ulvilla 19	2	39N22	77w51	5:11:24
Uneeda 3	18	38N02	81w47	5:27:08
Unger 33	2	39N26	78w15	5:13:00
Union 32	1	37N36	80w33	5:22:12
Union Addition 20	1	38N11	81w21	5:25:24
Union City 24	1	37N28	81w49	5:27:16
Union Ridge 6	1	38N35	82w11	5:28:44
Unus 13	1	37N56	80w23	5:21:32
Upland 27	1	38N34	81w59	5:27:56
Upper Addis Run 43	1	39N13	81w03	5:24:12
Upper Flats 27	1	38N54	81w56	5:27:44
Upperglade 51	1	38N24	80w31	5:22:04
Upper Leatherwood 8	1	38N23	81w07	5:24:28
Upper Mingo 42	1	38N30	80w03	5:20:12
Upper Tract 36	1	38N47	79w17	5:17:08
Upton Creek 20	18	38N23	81w49	5:27:16
Ury 41	1	37N38	81w19	5:25:16
Utica 18	1	39N08	81w44	5:26:56
Vadis 21	1	39N03	80w42	5:22:48
Vago 13	1	37N56	80w23	5:21:32
Vainville 2	27	39N28	77w58	5:11:52
Vale 13	1	37N52	80w51	5:23:24
Valley Bend 1	1	39N01	79w56	5:19:44
Valley Bend 42	1	38N47	79w55	5:19:40
Valley Chapel 21	1	39N07	80w30	5:22:00
Valley Fork 8	1	38N31	81w07	5:24:28
Valley Furnace 1	1	39N13	79w53	5:19:32
Valley Grove 35	6	40N06	80w34	5:22:16
Valley Head 42	1	38N33	80w02	5:20:08
Valley Point 39	12	39N30	79w39	5:18:36
Van 3	1	37N58	81w43	5:26:52
Vanclevesville 2	27	39N28	77w58	5:11:52
Vandalia 21	1	38N56	80w30	5:22:00
Vanderlip 14	1	39N21	78w45	5:15:00
Van Junction 3	1	37N58	81w43	5:26:52
Vanville 2	27	39N28	77w58	5:11:52
Van Voorhis 31	28	39N39	79w58	5:19:52
Varney 30	1	37N40	82w06	5:28:24
Varneytown 8	1	38N29	81w07	5:24:28
Vaucluse 37	1	39N24	81w12	5:24:48
Vaughan 34	1	38N14	81w12	5:24:48
Vegan 49	1	38N56	80w06	5:20:24
Verdunville 23	1	37N51	82w03	5:28:12
Verner 30	1	37N40	81w51	5:27:24
Victor 10	1	38N08	81w05	5:24:20
Victoria 39	12	39N24	79w52	5:19:28
Vienna 54	1	39N20	81w33	5:26:12
Viola 25	17	39N28	80w10	5:20:40
Viola 26	21	39N51	80w36	5:22:24
Virginia Heights 20	18	38N23	81w49	5:27:16
Virginville 5	32	40N24	80w33	5:22:12
Viropa 17	1	39N25	80w17	5:21:08
Volcano 54	1	39N11	81w23	5:25:32
Volga 1	1	39N05	80w08	5:20:32
Vulcan 30	1	37N33	82w08	5:28:32
Wadestown 31	17	39N41	80w20	5:21:20
Wadeville 54	1	39N08	81w44	5:26:56
Waggener 27	1	38N59	82w02	5:28:08
Wahoo 25	17	39N28	80w10	5:20:40
Wainville 51	1	38N25	80w33	5:22:12
Waiteville 32	1	37N29	80w26	5:21:44
Waldeck 21	1	39N03	80w28	5:21:52
Walker 54	1	39N13	81w21	5:25:24
Walker Lanes 54	1	39N16	81w40	5:26:40
Walkersville 21	1	38N52	80w28	5:21:52
Wallace 17	1	39N25	80w29	5:21:56
Wallace Heights 20	22	38N22	81w40	5:26:40
Wallback 8	1	38N33	81w07	5:24:28
Walnut 7	1	38N42	81w05	5:24:20
Walnut Bottom 16	1	39N03	79w00	5:16:00
Walnut Valley Acres 20	22	38N22	81w40	5:26:40
Walton 44	1	38N38	81w24	5:25:36
Wana 31	17	39N42	80w18	5:21:12
Wanda 23	1	37N52	81w54	5:27:36
Wapocomo 14	1	39N21	78w45	5:15:00
War 24	1	37N18	81w41	5:26:44
Ward 20	1	38N15	81w23	5:25:32
Warden 41	18	37N49	81w10	5:24:40
Wardensville 16	1	39N05	78w36	5:14:24
War Eagle 30	1	37N28	81w49	5:27:16
Warren 49	1	39N04	80w13	5:20:52
Warriormine 24	1	37N18	81w41	5:26:44
Warwood 35	34	40N04	80w42	5:22:48
Washburn 43	1	39N13	81w03	5:24:12
Washington 54	1	39N16	81w40	5:26:40
Washington Gardens 54	1	39N16	81w40	5:26:40
Washington Heights 3	18	38N04	81w49	5:27:16
Washington Lake 54	1	39N16	81w40	5:26:40
Waterloo 27	1	38N45	81w57	5:27:48
Watoga 38	1	38N11	80w08	5:20:32
Watson 25	17	39N28	80w10	5:20:40
Waverly 54	1	39N20	81w22	5:25:28
Wayne 50	1	38N13	82w27	5:29:48
Wayside 32	1	37N35	80w41	5:22:44
Weaver 42	1	39N01	79w56	5:19:44
Webb 50	1	37N54	82w27	5:29:48
Weberwood 20	14	38N21	81w42	5:26:48
Webster 46	14	39N20	80w01	5:20:04
Webster Springs 51	1	38N29	80w25	5:21:40
Weircrest 15	32	40N24	80w35	5:22:20
Weirton 15	32	40N24	80w35	5:22:20
Weirton Heights 15	32	40N24	80w35	5:22:20
Welch 24	1	37N26	81w35	5:26:20
Welch Glade 51	1	38N25	80w33	5:22:12
Wellford 20	1	38N29	81w21	5:25:24
Wellington Heights 1	1	39N09	80w03	5:20:12
Wellsburg 5	33	40N16	80w37	5:22:28
Welton 29	2	39N20	78w58	5:15:52
Wendel 46	1	39N18	80w06	5:20:24
Werner 1	1	39N01	79w56	5:19:44
Werth 34	1	38N17	80w51	5:23:24
West Columbia 27	1	38N59	82w04	5:28:16
West Dunbar 20	14	38N23	81w45	5:27:00
West End 25	17	39N28	80w10	5:20:40
West End 39	19	39N24	79w45	5:19:00
West Gilbert 30	1	37N37	81w52	5:27:28
West Grafton 46	14	39N20	80w01	5:20:04
West Hamlin 22	1	38N17	82w12	5:28:48
West Huntington 6	5	38N24	82w30	5:30:00
West Junction 3	1	37N58	81w43	5:26:52
West Liberty 35	6	40N10	80w36	5:22:24
West Logan 23	1	37N52	81w59	5:27:56
West Milford 17	1	39N12	80w24	5:21:36
Westmoreland 50	5	38N23	82w30	5:30:00
Weston 21	1	39N02	80w28	5:21:52
Westover 31	28	39N38	79w59	5:19:56
West Pea Ridge 6	5	38N25	82w25	5:29:40
West Raleigh 41	18	37N46	81w11	5:24:44
West Sabraton 31	28	39N39	79w58	5:19:52
West Union 9	1	39N18	80w47	5:23:08
West Vanvoorhis 31	28	39N41	79w59	5:19:56
West Williamson 30	1	37N41	82w16	5:29:04
Wharncliffe 30	1	37N33	81w58	5:27:52
Wharton 3	1	37N55	81w40	5:26:40
Wheeler 51	1	38N39	80w23	5:21:32
Wheeling 35	34	40N04	80w43	5:22:52
Wheeling Island 35	34	40N04	80w42	5:22:48
Whipple 10	1	37N57	81w10	5:24:40
Whirlwind 23	1	38N02	82w07	5:28:28
Whitby 41	1	37N40	81w11	5:24:44
Whitehall 25	17	39N28	80w10	5:20:40
White Oak 41	1	37N42	81w05	5:24:20
White Oak Springs 39	12	39N27	79w33	5:18:12
White Pine 7	1	38N55	81w06	5:24:24
White Rock 25	17	39N28	80w10	5:20:40
Whites Addition 23	1	37N51	82w01	5:28:04
Whites Creek 50	1	38N15	82w36	5:30:24
White Sulphur 13	14	37N48	80w17	5:21:08
White Sulphur Springs 13	14	37N48	80w18	5:21:12
Whitesville 3	18	37N59	81w32	5:26:08
Whitman 23	1	37N49	82w01	5:28:04
Whitmer 42	1	38N49	79w33	5:18:12
Whittaker 20	1	38N05	81w23	5:25:32
Wick 48	2	39N25	80w59	5:23:56
Wickham 41	18	37N47	81w11	5:24:44
Widen 8	1	38N28	80w52	5:23:28
Wihiteoak 43	1	39N11	80w57	5:23:48
Wikel 32	1	37N33	80w41	5:22:44
Wilbur 23	1	37N46	81w55	5:27:40
Wilbur 48	2	39N23	80w49	5:23:16
Wilcoe 24	1	37N23	81w34	5:26:16
Wildcat 21	1	38N45	80w27	5:21:48
Wilderness 34	1	38N10	80w50	5:23:20
Wilding 18	1	38N57	81w46	5:27:04
Wiley Ford 29	2	39N37	78w47	5:15:08
Wileyville 52	2	39N38	80w41	5:22:44
Wilkinson 23	1	37N51	82w00	5:28:00
Willard 17	1	39N24	80w18	5:21:12
William 47	1	39N09	79w30	5:18:00
Williams 54	1	39N20	81w28	5:25:52
Williamsburg 13	1	37N59	80w29	5:21:56
Williams Mountain 3	1	38N02	81w40	5:26:40
Williamson 30	1	37N41	82w17	5:29:08
Williamsport 12	1	39N20	78w55	5:15:40
Williamstown 54	1	39N24	81w27	5:25:48
Willis Branch 10	1	37N54	81w10	5:24:40
Willow Bend 32	1	37N32	80w32	5:22:08
Willow Island 37	1	39N21	81w19	5:25:16
Willowton 28	1	37N22	81w05	5:24:20
Wilmore 24	1	37N28	81w49	5:27:16
Wilsie 4	1	38N41	80w53	5:23:32
Wilson 12	1	39N15	79w24	5:17:36
Wilsonburg 17	14	39N18	80w24	5:21:36
Wilsondale 50	1	37N57	82w20	5:29:20
Wilsontown 49	1	38N50	80w21	5:21:24
Winding Gulf 41	1	37N41	81w15	5:25:00
Windsor Heights 5	9	40N12	80w40	5:22:40
Windy 53	1	39N04	81w24	5:25:36
Winebrenners Crossroad 2	27	39N28	77w58	5:11:52
Winfield 25	17	39N28	80w10	5:20:40
Winfield 40	1	38N32	81w54	5:27:36
Wingrove 10	1	37N57	81w10	5:24:40
Winifrede 20	1	38N10	81w34	5:26:16
Winifrede Junction 20	1	38N14	81w33	5:26:12
Winona 10	1	38N03	81w00	5:24:00
Wiseburg 18	1	38N54	81w40	5:26:40
Witcher 20	14	38N15	81w33	5:26:12
Wolfcreek 32	1	37N39	80w38	5:22:32
Wolfe 28	1	37N18	81w20	5:25:20
Wolf Pen 55	1	37N32	81w36	5:26:24
Wolf Run 26	21	39N50	80w34	5:22:16
Wolf Summit 17	1	39N17	80w28	5:21:52
Womelsdorf 42	1	38N54	79w58	5:19:52
Woodcliff Acres 54	1	39N16	81w40	5:26:40
Woodland 26	4	39N43	80w49	5:23:16
Woodland Park 25	17	39N28	80w10	5:20:40
Woodland Park 54	14	39N17	81w32	5:26:08
Woodlands 26	4	39N48	80w49	5:23:16
Woodrow 38	1	38N13	80w05	5:20:20
Woodruff 26	21	39N50	80w34	5:22:16
Woodville 22	1	38N10	81w54	5:27:36
Worth 24	1	37N25	81w23	5:25:32
Worthington 25	17	39N27	80w15	5:21:00
Wriston 10	18	38N03	81w06	5:24:24
Wyatt 17	1	39N26	80w21	5:21:24
Wyco 55	1	37N36	81w21	5:25:24
Wymer 42	1	38N54	79w37	5:18:28
Wyoma 27	1	38N47	82w12	5:28:48
Wyoming 55	1	37N35	81w36	5:26:24
Yards 28	1	37N17	81w19	5:25:16
Yates 6	1	38N26	82w13	5:28:52
Yawkey 22	1	38N14	81w58	5:27:52
Yolyn 23	1	37N50	81w52	5:27:28
Young 18	1	38N44	81w44	5:26:56
Youngs Bottom 20	1	38N26	81w29	5:25:56
Yukon 24	1	37N19	81w42	5:26:48
Zela 34	1	38N17	80w57	5:23:48
Zenith 32	1	37N27	80w40	5:22:40
Zevely 39	12	39N28	79w41	5:18:44
Zigler 36	1	38N39	79w20	5:17:20
Zinnia 9	1	39N17	80w34	5:22:16
Zion 49	1	38N53	80w18	5:21:12
Zona 44	1	38N48	81w21	5:25:24

WISCONSIN

TIME TABLES

WI # 1

Before 11/18/1883 LMT
11/18/1883 12:00 CST
3/31/1918 02:00 CWT
10/27/1918 02:00 CST
3/30/1919 02:00 CWT
10/26/1919 02:00 CST
2/09/1942 02:00 CWT
9/30/1945 02:00 CST
4/28/1957 02:00 CDT
9/29/1957 02:00 CST
4/27/1958 02:00 CDT
9/28/1958 02:00 CST
4/26/1959 02:00 CDT
9/27/1959 02:00 CST
4/24/1960 02:00 CDT
9/25/1960 02:00 CST
4/30/1961 02:00 CDT
9/24/1961 02:00 CST
4/29/1962 02:00 CDT
9/30/1962 02:00 CST
4/28/1963 02:00 CDT
9/29/1963 02:00 CST
4/26/1964 02:00 CDT
9/27/1964 02:00 CST
4/25/1965 02:00 CDT
10/31/1965 02:00 CST
4/24/1966 02:00 US#1

WI # 2

Before 11/18/1883 LMT
11/18/1883 12:00 CST
3/31/1918 02:00 CWT
10/27/1918 02:00 CST
3/30/1919 02:00 CWT
10/26/1919 02:00 CST
4/24/1921 02:00 CDT
10/30/1921 02:00 CST
2/09/1942 02:00 CWT
9/30/1945 02:00 CST
4/28/1957 02:00 CDT
9/29/1957 02:00 CST
4/27/1958 02:00 CDT
9/28/1958 02:00 CST
4/26/1959 02:00 CDT
9/27/1959 02:00 CST
4/24/1960 02:00 CDT
9/25/1960 02:00 CST
4/30/1961 02:00 CDT
9/24/1961 02:00 CST
4/29/1962 02:00 CDT
9/30/1962 02:00 CST
4/28/1963 02:00 CDT
9/29/1963 02:00 CST
4/26/1964 02:00 CDT
9/27/1964 02:00 CST
4/25/1965 02:00 CDT
10/31/1965 02:00 CST
4/24/1966 02:00 US#1

WI # 3

Before 11/18/1883 LMT
11/18/1883 12:00 CST
3/31/1918 02:00 CWT
10/27/1918 02:00 CST
3/30/1919 02:00 CWT
10/26/1919 02:00 CST
4/30/1922 02:00 CDT
10/24/1922 02:00 CST
4/29/1923 02:00 CDT
9/30/1923 02:00 CST
2/09/1942 02:00 CWT
9/30/1945 02:00 CST
4/28/1957 02:00 CDT
9/29/1957 02:00 CST
4/27/1958 02:00 CDT
9/28/1958 02:00 CST
4/26/1959 02:00 CDT
9/27/1959 02:00 CST
4/24/1960 02:00 CDT
9/25/1960 02:00 CST
4/30/1961 02:00 CDT
9/24/1961 02:00 CST
4/29/1962 02:00 CDT
9/30/1962 02:00 CST
4/28/1963 02:00 CDT
9/29/1963 02:00 CST
4/26/1964 02:00 CDT
9/27/1964 02:00 CST
4/25/1965 02:00 CDT
10/31/1965 02:00 CST
4/24/1966 02:00 US#1

WI # 4

Before 11/18/1883 LMT
11/18/1883 12:00 CST
3/31/1918 02:00 CWT
10/27/1918 02:00 CST
3/30/1919 02:00 CWT
10/26/1919 02:00 CST
4/24/1921 02:00 CDT
10/30/1921 02:00 CST
4/30/1922 02:00 CDT
10/24/1922 02:00 CST
4/29/1923 02:00 CDT
9/30/1923 02:00 CST
2/09/1942 02:00 CWT
9/30/1945 02:00 CST
4/28/1957 02:00 CDT
9/29/1957 02:00 CST
4/27/1958 02:00 CDT
9/28/1958 02:00 CST
4/26/1959 02:00 CDT
9/27/1959 02:00 CST
4/24/1960 02:00 CDT
9/25/1960 02:00 CST
4/30/1961 02:00 CDT
9/24/1961 02:00 CST
4/29/1962 02:00 CDT
9/30/1962 02:00 CST
4/28/1963 02:00 CDT
9/29/1963 02:00 CST
4/26/1964 02:00 CDT
9/27/1964 02:00 CST
4/25/1965 02:00 CDT
10/31/1965 02:00 CST
4/24/1966 02:00 US#1

WI # 5

Before 11/18/1883 LMT
11/18/1883 12:00 CST
3/31/1918 02:00 CWT
10/27/1918 02:00 CST
3/30/1919 02:00 CWT
10/26/1919 02:00 CST
4/24/1921 02:00 CDT
10/30/1921 02:00 CST
4/30/1922 02:00 CDT
10/24/1922 02:00 CST
4/29/1923 02:00 CDT
5/11/1923 02:00 CST
2/09/1942 02:00 CWT
9/30/1945 02:00 CST
4/28/1957 02:00 CDT
9/29/1957 02:00 CST
4/27/1958 02:00 CDT
9/28/1958 02:00 CST
4/26/1959 02:00 CDT
9/27/1959 02:00 CST
4/24/1960 02:00 CDT
9/25/1960 02:00 CST
4/30/1961 02:00 CDT
9/24/1961 02:00 CST
4/29/1962 02:00 CDT
9/30/1962 02:00 CST
4/28/1963 02:00 CDT
9/29/1963 02:00 CST
4/26/1964 02:00 CDT
9/27/1964 02:00 CST
4/25/1965 02:00 CDT
10/31/1965 02:00 CST
4/24/1966 02:00 US#1

WI # 6

Before 11/18/1883 LMT
11/18/1883 12:00 CST
3/31/1918 02:00 CWT
10/27/1918 02:00 CST
3/30/1919 02:00 CWT
10/26/1919 02:00 CST
2/09/1942 02:00 CWT
9/30/1945 02:00 CST
4/24/1955 02:00 CDT
9/25/1955 02:00 CST
4/29/1956 02:00 CDT
9/30/1956 02:00 CST
4/28/1957 02:00 CDT
9/29/1957 02:00 CST
4/27/1958 02:00 CDT
9/28/1958 02:00 CST
4/26/1959 02:00 CDT
9/27/1959 02:00 CST
4/24/1960 02:00 CDT
9/25/1960 02:00 CST
4/30/1961 02:00 CDT
9/24/1961 02:00 CST
4/29/1962 02:00 CDT
9/30/1962 02:00 CST
4/28/1963 02:00 CDT
9/29/1963 02:00 CST
4/26/1964 02:00 CDT
9/27/1964 02:00 CST
4/25/1965 02:00 CDT
10/31/1965 02:00 CST
4/24/1966 02:00 US#1

COUNTIES

1 Adams
2 Ashland
3 Barron
4 Bayfield
5 Brown
6 Buffalo
7 Burnett
8 Calumet
9 Chippewa
10 Clark
11 Columbia
12 Crawford
13 Dane
14 Dodge
15 Door
16 Douglas
17 Dunn
18 Eau Claire
19 Florence
20 Fond du Lac
21 Forest
22 Grant
23 Green
24 Green Lake
25 Iowa
26 Iron
27 Jackson
28 Jefferson
29 Juneau
30 Kenosha
31 Kewaunee
32 La Crosse
33 Lafayette
34 Langlade
35 Lincoln
36 Manitowoc
37 Marathon
38 Marinette
39 Marquette
40 Menominee
41 Milwaukee
42 Monroe
43 Oconto
44 Oneida
45 Outagamie
46 Ozaukee
47 Pepin
48 Pierce
49 Polk
50 Portage
51 Price
52 Racine
53 Richland
54 Rock
55 Rusk
56 St Croix
57 Sauk
58 Sawyer
59 Shawano
60 Sheboygan
61 Taylor
62 Trempealeau
63 Vernon
64 Vilas
65 Walworth
66 Washburn
67 Washington
68 Waukesha
69 Waupaca
70 Waushara
71 Winnebago
72 Wood

Place		Lat.	Long.	Time
Abbotsford 10	1	44N57	90w19	6:01:16
Abels Corners 65	1	42N41	88w33	5:54:12
Abrams 43	1	44N47	88w04	5:52:16
Ackerville 67	1	43N20	88w18	5:53:12
Ackley 34	1	45N10	89w15	5:57:00
Ada 60	1	43N53	87w54	5:51:36
Adams 1	1	43N57	89w49	5:59:16
Adams 65	1	42N48	88w24	5:53:36
Addison 67	1	43N25	88w22	5:53:28
Adell 60	1	43N37	87w57	5:51:48
Adrian 42	1	43N56	90w35	6:02:20
Advance 59	1	44N49	88w26	5:53:44
Afton 54	1	42N36	89w04	5:56:16
Agenda 2	1	46N03	90w22	6:01:28
Ahnapee 31	1	44N38	87w28	5:49:52
Ainsworth 34	1	45N23	88w59	5:55:56
Akan 53	1	43N20	90w35	6:02:20
Alaska 31	1	44N27	87w30	5:50:00
Alban 50	1	44N39	89w14	5:56:56
Albany 23	1	42N43	89w26	5:57:44
Albertville 9	1	45N00	91w44	6:06:56
Albion 13	1	42N50	89w04	5:56:16
Alden 49	1	45N15	92w31	6:10:04
Alderley 14	1	43N13	88w27	5:53:48
Algoma 31	1	44N36	87w27	5:49:48
Allen 18	1	44N35	91w24	6:05:36
Allen Grove 65	1	42N36	88w43	5:54:52
Allenton 67	1	43N25	88w20	5:53:20
Allenville 71	1	44N08	88w08	5:52:32
Allouez 5	1	44N27	88w04	5:52:16
Alma 6	1	44N20	91w55	6:07:40
Alma Center 27	1	44N26	90w54	6:03:36
Almena 3	1	45N25	92w05	6:08:20
Almon 59	1	44N54	89w03	5:56:12
Almond 50	1	44N16	89w25	5:57:40
Alpha 7	1	45N47	92w41	6:10:44
Altdorf 72	1	44N29	89w58	5:59:52
Alto 20	1	43N41	88w48	5:55:12
Altoona 18	1	44N48	91w27	6:05:48
Alvin 21	1	45N59	88w50	5:55:20
Amberg 38	1	45N30	88w00	5:52:00
Amery 49	1	45N19	92w22	6:09:28
Amherst 50	1	44N27	89w16	5:57:04
Amherst Junction 50	1	44N28	89w19	5:57:16
Amnicon 16	1	46N36	91w52	6:07:28
Amnicon Falls 16	1	46N36	91w50	6:07:20
Anacker 11	1	43N33	89w28	5:57:52
Angelica 59	1	44N41	88w19	5:53:16
Angelo 42	1	43N57	90w44	6:02:56
Angus 3	1	45N39	91w33	6:06:12
Aniwa 59	1	45N01	89w13	5:56:52
Annaton 22	1	42N56	90w37	6:02:28
Anson 9	1	45N00	91w15	6:05:00
Anston 5	1	44N36	88w10	5:52:40
Anthony 18	1	44N34	91w41	6:06:44
Antigo 34	1	45N09	89w09	5:56:36
Applecreek 45	1	44N16	88w23	5:53:32
Apple River 49	1	45N25	92w21	6:09:24
Appleton 45	1	44N16	88w25	5:53:40
Arbor Vitae 64	1	45N57	89w42	5:58:48
Arcade 20	1	43N51	88w50	5:55:20
Arcadia 62	1	44N15	91w30	6:06:00
Arena 25	1	43N10	89w55	5:59:40
Argonne 21	1	45N40	88w53	5:55:32
Argyle 33	1	42N42	89w52	5:59:28
Arkansaw 47	1	44N38	92w02	6:08:08
Arkdale 1	1	44N02	89w53	5:59:32
Arland 3	1	45N20	91w59	6:07:56
Arlington 11	1	43N20	89w23	5:57:32
Armenia 29	1	44N10	90w01	6:00:04
Armstrong 20	1	43N50	88w10	5:52:40
Armstrong 43	1	45N10	88w26	5:53:44
Armstrong Creek 21	1	45N40	88w30	5:54:00
Arnold 9	1	45N19	90w57	6:03:48
Arnott 50	1	44N27	89w27	5:57:48
Arpin 72	1	44N33	90w02	6:00:08
Arthur 9	1	45N04	91w09	6:04:36
Arthur 22	1	42N44	90w29	6:01:56
Ashford 20	1	43N35	88w20	5:53:20
Ashippun 14	1	43N13	88w31	5:54:04
Ashland 2	1	46N35	90w53	6:03:32
Ashland Junction 4	1	46N35	90w53	6:03:32
Ashley 37	1	44N52	89w42	5:58:48
Ash Ridge 53	1	43N30	90w40	6:02:40
Ashton 13	1	43N07	89w26	5:57:44
Ashton Corners 13	1	43N07	89w26	5:57:44
Ashwaubenon 5	1	44N28	88w05	5:52:20
Askeaton 5	1	44N19	88w06	5:52:24
Astico 14	1	43N20	88w56	5:55:44
Athelstane 38	1	45N25	88w06	5:52:24
Athens 37	1	45N02	90w05	6:00:20
Atlanta 55	1	45N31	91w20	6:05:20
Atlas 49	1	45N34	92w28	6:09:52
Attica 23	1	42N43	89w26	5:57:44
Atwater 14	1	43N30	88w43	5:54:52
Atwood 10	1	44N57	90w34	6:02:16
Auburndale 72	1	44N38	90w00	6:00:00
Augusta 18	1	44N41	91w07	6:04:28
Aurora 19	1	45N48	88w04	5:52:16
Auroraville	1	44N03	89w00	5:56:00
Avalanche 63	1	43N33	90w53	6:03:32
Avalon 54	1	42N38	88w52	5:55:28
Avoca 25	1	43N11	90w19	6:01:16
Avon 33	1	42N41	90w07	6:00:28
Avon 54	1	42N33	89w18	5:57:12
Aztalan 28	1	43N04	88w50	5:55:20
Babcock 72	1	44N18	90w07	6:00:28
Bad River Indian Reservation 2	1	46N35	90w53	6:03:32
Bagley 22	1	42N54	91w06	6:04:24
Baileys Harbor 15	1	45N04	87w08	5:48:32
Bakerville 72	1	44N33	89w58	5:59:52
Baldwin 56	1	44N58	92w22	6:09:28
Balsam Lake 49	1	45N27	92w27	6:09:48
Bancroft 50	1	44N19	89w31	5:58:04
Bangor 32	1	43N51	90w58	6:03:52
Baraboo 57	1	43N28	89w45	5:59:00
Barksdale 4	1	46N38	90w56	6:03:44
Barnes 4	1	46N20	91w29	6:05:56
Barneveld 25	1	43N01	89w54	5:59:36
Barnum 12	1	43N18	90w50	6:03:20
Barre 32	1	43N50	91w05	6:04:20
Barre Mills 32	1	43N49	91w14	6:04:56
Barron 3	1	45N24	91w51	6:07:24
Barronett 3	1	45N41	91w59	6:07:56
Barron Junction 3	1	45N24	91w51	6:07:24
Bartelme 59	1	44N54	88w55	5:55:40
Barton 67	1	43N27	88w13	5:52:52
Basco 13	1	42N52	89w33	5:58:12
Bashaw 7	1	45N46	91w58	6:07:52
Bass Bay 68	1	42N55	88w07	5:52:28
Bassett 30	1	42N32	88w13	5:52:52
Basswood 53	1	43N12	90w26	6:01:44
Batavia 60	1	43N36	88w03	5:52:12
Bateman 9	1	44N55	91w23	6:05:32
Bay City 48	1	44N35	92w27	6:09:48
Bayfield 4	1	46N49	90w49	6:03:16
Bay Mills 35	1	45N28	89w44	5:58:56
Bay Settlement 5	1	44N30	88w01	5:52:04
Bayside 41	1	43N10	87w54	5:51:36
Bayview 4	1	46N44	90w59	6:03:56

Bay View 41 1 42N59 87w54 5:51:36
Beachs Corners 62 1 44N11 91w16 6:05:04
Bear Bluff 27 1 44N13 90w21 6:01:24
Bear Creek 45 1 44N32 88w44 5:54:56
Bear Lake 55 1 45N36 91w50 6:07:20
Bear Trap 2 1 46N35 90w53 6:03:32
Bear Valley 53 1 43N26 90w07 6:00:28
Beaver 38 1 45N08 88w01 5:52:04
Beaver Brook 66 1 45N46 91w50 6:07:20
Beaver Dam 14 1 43N28 88w50 5:55:20
Beaver Dam Junction 14 1 43N27 88w51 5:55:24
Beaver Edge 14 1 43N27 88w51 5:55:24
Beecher 38 1 45N34 87w55 5:51:40
Beecher Lake 38 1 45N38 87w59 5:51:56
Beechwood 60 1 43N37 87w57 5:51:48
Beetown 22 1 42N48 90w53 6:03:32
Beldenville 48 1 44N46 92w30 6:10:00
Belgium 46 1 43N30 87w51 5:51:24
Bell 4 1 46N50 91w06 6:04:24
Bell Center 12 1 43N18 90w50 6:03:20
Belle Plaine 59 1 44N43 88w40 5:54:40
Belleville 13 1 42N52 89w32 5:58:08
Bellevue 5 1 44N27 87w55 5:51:40
Bellinger 61 1 44N57 90w48 6:03:12
Belmont 33 1 42N44 90w20 6:01:20
Beloit 54 1 42N31 89w02 5:56:08
Beloit North 54 1 42N31 89w03 5:56:12
Beloit West 54 1 42N31 89w03 5:56:12
Belt Line Junction 26 1 46N27 90w12 6:00:48
Belton 41 1 43N01 88w00 5:52:00
Belvidere 6 1 44N16 91w51 6:07:24
Benderville 16 1 44N37 87w51 5:51:24
Benoit 4 1 46N30 91w05 6:04:20
Benton 33 1 42N34 90w23 6:01:32
Berlin 24 1 43N58 88w57 5:55:48
Bern 37 1 45N03 90w08 6:00:32
Berry 13 1 43N10 89w40 5:58:40
Bethel 72 1 44N33 90w02 6:00:08
Bethesda 68 1 43N01 88w12 5:52:48
Bevent 37 1 44N49 89w25 5:57:40
Big Bend 68 1 42N53 88w13 5:52:52
Big Falls 69 1 44N37 89w01 5:56:04
Big Flats 1 1 44N07 89w46 5:59:04
Big Patch 22 1 42N44 90w29 6:01:56
Big Spring 1 1 43N40 89w38 5:58:32
Billings Park 16 1 46N42 92w05 6:08:20
Birch 2 1 46N37 90w41 6:02:44
Birch 35 1 45N20 89w36 5:58:24
Birch Creek 9 1 45N14 91w14 6:04:56
Birchwood 66 1 45N40 91w33 6:06:12
Birnamwood 59 1 44N56 89w13 5:56:52
Biron 72 1 44N26 89w47 5:59:08
Black Brook 49 1 45N15 92w21 6:09:24
Black Creek 45 1 44N29 88w27 5:53:48
Black Creek Junction 45 1 44N28 88w27 5:53:48
Black Earth 13 1 43N08 89w45 5:59:00
Black Hawk 57 1 43N16 89w56 5:59:44
Black River 60 1 43N44 87w46 5:51:04
Black River Falls 27 1 44N18 90w51 6:03:24
Blackwell 21 1 45N34 88w30 5:54:00
Black Wolf 71 1 43N57 88w31 5:54:04
Blaine 7 1 46N07 92w10 6:08:40
Blaine 50 1 44N17 89w23 5:57:32
Blair 62 1 44N18 91w14 6:04:56
Blanchard 33 1 42N48 89w54 5:59:36
Blanchardville 33 1 42N48 89w51 5:59:24
Blenker 72 1 44N37 89w55 5:59:40
Bloom 53 1 43N30 90w28 6:01:52
Bloom City 53 1 43N30 90w28 6:01:52
Bloomer 9 1 45N06 91w29 6:05:56
Bloomingdale 63 1 43N39 90w51 6:03:24
Bloomington 22 1 42N53 90w55 6:03:40
Bloomville 35 1 45N18 89w30 5:58:00
Blueberry 16 1 46N35 91w55 6:07:40
Blue Mounds 13 1 42N59 89w48 5:59:12
Blue River 22 1 43N11 90w34 6:02:16
Bluff Siding 6 1 44N07 91w41 6:06:44
Boardman 56 1 45N04 92w36 6:10:24
Boaz 53 1 43N20 90w32 6:02:08
Bohners Lake 52 1 42N38 88w17 5:53:08
Bohri 6 1 44N07 91w41 6:06:44
Bolt 31 1 44N21 87w50 5:51:20
Boltonville 67 1 43N31 88w14 5:52:56
Bonduel 59 1 44N44 88w27 5:53:48
Bone Lake 49 1 45N35 92w21 6:09:24
Borth 70 1 44N05 88w54 5:55:36
Boscobel 22 1 43N08 90w42 6:02:48
Bosstown 53 1 43N20 90w27 6:01:48
Boulder Junction 64 1 46N07 89w38 5:58:32
Bovina 45 1 44N28 88w33 5:54:12
Bowers 65 1 42N41 88w33 5:54:12
Bowler 59 1 44N52 88w59 5:55:56
Boyceville 17 1 45N03 92w02 6:08:08
Boyd 9 1 44N57 91w02 6:04:08
Boydtown 12 1 43N05 90w54 6:03:36
Brackett 18 1 44N42 91w21 6:05:24
Bradford 54 1 42N38 88w50 5:55:20
Bradley 35 1 45N29 89w44 5:58:56
Bradley 41 1 43N09 87w59 5:51:56
Branch 36 1 44N09 87w46 5:51:04
Brandon 20 1 43N44 88w47 5:55:08
Branstad 7 1 45N47 92w41 6:10:44
Brantwood 51 1 45N34 90w07 6:00:28
Brazeau 43 1 45N06 88w13 5:52:52
Breed 43 1 45N04 88w26 5:53:44
Briarton 59 1 44N40 88w15 5:53:00
Brickson Park 13 1 43N02 89w17 5:57:08
Bridge Creek 18 1 44N40 91w06 6:04:24
Bridgeport 12 1 43N01 91w04 6:04:16
Briggsville 39 1 43N39 89w35 5:58:20
Brigham 25 1 43N00 89w53 5:59:32
Brighton 30 1 42N41 88w07 5:52:28
Brill 3 1 45N36 91w40 6:06:40
Brillion 8 1 44N11 88w04 5:52:16
Bristol 30 1 42N34 88w03 5:52:12
Bristow 63 1 43N33 90w53 6:03:32
Brockville 36 1 44N09 87w49 5:51:16
Brockway 27 1 44N17 90w48 6:03:12
Brodhead 23 1 42N37 89w22 5:57:28
Brodtville 22 1 42N54 91w06 6:04:24
Brokaw 37 1 45N02 89w39 5:58:36
Brookfield 68 1 43N04 88w09 5:52:36
Brooklyn 23 1 42N51 89w23 5:57:32
Brooks 1 1 43N50 89w39 5:58:36
Brookside 1 1 43N57 89w49 5:59:16
Brookside 43 1 44N47 88w03 5:52:12
Brookville 56 1 44N57 92w18 6:09:12
Brookwood 13 1 43N04 89w27 5:57:48
Brothertown 8 1 43N58 88w19 5:53:16
Brown Deer 41 1 43N10 87w58 5:51:52
Browning 61 1 45N09 90w13 6:00:52
Browns Lake 52 1 42N41 88w14 5:52:56
Brownsville 14 1 43N37 88w30 5:54:00
Browntown 23 1 42N35 89w48 5:59:12
Bruce 55 1 45N28 91w16 6:05:04
Bruemmerville 31 1 44N36 87w26 5:49:44
Brule 16 1 46N33 91w34 6:06:16
Brunet 9 1 45N10 91w09 6:04:36
Brunswick 18 1 44N43 91w35 6:06:20
Brushville 70 1 44N09 89w05 5:56:20
Brussels 15 1 44N44 87w37 5:50:28
Bryant 34 1 45N13 89w01 5:56:04
Buchanan 45 1 44N15 88w18 5:53:12
Buckbee 69 1 44N38 88w46 5:55:04
Buckcreek 53 1 43N20 90w27 6:01:48
Buckman 5 1 44N21 87w50 5:51:20
Budd 63 1 43N33 90w53 6:03:32
Budsin 39 1 43N58 89w13 5:56:52
Buena Park 52 1 42N46 88w13 5:52:52
Buena Vista 68 1 43N04 88w21 5:53:24
Buffalo 6 1 44N14 91w51 6:07:24
Buffalo Shore Estates 39 1 43N46 89w28 5:57:52
Bunker Hill 53 1 43N31 90w11 6:00:44
Burke 13 1 43N10 89w18 5:57:12
Burkhardt 56 1 44N59 92w45 6:11:00
Burlington 52 1 42N41 88w17 5:53:08
Burnett 14 1 43N30 88w43 5:54:52
Burns 32 1 43N58 90w58 6:03:52
Burnside 62 1 44N25 91w28 6:05:52
Burton 22 1 42N41 90w42 6:02:48
Busseyville 28 1 42N50 89w04 5:56:16
Butler 41 1 43N06 88w05 5:52:20
Butte des Morts 71 1 44N02 88w36 5:54:24
Butternut 2 1 46N01 90w30 6:02:00
Byrds Creek 53 1 43N11 90w34 6:02:16
Byron 20 1 43N39 88w27 5:53:48
Cable 4 1 46N13 91w17 6:05:08
Caddy Vista 52 1 42N50 87w57 5:51:48
Cadiz 23 1 42N33 89w48 5:59:12
Cadott 9 1 44N57 91w09 6:04:36
Cady 56 1 44N54 92w12 6:08:48
Cainville 54 1 42N47 89w18 5:57:12
Calamine 33 1 42N45 90w10 6:00:40
Calamus 14 1 43N24 88w57 5:55:48
Caldwell 52 1 42N52 88w20 5:53:20
Caledonia 52 1 42N49 87w56 5:51:44
Callon 37 1 44N53 89w20 5:57:20
Calumet 20 1 43N56 88w15 5:53:00
Calumetville 20 1 43N52 88w17 5:53:08
Calvary 20 1 43N50 88w15 5:53:00
Cambria 11 1 43N33 89w07 5:56:28
Cambridge 13 1 43N00 89w01 5:56:04
Cameron 3 1 45N25 91w44 6:06:56
Campbell 32 1 43N51 91w16 6:05:04
Campbellsport 20 1 43N36 88w17 5:53:08
Camp Douglas 29 1 43N55 90w16 6:01:04
Campia 3 1 45N32 91w40 6:06:40
Camp Lake 30 1 42N32 88w08 5:52:32
Camp Leonard 13 1 43N02 89w17 5:57:08
Camp McCoy 42 1 43N56 90w49 6:03:16
Canton 3 1 45N26 91w40 6:06:40
Carey 26 1 46N19 90w13 6:00:52
Carlsville 15 1 44N57 87w21 5:49:24
Carlton 31 1 44N22 87w36 5:50:24
Carnot 15 1 44N42 87w29 5:49:56
Carol Beach Estates 30 1 42N35 87w51 5:51:24
Caroline 59 1 44N43 88w53 5:55:32
Carrollville 41 1 42N54 87w56 5:51:44
Carson 50 1 44N34 89w47 5:59:08
Carter 21 1 45N24 88w38 5:54:32
Cary 72 1 44N28 90w16 6:01:04
Caryville 17 1 44N45 91w41 6:06:44
Cascade 60 1 43N39 88w01 5:52:04
Casco 31 1 44N34 87w37 5:50:28
Casey 66 1 45N56 91w58 6:07:52
Cashton 42 1 43N44 90w47 6:03:08
Cassel 37 1 44N56 89w54 5:59:36
Cassell 57 1 43N15 89w44 5:58:56
Cassian 44 1 45N41 89w40 5:58:40
Cassville 22 1 42N43 90w59 6:03:56
Castle Rock 22 1 43N05 90w29 6:01:56
Caswell 21 1 45N40 88w39 5:54:36
Cataract 42 1 44N05 90w50 6:03:20
Catawba 51 1 45N32 90w32 6:02:08
Cato 36 1 44N06 87w52 5:51:28
Cavour 21 1 45N39 88w38 5:54:32
Cayuga 2 1 46N20 90w40 6:02:40
Cazenovia 53 1 43N31 90w12 6:00:48
Cecil 59 1 44N49 88w27 5:53:48
Cedar 26 1 46N29 90w25 6:01:40
Cedarburg 46 1 43N18 87w59 5:51:56
Cedar Creek 67 1 43N25 88w11 5:52:44
Cedar Falls 17 1 44N53 91w56 6:07:44
Cedar Grove 60 1 43N34 87w49 5:51:16
Cedar Lake 3 1 45N36 91w36 6:06:24
Cedar Rapids 55 1 45N35 90w51 6:03:24
Cedarville 38 1 45N23 87w57 5:51:48
Center House 24 1 43N42 88w59 5:55:56
Center Lake Woods 30 1 42N31 88w07 5:52:28
Center Valley 45 1 44N28 88w27 5:53:48
Centerville 25 1 43N03 90w23 6:01:32
Centerville 36 1 43N57 87w46 5:51:04
Centerville 62 1 44N06 91w21 6:05:24
Centuria 49 1 45N27 92w33 6:10:12
Chaffey 16 1 46N30 92w17 6:09:08
Chambers Island 15 1 45N08 87w15 5:49:00
Champion 5 1 44N31 87w56 5:51:44
Chapel Ridge Heights 5 1 44N30 88w01 5:52:04
Charlesburg 8 1 44N02 88w10 5:52:40
Charlestown 8 1 44N01 88w05 5:52:20
Charlie Bluff 54 1 42N47 88w57 5:55:48
Chase 43 1 44N44 88w10 5:52:40
Chaseburg 63 1 43N40 91w06 6:04:24
Chelsea 61 1 45N18 90w18 6:01:12
Chenequa 68 1 43N07 88w22 5:53:28
Chenequa North 68 1 43N06 88w25 5:53:40
Cherokee 37 1 44N55 90w18 6:01:12
Chester 14 1 43N36 88w43 5:54:52
Chetek 3 1 45N19 91w39 6:06:36
Chicago Corners 45 1 44N28 88w02 5:52:08
Chicog 66 1 46N02 91w58 6:07:52
Chili 10 1 44N38 90w21 6:01:24
Chilton 8 1 44N02 88w10 5:52:40
Chimney Rock 62 1 44N30 91w28 6:05:52
Chippewa 2 1 46N02 90w42 6:02:48
Chippewa Falls 9 1 44N56 91w24 6:05:36
Chittamo 66 1 46N06 91w50 6:07:20
Chiwaukee 30 1 42N35 87w51 5:51:24
Christie 10 1 44N39 90w36 6:02:24
Christilla Heights 54 1 42N31 89w03 5:56:12
Cicero 45 1 44N32 88w26 5:53:44
City Point 27 1 44N21 90w20 6:01:20
Clam Falls 49 1 45N41 92w21 6:09:24
Clam Lake 2 1 46N10 90w54 6:03:36
Clark 10 1 44N57 90w36 6:02:24
Clark Mills 36 1 44N09 87w52 5:51:28
Clarks Point 71 1 44N07 88w43 5:54:52
Clarno 23 1 42N32 89w39 5:58:36
Claybanks 15 1 44N44 87w22 5:49:28
Clayton 12 1 43N24 90w47 6:03:08
Clayton 49 1 45N20 92w10 6:08:40
Claywood 43 1 44N53 88w17 5:53:08
Clear Creek 18 1 44N39 91w21 6:05:24
Clearfield 29 1 43N56 90w08 6:00:32
Clear Lake 49 1 45N15 92w16 6:09:04
Clearwater Lake 44 1 45N46 89w11 5:56:44
Cleghorn 18 1 44N37 91w29 6:05:56
Cleveland 36 1 43N55 87w45 5:51:00
Clifford 51 1 45N33 90w00 6:00:00
Clifton 42 1 43N53 90w21 6:01:24
Clinton 54 1 42N34 88w52 5:55:28
Clintonville 69 1 44N37 88w46 5:55:04
Clover 4 1 46N48 91w14 6:04:56
Clover 36 1 44N06 87w41 5:50:44
Cloverdale 29 1 44N02 90w04 6:00:16
Clyde 25 1 43N08 90w13 6:00:52
Clyman 14 1 43N19 88w43 5:54:52
Cobb 25 1 42N58 90w20 6:01:20
Cobban 9 1 45N10 91w09 6:04:36
Cochrane 6 1 44N14 91w50 6:07:20
Coddington 50 1 44N27 89w33 5:58:12
Colburn 9 1 45N02 91w03 6:04:12
Colby 10 1 44N55 90w19 6:01:16
Coldspring 28 1 42N55 88w51 5:55:24
Cold Springs 28 1 42N51 88w43 5:54:52
Coleman 38 1 45N04 88w02 5:52:08
Colfax 17 1 45N00 91w44 6:06:56
Colgate 67 1 43N12 88w12 5:52:48
Collins 36 1 44N05 87w59 5:51:56
Coloma 70 1 44N02 89w31 5:58:04
Coloma Corners 70 1 44N02 89w31 5:58:04
Columbus 11 1 43N21 89w01 5:56:04
Combined Locks 45 1 44N19 89w00 5:56:00
Commonwealth 19 1 45N51 88w14 5:52:56
Como 65 1 42N37 88w29 5:53:56
Comstock 3 1 45N29 92w05 6:08:20
Concord 28 1 43N04 88w36 5:54:24
Connorsville 17 1 45N08 92w06 6:08:24
Conover 64 1 46N03 89w15 5:57:00
Conrath 55 1 45N23 91w02 6:04:08
Cooks Valley 9 1 45N04 91w36 6:06:24
Cooksville 54 1 42N50 89w14 5:56:56
Coomer 7 1 45N41 92w18 6:09:12
Coon 63 1 43N41 90w58 6:03:52
Coon Valley 63 1 43N42 91w01 6:04:04
Cooperstown 36 1 44N19 87w46 5:51:04
Coral City 62 1 44N24 91w19 6:05:16
Corinth 37 1 45N01 90w04 6:00:16
Cormier 5 1 44N30 88w01 5:52:04
Cornelia 22 1 42N44 90w29 6:01:56
Cornell 9 1 45N10 91w09 6:04:36
Corning 35 1 45N13 89w59 5:59:56
Cornucopia 4 1 46N51 91w06 6:04:24
Cottage Grove 13 1 43N04 89w11 5:56:44
Couderay 58 1 45N48 91w18 6:05:12
County Line 38 1 44N54 87w52 5:51:28
County Line 48 1 44N51 92w14 6:08:56
Courtland 11 1 43N30 89w04 5:56:16
Cox 9 1 45N10 90w48 6:03:12
Crandon 21 1 45N34 88w54 5:55:36
Cranmoor 72 1 44N21 90w00 6:00:00

Cream 6	1	44N20	91w55	6:07:40
Crescent 9	1	44N57	91w09	6:04:36
Crescent 44	1	45N36	89w29	5:57:56
Crescent Park 13	1	43N02	89w17	5:57:08
Crestview 52	1	42N48	87w49	5:51:16
Crestview 54	1	42N31	89w03	5:56:12
Crivitz 38	1	45N14	88w01	5:52:04
Cross 6	1	44N11	91w39	6:06:36
Cross Plains 13	1	43N04	89w40	5:58:40
Crystal 66	1	45N51	91w43	6:06:52
Crystal Lake Corners 69	1	44N21	89w05	5:56:20
Cuba City 22	1	42N36	90w26	6:01:44
Cudahy 41	1	42N58	87w52	5:51:28
Cumberland 3	1	45N32	92w01	6:08:04
Curran 27	1	44N22	91w06	6:04:24
Curran 31	1	44N21	87w50	5:51:20
Curtiss 10	1	44N57	90w26	6:01:44
Cushing 49	1	45N34	92w39	6:10:36
Custer 50	1	44N31	89w26	5:57:44
Cutler 29	1	44N03	90w15	6:01:00
Cutter 16	1	46N36	91w50	6:07:20
Cylon 56	1	45N10	92w21	6:09:24
Czechville 6	1	44N07	91w41	6:06:44
Dacada 46	1	43N33	87w58	5:51:52
Dairyland 16	1	46N13	92w09	6:08:36
Dakota 70	1	44N02	89w19	5:57:16
Dale 45	1	44N16	88w40	5:54:40
Daleyville 13	1	42N55	89w48	5:59:12
Dallas 3	1	45N16	91w51	6:07:24
Dalton 24	1	43N40	89w12	5:56:48
Danbury 7	1	46N01	92w22	6:09:28
Dancy 37	1	44N52	89w42	5:58:48
Dane 13	1	43N15	89w30	5:58:00
Daniels 7	1	45N46	92w28	6:09:52
Danville 14	1	43N20	89w01	5:56:04
Darboy 8	1	44N16	88w23	5:53:32
Darien 65	1	42N36	88w43	5:54:52
Darlington 33	1	42N41	90w07	6:00:28
Davis Corners 1	1	43N38	89w47	5:59:08
Day 37	1	44N50	90w02	6:00:08
Dayton 23	1	42N50	89w31	5:58:04
Deansville 13	1	43N11	89w04	5:56:16
Decatur 23	1	42N38	89w26	5:57:44
Deckers Corner 46	1	43N17	87w58	5:51:52
Decorah Prairie 62	1	44N06	91w21	6:05:24
Dedham 16	1	46N30	92w17	6:09:08
Deerbrook 34	1	45N14	89w09	5:56:36
Deerfield 13	1	43N03	89w04	5:56:16
Deer Park 56	1	45N11	92w23	6:09:32
De Forest 13	1	43N15	89w20	5:57:20
Dekorra 11	1	43N25	89w27	5:57:48
Delafield 68	1	43N04	88w24	5:53:36
Delavan 65	1	42N38	88w39	5:54:36
Delavan Lake 65	1	42N37	88w36	5:54:24
Dell 63	1	43N39	90w51	6:03:24
Dellona 57	1	43N36	89w54	5:59:36
Dell Prairie 1	1	43N42	89w45	5:59:00
Dellwood 1	1	43N59	89w56	5:59:44
Delmar 9	1	45N00	91w00	6:04:00
Delta 4	1	46N28	91w19	6:05:16
Delton 57	1	43N35	89w47	5:59:08
Denmark 5	1	44N21	87w50	5:51:20
Denoon 68	1	42N55	88w07	5:52:28
Denzer 57	1	43N27	89w52	5:59:28
De Pere 5	1	44N27	88w04	5:52:16
Deronda 49	1	45N18	92w26	6:09:44
De Soto 63	1	43N25	91w12	6:04:48
Devils Lake 57	1	43N28	89w45	5:59:00
Dewhurst 10	1	44N28	90w44	6:02:56
Dexter 72	1	44N23	90w07	6:00:28
Dexterville 72	1	44N23	90w07	6:00:28
Diamond Bluff 48	1	44N39	92w38	6:10:32
Dickeyville 22	1	42N38	90w36	6:02:24
Diefenbach Corners 67	1	43N20	88w18	5:53:12
Dilly 63	1	43N39	90w21	6:01:24
Disco 27	1	44N17	90w51	6:03:24
Dodge 62	1	44N08	91w33	6:06:12
Dodges Corners 68	1	42N52	88w20	5:53:20
Dodgeville 25	1	42N58	90w08	6:00:32
Doering 35	1	45N18	89w30	5:58:00
Donald 61	1	45N10	90w48	6:03:12
Dorchester 10	1	45N00	90w20	6:01:20
Doty 43	1	45N13	88w36	5:54:24
Dotyville 20	1	43N45	88w16	5:53:04
Douglas 39	1	43N41	89w33	5:58:12
Dousman 68	1	43N01	88w29	5:53:56
Dover 51	1	45N34	90w07	6:00:28
Dovre 3	1	45N15	91w37	6:06:28
Downing 17	1	45N03	92w07	6:08:28
Downing Junction 17	1	45N03	92w07	6:08:28
Downsville 17	1	44N47	91w56	6:07:44
Doyle 3	1	45N31	91w36	6:06:24
Doylestown 11	1	43N26	89w09	5:56:36
Drammen 18	1	44N38	91w35	6:06:20
Draper 58	1	45N54	90w48	6:03:12
Dresser 49	1	45N21	92w38	6:10:32
Drummond 4	1	46N20	91w15	6:05:00
Drywood 9	1	44N57	91w09	6:04:36
Duck Creek 5	1	44N30	88w01	5:52:04
Dudley 35	1	45N18	89w30	5:58:00
Dunbar 38	1	45N39	88w10	5:52:40
Dunbarton 33	1	42N34	90w14	6:00:56
Dundas 8	1	44N14	88w12	5:52:48
Dundee 20	1	43N36	88w17	5:53:08
Dunkirk 13	1	42N53	89w13	5:56:52
Duplainville 68	1	43N01	88w12	5:52:48
Dupont 69	1	44N38	88w55	5:55:40
Durand 47	1	44N38	91w58	6:07:52
Durham 68	1	42N56	88w02	5:52:08
Durham Hill 68	1	42N53	88w00	5:52:00
Duvall 31	1	44N32	87w42	5:50:48
Dyckesville 5	1	44N39	87w45	5:51:00
Eagle 68	1	42N53	88w29	5:53:56
Eagle Corners 53	1	43N12	90w26	6:01:44
Eagle Lake 52	1	42N41	88w07	5:52:28
Eagle Lake Manor 52	1	42N41	88w07	5:52:28
Eagle Point 9	1	45N02	91w21	6:05:24
Eagle River 64	1	45N55	89w15	5:57:00
Eagleton 9	1	45N04	91w23	6:05:32
Eagleville 68	1	42N52	88w20	5:53:20
Earl 66	1	45N55	91w46	6:07:04
East Bristol 13	1	43N20	89w01	5:56:04
East Delavan 65	1	42N37	88w37	5:54:28
East Ellsworth 48	1	44N44	92w29	6:09:56
East End 16	1	46N42	92w05	6:08:20
East Farmington 49	1	45N19	92w42	6:10:48
East Friesland 11	1	43N32	89w00	5:56:00
East Krok 31	1	44N27	87w30	5:50:00
Eastman 12	1	43N10	91w01	6:04:04
Eastmar 72	1	44N33	89w58	5:59:52
Easton 1	1	43N57	89w49	5:59:16
East Side 13	1	43N08	89w22	5:57:28
East Troy 65	1	42N47	88w24	5:53:36
East Waupun 14	1	43N38	88w44	5:54:56
Eastwin 36	1	44N09	87w35	5:50:20
Eau Claire 18	1	44N49	91w30	6:06:00
Eau Claire Southeast 18	1	44N48	91w29	6:05:56
Eau Galle 17	1	44N42	92w01	6:08:04
Eden 20	1	43N42	88w22	5:53:28
Edgar 37	1	44N55	89w59	5:59:56
Edgerton 54	1	42N50	89w04	5:56:16
Edgewater 58	1	45N45	91w28	6:05:52
Edgewood 68	1	43N04	88w18	5:53:12
Edithton Beach 30	1	42N35	87w51	5:51:24
Edmund 25	1	42N58	90w16	6:01:04
Edson 9	1	44N55	91w01	6:04:04
Edwards 60	1	43N55	87w45	5:51:00
Edwards Park 13	1	43N02	89w17	5:57:08
Egg Harbor 15	1	45N03	87w17	5:49:08
Eidsvold 10	1	44N58	90w56	6:03:44
Eileen 4	1	46N33	90w59	6:03:56
Eisenstein 51	1	45N57	90w18	6:01:12
Eland 59	1	44N52	89w13	5:56:52
Elba 14	1	43N19	88w57	5:55:48
Elcho 34	1	45N26	89w11	5:56:44
Elderon 37	1	44N47	89w15	5:57:00
Eldorado 20	1	43N51	88w35	5:54:20
Eleva 62	1	44N35	91w28	6:05:52
Elk 51	1	45N41	90w30	6:02:00
Elk Creek 62	1	44N23	91w26	6:05:44
Elkgrove 33	1	42N41	90w22	6:01:28
Elkhart Lake 60	1	43N50	88w01	5:52:04
Elkhorn 65	1	42N40	88w33	5:54:12
Elk Mound 17	1	44N52	91w42	6:06:48
Ella 47	1	44N32	92w03	6:08:12
Ellenboro 22	1	42N49	90w36	6:02:24
Ellington 45	1	44N22	88w33	5:54:12
Ellis 50	1	44N31	89w34	5:58:16
Ellison Bay 15	1	45N15	87w04	5:48:16
Ellisville 31	1	44N32	87w42	5:50:48
Ellsworth 48	1	44N44	92w29	6:09:56
Elm Grove 68	1	43N03	88w05	5:52:20
Elmhurst 34	1	45N09	89w08	5:56:32
Elm Island 52	1	42N46	88w13	5:52:52
Elmore 20	1	43N36	88w17	5:53:08
Elm Tree Corners 5	1	44N30	88w01	5:52:04
Elmwood 48	1	44N47	92w09	6:08:36
Elmwood Park 52	1	42N41	87w50	5:51:20
El Paso 48	1	44N44	92w20	6:09:20
Elroy 29	1	43N45	90w16	6:01:04
Elton	1	45N10	88w53	5:55:32
Embarrass 69	1	44N40	88w42	5:54:48
Emerald 56	1	45N05	92w20	6:09:20
Emerald Grove 54	1	42N41	89w01	5:56:04
Emery 51	1	45N43	90w07	6:00:28
Empire 20	1	43N45	88w21	5:53:24
Endeavor 39	1	43N43	89w29	5:57:56
Enterprise 44	1	45N31	89w18	5:57:12
Ephraim 15	1	45N09	87w10	5:48:40
Erdman 60	1	43N44	87w46	5:51:04
Erin 56	1	45N07	92w32	6:10:08
Erin 67	1	43N14	88w22	5:53:28
Erin Prairie 56	1	45N05	92w27	6:09:48
Esadore Lake 61	1	45N08	90w21	6:01:24
Esdaile 48	1	44N35	92w27	6:09:48
Esofea 63	1	43N39	90w51	6:03:24
Estella 9	1	45N09	91w07	6:04:28
Ettrick 62	1	44N10	91w16	6:05:04
Eureka 49	1	45N31	92w37	6:10:28
Eureka 71	1	44N00	88w51	5:55:24
Eureka Center 49	1	45N24	92w38	6:10:32
Euren 31	1	44N37	87w36	5:50:24
Evansville 54	1	42N47	89w18	5:57:12
Evergreen Park 60	1	43N44	87w46	5:51:04
Excelsior 53	1	43N11	90w34	6:02:16
Excelsior 57	1	43N31	89w53	5:59:32
Exeland 58	1	45N41	91w14	6:04:56
Exeter 23	1	42N50	89w31	5:58:04
Exile 48	1	44N38	92w12	6:08:48
Fairbanks 59	1	44N43	89w02	5:56:08
Fairburn 24	1	43N59	88w56	5:55:44
Fairchild 18	1	44N36	90w58	6:03:52
Fairfield 54	1	42N36	88w43	5:54:52
Fairfield 57	1	43N32	89w40	5:58:40
Fairplay 22	1	42N32	90w26	6:01:44
Fairview 6	1	44N25	92w00	6:08:00
Fairview 12	1	43N22	90w57	6:03:48
Fairview 41	1	43N00	88w00	5:52:00
Fairview Beach 71	1	44N01	88w33	5:54:12
Fair Water 20	1	43N44	88w52	5:55:28
Fall City 17	1	44N52	91w42	6:06:48
Fall Creek 18	1	44N46	91w17	6:05:08

Fall River 11	1	43N23	89w03	5:56:12
Falun 7	1	45N47	92w41	6:10:44
Fargo 63	1	43N33	90w53	6:03:32
Farmersville 14	1	43N31	88w34	5:54:16
Farmhill 48	1	44N47	92w09	6:08:36
Farmington 28	1	43N12	88w43	5:54:52
Fayette 33	1	42N46	90w01	6:00:04
Fence 19	1	45N45	88w25	5:53:40
Fennimore 22	1	42N59	90w39	6:02:36
Fenwood 37	1	44N52	90w01	6:00:04
Fern 19	1	45N51	88w23	5:53:32
Ferron Park 7	1	45N50	91w53	6:07:32
Ferryville 12	1	43N21	91w06	6:04:24
Fifield 51	1	45N53	90w25	6:01:40
Fillmore 67	1	43N28	87w57	5:51:48
Finley 29	1	44N12	90w08	6:00:32
Fish Creek 15	1	45N08	87w15	5:49:00
Fisk 71	1	44N01	88w33	5:54:12
Fitchburg 13	1	42N58	89w28	5:57:52
Five Corners 45	1	44N16	88w23	5:53:32
Five Corners 46	1	43N17	87w58	5:51:52
Fivepoints 53	1	43N11	90w34	6:02:16
Flambeau 55	1	45N13	91w07	6:04:28
Flintville 5	1	44N30	88w01	5:52:04
Florence 19	1	45N56	88w15	5:53:00
Folsom 63	1	43N24	90w47	6:03:08
Fond du Lac 20	2	43N47	88w27	5:53:48
Fontana 65	1	42N33	88w35	5:54:20
Fontana On Geneva Lake 65	1	42N33	88w34	5:54:16
Fontenoy 5	1	44N21	87w50	5:51:20
Footville 54	1	42N40	89w12	5:56:48
Ford 61	1	45N10	90w44	6:02:56
Forest 56	1	45N08	92w16	6:09:04
Forest Junction 8	1	44N13	88w09	5:52:36
Forestville 15	1	44N41	87w29	5:49:56
Fort Atkinson 28	1	42N56	88w50	5:55:20
Fort Winnebago 11	1	43N37	89w26	5:57:44
Forward 13	1	43N01	89w45	5:59:00
Foster 18	1	44N39	91w19	6:05:16
Fountain 29	1	43N51	90w14	6:00:56
Fountain City 6	1	44N08	91w43	6:06:52
Fountain Prairie 11	1	43N25	89w04	5:56:16
Four Corners 7	1	45N39	92w28	6:09:52
Foxboro 16	1	46N30	92w17	6:09:08
Fox Creek 49	1	45N27	92w27	6:09:48
Fox Lake 14	1	43N34	88w55	5:55:40
Fox Point 41	1	43N09	87w54	5:51:36
Fox River 30	1	42N40	88w16	5:53:04
Francis Creek 36	1	44N12	87w44	5:50:56
Franklin 27	1	44N13	91w07	6:04:28
Franklin 41	1	42N53	88w00	5:52:00
Franklin 60	1	43N44	87w59	5:51:56
Franksville 52	1	42N46	87w55	5:51:40
Franzen 37	1	44N49	89w18	5:57:12
Frazer 59	1	44N40	88w15	5:53:00
Frederic 49	1	45N40	92w28	6:09:52
Fred John 41	1	43N07	88w01	5:52:04
Fredonia 46	1	43N28	87w56	5:51:44
Freedom 45	1	44N23	88w17	5:53:08
Freeman 12	1	43N22	91w04	6:04:16
Freemans 34	1	45N19	88w51	5:55:24
Freistadt 46	1	43N08	87w57	5:51:48
Fremont 69	1	44N16	88w52	5:55:28
French Island 32	1	43N49	91w14	6:04:56
Frenchville 62	1	44N11	91w16	6:05:04
Friendship 1	1	43N58	89w49	5:59:16
Friesland 11	1	43N35	89w04	5:56:16
Frog Creek 66	1	46N07	91w42	6:06:48
Fulton 54	1	42N48	89w03	5:56:12
Fussville 68	1	43N10	88w07	5:52:28
Gale 62	1	44N07	91w19	6:05:16
Galesville 62	1	44N05	91w21	6:05:24
Galloway 37	1	44N43	89w16	5:57:04
Garden Valley 27	1	44N28	90w59	6:03:56
Garden Village 54	1	42N31	89w03	5:56:12
Gardner 15	1	44N48	87w35	5:50:20
Garfield 50	1	44N28	89w17	5:57:08
Gaslyn 7	1	45N53	92w22	6:09:28
Gays Mills 12	1	43N19	90w51	6:03:24
Genesee 68	1	42N57	88w22	5:53:28
Genesee Depot 68	1	42N58	88w22	5:53:28
Geneva 65	1	42N37	88w29	5:53:56
Genevesta 65	1	42N36	88w28	5:53:52
Genoa 63	1	43N35	91w13	6:04:52
Genoa City 65	1	42N30	88w20	5:53:20
Georgetown 22	1	42N36	90w26	6:01:44
Germania 26	1	46N26	90w15	6:01:00
Germania 39	1	43N53	89w16	5:57:04
Germantown 67	1	43N14	88w06	5:52:24
Gibbsville 60	1	43N42	87w49	5:51:16
Gibraltar 15	1	45N07	87w14	5:48:56
Gibson 36	1	44N17	87w43	5:50:52
Gile 26	1	46N26	90w15	6:01:00
Gillett 43	1	44N54	88w19	5:53:16
Gillingham 53	1	43N26	90w26	6:01:44
Gills Rock 15	1	45N17	87w01	5:48:04
Gilman 61	1	45N10	90w48	6:03:12
Gilmanton 6	1	44N28	91w41	6:06:44
Gingles 2	1	46N32	90w51	6:03:24
Glasgow 62	1	44N11	91w16	6:05:04
Gleason 35	1	45N18	89w30	5:58:00
Glenbeulah 60	1	43N46	88w03	5:52:12
Glencoe 6	1	44N17	91w35	6:06:20
Glendale 41	1	43N08	87w56	5:51:44
Glendale 42	1	43N47	90w22	6:01:28
Glen Flora 55	1	45N30	90w53	6:03:32
Glen Haven 22	1	42N50	91w04	6:04:16
Glenmore 5	1	44N22	87w57	5:51:48
Glenoak 39	1	43N48	89w19	5:57:16
Glenwood 56	1	45N05	92w12	6:08:48
Glenwood City 56	1	45N04	92w11	6:08:44
Glenwood-Downing 17	1	45N03	92w07	6:08:28

WISCONSIN

Place		Lat.	Long.	Time
Glidden 2	1	46N08	90w34	6:02:16
Goetz 9	1	44N59	91w08	6:04:32
Goldenthal 67	1	43N13	88w07	5:52:28
Goodman 38	1	45N38	88w21	5:53:24
Goodnow 44	1	45N40	89w39	5:58:36
Goodrich 61	1	45N09	90w05	6:00:20
Gooseville 60	1	43N33	87w58	5:51:52
Gordon 16	1	46N15	91w48	6:07:12
Gotham 53	1	43N13	90w18	6:01:12
Grafton 46	1	43N19	87w57	5:51:48
Grand Avenue Park 54	1	42N31	89w03	5:56:12
Grand Chute 45	1	44N17	88w25	5:53:40
Grand Marsh 1	1	43N53	89w42	5:58:48
Grand Rapids 72	1	44N23	89w46	5:59:04
Grand View 4	1	46N22	91w06	6:04:24
Grange Hall 48	1	44N33	92w19	6:09:16
Granton 10	1	44N35	90w28	6:01:52
Grantsburg 7	1	45N47	92w41	6:10:44
Gratiot 33	1	42N35	90w01	6:00:04
Gravesville 8	1	44N02	88w10	5:52:40
Green Bay 5	1	44N31	88w00	5:52:00
Greenbush 60	1	43N45	88w06	5:52:24
Greendale 41	1	42N57	87w59	5:51:56
Greenfield 41	1	42N58	88w00	5:52:00
Green Grove 10	1	44N54	90w29	6:01:56
Green Lake 24	1	43N51	88w58	5:55:52
Greenleaf	1	44N19	88w06	5:52:24
Greenridge Park 13	1	43N02	89w17	5:57:08
Greenstreet 36	1	44N17	87w49	5:51:16
Green Valley 59	1	44N48	88w16	5:53:04
Greenville 45	1	44N18	88w32	5:54:08
Greenwood 10	1	44N46	90w36	6:02:24
Grellton 28	1	43N12	88w43	5:54:52
Gresham 59	1	44N51	88w47	5:55:08
Grimms 36	1	44N09	87w57	5:51:48
Grow 55	1	45N26	90w58	6:03:52
Guenther 37	1	44N49	89w33	5:58:12
Gull Lake 66	1	46N01	91w43	6:06:52
Gurney 26	1	46N28	90w31	6:02:04
Guthrie 68	1	43N01	88w12	5:52:48
Hackett 51	1	45N36	90w19	6:01:16
Hager City 48	1	44N36	92w32	6:10:08
Halder 37	1	44N52	89w42	5:58:48
Hale 62	1	44N30	91w19	6:05:16
Hales Corners 41	1	42N56	88w03	5:52:12
Hallie 9	1	44N54	91w25	6:05:40
Halsey 37	1	45N03	90w01	6:00:04
Hamburg 37	1	45N05	89w53	5:59:32
Hamilton 32	1	43N55	91w05	6:04:20
Hammel 61	1	45N10	90w29	6:01:56
Hammond 56	1	44N59	92w27	6:09:48
Hampden 11	1	43N20	89w11	5:56:44
Hamples Corners 45	1	44N16	88w23	5:53:32
Hampton 41	1	43N07	88w00	5:52:00
Hancock 70	1	44N08	89w31	5:58:04
Haney 12	1	43N15	90w51	6:03:24
Hannibal 61	1	45N15	90w47	6:03:08
Hanover 54	1	42N38	89w10	5:56:40
Hansen 72	1	44N28	90w00	6:00:00
Happy Corners 22	1	42N36	90w26	6:01:44
Harbor 41	1	43N01	87w56	5:51:44
Harding 35	1	45N17	89w52	5:59:28
Harmony Corners 38	1	45N06	87w37	5:50:28
Harris 39	1	43N52	89w25	5:57:40
Harrison 35	1	45N18	89w30	5:58:00
Harrisville 39	1	43N53	89w29	5:57:56
Harshaw 44	1	45N40	89w39	5:58:36
Hartford 67	1	43N19	88w22	5:53:28
Hartland 68	1	43N06	88w21	5:53:24
Hatchville 17	1	44N53	91w56	6:07:44
Hatfield 27	1	44N25	90w44	6:02:56
Hatley 37	1	44N56	89w20	5:57:20
Hauer 58	1	45N51	91w32	6:06:08
Haugen 3	1	45N37	91w46	6:07:04
Haven 60	1	43N51	87w45	5:51:00
Hawkins 55	1	45N31	90w43	6:02:52
Hawthorne 16	1	46N30	91w52	6:07:28
Hayes 43	1	45N00	88w21	5:53:24
Hay River 17	1	45N05	91w57	6:07:48
Hayton 8	1	44N02	88w10	5:52:40
Hayward 58	1	46N01	91w29	6:05:56
Hazel Green 22	1	42N32	90w26	6:01:44
Hazelhurst 44	1	45N48	89w43	5:58:52
Heafford Junction 35	1	45N33	89w43	5:58:52
Heart Prairie 65	1	42N50	88w45	5:55:00
Hebel 5	1	44N21	87w50	5:51:20
Hebron 28	1	42N56	88w42	5:54:48
Heffron 70	1	44N17	89w23	5:57:32
Hegg 62	1	44N11	91w16	6:05:04
Helena 25	1	43N10	89w55	5:59:40
Helenville 28	1	43N01	88w41	5:54:44
Helvetia 69	1	44N33	89w03	5:56:12
Hendren 10	1	44N43	90w44	6:02:56
Henrietta 53	1	43N30	90w23	6:01:32
Henrysville 5	1	44N32	87w42	5:50:48
Herbster 4	1	46N50	91w16	6:05:04
Herman Center 14	1	43N31	88w34	5:54:16
Herold 6	1	44N20	91w55	6:07:40
Hersey 56	1	44N57	92w11	6:08:44
Hertel 7	1	45N49	92w11	6:08:44
Hewett 10	1	44N33	90w44	6:02:56
Hewitt 37	1	45N03	89w25	5:57:40
Hewitt 72	1	44N39	90w06	6:00:24
Hickory Corners 43	1	45N00	88w21	5:53:24
Hickory Grove 22	1	43N05	90w36	6:02:24
High Bridge 2	1	46N23	90w44	6:02:56
High Cliff 8	1	44N13	88w25	5:53:40
Highland 25	1	43N21	90w21	6:01:24
Highland Shore 71	1	44N01	88w33	5:54:12
Hika 36	1	43N55	87w45	5:51:00
Hilbert 8	1	44N09	88w10	5:52:40
Hilbert Junction 8	1	44N08	88w10	5:52:40
Hiles 21	1	45N43	88w59	5:55:56
Hill 51	1	45N26	90w13	6:00:52
Hillcrest 16	1	46N36	91w59	6:07:56
Hilldale 13	1	43N07	89w27	5:57:48
Hillpoint 57	1	43N26	90w07	6:00:28
Hillsboro 63	1	43N39	90w21	6:01:24
Hillsdale 3	1	45N19	91w52	6:07:28
Hillside 13	1	42N59	89w02	5:56:08
Hilltop 41	1	43N03	87w56	5:51:44
Hines 16	1	46N33	91w55	6:07:40
Hingham 60	1	43N38	87w55	5:51:40
Hintz 43	1	44N53	88w17	5:53:08
Hixon 10	1	44N59	90w37	6:02:28
Hixton 27	1	44N23	91w01	6:04:04
Hoard 10	1	44N59	90w30	6:02:00
Hobart 5	1	44N30	88w10	5:52:40
Hofa Park 59	1	44N31	88w20	5:53:20
Hoffman Corners 42	1	43N47	90w22	6:01:28
Holcombe 9	1	45N14	91w07	6:04:28
Holiday Hills 54	1	42N31	89w03	5:56:12
Holland 5	1	44N17	88w17	5:53:08
Hollandale 25	1	42N53	89w56	5:59:44
Hollister 34	1	45N15	88w48	5:55:12
Holmen 32	1	43N58	91w15	6:05:00
Holton 37	1	45N00	90w15	6:01:00
Holway 61	1	45N05	90w29	6:01:56
Holycross 46	1	43N30	87w51	5:51:24
Homestead 19	1	45N47	88w15	5:53:00
Honey Creek 57	1	43N19	89w55	5:59:40
Honey Creek 65	1	42N45	88w19	5:53:16
Honey Lake 52	1	42N40	88w16	5:53:04
Hoopers Mill 28	1	43N05	88w55	5:55:40
Hope 13	1	43N04	89w19	5:57:16
Horicon 14	1	43N27	88w38	5:54:32
Horns Corners 46	1	43N17	87w58	5:51:52
Horse Creek 49	1	45N12	92w32	6:10:08
Hortonia 45	1	44N21	88w40	5:54:40
Hortonville 45	1	44N20	88w38	5:54:32
Houghton 4	1	46N41	90w54	6:03:36
Houlton 56	1	44N59	92w47	6:11:08
How 43	1	44N59	88w25	5:53:40
Howard 5	1	44N31	88w03	5:52:12
Howards Grove 60	1	43N44	87w46	5:51:04
Hubbellton 28	1	43N12	88w43	5:54:52
Hub City 53	1	43N20	90w27	6:01:48
Hubertus 67	1	43N14	88w12	5:52:48
Hudson 56	1	44N58	92w45	6:11:00
Hughes 4	1	46N32	91w29	6:05:56
Hullsburg 14	1	43N20	88w27	5:53:48
Humbird 10	1	44N32	90w53	6:03:32
Humboldt 5	1	44N30	87w49	5:51:16
Hunter 58	1	45N55	91w13	6:04:52
Hunting 59	1	44N44	89w04	5:56:16
Huntington 56	1	45N07	92w32	6:10:08
Hurley 26	1	46N27	90w11	6:00:44
Huron 9	1	44N58	90w56	6:03:44
Hurricane 22	1	42N51	90w43	6:02:52
Husher 52	1	42N50	87w57	5:51:48
Hustisford 14	1	43N21	88w36	5:54:24
Hustler 29	1	43N52	90w16	6:01:04
Hutchins 59	1	44N59	89w02	5:56:08
Idlewild 15	1	44N50	87w22	5:49:28
Iduna 62	1	44N11	91w16	6:05:04
Imalone 55	1	45N27	91w17	6:05:08
Independence 62	1	44N22	91w25	6:05:40
Indian Creek 49	1	45N41	92w18	6:09:12
Indianford 54	1	42N50	89w04	5:56:16
Indian Shores 71	1	44N07	88w43	5:54:52
Ingersoll 37	1	44N52	89w12	5:56:48
Ingram 55	1	45N31	90w49	6:03:16
Inlet 65	1	42N37	88w37	5:54:28
Ino 4	1	46N26	91w04	6:04:16
Institute 15	1	44N54	87w17	5:49:08
Iola 69	1	44N30	89w08	5:56:32
Irma 35	1	45N21	89w40	5:58:40
Iron Belt 26	1	46N24	90w19	6:01:16
Iron Ridge 14	1	43N24	88w32	5:54:08
Iron River 4	1	46N34	91w24	6:05:36
Ironton 57	1	43N31	90w07	6:00:28
Irving 27	1	44N11	90w58	6:03:52
Irvington 17	1	44N53	91w56	6:07:44
Isaar 45	1	44N31	88w20	5:53:20
Isabelle 48	1	44N35	92w25	6:09:40
Island Beach 71	1	44N01	88w33	5:54:12
Island Lake 55	1	45N12	91w34	6:06:16
Island Park 71	1	44N02	88w44	5:54:56
Itasca 16	1	46N42	92w05	6:08:20
Ithaca 53	1	43N20	90w16	6:01:04
Ives 52	1	42N44	87w48	5:51:12
Ives Grove 52	1	42N44	87w52	5:51:28
Ixonia 28	1	43N09	88w36	5:54:24
Jackson 67	1	43N19	88w10	5:52:40
Jacksonport 15	1	44N59	87w11	5:48:44
Jacobs 2	1	46N07	90w35	6:02:20
Jamestown 22	1	42N34	90w36	6:02:24
Janesville 54	1	42N41	89w01	5:56:04
Jefferson 28	1	43N00	88w48	5:55:12
Jefferson Junction 28	1	43N00	88w48	5:55:12
Jeffris 35	1	45N18	89w30	5:58:00
Jennings 44	1	45N30	89w10	5:56:40
Jericho 8	1	44N02	88w10	5:52:40
Jericho 68	1	42N53	88w28	5:53:52
Jersey City 35	1	45N28	89w44	5:58:56
Jewett 56	1	45N07	92w32	6:10:08
Jim Falls 9	1	45N03	91w16	6:05:04
Joel 49	1	45N18	92w21	6:09:24
Johnsburg 20	1	43N53	88w18	5:53:12
Johnson 37	1	45N00	90w08	6:00:32
Johnson Creek 28	1	43N05	88w46	5:55:04
Johnsonville 60	1	43N42	87w49	5:51:16
Johnstown 54	1	43N11	90w19	6:01:16
Johnstown Center 54	1	42N42	88w51	5:55:24
Jonesdale 25	1	42N52	90w11	6:00:44
Jordan 23	1	42N39	89w46	5:59:04
Jordan 50	1	44N31	89w34	5:58:16
Juda 23	1	42N35	89w30	5:58:00
Jump River 61	1	45N20	90w44	6:02:56
Junction City 50	1	44N35	89w46	5:59:04
Juneau 14	1	43N24	88w42	5:54:48
Juneau 41	1	43N03	87w54	5:51:36
Kaiser 51	1	45N56	90w27	6:01:48
Kansasville 52	1	42N41	88w07	5:52:28
Karlsborg 7	1	45N53	92w22	6:09:28
Kaukauna 45	1	44N17	88w17	5:53:08
Keene 50	1	44N19	89w31	5:58:04
Keenville 71	1	44N01	88w33	5:54:12
Kekoskee 14	1	43N31	88w34	5:54:16
Kelley Brook 43	1	44N58	88w03	5:52:12
Kellner 50	1	44N22	89w44	5:58:56
Kellnersville 36	1	44N14	87w48	5:51:12
Kelly 4	1	46N27	90w59	6:03:56
Kelly 37	1	44N56	89w36	5:58:24
Kempster 34	1	45N18	89w10	5:56:40
Kendall 42	1	43N48	90w21	6:01:24
Kennan 51	1	45N37	90w37	6:02:28
Kenosha 30	3	42N35	87w49	5:51:16
Keshena 40	1	44N53	88w39	5:54:36
Keshena Falls 40	1	44N52	88w38	5:54:32
Kewaskum 67	1	43N31	88w14	5:52:56
Kewaunee 31	1	44N27	87w31	5:50:04
Keyesville 53	1	43N26	90w07	6:00:28
Keyser 11	1	43N15	89w21	5:57:24
Keystone 4	1	46N31	91w09	6:04:36
Keystone 9	1	45N10	91w09	6:04:36
Kickapoo 63	1	43N28	90w45	6:03:00
Kickapoo Center 63	1	43N30	90w40	6:02:40
Kiel 36	1	43N55	88w02	5:52:08
Kieler 22	1	42N40	90w36	6:02:24
Kildare 29	1	43N44	89w54	5:59:36
Kimball 26	1	46N29	90w17	6:01:08
Kimberly 45	1	44N16	88w20	5:53:20
King 35	1	45N31	89w36	5:58:24
King 69	1	44N20	89w08	5:56:32
Kingston 24	1	43N42	89w08	5:56:32
Kinnickinnic 56	1	44N54	92w33	6:10:12
Kirby 42	1	44N08	90w30	6:02:00
Kirchhayn 67	1	43N17	87w58	5:51:52
Klevenville 13	1	43N01	89w45	5:59:00
Klondike 43	1	45N04	88w02	5:52:08
Knapp 17	1	44N57	92w05	6:08:20
Kneeland 52	1	42N50	87w57	5:51:48
Knellsville 46	1	43N23	87w53	5:51:32
Knight 26	1	46N17	90w21	6:01:24
Knowles 14	1	43N34	88w30	5:54:00
Knowlton 37	1	44N49	89w40	5:58:40
Knox 51	1	45N32	90w06	6:00:24
Knox Mills 51	1	45N34	90w07	6:00:28
Kohlberg 15	1	44N42	87w29	5:49:56
Kohler 60	1	43N43	87w47	5:51:08
Kohlsville 67	1	43N25	88w11	5:52:44
Komensky 27	1	44N22	90w38	6:02:32
Koro 71	1	43N59	88w56	5:55:44
Koshkonong 54	1	42N53	88w50	5:55:20
Kossuth 36	1	44N12	87w44	5:50:56
Krakow 59	1	44N46	88w15	5:53:00
Kroghville 28	1	43N12	88w59	5:55:56
Krok 31	1	44N27	87w30	5:50:00
Kronenwetter 37	1	44N53	89w38	5:58:32
Kruger 7	1	45N53	92w22	6:09:28
Kunesh 5	1	44N40	88w15	5:53:00
Lac Courte Oreilles Indian R 58	1	46N35	90w53	6:03:32
Lac du Flambeau 64	1	45N58	89w53	5:59:32
Lac du Flambeau Indian Reser 26	1	46N35	90w53	6:03:32
Lac La Belle 68	1	43N09	88w31	5:54:04
La Crosse 32	4	43N48	91w15	6:05:00
Ladoga 20	1	43N38	88w44	5:54:56
Ladysmith 55	1	45N28	91w12	6:04:48
La Farge 63	1	43N35	90w38	6:02:32
La Follette 7	1	45N46	92w13	6:08:52
La Grange 65	1	42N48	88w36	5:54:24
Lake Beulah 65	1	42N49	88w19	5:53:16
Lake Butte des Morts 71	1	44N02	88w36	5:54:24
Lake Church 46	1	43N30	87w51	5:51:24
Lake Como Beach 65	1	42N36	88w28	5:53:52
Lake Delton 57	1	43N35	89w47	5:59:08
Lake Eau Claire 18	1	44N41	91w07	6:04:28
Lake Emily 50	1	44N28	89w17	5:57:08
Lakefield 46	1	43N19	87w58	5:51:52
Lake Five 67	1	43N12	88w16	5:53:04
Lake Geneva 65	1	42N36	88w26	5:53:44
Lake George 30	1	42N34	88w03	5:52:12
Lake George 44	1	45N38	89w25	5:57:40
Lake Hallie 9	1	44N55	91w23	6:05:32
Lake Holcombe 9	1	45N15	91w06	6:04:24
Lake Keesus 68	1	43N07	88w23	5:53:32
Lakeland 3	1	45N36	91w58	6:07:52
Lakeland College 60	1	43N44	87w46	5:51:04
Lake Michigan Estates 30	1	42N35	87w51	5:51:24
Lake Mills 28	1	43N05	88w55	5:55:40
Lake Nebagamon 16	1	46N31	91w42	6:06:48
Lakeshore 60	1	43N44	87w46	5:51:04
Lakeside 16	1	46N39	91w49	6:07:16
Lake Tomahawk 44	1	45N49	89w36	5:58:24
Laketown 49	1	45N35	92w35	6:10:20

Lake View 13 1 43N02 89w22 5:57:28
Lake View 60 1 43N44 87w46 5:51:04
Lake Wazeecha 72 1 44N23 89w46 5:59:04
Lake Windsor 13 1 43N13 89w20 5:57:20
Lake Wissota 9 1 44N55 91w18 6:05:12
Lakewood 43 1 45N18 88w31 5:54:04
Lamartine 20 1 43N44 88w34 5:54:16
Lamont 33 1 42N42 90w00 6:00:00
Lampson 66 1 45N59 91w50 6:07:20
Lanark 50 1 44N23 89w14 5:56:56
Lancaster 22 1 42N51 90w43 6:02:52
Land O)lakes 64 1 46N09 89w19 5:57:16
Land O'Lakes 64 1 46N10 89w13 5:56:52
Landstad 59 1 44N45 88w26 5:53:44
Langes 1 44N23 87w52 5:51:28
Langes Corner 5 1 44N21 87w50 5:51:20
Langlade 34 1 45N11 88w44 5:54:56
Lannon 68 1 43N09 88w10 5:52:40
Laona 21 1 45N34 88w40 5:54:40
La Pointe 2 1 46N47 90w47 6:03:08
La Prairie 54 1 42N38 88w56 5:55:44
Lark 5 1 44N19 88w06 5:52:24
Larrabee 69 1 44N39 88w49 5:55:16
Larsen 71 1 44N11 88w38 5:54:32
Larsons Beach 13 1 43N02 89w17 5:57:08
LaRue 57 1 43N27 89w52 5:59:28
Lasleys Point 71 1 44N07 88w43 5:54:52
Latto 25 1 42N58 90w08 6:00:32
Lauderdale 65 1 42N41 88w33 5:54:12
La Valle 57 1 43N35 90w08 6:00:32
LaVerne Dilweg 5 1 44N31 88w03 5:52:12
Lawrence 39 1 43N53 89w29 5:57:56
Layton Park 41 1 43N00 87w56 5:51:44
Leadmine 33 1 42N36 90w26 6:01:44
Lebanon 14 1 43N15 88w38 5:54:32
Leeds 11 1 43N19 89w18 5:57:12
Leeds Center 11 1 43N20 89w23 5:57:32
Leef 7 1 45N53 92w22 6:09:28
Leeman 45 1 44N27 88w34 5:54:16
Leipsig 14 1 43N27 88w51 5:55:24
Leland 57 1 43N20 89w57 5:59:48
Lemington 58 1 45N40 91w14 6:04:56
Lemonweir 29 1 43N47 90w01 6:00:04
Lena 43 1 44N57 88w03 5:52:12
Lenroot 58 1 46N07 91w26 6:05:44
Leola 1 1 44N13 89w39 5:58:36
Leon 42 1 43N53 90w51 6:03:24
Leonards Point 71 1 44N01 88w33 5:54:12
Leopolis 59 1 44N46 88w51 5:55:24
LeRoy 14 1 43N36 88w36 5:54:24
Lessor 59 1 44N37 88w25 5:53:40
Levis 10 1 44N28 90w37 6:02:28
Lewis 49 1 45N43 92w24 6:09:36
Lewiston 11 1 43N36 89w33 5:58:12
Leyden 54 1 42N44 89w08 5:56:32
Liberty Grove 15 1 45N13 87w03 5:48:12
Liberty Pole 63 1 43N29 90w55 6:03:40
Liddell 9 1 44N55 91w23 6:05:32
Lilly Lake 30 1 42N40 88w16 5:53:04
Lily 34 1 45N19 88w51 5:55:24
Lima Center 54 1 42N50 88w45 5:55:00
Limeridge 57 1 43N28 90w09 6:00:36
Lincoln 31 1 44N33 87w37 5:50:28
Lind 69 1 44N17 89w03 5:56:12
Lind Center 69 1 44N21 89w05 5:56:20
Linden 25 1 42N55 90w16 6:01:04
Lindina 29 1 43N46 90w08 6:00:32
Lindsey 72 1 44N33 89w58 5:59:52
Lindwerm 41 1 43N07 87w57 5:51:48
Linn 65 1 42N33 88w29 5:53:56
Linton 65 1 42N36 88w28 5:53:52
Linwood 50 1 44N29 89w40 5:58:40
Little Black 61 1 45N05 90w23 6:01:32
Little Chicago 37 1 44N57 89w50 5:59:20
Little Chute 45 1 44N17 88w18 5:53:12
Little Falls 42 1 44N05 90w51 6:03:24
Little Falls 49 1 45N18 92w21 6:09:24
Little Grant 22 1 42N54 90w50 6:03:20
Little Hope 69 1 44N21 89w05 5:56:20
Little Kohler 46 1 43N28 87w57 5:51:48
Little Prairie 65 1 42N53 88w28 5:53:52
Little Rapids 5 1 44N23 88w07 5:52:28
Little Rice 44 1 45N39 89w51 5:59:24
Little River 43 1 44N58 87w53 5:51:32
Little Rose 37 1 44N52 90w04 6:00:16
Little Sturgeon 15
1 44N44 87w37 5:50:28
Little Suamico 43 1 44N43 88w01 5:52:04
Little Wolf 69 1 44N28 88w56 5:55:44
Livingston 22 1 42N54 90w26 6:01:44
Lodi 11 1 43N19 89w32 5:58:08
Loganville 57 1 43N27 90w02 6:00:08
Lohrville 70 1 44N02 89w08 5:56:32
Lombard 10 1 44N57 90w48 6:03:12
Lomira 14 1 43N35 88w27 5:53:48
London 13 1 43N03 89w01 5:56:04
Lone Rock 29 1 43N55 90w16 6:01:04
Lone Rock 53 1 43N11 90w12 6:00:48
Long Lake 19 1 45N51 88w40 5:54:40
Longwood 10 1 44N53 90w36 6:02:24
Lookout 6 1 44N34 91w41 6:06:44
Loomis 38 1 45N04 87w45 5:51:00
Lorain 49 1 45N40 92w13 6:08:52
Loraine 49 1 45N32 92w02 6:08:08
Loretta 58 1 45N53 90w51 6:03:24
Lostcreek 48 1 44N44 92w29 6:09:56
Lost Lake 14 1 43N32 89w00 5:56:00
Louisburg 22 1 42N36 90w26 6:01:44
Louis Corners 36 1 43N55 88w02 5:52:08
Lowell 14 1 43N19 88w51 5:55:24
Lower Nemahbin Lake 68
1 43N06 88w29 5:53:56
Lowville 11 1 43N25 89w19 5:57:16
Loyal 10 1 44N44 90w30 6:02:00
Loyd 53 1 43N25 90w15 6:01:00
Lublin 61 1 45N05 90w43 6:02:52
Lucas 17 1 44N54 92w04 6:08:16
Luck 49 1 45N35 92w29 6:09:56
Ludington 18 1 44N50 91w08 6:04:32
Luger 51 1 45N37 90w21 6:01:24
Lugerville 51 1 45N37 90w21 6:01:24
Lund 47 1 44N28 92w15 6:09:00
Lunds 59 1 44N47 88w36 5:54:24
Luxemburg 31 1 44N33 87w42 5:50:48
Lykens 49 1 45N27 92w27 6:09:48
Lymantown 51 1 45N56 90w27 6:01:48
Lyndhurst 59 1 44N51 88w47 5:55:08
Lyndon Station 29 1 43N43 89w54 5:59:36
Lynn 10 1 44N33 90w22 6:01:28
Lynne 44 1 45N40 89w59 5:59:56
Lynxville 12 1 43N15 91w03 6:04:12
Lyons 65 1 42N39 88w21 5:53:24
Mackford 24 1 43N41 88w56 5:55:44
Mackville 45 1 44N21 88w25 5:53:40
Madge 66 1 45N45 91w43 6:06:52
Madison 13 1 43N04 89w24 5:57:36
Madsen 36 1 44N06 87w41 5:50:44
Magenta 18 1 44N48 91w29 6:05:56
Magnolia 54 1 42N43 89w18 5:57:12
Maiden Rock 48 1 44N34 92w18 6:09:12
Mallwood 54 1 42N50 89w04 5:56:16
Malone 20 1 43N52 88w17 5:53:08
Manawa 69 1 44N28 88w55 5:55:40
Manchester 24 1 43N41 89w03 5:56:12
Manitowish 26 1 46N08 90w01 6:00:04
Manitowish Waters 64
1 46N07 89w51 5:59:24
Manitowoc 36 1 44N05 87w41 5:50:44
Manitowoc Rapids 36
1 44N06 87w45 5:51:00
Manning 63 1 43N27 90w46 6:03:04
Manor Heights 60 1 42N54 91w06 6:04:24
Maple 16 1 46N37 91w42 6:06:48
Maple Bluff 13 1 43N07 89w22 5:57:28
Maple Creek 45 1 44N28 88w41 5:54:44
Mapledale 60 1 43N44 87w46 5:51:04
Maple Grove 36 1 44N09 87w57 5:51:48
Maplehurst 61 1 45N04 90w37 6:02:28
Maple Plain 3 1 45N36 92w06 6:08:24
Mapleton 68 1 43N06 88w29 5:53:56
Maple Valley 43 1 44N59 88w18 5:53:12
Maplewood 15 1 44N45 87w29 5:49:56
Marathon 37 1 44N56 89w50 5:59:20
Marathon City 37 1 44N57 89w50 5:59:20
Marblehead 20 1 43N42 88w22 5:53:28
Marcellon 11 1 43N36 89w18 5:57:12
Marengo 2 1 46N25 90w49 6:03:16
Maribel 36 1 44N17 87w48 5:51:12
Marietta 12 1 43N10 90w47 6:03:08
Marinette 38 1 45N06 87w38 5:50:32
Marion 69 1 44N39 88w54 5:55:36
Markesan 24 1 43N42 88w59 5:55:56
Markton 34 1 45N10 88w46 5:55:04
Marquette 24 1 43N44 89w07 5:56:28
Marshall 13 1 43N11 89w04 5:56:16
Marshfield 72 1 44N40 90w10 6:00:40
Marshland 6 1 44N07 91w41 6:06:44
Martell 48 1 44N50 92w24 6:09:36
Martinsville 13 1 43N11 89w35 5:58:20
Martintown 23 1 42N30 89w48 5:59:12
Marxville 13 1 43N11 89w48 5:59:12
Marytown 20 1 43N57 88w06 5:52:24
Mason 4 1 46N26 91w04 6:04:16
Mather 29 1 44N09 90w18 6:01:12
Matteson 69 1 44N38 88w41 5:54:44
Mattoon 59 1 45N01 89w02 5:56:08
Mauston 29 1 43N48 90w05 6:00:20
Maxville 6 1 44N33 91w57 6:07:48
Mayfair 41 1 43N03 88w02 5:52:08
Mayfield 67 1 43N19 88w10 5:52:40
Mayville 14 1 43N30 88w33 5:54:12
Mazomanie 13 1 43N11 89w48 5:59:12
McAllister 38 1 45N20 87w43 5:50:52
McCartney 22 1 42N43 91w00 6:04:00
McFarland 13 1 43N01 89w17 5:57:08
McMillan 37 1 44N49 90w07 6:00:28
McNaughton 44 1 45N44 89w33 5:58:12
Mead 10 1 44N49 90w44 6:02:56
Meadowbrook 58 1 45N41 91w07 6:04:28
Mecan 39 1 43N50 89w13 5:56:52
Medary 32 1 43N52 91w12 6:04:48
Medford 61 1 45N09 90w20 6:01:20
Medina 45 1 44N16 88w38 5:54:32
Meeham 50 1 44N27 89w33 5:58:12
Meeker 67 1 43N13 88w07 5:52:28
Meekers Grove 33 1 42N36 90w26 6:01:44
Meeme 36 1 43N56 87w52 5:51:28
Meenon 7 1 45N52 92w20 6:09:20
Meggers 36 1 43N57 88w06 5:52:24
Mellen 2 1 46N20 90w40 6:02:40
Melnik 36 1 44N09 87w49 5:51:16
Melrose 27 1 44N08 91w00 6:04:00
Melvina 42 1 43N48 90w47 6:03:08
Menasha 71 1 44N13 88w26 5:53:44
Menasha Junction 71
1 44N13 88w25 5:53:40
Menchalville 36 1 44N14 87w48 5:51:12
Menekaunee 38 1 45N06 87w37 5:50:28
Menominee 41 1 45N01 88w42 5:54:48
Menomonee Falls 68
1 43N11 88w07 5:52:28
Menomonie 17 1 44N53 91w55 6:07:40
Menomonie Junction 17
1 44N53 91w56 6:07:44
Mentor 10 1 44N33 90w52 6:03:28
Mequon 46 1 43N14 87w59 5:51:56
Mercer 26 1 46N10 90w04 6:00:16
Meridean 17 1 44N44 91w47 6:07:08
Merrill 35 1 45N11 89w41 5:58:44
Merrillan 27 1 44N27 90w50 6:03:20

Merrimac 57 1 43N22 89w37 5:58:28
Merton 68 1 43N09 88w19 5:53:16
Meteor 58 1 45N41 91w22 6:05:28
Metomen 20 1 43N46 88w49 5:55:16
Metz 71 1 44N15 88w53 5:55:32
Mid-city 41 1 43N03 87w58 5:51:52
Middle Inlet 38 1 45N18 88w00 5:52:00
Middle Ridge 32 1 43N53 90w59 6:03:56
Middleton 13 1 43N06 89w30 5:58:00
Midway 5 1 44N30 88w01 5:52:04
Midway 32 1 43N53 91w14 6:04:56
Mifflin 25 1 42N53 90w22 6:01:28
Mikana 3 1 45N36 91w36 6:06:24
Mikesville 71 1 44N01 88w33 5:54:12
Milan 37 1 44N59 90w11 6:00:44
Milford 28 1 43N09 88w51 5:55:24
Milladore 72 1 44N36 89w51 5:59:24
Millard 65 1 42N41 88w33 5:54:12
Millersville 60 1 43N44 87w46 5:51:04
Millhome 36 1 43N55 88w02 5:52:08
Mills Center 5 1 44N30 88w01 5:52:04
Millston 27 1 44N12 90w38 6:02:32
Milltown 49 1 45N32 92w30 6:10:00
Millville 22 1 43N01 90w57 6:03:48
Milton 54 1 42N47 88w56 5:55:44
Milton Junction 54
1 42N47 88w57 5:55:48
Milwaukee 41 5 43N02 87w55 5:51:40
Mindoro 32 1 44N01 91w06 6:04:24
Mineral Point 25 1 42N52 90w11 6:00:44
Minersville 2 1 46N25 90w49 6:03:16
Minnesota Junction 14
1 43N27 88w38 5:54:32
Minocqua 44 1 45N51 89w47 5:59:08
Minong 66 1 46N06 91w49 6:07:16
Misha Mokwa 6 1 44N38 91w58 6:07:52
Mishicot 36 1 44N14 87w38 5:50:32
Mitchell 60 1 43N40 88w06 5:52:24
Mitterhofer 61 1 44N57 90w48 6:03:12
Modena 6 1 44N27 91w47 6:07:08
Moeville 48 1 44N44 92w29 6:09:56
Mole Lake 21 1 45N29 88w59 5:55:56
Mole Lake Indian Reservation 21
1 46N35 90w53 6:03:32
Molitor 61 1 45N14 90w30 6:02:00
Monches 68 1 43N11 88w21 5:53:24
Mondovi 6 1 44N34 91w40 6:06:40
Monico 44 1 45N35 89w09 5:56:36
Monona 13 1 43N04 89w20 5:57:20
Monroe 23 1 42N36 89w38 5:58:32
Monroe Center 1 1 44N02 89w53 5:59:32
Montana 6 1 44N23 91w37 6:06:28
Montello 39 1 43N48 89w20 5:57:20
Monterey 68 1 43N10 88w30 5:54:00
Montfort 22 1 42N58 90w26 6:01:44
Monticello 23 1 42N45 89w36 5:58:24
Montpelier 31 1 44N27 87w42 5:50:48
Montreal 26 1 46N26 90w14 6:00:56
Montrose 13 1 42N55 89w34 5:58:16
Moon 37 1 44N52 89w42 5:58:48
Moquah 4 1 46N34 91w04 6:04:16
Morgan 43 1 44N49 88w11 5:52:44
Morgan 59 1 44N51 88w47 5:55:08
Morris 59 1 44N49 89w02 5:56:08
Morrison 5 1 44N17 87w57 5:51:48
Morrisonville 13 1 43N17 89w22 5:57:28
Morris Park 13 1 43N02 89w17 5:57:08
Morse 2 1 46N13 90w38 6:02:32
Moscow 25 1 42N52 89w54 5:59:36
Mosel 60 1 43N49 87w46 5:51:04
Mosinee 37 1 44N47 89w43 5:58:52
Mosinee Spur 16 1 46N15 91w48 6:07:12
Mosling 43 1 44N53 88w17 5:53:08
Moundville 39 1 43N41 89w27 5:57:48
Mountain 43 1 45N11 88w28 5:53:52
Mount Calvary 20 1 43N50 88w15 5:53:00
Mount Hope 22 1 42N58 90w51 6:03:24
Mount Horeb 13 1 43N00 89w45 5:59:00
Mount Ida 22 1 42N59 90w43 6:02:52
Mount Morris 70 1 44N07 89w11 5:56:44
Mount Sterling 12 1 43N19 90w56 6:03:44
Mount Tabor 63 1 43N47 90w22 6:01:28
Mount Vernon 13 1 43N01 89w45 5:59:00
Mount Zion 12 1 43N15 90w44 6:02:56
Mukwa 69 1 44N22 88w48 5:55:12
Mukwonago 68 1 42N52 88w20 5:53:20
Murphy Corner 45 1 44N17 88w17 5:53:08
Murry 55 1 45N35 91w19 6:05:16
Muscoda 22 1 43N11 90w27 6:01:48
Muskego 68 1 42N55 88w08 5:52:32
Myra 67 1 43N25 88w11 5:52:44
Nabob 67 1 43N25 88w11 5:52:44
Namekagon 4 1 46N13 91w03 6:04:12
Namur 15 1 44N44 87w37 5:50:28
Naples 6 1 44N33 91w35 6:06:20
Nasbro 14 1 43N37 88w30 5:54:00
Nasewaupee 15 1 44N49 87w27 5:49:48
Nash 4 1 46N35 90w53 6:03:32
Nashotah 68 1 43N06 88w24 5:53:36
Nashville 21 1 45N27 88w55 5:55:40
Nasonville 72 1 44N33 89w58 5:59:52
Navarino 59 1 44N37 88w30 5:54:00
Necedah 29 1 44N02 90w04 6:00:16
Neenah 71 1 44N11 88w28 5:53:52
Neillsville 10 1 44N34 90w36 6:02:24
Neith 60 1 43N48 88w01 5:52:04
Nekimi 71 1 43N57 88w36 5:54:24
Nekoosa 72 1 44N19 89w54 5:59:36
Nekoosa Junction 72
1 44N21 89w52 5:59:28
Nelma 21 1 46N06 88w39 5:54:36
Nelson 6 1 44N25 92w00 6:08:00
Nelsonville 50 1 44N30 89w16 5:57:04
Nenno 67 1 43N25 88w20 5:53:20
Neopit 40 1 44N59 88w50 5:55:20

WISCONSIN

Neosho 14	1	43N18	88w31	5:54:04
Nepeuskun 71	1	43N57	88w51	5:55:24
Neshkoro 39	1	43N58	89w13	5:56:52
Neuern 31	1	44N32	87w42	5:50:48
Neva 34	1	45N15	89w06	5:56:24
Neva Corners 34	1	45N14	89w09	5:56:36
Newald 21	1	45N44	88w42	5:54:48
New Amsterdam 32	1	43N58	91w15	6:05:00
Newark 54	1	42N33	89w11	5:56:44
New Auburn 9	1	45N12	91w33	6:06:12
New Berlin 68	1	42N59	88w06	5:52:24
Newbold 44	1	45N42	89w30	5:58:00
Newburg 67	1	43N26	88w03	5:52:12
Newburg Corners 32	1	43N53	90w59	6:03:56
New Centerville 56	1	44N58	92w23	6:09:32
New Chester 1	1	43N52	89w39	5:58:36
New Denmark 5	1	44N23	87w49	5:51:16
New Diggings 33	1	42N33	90w21	6:01:24
New Diggins	1	42N32	90w35	6:02:20
New Fane 20	1	43N31	88w14	5:52:56
New Franken 5	1	44N32	87w50	5:51:20
New Glarus 23	1	42N49	89w38	5:58:32
New Holstein 8	1	43N57	88w05	5:52:20
New Hope 50	1	44N33	89w15	5:57:00
New Johannesburg 56	1	45N07	92w32	6:10:08
New Lisbon 29	1	43N53	90w10	6:00:40
New London 69	1	44N23	88w45	5:55:00
New Lyme 42	1	44N07	90w45	6:03:00
New Miner 29	1	44N02	90w04	6:00:16
New Munster 30	1	42N35	88w14	5:52:56
Newport 11	1	43N37	89w42	5:58:48
New Post 58	1	45N48	91w18	6:05:12
New Prospect 20	1	43N36	88w17	5:53:08
New Richmond 56	1	45N07	92w32	6:10:08
New Rome 1	1	44N19	89w54	5:59:36
Newry 63	1	43N43	90w49	6:03:16
Newton 36	1	44N00	87w44	5:50:56
Newton 63	1	43N33	90w53	6:03:32
Newtonburg 36	1	44N06	87w41	5:50:44
Newville 54	1	42N50	89w04	5:56:16
Nghigh Bridge	1	46N24	90w44	6:02:56
Niagara 38	1	45N43	87w57	5:51:48
Nichols 45	1	44N34	88w28	5:53:52
Nippersink Manor 65	1	42N30	88w19	5:53:16
Nokomis 44	1	45N36	89w44	5:58:56
Nora 13	1	43N03	89w04	5:56:16
Nordheim 71	1	44N01	88w33	5:54:12
Norman 31	1	44N27	87w30	5:50:00
Norrie 37	1	44N56	89w17	5:57:08
Norske 69	1	44N30	89w07	5:56:28
North Andover 22	1	42N50	91w04	6:04:16
North Bay 52	1	42N46	87w47	5:51:08
North Beloit 54	1	42N31	89w03	5:56:12
North Bend 27	1	44N06	91w07	6:04:28
North Branch 27	1	44N26	90w54	6:03:36
North Bristol 13	1	43N12	89w13	5:56:52
North Cape 52	1	42N47	88w04	5:52:16
Northeim 36	1	44N00	87w44	5:50:56
Northfield 27	1	44N28	91w06	6:04:24
North Fond du Lac 20	1	43N48	88w29	5:53:56
North Freedom 57	1	43N28	89w52	5:59:28
North Hudson 56	1	45N00	92w45	6:11:00
North Lake 68	1	43N10	88w22	5:53:28
North Lancaster 22	1	42N54	90w43	6:02:52
Northland 69	1	44N30	89w07	5:56:28
North Leeds 11	1	43N20	89w23	5:57:32
North Lowell 14	1	43N24	88w42	5:54:48
North Menomonie 17	1	44N53	91w56	6:07:44
North Park 52	1	42N48	87w49	5:51:16
Northport 15	1	45N15	87w04	5:48:16
Northport 69	1	44N23	88w44	5:54:56
North Prairie 68	1	42N56	88w24	5:53:36
Northside 32	1	43N49	91w14	6:04:56
North Tomah 42	1	43N59	90w30	6:02:00
Northwoods Beach	1	45N55	91w24	6:05:36
North Woods Beach 58	1	46N01	91w29	6:05:56
North York 2	1	46N23	90w44	6:02:56
Norton 17	1	45N00	91w44	6:06:56
Norwalk 42	1	43N50	90w37	6:02:28
Norway 52	1	42N49	88w09	5:52:36
Norway Grove 13	1	43N15	89w21	5:57:24
Norway Ridge 42	1	44N08	90w30	6:02:00
Norwood 34	1	45N05	89w02	5:56:08
Nutterville 37	1	44N58	89w38	5:58:32
Nye 49	1	45N19	92w42	6:10:48
Oak Center 20	1	43N41	88w33	5:54:12
Oak Creek 41	1	42N52	87w55	5:51:40
Oakdale 42	1	43N58	90w23	6:01:32
Oakfield 20	1	43N41	88w33	5:54:12
Oak Grove 14	1	43N24	88w42	5:54:48
Oak Hill 28	1	42N52	88w35	5:54:20
Oakley 23	1	42N35	89w30	5:58:00
Oakridge 30	1	42N31	88w07	5:52:28
Oakwood 41	1	42N54	87w56	5:51:44
Oasis 70	1	44N12	89w24	5:57:36
Oconomowoc 68	1	43N07	88w30	5:54:00
Oconomowoc Lake 68	1	43N06	88w27	5:53:48
Oconomowoc Lake South 68	1	43N06	88w29	5:53:56
Oconto 43	1	44N53	87w52	5:51:28
Oconto Falls 43	1	44N53	88w08	5:52:32
Odanah 2	1	46N37	90w41	6:02:44
Ogdensburg 69	1	44N27	89w01	5:56:04
Ogema 51	1	45N27	90w18	6:01:12
Oil City 42	1	43N50	90w37	6:02:28
Ojibwa 58	1	45N48	91w07	6:04:28
Okauchee 68	1	43N07	88w27	5:53:48
Okauchee Lake 68	1	43N07	88w25	5:53:40
Okee 11	1	43N19	89w32	5:58:08
Old Albertville 9	1	45N00	91w44	6:06:56
Old Ashippun 14	1	43N14	88w31	5:54:04
Old Lebanon 14	1	43N12	88w43	5:54:52
Oliver 16	1	46N40	92w12	6:08:48
Olivet 48	1	44N51	92w14	6:08:56
Oma 26	1	46N17	90w02	6:00:08
Omro 71	1	44N02	88w45	5:55:00
Onalaska 32	1	43N53	91w14	6:04:56
Oneida 45	1	44N30	88w12	5:52:48
Oneida Indian Reservation 5	1	46N35	90w53	6:03:32
Ono 48	1	44N33	92w19	6:09:16
Ontario 63	1	43N43	90w35	6:02:20
Oostburg 60	1	43N37	87w48	5:51:12
Orange 29	1	43N56	90w15	6:01:00
Orange Mill 29	1	43N55	90w16	6:01:04
Oregon 13	1	42N56	89w23	5:57:32
Orfordville 54	1	42N38	89w16	5:57:04
Orienta 4	1	46N45	91w28	6:05:52
Orihula 71	1	44N15	88w53	5:55:32
Orion 53	1	43N15	90w21	6:01:24
Osborn 45	1	44N27	88w21	5:53:24
Osceola 49	1	45N19	92w42	6:10:48
Oshkosh 71	1	44N01	88w33	5:54:12
Osman 36	1	44N00	87w44	5:50:56
Osseo 62	1	44N35	91w13	6:04:52
Ostrander 69	1	44N23	88w44	5:54:56
Otsego 11	1	43N25	89w11	5:56:44
Ottawa 68	1	42N59	88w28	5:53:52
Oulu 4	1	46N38	91w30	6:06:00
Ourtown 60	1	43N42	87w49	5:51:16
Owen 10	1	44N57	90w33	6:02:12
Oxbo 58	1	45N53	90w51	6:03:24
Oxford 39	1	43N47	89w34	5:58:16
Pacific 11	1	43N30	89w24	5:57:36
Packwaukee 39	1	43N47	89w25	5:57:40
Paddock Lake 30	1	42N34	88w06	5:52:24
Padus 21	1	45N26	88w39	5:54:36
Palmyra 28	1	42N52	88w36	5:54:24
Paoli 13	1	42N52	89w33	5:58:12
Pardeeville 11	1	43N32	89w18	5:57:12
Parfreyville 69	1	44N21	89w05	5:56:20
Park Falls 51	1	45N56	90w27	6:01:48
Parkland 16	1	46N37	92w00	6:08:00
Parklawn 41	1	43N05	87w58	5:51:52
Park Mills 38	1	45N06	87w37	5:50:28
Park Ridge 50	1	44N31	89w32	5:58:08
Parrish 34	1	45N25	89w24	5:57:36
Parrish Junction 34	1	45N18	89w30	5:58:00
Patch Grove 22	1	42N56	90w58	6:03:52
Patzau 16	1	46N30	92w13	6:08:52
Pearson 34	1	45N22	89w01	5:56:04
Peck 34	1	45N15	89w14	5:56:56
Pecks Station 65	1	42N41	88w33	5:54:12
Peebles 20	1	44N17	88w21	5:53:24
Peeksville 2	1	46N07	90w29	6:01:56
Pelican 44	1	45N37	89w22	5:57:28
Pelican Lake 44	1	45N30	89w10	5:56:40
Pella 59	1	44N44	88w48	5:55:12
Pell Lake 65	1	42N32	88w21	5:53:24
Pembine 38	1	45N38	87w59	5:51:56
Pence 26	1	46N22	90w16	6:01:04
Peninsula Center 15	1	45N04	87w07	5:48:28
Pensaukee 43	1	44N50	87w55	5:51:40
Pepin 47	1	44N27	92w09	6:08:36
Peplin 37	1	44N52	89w42	5:58:48
Perida 7	1	45N53	92w22	6:09:28
Perkinstown 61	1	45N08	90w21	6:01:24
Perry 13	1	42N54	89w49	5:59:16
Perry Go Place 54	1	42N33	89w02	5:56:08
Pershing 61	1	45N15	90w51	6:03:24
Peru 50	1	44N34	89w15	5:57:00
Peshtigo 38	1	45N03	87w45	5:51:00
Petersburg 12	1	43N18	90w50	6:03:20
Pewaukee 68	1	43N05	88w16	5:53:04
Pewaukee West 68	1	43N04	88w20	5:53:20
Phantom Lake 68	1	42N52	88w20	5:53:20
Pheasant Branch 13	1	43N07	89w26	5:57:44
Phelps 64	1	46N04	89w05	5:56:20
Phillips 51	1	45N42	90w24	6:01:36
Phipps 58	1	46N01	91w29	6:05:56
Phlox 34	1	45N03	89w01	5:56:04
Piacenza 71	1	44N07	88w43	5:54:52
Pickerel 21	1	45N23	88w54	5:55:36
Pickett 71	1	43N54	88w44	5:54:56
Piehl 44	1	45N41	89w07	5:56:28
Pierce 31	1	44N32	87w30	5:50:00
Pigeon 62	1	44N26	91w13	6:04:52
Pigeon Falls 62	1	44N26	91w13	6:04:52
Pilsen 31	1	44N27	87w44	5:50:56
Pine Bluff 13	1	43N07	89w40	5:58:40
Pine Creek 62	1	44N08	91w33	6:06:12
Pine Grove 5	1	44N30	88w01	5:52:04
Pine Grove 50	1	44N18	89w33	5:58:12
Pinehill 27	1	44N17	90w51	6:03:24
Pine Knob 25	1	42N48	89w51	5:59:24
Pine Lake 26	1	46N27	90w12	6:00:48
Pine Lake 44	1	45N42	89w23	5:57:32
Pine River 35	1	45N10	89w33	5:58:12
Pine River 70	1	44N09	89w05	5:56:20
Pine Valley 10	1	44N33	90w37	6:02:28
Pipe 20	1	43N55	88w19	5:53:16
Pipersville 28	1	43N12	88w43	5:54:52
Pittsfield 5	1	44N38	88w11	5:52:44
Pittsville 72	1	44N27	90w08	6:00:32
Plain 57	1	43N15	90w03	6:00:12
Plainfield 70	1	44N13	89w30	5:58:00
Plainville 1	1	43N43	89w49	5:59:16
Plat 67	1	43N13	88w17	5:53:08
Platteville 22	1	42N44	90w29	6:01:56
Pleasant Prairie 30	1	42N32	87w52	5:51:28
Pleasant Ridge 25	1	42N58	90w08	6:00:32
Pleasant View 27	1	44N17	90w51	6:03:24
Pleasantville 62	1	44N37	91w14	6:04:56
Plover 50	1	44N27	89w33	5:58:12
Plugtown 12	1	43N08	90w42	6:02:48
Plum City 48	1	44N38	92w11	6:08:44
Plum Lake 64	1	46N02	89w31	5:58:04
Plymouth 60	1	43N45	87w59	5:51:56
Poland 5	1	44N30	88w01	5:52:04
Polar 34	1	45N10	88w59	5:55:56
Polifka Corners 36	1	44N09	87w49	5:51:16
Polk 67	1	43N20	88w15	5:53:00
Polley 61	1	45N10	90w48	6:03:12
Polonia 50	1	44N34	89w25	5:57:40
Poniatowski 37	1	44N57	89w57	5:59:48
Poplar 16	1	46N35	91w47	6:07:08
Popple Lake 9	1	44N55	91w23	6:05:32
Popple River 21	1	45N50	88w44	5:54:56
Porcupine 47	1	44N38	92w02	6:08:08
Portage 11	1	43N33	89w28	5:57:52
Portage Junction 11	1	43N33	89w28	5:57:52
Port Andrew 53	1	43N11	90w34	6:02:16
Port Edwards 72	1	44N21	89w52	5:59:28
Porter 54	1	42N48	89w11	5:56:44
Porterfield 38	1	45N09	87w48	5:51:12
Port Junction 46	1	43N23	87w53	5:51:32
Portland 14	1	43N12	88w59	5:55:56
Portland 42	1	43N46	90w47	6:03:08
Port Washington 46	1	43N23	87w53	5:51:32
Port Wing 4	1	46N47	91w23	6:05:32
Poskin 3	1	45N24	91w58	6:07:52
Post Lake 34	1	45N26	89w11	5:56:44
Postville 23	1	42N48	89w45	5:59:00
Potawatomi Indian Reservatio 21	1	46N35	90w53	6:03:32
Potosi 22	1	42N43	90w43	6:02:52
Potter 8	1	44N07	88w06	5:52:24
Potter Lake 65	1	42N48	88w24	5:53:36
Potts Corners 63	1	43N35	90w38	6:02:32
Pound 38	1	45N04	88w02	5:52:08
Powers Lake 30	1	42N33	88w17	5:53:08
Poygan 71	1	44N06	88w49	5:55:16
Poynette 11	1	43N24	89w24	5:57:36
Poy Sippi 70	1	44N08	89w00	5:56:00
Praag 6	1	44N20	91w55	6:07:40
Prairie Corners 22	1	42N32	90w26	6:01:44
Prairie du Chien 12	1	43N03	91w09	6:04:36
Prairie du Sac 57	1	43N17	89w43	5:58:52
Prairie Farm 3	1	45N14	91w59	6:07:56
Prairie Lake 3	1	45N21	91w43	6:06:52
Pratt 4	1	46N20	91w05	6:04:20
Pray 27	1	44N27	90w07	6:00:28
Preble 5	1	44N31	87w59	5:51:56
Prentice 51	1	45N33	90w17	6:01:08
Prescott 48	1	44N45	92w48	6:11:12
Presque Isle 64	1	46N15	89w44	5:58:56
Preston 22	1	42N59	90w39	6:02:36
Price 27	1	44N36	90w58	6:03:52
Price 34	1	45N15	88w59	5:55:56
Primrose 13	1	42N54	89w41	5:58:44
Princeton 24	1	43N51	89w08	5:56:32
Pulaski 5	1	44N41	88w15	5:53:00
Pulcifer 59	1	44N51	88w22	5:53:28
Purdy 63	1	43N33	90w53	6:03:32
Quarry 36	1	44N09	87w57	5:51:48
Quincy 1	1	43N54	89w55	5:59:40
Quinney 8	1	44N02	88w10	5:52:40
Racine 52	1	42N44	87w48	5:51:12
Radisson 58	1	45N46	91w13	6:04:52
Randall 7	1	45N47	92w41	6:10:44
Randall 30	1	42N32	88w15	5:53:00
Randolph 11	1	43N35	89w03	5:56:12
Random Lake 60	1	43N33	87w58	5:51:52
Range 49	1	45N24	92w17	6:09:08
Rankin 31	1	44N36	87w26	5:49:44
Rantoul 8	1	44N06	88w06	5:52:24
Rawson 41	1	42N55	87w54	5:51:36
Raymond 52	1	42N49	88w01	5:52:04
Readfield 69	1	44N16	88w46	5:55:04
Readstown 63	1	43N27	90w45	6:03:00
Red Banks 69	1	44N15	88w53	5:55:32
Red Cedar 17	1	44N53	91w50	6:07:20
Red Cliff 4	1	46N52	90w47	6:03:08
Red Cliff Indian Reservation 4	1	46N35	90w53	6:03:32
Redgranite 70	1	44N03	89w06	5:56:24
Red Mound 63	1	43N26	91w12	6:04:48
Red River 31	1	44N38	87w43	5:50:52
Red River 59	1	44N47	88w36	5:54:24
Red Springs 59	1	44N53	88w48	5:55:12
Redville 61	1	44N57	90w36	6:02:24
Reedsburg 57	1	43N32	90w00	6:00:00
Reedsville 36	1	44N09	87w57	5:51:48
Reeseville 14	1	43N18	88w51	5:55:24
Reeve 3	1	45N20	92w11	6:08:44
Reid 37	1	44N53	89w25	5:57:40
Reighmoor 71	1	44N02	88w44	5:54:56
Remington 72	1	44N18	90w11	6:00:44
Reseburg 10	1	44N54	90w44	6:02:56
Reserve 58	1	45N51	91w32	6:06:08
Retreat 63	1	43N26	91w12	6:04:48
Rewey 25	1	42N51	90w24	6:01:36
Rhine 60	1	43N49	87w58	5:51:52
Rhinelander 44	1	45N38	89w25	5:57:40
Rib Falls 37	1	44N58	89w54	5:59:36
Rib Lake 61	1	45N19	90w12	6:00:48
Rib Mountain 37	1	44N56	89w41	5:58:44

WISCONSIN

Place		Lat.	Long.	Time
Rice Lake 3	1	45N30	91w44	6:06:56
Richardson 49	1	45N20	92w11	6:08:44
Richfield 67	1	43N15	88w12	5:52:48
Richford 70	1	44N01	89w26	5:57:44
Richland Center 53	1	43N21	90w23	6:01:32
Richmond 65	1	42N37	88w37	5:54:28
Richwood 14	1	43N15	88w47	5:55:08
Ridgeland 17	1	45N12	91w54	6:07:36
Ridgeville 42	1	43N52	90w36	6:02:24
Ridgeway 25	1	43N00	90w00	6:00:00
Rief's Mills 36	1	44N09	87w49	5:51:16
Rietbrock 37	1	44N59	90w01	6:00:04
Rileys 13	1	42N59	89w32	5:58:08
Ring 71	1	44N01	88w33	5:54:12
Ringle 37	1	44N53	89w26	5:57:44
Rio 11	1	43N27	89w14	5:56:56
Rio Creek 31	1	44N35	87w32	5:50:08
Riplinger 10	1	44N50	90w24	6:01:36
Ripon 20	1	43N51	88w50	5:55:20
Ripon Junction 20	1	43N51	88w50	5:55:20
Rising Sun 12	1	43N21	91w06	6:04:24
River Falls 48	1	44N52	92w38	6:10:32
River Hills 41	1	43N10	87w56	5:51:44
Rivermoor 71	1	44N02	88w44	5:54:56
Riverside 33	1	42N34	90w01	6:00:04
Riverview 43	1	45N15	88w27	5:53:48
Roaringcreek 27	1	44N17	90w51	6:03:24
Roberts 56	1	44N59	92w33	6:10:12
Robinson 65	1	42N36	88w28	5:53:52
Rochester 52	1	42N44	88w15	5:53:00
Rockbridge 53	1	43N27	90w22	6:01:28
Rock Creek 17	1	44N43	91w43	6:06:52
Rockdale 13	1	42N58	89w03	5:56:12
Rock Elm 48	1	44N43	92w12	6:08:48
Rock Falls 17	1	44N43	91w42	6:06:48
Rock Falls 35	1	45N20	89w44	5:58:56
Rockfield 67	1	43N15	88w08	5:52:32
Rockland 32	1	43N54	90w55	6:03:40
Rock Springs 57	1	43N29	89w55	5:59:40
Rockton 63	1	43N35	90w38	6:02:32
Rockville 22	1	42N41	90w42	6:02:48
Rockville 36	1	43N55	88w02	5:52:08
Rockwood 36	1	44N06	87w41	5:50:44
Rodell 18	1	44N41	91w07	6:04:28
Rogersville 20	1	43N49	88w40	5:54:40
Rolling 34	1	45N05	89w09	5:56:36
Rolling Ground 12	1	43N24	90w47	6:03:08
Rolling Prairie 14	1	43N24	88w42	5:54:48
Romance 63	1	43N35	91w14	6:04:56
Rome 1	1	44N12	89w46	5:59:04
Rome 28	1	43N01	88w35	5:54:20
Roosevelt 44	1	45N38	89w25	5:57:40
Roosevelt 59	1	44N51	88w47	5:55:08
Rose 70	1	44N12	89w18	5:57:12
Rosecrans 36	1	44N17	87w49	5:51:16
Rose Lawn 59	1	44N31	88w20	5:53:20
Rosemere 36	1	44N06	87w41	5:50:44
Rosendale 20	1	43N49	88w41	5:54:44
Rosholt 50	1	44N38	89w18	5:57:12
Rosiere 31	1	44N33	87w37	5:50:28
Ross 21	1	45N44	88w44	5:54:56
Ross 63	1	43N33	90w53	6:03:32
Rostok 31	1	44N27	87w30	5:50:00
Rothschild 37	1	44N53	89w37	5:58:28
Round Lake 58	1	46N02	91w14	6:04:56
Rowleys Bay 15	1	45N15	87w04	5:48:16
Roxbury 13	1	43N15	89w41	5:58:44
Royalton 69	1	44N25	88w52	5:55:28
Rozellville 37	1	44N45	90w01	6:00:04
Rubicon 14	1	43N20	88w28	5:53:52
Ruby 9	1	45N14	90w59	6:03:56
Rudolph 72	1	44N30	89w48	5:59:12
Rural 69	1	44N21	89w05	5:56:20
Rushford 71	1	44N01	88w50	5:55:20
Rush Lake	1	43N56	88w51	5:55:24
Rush Lake Junction 71	1	43N51	88w50	5:55:20
Rush River 56	1	44N54	92w25	6:09:40
Rusk 17	1	44N54	91w50	6:07:20
Russell 62	1	44N23	91w26	6:05:44
Rutland 13	1	42N53	89w21	5:57:24
Sabin 53	1	43N20	90w27	6:01:48
Saint Anna 8	1	43N57	88w06	5:52:24
Saint Anthony 67	1	43N25	88w20	5:53:20
Saint Cloud 20	1	43N50	88w10	5:52:40
Saint Croix Falls 49	1	45N24	92w38	6:10:32
Saint Croix Indian Reservati 66	1	46N35	90w53	6:03:32
Saint Francis 41	1	42N58	87w52	5:51:28
Saint George 60	1	43N42	87w49	5:51:16
Saint Germain 64	1	45N55	89w29	5:57:56
Saint John 8	1	44N08	88w10	5:52:40
Saint Joseph 20	1	43N50	88w10	5:52:40
Saint Joseph 32	1	43N49	91w14	6:04:56
Saint Joseph 56	1	45N03	92w43	6:10:52
Saint Kilian 20	1	43N36	88w17	5:53:08
Saint Lawrence 67	1	43N19	88w23	5:53:32
Saint Lawrence 69	1	44N27	89w03	5:56:12
Saint Marie 24	1	43N54	89w05	5:56:20
Saint Martins 41	1	42N53	88w00	5:52:00
Saint Marys 42	1	43N46	90w47	6:03:08
Saint Michaels 67	1	43N31	88w14	5:52:56
Saint Nazianz 36	1	44N00	87w55	5:51:40
Saint Peter 20	1	43N52	88w17	5:53:08
Saint Vincent	1	13N15	61w12	4:04:48
Saint Wendel 36	1	43N55	87w45	5:51:00
Salem 30	1	42N34	88w06	5:52:24
Salem Oaks 30	1	42N34	88w06	5:52:24
Salmo 4	1	46N49	90w50	6:03:20
Salter 67	1	43N25	88w11	5:52:44
Salvatorian Center 8	1	43N57	88w06	5:52:24
Sampson 9	1	45N14	91w21	6:05:24
Sampson 43	1	44N43	88w04	5:52:16
Sanborn 2	1	46N33	90w40	6:02:40
Sand Bay 4	1	46N49	90w50	6:03:20
Sand Creek 17	1	45N10	91w41	6:06:44
Sandlake 49	1	45N21	92w38	6:10:32
Sand Prairie 53	1	43N11	90w34	6:02:16
Sandusky 57	1	43N26	90w07	6:00:28
Saratoga 72	1	44N18	89w49	5:59:16
Sarona 66	1	45N43	91w48	6:07:12
Sauk City 57	1	43N17	89w43	5:58:52
Saukville 46	1	43N23	87w56	5:51:44
Saxeville 70	1	44N11	89w07	5:56:28
Saxon 26	1	46N30	90w25	6:01:40
Saylesville 14	1	43N20	88w27	5:53:48
Saylesville 68	1	43N01	88w12	5:52:48
Sayner 64	1	45N59	89w32	5:58:08
Scandinavia 69	1	44N27	89w09	5:56:36
Scarboro 31	1	44N32	87w42	5:50:48
Schleswig 36	1	43N57	87w59	5:51:56
Schley 35	1	45N15	89w30	5:58:00
Schoepke 44	1	45N31	89w09	5:56:36
Schofield 37	1	44N54	89w36	5:58:24
School Hill 36	1	43N55	88w02	5:52:08
Sechlerville 27	1	44N22	91w01	6:04:04
Seeleys 58	1	46N01	91w29	6:05:56
Seif 10	1	44N38	90w44	6:02:56
Seneca 12	1	43N16	90w57	6:03:48
Sevastopol 15	1	44N54	87w20	5:49:20
Seven Mile Creek 29	1	43N41	90w01	6:00:04
Sextonville 53	1	43N17	90w17	6:01:08
Seymour 45	1	44N31	88w20	5:53:20
Shamrock 27	1	44N17	90w51	6:03:24
Shanagolden 2	1	46N07	90w45	6:03:00
Sharon 65	1	42N30	88w44	5:54:56
Shawano 59	1	44N47	88w36	5:54:24
Shawano North Beach 59	1	44N47	88w36	5:54:24
Sheboygan 60	1	43N46	87w45	5:51:00
Sheboygan Falls 60	1	43N42	87w49	5:51:16
Sheboygan South 60	1	43N44	87w46	5:51:04
Sheboygan West 60	1	43N44	87w46	5:51:04
Shelby 32	1	43N46	91w11	6:04:44
Sheldon 55	1	45N19	90w58	6:03:52
Shell Lake 66	1	45N45	91w55	6:07:40
Shennington 42	1	43N55	90w16	6:01:04
Shepley 59	1	44N49	89w10	5:56:40
Sheridan 69	1	44N24	89w12	5:56:48
Sherry 72	1	44N34	89w54	5:59:36
Sherwood 8	1	44N11	88w16	5:53:04
Shiocton 45	1	44N27	88w35	5:54:20
Shirley 5	1	44N28	88w02	5:52:08
Shopiere 54	1	42N33	88w52	5:55:28
Shoreview 30	1	42N31	88w07	5:52:28
Shorewood 41	1	43N05	87w54	5:51:36
Shorewood Hills 13	1	43N08	89w27	5:57:48
Shortville 10	1	44N33	90w35	6:02:20
Shoto 36	1	44N09	87w35	5:50:20
Shullsburg 33	1	42N34	90w14	6:00:56
Silica 20	1	43N52	88w17	5:53:08
Silver Cliff 38	1	45N26	88w21	5:53:24
Silvercreek 60	1	43N33	87w58	5:51:52
Silver Lake 30	1	42N33	88w10	5:52:40
Silver Lake 70	1	44N04	89w14	5:56:56
Sinsinawa 22	1	42N32	90w32	6:02:08
Sioux 4	1	46N41	90w54	6:03:36
Sioux Creek 3	1	45N15	91w43	6:06:52
Siren 7	1	45N47	92w24	6:09:36
Sister Bay 15	1	45N11	87w07	5:48:28
Skanawan 35	1	45N26	89w37	5:58:28
Slab City 59	1	44N45	88w26	5:53:44
Slabtown 28	1	43N00	88w48	5:55:12
Slades Corner 30	1	42N40	88w16	5:53:04
Slag Pile 56	1	44N57	92w18	6:09:12
Slinger 67	1	43N20	88w17	5:53:08
Slovan 31	1	44N27	87w30	5:50:00
Smelser 22	1	42N38	90w29	6:01:56
Sobieski 43	1	44N43	88w04	5:52:16
Sobieski Corners 43	1	44N43	88w04	5:52:16
Soldiers Grove 12	1	43N24	90w47	6:03:08
Solon Springs 16	1	46N22	91w49	6:07:16
Somers 30	1	42N38	87w55	5:51:40
Somerset 56	1	45N09	92w42	6:10:48
Somo 35	1	45N31	89w59	5:59:56
Soperton 21	1	45N26	88w39	5:54:36
South Beaver Dam 14	1	43N27	88w51	5:55:24
South Byron 20	1	43N38	88w29	5:53:56
South Chase 43	1	44N40	88w15	5:53:00
South Chippewa 9	1	44N55	91w23	6:05:32
South Fork 55	1	45N35	90w45	6:03:00
South Janesville 54	1	42N41	89w01	5:56:04
South Kenosha 30	1	42N35	87w51	5:51:24
South Lancaster 22	1	42N49	90w43	6:02:52
South Luxemburg 31	1	44N32	87w42	5:50:48
South Milwaukee 41	1	42N55	87w52	5:51:28
South Necedah 29	1	44N02	90w04	6:00:16
South Oshkosh 71	1	44N01	88w33	5:54:12
South Randolph 14	1	43N32	89w00	5:56:00
South Range 16	1	46N37	91w59	6:07:56
South Wayne 33	1	42N34	89w53	5:59:32
South Wisconsin Rapids 72	1	44N25	89w48	5:59:12
Sparta 42	1	43N56	90w49	6:03:16
Spaulding 27	1	44N27	90w07	6:00:28
Spencer 37	1	44N49	90w15	6:01:00
Spider Lake 58	1	46N07	91w11	6:04:44
Spirit 51	1	45N26	90w07	6:00:28
Spirit Falls 35	1	45N33	90w00	6:00:00
Split Rock 59	1	44N44	89w04	5:56:16
Spokeville 10	1	44N50	90w17	6:01:08
Spooner 66	1	45N50	91w53	6:07:32
Spread Eagle 19	1	45N53	88w08	5:52:32
Spring Bluff 1	1	44N02	89w31	5:58:04
Springbrook 66	1	45N57	91w41	6:06:44
Springdale 13	1	43N00	89w41	5:58:44
Springfield 65	1	42N39	88w25	5:53:40
Springfield Corners 13	1	43N15	89w30	5:58:00
Spring Green 57	1	43N11	90w04	6:00:16
Spring Grove 23	1	42N33	89w26	5:57:44
Spring Lake 48	1	44N48	92w14	6:08:56
Spring Lake 70	1	43N58	89w13	5:56:52
Spring Prairie 65	1	42N43	88w22	5:53:28
Springstead 26	1	45N56	90w27	6:01:48
Spring Valley 36	1	44N00	87w44	5:50:56
Spring Valley 48	1	44N51	92w14	6:08:56
Springville 1	1	43N47	89w47	5:59:08
Springville 63	1	43N33	90w53	6:03:32
Springwater 70	1	44N11	89w11	5:56:44
Spruce 43	1	44N59	88w11	5:52:44
Stadium 5	1	44N30	88w04	5:52:16
Stanbery 66	1	45N57	91w41	6:06:44
Standart 25	1	42N58	90w08	6:00:32
Stanfold 3	1	45N31	91w51	6:07:24
Stangelville 31	1	44N21	87w50	5:51:20
Stanley 9	1	44N58	90w56	6:03:44
Stark 36	1	44N21	87w50	5:51:20
Stark 63	1	43N36	90w38	6:02:32
Starks 44	1	45N38	89w25	5:57:40
Starlake 64	1	46N03	89w28	5:57:52
Star Prairie 56	1	45N12	92w32	6:10:08
Star Valley 12	1	43N24	90w47	6:03:08
State Street 52	1	42N44	87w48	5:51:12
Stella 44	1	45N41	89w14	5:56:56
Stephenson 38	1	45N16	88w06	5:52:24
Stephensville 45	1	44N20	88w37	5:54:28
Stetsonville 61	1	45N04	90w19	6:01:16
Stettin 37	1	44N59	89w46	5:59:04
Steuben 12	1	43N11	90w52	6:03:28
Stevens Point 50	1	44N31	89w34	5:58:16
Stevenstown 32	1	44N02	91w10	6:04:40
Stiles 43	1	44N52	88w03	5:52:12
Stiles Junction 43	1	44N58	88w03	5:52:12
Stinnett 66	1	46N01	91w37	6:06:28
Stitzer 22	1	42N56	90w37	6:02:28
Stockbridge 8	1	44N04	88w18	5:53:12
Stockbridge-Munsee Indian Re 59	1	46N35	90w53	6:03:32
Stockholm 47	1	44N29	92w16	6:09:04
Stockton 50	1	44N29	89w24	5:57:36
Stoddard 63	1	43N40	91w13	6:04:52
Stone 13	1	43N02	89w22	5:57:28
Stonebank 68	1	43N09	88w25	5:53:40
Stone Lake 66	1	45N51	91w32	6:06:08
Stoughton 13	1	42N55	89w13	5:56:52
Strader 18	1	44N41	91w07	6:04:28
Stratford 37	1	44N48	90w04	6:00:16
Strickland 55	1	45N25	91w29	6:05:56
Strongs Prairie 1	1	44N01	89w54	5:59:36
Strum 62	1	44N33	91w24	6:05:36
Stubbs 55	1	45N26	91w21	6:05:24
Sturgeon Bay 15	1	44N50	87w23	5:49:32
Sturtevant 52	1	42N42	87w54	5:51:36
Suamico 5	1	44N38	88w03	5:52:12
Sugar Bush 5	1	44N32	87w42	5:50:48
Sugar Bush 45	1	44N29	88w44	5:54:56
Sugar Camp 44	1	45N49	89w20	5:57:20
Sugar Creek 65	1	42N43	88w35	5:54:20
Sugar Grove 63	1	43N24	90w47	6:03:08
Sugar Island 14	1	43N12	88w43	5:54:52
Sullivan 28	1	42N59	88w38	5:54:32
Sullivan 32	1	43N53	91w14	6:04:56
Summit 42	1	43N50	90w37	6:02:28
Summit Corners 68	1	43N06	88w29	5:53:56
Summit Lake 34	1	45N23	89w12	5:56:48
Sumpter 57	1	43N21	89w46	5:59:04
Sun Prairie 13	1	43N11	89w13	5:56:52
Superior 16	1	46N44	92w06	6:08:24
Suring 43	1	45N00	88w21	5:53:24
Sussex 68	1	43N08	88w13	5:52:52
Swiss 7	1	46N01	92w17	6:09:08
Sylvan 53	1	43N25	90w38	6:02:32
Sylvania 52	1	42N44	87w52	5:51:28
Sylvester 23	1	42N39	89w32	5:58:08
Symco 69	1	44N31	88w54	5:55:36
Tabor 52	1	42N44	87w48	5:51:12
Taft 61	1	45N05	90w51	6:03:24
Tainter 17	1	45N00	91w51	6:07:24
Tamarack 62	1	44N16	91w30	6:06:00
Tannery 35	1	45N28	89w44	5:58:56
Tarrant 47	1	44N38	91w58	6:07:52
Taus 36	1	44N09	87w52	5:51:28
Taycheedah 20	1	43N51	88w20	5:53:20
Taylor 27	1	44N19	91w07	6:04:28
Teegarden 17	1	44N53	91w56	6:07:44
Tell 6	1	44N20	91w55	6:07:40
Templeton 68	1	43N08	88w13	5:52:52
Tennyson 22	1	42N41	90w41	6:02:44
Terrill 70	1	44N03	89w07	5:56:28
Tess Corners 68	1	42N56	88w02	5:52:08
Teutonia 41	1	43N04	87w56	5:51:44
Texas 37	1	45N03	89w35	5:58:20
Theresa 14	1	43N30	88w28	5:53:52
Thiel's Corner 67	1	43N17	87w58	5:51:52
Thiensville 46	1	43N14	87w59	5:51:56
Thirty Daems 31	1	44N32	87w42	5:50:48
Thompson 67	1	43N19	88w23	5:53:32
Thompsonville 52	1	42N46	87w55	5:51:40
Thornapple 55	1	45N30	91w12	6:04:48

WISCONSIN

Thornton 59	1	44N48	88w42	5:54:48
Thorp 10	1	44N57	90w48	6:03:12
Three Lakes 44	1	45N48	89w10	5:56:40
Tibbets 65	1	42N41	88w33	5:54:12
Tichigan 52	1	42N46	88w13	5:52:52
Tiffany 17	1	45N05	92w05	6:08:20
Tiffany 54	1	42N35	88w56	5:55:44
Tigerton 59	1	44N44	89w04	5:56:16
Tilden 9	1	45N00	91w26	6:05:44
Tilleda 59	1	44N49	88w55	5:55:40
Tipler 19	1	45N55	88w38	5:54:32
Tisch Mills 36	1	44N20	87w38	5:50:32
Token 13	1	43N15	89w21	5:57:24
Tomah 42	1	43N59	90w30	6:02:00
Tomahawk 35	1	45N28	89w44	5:58:56
Tonet 31	1	44N32	87w42	5:50:48
Tony 55	1	45N29	91w00	6:04:00
Towerville 12	1	43N24	90w47	6:03:08
Townsend 43	1	45N20	88w35	5:54:20
Trade Lake 7	1	45N41	92w36	6:10:24
Trade River 7	1	45N47	92w41	6:10:44
Trego 66	1	45N54	91w50	6:07:20
Trempealeau 62	1	44N00	91w26	6:05:44
Trevor 30	1	42N31	88w07	5:52:28
Tri City 41	1	42N54	87w56	5:51:44
Trimbelle 48	1	44N44	92w35	6:10:20
Tripoli 44	1	45N33	90w00	6:00:00
Tripp 4	1	46N38	91w22	6:05:28
Trout Run 27	1	44N17	90w51	6:03:24
Troy 65	1	42N48	88w24	5:53:36
Troy Center 65	1	42N49	88w28	5:53:52
True 55	1	45N31	90w53	6:03:32
Truesdell 30	1	42N35	87w51	5:51:24
Tuleta Hills 24	1	43N42	88w59	5:55:56
Tunnel City 42	1	44N00	90w34	6:02:16
Turtle 54	1	42N33	88w57	5:55:48
Turtle Lake 3	1	45N24	92w08	6:08:32
Tustin 70	1	44N10	88w54	5:55:36
Twelve Corners 45	1	44N28	88w27	5:53:48
Twin Bluffs 53	1	43N20	90w27	6:01:48
Twin Grove 23	1	42N35	89w30	5:58:00
Twin Lakes 30	1	42N31	88w15	5:53:00
Two Creeks 36	1	44N18	87w34	5:50:16
Two Rivers 36	1	44N09	87w34	5:50:16
Ubet 49	1	45N21	92w38	6:10:32
Underhill 43	1	44N54	88w25	5:53:40
Union 22	1	42N44	90w29	6:01:56
Union 54	1	42N47	89w18	5:57:12
Union Center 29	1	43N41	90w16	6:01:04
Union Church 52	1	42N46	87w55	5:51:40
Union Grove 52	1	42N41	88w03	5:52:12
Union Mills 25	1	42N58	90w08	6:00:32
Unity 37	1	44N51	90w19	6:01:16
University 13	1	43N06	89w24	5:57:36
Upham 34	1	45N20	89w11	5:56:44
Upper Third Street 41	1	43N04	87w55	5:51:40
Upson 26	1	46N22	90w24	6:01:36
Uptown 52	1	42N43	87w48	5:51:12
Urne 6	1	44N38	91w58	6:07:52
Utica 13	1	42N55	89w15	5:57:00
Utica 68	1	43N06	88w29	5:53:56
Valders 36	1	44N04	87w53	5:51:32
Valley 63	1	43N53	90w33	6:02:12
Valley Junction 42	1	43N59	90w30	6:02:00
Valmy 15	1	44N50	87w22	5:49:28
Valton 57	1	43N34	90w16	6:01:04
Van Buskirk 26	1	46N27	90w12	6:00:48
Vance Creek 3	1	45N14	92w07	6:08:28
Vandenbroek 45	1	44N18	88w19	5:53:16
Vandyne 20	1	43N53	88w30	5:54:00
Vaudreuil 27	1	44N19	90w48	6:03:12
Veedum 72	1	44N27	90w07	6:00:28
Vermont 13	1	43N04	89w48	5:59:12
Vernon 68	1	42N53	88w14	5:52:56
Verona 13	1	42N59	89w32	5:58:08
Vesper 72	1	44N29	89w58	5:59:52
Veterans Administration Hosp 13	1	43N07	89w27	5:57:48
Victory 63	1	43N29	91w13	6:04:52
Vienna 13	1	43N15	89w25	5:57:40
Vignes 15	1	44N50	87w22	5:49:28
Vilas 13	1	43N05	89w12	5:56:48
Vilas 34	1	45N15	89w21	5:57:24
Village Of Superior	1	46N40	92w06	6:08:24
Villard 41	1	43N07	87w57	5:51:48
Vinland 71	1	44N08	88w34	5:54:16
Viola 53	1	43N31	90w40	6:02:40
Viroqua 63	1	43N34	90w53	6:03:32
Wabeno 21	1	45N26	88w39	5:54:36
Wagner 38	1	45N19	87w44	5:50:56
Waino 16	1	46N33	91w34	6:06:16
Waldo 60	1	43N41	87w57	5:51:48
Waldwick 25	1	42N50	90w02	6:00:08
Wales 68	1	43N00	88w23	5:53:32
Walhain 31	1	44N32	87w42	5:50:48
Walsh 38	1	45N09	87w48	5:51:12
Walworth 65	6	42N33	88w37	5:54:28
Wandawega 65	1	42N41	88w33	5:54:12
Wanderoos 49	1	45N18	92w30	6:10:00
Warner 10	1	44N48	90w37	6:02:28
Warrens 42	1	44N08	90w30	6:02:00
Warrentown 48	1	44N33	92w19	6:09:16
Wascott 16	1	46N09	91w48	6:07:12
Washburn 4	1	46N40	90w54	6:03:36
Washington Island 15	1	45N24	86w56	5:47:44
Waterford 52	1	42N46	88w13	5:52:52
Waterford Woods 52	1	42N46	88w13	5:52:52
Waterloo 28	1	43N11	89w00	5:56:00
Watertown 28	1	43N12	88w43	5:54:52
Waterville 47	1	44N38	92w04	6:08:16
Waterville 68	1	43N06	88w29	5:53:56
Watterstown 22	1	43N09	90w36	6:02:24
Waubeek 47	1	44N39	91w59	6:07:56
Waubeesee 52	1	42N46	88w13	5:52:52
Waubeka 46	1	43N28	87w57	5:51:48
Waucousta 20	1	43N39	88w16	5:53:04
Waukau 71	1	44N00	88w46	5:55:04
Waukechon 59	1	44N43	88w32	5:54:08
Waukesha 68	1	43N01	88w14	5:52:56
Waumandee 6	1	44N18	91w43	6:06:52
Waunakee 13	1	43N11	89w27	5:57:48
Waupaca 69	1	44N21	89w05	5:56:20
Waupun 20	1	43N38	88w44	5:54:56
Wausau 37	1	44N58	89w38	5:58:32
Wausaukee 38	1	45N24	87w58	5:51:52
Wausau West 37	1	44N57	89w39	5:58:36
Wautoma 70	1	44N04	89w18	5:57:12
Wauwatosa 41	1	43N03	88w00	5:52:00
Wauzeka 12	1	43N06	90w56	6:03:44
Waverly 48	1	44N47	92w09	6:08:36
Wayne 67	1	43N36	88w17	5:53:08
Wayside 5	1	44N15	87w57	5:51:48
Webb Lake 7	1	46N02	92w06	6:08:24
Webster 5	1	44N30	88w01	5:52:04
Webster 7	1	45N53	92w22	6:09:28
Weirgor 58	1	45N42	91w14	6:04:56
Wellington 42	1	43N46	90w30	6:02:00
Wells 42	1	43N51	90w44	6:02:56
Wentworth 16	1	46N36	91w50	6:07:20
Werley 22	1	43N05	90w48	6:03:12
Wescott 59	1	44N49	88w33	5:54:12
West Allis 41	1	43N01	88w00	5:52:00
West Baraboo 57	1	43N28	89w46	5:59:04
West Bend 67	1	43N25	88w11	5:52:44
West Bloomfield 70	1	44N13	88w58	5:55:52
Westboro 61	1	45N21	90w18	6:01:12
Westby 63	1	43N39	90w51	6:03:24
Westchester 68	1	43N04	88w05	5:52:20
West De Pere 5	1	44N28	88w02	5:52:08
Western 41	1	43N04	87w58	5:51:52
Westfield 39	1	43N53	89w30	5:58:00
West Jacksonport 15	1	45N03	87w18	5:49:12
West Kewaunee 31	1	44N27	87w35	5:50:20
West Lima 53	1	43N35	90w38	6:02:32
West Marshland 7	1	45N53	92w37	6:10:28
West Milwaukee 41	1	43N01	87w59	5:51:56
Weston 17	1	44N49	92w04	6:08:16
Weston 37	1	44N56	89w36	5:58:24
West Plainfield 70	1	44N13	89w29	5:57:56
West Point 11	1	43N20	89w39	5:58:36
Westport 13	1	43N10	89w26	5:57:44
Westport 53	1	43N11	90w34	6:02:16
West Prairie 63	1	43N26	91w12	6:04:48
West Racine 52	1	42N44	87w50	5:51:20
Westrap 72	1	44N25	89w48	5:59:12
West Rosendale 20	1	43N49	88w40	5:54:40
West Salem 32	1	43N54	91w05	6:04:20
West Sussex 68	1	43N08	88w13	5:52:52
West Sweden 49	1	45N41	92w28	6:09:52
Weurtsburg 37	1	45N01	90w04	6:00:16
Weyauwega 69	1	44N19	88w56	5:55:44
Weyerhaeuser 55	1	45N26	91w25	6:05:40
Wheatland 30	1	42N40	88w16	5:53:04
Wheaton 9	1	44N54	91w32	6:06:08
Wheeler 17	1	45N03	91w55	6:07:40
Whitcomb 59	1	44N44	89w04	5:56:16
White Creek 1	1	43N50	89w52	5:59:28
Whitefish Bay 15	1	44N55	87w13	5:48:52
Whitefish Bay 41	1	43N23	87w55	5:51:40
Whitehall 62	1	44N22	91w19	6:05:16
White Lake 34	1	45N10	88w46	5:55:04
Whitelaw 36	1	44N09	87w49	5:51:16
White Oak Springs 33	1	42N31	90w16	6:01:04
White River 2	1	46N28	90w51	6:03:24
White River Village 65	1	42N36	88w28	5:53:52
Whitestown 63	1	43N41	90w35	6:02:20
Whitewater 65	1	42N50	88w44	5:54:56
Whiting 50	1	44N30	89w34	5:58:16
Whittlesey 61	1	45N14	90w20	6:01:20
Wien 37	1	44N56	90w01	6:00:04
Wild Rose 70	1	44N11	89w15	5:57:00
Wildwood 56	1	44N57	92w18	6:09:12
Wilkinson 55	1	45N31	91w28	6:05:52
Willard 10	1	44N44	90w43	6:02:52
Williams Bay 65	1	42N35	88w33	5:54:12
Williamstown 14	1	43N30	88w36	5:54:24
Willow 53	1	43N25	90w14	6:00:56
Willow Springs 33	1	42N45	90w09	6:00:36
Wilmot 30	1	42N31	88w11	5:52:44
Wilson 9	1	44N57	91w02	6:04:08
Wilson 56	1	44N57	92w11	6:08:44
Wilton 42	1	43N49	90w32	6:02:08
Winchester 64	1	46N13	89w54	5:59:36
Winchester 71	1	44N11	88w38	5:54:32
Wind Lake 52	1	42N46	88w13	5:52:52
Wind Point 52	1	42N47	87w46	5:51:04
Windsor 13	1	43N15	89w18	5:57:12
Winfield 57	1	43N37	90w01	6:00:04
Wingville 22	1	42N59	90w29	6:01:56
Winnebago 71	1	44N05	88w32	5:54:08
Winnebago Indian Reservation 32	1	46N35	90w53	6:03:32
Winnebago Mission 27	1	44N17	90w51	6:03:24
Winneconne 71	1	44N07	88w43	5:54:52
Winter 58	1	45N49	91w01	6:04:04
Wiota 33	1	42N39	89w57	5:59:48
Wiscona 41	1	43N07	87w57	5:51:48
Wisconsin Dells 11	1	43N38	89w46	5:59:04
Wisconsin Junction 21	1	45N40	88w53	5:55:32
Wisconsin Rapids 72	1	44N23	89w49	5:59:16
Wiswell 5	1	44N30	88w01	5:52:04
Withee 10	1	44N57	90w36	6:02:24
Wittenberg 59	1	44N49	89w10	5:56:40
Witwen 57	1	43N15	89w44	5:58:56
Wolfcreek 49	1	45N24	92w38	6:10:32
Wolf Lake 20	1	43N50	88w10	5:52:40
Wonewoc 29	1	43N41	90w14	6:00:56
Wood 41	1	43N07	88w01	5:52:04
Wood 72	1	44N28	90w08	6:00:32
Woodboro 44	1	45N37	89w33	5:58:12
Wooddale 58	1	45N39	91w33	6:06:12
Woodford 33	1	42N39	89w52	5:59:28
Woodhull 20	1	43N49	88w38	5:54:32
Woodhull Station 20	1	43N59	88w56	5:55:44
Woodland 14	1	43N22	88w31	5:54:04
Woodland 57	1	43N37	90w15	6:01:00
Woodman 22	1	43N07	90w48	6:03:12
Woodmohr 9	1	45N05	91w28	6:05:52
Wood River 7	1	45N46	92w35	6:10:20
Woodruff 44	1	45N54	89w42	5:58:48
Woodstock 53	1	43N26	90w26	6:01:44
Woodville 56	1	44N57	92w18	6:09:12
Woodworth 30	1	42N34	88w00	5:52:00
Worcester 51	1	45N42	90w21	6:01:24
Worden 10	1	44N54	90w52	6:03:28
Wrightstown 5	1	44N20	88w10	5:52:40
Wrightsville 27	1	44N26	90w54	6:03:36
Wyalusing 22	1	42N57	91w08	6:04:32
Wyeville 42	1	44N02	90w23	6:01:32
Wyocena 11	1	43N30	89w19	5:57:16
Yellow Lake 7	1	45N56	92w23	6:09:32
York 27	1	44N37	91w14	6:04:56
York Center 13	1	43N11	89w04	5:56:16
Yorkville 52	1	42N43	88w00	5:52:00
Young America 67	1	43N25	88w11	5:52:44
Yuba 53	1	43N33	90w26	6:01:44
Zachow 59	1	44N44	88w22	5:53:28
Zander 36	1	44N21	87w50	5:51:20
Zenda 65	6	42N31	88w29	5:53:56
Zion 71	1	44N02	88w44	5:54:56
Zittau 71	1	44N15	88w53	5:55:32

WYOMING

TIME TABLES

Before 11/18/1883		LMT
11/18/1883	12:00	MST
3/31/1918	02:00	MWT
10/27/1918	02:00	MST
3/30/1919	02:00	MWT
10/26/1919	02:00	MST
2/09/1942	02:00	MWT
9/30/1945	02:00	MST
4/30/1967	02:00	US#1

COUNTIES

1 Albany
2 Big Horn
3 Campbell
4 Carbon
5 Converse
6 Crook
7 Fremont
8 Goshen
9 Hot Springs
10 Johnson
11 Laramie
12 Lincoln
13 Natrona
14 Niobrara
15 Park
16 Platte
17 Sheridan
18 Sublette
19 Sweetwater
20 Teton
21 Uinta
22 Washakie
23 Weston

Place	Lat	Long	Time
Acme 17	44N55	106w59	7:07:56
Afton 12	42N44	110w56	7:23:44
Airport 11	41N08	104w49	6:59:16
Aladdin 6	44N38	104w11	6:56:44
Albany 1	41N11	106w08	7:04:32
Albin 11	41N25	104w06	6:56:24
Alcova 13	42N34	106w43	7:06:52
Allendale 13	42N49	106w19	7:05:16
Almy 21	41N20	111w00	7:24:00
Almy Junction 21	41N16	110w58	7:23:52
Alpine 12	43N11	111w03	7:24:12
Alpine Junction 12	42N55	111w00	7:24:00
Alta 20	43N46	110w59	7:23:56
Altamont	41N12	110w47	7:23:08
Alva 6	44N42	104w26	6:57:44
Arapahoe 7	42N58	108w29	7:13:56
Archer 11	41N08	104w49	6:59:16
Arminto 13	43N11	107w15	7:09:00
Arrow Head Lodge 17	44N48	106w57	7:07:48
Arvada 17	44N39	106w08	7:04:32
Aspen	41N13	110w45	7:23:00
Atlantic City 7	42N30	108w44	7:14:56
Auburn 12	42N48	111w00	7:24:00
Baggs 4	41N02	107w39	7:10:36
Bairoil 19	42N15	107w33	7:10:12
Banner 17	44N36	106w52	7:07:28
Basin 2	44N23	108w02	7:12:08
Bear Lodge 17	44N52	107w16	7:09:04
Beckton 17	44N48	106w57	7:07:48
Bedford 12	42N54	110w56	7:23:44
Beulah 6	44N33	104w05	6:56:20
Big Horn 17	44N41	107w00	7:08:00
Big Horn Central 2	44N32	108w11	7:12:44
Big Piney 18	42N32	110w07	7:20:28
Big Sandy 18	42N45	109w43	7:18:52
Bill 5	43N14	105w16	7:01:04
Bitter Creek 19	41N33	108w33	7:14:12
Blairtown 19	41N35	109w13	7:16:52
Bondurant 18	43N10	110w23	7:21:32
Bonneville 7	43N16	108w04	7:12:16
Bordeaux 16	42N03	104w57	6:59:48
Bosler 1	41N35	105w42	7:02:48
Boulder 18	42N45	109w43	7:18:52
Boxelder 5	42N51	105w52	7:03:28
Boysen	43N27	108w11	7:12:44
Bridger Valley 21	41N15	110w21	7:21:24
Bronx 18	42N52	110w04	7:20:16
Bryan 19	41N34	109w41	7:18:44
Buffalo 10	44N21	106w42	7:06:48
Buford 1	41N08	105w18	7:01:12
Burgess Junction 17	44N46	107w32	7:10:08
Burlington 2	44N27	108w26	7:13:44
Burns 11	41N12	104w21	6:57:24
Burntfork 19	41N02	109w56	7:19:44
Burris 7	43N22	109w16	7:17:04
Byron 2	44N48	108w30	7:14:00
Calpet 18	42N17	110w15	7:21:00
Canyon 15	44N30	110w30	7:22:00
Caribou Camp 10	44N21	106w42	7:06:48
Carlile 6	44N29	104w48	6:59:12
Carpenter 11	41N03	104w22	6:57:28
Carter 21	41N26	110w26	7:21:44
Casper 13	42N51	106w19	7:05:16
Cassa	42N24	104w57	6:59:48
Centennial 1	41N18	106w08	7:04:32
Chatham 22	44N01	107w57	7:11:48
Cheyenne 11	41N08	104w49	6:59:16
Cheyenne West 11	41N12	105w02	7:00:08
Chugwater 16	41N46	104w50	6:59:20
Church Butte 21	41N33	110w11	7:20:44
Clareton 23	43N42	104w42	6:58:48
Clark 15	44N55	109w11	7:16:44
Clay 23	43N59	104w25	6:57:40
Clay Spur 23	44N01	104w28	6:57:52
Clearmont 17	44N38	106w23	7:05:32
Cody 15	44N32	109w03	7:16:12
Cokeville 12	42N05	110w57	7:23:48
Colter Bay 20	43N29	110w46	7:23:04
Cora 18	42N56	109w59	7:19:56
Cottier 8	42N04	104w11	6:56:44
Cowley 2	44N53	108w28	7:13:52
C.r.a. Camp 13	43N25	106w16	7:05:04
Creston 19	41N42	107w45	7:11:00
Crowheart 7	43N19	109w11	7:16:44
Daniel 18	42N52	110w04	7:20:16
Dayton 17	44N53	107w16	7:09:04
Deaver 2	44N54	108w36	7:14:24
Devils Tower 6	44N35	104w42	6:58:48

Place	Lat	Long	Time
Diamond 16	41N45	104w49	6:59:16
Diamondville 12	41N47	110w32	7:22:08
Dickie 9	44N01	107w57	7:11:48
Dixon 4	41N02	107w32	7:10:08
Douglas 5	42N45	105w24	7:01:36
Downer Addition 17	44N48	106w57	7:07:48
Dubois 7	43N33	109w38	7:18:32
Duncan 7	43N32	109w38	7:18:32
Durham	41N12	104w36	6:58:24
Dwyer 16	42N15	104w58	6:59:52
East Thermopolis 9	43N39	108w12	7:12:48
Eden 19	42N03	109w26	7:17:44
Edgerton 13	43N25	106w15	7:05:00
Egbert 11	41N10	104w15	6:57:00
Elk	43N47	110w33	7:22:12
Elk Mountain 4	41N41	106w25	7:05:40
Elkol 12	41N43	110w37	7:22:28
Elmo 4	41N53	106w32	7:06:08
Emblem 2	44N30	108w23	7:13:32
Encampment 4	41N12	106w47	7:07:08
Ervay 13	42N50	106w23	7:05:32
Esterbrook 5	42N45	105w23	7:01:32
Ethete 7	43N02	108w47	7:15:08
Etna 12	43N02	111w01	7:24:04
Evanston 21	41N16	110w58	7:23:52
Evansville 13	42N52	106w16	7:05:04
Fairview 12	42N42	110w59	7:23:56
Farson 19	42N07	109w27	7:17:48
Federal 11	41N16	105w07	7:00:28
Fish Hatchery 4	41N27	106w48	7:07:12
Fishing Bridge 20	44N30	110w30	7:22:00
Five Mile Creek 7	43N26	108w54	7:15:36
Flattop 16	42N40	104w45	6:59:00
Fontenelle 12	41N48	110w32	7:22:08
Fort Bridger 21	41N19	110w23	7:21:32
Fort Laramie 8	42N13	104w31	6:58:04
Fort Steele 4	41N47	107w14	7:08:56
Fort Washakie 7	43N00	108w53	7:15:32
Four Corners 23	44N05	104w08	6:56:32
Fox Farm 11	41N07	104w47	6:59:08
Foxpark 1	41N05	106w09	7:04:36
Francis E. Warren Air Force 11	41N08	104w49	6:59:16
Frannie 15	44N58	108w37	7:14:28
Freedom 12	42N59	111w03	7:24:12
Frewen	41N39	108w04	7:12:16
Frontier 12	41N49	110w32	7:22:08
Garland 15	44N47	108w40	7:14:40
Garrett 1	42N06	105w39	7:02:36
Gas Camp 01 13	43N25	106w16	7:05:04
Gas Hills 7	43N02	108w23	7:13:32
Gebo 9	43N48	108w14	7:12:56
Gillette 3	44N18	105w30	7:02:00
Glendo 16	42N30	105w02	7:00:08
Glenrock 5	42N52	105w52	7:03:28
Goshen Hole 8	41N49	104w21	6:57:24
Granger 19	41N35	109w58	7:19:52
Granite Canon 11	41N06	105w09	7:00:36
Grants Village 20	44N30	110w30	7:22:00
Grass Creek 9	43N56	108w39	7:14:36
Green River 19	41N32	109w28	7:17:52
Greybull 2	44N30	108w03	7:12:12
Grover 12	42N48	110w56	7:23:44
Grovont 20	43N38	110w37	7:22:28
Guernsey 16	42N16	104w45	6:59:00
Halfway 18	42N33	110w07	7:20:28
Hallville	41N37	108w44	7:14:56
Hamilton Dome 9	43N46	108w35	7:14:20
Hamsfork 12	41N48	110w32	7:22:08
Hanna 4	41N52	106w34	7:06:16
Harriman 11	41N00	105w15	7:01:00
Hartville 16	42N20	104w44	6:58:56
Hat Creek 14	42N56	104w22	6:57:28
Hawk Springs 8	41N47	104w16	6:57:04
Heart Mountain 15	44N45	108w45	7:15:00
Hells Half Acre 13	42N58	107w02	7:08:08
Hiland 13	43N07	107w21	7:09:24
Hillsdale 11	41N13	104w29	6:57:56
Hilltop 13	42N50	106w23	7:05:32
Horse Creek 11	41N25	105w11	7:00:44
Hudson 7	42N54	108w35	7:14:20
Hulett 6	44N41	104w36	6:58:24
Huntley 8	41N56	104w09	6:56:36
Hyattville 2	44N15	107w36	7:10:24
Iron Mountain 11	41N33	105w13	7:00:52
Ishawooa 15	44N31	109w04	7:16:16
Jackson 20	43N29	110w46	7:23:04
Jackson Hole 20	43N32	110w44	7:22:56
James Town 19	41N31	109w28	7:17:52
Jay Em 8	42N28	104w22	6:57:28

Place	Lat	Long	Time
Jeffrey City 7	42N30	107w49	7:11:16
Jelm 1	41N04	106w01	7:04:04
Jenny Lake 20	43N40	110w43	7:22:52
Kane 2	44N50	108w23	7:13:32
Kaycee 10	43N43	106w38	7:06:32
Keeline 14	42N40	104w45	6:59:00
Kelly 20	43N38	110w37	7:22:28
Kemmerer 12	41N48	110w32	7:22:08
Kemmerer West 12	42N01	110w53	7:23:32
Kendall 18	42N56	109w59	7:19:56
Keystone 1	41N19	105w35	7:02:20
Kinnear 7	43N09	108w41	7:14:44
Kirby 9	43N48	108w11	7:12:44
Kirtley 14	42N45	104w27	6:57:48
Kortes Dam 4	42N12	106w52	7:07:28
La Barge 12	42N16	110w12	7:20:48
Lagrange 8	41N38	104w10	6:56:40
Lake 20	44N30	110w30	7:22:00
Lake Creek Resort 1	41N19	105w35	7:02:20
Lamont 4	42N13	107w29	7:09:56
Lance Creek 14	43N02	104w39	6:58:36
Lander 7	42N50	108w44	7:14:56
Laprele 5	42N45	105w23	7:01:32
Laramie 1	41N19	105w35	7:02:20
Laramie West 1	41N17	105w51	7:03:24
Latham	41N42	107w50	7:11:20
Leiter 17	44N43	106w16	7:05:04
Leo 4	41N52	106w33	7:06:12
Linch 10	43N37	106w12	7:04:48
Lindbergh 11	41N11	104w04	6:56:16
Lingle 8	42N08	104w21	6:57:24
Little America 19	41N33	109w51	7:19:24
Lonetree 21	41N03	110w09	7:20:36
Lookout 1	41N35	105w42	7:02:48
Lost Cabin 7	43N17	107w38	7:10:32
Lost Springs 5	42N46	104w56	6:59:44
Lovell 2	44N50	108w24	7:13:36
Lucerne 9	43N44	108w10	7:12:40
Lucky MacCamp 7	43N02	108w23	7:13:32
Lusk 14	42N46	104w27	6:57:48
Lyman 21	41N20	110w18	7:21:12
Lysite 7	43N16	107w41	7:10:44
Mammoth	44N59	110w42	7:22:48
Manderson 2	44N16	107w58	7:11:52
Mantua 15	44N45	108w45	7:15:00
Manville 14	42N47	104w37	6:58:28
Marbleton 18	42N34	110w06	7:20:24
Mayoworth 10	43N43	106w38	7:06:32
McFadden 4	41N39	106w08	7:04:32
McKinley 5	42N38	105w08	7:00:32
McKinnon 19	41N02	109w56	7:19:44
Medicine Bow 4	41N54	106w12	7:04:48
Meeteetse 15	44N09	108w52	7:15:28
Meriden 11	41N33	104w19	6:57:16
Merna 18	42N52	110w04	7:20:16
Midval 7	43N02	108w23	7:13:32
Midwest 13	43N25	106w16	7:05:04
Midwest Heights 13	42N50	106w23	7:05:32
Milford 7	42N53	108w47	7:15:08
Millburne 21	41N19	110w23	7:21:32
Mills 13	42N50	106w22	7:05:28
Monell	41N36	108w29	7:13:56
Moneta 7	43N10	107w43	7:10:52
Moorcroft 6	44N16	104w57	6:59:48
Moose 20	43N40	110w43	7:22:52
Moran 20	43N50	110w30	7:22:00
Morton 7	43N12	108w46	7:15:04
Moskee	44N16	104w11	6:56:44
Mountain Home 1	41N19	105w35	7:02:20
Mountain View 13	42N50	106w23	7:05:32
Mountain View 21	41N16	110w20	7:21:20
Muddy Gap 4	42N21	107w28	7:09:52
Mule Creek	43N19	104w08	6:56:32
Natrona 13	43N02	106w49	7:07:16
Newcastle 23	43N50	104w11	6:56:44
New Haven 6	44N45	104w51	6:59:24
Niobrara West 14	43N00	104w38	6:58:32
Node 14	42N43	104w18	6:57:12
Nutria	41N46	110w10	7:20:40
O'Donnell Spur 15	44N45	108w45	7:15:00
Old Faithful 20	44N30	110w30	7:22:00
Opal 12	41N46	110w19	7:21:16
Orchard Valley 11	41N06	104w49	6:59:16
Orin 5	42N39	105w12	7:00:48
Orpha 5	42N51	105w30	7:02:00
Osage 23	43N59	104w25	6:57:40
Oshoto 12	44N35	104w56	6:59:44
Osmond 12	42N44	110w56	7:23:44
Otto 2	44N24	108w16	7:13:04

Place	Lat.	Long.	Time
Pahaska 15	44N31	109w04	7:16:16
Paradise Valley 13	42N49	106w23	7:05:32
Parkerton 5	42N51	106w00	7:04:00
Parkman 17	44N58	107w20	7:09:20
Pavillion 7	43N15	108w42	7:14:48
Peru 19	41N33	109w35	7:18:20
Piedmont 21	41N13	110w38	7:22:32
Pine Bluffs 11	41N11	104w04	6:56:16
Pinedale 18	42N52	109w52	7:19:28
Point of Rocks 19	41N41	108w47	7:15:08
Powder River 13	43N02	106w59	7:07:56
Powell 15	44N45	108w46	7:15:04
Prairie Center 8	42N04	104w11	6:56:44
Quealy 19	41N32	109w13	7:16:52
Ragan	41N16	110w40	7:22:40
Ralston 15	44N43	108w52	7:15:28
Ranchester 17	44N54	107w10	7:08:40
Rawhide Creek 8	42N24	104w21	6:57:24
Rawlins 4	41N47	107w14	7:08:56
Raymond 12	42N05	110w57	7:23:48
Recluse 3	44N45	105w43	7:02:52
Redbird 14	42N45	104w27	6:57:48
Red Buttes 1	41N11	105w36	7:02:24
Red Buttes Village 13	42N50	106w23	7:05:32
Red Desert 19	41N40	107w58	7:11:52
Red Lane 9	43N39	108w12	7:12:48
Reliance 19	41N40	109w12	7:16:48
Richardson Acres 13	42N50	106w23	7:05:32
Riddle 15	44N31	109w04	7:16:16
Riner 19	41N44	107w33	7:10:12
Riverside 4	41N13	106w47	7:07:08
Riverton 7	43N02	108w23	7:13:32
Riverview 14	43N25	104w18	6:57:12
Robertson 21	41N11	110w25	7:21:40
Rockeagle 8	42N08	104w21	6:57:24
Rock River 1	41N44	105w58	7:03:52
Rock Springs 19	41N35	109w14	7:16:56
Rockypoint	44N55	105w06	7:00:24
Rozet 3	44N17	105w12	7:00:48
Ryan Park 4	41N20	106w30	7:06:00
Saddlestring 10	44N27	106w54	7:07:36
Sage 12	41N49	110w58	7:23:52
Sand Draw 7	42N46	108w11	7:12:44
Saratoga 4	41N27	106w49	7:07:16
Savery 4	41N02	107w27	7:09:48
Seminoe Dam 4	42N10	106w55	7:07:40
Shawnee 5	42N45	105w01	7:00:04
Shell 2	44N32	107w47	7:11:08
Sheridan 17	44N48	106w58	7:07:52
Sheridan Gardens 17	44N48	106w57	7:07:48
Sheridan West 17	44N52	107w11	7:08:44
Shoshoni 7	43N14	108w07	7:12:28
Sinclair 4	41N47	107w07	7:08:28
Slater 16	41N52	104w49	6:59:16
Smoot 12	42N37	110w55	7:23:40
Soda Well 3	44N38	105w20	7:01:20
South Laramie 1	41N19	105w35	7:02:20
South Pass City 7	42N28	108w48	7:15:12
South Superior 19	41N46	108w58	7:15:52
South Torrington 8	42N03	104w11	6:56:44
Spotted Horse 3	44N39	106w08	7:04:32
Stansbury	41N42	109w12	7:16:48
Star Valley 12	42N49	110w58	7:23:52
Story 17	44N35	106w53	7:07:32
Stroner	44N46	105w03	7:00:12
Sundance 6	44N24	104w23	6:57:32
Sunrise 16	42N20	104w42	6:58:48
Sunshine 15	44N09	108w52	7:15:28
Sunside 13	42N50	106w23	7:05:32
Superior 19	41N46	108w58	7:15:52
Sussex 10	43N42	106w18	7:05:12
Sussex Unit 10	43N37	106w12	7:04:48
Sweetwater 7	42N34	107w54	7:11:36
Sweetwater Station 7	42N50	108w45	7:15:00
Table Rock	41N37	108w23	7:13:32
Taylor 3	43N25	106w16	7:05:04
Teckla 3	44N18	105w30	7:02:00
Ten Sleep 22	44N02	107w27	7:09:48
Teton Village 20	43N30	110w53	7:23:32
Thayer Junction	41N41	108w55	7:15:40
Thayne 12	42N55	111w00	7:24:00
Thermopolis 9	43N39	108w13	7:12:52
Thermopolis West 9	43N45	108w24	7:13:36
Thumb 20	44N30	110w30	7:22:00
Tie Siding 1	41N05	105w31	7:02:04
Tipton 19	41N40	107w58	7:11:52
Torrington 8	42N04	104w11	6:56:44
Turnerville 12	42N54	110w56	7:23:44
Ucross 17	44N39	106w23	7:05:32
Ulm 17	44N39	106w35	7:06:20
University 1	41N19	105w35	7:02:20
Upton 23	44N06	104w38	6:58:32
Urie 21	41N20	110w18	7:21:12
Uva 16	42N03	104w57	6:59:48
Valley 15	44N11	109w36	7:18:24
Van Tassell 14	42N40	104w05	6:56:20
Verne 21	41N35	110w05	7:20:20
Veteran 8	41N58	104w23	6:57:32
Walcott 4	41N46	106w51	7:07:24
Waltman 13	43N04	107w12	7:08:48
Wamsutter 19	41N40	107w58	7:11:52
Wapiti 15	44N28	109w26	7:17:44
Warren 11	41N09	104w52	6:59:28
Wester Hills 11	41N08	104w49	6:59:16
West Lance Creek 14	43N02	104w39	6:58:36
West Laramie 1	41N19	105w35	7:02:20
Weston 3	44N38	105w20	7:01:20
West Poison Spider 13	42N50	106w23	7:05:32
Westvaco	41N37	109w48	7:19:12
Wheatland 16	42N03	104w58	6:59:52
Whitman 14	42N45	104w27	6:57:48
Wilcox	41N48	105w59	7:03:56
Willwood 15	44N45	108w45	7:15:00
Wilson 16	42N03	104w57	6:59:48
Winchester	43N52	108w10	7:12:40
Wind River 7	43N02	108w48	7:15:12
Wolf	44N46	107w14	7:08:56
Worland 22	44N01	107w57	7:11:48
Wyarno	44N49	106w46	7:07:04
Wyodak	44N17	105w22	7:01:28
Yoder 8	41N55	104w18	6:57:12

The American Ephemeris Series

Read what others have said about The American Ephemeris Series!

"Ephemerissimo! This is exciting! Neil Michelsen has produced the ultimate ephemeris. Everything is in it: the Sun and Moon longitude to the nearest second of arc; void-of-course Moon table; the true node of the Moon to the nearest minute of arc; the daily aspectarian; declinations and latitudes. The print is easily readable; the columns well organized in the right format. It's the best there is.... For people just beginning the study of astrology, it is hoped that their teachers will know about this new addition and recommend it over less accurate and informative but accumulatively more expensive publications. For those who already have ephemerides from 1931 to 1980, make the switch to Michelsen accuracy and convenience or watch for his planned addition of ephemerides of 1981 and beyond."

Astrology Now

"Both the book itself and the process by which it was compiled are impressive. Michelsen employed a new and sophisticated method of computer-controlled typesetting in which the data were 'dictated' to an entirely new printout device. The result is a greater degree of accuracy and completeness such as has hardly been previously possible without tremendous costs.... The quality, accuracy and amount of data in this series makes it an important tool for astrologers today."

Horoscope

"The new *American Ephemeris*...is, frankly, magnificient! ...Hand and Brackett [authors of the section on 'How to Cast a Natal Horoscope'] should be warmly congratulated on their clear and concise formulation, and the many tables are really quite an asset...There is no likelihood of there being anything to make you regret buying this volume. Neil Michelsen has made a supreme product, and it is truly a labour of love."

The Astrological Journal

Also by ACS Publications, Inc.

All About Astrology Series
The American Book of Nutrition & Medical Astrology (Nauman)
The American Book of Tables
The American Ephemeris Series 1901-2000
The American Ephemeris for the 20th Century [Midnight]
1900 to 2000
The American Ephemeris for the 20th Century [Noon] 1900 to 2000
The American Ephemeris for the 21st Century 2000-2049
The American Heliocentric Ephemeris 1901-2000
The American Midpoint Ephemeris 1986-1990 (Michelsen)
The American Sidereal Ephemeris 1976-2000
A New Awareness (Nast)
Asteroid Goddesses (George & Bloch)
Astro-Alchemy: Making the Most of Your Transits (Negus)
Astrological Games People Play (Ashman)
Astrological Insights into Personality (Lundsted)
Astrology: Old Theme, New Thoughts (March & McEvers)
Basic Astrology: A Guide for Teachers & Students (Negus)
Basic Astrology: A Workbook for Students (Negus)
The Body Says Yes (Kapel)
Comet Halley Ephemeris 1901-1996 (Michelsen)
Complete Horoscope Interpretation: Putting Together
Your Planetary Profile (Pottenger)
Cosmic Combinations: A Book of Astrological Exercises (Negus)
Easy Tarot Guide (Masino)
Expanding Astrology's Universe (Dobyns)
The Fortunes of Astrology: A New Complete Treatment of the
Arabic Parts (Granite)
The Gold Mine in Your Files (King)
Hands That Heal (Burns)
Healing with the Horoscope: A Guide to Counseling (Pottenger)
The Horary Reference Book (Ungar & Huber)
Horoscopes of the Western Hemisphere (Penfield)
Instant Astrology (Orser & Brightfields)
The International Atlas: World Latitudes, Longitudes and
Time Changes (Shanks)
Interpreting Solar Returns (Eshelman)
Interpreting the Eclipses (Jansky)
The Koch Book of Tables
The Mystery of Personal Identity (Mayer)
The Only Way to... Learn Astrology, Vol. I
Basic Principles (March & McEvers)
The Only Way to... Learn Astrology, Vol. II
Math & Interpretation Techniques (March & McEvers)
The Only Way to... Learn Astrology, Vol. III
Horoscope Analysis (March & McEvers)
Past Lives Future Growth (Marcotte & Druffel)
Planets in Combination (Burmyn)
The Psychic and the Detective (Druffel with Marcotte)
Psychology of the Planets (F. Gauquelin)
Secrets of the Palm (Hansen)
Seven Paths to Understanding (Dobyns & Wrobel)
Spirit Guides: We Are Not Alone (Belhayes)
Stalking the Wild Orgasm (Kilham)
Tomorrow Knocks (Brunton)
12 Times 12 (McEvers)

State Alpha Code Table

Code	State	Code	State	Code	State
AL	Alabama	LA	Louisiana	OK	Oklahoma
AK	Alaska	ME	Maine	OR	Oregon
AZ	Arizona	MD	Maryland	PA	Pennsylvania
AR	Arkansas	MA	Massachusetts	PR	Puerto Rico
CA	California	MI	Michigan	RI	Rhode Island
CO	Colorado	MN	Minnesota	SC	South Carolina
CT	Connecticut	MS	Mississippi	SD	South Dakota
DE	Delaware	MO	Missouri	TN	Tennessee
DC	District of Columbia	MT	Montana	TX	Texas
FL	Florida	NE	Nebraska	UT	Utah
GA	Georgia	NV	Nevada	VT	Vermont
HI	Hawaii	NH	New Hampshire	VA	Virginia
ID	Idaho	NJ	New Jersey	WA	Washington
IL	Illinois	NM	New Mexico	WV	West Virginia
IN	Indiana	NY	New York	WI	Wisconsin
IA	Iowa	NC	North Carolina	WY	Wyoming
KS	Kansas	ND	North Dakota		
KY	Kentucky	OH	Ohio		

Time Zones and Abbreviations

Abbr.	Name	Standard Meridian	Hours from Greenwich Mean Time Standard	Daylight (War)
A	Atlantic	60°	4:00	3:00
E	Eastern	75°	5:00	4:00
C	Central	90°	6:00	5:00
M	Mountain	105°	7:00	6:00
P	Pacific	120°	8:00	7:00
Y	Yukon	135°	9:00	8:00
AH	Alaska-Hawaii	150°	10:00	9:00
H	Hawaiian	157°30′	10:30	9:30
B	Bering	165°	11:00	10:00

Abbr.	Time Type
S	Standard
D	Daylight
W	War